BECKETT® BASKETBALL CARD PRICE GUIDE

NUMBER 20

THE HOBBY'S MOST RELIABLE AND RELIED UPON SOURCE™

Edited By Rob Springs with the staff of
BECKETT BASKETBALL

Founder & Advisor: Dr. James Beckett III

Manufactured in the United States of America
Published by Beckett Media LLC

Beckett Media LLC
4635 McEwen Road
Dallas, TX 75244
(972) 991-6657
www.beckett.com

First Printing
ISBN 978-193668190-7

There's No Comparison...

Services offered	Beckett	PSA	SGC
Authenticate, Grade & Encapsulate Cards	✓	☑	☑
Authenticate, Grade & Encapsulate Autographed Items	✓	☑	
Authenticate, Grade & Encapsulate Autographed Baseballs**	✓		
Authenticate, Grade & Encapsulate Photographs	✓		
Authenticate, Grade & Encapsulate Magazines	✓		
Authenticate, Grade & Encapsulate Programs	✓		
Authenticate, Grade & Encapsulate Pocket Schedules	✓		
Authenticate, Grade & Encapsulate Star Basketball Cards	✓		
Offers Both "Authentic" & "Authentic-Altered" Options In Lieu of Numerical Grading	✓		
Can Encapsulate Items Up To 8.5" x 11" & Up To 1/4" Thick	✓		
Same Grading Fee No Matter What The Value Of The Card Is	✓		
Completely Tamper-Resistant Holder	✓		
Custom Inner Sleeves To Protect Items From Movement Damage	✓		
Sub-Grades On BGS Cards Detailing Card Strengths & Weaknesses	✓		
Raw Card Review Grading At Trade Shows Across The United States	✓		
On-Time Or It's Free Money-Back Guarantee	✓		
Fee To Access Population Report	FREE	$49 to $189/yr.	FREE
Membership Fee To Submit	FREE	$49 to $189/yr.	FREE
Voted Grading Company Of The Year***	6 Times	0 Times	0 Times

*Beckett offers in conjunction with James Spence Authentication

***Six-time winner by Card Trade Magazine (the only company to ever win the award)

No One Offers More

BECKETT GRADING SERVICES

www.beckett.com/grading - 972-448-9188 - grading@beckett.com

Contents

HOW TO USE AND CONDITION GUIDE

Isn't it great? Every year this book gets bigger and better with all the new sets coming out. But even more exciting is that every year there are more attractive choices and, subsequently, more interest in the cards we love so much. This edition has been enhanced and expanded from the previous edition. The cards you collect—who appears on them, what they look like, where they are from, and (most important to most of you) what their current values are—are enumerated within. Many of the features contained in the other Beckett Price Guides have been incorporated into this volume since condition grading, terminology, and many other aspects of collecting are common to the card hobby in general. We hope you find the book both interesting and useful in your collecting pursuits.

The Beckett Basketball Card Price Guide has been successful where other attempts have failed because it is complete, current, and valid. This Price Guide contains not just one, but two prices by condition for all the basketball cards listed. These account for most of the basketball cards in existence. The prices were added to the card lists just prior to printing and reflect not the author's opinions or desires, but the going retail prices for each card based on the active market (sports memorabilia conventions and shows, sports card shops, mail-order catalogs, local club meetings, auction results, and other firsthand reports of actual realized prices).

What is the best price guide available on the market today? Of course card sellers will prefer the price guide with the highest prices, while card buyers will naturally prefer the one with the lowest prices. Accuracy, however, is the true test. Use the price guide used by more collectors and dealers than all the others combined because it's not the lowest and not the highest — but the most accurate guide, and is produced with integrity.

To facilitate your use of this book, read the complete introductory section on the following pages before going to the pricing pages. Every collectible field has its own terminology; we've tried to capture most of these terms and definitions in our glossary. Please read carefully the section on grading and the condition of your cards, as you will not be able to determine which price column is appropriate for a given card without first knowing its condition.

HOW TO COLLECT

Each collection is personal and reflects the individuality of its owner. There are no set rules on how to collect cards. Since card collecting is a hobby or leisure pastime, what you collect, how much you collect, and how much time and money you spend collecting are entirely up to you. The funds you have available for collecting and your own personal taste should determine how you collect.

It is impossible to collect every card ever produced. Therefore, beginners as well as intermediate and advanced collectors usually specialize in some way. One of the reasons this hobby is popular is that individual collectors can define and tailor their collecting methods to match their own tastes.

Many collectors select complete sets from particular years, acquire only certain players, some collectors are only interested in the first cards or Rookie Cards of certain players, and others collect cards by team.

Remember, this is a hobby so pick a style of collecting that appeals to you.

CONDITION GUIDE

The most widely used grades are defined to the right. Obviously, many cards will not perfectly fit one of the definitions. Therefore, categories between the major grades known as in-between grades are used, such as Good to Very Good (G-Vg), Very Good to Excellent (VgEx), and Excellent-Mint to Near Mint (ExMt-NrMt). Such grades indicate a card with all qualities of the lower category but with at least a few qualities of the higher category.

This Price Guide book lists each card and set in three grades, with the middle grade valued at about 40-45% of the top grade, and the bottom grade valued at about 10-15% of the top grade.

The value of cards that fall between the listed columns can also be calculated using a percentage of the top grade. For example, a card that falls between the top and middle grades (Ex, ExMt or NrMt in most cases) will generally be valued at anywhere from 50% to 90% of the top grade.

Similarly, a card that falls between the middle and bottom grades (G-Vg, Vg or VgEx in most cases) will generally be valued at anywhere from 20% to 40% of the top grade.

There are also cases where cards are in better condition than the top grade or worse than the bottom grade. Cards that grade worse than the lowest grade are generally valued at 5-10% of the top grade.

When a card exceeds the top grade by one — such as NrMt-Mt when the top grade is NrMt, or Mint when the top grade is NrMt-Mt — a premium of up to 50% is possible, with 10-20% the usual norm.

When a card exceeds the top grade by two — such as Mint when the top grade is NrMt, or NrMt-Mt when the top grade is ExMt — a premium of 25-50% is the usual norm. But certain condition sensitive cards or sets, particularly those from the prewar era, can bring premiums of up to 100% or even more.

Unopened packs, boxes and factory-collated sets are considered Mint in their unknown (and presumed perfect) state. Once opened, however, each card can be graded (and valued) in its own right by taking into account any defects that may be present in spite of the fact that the card has never been handled.

GENERAL CARD FLAWS

CENTERING

Current centering terminology uses numbers representing the percentage of border on either side of the main design. Obviously, centering is diminished in importance for borderless cards.

Slightly Off-Center (60/40): A slightly off-center card is one that upon close inspection is found to have one border bigger than the opposite border. This degree once was offensive to only purists, but now some hobbyists try to avoid cards that are anything other than perfectly centered.

Off-Center (70/30): An off-center card has one border that is noticeably more than twice as wide as the opposite border.

Badly Off-Center (80/20 or worse): A badly off-center card has virtually no border on one side of the card.

Miscut: A miscut card actually shows part of the adjacent card in its larger border and consequently a corresponding amount of its card is cut off.

GLOSSARY/LEGEND

Our glossary defines terms frequently used in the card collecting hobby. Many of these terms are also common to other types of sports memorabilia collecting. Some terms may have several meanings depending on use and context.

ABA – American Basketball Association
ACC – Accomplishment
ACO – Assistant Coach Card
AL – Active Leader
ART – All-Rookie Team
AS – All-Star
ASA – All-Star Advice
ASW – All-Star Weekend
AUTO or AU – Autograph.
AW – Award Winner
B – Bronze
BC – Bonus Card
BT – Beam Team or Breakaway Threats
CB – Collegiate Best
CBA – Continental Basketball Association
CL – Checklist card. Older checklist cards in Mint condition that have not been checked off are very desirable and command large premiums.
CO – Coach card
COMMON CARD – The typical card of any set; it has no premium value accruing from subject matter, numerical scarcity, popular demand, or anomaly.
COR – Corrected card. A version of an error card that was fixed by the manufacturer.
CY – City Lights
DIE-CUT – A card with part of its stock partially cut for ornamental reasons.
DISC – A circular-shaped card
DP – Double Print. A card that was printed in approximately double the quantity compared to other cards in the same series.
ERR – Error card. A card with erroneous information, spelling, or depiction on either side of the card.
EXCH – An exchange card that is inserted into packs that can be redeemed.
FIN – Finals
FLB – Flashback
FPM – Future Playoff MVP's
FSL – Future Scoring Leaders
FULL SHEET – A complete sheet of cards that has not been cut into individual cards by the manufacturer. Also called an uncut sheet.
G – Gold
GQ – Gentleman's Quarterly
GRA – Grace
HL – Highlight card
HOF – Hall of Fame, or Hall of Famer (also abbreviated HOFer).
HOR – Horizontal pose on a card as opposed to the standard vertical orientation found on most cards.
IA – In Action card. A special type of card depicting a player in an action photo, such as the 1982 Topps cards.
INSERT – A card of a different type, e.g., a poster, or any other sports collectible contained and sold in the same package along with a card or cards of a major set.
IS – Inside Stuff
JSY – Card contains a jersey swatch
JWA – John Wooden Award
MAG – Magic of SkyBox cards
MC – Members Choice
MEM – Memorial
MO – McDonald's Open
MINI – A small card or stamp (the 1991-92 SkyBox Canadian set, for example)
MVP – Most Valuable Player
NNO – No card number on back
NY – New York
OBVERSE – The front, face, or pictured side of the card
OLY – Olympic card
PANEL – An extended card that is composed of multiple individual cards
PC – Poster card
PF – Pacific Finest

CORNER WEAR

Corner wear is the most scrutinized grading criteria in the hobby.

Corner with a slight touch of wear: The corner still is sharp, but there is a slight touch of wear showing. On a dark-bordered card, this shows as a dot of white.

Fuzzy corner: The corner still comes to a point, but the point has just begun to fray. A slightly "dinged" corner is considered the same as a fuzzy corner.

Slightly rounded corner: The fraying of the corner has increased to where there is only a hint of a point. Mild layering may be evident. A "dinged" corner is considered the same as a slightly rounded corner.

Rounded corner: The point is completely gone. Some layering is noticeable.

Badly rounded corner: The corner is completely round and rough. Severe layering is evident.

CREASES

A third common defect is the crease. The degree of creasing in a card is difficult to show in a drawing or picture. On giving the specific condition of an expensive card for sale, the seller should note any creases additionally. Creases can be categorized as to severity according to the following scale.

Light Crease: A light crease is a crease that is barely noticeable upon close inspection. In fact, when cards are in plastic sheets or holders, a light crease may not be seen (until the card is taken out of the holder). A light crease on the front is much more serious than a light crease on the card back only.

Medium Crease: A medium crease is noticeable when held and studied at arm's length by the naked eye, but does not overly detract from the appearance of the card. It is an obvious crease, but not one that breaks the picture surface of the card.

Heavy Crease: A heavy crease is one that has torn or broken through the card's picture surface, e.g., puts a tear in the photo surface.

ALTERATIONS

Deceptive Trimming: This occurs when someone alters the card in order (1) to shave off edge wear, (2) to improve the sharpness of the corners, or (3) to improve centering — obviously their objective is to falsely increase the perceived value of the card to an unsuspecting buyer. The shrinkage usually is evident only if the trimmed card is compared to an adjacent full-sized card or if the trimmed card is itself measured.

Obvious Trimming: Obvious trimming is noticeable and unfortunate. It is usually performed by non-collectors who give no thought to the present or future value of their cards.

Deceptively Retouched Borders: This occurs when the borders (especially on those cards with dark borders) are touched up on the edges and corners with magic marker or crayons of appropriate color in order to make the card appear to be Mint.

MISCELLANEOUS CARD FLAWS

The following are common minor flaws that, depending on severity, lower a card's condition by one to four grades and often render it no better than Excellent-Mint: bubbles (lumps in surface), gum and wax stains, diamond cutting (slanted borders), notching, off-centered backs, paper wrinkles, scratched-off cartoons or puzzles on back, rubber band marks, scratches, surface impressions and warping.

The following are common serious flaws that, depending on severity, lower a card's condition at least four grades and often render it no better than Good: chemical or sun fading, erasure marks, mildew, miscutting (severe off-centering), holes, bleached or retouched borders, tape marks, tears, trimming, water or coffee stains and writing.

GRADES

Mint (Mt) – A card with no flaws or wear. The card has four perfect corners, 55/45 or better centering from top to bottom and from left to right, original gloss, smooth edges and original color borders. A Mint card does not have print spots, color or focus imperfections.

Near Mint-Mint (NrMt-Mt) – A card with one minor flaw. Any one of the following would lower a Mint card to Near Mint-Mint: one corner with a slight touch of wear, barely noticeable print spots, color or focus imperfections. The card must have 60/40 or better centering in both directions, original gloss, smooth edges and original color borders.

Near Mint (NrMt) – A card with one minor flaw. Any one of the following would lower a Mint card to Near Mint: one fuzzy corner or two to four corners with slight touches of wear, 70/30 to 60/40 centering, slightly rough edges, minor print spots, color or focus imperfections. The card must have original gloss and original color borders.

Excellent-Mint (ExMt) – A card with two or three fuzzy, but not rounded, corners and centering no worse than 80/20. The card may have no more than two of the following: slightly rough edges, very slightly discolored borders, minor print spots, color or focus imperfections. The card must have original gloss.

Excellent (Ex) – A card with four fuzzy but definitely not rounded corners and centering no worse than 70/30. The card may have a small amount of original gloss lost, rough edges, slightly discolored borders and minor print spots, color or focus imperfections.

Very Good (Vg) – A card that has been handled but not abused: slightly rounded corners with slight layering, slight notching on edges, a significant amount of gloss lost from the surface but no scuffing and moderate discoloration of borders. The card may have a few light creases.

Good (G), Fair (F), Poor (P) – A well-worn, mishandled or abused card: badly rounded and layered corners, scuffing, most or all original gloss missing, seriously discolored borders, moderate or heavy creases, and one or more serious flaws. The grade of Good, Fair or Poor depends on the severity of wear and flaws. Good, Fair and Poor cards generally are used only as fillers.

GLOSSARY/LEGEND

POY – Player of the Year
PROMOTIONAL SET – A set, usually containing a small number of cards, issued by a national card producer and distributed in limited quantities or to a select group of people, such as major show attendees or dealers with wholesale accounts. Also called a preview, prototype, promo, or test set.
QP – Quadruple Print. A card that was printed in approximately four times the quantity compared to other cards in the same series.
RC – Rookie Card. A player's first appearance on a regular issue card from one of the major card companies. With a few exceptions, each player has only one RC in any given set. A Rookie Card cannot be an All-Star, Highlight, In Action, League Leader, Super Action or Team Leader card. It can, however, be a coach card or draft pick card.
REGIONAL – A card issued and distributed only in a limited geographical area of the country.
REVERSE – The back or narrative side of the card
REV NEG – Reversed or flopped photo side of the card. This is a common type of error card, but only some are corrected
RIS – Rising Star
ROY – Rookie of the Year
S – Silver
SA – Super Action card. Similar to an In Action card
SAL – SkyBox Salutes
SERIES – The entire set of cards issued by a particular producer in a particular year, e.g., the 1978-79 Topps series. Also, within a particular set, series can refer to a group of (consecutively numbered) cards printed at the same time, e.g., the first series of the 1972-73 Topps set (#1 through #132).
SET – One each of an entire run of cards of the same type, produced by a particular manufacturer during a single season. In other words, if you have a complete set of 1989-90 Fleer cards, then you have every card from #1 up to and including #132; i.e., all the different cards that were produced.
SHOOT – Shooting Star
SKED – Schedules
SP – Single or Short Print. A card which was printed in lesser quantity compared to the other cards in the same series (also see DP).
SS – Star Stats.
STANDARD SIZE – The standard size for sports cards is 2 1/2 by 3 1/2 inches. All exceptions, such as 1969-70 Topps, are noted in card descriptions.
STOCK – The cardboard or paper on which the card is printed.
STY – Style
SY – Schoolyard Stars
TC – Team card or team checklist card
TD – Triple Double. A term used for having double digit totals in three categories.
TEAM CARD – A card that depicts an entire team, notably the 1989-90 and 1990-91 NBA Hoops Detroit Pistons championship cards and the 1991-92 NBA Hoops subset.
TEST SET – A set, usually containing a small number of cards, issued by a national producer and distributed in a limited section of the country or to a select group of people. Also called a promo or prototype set.
TFC – Team Fact card
TL – Team Leader
TO – Tip-off
TR – Traded card
TRIB – Tribune
TRV – Trivia
TT – Team Tickets card
UER – Uncorrected Error card
USA – Team USA.
VAR – Variation card. One of two or more cards from the same series, with the same card number (or player with identical pose, if the series is unnumbered) differing from one another in some aspect, from the printing, stock or other feature of the card. This is often caused when the manufacturer of the cards notices an error in a particular card, corrects the error and then resumes the print run.
VERT – Vertical pose on a card
XRC – Extended Rookie Card. A player's first appearance on a card, but issued in a set that was not distributed nationally nor in packs. In basketball sets, this term only refers to the 1983, '84 and '85 Star Company sets.
YB – Yearbook
20A – Twenty assist club
50P – Fifty point club
6M – Sixth Man
! – Condition sensitive card or set
* – Multi-sport set

HISTORY OF BASKETBALL CARDS

The earliest basketball collectibles known are team postcards issued at the turn of the 20th century. Many of these postcards feature collegiate or high school teams of that day. Postcards were intermittently issued throughout the first half of the 20th century, with the bulk of them coming out in the 1920s and '30s. Unfortunately, the cataloging of these collectibles is sporadic at best. In addition, many collectors consider these postcards as memorabilia more so than trading cards, thus their exclusion from this book.

In 1910, College Athlete Felts (catalog number B-33) made their debut. Of a total of 270 felts, 20 featured basketball plays.

The first true basketball trading cards were issued by Murad cigarettes in 1911. The "College Series" cards depict a number of various sports and colleges, including four basketball cards (Luther, Northwestern, Williams and Xavier). In addition to these small (2-by-3 inch) cards, Murad issued a large (8-by-5 inch) basketball card featuring Williams college (catalog number T-6) as part of another multisport set.

The first basketball cards ever to be issued in gum packs were distributed in 1933 by Goudey in its multisport Sport Kings set, which was the first issue to list individual and professional players. Four cards from the complete 48-card set feature Original Celtics basketball players Nat Holman, Ed Wachter, Joe Lapchick and Eddie Burke.

The period of growth that the NBA experienced from 1948 to 1951 marked the first initial boom, both for that sport and the cards that chronicle it. In 1948, Bowman created the first trading card set exclusively devoted to basketball cards, ushering in the modern era of hoops collectibles. The 72-card Bowman set contains the Rookie Card of HOFer George Mikan, one of the most valuable, and important, basketball cards in the hobby. Mikan, pro basketball's first dominant big man, set the stage for Bill Russell, Wilt Chamberlain and all the other legendary centers who have played the game since.

In addition to the Bowman release, Topps included 11 basketball cards in its 252-card multisport 1948 Magic Photo set. Five of the cards feature individual players (including collegiate great "Easy" Ed Macauley), another five feature colleges, and one additional card highlights a Manhattan-Dartmouth game. These 11 cards represent Topps first effort to produce basketball trading cards. Kellogg's also created an 18-card multisport set of trading cards in 1948 that were inserted into boxes of Pep cereal. The only basketball card in the set features Mikan. Throughout 1948 and 1949, the Exhibit Supply Company of Chicago issued oversized thick-stock multisport trading cards in conjunction with the 1948 Olympic games. Six basketball players were featured, including HOFers Mikan and Joe Fulks, among others. The cards were distributed through penny arcade machines.

In 1950-51, Scott's Chips issued a 13-card set featuring the Minneapolis Lakers. The cards were issued in Scott's Potato and Cheese Potato Chip boxes. The cards are extremely scarce today due to the fact that many were redeemed back in 1950-51 in exchange for game tickets and signed team pictures. This set contains possibly the scarcest Mikan issue in existence. In 1951, a Philadelphia-based meat company called Berk Ross issued a four-series, 72-card multisport set. The set contains five different basketball players, including the first cards of HOFers Bob Cousy and Bill Sharman.

Wheaties issued an oversized six-card multisport set on the backs of its cereal boxes in 1951. The only basketball player featured in the set is Mikan.

In 1952, Wheaties expanded the cereal box set to 30 cards, including six issues featuring basketball players of that day. Of these six cards, two feature Mikan (a portrait and an action shot). The 1952 cards are significantly smaller than the previous year's issue. That same year, the 32-card Bread for Health set was issued. The set was one of the few trading card issues of that decade exclusively devoted to the sport of basketball. The cards are actually bread end labels and were probably meant to be housed in an album. To date, the only companies known to have issued this set are Fisher's Bread in the New Jersey, New York and Pennsylvania areas and NBC Bread in the Michigan area.

One must skip ahead to 1957-58 to find the next major basketball issue, again produced by Topps. Its 80-card basketball set from that year is recognized within the hobby as the second major modern basketball issue, including Rookie Cards of all-time greats such as Bill Russell, Bob Cousy and Bob Pettit.

In 1960, Post cereal created a nine-card multisport set by devoting most of the back of the actual cereal boxes to full color picture frames of the athletes. HOFers Cousy and Pettit are the two featured basketball players.

In 1961-62, Fleer issued the third major modern basketball set. The 66-card set contains the Rookie Cards of all-time greats such as Wilt Chamberlain, Oscar Robertson and Jerry West. That same year, Bell Brand Potato Chips inserted trading cards (one per bag) featuring the L.A. Lakers team of that year including scarce, early issues of HOFers West and Elgin Baylor.

From 1963 to 1968 no major companies manufactured basketball cards. Kahn's, an Ohio-based meat company, issued small regional basketball sets from 1957-58 through 1965-66, including the first cards of Jerry West and Oscar Robertson in its 1960-61 set. All the Kahn's sets feature members of the Cincinnati Royals, except for the few issues featuring the Lakers' West.

In 1968, Topps printed a very limited quantity of standard-size black-and-white test issue cards, preluding its 1969-70 nationwide return to the basketball card market.

The 1969-70 Topps set began a 13-year run of producing nationally distributed basketball card sets which ended in 1981-82. This was about the time the league's popularity bottomed out and was about to begin its ascent to the lofty level it's at today.

Topps' run included several sets that are troublesome for today's collectors. The 1969-70, 1970-71 and 1976-77 sets are larger than standard size, making them hard to store and preserve. The 1980-81 set consists of standard-size panels containing three cards each separated by perforation lines. Completing and cataloging the 1980-81 set (which features the classic Larry Bird RC/Magic Johnson RC/Julius Erving panel) is challenging, to say the least.

In 1983, this basketball card void was filled by the Star Company, a small company which issued three attractive sets of basketball cards, along with a plethora of peripheral sets. Star's 1983-84 premiere offering was issued in four groups, with the first series (cards 1-100) very difficult to obtain, as many of the early team subsets were miscut and destroyed before release. The 1984-85 and 1985-86 sets were more widely and evenly distributed. Even so, players' initial appearances on any of the three Star Company sets are considered Extended Rookie Cards, not regular Rookie Cards, because of the relatively limited distribution. Chief among these is Michael Jordan's 1984-85 Star XRC, the most valuable sports card issued in a 1980s major set.

Then, in 1986, Fleer took over the rights to produce cards for the NBA. Their 1986-87, 1987-88 and 1988-89 sets each contain 132 attractive, colorful cards depicting mostly stars and superstars. They were sold in the familiar wax pack format (12 cards and one sticker per pack). Fleer increased its set size to 168 in 1989-90, and was joined by NBA Hoops, which produced a 300-card first series containing David Robinson's only Rookie Card and a 52-card second series. The demand for all three Star Company sets, along with the first four Fleer sets and the premiere NBA Hoops set, skyrocketed during the early part of 1990.

The basketball card market stabilized somewhat in 1990-91, with both Fleer and Hoops stepping up production tremendously. A new major set, SkyBox, also made a splash in the market with its unique "high-tech" cards featuring computer-generated backgrounds. Because of overproduction, none of the three major 1990-91 sets have experienced significant price growth, although the increased competition has led to higher quality and more innovative products. Another milestone in 1990-91 was the first-time inclusion of current rookies in update sets (NBA Hoops, SkyBox Series II and Fleer Update). The NBA Hoops and SkyBox issues contain just the 11 lottery picks, while Fleer's 100-card boxed set includes all rookies of any significance.

In 1991-92, the draft pick set market that Star Pics opened in 1990-91 expanded to include several competitors. More significantly, that season brought with it the three established NBA card brands plus Upper Deck, known throughout the hobby for its high quality card stock and photography in other sports. Upper Deck's first basketball set probably captured NBA action better than any previous set. But its value — like all other major 1990-91 and 1991-92 NBA sets — declined because of overproduction.

On the bright side, the historic entrance of NBA players to Olympic competition kept interest in basketball cards going long after the Chicago Bulls won their second straight NBA championship. So for at least one year, the basketball card market — probably the most seasonal of the four major team sports — remained in the spotlight for an extended period of time.

The 1992-93 season will be remembered as the year of Shaq — the debut campaign of the most heralded rookie in many years. Shaquille O'Neal headlined the most promising rookie class in NBA history, sparking unprecedented interest in basketball cards. Among O'Neal's many talented rookie companions were Alonzo Mourning, Jim Jackson and Latrell Sprewell.

Classic Games, known primarily for producing draft picks and minor league baseball cards, signed O'Neal to an exclusive contract through 1992, thus postponing the appearance of O'Neal's NBA-licensed cards.

Shaquille's Classic and NBA cards, particularly the inserts, became some of the most sought-after collectibles in years. As a direct result of O'Neal and his fellow rookie standouts, the basketball card market achieved a new level of popularity in 1993.

The hobby rode that crest of popularity throughout the 1993-94 season. Michael Jordan may have retired, but his absence only spurred interest in some of his tougher inserts. Another strong rookie class followed Shaq, and Reggie Miller elevated his collectibility to a superstar level. Hakeem Olajuwon, by leading the Rockets to an NBA title, boosted his early cards to levels surpassed only by Jordan. No new card makers came on board, but super premium Topps Finest raised the stakes, and the parallel set came into its own.

In 1994-95, the return of Michael Jordan, coupled with the high impact splash of Detroit Pistons rookie Grant Hill and Dallas Mavericks rookie Jason Kidd, kept collector interest high. In addition, the NBA granted all the licensed manufacturers the opportunity to create a fourth brand of basketball cards that year, allowing each company to create a selection of clearly defined niche products at different price points. The manufacturers also expanded the calendar release dates with 1994-95 cards being released on a consistent basis from August, 1994 all the way through June, 1995. The super-premium card market expanded greatly as the battle for the best selling five dollar (or more) pack reached epic levels by season's end.

The collecting year of 1996-97 brought even more to the table with a prominent mot of tough parallel sets and an influx of autographs available at lower ratio pulls. One of the greatest rookie classes in some time also carried the collecting season with players showing great promise: Allen Iverson, Kobe Bryant, Stephon Marbury, Antoine Walker and Steve Nash. Topps Chrome was also introduced bringing about a rookie frenzy not seen since the 1986-87 Fleer set.

In 1997-98, Kobe Bryant was viewed as the second coming of Michael Jordan and his cards gained in both value and popularity throughout the year. In addition, a stronger than expected rookie class gave collectors some new blood to chase after—including Tim Duncan and Tracy McGrady. Autographs, highlighted by Skybox Premium Autographics and SP Authentic Sign of the Times, and serial-numbered cards were the key

inserts to chase featuring numbering as low as one of one.

1998-99 forever changed the basketball hobby. While hoops cards had been steadily building steam over the previous decade or so, the player's strike crushed the growing basketball market and sent manufacturers reeling. Add to the equation a second Michael Jordan retirement, and enter the beginning of a slow decline that, spare a few market spikes here and there, would continue to haunt hoops collectibles up though the early 2000's. Many 1998-99 releases were cut back – or cut period. There was a bright spot once the season began—a great rookie class led by Vince Carter. And although the hobby benefited by combining the great class and products with shorter print runs (SP Authentic debuted the serially numbered rookie card—numbered to 3500), sales were still relatively softer than they had been pre-strike and pre-Jordan retirement.

The 1999-00 release year was also one of transition. Vince Carter became the most collected player in the hobby, and the big market NBA Champion Lakers helped to spike basketball card sales with the one-two combo of Kobe Bryant and Shaquille O'Neal. Another seemingly solid rookie class emerged, led by Steve Francis and Elton Brand, the likes of whom shared Rookie of the Year honors. 1999-00 products combined elements of short-printed and/or serially numbered rookies, autographs and game-worn materials. SP Authentic again led the way as far as consumer dollars were concerned, but many other brands also did extremely well, including E-X, Flair Showcase and SPx, which delivered the hobby's first serially numbered autograph rookie cards. The top hobby card of the year was the SPx Steve Francis RC, which is autographed and limited to 500 serially numbered copies.

With autographs and serially numbered cards already in the mix, card manufactures introduced a myriad of new concepts in 2000-01. Noteworthy issues include the first one-per-pack graded insert in Upper Deck Ultimate Collection, the first one-per-pack memorabilia release in SP Game Floor, the first one-per-box autograph jersey (an actual signed and numbered replica jersey) in Fleer Legacy and the first one-per-box 8x10 autograph canvas print in Topps Reserve. While some of these concepts have become commonplace over the course of the last year and a half, no card manufacturer had ever inserted these types of cards with such frequency. Also notable is a jump in average pack price—in 1999-00 the average pack cost about $3.20, and by the end of the 2000-01 release season, the average pack cost about $7.40.

2001-02 followed in the footsteps of previous years, as nearly every set issued had some type of memorabilia and/or autographed element to it. The hobby was shaken into a brief frenzy as Michael Jordan rose up out of retirement. Base Michael Jordan card values dominated sets, and at one point, $10 to $12 on the high end was a common value for base cards. Upper Deck followed the comeback of Michael Jordan with several commemorative issues such as MJ Jersey Collection, and MJ's Back Jerseys, which was inserted over several brands at the beginning of the release season. However, a soft rookie crop hurt overall sales as the current-day basketball card hobby is dominated by the new and exciting stars of the game.

With the arrival of the 2002-03 season came the path towards globalization of basketball trading cards. The 2002 NBA Draft boasts, to date, the highest number of foreign players drafted in the first round with ten; and the biggest push towards international card collecting was the number one draft choice, Yao Ming.

Though the number of products released during 2002-03 was lower than in previous years, rather than pocketing the money, manufacturers reinvested in better looking cards and more quality products. Topps released its first-ever all jersey set with Topps Jersey Edition and wowed collectors with its Bowman Signature Edition. Signature Edition includes one autograph rookie card per pack. Fleer concentrated on some of its bigger names like Hoops Hot Prospects and Flair. Upper Deck once again impressed the hobby with SP Authentic and SPx, but added a new hobby hit with Upper Deck Glass. UD Glass showcased glass cards of veteran stars and glass rookie cards sequentially numbered to 900, 500 and 250. Boxes also included one jumbo glass box topper-Magnifying Glass or a Magnifying Glass Autograph. Towards the end of the year, the basketball card hobby was abuzz with talk of LeBron James.

The incredible success of the 2003-04 rookie class, namely LeBron James, Carmelo Anthony and Dwyane Wade, brought basketball card collecting to new heights. Upper Deck signed an exclusive deal with LeBron at the beginning of the season for autographs and memorabilia, limiting his usage options for Fleer and Topps. The impact of LeBron James alone drove the high-end market, paving the way for some of the basketball hobby's highest priced super-premium sets. Upper Deck delivered Exquisite Collection ($500 per pack), which saw several sales above $30,000 for single cards. Topps answered with Contemporary Collection ($50 per pack), which delivered an array of autographs and memorabilia. Fleer issued Flair Final Edition (approximately $125 per pack), the only product where collectors had the opportunity to pull redemption cards for Draft Day memorabilia such as the team and player placards used on the actual NBA draft board and the ping pong balls from the draft lottery. Shaq's trade at the end of the season rejuvenated his cardboard career and also pushed the sales of Miami rookie, Dwyane Wade.

2004-05 provided a solid rookie class where a sleeper, Ben Gordon, who started out as a middle of the pack guy, ended the season as the most popular and expensive RC of the year. Other young and solid prospects from the class include Dwight Howard, Josh Smith, Josh Childress and Shaun Livingston. As for manufacturer highlights, it's an unfortunate fact that the year will be remembered for the closing down of Fleer/Skybox International at the beginning of the 2005 summer. Upper Deck made an offer and won the intellectual rights of the company, and the hobby is looking forward to what UD has in store for the brand names and trade marks. Aside from the Fleer purchase, UD made headlines with an unannounced return of Exquisite Collection, which ruled the hobby for months. Topps highlights included the return of the autographed Bowman and Bowman Chrome rookies, which find themselves atop the Hot List month in and month out, and introduced new brands Topps Luxury Box, which provided plenty of autographs and memorabilia along with Topps Total, a set that boasts the largest player roster of the year with 440-card base set.

2005-06 releases continued to build on the reputation that the basketball card market has established itself as the high-end market for sports cards. LeBron James' 2003-04 Exquisite Collection broke the $10,000 barrier, a first for any rookie card of any sport in the modern era of sports cards. During the release year, Upper Deck again issued Exquisite Collection ($500 per pack), Ultimate Collection ($100 per pa and Topps issued its first-time super premium product, Big Game ($75 per pack). To rookies from the 2005-06 crop include Chris Paul, Deron Williams and Andrew Bog Players from recent year's rookie classes made strong showings throughout the 20 06 season such as Dwight Howard and Kevin Martin, both of whom have huge NBA potential and the chance to be superstars. Miami phenom, Dwyane Wade won both his first NBA Title and first NBA Finals MVP, and dominated hot lists throughout the season and the summer of 2006.

While LeBron, Carmelo and Wade continue to be popular, the hobby suffered a lackluster 2006-07 release year. The two rookies who received unheralded hype, Adam Morrison and J.J. Redick, both disappointed and devastated collectibles durin the year. Both came out of the gate incredibly hot, but were met with nothing but do arrows in the price guides for most of the year. That said, a few youngsters stepped and salvaged what has otherwise been an inadequate rookie class: Brandon Roy, LaMarcus Aldridge, Andrea Bargnani and Tyrus Thomas. Product highlights include fourth Exquisite Collection release, the return of Hoops Hot Prospects under the Upper Deck umbrella and Topps Triple Threads—one of the most expensive and nicest premium products Topps has ever released.

2007-08 both opened and closed to the disappointment of basketball hobbyists. Before the start of the season, it was announced that number one draft pick, Greg Oden (a Topps exclusive), would miss the entire season with a knee injury that resulted in microfracture surgery. Highlights of the year include the moving of the Sea Supersonics and number two pick, Kevin Durant (a Upper Deck exclusive) to a very welcoming and hardcore fan base in Oklahoma City, and products such as Exquisit Collection, Chronology—which features one of the most comprehensive autograph player lists in several years and Topps Letterman, a product based around full letter swatches, both manufactured and taken from the nameplates on the back of player jerseys.

The 2008-09 release year will be remembered as one of transition and change. January 2009, the NBA made the announcement that Panini America will be the exclusive licensed producer of basketball cards in a multi-year deal starting October 1 2009. The deal leaves out longtime basketball card manufacturers Topps and Upper Deck. And, with Upper Deck holding the rights to all of the Fleer copyrights, 2009-1 marks the first year since 1985 that no licensed Fleer, Topps or Upper Deck product will be issued. In late September 2009, Panini America also announced that they ha reached a deal with Kobe Bryant, making their company the only one to insert his autograph into their card products. As a part of the licensing deal with the NBA, Panini purchased the card manufacturer previously known as Donruss/Playoff, so brand names familiar to baseball and football card enthusiasts, such as Elite, Prestige and Rookies and Stars, will make their basketball debut. Like so many other industries in the tough economy of 2009, the basketball card industry has been streamlined, and we anxiously await the result of such a big change.

Panini completed its run of 2009-10 basketball products in September 2010 with the issue of Hall of Fame. The year's highlights include the first-time issue of brands such as Absolute Memorabilia, Court Kings, Crown Royale and Playoff National Treasures. Each of the aforementioned brands was met favorably by hobbyists, and were big secondary market successes. Upper Deck and Topps released a handful c products in August and September 2009, including Exquisite Collection and Topps Chrome. In terms of the rookie class, it's been an interesting one. Number one over draft pick, Blake Griffin, did not play a single game due to injury, and players such a Brandon Jennings, Tyreke Evans and Stephen Curry emerged as the best in the class.

2010-11 was a return to prominence for basketball cards. Even though the rooki class was not as strong as many had hoped, it got an additional boost with the retu of 2009-10 rookie, Blake Griffin. Griffin set both the court and hobby on fire, sending collectors scrambling back to 2009-10 products. He was not the only player that exploded, as guys like Derrick Rose, Kevin Durant and Russell Westbrook heated up hobby for most of the year. Perhaps the largest hobby story of the year was from an old player, and some old manufactuers. Michael Jordan's late 1990's inserts and parallels exploded, pushing up those values to new heights. Panini remained the only fully licensed manufactuer, with Upper Deck producing a handful of sets featuring players in their college uniforms. As we look to the 2011-12 year, we can only hope the lockout resolves itself quickly, to not lose the momentum that basketball cards built up during this past season.

2011-12 was a rough time for collectors. The lockout not only had an impact on the court, but also in the hobby. Panini only released five new sets and none of ther featured the rookie draft class. They did, however, issue exchange cards in some products for players from that class. Leaf and Upper Deck also released a handful c sets, most notably Fleer Retro, by Upper Deck. This product was a nostalgia based nod to great inserts and autographs produced by Fleer from the 1990's and was one of the hottest products in recent memory. New products released for the 2012-13 se son by Panini feature a double rookie class, with players from the last two drafts.

Basketball **DEALER DIRECTORY**

ALASKA

BOSCO'S
2606 Spenard Rd
Anchorage, AK 99503-2309
(907) 274-4112
patmoe@boscos.com

Don's Sportscards
9900 Old Seward Hwy Ste 8
Anchorage, AK 99515-2249
(907) 349-8804
donssports@aol.com

ARKANSAS

HobbyTown USA
2614 S. Shackleford Rd. Suite C
Little Rock, AR 72205
(501) 228-4800
htulittlerock@comcast.net

ARIZONA

Sports Cards Etc.
2506 W Chilton St.
Chandler, AZ 85224-1108
(480) 777-2688
weedy@cox.net

Phoenix Card Co-Op
4326 West Bell Rd Suite# 7
Glendale, AZ 85308-3545
(602) 548-1254
phoenixcardcoop@cox.net

CALIFORNIA

The OC Dugout
5655 E. La Palma Ave #123
Anaheim Hills, CA 92807
(714) 997-1111
celebritysluggers@hotmail.com

Taylor Baseball Cards
8682 Beach Blvd Ste 101
Buena Park, CA 90620-4808
(714) 827-7746
taycard@aol.com

Teammates
4705 Manzanita Ave
Carmichael, CA 95608-0822
(916) 488-2303
teammates1@aol.com

Legacy Comics And Cards
123 W Wilson Ave
Glendale, CA 91203-2605
(818) 247-8803
legacycomics@hotmail.com

Best Variety Sportscards
358 W Foothill Blvd
Glendora, CA 91741
626-914-CARD
bestvarietycoinerrors.com

Best Variety Sportscards
358 W. Foothill Boulevard
Glendora, CA 91741
(626) 914-2273
bestvariety@hotmail.com

Baseball Cards Plus
6401 Edinger Ave
Huntington Beach, CA 92647-3341
(714) 898-5648
brian@surfcitycards.com

MVP Sportscards
24881 Alicia Pkwy Ste J
Laguna, CA 92653-4617
(949) 837-7830

South Bay Baseball Cards
1751 Pacific Coast Hwy
Lomita, CA 90717
SbayCards.com

Affordable Cards
2395 Hamner Ave Unit F
Norco, CA 92860
(951) 736-8552
affordcard@netzero.com

D and P Sports Cards
5968 S Land Park Dr
Sacramento, CA 95822-3313
(916) 391-8750
DNPcards@gmail.com

Clairemont Sportcards
4941 Clairemont Dr Ste C
San Diego, CA 92117-2731
(858) 270-4945
clairemontsc@netscape.net

Pro Star Sports and Gaming
414 N Capitol Ave
San Jose, CA 95133
(408) 259-6460
prostargaming@aol.com

COLORADO

Mike's Stadium Sports Cards
4022 S Parker Rd
Aurora, CO 80014
303-699-9808
cardmn5150@aol.com

Dale's Kardz And Koinz
4341 N Academy Blvd
Colorado Springs, CO 80918-6623
(719) 528-5959
dalezkardz@earthlink.net

Bill's Sports Collectibles
2335 S Broadway
Denver, CO 80210-5006
(303) 733-4878
billssportscolo@aol.com

FLORIDA

Jacksonville Sport Card Center
1370 Cassat Ave
Jacksonville, FL 32205-7063
(904) 387-0260

Orlando Sportscards South
9476 S Orange Blossom Trl
Orlando, FL 32837-8321
(407) 240-0384

Scott's Sportscards
6724 N University Dr
Tamarac, FL 33321
954-721-7141
scottysportscards@hotmail.com

GEORGIA

Sports Legends
310 N Glynn Street
Fayetteville, GA 30214
(678) 817-6769
sportslegendsusa.com

Champion Sportscards & Collectibles
840 Ernest Barrett Pkwy Suite#708
Kennesaw, GA 30144
(770) 427-2220
championsportscards@yahoo.com

IOWA

Midwest Collectibles
3541 N Fairmount St Ste A
Davenport, IA 52806
(563) 823-1975
midwestcoll@gmail.com

ILLINOIS

Baseball Card Exchange
21686 East Lincoln Hwy Unit C
Lynwood, IL 60411
800-598-8656
bbcexchange.com

Fred Copp
7948 North Octavia
Niles, IL 60714
(847) 967-7824
fcopp@sbcglobal.net

Southside Cards & Collectibles
11325 W 143rd ST
Orland Park, IL 60467
(708) 873-5088
www.southsidecards.com

The Baseball Card King
16030 Lincoln Hwy Unit 1
Plainfield, IL 60586
(815) 609-7777
thebaseballcardking@comcast.net

Primetime Sportscards
3398 Sheridan Rd
Zion, IL 60099-3661
(847) 746-2273
zioncards@aol.com

INDIANA

MCS Cards Comics and Gaming
107 1/2 W Wabash St;
Bluffton, IN 46714
(260) 824-4576
mcscardscomics@adamswells.com

More Fun Sportscards
706 Joliet St
Dyer, IN 46311-1720
(219) 322-5080
www.morefunsportscards.com

The Book Broker
2717 Covert Ave
Evansville, IN 47714-3950
(812) 479-5647

K&L Cards
265 S State Road 135
Greenwood, IN 46142-1421
(317) 883-2240
lscantcard@aol.com

The Sweet Spot
605 McCord Road Suite A
Valparaiso, IN 46383
219-242-8692
thevalposweetspot@comcast.net

KANSAS

Rock's Dugout
3232 N Rock Rd
Wichita, KS 67226-1313
(316) 682-7902
jcruocco@hotmail.com

KENTUCKY

Baseball Cards Warehouse
3323 Partner Pl Ste 9
Lexington, KY 40503-3505
(859) 223-7116
larrywatt@aol.com

LOUISIANA

Jason's Sports Cards
5734 S. Sherwood Forest Blvd.
Baton Rouge, LA 70726
(225) 291-4018

Louisianas Double Play
2834 S Sherwood Forest Blvd Ste C5
Baton Rouge, LA 70816-2246
(225) 296-5812
ladp@cox.net

MASSACHUSETTS

Slapshot Sportscards
184 Broadway
Saugus, MA 01906-1099
(781) 231-1800
slapshotsport@aol.com

MARYLAND

Baseball Card Outlet
7502 Eastern Ave
Baltimore, MD 21224-1919
(410) 284-7922
bcoutlet@aol.com

DugoutZone
9210 Baltimore National Pike
Ellicott City, MD 21042-2615
(410) 461-8664
www.dugoutzone.com

MICHIGAN

The Stadium
3980 East Wilder Rd
Bay City, MI 48706-2157
(989) 667-0450
dumars1935@charter.net

Kruk Cards
210 Campbell St
Rochester, MI 48307
248-656-6028
krukcards.com

Stadium Cards & Comics
2061 Golfside Dr
Ypsilanti, MI 48197-1303
(734) 434-0283
fennydude@aol.com

MINNESOTA

Tom Frantzen Sports-Collectibles
Mounds View Square Shopping Center
2559 Cty Rd 10
Mounds View, MN 55112
(763) 786-0014
tom@frantzensports.comcastbiz.net

Three Stars Sportscards
2801 Hamline Ave N
Roseville, MN 55113-1715
(651) 633-6041
wayne@threestarssportscards.com

MISSOURI

Show-Me Sports Cards Co
706 W. US Highway 40
Blue Springs, MO 64015-4651
(816) 224-3281
nitemayre1@sbcglobal.net

Fastbreak Sports
2825 S Glenstone Ave
Springfield, MO 65804-3732
(888) 543-3411
www.FastbreakSportsFansHQ.com

MISSISSIPPI

Gulf Coast Cards & Sports Memo
2600 Beach Blvd
Biloxi, MS 39531-4606
(228) 388-5178
gulfcoastcards@cableone.net

NEW JERSEY

The Hobby Shop
1077-C Hwy 34
Aberdeen, NJ 7747
(732) 583-0505
sales@hobbyshopnj.com

Rookies and Stars
1350 Saint Georges Ave
Avenel, NJ 07001-1134
(732) 396-3870
rookies_and_stars@comcast.net

East Coast Connection
288 Ridge Road
Lyndhurst, NJ 07071
201-438-4327
eastcoastconnection.net

NEVADA

Ultimate Sports Cards & Memorabilia
450 Fremont St #183
Las Vegas, NV 89101
702-363-7999
ultimatesportscardslv@yahoo.com

Ultimate Sportscards
3211 N Tenaya Way Ste 103
Las Vegas, NV 89129-7440
(702) 363-7999

NEW YORK

BP Sportscards & Memorabilia
38 N Main St
Florida, NY 10921-1319
(845) 651-1660
www.bpsportscards.com

Chameleon Comics
3 Maiden Ln
New York, NY 10038-4008
(212) 587-3411
steve@chameleoncomics.com

Dave & Adam's Card World
1595 Military Road
Niagra Falls, NY 14304
716-299-0777
dacardworld.com
Beckett Marketplace

Dave & Adam's Card World
3217F Southwestern Blvd
Orchard Park, NY 14127
716-677-1840
dacardworld.com
Beckett Marketplace

Dave & Adam's Card World
2217 Sheridan Drive
Tonawanda, NY 14223
716-837-4920
dacardworld.com
Beckett Marketplace

DCS Sportscards
3381C Merrick Rd
Wantagh, NY 11793
516-946-6334
dcssportscards.com

A&S Sports LLC
825 Carman Ave
Westbury, NY 11590
(516) 398-7800
www.nysportscards.com

BAB Collectibles
47 Mamaroneck Ave
White Plains, NY 10601
914-358-9494
brian31862000@yahoo.com

Dave & Adam's Card World
5575 Transit Rd
Williamsville, NY 14221
716-689-2273
dacardworld.com
Beckett Marketplace

NORTH CAROLINA

The Dugout Cards & Games
2109 Catawba Valley Blvd. SE
Hickory, NC 28602
(828) 322-4164
www.hickorydugout.com

NORTH DAKOTA

Big Nicks Sports Cards
3902 13th ave S Suite #100
West Acres Mall
Fargo, ND 58103
(701) 277-1989
bignickscards@cableone.net

OHIO

Sportmark
P O Box 805
Miamisburg, OH 45343
(937) 238-9771
sportmarkcards@gmail.com

OKLAHOMA

Al's Sportscards and Gaming
116 East 15th St
Edmond, OK 73013-4303
(405) 348-7583
Alscards7599@sbcglobal.net

Roundup Sportscards
211 North Perkins Road Suite 21
Stillwater, OK 74074
(719) 323-5900
brad_edwards52@yahoo.com

PENNSYLVANIA

Sports Vault
Exton Sq.Mall 229 Exton Sq. Prkwy.
Exton, PA 19341
(610) 561-6300
joe.deeney@strategicsports.com.

Steel City Collectibles
Westmoreland Mall
5256 Route 30
Greensburg, PA 15601
724-830-9369
steelcitycollect.com

Sportscard Playground
297 W County Line Rd
Hatboro, PA 19040-1719
(215) 675-6644
heidig@sportscardplayground.com

Shaffer's Trading Cards
2849 Westbranch Hwy
Lewisburg, PA 17837
570-524-4341
www.shafferstradingcards.com

Shaffer's Trading Cards
2849 Westbranch Hwy
Lewisburg, PA 17837
(570) 524-4341

Sports Cards Etc
110 West McMurray Road
McMurray, PA 15317
(724) 942-8085

Steel City Collectibles
Ross Park Mall
1000 Ross Park Mall Drive
Pittsburgh, PA 15237
412-366-5858
steelcitycollect.com

SOUTH DAKOTA

Heroes Sports Cards & Games
2425 A Mt. Rushmore Road
Rapid City, SD 57701
605-341-5280
heroes@rushmore.com

Triple Play Sports Cards
3816 S Western Ave
Sioux Falls, SD 57105-6511
(605) 332-4815
www.tpsc.net

TENNESSEE

Tennessee Card Company
2829 Bartlett Blvd.
Bartlett, TN 38134-4529
(901) 372-1408
tennesseecardco@bellsouth.net

Sports Treasures LLC
4819 N Broadway St
Knoxville, TN 37918-1708
(865) 688-2273
ebarkley23@comcast.net

TEXAS

Superior Sports Investments
P.O. Box 183613
Arlington, TX 76096
(817) 557-9196

Nick's Sportscards
7522 Campbell Road #119
Dallas, TX 75248-1726
(972) 248-2271
www.nickscards.net

Triple Cards & Collectibles
2452 Ave K
Plano, TX 75074-5911
(972) 509-5263
triplecard@sbcglobal.net

All American Sports Wear
3903 Eisenhauer Road
San Antonio, TX 78218-3408
(210) 393-5521
saallamerican@aol.com

Sports Cards Plus
2239 Lock Hill Selma Rd
San Antonio, TX 78230
(210) 524-2337
www.sportscardsplussa.com

Whats On Second
4177 Naco Perrin Blvd
San Antonio, TX 78217-2505
(210) 590-8444
whatsonsecond@stic.net

UTAH

House Of Cards & Coins
4700 S 900 E Ste 28
Salt Lake City, UT 84117-4980
(801) 485-7337
jeffj@pntgame.com

VIRGINIA

Blowout Cards
The Fantastic Store
14508 Lee Rd - Unit F
Chantilly, VA 20151
Blowoutcards.com

Jerseys Cards And Comics
1818 Todds Ln Ste G
Hampton, VA 23666-3139
(757) 890-2842

The Tenth Inning
3324 W. Mercury Blvd.
Hampton, VA 23666
(757) 827-1667
thetenthinning79@yahoo.com

WASHINGTON

Atomic Cards
2008 S 314th St
Federal Way, WA 98003-5475
(866) 440-9224
westcoastbryan@yahoo.com

D J's Sportcards & Comics
1630 Duvall Ave NE
Renton, WA 98059-3976
(425) 235-4357
dj@djssportscards.com

Card Exchange
14020 Aurora Ave N
Seattle, WA 98133-6915
(206) 440-5467
sportsryter@aol.com

Knutsen's Northwest-Sportscards
3816 Bridgeport Way West
University Place, WA 98466
(253) 564-9204
northwestsportscards@yahoo.com

WISCONSIN

Larry Fritsch Cards
735 Old Wausau Road
Stevens Point, WI 54481
866-595-8687
fritschcards.com

CANADA

Ramjak Sports
2401 Faithfull Avenue
Saskatoon, SK, CANADA S7K 4B5
306-974-7778
ramjak.sports@sasktel.net

ONLINE

Baseball Card Exchange
bbcexchange.com

Blowout Cards
Blowoutcards.com

CheckOutMyCards
checkoutmycards.com

Dave & Adam's Card World
dacardworld.com
Beckett Marketplace

DCS Sportscards
dcssportscards.com

GotBaseballCards.com
770-736-9998
gotbaseballcards.com

Pittsburgh Sports Cards
pittsburghsportscards.com

The Pit.com
thepit.com

**To be listed in the *Basketball Dealer Directory*,
please contact Bill Dumas at 972.448.9147 or bdumas@beckett.com**

BECKETT.
BASKETBALL
ONLINE PRICE GUIDE
Inventory and price all of your cards at the click of a button
WWW.BECKETT.COM/OPG
COMPUTER - THINKSTOCK PHOTO

1994 A Question of Sport UK

These cards are part of a British board game "A Question of Sport" in which participants attempt to name an athlete by seeing a picture of them. These white bordered, full color cards measure 2 1/4" by 3 1/2" and have a back that contains only the player's name surrounded by a blue border on white card stock. We've arranged the unnumbered cards alphabetically below.

COMPLETE SET (79) 20.00 50.00
37 Michael Jordan 3.20 8.00

1996 A Question of Sport Who Am I

This 100-card multi-sport set was from a game exclusively sold in England. Each front of the game cards features a blue and yellow border with a small color photo of the featured athlete on the top half. The player's name is listed below in light blue after a series of written clues about the player's identity. The only notable basketball player is Magic Johnson. The cards are not numbered and are checklisted below in alphabetical order.

COMPLETE SET (100) 30.00 75.00
48 Magic Johnson 3.20 8.00

1970-71 ABA All-Star 5x7 Picture Pack

his 12-card set featues black and white photos of ABA All-Stars from 1970-71. Each photo measures 5" by 7". The backs are blank and checklisted below in lphabetical order.

OMPLETE SET (12) 75.00 150.00
Rick Barry 20.00 40.00
John Brisker 5.00 10.00
George Carter 5.00 10.00
Mack Calvin 6.00 12.00
Joe Caldwell 6.00 12.00
Warren Jabali 7.50 15.00
Larry Jones 5.00 10.00
George Lehmann 5.00 10.00
Jim McDaniel 5.00 10.00
) Bill Melchionni 7.50 15.00
John Roche 5.00 10.00
George Thompson 5.00 10.00

2009-10 Absolute Memorabilia

1-141 PRINT RUN 499 SER.#'d SETS
Y AU RC PRINT RUNS LISTED IN CHECKLIST
Kobe Bryant 6.00 15.00
Dwight Howard 2.00 5.00
Rajon Rondo 1.50 4.00
Samuel Dalembert .75 2.00
eBron James 6.00 15.00
Chris Andersen 2.00 5.00
Dwyane Wade 2.50 6.00
Chris Bosh 1.25 3.00
Steve Nash 1.25 3.00
LaMarcus Aldridge 1.25 3.00
Danilo Gallinari 1.25 3.00
Joakim Noah 1.25 3.00
Brook Lopez 1.25 3.00
Tony Parker 1.25 3.00
Deron Williams 1.25 3.00
Marc Gasol 1.25 3.00
Joe Johnson 1.25 3.00
Dirk Nowitzki 1.50 4.00
Chris Paul 2.00 5.00
Chris Kaman 1.00 2.50
Kevin Love 2.00 5.00
Danny Granger 1.25 3.00
Antawn Jamison 1.25 3.00
Trevor Ariza .75 2.00
Carmelo Anthony 1.50 4.00
Monta Ellis 1.25 3.00
Al Horford 1.25 3.00
Kevin Durant 4.00 10.00
Brandon Roy 1.25 3.00
Corey Maggette 1.00 2.50
ndre Iguodala 1.25 3.00
ay Allen 1.25 3.00
haquille O'Neal 2.50 6.00
amal Crawford 1.00 2.50
erald Wallace 1.25 3.00
avid West 1.25 3.00
ach Randolph 1.00 2.50
odney Stuckey 1.25 3.00
errick Rose 4.00 10.00
m Duncan 2.00 5.00
avid Lee 1.00 2.50
mare Stoudemire 1.25 3.00
aron Brooks .75 2.00
mar Odom 1.25 3.00
n Wallace 1.25 3.00
J. Barea 1.50 4.00
neka Okafor 1.25 3.00
endan Haywood .75 2.00
ichael Beasley 1.25 3.00
len Iverson 1.50 4.00
drea Bargnani 1.00 2.50
ne 1.00 2.50
ul Pierce 1.50 4.00
Williams 1.00 2.50
son Thompson .75 2.00
56 Russell Westbrook 2.00 5.00
57 Andrew Bogut 1.25 3.00
58 Al Jefferson 1.25 3.00
59 Devin Harris 1.25 3.00
60 Vince Carter 1.50 4.00
61 Jason Kidd 1.25 3.00
62 Kevin Garnett 2.50 6.00
63 Rudy Gay 1.25 3.00
64 Stephen Jackson 1.00 2.50
65 Luol Deng 1.25 3.00
66 Carl Landry .75 2.00
67 Baron Davis 1.25 3.00
68 Ben Gordon 1.25 3.00
69 Al Harrington 1.00 2.50
70 Carlos Boozer 1.25 3.00
71 Pau Gasol 1.25 3.00
72 Luke Ridnour 1.00 2.50
73 Josh Smith 1.25 3.00
74 Raymond Felton 1.00 2.50
75 Kendrick Perkins 1.00 2.50
76 Dahntay Jones .75 2.00
77 Kevin Martin 1.25 3.00
78 Shawn Marion 1.25 3.00
79 Marcus Camby .75 2.00
80 Jermaine O'Neal 1.25 3.00
81 Manu Ginobili 1.25 3.00
82 Richard Hamilton 1.00 2.50
83 Rashard Lewis 1.00 2.50
84 Jason Richardson 1.25 3.00
85 Jeff Green 1.00 2.50
86 Elton Brand 1.25 3.00
87 Mehmet Okur .75 2.00
88 O.J. Mayo 1.25 3.00
89 Caron Butler 1.25 3.00
90 Rasheed Wallace 1.25 3.00
91 Jason Terry 1.00 2.50
92 Ron Artest 1.25 3.00
93 Jason Williams 1.00 2.50
94 Hedo Turkoglu 1.25 3.00
95 Yao Ming 1.50 4.00
96 Chauncey Billups 1.25 3.00
97 Nate Robinson 1.25 3.00
98 Mike Dunleavy .75 2.00
99 Louis Williams 1.00 2.50
100 Juwan Howard 1.00 2.50
101 Jalen Rose 1.25 3.00
102 Chris Webber 1.25 3.00
103 David Robinson 2.00 5.00
104 Chuck Person 1.25 3.00
105 Alvan Adams 1.25 3.00
106 Larry Bird 4.00 10.00
107 Scottie Pippen 2.50 6.00
108 Connie Hawkins 1.25 3.00
109 Magic Johnson 3.00 8.00
110 Bill Laimbeer 1.25 3.00
111 Shawn Bradley 1.25 3.00
112 Kelly Tripucka 1.25 3.00
113 Robert Horry 1.50 4.00
114 Spud Webb 1.25 3.00
115 World B. Free 1.25 3.00
116 Tim Hardaway 1.25 3.00
117 Sean Elliott 1.25 3.00
118 Anfernee Hardaway 3.00 8.00
119 Paul Westphal 1.25 3.00
120 Pete Maravich 4.00 10.00
121 Willis Reed 1.25 3.00
122 Nate Thurmond 1.25 3.00
123 Mychal Thompson 1.25 3.00
124 Kenny Anderson 1.25 3.00
125 Jerry West 1.50 4.00
126 Marcus Thornton RC 3.00 8.00
127 Jonas Jerebko RC 2.00 5.00
128 Wesley Matthews RC 3.00 8.00
129 A.J. Price RC 2.00 5.00
130 David Andersen RC 2.00 5.00
131 Serge Ibaka RC 5.00 12.00
132 Garrett Temple RC 2.00 5.00
133 Derrick Brown RC 2.00 5.00
134 Sundiata Gaines RC 2.00 5.00
135 Chris Hunter RC 2.00 5.00
136 Jon Brockman RC 2.00 5.00
137 Danny Green RC 3.00 8.00
138 Marcus Landry RC 2.00 5.00
139 Lester Hudson RC 2.00 5.00
140 Patrick Mills RC 2.50 6.00
141 Dante Cunningham RC 2.00 5.00
142 Brandon Jennings JSY AU/499 RC 12.00 30.00
143 Jonny Flynn JSY AU/349 RC 6.00 15.00
144 Stephen Curry JSY AU/499 RC 15.00 40.00
145 Omri Casspi JSY AU/499 RC 6.00 15.00
146 James Harden JSY AU/499 RC 20.00 50.00
147 Ty Lawson JSY AU/349 RC 10.00 25.00
148 Taj Gibson JSY AU/499 RC 8.00 20.00
149 Tyler Hansbrough JSY AU/499 RC 10.00 25.00
150 Chase Budinger JSY AU/499 RC 6.00 15.00
151 Sam Young JSY AU/299 RC 6.00 15.00
152 DeJuan Blair JSY AU/499 RC 8.00 20.00
153 Terrence Williams JSY AU/499 RC 6.00 15.00
154 Darren Collison JSY AU/499 RC 10.00 25.00
155 Toney Douglas JSY AU/499 RC 6.00 15.00
156 Wayne Ellington JSY AU/499 RC 6.00 15.00
157 Jrue Holiday JSY AU/499 RC 12.00 30.00
158 Eric Maynor JSY AU/499 RC 6.00 15.00
159 Rodrigue Beaubois JSY AU/349 RC 8.00 20.00
160 Austin Daye JSY AU/499 RC 6.00 15.00
161 Jodie Meeks JSY AU/499 RC 8.00 20.00
162 Jeff Pendergraph JSY AU/499 RC 6.00 15.00
163 Jordan Hill JSY AU/499 RC 6.00 15.00
164 DeMarre Carroll JSY AU/499 RC 6.00 15.00
165 Jeff Teague JSY AU/499 RC 8.00 20.00
166 Tyreke Evans JSY AU/499 RC 15.00 40.00
167 James Johnson JSY AU/349 RC 6.00 15.00
168 Earl Clark JSY AU/499 RC 6.00 15.00
169 Gerald Henderson JSY AU/499 RC 6.00 15.00
170 DaJuan Summers JSY AU/499 RC 6.00 15.00
171 Hasheem Thabeet JSY AU/499 RC 6.00 15.00
172 Blake Griffin JSY AU/499 RC 100.00 200.00
173 B.J. Mullens JSY AU/499 RC 6.00 15.00
174 Taylor Griffin JSY AU/499 RC 6.00 15.00
175 Jermaine Taylor JSY AU/299 RC 6.00 15.00
176 DeMar DeRozan JSY AU/499 RC 10.00 25.00

2009-10 Absolute Memorabilia Spectrum Gold

*GOLD: .6X TO 1.5X BASE HI
PRINT RUN 100 SER.#'d SETS

2009-10 Absolute Memorabilia Spectrum Platinum

*PLATINUM: 1.25X TO 3X BASE HI
PRINT RUN 25 SER.#'d SETS
118 Anfernee Hardaway 20.00 50.00

2009-10 Absolute Memorabilia Frequent Flyer

COMPLETE SET (19) 20.00 40.00
STATED PRINT RUN 100 SER.#'d SETS
1 Devin Harris 1.25 3.00
2 Elton Brand 1.25 3.00
3 Eric Gordon 1.25 3.00
5 Kobe Bryant 6.00 15.00
6 LeBron James 6.00 15.00
7 Kevin Martin 1.25 3.00
8 Shawn Marion 1.25 3.00
9 Vince Carter 1.50 4.00
10 DeMar DeRozan 2.00 5.00
11 Dwyane Wade 2.50 6.00
12 Nate Robinson 1.25 3.00
13 Allen Iverson 1.50 4.00
14 Amare Stoudemire 1.25 3.00
15 Gerald Wallace 1.25 3.00
16 Carmelo Anthony 1.50 4.00
17 Kevin Love 2.00 5.00
18 Ron Artest 1.25 3.00
19 Joe Johnson 1.25 3.00
20 Trevor Ariza .75 2.00

2009-10 Absolute Memorabilia Frequent Flyer Materials

STATED PRINT RUN 10 TO 100 SER.#'d SETS
SOME UNPRICED DUE TO SCARCITY
UNPRICED PRIME PRINT RUN 10 SER.#'d SETS
1 Devin Harris/100 3.00 8.00
2 Elton Brand/100 3.00 8.00
3 Eric Gordon/100 3.00 8.00
5 Kobe Bryant/100 10.00 25.00
6 LeBron James/100 10.00 25.00
7 Kevin Martin/100 3.00 8.00
8 Shawn Marion/100 3.00 8.00
9 Vince Carter/100 4.00 10.00
10 DeMar DeRozan/100 5.00 12.00
11 Dwyane Wade/50 6.00 15.00
12 Nate Robinson/100 3.00 8.00
13 Allen Iverson/25 8.00 20.00
15 Gerald Wallace/100 3.00 8.00
16 Carmelo Anthony/100 4.00 10.00
17 Kevin Love/100 5.00 12.00
19 Joe Johnson/100 3.00 8.00

2009-10 Absolute Memorabilia Frequent Flyer Materials Jersey Number

STATED PRINT RUN 5 TO 25 SER.#'d SETS
SOME UNPRICED DUE TO SCARCITY
UNPRICED PRIME PRINT RUN 5 SER.#'d SETS
1 Devin Harris/25 5.00 12.00
2 Elton Brand/25 5.00 12.00
3 Eric Gordon/25 5.00 12.00
5 Kobe Bryant/25 12.50 30.00
6 LeBron James/25 12.50 30.00
7 Kevin Martin/25 5.00 12.00
8 Shawn Marion/25 5.00 12.00
9 Vince Carter/25 6.00 15.00
10 DeMar DeRozan/25 8.00 20.00
11 Dwyane Wade/25 10.00 25.00
12 Nate Robinson/25 5.00 12.00
15 Gerald Wallace/25 5.00 12.00
16 Carmelo Anthony/25 6.00 15.00
17 Kevin Love/25 8.00 20.00
19 Joe Johnson/25 5.00 12.00

2009-10 Absolute Memorabilia Frequent Flyer Materials Jersey Number Signatures

STATED PRINT RUN 10 TO 25 SER.#'d SETS
UNPRICED PRIME PRINT RUN 5 SER.#'d SETS
1 Devin Harris/25 6.00 15.00
3 Eric Gordon/10 12.50 30.00
5 Kobe Bryant/25 100.00 200.00
17 Kevin Love/25 15.00 40.00

2009-10 Absolute Memorabilia Frequent Flyer Materials Signatures

STATED PRINT RUN 5 TO 25 SER.#'d SETS
UNPRICED PRIME PRINT RUN 5 SER.#'d SETS
1 Devin Harris/25 6.00 15.00
3 Eric Gordon/10 12.50 30.00
5 Kobe Bryant/25 100.00 200.00
10 DeMar DeRozan/25 15.00 40.00
17 Kevin Love/25 20.00 50.00

2009-10 Absolute Memorabilia Heroes

COMPLETE SET (14) 15.00 30.00
STATED PRINT RUN 100 SER.#'d SETS
1 Ray Allen 1.25 3.00
2 Rudy Fernandez 1.00 2.50
4 T.J. Ford .75 2.00
5 Brandon Jennings 2.50 6.00
6 Lamar Odom 1.25 3.00
7 Eric Gordon 1.25 3.00
8 Devin Harris 1.25 3.00
9 LeBron James 6.00 15.00
10 Russell Westbrook 2.00 5.00
11 Tyler Hansbrough 2.00 5.00
12 David Lee 1.00 2.50
13 Jason Kidd 1.25 3.00
14 Richard Hamilton 1.00 2.50
15 Kobe Bryant 6.00 15.00

2009-10 Absolute Memorabilia Heroes Materials

STATED PRINT RUN 50 TO 100 SETS
UNPRICED PRIME PRINT RUN 10 SER.#'d SETS
1 Ray Allen/100 3.00 8.00
2 Rudy Fernandez/100 2.50 6.00
4 T.J. Ford/100 2.00 5.00
5 Brandon Jennings/100 6.00 15.00
7 Eric Gordon/100 3.00 8.00
8 Devin Harris/100 3.00 8.00
9 LeBron James/100 8.00 20.00
10 Russell Westbrook/100 5.00 12.00
11 Tyler Hansbrough/100 5.00 12.00
12 David Lee/50 2.50 6.00
13 Jason Kidd/100 3.00 8.00
15 Kobe Bryant/100 8.00 20.00

2009-10 Absolute Memorabilia Heroes Materials Signatures

STATED PRINT RUN 5 TO 25 SER.#'d SETS
SOME UNPRICED DUE TO SCARCITY
UNPRICED PRIME PRINT RUN ONE TO 5 SETS
1 Ray Allen/25 20.00 50.00
4 T.J. Ford/25 6.00 15.00
5 Brandon Jennings/25 15.00 40.00
8 Devin Harris/25 6.00 15.00
10 Russell Westbrook/25 15.00 40.00
11 Tyler Hansbrough/25 10.00 25.00
13 Jason Kidd/25 12.50 30.00
15 Kobe Bryant/25 100.00 200.00

2009-10 Absolute Memorabilia Hoopla

COMPLETE SET (20) 25.00 50.00
STATED PRINT RUN 100 SER.#'d SETS
1 LeBron James 6.00 15.00
2 Dwyane Wade 2.50 6.00
3 Chris Paul 2.00 5.00
4 Kevin Durant 4.00 10.00
5 Dwight Howard 2.00 5.00
6 Gerald Wallace 1.25 3.00
7 Kobe Bryant 6.00 15.00
8 Steve Nash 1.25 3.00
9 Kevin Garnett 2.50 6.00
10 Dirk Nowitzki 1.50 4.00
11 Josh Smith 1.25 3.00
12 Chris Bosh 1.25 3.00
13 Carmelo Anthony 1.50 4.00
14 Brandon Roy 1.25 3.00
15 Derrick Rose 4.00 10.00
16 Tracy McGrady 1.25 3.00
17 Devin Harris 1.25 3.00
18 Tony Parker 1.25 3.00
19 Allen Iverson 1.50 4.00
20 Chris Andersen 2.00 5.00

2009-10 Absolute Memorabilia Hoopla Materials

STATED PRINT RUN 25 TO 100 SETS
UNPRICED PRIME PRINT RUN 10 SER.#'d SETS
1 LeBron James/100 10.00 25.00
2 Dwyane Wade/50 6.00 15.00
3 Chris Paul/100 5.00 12.00
4 Kevin Durant/100 10.00 25.00
5 Dwight Howard/100 5.00 12.00
6 Gerald Wallace/100 3.00 8.00
7 Kobe Bryant/100 10.00 25.00
9 Kevin Garnett/100 6.00 15.00
10 Dirk Nowitzki/100 4.00 10.00
11 Josh Smith/100 3.00 8.00
12 Chris Bosh/100 3.00 8.00
13 Carmelo Anthony/100 4.00 10.00
14 Brandon Roy/100 3.00 8.00
16 Tracy McGrady/100 3.00 8.00
17 Devin Harris/100 3.00 8.00
18 Tony Parker/50 3.00 8.00
19 Allen Iverson/25 8.00 20.00
20 Chris Andersen/100 5.00 12.00

2009-10 Absolute Memorabilia Hoopla Materials Jersey Number

STATED PRINT RUN 10 TO 25 SER.#'d SETS
SOME UNPRICED DUE TO SCARCITY
UNPRICED PRIME PRINT RUN 5 SER.#'d SETS
1 LeBron James/25 15.00 30.00
2 Dwyane Wade/25 10.00 25.00
3 Chris Paul/25 8.00 20.00
5 Dwight Howard/25 8.00 20.00
6 Gerald Wallace/25 5.00 12.00
7 Kobe Bryant/25 15.00 30.00
11 Josh Smith/25 5.00 12.00
13 Carmelo Anthony/25 6.00 15.00
16 Tracy McGrady/25 5.00 12.00
17 Devin Harris/25 5.00 12.00
18 Tony Parker/25 5.00 12.00
20 Chris Andersen/25 8.00 20.00

2009-10 Absolute Memorabilia Hoopla Materials Jersey Number Signatures

STATED PRINT RUN 5 TO 25 SER.#'d SETS
SOME NOT PRICED DUE TO SCARCITY
UNPRICED PRIME PRINT RUN 5 SER.#'d SETS
7 Kobe Bryant/25 125.00 225.00
16 Tracy McGrady/25 20.00 40.00
17 Devin Harris/25 6.00 15.00
18 Tony Parker/25 15.00 30.00

2009-10 Absolute Memorabilia Hoopla Materials Signatures

STATED PRINT RUN 25 SER.#'d SETS
UNPRICED PRIME PRINT RUN 5 SER.#'d SETS
7 Kobe Bryant 100.00 200.00
16 Tracy McGrady 15.00 30.00
17 Devin Harris 6.00 15.00
18 Tony Parker 15.00 30.00

2009-10 Absolute Memorabilia Marks of Fame

COMPLETE SET (10) 15.00 30.00
STATED PRINT RUN 100 SER.#'d SETS
1 LeBron James 6.00 15.00
2 Kareem Abdul-Jabbar 2.00 5.00
3 Allen Iverson 1.50 4.00
4 Magic Johnson 3.00 8.00
5 Ray Allen 1.25 3.00
6 Dikembe Mutombo 1.25 3.00
7 Dirk Nowitzki 1.50 4.00
8 Bill Russell 2.00 5.00
9 Kobe Bryant 6.00 15.00
10 Mark Price 1.25 3.00

2009-10 Absolute Memorabilia Marks of Fame Materials

STATED PRINT RUN 25 TO 100 SETS
UNPRICED PRIME PRINT RUN 10 SER.#'d SETS
1 LeBron James/100 8.00 20.00
2 Kareem Abdul-Jabbar/100 6.00 15.00
3 Allen Iverson/25 8.00 20.00
4 Magic Johnson/100 8.00 20.00
5 Ray Allen/100 3.00 8.00
6 Dikembe Mutombo/100 4.00 10.00
7 Dirk Nowitzki/100 4.00 10.00
9 Kobe Bryant/100 8.00 20.00
10 Mark Price/100 4.00 10.00

2009-10 Absolute Memorabilia Marks of Fame Materials Signatures

STATED PRINT RUN 8 TO 25 SER.#'d SETS
SOME NOT PRICED DUE TO SCARCITY
UNPRICED PRIME PRINT RUN 5 SER.#'d SETS
4 Magic Johnson/25 40.00 100.00
5 Ray Allen/25 25.00 50.00
9 Kobe Bryant/25 100.00 200.00

2009-10 Absolute Memorabilia Materials Prime Spectrum

STATED PRINT RUN ONE TO 25 SER.#'d SETS
SOME NOT PRICED DUE TO SCARCITY
1 Kobe Bryant/25 20.00 50.00
2 Dwight Howard/25 10.00 25.00
3 Rajon Rondo/25 10.00 25.00
4 Samuel Dalembert/25 4.00 10.00
5 LeBron James/25 20.00 50.00
6 Chris Andersen/25 10.00 25.00
7 Dwyane Wade/25 15.00 40.00
8 Chris Bosh/25 6.00 15.00
10 LaMarcus Aldridge/25 6.00 15.00
11 Danilo Gallinari/25 6.00 15.00
12 Joakim Noah/25 6.00 15.00
13 Brook Lopez/25 6.00 15.00
15 Deron Williams/25 6.00 15.00
16 Marc Gasol/25 6.00 15.00
17 Joe Johnson/25 6.00 15.00
18 Dirk Nowitzki/25 10.00 25.00
19 Chris Paul/25 10.00 25.00
21 Kevin Love/25 10.00 25.00
22 Danny Granger/25 6.00 15.00
25 Carmelo Anthony/25 8.00 20.00
27 Al Horford/25 6.00 15.00
28 Kevin Durant/25 20.00 50.00
29 Brandon Roy/25 6.00 15.00
30 Corey Maggette/25 5.00 12.00
31 Andre Iguodala/25 6.00 15.00
32 Ray Allen/25 6.00 15.00
33 Shaquille O'Neal/25 20.00 50.00
35 Gerald Wallace/25 6.00 15.00
36 David West/25 6.00 15.00
38 Rodney Stuckey/25 6.00 15.00
40 Tim Duncan/25 10.00 25.00
41 David Lee/25 5.00 12.00
46 J.J. Barea/25 12.50 30.00
47 Emeka Okafor/25 6.00 15.00
51 Andrea Bargnani/25 5.00 12.00
53 Paul Pierce/25 8.00 20.00
56 Russell Westbrook/25 10.00 25.00
57 Andrew Bogut/25 6.00 15.00
58 Al Jefferson/25 6.00 15.00
59 Devin Harris/25 6.00 15.00
60 Vince Carter/25 8.00 20.00
61 Jason Kidd/15 6.00 15.00
62 Kevin Garnett/25 12.00 30.00
63 Rudy Gay/25 6.00 15.00
65 Luol Deng/25 6.00 15.00
67 Baron Davis/25 6.00 15.00
70 Carlos Boozer/25 6.00 15.00
73 Josh Smith/25 6.00 15.00
74 Raymond Felton/25 5.00 12.00
77 Kevin Martin/25 6.00 15.00
79 Marcus Camby/25 4.00 10.00
81 Manu Ginobili/25 8.00 20.00
83 Rashard Lewis/25 5.00 12.00
85 Jeff Green/25 5.00 12.00
86 Elton Brand/25 6.00 15.00
87 Mehmet Okur/25 4.00 10.00
88 O.J. Mayo/25 6.00 15.00
90 Rasheed Wallace/25 6.00 15.00
91 Jason Terry/25 5.00 12.00
94 Hedo Turkoglu/25 6.00 15.00
96 Chauncey Billups/25 6.00 15.00
98 Mike Dunleavy/25 4.00 10.00
102 Chris Webber/25 15.00 40.00
104 Chuck Person/25 6.00 15.00
105 Alvan Adams/25 6.00 15.00
106 Larry Bird/25 15.00 30.00
109 Magic Johnson/25 15.00 30.00
113 Robert Horry/25 10.00 25.00
124 Kenny Anderson/25 6.00 15.00
125 Jerry West/15 15.00 40.00

2009-10 Absolute Memorabilia NBA Icons

COMPLETE SET (15) 40.00 70.00
STATED PRINT RUN 100 SER.#'d SETS
1 Jerry West 4.00 10.00
2 Patrick Ewing 4.00 10.00
3 Scottie Pippen 6.00 15.00
4 Reggie Lewis 3.00 8.00
5 Alonzo Mourning 4.00 10.00
6 Karl Malone 4.00 10.00
7 Dominique Wilkins 4.00 10.00
8 Willis Reed 3.00 8.00
9 Tim Hardaway 3.00 8.00
10 George Mikan 6.00 15.00
11 George Gervin 3.00 8.00
12 John Stockton 5.00 12.00
13 Bob Lanier 3.00 8.00
14 Mark Aguirre 3.00 8.00
15 Mark Eaton 3.00 8.00

2009-10 Absolute Memorabilia NBA Icons Materials

STATED PRINT RUN 5 TO 100 SETS
SOME NOT PRICED DUE TO SCARCITY
UNPRICED PRIME PRINT RUN 5 TO 10 SETS
UNPRICED SIG.MAT PRINT RUN 5 SETS
UNPRICED SIG.MAT PRIME PRINT RUN 5 SETS
2 Patrick Ewing/100 6.00 15.00
4 Reggie Lewis/100 10.00 25.00
6 Karl Malone/100 6.00 15.00
7 Dominique Wilkins/49 6.00 15.00
10 George Mikan/50 20.00 40.00
12 John Stockton/100 8.00 20.00
13 Bob Lanier/100 5.00 12.00
15 Mark Eaton/100 5.00 12.00

2009-10 Absolute Memorabilia Patches Jumbo Prime Spectrum

STATED PRINT RUN 25 SER.#'d SETS
1 Chris Paul 20.00 50.00
2 Danny Granger 12.00 30.00
3 Josh Smith 12.00 30.00
4 Marc Gasol 12.00 30.00
5 Kobe Bryant 60.00 150.00
6 Andre Iguodala 12.00 30.00
7 Kevin Garnett 30.00 80.00
8 Antawn Jamison 12.00 30.00
9 Raymond Felton 10.00 25.00
10 Marcus Camby 8.00 20.00

2009-10 Absolute Memorabilia Redemptions

EXCHANGES FOR FULL SIZE ITEMS
NNO Kobe Bryant Jersey/24 600.00 900.00
NNO Kobe Bryant Bsktbll/24 400.00 800.00

2009-10 Absolute Memorabilia Rookie Materials Jumbo Jersey Numbers Basketball

STATED PRINT RUN 25 SER.#'d SETS
UNPRICED PRIME PRINT RUN 10 SER.#'d SETS
UNPRICED PRIME SPECT.PRINT RUN 5 SETS
142 Brandon Jennings 10.00 25.00
143 Jonny Flynn 5.00 12.00
144 Stephen Curry 12.00 30.00
145 Omri Casspi 5.00 12.00
146 James Harden 15.00 40.00
147 Ty Lawson 8.00 20.00
148 Taj Gibson 6.00 15.00
149 Tyler Hansbrough 8.00 20.00
150 Chase Budinger 5.00 12.00
151 Sam Young 5.00 12.00
152 DeJuan Blair 6.00 15.00
153 Terrence Williams 5.00 12.00
154 Darren Collison 8.00 20.00
155 Toney Douglas 5.00 12.00
156 Wayne Ellington 5.00 12.00
157 Jrue Holiday 10.00 25.00
158 Eric Maynor 5.00 12.00
159 Rodrigue Beaubois 6.00 15.00
160 Austin Daye 5.00 12.00
161 Jodie Meeks 6.00 15.00
162 Jeff Pendergraph 5.00 12.00
163 Jordan Hill 5.00 12.00
164 DeMarre Carroll 5.00 12.00
165 Jeff Teague 6.00 15.00
166 Tyreke Evans 12.00 30.00
167 James Johnson 5.00 12.00
168 Earl Clark 5.00 12.00
169 Gerald Henderson 5.00 12.00
170 DaJuan Summers 5.00 12.00
171 Hasheem Thabeet 5.00 12.00
172 Blake Griffin 30.00 80.00
173 B.J. Mullens 5.00 12.00
174 Taylor Griffin 5.00 12.00
175 Jermaine Taylor 5.00 12.00
176 DeMar DeRozan 8.00 20.00

2009-10 Absolute Memorabilia Rookie Materials Jumbo Jersey Numbers Basketball Signatures

STATED PRINT RUN 25 SER.#'d SETS
UNPRICED PRIME PRINT RUN 5 SER.#'d SETS
UNPRICED PRIME SPECT.PRINT RUN 5 SETS
142 Brandon Jennings 20.00 50.00
143 Jonny Flynn 8.00 20.00
144 Stephen Curry 25.00 60.00
145 Omri Casspi 8.00 20.00
146 James Harden 25.00 60.00
147 Ty Lawson 12.00 30.00
148 Taj Gibson 10.00 25.00
149 Tyler Hansbrough 12.00 30.00
150 Chase Budinger 8.00 20.00
151 Sam Young 8.00 20.00
152 DeJuan Blair 10.00 25.00
153 Terrence Williams 8.00 20.00
154 Darren Collison 12.00 30.00
155 Toney Douglas 8.00 20.00
156 Wayne Ellington 8.00 20.00
157 Jrue Holiday 20.00 50.00
158 Eric Maynor 8.00 20.00
159 Rodrigue Beaubois 10.00 25.00
160 Austin Daye 8.00 20.00
161 Jodie Meeks 10.00 25.0
162 Jeff Pendergraph 8.00
163 Jordan Hill 8.0
164 DeMarre Carroll 8.00 20.00
165 Jeff Teague 10.00 25.00
166 Tyreke Evans 25.00 60.00
167 James Johnson 8.00 20.00
168 Earl Clark 8.00 20.00
169 Gerald Henderson 8.00 20.00
170 DaJuan Summers 8.00 20.00
171 Hasheem Thabeet 8.00 20.00
172 Blake Griffin 200.00 400.00
173 B.J. Mullens 8.00 20.00
174 Taylor Griffin 8.00 20.00
175 Jermaine Taylor 8.00 20.00
176 DeMar DeRozan 15.00 40.00

2009-10 Absolute Memorabilia Spectrum Signatures Gold

STATED PRINT RUN 20 TO 249 SETS
1 Kobe Bryant/99 75.00 150.00
14 Tony Parker/49 10.00 25.00
15 Deron Williams/49 10.00 25.00
21 Kevin Love/99 10.00 25.00
22 Danny Granger/49 5.00 12.00
31 Andre Iguodala/49 5.00 12.00
32 Ray Allen/49 15.00 40.00
43 Aaron Brooks/49 5.00 12.00
46 J.J. Barea/49 12.50 30.00
47 Emeka Okafor/49 5.00 12.00
51 Andrea Bargnani/49 5.00 12.00
56 Russell Westbrook/49 15.00 40.00
59 Devin Harris/49 5.00 12.00
61 Jason Kidd/49 10.00 25.00
67 Baron Davis/49 6.00 15.00
70 Carlos Boozer/49 5.00 12.00
80 Jermaine O'Neal/49 6.00 15.00
82 Richard Hamilton/49 5.00 12.00
92 Ron Artest/49 15.00 40.00
96 Chauncey Billups/20 8.00 20.00
101 Jalen Rose/49 10.00 25.00
105 Alvan Adams/49 6.00 15.00
106 Larry Bird/49 40.00 80.00
107 Scottie Pippen/49 100.00 200.00
108 Connie Hawkins/49 8.00 20.00
109 Magic Johnson/49 50.00 100.00
110 Bill Laimbeer/99 6.00 15.00
111 Shawn Bradley/49 8.00 20.00
114 Spud Webb/49 6.00 15.00
115 World B. Free/49 5.00 12.00
116 Tim Hardaway/49 10.00 25.00
117 Sean Elliott/49 15.00 30.00
119 Paul Westphal/40 10.00 25.00
122 Nate Thurmond/99 5.00 12.00
125 Jerry West/49 25.00 50.00
126 Marcus Thornton/249 10.00 25.00
127 Jonas Jerebko/249 6.00 15.00
128 Wesley Matthews/249 10.00 25.00
129 A.J. Price/249 5.00 12.00
131 Serge Ibaka/249 15.00 40.00
133 Derrick Brown/99 5.00 12.00
134 Sundiata Gaines/249 5.00 12.00
136 Jon Brockman/249 5.00 12.00
137 Danny Green/249 10.00 25.00
138 Marcus Landry/249 5.00 12.00
139 Lester Hudson/249 5.00 12.00
140 Patrick Mills/99 6.00 15.00
141 Dante Cunningham/249 5.00 12.00

2009-10 Absolute Memorabilia Spectrum Signatures Platinum

STATED PRINT RUN 5 TO 25 SER.#'d SETS
SOME UNPRICED DUE TO SCARCITY
1 Kobe Bryant/25 125.00 225.00
3 Rajon Rondo/25 25.00 50.00
14 Tony Parker/15 15.00 40.00
15 Deron Williams/25 12.00 30.00
21 Kevin Love/25 15.00 40.00
22 Danny Granger/25 6.00 15.00
31 Andre Iguodala/25 6.00 15.00
32 Ray Allen/25 25.00 50.00
43 Aaron Brooks/25 6.00 15.00
46 J.J. Barea/25 20.00 50.00
47 Emeka Okafor/25 6.00 15.00
51 Andrea Bargnani/25 6.00 15.00
56 Russell Westbrook/25 20.00 50.00
59 Devin Harris/25 6.00 15.00
61 Jason Kidd/25 15.00 30.00
67 Baron Davis/25 8.00 20.00
71 Pau Gasol/25 25.00 50.00
80 Jermaine O'Neal/25 8.00 20.00
82 Richard Hamilton/25 6.00 15.00
92 Ron Artest/25 20.00 50.00
101 Jalen Rose/25 15.00 30.00
105 Alvan Adams/25 8.00 20.00
106 Larry Bird/25 30.00 80.00
107 Scottie Pippen/25 100.00 200.00
108 Connie Hawkins/25 8.00 20.00
109 Magic Johnson/25 40.00 100.00
110 Bill Laimbeer/25 8.00 20.00
111 Shawn Bradley/25 10.00 25.00
114 Spud Webb/25 8.00 20.00
115 World B. Free/25 6.00 15.00
116 Tim Hardaway/25 15.00 40.00
117 Sean Elliott/25 20.00 40.00
119 Paul Westphal/25 12.50 30.00
121 Willis Reed/25 8.00 20.00
122 Nate Thurmond/25 8.00 20.00
125 Jerry West/25 30.00 60.00
126 Marcus Thornton/25 15.00 40.00
127 Jonas Jerebko/25 8.00
128 Wesley Matthews/25 12.00
129 A.J. Price/25
131 Serge Ibaka/25
133 Derrick Brown/25
134 Sundiata Gain
136 Jon Bro
137 D

2009-10 Absolute Memorabilia Star Gazing

COMPLETE SET (35) 40.00 80.00
STATED PRINT RUN 100 SER.#'d SETS
1 LeBron James 6.00 15.00
2 Kobe Bryant 6.00 15.00
3 Brandon Jennings 2.50 6.00
4 Tyreke Evans 3.00 8.00
5 Carmelo Anthony 1.50 4.00
6 Dwyane Wade 2.50 6.00
7 Chris Bosh 1.25 3.00
8 Pau Gasol 1.25 3.00
9 Jonny Flynn 1.25 3.00
10 Stephen Curry 3.00 8.00
11 Jason Kidd 1.25 3.00
12 Tony Parker 1.25 3.00
13 Danny Granger 1.25 3.00
14 Deron Williams 1.25 3.00
15 Dwight Howard 2.00 5.00
16 Kevin Durant 4.00 10.00
17 Blake Griffin 10.00 25.00
18 Omri Casspi 1.25 3.00
19 Kevin Garnett 2.50 6.00
20 Ray Allen 1.25 3.00
21 Shaquille O'Neal 2.50 6.00
22 Brandon Roy 1.25 3.00
23 Monta Ellis 1.25 3.00
24 Chris Paul 2.00 5.00
25 Dirk Nowitzki 1.50 4.00
26 David Lee 1.00 2.50
27 Tim Duncan 2.00 5.00
28 Antawn Jamison 1.25 3.00
29 Joe Johnson 1.25 3.00
30 Amare Stoudemire 1.25 3.00
31 Chris Kaman 1.00 2.50
32 Zach Randolph 1.00 2.50
33 Andrea Bargnani 1.00 2.50
34 Brook Lopez 1.25 3.00
35 Derrick Rose 4.00 10.00

2009-10 Absolute Memorabilia Star Gazing Jumbo Jersey Numbers

STATED PRINT RUN 10 TO 25 SER.#'d SETS
SOME NOT PRICED DUE TO SCARCITY
UNPRICED PRIME PRINT RUN ONE TO 10 SETS
1 LeBron James/25 15.00 40.00
2 Kobe Bryant/25 15.00 40.00
3 Brandon Jennings/25 10.00 25.00
4 Tyreke Evans/25 12.00 30.00
5 Carmelo Anthony/25 6.00 15.00
7 Chris Bosh/25 5.00 12.00
8 Pau Gasol/25 5.00 12.00
9 Jonny Flynn/25 5.00 12.00
10 Stephen Curry/25 12.00 30.00
11 Jason Kidd/25 5.00 12.00
13 Danny Granger/25 5.00 12.00
14 Deron Williams/25 5.00 12.00
15 Dwight Howard/25 8.00 20.00
16 Kevin Durant/25 12.00 30.00
17 Blake Griffin/25 30.00 80.00
18 Omri Casspi/25 5.00 12.00
19 Kevin Garnett/25 10.00 25.00
20 Ray Allen/25 5.00 12.00
21 Shaquille O'Neal/25 12.50 30.00
22 Brandon Roy/25 5.00 12.00
23 Monta Ellis/25 5.00 12.00
24 Chris Paul/25 8.00 20.00
25 Dirk Nowitzki/25 6.00 15.00
27 Tim Duncan/25 8.00 20.00
28 Antawn Jamison/25 5.00 12.00
29 Joe Johnson/25 5.00 12.00
33 Andrea Bargnani/25 4.00 10.00
34 Brook Lopez/25 5.00 12.00

2009-10 Absolute Memorabilia Star Gazing Jumbo Jersey Numbers Signatures

STATED PRINT RUN 10 TO 25 SER.#'d SETS
SOME UNPRICED DUE TO SCARCITY
UNPRICED PRIME PRINT RUN ONE TO 10 SETS
2 Kobe Bryant/25 100.00 200.00
3 Brandon Jennings/25 20.00 50.00
4 Tyreke Evans/25 25.00 60.00
8 Pau Gasol/25 30.00 60.00
9 Jonny Flynn/25 10.00 25.00
10 Stephen Curry/25 25.00 60.00
11 Jason Kidd/25 15.00 40.00
13 Danny Granger/25 10.00 25.00
14 Deron Williams/25 10.00 25.00
17 Blake Griffin/25 150.00 400.00
18 Omri Casspi/25 10.00 25.00
20 Ray Allen/25 25.00 60.00
33 Andrea Bargnani/25 20.00 40.00

2009-10 Absolute Memorabilia Star Gazing Jumbo Materials

STATED PRINT RUN 5 TO 25 SER.#'d SETS
UNPRICED PRIME SPECT.PRINT RUN 1 TO 5 SETS
1 LeBron James/25 15.00 40.00
2 Kobe Bryant/25 15.00 40.00
3 Brandon Jennings/25 10.00 25.00
4 Tyreke Evans/25 12.00 30.00
5 Carmelo Anthony/25 6.00 15.00
7 Chris Bosh/25 5.00 12.00
9 Jonny Flynn/25 5.00 12.00
10 Stephen Curry/25 12.00 30.00
11 Jason Kidd/25 5.00 12.00
13 Danny Granger/25 5.00 12.00
14 Deron Williams/25 5.00 12.00
15 Dwight Howard/25 8.00 20.00
16 Kevin Durant/25 12.00 30.00
17 Blake Griffin/25 30.00 80.00
18 Omri Casspi/25 5.00 12.00
19 Kevin Garnett/25 10.00 25.00
20 Ray Allen/25 10.00 25.00
21 Shaquille O'Neal/25 12.50 30.00
22 Brandon Roy/25 5.00 12.00
24 Chris Paul/25 8.00 20.00
25 Dirk Nowitzki/25 6.00 15.00
27 Tim Duncan/25 8.00 20.00
28 Antawn Jamison/25 5.00 12.00
29 Joe Johnson/25 5.00 12.00
33 Andrea Bargnani/25 4.00 10.00
34 Brook Lopez/25 5.00 12.00

2009-10 Absolute Memorabilia Star Gazing Materials

STATED PRINT RUN 10 TO 100 SER.#'d SETS
SOME NOT PRICED DUE TO SCARCITY
UNPRICED PRIME PRINT RUN 10 SER.#'d SETS
1 LeBron James/100 8.00 20.00
2 Kobe Bryant/100 8.00 20.00
3 Brandon Jennings/100 6.00 15.00
4 Tyreke Evans/100 8.00 20.00
5 Carmelo Anthony/100 4.00 10.00
6 Dwyane Wade/100 6.00 15.00
[illegible] 3.00 8.00
[illegible] 3.00 8.00
9 Jonny Flynn/100 3.00 8.00
10 Stephen Curry/100 8.00 20.00
11 Jason Kidd/100 3.00 8.00
12 Tony Parker/50 3.00 8.00
13 Danny Granger/100 3.00 8.00
14 Deron Williams/100 3.00 8.00
15 Dwight Howard/100 5.00 12.00
16 Kevin Durant/100 8.00 20.00
17 Blake Griffin/100 20.00 50.00
18 Omri Casspi/100 3.00 8.00
19 Kevin Garnett/100 6.00 15.00
20 Ray Allen/100 3.00 8.00
21 Shaquille O'Neal/100 6.00 15.00
22 Brandon Roy/100 3.00 8.00
23 Monta Ellis/100 3.00 8.00
24 Chris Paul/100 5.00 12.00
25 Dirk Nowitzki/100 4.00 10.00
26 David Lee/50 2.50 6.00
27 Tim Duncan/100 5.00 12.00
28 Antawn Jamison/100 3.00 8.00
29 Joe Johnson/100 3.00 8.00
31 Chris Kaman/25 2.50 6.00
33 Andrea Bargnani/100 2.50 6.00
34 Brook Lopez/100 3.00 8.00

2009-10 Absolute Memorabilia Star Gazing Materials Signatures

STATED PRINT RUN 25 SER.#'d SETS
UNPRICED PRIME PRINT RUN 5 SER.#'d SETS
2 Kobe Bryant 125.00 225.00
3 Brandon Jennings 20.00 50.00
4 Tyreke Evans 25.00 60.00
8 Pau Gasol 30.00 60.00
9 Jonny Flynn 10.00 25.00
10 Stephen Curry 25.00 60.00
11 Jason Kidd 15.00 40.00
12 Tony Parker 12.50 30.00
13 Danny Granger 10.00 25.00
14 Deron Williams 10.00 25.00
17 Blake Griffin 150.00 300.00
18 Omri Casspi 10.00 25.00
20 Ray Allen 20.00 50.00
33 Andrea Bargnani 10.00 25.00

2009-10 Absolute Memorabilia Team Quads TEAM Die Cut Materials

STATED PRINT RUN 25 TO 100 SER.#'d SETS
UNPRICED PRIME PRINT RUN 5 TO 10 SETS
1 Peja Stojakovic/100 6.00 15.00
David West
Emeka Okafor
Chris Paul
2 Hedo Turkoglu/100 6.00 15.00
Chris Bosh
Jose Calderon
Andrea Bargnani
3 Richard Hamilton/100 6.00 15.00
Tayshaun Prince
Ben Gordon
Rodney Stuckey
4 Andre Miller/100 6.00 15.00
LaMarcus Aldridge
Brandon Roy
Rudy Fernandez
5 Rasheed Wallace/100 15.00 30.00
Kevin Garnett
Paul Pierce
Rajon Rondo
6 Marcus Camby/100 6.00 15.00
Baron Davis
Chris Kaman
Eric Gordon
7 Shaquille O'Neal/25 8.00 20.00
Zydrunas Ilgauskas
LeBron James
Mo Williams
8 Vince Carter/100 6.00 15.00
Rashard Lewis
Dwight Howard
Jameer Nelson
9 Chris Andersen/100 6.00 15.00
Nene
Carmelo Anthony
J.R. Smith

2009-10 Absolute Memorabilia Team Tandems Materials

STATED PRINT RUN 100 SER.#'d SETS
UNPRICED PRIME PRINT RUN 10 SER.#'d SETS
1 David West 4.00 10.00
Emeka Okafor
2 Hedo Turkoglu 6.00 15.00
Jose Calderon
3 Chris Andersen 6.00 15.00
Nene
4 Andre Miller 4.00 10.00
Rudy Fernandez
5 Rajon Rondo 8.00 20.00
Rasheed Wallace
6 Boris Diaw 4.00 10.00
Raymond Felton
7 Brook Lopez 4.00 10.00
Devin Harris
8 Shaquille O'Neal 8.00 20.00
Zydrunas Ilgauskas
9 Jameer Nelson 4.00 10.00
Rashard Lewis

2009-10 Absolute Memorabilia Team Trios NBA Materials

STATED PRINT RUN 40 TO 100 SETS
UNPRICED PRIME PRINT RUN ONE TO 10 SETS
1 Joe Johnson/100 6.00 15.00
Josh Smith
Mike Bibby
2 Corey Maggett100 5.00 12.00
Monta Ellis
Stephen Curry
3 Marc Gasol/100 5.00 12.00
O.J. Mayo
Rudy Gay
4 Andre Iguodala/100 5.00 12.00
Elton Brand
Thaddeus Young
5 Kevin Garnett/100 10.00 25.00
Paul Pierce
Ray Allen
6 Al Jefferson/60 5.00 12.00
Kevin Love
Ryan Gomes
7 Jeff Green/100 10.00 25.00
Kevin Durant
Russell Westbrook
8 Carlos Boozer/40 6.00 15.00
Deron Williams
Paul Millsap
9 Aaron Brooks/100 5.00 12.00
Luis Scola
Shane Battier

2009-10 Absolute Memorabilia Tools of the Trade Materials Prime Black Spectrum

STATED PRINT RUN ONE TO 25 SER.#'d SETS
SOME UNPRICED DUE TO SCARCITY
*DOUBLE: .4X TO 1X BASE HI
DOUBLE PRINT RUN ONE TO 25 SETS
*TRIPLE: .6X TO 1.5X BASE HI
TRIPLE PRINT RUN ONE TO 25 SETS
2 Al Jefferson/25 6.00 15.00
3 Baron Davis/20 6.00 15.00
4 Brandon Roy/25 6.00 15.00
5 Carlos Boozer/25 6.00 15.00
8 D.J. Augustin/25 5.00 12.00
9 Elton Brand/25 6.00 15.00
10 Emeka Okafor/25 6.00 15.00
11 Kobe Bryant/25 20.00 50.00
12 LeBron James/25 20.00 50.00
15 Omri Casspi/25 6.00 15.00
16 Rajon Rondo/25 10.00 25.00
17 Ray Allen/25 8.00 20.00
20 Russell Westbrook/25 10.00 25.00
23 Stephen Curry/25 10.00 25.00

2009-10 Absolute Memorabilia Tools of the Trade Materials Prime Black Spectrum Jumbo

PRINT RUNS LISTED IN CHECKLIST
UNPRICED JSY NUMBER PRINT RUN 1 TO 10 SETS
2 Al Jefferson/25 10.00 25.00
3 Baron Davis/25 12.50 30.00
5 Carlos Boozer/25 10.00 25.00
9 Elton Brand/25 10.00 25.00
10 Emeka Okafor/25 10.00 25.00
11 Kobe Bryant/25 40.00 100.00
15 Omri Casspi/25 10.00 25.00
16 Rajon Rondo/25 20.00 40.00
17 Ray Allen/25 15.00 40.00
20 Russell Westbrook/25 20.00 50.00
23 Stephen Curry/25 25.00 60.00

2009-10 Absolute Memorabilia Tools of the Trade Materials Red

STATED PRINT RUN 150 TO 249 SETS
*BLUE: .4X TO 1X BASE HI
BLUE STATED PRINT RUN 30 TO 100 SETS
2 Al Jefferson/249 3.00 8.00
3 Baron Davis/249 3.00 8.00
4 Brandon Roy/249 3.00 8.00
5 Carlos Boozer/249 3.00 8.00
7 Chris Kaman/150 2.50 6.00
8 D.J. Augustin/249 2.50 6.00
9 Elton Brand/249 3.00 8.00
10 Emeka Okafor/249 3.00 8.00
11 Kobe Bryant/249 8.00 20.00
12 LeBron James/249 8.00 20.00
14 Nene/249 2.50 6.00
15 Omri Casspi/249 3.00 8.00
16 Rajon Rondo/249 4.00 10.00
17 Ray Allen/249 3.00 8.00
20 Russell Westbrook/249 5.00 12.00
22 Shane Battier/249 3.00 8.00
23 Stephen Curry/249 8.00 20.00
24 T.J. Ford/249 2.00 5.00

2010-11 Absolute Memorabilia

COMP.SET w/o SPs (100) 25.00 60.00
ROOKIE PRINT RUN 499 SER.#'d SETS
UNPRICED SPECT.BLACK PRINT RUN ONE SET
EXCH.EXPIRATION 9/16/2012
1 Kevin Durant 2.50 6.00
2 Derrick Rose 2.50 6.00
3 Blake Griffin 2.00 5.00
4 Dwight Howard 1.25 3.00
5 Kobe Bryant 4.00 10.00
6 Dwyane Wade 1.50 4.00
7 Chris Paul 1.25 3.00
8 Deron Williams .75 2.00
9 Paul Pierce 1.00 2.50
10 Stephen Curry 1.00 2.50
11 Amare Stoudemire .75 2.00
12 Dirk Nowitzki 1.00 2.50
13 Steve Nash .75 2.00
14 LeBron James 4.00 10.00
15 Carmelo Anthony 1.00 2.50
16 Brandon Jennings .75 2.00
17 Kevin Love 1.00 2.50
18 Joakim Noah .75 2.00
19 Tyreke Evans 1.00 2.50
20 Monta Ellis .75 2.00
21 Kevin Martin .75 2.00
22 Tim Duncan 1.25 3.00
23 Joe Johnson .75 2.00
24 LaMarcus Aldridge .75 2.00
25 Brook Lopez .75 2.00
26 Ray Allen .75 2.00
27 Stephen Jackson .60 1.50
28 Pau Gasol .75 2.00
29 Michael Beasley .75 2.00
30 Danny Granger .75 2.00
31 Chris Bosh .75 2.00
32 Tony Parker .75 2.00
33 Jrue Holiday .75 2.00
34 Vince Carter 1.00 2.50
35 DeMar DeRozan .75 2.00
36 Daniel Gibson .60 1.50
37 Marc Gasol .75 2.00
38 David West .75 2.00
39 David Lee .60 1.50
40 Ben Gordon .75 2.00
41 Andrew Bogut .75 2.00
42 Rajon Rondo 1.00 2.50
43 Luis Scola .60 1.50
44 Caron Butler .75 2.00
45 Andray Blatche .50 1.25
46 Antawn Jamison .75 2.00
47 O.J. Mayo .75 2.00
48 Paul Millsap .60 1.50
49 Eric Gordon .75 2.00
50 Andre Iguodala .75 2.00
51 Al Horford .60 1.50
52 Kevin Garnett 1.50 4.00
53 Luol Deng .75 2.00
54 DeJuan Blair .60 1.50
55 Mike Dunleavy .50 1.25
56 Al Thornton .60 1.50
57 Lamar Odom .75 2.00
58 Andrea Bargnani .60 1.50
59 Jason Richardson .75 2.00
60 Russell Westbrook 1.00 2.50
61 Tracy McGrady .75 2.00
62 Gerald Wallace .75 2.00
63 Jamal Crawford .60 1.50
64 Al Jefferson .75 2.00
65 Marcus Camby .50 1.25
66 Jonny Flynn .50 1.25
67 Jeff Green .60 1.50
68 Trevor Ariza .50 1.25
69 Rudy Gay .75 2.00
70 Aaron Brooks .50 1.25
71 Jason Kidd .75 2.00
72 Danilo Gallinari .75 2.00
73 Ty Lawson .75 2.00
74 Elton Brand .75 2.00
75 Terrence Williams .50 1.25
76 Richard Jefferson .75 2.00
77 J.J. Redick .75 2.00
78 Chris Kaman .60 1.50
79 Gerald Henderson .50 1.25
80 Jeff Teague .60 1.50
81 Drew Gooden .60 1.50
82 Juwan Howard .60 1.50
83 Tyler Hansbrough .75 2.00
84 Derek Fisher .60 1.50
85 Boris Diaw .60 1.50
86 Anderson Varejao .60 1.50
87 Toney Douglas .50 1.25
88 Robin Lopez .50 1.25
89 Zach Randolph .60 1.50
90 Carl Landry .50 1.25
91 Rashard Lewis .60 1.50
92 Darren Collison .75 2.00
93 Sasha Vujacic .50 1.25
94 Nene .60 1.50
95 Shaquille O'Neal 1.50 4.00
96 Emeka Okafor .75 2.00
97 Brandon Roy .75 2.00
98 Josh Smith .75 2.00
99 Devin Harris .75 2.00
100 Rodrigue Beaubois .60 1.50
101 M.L. Carr 1.50 4.00
102 Patrick Ewing 2.00 5.00
103 World B. Free 1.50 4.00
104 Tim Hardaway 1.50 4.00
105 Sam Perkins 1.50 4.00
106 Kenny Smith 1.50 4.00
107 Walt Bellamy 1.50 4.00
108 Scott Skiles 1.50 4.00
109 Robert Reid 1.50 4.00
110 Mitch Richmond 1.50 4.00
111 Nick Anderson 1.50 4.00
112 Shawn Kemp 2.50 6.00
113 Gary Payton 1.50 4.00
114 John Stockton 2.50 6.00
115 Ron Harper 1.50 4.00
116 Elgin Baylor 1.50 4.00
117 Darryl Dawkins 1.50 4.00
118 Bernard King 1.50 4.00
119 Bill Laimbeer 1.50 4.00
120 Tree Rollins 1.50 4.00
121 Bill Sharman 1.50 4.00
122 Danny Manning 1.50 4.00
123 Charles D. Smith 1.50 4.00
124 Wilt Chamberlain 3.00 8.00
125 Dan Majerle 1.50 4.00
126 Jeff Hornacek 1.50 4.00
127 George McGinnis 1.50 4.00
128 John Starks 1.50 4.00
129 Toni Kukoc 1.50 4.00
130 Byron Scott 1.50 4.00
131 Gus Williams 1.50 4.00
132 Jalen Rose 1.50 4.00
133 Campy Russell 1.50 4.00
134 Elvin Hayes 1.50 4.00
135 Kurt Rambis 1.50 4.00
136 Jeremy Lin RC 15.00 40.00
137 Terrico White RC 1.50 4.00
138 Timofey Mozgov RC 1.50 4.00
139 Sherron Collins RC 1.50 4.00
140 Ishmael Smith RC 1.50 4.00
141 Pape Sy RC 1.50 4.00
142 Jeremy Evans RC 1.50 4.00
143 Tiago Splitter RC 2.00 5.00
144 Landry Fields RC 2.50 6.00
145 Solomon Alabi RC 1.50 4.00
146 Derrick Caracter RC 1.50 4.00
147 Hamady N'diaye RC 1.50 4.00
148 Gary Neal RC 2.50 6.00
149 Armon Johnson RC 1.50 4.00
150 Omer Asik RC 2.00 5.00
151 John Wall JSY AU/499 RC 40.00 100.00
152 Evan Turner JSY AU/299 RC 12.00 30.00
153 Derrick Favors JSY AU/499 RC 8.00 20.00
154 Wesley Johnson JSY AU/499 RC 6.00 15.00
155 DeMarcus Cousins JSY AU/499 RC15.00 40.00
156 Ekpe Udoh JSY AU/499 RC 4.00 10.00
157 Greg Monroe JSY AU/499 RC 8.00 20.00
158 Al-Farouq Aminu JSY AU/399 RC4.00 10.00
159 Gordon Hayward JSY AU/499 RC8.00 20.00
160 Paul George JSY AU/499 RC 12.00 30.00
161 Cole Aldrich JSY AU/499 RC 4.00 10.00
162 Xavier Henry JSY AU/499 RC 5.00 12.00
163 Ed Davis JSY AU/499 RC 5.00 12.00
164 Patrick Patterson JSY AU/499 RC8.00 20.00
165 Larry Sanders JSY AU/299 RC 4.00 10.00
166 Luke Babbitt JSY AU/499 RC 4.00 10.00
167 Kevin Seraphin JSY AU/249 RC 5.00 12.00
168 Eric Bledsoe JSY AU/499 RC 8.00 20.00
169 Avery Bradley JSY AU/499 RC 8.00 20.00
170 James Anderson JSY AU/499 RC 4.00 10.00
171 Elliot Williams JSY AU/499 RC 4.00 10.00
172 Trevor Booker JSY AU/299 RC 4.00 10.00
173 Damion James JSY AU/299 RC 4.00 10.00
174 Dominique Jones JSY AU/299 RC4.00 10.00
175 Quincy Pondexter JSY AU/499 RC4.00 10.00
176 Jordan Crawford JSY AU/499 RC 6.00 15.00
177 Greivis Vasquez JSY AU/499 RC 5.00 12.00
178 Daniel Orton JSY AU/499 RC 5.00 12.00
179 Lazar Hayward JSY AU/299 RC 4.00 10.00
180 Dexter Pittman JSY AU/499 RC 4.00 10.00
181 Hassan Whiteside JSY AU/499 RC4.00 10.00
182 Andy Rautins JSY AU/499 RC 4.00 10.00
183 Lance Stephenson JSY AU/499 RC4.00 10.00
184 Devin Ebanks JSY AU/299 RC 5.00 12.00
185 Willie Warren JSY AU/299 RC 4.00 10.00

2010-11 Absolute Memorabilia Spectrum Gold

*GOLD 1-100: 1X TO 2.5X BASE HI
*GOLD 101-135: .5X TO 1.25X BASE HI
*GOLD 136-150: .6X TO 1.5X BASE HI
STATED PRINT RUN 100 SER.#'d SETS
136 Jeremy Lin 30.00 80.00

2010-11 Absolute Memorabilia Spectrum Platinum

*PLATINUM 1-100: 2X TO 5X BASE HI
*PLATINUM 101-135: 1X TO 2.5X BASE HI
*PLATINUM 136-150: 1X TO 2.5X BASE HI
STATED PRINT RUN 25 SER.#'d SETS
112 Shawn Kemp 75.00 150.00
113 Gary Payton 8.00 20.00
136 Jeremy Lin 50.00 125.00

2010-11 Absolute Memorabilia Absolute Heroes

COMPLETE SET (15) 12.50 25.00
STATED PRINT RUN 399 SER.#'d SETS
*SPECTRUM: 1X TO 2.5X BASE HI
SPECTRUM PRINT RUN 100 SER.#'d SETS
UNPRICED BLACK PRINT RUN ONE SET
1 Adrian Dantley 1.00 2.50
2 Alonzo Mourning 1.25 3.00
3 Bernard King 1.00 2.50
4 Bob Lanier 1.00 2.50
5 Detlef Schrempf 1.00 2.50
6 Glen Rice 1.00 2.50
7 Hakeem Olajuwon 1.25 3.00
8 Isiah Thomas 1.00 2.50
9 Karl Malone 1.25 3.00
10 Larry Bird 3.00 8.00
11 Larry Johnson 1.25 3.00
12 Magic Johnson 2.50 6.00
13 Mark Aguirre 1.00 2.50
14 Robert Parish 1.00 2.50
15 Toni Kukoc 1.00 2.50

2010-11 Absolute Memorabilia Absolute Heroes Materials

STATED PRINT RUN 25 TO 49 SER.#'d SETS
UNPRICED PRIME PRINT RUN 10 SETS
2 Alonzo Mourning/25 15.00 40.00
3 Bernard King/49 3.00 8.00
4 Bob Lanier/49 3.00 8.00
5 Detlef Schrempf/49 4.00 10.00
6 Glen Rice/49 3.00 8.00
7 Hakeem Olajuwon/49 4.00 10.00
8 Isiah Thomas/49 3.00 8.00
9 Karl Malone/49 4.00 10.00
10 Larry Bird/49 8.00 20.00
11 Larry Johnson/49 10.00 25.00
12 Magic Johnson/49 6.00 15.00
13 Mark Aguirre/49 3.00 8.00
14 Robert Parish/49 3.00 8.00
15 Toni Kukoc/49 5.00 12.00

2010-11 Absolute Memorabilia Absolute Heroes Materials Signatures

STATED PRINT RUN 5 TO 25 SER.#'d SETS
SOME UNPRICED DUE TO SCARCITY
UNPRICED PRIME PRINT RUN 5 SETS
4 Bob Lanier/25 8.00 20.00
5 Detlef Schrempf/25 8.00 20.00
6 Glen Rice/25 8.00 20.00
8 Isiah Thomas/25 15.00 40.00
10 Larry Bird/25 50.00 120.00
11 Larry Johnson/25 20.00 50.00
13 Mark Aguirre/25 10.00 25.00
14 Robert Parish/25 10.00 25.00
15 Toni Kukoc/25 20.00 50.00

2010-11 Absolute Memorabilia Absolute Patches Jumbo Prime Spectrum

STATED PRINT RUN 5 TO 25 SER.#'d SETS
SOME UNPRICED DUE TO SCARCITY
1 Bernard King/25 20.00 50.00
12 Robert Parish/25 12.00 30.00
13 Toni Kukoc/25 75.00 200.00

2010-11 Absolute Memorabilia Frequent Flyer

COMPLETE SET (20) 15.00 40.00
STATED PRINT RUN 399 SER.#'d SETS
*SPECTRUM: .6X TO 1.5X BASE HI
SPECTRUM PRINT RUN 100 SER.#'d SETS
UNPRICED BLACK PRINT RUN ONE SET
1 LeBron James 5.00 12.00
2 Kobe Bryant 5.00 12.00
3 Blake Griffin 2.50 6.00
4 Nate Robinson 1.00 2.50
5 Shannon Brown 1.00 2.50
6 DeMar DeRozan 1.00 2.50
7 Dwight Howard 1.50 4.00
8 Vince Carter 1.25 3.00
9 Jason Richardson 1.00 2.50
10 Andre Iguodala 1.00 2.50
11 Josh Smith 1.00 2.50
12 Rudy Gay 1.00 2.50
13 Derrick Rose 3.00 8.00
14 Gerald Wallace 1.00 2.50
15 J.R. Smith 1.00 2.50
16 Amare Stoudemire 1.00 2.50
17 Corey Brewer .60 1.50
18 David Thompson 1.50 4.00
19 Clyde Drexler 1.50 4.00
20 Dominique Wilkins 1.50 4.00

2010-11 Absolute Memorabilia Frequent Flyer Materials Jersey Number

STATED PRINT RUN 5 TO 25 SER.#'d SETS
SOME UNPRICED DUE TO SCARCITY
UNPRICED PRIME PRINT RUN ONE TO 5 SETS
1 LeBron James/25 15.00 40.00
2 Kobe Bryant/25 15.00 40.00
3 Blake Griffin/25 10.00 25.00
5 Shannon Brown/25 4.00 10.00
6 DeMar DeRozan/25 4.00 10.00
7 Dwight Howard/25 6.00 15.00
11 Josh Smith/25 4.00 10.00
12 Rudy Gay/25 4.00 10.00
15 J.R. Smith/25 4.00 10.00
20 Dominique Wilkins/25 5.00 12.00

2010-11 Absolute Memorabilia Frequent Flyer Materials Jersey Number Signatures

STATED PRINT RUN 5 TO 25 SER.#'d SETS
SOME UNPRICED DUE TO SCARCITY
UNPRICED PRIME PRINT RUN ONE TO 5 SETS
2 Kobe Bryant/25 100.00 200.00
3 Blake Griffin/25 75.00 150.00
6 DeMar DeRozan/25 10.00 25.00
20 Dominique Wilkins/25 15.00 40.00

2010-11 Absolute Memorabilia Frequent Flyer Materials Signatures

STATED PRINT RUN 5 TO 25 SER.#'d SETS
SOME UNPRICED DUE TO SCARCITY
UNPRICED PRIME PRINT RUN ONE TO 5 SETS
2 Kobe Bryant/25 100.00 200.00
3 Blake Griffin/25 75.00 150.00
6 DeMar DeRozan/25 10.00 25.00
20 Dominique Wilkins/25 15.00 40.00

2010-11 Absolute Memorabilia Hoopla

COMPLETE SET (20) 15.00 40.00
STATED PRINT RUN 399 SER.#'d SETS
*SPECTRUM: .6X TO 1.5X BASE HI
SPECTRUM PRINT RUN 100 SER.#'d SETS
UNPRICED BLACK PRINT RUN ONE SET
1 Andrew Bogut 1.00 2.50
2 Brook Lopez 1.00 2.50
3 Carmelo Anthony 1.25 3.00
4 Chauncey Billups 1.00 2.50
5 Chris Paul 1.50 4.00
6 Danilo Gallinari 1.00 2.50
7 Danny Granger 1.00 2.50
8 David Lee .75 2.00
9 Deron Williams 1.00 2.50
10 Dirk Nowitzki 1.25 3.00
11 Dwyane Wade 2.00 5.00
12 Gerald Wallace 1.00 2.50
13 Kobe Bryant 5.00 12.00
14 Kevin Durant 3.00 8.00
15 LeBron James 5.00 12.00
16 Monta Ellis 1.00 2.50
17 Derrick Rose 3.00 8.00
18 Rajon Rondo 1.25 3.00
19 Steve Nash 1.00 2.50
20 Tyreke Evans 1.25 3.00

2010-11 Absolute Memorabilia Hoopla Materials

STATED PRINT RUN 25 TO 49 SER.#'d SETS
UNPRICED PRIME PRINT RUN 5 TO 10 SETS
1 Andrew Bogut/49 3.00 8.00
3 Carmelo Anthony/25 5.00 12.00
4 Chauncey Billups/49 3.00 8.00
5 Chris Paul/49 5.00 12.00
6 Danilo Gallinari/49 3.00 8.00
8 David Lee/49 2.50 6.00
9 Deron Williams/49 3.00 8.00
10 Dirk Nowitzki/49 4.00 10.00
11 Dwyane Wade/49 6.00 15.00
13 Kobe Bryant/49 10.00 25.00
14 Kevin Durant/49 10.00 25.00
15 LeBron James/49 10.00 25.00
17 Derrick Rose/49 10.00 25.00
18 Rajon Rondo/49 4.00 10.00
19 Steve Nash/49 3.00 8.00
20 Tyreke Evans/49 4.00 10.00

2010-11 Absolute Memorabilia Hoopla Materials Jersey Number

STATED PRINT RUN 5 TO 25 SER.#'d SETS
SOME UNPRICED DUE TO SCARCITY
UNPRICED PRIME PRINT RUN 5 SETS
1 Andrew Bogut/25 4.00 10.00
3 Carmelo Anthony/25 5.00 12.00
4 Chauncey Billups/25 4.00 10.00
5 Chris Paul/25 6.00 15.00
8 David Lee/25 3.00 8.00
9 Deron Williams/25 4.00 10.00
10 Dirk Nowitzki/25 5.00 12.00
11 Dwyane Wade/25 8.00 20.00
13 Kobe Bryant/25 12.50 30.00
14 Kevin Durant/25 12.00 30.00
15 LeBron James/25 12.50 30.00
17 Derrick Rose/25 12.00 30.00
18 Rajon Rondo/25 5.00 12.00
20 Tyreke Evans/25 5.00 12.00

2010-11 Absolute Memorabilia Hoopla Materials Jersey Number Signatures

STATED PRINT RUN 5 TO 25 SER.#'d SETS
SOME UNPRICED DUE TO SCARCITY
UNPRICED PRIME PRINT RUN ONE TO 5 SETS
1 Andrew Bogut/25 8.00 20.00
13 Kobe Bryant/25 100.00 200.00
14 Kevin Durant/25 100.00 200.00

2010-11 Absolute Memorabilia Hoopla Materials Signatures

STATED PRINT RUN 5 TO 25 SER.#'d SETS
SOME UNPRICED DUE TO SCARCITY
UNPRICED PRIME PRINT RUN ONE TO 5 SETS
13 Kobe Bryant/25 100.00 200.00
14 Kevin Durant/25 100.00 200.00

2010-11 Absolute Memorabilia Marks of Fame

COMPLETE SET (10) 8.00 20.00
STATED PRINT RUN 399 SER.#'d SETS
*SPECTRUM: .75X TO 2X BASE HI
SPECTRUM PRINT RUN 100 SER.#'d SETS
UNPRICED BLACK PRINT RUN ONE SET
1 Magic Johnson 2.50 6.00
2 John Stockton 1.50 4.00
3 Hakeem Olajuwon 1.25 3.00
4 Isiah Thomas 1.00 2.50
5 Kareem Abdul-Jabbar 1.50 4.00
6 Karl Malone 1.25 3.00
7 Moses Malone 1.00 2.50
8 Robert Parish 1.00 2.50
9 Scottie Pippen 2.00 5.00
10 Xavier McDaniel 1.00 2.50

2010-11 Absolute Memorabilia Marks of Fame Materials

STATED PRINT RUN 49 SER.#'d SETS
UNPRICED PRIME PRINT RUN 10 SETS
1 Magic Johnson 6.00 15.00
2 John Stockton 6.00 15.00
3 Hakeem Olajuwon 5.00 12.00
4 Isiah Thomas 4.00 10.00
5 Kareem Abdul-Jabbar 6.00 15.00
6 Karl Malone 5.00 12.00
7 Moses Malone 4.00 10.00
8 Robert Parish 4.00 10.00
9 Scottie Pippen 8.00 20.00
10 Xavier McDaniel 4.00 10.00

2010-11 Absolute Memorabilia Marks of Fame Materials Signatures

STATED PRINT RUN 5 TO 25 SER.#'d SETS
SOME UNPRICED DUE TO SCARCITY
UNPRICED PRIME PRINT RUN ONE TO 5 SETS
4 Isiah Thomas/25 15.00 40.00
8 Robert Parish/25 10.00 25.00

2010-11 Absolute Memorabilia Materials Prime Spectrum

STATED PRINT RUN ONE TO 25 SER.#'d SETS
SOME UNPRICED DUE TO SCARCITY
3 Blake Griffin/25 15.00 40.00
9 Paul Pierce/25 8.00 20.00
13 Steve Nash/25 8.00 20.00
22 Tim Duncan/25 10.00 25.00
24 LaMarcus Aldridge/25 6.00 15.00
26 Ray Allen/25 8.00 20.00
29 Michael Beasley/25 6.00 15.00
32 Tony Parker/25 6.00 15.00
33 Jrue Holiday/25 6.00 15.00
35 DeMar DeRozan/25 6.00 15.00
38 David West/25 6.00 15.00
41 Andrew Bogut/25 6.00 15.00
43 Luis Scola/25 5.00 12.00
44 Caron Butler/25 6.00 15.00
47 O.J. Mayo/25 6.00 15.00
50 Andre Iguodala/25 6.00 15.00
51 Al Horford/25 5.00 12.00
52 Kevin Garnett/25 12.00 30.00
53 Luol Deng/25 6.00 15.00
54 DeJuan Blair/25 5.00 12.00
55 Mike Dunleavy/25 4.00 10.0
66 Jonny Flynn/25 4.00 10.0
71 Jason Kidd/25 10.00 25.0
73 Ty Lawson/25 6.00 15.0
74 Elton Brand/25 6.00 15.0
75 Terrence Williams/25 4.00 10.0
76 Richard Jefferson/25 6.00 15.0
77 J.J. Redick/25 6.00 15.0
78 Chris Kaman/25 5.00 12.0
79 Gerald Henderson/25 4.00 10.0
80 Jeff Teague/25 5.00 12.0
83 Tyler Hansbrough/25 6.00 15.0
85 Boris Diaw/25 5.00 12.0
87 Toney Douglas/25 4.00 10.0
94 Nene/25 5.00 12.0
95 Shaquille O'Neal/25 20.00 50.0
98 Josh Smith/25 6.00 15.0
99 Devin Harris/25 6.00 15.0
100 Rodrigue Beaubois/25 5.00 12.0
102 Patrick Ewing/25 15.00 40.0
105 Sam Perkins/25 6.00 15.0
110 Mitch Richmond/25 10.00 25.
111 Nick Anderson/25 6.00 15.
112 Shawn Kemp/25 75.00 200.
114 John Stockton/25 15.00 40.
118 Bernard King/25 6.00 15.
126 Jeff Hornacek/25 6.00 15.
129 Toni Kukoc/25 10.00 25.
132 Jalen Rose/25 8.00 20.
138 Timofey Mozgov/25 6.00 15.

2010-11 Absolute Memorabili

NBA Icons

COMPLETE SET (15) 15.00 30.
STATED PRINT RUN 399 SER.#'d SETS
*SPECTRUM: .75X TO 2X BASE HI
SPECTRUM PRINT RUN 100 SER.#'d SETS
UNPRICED BLACK PRINT RUN ONE SET
1 Larry Bird 3.00 8
2 Kareem Abdul-Jabbar 1.50 4
3 Patrick Ewing 1.25 3
4 David Robinson 1.50 4
5 Gary Payton 1.00 2
6 John Stockton 1.50 4
7 Magic Johnson 2.50 6
8 Kevin Durant 3.00 8
9 Kobe Bryant 5.00 12
10 Amare Stoudemire 1.00
11 Rajon Rondo 1.25
12 Carmelo Anthony 1.25
13 Chris Bosh 1.00
14 Steve Nash 1.00
15 Deron Williams 1.00

0-11 Absolute Memorabilia NBA Icons Materials

D PRINT RUN 25 TO 49 SER.#'d SETS
CED PRIME PRINT RUN 5 TO 10 SETS
Bird/49 10.00 25.00
em Abdul-Jabbar/49 5.00 12.00
k Ewing/49 8.00 20.00
d Robinson/49 5.00 12.00
Stockton/49 5.00 12.00
c Johnson/49 6.00 15.00
n Durant/49 10.00 25.00
Bryant/49 10.00 25.00
are Stoudemire/49 3.00 8.00
on Rondo/49 4.00 10.00
melo Anthony/25 5.00 12.00
is Bosh/49 3.00 8.00
ve Nash/49 3.00 8.00
on Williams/49 3.00 8.00

0-11 Absolute Memorabilia Icons Materials Signatures

D PRINT RUN 5 TO 25 SER.#'d SETS
CED PRIME PRINT RUN ONE TO 5 SETS
Bird/25 50.00 120.00
n Durant/25 100.00 200.00
Bryant/25 100.00 200.00

0-11 Absolute Memorabilia anini All Stars Rack Pack

OM INSERTS IN RETAIL PACKS
ht Howard 3.00 8.00
ne Wade 4.00 10.00
n Garnett 4.00 10.00
on James 10.00 25.00
n Rondo 2.50 6.00
e Stoudemire 2.00 5.00
ck Rose 6.00 15.00
Wall 8.00 20.00
Allen 2.00 5.00
is Bosh 2.00 5.00
l Pierce 2.50 6.00
quille O'Neal 4.00 10.00
kim Noah 2.00 5.00
melo Anthony 2.50 6.00
is Paul 3.00 8.00
in Durant 6.00 15.00
e Bryant 10.00 25.00
Ming 2.50 6.00
rew Bynum 2.50 6.00
ke Griffin 5.00 12.00
Nowitzki 2.50 6.00
nu Ginobili 2.00 5.00
Duncan 3.00 8.00
e 1.50 4.00
Gasol 2.00 5.00
ve Nash 2.00 5.00
Cousy 3.00 8.00
n Hayes 2.00 5.00
y West 2.50 6.00
n Havlicek 2.50 6.00
eem Abdul-Jabbar 3.00 8.00
l Malone 2.50 6.00
ry Bird 6.00 15.00
gic Johnson 5.00 12.00
ses Malone 2.00 5.00

0-11 Absolute Memorabilia kie Materials Jumbo Jersey Numbers Basketball

D PRINT RUN 25 SER.#'d SETS
CED PRIME PRINT RUN 10 SETS
hn Wall 20.00 50.00
an Turner 10.00 25.00
rrick Favors 10.00 25.00
esley Johnson 8.00 20.00
eMarcus Cousins 12.00 30.00
pe Udoh 5.00 12.00
eg Monroe 10.00 25.00
-Farouq Aminu 5.00 12.00
ordon Hayward 10.00 25.00
ul George 12.00 30.00
le Aldrich 5.00 12.00
vier Henry 6.00 15.00
Davis 6.00 15.00
trick Patterson 8.00 20.00
rry Sanders 5.00 12.00
ke Babbitt 5.00 12.00
evin Seraphin 6.00 15.00
ic Bledsoe 8.00 20.00
very Bradley 10.00 25.00
mes Anderson 5.00 12.00
iot Williams 5.00 12.00
evor Booker 5.00 12.00
amion James 5.00 12.00
ominique Jones 5.00 12.00
uincy Pondexter 5.00 12.00
rdan Crawford 8.00 20.00
reivis Vasquez 6.00 15.00
aniel Orton 5.00 12.00
azar Hayward 5.00 12.00
exter Pittman 5.00 12.00
assan Whiteside 5.00 12.00
ndy Rautins 5.00 12.00
ance Stephenson 5.00 12.00
evin Ebanks 6.00 15.00
illie Warren 5.00 12.00

0-11 Absolute Memorabilia kie Materials Jumbo Jersey nbers Basketball Signatures

D PRINT RUN 25 SER.#'d SETS
CED PRIME PRINT RUN 5 SETS
hn Wall 100.00 200.00
an Turner 20.00 50.00
rrick Favors 20.00 50.00
esley Johnson 15.00 40.00
eMarcus Cousins 30.00 80.00
pe Udoh 10.00 25.00
eg Monroe 20.00 50.00
-Farouq Aminu 10.00 25.00
ordon Hayward 20.00 50.00
aul George 25.00 60.00
ole Aldrich 10.00 25.00
avier Henry 12.00 30.00
l Davis 12.00 30.00
atrick Patterson 15.00 40.00
rry Sanders 10.00 25.00
ke Babbitt 10.00 25.00
evin Seraphin 12.00 30.00
ic Bledsoe 15.00 40.00
very Bradley 20.00 50.00
mes Anderson 10.00 25.00
liot Williams 10.00 25.00
evor Booker 10.00 25.00
amion James 10.00 25.00
ominique Jones 10.00 25.00
uincy Pondexter 10.00 25.00
rdan Crawford 15.00 40.00
eivis Vasquez 12.00 30.00

178 Daniel Orton 10.00 25.00
179 Lazar Hayward 10.00 25.00
180 Dexter Pittman 10.00 25.00
181 Hassan Whiteside 10.00 25.00
182 Andy Rautins 10.00 25.00
183 Lance Stephenson 10.00 25.00
184 Devin Ebanks 12.00 30.00
185 Willie Warren 10.00 25.00

2010-11 Absolute Memorabilia Spectrum Signatures Gold

STATED PRINT RUN ONE TO 199 SER.#'d SETS
SOME UNPRICED DUE TO SCARCITY
1 Kevin Durant/25 100.00 175.00
3 Blake Griffin/99 60.00 150.00
5 Kobe Bryant/25 100.00 200.00
8 Deron Williams/25 10.00 25.00
10 Stephen Curry/49 12.50 30.00
16 Brandon Jennings/99 8.00 20.00
18 Joakim Noah/99 8.00 20.00
19 Tyreke Evans/15 10.00 25.00
24 LaMarcus Aldridge/99 8.00 20.00
30 Danny Granger/99 4.00 10.00
31 Chris Bosh/25 20.00 50.00
33 Jrue Holiday/199 5.00 12.00
35 DeMar DeRozan/199 5.00 12.00
39 David Lee/99 4.00 10.00
40 Ben Gordon/199 4.00 10.00
44 Caron Butler/99 5.00 12.00
47 O.J. Mayo/49 5.00 12.00
51 Al Horford/49 5.00 12.00
54 DeJuan Blair/99 4.00 10.00
55 Mike Dunleavy/99 4.00 10.00
56 Al Thornton/199 4.00 10.00
57 Lamar Odom/99 8.00 20.00
58 Andrea Bargnani/99 4.00 10.00
60 Russell Westbrook/25 12.50 30.00
62 Gerald Wallace/199 4.00 10.00
64 Al Jefferson/25 5.00 12.00
70 Aaron Brooks/199 4.00 10.00
71 Jason Kidd/49 10.00 25.00
73 Ty Lawson/35 10.00 25.00
74 Elton Brand/25 5.00 12.00
75 Terrence Williams/99 4.00 10.00
77 J.J. Redick/99 5.00 12.00
78 Chris Kaman/99 4.00 10.00
79 Gerald Henderson/199 4.00 10.00
80 Jeff Teague/199 4.00 10.00
83 Tyler Hansbrough/99 6.00 15.00
84 Derek Fisher/99 8.00 20.00
85 Boris Diaw/199 4.00 10.00
87 Toney Douglas/199 4.00 10.00
88 Robin Lopez/99 4.00 10.00
89 Zach Randolph/99 4.00 10.00
90 Carl Landry/199 4.00 10.00
96 Emeka Okafor/99 4.00 10.00
97 Brandon Roy/99 6.00 15.00
99 Devin Harris/25 5.00 12.00
100 Rodrigue Beaubois/143 4.00 10.00
104 Tim Hardaway/49 8.00 20.00
105 Sam Perkins/99 4.00 10.00
121 Bill Sharman/99 4.00 10.00
122 Danny Manning/99 5.00 12.00
125 Dan Majerle/99 8.00 20.00
126 Jeff Hornacek/49 5.00 12.00
127 George McGinnis/49 4.00 10.00
128 John Starks/99 12.00 30.00
129 Toni Kukoc/25 20.00 50.00
130 Byron Scott/49 5.00 12.00
131 Gus Williams/99 4.00 10.00
133 Campy Russell/99 4.00 10.00
135 Kurt Rambis/49 6.00 15.00
136 Jeremy Lin/199 125.00 300.00
137 Terrico White/199 3.00 8.00
138 Timofey Mozgov/199 3.00 8.00
139 Sherron Collins/199 3.00 8.00
140 Ishmael Smith/199 3.00 8.00
142 Jeremy Evans/199 3.00 8.00
143 Tiago Splitter/199 12.00 30.00
144 Landry Fields/199 6.00 15.00
146 Derrick Caracter/199 4.00 10.00
149 Armon Johnson/199 3.00 8.00
150 Omer Asik/199 10.00 25.00

2010-11 Absolute Memorabilia Spectrum Signatures Platinum

STATED PRINT RUN ONE TO 25 SER.#'d SETS
SOME UNPRICED DUE TO SCARCITY
3 Blake Griffin/25 60.00 150.00
10 Stephen Curry/25 15.00 40.00
16 Brandon Jennings/25 10.00 25.00
18 Joakim Noah/25 12.50 30.00
19 Tyreke Evans/13 15.00 40.00
24 LaMarcus Aldridge/25 12.50 30.00
30 Danny Granger/25 6.00 15.00
33 Jrue Holiday/25 8.00 20.00
35 DeMar DeRozan/25 10.00 25.00
39 David Lee/25 6.00 15.00
40 Ben Gordon/25 6.00 15.00
44 Caron Butler/25 8.00 20.00
51 Al Horford/25 6.00 15.00
54 DeJuan Blair/25 6.00 15.00
55 Mike Dunleavy/25 6.00 15.00
56 Al Thornton/25 6.00 15.00
57 Lamar Odom/25 10.00 25.00
58 Andrea Bargnani/25 6.00 15.00
62 Gerald Wallace/25 6.00 15.00
64 Al Jefferson/25 6.00 15.00
70 Aaron Brooks/25 6.00 15.00
71 Jason Kidd/25 15.00 40.00
72 Danilo Gallinari/25 6.00 15.00

75 Terrence Williams/25 6.00 15.00
77 J.J. Redick/25 10.00 25.00
78 Chris Kaman/25 6.00 15.00
79 Gerald Henderson/25 6.00 15.00
80 Jeff Teague/25 6.00 15.00
83 Tyler Hansbrough/25 8.00 20.00
84 Derek Fisher/25 10.00 25.00
85 Boris Diaw/25 6.00 15.00
87 Toney Douglas/25 6.00 15.00
88 Robin Lopez/25 6.00 15.00
89 Zach Randolph/25 6.00 15.00
90 Carl Landry/25 6.00 15.00
92 Darren Collison/25 8.00 20.00
96 Emeka Okafor/25 6.00 15.00
97 Brandon Roy/25 8.00 20.00
100 Rodrigue Beaubois/25 6.00 15.00
104 Tim Hardaway/25 15.00 40.00
105 Sam Perkins/25 6.00 15.00
117 Darryl Dawkins/25 6.00 15.00
121 Bill Sharman/25 6.00 15.00
122 Danny Manning/25 10.00 25.00
125 Dan Majerle/25 15.00 40.00
127 George McGinnis/25 8.00 20.00
128 John Starks/25 15.00 40.00
130 Byron Scott/25 6.00 15.00
131 Gus Williams/25 8.00 20.00
133 Campy Russell/25 6.00 15.00
135 Kurt Rambis/25 8.00 20.00
136 Jeremy Lin/25 400.00 800.00
137 Terrico White/25 6.00 15.00
138 Timofey Mozgov/25 6.00 15.00
139 Sherron Collins/25 6.00 15.00
140 Ishmael Smith/25 6.00 15.00
142 Jeremy Evans/25 6.00 15.00
143 Tiago Splitter/25 20.00 50.00
144 Landry Fields/25 12.00 30.00
146 Derrick Caracter/25 8.00 20.00
149 Armon Johnson/25 6.00 15.00
150 Omer Asik/25 12.50 30.00

2010-11 Absolute Memorabilia Star Gazing

COMPLETE SET (35) 30.00 60.00
STATED PRINT RUN 399 SER.#'d SETS
*SPECTRUM: .6X TO 1.5X BASE HI
SPECTRUM PRINT RUN 100 SER.#'d SETS
UNPRICED BLACK PRINT RUN ONE SET
1 Kobe Bryant 5.00 12.00
2 Kevin Durant 3.00 8.00
3 Dwyane Wade 2.00 5.00
4 Amare Stoudemire 1.00 2.50
5 Dwight Howard 1.50 4.00
6 LeBron James 5.00 12.00
7 Pau Gasol 1.00 2.50
8 Rajon Rondo 1.25 3.00
9 Carmelo Anthony 1.25 3.00
10 Monta Ellis 1.00 2.50
11 Dirk Nowitzki 1.25 3.00
12 Derrick Rose 3.00 8.00
13 Kevin Martin 1.00 2.50
14 Russell Westbrook 1.25 3.00
15 Eric Gordon 1.00 2.50
16 Luis Scola .75 2.00
17 Michael Beasley 1.00 2.50
18 Rudy Gay 1.00 2.50
19 Deron Williams 1.00 2.50
20 Paul Pierce 1.25 3.00
21 Danny Granger 1.00 2.50
22 Paul Millsap .75 2.00
23 Kevin Garnett 2.00 5.00
24 Chris Paul 1.50 4.00
25 Brandon Roy 1.00 2.50
26 Kevin Love 1.25 3.00
27 Chris Bosh 1.00 2.50
28 Tony Parker 1.00 2.50
29 Steve Nash 1.00 2.50
30 Tyreke Evans 1.25 3.00
31 Joe Johnson 1.00 2.50
32 Ray Allen 1.00 2.50
33 Zach Randolph .75 2.00
34 Gerald Wallace 1.00 2.50
35 Brandon Jennings 1.00 2.50

2010-11 Absolute Memorabilia Star Gazing Materials Jumbo Jersey Number

STATED PRINT RUN 2 TO 25 SER.#'d SETS
SOME UNPRICED DUE TO SCARCITY
UNPRICED PRIME PRINT RUN 3 TO 10 SETS
1 Kobe Bryant/25 15.00 40.00
2 Kevin Durant/25 15.00 40.00
3 Dwyane Wade/25 10.00 25.00
5 Dwight Howard/25 8.00 20.00
6 LeBron James/25 15.00 40.00
7 Pau Gasol/25 5.00 12.00
8 Rajon Rondo/25 8.00 20.00
11 Dirk Nowitzki/25 6.00 15.00
12 Derrick Rose/25 15.00 40.00
14 Russell Westbrook/25 6.00 15.00
16 Luis Scola/25 4.00 10.00
19 Deron Williams/25 5.00 12.00
20 Paul Pierce/25 6.00 15.00
23 Kevin Garnett/25 10.00 25.00
24 Chris Paul/25 8.00 20.00
25 Brandon Roy/25 5.00 12.00
26 Kevin Love/25 6.00 15.00
27 Chris Bosh/25 5.00 12.00
28 Tony Parker/25 5.00 12.00
30 Tyreke Evans/25 6.00 15.00
31 Joe Johnson/25 5.00 12.00
35 Brandon Jennings/25 5.00 12.00

2010-11 Absolute Memorabilia Star Gazing Materials Jumbo Jersey Number Signatures

STATED PRINT RUN 5 TO 25 SER.#'d SETS
SOME UNPRICED DUE TO SCARCITY
UNPRICED PRIME PRINT RUN ONE TO 5 SETS
1 Kobe Bryant/25 125.00 250.00
2 Kevin Durant/25 100.00 200.00
14 Russell Westbrook/25 25.00 60.00
25 Brandon Roy/25 10.00 25.00
35 Brandon Jennings/25 12.50 30.00

2010-11 Absolute Memorabilia Star Gazing Materials

STATED PRINT RUN 5 TO 49 SER.#'d SETS
SOME UNPRICED DUE TO SCARCITY
UNPRICED PRIME PRINT RUN ONE TO 10 SETS
1 Kobe Bryant/49 10.00 25.00
2 Kevin Durant/49 10.00 25.00
3 Dwyane Wade/49 6.00 15.00
4 Amare Stoudemire/49 3.00 8.00
5 Dwight Howard/49 5.00 12.00
6 LeBron James/49 10.00 25.00
7 Pau Gasol/49 3.00 8.00
8 Rajon Rondo/49 4.00 10.00
9 Carmelo Anthony/25 5.00 12.00
11 Dirk Nowitzki/49 4.00 10.00
12 Derrick Rose/49 10.00 25.00
14 Russell Westbrook/49 4.00 10.00
16 Luis Scola/49 2.50 6.00
17 Michael Beasley/49 3.00 8.00
18 Rudy Gay/49 3.00 8.00
19 Deron Williams/49 3.00 8.00
20 Paul Pierce/49 4.00 10.00
23 Kevin Garnett/49 6.00 15.00
24 Chris Paul/49 5.00 12.00
25 Brandon Roy/49 3.00 8.00
26 Kevin Love/49 4.00 10.00
27 Chris Bosh/49 3.00 8.00
28 Tony Parker/49 3.00 8.00
29 Steve Nash/49 3.00 8.00
30 Tyreke Evans/49 4.00 10.00
31 Joe Johnson/49 3.00 8.00
32 Ray Allen/49 3.00 8.00
35 Brandon Jennings/49 3.00 8.00

2010-11 Absolute Memorabilia Star Gazing Materials Signatures

STATED PRINT RUN 5 TO 25 SER.#'d SETS
SOME UNPRICED DUE TO SCARCITY
UNPRICED PRIME PRINT RUN ONE TO 5 SETS
1 Kobe Bryant/25 100.00 200.00
2 Kevin Durant/25 100.00 200.00
14 Russell Westbrook/25 20.00 50.00
25 Brandon Roy/25 10.00 25.00
35 Brandon Jennings/25 10.00 25.00

2010-11 Absolute Memorabilia Team Quads TEAM Die Cut Materials

STATED PRINT RUN 100 SER.#'d SETS
UNPRICED PRIME PRINT RUN 10 SETS
1 Derek Fisher 15.00 40.00
Kobe Bryant
Lamar Odom
Pau Gasol
2 Kevin Garnett 12.00 30.00
Paul Pierce
Rajon Rondo
Ray Allen
3 Caron Butler 8.00 20.00
Dirk Nowitzki
Jason Kidd
Shawn Marion
4 Dwight Howard 6.00 15.00
J.J. Redick
Jameer Nelson
Jason Williams
5 Manu Ginobili 6.00 15.00
Richard Jefferson
Tim Duncan
Tony Parker

2010-11 Absolute Memorabilia Team Tandems Materials

STATED PRINT RUN 100 SER.#'d SETS
UNPRICED PRIME PRINT RUN 10 SETS
1 LeBron James 25.00 50.00
Dwyane Wade
2 Rajon Rondo 6.00 15.00
Paul Pierce
3 Pau Gasol 8.00 20.00
Kobe Bryant
4 Tony Parker 4.00 10.00
Tim Duncan
5 Russell Westbrook 10.00 25.00
Kevin Durant
6 Stephen Curry 4.00 10.00
David Lee
7 Derrick Rose 10.00 25.00
Joakim Noah
8 Brandon Jennings 4.00 10.00
Andrew Bogut
9 Carmelo Anthony 4.00 10.00
Chauncey Billups
10 Dirk Nowitzki 6.00 15.00
Jason Kidd

2010-11 Absolute Memorabilia Team Trios NBA Materials

STATED PRINT RUN 40 TO 100 SER.#'d SETS
UNPRICED PRIME PRINT RUN 10 SETS
1 Kobe Bryant 10.00 25.00
Pau Gasol
Lamar Odom
2 Dwyane Wade 30.00 80.00
LeBron James
Chris Bosh
3 Paul Pierce 12.00 30.00
Kevin Garnett
Rajon Rondo
4 Joe Johnson 5.00 12.00
Josh Smith
Al Horford
5 Carmelo Anthony 5.00 12.00
Chauncey Billups
Nene
6 Chris Paul 5.00 12.00
David West
Emeka Okafor
7 Stephen Curry/40 8.00 20.00
Andris Biedrins
David Lee
8 Derrick Rose 12.50 30.00
Joakim Noah
Luol Deng
9 Dirk Nowitzki 8.00 20.00
Jason Kidd
Jason Terry
10 Deron Williams 5.00 12.00
Andrei Kirilenko
Al Jefferson

2010-11 Absolute Memorabilia Tools of the Trade Materials Jumbo

STATED PRINT RUN ONE TO 99 SER.#'d SETS
SOME UNPRICED DUE TO SCARCITY
1 Kevin Durant/99 12.00 30.00
2 Brandon Jennings/99 4.00 10.00
3 Derrick Rose/49 12.00 30.00
4 LeBron James/49 15.00 40.00
5 Kobe Bryant/49 20.00 50.00
6 Deron Williams/99 4.00 10.00
7 Amare Stoudemire/49 4.00 10.00
8 Jonny Flynn/99 3.00 8.00
9 Chris Paul/49 6.00 15.00
10 Gary Payton/49 6.00 15.00
11 Anfernee Hardaway/99 12.50 30.00
12 Brook Lopez/99 4.00 10.00
13 Blake Griffin/99 10.00 25.00
14 LaMarcus Aldridge/99 4.00 10.00
15 Rajon Rondo/49 6.00 15.00
16 Dan Majerle/49 6.00 15.00
17 Mark Price/49 8.00 20.00
18 Dwight Howard/99 6.00 15.00
19 Ben Gordon/25 4.00 10.00
20 Stephen Curry/49 5.00 12.00
21 Carmelo Anthony/49 6.00 15.00
22 Dennis Rodman/99 10.00 25.00
23 Paul Pierce/99 5.00 12.00
24 Kevin Love/99 5.00 12.00
25 David Robinson/49 8.00 20.00
26 Hakeem Olajuwon/49 8.00 20.00
27 Joakim Noah/25 5.00 12.00
28 Dwyane Wade/99 8.00 20.00
29 Charles Oakley/99 4.00 10.00
30 Alonzo Mourning/25 15.00 40.00
31 Dirk Nowitzki/99 8.00 20.00
32 Steve Nash/99 5.00 12.00

2010-11 Absolute Memorabilia Tools of the Trade Materials Jumbo Jersey Numbers

STATED PRINT RUN ONE TO 99 SER.#'d SETS
SOME UNPRICED DUE TO SCARCITY
UNPRICED PRIME PRINT RUN 3 TO 10 SETS
1 Kevin Durant/99 12.00 30.00
2 Brandon Jennings/99 4.00 10.00
3 Derrick Rose/25 15.00 40.00
4 LeBron James/49 15.00 40.00
5 Kobe Bryant/49 20.00 50.00
6 Deron Williams/99 4.00 10.00
7 Amare Stoudemire/49 4.00 10.00
8 Jonny Flynn/49 3.00 8.00
9 Chris Paul/25 6.00 15.00
10 Gary Payton/49 6.00 15.00
11 Anfernee Hardaway/99 12.50 30.00
13 Blake Griffin/99 10.00 25.00
14 LaMarcus Aldridge/99 4.00 10.00
15 Rajon Rondo/49 6.00 15.00
16 Dan Majerle/25 10.00 25.00
17 Mark Price/49 10.00 25.00
18 Dwight Howard/99 6.00 15.00
21 Carmelo Anthony/49 6.00 15.00
22 Dennis Rodman/49 10.00 25.00
23 Paul Pierce/99 5.00 12.00
24 Kevin Love/99 5.00 12.00
25 David Robinson/25 8.00 20.00
26 Hakeem Olajuwon/49 8.00 20.00
27 Joakim Noah/25 6.00 15.00
28 Dwyane Wade/99 8.00 20.00
29 Charles Oakley/25 4.00 10.00
30 Alonzo Mourning/25 15.00 40.00
31 Dirk Nowitzki/49 6.00 15.00
32 Steve Nash/99 5.00 12.00

2010-11 Absolute Memorabilia Tools of the Trade Materials Prime Black Double Spectrum

STATED PRINT RUN ONE TO 25 SER.#'d SETS
SOME UNPRICED DUE TO SCARCITY
UNPRICED SIG.PRINT RUN ONE TO 5 SETS
11 Anfernee Hardaway/25 40.00 100.00
13 Blake Griffin/25 25.00 60.00
14 LaMarcus Aldridge/25 8.00 20.00
17 Mark Price/25 15.00 40.00
23 Paul Pierce/25 12.00 30.00
29 Charles Oakley/25 10.00 25.00

2010-11 Absolute Memorabilia Tools of the Trade Materials Prime Black Spectrum

STATED PRINT RUN ONE TO 25 SER.#'d SETS
SOME UNPRICED DUE TO SCARCITY
UNPRICED JUMBO PRINT RUN 3 TO 10 SETS
UNPRICED SIG.PRINT RUN ONE TO 10 SETS
11 Anfernee Hardaway/25 40.00 100.00
13 Blake Griffin/25 25.00 60.00
14 LaMarcus Aldridge/25 8.00 20.00
17 Mark Price/25 10.00 25.00
23 Paul Pierce/25 10.00 25.00
29 Charles Oakley/25 8.00 20.00

2010-11 Absolute Memorabilia Tools of the Trade Materials Prime Black Triple Spectrum

STATED PRINT RUN ONE TO 25 SER.#'d SETS
UNPRICED SIG.PRINT RUN ONE TO 5 SETS
8 Jonny Flynn/25 6.00 15.00
11 Anfernee Hardaway/25 40.00 100.00
13 Blake Griffin/25 30.00 80.00
14 LaMarcus Aldridge/25 10.00 25.00
17 Mark Price/25 15.00 40.00
23 Paul Pierce/25 15.00 40.00
29 Charles Oakley/25 15.00 40.00

2009-10 Absolute Memorabilia Retail

COMPLETE SET (125) 25.00 60.00
*RETAIL: .2X TO .5X HOBBY

2009-10 Absolute Memorabilia Retail Frequent Flyer

COMPLETE SET (20) 10.00 25.00
*RETAIL: .2X TO .5X HOBBY

2009-10 Absolute Memorabilia Retail Heroes

COMPLETE SET (15) 8.00 20.00
*RETAIL: .2X TO .5X HOBBY

2009-10 Absolute Memorabilia Retail Hoopla

COMPLETE SET (20) 10.00 25.00
*RETAIL: .2X TO .5X HOBBY

2009-10 Absolute Memorabilia Retail Marks of Fame

COMPLETE SET (10) 8.00 20.00
*RETAIL: .2X TO .5X HOBBY

2009-10 Absolute Memorabilia Retail NBA Icons

COMPLETE SET (15) 15.00 40.00
*RETAIL: .2X TO .5X HOBBY

2009-10 Absolute Memorabilia Retail Star Gazing

COMPLETE SET (35) 20.00 50.00
*RETAIL: .2X TO .5X HOBBY

1990 Action Packed Promos

Action Packed produced these cards in order to show the NBA what they could do with basketball cards. These unnumbered cards are numbered alphabetically for convenience in the checklist below. The cards are standard size, 2 1/2" by 3 1/2" with rounded corners. There are gold and white-bordered versions of this prototype set with the white being sold at a slight premium to the gold set. There is some question as to whether this is a legitimate set since Action Packed did not intend these to be sold.

COMPLETE SET (4) 100.00 200.00
1 Patrick Ewing 12.00 30.00
2 Magic Johnson 15.00 40.00
3 Michael Jordan 75.00 200.00

1993 Action Packed Hall of Fame

In conjunction with the Naismith Memorial Basketball Hall of Fame, Action Packed issued this 84-card standard-size set to honor the greatest basketball players and coaches of all time. The set was released in two separate series of 42 cards each. The first series contains 37 current Hall of Famers and a five-card subset devoted to Larry Bird, a Hall of Famer in waiting. The Julius Erving (72G) autographed card was numbered "x of 2500" on the card and was originally only available as a chiptopper in the second series hobby boxes, approximately found one per 20 boxes. The fronts display color photos featuring embossed, sculptured images of the player. The player's name and position are gold-foil stamped across the bottom. A Basketball Hall of Fame 25th anniversary logo in gold foil runs down the right edge. The backs display career highlights overlaid on a parquet basketball court design. Topical subsets featured are One On One (1-10), Coaches (11-16), and Larry Bird (17-21). The cards are numbered on the back. Card 24A is actually a preview card which was delivered to the hobby during January and February via Chiptoppers packed in every box of All-Madden football cards and Action Packed All-Star Gallery Series II baseball cards; it is distinguished from the regular cards by the fact that it has only black and gold print on the back and is not considered part of the complete set. The second series is subdivided into Hall of Fame players (43-51), Hall of Fame coaches (52-59), Class of 1993 (60-67), Dr.J. (68-72), College Days (74-78), and Players Who Coached (79-84).

COMPLETE SET (84) 8.00 20.00
COMPLETE SERIES 1 (42) 4.00 10.00
COMPLETE SERIES 2 (42) 4.00 10.00
1 Walt Frazier .20 .50
2 Jerry West .50 1.25
3 Dave Bing .08 .25
4 Earl Monroe .20 .50
5 Willis Reed .20 .50
6 Dave Cowens .20 .50
7 Bill Bradley .20 .50
8 Elgin Baylor .30 .75
9 Elvin Hayes .20 .50
10 Nate Thurmond .20 .50
11 Red Auerbach CO .30 .75
12 John Wooden CO .30 .75
13 Red Holzman CO .20 .50
14 Lou Carnesecca CO .08 .25
15 Bob Knight CO .20 .50
16 Dean Smith CO .20 .50
17 Larry Bird .60 1.50
Career Highlights
18 Larry Bird .60 1.50
Hometown Hero
19 Larry Bird .60 1.50
Larry's MVPs
20 Larry Bird .60 1.50
A Celtics' Tradition
21 Larry Bird .60 1.50
Larry The Legend
22 K.C. Jones .08 .25
23 Slater Martin .20 .50
24 Bob Wanzer .08 .25
25 Bob Davies .08 .25
26 Nate Archibald .20 .50
27 Bill Sharman .20 .50
28 Tom Gola .08 .25
29 Tom Heinsohn .20 .50
30 Clyde Lovellette .20 .50
31 Bob Pettit .20 .50
32 Dolph Schayes .20 .50
33 Jack Twyman .20 .50
34 Hal Greer .20 .50
35 Sam Jones .20 .50
36 Dave DeBusschere .20 .50
37 Connie Hawkins .20 .50
38 Jerry Lucas .20 .50
39 Pete Maravich .50 1.25
40 Oscar Robertson .40 1.00
41 Lenny Wilkens .20 .50
42 Bob Lanier .20 .50
43 Paul Arizin .20 .50
44 Harry Gallatin .20 .50
45 Frank Ramsey .20 .50
46 Ed Macauley .08 .25
47 Bob Kurland .08 .25
48 Rick Barry .20 .50
49 John Havlicek .30 .75
50 Hank Luisetti .08 .25
51 Wes Unseld .20 .50
52 Al McGuire .20 .50
53 Frank McGuire .08 .25
54 Ray Meyer .08 .25
55 Pete Newell .08 .25
56 Jack Ramsay .20 .50
57 Adolph Rupp .20 .50
58 Clarence Gaines .08 .25
59 Henry Iba .20 .50
60 Dan Issel .20 .50
61 Walt Bellamy .20 .50
62 Dick McGuire .08 .25
63 Calvin Murphy .20 .50
64 Uljana Semjonova .08 .25
65 Bill Walton .30 .75
66 Ann Meyers .08 .25
67 Julius Erving .40 1.00
68 Julius Erving .40 1.00
The Doctor is Born
69 Julius Erving .40 1.00
70 Julius Erving .40 1.00
The Virginia Squires
71 Julius Erving .40 1.00
Always an All-Star
72 Julius Erving .40 1.00
Erving in the NBA
73 Larry O'Brien .08 .25
74 Bill Bradley .20 .50
75 Pete Maravich .50 1.25
76 Elvin Hayes .20 .50
77 Jerry West .50 1.25
78 Oscar Robertson .40 1.00
79 K.C. Jones .20 .50
80 Tom Heinsohn .20 .50
81 Billy Cunningham .20 .50
82 Red Holzman .20 .50
83 Lenny Wilkens .20 .50
84 Bill Sharman .20 .50
XX Oscar Robertson PROMO 1.25 3.00

1993 Action Packed Hall of Fame 24K Gold

Randomly inserted in packs, these cards parallel the base set. The cards feature extra gold foil and a 24K logo on the card front.

*GOLD: 15X TO 40X VALUE
72G Julius Erving AU/2500 100.00 250.00

1995 Action Packed Hall of Fame

1995 Action Packed Hall of Fame Signature series I was released in January, with series II released in time for the playoffs. Except for Pete Maravich, every player in the set autographed at least 500 cards. Bill Russell and Bob Cousy are featured only on signed cards, not unsigned ones; thus, the regular set consists of 38 cards, but the signed set contains 40. Action Packed limited the product to 2,000 cases. "Greats of the Game" autograph cards were inserted one per case. The fronts feature either color or black-and- white embossed player photos inside gold borders. The player's name is reversed out in the top wider gold border. His facsimile autograph is inscribed in gold across the picture. On a ghosted version of the front photo, the backs present biography and career summary. The third series is subdivided as follows: Hall of Fame (1-31), Class of '94 (32-36), and Greats of the Game (37-40). Redeemed autograph cards are valued at 60 times the listed prices below. The autographed Russell and Cousy cards are priced individually below.

COMPLETE SET (38) 4.00 10.00
COMPLETE SERIES 1 (20) 2.00 5.00
COMPLETE SERIES 2 (18) 2.00 5.00
1 Nate Archibald .20 .50
2 Dick McGuire .20 .50
3 Lou Carnesecca .20 .50
4 Red Holzman .20 .50
5 Rick Barry .20 .50
6 Billy Cunningham .20 .50
7 Connie Hawkins .20 .50
8 Dan Issel .20 .50
9 Walt Bellamy .20 .50
10 Elvin Hayes .20 .50
11 Calvin Murphy .20 .50
12 Bob Knight .25 .60
13 Al McGuire .20 .50
14 K.C. Jones .20 .50
15 Jack Ramsay .20 .50
16 John Wooden .25 .60
17 Ray Meyer .20 .50
18 Lenny Wilkens .20 .50
19 Dean Smith .25 .60
20 Ed Macauley .20 .50
21 Nate Thurmond .20 .50
22 Dolph Schayes .20 .50
23 Bill Sharman .20 .50
24 Jerry Lucas .20 .50
25 Frank Ramsey .20 .50
26 Pete Maravich .60 1.50
27 Bob Pettit .20 .50
28 Hal Greer .20 .50
29 Bill Walton .20 .50
30 Bill Bradley .25 .60
31 Tom Gola .20 .50
32 Carol Blazejowski .20 .50
33 Denny Crum .20 .50
34 Chuck Daly .20 .50
35 Buddy Jeanette .20 .50
36 Cesare Rubini .20 .50
37 Bill Bradley .25 .60
38 Bill Walton .20 .50

1995 Action Packed Hall of Fame 24K Gold

Inserted one per box, these cards parallel the base set. The cards feature extra gold foil and a "24K" logo on the card front.

*GOLD: 8X TO 20X VALUE

1995 Action Packed Hall of Fame Autographs

Every box contained one autograph redemption card that were randomly inserted. Cousy and Russell only had autographed cards, thus, this set is complete at 40 cards, rather than 38.

COMPLETE SET (40) 400.00 700.00
1 Nate Archibald 8.00 20.00
2 Dick McGuire 8.00 20.00
3 Lou Carnesecca 8.00 20.00
4 Red Holzman 8.00 20.00
5 Rick Barry 8.00 20.00
6 Billy Cunningham 8.00 20.00
7 Connie Hawkins 8.00 20.00
8 Dan Issel 8.00 20.00
9 Walt Bellamy 8.00 20.00
10 Elvin Hayes 8.00 20.00
11 Calvin Murphy 8.00 20.00
12 Bob Knight 10.00 25.00
13 Al McGuire 8.00 20.00
14 K.C. Jones 8.00 20.00
15 Jack Ramsay 8.00 20.00
16 John Wooden 10.00 25.00
17 Ray Meyer 8.00 20.00
18 Lenny Wilkens 8.00 20.00

19 Dean Smith 10.00 25.00
20 Ed Macauley 10.00 25.00
21 Nate Thurmond 8.00 20.00
22 Dolph Schayes 8.00 20.00
23 Bill Sharman 8.00 20.00
24 Jerry Lucas 8.00 20.00
25 Frank Ramsey 8.00 20.00
26 Pete Maravich 25.00 60.00
27 Bob Pettit 8.00 20.00
28 Hal Greer 8.00 20.00
29 Bill Walton 8.00 20.00
30 Bill Bradley 10.00 25.00
31 Tom Gola 8.00 20.00
32 Carol Blazejowski 8.00 20.00
33 Denny Crum 8.00 20.00
34 Chuck Daly 8.00 20.00
35 Buddy Jeanette 8.00 20.00
36 Cesare Rubini 8.00 20.00
37 Bill Bradley 10.00 25.00
38 Bill Walton 8.00 20.00
39 Bob Cousy 20.00 50.00
40 Bill Russell 125.00 300.00

2009-10 Adrenalyn XL

COMPLETE SET (300) 30.00 80.00
1 Arron Afflalo .12 .30
2 Alexis Ajinca .12 .30
3 LaMarcus Aldridge .20 .50
4 Joe Alexander .12 .30
5 Ray Allen .20 .50
6 Rafer Alston .12 .30
7 Chris Andersen .30 .75
8 David Andersen RC .50 1.25
9 Ryan Anderson .20 .50
10 Carmelo Anthony .25 .60
11 Joel Anthony RC .50 1.25
12 Gilbert Arenas .20 .50
13 Trevor Ariza .12 .30
14 Hilton Armstrong .12 .30
15 Ron Artest .20 .50
16 Darrell Arthur .15 .40
17 D.J. Augustin .15 .40
18 Kelenna Azubuike .12 .30
19 Renaldo Balkman .12 .30
20 Leandro Barbosa .15 .40
21 J.J. Barea .25 .60
22 Andrea Bargnani .15 .40
23 Matt Barnes .12 .30
24 Brandon Bass .12 .30
25 Tony Battie .12 .30
26 Shane Battier .20 .50
27 Nicolas Batum .20 .50
28 Michael Beasley .20 .50
29 Rodrigue Beaubois RC .60 1.50
30 Raja Bell .15 .40
31 Charlie Bell .12 .30
32 Mike Bibby .15 .40
33 Andris Biedrins .12 .30
34 Chauncey Billups .20 .50
35 DeJuan Blair RC .60 1.50
36 Steve Blake .12 .30
37 Andray Blatche .12 .30
38 Andrew Bogut .20 .50
39 Matt Bonner .12 .30
40 Carlos Boozer .20 .50
41 Chris Bosh .20 .50
42 Elton Brand .20 .50
43 Corey Brewer .12 .30
44 Ronnie Brewer .15 .40
45 Primoz Brezec .12 .30
46 Aaron Brooks .12 .30
47 Derrick Brown .20 .50
48 Devin Brown .12 .30
49 Kobe Bryant 1.00 2.50
50 Rasual Butler .12 .30
51 Caron Butler .20 .50
52 Will Bynum .12 .30
53 Andrew Bynum .25 .60
54 Jose Calderon .15 .40
55 Marcus Camby .12 .30
56 Brian Cardinal .12 .30
57 DeMarre Carroll RC .50 1.25
58 Vince Carter .25 .60
59 Omri Casspi RC .50 1.25
60 Mario Chalmers .20 .50
61 Tyson Chandler .15 .40
62 Darren Collison RC .75 2.00
63 Mike Conley Jr. .15 .40
64 Daequan Cook .12 .30
65 Jamal Crawford .15 .40
66 Joe Crawford .12 .30
67 Stephen Curry RC 1.25 3.00
68 Samuel Dalembert .12 .30
69 Erick Dampier .12 .30
70 Glen Davis .15 .40
71 Baron Davis .20 .50
72 Austin Daye RC .50 1.25
73 Luol Deng .20 .50
74 DeMar DeRozan RC .75 2.00
75 Boris Diaw .15 .40
76 Dan Dickau .12 .30
77 Travis Diener .12 .30
78 Toney Douglas RC .50 1.25
79 Jared Dudley .12 .30
80 Chris Duhon .12 .30
81 Tim Duncan .30 .75
82 Mike Dunleavy .12 .30
83 Kevin Durant .60 1.50
84 Wayne Ellington RC .50 1.25
85 Monta Ellis .20 .50
86 Melvin Ely .12 .30
87 Maurice Evans .12 .30
88 Tyreke Evans RC 1.25 3.00
89 Reggie Evans .12 .30
90 Jordan Farmar .12 .30
91 Raymond Felton .15 .40
92 Rudy Fernandez .15 .40
93 Michael Finley .20 .50
94 Derek Fisher .15 .40
95 Jonny Flynn RC .50 1.25
96 T.J. Ford .12 .30
97 Jeff Foster .12 .30
98 Randy Foye .12 .30
99 Adonal Foyle .12 .30
100 Channing Frye .15 .40
101 Francisco Garcia .15 .40
102 Kevin Garnett .40 1.00
103 Pau Gasol .20 .50
104 Marc Gasol .20 .50
105 Rudy Gay .20 .50
106 Devean George .12 .30
107 Taj Gibson RC .60 1.50
108 Daniel Gibson .15 .40
109 Manu Ginobili .20 .50
110 Ryan Gomes .12 .30
111 Ben Gordon .20 .50
112 Eric Gordon .20 .50
113 Danny Granger .20 .50
114 Jeff Green .15 .40
115 Blake Griffin RC 6.00 15.00
116 Taylor Griffin RC .50 1.25
117 Richard Hamilton .15 .40
118 Tyler Hansbrough RC .75 2.00
119 James Harden RC 1.50 4.00
120 Matt Harpring .15 .40
121 Al Harrington .15 .40
122 Devin Harris .20 .50
123 Udonis Haslem .15 .40
124 Trenton Hassell .12 .30
125 Spencer Hawes .15 .40
126 Jarvis Hayes .12 .30
127 Brendan Haywood .12 .30
128 Gerald Henderson RC .50 1.25
129 Roy Hibbert .20 .50
130 Jordan Hill RC .50 1.25
131 Grant Hill .25 .60
132 Kirk Hinrich .20 .50
133 Jrue Holiday RC 1.00 2.50
134 Ryan Hollins .12 .30
135 Al Horford .20 .50
136 Eddie House .12 .30
137 Josh Howard .15 .40
138 Dwight Howard .30 .75
139 Lester Hudson RC .50 1.25
140 Larry Hughes .15 .40
141 Othello Hunter .12 .30
142 Lindsey Hunter .12 .30
143 Andre Iguodala .20 .50
144 Zydrunas Ilgauskas .12 .30
145 Didier Ilunga-Mbenga .12 .30
146 Ersan Ilyasova .15 .40
147 Allen Iverson .25 .60
148 Jarrett Jack .15 .40
149 Stephen Jackson .15 .40
150 LeBron James 1.00 2.50
151 Antawn Jamison .20 .50
152 Marko Jaric .12 .30
153 Al Jefferson .20 .50
154 Richard Jefferson .20 .50
155 Jared Jeffries .12 .30
156 Brandon Jennings RC 1.00 2.50
157 Yi Jianlian .15 .40
158 Joe Johnson .20 .50
159 Amir Johnson .12 .30
160 Dahntay Jones .12 .30
161 James Jones .20 .50
162 Chris Kaman .15 .40
163 Jason Kapono .12 .30
164 Jason Kidd .20 .50
165 Andrei Kirilenko .15 .40
166 Kyle Korver .15 .40
167 Kosta Koufos .12 .30
168 Nenad Krstic .12 .30
169 Carl Landry .12 .30
170 Acie Law .12 .30
171 Ty Lawson RC .75 2.00
172 Courtney Lee .15 .40
173 David Lee .15 .40
174 Rashard Lewis .15 .40
175 Shaun Livingston .12 .30
176 Brook Lopez .20 .50
177 Robin Lopez .12 .30
178 Kevin Love .30 .75
179 Kyle Lowry .15 .40
180 Corey Maggette .15 .40
181 Shawn Marion .20 .50
182 Kenyon Martin .20 .50
183 Kevin Martin .20 .50
184 Roger Mason .12 .30
185 Jason Maxiell .12 .30
186 Eric Maynor RC .50 1.25
187 O.J. Mayo .20 .50
188 Luc Mbah a Moute .12 .30
189 JaVale McGee .15 .40
190 Tracy McGrady .20 .50
191 Dominic McGuire .12 .30
192 Darko Milicic .12 .30
193 Brad Miller .15 .40
194 Andre Miller .15 .40
195 Mike Miller .20 .50
196 Paul Millsap .15 .40
197 Yao Ming .25 .60
198 Jamario Moon .12 .30
199 Anthony Morrow .12 .30
200 B.J. Mullens RC .50 1.25
201 Troy Murphy .12 .30
202 Steve Nash .20 .50
203 Jameer Nelson .15 .40
204 Nene .15 .40
205 Joakim Noah .20 .50
206 Andres Nocioni .12 .30
207 Steve Novak .12 .30
208 Dirk Nowitzki .25 .60
209 Patrick O'Bryant .12 .30
210 Greg Oden .15 .40
211 Lamar Odom .20 .50
212 Emeka Okafor .20 .50
213 Mehmet Okur .12 .30
214 Shaquille O'Neal .40 1.00
215 Jermaine O'Neal .20 .50
216 Travis Outlaw .15 .40
217 Zaza Pachulia .12 .30
218 Jannero Pargo .12 .30
219 Anthony Parker .12 .30
220 Tony Parker .20 .50
221 Chris Paul .30 .75
222 Sasha Pavlovic .12 .30
223 Jeff Pendergraph .20 .50
224 Kendrick Perkins .15 .40
225 Johan Petro .12 .30
226 Paul Pierce .25 .60
227 Mickael Pietrus .12 .30
228 James Posey .12 .30
229 Leon Powe .12 .30
230 Tayshaun Prince .20 .50
231 Joel Przybilla .12 .30
232 Chris Quinn .12 .30
233 Vladimir Radmanovic .12 .30
234 Zach Randolph .15 .40
235 Theo Ratliff .12 .30
236 Michael Redd .20 .50
237 J.J. Redick .20 .50
238 Quentin Richardson .15 .40
239 Jason Richardson .20 .50
240 Luke Ridnour .15 .40
241 Nate Robinson .20 .50
242 Rajon Rondo .25 .60
243 Derrick Rose .60 1.50
244 Brandon Roy .20 .50
245 Brandon Rush .15 .40
246 John Salmons .20 .50
247 Luis Scola .15 .40
248 Thabo Sefolosha .15 .40
249 Ramon Sessions .15 .40
250 Bobby Simmons .12 .30
251 Josh Smith .20 .50
252 J.R. Smith .20 .50
253 Craig Smith .12 .30
254 Jason Smith .12 .30
255 Marreese Speights .15 .40
256 Peja Stojakovic .20 .50
257 Amare Stoudemire .20 .50
258 Rodney Stuckey .20 .50
259 Jermaine Taylor RC .50 1.25
260 Jeff Teague RC .60 1.50
261 Sebastian Telfair .12 .30
262 Jason Terry .15 .40
263 Hasheem Thabeet RC .50 1.25
264 Tyrus Thomas .15 .40
265 Kurt Thomas .12 .30
266 Kenny Thomas .12 .30
267 Jason Thompson .12 .30
268 Al Thornton .15 .40
269 Marcus Thornton .30 .75
270 Ronny Turiaf .12 .30
271 Hedo Turkoglu .20 .50
272 Beno Udrih .12 .30
273 Anderson Varejao .15 .40
274 Charlie Villanueva .15 .40
275 Jake Voskuhl .12 .30
276 Sasha Vujacic .12 .30
277 Dwyane Wade .40 1.00
278 Rasheed Wallace .20 .50
279 Gerald Wallace .20 .50
280 Ben Wallace .20 .50
281 Luke Walton .12 .30
282 Hakim Warrick .15 .40
283 Kyle Weaver .12 .30
284 Delonte West .12 .30
285 David West .20 .50
286 Russell Westbrook .30 .75
287 D.J. White .12 .30
288 Chris Wilcox .12 .30
289 Marvin Williams .15 .40
290 Shelden Williams .12 .30
291 Mo Williams .15 .40
292 Shawne Williams .12 .30
293 Terrence Williams RC .50 1.25
294 Louis Williams .15 .40
295 Marcus Williams .12 .30
296 Deron Williams .20 .50
297 Julian Wright .12 .30
298 Antoine Wright .12 .30
299 Thaddeus Young .12 .30
300 Nick Young .15 .40

2009-10 Adrenalyn XL Extra

COMPLETE SET (30) 30.00 60.00
STATED ODDS 1:8 PACKS
1 Ron Artest 2.00 5.00
2 Michael Beasley 2.00 5.00
3 Chauncey Billups 2.00 5.00
4 Elton Brand 2.00 5.00
5 Jose Calderon 1.50 4.00
6 Vince Carter 2.50 6.00
7 Jamal Crawford 1.50 4.00
8 Boris Diaw 1.50 4.00
9 Mike Dunleavy 1.25 3.00
10 Monta Ellis 2.00 5.00
11 Kevin Garnett 4.00 10.00
12 Ryan Gomes 1.25 3.00
13 Ben Gordon 2.00 5.00
14 Eric Gordon 2.00 5.00
15 Antawn Jamison 2.00 5.00
16 David Lee 1.50 4.00
17 Brook Lopez 2.00 5.00
18 Andre Miller 1.50 4.00
19 Yao Ming 2.50 6.00
20 Steve Nash 2.00 5.00
21 Andres Nocioni 1.25 3.00
22 Mehmet Okur 1.25 3.00
23 Shaquille O'Neal 4.00 10.00
24 Tony Parker 2.00 5.00
25 Zach Randolph 1.50 4.00
26 John Salmons 2.00 5.00
27 Jason Terry 1.50 4.00
28 Hakim Warrick 1.50 4.00
29 David West 2.00 5.00
30 Russell Westbrook 3.00 8.00

2009-10 Adrenalyn XL Extra Signature

COMPLETE SET (30) 50.00 120.00
STATED ODDS 1:8 PACKS
1 Carmelo Anthony 4.00 10.00
2 Gilbert Arenas 3.00 8.00
3 Chris Bosh 3.00 8.00
4 Kobe Bryant 10.00 25.00
5 Tim Duncan 5.00 12.00
6 Kevin Durant 10.00 25.00
7 Rudy Gay 3.00 8.00
8 Danny Granger 3.00 8.00
9 Blake Griffin 12.00 30.00
10 Richard Hamilton 2.50 6.00
11 Devin Harris 3.00 8.00
12 Dwight Howard 5.00 12.00
13 Andre Iguodala 3.00 8.00
14 Stephen Jackson 2.50 6.00
15 LeBron James 10.00 25.00
16 Al Jefferson 3.00 8.00
17 Joe Johnson 3.00 8.00
18 Kevin Martin 3.00 8.00
19 Tracy McGrady 3.00 8.00
20 Dirk Nowitzki 4.00 10.00
21 Chris Paul 5.00 12.00
22 Paul Pierce 4.00 10.00
23 Michael Redd 3.00 8.00
24 Nate Robinson 3.00 8.00
25 Derrick Rose 10.00 25.00
26 Brandon Roy 3.00 8.00
27 Amare Stoudemire 3.00 8.00
28 Dwyane Wade 6.00 15.00
29 Gerald Wallace 3.00 8.00
30 Deron Williams 3.00 8.00

2009-10 Adrenalyn XL Special

COMPLETE SET (60) 15.00 30.00
STATED ODDS 1:2 PACKS
1 LaMarcus Aldridge .60 1.50
2 Ray Allen .60 1.50
3 Rafer Alston .40 1.00
4 Kelenna Azubuike .40 1.00
5 Andrea Bargnani .50 1.25
6 Shane Battier .60 1.50
7 Raja Bell .50 1.25
8 Mike Bibby .50 1.25
9 Andrew Bogut .60 1.50
10 Carlos Boozer .60 1.50
11 Caron Butler .60 1.50
12 Baron Davis .60 1.50
13 Raymond Felton .50 1.25
14 T.J. Ford .40 1.00
15 Randy Foye .40 1.00
16 Francisco Garcia .50 1.25
17 Marc Gasol .60 1.50
18 Pau Gasol .60 1.50
19 Manu Ginobili .60 1.50
20 Jeff Green .50 1.25
21 Al Harrington .50 1.25
22 Udonis Haslem .50 1.25
23 Spencer Hawes .50 1.25
24 Grant Hill .75 2.00
25 Larry Hughes .50 1.25
26 Zydrunas Ilgauskas .40 1.00
27 Richard Jefferson .60 1.50
28 Yi Jianlian .50 1.25
29 Jason Kidd .60 1.50
30 Andrei Kirilenko .50 1.25
31 Nenad Krstic .40 1.00
32 Rashard Lewis .50 1.25
33 Kevin Love 1.00 2.50
34 Corey Maggette .50 1.25
35 Shawn Marion .60 1.50
36 Kenyon Martin .60 1.50
37 O.J. Mayo .60 1.50
38 Troy Murphy .40 1.00
39 Jameer Nelson .50 1.25
40 Nene .50 1.25
41 Joakim Noah .60 1.50
42 Greg Oden .50 1.25
43 Lamar Odom .60 1.50
44 Emeka Okafor .60 1.50
45 Jermaine O'Neal .60 1.50
46 Tayshaun Prince .60 1.50
47 Jason Richardson .60 1.50
48 Luke Ridnour .50 1.25
49 Rajon Rondo .75 2.00
50 Luis Scola .50 1.25
51 Ramon Sessions .50 1.25
52 Josh Smith .60 1.50
53 Peja Stojakovic .60 1.50
54 Tyrus Thomas .50 1.25
55 Al Thornton .50 1.25
56 Hedo Turkoglu .60 1.50
57 Charlie Villanueva .50 1.25
58 Mo Williams .50 1.25
59 Louis Williams .50 1.25
60 Thaddeus Young .40 1.00

2009-10 Adrenalyn XL Ultimate Signature

COMPLETE SET (30) 60.00 120.00
STATED ODDS 1:23 PACKS
1 Carmelo Anthony 5.00 12.00
2 Gilbert Arenas 4.00 10.00
3 Chris Bosh 4.00 10.00
4 Kobe Bryant 15.00 40.00
5 Tim Duncan 6.00 15.00
6 Kevin Durant 12.00 30.00
7 Rudy Gay 4.00 10.00
8 Danny Granger 4.00 10.00
9 Blake Griffin 15.00 40.00
10 Richard Hamilton 3.00 8.00
11 Devin Harris 4.00 10.00
12 Dwight Howard 6.00 15.00
13 Andre Iguodala 4.00 10.00
14 Stephen Jackson 3.00 8.00
15 LeBron James 15.00 40.00
16 Al Jefferson 4.00 10.00
17 Joe Johnson 4.00 10.00
18 Kevin Martin 4.00 10.00
19 Tracy McGrady 4.00 10.00
20 Dirk Nowitzki 5.00 12.00
21 Chris Paul 6.00 15.00
22 Paul Pierce 5.00 12.00
23 Michael Redd 4.00 10.00
24 Nate Robinson 4.00 10.00
25 Derrick Rose 12.00 30.00
26 Brandon Roy 4.00 10.00
27 Amare Stoudemire 4.00 10.00
28 Dwyane Wade 8.00 20.00
29 Gerald Wallace 4.00 10.00
30 Deron Williams 4.00 10.00

2010-11 Adrenalyn XL

Released in January 2011, this interactive basketball game features a 300-card base set. Each card also features an online activation code to build a virtual collection.

COMPLETE SET (300) 25.00 60.00
1 Brendan Haywood .12 .30
2 Caron Butler .20 .50
3 Dirk Nowitzki .25 .60
4 Dominique Jones RC .50 1.25
5 J.J. Barea .20 .50
6 Jason Kidd .20 .50
7 Jason Terry .15 .40
8 Rodrigue Beaubois .15 .40
9 Shawn Marion .20 .50
10 Tyson Chandler .15 .40
11 Aaron Brooks .12 .30
12 Brad Miller .15 .40
13 Chase Budinger .12 .30
14 Courtney Lee .15 .40
15 Jordan Hill .12 .30
16 Kevin Martin .20 .50
17 Luis Scola .15 .40
18 Patrick Patterson RC .75 2.00
19 Shane Battier .15 .40
20 Yao Ming .25 .60
21 Acie Law .12 .30
22 Darrell Arthur .12 .30
23 DeMarre Carroll .15 .40
24 Hasheem Thabeet .12 .30
25 Marc Gasol .20 .50
26 Mike Conley Jr. .15 .40
27 O.J. Mayo .20 .50
28 Rudy Gay .20 .50
29 Xavier Henry RC .60 1.50
30 Zach Randolph .15 .40
31 Chris Paul .30 .75
32 David West .20 .50
33 Emeka Okafor .20 .50
34 Marco Belinelli .12 .30
35 Marcus Thornton .20 .50
36 Peja Stojakovic .20 .50
37 Pops Mensah-Bonsu .12 .30
38 Quincy Pondexter RC .50 1.25
39 Trevor Ariza .12 .30
40 Willie Green .12 .30
41 Antonio McDyess .15 .40
42 DeJuan Blair .15 .40
43 Garrett Temple .12 .30
44 George Hill .15 .40
45 James Anderson RC .50 1.25
46 Manu Ginobili .20 .50
47 Matt Bonner .12 .30
48 Richard Jefferson .20 .50
49 Tim Duncan .30 .75
50 Tony Parker .20 .50
51 Al Harrington .15 .40
52 Arron Afflalo .12 .30
53 Carmelo Anthony .25 .60
54 Chauncey Billups .20 .50
55 Chris Andersen .20 .50
56 J.R. Smith .20 .50
57 Kenyon Martin .20 .50
58 Nene .15 .40
59 Renaldo Balkman .12 .30
60 Ty Lawson .20 .50
61 Corey Brewer .12 .30
62 Darko Milicic .12 .30
63 Jonny Flynn .12 .30
64 Kevin Love .25 .60
65 Luke Ridnour .15 .40
66 Martell Webster .15 .40
67 Michael Beasley .20 .50
68 Sebastian Telfair .12 .30
69 Wayne Ellington .15 .40
70 Wesley Johnson RC .75 2.00
71 Andre Miller .15 .40
72 Brandon Roy .20 .50
73 Dante Cunningham .12 .30
74 Elliot Williams RC .50 1.25
75 Greg Oden .15 .40
76 LaMarcus Aldridge .20 .50
77 Luke Babbitt RC .50 1.25
78 Marcus Camby .12 .30
79 Patrick Mills .15 .40
80 Rudy Fernandez .15 .40
81 Cole Aldrich RC .50 1.25
82 Daequan Cook .12 .30
83 Eric Maynor .12 .30
84 James Harden .25 .60
85 Jeff Green .15 .40
86 Kevin Durant .60 1.50
87 Nenad Krstic .12 .30
88 Royal Ivey .12 .30
89 Russell Westbrook .25 .60
90 Serge Ibaka .25 .60
91 Al Jefferson .20 .50
92 Andrei Kirilenko .15 .40
93 C.J. Miles .12 .30
94 Deron Williams .20 .50
95 Gordon Hayward RC 1.00 2.50
96 Kyrylo Fesenko .12 .30
97 Mehmet Okur .12 .30
98 Paul Millsap .15 .40
99 Raja Bell .15 .40
100 Ronnie Price .12 .30
101 Andris Biedrins .12 .30
102 Brandan Wright .12 .30
103 Charlie Bell .12 .30
104 Dan Gadzuric .12 .30
105 David Lee .15 .40
106 Ekpe Udoh RC .50 1.25
107 Monta Ellis .20 .50
108 Reggie Williams RC .25 .60
109 Stephen Curry .25 .60
110 Vladimir Radmanovic .12 .30
111 Al-Farouq Aminu RC .50 1.25
112 Baron Davis .20 .50
113 Blake Griffin .50 1.25
114 Chris Kaman .15 .40
115 Craig Smith .12 .30
116 Eric Bledsoe RC .75 2.00
117 Eric Gordon .20 .50
118 Randy Foye .12 .30
119 Rasual Butler .12 .30
120 Ryan Gomes .12 .30
121 Andrew Bynum .25 .60
122 Derek Fisher .15 .40
123 Devin Ebanks RC .60 1.50
124 Kobe Bryant 1.00 2.50
125 Lamar Odom .20 .50
126 Luke Walton .12 .30
127 Pau Gasol .20 .50
128 Ron Artest .20 .50
129 Sasha Vujacic .12 .30
130 Theo Ratliff .12 .30
131 Channing Frye .15 .40
132 Earl Clark .12 .30
133 Goran Dragic .20 .50
134 Grant Hill .25 .60
135 Hakim Warrick .15 .40
136 Hedo Turkoglu .20 .50
137 Jared Dudley .12 .30
138 Jason Richardson .20 .50
139 Robin Lopez .12 .30
140 Steve Nash .20 .50
141 Beno Udrih .12 .30
142 Carl Landry .12 .30
143 DeMarcus Cousins RC 1.50 4.00
144 Donte Greene .12 .30
145 Francisco Garcia .15 .40
146 Hassan Whiteside RC .50 1.25
147 Jason Thompson .12 .30
148 Omri Casspi .12 .30
149 Samuel Dalembert .12 .30
150 Tyreke Evans .25 .60
151 Avery Bradley RC 1.00 2.50
152 Glen Davis .15 .40
153 Jermaine O'Neal .20 .50
154 Kendrick Perkins .15 .40
155 Kevin Garnett .40 1.00
156 Nate Robinson .20 .50
157 Paul Pierce .25 .60
158 Rajon Rondo .25 .60
159 Ray Allen .20 .50
160 Shaquille O'Neal .40 1.00
161 Anthony Morrow .12 .30
162 Brook Lopez .20 .50
163 Damion James RC .50 1.25
164 Derrick Favors RC 1.00 2.50
165 Devin Harris .20 .50
166 Jordan Farmar .12 .30
167 Quinton Ross .12 .30
168 Terrence Williams .12 .30
169 Travis Outlaw .15 .40
170 Troy Murphy .12 .30
171 Amare Stoudemire .20 .50
172 Andy Rautins RC .50 1.25
173 Anthony Randolph .15 .40
174 Danilo Gallinari .20 .50
175 Kelenna Azubuike .12 .30
176 Raymond Felton .15 .40
177 Ronny Turiaf .12 .30
178 Timofey Mozgov RC .50 1.25
179 Toney Douglas .12 .30
180 Wilson Chandler .15 .40
181 Andre Iguodala .20 .50
182 Andres Nocioni .12 .30
183 Elton Brand .20 .50
184 Evan Turner RC 1.00 2.50
185 Jason Kapono .12 .30
186 Jodie Meeks .20 .50
187 Jrue Holiday .20 .50
188 Louis Williams .15 .40
189 Spencer Hawes .15 .40
190 Thaddeus Young .12 .30
191 Andrea Bargnani .15 .40
192 David Andersen .12 .30
193 DeMar DeRozan .20 .50
194 Ed Davis RC .60 1.50
195 Jarrett Jack .15 .40
196 Jose Calderon .15 .40
197 Julian Wright .12 .30
198 Leandro Barbosa .15 .40
199 Linas Kleiza .12 .30
200 Reggie Evans .12 .30
201 C.J. Watson .12 .30
202 Carlos Boozer .20 .50
203 Derrick Rose .60 1.50
204 James Johnson .20 .50
205 Joakim Noah .20 .50
206 Keith Bogans .12 .30
207 Kyle Korver .15 .40
208 Luol Deng .20 .50
209 Ronnie Brewer .15 .40
210 Taj Gibson .15 .40
211 Anderson Varejao .15 .40
212 Antawn Jamison .20 .50
213 Anthony Parker .12 .30
214 Daniel Gibson .15 .40
215 J.J. Hickson .15 .40
216 Jamario Moon .12 .30
217 Leon Powe .12 .30
218 Mo Williams .15 .40
219 Ramon Sessions .15 .40
220 Ryan Hollins .12 .30
221 Austin Daye .12 .30
222 Ben Gordon .20 .50
223 Ben Wallace .20 .50
224 Charlie Villanueva .15 .40
225 Greg Monroe RC 1.00 2.50
226 Jason Maxiell .12 .30
227 Richard Hamilton .15 .40
228 Rodney Stuckey .20 .50
229 Tayshaun Prince .20 .50
230 Tracy McGrady .20 .50
231 Brandon Rush .15 .40
232 Dahntay Jones .12 .30
233 Danny Granger .20 .50
234 Darren Collison .20 .50
235 Jeff Foster .12 .30
236 Mike Dunleavy .12 .30
237 Paul George RC 1.25 3.00
238 Roy Hibbert .15 .40
239 T.J. Ford .12 .30
240 Tyler Hansbrough .20 .50
241 Andrew Bogut .20 .50
242 Brandon Jennings .20 .50
243 Carlos Delfino .12 .30
244 Chris Douglas-Roberts .12 .30
245 Drew Gooden .15 .40
246 Ersan Ilyasova .15 .40
247 John Salmons .20 .50
248 Larry Sanders RC .50 1.25
249 Luc Mbah a Moute .12 .30
250 Michael Redd .20 .50
251 Al Horford .15 .40
252 Jamal Crawford .15 .40
253 Jeff Teague .15 .40
254 Joe Johnson .20 .50
255 Jordan Crawford RC .75 2.00
256 Josh Smith .20 .50
257 Marvin Williams .15 .40
258 Maurice Evans .12 .30
259 Mike Bibby .15 .40
260 Zaza Pachulia .12 .30
261 Boris Diaw .15 .40
262 D.J. Augustin .15 .40
263 Derrick Brown .12 .30
264 Eduardo Najera .12 .30
265 Gerald Wallace .20 .50
266 Kwame Brown .12 .30
267 Matt Carroll .12 .30
268 Nazr Mohammed .12 .30
269 Stephen Jackson .15 .40
270 Tyrus Thomas .15 .40
271 Chris Bosh .20 .50
272 Dwyane Wade .40 1.00
273 Eddie House .12 .30
274 Joel Anthony .12 .30
275 Juwan Howard .15 .40
276 LeBron James 1.00 2.50
277 Mario Chalmers .20 .50
278 Mike Miller .20 .50
279 Udonis Haslem .15 .40
280 Zydrunas Ilgauskas .12 .30
281 Daniel Orton RC .50 1.25
282 Dwight Howard .30 .75
283 J.J. Redick .20 .50
284 Jameer Nelson .15 .40
285 Marcin Gortat .20 .50
286 Mickael Pietrus .12 .30
287 Quentin Richardson .15 .40
288 Rashard Lewis .15 .40
289 Ryan Anderson .15 .40
290 Vince Carter .25 .60
291 Al Thornton .15 .40
292 Andray Blatche .12 .30
293 Gilbert Arenas .20 .50
294 Hamady N'Diaye RC .50 1.25
295 JaVale McGee .15 .40
296 John Wall RC 2.00 5.00
297 Josh Howard .15 .40
298 Kevin Seraphin RC .60 1.50
299 Kirk Hinrich .20 .50
300 Yi Jianlian .15 .40

2010-11 Adrenalyn XL Extra

COMPLETE SET (30) 30.00 60.00
STATED ODDS 1:8 PACKS
1 Dirk Nowitzki 2.50 6.00
2 Luis Scola 1.50 4.00
3 Rudy Gay 2.00 5.00
4 Peja Stojakovic 2.00 5.00
5 Manu Ginobili 2.00 5.00
6 Nene 1.50 4.00
7 Martell Webster 1.50 4.00
8 Greg Oden 1.50 4.00
9 Jeff Green 1.50 4.00
10 Andrei Kirilenko 1.50 4.00
11 David Lee 1.50 4.00
12 Baron Davis 2.00 5.00
13 Ron Artest 2.00 5.00
14 Hedo Turkoglu 2.00 5.00
15 Omri Casspi 1.25 3.00
16 Jermaine O'Neal 2.00 5.00
17 Derrick Favors 4.00 10.00
18 Anthony Randolph 1.50 4.00
19 Elton Brand 2.00 5.00
20 DeMar DeRozan 2.00 5.00
21 Derrick Rose 6.00 15.00
22 Ramon Sessions 1.50 4.00
23 Richard Hamilton 1.50 4.00
24 T.J. Ford 1.25 3.00
25 John Salmons 2.00 5.00
26 Joe Johnson 2.00 5.00
27 Boris Diaw 1.50
28 Chris Bosh 2.00
29 Rashard Lewis 1.50
30 Gilbert Arenas 2.00

2010-11 Adrenalyn XL Extr Signature

COMPLETE SET (30) 60.00
STATED ODDS 1:8 PACKS
1 Jason Terry 2.50
2 Kevin Martin 3.00
3 Zach Randolph 2.50
4 David West 3.00
5 Tim Duncan 5.00
6 Chauncey Billups 3.00
7 Michael Beasley 3.00
8 Brandon Roy 3.00
9 Russell Westbrook 4.00
10 Al Jefferson 3.00
11 Monta Ellis 3.00
12 Blake Griffin 8.00
13 Pau Gasol 3.00
14 Jason Richardson 3.00
15 Carl Landry 2.00
16 Ray Allen 3.00
17 Devin Harris 3.00
18 Danilo Gallinari 3.00
19 Evan Turner 6.00
20 Leandro Barbosa 2.50
21 Joakim Noah 3.00
22 Antawn Jamison 3.00
23 Ben Gordon 3.00
24 Mike Dunleavy 2.00
25 Andrew Bogut 3.00
26 Mike Bibby 2.50
27 Gerald Wallace 3.00
28 Dwyane Wade 6.00
29 Vince Carter 4.00
30 Al Thornton 2.50

2010-11 Adrenalyn XL Speci

COMPLETE SET (60) 20.00
STATED ODDS 1:2 PACKS
1 Caron Butler .60
2 Tyson Chandler .50
3 Aaron Brooks .40
4 Courtney Lee .50
5 Marc Gasol .60
6 Mike Conley Jr. .50
7 Emeka Okafor .60
8 Marcus Thornton .60
9 George Hill .50
10 Richard Jefferson .60
11 Chris Andersen .60
12 Kenyon Martin .60
13 Darko Milicic .40
14 Wesley Johnson 1.00
15 Andre Miller .50
16 Rudy Fernandez .50
17 Cole Aldrich .60
18 James Harden .75
19 Mehmet Okur .40
20 Raja Bell .50
21 Charlie Bell .40
22 Reggie Williams .75
23 Eric Gordon .60
24 Randy Foye .40
25 Derek Fisher .50
26 Lamar Odom .60
27 Channing Frye .50
28 Robin Lopez .40
29 DeMarcus Cousins 2.00
30 Francisco Garcia .50
31 Kevin Garnett 1.25
32 Paul Pierce .75
33 Terrence Williams .40
34 Troy Murphy .40
35 Raymond Felton .50
36 Wilson Chandler .50
37 Andres Nocioni .40
38 Louis Williams .50
39 Ed Davis .75
40 Jose Calderon .50
41 Kyle Korver .50
42 Luol Deng .60
43 Anderson Varejao .50
44 Anthony Parker .40
45 Rodney Stuckey .60
46 Tracy McGrady .60
47 Darren Collison .60
48 Tyler Hansbrough .60
49 Chris Douglas-Roberts .40
50 Michael Redd .60
51 Jamal Crawford .50
52 Jeff Teague .50
53 D.J. Augustin .50
54 Nazr Mohammed .40
55 Mario Chalmers .60
56 Udonis Haslem .50
57 J.J. Redick .60
58 Jameer Nelson .50
59 JaVale McGee .50
60 Kirk Hinrich .60

2010-11 Adrenalyn XL Ultima Signature

COMPLETE SET (30) 150.00
STATED ODDS 1:23 PACKS
1 Jason Kidd 5.00
2 Yao Ming 6.00
3 O.J. Mayo 5.00
4 Chris Paul 8.00
5 Tony Parker 5.00
6 Carmelo Anthony 6.00
7 Kevin Love 6.00
8 LaMarcus Aldridge 5.00
9 Kevin Durant 15.00
10 Deron Williams 5.00
11 Stephen Curry 6.00
12 Chris Kaman 4.00
13 Kobe Bryant 25.00
14 Steve Nash 5.00
15 Tyreke Evans 6.00
16 Rajon Rondo 6.00
17 Brook Lopez 5.00
18 Amare Stoudemire 5.00
19 Andre Iguodala 5.00
20 Andrea Bargnani 4.00
21 Carlos Boozer 5.00
22 Mo Williams 4.00
23 Tayshaun Prince 5.00
24 Danny Granger 5.00
25 Brandon Jennings 5.00
26 Josh Smith 5.00
27 Stephen Jackson 4.00
28 LeBron James 15.00
29 Dwight Howard 8.00
30 John Wall 20.00

010 Adrenalyn XL All-Star Game

ırds were distributed via a wrapper redemption ıe NBA All-Star Jam Session in Dallas in y 2010. The card fronts feature the All-Star

ETE SET (10) 6.00 15.00
elo Anthony .60 1.50
Bryant 2.50 6.00
uncan .75 2.00
Garnett 1.00 2.50
t Howard .75 2.00
verson .60 1.50
n James 2.50 6.00
Nash .50 1.25
Stoudemire .60 1.50
ane Wade 1.00 2.50

011 Adrenalyn XL All-Star Game

ırds were distributed via a wrapper redemption he NBA All-Star Jam Session in Los Angeles in y 2011. The card fronts feature the All-Star

ETE SET (6) 10.00 20.00
n Wall 6.00 15.00
y Parker .60 1.50
phen Curry .75 2.00
ke Griffin 4.00 10.00
n Artest .60 1.50
be Bryant 3.00 8.00

09-10 Adrenalyn XL Italian

d in Italy, this 302-card set is a parallel to the American issue, but adds two cards that were ely available in the Italian Starter Kit, which are 301 and #302. The card fronts are identical to rican issue, but the backs contain both a larger he code and both the legal lines and web es are different.

ETE SET (302) 75.00 150.00
Afflalo .15 .40
Ajinca .15 .40
cus Aldridge .25 .60
exander .15 .40
llen .25 .60
Alston .15 .40
Andersen .40 1.00
Andersen .60 1.50
Anderson .25 .60
nelo Anthony .30 .75
Anthony .60 1.50
ert Arenas .25 .60
or Ariza .15 .40
n Armstrong .15 .40
Artest .25 .60
ell Arthur .20 .50
Augustin .20 .50
ana Azubuike .15 .40
ldo Balkman .15 .40
dro Barbosa .20 .50
Barea .30 .75
ea Bargnani .20 .50
Barnes .15 .40
don Bass .15 .40
Battie .15 .40
e Battier .25 .60
as Batum .25 .60
ael Beasley .25 .60
gue Beaubois .75 2.00
Bell .20 .50
ie Bell .15 .40
Bibby .20 .50
s Biedrins .15 .40
ncey Billups .25 .60
an Blair .75 2.00
e Blake .15 .40
ay Blatche .15 .40
ew Bogut .25 .60
Bonner .15 .40
s Boozer .25 .60
s Bosh .25 .60
Brand .25 .60
y Brewer .15 .40
ie Brewer .20 .50
oz Brezec .15 .40
n Brooks .15 .40
ck Brown .25 .60
n Brown .15 .40
Bryant 1.25 3.00
al Butler .15 .40
n Butler .25 .60
Bynum .15 .40
ew Bynum .30 .75
Calderon .20 .50
us Camby .15 .40
Cardinal .15 .40
arre Carroll .60 1.50
e Carter .30 .75
Casspi .60 1.50
o Chalmers .25 .60
n Chandler .20 .50
n Collison 1.00 2.50
Conley Jr. .20 .50
uan Cook .15 .40
l Crawford .20 .50
Crawford .15 .40
hen Curry 1.50 4.00
uel Dalembert .15 .40
Dampier .15 .40
Davis .20 .50
n Davis .25 .60
n Daye .60 1.50
Deng .25 .60
ar DeRozan 1.00 2.50
Diaw .20 .50
Dickau .15 .40
s Diener .15 .40
y Douglas .60 1.50
Dudley .15 .40
s Duhon .15 .40
Duncan .40 1.00
Dunleavy .15 .40
n Durant .75 2.00
ne Ellington .60 1.50
a Ellis .25 .60
in Ely .15 .40
rice Evans .15 .40
ke Evans 1.50 4.00
ie Evans .15 .40
an Farmar .15 .40
nond Felton .20 .50
Fernandez .20 .50
ael Finley .25 .60
k Fisher .20 .50
y Flynn .60 1.50
Ford .15 .40
Foster .15 .40
98 Randy Foye .15 .40
99 Adonal Foyle .15 .40
100 Channing Frye .20 .50
101 Francisco Garcia .20 .50
102 Kevin Garnett .50 1.25
103 Pau Gasol .25 .60
104 Marc Gasol .25 .60
105 Rudy Gay .25 .60
106 Devean George .15 .40
107 Taj Gibson .75 2.00
108 Daniel Gibson .20 .50
109 Manu Ginobili .25 .60
110 Ryan Gomes .15 .40
111 Ben Gordon .25 .60
112 Eric Gordon .25 .60
113 Danny Granger .25 .60
114 Jeff Green .20 .50
115 Blake Griffin 8.00 20.00
116 Taylor Griffin .60 1.50
117 Richard Hamilton .20 .50
118 Tyler Hansbrough 1.00 2.50
119 James Harden 2.00 5.00
120 Matt Harpring .20 .50
121 Al Harrington .20 .50
122 Devin Harris .25 .60
123 Udonis Haslem .20 .50
124 Trenton Hassell .15 .40
125 Spencer Hawes .20 .50
126 Jarvis Hayes .15 .40
127 Brendan Haywood .15 .40
128 Gerald Henderson .60 1.50
129 Roy Hibbert .25 .60
130 Jordan Hill .60 1.50
131 Grant Hill .30 .75
132 Kirk Hinrich .25 .60
133 Jrue Holiday 1.25 3.00
134 Ryan Hollins .15 .40
135 Al Horford .25 .60
136 Eddie House .15 .40
137 Josh Howard .20 .50
138 Dwight Howard .40 1.00
139 Lester Hudson .60 1.50
140 Larry Hughes .20 .50
141 Othello Hunter .15 .40
142 Lindsey Hunter .15 .40
143 Andre Iguodala .25 .60
144 Zydrunas Ilgauskas .15 .40
145 Didier Ilunga-Mbenga .15 .40
146 Ersan Ilyasova .20 .50
147 Allen Iverson .30 .75
148 Jarrett Jack .20 .50
149 Stephen Jackson .20 .50
150 LeBron James 1.25 3.00
151 Antawn Jamison .25 .60
152 Marko Jaric .15 .40
153 Al Jefferson .25 .60
154 Richard Jefferson .25 .60
155 Jared Jeffries .15 .40
156 Brandon Jennings 1.25 3.00
157 Yi Jianlian .20 .50
158 Joe Johnson .25 .60
159 Amir Johnson .15 .40
160 Dahntay Jones .15 .40
161 James Jones .25 .60
162 Chris Kaman .20 .50
163 Jason Kapono .15 .40
164 Jason Kidd .25 .60
165 Andrei Kirilenko .20 .50
166 Kyle Korver .20 .50
167 Kosta Koufos .15 .40
168 Nenad Krstic .15 .40
169 Carl Landry .15 .40
170 Acie Law .15 .40
171 Ty Lawson 1.00 2.50
172 Courtney Lee .20 .50
173 David Lee .20 .50
174 Rashard Lewis .20 .50
175 Shaun Livingston .15 .40
176 Brook Lopez .25 .60
177 Robin Lopez .15 .40
178 Kevin Love .40 1.00
179 Kyle Lowry .20 .50
180 Corey Maggette .20 .50
181 Shawn Marion .25 .60
182 Kenyon Martin .25 .60
183 Kevin Martin .25 .60
184 Roger Mason .15 .40
185 Jason Maxiell .15 .40
186 Eric Maynor .60 1.50
187 O.J. Mayo .25 .60
188 Luc Mbah a Moute .15 .40
189 JaVale McGee .20 .50
190 Tracy McGrady .25 .60
191 Dominic McGuire .15 .40
192 Darko Milicic .15 .40
193 Brad Miller .20 .50
194 Andre Miller .20 .50
195 Mike Miller .25 .60
196 Paul Millsap .20 .50
197 Yao Ming .30 .75
198 Jamario Moon .15 .40
199 Anthony Morrow .15 .40
200 B.J. Mullens .60 1.50
201 Troy Murphy .15 .40
202 Steve Nash .25 .60
203 Jameer Nelson .20 .50
204 Nene .20 .50
205 Joakim Noah .25 .60
206 Andres Nocioni .15 .40
207 Steve Novak .15 .40
208 Dirk Nowitzki .30 .75
209 Patrick O'Bryant .15 .40
210 Greg Oden .20 .50
211 Lamar Odom .25 .60
212 Emeka Okafor .25 .60
213 Mehmet Okur .15 .40
214 Shaquille O'Neal .50 1.25
215 Jermaine O'Neal .25 .60
216 Travis Outlaw .20 .50
217 Zaza Pachulia .15 .40
218 Jannero Pargo .15 .40
219 Anthony Parker .15 .40
220 Tony Parker .25 .60
221 Chris Paul .40 1.00
222 Sasha Pavlovic .15 .40
223 Jeff Pendergraph .25 .60
224 Kendrick Perkins .20 .50
225 Johan Petro .15 .40
226 Paul Pierce .30 .75
227 Mickael Pietrus .15 .40
228 James Posey .15 .40
229 Leon Powe .15 .40
230 Tayshaun Prince .25 .60
231 Joel Przybilla .15 .40
232 Chris Quinn .15 .40
233 Vladimir Radmanovic .15 .40
234 Zach Randolph .20 .50
235 Theo Ratliff .15 .40
236 Michael Redd .25 .60
237 J.J. Redick .25 .60
238 Quentin Richardson .20 .50
239 Jason Richardson .25 .60
240 Luke Ridnour .20 .50
241 Nate Robinson .25 .60
242 Rajon Rondo .30 .75
243 Derrick Rose .75 2.00
244 Brandon Roy .25 .60
245 Brandon Rush .20 .50
246 John Salmons .25 .60
247 Luis Scola .20 .50
248 Thabo Sefolosha .20 .50
249 Ramon Sessions .20 .50
250 Bobby Simmons .15 .40
251 Josh Smith .25 .60
252 J.R. Smith .25 .60
253 Craig Smith .15 .40
254 Jason Smith .15 .40
255 Marreese Speights .20 .50
256 Peja Stojakovic .25 .60
257 Amare Stoudemire .25 .60
258 Rodney Stuckey .25 .60
259 Jermaine Taylor .60 1.50
260 Jeff Teague .75 2.00
261 Sebastian Telfair .15 .40
262 Jason Terry .20 .50
263 Hasheem Thabeet .60 1.50
264 Tyrus Thomas .20 .50
265 Kurt Thomas .15 .40
266 Kenny Thomas .15 .40
267 Jason Thompson .15 .40
268 Al Thornton .20 .50
269 Marcus Thornton .40 1.00
270 Ronny Turiaf .15 .40
271 Hedo Turkoglu .25 .60
272 Beno Udrih .15 .40
273 Anderson Varejao .20 .50
274 Charlie Villanueva .20 .50
275 Jake Voskuhl .15 .40
276 Sasha Vujacic .15 .40
277 Dwyane Wade .50 1.25
278 Rasheed Wallace .25 .60
279 Gerald Wallace .25 .60
280 Ben Wallace .25 .60
281 Luke Walton .15 .40
282 Hakim Warrick .20 .50
283 Kyle Weaver .15 .40
284 Delonte West .15 .40
285 David West .25 .60
286 Russell Westbrook .40 1.00
287 D.J. White .15 .40
288 Chris Wilcox .15 .40
289 Marvin Williams .20 .50
290 Shelden Williams .15 .40
291 Mo Williams .20 .50
292 Shawne Williams .15 .40
293 Terrence Williams .60 1.50
294 Louis Williams .20 .50
295 Marcus Williams .15 .40
296 Deron Williams .25 .60
297 Julian Wright .15 .40
298 Antoine Wright .15 .40
299 Thaddeus Young .15 .40
300 Nick Young .20 .50
301 Marco Belinelli 1.25 3.00
Italian Starter Kit Exclusive
302 Danilo Gallinari 1.25 3.00
Italian Starter Kit Exclusive

1956 Adventure R749

The Adventure series produced by Gum Products in 1956, contains a wide variety of subject matter. Cards in the set measure the standard size. The color drawings are printed on a heavy thickness of cardboard and have large white borders. The backs contain the card number, the caption, and a short text. The most expensive cards in the series of 100 are those associated with sports (Louis, Tunney, etc.). In addition, card number 86 (Schmelling) is notorious and sold at a premium price because of the Nazi symbol printed on the card. Although this set is considered by many to be a topical or non-sport set, several boxers are featured (cards 11, 22, 31-35, 41-44, 76-80, 86-90). One of the few cards of Boston-area legend Harry Agannis is in this set. The sports-related cards are in greater demand than the non-sport cards. These cards came in one-card penny packs where were packed 240 to a box.

COMPLETE SET (100) 225.00 450.00
8 Baskets and Rebounds 12.50 25.00
Makes Points

2006-07 Albany Patroons CBA

Produced by the Albany Patroons, this 16-card set features photographs taken by team photographer, Chuck Miller, and a white bordered card stock. The sets were sold at Patroons home games.

COMPLETE SET (16) 2.50 6.00
1 Jamario Moon 2.00 5.00
2 Carl Mitchell .15 .40
3 Felipe Lopez .30 .75
4 Chris Sockwell .15 .40
5 T.J. Thompson .15 .40
6 Kwan Johnson .15 .40
7 Eric Williams .30 .75
8 Reggie Jessie .15 .40
9 Jordan Klaiber .15 .40
10 Kareem Reid .15 .40
11 Marvin Phillips .15 .40
12 Lucious Jordan .15 .40
13 John Strickland .15 .40
14 Michael Ray Richardson CO .40 1.00
15 Derrick Rowland ACO .15 .40
16 Lito The Panda Mascot .15 .40

1995-96 All-Star Jam Session David Robinson

This 4-card standard-size set was a wrapper redemption offer at the NBA All-Star Weekend Jam Session show (February 9-11) in San Antonio. Although each card features a distinctive design, they all carry the "All-Star Weekend, San Antonio '96" emblem on them. According to the backs, just 10,500 of each card were produced.

COMPLETE SET (4) 4.00 10.00
1 David Robinson Upper Deck 1.25 3.00
2 David Robinson Stadium Club 1.25 3.00
3 David Robinson Fleer 1.25 3.00
4 David Robinson SkyBox 1.25 3.00

1996-97 All-Star Jam Session Terrell Brandon

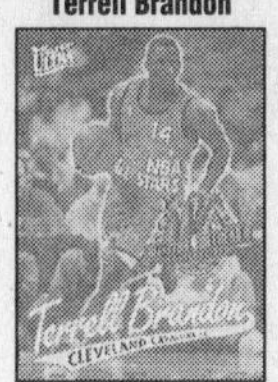

This three-card set was a wrapper redemption offer at the NBA All-Star Weekend Jam Session show (February 7-9) in Cleveland. Although each card features a distinctively different design, they all carry the "All-Star Weekend, Cleveland '97" emblem on them. According to the backs of the Ultra and SkyBox card, only 6,200 of each card were produced. The cards are numbered out of three.

COMPLETE SET (3) 2.00 4.00
1 Terrell Brandon Ultra .60 1.50
2 Terrell Brandon SkyBox .60 1.50
3 Terrell Brandon Stadium Club .60 1.50

1996-97 All-Star Jam Session Terrell Brandon Ticket

This ticket stub was used for admission into the Jam Session show during the 1997 NBA All-Star Weekend. The ticket carries the regular 1996-97 Ultra design.

NNO Terrell Brandon .40 1.00

1997-98 All-Star Jam Session Knicks Sheet A

Given away at the 1998 Jam Session in New York, collector's could receive this sheet by bringing three wrappers from any Fleer or SkyBox 1997-98 NBA product to the Fleer/SkyBox booth. The sheet features six Ultra cards. The sheets had a limited edition of 7500.

1 Knicks All-Star Sheet 2.00 5.00
Patrick Ewing
Larry Johnson
John Starks
Chris Dudley
Charlie Ward
Chris Mills

1997-98 All-Star Jam Session Knicks Sheet B

To obtain sheet B, collectors had to take three wrappers from any 1997-98 Fleer or SkyBox NBA product to a participating hobby dealer (or by mail) from a list that could be obtained at the Fleer/SkyBox booth at Jam Session. The sheet features SkyBox cards of Knick players. The sheet had a limited edition of 7500.

1 Knicks All-Star Sheet 2.50 6.00
Patrick Ewing
Larry Johnson
John Starks
Buck Williams
Chris Childs
Allan Houston

2007 Americana

COMPLETE SET (100) 30.00 60.00
74 Sheryl Swoopes .40 1.00

2007 Americana Gold Proofs

*GOLD PROOF: 2X TO 5X BASIC
RANDOM INSERTS IN HOBBY
STATED PRINT RUN 100 SERIAL #'d SETS

2007 Americana Platinum Proofs

*PLATINUM PROOF: 3X TO 8X BASIC
RANDOM INSERTS IN HOBBY
STATED PRINT RUN 25 SERIAL #'d SETS

2007 Americana Silver Proofs

*SILVER PROOF: 1.5X TO 4X BASIC
RANDOM INSERTS IN HOBBY
STATED PRINT RUN 250 SERIAL #'d SETS

2007 Americana Retail

COMPLETE SET (100) 20.00 50.00
*RETAIL: .3X TO .8X BASIC
ISSUED IN RETAIL PACKS

2007 Americana Gold Proofs Retail

*RETAIL GOLD: 2X TO 5X BASIC
RANDOM INSERTS IN RETAIL
STATED PRINT RUN 100 SERIAL #'d SETS

2007 Americana Platinum Proofs Retail

*RETAIL PLATINUM: 3X TO 8X BASIC
RANDOM INSERTS IN RETAIL
STATED PRINT RUN 25 SERIAL #'d SETS

2007 Americana Silver Proofs Retail

*RETAIL SILVER: 1.5X TO 4X BASIC
RANDOM INSERTS IN RETAIL
STATED PRINT RUN 250 SERIAL #'d SETS

2007 Americana Sports Legends

RANDOM INSERTS IN PACKS
STATED PRINT RUN 500 SERIAL #'d SETS
3 Walt Frazier 1.50 4.00
10 Larry Bird 4.00 10.00

2007 Americana Sports Legends Material

RANDOM INSERTS IN PACKS
PRINT RUNS B/WN 25-500 COPIES PER
3 Walt Frazier Jsy/500 4.00 10.00

2007 Americana Sports Legends Signature

RANDOM INSERTS IN PACKS
PRINT RUNS B/WN 25-50 COPIES PER
3 Walt Frazier/25 15.00 40.00
10 Larry Bird/25 70.00 120.00

2007 Americana Sports Legends Signature Material

*MTL: .5X TO 1.2X BASIC SIG
RANDOM INSERTS IN PACKS
PRINT RUNS B/WN 25-50 COPIES PER

2008 Americana II

201-270 ONE PER BOX
174 John Wooden .75 2.00
239 Lisa Leslie SP 2.00 5.00
242 Dick Vitale SP 2.00 5.00

2008 Americana II Gold Proofs

*GOLD 101-200: 2X TO 5X BASIC
101-200 PRINT RUN 100 SERIAL #'d SETS
201-270 PRINT RUN 10 SERIAL #'d SETS
201-270 NO PRICING DUE TO SCARCITY
RANDOM INSERTS IN HOBBY

2008 Americana II Platinum Proofs

*PLATINUM 101-200: 3X TO 8X BASIC
101-200 PRINT RUN 25 SERIAL #'d SETS
201-270 PRINT RUN 5 SERIAL #'d SETS
201-270 NO PRICING DUE TO SCARCITY
RANDOM INSERTS IN HOBBY

2008 Americana II Silver Proofs

*SILVER 101-200: 1.5X TO 4X BASIC
101-200 PRINT RUN 250 SERIAL #'d SETS
201-270 PRINT RUN 25 SERIAL #'d SETS
201-270 NO PRICING DUE TO SCARCITY
RANDOM INSERTS IN HOBBY

2008 Americana II Private Signings

RANDOM INSERTS IN PACKS
PRINT RUNS B/WN 1-1200 COPIES PER
NO PRICING ON QTY OF 14 OR LESS
EXCHANGE DEADLINE 01/16/10
174 John Wooden/79 50.00 100.00
239 Lisa Leslie/25 10.00 25.00
242 Dick Vitale/25 10.00 25.00

2008 Americana II Sports Legends

RANDOM INSERTS IN PACKS
STATED PRINT RUN 500 SERIAL #'d SETS
13 Dick Vitale 1.25 3.00
14 John Wooden 1.50 4.00

2008 Americana II Sports Legends Signature

RANDOM INSERTS IN PACKS
PRINT RUNS B/WN 50-100 COPIES PER
13 Dick Vitale/100 15.00 40.00
14 John Wooden/100 50.00 100.00

2008 Americana II Stars Signature Material

RANDOM INSERTS IN PACKS
PRINT RUNS B/WN 5-250 COPIES PER
NO PRICING ON QTY OF 10 OR LESS
239 Lisa Leslie/25 10.00 25.00

2000 American Express Postcards

This 4-card postcard set features Shaquille O'Neal, Walt Frazier, Allan Houston, and Marcus Camby. It was issued by "Max Racks", and distibuted to stores that carry "Max Racks" postcards.

COMPLETE SET (4) 2.50 6.00
1 Marcus Camby .40 1.00
2 Marcus Camby .80 2.00
Allan Houston
3 Walt Frazier .40 1.00
4 Shaquille O'Neal 2.00 5.00

1993 Anti-Gambling Postcards

COMPLETE SET (13) 6.00 15.00
6 Alex English BK .50 1.25
7 Alvin Robertson BK .50 1.25
8 Buck Williams BK .50 1.25

1991 Arena Holograms

The 1991 Arena Hologram cards were distributed through hobby dealers and feature famous athletes. According to Arena, production quantities were limited to 250,000 of each card. The standard-size hologram cards have on the horozontially oriented backs a color photo of the player in a tuxedo. Ken Griffey Jr. Frank Thomas, David Robinson, Joe Montana and Barry Sanders all signed cards with each being serial numbered by hand. A card-sized certificate of authenticity was also issued with each signed card.

COMPLETE SET (5) 3.20 8.00
5 David Robinson .40 1.00
AU5 David Robinson AU/250 40.00 75.00

1991 Arena Holograms 12th National

These standard-size cards have on their fronts a 3-D silver-colored emblem on a white background with orange borders. Though the back of each card salutes a different superstar, the players themselves are not pictured; instead, one finds pictures of a football; hockey stick and puck; basketball; and baseball in glove respectively. The cards are numbered on the front.

COMPLETE SET (4) 4.00 10.00
3 Michael Jordan 2.00 5.00

1979 Arizona Sports Collectors Show

COMPLETE SET (10) 7.50 15.00
8 Dick Van Arsdale 2.00 5.00
9 Tom Van Arsdale 2.00 5.00

2007-08 Artifacts

This 230-card set was released in October, 2007. The set was issued into the hobby in four-card packs which came 10 packs to a box and 20 boxes to a case. Cards numbered 1-100 feature NBA veterans while cards numbered 101-150 feature 2007-08 NBA rookies and cards numbered 151-200 feature retired greats. The cards numbered from 101-150 were issued to a stated print run of 699 serial numbered sets while cards 151-200 were issued to a stated print run of 999 serial numbered sets. The set concludes with cards 201-230 as Artifact Exclusives which were issued four cards per unopened box as a box topper.

COMP.SET w/o SP's (100) 15.00 40.00
101-110 PRINT RUN 699 SER.#'d SETS
111-150 PRINT RUN 1299 SER.#'d SETS
151-200 PRINT RUN 999 SER.#'d SETS
UNPRICED COPPER PRINT RUN 10 SETS
UNPRICED ARTIFACTS PRINT RUN ONE SET
1 Joe Johnson .40 1.00
2 Josh Smith .40 1.00
3 Marvin Williams .40 1.00
4 Josh Childress .30 .75
5 Al Jefferson .40 1.00
6 Paul Pierce .50 1.25
7 Gerald Green .30 .75
8 Adam Morrison .40 1.00
9 Gerald Wallace .40 1.00
10 Emeka Okafor .40 1.00
11 Raymond Felton .50 1.25
12 Ben Gordon .40 1.00
13 Luol Deng .40 1.00
14 Kirk Hinrich .40 1.00
15 Andres Nocioni .25 .60
16 LeBron James 2.00 5.00
17 Larry Hughes .30 .75
18 Zydrunas Ilgauskas .30 .75
19 Dirk Nowitzki .50 1.25
20 Josh Howard .30 .75
21 Jason Terry .30 .75
22 Carmelo Anthony .50 1.25
23 Allen Iverson .50 1.25
24 J.R. Smith .40 1.00
25 Richard Hamilton .30 .75
26 Tayshaun Prince .40 1.00
27 Chauncey Billups .40 1.00
28 Baron Davis .40 1.00
29 Monta Ellis .40 1.00
30 Jason Richardson .40 1.00
31 Yao Ming .50 1.25
32 Tracy McGrady .40 1.00
33 Rafer Alston .25 .60
34 Jermaine O'Neal .40 1.00
35 Jamaal Tinsley .25 .60
36 Mike Dunleavy .30 .75
37 Elton Brand .40 1.00
38 Cuttino Mobley .30 .75
39 Corey Maggette .30 .75
40 Kobe Bryant 2.00 5.00
41 Lamar Odom .40 1.00
42 Jordan Farmar .25 .60
43 Pau Gasol .40 1.00
44 Rudy Gay .40 1.00
45 Mike Miller .40 1.00
46 Shaquille O'Neal .75 2.00
47 Dwyane Wade 1.00 2.50
48 Jason Kapono .25 .60
49 Alonzo Mourning .50 1.25
50 Andrew Bogut .40 1.00
51 Michael Redd .40 1.00
52 Maurice Williams .30 .75
53 Kevin Garnett .75 2.00
54 Ricky Davis .30 .75
55 Randy Foye .40 1.00
56 Rashad McCants .25 .60
57 Jason Kidd .40 1.00
58 Vince Carter .50 1.25
59 Richard Jefferson .40 1.00
60 Peja Stojakovic .40 1.00
61 Chris Paul .75 2.00
62 David West .40 1.00
63 David Lee .30 .75
64 Stephon Marbury .30 .75
65 Eddy Curry .25 .60
66 Jamal Crawford .30 .75
67 Dwight Howard .60 1.50
68 Grant Hill .50 1.25
69 Jameer Nelson .30 .75
70 J.J. Redick .40 1.00
71 Andre Iguodala .40 1.00
72 Andre Miller .30 .75
73 Samuel Dalembert .25 .60
74 Steve Nash .50 1.25
75 Amare Stoudemire .40 1.00
76 Shawn Marion .40 1.00
77 Leandro Barbosa .30 .75
78 Zach Randolph .30 .75
79 Brandon Roy .50 1.25
80 LaMarcus Aldridge .50 1.25
81 Jarrett Jack .30 .75
82 Mike Bibby .40 1.00
83 Kevin Martin .40 1.00
84 Brad Miller .30 .75
85 Tim Duncan .60 1.50
86 Manu Ginobili .40 1.00
87 Tony Parker .40 1.00
88 Rashard Lewis .30 .75
89 Ray Allen .40 1.00
90 Chris Wilcox .25 .60
91 Chris Bosh .40 1.00
92 Andrea Bargnani .50 1.25
93 T.J. Ford .30 .75
94 Anthony Parker .25 .60
95 Deron Williams .60 1.50
96 Carlos Boozer .40 1.00
97 Mehmet Okur .25 .60
98 Gilbert Arenas .40 1.00
99 Caron Butler .40 1.00
100 Antawn Jamison .40 1.00
101 Greg Oden RC 2.00 5.00
102 Kevin Durant RC 12.00 30.00
103 Al Horford RC 2.00 5.00
104 Mike Conley Jr. RC 2.50 6.00
105 Jeff Green RC 2.00 5.00
106 Sun Yue RC 1.50 4.00
107 Corey Brewer RC 2.00 5.00
108 Brandan Wright RC 1.50 4.00
109 Joakim Noah RC 4.00 10.00
110 Spencer Hawes RC 1.50 4.00
111 Acie Law RC 1.50 4.00
112 Thaddeus Young RC 2.00 5.00
113 Julian Wright RC 1.50 4.00
114 Al Thornton RC 1.50 4.00
115 Rodney Stuckey RC 2.50 6.00
116 Nick Young RC 2.50 6.00
117 Sean Williams RC 1.50 4.00
118 Marco Belinelli RC 1.50 4.00
119 Javaris Crittenton RC 1.50 4.00
120 Jason Smith RC 1.50 4.00
121 Daequan Cook RC 1.50 4.00
122 Jared Dudley RC 1.50 4.00
123 Wilson Chandler RC 2.50 6.00
124 Morris Almond RC 1.50 4.00
125 Aaron Brooks RC 1.50 4.00
126 Arron Afflalo RC 2.00 5.00
127 Alando Tucker RC 1.50 4.00
128 Petteri Koponen RC 1.50 4.00
129 Carl Landry RC 1.50 4.00
130 Gabe Pruitt RC 1.50 4.00
131 Marcus Williams RC 1.50 4.00
132 Nick Fazekas RC 1.50 4.00
133 Glen Davis RC 2.50 6.00
134 Jermareo Davidson RC 1.50 4.00
135 Josh McRoberts RC 1.50 4.00
136 Chris Richard RC 1.50 4.00
137 Derrick Byars RC 1.50 4.00
138 Adam Haluska RC 1.50 4.00
139 Reyshawn Terry RC 1.50 4.00
140 Jared Jordan RC 1.50 4.00
141 Stephane Lasme RC 1.50 4.00
142 Dominic McGuire RC 1.50 4.00
143 Aaron Gray RC 1.50 4.00
144 JamesOn Curry RC 1.50 4.00
145 Taurean Green RC 1.50 4.00
146 Demetris Nichols RC 1.50 4.00
147 Herbert Hill RC 1.50 4.00
148 Ramon Sessions RC 2.50 6.00
149 Sammy Mejia RC 1.50 4.00
150 D.J. Strawberry RC 1.50 4.00
151 Bernard King 1.25 3.00
152 Bill Laimbeer 1.25 3.00
153 Bill Russell 2.00 5.00
154 Bill Sharman 1.25 3.00
155 Bill Walton 1.25 3.00
156 Billy Cunningham 1.25 3.00
157 Bob Cousy 2.00 5.00
158 Bob McAdoo 1.25 3.00
159 Bob Pettit 1.50 4.00
160 Chris Mullin 1.25 3.00
161 Clyde Drexler 1.50 4.00
162 Dave Bing 1.25 3.00
163 Dave Cowens 1.50 4.00
164 David Robinson 2.00 5.00
165 David Thompson 1.50 4.00
166 Dennis Rodman 2.00 5.00
167 Dolph Schayes 1.25 3.00
168 Earl Monroe 1.25 3.00
169 Elgin Baylor 1.25 3.00
170 Elvin Hayes 1.25 3.00
171 George Gervin 1.25 3.00
172 George Mikan 2.50 6.00
173 Hakeem Olajuwon 1.50 4.00
174 Hal Greer 1.25 3.00
175 Isiah Thomas 1.25 3.00
176 James Worthy 1.50 4.00
177 Jerry West 1.50 4.00
178 John Havlicek 1.25 3.00
179 John Stockton 2.00 5.00
180 Julius Erving 2.50 6.00
181 Karl Malone 1.50 4.00
182 Kevin McHale 1.50 4.00
183 Larry Bird 4.00 10.00
184 Lenny Wilkens 1.25 3.00
185 Magic Johnson 3.00 8.00
186 Michael Jordan 10.00 25.00
187 Moses Malone 1.25 3.00
188 Nate Archibald 1.25 3.00
189 Nate Thurmond 1.25 3.00
190 Oscar Robertson 1.25 3.00
191 Paul Arizin 1.25 3.00
192 Paul Westphal 1.50 4.00
193 Pete Maravich 4.00 10.00
194 Rick Barry 1.25 3.00
195 Robert Parish 1.25 3.00
196 Sam Jones 1.50 4.00
197 Walt Frazier 1.25 3.00
198 Wes Unseld 1.25 3.00
199 Willis Reed 1.25 3.00
200 Wilt Chamberlain 2.50 6.00
201 Yao Ming EX .75 2.00
202 Steve Nash EX .75 2.00
203 Chris Paul EX 1.25 3.00
204 Brandon Roy EX .75 2.00
205 Rudy Gay EX .60 1.50
206 Al Horford Uni EX .75 2.00
207 LaMarcus Aldridge EX .75 2.00
208 Tyrus Thomas EX .60 1.50
209 Julian Wright EX .60 1.50
210 Al Horford Suit EX .75 2.00
211 Corey Brewer EX .75 2.00
212 Joakim Noah EX 1.50 4.00
213 Mike Conley Jr. EX 1.00 2.50
214 Jeff Green EX .75 2.00
215 Kevin Durant Suit EX 5.00 12.00
216 Michael Jordan Red EX 5.00 12.00
217 Kobe Bryant Prpl EX 3.00 8.00
218 LeBron James Red EX 3.00 8.00
219 Kevin Durant Ball EX 5.00 12.00
220 Michael Jordan White EX 5.00 12.00

221 Kobe Bryant Yllw EX 3.00 8.00
222 LeBron James Blue EX 3.00 8.00
223 Kevin Durant Uni EX 5.00 12.00
224 Michael Jordan Red EX 5.00 12.00
225 Kobe Bryant Yllw EX 3.00 8.00
226 LeBron James White EX 3.00 8.00
227 Kevin Durant Back EX 5.00 12.00
228 Michael Jordan Black EX 5.00 12.00
229 Kobe Bryant Yllw EX 3.00 8.00
230 LeBron James Orange EX 3.00 8.00

2007-08 Artifacts Blue

*BLUE 1-100: 3X TO 8X BASE HI
*BLUE 101-150: 1.25X TO 3X
*BLUE 151-200: 2X TO 5X BASE HI
*BLUE 201-230: 4X TO 10X BASE HI
BLUE PRINT RUN 25 SER.#'d SETS

2007-08 Artifacts Gold

*GOLD 1-100: 1.25X TO 3X BASE HI
*GOLD 101-150: .75X TO 2X BASE HI
*GOLD 151-200: .75X TO 2X BASE HI
GOLD PRINT RUN 100 SER.#'d SETS

2007-08 Artifacts Red

*RED 1-100: 2X TO 5X BASE HI
*RED 101-150: 1X TO 2.5X BASE HI
*RED 151-200: 1.25X TO 3X BASE HI
RED PRINT RUN 50 SER.#'d SETS

2007-08 Artifacts Autofacts

APPROXIMATELY ONE PER BOX
AFAB Andrea Bargnani 5.00 12.00
AFAG Maurice Ager 4.00 10.00
AFAH Al Horford 10.00 25.00
AFAJ Antawn Jamison 4.00 10.00
AFAR Allan Ray 4.00 10.00
AFBA B.J. Armstrong 8.00 20.00
AFBB Bruce Bowen 4.00 10.00
AFBD Brad Daugherty 5.00 12.00
AFBG Ben Gordon 8.00 20.00
AFBJ Bobby Jones 4.00 10.00
AFBL Bill Laimbeer 5.00 12.00
AFBM Brad Miller 4.00 10.00
AFBR Brandon Roy 6.00 15.00
AFBW Bill Walton 8.00 20.00
AFCD Chris Duhon 4.00 10.00
AFCF Channing Frye 4.00 10.00
AFCH Connie Hawkins 8.00 20.00
AFCM Cedric Maxwell 4.00 10.00
AFCO Michael Cooper 5.00 12.00
AFCS Cedric Simmons 4.00 10.00
AFDB Dee Brown 4.00 10.00
AFDG Daniel Gibson 4.00 10.00
AFDL David Lee 5.00 12.00
AFDN David Noel 4.00 10.00
AFDR David Robinson 30.00 60.00
AFDU Kevin Durant 100.00 200.00
AFEC Eddy Curry 4.00 10.00
AFEV Maurice Evans 4.00 10.00
AFFE Raymond Felton 5.00 12.00
AFFG Francisco Garcia 4.00 10.00
AFGG George Gervin 6.00 15.00
AFGR Aaron Gray 6.00 15.00
AFIL Mile Ilic 4.00 10.00
AFJA James Augustine 4.00 10.00
AFJB Josh Boone 4.00 10.00
AFJE Julius Erving 30.00 60.00
AFJG Joey Graham 4.00 10.00
AFJK Jason Kapono 4.00 10.00
AFJM Jamaal Magloire 4.00 10.00
AFJR Jalen Rose 4.00 10.00
AFJS J.R. Smith 4.00 10.00
AFJW Julian Wright 6.00 15.00
AFKB Kobe Bryant 125.00 250.00
AFKI Jason Kidd 20.00 50.00
AFKL Kyle Lowry 4.00 10.00
AFLA LaMarcus Aldridge 6.00 15.00
AFLJ LeBron James 100.00 200.00
AFMA Corey Maggette 4.00 10.00
AFMB Mike Bibby 4.00 10.00
AFMC Mardy Collins 4.00 10.00
AFME Mark Eaton 5.00 12.00
AFMI Mike James 4.00 10.00
AFMJ Michael Jordan 300.00 525.00
AFMP Pops Mensah-Bonsu 4.00 10.00
AFMW Marcus Williams 4.00 10.00
AFNO Steve Novak 4.00 10.00
AFPD Paul Davis 4.00 10.00
AFPM Paul Millsap 5.00 12.00
AFPO Patrick O'Bryant 4.00 10.00
AFPP Paul Pierce 10.00 25.00
AFQR Quentin Richardson 4.00 10.00
AFRE Renaldo Balkman 4.00 10.00
AFRF Randy Foye 4.00 10.00
AFRG Rudy Gay 4.00 10.00
AFRH Ryan Hollins 4.00 10.00
AFRP Robert Parish 6.00 15.00
AFRR Rajon Rondo 10.00 25.00
AFSB Shannon Brown 4.00 10.00
AFSJ Solomon Jones 4.00 10.00
AFSL Shaun Livingston 4.00 10.00
AFSM Sean May 4.00 10.00
AFSN Steve Nash 30.00 80.00
AFSR Sergio Rodriguez 4.00 10.00
AFSS Saer Sene 4.00 10.00
AFST John Stockton 40.00 80.00
AFSW Shawne Williams 4.00 10.00
AFTC Tyson Chandler 4.00 10.00
AFTF T.J. Ford 4.00 10.00
AFTP Tayshaun Prince 5.00 12.00
AFTS Thabo Sefolosha 4.00 10.00
AFTT Tyrus Thomas 6.00 15.00
AFWE Martell Webster 4.00 10.00
AFWF Walt Frazier 8.00 20.00
AFYM Yao Ming 15.00 30.00

2007-08 Artifacts Conference Pairings

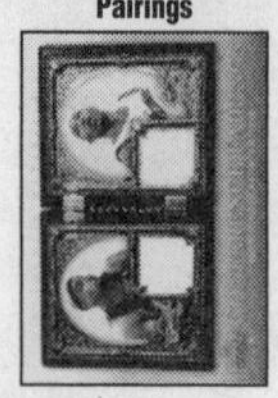

PRINT RUN 150 SER.#'d SETS
UNPRICED SILV.PATCH PRINT RUN 5 SETS
UNPRICED GOLD PATCH PRINT RUN ONE SET
CPAH Carmelo Anthony 6.00 15.00
Al Harrington
CPAJ Gilbert Arenas 3.00 8.00
Joe Johnson
CPAK Nenad Krstic 3.00 8.00
Trevor Ariza
CPAM Andrei Kirilenko 3.00 8.00
Brad Miller
CPAN Ray Allen 3.00 8.00
Jameer Nelson
CPAO LaMarcus Aldridge 3.00 8.00
Mehmet Okur
CPAS Tony Allen 5.00 12.00
John Starks
CPBA Shane Battier 3.00 8.00
Maurice Ager
CPBB Carlos Boozer 3.00 8.00
Shane Battier
CPBC Chris Bosh 6.00 15.00
Vince Carter
CPBE Larry Bird 15.00 30.00
Julius Erving
CPBG Francisco Garcia 3.00 8.00
Andrew Bynum
CPBH Chauncey Billups 3.00 8.00
Larry Hughes
CPBI Kobe Bryant 10.00 25.00
Allen Iverson
CPBN Andrea Bargnani 4.00 10.00
Andres Nocioni
CPBR Jordan Farmar 3.00 8.00
Brandon Roy
CPCB Corey Maggette 3.00 8.00
Carlos Boozer
CPCC Josh Childress 3.00 8.00
Jason Collins
CPCD Sam Cassell 3.00 8.00
Baron Davis
CPCO Marcus Camby 3.00 8.00
Mehmet Okur
CPCS Andrea Bargnani 4.00 10.00
Andrew Bogut
CPDC Mardy Collins 3.00 8.00
Ike Diogu
CPDF Baron Davis 3.00 8.00
Jordan Farmar
CPDM Michael Jordan 20.00 50.00
Dennis Rodman
CPDN Andres Nocioni 3.00 8.00
Ronald Dupree
CPDO Clyde Drexler 8.00 20.00
Hakeem Olajuwon
CPDR Mike Dunleavy 3.00 8.00
J.J. Redick
CPED Monta Ellis 3.00 8.00
Ricky Davis
CPEJ Monta Ellis 4.00 10.00
Jarrett Jack
CPES Elton Brand 3.00 8.00
Shane Battier
CPFG Randy Foye 3.00 8.00
Rudy Gay
CPFH Michael Finley 4.00 10.00
Juwan Howard
CPFR Raymond Felton 3.00 8.00
Michael Redd
CPGB Drew Gooden 3.00 8.00
Caron Butler
CPGH Manu Ginobili 4.00 10.00
Luther Head
CPGS Pau Gasol 4.00 10.00
Amare Stoudemire
CPGW Delonte West 3.00 8.00
Rudy Gay
CPHF Josh Howard 3.00 8.00
Michael Finley
CPHG Ben Gordon 3.00 8.00
Richard Hamilton
CPHH Kirk Hinrich 3.00 8.00
Richard Hamilton
CPHM Brendan Haywood 3.00 8.00
Sean May
CPHR Juwan Howard 5.00 12.00
Jalen Rose
CPIJ Andre Iguodala 3.00 8.00
Richard Jefferson
CPJF Joe Johnson 3.00 8.00
Raymond Felton
CPJJ LeBron James 40.00 70.00
Michael Jordan
CPJM Magic Johnson 20.00 40.00
Pete Maravich
CPJN Bobby Jones 3.00 8.00
David Noel
CPJP LeBron James 8.00 20.00
Tayshaun Prince
CPJR Jarrett Jack 3.00 8.00
Jalen Rose
CPJV Luke Jackson 3.00 8.00
Charlie Villanueva
CPJW Antawn Jamison 3.00 8.00
Marvin Williams
CPKA Kenyon Martin 3.00 8.00
Andrei Kirilenko
CPKM Jason Kidd 6.00 15.00
Stephon Marbury
CPMB Tracy McGrady 10.00 25.00
Kobe Bryant
CPMC Andre Miller 3.00 8.00
Jamal Crawford
CPMD Mike Bibby 3.00 8.00
Damon Stoudamire
CPMH Kevin Martin 6.00 15.00
Devin Harris
CPMK Chris Kaman 3.00 8.00
Brad Miller
CPMP Mickael Pietrus 5.00 12.00
Tony Parker
CPMW Sean May 3.00 8.00
Marvin Williams
CPNA Nene 3.00 8.00
Hilton Armstrong
CPNS Dirk Nowitzki 5.00 12.00
Peja Stojakovic
CPOB Lamar Odom 4.00 10.00
Elton Brand
CPOH Emeka Okafor 5.00 12.00
Dwight Howard
CPOO Shaquille O'Neal 5.00 12.00
Jermaine O'Neal
CPPD Mickael Pietrus 3.00 8.00
Boris Diaw
CPPH Paul Pierce 5.00 12.00
Kirk Hinrich
CPPL Johan Petro 3.00 8.00
Shawn Livingston
CPPM Tony Parker 4.00 10.00
Mike Miller
CPPW Deron Williams 5.00 12.00
Chris Paul
CPRA Quentin Richardson 3.00 8.00
Gilbert Arenas
CPRF Brandon Roy 3.00 8.00
Randy Foye
CPRH Quentin Richardson 3.00 8.00
Udonis Haslem
CPRL Ron Artest 3.00 8.00
Lamar Odom
CPRO David Robinson 10.00 25.00
Hakeem Olajuwon
CPRR Zach Randolph 3.00 8.00
Jason Richardson
CPSH J.R. Smith 3.00 8.00
Devin Harris
CPSJ Jose Calderon 3.00 8.00
Shannon Brown
CPSN Steve Nash 8.00 20.00
John Stockton
CPSS Cedric Simmons 3.00 8.00
Stromile Swift
CPTW Jason Terry 3.00 8.00
Luke Walton
CPWD Chris Wilcox 3.00 8.00
Boris Diaw
CPWK Jason Williams 5.00 12.00
Kyle Korver
CPWM Chris Webber 8.00 20.00
Alonzo Mourning
CPWO Ben Wallace 6.00 15.00
Shaquille O'Neal
CPWP Antoine Walker 3.00 8.00
Tayshaun Prince
CPWR Martell Webster 3.00 8.00
Luke Ridnour
CPWW Ben Wallace 4.00 10.00
Rasheed Wallace
CPYD Yao Ming 8.00 20.00
Tim Duncan

2007-08 Artifacts Divisional Artifacts

PRINT RUN 250 SER.#'d SETS
*BLUE: .6X TO 1.5X BASE HI
BLUE PRINT RUN 50 SER.#'d SETS
*COPPER: 1.25X TO 3X BASE HI
COPPER PRINT RUN 25 SER.#'d SETS
UNPRICED GOLD PRINT RUN ONE SET
*RED: .5X TO 1.25X BASE HI
RED PRINT RUN 100 SER.#'d SETS
UNPRICED SILVER PRINT RUN 10 SETS
*PATCH RED: 1.5X TO 4X BASE HI
PATCH RED PRINT RUN 29 SER.#'d SETS
UNPRICED PATCH SILV.PRINT RUN 5 SETS
UNPRICED PATCH GOLD PRINT RUN ONE SET
DAAB Andrew Bogut 3.00 8.00
DAAI Andre Iguodala 3.00 8.00
DAAJ Antawn Jamison 3.00 8.00
DAAK Andrei Kirilenko 2.50 6.00
DAAL Al Harrington 2.50 6.00
DAAM Alonzo Mourning 4.00 10.00
DAAR Allan Ray 2.00 5.00
DAAS Amare Stoudemire 3.00 8.00
DABC Brian Cardinal 2.00 5.00
DABD Boris Diaw 2.50 6.00
DABG Ben Gordon 3.00 8.00
DABI Chauncey Billups 3.00 8.00
DABJ Bobby Jones 2.00 5.00
DABR Brandon Roy 4.00 10.00
DABU Caron Butler 3.00 8.00
DACA Carmelo Anthony 4.00 10.00
DACB Chris Bosh 3.00 8.00
DACF Channing Frye 2.50 6.00
DACH Josh Childress 2.50 6.00
DACM Corey Maggette 2.50 6.00
DACP Chris Paul 6.00 15.00
DACS Cedric Simmons 2.50 6.00
DACW Chris Wilcox 2.00 5.00
DADA Baron Davis 3.00 8.00
DADH Dwight Howard 5.00 12.00
DADN David Noel 2.00 5.00
DADR David Robinson 5.00 12.00
DADS DeShawn Stevenson 2.00 5.00
DADW Deron Williams 5.00 12.00
DAEB Elton Brand 3.00 8.00
DAEO Emeka Okafor 3.00 8.00
DAGH Grant Hill 5.00 12.00
DAGW Gerald Wallace 3.00 8.00
DAHA Devin Harris 3.00 8.00
DAHO Josh Howard 2.50 6.00
DAIV Allen Iverson 4.00 10.00
DAJC Jose Calderon 2.50 6.00
DAJE Julius Erving 6.00 15.00
DAJH Juwan Howard 2.50 6.00
DAJK Jason Kidd 3.00 8.00
DAJM Jamaal Magloire 2.00 5.00
DAJO Jermaine O'Neal 3.00 8.00
DAJR J.J. Redick 3.00 8.00
DAJS Josh Smith 3.00 8.00
DAJT Jamaal Tinsley 2.00 5.00
DAKB Kobe Bryant 6.00 15.00
DAKE Kenyon Martin 3.00 8.00
DAKG Kevin Garnett 5.00 12.00
DAKT Kenny Thomas 2.00 5.00
DALA LaMarcus Aldridge 4.00 10.00
DALB Larry Bird 8.00 20.00
DALD Luol Deng 3.00 8.00
DALH Larry Hughes 2.50 6.00
DALJ LeBron James 8.00 20.00
DALO Lamar Odom 3.00 8.00
DALR Luke Ridnour 2.50 6.00
DALW Luke Walton 2.00 5.00
DAMA Sean May 2.00 5.00
DAMB Mike Bibby 3.00 8.00
DAMD Mike Dunleavy 2.50 6.00
DAMG Manu Ginobili 3.00 8.00
DAMJ Michael Jordan 25.00 60.00
DAMM Mike Miller 3.00 8.00
DAMO Mehmet Okur 2.00 5.00
DAMP Morris Peterson 2.00 5.00
DAMR Michael Redd 3.00 8.00
DAMW Marvin Williams 3.00 8.00
DANO Dirk Nowitzki 4.00 10.00
DANR Nate Robinson 3.00 8.00
DAPG Pau Gasol 3.00 8.00
DAPI Mickael Pietrus 2.00 5.00
DAPO Patrick O'Bryant 2.00 5.00
DAPP Paul Pierce 4.00 10.00
DAPS Peja Stojakovic 3.00 8.00
DARA Ray Allen 3.00 8.00
DARI Jason Richardson 3.00 8.00
DARJ Richard Jefferson 3.00 8.00
DARL Rashard Lewis 2.50 6.00
DARW Rasheed Wallace 3.00 8.00
DASC Sam Cassell 3.00 8.00
DASD Samuel Dalembert 2.00 5.00
DASH Shawn Marion 3.00 8.00
DASM Stephon Marbury 2.50 6.00
DASN Steve Nash 4.00 10.00
DASO Shaquille O'Neal 6.00 15.00
DAST John Stockton 5.00 12.00
DATD Tim Duncan 5.00 12.00
DATE Jason Terry 2.50 6.00
DATH J.R. Smith 3.00 8.00
DATM Tracy McGrady 3.00 8.00
DATP Tayshaun Prince 3.00 8.00
DAUD Beno Udrih 2.00 5.00
DAUH Udonis Haslem 2.50 6.00
DAVC Vince Carter 4.00 10.00
DAWA Ben Wallace 3.00 8.00
DAWF Walt Frazier 3.00 8.00
DAWR Bracey Wright 2.00 5.00
DAYM Yao Ming 4.00 10.00
DAZI Zydrunas Ilgauskas 2.50 6.00
DAZR Zach Randolph 2.50 6.00

2007-08 Artifacts Triple Jerseys

PRINT RUN 50 SER.#'d SETS
UNPRICED GOLD PRINT RUN ONE SET
BA Andrea Bargnani 6.00 15.00
AB Andrew Bogut 5.00 12.00
AI Allen Iverson 8.00 20.00
AJ Antawn Jamison 5.00 12.00
AK Andrei Kirilenko 4.00 10.00
AM Alonzo Mourning 12.50 30.00
AW Antoine Walker 4.00 10.00
BR Brandon Roy 6.00 15.00
CB Chauncey Billups 5.00 12.00
CD Clyde Drexler 15.00 40.00
DR David Robinson 20.00 40.00
DW Deron Williams 8.00 20.00
GG Gerald Green 4.00 10.00
HO Hakeem Olajuwon 6.00 15.00
JC Josh Childress 4.00 10.00
JE Julius Erving 10.00 25.00
JF Jordan Farmar 3.00 8.00
JK Jason Kidd 5.00 12.00
JO Jermaine O'Neal 5.00 12.00
JS John Stockton 8.00 20.00
JW Jason Williams 4.00 10.00
KB Kobe Bryant 15.00 40.00
KG Kevin Garnett 8.00 20.00
LA LaMarcus Aldridge 6.00 15.00
LB Larry Bird 15.00 40.00
LJ LeBron James 15.00 30.00
MG Manu Ginobili 5.00 12.00
MA Magic Johnson 12.00 30.00
MJ Michael Jordan 25.00 60.00
MR Michael Redd 5.00 12.00
PA Tony Parker 6.00 15.00
PM Pete Maravich 50.00 100.00
RH Richard Hamilton 4.00 10.00
RJ Richard Jefferson 5.00 12.00
RW Rasheed Wallace 5.00 12.00
SB Shane Battier 4.00 10.00
SM Josh Smith 5.00 12.00
TD Tim Duncan 8.00 20.00
TM Tracy McGrady 5.00 12.00
VC Vince Carter 6.00 15.00
YM Yao Ming 6.00 15.00
ZR Zach Randolph 4.00 10.00

1955 Ashland/Aetna Oil

The 1955 Ashland/Aetna Oil Basketball set contains 96 black and white, unnumbered cards each measuring 2 5/8" by 3 3/4". There are two different backs for each card front, one with an Ashland Oil ad, the other with an Aetna Oil ad. Aetna cards are considered to be worth an additional premium of 25 percent above the prices listed below. The backs contain a player's vital statistics, his home town, and his graduation class. These thin-stocked cards are difficult to obtain and have been numbered in the checklist below, by team and alphabetically within each team. The cards were distributed one at a time at Ashland (Kentucky and West Virginia) or Aetna (Ohio) gas stations in the region of the particular college. The set contains 12 players each from eight colleges: Eastern Kentucky 1-12, Kentucky 13-24, Louisville 25-36, Marshall 37-48, Morehead 49-60, Murray 61-72, Western Kentucky 73-84, and West Virginia 85-96. The cards of smaller school players within this set seem to be in shorter supply than the cards of the larger schools. However, the prices below reflect the smaller demand for the cards of players from the smaller schools. The key cards in the set are the first cards of Adolph Rupp, Hall of Famer and legendary coach of the Kentucky Wildcats, Ed Diddle, and Laker player/announcer Hot Rod Hundley. The catalog designation for this set is UO18.

COMPLETE SET (96) 4500.00 7500.00
COMMON CARD (1-36/73-84) 25.00 60.00
COMMON CARD (37-60) 35.00 70.00
COMMON CARD (61-72) 45.00 90.00
COMMON CARD (85-96) 50.00 100.00
1 Jack Adams 25.00 60.00
2 William Baxter 25.00 60.00
3 Jeffrey Brock 25.00 60.00
4 Paul Collins 25.00 60.00
5 Richard Culbertson 25.00 60.00
6 James Floyd 25.00 60.00
7 Harold Fraler 25.00 60.00
8 George Francis Jr. 25.00 60.00
9 Paul McBrayer CO 50.00 100.00
10 James Mitchell 25.00 60.00
11 Ronald Pellegrinon 25.00 60.00
12 Guy Strong 25.00 60.00
13 Earl Adkins 25.00 60.00
14 William Bibb 25.00 60.00
15 Jerry Bird 25.00 60.00
16 John Brewer 25.00 60.00
17 Robert Burrow 25.00 60.00
18 Gerry Calvert 25.00 60.00
19 William Evans 40.00 80.00
20 Phillip Grawemeyer 25.00 60.00
21 Ray Mills 25.00 60.00
22 Linville Puckett 25.00 60.00
23 Gayle Rose 40.00 80.00
24 Adolph Rupp CO 250.00 500.00
25 William Darragh 25.00 60.00
26 Vladimir Gastevich 25.00 60.00
27 Allan Glaza 25.00 60.00
28 Herbert Harrah 25.00 60.00
29 Bernard Peck Hickman CO 50.00 100.00
30 Richard Keffer 25.00 60.00
31 Gerald Moreman 25.00 60.00
32 James Morgan 25.00 60.00
33 John Prudhoe 25.00 60.00
34 Phillip Rollins 25.00 60.00
35 Roscoe Shackelford 25.00 60.00
36 Charles Tyra 50.00 100.00
37 Robert Ashley 35.00 70.00
38 Lewis Burns 35.00 70.00
39 Francis Crum 35.00 70.00
40 Raymond Frazier 35.00 70.00
41 Cam Henderson CO 40.00 75.00
42 Joseph Hunnicutt 35.00 70.00
43 Clarence Parkins 35.00 70.00
44 Jerry Pierson 35.00 70.00
45 David Robinson 35.00 70.00
46 Paul Underwood 35.00 70.00
47 Cebert Price 35.00 70.00
48 Charles Slack 35.00 70.00
49 David Breeze 35.00 70.00
50 Leonard Carpenter 35.00 70.00
51 Omar Fannin 35.00 70.00
52 Donnie Gaunce 35.00 70.00
53 Steve Hamilton 75.00 130.00
54 Bobby Laughlin CO 35.00 70.00
55 Jesse Mayabb 35.00 70.00
56 Jerry Riddle 35.00 70.00
57 Howard Shumate 35.00 70.00
58 Dan Swartz 35.00 70.00
59 Forrest Tolle 35.00 70.00
60 Donald Whitehouse 35.00 70.00
61 Rex Alexander CO 45.00 90.00
62 Jorgen Anderson 45.00 90.00
63 Jack Clutter 45.00 90.00
64 Howard Crittenden 45.00 90.00
65 James Gainey 45.00 90.00
66 Richard Kinder 45.00 90.00
67 Theo. Koenigsmark 45.00 90.00
68 Joseph Mikez 45.00 90.00
69 John Powless 50.00 100.00
70 Dolph Regelsky 45.00 90.00
71 Reinhard Tauck 45.00 90.00
72 Francis Watrous 45.00 90.00
73 Forrest Able 25.00 60.00
74 Tom Benbrook 25.00 60.00
75 Ronald Clark 25.00 60.00
76 Lynn Cole 25.00 60.00
77 Robert Daniels 25.00 60.00
78 Ed Diddle CO 125.00 250.00
79 Victor Harned 25.00 60.00
80 Dencil Miller 25.00 60.00
81 Ferrel Miller 25.00 60.00
82 George Orr 25.00 60.00
83 Jerry Weber 25.00 60.00
84 Jerry Whitsell 25.00 60.00
85 William Bergines 50.00 100.00
86 James Brennan 50.00 100.00
87 Marc Constantine 50.00 100.00
88 Michael Holt 50.00 100.00
89 Hot Rod Hundley 250.00 500.00
90 Clayce Kishbaugh 50.00 100.00
91 Ronald LaNeve 50.00 100.00
92 Gary Mullins 50.00 100.00
93 Fred Schaus CO 150.00 275.00
94 Frank Spadafore 50.00 100.00
95 Peter White 50.00 100.00
96 Paul Witting 50.00 100.00

1997 AT and T NBA PrePaid Phone Cards

These prepaid phone cards were made available through advertisements in AT and T and Chevron billing statements, as well as through various mailer coupon packs. The twelve 15-minute cards sold for $5.25 per card. Nine 30-minute cards at $10.50 per card and eight 60-minute cards at $21.00 per card were also available. One could purchase the entire 29 card set for $265.50. The offer was available through 8/31/97, but the prepaid cards have no expiration date. The card fronts have a blue background with a close-up of the player. The left side contains a somewhat blurred color action shot of the player with his name in white font running perpendicular on the side. Prices below are for cards that have unused phone time. Expired cards are 20 percent of the values listed below. The cards are unnumbered and listed below in alphabetical order within each section.

COMPLETE SET (29) 120.00 300.00
COMP.15 MINUTE SET (12) 20.00 50.00
COMP.30 MINUTE SET (9) 30.00 80.00
COMP.60 MINUTE SET (8) 80.00 200.00
1 Vin Baker 15 MIN 2.00 5.00
2 Shawn Bradley 15 MIN 2.00 5.00
3 Dale Ellis 15 MIN 2.00 5.00
4 Tom Gugliotta 15 MIN 2.00 5.00
5 Juwan Howard 15 MIN 2.00 5.00
6 Jim Jackson 15 MIN 2.00 5.00
7 Dikembe Mutombo 15 MIN 2.50 6.00
8 Bobby Phills 15 MIN 2.00 5.00
9 Dino Radja 15 MIN 2.00 5.00
10 Clifford Robinson 15 MIN 2.00 5.00
11 David Robinson 15 MIN 3.00 8.00
12 Latrell Sprewell 15 MIN 2.50 6.00
13 Greg Anthony 30 MIN 4.00 10.00
14 Brent Barry 30 MIN 4.00 10.00
15 Anfernee Hardaway 30 MIN 8.00 20.00
16 Kevin Johnson 30 MIN 5.00 12.00
17 Shawn Kemp 30 MIN 5.00 12.00
18 Karl Malone 30 MIN 8.00 20.00
19 Alonzo Mourning 30 MIN 6.00 15.00
20 Mitch Richmond 30 MIN 5.00 12.00
21 Clarence Weatherspoon 30 MIN 4.00 10.00
22 Clyde Drexler 60 MIN 12.00 30.00
23 Grant Hill 60 MIN 12.00 30.00
24 Eddie Jones 60 MIN 10.00 25.00
25 Toni Kukoc 60 MIN 10.00 25.00
26 Reggie Miller 60 MIN 12.00 30.00
27 Charles Oakley 60 MIN 8.00 20.00
28 Glen Rice 60 MIN 8.00 20.00
29 Damon Stoudamire 60 MIN 8.00 20.00

1992 Australian Futera NBL

This standard-size 96-card set was sponsored by Mitsubishi Motors. It consists of 12 teams with eight cards per team. The fronts display white-bordered player action shots with the team name and logo in the upper right corner and a different colored stripe for each team down the left side. The backs carry a color player portrait with biography and career statistics. The cards are unnumbered, arranged alphabetically by player, and checklisted alphabetically according to teams as follows: Adelaide 36ers (1-12), Brisbane Bullets (13-24), Canberra Cannons (25-36), Melbourne Tigers (37-48), North Melbourne Giants (49-60), Perth Wildcats (61-72), Southeast Melbourne Magic (73-84), and Sydney Kings (85-96).

COMPLETE SET (96) 15.00 40.00
1 Mark Bradtke .60 1.50
2 Mike Corkeron .20 .50
3 Mark Davis .40 1.00
4 Jerry Dennard .20 .50
5 Butch Hays .60 1.50
6 Graham Kubank .20 .50
7 Albert Leslie ACO .20 .50
8 Brett Maher .20 .50
9 Michael McKay .20 .50
10 Don Shipway CO .20 .50
11 Kym Taylor .20 .50
12 Brett Wheeler .20 .50
13 Adrian Branch 1.00 2.50
14 Lyndon Brieffies .20 .50
15 Greg Fox .20 .50
16 Luke Gribble .20 .50
17 Shane Heal .75 2.00
18 Brian Kerle CO .20 .50
19 Simon Kerle .20 .50
20 Leroy Loggins .75 2.00
21 Gordie McLeod ACO .20 .50
22 Andre Moore .40 1.00
23 Paul Rees .20 .50
24 Blair Smith .20 .50
25 Lachlan Armfield .20 .50
26 Barry Barnes CO .20 .50
27 Simon Cottrell .20 .50
28 Ian Ellis ACO .20 .50
29 Steve Hood .40 1.00
30 Jamie Kennedy .20 .50
31 Herb McEachin .20 .50
32 Jason Reese .20 .50
33 Phil Smyth .20 .50
34 John Stelzer .20 .50
35 Matt Witkowski .20 .50
36 Mat Zauner .20 .50
37 Lanard Copeland .60 1.50
38 Andrew Gaze 1.25 3.00
39 Lindsay Gaze CO .20 .50
40 Warrick Giddey .20 .50
41 Ray Gordon .20 .50
42 Steven Lunardon .20 .50
43 Nigel Purchase .20 .50
44 Robert Sibley .20 .50
45 David Simmons .40 1.00
46 Dean Vickerman .20 .50
47 Alan Westover ACO .20 .50
48 Steven Whitehead .30 .75
49 Glenn Binnes ACO .20 .50
50 Ray Borner .30 .75
51 Martin Clarke .20 .50
52 Scott Fisher .40 1.00
53 David Graham .20 .50
54 Rod Johnson .20 .50
55 Mark Leader .20 .50
56 Paul Maley .30 .75
57 Bruce Palmer CO .20 .50
58 Darryl Pearce .20 .50
59 Pat Reidy .20 .50
60 Andrew Simons .20 .50
61 Murray Arnold CO .20 .50
62 James Crawford .30 .75
63 Michael Ellis .20 .50
64 Ricky Grace .60
65 Dave Hancock ACO .20
66 Peter Hansen .20
67 Vince Hinchen .20
68 Griffin Longley .20
69 Tiny Pinder 1.25
70 Trevor Torrance .20
71 Andrew Vlahov .60
72 Eric Watterson .20
73 Lucas Agrums .20
74 Bruce Bolden .50
75 John Dorge .30
76 Brian Goorjian CO .20
77 Andrew Howey .20
78 Darren Lucas .20
79 Milt Newton .75
80 Scott Ninnis .20
81 Andrew Parkinson .20
82 Darren Perry .30
83 Tony Ronaldson .20
84 Ian Stacker .20
85 Jody Austin .20
86 Brad Dalton .20
87 Mark Dalton .20
88 Tony De Ambrosis .20
89 Peter Hill .20
90 Damian Keogh .20
91 Dwayne McClain .75
92 Ken McClary .20
93 Tim Morrissey .20
94 Cory Reader .20
95 Bob Turner CO .20
96 Dean Uthoff .75

1992 Australian Stops NB

This 92-card standard-size Australian National Basketball League set features black-bordered g color player action photos on the card fronts. Th player's name appears in white lettering in the n above each photo. The team name appears in w the margin below along with "Stops '92" in red. white back, the player's name, along with a brief biography, are shown in the top left, and in the t right, the NBL and Stops logos are displayed. A stat table appears underneath along with some c highlights. The player's team logo at the bottom rounds out the card. The cards are grouped by t follows: Adelaide 36ers (2-6, 26, 51), Brisbane (7-12), Canberra Cannons (13-16, 18), Hobart (17, 29-33), Geelong Supercats (19-22, 58), Go Coast Rollers (23-25, 27, 28), Melbourne Tigers 34-40, 80), Newcastle Falcons (41-44), North Melbourne Giants (45-50), Perth Wildcats (52- 91), Illawarra Hawks (60-64), South-East Melbo Magic (65-71), Sydney Kings (72-79), and Won NBL (82-87).

COMPLETE SET (92) 25.00
1 Ken Watson CO .40
2 Mark Bradtke .75
3 Mark Davis .50
4 Butch Hays .75
5 Michael McKay .20
6 Graham Kubank .20
7 Leroy Loggins .75
8 Andre Moore .75
9 Shane Heal 1.25
10 Simon Kerle .20
11 Greg Fox .20
12 Adrian Branch 1.50
13 Jamie Kennedy .20
14 Herb McEachin .20
15 Phil Smyth .20
16 Simon Cottrell .20
17 Jason Reese UER .40
(Card front says Canberra Cannons)
18 Steve Hood .60
19 Robert Locke .40
20 Cecil Exum .50
21 Matthew Alexander .40
22 Wayne Larkins .20
23 Mike Mitchell .75
24 Larry Sengstock .20
25 Andre LaFleur .60
26 Matthew Reece UER .20
(Card front says Gold Coast Rollers)
27 Ron Radliff .20
28 Rodger Smith .20
29 Cal Bruton CO .20
30 Wayne McDaniel .40
31 Justin Cass .20
32 Shane Froling .20
33 David Stiff .20
34 Lindsay Gaze CO .40
35 Andrew Gaze 2.00
36 David Simmons .50
37 Stephen Whitehead .50
38 Warrick Giddey .20
39 Lanard Copeland 1.25
40 Robert Sibley .20
41 Terry Dozier .75
42 Michael Johnson .20
43 Al Green .20
44 Paul Kuiper .20
45 Bruce Palmer CO .20
46 Scott Fisher .40
47 Ray Borner .20
48 Paul Maley .20
49 Pat Reidy .20
50 Mark Leader .20
51 Darryl Pearce UER .20
(Card front says North Melbourne Giants)
52 Murray Arnold CO .20
53 Ricky Grace .75
54 Andrew Vlahov .75
55 Tiny Pinder .75
56 James Crawford .60
57 Mike Ellis .20
58 Vince Hinchen UER .40
(Card front says Perth Wilcats)
59 Perth Team Photo .40
60 Justin Withers .40

g Hubbard .40 1.00
ck Harmison .75 2.00
vin Thomas .60 1.50
g Overton 1.50 4.00
n Goorjian CO .20 .50
e Bolden .60 1.50
en Lucas .20 .50
en Perry .40 1.00
n Dorge .20 .50
rew Parkinson .40 1.00
t Ninnis .40 1.00
Turner CO .20 .50
n Uthoff .75 2.00
nian Keogh .40 1.00
yne McClain 1.50 4.00
McClary .40 1.00
Morrissey .20 .50
k Dalton .20 .50
Jester .40 1.00
ey Kings mascot)
y Melbourne .40 1.00
s mascot)
e Crouch REF .20 .50
Pappas CO .20 .50
bie Black .20 .50
ine Moyle .20 .50
ralian Women's Team .40 1.00
e Burgess .20 .50
denong Rangers .40 1.00
Photo
Cooks .20 .50
at Miners
k Raiders .40 1.00
Photo
cklist .20 .50
y Grace SP 1.25 3.00
s Crawford (Back to Back Champions)
) Card SP .75 2.00

993 Australian Futera NBL

t series of the 1993 Australian Futera NBL set s of 110 standard-size cards. The fronts display ordered glossy color player action shots. Above oto, the player's name is displayed within a ay bar. Below the photo, the NBL logo appears ith the Mitsubishi name and logo. The backs e player's stats, career highlights and head within a light gray field. The player's name at the top within a darker gray bar. The cards cklisted below alphabetically according to s follows: Adelaide 36ers (1-7), Brisbane (8-16), Canberra Cannons (17-23), Geelong ts (24-30), Gold Coast Rollers (31-36), a Hawks (37-42), Hobart Devils (43-50), rne Tigers (51-58), Newcastle Falcons (59-67), elbourne Giants (68-76), Perth Wildcats (77- nsville Suns (85- 91), South-East Melbourne 92-102), and Sydney Kings (103-110).

ETE SET (110) 25.00 60.00
Blakemore .30 .75
Maher .20 .50
myth .20 .50
Ninnis .20 .50
Davis .40 1.00
McKay .20 .50
Dennard .20 .50
Purchase .20 .50
Heal .75 2.00
y Loggins .40 1.00
Colbert .20 .50
e Moore .40 1.00
er Smith .20 .50
Gribble .20 .50
e Froling .20 .50
lan Armfield .20 .50
Stelzer .20 .50
n Cottrell .20 .50
ey Monroe .75 2.00
Herzog .20 .50
Witkowski .20 .50
Kendrick .20 .50
n Withers .20 .50
ael Morrison .20 .50
Exum .40 1.00
Borner .20 .50
n Branch 1.00 2.50
e Larkins .20 .50
Hetenyi .20 .50
e Hinchen .20 .50
Mitchell .40 1.00
e LaFleur .40 1.00
ew Goodwin .20 .50
Fox .20 .50
ew Reece .20 .50
Hill .20 .50
k Harmison .50 1.25
e Hays .40 1.00
n Thomas .40 1.00
Steele .20 .50
MacDonald .20 .50
Corkeron .20 .50
e McDaniel .30 .75
Havrilla .20 .50
d Whiteside .20 .50
d Close .20 .50
Turner .20 .50
ony Stewart .20 .50
n Cass .20 .50
ew Svaldenis .20 .50
ck Giddey .20 .50
ew Gaze 1.00 2.50
Bradtke .50 1.25
rd Copeland .50 1.25
Gordon .20 .50
hen Whitehead .20 .50
rt Sibley .20 .50
d Simmons .30 .75
n Dennis .20 .50
ael Johnson .20 .50
tte Stephens .75 2.00
een .20 .50
t Kruger .20 .50
Joynes .20 .50
Dozier .60 1.50
Harvey .20 .50

67 Paul Kuiper .20 .50
68 Terry Johnson .20 .50
69 Darryl Pearce .20 .50
70 Mark Leader .20 .50
71 Larry Sengstock .20 .50
72 Pat Reidy .20 .50
73 Jason Reese .30 .75
74 Rod Johnson .20 .50
75 Paul Rees .20 .50
76 Paul Maley .20 .50
77 Scott Fisher .30 .75
78 James Crawford .20 .50
79 Andrew Vlahov .50 1.25
80 Eric Watterson .20 .50
81 Ricky Grace .40 1.00
82 Chris Carroll .20 .50
83 Trevor Torrance .20 .50
84 Steve Davis .20 .50
85 David Blades .20 .50
86 Rimas Kurtinaitias .30 .75
87 Ricky Jones .40 1.00
88 Lucas Agrums .20 .50
89 Graham Kubank .20 .50
90 Tonny Jensen .20 .50
91 Paul Simpson .20 .50
92 Darren Perry .20 .50
93 Bruce Bolden .40 1.00
94 Robert Rose .40 1.00
95 Darren Lucas .20 .50
96 Andrew Parkinson .20 .50
97 Tony Ronaldson .20 .50
98 Shane Bright .20 .50
99 David Graham .20 .50
100 Simon Kerle .20 .50
101 Andre Lemamis UER .20 .50
(Misspelled Andrej on back)
102 John Dorge .20 .50
103 Dwayne McClain .50 1.25
104 Damian Keogh .20 .50
105 Ken McClary .20 .50
106 Tony De Ambrosis .20 .50
107 Greg Hubbard .20 .50
108 Tim Morrissey .20 .50
109 Dean Uthoff .50 1.25
110 Mark Dalton .20 .50
NNO Melbourne Magic 8.00 20.00
NNO Herb McEachin 12.50 30.00
Legends Card

1993 Australian Futera Best of Both Worlds

The "Best of Both Worlds" redemption cards were randomly inserted in foil packs, and they could be redeemed for four cards featuring basketball players who have played in both the NBA and the NBL. Only 500 of each card were produced. The expiration date to redeem the cards in Australia was December 31, 1993. Each redeemed card was accompanied by a certification card. Inside white borders, the fronts show color action player photos, with the player's name printed across the top. The backs carry a color closeup above a player profile.

COMPLETE SET (4) 40.00 100.00
1 Terry Dozier 12.50 30.00
2 Dwayne McClain 12.50 30.00
3 Adrian Branch 15.00 35.00
4 Doug Overton 12.50 30.00

1993 Australian Futera Honours Awards

1,000 of each of these 11 standard-size cards were inserted in 1993 Futera packs. The fronts display full-color action photos framed by white borders. The top left corner of the picture is cut off and replaced by a set logo displaying the honor received. The backs have a narrowly-cropped closeup photo on the left and season summary on the right.

COMPLETE SET (11) 80.00 200.00
1 Scott Fisher MVP 6.00 15.00
2 Andrew Gaze MVP 10.00 25.00
3 Andrew Svaldenis MIP 3.00 8.00
4 Terry Dozier D-POY 6.00 15.00
5 Lachlan Armfield ROY 3.00 8.00
6 Brian Goorjian COY 3.00 8.00
7 Doug Overton 1st 8.00 20.00
8 Andrew Gaze 1st 10.00 25.00
9 Dwayne McClain 1st 6.00 15.00
10 Andrew Vlahov 1st 8.00 20.00
11 Scott Fisher 1st 6.00 15.00

1993 Australian Futera Super Gold

1,000 of each of these 14 standard-size cards were inserted in 1993 Futera packs. The fronts feature an color action shot surrounded by gold borders. The player's name is printed on a ghosted stripe along the left edge, while the title "Super Gold Card Series" appears across the top. The backs show gold borders and have a color photo, player profile, team logo and career stats.

COMPLETE SET (14) 50.00 125.00
1 John Dorge 3.00 8.00
2 Lanard Copeland 8.00 20.00
3 Pat Reidy 3.00 8.00
4 Cecil Exum 3.00 8.00
5 Melvin Thomas 6.00 15.00
6 Dean Uthoff 4.00 10.00
7 Terry Dozier 8.00 20.00
8 Mark Davis 8.00 20.00
9 Rimas Kurtinaitias 6.00 15.00
10 Shane Heal 10.00 25.00
11 Mike Mitchell 6.00 15.00
12 Justin Withers 3.00 8.00
13 Ricky Grace 10.00 25.00
14 Donald Whiteside 3.00 8.00

1993 Australian Stops NBL

This 92-card standard-size Australian National Basketball League set features white-bordered glossy color player action photos on the card fronts. The player's name appears in black lettering in the margin above each photo. The team name appears in black in the margin below along with "Stops '92" in red. On the white back, the player's name, along with a brief biography, are shown in the top left, and in the top right, the Stops logo is displayed. A short stat table appears underneath along with some career highlights. The player's team logo at the bottom and a picture of the front of the player's Rookie Card rounds out the card.

COMPLETE SET (92) 20.00 50.00
1 Terry Dozier .50 1.25
2 Steve Hood SD .40 1.00
3 Shane Heal 1.25 3.00
4 Tim Morrissey .20 .50
5 Cecil Exum .30 .75
6 Andrew Syaldenis .20 .50
7 Andrew Goodwin .20 .50
8 Al Green .20 .50
9 Wayne McDaniel .30 .75
10 Couch REF .20 .50
Mildenhall REF
11 Cal Bruton CO .20 .50
12 American All-Stars .40 1.00
13 Craig Adams .20 .50
14 Stephen Whitehead .20 .50
15 Michael Johnson .20 .50
16 Everette Stephens .75 2.00
17 Donald Whiteside .20 .50
18 Michael McKay .20 .50
19 Grant Kruger .20 .50
20 James Crawford .30 .75
21 Paul Maley .20 .50
22 Pat Reidy .20 .50
23 Australian Boomers .20 .50
24 Trevor Torrance .20 .50
25 Luc Longley 2.00 5.00
26 Chuck Harmison .60 1.50
27 Tony Ronaldson .20 .50
28 Tony De Ambrosis .20 .50
29 Mark Davis .40 1.00
30 Lanard Copeland SD .50 1.25
31 Darren Perry .40 1.00
32 Everette Stephens SD .50 1.25
33 Checklist .30 .75
34 Andrew Parkinson .20 .50
35 David Simmons .30 .75
36 Warrick Giddey .20 .50
37 Phil Smyth .20 .50
38 Scott Ninnis .20 .50
39 Leroy Loggins .60 1.50
40 Rodney Monroe .75 2.00
41 Lachlan Armfield .30 .75
42 Michael Morrison .30 .75
43 Ray Borner .20 .50
44 Mike Mitchell .60 1.50
45 Andre La Fleur .40 1.00
46 Andrew Vlahov .40 1.00
47 Scott Fisher .40 1.00
48 Dean Uthoff .50 1.25
49 Bruce Bolden .40 1.00
50 Greg Hubbard .30 .75
51 Damian Keogh .30 .75
52 Rimas Kurtinaitas .40 1.00
53 Adrian Branch 1.00 2.50
54 Vince Hinchen .20 .50
55 Ricky Jones .30 .75
56 Paris McCurdy .40 1.00
57 Brett Maher .20 .50
58 Shane Froling .20 .50
59 1992 Magic Champs .20 .50
60 Andre Moore .40 1.00
61 Fred Herzog .20 .50
62 Justin Withers .20 .50
63 Graham Kubank .20 .50
64 Wayne Larkins .20 .50
65 Lucas Agrums .20 .50
66 Matthew Reese .20 .50
67 Jim Havrilla .30 .75
68 Chris Steele .20 .50
69 Ray Gordan .20 .50
70 Mark Bradtke .50 1.25
71 Larry Sengstock .20 .50
72 Darryl Pearce .20 .50
73 Rod Johnson .20 .50
74 Brett Brown CO .20 .50
75 Jason Reese .20 .50
76 Ricky Grace .60 1.50
77 Darren Lucas .20 .50
78 Bruce Palmer CO .20 .50
79 Tigerman .30 .75
80 Robert Sibley .20 .50
81 Robert Rose .40 1.00
82 David Graham .20 .50
83 Ken McClary .20 .50
84 Dwayne McClain .75 2.00
85 Brian Goorjian CO .20 .50
86 Peter Hill .20 .50
87 Butch Hays .40 1.00
88 Andrew Gaze 1.25 3.00
89 Tonny Jensen .20 .50
90 Melvin Thomas .30 .75
91 Lanard Copeland .75 2.00
92 Checklist .40 1.00

1994 Australian Futera NBL Promos

This five-card cello-wrapped promo pack was given away at the 1994 National Sports Collectors Convention in Houston. Measuring the standard size, the fronts display full-bleed color action photos. Each card of the set is serially-numbered out of 5,000 sets produced. The cards are numbered on the back in gold foil in the upper right corner.

COMPLETE SET (5) 2.50 6.00
RC5 Andrew Gaze BK 1.00 2.50

1994 Australian Futera NBL

The 1994 Futera Australian NBL set consists of 220 standard-size cards. Foil packs contained nine cards, with 40 packs per display box and eight boxes per case. Australian and U.S. versions of the set were produced; the latter is distinguished by the silver foil "World Export Edition" seal on the card fronts. The fronts display white-bordered glossy color player action shots. A wooden basketball court stripe that cuts across the bottom of the picture and up the right edge carries the player's name and his team name. On a wooden basketball court background, the backs have a second color action photo, player profile, biography, and statistics. The cards are numbered on the back and checklisted below alphabetically according to teams as follows: Adelaide Sixers (1-6/111-116), Brisbane Bullets (7-13/117-121), Canberra Cannons (14-19/122-126), Geelong Supercats (20-25/127-130), Gold Coast Rollers (26-31/131-135), Hobart Devils (32-37/136-140), Illawarra Hawks (38-43/141-145), Melbourne Tigers (44-50/146-151), Newcastle Falcons (51-57/152-156), North Melbourne Giants (58-65/157-162), Perth Wildcats (66-72/163-167), South East Melbourne Magic (73-80/168-173), Sydney Kings (81-88/174-179), and Townsville Suns (89-96/180-183). The first series closes with NBL Honour Awards (97-106) and checklists (107-110).

COMPLETE SET (220) 30.00 60.00
COMPLETE SERIES 1 (110) 15.00 30.00
COMPLETE SERIES 2 (110) 15.00 30.00
1 Phil Smyth .20 .50
2 Scott Ninnis .20 .50
3 Brett Maher .20 .50
4 Michael McKay .20 .50
5 Mark Davis .40 1.00
6 David Robinson .40 1.00
7 Dave Colbert .20 .50
8 Shane Froling .20 .50
9 Rodger Smith .20 .50
10 Leroy Loggins .40 1.00
11 Andre Moore .30 .75
12 Shane Heal .60 1.50
13 Luke Gribble .20 .50
14 Rodney Monroe .40 1.00
15 Justin Withers .20 .50
16 Matt Witkowski .20 .50
17 Fred Herzog .20 .50
18 Lachlan Armfield .20 .50
19 John Stelzer .20 .50
20 Wayne Larkins .20 .50
21 Adrian Branch .75 2.00
22 Cecil Exum .25 .60
23 Ray Borner .20 .50
24 Michael Morrison .30 .75
25 Vince Hinchen .20 .50
26 Andrew Goodwin .20 .50
27 Andre LaFleur .20 .50
28 John Szigetti .20 .50
29 Matthew Reece .20 .50
30 Mike Mitchell .30 .75
31 Greg Fox .20 .50
32 Justin Cass .20 .50
33 David Close .20 .50
34 Andrew Svaldenis .20 .50
35 Donald Whiteside .30 .75
36 Wayne McDaniel .30 .75
37 Anthony Stewart .20 .50
38 Butch Hays .40 1.00
39 Chris Steele .20 .50
40 Melvin Thomas .30 .75
41 Dene MacDonald .20 .50
42 Chuck Harmison .50 1.25
43 Mike Corkeron .20 .50
44 Lanard Copeland .40 1.00
45 Stephen Whitehead .20 .50
46 Robert Sibley .20 .50
47 Mark Bradtke .50 1.25
48 Andrew Gaze .50 1.25
49 David Simmons .20 .50
50 Warrick Giddey .20 .50
51 Michael Johnson .20 .50
52 Al Green .20 .50
53 Peter Harvey .20 .50
54 Everette Stephens .30 .75
55 Grant Kruger .20 .50
56 Terry Dozier .40 1.00
57 Simon O'Donnell .20 .50
58 Paul Maley .20 .50
59 Darryl Pearce .20 .50
60 Mark Leader .20 .50
61 Jason Reese .20 .50
62 Rod Johnson .20 .50
63 Pat Reidy .20 .50
64 Paul Rees .20 .50
65 Larry Sengstock .20 .50
66 Trevor Torrance .20 .50
67 Andrew Vlahov .30 .75
68 James Crawford .20 .50
69 Ricky Grace .40 1.00
70 Scott Fisher .20 .50
71 Eric Watterson .20 .50
72 Chris Carroll .20 .50
73 Darren Lucas .20 .50
74 Bruce Bolden .30 .75
75 Robert Rose .40 1.00
76 John Dorge .20 .50
77 Andrew Parkinson .20 .50
78 David Graham .20 .50
79 Darren Perry .20 .50
80 Tony Ronaldson .20 .50
81 Greg Hubbard .20 .50
82 Dwayne McClain .40 1.00
83 Ken McClary .20 .50
84 Tim Morrissey .20 .50
85 Damian Keogh .20 .50
86 Tony De Ambrosis .20 .50
87 Dean Uthoff .50 1.25
88 Wayne Womack .20 .50
89 David Blades .20 .50
90 Ricky Jones .40 1.00
91 Rimas Kurtinaitias .20 .50
92 Brian Andrews .20 .50
93 Lucas Agrums .20 .50
94 Tonny Jensen .20 .50
95 Paul Simpson .20 .50
96 Darren Smith .20 .50
97 Robert Rose .30 .75
MVP Award
98 Andrew Gaze .40 1.00
Most Efficient Player
99 Andrew Gaze .40 1.00
Top Point Scorer
100 Terry Dozier .40 1.00
Best Defensive Player
101 Andre LaFleur .30 .75
Good Hands Award
102 Bruce Bolden .20 .50
Top Rebounder
103 Chris Blakemore .20 .50
Rookie of the Year
104 Scott Ninnis .20 .50
Most Improved Player
105 Andrew Vlahov .20 .50
Int'l. POY
106 Alan Black .20 .50
Coach of the Year
107 Checklist 1-37 .20 .50
108 Checklist 38-80 .20 .50
109 Checklist 81-110 .20 .50
110 Checklist Specials .20 .50
111 Robert Rose .40 1.00
112 Mark Davis .30 .75
113 Chris Blakemore .20 .50
114 Phil Smyth .20 .50
115 Brett Maher .20 .50
116 Mike McKay .20 .50
117 Dave Colbert .20 .50
118 Shane Heal .40 1.00
119 Leroy Loggins .40 1.00
120 Andre Moore .30 .75
121 Robert Sibley .20 .50
122 Jason Reese .20 .50
123 Lachlan Armfield .20 .50
124 Fred Herzog .20 .50
125 Justin Withers .20 .50
126 Adam Kendrick .20 .50
127 Everette Stephens .30 .75
128 Ray Borner .20 .50
129 Cecil Exum .30 .75
130 Simon Kerle .20 .50
131 Mike Mitchell .30 .75
132 Matthew Reece .20 .50
133 Tony De Ambrosis .20 .50
134 Andre LaFleur .30 .75
135 Peter Hill .20 .50
136 Calvin Talford .50 1.25
137 Darren Perry .20 .50
138 Wayne McDaniel .30 .75
139 Anthony Stewart .20 .50
140 Keith Nelson .20 .50
141 Butch Hays .30 .75
142 Melvin Thomas .30 .75
143 Chuck Harmison .50 1.25
144 Chris Steele .20 .50
145 Dene MacDonald .20 .50
146 Lanard Copeland .40 1.00
147 David Simmons .20 .50
148 Mark Bradtke .40 1.00
149 Andrew Gaze .50 1.25
150 Warrick Giddey .20 .50
151 Ray Gordon .20 .50
152 Derek Rucker .30 .75
153 Terry Dozier .40 1.00
154 Tonny Jensen .20 .50
155 Grant Kruger .20 .50
156 Paul Kuiper .20 .50
157 Darryl McDonald .60 1.50
158 Paul Maley .20 .50
159 Mark Leader .20 .50
160 Larry Sengstock .20 .50
161 Pat Reidy .20 .50
162 Paul Rees .20 .50
163 Ricky Grace .40 1.00
164 James Crawford .20 .50
165 Andrew Vlahov .30 .75
166 Scott Fisher .20 .50
167 Martin Cattalini .20 .50
168 Adonis Jordan .75 2.00
169 Darren Lucas .20 .50
171 Andrew Parkinson .20 .50
172 Tony Ronaldson .20 .50
173 David Graham .20 .50
174 Mario Donaldson .20 .50
175 Leon Trimmingham .60 1.50
176 Tim Morrissey .20 .50
177 Greg Hubbard .20 .50
178 Dean Uthoff .50 1.25
179 Damian Keogh .20 .50
180 Brendan LeGassick .20 .50
181 Ricky Jones .40 1.00
182 Lucas Agrums .20 .50
183 Graham Kubank .20 .50
184 1993 Finals Series .20 .50
Perth Defeats Brisbane
185 1993 Finals Series .20 .50
Melbourne Defeats SE Melbourne
186 1993 Finals Series .20 .50
Melbourne Leads Perth
187 1993 Finals Series .20 .50
Perth Squares the Series
188 1993 Finals Series .20 .50
Melbourne Defeats Perth
189 1993 Finals Series .20 .50
Grand Final MVP
190 1993 Finals Series .20 .50
Victory At Last
191 Lanard Copeland .40 1.00
Andrew Gaze
192 Ricky Grace .30 .75
James Crawford
193 Andre LaFleur .30 .75
Mike Mitchell
194 Shane Heal .30 .75
Leroy Loggins
195 Melvin Thomas .40 1.00
Butch Hays
196 Leon Trimmingham .30 .75
Mario Donaldson
197 Patrick Reidy .30 .75
Darryl McDonald
198 Sam MacKinnon .60 1.50
199 C.J. Bruton .20 .50
200 Aaron Trahair .40 1.00
201 Brad Williams .20 .50
202 Ryan Knights .20 .50
203 Darren Smith .20 .50
204 Opals Header .20 .50
204A Jenny Whittel .20 .50
205 Annie Burgess .20 .50
206 Sandy Brondello .20 .50
207 Allison Cook .20 .50
208 Michele Timms 1.00 2.50
209 Shelley Gorman .20 .50
210 Robyn Maher .20 .50
211 Trish Fallon .20 .50
212 Rachael Sporn .20 .50
213 Karen Dalton .20 .50
214 Michelle Brogan .20 .50
215 Samantha Thornton .20 .50
216 Tom Maher .20 .50
217 Checklist 111-151 .20 .50
218 Checklist 152-183 .20 .50
219 Checklist 184-220 .20 .50
220 Checklist Specials .20 .50

1994 Australian Futera Best of Both Worlds

Randomly inserted in foil packs, the "Best of Both Worlds" redemption cards feature basketball players who have played in both the NBA and the NBL. The odds of finding these standard-size cards were 1:300 foil packs. 1,000 of each card were produced, and the cards were individually numbered 0001-1000. The expiration date to redeem the first series cards in Australia was December 31, 1994. The second series cards' expiration date in Australia was August 31, 1995. Both the redemption and the certificate fronts show a ball, which displays the Australian and American flags, swishing through the net. The picture card shows an action and a portrait shot on the front, while the back contains biographical information.

COMPLETE SET (12) 125.00 250.00
BW1 Ricky Grace 12.50 30.00
Picture Card
BW2 Lanard Copeland 12.50 30.00
Picture Card
BW3 Andrew Gaze 15.00 40.00
Picture Card
BW4 Adonis Jordan 15.00 50.00
Picture Card
CC3 Andrew Gaze 10.00 20.00
Certification Card
CC4 Adonis Jordan 10.00 20.00
Certification Card
CD1 Ricky Grace 6.00 15.00
Certification Card
CD2 Lanard Copeland 8.00 20.00
Certification Card
RC3 Andrew Gaze 10.00 25.00
Redemption Card
RC4 Adonis Jordan 8.00 20.00
Redemption Card
RD1 Ricky Grace 8.00 20.00
Redemption Card
RD2 Lanard Copeland 8.00 20.00
Redemption Card

1994 Australian Futera Defensive Giants

Randomly inserted in second series foil packs, this seven-card standard-size set features the ABL's better defensive players. Just 3,000 of each card were produced, with each one individually numbered 0001-3000. The fronts display full-bleed color action photos; the letter D appears in the background in lightly ghosted lettering. The player's name is stamped in gold foil in the lower right corner. The backs have full-color photos in the left corner and a career summary on a light blue panel.

COMPLETE SET (7) 20.00 50.00
DG1 Terry Dozier 3.00 8.00
DG2 Robert Rose 6.00 15.00
DG3 Darren Lucas 2.00 5.00
DG4 Melvin Thomas 5.00 12.00
DG5 Derek Rucker 6.00 15.00
DG6 Mark Davis 5.00 12.00
DG7 Mark Bradtke 6.00 15.00

1994 Australian Futera Lords of the Ring

Randomly inserted in foil packs, this six-card standard-size set focuses on the NBL's best slam dunkers. The odds of finding these cards were 1:20 foil packs. Just 5,000 of each card were produced, with each one individually numbered 0001-5000. Against a brick wall (LR1-LR6) or textured (LR7-LR12) design, the fronts show these players dunking. The player's name is gold-foil stamped vertically along the left edge, and the Lords of the Ring logo is in the lower right corner. The backs feature player profiles.

COMPLETE SET (12) 25.00 60.00
LR1 Robert Rose 3.00 8.00
LR2 Lanard Copeland 3.00 8.00
LR3 Ricky Jones 1.50 4.00
LR4 Mark Bradtke 3.00 8.00
LR5 David Simmons 2.00 5.00
LR6 Andrew Vlahov 3.00 8.00
LR7 James Crawford 3.00 8.00
LR8 Bruce Bolden 3.00 8.00
LR9 Mike Mitchell 3.00 8.00
LR10 Darryl McDonald 5.00 12.00
LR11 Paul Maley 3.00 8.00
LR12 Leon Trimmingham 5.00 12.00

1994 Australian Futera NBL Heroes

Randomly inserted in foil packs, this 14-card standard-size set documents the careers of NBL legend Leroy Loggins in the first series and Scott Fisher in the second series. The odds of finding these cards were 1:17 foil packs. Just 5,000 of each card were produced, with each one individually numbered 0001-5000. Cards number NH2-NH7 and NH9-NH14 feature various action shots surrounded by black borders. The bottoms read "NBL 94" in white lettering against the black background while the word "Heroes" is stamped in gold foil. On a gray background, the backs carry a color drawing and summarize the player's career by year.

COMPLETE SET (14) 10.00 25.00
NH1 Leroy Loggins 1.50 4.00
Drawing
NH2 Leroy Loggins 1989 1.25 3.00
NH3 Leroy Loggins 1990 1.25 3.00
NH4 Leroy Loggins 1991 1.25 3.00
NH5 Leroy Loggins 1992 1.25 3.00
NH6 Leroy Loggins 1993 1.25 3.00
NH7 Leroy Loggins 1.25 3.00
Olympic Career
NH8 Scott Fisher 1.50 4.00
Drawing
NH9 Scott Fisher 1988 1.00 2.50
NH10 Scott Fisher 1989 1.00 2.50
NH11 Scott Fisher 1990 1.00 2.50
NH12 Scott Fisher 1991 1.00 2.50
NH13 Scott Fisher 1992 1.00 2.50
NH14 Scott Fisher 1993 1.00 2.50

1994 Australian Futera New Horizons

Randomly inserted in second series foil packs, this six-card standard-size set features young ABL stars. The fronts have the player's photo against their city skyline. In gold foil lettering, the player's first name runs across the left side while their last name is on the top. The words "New Horizons" are on the bottom. The backs feature a player photo and information against a street map of their city. According to the media release, only 3000 of each card was produced.

COMPLETE SET (6) 12.00 30.00
HZ1 Calvin Talford 4.00 10.00
HZ2 Darryl McDonald 5.00 12.00
HZ3 Leon Trimmingham 5.00 12.00
HZ4 Mario Donaldson 2.00 5.00
HZ5 Adonis Jordan 4.00 10.00
HZ6 Keith Jordan 2.00 5.00

1994 Australian Futera Offensive Threats

Randomly inserted in first series foil packs, this 14-card standard-size set features the highest point scorer from each NBL team. The odds of finding these cards were one per nine foil packs. Just 5,000 of each card were produced, with each one individually numbered 0001-5000. The fronts display full-bleed color action photos; the player's last name and scoring average appear in the background in lightly ghosted lettering. The backs have a full-color photo in the left corner and a career summary on a green panel.

COMPLETE SET (14) 20.00 50.00
OT1 Andrew Gaze 4.00 10.00
OT2 Ricky Jones 1.50 4.00
OT3 Adrian Branch 2.50 6.00
OT4 Jason Reese 1.50 4.00
OT5 Melvin Thomas 1.50 4.00
OT6 Rodney Monroe 2.50 6.00
OT7 Dwayne McClain 2.50 6.00
OT8 Scott Fisher 2.50 6.00
OT9 Leroy Loggins 2.50 6.00
OT10 Mike Mitchell 2.50 6.00
OT11 Mark Davis 1.50 4.00
OT12 Bruce Bolden 2.50 6.00
OT13 Everette Stephens 2.50 6.00
OT14 Wayne McDaniel 1.50 4.00

1994 Australian Futera Signature Series

Randomly inserted in second series foil packs, this seven-card standard-size set features signed cards of popular players. According to information provided on the media release, only 500 of each card was produced and each was individually numbered.

COMPLETE SET (7) 175.00 350.00
SS1 Checklist 8.00 20.00
SS2 Calvin Talford 24.00 60.00
SS3 Darryl McDonald 40.00 100.00
SS4 Mario Donaldson 20.00 50.00
SS5 Leon Trimmingham 50.00 125.00
SS6 Andrew Vhalov 24.00 60.00
SS7 Bruce Bolden 20.00 50.00

1995 Australian Futera NBL

The first series of the 1995 Futera Australian NBL set consists of 110 standard-size cards. Each display box contained forty 9-card foil packs. Each pack contains one card from an insert set, and one pack in each box featured only insert set cards. The fronts display full-bleed color action shots, with the player's name and team logo in an orangish-red stripe running along one of the sides. The backs have the player's name, a full-color inset photo, biographical information and NBL seasonal and career stats. All these elements are framed against a purple background on the left, a basketball in the middle and a wrap-around of the front photo on the right.

COMPLETE SET (110) 8.00 20.00
1 Darryl McDonald .40 1.00
2 Ricky Grace .30 .75
3 Fred Cofield .40 1.00
4 Brett Maher .07 .20
5 Lanard Copeland .40 1.00
6 Dean Uthoff .40 1.00
7 Everette Stephens .40 1.00
8 Andre LaFleur .25 .60
9 Graham Kubank .07 .20
10 Luke Gribble .07 .20
11 Darryl Johnson .20 .50
12 Mike Corkeron .07 .20
13 Keith Nelson .07 .20
14 Greg Hubbard .07 .20
15 Robert Rose .30 .75
16 Andrew Vlahov .30 .75
17 Paul Kuiper .07 .20
18 Wayne McDaniel .20 .50
19 Jason Reese .10 .30
20 Justin Cass .07 .20
21 Butch Hays .30 .75
22 Paul Maley .20 .50
23 Dave Simmons .07 .20
24 Mike Mitchell .20 .50
25 Bruce Bolden .30 .75
26 David Colbert .07 .20
27 Pat Reidy .08 .25
28 Mark Dalton .07 .20
29 Chris Blakemore .20 .50
30 Checklist 1-44 .07 .20
31 Simon Kerle .07 .20
32 Chris Steele .07 .20
33 Paul Rees .10 .30
34 Warrick Giddey .07 .20
35 Doug Peacock .07 .20
36 Damian Keogh .08 .25
37 Michael Johnson .07 .20
38 Justin Withers .08 .25
39 Aaron Trahair .20 .50
40 Leroy Loggins .30 .75
41 Mark Leader .07 .20
42 Anthony Stewart .08 .25
43 Adonis Jordan .75 2.00
44 Scott Ninnis .15 .40
45 Leon Trimmingham .50 1.25
46 David Blades .07 .20
47 Grant Kruger .07 .20
48 Robert Sibley .07 .20
49 Vince Hinchen .08 .25
50 Chuck Harmison .40 1.00
51 Matthew Alexander .07 .20
52 Simon Cottrell .07 .20
53 Tony De Ambrosis .07 .20
54 Calvin Talford .40 1.00
55 Sam MacKinnon .30 .75
56 Martin Cattalini .07 .20
57 Mike McKay .07 .20
58 Larry Sengstock .07 .20
59 Andrew Gaze .75 2.00
60 Checklist 45-88 .07 .20
61 Rodger Smith .07 .20
62 Melvin Thomas .20 .50
63 Peter Hill .07 .20
64 Mario Donaldson .07 .20
65 Darren Perry .08 .25
66 Matt Witkowski .08 .25
67 Derek Rucker .30 .75
68 Cecil Exum .30 .75
69 Lucas Agrums .07 .20
70 Darren Lucas .08 .25
71 Mark Bradtke .30 .75
72 Mark Davis .30 .75
73 Peter Harvey .07 .20
74 Ray Borner .08 .25
75 Dene MacDonald .07 .20
76 John Dorge .08 .25
77 Ricky Jones .30 .75
78 Shane Heal .40 1.00
79 Terry Dozier .40 1.00
80 Paul Crombie .07 .20
81 Stephen Whitehead .15 .40
82 Lachlan Armfield .10 .30
83 James Crawford .15 .40
84 Cameron Dickinson .07 .20
85 Tony Ronaldson .10 .30
86 Scott Fisher .15 .40
87 Andrew Parkinson .07 .20
88 Ray Gordon .07 .20
89 Checklist 89-110 .07 .20
90 Giants vs Magic Semi-Finals .07 .20
91 Sixers vs Tigers Semi-Finals .07 .20
92 Sixers vs Giants Semi-Finals .07 .20
93 Giants vs Sixers Semi-Finals .07 .20
94 N Melbourne Giants Championship Team .07 .20
95 Paul Rees .10 .30
96 Shane Heal .50 1.25
97 Derek Rucker .20 .50
98 Shane Heal .30 .75
99 Mark Bradtke .30 .75
100 Keith Nelson .10 .30
101 Andrew Gaze .75 2.00
102 Darryl McDonald .20 .50
103 Sam MacKinnon .20 .50
104 Brett Brown .10 .30
105 Andrew Gaze .75 2.00
106 Darren Lucas .10 .30
107 Chris Blakemore .20 .50
108 Mark Bradtke .30 .75
109 Checklist .07 .20
110 Checklist Specials .07 .20

1995 Australian Futera Airborne

Randomly inserted in first series foil packs, this nine-card standard-size set features players with exceptional jumping ability. The fronts show the featured player in the air against a speckled blue background. The player is identified in the lower left corner with set title above his name. The back is dedicated to a description of the player's leaping capabilities.

COMPLETE SET (9) 2.00 5.00
NA1 Sam MacKinnon .60 1.50
NA2 Butch Hays .30 .75
NA3 Paul Maley .30 .75
NA4 Calvin Talford .40 1.00
NA5 Mike Mitchell .40 1.00
NA6 Dave Simmons .20 .50
NA7 Ricky Jones .30 .75
NA8 Darryl McDonald .75 2.00
NA9 Checklist .20 .50

1995 Australian Futera Clutchmen

Randomly inserted in first series foil packs, this 15-card standard-size set features players who are considered "go-to" players. The fronts feature a color action shot framed by a brown geometric design. The identification of NBL Clutchmen runs vertically down either side while his name is printed across the bottom. The backs contain a player profile on the left, while the right side has a narrowly-cropped color photo.

COMPLETE SET (15) 5.00 12.00
CM1 Robert Rose .40 1.00
CM2 Leroy Loggins .75 2.00
CM3 Fred Cofield .40 1.00
CM4 Cecil Exum .30 .75
CM5 Doug Peacock .20 .50
CM6 Darren Perry .20 .50
CM7 Butch Hays .40 1.00
CM8 Andrew Gaze 1.00 2.50
CM9 Derek Rucker .75 2.00
CM10 Darryl McDonald .75 2.00
CM11 Ricky Grace .60 1.50
CM12 Tony Ronaldson .20 .50
CM13 Leon Trimmingham .30 .75
CM14 Cameron Dickinson 1.00 2.50
CM15 Checklist .20 .50

1995 Australian Futera Head To Head

Randomly inserted in first-series foil packs, these six die-cut double-sided cards feature 12 NBL stars. They were individually numbered out of 5000 and were inserted at a rate of one in every 23 packs. Each side features a color action photo, with a circular headshot gracing the top of the card and extending beyond the upper border. On each side the player's name is gold foil-stamped across the photo.

COMPLETE SET (6) 30.00 80.00
H1 Andrew Gaze 12.50 30.00
Darren Lucas
H2 Leroy Loggins 10.00 25.00
Robert Rose
H3 Leon Trimmingham 10.00 25.00
Ricky Jones
H4 Melvin Thomas 6.00 15.00
Keith Nelson
H5 Fred Cofield 5.00 12.00
Tonny Jensen
H6 Peter Hill 4.00 10.00
Simon Kerle

1995 Australian Futera Instant Impact

Randomly inserted in first series foil packs, this six-card standard-size set highlights players new to the NBL who have made a significant impact on the league. These cards are individually numbered out of 2,500 and were inserted one per 53 packs. The fronts show the player in action against a watercolor background. The set subtitle and the player's name are gold foil stamped on the fronts. The backs have player profile on the left with a narrowly-cropped closeup photo on the right.

COMPLETE SET (6) 25.00 60.00
II1 Darryl McDonald 6.00 15.00
II2 Sam MacKinnon 6.00 15.00
II3 Leon Trimmingham 8.00 20.00
II4 Chris Blakemore 4.00 10.00
II5 Derek Rucker 6.00 15.00
II6 Calvin Talford 4.00 10.00

1995 Australian Futera MVP/Rookie Redemption

Randomly inserted into first series foil packs, this three-card standard-size set features 1994-95 Australian MVP Andrew Gaze and 1994-95 Australian Rookie of the Year Sam MacKinnon. One in every 3,200 packs contained a redemption card for the special card signed by both players. Only 250 of these cards were produced. After a collector mailed in the redemption card, he received the special card, a certification card and the redemption card returned stamped.

COMPLETE SET (3) 125.00 250.00
MR1 Redemption Card 10.00 25.00
MR2 Andrew Gaze 100.00 250.00
Sam MacKinnon
MR3 Certification Card 10.00 25.00

1995 Australian Futera Star Challenge

Randomly inserted into first series foil packs, this ten-card standard-size set comprises of players who participated in the 1994 All-Star Challenge in Sydney. The cards were inserted one in every 16 packs and are individually numbered out of 5,000. The fronts have action shots in their all-star uniforms against a multi-colored background. The backs feature on the right side a color photo of the player in their all-star uniform, with game performance information directly beneath the picture.

COMPLETE SET (10) 15.00 40.00
NBL1 Tony Ronaldson 1.50 4.00
NBL2 Paul Rees 1.00 2.50
NBL3 Mark Bradtke 1.50 4.00
NBL4 Andrew Gaze 4.00 10.00
NBL5 Shane Heal 3.00 8.00
NBL6 Derek Rucker 2.50 6.00
NBL7 Butch Hays 1.50 4.00
NBL8 Mario Donaldson 1.00 2.50
NBL9 Leon Trimmingham 4.00 10.00
NBL10 Lanard Copeland 2.50 6.00

1995 Australian Futera 300 Club

Randomly inserted in first series foil packs, this 17-card standard-size set features players who have played in 300 or more NBL games. The fronts have player portraits which roll back in the lower right corner to reveal how many games each player appeared in. The backs show an action shot and a brief description of their career against a royal blue background.

COMPLETE SET (17) 2.50 6.00
GC1 Larry Sengstock .20 .50
GC2 Leroy Loggins .40 1.00
GC3 Damian Keogh .20 .50
GC4 Herb McEachin .20 .50
GC5 James Crawford .30 .75
GC6 Al Green .20 .50
GC7 Ray Borner .20 .50
GC8 Darryl Pearce .20 .50
GC9 Michael Johnson .20 .50
GC10 Phil Smyth .20 .50
GC11 Chuck Harmison .40 1.00
GC12 Mike Ellis .20 .50
GC13 Tim Morrissey .20 .50
GC14 Simon Cottrell .20 .50
GC15 Eric Waterson .20 .50
GC16 Mike McKay .20 .50
GC17 Checklist .20 .50

1995 Australian Futera Abdul-Jabbar Adidas Promo

This four-card standard-size set covers the career of NBA great Kareem Abdul-Jabbar. This set was issued to promote the 1995 Adidas streetball challenge. These cards are numbered individually out of 5,000. The fronts feature various color action shots of Kareem. The backs have descriptions of his career as well as a photo. Each card also has one line with his complete point totals.

COMPLETE SET (4) 15.00 40.00
COMMON CARD (K1-K4) 5.00 12.00

1996 Australian Futera NBL

This 100-card Series 1 set features big-name players and their respective teams on cards numbered 1-84. Cards numbered 85-89 honor women basketball players in the "Best of Both Worlds" subset. Cards numbered 90-98 feature the 1995 NBL Awards and the Finals Champions. The fronts feature full bleed borderless color action player photos. The backs carry player biographical and career information and statistics.

COMPLETE SET (100) 10.00 25.00
1 Mark Davis .40 1.00
2 Brett Maher .08 .25
3 Chris Blakemore .08 .25
4 Scott Ninnis .08 .25
5 Robert Rose .30 .75
6 Mike McKay .08 .25
7 Leroy Loggins .50 1.25
8 Mike Mitchell .20 .50
9 Robert Sibley .15 .40
10 Andrew Goodwin .08 .25
11 Shane Heal .30 .75
12 John Rillie .08 .25
13 Ray Borner .08 .25
14 Jamie Pearlman .08 .25
15 David Close .08 .25
16 Simon Dwight .08 .25
17 Lachlan Armfield .08 .25
18 Jervaughn Scales .20 .50
19 Andrew Svaldenis .08 .25
20 Cecil Exum .20 .50
21 Joey Wright .08 .25
22 Simon Kerle .08 .25
23 Greg Smith .08 .25
24 Justin Cass .08 .25
25 Trevor Torrance .08 .25
26 John Szigeti .08 .25
27 Peter Harvey .08 .25
28 Doug Peacock .08 .25
29 Tony De Ambrosis .08 .25
30 Steve Woodberry .60 1.50
31 Darren Smith .08 .25
32 Mark Nash .08 .25
33 Darren Perry .08 .25
34 David Stiff .08 .25
35 Andre Moore .30 .75
36 Jerome Scott .08 .25
37 Chuck Harmison .40 1.00
38 Terry Johnson .08 .25
39 Dene MacDonald .08 .25
40 Melvin Thomas .20 .50
41 Andre LaFleur .08 .25
42 Marc Brandon .08 .25
43 Andrew Gaze .75 2.00
44 Mark Bradtke .30 .75
45 Lanard Copeland .40 1.00
46 Blair Smith .08 .25
47 Dave Simmons .08 .25
48 Stephen Whitehead .08 .25
49 Butch Hays .30 .75
50 Michael Johnson .08 .25
51 Tonny Jensen .08 .25
52 Grant Kruger .08 .25
53 Martin McClean .08 .25
54 Matthew Alexander .08 .25
55 Darryl McDonald .08 .25
56 Paul Rees .08 .25
57 Larry Sengstock .08 .25
58 Paul Maley .08 .25
59 Pat Reidy .08 .25
60 Rod Johnson .08 .25
61 Andrew Vlahov .30 .75
62 Aaron Trahair .08 .25
63 Anthony Stewart .08 .25
64 Ricky Grace .40 1.00
65 Scott Fisher .50 1.25
66 James Crawford .30 .75
67 John Dorge .08 .25
68 Darren Lucas .08 .25
69 Tony Ronaldson .08 .25
70 Chris Anstey 1.25 3.00
71 Andrew Parkinson .08 .25
72 Sam MacKinnon .08 .25
73 Bruce Bolden .30 .75
74 Leon Trimmingham .30 .75
75 Justin Withers .08 .25
76 Brad Williams .08 .25
77 Greg Hubbard .08 .25
78 Mark Dalton .08 .25
79 Derek Rucker .08 .25
80 Clarence Tyson .15 .40
81 Shane Froling .08 .25
82 Cameron Dickinson .08 .25
83 David Blades .08 .25
84 Jason Cameron .08 .25
85 Michele Timms .60 1.50
86 Allison Cook .08 .25
87 Trish Fallon .08 .25
88 Sandy Brondello .08 .25
89 Shelley Gorman .08 .25
90 Andrew Gaze MVP .40 1.00
91 John Rillie ROY .20 .50
92 Darren Lucas .08 .25
93 Reggie Smith .20 .50
94 Tonny Jensen .08 .25
95 Darryl McDonald .08 .25
96 Andrew Gaze .40 1.00
97 Alan Black .08 .25
Tom Wisman CO
98 Championship Team .08 .25
Perth Wildcats
99 Checklist 1 .08 .25
100 Checklist 2 .08 .25

1996 Australian Futera NBL All-Stars

Randomly inserted in packs at a rate of one in 20, this 10-card set features the five starting players from the North vs South All-Star game. The fronts display a color player action cut-out on a metallic background that changes when the card is tilted slightly. The backs carry a small color player action photo with information about the player's performance in the All-Star game. Only 1,500 of each card was made and it's individual number is printed on the back.

COMPLETE SET (10) 25.00 60.00
ASN1 Shane Heal 6.00 15.00
ASN2 Derek Rucker 2.00 5.00
ASN3 Leroy Loggins 6.00 15.00
ASN4 Leon Trimmingham 2.00 5.00
ASN5 Clarence Tyson 2.00 5.00
ASS1 Andrew Gaze 10.00 25.00
ASS2 Darryl McDonald 2.00 5.00
ASS3 Mark Davis 2.00 5.00
ASS4 Andrew Vlahov 2.00 5.00
ASS5 John Dorge 2.00 5.00

1996 Australian Futera NBL Futera Dream Team

Randomly inserted in packs at a rate of one in 24, this 5-card set features five composite teams. Each team member contributed to his team's overall score by either points, rebounds, assists, steals or blocks. At the end of the season, the team's final score was calculated by using each player's '96 season average in his nominated category. The card with the winning team could be redeemed by mail for an uncut Series 1 sheet and was automatically entered into a drawing for a trip to the NBL Grand Final. The fronts display color action photos of each of the five members of the team indicated on the card with their names and categories below. The backs carry the instructions on how to arrive at the team's final score. The cards are listed below according to the team number on each card.

COMPLETE SET (5) 8.00 20.00
1 Andrew Gaze 5.00 12.00
Ray Borner
Peter Harvey
Brett Maher
Paul Rees
2 Derek Rucker 1.50 4.00
Andrew Vlahov
Butch Hays
Mike Mitchell
Blair Smith
3 Leon Trimmingham 1.50 4.00
David Simmons
Andre LaFleur
Leroy Loggins
Simon Dwight
4 Melvin Thomas 1.50 4.00
Bruce Bolden
Ricky Grace
Jamie Pearlman
Clarence Tyson
5 Lanard Copeland 2.50 6.00
Mark Davis
Darryl McDonald
Sam MacKinnon
John Dorge

1996 Australian Futera NBL Future Forces

Randomly inserted in packs at a rate of one in 12, this 10-card set features the five starting players from the Bucks vs Colts Coca-Cola Future Forces game. The fronts feature a color action player cut-out on a metallic blue, aqua, and silver-colored basketball background. The backs carry a color action player photo with information about the player's performance during the game. Only 2,500 of each card were printed and are individually numbered on the back.

COMPLETE SET (10) 15.00 40.00
FFB1 Chris Blakemore 2.00 5.00
FFB2 David Stiff 2.00 5.00
FFB3 John Rillie 2.00 5.00
FFB4 Jason Smith 2.00 5.00
FFB5 Rupert Sapwell 2.00 5.00
FFC1 Brett Maher 2.00 5.00
FFC2 Chris Anstey 8.00 20.00
FFC3 Terry Johnson 2.00 5.00
FFC4 Brad Williams 2.00 5.00
FFC5 Martin Catallini 2.00 5.00

1996 Australian Futera NBL Outer Limits

Randomly inserted in packs at a rate of one in 7, this 8-card set features the best three-point shooters in the league. The fronts display a color action player cut-out on a purple background which sparkles when tilted slightly. The backs carry information about the player over a faded player photo. Only 6,000 of each card was produced and are individually numbered on the back.

COMPLETE SET (8) 8.00 20.00
OL1 Shane Heal 1.50 4.00
OL2 Andrew Gaze 3.00 8.00
OL3 Aaron Trahair 1.25 3.00
OL4 Simon Kerle 1.25 3.00
OL5 Chris Jent 1.50 4.00
OL6 Derek Rucker 1.25 3.00
OL7 Terry Johnson 1.25 3.00
OL8 Andrew Parkinson 1.25 3.00

1996 Australian Futera NBL Ten Thousand Point Card

This one-card set commemorates the great achievement of Andrew Gaze and Leroy Loggins for reaching the milestone of scoring 10,000 points. Only 1,000 of the cards were produced, plus the first 150 redemption cards feature a gold seal entitling the holder to a rare dual-autograph version. The cards were randomly inserted at the rate of one in 300 packs with the rate of insertion for the dual-autograph redemption cards being one in 2,000 packs.

TTP2 Andrew Gaze 30.00 80.00
Leroy Loggins

1993-94 Avia Clyde Drexler

This six-card set was cosponsored by Avia and G.I.Joe's (The Sports and Auto Store). Inside white borders, the fronts display color action photos, with "Drexler" gold-foil stamped across the top. All team logos have been airbrushed off the photos. In black print on white background, the backs summarize milestones in Drexler's career. Biographical information on each card rounds out the back. The cards are numbered "X of 6." Between February 26 and March 5, 1994, the redemption card could be exchanged for three Drexler cards.

COMPLETE SET (6) 3.00 8.00
COMMON CARD 1.00 2.50
NNO Redemption Card .40 1.00

1993 Charles Barkley Collector's Edition

This unsightly 14-card set showcases NBA power forward Charles Barkley at various stages of his career. The set was printed by BD Production and Marketing Co. and was licensed by Barkley but not by the NBA as all league logos are removed. The cards full-color measure the standard size and was intended to be updated each year. We have yet to see any cards issued after 1993.

COMPLETE SET (14) 2.00 5.00
COMMON CARD (1-14) .20 .50

1994-95 Basketball USA

These cards were issued in the now defunct German Magazine entitled "Basketball USA". The cards are very similar in size and thickness as 5 Majuer however these cards seem to be a bit harder to locate. The cards have the same layout as 5 Majuer as well, but with purple borders on the front, and the backs are written in German. A few of the cards were issued with white borders and purple stars on the front. All cards have the Basketball USA logo on the bottom of the backs. Eight cards were issued in each bi-monthly magazine with four to a page perforated on the edge. The checklist below is believed to cover only half of the cards in existence. The cards listed are from issues #8 (July 1994) through #15 (September 1995). We hope to be able to provide a more complete listing in future price guides. The cards are unnumbered and listed below in alphabetical order.

COMPLETE SET (64) 150.00 300.00
1 Mahmoud Abdul-Rauf 1.25 3.00
2 Danny Ainge 2.00 5.00
3 Kenny Anderson 1.50 4.00
4 Nick Anderson 1.25 3.00
5 B.J. Armstrong 1.25
6 Stacey Augmon 1.50
7 Charles Barkley 6.00
8 Dana Barros 1.25
9 Muggsy Bogues 1.50
10 Cedric Ceballos 1.25
11 Derrick Coleman 1.50
12 Vlade Divac 2.00
13 Clyde Drexler 5.00
14 Joe Dumars 2.00
15 Sean Elliott 2.00
16 Patrick Ewing 5.00
17 Kendall Gill 1.25
18 Horace Grant 1.50
19 Anfernee Hardaway 3.00
20 Tim Hardaway 2.00
21 Carl Herrera 1.25
22 Jeff Hornacek 1.50
23 Robert Horry 2.00
24 Kevin Johnson 2.00
25 Larry Johnson 2.00
26 Michael Jordan 20.00
27 Shawn Kemp 2.00
28 Toni Kukoc 2.50
29 Christian Laettner 1.50
30 Dan Majerle 2.00
31 Karl Malone 6.00
32 Anthony Mason 1.25
33 Vernon Maxwell 1.25
34 Derrick McKey 1.25
35 Nate McMillan 1.25
36 Reggie Miller 5.00
37 Alonzo Mourning 5.00
38 Tracy Murray 1.25
39 Dikembe Mutombo 2.00
40 Charles Oakley 1.50
41 Hakeem Olajuwon 5.00
42 Shaquille O'Neal 8.00
43 Shaquille O'Neal 8.00
44 Billy Owens 1.25
45 Gary Payton 2.00
46 Sam Perkins 1.25
47 Ricky Pierce 1.25
48 Scottie Pippen 6.00
49 Mark Price 2.00
50 Glen Rice 2.00
51 Mitch Richmond 2.00
52 David Robinson 5.00
53 Dennis Rodman 6.00
54 Detlef Schrempf Dribbling 2.00
55 Detlef Schrempf Passing 2.00
56 Charles Smith 1.25
57 Rik Smits 1.50
58 Latrell Sprewell 2.50
59 John Starks 1.50
60 John Stockton 6.00
61 Rod Strickland 1.25
62 Otis Thorpe 1.25
63 Dominique Wilkins 4.00
64 Kevin Willis 1.25

1984-85 Bay State Bombardi

This oversized blank-backed card was released d the 1984-85 CBA season. The card features man the Bay State Bombardiers players and coaches. black and white card measures 8 3/4" x11".

1 John Ligums 4.00
Dave Cowens
Eddie Chavez
Joe Dawson
Pete DeBisschop
Mark Halsel
Kirk Richards
Kevin Springman
Kevin Williams
Leon Wilson

2003-04 Bazooka

Released in January 2004, Bazooka features 288 where numbers 1-220 are base veterans, some which have two uniform versions. Card numbers 275 feature rookies, some of which have two uni versions, and are inserted at the rate of one in th Cards 276-288 feature rookie players along with Bazooka Joe and are inserted at one in six. Bazo was packaged in 24-pack boxes where packs co six cards, one mini parallel card, one regular pa card (eight total) and one stick of gum. Packs ca suggested retail price of $2.

COMP.SET w/o RC's (220) 15.00
SOME CARDS HAVE HOME AND AWAY VERSI
B (AWAY) VERSION SAME VALUE AS A (HOME
1A Tracy McGrady Home .30
1B Tracy McGrady Away .30
2 DaJuan Wagner .15
3A Allen Iverson Home .40
3B Allen Iverson Away .40
4 Stromile Swift .15
5 Jalen Rose .20
6 Morris Peterson .15
7 Lamar Odom .25
8 Kobe Bryant 1.25
9 Chauncey Billups .25
10 Jason Kidd .40
11 Yao Ming .50
12 Stephon Marbury .20
13 Ricky Davis .20
14 Andrei Kirilenko .25
15 Courtney Alexander .15
16 Brad Miller .25
17 Bobby Jackson .15

hard Lewis .25 .60
an Howard .20 .50
n Houston .20 .50
in Garnett .50 1.25
n Terry .20 .50
son Richardson Home .25 .60
son Richardson Away .25 .60
y Stackhouse .20 .50
n Chandler .20 .50
v Gooden .20 .50
n Williams .20 .50
ie Jones .20 .50
ntin Richardson .20 .50
heed Wallace .25 .60
awn Marion Home .25 .60
awn Marion Away .25 .60
k Rose .15 .40
Wallace .25 .60
Pierce .30 .75
Harpring .20 .50
e Griffin .15 .40
i Kukoc .25 .60
e Bibby .25 .60
ame Brown .15 .40
Thomas .15 .40
Nowitzki .40 1.00
o Ratliff .15 .40
Allen .25 .60
hael Finley .25 .60
ious Harris .15 .40
ernee Hardaway .40 1.00
stian Laettner .15 .40
u Ginobili .30 .75
shaun Prince .25 .60
quille O'Neal .60 1.50
imir Radmanovic .15 .40
bert Cheaney .15 .40
Snow .15 .40
u Gasol Home .25 .60
u Gasol Away .25 .60
embe Mutombo .25 .60
n Williams .15 .40
iss Williamson .15 .40
rick Brown .15 .40
aal Tinsley .15 .40
is Webber .25 .60
yell Marshall .15 .40
rell Armstrong .15 .40
ny Thomas .15 .40
met Okur .20 .50
os Boozer .25 .60
nyon Martin Home .25 .60
nyon Martin Away .25 .60
edy Claxton .15 .40
t Barry .15 .40
Artest .25 .60
n Brand .25 .60
Hudson .15 .40
eve Nash Home .30 .75
eve Nash Away .30 .75
y Parker .25 .60
Boykins .15 .40
y Kittles .15 .40
wn Bradley .15 .40
y Delk .15 .40
runas Ilgauskas .20 .50
g Christie .15 .40
re Stoudemire .40 1.00
Fox .15 .40
n Skinner .15 .40
al Mashburn .20 .50
tel Woods .15 .40
Alston .15 .40
k Anderson .15 .40
re Miller .20 .50
ine Walker .25 .60
k Williams .15 .40
nce Carter Home .40 1.00
nce Carter Away .40 1.00
nell Harvey .15 .40
Lafrentz .15 .40
mond Mason .20 .50
ney Rogers .15 .40
Dixon• .15 .40
em Rush .15 .40
n Russell .15 .40
ndon Anderson .15 .40
an Giricek .15 .40
n Duncan .40 1.00
ch Randolph .25 .60
lik Allen .15 .40
hard Hamilton .20 .50
urice Taylor .15 .40
rko Jaric .15 .40
e Smith .20 .50
a Stojakovic .25 .60
hella Harrington .15 .40
thony Carter .15 .40
lly Szczerbiak .20 .50
y Murphy .25 .60
reef Abdur-Rahim .20 .50
ggie Miller .25 .60
Baker .15 .40
an Scalabrine .15 .40
c Piatkowski .15 .40
ttino Mobley .20 .50
ck Dampier .15 .40
lter Mccarty .15 .40
ron Butler .25 .60
von Dooling .15 .40
chael Redd .25 .60
nny Anderson .20 .50
. Brown .15 .40
vean George .15 .40
e Johnson .25 .60
rian Griffin .15 .40
nzi Wells .15 .40
sual Butler .15 .40
ron Davis .25 .60
sley Person .15 .40
ammond Williams .15 .40
onn Lue .15 .40
an Grant .15 .40
en Campbell .15 .40
n Rice .15 .40
chael Olowokandi .15 .40
thony Peeler .15 .40
ven Hunter .15 .40
dy Curry .20 .50
ome James .15 .40
vis Best .15 .40
r Mohammed .15 .40
ny Battie .15 .40
t Pollard .15 .40
nislav Medvedenko .15 .40
Jackson .15 .40
rcus Camby .20 .50
rcus Haislip .15 .40

150 Glenn Robinson .20 .50
151 Jerome Williams .15 .40
152 Greg Ostertag .15 .40
153 Stephen Jackson .20 .50
154 David Wesley .15 .40
155 Sam Cassell .20 .50
156 Hedo Turkoglu .25 .60
157 Al Harrington .20 .50
158 John Salmons .25 .60
159 Nikoloz Tskitishvili .15 .40
160 Samaki Walker .15 .40
161 Jake Tsakalidis .15 .40
162 Tim Thomas .15 .40
163 Ronald Murray .15 .40
164 Alonzo Mourning .30 .75
165 Chris Jefferies .15 .40
166 Darius Miles .15 .40
167 Kendall Gill .15 .40
168 Lonny Baxter .15 .40
169 Jonathan Bender .15 .40
170 Antawn Jamison .25 .60
171 Keon Clark .15 .40
172 Chris Wilcox .15 .40
173 Brendan Haywood .15 .40
174 Predrag Drobnjak .15 .40
175 Nene .20 .50
176 Casey Jacobsen .15 .40
177 Marcus Fizer .15 .40
178 Howard Eisley .15 .40
179 Damon Stoudamire .20 .50
180 Gary Payton .25 .60
181 Shane Battier .20 .50
182 Desagana Diop .15 .40
183 Antonio Davis .15 .40
184 Keith Van Horn .20 .50
185 Corey Maggette .20 .50
186 Jarron Collins .15 .40
187 James Posey .15 .40
188 Latrell Sprewell .20 .50
189 Aaron McKie .15 .40
190 Vlade Divac .20 .50
191 Pat Garrity .15 .40
192 Eric Williams .15 .40
193 Radoslav Nesterovic .15 .40
194 Dan Gadzuric .15 .40
195 Moochie Norris .15 .40
196 Clifford Robinson .15 .40
197 Richard Jefferson .25 .60
198 Lorenzen Wright .15 .40
199 Nick Van Exel .20 .50
200 Gilbert Arenas .25 .60
201 Robert Horry .20 .50
202 Scottie Pippen .40 1.00
203 Jon Barry .15 .40
204 Derrick Coleman .20 .50
205 Ron Mercer .15 .40
206 DeShawn Stevenson .15 .40
207 Ruben Patterson .15 .40
208 Rodney White .15 .40
209 Jamal Crawford .20 .50
210 Jermaine O'Neal .25 .60
211 Eduardo Najera .15 .40
212 Dan Dickau .15 .40
213 Antonio McDyess .20 .50
214 J.R. Bremer .15 .40
215 Dion Glover .15 .40
216 Lamond Murray .15 .40
217 Larry Hughes .20 .50
218 Mike Miller .25 .60
219 Mike Dunleavy .20 .50
220 Karl Malone .30 .75
221 David West RC .75 2.00
222 Steve Blake RC .75 2.00
223A LeBron James Home RC 6.00 15.00
223B LeBron James Away RC 6.00 15.00
224 Keith Bogans RC .60 1.50
225 Josh Howard RC .60 1.50
226A Chris Kaman Home RC .75 2.00
226B Chris Kaman Away RC .75 2.00
227A Marcus Banks Home RC .60 1.50
227B Marcus Banks Away RC .60 1.50
228A Chris Bosh Home RC 1.25 3.00
228B Chris Bosh Away RC 1.25 3.00
229 Troy Bell RC .60 1.50
230 Luke Walton RC .60 1.50
231 Francisco Elson RC .60 1.50
232 Ndudi Ebi RC .60 1.50
233 Maurice Williams RC 1.00 2.50
234 Kendrick Perkins RC 1.00 2.50
235 Dahntay Jones RC .60 1.50
236 Jason Kapono RC .60 1.50
237 Kyle Korver RC .75 2.00
238 Josh Moore RC .60 1.50
239 Travis Hansen RC .60 1.50
240A Carmelo Anthony Blue RC 1.50 4.00
240B Carmelo Anthony White RC 1.50 4.00
241 Keith McLeod RC .60 1.50
242 Zoran Planinic RC .60 1.50
243A Jarvis Hayes Home RC .60 1.50
243B Jarvis Hayes Away RC .60 1.50
244A Mickael Pietrus Home RC .60 1.50
244B Mickael Pietrus Away RC .60 1.50
245A Mike Sweetney Home RC .60 1.50
245B Mike Sweetney Away RC .60 1.50
246 Jerome Beasley RC .60 1.50
247 Zaza Pachulia RC .60 1.50
248 Ben Handlogten RC .60 1.50
249 Torraye Braggs RC .60 1.50
250A Nick Collison White RC .60 1.50
250B Nick Collison Green RC .60 1.50
251 Reece Gaines RC .60 1.50
252A Dwyane Wade Dribble RC 2.50 6.00
252B Dwyane Wade Layup RC 2.50 6.00
253 Devin Brown RC .60 1.50
254 Leandro Barbosa RC .75 2.00
255 Boris Diaw RC .75 2.00
256 Aleksandar Pavlovic RC .60 1.50
257 Udonis Haslem RC .75 2.00
258 Brian Cook RC .60 1.50
259 Maciej Lampe RC .60 1.50
260A T.J. Ford Home RC .75 2.00
260B T.J. Ford Away RC .75 2.00
261 Matt Carroll RC .60 1.50
262 James Jones RC .60 1.50
263 Brandon Hunter RC .60 1.50
264 Luke Ridnour RC .75 2.00
265 Theron Smith RC .60 1.50
266 Jon Stefansson RC .60 1.50
267 Zarko Cabarkapa RC .60 1.50
268 Marquis Daniels RC .60 1.50
269 Willie Green RC .60 1.50
270A Kirk Hinrich Left RC .75 2.00
270B Kirk Hinrich Right RC .75 2.00
271 Linton Johnson RC .60 1.50
272 Travis Outlaw RC .75 2.00
273 James Lang RC .60 1.50
274 Slavko Vranes RC .60 1.50
275A Darko Milicic Home RC .60 1.50
275B Darko Milicic Away RC .60 1.50
276 LeBron James BAZ 5.00 12.00
277 Darko Milicic BAZ .50 1.25
278 Carmelo Anthony BAZ 1.25 3.00
279 Chris Bosh BAZ 1.00 2.50
280 Dwyane Wade BAZ 2.00 5.00
281 Chris Kaman BAZ .60 1.50
282 Kirk Hinrich BAZ .60 1.50
283 T.J. Ford BAZ .60 1.50
284 Mike Sweetney BAZ .50 1.25
285 Jarvis Hayes BAZ .50 1.25
286 Mickael Pietrus BAZ .50 1.25
287 Nick Collison BAZ .50 1.25
288 Marcus Banks BAZ .50 1.25

2003-04 Bazooka Parallel

Inserted at the rate of one in one, this 288-card set parallels the base Bazooka set enhanced with metallic silver borders.
*PARALLEL SINGLES: .5X TO 1.25X BASE HI
*PARALLEL RCs: 1X TO 2X BASE HI
*PARALLEL BAZ. JOE: 1X TO 2.5X BASE HI

2003-04 Bazooka Mini

Inserted at the rate of one in three, this 288-card set parallels the base set in a mini-card format.
*MINI SINGLES: .6X TO 1.5X BASE HI
*MINI RCs: .5X TO 1.25X BASE HI
*MINI BAZ. JOE: .6X TO 1.5X BASE HI

2003-04 Bazooka Beginnings

Randomly inserted in packs at the rate of one in 26, this 24-card set features the new rookies on a white background with a swatch of memorabilia in the shape of the letter "B."
*PARALLEL: .75X TO 2X BASE HI
PARALLEL PRINT RUN 25 SER.#'d SETS
BC Brian Cook 2.50 6.00
CA Carmelo Anthony UER 6.00 15.00
Carmelo listed as #2 draft pick
CB Chris Bosh 5.00 12.00
CK Chris Kaman 3.00 8.00
DJ Dahntay Jones 2.50 6.00
DW Dwyane Wade 10.00 25.00
DWE David West 3.00 8.00
JH Jarvis Hayes 2.50 6.00
JHO Josh Howard 2.50 6.00
JK Jason Kapono 2.50 6.00
KH Kirk Hinrich 3.00 8.00
KP Kendrick Perkins 4.00 10.00
LB Leandro Barbosa 3.00 8.00
LR Luke Ridnour 3.00 8.00
LW Luke Walton 2.50 6.00
MB Marcus Banks 2.50 6.00
MP Mickael Pietrus 2.50 6.00
MS Mike Sweetney 2.50 6.00
NC Nick Collison 2.50 6.00
NE Ndudi Ebi 2.50 6.00
RG Reece Gaines 2.50 6.00
TB Troy Bell 2.50 6.00
TF T.J. Ford 3.00 8.00
TO Travis Outlaw 3.00 8.00

2003-04 Bazooka Blasts

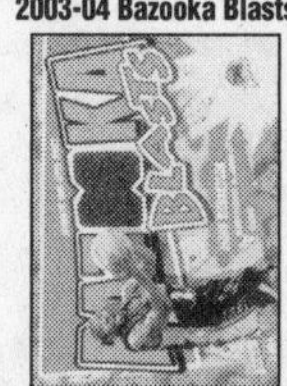

Randomly inserted in packs at the following rates, Group A one in 850, Group B one in 143, Group C one in 72, and Group D one in 15, this 59-card set is horizontally designed and looks like a comic strip. The letters "oo" in the word Bazooka are replaced with a memorabilia swatch. A Parallel set was also produced with cards sequentially numbered to 25.
*PARALLEL: 1X TO 2.5X BASE HI
SOME PARALLEL NOT PRICED DUE TO SCARCITY
JK Jason Kidd D 4.00 10.00
AG Adrian Griffin D 2.00 5.00
AHO Allan Houston C 2.00 5.00
AJ Avery Johnson D 2.00 5.00
AW Antoine Walker D 2.50 6.00
BD Baron Davis C 2.50 6.00
CB Caron Butler D 2.50 6.00
CM Cuttino Mobley C 2.00 5.00
CW Chris Wilcox D 2.00 5.00
DF Derek Fisher B 2.00 5.00
DM Dikembe Mutombo D 2.50 6.00
DW DaJuan Wagner D 2.00 5.00
EN Eduardo Najera D 2.00 5.00
FW Frank Williams D 2.00 5.00
GA Gilbert Arenas B 2.50 6.00
GP Gary Payton B 2.50 6.00
GR Glenn Robinson C 2.00 5.00
HT Hedo Turkoglu D 2.50 6.00
JD Juan Dixon B 2.00 5.00
JJ Joe Johnson B 2.50 6.00
JM Jamal Mashburn D 2.00 5.00
JO Jermaine O'Neal C 2.50 6.00
JR Jason Richardson D 2.50 6.00
JT Jamaal Tinsley D 2.00 5.00
KG Kevin Garnett C 5.00 12.00
KM Karl Malone D 3.00 8.00
KMA Kenyon Martin C 2.50 6.00
KR Kareem Rush D 2.00 5.00
LS Latrell Sprewell D 2.00 5.00
MB Mike Bibby D 2.50 6.00
MF Marcus Fizer B 2.00 5.00
MH Marcus Haislip C 2.00 5.00
MJ Marko Jaric/112 A 2.00 5.00
MP Morris Peterson B 1.50 4.00
MR Michael Redd D 2.50 6.00
N Nene D 2.00 5.00
NT Nikoloz Tskitishvili D 2.00 5.00
PP Paul Pierce D 3.00 8.00
PS Peja Stojakovic B 2.50 6.00
QR Quentin Richardson C 2.00 5.00
QW Qyntel Woods D 2.00 5.00
RA Ray Allen B 2.50 6.00
RJ Richard Jefferson D 2.50 6.00
RW Rasheed Wallace D 2.50 6.00
SAR Shareef Abdur-Rahim B 2.00 5.00
SF Steve Francis C 2.50 6.00
SM Stephon Marbury D 2.00 5.00
SMA Shawn Marion C 2.50 6.00
SN Steve Nash C 3.00 8.00
SO Shaquille O'Neal C 6.00 15.00
TAP Tayshaun Prince/182 A 2.50 6.00
TAW Tariq Abdul-Wahad D 2.00 5.00
TP Tony Parker D 2.50 6.00
VD Vlade Divac C 2.00 5.00
VR Vladimir Radmanovic C 2.00 5.00
WS Wally Szczerbiak B 2.00 5.00
YM Yao Ming D 5.00 12.00
ZI Zydrunas Ilgauskas D 2.00 5.00
ZR Zeljko Rebraca D 2.00 5.00

2003-04 Bazooka Boo-Yah

Randomly inserted at the following rates, Group A one in 850, Group B one in 143, Group C one in 72 and Group D one in 15, this 50-card set places a full-color player action photo on the left and the words BOO-YAH, where the letter "A" has been replaced with a swatch of jersey, along the right from top to bottom. A Parallel set was also produced and these cards are sequentially numbered to 25.
*PARALLEL: 1X TO 2.5X BASE HI
SOME PARALLEL NOT PRICED DUE TO SCARCITY
AI Allen Iverson/156 A
AK Andrei Kirilenko/97 A
AM Alonzo Mourning D 3.00 8.00
AS Amare Stoudemire D 4.00 10.00
AW Antoine Walker C 2.50 6.00
BD Baron Davis B 2.50 6.00
BW Ben Wallace B 2.50 6.00
CB Caron Butler C 2.50 6.00
CW Chris Webber B 2.50 6.00
DAM Darius Miles D 2.00 5.00
DG Devean George C 2.00 5.00
DM Dikembe Mutombo B 2.50 6.00
DN Dirk Nowitzki D 4.00 10.00
DW DaJuan Wagner B 2.00 5.00
EC Elden Campbell D 2.00 5.00
EG Eddie Griffin D 2.00 5.00
GA Gilbert Arenas D 2.50 6.00
JO Jermaine O'Neal B 2.50 6.00
JR Jason Richardson C 2.50 6.00
JS Jerry Stackhouse D 2.00 5.00
JT Jason Terry B 2.00 5.00
JW Jerome Williams D 2.00 5.00
KG Kevin Garnett C 5.00 12.00
KM Karl Malone B 3.00 8.00
KMA Kenyon Martin C 2.50 6.00
LO Lamar Odom B 2.50 6.00
LS Latrell Sprewell C 2.00 5.00
MF Michael Finley D 2.50 6.00
MFZ Marcus Fizer C 2.00 5.00
MO Michael Olowokandi D 2.00 5.00
N Nene D 2.00 5.00
NVE Nick Van Exel B 2.00 5.00
PG Pau Gasol D 2.50 6.00
PP Paul Pierce C 3.00 8.00
QR Quentin Richardson B 2.00 5.00
RA Ray Allen B 2.50 6.00
RJ Richard Jefferson C 2.50 6.00
RL Rashard Lewis C 2.50 6.00
RLA Raef Lafrentz A 2.00 5.00
RW Rasheed Wallace D 2.50 6.00
SB Shawn Bradley B 2.00 5.00
SF Steve Francis C 2.50 6.00
SM Shawn Marion C 2.50 6.00
SMA Stephon Marbury C 2.00 5.00
SN Steve Nash B 3.00 8.00
SO Shaquille O'Neal B 6.00 15.00
TC Tyson Chandler/164 A 2.00 5.00
TD Tim Duncan D 4.00 10.00
TMG Tracy McGrady B 3.00 8.00
YM Yao Ming D 5.00 12.00

2003-04 Bazooka Comics

Inserted at the rate of one in three, this set features 24 mini comics of NBA players.
COMPLETE SET (24) 8.00 20.00
1 Tracy McGrady .30 .75
2 Paul Pierce .30 .75
3 Allen Iverson .40 1.00
4 Amare Stoudemire .40 1.00
5 Jason Kidd .40 1.00
6 Allan Houston .20 .50
7 Shaquille O'Neal .60 1.50
8 Kobe Bryant 1.25 3.00
9 Yao Ming .50 1.25
10 Tim Duncan .40 1.00
11 Ben Wallace .25 .60
12 Karl Malone .30 .75
13 Kevin Garnett .50 1.25
14 Jason Richardson .25 .60
15 LeBron James 4.00 10.00
16 Darko Milicic .25 .60
17 Carmelo Anthony .60 1.50
18 T.J. Ford .30 .75
19 Kirk Hinrich .30 .75
20 Nick Collison .25 .60
21 Chris Bosh .50 1.25
22 Mike Sweetney .25 .60
23 Reece Gaines .25 .60
24 Luke Walten .25 .60

2003-04 Bazooka Four on One Stickers

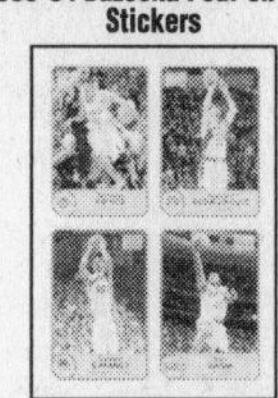

Inserted at the rate of one in four, this 55-card set places four player stickers on each front. The stickers themselves are done in the same design as the base Bazooka set.
COMPLETE SET (55) 15.00 40.00
1 Tim Duncan 1.25 3.00
Yao Ming
Shaquille O'Neal
Kevin Garnett
2 Tracy McGrady 1.50 4.00
Kobe Bryant
Vince Carter
Allen Iverson
3 Paul Pierce .50 1.25
Dirk Nowitzki
Chris Webber
Jamal Mashburn
4 Jason Kidd .50 1.25
Jayson Williams
Stephon Marbury
Gary Payton
5 Jamaal Tinsley .50 1.25
Jason Terry
Steve Nash
Andre Miller
6 Ben Wallace .50 1.25
Jermaine O'Neal
Brian Grant
Troy Murphy
7 Caron Butler .50 1.25
Amare Stoudemire
DaJuan Wagner
Drew Gooden
8 Gordon Giricek .50 1.25
Nene
Carlos Boozer
J.R. Bremer
9 Jason Richardson .50 1.25
Shawn Marian
Desmond Mason
Richard Jefferson
10 Allan Houston .50 1.25
Ray Allen
Troy Hudson
Reggie Miller
11 Michael Redd .50 1.25
Wesley Person
David Wesley
Wally Szczerbiak
12 Ron Artest .50 1.25
Kenyon Martin
Doug Christie
Scottie Pippen
13 Karl Malone .50 1.25
Juwan Howard
Rasheed Wallace
Elton Brand
14 Tony Parker .50 1.25
Baron Davis
Sam Cassell
Nick Van Exel
15 Keith Van Horn .50 1.25
Brad Miller
Matt Harpring
Christian Laettner
16 Pau Gasol .50 1.25
Marko Jaric
Peja Stojakovic
Andrei Kirilenko
17 Chauncey Billups .50 1.25
Bobby Jackson
Rodney Rodgers
Tim Thomas
18 Theo Ratliff .50 1.25
Shawn Bradley
Zydrunas Ilgauskas
Eddie Griffin
19 Mike Miller .50 1.25
Mike Dunleavy
Eddie Jones
Michael Finley
20 Stromile Swift .50 1.25
Jalen Rose
Morris Peterson
Lamar Odom
21 Ricky Davis .50 1.25
Courtney Alexander
Rashard Lewis
Jerry Stackhouse
22 Tyson Chandler .50 1.25
Kwame Brown
Qyntel Woods
Radoslav Nesterovic
23 Quentin Richardson .50 1.25
Malik Rose
Toni Kukoc
Mike Bibby
24 Kurt Thomas .50 1.25
Lucious Harris
Anfernee Hardaway
Manu Ginobili
25 Tayshaun Prince .50 1.25
Vladimir Radmanovic
Calbert Cheaney
Eric Snow
26 Dikembe Mutombo .50 1.25
Alvin Williams
Corliss Williamson
Kendrick Brown
27 Darrell Armstrong .50 1.25
Speedy Claxton
Brent Barry
Damon Stoudamire
28 Rafer Alston .50 1.25
Frank Williams
Juan Dixon
Tony Delk
29 Donyell Marshall .50 1.25
Kenny Thomas
Raef Lafrenz
Rick Fox
30 Antoine Walker .50 1.25
Richard Hamilton
Bonzi Wells
Glenn Robinson
31 Alonzo Mourning .50 1.25
Brendan Haywood
Vlade Divac
Michael Olowokandi
32 Kareem Rush .50 1.25
Zach Randolph
Devean George
Eddy Curry
33 Glenn Rice .50 1.25
Anthony Peeler
Robert Horry
Latrell Sprewell
34 Derrick Coleman .50 1.25
Dan Gadzuric
Keon Clark
Chris Wilcox
35 Casey Jacobsen .50 1.25
Nikoloz Tskitishvili
Shane Battier
Antonio McDyess
36 Gilbert Arenas .50 1.25
Corey Maggette
Dariuus Miles
Jamal Crawford
37 Eduardo Najera .50 1.25
Hidayet Turkoglu
Nazr Mohammed
Jake Tsakalidis
38 Joe Smith .50 1.25
P.J. Brown
Sharieef Abdur-Rahim
Jerome Williams
39 Antawn Jamison .50 1.25
Marcus Fizer
Maurice Taylor
Steven Hunter
40 Joe Johnson .50 1.25
DeSagana Diop
Scot Pollard
John Salmons
41 Moochie Norris .50 1.25
Rueben Patterson
Larry Hnughes
Keyon Dooling
42 Ron Mercer .50 1.25
Eric Williams
Derek Anderson
Cuttino Mobley
43 Earl Boykins .50 1.25
Tyrone Lue
Howard Eisley
Travis Best
44 Tony Battie .50 1.25
Jerome James
Clifford Robinson
Erick Dampier
45 Eric Piatkowski .50 1.25
Walter McCarty
Pat Garrity
Al Harrington
46 Marcus Haislip .50 1.25
Kendall Gill
Ronald Murray
Lorenzen Wright
47 DeShawn Stevenson .50 1.25
Kerry Kittles
James Posey
Aaron McKie
48 Brian Scalabrine .50 1.25
Kenny Anderson
Greg Ostertag
Shandon Anderson
49 Antonio Davis .50 1.25
Jarron Collins
Adrian Griffin
Jumaine Jones
50 LeBron James 4.00 10.00
Darko Milicic
Carmelo Anthony
Chris Bosh
51 Dwyane Wade 1.25 3.00
Chris Kaman
Kirk Hinrich
T.J. Ford
52 Mike Sweetney .50 1.25
Jarvis Hayes
Mickael Pietrus
Nick Collison
53 Marcus Banks .50 1.25
Luke Ridnour
Reece Gaines
Troy Bell
54 David West .50 1.25
Dahnay Jones
Travis Outlaw
Brian Cook
55 Ndudi Ebi .50 1.25
Kekndrick Perkins
Leandrinho Barbose
Josh Howard

2003-04 Bazooka Piece of Americana

Inserted in packs at the following rate: Group A one in 850, Group B one in 143, Group C one in 72 and Group D one in 15, this 27-card set features a horizontal design with black borders along the top and bottom, a copper background, color player photos on the left and a swatch of memorabilia on the right. A Parallel of this set was also inserted and those cards are sequentially numbered to 25.
*PARALLEL: 1X TO 2.5X BASE HI
SOME PARALLEL NOT PRICED DUE TO SCARCITY
AD Antonio Davis B 2.00 5.00
AH Allan Houston B 2.00 5.00
AM Alonzo Mourning C 3.00 8.00
AS Amare Stoudemire C 4.00 10.00
BH Brendan Haywood D 2.00 5.00
BM Brad Miller D 2.50 6.00
BW Ben Wallace C 2.50 6.00
CB Carlos Boozer D 2.50 6.00
DA Darrell Armstrong C 2.00 5.00
DD Dan Dickau/150 A 2.00 5.00
DM Darius Miles C 2.00 5.00
DW David Wesley D 2.00 5.00
ES Eric Snow B 2.00 5.00
GH Grant Hill D 3.00 8.00
JJ Jared Jeffries B 2.00 5.00
JT Jamaal Tinsley B 2.00 5.00
LO Lamar Odom/150 A 2.50 6.00
MD Mike Dunleavy D 2.00 5.00
MP Morris Peterson/150 A 1.50 4.00
PG Pat Garrity D 2.00 5.00
SB Shane Battier/44 A 2.00 5.00
SC Sam Cassell B 2.00 5.00
SO Shaquille O'Neal D 6.00 15.00
SS Steve Smith D 2.00 5.00
TD Tim Duncan D 4.00 10.00
TM Troy Murphy B 2.50 6.00
WP Wesley Person D 2.00 5.00

2003-04 Bazooka Signs

Inserted at the following rates: Group A one in 5840, Group B one in 4328 and Group C at one in 2000, this four card set features a full-color player photo that fades to white towards the bottom for authentic player autographs.
CA Carmelo Anthony/100 A 50.00 120.00
FW Frank Williams B 5.00 12.00
KH Kirk Hinrich/100 A 20.00 50.00
SO Shaquille O'Neal C 30.00 80.00

2003-04 Bazooka Stand Ups

One pop-up card was perforated on each box of Bazooka. Each has a full-color player photo and a two-tone colored background.
COMPLETE SET (4) 1.25 3.00
PRICES GIVEN FOR SEPARATED CARDS
NNO Carmelo Anthony .75 2.00
NNO T.J. Ford .40 1.00
NNO Kirk Hinrich .40 1.00
NNO Nick Collison .30 .75

2003-04 Bazooka Tattoos

Randomly inserted in packs at the rate of one in three, this 34-card set features temporary tattoos of team logos, the NBA logo, the Bazooka Logo and the Eastern and Western Conference logos.
COMPLETE SET (34) 5.00 12.00
1 Bazooka Logo .30 .75
2 Eastern Conference .30 .75
3 Western Conference .30 .75
4 NBA .30 .75
5 Atlanta Hawks .30 .75
6 Boston Celtics .30 .75
7 Charlotte Bobcats .30 .75
8 Chicago Bulls .30 .75
9 Cleveland Cavaliers .30 .75
10 Dallas Mavericks .30 .75
11 Denver Nuggets .30 .75
12 Detroit Pistons .30 .75
13 Golden State Warriors .30 .75
14 Houston Rockets .30 .75
15 Indiana Pacers .30 .75
16 Los Angeles Clippers .30 .75
17 Los Angeles Lakers .30 .75
18 Memphis Grizzlies .30 .75
19 Miami Heat .30 .75
20 Milwaukee Bucks .30 .75
21 Minnesota Timberwolves .30 .75
22 New Jersey Nets .30 .75
23 New Orleans Hornets .30 .75
24 New York Knicks .30 .75
25 Orlando Magic .30 .75
26 Philadelphia 76ers .30 .75
27 Phoenix Suns .30 .75
28 Portland Trailblazers .30 .75
29 Sacramento Kings .30 .75
30 San Antonio Spurs .30 .75
31 Seattle Supersonics .30 .75
32 Toronto Raptors .30 .75
33 Utah Jazz .30 .75
34 Washington Wizards .30 .75

2004-05 Bazooka

This 220-card set was released in January, 2005. The set was issued in eight-card packs with an $2 SRP and came 24 packs to a box. The first 165 cards feature active veterans while cards 166-220 feature Rookie Cards.
COMP.SET w/o RC's (165) 10.00 25.00
1 Shaquille O'Neal .60 1.50
2 Marquis Daniels .15 .40
3 Ben Wallace .25 .60
4 Jarvis Hayes .15 .40
5 Gerald Wallace .25 .60
6 Fred Jones .15 .40
7 Pau Gasol .25 .60
8 Latrell Sprewell .20 .50
9 Steve Francis .25 .60
10 Mike Bibby .25 .60
11 Chris Bosh .25 .60
12 Steve Nash .30 .75
13 Kirk Hinrich .25 .60
14 Richard Jefferson .25 .60
15 Zach Randolph .20 .50
16 Willie Green .15 .40
17 Al Harrington .20 .50
18 Rashard Lewis .25 .60
19 Ricky Davis .20 .50
20 Dwyane Wade .75 2.00
21 Tim Duncan .40 1.00
22 Eddy Curry .20 .50
23 Andre Miller .20 .50

24 Chris Wilcox .15 .40
25 Bobby Jackson .15 .40
26 Stephen Jackson .20 .50
27 Shane Battier .20 .50
28 Antawn Jamison .25 .60
29 Brent Barry .15 .40
30 Stephon Marbury .20 .50
31 Gordan Giricek .15 .40
32 Jamal Mashburn .25 .60
33 Allen Iverson .40 1.00
34 Paul Pierce .30 .75
35 Mike Dunleavy .20 .50
36 Gary Payton .25 .60
37 Brad Miller .25 .60
38 Eric Snow .15 .40
39 Theo Ratliff .15 .40
40 Richard Hamilton .20 .50
41 Dirk Nowitzki .40 1.00
42 Elton Brand .25 .60
43 Reggie Miller .25 .60
44 Baron Davis .25 .60
45 Jerome Williams .15 .40
46 Stromile Swift .15 .40
47 Andrei Kirilenko .20 .50
48 Jason Richardson .25 .60
49 Larry Hughes .20 .50
50 Yao Ming .50 1.25
51 Tim Thomas .15 .40
52 Erick Dampier .15 .40
53 Keith Van Horn .20 .50
54 Grant Hill .30 .75
55 Shareef Abdur-Rahim .20 .50
56 Amare Stoudemire .30 .75
57 David Wesley .15 .40
58 Chris Kaman .25 .60
59 Caron Butler .25 .60
60 Kenyon Martin .25 .60
61 Ray Allen .25 .60
62 Jerry Stackhouse .20 .50
63 Jason Kapono .15 .40
64 Mark Blount .15 .40
65 Hedo Turkoglu .25 .60
66 Carlos Boozer .25 .60
67 Kenny Thomas .15 .40
68 Manu Ginobili .30 .75
69 Kobe Bryant 1.25 3.00
70 Vince Carter .40 1.00
71 Troy Murphy .20 .50
72 Maurice Taylor .15 .40
73 Earl Boykins .15 .40
74 Boris Diaw .20 .50
75 Kerry Kittles .15 .40
76 Jamaal Tinsley .15 .40
77 Lamar Odom .25 .60
78 Jamaal Magloire .15 .40
79 Wally Szczerbiak .20 .50
80 Tayshaun Prince .25 .60
81 Mehmet Okur .20 .50
82 Eddie Jones .20 .50
83 Voshon Lenard .15 .40
84 Jamal Crawford .20 .50
85 Marko Jaric .15 .40
86 Ron Mercer .15 .40
87 Steve Smith .20 .50
88 Antoine Walker .25 .60
89 Kurt Thomas .15 .40
90 Ron Artest .25 .60
91 Luke Walton .15 .40
92 Dajuan Wagner .15 .40
93 Luke Ridnour .20 .50
94 Nene .20 .50
95 Josh Howard .25 .60
96 Juwan Howard .20 .50
97 David West .25 .60
98 Jonathan Bender .15 .40
99 Tony Parker .25 .60
100 LeBron James 1.50 4.00
101 Chris Webber .25 .60
102 Cuttino Mobley .20 .50
103 Rasheed Wallace .25 .60
104 Marcus Banks .15 .40
105 Ronald Murray .15 .40
106 Quentin Richardson .20 .50
107 Antonio McDyess .20 .50
108 Sam Cassell .20 .50
109 Allan Houston .20 .50
110 Leandro Barbosa .25 .60
111 Joe Smith .20 .50
112 Jason Kidd .40 1.00
113 Aleksandar Pavlovic .15 .40
114 Bruce Bowen .15 .40
115 Carmelo Anthony .50 1.25
116 Kwame Brown .15 .40
117 Mickael Pietrus .20 .50
118 Tony Battie .15 .40
119 Joe Johnson .25 .60
120 Damon Stoudamire .20 .50
121 Kevin Garnett .50 1.25
122 Michael Redd .25 .60
123 Doug Christie .15 .40
124 Darrell Armstrong .15 .40
125 James Posey .15 .40
126 Jim Jackson .15 .40
127 Udonis Haslem .20 .50
128 Drew Gooden .20 .50
129 Rasho Nesterovic .15 .40
130 Jermaine O'Neal .25 .60
131 Shawn Marion .25 .60
132 Samuel Dalembert .15 .40
133 Marcus Camby .20 .50
134 Devean George .15 .40
135 Darius Miles .15 .40
136 Michael Olowokandi .15 .40
137 Mike Miller .25 .60
138 Kareem Rush .15 .40
139 Jalen Rose .20 .50
140 Chauncey Billups .25 .60
141 Jason Williams .20 .50
142 Derek Fisher .20 .50
143 Donyell Marshall .15 .40
144 Alonzo Mourning .30 .75
145 T.J. Ford .20 .50
146 Tony Delk .15 .40
147 Gilbert Arenas .25 .60
148 Glenn Robinson .20 .50
149 Peja Stojakovic .25 .60
150 Tracy McGrady .30 .75
151 Rafer Alston .15 .40
152 Nazr Mohammed .15 .40
153 Corey Maggette .20 .50
154 Michael Doleac .15 .40
155 Zydrunas Ilgauskas .20 .50
156 Troy Hudson .15 .40
157 Vladimir Radmanovic .15 .40
158 Jason Collins .15 .40
159 Dikembe Mutombo .25 .60
160 Bonzi Wells .15 .40
161 Jason Terry .20 .50
162 Tyson Chandler .20 .50
163 Desmond Mason .20 .50
164 Carlos Arroyo .20 .50
165 Darko Milicic .15 .40
166 Ben Gordon RC .75 2.00
167 Kevin Martin RC .75 2.00
168 Jackson Vroman RC .60 1.50
169 Delonte West RC .75 2.00
170 Dorell Wright RC 1.00 2.50
171 Erik Daniels RC .60 1.50
172 Josh Childress RC .60 1.50
173 Anderson Varejao RC .75 2.00
174 Andre Emmett RC .60 1.50
175 Chris Duhon RC .60 1.50
176 Bernard Robinson RC .60 1.50
177 D.J. Mbenga RC .60 1.50
178 Kirk Snyder RC .60 1.50
179 Damien Wilkins RC .60 1.50
180 Andre Iguodala RC 1.00 2.50
181 Nenad Krstic RC .60 1.50
182 Pape Sow RC .60 1.50
183 Maurice Evans RC .60 1.50
184 John Edwards RC .60 1.50
185 Andres Nocioni RC .60 1.50
186 Arthur Johnson RC .60 1.50
187 Beno Udrih RC .60 1.50
188 Andris Biedrins RC .75 2.00
189 Kris Humphries RC .60 1.50
190 Trevor Ariza RC .60 1.50
191 Devin Harris RC 1.00 2.50
192 J.R. Smith RC .75 2.00
193 Romain Sato RC .60 1.50
194 Lionel Chalmers RC .60 1.50
195 Al Jefferson RC 1.00 2.50
196 Josh Smith RC 1.00 2.50
197 Antonio Burks RC .60 1.50
198 Tim Pickett RC .60 1.50
199 Justin Reed RC .60 1.50
200 Emeka Okafor RC 1.00 2.50
201 Sebastian Telfair RC .60 1.50
202 Sasha Vujacic RC .60 1.50
203 Royal Ivey RC .60 1.50
204 Rafael Araujo RC .60 1.50
205 Ibrahim Kutluay RC .60 1.50
206 Matt Freije RC .60 1.50
207 Jared Reiner RC .60 1.50
208 Luis Flores RC .60 1.50
209 Robert Swift RC .60 1.50
210 Shaun Livingston RC .60 1.50
211 Peter John Ramos RC .60 1.50
212 Luke Jackson RC .60 1.50
213 Luol Deng RC 1.00 2.50
214 Jameer Nelson RC .75 2.00
215 Tony Allen RC .75 2.00
216 Josh Davis RC .60 1.50
217 Yuta Tabuse RC 1.25 3.00
218 Donta Smith RC .60 1.50
219 David Harrison RC .60 1.50
220 Dwight Howard RC 2.00 5.00

2004-05 Bazooka Gold

Inserted at a stated rate of one per pack, this is a complete parallel of the basic Bazooka set. These cards can be differentiated from the regular cards with their gold foil.
*GOLD: .75X TO 2X BASE CARD HI

2004-05 Bazooka Mini

Inserted at a stated rate of one per pack, this is a complete parallel of the basic Bazooka set. These cards are differentiated from the basic card as they are much smaller than the regular cards The cards measure 1/4" by 3 1/8".
*MINI SINGLES: .5X TO 1.25X BASE HI
*MINI RC's: .6X TO 1.5X BASE HI

2004-05 Bazooka 4-on-1 Stickers

Randomly inserted into packs, these 55 stickers feature four-players each.
COMPLETE SET (55) 12.50 30.00
1 Shaquille O'Neal .75 2.00
Emeka Okafor
Kobe Bryant
Andre Iguodala
2 Ben Wallace .75 2.00
Tim Duncan
Yao Ming
Erick Dampier
3 Elton Brand .50 1.25
Chris Duhon
Shane Battier
Mike Dunleavy
4 Stephon Marbury .50 1.25
Shaun Livingston
Jason Kidd
5 Chris Webber .50 1.25
Jalen Rose
Juwan Howard
Jamal Crawford
6 Kevin Garnett 1.50 4.00
Tracy McGrady
LeBron James
Jermaine O'Neal
7 Vince Carter .75 2.00
Fred Jones
Jason Richardson
Desmond Mason
8 Pau Gasol .50 1.25
Dirk Nowitzki
Andrei Kirilenko
Peja Stojakovic
9 Carmelo Anthony .50 1.25
Ron Artest
Samuel Dalembert
Richard Hamilton
10 Carlos Boozer .50 1.25
Michael Redd
Cuttino Mobley
Rashard Lewis
11 Rafer Alston .50 1.25
Carlos Arroyo
Jason Williams
Steve Nash
12 Richard Jefferson .50 1.25
Luke Walton
Damon Stoudamire
Mike Bibby
13 Chris Wilcox .50 1.25
Steve Francis
Antawn Jamison
Jerry Stackhouse
14 Dwyane Wade 1.00 2.50
Kirk Hinrich
Allen Iverson
Gilbert Arenas
15 Shareef Abdur-Rahim .50 1.25
Nazr Mohammed
Hedo Turkoglu
Mehmet Okur
16 Rasheed Wallace .50 1.25
Kenyon Martin
Latrell Sprewell
Gary Payton
17 Dorell Wright .50 1.25
Marquis Daniels
Luke Ridnour
Jameer Nelson
18 Dwight Howard .75 2.00
Kwame Brown
Michael Olowokandi
Joe Smith
19 Reggie Miller .50 1.25
Jamal Mashburn
Sam Cassell
Jim Jackson
20 Amare Stoudemire .50 1.25
Eddy Curry
Zach Randolph
Tayshaun Prince
21 Jamaal Magloire .50 1.25
Chris Kaman
Tyson Chandler
Marcus Camby
22 Damien Wilkins .50 1.25
Robert Swift
David Harrison
Peter John Ramos
23 Tony Parker .75 2.00
Ben Gordon
Andre Miller
Devin Harris
24 Chris Bosh .50 1.25
Lamar Odom
Darius Miles
Shawn Marion
25 Luke Jackson .50 1.25
Jackson Vroman
Bobby Jackson
Stephen Jackson
26 Paul Pierce .50 1.25
Baron Davis
Corey Maggette
Jason Terry
27 Tim Thomas .60 1.50
Luol Deng
Mike Miller
Antoine Walker
28 Kris Humphries .50 1.25
Troy Murphy
Rafael Araujo
Brad Miller
29 Joe Johnson .50 1.25
Jarvis Hayes
Willie Green
Caron Butler
30 Kurt Thomas .60 1.50
Nene
Al Jefferson
Anderson Varejao
31 Troy Hudson .50 1.25
Ronald Murray
Marcus Banks
Earl Boykins
32 Mark Blount .50 1.25
Tony Battie
Rasho Nesterovic
Zydrunas Ilgauskas
33 Andre Emmett .50 1.25
Ray Allen
Allan Houston
Josh Childress
34 Quentin Richardson .50 1.25
Larry Hughes
Ricky Davis
Gerald Wallace
35 Keith Van Horn .50 1.25
Darko Milicic
Stromile Swift
Antonio McDyess
36 Josh Howard .50 1.25
Al Harrington
Jonathan Bender
Mickael Pietrus
37 J.R. Smith .75 2.00
Tony Allen
Sasha Vujacic
Kevin Martin
38 Kirk Snyder .50 1.25
Josh Smith
Bernard Robinson
Delonte West
39 Kareem Rush .50 1.25
Trevor Ariza
Pavel Podkolzine
Alonzo Mourning
40 Wally Szczerbiak .50 1.25
Brent Barry
Gordan Giricek
Jason Kapono
41 Bruce Bowen .50 1.25
Eric Snow
Kerry Kittles
Jamaal Tinsley
42 Kenny Thomas .50 1.25
Udonis Haslem
Drew Gooden
Manu Ginobili
43 Marko Jaric .50 1.25
Dajuan Wagner
Romain Sato
Lionel Chalmers
44 Devean George .50 1.25
Jerome Williams
David West
James Posey
45 Glenn Robinson .50 1.25
Chauncey Billups
Derek Fisher
Donyell Marshall
46 Michael Doleac .50 1.25
Theo Ratliff
Nenad Krstic
D.J. Mbenga
47 Leandro Barbosa .50 1.25
David Wesley
Eddie Jones
Boris Diaw
48 Andris Biedrins .75 2.00
Arthur Johnson
Beno Udrih
Yuta Tabuse
49 Voshon Lenard .50 1.25
Doug Christie
Darrell Armstrong
T.J. Ford
50 Bonzi Wells .50 1.25
Maurice Taylor
Steve Smith
Tony Delk
51 Jared Reiner .50 1.25
Luis Flores
Antonio Burks
Matt Freije
52 Aleksandar Pavlovic .50 1.25
Ron Mercer
Andres Nocioni
Vladimir Radmanovic
53 Pape Sow .50 1.25
Maurice Evans
John Edwards
Royal Ivey
54 Grant Hill .50 1.25
Jason Collins
Dikembe Mutombo
Josh Davis
55 Justin Reed .50 1.25
Ibrahim Kutluay
Erick Daniels
Donta Smith

2004-05 Bazooka Admissions

Randomly inserted into packs, these 23 cards featuring game-used swatches of leading rookies in the shape of an A. Since the players in group A and group B are inserted at different odds, we have notated which group they are a part of next to the player's name.
AE Andre Emmett B 2.00 5.00
AI Andre Iguodala A 3.00 8.00
AJ Al Jefferson B 3.00 8.00
AV Anderson Varejao B 2.50 6.00
BG Ben Gordon B 2.50 6.00
DH Devin Harris A 3.00 8.00
DW Dorell Wright B 3.00 8.00
EO Emeka Okafor B 3.00 8.00
JC Josh Childress B 2.00 5.00
JN Jameer Nelson B 2.50 6.00
JS Josh Smith B 3.00 8.00
KH Kris Humphries B 2.00 5.00
KM Kevin Martin B 2.50 6.00
KS Kirk Snyder B 2.00 5.00
LD Luol Deng B 3.00 8.00
LJ Luke Jackson B 2.00 5.00
SL Shaun Livingston B 2.00 5.00
ST Sebastian Telfair B 2.00 5.00
TA Tony Allen B 2.50 6.00
DHA David Harrison B 2.00 5.00
DHO Dwight Howard B 6.00 15.00
DWE Delonte West B 2.50 6.00
JRS J.R. Smith B 2.50 6.00

2004-05 Bazooka Adventures

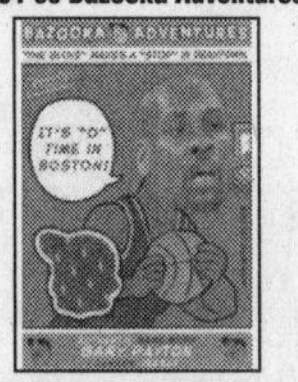

Randomly inserted into packs, these 23 cards featuring game-used swatches of leading veterans. Since the players in group A and group B are inserted at different odds, we have notated which group they are a part of next to the player's name.
BD Baron Davis B 2.50 6.00
CA Carmelo Anthony B 5.00 12.00
CB Carlos Boozer A 2.50 6.00
CM Cuttino Mobley B 2.00 5.00
FM Frank Williams B 2.00 5.00
GP Gary Payton B 2.50 6.00
JK Jason Kidd B 4.00 10.00
JM Jamaal Magloire A 2.00 5.00
JM2 Jamal Mashburn B 2.50 6.00
JO Jermaine O'Neal A 2.50 6.00
JS Joe Smith B 2.00 5.00
KH Kirk Hinrich B 2.50 6.00
MB Mike Bibby B 2.50 6.00
MG Manu Ginobili A 3.00 8.00
MP Morris Peterson B 2.00 5.00
PS Peja Stojakovic B 2.50 6.00
RJ Richard Jefferson B 2.50 6.00
SF Steve Francis B 2.50 6.00
SO Shaquille O'Neal B 6.00 15.00
TD Tim Duncan B 4.00 10.00
YM Yao Ming B 5.00 12.00
ZR Zach Randolph B 2.00 5.00

2004-05 Bazooka Back-Up

Randomly inserted into packs, these 24 cards featuring game-used relics of leading veterans who normally don't start. Since the players in group A and group B are inserted at different odds, we have notated which group they are a part of next to the player's name.
N Nene B 2.50 6.00
AM Antonio McDyess B 2.50 6.00
AP Aleksandar Pavlovic B 2.00 5.00
BD Boris Diaw B 2.50 6.00
CK Chris Kaman B 3.00 8.00
DC Derrick Coleman B 2.50 6.00
DF Derek Fisher B 2.50 6.00
DM Dikembe Mutombo B 3.00 8.00
DW David Wesley B 2.00 5.00
GR Glenn Robinson B 2.50 6.00
HG Horace Grant B 2.00 5.00
JC Jason Collins B 2.00 5.00
JJ Jim Jackson B 2.00 5.00
JK Jason Kapono B 2.00 5.00
MJ Marko Jaric B 2.00 5.00
MM Mike Miller B 3.00 8.00
PG Pat Garrity B 2.00 5.00
SP Scot Pollard B 2.00 5.00
TC Tyson Chandler B 2.50 6.00
VL Voshon Lenard B 2.00 5.00
VR Vladimir Radmanovic B 2.00 5.00
DWE David West B 3.00 8.00

2004-05 Bazooka Breakaway

Randomly inserted into packs, these 31 cards featuring game-used swatches of leading veterans. Since the players in group A and group B are inserted at different odds, we have notated which group they are a part of next to the player's name.
AF Anfernee Hardaway B 6.00 15.00
AI Allen Iverson B 4.00 10.00
AS Amare Stoudemire A 3.00 8.00
AW Antoine Walker B 2.50 6.00
BD Baron Davis B 2.50 6.00
BW Ben Wallace B 2.50 6.00
CA Chris Andersen B 4.00 10.00
CB Chris Bosh B 2.50 6.00
DM Desmond Mason B 2.00 5.00
DN Dirk Nowitzki B 4.00 10.00
EB Elton Brand A 2.50 6.00
JR Jason Richardson B 2.50 6.00
JS Jerry Stackhouse A 2.00 5.00
KH Kirk Hinrich B 2.50 6.00
LS Latrell Sprewell B 2.00 5.00
MJ Marko Jaric B 2.00 5.00
MR Michael Redd B 2.50 6.00
PG Pau Gasol B 2.50 6.00
PP Paul Pierce B 3.00 8.00
RA Ray Allen B 3.00 8.00
RH Richard Hamilton B 2.00 5.00
RJ Richard Jefferson B 2.50 6.00
SF Steve Francis B 2.50 6.00
SO Shaquille O'Neal B 6.00 15.00
TD Tim Duncan B 4.00 10.00
TM Tracy McGrady A 3.00 8.00
TP Tayshaun Prince B 2.50 6.00
UH Udonis Haslem B 2.00 5.00
YM Yao Ming B 5.00 12.00
SMA Stephon Marbury B 2.00 5.00
TOP Tony Parker B 2.50 6.00

2004-05 Bazooka Comics

Randomly inserted into packs, these 24 comics, done in the style of the old Bazooka comics, feature leading NBA superstars.
COMPLETE SET (24) 4.00 10.00
1 Tracy McGrady .25 .60
2 Peja Stojakovic .20 .50
3 Kevin Garnett .40 1.00
4 Ben Wallace .20 .50
5 Stephon Marbury .15 .40
6 Michael Redd .20 .50
7 Kenyon Martin .20 .50
8 Carmelo Anthony .40 1.00
9 Jermaine O'Neal .20 .50
10 LeBron James 1.25 3.00
11 Zach Randolph .15 .40
12 Vince Carter .30 .75
13 Andrei Kirilenko .15 .40
14 Pau Gasol .20 .50
15 Steve Francis .20 .50
16 Dwight Howard .60 1.50
17 Emeka Okafor .30 .75
18 Ben Gordon .25 .60
19 Shaun Livingston .20 .50
20 Devin Harris .30 .75
21 Luol Deng .30 .75
22 Andre Iguodala .30 .75
23 Sebastian Telfair .20 .50

2004-05 Bazooka Signs

Randomly inserted into packs, these 24 cards feature autograph of leading NBA players. Since the players in group A and group B are inserted at different odds, we have notated which group they are a part of next to the player's name.
SOME UNPRICED DUE TO SCARCITY
AB Andris Biedrins B 5.00 12.00
AJ Al Jefferson B 6.00 15.00
BG Ben Gordon B 5.00 12.00
DH Devin Harris B 6.00 15.00
EO Emeka Okafor C 6.00 15.00
JC Josh Childress B 4.00 10.00
JS Josh Smith B 6.00 15.00
LD Luol Deng B 6.00 15.00
ST Sebastian Telfair B 4.00 10.00
TD Tim Duncan A 40.00 100.00

2005-06 Bazooka

Released in November 2005, Topps Bazooka boasts a 220 card set where cards 1-165 feature veteran players, cards 166-215 feature rookies and cards 216-220 feature celebrities. Base cards have white borders and a red name box at the bottom of the card. Bazooka was packaged in 24-pack boxes containing eight cards each and carrying a SRP of $2.00.
COMPLETE SET (220) 15.00 40.00
UNPRICED BLUE PRINT RUN 5 SETS
1 Gilbert Arenas .25 .60
2 Josh Smith .25 .60
3 Carlos Boozer .25 .60
4 Al Jefferson .25 .60
5 Jalen Rose .25 .60
6 Primoz Brezec .15 .40
7 Rashard Lewis .25 .60
8 Ben Gordon .25 .60
9 Tony Parker .25 .60
10 Drew Gooden .20 .50
11 Mike Bibby .25 .60
12 Josh Howard .25 .60
13 Sebastian Telfair .20 .50
14 Earl Boykins .15 .40
15 Joe Johnson .25 .60
16 Rasheed Wallace .25 .60
17 Marc Jackson .15 .40
18 Baron Davis .25 .60
19 Dwight Howard .50 1.25
20 Tracy McGrady .30 .75
21 Trevor Ariza .15 .40
22 David Harrison .15 .40
23 J.R. Smith .25 .60
24 Chris Kaman .25 .60
25 Richard Jefferson .25 .60
26 Chris Mihm .15 .40
27 Sam Cassell .25 .60
28 Mike Miller .25 .60
29 Joe Smith .20 .50
30 Dwyane Wade .60 1.50
31 Tony Allen .15 .40
32 Antawn Jamison .25 .60
33 Eddy Curry .20 .50
34 Rafael Araujo .15 .40
35 Jerry Stackhouse .20 .50
36 Manu Ginobili .25 .60
37 Antonio McDyess .20 .50
38 Zach Randolph .20 .50
39 Mike James .15 .40
40 Chris Webber .25 .60
41 Bobby Simmons .15 .40
42 Jamal Crawford .20 .50
43 Pau Gasol .25 .60
44 Brian Scalabrine .15 .40
45 Desmond Mason .15 .40
46 Tyronn Lue .15 .40
47 Andrei Kirilenko .20 .50
48 Luke Ridnour .20 .50
49 Gerald Wallace .25 .60
50 LeBron James 1.25 3.00
51 Peja Stojakovic .25 .60
52 Andre Miller .20 .50
53 Quentin Richardson .20 .50
54 Mike Dunleavy .20 .50
55 Steve Francis .25 .60
56 Stephen Jackson .20 .50
57 P.J. Brown .15 .40
58 Caron Butler .25 .60
59 Keith Van Horn .20 .50
60 Shaquille O'Neal .50 1.25
61 Josh Childress .20 .50
62 Michael Doleac .15 .40
63 Lamar Odom .25 .60
64 Stephon Marbury .20 .50
65 Chris Duhon .15 .40
66 Shaun Livingston .15 .40
67 Eric Snow .15 .40
68 Travis Outlaw .20 .50
69 Ron Artest .25 .60
70 Emeka Okafor .25 .60
71 Chauncey Billups .25 .60
72 Jason Williams .20 .50
73 Jameer Nelson .20 .50
74 Eduardo Najera .15 .40
75 Speedy Claxton .15 .40
76 Kirk Snyder .15 .40
77 Rafer Alston .15 .40
78 Kobe Bryant 1.25 3.00
79 Michael Redd .25 .60
80 Tim Duncan .40 1.00
81 Tayshaun Prince .25 .60
82 Brendan Haywood .15 .40
83 Kyle Korver .20 .50
84 Tony Delk .15 .40
85 Luol Deng .25 .60
86 Elton Brand .25 .60
87 Jason Richardson .25 .60
88 Antoine Walker .20 .50
89 Ray Allen .25 .60
90 Yao Ming .30 .75
91 Damon Jones .15 .40
92 Anderson Varejao .20 .50
93 Kurt Thomas .15 .40
94 Latrell Sprewell .20 .50
95 Cuttino Mobley .20 .50
96 Chris Wilcox .15 .40
97 Devin Harris .25 .60
98 Jared Jeffries .15 .40
99 Nenad Krstic .15 .40
100 Steve Nash .30 .75
101 Reggie Evans .15 .40
102 Ben Wallace .25 .60
103 Allen Iverson .40 1.00
104 Bruce Bowen .15 .40
105 Paul Pierce .30 .75
106 Shareef Abdur-Rahim .20 .50
107 Vladimir Radmanovic .15 .40
108 Michael Finley .25 .60
109 Brent Barry .15 .40
110 Carmelo Anthony .50 1.25
111 Andre Iguodala .25 .60
112 Shane Battier .20 .50
113 Richard Hamilton .20 .50
114 Kenny Thomas .15 .40
115 Tyson Chandler .20
116 Jim Jackson .15
117 David Wesley .15
118 Grant Hill .30
119 Wally Szczerbiak .20
120 Dirk Nowitzki .40
121 Udonis Haslem .20
122 Jason Hart .15
123 Marcus Camby .20
124 Kirk Hinrich .25
125 Jermaine O'Neal .25
126 Derek Fisher .20
127 Donyell Marshall .15
128 Darius Miles .15
129 Kenyon Martin .25
130 Jason Kidd .40
131 Marquis Daniels .15
132 Kevin Garnett .50
133 Juwan Howard .20
134 Shawn Marion .25
135 Morris Peterson .15
136 Kevin Martin .25
137 Gary Payton .25
138 Maurice Williams .20
139 Eddie Jones .20
140 Vince Carter .40
141 Lorenzen Wright .15
142 Dan Dickau .15
143 Chucky Atkins .15
144 Mike Sweetney .15
145 Corey Maggette .20
146 Hedo Turkoglu .25
147 Jamaal Tinsley .15
148 Samuel Dalembert .15
149 Bob Sura .15
150 Amare Stoudemire .25
151 Troy Murphy .20
152 Joel Przybilla .15
153 Carlos Arroyo .20
154 Brad Miller .25
155 Jason Terry .20
156 Beno Udrih .15
157 Zydrunas Ilgauskas .20
158 Nick Collison .15
159 Andres Nocioni .15
160 Chris Bosh .25
161 Brevin Knight .15
162 Mehmet Okur .15
163 Ricky Davis .20
164 Larry Hughes .20
165 Al Harrington .20
166 Chris Paul RC 2.50
167 Danny Granger RC 1.25
168 Jarrett Jack RC .60
169 Wayne Simien RC .60
170 Deron Williams RC 1.50
171 Ryan Gomes RC .60
172 Daniel Ewing RC .60
173 Sean May RC .60
174 Alan Anderson RC .60
175 Hakim Warrick RC .75
176 Francisco Garcia RC .75
177 Nate Robinson RC .75
178 Luther Head RC .60
179 Joey Graham RC .60
180 Marvin Williams RC .75
181 Antoine Wright RC .60
182 Andrew Bynum RC 2.00
183 Johan Petro RC .60
184 Louis Williams RC 1.00
185 Andray Blatche RC .75
186 Sarunas Jasikevicius RC .60
187 Ike Diogu RC .60
188 Channing Frye RC .75
189 Julius Hodge RC .60
190 Rashad McCants RC .60
191 Yaroslav Korolev RC .60
192 C.J. Miles RC .75
193 Brandon Bass RC .75
194 Travis Diener RC .60
195 Monta Ellis RC 1.25
196 Linas Kleiza RC .60
197 Gerald Green RC .75
198 Jason Maxiell RC .60
199 David Lee RC 1.00
200 Andrew Bogut RC 1.00
201 Salim Stoudamire RC .60
202 Raymond Felton RC 1.00
203 Martell Webster RC .60
204 Chris Taft RC .60
205 Charlie Villanueva RC .75
206 Lawrence Roberts RC .60
207 Ersan Ilyasova RC .75
208 Martynas Andriuskevicius RC .60
209 Bracey Wright RC .60
210 Von Wafer RC .60
211 Eddie Basden RC .60
212 Dijon Thompson RC .60
213 Robert Whaley RC .60
214 Matt Walsh RC .60
215 Ricky Sanchez RC .60
216 Jay-Z .75
217 Shannon Elizabeth .75
218 Christie Brinkley .75
219 Jenny McCarthy .75
220 Carmen Electra .75

2005-06 Bazooka Gold

Inserted at one per pack, this 220-card set para base set enhanced with gold borders and a thic stock.
*1-165 GOLD: .6X TO 1.5X BASE HI
*166-220 GOLD: .75X TO 2X BASE HI

2005-06 Bazooka 4-on- Stickers

Inserted in packs at the rate of one in four, this set features mini stickers that are designed to p the best set design. Each sticker showcases fo players, hence the 4-on-1 set name.
1 Steve Nash .50
Emeka Okafor
Ben Gordon
Ben Wallace
2 Jermaine O'Neal .50

t Arenas
y Simmons
Randolph
Smith .50 1.25
Richardson
Barry
ond Mason
verson 1.50 4.00
Bryant
n James
e Stoudemire
owitzki .75 2.00
McGrady
Pierce
ne Wade
llen .50 1.25
n Richardson
el Redd
n Jones
ille O'Neal 1.25 3.00
uncan
Garnett
ing
Parker .50 1.25
on Marbury
inrich
tian Telfair
Bosh .50 1.25
rd Lewis
ed Wallace
n Jamison
May .50 1.25
and Felton
n Williams
d McCants
Webber .50 1.25
erson
t Howard
Brand
Davis .50 1.25
rtest
Sprewell
n Martin
haun Prince .50 1.25
Marion
Ginobili
i Kirilenko
Scalabrine .50 1.25
Brezec
Araujo
Kaman
Rose .50 1.25
Miller
l Wallace
en Jackson
Thomas .50 1.25
f Abdur-Rahim
Wilcox
Boozer
rrington .50 1.25
Maggette
ll Marshall
Thomas
Dunleavy .50 1.25
on Varejao
Childress
Livingston
n Davis .50 1.25
Bibby
Miller
Francis
Stojakovic .50 1.25
cey Billups
e Walker
Szczerbiak
1.00 2.50
Carter
Kidd
d Jefferson
Paul 1.25 3.00
Williams
obinson
Jack
Przybilla .50 1.25
as Ilgauskas
iller
Krstic
ew Bogut .75 2.00
ing Frye
v Bynum
Blatche
e Battier .50 1.25
Gooden
Evans
weetney
Wesley .50 1.25
ughes
ayton
Bowen
uis Daniels .50 1.25
effries
yder
Ariza
oykins .50 1.25
Lue
lston
Arroyo
Chandler .50 1.25
ollison
t Okur
en Wright
an Haywood .50 1.25
Haslem
Howard
ckson
Hill .50 1.25
o Anthony
guodala
nson
us Camby .50 1.25
Dalembert
aft
Villanueva
non Elizabeth 1.25 3.00
e Brinkley
McCarthy
n Elecktra
d Green .50 1.25
Hodge
e Wright
co Garcia
Crawford .50 1.25
ackhouse
Williams
Nelson
d Hamilton .50 1.25
ones
ith

Tony Allen
37 Eddy Curry .50 1.25
Marc Jackson
Chris Mihm
David Harrison
38 Lamar Odom .50 1.25
Antonio McDyess
Pau Gasol
Luol Deng
39 Darius Miles .50 1.25
Cuttino Mobley
Michael Finley
Caron Butler
40 Joe Smith .50 1.25
Andres Nocioni
Josh Howard
Kyle Korver
41 Martell Webster .50 1.25
Salim Stoudamire
Luther Head
Daniel Ewing
42 Luke Ridnour .50 1.25
Sam Cassell
Mike James
Chris Duhon
43 David Lee .50 1.25
Hakim Warrick
Danny Granger
Joey Graham
44 Jason Terry .50 1.25
Beno Udrih
Dan Dickau
Chucky Atkins
45 Devin Harris .50 1.25
Speedy Claxton
Kevin Martin
Maurice Williams
46 Alan Anderson .60 1.50
Linas Kleiza
Jason Maxiell
Wayne Simien
47 Ryan Gomes .50 1.25
Sarunas Jasikevicius
Yaroslav Korolev
Travis Diener
48 Troy Murphy .50 1.25
Keith Van Horn
Michael Doleac
Hedo Turkoglu
49 Derek Fisher .50 1.25
Eric Snow
Bob Sura
Brevin Knight
50 Tony Delk .75 2.00
Louis Williams
C.J. Miles
Monta Ellis
51 Travis Outlaw .50 1.25
Jason Hart
Morris Peterson
Jamaal Tinsley
52 P.J. Brown .50 1.25
Vladimir Radmanovic
Eduardo Najera
Nenad Krstic
53 Sean May .40 1.00
Johan Petro
Ike Diogu
Brandon Bass
54 Andrew Bogut .60 1.50
Tim Duncan
Shaquille O'Neal
Marvin Williams
55 Dwyane Wade 1.50 4.00
Allen Iverson
Jay-Z
Amare Stoudemire

2005-06 Bazooka All-Access Relics

Inserted in packs at the rate of one in 24, this 25-card set places small player photos and a circular swatch of memorabilia on a card with a blue and red background design.
AW Antoine Wright 3.00 8.00
CF Channing Frye 4.00 10.00
CP Chris Paul 10.00 25.00
CV Charlie Villanueva 4.00 10.00
DG Danny Granger 6.00 15.00
DL David Lee 5.00 12.00
DW Deron Williams 8.00 20.00
FG Francisco Garcia 4.00 10.00
GG Gerald Green 4.00 10.00
HW Hakim Warrick 4.00 10.00
JG Joey Graham 3.00 8.00
JH Julius Hodge 3.00 8.00
JJ Jarrett Jack 3.00 8.00
JM Jason Maxiell 3.00 8.00
LH Luther Head 3.00 8.00
ME Monta Ellis 6.00 15.00
MW Martell Webster 3.00 8.00
NR Nate Robinson 4.00 10.00
RF Raymond Felton 5.00 12.00
RG Ryan Gomes 3.00 8.00
RM Rashad McCants 3.00 8.00
SJ Sarunas Jasikevicius 3.00 8.00
SM Sean May 3.00 8.00
WS Wayne Simien 3.00 8.00
ABO Andrew Bogut 5.00 12.00

2005-06 Bazooka All-Star Relics

Seeded in packs at the rate of one in 46, this 20-cards set features NBA All-Stars along with a star-shaped swatch of memorabilia from All-Star Weekend. Backgrounds are blue and red and utilize several different star background elements.
AJ Antawn Jamison Shirt 3.00 8.00
BU Beno Udrih Shirt 2.00 5.00
BW Ben Wallace Warm 3.00 8.00
CA Chris Andersen Shorts 5.00 12.00
DH Dwight Howard Warm 6.00 15.00
EB Earl Boykins Warm 2.00 5.00
EO Emeka Okafor Shorts 3.00 8.00
GH Grant Hill Warm 4.00 10.00
JH Josh Howard Shorts 3.00 8.00
KH Kirk Hinrich Warm 3.00 8.00
KK Kyle Korver Shorts 2.50 6.00
LR Luke Ridnour 2.50 6.00
MG Manu Ginobili Warm 3.00 8.00
RA Ray Allen Shirt 3.00 8.00
RD Ronald Dupree 2.00 5.00
SM Shawn Marion Warm 3.00 8.00
SO Shaquille O'Neal Shorts 6.00 15.00
UH Udonis Haslem Shirt 2.50 6.00
YM Yao Ming Warm 4.00 10.00
AJE Al Jefferson Shorts 3.00 8.00

2005-06 Bazooka Blog Squad Relics

Inserted in packs at the rate of one in 37, this 25-card set features player photos and "B" shaped memorabilia swatches in the lower left hand corner.
AJ Al Jefferson 3.00 8.00
AN Andres Nocioni 2.00 5.00
AV Anderson Varejao 2.50 6.00
CA Carlos Arroyo 2.50 6.00
CB Caron Butler 3.00 8.00
CW Chris Wilcox 2.00 5.00
DW Dwyane Wade 6.00 15.00
GW Gerald Wallace 3.00 8.00
JC Josh Childress 2.50 6.00
JJ Joe Johnson 3.00 8.00
MD Marquis Daniels 2.00 5.00
NC Nick Collison 2.00 5.00
RA Ray Allen 3.00 8.00
RJ Richard Jefferson 3.00 8.00
SL Shaun Livingston 2.00 5.00
SO Shaquille O'Neal 6.00 15.00
ST Sebastian Telfair 2.50 6.00
UH Udonis Haslem 2.50 6.00
YM Yao Ming 4.00 10.00
DWE Delonte West 2.50 6.00
DWR Dorell Wright 2.00 5.00
MDU Mike Dunleavy 2.50 6.00
RAL Rafer Alston 2.00 5.00
RAR Ron Artest 3.00 8.00
SAR Shareef Abdur-Rahim 2.50 6.00

2005-06 Bazooka Comics

Inserted in packs at the rate of one in four, this 24-card set features NBA player themed comic cards.
COMPLETE SET (24) 10.00 25.00
1 Dwyane Wade 1.25 3.00
2 Steve Nash .60 1.50
3 Josh Smith .50 1.25
4 Emeka Okafor .50 1.25
5 Gilbert Arenas .50 1.25
6 Tim Duncan .75 2.00
7 Grant Hill .60 1.50
8 Ben Gordon .50 1.25
9 Dirk Nowitzki .75 2.00
10 Shaquille O'Neal 1.00 2.50
11 Ray Allen .50 1.25
12 Chris Bosh .50 1.25
13 Jason Richardson .50 1.25
14 Allen Iverson .75 2.00
15 Amare Stoudemire .50 1.25
16 LeBron James 2.50 6.00
17 Carmelo Anthony 1.00 2.50
18 Manu Ginobili .50 1.25
19 Andrew Bogut .75 2.00
20 Marvin Williams .60 1.50
21 Deron Williams 1.25 3.00
22 Raymond Felton .75 2.00
23 Channing Frye .60 1.50
24 Sean May .50 1.25

2005-06 Bazooka Minis

Inserted in packs at the rate of one in one, this set parallels the base Bazooka set on a smaller cut card.
*MINI STARS: .4X TO 1X BASE HI
*MINI RCs: .6X TO 1.5X HI

2005-06 Bazooka Power Relics

Randomly seeded in packs at the rate of one in 29, this 30-card set features full color player photos, a yellow name box along the bottom of the card and a circular swatch of memorabilia.

AK Andrei Kirilenko 2.50 6.00
BG Ben Gordon 3.00 8.00
BJ Bobby Jackson 2.00 5.00
BW Bonzi Wells 2.00 5.00
CA Carmelo Anthony 6.00 15.00
CB Carlos Boozer 3.00 8.00
DG Drew Gooden 2.50 6.00
DH Dwight Howard 6.00 15.00
DM Desmond Mason Shirt 2.00 5.00
EB Elton Brand 3.00 8.00
EO Emeka Okafor 3.00 8.00
JK Jason Kidd 5.00 12.00
JM Jamaal Magloire 2.00 5.00
JO Jermaine O'Neal 3.00 8.00
JR Jalen Rose 3.00 8.00
JS Josh Smith 3.00 8.00
LD Luol Deng 3.00 8.00
LH Larry Hughes 2.50 6.00
PG Pau Gasol 3.00 8.00
PS Peja Stojakovic 3.00 8.00
RA Rafael Araujo 2.00 5.00
RL Rashard Lewis 3.00 8.00
RM Ronald Murray 2.00 5.00
SF Steve Francis 3.00 8.00
SO Shaquille O'Neal 6.00 15.00
TD Tim Duncan 5.00 12.00
ZR Zach Randolph 2.50 6.00
CBO Chris Bosh 3.00 8.00
JRS J.R. Smith 3.00 8.00
KBR Kobe Bryant 8.00 20.00

2005-06 Bazooka Signs

Inserted in packs at the rate of one in 236, this 20-card set is designed to appear as though it's been printed on a page from a lined notebook. Cards are enhanced with silver autograph stickers.
AB Andrew Bogut 6.00 15.00
AI Allen Iverson 75.00 150.00
CA Carmelo Anthony 20.00 50.00
CB Christie Brinkley 40.00 80.00
DW Dwyane Wade 30.00 80.00
EO Emeka Okafor 5.00 12.00
GG Gerald Green 6.00 15.00
JM Jenny McCarthy 60.00 120.00
JN Jameer Nelson 5.00 12.00
JZ Jay-Z 30.00 80.00
ME Monta Ellis 8.00 20.00
RF Raymond Felton 6.00 15.00
SE Shannon Elizabeth 60.00 120.00
SM Stephon Marbury 8.00 20.00
DWI Deron Williams 12.00 30.00
SMA Sean May 5.00 12.00

2005-06 Bazooka Window Clings

Inserted in packs at the rate of one in four, these clear plastic window clings feature NBA team logos.
1 Atlanta Hawks .60 1.50
2 Boston Celtics .60 1.50
3 Charlotte Bobcats .60 1.50
4 Chicago Bulls .60 1.50
5 Cleveland Cavaliers .60 1.50
6 Dallas Mavericks .60 1.50
7 Denver Nuggets .60 1.50
8 Detroit Pistons .60 1.50
9 Golden State Warriors .60 1.50
10 Houston Rockets .60 1.50
11 Indiana Pacers .60 1.50
12 Los Angeles Clippers .60 1.50
13 Los Angeles Lakers .60 1.50
14 Memphis Grizzlies .60 1.50
15 Miami Heat .60 1.50
16 Milwaukee Bucks .60 1.50
17 Minnesota Timberwolves .60 1.50
18 New Jersey Nets .60 1.50
19 New Orleans Hornets .60 1.50
20 New York Knicks .60 1.50
21 Orlando Magic .60 1.50
22 Philadelphia 76ers .60 1.50
23 Phoenix Suns .60 1.50
24 Portland Trail Blazers .60 1.50
25 Sacramento Kings .60 1.50
26 San Antonio Spurs .60 1.50
27 Seattle SuperSonics .60 1.50
28 Toronto Raptors .60 1.50
29 Utah Jazz .60 1.50
30 Washington Wizards .60 1.50

1951 Berk Ross

The 1951 Berk Ross set consists of 72 cards (each measuring approximately 2 1/16" by 2 1/2") with tinted photographs, divided evenly into four series (designated in the checklist as A, B, C and D). The cards were marketed in boxes containing two card panels, without gum, and the set includes stars of other sports as well as baseball players. The set is sometimes still found in the original packaging. Intact panels command a premium over the listed prices. The catalog designation for this set is W532-1. In every series the first ten cards are baseball players; the set has a heavy emphasis on Yankees and Phillies players as they were in the World Series the year before. The set includes the first card of Bob Cousy as well as a card of Whitey Ford in his Rookie Card year.
COMPLETE SET (72) 900.00 1500.00
1-11 Bob Cousy Basketball 100.00 200.00
1-12 Dick Schnittker Basketball 5.00 10.00
2-11 Sherman White Basketball 5.00 10.00
3-11 Paul Unruh Basketball 5.00 10.00
4-11 Bill Sharman Basketball 20.00 40.00

1998-99 Black Diamond

The inaugural 120-card Black Diamond set was released in six-card packs with a suggested retail price of $3.99. The cards feature light f/x foil treatment with each sporting a single black diamond. The first 13 cards in the set commemorate Michael Jordan. The rookie card subset was inserted at one in four.
COMPLETE SET (120) 40.00 80.00
COMPLETE SET w/o RC (90) 20.00 40.00
1 Michael Jordan 1.25 3.00
2 Michael Jordan 1.25 3.00
3 Michael Jordan 1.25 3.00
4 Michael Jordan 1.25 3.00
5 Michael Jordan 1.25 3.00
6 Michael Jordan 1.25 3.00
7 Michael Jordan 1.25 3.00
8 Michael Jordan 1.25 3.00
9 Michael Jordan 1.25 3.00
10 Michael Jordan 1.25 3.00
11 Michael Jordan 1.25 3.00
12 Michael Jordan 1.25 3.00
13 Michael Jordan 1.25 3.00
14 Dikembe Mutombo .30 .75
15 Steve Smith .25 .60
16 Mookie Blaylock .20 .50
17 Antoine Walker .30 .75
18 Kenny Anderson .25 .60
19 Ron Mercer .25 .60
20 Glen Rice .30 .75
21 Derrick Coleman .25 .60
22 Michael Jordan 1.25 3.00
23 Toni Kukoc .30 .75
24 Brent Barry .25 .60
25 Brevin Knight .20 .50
26 Derek Anderson .20 .50
27 Shawn Kemp .30 .75
28 Shawn Bradley .20 .50
29 Michael Finley .30 .75
30 Nick Van Exel .25 .60
31 Chauncey Billups .40 1.00
32 Antonio McDyess .25 .60
33 Grant Hill .50 1.25
34 Jerry Stackhouse .30 .75
35 Bison Dele .20 .50
36 John Starks .25 .60
37 Chris Mills .20 .50
38 Scottie Pippen .50 1.25
39 Hakeem Olajuwon .40 1.00
40 Charles Barkley .50 1.25
41 Antonio Davis .20 .50
42 Reggie Miller .40 1.00
43 Mark Jackson .30 .75
44 Eddie Jones .30 .75
45 Shaquille O'Neal .75 2.00
46 Kobe Bryant 1.50 4.00
47 Rodney Rogers .20 .50
48 Maurice Taylor .20 .50
49 Tim Hardaway .30 .75
50 Jamal Mashburn .25 .60
51 Alonzo Mourning .40 1.00
52 Ray Allen .40 1.00
53 Terrell Brandon .20 .50
54 Glenn Robinson .25 .60
55 Joe Smith .25 .60
56 Stephon Marbury .40 1.00
57 Kevin Garnett .60 1.50
58 Kerry Kittles .20 .50
59 Jayson Williams .20 .50
60 Keith Van Horn .30 .75
61 Patrick Ewing .40 1.00
62 Allan Houston .25 .60
63 Latrell Sprewell .30 .75
64 Anfernee Hardaway .50 1.25
65 Horace Grant .25 .60
66 Allen Iverson .60 1.50
67 Tim Thomas .30 .75
68 Jason Kidd .50 1.25
69 Danny Manning .25 .60
70 Tom Gugliotta .20 .50
71 Damon Stoudamire .30 .75
72 Rasheed Wallace .30 .75
73 Isaiah Rider .20 .50
74 Corliss Williamson .20 .50
75 Chris Webber .30 .75
76 Tim Duncan .60 1.50
77 David Robinson .50 1.25
78 Sean Elliott .30 .75
79 Gary Payton .30 .75
80 Vin Baker .25 .60
81 John Wallace .20 .50
82 Tracy McGrady .50 1.25
83 Jeff Hornacek .25 .60
84 Karl Malone .40 1.00
85 John Stockton .40 1.00
86 Bryant Reeves .20 .50
87 Shareef Abdur-Rahim .30 .75
88 Rod Strickland .20 .50
89 Juwan Howard .25 .60
90 Mitch Richmond .30 .75
91 Michael Olowokandi RC 1.00 2.50
92 Dirk Nowitzki RC 5.00 12.00
93 Raef LaFrentz RC 1.00 2.50
94 Mike Bibby RC 2.00 5.00
95 Ricky Davis RC 1.25 3.00
96 Jason Williams RC 2.00 5.00
97 Al Harrington RC 1.25 3.00
98 Bonzi Wells RC .75 2.00
99 Keon Clark RC .75 2.00
100 Rashard Lewis RC 2.00 5.00
101 Paul Pierce RC 4.00 10.00
102 Antawn Jamison RC 2.00 5.00
103 Nazr Mohammed RC .75 2.00
104 Brian Skinner RC .75 2.00
105 Corey Benjamin RC .75 2.00
106 Peja Stojakovic RC 2.00 5.00
107 Bryce Drew RC .75 2.00
108 Matt Harpring RC 1.00 2.50
109 Toby Bailey RC .75 2.00
110 Tyronn Lue RC .75 2.00
111 Michael Dickerson RC .75 2.00
112 Roshown McLeod RC .75 2.00
113 Felipe Lopez RC .75 2.00
114 Michael Doleac RC .75 2.00
115 Ruben Patterson RC .75 2.00
116 Robert Traylor RC .75 2.00
117 Sam Jacobson RC .75 2.00
118 Larry Hughes RC 1.50 4.00
119 Pat Garrity RC .75 2.00
120 Vince Carter RC 4.00 10.00

1998-99 Black Diamond Double Diamond

Randomly inserted in packs, this 120-card set parallels the base set. The cards have red foil F/X treatment, rather than silver. The veteran cards (1-90) are serially numbered to 3000, while the rookies (91-120) are serially numbered to 2500. To ascertain values on individual cards, please refer to the multiplier in the header below, coupled with the value of the base card.
*STARS: 1X TO 2.5X BASE CARD HI
*RCs: .5X TO 1.25X BASE HI

1998-99 Black Diamond Triple Diamond

Randomly inserted in packs, this 120-card set parallels the base set. The cards have gold foil F/X treatment, rather than silver. The veteran cards (1-90) are serially numbered to 1500, while the rookies (91-120) are serially numbered to 1000. To ascertain values on individual cards, please refer to the multiplier in the header below, coupled with the value of the base card.
COMMON MJ (1-13/22) 6.00 15.00
*STARS: 1.5X TO 4X BASE CARD HI
*RCs: 1X TO 2.5X BASE CARD HI
92 Dirk Nowitzki 15.00 40.00

1998-99 Black Diamond Quadruple Diamond

Randomly inserted in packs, this 120-card set parallels the base set. The cards have green foil F/X treatment, rather than silver. The veteran cards (1-90) are serially numbered to 150, while the rookies (91-120) are serially numbered to 50. To ascertain values on individual cards, please refer to the multiplier in the header below, coupled with the value of the base card.
COMMON MJ (1-13/22) 30.00 80.00
*STARS: 15X TO 40X BASE CARD HI
*RCs: 4X TO 10X HI
92 Dirk Nowitzki 75.00 200.00

1998-99 Black Diamond Diamond Dominance

Randomly inserted in packs, this 30-card set features the most dominant players in the NBA. The cards are set against a bronze foil background. The cards are also serially numbered to 1000. Card backs carry a "D" prefix.
*EMERALD: 2.5X TO 6X HI COLUMN
EMERALD: PRINT RUN 100 SERIAL #'d SETS
D1 Steve Smith 1.50 4.00
D2 Paul Pierce 10.00 25.00
D3 Glen Rice 2.00 5.00
D4 Toni Kukoc 2.00 5.00
D5 Shawn Kemp 2.00 5.00
D6 Michael Finley 2.00 5.00
D7 Antonio McDyess 1.50 4.00
D8 Grant Hill 3.00 8.00
D9 Antawn Jamison 5.00 12.00
D10 Scottie Pippen 3.00 8.00
D11 Reggie Miller 2.50 6.00
D12 Michael Olowokandi 2.50 6.00
D13 Shaquille O'Neal 5.00 12.00
D14 Alonzo Mourning 2.50 6.00
D15 Ray Allen 2.50 6.00
D16 Stephon Marbury 2.50 6.00
D17 Keith Van Horn 2.00 5.00
D18 Allan Houston 1.50 4.00
D19 Anfernee Hardaway 3.00 8.00
D20 Allen Iverson 4.00 10.00
D21 Jason Kidd 3.00 8.00
D22 Damon Stoudamire 2.00 5.00
D23 Chris Webber 2.00 5.00
D24 Tim Duncan 4.00 10.00
D25 Gary Payton 2.00 5.00
D26 Vince Carter 10.00 25.00
D27 Karl Malone 2.50 6.00
D28 Mike Bibby 5.00 12.00
D29 Mitch Richmond 2.00 5.00
D30 Michael Jordan 20.00 50.00

1998-99 Black Diamond MJ Sheer Brilliance

Randomly inserted in hobby packs, this 30-card set focuses on Michael Jordan. The cards are serially numbered to 230 on the back. Card backs also contain a "B" prefix.
COMMON CARD (B1-B30) 25.00 60.00

1998-99 Black Diamond MJ Sheer Brilliance Extreme

Randomly inserted in hobby packs only, this 30-card set is a parallel of the MJ Sheer Brilliance insert. The cards are serially numbered to 23. Card backs contain a "B" prefix.
COMMON CARD (B1-B30) 100.00 250.00

1998-99 Black Diamond UD Authentics

Randomly inserted in packs, this five-card set features autographs from some of the top rookies in 1999. The cards are numbered out of 475.
AJ Antawn Jamison 15.00 40.00
BW Bonzi Wells 6.00 15.00
LH Larry Hughes 12.00 30.00
MB Mike Bibby 30.00 60.00
RT Robert Traylor 6.00 15.00

1999-00 Black Diamond

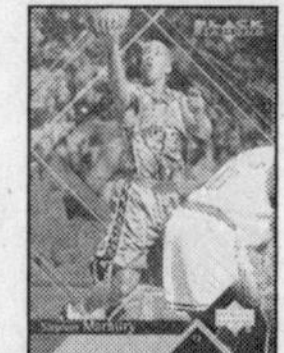

Upper Deck produced this year's Black Diamond with six-cards per pack that carried a suggested retail price of $3.99. The base set was made up of 120 cards, consisting of 90 veterans and a 30-card rookie subset that was inserted one in three packs.
COMPLETE SET (120) 25.00 50.00
COMPLETE SET w/o RC (90) 12.50 25.00
1 Dikembe Mutombo .30 .75
2 Alan Henderson .20 .50
3 Roshown McLeod .20 .50
4 Kenny Anderson .25 .60
5 Paul Pierce .50 1.25
6 Antoine Walker .30 .75
7 Eddie Jones .30 .75
8 Elden Campbell .20 .50
9 David Wesley .20 .50
10 Toni Kukoc .30 .75
11 Randy Brown .20 .50
12 Dickey Simpkins .20 .50
13 Shawn Kemp .30 .75
14 Zydrunas Ilgauskas .25 .60
15 Brevin Knight .20 .50
16 Michael Finley .30 .75
17 Dirk Nowitzki .60 1.50
18 Robert Pack .20 .50
19 Antonio McDyess .25 .60
20 Nick Van Exel .25 .60
21 Ron Mercer .25 .60
22 Grant Hill .40 1.00
23 Lindsey Hunter .20 .50
24 Jerry Stackhouse .30 .75
25 Antawn Jamison .30 .75
26 John Starks .30 .75
27 Donyell Marshall .20 .50
28 Hakeem Olajuwon .40 1.00
29 Charles Barkley .50 1.25
30 Cuttino Mobley .25 .60
31 Reggie Miller .30 .75
32 Rik Smits .30 .75
33 Jalen Rose .25 .60
34 Maurice Taylor .20 .50
35 Tyrone Nesby RC .30 .75
36 Michael Olowokandi .20 .50
37 Shaquille O'Neal .75 2.00
38 Kobe Bryant 1.50 4.00
39 Glen Rice .30 .75
40 P.J. Brown .20 .50
41 Tim Hardaway .30 .75
42 Alonzo Mourning .40 1.00
43 Jamal Mashburn .25 .60
44 Glenn Robinson .25 .60
45 Ray Allen .30 .75
46 Tim Thomas .25 .60
47 Kevin Garnett .60 1.50
48 Joe Smith .25 .60
49 Terrell Brandon .20 .50
50 Stephon Marbury .25 .60
51 Jayson Williams .20 .50
52 Keith Van Horn .25 .60
53 Latrell Sprewell .30 .75
54 Allan Houston .25 .60
55 Patrick Ewing .40 1.00
56 Marcus Camby .25 .60
57 Darrell Armstrong .20 .50
58 Bo Outlaw .20 .50
59 Michael Doleac .20 .50
60 Allen Iverson .60 1.50
61 Theo Ratliff .25 .60
62 Larry Hughes .25 .60
63 Anfernee Hardaway .50 1.25
64 Jason Kidd .50 1.25
65 Tom Gugliotta .20 .50
66 Brian Grant .20 .50
67 Damon Stoudamire .30 .75
68 Rasheed Wallace .30 .75
69 Jason Williams .40 1.00
70 Chris Webber .30 .75
71 Vlade Divac .30 .75
72 Tim Duncan .60 1.50
73 David Robinson .50 1.25
74 Avery Johnson .25 .60
75 Sean Elliott .30 .75
76 Gary Payton .30 .75
77 Vin Baker .30 .75
78 Brent Barry .25 .60
79 Vince Carter .60 1.50
80 Tracy McGrady .50 1.25
81 Doug Christie .25 .60
82 Karl Malone .40 1.00
83 John Stockton .40 1.00
84 Bryon Russell .20 .50
85 Shareef Abdur-Rahim .25 .60
86 Mike Bibby .30 .75
87 Felipe Lopez .20 .50
88 Juwan Howard .25 .60
89 Rod Strickland .20 .50
90 Mitch Richmond .30 .75
91 Elton Brand RC 1.00 2.50
92 Steve Francis RC 1.00 2.50
93 Baron Davis RC 1.25 3.00
94 Lamar Odom RC 1.25 3.00
95 Jonathan Bender RC .40 1.00
96 Wally Szczerbiak RC .75 2.00
97 Richard Hamilton RC 1.00 2.50
98 Andre Miller RC 1.00 2.50
99 Shawn Marion RC 1.00 2.50
100 Jason Terry RC 1.00 2.50
101 Trajan Langdon RC .40 1.00
102 Aleksandar Radojevic RC .40 1.00
103 Corey Maggette RC .75 2.00
104 William Avery RC .40 1.00
105 Ron Artest RC 1.00 2.50
106 Adrian Griffin RC .40 1.00
107 James Posey RC .40 1.00
108 Quincy Lewis RC .40 1.00
109 Dion Glover RC .40 1.00
110 Jeff Foster RC .40 1.00
111 Kenny Thomas RC .40 1.00
112 Devean George RC .40 1.00
113 Tim James RC .40 1.00
114 Vonteego Cummings RC .40 1.00
115 Jumaine Jones RC .40 1.00
116 Scott Padgett RC .40 1.00

117 Obinna Ekezie RC .40 1.00
118 Ryan Robertson RC .40 1.00
119 Chucky Atkins RC .40 1.00
120 A.J. Bramlett RC .40 1.00

1999-00 Black Diamond Diamond Cut

Randomly inserted in packs at one in six for the 90 veterans and one in 12 for the 30 rookies, this 120-card set parallels the base set. The cards feature Silver Light F/X and rainbow foil. To ascertain values on individual cards, please refer to the multiplier in the header below, coupled with the value of the base card.
COMPLETE SET (120) 40.00 100.00
*STARS: .75X TO 2X BASE CARD HI
*RCs: .6X TO 1.5X BASE HI

1999-00 Black Diamond Final Cut

Randomly inserted in packs, this 120-card set parallels the base set. The cards feature Gold Light F/X and were serially numbered. The veterans (1-90) were serially numbered to 100, while the rookies (91-120) were serially numbered to 50. To ascertain values on individual cards, please refer to the multiplier in the header below, coupled with the value of the base card.
*STARS: 10X TO 25X BASE CARD HI
*RCs: 6X TO 12X BASE HI

1999-00 Black Diamond A Piece of History

Randomly inserted in packs at one in 336 for regular cards and one in 144 for hobby-only, this 25-card set features a "single" piece of a game-used basketball that was used by that particular player.
*DOUBLE: 1.25X TO 3X BASE HI
DOUBLE STATED ODDS 1:864 H; 1:1008 H/R
*TRIPLE: 2.5X TO 6X HI
TRIPLE: PRINT RUN 25 SER.#'d SETS
AH Allan Houston H/R 4.00 10.00
AW Antoine Walker H 5.00 12.00
BD Baron Davis H 6.00 15.00
CB Charles Barkley H/R 15.00 40.00
CM Corey Maggette H/R 4.00 10.00
CW Chris Webber H 10.00 25.00
DG Devean George H 2.00 5.00
DR David Robinson H/R 8.00 20.00
GP Gary Payton H 6.00 15.00
HO Hakeem Olajuwon H 6.00 15.00
JB Jonathan Bender H 2.00 5.00
JS John Stockton H/R 6.00 15.00
JT Jason Terry H/R 5.00 12.00
JW Jason Williams H 6.00 15.00
KG Kevin Garnett H 10.00 25.00
KM Karl Malone H 6.00 15.00
KT Kenny Thomas H/R 2.00 5.00
MF Michael Finley H/R 5.00 12.00
PP Paul Pierce H/R 8.00 20.00
RM Reggie Miller H 5.00 12.00
SA Shareef Abdur-Rahim H/R 4.00 10.00
SF Steve Francis H 5.00 12.00
SO Shaquille O'Neal H/R 12.00 30.00
TB Terrell Brandon H 3.00 8.00
WS Wally Szczerbiak H/R 4.00 10.00

1999-00 Black Diamond Diamonation

Randomly inserted in packs at one in eight, this 10-card set features elite players who can take control of the game with their dominant play. Card backs carry a "D" prefix.
COMPLETE SET (10) 5.00 12.00
D1 Vince Carter 1.00 2.50
D2 Tim Duncan 1.00 2.50
D3 Kobe Bryant 2.50 6.00
D4 Stephon Marbury .40 1.00
D5 Ron Mercer .40 1.00
D6 Allen Iverson 1.00 2.50
D7 Shareef Abdur-Rahim .40 1.00
D8 Kevin Garnett 1.00 2.50
D9 Jason Kidd .75 2.00
D10 Allan Houston .40 1.00

1999-00 Black Diamond Jordan Diamond Gallery

Randomly inserted in packs at one in 12, this 10-card set featured candid portrait photography of Michael Jordan. Card backs carry a "DG" prefix.
COMPLETE SET (10) 15.00 30.00
COMMON CARD (DG1-DG10) 2.00 5.00
UNPRICED GOLD VERSION SERIAL #'d TO 1

1999-00 Black Diamond Might

Randomly inserted in packs at one in three, this 20-card set features some of the top powerhorses in the NBA. Card backs carry a "DM" prefix.
COMPLETE SET (20) 4.00 10.00
DM1 Shaquille O'Neal 1.00 2.50
DM2 Allan Houston .30 .75
DM3 Keith Van Horn .30 .75
DM4 Antonie Walker .40 1.00
DM5 Latrell Sprewell .40 1.00
DM6 Hakeem Olajuwon .50 1.25
DM7 David Robinson .60 1.50
DM8 Antonio McDyess .30 .75
DM9 Shawn Kemp .40 1.00
DM10 Ray Allen .40 1.00
DM11 Karl Malone .50 1.25
DM12 Tim Hardaway .40 1.00
DM13 Mike Bibby .40 1.00
DM14 Antawn Jamison .40 1.00
DM15 Dikembe Mutombo .40 1.00
DM16 Michael Finley .40 1.00
DM17 Juwan Howard .30 .75
DM18 Maurice Taylor .25 .60
DM19 Gary Payton .40 1.00
DM20 Shareef Abdur-Rahim .30 .75

1999-00 Black Diamond Myriad

Randomly inserted in packs at one in 24, this 10-card set highlights the NBA's biggest stars in action. Card backs carry a "M" prefix.
COMPLETE SET (10) 10.00 25.00
M1 Kobe Bryant 5.00 12.00
M2 Tim Duncan 2.00 5.00
M3 Kevin Garnett 2.00 5.00
M4 Keith Van Horn .75 2.00
M5 Vince Carter 2.00 5.00
M6 Grant Hill 1.25 3.00
M7 Anfernee Hardaway 1.50 4.00
M8 Karl Malone 1.25 3.00
M9 Allen Iverson 2.00 5.00
M10 Jason Williams 1.25 3.00

1999-00 Black Diamond Skills

Randomly inserted in packs at one in 24, this 10-card set takes a look at some of the most versatile athletes in the NBA. Card backs carry a "DS" prefix.
COMPLETE SET (10) 6.00 15.00
DS1 Stephon Marbury .75 2.00
DS2 Grant Hill 1.25 3.00
DS3 Reggie Miller 1.00 2.50
DS4 Jason Kidd 1.50 4.00
DS5 Mike Bibby 1.00 2.50
DS6 John Stockton 1.25 3.00
DS7 Jason Williams 1.25 3.00
DS8 Shaquille O'Neal 2.50 6.00
DS9 Antonio McDyess .75 2.00
DS10 Hakeem Olajuwon 1.25 3.00

2000-01 Black Diamond

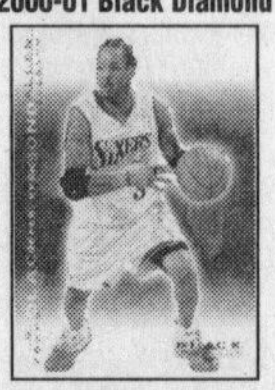

The 2000-01 Black Diamond product was released in March, 2001 and featured a 132-card base set that ws broken into tiers as follows: Base Veterans (1-90), and Rookies (91-132) that were broken into five groups. Group 1 (91-100) were serial numbered to 2000, Group 2 (101-110) were serial numbered to 1000, Group 3 (111-120) were serial numbered to 750, Group 4 (121-126) had a swatch of jersey and were serial numbered to 1750, and Group 5 (127-132) had a swatch of jersey and were serial numbered to 900. Each pack contained five cards, and carried a suggested retail price of $2.99.
COMP.SET w/o SP's (90) 8.00 20.00
1 Dikembe Mutombo .30 .75
2 Alan Henderson .20 .50
3 Jason Terry .30 .75
4 Paul Pierce .40 1.00
5 Antoine Walker .25 .60
6 Kenny Anderson .25 .60
7 Jamal Mashburn .25 .60
8 Derrick Coleman .25 .60
9 Baron Davis .30 .75
10 Elton Brand .30 .75
11 Ron Artest .30 .75
12 Ron Mercer .20 .50
13 Lamond Murray .20 .50
14 Andre Miller .25 .60
15 Matt Harpring .25 .60
16 Michael Finley .30 .75
17 Dirk Nowitzki .50 1.25
18 Steve Nash .50 1.25
19 Antonio McDyess .25 .60
20 Nick Van Exel .25 .60
21 Raef LaFrentz .20 .50
22 Jerry Stackhouse .25 .60
23 Joe Smith .25 .60
24 Chucky Atkins .20 .50
25 Antawn Jamison .30 .75
26 Larry Hughes .25 .60
27 Chris Mills .20 .50
28 Steve Francis .30 .75
29 Hakeem Olajuwon .40 1.00
30 Cuttino Mobley .25 .60
31 Reggie Miller .30 .75
32 Jalen Rose .25 .60
33 Jermaine O'Neal .30 .75
34 Austin Croshere .20 .50
35 Lamar Odom .30 .75
36 Corey Maggette .25 .60
37 Jeff McInnis .20 .50
38 Kobe Bryant 1.50 4.00
39 Shaquille O'Neal .75 2.00
40 Ron Harper .25 .60
41 Isaiah Rider .25 .60
42 Eddie Jones .30 .75
43 Tim Hardaway .30 .75
44 Brian Grant .20 .50
45 Glenn Robinson .25 .60
46 Sam Cassell .25 .60
47 Ray Allen .30 .75
48 Kevin Garnett .60 1.50
49 Terrell Brandon .20 .50
50 Wally Szczerbiak .25 .60
51 Stephon Marbury .25 .60
52 Keith Van Horn .25 .60
53 Kendall Gill .20 .50
54 Latrell Sprewell .25 .60
55 Allan Houston .25 .60
56 Marcus Camby .25 .60
57 Grant Hill .40 1.00
58 Tracy McGrady .50 1.25
59 Darrell Armstrong .20 .50
60 Allen Iverson .60 1.50
61 Toni Kukoc .25 .60
62 Theo Ratliff .20 .50
63 Jason Kidd .50 1.25
64 Shawn Marion .30 .75
65 Anfernee Hardaway .50 1.25
66 Scottie Pippen .50 1.25
67 Rasheed Wallace .30 .75
68 Damon Stoudamire .25 .60
69 Steve Smith .25 .60
70 Chris Webber .30 .75
71 Jason Williams .30 .75
72 Peja Stojakovic .30 .75
73 Tim Duncan .60 1.50
74 David Robinson .50 1.25
75 Derek Anderson .20 .50
76 Gary Payton .30 .75
77 Patrick Ewing .40 1.00
78 Rashard Lewis .30 .75
79 Vince Carter .60 1.50
80 Mark Jackson .25 .60
81 Antonio Davis .20 .50
82 Karl Malone .40 1.00
83 John Stockton .40 1.00
84 Bryon Russell .20 .50
85 Shareef Abdur-Rahim .25 .60
86 Michael Dickerson .20 .50
87 Mike Bibby .30 .75
88 Mitch Richmond .25 .60
89 Richard Hamilton .25 .60
90 Juwan Howard .25 .60
91 Eduardo Najera RC 1.25 3.00
92 Eddie House RC 1.25 3.00
93 Michael Redd RC 3.00 8.00
94 Ruben Wolkowyski RC 1.25 3.00
95 Dan Langhi RC 1.25 3.00
96 Mark Madsen RC 1.25 3.00
97 Speedy Claxton RC 1.25 3.00
98 Iakovos Tsakalidis RC 1.25 3.00
99 Dragan Tarlac RC 1.25 3.00
100 Donnell Harvey RC 1.25 3.00
101 Etan Thomas RC 1.50 4.00
102 Hedo Turkoglu RC 3.00 8.00
103 Mike Penberthy RC 1.50 4.00
104 Paul McPherson RC 1.50 4.00
105 Jason Collier RC 1.50 4.00
106 Hanno Mottola RC 1.50 4.00
107 A.J. Guyton RC 1.50 4.00
108 Daniel Santiago RC 2.50 6.00
109 Lavor Postell RC 1.50 4.00
110 Erick Barkley RC 1.50 4.00
111 Chris Porter RC 1.50 4.00
112 Mateen Cleaves RC 1.50 4.00
113 Marc Jackson RC 1.50 4.00
114 Joel Przybilla RC 1.50 4.00
115 Courtney Alexander RC 1.50 4.00
116 Khalid El-Amin RC 1.50 4.00
117 Keyon Dooling RC 1.50 4.00
118 Desmond Mason RC 2.00 5.00
119 Stephen Jackson RC 2.50 6.00
120 Morris Peterson RC 1.50 4.00
121 Jerome Moiso JSY RC 3.00 8.00
122 Jamal Crawford JSY RC 5.00 12.00
123 DeShawn Stevenson JSY RC 4.00 10.00
124 Quentin Richardson JSY RC 5.00 12.00
125 Marcus Fizer JSY RC 3.00 8.00
126 Mike Miller JSY RC 6.00 15.00
127 Jamaal Magloire JSY RC 4.00 10.00
128 Chris Mihm JSY RC 4.00 10.00
129 DerMarr Johnson JSY RC 4.00 10.00
130 Stromile Swift JSY RC 4.00 10.00
131 Darius Miles JSY RC 4.00 10.00
132 Kenyon Martin JSY RC 10.00 25.00

2000-01 Black Diamond Gold

This 132-card set is actually a complete gold-foil parallel of the 2000-01 Black Diamond base set. Each card in the set was broken into tiers as follows: Base Veterans (1-90) serial numbered to 500, and Rookies (91-132) that were broken into two groups. Group 1 (91-120) were serial numbered to 250, Group 2 (121-132) contained jersey swatches, and were serial numbered to 100.
*STARS 1-90: 1.5X TO 4X BASE HI
*GEMS 91-100: 1X TO 2.5X BASE HI
*GEMS 101-120: .8X TO 2X BASE HI
*JERSEY 121-126: .6X TO 1.5X BASE HI
*JERSEY 127-132: .5X TO 1.25X BASE HI

2000-01 Black Diamond Gold Jersey Autographs

Randomly inserted in packs at the rate of one in 280, this 12-card set parallels the Gold Rookie Jersey cards, numbers 121-132, and are enhanced with player autographs. Card print runs vary, and are all sequentially numbered to either 100, 150, or 200. Jamaal Magloire, card number 122A, and Kenyon Martin, card number 132A, were initially released as exchange cards.
121A Jerome Moiso/150 6.00 15.00
122A Jamal Crawford/200 10.00 25.00
123A DeShawn Stevenson/200 8.00 20.00
124A Quentin Richardson/150 10.00 25.00
125A Marcus Fizer/150 6.00 15.00
126A Mike Miller/150 12.00 30.00
130A Stromile Swift/100 6.00 15.00
131A Darius Miles/100 6.00 15.00

2000-01 Black Diamond Diamonation

Randomly inserted into packs at one in 10, this 14-card insert features players that dominate the game. Card backs carry a "D" prefix.
COMPLETE SET (14) 6.00 15.00
D1 Kobe Bryant 2.00 5.00
D2 Steve Francis .40 1.00
D3 Allen Iverson .75 2.00
D4 Kevin Garnett .75 2.00
D5 Tracy McGrady .60 1.50
D6 Michael Finley .40 1.00
D7 Paul Pierce .50 1.25
D8 Shaquille O'Neal 1.00 2.50
D9 Vince Carter .75 2.00
D10 Larry Hughes .30 .75
D11 Grant Hill .50 1.25
D12 Latrell Sprewell .30 .75
D13 Jerry Stackhouse .30 .75
D14 Tim Duncan .75 2.00

2000-01 Black Diamond Gallery

Randomly inserted into packs at one in 18, this 6-card insert features a gallery of talented players. Card backs carry a "DG" prefix.
COMPLETE SET (6) 3.00 8.00
DG1 Kobe Bryant 2.00 5.00
DG2 Vince Carter .75 2.00
DG3 Kevin Garnett .75 2.00
DG4 Shaquille O'Neal 1.00 2.50
DG5 Tim Duncan .75 2.00
DG6 Steve Francis .40 1.00

2000-01 Black Diamond Game Gear

Randomly inserted into hobby packs at one in 20, this 28-card insert features swatches of actual game-used memorabilia. Card backs carry the player's initials as numbering.
AH Anfernee Hardaway 5.00 12.00
AW Antoine Walker 2.50 6.00
BD Baron Davis 3.00 8.00
CP Chris Porter 3.00 8.00
DM Dikembe Mutombo 3.00 8.00
DN Dirk Nowitzki 5.00 12.00
DS DeShawn Stevenson 4.00 10.00
GH Grant Hill 4.00 10.00
GR Glen Rice 2.50 6.00
IR Isaiah Rider 2.50 6.00
JM Jamal Mashburn 2.50 6.00
KB Kobe Bryant 15.00 40.00
KE Khalid El-Amin 3.00 8.00
KG1 Kevin Garnett 6.00 15.00
KG2 Kevin Garnett 6.00 15.00
KM Karl Malone 4.00 10.00
LH Larry Hughes 2.50 6.00
LS Latrell Sprewell 2.50 6.00
MC Marcus Camby 2.50 6.00
MF Michael Finley 3.00 8.00
MM Mike Miller 6.00 15.00
PP Paul Pierce 4.00 10.00
RA Ron Artest 3.00 8.00
SM Stephon Marbury 2.50 6.00
TB Terrell Brandon 2.00 5.00
TG Tom Gugliotta 2.00 5.00
TM Tracy McGrady 5.00 12.00
WS Wally Szczerbiak 2.50 6.00

2000-01 Black Diamond Might

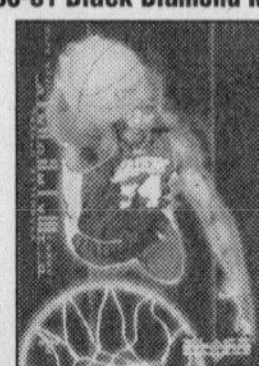
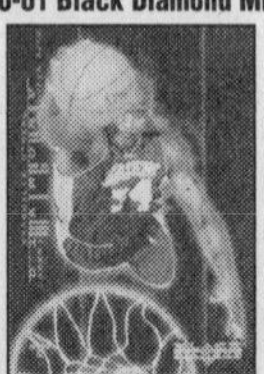

Randomly inserted into packs at one in 8, this 11-card insert features players that have the will to win. Card backs carry a "DM" prefix.
COMPLETE SET (11) 4.00 10.00
DM1 Shaquille O'Neal 1.00 2.50
DM2 Allen Iverson .75 2.00
DM3 Vince Carter .75 2.00
DM4 Chris Webber .40 1.00
DM5 Elton Brand .40 1.00
DM6 Karl Malone .50 1.25
DM7 Rasheed Wallace .40 1.00
DM8 Antawn Jamison .40 1.00
DM9 Kevin Garnett .75 2.00
DM10 Antonio McDyess .30 .75
DM11 Kobe Bryant 2.00 5.00

2000-01 Black Diamond Skills

Randomly inserted into packs at one in 8, this 11-card insert features some of the NBA's most skilled players. Card backs carry a "DS" prefix.
COMPLETE SET (11) 4.00 10.00
DS1 Kevin Garnett .75 2.00
DS2 Jason Kidd .60 1.50
DS3 Allen Iverson .75 2.00
DS4 Gary Payton .40 1.00
DS5 Tim Duncan .75 2.00
DS6 Eddie Jones .40 1.00
DS7 Grant Hill .50 1.25
DS8 Andre Miller .30 .75
DS9 Jason Williams .40 1.00
DS10 Kobe Bryant 2.00 5.00
DS11 Ray Allen .40 1.00

2003-04 Black Diamond

Released in December 2003, Black Diamond boasts a 198-card set divided up as follows: Single Diamond veterans are featured on card numbers 1-84; Double Diamond veterans, card numbers 85-117, are inserted at the rate of one in two; Double Diamond rookies, card numbers 118-126, are inserted at the rate of one in two, Triple Diamond veterans, card numbers 127-147, are inserted at the rate of one in eight; Triple Diamond rookies, card numbers 148-168, are inserted at the rate of one in eight; Quadruple Diamond veterans, card numbers 169-183, are inserted at the rate of one in 48; and Quadruple Diamond rookies, card numbers 184-198, are inserted at the rate of one in 48. Two players, Kyle Korver and Kerry Kittles are featured on two different cards in the set. All cards are printed on foil, feature full-color player action photos, and have diamonds in the lower right-hand corner for quick refernce to see if the card is a Single, Double, Triple or Quadruple Diamond Version. Black Diamond was packaged in 24-pack boxes of five-card packs and carried a suggested retail price of $3.99.
COMP.SET w/o SP's (84) 6.00 15.00
KORVER AND KITTLES HAVE 2 CARDS
UNPRICED RAINBOW PRINT RUN 10 SETS
1 Carlos Boozer .30 .75
2 Dajuan Wagner .20 .50
3 Steve Francis .30 .75
4 Michael Finley .30 .75
5 Jalen Rose .25 .60
6 Kenyon Martin .30 .75
7 Quentin Richardson .25 .60
8 Antoine Walker .30 .75
9 Drew Gooden .25 .60
10 Mike Bibby .30 .75
11 Zydrunas Ilgauskas .25 .60
12 Dan Dickau .20 .50
13 Steve Nash .40 1.00
14 Eduardo Najera .20 .50
15 Joe Smith .25 .60
16 Pau Gasol .30 .75
17 Anthony Mason .20 .50
18 Lamar Odom .30 .75
19 Sam Cassell .25 .60
20 Marko Jaric .20 .50
21 Marcus Fizer .20 .50
22 Jay Williams .20 .50
23 Jason Richardson .30 .75
24 Richard Jefferson .30 .75
25 Gerald Wallace .30 .75
26 Reggie Evans .20 .50
27 Jerome Williams .20 .50
28 Grant Hill .40 1.00
29 Darrell Armstrong .20 .50
30 Rasheed Wallace .30 .75
31 Shane Battier .25 .60
32 Richard Hamilton .25 .60
33 Antonio Davis .20 .50
34 Ray Allen .30 .75
35 Terrell Brandon .20 .50
36 Tim Thomas .20 .50
37 Al Harrington .25 .60
38 Brian Grant .20 .50
39 Zeljko Rebraca .20 .50
40 Kerry Kittles .20 .50
41 Maurice Taylor .20 .50
42 Jerry Stackhouse .25 .60
43 Nikoloz Tskitishvili .20 .50
44 Derrick Coleman .25 .60
45 Raef LaFrentz .20 .50
46 Dale Davis .20 .50
47 Andrei Kirilenko .30 .75
48 Melvin Ely .20 .50
49 Speedy Claxton .20 .50
50 Mike Miller .30 .75
51 Scot Pollard .20 .50
52 Popeye Jones .20 .50
53 Wesley Person .20 .50
54 Chris Wilcox .20 .50
55 Dikembe Mutombo .30 .75
56 Toni Kukoc .30 .75
57 Eddie Griffin .20 .50
58 Kedrick Brown .20 .50
59 Eddie Jones .25 .60
60 Jon Barry .20 .50
61 Jonathan Bender .20 .50
62 Larry Hughes .25 .60
63 Rodney White .20 .50
64 Eddy Curry .25 .60
65 Theo Ratliff .20 .50
66 Jamaal Tinsley .20 .50
67 Zach Randolph .30 .75
68 Alvin Williams .20 .50
69 Derek Fisher .25 .60
70 Vin Baker .20 .50
71 Juan Dixon .20 .50
72 Devean George .20 .50
73 Damon Stoudamire .25 .60
74 Joe Johnson .30 .75
75 Jared Jeffries .20 .50
76 Cuttino Mobley .25 .60
77 Vladimir Radmanovic .20 .50
78 Ron Mercer .20 .50
79 Kenny Thomas .20 .50
80 Nazr Mohammed .20 .50
81 Donyell Marshall .20 .50
82 Lorenzen Wright .20 .50
83 Nick Van Exel .25 .60
84 Jason Terry .25 .60
85 Ben Wallace .40 1.00
86 Glenn Robinson .30 .75
87 Gilbert Arenas .40 1.00
88 Caron Butler .40 1.00
89 Marcus Camby .30 .75
90 Jason Kidd .60 1.50
91 Antawn Jamison .40 1.00
92 Rashard Lewis .40 1.00
93 Juwan Howard .30 .75
94 Andre Miller .30 .75
95 Hedo Turkoglu .40 1.00
96 Jason Williams .30 .75
97 Chauncey Billups .40 1.00
98 P.J. Brown .25 .60
99 Tyson Chandler .30 .75
100 Jamal Mashburn .30 .75
101 Bonzi Wells .25 .60
102 Brad Miller .40 1.00
103 Gordan Giricek .25 .60
104 Nene .30 .75
105 Mike Dunleavy .30 .75
106 Kerry Kittles .25 .60
107 Jamaal Magloire .25 .60
108 Desmond Mason .30 .75
109 Corey Maggette .30 .75
110 Michael Olowokandi .25 .60
111 Tayshaun Prince .40 1.00
112 Earl Boykins .25 .60
113 Allan Houston .30 .75
114 Morris Peterson .25 .60
115 Ricky Davis .30 .75
116 Keith Van Horn .30 .75
117 Shareef Abdur-Rahim .30 .75
118 Willie Green RC 1.25 3.00
119 Kyle Korver RC 1.50 4.00
120 Brandon Hunter RC 1.25 3.00
121 Keith Bogans RC 1.25 3.00
122 Maurice Williams RC 2.00 5.00
123 James Lang RC 1.25 3.00
124 Zaur Pachulia RC 1.25 3.00
125 Slavko Vranes RC 1.25 3.00
126 Theron Smith RC 1.25 3.00
127 Paul Pierce 1.00 2.50
128 Alonzo Mourning 1.00 2.50
129 Elton Brand .75 2.00
130 Manu Ginobili 1.00 2.50
131 Peja Stojakovic .75 2.00
132 Latrell Sprewell .60 1.50
133 Baron Davis .75 2.00
134 Stephon Marbury .60 1.50
135 Darius Miles .50 1.25
136 Antonio McDyess .60 1.50
137 Jermaine O'Neal .75 2.00
138 Scottie Pippen 1.25 3.00
139 Wally Szczerbiak .60 1.50
140 Chris Webber .75 2.00
141 Reggie Miller .75 2.00
142 Tony Parker .75 2.00
143 Karl Malone 1.00 2.50
144 David Robinson 1.25 3.00
145 Matt Harpring .60 1.50
146 Shawn Marion .75 2.00
147 Tim Duncan 1.25 3.00
148 Dwyane Wade RC 6.00 15.00
149 Chris Kaman RC 2.00 5.00
150 Chris Bosh RC 3.00 8.00
151 Mickael Pietrus RC 1.50 4.00
152 Boris Diaw RC 2.00 5.00
153 Marcus Banks RC 1.50 4.00
154 Troy Bell RC 1.50 4.00
155 Zarko Cabarkapa RC 1.50 4.00
156 David West RC 2.00 5.00
157 Zoran Planinic RC 1.50 4.00
158 Aleksandar Pavlovic RC 1.50 4.00
159 Jerome Beasley RC 1.50 4.00
160 Kyle Korver 2.00 5.00
161 Travis Hansen RC 1.50 4.00
162 Steve Blake RC 2.00 5.00
163 Leandro Barbosa RC 2.00 5.00
164 Kendrick Perkins RC 2.50 6.00
165 Kirk Penney RC 1.50 4.00
166 Maciej Lampe RC 1.50 4.00
167 Jason Kapono RC 1.50 4.00
168 Luke Walton RC 1.50 4.00
169 Gary Payton 1.50 4.00
170 Wilt Chamberlain 3.00 8.00
171 Tracy McGrady 2.00 5.00
172 Amare Stoudemire 2.50 6.00
173 Vince Carter 2.50 6.00
174 Shaquille O'Neal 4.00 10.00
175 Larry Bird 5.00 12.00
176 Julius Erving 3.00 8.00
177 Magic Johnson 5.00 12.00
178 Dirk Nowitzki 2.50 6.00
179 Yao Ming 3.00 8.00
180 Allen Iverson 2.50 6.00
181 Kevin Garnett 3.00 8.00
182 Kobe Bryant 8.00 20.00
183 Michael Jordan 12.00 30.00
184 LeBron James RC 30.00 80.00
185 Darko Milicic RC 3.00 8.00
186 Carmelo Anthony RC 8.00 20.00
187 T.J. Ford RC 4.00 10.00
188 Mike Sweetney RC 3.00 8.00
189 Kirk Hinrich RC 4.00 10.00
190 Nick Collison RC 3.00 8.00
191 Travis Outlaw RC 4.00 10.00
192 Jarvis Hayes RC 3.00
193 Luke Ridnour RC 4.00
194 Reece Gaines RC 3.00
195 Ndudi Ebi RC 3.00
196 Dahntay Jones RC 3.00
197 Brian Cook RC 3.00
198 Josh Howard RC 3.00
NNO Lebron James PROMO 4.00
with product information

2003-04 Black Diamond Br

Randomly inserted in packs, this set parallels t
Black Diamond set enhanced with a bronze hu
card and sequential numbering to 100.
*1-84 SINGLES: 4X TO 10X BASE HI
*85-117 SINGLES: 3X TO 8X BASE HI
*118-126 RCs: 1.5X TO 4X BASE HI
*127-147 SINGLES: 1.5X TO 4X BASE HI
*148-168 RCs: 1.25X TO 3X BASE HI
*169-183 SINGLES: .75X TO 2X BASE HI
*184-198 RCs: .6X TO 1.5X BASE HI
148 Dwyane Wade 25.00
184 LeBron James 60.00

2003-04 Black Diamond G

This 198-card set parallels the base Black Diar
with a gold hue and sequential numbering to 2
*1-84 SINGLES: 10X TO 25X BASE HI
*85-117 SINGLES: 8X TO 20X BASE HI
*118-126 RCs: 2.5X TO 6X BASE HI
*127-147 SINGLES: 4X TO 10X BASE HI
*148-168 RCs: 2X TO 5X BASE HI
*169-183 SINGLES: 2.5X TO 6X BASE HI
*184-198 RCs: 1X TO 2.5X BASE HI
148 Dwyane Wade 50.00
184 LeBron James 100.00
186 Carmelo Anthony 25.00

2003-04 Black Diamond Karat Signatures

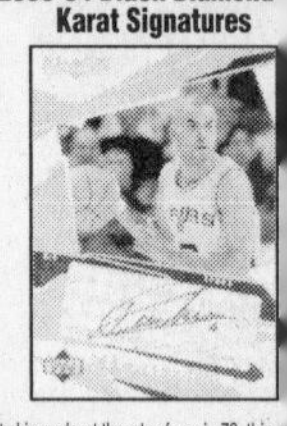

Inserted in packs at the rate of one in 72, this
set features a full color player action photo an
holofoil autograph sticker on a white and gold
background.
AJ Antawn Jamison 5.00
BA Marcus Banks 4.00
BE Jerome Beasley 4.00
BI Chauncey Billups 8.00
CA Carmelo Anthony/100 40.00
CB Caron Butler 8.00
CK Chris Kaman 5.00
CM Corey Maggette 4.00
CM Cuttino Mobley 4.00
DD Dan Dickau 4.00
DJ DerMarr Johnson 4.00
DM Darko Milicic/100 10.00
EB Earl Boykins 4.00
EG Eddie Griffin 4.00
GA Gilbert Arenas 8.00
GI Manu Ginobili 15.00
GP Gary Payton 12.50
JH Jarvis Hayes 4.00
JK Jason Kidd 15.00
JM Jerome Moiso 4.00
JR Jason Richardson 6.00
JS Jerry Stackhouse 6.00
KA Jason Kapono 4.00
KB Kobe Bryant/100 125.00
KE Keith Bogans 4.00
LJ LeBron James/100 350.00
LW Luke Walton 4.00
MB Mike Bibby 8.00
MJ Michael Jordan/23 300.00
ML Maciej Lampe 4.00
MS Mike Sweetney 4.00
PP Paul Pierce 15.00
PS Peja Stojakovic 8.00
RE Reggie Evans 4.00
RG Reece Gaines 4.00
RH Richard Hamilton 4.00
RJ Richard Jefferson 4.00
SB Shane Battier 5.00
SM Shawn Marion 5.00
TM Tracy McGrady/100 30.00
TP Tony Parker/100 12.50
YM Yao Ming/100 20.00

2003-04 Black Diamond Je

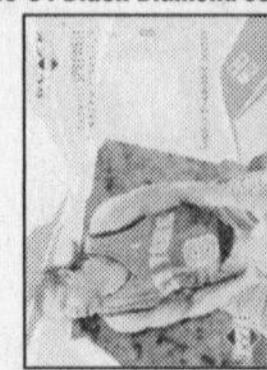

Inserted in packs at the rate of one in 14, this
set features a horizontal design with player ph
the left and jersey swatches on the right. The
backgrounds look like broken glass and acce
are set to match the player's team. A gold vers
also inserted with gold background highlights
cards sequentially numbered to 100.
*GOLD: .6X TO 1.5X BASE JSY HI
BDAD Antonio Davis 2.00
BDAH Anfernee Hardaway 4.00
BDAI Allen Iverson 4.00
BDAM Aaron McKie 2.00
BDAW Antoine Walker 2.50
BDBA Lonny Baxter 2.00
BDBW Ben Wallace 2.50
BDCB Caron Butler 2.50
BDCM Corey Maggette 2.00
BDCW Charlie Ward 2.00
BDDF Derek Fisher 2.00
BDDM Darius Miles 2.00
BDDN Dirk Nowitzki 4.00
BDDW David Wesley 2.00
BDEB Elton Brand 2.50
BDEC Eddy Curry 2.00

Manu Ginobili 3.00 8.00
Eddie Jones 2.00 5.00
Eric Snow 2.00 5.00
Frank Williams 2.00 5.00
Grant Hill SP 5.00 12.00
Glenn Robinson 2.00 5.00
Allan Houston 2.00 5.00
Robert Horry 2.00 5.00
Mark Jackson 2.50 6.00
Jonathan Bender 2.00 5.00
Joe Forte 2.00 5.00
Joe Johnson 2.50 6.00
Jason Kidd 4.00 10.00
Jamaal Magloire 2.00 5.00
Jason Richardson 2.50 6.00
Kobe Bryant SP 15.00 40.00
Kevin Garnett 5.00 12.00
Karl Malone 3.00 8.00
Kareem Rush 2.00 5.00
Keith Van Horn 2.00 5.00
Kenyon Martin 2.50 6.00
Larry Hughes 2.00 5.00
Lamar Odom 2.50 6.00
Latrell Sprewell 2.00 5.00
Jamal Mashburn 2.00 5.00
Mike Bibby 2.50 6.00
Marcus Camby 2.00 5.00
Marcus Fizer 2.00 5.00
Michael Jordan SP 40.00 100.00
Mike Miller 2.50 6.00
Michael Olowokandi 2.00 5.00
Alonzo Mourning 4.00 10.00
Dikembe Mutombo 2.50 6.00
Pau Gasol 2.50 6.00
Paul Pierce 3.00 8.00
Peja Stojakovic 2.50 6.00
Qyntel Woods 2.00 5.00
Ray Allen 2.50 6.00
Rashard Lewis 2.50 6.00
Reggie Miller 2.50 6.00
Rasheed Wallace 2.50 6.00
Joe Smith 2.00 5.00
Stephon Marbury 2.00 5.00
Tracy McGrady 3.00 8.00
Chris Webber 2.50 6.00
Chris Wilcox 2.00 5.00
Yao Ming 5.00 12.00

-04 Black Diamond Jerseys Double Diamond

nly seeded, this 26-card set parallels the base set enhanced with two diamonds in the lower and corner of the card and sequential ing to 250. A Gold version sequentially ed to 75 was also produced and is noticably by its gold background.
.6X TO 1.5X JSY HI
Antoine Walker 4.00 10.00
Carmelo Anthony 10.00 25.00
Caron Butler 4.00 10.00
Darius Miles 2.50 6.00
Elton Brand 4.00 10.00
Manu Ginobili 5.00 12.00
Gilbert Arenas 4.00 10.00
Grant Hill 5.00 12.00
Jason Richardson 4.00 10.00
Kobe Bryant 20.00 50.00
Kenyon Martin 4.00 10.00
LeBron James 50.00 120.00
Latrell Sprewell 3.00 8.00
Mike Bibby 4.00 10.00
Darko Milicic 4.00 10.00
Michael Jordan 50.00 120.00
Mike Miller 4.00 10.00
Pau Gasol 4.00 10.00
Paul Pierce 5.00 12.00
Ray Allen 4.00 10.00
Rashard Lewis 4.00 10.00
Reggie Miller 4.00 10.00
Rasheed Wallace 4.00 10.00
Stephon Marbury 3.00 8.00
Shaquille O'Neal 10.00 25.00
Tony Parker 4.00 10.00

-04 Black Diamond Jerseys Quadruple Diamond

ly seeded, this 6-card set parallels the base set enhanced with four diamonds in the lower nd corner of the card and sequential ng to 50. A Gold version sequentially d to 25 was also produced and is noticably by its gold background.
.6X TO 1.5X BASE HI
RINT RUN 25 SER.#'d SETS
llen Iverson 12.00 30.00
Kobe Bryant 40.00 100.00
LeBron James 80.00 200.00
Michael Jordan 100.00 225.00
Tracy McGrady 10.00 25.00
Yao Ming 15.00 40.00

-04 Black Diamond Jerseys Triple Diamond

y seeded, this 10-card set parallels the base set enhanced with three diamonds in the lower nd corner of the card and sequential ng to 100. A Gold version sequentially d to 50 was also produced and is noticably by its gold background.
6X TO 1.5X BASE JSY HI
Amare Stoudemire 8.00 20.00
Chris Webber 5.00 12.00
Dirk Nowitzki 8.00 20.00
Jason Kidd 8.00 20.00
Kobe Bryant 25.00 60.00
Kevin Garnett 10.00 25.00
LeBron James 80.00 200.00
Michael Jordan 60.00 150.00
Steve Nash 6.00 15.00
Tim Duncan 8.00 20.00

2004-05 Black Diamond

in March, Black Diamond consists of a 198- hat features four tiers for the veteran players or the rookies. The card design places a a card that is bordered only on the bottom and about a third of the way up on the left and right that contains the player's name, the card's highlight color and the diamond logo that indicates what tier the card falls into. Highlight colors are as follows: Single Dimond cards have blue highlights, Double Diamond cards have red highlights, Triple Diamond cards have green highlights and Quadruple Diamond cards have black highlights. The tiers break down as follows: cards 1-84 feature single Diamond Veterans, cards 85-126 are inserted at the rate of one in two packs and feature Double Diamond veterans, cards 127-147 are inserted at the rate of one in eight packs and feature Triple Diamond veterans, cards 148-162 are inserted at the rate of one in 30 packs and feature Quadruple Diamond veterans, cards 163-183 are inserted at the rate of one in eight packs and feature Triple Diamond rookies, and cards 184-198 are inserted at the rate of one in 30 packs and feature Quadruple Diamond rookies.

COMP.SET w/o SPs (84) 8.00 20.00
UNPRICED BLACK PRINT RUN 5 SETS
1 Tony Delk .20 .50
2 Boris Diaw .25 .60
3 Chris Crawford .20 .50
4 Ricky Davis .25 .60
5 Jiri Welsch .20 .50
6 Raef LaFrentz .20 .50
7 Jason Kapono .20 .50
8 Brevin Knight .20 .50
9 Bernard Robinson RC 1.25 3.00
10 Jahidi White .20 .50
11 Tyson Chandler .25 .60
12 Antonio Davis .20 .50
13 Andres Nocioni RC 1.25 3.00
14 Dajuan Wagner .20 .50
15 Zydrunas Ilgauskas .25 .60
16 Jeff McInnis .20 .50
17 Josh Howard .30 .75
18 Marquis Daniels .20 .50
19 Jason Terry .25 .60
20 Andre Miller .25 .60
21 Earl Boykins .20 .50
22 Carlos Delfino .30 .75
23 Ben Wallace .30 .75
24 Tayshaun Prince .30 .75
25 Mickael Pietrus .25 .60
26 Mike Dunleavy .25 .60
27 Speedy Claxton .20 .50
28 Jim Jackson .20 .50
29 Juwan Howard .25 .60
30 Maurice Taylor .20 .50
31 Tyronn Lue .20 .50
32 Jamaal Tinsley .20 .50
33 Stephen Jackson .25 .60
34 Fred Jones .20 .50
35 Kerry Kittles .20 .50
36 Marko Jaric .20 .50
37 Chris Kaman .30 .75
38 Caron Butler .30 .75
39 Kareem Rush .20 .50
40 Mike Miller .30 .75
41 James Posey .20 .50
42 Stromile Swift .20 .50
43 Eddie Jones .25 .60
44 Udonis Haslem .25 .60
45 Matt Freije RC 1.25 3.00
46 T.J. Ford .25 .60
47 Toni Kukoc .25 .60
48 Joe Smith .25 .60
49 Michael Olowokandi .20 .50
50 Wally Szczerbiak .25 .60
51 Troy Hudson .20 .50
52 Aaron Williams .20 .50
53 Alonzo Mourning .40 1.00
54 Nenad Krstic RC 1.25 3.00
55 Jamal Mashburn .30 .75
56 David Wesley .20 .50
57 Tim Pickett RC 1.25 3.00
58 Trevor Ariza RC 1.25 3.00
59 Tim Thomas .20 .50
60 Grant Hill .40 1.00
61 Hedo Turkoglu .30 .75
62 Kelvin Cato .20 .50
63 Kenny Thomas .20 .50
64 Aaron McKie .20 .50
65 Joe Johnson .30 .75
66 Quentin Richardson .25 .60
67 Damon Stoudamire .25 .60
68 Derek Anderson .20 .50
69 Nick Van Exel .25 .60
70 Doug Christie .20 .50
71 Bobby Jackson .20 .50
72 Malik Rose .20 .50
73 Rasho Nesterovic .20 .50
74 Romain Sato RC 1.25 3.00
75 Ronald Murray .20 .50
76 Luke Ridnour .25 .60
77 Pape Sow RC 1.25 3.00
78 Rafer Alston .20 .50
79 Morris Peterson .20 .50
80 Matt Harpring .25 .60
81 Mehmet Okur .25 .60
82 Larry Hughes .25 .60
83 Jarvis Hayes .20 .50
84 Kwame Brown .20 .50
85 Antoine Walker .50 1.25
86 Al Harrington .40 1.00
87 Gary Payton .50 1.25
88 Gerald Wallace .50 1.25
89 Eddy Curry .40 1.00
90 Kirk Hinrich .50 1.25
91 Drew Gooden .40 1.00
92 Michael Finley .50 1.25
93 Jerry Stackhouse .40 1.00
94 Kenyon Martin .50 1.25
95 Nene .40 1.00
96 Chauncey Billups .50 1.25
97 Richard Hamilton .40 1.00
98 Derek Fisher .40 1.00
99 Reggie Miller .50 1.25
100 Ron Artest .50 1.25
101 Corey Maggette .40 1.00
102 Lamar Odom .50 1.25
103 Karl Malone .60 1.50
104 Jason Williams .40 1.00
105 Bonzi Wells .30 .75
106 Desmond Mason .40 1.00
107 Sam Cassell .40 1.00
108 Jamaal Magloire .30 .75
109 Jamal Crawford .40 1.00
110 Allan Houston .40 1.00
111 Cuttino Mobley .40 1.00
112 Glenn Robinson .40 1.00
113 Shawn Marion .50 1.25
114 Darius Miles .30 .75
115 Zach Randolph .40 1.00
116 Chris Webber .50 1.25
117 Mike Bibby .50 1.25
118 Brad Miller .50 1.25
119 Manu Ginobili .60 1.50
120 Rashard Lewis .50 1.25
121 Jalen Rose .40 1.00
122 Chris Bosh .50 1.25
123 Carlos Boozer .50 1.25
124 Carlos Arroyo .40 1.00
125 Gilbert Arenas .50 1.25
126 Antawn Jamison .50 1.25
127 Paul Pierce 1.25 3.00
128 Dirk Nowitzki 1.50 4.00
129 Rasheed Wallace 1.00 2.50
130 Jason Richardson 1.00 2.50
131 Jermaine O'Neal 1.00 2.50
132 Elton Brand 1.00 2.50
133 Pau Gasol 1.00 2.50
134 Dwyane Wade 3.00 8.00
135 Michael Redd 1.00 2.50
136 Latrell Sprewell .75 2.00
137 Richard Jefferson 1.00 2.50
138 Baron Davis 1.00 2.50
139 Stephon Marbury .75 2.00
140 Steve Francis 1.00 2.50
141 Steve Nash 1.25 3.00
142 Shareef Abdur-Rahim .75 2.00
143 Peja Stojakovic 1.00 2.50
144 Tony Parker 1.00 2.50
145 Ray Allen 1.00 2.50
146 Vince Carter 1.50 4.00
147 Andrei Kirilenko .75 2.00
148 Larry Bird 5.00 12.00
149 Michael Jordan 12.00 30.00
150 LeBron James 10.00 25.00
151 Carmelo Anthony 3.00 8.00
152 Tracy McGrady 2.00 5.00
153 Yao Ming 3.00 8.00
154 Kobe Bryant 8.00 20.00
155 Magic Johnson 4.00 10.00
156 Shaquille O'Neal 4.00 10.00
157 Kevin Garnett 3.00 8.00
158 Jason Kidd 2.50 6.00
159 Allen Iverson 2.50 6.00
160 Julius Erving 3.00 8.00
161 Amare Stoudemire 2.00 5.00
162 Tim Duncan 2.50 6.00
163 Andris Biedrins RC 3.00 8.00
164 Robert Swift RC 2.50 6.00
165 Al Jefferson RC 4.00 10.00
166 Kirk Snyder RC 2.50 6.00
167 Dorell Wright RC 4.00 10.00
168 Pavel Podkolzine RC 2.50 6.00
169 Viktor Khryapa RC 2.50 6.00
170 Delonte West RC 3.00 8.00
171 Tony Allen RC 3.00 8.00
172 Kevin Martin RC 3.00 8.00
173 Sasha Vujacic RC 2.50 6.00
174 Beno Udrih RC 2.50 6.00
175 David Harrison RC 2.50 6.00
176 Anderson Varejao RC 3.00 8.00
177 Jackson Vroman RC 2.50 6.00
178 Peter John Ramos RC 2.50 6.00
179 Lionel Chalmers RC 2.50 6.00
180 Andre Emmett RC 2.50 6.00
181 Yuta Tabuse RC 5.00 12.00
182 Trevor Ariza RC 2.50 6.00
183 Chris Duhon RC 2.50 6.00
184 Dwight Howard RC 10.00 25.00
185 Emeka Okafor RC 5.00 12.00
186 Ben Gordon RC 4.00 10.00
187 Shaun Livingston RC 3.00 8.00
188 Devin Harris RC 5.00 12.00
189 Josh Childress RC 3.00 8.00
190 Luol Deng RC 5.00 12.00
191 Andre Iguodala RC 5.00 12.00
192 Luke Jackson RC 3.00 8.00
193 Sebastian Telfair RC 3.00 8.00
194 Kris Humphries RC 3.00 8.00
195 Josh Smith RC 5.00 12.00
196 J.R. Smith RC 4.00 10.00
197 Jameer Nelson RC 4.00 10.00
198 Rafael Araujo RC 3.00 8.00

2004-05 Black Diamond Green

Randomly inserted in packs, this 198-card set parallels the base set and is enhanced with a green background and sequential numbering to 25.
*1-84 SINGLE: 6X TO 15X BASE HI
*1-84 SINGLE RC: 2.5X TO 6X BASE HI
*85-126 DOUBLE: 4X TO 10X BASE HI
*127-147 TRIPLE: 2X TO 5X BASE HI
*148-162 QUAD: 1.25X TO 3X BASE HI
*163-183 RC TRIPLE: .75X TO 2X BASE HI
*184-198 RC QUAD: .6X TO 1.5X BASE HI
134 Dwyane Wade 20.00 50.00
149 Michael Jordan 50.00 125.00

2004-05 Black Diamond Red

Randomly inserted in packs, this 198-card set parallels the base set and is enhanced with a red background and sequential numbering to 100.
*1-84 SINGLE: 3X TO 8X BASE HI
*1-84 SINGLE RC: 1X TO 2.5X BASE HI
*85-126 DOUBLE: 2X TO 5X BASE HI
*127-147 TRIPLE: 1X TO 2.5X BASE HI
*148-162 QUAD: .6X TO 1.5X BASE HI
*163-183 RC TRIPLE: .5X TO 1.25X BASE HI
*184-198 RC QUAD: .4X TO 1X BASE HI
149 Michael Jordan 40.00 70.00

2004-05 Black Diamond Die Cuts

Inserted in packs at the rate of one in ten, this 42-card set features players in action on a card that is die cut on all four corners and a blue strip. This first die cut set is the single diamond version and a blue strip runs along the left side of the card. The double diamond version is inserted at one in 20 packs, utilizes the same card design but has a red strip along the left. The Triple Diamond version is inserted at one in 100 and has a green strip along the left side, and the quad version is inserted at one in 400 and has a black strip along the left.
*DC DOUBLE: .5X TO 1.25X BASE HI
*DC TRIPLE: .6X TO 1.5X BASE HI
*DC QUAD: 2X TO 5X BASE HI
DC1 LeBron James 8.00 20.00
DC2 Michael Jordan 10.00 25.00
DC3 Kobe Bryant 6.00 15.00
DC4 Dwight Howard 4.00 10.00
DC5 Tracy McGrady 1.50 4.00
DC6 Kevin Garnett 2.50 6.00
DC7 Emeka Okafor 2.00 5.00
DC8 Ben Gordon 1.50 4.00
DC9 Shaun Livingston 1.25 3.00
DC10 Devin Harris 2.00 5.00
DC11 Josh Childress 1.25 3.00
DC12 Luol Deng 2.00 5.00
DC13 Andre Iguodala 2.00 5.00
DC14 Sebastian Telfair 1.25 3.00
DC15 Josh Smith 2.00 5.00
DC16 J.R. Smith 1.50 4.00
DC17 Jameer Nelson 1.50 4.00
DC18 Larry Bird 4.00 10.00
DC19 Carmelo Anthony 2.50 6.00
DC20 Yao Ming 2.50 6.00
DC21 Magic Johnson 3.00 8.00
DC22 Shaquille O'Neal 3.00 8.00
DC23 Jason Kidd 2.00 5.00
DC24 Allen Iverson 2.00 5.00
DC25 Julius Erving 2.50 6.00
DC26 Amare Stoudemire 1.50 4.00
DC27 Tim Duncan 2.00 5.00
DC28 Paul Pierce 1.50 4.00
DC29 Dirk Nowitzki 2.00 5.00
DC30 Dwyane Wade 4.00 10.00
DC31 Baron Davis 1.25 3.00
DC32 Stephon Marbury 1.00 2.50
DC33 Steve Francis 1.25 3.00
DC34 Steve Nash 1.50 4.00
DC35 Peja Stojakovic 1.25 3.00
DC36 Tony Parker 1.25 3.00
DC37 Ray Allen 1.25 3.00
DC38 Vince Carter 2.00 5.00
DC39 Andrei Kirilenko 1.00 2.50
DC40 Mike Bibby 1.25 3.00
DC41 Ben Wallace 1.25 3.00
DC42 Manu Ginobili 1.50 4.00

2004-05 Black Diamond GemoGRAPHy

Seeded in packs at the rate of one in 20, this 36-card set is printed on foil board with a player image along the top of the card and an autograph box along the bottom. The autograph box is colored to match the feature player's team colors.
AH Al Harrington 4.00 10.00
AI Andre Iguodala 6.00 15.00
AK Andrei Kirilenko 4.00 10.00
AS Amare Stoudemire SP 12.50 30.00
BG Ben Gordon 5.00 12.00
BR Bernard Robinson 4.00 10.00
CA Carmelo Anthony SP 15.00 40.00
CB Carlos Boozer 6.00 15.00
DE Devin Harris 6.00 15.00
DH Dwight Howard 20.00 50.00
JC Josh Childress 4.00 10.00
JN Jameer Nelson 5.00 12.00
JR J.R. Smith 5.00 12.00
JS Josh Smith 6.00 15.00
KB Kobe Bryant SP 100.00 200.00
KG Kevin Garnett SP 20.00 50.00
KH Kris Humphries 4.00 10.00
LD Luol Deng 6.00 15.00
LJ LeBron James SP 100.00 200.00
LU Luke Jackson 4.00 10.00
MB Mike Bibby 4.00 10.00
MF Matt Freije 4.00 10.00
MJ Michael Jordan SP 250.00 500.00
PG Pau Gasol 10.00 25.00
PS Pape Sow 4.00 10.00
RA Rafael Araujo 4.00 10.00
RJ Richard Jefferson 4.00 10.00
RM Reggie Miller 40.00 100.00
RO Romain Sato 4.00 10.00
RS Robert Swift 4.00 10.00
SE Sebastian Telfair 4.00 10.00
SL Shaun Livingston 4.00 10.00
ST Stephon Marbury 6.00 15.00
TA Trevor Ariza 4.00 10.00
TM Tracy McGrady SP 20.00 50.00
ZR Zach Randolph 4.00 10.00

2004-05 Black Diamond Jerseys

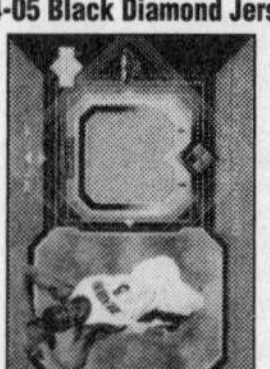

Inserted in packs at one in 13, this 42-card set is horizontally designed with a player photo on the left and a swatch of jersey on the right. The base level of this set is considered the single diamond, has the single diamond logo and highlight colors along the top and bottom of the card are in blue. There are three parallels to this set, Double Diamond, Triple Diamond and Quadruple Diamond, and for each progressive set, the jersey swatch gets larger. Doubles are highlighted with red, contain the double diamond logo and are squentially numbered to 250. Triples are highlighted with green, contain the double diamond logo and are squentially numbered to 100. Quads are highlighted with black, contain the double diamond logo, are squentially numbered to 10 and contain player autographs.
*DOUBLE: .5X TO 1.25X BASE HI
*TRIPLE: .6X TO 1.5X BASE HI
UNPRICED QUAD AU PRINT RUN 10 SETS
AI Allen Iverson 4.00 10.00
AN Andre Iguodala 4.00 10.00
AS Amare Stoudemire 3.00 8.00
AV Anderson Varejao 3.00 8.00
BD Baron Davis 2.50 6.00
BG Ben Gordon 3.00 8.00
CA Carmelo Anthony 5.00 12.00
CB Chauncey Billups 2.50 6.00
CD Chris Duhon 2.50 6.00
DA David Harrison 2.50 6.00
DB Elton Brand 2.50 6.00
DE Devin Harris 4.00 10.00
DH Dwight Howard 8.00 20.00
DN Dirk Nowitzki 4.00 10.00
DW Dajuan Wagner 2.00 5.00
EG Manu Ginobili 3.00 8.00
JC Jamal Crawford 2.00 5.00
JK Jason Kidd 4.00 10.00
JO Josh Childress 2.50 6.00
JR J.R. Smith 3.00 8.00
JS Josh Smith 4.00 10.00
JV Jackson Vroman 2.50 6.00
KB Kobe Bryant SP 10.00 25.00
KG Kevin Garnett 5.00 12.00
KM Kevin Martin 3.00 8.00
LC Lionel Chalmers 2.50 6.00
LD Luol Deng 4.00 10.00
LJ LeBron James SP 12.00 30.00
LU Luke Jackson 2.50 6.00
MJ Michael Jordan SP 30.00 80.00
RJ Richard Jefferson 2.50 6.00
RW Rasheed Wallace 2.50 6.00
SE Sebastian Telfair 2.50 6.00
SF Steve Francis 2.50 6.00
SL Shaun Livingston 2.50 6.00
SO Shaquille O'Neal 6.00 15.00
TA Tony Allen 3.00 8.00
TD Tim Duncan 4.00 10.00
TM Tracy McGrady 3.00 8.00
WE Delonte West 3.00 8.00
YT Yuta Tabuse 5.00 12.00
AU Andre Emmett 2.50 6.00

1994 Bleachers 23 Karat Promos

These standard-size promo cards were issued to promote two products licensed by Classic but produced by Bleachers, the 23K all-gold sculptured cards and Bleachers prototypical gold border cards. One promo card was included in each gold foil-stamped box that contained the all-gold sculptured card. These promo cards read "Original 23 Karat Genuine All-Gold Sculptured Trading Cards" at the bottom. Some of these card fronts have Bleachers logos while others have Classic logos. The other promo cards read "The Original 23 Karat Genuine Gold Border Basketball Cards" at the bottom. The fronts of show full-bleed color action player photos with an advertisement across the bottom. On a wood-grain background, the backs carry player profile and a facsimile autograph. The cards are unnumbered and checklisted below in alphabetical order.
COMPLETE SET (7) 1.00 2.50
1 Alonzo Mourning .08 .25
Bleachers All-Gold
(Jumping center in Georgetown uniform)
2 Shaquille O'Neal .20 .50
Classic All-Gold
(Squishing ball)
3 Shaquille O'Neal .20 .50
Classic All-Gold
(Running down court in white LSU uniform)
4 Shaquille O'Neal .20 .50
Classic Gold Border
(Running down court in purple LSU uniform)
5 Shaquille O'Neal .20 .50
Classic All-Gold
(Wearing South jersey)
6 Chris Webber .08 .25
Bleachers All-Gold
(Dunking in Michigan unform)
7 Class of '93 .20 .50
Bleachers All-Gold
Chris Webber
Anfernee Hardaway
Jamal Mashburn

1994-00 Bleachers 23 Karat Gold

This set of 23K all-gold sculptured cards was licensed by several different card companies but produced by Bleachers. Each standard-size card was packaged in a clear acrylic holder with a gold foil-stamped box and some included a promo card. Each card is reportedly limited to the amount listed per each card checklisted below; the serial number "X of X" is stamped on the back at the bottom. The card design features two thin gold-leaf sheets attached to a cardboard insert. The fronts display an embossed action shot inside an ornate picture frame. Some cards, like the Ultra Courtmasters series, are identical gold parallels to cards printed by card companies. The player's name or nickname is printed on the front. The backs present biography, college career highlights, and statistics. All card were issued at different times between 1994-2000. Except for serial numbers, the cards are unnumbered and thus are checklisted below in alphabetical order.
1 Larry Bird 6.00 15.00
Bleachers/10,000
2 Kobe Bryant 15.00 40.00
E-X2000/1996
3 Kobe Bryant 15.00 40.00
E-X2000 Purple Sig/1996
4 Kobe Bryant 15.00 40.00
E-X2000 Ball/1996
5 Chicago Bulls 6.00 15.00
Hoops Starting Five
6 Class of '93 8.00 20.00
Chris Webber
Anfernee Hardaway
Jamal Mashburn
7 Patrick Ewing 6.00 15.00
86/7 Fleer Red
Blue Border
8 Anfernee Hardaway 8.00 20.00
Ultra Courtmaster/10,000
9 Grant Hill 6.00 15.00
Classic/10,000
10 Grant Hill 6.00 15.00
96/7 Flair Showcase 23-K Gems
11 Grant Hill 6.00 15.00
Ultra Courtmasters/10,000
12 Grant Hill 10.00 25.00
Jason Kidd
Classic/10,000
13 Michael Jordan 15.00 40.00
Diamond Star
Upper Deck/25,000
14 Michael Jordan 20.00 50.00
86/7 Fleer
15 Michael Jordan 15.00 40.00
86/7 Fleer Stickers
16 Michael Jordan 15.00 40.00
96/7 Flair Showcase
17 Michael Jordan 20.00 50.00
Ultra Courtmasters/10,000
18 Michael Jordan 15.00 40.00
Ultra Starring Role
19 Michael Jordan 15.00 40.00
Upper Deck/25,000
20 Michael Jordan 15.00 40.00
Upper Deck/25,000
21 Michael Jordan 12.50 30.00
Upper Deck/50,000
22 Michael Jordan 15.00 40.00
Z-Force
23 Karl Malone 6.00 15.00
Ultra Courtmasters/10,000
24 Alonzo Mourning 6.00 15.00
Bleachers/10,000
25 Shaquille O'Neal (LSU) 12.50 30.00
Classic/10,000
26 Shaquille O'Neal (Orlando) 12.50 30.00
Classic/10,000
27 Shaquille O'Neal (Triple Image) 10.00 25.00
Classic/24,900
28 Shaquille O'Neal 10.00 25.00
Score Leader
Classic/25,000
29 Shaquille O'Neal JUMBO 12.50 30.00
Classic/10,000
30 Shaquille O'Neal 12.50 30.00
LAL Diam. Star
Classic/10,000
31 Shaquille O'Neal 12.50 30.00
ORL Diam. Star
Classic/10,000
32 Shaquille O'Neal 12.50 30.00
BK Rookies
Score Board/10,000
33 Shaquille O'Neal 12.50 30.00
Ultra Courtmasters/10,000
34 Scottie Pippen 8.00 20.00
Classic/10,000
35 Scottie Pippen 15.00 40.00
Classic/2,000
36 Scottie Pippen 8.00 20.00
Dennis Rodman
Bleachers/10,000
37 Scottie Pippen 8.00 20.00
Ultra Courtmasters/10,000
38 David Robinson 6.00 15.00
Classic/10,000
39 Glenn Robinson 8.00 20.00
Classic/4,996
40 Dennis Rodman(Rainbow Hair) 10.00 25.00
Bleachers/10,000
41 Dennis Rodman 10.00 25.00
Grn.Pink Hair)
Bleachers/10,000
42 Dennis Rodman 10.00 25.00
Diamond Star
Bleachers/10,000
43 Jerry Stackhouse 6.00 15.00
Classic/25,000
44 John Stockton 6.00 15.00
Ultra Courtmasters/10,000
45 Damon Stoudamire 10.00 25.00
Classic/4,996
46 Chris Webber 10.00 25.00
Bleachers/10,000
48 Kobe Bryant 15.00 40.00
E-X2000/5000
NNO Dennis Rodman 15.00 30.00
Michael Jordan
Scottie Pippen/72 Victories/10,000

1997 Bleachers/Fleer Gold Promos

This 2-card promo set was first released at the 1997 18th National Sports Collectors Convention in Cleveland, Ohio. The standard size cards are sculpted in Genuine 23 karat gold and are crafted to parallel these players' 1993-94 Fleer rookie cards. The backs have a "23 KT Gold Card" logo and are numbered "Prototype of 10,000". The cards were distributed individually in CD jewel cases. The actual set of 12 different Fleer rookie card parallels was not live at press time. Scheduled for release of 100,000 each are Michael Jordan, Karl Malone, Charles Barkley, Patrick Ewing, Hakeem Olajuwon, Clyde Drexler, Dennis Rodman, Scottie Pippen, Shawn Kemp, Shaquille O'Neal, Anfernee Hardaway and Grant Hill. The promo cards are unnumbered and listed below in alphabetical order.
COMPLETE SET (2) 2.00 5.00
1 Anfernee Hardaway 1.25 3.00
2 Grant Hill 1.25 3.00

1997 Bleachers/Fleer Gold

This 12-card set features embossed player images on 23 Karat all-gold sculptured cards. Each card was sold individually with a suggested retail price of $24.95 and packaged in a CD jewel case. The cards were packaged as six boxes per case with eight cards per box. The cards are unnumbered and checklisted below in alphabetical order. Each card is serially numbered with only 10,000 of each card produced. 17 matching serial number sets were also offered. These redemption cards were inserted at one in 2400 packs. The continuation line states the year of the player's original Fleer rookie card.
COMPLETE SET (12) 40.00 100.00
1 Charles Barkley 1986-87 5.00 12.00
2 Clyde Drexler 1986-87 4.00 10.00
3 Patrick Ewing 1986-87 4.00 10.00
4 Anfernee Hardaway 1993-94 5.00 12.00
5 Grant Hill 1994-95 5.00 12.00
6 Michael Jordan 1986-87 12.00 30.00
7 Shawn Kemp 1990-91 4.00 10.00
8 Karl Malone 1986-87 4.00 10.00
9 Hakeem Olajuwon 1986-87 4.00 10.00
10 Shaquille O'Neal 1992-93 8.00 20.00
11 Scottie Pippen 1988-89 5.00 12.00
12 Dennis Rodman 1988-89 6.00 15.00

1997 Bleachers/Fleer Gold Black Foil

Randomly inserted into packs at a rate of one in 50, this 12-card set parallels the basic set. The cards feature a black-foil facsimile autograph of each player. The cards are not numbered and listed below alphabetically.
COMPLETE SET (12) 60.00 150.00
1 Charles Barkley 1986-87 8.00 20.00
2 Clyde Drexler 1986-87 6.00 15.00
3 Patrick Ewing 1986-87 6.00 15.00
4 Anfernee Hardaway 1993-94 8.00 20.00
5 Grant Hill 1994-95 8.00 20.00
6 Michael Jordan 1986-87 20.00 50.00
7 Shawn Kemp 1990-91 6.00 15.00
8 Karl Malone 1986-87 6.00 15.00
9 Hakeem Olajuwon 1986-87 6.00 15.00
10 Shaquille O'Neal 1992-93 12.00 30.00
11 Scottie Pippen 1988-89 8.00 20.00
12 Dennis Rodman 1988-89 10.00 25.00

1997 Bleachers/Fleer Gold Holographic Foil

Randomly inserted into packs at a rate of one in 100, this 12-card set paralles the basic issue. The cards feature a holographic-foil facsimile autograph on the card front. The cards are not numbered and listed below in alphabetical order.
COMPLETE SET (12) 150.00 300.00
1 Charles Barkley 1986-87 12.00 30.00
2 Clyde Drexler 1986-87 10.00 25.00
3 Patrick Ewing 1986-87 10.00 25.00
4 Anfernee Hardaway 1993-94 12.00 30.00
5 Grant Hill 1994-95 12.00 30.00
6 Michael Jordan 1986-87 30.00 80.00
7 Shawn Kemp 1990-91 10.00 25.00
8 Karl Malone 1986-87 10.00 25.00
9 Hakeem Olajuwon 1986-87 10.00 25.00
10 Shaquille O'Neal 1992-93 20.00 50.00
11 Scottie Pippen 1988-89 12.00 30.00
12 Dennis Rodman 1988-89 15.00 40.00

1996-97 Blockbuster NBA at 50 Postcards

Distributed exclusively through Blockbuster music locations, this 5-card set features a colorful front with a post-card back. Collector's could mail in their postcard for a chance to win a trip for two to the 1997 NBA Conference Finals. The cards were available when purchasing the NBA at 50 - A Musical Celebration tapes or CD's. The cards are not numbered and listed in alphabetical order below.
COMPLETE SET (5) 4.00 10.00
1 Shareef Abdur-Rahim 2.00 5.00
2 Grant Hill 1.50 4.00
3 Hakeem Olajuwon 1.25 3.00
4 Scottie Pippen 1.50 4.00
5 Damon Stoudamire 1.00 2.50

1948 Bowman

The 1948 Bowman set of 72 cards was the company's only basketball issue. Five cards were issued in each pack. It was also the only major basketball issue until 1957-58 when Topps released a set. Cards in the set measure 2 1/16" by 2 1/2". The set is in color and features both player cards and diagram cards. The player cards in the second series are sometimes found without the red or blue printing on the card front, leaving only a gray background. These gray versions are more difficult to find, as they are printing errors where the printer apparently ran out of red or blue ink that was supposed to print on the player's uniform. The key Rookie Card in this set is George Mikan. Other Rookie Cards include Carl Braun, Joe Fulks, William Red Holzman, Jim Pollard, and Max Zaslofsky.
COMPLETE SET (72) 4000.00 6000.00
1 Ernie Calverley RC 75.00 150.00
2 Ralph Hamilton 40.00 60.00
3 Gale Bishop 40.00 60.00
4 Fred Lewis RC 50.00 75.00
5 Basketball Play 30.00 50.00
Single cut off post
6 Bob Feerick RC 50.00 75.00
7 John Logan 40.00 60.00
8 Mel Riebe 40.00 60.00
9 Andy Phillip RC 50.00 100.00
10 Bob Davies RC 50.00 100.00
11 Basketball Play 30.00 50.00
Single cut with return pass to post
12 Kenny Sailors RC 50.00 75.00
13 Paul Armstrong 40.00 60.00
14 Howard Dallmar RC 50.00 75.00
15 Bruce Hale RC 50.00 75.00
16 Sid Hertzberg 50.00 75.00
17 Basketball Play 30.00 50.00
Single cut
18 Red Rocha 40.00 60.00
19 Eddie Ehlers 40.00 60.00
20 Ellis(Gene) Vance 40.00 60.00
21 Fuzzy Levane RC 50.00 75.00
22 Earl Shannon 40.00 60.00
23 Basketball Play 30.00 50.00
Double cut off post
24 Leo (Crystal) Klier 40.00 60.00
25 George Senesky 40.00 60.00
26 Price Brookfield 40.00 60.00
27 John Norlander 40.00 60.00
28 Don Putman 40.00 60.00
29 Basketball Play 30.00 50.00
Double post
30 Jack Garfinkel 40.00 60.00
31 Chuck Gilmur 40.00 60.00

32 Red Holzman RC	125.00	225.00
33 Jack Smiley	40.00	60.00
34 Joe Fulks RC	90.00	150.00
35 Basketball Play	30.00	50.00
Screen play		
36 Hal Tidrick	40.00	60.00
37 Don (Swede) Carlson	60.00	90.00
38 Buddy Jeanette CO RC	80.00	135.00
39 Ray Kuka	60.00	90.00
40 Stan Miasek	60.00	90.00
41 Basketball Play	50.00	75.00
Double screen		
42 George Nostrand	60.00	90.00
43 Chuck Halbert RC	75.00	125.00
44 Arnie Johnson	60.00	90.00
45 Bob Doll	60.00	90.00
46 Bones McKinney RC	80.00	135.00
47 Basketball Play	50.00	75.00
Out of bounds		
48 Ed Sadowski	75.00	125.00
49 Bob Kinney	60.00	90.00
50 Charles (Hawk) Black	60.00	90.00
51 Jack Dwan	50.00	75.00
52 Connie Simmons RC	75.00	125.00
53 Basketball Play	50.00	75.00
Out of bounds		
54 Bud Palmer RC	100.00	150.00
55 Max Zaslofsky RC	125.00	200.00
56 Lee Roy Robbins	60.00	90.00
57 Arthur Spector	60.00	90.00
58 Arnie Risen RC	90.00	150.00
59 Basketball Play	50.00	75.00
Out of bounds play		
60 Ariel Maughan	60.00	90.00
61 Dick O'Keefe	60.00	90.00
62 Herman Schaefer	60.00	90.00
63 John Mahnken	60.00	90.00
64 Tommy Byrnes	60.00	90.00
65 Basketball Play	50.00	75.00
Held ball		
66 Jim Pollard RC	125.00	250.00
67 Lee Mogus	60.00	90.00
68 Lee Knorek	60.00	90.00
69 George Mikan RC	1500.00	2250.00
70 Walter Budko	60.00	90.00
71 Basketball Play	50.00	75.00
Guards Play		
72 Carl Braun RC	200.00	400.00

2003-04 Bowman

Released in October 2003 and marketed as two brands in one pack, Bowman and Bowman Chrome cards shared the same packs and boxes. The Bowman version features a 156-card set divided up into 110 base veteran cards with a red border around a centered picture surrounded by silver borders on the left and right and black borders on the top and the bottom. Cards 111-147 feature rookie players and have a blue border around their pictures and share the rest of the design elements with the base cards. Cards 148-157 are autographed rookie cards sequentially numbered to 250. Upon issue, card number 147 was not released. Bowman was packaged in 24-pack boxes with packs containing seven cards, four Bowman cards, four Bowman Chrome Cards and one Parallel, and carried a suggested retail price of $4.

COMP.SET w/o RC's (110)	15.00	40.00
1 Yao Ming	.60	1.50
2 Glenn Robinson	.25	.60
3 Antoine Walker	.30	.75
4 Jalen Rose	.25	.60
5 Ricky Davis	.25	.60
6 Juwan Howard	.25	.60
7 Kwame Brown	.20	.50
8 Mike Bibby	.30	.75
9 Wally Szczerbiak	.25	.60
10 Allen Iverson	.50	1.25
11 Shareef Abdur-Rahim	.25	.60
12 Jamal Mashburn	.25	.60
13 Stephon Marbury	.25	.60
14 Desmond Mason	.25	.60
15 Gordan Giricek	.20	.50
16 Caron Butler	.30	.75
17 Jermaine O'Neal	.30	.75
18 Kenyon Martin	.30	.75
19 Andrei Kirilenko	.30	.75
20 Dirk Nowitzki	.50	1.25
21 Richard Hamilton	.25	.60
22 Troy Murphy	.30	.75
23 Shawn Marion	.30	.75
24 Allan Houston	.25	.60
25 Keith Van Horn	.25	.60
26 Brian Grant	.20	.50
27 Mike Miller	.30	.75
28 Chris Webber	.30	.75
29 Brent Barry	.20	.50
30 Elton Brand	.30	.75
31 Juan Dixon	.20	.50
32 Karl Malone	.40	1.00
33 Darrell Armstrong	.20	.50
34 Rasheed Wallace	.30	.75
35 Michael Redd	.30	.75
36 Rashard Lewis	.30	.75
37 Ron Artest	.30	.75
38 P.J. Brown	.20	.50
39 Eddie Griffin	.20	.50
40 Tim Duncan	.50	1.25
41 Kurt Thomas	.20	.50
42 Raef Lafrentz	.20	.50
43 Ben Wallace	.30	.75
44 Lamar Odom	.30	.75
45 Vince Carter	.50	1.25
46 Derek Anderson	.20	.50
47 Stromile Swift	.20	.50
48 Bobby Jackson	.20	.50
49 Richard Jefferson	.30	.75
50 Shaquille O'Neal	.75	2.00
51 Calbert Cheaney	.20	.50
52 Troy Hudson	.20	.50
53 Ray Allen	.30	.75
54 Howard Eisley	.20	.50
55 Alonzo Mourning	.40	1.00
56 Sam Cassell	.25	.60
57 Derrick Coleman	.25	.60
58 Andre Miller	.25	.60
59 Antawn Jamison	.30	.75
60 Kevin Garnett	.60	1.50
61 Steve Francis	.30	.75
62 Tyson Chandler	.25	.60
63 Drew Gooden	.25	.60
64 Scottie Pippen	.50	1.25
65 Pau Gasol	.30	.75
66 Steve Nash	.40	1.00
67 DaJuan Wagner	.20	.50
68 Jason Terry	.25	.60
69 Reggie Miller	.30	.75
70 Tracy McGrady	.40	1.00
71 Nene Hilario	.25	.60
72 Morris Peterson	.20	.50
73 Peja Stojakovic	.30	.75
74 Eddie Jones	.25	.60
75 Tony Parker	.30	.75
76 Corliss Williamson	.20	.50
77 Vladimir Radmanovic	.20	.50
78 Amare Stoudemire	.50	1.25
79 Tony Delk	.20	.50
80 Jason Kidd	.50	1.25
81 Gary Payton	.30	.75
82 Corey Maggette	.25	.60
83 Darius Miles	.20	.50
84 Cuttino Mobley	.25	.60
85 Eric Snow	.20	.50
86 Matt Harpring	.25	.60
87 Manu Ginobili	.40	1.00
88 Latrell Sprewell	.25	.60
89 Alvin Williams	.20	.50
90 Paul Pierce	.40	1.00
91 Anfernee Hardaway	.50	1.25
92 Gilbert Arenas	.30	.75
93 Jerry Stackhouse	.25	.60
94 Tim Thomas	.20	.50
95 Nikoloz Tskitishvili	.20	.50
96 Doug Christie	.20	.50
97 Zydrunas Ilgauskas	.25	.60
98 Jamaal Tinsley	.20	.50
99 Theo Ratliff	.20	.50
100 Kobe Bryant	1.50	4.00
101 Chauncey Billups	.30	.75
102 Michael Finley	.30	.75
103 Jason Williams	.25	.60
104 Bonzi Wells	.20	.50
105 Voshon Lenard	.20	.50
106 Jason Richardson	.30	.75
107 Baron Davis	.30	.75
108 Radoslav Nesterovic	.20	.50
109 Eddy Curry	.25	.60
110 Michael Olowokandi	.20	.50
111 Josh Howard RC	1.50	4.00
112 Mario Austin RC	1.50	4.00
113 Rick Rickert RC	1.50	4.00
114 Tommy Smith RC	1.50	4.00
115 Dahntay Jones RC	1.50	4.00
116 Ndudi Ebi RC	1.50	4.00
117 Maurice Williams RC	2.50	6.00
118 Kendrick Perkins RC	2.50	6.00
119 Steve Blake RC	2.00	5.00
120 David West RC	2.00	5.00
121 Chris Kaman RC	2.00	5.00
122 Keith Bogans RC	1.50	4.00
123 LeBron James RC	15.00	40.00
124 Devin Brown RC	1.50	4.00
125 Jason Kapono RC	1.50	4.00
126 Zoran Planinic RC	1.50	4.00
127 Zaur Pachulia RC	1.50	4.00
128 Malick Badiane RC	1.50	4.00
129 Kyle Korver RC	2.00	5.00
130 Darko Milicic RC	1.50	4.00
131 Troy Bell RC	1.50	4.00
132 Luke Walton RC	1.50	4.00
133 Mike Sweetney RC	1.50	4.00
134 Jarvis Hayes RC	1.50	4.00
135 Leandro Barbosa RC	2.00	5.00
136 Carlos Delfino RC	2.00	5.00
137 Sofoklis Schortsanitis RC	1.50	4.00
138 Slavko Vranes RC	1.50	4.00
139 Travis Hansen RC	1.50	4.00
140 Carmelo Anthony RC	4.00	10.00
141 Reece Gaines RC	1.50	4.00
142 Maciej Lampe RC	1.50	4.00
143 Travis Outlaw RC	2.00	5.00
144 Jerome Beasley RC	1.50	4.00
145 Mickael Pietrus RC	1.50	4.00
146 Brian Cook RC	1.50	4.00
148 Kirk Hinrich AU RC	8.00	20.00
149 Dwyane Wade AU RC	40.00	100.00
150 Marcus Banks AU RC	6.00	15.00
151 Nick Collison AU RC	6.00	15.00
152 Boris Diaw AU RC	8.00	20.00
153 Chris Bosh AU RC	15.00	40.00
154 T.J. Ford AU RC	8.00	20.00
155 Luke Ridnour AU RC	8.00	20.00
156 A.Pavlovic AU RC	6.00	15.00
157 Z.Cabarkapa AU RC	6.00	15.00

2003-04 Bowman Gold

Inserted in packs at the rate of one in one, this 156-card set parallels the base set enhanced with gold highlights. Cards 148-157 were not autographed for this parallel set.

*1-110 GOLD: 1.25X TO 3X BASE HI
*111-146 GOLD RCs: .5X TO 1.25X BASE HI
*148-157 GOLD RCs: .1X TO .3X BASE HI
CARD 147 NOT RELEASED

149 Dwyane Wade	10.00	25.00

2003-04 Bowman Fabric of the Future

Inserted in packs at the rate of one in 37, this 25-card set places rookies in front of their new team logo with a swatch of memorabilia.

BC Brian Cook	3.00	8.00
CA Carmelo Anthony	8.00	20.00
CB Chris Bosh	6.00	15.00
CK Chris Kaman	4.00	10.00
DJ Dahntay Jones	3.00	8.00
DW Dwyane Wade	10.00	25.00
JH Jarvis Hayes	3.00	8.00
KB Keith Bogans	3.00	8.00
KH Kirk Hinrich	4.00	10.00
KP Kendrick Perkins	5.00	12.00
LB Leandro Barbosa	4.00	10.00
LR Luke Ridnour	4.00	10.00
LW Luke Walton	3.00	8.00
MB Marcus Banks	3.00	8.00
MP Mickael Pietrus	3.00	8.00
MS Mike Sweetney	3.00	8.00
NC Nick Collison	3.00	8.00
RG Reece Gaines	3.00	8.00
SB Steve Blake	4.00	10.00
SV Slavko Vranes	3.00	8.00
TB Troy Bell	3.00	8.00
TF T.J. Ford	4.00	10.00
TO Travis Outlaw	4.00	10.00
DWE David West	4.00	10.00
JHO Josh Howard	3.00	8.00

2003-04 Bowman Remembering Rookies

Inserted at the rate of one in 1282, this two card set features Elton Brand and Shaquille O'Neal with their authentic autographs.

RREB Elton Brand	8.00	20.00
RRSO Shaquille O'Neal	30.00	80.00

2003-04 Bowman Rookie Recalls

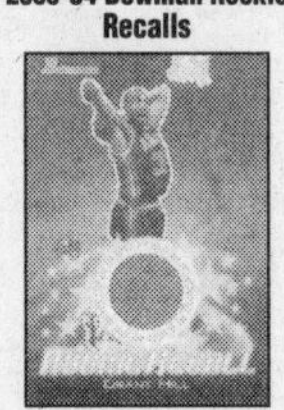

Inserted at the rate of one in 46, this 15-card set places players in action on a brown background with a circular swatch of memorabilia towards the bottom of the card.

RREAM Andre Miller	2.00	5.00
RREDM Darius Miles	2.00	5.00
RREEB Elton Brand	2.50	6.00
RREGH Grant Hill	3.00	8.00
RREGP Gary Payton	2.50	6.00
RREGR Glenn Robinson	2.00	5.00
RREKG Kevin Garnett	5.00	12.00
RREKM Karl Malone	3.00	8.00
RRELH Larry Hughes	2.00	5.00
RRERH Richard Hamilton	2.00	5.00
RRESF Steve Francis	2.50	6.00
RRETD Tim Duncan	4.00	10.00
RRETM Tracy McGrady	3.00	8.00

2003-04 Bowman Signs of the Future

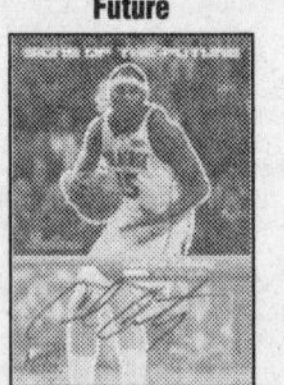

Seeded in packs at the rate of one in 171, this 37-card set features a white-out towards the bottom part of the card front for autographs of the 2003-04 Rookie Draft Class.

AP Aleksandar Pavlovic	4.00	10.00
BC Brian Cook	4.00	10.00
CA Carmelo Anthony	25.00	60.00
CB Chris Bosh	10.00	25.00
CD Carlos Delfino	5.00	12.00
DJ Dahntay Jones	4.00	10.00
DW Dwyane Wade	40.00	100.00
JB Jerome Beasley	4.00	10.00
JH Josh Howard	4.00	10.00
JK Jason Kapono	4.00	10.00
KB Keith Bogans	4.00	10.00
KH Kirk Hinrich	5.00	12.00
KP Kendrick Perkins	6.00	15.00
LB Leandro Barbosa	5.00	12.00
LR Luke Ridnour	5.00	12.00
LW Luke Walton	4.00	10.00
MA Mario Austin	4.00	10.00
MB Marcus Banks	4.00	10.00
ML Maciej Lampe	4.00	10.00
MP Mickael Pietrus	4.00	10.00
MS Mike Sweetney	4.00	10.00
NE Ndudi Ebi	4.00	10.00
NV Nick Collison	4.00	10.00
RG Reece Gaines	4.00	10.00
SB Steve Blake	5.00	12.00
SS Sofoklis Schortsianitis	4.00	10.00
SV Slavko Vranes	4.00	10.00
TB Troy Bell	4.00	10.00
TH Travis Hansen	4.00	10.00
TJ T.J. Ford	5.00	12.00
TO Travis Outlaw	5.00	12.00
TS Tommy Smith	4.00	10.00
ZP Zaur Pachulia	4.00	10.00
DWE David West	5.00	12.00
JHA Jarvis Hayes	4.00	10.00
MBA Malick Badiane	4.00	10.00
ZOP Zoran Planinic	4.00	10.00

2003-04 Bowman Sophomore Strands

Seeded at one in 46, this 10-card set focuses on players from the previous year's draft class. Each card places a full-color action photo above a square-shaped swatch of memorabilia.

AS Amare Stoudemire	4.00	10.00
CB Carlos Boozer	2.50	6.00
DG Drew Gooden	2.00	5.00
DW DaJuan Wagner	2.00	5.00
EG Manu Ginobili	3.00	8.00
JD Juan Dixon	2.00	5.00
MD Mike Dunleavy Jr.	2.00	5.00
MH Marcus Haislip	2.00	5.00
NH Nene Hilario	2.00	5.00
RH Ryan Humphrey	2.00	5.00
TP Tayshaun Prince	2.50	6.00
YM Yao Ming	5.00	12.00
CBU Caron Butler	2.50	6.00
JRB J.R. Bremer	2.00	5.00

2004-05 Bowman

Released in October of 2004 under the name Bowman Rookies and Stars again this year, packs contained an assortment of cards from both Bowman and Bowman Chrome, therefore they have been designated as such. Both sets contain 156 cards where cards 1-110 feature veteran players, cards 111-146 feature rookies, and card numbers 147-156 feature autographed rookie cards inserted at one in 105 packs for Bowman and are sequentially numbered to 250 for Bowman Chrome. All cards have gray borders, but the veteran players have red accents along the side borders and the rookies have blue accents. Boxes contained 24 packs of seven cards (four Bowman, two Bowman Chrome and one Bowman Gold Parallel) that carried a SRP of $4.00.

COMP.SET w/o RC's (110)	15.00	40.00
1 Yao Ming	.60	1.50
2 Eddy Curry	.25	.60
3 Stephon Marbury	.25	.60
4 Chris Webber	.30	.75
5 Jason Kidd	.50	1.25
6 Cuttino Mobley	.25	.60
7 Jermaine O'Neal	.30	.75
8 Kobe Bryant	1.50	4.00
9 Tony Parker	.30	.75
10 Gary Payton	.30	.75
11 T.J. Ford	.25	.60
12 Tim Duncan	.50	1.25
13 Glenn Robinson	.25	.60
14 Jason Richardson	.30	.75
15 Carmelo Anthony	.60	1.50
16 Pau Gasol	.30	.75
17 Kirk Hinrich	.30	.75
18 Kenyon Martin	.30	.75
19 Jamal Crawford	.25	.60
20 Elton Brand	.30	.75
21 Kevin Garnett	.60	1.50
22 Michael Redd	.30	.75
23 LeBron James	2.00	5.00
24 Andre Miller	.25	.60
25 Peja Stojakovic	.30	.75
26 Jarvis Hayes	.20	.50
27 David Wesley	.20	.50
28 Jason Kapono	.20	.50
29 Corey Maggette	.25	.60
30 Rasheed Wallace	.30	.75
31 Nene	.25	.60
32 Amare Stoudemire	.40	1.00
33 Allen Iverson	.50	1.25
34 Shaquille O'Neal	.75	2.00
35 Mike Dunleavy	.25	.60
36 Steve Nash	.40	1.00
37 Brad Miller	.30	.75
38 Chris Bosh	.30	.75
39 Boris Diaw	.25	.60
40 Steve Francis	.30	.75
41 Dirk Nowitzki	.50	1.25
42 Jason Williams	.25	.60
43 Gilbert Arenas	.30	.75
44 Keith Van Horn	.25	.60
45 Jamal Mashburn	.30	.75
46 Derek Fisher	.25	.60
47 Andrei Kirilenko	.25	.60
48 Ricky Davis	.25	.60
49 Gerald Wallace	.30	.75
50 Tracy McGrady	.40	1.00
51 Zach Randolph	.25	.60
52 Rafer Alston	.20	.50
53 Bobby Jackson	.20	.50
54 Desmond Mason	.25	.60
55 Tim Thomas	.20	.50
56 Jamaal Tinsley	.20	.50
57 Kwame Brown	.20	.50
58 Chauncey Billups	.30	.75
59 Brandon Hunter	.20	.50
60 Reggie Miller	.30	.75
61 Samuel Dalembert	.20	.50
62 James Posey	.20	.50
63 Erick Dampier	.20	.50
64 Carlos Arroyo	.25	.60
65 Reece Gaines	.20	.50
66 Darko Milicic	.20	.50
67 Sam Cassell	.25	.60
68 Dwyane Wade	1.00	2.50
69 Allan Houston	.25	.60
70 Ray Allen	.30	.75
71 Tyson Chandler	.25	.60
72 Bonzi Wells	.20	.50
73 Jalen Rose	.25	.60
74 Marquis Daniels	.20	.50
75 Zydrunas Ilgauskas	.25	.60
76 Tayshaun Prince	.30	.75
77 Lamar Odom	.30	.75
78 Luke Ridnour	.25	.60
79 Joe Johnson	.30	.75
80 Vince Carter	.50	1.25
81 Antoine Walker	.30	.75
82 Shareef Abdur-Rahim	.25	.60
83 Richard Jefferson	.30	.75
84 Maurice Taylor	.20	.50
85 Chris Kaman	.30	.75
86 Marcus Banks	.20	.50
87 Mike Bibby	.30	.75
88 Latrell Sprewell	.25	.60
89 Rashard Lewis	.30	.75
90 Baron Davis	.30	.75
91 Caron Butler	.30	.75
92 Michael Finley	.30	.75
93 Mike Miller	.30	.75
94 Al Harrington	.25	.60
95 Quentin Richardson	.25	.60
96 Jamaal Magloire	.20	.50
97 Darius Miles	.20	.50
98 Jeff Foster	.20	.50
99 Karl Malone	.40	1.00
100 Shawn Marion	.30	.75
101 Antawn Jamison	.30	.75
102 Manu Ginobili	.40	1.00
103 Ben Wallace	.30	.75
104 Paul Pierce	.40	1.00
105 Mike Sweetney	.20	.50
106 Ron Artest	.30	.75
107 Michael Olowokandi	.20	.50
108 Jason Terry	.25	.60
109 Gordan Giricek	.20	.50
110 Carlos Boozer	.30	.75
111 Romain Sato RC	1.00	2.50
112 Chris Duhon RC	1.00	2.50
113 Ben Gordon RC	1.25	3.00
114 Matt Freije RC	1.00	2.50
115 Al Jefferson RC	1.50	4.00
116 Beno Udrih RC	1.00	2.50
117 Kirk Snyder RC	1.00	2.50
118 Anderson Varejao RC	1.25	3.00
119 Devin Harris RC	1.50	4.00
120 Tony Allen RC	1.25	3.00
121 Ha Seung-Jin RC	1.00	2.50
122 J.R. Smith RC	1.25	3.00
123 Blake Stepp RC	1.00	2.50
124 Jameer Nelson RC	1.25	3.00
125 Kris Humphries RC	1.00	2.50
126 Josh Childress RC	1.00	2.50
127 Tim Pickett RC	1.00	2.50
128 Delonte West RC	1.25	3.00
129 Dwight Howard RC	3.00	8.00
130 Luke Jackson RC	1.00	2.50
131 Rickey Paulding RC	1.00	2.50
132 Andre Emmett RC	1.00	2.50
133 Josh Smith RC	1.50	4.00
134 Antonio Burks RC	1.00	2.50
135 Ricky Minard RC	1.00	2.50
136 Lionel Chalmers RC	1.00	2.50
137 Shaun Livingston RC	1.00	2.50
138 Trevor Ariza RC	1.00	2.50
139 Sergei Lishouk RC	1.00	2.50
140 Pape Sow RC	1.00	2.50
141 Rashad Wright RC	1.00	2.50
142 Jackson Vroman RC	1.00	2.50
143 Luis Flores RC	1.00	2.50
144 Royal Ivey RC	1.00	2.50
145 Kevin Martin RC	1.25	3.00
146 Andre Iguodala RC	1.50	4.00
147 Andris Biedrins AU RC	6.00	15.00
148 Pavel Podkolzine AU RC	5.00	12.00
149 Luol Deng AU RC	8.00	20.00
150 Robert Swift AU RC	5.00	12.00
151 Sebastian Telfair AU RC	5.00	12.00
152 Emeka Okafor AU RC	8.00	20.00
153 Dorell Wright AU RC	8.00	20.00
154 Sasha Vujacic AU RC	5.00	12.00
155 Rafael Araujo AU RC	5.00	12.00
156 David Harrison AU RC	5.00	12.00

2004-05 Bowman Gold

Inserted at one per pack, Bowman gold parallels the first 146 cards in the base Bowman set. The card is much thicker than the regular base cards and has gold borders.

*1-110 GOLD:1.25 X TO 3X BASE HI
*111-146 GOLD: .6X TO 1.5X BASE HI

147 Andris Biedrins	2.00	5.00
148 Pavel Podkolzine	1.50	4.00
149 Luol Deng	2.50	6.00
150 Robert Swift	1.50	4.00
151 Sebastian Telfair	1.50	4.00
152 Emeka Okafor	2.50	6.00
153 Dorell Wright	2.50	6.00
154 Sasha Vujacic	1.50	4.00
155 Rafael Araujo	1.50	4.00
156 David Harrison	1.50	4.00

2004-05 Bowman Cityscape Relics

Inserted in packs at the rate of one in 150, this 29-card set is horizontally designed with one player with a swatch of jersey on the left side, one player with a swatch of jersey on the right, a black border on the bottom of the card, and a city skyline background.

AR Ray Allen	3.00	8.00
Luke Ridnour		
BK Elton Brand	3.00	8.00
Chris Kaman		
CH Eddy Curry	3.00	8.00
Kirk Hinrich		
DG Tim Duncan	12.50	30.00
Manu Ginobili		
FG Steve Francis	3.00	8.00
Drew Gooden		
GJ Pau Gasol	3.00	8.00
Dahntay Jones		
GO Kevin Garnett	6.00	15.00
Michael Olowokandi		
IB Zydrunas Ilgauskas	3.00	8.00
Carlos Boozer		
IG Allen Iverson	6.00	15.00
Willie Green		
KJ Jason Kidd	6.00	15.00
Richard Jefferson		
MA Andre Miller	6.00	15.00
Carmelo Anthony		
MF Desmond Mason	3.00	8.00
T.J. Ford		
MM Tracy McGrady	8.00	20.00
Yao Ming		
MO Reggie Miller	6.00	15.00
Jermaine O'Neal		
MS Stephon Marbury	3.00	8.00
Mike Sweetney		
MW Jamal Mashburn	3.00	8.00
David West		
NH Dirk Nowitzki	3.00	8.00
Josh Howard		
OW Lamar Odom	6.00	15.00
Dwyane Wade		
PB Paul Pierce	3.00	8.00
Marcus Banks		
PR Gary Payton	3.00	8.00
Kareem Rush		
RP Jason Richardson	3.00	8.00
Mickael Pietrus		
TD Jason Terry	3.00	8.00
Boris Diaw		
WP Ben Wallace	3.00	8.00
Tayshaun Prince		
WS Chris Webber	3.00	8.00
Peja Stojakovic		
MAS Shawn Marion	5.00	12.00
Amare Stoudemire		
OWA Shaquille O'Neal	8.00	20.00
Luke Walton		
PEB Morris Peterson	3.00	8.00
Chris Bosh		

2004-05 Bowman Instant Impact Relics

Inserted in packs at one in 120, this 15-card set places full-color player action photos on a borderless card with a circular swatch of game worn memorabilia in the upper left corner.

AI Allen Iverson	4.00	10.00
AK Andrei Kirilenko	2.00	5.00
AS Amare Stoudemire	3.00	8.00
AW Antoine Walker	2.50	6.00
CA Carmelo Anthony	5.00	12.00
EB Elton Brand	2.50	6.00
JK Jason Kidd	4.00	10.00
JR Jason Richardson	2.50	6.00
PG Pau Gasol	2.50	6.00
SF Steve Francis	2.50	6.00
SM Stephon Marbury	2.00	5.00
SO Shaquille O'Neal	6.00	15.00
TD Tim Duncan	4.00	10.00
TP Tony Parker	2.50	6.00
YM Yao Ming	5.00	12.00

2004-05 Bowman Original Rookies

Serially numbered to 100, unless noted in the checklist, these are buybacks of each player's original Topps RC card and are enhanced by an embossed crimp stamp.

COMPLETE SET (8)	50.00	100.00
115 Tim Duncan	5.00	12.00
97-98 Topps		
138 Kobe Bryant	25.00	60.00
96-97 Topps		
171 Allen Iverson	6.00	15.00
96-97 Topps		
185 Yao Ming	5.00	12.00
02-03 Topps		
199 Vince Carter	5.00	12.00
98-99 Topps		
221 LeBron James	50.00	100.00
03-04 Topps/50		
225 Dwyane Wade	8.00	20.00
03-04 Topps		
237 Kevin Garnett	5.00	12.00
95-96 Topps		
362 Shaquille O'Neal	12.50	30.00
92-93 Topps		

2004-05 Bowman Remembering Rookies Autographs

Inserted at one in 658 packs for Group A and one in 1579 packs for Group B, this 13-card set features players and autographs on the Bowman card design for that year. If Bowman wasn't produced for basketball that year, Topps used the design from Bowman baseball.

AS Amare Stoudemire A	15.00	40.00
BD Baron Davis B	6.00	15.00
CA Carmelo Anthony A	25.00	50.00
JK Jason Kidd A	15.00	40.00
JO Jermaine O'Neal A	6.00	15.00
LO Lamar Odom A	6.00	15.00
PS Peja Stojakovic A	6.00	15.00
RH Richard Hamilton A	8.00	20.00
SM Shawn Marion A	6.00	15.00
SO Shaquille O'Neal A	40.00	80.00
TD Tim Duncan A	60.00	120.00
TM Tracy McGrady A	15.00	40.00
SMA Stephon Marbury B	15.00	40.00

2004-05 Bowman Rooki Registration Relics

Inserted in packs at the rate of one in 44, this 2 set features the 2004-05 rookie class on a hori designed card with a portrait photo on the left, worn jersey on the right and a white backgrour

AE Andre Emmett	2.50
AI Andre Iguodala	4.00
AJ Al Jefferson	4.00
AV Anderson Varejao	3.00
BG Ben Gordon	3.00
CD Chris Duhon	2.50
DH Dwight Howard	8.00
DW Dorell Wright	4.00
EO Emeka Okafor	4.00
JC Josh Childress	2.50
JN Jameer Nelson	3.00
JS Josh Smith	4.00
KH Kris Humphries	2.50
KM Kevin Martin	3.00
KS Kirk Snyder	2.50
LD Luol Deng	4.00
LJ Luke Jackson	2.50
RA Rafael Araujo	2.50
SL Shaun Livingston	2.50
ST Sebastian Telfair	2.50
TA Tony Allen	3.00
DEH Devin Harris	4.00
DHA David Harrison	2.50
DWE Delonte West	3.00
JRS J.R. Smith	3.00

2004-05 Bowman Signs of Future

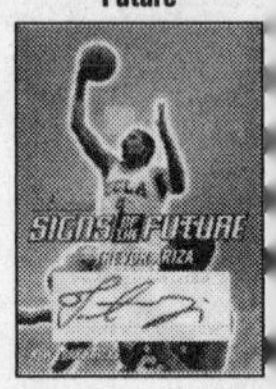

Seeded in packs at one in 38, this 34-card set the 2004-05 NBA draft class on a background match their new team's colors and has an auto a foil sticker.

DREJER AND MONIA NEVER ISSUED

AB Antonio Burks	4.00
AE Andre Emmett	4.00
AJ Al Jefferson	6.00
AV Anderson Varejao	5.00
BG Ben Gordon	5.00
BR Bernard Robinson	4.00
BS Blake Stepp	4.00
BU Beno Udrih	4.00
CD Chris Duhon	4.00
DH Devin Harris	6.00
DW Delonte West	5.00
EO Emeka Okafor	6.00
JN Jameer Nelson	5.00
JO Josh Childress	4.00
JR Justin Reed	4.00
JS Josh Smith	6.00
JV Jackson Vroman	4.00
KM Kevin Martin	5.00
KS Kirk Snyder	4.00
KY Kris Humphries	4.00
LJ Luke Jackson	4.00
MF Matt Freije	4.00
PS Pape Sow	4.00
RM Ricky Minard	4.00
RP Rickey Paulding	4.00
RS Romain Sato	4.00
RW Rashad Wright	4.00
SL Sergei Lishouk	4.00
TA Trevor Ariza	4.00
TP Tim Pickett	4.00
HSJ Ha Seung-Jin	4.00
JRS J.R. Smith	5.00
SLI Shaun Livingston	4.00
TAI Tony Allen	5.00

2004-05 Bowman Twice As Relics

Inserted in packs at one in 207, this nine card features colored background, a scale-colored photo in the background, a full-color photo ir foreground and a memorabilia swatch in the s the number 2.

CB Carlos Boozer	3.00
CM Cuttino Mobley	2.50
EN Eduardo Najera	2.00
GA Gilbert Arenas	3.00
MG Manu Ginobili	4.00
MJ Marko Jaric	2.00
MR Michael Redd	3.00
RL Rashard Lewis	3.00

2005-06 Bowman

ed as a two-in one product (Bowman Draft Picks
ospects) featuring both Bowman and Bowman
e cards, the Bowman portion of the set includes
rds where cards 1-110 picture veterans, cards
6 feature rookies, cards 147-151 feature
ties and cards 152-161 feature autographed
cards. Also included and randomly inserted is
DSBS featuring the NBA's Andrew Bogut and the
Alex Smith (both from Utah) along with their
phs and sequential numbering to 100. Base
eature white borders and red highlights on
cards and blue highlights on rookie cards. The
autographs showcase silver autograph stickers
ted odds of one in 63. Each pack contains seven
four bowman cards, two bowman chrome cards
hick gold parallel and carried a suggested retail
four dollars.

SET w/o RC's (110) 15.00 40.00
Nash .40 1.00
oz Brezec .20 .50
Davis .30 .75
rrington .25 .60
Butler .30 .75
us Camby .25 .60
s Boozer .30 .75
Gordon .30 .75
en Jackson .25 .60
Nowitzki .50 1.25
d Krstic .20 .50
n Richardson .30 .75
dan Haywood .20 .50
uncey Billups .30 .75
y Maggette .25 .60
Stojakovic .30 .75
t Hill .40 1.00
Gasol .30 .75
imir Radmanovic .20 .50
n Kidd .50 1.25
Duncan .50 1.25
d Harrison .20 .50
on James 1.50 4.00
nis Haslem .25 .60
Dickau .20 .50
no Mobley .25 .60
s Bosh .30 .75
stian Telfair .25 .60
ll Sprewell .25 .60
a Okafor .30 .75
James .20 .50
r Ariza .20 .50
Hughes .25 .60
mond Mason .20 .50
aun Prince .30 .75
u Ginobili .30 .75
Bibby .30 .75
e Iguodala .30 .75
al Magloire .20 .50
e Stoudemire .30 .75
Alston .20 .50
Brand .30 .75
e Francis .30 .75
ard Lewis .30 .75
zen Wright .20 .50
Hinrich .30 .75
ei Kirilenko .25 .60
Miller .30 .75
l Crawford .25 .60
uille O'Neal .60 1.50
n Livingston .20 .50
Murphy .25 .60
Gooden .25 .60
Pierce .40 1.00
Carter .50 1.25
Szczerbiak .25 .60
wn Jamison .30 .75
uis Daniels .20 .50
d Wallace .30 .75
Allen .30 .75
al Tinsley .20 .50
e Battier .25 .60
nas Ilgauskas .25 .60
et Okur .20 .50
eed Wallace .30 .75
ice Williams .25 .60
Howard .30 .75
Randolph .25 .60
Bryant 1.50 4.00
McGrady .40 1.00
Ridnour .25 .60
n Jones .20 .50
Allen .20 .50
Miller .30 .75
Cassell .30 .75
Wallace .30 .75
Sweetney .20 .50
Curry .25 .60
el Redd .30 .75
elo Anthony .60 1.50
t Howard .60 1.50
Smith .30 .75
d Jefferson .30 .75
d Hamilton .25 .60
Webber .30 .75
Marion .30 .75
Rose .30 .75
ura .20 .50
Dunleavy .25 .60
e Wade .75 2.00
Payton .30 .75
Deng .30 .75
n Martin .30 .75
Jdrih .20 .50
mith .30 .75
Odom .30 .75
Miller .25 .60
ne O'Neal .30 .75
ing .40 1.00
Iverson .50 1.25
tin Richardson .25 .60
t Arenas .30 .75
on Marbury .25 .60

104 Antoine Walker .25 .60
105 Jameer Nelson .25 .60
106 Joel Przybilla .20 .50
107 Devin Harris .30 .75
108 Tony Parker .30 .75
109 Josh Childress .25 .60
110 Kevin Garnett .60 1.50
111 Chris Paul RC 4.00 10.00
112 Danny Granger RC 2.00 5.00
113 Antoine Wright RC 1.00 2.50
114 Joey Graham RC 1.00 2.50
115 Wayne Simien RC 1.00 2.50
116 Channing Frye RC 1.25 3.00
117 Charlie Villanueva RC 1.25 3.00
118 Francisco Garcia RC 1.25 3.00
119 Ike Diogu RC 1.00 2.50
120 Jarrett Jack RC 1.00 2.50
121 Robert Whaley RC 1.00 2.50
122 C.J. Miles RC 1.25 3.00
123 Ryan Gomes RC 1.00 2.50
124 Nate Robinson RC 1.25 3.00
125 Daniel Ewing RC 1.00 2.50
126 Andray Blatche RC 1.25 3.00
127 Luther Head RC 1.00 2.50
128 Julius Hodge RC 1.00 2.50
129 Lawrence Roberts RC 1.00 2.50
130 Jason Maxiell RC 1.00 2.50
131 Martynas Andriuskevicius RC 1.00 2.50
132 Ersan Ilyasova RC 1.25 3.00
133 Martell Webster RC 1.00 2.50
134 Andrew Bynum RC 3.00 8.00
135 Louis Williams RC 1.50 4.00
136 Johan Petro RC 1.00 2.50
137 Brandon Bass RC 1.25 3.00
138 Travis Diener RC 1.00 2.50
139 Bracey Wright RC 1.00 2.50
140 Marvin Williams RC 1.25 3.00
141 Eddie Basden RC 1.00 2.50
142 Von Wafer RC 1.00 2.50
143 David Lee RC 1.50 4.00
144 Linas Kleiza RC 1.00 2.50
145 Luke Schenscher RC 1.00 2.50
146 Yaroslav Korolev RC 1.00 2.50
147 Carmen Electra 2.50 6.00
148 Christie Brinkley 2.50 6.00
149 Shannon Elizabeth 2.50 6.00
150 Jenny McCarthy 2.50 6.00
151 Jay-Z 2.50 6.00
152 Raymond Felton AU RC 6.00 15.00
153 Gerald Green AU RC 5.00 12.00
154 Rashad McCants AU RC 4.00 10.00
155 Andrew Bogut AU RC 6.00 15.00
156 Chris Taft AU RC 4.00 10.00
157 Sarunas Jasikevicius AU RC 4.00 10.00
158 Hakim Warrick AU RC 5.00 12.00
159 Deron Williams AU RC 15.00 30.00
160 Sean May AU RC 4.00 10.00
161 Monta Ellis AU RC 8.00 20.00
DSBS Andrew Bogut 60.00 120.00
Alex Smith (QB) AU/100

2005-06 Bowman Gold

Randomly inserted at the rate of one per pack, this 161-card set parallels the base Bowman set enahnced with thicker card stock and gold borders. Card numbers 152-161 are not autographed like their counterparts from the base set.
*1-110 GOLD: 1X TO 2.5X BASE HI
*111-151 GOLD: .6X TO 1.5X BASE HI

2005-06 Bowman Back to the Future Autographs

Inserted at the rate of one in 511 for group A and one in 8263 for group B, this 10-card set features top NBA players with full color action photos and a silver autograph sticker in the lower right-hand corner.

AI Allen Iverson B 40.00 100.00
BD Baron Davis B 8.00 20.00
BW Ben Wallace A 10.00 25.00
JK Jason Kidd B 15.00 40.00
LO Lamar Odom A 8.00 20.00
RH Richard Hamilton B 8.00 20.00
SM Stephon Marbury B 8.00 20.00
SO Shaquille O'Neal B ERR 30.00 75.00
card back RC listed as 1998-99
TD Tim Duncan A 75.00 150.00

2005-06 Bowman Beginnings Relics

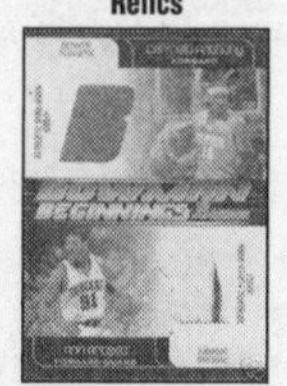

Inserted at the rate of one in 324, this cards showcases two players, one on the top and one on the bottom along with a "B" shaped swatch of memorabilia. Several different memorabilia swatches were used, see checklist for details.

AA Carmelo Anthony 5.00 12.00
Ron Artest
AI Gilbert Arenas Warm 5.00 12.00
Andre Iguodala
BM Chris Bosh 5.00 12.00
Stephon Marbury
DH Luol Deng 10.00 25.00
Grant Hill Warm
GH Ben Gordon 5.00 12.00
Richard Hamilton Warm
HF Devin Harris Shirt 5.00 12.00
Michael Finley
JW Antawn Jamison 5.00 12.00
Rasheed Wallace
OA Emeka Okafor 5.00 12.00
Ray Allen
PH Paul Pierce 10.00 25.00
Kirk Hinrich Shirt
DHO Tim Duncan Shirt 6.00 15.00
Josh Howard Shorts

2005-06 Bowman Bravo Relics

Inserted at the rate of one in 60, this 27-card set features both NBA players and celebrites on a card where full color photos appear on the top, and the word "Bravo!" appears on the bottom in big letters. The letter "A" from the word is actually a swatch of memorabilia. An autographed version sequentially numbered to nine was also products, but these cards are not priced due to scarcity.

UNPRICED AUTO PRINT RUN 9 SETS
AI Andre Iguodala 3.00 8.00
AK Andrei Kirilenko 2.50 6.00
AS Amare Stoudemire Shirt 3.00 8.00
AV Anderson Varejao 2.50 6.00
BG Ben Gordon 3.00 8.00
CA Carmelo Anthony 6.00 15.00
CB Christie Brinkley Jeans 8.00 20.00
CE Carmen Electra Jeans 10.00 25.00
DH Dwight Howard 6.00 15.00
DW Dwyane Wade 8.00 20.00
EO Emeka Okafor 3.00 8.00
GA Gilbert Arenas Shirt 3.00 8.00
JM Jenny McCarthy Jeans 10.00 25.00
JS Josh Smith 3.00 8.00
JZ Jay-Z Jeans 8.00 20.00
KB Kobe Bryant 10.00 25.00
KH Kirk Hinrich Shorts 3.00 8.00
LD Luol Deng 3.00 8.00
PG Pau Gasol 3.00 8.00
RL Rashard Lewis 3.00 8.00
RW Rasheed Wallace 3.00 8.00
SE Shannon Elizabeth Jeans 10.00 25.00
SO Shaquille O'Neal 6.00 15.00
TD Tim Duncan Warm 5.00 12.00
YM Yao Ming 4.00 10.00
ZR Zach Randolph 2.50 6.00
DHA Devin Harris 3.00 8.00

2005-06 Bowman Signs of the Future

Seeded in packs at the rate of one in 41, this 21-card set profiles some of the NBA's current-year rookies with full color photography and silver autograph stickers.

AB Andrew Bynum 15.00 40.00
AW Antoine Wright 5.00 12.00
BB Brandon Bass 6.00 15.00
CV Charlie Villanueva 6.00 15.00
DE Daniel Ewing 5.00 12.00
DG Danny Granger 10.00 25.00
DL David Lee 8.00 20.00
FG Francisco Garcia 6.00 15.00
ID Ike Diogu 5.00 12.00
JG Joey Graham 5.00 12.00
JH Julius Hodge 5.00 12.00
JJ Jarrett Jack 5.00 12.00
JM Jason Maxiell 5.00 12.00
JP Johan Petro 5.00 12.00
LH Luther Head 5.00 12.00
MW Martell Webster 5.00 12.00
RU Roko Ukic 5.00 12.00
SJ Sarunas Jasikevicius 5.00 12.00
TD Travis Diener 5.00 12.00
VW Von Wafer 5.00 12.00
WS Wayne Simien 5.00 12.00

2005-06 Bowman Skills Nation Relics

Randomly inserted at the rate of one in 81, this 20-card set places color player photos on the right side of the card and a red and black border on the left. Centered towards the bottom of the card is an "N" shaped swatch of memorabilia.

AI Allen Iverson 5.00 12.00
AM Andre Miller 2.50 6.00
BW Ben Wallace Warm 3.00 8.00
DM Desmond Mason 2.00 5.00
DW Dwyane Wade 8.00 20.00
FJ Fred Jones 2.00 5.00
JK Jason Kidd 5.00 12.00
JR Jason Richardson 3.00 8.00
JS Josh Smith 3.00 8.00
MB Mike Bibby 3.00 8.00
MC Marcus Camby 2.50 6.00
MR Michael Redd 3.00 8.00
PS Peja Stojakovic 3.00 8.00
QR Quentin Richardson 2.50 6.00
RA Ray Allen 3.00 8.00
SM Stephon Marbury 2.50 6.00
SN Steve Nash 4.00 10.00
SO Shaquille O'Neal 6.00 15.00
VL Voshon Lenard 2.00 5.00
DMU Dikembe Mutombo 4.00 10.00

2005-06 Bowman Welcome to the Show Relics

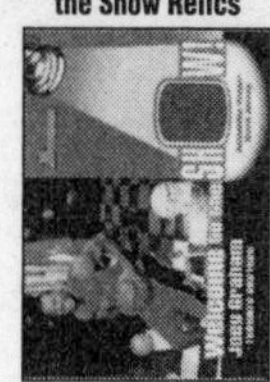

Found in packs at the rate of one in 41, this 27-card set features full-color player photos and a swatch of memorabilia worn at the NBA rookie photo shoot. Each card is horizontally designed with player photos on the left and memorabilia on the right. An autographed version sequentially numbered to five was also produced but is not priced due to scarcity.

AW Antoine Wright 3.00 8.00
BB Brandon Bass 4.00 10.00
CF Channing Frye 4.00 10.00
CP Chris Paul 10.00 25.00
CV Charlie Villanueva 4.00 10.00
DE Daniel Ewing 3.00 8.00
DG Danny Granger 6.00 15.00
DL David Lee 5.00 12.00
DW Deron Williams 8.00 20.00
EI Ersan Ilyasova 4.00 10.00
FG Francisco Garcia 4.00 10.00
GG Gerald Green 4.00 10.00
HW Hakim Warrick 4.00 10.00
JG Joey Graham 3.00 8.00
JH Julius Hodge 3.00 8.00
JJ Jarrett Jack 3.00 8.00
JM Jason Maxiell 3.00 8.00
LH Luther Head 3.00 8.00
MW Martell Webster 3.00 8.00
NR Nate Robinson 4.00 10.00
RF Raymond Felton 5.00 12.00
RM Rashad McCants 3.00 8.00
SJ Sarunas Jasikevicius 3.00 8.00
SM Sean May 3.00 8.00
WS Wayne Simien 3.00 8.00
ABO Andrew Bogut 5.00 12.00
CJM C.J. Miles 4.00 10.00

2006-07 Bowman

Packaged together with Bowman Chrome, Bowman features a 165-card set, showcasing veteran players on card numbers 1-110, NCAA coaches on card numbers 111-115 and rookie players on cards 116-165. All cards feature black borders, silver foil highlights and red color accents on veteran player cards and blue color accents on rookie player cards. Released late November 2006 under the product name of Bowman Rookies and Stars, boxes contain 18 packs where each pack has four Bowman cards, two Bowman Chrome cards and carried an original suggested retail price of $4.00 per pack.

COMPLETE SET (165) 20.00 50.00
COMP.SET w/o RC'S (115) 8.00 20.00
1 Gilbert Arenas .30 .75
2 Delonte West .25 .60
3 Gerald Wallace .30 .75
4 Ike Diogu .20 .50
5 Mike Miller .30 .75
6 Kobe Bryant 1.50 4.00
7 Richard Hamilton .25 .60
8 Vince Carter .40 1.00
9 Elton Brand .30 .75
10 Boris Diaw .25 .60
11 Carmelo Anthony .40 1.00
12 Jermaine O'Neal .30 .75
13 Al Harrington .25 .60
14 Dwight Howard .50 1.25
15 Chris Bosh .30 .75
16 Ben Gordon .30 .75
17 Josh Howard .25 .60
18 Yao Ming .40 1.00
19 David West .30 .75
20 Tim Duncan .50 1.25
21 Andre Iguodala .30 .75
22 LeBron James 1.50 4.00
23 Channing Frye .25 .60
24 Antoine Walker .25 .60
25 Ricky Davis .25 .60
26 Lamar Odom .30 .75
27 Amare Stoudemire .30 .75
28 Mike Bibby .30 .75
29 Allen Iverson .40 1.00
30 Marvin Williams .30 .75
31 Wally Szczerbiak .25 .60
32 Ben Wallace .30 .75
33 Nenad Krstic .20 .50
34 Deron Williams .50 1.25
35 Troy Murphy .20 .50
36 Raymond Felton .40 1.00
37 Jason Terry .25 .60
38 Zach Randolph .25 .60
39 Pau Gasol .30 .75
40 Larry Hughes .25 .60
41 Luol Deng .30 .75
42 Steve Francis .30 .75
43 Chauncey Billups .30 .75
44 Smush Parker .20 .50
45 Shareef Abdur-Rahim .25 .60
46 Andrei Kirilenko .25 .60
47 Shawn Marion .30 .75
48 Darko Milicic .20 .50
49 Shaquille O'Neal .60 1.50
50 Kevin Garnett .60 1.50
51 Michael Finley .30 .75
52 Peja Stojakovic .30 .75
53 Michael Redd .30 .75
54 Desmond Mason .20 .50
55 Luke Ridnour .25 .60
56 Kenyon Martin .30 .75
57 Morris Peterson .20 .50
58 Chris Kaman .25 .60
59 Jason Richardson .30 .75
60 Jason Kidd .50 1.25
61 Carlos Boozer .30 .75
62 Rashad McCants .20 .50
63 Nate Robinson .30 .75
64 Devin Harris .30 .75
65 Andrew Bogut .30 .75
66 Chris Duhon .20 .50
67 Drew Gooden .25 .60
68 Manu Ginobili .30 .75
69 Jameer Nelson .25 .60
70 Corey Maggette .25 .60
71 Charlie Villanueva .30 .75
72 Shane Battier .25 .60
73 Udonis Haslem .25 .60
74 Tracy McGrady .40 1.00
75 Bobby Simmons .20 .50
76 Baron Davis .30 .75
77 Zydrunas Ilgauskas .25 .60
78 Danny Granger .30 .75
79 Hakim Warrick .25 .60
80 Josh Smith .30 .75
81 Tayshaun Prince .30 .75
82 Rashard Lewis .30 .75
83 Luther Head .25 .60
84 Andre Miller .25 .60
85 T.J. Ford .25 .60
86 Sebastian Telfair .20 .50
87 Dirk Nowitzki .50 1.25
88 Kwame Brown .20 .50
89 Antawn Jamison .30 .75
90 Ron Artest .30 .75
91 Mehmet Okur .20 .50
92 Emeka Okafor .30 .75
93 Sam Cassell .30 .75
94 Chris Paul .60 1.50
95 Chris Webber .30 .75
96 Richard Jefferson .30 .75
97 Dwyane Wade .75 2.00
98 Tony Parker .30 .75
99 Paul Pierce .40 1.00
100 Marcus Camby .25 .60
101 Ray Allen .30 .75
102 Stephon Marbury .25 .60
103 Rasheed Wallace .30 .75
104 Brad Miller .30 .75
105 Kirk Hinrich .30 .75
106 Steve Nash .40 1.00
107 Sarunas Jasikevicius .25 .60
108 Darius Miles .20 .50
109 Joe Johnson .30 .75
110 Caron Butler .30 .75
111 John Wooden CO 1.25 3.00
112 Ben Howland CO 1.00 2.50
113 Jim Calhoun CO 1.00 2.50
114 Jim Boeheim CO 1.00 2.50
115 Roy Williams CO 1.00 2.50
116 LaMarcus Aldridge RC 2.50 6.00
117 Marcus Vinicius RC 1.00 2.50
118 Sergio Rodriguez RC 1.00 2.50
119 Will Blalock RC 1.00 2.50
120 Paul Millsap RC 1.50 4.00
121 Leon Powe RC 1.00 2.50
122 Rudy Gay RC 1.50 4.00
123 Tyrus Thomas RC 1.25 3.00
124 Brandon Roy RC 2.50 6.00
125 J.R. Pinnock RC 1.00 2.50
126 Kevin Pittsnogle RC 1.00 2.50
127 Mile Ilic RC 1.00 2.50
128 Mardy Collins RC 1.00 2.50
129 Craig Smith RC 1.00 2.50
130 Jordan Farmar RC 1.00 2.50
131 Quincy Douby RC 1.00 2.50
132 James Augustine RC 1.00 2.50
133 Josh Boone RC 1.00 2.50
134 Shannon Brown RC 1.50 4.00
135 David Noel RC 1.00 2.50
136 Kyle Lowry RC 1.25 3.00
137 Ryan Hollins RC 1.00 2.50
138 Renaldo Balkman RC 1.00 2.50
139 James White RC 1.00 2.50
140 Damir Markota RC 1.00 2.50
141 Paul Davis RC 1.00 2.50
142 Alexander Johnson RC 1.00 2.50
143 Steve Novak RC 1.00 2.50
144 P.J. Tucker RC 1.00 2.50
145 Saer Sene RC 1.00 2.50
146 Bobby Jones RC 1.00 2.50
147 Cedric Simmons RC 1.00 2.50
148 Allan Ray RC 1.00 2.50
149 Solomon Jones RC 1.00 2.50
150 Ronnie Brewer RC 1.25 3.00
151 Thabo Sefolosha RC 1.25 3.00
152 Maurice Ager RC 1.00 2.50
153 Daniel Gibson RC 1.25 3.00
154 Shawne Williams RC 1.00 2.50
155 Dee Brown RC 1.00 2.50
156 Andrea Bargnani RC 1.50 4.00
157 Patrick O'Bryant RC 1.00 2.50
158 Shelden Williams RC 1.00 2.50
159 Hilton Armstrong RC 1.00 2.50
160 Adam Morrison RC 1.25 3.00
161 Rodney Carney RC 1.00 2.50
162 Randy Foye RC 1.25 3.00
163 Rajon Rondo RC 4.00 10.00
164 Marcus Williams RC 1.00 2.50
165 J.J. Redick RC 1.25 3.00

2006-07 Bowman Bronze

*BRONZE 1-115: 4X TO 10X BASE HI
*BRONZE 116-165: 1.5X TO 4X BASE HI
STATED PRINT RUN 50 SER.#'d SETS

2006-07 Bowman Silver

*SILVER 1-115: 1.25X TO 3X BASE HI
*SILVER 116-165: .75X TO 2X BASE HI
STATED PRINT RUN 379 SER.#'d SETS

2006-07 Bowman McDonald's All-American Rookie Relics

STATED ODDS 1:60
1 Jordan Farmar 2.50 6.00
2 Rajon Rondo 6.00 15.00
3 Shannon Brown 4.00 10.00
4 Dee Brown 2.50 6.00
5 Paul Davis 2.50 6.00
6 J.J. Redick 3.00 8.00

2006-07 Bowman McDonald's All-American Rookie Relics Autographs

PRINT RUN 50 SER.#'d SETS
UNPRICED SUPER PRINT RUN ONE SET
1 Jordan Farmar 6.00 15.00
2 Rajon Rondo 30.00 80.00
3 Shannon Brown 10.00 25.00
4 Dee Brown 6.00 15.00
5 Paul Davis 6.00 15.00
6 J.J. Redick 8.00 20.00

2006-07 Bowman Power of 2 Autographs

PRINT RUN 10 TO 25 SER.#'d SETS
SOME NOT PRICED DUE TO SCARCITY
POWER OF 3 UNPRICED DUE TO SCARCITY
MW Adam Morrison B 50.00 125.00
Dwyane Wade

2006-07 Bowman Relics

GROUP A STATED ODDS 1:107
GROUP B STATED ODDS 1:19
*DUAL: .5X TO 1.25X BASE HI
DUAL PRINT RUN 249 SER.#'d SETS
*TRIPLE: .6X TO 1.5X BASE HI
TRIPLE PRINT RUN 50 SER.#'d SETS
AB Andrew Bogut B 2.50 6.00
AI Allen Iverson A 3.00 8.00
AJ Antawn Jamison A 2.50 6.00
AM Adam Morrison B 3.00 8.00
BJ Bobby Jones B 2.50 6.00
BW Ben Wallace A Shorts 2.50 6.00
CA Carmelo Anthony B 3.00 8.00
CB Chris Bosh B Shirt 2.50 6.00
CP Chris Paul B Shorts 5.00 12.00
CS Cedric Simmons B 2.50 6.00
CW Chris Webber A 2.50 6.00
DH Dwight Howard A 4.00 10.00
DN Dirk Nowitzki A Shorts 4.00 10.00
DW Dwyane Wade B 6.00 15.00
GA Gilbert Arenas B Shirt 2.50 6.00
HA Hilton Armstrong B 2.50 6.00
JB Josh Boone B 2.50 6.00
JF Jordan Farmar B 2.50 6.00
JS Josh Smith A 2.50 6.00
KB Kobe Bryant B 10.00 25.00
KG Kevin Garnett A Warm 5.00 12.00
LA LaMarcus Aldridge B 6.00 15.00
MB Mike Bibby B 2.50 6.00
MC Mardy Collins B 2.50 6.00
MW Marcus Williams B 2.50 6.00
PD Paul Davis B 2.50 6.00
PO Patrick O'Bryant B 2.50 6.00
PP Paul Pierce A Warm 3.00 8.00
QD Quincy Douby B 2.50 6.00
RA Ray Allen B 2.50 6.00
RB Renaldo Balkman B 2.50 6.00
RC Rodney Carney B 2.50 6.00
RF Randy Foye B 3.00 8.00
RG Rudy Gay B 4.00 10.00
RR Rajon Rondo B 6.00 15.00
RW Rasheed Wallace B 2.50 6.00
SJ Solomon Jones B 2.50 6.00
SM Shawn Marion A 2.50 6.00
SN Steve Nash A Warm 3.00 8.00
SO Shaquille O'Neal B 5.00 12.00
SW Shelden Williams B 2.50 6.00
TD Tim Duncan B 4.00 10.00
YM Yao Ming B 3.00 8.00
CSM Craig Smith B 2.50 6.00
DNO David Noel B 2.50 6.00
JJR J.J. Redick B 3.00 8.00
PJT P.J. Tucker B 2.50 6.00
RAR Ron Artest A 2.50 6.00
RBR Ronnie Brewer B 3.00 8.00
SNO Steve Novak B 2.50 6.00

2006-07 Bowman Rookie Snapshots Relics

PRINT RUN 199 SER.#'d SETS
AM Adam Morrison 4.00 10.00
CS Cedric Simmons 3.00 8.00
DB Dee Brown 3.00 8.00
HA Hilton Armstrong 3.00 8.00
JB Josh Boone 3.00 8.00
JF Jordan Farmar 3.00 8.00
JW James White 3.00 8.00
KL Kyle Lowry 4.00 10.00
KP Kevin Pittsnogle 3.00 8.00
LA LaMarcus Aldridge 8.00 20.00
MA Maurice Ager 3.00 8.00
MW Marcus Williams 3.00 8.00
PO Patrick O'Bryant 3.00 8.00
QD Quincy Douby 3.00 8.00
RB Renaldo Balkman 3.00 8.00
RC Rodney Carney 3.00 8.00
RF Randy Foye 4.00 10.00
RG Rudy Gay 5.00 12.00
RR Rajon Rondo 8.00 20.00
SB Shannon Brown 5.00 12.00
SW Shelden Williams 3.00 8.00
CSM Craig Smith 3.00 8.00
JJR J.J. Redick 4.00 10.00
RBR Ronnie Brewer 4.00 10.00
SWI Shawne Williams 3.00 8.00

2007-08 Bowman

This 160-card set was released in November, 2007. The set was issued into the hobby in six-card packs (2 of which were Bowman Chrome cards), with an $4 SRP, which came 18 packs per box and 12 boxes per case. Cards numbered 1-110 feature veterans while cards numbered 111-160 feature 2007-08 NBA rookies which were issued to a stated print run of 2999 serial numbered sets.

COMP.SET w/o SP's (110) 15.00 30.00
RC PRINT RUN 2999 SER.#'d SETS
UNPRICED PLATE PRINT RUN ONE SET
1 Gilbert Arenas .30 .75
2 Dwight Howard .50 1.25
3 Dwyane Wade .75 2.00
4 Chris Bosh .30 .75
5 Josh Smith .30 .75
6 Andrew Bogut .30 .75
7 Ben Gordon .30 .75
8 Deron Williams .50 1.25
9 Tony Parker .30 .75
10 Mike Bibby .30 .75
11 Yao Ming .40 1.00
12 Raymond Felton .40 1.00
13 Steve Nash .40 1.00
14 Jameer Nelson .25 .60
15 Carmelo Anthony .40 1.00
16 Pau Gasol .30 .75
17 Rashard Lewis .25 .60
18 Eddy Curry .20 .50
19 Luol Deng .30 .75
20 Kevin Garnett .60 1.50
21 Tim Duncan .50 1.25
22 Michael Redd .30 .75
23 LeBron James 1.50 4.00
24 Kobe Bryant 1.50 4.00
25 Al Jefferson .30 .75
26 Mike Dunleavy .25 .60
27 Tyson Chandler .25 .60
28 Zach Randolph .25 .60
29 Jason Richardson .30 .75
30 Rasheed Wallace .30 .75
31 Shawn Marion .30 .75
32 Shaquille O'Neal .60 1.50
33 Allen Iverson .40 1.00
34 Paul Pierce .40 1.00
35 Adam Morrison .30 .75
36 Mike Miller .30 .75
37 Larry Hughes .25 .60
38 Kevin Martin .30 .75
39 Charlie Villanueva .30 .75
40 Vince Carter .40 1.00
41 Dirk Nowitzki .40 1.00
42 Elton Brand .30 .75
43 Ray Allen .30 .75
44 Luke Walton .20 .50
45 Chris Paul .60 1.50
46 Marcus Camby .20 .50
47 Andrei Kirilenko .25 .60
48 J.J. Redick .30 .75
49 Richard Hamilton .25 .60
50 Emeka Okafor .30 .75
51 Manu Ginobili .30 .75
52 Monta Ellis .30 .75
53 Jorge Garbajosa .25 .60
54 Kyle Korver .25 .60
55 Jason Kidd .30 .75
56 Randy Foye .30 .75
57 Shane Battier .25 .60
58 Shaun Livingston .20 .50
59 Jason Terry .25 .60
60 Joe Johnson .30 .75
61 Lamar Odom .30 .75
62 Tayshaun Prince .30 .75
63 Chris Wilcox .20 .50
64 Leandro Barbosa .25 .60
65 Al Harrington .25 .60
66 Jamal Crawford .25 .60
67 Caron Butler .30 .75
68 Chauncey Billups .30 .75
69 Ricky Davis .25 .60
70 Andrea Bargnani .40 1.00
71 Samuel Dalembert .20 .50
72 LaMarcus Aldridge .40 1.00
73 Mehmet Okur .20 .50
74 Marcus Williams .20 .50
75 Andre Miller .25 .60
76 Rudy Gay .30 .75
77 Jermaine O'Neal .30 .75
78 Boris Diaw .25 .60
79 Ryan Gomes .20 .50
80 Gerald Wallace .30 .75
81 Udonis Haslem .25 .60
82 Mo Williams .25 .60
83 Jarrett Jack .25 .60
84 Chris Webber .30 .75
85 Trevor Ariza .20 .50
86 Kirk Hinrich .30 .75
87 Rafer Alston .20 .50
88 Danny Granger .30 .75
89 David West .30 .75
90 Drew Gooden .25 .60
91 Stephon Marbury .25 .60
92 Antawn Jamison .30 .75
93 Ron Artest .30 .75
94 Richard Jefferson .30 .75
95 Carlos Boozer .30 .75
96 Hakim Warrick .25 .60
97 T.J. Ford .25 .60
98 Desmond Mason .20 .50
99 Andre Iguodala .30 .75
100 Amare Stoudemire .30 .75
101 Tracy McGrady .30 .75
102 Jason Kapono .20 .50
103 Ben Wallace .30 .75
104 Marvin Williams .30 .75
105 Baron Davis .30 .75
106 Andrew Bynum .40 1.00
107 Brandon Roy .40 1.00
108 David Lee .25 .60
109 Corey Maggette .25 .60
110 Josh Howard .25 .60
111 Kevin Durant RC 12.00 30.00
112 Al Horford RC 2.00 5.00

113 Mike Conley Jr. RC 2.50 6.00
114 Jeff Green RC 2.00 5.00
115 Corey Brewer RC 2.00 5.00
116 Joakim Noah RC 4.00 10.00
117 Julian Wright RC 1.50 4.00
118 Ramon Sessions RC 2.50 6.00
119 Sammy Mejia RC 1.50 4.00
120 Luis Scola RC 2.50 6.00
121 Yi Jianlian RC 2.50 6.00
122 Arron Afflalo RC 2.00 5.00
123 Carl Landry RC 1.50 4.00
124 Alando Tucker RC 1.50 4.00
125 Gabe Pruitt RC 1.50 4.00
126 Marcus Williams RC 1.50 4.00
127 Spencer Hawes RC 1.50 4.00
128 Acie Law RC 1.50 4.00
129 Thaddeus Young RC 2.00 5.00
130 Nick Fazekas RC 1.50 4.00
131 Al Thornton RC 1.50 4.00
132 Rodney Stuckey RC 2.50 6.00
133 Nick Young RC 2.50 6.00
134 Glen Davis RC 2.50 6.00
135 Jermareo Davidson RC 1.50 4.00
136 JamesOn Curry RC 1.50 4.00
137 Jason Smith RC 1.50 4.00
138 Daequan Cook RC 1.50 4.00
139 Jared Dudley RC 1.50 4.00
140 Derrick Byars RC 1.50 4.00
141 Josh McRoberts RC 1.50 4.00
142 Adam Haluska RC 1.50 4.00
143 Reyshawn Terry RC 1.50 4.00
144 Aaron Gray RC 1.50 4.00
145 Herbert Hill RC 1.50 4.00
146 Jared Jordan RC 1.50 4.00
147 Wilson Chandler RC 2.50 6.00
148 Morris Almond RC 1.50 4.00
149 Aaron Brooks RC 1.50 4.00
150 Petteri Koponen RC 1.50 4.00
151 Dominic McGuire RC 1.50 4.00
152 Greg Oden RC 2.00 5.00
153 Stephane Lasme RC 1.50 4.00
154 D.J. Strawberry RC 1.50 4.00
155 Sean Williams RC 1.50 4.00
156 Marco Belinelli RC 1.50 4.00
157 Javaris Crittenton RC 1.50 4.00
158 Demetris Nichols RC 1.50 4.00
159 Taurean Green RC 1.50 4.00
160 Brandan Wright RC 1.50 4.00

2007-08 Bowman Copper

*COPPER: .5X TO 1.25X BASE HI
COPPER PRINT RUN 399 SER.#'d SETS
111 Kevin Durant 25.00 60.00

2007-08 Bowman Gold

*GOLD 1-110: 1.25X TO 3X BASE HI
*GOLD 111-160: 1.5X TO 4X BASE HI
GOLD PRINT RUN 99 SER.#'d SETS

2007-08 Bowman Silver

*SILVER: .75X TO 2X BASE HI
SILVER PRINT RUN 199 SER.#'d SETS

2007-08 Bowman Relics

*BRONZE: .6X TO 1.25X BASE HI
BRONZE PRINT RUN 50 SER.#'d SETS
*SILVER: .6X TO 1.5X BASE HI
SILVER PRINT RUN 25 SER.#'d SETS
UNPRICED GOLD PRINT RUN ONE SET
*DUAL: .5X TO 1.25X BASE HI
DUAL PRINT RUN 199 SER.#'d SETS
*DUAL BRONZE: .6X TO 1.5X HI
DUAL BRONZE PRINT RUN 50 SETS
*DUAL SILVER: .75X TO 2X BASE HI
DUAL SILVER PRINT RUN 25 SETS
UNPRICED DUAL GOLD PRINT RUN ONE SET
*TRIPLE: .6X TO 1.5X BASE HI
TRIPLE PRINT RUN 99 SER.#'d SETS
TRIPLE BRONZE: .75X TO 2X BASE HI
TRIPLE BRONZE PRINT RUN 50 SETS
*TRIPLE SILVER: 1X TO 2.5X BASE HI
TRIPLE SILVER PRINT RUN 25 SETS
UNPRICED TRIPLE GOLD PRINT RUN ONE SET
AH Al Horford 3.00 8.00
AIG Andre Iguodala 2.50 6.00
AL Acie Law 2.50 6.00
AM Adam Morrison 2.50 6.00
AS Amare Stoudemire 2.50 6.00
AT Al Thornton 2.50 6.00
BG Ben Gordon 2.50 6.00
BR Brandon Roy 3.00 8.00
BWR Brandan Wright 2.50 6.00
C Corey Brewer 3.00 8.00
CA Carmelo Anthony 3.00 8.00
CB Chris Bosh 2.50 6.00
DH Dwight Howard 4.00 10.00
DN Dirk Nowitzki 3.00 8.00
DW Dwyane Wade 5.00 12.00
DWI Deron Williams 4.00 10.00
EB Elton Brand 2.50 6.00
GO Greg Oden 3.00 8.00
GW Gerald Wallace 2.50 6.00
JC Javaris Crittenton 2.50 6.00
JG Jeff Green 3.00 8.00
JK Jason Kidd 2.50 6.00
JN Joakim Noah 6.00 15.00
JR Jason Richardson 2.50 6.00
JS Josh Smith 2.50 6.00
JSM Jason Smith 2.50 6.00
JW Julian Wright 2.50 6.00
KB Kobe Bryant 6.00 15.00
KG Kevin Garnett 5.00 12.00
LB Larry Bird 8.00 20.00
LD Luol Deng 2.50 6.00
MB Mike Bibby 2.50 6.00
MC Mike Conley Jr. 4.00 10.00
MJ Magic Johnson 6.00 15.00
NY Nick Young 4.00 10.00
PG Pau Gasol 2.50 6.00
RA Ray Allen 2.50 6.00
RH Richard Hamilton 2.00 5.00
RS Rodney Stuckey 4.00 10.00
SH Spencer Hawes 2.50 6.00
SM Shawn Marion 2.50 6.00
SN Steve Nash 3.00 8.00
SO Shaquille O'Neal 5.00 12.00
SW Sean Williams 2.50 6.00
TD Tim Duncan 4.00 10.00
TM Tracy McGrady 2.50 6.00
TP Tony Parker 2.50 6.00
TY Thaddeus Young 3.00 8.00
VC Vince Carter 3.00 8.00
YM Yao Ming 3.00 8.00

2008-09 Bowman

This set was released on October 29, 2008. The base set consists of 150 cards. Cards 1-110 feature veterans, and cards 111-150 are rookies.

COMPLETE SET (150) 25.00 60.00
UNPRICED PRESS PLATE PRINT RUN ONE SET
UNPRICED RED PRINT RUN ONE SET
1 Tracy McGrady .30 .75
2 Jason Kidd .30 .75
3 LeBron James 1.50 4.00
4 Chris Bosh .30 .75
5 Kevin Garnett .60 1.50
6 Josh Smith .30 .75
7 Richard Hamilton .25 .60
8 Monta Ellis .30 .75
9 Yi Jianlian .30 .75
10 Danny Granger .30 .75
11 Richard Jefferson .30 .75
12 Elton Brand .30 .75
13 Rudy Gay .30 .75
14 Andres Nocioni .20 .50
15 Carmelo Anthony .40 1.00
16 Pau Gasol .30 .75
17 Corey Brewer .25 .60
18 Hedo Turkoglu .30 .75
19 Andre Iguodala .30 .75
20 Raymond Felton .25 .60
21 Tim Duncan .50 1.25
22 Michael Redd .30 .75
23 Chris Paul .50 1.25
24 Kobe Bryant 1.50 4.00
25 Brandon Roy .30 .75
26 Carlos Boozer .30 .75
27 Jeff Green .25 .60
28 Luis Scola .25 .60
29 Al Thornton .25 .60
30 Gilbert Arenas .30 .75
31 Brandan Wright .25 .60
32 Shaquille O'Neal .60 1.50
33 Allen Iverson .40 1.00
34 Paul Pierce .40 1.00
35 Ben Gordon .30 .75
36 Jamal Crawford .25 .60
37 Andrew Bynum .40 1.00
38 Gerald Wallace .30 .75
39 Mike Conley Jr. .25 .60
40 Ben Wallace .30 .75
41 Dirk Nowitzki .40 1.00
42 David Lee .25 .60
43 Mo Williams .25 .60
44 Al Jefferson .30 .75
45 Tayshaun Prince .30 .75
46 Jameer Nelson .25 .60
47 Andrei Kirilenko .25 .60
48 David West .30 .75
49 Al Horford .30 .75
50 Steve Nash .30 .75
51 Ron Artest .30 .75
52 Greg Oden .30 .75
53 Sean Williams .25 .60
54 Jamario Moon .20 .50
55 Baron Davis .30 .75
56 Udonis Haslem .25 .60
57 Mike Dunleavy .25 .60
58 Shane Battier .25 .60
59 Andrew Bogut .30 .75
60 Ray Allen .30 .75
61 Nick Young .25 .60
62 Manu Ginobili .30 .75
63 Jason Richardson .30 .75
64 Mike Miller .30 .75
65 Leandro Barbosa .25 .60
66 Luol Deng .30 .75
67 Shawn Marion .30 .75
68 Peja Stojakovic .30 .75
69 Kevin Durant 1.25 3.00
70 Corey Maggette .25 .60
71 Chauncey Billups .30 .75
72 Josh Howard .25 .60
73 Kevin Martin .30 .75
74 Anderson Varejao .25 .60
75 Craig Smith .20 .50
76 Antawn Jamison .30 .75
77 Marcus Camby .20 .50
78 Andre Miller .25 .60
79 Zach Randolph .25 .60
80 Deron Williams .30 .75
81 Devin Harris .30 .75
82 Rashard Lewis .25 .60
83 Damien Wilkins .20 .50
84 LaMarcus Aldridge .30 .75
85 Larry Hughes .25 .60
86 Brad Miller .25 .60
87 Jermaine O'Neal .30 .75
88 Caron Butler .30 .75
89 Tyson Chandler .25 .60
90 Joe Johnson .30 .75
91 Amare Stoudemire .30 .75
92 Dwight Howard .60 1.50
93 Rajon Rondo .40 1.00
94 T.J. Ford .20 .50
95 Rodney Stuckey .40 1.00
96 Samuel Dalembert .20 .50
97 Tony Parker .30 .75
98 Vince Carter .40 1.00
99 Yao Ming .40 1.00
100 Dwyane Wade .60 1.50
101 Dominique Wilkins .40 1.00
102 Rick Barry .30 .75
103 John Stockton .50 1.25
104 Magic Johnson .75 2.00
105 George Gervin .40 1.00
106 Bill Russell .50 1.25
107 David Robinson .50 1.25
108 Dennis Rodman .50 1.25
109 Larry Bird 1.00 2.50
110 Jerry West .40 1.00
111 Derrick Rose RC 8.00 20.00
112 Michael Beasley RC 1.25 3.00
113 O.J. Mayo RC 1.25 3.00
114 Russell Westbrook RC 4.00 10.00
115 Kevin Love RC 3.00 8.00
116 Danilo Gallinari RC 1.25 3.00
117 Eric Gordon RC 2.00 5.00
118 Joe Alexander RC .75 2.00
119 D.J. Augustin RC .75 2.00
120 Brook Lopez RC 1.25 3.00
121 Jerryd Bayless RC .75 2.00
122 Jason Thompson RC .75 2.00
123 Anthony Randolph RC 1.00 2.50
124 Robin Lopez RC .75 2.00
125 Marreese Speights RC .75 2.00
126 Roy Hibbert RC 1.25 3.00
127 JaVale McGee RC 1.25 3.00
128 J.J. Hickson RC 1.00 2.50
129 Alexis Ajinca RC .75 2.00
130 Ryan Anderson RC 1.25 3.00
131 Courtney Lee RC 1.25 3.00
132 Kosta Koufos RC .75 2.00
133 Donte Greene RC .75 2.00
134 George Hill RC 1.25 3.00
135 D.J. White RC .75 2.00
136 J.R. Giddens RC .75 2.00
137 Joey Dorsey RC .75 2.00
138 Mario Chalmers RC 1.25 3.00
139 DeAndre Jordan RC 1.50 4.00
140 Chris Douglas-Roberts RC .75 2.00
141 Malik Hairston RC .75 2.00
142 Sean Singletary RC .75 2.00
143 Kyle Weaver RC .75 2.00
144 Patrick Ewing Jr. RC .75 2.00
145 Walter Sharpe RC .75 2.00
146 Sonny Weems RC .75 2.00
147 Shan Foster RC .75 2.00
148 Nicolas Batum RC 1.25 3.00
149 Brandon Rush RC .75 2.00
150 Darrell Arthur RC .75 2.00

2008-09 Bowman Blue

*BLUE 1-110: .75X TO 2X BASE HI
*BLUE 111-150: 1X TO 2.5X BASE HI
BLUE PRINT RUN 499 SER.#'d SETS
111 Derrick Rose 25.00 60.00

2008-09 Bowman Gold

*1-110 GOLD: 3X TO 8X BASE
*111-150 GOLD RC: 2X TO 5X BASE
GOLD PRINT RUN 50 SER.#'d SETS
111 Derrick Rose 50.00 125.00
114 Russell Westbrook 30.00 80.00

2008-09 Bowman Orange

*1-110 ORANGE: 1.25X TO 3X BASE
*111-150 ORANGE: 1.25X TO 3X BASE
ORANGE PRINT RUN 299 SETS
111 Derrick Rose 30.00 80.00

2008-09 Bowman Draft Day Issue Relics

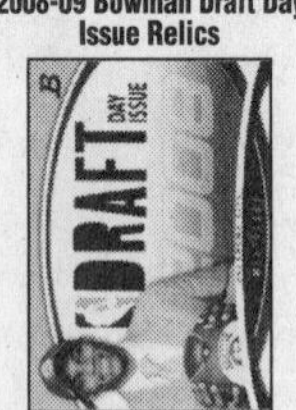

PRINT RUN 399 SER.#'d SETS
*BLUE: .5X TO 1.25X BASE HI
BLUE PRINT RUN 50 SER.#'d SETS
UNPRICED GOLD PRINT RUN 10 SER.#'d SETS
*ORANGE: .6X TO 1.5X BASE HI
ORANGE PRINT RUN 25 SETS
UNPRICED RED PRINT RUN ONE SET
DDIRAR Anthony Randolph 3.00 8.00
DDIRBL Brook Lopez 4.00 10.00
DDIRBR Brandon Rush 2.50 6.00
DDIRDG Danilo Gallinari 4.00 10.00
DDIRDJA D.J. Augustin 2.50 6.00
DDIRDR Derrick Rose 20.00 50.00
DDIREG Eric Gordon 6.00 15.00
DDIRJA Joe Alexander 2.50 6.00
DDIRJB Jerryd Bayless 2.50 6.00
DDIRJD Joey Dorsey 2.50 6.00
DDIRKL Kevin Love 10.00 25.00
DDIRMB Michael Beasley 4.00 10.00
DDIROJM O.J. Mayo 4.00 10.00
DDIRRL Robin Lopez 2.50 6.00
DDIRRW Russell Westbrook 12.00 30.00

2008-09 Bowman Draft Day Issue Relics Autographs

PRINT RUN 75 SER.#'d SETS
*BLUE: .5X TO 1.25X BASE HI
BLUE PRINT RUN 50 SER.#'d SETS
UNPRICED GOLD PRINT RUN 10 SETS
*ORANGE: .6X TO 1.5X BASE HI
ORANGE PRINT RUN 25 SER.#'d SETS
UNPRICED RED PRINT RUN ONE SET
DDIABL Brook Lopez 15.00 40.00
DDIADJA D.J. Augustin 10.00 25.00
DDIADR Derrick Rose 125.00 300.00
DDIAEG Eric Gordon 25.00 60.00
DDIAJA Joe Alexander 10.00 25.00
DDIAJB Jerryd Bayless 10.00 25.00
DDIAKL Kevin Love 40.00 100.00
DDIAMB Michael Beasley 15.00 40.00
DDIAOJM O.J. Mayo 15.00 40.00
DDIARW Russell Westbrook 50.00 125.00

2008-09 Bowman Draft Day Issue Relics Combos

*BLUE: .5X TO 1.25X BASE HI
BLUE PRINT RUN 50 SER.#'d SETS
UNPRICED GOLD PRINT RUN 10 SER.#'d SETS
*ORANGE: .6X TO 1.5X BASE HI
ORANGE PRINT RUN 25 SETS
UNPRICED RED PRINT RUN ONE SET
DDICAR Anthony Randolph 5.00 12.00
DDICBR Brandon Rush 4.00 10.00
DDICDG Danilo Gallinari 6.00 15.00
DDICJD Joey Dorsey 4.00 10.00
DDICRL Robin Lopez 4.00 10.00

2008-09 Bowman Draft Day Issue Relics Combos Autographs

PRINT RUN 75 SER.#'d SETS
*BLUE: .5X TO 1.25X BASE HI
BLUE PRINT RUN 50 SER.#'d SETS
UNPRICED GOLD PRINT RUN 10 SER.#'d SETS
*ORANGE: .6X TO 1.5X BASE HI
ORANGE PRINT RUN 25 SER.#'d SETS
UNPRICED RED PRINT RUN ONE SET
DDICABL Brook Lopez 15.00 40.00
DDICADJA D.J. Augustin 10.00 25.00
DDICADR Derrick Rose 125.00 300.00
DDICAEG Eric Gordon 25.00 60.00
DDICAJA Joe Alexander 10.00 25.00
DDICAJB Jerryd Bayless 10.00 25.00
DDICAKL Kevin Love 40.00 100.00
DDICAMB Michael Beasley 15.00 40.00
DDICAOJM O.J. Mayo 15.00 40.00
DDICARW Russell Westbrook 50.00 125.00

2008-09 Bowman Relics

STATED ODDS 1:13
*BLUE: .6X TO 1.5X BASE HI
BLUE PRINT RUN 50 SER.#'d SETS
UNPRICED GOLD PRINT RUN 10 SER.#'d SETS
*ORANGE: 1X TO 2.5X BASE HI
ORANGE PRINT RUN 25 SETS
UNPRICED RED PRINT RUN ONE SET
BRAH Al Horford 2.50 6.00
BRAI Allen Iverson 3.00 8.00
BRAJ Al Jefferson 2.50 6.00
BRAJA Antawn Jamison 2.50 6.00
BRAT Al Thornton 2.00 5.00
BRBR Brandon Roy 2.50 6.00
BRBW Ben Wallace 2.50 6.00
BRCA Carmelo Anthony 3.00 8.00
BRCB Chris Bosh 2.50 6.00
BRCBO Carlos Boozer 2.50 6.00
BRCBU Caron Butler 2.50 6.00
BRCM Corey Maggette 2.00 5.00
BRCP Chris Paul 4.00 10.00
BRDH Devin Harris 2.50 6.00
BRDHO Dwight Howard 5.00 12.00
BRDN Dirk Nowitzki 3.00 8.00
BRDW Dwyane Wade 5.00 12.00
BRDWI Deron Williams 2.50 6.00
BRJJ Joe Johnson 2.50 6.00
BRJO Jermaine O'Neal 2.50 6.00
BRJR Jason Richardson 2.50 6.00
BRKB Kobe Bryant 8.00 20.00
BRKG Kevin Garnett 5.00 12.00
BRLO Lamar Odom 2.50 6.00
BRMB Mike Bibby 2.00 5.00
BRMC Mike Conley Jr. 2.00 5.00
BRMG Manu Ginobili 2.50 6.00
BRMR Michael Redd 2.50 6.00
BRPG Pau Gasol 2.50 6.00
BRPP Paul Pierce 3.00 8.00
BRPS Peja Stojakovic 2.50 6.00
BRRA Ray Allen 2.50 6.00
BRRH Richard Hamilton 2.00 5.00
BRRL Rashard Lewis 2.00 5.00
BRRW Rasheed Wallace 2.50 6.00
BRSN Steve Nash 2.50 6.00
BRSO Shaquille O'Neal 5.00 12.00
BRTD Tim Duncan 4.00 10.00
BRTM Tracy McGrady 2.50 6.00
BRYM Yao Ming 3.00 8.00

2009-10 Bowman 48

COMPLETE SET (121) 40.00 80.00
COMP.SET w/o SP's (100) 10.00 25.00
101-114 RC PRINT RUN 2009 SER.#'d SETS
115-121 PRINT RUN 1948 SER.#'d SETS
UNPRICED RED PRINT RUN ONE SET
1 Al Horford .25 .60
2 Joe Johnson .25 .60
3 Josh Smith .25 .60
4 Paul Pierce .30 .75
5 Kevin Garnett .50 1.25
6 Ray Allen .25 .60
7 Rajon Rondo .30 .75
8 Gerald Wallace .25 .60
9 Emeka Okafor .25 .60
10 Ben Gordon .25 .60
11 Derrick Rose .75 2.00
12 John Salmons .25 .60
13 Mo Williams .20 .50
14 LeBron James 1.25 3.00
15 Anderson Varejao .20 .50
16 Dirk Nowitzki .30 .75
17 Jason Kidd .25 .60
18 Jason Terry .20 .50
19 Chauncey Billups .25 .60
20 Carmelo Anthony .30 .75
21 Richard Hamilton .20 .50
22 Allen Iverson .30 .75
23 Rasheed Wallace .25 .60
24 Monta Ellis .25 .60
25 Corey Maggette .20 .50
26 Anthony Randolph .20 .50
27 Tracy McGrady .25 .60
28 Yao Ming .30 .75
29 Ron Artest .25 .60
30 Danny Granger .25 .60
31 T.J. Ford .15 .40
32 Eric Gordon .25 .60
33 Baron Davis .25 .60
34 Marcus Camby .15 .40
35 Pau Gasol .25 .60
36 Kobe Bryant 1.25 3.00
37 Andrew Bynum .30 .75
38 Rudy Gay .25 .60
39 O.J. Mayo .25 .60
40 Michael Beasley .25 .60
41 Dwyane Wade .50 1.25
42 Jermaine O'Neal .25 .60
43 Michael Redd .25 .60
44 Richard Jefferson .25 .60
45 Al Jefferson .25 .60
46 Kevin Love .40 1.00
47 Mike Miller .25 .60
48 Vince Carter .30 .75
49 Devin Harris .25 .60
50 David West .25 .60
51 Chris Paul .40 1.00
52 Nate Robinson .25 .60
53 David Lee .20 .50
54 Kevin Durant .75 2.00
55 Russell Westbrook .40 1.00
56 Dwight Howard .40 1.00
57 Jameer Nelson .20 .50
58 Hedo Turkoglu .25 .60
59 Andre Iguodala .25 .60
60 Elton Brand .25 .60
61 Andre Miller .20 .50
62 Shaquille O'Neal .50 1.25
63 Amare Stoudemire .25 .60
64 Steve Nash .25 .60
65 Rudy Fernandez .20 .50
66 Brandon Roy .25 .60
67 LaMarcus Aldridge .25 .60
68 Spencer Hawes .20 .50
69 Kevin Martin .25 .60
70 Tony Parker .25 .60
71 Tim Duncan .40 1.00
72 Manu Ginobili .25 .60
73 Jose Calderon .20 .50
74 Chris Bosh .25 .60
75 Shawn Marion .25 .60
76 Carlos Boozer .25 .60
77 Deron Williams .25 .60
78 Caron Butler .25 .60
79 Antawn Jamison .25 .60
80 Gilbert Arenas .25 .60
81 Dominique Wilkins .30 .75
82 Bill Russell .40 1.00
83 Bob Cousy .40 1.00
84 Larry Bird .75 2.00
85 Rick Barry .25 .60
86 Elgin Baylor .25 .60
87 Jerry West .30 .75
88 Magic Johnson .60 1.50
89 Oscar Robertson .25 .60
90 George Mikan .50 1.25
91 Pete Maravich .75 2.00
92 Patrick Ewing .30 .75
93 Willis Reed .25 .60
94 Julius Erving .50 1.25
95 Moses Malone .25 .60
96 Wilt Chamberlain .50 1.25
97 Bill Walton .25 .60
98 Clyde Drexler .30 .75
99 Bob Pettit .25 .60
100 Karl Malone .30 .75
101 Blake Griffin RC 10.00 25.00
102 Jonny Flynn RC 1.50 4.00
103 Hasheem Thabeet RC 1.50 4.00
104 James Harden RC 5.00 12.00
105 DeMar DeRozan RC 2.50 6.00
106 Stephen Curry RC 4.00 10.00
107 Brandon Jennings RC 3.00 8.00
108 Jordan Hill RC 1.50 4.00
109 Earl Clark RC 1.50 4.00
110 Gerald Henderson RC 1.50 4.00
111 Tyreke Evans RC 4.00 10.00
112 Jrue Holiday RC 3.00 8.00
113 Tyler Hansbrough RC 2.50 6.00
114 Terrence Williams RC 1.50 4.00
115 Play Card 1.25 3.00
116 Play Card 1.25 3.00
117 Play Card 1.25 3.00
118 Play Card 1.25 3.00
119 Play Card 1.25 3.00
120 Play Card 1.25 3.00
121 Play Card 1.25 3.00

2009-10 Bowman 48 Black

*1-100 BLACK: 5X TO 12X BASE HI
*101-114 RC BLACK: 2X TO 5X BASE
*115-121 BLACK: 1X TO 2.5X BASE HI
BLACK PRINT RUN 48 SER.#'d SETS

2009-10 Bowman 48 Blue

*1-100 BLUE: 1.5X TO 4X BASE HI
*101-114 RC BLUE: .4X TO 1X BASE HI
*PLAY CARDS SAME VALUE AS BASE
BLUE PRINT RUN 1948 SER.#'d SETS

2009-10 Bowman 48 Autographs

STATED ODDS 1:9
*BLACK: .5X TO 1.25X BASE HI
BLACK PRINT RUN 48 SER.#'d SETS
48AAB Andrew Bynum 10.00 25.00
48AAJ Antawn Jamison 5.00 12.00
48ABG Ben Gordon 5.00 12.00
48ABR Bill Russell 40.00 100.00
48ABW Bill Walton SP 60.00 150.00
48ACA Carmelo Anthony 20.00 50.00
48ACM Corey Maggette 5.00 12.00
48ACP Chris Paul 20.00 50.00
48ADG Danny Granger 6.00 15.00
48ADH Dwight Howard 15.00 40.00
48ADL David Lee 5.00 12.00
48ADR Derrick Rose 50.00 120.00
48ADW Dwyane Wade 20.00 50.00
48AGO Greg Oden 6.00 15.00
48AJJ Jarrett Jack 5.00 12.00
48AJS Josh Smith 5.00 12.00
48AJW Jerry West 20.00 50.00
48AKH Kirk Hinrich 6.00 15.00
48AKL Kevin Love 12.00 30.00
48ALB Larry Bird SP 75.00 200.00
48ALD Luol Deng 5.00 12.00
48AMJ Magic Johnson 40.00 100.00
48AMW Mo Williams 5.00 12.00
48ARB Rick Barry 6.00 15.00
48AABA Andrea Bargnani 5.00 12.00
48AAIG Andre Iguodala 5.00 12.00
48ABRO Brandon Roy 8.00 20.00
48ADWI Dominique Wilkins 10.00 25.00
48AOJM O.J. Mayo 6.00 15.00
48ATJF T.J. Ford 5.00 12.00

2009-10 Bowman 48 Locker Room Collection Autograph Relics

PRINT RUN 41 SER.#'d SETS
UNPRICED BLACK PRINT RUN 8 SETS
*PATCHES: .75X TO 2X BASE HI
PATCH PRINT RUN 24 SER.#'d SETS
DRCARJW Jerry West 25.00 50.00
LRCARBR Bill Russell 50.00 125.00
LRCARCA Carmelo Anthony 25.00 50.00
LRCARCP Chris Paul 25.00 60.00
LRCARDG Danny Granger 10.00 25.00
LRCARDH Dwight Howard 20.00 50.00
LRCARDR Derrick Rose 50.00 120.00
LRCARDW Dwyane Wade 25.00 60.00
LRCARJS Josh Smith 10.00 25.00
LRCARLB Larry Bird 40.00 100.00
LRCARMJ Magic Johnson 40.00 80.00
LRCARAIG Andre Iguodala 10.00 25.00
LRCARBRO Brandon Roy 20.00 40.00
LRCARDWI Dominique Wilkins 20.00 50.00
LRCAROJM O.J. Mayo 20.00 40.00

2003-04 Bowman Chrome

Released in October 2003 and marketed as two brands in one pack, Bowman and Bowman Chrome cards shared the same packs and boxes. The Bowman version features a 156-card set divided up into 110 base veteran cards with a red border around a centered picture surrounded by silver borders on the left and right and black borders on the top and the bottom. Cards 111-147 feature rookie players and have a blue border around their pictures and share the rest of the design elements with the base cards. Cards 148-157 are autographed rookie cards sequentially numbered to 250. Upon issue, card number 147 was not released. Bowman was packaged in 24-pack boxes with packs containing seven cards, four Bowman cards, four Bowman Chrome Cards and one Parallel, and carried a suggested retail price of $4.

COMP.SET w/o RC's (110) 30.00 80.00
1 Yao Ming 1.00 2.50
2 Glenn Robinson .40 1.00
3 Antoine Walker .50 1.25
4 Jalen Rose .40 1.00
5 Ricky Davis .40 1.00
6 Juwan Howard .40 1.00
7 Kwame Brown .30 .75
8 Mike Bibby .50 1.25
9 Wally Szczerbiak .40 1.00
10 Allen Iverson .75 2.00
11 Shareef Abdur-Rahim .40 1.00
12 Jamal Mashburn .40 1.00
13 Stephon Marbury .40 1.00
14 Desmond Mason .40 1.00
15 Gordan Giricek .30 .75
16 Caron Butler .50 1.25
17 Jermaine O'Neal .50 1.25
18 Kenyon Martin .50 1.25
19 Andrei Kirilenko .50 1.25
20 Dirk Nowitzki .75 2.00
21 Richard Hamilton .40 1.00
22 Troy Murphy .50 1.25
23 Shawn Marion .50 1.25
24 Allan Houston .40 1.00
25 Keith Van Horn .40 1.00
26 Brian Grant .30 .75
27 Mike Miller .50 1.25
28 Chris Webber .50 1.25
29 Brent Barry .30 .75
30 Elton Brand .50 1.25
31 Juan Dixon .30 .75
32 Karl Malone .60 1.50
33 Darrell Armstrong .30 .75
34 Rasheed Wallace .50 1.25
35 Michael Redd .50 1.25
36 Rashard Lewis .50 1.25
37 Ron Artest .50 1.25
38 P.J. Brown .30 .75
39 Eddie Griffin .30 .75
40 Tim Duncan .75 2.00
41 Kurt Thomas .30 .75
42 Raef Lafrentz .30 .75
43 Ben Wallace .50 1.25
44 Lamar Odom .50 1.25
45 Vince Carter .75 2.00
46 Derek Anderson .30 .75
47 Stromile Swift .30 .75
48 Bobby Jackson .30 .75
49 Richard Jefferson .50 1.25
50 Shaquille O'Neal 1.25 3.00
51 Calbert Cheaney .30 .75
52 Troy Hudson .30 .75
53 Ray Allen .50 1.25
54 Howard Eisley .30 .75
55 Alonzo Mourning .60 1.50
56 Sam Cassell .40 1.00
57 Derrick Coleman .40 1.00
58 Andre Miller .40
59 Antawn Jamison .50
60 Kevin Garnett 1.00
61 Steve Francis .50
62 Tyson Chandler .40
63 Drew Gooden .40
64 Scottie Pippen .75
65 Pau Gasol .50
66 Steve Nash .60
67 DaJuan Wagner .30
68 Jason Terry .40
69 Reggie Miller .50
70 Tracy McGrady .60
71 Nene Hilario .40
72 Morris Peterson .30
73 Peja Stojakovic .50
74 Eddie Jones .40
75 Tony Parker .50
76 Corliss Williamson .30
77 Vladimir Radmanovic .30
78 Amare Stoudemire .75
79 Tony Delk .30
80 Jason Kidd .75
81 Gary Payton .50
82 Corey Maggette .40
83 Darius Miles .30
84 Cuttino Mobley .40
85 Eric Snow .30
86 Matt Harpring .40
87 Manu Ginobili .60
88 Latrell Sprewell .40
89 Alvin Williams .30
90 Paul Pierce .60
91 Anfernee Hardaway .75
92 Gilbert Arenas .50
93 Jerry Stackhouse .40
94 Tim Thomas .30
95 Nikoloz Tskitishvili .30
96 Doug Christie .30
97 Zydrunas Ilgauskas .40
98 Jamaal Tinsley .30
99 Theo Ratliff .30
100 Kobe Bryant 2.50
101 Chauncey Billups .50
102 Michael Finley .50
103 Jason Williams .40
104 Bonzi Wells .30
105 Voshon Lenard .30
106 Jason Richardson .50
107 Baron Davis .50
108 Radoslav Nesterovic .30
109 Eddy Curry .40
110 Michael Olowokandi .30
111 Josh Howard RC 3.00
112 Mario Austin RC 3.00
113 Rick Rickert RC 3.00
114 Tommy Smith RC 3.00
115 Dahntay Jones RC 3.00
116 Ndudi Ebi RC 3.00
117 Maurice Williams RC 5.00
118 Kendrick Perkins RC 5.00
119 Steve Blake RC 4.00
120 David West RC 4.00
121 Chris Kaman RC 4.00
122 Keith Bogans RC 3.00
123 LeBron James RC 30.00
124 Devin Brown RC 3.00
125 Jason Kapono RC 3.00
126 Zoran Planinic RC 3.00
127 Zaur Pachulia RC 3.00
128 Malick Badiane RC 3.00
129 Kyle Korver RC 4.00
130 Darko Milicic RC 3.00
131 Troy Bell RC 3.00
132 Luke Walton RC 3.00
133 Mike Sweetney RC 3.00
134 Jarvis Hayes RC 3.00
135 Leandro Barbosa RC 4.00
136 Carlos Delfino RC 4.00
137 Sofoklis Schortsanitis RC 3.00
138 Slavko Vranes RC 3.00
139 Travis Hansen RC 3.00
140 Carmelo Anthony RC 8.00
141 Reece Gaines RC 3.00
142 Maciej Lampe RC 3.00
143 Travis Outlaw RC 4.00
144 Jerome Beasley RC 3.00
145 Mickael Pietrus RC 3.00
146 Brian Cook RC 3.00
148 Kirk Hinrich AU RC 10.00
149 Dwyane Wade AU RC 175.00
150 Marcus Banks AU RC 8.00
151 Nick Collison AU RC 8.00
152 Boris Diaw AU RC 10.00
153 Chris Bosh AU RC 50.00
154 T.J. Ford AU RC 10.00
155 Luke Ridnour AU RC 10.00
156 Aleksander Pavlovic AU RC 8.00
157 Zarko Cabarkapa AU RC 8.00

2003-04 Bowman Chro Refractors

Randomly inserted in packs, this 156-card s the base Bowman Chrome set enhanced wit rainbow holofoil refractor effect. Cards 1-14 sequentially numbered to 300 and cards 148 sequentially numbered to 50.

*1-110: 1.5X TO 4X BASE CARD HI
*111-146: 1.25X TO 3X BASE HI
*148-157 AU RC REF: .75X TO 2X BASE HI
CARD 147 NOT RELEASED
100 Kobe Bryant 12.00
123 LeBron James 175.00
148 Kirk Hinrich AU 30.00
149 Dwyane Wade AU 500.00

2003-04 Bowman Chro Refractors Gold

Randomly inserted in packs, this 156-card s the base Bowman Chrome set enhanced wit refractor holofoil effect and sequential numb for cards 1-147 and sequential numbering to 148-157.

*1-110: 8X TO 20X BASE HI
*111-146 RC: 2X TO 5X BASE HI
CARD 147 NOT RELEASED
100 Kobe Bryant 60.00
123 LeBron James 800.00
140 Carmelo Anthony 125.00

2003-04 Bowman Chron fractors

Randomly inserted in packs, this 156-card s the base Bowman Chrome set enahnced wit (looks almost like confetti) refractor holofoil sequential numbering to 150 for cards 1-14 sequential numbering to 25 for cards 148-1

*1-110: 4X TO 10X BASE CARD HI
*111-146 RCs: 2X TO 5X BASE HI

57 RCs: 1.25X TO 3X BASE HI
47 NOT RELEASED
ron James 200.00 400.00
ane Wade AU 800.00 1300.00

004-05 Bowman Chrome

l in October of 2004 under the name Bowman and Stars again this year, packs contained an ent of cards from both Bowman and Bowman , therefore they have been designated as such. s contain 156 cards where cards 1-110 feature players, cards 111-146 feature rookies, and nbers 147-156 feature autographed rookie serted at one in 105 packs for Bowman and are ally numbered to 250 for Bowman Chrome. All ve gray borders, but the veteran players have nts along the side borders and the rookies e accents. Boxes contained 24 packs of seven ur Bowman, two Bowman Chrome and one Gold Parallel) that carried a SRP of $4.00.

ET w/o RCs (110) 25.00 60.00
ing 1.00 2.50
Curry .40 1.00
n Marbury .40 1.00
Webber .50 1.25
Kidd .75 2.00
Mobley .40 1.00
ne O'Neal .50 1.25
Bryant 2.50 6.00
Parker .50 1.25
Payton .50 1.25
ord .40 1.00
Duncan .75 2.00
n Robinson .40 1.00
Richardson .50 1.25
elo Anthony 1.00 2.50
Gasol .50 1.25
Hinrich .50 1.25
on Martin .50 1.25
l Crawford .40 1.00
Brand .50 1.25
Garnett 1.00 2.50
ael Redd .50 1.25
n James 3.00 8.00
Miller .40 1.00
Stojakovic .50 1.25
Hayes .30 .75
Wesley .30 .75
Kapono .30 .75
Maggette .40 1.00
eed Wallace .50 1.25
.40 1.00
e Stoudemire .60 1.50
Iverson .75 2.00
ille O'Neal 1.25 3.00
Dunleavy .40 1.00
Nash .60 1.50
Miller .50 1.25
Bosh .50 1.25
Diaw .40 1.00
Francis .50 1.25
Nowitzki .75 2.00
Williams .40 1.00
t Arenas .50 1.25
Van Horn .40 1.00
Mashburn .50 1.25
Fisher .40 1.00
i Kirilenko .40 1.00
Davis .40 1.00
l Wallace .50 1.25
McGrady .60 1.50
Randolph .40 1.00
Alston .30 .75
Jackson .30 .75
ond Mason .40 1.00
homas .30 .75
l Tinsley .30 .75
e Brown .30 .75
ncey Billups .50 1.25
on Hunter .30 .75
e Miller .50 1.25
el Dalembert .30 .75
s Posey .30 .75
Dampier .30 .75
s Arroyo .40 1.00
Gaines .30 .75
Milicic .30 .75
Cassell .40 1.00
ne Wade 1.50 4.00
Houston .40 1.00
len .50 1.25
Chandler .40 1.00
Wells .30 .75
Rose .40 1.00
is Daniels .30 .75
nas Ilgauskas .40 1.00
aun Prince .50 1.25
Odom .50 1.25
Ridnour .40 1.00
hnson .50 1.25
Carter .75 2.00
e Walker .50 1.25
ef Abdur-Rahim .40 1.00
d Jefferson .50 1.25
ce Taylor .30 .75
Kaman .50 1.25
s Banks .30 .75
Bibby .50 1.25
Sprewell .40 1.00
d Lewis .50 1.25
Davis .50 1.25
Butler .50 1.25
el Finley .50 1.25
Miller .50 1.25
ington .40 1.00
n Richardson .40 1.00
l Magloire .30 .75
Miles .30 .75
ster .30 .75
Malone .60 1.50
n Marion .50 1.25
n Jamison .50 1.25
Ginobili .60 1.50
Wallace .50 1.25
Pierce .60 1.50

105 Mike Sweetney .30 .75
106 Ron Artest .50 1.25
107 Michael Olowokandi .30 .75
108 Jason Terry .40 1.00
109 Gordan Giricek .30 .75
110 Carlos Boozer .50 1.25
111 Romain Sato RC 2.00 5.00
112 Chris Duhon RC 2.00 5.00
113 Ben Gordon RC 2.50 6.00
114 Matt Freije RC 2.00 5.00
115 Al Jefferson RC 3.00 8.00
116 Beno Udrih RC 2.00 5.00
117 Kirk Snyder RC 2.00 5.00
118 Anderson Varejao RC 2.50 6.00
119 Devin Harris RC 3.00 8.00
120 Tony Allen RC 2.50 6.00
121 Ha Seung-Jin RC 2.00 5.00
122 J.R. Smith RC 2.50 6.00
123 Blake Stepp RC 2.00 5.00
124 Jameer Nelson RC 2.50 6.00
125 Kris Humphries RC 2.00 5.00
126 Josh Childress RC 2.00 5.00
127 Tim Pickett RC 2.00 5.00
128 Delonte West RC 2.50 6.00
129 Dwight Howard RC 8.00 20.00
130 Luke Jackson RC 2.00 5.00
131 Rickey Paulding RC 2.00 5.00
132 Andre Emmett RC 2.00 5.00
133 Josh Smith RC 3.00 8.00
134 Antonio Burks RC 2.00 5.00
135 Ricky Minard RC 2.00 5.00
136 Lionel Chalmers RC 2.00 5.00
137 Shaun Livingston RC 2.00 5.00
138 Trevor Ariza RC 2.00 5.00
139 Sergei Lishouk RC 2.00 5.00
140 Pape Sow RC 2.00 5.00
141 Rashad Wright RC 2.00 5.00
142 Jackson Vroman RC 2.00 5.00
143 Luis Flores RC 2.00 5.00
144 Royal Ivey RC 2.00 5.00
145 Kevin Martin RC 2.50 6.00
146 Andre Iguodala RC 3.00 8.00
147 Andris Biedrins AU RC 10.00 25.00
148 Pavel Podkolzine AU RC 8.00 20.00
149 Luol Deng AU RC 12.00 30.00
150 Robert Swift AU RC 8.00 20.00
151 Sebastian Telfair AU RC 8.00 20.00
152 Emeka Okafor AU RC 12.00 30.00
153 Dorell Wright AU RC 12.00 30.00
154 Sasha Vujacic AU RC 8.00 20.00
155 Rafael Araujo AU RC 8.00 20.00
156 David Harrison AU RC 8.00 20.00

2004-05 Bowman Chrome Refractors

Randomly seeded in packs, this 156-card set parallels the base Bowman Chrome set and is enhanced by the rainbow holo-foil refractor effect. Cards 1-146 are sequentially numbered to 300 (inserted in packs at one in 18) and cards 147-156 are sequentially numbered to 50 (inserted in packs at one in 1579)

*1-110 REFRACTORS: 1.5X TO 4X BASE HI
*111-146 REFRACTORS: 1.25X TO 3X BASE HI
*147-156 REFRACTOR AU: 1X TO 2.5X BASE HI

2004-05 Bowman Chrome Refractors Gold

Randomly seeded in packs, this 156-card set parallels the base Bowman Chrome set enhanced with gold borders and a rainbow holofoil refractor effect. Card numbers 1-146 are sequentially numbered to 50 (inserted in packs at one in 59) and card number 147-156 are sequentially numbered to five.

*1-110 GOLD: 6X TO 15X BASE HI
*111-146 GOLD: 3X TO 8X BASE HI
23 LeBron James 60.00 150.00
129 Dwight Howard 100.00 200.00

2004-05 Bowman Chrome X-Fractors

Randomly inserted in packs, this 156-card set parallels the base set enhanced with Topps' rainbow holofoil refractor effect and has an extra treatment that breaks it down into cubes on the card. Numbers 1-146 are sequentially numbered to 150 and cards 147-156 are sequentially numbered to 25.

*1-110 X-FRACTORS: 4X TO 10X BASE HI
*111-146 X-FRACTORS: 2.5X TO 6X BASE HI
*147-156 X-FRACTORS AU: 1.5X TO 4X BASE HI

2005-06 Bowman Chrome

Randomly seeded in packs at the rate of two per, this 161-card set parallels the base set design and numbering of Bowman. Each card is finished in chrome and rookie autographs are sequentially numbered to 250.

COMP.SET w/o RC's (110) 25.00 60.00
UNPRICED SUPERFR.PRINT RUN ONE SET
1 Steve Nash .75 2.00
2 Primoz Brezec .40 1.00
3 Baron Davis .60 1.50
4 Al Harrington .50 1.25
5 Caron Butler .60 1.50
6 Marcus Camby .50 1.25
7 Carlos Boozer .60 1.50
8 Ben Gordon .60 1.50
9 Stephen Jackson .50 1.25
10 Dirk Nowitzki 1.00 2.50
11 Nenad Krstic .40 1.00
12 Jason Richardson .60 1.50
13 Brendan Haywood .40 1.00
14 Chauncey Billups .60 1.50
15 Corey Maggette .50 1.25
16 Peja Stojakovic .60 1.50
17 Grant Hill .75 2.00
18 Pau Gasol .60 1.50
19 Vladimir Radmanovic .40 1.00
20 Jason Kidd 1.00 2.50
21 Tim Duncan 1.00 2.50
22 David Harrison .40 1.00
23 LeBron James 3.00 8.00
24 Udonis Haslem .50 1.25
25 Dan Dickau .40 1.00
26 Cuttino Mobley .50 1.25
27 Chris Bosh .60 1.50
28 Sebastian Telfair .50 1.25
29 Latrell Sprewell .50 1.25
30 Emeka Okafor .60 1.50
31 Mike James .40 1.00
32 Trevor Ariza .40 1.00
33 Larry Hughes .50 1.25
34 Desmond Mason .40 1.00
35 Tayshaun Prince .60 1.50
36 Manu Ginobili .60 1.50
37 Mike Bibby .60 1.50
38 Andre Iguodala .60 1.50
39 Jamaal Magloire .40 1.00
40 Amare Stoudemire .60 1.50
41 Rafer Alston .40 1.00
42 Elton Brand .60 1.50
43 Steve Francis .60 1.50
44 Rashard Lewis .60 1.50
45 Lorenzen Wright .40 1.00
46 Kirk Hinrich .60 1.50
47 Andrei Kirilenko .50 1.25
48 Brad Miller .60 1.50
49 Jamal Crawford .50 1.25
50 Shaquille O'Neal 1.25 3.00
51 Shaun Livingston .40 1.00
52 Troy Murphy .50 1.25
53 Drew Gooden .50 1.25
54 Paul Pierce .75 2.00
55 Vince Carter 1.00 2.50
56 Wally Szczerbiak .50 1.25
57 Antawn Jamison .60 1.50
58 Marquis Daniels .40 1.00
59 Gerald Wallace .60 1.50
60 Ray Allen .60 1.50
61 Jamaal Tinsley .40 1.00
62 Shane Battier .50 1.25
63 Zydrunas Ilgauskas .50 1.25
64 Mehmet Okur .40 1.00
65 Rasheed Wallace .60 1.50
66 Maurice Williams .50 1.25
67 Josh Howard .60 1.50
68 Zach Randolph .50 1.25
69 Kobe Bryant 3.00 8.00
70 Tracy McGrady .75 2.00
71 Luke Ridnour .50 1.25
72 Damon Jones .40 1.00
73 Tony Allen .40 1.00
74 Mike Miller .60 1.50
75 Sam Cassell .60 1.50
76 Ben Wallace .60 1.50
77 Mike Sweetney .40 1.00
78 Eddy Curry .50 1.25
79 Michael Redd .60 1.50
80 Carmelo Anthony 1.25 3.00
81 Dwight Howard 1.25 3.00
82 Josh Smith .60 1.50
83 Richard Jefferson .60 1.50
84 Richard Hamilton .50 1.25
85 Chris Webber .60 1.50
86 Shawn Marion .60 1.50
87 Jalen Rose .60 1.50
88 Bob Sura .40 1.00
89 Mike Dunleavy .50 1.25
90 Dwyane Wade 1.50 4.00
91 Gary Payton .60 1.50
92 Luol Deng .60 1.50
93 Kenyon Martin .60 1.50
94 Beno Udrih .40 1.00
95 J.R. Smith .60 1.50
96 Lamar Odom .60 1.50
97 Andre Miller .50 1.25
98 Jermaine O'Neal .60 1.50
99 Yao Ming .75 2.00
100 Allen Iverson 1.00 2.50
101 Quentin Richardson .50 1.25
102 Gilbert Arenas .60 1.50
103 Stephon Marbury .50 1.25
104 Antoine Walker .50 1.25
105 Jameer Nelson .50 1.25
106 Joel Przybilla .40 1.00
107 Devin Harris .60 1.50
108 Tony Parker .60 1.50
109 Josh Childress .50 1.25
110 Kevin Garnett 1.25 3.00
111 Chris Paul RC 8.00 20.00
112 Danny Granger RC 4.00 10.00
113 Antoine Wright RC 2.00 5.00
114 Joey Graham RC 2.00 5.00
115 Wayne Simien RC 2.00 5.00
116 Channing Frye RC 2.50 6.00
117 Charlie Villanueva RC 2.50 6.00
118 Francisco Garcia RC 2.50 6.00
119 Ike Diogu RC 2.00 5.00
120 Jarrett Jack RC 2.00 5.00
121 Robert Whaley RC 2.00 5.00
122 C.J. Miles RC 2.50 6.00
123 Ryan Gomes RC 2.00 5.00
124 Nate Robinson RC 2.50 6.00
125 Daniel Ewing RC 2.00 5.00
126 Andray Blatche RC 2.50 6.00
127 Luther Head RC 2.00 5.00
128 Julius Hodge RC 2.00 5.00
129 Lawrence Roberts RC 2.00 5.00
130 Jason Maxiell RC 2.00 5.00
131 Martynas Andriuskevicius RC 2.00 5.00
132 Ersan Ilyasova RC 2.50 6.00
133 Martell Webster RC 2.00 5.00
134 Andrew Bynum RC 6.00 15.00
135 Louis Williams RC 3.00 8.00
136 Johan Petro RC 2.00 5.00
137 Brandon Bass RC 2.50 6.00
138 Travis Diener RC 2.00 5.00
139 Bracey Wright RC 2.00 5.00
140 Marvin Williams RC 2.50 6.00
141 Eddie Basden RC 2.00 5.00
142 Von Wafer RC 2.00 5.00
143 David Lee RC 3.00 8.00
144 Linas Kleiza RC 2.00 5.00
145 Luke Schenscher RC 2.00 5.00
146 Yaroslav Korolev RC 2.00 5.00
147 Carmen Electra 4.00 10.00
148 Christie Brinkley 4.00 10.00
149 Shannon Elizabeth 4.00 10.00
150 Jenny McCarthy 4.00 10.00
151 Jay-Z 4.00 10.00
152 Raymond Felton AU RC 10.00 25.00
153 Gerald Green AU RC 8.00 20.00
154 Rashad McCants AU RC 6.00 15.00
155 Andrew Bogut AU RC 10.00 25.00
156 Chris Taft AU RC 6.00 15.00
157 Sarunas Jasikevicius AU RC 6.00 15.00
158 Hakim Warrick AU RC 8.00 20.00
159 Deron Williams AU RC 20.00 50.00
160 Sean May AU RC 6.00 15.00
161 Monta Ellis AU RC 15.00 40.00

2005-06 Bowman Chrome Refractors

Randomly seeded in packs, this 161-card set parallels the Bowman Chrome set enahnced with the rainbow holofoil refractor effect and sequential numbering to 300 for cards 1-151 and sequential numbered to 50 for autographed cards 152-161.

*1-110: 1.5X TO 4X BASE HI
*111-151: 1X TO 2.5X BASE HI
*152-161: 1X TO 2.5X BASE HI

2005-06 Bowman Chrome Refractors Gold

Randomly seeded in packs, this 161-card set parallels the Bowman Chrome set enahnced with gold borders and the rainbow holofoil refractor effect and sequential numbering to 50 for cards 1-151 and sequential numbered to five for autographed cards 152-161.

*1-110 GOLD: 3X TO 8X BASE HI
*111-146 GOLD: 2X TO 5X BASE HI
23 LeBron James 30.00 80.00
69 Kobe Bryant 40.00 100.00
90 Dwyane Wade 20.00 50.00
111 Chris Paul 125.00 225.00

2005-06 Bowman Chrome X-Fractors

Randomly seeded in packs, this 161-card set parallels the Bowman Chrome set enahnced with the rainbow holofoil refractor effect and a checkered pattern background ,sequential numbering to 150 for cards 1-151 and sequential numbered to 25 for autographed cards 152-161.

*1-110: 2X TO 5X BASE HI
*111-146: 1.25X TO 3X BASE HI
*152-161 AU: 1.5X TO 4X BASE HI
23 LeBron James 20.00 50.00
69 Kobe Bryant 20.00 50.00

2006-07 Bowman Chrome

Packaged together with Bowman, Bowman Chrome features a 165-card set, showcasing veteran players on card numbers 1-110, NCAA coaches on card numbers 111-115, rookies on cards 116-125, and autograph sticker rookies on cards 126-165. All cards feature chromium foil card stock, black borders, and red color accents on veteran player cards and blue color accents on rookie player cards. Released late November 2006 under the product name of Bowman Rookies and Stars, boxes contain 18 packs where each pack has four Bowman cards, two Bowman Chrome cards and carried an original suggested retail price of $4.00 per pack.

COMP.SET w/o SP's (115) 35.00 70.00
116-125 RC APPROXIMATE ODDS 1:9
126-165 AU RC GROUP A ODDS 1:140
126-165 AU RC GROUP B ODDS 1:34
126-165 AU RC GROUP C ODDS 1:63
UNPRICED SUPERFR.PRINT RUN ONE SET
1 Gilbert Arenas .60 1.50
2 Delonte West .50 1.25
3 Gerald Wallace .60 1.50
4 Ike Diogu .40 1.00
5 Mike Miller .60 1.50
6 Kobe Bryant 3.00 8.00
7 Richard Hamilton .50 1.25
8 Vince Carter .75 2.00
9 Elton Brand .60 1.50
10 Boris Diaw .50 1.25
11 Carmelo Anthony .75 2.00
12 Jermaine O'Neal .60 1.50
13 Al Harrington .50 1.25
14 Dwight Howard 1.00 2.50
15 Chris Bosh .60 1.50
16 Ben Gordon .60 1.50
17 Josh Howard .50 1.25
18 Yao Ming .75 2.00
19 David West .60 1.50
20 Tim Duncan 1.00 2.50
21 Andre Iguodala .60 1.50
22 LeBron James 3.00 8.00
23 Channing Frye .50 1.25
24 Antoine Walker .50 1.25
25 Ricky Davis .50 1.25
26 Lamar Odom .60 1.50
27 Amare Stoudemire .60 1.50
28 Mike Bibby .60 1.50
29 Allen Iverson .75 2.00
30 Marvin Williams .60 1.50
31 Wally Szczerbiak .50 1.25
32 Ben Wallace .60 1.50
33 Nenad Krstic .40 1.00
34 Deron Williams 1.00 2.50
35 Troy Murphy .40 1.00
36 Raymond Felton .75 2.00
37 Jason Terry .50 1.25
38 Zach Randolph .50 1.25
39 Pau Gasol .60 1.50
40 Larry Hughes .50 1.25
41 Luol Deng .60 1.50
42 Steve Francis .60 1.50
43 Chauncey Billups .60 1.50
44 Smush Parker .40 1.00
45 Shareef Abdur-Rahim .50 1.25
46 Andrei Kirilenko .50 1.25
47 Shawn Marion .60 1.50
48 Darko Milicic .40 1.00
49 Shaquille O'Neal 1.25 3.00
50 Kevin Garnett 1.25 3.00
51 Michael Finley .60 1.50
52 Peja Stojakovic .60 1.50
53 Michael Redd .60 1.50
54 Desmond Mason .40 1.00
55 Luke Ridnour .50 1.25
56 Kenyon Martin .60 1.50
57 Morris Peterson .40 1.00
58 Chris Kaman .50 1.25
59 Jason Richardson .60 1.50
60 Jason Kidd 1.00 2.50
61 Carlos Boozer .60 1.50
62 Rashad McCants .40 1.00
63 Nate Robinson .60 1.50
64 Devin Harris .60 1.50
65 Andrew Bogut .60 1.50
66 Chris Duhon .40 1.00
67 Drew Gooden .50 1.25
68 Manu Ginobili .60 1.50
69 Jameer Nelson .50 1.25
70 Corey Maggette .50 1.25
71 Charlie Villanueva .60 1.50
72 Shane Battier .50 1.25
73 Udonis Haslem .50 1.25
74 Tracy McGrady .75 2.00
75 Bobby Simmons .40 1.00
76 Baron Davis .60 1.50
77 Zydrunas Ilgauskas .50 1.25
78 Danny Granger .60 1.50
79 Hakim Warrick .50 1.25
80 Josh Smith .60 1.50
81 Tayshaun Prince .60 1.50
82 Rashard Lewis .60 1.50
83 Luther Head .50 1.25
84 Andre Miller .50 1.25
85 T.J. Ford .50 1.25
86 Sebastian Telfair .40 1.00
87 Dirk Nowitzki 1.00 2.50
88 Kwame Brown .40 1.00
89 Antawn Jamison .60 1.50
90 Ron Artest .60 1.50
91 Mehmet Okur .40 1.00
92 Emeka Okafor .60 1.50
93 Sam Cassell .60 1.50
94 Chris Paul 1.25 3.00
95 Chris Webber .60 1.50
96 Richard Jefferson .60 1.50
97 Dwyane Wade 1.50 4.00
98 Tony Parker .60 1.50
99 Paul Pierce .75 2.00
100 Marcus Camby .50 1.25
101 Ray Allen .60 1.50
102 Stephon Marbury .50 1.25
103 Rasheed Wallace .60 1.50
104 Brad Miller .60 1.50
105 Kirk Hinrich .60 1.50
106 Steve Nash .75 2.00
107 Sarunas Jasikevicius .50 1.25
108 Darius Miles .40 1.00
109 Joe Johnson .60 1.50
110 Caron Butler .60 1.50
111 John Wooden CO 2.50 6.00
112 Ben Howland CO 2.00 5.00
113 Jim Calhoun CO 2.00 5.00
114 Jim Boeheim CO 2.00 5.00
115 Roy Williams CO 2.00 5.00
116 LaMarcus Aldridge RC 5.00 12.00
117 Marcus Vinicius RC 2.00 5.00
118 Sergio Rodriguez RC 2.00 5.00
119 Will Blalock RC 2.00 5.00
120 Paul Millsap RC 3.00 8.00
121 Leon Powe RC 2.00 5.00
122 Rudy Gay RC 3.00 8.00
123 Tyrus Thomas RC 2.50 6.00
124 Brandon Roy RC 5.00 12.00
125 J.R. Pinnock RC 2.00 5.00
126 Kevin Pittsnogle B AU RC 5.00 12.00
127 Mile Ilic C AU RC 5.00 12.00
128 Mardy Collins B AU RC 5.00 12.00
129 Craig Smith C AU RC 5.00 12.00
130 Jordan Farmar B AU RC 5.00 12.00
131 Quincy Douby B AU RC 5.00 12.00
132 James Augustine B AU RC 5.00 12.00
133 Josh Boone B AU RC 5.00 12.00
134 Shannon Brown B AU RC 8.00 20.00
135 David Noel B AU RC 5.00 12.00
136 Kyle Lowry B AU RC 6.00 15.00
137 Ryan Hollins C AU RC 5.00 12.00
138 Renaldo Balkman B AU RC 5.00 12.00
139 James White C AU RC 5.00 12.00
140 Damir Markota C AU RC 5.00 12.00
141 Paul Davis B AU RC 5.00 12.00
142 Alexander Johnson C AU RC 5.00 12.00
143 Steve Novak B AU RC 5.00 12.00
144 P.J. Tucker B AU RC 5.00 12.00
145 Saer Sene B AU RC 5.00 12.00
146 Bobby Jones B AU RC 5.00 12.00
147 Cedric Simmons B AU RC 5.00 12.00
148 Allan Ray C AU RC 5.00 12.00
149 Solomon Jones B AU RC 5.00 12.00
150 Ronnie Brewer A AU RC 6.00 15.00
151 Thabo Sefolosha B AU RC 6.00 15.00
152 Maurice Ager B AU RC 5.00 12.00
153 Daniel Gibson C AU RC 6.00 15.00
154 Shawne Williams B AU RC 5.00 12.00
155 Dee Brown B AU RC 5.00 12.00
156 Andrea Bargnani A AU RC 8.00 20.00
157 Patrick O'Bryant A AU RC 5.00 12.00
158 Shelden Williams A AU RC 5.00 12.00
159 Hilton Armstrong A AU RC 5.00 12.00
160 Adam Morrison A AU RC 6.00 15.00
161 Rodney Carney B AU RC 5.00 12.00
162 Randy Foye A AU RC 6.00 15.00
163 Rajon Rondo B AU RC 30.00 60.00
164 Marcus Williams A AU RC 5.00 12.00
165 J.J. Redick A AU RC 6.00 15.00

2006-07 Bowman Chrome Refractors

*1-115 REFRACTORS: 1X TO 2.5X BASE HI
*116-125 RC's: .75X TO 2X BASE HI
*126-165 RC's: .4X TO .8X BASE HI
REF.PRINT RUN 249 SER.#'d SETS
126-165 REF.RC's NOT AUTOGRAPHED

2006-07 Bowman Chrome Refractors Gold

*1-115 REF.GOLD: 3X TO 8X BASE HI
*116-125 REF.GOLD: 2.5X TO 6X BASE HI
*125-165 REF.GOLD: 1.25X TO 3X BASE HI
REF.GOLD PRINT RUN 50 SER.#'d SETS
136 Kyle Lowry AU 30.00 80.00
165 J.J. Redick AU 25.00 60.00

2006-07 Bowman Chrome X-Fractors

*1-115 X-FRACTORS: 1.5X TO 4X BASE HI
*116-125 RC's: 1.25X TO 3X BASE HI
*126-165 RC's: .5X TO 1.25X BASE HI
X-FRAC PRINT RUN 150 SER.#'d SETS
126-165 RC's NOT AUTOGRAPHED
22 LeBron James 15.00 40.00

2007-08 Bowman Chrome

This 160-card set was released in November, 2007. The set which has the same checklist as the basic Bowman set also is broken down into veterans (1-110) and rookies (111-160). The Rookie Cards were issued to a stated print run of 2999 serial numbered sets as well.

COMP.SET w/o SP's (110) 20.00 50.00
UNPRICED SUPERFRACT. PRINT RUN ONE SET
UNPRICED PRESS PLATE PRINT RUN ONE SET
1 Gilbert Arenas .60 1.50
2 Dwight Howard 1.00 2.50
3 Dwyane Wade 1.50 4.00
4 Chris Bosh .60 1.50
5 Josh Smith .60 1.50
6 Andrew Bogut .60 1.50
7 Ben Gordon .60 1.50
8 Deron Williams 1.00 2.50
9 Tony Parker .60 1.50
10 Mike Bibby .60 1.50
11 Yao Ming .75 2.00
12 Raymond Felton .75 2.00
13 Steve Nash .75 2.00
14 Jameer Nelson .50 1.25
15 Carmelo Anthony .75 2.00
16 Pau Gasol .60 1.50
17 Rashard Lewis .50 1.25
18 Eddy Curry .40 1.00
19 Luol Deng .60 1.50
20 Kevin Garnett 1.25 3.00
21 Tim Duncan 1.00 2.50
22 Michael Redd .60 1.50
23 LeBron James 3.00 8.00
24 Kobe Bryant 3.00 8.00
25 Al Jefferson .60 1.50
26 Mike Dunleavy .50 1.25
27 Tyson Chandler .50 1.25
28 Zach Randolph .50 1.25
29 Jason Richardson .60 1.50
30 Rasheed Wallace .60 1.50
31 Shawn Marion .60 1.50
32 Shaquille O'Neal 1.25 3.00
33 Allen Iverson .75 2.00
34 Paul Pierce .75 2.00
35 Adam Morrison .60 1.50
36 Mike Miller .60 1.50
37 Larry Hughes .50 1.25
38 Kevin Martin .60 1.50
39 Charlie Villanueva .60 1.50
40 Vince Carter .75 2.00
41 Dirk Nowitzki .75 2.00
42 Elton Brand .60 1.50
43 Ray Allen .60 1.50
44 Luke Walton .40 1.00
45 Chris Paul 1.25 3.00
46 Marcus Camby .40 1.00
47 Andrei Kirilenko .50 1.25
48 J.J. Redick .60 1.50
49 Richard Hamilton .50 1.25
50 Emeka Okafor .60 1.50
51 Manu Ginobili .60 1.50
52 Monta Ellis .60 1.50
53 Jorge Garbajosa .50 1.25
54 Kyle Korver .50 1.25
55 Jason Kidd .60 1.50
56 Randy Foye .60 1.50
57 Shane Battier .50 1.25
58 Shaun Livingston .40 1.00
59 Jason Terry .50 1.25
60 Joe Johnson .60 1.50
61 Lamar Odom .60 1.50
62 Tayshaun Prince .60 1.50
63 Chris Wilcox .40 1.00
64 Leandro Barbosa .50 1.25
65 Al Harrington .50 1.25
66 Jamal Crawford .50 1.25
67 Caron Butler .60 1.50
68 Chauncey Billups .60 1.50
69 Ricky Davis .50 1.25
70 Andrea Bargnani .75 2.00
71 Samuel Dalembert .40 1.00
72 LaMarcus Aldridge .75 2.00
73 Mehmet Okur .40 1.00
74 Marcus Williams .40 1.00
75 Andre Miller .50 1.25
76 Rudy Gay .60 1.50
77 Jermaine O'Neal .60 1.50
78 Boris Diaw .50 1.25
79 Ryan Gomes .40 1.00
80 Gerald Wallace .60 1.50
81 Udonis Haslem .50 1.25
82 Mo Williams .50 1.25
83 Jarrett Jack .50 1.25
84 Chris Webber .60 1.50
85 Trevor Ariza .40 1.00
86 Kirk Hinrich .60 1.50
87 Rafer Alston .40 1.00
88 Danny Granger .60 1.50
89 David West .60 1.50
90 Drew Gooden .50 1.25
91 Stephon Marbury .50 1.25
92 Antawn Jamison .60 1.50
93 Ron Artest .60 1.50
94 Richard Jefferson .60 1.50
95 Carlos Boozer .60 1.50
96 Hakim Warrick .50 1.25
97 T.J. Ford .50 1.25
98 Desmond Mason .40 1.00
99 Andre Iguodala .60 1.50
100 Amare Stoudemire .60 1.50
101 Tracy McGrady .60 1.50
102 Jason Kapono .40 1.00
103 Ben Wallace .60 1.50
104 Marvin Williams .60 1.50
105 Baron Davis .60 1.50
106 Andrew Bynum .75 2.00
107 Brandon Roy .75 2.00
108 David Lee .50 1.25
109 Corey Maggette .50 1.25
110 Josh Howard .50 1.25
111 Kevin Durant RC 25.00 60.00
112 Al Horford RC 3.00 8.00
113 Mike Conley Jr. RC 4.00 10.00
114 Jeff Green RC 3.00 8.00
115 Corey Brewer RC 3.00 8.00
116 Joakim Noah RC 6.00 15.00
117 Julian Wright RC 2.50 6.00
118 Ramon Sessions RC 4.00 10.00
119 Sammy Mejia RC 2.50 6.00
120 Luis Scola RC 4.00 10.00
121 Yi Jianlian RC 4.00 10.00
122 Arron Afflalo RC 3.00 8.00
123 Carl Landry RC 2.50 6.00
124 Alando Tucker RC 2.50 6.00
125 Gabe Pruitt RC 2.50 6.00
126 Marcus Williams RC 2.50 6.00
127 Spencer Hawes RC 2.50 6.00
128 Acie Law RC 2.50 6.00
129 Thaddeus Young RC 3.00 8.00
130 Nick Fazekas RC 2.50 6.00
131 Al Thornton RC 2.50 6.00
132 Rodney Stuckey RC 4.00 10.00
133 Nick Young RC 4.00 10.00
134 Glen Davis RC 4.00 10.00
135 Jermareo Davidson RC 2.50 6.00
136 JamesOn Curry RC 2.50 6.00
137 Jason Smith RC 2.50 6.00
138 Daequan Cook RC 2.50 6.00
139 Jared Dudley RC 2.50 6.00
140 Derrick Byars RC 2.50 6.00
141 Josh McRoberts RC 2.50 6.00
142 Adam Haluska RC 2.50 6.00
143 Reyshawn Terry RC 2.50 6.00
144 Aaron Gray AU RC 2.50 6.00
145 Herbert Hill RC 2.50 6.00
146 Jared Jordan RC 2.50 6.00
147 Wilson Chandler RC 4.00 10.00
148 Morris Almond RC 2.50 6.00
149 Aaron Brooks RC 2.50 6.00
150 Petteri Koponen RC 2.50 6.00
151 Dominic McGuire RC 2.50 6.00
152 Greg Oden RC 3.00 8.00
153 Stephane Lasme RC 2.50 6.00
154 D.J. Strawberry RC 2.50 6.00
155 Sean Williams RC 2.50 6.00
156 Marco Belinelli RC 2.50 6.00
157 Javaris Crittenton RC 2.50 6.00
158 Demetris Nichols RC 2.50 6.00
159 Taurean Green RC 2.50 6.00
160 Brandan Wright RC 2.50 6.00

2007-08 Bowman Chrome Refractors

*REFRACTORS: .6X TO 1.5X BASE HI
PRINT RUN 299 SER.#'d SETS
111 Kevin Durant 80.00 160.00

2007-08 Bowman Chrome Refractors Black

*BLACK 1-110: .75X TO 2X BASE HI
*BLACK 111-160: .75X TO 2X BASE HI
BLACK PRINT RUN 199 SER.#'d SETS
23 LeBron James 8.00 20.00
24 Kobe Bryant 8.00 20.00
111 Kevin Durant 125.00 200.00

2007-08 Bowman Chrome Refractors Gold

*GOLD 1-110: 1.5X TO 4X BASE HI
*GOLD 111-160: 1.5X TO 3X BASE HI
GOLD PRINT RUN 99 SER.#'d SETS
3 Dwyane Wade 8.00 20.00
23 LeBron James 25.00 60.00
24 Kobe Bryant 25.00 60.00
111 Kevin Durant 200.00 400.00

2007-08 Bowman Chrome X-Fractors

*X-FRAC 1-110: 1.5X TO 4X BASE HI
*X-FRAC 111-160: 1.5X TO 4X BASE HI
X-FRAC PRINT RUN 50 SER.#'d SETS
111 Kevin Durant 300.00 600.00

2007-08 Bowman Chrome Refractors Rookie Autographs

PRINT RUN 599 SER.#'d SETS
UNLESS LISTED IN CHECKLIST
*BLACK: .5X TO 1.25X BASE HI
BLACK PRINT RUN 99 SER.#'d SETS
*GOLD: .75X TO 2X BASE HI
GOLD PRINT RUN 50 SER.#'d SETS
UNPRICED SUPER PRINT RUN ONE SET
UNPRICED X-FRAC PRINT RUN 10 SETS
EXCH EXPIRATION 10/31/09
121 Yi Jianlian AU 8.00 20.00
122 Arron Afflalo AU 6.00 15.00
123 Carl Landry AU 5.00 12.00
124 Alando Tucker AU/479 5.00 12.00
125 Gabe Pruitt AU 5.00 12.00
126 Marcus Williams AU/479 5.00 12.00
127 Spencer Hawes AU/479 5.00 12.00
128 Acie Law AU/479 5.00 12.00
129 Thaddeus Young AU 6.00 15.00
130 Nick Fazekas AU 5.00 12.00
131 Al Thornton AU/479 5.00 12.00
132 Rodney Stuckey AU 8.00 20.00
133 Nick Young AU/479 8.00 20.00
134 Glen Davis AU 8.00 20.00
135 Jermareo Davidson AU 5.00 12.00
136 JamesOn Curry AU 5.00 12.00
137 Jason Smith AU 5.00 12.00
138 Daequan Cook AU 5.00 12.00
139 Jared Dudley AU 5.00 12.00
140 Derrick Byars AU 5.00 12.00
141 Josh McRoberts AU 5.00 12.00
142 Adam Haluska AU 5.00 12.00
143 Reyshawn Terry AU 5.00 12.00
144 Aaron Gray AU 5.00 12.00
145 Herbert Hill AU 5.00 12.00
146 Jared Jordan AU 5.00 12.00
147 Wilson Chandler AU 8.00 20.00
148 Morris Almond AU 5.00 12.00
149 Aaron Brooks AU 5.00 12.00
150 Petteri Koponen AU 5.00 12.00
151 Dominic McGuire AU 5.00 12.00
152 Greg Oden AU/479 10.00 25.00
153 Stephane Lasme AU 5.00 12.00
154 D.J. Strawberry AU 5.00 12.00
155 Sean Williams AU 5.00 12.00
156 Marco Belinelli AU 5.00 12.00
157 Javaris Crittenton AU/479 5.00 12.00
158 Demetris Nichols AU 5.00 12.00
159 Taurean Green AU 5.00 12.00
160 Brandan Wright AU/479 5.00 12.00

2008-09 Bowman Chrome

This set was released on October 29, 2008. The base set consists of 183 cards. Cards 1-110 feature veterans, and cards 111-150 are rookies. Cards 151-183 are autographed cards of most of the rookies.

COMP.SET w/o RC (110) 20.00 40.00
UNPRICED PRESS PLATE PRINT RUN ONE SET
UNPRICED RED PRINT RUN 5 SETS
UNPRICED SUPERFR.PRINT RUN ONE SET
1 Tracy McGrady .60 1.50
2 Jason Kidd .60 1.50
3 LeBron James 3.00 8.00
4 Chris Bosh .60 1.50
5 Kevin Garnett 1.25 3.00
6 Josh Smith .60 1.50
7 Richard Hamilton .50 1.25
8 Monta Ellis .60 1.50
9 Yi Jianlian .60 1.50
10 Danny Granger .60 1.50
11 Richard Jefferson .60 1.50
12 Elton Brand .60 1.50
13 Rudy Gay .60 1.50
14 Andres Nocioni .40 1.00
15 Carmelo Anthony .75 2.00
16 Pau Gasol .60 1.50
17 Corey Brewer .50 1.25
18 Hedo Turkoglu .60 1.50
19 Andre Iguodala .60 1.50
20 Raymond Felton .50 1.25
21 Tim Duncan 1.00 2.50
22 Michael Redd .60 1.50
23 Chris Paul 1.00 2.50
24 Kobe Bryant 3.00 8.00
25 Brandon Roy .60 1.50
26 Carlos Boozer .60 1.50
27 Jeff Green .50 1.25
28 Luis Scola .50 1.25
29 Al Thornton .50 1.25
30 Gilbert Arenas .60 1.50
31 Brandan Wright .50 1.25
32 Shaquille O'Neal 1.25 3.00
33 Allen Iverson .75 2.00
34 Paul Pierce .75 2.00
35 Ben Gordon .60 1.50
36 Jamal Crawford .50 1.25
37 Andrew Bynum .75 2.00
38 Gerald Wallace .60 1.50
39 Mike Conley Jr. .50 1.25
40 Ben Wallace .60 1.50
41 Dirk Nowitzki .75 2.00
42 David Lee .50 1.25
43 Mo Williams .50 1.25
44 Al Jefferson .60 1.50
45 Tayshaun Prince .60 1.50
46 Jameer Nelson .50 1.25
47 Andrei Kirilenko .50 1.25
48 David West .60 1.50
49 Al Horford .60 1.50
50 Steve Nash .60 1.50
51 Ron Artest .60 1.50
52 Greg Oden .60 1.50
53 Sean Williams .50 1.25
54 Jamario Moon .40 1.00
55 Baron Davis .60 1.50
56 Udonis Haslem .50 1.25
57 Mike Dunleavy .50 1.25
58 Shane Battier .50 1.25
59 Andrew Bogut .60 1.50
60 Ray Allen .60 1.50
61 Nick Young .50 1.25
62 Manu Ginobili .60 1.50
63 Jason Richardson .60 1.50
64 Mike Miller .60 1.50
65 Leandro Barbosa .50 1.25
66 Luol Deng .60 1.50
67 Shawn Marion .60 1.50
68 Peja Stojakovic .60 1.50
69 Kevin Durant 2.50 6.00
70 Corey Maggette .50 1.25
71 Chauncey Billups .60 1.50
72 Josh Howard .50 1.25
73 Kevin Martin .60 1.50
74 Anderson Varejao .50 1.25
75 Craig Smith .40 1.00
76 Antawn Jamison .60 1.50
77 Marcus Camby .40 1.00
78 Andre Miller .50 1.25
79 Zach Randolph .50 1.25
80 Deron Williams .60 1.50
81 Devin Harris .60 1.50
82 Rashard Lewis .50 1.25
83 Damien Wilkins .40 1.00
84 LaMarcus Aldridge .60 1.50
85 Larry Hughes .50 1.25
86 Brad Miller .50 1.25
87 Jermaine O'Neal .60 1.50
88 Caron Butler .60 1.50
89 Tyson Chandler .50 1.25
90 Joe Johnson .60 1.50
91 Amare Stoudemire .60 1.50
92 Dwight Howard 1.25 3.00
93 Rajon Rondo .75 2.00
94 T.J. Ford .40 1.00
95 Rodney Stuckey .75 2.00
96 Samuel Dalembert .40 1.00
97 Tony Parker .60 1.50
98 Vince Carter .75 2.00
99 Yao Ming .75 2.00
100 Dwyane Wade 1.25 3.00
101 Dominique Wilkins .75 2.00
102 Rick Barry .60 1.50
103 John Stockton 1.00 2.50
104 Magic Johnson 1.50 4.00
105 George Gervin .75 2.00
106 Bill Russell 1.00 2.50
107 David Robinson 1.00 2.50
108 Dennis Rodman 1.00 2.50
109 Larry Bird 2.00 5.00
110 Jerry West .75 2.00
111 Derrick Rose RC 20.00 50.00
112 Michael Beasley RC 2.50 6.00
113 O.J. Mayo RC 2.50 6.00
114 Russell Westbrook RC 8.00 20.00
115 Kevin Love RC 6.00 15.00
116 Danilo Gallinari RC 2.50 6.00
117 Eric Gordon RC 4.00 10.00
118 Joe Alexander RC 1.50 4.00
119 D.J. Augustin RC 1.50 4.00
120 Brook Lopez RC 2.50 6.00
121 Jerryd Bayless RC 1.50 4.00
122 Jason Thompson RC 1.50 4.00
123 Anthony Randolph RC 2.00 5.00
124 Robin Lopez RC 1.50 4.00
125 Marreese Speights RC 1.50 4.00
126 Roy Hibbert RC 2.50 6.00
127 JaVale McGee RC 2.50 6.00
128 J.J. Hickson RC 2.00 5.00
129 Alexis Ajinca RC 1.50 4.00
130 Ryan Anderson RC 2.50 6.00
131 Courtney Lee RC 2.50 6.00
132 Kosta Koufos RC 1.50 4.00
133 Donte Greene RC 1.50 4.00
134 George Hill RC 2.50 6.00
135 D.J. White RC 1.50 4.00
136 J.R. Giddens RC 1.50 4.00
137 Joey Dorsey RC 1.50 4.00
138 Mario Chalmers RC 2.50 6.00
139 DeAndre Jordan RC 3.00 8.00
140 Chris Douglas-Roberts RC 1.50 4.00
141 Malik Hairston RC 1.50 4.00
142 Sean Singletary RC 1.50 4.00
143 Kyle Weaver RC 1.50 4.00
144 Patrick Ewing Jr. RC 1.50 4.00
145 Walter Sharpe RC 1.50 4.00
146 Sonny Weems RC 1.50 4.00
147 Shan Foster RC 1.50 4.00
148 Nicolas Batum RC 2.50 6.00
149 Brandon Rush RC 1.50 4.00
150 Darrell Arthur RC 1.50 4.00
151 Derrick Rose AU A 300.00 500.00
152 Michael Beasley AU A 15.00 40.00
153 O.J. Mayo AU A 15.00 40.00
154 Russell Westbrook AU A 50.00 120.00
155 Kevin Love AU A 50.00 120.00
156 Danilo Gallinari AU A 10.00 25.00
157 Eric Gordon AU A 20.00 50.00
158 Joe Alexander AU A 5.00 12.00
159 D.J. Augustin AU B 5.00 12.00
160 Brook Lopez AU A 8.00 20.00
161 Jerryd Bayless AU A 5.00 12.00
162 Jason Thompson AU B 5.00 12.00
163 Anthony Randolph AU B 6.00 15.00
164 Robin Lopez AU B 5.00 12.00
165 Marreese Speights AU B 5.00 12.00
166 Roy Hibbert AU B 8.00 20.00
167 J.J. Hickson AU B 6.00 15.00
168 Ryan Anderson AU B 8.00 20.00
169 Courtney Lee AU B 8.00 20.00
170 Kosta Koufos AU B 5.00 12.00
171 George Hill AU B 8.00 20.00
172 D.J. White AU B 5.00 12.00
173 J.R. Giddens AU B 5.00 12.00
174 Joey Dorsey AU B 5.00 12.00
175 Mario Chalmers AU B 8.00 20.00
176 DeAndre Jordan AU B 12.00 30.00
177 Chris Douglas-Roberts AU B 5.00 12.00
178 JaVale McGee AU B 8.00 20.00
179 Kyle Weaver AU B 5.00 12.00
180 Patrick Ewing Jr. AU B 5.00 12.00
181 Sonny Weems AU B 5.00 12.00
182 Brandon Rush AU B 5.00 12.00
183 Darrell Arthur AU B 5.00 12.00

2008-09 Bowman Chrome Refractors

*1-110 REF: .6X TO 1.5X BASE HI
*101-150 REF: 75X TO 2X BASE HI
1-150 PRINT RUN 499 SER.#'d SETS
*151-183 AU.REF: .75X TO 2X BASE HI
151-183 AU PRINT RUN 50 SETS
3 LeBron James 10.00 25.00
24 Kobe Bryant 10.00 25.00
69 Kevin Durant 6.00 15.00
111 Derrick Rose 50.00 120.00
114 Russell Westbrook 20.00 50.00
115 Kevin Love 15.00 40.00
151 Derrick Rose AU 400.00 800.00
154 Russell Westbrook AU 125.00 300.00
155 Kevin Love AU 125.00 300.00

2008-09 Bowman Chrome Refractors Blue

*1-110 REF.BLUE: 2.5X TO 6X BASE HI
*111-150 REF.BLUE: 2X TO 5X BASE
PRINT RUN 99 SER.#'d SETS
100 Dwyane Wade 10.00 25.00
111 Derrick Rose 175.00 350.00

2008-09 Bowman Chrome Refractors Gold

*1-110 REF.GOLD: 4X TO 10X BASE
1-110 PRINT RUN 25 SER.#'d SETS
*111-150 REF.GOLD: 3X TO 8X BASE
111-150 PRINT RUN 50 SER.#'d SETS
*151-183 REF.GOLD: 1.5X TO 4X BASE
151-183 PRINT RUN 25 SER.#'d SETS
3 LeBron James 40.00 100.00
24 Kobe Bryant 50.00 125.00
114 Russell Westbrook 75.00 200.00
115 Kevin Love 75.00 150.00
152 Michael Beasley AU 75.00 200.00
153 O.J. Mayo AU 75.00 200.00
154 Russell Westbrook AU 300.00 600.00
155 Kevin Love AU 300.00 550.00
157 Eric Gordon AU 150.00 300.00

2008-09 Bowman Chrome X-Fractors

*X-FRACTORS 1-110: 1X TO 2.5X BASE HI
*X-FRACTORS 111-150: 1.25X TO 3X BASE HI
STATED PRINT RUN 299 SER.#'d SETS
3 LeBron James 12.00 30.00
24 Kobe Bryant 12.00 30.00
69 Kevin Durant 10.00 25.00
114 Russell Westbrook 30.00 80.00
115 Kevin Love 25.00 60.00

2006-07 Bowman Elevation

Bowman Elevation contains more insert and parallel sets of any product in the history of basketball cards--144 unique inserts and parallels were originally inserted. The base set features all-foil card stock, veteran players on cards 1-90 and rookies on cards 91-130 sequentially numbered to 999. Released in August 2006, Elevation boxes contained 16 packs of five cards each and carried an original suggested retail price of $10.00 per pack.

COMP.SET w/o SP's (90) 25.00 60.00
UNPRICED ONE OF ONE PARALLELS EXIST
1 Dwyane Wade 1.50 4.00
2 Elton Brand .60 1.50
3 Dwight Howard 1.00 2.50
4 Chris Bosh .60 1.50
5 Baron Davis .60 1.50
6 Marcus Camby .50 1.25
7 Rashard Lewis .60 1.50
8 Paul Pierce .75 2.00
9 Jermaine O'Neal .60 1.50
10 Gilbert Arenas .60 1.50
11 Larry Hughes .50 1.25
12 Manu Ginobili .60 1.50
13 Lamar Odom .60 1.50
14 Ron Artest .60 1.50
15 Carmelo Anthony .75 2.00
16 Deron Williams 1.00 2.50
17 Gerald Wallace .60 1.50
18 Peja Stojakovic .60 1.50
19 Vince Carter .75 2.00
20 Kevin Garnett 1.25 3.00
21 Yao Ming .75 2.00
22 Josh Howard .50 1.25
23 Michael Redd .60 1.50
24 Eddy Curry .50 1.25
25 Shawn Marion .60 1.50
26 Luol Deng .60 1.50
27 Ben Wallace .60 1.50
28 Sam Cassell .60 1.50
29 Steve Francis .60 1.50
30 Ray Allen .60 1.50
31 Andre Iguodala .60 1.50
32 Shaquille O'Neal 1.25 3.00
33 Pau Gasol .60 1.50
34 Jason Richardson .60 1.50
35 Ricky Davis .50 1.25
36 Joe Johnson .60 1.50
37 Dirk Nowitzki 1.00 2.50
38 Richard Hamilton .50 1.25
39 Troy Murphy .40 1.00
40 Charlie Villanueva .60 1.50
41 T.J. Ford .50 1.25
42 Zydrunas Ilgauskas .50 1.25
43 Andrei Kirilenko .50 1.25
44 Chris Paul 1.25 3.00
45 Grant Hill .75 2.00
46 Kobe Bryant 3.00 8.00
47 Tim Duncan 1.00 2.50
48 Raymond Felton .75 2.00
49 Antawn Jamison .60 1.50
50 Jason Kidd 1.00 2.50
51 Shareef Abdur-Rahim .50 1.25
52 Shane Battier .50 1.25
53 Kirk Hinrich .60 1.50
54 Jason Terry .50 1.25
55 Mehmet Okur .40 1.00
56 Stephon Marbury .50 1.25
57 Steve Nash .75 2.00
58 Mike Bibby .60 1.50
59 Sebastian Telfair .40 1.00
60 Richard Jefferson .60 1.50
61 Andre Miller .50 1.25
62 Delonte West .50 1.25
63 Tracy McGrady .75 2.00
64 Rasheed Wallace .60 1.50
65 Al Harrington .50 1.25
66 Emeka Okafor .60 1.50
67 Caron Butler .60 1.50
68 Andrew Bogut .60 1.50
69 Tony Parker .60 1.50
70 Zach Randolph .50 1.25
71 Allen Iverson .75 2.00
72 David West .60 1.50
73 Chris Webber .60 1.50
74 Ben Gordon .60 1.50
75 Corey Maggette .50 1.25
76 Sarunas Jasikevicius .50 1.25
77 Chauncey Billups .60 1.50
78 Amare Stoudemire .60 1.50
79 Luke Ridnour .50 1.25
80 LeBron James 3.00 8.00
81 Kenyon Martin .60 1.50
82 Marko Jaric .40 1.00
83 Antoine Walker .50 1.25
84 J.R. Smith .60 1.50
85 Mike Miller .60 1.50
86 Channing Frye .50 1.25
87 Smush Parker .40 1.00
88 Wally Szczerbiak .50 1.25
89 Morris Peterson .40 1.00
90 Luther Head .50 1.25
91 Randy Foye RC 2.50 6.00
92 Daniel Gibson RC 2.50 6.00
93 Hassan Adams RC 2.00 5.00
94 Hilton Armstrong RC 2.00 5.00
95 Marcus Williams RC 2.00 5.00
96 Paul Davis RC 2.00 5.00
97 Quincy Douby RC 2.00 5.00
98 Ronnie Brewer RC 2.50 6.00
99 Rodney Carney RC 2.00 5.00
100 Rudy Gay RC 3.00 8.00
101 Adam Morrison RC 2.50 6.00
102 Rajon Rondo RC 8.00 20.00
103 Steve Novak RC 2.00 5.00
104 Craig Smith RC 2.00 5.00
105 Leon Powe RC 2.00 5.00
106 James White RC 2.00 5.00
107 Josh Boone RC 2.00 5.00
108 J.J. Redick RC 2.50 6.00
109 Shelden Williams RC 2.00 5.00
110 Alexander Johnson RC 2.00 5.00
111 Guillermo Diaz RC 2.00 5.00
112 Maurice Ager RC 2.00 5.00
113 Jordan Farmar RC 2.00 5.00
114 Mardy Collins RC 2.00 5.00
115 Ryan Hollins RC 2.00 5.00
116 Kyle Lowry RC 2.50 6.00
117 James Augustine RC 2.00 5.00
118 Shawne Williams RC 2.00 5.00
119 LaMarcus Aldridge RC 5.00 12.00
120 Patrick O'Bryant RC 2.00 5.00
121 Cedric Simmons RC 2.00 5.00
122 P.J. Tucker RC 2.00 5.00
123 Brandon Roy RC 5.00 12.00
124 Tyrus Thomas RC 2.50 6.00
125 Andrea Bargnani RC 3.00 8.00
126 Dee Brown RC 2.00 5.00
127 Denham Brown RC 2.00 5.00
128 Saer Sene RC 2.00 5.00
129 Thabo Sefolosha RC 2.50 6.00
130 Shannon Brown RC 3.00 8.00

2006-07 Bowman Elevation Blue

*1-90 BLUE: .6X TO 1.5X BASE HI
*91-130 BLUE RC's SAME VALUE AS BASE
BLUE PRINT RUN 399 SER.#'d SETS

2006-07 Bowman Elevation Gold

*1-90 GOLD: 1X TO 2.5X BASE HI
*91-130 GOLD RC's: .6X TO 1.5X BASE HI
GOLD PRINT RUN 99 SER.#'d SETS

2006-07 Bowman Elevation Red

*1-90 RED: .75X TO 2X BASE HI
*91-130 RED RC's: .5X TO 1.25X BASE HI
PRINT RUN 299 SER.#'d SETS

2006-07 Bowman Elevation Board of Directors Relics

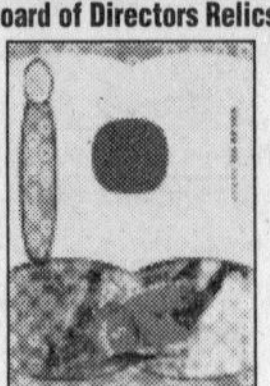

PRINT RUN 99 SER.#'d SETS
*RELICS BLUE SAME VALUE AS BASE
BLUE PRINT RUN 79 SER.#'d SETS
*RELICS GOLD: .75X TO 2X RELIC HI
GOLD PRINT RUN 25 SER.#'d SETS
*RELICS RED: .5X TO 1.25X RELIC HI
RED PRINT RUN 49 SER.#'d SETS
*RELICS DUAL: .5X TO 1.25 RELIC HI
DUAL PRINT RUN 99 SER.#'d SETS
*REL.DUAL BLUE: .5X TO 1.25X RELIC HI
DUAL BLUE PRINT RUN 79 SER.#'d SETS
*REL.DUAL GOLD: .75X TO 2X RELIC HI
DUAL GOLD PRINT RUN 25 SER.#'d SETS
*REL.DUAL RED: .6X TO 1.5X BASE HI
DUAL RED PRINT RUN 49 SER.#'d SETS
ONE OF ONES EXIST FOR RELICS AND DUAL
*PATCHES: 1.25X TO 3X RELIC HI
PATCH PRINT RUN 10 SER.#'d SETS
UNPRICED PATCH BLUE PRINT RUN 5 SETS
UNPRICED PATCH GOLD PRINT RUN 2 SETS
UNPRICED PATCH RED PRINT RUN 3 SETS
UNPRICED PATCH DUAL PRINT RUN 5 SETS
UNPRICED PATCH DUAL BLUE PRINT RUN 4 SETS
UNPRICED PATCH DUAL GOLD PRINT RUN 2 SETS
UNPRICED PATCH DUAL RED PRINT RUN 3 SETS
PATCH DUAL ONE OF ONE's EXIST
UNPRICED PATCH TRIPLE PRINT RUN 5 SETS
UNPRICED PATCH TRIP.BLUE PRINT RUN 4 SETS
UNPRICED PATCH TRIP.GOLD PRINT RUN 2 SETS
UNPRICED PATCH TRIP.RED PRINT RUN 3 SETS
PATCH TRIPLE ONE OF ONE'S EXIST
RAI Allen Iverson 4.00 10.00
RAM Andre Miller 2.50 6.00
RBB Brent Barry 2.00 5.00
RBM Brad Miller 3.00 8.00
RCB Chauncey Billups 3.00 8.00
RCM Corey Maggette 2.50 6.00
RDW David West 3.00 8.00
RGA Gilbert Arenas 3.00 8.00
RJK Jason Kidd 5.00 12.00
RJR Jason Richardson 3.00 8.00
RJS Josh Smith 3.00 8.00
RJT Jamaal Tinsley 2.00 5.00
RJW Jason Williams 2.50 6.00
RKH Kirk Hinrich 3.00 8.00
RLO Lamar Odom 3.00 8.00
RLR Luke Ridnour 2.50 6.00
RMG Manu Ginobili 3.00 8.00
RPG Pau Gasol 3.00 8.00
RPP Paul Pierce 4.00 10.00
RSM Sean May 2.00 5.00
RSO Shaquille O'Neal 6.00 15.00
RTM Tracy McGrady 4.00 10.00
RTP Tony Parker 3.00 8.00
RDWA Dwyane Wade 6.00 15.00
RDWE Delonte West 2.50 6.00
RSMA Stephon Marbury 2.50 6.00
RTJF T.J. Ford 2.50 6.00
RTPR Tayshaun Prince 3.00 8.00

2006-07 Bowman Elevation Board of Directors Relics Autographs

PRINT RUN 25 SER.#'d SETS
RTP Tony Parker 20.00 50.00
RDWA Dwyane Wade 75.00 150.00
RDWE Delonte West 12.50 30.00

2006-07 Bowman Elevation Board of Directors Relics Autographs Blue

PRINT RUN 19 SER.#'d SETS
UNPRICED RED PRINT RUN 9 SETS
UNPRICED GOLD PRINT RUN 5 SETS
ONE OF ONE'S EXIST
RLR Luke Ridnour 10.00 25.00
RSO Shaquille O'Neal 60.00 120.00
RTP Tony Parker 20.00 50.00
RDWE Delonte West 12.50 30.00

2006-07 Bowman Elevation Board of Directors Relics Dual Autographs

PRINT RUN 15 SER.#'d SETS
UNPRICED BLUE PRINT RUN 10 SETS
UNPRICED GOLD PRINT RUN 3 SETS
UNPRICED RED PRINT RUN 5 SETS
ONE OF ONE's EXIST
RAI Allen Iverson 75.00 150.00
RLR Luke Ridnour 10.00 25.00
RDWA Dwyane Wade 100.00 200.00
RDWE Delonte West 15.00 40.00
RTJF T.J. Ford 10.00 25.00

2006-07 Bowman Elevation Executive Level Relics

PRINT RUN 99 SER.#'d SETS
*RELICS BLUE SAME VALUE AS BASE
BLUE PRINT RUN 79 SER.#'d SETS
*RELICS GOLD: .75X TO 2X RELIC HI
GOLD PRINT RUN 25 SER.#'d SETS
*RELICS RED: .5X TO 1.25X RELIC HI
RED PRINT RUN 49 SER.#'d SETS
*RELICS DUAL: .5X TO 1.25 RELIC HI
DUAL PRINT RUN 99 SER.#'d SETS
*REL.DUAL BLUE: .5X TO 1.25X RELIC HI
DUAL BLUE PRINT RUN 79 SER.#'d SETS
*REL.DUAL GOLD: .75X TO 2X RELIC HI
DUAL GOLD PRINT RUN 25 SER.#'d SETS
*REL.DUAL RED: .6X TO 1.5X BASE HI
DUAL RED PRINT RUN 49 SER.#'d SETS
ONE OF ONES EXIST FOR RELICS AND DUAL
*PATCHES: 1.25X TO 3X RELIC HI
PATCH PRINT RUN 10 SER.#'d SETS
UNPRICED PATCH BLUE PRINT RUN 5 SETS
UNPRICED PATCH GOLD PRINT RUN 2 SETS
UNPRICED PATCH RED PRINT RUN 3 SETS
UNPRICED PATCH DUAL PRINT RUN 5 SETS
UNPRICED PATCH DUAL BLUE PRINT RUN 4 SETS
UNPRICED PATCH DUAL GOLD PRINT RUN 2 SETS
UNPRICED PATCH DUAL RED PRINT RUN 3 SETS
PATCH DUAL ONE OF ONE's EXIST
UNPRICED PATCH TRIP.PRINT RUN 5 SETS
UNPRICED PATCH TRIP.BLUE PRINT RUN 4 SETS
UNPRICED PATCH TRIP.GOLD PRINT RUN 2 SETS
UNPRICED PATCH TRIP.RED PRINT RUN 3 SETS
PAT.TRIPLE ONE OF ONE'S EXIST
RAB Andrew Bogut 3.00 8.00
RAI Allen Iverson 4.00 10.00
RAK Andrei Kirilenko 2.50 6.00
RBD Baron Davis 3.00 8.00
RBG Ben Gordon 3.00 8.00
RCA Carmelo Anthony 4.00 10.00
RCB Chris Bosh 3.00 8.00
RCP Chris Paul 6.00 15.00
RCV Charlie Villanueva 3.00 8.00
RDN Dirk Nowitzki 5.00 12.00
RDW Dwyane Wade 6.00 15.00
REB Elton Brand 3.00 8.00
REO Emeka Okafor 3.00 8.00
RJO Jermaine O'Neal 3.00 8.00
RKB Kobe Bryant 8.00 20.00
RKG Kevin Garnett 6.00 15.00
RLO Lamar Odom 3.00 8.00
RMB Mike Bibby 3.00 8.00
RNR Nate Robinson 3.00 8.00
RPG Pau Gasol 3.00 8.00
RPP Paul Pierce 4.00 10.00
RRA Ray Allen 3.00 8.00
RRH Richard Hamilton 2.50 6.00
RSB Shane Battier 2.50 6.00
RSM Sean May 2.00 5.00
RSN Steve Nash 4.00 10.00
RSO Shaquille O'Neal 6.00 15.00
RST Sebastian Telfair 2.00 5.00
RTD Tim Duncan 5.00 12.00
RVC Vince Carter 4.00 10.00
RYM Yao Ming 4.00 10.00
RRHO Robert Horry 2.50 6.00

2006-07 Bowman Elevation Executive Level Relics Autographs

RCV Charlie Villanueva 10.00 25.00
RDW Dwyane Wade 75.00 150.00
REO Emeka Okafor 10.00 25.00
RJO Jermaine O'Neal 10.00 25.00
RRH Richard Hamilton 10.00 25.00

2006-07 Bowman Elevation Executive Level Relics Autographs Blue

PRINT RUN 19 SER.#'d SETS
UNPRICED RED PRINT RUN 9 SETS
UNPRICED GOLD PRINT RUN 5 SETS
ONE OF ONE'S EXIST
RCV Charlie Villanueva 10.00 25.00
RDW Dwyane Wade 60.00 150.00
REO Emeka Okafor 10.00 25.00
RJO Jermaine O'Neal 10.00 25.00
RRH Richard Hamilton 10.00 25.00
RVC Vince Carter 25.00 50.00

2006-07 Bowman Elevation Executive Level Relics Dual Autographs

PRINT RUN 15 SER.#'d SETS
UNPRICED BLUE PRINT RUN 10 SER.#'d SETS
UNPRICED GOLD PRINT RUN 3 SER.#'d SETS
UNPRICED RED PRINT RUN 5 SER.#'d SETS
ONE OF ONE's EXIST
RDW Dwyane Wade 100.00 200.00
RVC Vince Carter 30.00 60.00

2006-07 Bowman Elevation Power Brokers Relics

PRINT RUN 99 SER.#'d SETS
*RELICS BLUE SAME VALUE AS BASE
BLUE PRINT RUN 79 SER.#'d SETS
*RELICS GOLD: .75X TO 2X RELIC HI
GOLD PRINT RUN 25 SER.#'d SETS
*RELICS RED: .5X TO 1.25X RELIC HI
RED PRINT RUN 49 SER.#'d SETS
*RELICS DUAL: .5X TO 1.25 RELIC HI
DUAL PRINT RUN 99 SER.#'d SETS
*REL.DUAL BLUE: .5X TO 1.25X RELIC HI
DUAL BLUE PRINT RUN 79 SER.#'d SETS
*REL.DUAL GOLD: .75X TO 2X RELIC HI
DUAL GOLD PRINT RUN 25 SER.#'d SETS
*REL.DUAL RED: .6X TO 1.5X BASE HI
DUAL RED PRINT RUN 49 SER.#'d SETS
ONE OF ONES EXIST FOR RELICS AND DUAL
*PATCHES: 1.25X TO 3X RELIC HI
PATCH PRINT RUN 10 SER.#'d SETS
UNPRICED PATCH BLUE PRINT RUN 5 SETS
UNPRICED PATCH GOLD PRINT RUN 2 SETS
UNPRICED PATCH RED PRINT RUN 3 SETS
UNPRICED PATCH DUAL PRINT RUN 5 SETS
UNPRICED PATCH DUAL BLUE PRINT RUN 4 SETS
UNPRICED PATCH DUAL GOLD PRINT RUN 2 SETS
UNPRICED PATCH DUAL RED PRINT RUN 3 SETS
PATCH DUAL ONE OF ONE's EXIST
UNPRICED PATCH TRIP.PRINT RUN 5 SETS
UNPRICED PATCH TRIP.BLUE PRINT RUN 4 SETS
UNPRICED PATCH TRIP.GOLD PRINT RUN 2 SETS
UNPRICED PATCH TRIP.RED PRINT RUN 3 SETS
PAT.TRIPLE ONE OF ONE'S EXIST
RAB Andrew Bogut 3.00 8.00
RAI Allen Iverson 4.00 10.00
RAJ Antawn Jamison 3.00 8.00
RBB Bruce Bowen 2.00 5.00
RBW Ben Wallace 3.00 8.00
RCB Chris Bosh 3.00 8.00
RCF Channing Frye 2.50 6.00
RCK Chris Kaman 2.50 6.00
RCV Charlie Villanueva 3.00 8.00
RCW Chris Webber 3.00 8.00
RDH Dwight Howard 5.00 12.00
RDW Dwyane Wade 6.00 15.00
REB Elton Brand 3.00 8.00
REO Emeka Okafor 3.00 8.00
RHW Hakim Warrick 2.50 6.00
RID Ike Diogu 2.00 5.00
RJO Jermaine O'Neal 3.00 8.00
RKB Kobe Bryant 8.00 20.00
RKG Kevin Garnett 6.00 15.00
RKM Kenyon Martin 3.00 8.00
RLD Luol Deng 3.00 8.00
RMC Marcus Camby 2.50 6.00
RRJ Richard Jefferson 3.00 8.00
RRL Rashard Lewis 3.00 8.00
RRW Rasheed Wallace 3.00 8.00
RSD Samuel Dalembert 2.00 5.00
RSM Shawn Marion 3.00 8.00
RSO Shaquille O'Neal 6.00 15.00
RTC Tyson Chandler 2.50 6.00
RTD Tim Duncan 5.00 12.00
RTP Tayshaun Prince 3.00 8.00
RYM Yao Ming 4.00 10.00
RAIG Andre Iguodala 3.00 8.00
RSAR Shareef Abdur-Rahim 2.50 6.00

2006-07 Bowman Elevation Power Brokers Relics Autographs

PRINT RUN 25 SER.#'d SETS
*BLUE: 4X TO 1X BASE HI
BLUE PRINT RUN 19 SER.#'d SETS
UNPRICED GOLD PRINT RUN 5 SETS
UNPRICED RED PRINT RUN 9 SETS
RAI Allen Iverson 75.00 150.00
RCB Chris Bosh 20.00 50.00
RCV Charlie Villanueva 10.00 25.00
RDW Dwyane Wade 75.00 150.00
REO Emeka Okafor 10.00 25.00
RHW Hakim Warrick 10.00 25.00
RLD Luol Deng 10.00 25.00

2006-07 Bowman Elevation Power Brokers Relics Dual Autographs

STATED PRINT RUN 15 SER.#'d SETS
UNPRICED BLUE PRINT RUN 10 SETS
UNPRICED GOLD PRINT RUN 3 SETS
UNPRICED RED PRINT RUN 5 SETS
ONE OF ONE'S EXIST
RAI Allen Iverson 75.00 150.00
RCB Chris Bosh 20.00 50.00
RCV Charlie Villanueva 10.00 25.00
RDW Dwyane Wade 75.00 150.00
RHW Hakim Warrick 10.00 25.00
RSO Shaquille O'Neal 75.00 150.00

2006-07 Bowman Elevation Rookie Writing Autographs

APPROXIMATE ODDS ONE PER BOX
AJ Alexander Johnson 3.00 8.00
AM Adam Morrison 4.00 10.00
AR Allan Ray 3.00 8.00
BJ Bobby Jones 3.00 8.00
CS Craig Smith 3.00 8.00
DB Denham Brown 3.00 8.00
DG Daniel Gibson 4.00 10.00
DN David Noel 3.00 8.00
GD Guillermo Diaz 3.00 8.00
HA Hassan Adams 3.00 8.00
JA James Augustine 3.00 8.00
JB Josh Boone 3.00 8.00
JF Jordan Farmar 3.00 8.00
KL Kyle Lowry 4.00 10.00
MA Maurice Ager 3.00 8.00
MC Mardy Collins 3.00 8.00
MW Marcus Williams 3.00 8.00
PD Paul Davis 3.00 8.00
QD Quincy Douby 3.00 8.00
RB Ronnie Brewer 4.00 10.00
RC Rodney Carney 3.00 8.00
RF Randy Foye 4.00 10.00
RH Ryan Hollins 3.00 8.00
RR Rajon Rondo 15.00 40.00
SJ Solomon Jones 3.00 8.00
SN Steve Novak 3.00 8.00
SW Shelden Williams 3.00 8.00
ABA Andrea Bargnani 6.00 15.00
CSI Cedric Simmons 3.00 8.00
DBR Dee Brown 3.00 8.00
HAR Hilton Armstrong 3.00 8.00
JJR J.J. Redick 4.00 10.00
PJT P.J. Tucker 3.00 8.00
POB Patrick O'Bryant 3.00 8.00
RBA Renaldo Balkman 3.00 8.00

2006-07 Bowman Elevation Rookie Writing Autographs Blue

*BLUE: .5X TO 1.25X HI COLUMN
STATED PRINT RUN 79 TO 139 SETS

2006-07 Bowman Elevation Rookie Writing Autographs Red

*RED: .6X TO 1.5X HI COLUMN
STATED PRINT RUN 59 TO 99 SETS

2006-07 Bowman Elevation Rookie Writing Autographs Gold

*GOLD: .75X TO 2X HI COLUMN
STATED PRINT RUN 29 TO 79 SETS
AM Adam Morrison/29 20.00 50.00
RR Rajon Rondo/39 50.00 100.00
JJR J.J. Redick/29 25.00 60.00

2007-08 Bowman Elevati

Released in April 2008, Bowman Elevation boa 100-card set where cards 1-100 picture both v and retired NBA players and cards 51-100 feat rookie players sequentially numbered to 999. than an all-foil card design that had been used previous years, 2007-08 Bowman Elevation fe cardboard stock with foil highlights incorporat the design. Elevation is packaged in 12-pack b five cards each and carried an intial suggested price of $9.75 per pack.

COMPLETE SET (100) 25.00
UNPRICED BLACK PRINT RUN ONE SET
UNPRICED GOLD PRINT RUN ONE SET
UNPRICED PLATE PRINT RUN ONE SET
1 Tracy McGrady .40
2 Shaquille O'Neal .75
3 Allen Iverson .50
4 Chris Bosh .40
5 Jason Kidd .40
6 Elton Brand .40
7 Brandon Roy .50
8 Tony Parker .40
9 Luol Deng .40
10 Gilbert Arenas .40
11 Amare Stoudemire .40
12 Dwight Howard .60
13 Deron Williams .60
14 Dirk Nowitzki .50
15 Vince Carter .50
16 Richard Hamilton .30
17 Baron Davis .40
18 Pau Gasol .40
19 Kevin Garnett .75
20 LeBron James 2.00
21 Tim Duncan .60
22 Steve Nash .50
23 Jason Richardson .40
24 Kobe Bryant 2.00
25 Josh Smith .40
26 Eddy Curry .25
27 Mike Bibby .40
28 Ray Allen .40
29 Andre Iguodala .40
30 Chris Paul .75
31 Yao Ming .50
32 Shawn Marion .40
33 Dwyane Wade 1.00
34 Paul Pierce .50
35 Carmelo Anthony .50
36 Jermaine O'Neal .40
37 Michael Redd .40
38 Gerald Wallace .40
39 Ben Gordon .40
40 Carlos Boozer .40
41 Larry Bird 2.00
42 Bill Walton .60
43 Kareem Abdul-Jabbar 1.00
44 John Havlicek .60
45 David Robinson 1.00
46 Bill Russell 1.00
47 Isiah Thomas .60
48 John Stockton 1.00
49 Dominique Wilkins .75
50 Magic Johnson 1.50
51 Nick Young RC 2.50
52 Greg Oden RC 2.00
53 Julian Wright RC 1.50
54 Dominic Mcguire RC 1.50
55 Acie Law RC 1.50
56 Luis Scola RC 2.50
57 Thaddeus Young RC 2.00
58 Rodney Stuckey RC 2.50
59 Jermareo Davidson RC 1.50
60 Daequan Cook RC 1.50
61 Josh McRoberts RC 1.50
62 Aaron Gray RC 1.50
63 Wilson Chandler RC 2.50
64 Chris Richard RC 1.50
65 Stephane Lasme RC 1.50
66 Kyrylo Fesenko RC 1.50
67 Taurean Green RC 1.50
68 Al Thornton RC 1.50
69 Corey Brewer RC \ 2.00
70 Ramon Sessions RC 2.50
71 Kevin Durant RC 12.00
72 Alando Tucker RC 1.50
73 Spencer Hawes RC 1.50
74 Nick Fazekas RC 1.50
75 Yi Jianlian RC 2.50
76 Juan Carlos Navarro RC 1.50
77 Jared Dudley RC 1.50
78 Adam Haluska RC 1.50
79 Herbert Hill RC 1.50
80 Kosta Perovic RC 1.50
81 JamesOn Curry RC 1.50
82 D.J. Strawberry RC 1.50
83 Javaris Crittenton RC 1.50
84 Al Horford RC 2.00
85 Mike Conley Jr. RC 2.50
86 Joakim Noah RC 4.00
87 Marco Belinelli RC 1.50
88 Arron Afflalo RC 2.00
89 Gabe Pruitt RC 1.50
90 Carl Landry RC 1.50
91 Jeff Green RC 2.00
92 Glen Davis RC 2.50
93 Jason Smith RC 1.50
94 Morris Almond RC 1.50
95 Cheik Samb RC 1.50
96 Brandon Wallace RC 1.50
97 Aaron Brooks RC 1.50
98 Brandan Wright RC 1.50
99 Sean Williams RC 1.50
100 Coby Karl RC 1.50

2007-08 Bowman Elevatio

*1-50 BLUE: 1X TO 2.5X BASE HI
*51-100 BLUE RCs: .5X TO 1.25X BASE HI
PRINT RUN 99 SER.#'d SETS
71 Kevin Durant 50.00

2007-08 Bowman Eleva Green

*1-40 GREEN: 4X TO 10X BASE HI
*41-50 GREEN: 3X TO 8X BASE HI

0 GREEN RCs: 1X TO 2.5X BASE HI
PRINT RUN 19 SER.#'d SETS
n Durant 200.00 400.00

7-08 Bowman Elevation Red

RED: 1.25X TO 3X BASE HI
) RED RCs: .6X TO 1.5X BASE HI
RUN 49 SER.#'d SETS

007-08 Bowman Elevation Autographs Patches

RUN 15 SER.#'d SETS
CED BLACK PRINT RUN ONE SET
CED BLUE PRINT RUN NINE SETS
CED GOLD PRINT RUN THREE SETS
CED GREEN PRINT RUN FIVE SETS
CED RED PRINT RUN SEVEN SETS
e Iguodala 15.00 30.00
on Davis 15.00 30.00
Gordon 8.00 20.00
Russell 100.00 200.00
melo Anthony 25.00 60.00
os Boozer 8.00 20.00
ris Bosh 20.00 40.00
rey Maggette 8.00 20.00
d Lee 8.00 20.00
id Robinson 50.00 100.00
wane Wade 50.00 120.00
ron Williams 20.00 40.00
ominique Wilkins 25.00 50.00
ald Wallace 15.00 30.00
Thomas 15.00 30.00
n Howard 8.00 20.00
n Stockton 60.00 150.00
Pierce 15.00 30.00
Barry 20.00 40.00
quille O'Neal 50.00 100.00

007-08 Bowman Elevation Relics

RUN 179 SER.#'d SETS
ED BLACK PRINT RUN ONE SET
.5X TO 1.25X BASE HI
RINT RUN 79 SER.#'d SETS
.75X TO 2X BASE HI
RINT RUN 19 SER.#'d SETS
: .6X TO 1.5X BASE HI
PRINT RUN 29 SER.#'d SETS
X TO 1.25X BASE HI
NT RUN 49 SER.#'d SETS
.5X TO 1.25X BASE HI
RINT RUN 79 SER.#'d SETS
ED DUAL BLACK PRINT RUN ONE SET
BLUE: .5X TO 1.25X BASE HI
LUE PRINT RUN 49 SER.#'d SETS
ED DUAL GOLD PRINT RUN 9 SETS
GREEN: .75X TO 2X BASE HI
REEN PRINT RUN 19 SER.#'d SETS
RED: .6X TO 1.5X BASE HI
ED PRINT RUN 29 SER.#'d SETS
: .6X TO 1.5X BASE HI
PRINT RUN 39 SER.#'d SETS
ED TRIP.BLACK PRINT RUN ONE SET
.UE: .6X TO 1.5X BASE HI
JE PRINT RUN 29 SER.#'d SETS
ED TRIP.GOLD PRINT RUN 5 SETS
ED TRIP.GREEN PRINT RUN 9 SETS
D: .75X TO 2X BASE HI
) PRINT RUN 19 SER.#'d SETS
ES: 1.25X TO 3X BASE HI
PRINT RUN 29 SER.#'d SETS
ED PATCH BLACK PRINT RUN ONE SET
UE: 1.5X TO 4X BASE HI
JE PRINT RUN 19 SER.#'d SETS
ED PAT.GOLD PRINT RUN 3 SETS
ED PAT.GREEN PRINT RUN 5 SETS
ED PAT.RED PRINT RUN 9 SETS
ED PAT.DUAL PRINT RUN 9 SETS
ED PAT.DUAL BLACK PRINT RUN ONE SET
ED PAT.DUAL BLUE PRINT RUN 5 SETS
ED PAT.DUAL GOLD PRINT RUN 2 SETS
ED PAT.DUAL GREEN PRINT RUN 3 SETS
ED PAT.DUAL RED PRINT RUN 4 SETS
ED PAT.TRIPLE PRINT RUN 9 SETS
ED PAT.TRIP.BLACK PRINT RUN ONE SET
ED PAT.TRIP.BLUE PRINT RUN 5 SETS
ED PAT.TRIP.GOLD PRINT RUN 2 SETS
ED PAT.TRIP.GREEN PRINT RUN 3 SETS
ED PAT.TRIP.RED PRINT RUN 4 SETS
ea Bargnani 4.00 10.00
Iguodala 3.00 8.00
ferson 3.00 8.00
awn Jamison 3.00 8.00
e Stoudemire 3.00 8.00
n Davis 3.00 8.00
ndon Roy 4.00 10.00
Wallace 3.00 8.00
uncey Billups 3.00 8.00
is Bosh 3.00 8.00
y Maggette 2.50 6.00
Paul 6.00 15.00
ht Howard 5.00 12.00
Lee 2.50 6.00
Nowitzki 4.00 10.00
d Robinson 5.00 12.00
ane Wade 6.00 15.00
on Williams 5.00 12.00
minique Wilkins 4.00 10.00
Brand 3.00 8.00
rt Arenas 3.00 8.00
Thomas 3.00 8.00
aine O'Neal 3.00 8.00
Richardson 3.00 8.00
Smith 3.00 8.00
Stockton 5.00 12.00
Bryant 8.00 20.00
Garnett 5.00 12.00
Bird 8.00 20.00
Deng 3.00 8.00
r Odom 3.00 8.00
c Johnson 6.00 15.00
ael Redd 3.00 8.00
Maravich 15.00 30.00

PP Paul Pierce 4.00 10.00
RA Ray Allen 3.00 8.00
RH Richard Hamilton 2.50 6.00
RL Rashard Lewis 2.50 6.00
SM Stephon Marbury 2.50 6.00
SN Steve Nash 4.00 10.00
SO Shaquille O'Neal 6.00 15.00
TD Tim Duncan 5.00 12.00
TM Tracy McGrady 3.00 8.00
TT Tyrus Thomas 3.00 8.00
YM Yao Ming 4.00 10.00

2007-08 Bowman Elevation Rookie Relics

PRINT RUN 199 SER.#'d SETS
*RELICS 99: SAME VALUE AS BASE
*RELICS 69: .5X TO 1.25X BASE
*RELICS 49: .5X TO 1.25X BASE
*RELICS 29: .6X TO 1.5X BASE
RELICS 1 UNPRICED DUE TO SCARCITY
*DUAL 99: .5X TO 1.25X BASE
*DUAL 79: .5X TO 1.25X BASE
*DUAL 29: .6X TO 1.5X BASE
*DUAL 19: .75X TO 2X BASE
DUAL 9 UNPRICED DUE TO SCARCITY
DUAL 1 UNPRICED DUE TO SCARCITY
*TRIPLE 49: .6X TO 1.5X BASE
*TRIPLE 39: .6X TO 1.5X BASE
*TRIPLE 29: .75X TO 2X BASE
*TRIPLE 19: 1X TO 2.5X BASE
TRIPLE 9 UNPRICED DUE TO SCARCITY
TRIPLE 1 UNPRICED DUE TO SCARCITY
AA Arron Afflalo 3.00 8.00
AB Aaron Brooks 2.50 6.00
AH Al Horford 3.00 8.00
AHA Adam Haluska 2.50 6.00
AL4 Acie Law 2.50 6.00
AT Al Thornton 2.50 6.00
ATU Alando Tucker 2.50 6.00
BW Brandan Wright 2.50 6.00
CB Corey Brewer 3.00 8.00
CL Carl Landry 2.50 6.00
CR Chris Richard 2.50 6.00
DC Daequan Cook 2.50 6.00
DJS D.J. Strawberry 2.50 6.00
DM Dominic McGuire 2.50 6.00
GD Glen Davis 4.00 10.00
GO Greg Oden 3.00 8.00
GP Gabe Pruitt 2.50 6.00
HH Herbert Hill 2.50 6.00
JC Javaris Crittenton 2.50 6.00
JD Jared Dudley 2.50 6.00
JDA Jermareo Davidson 2.50 6.00
JG Jeff Green 3.00 8.00
JN Joakim Noah 6.00 15.00
JS Jason Smith 2.50 6.00
JW Julian Wright 2.50 6.00
MA Morris Almond 2.50 6.00
MC Mike Conley Jr. 4.00 10.00
NF Nick Fazekas 2.50 6.00
NY Nick Young 4.00 10.00
RS Rodney Stuckey 4.00 10.00
SH Spencer Hawes 2.50 6.00
SW Sean Williams 2.50 6.00
TG Taurean Green 2.50 6.00
TY Thaddeus Young 3.00 8.00
WC Wilson Chandler 4.00 10.00

2007-08 Bowman Elevation Rookie Writings

STATED PRINT RUN 49 TO 299 SER.#'d SETS
UNPRICED BLACK PRINT RUN ONE SET
*BLUE: .5X TO 1.25X BASE
BLUE PRINT RUN 29 SER.#'d SETS
UNPRICED GOLD PRINT RUN NINE SETS
*GREEN: .6X TO 1.5X BASE
GREEN PRINT RUN 15 SER.#'d SETS
*RED: .6X TO 1.5X BASE
RED PRINT RUN 19 SER.#'d SETS
RWAA Arron Afflalo/299 5.00 12.00
RWAB Aaron Brooks/299 4.00 10.00
RWAG Aaron Gray/299 4.00 10.00
RWAH Adam Haluska/299 4.00 10.00
RWAL4 Acie Law/199 4.00 10.00
RWAT Al Thornton/199 4.00 10.00
RWCL Carl Landry/299 4.00 10.00
RWDJS D.J. Strawberry/299 4.00 10.00
RWGO Greg Oden/49 15.00 40.00
RWHH Herbert Hill/299 4.00 10.00
RWJC Javaris Crittenton/299 4.00 10.00
RWJD Jermareo Davidson/299 4.00 10.00
RWJS Jason Smith/199 4.00 10.00
RWMA Morris Almond/299 4.00 10.00
RWMB Marco Belinelli/299 4.00 10.00
RWNF Nick Fazekas/299 4.00 10.00
RWNY Nick Young/49 8.00 20.00
RWRS Rodney Stuckey/299 6.00 15.00
RWSW Sean Williams/299 4.00 10.00
RWTY Thaddeus Young/49 12.00 30.00
RWWC Wilson Chandler/199 6.00 15.00
RWYJ Yi Jianlian/49 12.00 30.00

2007-08 Bowman Elevation Rookie Writings Relics

STATED PRINT RUN 29 TO 169 SER.#'d SETS
UNPRICED BLACK PRINT RUN ONE SET
*BLUE: .5X TO 1.25X BASE HI
BLUE PRINT RUN 19 SER.#'d SETS
UNPRICED GOLD PRINT RUN FIVE SETS
UNPRICED GREEN PRINT RUN NINE SETS
*RED: .6X TO 1.5X BASE HI
RED PRINT RUN 15 SER.#'d SETS
RWAA Arron Afflalo/169 6.00 15.00
RWAB Aaron Brooks/169 5.00 12.00
RWAG Aaron Gray/169 5.00 12.00
RWAH Adam Haluska/169 5.00 12.00
RWAL4 Acie Law/79 5.00 12.00
RWAT Al Thornton/79 5.00 12.00
RWCL Carl Landry/169 5.00 12.00
RWDJS D.J. Strawberry/169 5.00 12.00
RWGO Greg Oden/29 30.00 80.00
RWHH Herbert Hill/169 5.00 12.00
RWJC Javaris Crittenton/169 5.00 12.00
RWJD Jermareo Davidson/169 5.00 12.00
RWJS Jason Smith/79 5.00 12.00
RWMA Morris Almond/169 5.00 12.00
RWMB Marco Belinelli/169 5.00 12.00
RWNF Nick Fazekas/169 5.00 12.00
RWNY Nick Young/29 15.00 40.00
RWRS Rodney Stuckey/169 8.00 20.00
RWSW Sean Williams/169 5.00 12.00
RWTY Thaddeus Young/29 15.00 40.00
RWWC Wilson Chandler/79 8.00 20.00
RWYJ Yi Jianlian/29 15.00 40.00

2007-08 Bowman Elevation Rookie Writings Patches

PRINT RUN 15 SER.#'d SETS
UNPRICED BLACK PRINT RUN ONE SET
UNPRICED BLUE PRINT RUN NINE SETS
UNPRICED GOLD PRINT RUN THREE SETS
UNPRICED GREEN PRINT RUN FIVE SETS
UNPRICED RED PRINT RUN SEVEN SETS
RWAA Arron Afflalo 10.00 25.00
RWAB Aaron Brooks 8.00 20.00
RWAG Aaron Gray 8.00 20.00
RWAH Adam Haluska 8.00 20.00
RWAL4 Acie Law 8.00 20.00
RWAT Al Thornton 8.00 20.00
RWCL Carl Landry 8.00 20.00
RWDJS D.J. Strawberry 8.00 20.00
RWGO Greg Oden 60.00 150.00
RWHH Herbert Hill 8.00 20.00
RWJC Javaris Crittenton 8.00 20.00
RWJD Jermareo Davidson 8.00 20.00
RWJS Jason Smith 8.00 20.00
RWMA Morris Almond 8.00 20.00
RWMB Marco Belinelli 8.00 20.00
RWNF Nick Fazekas 8.00 20.00
RWNY Nick Young 25.00 60.00
RWRS Rodney Stuckey 12.00 30.00
RWSW Sean Williams 8.00 20.00
RWTY Thaddeus Young 25.00 60.00
RWWC Wilson Chandler 12.00 30.00
RWYJ Yi Jianlian 30.00 80.00

2002-03 Bowman Signature Edition

Released in January 2003, Bowman Signature Edition boasts a 100-card set and is numbered to coincide with the featured player's initials. 45 rookie players were issued, numbered to 999, where all cards are autographed with some also containing jersey swatches-all of these cards were issued in uncirculated card holders with an irridescent tamper sticker along the top of the holder. Jay Williams is the only RC in the set who does not have an autographed card and his card is sequentially numbered to 1249. Signature Edition was packaged in six card packs, all containing one rookie autograph, with boxes of six packs each and a suggested retail price of $35 per pack.
SEAI Allen Iverson 1.25 3.00
SEAJ Antawn Jamison .75 2.00
SEAK Andrei Kirilenko .75 2.00
SEAM Alonzo Mourning 1.00 2.50
SEAS Amare Stoudemire JSY AU RC20.00 50.00
SEAW Antoine Walker .60 1.50
SEAKM Antonio McDyess .60 1.50
SEALM Andre Miller .60 1.50
SEBD Baron Davis .75 2.00
SEBN Bostjan Nachbar AU RC 4.00 10.00
SEBW Ben Wallace .75 2.00
SECB Curtis Borchardt AU RC 4.00 10.00
SECM Cuttino Mobley .60 1.50
SECO Chris Owens AU RC 4.00 10.00
SECT Cezary Trybanski AU RC 4.00 10.00
SECW Chris Wilcox JSY AU RC 4.00 10.00
SECBO Carlos Boozer JSY AU RC 8.00 20.00
SECBU Caron Butler JSY AU RC 6.00 15.00
SECJA Casey Jacobsen JSY AU RC 4.00 10.00
SECJE Chris Jefferies JSY AU RC 4.00 10.00
SEDD Dan Dickau AU RC 4.00 10.00
SEDN Dirk Nowitzki 1.25 3.00
SEDW DaJuan Wagner JSY AU RC 4.00 10.00
SEDGA Dan Gadzuric JSY AU RC 4.00 10.00
SEDGO Drew Gooden JSY AU RC 6.00 15.00
SEDLM Darius Miles .50 1.25
SEEB Elton Brand .75 2.00
SEEC Eddy Curry .60 1.50
SEEG Manu Ginobili AU RC 20.00 40.00
SEEJ Eddie Jones .60 1.50
SEER Efthimios Rentzias AU RC 4.00 10.00
SEFJ Fred Jones JSY AU RC 4.00 10.00
SEFR Frank Williams AU RC 4.00 10.00
SEGG Gordan Giricek AU RC 4.00 10.00
SEGP Gary Payton .75 2.00
SEGR Glenn Robinson .60 1.50
SEJB J.R. Bremer AU RC 4.00 10.00
SEJD Juan Dixon JSY AU RC 5.00 12.00
SEJJ Jared Jeffries JSY AU RC 4.00 10.00
SEJK Jason Kidd 1.25 3.00
SEJM Jamal Mashburn .60 1.50
SEJO Jermaine O'Neal .75 2.00
SEJP Jannero Pargo AU RC 4.00 10.00
SEJS John Salmons JSY AU RC 5.00 12.00
SEJT Jamaal Tinsley .50 1.25
SEJAW Jay Williams/1249 RC 2.50 6.00
SEJDS Jerry Stackhouse .60 1.50
SEJOS John Stockton 1.00 2.50
SEJWE Jiri Welsch AU RC 4.00 10.00
SEJWI Jerome Williams .50 1.25
SEKB Kobe Bryant 4.00 10.00
SEKG Kevin Garnett 1.50 4.00
SEKM Karl Malone 1.00 2.50
SEKR Kareem Rush JSY AU RC 4.00 10.00
SEKS Kenny Satterfield .50 1.25
SEKLM Kenyon Martin .75 2.00
SELS Latrell Sprewell .60 1.50
SEMB Mike Bibby .75 2.00
SEMD Mike Dunleavy JSY AU RC 5.00 12.00
SEME Melvin Ely JSY AU RC 4.00 10.00
SEMH Marcus Haislip JSY AU RC 4.00 10.00
SEMO Mehmet Okur AU RC 4.00 10.00
SEMCW Chris Webber .75 2.00
SEMJA Marko Jaric AU 4.00 10.00
SEMJJ Michael Jordan 6.00 15.00
SENH Nene Hilario JSY AU RC 5.00 12.00
SENT Nikoloz Tskitishvili JSY AU RC 4.00 10.00
SEPG Pau Gasol 1.00 2.50
SEPP Paul Pierce 1.00 2.50
SEPS Peja Stojakovic .75 2.00
SEPSA Predrag Savovic JSY AU RC 4.00 10.00
SEQR Quentin Richardson .60 1.50
SERA Robert Archibald JSY AU RC 4.00 10.00
SERA Ray Allen .75 2.00
SERB Rasual Butler AU RC 4.00 10.00
SERJ Richard Jefferson .75 2.00
SERL Rashard Lewis .75 2.00
SERW Rasheed Wallace .75 2.00
SERCH Richard Hamilton .60 1.50
SERHU Ryan Humphrey JSY AU RC 4.00 10.00
SERMA Roger Mason JSY AU RC 4.00 10.00
SERMU Ronald Murray JSY AU RC 4.00 10.00
SESA Shareef Abdur-Rahim .60 1.50
SESC Sam Clancy JSY AU RC 4.00 10.00
SESF Steve Francis .75 2.00
SESM Stephon Marbury .60 1.50
SESN Steve Nash 1.00 2.50
SESO Shaquille O'Neal 2.00 5.00
SESCB Shane Battier .75 2.00
SESDM Shawn Marion .75 2.00
SETC Tyson Chandler .60 1.50
SETD Tim Duncan 1.50 4.00
SETP Tayshaun Prince JSY AU RC 5.00 12.00
SETP Tony Parker 1.00 2.50
SETS Tamar Slay AU RC 4.00 10.00
SETLM Tracy McGrady 1.25 3.00
SEVC Vince Carter 1.25 3.00
SEVY Vincent Yarbrough JSY AU RC 4.00 10.00
SEWS Wally Szczerbiak .60 1.50
SEYM Yao Ming AU RC 30.00 60.00

2002-03 Bowman Signature Edition Parallel

Randomly inserted in packs, this 100-card set parallels the base Bowman Signature Edition set with a foil shift from silver to gold on the player's name, and silver borders on the top and bottom of the card. Rookie players are sequentially numbered to 99 and veterans are numbered to 249. Jay Williams is numbered to 249 because he did not sign any cards for this set.
*STARS: 1X TO 2.5X BASE CARD HI
*RCs: .6X TO 1.5X BASE CARD HI
SEAS Amare Stoudemire JSY AU 50.00 120.00
SECBU Caron Butler JSY AU 15.00 40.00
SEEG Manu Ginobili AU 50.00 120.00
SEJAW Jay Williams/249 6.00 15.00
SEMJJ Michael Jordan 20.00 50.00
SEYM Yao Ming AU 60.00 120.00

2003-04 Bowman Signature Edition

Released in January 2004, this 118-card set is divided up into 55 veteran player cards (numbers 1-55), five rookie cards sequentially numbered to 1250 (numbers 56-60), 16 autographed rookie cards sequentially numbered to 1250 unless noted in the checklist (numbers 61-76), 29 autograph jersey rookie cards sequentially numbered to 1250 unless noted in the checklist (numbers 77-105) and 13 autographed rookie cards sequentially numbered to 1250 (numbers 106-118). Bowman Signature Edition was packaged in six pack boxes with packs containing six cards, one of them being an uncirculated autograph or relic card, and carried a suggested retail price of $35.
COMP.SET w/o SP's (55) 25.00 60.00
UNPRICED BLUE PRINT RUN ONE SET
1 Tracy McGrady 1.00 2.50
2 Baron Davis .75 2.00
3 Allen Iverson 1.25 3.00
4 Bonzi Wells .50 1.25
5 Tony Parker .75 2.00
6 Morris Peterson .50 1.25
7 Jerry Stackhouse .60 1.50
8 Jason Terry .60 1.50
9 Tyson Chandler .60 1.50
10 Dirk Nowitzki 1.25 3.00
11 Nene .60 1.50
12 Antawn Jamison .75 2.00
13 Richard Hamilton .60 1.50
14 Steve Francis .75 2.00
15 Jermaine O'Neal .75 2.00
16 Elton Brand .75 2.00
17 Mike Miller .75 2.00
18 Caron Butler .75 2.00
19 Gary Payton .75 2.00
20 Shaquille O'Neal 2.00 5.00
21 Kevin Garnett 1.50 4.00
22 Desmond Mason .60 1.50
23 Jamal Mashburn .60 1.50
24 Drew Gooden .60 1.50
25 Eric Snow .50 1.25
26 Shawn Marion .75 2.00
27 Peja Stojakovic .75 2.00
28 Karl Malone 1.00 2.50
29 Shareef Abdur-Rahim .60 1.50
30 Paul Pierce 1.00 2.50
31 Dajuan Wagner .50 1.25
32 Steve Nash 1.00 2.50
33 Ben Wallace .75 2.00
34 Jason Richardson .75 2.00
35 Yao Ming 1.50 4.00
36 Ron Artest .75 2.00
37 Andre Miller .60 1.50
38 Kobe Bryant 4.00 10.00
39 Pau Gasol .75 2.00
40 Tim Duncan 1.25 3.00
41 Ray Allen .75 2.00
42 Vince Carter 1.25 3.00
43 Andrei Kirilenko .75 2.00
44 Chris Webber .75 2.00
45 Rasheed Wallace .75 2.00
46 Amare Stoudemire 1.25 3.00
47 Latrell Sprewell .60 1.50
48 Kenyon Martin .75 2.00
49 Wally Szczerbiak .60 1.50
50 Jason Kidd 1.25 3.00
51 Eddie Jones .60 1.50
52 Jalen Rose .60 1.50
53 Ricky Davis .60 1.50
54 Antoine Walker .75 2.00
55 Allan Houston .60 1.50
56 LeBron James RC 25.00 60.00
57 Darko Milicic RC 2.50 6.00
58 Chris Kaman RC 3.00 8.00
59 Kyle Korver RC 3.00 8.00
60 Willie Green RC 2.50 6.00
61 James Lang AU RC 3.00 8.00
62 Carl English AU RC 3.00 8.00
63 Devin Brown AU RC 3.00 8.00
64 Theron Smith AU RC 3.00 8.00
65 Rick Rickert AU RC 3.00 8.00
66 Zarko Cabarkapa AU RC 3.00 8.00
67 Derrick Zimmerman AU RC 3.00 8.00
68 Aleksandar Pavlovic AU RC 3.00 8.00
69 Malick Badiane AU RC 3.00 8.00
70 Boris Diaw AU RC 4.00 10.00
71 Zaur Pachulia AU RC 3.00 8.00
72 Zoran Planinic AU RC 3.00 8.00
73 Carlos Delfino AU RC 4.00 10.00
74 Maciej Lampe AU RC 3.00 8.00
75 Sofoklis Schortsanitis AU RC 3.00 8.00
76 Mario Austin AU RC 3.00 8.00
77 Carmelo Anthony/1170 JSY AU RC30.00 80.00
78 Chris Bosh JSY AU RC 12.00 30.00
79 Dwyane Wade JSY AU RC 50.00 125.00
80 Kirk Hinrich JSY AU RC 6.00 15.00
81 T.J. Ford JSY AU RC 6.00 15.00
82 David West/1245 JSY AU RC 6.00 15.00
83 Marcus Banks JSY AU RC 5.00 12.00
84 Dahntay Jones JSY AU RC 5.00 12.00
85 Luke Ridnour JSY AU RC 6.00 15.00
86 Reece Gaines JSY AU RC 5.00 12.00
87 Travis Outlaw/1075 JSY AU RC 6.00 15.00
88 Brian Cook/1063 JSY AU RC 5.00 12.00
89 Troy Bell JSY AU RC 5.00 12.00
90 Ndudi Ebi JSY AU RC 5.00 12.00
91 Kendrick Perkins/1238 JSY AU RC8.00 20.00
92 Leandro Barbosa JSY AU RC 6.00 15.00
93 Josh Howard/1111 JSY AU RC 5.00 12.00
94 Slavko Vranes JSY AU RC 5.00 12.00
95 Jason Kapono JSY AU RC 5.00 12.00
96 Luke Walton JSY AU RC 5.00 12.00
97 Mo Williams/1172 JSY AU RC 8.00 20.00
98 Matt Bonner/960 JSY AU RC 6.00 15.00
99 Travis Hansen JSY AU RC 5.00 12.00
100 Steve Blake JSY AU RC 6.00 15.00
101 Keith Bogans JSY AU RC 5.00 12.00
102 Mike Sweetney JSY AU RC 5.00 12.00
103 Jarvis Hayes JSY AU RC 5.00 12.00
104 Mickael Pietrus JSY AU RC 5.00 12.00
105 Nick Collison JSY AU RC 5.00 12.00
107 James Jones AU RC 3.00 8.00
108 Brandon Hunter AU RC 3.00 8.00
109 Tommy Smith AU RC 3.00 8.00
110 Marcus Hatten AU RC 3.00 8.00
111 Koko Archibong AU RC 3.00 8.00
112 Ime Udoka AU RC 5.00 12.00
113 Eric Chenowith AU RC 3.00 8.00
114 Stephane Pelle AU RC 3.00 8.00
115 Marquis Daniels AU RC 3.00 8.00
116 Paccelis Morlende AU RC 3.00 8.00
117 George Williams AU RC 3.00 8.00
118 Udonis Haslem AU RC 4.00 10.00

2003-04 Bowman Signature Edition Foil

Randomly inserted in packs, this 118-card set parallels the base Bowman Signature Edition set enhanced with a foil treatment and sequential numbering to 125. Please note that the rookie players who appeared in the base set with jerseys and autographs do not have either in this parallel.
*FOIL 1-55 SINGLES: 1.25X TO 3X BASE HI
*FOIL 56-60 SINGLES: 1X TO 2.5X BASE HI
*FOIL 61-76 SINGLES: .75X TO 2X BASE HI
*FOIL 77-105 SINGLES: .5X TO 1.25X BASE HI
*FOIL 106-118 SINGLES: .75X TO 2X BASE HI
77 Carmelo Anthony 15.00 40.00
78 Chris Bosh 12.00 30.00
79 Dwyane Wade 25.00 60.00

2003-04 Bowman Signature Edition Gold

Randomly inserted in packs, this 118-card set parallels the base Bowman Signature Edition set enhanced with gold highlights and sequential numbering to 99.
*GOLD 1-55 SINGLES: 1.5X TO 4X BASE HI
*GOLD 56-60 SINGLES: 1.25X TO 3X BASE HI
*GOLD 61-76 SINGLES: 1X TO 2.5X BASE HI
*GOLD 77-105 SINGLES: .75X TO 2X BASE HI
*GOLD 106-118 SINGLES: 1X TO 2.5X BASE HI
79 Dwyane Wade 200.00 400.00

2003-04 Bowman Signature Edition Silver

Randomly inserted in packs, this 118-card set parallels the base Bowman Signature Edition set enhanced with silver highlights and sequential numbering to 249.
*SLVR 1-55 SINGLES: 1X TO 2.5X BASE HI
*SLVR 56-60 SINGLES: .75X TO 2X BASE HI
*SLVR 61-76 SINGLES: .6X TO 1.5X BASE HI
*SLVR 77-105 SINGLES: .5X TO 1.25X BASE HI
*SLVR 106-118 SINGLES: .6X TO 1.5X BASE HI

2004-05 Bowman Signature Edition

Issued in early November 2004, Bowman Signature Edition consists of a 102-card set divided up into 55 veteran players, two jersey rookies (numbers 56 and 57) sequentially numbered to 100, jersey and autograped rookies (numbers 58-86) sequentially numbered to 399 and autographed rookies (numbers 87-103) sequentially numbered to 399. Veteran cards have red borders, while rookie cards have blue borders, and for the ones that include jerseys and autographs, the jerseys are in the shape of a star and the autographs are on foil stickers. Signature Edition was packaged in six pack boxes of six card packs (where one of the cards was Uncirculated in a sealed holder--all the rookies with jerseys and autographs were delivered sealed) and packs carred a $35.00 SRP. Card number 101 was not issued.
COMP.SET w/o SP's (55) 25.00 60.00
UNPRICED PARALLEL PRINT RUN ONE SET
1 Kevin Garnett 1.50 4.00
2 Eddy Curry .60 1.50
3 Ben Wallace .75 2.00
4 Cuttino Mobley .60 1.50
5 Vince Carter 1.25 3.00
6 Bonzi Wells .50 1.25
7 Jermaine O'Neal .75 2.00
8 Kobe Bryant 4.00 10.00
9 Stephon Marbury .60 1.50
10 Mike Bibby .75 2.00
11 Yao Ming 1.50 4.00
12 Richard Jefferson .75 2.00
13 Steve Nash 1.00 2.50
14 Luke Ridnour .60 1.50
15 Carmelo Anthony 1.50 4.00
16 Pau Gasol .75 2.00
17 Amare Stoudemire 1.00 2.50
18 Chris Webber .75 2.00
19 Sam Cassell .60 1.50
20 Tracy McGrady 1.00 2.50
21 Tim Duncan 1.25 3.00
22 Michael Redd .75 2.00
23 LeBron James 5.00 12.00
24 Baron Davis .75 2.00
25 Zach Randolph .60 1.50
26 Peja Stojakovic .75 2.00
27 Lamar Odom .75 2.00
28 Michael Finley .75 2.00
29 Zydrunas Ilgauskas .60 1.50
30 Rasheed Wallace .75 2.00
31 Mike Sweetney .50 1.25
32 Elton Brand .75 2.00
33 Steve Francis .75 2.00
34 Paul Pierce 1.00 2.50
35 Ray Allen .75 2.00
36 Tony Parker .75 2.00
37 Gerald Wallace .75 2.00
38 Chris Bosh .75 2.00
39 Desmond Mason .60 1.50
40 Allen Iverson 1.25 3.00
41 Dirk Nowitzki 1.25 3.00
42 Antoine Walker .75 2.00
43 Ron Artest .75 2.00
44 Jamaal Magloire .50 1.25
45 Kirk Hinrich .75 2.00
46 Jason Richardson .75 2.00
47 Andrei Kirilenko .60 1.50
48 Kenyon Martin .75 2.00
49 Carlos Boozer .75 2.00
50 Shaquille O'Neal 2.00 5.00
51 Shawn Marion .75 2.00
52 Kwame Brown .50 1.25
53 Corey Maggette .60 1.50
54 Dwyane Wade 2.50 6.00
55 Jason Kidd 1.25 3.00
56 Dwight Howard JSY RC 6.00 15.00
57 Andre Iguodala JSY RC 3.00 8.00
58 Andre Emmett JSY AU RC 5.00 12.00
59 Al Jefferson JSY AU RC 8.00 20.00
60 A.Varejao JSY AU RC 6.00 15.00
61 Ben Gordon JSY AU RC 6.00 15.00
62 David Harrison JSY AU RC 5.00 12.00
63 Delonte West JSY AU RC 6.00 15.00
64 Devin Harris JSY AU RC 8.00 20.00
65 Dorell Wright JSY AU RC 8.00 20.00
66 Ha Seung-Jin JSY AU RC 5.00 12.00
67 J.R. Smith JSY AU RC 6.00 15.00
68 Jackson Vroman JSY AU RC 5.00 12.00
69 Jameer Nelson JSY AU RC 6.00 15.00
70 Kris Humphries JSY AU RC 5.00 12.00
71 Josh Smith JSY AU RC 8.00 20.00
72 Kevin Martin JSY AU RC 6.00 15.00
73 Kirk Snyder JSY AU RC 5.00 12.00
74 Trevor Ariza JSY AU RC 5.00 12.00
75 Lionel Chalmers JSY AU RC 5.00 12.00
76 Luke Jackson JSY AU RC 5.00 12.00
77 Luol Deng JSY AU RC 8.00 20.00
78 Rafael Araujo JSY AU RC 5.00 12.00
79 Rickey Paulding JSY AU RC 5.00 12.00
80 Sebastian Telfair JSY AU RC 5.00 12.00
81 Shaun Livingston JSY AU RC 5.00 12.00
82 Tony Allen JSY AU RC 6.00 15.00
83 Josh Childress JSY AU RC 5.00 12.00
84 Emeka Okafor JSY AU RC 8.00 20.00
85 Ber.Robinson JSY AU RC 5.00 12.00
86 Chris Duhon JSY AU RC 5.00 12.00
87 Blake Stepp AU RC 3.00 8.00
88 Andris Biedrins AU RC 4.00 10.00
89 Donta Smith AU RC 3.00 8.00
90 Beno Udrih AU RC 3.00 8.00
91 Justin Reed AU RC 3.00 8.00
92 Pavel Podkolzine AU RC 3.00 8.00
93 Matt Freije AU RC 3.00 8.00
94 Pape Sow AU RC 3.00 8.00
95 Antonio Burks AU RC 3.00 8.00
96 Rashad Wright AU RC 3.00 8.00
97 Ricky Minard AU RC 3.00 8.00
98 Robert Swift AU RC 3.00 8.00
99 Romain Sato AU RC 3.00 8.00
100 Sasha Vujacic AU RC 3.00 8.00
102 Tim Pickett AU RC 3.00 8.00
103 Yuta Tabuse AU RC 12.50 30.00

2004-05 Bowman Signature Edition 169

Randomly seeded in packs, this 102-card set parallels the base set with veterans that have a copper border and rookies that have a blue border. All autographs and jerseys for the rookie players are the same as the base set. Each card is sequentially numbered to 169.
*1-55 169 SINGLES: 1.25X TO 3X BASE HI
*56-57 JSY 169: .4X TO 1X BASE HI
*58-86 JSY AU 169: .5X TO 1.25X BASE HI
*87-103 AU 169: .5X TO 1.25X BASE HI

2004-05 Bowman Signature Edition 50

Randomly seeded in packs, this 102-card set parallels the base set with veteran players having a gold border and rookie players having a silver border. Each card is sequentially numbered to 50.
*1-55 50 SINGLES: 1.5X TO 4X BASE HI
*56-57 JSY 50 SINGLES: .6X TO 1.5X BASE HI
*58-86 JSY AU 50: .75X TO 2X BASE HI
*87-103 AU 50: .6X TO 1.5X BASE HI
103 Yuta Tabuse AU 30.00 60.00

2004-05 Bowman Signature Edition Foil

Randomly inserted in boxes as a topper, this 102-card set parallels the base set enhanced with an all-foil card stock, red borders for the veterans, blue borders for the rookies, and Topps' holofoil refractor effect. None of the rookie players who appeared in the base set with autographs and jerseys have them in this parallel.
56 Dwight Howard 12.00 30.00
57 Andre Iguodala 6.00 15.00
58 Andre Emmett 4.00 10.00
59 Al Jefferson 6.00 15.00
60 Anderson Varejao 5.00 12.00
61 Ben Gordon 5.00 12.00
62 David Harrison 4.00 10.00
63 Delonte West 5.00 12.00
64 Devin Harris 6.00 15.00
65 Dorell Wright 6.00 15.00
66 Ha Seung-Jin 4.00 10.00
67 J.R. Smith 5.00 12.00
68 Jackson Vroman 4.00 10.00
69 Jameer Nelson 5.00 12.00
70 Kris Humphries 4.00 10.00
71 Josh Smith 6.00 15.00
72 Kevin Martin 5.00 12.00
73 Kirk Snyder 4.00 10.00
74 Trevor Ariza 4.00 10.00
75 Lionel Chalmers 4.00 10.00
76 Luke Jackson 4.00 10.00
77 Luol Deng 6.00 15.00
78 Rafael Araujo 4.00 10.00
79 Rickey Paulding 4.00 10.00
80 Sebastian Telfair 4.00 10.00
81 Shaun Livingston 4.00 10.00
82 Tony Allen 5.00 12.00
83 Josh Childress 4.00 10.00
84 Emeka Okafor 6.00 15.00
85 Bernard Robinson 4.00 10.00
86 Chris Duhon 4.00 10.00
87 Blake Stepp 4.00 10.00
88 Andris Biedrins 5.00 12.00
89 Donta Smith 4.00 10.00
90 Beno Udrih 4.00 10.00
91 Justin Reed 4.00 10.00
92 Pavel Podkolzine 4.00 10.00
93 Matt Freije 4.00 10.00
94 Pape Sow 4.00 10.00
95 Antonio Burks 4.00 10.00
96 Rashad Wright 4.00 10.00
97 Ricky Minard 4.00 10.00
98 Robert Swift 4.00 10.00
99 Romain Sato 4.00 10.00
100 Sasha Vujacic 4.00 10.00
102 Tim Pickett 4.00 10.00
103 Yuta Tabuse 8.00 20.00

2004-05 Bowman Signature Edition Flashback Autographs

Randomly inserted in packs, this 15-card set showcases players with images from earlier in their career and background colors to match their jersey colors. Each card has received the refractor treatment, contains both an autograph and a swatch of jersey and is sequentially numbered to 60. Two parallel versions of this set exist, one sequentially numbered to 10 and one where the cards are all numbered one of one.
AS Amare Stoudemire 25.00 60.00
BD Baron Davis 12.50 30.00
CA Carmelo Anthony 25.00 60.00
FJ Fred Jones 12.50 30.00
JK Jason Kidd 25.00 60.00
JO Jermaine O'Neal 12.50 30.00
LO Lamar Odom 12.50 30.00
PS Peja Stojakovic 12.50 30.00
RH Richard Hamilton 15.00 40.00
SM Stephon Marbury 15.00 40.00
SO Shaquille O'Neal 50.00 120.00
TD Tim Duncan 75.00 150.00
TM Tracy McGrady 25.00 60.00
SMA Shawn Marion 12.50 30.00

2006-07 Bowman Sterling

Released in early April 2006, Bowman Sterling features an interesting base set consisting of extra-thick all-foil card stock and an array of memorabilia, autographs and combos of the two. Card numbers 1-30 feature retired and veteran player jersey cards consisting of a player photo and a jersey swatch towards the bottom of

the front, card numbers 31-40 feature retired and veteran player jersey/memorabilia combo cards where the card is horizontally designed with a circular jersey swatch and a sticker autograph, card numbers 41-50 feature base rookies, card numbers 51-70 feature jersey rookies, card numbers 71-90 feature autograph rookies which place a sticker autograph below a player photo and card numbers 91-100 feature horizontally designed jersey/autograph combo rookies which showcase a circular swatch of memorabilia along with a sticker autograph. Bowman Sterling carried an initial suggested retail price of $50 per pack and each pack contains two base rookies, one retired/veteran relic, one autograph rookie and one rookie relic.
UNPRICED RED REF.PRINT RUN ONE SET
1 Ben Wallace JSY 3.00 8.00
2 Jason Richardson JSY 3.00 8.00
3 Steve Nash JSY 4.00 10.00
4 Pau Gasol JSY 3.00 8.00
5 Carmelo Anthony JSY 4.00 10.00
6 Kevin Garnett JSY 6.00 15.00
7 Tim Duncan JSY 5.00 12.00
8 Chauncey Billups JSY 3.00 8.00
9 Chris Paul JSY 6.00 15.00
10 Kobe Bryant JSY 10.00 25.00
11 Tony Parker JSY 3.00 8.00
12 Shaquille O'Neal JSY 6.00 15.00
13 Allen Iverson JSY 4.00 10.00
14 Dirk Nowitzki JSY 5.00 12.00
15 Paul Pierce JSY 4.00 10.00
16 Tracy McGrady JSY 4.00 10.00
17 Channing Frye JSY 3.00 8.00
18 Amare Stoudemire JSY 3.00 8.00
19 Dwight Howard JSY 5.00 12.00
20 Dwyane Wade JSY 8.00 20.00
21 Yao Ming JSY 4.00 10.00
22 Andrei Kirilenko JSY 3.00 8.00
23 Gilbert Arenas JSY 3.00 8.00
24 Shawn Marion JSY 3.00 8.00
25 Bob Lanier JSY 3.00 8.00
26 Pete Maravich JSY 15.00 40.00
27 Bill Walton JSY 3.00 8.00
28 Dennis Rodman JSY 5.00 12.00
29 Magic Johnson JSY 8.00 20.00
30 John Stockton JSY 5.00 12.00
31 Larry Bird JSY AU 60.00 120.00
32 Rick Barry JSY AU 12.50 30.00
33 Isiah Thomas JSY AU 12.50 30.00
34 Dominique Wilkins JSY AU 15.00 40.00
35 Ben Gordon JSY AU 10.00 25.00
36 Raymond Felton JSY AU 8.00 20.00
37 T.J. Ford JSY AU 8.00 20.00
38 Josh Howard JSY AU 8.00 20.00
39 Dwyane Wade JSY AU 30.00 60.00
40 Andre Iguodala JSY AU 8.00 20.00
41 Tarence Kinsey RC 2.00 5.00
42 Mickael Gelabale RC 2.00 5.00
43 Kelenna Azubuike RC 2.50 6.00
44 Pops Mensah-Bonsu RC 2.00 5.00
45 Walter Herrmann RC 2.00 5.00
46 Tyrus Thomas RC 2.50 6.00
47 Lynn Greer RC 2.00 5.00
48 Leon Powe RC 2.00 5.00
49 Yakhouba Diawara RC 2.00 5.00
50 Jose Barea RC 6.00 15.00
51 Saer Sene JSY RC 2.50 6.00
52 Steve Novak JSY RC 2.50 6.00
53 Josh Boone JSY RC 2.50 6.00
54 James White JSY RC 2.50 6.00
55 Rudy Gay JSY RC 4.00 10.00
56 David Noel JSY RC 2.50 6.00
57 Allan Ray JSY RC 2.50 6.00
58 Paul Davis JSY RC 2.50 6.00
59 Shawne Williams JSY RC 2.50 6.00
60 LaMarcus Aldridge JSY RC 6.00 15.00
61 Mardy Collins JSY RC 2.50 6.00
62 Solomon Jones JSY RC 2.50 6.00
63 Craig Smith JSY RC 2.50 6.00
64 Rajon Rondo JSY RC 10.00 25.00
65 Jorge Garbajosa JSY RC 2.50 6.00
66 Patrick O'Bryant JSY RC 2.50 6.00
67 Dee Brown JSY RC 2.50 6.00
68 Brandon Roy JSY RC 6.00 15.00
69 Bobby Jones JSY RC 2.50 6.00
70 Kyle Lowry JSY RC 3.00 8.00
71 Paul Millsap AU RC 6.00 15.00
72 Vassilis Spanoulis AU RC 4.00 10.00
73 Daniel Gibson AU RC 5.00 12.00
74 Marcus Vinicius AU RC 4.00 10.00
75 Ronnie Brewer AU RC 5.00 12.00
76 Damir Markota AU RC 4.00 10.00
77 Hilton Armstrong AU RC 4.00 10.00
78 Shannon Brown AU RC 6.00 15.00
79 Mile Ilic AU RC 4.00 10.00
80 Alexander Johnson AU RC 4.00 10.00
81 Will Blalock AU RC 4.00 10.00
82 P.J. Tucker AU RC 4.00 10.00
83 Sergio Rodriguez AU RC 4.00 10.00
84 Jordan Farmar AU RC 4.00 10.00
85 Renaldo Balkman AU RC 4.00 10.00
86 Quincy Douby AU RC 4.00 10.00
87 Hassan Adams AU RC 4.00 10.00
88 Chris Quinn AU RC 4.00 10.00
89 James Augustine AU RC 4.00 10.00
90 Ryan Hollins AU RC 4.00 10.00
91 J.J. Redick JSY AU RC 6.00 15.00
92 Adam Morrison JSY AU RC 6.00 15.00
93 Maurice Ager JSY AU RC 5.00 12.00
94 Shelden Williams JSY AU RC 5.00 12.00
95 Marcus Williams JSY AU RC 5.00 12.00
96 Andrea Bargnani JSY AU RC 8.00 20.00
97 Thabo Sefolosha JSY AU RC 6.00 15.00
98 Randy Foye JSY AU RC 6.00 15.00
99 Cedric Simmons JSY AU RC 5.00 12.00
100 Rodney Carney JSY AU RC 5.00 12.00

2006-07 Bowman Sterling Refractors

*1-30 REF: .5X TO 1.25X BASE HI
*31-40 AU REF SAME VALUE AS BASE
*41-100 RC REF: .5X TO 1.25X BASE HI
PRINT RUN 199 SER.#'d SETS
50 Jose Barea 12.50 30.00

2006-07 Bowman Sterling Refractors Black

*1-30 JSY REF.BLK: .75X TO 2X BASE HI
*31-40 JSY AU REF.BLK: .5X TO 1.25X HI
*42-100 RC REF.BLK: .75X TO 2X HI
PRINT RUN 25 SER.#'d SETS
50 Jose Barea 60.00 150.00

2006-07 Bowman Sterling Refractors Gold

*31-40 REF.GOLD: .5X TO 1.25X BASE HI
91-40 PRINT RUN 25 SER.#'d SETS
*71-90 REF.GOLD: .6X TO 1.5X BASE HI
71-90 PRINT RUN 219 TO 599 SETS
*91-100 REF.GOLD: .6X TO 1.5X BASE HI
91-100 PRINT RUN 25 SER.#'d SETS

2007-08 Bowman Sterling

Released in April 2008, Bowman Sterling features a 125-card set which mixes base cards, Jersey cards, Autograph cards, Autograph Jersey cards and Rookie cards--most cards are sequentially numbered and print runs are listed in the checklist. The card stock features an all-foil finish along with sticker autographs and circular jersey swatches. Sterling is packaged in six-pack boxes of five cards each, each pack contians two base cards, two relic cards and one autograph card, and carried an initial suggested retail price of $50 per pack.
UNPRICED SUPERFR.PRINT RUN ONE SET
UNPRICED X-FR BLACK PRINT RUN 10 SETS
UNPRICED X-FR GOLD PRNT RUN 10 SETS
UNPRICED X-FR RED PRINT RUN 10 SETS
AA Arron Afflalo JSY AU/218 RC 6.00 15.00
AB Andrea Bargnani JSY/385 2.50 6.00
ABR Aaron Brooks JSY AU/218 5.00 12.00
ABY Andrew Bynum JSY/385 5.00 12.00
AG Aaron Gray AU/412 RC 4.00 10.00
AH1 Al Horford RC 2.00 5.00
AH2 Al Horford JSY/975 4.00 10.00
AHA Al Harrington JSY/385 2.50 6.00
AHK Adam Haluska JSY AU/218 RC 5.00 12.00
AI Allen Iverson JSY/385 4.00 10.00
AIG Andre Iguodala JSY AU/190 6.00 15.00
AJ Al Jefferson JSY/385 2.50 6.00
AJA Antawn Jamison JSY/385 2.50 6.00
AL1 Acie Law JSY AU/113 5.00 12.00
AL2 Acie Law AU/412 RC 5.00 12.00
AS Amare Stoudemire JSY/385 4.00 10.00
AT1 Alando Tucker JSY AU/218 4.00 10.00
AT2 Alando Tucker AU/829 RC 5.00 12.00
ATH2 Al Thornton AU/412 RC 4.00 10.00
BD Baron Davis JSY AU/275 6.00 15.00
BG Ben Gordon JSY/385 2.50 6.00
BK Bernard King JSY/385 3.00 8.00
BL Bill Laimbeer JSY/385 3.00 8.00
BR Brandon Roy JSY/385 3.00 8.00
BRU Bill Russell JSY AU/15 100.00 200.00
BWR1 Brandan Wright JSY AU/21 12.00 30.00
BWR2 Brandan Wright JSY/975 RC 2.50 6.00
CA Carmelo Anthony JSY AU/15 25.00 50.00
CB1 Corey Brewer RC 2.00 5.00
CB2 Corey Brewer JSY/975 3.00 8.00
CBO Chris Bosh JSY AU/89 8.00 20.00
CBZ Carlos Boozer JSY AU/340 6.00 15.00
CD Clyde Drexler JSY/385 4.00 10.00
CK Coby Karl AU/829 RC 5.00 12.00
CL Carl Landry JSY AU/218 RC 6.00 15.00
CM Corey Maggette JSY/385 2.50 6.00
CP Chris Paul JSY/385 4.00 10.00
CR Chris Richard RC 1.50 4.00
CR2 Chris Richard JSY/975 2.50 6.00
DC Daequan Cook JSY AU/113 RC 5.00 12.00
DH Dwight Howard JSY AU/89 20.00 40.00
DJS1 D.J. Strawberry JSY AU/218 5.00 12.00
DJS2 D.J. Strawberry AU/829 RC 5.00 12.00
DM Dominic McGuire JSY AU/113 RC5.00 12.00
DN Dirk Nowitzki JSY/385 3.00 8.00
DNI Demetris Nichols JSY AU/218 RC5.00 12.00
DR David Robinson JSY AU/15 50.00 120.00
DRO Dennis Rodman JSY AU/89 30.00 60.00
DW Dwyane Wade JSY AU/15 40.00 80.00
DWI Dominique Wilkins JSY AU/27512.00 30.00
EM Earl Monroe JSY/385 3.00 8.00
GA1 Gilbert Arenas JSY/385 2.50 6.00
GD1 Glen Davis JSY AU/218 8.00 20.00
GD2 Glen Davis AU/829 RC 5.00 12.00
GG George Gervin JSY/385 4.00 10.00
GO1 Greg Oden JSY AU/21 50.00 125.00
GO2 Greg Oden JSY/975 RC 4.00 10.00
GP1 Gabe Pruitt JSY AU/218 5.00 12.00
GP2 Gabe Pruitt AU/829 RC 5.00 12.00
HH1 Herbert Hill JSY AU/218 5.00 12.00
HH2 Herbert Hill AU/829 RC 5.00 12.00
IT Isiah Thomas JSY AU/89 15.00 30.00
JC1 Javaris Crittenton JSY/218 AU 5.00 12.00
JC2 Javaris Crittenton AU/412 RC 5.00 12.00
JCN Juan Navarro AU/129 RC 5.00 12.00
JD Jared Dudley JSY AU/218 RC 5.00 12.00
JDA Jermareo Davidson JSY AU/218 RC5.00 12.00
JG1 Jeff Green RC 2.00 5.00
JG2 Jeff Green JSY/975 4.00 10.00
JJ Joe Johnson JSY/385 2.50 6.00
JK Jason Kidd JSY/385 2.50 6.00
JMC Josh McRoberts JSY AU/218 RC5.00 12.00
JN1 Joakim Noah RC 4.00 10.00
JN2 Joakim Noah JSY/975 5.00 12.00
JO Jermaine O'Neal JSY/385 2.50 6.00
JOC JamesOn Curry AU/412 RC 5.00 12.00
JR Jason Richardson JSY/385 2.50 6.00
JS Jason Smith JSY AU/113 RC 5.00 12.00
JW1 Julian Wright RC 1.50 4.00
JW2 Julian Wright JSY/975 2.50 6.00
KB Kobe Bryant JSY/385 8.00 20.00
KD Kevin Durant RC 12.00 30.00
KG Kevin Garnett JSY/385 5.00 12.00
KMA Karl Malone JSY/385 5.00 12.00
LB Larry Bird JSY AU/15 75.00 150.00
LD Luol Deng JSY/385 2.50 6.00
LS Luis Scola RC 2.50 6.00
MA Morris Almond JSY AU/113 RC 5.00 12.00
MB Mike Bibby JSY/385 2.50 6.00
MBE Marco Belinelli AU/129 RC 5.00 12.00
MC1 Mike Conley Jr. RC 2.50 6.00
MC2 Mike Conley Jr. JSY/975 4.00 10.00
MCO Michael Cooper JSY/385 3.00 8.00
MG Marcin Gortat AU/829 RC 6.00 15.00
MG Manu Ginobili JSY/385 3.00 8.00
MJ Magic Johnson JSY AU/15 75.00 150.00
MM Mike Miller JSY/385 2.50 6.00
MR Michael Redd JSY/385 2.50 6.00
NF Nick Fazekas JSY AU/218 RC 5.00 12.00
NTA Nate Archibald JSY/385 3.00 8.00
NY2 Nick Young JSY RC 4.00 10.00
PG Pau Gasol JSY/385 2.50 6.00
PP Paul Pierce JSY AU/190 15.00 30.00
RA Ray Allen JSY AU/190 15.00 40.00
RB Rick Barry JSY AU/340 10.00 25.00
RH Richard Hamilton JSY/385 2.50 6.00
RS Rodney Stuckey JSY AU/218 RC 15.00 40.00
RS Ramon Sessions RC 2.50 6.00
SH Spencer Hawes JSY AU/113 RC 5.00 12.00
SM Stephon Marbury JSY/385 2.50 6.00
SMA Shawn Marion JSY/385 2.50 6.00
SN Steve Nash JSY/385 4.00 10.00
SO Shaquille O'Neal JSY AU/15 100.00 200.00
SW Sean Williams JSY AU/218 RC 5.00 12.00
TD Tim Duncan JSY/385 4.00 10.00
TG Taurean Green JSY AU/218 RC 5.00 12.00
TM Tracy McGrady JSY/385 2.50 6.00
TY Thaddeus Young JSY AU/21 RC 50.00 100.00
VC Vince Carter JSY AU/89 15.00 40.00
WC Wilson Chandler JSY AU/218 RC 6.00 15.00
YJ Yi Jianlian AU/129 RC 10.00 25.00
YM Yao Ming JSY/385 3.00 8.00

2007-08 Bowman Sterling Refractors

*RC REFRACTORS: .6X TO 1.5X BASE
*AU REFRACTOR: .5X TO 1.25X BASE
AUTO PRINT RUN 99 SER.#'d SETS
*JSY REFRACTOR: .5X TO 1.25X BASE
JSY.REF.PRINT RUN 199 SER.#'d SETS
JSY AU REF.PRINT RUN 10 SETS
JSY AU REF.UNPRICED DUE TO SCARCITY
ATH1 Al Thornton JSY AU/19 10.00 25.00
ATH2 Al Thornton AU/99 8.00 20.00
JW1 Julian Wright 2.50 6.00
KD Kevin Durant 40.00 80.00
NY1 Nick Young JSY AU/19 15.00 40.00
RS Ramon Sessions 4.00 10.00
TY Thaddeus Young JSY AU/19 60.00 120.00

2007-08 Bowman Sterling Refractors Black

*RC REF.: .75X TO 2X BASE
*AU REF.: .6X TO 1.5X BASE
AUTO PRINT RUN 25 SER.#'d SETS
*JSY REF.: .6X TO 1.5X BASE
JSY.REF.PRINT RUN 199 SER.#'d SETS
JSY AU REF.PRINT RUN 5 SETS
JSY AU REF.UNPRICED DUE TO SCARCITY
ATH2 Al Thornton AU 12.50 30.00
KD Kevin Durant 40.00 100.00

2007-08 Bowman Sterling Refractors Gold

*RC REF.: 1.25X TO 3X BASE
UNPRICED AU.REF.PRINT RUN 10 SETS
*JSY REF.: 1X TO 2.5X BASE
JSY.REF.PRINT RUN 25 SETS
JSY AU REF.PRINT RUN ONE SET
JSY AU REF.UNPRICED DUE TO SCARCITY

2007-08 Bowman Sterling Refractors Red

*RC REF.: 1.25X TO 3X BASE
REF.AU/JSY PRINT RUN ONE SET
REF.AU/JSY UNPRICED DUE TO SCARCITY

2007-08 Bowman Sterling X-Fractors

*RC X-FRAC: 1.5X TO 4X BASE
PRINT RUN 25 SER.#'d SETS
KD Kevin Durant 300.00 600.00

2007-08 Bowman Sterling Box Loaders

*REFRACTORS: .75X TO 2X BASE
REF.PRINT RUN 50 SER.#'d SETS
*REF.BLACK: 1.5X TO 4X BASE
REF.BLACK PRINT RUN 25 SER.#'d SETS
*REF.GOLD: 2X TO 5X BASE
REF.GOLD PRINT RUN 15 SER.#'d SETS
UNPRICED REF.RED PRINT RUN ONE SET
BL1 Acie Law/199 1.50 4.00
BL2 Yi Jianlian/199 2.50 6.00
BL3 Brandan Wright/99 1.50 4.00
BL4 Corey Brewer/99 2.00 5.00
BL5 Greg Oden/199 2.00 5.00
BL6 Javaris Crittenton/99 1.50 4.00
BL7 Nick Young/199 2.50 6.00
BL8 Julian Wright/99 1.50 4.00
BL9 Thaddeus Young/199 2.00 5.00
BL10 Kevin Durant/199 15.00 40.00
BL11 Al Horford/199 2.00 5.00
BL12 Mike Conley Jr./199 2.50 6.00
BL13 Joakim Noah/99 4.00 10.00
BL14 Jeff Green/199 2.00 5.00

2007-08 Bowman Sterling Relics Autographs Dual

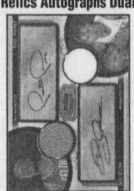

REFRACTOR PRINT RUN FIVE SETS
REF.BLACK PRINT RUN FIVE SETS
REF.GOLD PRINT RUN ONE SET
REF.RED PRINT RUN FIVE SETS
REFRACTORS UNPRICED DUE TO SCARCITY
SOME UNPRICED DUE TO SCARCITY
BC Chris Bosh/25 30.00 80.00
Vince Carter
BJ Chauncey Billups/85 12.50 30.00
Joe Johnson
BW Carlos Boozer/85 20.00 50.00
Deron Williams
CJ Vince Carter/85 20.00 50.00
Antawn Jamison
HB John Havlicek/15 50.00 100.00
Elgin Baylor
HM Dwight Howard/85 30.00 60.00
Moses Malone
IW Andre Iguodala/85 12.50 30.00
Luke Walton
JO Yi Jianlian 30.00 80.00
Greg Oden
LM David Lee/85 12.50 30.00
Mike Miller
PA Paul Pierce/25 50.00 120.00
Ray Allen
RR David Robinson/15 100.00 200.00
Dennis Rodman
WB Jerry West/15 100.00 200.00
Elgin Baylor
WW Spud Webb/85 25.00 60.00
Dominique Wilkins

1996-97 Bowman's Best

The premier edition of 1996-97 Bowman's Best set was issued in one series totalling 125 cards. The basic set consists of 80 veterans on a gold foil card background, 25 rookies on a silver foil card background and 20 throwback cards on a black and white card background. Each six-card pack had a suggested retail price of $3.99.
COMPLETE SET (125) 25.00 50.00
1 Scottie Pippen .60 1.50
2 Glen Rice .40 1.00
3 Bryant Stith .25 .60
4 Dino Radja .30 .75
5 Horace Grant .30 .75
6 Mahmoud Abdul-Rauf .25 .60
7 Mookie Blaylock .25 .60
8 Clifford Robinson .25 .60
9 Vin Baker .30 .75
10 Grant Hill .60 1.50
11 Terrell Brandon .25 .60
12 P.J. Brown .25 .60
13 Kendall Gill .25 .60
14 Brent Barry .30 .75
15 Hakeem Olajuwon .50 1.25
16 Allan Houston .30 .75
17 Elden Campbell .25 .60
18 Latrell Sprewell .40 1.00
19 Jerry Stackhouse .50 1.25
20 Robert Horry .30 .75
21 Mitch Richmond .40 1.00
22 Gary Payton .40 1.00
23 Rik Smits .30 .75
24 Jim Jackson .25 .60
25 Damon Stoudamire .40 1.00
26 Bobby Phills .25 .60
27 Chris Webber .50 1.25
28 Shawn Bradley .25 .60
29 Arvydas Sabonis .30 .75
30 John Stockton .50 1.25
31 Anfernee Hardaway .60 1.50
32 Christian Laettner .30 .75
33 Juwan Howard .30 .75
34 Anthony Mason .25 .60
35 Tom Gugliotta .25 .60
36 Avery Johnson .30 .75
37 Cedric Ceballos .25 .60
38 Patrick Ewing .50 1.25
39 Joe Smith .30 .75
40 Dennis Rodman .75 2.00
41 Alonzo Mourning .50 1.25
42 Kevin Garnett 1.00 2.50
43 Antonio McDyess .40 1.00
44 Detlef Schrempf .40 1.00
45 Reggie Miller .50 1.25
46 Charles Barkley .60 1.50
47 Derrick Coleman .30 .75
48 Brian Grant .30 .75
49 Kenny Anderson .30 .75
50 Otis Thorpe .25 .60
51 Rod Strickland .25 .60
52 Eric Williams .25 .60
53 Rony Seikaly .30 .75
54 Danny Manning .30 .75
55 Karl Malone .50 1.25
56 B.J. Armstrong .25 .60
57 Greg Anthony .25 .60
58 Larry Johnson .40 1.00
59 Loy Vaught .25 .60
60 Sean Elliott .40 1.00
61 Dikembe Mutombo .40 1.00
62 Clarence Weatherspoon .25 .60
63 Jamal Mashburn .30 .75
64 Bryant Reeves .25 .60
65 Vlade Divac .40 1.00
66 Shawn Kemp .40 1.00
67 LaPhonso Ellis .25 .60
68 Tyrone Hill .25 .60
69 David Robinson .60 1.50
70 Shaquille O'Neal 1.00 2.50
71 Doug Christie .25 .60
72 Jayson Williams .25 .60
73 Michael Finley .50 1.25
74 Tim Hardaway .40 1.00
75 Clyde Drexler .50 1.25
76 Joe Dumars .40 1.00
77 Glenn Robinson .40 1.00
78 Dana Barros .25 .60
79 Jason Kidd .60 1.50
80 Michael Jordan 3.00 8.00
R1 Allen Iverson RC 3.00 8.00
R2 Stephon Marbury RC 1.50 4.00
R3 Shareef Abdur-Rahim RC 1.25 3.00
R4 Marcus Camby RC 1.00 2.50
R5 Ray Allen RC 2.50 6.00
R6 Antoine Walker RC 1.25 3.00
R7 Lorenzen Wright RC .60 1.50
R8 Kerry Kittles RC .60 1.50
R9 Samaki Walker RC .60 1.50
R10 Tony Delk RC .60 1.50
R11 Vitaly Potapenko RC .60 1.50
R12 Jerome Williams RC .60 1.50
R13 Todd Fuller RC .60 1.50
R14 Erick Dampier RC .60 1.50
R15 Derek Fisher RC 1.25 3.00
R16 Donald Whiteside RC .60 1.50
R17 John Wallace RC .60 1.50
R18 Steve Nash RC 3.00 8.00
R19 Brian Evans RC .60 1.50
R20 Jermaine O'Neal RC 1.50 4.00
R21 Roy Rogers RC .60 1.50
R22 Priest Lauderdale RC .60 1.50
R23 Kobe Bryant RC 12.00 30.00
R24 Martin Muursepp RC .60 1.50
R25 Zydrunas Ilgauskas RC 1.00 2.50
TB1 Avery Johnson RET .15 .40
TB2 Chris Webber RET .25 .60
TB3 Sean Elliott RET .20 .50
TB4 Joe Dumars RET .20 .50
TB5 Grant Hill RET .30 .75
TB6 Gary Payton RET .20 .50
TB7 Shawn Kemp RET .20 .50
TB8 Shaquille O'Neal RET .50 1.25
TB9 Eddie Jones RET .20 .50
TB10 John Wallace RET .30 .75
TB11 Patrick Ewing RET .25 .60
TB12 Jerry Stackhouse RET .25 .60
TB13 Allen Iverson RET 1.50 4.00
TB14 Latrell Sprewell RET .20 .50
TB15 Dino Radja RET .15 .40
TB16 David Wesley RET .12 .30
TB17 Joe Smith RET .15 .40
TB18 Damon Stoudamire RET .20 .50
TB19 Marcus Camby RET .50 1.25
TB20 Juwan Howard RET .15 .40

1996-97 Bowman's Best Refractors

Randomly inserted in packs at a rate of one in 12, this 125-card set parallels the basic set with the traditional "refractor-type" foil. To ascertain values on individual cards, please refer to the multiplier in the header below, coupled with the value of the base card.
*STARS: 4X TO 10X BASE CARD HI
*RCs/RET RCs: 2X TO 5X BASE HI
*RETRO STARS: 8X TO 20X BASE HI
79 Jason Kidd 8.00 20.00
80 Michael Jordan 40.00 100.00

1996-97 Bowman's Best Atomic Refractors

Randomly inserted in packs at a rate of one in 24, this 80-card set parallels the Refractor insert. The only difference is the use of the "hyper-plaid" atomic refractor technology. To ascertain values on individual cards, please refer to the multiplier in the header below, coupled with the value of the base card.
*STARS: 8X TO 20X HI COLUMN
*RCs/RET RCs: 4X TO 10X HI
*RETRO STARS: 15X TO 40X HI
79 Jason Kidd 15.00 40.00
80 Michael Jordan 150.00 300.00
R23 Kobe Bryant 250.00 500.00

1996-97 Bowman's Best Cuts

Randomly inserted in packs at a rate of one in 24, this 20-card set features the best in the NBA against a die-cut chromium background. Each card front also contains a facsimile autograph of the player. Card backs are numbered with a "BC" prefix.
COMPLETE SET (20) 40.00 100.00
*ATOMIC REFRACTORS: 3X TO 8X HI
ATO: STATED ODDS 1:192 HOB, 1:320 RET
*REFRACTORS: 1.5X TO 4X HI COLUMN
REF: STATED ODDS 1:96 HOB, 1:160 RET
BC1 Karl Malone 2.00 5.00
BC2 Michael Jordan 12.00 30.00
BC3 Juwan Howard 1.25 3.00
BC4 Charles Barkley 2.50 6.00
BC5 Jerry Stackhouse 2.00 5.00
BC6 Anfernee Hardaway 2.50 6.00
BC7 Shaquille O'Neal 4.00 10.00
BC8 Alonzo Mourning 2.00 5.00
BC9 Shawn Kemp 1.50 4.00
BC10 Scottie Pippen 2.50 6.00
BC11 David Robinson 2.50 6.00
BC12 Kevin Garnett 4.00 10.00
BC13 Patrick Ewing 2.00 5.00
BC14 Hakeem Olajuwon 2.00 5.00
BC15 Damon Stoudamire 1.50 4.00
BC16 Grant Hill 2.50 6.00
BC17 Dennis Rodman 3.00 8.00
BC18 Chris Webber 2.00 5.00
BC19 Gary Payton 1.50 4.00
BC20 John Stockton 2.00 5.00

1996-97 Bowman's Best Honor Roll

Randomly inserted in packs at a rate of one in 48, this 10-card set showcases some of the top draft pick combos all the way back to 1984. Card backs are numbered with a "HR" prefix.
COMPLETE SET (10) 30.00 80.00
*REFRACTORS: 1.25X TO 3X HI COLUMN
REF: STATED ODDS 1:192 HOB, 1:320 RET
HR1 Charles Barkley 4.00 10.00
John Stockton
HR2 Michael Jordan 15.00 40.00
Hakeem Olajuwon
HR3 Patrick Ewing 4.00 10.00
Karl Malone
HR4 Dennis Rodman 2.50 6.00
Arvydas Sabonis
HR5 Scottie Pippen 10.00 20.00
David Robinson
HR6 Glen Rice 2.50 6.00
Shawn Kemp
HR7 Shaquille O'Neal 6.00 15.00
Alonzo Mourning
HR8 Anfernee Hardaway 4.00 10.00
Chris Webber
HR9 Grant Hill 3.00 8.00
Juwan Howard
HR10 Kevin Garnett 5.00 12.00
Jerry Stackhouse

1996-97 Bowman's Best Honor Roll Atomic Refractors

Randomly inserted in packs at a rate of one in 384, this 10-card set parallels the Honor Roll Refractor insert. Cards feature the hyper-plaid Atomic Refractor design. Card backs are numbered with a "HR" prefix. To ascertain values on individual cards, please refer to the multiplier in the header below, coupled with the value of the base card.
*STARS: 2.5X TO 6X VALUE
HR2 Michael Jordan 150.00 300.00
Hakeem Olajuwon

1996-97 Bowman's Best Picks

Randomly inserted in packs at a rate of one in 24, this 10-card set features some of the best players from the class of 1996. Card fronts also contain a facsimile autograph of each player. Card backs are numbered with a "BP" prefix.
COMPLETE SET (10) 20.00 50.00
*REFRACTORS: 1.25X TO 3X HI COLUMN
REF: STATED ODDS 1:96 HOB, 1:160 RET
BP1 Stephon Marbury 2.50 6.00
BP2 Marcus Camby 1.50 4.00
BP3 Lorenzen Wright 1.00 2.50
BP4 John Wallace 1.00 2.50
BP5 Ray Allen 4.00 10.00
BP6 Kerry Kittles 1.00 2.50
BP7 Shareef Abdur-Rahim 2.00 5.00
BP8 Todd Fuller 1.00 2.50
BP9 Allen Iverson 5.00 12.00
BP10 Kobe Bryant 15.00 40.00

1996-97 Bowman's Best Picks Atomic Refractors

Randomly inserted in packs at a rate of one in 96, this 10-card set parallels the Best Pick Refractor insert. Cards feature the "hyper-plaid" Atomic Refractor technology. Card backs are numbered with a "BP" prefix. To ascertain values on individual cards, please refer to the multiplier in the header below, coupled with the value of the base card.
*ATOMIC: 2.5X TO 6X VALUE
BP10 Kobe Bryant 200.00 400.00

1996-97 Bowman's Best Shots

Randomly inserted in packs at a rate of one in 12, this 10-card set features some of the top NBA superstars on crystal clear chromium cards. Card backs are numbered with a "BS" prefix.
COMPLETE SET (10) 20.00 40.00
*ATOMIC REFRACTORS: 2X TO 5X HI
ATO: STATED ODDS 1:96 HOB, 1:160 RET
*REFRACTORS: .75X TO 2X HI COLUMN
REF: STATED ODDS 1:48 HOB, 1:80 RET
BS1 Scottie Pippen 2.00 5.00
BS2 Gary Payton 1.25 3.00
BS3 Shaquille O'Neal 3.00 8.00
BS4 Hakeem Olajuwon 1.50 4.00
BS5 Kevin Garnett 3.00 8.00
BS6 Michael Jordan 10.00 25.00
BS7 Anfernee Hardaway 2.00 5.00
BS8 Grant Hill 2.00 5.00
BS9 Shawn Kemp 1.25 3.00
BS10 Dennis Rodman 2.50 6.00

1997-98 Bowman's Best

The 1997-98 Bowman's Best set was issued in one series totalling 125 cards. The basic set consists of 90 veterans, a 10 card Best Performances subset and 25 rookie cards. Each six-card pack had a suggested retail price of $3.99.
COMPLETE SET (125) 15.00 40.00
1 Scottie Pippen .50 1.25
2 Michael Finley .30 .75
3 David Wesley .20 .50
4 Brent Barry .25 .60
5 Gary Payton .30 .75
6 Christian Laettner .25 .60
7 Grant Hill .50 1.25
8 Glenn Robinson .25 .60
9 Reggie Miller .40 1.00
10 Tyus Edney .20 .50
11 Jim Jackson .20 .50
12 John Stockton .40 1.00
13 Karl Malone .40 1.00
14 Samaki Walker .20 .50
15 Bryant Stith .20 .50
16 Clyde Drexler .40 1.00
17 Danny Ferry .20 .50
18 Shawn Bradley .20 .50
19 Bryant Reeves .20 .50
20 John Starks .25 .60
21 Joe Dumars .30 .75
22 Checklist .20 .50
23 Antonio McDyess .25 .60
24 Jeff Hornacek .25 .60
25 Terrell Brandon .20 .50
26 Kendall Gill .20 .50
27 LaPhonso Ellis .20 .50
28 Shaquille O'Neal .75 2.00
29 Mahmoud Abdul-Rauf .20 .50
30 Eric Williams .20 .50
31 Lorenzen Wright .20 .50
32 Shareef Abdur-Rahim .30 .75
33 Avery Johnson .25 .60
34 Juwan Howard .25 .60
35 Vin Baker .25 .60
36 Dikembe Mutombo .30 .75
37 Patrick Ewing .40 1.00
38 Allen Iverson .60 1.50
39 Alonzo Mourning .40 1.00
40 Travis Knight .20
41 Ray Allen .40
42 Detlef Schrempf .30
43 Kevin Johnson .30
44 David Robinson .50
45 Tim Hardaway .30
46 Shawn Kemp .30
47 Marcus Camby .30
48 Rony Seikaly .25
49 Eddie Jones .30
50 Rik Smits .25
51 Jayson Williams .20
52 Malik Sealy .20
53 Chris Mullin .30
54 Larry Johnson .30
55 Isaiah Rider .20
56 Dennis Rodman .60
57 Bob Sura .20
58 Hakeem Olajuwon .40
59 Steve Smith .25
60 Michael Jordan 2.50
61 Jerry Stackhouse .30
62 Joe Smith .25
63 Walt Williams .20
64 Anthony Peeler .20
65 Charles Barkley .50
66 Erick Dampier .20
67 Horace Grant .25
68 Anthony Mason .20
69 Anfernee Hardaway .50
70 Elden Campbell .20
71 Cedric Ceballos .20
72 Allan Houston .25
73 Kerry Kittles .20
74 Antoine Walker .30
75 Sean Elliott .30
76 Jamal Mashburn .25
77 Mitch Richmond .30
78 Damon Stoudamire .30
79 Tom Gugliotta .20
80 Jason Kidd .50
81 Chris Webber .30
82 Glen Rice .30
83 Loy Vaught .20
84 Olden Polynice .20
85 Kenny Anderson .25
86 Stephon Marbury .40
87 Calbert Cheaney .20
88 Kobe Bryant 1.50
89 Arvydas Sabonis .25
90 Kevin Garnett .60
91 Grant Hill BP .25
92 Clyde Drexler BP .20
93 Patrick Ewing BP .20
94 Shawn Kemp BP .15
95 Shaquille O'Neal BP .40
96 Michael Jordan BP 1.25
97 Karl Malone BP .20
98 Allen Iverson BP .30
99 Shareef Abdur-Rahim BP .15
100 Dikembe Mutombo BP .15
101 Bobby Jackson RC .40
102 Tony Battie RC .40
103 Keith Booth RC .30
104 Keith Van Horn RC .60
105 Paul Grant RC .30
106 Tim Duncan RC 2.00
107 Scot Pollard RC .30
108 Maurice Taylor RC .30
109 Antonio Daniels RC .30
110 Austin Croshere RC .30
111 Tracy McGrady RC 1.50
112 Charles O'Bannon RC .30
113 Rodrick Rhodes RC .30
114 Johnny Taylor RC .30
115 Danny Fortson RC .30
116 Chauncey Billups RC 1.25
117 Tim Thomas RC .60
118 Derek Anderson RC .30
119 Ed Gray RC .30
120 Jacque Vaughn RC .30
121 Kelvin Cato RC .30
122 Tariq Abdul-Wahad RC .30
123 Ron Mercer RC .40
124 Brevin Knight RC .30
125 Adonal Foyle RC .30

1997-98 Bowman's Best Refractors

This 125-card parallel set was randomly inserte packs at a rate of one in 12 packs and features "classic" refractor technology. To ascertain valu individual cards, please refer to the multiplier li below coupled with the value of the base card.
*STARS: 4X TO 10X BASE CARD HI
*SUBSET: 6X TO 15X BASE HI
*RCs: 1.5X TO 4X BASE HI
96 Michael Jordan BP 25.00
106 Tim Duncan 12.00

1997-98 Bowman's Best Ato Refractors

Randomly inserted into packs at a rate of one ir this 125-card set parallels the basic issue. The feature the "hyper-plaid" refractor pattern. To as values on individual cards, please refer to the multiplier in the header below, coupled with the of the base card.
*STARS: 6X TO 15X BASE CARD HI
*SUBSET: 10X TO 25X BASE HI
*RCs: 3X TO 8X BASE HI
1 Scottie Pippen 10.00
60 Michael Jordan 100.00
88 Kobe Bryant 30.00
96 Michael Jordan BP 50.00
106 Tim Duncan 20.00

1997-98 Bowman's Bes Autographs

Randomly inserted into packs at a rate of one i this 11-card set features autographs on the reg player cards. The only exception is Karl Malone has a regular autograph and a special MVP car autograph. There is no special insertion rate fo MVP card.
*REFRACTORS: .75X TO 2X HI COLUMN
REF: STATED ODDS 1:1,987 H, 1:3,974 R
*ATOMIC REFRACTORS: 2X TO 5X HI
ATO: STATED ODDS 1:5,961 H, 1:11,922 R
8 Glenn Robinson 10.00
13 Karl Malone 75.00
36 Dikembe Mutombo 12.00
59 Steve Smith 6.00
77 Mitch Richmond 12.50
102 Tony Battie 6.00
104 Keith Van Horn 10.00
116 Chauncey Billups 15.00

Mercer	8.00	20.00
nal Foyle	6.00	15.00
Malone MVP	75.00	150.00

97-98 Bowman's Best Cuts

ly inserted into packs at one in 24, this 10-er cut set features ten of the hottest players in e today. Card backs feature a "BC" prefix.

ETE SET (10)	20.00	50.00
C REFRACTORS: 1.25X TO 3X HI		
ATED ODDS 1:96 HOB, 1:160 RET		
CTORS: .6X TO 1.5X HI COLUMN		
ATED ODDS 1:48 HOB, 1:80 RET		
Baker	1.50	4.00
rick Ewing	2.50	6.00
ottie Pippen	3.00	8.00
l Malone	2.50	6.00
vin Garnett	4.00	10.00
fernee Hardaway	3.00	8.00
awn Kemp	2.00	5.00
arles Barkley	3.00	8.00
phon Marbury	2.50	6.00
aquille O'Neal	5.00	12.00

7-98 Bowman's Best Mirror Image

ly inserted into packs at a rate of one in 48, card set features two veterans and two rookies on double-sided cards. The cards look similar ng cards". Card backs carry a "MI" prefix.

ETE SET (10)	30.00	80.00
C REFRACTORS: 1.25X TO 3X HI		
ATED ODDS 1:192 HOB, 1:320 RET		
CTORS: .6X TO 1.5X HI COLUMN		
ATED ODDS 1:96 HOB, 1:160 RET		
hael Jordan	12.00	30.00
ercer		
on Marbury		
Payton		
Thomas	5.00	12.00
Webber		
ille O'Neal		
l Foyle		
Hardaway	6.00	15.00
verson		
Jackson		
Kidd		
ttie Pippen	10.00	25.00
Van Horn		
Bryant		
Ceballos		
nt Hill	5.00	12.00
McGrady		
ef Abdur-Rahim		
Garnett		
wn Kemp	6.00	15.00
s Camby		
uncan		
Robinson		
Allen	2.50	6.00
Smith		
on Anderson		
Elliott		
uncey Billups	3.00	8.00
Brandon		
io Daniels		
Johnson		
y Kittles	3.00	8.00
e Miller		
Battie		
m Olajuwon		
rry Johnson	2.50	6.00
e Walker		
e Taylor		
ker		

7-98 Bowman's Best Picks

ly inserted into packs at a rate of one in 24, card set features some of the top rookies from class. Card backs carry a "BP" prefix.

ETE SET (10)	8.00	20.00
C REFRACTORS: 1.5X TO 4X HI		
ATED ODDS 1:96 HOB, 1:160 RET		
CTORS: .75X TO 2X HI COLUMN		
ATED ODDS 1:48 HOB, 1:80 RET		
nal Foyle	.50	1.25
urice Taylor	.50	1.25
tin Croshere	.50	1.25
y McGrady	2.50	6.00
onio Daniels	.50	1.25
y Battie	.60	1.50
uncey Billups	2.00	5.00
Duncan	3.00	8.00
Mercer	.60	1.50
th Van Horn	1.00	2.50

1997-98 Bowman's Best Techniques

Randomly inserted into packs at a rate of one in 12, this 10-card set focuses on some of the NBA's top players at their positions. Card backs carry a "T" prefix.

COMPLETE SET (10)	12.50	30.00
*ATOMIC REFRACTORS: 1.5X TO 4X HI		
ATO: STATED ODDS 1:96 HOB, 1:160 RET		
*REFRACTORS: .75X TO 2X HI COLUMN		
REF: STATED ODDS 1:48 HOB, 1:80 RET		
T1 Dikembe Mutombo	1.00	2.50
T2 Michael Jordan	8.00	20.00
T3 Grant Hill	1.50	4.00
T4 Kobe Bryant	5.00	12.00
T5 Gary Payton	1.00	2.50
T6 Glen Rice	1.00	2.50
T7 Dennis Rodman	2.00	5.00
T8 Hakeem Olajuwon	1.25	3.00
T9 Allen Iverson	2.00	5.00
T10 John Stockton	1.25	3.00

1998-99 Bowman's Best

Released as a 125-card set, this product was distributed in six card packs with a suggested retail price of $5.00. The set was broken up into 100 veterans and 25 rookies. The veterans were issued against gold backgrounds, while the rookies were issued against silver backgrounds. The rookies were also inserted one in four packs.

COMPLETE SET (125)	50.00	100.00
COMPLETE SET w/o SP (100)	10.00	20.00
1 Jason Kidd	.50	1.25
2 Dikembe Mutombo	.30	.75
3 Chris Mullin	.30	.75
4 Terrell Brandon	.20	.50
5 Cedric Ceballos	.20	.50
6 Rod Strickland	.20	.50
7 Darrell Armstrong	.20	.50
8 Anfernee Hardaway	.50	1.25
9 Eddie Jones	.30	.75
10 Allen Iverson	.60	1.50
11 Kenny Anderson	.25	.60
12 Toni Kukoc	.30	.75
13 Lawrence Funderburke	.20	.50
14 P.J. Brown	.20	.50
15 Jeff Hornacek	.25	.60
16 Mookie Blaylock	.20	.50
17 Avery Johnson	.25	.60
18 Donyell Marshall	.20	.50
19 Detlef Schrempf	.30	.75
20 Joe Dumars	.30	.75
21 Charles Barkley	.50	1.25
22 Maurice Taylor	.20	.50
23 Chauncey Billups	.40	1.00
24 Lee Mayberry	.20	.50
25 Glen Rice	.30	.75
26 John Stockton	.40	1.00
27 Rik Smits	.25	.60
28 LaPhonso Ellis	.20	.50
29 Kerry Kittles	.20	.50
30 Damon Stoudamire	.30	.75
31 Kevin Garnett	.60	1.50
32 Chris Mills	.20	.50
33 Kendall Gill	.20	.50
34 Tim Thomas	.30	.75
35 Derek Anderson	.20	.50
36 Billy Owens	.20	.50
37 Bobby Jackson	.25	.60
38 Allan Houston	.25	.60
39 Horace Grant	.25	.60
40 Ray Allen	.40	1.00
41 Shawn Bradley	.20	.50
42 Arvydas Sabonis	.25	.60
43 Rex Chapman	.20	.50
44 Larry Johnson	.30	.75
45 Jayson Williams	.20	.50
46 Joe Smith	.25	.60
47 Ron Mercer	.25	.60
48 Rodney Rogers	.20	.50
49 Corliss Williamson	.20	.50
50 Tim Duncan	.60	1.50
51 Rasheed Wallace	.30	.75
52 Vin Baker	.25	.60
53 Reggie Miller	.40	1.00
54 Patrick Ewing	.40	1.00
55 Michael Finley	.30	.75
56 Bryant Reeves	.20	.50
57 Glenn Robinson	.25	.60
58 Walter McCarty	.20	.50
59 Brent Barry	.25	.60
60 John Starks	.25	.60
61 Clarence Weatherspoon	.20	.50
62 Calbert Cheaney	.20	.50
63 Lamond Murray	.20	.50
64 Zydrunas Ilgauskas	.30	.75
65 Anthony Mason	.20	.50
66 Bryon Russell	.20	.50
67 Dean Garrett	.20	.50
68 Tom Gugliotta	.20	.50
69 Dennis Rodman	.60	1.50
70 Keith Van Horn	.30	.75
71 Jamal Mashburn	.25	.60
72 Steve Smith	.25	.60
73 David Wesley	.20	.50
74 Chris Webber	.30	.75
75 Isaiah Rider	.20	.50
76 Stephon Marbury	.40	1.00
77 Tim Hardaway	.30	.75
78 Jerry Stackhouse	.30	.75
79 John Wallace	.20	.50
80 Karl Malone	.40	1.00
81 Juwan Howard	.25	.60
82 Antonio McDyess	.25	.60
83 David Robinson	.50	1.25
84 Bobby Phills	.20	.50
85 Scottie Pippen	.50	1.25
86 Brevin Knight	.20	.50
87 Alan Henderson	.20	.50
88 Kobe Bryant	1.50	4.00
89 Shawn Kemp	.30	.75
90 Antoine Walker	.30	.75
91 Tracy McGrady	.50	1.25
92 Hakeem Olajuwon	.40	1.00
93 Mark Jackson	.30	.75
94 Bison Dele	.20	.50
95 Gary Payton	.30	.75
96 Ron Harper	.25	.60
97 Shareef Abdur-Rahim	.30	.75
98 Alonzo Mourning	.40	1.00
99 Grant Hill	.50	1.25
100 Shaquille O'Neal	.75	2.00
101 Michael Olowokandi RC	1.25	3.00
102 Mike Bibby RC	2.50	6.00
103 Raef LaFrentz RC	1.25	3.00
104 Antawn Jamison RC	2.50	6.00
105 Vince Carter RC	5.00	12.00
106 Robert Traylor RC	1.00	2.50
107 Jason Williams RC	2.50	6.00
108 Larry Hughes RC	2.00	5.00
109 Dirk Nowitzki RC	6.00	15.00
110 Paul Pierce RC	5.00	12.00
111 Bonzi Wells RC	1.00	2.50
112 Michael Doleac RC	1.00	2.50
113 Keon Clark RC	1.00	2.50
114 Michael Dickerson RC	1.00	2.50
115 Matt Harpring RC	1.25	3.00
116 Bryce Drew RC	1.00	2.50
117 Pat Garrity RC	1.00	2.50
118 Roshown McLeod RC	1.00	2.50
119 Ricky Davis RC	1.50	4.00
120 Brian Skinner RC	1.00	2.50
121 Tyronn Lue RC	1.00	2.50
122 Felipe Lopez RC	1.00	2.50
123 Al Harrington RC	1.50	4.00
124 Corey Benjamin RC	1.00	2.50
125 Nazr Mohammed RC	1.00	2.50

1998-99 Bowman's Best Refractors

Randomly inserted in packs at one in 25, this 125-card set parallels the base set using the classic Refractor technology. The cards are serially numbered to 400. To ascertain values for individual cards, refer to the multiplier in the header below, coupled with the value of the base card.

*STARS: 5X TO 12X BASE CARD HI		
*RCs: 1.25X TO 3X BASE HI		
105 Vince Carter	25.00	60.00
109 Dirk Nowitzki	35.00	70.00

1998-99 Bowman's Best Atomic Refractors

Randomly inserted in packs at one in 100, this 125-card set parallels the base set using the classic Atomic Refractor technology. The cards are serially numbered to 100. To ascertain values for individual cards, refer to the multiplier in the header below, coupled with the value of the base card.

*STARS: 15X TO 40X BASE CARD HI		
*RCs: 3X TO 8X BASE HI		
1 Jason Kidd	25.00	60.00
8 Anfernee Hardaway	25.00	60.00
21 Charles Barkley	25.00	60.00
26 John Stockton	20.00	50.00
31 Kevin Garnett	40.00	100.00
40 Ray Allen	20.00	50.00
69 Dennis Rodman	40.00	100.00
85 Scottie Pippen	25.00	60.00
95 Gary Payton	15.00	40.00
99 Grant Hill	25.00	60.00
100 Shaquille O'Neal	40.00	100.00
105 Vince Carter	80.00	200.00
109 Dirk Nowitzki	80.00	200.00
110 Paul Pierce	50.00	120.00

1998-99 Bowman's Best Autographs

Randomly inserted in packs, this 9-card set features autographs of five current favorties and five future superstars. The veterans were inserted at one in 628, while the rookies were inserted at one in 598. Card backs carry an "A" prefix. Card "A7" does not exist.

A1 Kobe Bryant	75.00	150.00
A2 Tim Duncan	50.00	125.00
A3 Eddie Jones	12.50	30.00
A4 Gary Payton	12.50	30.00
A5 Antoine Walker	6.00	15.00
A6 Antawn Jamison	10.00	25.00
A8 Mike Bibby	6.00	15.00
A9 Vince Carter	30.00	80.00
A10 Michael Doleac	5.00	12.00

1998-99 Bowman's Best Autographs Atomic Refractors

Randomly inserted in packs at one in 10,073 for veterans and one in 12,515 for rookies, this 9-card set parallels the Autograph insert. Card backs carry an "A" prefix. Card "A7" does not exist. To ascertain values on individual cards, please refer to the multiplier in the header, coupled with the value of the base insert.

*ATO.REF: 2X TO 5X VALUE		
A9 Vince Carter	500.00	1000.00

1998-99 Bowman's Best Autographs Refractors

Randomly inserted in packs at one in 3,358 for veterans and one in 4,172 for rookies, this 9-card set parallels the Autograph insert using Refractor technology. Card backs carry an "A" prefix. Card "A7" does not exist. To ascertain values on individual cards, please refer to the multiplier in the header, coupled with the value of the base insert.

*REF: .75X TO 2X VALUE		
A9 Vince Carter	125.00	250.00

1998-99 Bowman's Best Franchise Best

Randomly inserted in packs at one in 23, this 10-card set highlights some of the best to ever play in the NBA. The cards are printed on 26-pt. stock and carry a "FB" prefix.

COMPLETE SET (10)	10.00	25.00
FB1 Michael Jordan	6.00	15.00
FB2 Karl Malone	1.00	2.50
FB3 Antoine Walker	.75	2.00
FB4 Grant Hill	1.25	3.00
FB5 Kevin Garnett	1.50	4.00
FB6 Shaquille O'Neal	2.00	5.00
FB7 Gary Payton	.75	2.00
FB8 Keith Van Horn	.75	2.00
FB9 Tim Duncan	1.50	4.00
FB10 Allen Iverson	1.50	4.00

1998-99 Bowman's Best Mirror Image

Randomly inserted in packs at one in 12, this 20-card set features a player from both the Western Conference and Eastern Conference on a die cut design. Card backs carry a "MI" prefix.

COMPLETE SET (20)	20.00	40.00
*REF: 6X TO 15X HI COLUMN		
REF: PRINT RUN 100 SERIAL #'d SETS		
*ATO.REF: 25X TO 60X HI		
ATO.REF: PRINT RUN 25 SERIAL #'d SETS		
MI1 Tim Hardaway	.75	2.00
Brevin Knight		
MI2 Gary Payton	.75	2.00
Damon Stoudamire		
MI3 Anfernee Hardaway	2.00	5.00
Allen Iverson		
MI4 John Stockton	1.00	2.50
Stephon Marbury		
MI5 Ray Allen	1.00	2.50
Kerry Kittles		
MI6 Eddie Jones	4.00	10.00
Kobe Bryant		
MI7 Steve Smith	.60	1.50
Ron Mercer		
MI8 Isaiah Rider	.75	2.00
Michael Finley		
MI9 Latrell Sprewell	.75	2.00
Antoine Walker		
MI10 Detlef Schrempf	.75	2.00
Shareef Abdur-Rahim		
MI11 Grant Hill	1.25	3.00
Tim Thomas		
MI12 Scottie Pippen	2.00	5.00
Kevin Garnett		
MI13 Jayson Williams	.60	1.50
Juwan Howard		
MI14 Vin Baker	.60	1.50
Antonio McDyess		
MI15 Shawn Kemp	.75	2.00
Keith Van Horn		
MI16 Karl Malone	1.50	4.00
Tim Duncan		
MI17 Alonzo Mourning	1.00	2.50
Zydrunas Ilgauskas		
MI18 Shaquille O'Neal	2.00	5.00
Bryant Reeves		
MI19 Dikembe Mutombo	.75	2.00
Theo Ratliff		
MI20 David Robinson	1.25	3.00
Greg Ostertag		

1998-99 Bowman's Best Performers

Randomly inserted at one in 12, this 10-card set highlights five veterans with some of last season's best stats, plus five rookies with the best collegiate stats. Card backs carry a "BP" prefix.

COMPLETE SET (10)	10.00	20.00
*REF: 4X TO 10X HI COLUMN		
REF: PRINT RUN 200 SERIAL #'d SETS		
*ATO.REF: 12X TO 30X HI		
ATO.REF: PRINT RUN 50 SERIAL #'d SETS		
BP1 Shaquille O'Neal	2.00	5.00
BP2 Kevin Garnett	1.50	4.00
BP3 Dikembe Mutombo	.75	2.00
BP4 Grant Hill	1.25	3.00
BP5 Tim Duncan	1.50	4.00
BP6 Antawn Jamison	1.00	2.50
BP7 Raef LaFrentz	.50	1.25
BP8 Mike Bibby	1.00	2.50
BP9 Paul Pierce	2.00	5.00
BP10 Jason Williams	1.00	2.50

1999-00 Bowman's Best

This year's version of Bowman's Best was issued as a 133-card set. Each pack contained five regular cards and one rookie card and carried a suggested retail price of $5. The set was broken into the following categories: 90 veterans, 10 Best Performers (subset) and 33 rookies.

COMPLETE SET (133)	30.00	60.00
1 Vince Carter	.60	1.50
2 Dikembe Mutombo	.30	.75
3 Steve Nash	.50	1.25
4 Matt Harpring	.25	.60
5 Stephon Marbury	.25	.60
6 Chris Webber	.30	.75
7 Jason Kidd	.50	1.25
8 Theo Ratliff	.25	.60
9 Damon Stoudamire	.30	.75
10 Shareef Abdur-Rahim	.25	.60
11 Rod Strickland	.20	.50
12 Jeff Hornacek	.25	.60
13 Vin Baker	.30	.75
14 Joe Smith	.25	.60
15 Alonzo Mourning	.40	1.00
16 Isaiah Rider	.20	.50
17 Shaquille O'Neal	.75	2.00
18 Chris Mullin	.30	.75
19 Charles Barkley	.50	1.25
20 Grant Hill	.40	1.00
21 Chris Mills	.20	.50
22 Antonio McDyess	.25	.60
23 Brevin Knight	.20	.50
24 Toni Kukoc	.30	.75
25 Antoine Walker	.30	.75
26 Eddie Jones	.30	.75
27 Tim Thomas	.25	.60
28 Latrell Sprewell	.30	.75
29 Larry Hughes	.25	.60
30 Tim Duncan	.60	1.50
31 Horace Grant	.25	.60
32 John Stockton	.40	1.00
33 Mike Bibby	.30	.75
34 Mitch Richmond	.30	.75
35 Allan Houston	.25	.60
36 Terrell Brandon	.20	.50
37 Glenn Robinson	.25	.60
38 Tyrone Nesby RC	.30	.75
39 Glen Rice	.30	.75
40 Hakeem Olajuwon	.40	1.00
41 Jerry Stackhouse	.30	.75
42 Elden Campbell	.20	.50
43 Ron Harper	.20	.50
44 Kenny Anderson	.25	.60
45 Michael Finley	.30	.75
46 Scottie Pippen	.50	1.25
47 Lindsey Hunter	.20	.50
48 Michael Olowokandi	.20	.50
49 P.J. Brown	.20	.50
50 Keith Van Horn	.25	.60
51 Michael Doleac	.20	.50
52 Anfernee Hardaway	.50	1.25
53 Rasheed Wallace	.30	.75
54 Nick Anderson	.20	.50
55 Gary Payton	.30	.75
56 Tracy McGrady	.50	1.25
57 Ray Allen	.30	.75
58 Kobe Bryant	1.50	4.00
59 Ron Mercer	.25	.60
60 Shawn Kemp	.30	.75
61 Anthony Mason	.20	.50
62 Tim Hardaway	.30	.75
63 Antawn Jamison	.30	.75
64 Mark Jackson	.30	.75
65 Tom Gugliotta	.20	.50
66 Marcus Camby	.25	.60
67 Kerry Kittles	.20	.50
68 Vlade Divac	.30	.75
69 Avery Johnson	.25	.60
70 Karl Malone	.40	1.00
71 Juwan Howard	.25	.60
72 Alan Henderson	.20	.50
73 Hersey Hawkins	.20	.50
74 Darrell Armstrong	.20	.50
75 Allen Iverson	.60	1.50
76 Maurice Taylor	.20	.50
77 Gary Trent	.20	.50
78 John Starks	.30	.75
79 Paul Pierce	.50	1.25
80 Kevin Garnett	.60	1.50
81 Patrick Ewing	.40	1.00
82 Steve Smith	.20	.50
83 Jason Williams	.40	1.00
84 David Robinson	.50	1.25
85 Charles Oakley	.25	.60
86 Bryant Reeves	.20	.50
87 Nick Van Exel	.25	.60
88 Reggie Miller	.30	.75
89 Chris Gatling	.20	.50
90 Brian Grant	.20	.50
91 Allen Iverson BP	.60	1.50
92 Tim Duncan BP	.60	1.50
93 Keith Van Horn BP	.25	.60
94 Kevin Garnett BP	.60	1.50
95 Kobe Bryant BP	1.50	4.00
96 Elton Brand BP	.75	2.00
97 Baron Davis BP	1.00	2.50
98 Lamar Odom BP	1.00	2.50
99 Wally Szczerbiak BP	.60	1.50
100 Jason Terry BP	.75	2.00
101 Elton Brand RC	1.00	2.50
102 Steve Francis RC	1.00	2.50
103 Baron Davis RC	1.25	3.00
104 Lamar Odom RC	1.25	3.00
105 Jonathan Bender RC	.40	1.00
106 Wally Szczerbiak RC	.75	2.00
107 Richard Hamilton RC	1.00	2.50
108 Andre Miller RC	1.00	2.50
109 Shawn Marion RC	1.00	2.50
110 Jason Terry RC	1.00	2.50
111 Trajan Langdon RC	.40	1.00
112 Aleksandar Radojevic RC	.40	1.00
113 Corey Maggette RC	.75	2.00
114 William Avery RC	.40	1.00
115 DeMarco Johnson RC	.40	1.00
116 Ron Artest RC	1.00	2.50
117 Cal Bowdler RC	.40	1.00
118 James Posey RC	.40	1.00
119 Quincy Lewis RC	.40	1.00
120 Dion Glover RC	.40	1.00
121 Jeff Foster RC	.40	1.00
122 Kenny Thomas RC	.40	1.00
123 Devean George RC	.40	1.00
124 Tim James RC	.40	1.00
125 Vonteego Cummings RC	.40	1.00
126 Jumaine Jones RC	.40	1.00
127 Scott Padgett RC	.40	1.00
128 Anthony Carter RC	.40	1.00
129 Chris Herren RC	.40	1.00
130 Todd MacCulloch RC	.40	1.00
131 John Celestand RC	.40	1.00
132 Adrian Griffin RC	.40	1.00
133 Mirsad Turkcan RC	.40	1.00

1999-00 Bowman's Best Atomic Refractors

Randomly inserted in packs at one in 33, this 133-card set parallels the base set. The cards featured the Atomic Refractor technology. The cards were serially numbered to 100. To ascertain values on individual cards, please refer to the multiplier in the header, coupled with the value of the base card.

*STARS: 10X TO 25X BASE CARD HI
*RCs: 5X TO 12X BASE HI

1999-00 Bowman's Best Refractors

Randomly inserted in packs at one in eight, this 133-card set parallels the base set. The cards featured the "classic" Refractor technology. The cards were serially numbered to 400. To ascertain values on individual cards, please refer to the multiplier in the header, coupled with the value of the base card.

*STARS: 3X TO 8X BASE CARD HI		
*RCs: 2X TO 5X BASE HI		
58 Kobe Bryant	15.00	40.00

1999-00 Bowman's Best Autographs

Randomly inserted in packs at one in 79, this 11-card set features autographs of top players and rookies. Each card features the Topps "Certified Autograph Issue" logo and Topps 3M sticker. Card backs carry a "BBA" prefix.

BBA1 Mitch Richmond	5.00	12.00
BBA2 Damon Stoudamire	4.00	10.00
BBA3 Antoine Walker	4.00	10.00
BBA4 Antonio McDyess	4.00	10.00
BBA5 Trajan Langdon	4.00	10.00
BBA6 Jumaine Jones	4.00	10.00
BBA7 Andre Miller	6.00	15.00
BBA8 Richard Hamilton	6.00	15.00
BBA9 Jonathan Bender	4.00	10.00
BBA10 William Avery	4.00	10.00
BBA11 Shawn Marion	6.00	15.00

1999-00 Bowman's Best Class Photo

Randomly inserted in packs at one in 100, this set features the star members of the 1999 NBA Rookie Class on one card. The card was also available as a Refractor (one in 3478 and serially numbered to 125) and as an Atomic Refractor (one in 12420 and serially numbered to 35).

CS1 Draft Picks	3.00	8.00
Richard Hamilton		
Corey Maggette		
Lamar Odom		
Wally Szczerbiak		
Jonathan Bender		
Trajan Langdon		
Aleksandar Radojevic		
Baron Davis		
Shawn Marion		
Jason Terry		
Andre Miller		
Steve Francis		
Elton Brand		
CS1 Draft Picks Refractor	25.00	60.00
Richard Hamilton		
Corey Maggette		
Lamar Odom		
Wally Szczerbiak		
Jonathan Bender		
Trajan Langdon		
Aleksandar Radojevic		
Baron Davis		
Shawn Marion		
Jason Terry		
Andre Miller		
Steve Francis		
Elton Brand		
CS1 Draft Picks Atomic Refractor	100.00	200.00
Richard Hamilton		
Corey Maggette		
Lamar Odom		
Wally Szczerbiak		
Jonathan Bender		
Trajan Langdon		
Aleksandar Radojevic		
Baron Davis		
Shawn Marion		
Jason Terry		
Andre Miller		
Steve Francis		
Elton Brand		

1999-00 Bowman's Best Franchise Favorites

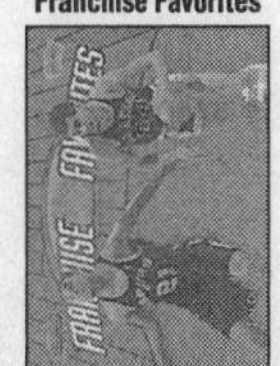

Randomly inserted in packs at one in 14, this three-card set honors the 1998-99 NBA Champion San Antonio Spurs. Autographs of all three cards were also available. The Duncan auto was inserted at one in 2174, the Gervin auto was inserted at one in 966 and the combo auto was inserted at one in 8694.

COMPLETE SET (3)	1.50	4.00
FR1A Tim Duncan	.75	2.00
FR1B George Gervin	.40	1.00
FR1C Tim Duncan	1.25	3.00
George Gervin		
FRA1A Tim Duncan AU	100.00	175.00
FRA1B George Gervin AU	8.00	20.00
FRA1C Tim Duncan AU	125.00	250.00
George Gervin AU		

1999-00 Bowman's Best Franchise Foundations

Randomly inserted in packs at one in 21, this 13-card set features greats of the game posed against the skyline of their team's home city. The cards are die cut and carry a "FF" prefix.

COMPLETE SET (13)	12.50	30.00
FF1 Allen Iverson	2.00	5.00
FF2 Tim Duncan	2.00	5.00
FF3 Kevin Garnett	2.00	5.00
FF4 Shareef Abdur-Rahim	.75	2.00
FF5 Kobe Bryant	5.00	12.00
FF6 Grant Hill	1.25	3.00
FF7 Keith Van Horn	.75	2.00
FF8 Vince Carter	2.00	5.00
FF9 Antoine Walker	1.00	2.50
FF10 Shaquille O'Neal	2.50	6.00
FF11 Jason Williams	1.25	3.00
FF12 Stephon Marbury	.75	2.00
FF13 Antonio McDyess	.75	2.00

1999-00 Bowman's Best Franchise Futures

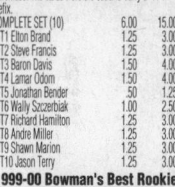

Randomly inserted at one in 27, this 10-card set showcases the future leaders of their respective franchises. The cards were die cut and carry a "FFT" prefix.

COMPLETE SET (10)	6.00	15.00
FFT1 Elton Brand	1.25	3.00
FFT2 Steve Francis	1.25	3.00
FFT3 Baron Davis	1.50	4.00
FFT4 Lamar Odom	1.50	4.00
FFT5 Jonathan Bender	.50	1.25
FFT6 Wally Szczerbiak	1.00	2.50
FFT7 Richard Hamilton	1.25	3.00
FFT8 Andre Miller	1.25	3.00
FFT9 Shawn Marion	1.25	3.00
FFT10 Jason Terry	1.25	3.00

1999-00 Bowman's Best Rookie Locker Room Collection

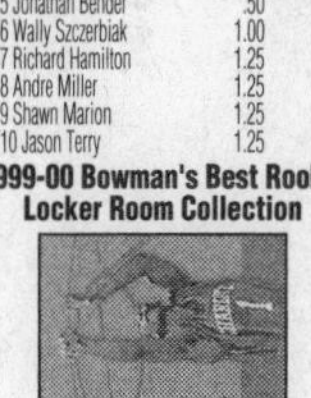

Randomly inserted in packs, this nine-card set features jerseys and autographs of the top rookies. All cards feature the Topps 3M sticker to verify authenticity. The autographed cards were inserted at one in 174, while the jersey cards were inserted at one in 197. Card backs carry either a "LRCA" prefix or "LRCJ" prefix.

LRCA1 Elton Brand AU	8.00	20.00
LRCA2 Steve Francis AU	8.00	20.00
LRCA3 Wally Szczerbiak AU	6.00	15.00
LRCA4 Baron Davis AU	10.00	25.00
LRCA5 Corey Maggette AU	6.00	15.00
LRCJ1 Elton Brand	5.00	12.00
LRCJ2 Steve Francis	5.00	12.00
LRCJ3 Wally Szczerbiak	4.00	10.00
LRCJ4 Baron Davis	6.00	15.00

1999-00 Bowman's Best Techniques

Randomly inserted in packs at one in 21, this 13-card set features the NBA's most spectacular players and their patented moves. Card backs carry a "BT" prefix.

COMPLETE SET (13)	8.00	20.00
BT1 Tim Duncan	2.00	5.00
BT2 Tim Hardaway	1.00	2.50
BT3 Shaquille O'Neal	2.50	6.00
BT4 Vince Carter	2.00	5.00
BT5 Dikembe Mutombo	1.00	2.50
BT6 Grant Hill	1.25	3.00

BT7 Gary Payton	1.00	2.50
BT8 Jason Williams	1.25	3.00
BT9 Stephon Marbury	.75	2.00
BT10 Reggie Miller	1.00	2.50
BT11 Scottie Pippen	1.50	4.00
BT12 John Stockton	1.25	3.00
BT13 Karl Malone	1.25	3.00

1999-00 Bowman's Best World's Best

Randomly inserted in packs at one in 30, this nine-card set features nine members of the Men's Team USA squad that competed in the 2000 Summer Olympic Games. Card backs carry a "WB" prefix.

COMPLETE SET (9)	5.00	12.00
WB1 Allan Houston	.75	2.00
WB2 Kevin Garnett	2.00	5.00
WB3 Gary Payton	1.00	2.50
WB4 Steve Smith	.60	1.50
WB5 Tim Hardaway	1.00	2.50
WB6 Tim Duncan	2.00	5.00
WB7 Jason Kidd	1.50	4.00
WB8 Tom Gugliotta	.60	1.50
WB9 Vin Baker	1.00	2.50

2000-01 Bowman's Best Promos

This six-card standard-size set was sent to dealers as a promotional set for the 2000-01 Bowman's Best issue. The cards carry a "PP" prefix.

COMPLETE SET (6)	1.25	3.00
PP1 Jason Kidd	.50	1.25
PP2 Alonzo Mourning	.40	1.00
PP3 John Stockton	.40	1.00
PP4 Antoine Walker	.25	.60
PP5 Scottie Pippen	.50	1.25
PP6 Allan Houston	.25	.60

2000-01 Bowman's Best

The 2000-01 Bowman's Best product was released in February, 2001 and features a 133-card base set. The set is broken into tiers as follows. Base Veterans (1-100), and Rookies (101-133) that are individually serial numbered to 499. Please note that there are three different versions of each rookie card, and that each version is serial numbered to 499. Please note that version "A" cards are blue, Version "B" cards are black, and Version "C" cards are blue-black. Each pack contains five cards and carries a suggested retail price of 2.99.

COMPLETE SET w/o RC (100)	15.00	30.00
1 Allen Iverson	.60	1.50
2 Darrell Armstrong	.20	.50
3 Kendall Gill	.20	.50
4 Marcus Camby	.25	.60
5 Glen Rice	.25	.60
6 Eddie Jones	.30	.75
7 Wally Szczerbiak	.25	.60
8 Antawn Jamison	.30	.75
9 Raef LaFrentz	.20	.50
10 Steve Francis	.30	.75
11 Tracy McGrady	.50	1.25
12 Brian Grant	.20	.50
13 Vlade Divac	.25	.60
14 Gary Payton	.30	.75
15 Vince Carter	.60	1.50
16 John Stockton	.40	1.00
17 Mike Bibby	.30	.75
18 Derek Anderson	.20	.50
19 Juwan Howard	.25	.60
20 Allan Houston	.25	.60
21 Kevin Garnett	.60	1.50
22 Michael Olowokandi	.20	.50
23 Maurice Taylor	.20	.50
24 Jerry Stackhouse	.25	.60
25 Nick Van Exel	.25	.60
26 Andre Miller	.25	.60
27 Michael Finley	.30	.75
28 Jamal Mashburn	.25	.60
29 Ron Mercer	.20	.50
30 Jim Jackson	.20	.50
31 Kenny Anderson	.25	.60
32 Karl Malone	.40	1.00
33 Rod Strickland	.25	.60
34 Shaquille O'Neal	.75	2.00
35 Glenn Robinson	.25	.60
36 Keith Van Horn	.25	.60
37 Grant Hill	.40	1.00
38 Eric Snow	.20	.50
39 Anfernee Hardaway	.50	1.25
40 Scottie Pippen	.50	1.25
41 Jason Williams	.30	.75
42 Elton Brand	.30	.75
43 Stephon Marbury	.25	.60
44 David Robinson	.50	1.25
45 Antonio Davis	.20	.50
46 Michael Dickerson	.20	.50
47 Mitch Richmond	.25	.60
48 Rashard Lewis	.30	.75
49 Jermaine O'Neal	.30	.75
50 Tim Duncan	.60	1.50
51 Tom Gugliotta	.20	.50
52 Theo Ratliff	.20	.50
53 Joe Smith	.25	.60
54 Tim Thomas	.20	.50
55 Brevin Knight	.20	.50
56 Dale Davis	.20	.50
57 Cuttino Mobley	.25	.60
58 Cedric Ceballos	.20	.50
59 Christian Laettner	.20	.50
60 Dirk Nowitzki	.50	1.25
61 Paul Pierce	.40	1.00
62 Derrick Coleman	.25	.60
63 Dikembe Mutombo	.30	.75
64 Lamond Murray	.20	.50
65 Antonio McDyess	.25	.60
66 Reggie Miller	.30	.75
67 Hakeem Olajuwon	.40	1.00
68 Corey Maggette	.25	.60
69 Lamar Odom	.30	.75
70 Larry Hughes	.25	.60
71 Anthony Mason	.20	.50
72 Sam Cassell	.25	.60
73 Terrell Brandon	.20	.50
74 Latrell Sprewell	.25	.60
75 Kobe Bryant	1.50	4.00
76 Tim Hardaway	.30	.75
77 Mark Jackson	.25	.60
78 Vin Baker	.25	.60
79 Jonathan Bender	.20	.50
80 Chris Webber	.30	.75
81 Rasheed Wallace	.30	.75
82 Shawn Marion	.30	.75
83 Toni Kukoc	.25	.60
84 Patrick Ewing	.40	1.00
85 Ray Allen	.30	.75
86 Isaiah Rider	.25	.60
87 Danny Fortson	.20	.50
88 Jerome Williams	.20	.50
89 Shawn Kemp	.30	.75
90 Ron Artest	.30	.75
91 P.J. Brown	.20	.50
92 Baron Davis	.30	.75
93 Antoine Walker	.25	.60
94 Jason Terry	.30	.75
95 Jalen Rose	.25	.60
96 Avery Johnson	.25	.60
97 Shareef Abdur-Rahim	.25	.60
98 Bryon Russell	.20	.50
99 Richard Hamilton	.25	.60
100 Jason Kidd	.50	1.25
101A Kenyon Martin RC	2.50	6.00
101B Kenyon Martin RC	2.50	6.00
101C Kenyon Martin RC	2.50	6.00
102A Stromile Swift RC	1.00	2.50
102B Stromile Swift RC	1.00	2.50
102C Stromile Swift RC	1.00	2.50
103A Darius Miles RC	1.00	2.50
103B Darius Miles RC	1.00	2.50
103C Darius Miles RC	1.00	2.50
104A Marcus Fizer RC	1.00	2.50
104B Marcus Fizer RC	1.00	2.50
104C Marcus Fizer RC	1.00	2.50
105A Mike Miller RC	2.00	5.00
105B Mike Miller RC	2.00	5.00
105C Mike Miller RC	2.00	5.00
106A DerMarr Johnson RC	1.00	2.50
106B DerMarr Johnson RC	1.00	2.50
106C DerMarr Johnson RC	1.00	2.50
107A Chris Mihm RC	1.00	2.50
107B Chris Mihm RC	1.00	2.50
107C Chris Mihm RC	1.00	2.50
108A Jamal Crawford RC	1.50	4.00
108B Jamal Crawford RC	1.50	4.00
108C Jamal Crawford RC	1.50	4.00
109A Joel Przybilla RC	1.00	2.50
109B Joel Przybilla RC	1.00	2.50
109C Joel Przybilla RC	1.00	2.50
110A Keyon Dooling RC	1.00	2.50
110B Keyon Dooling RC	1.00	2.50
110C Keyon Dooling RC	1.00	2.50
111A Jerome Moiso RC	1.00	2.50
111B Jerome Moiso RC	1.00	2.50
111C Jerome Moiso RC	1.00	2.50
112A Etan Thomas RC	1.00	2.50
112B Etan Thomas RC	1.00	2.50
112C Etan Thomas RC	1.00	2.50
113A Courtney Alexander RC	1.00	2.50
113B Courtney Alexander RC	1.00	2.50
113C Courtney Alexander RC	1.00	2.50
114A Mateen Cleaves RC	1.00	2.50
114B Mateen Cleaves RC	1.00	2.50
114C Mateen Cleaves RC	1.00	2.50
115A Jason Collier RC	1.00	2.50
115B Jason Collier RC	1.00	2.50
115C Jason Collier RC	1.00	2.50
116A Hedo Turkoglu RC	2.00	5.00
116B Hedo Turkoglu RC	2.00	5.00
116C Hedo Turkoglu RC	2.00	5.00
117A Desmond Mason RC	1.25	3.00
117B Desmond Mason RC	1.25	3.00
117C Desmond Mason RC	1.25	3.00
118A Quentin Richardson RC	1.50	4.00
118B Quentin Richardson RC	1.50	4.00
118C Quentin Richardson RC	1.50	4.00
119A Jamaal Magloire RC	1.00	2.50
119B Jamaal Magloire RC	1.00	2.50
119C Jamaal Magloire RC	1.00	2.50
120A Speedy Claxton RC	1.00	2.50
120B Speedy Claxton RC	1.00	2.50
120C Speedy Claxton RC	1.00	2.50
121A Morris Peterson RC	1.00	2.50
121B Morris Peterson RC	1.00	2.50
121C Morris Peterson RC	1.00	2.50
122A Donnell Harvey RC	1.00	2.50
122B Donnell Harvey RC	1.00	2.50
122C Donnell Harvey RC	1.00	2.50
123A DeShawn Stevenson RC	1.25	3.00
123B DeShawn Stevenson RC	1.25	3.00
123C DeShawn Stevenson RC	1.25	3.00
124A Dalibor Bagaric RC	1.00	2.50
124B Dalibor Bagaric RC	1.00	2.50
124C Dalibor Bagaric RC	1.00	2.50
125A Iakovos Tsakalidis RC	1.00	2.50
125B Iakovos Tsakalidis RC	1.00	2.50
125C Iakovos Tsakalidis RC	1.00	2.50
126A Mamadou N'Diaye RC	1.00	2.50
126B Mamadou N'Diaye RC	1.00	2.50
126C Mamadou N'Diaye RC	1.00	2.50
127A Lavor Postell RC	1.00	2.50
127B Lavor Postell RC	1.00	2.50
127C Lavor Postell RC	1.00	2.50
128A Erick Barkley RC	1.00	2.50
128B Erick Barkley RC	1.00	2.50
128C Erick Barkley RC	1.00	2.50
129A Mark Madsen RC	1.00	2.50
129B Mark Madsen RC	1.00	2.50
129C Mark Madsen RC	1.00	2.50
130A Khalid El-Amin RC	1.00	2.50
130B Khalid El-Amin RC	1.00	2.50
130C Khalid El-Amin RC	1.00	2.50
131A A.J. Guyton RC	1.00	2.50
131B A.J. Guyton RC	1.00	2.50
131C A.J. Guyton RC	1.00	2.50
132A Stephen Jackson RC	1.50	4.00
132B Stephen Jackson RC	1.50	4.00
132C Stephen Jackson RC	1.50	4.00
133A Michael Redd RC	2.50	6.00
133B Michael Redd RC	2.50	6.00
133C Michael Redd RC	2.50	6.00
LCP1 Kenyon Martin	4.00	10.00
Stromile Swift		
Darius Miles		
Marcus Fizer		
Mike Miller		
DerMarr Johnson		
Chris Mihm		
Jamal Crawford		
Joel Przybilla		
Keyon Dooling		
Jerome Moiso		
Etan Thomas		
Courtney Alexander		

2000-01 Bowman's Best Elements of the Game

Randomly inserted into packs at one in 12, this 13-card insert features players that have all of the elements to make them superstars. Card backs carry an "EG" prefix.

COMPLETE SET (13)	12.50	25.00
EG1 Shaquille O'Neal	1.50	4.00
EG2 Allen Iverson	1.25	3.00
EG3 Vince Carter	1.25	3.00
EG4 Jason Kidd	1.00	2.50
EG5 Kevin Garnett	1.25	3.00
EG6 Tracy McGrady	1.00	2.50
EG7 Tim Duncan	1.25	3.00
EG8 Gary Payton	.60	1.50
EG9 Larry Hughes	.50	1.25
EG10 Lamar Odom	.60	1.50
EG11 Jason Williams	.60	1.50
EG12 Kobe Bryant	3.00	8.00
EG13 Karl Malone	.75	2.00

2000-01 Bowman's Best Expressions

Randomly inserted into packs at one in 8, this 20-card insert features players that express themselves very well on the basketball court. Card backs carry an "E" prefix.

COMPLETE SET (20)	12.50	25.00
E1 Shaquille O'Neal	1.50	4.00
E2 Kevin Garnett	1.25	3.00
E3 Allen Iverson	1.25	3.00
E4 Antonio McDyess	.50	1.25
E5 Rasheed Wallace	.60	1.50
E6 Steve Francis	.60	1.50
E7 Kobe Bryant	3.00	8.00
E8 Vince Carter	1.25	3.00
E9 Chris Webber	.60	1.50
E10 Gary Payton	.60	1.50
E11 Latrell Sprewell	.50	1.25
E12 Tracy McGrady	1.00	2.50
E13 Reggie Miller	.60	1.50
E14 Antoine Walker	.50	1.25
E15 Jason Williams	.60	1.50
E16 Michael Finley	.60	1.50
E17 Patrick Ewing	.75	2.00
E18 Karl Malone	.75	2.00
E19 Elton Brand	.60	1.50
E20 Lamar Odom	.60	1.50

2000-01 Bowman's Best Franchise Favorites

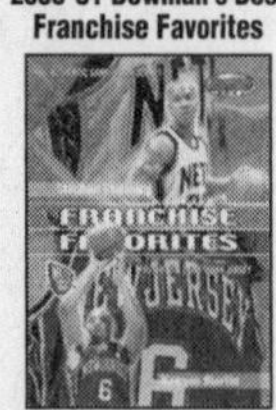

Randomly inserted into packs, this 10-card insert features seven dual-player jersey cards of superstar teammates. The set also includes autographed cards of Shaquille O'Neal, Magic Johnson, and a Shaquille O'Neal/Magic Johnson co-signer. Card backs carry an "FFJ" prefix.

FFA1 Shaquille O'Neal AU	40.00	80.00
FFA2 Magic Johnson AU	40.00	100.00
FFA3 Shaquille O'Neal AU	125.00	250.00
Magic Johnson AU		
FFJ1 Tracy McGrady	10.00	25.00
Grant Hill JSY		
FFJ2 Antoine Walker	12.00	30.00
Paul Pierce JSY		
FFJ3 Darius Miles	8.00	20.00
Keyon Dooling JSY		
FFJ4 Stephon Marbury	8.00	20.00
Kenyon Martin JSY		
FFJ5 Jason Kidd	20.00	50.00
Anfernee Hardaway JSY		
FFJ6 Shareef Abdur-Rahim	8.00	20.00
Stromile Swift JSY		

2000-01 Bowman's Best Rookie Locker Room Collection

Randomly inserted into packs, this 58-card insert is broken into four tiers. The first tier features (15) rookies from the 2000-01 season (1:4), the second tier features an autographed version of the these (15) cards (1:32), the third tier features (25) rookies with a swatch of jersey worn at the Rookie Photo Shoot. (1:41), and the fourth tier features (3) autographed cards of Steve Francis and Elton Brand (1:274). Card backs carry an "LRC" prefix.

LRC1 Kenyon Martin	.75	2.00
LRC2 Stromile Swift	.30	.75
LRC3 Darius Miles	.30	.75
LRC4 Marcus Fizer	.30	.75
LRC5 Mike Miller	.60	1.50
LRC6 DerMarr Johnson	.30	.75
LRC7 Chris Mihm	.30	.75
LRC8 Jamal Crawford	.50	1.25
LRC9 Joel Przybilla	.30	.75
LRC10 Keyon Dooling	.30	.75
LRC11 Jerome Moiso	.30	.75
LRC12 Courtney Alexander	.30	.75
LRC13 Mateen Cleaves	.30	.75
LRC14 Speedy Claxton	.30	.75
LRC15 DeShawn Stevenson	.40	1.00
LRCA1 Jamal Crawford AU	6.00	15.00
LRCA2 Courtney Alexander AU	4.00	10.00
LRCA3 Keyon Dooling AU	4.00	10.00
LRCA4 Mateen Cleaves AU	4.00	10.00
LRCA5 A.J. Guyton AU	4.00	10.00
LRCA6 Khalid El-Amin AU	4.00	10.00
LRCA7 Desmond Mason AU	5.00	12.00
LRCA8 Erick Barkley AU	4.00	10.00
LRCA9 Larry Hughes AU	4.00	10.00
LRCA10 Maurice Taylor AU	4.00	10.00
LRCA11 Tim Thomas AU	4.00	10.00
LRCA12 Antawn Jamison AU	6.00	15.00
LRCA13 Jonathan Bender AU	4.00	10.00
LRCA14 Baron Davis AU	5.00	12.00
LRCA15 Mike Bibby AU	5.00	12.00
LRCF1 Steve Francis AU	6.00	15.00
LRCF2 Elton Brand AU	5.00	12.00
LRCF3 Steve Francis AU	12.50	30.00
Elton Brand AU		
LRCR1 Kenyon Martin JSY	6.00	15.00
LRCR2 Stromile Swift JSY	2.50	6.00
LRCR3 Darius Miles JSY	2.50	6.00
LRCR4 Marcus Fizer JSY	2.50	6.00
LRCR5 Mike Miller JSY	5.00	12.00
LRCR6 DerMarr Johnson JSY	2.50	6.00
LRCR7 Chris Mihm JSY	2.50	6.00
LRCR8 Mark Madsen JSY	2.50	6.00
LRCR9 Joel Przybilla JSY	2.50	6.00
LRCR10 Keyon Dooling JSY	2.50	6.00
LRCR11 Jerome Moiso JSY	2.50	6.00
LRCR12 Etan Thomas JSY	2.50	6.00
LRCR13 Courtney Alexander JSY	2.50	6.00
LRCR14 Mateen Cleaves JSY	2.50	6.00
LRCR15 Jason Collier JSY	2.50	6.00
LRCR16 Desmond Mason JSY	3.00	8.00
LRCR17 Quentin Richardson JSY	4.00	10.00
LRCR18 Jamaal Magloire JSY	2.50	6.00
LRCR19 Speedy Claxton JSY	2.50	6.00
LRCR20 Morris Peterson JSY	2.50	6.00
LRCR21 Donnell Harvey JSY	2.50	6.00
LRCR22 DeShawn Stevenson JSY	3.00	8.00
LRCR23 Mamadou N'Diaye JSY	2.50	6.00
LRCR24 Erick Barkley JSY	2.50	6.00
LRCR25 Hedo Turkoglu JSY	5.00	12.00

1974-75 Braves Buffalo Linnett

These three charcoal drawings are skillfully executed facial portraits of Buffalo Braves players. They were drawn by noted sports artist Charles Linnett and measure approximately 8 1/2" by 11". In the lower right corner, a facsimile autograph of the player is written across the portrait. The backs are blank. The drawings are unnumbered and are checklisted below in alphabetical order.

COMPLETE SET (3)	10.00	20.00
1 Ernie DiGregorio	5.00	10.00
2 Garfield Heard	2.50	6.00
3 Jim McMillian	2.50	6.00

1976-77 Braves Team Issue

These 8" by 10" blank-backed black and white glossy photos feature members of the 1976-77 Buffalo Braves. Since these photos are unnumbered, we have sequenced them in alphabetical order.

COMPLETE SET (14)	15.00	30.00
1 Don Adams	.75	2.00
2 Bird Averitt	.75	2.00
3 Gary Brewster	.75	2.00
4 Fred Foster	.75	2.00
5 George Jackson	.75	2.00
6 Greg Jackson	.75	2.00
7 Bob McAdoo	5.00	10.00
8 John Neumann	.75	2.00
9 Dale Schlueter	.75	2.00
10 Randy Smith	2.50	6.00
11 John Shumate	1.00	2.50
12 Claude Terry	.75	2.00
13 Bob MacKinnon GM	.75	2.00
Tates Locke CO		
14 Charlie Harrison ACO	.75	2.00
Ray Melchiorre TR		

1951 Bread For Energy

The 1951 Bread for Energy bread end labels set contains 11 known labels of players in the National Football League, professional basketball, pro boxing, and famous actors. Each measures approximately 2 3/4" by 2 3/4" with the corners cut out in typical bread label style. These labels are not usually found in top condition due to the difficulty in removing them from the bread package. While all the bakeries who issued this set are not presently known, Junge's Brand Bread in the New England area is one bakery that has been confirmed. As with many of the bread label sets of the early 1950's, an album to house the set was probably issued. Each label was printed with a red, yellow, and blue background. The cards are unnumbered but are arranged alphabetically within subject below.

24 Bob Davies BK	600.00	1000.00
25 Joe Fulks BK	1000.00	1500.00
26 Dick McGuire BK	600.00	1000.00
27 George Mikan BK	6000.00	9000.00

1950-51 Bread for Health

The 1950-51 Bread for Health basketball set consists of 32 bread end labels (each measuring approximately 2 3/4" by 2 3/4") of players in the National Basketball Association. While all the bakeries who issued this set are not present known, Fisher's Bread in the New Jersey, New York and Pennsylvania area and NBC Bread in the Michigan area are two of the bakeries that have been confirmed to date. As with many of the bread label sets of the early '50s, an album to house the set was probably issued. Each label contains the B.E.B. copyright found on so many of the labels of this period. Labels which contain "Bread for Energy" at the bottom are not a part of the set but part of a series of movie, western and sports stars issued during the same approximate time period. The American Card Catalog does not designate a number to this series; however, based on its similarity to a corresponding football issue, it is referenced as D290-15A. The set is dated by the fact that 1949-50 was Buddy Jeanette and Bob Kinney's last active year and Vince Boryla, Tony Lavelli, and Vern Mikkelsen's first active year.

COMPLETE SET (32)	16000.00	21000.00
1 Paul Armstrong	250.00	450.00
2 Ralph Beard	400.00	750.00
3 Vince Boryla	300.00	600.00
4 Walter Budko	250.00	450.00
5 Al Cervi	250.00	450.00
6 Bob Davies	600.00	950.00
7 Dwight Eddleman	300.00	600.00
8 Arnold Ferrin	300.00	600.00
9 Joe Fulks	800.00	1200.00
10 Harry Gallatin	400.00	650.00
11 Chuck Gilmur	250.00	450.00
12 Alex Groza	400.00	750.00
13 Bruce Hale	300.00	600.00
14 Paul Hoffman	250.00	450.00
15 Buddy Jeanette	400.00	750.00
16 Bob Kinney	250.00	450.00
17 Tony Lavelli	250.00	450.00
18 Ron Livingstone	250.00	450.00
19 Horace McKinney	400.00	700.00
20 Stan Miasek	250.00	450.00
21 George Mikan	2300.00	3300.00
22 Andy Phillip	300.00	600.00
23 Arnie Risen	400.00	750.00
24 Fred Schaus	400.00	700.00
25 Dolph Schayes	1100.00	1500.00
26 Fred Scolari	250.00	450.00
27 George Senesky	250.00	450.00
28 Paul Seymour	300.00	600.00
29 Cornelius Simmons	300.00	600.00
30 Gene Vance	250.00	450.00
31 Brady Walker	250.00	450.00
32 Max Zaslofsky	300.00	600.00

1976 Buckmans Discs

The 1976 Buckmans Discs set contains 20 unnumbered discs measuring approximately 3 3/8" in diameter. The discs have various color borders containing brief biographical information and feature black and white drawings of the players with fascimile signatures. This set was distributed through Buckmans Ice Cream Village in Rochester, New York. The discs can be found with Buckmans backs or blank backs with the Buckmans backs being harder to find and carrying a 50 percent premium above the prices listed below. The cards are listed alphabetically in the checklist below. The set was also issued with Crane Potato Chips; the Crane Potato Chips advertisement on the backs is printed in red and blue on a white background. The Crane variations show Crane at the top of the disc rather than four stars; the Crane discs are harder to find and are valued at approximately six times the Buckmans prices listed below.

COMPLETE SET (20)	25.00	50.00
1 Kareem Abdul-Jabbar	4.00	10.00
2 Nate Archibald	2.00	5.00
3 Rick Barry	2.00	5.00
4 Tom Boerwinkle	.75	2.00
5 Bill Bradley	2.50	6.00
6 Dave Cowens	2.50	6.00
7 Bob Dandridge	1.00	2.50
8 Walt Frazier	2.50	6.00
9 Gail Goodrich	2.50	6.00
10 John Havlicek	3.00	8.00
11 Connie Hawkins	2.50	6.00
12 Lou Hudson	1.25	3.00
13 Sam Lacey	.75	2.00
14 Bob Lanier	2.00	5.00
15 Bob Love	1.50	4.00
16 Bob McAdoo	1.50	4.00
17 Earl Monroe	2.00	5.00
18 Jerry Sloan	2.00	5.00
19 Norm Van Lier	1.25	3.00
20 Jo Jo White	1.25	3.00

1977-78 Bucks Action Photos

These glossy action photos featuring members of the Milwaukee Bucks measure approximately 5" by 7" and are printed on very thin paper. The photos are in full color and borderless. The players are identified only by their facsimile autographs inscribed across the picture. The backs are blank.

COMPLETE SET (10)	6.00	15.00
1 Kent Benson	.75	2.00
2 Junior Bridgeman	.75	2.00
3 Quinn Buckner	1.00	2.50
4 Alex English	3.00	8.00
5 John Gianelli	.60	1.50
6 Ernie Grunfeld	1.00	2.50
7 Marques Johnson	2.00	5.00
8 Dave Meyers	.75	2.00
9 Lloyd Walton	.60	1.50
10 Brian Winters	1.00	2.50

1985 Bucks Card Night/Star

This 13-card set was given away during the Milwaukee Bucks "Card Night" on January 21, 1985. Card number 10 Larry Micheaux was withdrawn at the request of the Bucks management due to his Free Agent signing after the printing of the cards. Cards measure 2 1/2" by 3 1/2" and have a green border around the fronts of the cards and green printing on the backs. Cards feature Star '85 logo on the fronts.

COMPLETE SET (13)	20.00	50.00
1 Don Nelson CO	1.50	4.00
2 Randy Breuer	.75	2.00
3 Terry Cummings	2.00	5.00
4 Charlie Davis	.75	2.00
5 Mike Dunleavy	1.50	4.00
6 Kenny Fields	.75	2.00
7 Kevin Grevey	.75	2.00
8 Craig Hodges	1.25	3.00
9 Alton Lister	.75	2.00
10 Larry Micheaux SP	15.00	30.00
11 Paul Mokeski	1.25	3.00
12 Sidney Moncrief	2.50	6.00
13 Paul Pressey	1.25	3.00

1988-89 Bucks Green Border

This 16-card set was issued in sheet form: four rows of four cards each; after perforation, the cards measure approximately 2 3/4" by 4". Each of the four strips was given away at a different Milwaukee Bucks home game. The fronts feature a color action player photo, with a thin black border on medium green background. In white lettering the team and player name are given below the picture. The back has the Milwaukee Bucks logo in the upper left corner and biographical information given in tabular format. Whole sheets carry a slight premium on the set price.

COMPLETE SET (16)	12.50	30.00
1 Kareem Abdul-Jabbar	5.00	12.00
2 Randy Breuer	.75	2.00
3 Terry Cummings	1.50	4.00
4 Jeff Grayer	.75	2.00
5 Del Harris CO	1.25	3.00
6 Tito Horford	.75	2.00
7 Jay Humphries	1.25	3.00
8 Larry Krystkowiak	.75	2.00
9 Paul Mokeski	.75	2.00
10 Sidney Moncrief	2.00	5.00
11 Ricky Pierce	1.25	3.00
12 Paul Pressey	.75	2.00
13 Fred Roberts	.75	2.00
14 Jack Sikma	1.50	4.00
15 The Bradley Center	.75	2.00
16 Del Harris CO	1.00	2.50
Frank Hamblen ACO		
Mack Calvin ACO		
Mike Dunleavy ACO		
Jeff Snedeker TR		

1986 Bucks Lifebuoy/Star

The 1986 Star Lifebuoy Milwaukee Bucks set contains 13 cards, one for each of the 12 players plus a coaching staff card. The set's basic design is identical to those of the Star Company's regular NBA sets. The front borders are lime green, and the backs show each player's NBA statistics (collegiate for number 13 Jerry Reynolds). The cards show a Star '86 logo in the right corner. The cards measure approximately 2 by 3 1/2". The cards are numbered in the upper corner of the reverse; the numbering correspon alphabetical order by player.

COMPLETE SET (13)	6.00
1 Don Nelson CO	1.25
2 Randy Breuer	.60
3 Terry Cummings	1.25
4 Charlie Davis	.60
5 Kenny Fields	.60
6 Craig Hodges	.75
7 Jeff Lamp	.75
8 Alton Lister	.60
9 Paul Mokeski	.75
10 Sidney Moncrief	1.50
11 Ricky Pierce	.75
12 Paul Pressey	.75
13 Jerry Reynolds	.60

1973-74 Bucks Linnett

Measuring 8 1/2" by 11", these six charcoal dra are facial portraits by noted sports artist Charles Linnett. The player's facsimile autograph is insc across the lower right corner. The backs are bla Three portraits were included in each package, suggested retail price of 99 cents. The portraits unnumbered and checklisted below in alphabet order. The set is dated by the fact that 1973-74 Oscar Robertson's last year with the Bucks and Driscoll's first year with the Bucks.

COMPLETE SET (6)	20.00
1 Kareem Abdul-Jabbar	12.50
2 Lucius Allen	1.50
3 Terry Driscoll	1.25
4 Russell Lee	1.25
5 Curtis Perry	1.25
6 Oscar Robertson	10.00

1974-75 Bucks Linnett

These ten charcoal drawings are skillfully execu facial portraits of Milwaukee Bucks players. The drawn by noted sports artist Charles Linnett and measure approximately 8 1/2" by 11". In the low corner, a facsimile autograph of the player is w across the portrait. The backs are blank. The dr are unnumbered and we have checklisted them in alphabetical order. The set is dated by the fac 1974-75 was Gary Brokaw and Kevin Restani's active year and Steve Kuberski and George Thompson's only year with the Bucks.

COMPLETE SET (10)	25.00
1 Kareem Abdul-Jabbar	12.50
2 Gary Brokaw	1.25
3 Bob Dandridge	1.50
4 Mickey Davis	1.00
5 Steve Kuberski	1.00
6 Jon McGlocklin	1.50
7 Jim Price	1.00
8 Kevin Restani	1.00
9 George Thompson	1.00
10 Cornell Warner	1.00

1976-77 Bucks Playing Ca

The 55-card deck of playing cards was co-spo by White Hen Pantry and Coca-Cola. The cards measure approximately 2 1/4" by 3 1/2" and ha rounded corners. The fronts feature black-and- action shots with coach or player identification background and statistics below the picture. Th have a brown, red and yellow design with a bas in the center. The two sponsors logos appear t opposite diagonal corners of the card. The set checklisted below as if it was a playing card se checklist, C means Clubs, D means Diamonds means Hearts and S means Spades. The cards checklisted in playing card order by suits and are assigned to Aces (1), Jacks (11), Queens (Kings (13). Two coaches cards that could be u jokers and a filler card with a color Bucks logo White Hen Pantry ad are listed at the end. Key include the first ever of Quinn Buckner and Ale English.

COMP.FACT SET (55)	35.00
C1 Bucks Logo	.30
C2 Brian Winters	1.25
C3 Lloyd Walton	.30
C4 Junior Bridgeman	.75
C5 Alex English	5.00
C6 Quinn Buckner	1.25
C7 David Meyers	.75
C8 Swen Nater	.75
C9 Scott Lloyd	.30
C10 Bob Dandridge	1.00
C11 Kevin Restani	.40
C12 Rowland Garrett	.30
C13 Fred Carter	1.25
D1 Bucks Logo	.30
D2 Fred Carter	.75
D3 Rowland Garrett	.30
D4 Kevin Restani	.40
D5 Bob Dandridge	1.00
D6 Scott Lloyd	.30
D7 Swen Nater	.75
D8 David Meyers	.75
D9 Quinn Buckner	1.25
D10 Alex English	5.00
D11 Junior Bridgeman	1.00
D12 Lloyd Walton	.75
D13 Brian Winters	1.00
H1 Bucks Logo	.30
H2 Fred Carter	.60

H3 Rowland Garrett	.30	.75
H4 Kevin Restani	.40	1.00
H5 Bob Dandridge	1.00	2.50
H6 Scott Lloyd	.30	.75
H7 Swen Nater	.75	2.00
H8 David Meyers	.75	2.00
H9 Quinn Buckner	1.25	3.00
H10 Alex English	5.00	10.00
H11 Junior Bridgeman	1.00	2.50
H12 Lloyd Walton	.30	.75
H13 Brian Winters	1.25	3.00
S1 Bucks Logo	.30	.75
S2 Brian Winters	1.25	3.00
S3 Lloyd Walton	.30	.75
S4 Junior Bridgeman	1.00	2.50
S5 Alex English	5.00	10.00
S6 Quinn Buckner	1.25	3.00
S7 David Meyers	.75	2.00
S8 Swen Nater	.75	2.00
S9 Scott Lloyd	.30	.75
S10 Bob Dandridge	1.00	2.50
S11 Kevin Restani	.40	1.00
S12 Rowland Garrett	.30	.75
S13 Fred Carter	.75	2.00
NNO Don Nelson CO	2.50	6.00
NNO K.C. Jones ACO	2.00	5.00
NNO Bucks Logo	.30	.75
White Hen Pantry Ad		

1987-88 Bucks Polaroid

The 1987-88 Polaroid Milwaukee Bucks set contains 16 cards each measuring approximately 2 3/4" by 4". There are 14 player cards plus one coaching staff card and one title card. The cards were distributed in sheet orm with perforations. The front borders are deep green and the backs feature biographical information. Whole sheets carry a slight premium on the set price.

COMPLETE SET (16)	12.50	30.00
2 Junior Bridgeman	1.25	3.00
Pace Mannion	.75	2.00
Sidney Moncrief	2.50	6.00
0 John Lucas	2.00	5.00
5 Craig Hodges	1.25	3.00
1 Conner Henry	1.00	2.50
5 Paul Pressey	1.25	3.00
4 Terry Cummings	2.00	5.00
5 Jerry Reynolds	.75	2.00
2 Larry Krystkowiak	1.25	3.00
3 Jack Sikma	2.00	5.00
4 Paul Mokeski	.75	2.00
5 Randy Breuer	.75	2.00
4 John Stroeder	.75	2.00
NO Del Harris CO	1.25	3.00
Frank Hamblen ACO		
Mack Calvin ACO		
Mike Dunleavy ACO		
Jeff Snedeker TR		
NO Title Card (discount offer detailed on back)	1.00	2.50

1979-80 Bucks Police/Spic'n'Span

s set contains 12 standard-size cards measuring uring the Milwaukee Bucks. Card backs contain ty tips ("Game Plan Tip"). The cards are numbered he back next to the facsimile autograph. The cards ure full-color fronts and black printing on a white stock back. The set was sponsored by 'N'Span. The cards were available one per cleaning r or were available (originally) for sale as a set the Wisconsin Sports Collectors Association for postpaid. A coupon card was also available which good for 1.00 discount on cleaning.

PLETE SET (13)	45.00	90.00
nior Bridgeman	3.00	8.00
dney Moncrief	12.50	25.00
Cummings	2.00	5.00
ve Meyers	5.00	10.00
rques Johnson	8.00	20.00
oyd Walton	2.00	5.00
uinn Buckner	2.50	6.00
chard Washington	2.50	6.00
ian Winters	3.00	8.00
arvey Catchings	2.00	5.00
ent Benson	2.50	6.00
Don Nelson CO and n Killilea ACO	5.00	10.00
Coupon Card	10.00	25.00

1972-73 Bucks Ruler

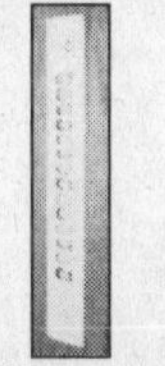

tandard 12" ruler features a head shot of the s from the 1972-3 Milwaukee Bucks. Similar to er, we have identified the rulers using the left to method.

em Abdul-Jabbar	5.00	10.00
McGlocklin		
s Perry		

Dick Cunningham
Russell Lee
Oscar Robertson
Mickey Davis
Lucius Allen
Terry Driscoll
Bob Dandridge
Bill Bates TR
Hubie Brown ACO
Larry Costello CO

1970-71 Bucks Team Issue

Each of these team-issued photos measure approximately 5" by 7" and feature black and white player portraits. The player's name is listed below the photo. The backs are blank. The photos are unnumbered and listed below alphabetically.

COMPLETE SET (10)	25.00	50.00
1 Lew Alcindor	12.50	25.00
2 Lucius Allen	2.00	5.00
3 Bob Boozer	1.50	4.00
4 Larry Costello CO	1.25	3.00
5 Dick Cunningham	.75	2.00
6 Bob Dandridge	2.00	5.00
7 Bob Greacen	.75	2.00
8 Jon McGlocklin	1.50	4.00
9 Oscar Robertson	10.00	20.00
10 Greg Smith	.75	2.00

1971-72 Bucks Team Issue

Each of these team-issued photos measure approximately 5" by 6 3/4" and feature black and white player portraits. The player's name is listed below the photo. The backs are blank. The photos are unnumbered and listed below alphabetically.

COMPLETE SET (12)	25.00	50.00
1 Kareem Abdul-Jabbar	10.00	20.00
2 Lucius Allen	1.50	4.00
3 John Block	.75	2.00
4 Larry Costello CO	1.00	2.50
5 Bob Dandridge	1.50	4.00
6 Toby Kimball	.75	2.00
7 Jon McGlocklin	1.25	3.00
8 McCoy McLemore	.75	2.00
9 Barry Nelson	.75	2.00
10 Oscar Robertson	8.00	20.00
11 Greg Smith	.75	2.00
12 Jeff Webb	.75	2.00

1992-93 Bullets Crown/Topps

Subtitled "Great Bullets Past and Present," this set of nine standard-size player cards was a promotion only at Crown Gasoline Stations. The cards were distributed one strip for 29 cents with a fill-up of gas. The cards were issued in vertical strips of three players (1-3, 4-6, and 7-9) and a coupon/checklist card. Each strip contained two current Bullets players and one ex-Bullets star. The design was identical to the 1992-93 Topps regular series. The distinctive characteristic of the cards is that they are numbered with a "WB" prefix on their backs.

COMPLETE SET (12)	2.50	6.00
WB1 Tom Gugliotta	.75	2.00
WB2 Rex Chapman	.30	.75
WB3 Phil Chenier	.20	.50
WB4 Pervis Ellison	.20	.50
WB5 Brent Price	.20	.50
WB6 Wes Unseld	.60	1.50
WB7 Michael Adams	.20	.50
WB8 Harvey Grant	.20	.50
WB9 Elvin Hayes	1.00	2.50
NNO Crown Gasoline Coupon 1	.08	.25
NNO Crown Gasoline Coupon 2	.08	.25
NNO Crown Gasoline Coupon 3	.08	.25

1954-55 Bullets Gunther Beer

This 11-card set of Baltimore Bullets was sponsored by Gunther Beer. These black and white cards measure approximately 2 5/8" by 3 5/8". The fronts feature a black and white posed player photo. The question "What's the good word," is written across the card top. A Gunther Beer bottle cap and the player's name are superimposed on the player's chest. The back has the words "Follow the Bullets with Gunther Beer" at the top, with biographical information and career summary below. A radio and TV notice on the bottom round out the card back. The cards are unnumbered and are checklisted below in alphabetical order. The cards are frequently found personally autographed. The catalog designation for this set is H805.

COMPLETE SET (11)	2000.00	3700.00
1 Leo Barnhorst	150.00	300.00
2 Clair Bee CO	400.00	800.00
3 Bill Bolger	150.00	300.00
4 Ray Felix	250.00	500.00
5 Jim Fritsche	150.00	300.00
6 Rollen Hans	150.00	300.00
7 Paul Hoffman	200.00	400.00
8 Bob Houbregs	250.00	500.00
9 Ed Miller	150.00	300.00
10 Al Roges	150.00	300.00
11 Harold Uplinger	150.00	300.00

1995-96 Bullets Police

Presented by NationsBank, this 6-card standard-size "Kids 'N Cops" set was issued by the Washington Bullets in conjunction with the District of Columbia Metropolitan Police Department. Youths ages 6-16 who introduced themselves to a Metropolitan police officer received a player card. By completing the 6-card set and turning in the Hoops mascot card to any DC precinct, one received a coupon good for two tickets to a Bullets home game. The offer began on February 11 and ran through April 8. The fronts display glossy full-bleed color action photos. A red vertical bar at the upper left carries the set title and NationsBank emblem. On a white card face, the backs carry a circular headshot, biography, facsimile autograph, conflict resolution message, and sponsor logos. The set is designed so that the first letter of each conflict resolution-message spells out POWER. The cards are unnumbered and checklisted below in alphabetical order.

COMPLETE SET (6)	4.00	10.00
1 Calbert Cheaney	.40	1.00
2 Juwan Howard	.75	2.00
3 Gheorghe Muresan	.40	1.00
4 Robert Pack	.40	1.00
5 Rasheed Wallace	1.50	4.00
6 Chris Webber	2.50	6.00
NNO Hoops Mascot Card	.40	1.00

1973-74 Bullets Standups

These 12 player cards were issued by Johnny Pro Enterprises in an album, with six players per 11 1/4" by 14" sheet. Reportedly 6,000 albums were produced for distribution in a promotion at the Bullets' February 16th game at the Capital Centre. After perforation, the cards measure approximately 3 3/4" by 7 1/16". The cards are die cut, allowing the player pictures and bases to be pushed out and displayed as stand-ups. The fronts feature a color photo of the player, either dribbling or shooting the ball. The backs are blank. The cards are unnumbered and are checklisted below in alphabetical order. A card set, still intact in the album, would be valued at double the values listed below.

COMPLETE SET (12)	25.00	50.00
1 Phil Chenier	2.00	5.00
2 Archie Clark	2.00	5.00
3 Elvin Hayes	10.00	20.00
4 Tom Kozelko	1.25	3.00
5 Manny Leaks	1.25	3.00
6 Louie Nelson	1.25	3.00
7 Kevin Porter	1.50	4.00
8 Mike Riordan	1.50	4.00
9 Dave Stallworth	1.50	4.00
10 Wes Unseld	7.50	15.00
11 Nick Weatherspoon	1.25	3.00
12 Walt Wesley	1.25	3.00

1977-78 Bullets Standups

These 11 player cards were issued by Johnny Pro Enterprises in conjunction with Dart Drugs. The cards were issued in a four-page colorful album and were given out at the Bullets game on March 25, 1978. The cards are die cut, allowing the player pictures and bases to be pushed out and displayed as stand-ups. The backs are blank. The cards are unnumbered and are checklisted below in alphabetical order. A card set, still intact in the album, would be valued at double the values listed below.

COMPLETE SET (11)	15.00	30.00
1 Greg Ballard	.75	2.00
2 Phil Chenier	1.50	4.00
3 Bob Dandridge	1.25	3.00
4 Kevin Grevey	1.25	3.00
5 Elvin Hayes	7.50	15.00
6 Tom Henderson	.75	2.00
7 Mitch Kupchak	1.50	4.00
8 Joe Pace	.75	2.00
9 Wes Unseld	5.00	10.00
10 Phil Walker	.75	2.00
11 Larry Wright	.75	2.00

1964-65 Bullets Team Issue

These blank-backed photos, which measure 8" by 11" and have blank backs, Since these photos are unnumbered, we have sequenced them in alphabetical order.

COMPLETE SET (7)	75.00	150.00
1 Gary Bradds	10.00	20.00
2 Bob Ferry	12.50	25.00
3 Si Green	10.00	20.00
4 Les Hunter	10.00	20.00
5 Wally Jones	12.50	25.00
6 Kevin Loughery	20.00	40.00
7 Don Ohl	10.00	20.00

1968-69 Bullets Team Issue

This set is complete at 12 pieces and is measured at 8 1/2 by 11 1/2. The items were printed on thin paper stock (newsprint type quality, but thicker than ordinary writing paper) in black and white and feature a facsimile signature on the front with a blank back.

COMPLETE SET (12)	150.00	300.00
1 Leroy Ellis	15.00	30.00
2 Bob Ferry	15.00	30.00
3 Gus Johnson	15.00	30.00
4 Kevin Loughery	15.00	30.00
5 Jack Marin	15.00	30.00
6 Earl Monroe	25.00	50.00
7 Barry Orms	15.00	30.00
8 Bob Quick	15.00	30.00
9 Ray Scott	15.00	30.00
10 Gene Shue	15.00	30.00
11 Wes Unseld	20.00	50.00
12 Tom Workman	15.00	30.00

1969-70 Bullets Team Issue

Each of these team-issued photos measure approximately 8" by 10" and feature black and white player portraits. The player's name is listed below the photo. Each photo also contains a facsimile autograph. The backs are blank. The photos are unnumbered and listed below alphabetically.

COMPLETE SET (12)	25.00	50.00
1 Mike Davis	.75	2.00
2 Fred Carter	2.00	5.00
3 Leroy Ellis	1.25	3.00
4 Gus Johnson	2.00	5.00
5 Kevin Loughery	2.00	5.00
6 Ed Manning	1.25	3.00
7 Jack Marin	1.25	3.00
8 Earl Monroe	7.50	15.00
9 Bob Quick	.75	2.00
10 Ray Scott	.75	2.00
11 Gene Shue CO	2.00	5.00
12 Wes Unseld	6.00	12.00

1975-76 Bullets Team Issue

Each of these 11 team-issued photos measure approximately 5" by 7" and feature black and white player portraits. The backs are blank. The photos are unnumbered and listed below alphabetically.

COMPLETE SET (11)	20.00	35.00
1 Dave Bing	2.50	6.00
2 Bernie Bickerstaff ACO	2.00	5.00
3 Clem Haskins	1.25	3.00
4 Elvin Hayes	6.00	12.00
5 Jimmy Jones	.75	2.00
6 K.C. Jones CO	1.25	3.00
7 Tom Kozelko	.75	2.00
8 Mike Riordan	1.00	2.50
9 Leonard Robinson	1.25	3.00
10 Nick Weatherspoon	.75	2.00
11 Wes Unseld	2.50	6.00

1976-77 Bullets Team Issue

Each of these team-issued photos measure approximately 5" by 7" and feature black and white player portraits. The player's name is listed below the photo. The backs are blank. The photos are unnumbered and listed below alphabetically.

COMPLETE SET (15)	20.00	40.00
1 Bernie Bickerstaff ACO	.75	2.00
2 Dave Bing	1.50	4.00
3 Phil Chenier	1.25	3.00
4 Leonard Gray	.60	1.50
5 Kevin Grevey	1.25	3.00
6 Elvin Hayes	5.00	10.00
7 Jimmy Jones	.60	1.50
8 Mitch Kupchak	1.50	4.00
9 Dick Motta CO	.75	2.00
10 Joe Pace	.60	1.50
11 Mike Riordan	.75	2.00
12 Len Robinson	.75	2.00
13 Wes Unseld	2.00	5.00
14 Bob Weiss	.75	2.00
15 Larry Wright	.60	1.50

1977-78 Bullets Team Issue 5 x 7

This 5" x7" set was produced for the Washington Bullets during the 1977-78 season. The set features 12 black and white cards of the team's players and coaches.

COMPLETE SET (12)	20.00	40.00
1 Greg Ballard	1.25	3.00
2 Bernie Bickerstaff ACO	1.25	3.00
3 Phil Chenier	1.50	4.00
4 Bob Dandridge	2.00	5.00
5 Elvin Hayes	2.50	6.00
6 Tom Henderson	1.25	3.00
7 Mitch Kupchak	1.50	4.00
8 Dick Motta CO	1.50	4.00
9 Joe Pace	1.25	3.00
10 Wes Unseld	2.00	5.00
11 Phil Walker	1.25	3.00
12 Larry Wright	1.25	3.00

1977-78 Bullets Team Issue

These black and white glossy blank-backed photos, which measure 8" by 10" feature members of the World Championship Washington Bullets team. Since these photos are unnumbered, we have sequenced them in alphabetical order.

COMPLETE SET (13)	15.00	30.00
1 Greg Ballard	.75	2.00
2 Dave Corzine	.75	2.00
3 Bob Dandridge	1.00	2.50
4 Kevin Grevey	1.00	2.50
5 Elvin Hayes	2.50	6.00
6 Tom Henderson	.75	2.00
7 Charles Johnson	.75	2.00
8 Mitch Kupchak	1.00	2.50
9 Dick Motta CO	1.00	2.50
10 Roger Phegley	.75	2.00
11 Wes Unseld	2.00	5.00
12 Larry Wright	.75	2.00
13 Bernie Bickerstaff ACO John Lally TR	1.00	2.50

1989-90 Bulls Dairy Council

Sponsored by the Dairy Council of Wisconsin Inc., this six-card set was issued to promote the consumption of milk by educating the public to its health benefits. The cards are printed on thin card stock and measure approximately 4" by 8". Each front has a color cartoon drawing of the player posed with a basketball. The size of each player's head is exaggerated, and a plackard overlaying a portion of the picture reads "Grow Like a Pro." At the bottom of each card are pictures of an apple, a glass of milk, a slice of bread, and a steak, representing the four major food groups. As indicated by the subtitles listed below, the backs extol the health benefits of drinking milk. The cards are unnumbered and checklisted alphabetically below.

COMPLETE SET (6)	75.00	150.00
1 Bill Cartwright (Milk is Good for Snacks)	2.50	6.00
2 Horace Grant (Milk is Good for Teeth)	3.00	8.00
3 Michael Jordan (Milk is Good for Breakfast)	50.00	100.00
4 Stacey King (Milk is Good for Skin)	1.50	4.00
5 John Paxson (Milk is Good for Bones)	3.00	7.00
6 Scottie Pippen (Milk is Good for Eyes)	12.50	30.00

1987-88 Bulls Entenmann's

The 1987-88 Entenmann's Chicago Bulls set contains 12 blank-backed cards measuring approximately 2 5/8" by 4". The complete set was given to each attending fan at a specific Bulls home game during the 1987-88 season. There are 11 player cards and one coach card in this set. The cards are unnumbered except for uniform number; they are ordered and numbered below by uniform number. The set features the first professional cards of Horace Grant and Scottie Pippen.

COMPLETE SET (12)	40.00	100.00
2 Rory Sparrow	.75	2.00
3 Sedale Threatt	1.25	2.50
5 John Paxson	2.00	5.00
6 Brad Sellers	.75	2.00
17 Mike Brown	1.25	3.00
23 Michael Jordan	30.00	60.00
31 Granville Waiters	1.25	3.00
33 Scottie Pippen	12.50	30.00
34 Charles Oakley	2.00	5.00
40 Dave Corzine	.75	2.00
54 Horace Grant	4.00	10.00
NNO Doug Collins CO	2.50	6.00

1988-89 Bulls Entenmann's

The 1988-89 Entenmann's Chicago Bulls set contains 12 blank-backed player cards each measuring approximately 2 5/8" by 4". The complete set was given to each attending fan at a specific Bulls home game during the 1988-89 season. The cards are unnumbered except for uniform number; they are ordered and numbered below by uniform number.

COMPLETE SET (12)	30.00	75.00
2 Brad Sellers	.60	1.50
5 John Paxson	1.50	4.00
11 Sam Vincent	.75	2.00
14 Craig Hodges	.75	2.00
15 Jack Haley	.75	2.00
22 Charles Davis	.75	2.00
23 Michael Jordan	20.00	45.00
24 Bill Cartwright	1.50	4.00
32 Will Perdue	.75	2.00
33 Scottie Pippen	8.00	20.00
40 Dave Corzine	.75	2.00
54 Horace Grant	2.00	5.00

1989-90 Bulls Equal

This 12-card set was sponsored by Equal Brand sweetener, and its company logo appears in the lower right corner of the card face. It has been reported that 10,000 sets were given away to fans attending the April 17th Chicago Bulls home game, although reportedly additional sets later made their way into the hobby. These oversized cards measure approximately 3" by 4 1/4". The fronts feature a borderless color action photo. The player's number, name, height, and position are given in the white stripe below the picture. Except for the sponsor's trademark notice, the backs are blank. The cards are unnumbered and checklisted below in alphabetical order. The set contains the first professional cards of B.J. Armstrong and Stacey King.

COMPLETE SET (12)	8.00	20.00
1 B.J. Armstrong	.75	2.00
2 Bill Cartwright	.60	1.50
3 Charles Davis	.30	.75
4 Horace Grant	1.00	2.50
5 Craig Hodges	.40	1.00
6 Michael Jordan	4.00	10.00
7 Stacey King	.60	1.50
8 Ed Nealy	.30	.75
9 John Paxson	.75	2.00
10 Will Perdue	.40	1.00
11 Scottie Pippen	2.00	5.00
12 Jeff Sanders	.30	.75

1990-91 Bulls Equal/Star

This 16-card standard-size set was sponsored by Equal brand sweetener and celebrates the 25th anniversary of the Chicago Bulls franchise. The set was produced (reportedly 10,000 complete sets) by Star Company and was distributed at the April 9th Chicago Bulls home game, although additional sets later made their way into the hobby. The cards feature color action player photos for current Bull players, and blue-tinted photos for past Bull players. The team logo and the words "The Silver Season" overlay the top of the picture. The card background is in silver, and the player's name appears in a gray diagonal stripe traversing the bottom of the picture. The sponsor logo appears in blue print at the card bottom. The back has brief biographical information and statistics, in black print on a pink background. There was also a glossy version reportedly reproduced in 1997 which is valued at two to three times the values listed below.

COMPLETE SET (16)	5.00	12.00
2 Tom Boerwinkle	.20	.50
3 Bob Boozer	.20	.50
4 Bill Cartwright	.30	.75
5 Artis Gilmore	.40	1.00
6 Horace Grant	.40	1.00
7 Phil Jackson CO	.40	1.00
8 Johnny Kerr	.40	1.00
9 Bob Love	.40	1.00
10 Dick Motta CO	.20	.50
11 John Paxson	.40	1.00
12 Scottie Pippen	.75	2.00
13 Guy Rodgers	.20	.50
14 Jerry Sloan	.60	1.50
15 Norm Van Lier	.20	.50
16 Chet Walker	.40	1.00
1 Michael Jordan	1.50	4.00

1970-71 Bulls Hawthorne Milk

This six-card set was issued on the side panels of Hawthorne Milk cartons. The cards were intended to be cut from the carton and measure approximately 3 1/4" by 3 3/8" and feature on the front a posed head shot of the player within a circular picture frame. The second Weiss card measures 4 11/16" by 2 7/8". The backs are blank. The cards are unnumbered and are checklisted below in alphabetical order. The player photo is printed in blue but the outer border of the card is bright red.

COMPLETE SET (6)	1000.00	1800.00
1 Bob Love	250.00	450.00
2 Jerry Sloan/(Photo in blue gray with red border)	250.00	450.00
3 Jerry Sloan/(Photo in red tint with red border)	250.00	450.00
4 Chet Walker	200.00	350.00
5 Bob Weiss (Regular size)	125.00	225.00
6 Bob Weiss (Large size)	125.00	250.00

1985 Bulls Interlake

These glossy color action photos measure approximately 5" by 7" and are printed on thin card stock. The player photo image has rounded corners and a red border on a white card face. Player information appears beneath the picture, between two circles. The left circle has a Boy Scout emblem, while the right one has the words "An Interlake Youth Incentive Program." Supposedly the cards were given out in the fall of 1985 as an incentive to join the Boy Scouts. The Chicago Bulls sponsored a dinner for the Boy Scouts and Michael Jordan was the guest speaker. The backs are blank. The Jordan card has been heavily counterfeited so buyer beware when attempting to purchase one. The counterfeits are very glossy, made with very thin stock and are cut slightly smaller than the real cards.

COMPLETE SET (2)	75.00	150.00
1 Michael Jordan	75.00	150.00
2 Orlando Woolridge	4.00	10.00

1969-70 Bulls Pepsi

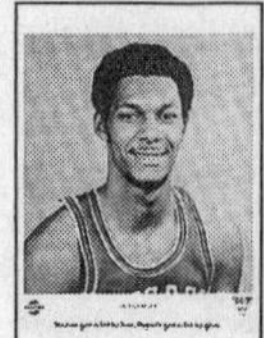

Sponsored by Pepsi, this 13-card set measures 8" by 10" and features members of the 1969-70 Chicago Bulls. The fronts have black-and-white player portraits with white borders. The player's name and height appear under the photo, along with team and sponsor logos, and the slogan "You've got a lot to live, Pepsi's got a lot to give." The backs are blank. The cards are unnumbered and checklisted below in alphabetical order.

COMPLETE SET (13)	75.00	150.00
1 Tom Boerwinkle	6.00	12.00
2 Shaler Halimon	2.50	6.00
3 Clem Haskins	5.00	10.00
4 Bob Kauffman	2.50	6.00
5 Bob Love	20.00	40.00
6 Ed Manning	3.00	8.00
7 Dick Motta CO	5.00	10.00
8 Loy Petersen	2.50	6.00
9 Jerry Sloan	15.00	30.00
10 Al Tucker	2.50	6.00
11 Chet Walker	12.50	25.00
12 Bob Weiss	5.00	12.00
13 Walt Wesley	3.00	8.00

1979-80 Bulls Police

This set contains 16 cards measuring approximately 2 5/8" by 4 1/8" featuring the Chicago Bulls. Cards in the set have either rounded or squared corners. Backs contain safety tips and are written in black ink with blue accent. The set was also sponsored by La Margarita Mexican Restaurants and Azteca Tortillas. The card backs are subtitled Kiwanis Cue Cards. Cards are unnumbered except for uniform number; they are checklisted below by uniform number. The cards of Coby Dietrick and (especially) Reggie Theus are considered more difficult to find and are marked as SP in the listings below.

COMPLETE SET (16)	40.00	70.00
1 Delmer Beshore	1.25	3.00
13 Dwight Jones	1.25	3.00
15 John Mengelt	1.25	3.00
17 Scott May	1.50	4.00
20 Dennis Awtrey	1.25	3.00
24 Reggie Theus SP	15.00	30.00
26 Coby Dietrick SP	7.50	15.00
27 Ollie Johnson	1.25	3.00
28 Sam Smith	1.25	3.00
34 David Greenwood	2.50	6.00
40 Ricky Sobers	1.50	4.00
53 Artis Gilmore	3.00	8.00
54 Mark Landsberger	1.50	4.00
NNO Jerry Sloan CO	3.00	8.00
NNO Phil Johnson ACO	1.50	4.00
NNO Luv-A-Bull	1.25	3.00

1976-77 Bulls Team Issue

These black and white blank-backed glossy ph which measure 8" by 10", feature members 1976-77 Chicago Bulls. Since these ph

unnumbered, we have sequenced them in alphabetical order.
COMPLETE SET (17) 17.50 35.00
1 Ed Badger CO 1.00 2.50
2 Leon Benbow .75 2.00
3 Tom Boerwinkle 1.00 2.50
4 Eric Fernsten .75 2.00
5 Mickey Johnson .75 2.00
6 Tom Kropp .75 2.00
7 John Laskowski .75 2.00
8 Bob Love 1.25 3.00
9 Jack Marin 1.00 2.50
10 Scott May 1.00 2.50
11 Cliff Pondexter .75 2.00
12 Jerry Sloan 1.50 4.00
13 Willie Smith .75 2.00
14 Keith Starr .75 2.00
15 Norm Van Lier 1.00 2.50
16 Bob Wilson .75 2.00
17 Doug Atkinson TR .75 2.00
Gene Tormohlen ACO

1985-86 Bulls Team Issue

Each of these team-issued photos measure approximately 8" by 10" and feature black and white player portraits on two sheets. The player's name is listed below the photo. Both sheets contain eight individual player portraits. The backs are blank. The photos are unnumbered and listed below alphabetically.
COMPLETE SET (2) 20.00 50.00
1 Sidney Green 20.00 50.00
Michael Jordan
Kyle Macy
Billy McKinney
Charles Oakley
Jawann Oldham
Mike Smrek
Orlando Woolridge
2 Stan Albeck CO 4.00 10.00
Murray Arnold ACO
Gene Banks
Dave Corzine
George Gervin
Jerry Krause GM
Mike Thibault ACO
Tex Winter ACO

2008-09 Bulls Upper Deck

COMPLETE SET (14) 8.00 20.00
1 Luol Deng .30 .75
2 Ben Gordon .30 .75
3 Kirk Hinrich .30 .75
4 Drew Gooden .25 .60
5 Larry Hughes .25 .60
6 Andres Nocioni .20 .50
7 Thabo Sefolosha .25 .60
8 Joakim Noah .30 .75
9 Tyrus Thomas .25 .60
10 Aaron Gray .20 .50
11 Cedric Simmons .25 .60
12 Derrick Rose 6.00 15.00
13 Vinny Del Negro CO .30 .75
14 Michael Jordan 2.50 6.00

1977-78 Bulls White Hen Pantry

These high gloss player photos are printed on very thin paper and measure approximately 5" by 7". The fronts feature borderless color game action photos with a facsimile autograph; the backs are blank. The photos are unnumbered and we have checklisted them below in alphabetical order.
COMPLETE SET (7) 6.00 12.00
1 Tom Boerwinkle .75 2.00
2 Artis Gilmore 2.00 5.00
3 Wilbur Holland .60 1.50
4 Mickey Johnson .75 2.00
5 Scott May 1.00 2.50
6 John Mengelt .60 1.50
7 Norm Van Lier 1.00 2.50

1932 Briggs Chocolate

This set was issued by C.A. Briggs Chocolate company in 1932. The cards feature 31-different sports with each card including an artist's rendering of a sporting event. Although players are not named, it is thought that most were modeled after famous athletes of the time. The cardbacks include a written portion about the sport and an offer from Briggs for free baseball equipment for building a compete set of cards.
8 Basketball 125.00 250.00

1992 Canadian Kraft Olympic 3D

This set of 10 3D-action cards celebrate various Olympic sports. Through a mail-in offer, collectors could obtain three cards by sending in one UPC symbol and $3.00 for shipping and handling. The cards measure the standard size and consist of three thin sheets attached at the top. The first sheet provides ...und. The second sheet is a color player ...erted into sheet one, thus "locking" ...action. In a bilingual format, the ...history of the sport as an ...ver consists of a montage ...al backs list medal ...s Olympic games.
... 2.00 5.00
... .40 1.00

1989 CAO Muflon Yugoslavian

This 73-card set was issued in 2-card packs in Yugoslavia. The cards measure at 2 1/2" by 3 3/16". Aside from the checklist below very little is known about this product. It is believed to have been produced by a company in Belgrade.
COMPLETE SET (73) 4000.00 5200.00
1 Magic Johnson 12.50 30.00
Pat Riley
2 Mitch Richmond 6.00 15.00
3 Mark Jackson 3.00 8.00
4 Moses Malone 2.50 6.00
5 Mark Price 2.00 5.00
6 Vern Fleming 1.25 3.00
7 Spud Webb 2.00 5.00
8 Rumeal Robinson 1.25 3.00
9 Lionel Simmons 1.25 3.00
10 John Stockton 10.00 25.00
11 Michael Adams 1.25 3.00
12 Fat Lever 1.25 3.00
13 Muggsy Bogues 2.50 6.00
14 Maurice Cheeks 2.50 6.00
15 Kenny Smith 2.00 5.00
16 Larry Bird 12.50 30.00
James Worthy
17 Gerald Wilkins 1.25 3.00
18 Rolando Blackman 1.25 3.00
19 Arijan Komazec 1.25 3.00
20 Kevin Johnson 2.00 5.00
21 Zoran Radovic 1.25 3.00
22 Sarunas Marcilionis 1.50 4.00
23 Mario Primorac 1.25 3.00
24 Clyde Drexler 12.50 30.00
25 Jure Zdovc 1.25 3.00
26 Drazen Petrovic 15.00 30.00
27 Predrag Danilovic 1.50 4.00
28 Dale Ellis 1.50 4.00
29 John Battle 1.25 3.00
30 Nikos Galis 2.50 6.00
31 Antdanelo Riva 1.50 4.00
32 Toni Kukoc 6.00 15.00
33 Zoran Cutura 1.25 3.00
34 Kevin McHale 4.00 10.00
35 Valdemar Homicus 1.25 3.00
36 Charles Barkley 12.50 30.00
37 Detlef Schrempf 2.00 5.00
38 Larry Nance 2.00 5.00
39 Danny Manning 2.50 6.00
40 Mark Aguirre 4.00 10.00
Magic Johnson
41 Chris Mullin 4.00 10.00
Kevin McHale
42 Chuck Person 1.25 3.00
43 A.C. Green 3.00 8.00
Bill Laimbeer
44 Dominique Wilkins 6.00 15.00
45 Jack Sikma 1.25 3.00
46 James Worthy 10.00 25.00
Larry Bird
47 Otis Thorpe 1.25 3.00
48 Adrian Dantley 8.00 20.00
Larry Bird
49 Karl Malone 10.00 25.00
50 Alex English 2.00 5.00
51 Terry Cummings 1.25 3.00
52 Willie Anderson 1.25 3.00
53 Zarko Paspalj 2.00 5.00
54 Robert Parish 3.00 8.00
55 Patrick Ewing 6.00 15.00
56 Dusko Ivanovic 1.25 3.00
57 Pat Cummings 1.25 3.00
58 Bill Laimbeer 2.50 6.00
59 Craig Hodges 1.25 3.00
60 Moses Malone 3.00 8.00
61 Hakeem Olajuwon 10.00 25.00
Karl Malone
62 Julius Erving 10.00 25.00
63 Kareem Abdul-Jabbar 6.00 15.00
64 Manute Bol 1.25 3.00
65 Stefan Ostrowski 1.25 3.00
66 San Epifanio 1.25 3.00
67 Arvydas Sabonis 4.00 10.00
68 Dino Radja 1.50 4.00
69 Isiah Thomas 4.00 10.00
70 Vlade Divac 3.00 8.00
72 Michael Jordan 3000.00 5000.00
73 Magic Johnson 15.00 40.00

1975 Carvel Discs

The 1975 Carvel NBA Basketball Discs set contains 36 unnumbered discs measuring approximately 3 3/8" in diameter. The blank-backed discs have various (five different colors) color borders, and feature black and white drawings of the players with fascimile signatures. There are also white (colorless) border variations, which can be found with or without Carvel at the top, which are very difficult to find. A poster was produced which provided circular places for each of the 36 discs to be taped or glued onto. Since the discs are unnumbered, they are checklisted below in alphabetical order. The set is dated by the fact that 1974-75 was Happy Hairston and Chet Walker's last active year in the NBA.
COMPLETE SET (36) 45.00 90.00
1 Kareem Abdul-Jabbar 4.00 10.00
2 Nate Archibald 3.00 6.00
3 Bill Bradley 2.50 6.00
4 Don Chaney 1.25 3.00
5 Dave Cowens 2.50 6.00
6 Bob Dandridge 1.00 2.50
7 Ernie DiGregorio 1.25 3.00
8 Walt Frazier 2.50 6.00
9 John Gianelli .75 2.00
10 Gail Goodrich 2.50 6.00
11 Happy Hairston 1.25 3.00
12 John Havlicek 4.00 10.00
13 Spencer Haywood 1.25 3.00
14 Garfield Heard .75 2.00
15 Lou Hudson 1.00 2.50
16 Phil Jackson 2.50 6.00
17 Sam Lacey .75 2.00
18 Bob Lanier 3.00 6.00
19 Bob Love 1.50 4.00
20 Bob McAdoo 2.00 5.00
21 Jim McMillian 1.25 3.00
22 Dean Meminger .75 2.00
23 Earl Monroe 2.50 6.00
24 Don Nelson 1.50 4.00
25 Jim Price .75 2.00
26 Clifford Ray .75 2.00
27 Charlie Scott 1.00 2.50
28 Paul Silas 1.50 4.00
29 Jerry Sloan 2.00 5.00
30 Randy Smith 1.25 3.00
31 Dick Van Arsdale 1.25 3.00
32 Norm Van Lier 1.25 3.00
33 Chet Walker 1.25 3.00
34 Paul Westphal 2.00 5.00
35 Jo Jo White 1.25 3.00
36 Hawthorne Wingo .75 2.00

1993-94 Cavaliers Nickles Bread

One card from this 13-card set was inserted in every loaf of Nickles brand bread. The bakery does an annual card promotion in the greater Cleveland area.
COMPLETE SET (13) 6.00 15.00
1 John Battle .40 1.00
2 Terrell Brandon .75 2.00
3 Brad Daugherty .40 1.00
4 Danny Ferry .40 1.00
5 Jay Guidinger .40 1.00
6 Tyrone Hill .40 1.00
7 Gerald Madkins .40 1.00
8 Chris Mills .60 1.50
9 Larry Nance .75 2.00
10 Bobby Phills .40 1.00
11 Mark Price .75 2.00
12 Gerald Wilkins .50 1.25
13 John Williams .40 1.00

1973-74 Cavaliers Postcards

This eight-card set was released during the 1973-74 season, and features many of the Cleveland Cavalier players from that year. Please note that these postcards measure 3 1/2"x5 1/4".
COMPLETE SET (8) 20.00 40.00
1 Lenny Wilkens CO 2.50 6.00
2 Austin Carr 1.50 4.00
3 Barry Clemens 1.25 3.00
4 Bobby Smith 1.25 3.00
5 Jim Brewer 1.25 3.00
6 Dwight Davis 1.25 3.00
7 Steve Patterson 1.25 3.00
8 Fred Foster 1.25 3.00
9 Jim Cleamons 1.50 4.00
10 Luke Witte 1.25 3.00
11 Bob Rule 1.25 3.00
12 John Warren 1.25 3.00

1976 Cavaliers Royal Crown Cola Cans

The 1976 Royal Crown Cola Cleveland Cavaliers Cans team issue contains at least seven standard-sized cans. Each can contains a facsimile autograph, except one - Dick Snyder has cans with and without an autograph. There is no number given, thus the set is listed below alphabetically. Cans opened from the bottom command up to a 25 percent premium over the prices below. The checklist below is thought to be incomplete--any additional input on this series would be appreciated.
COMPLETE SET (7) 20.00 40.00
1 Jim Brewer 2.00 5.00
2 Austin Carr 3.00 8.00
3 Bill Fitch CO 2.50 6.00
4 Jim Chones 2.50 6.00
5 Jim Cleamons 2.50 6.00
6 Dick Snyder 2.00 5.00
with autograph
6A Dick Snyder 2.00 5.00
without autograph
7 Bingo Smith 2.50 6.00

1980-81 Cavaliers Team Issue

This 5 1/2"x 8 1/2" set was produced for the Cleveland Cavaliers during the 1980-81 season. The set features 10 black and white cards of the team's players.
COMPLETE SET (10) 15.00 30.00
1 Kenny Carr 1.25 3.00
2 Mack Calvin 1.50 4.00
3 Mike Bratz 1.25 3.00
4 Geoff Huston 1.25 3.00
5 Walter Jordan 1.25 3.00
6 Bill Laimbeer 2.50 6.00
7 Don Ford 1.25 3.00
8 Mike Mitchell 1.50 4.00
9 Roger Phegley 1.25 3.00
10 Randy Smith 1.50 4.00

2008-09 Cavaliers Upper Deck

COMPLETE SET (14) 2.50 6.00
1 LeBron James 1.50 4.00
2 Delonte West .25 .60
3 Daniel Gibson .30 .75
4 Zydrunas Ilgauskas .25 .60
5 Anderson Varejao .25 .60
6 Ben Wallace .30 .75
7 Aleksandar Pavlovic .20 .50
8 Lorenzen Wright .20 .50
9 Wally Szczerbiak .25 .60
10 Eric Snow .20 .50
11 Mo Williams .25 .60
12 J.J. Hickson .40 1.00
13 Mike Brown CO .20 .50
14 Mark Price .50 1.25

2008-09 Cavaliers Upper Deck LeBron James

COMPLETE SET (10) 8.00 20.00
COMMON CARD 1.00 2.50

2007 Cavaliers Upper Deck Rite Aid

COMPLETE SET (16) 5.00 12.00
1 Shannon Brown .60 1.50
2 Daniel Gibson .40 1.00
3 Drew Gooden .40 1.00
4 Larry Hughes .60 1.50
5 Zydrunas Ilgauskas .60 1.50
6 LeBron James 3.00 8.00
7 Damon Jones .40 1.00
8 Dwayne Jones .40 1.00
9 Donyell Marshall .40 1.00
10 Ira Newble .40 1.00
11 Aleksandar Pavlovic .40 1.00
12 Scot Pollard .40 1.00
13 Eric Snow .40 1.00
14 Anderson Varejao .60 1.50
15 David Wesley .40 1.00
16 Mike Brown .40 1.00

2008 Celebrity Cuts

COMPLETE SET (100) 125.00 200.00
STATED PRINT RUN 499 SERIAL #'d SETS
47 John Wooden 1.50 4.00
48 Larry Bird 2.00 5.00
92 Walt Frazier 1.50 4.00

2008 Celebrity Cuts Century Gold

*GOLD: .75X TO 2X BASIC
RANDOM INSERTS IN PACKS
STATED PRINT RUN 25 SERIAL #'d SETS

2008 Celebrity Cuts Century Silver

*SILVER: .6X TO 1.5X BASIC
RANDOM INSERTS IN PACKS
STATED PRINT RUN 50 SERIAL #'d SETS

2008 Celebrity Cuts Century Material

RANDOM INSERTS IN PACKS
PRINT RUNS B/WN 5-100 COPIES
NO PRICING ON QTY OF 5
48 Larry Bird/100 6.00 15.00
92 Walt Frazier/100 4.00 10.00

2008 Celebrity Cuts Century Material Prime

RANDOM INSERTS IN PACKS
PRINT RUNS B/WN 1-50 COPIES PER
NO PRICING ON QTY OF 12 OR LESS
48 Larry Bird/50 10.00 25.00
92 Walt Frazier/50 6.00 15.00

2008 Celebrity Cuts Century Material Combo

RANDOM INSERTS IN PACKS
PRINT RUNS B/WN 5-50 COPIES PER
NO PRICING ON QTY OF 10 OR LESS
48 Larry Bird/50 10.00 25.00
92 Walt Frazier/50 6.00 15.00

2008 Celebrity Cuts Century Signature Gold

RANDOM INSERTS IN PACKS
PRINT RUNS B/WN 1-200 COPIES PER
NO PRICING ON QTY OF 14 OR LESS
47 John Wooden/25 75.00 150.00
48 Larry Bird/50 40.00 70.00
92 Walt Frazier/50 10.00 25.00

2008 Celebrity Cuts Century Signature Material

RANDOM INSERTS IN PACKS
PRINT RUNS B/WN 1-50 COPIES PER
NO PRICING ON QTY OF 14 OR LESS
48 Larry Bird/50 50.00 80.00
92 Walt Frazier/50 10.00 25.00

2008 Celebrity Cuts Century Signature Material Prime

48 Larry Bird/50 60.00 100.00

1977-78 Celtics Citgo

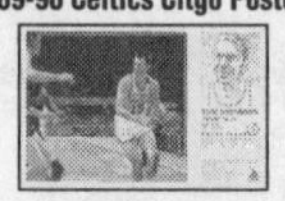

Sponsored by Citgo Gas, the 17 photos in this set each measure approximately 8 1/2" by 11". The fronts feature full bleed glossy color action pictures. Most card backs carry player information for the featured player including biography, career summary, amd complete statistics. The back of card number 5 exhibits a chart titled "Celtics vs. NBA Opponents Over The Years" (1946-1977), while the back of card number 6 lists the Celtics' roster for the 1977-78 season. Only the Kermit Washington photo is a non-action, portrait shot, suggesting that he may have been added to the set later. The photos are unnumbered and ordered below in alphabetical order.
COMPLETE SET (17) 40.00 75.00
1 Dave Bing 2.50 6.00
2 Tommy Boswell 1.25 3.00
3 Don Chaney 2.00 5.00
4 Dave Cowens 3.00 8.00
5 Dave Cowens 3.00 8.00
(With John Havlicek and Curtis Rowe)
6 Dave Cowens 3.00 8.00
(With Charlie Scott)
7 John Havlicek 7.50 15.00
8 Sam Jones 2.50 6.00
9 Cedric Maxwell 1.50 4.00
10 Curtis Rowe 2.00 5.00
11 Tom Sanders CO 1.50 4.00
12 Fred Saunders 1.25 3.00
13 Kevin Stacom 1.25 3.00
14 Kermit Washington 1.25 3.00
15 Jo Jo White 2.50 6.00
16 Sidney Wicks 2.50 6.00
17 Ballboy Contest 1.25 3.00

1988-89 Celtics Citgo

Sponsored by Citgo Gas, these approximately 10 1/2" by 12 1/2" color illustrations are bordered in white and printed on thin glossy paper. The players are pictured in a color action pose in Boston Garden. Bird is pictured shooting his patented outside jumper; an unidentified Golden State Warrior (uniform number 34) extends his right arm in a vain effort to block the shot. The wider bottom white border carries a facsimile autograph and a brief player profile. The pictures are unnumbered and blank on the back.
COMPLETE SET (7) 12.50 30.00
1 Danny Ainge 2.50 6.00
2 Larry Bird 6.00 15.00
3 Dennis Johnson 2.00 5.00
4 Reggie Lewis 2.00 5.00
5 Kevin McHale 3.00 8.00
6 Robert Parish 2.50 6.00
7 Team Picture 3.00 8.00

1989-90 Celtics Citgo Posters

Sponsored by Citgo Petroleum Corp. of Tulsa, Oklahoma, this set of posters was produced with each player's permission and the cooperation of the Boston Celtics and The Sports Museum of New England. Each poster measures 17" by 11" and is printed on glossy paper stock. The left two-thirds of the poster consists of a color painting of an action scene by artist Mike Wimmer. On the right third are a portrait (in blank ink), biographical information, and career summary. The Citgo emblem in the lower right corner rounds out the front. The backs are blank. The posters are unnumbered and checklisted below alphabetically according to player's last name.
COMPLETE SET (6) 8.00 20.00
1 Bob Cousy 3.00 8.00
1 Dave Cowens 2.50 6.00
2 Tom Heinsohn 2.50 6.00
3 Sam Jones 2.50 6.00
4 Tom Sanders 1.25 3.00
5 Paul Silas 1.50 4.00

1986 Celtics Cups

Issued by Nestle, this set is comprised of four white plastic souvenir cups. Along the top rim of the cups, in red letters, the words "Sharpshooters" appear, and below are color portraits of Celtics players. Each cup features two players, the Celtics logo, the years the Celtics won championships, and the Nestle Crunch and Chunky logos.
COMPLETE SET (4) 8.00 20.00
1 Dennis Johnson 1.25 3.00
Greg Kite
2 Bill Walton 2.00 5.00
Jerry Sichting
3 Larry Bird 4.00 10.00
Danny Ainge
4 Robert Parish 2.50 6.00
Kevin McHale

1974-75 Celtics Linnett

These charcoal drawings are skillfully executed facial portraits of Boston Celtic players. They were drawn by noted sports artist Charles Linnett and measure approximately 8 1/2" by 11". A facsimile autograph of the player is written across the lower right, the Celtics' logo appears in the lower left, and the backs are blank. The drawings are unnumbered and checklisted below in alphabetical order. The set is very similar to the Linnett Milwaukee Bucks set of the same year. A 1969 NBA Properties copyright is printed in the lower left corner of the card and a 1973 NBAPA copyright is printed on the wrapper of the two-card package in which they were sold. The set is dated by the fact that Steve Downing and Phil Hankinson's first year with the Boston Celtics was 1973-74.
COMPLETE SET (9) 30.00 60.00
1 Don Chaney 2.50 6.00
2 Dave Cowens 7.50 15.00
3 Steve Downing 2.00 5.00
4 Henry Finkel 2.50 6.00
5 Phil Hankinson 2.00 5.00
6 John Havlicek 10.00 20.00
7 Don Nelson 5.00 10.00
8 Paul Silas 3.00 8.00
9 Jo Jo White 3.00 8.00

1975-76 Celtics Linnett Green Borders

Packaged in cello wrap, these three cards measure approximately 4" by 6" and feature artwork by Charles Linnett. The fronts feature a charcoal portrait of the player surrounded by a green border displaying players from various sports. The team logo, player's name, and facsimile autograph appear across the lower portion of the front. The backs are blank. The cards are unnumbered and checklisted below in alphabetical order.
COMPLETE SET (3) 8.00 20.00
1 Dave Cowens 3.00 8.00
2 John Havlicek 4.00 10.00
3 Jo Jo White 2.50 6.00

1956-57 Celtics Photos

This ten card oversized blank backed set was released during the 1956-57 season, and features such Celtics stars as Bob Cousy and Bill Sharman. Please note that these black and white cards measure 6.5"x 8".
COMPLETE SET (10) 1000.00 2000.00
1 Bob Cousy 250.00 500.00
2 Tom Heinsohn 200.00 400.00
3 Dick Hemric 75.00 150.00
4 Jim Loscutoff 100.00 200.00
5 Jack Nichols 75.00 150.00
6 Togo Palazzi 75.00 150.00
7 Andy Phillip 100.00 200.00
8 Arnie Risen 100.00 200.00
9 Bill Sharman 150.00 300.00
10 Lou Tsioropoulos 75.00 150.00

1976-77 Celtics Team Issue

These black and white blank-backed photos, which measure 8" by 10" feature members of the 1976-77 Boston Celtics. Since these photos are unnumbered, we have sequenced them in alphabetical order.
COMPLETE SET (12) 15.00 30.00
1 Jerome Anderson .75 2.00
2 Jim Ard .75 2.00
3 Tom Boswell .75 2.00
4 Norm Cook .75 2.00
5 John Havlicek 3.00 8.00
6 Steve Kuberski .75 2.00
7 Glenn McDonald .75 2.00
8 Curtis Rowe 1.00 2.50
9 Fred Saunders .75 2.00
10 Paul Silas 1.50 4.00
11 Kevin Stacom .75 2.00
12 Sidney Wicks 1.00 2.50

2001-02 Celtics Topps

Released by Topps in conjunction with Dunkin' Donuts, this 10-card set is horizontally designed with the Celtics logo in the background and was given away at a game during the 2001-02 season.
COMPLETE SET (10) 2.50 6.00
BC1 Antoine Walker .50 1.25
BC2 Paul Pierce .75 2.00
BC3 Kenny Anderson .50 1.25
BC4 Bryant Stith .40 1.00
BC5 Vitaly Potapenko .40 1.00
BC6 Eric Williams .40 1.00
BC7 Mark Blount .40 1.00
BC8 Tony Battie .40 1.00
BC9 Jerome Moiso .40 1.00
BC10 Randy Brown .40 1.00

1994-95 Celtics Tribute

This set of eight was issued to commemorate tributes in the Boston Garden at various dates during the 1994-95 season. Though each measures 8 1/2" by 11" and is printed on thin glossy paper, Bird and McHale are photos taken by photographer Steve Lipofsky, while the other players and coaches are portrayed by canvas paintings by Boston-based sports artist Paul Balmer. Each picture has a white border and a Boston Celtics "Honor the Tradition" logo superposed at the lower left corner. The backs give the date the player or coach was honored, a detailed career summary, and season-by-season statistics. Only the Bird photo was sponsored by CellularOne, and only McHale's photo includes an anti-smoking message sponsored by the Massachusetts Department of Public Health. The pictures are listed in alphabetical order.
COMPLETE SET (8) 8.00 20.00
1 Red Auerbach CO 2.00 5.00
2 Larry Bird 3.00 8.00
3 Bob Cousy 1.50 4.00
4 Dave Cowens 1.25 3.00
5 John Havlicek 1.50 4.00
6 Tom Heinsohn 1.25 3.00
7 K.C. Jones 1.25 3.00
8 Kevin McHale 1.50 4.00

2008-09 Celtics Upper Deck

COMPLETE SET (14) 2.50 6.00
1 Paul Pierce .40 1.00
2 Kevin Garnett .60 1.50
3 Ray Allen .30 .75
4 Rajon Rondo .40 1.00
5 Kendrick Perkins .25 .60
6 Leon Powe .20 .50
7 Glen Davis .25 .60
8 Sam Cassell .30 .75
9 Patrick O'Bryant .20 .50
10 Eddie House .20 .50
11 Gabe Pruitt .20 .50
12 J.R. Giddens .30 .75
13 Doc Rivers CO .30 .75
14 Larry Bird 1.00 2.50

1992-93 Center Court

This 53-card set was produced by Capital Cards and Forgotten Heroes for the Basketball Hall of Fame. The production run was limited to 10,000 (each card of the set is numbered "X of 10,000" on the back). The cards are postcard size measuring approximately 3 1/2" by 5 1/2". Inside white borders, the fronts display glossy color player portraits by noted sports artist Ron Lewis. The horizontally oriented backs have the player's name and the year he was elected to the Hall of Fame. The cards are numbered on the back. A second series (27-52) was issued in 1993, which included a card (PD1) honoring George Mikan as the Player of the Decade of the 40's.
COMPLETE SET (53) 60.00 120.00
COMPLETE SERIES 1 (26) 25.00 60.00
COMPLETE SERIES 2 (27) 25.00 60.00
1 George Mikan 2.50 6.00
2 Bill Bradley 2.00 5.00
3 Bobby Wanzer 1.50 4.00
4 Ed Macauley 1.50 4.00
5 Harry Gallatin 1.50 4.00
6 William (Pop) Gates 1.50 4.00
7 Bobby Knight CO 2.00 5.00
8 Dolph Schayes 1.50 4.00
9 Bob Pettit 1.50 4.00
10 Walt Frazier 1.50 4.00
11 Elvin Hayes 1.25 3.00
12 Paul Arizin 1.50 4.00
13 Forrest (Phog) Allen CO 1.50 4.00
14 Oscar Robertson 2.00 5.00
15 John Wooden CO 2.00 5.00
16 Red Holzman CO 1.50 4.00
17 Jack Twyman 1.50 4.00
18 Dean Smith CO 2.00 5.00
19 John Nucatola 1.50 4.00
20 Elgin Baylor 1.50 4.00
21 Dave Bing 1.50 4.00
22 Lester Harrison 1.50 4.00
23 Joe Lapchick 1.25 3.00
24 Rick Barry 1.50 4.00
25 Lou Carnesecca CO 1.50 4.00
26 Checklist Card 1.50 4.00
27 Red Auerbach 2.00 5.00
28 Dave DeBusschere 1.50 4.0
29 Clarence Gaines 1.25 3.0
30 Tom Gola 1.50 4.0
31 Hal Greer 1.50 4.0
32 Lusia Harris-Stewart 2.00 5.0
33 K.C. Jones 1.50 4.0
34 Sam Jones 1.50 4.0
35 Robert Davies 1.25 3.0
36 Harry Litwack 1.50 4.0
37 Clyde Lovellette 1.50 4.0
38 Slater Martin 1.50 4.0
39 Al McGuire 1.50 4.0
40 Ray Meyer 1.50 4.0
41 Earl Monroe 1.50 4.0
42 Andy Phillip 1.50 4.0
43 Jim Pollard 1.50 4.0
44 Bill Sharman 1.50 4.0
45 J.Dallas Shirley 1.50 4.0
46 Nate Thurmond 1.50 4.0
47 Stan Watts 1.50 4.0
48 Bobby McDermott 1.50 4.0
49 Clair Bee 1.50 4.0
50 Willis Reed 1.50 4.0
51 Larry O'Brien 1.25 3.0
52 Checklist Card 1.25 3.0
PD1 George Mikan 2.00 5.

2009-10 Certified

COMP.SET w/o SPs (150) 50.00 100.
151-170 PRINT RUN 500 SER.#'d SETS
171-200 RC PRINT RUN 399 SER.#'d SETS
UNPRICED BLACK PRINT RUN ONE SET
UNPRICED EMERALD PRINT RUN 3 TO 5 SETS
1 Dirk Nowitzki 1.00
2 Jason Kidd .75
3 Jason Terry .60
4 J.J. Barea 1.00
5 Josh Howard .60
6 Shawn Marion .75
7 Luis Scola .60
8 Shane Battier .75
9 Tracy McGrady .75
10 Trevor Ariza .50
11 Yao Ming 1.00
12 Allen Iverson 1.00
13 Marc Gasol .75
14 O.J. Mayo .75
15 Rudy Gay .75
16 Zach Randolph .60
17 Chris Paul 1.25
18 David West .75
19 Emeka Okafor .75
20 James Posey .50
21 Peja Stojakovic .75
22 Manu Ginobili .75
23 Michael Finley .75
24 Richard Jefferson .75
25 Tim Duncan 1.25
26 Tony Parker .75
27 Carmelo Anthony 1.00
28 Chauncey Billups .75
29 Chris Andersen 1.25
30 J.R. Smith .75
31 Kenyon Martin .75
32 Nene .60
33 Al Jefferson .75
34 Kevin Love 1.25
35 Ramon Sessions .60
36 Ryan Gomes .50
37 Andre Miller .60
38 Brandon Roy .75
39 Greg Oden .60
40 LaMarcus Aldridge .75
41 Rudy Fernandez .60
42 Jeff Green .60
43 Kevin Durant 2.50
44 Nick Collison .50
45 Russell Westbrook 1.25
46 Andrei Kirilenko .60
47 Carlos Boozer .75

48 Deron Williams .75 2.00
49 Mehmet Okur .50 1.25
50 Paul Millsap .60 1.50
51 Andris Biedrins .50 1.25
52 Anthony Randolph .60 1.50
53 Corey Maggette .60 1.50
54 Devean George .50 1.25
55 Kelenna Azubuike .50 1.25
56 Stephen Jackson .60 1.50
57 Al Thornton .60 1.50
58 Baron Davis .75 2.00
59 Chris Kaman .60 1.50
60 Eric Gordon .75 2.00
61 Marcus Camby .50 1.25
62 Andrew Bynum 1.00 2.50
63 Derek Fisher .60 1.50
64 Kobe Bryant 4.00 10.00
65 Lamar Odom .75 2.00
66 Luke Walton .50 1.25
67 Pau Gasol .75 2.00
68 Ron Artest .75 2.00
69 Amare Stoudemire .75 2.00
70 Grant Hill 1.00 2.50
71 Jason Richardson .75 2.00
72 Leandro Barbosa .60 1.50
73 Steve Nash .75 2.00
74 Andres Nocioni .50 1.25
75 Francisco Garcia .60 1.50
76 Kevin Martin .75 2.00
77 Sean May .50 1.25
78 Kevin Garnett 1.50 4.00
79 Paul Pierce 1.00 2.50
80 Rajon Rondo 1.00 2.50
81 Rasheed Wallace .75 2.00
82 Ray Allen .75 2.00
83 Brook Lopez .75 2.00
84 Courtney Lee .60 1.50
85 Devin Harris .75 2.00
86 Yi Jianlian .60 1.50
87 Al Harrington .60 1.50
88 Chris Duhon .50 1.25
89 Danilo Gallinari .75 2.00
90 Darko Milicic .50 1.25
91 David Lee .60 1.50
92 Nate Robinson .75 2.00
93 Andre Iguodala .75 2.00
94 Elton Brand .75 2.00
95 Samuel Dalembert .50 1.25
96 Thaddeus Young .50 1.25
97 Andrea Bargnani .60 1.50
98 Chris Bosh .75 2.00
99 Hedo Turkoglu .75 2.00
100 Jarrett Jack .60 1.50
101 Jose Calderon .60 1.50
102 Derrick Rose 2.50 6.00
103 Joakim Noah .75 2.00
104 Luol Deng .75 2.00
105 Tyrus Thomas .60 1.50
106 Anderson Varejao .60 1.50
107 LeBron James 4.00 10.00
108 Mo Williams .60 1.50
109 Shaquille O'Neal 1.50 4.00
110 Zydrunas Ilgauskas .50 1.25
111 Ben Gordon .75 2.00
112 Ben Wallace .75 2.00
113 Charlie Villanueva .60 1.50
114 Richard Hamilton .60 1.50
115 Rodney Stuckey .75 2.00
116 Tayshaun Prince .75 2.00
117 Danny Granger .75 2.00
118 Jeff Foster .50 1.25
119 T.J. Ford .50 1.25
120 Troy Murphy .50 1.25
121 Andrew Bogut .75 2.00
122 Hakim Warrick .60 1.50
123 Luke Ridnour .60 1.50
124 Michael Redd .75 2.00
125 Al Horford .75 2.00
126 Jamal Crawford .60 1.50
127 Joe Johnson .75 2.00
128 Josh Smith .75 2.00
129 Mike Bibby .60 1.50
130 Boris Diaw .60 1.50
131 D.J. Augustin .60 1.50
132 Gerald Wallace .75 2.00
133 Raja Bell .60 1.50
134 Raymond Felton .60 1.50
135 Tyson Chandler .60 1.50
136 Dwyane Wade 1.50 4.00
137 Jermaine O'Neal .75 2.00
138 Mario Chalmers .75 2.00
139 Michael Beasley .75 2.00
140 Quentin Richardson .60 1.50
141 Udonis Haslem .60 1.50
142 Dwight Howard 1.25 3.00
143 J.J. Redick .75 2.00
144 Jameer Nelson .60 1.50
145 Mickael Pietrus .50 1.25
146 Rashard Lewis .60 1.50
147 Antawn Jamison .75 2.00
148 Caron Butler .75 2.00
149 Gilbert Arenas .75 2.00
150 Randy Foye .50 1.25
151 Isiah Thomas 1.50 4.00
152 Byron Scott 1.50 4.00
153 Frank Ramsey 1.50 4.00
154 Dikembe Mutombo 1.50 4.00
155 Alonzo Mourning 2.00 5.00
156 John Starks 1.50 4.00
157 Adrian Dantley 1.50 4.00
158 Bailey Howell 1.50 4.00
159 Al Attles 1.50 4.00
160 Walt Frazier 1.50 4.00
161 Tim Hardaway 1.50 4.00
162 Pat Riley 1.50 4.00
163 Paul Westphal 1.50 4.00
164 Bill Walton 1.50 4.00
165 Jack Sikma 1.50 4.00
166 Magic Johnson 4.00 10.00
167 Spud Webb 1.50 4.00
168 Wilt Chamberlain 3.00 8.00
169 Wes Unseld 1.50 4.00
170 James Worthy 2.00 5.00
171 Blake Griffin JSY AU RC 75.00 150.00
172 Hasheem Thabeet JSY AU RC 5.00 12.00
173 James Harden JSY AU RC 15.00 40.00
174 Tyreke Evans JSY AU RC 15.00 40.00
175 Jonny Flynn JSY AU RC 5.00 12.00
176 Stephen Curry JSY AU RC 15.00 40.00
177 Jordan Hill JSY AU RC 5.00 12.00
178 Brandon Jennings JSY AU RC 10.00 25.00
179 Terrence Williams JSY AU RC 5.00 12.00
180 Gerald Henderson JSY AU RC 5.00 12.00
181 Tyler Hansbrough JSY AU RC 8.00 20.00
182 Earl Clark JSY AU RC 5.00 12.00
183 Austin Daye JSY AU RC 5.00 12.00
184 James Johnson JSY AU RC 5.00 12.00
185 Jrue Holiday JSY AU RC 10.00 25.00
186 Ty Lawson JSY AU RC 8.00 20.00
187 Jeff Teague JSY AU RC 6.00 15.00
188 Eric Maynor JSY AU RC 5.00 12.00
189 Darren Collison JSY AU RC 8.00 20.00
190 Omri Casspi JSY AU RC 5.00 12.00
191 B.J. Mullens JSY AU RC 5.00 12.00
192 Rodrigue Beaubois JSY AU RC 6.00 15.00
193 Taj Gibson JSY AU RC 6.00 15.00
194 DeMarre Carroll JSY AU RC 5.00 12.00
195 Wayne Ellington JSY AU RC 5.00 12.00
196 Toney Douglas JSY AU RC 5.00 12.00
197 Jeff Pendergraph JSY AU RC 5.00 12.00
198 Jermaine Taylor JSY AU RC 5.00 12.00
199 DeJuan Blair JSY AU RC 6.00 15.00
200 Jodie Meeks JSY AU RC 6.00 15.00

2009-10 Certified Mirror Blue

*BLUE 1-150: 1X TO 2.5X BASE HI
*BLUE 151-170: .6X TO 1.5X BASE HI
BLUE 1-170 PRINT RUN 100 SER.#'d SETS
*BLUE RC 171-200: .6X TO 1.5X BASE HI
BLUE RC PRINT RUN 50 SER.#'d SETS

2009-10 Certified Mirror Blue Materials

STATED PRINT RUN 10 TO 50 SER.#'d SETS
SOME UNPRICED DUE TO SCARCITY
1 Dirk Nowitzki/50 5.00 12.00
2 Jason Kidd/50 4.00 10.00
3 Jason Terry/50 3.00 8.00
4 J.J. Barea/50 10.00 25.00
5 Josh Howard/50 3.00 8.00
6 Shawn Marion/50 4.00 10.00
7 Luis Scola/25 3.00 8.00
8 Shane Battier/50 4.00 10.00
9 Tracy McGrady/50 4.00 10.00
11 Yao Ming/25 5.00 12.00
14 O.J. Mayo/25 4.00 10.00
17 Chris Paul/50 6.00 15.00
18 David West/50 4.00 10.00
25 Tim Duncan/50 6.00 15.00
27 Carmelo Anthony/50 5.00 12.00
28 Chauncey Billups/25 4.00 10.00
29 Chris Andersen/25 6.00 15.00
31 Kenyon Martin/50 4.00 10.00
32 Nene/25 3.00 8.00
33 Al Jefferson/50 4.00 10.00
34 Kevin Love/50 6.00 15.00
36 Ryan Gomes/25 2.50 6.00
38 Brandon Roy/50 4.00 10.00
39 Greg Oden/50 3.00 8.00
40 LaMarcus Aldridge/25 4.00 10.00
46 Andrei Kirilenko/50 3.00 8.00
47 Carlos Boozer/50 4.00 10.00
48 Deron Williams/50 4.00 10.00
49 Mehmet Okur/50 2.50 6.00
50 Paul Millsap/25 3.00 8.00
59 Chris Kaman/50 3.00 8.00
62 Andrew Bynum/50 5.00 12.00
64 Kobe Bryant/50 15.00 30.00
67 Pau Gasol/50 4.00 10.00
74 Andres Nocioni/25 2.50 6.00
78 Kevin Garnett/25 8.00 20.00
79 Paul Pierce/25 5.00 12.00
82 Ray Allen/25 4.00 10.00
87 Al Harrington/25 3.00 8.00
89 Danilo Gallinari/50 4.00 10.00
91 David Lee/50 3.00 8.00
92 Nate Robinson/25 4.00 10.00
93 Andre Iguodala/50 4.00 10.00
94 Elton Brand/25 4.00 10.00
95 Samuel Dalembert/50 2.50 6.00
96 Thaddeus Young/50 2.50 6.00
97 Andrea Bargnani/50 3.00 8.00
98 Chris Bosh/50 4.00 10.00
101 Jose Calderon/50 3.00 8.00
102 Derrick Rose/50 12.00 30.00
107 LeBron James/25 15.00 40.00
108 Mo Williams/25 3.00 8.00
109 Shaquille O'Neal/50 8.00 20.00
110 Zydrunas Ilgauskas/50 2.50 6.00
111 Ben Gordon/50 4.00 10.00
113 Charlie Villanueva/50 3.00 8.00
114 Richard Hamilton/50 3.00 8.00
116 Tayshaun Prince/50 4.00 10.00
118 Jeff Foster/50 2.50 6.00
125 Al Horford/50 4.00 10.00
127 Joe Johnson/25 4.00 10.00
128 Josh Smith/25 4.00 10.00
130 Boris Diaw/25 3.00 8.00
131 D.J. Augustin/50 3.00 8.00
132 Gerald Wallace/50 4.00 10.00
134 Raymond Felton/25 3.00 8.00
136 Dwyane Wade/50 8.00 20.00
137 Jermaine O'Neal/25 4.00 10.00
139 Michael Beasley/25 4.00 10.00
141 Udonis Haslem/25 3.00 8.00
142 Dwight Howard/50 6.00 15.00
146 Rashard Lewis/25 3.00 8.00
147 Antawn Jamison/50 4.00 10.00
149 Gilbert Arenas/50 4.00 10.00
151 Isiah Thomas/50 4.00 10.00
154 Dikembe Mutombo/50 6.00 15.00
157 Adrian Dantley/50 4.00 10.00
166 Magic Johnson/50 10.00 25.00

2009-10 Certified Mirror Gold

*1-150: 2.5X TO 6X BASE HI
*151-170: 1.5X TO 4X BASE HI
*171-200 RC: 1X TO 2.5X BASE HI
STATED PRINT RUN 25 SER.#'d SETS
174 Tyreke Evans JSY AU 50.00 120.00
176 Stephen Curry JSY AU 50.00 120.00
178 Brandon Jennings JSY AU 30.00 80.00
180 Gerald Henderson JSY AU 15.00 40.00
185 Jrue Holiday JSY AU 30.00 80.00

2009-10 Certified Mirror Gold Materials Prime

STATED PRINT RUN 5 TO 25 SER.#'d SETS
SOME UNPRICED DUE TO SCARCITY
1 Dirk Nowitzki/25 10.00 25.00
2 Jason Kidd/25 8.00 20.00
3 Jason Terry/25 6.00 15.00
4 J.J. Barea/25 12.50 30.00
6 Shawn Marion/25 8.00 20.00
8 Shane Battier/25 8.00 20.00
25 Tim Duncan/25 12.00 30.00
33 Al Jefferson/25 8.00 20.00
34 Kevin Love/25 12.00 30.00
46 Andrei Kirilenko/25 6.00 15.00
59 Chris Kaman/25 6.00 15.00
64 Kobe Bryant/25 25.00 60.00
87 Al Harrington/15 6.00 15.00
89 Danilo Gallinari/25 8.00 20.00
91 David Lee/25 6.00 15.00
93 Andre Iguodala/25 8.00 20.00
95 Samuel Dalembert/25 5.00 12.00
96 Thaddeus Young/25 5.00 12.00
109 Shaquille O'Neal/25 20.00 50.00
110 Zydrunas Ilgauskas/25 5.00 12.00
118 Jeff Foster/25 5.00 12.00
125 Al Horford/25 8.00 20.00
131 D.J. Augustin/25 6.00 15.00
151 Isiah Thomas/25 8.00 20.00
154 Dikembe Mutombo/25 10.00 25.00
157 Adrian Dantley/25 8.00 20.00
166 Magic Johnson/25 20.00 50.00

2009-10 Certified Mirror Gold Signatures

STATED PRINT RUN 10 TO 25 SER.#'d SETS
SOME UNPRICED DUE TO SCARCITY
5 Josh Howard/25 6.00 15.00
19 Emeka Okafor/25 6.00 15.00
26 Tony Parker/25 15.00 30.00
34 Kevin Love/25 20.00 50:00
36 Ryan Gomes/25 6.00 15.00
45 Russell Westbrook/25 20.00 50.00
47 Carlos Boozer/25 8.00 20.00
48 Deron Williams/25 15.00 30.00
59 Chris Kaman/25 6.00 15.00
60 Eric Gordon/25 10.00 25.00
64 Kobe Bryant/25 125.00 225.00
80 Rajon Rondo/25 20.00 50.00
82 Ray Allen/25 25.00 50.00
85 Devin Harris/25 10.00 25.00
91 David Lee/15 15.00 30.00
93 Andre Iguodala/25 8.00 20.00
94 Elton Brand/25 8.00 20.00
113 Charlie Villanueva/25 6.00 15.00
117 Danny Granger/25 8.00 20.00
137 Jermaine O'Neal/25 8.00 20.00
150 Randy Foye/25 6.00 15.00
152 Byron Scott/25 8.00 20.00
153 Frank Ramsey/25 6.00 15.00
157 Adrian Dantley/25 8.00 20.00
158 Bailey Howell/25 8.00 20.00
164 Bill Walton/25 12.00 30.00
170 James Worthy/25 20.00 40.00

2009-10 Certified Mirror Red

*1-170: .5X TO 1.25X BASE HI
PRINT RUN 250 SER.#'d SETS
*171-200 RC: .5X TO 1.25X BASE HI
171-200 RC PRINT RUN 100 SER.#'d SETS

2009-10 Certified Champions

COMPLETE SET (25) 20.00 40.00
PRINT RUN 500 SER.#'d SETS
UNPRICED BLACK PRINT RUN ONE SET
*BLUE: .6X TO 1.5X BASE HI
BLUE PRINT RUN 100 SER.#'d SETS
UNPRICED EMERALD PRINT RUN 5 SETS
*GOLD: 1.25X TO 3X BASE HI
GOLD PRINT RUN 25 SER.#'d SETS
*RED: .5X TO 1.25X BASE HI
RED PRINT RUN 250 SER.#'d SETS
1 Kobe Bryant 5.00 12.00
2 Bill Laimbeer 1.00 2.50
3 Bill Russell 1.50 4.00
4 Bill Walton 1.00 2.50
5 Dwyane Wade 2.00 5.00
6 Hakeem Olajuwon 1.25 3.00
7 Isiah Thomas 1.00 2.50
8 Jerry West 1.25 3.00
9 John Havlicek 1.00 2.50
10 Kevin Garnett 2.00 5.00
11 Magic Johnson 2.50 6.00
12 Oscar Robertson 1.00 2.50
13 Rick Barry 1.00 2.50
14 Shaquille O'Neal 2.00 5.00
15 Tim Duncan 1.50 4.00
16 Walt Frazier 1.00 2.50
17 Chauncey Billups 1.00 2.50
18 Tony Parker 1.00 2.50
19 Wes Unseld 1.00 2.50
20 Willis Reed 1.00 2.50
21 Kareem Abdul-Jabbar 1.50 4.00
22 Joe Dumars 1.00 2.50
23 Paul Pierce 1.25 3.00
24 Dolph Schayes 1.00 2.50
25 Arnie Risen 1.00 2.50

2009-10 Certified Champions Materials

STATED PRINT RUN 10 TO 99 SER.#'d SETS
SOME UNPRICED DUE TO SCARCITY
*PRIME: .6X TO 1.5X HI COLUMN
PRIME PRINT RUN ONE TO 25 SETS
1 Kobe Bryant/99 10.00 25.00
5 Dwyane Wade/99 6.00 15.00
6 Hakeem Olajuwon/99 5.00 12.00
7 Isiah Thomas/99 4.00 10.00
8 Jerry West/99 5.00 12.00
9 John Havlicek/50 6.00 15.00
10 Kevin Garnett/50 6.00 15.00
11 Magic Johnson/99 8.00 20.00
15 Tim Duncan/99 5.00 12.00
22 Joe Dumars/99 4.00 10.00
23 Paul Pierce/99 4.00 10.00

2009-10 Certified Champions Signatures

STATED PRINT RUN 10 TO 50 SER.#'d SETS
SOME UNPRICED DUE TO SCARCITY
1 Kobe Bryant/50 100.00 200.00
2 Bill Laimbeer/50 8.00 20.00
3 Bill Russell/50 50.00 100.00
4 Bill Walton/50 8.00 20.00
7 Isiah Thomas/50 10.00 25.00
8 Jerry West/35 25.00 50.00
9 John Havlicek/50 15.00 40.00
12 Oscar Robertson/50 30.00 80.00
13 Rick Barry/50 8.00 20.00
18 Tony Parker/50 15.00 30.00
19 Wes Unseld/25 8.00 20.00
20 Willis Reed/50 15.00 30.00
21 Kareem Abdul-Jabbar/25 40.00 100.00
24 Dolph Schayes/50 8.00 20.00
25 Arnie Risen/50 8.00 20.00

2009-10 Certified Fabric of the Game

STATED PRINT RUN 10 TO 250 SETS
*JSY NUMBER: .5X TO 1.25X BASE HI
JSY NUMBER PRINT RUN 10 TO 99 SETS
*JSY NUM.PRIME: .75X TO 2X BASE HI
JSY NUM.PRIME PRINT RUN ONE TO 25 SETS
*NBA DC: .6X TO 1.5X BASE HI
NBA DC STATED PRINT RUN 5 TO 50 SETS
*NBA DC PRIME: 1.5X TO 4X BASE HI
NBA DC PRIME PRINT RUN ONE TO 25 SETS
*PRIME: .75X TO 2X BASE HI
PRIME STATED PRINT RUN ONE TO 25 SETS
*TEAM DC: 1X TO 2.5X BASE HI
TEAM DC STATED PRINT RUN ONE TO 25 SETS
UNPRICED TEAM DC PRIME PRINT RUN 1 TO 10 SETS
1 Dirk Nowitzki/250 4.00 10.00
2 Jason Kidd/250 3.00 8.00
3 Jason Terry/250 2.50 6.00
4 J.J. Barea/250 5.00 12.00
5 Josh Howard/250 2.50 6.00
6 Shawn Marion/250 3.00 8.00
7 Luis Scola/250 2.50 6.00
8 Shane Battier/250 3.00 8.00
9 Tracy McGrady/250 3.00 8.00
11 Yao Ming/250 4.00 10.00
14 O.J. Mayo/100 3.00 8.00
17 Chris Paul/250 5.00 12.00
18 David West/250 3.00 8.00
21 Peja Stojakovic/100 3.00 8.00
25 Tim Duncan/250 5.00 12.00
27 Carmelo Anthony/250 4.00 10.00
28 Chauncey Billups/250 3.00 8.00
29 Chris Andersen/250 5.00 12.00
31 Kenyon Martin/250 3.00 8.00
32 Nene/250 2.50 6.00
33 Al Jefferson/250 3.00 8.00
34 Kevin Love/250 5.00 12.00
36 Ryan Gomes/250 2.00 5.00
38 Brandon Roy/50 3.00 8.00
39 Greg Oden/250 2.50 6.00
40 LaMarcus Aldridge/250 3.00 8.00
46 Andrei Kirilenko/250 2.50 6.00
47 Carlos Boozer/250 3.00 8.00
48 Deron Williams/250 3.00 8.00
49 Mehmet Okur/250 2.00 5.00
50 Paul Millsap/250 2.50 6.00
59 Chris Kaman/250 2.50 6.00
62 Andrew Bynum/100 4.00 10.00
64 Kobe Bryant/250 10.00 25.00
67 Pau Gasol/250 3.00 8.00
74 Andres Nocioni/50 2.00 5.00
78 Kevin Garnett/250 6.00 15.00
79 Paul Pierce/250 4.00 10.00
80 Rajon Rondo/100 4.00 10.00
82 Ray Allen/100 3.00 8.00
87 Al Harrington/25 2.50 6.00
89 Danilo Gallinari/250 3.00 8.00
91 David Lee/250 2.50 6.00
92 Nate Robinson/250 3.00 8.00
93 Andre Iguodala/250 3.00 8.00
94 Elton Brand/250 3.00 8.00
95 Samuel Dalembert/250 2.00 5.00
96 Thaddeus Young/250 2.00 5.00
97 Andrea Bargnani/250 2.50 6.00
98 Chris Bosh/250 3.00 8.00
101 Jose Calderon/250 2.50 6.00
102 Derrick Rose/100 10.00 25.00
107 LeBron James/250 8.00 20.00
108 Mo Williams/250 2.50 6.00
109 Shaquille O'Neal/250 8.00 20.00
110 Zydrunas Ilgauskas/250 2.00 5.00
111 Ben Gordon/250 3.00 8.00
113 Charlie Villanueva/250 2.50 6.00
114 Richard Hamilton/250 2.50 6.00
116 Tayshaun Prince/250 3.00 8.00
118 Jeff Foster/250 2.00 5.00
124 Michael Redd/100 3.00 8.00
125 Al Horford/250 3.00 8.00
127 Joe Johnson/100 3.00 8.00
128 Josh Smith/250 3.00 8.00
129 Mike Bibby/100 2.50 6.00
130 Boris Diaw/250 2.50 6.00
131 D.J. Augustin/250 2.50 6.00
132 Gerald Wallace/250 3.00 8.00
134 Raymond Felton/250 2.50 6.00
136 Dwyane Wade/250 6.00 15.00
137 Jermaine O'Neal/25 3.00 8.00
139 Michael Beasley/250 3.00 8.00
141 Udonis Haslem/250 2.50 6.00
142 Dwight Howard/250 5.00 12.00
146 Rashard Lewis/250 2.50 6.00
147 Antawn Jamison/100 3.00 8.00
149 Gilbert Arenas/250 3.00 8.00
151 Isiah Thomas/250 3.00 8.00
154 Dikembe Mutombo/250 5.00 12.00
157 Adrian Dantley/50 3.00 8.00
160 Walt Frazier/50 3.00 8.00
166 Magic Johnson/250 8.00 20.00
171 Blake Griffin/250 12.00 30.00
172 Hasheem Thabeet/250 2.00 5.00
173 James Harden/250 6.00 15.00
174 Tyreke Evans/250 5.00 12.00
175 Jonny Flynn/250 2.00 5.00
176 Stephen Curry/250 5.00 12.00
177 Jordan Hill/250 2.00 5.00
178 Brandon Jennings/250 4.00 10.00
179 Terrence Williams/250 2.00 5.00
180 Gerald Henderson/250 2.00 5.00
181 Tyler Hansbrough/250 3.00 8.00
182 Earl Clark/250 2.00 5.00
183 Austin Daye/250 2.00 5.00
184 James Johnson/250 2.00 5.00
185 Jrue Holiday/250 4.00 10.00
186 Ty Lawson/250 3.00 8.00
187 Jeff Teague/250 2.50 6.00
188 Eric Maynor/250 2.00 5.00
189 Darren Collison/250 3.00 8.00
190 Omri Casspi/250 2.00 5.00
191 B.J. Mullens/250 2.00 5.00
192 Rodrigue Beaubois/250 2.50 6.00
193 Taj Gibson/250 2.50 6.00
194 DeMarre Carroll/250 2.00 5.00
195 Wayne Ellington/250 2.00 5.00
196 Toney Douglas/250 2.00 5.00
197 Jeff Pendergraph/250 2.00 5.00
198 Jermaine Taylor/250 2.00 5.00
199 DeJuan Blair/250 2.50 6.00
200 Jodie Meeks/250 2.50 6.00

2009-10 Certified Fabric of the Game Jersey Number Signatures

STATED PRINT RUN ONE TO 25 SER.#'d SETS
SOME UNPRICED DUE TO SCARCITY
UNPRICED PRIME SIG. PRINT RUN ONE TO 10 SETS
2 Jason Kidd/25 20.00 50.00
5 Josh Howard/25 8.00 20.00
34 Kevin Love/25 20.00 50.00
36 Ryan Gomes/25 8.00 20.00
48 Deron Williams/25 15.00 40.00
59 Chris Kaman/25 8.00 20.00
64 Kobe Bryant/25 125.00 250.00
67 Pau Gasol/25 20.00 50.00
91 David Lee/25 8.00 20.00
93 Andre Iguodala/25 8.00 20.00
98 Chris Bosh/25 15.00 40.00
113 Charlie Villanueva/25 8.00 20.00
137 Jermaine O'Neal/25 8.00 20.00
139 Michael Beasley/25 10.00 25.00
151 Isiah Thomas/25 15.00 30.00
154 Dikembe Mutombo/25 25.00 60.00
157 Adrian Dantley/25 8.00 20.00
171 Blake Griffin/25 175.00 350.00
172 Hasheem Thabeet/25 8.00 20.00
173 James Harden/25 25.00 60.00
174 Tyreke Evans/25 25.00 60.00
175 Jonny Flynn/25 8.00 20.00
176 Stephen Curry/25 25.00 60.00
177 Jordan Hill/25 8.00 20.00
178 Brandon Jennings/25 15.00 40.00
179 Terrence Williams/25 8.00 20.00
180 Gerald Henderson/25 8.00 20.00
181 Tyler Hansbrough/25 12.00 30.00
182 Earl Clark/25 8.00 20.00
183 Austin Daye/25 8.00 20.00
184 James Johnson/25 8.00 20.00
185 Jrue Holiday/25 15.00 40.00
186 Ty Lawson/25 12.00 30.00
187 Jeff Teague/25 10.00 25.00
188 Eric Maynor/25 8.00 20.00
189 Darren Collison/25 12.00 30.00
190 Omri Casspi/25 8.00 20.00
191 B.J. Mullens/25 8.00 20.00
192 Rodrigue Beaubois/25 10.00 25.00
193 Taj Gibson/25 10.00 25.00
194 DeMarre Carroll/25 8.00 20.00
195 Wayne Ellington/25 8.00 20.00
196 Toney Douglas/25 8.00 20.00
197 Jeff Pendergraph/25 8.00 20.00
198 Jermaine Taylor/25 8.00 20.00
199 DeJuan Blair/25 10.00 25.00
200 Jodie Meeks/25 10.00 25.00

2009-10 Certified Gold Team

COMPLETE SET (25) 10.00 25.00
PRINT RUN 500 SER.#'d SETS
UNPRICED BLACK PRINT RUN ONE SET
*BLUE: .6X TO 1.5X BASE HI
BLUE PRINT RUN 100 SER.#'d SETS
UNPRICED EMERALD PRINT RUN 5 SETS
*GOLD: 1.25X TO 3X BASE HI
GOLD PRINT RUN 25 SER.#'d SETS
*RED: .5X TO 1.25X BASE HI
RED PRINT RUN 250 SER.#'d SETS
1 Kobe Bryant 5.00 12.00
2 Dwyane Wade 2.00 5.00
3 Chris Paul 1.50 4.00
4 Dwight Howard 1.50 4.00
5 Danny Granger 1.00 2.50
6 Deron Williams 1.00 2.50
7 Carmelo Anthony 1.25 3.00
8 Kevin Durant 3.00 8.00
9 Paul Pierce 1.25 3.00
10 LeBron James 5.00 12.00

2009-10 Certified Gold Team Materials

STATED PRINT RUN 99 SER.#'d SETS
*PRIME: 1X TO 2.5X HI COLUMN
PRIME PRINT RUN ONE TO 25 SETS
1 Kobe Bryant 10.00 25.00
2 Dwyane Wade 6.00 15.00
3 Chris Paul 5.00 12.00
4 Dwight Howard 5.00 12.00
6 Deron Williams 3.00 8.00
7 Carmelo Anthony 4.00 10.00
9 Paul Pierce 4.00 10.00
10 LeBron James 10.00 25.00

2009-10 Certified Gold Team Signatures

STATED PRINT RUN 25 TO 50 SER.#'d SETS
1 Kobe Bryant/50 100.00 200.00
5 Danny Granger/25 8.00 20.00
6 Deron Williams/50 10.00 25.00

2009-10 Certified Imports

COMPLETE SET (15) 7.50 15.00
STATED PRINT RUN 500 SER.#'d SETS
UNPRICED BLACK PRINT RUN ONE SET
*BLUE: .6X TO 1.5X BASE HI
BLUE PRINT RUN 100 SER.#'d SETS
UNPRICED EMERALD PRINT RUN 5 SETS
*GOLD: 1.25X TO 3X BASE HI
GOLD PRINT RUN 25 SER.#'d SETS
*RED: .5X TO 1.25X BASE HI
RED PRINT RUN 250 SER.#'d SETS
1 Andrea Bargnani .75 2.00
2 Andrew Bogut 1.00 2.50
3 Boris Diaw .75 2.00
4 Dirk Nowitzki 1.25 3.00
5 Hasheem Thabeet 1.00 2.50
6 Hedo Turkoglu 1.00 2.50
7 Kelenna Azubuike .60 1.50
8 Manu Ginobili 1.00 2.50
9 Nene .75 2.00
10 Omri Casspi 1.00 2.50
11 Pau Gasol 1.00 2.50
12 Steve Nash 1.00 2.50
13 Yao Ming 1.25 3.00
14 Zydrunas Ilgauskas .60 1.50
15 Andrei Kirilenko .75 2.00

2009-10 Certified Imports Materials

STATED PRINT RUN 25 TO 99 SER.#'d SETS
*PRIME: .75X TO 2X BASE HI
PRIME PRINT RUN 5 TO 25 SER.#'d SETS
1 Andrea Bargnani/25 2.50 6.00
3 Boris Diaw/50 2.50 6.00
4 Dirk Nowitzki/99 4.00 10.00
5 Hasheem Thabeet/99 3.00 8.00
8 Manu Ginobili/25 3.00 8.00
9 Nene/99 2.50 6.00
10 Omri Casspi/99 3.00 8.00
11 Pau Gasol/99 3.00 8.00
13 Yao Ming/99 4.00 10.00
14 Zydrunas Ilgauskas/99 2.00 5.00
15 Andrei Kirilenko/99 2.50 6.00

2009-10 Certified Imports Signatures

STATED PRINT RUN 10 TO 50 SER.#'d SETS
SOME UNPRICED DUE TO SCARCITY
5 Hasheem Thabeet/50 8.00 20.00
10 Omri Casspi/50 8.00 20.00
11 Pau Gasol/25 25.00 50.00

2009-10 Certified Potential

COMPLETE SET (35)
STATED PRINT RUN 500 SER.#'d SETS
UNPRICED BLACK PRINT RUN ONE SET
*BLUE STARS: .75X TO 2X BASE HI
*BLUE RCs: 1X TO 2.5X BASE HI
BLUE PRINT RUN 50 SER.#'d SETS
UNPRICED EMERALD PRINT RUN 5 SETS
*RED STARS: .6X TO 1.5X BASE HI
*RED RCs: .75X TO 2X BASE HI
RED PRINT RUN 100 SER.#'d SETS
1 Anthony Morrow .60 1.50
2 Anthony Randolph .75 2.00
3 Brook Lopez 1.00 2.50
4 D.J. Augustin .75 2.00
5 Derrick Rose 3.00 8.00
6 Eric Gordon 1.00 2.50
7 Greg Oden .75 2.00
8 Jason Thompson .60 1.50
9 Kevin Love 1.50 4.00
10 Marc Gasol 1.00 2.50
11 Mario Chalmers 1.00 2.50
12 Michael Beasley 1.00 2.50
13 O.J. Mayo 1.00 2.50
14 Rudy Fernandez .75 2.00
15 Russell Westbrook 1.50 4.00
16 Brandon Rush .75 2.00
17 Courtney Lee .75 2.00
18 Luc Mbah a Moute .60 1.50
19 Ryan Anderson 1.00 2.50
20 Blake Griffin 6.00 15.00
21 Brandon Jennings 2.00 5.00
22 DeMar DeRozan 1.50 4.00
23 Earl Clark 1.00 2.50
24 Gerald Henderson 1.00 2.50
25 James Harden 3.00 8.00
26 Jordan Hill 1.00 2.50
27 Stephen Curry 2.50 6.00
28 Tyreke Evans 2.50 6.00
29 DeJuan Blair 1.25 3.00
30 Jeff Teague 1.25 3.00
31 Sam Young 1.00 2.50
32 Taj Gibson 1.25 3.00
33 Chase Budinger 1.00 2.50
34 Hasheem Thabeet 1.00 2.50
35 Jonny Flynn 1.00 2.50

2009-10 Certified Potential Gold

*GOLD STARS: 1.25X TO 3X BASE HI
*GOLD RCs: 1.5X TO 4X BASE HI
STATED PRINT RUN 25 SER.#'d SETS
20 Blake Griffin 75.00 150.00

2009-10 Certified Potential Materials

STATED PRINT RUN 100 TO 599 SETS
*PRIME STARS: .75X TO 2X BASE HI
*PRIME RCs: 1X TO 2.5X BASE HI
PRIME PRINT RUN 5 TO 25 SER.#'d SETS
4 D.J. Augustin/100 2.50 6.00
5 Derrick Rose/100 10.00 25.00
7 Greg Oden/100 2.50 6.00
9 Kevin Love/599 5.00 12.00
12 Michael Beasley/250 3.00 8.00
20 Blake Griffin/599 8.00 20.00
21 Brandon Jennings/599 4.00 10.00
22 DeMar DeRozan/599 3.00 8.00
23 Earl Clark/599 2.00 5.00
24 Gerald Henderson/599 2.00 5.00
25 James Harden/599 6.00 15.00
26 Jordan Hill/599 2.00 5.00
27 Stephen Curry/599 5.00 12.00
28 Tyreke Evans/599 5.00 12.00
29 DeJuan Blair/599 2.50 6.00
30 Jeff Teague/599 2.50 6.00
31 Sam Young/599 2.00 5.00
32 Taj Gibson/599 2.50 6.00
33 Chase Budinger/599 2.00 5.00
34 Hasheem Thabeet/599 2.00 5.00
35 Jonny Flynn/599 2.00 5.00

2009-10 Certified Potential Signatures

STATED PRINT RUN 25 SER.#'d SETS
6 Eric Gordon 8.00 20.00
9 Kevin Love 15.00 40.00
12 Michael Beasley 15.00 30.00
15 Russell Westbrook 15.00 40.00
20 Blake Griffin 150.00 300.00
21 Brandon Jennings 15.00 40.00
23 Earl Clark 8.00 20.00
24 Gerald Henderson 8.00 20.00
25 James Harden 25.00 60.00
26 Jordan Hill 8.00 20.00
27 Stephen Curry 20.00 50.00
28 Tyreke Evans 20.00 50.00
29 DeJuan Blair 10.00 25.00
30 Jeff Teague 10.00 25.00
31 Sam Young 8.00 20.00
32 Taj Gibson 10.00 25.00
34 Hasheem Thabeet 8.00 20.00
35 Jonny Flynn 8.00 20.00

2009-10 Certified Shirt Off My Back Combos

STATED PRINT RUN 25 TO 99 SER.#'d SETS
1 Rajon Rondo/99 8.00 20.00
Ray Allen
2 Jason Kidd/99 5.00 12.00
Josh Howard
3 Shane Battier/99 4.00 10.00
Tracy McGrady
7 Jermaine O'Neal/49 4.00 10.00
Michael Beasley
8 Al Jefferson/99 4.00 10.00
Ryan Gomes
9 Andre Iguodala/99 4.00 10.00
Elton Brand
10 Andrea Bargnani/99 5.00 12.00
Chris Bosh
12 Kevin McHale/99 8.00 20.00
Robert Parish
13 Artis Gilmore/99 6.00 15.00
George Gervin
14 Clyde Drexler/99 15.00 30.00
Scottie Pippen
15 Patrick Ewing/25 25.00 60.00
Walt Frazier

2009-10 Certified Shirt Off My Back Combos Prime

*PRIME: .75X TO 2X BASE HI
STATED PRINT RUN 10 TO 25 SER.#'d SETS
SOME UNPRICED DUE TO SCARCITY
UNPRICED SIG.PRIME PRINT RUN ONE SET
UNPRICED SIGNATURE PRINT RUN 5 SETS
14 Clyde Drexler/25 30.00 80.00
Scottie Pippen

2010 Certified National Convention

COMPLETE SET (4) 6.00 15.00
ET Evan Turner 2.50 6.00
KB Kobe Bryant 5.00 12.00
LB Larry Bird 3.00 8.00
RR Rajon Rondo 1.25 3.00

2010 Certified National Convention Blue

COMPLETE SET (5) 40.00 80.00
ANNOUNCED PRINT RUN 25 SETS
ET Evan Turner 8.00 20.00
JW John Wall 12.00 30.00
KB Kobe Bryant 10.00 25.00
LB Larry Bird 6.00 15.00
RR Rajon Rondo 2.50 6.00

2010 Certified National Convention Green

COMPLETE SET (5) 15.00 30.00
ANNOUNCED PRINT RUN 50 SETS
ET Evan Turner 3.00 8.00
JW John Wall 5.00 12.00
KB Kobe Bryant 6.00 15.00
LB Larry Bird 4.00 10.00
RR Rajon Rondo 1.50 4.00

1992 Champion HOF Inductees

This ten-card standard-size set honors the 1992 Basketball Hall of Fame Inductees. The fronts feature black-and-white photos on a white face. A wide gray stripe cuts across the side borders, carrying a row of white stars that edge each side of the picture. The set title appears in the top white border, while the player's name is printed in the white border beneath the picture. The horizontal backs present biography, statistics or coaching record, and a list of career highlights. The cards are numbered in the upper right corner.

COMPLETE SET (10) 25.00 60.00
1 Bob Lanier 5.00 12.00
2 Sergei Belov 3.00 8.00
3 Lou Carnesecca CO 3.00 8.00
4 Connie Hawkins 6.00 15.00
5 Al McGuire CO 3.00 8.00
6 Jack Ramsay CO 2.50 6.00
7 Nera White 2.00 5.00
8 Phil Woolpert CO 2.00 5.00
9 Lusia Harris-Stewart 2.50 6.00
10 Title card 3.00 8.00

1989-90 Chicle Metalicas Spanish Stickers

If you have more information on this checklist, please feel free to send it to us at basketballmag@beckett.com

JW James Worthy 20.00 40.00
LB Larry Bird IA
MA Magic Johnson IA
RH Ron Harper
DW1 Dominique Wilkins
DW2 Dominique Wilkins IA
MJ1 Michael Jordan 150.00 300.00
MJ2 Michael Jordan IA 125.00 250.00

1993 Chicle Metalicas Spanish Wrappers

BW Buck Williams with Michael Jordan 100.00 200.00
MJ Michael Jordan guarded by #20 100.00 200.00
MJP Michael Jordan Portrait 100.00 200.00

2006-07 Chronology

1-100 PRINT RUN 199 SER.#'d SETS
101-142 PRINT RUN 99 SER.#'d SETS
143-148 NOT ISSUED IN PACKS
149-184 PRINT RUN 99 SER.#'d SETS
185-226 PRINT RUN 40 SER.#'d SETS
227-246 PRINT RUN 50 SER.#'d SETS
247-276 PRINT RUN 250 SER.#'d SETS
1 Slick Watts 2.50 6.00
2 Louie Dampier 2.50 6.00
3 Al Attles 2.50 6.00
4 Alvin Robertson 2.50 6.00
5 Detlef Schrempf 2.50 6.00
6 Artis Gilmore 2.50 6.00
7 Austin Carr 2.50 6.00
8 Avery Johnson 2.50 6.00
9 B.J. Armstrong 2.50 6.00
10 Dave Bing 2.50 6.00
11 Bingo Smith 2.50 6.00
12 Bob Dandridge 3.00 8.00
13 Bill Bradley 3.00 8.00
14 Bobby Jones 2.50 6.00
15 Brad Daugherty 2.50 6.00
16 Byron Scott 2.50 6.00
17 Cazzie Russell 2.50 6.00
18 Cedric Maxwell 2.50 6.00
19 Charles Oakley 2.50 6.00
20 Chet Walker 2.50 6.00
21 Chuck Share 2.50 6.00
22 Dan Majerle 3.00 8.00
23 Danny Ainge 2.50 6.00
24 Danny Manning 2.50 6.00
25 Darrell Griffith 2.50 6.00
26 Darryl Dawkins 2.50 6.00
27 Dennis Johnson 3.00 8.00
28 Gheorghe Muresan 2.50 6.00
29 Dick Barnett 3.00 8.00
30 Dick Van Arsdale 2.50 6.00
31 Dominique Wilkins 3.00 8.00
32 Don Buse 2.50 6.00
33 Don Ohl 2.50 6.00
34 Ernie DiGregorio 2.50 6.00
35 Fred Brown 2.50 6.00
36 Julius Erving 5.00 12.00
37 George McGinnis 2.50 6.00
38 Calvin Natt 2.50 6.00
39 Rick Mahorn 2.50 6.00
40 Gus Williams 2.50 6.00
41 Jack Sikma 2.50 6.00
42 Jamaal Wilkes 2.50 6.00
43 James Edwards 2.50 6.00
44 Jerry Sloan 2.50 6.00
45 Jim Loscutoff 3.00 8.00
46 Jo Jo White 2.50 6.00
47 John Johnson 2.50 6.00
48 Johnny Kerr 3.00 8.00

49 Karl Malone 3.00 8.00
50 Junior Bridgeman 2.50 6.00
51 Kiki Vandeweghe 2.50 6.00
52 Kurt Rambis 2.50 6.00
53 Larry Nance 2.50 6.00
54 Lonnie Shelton 2.50 6.00
55 Lou Hudson 2.50 6.00
56 Kevin McHale 3.00 8.00
57 Tree Rollins 2.50 6.00
58 George Karl 3.00 8.00
59 Maurice Lucas 2.50 6.00
60 Mel Daniels 2.50 6.00
61 Michael Cooper 2.50 6.00
62 Mitch Richmond 2.50 6.00
63 Joe Dumars 2.50 6.00
64 Mike Dunleavy Sr. 2.50 6.00
65 Moses Malone 2.50 6.00
66 Muggsy Bogues 2.50 6.00
67 Norm Nixon 2.50 6.00
68 Norm Van Lier 3.00 8.00
69 Oscar Robertson 2.50 6.00
70 Paul Arizin 2.50 6.00
71 Paul Westphal 2.50 6.00
72 Phil Chenier 2.50 6.00
73 Phil Ford 2.50 6.00
74 John Starks 2.50 6.00
75 Richie Guerin 2.50 6.00
76 Rolando Blackman 2.50 6.00
77 World B. Free 2.50 6.00
78 Rudy Tomjanovich 2.50 6.00
79 Sam Perkins 2.50 6.00
80 Sean Elliott 2.50 6.00
81 Ricky Pierce 2.50 6.00
82 Sidney Moncrief 2.50 6.00
83 Horace Grant 2.50 6.00
84 Spencer Haywood 2.50 6.00
85 Steve Kerr 2.50 6.00
86 Terry Dischinger 2.50 6.00
87 Mitch Kupchak 2.50 6.00
88 Tom Chambers 2.50 6.00
89 Tom Sanders 2.50 6.00
90 Michael Ray Richardson 2.50 6.00
91 Terry Cummings 2.50 6.00
92 Spud Webb 2.50 6.00
93 Walter Davis 2.50 6.00
94 Wayman Tisdale 2.50 6.00
95 Wayne Embry 2.50 6.00
96 Wilt Chamberlain 5.00 12.00
97 Jeff Hornacek 2.50 6.00
98 Eddie Johnson 2.50 6.00
99 Xavier McDaniel 2.50 6.00
100 Zelmo Beaty 2.50 6.00
101 Allan Ray JSY AU RC 6.00 15.00
102 Andrea Bargnani JSY AU RC 15.00 40.00
103 Bobby Jones JSY AU RC 6.00 15.00
104 Brandon Roy JSY AU RC 30.00 80.00
105 Cedric Simmons JSY AU RC 6.00 15.00
106 Craig Smith JSY AU RC 6.00 15.00
107 Daniel Gibson JSY AU RC 12.00 30.00
108 Dee Brown JSY AU RC 6.00 15.00
109 Damir Markota JSY AU RC 6.00 15.00
110 Hilton Armstrong JSY AU RC 6.00 15.00
111 James Augustine JSY AU RC 6.00 15.00
112 James White JSY AU RC 6.00 15.00
113 Hassan Adams JSY AU RC 6.00 15.00
114 Jorge Garbajosa JSY AU RC 6.00 15.00
115 Josh Boone JSY AU RC 6.00 15.00
116 Kyle Lowry JSY AU RC 8.00 20.00
117 LaMarcus Aldridge JSY AU RC 25.00 60.00
118 David Noel JSY AU RC 6.00 15.00
119 Marcus Williams JSY AU RC 6.00 15.00
120 Mardy Collins JSY AU RC 6.00 15.00
121 Maurice Ager JSY AU RC 6.00 15.00
122 P.J. Tucker JSY AU RC 6.00 15.00
123 Patrick O'Bryant JSY AU RC 6.00 15.00
124 Paul Davis JSY AU RC 6.00 15.00
125 Paul Millsap JSY AU RC 10.00 25.00
126 Q.Douby JSY AU RC 6.00 15.00
127 Rajon Rondo JSY AU RC 40.00 100.00
128 Randy Foye JSY AU RC 8.00 20.00
129 Renaldo Balkman JSY AU RC 6.00 15.00
130 Yakhouba Diawara JSY AU RC 6.00 15.00
131 Rodney Carney JSY AU RC 6.00 15.00
132 Ronnie Brewer JSY AU RC 8.00 20.00
133 Rudy Gay JSY AU RC 15.00 40.00
134 Saer Sene JSY AU RC 6.00 15.00
135 Sergio Rodriguez JSY AU RC 6.00 15.00
136 Shannon Brown JSY AU RC 15.00 30.00
137 Shawne Williams JSY AU RC 8.00 20.00
138 Shelden Williams JSY AU RC 6.00 15.00
139 Solomon Jones JSY AU RC 6.00 15.00
140 Thabo Sefolosha JSY AU RC 8.00 20.00
141 Tyrus Thomas JSY AU RC 10.00 25.00
142 Steve Novak JSY AU RC 6.00 15.00
149 Al Cervi JSY AU 10.00 25.00
150 Alex English JSY AU 10.00 25.00
151 Arnie Risen JSY AU 10.00 25.00
152 Bailey Howell JSY AU 10.00 25.00
153 Bill Sharman JSY AU 10.00 25.00
154 Don Nelson JSY AU 20.00 40.00
155 Bob Lanier JSY AU 15.00 30.00
156 Bob McAdoo JSY AU 25.00 50.00
157 Bob Pettit JSY AU 15.00 40.00
158 Bobby Wanzer JSY AU 10.00 25.00
159 Calvin Murphy JSY AU 10.00 25.00
160 Clyde Lovellette JSY AU 15.00 40.00
161 Bill Laimbeer JSY AU 25.00 50.00
162 Dave Cowens JSY AU 10.00 25.00
163 David Thompson JSY AU 10.00 25.00
164 Dick McGuire JSY AU 10.00 25.00
165 John Wooden JSY AU 125.00 250.00
166 Ed Macauley JSY AU 15.00 40.00
167 Elgin Baylor JSY AU 40.00 100.00
168 Elvin Hayes JSY AU 15.00 30.00
169 Frank Ramsey JSY AU 15.00 40.00
170 Gail Goodrich JSY AU 15.00 40.00
171 Hal Greer JSY AU 15.00 40.00
172 Adrian Dantley JSY AU 15.00 30.00
173 Jerry Lucas JSY AU 12.50 30.00
174 Reggie Theus JSY AU 10.00 25.00
175 Charlie Scott JSY AU 12.00 30.00
176 Nate Archibald JSY AU 15.00 40.00
177 Nate Thurmond JSY AU 10.00 25.00
178 Rick Barry JSY AU 15.00 40.00
179 Slater Martin JSY AU 25.00 50.00
180 Tom Heinsohn JSY AU 15.00 30.00
181 Vern Mikkelsen JSY AU 25.00 50.00
182 Walt Bellamy JSY AU 10.00 25.00
183 Walt Frazier JSY AU 25.00 50.00
184 Rod Hundley JSY AU 15.00 40.00
185 Ralph Sampson JSY AU 15.00 40.00
186 Bill Russell JSY AU 150.00 300.00
7 Julius Erving JSY AU 80.00 200.00
arry Bird JSY AU 100.00 200.00
es Worthy JSY AU 50.00 120.00
m Abdul-Jabbar JSY AU 50.00 100.00
rexler JSY AU 40.00 80.00
nson JSY AU 80.00 160.00

193 Wes Unseld JSY AU 15.00 40.00
194 John Stockton JSY AU 60.00 120.00
195 George Gervin JSY AU 15.00 40.00
197 David Robinson JSY AU 80.00 160.00
198 Sam Jones JSY AU 50.00 100.00
199 Bill Walton JSY AU 15.00 40.00
200 Earl Lloyd JSY AU 15.00 40.00
201 Mark Price JSY AU 40.00 80.00
202 John Havlicek JSY AU 50.00 100.00
203 Cliff Hagan JSY AU 15.00 40.00
204 Dolph Schayes JSY AU 25.00 50.00
205 Harry Gallatin JSY AU 15.00 40.00
206 Jerry West JSY AU 50.00 120.00
207 Connie Hawkins JSY AU 15.00 40.00
208 Lenny Wilkens JSY AU 15.00 40.00
209 Michael Jordan JSY AU 500.00 850.00
210 Hakeem Olajuwon JSY AU 50.00 100.00
211 Dan Issel JSY AU 15.00 40.00
212 Robert Parish JSY AU 20.00 50.00
213 Dennis Rodman JSY AU 75.00 150.00
214 Pat Riley JSY AU 30.00 80.00
215 Maurice Cheeks JSY AU 15.00 40.00
216 Bob Houbregs JSY AU 15.00 40.00
217 Tracy McGrady JSY AU 50.00 100.00
218 Yao Ming JSY AU 30.00 80.00
219 Paul Pierce JSY AU 25.00 60.00
220 Ben Gordon JSY AU 30.00 80.00
221 Kobe Bryant JSY AU 200.00 450.00
222 Steve Nash JSY AU 100.00 200.00
223 LeBron James JSY AU 200.00 450.00
224 Carmelo Anthony JSY AU 40.00 100.00
225 Jason Kidd JSY AU 40.00 100.00
226 Chris Paul JSY AU 30.00 80.00
227 Bill Fitch AU 10.00 25.00
228 Jack Ramsay AU 15.00 30.00
229 John Kundla AU 50.00 100.00
230 Dean Smith AU 25.00 60.00
231 Pat Riley AU 15.00 30.00
232 Jerry Sloan AU 15.00 30.00
233 Don Haskins AU 20.00 40.00
234 Rick Pitino AU 20.00 40.00
235 John Chaney AU 15.00 40.00
238 Lenny Wilkens AU 10.00 25.00
239 Chuck Daly AU 25.00 50.00
240 George Karl AU 20.00 40.00
241 John Wooden AU 100.00 200.00
242 Digger Phelps AU 10.00 25.00
243 Jud Heathcote AU 20.00 40.00
244 Dick Motta AU 10.00 25.00
245 Gene Shue AU 10.00 25.00
246 Jim Calhoun AU 10.00 25.00
247 Greg Oden XRC 8.00 20.00
248 Kevin Durant AU XRC 200.00 400.00
249 Al Horford XRC 8.00 20.00
250 Mike Conley Jr. XRC 8.00 20.00
251 Jeff Green XRC 8.00 20.00
252 Yi Jianlian XRC 10.00 25.00
253 Corey Brewer XRC 8.00 20.00
254 Brandan Wright XRC 6.00 15.00
255 Joakim Noah XRC 15.00 40.00
256 Spencer Hawes XRC 6.00 15.00
257 Acie Law XRC 6.00 15.00
258 Thaddeus Young XRC 8.00 20.00
259 Julian Wright XRC 6.00 15.00
260 Al Thornton XRC 6.00 15.00
261 Rodney Stuckey XRC 10.00 25.00
262 Nick Young XRC 10.00 25.00
263 Sean Williams XRC 6.00 15.00
264 Marco Belinelli XRC 6.00 15.00
265 Javaris Crittenton XRC 6.00 15.00
266 Jason Smith XRC 6.00 15.00
267 Daequan Cook XRC 6.00 15.00
268 Jared Dudley XRC 6.00 15.00
269 Wilson Chandler XRC 10.00 25.00
270 Morris Almond XRC 6.00 15.00
271 Arron Afflalo XRC 8.00 20.00
272 Aaron Brooks XRC 6.00 15.00
273 Alando Tucker XRC 6.00 15.00
274 Marcus Williams XRC 6.00 15.00
275 Carl Landry XRC 6.00 15.00
276 Gabe Pruitt XRC 6.00 15.00

2006-07 Chronology 2007-08 Rookie Draft Redemptions Silver

*SILVER: .6X TO 1.5X BASE HI
SILVER PRINT RUN 50 SER.#'d SETS
UNPRICED GOLD PRINT RUN 10 SETS

2006-07 Chronology 20,000 Point Club

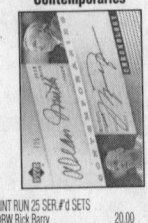

PRINT RUN 25 SER.#'d SETS
20KAD Adrian Dantley 15.00 30.00
20KAE Alex English 15.00 30.00
20KBP Bob Pettit 20.00 50.00
20KCD Clyde Drexler 30.00 80.00
20KDR David Robinson 60.00 120.00
20KEB Elgin Baylor 30.00 60.00
20KEH Elvin Hayes 15.00 30.00
20KGG George Gervin 30.00 60.00
20KHG Hal Greer 20.00 50.00
20KHO Hakeem Olajuwon 25.00 50.00
20KJH John Havlicek 30.00 60.00
20KJW Jerry West 60.00 150.00
20KKA Kareem Abdul-Jabbar 60.00 120.00
20KLB Larry Bird 50.00 100.00
20KMJ Michael Jordan 300.00 500.00
20KRP Robert Parish 20.00 40.00
20KTC Tom Chambers 15.00 30.00
20KWB Walt Bellamy 20.00 40.00

2006-07 Chronology Autographs

APPROXIMATELY ONE PER PACK
UNPRICED GOLD PRINT RUN 10 SETS
1 Slick Watts 6.00 15.00
1a Slick Watts Slick only 10.00 25.00
2 Louie Dampier 15.00 40.00
3 Al Attles 6.00 15.00
4 Alvin Robertson 6.00 15.00
6 Artis Gilmore 6.00 15.00
7 Austin Carr 8.00 20.00
8 Avery Johnson 6.00 15.00
9 B.J. Armstrong 8.00 20.00
12 Bob Dandridge 10.00 25.00
14 Bobby Jones 8.00 20.00
15 Brad Daugherty 6.00 15.00
16 Byron Scott 8.00 20.00
16a Byron Scott 3 Time Champs 30.00 60.00
17 Cazzie Russell 6.00 15.00
18 Cedric Maxwell 6.00 15.00
20 Chet Walker 8.00 20.00
21 Chuck Share 6.00 15.00
24 Danny Manning 8.00 20.00
25 Darrell Griffith 6.00 15.00
26 Darryl Dawkins Silver 8.00 20.00
29 Dick Barnett 10.00 25.00
30 Dick Van Arsdale 15.00 30.00
30a Dick Van Arsdale Orig.Sun 25.00 50.00
32 Don Buse 8.00 20.00
33 Don Ohl 10.00 25.00
34 Ernie DeGregorio 15.00 40.00
35 Fred Brown 6.00 15.00
37 George McGinnis 8.00 20.00
39 Rick Mahorn 8.00 20.00
40 Gus Williams 8.00 20.00
41 Jack Sikma 6.00 15.00
42 Jamaal Wilkes 6.00 15.00
44 Jerry Sloan 12.00 30.00
44a Jerry Sloan Spider 30.00 60.00
45 Jim Loscutoff 6.00 15.00
46 Jo Jo White 6.00 15.00
47 John Johnson 6.00 15.00
48 Johnny Kerr 12.50 30.00
50 Junior Bridgeman 8.00 20.00
51 Kiki Vandeweghe 6.00 15.00
53 Larry Nance 6.00 15.00
54 Lonnie Shelton 8.00 20.00
55 Lou Hudson 6.00 15.00
57 Tree Rollins 6.00 15.00
58 George Karl 20.00 35.00
59 Maurice Lucas 6.00 15.00
60 Mel Daniels 10.00 25.00
61 Michael Cooper 8.00 20.00
61a Michael Cooper Gold 10.00 25.00
66 Muggsy Bogues 8.00 20.00
67 Norm Nixon 6.00 15.00
68 Norm Van Lier 15.00 30.00
71 Paul Westphal 6.00 15.00
72 Phil Chenier 6.00 15.00
73 Phil Ford 8.00 20.00
73a Phil Ford UNC 10.00 25.00
75 Richie Guerin 6.00 15.00
76 Rolando Blackman 8.00 20.00
78 Rudy Tomjanovich Rudy T. 8.00 20.00
78a Rudy Tomjanovich signed twice 15.00 30.00
79 Sam Perkins 6.00 15.00
80 Sean Elliott 10.00 25.00
82 Sidney Moncrief 6.00 15.00
83 Horace Grant 25.00 60.00
84 Spencer Haywood 6.00 15.00
85 Steve Kerr 10.00 25.00
85a Steve Kerr 5 Time Champ 35.00 70.00
86 Terry Dischinger 8.00 20.00
88 Tom Chambers 6.00 15.00
89 Tom Sanders 10.00 25.00
90 Michael Ray Richardson 6.00 15.00
91 Terry Cummings 6.00 15.00
93 Walter Davis 6.00 15.00
94 Wayman Tisdale 8.00 20.00
97 Jeff Hornacek 10.00 25.00
98 Eddie Johnson 6.00 15.00
99 Xavier McDaniel 6.00 15.00
100 Zelmo Beaty 10.00 25.00
100a Zelmo Beaty Big E only 10.00 25.00

2006-07 Chronology Contemporaries

PRINT RUN 25 SER.#'d SETS
COBW Rick Barry / Jamaal Wilkes 20.00 40.00
COCE Maurice Cheeks / Julius Erving 50.00 100.00
CODH Dave Cowens / John Havlicek 50.00 100.00
CODO Clyde Drexler / Hakeem Olajuwon 80.00 160.00
COFA Walt Frazier / Nate Archibald 30.00 60.00
COFB Bill Fitch / Larry Bird 100.00 225.00
COGB Horace Grant / Kobe Bryant 100.00 225.00
COGC Hal Greer / Elgin Baylor 40.00 80.00
COGD Darrell Griffith / Darryl Dawkins 20.00 40.00
COGT George Gervin / David Thompson 20.00 40.00
COGW Gail Goodrich / Jerry West 60.00 150.00
COHL Connie Hawkins / Bob Lanier 25.00 50.00
COHS Tom Heinsohn / Bill Sharman 25.00 50.00
COHU Elvin Hayes / Wes Unseld 25.00 50.00
COHW Lou Hudson / Lenny Wilkens 20.00 40.00
COJH Magic Johnson / Jud Heathcote 50.00 100.00
COKM John Kundla / Vern Mikkelsen 20.00 40.00
COKS Johnny Kerr / Dolph Schayes 40.00 80.00
COLW Maurice Lucas / Bill Walton 30.00 60.00
COMM Slater Martin / Vern Mikkelsen 50.00 100.00
CORE David Robinson / Sean Elliott 80.00 160.00
CORL Dennis Rodman / Bill Laimbeer 40.00 80.00
CORS Pat Riley / Bill Sharman 40.00 80.00
COSJ Dean Smith / Michael Jordan 500.00 800.00
COSO Ralph Sampson / Hakeem Olajuwon 20.00 40.00
COWA John Wooden / Kareem Abdul-Jabbar 200.00 350.00

2006-07 Chronology Cut Signatures

STATED PRINT RUN 6 TO 17 SER.#'d SETS
MOST UNPRICED DUE TO SCARCITY
CSDD Dave DeBusschere/17 150.00 300.00

2006-07 Chronology HOF Inscriptions

PRINT RUN 50 SER.#'d SETS
HOFAE Alex English 6.00 15.00
HOFBH Bailey Howell 10.00 25.00
HOFBW Bobby Wanzer 20.00 40.00
HOFCD Clyde Drexler 30.00 60.00
HOFCH Cliff Hagan 25.00 50.00
HOFCL Clyde Lovellette 25.00 60.00
HOFCM Calvin Murphy 6.00 15.00
HOFDI Dan Issel 12.00 30.00
HOFDM Dick McGuire 10.00 25.00
HOFFR Frank Ramsey 25.00 50.00
HOFHG Hal Greer 20.00 50.00
HOFJE Julius Erving 40.00 80.00
HOFKA Kareem Abdul-Jabbar 40.00 80.00
HOFLB Larry Bird 50.00 100.00
HOFMJ Magic Johnson 50.00 100.00
HOFNT Nate Thurmond 15.00 40.00

2006-07 Chronology MVP Winners

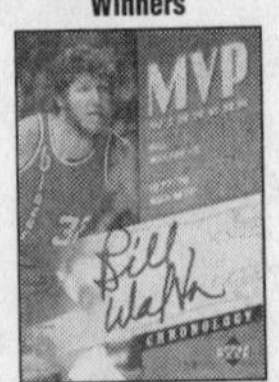

PRINT RUN 50 SER.#'d SETS
MVPAG Artis Gilmore 15.00 40.00
MVPBL Bob Lanier 10.00 25.00
MVPBM Bob McAdoo 25.00 50.00
MVPBP Bob Pettit 20.00 40.00
MVPBR Bill Russell 80.00 160.00
MVPBS Bill Sharman 10.00 25.00
MVPBW Bill Walton 15.00 30.00
MVPCM Cedric Maxwell 10.00 25.00
MVPDC Dave Cowens 15.00 30.00
MVPDT David Thompson 15.00 30.00
MVPEB Elgin Baylor 25.00 50.00
MVPEM Ed Macauley 25.00 50.00
MVPGG George Gervin 15.00 40.00
MVPHG Hal Greer 12.50 30.00
MVPHO Hakeem Olajuwon 20.00 40.00
MVPJL Jerry Lucas 15.00 40.00
MVPJS John Stockton 60.00 120.00
MVPJW James Worthy 30.00 80.00
MVPLJ LeBron James 100.00 225.00
MVPLW Lenny Wilkens 10.00 25.00
MVPMJ Michael Jordan 300.00 525.00
MVPNA Nate Archibald 12.50 30.00
MVPRB Rick Barry 12.50 30.00
MVPRS Ralph Sampson 10.00 25.00
MVPSH Spencer Haywood 10.00 25.00
MVPTC Tom Chambers 10.00 25.00
MVPWE Jerry West 30.00 80.00
MVPWF Walt Frazier 15.00 30.00
MVPWH Jo Jo White 15.00 30.00
MVPWU Wes Unseld 15.00 30.00

2006-07 Chronology Retired Numbers

STATED PRINT RUN ONE TO 44 SER.#'d SETS
SOME UNPRICED DUE TO SCARCITY
RNBL Bill Laimbeer/40 20.00 50.00
RNDG Darrell Griffith/35 8.00 20.00
RNGG Gail Goodrich/25 20.00 50.00
RNGM George McGinnis/30 20.00 40.00
RNHG Hal Greer/32 25.00 50.00
RNLB Larry Bird/33 60.00 120.00
RNLN Larry Nance/22 15.00 30.00
RNMP Mark Price/25 25.00 50.00
RNPW Paul Westphal/44 15.00 30.00
RNRB Rolando Blackman/22 20.00 40.00
RNTH Tom Heinsohn/15 20.00 50.00
RNTS Tom Sanders/25 20.00 40.00

2006-07 Chronology Signature Decades

STATED PRINT RUN 50 TO 90 SER.#'d SETS
DAC Al Cervi/50 25.00 50.00
DAE Alex English/80 8.00 20.00
DAM Alonzo Mourning/90 20.00 50.00
DAR Arnie Risen/50 20.00 50.00
DBH Bob Houbregs/50 25.00 50.00
DBL Bob Lanier/70 8.00 20.00
DBM Bob McAdoo/70 25.00 50.00
DBP Bob Pettit/60 15.00 40.00
DBS Bill Sharman/50 10.00 25.00
DBW Bill Walton/80 12.50 30.00
DCD Clyde Drexler/90 20.00 40.00
DCH Cliff Hagan/60 15.00 40.00
DCL Clyde Lovellette/50 25.00 50.00
DCM Calvin Murphy/70 8.00 20.00
DDC Dave Cowens/70 8.00 20.00
DDD Darryl Dawkins/80 8.00 20.00
DDM Dick McGuire/50 10.00 25.00
DDR David Robinson/90 40.00 80.00
DDS Dolph Schayes/50 20.00 50.00
DDT David Thompson/70 10.00 25.00
DEB Elgin Baylor/60 20.00 40.00
DEH Elvin Hayes/70 12.50 30.00
DFR Frank Ramsey/50 20.00 40.00
DGG George Gervin/70 10.00 25.00
DGR Hal Greer/60 15.00 30.00
DHG Harry Gallatin/50 15.00 40.00
DHO Bailey Howell/60 10.00 25.00
DJH John Havlicek/70 20.00 40.00
DJK Jason Kidd/90 15.00 30.00
DJL Jerry Lucas/70 15.00 30.00
DJO Mark Price/90 25.00 60.00
DJW James Worthy/80 25.00 60.00
DLA Bill Laimbeer/80 8.00 20.00
DMA Dan Majerle/90 25.00 50.00
DMC Maurice Cheeks/80 8.00 20.00
DMR Mitch Richmond/90 15.00 30.00
DNA Nate Archibald/70 15.00 30.00
DNT Nate Thurmond/60 15.00 30.00
DOL Hakeem Olajuwon/90 15.00 30.00
DRO Dennis Rodman/90 30.00 80.00
DRP Robert Parish/80 10.00 25.00
DSE Sean Elliott/90 15.00 30.00
DSJ Sam Jones/60. 15.00 40.00
DSM Slater Martin/50 25.00 60.00
DTH Tom Heinsohn/60 15.00 30.00
DWB Walt Bellamy/60 8.00 20.00
DWD Walter Davis/80 10.00 25.00
DWF Walt Frazier/70 15.00 30.00

2006-07 Chronology Stitches in Time

PRINT RUN 199 SER.#'d SETS
*GOLD: .5X TO 1.25X BASE HI
GOLD PRINT RUN 75 SER.#'d SETS
SITAB Andrea Bargnani 5.00 12.00
SITAI Allen Iverson 4.00 10.00
SITBR Brandon Roy 6.00 15.00
SITCA Carmelo Anthony 4.00 10.00
SITDR Dennis Rodman 5.00 12.00
SITHO Hakeem Olajuwon 4.00 10.00
SITJE Julius Erving 6.00 15.00
SITJO Magic Johnson 8.00 20.00
SITJR J.J. Redick 4.00 10.00
SITJS John Stockton 5.00 12.00
SITJW Jerry West 4.00 10.00
SITKB Kobe Bryant 8.00 20.00
SITKG Kevin Garnett 6.00 15.00
SITKM Kevin McHale 4.00 10.00
SITLA LaMarcus Aldridge 6.00 15.00
SITLB Larry Bird 10.00 25.00
SITLJ LeBron James 10.00 25.00
SITMJ Michael Jordan 25.00 60.00
SITPM Pete Maravich 20.00 50.00
SITRB Ronnie Brewer 4.00 10.00
SITRF Randy Foye 4.00 10.00
SITRG Rudy Gay 5.00 12.00
SITSO Shaquille O'Neal 6.00 15.00
SITSW Shelden Williams 3.00 8.00
SITTD Tim Duncan 5.00 12.00
SITTM Tracy McGrady 4.00 10.00
SITTS Thabo Sefolosha 4.00 10.00
SITTT Tyrus Thomas 4.00 10.00
SITVC Vince Carter 4.00 10.00
SITYM Yao Ming 4.00 10.00

2006-07 Chronology Stitches in Time Autographs

PRINT RUN 25 SER.#'d SETS
SITSAB Andrea Bargnani 15.00 40.00
SITSBR Brandon Roy 25.00 60.00
SITSCA Carmelo Anthony 30.00 80.00
SITSDR Dennis Rodman 40.00 80.00
SITSHO Hakeem Olajuwon 25.00 50.00
SITSJE Julius Erving 75.00 150.00
SITSJO Michael Jordan 400.00 650.00
SITSJS John Stockton 50.00 100.00
SITSKB Kobe Bryant 150.00 300.00
SITSLA LaMarcus Aldridge 25.00 60.00
SITSLB Larry Bird 60.00 120.00
SITSLJ LeBron James 150.00 300.00
SITSMJ Magic Johnson 60.00 120.00
SITSRF Randy Foye 15.00 40.00
SITSRG Rudy Gay 15.00 40.00
SITSTM Tracy McGrady 25.00 50.00
SITSTT Tyrus Thomas 20.00 50.00
SITSVC Vince Carter 30.00 80.00
SITSYM Yao Ming 30.00 80.00

2006-07 Chronology Stitches in Time Dual

PRINT RUN 75 SER.#'d SETS
SITDAR LaMarcus Aldridge / Brandon Roy 10.00 25.00
SITDBJ Larry Bird / Magic Johnson 20.00 50.00
SITDIA Allen Iverson / Carmelo Anthony 10.00 25.00
SITDJB Magic Johnson / Kobe Bryant 20.00 40.00
SITDJE Michael Jordan / Julius Erving 30.00 80.00
SITDJJ LeBron James / Michael Jordan 40.00 80.00
SITDMM Tracy McGrady / Yao Ming 6.00 15.00
SITDOD Shaquille O'Neal / Tim Duncan 10.00 25.00
SITDTS Tyrus Thomas / Thabo Sefolosha 6.00 15.00
SITDWS Jerry West / John Stockton 15.00 30.00

2007-08 Chronology

1-100 PRINT RUN 250 SER.#'d SETS
101-130 AU PRINT RUN 25 SER.#'d SETS
131-214 AU PRINT RUN 99 SER.#'d SETS
215-244 AU RC PRINT RUN 99 SER.#'d SETS
245-250 RC PRINT RUN 99 SER.#'d SETS
251-283 XRC PRINT RUN 250 SER.#'d SETS
1 Andrew Toney 2.50 6.00
2 Artis Gilmore 2.50 6.00
3 B.J. Armstrong 2.50 6.00
4 Bernard King 2.50 6.00
5 Bill Cartwright 2.50 6.00
6 Bill Laimbeer 2.50 6.00
7 Bill Russell 4.00 10.00
8 Bill Walton 2.50 6.00
9 Bill Wennington 2.50 6.00
10 Billy Cunningham 2.50 6.00
11 Bob Cousy 4.00 10.00
12 Bob McAdoo 2.50 6.00
13 Brad Davis 2.50 6.00
14 Byron Scott 2.50 6.00
15 Cedric Maxwell 2.50 6.00
16 Charles Oakley 2.50 6.00
17 Clyde Drexler 3.00 8.00
18 Clyde Lovellette 2.50 6.00
19 Dan Issel 2.50 6.00
20 Danny Ainge 2.50 6.00
21 Darrell Walker 2.50 6.00
22 Dave Bing 2.50 6.00
23 Dave Cowens 3.00 8.00
24 Dave DeBusschere 3.00 8.00
25 David Robinson 4.00 10.00
26 Dennis Rodman 4.00 10.00
27 Derrick Coleman 2.50 6.00
28 Dino Radja 3.00 8.00
29 Doc Rivers 2.50 6.00
30 Dominique Wilkins 3.00 8.00
31 Earl Monroe 2.50 6.00
32 Elgin Baylor 2.50 6.00
33 Freddie Lewis 2.50 6.00
34 George Gervin 2.50 6.00
35 George Mikan 5.00 12.00
36 Gheorghe Muresan 2.50 6.00
37 Gus Williams 2.50 6.00
38 Hakeem Olajuwon 3.00 8.00
39 Hal Greer 2.50 6.00
40 Harry Gallatin 2.50 6.00
41 Horace Grant 2.50 6.00
42 Isiah Thomas 2.50 6.00
43 Jack Sikma 2.50 6.00
44 James Worthy 3.00 8.00
45 Jay Vincent 2.50 6.00
46 Jerry Lucas 2.50 6.00
47 Jerry West 3.00 8.00
48 Jim Paxson 2.50 6.00
49 Jim Price 2.50 6.00
50 Joe Dumars 2.50 6.00
51 John Havlicek 2.50 6.00
52 John Paxson 2.50 6.00
53 John Salley 2.50 6.00
54 Julius Erving 5.00 12.00
55 Kareem Abdul-Jabbar 4.00 10.00
56 Karl Malone 3.00 8.00
57 Kenny Smith 2.50 6.00
58 Kermit Washington 2.50 6.00
59 Kevin McHale 3.00 8.00
60 Kurt Rambis 3.00 8.00
61 Larry Bird 8.00 20.00
62 Lenny Wilkens 2.50 6.00
63 Lionel Hollins 2.50 6.00
64 Luc Longley 2.50 6.00
65 Magic Johnson 6.00 15.00
66 Manute Bol 3.00 8.00
67 Mark Aguirre 2.50 6.00
68 Marques Johnson 2.50 6.00
69 Michael Jordan 25.00 60.00
70 Michael Ray Richardson 2.50 6.00
71 Moses Malone 2.50 6.00
72 Nate Archibald 2.50 6.00
73 Oscar Robertson 2.50 6.00
74 Paul Arizin 2.50 6.00
75 Paul Silas 2.50 6.00
76 Paul Westphal 3.00 8.00
77 Pete Maravich 8.00 20.00
78 Phil Jackson 3.00 8.00
79 Pooh Richardson 2.50 6.00
80 Reggie Miller 4.00 10.00
81 Rick Barry 2.50 6.00
82 Ron Harper 2.50 6.00
83 Joe Barry Carroll 2.50 6.00
84 Spencer Haywood 2.50 6.00
85 Stacey Augmon 2.50 6.00
86 Steve Kerr 2.50 6.00
87 Swen Nater 2.50 6.00
88 Lonnie Shelton 2.50 6.00
89 Thurl Bailey 2.50 6.00
90 Tom Chambers 2.50 6.00
91 Tom Sanders 2.50 6.00
92 Toni Kukoc 3.00 8.00
93 Vernon Maxwell 2.50 6.00
94 Vlade Divac 2.50 6.00
95 Walt Bellamy 2.50 6.00
96 Will Perdue 2.50 6.00
97 Reggie Theus 2.50 6.00
98 Willis Reed 2.50 6.00
99 Wilt Chamberlain 5.00 12.00
100 Xavier McDaniel 2.50 6.00
101 James Silas AU 12.00 30.00
102 Steve Nash AU 50.00 125.00
103 Yao Ming AU 25.00 60.00
104 Kevin Durant AU 300.00 600.00
106 Carmelo Anthony AU 20.00 40.00
108 Chris Paul AU 40.00 100.00
109 Dwight Howard AU 25.00 60.00
110 Vince Carter AU 50.00 120.00
111 Bill Laimbeer AU 15.00 40.00
112 Rick Barry AU 20.00 50.00
113 Spencer Haywood AU 12.00 30.00
114 Paul Pierce AU 20.00 40.00
116 Wes Unseld AU 12.00 30.00
117 Artis Gilmore AU 12.00 30.00
118 Tracy McGrady AU 20.00 50.00
119 David Robinson AU 40.00 80.00
120 Moses Malone AU 12.00 30.00
121 Dennis Rodman AU 40.00 80.00
122 Pat Riley AU 15.00 40.00
123 Michael Jordan AU 500.00 1000.00
124 LaMarcus Aldridge AU 12.00 30.00
125 Randy Foye AU 12.00 30.00
126 Jermaine O'Neal AU 12.00 30.00
127 Brad Daugherty AU 12.00 30.00
128 Muggsy Bogues AU 12.00 30.00
129 Kiki Vandeweghe AU 12.00 30.00
130 Micheal Ray Richardson AU 12.00 30.00
131 David Robinson AU 30.00 60.00
132 Kobe Bryant AU 150.00 300.00
133 Vince Carter AU 50.00 120.00
134 Kobe Bryant AU 200.00 400.00
135 Kevin Durant AU 250.00 450.00
136 Michael Jordan AU Blue 400.00 800.00
137 Magic Johnson AU 60.00 150.00
138 Michael Jordan AU 400.00 800.00
139 Jerry West AU 30.00 60.00
140 Tom Chambers AU 10.00 25.00
141 Bill Laimbeer AU 10.00 25.00
142 Julius Erving AU 100.00 200.00
143 Spud Webb AU 20.00 50.00
144 Clyde Drexler AU 40.00 70.00
145 Sean Elliott AU 10.00 25.00
146 Dominique Wilkins AU 20.00 50.00
147 Magic Johnson AU 60.00 150.00
148 John Wooden AU 75.00 150.00
149 Kareem Abdul-Jabbar AU 30.00 80.00
150 Larry Bird / Magic Johnson AU 175.00 350.00
151 Steve Kerr AU 12.00 30.0
152 Rick Barry AU 20.00 50.0
153 James Worthy AU 25.00 60.0
154 John Paxson AU 15.00 30.0
155 Baron Davis AU 20.00 50.0
156 Chris Paul AU 40.00 100.0
157 LeBron James AU 175.00 350.0
158 Kobe Bryant AU 150.00 300.0
159 Kevin Durant AU 250.00 450.0
160 Kevin Garnett AU 50.00 100.0
161 Bailey Howell AU 12.00 30.0
162 Bob Love AU 12.00 30.0
162a Bob Love #10 15.00 30.0
163 Norm Nixon AU 10.00 25.0
164 Horace Grant AU 20.00 50.0
165 Darrell Griffith AU 10.00 25.0
165a Darrell Griffith AU Dr. Dunk 20.00 40.
166 Dick McGuire AU 10.00 25.
167 Chet Walker AU 10.00 25.
168 Clyde Drexler AU 40.00 70.
169 Gail Goodrich AU 12.00 30.
170 Walt Frazier AU 20.00 50.
171 George Gervin AU 15.00 40.
172 Hal Greer AU 12.00 30.
173 Sam Jones AU 20.00 50.
174 Jerry Lucas AU 15.00 30.
175 Hakeem Olajuwon AU 40.00 100.
175a Hakeem Olajuwon AU 94 MVP 40.00 100.
176 Robert Parish AU 12.00 30
177 Bob Pettit AU 15.00 40
178 Spud Webb AU 25.00 60
179 Pat Riley AU 20.00 50
180 Bill Sharman AU 15.00 40
180a Bill Sharman WW2 Vet 25.00 50
181 John Stockton AU 50.00 125
182 Nate Thurmond AU 10.00 25
183 Wes Unseld AU 15.00 40
184 Bill Walton AU 15.00 30
185 Sam Perkins AU 20.00 40
186 Lenny Wilkens AU 12.00 30
187 Rudy Tomjanovich AU 12.00 30
188 Artis Gilmore AU 12.00 30
189 Adrian Dantley AU 10.00 25
190 David Thompson AU 12.00 30
190a David Thompson AU Skywalker 15.00 30
190b David Thompson AU Wolfpack 15.00 3
191 Dominique Wilkins AU 20.00 5
192 Dennis Rodman AU 30.00 8
193 Kiki Vandeweghe AU 10.00 2
194 Bob McAdoo AU 15.00 4
195 Alex English AU 10.00 2
196 George McGinnis AU 10.00 2
196a George McGinnis AU 75 ABA MVP 15.00 4
197 Vern Mikkelsen AU 10.00 2
198 Walt Bellamy AU 10.00 2
199 Bob Lanier AU 10.00 2
199a Bob Lanier AU MVP 25.00
200 Connie Hawkins AU 10.00
201 Bobby Wanzer AU 15.00
202 Tom Heinsohn AU 15.00
203 Slater Martin AU 15.00
204 Michael Cooper AU 10.00

205 Darryl Dawkins AU 12.00 30.00
206 Bobby Jones AU 12.00 30.00
207 Dolph Schayes AU 10.00 25.00
208 Louie Dampier AU 10.00 25.00
209 Don Nelson AU 12.00 30.00
210 Marques Johnson AU 10.00 25.00
211 Moses Malone AU 20.00 50.00
212 Dick Barnett AU 12.00 30.00
213 Cliff Hagan AU 15.00 30.00
214 Meadowlark Lemon AU 25.00 60.00
215 Kevin Durant AU RC 300.00 600.00
216 Al Horford AU RC 15.00 40.00
217 Corey Brewer AU RC 8.00 20.00
218 Mike Conley Jr. AU RC 10.00 25.00
218a Mike Conley Jr. AU Go Buckeyes 25.00 50.00
219 Joakim Noah AU RC 25.00 60.00
220 Julian Wright AU RC 6.00 15.00
220a Julian Wright AU Go Jayhawks 20.00 40.00
221 Jeff Green AU RC 12.50 30.00
222 Spencer Hawes AU RC 6.00 15.00
222a Spencer Hawes AU Go Huskies 15.00 30.00
223 Acie Law AU RC 6.00 15.00
224 Al Thornton AU RC 10.00 25.00
225 Rodney Stuckey AU RC 15.00 40.00
226 Sean Williams AU RC 6.00 15.00
226a Sean Williams AU Area 51 6.00 15.00
227 Marco Belinelli AU RC 6.00 15.00
228 Javaris Crittenton AU RC 6.00 15.00
229 Jason Smith AU RC 6.00 15.00
230 Daequan Cook AU RC 10.00 25.00
231 Jared Dudley AU RC 6.00 15.00
232 Wilson Chandler AU RC 10.00 25.00
233 Morris Almond AU RC 6.00 15.00
234 Aaron Brooks AU RC 6.00 15.00
235 Arron Afflalo AU RC 8.00 20.00
235a Arron Afflalo AU Go Bruins 20.00 40.00
236 Alando Tucker AU RC 6.00 15.00
237 Jermareo Davidson AU RC 6.00 15.00
239 Gabe Pruitt AU RC 6.00 15.00
240 Dominic McGuire AU RC 6.00 15.00
241 Glen Davis AU RC 12.00 30.00
241a Glen Davis AU Big Baby 20.00 40.00
242 Josh McRoberts AU RC 6.00 15.00
43 Luis Scola AU RC 10.00 25.00
44 Juan Navarro AU RC 6.00 15.00
45 Greg Oden RC 5.00 12.00
46 Yi Jianlian RC 6.00 15.00
47 Brandan Wright RC 4.00 10.00
48 Nick Young RC 6.00 15.00
49 Thaddeus Young RC 5.00 12.00
50 Kyrylo Fesenko RC 4.00 10.00
51 Derrick Rose XRC 40.00 100.00
52 Michael Beasley XRC 8.00 20.00
53 O.J. Mayo XRC 8.00 20.00
54 Russell Westbrook XRC 25.00 60.00
55 Kevin Love XRC 20.00 50.00
56 Danilo Gallinari XRC 8.00 20.00
57 Eric Gordon XRC 10.00 25.00
58 Joe Alexander XRC 5.00 12.00
9 D.J. Augustin XRC 5.00 12.00
0 Brook Lopez XRC 8.00 20.00
1 Jerryd Bayless XRC 5.00 12.00
2 Jason Thompson XRC 5.00 12.00
3 Brandon Rush XRC 5.00 12.00
4 Anthony Randolph XRC 6.00 15.00
5 Robin Lopez XRC 5.00 12.00
6 Marreese Speights XRC 5.00 12.00
7 Roy Hibbert XRC 8.00 20.00
8 JaVale McGee XRC 8.00 20.00
9 J.J. Hickson XRC 6.00 15.00
Alexis Ajinca XRC 5.00 12.00
Ryan Anderson XRC 8.00 20.00
Courtney Lee XRC 8.00 20.00
Kosta Koufos XRC 5.00 12.00
Kyle Weaver XRC 5.00 12.00
Nicolas Batum XRC 6.00 15.00
George Hill XRC 8.00 20.00
Darrell Arthur XRC 5.00 12.00
Donte Greene XRC 5.00 12.00
D.J. White XRC 5.00 12.00
J.R. Giddens XRC 5.00 12.00
Mario Chalmers XRC 8.00 20.00
Walter Sharpe XRC 5.00 12.00
DeAndre Jordan XRC 10.00 25.00

2007-08 Chronology Rookie Redemptions Gold

D: .75X TO 2X BASE HI
TED PRINT RUN 25 SER.#'d SETS

2007-08 Chronology Rookie Redemptions Silver

VER: .5X TO 1.25X BASE
TED PRINT RUN 99 SER.#'d SETS
Derrick Rose 80.00 200.00

07-08 Chronology Autographs

OM INSERTS IN PACKS
ICED GOLD PRINT RUN 10 SER.#'d SETS
s Gilmore 6.00 15.00
Armstrong 6.00 15.00
ard King 10.00 25.00
Cartwright 20.00 40.00
Laimbeer 6.00 15.00
Walton Grateful Red 30.00 80.00
Wennington 8.00 20.00
McAdoo 15.00 30.00
d Davis 6.00 15.00
on Scott 6.00 15.00
dric Maxwell 6.00 15.00
de Drexler 15.00 40.00
de Lovellette 8.00 20.00
Issel 6.00 15.00
ell Walker 6.00 15.00
e Cowens 6.00 15.00
id Robinson 30.00 60.00
Radja 6.00 15.00
o Radja All Rookie 8.00 20.00
Baylor 15.00 30.00
in Baylor 77 HOF 25.00 50.00
in Baylor Kappa Alpha Psi 30.00 60.00
die Lewis 6.00 15.00
ge Gervin 10.00 25.00

36 Gheorghe Muresan 6.00 15.00
37 Gus Williams 6.00 15.00
38 Hakeem Olajuwon 12.50 30.00
39 Hal Greer 8.00 20.00
40 Harry Gallatin 6.00 15.00
41 Horace Grant 10.00 25.00
43 Jack Sikma 6.00 15.00
45 Jay Vincent 6.00 15.00
46 Jerry Lucas 15.00 40.00
47 Jerry West 30.00 60.00
48 Jim Paxson 6.00 15.00
49 Jim Price 6.00 15.00
50 Joe Dumars 15.00 30.00
52 John Paxson 12.50 30.00
53 John Salley 6.00 15.00
54 Julius Erving 30.00 60.00
55 Kareem Abdul-Jabbar 60.00 120.00
57 Kenny Smith 8.00 20.00
58 Kermit Washington 6.00 15.00
61 Larry Bird 75.00 150.00
62 Lenny Wilkens 10.00 25.00
63 Lionel Hollins 6.00 15.00
65 Magic Johnson 40.00 80.00
68 Marques Johnson 6.00 15.00
69 Michael Jordan 300.00 400.00
70 Michael Ray Richardson 6.00 15.00
71 Moses Malone 8.00 20.00
72 Nate Archibald 8.00 20.00
76 Paul Westphal 6.00 15.00
79 Pooh Richardson 6.00 15.00
81 Rick Barry 6.00 15.00
82 Ron Harper 30.00 60.00
84 Spencer Haywood 6.00 15.00
85 Stacey Augmon 6.00 15.00
86 Steve Kerr 6.00 15.00
87 Swen Nater 6.00 15.00
88 Lonnie Shelton 6.00 15.00
89 Thurl Bailey 6.00 15.00
90 Tom Chambers 6.00 15.00
91 Tom Sanders 8.00 20.00
92 Toni Kukoc 12.50 30.00
94 Vlade Divac 20.00 50.00
95 Walt Bellamy 6.00 15.00
96 Will Perdue 8.00 20.00
97 Reggie Theus 6.00 15.00
100 Xavier McDaniel 6.00 15.00

2007-08 Chronology Dedications

PRINT RUN 50 SER.#'d SETS
UNPRICED GOLD PRINT RUN 10 SETS
DAC Al Cervi 6.00 15.00
DAD Adrian Dantley 6.00 15.00
DAE Alex English 6.00 15.00
DAG Artis Gilmore 6.00 15.00
DBL Bob Lanier 8.00 20.00
DBM Bob McAdoo 15.00 30.00
DBP Bob Pettit 15.00 30.00
DBS Bill Sharman 8.00 20.00
DBW Bill Walton 8.00 20.00
DCD Clyde Drexler 30.00 60.00
DCW Chet Walker 6.00 15.00
DDC Dave Cowens 10.00 25.00
DDG Darrell Griffith 6.00 15.00
DDT David Thompson 6.00 15.00
DGE George Gervin 8.00 20.00
DGG Gail Goodrich 8.00 20.00
DHG Hal Greer 8.00 20.00
DJR Jack Ramsay 8.00 20.00
DLA Bill Laimbeer 10.00 25.00
DLW Lenny Wilkens 6.00 15.00
DMC Maurice Cheeks 6.00 15.00
DNN Norm Nixon 6.00 15.00
DRB Rick Barry 10.00 25.00
DRO Rolando Blackman 10.00 25.00
DRP Robert Parish 8.00 20.00
DSM Sidney Moncrief 6.00 15.00
DTH Tom Heinsohn 10.00 25.00
DWU Wes Unseld 8.00 20.00

2007-08 Chronology Era Associates

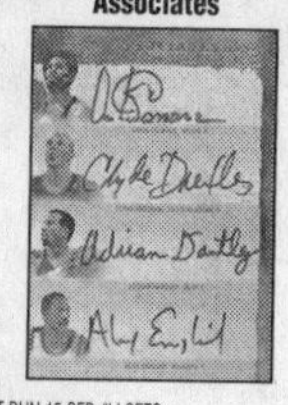

PRINT RUN 15 SER.#'d SETS
EJBJ Larry Bird 800.00 1000.00
Julius Erving
Magic Johnson
Michael Jordan
GDDE Artis Gilmore 100.00 225.00
Clyde Drexler
Adrian Dantley
Alex English
JCHP Antawn Jamison 100.00 200.00
Vince Carter
Larry Hughes
Paul Pierce
MHSD Amare Stoudemire 150.00 300.00
Kevin Durant
Dwight Howard
Yao Ming
MLAW Kareem Abdul-Jabbar 125.00 225.00
Bob McAdoo
Bill Walton
Bob Lanier
ORMP Moses Malone 100.00 250.00
Robert Parish
Hakeem Olajuwon
David Robinson
PSHS Bob Pettit 50.00 100.00
Tom Heinsohn
Bill Sharman
Dolph Schayes

2007-08 Chronology Freshman Registry

PRINT RUN 25 SER.#'d SETS
BCB Buck Williams 30.00 60.00
Tom Chambers
Rolando Blackman
DGC Kevin Durant 75.00 150.00
Jeff Green
Mike Conley Jr.
DHP Brad Daugherty 50.00 100.00
Ron Harper
Mark Price
HBN Al Horford 30.00 60.00
Corey Brewer
Joakim Noah
HWN John Havlicek 30.00 60.00
Chet Walker
Don Nelson
LTC Bob Lanier 40.00 80.00
Rudy Tomjanovich
Dave Cowens
MKS Bernard King 15.00 40.00
Jack Sikma
Cedric Maxwell
PKG Bob Pettit 30.00 80.00
Johnny Kerr
Richie Guerin
RHJ Tom Heinsohn 200.00 300.00
Bill Russell
Sam Jones
SSD Ralph Sampson 40.00 80.00
Byron Scott
Clyde Drexler
WCW James Worthy 40.00 80.00
Terry Cummings
Dominique Wilkins
WSW Jerry West 50.00 100.00
Lenny Wilkens
Tom Sanders
WWW Bill Walton 30.00 80.00
Brian Winters
Jamaal Wilkes

2007-08 Chronology Historically Accurate

PRINT RUN 50 SER.#'d SETS
UNPRICED GOLD PRINT RUN 10 SETS
HAAD Adrian Dantley 6.00 15.00
HAAG Artis Gilmore 6.00 15.00
HABA B.J. Armstrong 10.00 25.00
HACM Cedric Maxwell 10.00 25.00
HADI Dan Issel 6.00 15.00
HAJR Jeff Ruland 6.00 15.00
HAKV Kiki Vandeweghe 6.00 15.00
HAMP Mark Price 25.00 60.00
HASK Steve Kerr 12.50 30.00

2007-08 Chronology My Generation

STATED PRINT RUN 62 TO 75 SER.#'d SETS
UNPRICED GOLD PRINT RUN 10 SETS
MGAG Artis Gilmore/71 8.00 20.00
MGBL Bob Love/67 8.00 20.00
MGBM Bob McAdoo/72 15.00 30.00
MGBW Bill Walton/74 15.00 30.00
MGCW Chet Walker/62 8.00 20.00
MGDI Dan Issel/70 8.00 20.00
MGDT David Thompson/75 8.00 20.00
MGGG George Gervin/72 8.00 20.00
MGGM George McGinnis/71 10.00 25.00
MGJL Jerry Lucas/71 8.00 20.00
MGJS James Silas/72 8.00 20.00
MGJW Jamaal Wilkes/74 8.00 20.00
MGLD Louie Dampier/69 8.00 20.00
MGMD Mel Daniels/67 8.00 20.00
MGMM Moses Malone/74 15.00 30.00
MGRB Rick Barry/65 10.00 25.00
MGSH Spencer Haywood/69 8.00 20.00
MGSN Swen Nater/73 8.00 20.00
MGWF Walt Frazier/67 8.00 20.00

2007-08 Chronology Seriatim

STATED PRINT RUN 8 TO 90 SER.#'d SETS
SOME UNPRICED DUE TO SCARCITY
AM Nate Archibald/80 8.00 20.00
Cedric Maxwell
BH Bill Hodges/70 40.00 80.00
Larry Bird
BT Nate Thurmond/70 20.00 40.00
Rick Barry
CA Dave Cowens/70 15.00 30.00
Nate Archibald
CC Mike Conley Sr./80 10.00 25.00
Mike Conley Jr.
CL Bob Lanier/70 8.00 20.00
ML Carr
DD Adrian Dantley/80 8.00 20.00
Walter Davis
DF Walter Davis/80 15.00 40.00
Phil Ford
DS Dominique Wilkins/80 20.00 40.00
Spud Webb
FR Walt Frazier/60 20.00 40.00
Cazzie Russell
FW Walt Frazier/60 20.00 40.00
Bobby Wanzer
GA George Gervin/80 20.00 40.00
Nate Archibald
GC Horace Grant/90 20.00 40.00
Bill Cartwright
GG Artis Gilmore/80 15.00 30.00
George Gervin
GW Darrell Griffith/80 15.00 30.00
Deron Williams
HB Spencer Haywood/70 15.00 30.00
Fred Brown
HH Alfredo Horford/80 8.00 20.00
Al Horford
HK Toni Kukoc/90 25.00 50.00
Ron Harper
HR Richie Guerin/50 8.00 20.00
Harry Gallatin
IN George McGinnis/80 12.50 30.00
Mel Daniels
IW Bill Walton/70 15.00 40.00
Dan Issel
KA Steve Kerr/90 12.50 30.00
B.J. Armstrong
KG Kevin Garnett/90 40.00 80.00
Jason Kidd
KP Steve Kerr/90 25.00 50.00
John Paxson
LC Dave Cowens/70 12.50 30.00
Bob Lanier
LD Bill Laimbeer/80 15.00 30.00
Adrian Dantley
LH Hal Greer/70 15.00 40.00
Chet Walker
MK Bob McAdoo/70 20.00 40.00
George Karl
MM Vern Mikkelsen/50 20.00 40.00
Slater Martin
NN Ernie Vandeweghe/50 10.00 25.00
Kiki Vandeweghe
OD Clyde Drexler/80 30.00 60.00
Hakeem Olajuwon
OR David Robinson/90 40.00 100.00
Hakeem Olajuwon
PW Will Perdue/90 20.00 40.00
Bill Wennington
RB Robert Parish/80 20.00 40.00
Bill Walton
RG Gail Goodrich/70 10.00 25.00
Cazzie Russell
RJ Sam Jones/50 75.00 200.00
Bill Russell
RL Dennis Rodman/80 20.00 50.00
Bill Laimbeer
RS Bill Sharman/50 10.00 25.00
Arnie Risen
SH Tom Sanders/60 10.00 25.00
Tom Heinsohn
SK Dolph Schayes/60 12.50 30.00
Johnny Kerr
TE Alex English/80 15.00 40.00
David Thompson
TG George Gervin/80 15.00 30.00
David Thompson
WC James Worthy/80 25.00 50.00
Michael Cooper
WL Jerry Lucas/60 25.00 50.00
Jerry West
WP Robert Parish/80 25.00 50.00
James Worthy
WR Lenny Wilkens/70 10.00 25.00
Jack Ramsay
WS Jamaal Wilkes/80 15.00 30.00
Byron Scott

2007-08 Chronology Stitches in Time

PRINT RUN 99 SER.#'d SETS
*STITCH 50: .5X TO 1.25X BASE HI
STITCH 50 PRINT RUN 50 SETS
*STITCH 15: .75X TO 2X BASE HI
STITCH 15 PRINT RUN 15 SETS
STITCH FIVE UNPRICED DUE TO SCARCITY
STITCH ONE UNPRICED DUE TO SCARCITY
AB Aaron Brooks R 4.00 10.00
AD Adrian Dantley L 4.00 10.00
AH Al Horford R 5.00 12.00
AI Allen Iverson V 5.00 12.00
AL Acie Law R 4.00 10.00
AT Al Thornton R 4.00 10.00
BG Ben Gordon V 4.00 10.00
BI Bill Russell L 10.00 25.00
BR Brandon Roy V 5.00 12.00
BW Bill Walton L 4.00 10.00
CA Carmelo Anthony V 5.00 12.00
CB Corey Brewer R 5.00 12.00
CD Clyde Drexler L 5.00 12.00
CK Maurice Cheeks L 4.00 10.00
CM Chris Mullin L 4.00 10.00
CP Chris Paul V 8.00 20.00
DC Daequan Cook R 4.00 10.00
DE Deron Williams V 6.00 15.00
DH Dwight Howard V 6.00 15.00
DR Dennis Rodman L 6.00 15.00
DW Dominique Wilkins L 5.00 12.00
GD Glen Davis R 6.00 15.00
GG George Gervin L 4.00 10.00
HO Hakeem Olajuwon L 6.00 15.00
JA Jason Smith R 4.00 10.00
JC Javaris Crittenton R 4.00 10.00
JD Jared Dudley R 4.00 10.00
JE Julius Erving L 8.00 20.00
JG Jeff Green R 5.00 12.00
JK Jason Kidd V 4.00 10.00
JN Joakim Noah R 10.00 25.00
JO Michael Jordan L 50.00 125.00
JS John Stockton L 6.00 15.00
JW Julian Wright R 4.00 10.00
KA Kareem Abdul-Jabbar L 6.00 15.00
KB Kobe Bryant V 15.00 30.00
KD Kevin Durant R 25.00 60.00
KG Kevin Garnett V 8.00 20.00
KH Kirk Hinrich V 4.00 10.00
LB Larry Bird L 10.00 25.00
LJ LeBron James V 15.00 40.00
MA Morris Almond R 4.00 10.00
MC Mike Conley Jr. R 6.00 15.00
MI Michael Cooper L 4.00 10.00
MJ Magic Johnson L 8.00 20.00
MM Moses Malone L 4.00 10.00
PP Paul Pierce V 5.00 12.00
RO David Robinson L 6.00 15.00
RS Rodney Stuckey R 6.00 15.00
SH Spencer Hawes R 4.00 10.00
SN Steve Nash V 5.00 12.00
SO Shaquille O'Neal V 8.00 20.00
SW Sean Williams R 4.00 10.00
TM Tracy McGrady V 4.00 10.00
TP Tony Parker V 4.00 10.00
VC Vince Carter V 5.00 12.00
WA Dwyane Wade V 10.00 25.00
WC Wilson Chandler R 6.00 15.00
WF Walt Frazier L 4.00 10.00
YM Yao Ming V 5.00 12.00

2007-08 Chronology Stitches in Time Patches Autographs

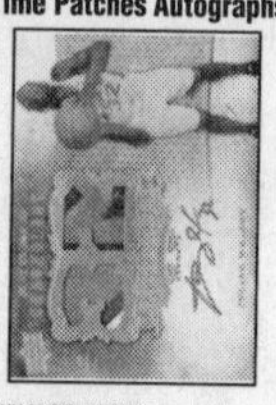

PRINT RUN 35 SER.#'d SETS
*STITCH AUTO 25: .5X TO 1.25X HI
STITCH AUTO 25 PRINT RUN 25 SER.#'d SETS
*STITCH AUTO 15: .6X TO 1.5X HI
STITCH AUTO 15 PRINT RUN 15 SER.#'d SETS
STITCH AUTO 5 UNPRICED DUE TO SCARCITY
STITCH AUTO 1 UNPRICED DUE TO SCARCITY
AB Aaron Brooks 8.00 20.00
AD Adrian Dantley 15.00 40.00
AH Al Horford 10.00 25.00
AL Acie Law 8.00 20.00
CB Corey Brewer 10.00 25.00
CM Chris Mullin 60.00 120.00
DC Daequan Cook 8.00 20.00
DE Deron Williams 25.00 50.00
GD Glen Davis 12.00 30.00
JA Jason Smith 8.00 20.00
JC Javaris Crittenton 8.00 20.00
JD Jared Dudley 8.00 20.00
JG Jeff Green 10.00 25.00
JN Joakim Noah 20.00 50.00
JW Julian Wright 8.00 20.00
KB Kobe Bryant 250.00 500.00
KD Kevin Durant 500.00 1000.00
KG Kevin Garnett 100.00 175.00
KH Kirk Hinrich 15.00 30.00
LJ LeBron James 200.00 350.00
MA Morris Almond 8.00 20.00
MC Mike Conley Jr. 12.00 30.00
MM Moses Malone 25.00 50.00
RS Rodney Stuckey 12.00 30.00
SH Spencer Hawes 8.00 20.00
SW Sean Williams 8.00 20.00
WC Wilson Chandler 12.00 30.00
WF Walt Frazier 25.00 60.00

2007-08 Chronology The LeBrons

RANDOM INSERTS IN PACKS
LJ LeBron James 6.00 15.00
Blue Border
LJ LeBron James 4.00 10.00
Red Border

2007-08 Chronology Through the Years

PRINT RUN 50 SER.#'d SETS
UNPRICED GOLD PRINT RUN 10 SETS
TEAD Adrian Dantley 10.00 25.00
TEAG Artis Gilmore 10.00 25.00
TEBC Bill Cartwright 20.00 40.00
TEBL Bill Laimbeer 10.00 25.00
TEBM Bob McAdoo 15.00 30.00
TEBO Bob Lanier 10.00 25.00
TECD Clyde Drexler 25.00 60.00
TEDR Dennis Rodman 25.00 60.00
TEDT David Thompson 15.00 40.00
TEDW Dominique Wilkins 20.00 40.00
TEHG Horace Grant 15.00 40.00
TEJE Julius Erving 30.00 60.00
TEJP John Paxson 10.00 25.00
TEJS Jack Sikma 10.00 25.00
TERB Rick Barry 12.00 30.00
TERP Robert Parish 15.00 40.00
TESP Sam Perkins 15.00 30.00
TEVD Vlade Divac 25.00 60.00

2007-08 Chronology Uniformity

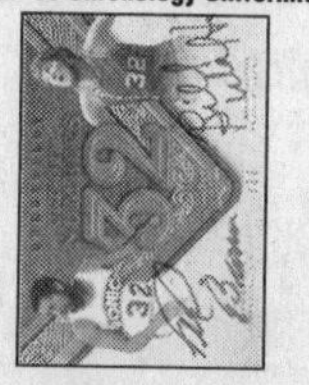

STATED PRINT RUN 2 TO 44 SER.#'d SETS
SOME UNPRICED DUE TO SCARCITY
UNPRICED GOLD PRINT RUN 10 SETS
UNBA Kareem Abdul-Jabbar/33 100.00 225.00
Larry Bird
UNBJ Sam Jones/24 20.00 50.00
Rick Barry
UNDS Brad Daugherty/43 15.00 30.00
Jack Sikma
UNFW Fred Brown/32 15.00 30.00
Bill Walton
UNGH Hal Greer/15 25.00 60.00
Tom Heinsohn
UNGW George Gervin/44 40.00 80.00
Jerry West
UNIW Dan Issel/44 20.00 40.00
Paul Westphal
UNJB Kobe Bryant/24 125.00 250.00
Sam Jones
UNKM Bernard King/30 20.00 50.00
George McGinnis
UNTW James Worthy/42 25.00 50.00
Nate Thurmond
UNWN Don Nelson/19 20.00 40.00
Lenny Wilkens

1996 Classic Legends of the Final Four

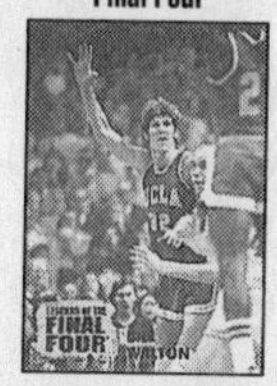

Sponsored by Sears, official NCAA corporate sponsor, this 32-card set spotlights players and coaches who participated in the Final Four. Each 7-card pack contained six player cards and one "Coaches vs. Cancer" card. The fronts feature full-bleed glossy color action player photos. The set title "Legends of the Final Four"and the player's name are gold foil stamped across the bottom. On a mustard card face accented with orange, the backs carry a profile as well as NCAA Tournament record statistics. The set subdivides into four parts: female players (1-10), male players (11-20), male coaches (MC1-MC5), and female coaches (WC1-WC5). The set concludes with an unnumbered checklist card and a "Coaches vs. Cancer" card. The wrapper itself entitled the holder to 10% off the purchase of Craftsman hand tools. The offer expired 12/31/96.

COMPLETE SET (32) 12.00 30.00
1 Sheryl Swoopes 3.00 8.00
2 Cheryl Miller 3.00 8.00
3 Rebecca Lobo 2.00 5.00
4 Jennifer Azzi 1.50 4.00
5 Dawn Staley 2.00 5.00
6 Charlotte Smith 1.00 2.50
7 Bridgette Gordon .40 1.00
8 Erica Westbrooks .20 .50
9 Tracy Claxton .20 .50
10 Clarissa Davis .20 .50
11 Kareem Abdul-Jabbar .40 1.00
12 Hakeem Olajuwon .40 1.00
13 Bill Walton .40 1.00
14 James Worthy .40 1.00
15 Isiah Thomas .40 1.00
16 Darrell Griffith .20 .50
17 Bobby Hurley .20 .50
18 Glen Rice .20 .50
19 Ed Pinckney .20 .50
20 Danny Manning .20 .50
MC1 John Wooden 1.00 2.50
MC2 Dean Smith .60 1.50
MC3 Nolan Richardson .40 1.00
MC4 Mike Krzyzewski .60 1.50
MC5 John Thompson .40 1.00
WC1 Tara Vanderveer .40 1.00
WC2 Pat Summitt 3.00 8.00
WC3 Marianne Stanley .40 1.00
WC4 Sylvia Hatchell .40 1.00
WC5 Geno Auriemma .40 1.00
NNO Checklist .20 .50
(Sears Trophy)
NNO Coaches vs. Cancer DP .20 .50

2002 Classic Signature Series Shaquille O'Neal

This 2 1/2" by 4 3/4" card shows Shaquille O'Neal dunking a basketball with a silver facsimile signature across the card. The borders are gold, and along the bottom of the card, the stated print run is 24,900 total cards. According to hobbyists, this card was only available through Home Shopping Network.

SS1 Shaquille O'Neal 6.00 15.00

2009-10 Classics

COMP.SET w/o SP's (100) 15.00 30.00
101-160 PRINT RUN 999 SER.#'d SETS
161-200 PRINT RUNS LISTED IN CHECKLIST
1 Kevin Garnett 1.00 2.50
2 Rasheed Wallace .50 1.25
3 Paul Pierce .60 1.50
4 Kendrick Perkins .40 1.00
5 Brook Lopez .50 1.25
6 Devin Harris .50 1.25
7 Chris Douglas-Roberts .30 .75
8 Al Harrington .40 1.00
9 David Lee .40 1.00
10 Danilo Gallinari .50 1.25
11 Andre Iguodala .50 1.25
12 Louis Williams .40 1.00
13 Elton Brand .50 1.25
14 Chris Bosh .50 1.25
15 Andrea Bargnani .40 1.00
16 Hedo Turkoglu .50 1.25
17 Jose Calderon .40 1.00
18 Dirk Nowitzki .60 1.50
19 Shawn Marion .50 1.25
20 Drew Gooden .40 1.00
21 J.J. Barea .60 1.50
22 Shane Battier .50 1.25
23 Aaron Brooks .30 .75
24 Trevor Ariza .30 .75
25 Rudy Gay .50 1.25
26 Zach Randolph .40 1.00
27 O.J. Mayo .50 1.25
28 Chris Paul .75 2.00
29 David West .50 1.25
30 Emeka Okafor .50 1.25
31 Tim Duncan .75 2.00
32 Tony Parker .50 1.25
33 Richard Jefferson .50 1.25
34 Manu Ginobili .50 1.25
35 Luol Deng .50 1.25
36 Derrick Rose 1.50 4.00
37 John Salmons .50 1.25
38 LeBron James 2.50 6.00
39 Mo Williams .40 1.00
40 Shaquille O'Neal 1.00 2.50
41 Anderson Varejao .40 1.00
42 Ben Gordon .50 1.25
43 Rodney Stuckey .50 1.25
44 Charlie Villanueva .40 1.00
45 Danny Granger .50 1.25
46 Mike Dunleavy .30 .75
47 Dahntay Jones .30 .75
48 Andrew Bogut .50 1.25
49 Michael Redd .50 1.25
50 Hakim Warrick .40 1.00
51 Carmelo Anthony .60 1.50
52 Chauncey Billups .50 1.25
53 Nene .40 1.00
54 Chris Andersen .75 2.00
55 Al Jefferson .50 1.25
56 Corey Brewer .30 .75
57 Ryan Gomes .30 .75
58 Brandon Roy .50 1.25
59 LaMarcus Aldridge .50 1.25
60 Andre Miller .40 1.00
61 Kevin Durant 1.50 4.00
62 Russell Westbrook .75 2.00
63 Jeff Green .40 1.00
64 Carlos Boozer .50 1.25
65 Deron Williams .50 1.25
66 Andrei Kirilenko .40 1.00
67 Joe Johnson .50 1.25
68 Josh Smith .50 1.25
69 Jamal Crawford .40 1.00
70 Stephen Jackson .40 1.00
71 Raymond Felton .40 1.00
72 Gerald Wallace .50 1.25
73 Dwyane Wade 1.00 2.50
74 Jermaine O'Neal .50 1.25
75 Michael Beasley .50 1.25
76 Udonis Haslem .40 1.00
77 Vince Carter .60 1.50
78 Dwight Howard .75 2.00
79 Rashard Lewis .40 1.00
80 J.J. Redick .50 1.25
81 Antawn Jamison .50 1.25
82 Caron Butler .50 1.25
83 Randy Foye .30 .75
84 Monta Ellis .50 1.25
85 Corey Maggette .40 1.00
86 Anthony Randolph .40 1.00
87 Chris Kaman .40 1.00
88 Eric Gordon .50 1.25
89 Baron Davis .50 1.25
90 Kobe Bryant 2.50 6.00
91 Andrew Bynum .60 1.50
92 Lamar Odom .50 1.25
93 Ron Artest .50 1.25
94 Amare Stoudemire .50 1.25
95 Jason Richardson .50 1.25
96 Steve Nash .50 1.25
97 Grant Hill .60 1.50
98 Kevin Martin .50 1.25
99 Beno Udrih .30 .75
100 Jason Thompson .30 .75
101 Larry Bird 4.00 10.00
102 Gail Goodrich 1.25 3.00
103 Harry Gallatin 1.25 3.00
104 Chris Webber 1.25 3.00
105 Nate McMillan 1.25 3.00
106 George Mikan 2.50 6.00
107 Drazen Petrovic 2.50 6.00
108 Jalen Rose 1.25 3.00
109 Mitch Richmond 1.25 3.00
110 Mark Price 1.25 3.00
111 David Robinson 2.00 5.00
112 Rick Barry 1.25 3.00
113 Lenny Wilkens 1.25 3.00
114 Robert Horry 1.50 4.00
115 Walt Frazier 1.25 3.00
116 Buck Williams 1.25 3.00
117 Patrick Ewing 1.50 4.00
118 Danny Manning 1.25 3.00
119 Dennis Johnson 1.25 3.00
120 Rony Seikaly 1.25 3.00
121 Chris Mullin 1.25 3.00
122 Hakeem Olajuwon 1.50 4.00
123 George Gervin 1.25 3.00
124 Rex Chapman 1.25 3.00
125 Bob McAdoo 1.25 3.00
126 Dana Barros 1.25 3.00
127 B.J. Armstrong 1.25 3.00
128 Danny Roundfield 1.25 3.00
129 Oscar Robertson 1.25 3.00
130 Bill Russell 2.00 5.00
131 Doc Rivers 1.25 3.00
132 Clyde Drexler 1.50 4.00
133 Kareem Abdul-Jabbar 2.00 5.00
134 Bernard King 1.25 3.00
135 Don Nelson 1.25 3.00
136 John Salley 1.25 3.00
137 Jerry Sloan 1.25 3.00
138 Joe Dumars 1.25 3.00
139 Karl Malone 1.50 4.00
140 Magic Johnson 3.00 8.00
141 Dominique Wilkins 1.50 4.00
142 Jack Sikma 1.25 3.00
143 Wes Unseld 1.25 3.00
144 Sidney Moncrief 1.25 3.00
145 Sleepy Floyd 1.25 3.00
146 Spencer Haywood 1.25 3.00
147 Kevin McHale 1.25 3.00
148 Glen Rice 1.25 3.00
149 Isiah Thomas 1.25 3.00
150 Jerry West 1.50 4.00
151 Willis Reed 1.25 3.00
152 Bob Lanier 1.25 3.00
153 Elgin Baylor 1.25 3.00
154 Scottie Pippen 2.50 6.00
155 Elvin Hayes 1.25 3.00
156 Scott Skiles 1.25 3.00

157 Ed Macauley 1.25 3.00
158 Pete Maravich 4.00 10.00
159 Bob Cousy 2.00 5.00
160 Wilt Chamberlain 2.50 6.00
161 Blake Griffin AU/499 RC 125.00 225.00
162 Hasheem Thabeet AU/499 RC 5.00 12.00
163 James Harden AU/499 RC 15.00 40.00
164 Tyreke Evans AU/499 RC 12.00 30.00
165 Jonny Flynn AU/499 RC 5.00 12.00
166 Stephen Curry AU/499 RC 12.00 30.00
167 Jordan Hill AU/469 RC 5.00 12.00
168 Brandon Jennings AU/499 RC 10.00 25.00
169 Terrence Williams AU/499 RC 5.00 12.00
170 Gerald Henderson AU/499 RC 5.00 12.00
171 Tyler Hansbrough AU/499 RC 8.00 20.00
172 Earl Clark AU/571 RC 5.00 12.00
173 Austin Daye AU/598 RC 5.00 12.00
174 James Johnson AU/199 RC 5.00 12.00
175 Jrue Holiday AU/499 RC 10.00 25.00
176 Ty Lawson AU/599 RC 8.00 20.00
177 Jeff Teague AU/553 RC 6.00 15.00
178 Eric Maynor AU/599 RC 5.00 12.00
179 Darren Collison AU/799 RC 8.00 20.00
180 Omri Casspi AU/862 RC 5.00 12.00
181 B.J. Mullens AU/872 RC 5.00 12.00
182 Rodrigue Beaubois AU/199 RC 6.00 15.00
183 Taj Gibson AU/823 RC 6.00 15.00
184 DeMarre Carroll AU/864 RC 5.00 12.00
185 Wayne Ellington AU/575 RC 5.00 12.00
186 Toney Douglas AU/933 RC 5.00 12.00
187 DeJuan Blair AU/999 RC 6.00 15.00
188 Sam Young AU/249 RC 5.00 12.00
189 A.J. Price AU/999 RC 5.00 12.00
190 Chase Budinger AU/999 RC 5.00 12.00
191 David Andersen AU/99 RC 10.00 25.00
192 Jonas Jerebko AU/999 RC 5.00 12.00
193 Marcus Landry AU/999 RC 5.00 12.00
194 Serge Ibaka AU/99 RC 40.00 80.00
195 Patrick Mills AU/99 RC 25.00 60.00
196 Wesley Matthews AU/99 RC 30.00 80.00
197 Taylor Griffin AU/999 RC 5.00 12.00
198 Jermaine Taylor AU/999 RC 5.00 12.00
199 Jodie Meeks AU/249 RC 6.00 15.00
200 DaJuan Summers AU/999 RC 5.00 12.00

2009-10 Classics Timeless Tributes Gold

*1-100 GOLD: 2X TO 5X BASE HI
*101-160 GOLD: .75X TO 2X BASE HI
*161-200 GOLD: .6X TO 1.5X SILVER HI
GOLD PRINT RUN 50 SER.#'d SETS
161 Blake Griffin 30.00 80.00

2009-10 Classics Timeless Tributes Platinum

*1-100 PLATINUM: 3X TO 8X BASE HI
*101-160 PLATINUM: 1.25X TO 3X BASE HI
*161-200 PLAT: .75X TO 2X SILVER HI
PLATINUM PRINT RUN 25 SER.#'d SETS
107 Drazen Petrovic 10.00 25.00

2009-10 Classics Timeless Tributes Silver

*1-100 SILVER: 1.25X TO 3X BASE HI
*101-160 SILVER: .5X TO 1.25X BASE HI
SILVER PRINT RUN 100 SER.#'d SETS
161 Blake Griffin 15.00 40.00
162 Hasheem Thabeet 2.50 6.00
163 James Harden 8.00 20.00
164 Tyreke Evans 6.00 15.00
165 Jonny Flynn 2.50 6.00
166 Stephen Curry 6.00 15.00
167 Jordan Hill 2.50 6.00
168 Brandon Jennings 5.00 12.00
169 Terrence Williams 2.50 6.00
170 Gerald Henderson 2.50 6.00
171 Tyler Hansbrough 4.00 10.00
172 Earl Clark 2.50 6.00
173 Austin Daye 2.50 6.00
174 James Johnson 2.50 6.00
175 Jrue Holiday 5.00 12.00
176 Ty Lawson 4.00 10.00
177 Jeff Teague 3.00 8.00
178 Eric Maynor 2.50 6.00
179 Darren Collison 4.00 10.00
180 Omri Casspi 2.50 6.00
181 B.J. Mullens 2.50 6.00
182 Rodrigue Beaubois 3.00 8.00
183 Taj Gibson 3.00 8.00
184 DeMarre Carroll 2.50 6.00
185 Wayne Ellington 2.50 6.00
186 Toney Douglas 2.50 6.00
187 DeJuan Blair 3.00 8.00
188 Sam Young 2.50 6.00
189 A.J. Price 2.50 6.00
190 Chase Budinger 2.50 6.00
191 David Andersen 2.50 6.00
192 Jonas Jerebko 2.50 6.00
193 Marcus Landry 2.50 6.00
194 Serge Ibaka 6.00 15.00
195 Patrick Mills 3.00 8.00
196 Wesley Matthews 4.00 10.00
197 Taylor Griffin 2.50 6.00
198 Jermaine Taylor 2.50 6.00
199 Jodie Meeks 3.00 8.00
200 DaJuan Summers 2.50 6.00

2009-10 Classics Blast From The Past Jerseys

STATED PRINT RUN 25 TO 199 SETS
1 Dan Issel/99 4.00 10.00
2 Adrian Dantley/99 4.00 10.00
3 Anfernee Hardaway/199 10.00 25.00
4 Bernard King/199 4.00 10.00
5 Clyde Drexler/199 5.00 12.00
6 Glen Rice/199 4.00 10.00
7 John Stockton/25 8.00 20.00
8 Robert Horry/199 5.00 12.00
9 Karl Malone/199 5.00 12.00
10 Larry Johnson/199 10.00 25.00
11 Danny Manning/199 4.00 10.00
12 Reggie Lewis/199 10.00 25.00
13 Kevin Johnson/199 4.00 10.00
14 Sleepy Floyd/199 4.00 10.00
15 Tom Heinsohn/99 4.00 10.00
16 Xavier McDaniel/199 4.00 10.00
17 Artis Gilmore/199 4.00 10.00
18 Toni Kukoc/199 5.00 12.00
19 Chuck Person/199 4.00 10.00
20 Bob Lanier/199 4.00 10.00
21 Dominique Wilkins/199 5.00 12.00
22 Hakeem Olajuwon/199 5.00 12.00
23 Sam Perkins/199 4.00 10.00
24 Chris Mullin/199 4.00 10.00
25 Michael Cage/199 4.00 10.00

2009-10 Classics Blast From The Past Jerseys Prime

*PRIME: .6X TO 1.5X HI COLUMN
STATED PRINT RUN 10 TO 30 SER.#'d SETS
5 Clyde Drexler/30 12.00 30.00
6 Glen Rice/30 15.00 30.00
9 Karl Malone/30 15.00 30.00
10 Larry Johnson/30 30.00 80.00
11 Danny Manning/30 15.00 30.00
12 Reggie Lewis/30 30.00 60.00
13 Kevin Johnson/30 8.00 20.00
18 Toni Kukoc/30 10.00 25.00
21 Dominique Wilkins/30 10.00 25.00
22 Hakeem Olajuwon/30 10.00 25.00
24 Chris Mullin/30 10.00 25.00

2009-10 Classics Blast From The Past Jerseys Signatures

PRINT RUN 25 SER.#'d SETS
1 Dan Issel 8.00 20.00
2 Adrian Dantley 8.00 20.00
3 Anfernee Hardaway 60.00 120.00
4 Bernard King 8.00 20.00
5 Clyde Drexler 20.00 50.00
6 Glen Rice 20.00 50.00
10 Larry Johnson 40.00 100.00
11 Danny Manning 15.00 30.00
13 Kevin Johnson 30.00 80.00
14 Sleepy Floyd 8.00 20.00
16 Xavier McDaniel 8.00 20.00
17 Artis Gilmore 8.00 20.00
18 Toni Kukoc 25.00 60.00
23 Sam Perkins 8.00 20.00

2009-10 Classics Blast From The Past Jerseys Prime Signatures

PRINT RUNS LISTED IN CHECKLIST
2 Adrian Dantley/25 12.50 30.00
3 Anfernee Hardaway/25 75.00 150.00
6 Glen Rice/25 25.00 60.00
10 Larry Johnson/25 50.00 120.00
11 Danny Manning/25 20.00 40.00
13 Kevin Johnson/25 50.00 100.00
14 Sleepy Floyd/25 15.00 40.00
16 Xavier McDaniel/25 12.50 30.00
18 Toni Kukoc/25 30.00 80.00
23 Sam Perkins/25 12.50 30.00

2009-10 Classics Classic Combos

COMPLETE SET (10) 10.00 25.00
*GOLD: .75X TO 2X BASE HI
GOLD PRINT RUN 100 SER.#'d SETS
*PLATINUM: 1.5X TO 4X BASE HI
PLATINUM PRINT RUN 25 SER.#'d SETS
*SILVER: .5X TO 1.25X BASE HI
SILVER PRINT RUN 250 SER.#'d SETS
1 Kobe Bryant / Lamar Odom 4.00 10.00
2 LeBron James / Shaquille O'Neal 4.00 10.00
3 Paul Pierce / Kevin Garnett 1.50 4.00
4 Dirk Nowitzki / Shawn Marion 1.00 2.50
5 Dwyane Wade / Jermaine O'Neal 1.50 4.00
6 Bill Russell / Bill Sharman 1.25 3.00
7 Alonzo Mourning / Tim Hardaway 1.00 2.50
8 Hakeem Olajuwon / Clyde Drexler 1.00 2.50
9 Isiah Thomas / Joe Dumars .75 2.00
10 John Stockton / Karl Malone 1.25 3.00

2009-10 Classics Classic Combos Jerseys

STATED PRINT RUN ONE TO 99 SER.#'d SETS
2 LeBron James/99 / Shaquille O'Neal 10.00 25.00
3 Paul Pierce/99 / Kevin Garnett 6.00 15.00
4 Dirk Nowitzki/99 / Shawn Marion 6.00 15.00
8 Hakeem Olajuwon/99 / Clyde Drexler 6.00 15.00
9 Isiah Thomas/99 / Joe Dumars 8.00 20.00
10 John Stockton/99 / Karl Malone 6.00 15.00

2009-10 Classics Classic Combos Jerseys Prime

*PRIME: 1X TO 2.5X BASE HI
PRINT RUN 25 SER.#'d SETS
2 LeBron James / Shaquille O'Neal 30.00 80.00
3 Paul Pierce / Kevin Garnett 12.00 30.00
9 Isiah Thomas / Joe Dumars 10.00 25.00

2009-10 Classics Classic Confrontations

COMPLETE SET (10) 10.00 25.00
*GOLD: ..75X TO 2X BASE HI
GOLD PRINT RUN 50 SER.#'d SETS
*PLATINUM: 1.5X TO 4X BASE HI
PLATINUM PRINT RUN 25 SER.#'d SETS
*SILVER: .5X TO 1.25X BASE HI
SILVER PRINT RUN 250 SER.#'d SETS
1 Larry Bird / Magic Johnson 2.50 6.00
2 Earl Monroe / Walt Frazier .75 2.00
3 Willis Reed / Kareem Abdul-Jabbar 1.25 3.00
4 James Worthy / Robert Parish 1.00 2.50
5 Kobe Bryant / LeBron James 4.00 10.00
6 Dirk Nowitzki / Tim Duncan 1.25 3.00
7 Chris Paul / Dwyane Wade 1.50 4.00
8 Kevin Garnett / Shaquille O'Neal 1.50 4.00
9 Jason Kidd / Steve Nash .75 2.00
10 Jerry West / Oscar Robertson 1.00 2.50

2009-10 Classics Classic Confrontations Jerseys

STATED PRINT RUN 199 SER.#'d SETS
*PRIME: 1X TO 2.5X BASE HI
PRIME PRINT RUN 25 SER.#'d SETS
1 Larry Bird / Magic Johnson 12.50 30.00
5 Kobe Bryant / LeBron James 10.00 25.00
6 Dirk Nowitzki / Tim Duncan 5.00 12.00
7 Chris Paul / Dwyane Wade 5.00 12.00
8 Kevin Garnett / Shaquille O'Neal 10.00 25.00

2009-10 Classics Classic Confrontations Jerseys Signatures

STATED PRINT RUN 25 SER.#'d SETS
*PRIME: .5X TO 1.25X BASE HI
PRIME PRINT RUN 25 SER.#'d SETS
1 Larry Bird / Magic Johnson 100.00 200.00

2009-10 Classics Classic Greats

COMPLETE SET (30) 25.00 50.00
*GOLD: .6X TO 1.5X BASE HI
GOLD PRINT RUN 100 SER.#'d SETS
*PLATINUM: 1X TO 2.5X BASE HI
PLATINUM PRINT RUN 25 SER.#'d SETS
*SILVER: .5X TO 1.25X BASE HI
SILVER PRINT RUN 250 SER.#'d SETS
1 Bill Russell 2.00 5.00
2 Bill Sharman 1.25 3.00
3 Bill Walton 1.25 3.00
4 Bob Cousy 2.00 5.00
5 Clyde Drexler 1.50 4.00
6 Dave Cowens 1.25 3.00
7 Earl Monroe 1.25 3.00
8 Elvin Hayes 1.25 3.00
9 George Gervin 1.25 3.00
10 Hakeem Olajuwon 1.50 4.00
11 Hal Greer 1.25 3.00
12 Isiah Thomas 1.25 3.00
13 James Worthy 1.50 4.00
14 Jerry West 1.50 4.00
15 John Havlicek 1.25 3.00
16 Kareem Abdul-Jabbar 2.00 5.00
17 Karl Malone 1.50 4.00
18 Kevin McHale 1.25 3.00
19 Larry Bird 4.00 10.00
20 Lenny Wilkens 1.25 3.00
21 Magic Johnson 3.00 8.00
22 Moses Malone 1.25 3.00
23 Nate Archibald 1.25 3.00
24 Nate Thurmond 1.25 3.00
25 Oscar Robertson 1.25 3.00
26 Rick Barry 1.25 3.00
27 Robert Parish 1.25 3.00
28 Walt Frazier 1.25 3.00
29 Wes Unseld 1.25 3.00
30 Willis Reed 1.25 3.00

2009-10 Classics Classic Greats Jerseys

STATED PRINT RUN 10 TO 99 SER.#'d SETS
SOME UNPRICED DUE TO SCARCITY
5 Clyde Drexler/99 6.00 15.00
6 Dave Cowens/99 4.00 10.00
7 Earl Monroe/99 4.00 10.00
10 Hakeem Olajuwon/99 5.00 12.00
12 Isiah Thomas/99 4.00 10.00
15 John Havlicek/49 4.00 10.00
16 Kareem Abdul-Jabbar/99 8.00 20.00
17 Karl Malone/99 5.00 12.00
18 Kevin McHale/99 4.00 10.00
19 Larry Bird/99 10.00 25.00
21 Magic Johnson/99 6.00 15.00
22 Moses Malone/25 6.00 15.00
26 Rick Barry/99 4.00 10.00
27 Robert Parish/99 4.00 10.00

2009-10 Classics Classic Greats Jerseys Prime

*PRIME: .6X TO 1.5X HI COLUMN
STATED PRINT RUN 10 TO 25 SER.#'d SETS
SOME UNPRICED DUE TO SCARCITY
6 Dave Cowens/25 8.00 20.00
15 John Havlicek/25 8.00 20.00
21 Magic Johnson/25 12.50 30.00
26 Rick Barry/25 6.00 15.00

2009-10 Classics Classic Greats Jerseys Signatures

STATED PRINT RUN 5 TO 25 SER.#'d SETS
SOME UNPRICED DUE TO SCARCITY
5 Clyde Drexler/25 25.00 60.00
6 Dave Cowens/25 10.00 25.00
7 Earl Monroe/25 15.00 40.00
12 Isiah Thomas/25 12.50 30.00
16 Kareem Abdul-Jabbar/25 30.00 80.00
18 Kevin McHale/25 40.00 100.00
19 Larry Bird/25 40.00 100.00
21 Magic Johnson/25 40.00 100.00
26 Rick Barry/25 12.50 30.00
27 Robert Parish/25 10.00 25.00

2009-10 Classics Classic Greats Jerseys Prime Signatures

STATED PRINT RUN 5 TO 25 SER.#'d SETS
SOME UNPRICED DUE TO SCARCITY
6 Dave Cowens/25 12.50 30.00
7 Earl Monroe/25 15.00 40.00
12 Isiah Thomas/25 15.00 40.00
16 Kareem Abdul-Jabbar/25 50.00 120.00
18 Kevin McHale/25 50.00 120.00
19 Larry Bird/25 50.00 120.00
21 Magic Johnson/25 40.00 100.00
26 Rick Barry/25 12.50. 30.00
27 Robert Parish/25 12.50 30.00

2009-10 Classics Dress Code

COMPLETE SET (25) 20.00 40.00
*GOLD: .6X TO 1.5X BASE HI
GOLD PRINT RUN 100 SER.#'d SETS
*PLATINUM: 1.25X TO 3X BASE HI
PLATINUM PRINT RUN 25 SER.#'d SETS
*SILVER: .5X TO 1.25X BASE HI
SILVER PRINT RUN 250 SER.#'d SETS
1 Al Horford .75 2.00
2 Alex English .75 2.00
3 Andre Iguodala .75 2.00
4 Yao Ming 1.00 2.50
5 Tracy McGrady .75 2.00
6 Tim Duncan 1.25 3.00
7 Thaddeus Young .50 1.25
8 Shawn Marion .75 2.00
9 Samuel Dalembert .50 1.25
10 Sam Perkins .75 2.00
11 David Lee .60 1.50
12 Dwight Howard 1.25 3.00
13 Erick Dampier .50 1.25
14 Randy Foye .50 1.25
15 Jeff Hornacek .75 2.00
16 Kevin Garnett 1.50 4.00
17 Kobe Bryant 4.00 10.00
18 LeBron James 4.00 10.00
19 Mark Price .75 2.00
20 Mehmet Okur .50 1.25
21 Mitch Richmond .75 2.00
22 Nene .60 1.50
23 Patrick Ewing 1.00 2.50
24 Carlos Boozer .75 2.00
25 Chauncey Billups .75 2.00

2009-10 Classics Dress Code Jerseys

STATED PRINT RUN 49 TO 199 SER.#'d SETS
1 Al Horford/199 3.00 8.00
2 Alex English/199 3.00 8.00
3 Andre Iguodala/199 3.00 8.00
4 Yao Ming/99 4.00 10.00
5 Tracy McGrady/199 3.00 8.00
6 Tim Duncan/199 5.00 12.00
7 Thaddeus Young/199 2.00 5.00
8 Shawn Marion/199 3.00 8.00
9 Samuel Dalembert/199 2.00 5.00
10 Sam Perkins/199 3.00 8.00
11 David Lee/49 2.50 6.00
12 Dwight Howard/199 5.00 12.00
13 Erick Dampier/199 2.00 5.00
14 Randy Foye/199 2.00 5.00
15 Jeff Hornacek/199 3.00 8.00
16 Kevin Garnett/199 6.00 15.00
17 Kobe Bryant/99 10.00 25.00
18 LeBron James/199 8.00 20.00
19 Mark Price/199 6.00 15.00
21 Mitch Richmond/199 3.00 8.00
22 Nene/199 2.50 6.00
23 Patrick Ewing/199 10.00 25.00
24 Carlos Boozer/199 3.00 8.00
25 Chauncey Billups/199 3.00 8.00

2009-10 Classics Dress Code Jerseys Prime

*PRIME: .75X TO 2X BASE HI
STATED PRINT RUN 5 TO 25 SER.#'d SETS
SOME UNPRICED DUE TO SCARCITY
23 Patrick Ewing/25 30.00 80.00

2009-10 Classics Dress Code Jerseys Signatures

STATED PRINT RUN 10 TO 25 SER.#'d SETS
SOME UNPRICED DUE TO SCARCITY
2 Alex English/25 8.00 20.00
3 Andre Iguodala/25 6.00 15.00
10 Sam Perkins/25 6.00 15.00
15 Jeff Hornacek/25 8.00 20.00
17 Kobe Bryant/25 100.00 200.00
24 Carlos Boozer/25 6.00 15.00
25 Chauncey Billups/25 12.50 30.00

2009-10 Classics Dress Code Jerseys Prime Signatures

STATED PRINT RUN 10 TO 25 SER.#'d SETS
SOME UNPRICED DUE TO SCARCITY
2 Alex English/25 10.00 25.00
3 Andre Iguodala/25 8.00 20.00
10 Sam Perkins/25 12.50 30.00
11 David Lee/25 10.00 25.00
15 Jeff Hornacek/25 10.00 25.00
24 Carlos Boozer/25 8.00 20.00
25 Chauncey Billups/25 15.00 40.00

2009-10 Classics Significant Signatures Gold

STATED PRINT RUN 13 TO 50 SER.#'d SETS
ASTERISK CARDS FROM SEASON UPDATE
6 Devin Harris/50 5.00 12.00
22 Shane Battier/50 5.00 12.00
23 Aaron Brooks/50 5.00 12.00
24 Trevor Ariza/27 5.00 12.00
30 Emeka Okafor/50 6.00 15.00
32 Tony Parker/50 10.00 25.00
44 Charlie Villanueva/50 5.00 12.00
45 Danny Granger/39 10.00 25.00
57 Ryan Gomes/50 5.00 12.00
74 Jermaine O'Neal/13 10.00 25.00
88 Eric Gordon/50 8.00 20.00
90 Kobe Bryant/50 100.00 200.00
101 Larry Bird/50 40.00 100.00
102 Gail Goodrich/50 10.00 25.00
103 Harry Gallatin/50 5.00 12.00
108 Jalen Rose/50 8.00 20.00
112 Rick Barry/50 8.00 20.00
113 Lenny Wilkens/50 8.00 20.00
114 Robert Horry/50* 20.00 50.00
115 Walt Frazier/50 10.00 25.00
118 Danny Manning/50 10.00 25.00
121 Chris Mullin/50 25.00 50.00
123 George Gervin/50 8.00 20.00
125 Bob McAdoo/50 15.00 30.00
129 Oscar Robertson/50 60.00 120.00
130 Bill Russell/50 80.00 160.00
131 Doc Rivers/50 10.00 25.00
132 Clyde Drexler/50 25.00 60.00
133 Kareem Abdul-Jabbar/50 50.00 120.00
134 Bernard King/50 8.00 20.00
138 Joe Dumars/50 20.00 50.00
140 Magic Johnson/49 50.00 120.00
141 Dominique Wilkins/50 12.50 30.00
143 Wes Unseld/45 10.00 25.00
144 Sidney Moncrief/50* 8.00 20.00
145 Sleepy Floyd/48 8.00 20.00
146 Spencer Haywood/50 5.00 12.00
147 Kevin McHale/50 30.00 60.00
148 Glen Rice/50 12.50 30.00
149 Isiah Thomas/50 12.50 30.00
150 Jerry West/50 30.00 80.00
151 Willis Reed/50 12.50 30.00
153 Elgin Baylor/50 15.00 40.00
154 Scottie Pippen/50 125.00 225.00
155 Elvin Hayes/50 10.00 25.00
159 Bob Cousy/50 20.00 50.00

2009-10 Classics Significant Signatures Platinum

STATED PRINT RUN ONE TO 25 SER.#'d SETS
SOME UNPRICED DUE TO SCARCITY
6 Devin Harris/25 6.00 15.00
22 Shane Battier/25 6.00 15.00
23 Aaron Brooks/25 6.00 15.00
24 Trevor Ariza/25 6.00 15.00
30 Emeka Okafor/25 8.00 20.00
32 Tony Parker/25 15.00 40.00
44 Charlie Villanueva/25 6.00 15.00
45 Danny Granger/25 12.50 30.00
57 Ryan Gomes/25 6.00 15.00
74 Jermaine O'Neal/25 8.00 20.00
88 Eric Gordon/25 10.00 25.00
90 Kobe Bryant/25 125.00 225.00
101 Larry Bird/25 50.00 120.00
102 Gail Goodrich/25 12.50 30.00
103 Harry Gallatin/25 6.00 15.00
108 Jalen Rose/25 10.00 25.00
110 Mark Price/25* 25.00 60.00
112 Rick Barry/25 10.00 25.00
113 Lenny Wilkens/25 10.00 25.00
114 Robert Horry/25* 25.00 60.00
115 Walt Frazier/24 12.50 30.00
118 Danny Manning/25 12.50 30.00
121 Chris Mullin/25 25.00 60.00
122 Hakeem Olajuwon/25 30.00 80.00
123 George Gervin/25 10.00 25.00
125 Bob McAdoo/25 20.00 40.00
129 Oscar Robertson/25 75.00 150.00
130 Bill Russell/25 80.00 200.00
131 Doc Rivers/25 15.00 40.00
132 Clyde Drexler/25 30.00 80.00
133 Kareem Abdul-Jabbar/25 60.00 150.00
134 Bernard King/25 10.00 25.00
140 Magic Johnson/25 60.00 150.00
141 Dominique Wilkins/25 20.00 50.00
143 Wes Unseld/25 12.50 30.00
145 Sleepy Floyd/25 10.00 25.00
146 Spencer Haywood/25 8.00 20.00
147 Kevin McHale/25 40.00 80.00
148 Glen Rice/25 15.00 40.00
149 Isiah Thomas/25 15.00 40.00
150 Jerry West/25 40.00 100.00
151 Willis Reed/25 15.00 40.00
154 Scottie Pippen/25 150.00 250.00
155 Elvin Hayes/25 12.50 30.00
159 Bob Cousy/25 25.00 60.00

2009-10 Classics Timeless Threads

STATED PRINT RUN ONE TO 265 SETS
SOME UNPRICED DUE TO SCARCITY
1 Kevin Garnett/199 6.00 15.00
3 Paul Pierce/199 4.00 10.00
9 David Lee/49 2.50 6.00
10 Danilo Gallinari/25 3.00 8.00
11 Andre Iguodala/199 3.00 8.00
13 Elton Brand/199 3.00 8.00
14 Chris Bosh/199 3.00 8.00
15 Andrea Bargnani/25 2.50 6.00
17 Jose Calderon/299 2.50 6.00
18 Dirk Nowitzki/199 4.00 10.00
19 Shawn Marion/199 3.00 8.00
21 J.J. Barea/199 5.00 12.00
22 Shane Battier/199 3.00 8.00
23 Aaron Brooks/199 2.00 5.00
27 O.J. Mayo/199 3.00 8.00
28 Chris Paul/199 5.00 12.00
29 David West/199 3.00 8.00
31 Tim Duncan/199 5.00 12.00
32 Tony Parker/25 6.00 15.00
38 LeBron James/199 10.00 25.00
39 Mo Williams/99 2.50 6.00
40 Shaquille O'Neal/199 6.00 15.00
44 Charlie Villanueva/199 2.50 6.00
51 Carmelo Anthony/199 4.00 10.00
52 Chauncey Billups/199 3.00 8.00
53 Nene/299 2.50 6.00
55 Al Jefferson/199 3.00 8.00
57 Ryan Gomes/299 2.00 5.00
58 Brandon Roy/199 3.00 8.00
59 LaMarcus Aldridge/199 3.00 8.00
61 Kevin Durant/199 8.00 20.00
64 Carlos Boozer/199 3.00 8.00
65 Deron Williams/199 3.00 8.00
66 Andrei Kirilenko/199 2.50 6.00
68 Josh Smith/199 3.00 8.00
72 Gerald Wallace/199 3.00 8.00
73 Dwyane Wade/199 6.00 15.00
75 Michael Beasley/99 3.00 8.00
76 Udonis Haslem/199 2.50 6.00
78 Dwight Howard/199 5.00 12.00
79 Rashard Lewis/199 2.50 6.00
81 Antawn Jamison/199 3.00 8.00
83 Randy Foye/199 2.00 5.00
87 Chris Kaman/199 2.50 6.00
90 Kobe Bryant/99 8.00 20.00
109 Mitch Richmond/99 4.00 10.00
110 Mark Price/99 8.00 20.00
112 Rick Barry/99 6.00 15.00
117 Patrick Ewing/99 12.50 30.00
119 Dennis Johnson/99 10.00 25.00
121 Chris Mullin/99 6.00 15.00
122 Hakeem Olajuwon/99 6.00 15.00
132 Clyde Drexler/99 8.00 20.00
133 Kareem Abdul-Jabbar/99 6.00 15.00
138 Joe Dumars/49 4.00 10.00
139 Karl Malone/99 8.00 20.00
140 Magic Johnson/99 6.00 15.00
141 Dominique Wilkins/49 6.00 15.00
147 Kevin McHale/99 6.00 15.00
149 Isiah Thomas/99 4.00 10.00
150 Jerry West/49 6.00 15.00
161 Blake Griffin/265 12.00 30.00
162 Hasheem Thabeet/265 2.00 5.00
163 James Harden/265 6.00 15.00
164 Tyreke Evans/265 5.00 12.00
165 Jonny Flynn/265 2.00 5.00
166 Stephen Curry/265 5.00 12.00
167 Jordan Hill/265 2.00 5.00
168 Brandon Jennings/265 4.00 10.00
169 Terrence Williams/265 2.00 5.00
170 Gerald Henderson/265 2.00 5.00
171 Tyler Hansbrough/265 3.00 8.00
172 Earl Clark/265 2.00 5.00
173 Austin Daye/265 2.00 5.00
174 James Johnson/265 2.00 5.00
175 Jrue Holiday/265 4.00 10.00
176 Ty Lawson/265 3.00 8.00
177 Jeff Teague/265 2.50 6.00
178 Eric Maynor/265 2.00 5.00
179 Darren Collison/265 3.00 8.00
180 Omri Casspi/265 2.00 5.00
181 B.J. Mullens/265 2.00 5.00
182 Rodrigue Beaubois/265 2.50 6.00
183 Taj Gibson/265 2.50 6.00
184 DeMarre Carroll/265 2.00 5.00
185 Wayne Ellington/265 2.00 5.00
186 Toney Douglas/265 2.00 5.00
187 DeJuan Blair/265 2.50 6.00
188 Sam Young/265 2.00 5.00
190 Chase Budinger/265 2.00 5.00
197 Taylor Griffin/265 2.00 5.00
198 Jermaine Taylor/265 2.00 5.00
199 Jodie Meeks/265 2.50 6.00
200 DaJuan Summers/265 2.00 5.00

2009-10 Classics Timeless Threads Prime

*PRIME: .75X TO 2X HI COLUMN
*PRIME RCs: 1X TO 2.5X HI COLUMN
STATED PRINT RUN ONE TO 25 SER.#'d SETS
SOME UNPRICED DUE TO SCARCITY
21 J.J. Barea/25 12.50 30.00
40 Shaquille O'Neal/25 20.00 50.00
161 Blake Griffin/25 30.00 80.00

2010-11 Classics

COMP.SET w/o SPs (100) 15.00 30.00
RETIRED PRINT RUN 999 SER.#'d SETS
AU RC PRINT RUN 199 TO 699 SER.#'d SETS
EXCH.EXPIRATION 10/13/2012
UNPRICED BLACK PRINT RUN ONE SET
1 Dirk Nowitzki .60 1.50
2 Caron Butler .50 1.25
3 Tyson Chandler .40 1.00
4 Ian Mahinmi RC .50 1.25
5 George Hill .40 1.00
6 Tim Duncan .75 2.00
7 Manu Ginobili .50 1.25
8 Chris Paul .75 2.00
9 Marco Belinelli .30 .75
10 David West .50 1.25
11 Marc Gasol .50 1.25
12 Zach Randolph .40 1.00
13 Mike Conley Jr. .40 1.00
14 Aaron Brooks .30 .75
15 Kevin Martin .50 1.25
16 Luis Scola .40 1.00
17 Kobe Bryant 2.50 6.00
18 Derek Fisher .40 1.00
19 Pau Gasol .50 1.25
20 Lamar Odom .50 1.25
21 Eric Gordon .50 1.25
22 Blake Griffin 1.25 3.00
23 Chris Kaman .40 1.00
24 Steve Nash .50 1.25
25 Vince Carter .60 1.50
26 Channing Frye .40 1.00
27 Stephen Curry .60 1.50
28 Monta Ellis .50 1.25
29 David Lee .40 1.00
30 Tyreke Evans .60 1.50
31 Beno Udrih .30 .75
32 Carl Landry .30 .75
33 Kevin Durant 1.50 4.00
34 Jeff Green .40 1.00
35 Russell Westbrook .60 1.50
36 Michael Beasley .50 1.25
37 Kevin Love .60 1.50
38 Corey Brewer .30 .75
39 Carmelo Anthony .60 1.50
40 Nene .40 1.00
41 Chauncey Billups .50 1.25
42 Arron Afflalo .30 .75
43 Brandon Roy .50 1.25
44 Wesley Matthews .50 1.25
45 LaMarcus Aldridge .50 1.25
46 Rudy Fernandez .40 1.00
47 Al Jefferson .50 1.25
48 Deron Williams .50 1.25
49 Andrei Kirilenko .40 1.00
50 Rajon Rondo .60 1.50
51 Paul Pierce .60 1.50
52 Kevin Garnett 1.00 2.50
53 Ray Allen .50 1.25
54 Amare Stoudemire .50 1.25
55 Raymond Felton .40 1.00
56 Toney Douglas .30 .75
57 Danilo Gallinari .50 1.25
58 Bill Walker .30 .75
59 Andrea Bargnani .40 1.00
60 Sonny Weems .30 .75
61 DeMar DeRozan .50 1.25
62 Jrue Holiday .50 1.25
63 Elton Brand .50 1.25
64 Andre Iguodala .50 1.25
65 Brook Lopez .50 1.25
66 Anthony Morrow .30 .75
67 Devin Harris .50 1.25
68 Derrick Rose 1.50 4.00
69 Luol Deng .50 1.25
70 Carlos Boozer .50 1.25
71 Joakim Noah .50 1.25
72 Danny Granger .50 1.25
73 Darren Collison .50 1.25
74 Roy Hibbert .40 1.00
75 J.J. Hickson .40 1.00
76 Antawn Jamison .50 1.25
77 Mo Williams .40 1.00
78 Andrew Bogut .50 1.25
79 Brandon Jennings .50 1.25
80 John Salmons .50 1.25
81 Tayshaun Prince .50 1.25
82 Rodney Stuckey .50 1.25
83 Charlie Villanueva .40 1.00
84 Dwight Howard .75 2.00
85 Jameer Nelson .40 1.00
86 Hedo Turkoglu .50 1.25
87 Jason Richardson .50 1.25
88 Stephen Jackson .40 1.00
89 Boris Diaw .40 1.00
90 Gerald Wallace .50 1.25
91 Jamal Crawford .40 1.00
92 Josh Smith .50 1.25
93 Joe Johnson .50 1.25
94 Dwyane Wade 1.00 2.50
95 LeBron James 2.50 6.00
96 Chris Bosh .50 1.25
97 Erick Dampier .30 .75
98 Nick Young .40 1.00
99 Andray Blatche .30 .75
100 Kirk Hinrich .50 1.25
101 Bill Walton 1.00 2.50
102 Byron Scott 1.00 2.50
103 Mark Aguirre 1.00 2.50
104 Michael Finley 1.00 2.50
105 Nate McMillan 1.00 2.50
106 Nick Anderson 1.00 2.50
107 Artis Gilmore 1.00 2.50
108 Jamal Mashburn 1.00 2.50
109 Larry Bird 3.00 8.00
110 Julius Erving 2.00 5.00
111 Sidney Moncrief 1.00 2.50
112 Rony Seikaly 1.00 2.50
113 Jalen Rose 1.00 2.50
114 Rickey Green 1.00 2.50
115 Robert Horry 1.25 3.00
116 Rex Chapman 1.00 2.50
117 Jack Sikma 1.00 2.50
118 Nate Thurmond 1.00 2.50
119 Glenn Robinson 1.00 2.50
120 Doc Rivers 1.00 2.50
121 David Robinson 1.50 4.00
122 Michael Cooper 1.00 2.50
123 Al Attles 1.00 2.50
124 Alonzo Mourning 1.25 3.00
125 Dave Bing 1.00 2.50
126 Bobby Jones 1.00 2.50
127 Moses Malone 1.00 2.50
128 Tim Hardaway 1.00 2.50
129 Tom Heinsohn 1.00 2.50
130 Chris Webber 1.00 2.50
131 Gus Williams 1.00 2.50
132 Campy Russell 1.00 2.50
133 Charles D. Smith 1.00 2.50
134 Magic Johnson 2.50 6.00
135 Spud Webb 1.00 2.50
136 Charles Oakley 1.00 2.50
137 Pete Maravich 3.00 8.0
138 Jerry West 1.25 3.0
139 Derek Harper 1.00 2.5
140 Hakeem Olajuwon 1.25 3.0
141 Luke Babbitt/699 AU RC 5.00 12.0
142 Kevin Seraphin/699 AU RC 6.00 15.0
143 Eric Bledsoe/699 AU RC 8.00 20.0
144 Avery Bradley/699 AU RC 10.00 25.0
145 James Anderson/699 AU RC 5.00 12.0
146 Elliot Williams/699 AU RC 5.00 12.0
147 Trevor Booker/699 AU RC 5.00 12.0
148 Damion James/699 AU RC 5.00 12.0
149 Dominique Jones/689 AU RC 5.00 12.0
150 Quincy Pondexter/699 AU RC 5.00 12.0
151 Jordan Crawford/699 AU RC 8.00 20.0
152 Greivis Vasquez/699 AU RC 6.00 15.0
153 Daniel Orton/699 AU RC 5.00 12.
154 Lazar Hayward/599 AU RC 5.00 12.
155 John Wall/199 AU RC 125.00 250.
156 Evan Turner/299 AU RC 12.00 30.
157 Derrick Favors/299 AU RC 10.00 25.
158 Wesley Johnson/299 AU RC 8.00 20.
159 DeMarcus Cousins/349 AU RC 20.00 50.
160 Ekpe Udoh/399 AU RC 5.00 12.
161 Greg Monroe/399 AU RC 10.00 25.
162 Al-Farouq Aminu/699 AU RC 5.00 12.
163 Gordon Hayward/449 AU RC 10.00 25.
164 Paul George/449 AU RC 12.00 30
165 Cole Aldrich/449 AU RC 5.00 12
166 Xavier Henry/449 AU RC 6.00 15
167 Ed Davis/449 AU RC 6.00 15
168 Patrick Patterson/449 AU RC 8.00 20
169 Larry Sanders/699 AU RC 5.00 12
170 Luke Harangody/699 AU RC 5.00 12
171 Dexter Pittman/699 AU RC 5.00 12
172 Hassan Whiteside/699 AU RC 5.00 12
173 Andy Rautins/699 AU RC 5.00 12
174 Lance Stephenson/699 AU RC 5.00 12
175 Armon Johnson/699 AU RC 5.00 12
176 Terrico White/699 AU RC 5.00 12
177 Sherron Collins/699 AU RC EXCH 5.00 12
178 Landry Fields/699 AU RC 8.00 20
179 Jeremy Lin/699 AU RC 75.00 20
180 Timofey Mozgov/699 AU RC 5.00 1

2010-11 Classics Timeless Tributes Gold

*STARS: 1.25X TO 3X BASE HI
*RETIRED: .6X TO 1.5X BASE HI
124 Alonzo Mourning 5.00 1

2010-11 Classics Timeless Tributes Platinum

*STARS: 3X TO 8X BASE HI
*RETIRED: 1.5X TO 4X BASE HI
124 Alonzo Mourning 10.00 2

2010-11 Classics Timeless Tributes Silver

*STARS: 1X TO 2.5X BASE HI
*RETIRED: .5X TO 1.25X BASE HI

2010-11 Classics Blast Fro The Past

COMPLETE SET (25) 10.00
RANDOM INSERTS IN PACKS
1 Amare Stoudemire .75
2 Al Jefferson .75
3 LeBron James 4.00
4 David Lee .60

os Boozer .75 2.00
Murphy .50 1.25
Hinrich .75 2.00
Martin .75 2.00
n Durant 2.50 6.00
h Howard .60 1.50
o Turkoglu .75 2.00
on Butler .75 2.00
on Kidd .75 2.00
hael Beasley .75 2.00
n Salmons .75 2.00
ce Carter 1.00 2.50
lianlian .60 1.50
Harrington .60 1.50
dres Nocioni .50 1.25
awn Jamison .75 2.00
hony Randolph .60 1.50
is Bosh .75 2.00
entin Richardson .60 1.50
e Robinson .75 2.00
eem Abdul-Jabbar 1.25 3.00

010-11 Classics Blast From The Past Jerseys

D PRINT RUN 99 TO 199 SER.#'d SETS
re Stoudemire/199 2.50 6.00
fferson/199 2.50 6.00
on James/199 8.00 20.00
d Lee/199 2.00 5.00
os Boozer/199 2.50 6.00
Murphy/99 2.00 5.00
Hinrich/199 2.50 6.00
n Martin/199 2.50 6.00
n Durant/199 8.00 20.00
sh Howard/199 2.00 5.00
do Turkoglu/199 2.50 6.00
on Butler/199 2.50 6.00
on Kidd/199 2.50 6.00
chael Beasley/199 2.50 6.00
n Salmons/199 2.50 6.00
ce Carter/199 3.00 8.00
lianlian/199 2.00 5.00
Harrington/199 2.00 5.00
dres Nocioni/199 2.00 5.00
awn Jamison/199 2.50 6.00
thony Randolph/199 2.00 5.00
ris Bosh/199 2.50 6.00
entin Richardson/199 2.00 5.00
e Robinson/199 2.50 6.00
eem Abdul-Jabbar/99 4.00 10.00

010-11 Classics Blast From The Past Jerseys Prime

E: 1X TO 2.5X BASE HI
D PRINT RUN ONE TO 25 SER.#'d SETS
UNPRICED DUE TO SCARCITY
ce Carter/25 12.50 30.00

010-11 Classics Blast From he Past Jerseys Signatures

D PRINT RUN 5 TO 25 SER.#'d SETS
UNPRICED DUE TO SCARCITY
re Stoudemire/25 15.00 40.00
efferson/25 6.00 15.00
d Lee/25 6.00 15.00
n Durant/25 125.00 250.00
ron Butler/25 8.00 20.00
on Kidd/25 15.00 40.00
thony Randolph/25 6.00 15.00

010-11 Classics Blast From The Past Jerseys Prime Signatures

D PRINT RUN 5 TO 25 SER.#'d SETS
UNPRICED DUE TO SCARCITY
efferson/25 8.00 20.00
d Lee/25 8.00 20.00
n Durant/15 200.00 400.00
ron Butler/25 10.00 25.00
son Kidd/25 20.00 50.00
thony Randolph/25 8.00 20.00

2010-11 Classics Classic Combos

PLETE SET (10) 6.00 15.00
OM INSERTS IN PACKS
D: 1X TO 2.5X BASE HI
PRINT RUN 100 SER.#'d SETS
TINUM: 1.25X TO 3X BASE HI
NUM PRINT RUN 25 SER.#'d SETS
ER: .5X TO 1.25X BASE HI
R PRINT RUN 250 SER.#'d SETS
ICED BLACK PRINT RUN ONE SET
y Bird 2.50 6.00
bert Parish
nes Worthy 2.00 5.00
gic Johnson
n Stockton 1.25 3.00
Malone
eem Abdul-Jabbar 1.25 3.00
ar Robertson
l Goodrich 1.00 2.50
y West
t Frazier .75 2.00
lis Reed
h Thomas .75 2.00
Dumars
e Thurmond .75 2.00
k Barry
nis Rodman 1.50 4.00
ottie Pippen
an Issel 1.00 2.50
id Thompson

2010-11 Classics Classic Combos Jerseys

ED PRINT RUN 99 SER.#'d SETS
ME: 1X TO 2.5X BASE HI
E PRINT RUN 25 SER.#'d SETS
y Bird 10.00 25.00
bert Parish
nes Worthy 8.00 20.00
gic Johnson
n Stockton 6.00 15.00
Malone
h Thomas 5.00 12.00
Joe Dumars
9 Dennis Rodman 15.00 40.00
Scottie Pippen

2010-11 Classics Classic Greats

COMPLETE SET (30) 15.00 40.00
RANDOM INSERTS IN PACKS
*SILVER: .6X TO 1.5X BASE HI
SILVER PRINT RUN 250 SER.#'d SETS
UNPRICED BLACK PRINT RUN ONE SET
1 Bill Russell 1.50 4.00
2 Adrian Dantley 1.00 2.50
3 Nate Archibald 1.00 2.50
4 Patrick Ewing 1.25 3.00
5 Kevin McHale 1.00 2.50
6 Magic Johnson 2.50 6.00
7 Sam Jones 1.00 2.50
8 Walter Berry 1.00 2.50
9 Spencer Haywood 1.00 2.50
10 Alonzo Mourning 1.25 3.00
11 Artis Gilmore 1.00 2.50
12 James Worthy 1.25 3.00
13 Paul Westphal 1.00 2.50
14 Scottie Pippen 2.00 5.00
15 Shawn Kemp 1.50 4.00
16 Larry Bird 3.00 8.00
17 Lenny Wilkens 1.00 2.50
18 Mark Jackson 1.00 2.50
19 Toni Kukoc 1.00 2.50
20 Dennis Rodman 1.50 4.00
21 Chris Mullin 1.00 2.50
22 Dominique Wilkins 1.25 3.00
23 Rolando Blackman 1.00 2.50
24 Walt Frazier 1.00 2.50
25 Cliff Hagan 1.00 2.50
26 Connie Hawkins 1.00 2.50
27 Gary Payton 1.00 2.50
28 George Gervin 1.00 2.50
29 Maurice Cheeks 1.00 2.50
30 Moses Malone 1.00 2.50

2010-11 Classics Classic Greats Gold

*GOLD: .75X TO 2X BASE HI
STATED PRINT RUN 100 SER.#'d SETS
4 Patrick Ewing 4.00 10.00
10 Alonzo Mourning 5.00 12.00
15 Shawn Kemp 12.50 30.00

2010-11 Classics Classic Greats Platinum

*PLATINUM: 1.25X TO 3X BASE HI
STATED PRINT RUN 25 SER.#'d SETS
4 Patrick Ewing 10.00 25.00
10 Alonzo Mourning 10.00 25.00
15 Shawn Kemp 40.00 100.00

2010-11 Classics Classic Greats Signatures

STATED PRINT RUN 5 TO 99 SER.#'d SETS
SOME UNPRICED DUE TO SCARCITY
2 Adrian Dantley/49 12.50 30.00
3 Nate Archibald/49 8.00 20.00
7 Sam Jones/25 25.00 60.00
8 Walter Berry/99 6.00 15.00
12 James Worthy/25 20.00 50.00
13 Paul Westphal/49 6.00 15.00
17 Lenny Wilkens/49 6.00 15.00
19 Toni Kukoc/25 25.00 60.00
23 Rolando Blackman/25 8.00 20.00
26 Connie Hawkins/99 12.50 30.00
28 George Gervin/25 12.50 30.00
29 Maurice Cheeks/49 6.00 15.00

2010-11 Classics Classic Moments

COMPLETE SET (10) 10.00 25.00
RANDOM INSERTS IN PACKS
*GOLD: .75X TO 2X BASE HI
GOLD PRINT RUN 100 SER.#'d SETS
*PLATINUM: 1.25X TO 3X BASE HI
PLATINUM PRINT RUN 25 SER.#'d SETS
*SILVER: .5X TO 1.25X BASE HI
SILVER PRINT RUN 250 SER.#'d SETS
UNPRICED BLACK PRINT RUN ONE SET
1 Wilt Chamberlain 1.50 4.00
2 Magic Johnson 2.00 5.00
3 Brandon Jennings .75 2.00
4 LeBron James 4.00 10.00
5 Rajon Rondo 1.00 2.50
6 Kevin Durant 2.50 6.00
7 Kareem Abdul-Jabbar 1.25 3.00
8 John Havlicek 1.00 2.50
9 Kobe Bryant 4.00 10.00
10 Blake Griffin 2.00 5.00

2010-11 Classics Classic Moments Signatures

STATED PRINT RUN 5 TO 99 SER.#'d SETS
SOME UNPRICED DUE TO SCARCITY
5 Rajon Rondo/25 25.00 60.00
6 Kevin Durant/25 125.00 225.00
9 Kobe Bryant/99 100.00 200.00
10 Blake Griffin/25 60.00 150.00

2010-11 Classics Dress Code

COMPLETE SET (25) 12.50 30.00
RANDOM INSERTS IN PACKS
*GOLD: .75X TO 2X BASE HI
GOLD PRINT RUN 100 SER.#'d SETS
*PLATINUM: 1.25X TO 3X BASE HI
PLATINUM PRINT RUN 25 SER.#'d SETS
*SILVER: .5X TO 1.25X BASE HI
SILVER PRINT RUN 250 SER.#'d SETS
UNPRICED BLACK PRINT RUN ONE SET
1 Kobe Bryant 4.00 10.00
2 Andre Iguodala .75 2.00
3 Nene .60 1.50
4 Mo Williams .60 1.50
5 Tim Duncan 1.25 3.00
6 Jason Kidd .75 2.00
7 Gerald Wallace .75 2.00
8 Dwight Howard 1.25 3.00
9 David Lee .60 1.50
10 Brandon Jennings .75 2.00
11 Brook Lopez .75 2.00
12 Toney Douglas .50 1.25
13 Shawn Marion .75 2.00
14 Marc Gasol .75 2.00
15 Luol Deng .75 2.00
16 Kevin Love 1.00 2.50
17 Jrue Holiday .75 2.00
18 Dirk Nowitzki 1.00 2.50
19 Stephen Curry 1.00 2.50
20 Dwyane Wade 1.50 4.00
21 Blake Griffin 2.00 5.00
22 Amare Stoudemire .75 2.00
23 Joe Johnson .75 2.00
24 Andrea Bargnani .60 1.50
25 Andrew Bogut .75 2.00

2010-11 Classics Dress Code Jerseys

STATED PRINT RUN 25 TO 199 SER.#'d SETS
*PRIME: 1X TO 2.5X BASE HI
PRIME PRINT RUN 5 TO 25 SETS
SOME PRIME UNPRICED DUE TO SCARCITY
1 Kobe Bryant/199 10.00 25.00
2 Andre Iguodala/199 2.50 6.00
3 Nene/199 2.00 5.00
5 Tim Duncan/199 4.00 10.00
6 Jason Kidd/199 2.50 6.00
7 Gerald Wallace/199 2.50 6.00
8 Dwight Howard/199 4.00 10.00
9 David Lee/199 2.00 5.00
10 Brandon Jennings/199 2.50 6.00
11 Brook Lopez/199 2.50 6.00
12 Toney Douglas/199 1.50 4.00
13 Shawn Marion/199 2.50 6.00
14 Marc Gasol/199 2.50 6.00
15 Luol Deng/199 2.50 6.00
16 Kevin Love/199 3.00 8.00
17 Jrue Holiday/199 2.50 6.00
18 Dirk Nowitzki/199 3.00 8.00
19 Stephen Curry/25 3.00 8.00
20 Dwyane Wade/199 5.00 12.00
21 Blake Griffin/199 6.00 15.00
22 Amare Stoudemire/199 2.50 6.00
23 Joe Johnson/199 2.50 6.00
24 Andrea Bargnani/199 2.00 5.00
25 Andrew Bogut/199 2.50 6.00

2010-11 Classics Dress Code Jerseys Signatures

STATED PRINT RUN 10 TO 25 SER.#'d SETS
SOME UNPRICED DUE TO SCARCITY
1 Kobe Bryant/25 100.00 200.00
2 Andre Iguodala/25 6.00 15.00
6 Jason Kidd/25 15.00 40.00
7 Gerald Wallace/25 8.00 20.00
9 David Lee/25 6.00 15.00
10 Brandon Jennings/25 15.00 40.00
12 Toney Douglas/25 6.00 15.00
14 Marc Gasol/25 EXCH 15.00 40.00
16 Kevin Love/25 12.50 30.00
17 Jrue Holiday/25 6.00 15.00
19 Stephen Curry/25 15.00 40.00
21 Blake Griffin/25 75.00 150.00
22 Amare Stoudemire/25 20.00 50.00
24 Andrea Bargnani/25 8.00 20.00
25 Andrew Bogut/25 8.00 20.00

2010-11 Classics Dress Code Jerseys Prime Signatures

STATED PRINT RUN 10 TO 25 SER.#'d SETS
SOME UNPRICED DUE TO SCARCITY
1 Kobe Bryant/25 125.00 225.00
2 Andre Iguodala/25 10.00 25.00
7 Gerald Wallace/25 10.00 25.00
9 David Lee/25 8.00 20.00
11 Brook Lopez/25 8.00 20.00
12 Toney Douglas/25 8.00 20.00
16 Kevin Love/25 15.00 40.00
17 Jrue Holiday/25 10.00 25.00
19 Stephen Curry/25 20.00 50.00
21 Blake Griffin/20 100.00 200.00
23 Joe Johnson/25 10.00 25.00
24 Andrea Bargnani/25 10.00 25.00
25 Andrew Bogut/25 12.50 30.00

2010-11 Classics Hoops Previews

COMPLETE SET (20) 20.00 50.00
RANDOM INSERTS IN RACK PACKS
1 Amare Stoudemire 1.00 2.50
2 Blake Griffin 2.50 6.00
3 Carmelo Anthony 1.25 3.00
4 Dirk Nowitzki 1.25 3.00
5 Dwight Howard 1.50 4.00
6 Dwyane Wade 2.00 5.00
7 John Wall 4.00 10.00
8 Kevin Durant 3.00 8.00
9 Kobe Bryant 5.00 12.00
10 LeBron James 5.00 12.00
11 Monta Ellis 1.00 2.50
12 Derrick Rose 3.00 8.00
13 Eric Gordon 1.00 2.50
14 Russell Westbrook 1.25 3.00
15 Kevin Love 1.25 3.00
16 Chris Paul 1.50 4.00
17 LaMarcus Aldridge 1.00 2.50
18 Paul Pierce 1.25 3.00
19 Steve Nash 1.00 2.50
20 Stephen Curry 1.25 3.00

2010-11 Classics Membership Materials

STATED PRINT RUN 100 TO 499 SER.#'d SETS
1 Mike Bibby/499 2.00 5.00
2 Paul Pierce/499 3.00 8.00
3 Larry Johnson/499 5.00 12.00
4 Scottie Pippen/499 5.00 12.00
5 Dirk Nowitzki/499 3.00 8.00
6 Nene/499 2.00 5.00
7 Tayshaun Prince/499 2.50 6.00
8 Chris Mullin/250 2.50 6.00
9 Yao Ming/499 3.00 8.00
10 Chuck Person/499 2.50 6.00
11 Blake Griffin/499 6.00 15.00
12 Kobe Bryant/499 8.00 20.00
13 O.J. Mayo/499 2.50 6.00
14 Dwyane Wade/499 5.00 12.00
15 Andrew Bogut/499 2.50 6.00
16 Kevin Love/499 3.00 8.00
17 Derrick Coleman/499 2.50 6.00
18 Chris Paul/499 4.00 10.00
19 Charles Oakley/250 2.50 6.00
20 Jameer Nelson/499 2.00 5.00
21 Andre Iguodala/499 2.50 6.00
22 Anfernee Hardaway/499 6.00 15.00
23 LaMarcus Aldridge/499 2.50 6.00
24 Tyreke Evans/499 3.00 8.00
25 Tim Duncan/499 4.00 10.00
26 Karl Malone/499 3.00 8.00
27 Alex English/499 2.50 6.00
28 Kevin Johnson/499 2.50 6.00
29 Clyde Drexler/499 3.00 8.00
30 John Stockton/250 4.00 10.00
31 Kevin McHale/250 2.50 6.00
32 David West/499 2.50 6.00
33 Dwight Howard/250 4.00 10.00
34 Deron Williams/499 2.50 6.00
35 Pau Gasol/499 2.50 6.00
36 Dominique Wilkins/250 3.00 8.00
37 Robert Parish/499 2.50 6.00
38 Dennis Rodman/100 10.00 25.00
39 Shawn Marion/499 2.50 6.00
40 Carmelo Anthony/250 3.00 8.00
41 Dikembe Mutombo/250 3.00 8.00
42 Richard Hamilton/499 2.00 5.00
43 Magic Johnson/100 6.00 15.00
44 Tim Hardaway/499 2.50 6.00
45 Patrick Ewing/499 3.00 8.00
46 Brandon Roy/100 2.50 6.00
47 Chris Webber/499 2.50 6.00
48 David Robinson/100 4.00 10.00
49 Gary Payton/250 3.00 8.00
50 Kevin Durant/499 6.00 15.00

2010-11 Classics Membership Materials Prime

*PRIME: 1X TO 2.5X BASE HI
STATED PRINT RUN 2 TO 49 SER.#'d SETS
SOME UNPRICED DUE TO SCARCITY
3 Larry Johnson/49 15.00 40.00
4 Scottie Pippen/49 20.00 50.00
26 Karl Malone/49 10.00 25.00
42 Richard Hamilton/25 6.00 15.00
44 Tim Hardaway/49 12.50 30.00
45 Patrick Ewing/49 12.50 30.00

2010-11 Classics Significant Signatures

STATED PRINT RUN 10 TO 99 SER.#'d SETS
SOME UNPRICED DUE TO SCARCITY
1 A.C. Green/99 12.00 30.00
2 Adrian Dantley/99 10.00 25.00
3 Al Jefferson/49 8.00 20.00
4 Alonzo Mourning/49 30.00 80.00
5 Amare Stoudemire/49 20.00 50.00
6 Andre Iguodala/99 6.00 15.00
7 Andre Miller/99 6.00 15.00
8 Andrea Bargnani/99 6.00 15.00
9 Artis Gilmore/99 8.00 20.00
10 Bailey Howell/99 10.00 25.00
11 Bill Cartwright/49 15.00 40.00
12 Bob Lanier/99 6.00 15.00
13 Brandon Jennings/99 12.50 30.00
14 David Lee/99 6.00 15.00
15 Dennis Rodman/49 40.00 100.00
16 Dolph Schayes/99 8.00 20.00
17 Dominique Wilkins/49 20.00 50.00
18 Elvin Hayes/49 8.00 20.00
19 Joakim Noah/99 12.50 30.00
20 Kevin Durant/49 100.00 200.00
21 Kobe Bryant/99 100.00 200.00
22 Larry Johnson/99 25.00 60.00
23 Lenny Wilkens/99 6.00 15.00
24 Marc Gasol/99 15.00 40.00
25 Paul Westphal/99 12.50 30.00
26 Rick Barry/49 12.50 30.00
27 Robert Horry/99 15.00 40.00
28 Rolando Blackman/99 8.00 20.00
29 Sam Perkins/49 8.00 20.00
30 Oscar Robertson/49 50.00 120.00
31 Sean Elliott/99 10.00 25.00
32 Shane Battier/49 6.00 15.00
34 Larry Bird/33 75.00 150.00
35 Sam Jones/49 12.50 30.00
36 Spud Webb/99 8.00 20.00
37 Stephen Curry/49 17.50 35.00
38 Toni Kukoc/49 20.00 50.00
39 Tyreke Evans/49 15.00 40.00
40 Jason Kidd/49 20.00 50.00
41 Andrew Bynum/49 15.00 40.00
42 Andrew Bogut/49 12.00 30.00
43 Blake Griffin/99 75.00 150.00
44 Magic Johnson/32 75.00 150.00
45 Gary Payton/49 15.00 40.00
46 Jerry West/35 40.00 100.00
47 Chris Bosh/99 12.50 30.00
49 Devin Harris/99 8.00 20.00
50 Rajon Rondo/49 25.00 60.00
51 Kareem Abdul-Jabbar/25 40.00 100.00
52 Pau Gasol/99 20.00 50.00
53 Bill Walton/49 10.00 25.00
54 Carmelo Anthony/20 25.00 60.00
55 Derrick Rose/25 EXCH
57 Deron Williams/99 10.00 25.00
58 Darren Collison/99 6.00 15.00
59 Steve Nash/25 30.00 80.00
60 Elgin Baylor/25 20.00 50.00

1989 Cleo Michael Jordan Valentines

COMMON CARD .40 1.00

1991 Cleo Michael Jordan Valentines

These blank-backed red- or pink-bordered valentine cards came in 32- and 38-card boxes of Cleo Valentines and feature action and posed color photos of Michael Jordan. The valentines are printed on thin white card stock, with cards 2-5, 7 and 11 measuring 2 1/2" by 3 1/4" and cards 1, 6, 8-10 measuring 2 1/4" by 5". The cards come in perforated groups of two or three. The back of the box features three bonus cutouts that are otherwise identical to cards 7, 10 and 11 except they are printed on gray cardboard stock. Non-mailable envelopes were included in the boxes. The cards are unnumbered and are listed below alphabetically by the valentine messages that are printed in the red hearts on the cards.
COMPLETE SET (11) 2.00 5.00
COMMON CARD (1-11) .30 .75

1978-79 Clippers Handyman

The 1978-79 San Diego Clippers Handyman set contains nine cards measuring approximately 2" by 4 1/4". The cards are "3-D" and are similar to the 1970s Kelloggs baseball sets. Each card has a coupon tab attached (included in the dimensions given above). Coach Gene Shue's card was apparently not distributed (as it was the grand prize winner of the contest) with the other cards but it does exist. Some veteran collectors and dealers also consider Kunnert to be somewhat tougher to find. In addition there is a second version of the Lloyd Free card with a signature variation. The set price below does not include the Gene Shue card.
COMPLETE SET (9) 25.00 50.00
1 Randy Smith 9 2.50 6.00
2 Nick Weatherspoon 12 2.00 5.00
3 Freeman Williams 20 1.50 4.00
4 Sidney Wicks 21 3.00 8.00
5A Lloyd Free 24 2.50 6.00
5B Lloyd Free 24 10.00 20.00
(Signature variation)
6 Swen Nater 31 2.00 5.00
7 Jerome Whitehead 33 1.25 3.00
8 Kermit Washington 42 1.50 4.00
9 Kevin Kunnert 44 10.00 20.00
NNO Gene Shue CO SP 750.00 1500.00

1990-91 Clippers Star

This 12-card set of Los Angeles Clippers was produced by the Star Company and measures the standard size. The fronts feature color action shots, with red borders that wash out in the middle of the card face. The horizontally oriented backs are printed in red and blue on white and have biographical as well as statistical information. The cards are unnumbered and are checklisted below in alphabetical order. Benoit Benjamin and Mike Smrek were apparently planned for the set but were not released with the other cards listed below.
COMPLETE SET (12) 1.50 4.00
1 Ken Bannister .08 .25
2 Winston Garland .08 .25
3 Tom Garrick .08 .25
4 Gary Grant .08 .25
5 Ron Harper .60 1.50
6 Bo Kimble .08 .25
7 Danny Manning .60 1.50
8 Jeff Martin .08 .25
9 Ken Norman .08 .25
10 Mike Schuler CO .08 .25
11 Charles Smith .08 .25
12 Loy Vaught .60 1.50

2000-01 Clippers Topps

COMPLETE SET (10) 2.00 5.00
NNO AT&T Wireless Sponsor Card .20 .50
LC1 Lamar Odom .50 1.25
LC10 Quentin Richardson .75 2.00
LC2 Michael Olowokandi .30 .75
LC3 Corey Maggette .40 1.00
LC4 Alvin Gentry CO .30 .75
LC6 Eric Piatkowski .30 .75
LC7 Brian Skinner .30 .75
LC8 Darius Miles .50 1.25
LC9 Keyon Dooling .50 1.25

2001-02 Clippers Topps

Issued by Topps, this six-card set was given away at a game during the 2001-02 Clippers season.
COMPLETE SET (6) 1.50 4.00
LC2 Michael Olowokandi .40 1.00
LC3 Corey Maggette .50 1.25
LC4 Alvin Gentry CO .40 1.00
LC6 Eric Piatkowski .40 1.00
LC7 Brian Skinner .40 1.00
LC8 Darius Miles .40 1.00

2005-06 Clippers Topps

Sponsored by Jet Blue Airways, this 15-card set was given away at a 2005-06 Los Angeles Clippers home game.
COMPLETE SET (15) 5.00 12.00
NNO Jet Blue Airways Sponsor Card .40 1.00
LAC1 Elton Brand .60 1.50
LAC10 Vladimir Radmanovic .40 1.00
LAC11 Zeljko Rebraca .40 1.00
LAC12 Quinton Ross .40 1.00
LAC13 James Singleton .60 1.50
LAC14 Mike Dunleavy, Sr. CO .60 1.50
LAC2 Sam Cassell .60 1.50
LAC3 Daniel Ewing .60 1.50
LAC4 Chris Kaman .60 1.50
LAC5 Yaroslav Korolev .60 1.50
LAC6 Corey Maggette .50 1.25
LAC7 Walter McCarty .40 1.00
LAC8 Cuttino Mobley .50 1.25
LAC9 Shaun Livingston .40 1.00

2001-02 Clippers Upper Deck

Released by Upper Deck in conjunction with AT&T Wireless, this 10-card set features the Clippers and was given away during the 2001-02 season.
COMPLETE SET (10) 2.50 6.00
NNO AT&T Wireless Sponsor Card .25 .60
LAC1 Elton Brand .60 1.50
LAC2 Darius Miles .40 1.00
LAC3 Lamar Odom .60 1.50
LAC4 Corey Maggette .50 1.25
LAC5 Quentin Richardson .50 1.25
LAC6 Keyon Dooling .40 1.00
LAC7 Jeff McInnis .40 1.00
LAC8 Eric Piatkowski .40 1.00
LAC9 Michael Olowokandi .40 1.00

2006-07 Clippers Upper Deck JetBlue

COMPLETE SET (14) 3.00 8.00
1 Elton Brand .60 1.50
2 Sam Cassell .60 1.50
3 Paul Davis .60 1.50
4 Daniel Ewing .40 1.00
5 Chris Kaman .50 1.25
6 Shaun Livingston .40 1.00
7 Corey Maggette .50 1.25
8 Cuttino Mobley .50 1.25
9 Quinton Ross .40 1.00
10 James Singleton .40 1.00
11 Tim Thomas .40 1.00
12 Aaron Williams .40 1.00
13 Mike Dunleavy Coach .40 1.00
14 Clipper Nation .20 .50

1994-95 Collector's Choice

These 420 standard-size cards, issued in two separate series of 210-cards each, comprise Upper Deck's '94-95 Collector's Choice set. Cards were issued in 12-card hobby packs (suggested retail of ninety-nine cents), 13-card retail packs (suggested retail of $1.18), and 20-card retail jumbo packs. White bordered fronts feature color player action shots. The player's name, team, and position appear in a lower corner. The back carries another color player action shot at the top, with statistics and career highlights displayed below. The following subsets are included in this set: Tip-Off (166-192), All-Star Advice (193-198), NBA Profiles (199-206), Blueprints (372-398), Trivia (399-406), and Draft Class (407-416). Rookie Cards in this set include Grant Hill, Juwan Howard, Eddie Jones, Jason Kidd and Glenn Robinson.
COMPLETE SET (420) 15.00 40.00
COMPLETE SERIES 1 (210) 8.00 20.00
COMPLETE SERIES 2 (210) 8.00 20.00
1 Anfernee Hardaway .20 .50
2 Mark Macon .07 .20
3 Steve Smith .10 .25
4 Chris Webber .20 .50
5 Donald Royal .07 .20
6 Avery Johnson .10 .25
7 Kevin Johnson .12 .30
8 Doug Christie .07 .20
9 Derrick McKey .07 .20
10 Dennis Rodman .25 .60
11 Scott Skiles UER .07 .20
(Listed as playing with Cavaliers instead of Pacers in '87-'88, '88-'89)
12 Johnny Dawkins .07 .20
13 Kendall Gill .07 .20
14 Jeff Hornacek .10 .25
15 Latrell Sprewell .15 .40
16 Lucious Harris .07 .20
17 Chris Mullin .12 .30
18 John Williams .07 .20
19 Tony Campbell .07 .20
20 LaPhonso Ellis .07 .20
21 Gerald Wilkins .07 .20
22 Clyde Drexler .15 .40
23 Michael Jordan BB 1.00 2.50
24 George Lynch .07 .20
25 Mark Price .12 .30
26 James Robinson .07 .20
27 Elmore Spencer .07 .20
28 Stacey King .07 .20
29 Corie Blount .07 .20
30 Dell Curry .07 .20
31 Reggie Miller .15 .40
32 Karl Malone .15 .40
33 Scottie Pippen .25 .60
34 Hakeem Olajuwon .15 .40
35 Clarence Weatherspoon .07 .20
36 Kevin Edwards .07 .20
37 Pete Myers .07 .20
38 Jeff Turner .07 .20
39 Ennis Whatley .07 .20
40 Calbert Cheaney .07 .20
41 Glen Rice .12 .30
42 Vin Baker .12 .30
43 Grant Long .07 .20
44 Derrick Coleman .10 .25
45 Rik Smits .10 .25
46 Chris Smith .07 .20
47 Carl Herrera .07 .20
48 Bob Martin .07 .20
49 Terrell Brandon .07 .20
50 David Robinson .20 .50
51 Danny Ferry .07 .20
52 Buck Williams .07 .20
53 Josh Grant .07 .20
54 Ed Pinckney .07 .20
55 Dikembe Mutombo .12 .30
56 Clifford Robinson .07 .20
57 Luther Wright .07 .20
58 Scott Burrell .07 .20
59 Stacey Augmon .10 .25
60 Jeff Malone .07 .20
61 Byron Houston .07 .20
62 Anthony Peeler .07 .20
63 Michael Adams .07 .20
64 Negele Knight .07 .20
65 Terry Cummings .12 .30
66 Christian Laettner .10 .25
67 Tracy Murray .07 .20
68 Sedale Threatt .07 .20
69 Dan Majerle .12 .30
70 Frank Brickowski .07 .20
71 Ken Norman .07 .20
72 Charles Smith .07 .20
73 Adam Keefe .07 .20
74 P.J. Brown .07 .20
75 Kevin Duckworth .07 .20
76 Shawn Bradley UER .07 .20
Bradely on back
77 Darnell Mee .07 .20
78 Nick Anderson .07 .20
79 Mark West .07 .20
80 B.J. Armstrong .07 .20
81 Dennis Scott .07 .20
82 Lindsey Hunter .07 .20
83 Derek Strong .07 .20
84 Mike Brown .07 .20
85 Antonio Harvey .07 .20
86 Anthony Bonner .07 .20
87 Sam Cassell .12 .30
88 Harold Miner .07 .20
89 Spud Webb .12 .30
90 Mookie Blaylock .07 .20
91 Greg Anthony .07 .20
92 Richard Petruska .07 .20
93 Sean Rooks .07 .20
94 Ervin Johnson .07 .20
95 Randy Brown .07 .20
96 Orlando Woolridge .07 .20
97 Charles Oakley .10 .25
98 Craig Ehlo .07 .20
99 Derek Harper .10 .25
100 Doug Edwards .07 .20
101 Muggsy Bogues .10 .25
102 Mitch Richmond .12 .30
103 Mahmoud Abdul-Rauf .07 .20
104 Joe Dumars .12 .30
105 Eric Riley .07 .20
106 Terry Mills .07 .20
107 Toni Kukoc .15 .40
108 Jon Koncak .07 .20
109 Haywoode Workman .07 .20
110 Todd Day .07 .20
111 Detlef Schrempf .12 .30
112 David Wesley .07 .20
113 Mark Jackson .12 .30
114 Doug Overton .07 .20
115 Vinny Del Negro .07 .20
116 Loy Vaught .07 .20
117 Mike Peplowski .07 .20
118 Bimbo Coles .07 .20
119 Rex Walters .07 .20
120 Sherman Douglas .07 .20
121 David Benoit .07 .20
122 John Salley .07 .20
123 Cedric Ceballos .07 .20
124 Chris Mills .07 .20
125 Robert Horry .12 .30
126 Johnny Newman .07 .20
127 Malcolm Mackey .07 .20
128 Terry Dehere .07 .20
129 Dino Radja .10 .25
130 Reggie Williams .07 .20
131 Xavier McDaniel .07 .20
132 Bobby Hurley .12 .30
133 Alonzo Mourning .15 .40
134 Isaiah Rider .12 .30
135 Antoine Carr .07 .20
136 Robert Pack .07 .20
137 Walt Williams .07 .20
138 Tyrone Corbin .07 .20
139 Popeye Jones .07 .20
140 Shawn Kemp .12 .30
141 Thurl Bailey .07 .20
142 James Worthy .15 .40
143 Scott Haskin .07 .20
144 Hubert Davis .07 .20
145 A.C. Green .12 .30
146 Dale Davis .07 .20
147 Nate McMillan .07 .20
148 Chris Morris .07 .20
149 Will Perdue .07 .20
150 Felton Spencer .07 .20
151 Rod Strickland .07 .20
152 Blue Edwards .07 .20
153 John Williams .07 .20
154 Rodney Rogers .07 .20

155 Acie Earl .07 .20
156 Hersey Hawkins .07 .20
157 Jamal Mashburn .12 .30
158 Don MacLean .07 .20
159 Micheal Williams .07 .20
160 Kenny Gattison .07 .20
161 Rich King .07 .20
162 Allan Houston .12 .30
163 Hoop-it up .07 .20
Men's Champions
164 Hoop-it up .07 .20
Women's Champions
Lisa Harrison
165 Hoop-it up .07 .20
Slam-Dunk Champions
Corey Etheridge
166 Danny Manning TO .10 .25
167 Robert Parish TO .12 .30
168 Alonzo Mourning TO .15 .40
169 Scottie Pippen TO .25 .60
170 Mark Price TO .12 .30
171 Jamal Mashburn TO .12 .30
172 Dikembe Mutombo TO .12 .30
173 Joe Dumars TO .12 .30
174 Chris Webber TO .20 .50
175 Hakeem Olajuwon TO .15 .40
176 Reggie Miller TO .15 .40
177 Ron Harper TO .10 .25
178 Nick Van Exel TO .12 .30
179 Steve Smith TO .10 .25
180 Vin Baker TO .12 .30
181 Isaiah Rider TO .12 .30
182 Derrick Coleman TO .10 .25
183 Patrick Ewing TO .15 .40
184 Shaquille O'Neal TO .30 .75
185 Clarence Weatherspoon TO .07 .20
186 Charles Barkley TO .20 .50
187 Clyde Drexler TO .15 .40
188 Mitch Richmond TO .12 .30
189 David Robinson TO .20 .50
190 Shawn Kemp TO .12 .30
191 Karl Malone TO .15 .40
192 Tom Gugliotta TO .07 .20
193 Kenny Anderson ASA .10 .25
194 Alonzo Mourning ASA .15 .40
195 Mark Price ASA .12 .30
196 John Stockton ASA .15 .40
197 Shaquille O'Neal ASA .30 .75
198 Latrell Sprewell ASA .15 .40
199 Charles Barkley PRO .20 .50
200 Chris Webber PRO .20 .50
201 Patrick Ewing PRO .15 .40
202 Dennis Rodman PRO .25 .60
203 Shawn Kemp PRO .12 .30
204 Michael Jordan PRO 1.00 2.50
205 Shaquille O'Neal PRO .30 .75
206 Larry Johnson PRO .12 .30
207 Tim Hardaway CL .12 .30
208 John Stockton CL .15 .40
209 Harold Miner CL .07 .20
210 B.J. Armstrong CL .07 .20
211 Vernon Maxwell .07 .20
212 John Stockton .15 .40
213 Luc Longley .07 .20
214 Sam Perkins .07 .20
215 Pooh Richardson .07 .20
216 Tyrone Corbin .07 .20
217 Mario Elie .07 .20
218 Bobby Phills .07 .20
219 Grant Hill RC .60 1.50
220 Gary Payton .12 .30
221 Tom Hammonds .07 .20
222 Danny Ainge .12 .30
223 Gary Grant .07 .20
224 Jim Jackson .07 .20
225 Chris Gatling .07 .20
226 Sergei Bazarevich RC .12 .30
227 Tony Dumas RC .12 .30
228 Andrew Lang .07 .20
229 Wesley Person RC .12 .30
230 Terry Porter .07 .20
231 Duane Causwell .07 .20
232 Shaquille O'Neal .30 .75
233 Antonio Davis .07 .20
234 Charles Barkley .20 .50
235 Tony Massenburg .07 .20
236 Ricky Pierce .07 .20
237 Scott Skiles .07 .20
238 Jalen Rose RC .30 .75
239 Charlie Ward RC .12 .30
240 Michael Jordan COMM 1.00 2.50
241 Elden Campbell .07 .20
242 Bill Cartwright .10 .25
243 Armon Gilliam UER .07 .20
Card numbered 372
244 Rick Fox .07 .20
245 Tim Breaux .07 .20
246 Monty Williams RC .12 .30
247 Dominique Wilkins .15 .40
248 Robert Parish .12 .30
249 Mark Jackson .12 .30
250 Jason Kidd RC .60 1.50
251 Andres Guibert .07 .20
252 Matt Geiger .07 .20
253 Stanley Roberts .07 .20
254 Jack Haley .07 .20
255 David Wingate .07 .20
256 John Crotty .07 .20
257 Brian Grant RC .20 .50
258 Otis Thorpe .07 .20
259 Clifford Rozier RC .12 .30
260 Grant Long .07 .20
261 Eric Mobley RC .12 .30
262 Dickey Simpkins RC .12 .30
263 J.R. Reid .07 .20
264 Kevin Willis .07 .20
265 Scott Brooks .07 .20
266 Glenn Robinson RC .25 .60
267 Dana Barros .07 .20
268 Ken Norman .07 .20
269 Herb Williams .07 .20
270 Dee Brown .07 .20
271 Steve Kerr .10 .25
272 Jon Barry .07 .20
273 Sean Elliott .12 .30
274 Elliot Perry .07 .20
275 Kenny Smith .10 .25
276 Sean Rooks .07 .20
277 Gheorghe Muresan .07 .20
278 Juwan Howard RC .20 .50
279 Steve Smith .10 .25
280 Anthony Bowie .07 .20
281 Moses Malone .12 .30
282 Olden Polynice .07 .20
283 Jo Jo English .07 .20
284 Marty Conlon .07 .20
285 Sam Mitchell .07 .20
286 Doug West .07 .20
287 Cedric Ceballos .07 .20
288 Lorenzo Williams .07 .20
289 Harold Ellis .07 .20
290 Doc Rivers .10 .25
291 Keith Tower .07 .20
292 Mark Bryant .07 .20
293 Oliver Miller .07 .20
294 Michael Adams .07 .20
295 Tree Rollins .07 .20
296 Eddie Jones RC .40 1.00
297 Malik Sealy .07 .20
298 Blue Edwards .07 .20
299 Brooks Thompson RC .12 .30
300 Benoit Benjamin .07 .20
301 Avery Johnson .10 .25
302 Larry Johnson .12 .30
303 John Starks .10 .25
304 Byron Scott .10 .25
305 Eric Murdock .07 .20
306 Jay Humphries .07 .20
307 Kenny Anderson .10 .25
308 Brian Williams .07 .20
309 Nick Van Exel .12 .30
310 Tim Hardaway .12 .30
311 Lee Mayberry .07 .20
312 Vlade Divac .12 .30
313 Donyell Marshall RC .12 .30
314 Anthony Mason .07 .20
315 Danny Manning .10 .25
316 Tyrone Hill .07 .20
317 Vincent Askew .07 .20
318 Khalid Reeves RC .12 .30
319 Ron Harper .10 .25
320 Brent Price .07 .20
321 Byron Houston .07 .20
322 Lamond Murray RC .12 .30
323 Bryant Stith .07 .20
324 Tom Gugliotta .07 .20
325 Jerome Kersey .07 .20
326 B.J.Tyler RC .12 .30
327 Antonio Lang RC .12 .30
328 Carlos Rogers RC .12 .30
329 Wayman Tisdale .07 .20
330 Kevin Gamble .07 .20
331 Eric Piatkowski RC .15 .40
332 Mitchell Butler .07 .20
333 Patrick Ewing .15 .40
334 Doug Smith .07 .20
335 Joe Kleine .07 .20
336 Keith Jennings .07 .20
337 Bill Curley RC .12 .30
338 Johnny Newman .07 .20
339 Howard Eisley RC .12 .30
340 Willie Anderson .07 .20
341 Aaron McKie RC .12 .30
342 Tom Chambers .12 .30
343 Scott Williams .07 .20
344 Harvey Grant .07 .20
345 Billy Owens .07 .20
346 Sharone Wright RC .12 .30
347 Michael Cage .07 .20
348 Vern Fleming .07 .20
349 Darrin Hancock RC .12 .30
350 Matt Fish .07 .20
351 Rony Seikaly .10 .25
352 Victor Alexander .07 .20
353 Anthony Miller RC .12 .30
354 Horace Grant .10 .25
355 Jayson Williams .07 .20
356 Dale Ellis .07 .20
357 Sarunas Marciulionis .07 .20
358 Anthony Avent .07 .20
359 Rex Chapman .07 .20
360 Askia Jones RC .12 .30
361 Bo Outlaw RC .12 .30
362 Chuck Person .10 .25
363 Danny Schayes .07 .20
364 Morlon Wiley .07 .20
365 Dontonio Wingfield RC .12 .30
366 Tony Smith .07 .20
367 Bill Wennington .07 .20
368 Bryon Russell .07 .20
369 Geert Hammink .07 .20
370 Eric Montross RC .12 .30
371 Cliff Levingston .07 .20
372 Stacey Augmon BP .10 .25
373 Eric Montross BP .07 .20
374 Alonzo Mourning BP .15 .40
375 Scottie Pippen BP .25 .60
376 Mark Price BP .12 .30
377 Jason Kidd BP .40 1.00
378 Jalen Rose BP .20 .50
379 Grant Hill BP .40 1.00
380 Latrell Sprewell BP .15 .40
381 Hakeem Olajuwon BP .15 .40
382 Reggie Miller BP .15 .40
383 Lamond Murray BP .07 .20
384 Eddie Jones BP .25 .60
385 Khalid Reeves BP .07 .20
386 Glenn Robinson BP .15 .40
387 Donyell Marshall BP .07 .20
388 Derrick Coleman BP .10 .25
389 Patrick Ewing BP .15 .40
390 Shaquille O'Neal BP .30 .75
391 Sharone Wright BP .07 .20
392 Charles Barkley BP .20 .50
393 Aaron McKie BP .07 .20
394 Brian Grant BP .12 .30
395 David Robinson BP .20 .50
396 Shawn Kemp BP .12 .30
397 Karl Malone BP .15 .40
398 Tom Gugliotta BP .07 .20
399 Hakeem Olajuwon TRIV .15 .40
400 Shaquille O'Neal TRIV .30 .75
401 Chris Webber TRIV .20 .50
402 Michael Jordan TRIV 1.00 2.50
403 David Robinson TRIV .20 .50
404 Shawn Kemp TRIV .12 .30
405 Patrick Ewing TRIV .15 .40
406 Charles Barkley TRIV .20 .50
407 Glenn Robinson DC .15 .40
408 Jason Kidd DC .40 1.00
409 Grant Hill DC .40 1.00
410 Donyell Marshall DC .07 .20
411 Sharone Wright DC .07 .20
412 Lamond Murray DC .07 .20
413 Brian Grant DC .12 .30
414 Eric Montross DC .07 .20
415 Eddie Jones DC .25 .60
416 Carlos Rogers DC .07 .20
417 Shawn Kemp CL .12 .30
418 Bobby Hurley CL .12 .30
419 Shawn Bradley CL .07 .20
420 Michael Jordan CL .40 1.00

1994-95 Collector's Choice Silver Signature

Issued one per Collector's Choice 12-card hobby pack, two per 13-card retail pack, and three per 20-card retail jumbo pack, these 420 standard-size cards parallel that of the basic 1994-95 Collector's Choice set. The difference is the player's facsimile autograph appears in silver-foil near the bottom and the front borders are colored in silver. A handful of first year players were not available for facsimile autographs and have team names scripted in silver foil instead. Please refer to the multiplier provided (and the values listed for the regular-issue 1994-95 Collector's Choice cards) to ascertain the value of the silver cards.

COMPLETE SET (420) 50.00 100.00
COMPLETE SERIES 1 (210) 20.00 40.00
COMPLETE SERIES 2 (210) 30.00 60.00
*STARS: 1.25X TO 3X BASE CARD HI
*RCs: 1X TO 2.5X BASE HI
*SUBSETS: .6X TO 1.5X BASE HI

1994-95 Collector's Choice Gold Signature

Issued one in every 36 first series 12-card hobby packs and 13-card retail packs, and one in every twenty 20-card retail jumbo packs, these 420 standard-size cards parallel that of the basic 1994-95 Collector's Choice set. The difference is the player's facsimile autograph which appears in gold-foil near the bottom and the front borders are colored in gold. To ascertain values on indivdual cards, please refer to the multiplier in the header, coupled with the value of the base card.

*STARS: 10X TO 25X BASE CARD HI
*RCs: 8X TO 20X BASE HI
*SUBSETS: 5X TO 12X BASE HI
1 Anfernee Hardaway 6.00 15.00
4 Chris Webber 6.00 15.00
23 Michael Jordan BB 30.00 80.00
140 Shawn Kemp 5.00 12.00
204 Michael Jordan PRO 15.00 40.00
240 Michael Jordan COMM 30.00 80.00
402 Michael Jordan TRIV 15.00 40.00
420 Michael Jordan CL 8.00 20.00

1994-95 Collector's Choice Blow-Ups

One of these oversized (5" by 7") cards was inserted exclusively into each series 2 hobby box. Each Blow-Up is identical in design and numbering to their corresponding basic issue card. According to information provided by Upper Deck at least 3,000 of these cards were autographed and randomly seeded into boxes. There are far fewer autographed Michael Jordan Blow-Ups than the other four players featured.

COMPLETE SET (5) 5.00 10.00
23 Michael Jordan BB 3.00 8.00
40 Calbert Cheaney .25 .60
76 Shawn Bradley .25 .60
132 Bobby Hurley .40 1.00
140 Shawn Kemp .40 1.00
A23 Michael Jordan AU 3500.00 5000.00
A40 Calbert Cheaney AU 15.00 30.00
A76 Shawn Bradley AU 15.00 30.00
A132 Bobby Hurley AU 15.00 30.00
A140 Shawn Kemp AU 40.00 100.00

1994-95 Collector's Choice Crash the Game Assists

These fifteen standard-size Crash the Game Assists cards were randomly inserted exclusively into first series retail packs at a rate of one in 20. Cards that featured players who tallied 750 or more assists during the 1994-95 campaign were redeemable for a 15-card parallel Crash the Game Assists Redemption set. Only John Stockton eclipsed the mark. The fronts feature a color-action photo with the background of the game in black and white. The top has the player's name in a box the color of his team and the bottom has the words "You Crash The Game" in foil with the player's position behind it in his team's color. The back says 750 assists at the top below his name surrounded by the player's team color. There are instructions on how to redeem your cards if you win. The exchange deadline was June 16th, 1995. The redemption cards were delayed in shipping until late October, 1995.

COMPLETE SET (15) 4.00 10.00
*RED.CARDS: .2X TO .5X HI COLUMN
A1 Michael Adams .40 1.00
A2 Kenny Anderson .50 1.25
A3 Mookie Blaylock .40 1.00
A4 Muggsy Bogues .50 1.25
A5 Sherman Douglas .40 1.00
A6 Anfernee Hardaway 1.00 2.50
A7 Tim Hardaway .60 1.50
A8 Lindsey Hunter .40 1.00
A9 Mark Jackson .60 1.50
A10 Kevin Johnson .60 1.50
A11 Eric Murdock .40 1.00
A12 Mark Price .60 1.50
A13 John Stockton .75 2.00
A14 Rod Strickland .40 1.00
A15 Micheal Williams .40 1.00

1994-95 Collector's Choice Crash the Game Rebounds

These fifteen standard-size Crash the Game Rebounds cards were randomly inserted exclusively into second series retail packs at a rate of one in 20. Cards that featured players who grabbed 1,000 or more rebounds during the 1994-95 campaign were redeemable for a 15-card parallel Crash the Game Rebounds Redemption set. The card design is the same as the Assists set except on the back it says 1,000 Rebounds. Only Dikembe Mutombo eclipsed the mark. The exchange deadline was June 30, 1995. The redemption cards were delayed in shipping until late October, 1995.

COMPLETE SET (15) 6.00 15.00
*RED.CARDS: .2X TO .5X HI COLUMN
R1 Derrick Coleman .50 1.25
R2 Patrick Ewing .75 2.00
R3 Horace Grant .50 1.25
R4 Shawn Kemp .60 1.50
R5 Karl Malone .75 2.00
R6 Alonzo Mourning .75 2.00
R7 Dikembe Mutombo .60 1.50
R8 Charles Oakley .50 1.25
R9 Hakeem Olajuwon .75 2.00
R10 Shaquille O'Neal 1.50 4.00
R11 Olden Polynice .40 1.00
R12 David Robinson 1.00 2.50
R13 Dennis Rodman 1.25 3.00
R14 Otis Thorpe .40 1.00
R15 Kevin Willis .40 1.00

1994-95 Collector's Choice Crash the Game Rookie Scoring

These fifteen standard-size Crash the Game Rookie Scoring cards were randomly inserted exclusively into second series hobby packs at a rate of one in 20. Cards that featured rookies who scored more than 1,250 points during the 1994-95 campaign were redeemable for a 15-card parallel Crash the Game Rookie Scoring Redemption set. The card design is the same as the Assists set except on the back it says 1,250 Points. Only Grant Hill and Glenn Robinson eclipsed the mark. The exchange deadline was June 30th, 1995. The redemption cards were delayed in shipping until late October, 1995.

COMPLETE SET (15) 4.00 10.00
*RED.CARDS: .2X TO .5X HI COLUMN
S1 Tony Dumas .25 .60
S2 Brian Grant .40 1.00
S3 Grant Hill 1.25 3.00
S4 Juwan Howard .40 1.00
S5 Eddie Jones .75 2.00
S6 Jason Kidd 1.25 3.00
S7 Donyell Marshall .25 .60
S8 Eric Montross .25 .60
S9 Lamond Murray .25 .60
S10 Khalid Reeves .25 .60
S11 Glenn Robinson .50 1.25
S12 Jalen Rose .60 1.50
S13 Dickey Simpkins .25 .60
S14 Charlie Ward .25 .60
S15 Sharone Wright .25 .60

1994-95 Collector's Choice Crash the Game Scoring

These fifteen standard-size Crash the Game Scoring cards were randomly inserted exclusively into first series hobby packs at a rate of one in 20. Cards that featured players who posted 2,000 or more points during the 1994-95 campaign were redeemable for a 15-card parallel Crash the Game Scoring Redemption set. The card design is the same as the Assists set except on the back it says 2,000 Points. Karl Malone, Shaquille O'Neal, Hakeem Olajuwon and David Robinson all eclipsed the mark. The exchange deadline was June 30, 1995. The redemption cards were delayed in shipping until late October, 1995.

COMPLETE SET (15) 6.00 15.00
*RED.CARDS: .2X TO .5X HI COLUMN
S1 Charles Barkley 1.00 2.50
S2 Derrick Coleman .50 1.25
S3 Joe Dumars .60 1.50
S4 Patrick Ewing .75 2.00
S5 Karl Malone .75 2.00
S6 Reggie Miller .75 2.00
S7 Shaquille O'Neal 1.50 4.00
S8 Hakeem Olajuwon .75 2.00
S9 Scottie Pippen 1.25 3.00
S10 Glen Rice .60 1.50
S11 Mitch Richmond .60 1.50
S12 David Robinson 1.00 2.50
S13 Latrell Sprewell .75 2.00
S14 Chris Webber 1.00 2.50
S15 Dominique Wilkins .75 2.00

1994-95 Collector's Choice Draft Trade

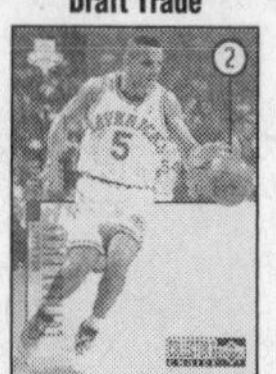

This 10-card set was available only by redeeming a Draft Trade card that was randomly seeded into one in every 36 first series Collector's Choice hobby or retail packs. The fronts have a color-action photo with the top-half having the background of the game in black and white. The bottom of the card has a white background. On the left side of the card are the words "NBA Draft Lottery Picks" with the player's name above it. The backs have the player's name and information set against the colors of his team. The expiration date on the redemption was June 16th, 1995.

COMPLETE SET (10) 2.50 6.00
1 Glenn Robinson .40 1.00
2 Jason Kidd 1.00 2.50
3 Grant Hill 1.00 2.50
4 Donyell Marshall .20 .50
5 Juwan Howard .30 .75
6 Sharone Wright .20 .50
7 Lamond Murray .20 .50
8 Brian Grant .30 .75
9 Eric Montross .20 .50
10 Eddie Jones .60 1.50

1995-96 Collector's Choice

These 410-standard size cards, issued in two seperate series of 210 and 200 cards respectively, comprise Upper Deck's 1995-96 Collector's Choice set. Cards were primarily issued in 12-card hobby and retail packs (suggested retail price of ninety-nine cents) and five-card retail mini-packs. In addition, large retail chain stores received complete factory sets around the end of the season (SRP $29.97). Each factory set contains a basic 410 card set, four Collector's Choice Jordan Collection inserts, four Player's Club Platinum inserts and a special 5" by 7" Bulls Commemorative card celebrating their 70 win season. Regular issue cards feature white-bordered fronts with color player action shots. The backs have a color photo and statistics. The following subsets are included: Fun Facts (166-194), Professor Dunk (195-208), Scouting Report (321-349), Playoff Time (350-365), I Love this Team (366-394), Photo Gallery (395-403) and Shawn Kemp's Top 40 (404-408). Special Crash Packs containing only inserts (an assortion of Player's Club, Player's Club Platinum and Crash the Game cards) were randomly inserted into one in every 175 12-card packs. Rookie Cards of note include Michael Finley, Kevin Garnett, Joe Smith, Jerry Stackhouse and Damon Stoudamire.

COMPLETE SET (410) 17.50 35.00
COMPLETE FACT.SET (419) 25.00 35.00
COMPLETE SERIES 1 (210) 7.50 15.00
COMPLETE SERIES 2 (200) 10.00 20.00
1 Rod Strickland .07 .20
2 Larry Johnson .12 .30
3 Mahmoud Abdul-Rauf .07 .20
4 Joe Dumars .12 .30
5 Jason Kidd .20 .50
6 Avery Johnson .10 .25
7 Dee Brown .07 .20
8 Brian Williams .07 .20
9 Nick Van Exel .12 .30
10 Dennis Rodman .25 .60
11 Rony Seikaly .10 .25
12 Harvey Grant .07 .20
13 Craig Ehlo .07 .20
14 Derek Harper .10 .25
15 Oliver Miller .07 .20
16 Dennis Scott .07 .20
17 Ed Pinckney .07 .20
18 Eric Piatkowski .10 .25
19 B.J. Armstrong .07 .20
20 Tyrone Hill .07 .20
21 Malik Sealy .07 .20
22 Clyde Drexler .15 .40
23 Aaron McKie .07 .20
24 Harold Miner .07 .20
25 Bobby Hurley .12 .30
26 Dell Curry .07 .20
27 Micheal Williams .07 .20
28 Adam Keefe .07 .20
29 Antonio Harvey .07 .20
30 Billy Owens .07 .20
31 Nate McMillan .07 .20
32 J.R. Reid .07 .20
33 Grant Hill .20 .50
34 Charles Barkley .20 .50
35 Tyrone Corbin .07 .20
36 Don MacLean .07 .20
37 Kenny Smith .10 .25
38 Juwan Howard .12 .30
39 Charles Smith .07 .20
40 Shawn Kemp .12 .30
41 Dana Barros .07 .20
42 Vin Baker .10 .25
43 Armon Gilliam .07 .20
44 Spud Webb .12 .30
45 Michael Jordan 1.00 2.50
46 Scott Williams .07 .20
47 Vlade Divac .12 .30
48 Roy Tarpley .07 .20
49 Bimbo Coles .07 .20
50 David Robinson .20 .50
51 Terry Dehere .07 .20
52 Bobby Phills .07 .20
53 Sherman Douglas .07 .20
54 Rodney Rogers .07 .20
55 Detlef Schrempf .12 .30
56 Calbert Cheaney .07 .20
57 Tom Gugliotta .07 .20
58 Jeff Turner .07 .20
59 Mookie Blaylock .07 .20
60 Bill Curley .07 .20
61 Chris Dudley .07 .20
62 Popeye Jones .07 .20
63 Scott Burrell .07 .20
64 Dale Davis .07 .20
65 Mitchell Butler .07 .20
66 Pervis Ellison .07 .20
67 Todd Day .07 .20
68 Carl Herrera .07 .20
69 Jeff Hornacek .10 .25
70 Vincent Askew .07 .20
71 A.C. Green .12 .30
72 Kevin Gamble .07 .20
73 Chris Gatling .07 .20
74 Otis Thorpe .07 .20
75 Michael Cage .07 .20
76 Carlos Rogers .07 .20
77 Gheorghe Muresan .07 .20
78 Olden Polynice .07 .20
79 Grant Long .07 .20
80 Allan Houston .10 .25
81 Bo Outlaw .07 .20
82 Clarence Weatherspoon .07 .20
83 Tony Dumas .07 .20
84 Herb Williams .07 .20
85 P.J. Brown .07 .20
86 Robert Horry .10 .25
87 Byron Scott .10 .25
88 Horace Grant .10 .25
89 Dominique Wilkins .15 .40
90 Doug West .07 .20
91 Antoine Carr .07 .20
92 Dickey Simpkins .07 .20
93 Elden Campbell .07 .20
94 Kevin Johnson .12 .30
95 Rex Chapman .07 .20
96 John Williams .07 .20
97 Tim Hardaway .12 .30
98 Rik Smits .10 .25
99 Rex Walters .07 .20
100 Robert Parish .12 .30
101 Isaiah Rider .12 .30
102 Sarunas Marciulionis .07 .20
103 Andrew Lang .07 .20
104 Eric Mobley .07 .20
105 Randy Brown .07 .20
106 John Stockton .15 .40
107 Lamond Murray .07 .20
108 Will Perdue .07 .20
109 Wayman Tisdale .07 .20
110 John Starks .10 .25
111 John Salley .07 .20
112 Lucious Harris .07 .20
113 Jeff Malone .07 .20
114 Anthony Bowie .07 .20
115 Vinny Del Negro .07 .20
116 Michael Adams .07 .20
117 Chris Mullin .12 .30
118 Benoit Benjamin .07 .20
119 Byron Houston .07 .20
120 LaPhonso Ellis .07 .20
121 Doug Overton .07 .20
122 Jerome Kersey .07 .20
123 Greg Minor .07 .20
124 Christian Laettner .10 .25
125 Mark Price .12 .30
126 Kevin Willis .07 .20
127 Kenny Anderson .10 .25
128 Marty Conlon .07 .20
129 Blue Edwards .07 .20
130 Danny Schayes .07 .20
131 Duane Ferrell .07 .20
132 Charles Oakley .10 .25
133 Brian Grant .10 .25
134 Reggie Williams .07 .20
135 Steve Kerr .10 .25
136 Khalid Reeves .07 .20
137 David Benoit .07 .20
138 Derrick Coleman .10 .25
139 Anthony Peeler .07 .20
140 Jim Jackson .07 .20
141 Stacey Augmon .10 .25
142 Sam Cassell .12 .30
143 Derrick McKey .07 .20
144 Danny Ferry .07 .20
145 Anfernee Hardaway .20 .50
146 Clifford Robinson .07 .20
147 B.J. Tyler .07 .20
148 Mark West .07 .20
149 David Wingate .07 .20
150 Willie Anderson .07 .20
151 Hersey Hawkins .07 .20
152 Bryant Stith .07 .20
153 Dan Majerle .12 .30
154 Chris Smith .07 .20
155 Donyell Marshall .07 .20
156 Loy Vaught .07 .20
157 Reggie Miller .15 .40
158 Hubert Davis .07 .20
159 Ron Harper .10 .25
160 Lee Mayberry .07 .20
161 Eddie Jones .15 .40
162 Shawn Bradley .07 .20
163 Nick Anderson .07 .20
164 Ervin Johnson .07 .20
165 Walt Williams .07 .20
166 Steve Smith FF .10 .25
167 Dino Radja FF .10 .25
168 Alonzo Mourning FF .15 .40
169 Michael Jordan FF 1.00 2.50
170 Tyrone Hill FF .07 .20
171 Jamal Mashburn FF .12 .30
172 Dikembe Mutombo FF .12 .30
173 Grant Hill FF .20 .50
with Michael Jordan
174 Latrell Sprewell FF .12 .30
175 Hakeem Olajuwon FF .15 .40
176 Reggie Miller FF .15 .40
177 Pooh Richardson FF .07 .20
178 Cedric Ceballos FF .07 .20
179 Glen Rice FF .12 .30
180 Glenn Robinson FF .12 .30
181 Isaiah Rider FF .12 .30
182 Derrick Coleman FF .10 .25
183 Patrick Ewing FF .15 .40
184 Shaquille O'Neal FF .30 .75
185 Dana Barros FF .07 .20
186 Dan Majerle FF .12 .30
187 Clifford Robinson FF .07 .20
188 Mitch Richmond FF .12 .30
189 David Robinson FF .20 .50
190 Gary Payton FF .12 .30
191 Oliver Miller FF .07 .20
192 Karl Malone FF .15 .40
193 Kevin Pritchard FF .07 .20
194 Chris Webber FF .15 .40
195 Michael Jordan PD 1.00 2.50
196 Hakeem Olajuwon PD .15 .40
197 Vin Baker PD .10 .25
198 Grant Hill PD .20 .50
199 Clyde Drexler PD .15 .40
200 Chris Webber PD .15 .40
201 Shawn Kemp PD .12 .30
202 Shaquille O'Neal PD .30 .75
203 Stacey Augmon PD .10 .25
204 David Benoit PD .07 .20
205 Rodney Rogers PD .07 .20
206 Latrell Sprewell PD .12 .30
207 Brian Grant PD .10 .25
208 Lamond Murray PD .07 .20
209 Shawn Kemp CL .10 .25
210 Michael Jordan CL .40 1.00
211 Cory Alexander RC .12 .30
212 Vernon Maxwell .07 .20
213 George Lynch .07 .20
214 Terry Mills .07 .20
215 Scottie Pippen .20 .50
216 Donald Royal .07 .20
217 Wesley Person .07 .20
218 Antonio Davis .07 .20
219 Glenn Robinson .12 .30
220 Jerry Stackhouse RC .40 1.00
221 James Robinson .07 .20
222 Chris Mills .07 .20
223 Chuck Person .10 .25
224 Duane Causwell .07 .20
225 Gary Payton .12 .30
226 Eric Montross .07 .20
227 Felton Spencer .07 .20
228 Scott Skiles .07 .20
229 Latrell Sprewell .12 .30
230 Sedale Threatt .07 .20
231 Mark Bryant .07 .20
232 Buck Williams .07 .20
233 Brian Williams .07 .20
234 Sharone Wright .07 .20
235 Karl Malone .15 .40
236 Kevin Edwards .07 .20
237 Muggsy Bogues .10 .25
238 Mario Elie .07 .20
239 Rasheed Wallace RC .40 1.00
240 George Zidek RC .12 .30
241 Cedric Ceballos .07 .20
242 Alan Henderson RC .12 .30
243 Joe Kleine .07 .20
244 Patrick Ewing .15 .40
245 Sasha Danilovic RC .12 .30
246 Bill Wennington .07 .20
247 Steve Smith .10 .25
248 Bryant Stith .07 .20
249 Dino Radja .10 .25
250 Monty Williams .07 .20
251 Andrew DeClercq RC .12 .30
252 Sean Elliott .12 .30
253 Rick Fox .07 .20
254 Lionel Simmons .07 .20
255 Dikembe Mutombo .12 .30
256 Lindsey Hunter .07 .20
257 Terrell Brandon .07 .20
258 Shawn Respert RC .12 .30
259 Rodney Rogers .07
260 Bryon Russell .07
261 David Wesley .07
262 Ken Norman .07
263 Mitch Richmond .12
264 Sam Perkins .07
265 Hakeem Olajuwon .15
266 Brian Shaw .07
267 B.J. Armstrong .07
268 Jalen Rose .15
269 Bryant Reeves RC .12
270 Cherokee Parks RC .12
271 Dennis Rodman .25
272 Kendall Gill .07
273 Elliot Perry .07
274 Anthony Mason .07
275 Kevin Garnett RC 1.00
276 Damon Stoudamire RC .30
277 Lawrence Moten RC .12
278 Ed O'Bannon RC .12
279 Toni Kukoc .12
280 Greg Ostertag RC .12
281 Tom Hammonds .07
282 Yinka Dare .07
283 Michael Smith .07
284 Clifford Rozier .07
285 Gary Trent RC .12
286 Shaquille O'Neal .30
287 Luc Longley .07
288 Bob Sura RC .12
289 Dana Barros .07
290 Lorenzo Williams .07
291 Haywoode Workman .07
292 Randolph Childress RC .12
293 Doc Rivers .10
294 Chris Webber .15
295 Kurt Thomas RC .12
296 Greg Anthony .07
297 Tyus Edney RC .12
298 Danny Manning .10
299 Brent Barry RC .20
300 Joe Smith RC .25
301 Pooh Richardson .07
302 Mark Jackson .12
303 Richard Dumas .07
304 Michael Finley RC .40
305 Theo Ratliff RC .20
306 Gary Grant .07
307 Jamal Mashburn .12
308 Corliss Williamson RC .12
309 Eric Williams RC .12
310 Zan Tabak .07
311 Eric Murdock .07
312 Sherrell Ford RC .12
313 Terry Davis .07
314 Vern Fleming .07
315 Jason Caffey RC .12
316 Mario Bennett RC .12
317 David Vaughn RC .12
318 Loren Meyer RC .12
319 Travis Best RC .12
320 Byron Scott .10
321 Mookie Blaylock SR .07
322 Dee Brown SR .07
323 Alonzo Mourning SR .15
324 Michael Jordan SR 1.00
325 Terrell Brandon SR .07
326 Jim Jackson SR .07
327 Dikembe Mutombo SR .12
328 Grant Hill SR .20
329 Joe Smith SR UER .15
Team stats say Seattle
Should be Golden State
330 Clyde Drexler SR .15
331 Reggie Miller SR .15
332 Lamond Murray SR .07
333 Nick Van Exel SR .12
334 Glen Rice SR .12
335 Glenn Robinson SR .12
336 Christian Laettner SR .10
337 Kenny Anderson SR .10
338 Patrick Ewing SR .15
339 Shaquille O'Neal SR .30
340 Jerry Stackhouse SR .25
341 Charles Barkley SR .20
342 Clifford Robinson SR .07
343 Brian Grant SR .10
344 David Robinson SR .20
345 Shawn Kemp SR .12
346 Damon Stoudamire SR .20
347 Karl Malone SR .15
348 Bryant Reeves SR .07
349 Juwan Howard SR .12
350 Nick Anderson .07
Dee Brown PT
351 Rik Smits PT .10
352 Herb Williams .07
Greg Dreiling PT
353 Michael Jordan PT 1.00
354 David Robinson PT .20
355 Terry Porter .12
Kevin Johnson PT
356 Clyde Drexler PT .15
357 Cedric Ceballos PT .07
358 Horace Grant .10
Group PT
359 Reggie Miller PT .15
360 Avery Johnson .12
Nick Van Exel PT
361 Hakeem Olajuwon .15
Robert Horry PT
362 Rik Smits PT .10
363 David Robinson .20
Hakeem Olajuwon PT
364 Robert Horry PT .10
365 Kenny Smith PT .10
366 Stacey Augmon LOVE .10
367 Sherman Douglas LOVE .07
368 Larry Johnson LOVE .12
369 Scottie Pippen LOVE .20
370 Tyrone Hill LOVE .07
371 Jamal Mashburn LOVE .12
372 Mahmoud Abdul-Rauf LOVE .07
373 Grant Hill LOVE .20
374 Latrell Sprewell LOVE .12
375 Sam Cassell LOVE .12
376 Rik Smits LOVE .10
377 Terry Dehere LOVE .07
378 Eddie Jones LOVE .15
379 Billy Owens LOVE .07
380 Vin Baker LOVE .10
381 Isaiah Rider LOVE .12
382 Kenny Anderson LOVE .10
383 John Starks LOVE .10
384 Anfernee Hardaway LOVE .20
385 Sharone Wright LOVE .07
386 Charles Barkley LOVE .20
387 Clifford Robinson LOVE .07

lt Williams LOVE .07 .20
n Elliott LOVE .12 .30
y Payton LOVE .12 .30
los Rogers LOVE .07 .20
n Stockton LOVE .15 .40
g Anthony LOVE .07 .20
is Webber LOVE .15 .40
y Payton PG .12 .30
okie Blaylock PG .07 .20
arles Barkley PG .20 .50
ant Hill PG .20 .50
fernee Hardaway PG .20 .50
nny Anderson PG .10 .25
rk Jackson PG .12 .30
l Malone PG .15 .40
ery Johnson PG .10 .25
ry Johnson 40 .12 .30
k Van Exel 40 .12 .30
Baker 40 .10 .25
son Kidd 40 .20 .50
vid Robinson 40 .20 .50
awn Kemp CL .08 .25
chael Jordan CL .40 1.00
ulls Comm. Card 2.50 6.00
d with Factory set

995-96 Collector's Choice Player's Club

one per pack in both first and second series or's Choice 12-card packs, these 410 standard-rds parallel the basic 1995-96 Collector's set. Unlike the basic issue cards, Player's Club nts feature silver borders (except on the ess subset cards) and Player's Club logo. efer to the multiplier provided below (and the isted for the regular issue 1995-96 Collector's cards) to ascertain the value of individual s Club cards.

LETE SET (410) 35.00 70.00
LETE SERIES 1 (210) 15.00 30.00
LETE SERIES 2 (200) 20.00 40.00
S: 1.25X TO 3X BASE CARD HI
1X TO 2.5X BASE HI
ETS: .75X TO 2X BASE HI

995-96 Collector's Choice Player's Club Platinum

randomly one in every thirty-five first and series 12-card packs (and also packaged four il factory set at the end of the season), these ndard-size cards parallel the basic 1995-96 or's Choice series. Unlike the basic issue cards, s Club Platinum card fronts feature a special foil paper stock and Player's Club Platinum o ascertain values on individual cards, please the multiplier in the header, coupled with the f the base card.

S: 12.5X TO 30X BASE CARD HI
8X TO 20X BASE HI
ETS: 8X TO 20X BASE HI
ant Hill FF 8.00 20.00
Michael Jordan

995-96 Collector's Choice Crash the Game Assists/Rebounds

randomly into one in every five second series d packs, cards from this 90-card set feature eparate versions of thirty different player cards. layer was given three separate specific game if the player depicted on the card tallied 10 or ssists or rebounds on that date, the card was able for a special 30-card Crash the Game /Rebounds Silver Trade set. Losing cards are d with an "L" and winning cards with a "W". The g cards are actually in shorter supply than cards due to the fact that many of them were in for redemption and then destroyed.

CARDS: 1.25X TO 3X HI COLUMN
SER.2 STATED ODDS 1:49
R RED.CARDS: .2X TO .5X HI COLUMN
RED.CARDS: 1.5X TO 4X SILVER RED.
ED.SET PER WINNER BY MAIL
chael Jordan 1/30 L 4.00 10.00
ichael Jordan 2/22 L 4.00 10.00
ichael Jordan 3/19 L 4.00 10.00
Hardaway 2/4 L .50 1.25
m Hardaway 3/12 L .50 1.25
m Hardaway 4/11 W .50 1.25
van Howard 2/2 L .50 1.25
wan Howard 2/21 L .50 1.25
wan Howard 3/30 L .50 1.25
wn Kemp 1/29 L .50 1.25
hawn Kemp 3/15 W .50 1.25
hawn Kemp 4/3 L .50 1.25
k Van Exel 2/4 L .50 1.25
ick Van Exel 2/21 L .50 1.25
ick Van Exel 4/14 L .50 1.25
okie Blaylock 2/16 L .30 .75
ookie Blaylock 3/8 L .30 .75
ookie Blaylock 4/20 L .30 .75
n Stockton 2/13 W .60 1.50
ohn Stockton 3/6 W .60 1.50
ohn Stockton 4/14 W .60 1.50
ottie Pippen 1/28 L .75 2.00
cottie Pippen 3/15 L .75 2.00
cottie Pippen 4/11 L .75 2.00
Baker 2/3 L .40 1.00
in Baker 3/4 W .40 1.00
in Baker 4/5 W .40 1.00
amond Murray 2/3 L .30 .75
Lamond Murray 2/17 L .30 .75
Lamond Murray 3/30 L .30 .75
avid Robinson 2/15 W .75 2.00
David Robinson 3/14 W .75 2.00
David Robinson 4/13 W .75 2.00
ason Kidd 2/6 L .75 2.00
Jason Kidd 3/19 L .75 2.00
Jason Kidd 4/13 W .75 2.00
od Strickland 2/15 L .30 .75
Rod Strickland 3/8 W .30 .75
Rod Strickland 4/5 L .30 .75
len Rice 1/29 L .50 1.25
Glen Rice 2/28 L .50 1.25
Glen Rice 4/2 L .50 1.25
nfernee Hardaway 2/4 W .75 2.00
Anfernee Hardaway 3/31 L .75 2.00
Anfernee Hardaway 4/21 W .75 2.00
akeem Olajuwon 2/15 L .60 1.50
Hakeem Olajuwon 3/8 L .60 1.50
Hakeem Olajuwon 4/15 W .60 1.50
enny Anderson 2/14 W .40 1.00
Kenny Anderson 2/29 W .40 1.00
Kenny Anderson 3/29 L .40 1.00
harone Wright 2/14 L .30 .75
Sharone Wright 3/22 L .30 .75
Sharone Wright 4/17 L .30 .75
C19 Dikembe Mutombo 2/16 L .50 1.25
C19B Dikembe Mutombo 3/2 W .50 1.25
C19C Dikembe Mutombo 4/5 W .50 1.25
C20 Muggsy Bogues 2/1 L .40 1.00
C20B Muggsy Bogues 2/21 L .40 1.00
C20C Muggsy Bogues 3/20 L .40 1.00
C21 Reggie Miller 2/18 L .60 1.50
C21B Reggie Miller 3/5 L .60 1.50
C21C Reggie Miller 4/8 L .60 1.50
C22 Danny Manning 2/6 L .40 1.00
C22B Danny Manning 3/3 L .40 1.00
C22C Danny Manning 4/16 L .40 1.00
C23 Christian Laettner 2/5 L .40 1.00
C23B Christian Laettner 3/10 L .40 1.00
C23C Christian Laettner 3/27 W .40 1.00
C24 Eric Montross 2/14 L .30 .75
C24B Eric Montross 3/8 L .30 .75
C24C Eric Montross 3/31 L .30 .75
C25 Patrick Ewing 2/21 L .60 1.50
C25B Patrick Ewing 3/29 W .60 1.50
C25C Patrick Ewing 4/3 W .60 1.50
C26 Damon Stoudamire 1/30 L 1.25 3.00
C26B Damon Stoudamire 3/10 L 1.25 3.00
C26C Damon Stoudamire 3/22 W 1.25 3.00
C27 Bryant Reeves 2/28 L .50 1.25
C27B Bryant Reeves 3/31 L .50 1.25
C27C Bryant Reeves 4/9 L .50 1.25
C28 Joe Dumars 2/15 L .50 1.25
C28B Joe Dumars 3/22 L .50 1.25
C28C Joe Dumars 4/13 L .50 1.25
C29 Tyrone Hill 2/6 L .30 .75
C29B Tyrone Hill 3/10 L .30 .75
C29C Tyrone Hill 4/20 L .30 .75
C30 Brian Grant 2/13 L .40 1.00
C30B Brian Grant 3/20 L .40 1.00
C30C Brian Grant 4/21 L .40 1.00

1995-96 Collector's Choice Crash the Game Scoring

Issued randomly into one in every five first series 12-card packs, cards from this 81-card set features three separate versions of twenty-seven different player cards. Each player is matched up against three different teams (two within their conference and one outside of their conference). If the player depicted on the card scored 30 or more points versus the team depicted on the card, the card was redeemable for a special 30-card Crash the Game Scoring Silver Trade set. Losing cards are signified with an "L" and winning cards are signified with a "W". The winning cards are actually in shorter supply than losing cards due to the fact that many of them were mailed in for redemption and then destroyed.

*GOLD CARDS: 1.5X TO 4X HI COLUMN
GOLD: SER.1 STATED ODDS 1:50
*SILVER RED.CARDS: .2X TO .5X HI COLUMN
*GOLD RED.CARDS: 1.5X TO 4X SILVER RED.
ONE RED.SET PER WINNER BY MAIL
C1 Michael Jordan HOU W 4.00 10.00
C1B Michael Jordan NY W 4.00 10.00
C1C Michael Jordan ORL W 4.00 10.00
C2 Kenny Anderson CLE L .40 1.00
C2B Kenny Anderson LAC L .40 1.00
C2C Kenny Anderson MIA L .40 1.00
C3 Charles Barkley CLE L .75 2.00
C3B Charles Barkley GS W .75 2.00
C3C Charles Barkley SA W .75 2.00
C4 Dana Barros ATL L .30 .75
C4B Dana Barros BOS W .30 .75
C4C Dana Barros LAL L .30 .75
C5 Anfernee Hardaway CHI W .75 2.00
C5B Anfernee Hardaway SA W .75 2.00
C5C Anfernee Hardaway MIL W .75 2.00
C6 Mookie Blaylock DAL L .30 .75
C6B Mookie Blaylock DET L .30 .75
C6C Mookie Blaylock TOR L .30 .75
C7 Lamond Murray ATL L .30 .75
C7B Lamond Murray MIN L .30 .75
C7C Lamond Murray VAN L .30 .75
C8 Karl Malone HOU L .60 1.50
C8B Karl Malone NY L .60 1.50
C8C Karl Malone POR W .60 1.50
C9 Alonzo Mourning CHI L .60 1.50
C9B Alonzo Mourning IND L .60 1.50
C9C Alonzo Mourning WASH W .60 1.50
C10 Hakeem Olajuwon LAL W .60 1.50
C10B Hakeem Olajuwon ORL W .60 1.50
C10C Hakeem Olajuwon POR W .60 1.50
C11 Mark Price CHI L .50 1.25
C11B Mark Price NJ L .50 1.25
C11C Mark Price SEA L .50 1.25
C12 Isaiah Rider BOS L .50 1.25
C12B Isaiah Rider PHO L .50 1.25
C12C Isaiah Rider SAC L .50 1.25
C13 Glen Rice NJ W .50 1.25
C13B Glen Rice SAC W .50 1.25
C13C Glen Rice WASH W .50 1.25
C14 Mitch Richmond LAL L .50 1.25
C14B Mitch Richmond MIN W .50 1.25
C14C Mitch Richmond NJ L .50 1.25
C15 Chris Webber GS W .60 1.50
C15B Chris Webber IND L .60 1.50
C15C Chris Webber PHI L .60 1.50
C16 Nick Van Exel DAL L .50 1.25
C16B Nick Van Exel MIL L .50 1.25
C16C Nick Van Exel SAC L .50 1.25
C17 Mahmoud Abdul-Rauf CHA L .30 .75
C17B Mahmoud Abdul-Rauf PHO W .30 .75
C17C Mahmoud Abdul-Rauf SEA L .30 .75
C18 Dominique Wilkins PHI L .60 1.50
C18B Dominique Wilkins POR L .60 1.50
C18C Dominique Wilkins TOR L .60 1.50
C19 Patrick Ewing BOS W .60 1.50
C19B Patrick Ewing CHA L .60 1.50
C19C Patrick Ewing PHO L .60 1.50
C20 David Robinson DEN W .75 2.00
C20B David Robinson SEA W .75 2.00
C20C David Robinson WASH W .75 2.00
C21 Shawn Kemp DEN L .50 1.25
C21B Shawn Kemp DET L .50 1.25
C21C Shawn Kemp UTAH L .50 1.25
C22 Jason Kidd IND W .75 2.00
C22B Jason Kidd IND L .75 2.00
C22C Jason Kidd SA L .75 2.00
C23 Glenn Robinson ATL W .50 1.25
C23B Glenn Robinson CHA L .50 1.25
C23C Glenn Robinson VAN L .50 1.25
C24 Reggie Miller MIN L .60 1.50
C24B Reggie Miller NY L .60 1.50
C24C Reggie Miller ORL L .60 1.50
C25 Joe Dumars CLE L .50 1.25
C25B Joe Dumars MIL L .50 1.25
C25C Joe Dumars UTAH L .50 1.25
C26 Latrell Sprewell DAL L .50 1.25
C26B Latrell Sprewell HOU L .50 1.25
C26C Latrell Sprewell MIA L .50 1.25
C27 Clifford Robinson LAC L .30 .75
C27B Clifford Robinson PHI L .30 .75
C27C Clifford Robinson UTAH W .30 .75
XC28 Damon Stoudamire 1.25 3.00
XC29 Bryant Reeves .50 1.25
XC30 Michael Jordan 4.00 10.00

1995-96 Collector's Choice Debut Trade

This 30-card set was only available by redeeming the Collector's Choice Debut Trade card, which was randomly seeded into second series 12-card packs at a rate of one in 30. The 30-card set primarily consists of a selection of player's traded during the 1995-96 season. The prices listed below are for the more common regular issue cards. The Debut Trade card program expired on May 8th, 1996. Collectors started receiving their cards around late June, 1996. It's interesting to note that rookies Antonio McDyess and Arvydas Sabonis were left out of the regular issue Collector's Choice set but included here in the Debut Trade set.

*PLAYER'S CLUB: .75X TO 2X HI COLUM
PC TRADE: SER.2 STATED ODDS 1:144
*PC PLATINUM STARS: 8X TO 20X HI COLUMN
*PC PLATINUM RCs: 6X TO 15X HI
PCP TRADE: SER.2 STATED ODDS 1:720
T1 Magic Johnson .40 1.00
T2 Arvydas Sabonis .30 .75
T3 Kenny Anderson .12 .30
T4 Antonio McDyess .40 1.00
T5 Sherman Douglas .10 .25
T6 Spud Webb .15 .40
T7 Glen Rice .15 .40
T8 Todd Day .10 .25
T9 John Williams .10 .25
T10 Chris Morris .10 .25
T11 Shawn Bradley .10 .25
T12 Dan Majerle .15 .40
T13 George McCloud .10 .25
T14 Derrick Coleman .12 .30
T15 Kendall Gill .10 .25
T16 Ricky Pierce .10 .25
T17 Robert Pack .10 .25
T18 Alonzo Mourning .20 .50
T19 Matt Geiger .10 .25
T20 Don MacLean .10 .25
T21 Willie Anderson .10 .25
T22 Oliver Miller .10 .25
T23 Tracy Murray .10 .25
T24 Ed Pinckney .10 .25
T25 Alvin Robertson .10 .25
T26 Anthony Avent .10 .25
T27 Blue Edwards .10 .25
T28 Kenny Gattison .10 .25
T29 Chris King .10 .25
T30 Eric Murdock .10 .25

1995-96 Collector's Choice Draft Trade

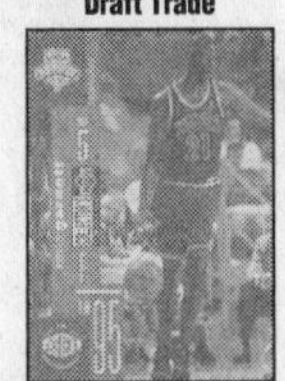

This 10-card set was only available by redeeming a Collector's Choice Draft Trade card, which was randomly inserted into series one packs at a rate of one in 144 packs. The 10-card set consists of the top rookies from the 1995-96 season. Card fronts contain a photo with the player's name, draft pick number and position. Card backs contain biographical and statistical information from the player's college/high school year(s) and are numbered with a "D" prefix. The Draft Trade card program expired on June 7, 1996.

COMPLETE SET (10) 6.00 15.00
D1 Joe Smith 1.00 2.50
D2 Antonio McDyess 1.25 3.00
D3 Jerry Stackhouse 1.50 4.00
D4 Rasheed Wallace 1.50 4.00
D5 Kevin Garnett 4.00 10.00
D6 Bryant Reeves .50 1.25
D7 Damon Stoudamire 1.25 3.00
D8 Shawn Respert .50 1.25
D9 Ed O'Bannon .50 1.25
D10 Kurt Thomas .50 1.25

1995-96 Collector's Choice Jordan He's Back

Inserted one per special retail pack, this five-card set commemorates Michael Jordan coming back in the 1994-95 season. Each card focuses on a particular moment/game.

COMMON JORDAN (M1-M5) .60 1.50

1995-96 Collector's Choice Jordan He's Back Jumbos

COMPLETE SET (3) 4.00 10.00
COMMON CARD 2.00 5.00

1995-96 Collector's Choice Jordan Collection

Randomly inserted into one in every 11 first and second series 12-card packs, these eight standard-size cards comprise the first and third parts of a 24-card set, spanning across all of Upper Deck's 1995-96 basketball products, highlighting the career of Michael Jordan. The fronts have a full-color photo with a gold-foil picture of Jordan in the lower left hand corner wearing number 45. The backs have a color photo at the top with information about the highlight and statistics from that year at the bottom.

COMPLETE SET (8) 8.00 20.00
COMPLETE SER.1 SET (4) 4.00 10.00
COMPLETE SER.2 SET (4) 4.00 10.00
COMMON SER.1 (JC1-JC8) 1.50 4.00
COMMON SER.2 (JC9-JC12) 1.50 4.00

1996-97 Collector's Choice

These 400-standard size cards, comprise Upper Deck's 1996-97 Collector's Choice series one and two set. Cards were primarily issued in 12-card hobby and retail packs with a suggested retail price of ninety-nine cents. Regular issue cards feature white-bordered fronts with color player action shots. The backs have a color photo and statistics. A Factory Set was also issued in early May 1997. The set contained all the basic cards from both series, five Gold Mini-Cards (randomly inserted) and one of four commemorative cards (measuring 3 1/2" by 5") featuring either Shawn Kemp, Michael Jordan, Anfernee Hardaway or a Jordan/Hardaway dual card. The set was issued as a 406-card factory set with a suggested retail price of $29.99. Also included as an insert in packs (1:4 packs) was a game piece for Upper Deck's Meet the Stars promotion. Each game piece was a multiple choice trivia card about basketball. The collector would scratch off the box next to the answer that they felt best matched the question to determine if they won. Instant win game pieces were also inserted one in 72 packs. Winning game pieces could be sent into Upper Deck for a prize drawing. The Grand Prize was a chance to meet Michael Jordan. Prizes for 2nd through 4th were for Upper Deck Authenticated shopping sprees. The 5th prize was two special Michael Jordan Meet the Stars cards. The blank back cards measure 5" by 7" and are titled Dynamic Debut and Magic Memories. These two cards are priced at the bottom of the base set.

COMPLETE SET (400) 30.00 30.00
COMP.FACT.SET (406) 15.00 35.00
COMPLETE SERIES 1 (200) 7.50 15.00
COMPLETE SERIES 2 (200) 7.50 15.00
COMP.UPDATE SET (30) 4.00 10.00
1 Mookie Blaylock .07 .20
2 Grant Long .07 .20
3 Christian Laettner .10 .25
4 Craig Ehlo .07 .20
5 Ken Norman .07 .20
6 Stacey Augmon .10 .25
7 Dana Barros .07 .20
8 Dino Radja .10 .25
9 Rick Fox .07 .20
10 Eric Montross .07 .20
11 David Wesley .07 .20
12 Eric Williams .07 .20
13 Glen Rice .12 .30
14 Dell Curry .07 .20
15 Matt Geiger .07 .20
16 Scott Burrell .07 .20
17 George Zidek .07 .20
18 Muggsy Bogues .10 .25
19 Ron Harper .10 .25
20 Steve Kerr .10 .25
21 Toni Kukoc .12 .30
22 Dennis Rodman .25 .60
23 Michael Jordan 1.00 2.50
24 Luc Longley .07 .20
25 Michael Jordan 1.00 2.50
Vlade Divac VT
26 Michael Jordan Bulls VT 1.00 2.50
27 Luc Longley Bulls VT .07 .20
28 Scottie Pippen Bulls VT .20 .50
29 Toni Kukoc .12 .30
Juwan Howard VT
30 Terrell Brandon .07 .20
31 Bobby Phills .07 .20
32 Tyrone Hill .07 .20
33 Michael Cage .07 .20
34 Bob Sura .07 .20
35 Tony Dumas .07 .20
36 Jim Jackson .07 .20
37 Loren Meyer .07 .20
38 Cherokee Parks .07 .20
39 Jamal Mashburn .10 .25
40 Popeye Jones .07 .20
41 LaPhonso Ellis .07 .20
42 Jalen Rose .10 .25
43 Antonio McDyess .12 .30
44 Tom Hammonds .07 .20
45 Mahmoud Abdul-Rauf .07 .20
46 Dale Ellis .07 .20
47 Joe Dumars .12 .30
48 Theo Ratliff .07 .20
49 Lindsey Hunter .07 .20
50 Terry Mills .07 .20
51 Don Reid .07 .20
52 B.J. Armstrong .07 .20
53 Bimbo Coles .07 .20
54 Joe Smith .10 .25
55 Chris Mullin .12 .30
56 Rony Seikaly .10 .25
57 Donyell Marshall .07 .20
58 Hakeem Olajuwon .15 .40
59 Robert Horry .10 .25
60 Mario Elie .07 .20
61 Mark Bryant .07 .20
62 Chucky Brown .07 .20
63 Rik Smits .10 .25
64 Derrick McKey .07 .20
65 Eddie Johnson .07 .20
66 Mark Jackson .12 .30
67 Ricky Pierce .07 .20
68 Travis Best .07 .20
69 Rodney Rogers .07 .20
70 Brent Barry .10 .25
71 Lamond Murray .07 .20
72 Eric Piatkowski .10 .25
73 Pooh Richardson .07 .20
74 Cedric Ceballos .07 .20
75 Eddie Jones .12 .30
76 Anthony Peeler .07 .20
77 George Lynch .07 .20
78 Vlade Divac .12 .30
79 Rex Chapman .07 .20
80 Sasha Danilovic .07 .20
81 Kurt Thomas .07 .20
82 Keith Askins .07 .20
83 Walt Williams .07 .20
84 Vin Baker .10 .25
85 Shawn Respert .07 .20
86 Sherman Douglas .07 .20
87 Marty Conlon .07 .20
88 Johnny Newman .07 .20
89 Kevin Garnett .30 .75
90 Andrew Lang .07 .20
91 Terry Porter .07 .20
92 Sam Mitchell .07 .20
93 Tom Gugliotta .07 .20
94 Spud Webb .12 .30
95 Kendall Gill .07 .20
96 Vern Fleming .07 .20
97 Shawn Bradley .07 .20
98 Yinka Dare .07 .20
99 Jayson Williams .07 .20
100 Kevin Edwards .07 .20
101 Charles Oakley .10 .25
102 Anthony Mason .07 .20
103 John Starks .10 .25
104 J.R. Reid .07 .20
105 Hubert Davis .07 .20
106 Gary Grant .07 .20
107 Nick Anderson .07 .20
108 Donald Royal .07 .20
109 Brian Shaw .07 .20
110 Brooks Thompson .07 .20
111 Anfernee Hardaway .20 .50
112 Dennis Scott .07 .20
113 Anfernee Hardaway PEN .20 .50
114 Anfernee Hardaway PEN .20 .50
115 Anfernee Hardaway PEN .20 .50
116 Anfernee Hardaway PEN .20 .50
117 Anfernee Hardaway PEN .20 .50
118 Derrick Coleman .10 .25
119 Rex Walters .07 .20
120 Sean Higgins .07 .20
121 Clarence Weatherspoon .07 .20
122 Jerry Stackhouse .15 .40
123 Elliot Perry .07 .20
124 Wayman Tisdale .07 .20
125 Wesley Person .07 .20
126 Charles Barkley .20 .50
127 A.C. Green .12 .30
128 Harvey Grant .07 .20
129 Arvydas Sabonis .10 .25
130 Aaron McKie .07 .20
131 Gary Trent .07 .20
132 Buck Williams .07 .20
133 Billy Owens .07 .20
134 Brian Grant .10 .25
135 Corliss Williamson .07 .20
136 Tyus Edney .07 .20
137 Olden Polynice .07 .20
138 Avery Johnson .10 .25
139 Vinny Del Negro .07 .20
140 Sean Elliott .12 .30
141 Chuck Person .10 .25
142 Will Perdue .07 .20
143 Nate McMillan .07 .20
144 Vincent Askew .07 .20
145 Detlef Schrempf .12 .30
146 Hersey Hawkins .07 .20
147 Sharone Wright .07 .20
148 Zan Tabak .07 .20
149 Oliver Miller .07 .20
150 Doug Christie .07 .20
151 Damon Stoudamire .12 .30
152 Jeff Hornacek .10 .25
153 Chris Morris .07 .20
154 Antoine Carr .07 .20
155 Karl Malone .15 .40
156 Adam Keefe .07 .20
157 Greg Anthony .07 .20
158 Blue Edwards .07 .20
159 Bryant Reeves .07 .20
160 Anthony Avent .07 .20
161 Lawrence Moten .07 .20
162 Calbert Cheaney .07 .20
163 Chris Webber .15 .40
164 Tim Legler .07 .20
165 Gheorghe Muresan .07 .20
166 Stacey Augmon FUND .10 .25
167 Dee Brown FUND .07 .20
168 Glen Rice FUND .12 .30
169 Scottie Pippen FUND .20 .50
170 Danny Ferry FUND .07 .20
171 Jason Kidd FUND .20 .50
172 LaPhonso Ellis FUND .07 .20
173 Grant Hill FUND .20 .50
174 Chris Mullin FUND .12 .30
175 Clyde Drexler FUND .15 .40
176 Rik Smits FUND .10 .25
177 Loy Vaught FUND .07 .20
178 Nick Van Exel FUND .12 .30
179 Alonzo Mourning FUND .15 .40
180 Glenn Robinson FUND .12 .30
181 Isaiah Rider FUND .10 .25
182 Ed O'Bannon FUND .07 .20
183 Patrick Ewing FUND .15 .40
184 Shaquille O'Neal FUND .30 .75
185 Derrick Coleman FUND .10 .25
186 Danny Manning FUND .10 .25
187 Clifford Robinson FUND .07 .20
188 Mitch Richmond FUND .12 .30
189 David Robinson FUND .20 .50
190 Shawn Kemp FUND .12 .30
191 Oliver Miller FUND .07 .20
192 John Stockton FUND .15 .40
193 Greg Anthony FUND .07 .20
194 Rasheed Wallace FUND .15 .40
195 Michael Jordan FUND 1.00 2.50
196 Michael Jordan .20 .50
Matt Geiger CL
197 Eddie Jones .07 .20
Antonio McDyess CL
198 Anfernee Hardaway .20 .50
Kevin Garnett CL
199 Damon Stoudamire .07 .20
Avery Johnson CL
200 David Robinson .12 .30
Chris Mullin CL
201 Alan Henderson .07 .20
202 Steve Smith .10 .25
203 Donnie Boyce RC .12 .30
204 Priest Lauderdale RC .12 .30
205 Dikembe Mutombo .12 .30
206 Dee Brown .07 .20
207 Junior Burrough .07 .20
208 Todd Day .07 .20
209 Pervis Ellison .07 .20
210 Greg Minor .07 .20
211 Antoine Walker RC .25 .60
212 Rafael Addison .07 .20
213 Tony Delk RC .12 .30
214 Vlade Divac .12 .30
215 Anthony Goldwire .07 .20
216 Anthony Mason .07 .20
217 Dickey Simpkins .07 .20
218 Randy Brown .07 .20
219 Jud Buechler .07 .20
220 Jason Caffey .07 .20
221 Scottie Pippen .20 .50
222 Bill Wennington .07 .20
223 Danny Ferry .07 .20
224 Antonio Lang .07 .20
225 Chris Mills .07 .20
226 Vitaly Potapenko RC .12 .30
227 Terry Davis .07 .20
228 Chris Gatling .07 .20
229 Jason Kidd .20 .50
230 George McCloud .07 .20
231 Eric Montross .07 .20
232 Samaki Walker RC .12 .30
233 Mark Jackson .12 .30
234 Ervin Johnson .07 .20
235 Sarunas Marciulionis .07 .20
236 Eric Murdock .07 .20
237 Ricky Pierce .07 .20
238 Bryant Stith .07 .20
239 Stacey Augmon .10 .25
240 Grant Hill .20 .50
241 Otis Thorpe .07 .20
242 Jerome Williams RC .12 .30
243 Andrew DeClercq .07 .20
244 Todd Fuller RC .12 .30
245 Mark Price .12 .30
246 Clifford Rozier .07 .20
247 Latrell Sprewell .12 .30
248 Charles Barkley .20 .50
249 Clyde Drexler .15 .40
250 Othella Harrington RC .12 .30
251 Sam Mack .07 .20
252 Kevin Willis .07 .20
253 Erick Dampier RC .12 .30
254 Antonio Davis .07 .20
255 Dale Davis .07 .20
256 Duane Ferrell .07 .20
257 Reggie Miller .15 .40
258 Jalen Rose .10 .25
259 Reggie Williams .07 .20
260 Terry Dehere .07 .20
261 Bo Outlaw .07 .20
262 Stanley Roberts .07 .20
263 Malik Sealy .07 .20
264 Loy Vaught .07 .20
265 Lorenzen Wright RC .12 .30
266 Corie Blount .07 .20
267 Kobe Bryant RC 2.00 5.00
268 Elden Campbell .07 .20
269 Derek Fisher RC .25 .60
270 Shaquille O'Neal .30 .75
271 Nick Van Exel .12 .30
272 P.J. Brown .07 .20
273 Tim Hardaway .12 .30
274 Voshon Lenard RC .12 .30
275 Dan Majerle .12 .30
276 Alonzo Mourning .15 .40
277 Martin Muursepp RC .12 .30
278 Ray Allen RC .50 1.25
279 Elliot Perry .07 .20
280 Glenn Robinson .12 .30
281 Stephon Marbury RC .30 .75
282 Cherokee Parks .07 .20
283 Doug West .07 .20
284 Micheal Williams .07 .20
285 Kerry Kittles RC .12 .30
286 Ed O'Bannon .07 .20
287 Robert Pack .07 .20
288 Khalid Reeves .07 .20
289 David Benoit .07 .20
290 Patrick Ewing .15 .40
291 Allan Houston .10 .25
292 Larry Johnson .12 .30
293 Dontae' Jones RC .12 .30
294 Walter McCarty RC .12 .30
295 John Wallace RC .12 .30
296 Charlie Ward .07 .20
297 Brian Evans RC .12 .30
298 Horace Grant .10 .25
299 Jon Koncak .07 .20
300 Felton Spencer .07 .20
301 Allen Iverson RC .60 1.50
302 Don MacLean .07 .20
303 Scott Williams .07 .20
304 Sam Cassell .10 .25
305 Michael Finley .15 .40
306 Robert Horry .10 .25
307 Kevin Johnson .12 .30
308 Joe Kleine .07 .20
309 Danny Manning .10 .25
310 Steve Nash RC .60 1.50
311 John Williams .07 .20
312 Kenny Anderson .10 .25
313 Randolph Childress .07 .20
314 Chris Dudley .07 .20
315 Jermaine O'Neal RC .30 .75
316 Isaiah Rider .10 .25
317 Clifford Robinson .07 .20
318 Rasheed Wallace .15 .40
319 Mahmoud Abdul-Rauf .07 .20
320 Duane Causwell .07 .20
321 Bobby Hurley .12 .30
322 Mitch Richmond .12 .30
323 Lionel Simmons .07 .20
324 Michael Smith .07 .20
325 Dominique Wilkins .15 .40
326 Cory Alexander .07 .20
327 Greg Anderson .07 .20
328 Carl Herrera .07 .20
329 David Robinson .20 .50
330 Charles Smith .07 .20
331 Craig Ehlo .07 .20
332 Sherrell Ford .07 .20
333 Shawn Kemp .12 .30
334 Jim McIlvaine .07 .20
335 Gary Payton .12 .30
336 Sam Perkins .07 .20
337 Eric Snow RC .12 .30
338 David Wingate .07 .20
339 Marcus Camby RC .20 .50
340 Acie Earl .07 .20
341 Carlos Rogers .07 .20
342 Greg Ostertag .07 .20
343 Bryon Russell .07 .20
344 John Stockton .15 .40
345 Jamie Watson .07 .20
346 Shareef Abdur-Rahim RC .25 .60
347 Doug Edwards .07 .20
348 George Lynch .07 .20
349 Eric Mobley .07 .20
350 Anthony Peeler .07 .20
351 Roy Rogers RC .12 .30
352 Juwan Howard .10 .25
353 Harvey Grant .07 .20
354 Tracy Murray .07 .20
355 Rod Strickland .07 .20
356 Anfernee Hardaway .50 1.25
Michael Jordan ONE
357 Hakeem Olajuwon .25 .60
Shaquille O'Neal ONE
358 Joe Smith .15 .40
Shawn Kemp ONE
359 Detlef Schrempf .08 .25
Toni Kukoc ONE
360 Jim Jackson .15 .40
Jerry Stackhouse ONE
361 Kobe Bryant .40 1.00
Shareef Abdur-Rahim ONE
362 Nick Anderson .30 .75
Michael Jordan AJ
363 Joe Dumars .30 .75
Michael Jordan AJ
364 John Starks .30 .75
Michael Jordan AJ
365 Reggie Miller .50 1.25
Michael Jordan AJ
366 Gary Payton .40 1.00
Michael Jordan AJ
367 Mookie Blaylock PLAY .07 .20
368 Dino Radja .07 .20
Rick Fox
David Wesley PLAY
369 Glen Rice PLAY .12 .30
370 Michael Jordan .50 1.25
Scottie Pippen PLAY
371 Terrell Brandon PLAY .07 .20
372 Jason Kidd PLAY .20 .50
373 Antonio McDyess PLAY .12 .30
374 Grant Hill PLAY .20 .50
375 Joe Smith PLAY .10 .25
376 Charles Barkley .30 .75
Hakeem Olajuwon
Clyde Drexler PLAY
377 Reggie Miller PLAY .15 .40
378 L.A. Clippers PLAY .07 .20
379 Nick Van Exel PLAY .12 .30
380 Alonzo Mourning PLAY .15 .40
381 Ray Allen PLAY .25 .60
382 Stephon Marbury PLAY .25 .60
383 Shawn Bradley PLAY .07 .20
384 Patrick Ewing PLAY .15 .40
385 Anfernee Hardaway PLAY .20 .50
386 Jerry Stackhouse PLAY .15 .40
387 Danny Manning PLAY .10 .25
388 Clifford Robinson PLAY .07 .20
389 Tyus Edney PLAY .07 .20
390 San Antonio Spurs PLAY .07 .20
391 Shawn Kemp PLAY .12 .30
392 Toronto Raptors PLAY .07 .20
393 John Stockton PLAY .15 .40
394 Greg Anthony PLAY .07 .20
395 Gheorghe Muresan PLAY .07 .20
396 Checklist .07 .20
397 Checklist .07 .20
398 Checklist .07 .20
399 Checklist .07 .20
400 Checklist .07 .20
401 Henry James TRADE .20 .50
402 Shawn Bradley TRADE .20 .50
403 Sasha Danilovic TRADE .20 .50
404 Michael Finley TRADE .40 1.00
405 A.C. Green TRADE .30 .75
406 Derek Harper TRADE .25 .60
407 Khalid Reeves TRADE .20 .50
408 Aaron McKie TRADE .20 .50
409 Matt Maloney TRADE RC .30 .75
410 Darrick Martin TRADE .20 .50
411 Robert Horry TRADE .25 .60
412 Travis Knight TRADE RC .30 .75
413 Isaac Austin TRADE .20 .50
414 Jamal Mashburn TRADE .25 .60
415 Armon Gilliam TRADE .20 .50
416 Chris Carr TRADE RC .30 .75
417 Dean Garrett TRADE RC .30 .75
418 Shane Heal TRADE RC .30 .75
419 Sam Cassell TRADE .25 .60
420 Chris Gatling TRADE .20 .50
421 Jim Jackson TRADE .20 .50
422 Chris Childs TRADE .20 .50
423 Rony Seikaly TRADE .25 .60
424 Gerald Wilkins TRADE .20 .50
425 Cedric Ceballos TRADE .20 .50
426 Tony Dumas TRADE .20 .50
427 Jason Kidd TRADE .50 1.25
428 Popeye Jones TRADE .20 .50
429 Walt Williams TRADE .20 .50
430 Jaren Jackson TRADE .20 .50
NNO Update Trade Card 2.00 5.00
NNO Michael Jordan 5x7 MM 4.00 10.00
NNO Michael Jordan 5x7 DD 4.00 10.00

1996-97 Collector's Choice Crash the Game Scoring 1

Randomly inserted into first series packs at a rate of one in 5, this 60-card silver set features two separate versions of thirty different player cards. Each player is given two seperate weeks to score 30 points in any given game during that time period. If the player depicted on the card scores 30 or more points in the given week, the card can be redeemed for one premium quality silver card of the depicted player. The expiration date for the cards was May 9, 1997.

COMPLETE SILVER SET (60) 20.00 50.00
*GOLD CARDS: 1.25X TO 3X HI COLUMN
GOLD: SER.1 STATED ODDS 1:49
*SILVER RED.CARDS: .5X TO 1.25X SILVER HI

*GOLD RED.CARDS: 1.5X TO 4X SILVER HI
ONE RED.CARD PER WINNER BY MAIL

C1 Mookie Blaylock 11/4 L	.40	1.00
C1B Mookie Blaylock 12/16 L	.40	1.00
C2 Dino Radja 11/18 L	.50	1.25
C2B Dino Radja 1/6 L	.50	1.25
C3 Glen Rice 11/18 L	.60	1.50
C3B Glen Rice 1/27 W	.60	1.50
C4 Scottie Pippen 12/2 L	1.00	2.50
C4B Scottie Pippen 1/13 L	1.00	2.50
C5 Terrell Brandon 11/4 L	.40	1.00
C5B Terrell Brandon 1/13 L	.40	1.00
C6 Jason Kidd 12/9 L	1.00	2.50
C6B Jason Kidd 12/23 L	1.00	2.50
C7 Antonio McDyess 11/11 L	.60	1.50
C7B Antonio McDyess 12/23 L	.60	1.50
C8 Joe Dumars 12/9 L	.60	1.50
C8B Joe Dumars 1/13 L	.60	1.50
C9 Joe Smith 12/2 L	.50	1.25
C9B Joe Smith 12/23 W	.50	1.25
C10 Hakeem Olajuwon 11/4 W	.75	2.00
C10B Hakeem Olajuwon 12/23 W	.75	2.00
C11 Reggie Miller 12/9 L	.75	2.00
C11B Reggie Miller 1/27 W	.75	2.00
C12 Loy Vaught 11/18 L	.40	1.00
C12B Loy Vaught 1/6 L	.40	1.00
C13 Cedric Ceballos 12/2 L	.40	1.00
C13B Cedric Ceballos 1/27 L	.40	1.00
C14 Alonzo Mourning 11/11 L	.75	2.00
C14B Alonzo Mourning 1/6 W	.75	2.00
C15 Vin Baker 12/9 L	.50	1.25
C15B Vin Baker 1/27 L	.50	1.25
C16 Kevin Garnett 11/18 L	1.50	4.00
C16B Kevin Garnett 1/13 L	1.50	4.00
C17 Ed O'Bannon 12/2 L	.40	1.00
C17B Ed O'Bannon 1/6 L	.40	1.00
C18 Patrick Ewing 11/4 W	.75	2.00
C18B Patrick Ewing 1/13 L	.75	2.00
C19 Anfernee Hardaway 12/23 L	1.00	2.50
C19B Anfernee Hardaway 1/27 W	1.00	2.50
C20 Clarence Weatherspoon 12/16 L	.40	1.00
C20B Clarence Weatherspoon 1/13 W	.40	1.00
C21 Kevin Johnson 11/11 L	.60	1.50
C21B Kevin Johnson 1/27 L	.60	1.50
C22 Clifford Robinson 12/16 L	.40	1.00
C22B Clifford Robinson 1/6 L	.40	1.00
C23 Mitch Richmond 12/16 W	.60	1.50
C23B Mitch Richmond 1/27 W	.60	1.50
C24 Sean Elliott 11/4 L	.60	1.50
C24B Sean Elliott 1/6 L	.60	1.50
C25 Shawn Kemp 12/16 L	.60	1.50
C25B Shawn Kemp 1/13 L	.60	1.50
C26 Damon Stoudamire 12/9 W	.60	1.50
C26B Damon Stoudamire 1/6 L	.60	1.50
C27 John Stockton 11/11 L	.75	2.00
C27B John Stockton 12/23 L	.75	2.00
C28 Bryant Reeves 12/2 L	.40	1.00
C28B Bryant Reeves 1/27 W	.40	1.00
C29 Rasheed Wallace 11/18 L	.75	2.00
C29B Rasheed Wallace 1/13 L	.75	2.00
C30 Michael Jordan 11/11 W	5.00	12.00
C30B Michael Jordan 12/23 W	5.00	12.00

1996-97 Collector's Choice Crash the Game Scoring 2

Randomly inserted into second series packs at a rate of one in five, this 60-card silver set features two separate versions of thirty different player cards. Each player is given two seperate weeks to score 30 points in any given game during that time period. If the player depicted on the card scores 30 or more points in the given week, the card can be redeemed for one premium quality silver card of the depicted player. The expiration date for the cards was July 1, 1997.
*GOLD CARDS: 1.25X TO 3X HI COLUMN
GOLD: SER.2 STATED ODDS 1:49
*SILVER RED.CARDS: .5X TO 1.25X SILVER HI
*GOLD RED.CARDS: 1.5X TO 4X SILVER HI
ONE RED.CARD PER WINNER BY MAIL

C1 Steve Smith 2/17 L	.50	1.25
C1B Steve Smith 4/14 W	.50	1.25
C2 Dana Barros 3/3 L	.40	1.00
C2B Dana Barros 3/31 L	.40	1.00
C3 Tony Delk 2/24 L	.60	1.50
C3B Tony Delk 4/7 L	.60	1.50
C4 Toni Kukoc 3/10 L	.60	1.50
C4B Toni Kukoc 3/31 L	.60	1.50
C5 Bobby Phills 2/24 L	.40	1.00
C5B Bobby Phills 3/17 L	.40	1.00
C6 Jamal Mashburn 3/3 L	.50	1.25
C6B Jamal Mashburn 3/31 L	.50	1.25
C7 LaPhonso Ellis 2/24 W	.40	1.00
C7B LaPhonso Ellis 3/31 L	.40	1.00
C8 Jerome Williams 2/17 L	.60	1.50
C8B Jerome Williams 4/7 L	.60	1.50
C9 Latrell Sprewell 3/3 L	.60	1.50
C9B Latrell Sprewell 4/7 L	.60	1.50
C10 Clyde Drexler 2/24 L	.75	2.00
C10B Clyde Drexler 4/7 L	.75	2.00
C11 Dale Davis 3/3 L	.40	1.00
C11B Dale Davis 3/24 L	.40	1.00
C12 Brent Barry 3/3 L	.50	1.25
C12B Brent Barry 4/14 L	.50	1.25
C13 Nick Van Exel 3/10 L	.60	1.50
C13B Nick Van Exel 4/7 L	.60	1.50
C14 Sasha Danilovic 2/17 L	.40	1.00
C14B Sasha Danilovic 3/17 L	.40	1.00
C15 Glenn Robinson 2/24 L	.60	1.50
C15B Glenn Robinson 3/17 L	.60	1.50
C16 Stephon Marbury 2/17 L	1.50	4.00
C16B Stephon Marbury 3/31 L	1.50	4.00
C17 Shawn Bradley 3/10 W	.40	1.00
C17B Shawn Bradley 3/24 L	.40	1.00
C18 John Wallace 3/3 L	.60	1.50
C18B John Wallace 4/14 L	.60	1.50
C19 Anfernee Hardaway 2/24 L	1.00	2.50
C19B Anfernee Hardaway 4/14 L	1.00	2.50
C20 Jerry Stackhouse 3/10 W	.75	2.00
C20B Jerry Stackhouse 3/31 W	.75	2.00
C21 Danny Manning 2/17 L	.50	1.25
C21B Danny Manning 3/24 L	.50	1.25
C22 Arvydas Sabonis 2/24 L	.50	1.25
C22B Arvydas Sabonis 3/31 L	.50	1.25
C23 Brian Grant 3/3 L	.50	1.25
C23B Brian Grant 3/31 L	.50	1.25
C24 David Robinson 2/24 L	1.00	2.50
C24B David Robinson 3/24 L	1.00	2.50
C25 Gary Payton 3/3 L	.60	1.50
C25B Gary Payton 4/14 L	.60	1.50
C26 Marcus Camby 3/3 L	1.00	2.50
C26B Marcus Camby 4/7 L	1.00	2.50
C27 Karl Malone 2/24 W	.75	2.00
C27B Karl Malone 4/14 W	.75	2.00
C28 Shareef Abdur-Rahim 2/24 L	1.25	3.00
C28B Shareef Abdur-Rahim 3/17 L	1.25	3.00
C29 Juwan Howard 2/17 L	.50	1.25
C29B Juwan Howard 4/7 L	.50	1.25
C30 Michael Jordan 3/9 W	5.00	12.00
C30B Michael Jordan 4/14 W	5.00	12.00

1996-97 Collector's Choice Draft Trade

This 10-card set was available by exchanging a Draft Trade card, inserted at a rate of one in 144 in the series one set. The trade card expired May 9, 1997. Each card has a full portrait shot of the player and career information on the back. The cards are numbered with a "DR" prefix.

COMPLETE SET (10)	10.00	20.00
DR1 Allen Iverson	3.00	8.00
DR2 Marcus Camby	1.00	2.50
DR3 Shareef Abdur-Rahim	1.25	3.00
DR4 Stephon Marbury	1.50	4.00
DR5 Ray Allen	2.50	6.00
DR6 Antoine Walker	1.25	3.00
DR7 Lorenzen Wright	.60	1.50
DR8 Kerry Kittles	.60	1.50
DR9 Samaki Walker	.60	1.50
DR10 Erick Dampier	.60	1.50
NNO Expired Trade Card	.40	1.00

1996-97 Collector's Choice Factory Blow-Ups

Inserted one per 1996-97 Collector's Choice Factory set, this 4-card set measures 3 1/2" by 5" and features the Upper Deck spokesmen.

COMPLETE SET (4)	2.50	6.00
1 Michael Jordan	2.00	5.00
2 Shawn Kemp	.25	.60
3 Anfernee Hardaway	.40	1.00
4 Michael Jordan	1.50	4.00
Anfernee Hardaway		

1996-97 Collector's Choice Game Face

Inserted one per special retail pack, this 10-card set is standard-sized with white bordered fronts and the logo "Game Face" in gold on the front. Card backs include a inset photo of the player with commentary. Cards are numbered with a "GF" prefix.

COMPLETE SET (10)	4.00	10.00
GF1 Anfernee Hardaway	.60	1.50
GF2 Michael Jordan	3.00	8.00
GF3 Shawn Kemp	.40	1.00
GF4 Alonzo Mourning	.50	1.25
GF5 Cherokee Parks	.25	.60
GF6 Avery Johnson	.30	.75
GF7 LaPhonso Ellis	.25	.60
GF8 Rasheed Wallace	.50	1.25
GF9 Jim Jackson	.25	.60
GF10 Larry Johnson	.40	1.00

1996-97 Collector's Choice Jordan A Cut Above

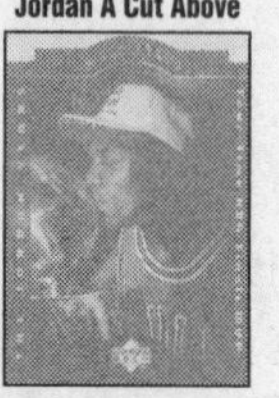

One of these ten Jordan ACA cards was inserted into every special Wal-Mart ninety-nine cent series one retail pack. This 10-card set focuses on Michael Jordan's career feats. Each card front is die cut at the top with the set name "A Cut Above" in gold foil. Card backs feature a head shot with a summary of each feat.

COMPLETE SET (10)	8.00	20.00
COMMON JORDAN (CA1-CA10)	1.00	2.50

1996-97 Collector's Choice Jordan A Cut Above Jumbos

Released in complete set form in retail outlets, this 10-card set parallels the A Cut Above insert from 1996-97 Collector's Choice packs. Card backs carry a "CA" prefix.

COMP.FACT SET (10)	8.00	20.00
COMMON CARD (CA1-CA10)	1.00	2.50

1996-97 Collector's Choice Memorable Moments

Inserted one per special series two retail pack, this 10-card set features memorable moments from the 1996 NBA season. The cards have a die cut design on both the top and bottom of the card with gold foil running along each of those die cut borders. Card backs describe the moment.

COMPLETE SET (10)	5.00	12.00
1 Michael Jordan	3.00	8.00
2 Nick Van Exel	.40	1.00
3 Karl Malone	.50	1.25
4 Latrell Sprewell	.40	1.00
5 Anfernee Hardaway	.60	1.50
6 Glenn Robinson	.40	1.00
7 Shaquille O'Neal	1.00	2.50
8 Damon Stoudamire	.40	1.00
9 Clyde Drexler	.50	1.25
10 Shawn Kemp	.40	1.00

1996-97 Collector's Choice Mini-Cards

Inserted in both series at a rate of one per pack, this 60-card set is comprised of 180 different "mini-cards". Three of these mini-cards form one standard-sized card and are issued in that form. Card fronts feature perforated panels of three players with silver foil. Card backs feature a brief commentary on each player. Each card contains it's own individual number, with an "M" prefix and is ordered below by the far left number on the card back. Also, card number M106 was never issued. Both Bob Sura and Bryant Stith were numbered M112.

COMPLETE SET (60)	8.00	20.00
COMPLETE SERIES 1 (30)	3.00	8.00
COMPLETE SERIES 2 (30)	5.00	12.00
*GOLD: 2.5X TO 6X HI COLUMN		
GOLD: SER.1/2 STATED ODDS 1:35		
M2 Rex Walters	.15	.40
Jeff Hornacek		
Mookie Blaylock		
M5 Detlef Schrempf	.20	.50
Toni Kukoc		
Dino Radja		
M6 Ashraf Amaya	.12	.30
Sharone Wright		
Eric Williams		
M10 Tyus Edney	.12	.30
Ed O'Bannon		
George Zidek		
M13 Theo Ratliff	.12	.30
Shawn Bradley		
Luc Longley		
M22 Bobby Phills	.15	.40
Avery Johnson		
Mahmoud Abdul-Rauf		
M23 Popeye Jones	.12	.30
Chris Morris		
Tom Hammonds		
M25 Bobby Hurley	.30	.75
Christian Laettner		
Grant Hill		
M28 Sherman Douglas	.15	.40
Derrick Coleman		
Rony Seikaly		
M30 Nick Van Exel	.20	.50
John Starks		
Sam Cassell		
M33 Matt Geiger	.12	.30
Dennis Scott		
Travis Best		
M36 Cedric Ceballos	.15	.40
Isaiah Rider		
Brent Barry		
M37 Jason Kidd	.30	.75
Kevin Johnson		
Lamond Murray		
M38 Chris Mullin	.20	.50
Jayson Williams		
Terry Dehere		
M39 Arvedas Sabonis	.20	.50
Sasha Danilovic		
Vlade Divac		
M43 Tyrone Hill	.15	.40
Brian Grant		
Kurt Thomas		
M44 Derrick McKey	.15	.40
Robert Horry		
Keith Askins		
M46 Randolph Childress	.30	.75
David Robinson		
Shawn Respert		
M49 Todd Day	.12	.30
Oliver Miller		
Andrew Lang		
M56 Dell Curry	.15	.40
Bimbo Coles		
Charles Oakley		
M57 Rasheed Wallace	.25	.60
Jerry Stackhouse		
J.R. Reid		
M66 Joe Dumars	.25	.60
Clyde Drexler		
A.C. Green		
M67 Kendall Gill	.12	.30
Nick Anderson		
Aaron McKie		
M75 Danny Ferry	.20	.50
Mark Jackson		
Doc Rivers		
M78 Michael Jordan	1.50	4.00
Anfernee Hardaway		
Shawn Kemp		
M79 Jalen Rose	.25	.60
Chris Webber		
Jimmy King		
M83 Dennis Rodman	.75	2.00
Charles Barkley		
Karl Malone		
M85 Stacey Augmon	.20	.50
Larry Johnson		
Greg Anthony		
M86 Nate McMillan	.12	.30
Tom Gugliotta		
Blue Edwards		
M90 Jim Jackson	.20	.50
Glenn Robinson		
Calbert Cheaney		
M92 Ken Norman	.12	.30
Doug West		
Kevin Edwards		
M93 Steve Smith	.20	.50
Tim Hardaway		
BJ Armstrong		
M99 Glen Rice	.20	.50
Danny Manning		
Sam Perkins		
M102 Steve Kerr	.25	.60
Reggie Miller		
Dana Barros		
M109 Samaki Walker	.20	.50
Lorenzen Wright		
Greg Minor		
M110 LaPhonso Ellis	.12	.30
Kevin Willis		
Clarence Weatherspoon		
M111 Antonio McDyess	.20	.50
Latrell Sprewell		
Jason Caffey		
M112A Bryant Stith	.15	.40
Vinny Del Negro		
Kenny Anderson		
M112B Bob Sura	.12	.30
Rodney Rogers		
Olden Polynice		
M113 Lindsey Hunter	.20	.50
Eddie Jones		
Ron Harper		
M115 Otis Thorpe	.25	.60
John Stockton		
Antoine Carr		
M125 Rik Smits	.25	.60
Hakeem Olajuwon		
Gheorghe Muresan		
M129 Kobe Bryant	2.50	6.00
Jermaine O'Neal		
Kevin Garnett		
M135 Alonzo Mourning	.25	.60
Dikembe Mutombo		
Patrick Ewing		
M137 Vin Baker	.30	.75
Jamal Mashburn		
Scottie Pippen		
M140 Stephon Marbury	.50	1.25
Darrin Hancock		
Wesley Person		
M146 Allan Houston	.30	.75
Marcus Camby		
Kerry Kittles		
M148 John Wallace	.40	1.00
Walter McCarty		
Antoine Walker		
M149 Horace Grant	.15	.40
Elden Campbell		
Dale Davis		
M150 Donald Royal	.12	.30
Tim Legler		
Mario Elie		
M151 Brian Shaw	.12	.30
Antonio Davis		
P.J. Brown		
M152 Allen Iverson	1.00	2.50
Joe Smith		
Shaquille O'Neal		
M159 Cliff Robinson	.75	2.00
Scott Burrell		
Ray Allen		
M161 Mitch Richmond	.20	.50
Will Perdue		
Hersey Hawkins		
M167 Gary Payton	.20	.50
Terrell Brandon		
Sean Elliott		
M170 Doug Christie	.12	.30
Johnny Newman		
Tony Dumas		
M175 Shareef Abdur-Rahim	.40	1.00
Chris Mills		
Khalid Reeves		
M176 Lawrence Moten	.12	.30
Michael Smith		
Bryon Russell		
M177 Bryant Reeves	.25	.60
Michael Finley		
Damon Stoudamire		
M178 Juwan Howard	.15	.40
Loy Vaught		
Terry Mills		

1996-97 Collector's Choice Stick-Ums 1

Randomly inserted into first series packs at a rate of one in 4, this 30-card set features separate removable stickers of the actual player, the player's name and the given statistical categories. Card backs are black and white and feature set information including the complete Stick-Um checklist. Card stock is noticeably thin. Cards are numbered with an "S" prefix.

COMPLETE SET (30)	3.00	8.00
S1 Mookie Blaylock	.12	.30
S2 Dana Barros	.12	.30
S3 Scott Burrell	.12	.30
S4 Dennis Rodman	.40	1.00
S5 Terrell Brandon	.12	.30
S6 Jamal Mashburn	.15	.40
S7 LaPhonso Ellis	.12	.30
S8 Grant Hill	.30	.75
S9 Joe Smith	.15	.40
S10 Hakeem Olajuwon	.25	.60
S11 Rik Smits	.15	.40
S12 Brent Barry	.15	.40
S13 Nick Van Exel	.20	.50
S14 Sasha Danilovic	.12	.30
S15 Vin Baker	.15	.40
S16 Kevin Garnett	.50	1.25
S17 Shawn Bradley	.12	.30
S18 Patrick Ewing	.25	.60
S19 Anfernee Hardaway	.30	.75
S20 Clarence Weatherspoon	.12	.30
S21 Charles Barkley	.30	.75
S22 Clifford Robinson	.12	.30
S23 Mitch Richmond	.20	.50
S24 David Robinson	.30	.75
S25 Shawn Kemp	.20	.50
S26 Damon Stoudamire	.20	.50
S27 Karl Malone	.25	.60
S28 Bryant Reeves	.12	.30
S29 Gheorghe Muresan	.12	.30
S30 Michael Jordan	1.50	4.00

1996-97 Collector's Choice Stick-Ums 2

Randomly inserted into second series packs at a rate of one in 3, this 30-card set features separate removable stickers of the actual player, the player's name and the given statistical categories. Card backs are black and white and feature set information including the complete Stick-Um checklist. Card stock is noticeably thin. Cards are numbered with an "S" prefix.

COMPLETE SET (30)	3.00	8.00
S1 Steve Smith	.15	.40
S2 Dino Radja	.15	.40
S3 Glen Rice	.20	.50
S4 Toni Kukoc	.20	.50
S5 Bobby Phills	.12	.30
S6 Jason Kidd	.30	.75
S7 Antonio McDyess	.20	.50
S8 Joe Dumars	.20	.50
S9 Latrell Sprewell	.20	.50
S10 Clyde Drexler	.25	.60
S11 Reggie Miller	.25	.60
S12 Loy Vaught	.12	.30
S13 Eddie Jones	.20	.50
S14 Alonzo Mourning	.25	.60
S15 Glenn Robinson	.20	.50
S16 Tom Gugliotta	.12	.30
S17 Ed O'Bannon	.12	.30
S18 John Starks	.15	.40
S19 Anfernee Hardaway	.30	.75
S20 Jerry Stackhouse	.25	.60
S21 Kevin Johnson	.20	.50
S22 Arvydas Sabonis	.15	.40
S23 Brian Grant	.15	.40
S24 Sean Elliott	.20	.50
S25 Gary Payton	.20	.50
S26 Zan Tabak	.12	.30
S27 John Stockton	.25	.60
S28 Greg Anthony	.12	.30
S29 Juwan Howard	.15	.40
S30 Michael Jordan	1.50	4.00

1996-97 Collector's Choice Chicago Bulls

Issued with a suggested retail price of $2.99, this set features nine players from the above team. In addition, each team set contained two bonus Collector's Choice Gold Mini-Cards. These differed from the regular Gold Mini-Cards with each having the same card number on each panel and the cards being numbered B1 and B2.

COMP.FACT SET (11)	3.00	8.00
B1 Ron Harper	1.50	4.00
Michael Jordan		
Steve Kerr		
B2 Toni Kukoc	1.25	3.00
Scottie Pippen		
Dennis Rodman		
CH1 Jason Caffey	.20	.50
CH2 Ron Harper	.25	.60
CH3 Michael Jordan	1.50	4.00
CH4 Steve Kerr	.25	.60
CH5 Toni Kukoc	.30	.75
CH6 Luc Longley	.20	.50
CH7 Scottie Pippen	.50	1.25
CH8 Dennis Rodman	.60	1.50
CH9 Bill Wennington	.20	.50

1996-97 Collector's Choice Houston Rockets

Issued with a suggested retail price of $2.99, this set features nine players from the above team. In addition, each team set contained a replica blow-up card of the Building A Winner subset from the 1996-97 Upper Deck set.

COMP.FACT SET (9)	1.50	4.00
HT1 Charles Barkley	.50	1.25
HT2 Matt Bullard	.20	.50
HT3 Clyde Drexler	.40	1.00
HT4 Mario Elie	.20	.50
HT5 Othella Harrington	.30	.75
HT6 Sam Mack	.20	.50
HT7 Matt Maloney	.30	.75
HT8 Hakeem Olajuwon	.40	1.00
HT9 Kevin Willis	.20	.50
NNO Houston Rockets Blow-Up	.75	2.00

1996-97 Collector's Choice Los Angeles Lakers

Issued with a suggested retail price of $2.99, this set features nine players from the above team. In addition, each team set contained two bonus Collector's Choice Gold Mini-Cards. These differed from the regular Gold Mini-Cards with each having the same card number on each panel and the cards being numbered L1 and L2.

COMP.FACT SET (11)	8.00	20.00
L1 Kobe Bryant	2.00	5.00
Elden Campbell		
Derek Fisher		
L2 Eddie Jones	.75	2.00
Shaquille O'Neal		
Nick Van Exel		
LA1 Corie Blount	.20	.50
LA2 Kobe Bryant	6.00	15.00
LA3 Elden Campbell	.20	.50
LA4 Derek Fisher	.60	1.50
LA5 Eddie Jones	.30	.75
LA6 Travis Knight	.30	.75
LA7 Shaquille O'Neal	.75	2.00
LA8 Byron Scott	.25	.60
LA9 Nick Van Exel	.30	.75

1996-97 Collector's Choice Miami Heat Team Set

Issued with a suggested retail price of $2.99, this set features nine players from the above team. In addition, each team set contained a replica blow-up card of the Building A Winner subset from the 1996-97 Upper Deck set.

COMP.FACT SET (9)	1.50	4.00
MI1 Keith Askins	.20	.50
MI2 P.J. Brown	.20	.50
MI3 Sasha Danilovic	.20	.50
MI4 Tim Hardaway	.30	.75
MI5 Voshon Lenard	.30	.75
MI6 Dan Majerle	.30	.75
MI7 Alonzo Mourning	.40	1.00
MI8 Martin Muursepp	.30	.75
MI9 Kurt Thomas	.20	.50
NNO Miami Heat BW Blow-Up	.60	1.50

1996-97 Collector's Choice Orlando Magic Team Set

Issued with a suggested retail price of $2.99, this set features nine players from the above team. In addition, each team set contained two bonus Collector's Choice Gold Mini-Cards. These differed from the regular Gold Mini-Cards with each having the same card number on each panel and the cards being numbered O1 and O2.

COMP. FACT SET (11)	1.50	4.00
O1 Nick Anderson	.40	1.00
Horace Grant		
Anfernee Hardaway		
O2 Dennis Scott	.20	.50
Rony Seikaly		
Brian Shaw		
OR1 Nick Anderson	.20	.50
OR2 Brian Evans	.30	.75
OR3 Horace Grant	.25	.60
OR4 Anfernee Hardaway	.50	1.25
OR5 Derek Strong	.20	.50
OR6 Rony Seikaly	.25	.60
OR7 Dennis Scott	.20	.50
OR8 Brian Shaw	.20	.50
OR9 Gerald Wilkins	.20	.50

1996-97 Collector's Choice Penny! Blow Ups

Inserted one per special series one retail box as chiptoppers, these cards are blown-up parallels of the Penny! 5-card subset from the 1996-97 Collector's Choice series one set. The fronts and backs are identical to that of the regular standard-sized cards.

COMPLETE SET (5)	5.00	12.00
COMMON CARD (113-117)	1.25	3.00

1996-97 Collector's Choice San Antoino Spurs

Issued with a suggested retail price of $2.99, this set features nine players from the above team. In addition, each team set contained a replica blow-up card of the Building A Winner subset from the 1996-97 Upper Deck set.

COMP.FACT SET (9)	1.50	4.00
ST1 Cory Alexander	.20	.50
ST2 Vinny Del Negro	.20	.50
ST3 Sean Elliott	.30	.75
ST4 Carl Herrera	.20	.50
ST5 Avery Johnson	.25	.60
ST6 Will Perdue	.20	.50
ST7 David Robinson	.50	1.25
ST8 Charles Smith	.20	.50
ST9 Dominique Wilkins	.40	1.00
NNO San Antonio Spurs Blow-Up	.60	1.50

1996-97 Collector's Choice Seattle Supersonics

Issued with a suggested retail price of $2.99, this set features nine players from the above team. In addition, each team set contained two bonus Collector's Choice Gold Mini-Cards. These differed from the regular Gold Mini-Cards with each having the same card number on each panel and the cards being numbered B1 and B2.

COMP.FACT SET (11)	1.50	4.00
B1 Hersey Hawkins	.60	1.50
Shawn Kemp		
Nate McMillan		
B2 Gary Payton	.40	1.00
Sam Perkins		
Detlef Schrempf		
ST1 Craig Ehlo	.20	.50
ST2 Hersey Hawkins	.20	.50
ST3 Shawn Kemp	.30	.75
ST4 Jim McIlvaine	.20	.50
ST5 Nate McMillan	.20	.50
ST6 Gary Payton	.30	.75
ST7 Sam Perkins	.20	.50
ST8 Detlef Schrempf	.30	.75
ST9 Eric Snow	.30	.75

1997-98 Collector's Choice

The 1997-98 Collector's Choice issue totaled 400 cards with each series containing 200. Each pack contained 14 cards and carried a suggested retail price of $1.29. The set contains the topical subsets: Game Night (156-185), Catch 23 (186-195), Hot Properties (356-385) and Michael's Magic (386-395). The fronts feature color action player photos in a white border. The backs carry player information. Checklist cards 196-200 were Challenge cards which when filled in correctly could be redeemed for a set of the Top 10 Picks in the 1997 NBA Draft. A factory set was also released, which contained not only the 400 basic cards, but also five Miniatures, and 10 special StarQuest cards that were available only in the factory set.

COMPLETE SET (400)	15.00	30.00
COMP.FACTORY SET (415)	25.00	40.00
COMPLETE SERIES 1 (200)	7.50	15.00
COMPLETE SERIES 2 (200)	7.50	15.00
1 Mookie Blaylock	.07	.20
2 Dikembe Mutombo	.12	.30
3 Eldridge Recasner	.07	.20
4 Christian Laettner	.10	.25
5 Tyrone Corbin	.07	.20
6 Antoine Walker	.12	.30
7 Eric Williams	.07	.20
8 Dana Barros	.07	.20
9 David Wesley	.07	.20
10 Dino Radja	.10	.25
11 Vlade Divac	.12	.30
12 Dell Curry	.07	.20
13 Muggsy Bogues	.10	.25
14 Tony Smith	.07	.20
15 Glen Rice	.12	.30
16 Anthony Mason	.07	.20
17 Dennis Rodman	.25	.60
18 Brian Williams	.07	.20
19 Toni Kukoc	.12	.30
20 Jason Caffey	.07	.20
21 Steve Kerr	.10	.25
22 Luc Longley	.07	.20
23 Michael Jordan	1.00	2.50
24 Chris Mills	.07	.20
25 Tyrone Hill	.07	.20
26 Vitaly Potapenko	.07	.20
27 Bob Sura	.07	.20
28 Robert Pack	.07	.20
29 Ed O'Bannon	.07	.20
30 Michael Finley	.12	.30
31 Shawn Bradley	.07	.20
32 Khalid Reeves	.07	.20
33 Antonio McDyess	.10	.25
34 Ervin Johnson	.07	.20
35 Dale Ellis	.07	.20
36 Bryant Stith	.07	.20
37 Tom Hammonds	.07	.20
38 Otis Thorpe	.07	.20
39 Lindsey Hunter	.07	.20
40 Grant Long	.07	.20
41 Aaron McKie	.07	.20
42 Randolph Childress	.07	.20
43 Scott Burrell	.07	.20
44 Bimbo Coles	.07	.20
45 B.J. Armstrong	.07	.20
46 Mark Price	.12	.30
47 Latrell Sprewell	.12	.30
48 Felton Spencer	.07	.20
49 Charles Barkley	.20	.50
50 Mario Elie	.07	.20
51 Clyde Drexler	.15	.40
52 Kevin Willis	.07	.20
53 Antonio Davis	.07	.20
54 Reggie Miller	.15	.40
55 Dale Davis	.07	.20
56 Mark Jackson	.12	.30
57 Erick Dampier	.07	.20
58 Pooh Richardson	.07	.20
59 Terry Dehere	.07	.20
60 Brent Barry	.10	.25
61 Loy Vaught	.07	.20

62 Lorenzen Wright	.07
63 Eddie Jones	.12
64 Kobe Bryant	.60
65 Elden Campbell	.07
66 Corie Blount	.07
67 Shaquille O'Neal	.30
68 Dan Majerle	.12
69 P.J. Brown	.07
70 Tim Hardaway	.12
71 Isaac Austin	.07
72 Jamal Mashburn	.10
73 Ray Allen	.15
74 Glenn Robinson	.10
75 Armon Gilliam	.07
76 Johnny Newman	.07
77 Elliot Perry	.07
78 Sherman Douglas	.07
79 Doug West	.07
80 Kevin Garnett	.25
81 Sam Mitchell	.07
82 Tom Gugliotta	.07
83 Terry Porter	.07
84 Chris Carr	.07
85 Kevin Edwards	.07
86 Jayson Williams	.07
87 Kendall Gill	.07
88 Kerry Kittles	.07
89 Chris Gatling	.07
90 John Starks	.10
91 Charlie Ward	.07
92 Larry Johnson	.12
93 Charles Oakley	.10
94 Chris Childs	.07
95 Allan Houston	.10
96 Horace Grant	.10
97 Darrell Armstrong	.07
98 Rony Seikaly	.10
99 Dennis Scott	.07
100 Anfernee Hardaway	.20
101 Brian Shaw	.07
102 Jerry Stackhouse	.12
103 Rex Walters	.07
104 Don MacLean	.07
105 Derrick Coleman	.10
106 Lucious Harris	.07
107 Clarence Weatherspoon	.07
108 Cedric Ceballos	.07
109 Danny Manning	.10
110 Jason Kidd	.20
111 Loren Meyer	.07
112 Wesley Person	.07
113 Steve Nash	.25
114 Isaiah Rider	.07
115 Stacey Augmon	.10
116 Arvydas Sabonis	.10
117 Kenny Anderson	.10
118 Jermaine O'Neal	.15
119 Gary Trent	.07
120 Michael Smith	.07
121 Kevin Gamble	.07
122 Olden Polynice	.07
123 Billy Owens	.07
124 Corliss Williamson	.07
125 Cory Alexander	.07
126 Vinny Del Negro	.07
127 Sean Elliott	.12
128 Will Perdue	.07
129 Carl Herrera	.07
130 Shawn Kemp	.12
131 Hersey Hawkins	.07
132 Nate McMillan	.07
133 Craig Ehlo	.07
134 Detlef Schrempf	.12
135 Sam Perkins	.07
136 Sharone Wright	.07
137 Doug Christie	.07
138 Popeye Jones	.07
139 Shawn Respert	.07
140 Marcus Camby	.12
141 Adam Keefe	.07
142 Karl Malone	.15
143 John Stockton	.15
144 Greg Ostertag	.07
145 Chris Morris	.07
146 Shareef Abdur-Rahim	.12
147 Roy Rogers	.07
148 George Lynch	.07
149 Anthony Peeler	.07
150 Lee Mayberry	.07
151 Calbert Cheaney	.07
152 Harvey Grant	.07
153 Rod Strickland	.07
154 Tracy Murray	.07
155 Chris Webber	.12
156 Mookie Blaylock	.12
Christian Laettner	
Dikembe Mutombo	
Steve Smith	
157 Antoine Walker	.12
Dana Barros	
David Wesley	
158 Glen Rice	.12
Anthony Mason	
Tony Delk	
Vlade Divac	
159 Michael Jordan	1.00
Toni Kukoc	
Scottie Pippen	
Dennis Rodman	
160 Tyrone Hill	.07
Terrell Brandon	
Bob Sura	
161 Shawn Bradley	.12
Michael Finley	
Ed O'Bannon	
Robert Pack	
162 Antoino McDyess	.10
Ervin Johnson	
Dale Ellis	
LaPhonso Ellis	
163 Grant Hill	.20
Joe Dumars	
Theo Ratliff	
Lindsey Hunter	
164 Latrell Sprewell	.12
Chris Mullin	
Joe Smith	
165 Hakeem Olajuwon	.20
Clyde Drexler	
Charles Barkley	
Kevin Willis	
166 Reggie Miller	.15
Antonio Davis	
Dale Davis	
167 Loy Vaught	.10
Terry Dehere	
Pooh Richardson	
Brent Barry	

ldie Jones .60 1.50
uille O'Neal
Bryant
Van Exel
n Hardaway .15 .40
zo Mourning
Brown
al Mashburn
n Baker .15 .40
Allen
t Perry
ny Newman
n Robinson
evin Garnett .25 .60
hon Marbury
Porter
Gugliotta
ndall Gill .07 .20
lackson
s Gatling
on Williams
atrick Ewing .15 .40
Houston
les Oakley
Johnson
lie Ward
fernee Hardaway .20 .50
ce Grant
Shaw
Seikaly
len Iverson .25 .60
Stackhouse
ick Coleman
Walters
son Kidd .20 .50
ny Manning
ley Person
n Johnson
asheed Wallace .12 .30
ay Anderson
h Rider
das Sabonis
litch Richmond .12 .30
n Polynice
Owens
moud Abdul-Rauf
ean Elliott .20 .50
y Johnson
d Robinson
Alexander
ary Payton .12 .30
ef Schrempf
wn Kemp
ey Hawkins
amon Stoudamire .12 .30
cus Camby
Tabak
g Christie
arl Malone .15 .40
Stockton
Hornacek
hareef Abdur-Rahim .12 .30
Rogers
ony Peeler
nt Reeves
hris Webber .12 .30
an Howard
ert Cheaney
Strickland
997 NBA Finals 1.00 2.50
e Night
hael Jordan
Malone
nis Rodman
Stockton
lichael Jordan .50 1.25
h 23 Fast Break
lichael Jordan .50 1.25
h 23 Finger Roll
lichael Jordan .50 1.25
h 23 Favorite Pastimes
lichael Jordan .50 1.25
h 23 Championship Drive
lichael Jordan .50 1.25
h 23 Road Show
lichael Jordan .50 1.25
h 23 Media Circus
lichael Jordan .50 1.25
h 23 Jump Shot
lichael Jordan .50 1.25
h 23 Shake and Bake
lichael Jordan .50 1.25
h 23 Strong Finish
lichael Jordan .50 1.25
h 23 Leader
hecklist #1 .07 .20
hecklist #2 .07 .20
hecklist #3 .07 .20
hecklist #4 .07 .20
hecklist #5 .07 .20
teve Smith .10 .25
hris Crawford RC .12 .30
d Gray RC .12 .30
lan Henderson .07 .20
Valter McCarty .07 .20
ee Brown .07 .20
hauncey Billups RC .50 1.25
on Mercer RC .15 .40
ravis Knight .07 .20
ndrew DeClercq .07 .20
yus Edney .07 .20
Matt Geiger .07 .20
ony Delk .07 .20
R. Reid .07 .20
obby Phills .07 .20
avid Wesley .07 .20
on Harper .10 .25
cottie Pippen .20 .50
cott Burrell .07 .20
eith Booth RC .12 .30
ill Wennington .07 .20
hawn Kemp .12 .30
ydrunas Ilgauskas .12 .30
revin Knight RC .12 .30
anny Ferry .07 .20
erek Anderson RC .12 .30
Vesley Person .07 .20
.C. Green .12 .30
amaki Walker .07 .20
lubert Davis .07 .20
rick Strickland RC .12 .30
ennis Scott .07 .20
ony Battie RC .15 .40
aPhonso Ellis .07 .20
ric Williams .07 .20
obby Jackson RC .15 .40
nthony Goldwire .07 .20
anny Fortson RC .12 .30

239 Joe Dumars .12 .30
240 Grant Hill .20 .50
241 Malik Sealy .07 .20
242 Brian Williams .07 .20
243 Theo Ratliff .10 .25
244 Scot Pollard RC .12 .30
245 Erick Dampier .07 .20
246 Duane Ferrell .07 .20
247 Joe Smith .10 .25
248 Todd Fuller .07 .20
249 Adonal Foyle RC .12 .30
250 Othella Harrington .07 .20
251 Matt Maloney .07 .20
252 Hakeem Olajuwon .15 .40
253 Rodrick Rhodes RC .12 .30
254 Eddie Johnson .07 .20
255 Brent Price .07 .20
256 Austin Croshere RC .12 .30
257 Derrick McKey .07 .20
258 Chris Mullin .12 .30
259 Rik Smits .10 .25
260 Jalen Rose .10 .25
261 Darrick Martin .07 .20
262 Lamond Murray .07 .20
263 Maurice Taylor RC .12 .30
264 Rodney Rogers .07 .20
265 James Robinson .07 .20
266 Rick Fox .07 .20
267 Nick Van Exel .10 .25
268 Sean Rooks .07 .20
269 Derek Fisher .12 .30
270 Jon Barry .07 .20
271 Robert Horry .10 .25
272 Terry Mills .07 .20
273 Charles Smith RC .12 .30
274 Alonzo Mourning .15 .40
275 Voshon Lenard .07 .20
276 Todd Day .07 .20
277 Ervin Johnson .07 .20
278 Terrell Brandon .07 .20
279 Michael Curry .07 .20
280 Andrew Lang .07 .20
281 Tyrone Hill .07 .20
282 Stephon Marbury .15 .40
283 Cherokee Parks .07 .20
284 Stanley Roberts .07 .20
285 Paul Grant RC .12 .30
286 David Benoit .07 .20
287 Lucious Harris .07 .20
288 Don MacLean .07 .20
289 Sam Cassell .10 .25
290 Keith Van Horn RC .25 .60
291 Patrick Ewing .15 .40
292 Walter McCarty .07 .20
293 Chris Dudley .07 .20
294 Chris Mills .07 .20
295 Buck Williams .07 .20
296 Nick Anderson .07 .20
297 Derek Strong .07 .20
298 Gerald Wilkins .07 .20
299 Johnny Taylor RC .12 .30
300 Derek Harper .10 .25
301 Anthony Parker RC .12 .30
302 Allen Iverson .25 .60
303 Jim Jackson .07 .20
304 Eric Montross .07 .20
305 Tim Thomas RC .25 .60
306 Kebu Stewart RC .12 .30
307 Rex Chapman .07 .20
308 Tom Chambers .12 .30
309 Kevin Johnson .12 .30
310 John Williams .07 .20
311 Clifford Robinson .07 .20
312 Antonio McDyess .10 .25
313 Rasheed Wallace .12 .30
314 Brian Grant .07 .20
315 Dontonio Wingfield .07 .20
316 Kelvin Cato RC .12 .30
317 Mahmoud Abdul-Rauf .07 .20
318 Lawrence Funderburke RC .12 .30
319 Mitch Richmond .12 .30
320 Tariq Abdul-Wahad RC .12 .30
321 Terry Dehere .07 .20
322 Michael Stewart RC .12 .30
323 Tim Duncan RC .75 2.00
324 Avery Johnson .10 .25
325 David Robinson .20 .50
326 Charles Smith .07 .20
327 Chuck Person .10 .25
328 Monty Williams .07 .20
329 Jim McIlvaine .07 .20
330 Gary Payton .12 .30
331 Eric Snow .07 .20
332 Dale Ellis .07 .20
333 Vin Baker .10 .25
334 Walt Williams .07 .20
335 Tracy McGrady RC .60 1.50
336 Damon Stoudamire .12 .30
337 Carlos Rogers .07 .20
338 John Wallace .07 .20
339 Shandon Anderson .07 .20
340 Jeff Hornacek .10 .25
341 Howard Eisley .07 .20
342 Jacque Vaughn RC .12 .30
343 Bryon Russell .07 .20
344 Antoine Carr .07 .20
345 Antonio Daniels RC .12 .30
346 Pete Chilcutt .07 .20
347 Blue Edwards .07 .20
348 Bryant Reeves .07 .20
349 Chris Robinson RC .12 .30
350 Otis Thorpe .07 .20
351 Tim Legler .07 .20
352 Juwan Howard .10 .25
353 God Shammgod RC .12 .30
354 Gheorghe Muresan .07 .20
355 Chris Whitney .07 .20
356 Dikembe Mutombo HP .12 .30
357 Antoine Walker HP .12 .30
358 Glen Rice HP .12 .30
359 Scottie Pippen HP .20 .50
360 Derek Anderson HP .12 .30
361 Michael Finley HP .12 .30
362 LaPhonso Ellis HP .07 .20
363 Grant Hill HP .20 .50
364 Joe Smith HP .10 .25
365 Charles Barkley HP .20 .50
366 Reggie Miller HP .15 .40
367 Loy Vaught HP .07 .20
368 Shaquille O'Neal HP .30 .75
369 Alonzo Mourning HP .15 .40
370 Glenn Robinson HP .10 .25
371 Kevin Garnett HP .25 .60
372 Kendall Gill HP .07 .20
373 Allan Houston HP .10 .25
374 Anfernee Hardaway HP .20 .50
375 Tim Thomas HP .25 .60
376 Jason Kidd HP .20 .50
377 Kenny Anderson HP .10 .25
378 Mitch Richmond HP .12 .30
379 Tim Duncan HP .75 2.00
380 Gary Payton HP .12 .30
381 Marcus Camby HP .12 .30
382 Karl Malone HP .15 .40
383 Shareef Abdur-Rahim HP .12 .30
384 Chris Webber HP .12 .30
385 Michael Jordan HP 1.00 2.50
386 Michael Jordan MM .50 1.25
387 Michael Jordan MM .50 1.25
388 Michael Jordan MM .50 1.25
389 Michael Jordan MM .50 1.25
390 Michael Jordan MM .50 1.25
391 Michael Jordan MM .50 1.25
392 Michael Jordan MM .50 1.25
393 Michael Jordan MM .50 1.25
394 Michael Jordan MM .50 1.25
395 Michael Jordan MM .50 1.25
396 Checklist #1 .07 .20
397 Checklist #2 .07 .20
398 Checklist #3 .07 .20
399 Checklist #4 .07 .20
400 Checklist #5 .07 .20

1997-98 Collector's Choice Crash the Game Scoring

Randomly inserted in series one packs at the rate of one in five, this 30-card set features color action player photos in white borders. If the player pictured on the card scored 30 or more points in the week they were designated, the card was a winner and could be redeemed for a complete 30-card redemption set. The expiration date for the game was July 1, 1998. Card backs are numbered with a "C" prefix.

COMPLETE SET (60) 25.00 50.00
*RED.CARDS: .25X TO .6X HI COLUMN
ONE RED.SET PER WINNER BY MAIL
ONE RED.SET PER 15 NON-WIN BY MAIL
C1A Dikembe Mutombo 11/17 L .50 1.25
C1B Dikembe Mutombo 1/12 L .50 1.25
C2A Dana Barros 12/1 L .30 .75
C2B Dana Barros 12/22 L .30 .75
C3A Glen Rice 12/15 W .50 1.25
C3B Glen Rice 1/19 W .50 1.25
C4A Scottie Pippen 11/10 L .75 2.00
C4B Scottie Pippen 1/5 L .75 2.00
C5A Terrell Brandon 11/17 L .30 .75
C5B Terrell Brandon 1/5 L .30 .75
C6A Shawn Bradley 12/1 L .30 .75
C6B Shawn Bradley 12/22 L .30 .75
C7A Antonio McDyess 12/8 L .40 1.00
C7B Antonio McDyess 1/19 L .40 1.00
C8A Lindsey Hunter 12/8 L .30 .75
C8B Lindsey Hunter 12/22 L .30 .75
C9A Joe Smith 11/17 L .40 1.00
C9B Joe Smith 1/19 W .40 1.00
C10A Hakeem Olajuwon 11/17 L .60 1.50
C10B Hakeem Olajuwon 1/5 L .60 1.50
C11A Reggie Miller 11/24 W .60 1.50
C11B Reggie Miller 12/29 L .60 1.50
C12A Rodney Rogers 11/24 L .30 .75
C12B Rodney Rogers 1/19 L .30 .75
C13A Nick Van Exel 12/1 L .40 1.00
C13B Nick Van Exel 1/5 L .40 1.00
C14A Tim Hardaway 12/8 L .50 1.25
C14B Tim Hardaway 12/29 L .50 1.25
C15A Glenn Robinson 11/17 L .40 1.00
C15B Glenn Robinson 1/5 L .40 1.00
C16A Kevin Garnett 11/10 L 1.00 2.50
C16B Kevin Garnett 12/15 L 1.00 2.50
C17A Kerry Kittles 11/24 L .30 .75
C17B Kerry Kittles 12/29 L .30 .75
C18A Larry Johnson 12/1 L .50 1.25
C18B Larry Johnson 1/12 L .50 1.25
C19A Anfernee Hardaway 11/24 L .75 2.00
C19B Anfernee Hardaway 1/5 L .75 2.00
C20A Allen Iverson 12/1 L 1.00 2.50
C20B Allen Iverson 1/12 W 1.00 2.50
C21A Jason Kidd 11/24 L .75 2.00
C21B Jason Kidd 12/29 L .75 2.00
C22A Arvydas Sabonis 11/17 L .40 1.00
C22B Arvydas Sabonis 1/19 W .40 1.00
C23A Mitch Richmond 12/8 W .50 1.25
C23B Mitch Richmond 1/5 L .50 1.25
C24A David Robinson 11/10 W .75 2.00
C24B David Robinson 12/29 L .75 2.00
C25A Gary Payton 12/1 L .50 1.25
C25B Gary Payton 12/22 L .50 1.25
C26A Marcus Camby 12/15 L .50 1.25
C26B Marcus Camby 1/12 L .50 1.25
C27A Karl Malone 12/8 W .60 1.50
C27B Karl Malone 1/19 W .60 1.50
C28A Bryant Reeves 11/17 L .30 .75
C28B Bryant Reeves 1/5 L .30 .75
C29A Chris Webber 12/8 W .50 1.25
C29B Chris Webber 1/12 W .50 1.25
C30A Michael Jordan 11/24 W 4.00 10.00
C30B Michael Jordan 12/29 W 4.00 10.00

1997-98 Collector's Choice Draft Trade

Available only through the checklist challenge redemption from series one, this 10-card set features the top picks from the 1997 Draft.

COMPLETE SET (10) 60.00 150.00
1 Tim Duncan 20.00 50.00
2 Keith Van Horn 6.00 15.00
3 Chauncey Billups 12.00 30.00
4 Antonio Daniels 3.00 8.00
5 Tony Battie 4.00 10.00
6 Ron Mercer 4.00 10.00
7 Tim Thomas 6.00 15.00
8 Adonal Foyle 3.00 8.00
9 Tracy McGrady 15.00 40.00
10 Danny Fortson 3.00 8.00

1997-98 Collector's Choice Factory All StarQuest

Inserted into factory sets only, this 10-card set featues some of the top players in the NBA. The set utilizes the same design as the regular StarQuest set, but has "All StarQuest" at the bottom of the card.

COMPLETE SET (10) 5.00 12.00
AS1 Kobe Bryant 1.50 4.00
AS2 Gary Payton .30 .75
AS3 Kevin Garnett .60 1.50
AS4 Karl Malone .40 1.00
AS5 Shaquille O'Neal .75 2.00
AS6 Michael Jordan 2.50 6.00
AS7 Anfernee Hardaway .50 1.25
AS8 Grant Hill .50 1.25
AS9 Shawn Kemp .30 .75
AS10 Dikembe Mutombo .30 .75

1997-98 Collector's Choice Memorable Moments

Distributed one per series two Anco pack, this 10-card set features some of the most memorable moments for each player from the previous season.

COMPLETE SET (10) 6.00 15.00
1 Michael Jordan 3.00 8.00
2 Grant Hill .60 1.50
3 Anfernee Hardaway .60 1.50
4 Kobe Bryant 2.00 5.00
5 Kevin Garnett .75 2.00
6 Jason Kidd .60 1.50
7 Karl Malone .50 1.25
8 Hakeem Olajuwon .50 1.25
9 Gary Payton .40 1.00
10 Dennis Rodman .75 2.00

1997-98 Collector's Choice Miniatures

Randomly inserted into series two packs at a rate of one in 3, this 30-card set features one player from all 29 teams on a mini-standee card. Each card is die cut. Each factory set also included five random cards from this set. Card backs carry a "M" prefix.

COMPLETE SET (30) 4.00 10.00
M1 Mookie Blaylock .10 .25
M2 Chauncey Billups .60 1.50
M3 Glen Rice .15 .40
M4 Scottie Pippen .25 .60
M5 Bob Sura .10 .25
M6 Erick Strickland .15 .40
M7 Tony Battie .20 .50
M8 Joe Dumars .15 .40
M9 Adonal Foyle .15 .40
M10 Charles Barkley .25 .60
M11 Dale Davis .10 .25
M12 Lamond Murray .10 .25
M13 Kobe Bryant .75 2.00
M14 Tim Hardaway .15 .40
M15 Glenn Robinson .12 .30
M16 Kevin Garnett .30 .75
M17 Keith Van Horn .30 .75
M18 Patrick Ewing .20 .50
M19 Anfernee Hardaway .25 .60
M20 Tim Thomas .30 .75
M21 Jason Kidd .25 .60
M22 Isaiah Rider .10 .25
M23 Mahmoud Abdul-Rauf .10 .25
M24 Tim Duncan 1.00 2.50
M25 Detlef Schrempf .15 .40
M26 Damon Stoudamire .15 .40
M27 John Stockton .20 .50
M28 Bryant Reeves .10 .25
M29 Juwan Howard .12 .30
M30 Michael Jordan 1.25 3.00

1997-98 Collector's Choice MJ Bullseye

Randomly inserted into series two packs at a rate of one in five, this 30-card set features a double Crash the Game theme focused solely on Michael Jordan. Each card had two ways to win, by either matching between the given range Jordan's total points from the 1997-98 season or by having Jordan score 100 points in the given week. Winning cards were redeemable for either individual cards from a 13-card Blow-up Jordan Rewind redemption set or the complete set. The game ended on June 1, 1998.

COMMON JORDAN (B1-B30) 2.00 5.00

1997-98 Collector's Choice MJ Rewind Redemption

This 13-card set was available via redemption from winning 1997-98 Collector's Choice Crash the Game MJ Bullseye cards. Each winning card returned either an individual card or a complete set. The cards are oversized and feature key moments and photography from each of Michael Jordan's NBA seasons. Card backs are numbered with a "R" prefix.

COMPLETE SET (13) 15.00 40.00
COMMON CARD (R1-R13) 1.50 4.00

1997-98 Collector's Choice Star Attractions

Inserted one per special Collector's Choice series one and two Anco pack, this 20-card set was divided up into two sets of ten cards. The cards feature a silver metallic background on the die cut front with the theme "Star Attractions" logo located at the top. Card backs are numbered with a "SA" prefix.

COMPLETE SET (20) 15.00 40.00
COMPLETE SERIES 1 (10) 10.00 25.00
COMPLETE SERIES 2 (10) 6.00 15.00
*GOLD: 2X TO 5X HI COLUMN
GOLD: SER.1/2 STATED ODDS 1:20 SPEC.
SA1 Michael Jordan 5.00 12.00
SA2 Joe Smith .50 1.25
SA3 Karl Malone .75 2.00
SA4 Chauncey Billups 1.25 3.00
SA5 Charles Barkley 1.00 2.50
SA6 Shaquille O'Neal 1.50 4.00
SA7 Jason Kidd 1.00 2.50
SA8 Chris Webber .60 1.50
SA9 Allen Iverson 1.25 3.00
SA10 Patrick Ewing .75 2.00
SA11 Tim Duncan 2.00 5.00
SA12 Kevin Garnett 1.25 3.00
SA13 Tony Battie .40 1.00
SA14 Gary Payton .60 1.50
SA15 Hakeem Olajuwon .75 2.00
SA16 Antonio Daniels .30 .75
SA17 Grant Hill 1.00 2.50
SA18 Anfernee Hardaway 1.00 2.50
SA19 Scottie Pippen 1.00 2.50
SA20 Keith Van Horn .60 1.50

1997-98 Collector's Choice StarQuest

Randomly inserted both series packs, this 180-card set features color action photos of the top players of the game. Both 90-card series features tiering, containing bronze, silver, gold, and platinum levels. The bronze tier contains 90 players with an insertion rate of 1:1; silver has 40 players with an insertion rate of 1:21; gold contains 30 players with a 1:71 insertion rate; the top twenty stars are in the platinum tier with a 1:145 insertion rate. Card backs are numbered with a "SQ" prefix.

1 Dale Davis .15 .40
2 Jamal Mashburn .20 .50
3 Christian Laettner .20 .50
4 Billy Owens .15 .40
5 Vlade Divac .25 .60
6 Sean Elliott .25 .60
7 Marcus Camby .25 .60
8 Dana Barros .15 .40
9 Rod Strickland .15 .40
10 Jim Jackson .15 .40
11 Tyrone Hill .15 .40
12 Ervin Johnson .15 .40
13 Antoine Walker .25 .60
14 Lorenzen Wright .15 .40
15 Shawn Bradley .15 .40
16 John Starks .20 .50
17 Corliss Williamson .15 .40
18 Steve Smith .20 .50
19 Chris Mills .15 .40
20 Vinny Del Negro .15 .40
21 Jayson Williams .15 .40
22 Anthony Mason .15 .40
23 Dennis Scott .15 .40
24 Mark Jackson .25 .60
25 Dino Radja .20 .50
26 Greg Ostertag .15 .40
27 Anthony Peeler .15 .40
28 Toni Kukoc .25 .60
29 Michael Finley .25 .60
30 Brent Barry .20 .50
31 Wesley Person .15 .40
32 Horace Grant .20 .50
33 Walt Williams .15 .40
34 Bryant Stith .15 .40
35 Ray Allen .30 .75
36 Otis Thorpe .15 .40
37 Rasheed Wallace .25 .60
38 Charles Oakley .20 .50
39 Robert Pack .15 .40
40 Kendall Gill .15 .40
41 Lindsey Hunter .15 .40
42 Cedric Ceballos .15 .40
43 Allan Houston .20 .50
44 Bryant Reeves .15 .40
45 Derrick Coleman .20 .50
46 Isaiah Rider .75 2.00
47 Detlef Schrempf 1.25 3.00
48 Antonio McDyess 1.00 2.50
49 Glenn Robinson 1.00 2.50
50 Damon Stoudamire 1.25 3.00
51 Terrell Brandon .75 2.00
52 Joe Smith 1.00 2.50
53 Tom Gugliotta .75 2.00
54 Loy Vaught .75 2.00
55 Kenny Anderson 1.00 2.50
56 Dikembe Mutombo 1.25 3.00
57 Tim Hardaway 1.25 3.00
58 Chris Webber 1.25 3.00
59 Nick Van Exel 1.00 2.50
60 Kerry Kittles .75 2.00
61 Chris Mullin 1.25 3.00
62 Stephon Marbury 1.50 4.00
63 Juwan Howard 1.00 2.50
64 Larry Johnson 1.25 3.00
65 Shareef Abdur-Rahim 1.25 3.00
66 Dennis Rodman 4.00 10.00
67 Vin Baker 1.50 4.00
68 Clyde Drexler 2.50 6.00
69 Eddie Jones 2.00 5.00
70 Jerry Stackhouse 2.00 5.00
71 Karl Malone 2.50 6.00
72 Mitch Richmond 2.00 5.00
73 Glen Rice 2.00 5.00
74 Jason Kidd 3.00 8.00
75 Latrell Sprewell 2.00 5.00
76 David Robinson 3.00 8.00
77 Charles Barkley 3.00 8.00
78 Gary Payton 2.00 5.00
79 Scottie Pippen 3.00 8.00
80 Reggie Miller 2.50 6.00
81 Alonzo Mourning 3.00 8.00
82 Allen Iverson 5.00 12.00
83 Michael Jordan 20.00 50.00
84 Shawn Kemp 2.50 6.00
85 Kevin Garnett 5.00 12.00
86 Grant Hill 4.00 10.00
87 Anfernee Hardaway 4.00 10.00
88 Shaquille O'Neal 6.00 15.00
89 John Stockton 3.00 8.00
90 Hakeem Olajuwon 3.00 8.00
91 Billy Owens .15 .40
92 Derek Anderson .25 .60
93 Hersey Hawkins .15 .40
94 Bryon Russell .15 .40
95 Rik Smits .20 .50
96 Tracy McGrady 1.25 3.00
97 Kendall Gill .15 .40
98 Tim Thomas .50 1.25
99 Robert Horry .20 .50
100 Marcus Camby .25 .60
101 Rodney Rogers .15 .40
102 Danny Manning .20 .50
103 John Starks .20 .50
104 Mahmoud Abdul-Rauf .15 .40
105 Chris Childs .15 .40
106 Antonio Davis .15 .40
107 Lamond Murray .15 .40
108 Nick Anderson .15 .40
109 Antoine Walker .25 .60
110 Christian Laettner .20 .50
111 Gary Trent .15 .40
112 Tony Battie .30 .75
113 Vlade Divac .25 .60
114 Kevin Johnson .25 .60
115 Erick Strickland .25 .60
116 Ray Allen .30 .75
117 Antonio Daniels .25 .60
118 Sean Elliott .25 .60
119 Horace Grant .20 .50
120 Walt Williams .15 .40
121 Rony Seikaly .20 .50
122 Allan Houston .20 .50
123 Michael Finley .25 .60
124 Rasheed Wallace .25 .60
125 Doug Christie .15 .40
126 Danny Ferry .15 .40
127 Arvydas Sabonis .20 .50
128 Shandon Anderson .15 .40
129 Otis Thorpe .15 .40
130 Adonal Foyle .25 .60
131 Bryant Reeves .15 .40
132 Theo Ratliff .20 .50
133 Matt Maloney .15 .40
134 Voshon Lenard .15 .40
135 Danny Fortson .25 .60
136 Joe Smith 1.00 2.50
137 Mookie Blaylock .75 2.00
138 Loy Vaught .75 2.00
139 Tom Gugliotta .75 2.00
140 Damon Stoudamire 1.25 3.00
141 Antonio McDyess 1.00 2.50
142 Kobe Bryant 10.00 25.00
143 Juwan Howard 1.00 2.50
144 Tim Hardaway 1.25 3.00
145 Ron Mercer 1.50 4.00
146 Joe Dumars 1.25 3.00
147 Clyde Drexler 1.50 4.00
148 Shareef Abdur-Rahim 1.25 3.00
149 LaPhonso Ellis .75 2.00
150 Dikembe Mutombo 1.25 3.00
151 Chauncey Billups 5.00 12.00
152 Chris Webber 1.25 3.00
153 Glenn Robinson 1.00 2.50
154 Patrick Ewing 1.50 4.00
155 Stephon Marbury 1.50 4.00
156 Keith Van Horn 4.00 10.00
157 Karl Malone 2.50 6.00
158 Terrell Brandon 1.25 3.00
159 Sam Cassell 1.50 4.00
160 Jerry Stackhouse 2.00 5.00
161 Vin Baker 1.50 4.00
162 Jason Kidd 3.00 8.00
163 Charles Barkley 3.00 8.00
164 Reggie Miller 2.50 6.00
165 Alonzo Mourning 2.50 6.00
166 Scottie Pippen 3.00 8.00
167 Glen Rice 2.00 5.00
168 Allen Iverson 4.00 10.00
169 David Robinson 3.00 8.00
170 Shawn Kemp 2.00 5.00
171 Michael Jordan 20.00 50.00
172 Tim Duncan 15.00 40.00
173 Anfernee Hardaway 4.00 10.00
174 Shaquille O'Neal 6.00 15.00
175 John Stockton 3.00 8.00
176 Gary Payton 2.50 6.00
177 Mitch Richmond 2.50 6.00
178 Kevin Garnett 5.00 12.00
179 Hakeem Olajuwon 3.00 8.00
180 Grant Hill 4.00 10.00

1997-98 Collector's Choice Stick-Ums

Randomly inserted in series one packs at the rate of one in three, this 30-sticker set features color action images of a player from each NBA team in the middle of a dunk and can be stuck anywhere. Card backs carry a checklist for the set and are numbered with a "S" prefix.

COMPLETE SET (30) 3.00 8.00
S1 Steve Smith .12 .30
S2 Antoine Walker .15 .40
S3 Anthony Mason .10 .25
S4 Dennis Rodman .30 .75
S5 Terrell Brandon .10 .25
S6 Michael Finley .15 .40
S7 Antonio McDyess .12 .30
S8 Grant Hill .25 .60
S9 Joe Smith .12 .30
S10 Hakeem Olajuwon .20 .50
S11 Reggie Miller .20 .50
S12 Loy Vaught .10 .25
S13 Shaquille O'Neal .40 1.00
S14 Alonzo Mourning .20 .50
S15 Vin Baker .12 .30
S16 Stephon Marbury .20 .50
S17 Jim Jackson .10 .25
S18 John Starks .12 .30
S19 Anfernee Hardaway .25 .60
S20 Allen Iverson .30 .75
S21 Jason Kidd .25 .60
S22 Kenny Anderson .12 .30
S23 Mitch Richmond .15 .40
S24 David Robinson .25 .60
S25 Shawn Kemp .15 .40
S26 Damon Stoudamire .15 .40
S27 Karl Malone .20 .50
S28 Bryant Reeves .10 .25
S29 Juwan Howard .12 .30
S30 Michael Jordan 1.25 3.00

1997-98 Collector's Choice The Jordan Dynasty

Randomly inserted in series one packs, this five-card insert set features color player photos of Michael Jordan and celebrates the five NBA championships he and the Bulls have brought to Chicago. Each card contains a detailed summary of the highlights of each of the five seasons. Only 23,000 of each card was produced.

COMPLETE SET (5) 15.00 40.00
COMMON CARD (1-5) 6.00 15.00

1997-98 Collector's Choice Catch 23

This 10-card set measures approximately 5" by 7" and features 10 cards that are a larger version of the "Catch 23" subset from 1997-98 Collector's Choice. The cards were inserted one per retail blister package with two 1997-98 Collector's Choice packs. Those blister packs retailed for $2.99. The card backs are numbered with a "C" prefix.

COMPLETE SET (10) 10.00 25.00
COMMON CARD (C1-C10) 1.25 3.00

1997-98 Collector's Choice Jumbos

This 15-card set measures approximately 7" by 11" and features color player photos on the fronts. The first 10 cards listed are a jumbo version of the "Catch 23" set and display a Michael Jordan photo with a paragraph on the back explaining the picture. The last five cards honor five top teams from the 1996-97 NBA season and feature color action photos of the top team members with their statistics. The cards were inserted as chiptoppers in retail boxes.

COMPLETE SET (15) 15.00 40.00
1 Michael Jordan 2.00 5.00
Natural-Born Leader
2 Michael Jordan 2.00 5.00
Strong Finish
3 Michael Jordan 2.00 5.00
Shake and Bake
4 Michael Jordan 2.00 5.00
Classic Jump Shot
5 Michael Jordan 2.00 5.00
Media Circus
6 Michael Jordan 2.00 5.00
Traveling Road Show
7 Michael Jordan 2.00 5.00
Championship Drive
8 Michael Jordan 2.00 5.00
Favorite Pastimes
9 Michael Jordan 2.00 5.00
Finger Roll

10 Michael Jordan Fast Break 2.00 5.00
GN1 Utah Jazz Game Night 1.25 3.00
GN2 Los Angeles Lakers Game Night 1.50 4.00
GN3 Minnesota Timberwolves Game Night 1.25 3.00
GN4 Orlando Magic Game Night 1.25 3.00
GN5 Chicago Bulls Game Night 2.00 5.00

1995-96 Collector's Choice European Stickers

Distributed in 100-pack boxes, this 212-card set utilizes the design of both the 1994-95 Collector's Chioce American and the 1995-96 Collector's Choice American (though the 1994-95 design is used primarily throughout the set.) The cards, which are smaller than standard size, feature identical fronts to the American version. The backs feature the NBA Logo, the Collector's Choice/Upper Deck Logo, the card number in a black circle and copyright information. Team logo stickers are also available in the set.

COMPLETE SET (212) 20.00 50.00
1 Golden State Warriors Logo .10 .25
2 Latrell Sprewell .40 1.00
3 Ricky Pierce .25 .60
4 Tim Hardaway .40 1.00
5 Chris Mullin .40 1.00
6 Donyell Marshall .25 .60
7 Clifford Rozier .25 .60
8 Carlos Rogers .25 .60
9 Rony Seikaly .30 .75
10 Los Angeles Clippers Logo .10 .25
11 Pooh Richardson .25 .60
12 Terry Dehere .25 .60
13 Eric Piatkowski .30 .75
14 Loy Vaught .25 .60
15 Malik Sealy .25 .60
16 Lamond Murray .25 .60
17 Los Angeles Lakers Logo .10 .25
18 Sedale Threatt .25 .60
19 Nick Van Exel .40 1.00
20 Cedric Ceballos .25 .60
21 George Lynch .25 .60
22 Eddie Jones .50 1.25
23 Elden Campbell .25 .60
24 Vlade Divac .40 1.00
25 Phoenix Suns Logo .10 .25
26 Kevin Johnson .40 1.00
27 Wesley Person .25 .60
28 Dan Majerle .40 1.00
29 A.C. Green .40 1.00
30 Charles Barkley .60 1.50
31 Danny Manning .30 .75
32 Wayman Tisdale .25 .60
33 Portland Trail Blazers Logo .10 .25
34 Rod Strickland .25 .60
35 Terry Porter .25 .60
36 Aaron McKie .25 .60
37 Otis Thorpe .25 .60
38 Buck Williams .25 .60
39 Clifford Robinson .25 .60
40 Harvey Grant .25 .60
41 Sacramento Kings Logo .10 .25
42 Randy Brown .25 .60
43 Mitch Richmond .40 1.00
44 Bobby Hurley .40 1.00
45 Walt Williams .25 .60
46 Brian Grant .30 .75
47 Olden Polynice .25 .60
48 Duane Causwell .25 .60
49 Seattle Supersonics Logo .10 .25
50 Kendall Gill .25 .60
51 Gary Payton .40 1.00
52 Sarunas Marciulionis .25 .60
53 Nate McMillan .25 .60
54 Detlef Schrempf .40 1.00
55 Shawn Kemp .40 1.00
56 Sam Perkins .25 .60
57 Dallas Mavericks Logo .10 .25
58 Jim Jackson .25 .60
59 Jason Kidd .60 1.50
60 Tony Dumas .25 .60
61 Jamal Mashburn .40 1.00
62 Doug Smith .25 .60
63 Popeye Jones .25 .60
64 Denver Nuggets Logo .10 .25
65 Robert Pack .25 .60
66 Bryant Stith .25 .60
67 Mahmoud Abdul-Rauf .25 .60
68 Jalen Rose .50 1.25
69 Reggie Williams .25 .60
70 LaPhonso Ellis .25 .60
71 Dikembe Mutombo .40 1.00
72 Houston Rockets Logo .10 .25
73 Sam Cassell .40 1.00
74 Kenny Smith .30 .75
75 Clyde Drexler .50 1.25
76 Carl Herrera .25 .60
77 Robert Horry .30 .75
78 Otis Thorpe .25 .60
79 Hakeem Olajuwon .50 1.25
80 Minnesota Timberwolves Logo .10 .25
81 Chris Smith .25 .60
82 Micheal Williams .25 .60
83 Doug West .25 .60
84 Isaiah Rider .40 1.00
85 Christian Laettner .30 .75
86 Tom Gugliotta .25 .60
87 San Antonio Spurs Logo .10 .25
88 Avery Johnson .30 .75
89 Vinny Del Negro .25 .60
90 Dennis Rodman .75 2.00
91 Sean Elliott .40 1.00
92 Chuck Person .30 .75
93 J.R. Reid .25 .60
94 David Robinson .60 1.50
95 Utah Jazz Logo .10 .25
96 Jeff Hornacek .30 .75
97 John Stockton .50 1.25
98 David Benoit .25 .60
99 Karl Malone .50 1.25
100 Tom Chambers .40 1.00
101 Antoine Carr .25 .60
102 Felton Spencer .25 .60
103 Atlanta Hawks Logo .10 .25
104 Mookie Blaylock .25 .60
105 Craig Ehlo .25 .60
106 Steve Smith .30 .75
107 Stacey Augmon .30 .75
108 Grant Long .25 .60
109 Ken Norman .25 .60
110 Jon Koncak .25 .60
111 Charlotte Hornets Logo .10 .20
112 Hersey Hawkins .25 .60
113 Dell Curry .25 .60
114 Muggsy Bogues .30 .75
115 Scott Burrell .25 .60
116 Larry Johnson .40 1.00
117 Robert Parish .40 1.00
118 Alonzo Mourning .50 1.25
119 Chicago Bulls Logo .10 .25
120 Michael Jordan 3.00 8.00
121 Ron Harper .30 .75
122 Toni Kukoc .40 1.00
123 Scottie Pippen .60 1.50
124 Dickey Simpkins .25 .60
125 Will Perdue .25 .60
126 Cleveland Cavaliers Logo .10 .25
127 Gerald Wilkins .25 .60
128 Mark Price .40 1.00
129 Terrell Brandon .25 .60
130 Bobby Phills .25 .60
131 Chris Mills .25 .60
132 Tyrone Hill .25 .60
133 John Williams .25 .60
134 Detroit Pistons Logo .10 .25
135 Lindsey Hunter .25 .60
136 Joe Dumars .40 1.00
137 Allan Houston .30 .75
138 Terry Mills .25 .60
139 Grant Hill .60 1.50
140 Mark West .25 .60
141 Indiana Pacers Logo .10 .25
142 Reggie Miller .50 1.25
143 Mark Jackson .40 1.00
144 Duane Ferrell .25 .60
145 Derrick McKey .25 .60
146 Dale Davis .25 .60
147 Antonio Davis .25 .60
148 Rik Smits .30 .75
149 Milwaukee Bucks Logo .10 .25
150 Lee Mayberry .25 .60
151 Todd Day .25 .60
152 Vin Baker .30 .75
153 Glenn Robinson .40 1.00
154 Marty Conlon .25 .60
155 Johnny Newman .25 .60
156 Eric Mobley .25 .60
157 Boston Celtics Logo .10 .25
158 Sherman Douglas .25 .60
159 Dee Brown .25 .60
160 Rick Fox .25 .60
161 Dino Radja .30 .75
162 Xavier McDaniel .25 .60
163 Dominique Wilkins .50 1.25
164 Eric Montross .25 .60
165 Miami Heat Logo .10 .25
166 Bimbo Coles .25 .60
167 Khalid Reeves .25 .60
168 Glen Rice .40 1.00
169 Billy Owens .25 .60
170 Kevin Willis .25 .60
171 Matt Geiger .25 .60
172 New Jersey Nets Logo .10 .25
173 Kevin Edwards .25 .60
174 Rex Walters .25 .60
175 Kenny Anderson .30 .75
176 Derrick Coleman .30 .75
177 Chris Morris .25 .60
178 Armon Gilliam .25 .60
179 P.J. Brown .25 .60
180 New York Knicks Logo .10 .25
181 Derek Harper .30 .75
182 Charlie Ward .25 .60
183 John Starks .30 .75
184 Charles Smith .25 .60
185 Charles Oakley .30 .75
186 Anthony Mason .25 .60
187 Patrick Ewing .50 1.25
188 Orlando Magic Logo .10 .25
189 Anthony Bowie .25 .60
190 Anfernee Hardaway .60 1.50
191 Nick Anderson .25 .60
192 Dennis Scott .25 .60
193 Donald Royal .25 .60
194 Horace Grant .30 .75
195 Shaquille O'Neal 1.00 2.50
196 Philadelphia 76ers Logo .10 .25
197 Jeff Malone .25 .60
198 Dana Barros .25 .60
199 Clarence Weatherspoon .25 .60
200 Scott Williams .25 .60
201 Sharone Wright .25 .60
202 Shawn Bradley .25 .60
203 Washington Bullets Logo .10 .25
204 Scott Skiles .25 .60
205 Mitchell Butler .25 .60
206 Calbert Cheaney .25 .60
207 Don MacLean .25 .60
208 Juwan Howard .40 1.00
209 Kevin Duckworth .25 .60
210 Gheorghe Muresan .25 .60
211 Toronto Raptors Logo 1.00 .25
212 Vancouver Grizzlies Logo .10 .25

1995-96 Collector's Choice European Stickers Michael Jordan

Randomly inserted into packs of 1995-96 Collector's Choice European at roughly one in five, this nine-card set is identical in design to the 1995-96 Collector's Choice Jordan Collection and the 1995-96 Collector's Choice He's Back sets. These stickers have a "MJ" prefix on the back.

COMPLETE SET (9) 12.00 30.00
COMMON STICKER (1-9) 1.60 4.00

1996 Collector's Choice Hula Hoops European

This 40-card set was distributed in the United Kingdom under the promoter of KP Foods. The cards are designed like the Collector's Choice set, but are mini in size. Card backs are numbered with a "HH" prefix.

COMPLETE SET (40) 125.00 250.00
HH1 Mookie Blaylock 3.00 8.00
HH2 Dana Barros 3.00 8.00
HH3 Toni Kukoc 5.00 12.00
HH4 Terrell Brandon 3.00 8.00
HH5 Jamal Mashburn 4.00 10.00
HH6 Antonio McDyess 5.00 12.00
HH7 Chris Mullin 5.00 12.00
HH8 Hakeem Olajuwon 6.00 15.00
HH9 Brent Barry 4.00 10.00
HH10 Eddie Jones 5.00 12.00
HH11 Kurt Thomas 3.00 8.00
HH12 Kevin Garnett 12.00 30.00
HH13 Kendall Gill 3.00 8.00
HH14 John Starks 4.00 10.00
HH15 Dennis Scott 3.00 8.00
HH16 Jerry Stackhouse 6.00 15.00
HH17 Arvydas Sabonis 4.00 10.00
HH18 Billy Owens 3.00 8.00
HH19 Avery Johnson 4.00 10.00
HH20 Damon Stoudamire 5.00 12.00
HH21 Christian Laettner 4.00 10.00
HH22 Dino Radja 4.00 10.00
HH23 Dennis Rodman 10.00 25.00
HH24 Jim Jackson 3.00 8.00
HH25 LaPhonso Ellis 3.00 8.00
HH26 Joe Dumars 5.00 12.00
HH27 Joe Smith 4.00 10.00
HH28 Rik Smits 4.00 10.00
HH29 Cedric Ceballos 3.00 8.00
HH30 Sasha Danilovic 3.00 8.00
HH31 Vin Baker 4.00 10.00
HH32 Shawn Bradley 3.00 8.00
HH33 Charles Oakley 4.00 10.00
HH34 Anfernee Hardaway 8.00 20.00
HH35 Derrick Coleman 4.00 10.00
HH36 Wesley Person 3.00 8.00
HH37 Brian Grant 4.00 10.00
HH38 Sean Elliott 5.00 12.00
HH39 Detlef Schrempf 5.00 12.00
HH40 Karl Malone 6.00 15.00

1994-95 Collector's Choice International French

This 429-card standard size set was issued in two separate series of 210 and 219 cards by Upper Deck for the French, German and Italian markets. Cards were distributed for all countries in 10-card packs and 30 pack boxes (featuring Michael Jordan on both the wrapper and the box). The first 210 cards are similar in design and numbering to the American 1994-95 Collector's Choice set. The following subsets are included in this set: Tip-Off (166-192), All-Star Advice (193-198), NBA Profiles (199-206), Checklists (207-210, 417-420), Michael Jordan Heroes (211-219), Blueprints (372-398), Trivia (399-406) and Draft Class (407-416). The Michael Jordan Heroes subset cards are believed to be tougher to pull from packs than other regular issue cards. White-bordered fronts feature color player action shots. The player's name, team and position appear in a lower corner. The back carries another color player action shot at the top, with statistics and career highlights displayed below. All cards feature bilingual information. This product has been made readily available to the U.S. market through closeouts.

COMPLETE SET (429) 20.00 50.00
COMPLETE SERIES 1 (219) 10.00 25.00
COMPLETE SERIES 2 (210) 10.00 25.00
1 Anfernee Hardaway .50 1.25
2 Mark Macon .20 .50
3 Steve Smith .25 .60
4 Chris Webber .50 1.25
5 Donald Royal .20 .50
6 Avery Johnson .25 .60
7 Kevin Johnson .30 .75
8 Doug Christie .20 .50
9 Derrick McKey .20 .50
10 Dennis Rodman .60 1.50
11 Scott Skiles .20 .50
12 Johnny Dawkins .20 .50
13 Kendall Gill .20 .50
14 Jeff Hornacek .25 .60
15 Latrell Sprewell .40 1.00
16 Lucious Harris .20 .50
17 Chris Mullin .30 .75
18 John Williams .20 .50
19 Tony Campbell .20 .50
20 LaPhonso Ellis .20 .50
21 Gerald Wilkins .20 .50
22 Clyde Drexler .40 1.00
23 Michael Jordan BB 2.50 6.00
24 George Lynch .20 .50
25 Mark Price .30 .75
26 James Robinson .20 .50
27 Elmore Spencer .20 .50
28 Stacey King .20 .50
29 Corie Blount .20 .50
30 Dell Curry .20 .50
31 Reggie Miller .40 1.00
32 Karl Malone .40 1.00
33 Scottie Pippen .60 1.50
34 Hakeem Olajuwon .40 1.00
35 Clarence Weatherspoon .20 .50
36 Kevin Edwards .20 .50
37 Pete Myers .20 .50
38 Jeff Turner .20 .50
39 Ennis Whatley .20 .50
40 Calbert Cheaney .20 .50
41 Glen Rice .30 .75
42 Vin Baker .30 .75
43 Grant Long .20 .50
44 Derrick Coleman .25 .60
45 Rik Smits .25 .60
46 Chris Smith .20 .50
47 Carl Herrera .20 .50
48 Bob Martin .20 .50
49 Terrell Brandon .20 .50
50 David Robinson .50 1.25
51 Danny Ferry .20 .50
52 Buck Williams .20 .50
53 Josh Grant .20 .50
54 Ed Pinckney .20 .50
55 Dikembe Mutombo .30 .75
56 Clifford Robinson .20 .50
57 Luther Wright .20 .50
58 Scott Burrell .20 .50
59 Stacey Augmon .25 .60
60 Jeff Malone .20 .50
61 Byron Houston .20 .50
62 Anthony Peeler .20 .50
63 Michael Adams .20 .50
64 Negele Knight .20 .50
65 Terry Cummings .30 .75
66 Christian Laettner .25 .60
67 Tracy Murray .20 .50
68 Sedale Threatt .20 .50
69 Dan Majerle .30 .75
70 Frank Brickowski .20 .50
71 Ken Norman .20 .50
72 Charles Smith .20 .50
73 Adam Keefe .20 .50
74 P.J. Brown .20 .50
75 Kevin Duckworth .20 .50
76 Shawn Bradley .20 .50
77 Darnell Mee .20 .50
78 Nick Anderson .20 .50
79 Mark West .20 .50
80 B.J. Armstrong .20 .50
81 Dennis Scott .20 .50
82 Lindsey Hunter .20 .50
83 Derek Strong .20 .50
84 Mike Brown .20 .50
85 Antonio Harvey .20 .50
86 Anthony Bonner .20 .50
87 Sam Cassell .30 .75
88 Harold Miner .20 .50
89 Spud Webb .30 .75
90 Mookie Blaylock .20 .50
91 Greg Anthony .20 .50
92 Richard Petruska .20 .50
93 Sean Rooks .20 .50
94 Ervin Johnson .20 .50
95 Randy Brown .20 .50
96 Orlando Woolridge .20 .50
97 Charles Oakley .25 .60
98 Craig Ehlo .20 .50
99 Derek Harper .25 .60
100 Doug Edwards .20 .50
101 Muggsy Bogues .25 .60
102 Mitch Richmond .30 .75
103 Mahmoud Abdul-Rauf .20 .50
104 Joe Dumars .30 .75
105 Eric Riley .20 .50
106 Terry Mills .20 .50
107 Toni Kukoc .40 1.00
108 Jon Koncak .20 .50
109 Haywoode Workman .20 .50
110 Todd Day .20 .50
111 Detlef Schrempf .30 .75
112 David Wesley .20 .50
113 Mark Jackson .30 .75
114 Doug Overton .20 .50
115 Vinny Del Negro .20 .50
116 Loy Vaught .20 .50
117 Mike Peplowski .20 .50
118 Bimbo Coles .20 .50
119 Rex Walters .20 .50
120 Sherman Douglas .20 .50
121 David Benoit .20 .50
122 John Salley .20 .50
123 Cedric Ceballos .20 .50
124 Chris Mills .20 .50
125 Robert Horry .30 .75
126 Johnny Newman .20 .50
127 Malcolm Mackey .20 .50
128 Terry Dehere .20 .50
129 Dino Radja .25 .60
130 Reggie Williams .20 .50
131 Xavier McDaniel .20 .50
132 Bobby Hurley .30 .75
133 Alonzo Mourning .40 1.00
134 Isaiah Rider .30 .75
135 Antoine Carr .20 .50
136 Robert Pack .20 .50
137 Walt Williams .20 .50
138 Tyrone Corbin .20 .50
139 Popeye Jones .20 .50
140 Shawn Kemp .30 .75
141 Thurl Bailey .20 .50
142 James Worthy .40 1.00
143 Scott Haskin .20 .50
144 Hubert Davis .20 .50
145 A.C. Green .30 .75
146 Dale Davis .20 .50
147 Nate McMillan .20 .50
148 Chris Morris .20 .50
149 Will Perdue .20 .50
150 Felton Spencer .20 .50
151 Rod Strickland .20 .50
152 Blue Edwards .20 .50
153 John S. Williams .20 .50
154 Rodney Rogers .20 .50
155 Acie Earl .20 .50
156 Hersey Hawkins .20 .50
157 Jamal Mashburn .30 .75
158 Don MacLean .20 .50
159 Micheal Williams .20 .50
160 Kenny Gattison .20 .50
161 Rich King .20 .50
162 Allan Houston .30 .75
163 John Stockton .40 1.00
164 Kenny Anderson .25 .60
165 Shaquille O'Neal .75 2.00
166 Danny Manning TO .25 .60
167 Dee Brown TO .20 .50
168 Alonzo Mourning TO .40 1.00
169 Scottie Pippen TO .60 1.50
170 Mark Price TO .30 .75
171 Jamal Mashburn TO .30 .75
172 Dikembe Mutombo TO .30 .75
173 Joe Dumars TO .30 .75
174 Chris Webber TO .50 1.25
175 Hakeem Olajuwon TO .40 1.00
176 Reggie Miller TO .40 1.00
177 Ron Harper TO .25 .60
178 Nick Van Exel TO .30 .75
179 Steve Smith TO .25 .60
180 Vin Baker TO .30 .75
181 Isaiah Rider TO .30 .75
182 Derrick Coleman TO .25 .60
183 Patrick Ewing TO .40 1.00
184 Shaquille O'Neal TO .75 2.00
185 Clarence Weatherspoon TO .20 .50
186 Charles Barkley TO .50 1.25
187 Clyde Drexler TO .40 1.00
188 Mitch Richmond TO .30 .75
189 David Robinson TO .50 1.25
190 Shawn Kemp TO .30 .75
191 Karl Malone TO .40 1.00
192 Tom Gugliotta TO .20 .50
193 Kenny Anderson ASA .25 .60
194 Alonzo Mourning ASA .40 1.00
195 Mark Price ASA .30 .75
196 John Stockton ASA .40 1.00
197 Shaquille O'Neal ASA .75 2.00
198 Latrell Sprewell ASA .40 1.00
199 Charles Barkley PRO .50 1.25
200 Chris Webber PRO .50 1.25
201 Patrick Ewing PRO .40 1.00
202 Dennis Rodman PRO .60 1.50
203 Shawn Kemp PRO .30 .75
204 Michael Jordan PRO 2.50 6.00
205 Shaquille O'Neal PRO .75 2.00
206 Larry Johnson PRO .30 .75
207 Tim Hardaway CL .30 .75
208 John Stockton CL .40 1.00
209 Harold Miner CL .20 .50
210 B.J. Armstrong CL .20 .50
211 Michael Jordan ROY 2.50 6.00
212 Michael Jordan 63-Pt. Game 2.50 6.00
213 Michael Jordan Slam-Dunk 2.50 6.00
214 Michael Jordan MVP 2.50 6.00
215 Michael Jordan All-Star 2.50 6.00
216 Michael Jordan 3,000-Points 2.50 6.00
217 Michael Jordan Champ. 2.50 6.00
218 Michael Jordan 1985-94 M.J.'s Decade of Dominanc 2.50 6.00
219 Michael Jordan CL 2.50 6.00
220 Gary Payton .30 .75
221 Tom Hammonds .20 .50
222 Danny Ainge .30 .75
223 Gary Grant .20 .50
224 Jim Jackson .20 .50
225 Chris Gatling .20 .50
226 Sergei Bazarevich .30 .75
227 Tony Dumas .30 .75
228 Andrew Lang .20 .50
229 Wesley Person .30 .75
230 Terry Porter .20 .50
231 Duane Causwell .20 .50
232 Shaquille O'Neal .75 2.00
233 Antonio Davis .20 .50
234 Charles Barkley .50 1.25
235 Tony Massenburg .20 .50
236 Ricky Pierce .20 .50
237 Scott Skiles .20 .50
238 Jalen Rose .75 2.00
239 Charlie Ward .30 .75
240 Michael Jordan COMM 2.50 6.00
241 Elden Campbell .20 .50
242 Bill Cartwright .25 .60
243 Armon Gilliam UER Card numbered 372 .20 .50
244 Rick Fox .20 .50
245 Tim Breaux .20 .50
246 Monty Williams .30 .75
247 Dominique Wilkins .40 1.00
248 Robert Parish .30 .75
249 Mark Jackson .30 .75
250 Jason Kidd 1.50 4.00
251 Andres Guibert .20 .50
252 Matt Geiger .20 .50
253 Stanley Roberts .20 .50
254 Jack Haley .20 .50
255 David Wingate .20 .50
256 John Crotty .20 .50
257 Brian Grant .50 1.25
258 Otis Thorpe .20 .50
259 Clifford Rozier .30 .75
260 Grant Long .20 .50
261 Eric Mobley .30 .75
262 Dickey Simpkins .30 .75
263 J.R. Reid .20 .50
264 Kevin Willis .20 .50
265 Scott Brooks .20 .50
266 Glenn Robinson .60 1.50
267 Dana Barros .20 .50
268 Ken Norman .20 .50
269 Herb Williams .20 .50
270 Dee Brown .20 .50
271 Steve Kerr .25 .60
272 Jon Barry .20 .50
273 Sean Elliott .30 .75
274 Elliot Perry .20 .50
275 Kenny Smith .25 .60
276 Sean Rooks .20 .50
277 Gheorghe Muresan .20 .50
278 Juwan Howard .50 1.25
279 Steve Smith .25 .60
280 Anthony Bowie .20 .50
281 Moses Malone .30 .75
282 Olden Polynice .20 .50
283 Jo Jo English .20 .50
284 Marty Conlon .20 .50
285 Sam Mitchell .20 .50
286 Doug West .20 .50
287 Cedric Ceballos .20 .50
288 Lorenzo Williams .20 .50
289 Harold Ellis .20 .50
290 Doc Rivers .25 .60
291 Keith Tower .20 .50
292 Mark Bryant .20 .50
293 Oliver Miller .20 .50
294 Michael Adams .20 .50
295 Tree Rollins .20 .50
296 Eddie Jones 1.00 2.50
297 Malik Sealy .20 .50
298 Blue Edwards .20 .50
299 Brooks Thompson .30 .75
300 Benoit Benjamin .20 .50
301 Avery Johnson .25 .60
302 Larry Johnson .30 .75
303 John Starks .25 .60
304 Byron Scott .25 .60
305 Eric Murdock .20 .50
306 Jay Humphries .20 .50
307 Kenny Anderson .25 .60
308 Brian Williams .20 .50
309 Nick Van Exel .30 .75
310 Tim Hardaway .30 .75
311 Lee Mayberry .20 .50
312 Vlade Divac .30 .75
313 Donyell Marshall .30 .75
314 Anthony Mason .20 .50
315 Danny Manning .25 .60
316 Tyrone Hill .20 .50
317 Vincent Askew .20 .50
318 Khalid Reeves .30 .75
319 Ron Harper .25 .60
320 Brent Price .20 .50
321 Byron Houston .20 .50
322 Lamond Murray .30 .75
323 Bryant Stith .20 .50
324 Tom Gugliotta .20 .50
325 Jerome Kersey .20 .50
326 B.J. Tyler .30 .75
327 Antonio Lang .30 .75
328 Carlos Rogers .30 .75
329 Wayman Tisdale .20 .50
330 Kevin Gamble .20 .50
331 Eric Piatkowski .40 1.00
332 Mitchell Butler .20 .50
333 Patrick Ewing .40 1.00
334 Doug Smith .20 .50
335 Joe Kleine .20 .50
336 Keith Jennings .20 .50
337 Bill Curley .30 .75
338 Johnny Newman .20 .50
339 Howard Eisley .30 .75
340 Willie Anderson .20 .50
341 Aaron McKie .30 .75
342 Tom Chambers .30 .75
343 Scott Williams .20 .50
344 Harvey Grant .20 .50
345 Billy Owens .20 .50
346 Sharone Wright .30 .75
347 Michael Cage .20 .50
348 Vern Fleming .20 .50
349 Darrin Hancock .30 .75
350 Matt Fish .20 .50
351 Rony Seikaly .25 .60
352 Victor Alexander .20 .50
353 Anthony Miller .30 .75
354 Horace Grant .25 .60
355 Jayson Williams .20 .50
356 Dale Ellis .20 .50
357 Sarunas Marciulionis .20 .50
358 Anthony Avent .20 .50
359 Rex Chapman .20 .50
360 Askia Jones .30 .75
361 Bo Outlaw .30 .75
362 Chuck Person .25 .60
363 Danny Schayes .20 .50
364 Morlon Wiley .20 .50
365 Dontonio Wingfield .30 .75
366 Tony Smith .20 .50
367 Bill Wennington .20 .50
368 Bryon Russell .20 .50
369 Geert Hammink .20 .50
370 Eric Montross .30 .75
371 Cliff Levingston .20 .50
372 Stacey Augmon BP .25 .60
373 Eric Montross BP .20 .50
374 Alonzo Mourning BP .40 1.00
375 Scottie Pippen BP .60 1.50
376 Mark Price BP .30 .75
377 Jason Kidd BP 1.00 2.50
378 Jalen Rose BP .50 1.25
379 Grant Hill BP 1.00 2.50
380 Latrell Sprewell BP .40 1.00
381 Hakeem Olajuwon BP .40 1.00
382 Reggie Miller BP .40 1.00
383 Lamond Murray BP .20 .50
384 Eddie Jones BP .60 1.50
385 Khalid Reeves BP .20 .50
386 Glenn Robinson BP .40 1.00
387 Donyell Marshall BP .20 .50
388 Derrick Coleman BP .25 .60
389 Patrick Ewing BP .40 1.00
390 Shaquille O'Neal BP .75 2.00
391 Sharone Wright BP .20 .50
392 Charles Barkley BP .50 1.25
393 Aaron McKie BP .20 .50
394 Brian Grant BP .30 .75
395 David Robinson BP .50 1.25
396 Shawn Kemp BP .30 .75
397 Karl Malone BP .40 1.00
398 Tom Gugliotta BP .20 .50
399 Hakeem Olajuwon TRIV .40 1.00
400 Shaquille O'Neal TRIV .75 2.00
401 Chris Webber TRIV .50 1.25
402 Michael Jordan TRIV 2.50 6.00
403 David Robinson TRIV .50 1.25
404 Shawn Kemp TRIV .30 .75
405 Patrick Ewing TRIV .40 1.00
406 Charles Barkley TRIV .50 1.25
407 Glenn Robinson DC .40 1.00
408 Jason Kidd DC 1.00 2.50
409 Grant Hill DC 1.00 2.50
410 Donyell Marshall DC .20 .50
411 Sharone Wright DC .20 .50
412 Lamond Murray DC .20 .50
413 Brian Grant DC .30 .75
414 Eric Montross DC .20 .50
415 Eddie Jones DC .60 1.50
416 Carlos Rogers DC .20 .50
417 Shawn Kemp CL .30 .75
418 Bobby Hurley CL .30 .75
419 Shawn Bradley CL .20 .50
420 Michael Jordan CL 2.50 6.00
421 Vernon Maxwell .20 .50
422 John Stockton .40 1.00
423 Luc Longley .20 .50
424 Sam Perkins .20 .50
425 Pooh Richardson .20 .50
426 Tyrone Corbin .20 .50
427 Mario Elie .20 .50
428 Bobby Phills .20 .50
429 Grant Hill 1.50 4.00

1994-95 Collector's Choice International French Gold Signatures

Cards from this 72-card parallel, skip-numbered insert set were randomly seeded in both series packs of French, German and Italian Collector's Choice. Only first series Spanish packs contained these inserts. The 27 Gold Signatures issued in first series packs parallel the basic issue Tip-Offs subset cards. These cards were seeded at rate of 1:5 packs. The 45 Gold Signatures issued in second series packs parallel the basic issue Blueprints, Trivia and Draft Class subset cards. These cards were seeded at a rate of 1:3 packs. Unlike the basic issue cards these inserts feature a gold foil facsimile signature stamped on the front.

COMPLETE SET (72) 55.00 130.00
COMPLETE SERIES 1 (27) 15.00 30.00
COMPLETE SERIES 2 (45) 40.00 100.00
166 Danny Manning TO 1.00 2.50
167 Dee Brown TO .75 2.00
168 Alonzo Mourning TO 1.50 4.00
169 Scottie Pippen TO 2.50 6.00
170 Mark Price TO 1.25 3.00
171 Jamal Mashburn TO 1.25 3.00
172 Dikembe Mutombo TO 1.25 3.00
173 Joe Dumars TO 1.25 3.00
174 Chris Webber TO 2.00 5.00
175 Hakeem Olajuwon TO 1.50 4.00
176 Reggie Miller TO 1.50 4.00
177 Ron Harper TO 1.00 2.50
178 Nick Van Exel TO 1.25 3.00
179 Steve Smith TO 1.00 2.50
180 Vin Baker TO 1.25 3.00
181 Isaiah Rider TO 1.25 3.00
182 Derrick Coleman TO 1.00 2.50
183 Patrick Ewing TO 1.50 4.00
184 Shaquille O'Neal TO 3.00 8.00
185 Clarence Weatherspoon TO .75 2.00
186 Charles Barkley TO 2.00 5.00
187 Clyde Drexler TO 1.50 4.00
188 Mitch Richmond TO 1.25 3.00
189 David Robinson TO 2.00 5.00
190 Shawn Kemp TO 1.25 3.00
191 Karl Malone TO 1.50 4.00
192 Tom Gugliotta TO .75 2.00
372 Stacey Augmon BP 1.00 2.50
373 Eric Montross BP .60 1.50
374 Alonzo Mourning BP 1.50 4.00
375 Scottie Pippen BP 2.50 6.00
376 Mark Price BP 1.25 3.00
377 Jason Kidd BP 3.00 8.00
378 Jalen Rose BP 1.50 4.00
379 Grant Hill BP 3.00 8.00
380 Latrell Sprewell BP 1.50 4.00
381 Hakeem Olajuwon BP 1.50 4.00
382 Reggie Miller BP 1.50 4.00
383 Lamond Murray BP .60
384 Eddie Jones BP 2.00
385 Khalid Reeves BP .60
386 Glenn Robinson BP 1.25
387 Donyell Marshall BP .60
388 Derrick Coleman BP 1.00
389 Patrick Ewing BP 1.50
390 Shaquille O'Neal BP 3.00
391 Sharone Wright BP .60
392 Charles Barkley BP 2.00
393 Aaron McKie BP .60
394 Brian Grant BP 1.00
395 David Robinson BP 2.00
396 Shawn Kemp BP 1.25
397 Karl Malone BP 1.50
398 Tom Gugliotta BP .75
399 Hakeem Olajuwon TRIV 1.50
400 Shaquille O'Neal TRIV 3.00
401 Chris Webber TRIV 2.00
402 Michael Jordan TRIV 10.00
403 David Robinson TRIV 2.00
404 Shawn Kemp TRIV 1.25
405 Patrick Ewing TRIV 1.50
406 Charles Barkley TRIV 2.00
407 Glenn Robinson DC 1.25
408 Jason Kidd DC 3.00
409 Grant Hill DC 3.00
410 Donyell Marshall DC .60
411 Sharone Wright DC .60
412 Lamond Murray DC .60
413 Brian Grant DC 1.00
414 Eric Montross DC .60
415 Eddie Jones DC 2.00
416 Carlos Rogers DC .60

1994-95 Collector's Choice International French Decade Dominance

Issued approximately one in every five packs of se[...] series French, German, Italian and Spanish and o[...] every three second series Japanese packs, these t[...] standard-size cards are derived from the Decade o[...] Dominance subset within the American 1994 Upp[...] Deck Rare Air boxed set. The card backs are biling[...] and the numbering differs from their American counterparts in the Rare Air boxed set. The horizo[...] fronts feature on the left a photo of Jordan dunking while the right side features various highlights fro[...] Jordan's career.

COMPLETE SET (10) 12.00
J1 Michael Jordan Career Stats 1.50
J2 Michael Jordan '84 NBA ROY 1.50
J3 Michael Jordan '87 Slam-Dunk Champion 1.50
J4 Michael Jordan NBA All-Star Game Stats 1.50
J5 Michael Jordan Efficient Scorer 1.50
J6 Michael Jordan '88 NBA Defensive POY 1.50
J7 Michael Jordan 1991 NBA Title 1.50
J8 Michael Jordan Unstoppable 1.50
J9 Michael Jordan All-NBA First Team 1.50
J10 Michael Jordan Averaging over 30 ppg 1.50

1994-95 Collector's Choice International German

COMPLETE SET (429) 20.00
COMPLETE SERIES 1 (219) 10.00
COMPLETE SERIES 2 (210) 10.00
*GERMAN: SAME VALUE AS FRENCH

1994-95 Collector's Choice International German Gold Signatures

COMPLETE SET (72) 55.00
COMPLETE SERIES 1 (27) 15.00
COMPLETE SERIES 2 (45) 40.00
*GERMAN: SAME VALUE AS FRENCH

1994-95 Collector's Choice International German Decade Dominance

COMPLETE SET (10) 12.00
*GERMAN: SAME VALUE AS FRENCH

1994-95 Collector's Choice International Italian

COMPLETE SET (429) 20.00
COMPLETE SERIES 1 (219) 10.00
COMPLETE SERIES 2 (210) 10.00
*ITALIAN: SAME VALUE AS FRENCH

1994-95 Collector's Choice International Italian Gold Signatures

COMPLETE SET (72) 55.00
COMPLETE SERIES 1 (27) 15.00
COMPLETE SERIES 2 (45) 40.00
*ITALIAN: SAME VALUE AS FRENCH

1994-95 Collector's Choice International Italian Decade Dominance

COMPLETE SET (10) 12.00
*ITALIAN: SAME VALUE AS FRENCH

1994-95 Collector's Choice International Japanese I

Collector's Choice Japanese is a two series set wh[...] series one is a 219-card standard size set issued b[...] Upper Deck for the Japanese market. Cards were distributed primarily in 10-card packs (with an ord[...] form card inserted into each pack) and 30 pack box[...] Suggested retail price per pack was 300 yen (approximately three dollars in American funds). Complete Japanese 1 sets were also available in a glossy binder designed for and distributed in nine-sheets. The cards are similar in design and numbe[...] to the American 1994-95 Collector's Choice series set. White-bordered fronts feature color player actic[...] shots. The player's name, team and position appea[...] a lower corner. The back carries another color play[...] action shot at the top, with statistics and career highlights displayed below. The following subsets [...] included in this set: Tip-Off (166-192), All-Star Adv[...] (193-198), NBA Profiles (199-206), Checklists (20[...] 210), and Michael Jordan Heroes (211-219). The l[...] nine cards in the set are derived from the American 1994-95 Upper Deck Michael Jordan Heroes inser[...] and are believed to be somewhat tougher to pull fr[...] packs. All cards feature information only in Japane[...] except for the subset cards which have informatior[...] both English and Japanese.

ETE SET (219) 50.00 100.00
nee Hardaway .60 1.50
Macon .25 .60
Smith .30 .75
Webber .60 1.50
d Royal .25 .60
Johnson .30 .75
Johnson .40 1.00
Christie .25 .60
k McKey .25 .60
nis Rodman .75 2.00
t Skiles .25 .60
nny Dawkins .25 .60
tall Gill .25 .60
Hornacek .30 .75
ell Sprewell .50 1.25
ous Harris .25 .60
s Mullin .40 1.00
n Williams .25 .60
y Campbell .25 .60
nonso Ellis .25 .60
ld Wilkins .25 .60
le Drexler .50 1.25
nael Jordan BB 3.00 8.00
rge Lynch .25 .60
k Price .40 1.00
es Robinson .25 .60
ore Spencer .25 .60
ey King .25 .60
e Blount .25 .60
Curry .25 .60
gie Miller .50 1.25
Malone .50 1.25
ttie Pippen .75 2.00
eem Olajuwon .50 1.25
ence Weatherspoon .25 .60
n Edwards .25 .60
Myers .25 .60
Turner .25 .60
is Whatley .25 .60
pert Cheaney .25 .60
Rice .40 1.00
Baker .40 1.00
nt Long .25 .60
ick Coleman .30 .75
Smits .30 .75
s Smith .25 .60
Herrera .25 .60
Martin .25 .60
ell Brandon .25 .60
id Robinson .60 1.50
ny Ferry .25 .60
k Williams .25 .60
n Grant .25 .60
Pinckney .25 .60
embe Mutombo .40 1.00
fford Robinson .25 .60
ver Wright .25 .60
tt Burrell .25 .60
ey Augmon .30 .75
Malone .25 .60
vn Houston .25 .60
nony Peeler .25 .60
hael Adams .25 .60
ele Knight .25 .60
y Cummings .40 1.00
istian Laettner .30 .75
y Murray .25 .60
ale Threatt .25 .60
Majerle .40 1.00
k Brickowski .25 .60
Norman .25 .60
rles Smith .25 .60
m Keefe .25 .60
Brown .25 .60
n Duckworth .25 .60
wn Bradley .25 .60
nell Mee .25 .60
k Anderson .25 .60
k West .25 .60
Armstrong .25 .60
nis Scott .25 .60
lsey Hunter .25 .60
ek Strong .25 .60
e Brown .25 .60
onio Harvey .25 .60
hony Bonner .25 .60
Cassell .40 1.00
old Miner .25 .60
d Webb .40 1.00
okie Blaylock .25 .60
g Anthony .25 .60
nard Petruska .25 .60
Rooks .25 .60
n Johnson .25 .60
dy Brown .25 .60
ndo Woolridge .25 .60
rles Oakley .30 .75
g Ehlo .25 .60
ek Harper .30 .75
ug Edwards .25 .60
ggsy Bogues .30 .75
tch Richmond .40 1.00
hmoud Abdul-Rauf .25 .60
e Dumars .40 1.00
ric Riley .25 .60
rry Mills .25 .60
ni Kukoc .50 1.25
n Koncak .25 .60
ywoode Workman .25 .60
dd Day .25 .60
tlef Schrempf .40 1.00
vid Wesley .25 .60
ark Jackson .40 1.00
ug Overton .25 .60
ny Del Negro .25 .60
y Vaught .25 .60
ke Peplowski .25 .60
mbo Coles .25 .60
x Walters .25 .60
erman Douglas .25 .60
vid Benoit .25 .60
hn Salley .25 .60
dric Ceballos .25 .60
ris Mills .25 .60
bert Horry .40 1.00
nny Newman .25 .60
alcolm Mackey .25 .60
rry Dehere .25 .60
no Radja .30 .75
ggie Williams .25 .60
vier McDaniel .25 .60
bby Hurley .40 1.00
nzo Mourning .50 1.25
aiah Rider .40 1.00
toine Carr .25 .60
bert Pack .25 .60
alt Williams .25 .60
138 Tyrone Corbin .25 .60
139 Popeye Jones .25 .60
140 Shawn Kemp .40 1.00
141 Thurl Bailey .25 .60
142 James Worthy .50 1.25
143 Scott Haskin .25 .60
144 Hubert Davis .25 .60
145 A.C. Green .40 1.00
146 Dale Davis .25 .60
147 Nate McMillan .25 .60
148 Chris Morris .25 .60
149 Will Perdue .25 .60
150 Felton Spencer .25 .60
151 Rod Strickland .25 .60
152 Blue Edwards .25 .60
153 John S. Williams .25 .60
154 Rodney Rogers .25 .60
155 Acie Earl .25 .60
156 Hersey Hawkins .25 .60
157 Jamal Mashburn .40 1.00
158 Don MacLean .25 .60
159 Micheal Williams .25 .60
160 Kenny Gattison .25 .60
161 Rich King .25 .60
162 Allan Houston .40 1.00
163 John Stockton .50 1.25
164 Kenny Anderson .30 .75
165 Shaquille O'Neal 1.00 2.50
166 Danny Manning TO .25 .60
167 Dee Brown TO .25 .60
168 Alonzo Mourning TO .50 1.25
169 Scottie Pippen TO .75 2.00
170 Mark Price TO .25 .60
171 Jamal Mashburn TO .40 1.00
172 Dikembe Mutombo TO .40 1.00
173 Joe Dumars TO .40 1.00
174 Chris Webber TO .60 1.50
175 Hakeem Olajuwon TO .50 1.25
176 Reggie Miller TO .50 1.25
177 Ron Harper TO .30 .75
178 Nick Van Exel TO .40 1.00
179 Steve Smith TO .30 .75
180 Vin Baker TO .40 1.00
181 Isaiah Rider TO .40 1.00
182 Derrick Coleman TO .30 .75
183 Patrick Ewing TO .50 1.25
184 Shaquille O'Neal TO 1.00 2.50
185 Clarence Weatherspoon TO .25 .60
186 Charles Barkley TO .60 1.50
187 Clyde Drexler TO .50 1.25
188 Mitch Richmond TO .40 1.00
189 David Robinson TO .60 1.50
190 Shawn Kemp TO .40 1.00
191 Karl Malone TO .50 1.25
192 Tom Gugliotta TO .25 .60
193 Kenny Anderson ASA .30 .75
194 Alonzo Mourning ASA .50 1.25
195 Mark Price ASA .40 1.00
196 John Stockton ASA .50 1.25
197 Shaquille O'Neal ASA 1.00 2.50
198 Latrell Sprewell ASA .50 1.25
199 Charles Barkley PRO .60 1.50
200 Chris Webber PRO .60 1.50
201 Patrick Ewing PRO .50 1.25
202 Dennis Rodman PRO .75 2.00
203 Shawn Kemp PRO .40 1.00
204 Michael Jordan PRO 3.00 8.00
205 Shaquille O'Neal PRO 1.00 2.50
206 Larry Johnson PRO .40 1.00
207 Tim Hardaway CL .40 1.00
208 John Stockton CL .50 1.25
209 Harold Miner CL .25 .60
210 B.J.Armstrong CL .25 .60
211 Michael Jordan ROY 3.00 8.00
212 Michael Jordan 63-Pt. Game 3.00 8.00
213 Michael Jordan Slam-Dunk 3.00 8.00
214 Michael Jordan MVP 3.00 8.00
215 Michael Jordan All-Star 3.00 8.00
216 Michael Jordan 3,000-Points 3.00 8.00
217 Michael Jordan Champ. 3.00 8.00
218 Michael Jordan Decade 3.00 8.00
219 Michael Jordan CL 3.00 8.00

1994-95 Collector's Choice International Japanese II

This 210-card standard size, skip-numbered set was issued by Upper Deck for the Japanese market. Cards were distributed in 10-card packs (with an order form card in each pack) and 30-pack boxes (featuring Michael Jordan on both the wrapper and the box). Suggested retail price per pack was 300 yen (approximately three dollars in American funds). The cards are similar (though not identical) in design and numbering to the American 1994-95 Collector's Choice series 2 set. The following subsets are included in this set: Blueprints (153-179), World of Trivia (399-406), Draft Class (407-416) and Checklists (417-420). Please note that the Blueprints subset is numbered out of order in relation to the rest of the set and may be a source of confusion for collectors assembling both first and second series sets. Also, there are no cards issued between numbers 371 and 399. White-bordered fronts feature color player action shots. The player's name, team and position appear in a lower corner. The back carries another color player action shot at the top, with statistics and career highlights displayed below. All cards feature information only in Japanese except for the subset cards which have information in both English and Japanese. A special Michael Jordan Trade card (T1) was randomly inserted into 1:35 packs. The card was redeemable for a special 3 1/2" by 5" Michael Jordan "C" Sheet jumbo card.

COMPLETE SET (210) 35.00 75.00
220 Gary Payton .40 1.00
221 Tom Hammonds .25 .60
222 Danny Ainge .40 1.00
223 Gary Grant .25 .60
224 Jim Jackson .25 .60
225 Chris Gatling .25 .60
226 Sergei Bazarevich .40 1.00
227 Tony Dumas .40 1.00
228 Andrew Lang .25 .60
229 Wesley Person .40 1.00
230 Terry Porter .25 .60
231 Duane Causwell .25 .60
232 Shaquille O'Neal 1.00 2.50
233 Antonio Davis .25 .60
234 Charles Barkley .60 1.50
235 Tony Massenburg .25 .60
236 Ricky Pierce .25 .60
237 Scott Skiles .25 .60
238 Jalen Rose 1.00 2.50
239 Charlie Ward .40 1.00
240 Michael Jordan COMM 3.00 8.00
241 Elden Campbell .25 .60
242 Bill Cartwright .30 .75
243 Armon Gilliam UER .25 .60
Card numbered 372
244 Rick Fox .25 .60
245 Tim Breaux .25 .60
246 Monty Williams .40 1.00
247 Dominique Wilkins .50 1.25
248 Robert Parish .40 1.00
249 Mark Jackson .40 1.00
250 Jason Kidd 2.00 5.00
251 Andres Guibert .25 .60
252 Matt Geiger .25 .60
253 Stanley Roberts .25 .60
254 Jack Haley .25 .60
255 David Wingate .25 .60
256 John Crotty .25 .60
257 Brian Grant .60 1.50
258 Otis Thorpe .25 .60
259 Clifford Rozier .40 1.00
260 Grant Long .25 .60
261 Eric Mobley .40 1.00
262 Dickey Simpkins .40 1.00
263 J.R. Reid .25 .60
264 Kevin Willis .25 .60
265 Scott Brooks .25 .60
266 Glenn Robinson .75 2.00
267 Dana Barros .25 .60
268 Ken Norman .25 .60
269 Herb Williams .25 .60
270 Dee Brown .25 .60
271 Steve Kerr .30 .75
272 Jon Barry .25 .60
273 Sean Elliott .40 1.00
274 Elliot Perry .25 .60
275 Kenny Smith .30 .75
276 Sean Rooks .25 .60
277 Gheorghe Muresan .25 .60
278 Juwan Howard .60 1.50
279 Steve Smith .30 .75
280 Anthony Bowie .25 .60
281 Moses Malone .40 1.00
282 Olden Polynice .25 .60
283 Jo Jo English .25 .60
284 Marty Conlon .25 .60
285 Sam Mitchell .25 .60
286 Doug West .25 .60
287 Cedric Ceballos .25 .60
288 Lorenzo Williams .25 .60
289 Harold Ellis .25 .60
290 Doc Rivers .30 .75
291 Keith Tower .25 .60
292 Mark Bryant .25 .60
293 Oliver Miller .25 .60
294 Michael Adams .25 .60
295 Tree Rollins .25 .60
296 Eddie Jones 1.25 3.00
297 Malik Sealy .25 .60
298 Blue Edwards .25 .60
299 Brooks Thompson .40 1.00
300 Benoit Benjamin .25 .60
301 Avery Johnson .30 .75
302 Larry Johnson .40 1.00
303 John Starks .30 .75
304 Byron Scott .30 .75
305 Eric Murdock .25 .60
306 Jay Humphries .25 .60
307 Kenny Anderson .30 .75
308 Brian Williams .25 .60
309 Nick Van Exel .40 1.00
310 Tim Hardaway .40 1.00
311 Lee Mayberry .25 .60
312 Vlade Divac .40 1.00
313 Donyell Marshall .40 1.00
314 Anthony Mason .30 .75
315 Danny Manning .30 .75
316 Tyrone Hill .25 .60
317 Vincent Askew .25 .60
318 Khalid Reeves .25 .60
319 Ron Harper .30 .75
320 Brent Price .25 .60
321 Byron Houston .25 .60
322 Lamond Murray .40 1.00
323 Bryant Stith .25 .60
324 Tom Gugliotta .25 .60
325 Jerome Kersey .25 .60
326 B.J. Tyler .40 1.00
327 Antonio Lang .40 1.00
328 Carlos Rogers .40 1.00
329 Wayman Tisdale .25 .60
330 Kevin Gamble .25 .60
331 Eric Piatkowski .50 1.25
332 Mitchell Butler .25 .60
333 Patrick Ewing .50 1.25
334 Doug Smith .25 .60
335 Joe Kleine .25 .60
336 Keith Jennings .25 .60
337 Bill Curley .40 1.00
338 Johnny Newman .25 .60
339 Howard Eisley .40 1.00
340 Willie Anderson .25 .60
341 Aaron McKie .40 1.00
342 Tom Chambers .40 1.00
343 Scott Williams .25 .60
344 Harvey Grant .25 .60
345 Billy Owens .25 .60
346 Sharone Wright .40 1.00
347 Michael Cage .25 .60
348 Vern Fleming .25 .60
349 Darrin Hancock .40 1.00
350 Matt Fish .25 .60
351 Rony Seikaly .30 .75
352 Victor Alexander .25 .60
353 Anthony Miller .40 1.00
354 Horace Grant .30 .75
355 Jayson Williams .25 .60
356 Dale Ellis .25 .60
357 Sarunas Marciulionis .25 .60
358 Anthony Avent .25 .60
359 Rex Chapman .25 .60
360 Askia Jones .25 .60
361 Bo Outlaw .25 .60
362 Chuck Person .30 .75
363 Danny Schayes .25 .60
364 Morlon Wiley .25 .60
365 Dontonio Wingfield .40 1.00
366 Tony Smith .25 .60
367 Bill Wennington .25 .60
368 Bryon Russell .25 .60
369 Geert Hammink .25 .60
370 Eric Montross .40 1.00
371 Cliff Levingston .25 .60
372 Stacey Augmon BP .25 .60
373 Eric Montross BP .30 .75
374 Alonzo Mourning BP .50 1.25
375 Scottie Pippen BP .75 2.00
376 Mark Price BP .25 .60
377 Jason Kidd BP 1.50 4.00
378 Jalen Rose BP .60 1.50
379 Grant Hill BP 1.50 4.00
380 Latrell Sprewell BP .50 1.25
381 Hakeem Olajuwon BP .50 1.25
382 Reggie Miller BP .50 1.25
383 Lamond Murray BP .30 .75
384 Eddie Jones BP 1.00 2.50
385 Khalid Reeves BP .30 .75
386 Glenn Robinson BP .60 1.50
387 Donyell Marshall BP .30 .75
388 Derrick Coleman BP .30 .75
389 Patrick Ewing BP .50 1.25
390 Shaquille O'Neal BP 1.00 2.50
391 Sharone Wright BP .30 .75
392 Charles Barkley BP .60 1.50
393 Aaron McKie BP .30 .75
394 Brian Grant BP .50 1.25
395 David Robinson BP .60 1.50
396 Shawn Kemp BP .40 1.00
397 Karl Malone BP .50 1.25
398 Tom Gugliotta BP .25 .60
399 Hakeem Olajuwon TRIV .50 1.25
400 Shaquille O'Neal TRIV 1.00 2.50
401 Chris Webber TRIV .60 1.50
402 Michael Jordan TRIV 3.00 8.00
403 David Robinson TRIV .60 1.50
404 Shawn Kemp TRIV .40 1.00
405 Patrick Ewing TRIV .50 1.25
406 Charles Barkley TRIV .60 1.50
407 Glenn Robinson DC .60 1.50
408 Jason Kidd DC 1.50 4.00
409 Grant Hill DC 1.50 4.00
410 Donyell Marshall DC .30 .75
411 Sharone Wright DC .30 .75
412 Lamond Murray DC .30 .75
413 Brian Grant DC .50 1.25
414 Eric Montross DC .30 .75
415 Eddie Jones DC 1.00 2.50
416 Carlos Rogers DC .30 .75
417 Shawn Kemp CL .40 1.00
418 Bobby Hurley CL .40 1.00
419 Shawn Bradley CL .25 .60
420 Michael Jordan CL 3.00 8.00
421 Vernon Maxwell .25 .60
422 John Stockton .50 1.25
423 Luc Longley .25 .60
424 Sam Perkins .25 .60
425 Pooh Richardson .25 .60
426 Tyrone Corbin .25 .60
427 Mario Elie .25 .60
428 Bobby Phills .25 .60
429 Grant Hill 2.00 5.00

1994-95 Collector's Choice International Japanese I Gold Signatures

Issued approximately one in every 30 Collector's Choice Japanese 1 packs, these 27 standard size cards parallel that of the basic issue Tip-Offs subset. Unlike the basic cards these inserts feature a gold foil facsimile signature stamped on the front of each card. The borderless fronts feature a full-color shot with the words "Tip Offs" in the lower left corner and Collector's Choice logo in the upper left corner. The backs feature all the information in a bilingual format with a small inset player photo in the upper right corner. The set is arranged in alphabetical order by team.

COMPLETE SET (27) 125.00 250.00
166 Danny Manning 3.00 8.00
167 Dee Brown 2.50 6.00
168 Alonzo Mourning 5.00 12.00
169 Scottie Pippen 8.00 20.00
170 Mark Price 4.00 10.00
171 Jamal Mashburn 4.00 10.00
172 Dikembe Mutombo 4.00 10.00
173 Joe Dumars 4.00 10.00
174 Chris Webber 6.00 15.00
175 Hakeem Olajuwon 5.00 12.00
176 Reggie Miller 5.00 12.00
177 Ron Harper 3.00 8.00
178 Nick Van Exel 4.00 10.00
179 Steve Smith 3.00 8.00
180 Vin Baker 4.00 10.00
181 Isaiah Rider 4.00 10.00
182 Derrick Coleman 3.00 8.00
183 Patrick Ewing 5.00 12.00
184 Shaquille O'Neal 10.00 25.00
185 Clarence Weatherspoon 2.50 6.00
186 Charles Barkley 6.00 15.00
187 Clyde Drexler 5.00 12.00
188 Mitch Richmond 4.00 10.00
189 David Robinson 6.00 15.00
190 Shawn Kemp 4.00 10.00
191 Karl Malone 5.00 12.00
192 Tom Gugliotta 2.50 6.00

1994-95 Collector's Choice International Japanese II Gold Signatures

Issued approximately one in every five Collector's Choice Japanese 2 packs, these 44 standard size, skip-numbered cards parallel that of the basic issue Blueprints, World of Trivia and Draft Class subsets. Unlike the basic issue cards, these inserts feature a gold foil facsimile signature stamped on the front of each card.

COMPLETE SET (44) 200.00 400.00
372 Stacey Augmon BP 3.00 8.00
373 Eric Montross BP 2.00 5.00
374 Alonzo Mourning BP 5.00 12.00
375 Scottie Pippen BP 8.00 20.00
376 Mark Price BP 4.00 10.00
377 Jason Kidd BP 10.00 25.00
378 Jalen Rose BP 5.00 12.00
379 Grant Hill BP 10.00 25.00
380 Latrell Sprewell BP 5.00 12.00
381 Hakeem Olajuwon BP 5.00 12.00
382 Reggie Miller BP 5.00 12.00
383 Lamond Murray BP 2.00 5.00
384 Eddie Jones BP 6.00 15.00
385 Khalid Reeves BP 2.00 5.00
386 Glenn Robinson BP 4.00 10.00
387 Donyell Marshall BP 2.00 5.00
388 Derrick Coleman BP 3.00 8.00
389 Patrick Ewing BP 5.00 12.00
390 Shaquille O'Neal BP 10.00 25.00
391 Sharone Wright BP 2.00 5.00
392 Charles Barkley BP 6.00 15.00
393 Aaron McKie BP 2.00 5.00
394 Brian Grant BP 3.00 8.00
395 David Robinson BP 6.00 15.00
396 Shawn Kemp BP 4.00 10.00
397 Karl Malone BP 5.00 12.00
398 Tom Gugliotta BP 2.50 6.00
400 Shaquille O'Neal TRIV 10.00 25.00
401 Chris Webber TRIV 6.00 15.00
402 Michael Jordan TRIV 30.00 80.00
403 David Robinson TRIV 6.00 15.00
404 Shawn Kemp TRIV 4.00 10.00
405 Patrick Ewing TRIV 5.00 12.00
406 Charles Barkley TRIV 6.00 15.00
407 Glenn Robinson DC 4.00 10.00
408 Jason Kidd DC 10.00 25.00
409 Grant Hill DC 10.00 25.00
410 Donyell Marshall DC 2.00 5.00
411 Sharone Wright DC 2.00 5.00
412 Lamond Murray DC 2.00 5.00
413 Brian Grant DC 3.00 8.00
414 Eric Montross DC 2.00 5.00
415 Eddie Jones DC 6.00 15.00
416 Carlos Rogers DC 2.00 5.00

1994-95 Collector's Choice International Japanese Silver Signatures

Issued one per Collector's Choice Japanese 1 packs, these 25 standard size cards parallel that of the basic issue Tip-Offs subset. Unlike the basic cards these inserts feature a silver foil facsimile signature stamped on the front of each card. The borderless fronts feature a full-color shot with the words "Tip Offs" in the lower left corner and Collector's Choice logo in the upper left corner. The backs feature all the information in a bilingual format with a small inset player photo in the upper right corner. The set is arranged in alphabetical order by team.

COMPLETE SET (25) 6.00 15.00
166 Danny Manning TO .50 1.25
167 Dee Brown TO .40 1.00
168 Alonzo Mourning TO .75 2.00
169 Scottie Pippen TO 1.25 3.00
170 Mark Price TO .60 1.50
171 Jamal Mashburn TO .60 1.50
172 Dikembe Mutombo TO .60 1.50
173 Joe Dumars TO .60 1.50
174 Chris Webber TO 1.00 2.50
175 Hakeem Olajuwon TO .75 2.00
177 Ron Harper TO .50 1.25
178 Nick Van Exel TO .60 1.50
179 Steve Smith TO .50 1.25
180 Vin Baker TO .60 1.50
181 Isaiah Rider TO .60 1.50
182 Derrick Coleman TO .50 1.25
183 Patrick Ewing TO .75 2.00
184 Shaquille O'Neal TO 1.50 4.00
185 Clarence Weatherspoon TO .40 1.00
187 Clyde Drexler TO .75 2.00
188 Mitch Richmond TO .60 1.50
189 David Robinson TO 1.00 2.50
190 Shawn Kemp TO .60 1.50
191 Karl Malone TO .75 2.00
192 Tom Gugliotta TO .40 1.00

1994-95 Collector's Choice International Japanese Decade of Dominance

COMPLETE SET (10) 30.00 80.00
COMMON CARD 4.00 10.00

1994-95 Collector's Choice International Spanish I

This 219-card standard size set was issued by Upper Deck for the Spanish market. Cards were distributed in 10-card packs and 30 pack boxes (featuring Michael Jordan on both wrappers and boxes). Cards were distributed in 10-card packs and 30 pack boxes (featuring Michael Jordan on both wrappers and boxes). The first 210 cards are similar in design and numbering to the American 1994-95 Collector's Choice set. White-bordered fronts feature color player action shots. The player's name, team and position appear in a lower corner. The back carries another color player action shot at the top, with statistics and career highlights displayed below. The following subsets are included in this set: Tip-Off (166-192), All-Star Advice (193-198), NBA Profiles (199-206), Checklists (207-210), and Michael Jordan Heroes (211-219). The last nine cards in the set are derived from the American 1994-95 Upper Deck Michael Jordan Heroes insert set. All cards feature bilingual information (Spanish and English). This product has been made readily available to the U.S. market through closeouts.

COMPLETE SET (219) 10.00 25.00
*SPANISH: SAME VALUE AS FRENCH

1994-95 Collector's Choice International Spanish II

This 210-card standard-size set was issued by Upper Deck for the Spanish market. Cards were issued in 6-card packs and 50-pack boxes (featuring Shawn Kemp on both the wrapper and box). The cards are similar in design to the American 1994-95 Collector's Choice set. Spanish 2 card sequencing from 1-201 mirrors the American Collector's Choice from 220-420 and Spanish 2 card sequencing from 202-210 mirror the American cards 211-219. The numbering may be a source of confusion for collectors assembling both first and second series Spanish cards. White-bordered fronts feature color player action shots. The player's name, team, and position appear in a lower corner. The back carries another color player action shot at the top, with statistics and career highlights displayed below. The cards all have bilingual (English and Spanish) information on the back. The following subsets are included in the set: Blueprint for Success (153-179), Dr. Basketball's World of Trivia (180-187), 1994 Draft Class (188-197), and Checklists (198-201). This product has been made readily available through closeouts.

COMPLETE SET (210) 10.00 20.00
*SPANISH: SAME VALUE AS FRENCH

1994-95 Collector's Choice International Spanish Gold Signatures

COMPLETE SET (72) 55.00 130.00
COMPLETE SERIES 1 (27) 15.00 30.00
COMPLETE SERIES 2 (45) 40.00 100.00
*SPANISH: SAME VALUE AS FRENCH

1994-95 Collector's Choice International Spanish Decade of Dominance

COMPLETE SET (10) 12.00 30.00
*SPANISH: SAME VALUE AS FRENCH

1995-96 Collector's Choice International French I

Consisting of 210 cards, the 1995-96 Collector's Choice International set was distributed in France, Germany, Italy, Latin America, Northern Europe, Portugal and Spain. These cards are identical in design to the 1995-96 Collector's Choice American cards except for bilingual text for the respective countries and the regular card numbering. The first series subsets replicate the exact numbering used for the first series American issue. All countries received 10-card packs and 30-pack boxes. This product has been made available to the U.S. market through closeouts.

COMPLETE SET (210) 8.00 20.00
1 Craig Ehlo .10 .25
2 Tyrone Corbin .10 .25
3 Mookie Blaylock .10 .25
4 Grant Long .10 .25
5 Andrew Lang .10 .25
6 Stacey Augmon .12 .30
7 Dee Brown .10 .25
8 Sherman Douglas .10 .25
9 Pervis Ellison .10 .25
10 Dominique Wilkins .20 .50
11 Greg Minor .10 .25
12 Larry Johnson .15 .40
13 Dell Curry .10 .25
14 Scott Burrell .10 .25
15 Robert Parish .15 .40
16 Michael Adams .10 .25
17 David Wingate .10 .25
18 Hersey Hawkins .10 .25
19 B.J. Armstrong .10 .25
20 Michael Jordan 1.25 3.00
21 Dickey Simpkins .10 .25
22 Will Perdue .10 .25
23 Steve Kerr .12 .30
24 Ron Harper .12 .30
25 Tyrone Hill .10 .25
26 Bobby Phills .10 .25
27 Michael Cage .10 .25
28 John Williams .10 .25
29 Mark Price .15 .40
30 Danny Ferry .10 .25
31 Jason Kidd .25 .60
32 Roy Tarpley .10 .25
33 Popeye Jones .10 .25
34 Tony Dumas .10 .25
35 Lucious Harris .10 .25
36 Jim Jackson .10 .25
37 Mahmoud Abdul-Rauf .10 .25
38 Brian Williams .10 .25
39 Rodney Rogers .10 .25
40 LaPhonso Ellis .10 .25
41 Reggie Williams .10 .25
42 Bryant Stith .10 .25
43 Joe Dumars .15 .40
44 Oliver Miller .10 .25
45 Grant Hill .25 .60
46 Bill Curley .10 .25
47 Allan Houston .12 .30
48 Mark West .10 .25
49 Rony Seikaly .12 .30
50 Chris Gatling .10 .25
51 Carlos Rogers .10 .25
52 Tim Hardaway .15 .40
53 Chris Mullin .15 .40
54 Donyell Marshall .10 .25
55 Clyde Drexler .20 .50
56 Kenny Smith .12 .30
57 Carl Herrera .10 .25
58 Robert Horry .12 .30
59 Sam Cassell .15 .40
60 Dale Davis .10 .25
61 Byron Scott .12 .30
62 Rik Smits .12 .30
63 Duane Ferrell .10 .25
64 Derrick McKey .10 .25
65 Reggie Miller .20 .50
66 Eric Piatkowski .12 .30
67 Malik Sealy .10 .25
68 Terry Dehere .10 .25
69 Bo Outlaw .10 .25
70 Lamond Murray .10 .25
71 Loy Vaught .10 .25
72 Nick Van Exel .15 .40
73 Antonio Harvey .10 .25
74 Vlade Divac .15 .40
75 Elden Campbell .10 .25
76 Anthony Peeler .10 .25
77 Eddie Jones .20 .50
78 Harold Miner .10 .25
79 Billy Owens .10 .25
80 Bimbo Coles .10 .25
81 Kevin Gamble .10 .25
82 John Salley .10 .25
83 Kevin Willis .10 .25
84 Khalid Reeves .10 .25
85 Ed Pinckney .10 .25
86 Vin Baker .12 .30
87 Todd Day .10 .25
88 Eric Mobley .10 .25
89 Marty Conlon .10 .25
90 Lee Mayberry .10 .25
91 Micheal Williams .10 .25
92 Tom Gugliotta .10 .25
93 Doug West .10 .25
94 Isaiah Rider .15 .40
95 Christian Laettner .12 .30
96 Chris Smith .10 .25
97 Armon Gilliam .10 .25
98 P.J. Brown .10 .25
99 Rex Walters .10 .25
100 Benoit Benjamin .10 .25
101 Kenny Anderson .12 .30
102 Derrick Coleman .12 .30
103 Derek Harper .12 .30
104 Charles Smith .10 .25
105 Herb Williams .10 .25
106 John Starks .12 .30
107 Charles Oakley .12 .30
108 Hubert Davis .10 .25
109 Dennis Scott .10 .25
110 Jeff Turner .10 .25
111 Horace Grant .12 .30
112 Anthony Bowie .10 .25
113 Anfernee Hardaway .25 .60
114 Nick Anderson .10 .25
115 Dana Barros .10 .25
116 Scott Williams .10 .25
117 Clarence Weatherspoon .10 .25
118 Jeff Malone .10 .25
119 B.J. Tyler .10 .25
120 Shawn Bradley .10 .25
121 Charles Barkley .25 .60
122 A.C. Green .15 .40
123 Kevin Johnson .15 .40
124 Wayman Tisdale .10 .25
125 Danny Schayes .10 .25
126 Dan Majerle .15 .40
127 Rod Strickland .10 .25
128 Harvey Grant .10 .25
129 Aaron McKie .10 .25
130 Chris Dudley .10 .25
131 Otis Thorpe .10 .25
132 Jerome Kersey .10 .25
133 Clifford Robinson .10 .25
134 Bobby Hurley .15 .40
135 Spud Webb .15 .40
136 Olden Polynice .10 .25
137 Randy Brown .10 .25
138 Brian Grant .12 .30
139 Walt Williams .10 .25
140 Avery Johnson .12 .30
141 Dennis Rodman .30 .75
142 J.R. Reid .10 .25
143 David Robinson .25 .60
144 Vinny Del Negro .10 .25
145 Willie Anderson .10 .25
146 Nate McMillan .10 .25
147 Shawn Kemp .15 .40
148 Detlef Schrempf .15 .40
149 Vincent Askew .10 .25
150 Sarunas Marciulionis .10 .25
151 Byron Houston .10 .25
152 Ervin Johnson .10 .25
153 Adam Keefe .10 .25
154 Jeff Hornacek .12 .30
155 Antoine Carr .10 .25
156 John Stockton .20 .50
157 Blue Edwards .10 .25
158 David Benoit .10 .25
159 Don MacLean .10 .25
160 Juwan Howard .15 .40
161 Calbert Cheaney .10 .25
162 Mitchell Butler .10 .25
163 Gheorghe Muresan .10 .25
164 Rex Chapman .10 .25
165 Doug Overton .10 .25
166 Steve Smith FF .12 .30
167 Dino Radja FF .12 .30
168 Alonzo Mourning FF .20 .50
169 Michael Jordan FF 1.25 3.00
170 Tyrone Hill FF .10 .25
171 Jamal Mashburn FF .15 .40
172 Dikembe Mutombo FF .15 .40
173 Grant Hill FF .40 1.00
with Michael Jordan
174 Latrell Sprewell FF .15 .40
175 Hakeem Olajuwon FF .20 .50
176 Reggie Miller FF .20 .50
177 Pooh Richardson FF .10 .25
178 Cedric Ceballos FF .10 .25
179 Glen Rice FF .15 .40
180 Glenn Robinson FF .15 .40
181 Isaiah Rider FF .15 .40
182 Derrick Coleman FF .12 .30
183 Patrick Ewing FF .20 .50
184 Shaquille O'Neal FF .40 1.00
185 Dana Barros FF .10 .25
186 Dan Majerle FF .15 .40
187 Clifford Robinson FF .10 .25
188 Mitch Richmond FF .15 .40
189 David Robinson FF .25 .60
190 Gary Payton FF .15 .40
191 Oliver Miller FF .10 .25
192 Karl Malone FF .20 .50
193 Kevin Pritchard FF .10 .25
194 Chris Webber FF .20 .50
195 Michael Jordan PD 1.25 3.00
196 Hakeem Olajuwon PD .20 .50
197 Ron Harper PD .12 .30
198 Grant Hill PD .25 .60
199 Clyde Drexler PD .20 .50
200 Chris Webber PD .20 .50
201 Shawn Kemp PD .15 .40
202 Shaquille O'Neal PD .40 1.00
203 Stacey Augmon PD .12 .30
204 David Benoit PD .10 .25
205 Rodney Rogers PD .10 .25
206 Latrell Sprewell PD .15 .40
207 Brian Grant PD .12 .30
208 Lamond Murray PD .10 .25
209 Shawn Kemp CL .15 .40
210 Michael Jordan CL 1.25 3.00

1995-96 Collector's Choice International French II

The series two Collector's Choice International set contains 200-cards and was distributed in France, Germany, Italy, Latin America, Northern Europe, Portugal and Spain. Packs contained 10 cards and boxes contained 30 packs. Though player content is the same as the American series two Collector's Choice the order of the cards and numbering is entirely different. Unlike the American cards, basic issue cards were placed in team order alphabetically by the city. Also, unlike the American issue, the cards are not numbered as a continuation of the first series. The second series set was numbered 1-200, which may create some confusion for collectors who have obtained both first and second series cards. This product has been made available to the U.S. market through closeouts.

COMPLETE SET (200) 8.00 20.00
1 Alan Henderson .15 .40
2 Steve Smith .12 .30
3 Ken Norman .10 .25
4 Eric Montross .10 .25
5 Dino Radja .12 .30
6 Rick Fox .10 .25
7 David Wesley .10 .25
8 Dana Barros .10 .25
9 Eric Williams .15 .40
10 George Zidek .10 .25
11 Muggsy Bogues .12 .30
12 Kendall Gill .10 .25
13 Scottie Pippen .25 .60
14 Bill Wennington .10 .25
15 Dennis Rodman .30 .75
16 Toni Kukoc .15 .40
17 Luc Longley .10 .25
18 Jason Caffey .15 .40
19 Chris Mills .10 .25
20 Terrell Brandon .10 .25
21 Bob Sura .15 .40
22 Cherokee Parks .15 .40
23 Lorenzo Williams .10 .25
24 Jamal Mashburn .15 .40
25 Terry Davis .10 .25
26 Loren Meyer .15 .40
27 Bryant Stith .10 .25
28 Dikembe Mutombo .15 .40
29 Jalen Rose .20 .50
30 Tom Hammonds .10 .25
31 Terry Mills .10 .25
32 Lindsey Hunter .10 .25
33 Theo Ratliff .25 .60
34 Latrell Sprewell .15 .40
35 Andrew DeClercq .15 .40
36 B.J. Armstrong .10 .25
37 Clifford Rozier .10 .25
38 Joe Smith .30 .75
39 Mark Bryant .10 .25
40 Mario Elie .10 .25
41 Hakeem Olajuwon .20 .50
42 Antonio Davis .10 .25
43 Haywoode Workman .10 .25
44 Mark Jackson .15 .40
45 Travis Best .15 .40
46 Brian Williams .10 .25

47 Rodney Rogers .10 .25
48 Brent Barry .25 .60
49 Pooh Richardson .10 .25
50 Gary Grant .10 .25
51 George Lynch .10 .25
52 Sedale Threatt .10 .25
53 Cedric Ceballos .10 .25
54 Sasha Danilovic .15 .40
55 Kurt Thomas .15 .40
56 Glenn Robinson .15 .40
57 Shawn Respert .15 .40
58 Eric Murdock .10 .25
59 Kevin Garnett 1.25 3.00
60 Kevin Edwards .10 .25
61 Ed O'Bannon .15 .40
62 Yinka Dare .10 .25
63 Vern Fleming .10 .25
64 Patrick Ewing .20 .50
65 Monty Williams .10 .25
66 Anthony Mason .10 .25
67 Donald Royal .10 .25
68 Brian Shaw .10 .25
69 Shaquille O'Neal .40 1.00
70 David Vaughn .15 .40
71 Vernon Maxwell .10 .25
72 Jerry Stackhouse .50 1.25
73 Sharone Wright .10 .25
74 Richard Dumas .10 .25
75 Wesley Person .10 .25
76 Joe Kleine .10 .25
77 Elliot Perry .10 .25
78 Danny Manning .12 .30
79 Michael Finley .50 1.25
80 Mario Bennett .15 .40
81 James Robinson .10 .25
82 Buck Williams .10 .25
83 Gary Trent .15 .40
84 Randolph Childress .15 .40
85 Duane Causwell .10 .25
86 Lionel Simmons .10 .25
87 Mitch Richmond .15 .40
88 Michael Smith .10 .25
89 Tyus Edney .15 .40
90 Corliss Williamson .15 .40
91 Cory Alexander .15 .40
92 Chuck Person .12 .30
93 Sean Elliott .15 .40
94 Doc Rivers .12 .30
95 Gary Payton .15 .40
96 Sam Perkins .10 .25
97 Sherrell Ford .15 .40
98 Damon Stoudamire .40 1.00
99 Zan Tabak .10 .25
100 Felton Spencer .10 .25
101 Karl Malone .20 .50
102 Bryon Russell .10 .25
103 Greg Ostertag .15 .40
104 Bryant Reeves .15 .40
105 Lawrence Moten .15 .40
106 Greg Anthony .10 .25
107 Byron Scott .12 .30
108 Scott Skiles .10 .25
109 Rasheed Wallace .50 1.25
110 Chris Webber .20 .50
111 Mookie Blaylock SR .10 .25
112 Dee Brown SR .10 .25
113 Alonzo Mourning SR .20 .50
114 Michael Jordan SR 1.25 3.00
115 Terrell Brandon SR .10 .25
116 Jim Jackson SR .10 .25
117 Dikembe Mutombo SR .15 .40
118 Grant Hill SR .25 .60
119 Joe Smith SR .30 .75
120 Clyde Drexler SR .20 .50
121 Reggie Miller SR .20 .50
122 Lamond Murray SR .10 .25
123 Nick Van Exel SR .15 .40
124 Glen Rice SR .15 .40
125 Glenn Robinson SR .15 .40
126 Christian Laettner SR .12 .30
127 Kenny Anderson SR .12 .30
128 Patrick Ewing SR .20 .50
129 Shaquille O'Neal SR .40 1.00
130 Jerry Stackhouse SR .50 1.25
131 Charles Barkley SR .25 .60
132 Clifford Robinson SR .10 .25
133 Brian Grant SR .12 .30
134 David Robinson SR .25 .60
135 Shawn Kemp SR .15 .40
136 Damon Stoudamire SR .40 1.00
137 Karl Malone SR .20 .50
138 Bryant Reeves SR .15 .40
139 Juwan Howard SR .15 .40
140 Nick Anderson .10 .25
Dee Brown PT
141 Rik Smits PT .12 .30
142 Herb Williams .10 .25
Tom Tolbert PT
143 Michael Jordan PT 1.25 3.00
144 David Robinson PT .25 .60
145 Terry Porter .15 .40
Kevin Johnson PT
146 Clyde Drexler PT .20 .50
147 Cedric Ceballos PT .10 .25
148 Horace Grant .12 .30
Group PT
149 Reggie Miller PT .20 .50
150 Avery Johnson .15 .40
Nick Van Exel PT
151 Hakeem Olajuwon .20 .50
Robert Horry PT
152 Rik Smits PT .12 .30
153 David Robinson .25 .60
Hakeem Olajuwon PT
154 Robert Horry PT .12 .30
155 Kenny Smith PT .12 .30
156 Stacey Augmon LOVE .12 .30
157 Sherman Douglas LOVE .10 .25
158 Larry Johnson LOVE .15 .40
159 Scottie Pippen LOVE .25 .60
160 Tyrone Hill LOVE .10 .25
161 Jamal Mashburn LOVE .15 .40
162 Mahmoud Abdul-Rauf LOVE .10 .25
163 Grant Hill LOVE .25 .60
164 Latrell Sprewell LOVE .15 .40
165 Sam Cassell LOVE .15 .40
166 Rik Smits LOVE .12 .30
167 Terry Dehere LOVE .10 .25
168 Eddie Jones LOVE .20 .50
169 Billy Owens LOVE .10 .25
170 Vin Baker LOVE .12 .30
171 Isaiah Rider LOVE .15 .40
172 Kenny Anderson LOVE .12 .30
173 John Starks LOVE .12 .30
174 Anfernee Hardaway LOVE .25 .60
175 Sharone Wright LOVE .10 .25
176 Charles Barkley LOVE .25 .60
177 Clifford Robinson LOVE .10 .25
178 Walt Williams LOVE .10 .25
179 Sean Elliott LOVE .15 .40
180 Gary Payton LOVE .15 .40
181 Carlos Rogers LOVE .10 .25
182 John Stockton LOVE .20 .50
183 Greg Anthony LOVE .10 .25
184 Chris Webber LOVE .20 .50
185 Gary Payton PG .15 .40
186 Mookie Blaylock PG .10 .25
187 Charles Barkley PG .25 .60
188 Grant Hill PG .25 .60
189 Anfernee Hardaway PG .25 .60
190 Kenny Anderson PG .12 .30
191 Mark Jackson PG .15 .40
192 Karl Malone PG .20 .50
193 Avery Johnson PG .12 .30
194 Larry Johnson 40 .15 .40
195 Nick Van Exel 40 .15 .40
196 Vin Baker 40 .12 .30
197 Jason Kidd 40 .25 .60
198 David Robinson 40 .25 .60
199 Shawn Kemp CL .15 .40
200 Michael Jordan CL 1.25 3.00

1995-96 Collector's Choice International French Jordan Collection

Randomly inserted into one in every eleven second series packs of French, German, Italian, Japanese, Latin, Northern European and Portugese packs. These cards are based upon the American second series Collector's Choice Jordan Collection inserts, but were renumbered in the European issue.

COMPLETE SET (4) 5.00 12.00
COMMON CARD (J1-J4) 1.50 4.00

1995-96 Collector's Choice International French NBA Extremes

Randomly inserted into one in every ten second series packs of French, German, Italian, Japanese, Latin, Northern European and Portugese. These cards were exclusive to the International product line and were not derived from any previous American Upper Deck issue.

COMPLETE SET (9) 1.50 4.00
E1 Muggsy Bogues .40 1.00
E2 Spud Webb .50 1.25
E3 Dana Barros .30 .75
E4 Avery Johnson .40 1.00
E5 Vlade Divac .50 1.25
E6 Dikembe Mutombo .50 1.25
E7 Rik Smits .40 1.00
E8 Shawn Bradley .30 .75
E9 Gheorghe Muresan .30 .75

1995-96 Collector's Choice International French Special Edition Holograms

Randomly inserted in all first series International foil packs, this set of nine holograms was based upon the American 1994-95 Upper Deck Special Edition inserts. The cards were randomly seeded into 1:5 packs of French, German, Italian and Japanese and 1:10 packs of Latin and Spanish. Unlike the American cards, the fronts display full-bleed holograms except at the upper left, where a black stripe carries the player's name (in gold foil) and position. The backs carry a color action photo and 1994-95 season statistics.

COMPLETE SET (9) 4.00 10.00
H1 Larry Johnson .60 1.50
H2 Scottie Pippen 1.00 2.50
H3 Grant Hill 1.00 2.50
H4 Reggie Miller .75 2.00
H5 Glenn Robinson .60 1.50
H6 Patrick Ewing .75 2.00
H7 Shaquille O'Neal 1.50 4.00
H8 John Stockton .75 2.00
H9 Chris Webber .75 2.00

1995-96 Collector's Choice International German I

COMPLETE SET (210) 8.00 20.00
*GERMAN: SAME VALUE AS FRENCH

1995-96 Collector's Choice International German II

COMPLETE SET (200) 8.00 20.00
*GERMAN: SAME VALUE AS FRENCH

1995-96 Collector's Choice International German Jordan Collection

COMPLETE SET (4) 5.00 12.00
*GERMAN: SAME VALUE AS FRENCH

1995-96 Collector's Choice International German NBA Extremes

COMPLETE SET (9) 1.50 4.00
*GERMAN: SAME VALUE AS FRENCH

1995-96 Collector's Choice International German Special Edition Holograms

COMPLETE SET (9) 4.00 10.00
*GERMAN: SAME VALUE AS FRENCH

1995-96 Collector's Choice International Italian I

COMPLETE SET (210) 8.00 20.00
*ITALIAN: SAME VALUE AS FRENCH

1995-96 Collector's Choice International Italian II

COMPLETE SET (200) 8.00 20.00
*ITALIAN: SAME VALUE AS FRENCH

1995-96 Collector's Choice International Italian Jordan Collection

COMPLETE SET (4) 5.00 12.00
*ITALIAN: SAME VALUE AS FRENCH

1995-96 Collector's Choice International Italian NBA Extremes

COMPLETE SET (9) 1.50 4.00
*ITALIAN: SAME VALUE AS FRENCH

1995-96 Collector's Choice International Italian Special Edition Holograms

COMPLETE SET (9) 4.00 10.00
*ITALIAN: SAME VALUE AS FRENCH

1995-96 Collector's Choice International Japanese

Consisting of 410 cards released in two separate series of 210 and 200 cards respectively, the 1995-96 Collector's Choice Japanese set is identical in design (excexcept for bilingual text) and numbering to the cards released in the 1995-96 American series. The cards were sold in 10-card packs and 30-pack boxes.

COMPLETE SET (410) 110.00 220.00
COMPLETE SERIES 1 (210) 50.00 100.00
COMPLETE SERIES 2 (200) 60.00 120.00
1 Craig Ehlo .40 1.00
2 Tyrone Corbin .40 1.00
3 Mookie Blaylock .40 1.00
4 Grant Long .40 1.00
5 Andrew Lang .40 1.00
6 Stacey Augmon .50 1.25
7 Dee Brown .40 1.00
8 Sherman Douglas .40 1.00
9 Pervis Ellison .40 1.00
10 Dominique Wilkins .75 2.00
11 Greg Minor .40 1.00
12 Larry Johnson .60 1.50
13 Dell Curry .40 1.00
14 Scott Burrell .40 1.00
15 Robert Parish .60 1.50
16 Michael Adams .40 1.00
17 David Wingate .40 1.00
18 Hersey Hawkins .40 1.00
19 B.J. Armstrong .40 1.00
20 Michael Jordan 5.00 12.00
21 Dickey Simpkins .40 1.00
22 Will Perdue .40 1.00
23 Steve Kerr .50 1.25
24 Ron Harper .50 1.25
25 Tyrone Hill .40 1.00
26 Bobby Phills .40 1.00
27 Michael Cage .40 1.00
28 John Williams .40 1.00
29 Mark Price .60 1.50
30 Danny Ferry .40 1.00
31 Jason Kidd 1.00 2.50
32 Roy Tarpley .40 1.00
33 Popeye Jones .40 1.00
34 Tony Dumas .40 1.00
35 Lucious Harris .40 1.00
36 Jim Jackson .40 1.00
37 Mahmoud Abdul-Rauf .40 1.00
38 Brian Williams .40 1.00
39 Rodney Rogers .40 1.00
40 LaPhonso Ellis .40 1.00
41 Reggie Williams .40 1.00
42 Bryant Stith .40 1.00
43 Joe Dumars .60 1.50
44 Oliver Miller .40 1.00
45 Grant Hill 1.00 2.50
46 Bill Curley .40 1.00
47 Allan Houston .50 1.25
48 Mark West .40 1.00
49 Rony Seikaly .50 1.25
50 Chris Gatling .40 1.00
51 Carlos Rogers .40 1.00
52 Tim Hardaway .60 1.50
53 Chris Mullin .60 1.50
54 Donyell Marshall .40 1.00
55 Clyde Drexler .75 2.00
56 Kenny Smith .50 1.25
57 Carl Herrera .40 1.00
58 Robert Horry .50 1.25
59 Sam Cassell .60 1.50
60 Dale Davis .40 1.00
61 Byron Scott .50 1.25
62 Rik Smits .50 1.25
63 Duane Ferrell .40 1.00
64 Derrick McKey .40 1.00
65 Reggie Miller .75 2.00
66 Eric Piatkowski .50 1.25
67 Malik Sealy .40 1.00
68 Terry Dehere .40 1.00
69 Bo Outlaw .40 1.00
70 Lamond Murray .40 1.00
71 Loy Vaught .40 1.00
72 Nick Van Exel .60 1.50
73 Antonio Harvey .40 1.00
74 Vlade Divac .60 1.50
75 Elden Campbell .40 1.00
76 Anthony Peeler .40 1.00
77 Eddie Jones .75 2.00
78 Harold Miner .40 1.00
79 Billy Owens .40 1.00
80 Bimbo Coles .40 1.00
81 Kevin Gamble .40 1.00
82 John Salley .40 1.00
83 Kevin Willis .40 1.00
84 Khalid Reeves .40 1.00
85 Ed Pinckney .40 1.00
86 Vin Baker .50 1.25
87 Todd Day .40 1.00
88 Eric Mobley .40 1.00
89 Marty Conlon .40 1.00
90 Lee Mayberry .40 1.00
91 Micheal Williams .40 1.00
92 Tom Gugliotta .40 1.00
93 Doug West .40 1.00
94 Isaiah Rider .60 1.50
95 Christian Laettner .50 1.25
96 Chris Smith .40 1.00
97 Armon Gilliam .40 1.00
98 P.J. Brown .40 1.00
99 Rex Walters .40 1.00
100 Benoit Benjamin .40 1.00
101 Kenny Anderson .50 1.25
102 Derrick Coleman .50 1.25
103 Derek Harper .50 1.25
104 Charles Smith .40 1.00
105 Herb Williams .40 1.00
106 John Starks .50 1.25
107 Charles Oakley .50 1.25
108 Hubert Davis .40 1.00
109 Dennis Scott .40 1.00
110 Jeff Turner .40 1.00
111 Horace Grant .50 1.25
112 Anthony Bowie .40 1.00
113 Anfernee Hardaway 1.00 2.50
114 Nick Anderson .40 1.00
115 Dana Barros .40 1.00
116 Scott Williams .40 1.00
117 Clarence Weatherspoon .40 1.00
118 Jeff Malone .40 1.00
119 B.J. Tyler .40 1.00
120 Shawn Bradley .40 1.00
121 Charles Barkley 1.00 2.50
122 A.C. Green .60 1.50
123 Kevin Johnson .60 1.50
124 Wayman Tisdale .40 1.00
125 Danny Schayes .40 1.00
126 Dan Majerle .60 1.50
127 Rod Strickland .40 1.00
128 Harvey Grant .40 1.00
129 Aaron McKie .40 1.00
130 Chris Dudley .40 1.00
131 Otis Thorpe .40 1.00
132 Jerome Kersey .40 1.00
133 Clifford Robinson .40 1.00
134 Bobby Hurley .60 1.50
135 Spud Webb .60 1.50
136 Olden Polynice .40 1.00
137 Randy Brown .40 1.00
138 Brian Grant .50 1.25
139 Walt Williams .40 1.00
140 Avery Johnson .50 1.25
141 Dennis Rodman 1.25 3.00
142 J.R. Reid .40 1.00
143 David Robinson 1.00 2.50
144 Vinny Del Negro .40 1.00
145 Willie Anderson .40 1.00
146 Nate McMillan .40 1.00
147 Shawn Kemp .60 1.50
148 Detlef Schrempf .60 1.50
149 Vincent Askew .40 1.00
150 Sarunas Marciulionis .40 1.00
151 Byron Houston .40 1.00
152 Ervin Johnson .40 1.00
153 Adam Keefe .40 1.00
154 Jeff Hornacek .50 1.25
155 Antoine Carr .40 1.00
156 John Stockton .75 2.00
157 Blue Edwards .40 1.00
158 David Benoit .40 1.00
159 Don MacLean .40 1.00
160 Juwan Howard .60 1.50
161 Calbert Cheaney .40 1.00
162 Mitchell Butler .40 1.00
163 Gheorghe Muresan .40 1.00
164 Rex Chapman .40 1.00
165 Doug Overton .40 1.00
166 Steve Smith FF .25 .60
167 Dino Radja FF .25 .60
168 Alonzo Mourning FF .40 1.00
169 Michael Jordan FF 2.50 6.00
170 Tyrone Hill FF .20 .50
171 Jamal Mashburn FF .30 .75
172 Dikembe Mutombo FF .30 .75
173 Grant Hill FF 1.00 2.50
w/Michael Jordan
174 Latrell Sprewell FF .30 .75
175 Hakeem Olajuwon FF .40 1.00
176 Reggie Miller FF .40 1.00
177 Pooh Richardson FF .20 .50
178 Cedric Ceballos FF .20 .50
179 Glen Rice FF .30 .75
180 Glenn Robinson FF .30 .75
181 Isaiah Rider FF .30 .75
182 Derrick Coleman FF .25 .60
183 Patrick Ewing FF .40 1.00
184 Shaquille O'Neal FF .75 2.00
185 Dana Barros FF .20 .50
186 Dan Majerle FF .30 .75
187 Clifford Robinson FF .20 .50
188 Mitch Richmond FF .30 .75
189 David Robinson FF .50 1.25
190 Gary Payton FF .30 .75
191 Oliver Miller FF .20 .50
192 Karl Malone FF .40 1.00
193 Kevin Pritchard FF .20 .50
194 Chris Webber FF .40 1.00
195 Michael Jordan PD 2.50 6.00
196 Hakeem Olajuwon PD .40 1.00
197 Vin Baker PD .25 .60
198 Grant Hill PD .50 1.25
199 Clyde Drexler PD .40 1.00
200 Chris Webber PD .40 1.00
201 Shawn Kemp PD .30 .75
202 Shaquille O'Neal PD .75 2.00
203 Stacey Augmon PD .25 .60
204 David Benoit PD .20 .50
205 Rodney Rogers PD .20 .50
206 Latrell Sprewell PD .30 .75
207 Brian Grant PD .25 .60
208 Lamond Murray PD .20 .50
209 Shawn Kemp CL .30 .75
210 Michael Jordan CL 2.50 6.00
211 Cory Alexander .60 1.50
212 Vernon Maxwell .40 1.00
213 George Lynch .40 1.00
214 Terry Mills .40 1.00
215 Scottie Pippen 1.00 2.50
216 Donald Royal .40 1.00
217 Wesley Person .40 1.00
218 Antonio Davis .40 1.00
219 Glenn Robinson .60 1.50
220 Jerry Stackhouse 2.00 5.00
221 James Robinson .40 1.00
222 Chris Mills .40 1.00
223 Chuck Person .50 1.25
224 Duane Causwell .40 1.00
225 Gary Payton .60 1.50
226 Eric Montross .40 1.00
227 Felton Spencer .40 1.00
228 Scott Skiles .40 1.00
229 Latrell Sprewell .60 1.50
230 Sedale Threatt .40 1.00
231 Mark Bryant .40 1.00
232 Buck Williams .40 1.00
233 Brian Williams .40 1.00
234 Sharone Wright .40 1.00
235 Karl Malone .75 2.00
236 Kevin Edwards .40 1.00
237 Muggsy Bogues .50 1.25
238 Mario Elie .40 1.00
239 Rasheed Wallace 2.00 5.00
240 George Zidek .60 1.50
241 Cedric Ceballos .40 1.00
242 Alan Henderson .60 1.50
243 Joe Kleine .40 1.00
244 Patrick Ewing .75 2.00
245 Sasha Danilovic .60 1.50
246 Bill Wennington .40 1.00
247 Steve Smith .50 1.25
248 Bryant Stith .40 1.00
249 Dino Radja .50 1.25
250 Monty Williams .40 1.00
251 Andrew DeClercq .60 1.50
252 Sean Elliott .60 1.50
253 Rick Fox .40 1.00
254 Lionel Simmons .40 1.00
255 Dikembe Mutombo .60 1.50
256 Lindsey Hunter .40 1.00
257 Terrell Brandon .40 1.00
258 Shawn Respert .60 1.50
259 Rodney Rogers .40 1.00
260 Bryon Russell .40 1.00
261 David Wesley .40 1.00
262 Ken Norman .40 1.00
263 Mitch Richmond .60 1.50
264 Sam Perkins .40 1.00
265 Hakeem Olajuwon .75 2.00
266 Brian Shaw .40 1.00
267 B.J. Armstrong .40 1.00
268 Jalen Rose .75 2.00
269 Bryant Reeves .60 1.50
270 Cherokee Parks .60 1.50
271 Dennis Rodman 1.25 3.00
272 Kendall Gill .40 1.00
273 Elliot Perry .40 1.00
274 Anthony Mason .40 1.00
275 Kevin Garnett 5.00 12.00
276 Damon Stoudamire 1.50 4.00
277 Lawrence Moten .60 1.50
278 Ed O'Bannon .60 1.50
279 Toni Kukoc .60 1.50
280 Greg Ostertag .60 1.50
281 Tom Hammonds .40 1.00
282 Yinka Dare .40 1.00
283 Michael Smith .40 1.00
284 Clifford Rozier .40 1.00
285 Gary Trent .60 1.50
286 Shaquille O'Neal 1.50 4.00
287 Luc Longley .40 1.00
288 Bob Sura .60 1.50
289 Dana Barros .40 1.00
290 Lorenzo Williams .40 1.00
291 Haywoode Workman .40 1.00
292 Randolph Childress .60 1.50
293 Doc Rivers .50 1.25
294 Chris Webber .75 2.00
295 Kurt Thomas .60 1.50
296 Greg Anthony .40 1.00
297 Tyus Edney .60 1.50
298 Danny Manning .50 1.25
299 Brent Barry 1.00 2.50
300 Joe Smith 1.25 3.00
301 Pooh Richardson .40 1.00
302 Mark Jackson .60 1.50
303 Richard Dumas .40 1.00
304 Michael Finley 2.00 5.00
305 Theo Ratliff 1.00 2.50
306 Gary Grant .40 1.00
307 Jamal Mashburn .60 1.50
308 Corliss Williamson .60 1.50
309 Eric Williams .60 1.50
310 Zan Tabak .40 1.00
311 Eric Murdock .40 1.00
312 Sherrell Ford .60 1.50
313 Terry Davis .40 1.00
314 Vern Fleming .40 1.00
315 Jason Caffey .60 1.50
316 Mario Bennett .60 1.50
317 David Vaughn .60 1.50
318 Loren Meyer .60 1.50
319 Travis Best .60 1.50
320 Byron Scott .50 1.25
321 Mookie Blaylock SR .20 .50
322 Dee Brown SR .20 .50
323 Alonzo Mourning SR .40 1.00
324 Michael Jordan SR 2.50 6.00
325 Terrell Brandon SR .20 .50
326 Jim Jackson SR .20 .50
327 Dikembe Mutombo SR .30 .75
328 Grant Hill SR .50 1.25
329 Joe Smith SR .60 1.50
330 Clyde Drexler SR .40 1.00
331 Reggie Miller SR .40 1.00
332 Lamond Murray SR .20 .50
333 Nick Van Exel SR .30 .75
334 Glen Rice SR .30 .75
335 Glenn Robinson SR .30 .75
336 Christian Laettner SR .25 .60
337 Kenny Anderson SR .25 .60
338 Patrick Ewing SR .40 1.00
339 Shaquille O'Neal SR .75 2.00
340 Jerry Stackhouse SR 1.00 2.50
341 Charles Barkley SR .50 1.25
342 Clifford Robinson SR .20 .50
343 Brian Grant SR .25 .60
344 David Robinson SR .50 1.25
345 Shawn Kemp SR .30 .75
346 Damon Stoudamire SR .75 2.00
347 Karl Malone SR .40 1.00
348 Bryant Reeves SR .30 .75
349 Juwan Howard SR .30 .75
350 Nick Anderson .20 .50
Dee Brown PT
351 Rik Smits PT .25 .60
352 Herb Williams .20 .50
Tom Tolbert PT
353 Michael Jordan PT 2.50 6.00
354 David Robinson PT .50 1.25
355 Terry Porter .30 .75
Kevin Johnson PT
356 Clyde Drexler PT .40 1.00
357 Cedric Ceballos PT .20 .50
358 Horace Grant .25 .60
Group PT
359 Reggie Miller PT .40 1.00
360 Avery Johnson .30 .75
Nick Van Exel PT
361 Hakeem Olajuwon .40 1.00
Robert Horry PT
362 Rik Smits PT .25 .60
363 David Robinson .50 1.25
Hakeem Olajuwon PT
364 Robert Horry PT .25 .60
365 Kenny Smith PT .25 .60
366 Stacey Augmon LOVE .25 .60
367 Sherman Douglas LOVE .20 .50
368 Larry Johnson LOVE .30 .75
369 Scottie Pippen LOVE .50 1.25
370 Tyrone Hill LOVE .20 .50
371 Jamal Mashburn LOVE .30 .75
372 Mahmoud Abdul-Rauf LOVE .20 .50
373 Grant Hill LOVE .50 1.25
374 Latrell Sprewell LOVE .30 .75
375 Sam Cassell LOVE .30 .75
376 Rik Smits LOVE .25 .60
377 Terry Dehere LOVE .20 .50
378 Eddie Jones LOVE .40 1.00
379 Billy Owens LOVE .20 .50
380 Vin Baker LOVE .25 .60
381 Isaiah Rider LOVE .30 .75
382 Kenny Anderson LOVE .25 .60
383 John Starks LOVE .25 .60
384 Anfernee Hardaway LOVE .50 1.25
385 Sharone Wright LOVE .20 .50
386 Charles Barkley LOVE .50 1.25
387 Clifford Robinson LOVE .20 .50
388 Walt Williams LOVE .20 .50
389 Sean Elliott LOVE .30 .75
390 Gary Payton LOVE .30 .75
391 Carlos Rogers LOVE .20 .50
392 John Stockton LOVE .40 1.00
393 Greg Anthony LOVE .20 .50
394 Chris Webber LOVE .40 1.00
395 Gary Payton PG .30 .75
396 Mookie Blaylock PG .20 .50
397 Charles Barkley PG .50 1.25
398 Grant Hill PG .50 1.25
399 Anfernee Hardaway PG .50 1.25
400 Kenny Anderson PG .25 .60
401 Mark Jackson PG .30 .75
402 Karl Malone PG .40 1.00
403 Avery Johnson PG .25 .60
404 Larry Johnson 40 .30 .75
405 Nick Van Exel 40 .30 .75
406 Vin Baker 40 .25 .60
407 Jason Kidd 40 .50 1.25
408 David Robinson 40 .50 1.25
409 Shawn Kemp CL .30 .75
410 Michael Jordan CL 2.50 6.00

1995-96 Collector's Choice International Japanese Jordan Collection

COMPLETE SET (4) 8.00 20.00
COMMON CARD (J1-J4) 2.50 6.00

1995-96 Collector's Choice International Japanese NBA Extremes

COMPLETE SET (9) 2.50 6.00
E1 Muggsy Bogues .60 1.50
E2 Spud Webb .75 2.00
E3 Dana Barros .50 1.25
E4 Avery Johnson .60 1.50
E5 Vlade Divac .75 2.00
E6 Dikembe Mutombo .75 2.00
E7 Rik Smits .60 1.50
E8 Shawn Bradley .50 1.25
E9 Gheorghe Muresan .50 1.25

1995-96 Collector's Choice International Japanese Special Edition Holograms

COMPLETE SET (9) 6.00 15.00
H1 Larry Johnson 1.00 2.50
H2 Scottie Pippen 1.50 4.00
H3 Grant Hill 1.50 4.00
H4 Reggie Miller 1.25 3.00
H5 Glenn Robinson 1.00 2.50
H6 Patrick Ewing 1.25 3.00
H7 Shaquille O'Neal 2.50 6.00
H8 John Stockton 1.25 3.00
H9 Chris Webber 1.25 3.00

1995-96 Collector's Choice International Portuguese I

COMPLETE SET (210) 8.00 20.00
*PORTUGUESE: SAME VALUE AS FRENCH

1995-96 Collector's Choice International Portuguese II

COMPLETE SET (200) 8.00 20.00
*PORTUGUESE: SAME VALUE AS FRENCH

1995-96 Collector's Choice International Portuguese Jordan Collection

COMPLETE SET (4) 5.00 12.00
*PORTUGUESE: SAME VALUE AS FRENCH

1995-96 Collector's Choice International Portuguese NBA Extremes

COMPLETE SET (9) 1.50 4.00
*PORTUGUESE: SAME VALUE AS FRENCH

1995-96 Collector's Choice International Portuguese Special Edition Holograms

COMPLETE SET (9) 4.00 10.00
*PORTUGUESE: SAME VALUE AS FRENCH

1995-96 Collector's Choice International Spanish I

COMPLETE SET (210) 8.00 20.00
*SPANISH: SAME VALUE AS FRENCH

1995-96 Collector's Choice International Spanish II

COMPLETE SET (200) 8.00 20.00
*SPANISH: SAME VALUE AS FRENCH

1995-96 Collector's Choice International Spanish Jordan Collection

COMPLETE SET (4) 5.00 12.00
*SPANISH: SAME VALUE AS FRENCH

1995-96 Collector's Choice International Spanish NBA Extremes

COMPLETE SET (9) 1.50 4.00
*SPANISH: SAME VALUE AS FRENCH

1995-96 Collector's Choice International Spanish Special Edition Holograms

COMPLETE SET (9) 4.00 10.00
*SPANISH: SAME VALUE AS FRENCH

1996-97 Collector's Choice International English Jordan's Journal

COMPLETE SET (6) 8.00 20.00
COMMON CARD (J1-J6) 2.00 5.00

1996-97 Collector's Choice International French

COMPLETE SET (200) 20.00 40.00
1 Mookie Blaylock .15 .40
2 Grant Long .15 .40
3 Christian Laettner .20 .50
4 Craig Ehlo .15 .40
5 Ken Norman .15 .40
6 Stacey Augmon .20 .50
7 Dana Barros .15 .40
8 Dino Radja .20 .50
9 Rick Fox .15 .40
10 Eric Montross .15 .40
11 David Wesley .15 .40
12 Eric Williams .15 .40
13 Glen Rice .25 .60
14 Dell Curry .15 .40
15 Matt Geiger .15 .40
16 Scott Burrell .15 .40
17 George Zidek .15 .40
18 Muggsy Bogues .20 .50
19 Ron Harper .20 .50
20 Steve Kerr .20 .50
21 Toni Kukoc .25 .60
22 Dennis Rodman .50 1.25
23 Michael Jordan 2.00 5.00
24 Luc Longley .15 .40
25 Michael Jordan VT 2.00 5.00
26 Michael Jordan VT 2.00 5.00
27 Luc Longley VT .15 .40
28 Scottie Pippen VT .40 1.00
29 Toni Kukoc VT .25 .60
30 Terrell Brandon .15 .40
31 Bobby Phills .15 .40
32 Tyrone Hill .15 .40
33 Michael Cage .15 .40
34 Bob Sura .15
35 Tony Dumas .15
36 Jim Jackson .15
37 Loren Meyer .15
38 Cherokee Parks .15
39 Jamal Mashburn .20
40 Popeye Jones .15
41 LaPhonso Ellis .15
42 Jalen Rose .20
43 Antonio McDyess .25
44 Tom Hammonds .15
45 Mahmoud Abdul-Rauf .15
46 Dale Ellis .15
47 Joe Dumars .25
48 Theo Ratliff .15
49 Lindsey Hunter .15
50 Terry Mills .15
51 Don Reid .15
52 B.J. Armstrong .15
53 Bimbo Coles .15
54 Joe Smith .20
55 Chris Mullin .25
56 Rony Seikaly .20
57 Donyell Marshall .15
58 Hakeem Olajuwon .30
59 Robert Horry .20
60 Mario Elie .15
61 Mark Bryant .15
62 Chucky Brown .15
63 Rik Smits .20
64 Derrick McKey .15
65 Eddie Johnson .15
66 Mark Jackson .25
67 Ricky Pierce .15
68 Travis Best .15
69 Rodney Rogers .15
70 Brent Barry .20
71 Lamond Murray .15
72 Eric Piatkowski .20
73 Pooh Richardson .15
74 Cedric Ceballos .15
75 Eddie Jones .25
76 Anthony Peeler .15
77 George Lynch .15
78 Vlade Divac .25
79 Rex Chapman .15
80 Sasha Danilovic .15
81 Kurt Thomas .15
82 Keith Askins .15
83 Walt Williams .15
84 Vin Baker .20
85 Shawn Respert .15
86 Sherman Douglas .15
87 Marty Conlon .15
88 Johnny Newman .15
89 Kevin Garnett .60
90 Andrew Lang .15
91 Terry Porter .15
92 Sam Mitchell .15
93 Tom Gugliotta .15
94 Spud Webb .25
95 Kendall Gill .15
96 Vern Fleming .15
97 Shawn Bradley .15
98 Yinka Dare .15
99 Jayson Williams .15
100 Kevin Edwards .15
101 Charles Oakley .20
102 Anthony Mason .15
103 John Starks .20
104 J.R. Reid .15
105 Hubert Davis .15
106 Gary Grant .15
107 Nick Anderson .15
108 Donald Royal .15
109 Brian Shaw .15
110 Brooks Thompson .15
111 Anfernee Hardaway .40
112 Dennis Scott .15
113 Anfernee Hardaway .40
114 Anfernee Hardaway .40
115 Anfernee Hardaway .40
116 Anfernee Hardaway .40
117 Anfernee Hardaway .40
118 Derrick Coleman .20
119 Rex Walters .15
120 Sean Higgins .15
121 Clarence Weatherspoon .15
122 Jerry Stackhouse .30
123 Elliot Perry .15
124 Wayman Tisdale .15
125 Wesley Person .15
126 Charles Barkley .40
127 A.C. Green .25
128 Harvey Grant .15
129 Arvydas Sabonis .20
130 Aaron McKie .15
131 Gary Trent .15
132 Buck Williams .15
133 Billy Owens .15
134 Brian Grant .20
135 Corliss Williamson .15
136 Tyus Edney .15
137 Olden Polynice .15
138 Avery Johnson .20
139 Vinny Del Negro .15
140 Sean Elliott .25
141 Chuck Person .20
142 Will Perdue .15
143 Nate McMillan .15
144 Vincent Askew .15
145 Detlef Schrempf .25
146 Hersey Hawkins .15
147 Sharone Wright .15
148 Zan Tabak .15
149 Oliver Miller .15
150 Doug Christie .15
151 Damon Stoudamire .25
152 Jeff Hornacek .20
153 Chris Morris .15
154 Antoine Carr .15
155 Karl Malone .30
156 Adam Keefe .15
157 Greg Anthony .15
158 Blue Edwards .15
159 Bryant Reeves .15
160 Anthony Avent .15
161 Lawrence Moten .15
162 Calbert Cheaney .15
163 Chris Webber .30
164 Tim Legler .15
165 Gheorghe Muresan .15
166 Stacey Augmon FUND .20
167 Dee Brown FUND .15
168 Glen Rice FUND .25
169 Scottie Pippen FUND .40

Danny Ferry FUND .15 .40
Jason Kidd FUND .40 1.00
Tom Hammonds FUND .15 .40
Grant Hill FUND .40 1.00
Chris Mullin FUND .25 .60
Clyde Drexler FUND .30 .75
Rik Smits FUND .20 .50
Lamond Murray FUND .15 .40
Nick Van Exel FUND .25 .60
Alonzo Mourning FUND .30 .75
Glenn Robinson FUND .25 .60
Isaiah Rider FUND .20 .50
Ed O'Bannon FUND .15 .40
Patrick Ewing FUND .30 .75
Shaquille O'Neal FUND .60 1.50
Derrick Coleman FUND .20 .50
Danny Manning FUND .20 .50
Clifford Robinson FUND .15 .40
Mitch Richmond FUND .25 .60
David Robinson FUND .40 1.00
Shawn Kemp FUND .25 .60
Oliver Miller FUND .15 .40
John Stockton FUND .30 .75
Greg Anthony FUND .15 .40
Rasheed Wallace FUND .30 .75
Michael Jordan FUND 2.00 5.00
Checklist .40 1.00
Checklist .15 .40
Checklist .40 1.00
Checklist .15 .40
Checklist .25 .60

1996-97 Collector's Choice International French Crash the Game Scoring

PLETE SET (60) 40.00 80.00
Mookie Blaylock .60 1.50
Mookie Blaylock .60 1.50
Dino Radja .75 2.00
Dino Radja .75 2.00
Glen Rice 1.00 2.50
Glen Rice 1.00 2.50
Scottie Pippen 1.50 4.00
Scottie Pippen 1.50 4.00
Terrell Brandon .60 1.50
Terrell Brandon .60 1.50
Jason Kidd 1.50 4.00
Jason Kidd 1.50 4.00
Antonio McDyess 1.00 2.50
Antonio McDyess 1.00 2.50
Joe Dumars 1.00 2.50
Joe Dumars 1.00 2.50
Joe Smith .75 2.00
Joe Smith .75 2.00
A Hakeem Olajuwon 1.25 3.00
B Hakeem Olajuwon 1.25 3.00
A Reggie Miller 1.25 3.00
B Reggie Miller 1.25 3.00
A Loy Vaught .60 1.50
B Loy Vaught .60 1.50
A Cedric Ceballos .60 1.50
B Cedric Ceballos .60 1.50
A Alonzo Mourning 1.25 3.00
B Alonzo Mourning 1.25 3.00
A Vin Baker .75 2.00
B Vin Baker .75 2.00
A Kevin Garnett 2.50 6.00
B Kevin Garnett 2.50 6.00
A Ed O'Bannon .60 1.50
B Ed O'Bannon .60 1.50
A Patrick Ewing 1.25 3.00
B Patrick Ewing 1.25 3.00
A Anfernee Hardaway 1.50 4.00
B Anfernee Hardaway 1.50 4.00
A Clarence Weatherspoon .60 1.50
B Clarence Weatherspoon .60 1.50
A Kevin Johnson 1.00 2.50
B Kevin Johnson 1.00 2.50
A Clifford Robinson .60 1.50
B Clifford Robinson .60 1.50
A Mitch Richmond 1.00 2.50
B Mitch Richmond 1.00 2.50
A Sean Elliott 1.00 2.50
B Sean Elliott 1.00 2.50
A Shawn Kemp 1.00 2.50
B Shawn Kemp 1.00 2.50
A Damon Stoudamire 1.00 2.50
B Damon Stoudamire 1.00 2.50
A John Stockton 1.25 3.00
B John Stockton 1.25 3.00
A Bryant Reeves .60 1.50
B Bryant Reeves .60 1.50
A Rasheed Wallace 1.25 3.00
B Rasheed Wallace 1.25 3.00
A Michael Jordan 8.00 20.00
B Michael Jordan 8.00 20.00

1996-97 Collector's Choice International French Jordan's Journal

PLETE SET (6) 8.00 20.00
MON CARD 2.00 5.00

1996-97 Collector's Choice International French Mini-Cards

PLETE SET (30) 6.00 15.00
Mookie Blaylock .30 .75
Hornacek
Walters
Dino Radja .40 1.00
ni Kukoc
lef Schrempf
ric Williams .25 .60
arone Wright
raf Amaya
George Zidek .25 .60
O'Bannon
is Edney
Luc Longley .25 .60
awn Bradley
eo Ratliff
Mahmoud Abdul-Rauf .30 .75
ery Johnson
bby Phills
Tom Hammonds .25 .60
is Morris
peye Jones
Grant Hill .60 1.50
ristian Laettner
bby Hurley
Rony Seikaly .30 .75
rick Coleman
rman Douglas
Sam Cassell .40 1.00
n Starks
k Van Exel
Travis Best .25 .60
nis Scott
t Geiger

M36 Brent Barry .30 .75
Isaiah Rider
Cedric Ceballos
M37 Lamond Murray .60 1.50
Kevin Johnson
Jason Kidd
M38 Terry Dehere .40 1.00
Jayson Williams
Chris Mullin
M39 Vlade Divac .40 1.00
Sasha Danilovic
Arvydas Sabonis
M43 Kurt Thomas .30 .75
Brian Grant
Tyrone Hill
M44 Keith Askins .30 .75
Robert Horry
Derrick McKey
M46 Shawn Respert .60 1.50
David Robinson
Randolph Childress
M49 Andrew Lang .25 .60
Oliver Miller
Todd Day
M56 Charles Oakley .30 .75
Bimbo Coles
Dell Curry
M57 J.R. Reid .50 1.25
Jerry Stackhouse
Rasheed Wallace
M66 A.C. Green .50 1.25
Clyde Drexler
Joe Dumars
M67 Aaron McKie .25 .60
Nick Anderson
Kendall Gill
M75 Doc Rivers .40 1.00
Mark Jackson
Danny Ferry
M78 Shawn Kemp 3.00 8.00
Anfernee Hardaway
Michael Jordan
M79 Jimmy King .50 1.25
Chris Webber
Jalen Rose
M83 Karl Malone .75 2.00
Charles Barkley
Dennis Rodman
M85 Greg Anthony .40 1.00
Larry Johnson
Stacey Augmon
M86 Blue Edwards .25 .60
Tom Gugliotta
Nate McMillan
M90 Calbert Cheaney .40 1.00
Glenn Robinson
Jim Jackson

1996-97 Collector's Choice International French Stick Ums

COMPLETE SET (30) 8.00 20.00
S1 Mookie Blaylock .25 .60
S2 Dana Barros .25 .60
S3 Scott Burrell .25 .60
S4 Dennis Rodman .75 2.00
S5 Terrell Brandon .25 .60
S6 Jamal Mashburn .30 .75
S7 LaPhonso Ellis .25 .60
S8 Grant Hill .60 1.50
S9 Joe Smith .30 .75
S10 Hakeem Olajuwon .50 1.25
S11 Rik Smits .30 .75
S12 Brent Barry .30 .75
S13 Nick Van Exel .40 1.00
S14 Sasha Danilovic .25 .60
S15 Vin Baker .30 .75
S16 Kevin Garnett 1.00 2.50
S17 Shawn Bradley .25 .60
S18 Patrick Ewing .50 1.25
S19 Anfernee Hardaway .60 1.50
S20 Clarence Weatherspoon .25 .60
S21 Charles Barkley .60 1.50
S22 Clifford Robinson .25 .60
S23 Mitch Richmond .40 1.00
S24 David Robinson .60 1.50
S25 Shawn Kemp .40 1.00
S26 Damon Stoudamire .40 1.00
S27 Karl Malone .50 1.25
S28 Bryant Reeves .25 .60
S29 Gheorghe Muresan .25 .60
S30 Michael Jordan 3.00 8.00

1996-97 Collector's Choice International German

COMPLETE SET (200) 20.00 40.00
*GERMAN: SAME VALUE AS FRENCH

1996-97 Collector's Choice International German Jordan's Journal

COMPLETE SET (6) 8.00 20.00
COMMON CARD 2.00 5.00

1996-97 Collector's Choice International German Mini-Cards

COMPLETE SET (30) 6.00 15.00
*GERMAN: SAME VALUE AS FRENCH

1996-97 Collector's Choice International German Stick Ums

COMPLETE SET (30) 8.00 20.00
*GERMAN: SAME VALUE AS FRENCH

1996-97 Collector's Choice International Italian

Consisting of 200 cards, the 1996-97 Collector's Choice International set was distributed in Italy and possibly other countries. We currently only have a checklist for the Italian. These cards are identical in design to the 1996-97 Collector's Choice American cards except for bilingual text for the respective countries and the regular card numbering.
COMPLETE SET (200) 20.00 40.00
*ITALIAN: SAME VALUE AS FRENCH

1996-97 Collector's Choice International Italian Crash the Game Scoring

Randomly inserted into first series Italian packs, this 60-card silver set features two separate versions of thirty different player cards. Each player is given two separate weeks to score 30 points in any given game during that time period. If the player depicted on the card scores 30 or more points in the given week, the card could be redeemed for one premium quality silver card of the depicted player. The expiration date for the cards was June 7, 1997.
COMPLETE SET (60) 40.00 80.00
*ITALIAN: SAME VALUE AS FRENCH

1996-97 Collector's Choice International Italian Jordan's Journal

This six-card set was randomly inserted into packs of 1996-97 Collector's Choice International Italian basketball.
COMPLETE SET (6) 8.00 20.00
COMMON CARD 2.00 5.00

1996-97 Collector's Choice International Italian Mini-Cards

Inserted at a rate of one per series one pack, this 30-card set is comprised of 90 different "mini-cards". Three of these mini-cards form one standard-sized card and are issued in that form. Card fronts feature perforated panels of three players with silver foil. Card backs feature a brief commentary on each player. Each card contains it's own individual number, with an "M" prefix and is ordered below by the far left number on the card back.
COMPLETE SET (30) 6.00 15.00
*ITALIAN: SAME VALUE AS FRENCH
M2 Mookie Blaylock .30 .75
Jeff Hornacek
Rex Walters
M5 Dino Radja .40 1.00
Toni Kukoc
Detlef Schrempf
M6 Eric Williams .25 .60
Sharone Wright
Ashraf Amaya
M10 George Zidek .25 .60
Ed O'Bannon
Tyus Edney
M13 Luc Longley .25 .60
Shawn Bradley
Theo Ratliff
M22 Mahmoud Abdul-Rauf .30 .75
Avery Johnson
Bobby Phills
M23 Tom Hammonds .25 .60
Chris Morris
Popeye Jones
M25 Grant Hill .60 1.50
Christian Laettner
Bobby Hurley
M28 Rony Seikaly .30 .75
Derrick Coleman
Sherman Douglas
M30 Sam Cassell .40 1.00
John Starks
Nick Van Exel
M33 Travis Best .25 .60
Dennis Scott
Matt Geiger
M36 Brent Barry .30 .75
Isaiah Rider
Cedric Ceballos
M37 Lamond Murray .60 1.50
Kevin Johnson
Jason Kidd
M38 Terry Dehere .40 1.00
Jayson Williams
Chris Mullin
M39 Vlade Divac .40 1.00
Sasha Danilovic
Arvydas Sabonis
M43 Kurt Thomas .30 .75
Brian Grant
Tyrone Hill
M44 Keith Askins .30 .75
Robert Horry
Derrick McKey
M46 Shawn Respert .60 1.50
David Robinson
Randolph Childress
M49 Andrew Lang .25 .60
Oliver Miller
Todd Day
M56 Charles Oakley .30 .75
Bimbo Coles
Dell Curry
M57 J.R. Reid .50 1.25
Jerry Stackhouse
Rasheed Wallace
M66 A.C. Green .50 1.25
Clyde Drexler
Joe Dumars
M67 Aaron McKie .25 .60
Nick Anderson
Kendall Gill
M75 Doc Rivers .40 1.00
Mark Jackson
Danny Ferry
M78 Shawn Kemp 3.00 8.00
Anfernee Hardaway
Michael Jordan
M79 Jimmy King .50 1.25
Chris Webber
Jalen Rose
M83 Karl Malone .75 2.00
Charles Barkley
Dennis Rodman
M85 Greg Anthony .40 1.00
Larry Johnson
Stacey Augmon
M86 Blue Edwards .25 .60
Tom Gugliotta
Nate McMillan
M90 Calbert Cheaney .40 1.00
Glenn Robinson
Jim Jackson

1996-97 Collector's Choice International Italian Stick Ums

This 30-card set was randomly inserted into packs of 1996-97 Collector's Choice International Italian basketball. The checklist mirrors the American 1996-97 Collector's Choice series one Stick-Um set. The card design is the same with different language text on the card back.
COMPLETE SET (30) 8.00 20.00
*ITALIAN: SAME VALUE AS FRENCH

1996-97 Collector's Choice International Japanese Coast to Coast

CC2 Michael Jordan 40.00 100.00

1996-97 Collector's Choice International Spanish

COMPLETE SET (200) 20.00 40.00
*SPANISH: SAME VALUE AS FRENCH

1996-97 Collector's Choice International Spanish Crash the Game Scoring

COMPLETE SET (60) 40.00 80.00
*SPANISH: SAME VALUE AS FRENCH

1996-97 Collector's Choice International Spanish Jordan's Journal

COMPLETE SET (6) 8.00 20.00
COMMON CARD 2.00 5.00

1996-97 Collector's Choice International Spanish Stick Ums

COMPLETE SET (30) 8.00 20.00
*SPANISH: SAME VALUE AS FRENCH

1971-72 Colonels Marathon Oil

This set of Marathon Oil Pro Star Portraits consists of colorful portraits by distinguished artist Nicholas Volpe. Each (ABA Kentucky Colonels) portrait measures approximately 7 1/2" by 9 7/8" and features a painting of the player's face on a black background, with an action painting superimposed to the side. A facsimile autograph in white appears at the bottom of the portrait. At the bottom of each portrait is a postcard measuring 7 1/2" by 4" after perforation. While the back of the portrait has offers for a basketball photo album, autographed tumblers, and a poster, the postcard itself could also be used to apply for a Marathon credit card. The portraits are unnumbered and checklisted below in alphabetical order. Tumblers featuring these drawings are valued at 3x the listed prices. The key card in the set is Dan Issel during his Rookie Card year.
COMPLETE SET (11) 50.00 100.00
1 Darrell Carrier 5.00 10.00
2 Bobby Croft 3.00 8.00
3 Louie Dampier 10.00 25.00
4 Les Hunter 3.00 8.00
5 Dan Issel 20.00 40.00
6 Jim Ligon 3.00 8.00
7 Cincy Powell 5.00 12.00
8 Mike Pratt 5.00 10.00
9 Walt Simon 3.00 8.00
10 Sam Smith 3.00 8.00
11 Howard Wright 3.00 8.00

1959 Comet Sweets Olympic Achievements

Celebrating various Olympic events, ceremonies, and their history, this 25-card set was issued by Comet Sweets. The cards are printed on thin cardboard stock and measure 1 7/16" by 2 9/16". Inside white borders, the fronts display water color paintings of various Olympic events. Some cards are horizontally oriented; others are vertically oriented. The set title "Olympic Achievements" appears at the top on the backs, with a discussion of the event below. This set is the first series; the cards are numbered "X to 25."
COMPLETE SET (25) 30.00 60.00
12 Basketball 2.50 5.00

1972-73 Comspec

This 36-card set is printed on thin card stock, and each card measures approximately 2 1/4" by 3 1/2". The fronts display posed color player photos bordered in white. The photos have different color backgrounds (blue, green, orange, pink, red, or yellow). The only card that contains a genuine action shot from a game is that of Chet Walker. The team name, player's name, and his position appear in the white border beneath each picture. The horizontally oriented backs have biography and career statistics. The cards are unnumbered and checklisted below in alphabetical order.
COMPLETE SET (36) 2200.00 2800.00
1 Kareem Abdul-Jabbar 150.00 300.00
2 Rick Adelman 20.00 45.00
3 Nate Archibald 40.00 80.00
4 Rick Barry 40.00 80.00
5 Walt Bellamy 20.00 50.00
6 Dave Bing 30.00 75.00
7 Austin Carr 15.00 40.00
8 Wilt Chamberlain 250.00 500.00
9 Dave Cowens 40.00 80.00
10 Walt Frazier 40.00 80.00
11 Gail Goodrich 30.00 75.00
12 John Havlicek 100.00 225.00
13 Connie Hawkins 45.00 90.00
14 Elvin Hayes 30.00 75.00
15 Spencer Haywood 15.00 40.00
16 John Hummer 12.50 30.00
17 Don Kojis 15.00 40.00
18 Bob Lanier 40.00 80.00
19 Kevin Loughery 15.00 40.00
20 Jerry Lucas 30.00 75.00
21 Pete Maravich 250.00 500.00
22 Jack Marin 15.00 40.00
23 Calvin Murphy 30.00 60.00
24 Geoff Petrie 25.00 50.00
25 Willis Reed 40.00 80.00
26 Oscar Robertson 100.00 225.00
27 Cazzie Russell 20.00 40.00
28 Elmore Smith 12.50 30.00
29 Dick Snyder 12.50 30.00
30 Wes Unseld 30.00 75.00
31 Dick Van Arsdale 25.00 50.00
32 Tom Van Arsdale 12.50 30.00
33 Norm Van Lier 30.00 60.00
34 Chet Walker 30.00 60.00
35 Jerry West 150.00 300.00
36 Lenny Wilkens 45.00 90.00

1971-72 Condors Pittsburgh Team Issue

This set of 11 photos features the Pittsburgh Condors of the American Basketball Association. The cards measure approximately 5 1/2" by 7". The froots carry black-and-white posed action photos with a white border. The player's name and the team name appear under the picture. The backs are blank. The photos are unnumbered and checklisted below in alphabetical order.
COMPLETE SET (11) 35.00 70.00
1 John Brisker 5.00 10.00
2 George Carter 3.00 8.00
3 Mickey Davis 2.50 6.00
4 Stew Johnson 2.50 6.00
5 Arvesta Kelly 2.50 6.00
6 Dave Lattin 5.00 10.00
7 Mike Lewis 2.50 6.00
8 Jimmy O'Brien 4.00 10.00
9 Paul Ruffner 2.50 6.00
10 Skeeter Swift 3.00 8.00
11 George Thompson 5.00 10.00

1971-72 Condors Pittsburgh Team Photo

Each of these team-issued photos measure approximately 8" by 10" and feature black and white player portraits on two different sheets. The player's name is listed below the photo. Each sheet contains eight player portraits. The backs are blank. The photos are unnumbered and listed below alphabetically.
COMPLETE SET (2) 20.00 40.00
1 John Brisker 12.50 25.00
George Carter
Mickey Davis
Mike Lewis
Jimmy O'Brien
Paul Ruffner
Skeeter Swift
George Thompson
2 Don Bezahler 10.00 20.00
Mark Binstein
Stew Johnson
Arvesta Kelly
David Lattin
Jack McMahon
Ray Melchiorre
Walt Szczerbiak

1969-70 Converse Staff

This ten-card set was sponsored by Converse Shoes. The cards measure approximately 2 1/4" by 2 3/4". The fronts feature a drawn player portrait and basketball tip. The backs are blank. The cards are unnumbered and are checklisted below in alphabetical order.
COMPLETE SET (10) 150.00 300.00
1 Bob Davies 30.00 60.00
2 Joe Dean 10.00 25.00
3 Gib Ford 10.00 25.00
4 Bob Houbregs 15.00 40.00
5 Rod Hundley 30.00 60.00
6 Stu Inman 15.00 30.00
7 Bunny Levitt 15.00 40.00
8 Earl Lloyd 15.00 30.00
9 John Norlander 15.00 30.00
10 Phil Rollins 10.00 25.00

1989 Converse

This 15-card standard-size set was sponsored by Converse. The color action player photo on the front of the card is outlined by a thin black border against a white background. At the top, the words "Converse, Official Shoe of the NBA" is printed in blue lettering, as is the player's name and number below the picture. The NBA logo in the upper right corner rounds out the card face. The back presents a brief biography, career highlights, and a tip from the player and Converse in the form of an anti-drug or alcohol message. The cards are unnumbered and checklisted below in alphabetical order. Mark Aguirre is misspelled Aquirre on the checklist card. The set originally included a free video offer card; for 3.95 to cover shipping and handling, the collector could receive a video of Converse basketball tips, featuring Julius Erving, Kevin McHale, and Dale Brown. The cards were reportedly intended for distribution at youth basketball clinics sponsored by Converse but it is apparent that much remainder stock has been made available to the hobby thus greatly increasing the supply.
COMPLETE SET (15) 4.00 10.00
1 Mark Aguirre .20 .50
2 Larry Bird 2.50 6.00
3 Rolando Blackman .30 .75
4 Muggsy Bogues .40 1.00
5 Rex Chapman .40 1.00
6 Magic Johnson 1.25 3.00
7 Bernard King .30 .75
8 Bill Laimbeer .30 .75
9 Karl Malone 1.00 2.50
10 Kevin McHale .50 1.25
11 Mark Price .40 1.00
12 Jack Sikma .20 .50
13 Reggie Theus .30 .75
14 Title Card .20 .50
NNO Free Video Offer .20 .50

1993-94 Costacos Brothers Poster Cards

COMPLETE SET (18) 10.00 20.00
3 Charles Barkley .60 1.50
Sir Charles
14 Alonzo Mourning .30 .75
Zo
15 Shaquille O'Neal 1.25 3.00
Shaq

1969-70 Cougars Carolina Team Issue

Each of these team-issued photos measure approximately 8" by 10" and feature black and white player portraits. The player's name is listed below the photo and the fronts feature a facsimile autograph. The backs are blank. The photos are unnumbered and listed below alphabetically.
COMPLETE SET (15) 50.00 100.00
1 Carolina Cougars 5.00 10.00
Team Photo
2 Bill Bunting 2.50 6.00
3 Cal Fowler 2.50 6.00
4 Steve Kramer 2.50 6.00
5 Gene Littles 3.00 8.00
6 Randy Mahaffey 2.50 6.00
7 Bones McKinney CO 5.00 10.00
8 Larry Miller 3.00 8.00
9 Doug Moe 5.00 10.00
10 Rich Niemann 2.50 6.00
11 George Peeples 2.50 6.00
12 Ron Perry 2.50 6.00
13 George Sutor 2.50 6.00
14 Bob Verga 3.00 8.00
15 Hank Whitney 2.50 6.00

1970-71 Cougars Team Issue

These photos were issued by the Carolina Cougars. They feature members of the 1970-71 Cougars team. This list may not be complete so any additions are appreciated. Jim McDaniel was signed out of college and was going to be the star rookie the next season. Also please note the Larry Steele never played for the Cougars.
COMPLETE SET 12.50 25.00
1 Gary Bradds 2.00 5.00
2 Jim McDaniels 2.50 6.00
3 Dave Newmark 2.00 5.00
4 George Peeples 2.00 5.00
5 Larry Steele 3.00 8.00

2009-10 Court Kings

COMP.SET w/o RC's (120) 50.00 100.00
1-120 PRINT RUN 450 SER.#'d SETS
ROOKIE PRINT RUN 649 SER.#'d SETS
1 Carmelo Anthony 1.25 3.00
2 Chris Andersen 1.50 4.00
3 J.R. Smith 1.00 2.50
4 Chauncey Billups 1.00 2.50
5 Kevin Love 1.50 4.00
6 Al Jefferson 1.00 2.50
7 Corey Brewer .60 1.50
8 Kevin Durant 3.00 8.00
9 Russell Westbrook 1.50 4.00
10 Jeff Green .75 2.00
11 Brandon Roy 1.00 2.50
12 LaMarcus Aldridge 1.00 2.50
13 Juwan Howard .75 2.00
14 Deron Williams 1.00 2.50
15 Carlos Boozer 1.00 2.50
16 Paul Millsap .75 2.00
17 Dirk Nowitzki 1.25 3.00
18 Jason Kidd 1.00 2.50
19 Drew Gooden .75 2.00
20 J.J. Barea 1.25 3.00
21 Trevor Ariza .60 1.50
22 Aaron Brooks .60 1.50
23 Carl Landry .60 1.50
24 Tony Parker 1.00 2.50
25 Richard Jefferson 1.00 2.50
26 Tim Duncan 1.50 4.00
27 Marc Gasol 1.00 2.50
28 Rudy Gay 1.00 2.50
29 Zach Randolph .75 2.00
30 Emeka Okafor 1.00 2.50
31 Chris Paul 1.50 4.00
32 David West 1.00 2.50
33 Jason Thompson .60 1.50
34 Kevin Martin 1.00 2.50
35 Spencer Hawes .75 2.00
36 Amare Stoudemire 1.00 2.50
37 Channing Frye .75 2.00
38 Steve Nash 1.00 2.50
39 Pau Gasol 1.00 2.50
40 Kobe Bryant 5.00 12.00
41 Derek Fisher .75 2.00
42 Andrew Bynum 1.25 3.00
43 Monta Ellis 1.00 2.50
44 Anthony Morrow .60 1.50
45 Corey Maggette .75 2.00
46 Baron Davis 1.00 2.50
47 Chris Kaman .75 2.00
48 Eric Gordon 1.00 2.50
49 Kevin Garnett 2.00 5.00
50 Ray Allen 1.00 2.50
51 Paul Pierce 1.25 3.00
52 Kendrick Perkins .75 2.00
53 Nate Robinson 1.00 2.50
54 Chris Duhon .60 1.50
55 David Lee .75 2.00
56 Danilo Gallinari 1.00 2.50
57 Allen Iverson 1.25 3.00
58 Andre Iguodala 1.00 2.50
59 Louis Williams .75 2.00
60 Elton Brand 1.00 2.50
61 Andrea Bargnani .75 2.00
62 Chris Bosh 1.00 2.50
63 Hedo Turkoglu 1.00 2.50
64 Brook Lopez 1.00 2.50
65 Rafer Alston .60 1.50
66 Devin Harris 1.00 2.50
67 LeBron James 5.00 12.00
68 Anderson Varejao .75 2.00
69 Delonte West .60 1.50
70 Shaquille O'Neal 2.00 5.00
71 Ben Gordon 1.00 2.50
72 Rodney Stuckey 1.00 2.50
73 Ben Wallace 1.00 2.50
74 Danny Granger 1.00 2.50
75 Troy Murphy .60 1.50
76 Dahntay Jones .60 1.50
77 Andrew Bogut 1.00 2.50
78 Luke Ridnour .75 2.00
79 Hakim Warrick .75 2.00
80 Luol Deng 1.00 2.50
81 Derrick Rose 3.00 8.00
82 Joakim Noah 1.00 2.50
83 John Salmons 1.00 2.50
84 Joe Johnson 1.00 2.50
85 Al Horford 1.00 2.50
86 Jamal Crawford .75 2.00
87 Marvin Williams .75 2.00
88 Dwyane Wade 2.00 5.00
89 Jermaine O'Neal 1.00 2.50
90 Michael Beasley 1.00 2.50
91 Gerald Wallace 1.00 2.50
92 Stephen Jackson .75 2.00
93 Raymond Felton .75 2.00
94 Dwight Howard 1.50 4.00
95 Vince Carter 1.25 3.00
96 Rashard Lewis .75 2.00
97 Jason Williams .75 2.00
98 Antawn Jamison 1.00 2.50
99 Mike Miller 1.00 2.50
100 Caron Butler 1.00 2.50
101 Harry Gallatin 1.00 2.50
102 Nate Archibald 1.00 2.50
103 Elgin Baylor 1.00 2.50
104 Walt Bellamy 1.00 2.50
105 Dave Bing 1.00 2.50
106 Louie Dampier 1.00 2.50
107 Clyde Drexler 1.25 3.00
108 Mark Eaton 1.00 2.50
109 John Havlicek 1.00 2.50
110 Jerry Lucas 1.00 2.50
111 George McGinnis 1.00 2.50
112 Sidney Moncrief 1.00 2.50
113 Kurt Rambis 1.00 2.50
114 Bill Sharman 1.00 2.50
115 Lenny Wilkens 1.00 2.50
116 Elvin Hayes 1.00 2.50
117 Walt Frazier 1.00 2.50
118 Connie Hawkins 1.00 2.50
119 Spencer Haywood 1.00 2.50
120 Dell Curry 1.00 2.50
121 Jrue Holiday AU RC 8.00 20.00
122 James Johnson AU RC 4.00 10.00
123 Taj Gibson AU RC 5.00 12.00
124 Brandon Jennings AU RC 10.00 25.00
125 Jeff Teague AU RC 5.00 12.00
126 Earl Clark AU RC 4.00 10.00
127 Jordan Hill AU RC 4.00 10.00
128 Toney Douglas AU RC 4.00 10.00
129 Stephen Curry AU RC 12.00 30.00
130 Austin Daye AU RC 4.00 10.00
131 Jonas Jerebko AU RC 4.00 10.00
132 Jonny Flynn AU RC 4.00 10.00
133 Wayne Ellington AU RC 4.00 10.00
134 Ty Lawson AU RC 8.00 20.00
135 Chase Budinger AU RC 4.00 10.00
136 DeJuan Blair AU RC 5.00 12.00
137 Tyler Hansbrough AU RC 6.00 15.00
138 DeMarre Carroll AU RC 4.00 10.00
139 Hasheem Thabeet AU RC 4.00 10.00
140 Terrence Williams AU RC 4.00 10.00
141 Darren Collison AU RC 6.00 15.00
142 Marcus Thornton AU RC 6.00 15.00
143 Derrick Brown AU RC 4.00 10.00
144 Gerald Henderson AU RC 4.00 10.00
145 James Harden AU RC 12.00 30.00
146 DeMar DeRozan AU RC 6.00 15.00
147 Tyreke Evans AU RC 12.00 30.00
148 Omri Casspi AU RC 4.00 10.00
149 Eric Maynor AU RC 4.00 10.00
150 Blake Griffin AU RC 100.00 175.00

2009-10 Court Kings Bronze

*BRONZE: .5X TO 1.25X BASE HI
STATED PRINT RUN 149 SER.#'d SETS

2009-10 Court Kings Silver

*SILVER: .75X TO 2X BASE HI
STATED PRINT RUN 99 SER.#'d SETS

2009-10 Court Kings Artistry

COMPLETE SET (30) 20.00 40.00
STATED PRINT RUN 249 SER.#'d SETS
UNPRICED BLACK PRINT RUN ONE SET
*BRONZE: .5X TO 1.25X BASE HI
BRONZE PRINT RUN 199 SER.#'d SETS
*SILVER: .6X TO 1.5X BASE HI
SILVER PRINT RUN 99 SER.#'d SETS
1 Josh Smith .75 2.00
2 Kevin Garnett 1.50 4.00
3 Gerald Wallace .75 2.00
4 Derrick Rose 2.50 6.00
5 LeBron James 4.00 10.00
6 Jason Terry .60 1.50
7 Carmelo Anthony 1.00 2.50
8 Rodney Stuckey .75 2.00
9 Monta Ellis .75 2.00
10 Carl Landry .50 1.25
11 Dahntay Jones .50 1.25
12 Chris Kaman .60 1.50
13 Kobe Bryant 4.00 10.00
14 Rudy Gay .75 2.00
15 Dwyane Wade 1.50 4.00
16 Ersan Ilyasova .60 1.50
17 Al Jefferson .75 2.00
18 Brook Lopez .75 2.00
19 David West .75 2.00
20 Danilo Gallinari .75 2.00
21 Kevin Durant 2.50 6.00
22 Dwight Howard 1.25 3.00

23 Andre Iguodala .75 2.00
24 Jason Richardson .75 2.00
25 Brandon Roy .75 2.00
26 Jason Thompson .50 1.25
27 Tim Duncan 1.25 3.00
28 Chris Bosh .75 2.00
29 Carlos Boozer .75 2.00
30 Andrew Bogut .75 2.00

2009-10 Court Kings Artistry Materials

PRINT RUN ONE TO 299 SER.#'d SETS
SOME UNPRICED DUE TO SCARCITY
1 Josh Smith/299 2.50 6.00
2 Kevin Garnett/299 5.00 12.00
3 Gerald Wallace/299 2.50 6.00
5 LeBron James/299 8.00 20.00
6 Jason Terry/299 2.00 5.00
7 Carmelo Anthony/299 3.00 8.00
8 Rodney Stuckey/299 2.50 6.00
9 Monta Ellis/299 2.50 6.00
12 Chris Kaman/299 2.00 5.00
13 Kobe Bryant/299 8.00 20.00
14 Rudy Gay/299 2.50 6.00
15 Dwyane Wade/299 5.00 12.00
17 Al Jefferson/299 2.50 6.00
18 Brook Lopez/299 2.50 6.00
19 David West/299 2.50 6.00
20 Danilo Gallinari/49 2.50 6.00
21 Kevin Durant/299 6.00 15.00
22 Dwight Howard/299 4.00 10.00
23 Andre Iguodala/299 2.50 6.00
24 Jason Richardson/299 2.50 6.00
25 Brandon Roy/299 2.50 6.00
27 Tim Duncan/299 4.00 10.00
28 Chris Bosh/299 2.50 6.00
29 Carlos Boozer/299 2.50 6.00
30 Andrew Bogut/299 2.50 6.00

2009-10 Court Kings Artistry Signatures

STATED PRINT RUN 5 TO 99 SER.#'d SETS
SOME UNPRICED DUE TO SCARCITY
13 Kobe Bryant/99 100.00 200.00
23 Andre Iguodala/99 5.00 12.00
25 Brandon Roy/49 8.00 20.00

2009-10 Court Kings Dribble Kings

COMPLETE SET (15) 15.00 30.00
STATED PRINT RUN 149 SER.#'d SETS
UNPRICED BLACK PRINT RUN ONE SET
1 Steve Nash 1.25 3.00
2 Tony Parker 1.25 3.00
3 Chris Paul 2.00 5.00
4 Deron Williams 1.25 3.00
5 Pete Maravich 4.00 10.00
6 John Stockton 2.00 5.00
7 Jerry West 1.50 4.00
8 Carmelo Anthony 1.50 4.00
9 Dwyane Wade 2.50 6.00
10 Bob Cousy 1.50 4.00
11 Rafer Alston .75 2.00
12 Jason Kidd 1.25 3.00
13 Earl Monroe 1.25 3.00
14 Oscar Robertson 1.25 3.00
15 Kobe Bryant 6.00 15.00

2009-10 Court Kings Dribble Kings Materials

STATED PRINT RUN 99 TO 299 SER.#'d SETS
1 Steve Nash/199 2.50 6.00
2 Tony Parker/199 2.50 6.00
3 Chris Paul/299 4.00 10.00
4 Deron Williams/299 2.50 6.00
6 John Stockton/299 4.00 10.00
8 Carmelo Anthony/299 3.00 8.00
9 Dwyane Wade/299 5.00 12.00
11 Rafer Alston/299 2.00 5.00
12 Jason Kidd/299 2.50 6.00
13 Earl Monroe/299 3.00 8.00
15 Kobe Bryant/99 15.00 30.00

2009-10 Court Kings Dribble Kings Signatures

STATED PRINT RUN 5 TO 49 SER.#'d SETS
SOME UNPRICED DUE TO SCARCITY
2 Tony Parker/49 8.00 20.00
12 Jason Kidd/49 12.50 30.00
15 Kobe Bryant/49 100.00 200.00

2009-10 Court Kings Gallery of Stars

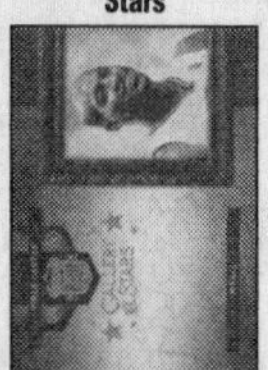

COMPLETE SET (20) 15.00 30.00
STATED PRINT RUN 249 SER.#'d SETS
UNPRICED BLACK PRINT RUN ONE SET
*BRONZE: .6X TO 1.5X BASE HI
BRONZE PRINT RUN 149 SER.#'d SETS
*SILVER: .75X TO 2X BASE HI
SILVER PRINT RUN 49 SER.#'d SETS
1 Aaron Brooks .75 2.00
2 Al Jefferson 1.25 3.00
3 Danny Granger 1.25 3.00
4 Devin Harris 1.25 3.00
5 Chauncey Billups 1.25 3.00
6 David Lee 1.00 2.50
7 Josh Howard 1.00 2.50
8 Luol Deng 1.25 3.00
9 Lamar Odom 1.25 3.00
10 Marc Gasol 1.25 3.00
11 Rajon Rondo 1.50 4.00
12 Ron Artest 1.25 3.00
13 Russell Westbrook 2.00 5.00
14 Shane Battier 1.25 3.00
15 Stephen Jackson 1.00 2.50
16 Tayshaun Prince 1.25 3.00
17 Vince Carter 1.50 4.00
18 Al Harrington 1.00 2.50
19 Joakim Noah 1.25 3.00
20 Kevin Love 2.00 5.00

2009-10 Court Kings Gallery of Stars Materials

STATED PRINT RUN 25 TO 299 SER.#'d SETS
1 Aaron Brooks/299 1.50 4.00
2 Al Jefferson/299 2.50 6.00
3 Danny Granger/299 2.50 6.00
4 Devin Harris/299 2.50 6.00
5 Chauncey Billups/299 2.50 6.00
6 David Lee/199 2.00 5.00
7 Josh Howard/299 2.00 5.00
8 Luol Deng/299 2.00 5.00
10 Marc Gasol/299 2.50 6.00
11 Rajon Rondo/299 3.00 8.00
12 Ron Artest/299 2.50 6.00
13 Russell Westbrook/299 4.00 10.00
14 Shane Battier/299 2.50 6.00
16 Tayshaun Prince/299 2.50 6.00
17 Vince Carter/299 3.00 8.00
18 Al Harrington/25 3.00 8.00
19 Joakim Noah/299 2.50 6.00
20 Kevin Love/299 4.00 10.00

2009-10 Court Kings Gallery of Stars Signatures

STATED PRINT RUN 49 TO 99 SER.#'d SETS
1 Aaron Brooks/99 4.00 10.00
4 Devin Harris/49 4.00 10.00
5 Chauncey Billups/49 8.00 20.00
7 Josh Howard/49 4.00 10.00
11 Rajon Rondo/49 10.00 25.00
13 Russell Westbrook/49 12.50 30.00
14 Shane Battier/49 5.00 12.00
17 Vince Carter/49 15.00 40.00
20 Kevin Love/49 12.50 30.00

2009-10 Court Kings Hardwood Heroes

COMPLETE SET (20) 20.00 40.00
STATED PRINT RUN 249 SER.#'d SETS
UNPRICED BLACK PRINT RUN ONE SET
1 LeBron James 5.00 12.00
2 Magic Johnson 2.50 6.00
3 Allen Iverson 1.25 3.00
4 Steve Nash 1.00 2.50
5 Patrick Ewing 1.25 3.00
6 Carmelo Anthony 1.25 3.00
7 Kevin Durant 3.00 8.00
8 Oscar Robertson 1.00 2.50
9 Dirk Nowitzki 1.25 3.00
10 Kobe Bryant 5.00 12.00
11 Scottie Pippen 2.00 5.00
12 Deron Williams 1.00 2.50
13 Dwyane Wade 2.00 5.00
14 Ty Lawson 1.50 4.00
15 Bill Russell 1.50 4.00
16 Shaquille O'Neal 2.00 5.00
17 Chris Paul 1.50 4.00
18 Derrick Rose 3.00 8.00
19 Larry Bird 3.00 8.00
20 Blake Griffin 6.00 15.00

2009-10 Court Kings Hardwood Heroes Materials

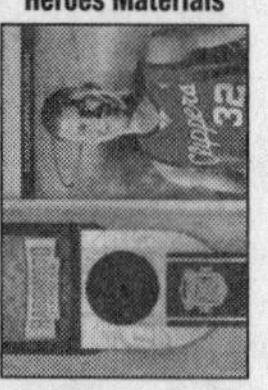

STATED PRINT RUN ONE TO 299 SER.#'d SETS
SOME UNPRICED DUE TO SCARCITY
1 LeBron James/299 10.00 25.00
2 Magic Johnson/299 8.00 20.00
3 Allen Iverson/99 4.00 10.00
4 Steve Nash/199 3.00 8.00
5 Patrick Ewing/299 3.00 8.00
6 Carmelo Anthony/299 4.00 10.00
7 Kevin Durant/299 6.00 15.00
9 Dirk Nowitzki/299 4.00 10.00
10 Kobe Bryant/299 8.00 20.00
11 Scottie Pippen/299 6.00 15.00
12 Deron Williams/299 3.00 8.00
13 Dwyane Wade/299 5.00 12.00
14 Ty Lawson/299 5.00 12.00
16 Shaquille O'Neal/299 6.00 15.00
17 Chris Paul/299 5.00 12.00
19 Larry Bird/99 10.00 25.00
20 Blake Griffin/299 10.00 25.00

2009-10 Court Kings Hardwood Heroes Signatures

STATED PRINT RUN ONE TO 49 SER.#'d SETS
SOME UNPRICED DUE TO SCARCITY
10 Kobe Bryant/49 100.00 200.00
11 Scottie Pippen/49 75.00 150.00

2009-10 Court Kings Jumbo Boxtoppers

COMPLETE SET (50) 100.00 200.00
STATED PRINT RUN 349 SER.#'d SETS
1 Ray Allen 2.00 5.00
2 Tracy McGrady 2.00 5.00
3 Bob Cousy 3.00 8.00
4 Pau Gasol 2.00 5.00
5 Dirk Nowitzki 2.50 6.00
6 Alonzo Mourning 2.50 6.00
7 Bill Walton 2.00 5.00
8 Vince Carter 2.50 6.00
9 Tyreke Evans 6.00 15.00
10 David Lee 1.50 4.00
11 Andrew Bogut 2.00 5.00
12 Pete Maravich 6.00 15.00
13 Cedric Maxwell 2.00 5.00
14 Shaquille O'Neal 4.00 10.00
15 Baron Davis 2.00 5.00
16 Kevin Love 3.00 8.00
17 Artis Gilmore 2.00 5.00
18 Connie Hawkins 2.00 5.00
19 Jermaine O'Neal 2.00 5.00
20 Kevin Durant 6.00 15.00
21 Magic Johnson 5.00 12.00
22 Patrick Ewing 2.50 6.00
23 LeBron James 10.00 25.00
24 Jason Kidd 2.00 5.00
25 Rajon Rondo 2.50 6.00
26 Al Attles 2.00 5.00
27 David Thompson 2.50 6.00
28 Chris Bosh 2.00 5.00
29 Lamar Odom 2.00 5.00
30 Tim Duncan 3.00 8.00
31 Dan Majerle 2.00 5.00
32 Isiah Thomas 2.00 5.00
33 Kareem Abdul-Jabbar 3.00 8.00
34 Stephen Curry 5.00 12.00
35 Deron Williams 2.00 5.00
36 Carmelo Anthony 2.50 6.00
37 Darryl Dawkins 2.00 5.00
38 John Thompson 2.00 5.00
39 Bob McAdoo 2.00 5.00
40 Brandon Jennings 4.00 10.00
41 Trevor Ariza 1.25 3.00
42 Kevin McHale 2.00 5.00
43 Brandon Roy 2.00 5.00
44 Danny Granger 2.00 5.00
45 Jalen Rose 2.00 5.00
46 Devin Harris 2.00 5.00
47 Elton Brand 2.00 5.00
48 Lenny Wilkens 2.00 5.00
49 Larry Bird 6.00 15.00
50 Kobe Bryant 10.00 25.00

2009-10 Court Kings Jumbo Boxtoppers Autographs

STATED PRINT RUN 10 TO 75 SER.#'d SETS
SOME UNPRICED DUE TO SCARCITY
5 Dirk Nowitzki/20 30.00 80.00
6 Alonzo Mourning/49 40.00 80.00
7 Bill Walton/49 12.50 30.00
8 Vince Carter/49 30.00 60.00
9 Tyreke Evans/75 40.00 100.00
10 David Lee/74 10.00 25.00
11 Andrew Bogut/75 10.00 25.00
13 Cedric Maxwell/75 10.00 25.00
15 Baron Davis/75 10.00 25.00
16 Kevin Love/75 15.00 40.00
17 Artis Gilmore/75 15.00 30.00
18 Connie Hawkins/75 15.00 30.00
19 Jermaine O'Neal/49 10.00 25.00
21 Magic Johnson/15 75.00 200.00
24 Jason Kidd/49 20.00 40.00
25 Rajon Rondo/75 25.00 60.00
26 Al Attles/75 10.00 25.00
27 David Thompson/74 10.00 25.00
28 Chris Bosh/49 15.00 40.00
29 Lamar Odom/75 15.00 30.00
31 Dan Majerle/75 20.00 40.00
32 Isiah Thomas/75 20.00 50.00
34 Stephen Curry/64 40.00 100.00
35 Deron Williams/49 15.00 30.00
37 Darryl Dawkins/75 10.00 25.00
39 Bob McAdoo/75 12.50 30.00
40 Brandon Jennings/75 25.00 50.00
41 Trevor Ariza/75 10.00 25.00
42 Kevin McHale/20 30.00 80.00
43 Brandon Roy/49 15.00 30.00
44 Danny Granger/75 10.00 25.00
45 Jalen Rose/75 10.00 25.00
46 Devin Harris/75 10.00 25.00
48 Lenny Wilkens/75 10.00 25.00
49 Larry Bird/15 75.00 150.00
50 Kobe Bryant/75 125.00 225.00

2009-10 Court Kings Kobe Bryant Lithographs

COMMON EXCH (1-5) 250.00 500.00
STATED PRINT RUN 24 SER.#'d SETS

2009-10 Court Kings Le Cinque Piu Belle

COMPLETE SET (5) 40.00 100.00
COMMON CARD (1-5) 12.00 30.00
STATED PRINT RUN 149 SER.#'d SETS

2009-10 Court Kings Le Cinque Piu Belle Signatures

COMMON CARD (1-5) 200.00 400.00
STATED PRINT RUN 24 SER.#'d SETS

2009-10 Court Kings Masterpieces

COMPLETE SET (20) 30.00 60.00
STATED PRINT RUN 149 SER.#'d SETS
UNPRICED BLACK PRINT RUN ONE SET
1 Nate Robinson 2.00 5.00
2 Dwight Howard 3.00 8.00
3 Josh Smith 2.00 5.00
4 Jason Richardson 2.00 5.00
5 Vince Carter 2.50 6.00
6 Kobe Bryant 10.00 25.00
7 Cedric Ceballos 2.00 5.00
8 Dee Brown 2.00 5.00
9 Dominique Wilkins 2.50 6.00
10 Kenny Walker 2.00 5.00
11 Spud Webb 2.00 5.00
12 Larry Nance 2.00 5.00
13 Carmelo Anthony 2.50 6.00
14 Andre Iguodala 2.00 5.00
15 J.R. Smith 2.00 5.00
16 LeBron James 10.00 25.00
17 Larry Johnson 2.00 5.00
18 Kenny Smith 2.00 5.00
19 Clyde Drexler 2.50 6.00
20 Amare Stoudemire 2.00 5.00

2009-10 Court Kings Masterpieces Materials

STATED PRINT RUN 199 TO 299 SER.#'d SETS
2 Dwight Howard/299 4.00 10.00
3 Josh Smith/299 2.50 6.00
4 Jason Richardson/299 2.50 6.00
5 Vince Carter/299 4.00 10.00
6 Kobe Bryant/199 10.00 25.00
9 Dominique Wilkins/299 3.00 8.00
13 Carmelo Anthony/299 3.00 8.00
14 Andre Iguodala/299 2.50 6.00
15 J.R. Smith/299 2.50 6.00
16 LeBron James/299 8.00 20.00
19 Clyde Drexler/299 4.00 10.00
20 Amare Stoudemire/299 2.50 6.00

2009-10 Court Kings Masterpieces Signatures

STATED PRINT RUN 5 TO 49 SER.#'d SETS
SOME UNPRICED DUE TO SCARCITY
5 Vince Carter/49 12.50 30.00
6 Kobe Bryant/49 100.00 200.00
10 Kenny Walker/49 10.00 25.00
11 Spud Webb/49 10.00 25.00
14 Andre Iguodala/49 10.00 25.00
17 Larry Johnson/49 20.00 50.00
19 Clyde Drexler/49 20.00 50.00

2009-10 Court Kings Materials

STATED PRINT RUN 25 TO 149 SER.#'d SETS
1 Carmelo Anthony/149 4.00 10.00
2 Chris Andersen/149 5.00 12.00
3 J.R. Smith/149 3.00 8.00
4 Chauncey Billups/149 3.00 8.00
5 Kevin Love/149 5.00 12.00
6 Al Jefferson/149 3.00 8.00
8 Kevin Durant/149 8.00 20.00
9 Russell Westbrook/149 5.00 12.00
10 Jeff Green/149 2.50 6.00
11 Brandon Roy/149 3.00 8.00
12 LaMarcus Aldridge/149 3.00 8.00
13 Juwan Howard/149 2.50 6.00
14 Deron Williams/149 3.00 8.00
15 Carlos Boozer/149 3.00 8.00
16 Paul Millsap/99 2.50 6.00
17 Dirk Nowitzki/149 4.00 10.00
18 Jason Kidd/149 3.00 8.00
20 J.J. Barea/149 5.00 12.00
22 Aaron Brooks/149 2.00 5.00
24 Tony Parker/149 3.00 8.00
25 Richard Jefferson/149 3.00 8.00
26 Tim Duncan/149 5.00 12.00
27 Marc Gasol/149 3.00 8.00
28 Rudy Gay/149 3.00 8.00
30 Emeka Okafor/149 3.00 8.00
31 Chris Paul/149 5.00 12.00
32 David West/149 3.00 8.00
34 Kevin Martin/149 3.00 8.00
36 Amare Stoudemire/149 3.00 8.00
37 Channing Frye/149 2.50 6.00
38 Steve Nash/149 3.00 8.00
39 Pau Gasol/149 3.00 8.00
40 Kobe Bryant/149 10.00 25.00
41 Derek Fisher/149 2.50 6.00
42 Andrew Bynum/149 4.00 10.00
43 Monta Ellis/149 3.00 8.00
45 Corey Maggette/149 3.00 8.00
46 Baron Davis/149 3.00 8.00
47 Chris Kaman/149 2.50 6.00
48 Eric Gordon/149 3.00 8.00
49 Kevin Garnett/149 6.00 15.00
50 Ray Allen/149 3.00 8.00
51 Paul Pierce/149 4.00 10.00
54 Chris Duhon/149 2.00 5.00
55 David Lee/149 2.50 6.00
56 Danilo Gallinari/49 5.00 12.00
57 Allen Iverson/99 4.00 10.00
58 Andre Iguodala/149 3.00 8.00
60 Elton Brand/149 3.00 8.00
61 Andrea Bargnani/149 2.50 6.00
62 Chris Bosh/149 3.00 8.00
63 Hedo Turkoglu/149 3.00 8.00
64 Brook Lopez/149 3.00 8.00
65 Rafer Alston/149 2.00 5.00
66 Devin Harris/149 3.00 8.00
67 LeBron James/149 10.00 25.00
70 Shaquille O'Neal/149 8.00 20.00
71 Ben Gordon/149 3.00 8.00
72 Rodney Stuckey/149 3.00 8.00
74 Danny Granger/149 3.00 8.00
75 Troy Murphy/149 2.00 5.00
77 Andrew Bogut/149 3.00 8.00
80 Luol Deng/149 3.00 8.00
81 Derrick Rose/149 10.00 25.00
82 Joakim Noah/149 3.00 8.00
83 John Salmons/149 3.00 8.00
84 Joe Johnson/149 3.00 8.00
85 Al Horford/149 3.00 8.00
87 Marvin Williams/149 2.50 6.00
88 Dwyane Wade/149 6.00 15.00
89 Jermaine O'Neal/149 4.00 10.00
90 Michael Beasley/149 3.00 8.00
91 Gerald Wallace/149 3.00 8.00
93 Raymond Felton/149 2.50 6.00
94 Dwight Howard/149 6.00 15.00
95 Vince Carter/149 4.00 10.00
96 Rashard Lewis/149 2.50 6.00
97 Jason Williams/149 2.50 6.00
98 Antawn Jamison/149 3.00 8.00
99 Mike Miller/149 3.00 8.00
100 Caron Butler/149 3.00 8.00
107 Clyde Drexler/149 6.00 15.00
108 Mark Eaton/149 5.00 12.00
109 John Havlicek/99 6.00 15.00
117 Walt Frazier/25 8.00 20.00

2009-10 Court Kings Portraits

COMPLETE SET (20) 15.00 30.00
STATED PRINT RUN 149 SER.#'d SETS
UNPRICED BLACK PRINT RUN ONE SET
1 Chris Andersen 1.50 4.00
2 Ron Artest 1.00 2.50
3 Kobe Bryant 5.00 12.00
4 LeBron James 5.00 12.00
5 Dirk Nowitzki 1.25 3.00
6 Joakim Noah 1.00 2.50
7 Dwight Howard 1.50 4.00
8 Allen Iverson 1.25 3.00
9 Steve Nash 1.00 2.50
10 Tony Parker 1.00 2.50
11 Shaquille O'Neal 2.00 5.00
12 Chris Bosh 1.00 2.50
13 Rasheed Wallace 1.00 2.50
14 Jason Kidd 1.00 2.50
15 Nene .75 2.00
16 Richard Hamilton .75 2.00
17 Zach Randolph .75 2.00
18 Chris Paul 1.50 4.00
19 David Lee .75 2.00
20 Vince Carter 1.25 3.00

2009-10 Court Kings Portraits Materials

STATED PRINT RUN 49 TO 299 SER.#'d SETS
1 Chris Andersen/299 5.00 12.00
3 Kobe Bryant/99 10.00 25.00
4 LeBron James/99 10.00 25.00
5 Dirk Nowitzki/299 4.00 10.00
6 Joakim Noah/299 3.00 8.00
7 Dwight Howard/299 5.00 12.00
8 Allen Iverson/99 4.00 10.00
9 Steve Nash/199 3.00 8.00
10 Tony Parker/199 3.00 8.00
11 Shaquille O'Neal/299 6.00 15.00
12 Chris Bosh/299 3.00 8.00
13 Rasheed Wallace/299 3.00 8.00
14 Jason Kidd/299 3.00 8.00
15 Nene/299 2.50 6.00
16 Richard Hamilton/49 2.50 6.00
18 Chris Paul/299 5.00 12.00
19 David Lee/199 2.50 6.00
20 Vince Carter/299 4.00 10.00

2009-10 Court Kings Portraits Signatures

STATED PRINT RUN 49 SER.#'d SETS
1 Chris Andersen 20.00 40.00
3 Kobe Bryant 125.00 225.00
10 Tony Parker 6.00 15.00
14 Jason Kidd 10.00 25.00
16 Richard Hamilton 6.00 15.00
20 Vince Carter 20.00 40.00

2009-10 Court Kings Signatures

STATED PRINT RUN 5 TO 49 SER.#'d SETS
SOME UNPRICED DUE TO SCARCITY
2 Chris Andersen/49 20.00 40.00
4 Chauncey Billups/49 8.00 20.00
5 Kevin Love/49 20.00 50.00
9 Russell Westbrook/49 20.00 50.00
11 Brandon Roy/49 10.00 25.00
18 Jason Kidd/49 12.00 30.00
20 J.J. Barea/49 15.00 40.00
22 Aaron Brooks/49 5.00 12.00
24 Tony Parker/49 12.00 30.00
26 Emeka Okafor/49 5.00 12.00
40 Kobe Bryant/49 100.00 200.00
42 Andrew Bynum/49 8.00 20.00
46 Baron Davis/49 8.00 20.00
48 Eric Gordon/49 6.00 15.00
58 Andre Iguodala/49 5.00 12.00
61 Andrea Bargnani/49 5.00 12.00
66 Devin Harris/49 5.00 12.00
89 Jermaine O'Neal/49 6.00 15.00
90 Michael Beasley/49 6.00 15.00
95 Vince Carter/49 15.00 40.00
101 Harry Gallatin/49 6.00 15.00
102 Nate Archibald/49 6.00 15.00
111 George McGinnis/49 6.00 15.00
112 Sidney Moncrief/49 6.00 15.00
114 Bill Sharman/49 5.00 12.00
115 Lenny Wilkens/49 6.00 15.00
116 Elvin Hayes/49 10.00 25.00
117 Walt Frazier/49 10.00 25.00
120 Dell Curry/49 5.00 12.00

2009-10 Court Kings Supreme Court

COMPLETE SET (20) 20.00 40.00
STATED PRINT RUN 149 SER.#'d SETS
UNPRICED BLACK PRINT RUN ONE SET
1 Vince Carter 1.25 3.00
2 Carmelo Anthony 1.25 3.00
3 Chris Bosh 1.00 2.50
4 David Lee .75 2.00
5 Tyreke Evans 2.50 6.00
6 Dirk Nowitzki 1.25 3.00
7 Kevin Durant 3.00 8.00
8 Gerald Wallace 1.00 2.50
9 Kevin Garnett 2.00 5.00
10 Kobe Bryant 5.00 12.00
11 Dwyane Wade 2.00 5.00
12 Dwight Howard 1.50 4.00
13 Shaquille O'Neal 2.00 5.00
14 Danny Granger 1.00 2.50
15 Tony Parker 1.00 2.50
16 Brandon Jennings 2.00 5.00
17 LeBron James 5.00 12.00
18 Chris Paul 1.50 4.00
19 Ray Allen 1.00 2.50
20 Allen Iverson 1.25 3.00

2009-10 Court Kings Supreme Court Materials

STATED PRINT RUN 99 TO 299 SER.#'d SETS
1 Vince Carter/299 4.00 10.00
2 Carmelo Anthony/299 4.00 10.00
3 Chris Bosh/299 3.00 8.00
4 David Lee/199 2.50 6.00
5 Tyreke Evans/299 6.00 15.00
6 Dirk Nowitzki/299 4.00 10.00
7 Kevin Durant/299 6.00 15.00
8 Gerald Wallace/299 3.00 8.00
9 Kevin Garnett/299 6.00 15.00
10 Kobe Bryant/99 10.00 25.00
11 Dwyane Wade/299 5.00 12.00
12 Dwight Howard/299 5.00 12.00
13 Shaquille O'Neal/299 6.00 15.00
14 Danny Granger/299 3.00 8.00
15 Tony Parker/199 3.00 8.00
16 Brandon Jennings/299 6.00 15.00
17 LeBron James/99 10.00 25.00
18 Chris Paul/299 5.00 12.00
19 Ray Allen/299 3.00 8.00
20 Allen Iverson/99 4.00 10.00

2009-10 Court Kings Supreme Court Signatures

STATED PRINT RUN 10 TO 49 SER.#'d SETS
SOME NOT PRICED DUE TO SCARCITY
1 Vince Carter/49 20.00 50.00
4 David Lee/49 8.00 20.00
5 Tyreke Evans/49 20.00 50.00
10 Kobe Bryant/49 100.00 200.00
14 Danny Granger/49 8.00 20.00
15 Tony Parker/49 8.00 20.00
16 Brandon Jennings/49 20.00 50.00
19 Ray Allen/49 25.00 60.00

1991 Cousy Collection Preview

This five-card "preview" standard-size set was issued to honor Bob Cousy, who sparked the Boston Celtics to six world championships during his thirteen year career. The front features vintage black and white photos that highlight Bob Cousy's career. The lettering is in green and white on a black background. The back presents biographical information and is printed in black lettering on gray, with black and green stripes traversing the top of the card. The cards are numbered on the back. The preview cards have a copyright date of 1991 on the card back whereas the regular issue set has a copyright date of 1992.

COMPLETE SET (5) 2.00 5.00
COMMON CARD (1-5) .60 1.50
1 Rookie Card 1.00 2.50

1992 Cousy Collection

Publicist Milton Kahn produced this 25-card set to chronicle the career of former Boston Celtic great and Basketball Hall of Fame Bob Cousy. Production quantities of the standard-size cards were limited to 100,000 sets. The cards were only available in complete set form. The fronts feature black and white photos that capture various moments in Cousy's career. The photos are bordered on the top by a green stripe and by black on the other three sides. The backs have a similar design to the fronts. On a gray background, they have captions for the photos and a card number in the upper left corner. On the back, each card of the set bears a unique serial number. The preview cards have a copyright date of 1991 on the card back whereas the regular issue set has a copyright date of 1992.

COMPLETE SET (25) 2.50 6.00
COMMON CARD (1-25) .20 .50
1 Rookie Card 1.00 2.50
7 Double Trouble .40 1.00
w/Bill Sharman
9 Stan the Man 1955 1.00 2.50
10 Timely Idea 1955 .40 1.00
14 Four Plan 1958-1959 .40 1.00
w/Bill Sharman
16 Victory Watch/1961-1962 .40 1.00
(With Red Auerbach and Tom Heinsohn)
17 Visit with J.F.K./1961-1962 .60 1.50
(With Red Auerbach)
21 Author 1965 .40 1.00
(With Howard Cosell)
22 Podnuhs 1965 .40 1.00

2009-10 Crown Royale

COMP.SET w/o SPs (100) 60.00 120.00
101-140 RC PRINT RUNS LISTED BELOW
1 Kevin Garnett 3.00 8.00
2 Paul Pierce 2.00 5.00
3 Rasheed Wallace 1.50 4.00
4 Ray Allen 1.50 4.00
5 Brook Lopez 1.50 4.00
6 Devin Harris 1.50 4.00
7 Yi Jianlian 1.25 3.00
8 Al Harrington 1.25 3.00
9 Danilo Gallinari 1.50 4.00
10 David Lee 1.25 3.00
11 Nate Robinson 1.50 4.00
12 Allen Iverson 2.00 5.00
13 Andre Iguodala 1.50 4.00
14 Elton Brand 1.50 4.00
15 Louis Williams 1.25 3.00
16 Andrea Bargnani 1.25 3.00
17 Chris Bosh 1.50 4.00
18 Hedo Turkoglu 1.25 3.00
19 Dirk Nowitzki 2.00 5.00
20 J.J. Barea 2.00 5.00
21 Jason Kidd 1.50 4.00
22 Jason Terry 1.25 3.00
23 Aaron Brooks 1.00 2.50
24 Carl Landry 1.00 2.50
25 Trevor Ariza 1.00 2.50
26 O.J. Mayo 1.50 4.00
27 Rudy Gay 1.50 4.00
28 Zach Randolph 1.25 3.00
29 Chris Paul 2.50 6.00
30 David West 1.50 4.00
31 Peja Stojakovic 1.25 3.00
32 Manu Ginobili 1.50 4.00
33 Tim Duncan 2.50 6.00
34 Tony Parker 1.50 4.00
35 Derrick Rose 5.00 12.00
36 John Salmons 1.50 4.00
37 Luol Deng 1.25 3.00
38 LeBron James 8.00 20.00
39 Mo Williams 1.25 3.00
40 Shaquille O'Neal 3.00 8.00
41 Ben Gordon 1.50 4.00
42 Charlie Villanueva 1.25 3.00
43 Richard Hamilton 1.25
44 Rodney Stuckey 1.50
45 Dahntay Jones 1.00
46 Danny Granger 1.50
47 Troy Murphy 1.00
48 Andrew Bogut 1.50
49 Hakim Warrick 1.25
50 Luke Ridnour 1.25
51 Carmelo Anthony 2.00
52 Chauncey Billups 1.50
53 J.R. Smith 1.50
54 Nene 1.25
55 Al Jefferson 1.50
56 Corey Brewer 1.00
57 Kevin Love 2.50
58 Andre Miller 1.25
59 Brandon Roy 1.50
60 LaMarcus Aldridge 1.50
61 Jeff Green 1.25
62 Kevin Durant 5.00
63 Russell Westbrook 2.50
64 Carlos Boozer 1.50
65 Deron Williams 1.50
66 Mehmet Okur 1.00
67 Al Horford 1.50
68 Jamal Crawford 1.25
69 Joe Johnson 1.50
70 Josh Smith 1.50
71 Gerald Wallace 1.50
72 Raymond Felton 1.25
73 Stephen Jackson 1.25
74 Dwyane Wade 3.00
75 Jermaine O'Neal 1.50
76 Michael Beasley 1.50
77 Dwight Howard 2.50
78 J.J. Redick 1.50
79 Rashard Lewis 1.25
80 Vince Carter 2.00
81 Antawn Jamison 1.50
82 Caron Butler 1.50
83 Randy Foye 1.00
84 Corey Maggette 1.25
85 Kelenna Azubuike 1.00
86 Monta Ellis 1.25
87 Al Thornton 1.25
88 Baron Davis 1.50
89 Chris Kaman 1.25
90 Eric Gordon 1.50
91 Andrew Bynum 2.00
92 Kobe Bryant 8.00
93 Pau Gasol 1.50
94 Ron Artest 1.50
95 Amare Stoudemire 2.50
96 Jason Richardson 1.50
97 Steve Nash 2.00
98 Beno Udrih 1.00
99 Jason Thompson 1.50
100 Kevin Martin 1.50
101 Tyreke Evans AU/399 RC 15.00
102 Brandon Jennings AU/399 RC 12.00
103 Stephen Curry AU/399 RC 15.00
104 James Harden AU/599 RC 20.00
105 Jonny Flynn AU/149 RC 10.00
106 Ty Lawson AU/599 RC 10.00
107 DeJuan Blair AU/699 RC 8.00
108 Blake Griffin AU/399 RC 125.00 25
109 Hasheem Thabeet AU/149 RC 6.00
110 Omri Casspi AU/650 RC 6.00
111 Gerald Henderson AU/599 RC 6.00
112 Taj Gibson AU/599 RC 8.00
113 Jrue Holiday AU/599 RC 12.00
114 Rodrigue Beaubois AU/599 RC 8.00
115 Jeff Teague AU/599 RC 8.00
116 Earl Clark AU/599 RC 6.00
117 Chase Budinger AU/699 RC 6.00
118 Jordan Hill AU/599 RC 6.00
119 Terrence Williams AU/599 RC 6.00
120 Tyler Hansbrough AU/612 RC 10.00
121 Austin Daye AU/599 RC 6.00
122 Wayne Ellington AU/658 RC 6.00
123 Darren Collison AU/599 RC 10.00
124 James Johnson AU/599 RC 6.00
125 B.J. Mullens AU/699 RC 6.00
126 Toney Douglas AU/699 RC 6.00
127 DeMarre Carroll AU/699 RC 6.00
128 DaJuan Summers AU/699 RC 6.00
129 Jodie Meeks AU/699 RC 8.00
130 DeMar DeRozan AU/699 RC 10.00
131 Jermaine Taylor AU/699 RC 6.00
132 Jon Brockman AU/699 RC 6.00
133 Marcus Thornton AU/669 RC 10.00
134 Jonas Jerebko AU/699 RC 6.00
135 Sam Young AU/149 RC 12.50
136 Wesley Matthews AU/699 RC 10.00
137 Jeff Pendergraph AU/149 RC 8.00
138 Serge Ibaka AU/699 RC 15.00
139 David Andersen AU/149 RC 8.00
140 Dante Cunningham AU/699 RC 6.00

2009-10 Crown Royale All-St

COMPLETE SET (25) 15.00
RANDOM INSERTS IN PACKS
1 Kobe Bryant 4.00
2 LeBron James 4.00
3 Allen Iverson 1.50
4 Kevin Garnett 1.50
5 Rajon Rondo 1.00
6 Al Horford .75
7 Brook Lopez .75
8 Chauncey Billups .75
9 Danny Granger .75
10 David Lee .60
11 Gerald Wallace .75
12 Pau Gasol .75
13 Tony Parker .75
14 Zach Randolph .60
15 Aaron Brooks .60
16 Al Jefferson .75
17 Antawn Jamison .75
18 Chris Kaman .60
19 Corey Maggette .60
20 David West .75
21 Kevin Martin .75

Mayo .75 2.00
hard Lewis .60 1.50
ney Stuckey .75 2.00
hen Jackson .60 1.50

9-10 Crown Royale All-Stars Materials

D PRINT RUN 25 TO 599 SER.#'d SETS
Bryant/599 8.00 20.00
n James/99 10.00 25.00
Iverson/100 5.00 12.00
Garnett/599 5.00 12.00
Rondo/599 3.00 8.00
rford/599 2.50 6.00
Lopez/599 2.50 6.00
ncey Billups/100 2.50 6.00
y Granger/599 2.50 6.00
ald Wallace/599 2.50 6.00
Gasol/299 2.50 6.00
Parker/599 2.50 6.00
n Brooks/25 3.00 8.00
efferson/599 2.50 6.00
ey Maggette/599 2.00 5.00
d West/599 2.50 6.00
n Martin/599 2.50 6.00
Mayo/599 2.50 6.00
ard Lewis/399 2.00 5.00
ney Stuckey/599 2.50 6.00
hen Jackson/599 2.00 5.00

9-10 Crown Royale All-Stars Materials Prime

1.25X TO 3X BASE HI
PRINT RUN ONE TO 25 SER.#'d SETS
NPRICED DUE TO SCARCITY
Iverson/25 20.00 50.00
Rondo/25 12.50 30.00

9-10 Crown Royale King on the Court

ETE SET (10) 15.00 30.00
M INSERTS IN PACKS
n James 5.00 12.00
n Noah 1.00 2.50
Duncan 1.50 4.00
Paul 1.50 4.00
Durant 3.00 8.00
ne Wade 2.00 5.00
Pierce 1.25 3.00
Bosh 1.00 2.50
e Evans 2.50 6.00
e Bryant 5.00 12.00

9-10 Crown Royale King on the Court Materials

D PRINT RUN 149 SER.#'d SETS
ED PRIME PRINT RUN 10 SER.#'d SETS
n James 10.00 25.00
n Noah 3.00 8.00
Duncan 5.00 12.00
Paul 5.00 12.00
Durant 8.00 20.00
ne Wade 6.00 15.00
Pierce 4.00 10.00
Bosh 3.00 8.00
e Evans 8.00 20.00
e Bryant 10.00 25.00

09-10 Crown Royale Living Legends

ETE SET (25) 25.00 50.00
M INSERTS IN PACKS
ove 1.50 4.00
Daugherty 1.50 4.00
English 1.50 4.00
Pierce 1.50 4.00
k Ewing 2.00 5.00
Webber 1.50 4.00
Johnson 4.00 10.00
ackson 2.00 5.00
tte Lever 1.50 4.00
Bird 5.00 12.00
k Aguirre 1.50 4.00
hal Thompson 1.50 4.00
Davis 1.50 4.00
r Robertson 1.50 4.00
Carr 1.50 4.00
Malone 2.00 5.00
d Robinson 2.50 6.00
n Baylor 1.50 4.00
rice Lucas 1.50 4.00
tie Pippen 3.00 8.00
West 2.00 5.00
Majerle 1.50 4.00
em Olajuwon 2.00 5.00
Stockton 2.50 6.00
ge Gervin 1.50 4.00

2009-10 Crown Royale Living Legends Materials

STATED PRINT RUN 25 TO 499 SER.#'d SETS
3 Alex English/499 4.00 10.00
5 Patrick Ewing/299 5.00 12.00
6 Chris Webber/499 4.00 10.00
7 Magic Johnson/99 10.00 25.00
10 Larry Bird/25 10.00 25.00
16 Karl Malone/499 5.00 12.00
19 Maurice Lucas/499 4.00 10.00
20 Scottie Pippen/499 6.00 15.00
21 Jerry West/25 8.00 20.00
23 Hakeem Olajuwon/499 5.00 12.00
24 John Stockton/199 5.00 12.00

2009-10 Crown Royale Living Legends Materials Prime

*PRIME: .75X TO 2X BASE HI
STATED PRINT RUN 5 TO 25 SER.#'d SETS
SOME UNPRICED DUE TO SCARCITY
3 Alex English/25 12.00 30.00
5 Patrick Ewing/25 15.00 30.00
7 Magic Johnson/25 15.00 40.00
20 Scottie Pippen/25 20.00 50.00
24 John Stockton/25 15.00 40.00
25 George Gervin/25 8.00 20.00

2009-10 Crown Royale Majestic Signatures

STATED PRINT RUN 10 TO 99 SER.#'d SETS
AA Alvan Adams/199 6.00 15.00
AB Andrew Bogut/199 10.00 25.00
AI Allen Iverson/25 175.00 325.00
AM Alonzo Mourning/99 25.00 60.00
BD Bob Dandridge/199 6.00 15.00
BJ Bobby Jackson/199 6.00 15.00
BR Bill Russell/49 75.00 150.00
CA Chris Andersen/99 40.00 80.00
CR Cazzie Russell/196 6.00 15.00
CV Charlie Villanueva/196 6.00 15.00
DA D.J. Augustin/199 6.00 15.00
DF Derek Fisher/199 12.00 30.00
DG Danny Granger/99 8.00 20.00
DH Devin Harris/199 6.00 15.00
DL David Lee/199 6.00 15.00
DR Doc Rivers/199 10.00 25.00
DS Detlef Schrempf/199 8.00 20.00
DT David Thompson/199 6.00 15.00
EG Eric Gordon/198 8.00 20.00
EO Emeka Okafor/99 8.00 20.00
GM George McGinnis/199 6.00 15.00
GP Gary Payton/99 12.50 30.00
HH Hersey Hawkins/199 8.00 20.00
JB J.J. Barea/199 12.50 30.00
JH John Havlicek/25 25.00 50.00
JK Jason Kidd/49 15.00 40.00
JO Jermaine O'Neal/99 12.50 30.00
JR Jalen Rose/199 6.00 15.00
KB Kobe Bryant/199 100.00 200.00
KL Kevin Love/99 12.00 30.00
LB Larry Bird/25 50.00 120.00
LO Lamar Odom/99 10.00 25.00
MB Michael Beasley/99 8.00 20.00
MJ Magic Johnson/23 60.00 120.00
MW Mo Williams/99 6.00 15.00
OR Oscar Robertson/25 100.00 200.00
PG Pau Gasol/30 30.00 80.00
RA Ray Allen/49 30.00 80.00
RH Robert Horry/99 40.00 80.00
RR Rajon Rondo/199 15.00 40.00
RW Russell Westbrook/99 12.50 30.00
SB Shawn Bradley/199 6.00 15.00
SE Sean Elliott/199 10.00 25.00
SH Spencer Haywood/199 6.00 15.00
SN Steve Nash/96 40.00 80.00
SO Shaquille O'Neal/25 150.00 300.00
SP Scottie Pippen/99 80.00 160.00
TM Tracy McGrady/25 30.00 60.00
TP Tony Parker/99 12.00 30.00
VC Vince Carter/99 20.00 50.00
AI2 Andre Iguodala/199 6.00 15.00
DLM Dan Majerle/199 10.00 25.00
DMW Deron Williams/99 10.00 25.00

2009-10 Crown Royale Nothing But Net

COMPLETE SET (10) 6.00 15.00
RANDOM INSERTS IN PACKS
1 Danilo Gallinari 1.00 2.50
2 Channing Frye .75 2.00
3 Aaron Brooks .60 1.50
4 Peja Stojakovic 1.00 2.50
5 Martell Webster .75 2.00
6 Rashard Lewis .75 2.00
7 Mo Williams .75 2.00
8 Jason Kidd 1.00 2.50
9 LeBron James 5.00 12.00
10 Chauncey Billups 1.00 2.50

2009-10 Crown Royale Nothing But Net Materials

STATED PRINT RUN 25 TO 499 SER.#'d SETS
*PRIME: .75X TO 2X HI COLUMN
PRIME PRINT RUN ONE TO 25 SETS
3 Aaron Brooks/25 3.00 8.00
4 Peja Stojakovic/499 3.00 8.00
6 Rashard Lewis/299 2.50 6.00
8 Jason Kidd/399 3.00 8.00
9 LeBron James/99 10.00 25.00
10 Chauncey Billups/100 3.00 8.00

2009-10 Crown Royale Rookie Royalty

COMPLETE SET (10) 8.00 20.00
RANDOM INSERTS IN PACKS
1 Brandon Jennings 2.50 6.00
Stephen Curry
Tyreke Evans
2 Darren Collison 1.50 4.00
Jonny Flynn
Ty Lawson
3 Blake Griffin 6.00 15.00
DeJuan Blair
Taj Gibson
4 Chase Budinger 3.00 8.00
DeMar DeRozan
James Harden
5 Austin Daye 1.00 2.50
Earl Clark
Omri Casspi
6 Eric Maynor 2.00 5.00
Jeff Teague
Jrue Holiday
7 Blake Griffin 6.00 15.00
Hasheem Thabeet
James Harden
8 Ty Lawson 1.50 4.00
Tyler Hansbrough
Wayne Ellington
9 DeMarre Carroll 1.00 2.50
Hasheem Thabeet
Sam Young
10 James Johnson 1.00 2.50
Jeff Pendergraph
Jordan Hill

2009-10 Crown Royale Rookie Royalty Materials

STATED PRINT RUN 499 SER.#'d SETS
1 Brandon Jennings 8.00 20.00
Stephen Curry
Tyreke Evans
2 Darren Collison 5.00 12.00
Jonny Flynn
Ty Lawson
3 Blake Griffin 10.00 25.00
DeJuan Blair
Taj Gibson
4 Chase Budinger 5.00 12.00
DeMar DeRozan
James Harden
5 Austin Daye 4.00 10.00
Earl Clark
Omri Casspi
6 Eric Maynor 5.00 12.00
Jeff Teague
Jrue Holiday
7 Blake Griffin 10.00 25.00
Hasheem Thabeet
James Harden
8 Ty Lawson 5.00 12.00
Tyler Hansbrough
Wayne Ellington
9 DeMarre Carroll 4.00 10.00
Hasheem Thabeet
Sam Young
10 James Johnson 4.00 10.00
Jeff Pendergraph
Jordan Hill

2009-10 Crown Royale Rookie Royalty Materials Prime

*PRIME: .75X TO 2X BASE HI
STATED PRINT RUN 25 SER.#'d SETS
1 Brandon Jennings 20.00 50.00
Stephen Curry
Tyreke Evans
2 Darren Collison 20.00 50.00
Jonny Flynn
Ty Lawson
3 Blake Griffin 25.00 60.00
DeJuan Blair
Taj Gibson
4 Chase Budinger 12.50 30.00
DeMar DeRozan
James Harden
6 Eric Maynor 12.50 30.00
Jeff Teague
Jrue Holiday
7 Blake Griffin 25.00 60.00
Hasheem Thabeet
James Harden
8 Ty Lawson 20.00 50.00
Tyler Hansbrough
Wayne Ellington

2009-10 Crown Royale Royalty

COMPLETE SET (20) 15.00 30.00
RANDOM INSERTS IN PACKS
1 Kobe Bryant 4.00 10.00
2 LeBron James 4.00 10.00
3 Dwyane Wade 1.50 4.00
4 Carmelo Anthony 1.00 2.50
5 Kevin Durant 2.50 6.00
6 Monta Ellis .75 2.00
7 Dirk Nowitzki 1.00 2.50
8 Chris Bosh .75 2.00
9 Brandon Roy .75 2.00
10 Joe Johnson .75 2.00
11 Dwight Howard 1.25 3.00
12 Steve Nash .75 2.00
13 Chris Paul 1.25 3.00
14 Tim Duncan 1.25 3.00
15 Paul Pierce 1.00 2.50
16 Shaquille O'Neal 1.50 4.00
17 Amare Stoudemire .75 2.00
18 Derrick Rose 2.50 6.00
19 Deron Williams .75 2.00
20 Vince Carter 1.00 2.50

2009-10 Crown Royale Royalty Materials

STATED PRINT RUN 99 TO 499 SER.#'d SETS
1 Kobe Bryant/499 8.00 20.00
2 LeBron James/99 10.00 25.00
4 Carmelo Anthony/499 4.00 10.00
5 Kevin Durant/499 6.00 15.00
7 Dirk Nowitzki/499 4.00 10.00
8 Chris Bosh/499 3.00 8.00
9 Brandon Roy/499 3.00 8.00
10 Joe Johnson/499 3.00 8.00
11 Dwight Howard/499 5.00 12.00
13 Chris Paul/499 5.00 12.00
14 Tim Duncan/499 5.00 12.00
15 Paul Pierce/499 4.00 10.00
16 Shaquille O'Neal/499 6.00 15.00
18 Derrick Rose/499 6.00 15.00
19 Deron Williams/499 3.00 8.00
20 Vince Carter/499 4.00 10.00

2009-10 Crown Royale Royalty Materials Prime

PRIME: 1X TO 2.5X BASE HI
STATED PRINT RUN 5 TO 25 SER.#'d SETS
SOME UNPRICED DUE TO SCARCITY
3 Dwyane Wade/25 15.00 40.00

2010 Crown Royale National Convention VIP

COMPLETE SET (6) 5.00 12.00
VIP1 Kobe Bryant 3.00 8.00
VIP2 Carmelo Anthony .75 2.00
VIP3 Derrick Rose 2.00 5.00
VIP4 Brandon Jennings .75 2.00
VIP5 Wesley Johnson 1.00 2.50
VIP6 Evan Turner 1.50 4.00

2010 Crown Royale National Convention VIP Blue

COMPLETE SET (6) 40.00 80.00
*BLUE: 2X TO 5X BASE HI
ANNOUNCED PRINT RUN 25 SETS

2010 Crown Royale National Convention VIP Green

COMPLETE SET (6) 10.00 25.00
*GREEN: .75X TO 2X BASE HI
ANNOUNCED PRINT RUN 50 SETS

2002-03 Dakota Wizards CBA

Produced by United Digital Printing and Mailing, this 15-card set features color photos and blue borders and was given away at home games as a promotion and also sold by the team.

COMPLETE SET (15) 1.50 4.00
1 Shawn Daniels .15 .40
2 Khalid El-Amin .30 .75
3 Rico Hill .15 .40
4 Courtney James .15 .40
5 Dave Joerger CO .30 .75
6 Ken Johnson .15 .40
7 Mike Johnson .15 .40
8 Casey Owens ACO .15 .40
9 Chris Porter .30 .75
10 Kevin Rice .15 .40
11 Miles Simon .15 .40
12 Marketing Team .15 .40
13 President/Vice President .15 .40
14 Dance Team .15 .40
15 Mascot .15 .40

1991-92 David Robinson Fan Club

Produced by TRG Inc., these two standard-size cards were issued in consecutive years. Card number 1, released in 1991, was designed by David Robinson and features a posed color photo of Robinson with his saxophone. A signed basketball is in the upper left corner and five stars in a circle pattern are in the upper right. Navy blue border stripes at the bottom contain Robinson's nickname "The Admiral," and the words "Inaugural" and "Leisure Series No. 1 '91" in white lettering. The back is beige and displays a close-up photo and player information. Card number 2, released in 1992, features a full-bleed photo of Robinson balancing a basketball on one finger. The words "The Admiral Leisure Series No. 2 '92" are printed in an arch at the top. The back shows a blue tinted photo of Robinson playing golf and includes biography and player information with a facsimile autograph at the bottom. The cards are numbered on the front. These cards were offered directly by The Robinson Group to members of the David Robinson Fan Club, as well as via a mail-in order form included in Strand's "The Story of a Game" video. Reportedly 50,000 complete Leisure Series sets were produced.

COMPLETE SET (2) 4.00 10.00
COMMON CARD (1-2) 2.00 5.00

1977-78 Dell Flipbooks

This set of flipbooks was produced by Pocket Money Basketball Co. and were sold in most retail outlets and toy stores. The retail display featured eight complete sets of six booklets or 48 books individually for sale at a suggested retail price of 50 cents. These flipbooks measure approximately 4" by 3 1/8" and are 24 pages in length. They have color action player photos and career statistics. The booklets are unnumbered and are checklisted below in alphabetical order by subject. The front has a white stripe at the top, and a color head and shoulders shot of the player on a color background. The inside front cover has a table of contents, while the inside back cover has the logos of all 22 NBA teams. Each flipbook features a different play or move by the player; e.g., the Maravich flipbook is titled, "Pete The Pistol Maravich and his Fancy Dribble." When the odd-numbered pages are flipped in a smooth movement from front to back, they form a color "motion picture-- of Maravich crossing over his dribble through his legs. The even-numbered pages present a variety of information on Maravich, his team (New Orleans Jazz), and the 1976-77 NBA season.

COMPLETE SET (6) 40.00 80.00
1 Kareem Abdul-Jabbar 7.50 15.00
2 Dave Cowens 6.00 12.00
3 Julius Erving 7.50 15.00
4 Pete Maravich 20.00 40.00
5 David Thompson 6.00 12.00
6 Bill Walton 6.00 12.00

1970 Detroit Free Press

These color clippings came from the Detroit Free Press News in 1970. The set features six known players (as listed below), but it is assumed that there are more players in the set. We are still looking for additional players to add to the checklist, thus if you know of any, please contact us. The clippings are not numbered and checklisted below in alphabetical order.

COMPLETE SET (6) 30.00 60.00
1 Dave Bing 12.50 25.00
2 Howard Komives 3.00 8.00
3 Eddie Miles 3.00 8.00
4 Ralph Simpson 6.00 12.00
5 Rudy Tomjanovich 10.00 20.00
6 Jimmy Walker 5.00 10.00

2010-11 Donruss

COMPLETE SET (295) 20.00 50.00
EXCHANGE EXP: 6/20/2012
1 Rajon Rondo .40 1.00
2 Kevin Garnett .60 1.50
3 Shaquille O'Neal .60 1.50
4 Ray Allen .30 .75
5 Paul Pierce .40 1.00
6 Kendrick Perkins .25 .60
7 Nate Robinson .30 .75
8 Jermaine O'Neal .30 .75
9 Jordan Farmar .20 .50
10 Brook Lopez .30 .75
11 Terrence Williams .20 .50
12 Devin Harris .30 .75
13 Troy Murphy .20 .50
14 Anthony Morrow .20 .50
15 Danilo Gallinari .30 .75
16 Amare Stoudemire .30 .75
17 Raymond Felton .25 .60
18 Toney Douglas .25 .60
19 Wilson Chandler .25 .60
20 Anthony Randolph .25 .60
21 Kelenna Azubuike .20 .50
22 Jrue Holiday .30 .75
23 Andres Nocioni .20 .50
24 Elton Brand .30 .75
25 Andre Iguodala .30 .75
26 Spencer Hawes .25 .60
27 Thaddeus Young .20 .50
28 Louis Williams .25 .60
29 Jason Kapono .20 .50
30 Leandro Barbosa .25 .60
31 Andrea Bargnani .25 .60
32 Jose Calderon .25 .60
33 Jarrett Jack .25 .60
34 DeMar DeRozan .30 .75
35 Amir Johnson .20 .50
36 Sonny Weems .20 .50
37 Derrick Rose 1.00 2.50
38 Taj Gibson .30 .75
39 Joakim Noah .30 .75
40 Luol Deng .30 .75
41 C.J. Watson .20 .50
42 Kyle Korver .30 .75
43 James Johnson .20 .50
44 Carlos Boozer .30 .75
45 Mo Williams .25 .60
46 Antawn Jamison .30 .75
47 Daniel Gibson .25 .60
48 Anderson Varejao .25 .60
49 Ramon Sessions .25 .60
50 Anthony Parker .20 .50
51 Ryan Hollins .20 .50
52 Ben Gordon .30 .75
53 Tracy McGrady .30 .75
54 Jonas Jerebko .20 .50
55 Richard Hamilton .20 .50
56 Ben Wallace .20 .50
57 Charlie Villanueva .25 .60
58 Tayshaun Prince .30 .75
59 Mike Dunleavy .20 .50
60 Dahntay Jones .20 .50
61 T.J. Ford .20 .50
62 Roy Hibbert .25 .60
63 Darren Collison .25 .60
64 Danny Granger .30 .75
65 Tyler Hansbrough .30 .75
66 Brandon Rush .25 .60
67 Andrew Bogut .30 .75
68 Brandon Jennings .30 .75
69 John Salmons .30 .75
70 Corey Maggette .25 .60
71 Carlos Delfino .20 .50
72 Michael Redd .30 .75
73 Drew Gooden .25 .60
74 Rodrigue Beaubois .25 .60
75 Dirk Nowitzki .40 1.00
76 Caron Butler .30 .75
77 Tyson Chandler .25 .60
78 Jason Kidd .30 .75
79 Shawn Marion .30 .75
80 Brendan Haywood .20 .50
81 Jason Terry .25 .60
82 Aaron Brooks .20 .50
83 Yao Ming .40 1.00
84 Jordan Hill .20 .50
85 Courtney Lee .25 .60
86 Kevin Martin .30 .75
87 Shane Battier .25 .60
88 Luis Scola .25 .60
89 Brad Miller .25 .60
90 O.J. Mayo .30 .75
91 Marc Gasol .30 .75
92 Rudy Gay .30 .75
93 Zach Randolph .25 .60
94 Sam Young .30 .75
95 Mike Conley Jr. .25 .60
96 Hasheem Thabeet .20 .50
97 Darrell Arthur .20 .50
98 Chris Paul .50 1.25
99 David West .30 .75
100 Trevor Ariza .20 .50
101 Emeka Okafor .30 .75
102 Marcus Thornton .30 .75
103 Peja Stojakovic .30 .75
104 Marco Belinelli .20 .50
105 DeJuan Blair .25 .60
106 Tim Duncan .50 1.25
107 George Hill .25 .60
108 Antonio McDyess .25 .60
109 Richard Jefferson .30 .75
110 Tony Parker .30 .75
111 Manu Ginobili .30 .75
112 Carmelo Anthony .40 1.00
113 Chris Andersen .30 .75
114 Ty Lawson .30 .75
115 Chauncey Billups .30 .75
116 Al Harrington .25 .60
117 Nene' .25 .60
118 Kenyon Martin .30 .75
119 J.R. Smith .30 .75
120 Michael Beasley .30 .75
121 Jonny Flynn .20 .50
122 Kevin Love .40 1.00
123 Luke Ridnour .25 .60
124 Darko Milicic .20 .50
125 Anthony Tolliver .20 .50
126 Corey Brewer .20 .50
127 Marcus Camby .20 .50
128 LaMarcus Aldridge .30 .75
129 Rudy Fernandez .25 .60
130 Brandon Roy .30 .75
131 Andre Miller .25 .60
132 Greg Oden .25 .60
133 Nicolas Batum .30 .75
134 Kevin Durant 1.00 2.50
135 Jeff Green .25 .60
136 Russell Westbrook .40 1.00
137 Serge Ibaka .40 1.00
138 James Harden .40 1.00
139 Nenad Krstic .20 .50
140 Daequan Cook .20 .50
141 Eric Maynor .20 .50
142 Deron Williams .30 .75
143 Al Jefferson .30 .75
144 C.J. Miles .20 .50
145 Raja Bell .25 .60
146 Paul Millsap .25 .60
147 Mehmet Okur .20 .50
148 Andrei Kirilenko .25 .60
149 Joe Johnson .30 .75
150 Jeff Teague .25 .60
151 Mike Bibby .25 .60
152 Josh Smith .30 .75
153 Al Horford .25 .60
154 Marvin Williams .25 .60
155 Jamal Crawford .25 .60
156 Maurice Evans .20 .50
157 Gerald Wallace .30 .75
158 Gerald Henderson .20 .50
159 D.J. Augustin .25 .60
160 Eduardo Najera .20 .50
161 Stephen Jackson .25 .60
162 Tyrus Thomas .25 .60
163 Boris Diaw .25 .60
164 Derrick Brown .20 .50
165 LeBron James 1.50 4.00
166 Dwyane Wade .60 1.50
167 Chris Bosh .30 .75
168 Mike Miller .30 .75
169 Mario Chalmers .30 .75
170 Udonis Haslem .25 .60
171 Juwan Howard .25 .60
172 Carlos Arroyo .25 .60
173 Dwight Howard .50 1.25
174 Vince Carter .40 1.00
175 Chris Duhon .20 .50
176 Jason Williams .25 .60
177 J.J. Redick .30 .75
178 Quentin Richardson .25 .60
179 Jameer Nelson .25 .60
180 Rashard Lewis .25 .60
181 Al Thornton .25 .60
182 Kirk Hinrich .30 .75
183 Josh Howard .25 .60
184 Yi Jianlian .25 .60
185 Nick Young .25 .60
186 Gilbert Arenas .30 .75
187 Andray Blatche .20 .50
188 JaVale McGee .25 .60
189 Stephen Curry .40 1.00
190 Monta Ellis .30 .75
191 David Lee .25 .60
192 Andris Biedrins .20 .50
193 Reggie Williams RC .75 2.00
194 Charlie Bell .20 .50
195 Vladimir Radmanovic .20 .50
196 Eric Gordon .30 .75
197 Blake Griffin .75 2.00
198 Chris Kaman .25 .60
199 Baron Davis .30 .75
200 Craig Smith .20 .50
201 Ryan Gomes .20 .50
202 Rasual Butler .20 .50
203 Kobe Bryant 1.50 4.00
204 Derek Fisher .25 .60
205 Lamar Odom .30 .75
206 Pau Gasol .30 .75
207 Andrew Bynum .40 1.00
208 Shannon Brown .30 .75
209 Ron Artest .30 .75
210 Luke Walton .20 .50
211 Sasha Vujacic .20 .50
212 Steve Nash .30 .75
213 Hedo Turkoglu .30 .75
214 Channing Frye .25 .60
215 Robin Lopez .20 .50
216 Earl Clark .20 .50
217 Grant Hill .40 1.00
218 Jared Dudley .20 .50
219 Jason Richardson .30 .75
220 Tyreke Evans .40 1.00
221 Carl Landry .20 .50
222 Francisco Garcia .25 .60
223 Omri Casspi .20 .50
224 Jason Thompson .20 .50
225 Samuel Dalembert .20 .50
226 Beno Udrih .20 .50
227 Antoine Wright .20 .50
228 John Wall RC 2.50 6.00
229 Evan Turner RC 1.25 3.00
230 Derrick Favors RC 1.25 3.00
231 Wesley Johnson RC 1.00 2.50
232 DeMarcus Cousins RC 2.00 5.00
233 Ekpe Udoh RC .60 1.50
234 Greg Monroe RC 1.25 3.00
235 Al-Farouq Aminu RC .60 1.50
236 Gordon Hayward RC 1.25 3.00
237 Paul George RC 1.50 4.00
238 Cole Aldrich RC .60 1.50
239 Xavier Henry RC .75 2.00
240 Ed Davis RC .75 2.00
241 Patrick Patterson RC 1.00 2.50
242 Larry Sanders RC .60 1.50
243 Luke Babbitt RC .60 1.50
244 Kevin Seraphin RC .75 2.00
245 Eric Bledsoe RC 1.00 2.50
246 Avery Bradley RC 1.25 3.00
247 James Anderson RC .60 1.50
248 Craig Brackins RC .60 1.50
249 Elliot Williams RC .60 1.50
250 Trevor Booker RC .60 1.50
251 Damion James RC .60 1.50
252 Dominique Jones RC .60 1.50
253 Quincy Pondexter RC .60 1.50
254 Jordan Crawford RC 1.00 2.50
255 Greivis Vasquez RC .75 2.00
256 Daniel Orton RC .60 1.50
257 Lazar Hayward RC .60 1.50
258 Dexter Pittman RC .60 1.50
259 Hassan Whiteside RC .60 1.50
260 Andy Rautins RC .60 1.50
261 Luke Harangody RC .60 1.50
262 Timofey Mozgov RC .60 1.50
263 Boston Celtics CL .60 1.50
264 New Jersey Nets CL .40 1.00
265 New York Knicks CL .40 1.00
266 Philadelphia 76ers CL .40 1.00
267 Toronto Raptors CL .40 1.00
268 Chicago Bulls CL .40 1.00
269 Cleveland Cavaliers CL .40 1.00
270 Detroit Pistons CL .40 1.00
271 Indiana Pacers CL .40 1.00
272 Milwaukee Bucks CL .40 1.00
273 Atlanta Hawks CL .40 1.00
274 Charlotte Bobcats CL .40 1.00
275 Miami Heat CL .60 1.50
276 Orlando Magic CL .40 1.00
277 Washington Wizards CL .75 2.00
278 Dallas Mavericks CL .40 1.00
279 Houston Rockets CL .40 1.00
280 Memphis Grizzlies CL .40 1.00
281 New Orleans Hornets CL .40 1.00
282 San Antonio Spurs CL .40 1.00
283 Denver Nuggets CL .40 1.00
284 Minnesota Timberwolves CL .40 1.00
285 Portland Trail Blazers CL .40 1.00
286 Oklahoma City Thunder CL .40 1.00
287 Utah Jazz CL .40 1.00
288 Golden State Warriors CL .40 1.00
289 Los Angeles Clippers CL .40 1.00
290 Los Angeles Lakers CL .60 1.50
291 Phoenix Suns CL .40 1.00
292 Sacramento Kings CL .40 1.00
293 Kobe Bryant CL .75 2.00
294 Chris Bosh CL .15 .40
295 Kevin Durant CL .50 1.25

2010-11 Donruss Die Cuts Emerald

*VETS/CL: .75X TO 2X BASE HI
*ROOKIES: .6X TO 1.5X BASE HI
RANDOM INSERTS IN PACKS

2010-11 Donruss Die Cuts Ruby

*VETS/CL: 5X TO 12X BASE HI
*ROOKIES: 2.5X TO 6X BASE HI
*PL CL 293-295: 10X TO 25X BASE HI
STATED PRINT RUN 25 SER.#'d SETS
RANDOMLY INSERTED IN RETAIL PACKS

2010-11 Donruss Die Cuts Sapphire

*VETS/CL: 3X TO 8X BASE HI
*ROOKIES: 2X TO 5X BASE HI
*PL CL 293-295: 6X TO 15X BASE HI
STATED PRINT RUN 49 SER.#'d SETS

2010-11 Donruss Press Proofs

*VETS/CL: 2.5X TO 6X BASE HI
*ROOKIES: 1.5X TO 4X BASE HI
*PL CL 293-295: 5X TO 12X BASE HI
STATED PRINT RUN 100 SER.#'d SETS

2010-11 Donruss Craftsmen

COMPLETE SET (15) 12.50 25.00
STATED PRINT RUN 999 SER.#'d SETS
*DC EMERALD: .5X TO 1.25X HI
DC EMERALD RANDOM INSERTS IN PACKS
*DC RUBY: 1.5X TO 4X HI
DC RUBY PRINT RUN 25 SETS
*DC SAPPHIRE: 1X TO 2.5X HI
DC SAPPHIRE PRINT RUN 49 SETS
*PRESS PROOFS: .75X TO 2X HI
PRESS PROOFS PRINT RUN 100 SETS
1 Kobe Bryant 4.00 10.00
2 Kevin Durant 2.50 6.00
3 LeBron James 4.00 10.00
4 Dwight Howard 1.25 3.00
5 Carmelo Anthony 1.00 2.50
6 Dwyane Wade 1.50 4.00
7 Dirk Nowitzki 1.00 2.50
8 Amare Stoudemire .75 2.00
9 Steve Nash .75 2.00
10 Deron Williams .75 2.00
11 Andrew Bogut .75 2.00
12 Joe Johnson .75 2.00
13 Brandon Roy .75 2.00
14 Pau Gasol .75 2.00
15 Tim Duncan 1.25 3.00

2010-11 Donruss Craftsmen Materials

STATED PRINT RUN 99 TO 299 SER.#'d SETS
*PRIME: .75X TO 2X HI
PRIME PRINT RUN 5 TO 25 SER.#'d SETS
SOME PRIME UNPRICED DUE TO SCARCITY
1 Kobe Bryant/299 8.00 20.00
2 Kevin Durant/299 6.00 15.00
3 LeBron James/299 8.00 20.00
4 Dwight Howard/299 5.00 12.00
5 Carmelo Anthony/99 4.00 10.00
6 Dwyane Wade/299 6.00 15.00
7 Dirk Nowitzki/299 4.00 10.00
8 Amare Stoudemire/299 3.00 8.00
9 Steve Nash/299 3.00 8.00
10 Deron Williams/299 3.00 8.00
11 Andrew Bogut/99 3.00 8.00
12 Joe Johnson/299 3.00 8.00
13 Brandon Roy/99 3.00 8.00
14 Pau Gasol/299 3.00 8.00
15 Tim Duncan/299 5.00 12.00

2010-11 Donruss Craftsmen Materials Signatures

STATED PRINT RUN ONE TO 25 SER.#'d SETS
SOME UNPRICED DUE TO SCARCITY
UNPRICED SIG.PRIME PRINT RUN 1 TO 5 SETS
1 Kobe Bryant/25 100.00 200.00
8 Amare Stoudemire/25 25.00 60.00
11 Andrew Bogut/25 8.00 20.00
12 Joe Johnson/25 10.00 25.00

2010-11 Donruss Craftsmen Signatures

STATED PRINT RUN ONE TO 49 SER.#'d SETS
SOME UNPRICED DUE TO SCARCITY
1 Kobe Bryant/49 100.00 200.00
8 Amare Stoudemire/25 20.00 50.00
11 Andrew Bogut/25 6.00 15.00
12 Joe Johnson/25 8.00 20.00

2010-11 Donruss Duos

COMPLETE SET (5) 7.50 15.00
RANDOM INSERTS IN PACKS
1 Kobe Bryant 3.00 8.00
LeBron James
2 Larry Bird 3.00 8.00
Magic Johnson
3 Amare Stoudemire 1.25 3.00
Dwight Howard
4 Blake Griffin 4.00 10.00
John Wall
5 Dwyane Wade 2.50 6.00
Kevin Durant

2010-11 Donruss Gamers

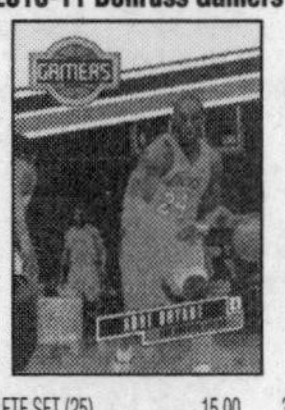

COMPLETE SET (25) 15.00 30.00
STATED PRINT RUN 999 SER.#'d SETS
*DC EMERALD: .5X TO 1.25X HI
DC EMERALD RANDOM INSERTS IN PACKS
*DC RUBY: 1.5X TO 4X HI
DC RUBY PRINT RUN 25 SETS
*DC SAPPHIRE: 1X TO 2.5X HI
DC SAPPHIRE PRINT RUN 49 SETS
*PRESS PROOFS: .75X TO 2X HI
PRESS PROOFS PRINT RUN 100 SETS
1 Derrick Rose 2.50 6.00
2 Kobe Bryant 4.00 10.00
3 LeBron James 4.00 10.00
4 Kevin Garnett 1.50 4.00
5 Dwight Howard 1.25 3.00
6 Brook Lopez .75 2.00
7 Robin Lopez .50 1.25
8 Eric Gordon .75 2.00
9 David Lee .60 1.50
10 Al Jefferson .75 2.00
11 Russell Westbrook 1.00 2.50
12 Marcus Camby .50 1.25
13 Jonny Flynn .50 1.25
14 Carmelo Anthony 1.00 2.50
15 Manu Ginobili .75 2.00
16 David West .75 2.00
17 Zach Randolph .60 1.50
18 Luis Scola .60 1.50
19 Jason Terry .60 1.50
20 Stephen Jackson .60 1.50
21 Josh Smith .75 2.00
22 Ben Wallace .75 2.00
23 Anderson Varejao .60 1.50
24 Andre Iguodala .75 2.00
25 Amare Stoudemire .75 2.00

2010-11 Donruss Gamers Materials

STATED PRINT RUN 99 TO 299 SER.#'d SETS
*PRIME: .75X TO 2X HI
PRIME PRINT RUN 5 TO 49 SER.#'d SETS
SOME PRIME UNPRICED DUE TO SCARCITY
1 Derrick Rose/299 6.00 15.00
2 Kobe Bryant/299 8.00 20.00
3 LeBron James/299 8.00 20.00
4 Kevin Garnett/299 6.00 15.00
5 Dwight Howard/299 5.00 12.00
6 Brook Lopez/299 3.00 8.00
7 Robin Lopez/299 2.00 5.00
8 Eric Gordon/299 3.00 8.00
9 David Lee/299 2.50 6.00
10 Al Jefferson/299 3.00 8.00
11 Russell Westbrook/299 4.00 10.00
12 Marcus Camby/99 2.00 5.00
13 Jonny Flynn/299 2.00 5.00
14 Carmelo Anthony/99 4.00 10.00
15 Manu Ginobili/299 3.00 8.00
16 David West/299 3.00 8.00
17 Zach Randolph/299 2.50 6.00
18 Luis Scola/199 2.50 6.00
19 Jason Terry/299 2.50 6.00
20 Stephen Jackson/299 2.50 6.00
21 Josh Smith/99 3.00 8.00
24 Andre Iguodala/299 3.00 8.00
25 Amare Stoudemire/299 3.00 8.00

2010-11 Donruss Gamers Materials Signatures

STATED PRINT RUN 5 TO 49 SER.#'d SETS
SOME UNPRICED DUE TO SCARCITY
2 Kobe Bryant/25 100.00 200.00
6 Brook Lopez/25 8.00 20.00
7 Robin Lopez/49 5.00 12.00
9 David Lee/25 8.00 20.00
10 Al Jefferson/25 10.00 25.00
11 Russell Westbrook/25 25.00 60.00
13 Jonny Flynn/25 6.00 15.00
25 Amare Stoudemire/25 20.00 50.00

2010-11 Donruss Gamers Materials Signatures Prime

STATED PRINT RUN 5 TO 25 SER.#'d SETS
SOME UNPRICED DUE TO SCARCITY
7 Robin Lopez/25 6.00 15.00
13 Jonny Flynn/25 8.00 20.00

2010-11 Donruss Gamers Signatures

STATED PRINT RUN 5 TO 99 SER.#'d SETS
SOME UNPRICED DUE TO SCARCITY
2 Kobe Bryant/49 100.00 200.00
6 Brook Lopez/25 5.00 12.00
7 Robin Lopez/99 4.00 10.00
9 David Lee/25 6.00 15.00
10 Al Jefferson/49 4.00 10.00
11 Russell Westbrook/25 12.50 30.00
13 Jonny Flynn/49 4.00 10.00
25 Amare Stoudemire/25 20.00 50.00

2010-11 Donruss Jersey Kings

COMPLETE SET (25) 15.00 40.00
STATED PRINT RUN 999 SER.#'d SETS
*DC EMERALD: .5X TO 1.25X HI
DC EMERALD RANDOM INSERTS IN PACKS
*DC RUBY: 1.5X TO 4X HI
DC RUBY PRINT RUN 25 SETS
*DC SAPPHIRE: 1X TO 2.5X HI
DC SAPPHIRE PRINT RUN 49 SETS
*PRESS PROOFS: .75X TO 2X HI
PRESS PROOFS PRINT RUN 100 SETS
1 Allen Iverson 1.50 4.00
2 Andre Miller 1.00 2.50
3 Ben Gordon 1.25 3.00
4 Xavier McDaniel 1.25 3.00
5 Vince Carter 1.50 4.00
6 Luis Scola 1.00 2.50
7 J.J. Redick 1.25 3.00
8 Thaddeus Young .75 2.00
9 Baron Davis 1.25 3.00
10 Kevin Love 1.50 4.00
11 Danilo Gallinari 1.25 3.00
12 Joe Dumars 1.25 3.00
13 Maurice Cheeks 1.25 3.00
14 Dennis Rodman 2.00 5.00
15 Tayshaun Prince 1.25 3.00
16 Andrew Bogut 1.25 3.00
17 Cedric Maxwell 1.25 3.00
18 Jonny Flynn .75 2.00
19 LaMarcus Aldridge 1.25 3.00
20 Mitch Richmond 1.25 3.00
21 Toni Kukoc 1.25 3.00
22 Luol Deng 1.25 3.00
23 Al Horford 1.00 2.50
24 Richard Hamilton 1.00 2.50
25 Dan Majerle 1.25 3.00

2010-11 Donruss Jersey Kings Materials

STATED PRINT RUN 99 TO 299 SER.#'d SETS
*PRIME: .75X TO 2X HI
PRIME PRINT RUN 5 TO 49 SER.#'d SETS
SOME PRIME UNPRICED DUE TO SCARCITY
1 Allen Iverson/99 4.00 10.00
2 Andre Miller/299 2.50 6.00
3 Ben Gordon/299 3.00 8.00
4 Xavier McDaniel/299 3.00 8.00
5 Vince Carter/299 4.00 10.00
6 Luis Scola/199 2.50 6.00
7 J.J. Redick/299 3.00 8.00
8 Thaddeus Young/299 2.00 5.00
9 Baron Davis/99 3.00 8.00
10 Kevin Love/299 4.00 10.00
11 Danilo Gallinari/299 3.00 8.00
12 Joe Dumars/199 3.00 8.00
13 Maurice Cheeks/299 3.00 8.00
14 Dennis Rodman/299 8.00 20.00
15 Tayshaun Prince/299 3.00 8.00
16 Andrew Bogut/99 3.00 8.00
18 Jonny Flynn/299 2.00 5.00
19 LaMarcus Aldridge/299 3.00 8.00
20 Mitch Richmond/299 3.00 8.00
21 Toni Kukoc/299 3.00 8.00
22 Luol Deng/299 3.00 8.00
23 Al Horford/299 2.50 6.00
24 Richard Hamilton/299 2.50 6.00
25 Dan Majerle/299 3.00 8.00

2010-11 Donruss Jersey Kings Materials Signatures

STATED PRINT RUN 10 TO 49 SER.#'d SETS
SOME UNPRICED DUE TO SCARCITY
3 Ben Gordon/25 6.00 15.00
4 Xavier McDaniel/49 8.00 20.00
7 J.J. Redick/25 10.00 25.00
10 Kevin Love/25 12.50 30.00
11 Danilo Gallinari/49 8.00 20.00
12 Joe Dumars/49 15.00 40.00
13 Maurice Cheeks/49 8.00 20.00
14 Dennis Rodman/49 25.00 60.00
16 Andrew Bogut/25 8.00 20.00
18 Jonny Flynn/49 6.00 15.00
21 Toni Kukoc/49 15.00 40.00
24 Richard Hamilton/25 12.50 30.00
25 Dan Majerle/49 12.50 30.00

2010-11 Donruss Jersey Kings Materials Signatures Prime

STATED PRINT RUN 5 TO 25 SER.#'d SETS
SOME UNPRICED DUE TO SCARCITY
4 Xavier McDaniel/25 12.50 30.00
7 J.J. Redick/25 25.00 60.00
10 Kevin Love/25 25.00 60.00
12 Joe Dumars/25 20.00 50.00
13 Maurice Cheeks/25 10.00 25.00
14 Dennis Rodman/25 30.00 80.00
18 Jonny Flynn/25 8.00 20.00
21 Toni Kukoc/25 30.00 80.00
25 Dan Majerle/25 25.00 60.00

2010-11 Donruss Jersey Kings Signatures

STATED PRINT RUN 10 TO 99 SER.#'d SETS
SOME UNPRICED DUE TO SCARCITY
3 Ben Gordon/25 6.00 15.00
4 Xavier McDaniel/75 6.00 15.00
7 J.J. Redick/49 6.00 15.00
10 Kevin Love/25 10.00 25.00
11 Danilo Gallinari/25 6.00 15.00
12 Joe Dumars/25 12.50 30.00
13 Maurice Cheeks/49 5.00 12.00
14 Dennis Rodman/49 20.00 50.00
16 Andrew Bogut/25 8.00 20.00
17 Cedric Maxwell/49 4.00 10.00
18 Jonny Flynn/49 4.00 10.00
21 Toni Kukoc/25 20.00 50.00
24 Richard Hamilton/49 4.00 10.00
25 Dan Majerle/99 10.00 25.00

2010-11 Donruss Magicians

COMPLETE SET (10) 7.50 15.00
STATED PRINT RUN 999 SER.#'d SETS
*DC EMERALD: .5X TO 1.25X HI
DC EMERALD RANDOM INSERTS IN PACKS
*DC RUBY: 1.5X TO 4X HI
DC RUBY PRINT RUN 25 SETS
*DC SAPPHIRE: 1X TO 2.5X HI
DC SAPPHIRE PRINT RUN 49 SETS
*PRESS PROOFS: .75X TO 2X HI
PRESS PROOFS PRINT RUN 100 SETS
1 Steve Nash 1.00 2.50
2 Jason Kidd 1.00 2.50
3 Chris Paul 1.50 4.00
4 Deron Williams 1.00 2.50
5 Rajon Rondo 1.25 3.00
6 Stephen Curry 1.25 3.00
7 Derrick Rose 3.00 8.00
8 John Stockton 1.50 4.00
9 Pete Maravich 3.00 8.00
10 Isiah Thomas 1.00 2.50

2010-11 Donruss Magicians Materials

STATED PRINT RUN 299 SER.#'d SETS
1 Steve Nash 3.00 8.00
2 Jason Kidd 3.00 8.00
3 Chris Paul 5.00 12.00
4 Deron Williams 3.00 8.00
5 Rajon Rondo 4.00 10.00
6 Stephen Curry 4.00 10.00
7 Derrick Rose 6.00 15.00
8 John Stockton 5.00 12.00

2010-11 Donruss Magicians Materials Prime

STATED PRINT RUN 10 TO 49 SER.#'d SETS
SOME UNPRICED DUE TO SCARCITY
1 Steve Nash/25 8.00 20.00
8 John Stockton/49 10.00 25.00
10 Isiah Thomas/49 6.00 15.00

2010-11 Donruss Masters

COMPLETE SET (10) 7.50 15.00
STATED PRINT RUN 999 SER.#'d SETS
*DC EMERALD: .5X TO 1.25X HI
DC EMERALD RANDOM INSERTS IN PACKS
*DC RUBY: 2X TO 5X HI
DC RUBY PRINT RUN 25 SETS
*DC SAPPHIRE: 1X TO 2.5X HI
DC SAPPHIRE PRINT RUN 49 SETS
*PRESS PROOFS: .75X TO 2X HI
PRESS PROOFS PRINT RUN 100 SETS
1 Magic Johnson 2.50 6.00
2 Larry Bird 3.00 8.00
3 Artis Gilmore 1.00 2.50
4 Chris Mullin 1.00 2.50
5 Clyde Drexler 1.25 3.00
6 Kevin McHale 1.00 2.50
7 Patrick Ewing 1.25 3.00
8 Rolando Blackman 1.00 2.50
9 Scottie Pippen 2.00 5.00
10 Walt Frazier 1.00 2.50

2010-11 Donruss Masters Materials

STATED PRINT RUN 49 TO 299 SER.#'d SETS
1 Magic Johnson/299 6.00 15.00
2 Larry Bird/299 8.00 20.00
3 Artis Gilmore/49 3.00 8.00
4 Chris Mullin/299 3.00 8.00
5 Clyde Drexler/299 4.00 10.00
6 Kevin McHale/299 3.00 8.00
7 Patrick Ewing/299 4.00 10.00
8 Rolando Blackman/49 3.00 8.00
9 Scottie Pippen/299 6.00 15.00

2010-11 Donruss Masters Materials Prime

*PRIME: .75X TO 2X BASE HI
STATED PRINT RUN 5 TO 49 SER.#'d SETS
SOME UNPRICED DUE TO SCARCITY
7 Patrick Ewing/49 12.50 30.00
9 Scottie Pippen/49 30.00 60.00

2010-11 Donruss Masters Materials Signatures

STATED PRINT RUN ONE TO 49 SER.#'d SETS
SOME UNPRICED DUE TO SCARCITY
3 Artis Gilmore/49 8.00 20.00
4 Chris Mullin/49 12.50 30.00
5 Clyde Drexler/49 15.00 40.00
8 Rolando Blackman/49 8.00 20.00

2010-11 Donruss Masters Materials Signatures Prime

STATED PRINT RUN ONE TO 25 SER.#'d SETS
SOME UNPRICED DUE TO SCARCITY
3 Artis Gilmore/25 15.00 40.00
4 Chris Mullin/25 25.00 60.00
5 Clyde Drexler/25 25.00 60.00
8 Rolando Blackman/25 15.00 40.00

2010-11 Donruss Masters Signatures

STATED PRINT RUN ONE TO 99 SER.#'d SETS
SOME UNPRICED DUE TO SCARCITY
3 Artis Gilmore/49 6.00 15.00
4 Chris Mullin/99 10.00 25.00
5 Clyde Drexler/25 25.00 60.00
8 Rolando Blackman/25 8.00 20.00

2010-11 Donruss Production Line

COMPLETE SET (100) 50.00 100.00
STATED PRINT RUN 999 SER.#'d SETS
*DC EMERALD: .5X TO 1.25X HI
DC EMERALD RANDOM INSERTS IN PACKS
*DC RUBY: 1.5X TO 4X HI
DC RUBY PRINT RUN 25 SETS
*DC SAPPHIRE: 1X TO 2.5X HI
DC SAPPHIRE PRINT RUN 49 SETS
*PRESS PROOFS: .75X TO 2X HI
PRESS PROOFS PRINT RUN 100 SETS
*RACK PACK: .4X TO 1X BASE HI
RACK PACK RANDOM INSERTS IN RACK PACKS
1 Kevin Durant 2.50 6.00
2 LeBron James 4.00 10.00
3 Carmelo Anthony 1.00 2.50
4 Kobe Bryant 4.00 10.00
5 Dwyane Wade 1.50 4.00
6 Monta Ellis .75 2.00
7 Dirk Nowitzki 1.00 2.50
8 Danny Granger .75 2.00
9 Chris Bosh .75 2.00
10 Amare Stoudemire .75 2.00
11 Gilbert Arenas .75 2.00
12 Brandon Roy .75 2.00
13 Joe Johnson .75 2.00
14 Derrick Rose 2.50 6.00
15 Zach Randolph .60 1.50
16 Stephen Jackson .60 1.50
17 Kevin Martin .75 2.00
18 David Lee .60 1.50
19 Tyreke Evans 1.00 2.50
20 Corey Maggette .60 1.50
21 Dwight Howard 1.25 3.00
22 Marcus Camby .50 1.25
23 Zach Randolph .60 1.50
24 David Lee .60 1.50
25 Pau Gasol .75 2.00
26 Carlos Boozer .75 2.00
27 Joakim Noah .75 2.00
28 Kevin Love 1.00 2.50
29 Chris Bosh .75 2.00
30 Troy Murphy .50 1.25
31 Andrew Bogut .75 2.00
32 Tim Duncan 1.25 3.00
33 Gerald Wallace .75 2.00
34 Al Horford .60 1.50
35 Lamar Odom .75 2.00
36 Samuel Dalembert .50 1.25
37 Kenyon Martin .75 2.00
38 Brendan Haywood .50 1.25
39 Marc Gasol .75 2.00
40 Chris Kaman .60 1.50
41 Steve Nash .75 2.00
42 Chris Paul 1.25 3.00
43 Deron Williams .75 2.00
44 Rajon Rondo 1.00 2.50
45 Jason Kidd .75 2.00
46 LeBron James 4.00 10.00
47 Baron Davis .75 2.00
48 Russell Westbrook 1.00 2.50
49 Gilbert Arenas .75 2.00
50 Devin Harris .75 2.00
51 Dwyane Wade 1.50 4.00
52 Derrick Rose 2.50 6.00
53 Jose Calderon .60 1.50
54 Stephen Curry 1.00 2.50
55 Andre Iguodala .75 2.00
56 Tyreke Evans 1.00 2.50
57 Brandon Jennings .75 2.00
58 Darren Collison .75 2.00
59 Tony Parker .75 2.00
60 Dwight Howard 1.25 3.00
61 Andrew Bogut .75 2.00
62 Greg Oden .60 1.50
63 Josh Smith .75 2.00
64 Brendan Haywood .50 1.25
65 Marcus Camby .50 1.25
66 Chris Andersen .75 2.00
67 Samuel Dalembert .50 1.25
68 Pau Gasol .75 2.00
69 Brook Lopez .75 2.00
70 Kendrick Perkins .60 1.50
71 JaVale McGee .60 1.50
72 Roy Hibbert .60 1.50
73 Marc Gasol .75 2.00
74 Tyrus Thomas .60 1.50
75 Joakim Noah .75 2.00
76 Rajon Rondo 1.00 2.50
77 Monta Ellis .75 2.00
78 Chris Paul 1.25 3.00
79 Stephen Curry 1.00 2.50
80 Dwyane Wade 1.50 4.00
81 Jason Kidd .75 2.00
82 Trevor Ariza .50 1.25
83 Andre Iguodala .75 2.00
84 Baron Davis .75 2.00
85 LeBron James 4.00 10.00
86 Stephen Jackson .60 1.50
87 Josh Smith .75 2.00
88 C.J. Watson .50 1.25
89 Ronnie Brewer .60 1.50
90 Caron Butler .75 2.00
91 Aaron Brooks .50 1.25
92 Danilo Gallinari .75 2.00
93 Jason Kidd .75 2.00
94 Channing Frye .60 1.50
95 Rashard Lewis .60 1.50
96 Stephen Curry 1.00 2.50
97 Jamal Crawford .60 1.50
98 Mo Williams .60 1.50
99 Danny Granger .75 2.00
100 J.R. Smith .75 2.00

2010-11 Donruss Production Line Materials

STATED PRINT RUN 49 TO 399 SER.#'d SETS
*STAT DC: .4X TO 1X BASE HI
STAT DC PRINT RUN 49 TO 399 SER.#'d SETS
*PRIME: .75X TO 2X HI
PRIME PRINT RUN 5 TO 49 SER.#'d SETS
*STAT DC PRIME: .75X TO 2X HI
STAT DC PRIME PRINT RUN 5 TO 49 SETS
SOME PRIME UNPRICED DUE TO SCARCITY
1 Kevin Durant/399 6.00 15.00
2 LeBron James/399 8.00 20.00
3 Carmelo Anthony/299 4.00 10.00
4 Kobe Bryant/399 8.00 20.00
5 Dwyane Wade/399 6.00 15.00
7 Dirk Nowitzki/399 4.00 10.00
9 Chris Bosh/399 3.00 8.00
10 Amare Stoudemire/399 3.00 8.00
11 Gilbert Arenas/399 3.00 8.00
12 Brandon Roy/99 3.00 8.00
13 Joe Johnson/399 3.00 8.00
14 Derrick Rose/399 8.00 20.00
15 Zach Randolph/399 2.50 6.00
16 Stephen Jackson/399 2.50 6.00
18 David Lee/399 2.50 6.00
19 Tyreke Evans/399 4.00 10.00
20 Corey Maggette/49 2.50 6.00
21 Dwight Howard/399 5.00 12.00
22 Marcus Camby/49 2.00 5.00
23 Zach Randolph/399 2.50 6.00
24 David Lee/399 2.50 6.00
25 Pau Gasol/399 3.00 8.00
26 Carlos Boozer/299 3.00 8.00
27 Joakim Noah/199 3.00 8.00
28 Kevin Love/399 4.00 10.00
29 Chris Bosh/399 3.00 8.00
31 Andrew Bogut/199 3.00 8.00
32 Tim Duncan/399 5.00 12.00
33 Gerald Wallace/399 3.00 8.00
34 Al Horford/299 2.50 6.00
35 Lamar Odom/399 3.00 8.00
36 Samuel Dalembert/299 2.00 5.00
37 Kenyon Martin/399 3.00 8.00
38 Brendan Haywood/199 2.00 5.00
39 Marc Gasol/399 3.00 8.00
40 Chris Kaman/399 2.50 6.00
41 Steve Nash/399 3.00 8.00
42 Chris Paul/399 5.00 12.00
43 Deron Williams/399 3.00 8.00
44 Rajon Rondo/399 4.00 10.00
45 Jason Kidd/399 3.00 8.00
46 LeBron James/399 8.00 20.00
47 Baron Davis/99 3.00 8.00
48 Russell Westbrook/399 4.00 10.00
49 Gilbert Arenas/399 3.00 8.00
51 Dwyane Wade/399 6.00 15.00
52 Derrick Rose/399 8.00 20.00
53 Jose Calderon/399 2.50 6.00
54 Stephen Curry/399 4.00 10.00
55 Andre Iguodala/299 3.00 8.00
56 Tyreke Evans/399 4.00 10.00
57 Brandon Jennings/399 3.00 8.00
58 Darren Collison/199 3.00 8.00
59 Tony Parker/99 3.00 8.00
60 Dwight Howard/399 5.00 12.00
61 Andrew Bogut/199 3.00 8.00
62 Greg Oden/299 2.50 6.00
63 Josh Smith/99 3.00 8.00
64 Brendan Haywood/199 2.00 5.00
65 Marcus Camby/49 2.00 5.00
66 Chris Andersen/399 3.00 8.00
67 Samuel Dalembert/299 2.00 5.00
68 Pau Gasol/399 3.00 8.00
69 Brook Lopez/399 3.00 8.00
73 Marc Gasol/399 3.00 8.00
75 Joakim Noah/199 3.00 8.00
76 Rajon Rondo/399 4.00 10.00
78 Chris Paul/399 5.00 12.00
79 Stephen Curry/399 4.00 10.00
80 Dwyane Wade/399 6.00 15.00
81 Jason Kidd/399 3.00 8.00
83 Andre Iguodala/299 3.00 8.00
84 Baron Davis/99 3.00 8.00
85 LeBron James/399 8.00 20.00
86 Stephen Jackson/399 2.50 6.00
87 Josh Smith/99 3.00 8.00
90 Caron Butler/399 3.00 8.00
92 Danilo Gallinari/399 3.00 8.00
93 Jason Kidd/399 3.00 8.00
94 Channing Frye/74 2.50 6.00
95 Rashard Lewis/399 2.50 6.00
96 Stephen Curry/399 4.00 10.00
100 J.R. Smith/399 3.00 8.00

2010-11 Donruss Production Line Materials Signatures

STATED PRINT RUN ONE TO 25 SER.#'d SETS
SOME UNPRICED DUE TO SCARCITY
4 Kobe Bryant/25 100.00 200.00
9 Chris Bosh/25 20.00 50.00
10 Amare Stoudemire/25 25.00 60.00
13 Joe Johnson/25 15.00 40.00
18 David Lee/25 8.00 20.00
19 Tyreke Evans/25 15.00 40.00
24 David Lee/25 8.00 20.00
27 Joakim Noah/25 12.50 30.00
28 Kevin Love/25 12.50 30.00
29 Chris Bosh/25 20.00 50.00
31 Andrew Bogut/25 8.00 20.00
39 Marc Gasol/25 12.50 30.00
48 Russell Westbrook/25 15.00 40.00
56 Tyreke Evans/25 15.00 40.00
59 Tony Parker/25 10.00 25.00
61 Andrew Bogut/25 8.00 20.00
66 Chris Andersen/25 20.00 50.00
69 Brook Lopez/25 8.00 20.00
73 Marc Gasol/25 12.50 30.00
75 Joakim Noah/25 12.50 30.00
90 Caron Butler/15 10.00 25.00
92 Danilo Gallinari/25 8.00 20.00
94 Channing Frye/25 8.00 20.00
100 J.R. Smith/25 8.00 20.00

2010-11 Donruss Production Line Materials Signatures Prime

STATED PRINT RUN ONE TO 49 SER.#'d SETS
SOME UNPRICED DUE TO SCARCITY
50 Devin Harris/49 10.00 25.00
90 Caron Butler/15 12.50 30.00
94 Channing Frye/25 10.00 25.00
100 J.R. Smith/25 10.00 25.00

2010-11 Donruss Production Line Signatures

STATED PRINT RUN ONE TO 99 SER.#'d SETS
SOME UNPRICED DUE TO SCARCITY
4 Kobe Bryant/49 100.00 200.00
8 Danny Granger/25 6.00 15.00
9 Chris Bosh/25 12.50 30.00
10 Amare Stoudemire/25 20.00 50.00
13 Joe Johnson/25 8.00 20.00
18 David Lee/25 6.00 15.00
19 Tyreke Evans/49 10.00 25.00
24 David Lee/25 6.00 15.00
27 Joakim Noah/25 10.00 25.00
28 Kevin Love/25 10.00 25.00
29 Chris Bosh/25 12.50 30.00
31 Andrew Bogut/25 6.00 15.00
39 Marc Gasol/25 10.00 25.00
48 Russell Westbrook/25 15.00 40.00
50 Devin Harris/25 6.00 15.00
56 Tyreke Evans/49 10.00 25.00
58 Darren Collison/25 6.00 15.00
59 Tony Parker/25 6.00 15.00
61 Andrew Bogut/25 6.00 15.00
66 Chris Andersen/25 12.50 30.00
69 Brook Lopez/25 4.00 10.00
73 Marc Gasol/25 10.00 25.00
75 Joakim Noah/25 10.00 25.00
89 Ronnie Brewer/99 4.00 10.00
90 Caron Butler/15 8.00 20.00
91 Aaron Brooks/99 4.00 10.00
92 Danilo Gallinari/49 4.00 10.00
94 Channing Frye/25 4.00 10.00
98 Mo Williams/25 4.00 10.00
99 Danny Granger/25 6.00 15.00
100 J.R. Smith/49 4.00 10.00

2010-11 Donruss Production Line Stat Die Cuts Materials

STATED PRINT RUN 5 TO 49 SER.#'d SETS
SOME UNPRICED DUE TO SCARCITY
1 Kevin Durant/399 6.00 15.00
2 LeBron James/399 8.00 20.00
3 Carmelo Anthony/299 4.00 10.00
4 Kobe Bryant/399 8.00 20.00
5 Dwyane Wade/399 6.00 15.00
7 Dirk Nowitzki/399 4.00 10.00
9 Chris Bosh/399 3.00 8.00
10 Amare Stoudemire/399 3.00 8.00
11 Gilbert Arenas/399 3.00 8.00
12 Brandon Roy/99 3.00 8.00
13 Joe Johnson/399 3.00 8.00
14 Derrick Rose/399 8.00 20.00
15 Zach Randolph/399 2.50 6.00
16 Stephen Jackson/399 2.50 6.00
18 David Lee/399 2.50 6.00
19 Tyreke Evans/399 4.00 10.00
20 Corey Maggette/49 2.50 6.00
21 Dwight Howard/399 5.00 12.00
22 Marcus Camby/49 2.00 5.00
23 Zach Randolph/399 2.50 6.00
24 David Lee/399 2.50 6.00
25 Pau Gasol/399 3.00 8.00
26 Carlos Boozer/299 3.00 8.00
27 Joakim Noah/199 3.00 8.00
28 Kevin Love/399 4.00 10.00
29 Chris Bosh/399 3.00 8.00
31 Andrew Bogut/199 3.00 8.00
32 Tim Duncan/399 5.00 12.00
33 Gerald Wallace/399 3.00 8.00
34 Al Horford/299 2.50 6.00
35 Lamar Odom/399 3.00 8.00
36 Samuel Dalembert/299 2.00 5.00
37 Kenyon Martin/399 3.00 8.00
38 Brendan Haywood/199 2.00 5.00
39 Marc Gasol/399 3.00 8.00
40 Chris Kaman/399 2.50 6.00
41 Steve Nash/399 3.00 8.00
42 Chris Paul/399 5.00 12.00
43 Deron Williams/399 3.00 8.00
44 Rajon Rondo/399 4.00 10.00
45 Jason Kidd/399 3.00 8.00
46 LeBron James/399 8.00 20.00
47 Baron Davis/99 3.00 8.00
48 Russell Westbrook/399 4.00 10.00
49 Gilbert Arenas/399 3.00 8.00
51 Dwyane Wade/399 6.00 15.00
52 Derrick Rose/399 8.00 20.00
53 Jose Calderon/399 2.50 6.00
54 Stephen Curry/399 4.00 10.00
55 Andre Iguodala/299 3.00 8.00
56 Tyreke Evans/399 4.00 10.00
57 Brandon Jennings/399 3.00 8.00
58 Darren Collison/199 3.00 8.00
59 Tony Parker/99 3.00 8.00
60 Dwight Howard/399 5.00 12.00
61 Andrew Bogut/199 3.00 8.00
62 Greg Oden/299 2.50 6.00
63 Josh Smith/99 3.00 8.00
64 Brendan Haywood/199 2.00 5.00
65 Marcus Camby/49 2.00 5.00
66 Chris Andersen/399 3.00 8.00
67 Samuel Dalembert/299 2.00 5.00
68 Pau Gasol/399 3.00 8.00
69 Brook Lopez/399 3.00 8.00
73 Marc Gasol/399 3.00 8.00
75 Joakim Noah/199 3.00 8.00
76 Rajon Rondo/399 4.00 10.00
78 Chris Paul/399 5.00 12.00
79 Stephen Curry/399 4.00 10.00
80 Dwyane Wade/399 6.00 15.00
81 Jason Kidd/399 3.00 8.00
83 Andre Iguodala/299 3.00 8.00
84 Baron Davis/99 3.00 8.00
85 LeBron James/399 8.00 20.00
87 Josh Smith/99 3.00 8.00
90 Caron Butler/399 3.00 8.00
92 Danilo Gallinari/399 3.00 8.00
93 Jason Kidd/399 3.00 8.00
94 Channing Frye/99 2.50 6.00
95 Rashard Lewis/399 2.50 6.00
96 Stephen Curry/399 4.00 10.00
100 J.R. Smith/399 3.00 8.00

2010-11 Donruss Signature

STATED PRINT RUN ONE TO 599 SER.#'d SETS
SOME UNPRICED DUE TO SCARCITY
6 Kendrick Perkins/49 6.00
10 Brook Lopez/25 6.00
11 Terrence Williams/199 4.00
12 Devin Harris/49 4.00
15 Danilo Gallinari/25 5.00
18 Toney Douglas/199 4.00
20 Anthony Randolph/49 4.00
22 Jrue Holiday/199 5.00
31 Andrea Bargnani/49 4.00
34 DeMar DeRozan/99 5.00
36 Sonny Weems/99 4.00
39 Joakim Noah/25 12.50
45 Mo Williams/25 4.00
52 Ben Gordon/25 6.00
54 Jonas Jerebko/199 4.00
55 Richard Hamilton/25 5.00
57 Charlie Villanueva/49 4.00
59 Mike Dunleavy/49 4.00
61 T.J. Ford/49 4.00
63 Darren Collison/25 5.00
64 Danny Granger/25 6.00
65 Tyler Hansbrough/99 4.00
67 Andrew Bogut/25 6.00
74 Rodrigue Beaubois/199 5.00
76 Caron Butler/25 6.00
82 Aaron Brooks/49 4.00
84 Jordan Hill/49 4.00
91 Marc Gasol/49 10.00
94 Sam Young/299 4.00
96 Hasheem Thabeet/199 4.00
101 Emeka Okafor/49 4.00
102 Marcus Thornton/199 5.00
105 DeJuan Blair/99 4.00
110 Tony Parker/25 6.00
113 Chris Andersen/25 12.50
114 Ty Lawson/149 5.00
115 Chauncey Billups/25 5.00
119 J.R. Smith/49 4.00
121 Jonny Flynn/99 5.00
122 Kevin Love/25 10.00
136 Russell Westbrook/25 15.00
138 James Harden/49 8.00
141 Eric Maynor/199 4.00
143 Al Jefferson/49 4.00
149 Joe Johnson/25 8.00
150 Jeff Teague/199 4.00
151 Mike Bibby/25 6.00
158 Gerald Henderson/99 4.00
159 D.J. Augustin/49 4.00
164 Derrick Brown/399 4.00
167 Chris Bosh/25 15.00
177 J.J. Redick/49 10.00
181 Al Thornton/49 4.00
183 Josh Howard/49 4.00
191 David Lee/25 6.00
197 Blake Griffin/25 75.00
203 Kobe Bryant/49 100.00
214 Channing Frye/25 4.00
215 Robin Lopez/49 4.00
216 Earl Clark/199 4.00
220 Tyreke Evans/49 12.50
221 Carl Landry/49 4.00
223 Omri Casspi/199 4.00
228 John Wall/299 30.00
229 Evan Turner/199 8.00
230 Derrick Favors/299 8.00
231 Wesley Johnson/99 6.00
232 DeMarcus Cousins/299 15.00
233 Ekpe Udoh/399 4.00
234 Greg Monroe/399 8.00
235 Al-Farouq Aminu/399 4.00
236 Gordon Hayward/299 8.00
237 Paul George/399 10.00
238 Cole Aldrich/399 4.00
239 Xavier Henry/399 5.00
240 Ed Davis/399 5.00
241 Patrick Patterson/499 6.00
242 Larry Sanders/399 4.00
243 Luke Babbitt/399 4.00
244 Kevin Seraphin/399 5.00
245 Eric Bledsoe/399 8.00
246 Avery Bradley/399 8.00
247 James Anderson/499 4.00
248 Craig Brackins/499 4.00
249 Elliot Williams/499 4.00
250 Trevor Booker/499 4.00
251 Damion James/399 4.00
252 Dominique Jones/399 4.00
253 Quincy Pondexter/599 4.00
254 Jordan Crawford/499 6.00
255 Greivis Vasquez/599 5.00
256 Daniel Orton/499 4.00
257 Lazar Hayward/599 4.00
258 Dexter Pittman/599 4.00
259 Hassan Whiteside/599 4.00
260 Andy Rautins/499 4.00
261 Luke Harangody/499 4.00
262 Timofey Mozgov/599 4.00

2009-10 Donruss Elite

COMP.SET w/o SPs (120) 25.00
121-160 PRINT RUN 499 SER.#'d SETS
161-200 PRINT RUN 499 SER.#'d SETS
UNLESS LISTED IN CHECKLIST
1 Joe Johnson .50
2 Jamal Crawford .40
3 Josh Smith .50
4 Mike Bibby .40
5 Paul Pierce .60
6 Kevin Garnett 1.00
7 Ray Allen .50
8 Rajon Rondo .60
9 Gerald Wallace .50
10 Boris Diaw .40
11 Raymond Felton .40
12 Derrick Rose 1.50
13 John Salmons .50
14 Brad Miller .40
15 Tyrus Thomas .40
16 LeBron James 2.50
17 Shaquille O'Neal 1.00

Williams .40 1.00
onte West .30 .75
k Nowitzki .60 1.50
on Kidd .50 1.25
on Terry .40 1.00
wn Marion .50 1.25
melo Anthony .60 1.50
uncey Billups .50 1.25
yon Martin .50 1.25
ne .40 1.00
Gordon .50 1.25
hard Hamilton .40 1.00
arlie Villanueva .40 1.00
shaun Prince .50 1.25
phen Jackson .40 1.00
nta Ellis .50 1.25
rey Maggette .40 1.00
enna Azubuike .30 .75
cy McGrady .50 1.25
ne Battier .50 1.25
s Scola .40 1.00
vor Ariza .30 .75
ny Granger .50 1.25
ke Dunleavy .30 .75
y Murphy .30 .75
Ford .30 .75
Gordon .50 1.25
hornton .40 1.00
on Davis .50 1.25
cus Camby .30 .75
be Bryant 2.50 6.00
n Artest .50 1.25
Gasol .50 1.25
rew Bynum .60 1.50
h Randolph .40 1.00
y Gay .50 1.25
. Mayo .50 1.25
c Gasol .50 1.25
vane Wade 1.00 2.50
chael Beasley .50 1.25
maine O'Neal .50 1.25
quan Cook .30 .75
ntin Richardson .40 1.00
chael Redd .50 1.25
im Warrick .40 1.00
drew Bogut .50 1.25
e Ridnour .40 1.00
Jefferson .50 1.25
n Gomes .30 .75
in Love .75 2.00
in Harris .50 1.25
ok Lopez .50 1.25
ianlian .40 1.00
er Alston .30 .75
is Paul .75 2.00
id West .50 1.25
a Stojakovic .50 1.25
nes Posey .30 .75
eka Okafor .50 1.25
e Robinson .50 1.25
id Lee .40 1.00
Harrington .40 1.00
y Hughes .40 1.00
in Durant 1.50 4.00
sell Westbrook .75 2.00
Green .40 1.00
ad Krstic .30 .75
ght Howard .75 2.00
e Carter .60 1.50
hard Lewis .40 1.00
eer Nelson .40 1.00
n Brand .50 1.25
re Iguodala .50 1.25
ddeus Young .30 .75
are Stoudemire .50 1.25
e Nash .50 1.25
n Richardson .50 1.25
t Hill .60 1.50
ndon Roy .50 1.25
arcus Aldridge .50 1.25
e Blake .30 .75
re Miller .40 1.00
eg Oden .40 1.00
vin Martin .50 1.25
dres Nocioni .30 .75
ncisco Garcia .40 1.00
encer Hawes .40 1.00
ny Parker .50 1.25
n Duncan .75 2.00
anu Ginobili .50 1.25
chard Jefferson .50 1.25
ris Bosh .50 1.25
se Calderon .40 1.00
drea Bargnani .40 1.00
do Turkoglu .50 1.25
ron Williams .50 1.25
hmet Okur .30 .75
drei Kirilenko .40 1.00
rlos Boozer .50 1.25
twn Jamison .50 1.25
ron Butler .50 1.25
bert Arenas .50 1.25
ndy Foye .30 .75
lis Reed .75 2.00
ris Mullin .75 2.00
vin Johnson .75 2.00
encer Haywood .75 2.00
vid Robinson 1.25 3.00
l Jackson 1.00 2.50
gic Johnson 2.00 5.00
l Westphal .75 2.00
x English .75 2.00
reem Abdul-Jabbar 1.25 3.00
n Rice .75 2.00
e McMillan .75 2.00
o Cousy 1.25 3.00
ch Richmond .75 2.00
ly Tripucka .75 2.00
dric Maxwell .75 2.00
nny Wilkens .75 2.00
Russell 1.25 3.00
n Elliott .75 2.00
sey Hawkins .75 2.00
de Drexler 1.00 2.50
y Bird 2.50 6.00
nnie Hawkins .75 2.00
Hudson .75 2.00
ar Robertson .75 2.00
y Lucas .75 2.00
n McHale .75 2.00
hael Cage .75 2.00
e Divac .75 2.00
West 1.00 2.50
Walton .75 2.00
Barry .75 2.00
Gilmore .75 2.00
Monroe .75 2.00
er McDaniel .75 2.00

156 Jalen Rose .75 2.00
157 Walt Frazier .75 2.00
158 Isiah Thomas .75 2.00
159 James Worthy 1.00 2.50
160 Karl Malone 1.00 2.50
161 Blake Griffin AU RC 100.00 200.00
162 Hasheem Thabeet AU RC 5.00 12.00
163 James Harden/479 AU RC 15.00 40.00
164 Tyreke Evans AU RC 12.00 30.00
165 Jonny Flynn AU RC 5.00 12.00
166 Stephen Curry AU RC 12.00 30.00
167 Jordan Hill AU RC 5.00 12.00
168 Danny Green AU RC 8.00 20.00
169 Brandon Jennings AU RC 10.00 25.00
170 Terrence Williams AU RC 5.00 12.00
171 Gerald Henderson AU RC 5.00 12.00
172 Tyler Hansbrough AU RC 8.00 20.00
173 Earl Clark AU RC 5.00 12.00
174 Austin Daye AU RC 5.00 12.00
175 James Johnson AU RC 5.00 12.00
176 Jrue Holiday AU RC 10.00 25.00
177 Ty Lawson AU RC 8.00 20.00
178 Jeff Teague AU RC 6.00 15.00
179 Eric Maynor/199 AU RC 5.00 12.00
180 Darren Collison/199 AU RC 8.00 20.00
181 Omri Casspi AU RC 5.00 12.00
182 B.J. Mullens AU RC 5.00 12.00
183 Rodrigue Beaubois AU RC 6.00 15.00
184 Taj Gibson/199 AU RC 6.00 15.00
185 DeMarre Carroll AU RC 5.00 12.00
186 Wayne Ellington/199 AU RC 5.00 12.00
187 Toney Douglas AU RC 5.00 12.00
188 Jeff Pendergraph AU RC 5.00 12.00
189 Jermaine Taylor AU RC 5.00 12.00
190 Dante Cunningham/199 AU RC 5.00 12.00
191 DaJuan Summers AU RC 5.00 12.00
192 Sam Young/199 AU RC 5.00 12.00
193 DeJuan Blair AU RC 6.00 15.00
194 Jon Brockman AU RC 5.00 12.00
195 A.J. Price AU RC 5.00 12.00
196 Derrick Brown/199 AU RC 5.00 12.00
197 Jodie Meeks AU RC 6.00 15.00
198 Marcus Thornton/199 AU RC 8.00 20.00
199 Chase Budinger AU RC 5.00 12.00
200 Taylor Griffin AU RC 5.00 12.00

2009-10 Donruss Elite Aspirations

*1-120/10-29: 3X TO 8X BASE HI
*1-120/30-55: 2X TO 5X BASE HI
*121-160/10-29: 1.5X TO 4X BASE HI
*121-160/30-55: 1.25X TO 3X BASE HI
PRINT RUNS LISTED IN CHECKLIST
SOME ROOKIES UNPRICED DUE TO SCARCITY
7 Ray Allen/20 5.00 12.00
93 Steve Nash/13 6.00 15.00
95 Grant Hill/33 12.50 30.00
161 Blake Griffin/32 50.00 120.00
162 Hasheem Thabeet/34 2.00 5.00
166 Stephen Curry/30 30.00 80.00
167 Jordan Hill/43 2.00 5.00
169 Brandon Jennings/3
171 Gerald Henderson/15 4.00 10.00
172 Tyler Hansbrough/50 3.00 8.00
173 Earl Clark/55 2.00 5.00
175 James Johnson/16 4.00 10.00
181 Omri Casspi/18 4.00 10.00
182 B.J. Mullens/23 4.00 10.00
184 Taj Gibson/22 5.00 12.00
186 Wayne Ellington/19 4.00 10.00
187 Toney Douglas/23 4.00 10.00
190 Dante Cunningham/33 2.00 5.00
191 DaJuan Summers/35 2.00 5.00
193 DeJuan Blair/45 2.50 6.00
194 Jon Brockman/40 2.00 5.00
195 A.J. Price/22 4.00 10.00
197 Jodie Meeks/23 5.00 12.00
200 Taylor Griffin/32 2.00 5.00

2009-10 Donruss Elite Status

*1-120/45-75: 1.5X TO 4X BASE HI
*1-120/76-99: 1.25X TO 3X BASE HI
*121-160/45-75: 1.25 TO 3X BASE HI
*121-160/76-99: .75X TO 2X BASE HI
PRINT RUNS LISTED IN CHECKLIST
95 Grant Hill/67 6.00 15.00
161 Blake Griffin/68 30.00 80.00
162 Hasheem Thabeet/66 2.00 5.00
163 James Harden/87 10.00 25.00
164 Tyreke Evans/87 10.00 25.00
165 Jonny Flynn/90 2.00 5.00
166 Stephen Curry/70 10.00 25.00
167 Jordan Hill/57 2.00 5.00
168 Danny Green/86 3.00 8.00
169 Brandon Jennings/97 4.00 10.00
170 Terrence Williams/92 2.00 5.00
171 Gerald Henderson/85 2.00 5.00
172 Tyler Hansbrough/50 3.00 8.00
173 Earl Clark/45 2.00 5.00
174 Austin Daye/95 2.00 5.00
175 James Johnson/84 2.00 5.00
176 Jrue Holiday/89 4.00 10.00
177 Ty Lawson/97 3.00 8.00
178 Jeff Teague/99 2.50 6.00
179 Eric Maynor/97 2.00 5.00
180 Darren Collison/98 3.00 8.00
181 Omri Casspi/82 2.00 5.00
182 B.J. Mullens/77 2.00 5.00
183 Rodrigue Beaubois/97 2.50 6.00
184 Taj Gibson/78 2.50 6.00
185 DeMarre Carroll/99 2.00 5.00
186 Wayne Ellington/81 2.00 5.00
187 Toney Douglas/77 2.00 5.00
188 Jeff Pendergraph/96 2.00 5.00
189 Jermaine Taylor/92 2.00 5.00
190 Dante Cunningham/67 2.00 5.00
191 DaJuan Summers/65 2.00 5.00
192 Sam Young/96 2.00 5.00
193 DeJuan Blair/55 2.50 6.00
194 Jon Brockman/60 2.00 5.00
195 A.J. Price/78 2.00 5.00
196 Derrick Brown/96 2.00 5.00
197 Jodie Meeks/77 2.50 6.00
198 Marcus Thornton/95 3.00 8.00
199 Chase Budinger/90 2.00 5.00
200 Taylor Griffin/68 2.00 5.00

2009-10 Donruss Elite Status Gold

*1-120: 4X TO 10X BASE HI
*121-160: 2X TO 5X BASE HI
GOLD PRINT RUN 24 SER.#'d SETS
93 Steve Nash 6.00 15.00
95 Grant Hill 12.50 30.00
125 David Robinson 8.00 20.00
161 Blake Griffin 125.00 250.00
162 Hasheem Thabeet 5.00 12.00
163 James Harden 20.00 50.00
164 Tyreke Evans 20.00 50.00
165 Jonny Flynn 5.00 12.00
166 Stephen Curry 20.00 50.00
167 Jordan Hill 5.00 12.00
168 Danny Green 8.00 20.00
169 Brandon Jennings 10.00 25.00
170 Terrence Williams 5.00 12.00
171 Gerald Henderson 5.00 12.00
172 Tyler Hansbrough 8.00 20.00
173 Earl Clark 5.00 12.00
174 Austin Daye 5.00 12.00
175 James Johnson 5.00 12.00
176 Jrue Holiday 10.00 25.00
177 Ty Lawson 8.00 20.00
178 Jeff Teague 6.00 15.00
179 Eric Maynor 5.00 12.00
180 Darren Collison 8.00 20.00
181 Omri Casspi 5.00 12.00
182 B.J. Mullens 5.00 12.00
183 Rodrigue Beaubois 6.00 15.00
184 Taj Gibson 6.00 15.00
185 DeMarre Carroll 5.00 12.00
186 Wayne Ellington 5.00 12.00
187 Toney Douglas 5.00 12.00
188 Jeff Pendergraph 5.00 12.00
189 Jermaine Taylor 5.00 12.00
190 Dante Cunningham 5.00 12.00
191 DaJuan Summers 5.00 12.00
192 Sam Young 5.00 12.00
193 DeJuan Blair 6.00 15.00
194 Jon Brockman 5.00 12.00
195 A.J. Price 5.00 12.00
196 Derrick Brown 5.00 12.00
197 Jodie Meeks 6.00 15.00
198 Marcus Thornton 8.00 20.00
199 Chase Budinger 5.00 12.00
200 Taylor Griffin 5.00 12.00

2009-10 Donruss Elite Status Gold Autographs

STATED PRINT RUN 5 TO 24 SER.#'d SETS
SOME UNPRICED DUE TO SCARCITY
UNPRICED BLACK PRINT RUN ONE SET
4 Mike Bibby 8.00 20.00
20 Dirk Nowitzki 50.00 120.00
21 Jason Kidd 15.00 40.00
30 Charlie Villanueva 8.00 20.00
37 Shane Battier 8.00 20.00
40 Danny Granger 8.00 20.00
51 Andrew Bynum 10.00 25.00
57 Michael Beasley 12.00 30.00
67 Kevin Love 15.00 40.00
68 Devin Harris 10.00 25.00
90 Andre Iguodala 8.00 20.00
116 Carlos Boozer 8.00 20.00
121 Willis Reed 15.00 40.00
122 Chris Mullin 20.00 50.00
124 Spencer Haywood 8.00 20.00
129 Alex English 8.00 20.00
133 Bob Cousy 12.50 30.00
137 Lenny Wilkens 8.00 20.00
138 Bill Russell 50.00 120.00
139 Sean Elliott 25.00 60.00
143 Connie Hawkins 10.00 25.00
145 Oscar Robertson 30.00 80.00
150 Jerry West 30.00 80.00
151 Bill Walton 10.00 25.00
152 Rick Barry 8.00 20.00
153 Artis Gilmore 10.00 25.00
157 Walt Frazier 10.00 25.00
161 Blake Griffin 200.00 400.00
162 Hasheem Thabeet 10.00 25.00
163 James Harden 50.00 120.00
164 Tyreke Evans 50.00 120.00
165 Jonny Flynn 10.00 25.00
166 Stephen Curry 50.00 120.00
167 Jordan Hill 10.00 25.00
168 Danny Green 15.00 40.00
169 Brandon Jennings 25.00 60.00
170 Terrence Williams 10.00 25.00
171 Gerald Henderson 10.00 25.00
172 Tyler Hansbrough 20.00 50.00
173 Earl Clark 10.00 25.00
174 Austin Daye 10.00 25.00
175 James Johnson 10.00 25.00
176 Jrue Holiday 25.00 60.00
177 Ty Lawson 20.00 50.00
178 Jeff Teague 12.00 30.00
179 Eric Maynor 10.00 25.00
180 Darren Collison 15.00 40.00
181 Omri Casspi 10.00 25.00
182 B.J. Mullens 10.00 25.00
183 Rodrigue Beaubois 12.00 30.00
184 Taj Gibson 12.00 30.00
185 DeMarre Carroll 10.00 25.00
186 Wayne Ellington 15.00 40.00
187 Toney Douglas 10.00 25.00
188 Jeff Pendergraph 10.00 25.00
189 Jermaine Taylor 10.00 25.00
190 Dante Cunningham 10.00 25.00
191 DaJuan Summers 10.00 25.00
192 Sam Young 10.00 25.00
193 DeJuan Blair 15.00 40.00
194 Jon Brockman 10.00 25.00
195 A.J. Price 10.00 25.00
196 Derrick Brown 10.00 25.00
197 Jodie Meeks 12.00 30.00
198 Marcus Thornton 15.00 40.00
199 Chase Budinger 10.00 25.00
200 Taylor Griffin 10.00 25.00

2009-10 Donruss Elite ARCeologists

COMPLETE SET (15) 6.00 15.00
*BLACK: 2X TO 5X BASE HI
BLACK PRINT RUN 25 SER.#'d SETS
*GOLD: 1.25X TO 3X BASE HI
GOLD PRINT RUN 100 SER.#'d SETS
*GREEN: .4X TO 1X BASE HI
GREEN RANDOM INSERTS IN RETAIL PACKS
*RED: .6X TO 1.5X BASE HI
RED PRINT RUN 249 SER.#'d SETS
1 Ray Allen .75 2.00
2 Steve Nash .75 2.00
3 Roger Mason .50 1.25
4 Chauncey Billups .75 2.00
5 Rashard Lewis .60 1.50
6 Ben Gordon .75 2.00
7 Kobe Bryant 4.00 10.00
8 Troy Murphy .50 1.25
9 Jason Kidd .75 2.00
10 Mike Bibby .60 1.50
11 Daequan Cook .50 1.25
12 Vince Carter 1.00 2.50
13 Peja Stojakovic .75 2.00
14 Michael Finley .75 2.00
15 O.J. Mayo .75 2.00

2009-10 Donruss Elite ARCeologists Autographs

STATED PRINT RUN 25 TO 50 SER.#'d SETS
7 Kobe Bryant/47 100.00 200.00
9 Jason Kidd/25 15.00 30.00
10 Mike Bibby/50 8.00 20.00

2009-10 Donruss Elite ARCeologists Jerseys

STATED PRINT RUN 99 TO 299 SER.#'d SETS
1 Ray Allen/299 3.00 8.00
5 Rashard Lewis/299 2.50 6.00
7 Kobe Bryant/99 12.50 30.00
9 Jason Kidd/299 3.00 8.00
10 Mike Bibby/299 2.50 6.00
13 Peja Stojakovic/299 3.00 8.00
15 O.J. Mayo/140 3.00 8.00

2009-10 Donruss Elite ARCeologists Jerseys Prime

*PRIME: .75X TO 2X BASE HI
STATED PRINT RUN 24-50 SER.#'d SETS
2 Steve Nash/25 10.00 25.00
7 Kobe Bryant/24 20.00 40.00

2009-10 Donruss Elite Clutch Performers

COMPLETE SET (20) 15.00 30.00
*BLACK: 1.5X TO 4X BASE HI
PRINT RUN 25 SER.#'d SETS
*GOLD: 1X TO 2.5X BASE HI
GOLD PRINT RUN 100 SER.#d SETS
*GREEN: .4X TO 1X BASE HI
GREEN RANDOM INSERTS IN RETAIL PACKS
*RED: .5X TO 1.25X BASE HI
RED PRINT RUN 249 SER.#'d SETS
1 Paul Pierce 1.25 3.00
2 LeBron James 5.00 12.00
3 Jason Terry .75 2.00
4 Manu Ginobili 1.00 2.50
5 Kobe Bryant 5.00 12.00
6 Brandon Roy 1.00 2.50
7 Dwyane Wade 2.00 5.00
8 Deron Williams 1.00 2.50
9 Andre Iguodala 1.00 2.50
10 Carmelo Anthony 1.25 3.00
11 Chris Paul 1.50 4.00
12 Tracy McGrady 1.00 2.50
13 Ray Allen 1.00 2.50
14 Stephen Jackson .75 2.00
15 Devin Harris 1.00 2.50
16 Gilbert Arenas 1.00 2.50
17 Al Jefferson 1.00 2.50
18 Richard Hamilton .75 2.00
19 Dirk Nowitzki 1.25 3.00
20 Joe Johnson 1.00 2.50

2009-10 Donruss Elite Clutch Performers Jerseys

STATED PRINT RUN 35 TO 299 SER.#'d SETS
1 Paul Pierce/299 4.00 10.00
2 LeBron James/199 8.00 20.00
3 Jason Terry/299 2.50 6.00
5 Kobe Bryant/99 10.00 25.00
6 Brandon Roy/125 3.00 8.00
7 Dwyane Wade/199 6.00 15.00
8 Deron Williams/299 3.00 8.00
9 Andre Iguodala/299 3.00 8.00
10 Carmelo Anthony/199 4.00 10.00
11 Chris Paul/199 5.00 12.00
12 Tracy McGrady/299 3.00 8.00
13 Ray Allen/299 3.00 8.00
14 Stephen Jackson/299 2.50 6.00
15 Devin Harris/70 3.00 8.00
17 Al Jefferson/299 3.00 8.00
19 Dirk Nowitzki/35 6.00 15.00
20 Joe Johnson/299 3.00 8.00

2009-10 Donruss Elite Clutch Performers Jerseys Prime

*PRIME: .75X TO 2X BASE HI
STATED PRINT RUN 10 TO 50 SER.#'d SETS
SOME UNPRICED DUE TO SCARCITY
4 Manu Ginobili/50 6.00 15.00
6 Brandon Roy/15 10.00 25.00
7 Dwyane Wade/15 15.00 40.00

2009-10 Donruss Elite In the Zone

COMPLETE SET (20) 20.00 40.00
*BLACK: 1.5X TO 4X BASE HI
BLACK PRINT RUN 25 SER.#'d SETS
*GOLD: 1X TO 2.5X BASE HI
GOLD PRINT RUN 100 SER.#'d SETS
*GREEN: .4X TO 1X BASE HI
GREEN RANDOM INSERTS IN RETAIL PACKS
*RED: .5X TO 1.25X BASE HI
RED PRINT RUN 249 SER.#'d SETS
1 Shaquille O'Neal 2.00 5.00
2 Nene .75 2.00
3 Dwight Howard 1.50 4.00
4 Pau Gasol 1.00 2.50
5 Emeka Okafor 1.00 2.50
6 David Lee .75 2.00
7 Yao Ming 1.25 3.00
8 Amare Stoudemire 1.00 2.50
9 Kevin Garnett 2.00 5.00
10 Al Horford 1.00 2.50
11 Tony Parker 1.00 2.50
12 Rajon Rondo 1.25 3.00
13 Tim Duncan 1.50 4.00
14 Steve Nash 1.00 2.50
15 Chris Paul 1.50 4.00
16 Jose Calderon .75 2.00
17 Al Jefferson 1.00 2.50
18 Dwyane Wade 2.00 5.00
19 LeBron James 5.00 12.00
20 LaMarcus Aldridge 1.00 2.50

2009-10 Donruss Elite In the Zone Jerseys

PRINT RUNS 199 OR 299 SER.#'d SETS
*PRIME: .75X TO 2X BASE HI
PRIME PRINT RUNS 15-50 SER.#'d SETS
3 Dwight Howard 5.00 12.00
4 Pau Gasol/199 3.00 8.00
6 David Lee 2.50 6.00
7 Yao Ming 4.00 10.00
8 Amare Stoudemire 3.00 8.00
9 Kevin Garnett 6.00 15.00
10 Al Horford 3.00 8.00
12 Rajon Rondo 4.00 10.00
13 Tim Duncan 5.00 12.00
15 Chris Paul/199 5.00 12.00
16 Jose Calderon 2.50 6.00
17 Al Jefferson 3.00 8.00
18 Dwyane Wade/199 6.00 15.00
19 LeBron James/199 8.00 20.00
20 LaMarcus Aldridge 3.00 8.00

2009-10 Donruss Elite Jerseys

STATED PRINT RUN 99 SER.#'d SETS
3 Josh Smith 3.00 8.00
4 Mike Bibby 2.50 6.00
5 Paul Pierce 4.00 10.00
6 Kevin Garnett 6.00 15.00
8 Rajon Rondo 4.00 10.00
16 LeBron James 10.00 25.00
21 Jason Kidd 3.00 8.00
22 Jason Terry 2.50 6.00
26 Kenyon Martin 3.00 8.00
31 Tayshaun Prince 3.00 8.00
32 Stephen Jackson 2.50 6.00
36 Tracy McGrady 3.00 8.00
37 Shane Battier 3.00 8.00
38 Luis Scola 2.50 6.00
48 Kobe Bryant 10.00 25.00
50 Pau Gasol 3.00 8.00
51 Andrew Bynum 4.00 10.00
56 Dwyane Wade 6.00 15.00
57 Michael Beasley 3.00 8.00
58 Jermaine O'Neal 3.00 8.00
63 Andrew Bogut 3.00 8.00
65 Al Jefferson 3.00 8.00
67 Kevin Love 5.00 12.00
72 Chris Paul 5.00 12.00
74 Peja Stojakovic 3.00 8.00
77 Nate Robinson 3.00 8.00
78 David Lee 2.50 6.00
85 Dwight Howard 5.00 12.00
87 Rashard Lewis 2.50 6.00
89 Elton Brand 3.00 8.00
91 Thaddeus Young 2.00 5.00
97 LaMarcus Aldridge 3.00 8.00
102 Andres Nocioni 2.00 5.00
106 Tim Duncan 5.00 12.00
109 Chris Bosh 3.00 8.00
110 Jose Calderon 2.50 6.00
111 Andrea Bargnani 2.50 6.00
113 Deron Williams 3.00 8.00
114 Mehmet Okur 2.00 5.00
115 Andrei Kirilenko 2.50 6.00
116 Carlos Boozer 3.00 8.00
122 Chris Mullin 3.00 8.00
123 Kevin Johnson 3.00 8.00
141 Clyde Drexler 4.00 10.00
142 Larry Bird 10.00 25.00
147 Kevin McHale 3.00 8.00
157 Walt Frazier 3.00 8.00
158 Isiah Thomas 3.00 8.00
160 Karl Malone 4.00 10.00

2009-10 Donruss Elite Jerseys Prime

*PRIME: .75X TO 2X BASE HI
STATED PRINT RUN 15 TO 50 SER.#'d SETS
56 Dwyane Wade/15 15.00 40.00
122 Chris Mullin/50 8.00 20.00
123 Kevin Johnson/50 8.00 20.00
142 Larry Bird/50 20.00 40.00
147 Kevin McHale/50 10.00 25.00
158 Isiah Thomas/50 8.00 20.00

2009-10 Donruss Elite Passing the Torch

COMPLETE SET (15) 20.00 50.00
*BLACK: 1.5X TO 4X BASE HI
BLACK PRINT RUN 25 SER.#'d SETS
*GOLD: .75X TO 2X BASE HI
GOLD PRINT RUN 100 SER.#'d SETS
*GREEN: .4X TO 1X BASE HI
GREEN RANDOM INSERTS IN RETAIL PACKS
*RED: .6X TO 1.5X BASE HI
RED PRINT RUN 249 SER.#'d SETS
1 Magic Johnson 4.00 10.00
Kobe Bryant
2 Bill Russell 3.00 8.00
Robert Parish
3 Larry Bird 3.00 8.00
Ray Allen
4 Bill Walton 2.00 5.00
Luke Walton
5 Moses Malone 2.00 5.00
Yao Ming
6 David Thompson 2.00 5.00
Vince Carter
7 Dennis Rodman 2.50 6.00
Chris Andersen
8 Moses Malone 3.00 8.00
Shaquille O'Neal
9 David Robinson 3.00 8.00
Tim Duncan
10 Dell Curry 2.50 6.00
Stephen Curry
11 Tyler Hansbrough 4.00 10.00
Blake Griffin
12 Dan Majerle 2.00 5.00
Chris Kaman
13 George Gervin 2.50 6.00
Tony Parker
14 George McGinnis 2.50 6.00
Tyler Hansbrough
15 Kareem Abdul-Jabbar 4.00 10.00
Kobe Bryant

2009-10 Donruss Elite Passing the Torch Autographs

STATED PRINT RUN 25 SER.#'d SETS
1 Magic Johnson 125.00 250.00
Kobe Bryant
2 Bill Russell 60.00 120.00
Robert Parish
3 Larry Bird 60.00 120.00
Ray Allen
10 Dell Curry 40.00 100.00
Stephen Curry
11 Tyler Hansbrough 100.00 200.00
Blake Griffin
12 Dan Majerle 15.00 40.00
Chris Kaman
13 George Gervin 20.00 50.00
Tony Parker
14 George McGinnis 20.00 50.00
Tyler Hansbrough
15 Kareem Abdul-Jabbar 125.00 250.00
Kobe Bryant

2009-10 Donruss Elite Prime Targets

COMPLETE SET (20) 10.00 25.00
*BLACK: 2X TO 5X BASE HI
BLACK PRINT RUN 25 SER.#'d SETS
*GOLD: 1.25X TO 3X BASE HI
GOLD PRINT RUN 100 SER.#'d SETS
*GREEN: .4X TO 1X BASE HI
GREEN RANDOM INSERTS IN RETAIL PACKS
*RED: .6X TO 1.5X BASE HI
RED PRINT RUN 249 SER.#'d SETS
1 Dwyane Wade 1.50 4.00
2 Kobe Bryant 4.00 10.00
2AU Kobe Bryant AU/39
3 Dirk Nowitzki 1.00 2.50
4 LeBron James 4.00 10.00
5 Antawn Jamison .75 2.00
6 Joe Johnson .75 2.00
7 Kevin Durant 2.50 6.00
8 Vince Carter 1.00 2.50
9 Brandon Roy .75 2.00
10 Ben Gordon .75 2.00
11 David West .75 2.00
12 O.J. Mayo .75 2.00
13 Danny Granger .75 2.00
14 Chris Bosh .75 2.00
15 Tony Parker .75 2.00
16 Rudy Gay .75 2.00
17 Chris Paul 1.25 3.00
18 LaMarcus Aldridge .75 2.00
19 Al Harrington .60 1.50
20 Raymond Felton .60 1.50

2009-10 Donruss Elite Prime Targets Jerseys

STATED PRINT RUN 99 TO 299 SER.#'d SETS
1 Dwyane Wade/199 6.00 15.00
2 Kobe Bryant/99 10.00 25.00
4 LeBron James/199 8.00 20.00
6 Joe Johnson/299 3.00 8.00
12 O.J. Mayo/299 3.00 8.00
14 Chris Bosh/299 3.00 8.00
17 Chris Paul/199 5.00 12.00
18 LaMarcus Aldridge/299 3.00 8.00
19 Al Harrington/145 2.50 6.00

2009-10 Donruss Elite Prime Targets Jerseys Prime

*PRIME: .75X TO 2X BASE HI
STATED PRINT RUN 2 TO 50 SER.#'d SETS
SOME UNPRICED DUE TO SCARCITY
7 Kevin Durant/25 15.00 30.00
9 Brandon Roy/50 6.00 15.00
15 Tony Parker/15 10.00 25.00

2009-10 Donruss Elite Series

COMPLETE SET (20) 25.00 50.00
*BLACK: 1.5X TO 4X BASE HI
BLACK PRINT RUN 25 SER.#'d SETS
*GOLD: 1X TO 2.5X BASE HI
GOLD PRINT RUN 100 SER.#'d SETS
*GREEN: .4X TO 1X BASE HI
GREEN RANDOM INSERTS IN RETAIL PACKS
*RED: .6X TO 1.5X BASE HI
RED PRINT RUN 249 SER.#'d SETS
1 Joe Johnson 1.00 2.50
2 Paul Pierce 1.25 3.00
3 Gerald Wallace 1.00 2.50
4 Derrick Rose 3.00 8.00
5 LeBron James 5.00 12.00
6 Dirk Nowitzki 1.25 3.00
7 Carmelo Anthony 1.25 3.00
8 Richard Hamilton .75 2.00
9 Stephen Jackson .75 2.00
10 Yao Ming 1.25 3.00
11 Danny Granger 1.00 2.50
12 Marcus Camby .60 1.50
13 Kobe Bryant 5.00 12.00
14 O.J. Mayo 1.00 2.50
15 Dwyane Wade 2.00 5.00
16 Michael Redd 1.00 2.50
17 Al Jefferson 1.00 2.50
18 Devin Harris 1.00 2.50
19 Chris Paul 1.50 4.00
20 David Lee .75 2.00
21 Kevin Durant 3.00 8.00
22 Dwight Howard 1.50 4.00
23 Andre Iguodala 1.00 2.50
24 Amare Stoudemire 1.00 2.50
25 Brandon Roy 1.00 2.50
26 Kevin Martin 1.00 2.50
27 Tim Duncan 1.50 4.00
28 Chris Bosh 1.00 2.50
29 Deron Williams 1.00 2.50
30 Antawn Jamison 1.00 2.50

2009-10 Donruss Elite Series Jerseys

STATED PRINT RUN 5 TO 299 SER.#'d SETS
SOME UNPRICED DUE TO SCARCITY
1 Joe Johnson/225 3.00 8.00
2 Paul Pierce/299 4.00 10.00
5 LeBron James/199 8.00 20.00
9 Stephen Jackson/299 2.50 6.00
10 Yao Ming/149 4.00 10.00
13 Kobe Bryant/99 12.50 30.00
14 O.J. Mayo/299 3.00 8.00
15 Dwyane Wade/199 6.00 15.00
16 Michael Redd/249 3.00 8.00
17 Al Jefferson/299 3.00 8.00
19 Chris Paul/199 5.00 12.00
20 David Lee/299 2.50 6.00
22 Dwight Howard/299 5.00 12.00
23 Andre Iguodala/299 3.00 8.00
25 Brandon Roy/299 3.00 8.00
27 Tim Duncan/299 5.00 12.00
28 Chris Bosh/299 3.00 8.00
29 Deron Williams/299 3.00 8.00

2009-10 Donruss Elite Series Jerseys Prime

*PRIME: .75X TO 2X BASE HI
STATED PRINT RUN 10 TO 50 SER.#'d SETS
SOME UNPRICED DUE TO SCARCITY
18 Devin Harris/50 6.00 15.00
19 Chris Paul/15 10.00 25.00
21 Kevin Durant/25 15.00 30.00
24 Amare Stoudemire/50 6.00 15.00
26 Kevin Martin/25 6.00 15.00
27 Tim Duncan/50 10.00 25.00

2009-10 Donruss Elite Teamwork Combos

*BLACK: 1.5X TO 4X BASE HI
BLACK PRINT RUN 25 SER.#'d SETS
*GOLD: 1X TO 2.5X BASE HI
GOLD PRINT RUN 100 SER.#'d SETS
*GREEN: .4X TO 1X BASE HI
GREEN RANDOM INSERTS IN RETAIL PACKS
*RED: .5X TO 1.25X BASE HI
RED PRINT RUN 249 SER.#'d SETS
1 Joe Johnson 1.00 2.50
Mike Bibby
2 Kevin Garnett 2.00 5.00
Paul Pierce
3 Gerald Henderson 1.00 2.50
Raymond Felton
4 Derrick Rose 3.00 8.00
John Salmons
5 LeBron James 5.00 12.00
Shaquille O'Neal
6 Dirk Nowitzki 1.25 3.00
Jason Kidd
7 Carmelo Anthony 1.25 3.00
Chauncey Billups
8 Ben Gordon 1.00 2.50
Richard Hamilton
9 Monta Ellis 1.00 2.50
Stephen Jackson
10 Shane Battier 1.00 2.50
Tracy McGrady
11 Danny Granger 1.00 2.50
Mike Dunleavy
12 Al Thornton 1.00 2.50
Eric Gordon
13 Kobe Bryant 5.00 12.00
Pau Gasol
14 O.J. Mayo 1.00 2.50
Zach Randolph
15 Dwyane Wade 2.00 5.00
Michael Beasley
16 Andrew Bogut 1.00 2.50
Michael Redd
17 Al Jefferson 1.00 2.50
Ryan Gomes
18 Brook Lopez 1.00 2.50
Devin Harris
19 Chris Paul 1.50 4.00
David West
20 David Lee 1.00 2.50
Nate Robinson
21 Kevin Durant 3.00 8.00
Russell Westbrook
22 Dwight Howard 1.50 4.00
Vince Carter
23 Andre Iguodala 1.00 2.50
Elton Brand
24 Amar'e Stoudemire 1.00 2.50
Steve Nash
25 Andre Miller 1.00 2.50
Brandon Roy
26 Andres Nocioni 1.00 2.50
Kevin Martin
27 Tim Duncan 1.50 4.00
Tony Parker
28 Andrea Bargnani .75 2.00
Jose Calderon
29 Deron Williams 1.00 2.50
Mehmet Okur
30 Antawn Jamison 1.00 2.50
Gilbert Arenas

2009-10 Donruss Elite Teamwork Combos Autographs

STATED PRINT RUN 50 SER.#'d SETS
6 Dirk Nowitzki 75.00 150.00
Jason Kidd
13 Kobe Bryant 100.00 200.00
Pau Gasol
23 Andre Iguodala 20.00 40.00
Elton Brand

2009-10 Donruss Elite Threads

STATED PRINT RUN 15 TO 99 SER.#'d SESTS
1 Joe Johnson/99 3.00 8.00
2 Mike Bibby/99 2.50 6.00
3 Al Horford/99 3.00 8.00
4 Kevin Garnett/99 6.00 15.00
5 Ray Allen/99 3.00 8.00
6 Gerald Wallace/99 3.00 8.00
7 Derrick Rose/99 10.00 25.00
8 LeBron James/99 10.00 25.00
9 Josh Howard/99 2.50 6.00
10 Dirk Nowitzki/99 4.00 10.00
11 Jason Kidd/99 3.00 8.00
12 Jason Terry/99 2.50 6.00
13 Carmelo Anthony/99 4.00 10.00
14 Kenyon Martin/99 3.00 8.00
15 Austin Daye/99 3.00 8.00
17 Stephen Jackson/99 2.50 6.00
18 Tracy McGrady/99 3.00 8.00
19 Tyler Hansbrough/99 5.00 12.00
20 Blake Griffin/99 15.00 40.00
21 Kobe Bryant/99 10.00 25.00
22 Andrew Bynum/99 4.00 10.00
23 Pau Gasol/99 3.00 8.00
25 O.J. Mayo/99 3.00 8.00
26 Dwyane Wade/99 6.00 15.00
27 Michael Beasley/99 3.00 8.00
28 Michael Redd/99 3.00 8.00
29 Al Jefferson/99 3.00 8.00
31 Chris Paul/99 5.00 12.00
32 David West/99 3.00 8.00
33 Nate Robinson/99 3.00 8.00
35 Dwight Howard/99 5.00 12.00
37 Elton Brand/99 3.00 8.00
38 Andre Iguodala/99 3.00 8.00
39 Amare Stoudemire/99 3.00 8.00
40 Steve Nash/15 8.00 20.00
41 Brandon Roy/99 3.00 8.00
42 Tyreke Evans/99 8.00 20.00
44 Tim Duncan/99 5.00 12.00
45 Manu Ginobili/45 3.00 8.00
46 Chris Bosh/99 3.00 8.00
47 Deron Williams/99 3.00 8.00
48 Carlos Boozer/99 3.00 8.00
49 Andrei Kirilenko/99 2.50 6.00
50 Tayshaun Prince/99 3.00 8.00

2009-10 Donruss Elite Threads Autographs

STATED PRINT RUN 25 SER.#'d SETS
2 Mike Bibby 6.00 15.00
10 Dirk Nowitzki 50.00 120.00
11 Jason Kidd 15.00 40.00
15 Austin Daye 6.00 15.00
19 Tyler Hansbrough 12.50 30.00
20 Blake Griffin 150.00 350.00
21 Kobe Bryant 125.00 225.00
38 Andre Iguodala 6.00 15.00
42 Tyreke Evans 25.00 60.00
48 Carlos Boozer 6.00 15.00

2009-10 Donruss Elite Threads Prime

*PRIME: .75X TO 2X BASE HI
STATED PRINT RUN 10 TO 50 SER.#'d SETS
SOME UNPRICED DUE TO SCARCITY
30 Devin Harris/50 6.00 15.00
34 Kevin Durant/25 20.00 50.00
40 Steve Nash/25 10.00 25.00
43 Tony Parker/50 8.00 20.00

2009-10 Donruss Elite Retail

These cards differ from the hobby version by utilizing a conventional type of cardboard, rather than the traditional metal board. The set is complete at 120 cards and contains no legends or rookies, like the standard Hobby set.
COMPLETE SET (120) 10.00 25.00
*RETAIL: .2X TO .5X HOBBY

2007 Donruss Elite Extra Edition

COMPLETE SET (142)
COMP.SET w/o AU's (92) 8.00 20.00
COMMON CARD (1-92) .20 .50
COMMON AU (92-142) 4.00 10.00
OVERALL AUTO/MEM ODDS 1:5
AU PRINT RUNS B/WN 374-999 COPIES PER
EXCHANGE DEADLINE 07/01/2009
56 Demetris Nichols .20 .50
57 Aaron Gray .20 .50
58 Daequan Cook .20 .50
59 Derrick Byars .20 .50
60 Reyshawn Terry .20 .50
61 Taurean Green .20 .50
62 Don Haskins .20 .50
63 Jerry Tarkanian .20 .50
64 Rick Majerus .20 .50
65 Rollie Massimino .20 .50
67 Dale Brown .20 .50
68 Dean Smith .20 .50
69 Eddie Sutton .20 .50
71 Gene Keady .20 .50
72 Jim Boeheim .20 .50
73 Norm Stewart .20 .50
80 Rebecca Lobo .20 .50
83 Elvin Hayes .20 .50
85 Bill Walton .20 .50
86 Sidney Moncrief .20 .50
87 Dominique Wilkins .20 .50
90 Muggsy Bogues .20 .50
137 Alando Tucker AU/494 4.00 10.00
139 Marc Gasol AU/474 5.00 12.00
140 Stephane Lasme AU/674 4.00 10.00

2007 Donruss Elite Extra Edition Aspirations

*ASP 1-92: 3X TO 8X BASIC
OVERALL INSERT ODDS 1:4
STATED PRINT RUN 100 SER.#'d SETS
136 D. J. Strawberry 2.00 5.00
137 Alando Tucker 1.50 4.00
138 Jared Jordan 1.50 4.00
139 Marc Gasol 2.00 5.00
140 Stephane Lasme 1.50 4.00

2007 Donruss Elite Extra Edition Status

*STATUS 1-92: 4X TO 10X BASIC
OVERALL INSERT ODDS 1:4
STATED PRINT RUN 50 SER.#'d SETS
136 D. J. Strawberry 2.50 6.00
137 Alando Tucker 2.00 5.00
138 Jared Jordan 2.00 5.00
139 Marc Gasol 3.00 8.00
140 Stephane Lasme 2.00 5.00

2007 Donruss Elite Extra Edition College Ties

STATED PRINT RUN 1500 SER.#'d SETS
*GOLD: .6X TO 1.5X BASIC
GOLD PRINT RUN 500 SER.#'d SETS
*RED: 1X TO 2.5X BASIC
RED PRINT RUN 100 SER.#'d SETS
OVERALL INSERT ODDS 1:4
5 Taurean Green 1.25 3.00
Matt LaPorta
7 Jim Boeheim .75 2.00
Demetris Nichols
11 Daequan Cook .75 2.00
Cory Luebke
12 D. J. Strawberry .75 2.00
Brett Cecil

2007 Donruss Elite Extra Edition College Ties Autographs

OVERALL AUTO/MEM ODDS 1:5
PRINT RUNS B/WN 50-100 COPIES PER
EXCHANGE DEADLINE 07/01/2009
5 Taurean Green 10.00 25.00
Matt LaPorta
7 Jim Boeheim 6.00 15.00
Demetris Nichols EXCH
11 Daequan Cook 10.00 25.00
Cory Luebke
12 D. J. Strawberry 6.00 15.00
Brett Cecil EXCH

2007 Donruss Elite Extra Edition Collegiate Patches

OVERALL AUTO/MEM ODDS 1:5
PRINT RUNS B/WN 25-250 COPIES PER
NO PRICING ON QTY 25 OR LESS
5 Dale Brown/250 12.50 30.00
6 Dean Smith/250 30.00 60.00
7 Eddie Sutton/250 10.00 25.00
9 Gene Keady/250 10.00 25.00
11 Jim Boeheim/250 10.00 25.00
12 Sheryl Swoopes/250 12.50 30.00
13 Norm Stewart/250 10.00 25.00
14 Rebecca Lobo/250 10.00 25.00
21 Bill Walton/50 15.00 40.00
22 Sidney Moncrief/250 6.00 15.00
23 Dominique Wilkins/100 10.00 25.00
43 Aaron Gray/250 6.00 15.00
44 Daequan Cook/250 6.00 15.00
46 Rick Majeras/250 EXCH 6.00 15.00
47 Taurean Green/250 6.00 15.00
49 Bobby Hurley/250 EXCH 10.00 25.00
50 Muggsy Bogues/250 10.00 25.00
51 Jerry Tarkanian/250 6.00 15.00
53 Lynette Woodard/249 6.00 15.00

2007 Donruss Elite Extra Edition School Colors

OVERALL INSERT ODDS 1:4
STATED PRINT RUN 1500 SER.#'d SETS
8 Alando Tucker .75 2.00
9 Daequan Cook .75 2.00
10 Eddie Sutton .75 2.00
11 Dean Smith .75 2.00
14 Don Haskins .75 2.00
15 Jerry Tarkanian .75 2.00
16 Rick Majerus .75 2.00
17 Rollie Massimino .75 2.00
19 Dale Brown .75 2.00
21 Gene Keady .75 2.00
22 Jim Boeheim .75 2.00
23 Norm Stewart .75 2.00
25 Bill Walton .75 2.00

2007 Donruss Elite Extra Edition School Colors Autographs

OVERALL AUTO/MEM ODDS 1:5
PRINT RUNS B/WN 10-50 COPIES PER
NO PRICING ON QTY 25 OR LESS
EXCHANGE DEADLINE 07/01/2009
8 Alando Tucker/50 6.00 15.00
9 Daequan Cook/50 6.00 15.00
14 Don Haskins/25 12.50 30.00
21 Gene Keady/25 12.50 30.00
25 Bill Walton/25 15.00 40.00

2007 Donruss Elite Extra Edition Signature Aspirations

OVERALL AU/MEM ODDS 1:5
PRINT RUNS B/WN 5-100 COPIES PER
NO PRICING ON QTY 25 OR LESS
EXCHANGE DEADLINE 07/01/2007
57 Aaron Gray/100 4.00 10.00
58 Daequan Cook/50 10.00 25.00
61 Taurean Green/75 4.00 10.00
62 Don Haskins/100 4.00 10.00
63 Jerry Tarkanian/50 5.00 12.00
64 Rick Majerus/100 4.00 10.00
69 Eddie Sutton/50 5.00 12.00
71 Gene Keady/50 5.00 12.00
72 Jim Boeheim/100 5.00 12.00
80 Rebecca Lobo/100 6.00 15.00
83 Elvin Hayes/100 4.00 10.00
85 Bill Walton/100 6.00 15.00
86 Sidney Moncrief/50 5.00 12.00
87 Dominique Wilkins/50 10.00 25.00
90 Muggsy Bogues/100 4.00 10.00
137 Alando Tucker/50 5.00 12.00
139 Marc Gasol/50 EXCH 10.00 25.00
140 Stephane Lasme/100 4.00 10.00

2007 Donruss Elite Extra Edition Signature Status

OVERALL AU/MEM ODDS 1:5
PRINT RUNS B/WN 1-50 COPIES PER
NO PRICING ON QTY 25 OR LESS
EXCHANGE DEADLINE 07/01/2007
57 Aaron Gray/50 6.00 15.00
61 Taurean Green/29 6.00 15.00
62 Don Haskins/50 6.00 15.00
64 Rick Majerus/50 6.00 15.00
69 Eddie Sutton/25 12.50 30.00
72 Jim Boeheim/50 8.00 20.00
80 Rebecca Lobo/50 10.00 25.00
83 Elvin Hayes/50 6.00 15.00
85 Bill Walton/50 10.00 25.00
86 Sidney Moncrief/25 6.00 15.00
87 Dominique Wilkins/25 20.00 50.00
90 Muggsy Bogues/50 6.00 15.00
140 Stephane Lasme/50 6.00 15.00

2007 Donruss Elite Extra Edition Signature Turn of the Century

OVERALL AU/MEM ODDS 1:5
PRINT RUNS B/WN 10-500 COPIES PER
NO PRICING ON QTY 25 OR LESS
EXCHANGE DEADLINE 07/01/2007
57 Aaron Gray/500 4.00 10.00
58 Daequan Cook/494 4.00 10.00
61 Taurean Green/500 4.00 10.00
62 Don Haskins/194 5.00 12.00
63 Jerry Tarkanian/144 5.00 12.00
64 Rick Majerus/194 5.00 12.00
67 Dale Brown/89 6.00 15.00
69 Eddie Sutton/144 6.00 15.00
71 Gene Keady/144 5.00 12.00
80 Rebecca Lobo/234 6.00 15.00
83 Elvin Hayes/344 4.00 10.00
86 Sidney Moncrief/169 4.00 10.00
90 Muggsy Bogues/94 6.00 15.00
137 Alando Tucker/100 4.00 10.00
140 Stephane Lasme/145 5.00 12.00

2007 Donruss Elite Extra Edition Throwback Threads

OVERALL AUTO/MEM ODDS 1:5
PRINT RUNS B/WN 44-500 COPIES PER
21 Dale Brown/500 3.00 8.00
22 Don Haskins/500 3.00 8.00

2007 Donruss Elite Extra Edition Throwback Threads Prime

*PRIME: .75X TO 2X BASIC
OVERALL AUTO/MEM ODDS 1:5
PRINT RUNS B/WN 3-50 COPIES PER
NO PRICING ON QTY 25 OR LESS

2007 Donruss Elite Extra Edition Throwback Threads Autographs

OVERALL AUTO/MEM ODDS 1:5
PRINT RUNS B/WN 50-100 COPIES PER
EXCHANGE DEADLINE 07/01/2009
21 Dale Brown/50 6.00 15.00
22 Don Haskins/100 12.50 30.00

2008 Donruss Elite Extra Edition

This set was released on November 26, 2008. The base set consists of 199 cards.
COMP.SET w/o AU's (100) 10.00 25.00
COMMON CARD (1-100) .20 .50
COMMON AU (101-200) 3.00 8.00
RANDOM INSERTS IN PACKS
PRINT RUNS B/WN 99-1495
EXCH DEADLINE 5/26/2010
198 Derrick Rose AU/99 125.00 250.00
199 Michael Beasley AU/99 30.00 60.00
200 O.J. Mayo AU/99 40.00 80.00

2008 Donruss Elite Extra Edition Aspirations

*ASP 1-100: 2.5X TO 6X BASIC
RANDOM INSERTS IN PACKS
STATED PRINT RUN 150 SER.#'d SETS
198 Derrick Rose 20.00 50.00
199 Michael Beasley 6.00 15.00
200 O.J. Mayo 3.00 8.00

2008 Donruss Elite Extra Edition Status

*STATUS 1-100: 4X TO 10X BASIC
*STATUS 101-200: .6X TO 1.5X ASP
RANDOM INSERTS IN PACKS
STATED PRINT RUN 50 SER.#'d SETS
198 Derrick Rose 40.00 80.00
199 Michael Beasley 10.00 25.00
200 O.J. Mayo 6.00 15.00

2008 Donruss Elite Extra Edition Collegiate Patches Autographs

OVERALL AUTO/MEM ODDS 1:5
PRINT RUNS B/WN 20-255 COPIES PER
NO PRICING ON QTY 25 OR LESS
EXCH DEADLINE 5/26/2010
4 O.J. Mayo/50 20.00 50.00
7 Michael Beasley/100 15.00 40.00

2008 Donruss Elite Extra Edition School Colors

OVERALL INSERT ODDS 1:2
STATED PRINT RUN 1500 SER.#'d SET
4 O.J. Mayo 1.25 3.00
7 Michael Beasley 1.25 3.00
9 Derrick Rose 5.00 12.00

2008 Donruss Elite Extra Edition School Colors Autographs

OVERALL AUTO/MEM ODDS 1:5
PRINT RUNS B/WN 25-50 COPIES PER
NO PRICING ON QTY 25 OR LESS
EXCH DEADLINE 5/26/2010
4 O.J. Mayo/25 20.00 50.00
7 Michael Beasley/25 20.00 50.00
9 Derrick Rose/25 60.00 150.00

2008 Donruss Elite Extra Edition School Colors Materials

OVERALL AU/MEM ODDS 1:5
STATED PRINT RUN 100 SER.#'d SETS
4 O.J. Mayo 6.00 15.00
7 Michael Beasley 6.00 15.00
9 Derrick Rose 20.00 50.00

2008 Donruss Elite Extra Edition Signature Aspirations

OVERALL AU/MEM ODDS 1:5
PRINT RUN B/WN 5-100 COPIES PER
NO PRICING ON QTY 25 OR LESS
EXCH DEADLINE 5/26/2010
200 O.J. Mayo/25 20.00 50.00

2008 Donruss Elite Extra Edition Signature Status

OVERALL AUTO/MEM ODDS 1:5
PRINT RUN B/WN 5-50 COPIES PER
NO PRICING ON QTY 25 OR LESS
EXCH DEADLINE 5/26/2010

2008 Donruss Elite Extra Edition Signature Turn of the Century

OVERALL AUTO/MEM ODDS 1:5
PRINT RUNS B/WN 8-999 COPIES PER
EXCH DEADLINE 5/26/2010
198 Derrick Rose/25 125.00 250.00
199 Michael Beasley/25 30.00 80.00
200 O.J. Mayo/25 30.00 80.00

2008 Donruss Elite Extra Edition Throwback Threads

OVERALL AU/MEM ODDS 1:5
PRINT RUNS B/WN 15-500 COPIES PER
NO PRICING ON QTY 25 OR LESS
10 Derrick Rose/500 12.50 30.00
11 Michael Beasley/500 8.00 20.00
12 O.J. Mayo/400 6.00 15.00

2008 Donruss Elite Extra Edition Throwback Threads Prime

OVERALL AU/MEM ODDS 1:5
PRINT RUNS B/WN 1-50 COPIES PER
NO PRICING ON QTY 10 OR LESS

2008 Donruss Elite Extra Edition Throwback Threads Autographs

OVERALL AUTO/MEM ODDS 1:5
PRINT RUNS B/WN 4-100 COPIES PER
NO PRICING ON QTY 25 OR LESS
EXCH DEADLINE 5/26/2010
10 Derrick Rose/25 125.00 250.00
11 Michael Beasley/25 20.00 50.00
12 O.J. Mayo/25 20.00 50.00

2008 Donruss Elite Extra Edition Throwback Threads Autographs Prime

OVERALL AUTO/MEM ODDS 1:5
PRINT RUNS B/WN 1-25 COPIES PER
NO PRICING DUE TO SCARCITY
EXCH DEADLINE 5/26/2010

2010 Donruss Elite National Convention

ANNOUNCED PRINT RUN 499 SETS
21 Blake Griffin 2.00 5.00
22 Brandon Jennings 1.25 3.00
23 Carmelo Anthony 1.25 3.00
24 Chris Bosh 2.00 5.00
25 DeMarcus Cousins 6.00 15.00
26 Derrick Favors 4.00 10.00
27 Derrick Rose 2.00 5.00
28 Dirk Nowitzki 1.25 3.00
29 Dwight Howard 1.25 3.00
30 Dwyane Wade 2.00 5.00
31 Evan Turner 4.00 10.00
32 John Wall 10.00 25.00
33 Kevin Durant 2.00 5.00
34 Kobe Bryant 3.00 8.00
35 Larry Bird 2.00 5.00
36 LeBron James 8.00 20.00
37 Magic Johnson 1.50 4.00
38 Rajon Rondo 1.25 3.00
39 Tyreke Evans 1.25 3.00
40 Wesley Johnson 3.00 8.00

2010 Donruss Elite National Convention Aspirations

*ASPIRATIONS: .8X TO 2X BASIC CARDS
ANNOUNCED PRINT RUN 50

2010 Donruss Elite National Convention Status

*STATUS: .8X TO 2X BASIC CARDS
ANNOUNCED PRINT RUN 25

2010 Donruss Elite National Convention Autographs

STATED PRINT RUN 1-25
21 Blake Griffin/25 80.00 200.00
22 Brandon Jennings/25 15.00 40.00
25 DeMarcus Cousins/25 40.00 100.00
40 Wesley Johnson/25 20.00 50.00

2011 Donruss Elite National Convention

ANNOUNCED PRINT RUN 500 SETS
*BLUE/10: 2X TO 5X BASIC CARDS
*RED/25: 1.5X TO 4X BASIC CARDS
8 Blake Griffin 1.50 4.00
9 Dirk Nowitzki 1.25 3.00
10 John Wall 1.50 4.00
11 Kevin Durant 1.50 4.00
12 Kobe Bryant 1.50 4.00

1996 Donruss Kazaam Promo

The front of this standard-size card has a white background with a color picture of Shaquille O'Neal as "Kazaam" emanating from an oversized stereo. The kid actor from the movie sits perched on the stereo. The back has a yellow background with another picture of "Kazzam" and a promotional blurb about the forthcoming Donruss Kazaam set. The word "prototype" appears in purple in the top left corner. The card is not numbered.
NNO Shaquille O'Neal 1.50 4.00
(as Kazaam)

2008 Donruss Sports Legends

This set was released on December 10, 2008. The base set consists of 144 cards and features cards of players from various sports.
COMPLETE SET (144) 40.00 100.00
3 Larry Bird 1.25 3.00
7 Oscar Robertson .60 1.50
12 John Wooden .75 2.00
14 Clyde Lovellette .50 1.25
19 Dan Issel .50 1.25
22 Elvin Hayes .60 1.50
25 Kevin McHale .60 1.50
26 Sidney Moncrief .50 1.25
32 Walt Frazier .50 1.25
39 Bobby Wanzer .50 1.25
42 Marques Haynes .50 1.25
44 Dolph Schayes .50 1.25
47 Dominique Wilkins .60 1.50
49 Alex English .50 1.25
52 Robert Parish .50 1.25
55 Bailey Howell .40 1.00
57 Don Haskins .40 1.00
61 Dean Smith .50 1.25
62 Rollie Massimino .50 1.25
67 Dick Vitale .50 1.25
72 Rick Majerus .50 1.25
74 Al Cervi .40 1.00
76 Lisa Leslie .60 1.50
77 Jerry West .75 2.00
86 Wes Unseld .50 1.25
87 Bill Walton .60 1.50
89 Arnie Risen .50 1.25
92 Dennis Rodman .60 1.50
97 Jim Boeheim .40 1.00
102 Jerry Tarkanian .50 1.25
107 Lynette Woodard .40 1.00
112 Muggsy Bogues .50 1.25
117 Sheryl Swoopes .60 1.50
121 Nate Thurmond .50 1.25
124 Cliff Hagan .50 1.25
134 George Gervin .50 1.25
146 Bobby Hurley .50 1.25
147 Eddie Sutton .50 1.25
149 David Thompson .60 1.50

2008 Donruss Sports Legends Mirror Blue

*BLUE/100: 2X TO 5X BASIC CARDS
STATED PRINT RUN 100 SER.#'d SETS

2008 Donruss Sports Legends Mirror Gold

*GOLD/25: 3X TO 8X BASIC CARDS
STATED PRINT RUN 25 SER.#'d SETS

2008 Donruss Sports Legends Mirror Red

*RED/250: 1.5X TO 4X BASIC CARDS
STATED PRINT RUN 250 SER.#'d SETS

2008 Donruss Sports Legends Museum Collection

SILVER PRINT RUN 1000 SER.#'d SETS
*GOLD/100: .6X TO 1.5X SILVER/1000
GOLD PRINT RUN 100 SER.#'d SETS
19 Robert Parish 1.25 3.00
23 Dominique Wilkins 1.50 4.00
30 Bill Walton 1.50 4.00

2008 Donruss Sports Legends Museum Collection Materials

STATED PRINT RUN 25-250
*PRIME/25: .6X TO 1.5X BASIC MATERIAL
PRIME PRINT RUN 1-25
SERIAL #'d UNDER 25 NOT PRICED
23 Dominique Wilkins/100 5.00 12.00

2008 Donruss Sports Legends Certified Cuts

STATED PRINT RUN 1-100
SERIAL #'d TO 1 NOT PRICED
1 Jerry West/50 30.00 60.00
4 Nate Thurmond 15.00 40.00
Nate the Great/49
6 Larry Bird/50 50.00 100.00
7a Dennis Rodman 30.00 60.00
The Worm/40
7b Dennis Rodman 30.00 60.00
Double Team/20
8a Dick Vitale 30.00 60.00
Call the Fire Chief/10
8b Dick Vitale 30.00 60.00
Cyclops/10
8c Dick Vitale 30.00 60.00
Diaper Dandy/10
8d Dick Vitale 30.00 60.00
Dickie V/10
8e Dick Vitale 30.00 60.00
It's Awesome Baby/10
8f Dick Vitale 30.00 60.00
Maalox Masher/10
8g Dick Vitale 30.00 60.00
Mr. College Basketball/10
8h Dick Vitale 30.00 60.00
PTPer/10
8i Dick Vitale 30.00 60.00
Dipsy Doo Dunkeroo/10
8j Dick Vitale 30.00 60.00
Slap A Lapper/10
8k Dick Vitale 30.00 60.00
Trifecta/10
9a Marques Haynes 25.00 50.00
Harlem Globetrotters/20
9b Marques Haynes 25.00 50.00
HOF '98/20
10 Oscar Robertson/50 60.00 100.00
11 Robert Parish/100 8.00 20.00
12 John Wooden/20 125.00 250.00
23 George Gervin 25.00 50.00
Iceman/50

2008 Donruss Sports Legends Champions

SILVER PRINT RUN 1000 SER.#'d SETS
*GOLD/100: .6X TO 1.5X SILVER/1000
GOLD PRINT RUN 100 SER.#'d SETS
1 Jerry West 2.00 5.00
7 Larry Bird 3.00 8.00
10 Dolph Schayes 1.25 3.00
13 Cliff Hagan 1.25 3.00
15 Bill Walton 1.50 4.00
16 Dan Issel 1.25 3.00

2008 Donruss Sports Legends Champions Materials

STATED PRINT RUN 10-250
1 Jerry West Jsy/250 6.00 15.00
16 Dan Issel Jsy/100 4.00 10.00

2008 Donruss Sports Legends Champions Signatures

STATED PRINT RUN 1-100
SERIAL #'d UNDER 25 NOT PRICED
1 Jerry West/50 30.00 50.00
10 Dolph Schayes/100 8.00 20.00
13 Cliff Hagan/100 6.00 15.00
15 Bill Walton/25 25.00 50.00
16 Dan Issel/100 6.00 15.00

2008 Donruss Sports Legends College Heroes

SILVER PRINT RUN 1000 SER.#'d SETS
*GOLD/100: .6X TO 1.5X SILVER/1000
GOLD PRINT RUN 100 SER.#'d SETS
6 Oscar Robertson 1.50 4.00
7 Elvin Hayes 1.50 4.00
9 Dan Issel 1.25 3.00

2008 Donruss Sports Legends College Heroes Materials

STATED PRINT RUN 50-250
6 Oscar Robertson Jsy/250 5.00 12.00
7 Elvin Hayes Jsy/250 5.00 12.00
9 Dan Issel Jsy/250 4.00 10.00

2008 Donruss Sports Legends College Heroes Signatures

STATED PRINT RUN 25-100
6 Oscar Robertson/25 20.00 40.00
7 Elvin Hayes/100 6.00 15.00
9 Dan Issel/100 6.00 15.00

2008 Donruss Sports Legends Collegiate Legends Patch Autographs

STATED PRINT RUN 25-250
4 Lisa Leslie/250 8.00 20.00
5 Oscar Robertson/50 60.00 100.00
6 Jerry West/52 30.00 60.00
10 Arnie Risen/98 8.00 20.00
11 John Wooden/100 75.00 150.00
13 John Wooden/25 75.00 150.00
15 Dan Issel/100 20.00 40.00
16 Elvin Hayes/100 15.00 40.00
17 Clyde Lovellette/100 8.00 20.00
18 Alex English/100 EXCH 12.00 30.00
19 David Thompson/100 15.00 40.00
20 Cliff Hagan/99 15.00 40.00
23 Wes Unseld/100 10.00 25.00

2008 Donruss Sports Legends Legends of the Game Combos

STATED PRINT RUN 25-100
UNPRICED PRIME PRINT RUN 1-10
6 Ted Williams Jsy 30.00 60.00
Larry Bird Jsy/25
8 Earl Campbell JsyII 6.00 15.00
Elvin Hayes Jsy
9 Hank Aaron Bat 8.00 20.00
Dominique Wilkins Jsy

2008 Donruss Sports Legends Materials Mirror Blue

*MIRROR BLUE: .5X TO 1.2X MIRROR RED
MIRROR BLUE PRINT RUN 5-250
SERIAL #'d UNDER 15 NOT PRICED
3 Larry Bird/25 10.00 25.00
72 Rick Majerus/100 5.00 12.00

2008 Donruss Sports Legends Materials Mirror Gold

*GOLD/25: .8X TO 2X MIRROR RED
GOLD PRINT RUN 1-25 SER.#'d SETS
SERIAL #'d UNDER 20 NOT PRICED
76 Lisa Leslie/20 5.00 12.00

2008 Donruss Sports Legends Materials Mirror Red

MIRROR RED PRINT RUN 10-500
SERIAL #'d UNDER 25 NOT PRICED
*GOLD/25: .8X TO 2X MIRROR RED
UNPRICED MIRROR EMERALD PRINT RUN 1-5
UNPRICED MIRROR BLACK PRINT RUN 1
7 Oscar Robertson Jsy/500 4.00 10.00
19 Dan Issel Jsy/500 4.00 10.00
22 Elvin Hayes Jsy/500 4.00 10.00
26 Sidney Moncrief Jsy/475 4.00 10.00
32 Walt Frazier Jsy/500 3.00 8.00
42 Marques Haynes Jsy/500 3.00 8.00
47 Dominique Wilkins Jsy/300 4.00 10.00
52 Robert Parish Jsy/350 3.00 8.00
55 Bailey Howell Jsy/500 2.50 6.00
57 Don Haskins Shirt/475 2.50 6.00
62 Rollie Massimino Shirt/500 3.00 8.00
72 Rick Majerus Sweater/400 3.00 8.00
77 Jerry West Jsy/500 5.00 12.00
86 Wes Unseld Jsy/500 3.00 8.00
112 Muggsy Bogues Jsy/500 3.00 8.00

2008 Donruss Sports Legends Museum Curator Collection Materials

STATED PRINT RUN 10-100
*PRIME/25: .6X TO 1.5X BASIC MATERIAL
PRIME PRINT RUN 1-25
SERIAL #'d UNDER 25 NOT PRICED
23 Dominique Wilkins/25 8.00 20.00

2008 Donruss Sports Legends Museum Collection Signatures

STATED PRINT RUN 1-250
SERIAL #'d UNDER 25 NOT PRICED
19 Robert Parish/50 10.00 25.00
30 Bill Walton/25 25.00 50.00

2008 Donruss Sports Legends Signature Connection Combos

STATED PRINT RUN 25-100
1 Larry Bird 90.00 150.00
Kevin McHale
5 Elvin Hayes 20.00 40.00
Earl Campbell
6 Gale Sayers 20.00 40.00
Lynette Woodard
8 Lance Alworth 90.00 150.00
Sidney Moncrief/10
9 Bill Walton 100.00 200.00
John Wooden
12 Troy Aikman 60.00 100.00
Bill Walton

2008 Donruss Sports Legends Signature Connection Triples

STATED PRINT RUN 25-250
1 Larry Bird 150.00 250.00
Robert Parish
Kevin McHale/25
3 Lynette Woodard 30.00 60.00
Marques Haynes
Bob Gibson/50

2008 Donruss Sports Legends Signatures Mirror Blue

MIRROR BLUE PRINT RUN 2-250
SERIAL #'d UNDER 10 NOT PRICED
UNPRICED MIRROR EMERALD PRINT RUN 1-5
UNPRICED MIRROR BLACK PRINT RUN 1
3 Larry Bird/2
7 Oscar Robertson/15 20.00 50.00
12 John Wooden/25 100.00 200.00
14 Clyde Lovellette/150 5.00 12.00
19 Dan Issel/100 6.00 15.00
22 Elvin Hayes/25 10.00 25.00
25 Kevin McHale/100 40.00 80.00
32 Walt Frazier/50 8.00 20.00
39 Bobby Wanzer/250 5.00 12.00
42 Marques Haynes/50 12.00 30.00
44 Dolph Schayes/150 8.00 20.00
52 Robert Parish/50 10.00 25.00
55 Bailey Howell/250 4.00 10.00
62 Rollie Massimino/50 6.00 15.00
67 Dick Vitale/25 15.00 40.00
72 Rick Majerus/15 8.00 20.00
74 Al Cervi/250 4.00 10.00
76 Lisa Leslie/100 8.00 20.00
77 Jerry West/25 30.00 60.00
86 Wes Unseld/50 5.00 12.00
87 Bill Walton/25 20.00 40.00
89 Arnie Risen/250 6.00 15.00
92 Dennis Rodman/50 15.00 40.00
107 Lynette Woodard/50 10.00 25.00
121 Nate Thurmond/100 6.00 15.00
124 Cliff Hagan/150 6.00 15.00
134 George Gervin/50 6.00 15.00
147 Eddie Sutton/27 8.00 20.00
149 David Thompson/250 5.00 12.00

2008 Donruss Sports Legends Signatures Mirror Gold

MIRROR GOLD PRINT RUN 4-25
SERIAL #'d UNDER 10 NOT PRICED
3 Larry Bird/10
7 Oscar Robertson/10 25.00 60.00
12 John Wooden/10 125.00 250.00
14 Clyde Lovellette/25 8.00 20.00
19 Dan Issel/25 8.00 20.00
22 Elvin Hayes/10 12.00 30.00
25 Kevin McHale/25 50.00 100.00
32 Walt Frazier/25 10.00 25.00
39 Bobby Wanzer/25 8.00 20.00
42 Marques Haynes/25 15.00 40.00
44 Dolph Schayes/25 12.00 30.00
52 Robert Parish/25 12.00 30.00
55 Bailey Howell/25 6.00 15.00
62 Rollie Massimino/25 8.00 20.00
67 Dick Vitale/10 20.00 50.00
72 Rick Majerus/10 10.00 25.00
74 Al Cervi/25 6.00 15.00
76 Lisa Leslie/25 10.00 25.00
77 Jerry West/10 30.00 80.00
86 Wes Unseld/25 6.00 15.00
87 Bill Walton/10 20.00 50.00
89 Arnie Risen/25 10.00 25.00
92 Dennis Rodman/25 20.00 50.00
107 Lynette Woodard/25 12.00 30.00
121 Nate Thurmond/25 8.00 20.00
124 Cliff Hagan/25 10.00 25.00
134 George Gervin/25 8.00 20.00
147 Eddie Sutton/10 10.00 25.00
149 David Thompson/25 8.00 20.00

2008 Donruss Sports Legends Signatures Mirror Red

*MIRROR RED: .3X TO .8X MIRROR BLUE
MIRROR RED PRINT RUN 25-1370
7 Oscar Robertson/25 15.00 40.00
12 John Wooden/25 100.00 200.00
14 Clyde Lovellette/659 4.00 10.00
19 Dan Issel/501 5.00 12.00
22 Elvin Hayes/79 8.00 20.00
25 Kevin McHale/369 25.00 60.00
32 Walt Frazier/158 6.00 15.00
39 Bobby Wanzer/658 4.00 10.00
42 Marques Haynes/337 10.00 25.00
44 Dolph Schayes/655 6.00 15.00
52 Robert Parish/211 8.00 20.00
55 Bailey Howell/664 3.00 8.00
62 Rollie Massimino/333 5.00 12.00
67 Dick Vitale/133 12.00 30.00
74 Al Cervi/619 3.00 8.00
76 Lisa Leslie/396 6.00 15.00
77 Jerry West/25 25.00 60.00
86 Wes Unseld/283 4.00 10.00
87 Bill Walton/259 12.00 30.00
89 Arnie Risen/558 5.00 12.00
92 Dennis Rodman/179 12.00 30.00
107 Lynette Woodard/112 8.00 20.00
121 Nate Thurmond/270 5.00 12.00
124 Cliff Hagan/556 5.00 12.00
134 George Gervin/287 5.00 12.00
149 David Thompson/767 4.00 10.00

2008 Donruss Threads Diamond Kings

RANDOM INSERTS IN PACKS
*GOLD: .6X TO 1.5X BASIC
GOLD RANDOMLY INSERTED
GOLD PRINT RUN 100 SER.#'d SETS
FRM.BLK.RANDOMLY INSERTED
FRM.BLK.PRINT RUN 10 SER.#'d SETS
NO FRM.BLK PRINCING AVAILABLE
*FRM.BLUE: .75X TO 2X BASIC
FRM.BLUE RANDOMLY INSERTS
FRM.BLUE PRINT RUN 50 SER.#'d SETS
FRM.GRN.RANDOMLY INSERTED
FRM.GRN.PRINT RUN 25 SER.#'d SETS
NO FRM.GRN PRINCING AVAILABLE
*FRM.RED: .6X TO 1.5X BASIC
FRM.RED RANDOMLY INSERTS
FRM.RED PRINT RUN 100 SER.#'d SETS
PLAT.RANDOMLY INSERTED
PLAT.PRINT RUN 25 SER.#'d SETS
NO PLAT.PRINCING AVAILABLE
*SILVER: .5X TO 1.2X.BASIC
SILVER RANDOMLY INSERTS
SILVER PRINT RUN 250 SER.#'d SETS
53 Derrick Rose 1.50 4.00
54 Michael Beasley 1.50 4.00
55 O.J. Mayo 1.50 4.00

2008 Donruss Threads Diam Kings Signatures

RANDOM INSERTS IN PACKS
PRINT RUNS B/WN 5-500 COPIES PER
NO PRICING ON QTY 25 OR LESS
53 Derrick Rose/60 100.00 2

1990 88's Calgary WBL

Measuring roughly 13 1/2" by 20 1/4", this shee player cards (and 6 game ticket discount coupor features the Calgary 88's of the World Basketbal League. The sheet was perforated longitudinally, yielding four 6-card strips and a strip of 6 coupo the sheet was perforated and the cards cut, they measure the standard size. On a white card face, fronts feature posed color player photos or color shots. The team logo and various sponsor logos overlay the pictures at each corner. In black prin white, the backs carry biography, statistics, or pl profile. The coupons entitled the holder to $2.0 any $5.00 or $7.00 seat at any 1990 regular sea home game.
COMPLETE SET (24) 15.00
1 David Boone .60
2 Scott Hicks .60
3 Dwayne McClain 1.25
4 Chip Engelland 2.00
Driving to hoop)
5 Perry Young 1.25
6 Chip Engelland 1.50
7 Steve Smith .60
8 Jim Thomas .75
(Setting up play)
9 George Jackson .60
(Dunking)
10 George Jackson .60
11 Perry Young .60
12 Carlos Clark 1.25
(Dribbling)
13 Dave Henderson .60
(Shooting)
14 Carlos Clark 1.25
15 John Hegwood .60
16 Perry Young .60
(Shooting)
17 Chip Engelland 1.50
(Shooting)
18 Sean Chambers .60
19 Carlos Clark 1.25
(Shooting)
20 1989 WBL Playoffs .75
(Jim Thomas)
21 1989 WBL Playoffs .60
(Final Standings on back)
22 Jim Thomas .75
23 Team Photo .60
24 Perry Young .60
(Rebounding)

2010-11 Elite Black Box

STATED PRINT RUN 99 SER.#'d SETS
UNPRICED ASPIRATIONS PRINT RUN 5 SETS
1 LeBron James 10.00
2 Dirk Nowitzki 2.50
3 Kevin Durant 6.00
4 Kobe Bryant 10.00
5 Carmelo Anthony 2.50
6 LaMarcus Aldridge 2.00
7 Al Horford 1.50
8 Kevin Garnett 4.00
9 Chris Paul 3.00
10 Dwight Howard 3.00
11 Dwyane Wade 4.00
12 Blake Griffin 5.00
13 Andrea Bargnani 1.50
14 Kevin Love 2.50
15 Zach Randolph 1.50
16 Ray Allen 2.00
17 Derrick Rose 6.00
18 Monta Ellis 2.00
19 Danny Granger 2.00
20 Ty Lawson 2.00
21 Tony Parker 2.00
22 Brook Lopez 2.00
23 Eric Gordon 2.00
24 Russell Westbrook 2.50
25 Tyson Chandler 1.50
26 Vince Carter 2.50
27 Amare Stoudemire 2.00
28 Kevin Martin 2.00
29 Joe Johnson 2.00
30 Stephen Jackson 1.50
31 JaVale McGee 1.50
32 Chauncey Billups 2.00
33 Paul Pierce 2.50
34 Darren Collison 2.00
35 Serge Ibaka 2.50
36 J.J. Barea 2.00
37 Chris Bosh 2.00
38 Al Jefferson 2.00
39 Rudy Gay 2.00
40 Deron Williams 2.00
41 David West 2.00
42 Luis Scola 1.50
43 Antawn Jamison 2.00
44 Brandon Jennings 2.00
45 Stephen Curry 2.50
46 Steve Nash 2.00
47 Chris Kaman 1.50

dre Iguodala 2.00 5.00
akim Noah 2.00 5.00
andon Roy 2.00 5.00
drei Kirilenko 1.50 4.00
meer Nelson 1.50 4.00
e Holiday 2.00 5.00
n Gordon 2.00 5.00
rc Gasol 2.00 5.00
rald Wallace 2.00 5.00
jon Rondo 2.50 6.00
n Duncan 3.00 8.00
u Gasol 2.00 5.00
chael Beasley 2.00 5.00
reke Evans 2.50 6.00
vid Lee 1.50 4.00
Mar DeRozan 2.00 5.00
esley Matthews 2.00 5.00
sh Smith 2.00 5.00
wan Howard 1.50 4.00
ne 1.50 4.00
mes Harden 2.50 6.00
vin Harris 2.00 5.00
on Brand 2.00 5.00
neka Okafor 2.00 5.00
son Terry 1.50 4.00
ol Deng 2.00 5.00
ck Young 1.50 4.00
nilo Gallinari 2.00 5.00
rlos Boozer 2.00 5.00
drew Bogut 2.00 5.00
ymond Felton 1.50 4.00
ron Davis 2.00 5.00
nu Ginobili 2.00 5.00
mal Crawford 1.50 4.00
n Wallace 2.00 5.00
son Kidd 2.00 5.00
vor Ariza 1.25 3.00
ndrick Perkins 1.50 4.00
drew Bynum 2.50 6.00
ron Brooks 1.25 3.00
y Hibbert 1.50 4.00
ck Collison 1.25 3.00
. Redick 2.00 5.00
. Smith 2.00 5.00
s Humphries 1.25 3.00
nny Flynn 1.25 3.00
andon Bass 1.25 3.00
Gibson 1.50 4.00
rald Henderson 1.25 3.00
n Davis 1.50 4.00
Juan Blair 1.50 4.00
acy McGrady 2.00 5.00
amuel Dalembert 1.25 3.00
Vilt Chamberlain 5.00 12.00
arl Malone 2.50 6.00
ulius Erving 4.00 10.00
alen Rose 2.00 5.00
lex English 2.00 5.00
lonzo Mourning 2.50 6.00
avid Robinson 3.00 8.00
evin Johnson 2.00 5.00
evin McHale 2.00 5.00
haquille O'Neal 4.00 10.00
es Unseld 2.00 5.00
alt Frazier 2.00 5.00
eorge Gervin 2.00 5.00
ary Payton 2.00 5.00
gin Baylor 2.00 5.00
ob McAdoo 2.00 5.00
ominique Wilkins 2.50 6.00
eorge Mikan 4.00 10.00
enny Wilkens 2.00 5.00
rry West 2.50 6.00
akeem Olajuwon 2.50 6.00
enny Smith 2.00 5.00
lyde Drexler 2.50 6.00
ate Thurmond 2.00 5.00
hn Havlicek 2.50 6.00
arryl Dawkins 2.00 5.00
arrell Griffith 2.00 5.00
anny Manning 2.00 5.00
an Issel 2.00 5.00
rry Bird 6.00 15.00
m Perkins 2.00 5.00
ll Laimbeer 2.00 5.00
hawn Bradley 2.00 5.00
mes Worthy 2.50 6.00
edric Maxwell 2.00 5.00
ailey Howell 2.00 5.00
agic Johnson 5.00 12.00
elly Tripucka 2.00 5.00
kembe Mutombo 2.00 5.00
ristian Laettner 2.50 6.00
ob Lanier 2.00 5.00
ark Eaton 2.00 5.00
oni Kukoc 2.00 5.00
arl Monroe 2.00 5.00
en Rice 2.00 5.00
arry Johnson 2.50 6.00
ki Vandeweghe 2.00 5.00
hris Webber 2.00 5.00
n Harper 2.00 5.00
reem Abdul-Jabbar 3.00 8.00
m Jones 2.00 5.00
pencer Haywood 2.00 5.00
ennis Scott 2.00 5.00
vin Hayes 2.00 5.00
obert Horry 2.50 6.00
anute Bol 2.00 5.00
evin Willis 2.00 5.00
hris Mullin 2.00 5.00
ah Thomas 2.00 5.00
ve Cowens 2.00 5.00
car Robertson 2.50 6.00
ck Barry 2.00 5.00
van Adams 2.00 5.00
avier McDaniel 2.00 5.00
eepy Floyd 2.00 5.00
ark Aguirre 2.00 5.00
ark Price 2.00 5.00
ernard King 2.00 5.00
e Dumars 2.00 5.00
eggie Lewis 2.00 5.00
chael Cooper 2.00 5.00
obert Parish 2.00 5.00
anny Ainge 2.00 5.00
aurice Cheeks 2.00 5.00
dney Moncrief 2.00 5.00
tis Gilmore 2.00 5.00
ff Hornacek 2.00 5.00
ennis Rodman 8.00 20.00
m Chambers 2.00 5.00
n Hardaway 2.00 5.00
tch Richmond 2.00 5.00
e Maravich 6.00 15.00
trick Ewing 2.50 6.00

184 Walt Bellamy 2.00 5.00
185 Vlade Divac 2.00 5.00
186 Steve Smith 2.00 5.00
187 Rolando Blackman 2.00 5.00
188 M.L. Carr 2.00 5.00
189 Kurt Rambis 2.00 5.00
190 Kenny Walker 2.00 5.00
191 Jamal Mashburn 2.00 5.00
192 Connie Hawkins 2.00 5.00
193 Dan Majerle 2.00 5.00
194 Adrian Dantley 2.00 5.00
195 Al Attles 2.00 5.00
196 Ralph Sampson 2.00 5.00
197 Walter Berry 2.00 5.00
198 Bill Russell 3.00 8.00
199 Bill Walton 2.00 5.00
200 World B. Free 2.00 5.00

2010-11 Elite Black Box All-Star Matchups Materials Prime

STATED PRINT RUN 25 SER.#'d SETS
1 Chris Bosh 125.00 250.00
Dwyane Wade
Kevin Durant
Russell Westbrook
2 Tim Duncan 40.00 100.00
Yao Ming
Dwight Howard
Kevin Garnett
3 Allen Iverson 75.00 150.00
Vince Carter
Kevin Garnett
Shaquille O'Neal
4 Karl Malone 100.00 200.00
Shawn Kemp
Joe Dumars
Tim Hardaway
5 Alex English 40.00 100.00
Magic Johnson
Julius Erving
Robert Parish

2010-11 Elite Black Box All-Star Matchups Signatures

STATED PRINT RUN 5 TO 25 SER.#'d SETS
SOME UNPRICED DUE TO SCARCITY
1 Paul Pierce/25 EXCH 200.00 400.00
Ray Allen
Kobe Bryant
Pau Gasol
2 Carmelo Anthony/5
Steve Nash
Jason Kidd
Joe Johnson
3 Vince Carter/25 200.00 400.00
Grant Hill
David Robinson
Gary Payton
4 Chris Mullin/25 EXCH 100.00 200.00
Clyde Drexler
Dominique Wilkins
Isiah Thomas
5 Walt Frazier/25 50.00 120.00
Wes Unseld
Rick Barry
Spencer Haywood

2010-11 Elite Black Box All-Time Matchups Materials Prime

STATED PRINT RUN 10 TO 25 SER.#'d SETS
SOME UNPRICED DUE TO SCARCITY
1 Wilt Chamberlain/10
Bob Lanier
2 Julius Erving/25 40.00 100.00
Magic Johnson
3 Karl Malone/25 40.00 100.00
Hakeem Olajuwon
4 David Robinson/25 60.00 150.00
Patrick Ewing
5 Kareem Abdul-Jabbar/25 35.00 70.00
Robert Parish

2010-11 Elite Black Box All-Time Matchups Signatures

STATED PRINT RUN 10 TO 25 SER.#'d SETS
SOME UNPRICED DUE TO SCARCITY
1 Bill Russell/10
Jerry West
2 Larry Bird/10
Magic Johnson
3 Kareem Abdul-Jabbar/25 40.00 100.00
Elvin Hayes
4 Clyde Drexler/25 40.00 100.00
Dominique Wilkins
5 Elgin Baylor/25 25.00 60.00
Nate Thurmond

2010-11 Elite Black Box Award Winners Materials Prime

STATED PRINT RUN 15 TO 25 SER.#'d SETS
1 Derrick Rose/25 150.00 250.00
LeBron James
Kobe Bryant
Dirk Nowitzki
2 Larry Bird/15 75.00 150.00
Moses Malone
Julius Erving
Kareem Abdul-Jabbar
3 Karl Malone/25 75.00 150.00
David Robinson
Hakeem Olajuwon
Magic Johnson

2010-11 Elite Black Box Award Winners Signatures

STATED PRINT RUN 5 TO 25 SER.#'d SETS
SOME UNPRICED DUE TO SCARCITY
1 Blake Griffin/5
Tyreke Evans
Derrick Rose
Kevin Durant
2 Kobe Bryant/5
Steve Nash
Bill Walton
Bill Russell
3 Wes Unseld/25 75.00 150.00
Earl Monroe
Rick Barry
Willis Reed

2010-11 Elite Black Box Black and Blue Signatures

STATED PRINT RUN 10 TO 40 SER.#'d SETS
SOME UNPRICED DUE TO SCARCITY
1 Kobe Bryant/37 100.00 200.00
2 Blake Griffin/25 100.00 200.00
3 Derrick Rose/10
4 Chris Bosh/10
5 Zach Randolph/39 10.00 25.00
6 Monta Ellis/39 10.00 25.00
7 Kevin Martin/49 10.00 25.00
8 LaMarcus Aldridge/39 12.00 30.00
9 Tyreke Evans/25 15.00 40.00
10 Stephen Curry/39 15.00 40.00
11 Kevin Love/40 15.00 40.00
12 Eric Gordon/39 12.50 30.00
13 Paul Pierce/25 EXCH 25.00 60.00
14 Joe Johnson/25 15.00 40.00
15 Andrea Bargnani/39 10.00 25.00
16 Larry Bird/10
17 Magic Johnson/10
18 Oscar Robertson/25 75.00 150.00
19 Bill Russell/10
20 Kareem Abdul-Jabbar/10

2010-11 Elite Black Box Champions Materials Prime

STATED PRINT RUN ONE TO 25 SER.#'d SETS
SOME UNPRICED DUE TO SCARCITY
1 Andrew Bynum/25 125.00 250.00
Derek Fisher
Kobe Bryant
Lamar Odom
2 Danny Ainge/25 60.00 150.00
Kevin McHale
Larry Bird
Robert Parish
3 David Robinson/25 100.00 200.00
Manu Ginobili
Tim Duncan
Tony Parker
4 Ron Harper/25 175.00 300.00
Scottie Pippen
Toni Kukoc
Dennis Rodman
5 Isiah Thomas/1
Joe Dumars
Bill Laimbeer
Adrian Dantley

2010-11 Elite Black Box Champions Signatures

STATED PRINT RUN 10 TO 25 SER.#'d SETS
SOME UNPRICED DUE TO SCARCITY
1 Kareem Abdul-Jabbar/10
Byron Scott
James Worthy
Magic Johnson
Michael Cooper
2 Bill Russell/10
John Havlicek
Bailey Howell
Sam Jones
Tom Heinsohn
3 Bill Russell/10
Bill Sharman
K.C. Jones
Frank Ramsey
Tom Heinsohn
4 Bill Walton/25 150.00 300.00
Rick Carlisle
Kevin McHale
Larry Bird
Robert Parish
5 Bill Laimbeer/25 75.00 150.00
Dennis Rodman
Isiah Thomas
Joe Dumars
Mark Aguirre

2010-11 Elite Black Box Crusade

STATED PRINT RUN 25 SER.#'d SETS
1 Derrick Rose 12.00 30.00
2 John Wall 15.00 40.00
3 Dwyane Wade 10.00 25.00
4 Chauncey Billups 4.00 10.00
5 Kevin Garnett 8.00 20.00
6 LeBron James 40.00 100.00
7 Carmelo Anthony 5.00 12.00
8 Deron Williams 4.00 10.00
9 Rajon Rondo 5.00 12.00
10 David Lee 3.00 8.00
11 Brook Lopez 4.00 10.00
12 Dwight Howard 6.00 15.00
13 Steve Nash 4.00 10.00
14 Jameer Nelson 3.00 8.00
15 Al Horford 3.00 8.00
16 Pau Gasol 4.00 10.00
17 Anderson Varejao 3.00 8.00
18 Marc Gasol 4.00 10.00
19 Beno Udrih 2.50 6.00
20 Ray Allen 4.00 10.00
21 Tim Duncan 8.00 20.00
22 Rudy Gay 4.00 10.00
23 Jason Richardson 4.00 10.00
24 Kobe Bryant 20.00 50.00
25 Al Jefferson 4.00 10.00
26 Chris Kaman 3.00 8.00
27 Danny Granger 4.00 10.00
28 Elton Brand 4.00 10.00
29 Emeka Okafor 4.00 10.00
30 Stephen Curry 5.00 12.00
31 Jason Terry 3.00 8.00
32 Blake Griffin 10.00 25.00
33 Grant Hill 10.00 25.00
34 Paul Pierce 5.00 12.00
35 Kevin Durant 12.00 30.00
36 Boris Diaw 3.00 8.00
37 Nene 3.00 8.00
38 David West 4.00 10.00
39 Paul Millsap 3.00 8.00
40 Andre Miller 3.00 8.00
41 Dirk Nowitzki 8.00 20.00
42 Kevin Love 5.00 12.00
43 Kris Humphries 2.50 6.00
44 Tayshaun Prince 4.00 10.00
45 J.J. Hickson 3.00 8.00
46 Manu Ginobili 4.00 10.00
47 Raymond Felton 3.00 8.00
48 Andrew Bynum 5.00 12.00
49 John Salmons 4.00 10.00
50 Zach Randolph 3.00 8.00
51 DeMarcus Cousins 12.00 30.00
52 D.J. Augustin 3.00 8.00
53 Tyreke Evans 5.00 12.00
54 James Harden 5.00 12.00
55 Roy Hibbert 3.00 8.00
56 Luke Ridnour 3.00 8.00
57 Joakim Noah 4.00 10.00
58 Kevin Martin 4.00 10.00
59 LaMarcus Aldridge 4.00 10.00
60 Jrue Holiday 4.00 10.00
61 Mike Conley Jr. 3.00 8.00
62 DeMar DeRozan 4.00 10.00
63 Eric Gordon 4.00 10.00
64 Andre Iguodala 4.00 10.00
65 Tony Parker 4.00 10.00
66 Luol Deng 4.00 10.00
67 Michael Beasley 4.00 10.00
68 Monta Ellis 4.00 10.00
69 Jose Calderon 3.00 8.00
70 Danilo Gallinari 4.00 10.00
71 Channing Frye 3.00 8.00
72 Andrea Bargnani 3.00 8.00
73 Lamar Odom 4.00 10.00
74 Kyle Lowry 3.00 8.00
75 Andray Blatche 2.50 6.00
76 Andrew Bogut 4.00 10.00
77 Devin Harris 4.00 10.00
78 Josh Smith 4.00 10.00
79 Carlos Boozer 4.00 10.00
80 Antawn Jamison 4.00 10.00
81 Luis Scola 3.00 8.00
82 Caron Butler 4.00 10.00
83 Gerald Wallace 4.00 10.00
84 Chris Paul 6.00 15.00
85 Baron Davis 4.00 10.00
86 Ramon Sessions 3.00 8.00
87 Brandon Jennings 4.00 10.00
88 Rodney Stuckey 4.00 10.00
89 Wesley Matthews 4.00 10.00
90 Joe Johnson 4.00 10.00
91 Mo Williams 3.00 8.00
92 Darren Collison 4.00 10.00
93 Jason Kidd 4.00 10.00
94 Dorell Wright 2.50 6.00
95 Chris Bosh 4.00 10.00
96 Nick Young 3.00 8.00
97 Amare Stoudemire 4.00 10.00
98 Stephen Jackson 3.00 8.00
99 Shawn Marion 4.00 10.00
100 Russell Westbrook 5.00 12.00

2010-11 Elite Black Box Crusade Materials

STATED PRINT RUN 99 SER.#'d SETS
1 Derrick Rose 12.00 30.00
2 John Wall 10.00 25.00
3 Dwyane Wade 8.00 20.00
4 Chauncey Billups 4.00 10.00
5 Kevin Garnett 8.00 20.00
6 LeBron James 15.00 40.00
7 Carmelo Anthony 5.00 12.00
8 Deron Williams 4.00 10.00
9 Rajon Rondo 5.00 12.00
10 David Lee 3.00 8.00
11 Brook Lopez 4.00 10.00
12 Dwight Howard 6.00 15.00
13 Steve Nash 4.00 10.00
14 Jameer Nelson 3.00 8.00
15 Al Horford 3.00 8.00
16 Pau Gasol 4.00 10.00
17 Anderson Varejao 3.00 8.00
18 Marc Gasol 4.00 10.00
19 Beno Udrih 2.50 6.00
20 Ray Allen 4.00 10.00
21 Tim Duncan 6.00 15.00
22 Rudy Gay 4.00 10.00
23 Jason Richardson 4.00 10.00
24 Kobe Bryant 12.00 30.00
25 Al Jefferson 4.00 10.00
26 Chris Kaman 3.00 8.00
27 Danny Granger 4.00 10.00
28 Elton Brand 4.00 10.00
29 Emeka Okafor 4.00 10.00
30 Stephen Curry 5.00 12.00
31 Jason Terry 3.00 8.00
32 Blake Griffin 10.00 25.00
33 Grant Hill 10.00 25.00
34 Paul Pierce 5.00 12.00
35 Kevin Durant 12.00 30.00
36 Boris Diaw 3.00 8.00
37 Nene 3.00 8.00
38 David West 4.00 10.00
39 Paul Millsap 3.00 8.00
40 Andre Miller 3.00 8.00
41 Dirk Nowitzki 5.00 12.00
42 Kevin Love 5.00 12.00
44 Tayshaun Prince 4.00 10.00
46 Manu Ginobili 4.00 10.00
48 Andrew Bynum 5.00 12.00
49 John Salmons 4.00 10.00
50 Zach Randolph 3.00 8.00
51 DeMarcus Cousins 8.00 20.00
52 D.J. Augustin 3.00 8.00
53 Tyreke Evans 5.00 12.00
54 James Harden 5.00 12.00
55 Roy Hibbert 3.00 8.00
56 Luke Ridnour 3.00 8.00
57 Joakim Noah 4.00 10.00
58 Kevin Martin 4.00 10.00
59 LaMarcus Aldridge 4.00 10.00
60 Jrue Holiday 4.00 10.00
61 Mike Conley Jr. 3.00 8.00
62 DeMar DeRozan 4.00 10.00
63 Eric Gordon 4.00 10.00
64 Andre Iguodala 4.00 10.00
65 Tony Parker 4.00 10.00
66 Luol Deng 4.00 10.00
67 Michael Beasley 4.00 10.00
68 Monta Ellis 4.00 10.00
69 Jose Calderon 3.00 8.00
70 Danilo Gallinari 4.00 10.00
71 Channing Frye 3.00 8.00
72 Andrea Bargnani 3.00 8.00
73 Lamar Odom 4.00 10.00
74 Kyle Lowry 3.00 8.00
76 Andrew Bogut 4.00 10.00
77 Devin Harris 4.00 10.00
78 Josh Smith 4.00 10.00
79 Carlos Boozer 4.00 10.00
80 Antawn Jamison 4.00 10.00
81 Luis Scola 3.00 8.00
82 Caron Butler 4.00 10.00
84 Chris Paul 6.00 15.00
86 Ramon Sessions 3.00 8.00
87 Brandon Jennings 4.00 10.00
89 Wesley Matthews 4.00 10.00
90 Joe Johnson 4.00 10.00
91 Mo Williams 3.00 8.00
92 Darren Collison 4.00 10.00
93 Jason Kidd 4.00 10.00
95 Chris Bosh 4.00 10.00
96 Nick Young 3.00 8.00
97 Amare Stoudemire 4.00 10.00
98 Stephen Jackson 3.00 8.00
99 Shawn Marion 4.00 10.00
100 Russell Westbrook 5.00 12.00

2010-11 Elite Black Box Crusade Materials Signatures

STATED PRINT RUN 5 TO 25 SER.#'d SETS
SOME UNPRICED DUE TO SCARCITY
10 David Lee/25 5.00 12.00
11 Brook Lopez/25 8.00 20.00
14 Jameer Nelson/25 5.00 12.00
15 Al Horford/25 6.00 15.00
17 Anderson Varejao/25 5.00 12.00
19 Beno Udrih/25 5.00 12.00
22 Rudy Gay/25 8.00 20.00
24 Kobe Bryant/25 100.00 200.00
25 Al Jefferson/25 6.00 15.00
26 Chris Kaman/25 5.00 12.00
27 Danny Granger/25 8.00 20.00
29 Emeka Okafor/25 5.00 12.00
30 Stephen Curry/25 12.50 30.00
31 Jason Terry/25 10.00 25.00
33 Grant Hill/25 75.00 150.00
36 Boris Diaw/25 5.00 12.00
39 Paul Millsap/25 10.00 25.00
40 Andre Miller/25 6.00 15.00
50 Zach Randolph/25 12.50 30.00
51 DeMarcus Cousins/25 20.00 50.00
52 D.J. Augustin/25 5.00 12.00
53 Tyreke Evans/25 12.50 30.00
54 James Harden/25 15.00 40.00
55 Roy Hibbert/25 5.00 12.00
56 Luke Ridnour/25 5.00 12.00
57 Joakim Noah/25 EXCH 10.00 25.00
58 Kevin Martin/25 5.00 12.00
59 LaMarcus Aldridge/25 10.00 25.00
60 Jrue Holiday/25 5.00 12.00
61 Mike Conley Jr./25 8.00 20.00
62 DeMar DeRozan/25 8.00 20.00
63 Eric Gordon/25 8.00 20.00
64 Andre Iguodala/25 5.00 12.00
68 Monta Ellis/25 12.00 30.00
69 Jose Calderon/25 10.00 25.00
70 Danilo Gallinari/25 5.00 12.00
71 Channing Frye/20 5.00 12.00
72 Andrea Bargnani/25 6.00 15.00
76 Andrew Bogut/25 12.50 30.00
77 Devin Harris/25 6.00 15.00
78 Josh Smith/25 10.00 25.00
79 Carlos Boozer/25 EXCH 10.00 25.00
80 Antawn Jamison/25 5.00 12.00
81 Luis Scola/25 EXCH 6.00 15.00
82 Caron Butler/25 8.00 20.00
87 Brandon Jennings/25 10.00 25.00
89 Wesley Matthews/25 8.00 20.00
90 Joe Johnson/25 8.00 20.00
91 Mo Williams/25 5.00 12.00
92 Darren Collison/25 5.00 12.00
98 Stephen Jackson/25 5.00 12.00
100 Russell Westbrook/25 25.00 60.00

2010-11 Elite Black Box Crusade Signatures

STATED PRINT RUN 5 TO 149 SER.#'d SETS
SOME UNPRICED DUE TO SCARCITY
10 David Lee/25 10.00 25.00
11 Brook Lopez/25 10.00 25.00
14 Jameer Nelson/25 8.00 20.00
17 Anderson Varejao/49 5.00 12.00
19 Beno Udrih/99 5.00 12.00
22 Rudy Gay/49 6.00 15.00
24 Kobe Bryant/149 75.00 150.00
26 Chris Kaman/49 5.00 12.00
30 Stephen Curry/49 17.50 35.00
31 Jason Terry/25 EXCH 12.50 30.00
36 Boris Diaw/99 5.00 12.00
39 Paul Millsap/99 6.00 15.00
40 Andre Miller/49 5.00 12.00
43 Kris Humphries/99 5.00 12.00
47 Raymond Felton/49 5.00 12.00
50 Zach Randolph/25 12.50 30.00
51 DeMarcus Cousins/25 40.00 100.00
52 D.J. Augustin/25 5.00 12.00
54 James Harden/25 20.00 50.00
55 Roy Hibbert/99 5.00 12.00
56 Luke Ridnour/49 8.00 20.00
58 Kevin Martin/59 5.00 12.00
59 LaMarcus Aldridge/25 15.00 40.00
60 Jrue Holiday/99 8.00 20.00
61 Mike Conley Jr./49 5.00 12.00
62 DeMar DeRozan/25 12.00 30.00
63 Eric Gordon/49 10.00 25.00
64 Andre Iguodala/25 6.00 15.00
68 Monta Ellis/49 10.00 25.00
69 Jose Calderon/49 10.00 25.00
71 Channing Frye/49 5.00 12.00
72 Andrea Bargnani/25 6.00 15.00
77 Devin Harris/25 6.00 15.00
78 Josh Smith/25 12.00 30.00
79 Carlos Boozer/49 12.50 30.00
80 Antawn Jamison/49 6.00 15.00
81 Luis Scola/49 8.00 20.00
82 Caron Butler/25 12.50 30.00
83 Gerald Wallace/25 12.50 30.00
87 Brandon Jennings/25 15.00 40.00
89 Wesley Matthews/99 5.00 12.00
92 Darren Collison/99 6.00 15.00
95 Chris Bosh/20 25.00 60.00
98 Stephen Jackson/99 5.00 12.00
100 Russell Westbrook/25 25.00 60.00

2010-11 Elite Black Box Draft Classes Materials Prime

STATED PRINT RUN 15 TO 99 SER.#'d SETS
1 Magic Johnson/99 12.50 30.00
Mark Eaton
Bill Laimbeer
2 Mark Aguirre/15 12.50 30.00
Isiah Thomas
Rolando Blackman
3 James Worthy/99 10.00 25.00
Dominique Wilkins
Sleepy Floyd
5 Blake Griffin/99 20.00 50.00
Stephen Curry
Darren Collison

2010-11 Elite Black Box Draft Classes Signatures

STATED PRINT RUN 10 TO 49 SER.#'d SETS
SOME UNPRICED DUE TO SCARCITY
2 Mark Aguirre/49 20.00 50.00
Isiah Thomas
Rolando Blackman
3 James Worthy/25 30.00 80.00
Dominique Wilkins
Sleepy Floyd
4 David Robinson/25 40.00 100.00
Kenny Smith
Kevin Johnson
5 Blake Griffin/25 50.00 120.00
Stephen Curry
Darren Collison

2010-11 Elite Black Box Dream Team Materials Prime

STATED PRINT RUN 99 SER.#'d SETS
UNPRICED AUTO PRINT RUN 10 SETS
1 Clyde Drexler 30.00 80.00
John Stockton
Magic Johnson
2 Chris Mullin 30.00 80.00
Larry Bird
David Robinson

2010-11 Elite Black Box Elite Series Materials Prime

STATED PRINT RUN ONE TO 49 SER.#'d SETS
SOME UNPRICED DUE TO SCARCITY
UNPRICED PRIME SIG PRINT RUN 5 SETS
UNPRICED SIG PRINT RUN 5 TO 10 SETS
1 Julius Erving/25 12.00 30.00
2 Magic Johnson/49 15.00 40.00
3 Chris Mullin/49 8.00 20.00
5 Kevin McHale/49 6.00 15.00
6 Nate Thurmond/25 25.00 60.00
10 Mark Price/49 10.00 25.00
11 David Robinson/49 10.00 25.00
12 Michael Cooper/49 6.00 15.00
14 Charles Oakley/49 8.00 20.00
18 Spencer Haywood/49 12.50 30.00
19 Robert Parish/25 6.00 15.00
20 Mark Eaton/49 6.00 15.00
21 Bill Laimbeer/25 6.00 15.00
23 Bernard King/25 6.00 15.00
24 Dennis Rodman/25 20.00 50.00
26 Kareem Abdul-Jabbar/25 10.00 25.00
29 Dominique Wilkins/25 10.00 25.00
30 Gary Payton/25 10.00 25.00
31 Jalen Rose/49 6.00 15.00
34 Alex English/25 6.00 15.00
35 Alonzo Mourning/25 25.00 60.00
37 Dan Issel/25 6.00 15.00
38 Kelly Tripucka/49 6.00 15.00
39 Larry Johnson/49 20.00 50.00
40 Mitch Richmond/49 15.00 40.00
42 Sam Perkins/25 8.00 20.00
44 George Gervin/25 6.00 15.00
46 Hakeem Olajuwon/49 8.00 20.00
48 Maurice Cheeks/25 6.00 15.00
49 Nick Van Exel/49 8.00 20.00
50 Robert Horry/25 8.00 20.00
51 Kobe Bryant/25 25.00 60.00
52 Kevin Durant/25 20.00 50.00
53 Blake Griffin/49 20.00 50.00
55 Kevin Love/25 8.00 20.00
56 Zach Randolph/25 5.00 12.00
57 Derrick Rose/25 25.00 60.00
59 Tony Parker/25 10.00 25.00
60 Paul Pierce/25 8.00 20.00
61 Lamar Odom/25 6.00 15.00
63 Eric Gordon/25 6.00 15.00
64 Carlos Boozer/25 6.00 15.00
65 Danny Granger/25 6.00 15.00
66 Jason Kidd/25 10.00 25.00
67 Kevin Martin/25 6.00 15.00
68 LaMarcus Aldridge/25 6.00 15.00
69 Pau Gasol/15 10.00 25.00
70 Ray Allen/25 8.00 20.00
71 Rudy Gay/25 6.00 15.00
72 Stephen Curry/25 8.00 20.00
73 Ben Gordon/15 6.00 15.00
74 Brandon Jennings/25 6.00 15.00
76 Tyreke Evans/25 8.00 20.00
77 Ty Lawson/25 6.00 15.00
78 Joe Johnson/25 6.00 15.00
79 Andre Miller/25 5.00 12.00
80 Chris Bosh/25 6.00 15.00
81 Chauncey Billups/25 6.00 15.00
84 Jeff Teague/25 5.00 12.00
88 Marc Gasol/25 6.00 15.00
89 Samuel Dalembert/25 4.00 10.00
91 Grant Hill/25 20.00 50.00
93 DeMar DeRozan/25 6.00 15.00
94 Caron Butler/25 6.00 15.00
95 Monta Ellis/25 6.00 15.00
96 Taj Gibson/25 5.00 12.00
97 O.J. Mayo/25 6.00 15.00
98 Trevor Ariza/25 4.00 10.00
99 Jrue Holiday/25 6.00 15.00
100 Steve Nash/25 10.00 25.00

2010-11 Elite Black Box Flag Patches Signatures

STATED PRINT RUN 5 TO 149 SER.#'d SETS
SOME UNPRICED DUE TO SCARCITY
4 Toni Kukoc/99 15.00 40.00
7 Peja Stojakovic/25 25.00 60.00
11 Dikembe Mutombo/99 12.00 30.00
12 Al Horford/25 8.00 20.00
14 Boris Diaw/99 10.00 25.00
15 Shawn Bradley/149 6.00 15.00
16 Chris Kaman/25 10.00 25.00
17 Detlef Schrempf/149 6.00 15.00
19 Andrea Bargnani/25 10.00 25.00
20 Roy Hibbert/149 8.00 20.00
21 Serge Ibaka/99 10.00 25.00
22 Vlade Divac/149 EXCH 8.00 20.00
23 Nenad Krstic/149 6.00 15.00
24 Darko Milicic/149 6.00 15.00
25 Goran Dragic/149 12.00 30.00
26 Jose Calderon/49 8.00 20.00
29 Hedo Turkoglu/49 6.00 15.00
34 Kobe Bryant/99 100.00 200.00
49 Bill Walton/25 12.50 30.00
50 Brook Lopez/25 6.00 15.00
51 Byron Scott/149 6.00 15.00
52 Caron Butler/25 10.00 25.00
56 Dan Majerle/149 8.00 20.00
57 Dave Cowens/25 10.00 25.00
58 David Lee/25 8.00 20.00
59 Dell Curry/149 6.00 15.00
62 Elgin Baylor/25 15.00 40.00
74 Larry Johnson/149 12.50 30.00
75 Lenny Wilkens/25 15.00 40.00

76 Mark Price/149 8.00 20.00
77 Monta Ellis/99 6.00 15.00
83 Robert Horry/99 10.00 25.00
84 Shane Battier/49 6.00 15.00
85 Stephen Curry/99 12.50 30.00
86 Tim Hardaway/149 10.00 25.00
87 Tyson Chandler/25 10.00 25.00
88 A.C. Green/99 8.00 20.00
89 Adrian Dantley/99 6.00 15.00
90 Bernard King/99 8.00 20.00
91 Bill Laimbeer/149 6.00 15.00
92 Cedric Maxwell/149 6.00 15.00
93 Darryl Dawkins/149 6.00 15.00
94 Gail Goodrich/25 12.50 30.00
95 Glen Rice/99 10.00 25.00
96 Jeff Hornacek/149 8.00 20.00
97 Nate Archibald/25 6.00 15.00
98 Nate Thurmond/25 12.00 30.00
99 Sam Perkins/99 6.00 15.00
100 Sean Elliott/149 8.00 20.00

2010-11 Elite Black Box Hall of Fame Materials Prime

STATED PRINT RUN 99 SER.#'d SETS
3 James Worthy 12.50 30.00
Alex English
Dominique Wilkins
4 Joe Dumars 25.00 60.00
Clyde Drexler
David Robinson

2010-11 Elite Black Box Hall of Fame Signatures

STATED PRINT RUN 10 TO 49 SER.#'d SETS
SOME UNPRICED DUE TO SCARCITY
3 James Worthy/25 25.00 60.00
Alex English
Dominique Wilkins
6 Sam Jones/49 25.00 60.00
Nate Thurmond
Billy Cunningham
7 George Gervin/49 25.00 60.00
Bailey Howell
Arnie Risen
8 Chris Mullin/25 100.00 200.00
Artis Gilmore
Dennis Rodman

2010-11 Elite Black Box Materials

STATED PRINT RUN 2 TO 99 SER.#'d SETS
SOME UNPRICED DUE TO SCARCITY
1 LeBron James/99 12.00 30.00
2 Dirk Nowitzki/99 5.00 12.00
3 Kevin Durant/99 12.00 30.00
4 Kobe Bryant/99 12.00 30.00
5 Carmelo Anthony/99 5.00 12.00
6 LaMarcus Aldridge/99 4.00 10.00
7 Al Horford/99 3.00 8.00
8 Kevin Garnett/99 8.00 20.00
9 Chris Paul/99 6.00 15.00
10 Dwight Howard/99 6.00 15.00
11 Dwyane Wade/99 8.00 20.00
12 Blake Griffin/99 10.00 25.00
13 Andrea Bargnani/99 3.00 8.00
14 Kevin Love/99 5.00 12.00
15 Zach Randolph/99 3.00 8.00
16 Ray Allen/99 4.00 10.00
17 Derrick Rose/99 12.00 30.00
18 Monta Ellis/99 4.00 10.00
19 Danny Granger/99 4.00 10.00
20 Ty Lawson/99 4.00 10.00
21 Tony Parker/99 4.00 10.00
22 Brook Lopez/99 4.00 10.00
23 Eric Gordon/99 4.00 10.00
24 Russell Westbrook/99 5.00 12.00
25 Tyson Chandler/99 3.00 8.00
26 Vince Carter/99 5.00 12.00
27 Amare Stoudemire/99 4.00 10.00
28 Kevin Martin/99 4.00 10.00
29 Joe Johnson/99 4.00 10.00
30 Stephen Jackson/99 3.00 8.00
31 JaVale McGee/99 3.00 8.00
32 Chauncey Billups/99 4.00 10.00
33 Paul Pierce/99 5.00 12.00
34 Darren Collison/99 4.00 10.00
35 Serge Ibaka/99 5.00 12.00
36 J.J. Barea/99 4.00 10.00
37 Chris Bosh/99 4.00 10.00
38 Al Jefferson/99 4.00 10.00
39 Rudy Gay/99 4.00 10.00
40 Deron Williams/99 4.00 10.00
41 David West/99 4.00 10.00
42 Luis Scola/99 3.00 8.00
43 Antawn Jamison/99 4.00 10.00
44 Brandon Jennings/99 4.00 10.00
45 Stephen Curry/99 5.00 12.00
46 Steve Nash/99 4.00 10.00
47 Chris Kaman/99 3.00 8.00
48 Andre Iguodala/99 4.00 10.00
49 Joakim Noah/99 4.00 10.00
50 Brandon Roy/99 4.00 10.00
51 Andrei Kirilenko/99 3.00 8.00
52 Jameer Nelson/99 3.00 8.00
53 Jrue Holiday/99 4.00 10.00
54 Ben Gordon/99 4.00 10.00
55 Marc Gasol/99 4.00 10.00
56 Gerald Wallace/99 4.00 10.00
57 Rajon Rondo/99 5.00 12.00
58 Tim Duncan/99 6.00 15.00
59 Pau Gasol/99 4.00 10.00
60 Michael Beasley/99 4.00 10.00
61 Tyreke Evans/99 5.00 12.00
62 David Lee/99 3.00 8.00
63 DeMar DeRozan/99 4.00 10.00
64 Wesley Matthews/99 4.00 10.00
65 Josh Smith/99 4.00 10.00
67 Nene/99 3.00 8.00
68 James Harden/99 5.00 12.00
69 Devin Harris/99 4.00 10.00
70 Elton Brand/99 4.00 10.00
71 Emeka Okafor/99 4.00 10.00
72 Jason Terry/99 3.00 8.00
73 Luol Deng/99 4.00 10.00
74 Nick Young/99 3.00 8.00
75 Danilo Gallinari/99 4.00 10.00
76 Carlos Boozer/99 4.00 10.00
77 Andrew Bogut/99 4.00 10.00
80 Manu Ginobili/99 4.00 10.00
82 Ben Wallace/99 4.00 10.00
83 Jason Kidd/99 4.00 10.00
84 Trevor Ariza/99 2.50 6.00
86 Andrew Bynum/99 5.00 12.00
88 Roy Hibbert/99 3.00 8.00
90 J.J. Redick/99 4.00 10.00
91 J.R. Smith/49 4.00 10.00
93 Jonny Flynn/99 2.50 6.00
94 Brandon Bass/99 2.50 6.00
95 Taj Gibson/99 3.00 8.00
97 Glen Davis/99 3.00 8.00
98 DeJuan Blair/99 3.00 8.00
99 Tracy McGrady/99 4.00 10.00
100 Samuel Dalembert/99 2.50 6.00
102 Karl Malone/99 5.00 12.00
103 Julius Erving/49 8.00 20.00
104 Jalen Rose/99 4.00 10.00
105 Alex English/99 4.00 10.00
106 Alonzo Mourning/99 5.00 12.00
107 David Robinson/99 6.00 15.00
108 Kevin Johnson/99 5.00 12.00
109 Kevin McHale/99 4.00 10.00
110 Shaquille O'Neal/99 8.00 20.00
114 Gary Payton/25 8.00 20.00
117 Dominique Wilkins/99 5.00 12.00
118 George Mikan/49 10.00 25.00
120 Jerry West/25 8.00 20.00
121 Hakeem Olajuwon/99 5.00 12.00
123 Clyde Drexler/99 5.00 12.00
124 Nate Thurmond/25 4.00 10.00
127 Darrell Griffith/99 4.00 10.00
128 Danny Manning/99 4.00 10.00
129 Dan Issel/99 4.00 10.00
130 Larry Bird/99 12.00 30.00
132 Bill Laimbeer/99 4.00 10.00
133 Shawn Bradley/99 4.00 10.00
134 James Worthy/99 5.00 12.00
135 Cedric Maxwell/99 4.00 10.00
136 Bailey Howell/25 4.00 10.00
137 Magic Johnson/25 10.00 25.00
138 Kelly Tripucka/99 4.00 10.00
139 Dikembe Mutombo/99 4.00 10.00
142 Mark Eaton/99 4.00 10.00
143 Toni Kukoc/99 4.00 10.00
144 Earl Monroe/99 4.00 10.00
145 Glen Rice/99 4.00 10.00
146 Larry Johnson/99 6.00 15.00
147 Kiki Vandeweghe/99 4.00 10.00
148 Chris Webber/99 4.00 10.00
149 Ron Harper/99 4.00 10.00
150 Kareem Abdul-Jabbar/49 6.00 15.00
151 Sam Jones/49 4.00 10.00
152 Spencer Haywood/49 4.00 10.00
153 Dennis Scott/99 4.00 10.00
155 Robert Horry/49 5.00 12.00
156 Manute Bol/99 4.00 10.00
157 Kevin Willis/99 4.00 10.00
158 Chris Mullin/49 4.00 10.00
159 Isiah Thomas/99 4.00 10.00
163 Alvan Adams/99 4.00 10.00
164 Xavier McDaniel/99 4.00 10.00
165 Sleepy Floyd/99 4.00 10.00
166 Mark Aguirre/99 4.00 10.00
167 Mark Price/25 6.00 15.00
168 Bernard King/25 4.00 10.00
169 Joe Dumars/99 4.00 10.00
170 Reggie Lewis/99 12.50 30.00
171 Michael Cooper/99 4.00 10.00
172 Robert Parish/99 4.00 10.00
173 Danny Ainge/99 4.00 10.00
174 Maurice Cheeks/99 4.00 10.00
177 Jeff Hornacek/25 4.00 10.00
179 Tom Chambers/99 4.00 10.00
181 Mitch Richmond/99 4.00 10.00
183 Patrick Ewing/99 8.00 20.00
186 Steve Smith/99 4.00 10.00
193 Dan Majerle/99 4.00 10.00

2010-11 Elite Black Box Passing the Torch Materials

STATED PRINT RUN 5 TO 99 SER.#'d SETS
SOME UNPRICED DUE TO SCARCITY
1 Jerry West/25 30.00 80.00
Kobe Bryant
2 Shawn Kemp/99 25.00 60.00
Kevin Durant
5 Julius Erving/99 12.50 30.00
Andre Iguodala
6 Mitch Richmond/99 8.00 20.00
Monta Ellis
8 Clyde Drexler/99 10.00 25.00
Kevin Martin
9 Chris Mullin/75 8.00 20.00
David Lee
10 Dominique Wilkins/99 10.00 25.00
Joe Johnson
13 Jalen Rose/99 6.00 15.00
Darren Collison
15 Dennis Rodman/99 15.00 40.00
Kevin Love
16 Mark Eaton/99 6.00 15.00
Andrew Bogut
18 Joe Dumars/99 6.00 15.00
Greg Monroe
20 Alonzo Mourning/99 15.00 40.00
Chris Bosh
22 Kevin Johnson/99 10.00 25.00
Steve Nash
24 Robert Parish/99 6.00 15.00
Marcus Camby
26 Ray Allen/99 10.00 25.00
Stephen Curry
27 Gary Payton/99 10.00 25.00
Eric Gordon
28 Gary Payton/99 10.00 25.00
Russell Westbrook
30 David Robinson/99 12.00 30.00
Andrew Bynum
31 John Stockton/99 15.00 40.00
J.J. Barea
32 George Gervin/75 15.00 40.00
Kevin Durant
34 Kobe Bryant/99 20.00 50.00
Andre Iguodala
36 Elgin Baylor/25 35.00 70.00
Kobe Bryant
38 Toni Kukoc/99 12.00 30.00
Joakim Noah
39 John Havlicek/25 20.00 50.00
Paul Pierce
41 Darrell Griffith/99 6.00 15.00
Devin Harris
42 Isiah Thomas/99 10.00 25.00
Ben Gordon
45 Alex English/25 10.00 25.00
J.R. Smith
48 Dikembe Mutombo/99 8.00 20.00
Josh Smith
49 Kelly Tripucka/99 6.00 15.00
Derrick Favors
50 Glen Rice/85 8.00 20.00
Stephen Jackson

2010-11 Elite Black Box Passing the Torch Signatures

STATED PRINT RUN 3 TO 149 SER.#'d SETS
SOME UNPRICED DUE TO SCARCITY
4 Walt Frazier/25 25.00 60.00
Chauncey Billups
6 Mitch Richmond/149 20.00 50.00
Monta Ellis
9 Chris Mullin/149 20.00 50.00
David Lee
11 Adrian Dantley/149 10.00 25.00
Greg Monroe
13 Jalen Rose/149 10.00 25.00
Darren Collison
16 Mark Eaton/149 10.00 25.00
Andrew Bogut
17 Sam Perkins/99 10.00 25.00
Zach Randolph
18 Joe Dumars/149 15.00 40.00
Greg Monroe
19 Nate Archibald/49 20.00 50.00
Brandon Jennings
21 Elvin Hayes/25 15.00 40.00
LaMarcus Aldridge
24 Robert Parish/99 15.00 40.00
Marcus Camby
25 World B. Free/99 10.00 25.00
Monta Ellis
26 Ray Allen/25 30.00 80.00
Stephen Curry
29 David Thompson/99 10.00 25.00
Jordan Crawford
33 Nate Archibald/99 10.00 25.00
Derek Fisher
34 Kobe Bryant/99 100.00 200.00
Andre Iguodala
36 Elgin Baylor/99 150.00 300.00
Kobe Bryant
37 Sam Perkins/25 12.00 30.00
Tyson Chandler
38 Toni Kukoc/25 30.00 80.00
Joakim Noah
41 Darrell Griffith/99 10.00 25.00
Devin Harris
43 Bernard King/149 15.00 40.00
Landry Fields
44 Darryl Dawkins/49 10.00 25.00
Brook Lopez
45 Alex English/99 10.00 25.00
J.R. Smith
46 Rolando Blackman/49 12.00 30.00
Jason Terry
48 Dikembe Mutombo/99 20.00 50.00
Josh Smith
49 Kelly Tripucka/99 10.00 25.00
Derrick Favors
50 Glen Rice/99 10.00 25.00
Stephen Jackson

2010-11 Elite Black Box Private Signings

STATED PRINT RUN 10 TO 199 SER.#'d SETS
SOME UNPRICED DUE TO SCARCITY
2 Artis Gilmore/148 6.00 15.00
3 Dirk Nowitzki/51 100.00 200.00
4 Gail Goodrich/49 5.00 12.00
5 Jack Twyman/99 15.00 40.00
6 Bill Laimbeer/148 5.00 12.00
7 Rolando Blackman/149 8.00 20.00
8 Sean Elliott/199 8.00 20.00
9 Mark Eaton/199 5.00 12.00

2010-11 Elite Black Box Reigning Threes Materials Prime

STATED PRINT RUN 24 TO 49 SER.#'d SETS
1 Kobe Bryant/24 30.00 70.00
2 Kevin Durant/49 25.00 60.00
3 Stephen Curry/49 10.00 25.00
4 Ty Lawson/49 8.00 20.00
5 Ray Allen/49 8.00 20.00
6 Channing Frye/49 6.00 15.00
7 Jason Terry/49 6.00 15.00
8 Danny Granger/49 8.00 20.00
9 Kevin Martin/49 8.00 20.00
10 Toney Douglas/49 5.00 12.00

2010-11 Elite Black Box Reigning Threes Signatures

STATED PRINT RUN 10 TO 99 SER.#'d SETS
SOME UNPRICED DUE TO SCARCITY
1 Kobe Bryant/99 100.00 175.00
3 Stephen Curry/99 10.00 25.00
4 Ty Lawson/99 8.00 20.00
6 Channing Frye/99 5.00 12.00
7 Jason Terry/49 EXCH 10.00 25.00
8 Danny Granger/49 5.00 12.00
9 Kevin Martin/99 5.00 12.00
10 Toney Douglas/49 5.00 12.00

2010-11 Elite Black Box Signatures

STATED PRINT RUN 5 TO 149 SER.#'d SETS
SOME UNPRICED DUE TO SCARCITY
4 Kobe Bryant/99 75.00 150.00
6 LaMarcus Aldridge/24 8.00 20.00
7 Al Horford/24 6.00 15.00
13 Andrea Bargnani/24 4.00 10.00
14 Kevin Love/24 15.00 40.00
15 Zach Randolph/24 8.00 20.00
18 Monta Ellis/149 8.00 20.00
19 Danny Granger/24 6.00 15.00
20 Ty Lawson/149 5.00 12.00
22 Brook Lopez/24 4.00 10.00
23 Eric Gordon/149 6.00 15.00
24 Russell Westbrook/24 15.00 40.00
25 Tyson Chandler/24 6.00 15.00
28 Kevin Martin/149 4.00 10.00
30 Stephen Jackson/49 4.00 10.00
31 JaVale McGee/149 4.00 10.00
34 Darren Collison/149 4.00 10.00
35 Serge Ibaka/149 8.00 20.00
36 J.J. Barea/149 10.00 25.00
39 Rudy Gay/49 EXCH 5.00 12.00
43 Antawn Jamison/49 4.00 10.00
45 Stephen Curry/49 10.00 25.00
47 Chris Kaman/24 4.00 10.00
48 Andre Iguodala/24 5.00 12.00
51 Andrei Kirilenko/24 6.00 15.00
52 Jameer Nelson/24 4.00 10.00
53 Jrue Holiday/49 8.00 20.00
56 Gerald Wallace/24 10.00 25.00
62 David Lee/24 5.00 12.00
63 DeMar DeRozan/24 6.00 15.00
64 Wesley Matthews/99 5.00 12.00
65 Josh Smith/24 8.00 20.00
66 Juwan Howard/99 4.00 10.00
68 James Harden/24 12.00 30.00
69 Devin Harris/24 4.00 10.00
76 Carlos Boozer/24 6.00 15.00
77 Andrew Bogut/149 8.00 20.00
78 Raymond Felton/24 4.00 10.00
79 Baron Davis/24 5.00 12.00
84 Trevor Ariza/24 4.00 10.00
85 Kendrick Perkins/49 5.00 12.00
86 Andrew Bynum/24 8.00 20.00
87 Aaron Brooks/49 4.00 10.00
88 Roy Hibbert/149 5.00 12.00
90 J.J. Redick/99 5.00 12.00
92 Kris Humphries/99 4.00 10.00
93 Jonny Flynn/99 4.00 10.00
95 Taj Gibson/99 5.00 12.00
96 Gerald Henderson/149 4.00 10.00
98 DeJuan Blair/149 4.00 10.00
100 Samuel Dalembert/99 4.00 10.00
105 Alex English/99 4.00 10.00
111 Wes Unseld/24 4.00 10.00
112 Walt Frazier/24 10.00 25.00
113 George Gervin/24 8.00 20.00
115 Elgin Baylor/24 EXCH 10.00 25.00
116 Bob McAdoo/99 10.00 25.00
119 Lenny Wilkens/24 6.00 15.00
122 Kenny Smith/24 4.00 10.00
124 Nate Thurmond/24 12.00 30.00
126 Darryl Dawkins/149 4.00 10.00
127 Darrell Griffith/149 4.00 10.00
128 Danny Manning/24 8.00 20.00
129 Dan Issel/149 6.00 15.00
131 Sam Perkins/99 5.00 12.00
132 Bill Laimbeer/149 4.00 10.00
133 Shawn Bradley/149 4.00 10.00
135 Cedric Maxwell/149 4.00 10.00
136 Bailey Howell/99 8.00 20.00
138 Kelly Tripucka/149 4.00 10.00
139 Dikembe Mutombo/99 10.00 25.00
142 Mark Eaton/149 4.00 10.00
143 Toni Kukoc/99 8.00 20.00
144 Earl Monroe/24 12.00 30.00
145 Glen Rice/49 10.00 25.00
146 Larry Johnson/149 10.00 25.00
147 Kiki Vandeweghe/149 4.00 10.00
149 Ron Harper/149 10.00 25.00
151 Sam Jones/24 10.00 25.00
152 Spencer Haywood/149 4.00 10.00
154 Elvin Hayes/24 5.00 12.00
155 Robert Horry/99 10.00 25.00
156 Manute Bol/49 15.00 40.00
157 Kevin Willis/149 6.00 15.00
158 Chris Mullin/99 10.00 25.00
159 Isiah Thomas/24 EXCH 10.00 25.00
160 Dave Cowens/24 6.00 15.00
162 Rick Barry/24 8.00 20.00
163 Alvan Adams/99 4.00 10.00
164 Xavier McDaniel/149 4.00 10.00
165 Sleepy Floyd/149 5.00 12.00
166 Mark Aguirre/149 6.00 15.00
167 Mark Price/149 10.00 25.00
168 Bernard King/99 4.00 10.00
169 Joe Dumars/24 10.00 25.00
171 Michael Cooper/99 8.00 20.00
172 Robert Parish/24 6.00 15.00
174 Maurice Cheeks/149 4.00 10.00
175 Sidney Moncrief/149 4.00 10.00
176 Artis Gilmore/24 8.00 20.00
177 Jeff Hornacek/149 4.00 10.00
180 Tim Hardaway/99 8.00 20.00
181 Mitch Richmond/99 EXCH 12.50 30.00
184 Walt Bellamy/24 5.00 12.00
185 Vlade Divac/149 8.00 20.00
186 Steve Smith/149 4.00 10.00
187 Rolando Blackman/149 4.00 10.00
188 M.L. Carr/149 6.00 15.00
189 Kurt Rambis/149 10.00 25.00
190 Kenny Walker/99 12.50 30.00
191 Jamal Mashburn/149 10.00 25.00
192 Connie Hawkins/99 8.00 20.00
193 Dan Majerle/149 EXCH 6.00 15.00
194 Adrian Dantley/99 4.00 10.00
195 Al Attles/149 4.00 10.00
196 Ralph Sampson/149 5.00 12.00
197 Walter Berry/149 4.00 10.00
199 Bill Walton/24 6.00 15.00
200 World B. Free/24 6.00 15.00

2010-11 Elite Black Box Teammates Materials Prime

STATED PRINT RUN 49 SER.#'d SETS
1 Kevin Durant 40.00 100.00
Russell Westbrook
Serge Ibaka
2 Blake Griffin 25.00 60.00
Eric Gordon
Mo Williams
3 Paul Pierce 25.00 60.00
Ray Allen
Rajon Rondo
4 LeBron James 150.00 300.00
Dwyane Wade
Chris Bosh
5 Kobe Bryant 50.00 120.00
Pau Gasol
Derek Fisher
6 Kareem Abdul-Jabbar 30.00 80.00
Magic Johnson
James Worthy
8 Larry Bird 25.00 60.00
Kevin McHale
Robert Parish

2010-11 Elite Black Box Teammates Signatures

STATED PRINT RUN 10 TO 25 SER.#'d SETS
SOME UNPRICED DUE TO SCARCITY
2 Blake Griffin/25 60.00 150.00
Eric Gordon
Mo Williams
5 Kobe Bryant/25 125.00 225.00
Pau Gasol
Derek Fisher
10 Hakeem Olajuwon/25 75.00 150.00
Clyde Drexler
Robert Horry

2010-11 Elite Black Box The Rookies Materials Dual Prime

STATED PRINT RUN 20 TO 25 SER.#'d SETS
1 John Wall/25 40.00 80.00
DeMarcus Cousins
2 Landry Fields/25 15.00 40.00
John Wall
4 Wesley Johnson/20 8.00 20.00
Lazar Hayward
5 DeMarcus Cousins/25 12.50 30.00
Landry Fields
7 Blake Griffin/25 25.00 60.00
John Wall
9 Gordon Hayward/25 15.00 40.00
Derrick Favors
10 Wesley Johnson/25 10.00 25.00
Evan Turner

2010-11 Elite Black Box The Rookies Materials Prime

STATED PRINT RUN 15 TO 99 SER.#'d SETS
1 John Wall/99 15.00 40.00
2 Landry Fields/99 6.00 15.00
3 DeMarcus Cousins/99 12.00 30.00
4 Greg Monroe/99 8.00 20.00
5 Gary Neal/35 6.00 15.00
6 Eric Bledsoe/37 8.00 20.00
7 Paul George/20 12.00 30.00
8 Gordon Hayward/99 8.00 20.00
9 Greivis Vasquez/15 6.00 15.00

2010-11 Elite Black Box The Rookies Materials Triple

STATED PRINT RUN 49 SER.#'d SETS
1 Blake Griffin 20.00 50.00
John Wall
DeMarcus Cousins
2 Evan Turner 10.00 25.00
Derrick Favors
Wesley Johnson
3 Ekpe Udoh 8.00 20.00
Greg Monroe
Al-Farouq Aminu
4 Gordon Hayward 6.00 15.00
Paul George
Ed Davis
6 Blake Griffin 12.00 30.00
Al-Farouq Aminu
Willie Warren
7 Landry Fields 10.00 25.00
Gary Neal
Greg Monroe
9 John Wall 12.50 30.00
Landry Fields
Greg Monroe

2010-11 Elite Black Box The Rookies Signatures

STATED PRINT RUN 10 TO 149 SER.#'d SETS
SOME UNPRICED DUE TO SCARCITY
1 John Wall/25 125.00 250.00
2 Landry Fields/149 8.00 20.00
3 DeMarcus Cousins/49 25.00 60.00
4 Greg Monroe/149 10.00 25.00
5 Gary Neal/149 8.00 20.00
6 Eric Bledsoe/149 8.00 20.00
7 Paul George/149 15.00 40.00
8 Gordon Hayward/149 12.00 30.00
9 Greivis Vasquez/149 8.00 20.00

2010-11 Elite Black Box The Rookies Signatures Dual

STATED PRINT RUN 10 TO 99 SER.#'d SETS
SOME UNPRICED DUE TO SCARCITY
3 Eric Bledsoe/99 10.00 25.00
Al-Farouq Aminu
4 Wesley Johnson/25 10.00 25.00
Lazar Hayward
5 DeMarcus Cousins/25 25.00 60.00
Landry Fields
6 Ed Davis/25 12.50 30.00
Paul George
9 Gordon Hayward/49 15.00 40.00
Derrick Favors
10 Wesley Johnson/10
Evan Turner

2010-11 Elite Black Box The Rookies Signatures Triple

STATED PRINT RUN 49 SER.#'d SETS
1 Blake Griffin 200.00 350.00
John Wall
DeMarcus Cousins
2 Evan Turner 30.00 80.00
Derrick Favors
Wesley Johnson
3 Ekpe Udoh 15.00 40.00
Greg Monroe
Al-Farouq Aminu
4 Gordon Hayward 20.00 50.00
Paul George
Ed Davis
5 John Wall 60.00 150.00
DeMarcus Cousins
Eric Bledsoe
6 Blake Griffin 40.00 100.00
Al-Farouq Aminu
Willie Warren
7 Landry Fields 15.00 40.00
Gary Neal
Greg Monroe
8 Derrick Favors 15.00 40.00
Gordon Hayward
Jeremy Evans
9 John Wall 60.00 150.00
Landry Fields
Greg Monroe
10 DeMarcus Cousins 15.00 40.00
Gary Neal
Jeremy Evans

2010-11 Elite Black Box Thunderstruck Signatures

COMMON CARD (1-10) 125.00 300.00
STATED PRINT RUN 10 SER.#'d SETS

2010-11 Elite Black Box USA Basketball Materials Prime Signatures

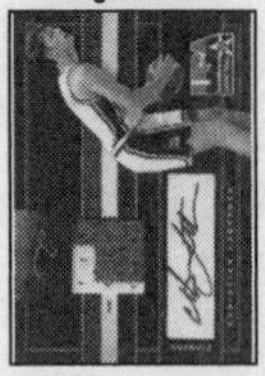

STATED PRINT RUN 25 TO 49 SER.#'d SETS
1 Alonzo Mourning/25 75.00
2 Carlos Boozer/25 12.50
3 Christian Laettner/49 30.00
4 Clyde Drexler/25 50.00
5 Dan Majerle/49 25.00
6 Dominique Wilkins/25 30.00
7 Joe Dumars/49 15.00
8 Kevin Johnson/49 25.00
9 Larry Johnson/49 25.00
10 Steve Smith/49 15.00

2010-11 Elite Black Box USA Basketball Materials Signatures

STATED PRINT RUN 25 TO 49 SER.#'d SETS
1 Alonzo Mourning/25 40.00
2 Carlos Boozer/25 12.50
3 Christian Laettner/49 20.00
5 Dan Majerle/49 12.50
6 Dominique Wilkins/25 25.00
7 Joe Dumars/49 10.00
9 Larry Johnson/49 20.00
10 Steve Smith/49 10.00

2010-11 Elite Black Box USA Basketball Patches Signatures

STATED PRINT RUN 5 TO 49 SER.#'d SETS
SOME UNPRICED DUE TO SCARCITY
2 Chris Mullin/49 20.00
6 Isiah Thomas/49 EXCH 15.00
11 Kevin Love/25 15.00
12 Kobe Bryant/49 100.00
17 Sean Elliott/49 12.00
18 Tyson Chandler/25 12.00
20 Walt Bellamy/25 12.00

1994-95 Embossed

Featuring 121 double-sided, standard-size embo cards, the 1994-95 Embossed set marks the pre a new product for Topps. Each six-card pack con five basic cards and one Golden Idols parallel go card, with a suggested retail of 3.00 per pack. Th fronts display a color embossed player photo fra by a textured border. The backs carry a second embossed player photo, biography, statistics, an special "Did You Know" section containing uniqu information not found on other Topps cards. The are grouped alphabetically within teams. The set with a silver foil Draft Picks subset (101-120) fo by a Michael Jordan card that was added at the l minute. In addition to the Draft Picks, all of the Houston Rockets cards were given a foil backgrc treatment. Rookie Cards of note in this set incluc Grant Hill, Juwan Howard, Jason Kidd and Glenn Robinson.

COMPLETE SET (121) 10.00
1 Stacey Augmon .20
2 Mookie Blaylock .15
3 Ken Norman .15
4 Steve Smith .20
5 Dee Brown .15
6 Blue Edwards .15
7 Dino Radja .20
8 Dominique Wilkins .30
9 Muggsy Bogues .20
10 Dell Curry .15
11 Larry Johnson .25
12 Alonzo Mourning .30
13 B.J. Armstrong .15
14 Ron Harper .20
15 Toni Kukoc .30
16 Scottie Pippen .50
17 Tyrone Hill .15
18 Mark Price .25
19 John Williams .15
20 Jim Jackson .15
21 Popeye Jones .15
22 Jamal Mashburn .25
23 Mahmoud Abdul-Rauf .15
24 LaPhonso Ellis .15
25 Dikembe Mutombo .25
26 Rodney Rogers .15
27 Joe Dumars .25
28 Lindsey Hunter .15
29 Oliver Miller .15
30 Terry Mills .15
31 Tom Gugliotta .15
32 Tim Hardaway .25
33 Chris Mullin .25
34 Latrell Sprewell .30
35 Sam Cassell FOIL .25
36 Robert Horry FOIL .25
37 Vernon Maxwell FOIL .15
38 Hakeem Olajuwon FOIL .30
39 Otis Thorpe FOIL .15

rk Jackson .25 .60
gie Miller .30 .75
Smits .20 .50
y Dehere .15 .40
nley Roberts .15 .40
Vaught .15 .40
de Divac .25 .60
rge Lynch .15 .40
k Van Exel .25 .60
y Owens .15 .40
n Rice .25 .60
in Willis .15 .40
Baker .25 .60
d Day .15 .40
Murdock .15 .40
istian Laettner .20 .50
ah Rider .25 .60
heal Williams .15 .40
ny Anderson .20 .50
Brown .15 .40
ick Coleman .20 .50
is Morris .15 .40
ick Ewing .30 .75
ek Harper .20 .50
hony Mason .15 .40
rles Oakley .20 .50
n Starks .20 .50
ace Grant .20 .50
ernee Hardaway .40 1.00
quille O'Neal .60 1.50
nis Scott .15 .40
wn Bradley .15 .40
Malone .15 .40
ence Weatherspoon .15 .40
rles Barkley .40 1.00
in Johnson .25 .60
Majerle .25 .60
ny Manning .20 .50
man Tisdale .15 .40
de Drexler .30 .75
ford Robinson .15 .40
Strickland .15 .40
by Hurley .25 .60
n Polynice .15 .40
h Richmond .25 .60
d Webb .25 .60
Elliott .25 .60
ck Person .20 .50
id Robinson .40 1.00
nis Rodman .50 1.25
dall Gill .15 .40
wn Kemp .25 .60
nas Marciulionis .15 .40
Payton .25 .60
f Schrempf .25 .60
Hornacek .20 .50
Malone .30 .75
Stockton .30 .75
MacLean .15 .40
t Skiles .15 .40
is Webber .40 1.00
nn Robinson FOIL RC .50 1.25
on Kidd FOIL RC 1.25 3.00
nt Hill FOIL RC 1.25 3.00
nyell Marshall FOIL RC .25 .60
an Howard FOIL RC .40 1.00
arone Wright FOIL RC .25 .60
nond Murray FOIL RC .25 .60
an Grant FOIL RC .40 1.00
Montross FOIL RC .25 .60
die Jones FOIL RC .75 2.00
los Rogers FOIL RC .25 .60
lid Reeves FOIL RC .25 .60
n Rose FOIL RC .60 1.50
a Dare FOIL RC .25 .60
Piatkowski FOIL RC .30 .75
ford Rozier FOIL RC .25 .60
n McKie FOIL RC .25 .60
Mobley FOIL RC .25 .60
y Dumas FOIL RC .25 .60
Tyler FOIL RC .25 .60
hael Jordan 4.00 10.00

-95 Embossed Golden Idols

one per pack, this 121-card set parallels the 1994-95 Embossed issue. The only difference gold foil treatment on each card front. Please he multipliers provided below for individual ues.

TE SET (121) 25.00 60.00
.8X TO 2X BASIC CARDS

1994-95 Emotion

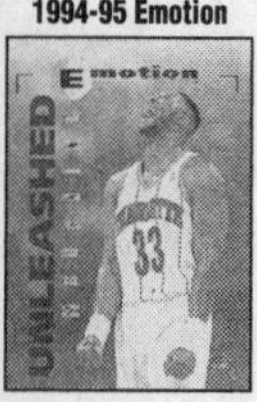

plete 1994-95 Emotion set (produced by consists of 121 standard size cards. The cards ed in eight-card packs with 36 packs per box. d retail price was $4.99 per pack. The fronts -bleed color photos. Predominantly placed in le is a one word description of the player. The ve career statistics and player information two photo background. The cards are alphabetically within teams. The set closes topical subsets: Rookies (101-110) and 111-120). A Grant Hill SkyMotion card was those who sent in two wrappers and a check order for 24.99 before December 31st, 1995. shows three seconds of a Hill dunk. Rookie note in this set include Grant Hill, Juwan Eddie Jones, Jason Kidd and Glenn Robinson.

TE SET (121) 20.00 50.00
Augmon .30 .75
Blaylock .25 .60
mith .30 .75
inor RC .40 1.00
ontross RC .40 1.00
adja .30 .75
que Wilkins .50 1.25
y Bogues .30 .75
ohnson .40 1.00
Mourning .50 1.25
rmstrong .25 .60
ukoc .50 1.25
Pippen .75 2.00
Simpkins RC .40 1.00
15 Tyrone Hill .25 .60
16 Chris Mills .25 .60
17 Mark Price .40 1.00
18 Tony Dumas RC .40 1.00
19 Jim Jackson .25 .60
20 Jason Kidd RC 2.00 5.00
21 Jamal Mashburn .40 1.00
22 LaPhonso Ellis .25 .60
23 Dikembe Mutombo .40 1.00
24 Rodney Rogers .25 .60
25 Jalen Rose RC 1.00 2.50
26 Bill Curley RC .40 1.00
27 Joe Dumars .40 1.00
28 Grant Hill RC 2.00 5.00
29 Tim Hardaway .40 1.00
30 Donyell Marshall RC .40 1.00
31 Chris Mullin .40 1.00
32 Carlos Rogers RC .40 1.00
33 Clifford Rozier RC .40 1.00
34 Latrell Sprewell .50 1.25
35 Sam Cassell .40 1.00
36 Clyde Drexler .50 1.25
37 Robert Horry .40 1.00
38 Hakeem Olajuwon .50 1.25
39 Mark Jackson .40 1.00
40 Reggie Miller .50 1.25
41 Rik Smits .30 .75
42 Lamond Murray RC .40 1.00
43 Eric Piatkowski RC .50 1.25
44 Loy Vaught .25 .60
45 Cedric Ceballos .25 .60
46 Eddie Jones RC 1.25 3.00
47 George Lynch .25 .60
48 Nick Van Exel .40 1.00
49 Harold Miner .25 .60
50 Khalid Reeves RC .40 1.00
51 Glen Rice .40 1.00
52 Kevin Willis .25 .60
53 Vin Baker .40 1.00
54 Eric Mobley RC .40 1.00
55 Eric Murdock .25 .60
56 Glenn Robinson RC .75 2.00
57 Tom Gugliotta .25 .60
58 Christian Laettner .30 .75
59 Isaiah Rider .40 1.00
60 Kenny Anderson .30 .75
61 Derrick Coleman .30 .75
62 Yinka Dare RC .40 1.00
63 Patrick Ewing .50 1.25
64 John Starks .30 .75
65 Charlie Ward RC .40 1.00
66 Monty Williams RC .40 1.00
67 Nick Anderson .25 .60
68 Horace Grant .30 .75
69 Anfernee Hardaway .60 1.50
70 Shaquille O'Neal 1.00 2.50
71 Brooks Thompson RC .40 1.00
72 Dana Barros .25 .60
73 Shawn Bradley .25 .60
74 B.J. Tyler RC .40 1.00
75 Clarence Weatherspoon .25 .60
76 Sharone Wright RC .40 1.00
77 Charles Barkley .60 1.50
78 Kevin Johnson .40 1.00
79 Dan Majerle .40 1.00
80 Danny Manning .30 .75
81 Wesley Person RC .40 1.00
82 Aaron McKie RC .40 1.00
83 Clifford Robinson .25 .60
84 Rod Strickland .25 .60
85 Brian Grant RC .60 1.50
86 Bobby Hurley .40 1.00
87 Mitch Richmond .40 1.00
88 Sean Elliott .40 1.00
89 David Robinson .60 1.50
90 Dennis Rodman .75 2.00
91 Shawn Kemp .40 1.00
92 Gary Payton .40 1.00
93 Dontonio Wingfield RC .40 1.00
94 Jeff Hornacek .30 .75
95 Karl Malone .50 1.25
96 John Stockton .50 1.25
97 Calbert Cheaney .25 .60
98 Juwan Howard RC .60 1.50
99 Chris Webber .60 1.50
100 Michael Jordan 5.00 12.00
101 Brian Grant ROO .30 .75
102 Grant Hill ROO 1.00 2.50
103 Juwan Howard ROO .30 .75
104 Eddie Jones ROO .60 1.50
105 Jason Kidd ROO 1.00 2.50
106 Eric Montross ROO .20 .50
107 Lamond Murray ROO .20 .50
108 Wesley Person ROO .20 .50
109 Glenn Robinson ROO .40 1.00
110 Sharone Wright ROO .20 .50
111 Anfernee Hardaway MAS .30 .75
112 Shawn Kemp MAS .20 .50
113 Karl Malone MAS .25 .60
114 Alonzo Mourning MAS .25 .60
115 Shaquille O'Neal MAS .50 1.25
116 Hakeem Olajuwon MAS .25 .60
117 Scottie Pippen MAS .40 1.00
118 David Robinson MAS .30 .75
119 Latrell Sprewell MAS .25 .60
120 Chris Webber MAS .30 .75
121 Checklist .25 .60
NNO Grant Hill 20.00 50.00
SkyMotion Exchange
NNO Grant Hill 1.00 2.50
David Robinson Promo

1994-95 Emotion N-Tense

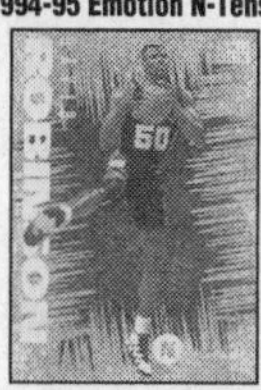

Cards from this 10-card standard-size set were randomly inserted in Emotion packs at a rate of one in 18. The set contains a selection of some of the top players in the NBA. The fronts have full-bleed color photos and the player's name down the left in a hologram set against a sparkling gold background. The backs have two color action photos with the players name across the middle against a black background. The set is sequenced in alphabetical order.

COMPLETE SET (10) 25.00 60.00
N1 Charles Barkley 3.00 8.00
N2 Patrick Ewing 2.50 6.00
N3 Michael Jordan 15.00 40.00
N4 Shawn Kemp 2.00 5.00
N5 Karl Malone 2.50 6.00
N6 Alonzo Mourning 2.50 6.00
N7 Shaquille O'Neal 5.00 12.00
N8 Hakeem Olajuwon 2.50 6.00
N9 David Robinson 3.00 8.00
N10 Glenn Robinson 2.00 5.00

1994-95 Emotion X-Cited

Cards from this 20-card standard-size set were randomly inserted in Emotion packs at a rate of one in four. The set features a selection of the top guards and small forwards in the NBA. The fronts have full-bleed color photos and the player's last name across the top set against a sparkling background. The backs have two color action photos set against a black background. The set is sequenced in alphabetical order.

COMPLETE SET (20) 15.00 40.00
X1 Kenny Anderson 1.00 2.50
X2 Anfernee Hardaway 2.00 5.00
X3 Tim Hardaway 1.25 3.00
X4 Grant Hill 4.00 10.00
X5 Jim Jackson .75 2.00
X6 Eddie Jones 2.50 6.00
X7 Jason Kidd 4.00 10.00
X8 Dan Majerle 1.25 3.00
X9 Jamal Mashburn 1.25 3.00
X10 Lamond Murray .75 2.00
X11 Gary Payton .75 2.00
X12 Wesley Person .75 2.00
X13 Scottie Pippen 2.50 6.00
X14 Mark Price 1.25 3.00
X15 Mitch Richmond 1.25 3.00
X16 Isaiah Rider 1.25 3.00
X17 Latrell Sprewell 1.50 4.00
X18 John Stockton 1.50 4.00
X19 Rod Strickland .75 2.00
X20 Nick Van Exel 1.25 3.00

2001 eTopps

eTopps was introduced to the hobby via a special "Topps Trading Floor" on eBay with opening prices of $4.00, $6.50, or $9.50 per card. Six different cards were available each week, and once purchased, the buyer had the option of keeping the cards in his/her portfolio for resale, or delivered in a tamper-proof acrylic case. The eTopps floor was run very similar to the workings of the stock market.

1 Darius Miles/795 1.00 2.50
2 Glenn Robinson/474 3.00 8.00
3 Allen Iverson/4368 1.00 2.50
4 Derek Anderson/635 1.00 2.50
5 David Robinson/931 4.00 10.00
6 Gary Payton/640 2.50 6.00
7 Baron Davis/521 2.50 6.00
8 Antoine Walker/763 1.25 3.00
9 Jerry Stackhouse/400 6.00 15.00
10 Vince Carter/2871 1.00 2.50
11 Shawn Marion/2000 1.00 2.50
12 Grant Hill/542 2.50 6.00
13 Kenyon Martin/646 1.50 4.00
14 Eddie Jones/572 1.00 2.50
15 Kobe Bryant/5000 4.00 10.00
16 Michael Finley/1880 1.00 2.50
17 Andre Miller/688 1.25 3.00
18 Peja Stojakovic/1151 1.00 2.50
19 Richard Hamilton/1237 1.00 2.50
20 Steve Francis/841 1.50 4.00
21 Tracy McGrady/758 1.50 4.00
22 Jason Kidd/722 1.25 3.00
23 Lamar Odom/497 1.50 4.00
24 Antawn Jamison/451 2.50 6.00
25 Paul Pierce/797 1.50 4.00
26 Alonzo Mourning/519 2.50 6.00
27 Marcus Camby/810 1.25 3.00
28 Stephon Marbury/418 15.00 30.00
29 Morris Peterson/642 1.25 3.00
30 Tim Duncan/608 5.00 12.00
31 Jason Terry/605 1.25 3.00
32 Reggie Miller/678 6.00 15.00
33 Patrick Ewing/1497 1.25 3.00
34 Shaquille O'Neal/2270 1.50 4.00
35 Ray Allen/1153 1.25 3.00
36 Allan Houston/459 2.50 6.00
37 Dikembe Mutombo/532 2.00 5.00
38 Mike Bibby/638 1.25 3.00
39 Karl Malone/1015 8.00 20.00
40 Chris Webber/473 2.50 6.00
41 Wang Zhizhi/927 1.50 4.00
42 Elton Brand/648 1.50 4.00
43 Antonio McDyess/424 4.00 10.00
44 Shareef Abdur-Rahim/531 2.50 6.00
45 Jamal Mashburn/490 2.00 5.00
46 Jermaine O'Neal/561 2.50 6.00
47 Latrell Sprewell/1009 1.00 2.50
48 Mike Miller/625 2.50 6.00
49 John Stockton/797 2.50 6.00
50 Kevin Garnett/855 4.00 10.00
51 Hakeem Olajuwon/422 8.00 20.00
52 Dirk Nowitzki/1051 3.00 8.00
53 Rasheed Wallace/664 1.25 3.00
54 Kwame Brown/2640 1.00 2.50
55 Tyson Chandler/953 1.00 2.50
56 Pau Gasol/2262 1.25 3.00
57 Eddy Curry/894 1.00 2.50
58 Jason Richardson/1689 1.00 2.50
59 Shane Battier/1784 1.00 2.50
60 Eddie Griffin/869 15.00 40.00
61 Desagana Diop/649 1.00 2.50
62 Rodney White/491 1.50 4.00
63 Joe Johnson/2005 1.00 2.50
64 Kedrick Brown/573 1.25 3.00
65 Vladimir Radmanovic/711 1.00 2.50
66 Richard Jefferson/1915 1.00 2.50
67 Troy Murphy/545 1.25 3.00
68 Joseph Forte/640 1.25 3.00
69 Gerald Wallace/906 1.25 3.00
70 Tony Parker/2165 1.25 3.00
71 Jamaal Tinsley/2423 1.00 2.50
72 Loren Woods/594 1.00 2.50

2001 eTopps Test Run

This version of eTopps came out three months before regular eTopps IPO's were offered for basketball. Price information is limited so this set remains unpriced.

DD DeSagana Diop
EC Eddy Curry
EG Eddie Griffin
JF Joseph Forte
KB Kwame Brown
LW Loren Woods
RJ Richard Jefferson
RW Rodney White
TM Troy Murphy

2002 eTopps

1 Shaquille O'Neal/2273 2.00 5.00
2 Richard Jefferson/1349 1.00 2.50
3 Tracy McGrady/2090 1.00 2.50
4 Steve Francis/1075 1.00 2.50
5 Dirk Nowitzki/2140 1.25 3.00
6 Paul Pierce/1500 1.00 2.50
7 Ben Wallace/1682 1.00 2.50
8 Ray Allen/1129 1.00 2.50
9 Kevin Garnett/1707 1.00 2.50
10 Jermaine O'Neal/1177 1.00 2.50
11 Vince Carter/1889 1.00 2.50
12 Tim Duncan/1089 1.25 3.00
13 Nikoloz Tskitishvili/1468 1.00 2.50
14 Juan Dixon/3000 1.00 2.50
15 Marcus Haislip/1801 1.00 2.50
16 Mike Dunleavy/2859 1.00 2.50
17 Dan Dickau/2000 1.00 2.50
18 Nene Hilario/3000 1.00 2.50
19 Kareem Rush/2000 1.00 2.50
20 Caron Butler/3000 1.00 2.50
21 Jason Terry/1500 1.00 2.50
22 Elton Brand/801 1.00 2.50
23 Shane Battier/1415 1.00 2.50
24 Kenyon Martin/1087 1.00 2.50
25 Jerry Stackhouse/911 1.00 2.50
26 Eddy Curry/1500 1.00 2.50
27 Allen Iverson/1212 1.00 2.50
28 Chris Webber/1500 1.00 2.50
29 Gary Payton/1089 1.00 2.50
30 Mike Bibby/1280 1.00 2.50
31 Wally Szczerbiak/1072 1.50 4.00
32 Shawn Marion/1906 1.00 2.50
33 Jared Jeffries/1875 1.00 2.50
34 Fred Jones/2000 1.00 2.50
35 Drew Gooden/4000 1.00 2.50
36 Jay Williams/3000 1.00 2.50
37 Frank Williams/1864 1.00 2.50
38 Qyntel Woods/2000 1.00 2.50
39 Chris Wilcox/2000 1.00 2.50
40 Casey Jacobsen/1973 1.00 2.50
41 John Stockton/1500 1.00 2.50
42 Rasheed Wallace/762 1.00 2.50
43 Baron Davis/1000 1.00 2.50
44 Grant Hill/1093 1.00 2.50
45 Kobe Bryant/2000 4.00 10.00
46 Jason Richardson/1370 1.00 2.50
47 Andre Miller/722 1.00 2.50
48 Antoine Walker/1585 1.00 2.50
49 Shareef Abdur-Rahim/700 1.00 2.50
50 Tony Parker/1378 2.00 5.00
51 Jason Kidd/1266 1.00 2.50
52 Darius Miles/1108 1.00 2.50
53 Yao Ming/6000 1.00 2.50
54 Manu Ginobili/2000 1.00 2.50
55 John Salmons/1268 1.00 2.50
56 Melvin Ely/1611 1.00 2.50
57 Dajuan Wagner/4000 1.00 2.50
58 Amare Stoudemire/4000 1.00 2.50
59 Bostjan Nachbar/1851 1.00 2.50
60 Marko Jaric/1533 1.00 2.50
61 Antonio McDyess/951 1.00 2.50
62 Pau Gasol/1097 1.00 2.50
63 Steve Nash/2675 1.00 2.50
64 Karl Malone/1500 1.00 2.50
65 Richard Hamilton/738 1.00 2.50
66 Peja Stojakovic/1507 1.00 2.50
67 Jamal Mashburn/641 2.00 5.00
68 Glenn Robinson/1000 1.25 3.00
69 Jamaal Tinsley/1034 1.25 3.00
70 Tyson Chandler/1500 1.00 2.50
71 Jerome Williams/1219 1.00 2.50
72 Latrell Sprewell/1000 1.00 2.50
73 Scottie Pippen/1050 1.50 4.00
74 Ricky Davis/1145 1.00 2.50
75 Carlos Boozer/2309 1.00 2.50
76 Andrei Kirilenko/1254 1.00 2.50
77 Gordan Giricek/1573 1.00 2.50
78 Gilbert Arenas/2000 1.00 2.50

2002 eTopps Event Series

ES3 Shaquille O'Neal/3000 2.50 6.00
Lakers Champs

2003 eTopps

1 Tim Duncan/740 1.50 4.00
2 Michael Redd/853 1.00 2.50
3 Antawn Jamison/500 1.00 2.50
4 Allan Houston/532 1.00 2.50
5 Kobe Bryant/1371 4.00 10.00
6 Matt Harpring/635 1.25 3.00
7 Kevin Garnett/664 2.50 6.00
8 Dirk Nowitzki/1000 1.00 2.50
10 Jason Richardson/764 1.00 2.50
11 Amare Stoudemire/554 2.00 5.00
12 Chris Webber/589 2.50 6.00
13 Larry Hughes/717 1.00 2.50
14 Alonzo Mourning/1000 1.00 2.50
15 Yao Ming/1105 1.50 4.00
16 Ron Artest/450 2.50 6.00
17 Kenyon Martin/760 1.00 2.50
19 Stephon Marbury/509 1.25 3.00
20 Shaquille O'Neal/1070 2.00 5.00
21 Jermaine O'Neal/934 1.25 3.00
22 Drew Gooden/392 3.00 8.00
23 Tony Parker/626 3.00 8.00
24 Vince Carter/622 1.25 3.00
25 Jason Kidd/693 1.00 2.50
26 Caron Butler/602 1.50 4.00
27 Paul Pierce/775 1.25 3.00
28 Steve Nash/615 1.00 2.50
29 Al Harrington/642 1.00 2.50
30 Allen Iverson/949 1.25 3.00
31 Troy Hudson/803 1.00 2.50
32 Troy Murphy/607 1.00 2.50
33 Nene/744 1.00 2.50
34 Zydrunas Ilgauskas/558 1.00 2.50
35 Steve Francis/675 1.00 2.50
36 Ray Allen/900 1.00 2.50
37 Bobby Jackson/562 1.00 2.50
38 Ben Wallace/1000 1.00 2.50
39 Quentin Richardson/605 1.00 2.50
40 Tracy McGrady/812 1.00 2.50
41 Shareef Abdur-Rahim/546 6.00 15.00
42 Gary Payton/1000 1.00 2.50
43 LeBron James/10000 15.00 30.00
44 Darko Milicic/1789 1.00 2.50
45 Carmelo Anthony/5000 4.00 10.00
46 Chris Bosh/1571 5.00 12.00
47 Dwyane Wade/1208 15.00 40.00
48 Chris Kaman/641 1.50 4.00
49 Kirk Hinrich/686 1.25 3.00
50 T.J. Ford/1500 1.00 2.50
51 Mike Sweetney/910 1.00 2.50
52 Jarvis Hayes/922 1.00 2.50
53 Mickael Pietrus/902 1.50 4.00
54 Nick Collison/1000 1.00 2.50
55 Marcus Banks/687 1.00 2.50
56 Luke Ridnour/874 1.00 2.50
57 Reece gaines/982 1.00 2.50
58 Troy Bell/821 1.00 2.50
59 Zarko Cabarkapa/641 1.25 3.00
60 David West/876 1.00 2.50
61 Aleksandar Pavlovic/618 1.00 2.50
62 Dahntay Jones/798 1.00 2.50
63 Boris Diaw/701 1.00 2.50
64 Zoran Planinic/573 1.00 2.50
65 Travis Outlaw/798 1.00 2.50
66 Brian Cook/768 1.00 2.50
67 Ndudi Ebi/1000 1.00 2.50
68 Kendrick Perkins/857 1.00 2.50
69 Jason Kapono/547 1.00 2.50
70 Luke Walton/1203 1.00 2.50
71 Leandro Barbosa/1000 1.00 2.50
72 Steve Blake/690 1.00 2.50
73 Josh Howard/1000 1.00 2.50
74 Carlos Arroyo/1000 1.00 2.50
75 Zach Randolph/1250 1.00 2.50
76 Brad Miller/1000 1.00 2.50
77 Desmond Mason/918 1.00 2.50
78 Chauncey Billups/977 1.00 2.50
79 Sam Cassell/1000 1.00 2.50
80 Rashard Lewis/923 1.00 2.50

2004 eTopps

1 Miami Heat/1000 1.00 2.50
2 Detroit Pistons/1000 1.00 2.50
3 Cleveland Cavaliers/1000 1.00 2.50
4 Denver Nuggets/1000 1.00 2.50
5 New York Knicks/605 1.00 2.50
6 Dallas Mavericks/1000 1.00 2.50
7 Minnesota Timberwolves/928 1.00 2.50
8 Phoenix Suns/945 1.00 2.50
9 Toronto Raptors/559 2.00 5.00
10 Seattle Supersonics/925 1.50 4.00
11 Utah Jazz/748 1.50 4.00
12 Boston Celtics/688 1.00 2.50
13 Sacramento Kings/766 1.00 2.50
14 Orlando Magic/770 1.00 2.50
15 Indiana Pacers/745 1.00 2.50
16 San Antonio Spurs/950 1.00 2.50
17 Memphis Grizzlies/640 1.00 2.50
18 Los Angeles Lakers/850 1.00 2.50
19 Charlotte Bobcats/950 1.00 2.50
20 Houston Rockets/511 1.50 4.00
21 Golden State Warriors/531 2.00 5.00
22 Chicago Bulls/750 1.50 4.00
23 Atlanta Hawks/499 8.00 20.00
24 Los Angeles Clippers/719 1.00 2.50
25 Milwaukee Bucks/654 1.00 2.50
26 New Jersey Nets/673 1.00 2.50
27 New Orleans Hornets/688 1.00 2.50
28 Philadelphia 76ers/700 1.00 2.50
29 Portland Trail Blazers/700 1.00 2.50
30 Washington Wizards/700 1.00 2.50
31 Tracy McGrady/1000 1.00 2.50
32 Kenyon Martin/1000 1.00 2.50
33 LeBron James/2000 5.00 12.00
34 Carmelo Anthony/2000 1.00 2.50
35 Dwight Howard/3000 4.00 10.00
36 Emeka Okafor/3000 1.00 2.50
37 Shaquille O'Neal/2000 1.00 2.50
38 Ben Gordon/2000 1.00 2.50
39 Devin Harris/1362 1.00 2.50
40 Kris Humphries/839 1.00 2.50
41 Andre Iguodala/982 1.50 4.00
42 Luke Jackson/1366 1.00 2.50
43 Al Jefferson/1000 1.00 2.50
44 Josh Childress/1220 1.00 2.50
45 Jameer Nelson/1000 2.00 5.00
46 Kobe Bryant/1000 2.00 5.00
47 Kirk Snyder/896 1.00 2.50
48 Sebastian Telfair/1756 1.00 2.50
49 Andris Biedrins/868 1.50 4.00
50 Shaun Livingston/2000 1.00 2.50
51 Robert Swift/813 1.00 2.50
52 Rafael Araujo/877 1.00 2.50
53 Lamar Odom/560 1.00 2.50
54 Luol Deng/1000 1.00 2.50
55 J.R. Smith/1000 1.00 2.50
56 Trevor Ariza/1000 1.00 2.50
57 Dwyane Wade/2000 4.00 10.00
58 Peter John Ramos/626 1.00 2.50
59 Carlos Arroyo/633 1.00 2.50
60 Amare Stoudemire/1000 1.00 2.50
61 Jamal Crawford/739 1.00 2.50
62 Quentin Richardson/548 1.00 2.50
63 Marquis Daniels/688 1.00 2.50
64 Corey Maggette/672 1.00 2.50
65 Yao Ming/1000 1.25 3.00
66 Samuel Dalembert/578 1.50 4.00
67 David Harrison/814 1.00 2.50
68 Chris Duhon/963 1.00 2.50
69 Bonzi Wells/580 1.00 2.50
70 Kevin Garnett/1000 1.00 2.50
71 Dirk Nowitzki/907 1.00 2.50
72 Josh Smith/800 2.00 5.00
73 Allen Iverson/604 1.00 2.50
74 Tim Duncan/1000 1.25 3.00
75 Kyle Korver/800 1.00 2.50
76 Rashard Lewis/800 1.00 2.50
78 Stephon Marbury/800 1.00 2.50

2004 eTopps ECON Cleveland

These cards were given away to VIP attendees to the 2004 edition of The National Sports Collectors Convention in Cleveland. Each card features a famous Cleveland area athlete with The National logo at the top of the card and the eTopps and player names at the bottom.

2 Larry Nance/860 1.50 4.00

2005 eTopps

1 Al Harrington/463 1.25 3.00
2 Paul Pierce/527 3.00 8.00
3 Emeka Okafor/672 1.00 2.50
4 Kirk Hinrich/690 1.00 2.50
5 Lebron James/1000 3.00 8.00
6 Dirk Nowitzki/577 1.50 4.00
7 Carmelo Anthony/1000 1.00 2.50
8 Ben Wallace/605 1.00 2.50
9 Baron Davis/594 1.00 2.50
10 Yao Ming/695 2.00 5.00
11 Jermaine O'Neal/602 2.00 5.00
12 Elton Brand/620 1.00 2.50
13 Kobe Bryant/1000 2.00 5.00
14 Pau Gasol/551 1.00 2.50
15 Dwyane Wade/1500 1.25 3.00
16 Desmond Mason/461 1.50 4.00
17 Kevin Garnett/1000 1.25 3.00
18 Vince Carter/645 1.00 2.50
19 J.R. Smith/534 10.00 25.00
20 Stephon Marbury/529 1.00 2.50
21 Dwight Howard/937 1.25 3.00
22 Allen Iverson/905 1.00 2.50
23 Steve Nash/641 1.00 2.50
24 Zach Randolph/481 1.25 3.00
25 Mike Bibby/564 1.00 2.50
26 Tim Duncan/983 1.25 3.00
27 Ray Allen/602 1.25 3.00
28 Chris Bosh/525 1.50 4.00
29 Carlos Boozer/490 1.25 3.00
30 Gilbert Arenas/702 1.00 2.50
31 Bobby Simmons/504 1.00 2.50
32 Andres Nocioni/590 1.00 2.50
33 Udonis Haslem/544 1.00 2.50
34 Tayshaun Prince/685 1.00 2.50
35 Primoz Brezec/512 1.00 2.50
36 Nenad Krstic/554 1.00 2.50
37 Rafer Alston/493 1.00 2.50
38 Damon Jones/528 1.00 2.50
39 Brent Barry/525 1.00 2.50
40 Earl Boykins/500 1.50 4.00
41 Gerald Green/1500 1.00 2.50
42 Francisco Garcia/1000 1.00 2.50
43 Joey Graham/579 1.00 2.50
44 Deron Williams/1334 2.00 5.00
45 Andrew Bogut/2000 1.00 2.50
46 Chris Paul/2000 4.00 10.00
47 Hakim Warrick/1000 1.00 2.50
48 Antoine Wright/662 1.00 2.50
49 Rashad McCants/1000 1.00 2.50
50 Sarunas Jasikevicius/847 1.00 2.50
51 Channing Frye/1000 1.00 2.50
52 Ike Diogu/945 1.00 2.50
53 Danny Granger/1000 3.00 8.00
54 Charlie Villanueva/906 1.00 2.50
55 Andrew Bynum/844 4.00 10.00
56 Marvin Williams/2000 1.00 2.50
57 Raymond Felton/1156 1.00 2.50
58 Martell Webster/1000 1.00 2.50
59 Sean May/1000 1.00 2.50
60 Julius Hodge/565 1.00 2.50

2005 eTopps Autographs

AI1 Allen Iverson 50.00 125.00
2001 eTopps/40
AI2 Allen Iverson 50.00 125.00
2002 eTopps/40
AI3 Allen Iverson 50.00 125.00
2003 eTopps/40
AI4 Allen Iverson
2004 eTopps/30
BG1 Ben Gordon
2004 eTopps/50
DW1 Dwyane Wade 75.00 150.00
2003 eTopps/63
DW2 Dwyane Wade
2004 eTopps/33
ES1 Steve Nash 200.00 350.00
Dwyane Wade
2005 eTopps Event Series
ST1 Sebastian Telfair
2004 eTopps/105

2005 eTopps Classic

1 Bill Russell/1500 2.50 6.00
2 Elgin Baylor/925 3.00 8.00
4 Oscar Robertson/934 3.00 8.00
5 Willis Reed/672 2.50 6.00
6 Spud Webb/506 3.00 8.00
7 Bill Walton/768 3.00 8.00
8 Chris Mullin/525 3.00 8.00
9 Darryl Dawkins/537 3.00 8.00
10 Earl Monroe/562 3.00 8.00
11 Hal Greer/563 3.00 8.00
12 John Havlicek/759 3.00 8.00
13 Moses Malone/670 2.50 6.00
14 Phil Jackson/589 3.00 8.00
15 Robert Parish/586 2.50 6.00
16 Gail Goodrich/485 5.00 12.00
17 Dolph Schayes/579 2.50 6.00
18 Manute Bol/519 2.50 6.00
19 Bob Pettit/496 4.00 10.00
20 Tom Heinsohn/592 3.00 8.00
21 Magic Johnson/1000 4.00 10.00
22 Dominique Wilkins/635 3.00 8.00
23 Isiah Thomas/941 3.00 8.00
24 Dennis Rodman/849 4.00 10.00

2005 eTopps Playoffs

1 Suns and Heat Complete Sweep/5141.25 3.00
2 Steve Nash/679 .75 2.00
3 Reggie Miller/1000 2.50 6.00
4 Tony Parker/706 .75 2.00
5 Rasheed Wallace/560 1.00 2.50
6 Robert Horry/609 1.25 3.00
7 Spurs Regain the Throne/1000 .75 2.00
8 Tim Duncan/950 1.25 3.00

2006 eTopps

1 Dwyane Wade/999 1.50 4.00
1 Amare Stoudemire/425 2.50 6.00
2 Chris Paul/999 1.00 2.50
3 Andrea Bargnani/1499 1.00 2.50
4 Randy Foye/999 1.00 2.50
5 Craig Smith/799 1.00 2.50
6 Allen Iverson/655 1.00 2.50
7 Lebron James/999 3.00 8.00
8 Tyrus Thomas/799 1.00 2.50
9 Adam Morrison/999 1.00 2.50
10 Jordan Farmar/799 8.00 20.00
11 Marcus Williams/799 1.00 2.50
12 Brandon Roy/799 2.50 6.00
13 Dirk Nowitzki/499 2.50 6.00
14 Kevin Garnett/799 1.25 3.00
15 Rudy Gay/999 1.25 3.00
16 Rajon Rondo/1025 4.00 10.00
17 Shelden Williams/799 1.00 2.50
19 Kobe Bryant/999 2.00 5.00
20 Lamarcus Aldridge/799 2.50 6.00
21 Allan Ray/799 1.00 2.50
22 J.J. Redick/799 1.00 2.50
23 Rodney Carney/799 1.00 2.50
24 Tim Duncan/405 4.00 10.00
25 Vince Carter/699 1.00 2.50
26 Tracy McGrady/699 1.00 2.50
27 Renaldo Balkman/699 1.00 2.50
28 Josh Boone/699 1.00 2.50
29 Daniel Gibson/699 1.00 2.50
30 Shaquille O'Neal/413 6.00 15.00
31 Carmelo Anthony/699 1.00 2.50
32 Ronnie Brewer/699 1.00 2.50
33 Patrick O'Bryant/699 1.00 2.50
34 Hilton Armstrong/699 1.00 2.50
35 Alexander Johnson/699 1.00 2.50
36 Steve Nash/434 2.00 5.00
37 David Lee/499 1.50 4.00
38 Paul Millsap/699 1.00 2.50
39 Thabo Sefolosha/699 1.00 2.50
40 Kyle Lowry/599 1.50 4.00
41 Jorge Garbajosa/699 1.00 2.50
42 Yao Ming/399 6.00 15.00

2006 eTopps Event Series National VIP Promos

DW Dwyane Wade 2.00 5.00

2006 eTopps Playoffs

9 Dwyane Wade/1161 1.00 2.50

2006 eTopps Autographs

CA1 Carmelo Anthony 25.00 60.00
2006 eTopps McDonald's/72
CC1 Chris Collins
2006 eTopps McDonald's/29
CP1 Chris Paul 25.00 60.00
2006 eTopps McDonald's/112
CV1 Charlie Villanueva
2006 eTopps McDonald's/42
DR1 Dennis Rodman 20.00 50.00
2005 eTopps Classic/50
JO1 Jermaine O'Neal
2006 eTopps McDonald's/67
MJ1 Magic Johnson
2005 eTopps Classic/52
MJ2 Magic Johnson
2006 eTopps McDonald's/97
SH1 Shaheen Holloway
2006 eTopps McDonald's/35
VC1 Vince Carter
2001 eTopps/34
VC2 Vince Carter
2002 eTopps/19
VC3 Vince Carter
2003 eTopps/14
VC4 Vince Carter
2005 eTopps/34

2006 eTopps McDonald's

1 Jermaine O'Neal 2.00 5.00
2 Chris Paul 1.00 2.50
3 Kenny Smith 3.00 8.00
4 Carmelo Anthony 2.50 6.00
5 Shaheen Holloway 3.00 8.00
6 Shaquille O'Neal 1.50 4.00
7 Magic Johnson 1.50 4.00
10 Elton Brand 2.00 5.00
11 Chris Collins 2.00 5.00
12 Tommy Amaker 2.00 5.00
13 Richard Hamilton 1.50 4.00
14 Vince Carter 1.50 4.00
15 Corey Maggette 1.50 4.00
16 Charlie Villanueva 1.50 4.00

2007 eTopps

1 Jermaine O'Neal/699 1.25 3.00
2 Rashard Lewis/699 1.00 2.50
3 Al Horford/999 1.50 4.00
4 Luis Scola/799 1.00 2.50
5 Mike Conley Jr./999 1.00 2.50
6 Kevin Garnett/544 2.00 5.00
7 Chris Paul/699 1.00 2.50
8 Yi Jianlian/999 1.00 2.50
9 Sean Williams/699 1.00 2.50
10 Ray Allen/699 1.00 2.50
11 Greg Oden/1499 1.25 3.00
12 Javaris Crittenton/599 1.00 2.50
13 Dwight Howard/749 1.25 3.00
14 Carmelo Anthony/699 1.25 3.00
15 Glen Davis/749 1.25 3.00
16 Nick Young/749 1.25 3.00
17 Jason Richardson/699 1.00 2.50
18 Kobe Bryant/999 2.50 6.00
19 Kevin Durant/1499 15.00 40.00
20 Zach Randolph/352 8.00 20.00
21 Julian Wright/749 1.00 2.50
22 Joakim Noah/749 1.50 4.00
23 Deron Williams/699 1.25 3.00
24 Chris Bosh/699 1.00 2.50
25 Rodney Stuckey/749 1.00 2.50
26 D.J. Strawberry/749 1.00 2.50
27 Dwyane Wade/899 1.50 4.00
28 Arron Afflalo/699 1.00 2.50
29 Al Thornton/1060 1.00 2.50
30 Tony Parker/499 2.00 5.00
31 Shaquille O'Neal/499 2.00 5.00
32 Brandan Wright/699 1.00 2.50
33 Acie Law/499 1.00 2.50
34 LeBron James/999 3.00 8.00
35 Allen Iverson/649 1.00 2.50
36 Dirk Nowitzki/649 1.00 2.50
37 Corey Brewer/699 1.00 2.50
38 Jeff Green/699 1.25 3.00
39 Jason Kidd/439 2.00 5.00
40 Vince Carter/599 1.00 2.50
41 Thaddeus Young/749 1.00 2.50
42 Jason Smith/709 1.00 2.50
43 Spencer Hawes/499 6.00 15.00
44 Daequan Cook/699 1.00 2.50

2007 eTopps Autographs

BR1 Bill Russell 125.00 250.00
2005 eTopps Classic/50
SO1 Shaquille O'Neal
2006 eTopps McDonald's/83
VC5 Vince Carter 25.00 60.00
2006 eTopps McDonald's/75

2008 eTopps

1 Chris Paul/599 1.50 4.00
2 Eric Gordon/749 3.00 8.00
3 Michael Beasley/999 2.00 5.00
4 Kevin Love/749 8.00 20.00
5 Brook Lopez/749 2.50 6.00
6 Dwight Howard/699 2.00 5.00
7 Marc Gasol/699 3.00 8.00
8 Sun Yue/699 1.00 2.50
9 Joe Johnson/639 2.50 6.00
10 Kevin Garnett/699 2.00 5.00
11 Allen Iverson/670 1.25 3.00
12 Kobe Bryant/484 10.00 25.00
13 O.J. Mayo/899 2.50 6.00
14 Chris Bosh/499 2.00 5.00
15 D.J. Augustin/699 1.25 3.00
16 Danilo Gallinari/561 3.00 8.00
17 Russell Westbrook/699 12.00 30.00
18 Carmelo Anthony/499 2.50 6.00
19 Derrick Rose/999 15.00 40.00
20 Rudy Fernandez/649 1.25 3.00
21 Marreese Speights/599 1.00 2.50
22 Dwyane Wade/499 5.00 12.00
23 Mario Chalmers/599 1.50 4.00
24 Jason Thompson/499 1.50 4.00
25 Shaquille O'Neal/499 2.50 6.00
26 Roy Hibbert/574 2.00 5.00
27 Ray Allen/649 1.50 4.00
28 Deron Williams/649 1.00 2.50

29 Kevin Durant/799	4.00	10.00
30 Anthony Morrow/649	1.50	4.00
31 Luc Mbah A Moute/649	1.00	2.50
32 LeBron James/529	10.00	25.00
44P Barack Obama/999	8.00	20.00

1995-96 E-XL

The 1995-96 Skybox E-XL set was issued in one series totalling 100 cards. Only the top veterans and rookies in the league were selected for inclusion within this premium brand set. The 6-card packs retailed for $4.99 each. Cards are numbered alphabetically within teams. The only subset is Untouchable (91-99). The product picks up where the 1994-95 SkyBox Emotion issue left off. Each player card features silhouetted action photo over a multi-colored background, framed by one of five different shaped die cut window designs. Only the player image and multi-colored backgrounds are UV coated. The rest of the card is non-UV coated, giving the card a unique look and feel. A non-numbered Grant Hill promo card was issued to preview the set.

COMPLETE SET (100)	15.00	40.00
1 Stacey Augmon	.30	.75
2 Mookie Blaylock	.25	.60
3 Christian Laettner	.30	.75
4 Dana Barros	.25	.60
5 Dino Radja	.30	.75
6 Eric Williams RC	.40	1.00
7 Kenny Anderson	.30	.75
8 Larry Johnson	.40	1.00
9 Glen Rice	.40	1.00
10 Michael Jordan	3.00	8.00
11 Toni Kukoc	.40	1.00
12 Scottie Pippen	.60	1.50
13 Dennis Rodman	.75	2.00
14 Terrell Brandon	.25	.60
15 Bobby Phills	.25	.60
16 Bob Sura RC	.40	1.00
17 Jim Jackson	.25	.60
18 Jason Kidd	.60	1.50
19 Jamal Mashburn	.40	1.00
20 Mahmoud Abdul-Rauf	.25	.60
21 Antonio McDyess RC	1.00	2.50
22 Dikembe Mutombo	.40	1.00
23 Joe Dumars	.40	1.00
24 Grant Hill	.60	1.50
25 Allan Houston	.30	.75
26 Joe Smith RC	.75	2.00
27 Latrell Sprewell	.40	1.00
28 Kevin Willis	.25	.60
29 Sam Cassell	.40	1.00
30 Clyde Drexler	.50	1.25
31 Robert Horry	.30	.75
32 Hakeem Olajuwon	.50	1.25
33 Derrick McKey	.25	.60
34 Reggie Miller	.50	1.25
35 Rik Smits	.30	.75
36 Brent Barry RC	.60	1.50
37 Loy Vaught	.25	.60
38 Brian Williams	.25	.60
39 Cedric Ceballos	.25	.60
40 Magic Johnson	1.00	2.50
41 Nick Van Exel	.40	1.00
42 Tim Hardaway	.40	1.00
43 Alonzo Mourning	.50	1.25
44 Kurt Thomas RC	.40	1.00
45 Walt Williams	.25	.60
46 Vin Baker	.30	.75
47 Shawn Respert RC	.40	1.00
48 Glenn Robinson	.40	1.00
49 Kevin Garnett RC	3.00	8.00
50 Tom Gugliotta	.25	.60
51 Isaiah Rider	.40	1.00
52 Shawn Bradley	.25	.60
53 Chris Childs	.25	.60
54 Ed O'Bannon RC	.40	1.00
55 Patrick Ewing	.50	1.25
56 Anthony Mason	.25	.60
57 Charles Oakley	.30	.75
58 Horace Grant	.30	.75
59 Anfernee Hardaway	.60	1.50
60 Shaquille O'Neal	1.00	2.50
61 Derrick Coleman	.30	.75
62 Jerry Stackhouse RC	1.25	3.00
63 Clarence Weatherspoon	.25	.60
64 Charles Barkley	.60	1.50
65 Michael Finley RC	1.25	3.00
66 Kevin Johnson	.40	1.00
67 Clifford Robinson	.25	.60
68 Arvydas Sabonis RC	.75	2.00
69 Rod Strickland	.25	.60
70 Tyus Edney RC	.40	1.00
71 Billy Owens	.25	.60
72 Mitch Richmond	.40	1.00
73 Sean Elliott	.40	1.00
74 Avery Johnson	.30	.75
75 David Robinson	.60	1.50
76 Shawn Kemp	.40	1.00
77 Gary Payton	.40	1.00
78 Detlef Schrempf	.40	1.00
79 Tracy Murray	.25	.60
80 Damon Stoudamire RC	1.00	2.50
81 Sharone Wright	.25	.60
82 Jeff Hornacek	.30	.75
83 Karl Malone	.50	1.25
84 John Stockton	.50	1.25
85 Greg Anthony	.25	.60
86 Bryant Reeves RC	.40	1.00
87 Byron Scott	.30	.75
88 Juwan Howard	.40	1.00
89 Gheorghe Muresan	.25	.60
90 Rasheed Wallace RC	1.25	3.00
91 Steve Smith UNT	.15	.40
92 Dikembe Mutombo UNT	.20	.50
93 Brent Barry UNT	.30	.75
94 Glenn Robinson UNT	.20	.50
95 Armon Gilliam UNT	.12	.30
96 Nick Anderson UNT	.12	.30
97 Gary Trent UNT	.20	.50
98 Brian Grant UNT	.15	.40
99 Bryant Reeves UNT	.20	.50
100 Checklist	.25	.60
NNO Grant Hill Promo	1.00	2.50

1995-96 E-XL Blue

Randomly inserted at a rate of slightly more than one card per pack, this 100-card set is a parallel of the basic SkyBox E-XL set. Card fronts are identical to the basic issue except the black border is replaced with a blue border. Card backs are also identical. Please refer to the multipliers listed below to ascertain values.

COMPLETE SET (100)	40.00	100.00

*STARS: 1X TO 2.5X BASE CARD HI
*RCs: .75X TO 2X BASE HI

1995-96 E-XL A Cut Above

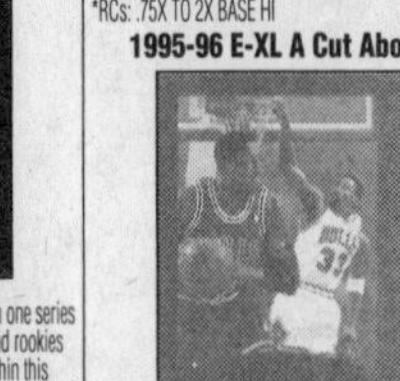

Randomly inserted in hobby and retail packs at a rate of one in 130, this 10-card die-cut insert set features a selection of the NBA's elite stars. Each card front features a unique framing of two different, die-cut photos surrounded by a blue border. Card backs contain an action photo and brief commentary and are numbered as "X of 10".

COMPLETE SET (10)	60.00	120.00
1 Scottie Pippen	8.00	20.00
2 Jason Kidd	8.00	20.00
3 Grant Hill	8.00	20.00
4 Joe Smith	5.00	12.00
5 Hakeem Olajuwon	6.00	15.00
6 Magic Johnson	12.00	30.00
7 Shaquille O'Neal	12.00	30.00
8 Jerry Stackhouse	8.00	20.00
9 Charles Barkley	8.00	20.00
10 David Robinson	8.00	20.00

1995-96 E-XL Natural Born Thrillers

Randomly inserted in hobby and retail packs at a rate of one in 48, this 10-card set highlights a selection of crowd-pleasing players who do incredible things on the court. Each card features a multi-layered die-cut design. Card backs are black and textured with the player's name and a brief commentary in gold foil. The cards are numbered as "X of 10". A non-numbered Jerry Stackhouse card was sent out to preview the set.

COMPLETE SET (10)	100.00	200.00
1 Michael Jordan	75.00	150.00
2 Antonio McDyess	4.00	10.00
3 Grant Hill	5.00	12.00
4 Clyde Drexler	4.00	10.00
5 Kevin Garnett	12.00	30.00
6 Anfernee Hardaway	5.00	12.00
7 Jerry Stackhouse	5.00	12.00
8 Michael Finley	5.00	12.00
9 Shawn Kemp	3.00	8.00
10 Damon Stoudamire	4.00	10.00
NNO Jerry Stackhouse PROMO	2.50	6.00

1995-96 E-XL No Boundaries

Randomly inserted exclusively in hobby packs at a rate of one in 18, this 10-card set features players that can bust open a game on a special die cut designed card. Card fronts have metallic backgrounds with an action shot of the player and the player's name which is written in gold foil. Card backs feature the a head shot of the player in a die-cut circle. The cards are numbered as "X of 10".

COMPLETE SET (10)	25.00	60.00
1 Michael Jordan	12.00	30.00
2 Antonio McDyess	2.50	6.00
3 Hakeem Olajuwon	2.50	6.00
4 Magic Johnson	5.00	12.00
5 Vin Baker	1.50	4.00
6 Patrick Ewing	2.50	6.00
7 Anfernee Hardaway	3.00	8.00
8 Jerry Stackhouse	3.00	8.00
9 Gary Payton	2.00	5.00
10 Damon Stoudamire	2.50	6.00

1995-96 E-XL Unstoppable

Randomly inserted in hobby and retail packs at a rate of one in 6, this 20-card set features 10 players who are "unstoppable" inside the paint and 10 who are "unstoppable" from outside. Card fronts have a large action shot of the player with the player's name written vertically along the border. Card backs have a textured background photo with a brief commentary on the player. The cards are numbered as "X of 20".

COMPLETE SET (20)	20.00	50.00
1 Alan Henderson	1.00	2.50
2 Glen Rice	1.50	4.00
3 Scottie Pippen	2.50	6.00
4 Dennis Rodman	3.00	8.00
5 Terrell Brandon	1.00	2.50
6 Jason Kidd	2.50	6.00
7 Grant Hill	2.50	6.00
8 Joe Smith	2.00	5.00
9 Sam Cassell	1.50	4.00
10 Reggie Miller	2.00	5.00
11 Alonzo Mourning	2.00	5.00
12 Shaquille O'Neal	4.00	10.00
13 Charles Barkley	2.50	6.00
14 Clifford Robinson	1.00	2.50
15 Sean Elliott	1.50	4.00
16 David Robinson	2.50	6.00
17 Shawn Kemp	1.50	4.00
18 Karl Malone	2.00	5.00
19 John Stockton	2.00	5.00
20 Juwan Howard	1.50	4.00

1996-97 E-X2000

The SkyBox E-X2000 set was issued in one series totalling 80 cards. Cards were available in 2-card packs with a suggested retail price of $3.99. Card designs are similar to the 1995-96 Hoops SkyView insert with a clear plastic design inside of a frame with a photo of the player overlapped. The cards are designated as Condition Sensitive due to the easy nature of damaging the cards. A Grant Hill Emerald exchange card was also inserted at one in 500 packs. This card was exchangeable for a Grant Hill autographed ball. Reportedly, only 75 balls were signed for the promotion. Also available to dealers who purchased a case was a blow-up Grant Hill E-X2000 card which was serial numbered to 3000. A regular issue-size Grant Hill promo card was also released and is listed below at the end of the set.

COMPLETE SET (82)	60.00	120.00
1 Christian Laettner	.50	1.25
2 Dikembe Mutombo	.60	1.50
3 Steve Smith	.50	1.25
4 Antoine Walker RC	2.00	5.00
5 David Wesley	.40	1.00
6 Tony Delk RC	1.00	2.50
7 Anthony Mason	.40	1.00
8 Glen Rice	.60	1.50
9 Michael Jordan	8.00	20.00
10 Scottie Pippen	1.00	2.50
11 Dennis Rodman	1.25	3.00
12 Terrell Brandon	.40	1.00
13 Chris Mills	.40	1.00
14 Shawn Bradley	.40	1.00
15 Michael Finley	.75	2.00
16 Dale Ellis	.40	1.00
17 Antonio McDyess	.60	1.50
18 Joe Dumars	.60	1.50
19 Grant Hill	1.00	2.50
20 Chris Mullin	.60	1.50
21 Joe Smith	.50	1.25
22 Latrell Sprewell	.60	1.50
23 Charles Barkley	1.00	2.50
24 Clyde Drexler	.75	2.00
25 Hakeem Olajuwon	.75	2.00
26 Erick Dampier RC	1.00	2.50
27 Reggie Miller	.75	2.00
28 Loy Vaught	.40	1.00
29 Lorenzen Wright RC	1.00	2.50
30 Kobe Bryant RC	30.00	65.00
31 Eddie Jones	.60	1.50
32 Shaquille O'Neal	1.50	4.00
33 Nick Van Exel	.60	1.50
34 Tim Hardaway	.60	1.50
35 Jamal Mashburn	.50	1.25
36 Alonzo Mourning	.75	2.00
37 Ray Allen RC	4.00	10.00
38 Vin Baker	.50	1.25
39 Glenn Robinson	.60	1.50
40 Kevin Garnett	1.50	4.00
41 Tom Gugliotta	.40	1.00
42 Stephon Marbury RC	2.50	6.00
43 Kendall Gill	.40	1.00
44 Jim Jackson	.40	1.00
45 Kerry Kittles RC	1.00	2.50
46 Patrick Ewing	.75	2.00
47 Larry Johnson	.60	1.50
48 John Wallace RC	1.00	2.50
49 Nick Anderson	.40	1.00
50 Horace Grant	.50	1.25
51 Anfernee Hardaway	1.00	2.50
52 Derrick Coleman	.50	1.25
53 Allen Iverson RC	6.00	15.00
54 Jerry Stackhouse	.75	2.00
55 Cedric Ceballos	.40	1.00
56 Kevin Johnson	.60	1.50
57 Jason Kidd	1.00	2.50
58 Clifford Robinson	.40	1.00
59 Arvydas Sabonis	.50	1.25
60 Rasheed Wallace	.75	2.00
61 Mahmoud Abdul-Rauf	.40	1.00
62 Brian Grant	.50	1.25
63 Mitch Richmond	.60	1.50
64 Sean Elliott	.60	1.50
65 David Robinson	1.00	2.50
66 Dominique Wilkins	.75	2.00
67 Shawn Kemp	.60	1.50
68 Gary Payton	.60	1.50
69 Detlef Schrempf	.60	1.50
70 Marcus Camby RC	1.50	4.00
71 Damon Stoudamire	.60	1.50
72 Walt Williams	.40	1.00
73 Shandon Anderson RC	1.00	2.50
74 Karl Malone	.75	2.00
75 John Stockton	.75	2.00
76 Shareef Abdur-Rahim RC	2.00	5.00
77 Bryant Reeves	.40	1.00
78 Roy Rogers RC	1.00	2.50
79 Juwan Howard	.50	1.25
80 Chris Webber	.75	2.00
81 Checklist	.25	.60
82 Checklist	.25	.60
NNO Grant Hill AU Ball/75	100.00	200.00
NNO Grant Hill Blow-Up/3000	8.00	20.00
NNO Grant Hill PROMO	1.00	2.50

1996-97 E-X2000 Credentials

Randomly inserted in packs, this 80-card set is a parallel to the basic set. Numbered out of 499, these cards feature an alternate foil and background image. The cards are considered Condition Sensitive due to the easy nature of damaging the cards. To ascertain values on individual cards, please refer to the multiplier in the header below, coupled with the value of the base card.

*STARS: 8X TO 20X BASE CARD HI
*RCs: 2.5X TO 6X BASE HI

9 Michael Jordan	400.00	700.00
10 Scottie Pippen	40.00	70.00
11 Dennis Rodman	40.00	80.00
19 Grant Hill	25.00	60.00
22 Latrell Sprewell	25.00	60.00
23 Charles Barkley	25.00	60.00
27 Reggie Miller	25.00	60.00
30 Kobe Bryant	750.00	1250.00
32 Shaquille O'Neal	40.00	100.00
37 Ray Allen	60.00	120.00
42 Stephon Marbury	20.00	50.00
47 Larry Johnson	15.00	40.00
51 Anfernee Hardaway	30.00	80.00
53 Allen Iverson	100.00	200.00
67 Shawn Kemp	15.00	40.00
68 Gary Payton	15.00	40.00
75 John Stockton	20.00	50.00
76 Shareef Abdur-Rahim	15.00	40.00

1996-97 E-X2000 A Cut Above

Randomly inserted in packs at a rate of one in 288, this 10-card set features a sawblade die cut at the top of the card.

COMPLETE SET (10)	700.00	1200.00
1 Kevin Garnett	60.00	150.00
2 Anfernee Hardaway	100.00	175.00
3 Grant Hill	50.00	120.00
4 Allen Iverson	50.00	125.00
5 Michael Jordan	500.00	850.00
6 Shawn Kemp	50.00	120.00
7 Hakeem Olajuwon	30.00	80.00
8 Shaquille O'Neal	60.00	150.00
9 Glenn Robinson	25.00	60.00
10 Dennis Rodman	50.00	125.00

1996-97 E-X2000 Net Assets

Randomly inserted in packs at a rate of one in 20, this 20-card set features a precision cut net in the background of the card.

COMPLETE SET (20)	60.00	150.00
1 Ray Allen	4.00	10.00
2 Charles Barkley	3.00	8.00
3 Patrick Ewing	2.50	6.00
4 Kevin Garnett	5.00	12.00
5 Anfernee Hardaway	3.00	8.00
6 Grant Hill	3.00	8.00
7 Allen Iverson	5.00	12.00
8 Michael Jordan	50.00	125.00
9 Jason Kidd	3.00	8.00
10 Kerry Kittles	1.00	2.50
11 Karl Malone	2.50	6.00
12 Alonzo Mourning	2.50	6.00
13 Shaquille O'Neal	5.00	12.00
14 Gary Payton	2.00	5.00
15 Bryant Reeves	1.25	3.00
16 David Robinson	3.00	8.00
17 Dennis Rodman	4.00	10.00
18 Joe Smith	1.50	4.00
19 Damon Stoudamire	2.00	5.00
20 Chris Webber	2.50	6.00

1996-97 E-X2000 Star Date 2000

Randomly inserted in packs at a rate of one in 9, this 15-card set features many of the players from the 1996-97 rookie class on a futuristic outer space background.

COMPLETE SET (15)	20.00	50.00
1 Shareef Abdur-Rahim	1.25	3.00
2 Ray Allen	2.50	6.00
3 Kobe Bryant	12.50	30.00
4 Marcus Camby	1.00	2.50
5 Erick Dampier	.60	1.50
6 Juwan Howard	.75	2.00
7 Allen Iverson	3.00	8.00
8 Jason Kidd	1.50	4.00
9 Kerry Kittles	.60	1.50
10 Stephon Marbury	1.50	4.00
11 Jamal Mashburn	.75	2.00
12 Antonio McDyess	1.00	2.50
13 Joe Smith	.75	2.00
14 Damon Stoudamire	1.00	2.50
15 Antoine Walker	1.25	3.00

1997-98 E-X2001

The 1997-98 SkyBox E-X2001 hobby set only was issued in one series totalling 82 cards - 80 basic and two checklists. Each pack contained two cards that carried a suggested retail price of $3.99. The cards feature a semi-clear plastic background with the player die cut over the top of the card. A Grant Hill sample card was also released and is listed at the end of the base set.

COMPLETE SET (82)	20.00	50.00
1 Grant Hill	.75	2.00
2 Kevin Garnett	1.00	2.50
3 Allen Iverson	1.00	2.50
4 Anfernee Hardaway	.75	2.00
5 Dennis Rodman	1.00	2.50
6 Shawn Kemp	.50	1.25
7 Shaquille O'Neal	1.25	3.00
8 Kobe Bryant	2.50	6.00
9 Michael Jordan	4.00	10.00
10 Marcus Camby	.50	1.25
11 Scottie Pippen	.75	2.00
12 Antoine Walker	.50	1.25
13 Stephon Marbury	.60	1.50
14 Shareef Abdur-Rahim	.50	1.25
15 Jerry Stackhouse	.50	1.25
16 Eddie Jones	.50	1.25
17 Charles Barkley	.75	2.00
18 David Robinson	.75	2.00
19 Karl Malone	.60	1.50
20 Damon Stoudamire	.50	1.25
21 Patrick Ewing	.60	1.50
22 Kerry Kittles	.30	.75
23 Gary Payton	.50	1.25
24 Glenn Robinson	.40	1.00
25 Hakeem Olajuwon	.60	1.50
26 John Starks	.40	1.00
27 John Stockton	.60	1.50
28 Vin Baker	.40	1.00
29 Reggie Miller	.60	1.50
30 Clyde Drexler	.60	1.50
31 Alonzo Mourning	.60	1.50
32 Juwan Howard	.40	1.00
33 Ray Allen	.60	1.50
34 Christian Laettner	.40	1.00
35 Terrell Brandon	.30	.75
36 Sean Elliott	.50	1.25
37 Rod Strickland	.30	.75
38 Rodney Rogers	.30	.75
39 Donyell Marshall	.30	.75
40 David Wesley	.30	.75
41 Sam Cassell	.40	1.00
42 Cedric Ceballos	.30	.75
43 Mahmoud Abdul-Rauf	.30	.75
44 Rik Smits	.40	1.00
45 Lindsey Hunter	.30	.75
46 Michael Finley	.50	1.25
47 Steve Smith	.40	1.00
48 Larry Johnson	.50	1.25
49 Dikembe Mutombo	.50	1.25
50 Tom Gugliotta	.30	.75
51 Joe Dumars	.50	1.25
52 Glen Rice	.50	1.25
53 Bryant Reeves	.30	.75
54 Tim Hardaway	.50	1.25
55 Isaiah Rider	.30	.75
56 Rasheed Wallace	.50	1.25
57 Jason Kidd	.75	2.00
58 Joe Smith	.40	1.00
59 Chris Webber	.50	1.25
60 Mitch Richmond	.50	1.25
61 Antonio McDyess	.40	1.00
62 Bobby Jackson RC	.75	2.00
63 Derek Anderson RC	.60	1.50
64 Kelvin Cato RC	.60	1.50
65 Jacque Vaughn RC	.60	1.50
66 Tariq Abdul-Wahad RC	.60	1.50
67 Johnny Taylor RC	.60	1.50
68 Chris Anstey RC	.60	1.50
69 Maurice Taylor RC	.60	1.50
70 Antonio Daniels RC	.60	1.50
71 Chauncey Billups RC	2.50	6.00
72 Austin Croshere RC	.60	1.50
73 Brevin Knight RC	.60	1.50
74 Keith Van Horn RC	1.25	3.00
75 Tim Duncan RC	4.00	10.00
76 Danny Fortson RC	.60	1.50
77 Tim Thomas RC	1.25	3.00
78 Tony Battie RC	.75	2.00
79 Tracy McGrady RC	3.00	8.00
80 Ron Mercer RC	.75	2.00
81 Checklist (1-82)	.30	.75
82 Checklist (inserts)	.30	.75
S1 Grant Hill SAMPLE	1.25	3.00

1997-98 E-X2001 Essential Credentials Future

Randomly inserted into packs, the Essential Credential Future features multi-tiered serial numbering cards. These cards are distinguished by their orange/pink glow edge stock. Each card is sequentially numbered with the amount of cards being equal to the opposite of their Essential Credentials Now card. For example, card number 1 has 80 serial numbered cards, while card number 80 has only one card. The tougher cards are not priced.

*VETS #'d 41-80: 25X TO 60X BASE HI
*VETS #'d 20-40: 30X TO 80X BASE HI

1 Grant Hill/80	150.00	300.00
2 Kevin Garnett/79	150.00	300.00
3 Allen Iverson/78	150.00	300.00
4 Anfernee Hardaway/77	100.00	200.00
5 Dennis Rodman/76	200.00	400.00
6 Shawn Kemp/75	40.00	100.00
7 Shaquille O'Neal/74	200.00	400.00
8 Kobe Bryant/73	800.00	1300.00
9 Michael Jordan/72	1400.00	2200.00
11 Scottie Pippen/70	125.00	250.00
15 Jerry Stackhouse/66	40.00	100.00
17 Charles Barkley/64	75.00	150.00
18 David Robinson/63	75.00	150.00
19 Karl Malone/62	75.00	150.00
23 Gary Payton/58	60.00	150.00
25 Hakeem Olajuwon/56	75.00	200.00
29 Reggie Miller/52	125.00	225.00
30 Clyde Drexler/51	50.00	120.00
31 Alonzo Mourning/50	75.00	150.00
57 Jason Kidd/24	125.00	250.00
59 Chris Webber/22	175.00	350.00
61 Antonio McDyess/20	80.00	200.00

1997-98 E-X2001 Essential Credentials Now

Randomly inserted into packs, the Essential Credential Now features multi-tiered serial numbering cards. These cards are distinguished by their yellow/green glow edge stock. Each card is sequentially numbered with the amount of cards being equal to the player's card number. For example, card number 1 has only one card and card number 80 has eighty serial number cards. The tougher cards have not been priced.

*VETS #'d 20-30: 30X TO 80X BASE HI
*VETS #'d 31-50: 25X TO 60X BASE HI
*VETS #'d 51-61: 20X TO 50X BASE HI
*RCs #'d 62-80: 10X TO 25X BASE HI

21 Patrick Ewing/21	75.00	150.00
23 Gary Payton/23	100.00	200.00
25 Hakeem Olajuwon/25	125.00	250.00
27 John Stockton/27	75.00	150.00
29 Reggie Miller/29	125.00	250.00
30 Clyde Drexler/30	75.00	150.00
31 Alonzo Mourning/31	125.00	250.00
33 Ray Allen/33	60.00	120.00
52 Glen Rice/52	30.00	80.00
57 Jason Kidd/57	100.00	200.00
59 Chris Webber/59	75.00	150.00
75 Tim Duncan/75	250.00	450.00

1997-98 E-X2001 Gravity Denied

Randomly inserted into packs at a rate of one in 24, this 20-card set features two die cut pieces, that form an "aerodynamic" photo of these NBA players in three separate windows.

COMPLETE SET (20)	40.00	100.00
1 Vin Baker	1.25	3.00
2 Charles Barkley	2.50	6.00
3 Tony Battie	1.25	3.00
4 Kobe Bryant	10.00	25.00
5 Patrick Ewing	2.00	5.00
6 Kevin Garnett	3.00	8.00
7 Anfernee Hardaway	2.50	6.00
8 Grant Hill	2.50	6.00
9 Michael Jordan	20.00	50.00
10 Shawn Kemp	1.50	4.00
11 Kerry Kittles	1.00	2.50
12 Karl Malone	2.00	5.00
13 Tracy McGrady	5.00	12.00
14 Hakeem Olajuwon	2.00	5.00
15 Shaquille O'Neal	4.00	10.00
16 Scottie Pippen	2.50	6.00
17 Jerry Stackhouse	1.50	4.00
18 Tim Thomas	2.00	5.00
19 Antoine Walker	1.50	4.00
20 Chris Webber	1.50	4.00

1997-98 E-X2001 Jambalaya

Randomly inserted into packs at a rate of one in 720, this 15-card set features the NBA's best jammers on a die cut background in the shape of an oval.

1 Allen Iverson	100.00	250.00
2 Anfernee Hardaway	100.00	250.00
3 Dennis Rodman	250.00	500.00
4 Grant Hill	100.00	250.00
5 Kevin Garnett	175.00	350.00
6 Michael Jordan	2000.00	3500.00
7 Shaquille O'Neal	150.00	300.00
8 Tim Duncan	200.00	400.00
9 Keith Van Horn	30.00	80.00
10 Stephon Marbury	50.00	125.00
11 Shareef Abdur-Rahim	40.00	100.00
12 Kobe Bryant	1000.00	1800.00
13 Damon Stoudamire	40.00	100.00
14 Scottie Pippen	200.00	400.00
15 Eddie Jones	75.00	150.00

1997-98 E-X2001 Star Date 2001

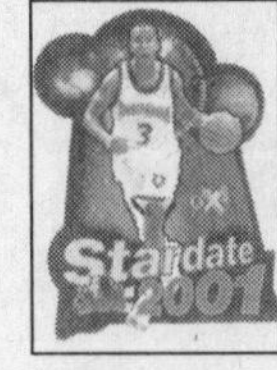

Randomly inserted into packs at a rate of one in 12, this 15-card set features some of the best young stars in the NBA. The cards have a die cut "galaxy" background with silver rainbow holofoil.

COMPLETE SET (15)	12.50	30.00
1 Shareef Abdur-Rahim	.75	2.00
2 Tony Battie	.60	1.50
3 Kobe Bryant	4.00	10.00
4 Antonio Daniels	.50	1.25
5 Tim Duncan	3.00	8.00
6 Adonal Foyle	.50	1.25
7 Allen Iverson	1.50	4.00
8 Matt Maloney	.50	1.25
9 Stephon Marbury	1.00	2.50
10 Tracy McGrady	2.50	6.00
11 Ron Mercer	.60	1.50
12 Tim Thomas	1.00	2.50
13 Keith Van Horn	1.00	2.50
14 Jacque Vaughn	.50	1.25
15 Antoine Walker	.75	2.00

1997-98 E-X2001 Grant Hi Hawaii

This card, virtually identical to the basic Grant H SkyBox E-X2001 basic card, was given away to who attended the annual 1998 Kit Young Hawaii Convention. The card is differentiated by a "Haw palm tree" in gold foil on the front. The card bac numbered, but listed as "sample".

S1 Grant Hill	6.00

1998-99 E-X Century

Continuing with the name change philosophy, t year's Fleer/SkyBox super premium set E-X Cer was released in three-card packs with a suggest retail price of $5.99. This 90 card set features 60 veterans and 30 prospects, which were slightly i at one in 1.5.

COMPLETE SET (1-90)	40.00
1 Keith Van Horn	.40
2 Scottie Pippen	.60
3 Tim Thomas	.40
4 Stephon Marbury	.50
5 Allen Iverson	.75
6 Grant Hill	.60
7 Tim Duncan	.75
8 Latrell Sprewell	.40
9 Ron Mercer	.30
10 Kobe Bryant	2.00
11 Antoine Walker	.40
12 Reggie Miller	.50
13 Kevin Garnett	.75
14 Shaquille O'Neal	1.00
15 Karl Malone	.50
16 Dennis Rodman	.75
17 Tracy McGrady	.60
18 Anfernee Hardaway	.60
19 Shareef Abdur-Rahim	.40
20 Marcus Camby	.30
21 Eddie Jones	.40
22 Vin Baker	.30
23 Charles Barkley	.60
24 Patrick Ewing	.50
25 Jason Kidd	.60
26 Mitch Richmond	.40
27 Tim Hardaway	.40
28 Glen Rice	.40
29 Shawn Kemp	.40
30 John Stockton	.50
31 Ray Allen	.50
32 Brevin Knight	.25
33 David Robinson	.60
34 Juwan Howard	.30
35 Alonzo Mourning	.50
36 Hakeem Olajuwon	.50
37 Gary Payton	.40
38 Damon Stoudamire	.40
39 Steve Smith	.30
40 Chris Webber	.40
41 Michael Finley	.40
42 Jayson Williams	.25
43 Maurice Taylor	.25
44 Jalen Rose	.30
45 Sam Cassell	.30
46 Jerry Stackhouse	.40
47 Toni Kukoc	.40
48 Charles Oakley	.30
49 Jim Jackson	.25
50 Dikembe Mutombo	.40
51 Wesley Person	.25
52 Antonio Daniels	.25
53 Isaiah Rider	.25
54 Tom Gugliotta	.25
55 Antonio McDyess	.30
56 Jeff Hornacek	.30
57 Joe Dumars	.40
58 Jamal Mashburn	.30
59 Donyell Marshall	.25
60 Glenn Robinson	.30
61 Jelani McCoy RC	1.00
62 Peja Stojakovic RC	2.50
63 Randell Jackson RC	1.00
64 Brad Miller RC	2.50
65 Corey Benjamin RC	1.00
66 Toby Bailey RC	1.00
67 Nazr Mohammed RC	1.00
68 Dirk Nowitzki RC	6.00
69 Andrae Patterson RC	1.00
70 Michael Dickerson RC	1.00
71 Cory Carr RC	1.00
72 Brian Skinner RC	1.00
73 Pat Garrity RC	1.00
74 Ricky Davis RC	1.50
75 Roshown McLeod RC	1.00
76 Matt Harpring RC	1.25
77 Jason Williams RC	2.50
78 Keon Clark RC	1.00
79 Al Harrington RC	1.50
80 Felipe Lopez RC	1.00
81 Michael Doleac RC	1.00
82 Paul Pierce RC	5.00
83 Robert Traylor RC	1.00
84 Raef LaFrentz RC	1.25
85 Michael Olowokandi RC	1.25
86 Mike Bibby RC	2.50
87 Antawn Jamison RC	2.50
88 Bonzi Wells RC	1.00
89 Vince Carter RC	5.00
90 Larry Hughes RC	2.00

98-99 E-X Century Essential Credentials Future

mly inserted in packs, this 90-card set is a
l to the base set. Each card carries unique
y numbering, which is opposite the players card
r. Thus, card number 1 is serially numbered to
ile card number 90 is serially numbered to 1.
with a limited print run are not priced.
#'d 71-90: 20X TO 50X BASE HI
#'d 41-70: 25X TO 60X BASE HI
#'d 31-40: 30X TO 80X BASE HI
#'d 15-30: 6X TO 15X BASE HI
tie Pippen/89 100.00 250.00
Iverson/86 50.00 125.00
t Hill/85 75.00 150.00
e Bryant/81 600.00 1000.00
nis Rodman/75 125.00 250.00
cy McGrady/74 40.00 100.00
ernee Hardaway/73 60.00 120.00
wn Kemp/62 50.00 100.00
n Stockton/61 40.00 100.00
Allen/60 40.00 100.00
nzo Mourning/56 50.00 125.00
eem Olajuwon/55 50.00 120.00
Payton/54 50.00 100.00
s Webber/51 50.00 120.00
i Kukoc/44 100.00 175.00

98-99 E-X Century Essential Credentials Now

mly inserted in packs, this 90-card set is a
to the base set. Each card carries unique
numbering, which is the same as the players
umber. Thus, card number 1 is serially
red to 1, while card number 90 is serially
red to 90. Cards with a print run of 25 or less
priced due to lack of market information.
#'d 16-30: 40X TO 100X BASE HI
#'d 31-40: 30X TO 80X BASE HI
#'d 41-60: 25X TO 60X BASE HI
'd 61-90: 4X TO 10X BASE HI
nis Rodman/16 300.00 600.00
y McGrady/17 100.00 200.00
ernee Hardaway/18 150.00 300.00
ie Jones/21 75.00 150.00
wn Kemp/29 75.00 150.00
n Stockton/30 75.00 150.00
Allen/31 50.00 120.00
nzo Mourning/35 75.00 150.00
eem Olajuwon/36 60.00 150.00
Payton/37 65.00 125.00
s Webber/40 60.00 150.00
i Kukoc/47 100.00 175.00
Nowitzki/68 200.00 400.00
n Williams/77 40.00 100.00
Pierce/82 75.00 200.00
e Bibby/86 40.00 80.00
e Carter/89 150.00 300.00

98-99 E-X Century Authen-Kicks

nly inserted in packs, this 12-card set features
pieces of game worn shoes inserted into the
e cards are sequentially numbered, with each
aving a different serial number due to different
es.
n Jamison/225 15.00 40.00
McGrady/225 30.00 80.00
Mercer/180 15.00 40.00
ne Walker/125 20.00 50.00
Bibby/165 25.00 50.00
el Dickerson/230 15.00 40.00
Hughes/115 30.00 60.00
aFrentz/160 15.00 40.00
Van Horn/125 30.00 60.00
th Van Horn AU/44 50.00 120.00
Thomas/215 15.00 40.00
Iverson/165 50.00 120.00
rt Traylor/215 15.00 40.00

3-99 E-X Century Dunk 'N Go Nuts

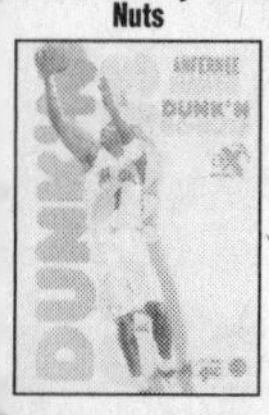

y inserted in packs at one in 36, this 20-card
res players who spend most of their time
. The card design is very similar to a "Dunkin'
box.
ETE SET (20) 250.00 500.00
omas 5.00 12.00
Hill 8.00 20.00
f Abdur-Rahim 5.00 12.00
uncan 12.00 30.00
verson 10.00 25.00
Bryant 50.00 120.00
e Walker 5.00 12.00
Garnett 10.00 25.00
ille O'Neal 12.00 30.00
McGrady 8.00 20.00
n Jamison 12.00 30.00
Carter 25.00 60.00
t Traylor 5.00 12.00
e Pippen 8.00 20.00
ael Jordan 150.00 300.00
ael Olowokandi 6.00 15.00
nee Hardaway 10.00 25.00
ael Dickerson 5.00 12.00
Mercer 4.00 10.00
Lopez 5.00 12.00

-99 E-X Century Generation E-X

inserted in packs at one in 18, this 15-card
s on top rookies and young players. The
cards feature a black bordered background.
COMPLETE SET (15) 12.50 30.00
1 Larry Hughes 1.00 2.50
2 Michael Olowokandi .60 1.50
3 Tim Duncan 1.50 4.00
4 Vince Carter 2.50 6.00
5 Antawn Jamison 1.25 3.00
6 Kevin Garnett 1.50 4.00
7 Al Harrington .75 2.00
8 Mike Bibby 1.25 3.00
9 Raef LaFrentz .60 1.50
10 Ron Mercer .60 1.50
11 Tracy McGrady 1.25 3.00
12 Kobe Bryant 6.00 15.00
13 Keith Van Horn .75 2.00
14 Stephon Marbury 1.00 2.50
15 Allen Iverson 1.50 4.00

1999-00 E-X

The 1999-00 E-X set was released in March,2000 as a 90-card set, with 60 veterans and 30 rookies. Each of the rookies were serial numbered to 3499. Each pack contained 3-cards and carried a suggested retail price of 3.99.

COMPLETE SET (90) 40.00 100.00
COMPLETE SET w/o RC (60) 15.00 30.00
1 Stephon Marbury .30 .75
2 Antawn Jamison .40 1.00
3 Patrick Ewing .50 1.25
4 Nick Anderson .25 .60
5 Charles Barkley .60 1.50
6 Marcus Camby .30 .75
7 Ron Mercer .30 .75
8 Avery Johnson .30 .75
9 Maurice Taylor .25 .60
10 Isaiah Rider .25 .60
11 Dirk Nowitzki .75 2.00
12 Damon Stoudamire .40 1.00
13 Alonzo Mourning .50 1.25
14 Jason Kidd .60 1.50
15 Juwan Howard .30 .75
16 Vince Carter .75 2.00
17 Tim Duncan .75 2.00
18 Paul Pierce .60 1.50
19 Tim Hardaway .40 1.00
20 Grant Hill .50 1.25
21 Keith Van Horn .30 .75
22 Shaquille O'Neal 1.00 2.50
23 Jason Williams .50 1.25
24 Shareef Abdur-Rahim .30 .75
25 Kobe Bryant 2.00 5.00
26 David Robinson .60 1.50
27 Anfernee Hardaway .60 1.50
28 Vin Baker .40 1.00
29 Hakeem Olajuwon .50 1.25
30 Michael Olowokandi .25 .60
31 Mike Bibby .40 1.00
32 Tracy McGrady .60 1.50
33 Antoine Walker .40 1.00
34 Larry Hughes .30 .75
35 Chris Webber .40 1.00
36 Ray Allen .40 1.00
37 Danny Fortson .25 .60
38 Shawn Kemp .40 1.00
39 Michael Doleac .25 .60
40 Gary Payton .40 1.00
41 Toni Kukoc .40 1.00
42 Kevin Garnett .75 2.00
43 Steve Smith .25 .60
44 Scottie Pippen .60 1.50
45 Allen Iverson .75 2.00
46 Latrell Sprewell .40 1.00
47 Matt Harpring .30 .75
48 Lindsey Hunter .25 .60
49 Karl Malone .50 1.25
50 Michael Finley .40 1.00
51 Jerry Stackhouse .40 1.00
52 Cedric Ceballos .25 .60
53 Brent Barry .30 .75
54 Elden Campbell .25 .60
55 Glenn Robinson .30 .75
56 Eddie Jones .40 1.00
57 Reggie Miller .40 1.00
58 Mitch Richmond .40 1.00
59 Raef LaFrentz .30 .75
60 John Starks .40 1.00
61 Elton Brand RC 2.00 5.00
62 William Avery RC .75 2.00
63 Cal Bowdler RC .75 2.00
64 Dion Glover RC .75 2.00
65 Lamar Odom RC 2.50 6.00
66 Richard Hamilton RC 2.00 5.00
67 Kenny Thomas RC .75 2.00
68 Shawn Marion RC 2.00 5.00
69 Baron Davis RC 2.50 6.00
70 Wally Szczerbiak RC 1.50 4.00
71 Scott Padgett RC .75 2.00
72 Jason Terry RC 2.00 5.00
73 Trajan Langdon RC .75 2.00
74 Andre Miller RC 2.00 5.00
75 Jeff Foster RC .75 2.00
76 Tim James RC .75 2.00
77 Aleksandar Radojevic RC .75 2.00
78 Quincy Lewis RC .75 2.00
79 James Posey RC .75 2.00
80 Steve Francis RC 2.00 5.00
81 Jonathan Bender RC .75 2.00
82 Corey Maggette RC 1.50 4.00
83 Obinna Ekezie RC .75 2.00
84 Laron Profit RC .75 2.00
85 Devean George RC .75 2.00
86 Ron Artest RC 2.00 5.00
87 Rafer Alston RC 1.00 2.50
88 Vonteego Cummings RC .75 2.00
89 Evan Eschmeyer RC .75 2.00
90 Jumaine Jones RC .75 2.00
S16 Vince Carter PROMO 1.25 3.00

1999-00 E-X Essential Credentials Future

Randomly inserted in packs, this 90-card set parallels the base set. Each card is individually serial numbered opposite their card number in the base set. The veterans are numbered 1-60, while the rookies are numbered 1-30. The cards are printed on blue plastic stock. The print runs are listed below. Please note that some cards are not priced due to lack of market activity.
*VETS #'d 36-60: 20X TO 50X BASE HI
*VETS #'d 21-35: 25X TO 60X BASE HI
*RC #'d 21-30: 8X TO 20X BASE HI
17 Tim Duncan/44 60.00 150.00
20 Grant Hill/41 40.00 100.00
25 Kobe Bryant/36 200.00 350.00
35 Chris Webber/26 60.00 150.00
36 Ray Allen/25 40.00 100.00
38 Shawn Kemp/23 50.00 120.00

1999-00 E-X Essential Credentials Now

Randomly inserted in packs, this 90-card set parallels the base set. Each card is individually serial numbered the same as their card number in the base set. The veterans are numbered 1-60, while the rookies are numbered 1-30. The cards are printed on red plastic stock. The print runs are listed below. Some cards are not priced due to lack of market activity.
*VETS #'d 36-60: 20X TO 50X BASE HI
*VETS #'d 21-35: 25X TO 60X BASE HI
*RCs #'d 21-30: 8X TO 20X BASE HI
22 Shaquille O'Neal/22 150.00 300.00
25 Kobe Bryant/25 200.00 400.00
27 Anfernee Hardaway/27 50.00 120.00
29 Hakeem Olajuwon/29 40.00 100.00
35 Chris Webber/35 50.00 120.00
36 Ray Allen/36 30.00 80.00
38 Shawn Kemp/38 40.00 100.00
44 Scottie Pippen/44 100.00 200.00

1999-00 E-X E-Xceptional Red

Randomly inserted in packs at one in 16, this 15-card set features some of the game's best on die cut, foil-stamped Warp Tech technology. Card backs carry a "XC" prefix.
COMPLETE SET (15) 75.00 150.00
*GREEN: 1X TO 2.5X HI COLUMN
GREEN: PRINT RUN 500 SERIAL #'d SETS
XC1 Jason Williams 4.00 10.00
XC2 Kevin Garnett 6.00 15.00
XC3 Allen Iverson 6.00 15.00
XC4 Paul Pierce 5.00 12.00
XC5 Keith Van Horn 2.50 6.00
XC6 Grant Hill 4.00 10.00
XC7 Scottie Pippen 5.00 12.00
XC8 Stephon Marbury 2.50 6.00
XC9 Tim Duncan 6.00 15.00
XC10 Kobe Bryant 25.00 60.00
XC11 Vince Carter 6.00 15.00
XC12 Shaquille O'Neal 8.00 20.00
XC13 Steve Francis 3.00 8.00
XC14 Elton Brand 3.00 8.00
XC15 Lamar Odom 4.00 10.00

1999-00 E-X E-Xceptional Blue

Randomly inserted in packs, this 15-card set parallels the E-Xceptional red set. The cards feature a blue background and are serially numbered to 250. To ascertain values on individual cards, please refer to the multiplier in the header, coupled with the value of the base insert.
*BLUE STARS: 3X TO 8X HI COLUMN
*BLUE RCs: 2.5X TO 6X HI COLUMN
XC10 Kobe Bryant 300.00 600.00

1999-00 E-X E-Xciting

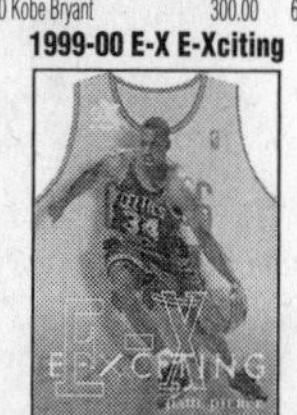

Randomly inserted in packs at one in 24, this 10-card set features jersey-shaped cards on felt stock. Card backs carry a "XCT" prefix.
COMPLETE SET (10) 15.00 40.00
XCT1 Jason Williams 1.50 4.00
XCT2 Vince Carter 2.50 6.00
XCT3 Allen Iverson 2.50 6.00
XCT4 Kevin Garnett 2.50 6.00
XCT5 Shaquille O'Neal 3.00 8.00
XCT6 Larry Hughes 1.00 2.50
XCT7 Tim Duncan 2.50 6.00
XCT8 Kobe Bryant 8.00 20.00
XCT9 Grant Hill 1.50 4.00
XCT10 Paul Pierce 2.00 5.00

1999-00 E-X E-Xplosive

Randomly inserted in packs, this 10-card set features the most explosive players in the NBA on foil-stamped fronts. Each card is serially numbered to 1999. The first 99 cards for each player feature autographs. Card backs carry a "XP" prefix.
XP1 William Avery .75 2.00
XP1A William Avery AU 8.00 20.00
XP2 Baron Davis 2.50 6.00
XP2A Baron Davis AU 25.00 60.00
XP3 Richard Hamilton 2.00 5.00
XP3A Richard Hamilton AU 20.00 50.00
XP4 Trajan Langdon .75 2.00
XP4A Trajan Langdon AU 8.00 20.00
XP5 Wally Szczerbiak 1.50 4.00
XP5A Wally Szczerbiak AU 15.00 40.00
XP6 Jason Terry 2.00 5.00
XP6A Jason Terry AU 20.00 50.00
XP7 Shawn Marion 2.00 5.00
XP7A Shawn Marion AU 20.00 50.00
XP8 James Posey .75 2.00
XP8A James Posey AU 8.00 20.00
XP9 Lamar Odom 2.50 6.00
XP9A Lamar Odom AU 25.00 60.00
XP10 Quincy Lewis .75 2.00
XP10A Quincy Lewis AU 8.00 20.00

1999-00 E-X Generation E-X

Randomly inserted in packs at one in eight, this 15-card set focuses on young talent. The cards feature foil-stamped plastic with a holographic metallized background. Card backs carry a "GX" prefix.
COMPLETE SET (15) 8.00 20.00
GX1 Michael Olowokandi .40 1.00
GX2 Kobe Bryant 3.00 8.00
GX3 Allen Iverson 1.25 3.00
GX4 Tim Duncan 1.25 3.00
GX5 Vince Carter 1.25 3.00
GX6 Paul Pierce 1.00 2.50
GX7 Jason Williams .75 2.00
GX8 Steve Francis 1.50 4.00
GX9 Lamar Odom 2.00 5.00
GX10 Elton Brand 1.50 4.00
GX11 Larry Hughes .50 1.25
GX12 Antawn Jamison .60 1.50
GX13 Mike Bibby .60 1.50
GX14 Keith Van Horn .50 1.25
GX15 Raef LaFrentz .50 1.25

1999-00 E-X Genuine Coverage

Randomly inserted in packs at one in 72, this 20-card set features fan favorites on cards featuring game-worn memorabilia. Card backs carry a "GC" prefix.
GC1 Shaquille O'Neal 12.00 30.00
GC2 Vince Carter 10.00 25.00
GC3 Jason Kidd 8.00 20.00
GC4 Karl Malone 6.00 15.00
GC5 Joe Smith 4.00 10.00
GC6 Terrell Brandon 3.00 8.00
GC7 John Stockton 6.00 15.00
GC8 Lamar Odom 6.00 15.00
GC9 Shareef Abdur-Rahim 4.00 10.00
GC10 David Robinson 8.00 20.00
GC11 Larry Hughes 4.00 10.00
GC12 Michael Olowokandi 3.00 8.00
GC13 Antonio McDyess 4.00 10.00
GC14 Mike Bibby 5.00 12.00
GC15 Stephon Marbury 4.00 10.00
GC16 Michael Finley 5.00 12.00
GC17 Gary Payton 5.00 12.00
GC18 Keith Van Horn 4.00 10.00
GC19 Jamal Mashburn 4.00 10.00
GC20 Grant Hill 6.00 15.00

2000-01 E-X

The 2000-01 E-X product was released in February, 2001 and featured a 130-card base set that was broken into tiers as follows: Base Veterans (1-100), and Rookies (101-130). The rookies were serial numbered as follows: 101-110 were serial numbered to 1000, 111-120 were serial numbered to 1250, and 121-130 were serial numbered to 1500.
COMPLETE SET w/o RC (100) 12.50 30.00
1 Dikembe Mutombo .40 1.00
2 Jim Jackson .25 .60
3 Jason Terry .40 1.00
4 Kenny Anderson .30 .75
5 Antoine Walker .30 .75
6 Paul Pierce .50 1.25
7 Jamal Mashburn .30 .75
8 Baron Davis .40 1.00
9 Derrick Coleman .30 .75
10 Elton Brand .40 1.00
11 Ron Artest .40 1.00
12 Andre Miller .30 .75
13 Brevin Knight .25 .60
14 Trajan Langdon .25 .60
15 Lamond Murray .25 .60
16 Dirk Nowitzki .60 1.50
17 Michael Finley .40 1.00
18 Nick Van Exel .30 .75
19 Antonio McDyess .30 .75
20 Raef LaFrentz .25 .60
21 Tariq Abdul-Wahad .25 .60
22 Cedric Ceballos .25 .60
23 Jerry Stackhouse .30 .75
24 Jerome Williams .25 .60
25 Larry Hughes .30 .75
26 Antawn Jamison .40 1.00
27 Mookie Blaylock .30 .75
28 Steve Francis .40 1.00
29 Hakeem Olajuwon .50 1.25
30 Maurice Taylor .25 .60
31 Jonathan Bender .25 .60
32 Reggie Miller .40 1.00
33 Austin Croshere .25 .60
34 Travis Best .25 .60
35 Jalen Rose .30 .75
36 Lamar Odom .40 1.00
37 Corey Maggette .30 .75
38 Shaquille O'Neal 1.00 2.50
39 Kobe Bryant 2.00 5.00
40 Horace Grant .30 .75
41 Isaiah Rider .30 .75
42 Brian Grant .25 .60
43 Eddie Jones .40 1.00
44 Tim Hardaway .40 1.00
45 Anthony Mason .25 .60
46 Glenn Robinson .30 .75
47 Ray Allen .40 1.00
48 Sam Cassell .30 .75
49 Tim Thomas .25 .60
50 Kevin Garnett .75 2.00
51 Terrell Brandon .25 .60
52 Joe Smith .30 .75
53 Wally Szczerbiak .30 .75
54 Chauncey Billups .40 1.00
55 Stephon Marbury .30 .75
56 Keith Van Horn .30 .75
57 Kerry Kittles .25 .60
58 Allan Houston .30 .75
59 Latrell Sprewell .30 .75
60 Larry Johnson .40 1.00
61 Glen Rice .30 .75
62 Grant Hill .50 1.25
63 Tracy McGrady .60 1.50
64 Darrell Armstrong .25 .60
65 Allen Iverson .75 2.00
66 Toni Kukoc .30 .75
67 Theo Ratliff .25 .60
68 Jason Kidd .60 1.50
69 Anfernee Hardaway .60 1.50
70 Tom Gugliotta .25 .60
71 Clifford Robinson .25 .60
72 Shawn Kemp .40 1.00
73 Scottie Pippen .60 1.50
74 Rasheed Wallace .40 1.00
75 Steve Smith .30 .75
76 Chris Webber .40 1.00
77 Jason Williams .40 1.00
78 Peja Stojakovic .40 1.00
79 Tim Duncan .75 2.00
80 David Robinson .60 1.50
81 Sean Elliott .30 .75
82 Derek Anderson .25 .60
83 Vin Baker .30 .75
84 Rashard Lewis .40 1.00
85 Gary Payton .40 1.00
86 Patrick Ewing .50 1.25
87 Vince Carter .75 2.00
88 Mark Jackson .30 .75
89 Antonio Davis .25 .60
90 Karl Malone .50 1.25
91 John Stockton .50 1.25
92 Bryon Russell .25 .60
93 Donyell Marshall .25 .60
94 Shareef Abdur-Rahim .30 .75
95 Mike Bibby .40 1.00
96 Michael Dickerson .25 .60
97 Mitch Richmond .30 .75
98 Juwan Howard .30 .75
99 Richard Hamilton .30 .75
100 Rod Strickland .30 .75
101 DerMarr Johnson RC 1.50 4.00
102 Kenyon Martin RC 4.00 10.00
103 Marcus Fizer RC 1.50 4.00
104 Courtney Alexander RC 1.50 4.00
105 Stromile Swift RC 1.50 4.00
106 Darius Miles RC 1.50 4.00
107 Mike Miller RC 3.00 8.00
108 Jamal Crawford RC 2.50 6.00
109 Speedy Claxton RC 1.50 4.00
110 Quentin Richardson RC 2.50 6.00
111 Keyon Dooling RC 1.50 4.00
112 Desmond Mason RC 2.00 5.00
113 Mateen Cleaves RC 1.50 4.00
114 Morris Peterson RC 1.50 4.00
115 Hedo Turkoglu RC 3.00 8.00
116 Donnell Harvey RC 1.50 4.00
117 Jerome Moiso RC 1.50 4.00
118 Jason Collier RC 1.50 4.00
119 Jamaal Magloire RC 1.50 4.00
120 Erick Barkley RC 1.50 4.00
121 Etan Thomas RC 1.50 4.00
122 DeShawn Stevenson RC 2.00 5.00
123 Dan Langhi RC 1.50 4.00
124 Mark Madsen RC 1.50 4.00
125 Khalid El-Amin RC 1.50 4.00
126 Lavor Postell RC 1.50 4.00
127 Eddie House RC 1.50 4.00
128 Michael Redd RC 4.00 10.00
129 Chris Porter RC 1.50 4.00
130 Mike Smith RC 1.50 4.00

2000-01 E-X Essential Credentials

Randomly inserted in packs at one in 42, this 130-card set parallels the E-X base set. Please note that this set was also broken into two tiers: Veterans (1-100) serial numbered to 201, and Rookies (101-130) serial numbered to 21.
*STARS: 6X TO 15X BASE CARD HI
*RCs: 2.5X TO 6X BASE HI
38 Shaquille O'Neal 20.00 50.00
39 Kobe Bryant 50.00 120.00
47 Ray Allen 8.00 20.00
72 Shawn Kemp 15.00 40.00
76 Chris Webber 8.00 20.00
77 Jason Williams 8.00 20.00
101 DerMarr Johnson 10.00 25.00
102 Kenyon Martin 25.00 60.00
103 Marcus Fizer 10.00 25.00
104 Courtney Alexander 10.00 25.00
105 Stromile Swift 10.00 25.00
106 Darius Miles 10.00 25.00
107 Mike Miller 20.00 50.00
108 Jamal Crawford 15.00 40.00
109 Speedy Claxton 10.00 25.00
110 Quentin Richardson 15.00 40.00
111 Keyon Dooling 10.00 25.00
112 Desmond Mason 12.00 30.00
113 Mateen Cleaves 10.00 25.00
114 Morris Peterson 10.00 25.00
115 Hedo Turkoglu 20.00 50.00
116 Donnell Harvey 10.00 25.00
117 Jerome Moiso 10.00 25.00
118 Jason Collier 10.00 25.00
119 Jamaal Magloire 10.00 25.00
120 Erick Barkley 10.00 25.00
121 Etan Thomas 10.00 25.00
122 DeShawn Stevenson 12.00 30.00
123 Dan Langhi 10.00 25.00
124 Mark Madsen 10.00 25.00
125 Khalid El-Amin 10.00 25.00
126 Lavor Postell 10.00 25.00
127 Eddie House 10.00 25.00
128 Michael Redd 25.00 60.00
129 Chris Porter 10.00 25.00
130 Mike Smith 10.00 25.00

2000-01 E-X Rookie Memorabilia

Randomly inserted into packs, this 28-card insert set is actually a partial-parallel of the rookies from the 2000-01 E-X base set. Please note that each of these cards feature either: an autograph (numbered to 500 or 250), a jersey swatch (numbered to 275), or a ball swatch (numbered to 275).
101 DerMarr Johnson JSY/275 3.00 8.00
102 Kenyon Martin JSY/275 8.00 20.00
103 Marcus Fizer BALL/275 3.00 8.00
104 Courtney Alexander AU/500 3.00 8.00
105 Stromile Swift JSY/275 3.00 8.00
106 Darius Miles JSY/275 3.00 8.00
107 Mike Miller JSY/275 6.00 15.00
108 Jamal Crawford AU/250 5.00 12.00
109 Speedy Claxton JSY/275 3.00 8.00
110 Quentin Richardson JSY/275 5.00 12.00
111 Keyon Dooling AU/250 3.00 8.00
112 Desmond Mason AU/500 4.00 10.00
113 Mateen Cleaves AU/500 3.00 8.00
114 Morris Peterson JSY/275 3.00 8.00
115 Hedo Turkoglu AU/250 6.00 15.00
116 Donnell Harvey AU/250 3.00 8.00
117 Jerome Moiso JSY/275 3.00 8.00
118 Jason Collier AU/250 3.00 8.00
120 Erick Barkley AU/250 3.00 8.00
121 Etan Thomas JSY/275 3.00 8.00
122 DeShawn Stevenson JSY/275 4.00 10.00
123 Dan Langhi AU/500 3.00 8.00
125 Khalid El-Amin AU/500 3.00 8.00
126 Lavor Postell AU/500 3.00 8.00
127 Eddie House AU/500 3.00 8.00
128 Michael Redd AU/500 10.00 25.00
129 Chris Porter AU/500 3.00 8.00
130 Mike Smith AU/500 3.00 8.00

2000-01 E-X Vince Carter Rookie Remnants

This three-card insert was randomly inserted into 2000-01 Fleer products. The set includes a Vince Carter floor card (numbered to 100), a Vince Carter floor/jersey card (numbered to 15), and finally an autographed Vince Carter floor/jersey card (numbered 1 of 1).
NNO Vince Carter FLR/100 12.50 30.00

2000-01 E-X Generation E-X

Randomly inserted into packs at one in 24, this 21-card insert set focuses on players that appear to be among the next generation of star athletes in the NBA. Card backs carry a "GE" prefix.
GE1 Vince Carter 2.00 5.00
GE2 Grant Hill 1.25 3.00
GE3 Lamar Odom 1.00 2.50
GE4 Allen Iverson 2.00 5.00
GE5 Keith Van Horn .75 2.00
GE6 Shareef Abdur-Rahim .75 2.00
GE7 Dirk Nowitzki 1.50 4.00
GE8 Morris Peterson 1.00 2.50
GE9 Mike Miller 2.00 5.00
GE10 Darius Miles 1.00 2.50
GE11 Speedy Claxton 1.00 2.50
GE12 Kenyon Martin 2.50 6.00
GE13 Stromile Swift 1.00 2.50
GE14 Courtney Alexander 1.00 2.50
GE15 Vince Carter / Morris Peterson 2.00 5.00
GE16 Grant Hill / Mike Miller 2.00 5.00
GE17 Lamar Odom / Darius Miles 1.00 2.50
GE18 Allen Iverson / Speedy Claxton 2.00 5.00
GE19 Keith Van Horn / Kenyon Martin 2.50 6.00
GE20 Shareef Abdur-Rahim / Stromile Swift 1.00 2.50
GE21 Dirk Nowitzki / Courtney Alexander 1.50 4.00

2000-01 E-X Generation E-X Game Jerseys

Randomly inserted into packs at one in 85, this 21-card insert set is actually a complete parallel of the Generation E-X insert set. Each of these cards feature a swatch of actual game-used jersey. Card backs carry a "GE" prefix. Please note that cards containing a single-jersey swatch were serial numbered to 600, while dual-jersey cards were serial numbered to 100.
GE1 Vince Carter 6.00 15.00
GE2 Grant Hill 4.00 10.00
GE3 Lamar Odom 3.00 8.00
GE4 Allen Iverson 6.00 15.00
GE5 Keith Van Horn 2.50 6.00
GE6 Shareef Abdur-Rahim 2.50 6.00
GE7 Dirk Nowitzki 5.00 12.00
GE9 Mike Miller 5.00 12.00
GE10 Darius Miles 2.50 6.00
GE11 Speedy Claxton 2.50 6.00
GE12 Kenyon Martin 6.00 15.00
GE13 Stromile Swift 2.50 6.00
GE16 Grant Hill / Mike Miller 6.00 15.00
GE17 Lamar Odom / Darius Miles 4.00 10.00
GE18 Allen Iverson / Speedy Claxton 6.00 15.00
GE19 Keith Van Horn / Kenyon Martin 6.00 15.00
GE20 Shareef Abdur-Rahim / Stromile Swift 4.00 10.00

2000-01 E-X Gravity Denied

Randomly inserted into packs at one in 48, this 10-card insert set focuses on players that defy the laws of gravity. Card backs carry a "GD" prefix.
COMPLETE SET (10) 20.00 40.00
GD1 Vince Carter 3.00 8.00
GD2 Jason Kidd 2.50 6.00
GD3 Eddie Jones 1.50 4.00
GD4 Tracy McGrady 2.50 6.00
GD5 Kobe Bryant 8.00 20.00
GD6 Grant Hill 2.00 5.00
GD7 Lamar Odom 1.50 4.00
GD8 Steve Francis 1.50 4.00
GD9 Kevin Garnett 3.00 8.00
GD10 Allen Iverson 3.00 8.00

2000-01 E-X NBA Debut Postmarks

Randomly inserted into packs at one in 288, this 11-card insert set features U.S. postal marks from the actual day that each of these rookies made their NBA debuts. Card backs carry a "PM" prefix.
PM1 Kenyon Martin 8.00 20.00
PM3 Darius Miles 3.00 8.00
PM4 Marcus Fizer 3.00 8.00
PM5 Mike Miller 6.00 15.00
PM6 Dermarr Johnson 3.00 8.00
PM7 Jamal Crawford 5.00 12.00
PM8 Jerome Moiso 3.00 8.00
PM9 Courtney Alexander 3.00 8.00
PM11 Hedo Turkoglu 6.00 15.00
PM13 Jamaal Magloire 3.00 8.00
PM14 Keyon Dooling 3.00 8.00

2000-01 E-X Net Assets

Randomly inserted into packs at one in 8, this 20-card insert set focuses on players that rip it through the net on a very consistent basis. Card backs carry a "NA" prefix.
COMPLETE SET (20) 15.00 30.00
NA1 Vince Carter 1.50 4.00
NA2 Reggie Miller .75 2.00
NA3 Karl Malone 1.00 2.50
NA4 Ray Allen .75 2.00
NA5 Dirk Nowitzki 1.25 3.00
NA6 Scottie Pippen 1.25 3.00
NA7 Tracy McGrady 1.25 3.00
NA8 Kobe Bryant 4.00 10.00
NA9 Larry Hughes .60 1.50
NA10 Shareef Abdur-Rahim .60 1.50
NA11 Tim Duncan 1.50 4.00
NA12 Gary Payton .75 2.00
NA13 Eddie Jones .75 2.00
NA14 Steve Francis .75 2.00
NA15 Antoine Walker .60 1.50
NA16 Kevin Garnett 1.50 4.00
NA17 Chris Webber .75 2.00
NA18 Shaquille O'Neal 2.00 5.00
NA19 Jason Kidd 1.25 3.00
NA20 Elton Brand .75 2.00

2000-01 E-X No Boundaries

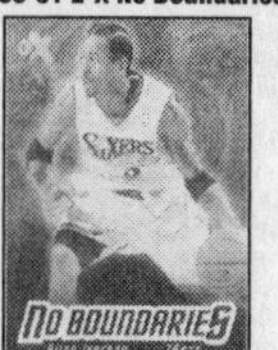

Randomly inserted into packs at one in 12, this 10-card insert set focuses on players that have no boundaries as to where their talent may take them. Card backs carry a "NB" prefix.
COMPLETE SET (10) 10.00 25.00
NB1 Vince Carter 1.50 4.00
NB2 Shareef Abdur-Rahim .60 1.50
NB3 Elton Brand .75 2.00
NB4 Shaquille O'Neal 2.00 5.00
NB5 Kobe Bryant 4.00 10.00
NB6 Allen Iverson 1.50 4.00
NB7 Tim Duncan 1.50 4.00

NB8 Steve Francis .75 2.00
NB9 Kevin Garnett 1.50 4.00
NB10 Grant Hill 1.00 2.50

2001-02 E-X

Released in late February 2002, this 130-card set is comprised of 100 veteran cards (card numbers 1-60 Base, 61-80 Role Players, 81-100 Leading Men) and 30 short printed rookie player cards. Base cards feature full color player action photos with true life backgrounds containing an embossed basketball pattern and a color shift to match the featured player's jersey colors. The upper left and lower right hand corners of the cards are colored in, and the different colors are as follows. Card numbers 1-60 are white, card numbers 61-80 are bronze, card numbers 81-100 are gold, and card numbers 101-130 are purple. The rookies are staggered numbered to 1750, 1250 and 750 in no particular order, so print runs are listed below. E-X was packaged in four card packs with 24 packs per box.

COMPLETE SET (130) 100.00 200.00
COMP.SET w/o SP's (100) 15.00 40.00
1 Shareef Abdur-Rahim .30 .75
2 DerMarr Johnson .25 .60
3 Jason Terry .40 1.00
4 Paul Pierce .50 1.25
5 Antoine Walker .30 .75
6 Baron Davis .40 1.00
7 Jamal Mashburn .30 .75
8 Chris Mihm .25 .60
9 Andre Miller .30 .75
10 Dirk Nowitzki .60 1.50
11 Michael Finley .40 1.00
12 Raef LaFrentz .25 .60
13 Antonio McDyess .30 .75
14 Jerry Stackhouse .30 .75
15 Antawn Jamison .40 1.00
16 Steve Francis .40 1.00
17 Jalen Rose .30 .75
18 Elton Brand .40 1.00
19 Darius Miles .25 .60
20 Lamar Odom .40 1.00
21 Mitch Richmond .30 .75
22 Michael Dickerson .25 .60
23 Stromile Swift .25 .60
24 Alonzo Mourning .50 1.25
25 Courtney Alexander .25 .60
26 Ray Allen .40 1.00
27 Glenn Robinson .30 .75
28 Terrell Brandon .25 .60
29 Wally Szczerbiak .30 .75
30 Joe Smith .30 .75
31 Jason Kidd .60 1.50
32 Kenyon Martin .40 1.00
33 Keith Van Horn .30 .75
34 Grant Hill .50 1.25
35 Tracy McGrady .60 1.50
36 Mike Miller .40 1.00
37 Allen Iverson .75 2.00
38 Speedy Claxton .25 .60
39 Dikembe Mutombo .40 1.00
40 Tom Gugliotta .25 .60
41 Penny Hardaway .60 1.50
42 Stephon Marbury .30 .75
43 Shawn Marion .40 1.00
44 Rasheed Wallace .40 1.00
45 Peja Stojakovic .40 1.00
46 Mike Bibby .40 1.00
47 Chris Webber .40 1.00
48 David Robinson .60 1.50
49 Vin Baker .30 .75
50 Rashard Lewis .40 1.00
51 Desmond Mason .30 .75
52 Gary Payton .40 1.00
53 Vince Carter .60 1.50
54 Antonio Davis .25 .60
55 Hakeem Olajuwon .50 1.25
56 Morris Peterson .25 .60
57 Karl Malone .50 1.25
58 DeShawn Stevenson .25 .60
59 John Stockton .50 1.25
60 Richard Hamilton .30 .75
61 Corey Maggette .30 .75
62 Steve Smith .30 .75
63 Tim Thomas .25 .60
64 Lindsey Hunter .25 .60
65 Jermaine O'Neal .40 1.00
66 Cuttino Mobley .30 .75
67 Nick Van Exel .30 .75
68 Juwan Howard .30 .75
69 James Posey .25 .60
70 David Wesley .25 .60
71 Marcus Fizer .25 .60
72 Jumaine Jones .25 .60
73 Tim Hardaway .40 1.00
74 Danny Fortson .25 .60
75 Jonathan Bender .25 .60
76 Quentin Richardson .30 .75
77 Eddie House .25 .60
78 Kurt Thomas .25 .60
79 Anthony Mason .25 .60
80 Theo Ratliff .25 .60
81 Allan Houston .30 .75
82 Latrell Sprewell .30 .75
83 Jason Williams .30 .75
84 Eddie Jones .30 .75
85 Damon Stoudamire .30 .75
86 Sam Cassell .30 .75
87 Cliff Robinson .30 .75
88 Patrick Ewing .50 1.25
89 Tim Duncan .75 2.00
90 Marcus Camby .30 .75
91 Brian Grant .25 .60
92 Kobe Bryant 2.00 5.00
93 Ron Mercer .25 .60
94 Reggie Miller .40 1.00
95 Shaquille O'Neal 1.00 2.50
96 Kevin Garnett 1.00 2.50
97 Scottie Pippen .60 1.50
98 Michael Jordan 6.00 15.00
99 Steve Nash .60 1.50
100 Derek Anderson .25 .60
101 Kedrick Brown/1750 RC 1.00 2.50
102 Joseph Forte/1750 RC 1.00 2.50
103 Joe Johnson/1250 RC 3.00 8.00
104 Kirk Haston/1750 RC 1.00 2.50
105 Tyson Chandler/750 RC 3.00 8.00
106 Eddy Curry/1250 RC 2.00 5.00
107 DeSagana Diop/1750 RC 1.00 2.50
108 Trenton Hassell/1250 RC 1.25 3.00
109 Zeljko Rebraca/1250 RC 1.25 3.00
110 Rodney White/1750 RC 1.00 2.50
111 Troy Murphy/1250 RC 2.00 5.00
112 Jason Richardson/750 RC 4.00 10.00
113 Eddie Griffin/750 RC 2.00 5.00
114 Terence Morris/1750 RC 1.00 2.50
115 Oscar Torres/1250 RC 1.25 3.00
116 Jamaal Tinsley/750 RC 2.50 6.00
117 Pau Gasol/750 RC 6.00 15.00
118 Shane Battier/750 RC 4.00 10.00
119 Brandon Armstrong/1250 RC 1.25 3.00
120 Richard Jefferson/750 RC 4.00 10.00
121 Steven Hunter/1250 RC 1.25 3.00
122 Samuel Dalembert/1750 RC 1.25 3.00
123 Zach Randolph/750 RC 3.00 8.00
124 Gerald Wallace/1750 RC 1.50 4.00
125 Tony Parker/750 RC 8.00 20.00
126 Vladimir Radmanovic/1250 RC 1.25 3.00
127 Michael Bradley/1750 RC 1.00 2.50
128 Jarron Collins/1750 RC 1.00 2.50
129 Andrei Kirilenko/750 RC 5.00 12.00
130 Kwame Brown/750 RC 2.00 5.00

2001-02 E-X Essential Credentials Future

Randomly inserted in packs, this 130-card set parallels the base set enhanced with blue borders. Each card is sequentially numbered, and print runs appear below.

*STARS #'d 21-40: 10X TO 25X BASE CARD HI
*STARS #'d 41-60: 6X TO 15X BASE CARD HI
*STARS #'d 61-70: 5X TO 12X BASE CARD HI
103 Joe Johnson/28 50.00 125.00
105 Tyson Chandler/26 30.00 80.00
106 Eddy Curry/25 30.00 80.00
108 Trenton Hassell/23 20.00 50.00

2001-02 E-X Essential Credentials Future Memorabilia

Randomly inserted in packs, this 130-card set parallels the base set enhanced with blue borders and a swatch of memorabilia. Each card is sequentially numbered, and print runs appear below.

*STARS #'d 21-40: 10X TO 25X BASE CARD HI
*STARS #'d 41-60: 12X TO 30X BASE HI
LOWER PRINT RUNS NOT PRICED

2001-02 E-X Essential Credentials Now

Randomly inserted in packs, this 130-card set parallels the base set enhanced with red borders. Each card is sequentially numbered, and print runs appear below.

*STARS #'d 21-40: 10X TO 25X BASE CARD HI
*STARS #'d 41-60: 6X TO 15X BASE CARD HI
LOWER PRINT RUNS NOT PRICED
103 Joe Johnson/43 30.00 80.00
104 Kirk Haston/44 12.00 30.00
105 Tyson Chandler/45 20.00 50.00
106 Eddy Curry/46 20.00 50.00
107 DeSagana Diop/47 12.00 30.00
108 Trenton Hassell/48 12.00 30.00
109 Zeljko Rebraca/49 12.00 30.00
110 Rodney White/50 12.00 30.00
111 Troy Murphy/51 20.00 50.00
112 Jason Richardson/52 25.00 60.00
113 Eddie Griffin/53 12.00 30.00
114 Terence Morris/54 12.00 30.00
115 Oscar Torres/55 12.00 30.00
116 Jamaal Tinsley/56 15.00 40.00
117 Pau Gasol/57 40.00 100.00
118 Shane Battier/58 25.00 60.00
119 Brandon Armstrong/59 12.00 30.00
120 Richard Jefferson/60 25.00 60.00
121 Steven Hunter/61 12.00 30.00
122 Samuel Dalembert/62 15.00 40.00
123 Zach Randolph/63 30.00 80.00
124 Gerald Wallace/64 20.00 50.00
125 Tony Parker/65 50.00 125.00
126 Vladimir Radmanovic/66 12.00 30.00
127 Michael Bradley/67 12.00 30.00
128 Jarron Collins/68 12.00 30.00
129 Andrei Kirilenko/69 30.00 80.00
130 Kwame Brown/70 12.00 30.00

2001-02 E-X Essential Credentials Now Memorabilia

Randomly inserted in packs, this 130-card set parallels the base set enhanced with red borders and a swatch of memorabilia. Each card is sequentially numbered, and print runs appear below.

*STARS #'d 21-40: 12X TO 30X BASE CARD HI
*STARS #'d 41-60: 10X TO 25X BASE HI
LOWER PRINT RUNS NOT PRICED
47 Chris Webber/47 12.00 30.00

2001-02 E-X Behind the Numbers

Randomly inserted in packs at the rate of one in 288, this 15-card set is designed horizontally with full color player action photo centered and a portrait style "black and white" photo in the upper left hand corner. The player's number appears on the right side of the card, and background color is set to match the featured player's jersey colors.

1 Larry Bird 20.00 50.00
2 Allen Iverson 12.00 30.00
3 David Robinson 10.00 25.00
4 Karl Malone 8.00 20.00
5 Tracy McGrady 10.00 25.00
6 Steve Francis 6.00 15.00
7 Jason Terry 6.00 15.00
8 Antoine Walker 5.00 12.00
9 Grant Hill 8.00 20.00
10 Michael Finley 6.00 15.00
11 Jason Kidd 10.00 25.00
12 Alonzo Mourning 8.00 20.00
13 Darius Miles 4.00 10.00
14 Ray Allen 6.00 15.00
15A Vince Carter 10.00 25.00
15B Vince Carter AU 15.00 40.00

2001-02 E-X Behind the Numbers Jerseys

Randomly inserted in packs at the rate of one in 24, this 18-card set parallels the design of the base Behind the Numbers set enhanced with a jersey swatch in the shape of the player's number. Gary Payton, Paul Pierce and Michael Finley did not appear in the base set, but have versions in this jersey set.

1 Larry Bird 12.00 30.00
2 Vince Carter 6.00 15.00
3 Baron Davis 4.00 10.00
4 Michael Finley 4.00 10.00
5 Steve Francis 4.00 10.00
6 Grant Hill 5.00 12.00
7 Allen Iverson 8.00 20.00
8 Jason Kidd 6.00 15.00
9 Karl Malone 5.00 12.00
10 Kenyon Martin 4.00 10.00
11 Tracy McGrady 6.00 15.00
12 Darius Miles 2.50 6.00
13 Alonzo Mourning 6.00 15.00
14 Dirk Nowitzki 6.00 15.00
15 Gary Payton 4.00 10.00
16 Paul Pierce 5.00 12.00
17 Jason Terry 4.00 10.00
18 Antoine Walker 3.00 8.00

2001-02 E-X Behind the Numbers Jerseys Autographs

Randomly inserted in packs, this set parallels the design of the Behind the Numbers Jersey set enhanced with player autographs. Each card is sequentially numbered to the featured player's jersey number.

SOME UNPRICED DUE TO SCARCITY
1 Larry Bird/33 125.00 250.00
2 Vince Carter/15 75.00 200.00

2001-02 E-X Box Office Draws

Randomly seeded in packs at the rate of one in 24, this 20-card set is designed to resemble a movie poster. Each card has three photos of the featured player, two in action, and one portrait, and the background color is set to match each player's jersey color.

COMPLETE SET (20) 15.00 40.00
1 Shareef Abdur-Rahim 1.00 2.50
2 John Stockton 1.50 4.00
3 Peja Stojakovic 1.25 3.00
4 Elton Brand 1.25 3.00
5 Stephon Marbury 1.00 2.50
6 Eddie Jones 1.00 2.50
7 Baron Davis 1.25 3.00
8 Keith Van Horn 1.00 2.50
9 Paul Pierce 1.50 4.00
10 Gary Payton 1.25 3.00
11 Grant Hill 1.50 4.00
12 Chris Webber 1.25 3.00
13 Latrell Sprewell 1.25 3.00
14 Jerry Stackhouse 1.00 2.50
15 Vince Carter 2.00 5.00
16 Allen Iverson 2.50 6.00
17 Dirk Nowitzki 2.00 5.00
18 Shawn Marion 1.25 3.00
19 Steve Francis 1.25 3.00
20 Richard Hamilton 1.00 2.50

2001-02 E-X Box Office Draws Memorabilia

Randomly inserted in packs at the rate of one in 33, this 19-card set parallels the base Box Office Draws insert set enhanced with a swatch of either shorts or a warm-up.

1 Shareef Abdur-Rahim Warm 3.00 8.00
2 Elton Brand Warm 4.00 10.00
3 Vince Carter Shorts 6.00 15.00
4 Michael Finley Shorts 4.00 10.00
5 Steve Francis Shorts 4.00 10.00
6 Richard Hamilton Shorts 3.00 8.00
7 Grant Hill Shorts 5.00 12.00
8 Allen Iverson Shorts 8.00 20.00
9 Stephon Marbury Warm 3.00 8.00
10 Shawn Marion Shorts 4.00 10.00
11 Tracy McGrady Shorts 6.00 15.00
12 Dirk Nowitzki Shorts 6.00 15.00
13 Lamar Odom Shorts 4.00 10.00
14 Paul Pierce Warm 5.00 12.00
15 Jerry Stackhouse Warm 3.00 8.00
16 John Stockton Warm 5.00 12.00
17 Peja Stojakovic Warm 4.00 10.00
18 Keith Van Horn Warm 3.00 8.00
19 Chris Webber Warm 4.00 10.00

2001-02 E-X Net Assets

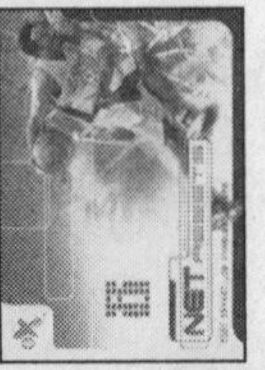

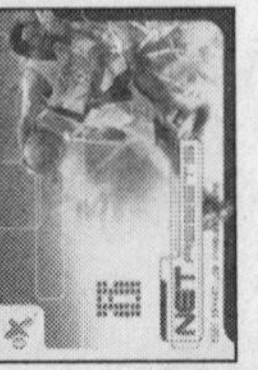

Randomly inserted in packs at the rate of one in 12, this 15-card set features a horizontal card design with player action photos on the right side set against a portrait style photo and a photo of the net from a basketball hoop. Background color is set to match the pictured player's jersey colors.

1 Kobe Bryant 5.00 12.00
2 Kwame Brown 1.00 2.50
3 Kevin Garnett 2.00 5.00
4 Eddie Griffin 1.00 2.50
5 Shaquille O'Neal 2.50 6.00
6 Tim Duncan 2.00 5.00
7 Tyson Chandler 1.50 4.00
8 Allen Iverson 2.00 5.00
9 Grant Hill 1.25 3.00
10 Michael Jordan 8.00 20.00
11 Ray Allen 1.00 2.50
12 Jason Richardson 2.00 5.00
13 Eddy Curry 1.50 4.00
14 Dirk Nowitzki 1.50 4.00
15 Vince Carter 1.50 4.00

2003-04 E-X

Issued in September of 2003, E-X consisted of a 102-card base set divided up into 72 veteran players and 30 rookies. Cards are printed on acetate plastic and feature a full-color player action photo along with the player's name and number and colored backgrounds to match the player's team colors. E-X was packaged in 3-card packs and 20-pack boxes and carried a suggested retail price of $5.99.

COMP.SET w/o SP's (72) 20.00 50.00
1 Shareef Abdur-Rahim .30 .75
2 Ray Allen .40 1.00
3 Gilbert Arenas .40 1.00
4 Ron Artest .40 1.00
5 Mike Bibby .40 1.00
6 Chauncey Billups .40 1.00
7 Elton Brand .40 1.00
8 Kwame Brown .25 .60
9 Kobe Bryant 2.00 5.00
10 Caron Butler .40 1.00
11 Vince Carter .60 1.50
12 Eddy Curry .30 .75
13 Ricky Davis .30 .75
14 Baron Davis .40 1.00
15 Tim Duncan .60 1.50
16 Michael Finley .40 1.00
17 Steve Francis .40 1.00
18 Kevin Garnett .75 2.00
19 Pau Gasol .40 1.00
20 Manu Ginobili .50 1.25
21 Drew Gooden .30 .75
22 Nene .30 .75
23 Grant Hill .50 1.25
24 Allan Houston .30 .75
25 Juwan Howard .30 .75
26 Zydrunas Ilgauskas .30 .75
27 Allen Iverson .60 1.50
28 Antawn Jamison .40 1.00
29 Richard Jefferson .40 1.00
30 Eddie Jones .30 .75
31 Jason Kidd .60 1.50
32 Andrei Kirilenko .40 1.00
33 Rashard Lewis .40 1.00
34 Corey Maggette .30 .75
35 Karl Malone .50 1.25
36 Stephon Marbury .30 .75
37 Shawn Marion .40 1.00
38 Kenyon Martin .40 1.00
39 Jamal Mashburn .30 .75
40 Tracy McGrady .50 1.25
41 Reggie Miller .40 1.00
42 Mike Miller .40 1.00
43 Yao Ming .75 2.00
44 Cuttino Mobley .30 .75
45 Steve Nash .50 1.25
46 Dirk Nowitzki .60 1.50
47 Jermaine O'Neal .40 1.00
48 Shaquille O'Neal 1.00 2.50
49 Tony Parker .40 1.00
50 Gary Payton .40 1.00
51 Morris Peterson .25 .60
52 Paul Pierce .50 1.25
53 Scottie Pippen .60 1.50
54 Tayshaun Prince .40 1.00
55 Vladimir Radmanovic .25 .60
56 Michael Redd .40 1.00
57 Jason Richardson .40 1.00
58 Glenn Robinson .30 .75
59 Jalen Rose .30 .75
60 Latrell Sprewell .30 .75
61 Jerry Stackhouse .30 .75
62 Peja Stojakovic .40 1.00
63 Amare Stoudemire .60 1.50
64 Wally Szczerbiak .30 .75
65 Jason Terry .30 .75
66 Keith Van Horn .30 .75
67 Dajuan Wagner .25 .60
68 Antoine Walker .40 1.00
69 Ben Wallace .40 1.00
70 Rasheed Wallace .40 1.00
71 Chris Webber .40 1.00
72 Bonzi Wells .25 .60
73 Carmelo Anthony RC 8.00 20.00
74 Ndudi Ebi RC 3.00 8.00
75 Luke Ridnour RC 4.00 10.00
76 Josh Howard RC 4.00 10.00
77 Marcus Banks RC 3.00 8.00
78 Zarko Cabarkapa RC 3.00 8.00
79 Kendrick Perkins RC 5.00 12.00
80 Leandro Barbosa RC 4.00 10.00
81 David West RC 4.00 10.00
82 Boris Diaw RC 4.00 10.00
83 Carlos Delfino RC 4.00 10.00
84 Mickael Pietrus RC 3.00 8.00
85 Troy Bell RC 3.00 8.00
86 Reece Gaines RC 3.00 8.00
87 Brian Cook RC 3.00 8.00
88 Kirk Hinrich RC 4.00 10.00
89 Travis Outlaw RC 4.00 10.00
90 Dwyane Wade RC 12.00 30.00
91 Luke Walton RC 3.00 8.00
92 Chris Bosh RC 6.00 15.00
93 Jarvis Hayes RC 3.00 8.00
94 Maciej Lampe RC 3.00 8.00
95 Mike Sweetney RC 3.00 8.00
96 Sofoklis Schortsanitis RC 3.00 8.00
97 Dahntay Jones RC 3.00 8.00
98 Nick Collison RC 3.00 8.00
99 Chris Kaman RC 4.00 10.00
100 Darko Milicic RC 3.00 8.00
101 T.J. Ford RC 4.00 10.00
102 LeBron James RC 30.00 80.00

2003-04 E-X Essential Credentials Future

Inserted at one in 28, this 102-card set is a parallel of the base E-X set and is enhanced with sequentially numbered cards and slightly different color schemes. Print runs are listed below.

*SINGLES #'d 25-30: 2.5X TO 6X BASE HI
*SINGLES #'d 31-40: 10X TO 25X BASE HI
*SINGLES #'d 41-60: 8X TO 20X BASE HI
*SINGLES #'d 61-80: 6X TO 15X BASE HI
*SINGLES #'d 81-102: 5X TO 12X BASE HI
SOME NOT PRICED DUE TO SCARCITY
2 Ray Allen/101 8.00 20.00
9 Kobe Bryant/94 75.00 150.00
18 Kevin Garnett/85 15.00 40.00
23 Grant Hill/80 8.00 20.00
73 Carmelo Anthony/30 100.00 200.00

2003-04 E-X Essential Credentials Now

Inserted at one in 28, this 102-card set is a parallel of the base E-X set and is enhanced with sequentially numbered cards and slightly different color schemes. Print runs are listed below.

*SINGLES #'d 25-40: 12.5X TO 30X BASE HI
*SINGLES #'d 41-60: 10X TO 25X BASE HI
*SINGLES #'d 61-72: 6X TO 15X BASE HI
*SINGLES #'d 73-102: 1.5X TO 4X BASE HI
SOME NOT PRICED DUE TO SCARCITY
35 Karl Malone/35 25.00 60.00
40 Tracy McGrady/40 20.00 50.00
73 Carmelo Anthony/73 40.00 100.00
102 LeBron James/102 150.00 400.00

2003-04 E-X Behind the Numbers

Inserted in packs at the rate of one in 80, this 15-card set features a horizontal design with player images on the right and the player's number on the left.

COMPLETE SET (15) 15.00 40.00
1 Dirk Nowitzki 2.00 5.00
2 Antoine Walker 1.25 3.00
3 Tayshaun Prince 1.25 3.00
4 Jason Kidd 2.00 5.00
5 Tracy McGrady 1.50 4.00
6 Allen Iverson 2.00 5.00
7 Pau Gasol 1.25 3.00
8 Eddy Curry 1.00 2.50
9 Elton Brand 1.25 3.00
10 Amare Stoudemire 2.00 5.00
11 Manu Ginobili 1.50 4.00
12 Andrei Kirilenko 1.25 3.00
13 Kevin Garnett 2.50 6.00
14 Peja Stojakovic 1.25 3.00
15 Kenyon Martin 1.25 3.00

2003-04 E-X Behind the Numbers Game-Used

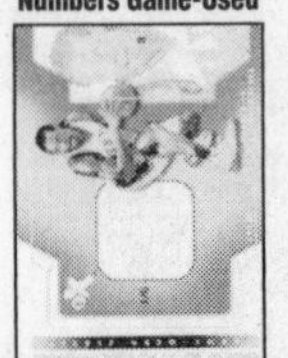

Seeded at one in 10 packs, this 25-card set parallels the design of the non-jersey version of the Behind the Numbers set. Each card replaces the printed player's number with a swatch of game-worn memorabilia in the shape of the featured player's number.

*GOLD: .5X TO 1.25X BASE HI
GOLD PRINT RUN 150 SER.#'d SETS
1 Dirk Nowitzki 4.00 10.00
2 Antoine Walker 2.50 6.00
3 Tayshaun Prince 2.50 6.00
4 Jason Kidd 4.00 10.00
5 Tracy McGrady 3.00 8.00
6 Allen Iverson 4.00 10.00
7 Pau Gasol 2.50 6.00
8 Eddy Curry 2.00 5.00
9 Elton Brand 2.50 6.00
10 Amare Stoudemire 4.00 10.00
11 Manu Ginobili 3.00 8.00
12 Andrei Kirilenko 2.50 6.00
13 Kevin Garnett 5.00 12.00
14 Peja Stojakovic 2.50 6.00
15 Kenyon Martin 2.50 6.00
16 Tyson Chandler 2.00 5.00
17 Latrell Sprewell 2.50 6.00
18 Caron Butler 2.50 6.00
19 Drew Gooden 2.00 5.00
20 Marcus Haislip 2.00 5.00
21 Kwame Brown 2.00 5.00
22 Vince Carter 4.00 10.00
23 Jermaine O'Neal 2.50 6.00
24 Joe Johnson 2.50 6.00
25 Yao Ming 5.00 12.00

2003-04 E-X Buzzer Beaters

Seeded at the rate of one in 240 packs, this 10-card set is printed horizontally on clear acetate plastic. The backgroud is that of an NBA backboard while full-color player photos appear in the foreground.

COMPLETE SET (10) 40.00 80.00
1 Vince Carter 6.00 15.00
2 Ben Wallace 4.00 10.00
3 Amare Stoudemire 6.00 15.00
4 Tony Parker 4.00 10.00
5 Kenyon Martin 4.00 10.00
6 Tracy McGrady 5.00 12.00
7 Dirk Nowitzki 6.00 15.00
8 Gilbert Arenas 4.00 10.00
9 Kevin Garnett 8.00 20.00
10 Elton Brand 4.00 10.00

2003-04 E-X Buzzer Beaters Autographs

A Parallel of the base Buzzer Beaters set, these 11 cards are enhanced with a foil sticker on which appears the player's autograph.

1 Ben Wallace/299 12.50 30.00
2 Amare Stoudemire/99 20.00 40.00
5 Tracy McGrady/299 15.00 40.00
6 Gilbert Arenas/99 15.00 40.00
7 Carmelo Anthony/299 25.00 60.00
8 Mike Sweetney/299 8.00 20.00
9 Chris Bosh/299 15.00 40.00
10 Dwyane Wade/299 50.00 100.00

2003-04 E-X Jambalaya

Jambalaya was one of the most popular insert sets upon its release and through the 2003-04 season. Cards are die cut into ovals and appear on an almost 3-D background. Stated odds for the set were one in 480 packs.

1 LeBron James 300.00 600.00
2 Carmelo Anthony 60.00 120.00
3 Dwyane Wade 75.00 200.00
4 Darko Milicic 10.00 25.00
5 T.J. Ford 12.00 30.00
6 Chris Bosh 40.00 100.00
7 Mike Sweetney 10.00 25.00
8 Kobe Bryant 400.00 650.00
9 Jermaine O'Neal 25.00 60.00
10 Vince Carter 40.00 100.00
11 Allen Iverson 60.00 120.00
12 Tracy McGrady 40.00 100.00
13 Yao Ming 40.00 100.00
14 Shaquille O'Neal 50.00 120.00
15 Tim Duncan 50.00 120.00

2003-04 E-X Net Assets

Inserted at the rate of one in 32, the 10-card Net Assets insert set places full-color player images against a background that features both the team's colors and a close-up of the net from a basket.

COMPLETE SET (10) 8.00 20.00
1 Kobe Bryant 4.00 10.00
2 Jason Richardson .75 2.00
3 Tim Duncan 1.25 3.00
4 Chris Webber .75 2.00
5 Jason Kidd 1.25 3.00
6 Steve Nash 1.00 2.50
7 Allen Iverson 1.25 3.00
8 Steve Francis .75 2.00
9 Paul Pierce 1.00 2.50
10 Shaquille O'Neal 2.00 5.00

2003-04 E-X Net Assets Game-Used

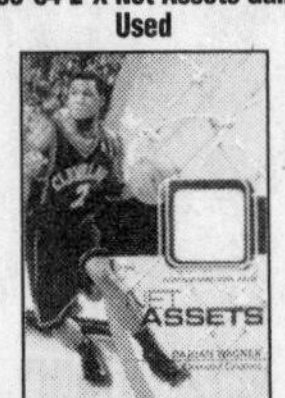

Seeded at one in 12, this 15-card set parallels the base Net Assets insert set enhanced with a swatch of game-worn memorabilia.

1 Chris Webber 2.50 6.00
2 Jason Kidd 4.00 10.00
3 Steve Nash 3.00 8.00
4 Allen Iverson 4.00 10.00
5 Steve Francis 2.50 6.00
6 Paul Pierce 3.00 8.00
7 Jerry Stackhouse 2.50 6.00
8 Reggie Miller 2.50 6.00
9 Bonzi Wells 2.00 5.00
10 Shane Battier 2.00 5.00
11 Dajuan Wagner 2.00 5.00
12 Andre Miller 2.00 5.00
13 Nene Hilario 2.00 5.00
14 Tony Parker 2.50 6.00
15 Jamal Mashburn 2.00 5.00

2003-04 E-X Net Assets Patch

Seeded at one in 12, this 15-card set parallels the base Net Assets insert set enhanced with a premium swatch of game-worn patches.

*PATCH: 1.25X TO 3X BASE GU HI
1 Chris Webber 12.00 30.00
4 Allen Iverson 15.00 40.00
8 Reggie Miller 15.00 40.00

2004-05 E-XL

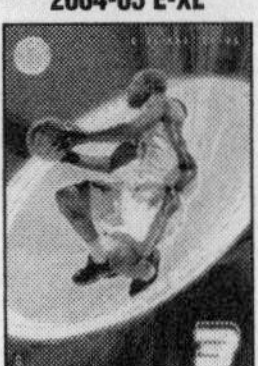

Released in December 2004, E-XL consists of a 1 card based set divided up into 70 veteran players two tiers of rookies. The first tier, cards 71-94 are sequentially numbered to 399 and the second tier cards 95-107 are sequentially numbered to 899. cards feature player action photos centered by a of white with colored backgrounds and bronze foil highlights. E-XL was packaged in both Hobby an Retail formats. Hobby boxes contain 18 packs of cards each while Retail boxes contain 24 packs o cards each.

COMP.SET w/o SP's (70) 15.00
1 Dwyane Wade 1.25
2 Kobe Bryant 2.00
3 Mike Bibby .40
4 Michael Finley .40
5 Jamal Mashburn .40
6 Carmelo Anthony .75
7 Jason Kidd .60
8 Andrei Kirilenko .40
9 Ron Artest .40
10 Peja Stojakovic .40
11 Yao Ming .75
12 Shawn Marion .40
13 Desmond Mason .30
14 Paul Pierce .50
15 Pau Gasol .40
16 Tim Duncan .60
17 Andre Miller .30
18 Allan Houston .30
19 Ben Wallace .40
20 Stephon Marbury .40
21 Gilbert Arenas .40
22 Luke Walton .25
23 Rashard Lewis .40
24 Elton Brand .40
25 Zach Randolph .30
26 Eddy Curry .30
27 Richard Jefferson .40
28 Kirk Hinrich .40
29 Jason Terry .30
30 Ray Allen .40
31 Mike Dunleavy .30
32 Glenn Robinson .30
33 Darko Milicic .25
34 Steve Francis .40
35 Antawn Jamison .40
36 Jason Williams .30
37 Tracy McGrady .50
38 Steve Nash .50
39 Gary Payton .40
40 Sam Cassell .30
41 Gerald Wallace .40
42 Shaquille O'Neal 1.00
43 Tony Parker .40
44 Richard Hamilton .30
45 Kenyon Martin .40
46 Baron Davis .40
47 Jarvis Hayes .25
48 Chris Kaman .40
49 Manu Ginobili .50
50 Jermaine O'Neal .40
51 Amare Stoudemire .50
52 Latrell Sprewell .30
53 LeBron James 2.50
54 Michael Redd .40
55 Chris Bosh .40
56 Juwan Howard .30
57 Jason Richardson .40
58 Allen Iverson .60
59 Antoine Walker .40
60 Eddie Jones .30
61 Carlos Arroyo .30
62 Lamar Odom .40
63 Chris Webber .40
64 Drew Gooden .25
65 Jamaal Magloire .25
66 Dirk Nowitzki .60
67 Kevin Garnett .75
68 Vince Carter .60
69 Reggie Miller .40
70 Shareef Abdur-Rahim .30
71 Emeka Okafor RC 4.00
72 Pavel Podkolzine RC 2.50
73 Kris Snyder RC 2.50
74 Ben Gordon RC 3.00
75 Devin Harris RC 4.00
76 Josh Childress RC 2.50
77 Dorell Wright RC 4.00
78 Dwight Howard RC 8.00
79 Andre Iguodala RC 4.00
80 Viktor Khryapa RC 2.50
81 Al Jefferson RC 4.00
82 Kevin Martin RC 3.00
83 Delonte West RC 3.00
84 Josh Smith RC 4.00
85 Luol Deng RC 4.00
86 Kris Humphries RC 2.50
87 Sebastian Telfair RC 2.50
88 Rafael Araujo RC 2.50
89 Jameer Nelson RC 3.00
90 Shaun Livingston RC 3.00
91 Andris Biedrins RC 2.50
92 Robert Swift RC 2.50
93 Luke Jackson RC 2.50
94 J.R. Smith RC 3.00
95 Tony Allen RC 2.00
96 Sasha Vujacic RC 1.50
97 David Harrison RC 1.50
98 Anderson Varejao RC 2.00
99 Jackson Vroman RC 1.50
100 Peter John Ramos RC 1.50
101 Lionel Chalmers RC 1.50
102 Donta Smith RC 1.50
103 Andre Emmett RC 1.50
104 Trevor Ariza RC 1.50
105 Tim Pickett RC 1.50
106 Bernard Robinson RC 1.50
107 Matt Freije RC 1.50

2004-05 E-XL Essentia Credentials Future

Randomly inserted in packs, this 107-card se the base set enhanced with red foil and seque

ering. The numbering system starts at 107 on
one and decreases by one number for each
cutive card to where card number 107 is a one of

GLES #'d 81-107: 4X TO 10X BASE HI
LES #'d 61-80: 5X TO 12X BASE HI
GLES #'d 38-60: 6X TO 15X BASE HI
#'d 26-37: 1.5X TO 4X BASE HI
#'d 15-25: 2X TO 5X BASE HI
e Bryant/106 25.00 60.00
y Allen/78 6.00 15.00
ris Webber/45 8.00 20.00

2004-05 E-XL Essential Credentials Now

mly inserted in packs, this 107-card set parallels
se set enhanced with blue foil and sequential
ering. The numbering system starts at 1 on card
d increases by one number for each consecutive
o where card number 107 is serially numbered to

LES #'d 15-25: 10X TO 25X BASE HI
LES #'d 26-40: 8X TO 20X BASE HI
LES #'d 41-60: 6X TO 15X BASE HI
LES #'d 60-70: 5X TO 12X BASE HI
#'d 71-94: .6X TO 1.5X BASE HI
#'d 95-107: .5 TO 1.25 BASE HI
Allen/30 10.00 25.00
ris Webber/63 6.00 15.00

04-05 E-XL Rookies Die Cuts

y numbered to the same amounts as their RC
counterparts, this 30 card set features rounded
rners and die cutting on the top and bottom of
d.
CUTS: .4X TO 1X BASE HI
STATED PRINT RUN 399 SETS
7 STATED PRINT RUN 899 SETS

2004-05 E-XL ConnEXions Autographs

mly inserted and limited to varying amounts, this
d set is designed horizontally and features player
aphs on the left, one on top of the other, and
e corresponding player's photo along the right
f the card.
Howard/100 8.00 20.00
quis Daniels
ei Kirilenko 6.00 15.00
ei Monia
haun Prince/20 15.00 40.00
ncey Billups
Randolph/20 20.00 50.00
n Richardson
kael Pietrus 12.50 30.00
Parker
nu Ginobili 60.00 120.00
s Arroyo
ce Carter/100 20.00 50.00
wn Jamison
on Richardson 15.00 40.00
Jones
h Smith/20 30.00 80.00
Smith
Gordon 12.50 30.00
eer Nelson
n Brand/50 20.00 50.00
s Boozer

2004-05 E-XL ConnEXions Jerseys

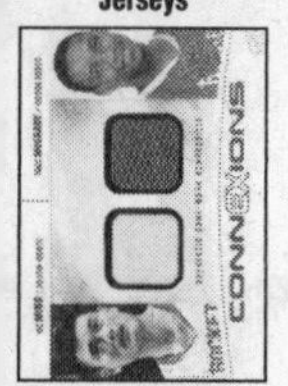

nly inserted, this 25-card set places two player
s on the right and left of each card, two square
es of memorabilia in the middle and sequential
ing to 22. One of one versions also exist.
ne Wade 20.00 50.00
elo Anthony
wn Jamison 15.00 40.00
Carter
Bibby 15.00 40.00
Stojakovic
ne Wade 25.00 60.00
uille O'Neal
on Marbury 10.00 25.00
tian Telfair
Mashburn 10.00 25.00
al Magloire
uille O'Neal 25.00 60.00
uncan
n Garnett 12.50 30.00
e Stoudemire
Gordon 12.50 30.00
Deng
Ming 15.00 40.00
McGrady
Wallace 10.00 25.00
eed Wallace
McGrady 30.00 80.00
Carter

2004-05 E-XL Court Authentics

Inserted in packs, this 35-card set places portrait style photos of players on the top of the card and a square swatch of memorabilia in the lower left of the card. Each is highlighted with red foil and is sequentially numbered to 500. Several parallel versions of this set were issued and are as follows: Die Cuts with rounded out corners serially numbered to 75, Namplates that include a swatch of letter from the players nameplate serially numbered to the letters in the player's last name, Patches containing a patch swatch serially numbered to 70, Patches 50 serially numbered to 50, Patches Dual with two patch swatches serially numbered to 50, Patches triple with three patch swatches serially numbered to 13, Patches/Jersey serially numbered to 35, Patches/Warmup serially numbered to 44, Patches/Warmup/Jersey serially numbered to eight.

AI Allen Iverson 4.00 10.00
AS Amare Stoudemire 3.00 8.00
BD Baron Davis 2.50 6.00
BG Ben Gordon 3.00 8.00
BW Ben Wallace 2.50 6.00
CA Carmelo Anthony 5.00 12.00
CB Chris Bosh 2.50 6.00
CW Chris Webber 3.00 8.00
DH Dwight Howard 8.00 20.00
DH2 Devin Harris 4.00 10.00
DM Darko Milicic 2.00 5.00
DN Dirk Nowitzki 4.00 10.00
DW Dwyane Wade 8.00 20.00
EB Elton Brand 2.50 6.00
JK Jason Kidd 4.00 10.00
JO Jermaine O'Neal 2.50 6.00
JR Jason Richardson 2.50 6.00
KG Kevin Garnett 5.00 12.00
KH Kirk Hinrich 2.50 6.00
KM Kenyon Martin 2.50 6.00
LD Luol Deng 4.00 10.00
MB Mike Bibby 2.50 6.00
PP Paul Pierce 3.00 8.00
RA Ray Allen 2.50 6.00
SF Steve Francis 2.50 6.00
SL Shaun Livingston 2.50 6.00
SM Stephon Marbury 2.00 5.00
SM2 Shawn Marion 2.50 6.00
SN Steve Nash 3.00 8.00
SO Shaquille O'Neal 6.00 15.00
TD Tim Duncan 4.00 10.00
TM Tracy McGrady 3.00 8.00
TP Tony Parker 2.50 6.00
VC Vince Carter 4.00 10.00
YM Yao Ming 5.00 12.00

2004-05 E-XL Court Authentics Signatures

This is the set redeemed from the Autograph Redemptions. The cards look like the Court Authentics set only they feature an autograph instead of a memorabilia swatch and are sequentially numbered from 100 to 200.

COMMON CARD 4.00 10.00
PRINT RUN 100 TO 200 SETS
UNPRICED PARALLEL PRINT RUN 10 SETS
AE Andre Emmett/200 4.00 10.00
AJ Al Jefferson/100 6.00 15.00
CD Carlos Delfino/200 4.00 10.00
JC Josh Childress/100 4.00 10.00
LC Lionel Chalmers/200 4.00 10.00
LD Luol Deng/200 6.00 15.00
NC Nick Collison/100 4.00 10.00

2004-05 E-XL Court Authentics Signatures Jerseys

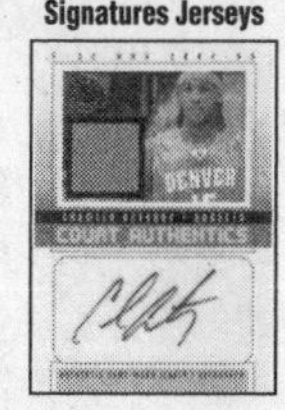

Randomly inserted in packs, this 40-card set parallels the design of the base Court Authentics set with both a jersey swatch and an autograph and is sequentially numbered from 50 to 70. Several different parallel versions of this set were issued and are as follows: Jersey/Warmup serially numbered to 30, Logos numbered one of one, Patches serially numbered to the player's jersey number and Tags that feature the tags off the jersey and are serially numbered to 5.

*SIG.JSY/WARM: .5X TO 1.25X BASE HI
AB Andris Biedrins 12.00 30.00
BG Ben Gordon 12.00 30.00
CA Carmelo Anthony 20.00 50.00
CB Chris Bosh 12.50 30.00
DH Devin Harris 15.00 40.00
DW Dwyane Wade 40.00 100.00
JC Josh Childress 10.00 25.00
JK Jason Kidd 20.00 50.00
JN Jameer Nelson 12.00 30.00
JO Jermaine O'Neal/67 10.00 25.00
LD Luol Deng 15.00 40.00
LJ Luke Jackson 10.00 25.00
LO Lamar Odom 12.50 30.00
MB Mike Bibby 10.00 25.00
PP Paul Pierce 12.50 30.00
RA Ray Allen 15.00 40.00
RJ Richard Jefferson 10.00 25.00
SL Shaun Livingston 10.00 25.00
SM Stephon Marbury 15.00 40.00
TF T.J. Ford/50 10.00 25.00
VC Vince Carter 20.00 50.00

2004-05 E-XL E-Xceptional

Inserted in packs at the rate of one in 54, this 10-card set features a foil board card stock with a rainbow holofoil effect, full color player photos and gold foil highlights.

COMPLETE SET (10) 30.00 80.00
*XL PARALLEL: .75X TO 2X BASE
1 Shaquille O'Neal 5.00 12.00
2 LeBron James 12.00 30.00
3 Vince Carter 3.00 8.00
4 Kobe Bryant 10.00 25.00
5 Dwyane Wade 6.00 15.00
6 Kevin Garnett 4.00 10.00
7 Allen Iverson 3.00 8.00
8 Tim Duncan 3.00 8.00
9 Jason Kidd 3.00 8.00
10 Yao Ming 4.00 10.00

2004-05 E-XL Jambalaya

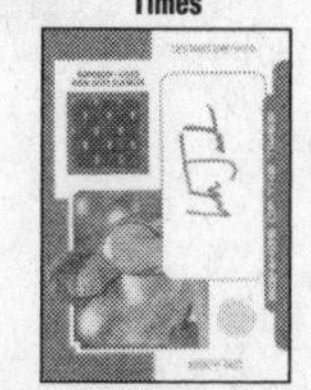

Inserted in packs at the rate of one in 216, this 10-card set features the normal oval-design/split background color for which Jambalaya has come to be known. Cards also have a circular gold logo in the upper right corner. An X-L version of the card was also made. These were inserted at the rate of one in 2160 and are differentiated by holofoil highlights instead of the gold foil.

*XL: .6X TO 1.5X BASE HI
XL STATED ODDS 1:2160
1 Carmelo Anthony 40.00 100.00
2 Shaquille O'Neal 50.00 125.00
3 Kobe Bryant 175.00 350.00
4 Vince Carter 30.00 80.00
5 Tracy McGrady 25.00 60.00
6 Kevin Garnett 40.00 100.00
7 Amare Stoudemire 25.00 60.00
8 Allen Iverson 50.00 120.00
9 LeBron James 175.00 350.00
10 Tim Duncan 30.00 80.00

2004-05 E-XL Signings of the Times

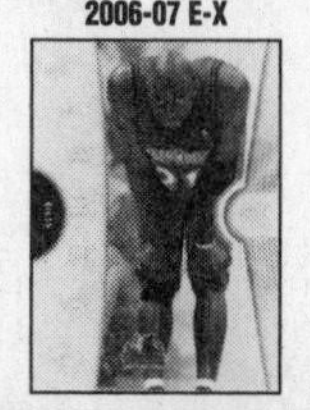

Randomly inserted, this 26-card set features a horizontal design, a black and white picture of the player on the left, a square jersey swatch on the right and an autograph along the bottom. Each card is sequentially numbered to 100. Several different parallels were issued for this set and are sequentially numbered to 50, 25 and one of one.

*SIGS 50: .5X TO 1.25X BASE HI
*SIGS 25: .6X TO 1.5X BASE HI
AB Andris Biedrins 8.00 20.00
AJ Al Jefferson 10.00 25.00
AV Anderson Varejao 8.00 20.00
BG Ben Gordon 8.00 20.00
CD Chris Duhon 6.00 15.00
DH Devin Harris 10.00 25.00
DH David Harrison 6.00 15.00
DW Delonte West 8.00 20.00
DW Dorell Wright 10.00 25.00
JC Josh Childress 6.00 15.00
JN Jameer Nelson 8.00 20.00
JS Josh Smith 10.00 25.00
JS2 J.R. Smith 8.00 20.00
KM Kevin Martin
KS Kirk Snyder 6.00 15.00
LC Lionel Chalmers 6.00 15.00
LD Luol Deng 10.00 25.00
LJ Luke Jackson 6.00 15.00
PP Pavel Podkolzine 6.00 15.00
RA Rafael Araujo 6.00 15.00
RS Robert Swift 6.00 15.00
SL Shaun Livingston 6.00 15.00
ST Sebastian Telfair 6.00 15.00
TA Tony Allen 8.00 20.00

2006-07 E-X

Released in mid March 2007, E-X boasts an 80-card base set where veteran players are featured on cards 1-40, rookies sequentially numbered to 99 are featured on cards 41-46 and autograph rookies are featured on cards 47-80. Base cards consist of a combination of acetate plastic with foil-board highlights and all rookie autographs are signed directly on the cards (see checklist for print runs). E-X carried an initial suggested retail price of $14.99; boxes contain eight packs of five cards each.

COMP.SET w/o RC's (40) 12.50 30.00
1 Joe Johnson .50 1.25
2 Paul Pierce .60 1.50
3 Emeka Okafor .50 1.25
4 Michael Jordan 4.00 10.00
5 Ben Gordon .50 1.25
6 LeBron James 2.50 6.00
7 Dirk Nowitzki .75 2.00
8 Jason Terry .40 1.00
9 Carmelo Anthony .60 1.50
10 Chauncey Billups .50 1.25
11 Ben Wallace .50 1.25
12 Baron Davis .50 1.25
13 Jason Richardson .50 1.25
14 Yao Ming .60 1.50
15 Jermaine O'Neal .50 1.25
16 Elton Brand .50 1.25
17 Kobe Bryant 2.50 6.00
18 Pau Gasol .50 1.25
19 Tracy McGrady .60 1.50
20 Shaquille O'Neal 1.00 2.50
21 Dwyane Wade 1.25 3.00
22 Andrew Bogut .50 1.25
23 Kevin Garnett 1.00 2.50
24 Vince Carter .60 1.50
25 Jason Kidd .75 2.00
26 Chris Paul 1.00 2.50
27 Stephon Marbury .40 1.00
28 Dwight Howard .75 2.00
29 Allen Iverson .60 1.50
30 Steve Nash .60 1.50
31 Shawn Marion .50 1.25
32 Martell Webster .40 1.00
33 Mike Bibby .50 1.25
34 Ron Artest .50 1.25
35 Tim Duncan .75 2.00
36 Manu Ginobili .50 1.25
37 Ray Allen .50 1.25
38 Chris Bosh .50 1.25
39 Andrei Kirilenko .40 1.00
40 Gilbert Arenas .50 1.25
41 J.J. Redick/99 RC 8.00 20.00
42 Adam Morrison/99 RC 8.00 20.00
43 Jorge Garbajosa/99 RC 6.00 15.00
44 Saer Sene/99 RC 6.00 15.00
45 Renaldo Balkman/99 RC 6.00 15.00
46 Thabo Sefolosha/99 RC 8.00 20.00
47 Kevin Pittsnogle/899 AU RC 4.00 10.00
48 Daniel Gibson/899 AU RC 5.00 12.00
49 Dee Brown/899 AU RC 4.00 10.00
50 Sergio Rodriguez/899 AU RC 4.00 10.00
51 Bobby Jones/899 AU RC 4.00 10.00
52 Craig Smith/899 AU RC 4.00 10.00
53 David Noel/899 AU RC 4.00 10.00
54 Denham Brown/899 AU RC 4.00 10.00
55 James White/899 AU RC 4.00 10.00
56 Paul Davis/899 AU RC 4.00 10.00
57 P.J. Tucker/899 AU RC 4.00 10.00
58 Solomon Jones/899 AU RC 4.00 10.00
59 Steve Novak/899 AU RC 4.00 10.00
60 Allan Ray/899 AU RC 4.00 10.00
61 Jordan Farmar/899 AU RC 4.00 10.00
62 Josh Boone/899 AU RC 4.00 10.00
63 Mardy Collins/899 AU RC 4.00 10.00
64 Rodney Carney/399 AU RC 6.00 15.00
65 Quincy Douby/399 AU RC 6.00 15.00
66 Shannon Brown/399 AU RC 10.00 25.00
67 Rajon Rondo/399 AU RC 25.00 60.00
68 Maurice Ager/399 AU RC 6.00 15.00
69 Ronnie Brewer/399 AU RC 8.00 20.00
70 Marcus Williams/399 AU RC 6.00 15.00
71 Kyle Lowry/399 AU RC 8.00 20.00
72 Cedric Simmons/399 AU RC 6.00 15.00
73 Patrick O'Bryant/399 AU RC 6.00 15.00
74 Hilton Armstrong/399 AU RC 6.00 15.00
75 Rudy Gay/199 AU RC 12.00 30.00
76 Brandon Roy/199 AU RC 20.00 50.00
77 Shelden Williams/199 AU RC 8.00 20.00
78 Tyrus Thomas/199 AU RC 10.00 25.00
79 LaMarcus Aldridge/199 AU RC 20.00 50.00
80 Andrea Bargnani/199 AU RC 12.00 30.00

2006-07 E-X Behind the Numbers

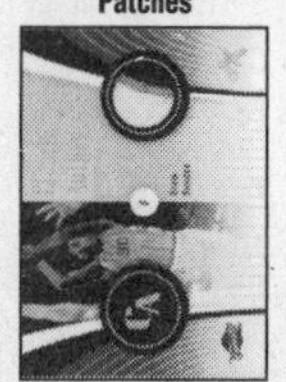

APPROXIMATE ODDS 1:8
BNAI Andre Iguodala 3.00 8.00
BNBD Baron Davis 3.00 8.00
BNBH Brendan Haywood 2.00 5.00
BNBM Brad Miller 3.00 8.00
BNBW Ben Wallace 3.00 8.00
BNCA Carmelo Anthony 4.00 10.00
BNCB Chauncey Billups 3.00 8.00
BNCM Corey Maggette 2.50 6.00
BNCW Chris Webber 3.00 8.00
BNDW David West 3.00 8.00
BNGA Gilbert Arenas 3.00 8.00
BNJG Joey Graham 2.00 5.00
BNJR Jason Richardson 3.00 8.00
BNJS J.R. Smith 3.00 8.00
BNKB Kobe Bryant 10.00 25.00
BNKH Kirk Hinrich 3.00 8.00
BNKK Kyle Korver 2.50 6.00
BNLJ LeBron James 10.00 25.00
BNLW Luke Walton 2.00 5.00
BNMA Sean May 2.00 5.00
BNPP Paul Pierce 4.00 10.00
BNRI Royal Ivey 2.00 5.00
BNSL Shaun Livingston 2.00 5.00
BNSM Shawn Marion 3.00 8.00
BNSN Steve Nash 4.00 10.00
BNTC Tyson Chandler 2.50 6.00
BNTP Tony Parker 3.00 8.00
BNWS Wally Szczerbiak 2.50 6.00
BNZI Zydrunas Ilgauskas 2.50 6.00

2006-07 E-X Behind the Numbers Autographs

SOME UNPRICED DUE TO SCARCITY
BNCA Carmelo Anthony/15 30.00 80.00
BNJG Joey Graham/14 8.00 20.00
BNLJ LeBron James/23 200.00 400.00
BNPP Paul Pierce/34 20.00 50.00
BNSN Steve Nash/13 40.00 100.00

2006-07 E-X Clearly Authentics Autographs

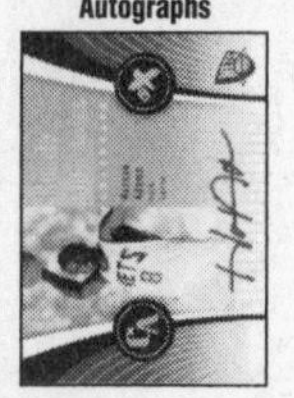

APPROXIMATE ODDS 1:8
UNPRICED GOLD PRINT RUN FIVE SETS
UNPRICED JSY/TAG PRINT RUN TEN SETS
CAAAB Andrew Bogut 8.00 20.00
CAAAI Andre Iguodala 4.00 10.00
CAAAJ Al Jefferson 3.00 8.00
CAAAM Amir Johnson 3.00 8.00
CAAAU James Augustine 3.00 8.00
CAABA Brent Barry 5.00 12.00
CAABB Brandon Bass 3.00 8.00
CAABD Baron Davis SP 6.00 15.00
CAABG Ben Gordon SP 12.50 30.00
CAABI Chauncey Billups 8.00 20.00
CAABJ Bobby Jackson 3.00 8.00
CAABO Bruce Bowen 5.00 12.00
CAABS Bobby Simmons 3.00 8.00
CAACA Carmelo Anthony SP 20.00 40.00
CAACB Charlie Bell 3.00 8.00
CAACD Chris Duhon 3.00 8.00
CAACH Chuck Hayes 3.00 8.00
CAACK Chris Kaman 3.00 8.00
CAACM Cedric Maxwell 6.00 15.00
CAACP Chris Paul SP 20.00 50.00
CAADA Damir Markota 3.00 8.00
CAADB Dee Brown 3.00 8.00
CAADD Dan Dickau 3.00 8.00
CAADG Danny Granger 3.00 8.00
CAADH Dwight Howard 12.50 30.00
CAADO Donyell Marshall 3.00 8.00
CAAEC Eddy Curry 3.00 8.00
CAAEI Ersan Ilyasova 3.00 8.00
CAAFG Francisco Garcia 3.00 8.00
CAAGG Gerald Green 3.00 8.00
CAAGW Gerald Wallace 3.00 8.00
CAAHA Hassan Adams 3.00 8.00
CAAIU Ime Udoka 3.00 8.00
CAAJA Antawn Jamison 6.00 15.00
CAAJC Josh Childress 3.00 8.00
CAAJG Joey Graham 3.00 8.00
CAAJK Jason Kapono 3.00 8.00
CAAJR Jalen Rose 4.00 10.00
CAAJS J.R. Smith 4.00 10.00
CAAKD Keyon Dooling 3.00 8.00
CAAKG Kevin Garnett 20.00 50.00
CAAKH Kirk Hinrich 10.00 25.00
CAAKI Jason Kidd SP 15.00 40.00
CAAKK Kyle Korver 5.00 12.00
CAALH Larry Hughes 3.00 8.00
CAALJ LeBron James SP 125.00 250.00
CAALR Lawrence Roberts 3.00 8.00
CAALW Louis Williams 3.00 8.00
CAAMB Mike Bibby 6.00 15.00
CAAMD Marquis Daniels 3.00 8.00
CAAMM Chris Mihm 3.00 8.00
CAAMO Cuttino Mobley 3.00 8.00
CAAMW Martell Webster 3.00 8.00
CAAPO Patrick O'Bryant 3.00 8.00
CAAPP Paul Pierce 10.00 25.00
CAAPS Peja Stojakovic 5.00 12.00
CAAQR Quentin Richardson 3.00 8.00
CAARF Raymond Felton 4.00 10.00
CAARI Luke Ridnour 3.00 8.00
CAARM Rashad McCants 3.00 8.00
CAARW Mile Ilic 3.00 8.00
CAASA Shareef Abdur-Rahim 3.00 8.00
CAASC Speedy Claxton 3.00 8.00
CAASG Stephen Graham 3.00 8.00
CAASI James Singleton 3.00 8.00
CAASL Shaun Livingston 3.00 8.00
CAASN Steve Nash SP 60.00 120.00
CAASS Salim Stoudamire 3.00 8.00
CAAST DeShawn Stevenson 3.00 8.00
CAATA Tony Allen 3.00 8.00
CAATE Sebastian Telfair 3.00 8.00
CAATF T.J. Ford 3.00 8.00
CAATM Tracy McGrady SP 15.00 40.00
CAATP Tayshaun Prince 5.00 12.00
CAAWB Will Blalock 3.00 8.00
CAAWI Marvin Williams 5.00 12.00
CAAWL Damien Wilkins 3.00 8.00
CAAWM Maurice Williams 3.00 8.00
CAAYM Yao Ming SP 20.00 50.00

2006-07 E-X Clearly Authentics Patches

PRINT RUN 75 SER.#'d SETS
CAAB Andrew Bogut 5.00 12.00
CAAI Andre Iguodala 5.00 12.00
CAAJ Al Jefferson 5.00 12.00
CAAL Ray Allen 5.00 12.00
CAAS Amare Stoudemire 5.00 12.00
CABD Baron Davis 5.00 12.00
CABI Chauncey Billups 5.00 12.00
CABM Brad Miller 5.00 12.00
CABO Bruce Bowen 3.00 8.00
CABR Kobe Bryant 25.00 60.00
CABW Ben Wallace 5.00 12.00
CACA Carmelo Anthony 6.00 15.00
CACB Carlos Boozer 5.00 12.00
CACF Channing Frye 4.00 10.00
CACM Corey Maggette 4.00 10.00
CACP Chris Paul 10.00 25.00
CACW Chris Webber 5.00 12.00
CADG Danny Granger 5.00 12.00
CADH Dwight Howard 8.00 20.00
CADM Donyell Marshall 3.00 8.00
CADN Dirk Nowitzki 8.00 20.00
CADW Deron Williams 8.00 20.00
CAEB Elton Brand 5.00 12.00
CAEC Eddy Curry 4.00 10.00
CAEI Ersan Ilyasova 3.00 8.00
CAEO Emeka Okafor 5.00 12.00
CAFG Francisco Garcia 4.00 10.00
CAGG Gerald Green 4.00 10.00
CAGH Grant Hill 20.00 50.00
CAGO Drew Gooden 4.00 10.00
CAHA Devin Harris 5.00 12.00
CAHE Luther Head 4.00 10.00
CAHW Hakim Warrick 4.00 10.00
CAID Ike Diogu 3.00 8.00
CAIV Royal Ivey 3.00 8.00
CAJA Antawn Jamison 5.00 12.00
CAJC Josh Childress 4.00 10.00
CAJG Joey Graham 3.00 8.00
CAJK Jason Kidd 8.00 20.00
CAJM Jamaal Magloire 3.00 8.00
CAJO Jermaine O'Neal 5.00 12.00
CAJR Jalen Rose 4.00 10.00
CAJS J.R. Smith 5.00 12.00
CAJT Jason Terry 4.00 10.00
CAKB Kwame Brown 3.00 8.00
CAKG Kevin Garnett 10.00 25.00
CAKH Kirk Hinrich 5.00 12.00
CAKK Kyle Korver 4.00 10.00
CALB Leandro Barbosa 4.00 10.00
CALD Luol Deng 5.00 12.00
CALH Larry Hughes 4.00 10.00
CALJ LeBron James 20.00 50.00
CALO Lamar Odom 5.00 12.00
CALR Luke Ridnour 4.00 10.00
CAMA Stephon Marbury 4.00 10.00
CAMB Mike Bibby 5.00 12.00
CAMD Marquis Daniels 3.00 8.00
CAMG Manu Ginobili 5.00 12.00
CAMR Michael Redd 5.00 12.00
CAMW Martell Webster 4.00 10.00
CANE Nene 4.00 10.00
CANR Nate Robinson 5.00 12.00
CAPG Pau Gasol 5.00 12.00
CAPP Paul Pierce 6.00 15.00
CAPS Peja Stojakovic 5.00 12.00
CAPT Tayshaun Prince 5.00 12.00
CAQR Quentin Richardson 4.00 10.00
CARA Ron Artest 5.00 12.00
CARF Raymond Felton 6.00 15.00
CARH Richard Hamilton 4.00 10.00
CARI Jason Richardson 5.00 12.00
CARJ Richard Jefferson 5.00 12.00
CARM Rashad McCants 3.00 8.00
CASI Wayne Simien 3.00 8.00
CASJ Sarunas Jasikevicius 4.00 10.00
CASL Shaun Livingston 3.00 8.00
CASM Sean May 3.00 8.00
CASN Steve Nash 6.00 15.00
CASO Shaquille O'Neal 10.00 25.00
CASS Stromile Swift 3.00 8.00
CAST Sebastian Telfair 3.00 8.00
CATC Tyson Chandler 4.00 10.00
CATM Tracy McGrady 6.00 15.00
CATP Tony Parker 5.00 12.00
CAVC Vince Carter 6.00 15.00
CAWE Delonte West 4.00 10.00
CAWS Wally Szczerbiak 4.00 10.00
CAYM Yao Ming 6.00 15.00
CAZI Zydrunas Ilgauskas 4.00 10.00

2006-07 E-X Clearly Authentics Patches Autographs

PRINT RUN 25 SER.#'d SETS
CAAB Andrew Bogut 15.00 40.00
CAAI Andre Iguodala 12.50 30.00
CAAJ Al Jefferson 10.00 25.00
CABD Baron Davis 8.00 20.00
CABI Chauncey Billups 10.00 25.00
CABO Bruce Bowen 8.00 20.00
CACA Carmelo Anthony 40.00 80.00
CACB Carlos Boozer 20.00 50.00
CACF Channing Frye 10.00 25.00
CADG Danny Granger 10.00 25.00
CADH Dwight Howard 30.00 75.00
CADM Donyell Marshall 8.00 20.00
CADW Deron Williams 15.00 40.00
CAEI Ersan Ilyasova 8.00 20.00
CAEO Emeka Okafor 8.00 20.00
CAGG Gerald Green 12.50 30.00
CAHW Hakim Warrick 8.00 20.00
CAJA Antawn Jamison 8.00 20.00
CAJC Josh Childress 8.00 20.00
CAJG Joey Graham 8.00 20.00
CAJK Jason Kidd 12.00 30.00
CAJS J.R. Smith 10.00 25.00
CAKH Kirk Hinrich 15.00 40.00
CAKK Kyle Korver 10.00 25.00
CALB Leandro Barbosa 10.00 25.00
CALJ LeBron James 150.00 300.00
CALR Luke Ridnour 10.00 25.00
CAMB Mike Bibby 10.00 25.00
CAMW Martell Webster 8.00 20.00
CANR Nate Robinson 10.00 25.00
CAPS Peja Stojakovic 10.00 25.00
CAPT Tayshaun Prince 10.00 25.00
CARA Ron Artest 8.00 20.00
CARF Raymond Felton 10.00 25.00
CARJ Richard Jefferson 8.00 20.00
CASL Shaun Livingston 8.00 20.00
CASM Sean May 8.00 20.00
CASN Steve Nash 80.00 160.00
CAST Sebastian Telfair 8.00 20.00
CATC Tyson Chandler 8.00 20.00
CATM Tracy McGrady 30.00 80.00
CAVC Vince Carter 60.00 120.00
CAYM Yao Ming 30.00 75.00

2006-07 E-X ConnEXions

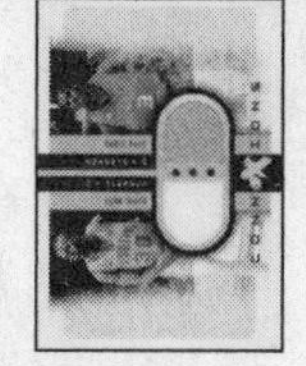

PRINT RUN 199 SER.#'d SETS
CNAR Ray Allen 3.00 8.00
Luke Ridnour
CNBG Chris Bosh 3.00 8.00
Joey Graham
CNBO Lamar Odom 3.00 8.00
Kwame Brown
CNBW Carlos Boozer 5.00 12.00
Deron Williams
CNCK Vince Carter 8.00 20.00
Nenad Krstic
CNDN Luol Deng 3.00 8.00
Andres Nocioni
CNDP Tim Duncan 6.00 15.00
Tony Parker
CNGJ Danny Granger 3.00 8.00
Sarunas Jasikevicius
CNGM Kevin Garnett 5.00 12.00
Rashad McCants
CNHB Richard Hamilton 3.00 8.00
Chauncey Billups
CNIJ Zydrunas Ilgauskas 10.00 25.00
LeBron James
CNJA Antawn Jamison 3.00 8.00
Gilbert Arenas
CNJW Dahntay Jones 3.00 8.00
Hakim Warrick
CNMB Corey Maggette 3.00 8.00
Elton Brand
CNMM Tracy McGrady 5.00 12.00
Yao Ming
CNNB Andrew Bogut 3.00 8.00
David Noel
CNNH Dirk Nowitzki 4.00 10.00
Devin Harris
CNNM Steve Nash 5.00 12.00
Shawn Marion
CNOF Emeka Okafor 3.00 8.00
Raymond Felton
CNRF Quentin Richardson 3.00 8.00
Channing Frye
CNRR Quentin Richardson 3.00 8.00
Nate Robinson
CNSH Stromile Swift 3.00 8.00
Hakim Warrick
CNSI Josh Smith 3.00 8.00
Royal Ivey
CNSO Wayne Simien 5.00 12.00
Shaquille O'Neal
CNSW Josh Smith 3.00 8.00
Marvin Williams
CNTH Jason Terry 3.00 8.00
Devin Harris
CNTW Ben Wallace 4.00 10.00
Tyrus Thomas
CNWI Chris Webber 3.00 8.00
Andre Iguodala
CNWP David West 4.00 10.00
Chris Paul
CNWS Wally Szczerbiak 3.00 8.00
Delonte West

2006-07 E-X ConnEXions Autographs

PRINT RUN 25 SER.#'d SETS
CNBG Chris Bosh 20.00 50.00
Joey Graham
CNBW Carlos Boozer 25.00 60.00
Deron Williams
CNMM Tracy McGrady 40.00 100.00
Yao Ming
CNNB David Noel 12.00 30.00
Andrew Bogut
CNOF Emeka Okafor 10.00 25.00
Raymond Felton

2006-07 E-X Essential Credentials Future

SOME UNPRICED DUE TO SCARCITY
1 Joe Johnson/80 6.00 15.00
2 Paul Pierce/79 8.00 20.00
3 Emeka Okafor/78 6.00 15.00
4 Michael Jordan/77 300.00 550.00
5 Ben Gordon/76 6.00 15.00
6 LeBron James/75 30.00 80.00
7 Dirk Nowitzki/74 10.00 25.00
8 Jason Terry/73 5.00 12.00
9 Carmelo Anthony/72 8.00 20.00
10 Chauncey Billups/71 6.00 15.00
11 Ben Wallace/70 6.00 15.00
12 Baron Davis/69 6.00 15.00
13 Jason Richardson/68 6.00 15.00
14 Yao Ming/67 8.00 20.00
15 Jermaine O'Neal/66 6.00 15.00
16 Elton Brand/65 6.00 15.00
17 Kobe Bryant/64 60.00 150.00
18 Pau Gasol/63 6.00 15.00
19 Tracy McGrady/62 8.00 20.00
20 Shaquille O'Neal/61 12.00 30.00
21 Dwyane Wade/60 20.00 50.00
22 Andrew Bogut/59 8.00 20.00
23 Kevin Garnett/58 15.00 40.00
24 Vince Carter/57 10.00 25.00
25 Jason Kidd/56 12.00 30.00
26 Chris Paul/55 20.00 50.00
27 Stephon Marbury/54 6.00 15.00
28 Dwight Howard/53 15.00 40.00
29 Allen Iverson/52 10.00 25.00
30 Steve Nash/51 10.00 25.00
31 Shawn Marion/50 8.00 20.00

32 Martell Webster/49	6.00	15.00
33 Mike Bibby/48	8.00	20.00
34 Ron Artest/47	8.00	20.00
35 Tim Duncan/46	12.00	30.00
36 Manu Ginobili/45	8.00	20.00
37 Ray Allen/44	10.00	25.00
38 Chris Bosh/43	8.00	20.00
39 Andrei Kirilenko/42	6.00	15.00
40 Gilbert Arenas/41	8.00	20.00
41 J.J. Redick/40	10.00	25.00
42 Adam Morrison/39	10.00	25.00
43 Jorge Garbajosa/38	8.00	20.00
44 Saer Sene/37	8.00	20.00
45 Renaldo Balkman/36	8.00	20.00
46 Thabo Sefolosha/35	10.00	25.00
47 Kevin Pittsnogle AU/34	8.00	20.00
48 Daniel Gibson AU/33	10.00	25.00
49 Dee Brown AU/32	8.00	20.00
50 Sergio Rodriguez AU/31	8.00	20.00
52 Craig Smith AU/29	8.00	20.00
53 David Noel AU/28	8.00	20.00
54 Denham Brown AU/27	8.00	20.00
55 James White AU/26	8.00	20.00
56 Paul Davis AU/25	8.00	20.00
57 P.J. Tucker AU/24	8.00	20.00
58 Solomon Jones AU/23	8.00	20.00
59 Steve Novak AU/22	8.00	20.00
60 Allan Ray AU/21	8.00	20.00
61 Jordan Farmar AU/20	8.00	20.00
62 Josh Boone AU/19	8.00	20.00
63 Mardy Collins AU/18	8.00	20.00
64 Rodney Carney AU/17	8.00	20.00
65 Quincy Douby AU/16	8.00	20.00
66 Shannon Brown AU/15	12.00	30.00

2006-07 E-X Essential Credentials Now

SOME UNPRICED DUE TO SCARCITY

15 Jermaine O'Neal/15	15.00	40.00
16 Elton Brand/16	15.00	40.00
17 Kobe Bryant/17	200.00	400.00
18 Pau Gasol/18	15.00	40.00
19 Tracy McGrady/19	20.00	50.00
20 Shaquille O'Neal/20	60.00	150.00
21 Dwyane Wade/21	100.00	250.00
22 Andrew Bogut/22	15.00	40.00
23 Kevin Garnett/23	30.00	80.00
24 Vince Carter/24	20.00	50.00
25 Jason Kidd/25	25.00	60.00
26 Chris Paul/26	50.00	125.00
27 Stephon Marbury/27	12.00	30.00
28 Dwight Howard/28	25.00	60.00
29 Allen Iverson/29	20.00	50.00
30 Steve Nash/30	20.00	50.00
31 Shawn Marion/31	8.00	20.00
32 Martell Webster/32	6.00	15.00
33 Mike Bibby/33	8.00	20.00
34 Ron Artest/34	8.00	20.00
35 Tim Duncan/35	20.00	50.00
36 Manu Ginobili/36	8.00	20.00
37 Ray Allen/37	10.00	25.00
38 Chris Bosh/38	8.00	20.00
39 Andrei Kirilenko/39	6.00	15.00
40 Gilbert Arenas/40	8.00	20.00
41 J.J. Redick/41	10.00	25.00
42 Adam Morrison/42	10.00	25.00
43 Jorge Garbajosa/43	8.00	20.00
44 Saer Sene/44	8.00	20.00
45 Renaldo Balkman/45	8.00	20.00
46 Thabo Sefolosha/46	10.00	25.00
47 Kevin Pittsnogle AU/47	6.00	15.00
48 Daniel Gibson AU/48	8.00	20.00
49 Dee Brown AU/49	6.00	15.00
50 Sergio Rodriguez AU/50	6.00	15.00
51 Bobby Jones AU/51	6.00	15.00
52 Craig Smith AU/52	6.00	15.00
53 David Noel AU/53	6.00	15.00
54 Denham Brown AU/54	6.00	15.00
55 James White AU/55	6.00	15.00
56 Paul Davis AU/56	6.00	15.00
57 P.J. Tucker AU/57	6.00	15.00
58 Solomon Jones AU/58	6.00	15.00
59 Steve Novak AU/59	6.00	15.00
60 Allan Ray AU/60	6.00	15.00
61 Jordan Farmar AU/61	6.00	15.00
62 Josh Boone AU/62	6.00	15.00
63 Mardy Collins AU/63	6.00	15.00
64 Rodney Carney AU/64	6.00	15.00
65 Quincy Douby AU/65	6.00	15.00
66 Shannon Brown AU/66	10.00	25.00
67 Rajon Rondo AU/67	30.00	80.00
68 Maurice Ager AU/68	6.00	15.00
69 Ronnie Brewer AU/69	8.00	20.00
70 Marcus Williams AU/70	6.00	15.00
71 Kyle Lowry AU/71	10.00	25.00
72 Cedric Simmons AU/72	6.00	15.00
73 Patrick O'Bryant AU/73	6.00	15.00
74 Hilton Armstrong AU/74	6.00	15.00
75 Rudy Gay AU/75	20.00	50.00
76 Brandon Roy AU/76	20.00	50.00
77 Shelden Williams AU/77	6.00	15.00
78 Tyrus Thomas AU/78	10.00	25.00
79 LaMarcus Aldridge AU/79	30.00	60.00
80 Andrea Bargnani AU/80	20.00	50.00

2006-07 E-X Jambalaya

APPROXIMATE ODDS 1:48

JAI Allen Iverson	40.00	100.00
JBR Bill Russell	60.00	150.00
JCD Clyde Drexler	40.00	100.00
JDH Dwight Howard	30.00	80.00
JDR David Robinson	75.00	200.00
JDW Dwyane Wade	125.00	250.00
JHO Hakeem Olajuwon	50.00	125.00
JJE Julius Erving	50.00	125.00
JJK Jason Kidd	40.00	100.00
JJO Magic Johnson	60.00	120.00
JJS John Stockton	40.00	100.00
JLB Larry Bird	60.00	150.00
JLJ LeBron James	125.00	300.00
JMG Manu Ginobili	50.00	125.00
JMJ Michael Jordan	1200.00	2000.00
JPP Paul Pierce	40.00	100.00
JPS Peja Stojakovic	25.00	60.00
JSM Stephon Marbury	25.00	60.00
JTD Tim Duncan	50.00	125.00
JTM Tracy McGrady	30.00	80.00

1967-73 Equitable Sports Hall of Fame

This set consists of copies of art work found over a number of years in many national magazines, especially "Sports Illustrated," honoring sports heroes that Equitable Life Assurance Society selected to be in its very own Sports Hall of Fame. The cards consists of charcoal-type drawings on white backgrounds by artists, George Loh and Robert Riger, and measure approximately 11" by 7 3/4". The unnumbered cards have been assigned numbers below using a sport prefix (BB- baseball, BK- basketball, FB- football, HK- hockey, OT-other).

COMPLETE SET (95)	250.00	500.00
BK1 Elgin Baylor	3.00	6.00
BK2 Wilt Chamberlain	5.00	10.00
BK3 Bob Cousy	3.00	6.00
BK4 Hal Grier	2.00	4.00
BK5 Jerry Lucas	2.00	4.00
BK6 George Mikan	3.00	6.00
BK7 Bob Pettit	3.00	6.00
BK8 Willis Reed	2.00	4.00
BK9 Bill Russell	5.00	10.00
BK10 Dolph Schayes	2.00	4.00

2003-04 Exquisite Collection

Released in early June 2004, UD Exquisite Collection's base set includes 78 cards divided up as follows: 42 base veteran, rookie and retired player cards sequentially numbered to 225; 29 autographed jersey rookie cards, numbers 44-73, sequentially numbered to 225; six autographed jersey rookie cards, number 43 and 74-78, sequentially numbered to 99. Base veteran rookie and retired player cards have white borders on the left and right of the card with full color player photos through the middle and rookie cards place a small action photo on the top of the card below which appears an "R" shaped swatch of memorabilia and an autograph. Exquisite boxes consisted of a single pack in an engraved wooden box and contained five cards with a suggested retail price of $500. Also released were a gold parallel of the veteran cards, a partial jersey parallel of the veteran cards sequentially numbered to 25 and a partial patch parallel sequentially numbered to 10.

UNPRICED RAINBOW PRINT RUN ONE SET

1 Jason Terry	12.00	30.00
2 Paul Pierce	20.00	50.00
3 Michael Jordan	350.00	650.00
4 Kirk Hinrich RC	20.00	50.00
5 Dajuan Wagner	10.00	25.00
6 Dirk Nowitzki	30.00	80.00
7 Steve Nash	20.00	50.00
8 Andre Miller	12.00	30.00
9 Ben Wallace	15.00	40.00
10 Jason Richardson	15.00	40.00
11 Steve Francis	15.00	40.00
12 Yao Ming	30.00	80.00
13 Jermaine O'Neal	15.00	40.00
14 Elton Brand	15.00	40.00
15 Kobe Bryant	125.00	300.00
16 Gary Payton	15.00	40.00
17 Shaquille O'Neal	50.00	125.00
18 Pau Gasol	15.00	40.00
19 Lamar Odom	15.00	40.00
20 T.J. Ford RC	20.00	50.00
21 Kevin Garnett	30.00	80.00
22 Latrell Sprewell	15.00	40.00
23 Jason Kidd	25.00	60.00
24 Richard Jefferson	15.00	40.00
25 Baron Davis	15.00	40.00
26 Allan Houston	12.00	30.00
27 Stephon Marbury	12.00	30.00
28 Tracy McGrady	20.00	50.00
29 Allen Iverson	40.00	100.00
30 Shawn Marion	15.00	40.00
31 Amare Stoudemire	25.00	60.00
32 Shareef Abdur-Rahim	12.00	30.00
33 Mike Bibby	15.00	40.00
34 Chris Webber	20.00	50.00
35 Tim Duncan	25.00	60.00
36 Manu Ginobili	20.00	50.00
37 Ray Allen	20.00	50.00
38 Nick Collison RC	20.00	50.00
39 Vince Carter	25.00	60.00
40 Andrei Kirilenko	15.00	40.00
41 Gilbert Arenas	15.00	40.00
42 Jerry Stackhouse	15.00	40.00
43 Udonis Haslem JSY AU RC	100.00	225.00
44 Mo Williams JSY AU RC	40.00	100.00
45 Keith Bogans JSY AU RC	15.00	40.00
46 Travis Hansen JSY AU RC	15.00	40.00
47 Jason Kapono JSY AU RC	15.00	40.00
48 Zaza Pachulia JSY AU RC	15.00	40.00
49 Zarko Cabarkapa JSY AU RC	15.00	40.00
50 Kyle Korver JSY AU RC	20.00	50.00
51 Luke Walton JSY AU RC	25.00	60.00
52 Maciej Lampe JSY AU RC	20.00	50.00
53 Josh Howard JSY AU RC	40.00	100.00
54 Leandro Barbosa JSY AU RC	40.00	80.00
55 Kendrick Perkins JSY AU RC	40.00	80.00
56 Ndudi Ebi JSY AU RC	15.00	40.00
57 Jerome Beasley JSY AU RC	15.00	40.00
58 Brian Cook JSY AU RC	15.00	40.00
59 Travis Outlaw JSY AU RC	20.00	50.00
60 Zoran Planinic JSY AU RC	15.00	40.00
61 Boris Diaw JSY AU RC	40.00	100.00
62 Steve Blake JSY AU RC	40.00	80.00
63 Aleksandar Pavlovic JSY AU RC	15.00	40.00
64 David West JSY AU RC	90.00	180.00
65 Mike Sweetney JSY AU RC	15.00	40.00
66 Troy Bell JSY AU RC	15.00	40.00
67 Reece Gaines JSY AU RC	15.00	40.00
68 Luke Ridnour JSY AU RC	25.00	60.00
69 Marcus Banks JSY AU RC	15.00	40.00
70 Dahntay Jones JSY AU RC	25.00	60.00
71 Mickael Pietrus JSY AU RC	30.00	80.00
72 Chris Kaman JSY AU RC	25.00	60.00
73 Jarvis Hayes JSY AU RC	20.00	50.00
74 Dwyane Wade JSY AU RC	2500.00	4000.00
75 Chris Bosh JSY AU RC	1200.00	1900.00
76 Carmelo Anthony JSY AU RC	1500.00	2500.00
77 Darko Milicic JSY AU RC	100.00	200.00
78 LeBron James JSY AU RC	8000.00	12000.00

2003-04 Exquisite Collection Gold

Randomly inserted, this 78-card set is a parallel of the base set enhanced with gold foil highlights and sequential numbering to 25.

*GOLD 1-42: 1X TO 2.5X BASE HI

GOLD RCs DO NOT CONTAIN AU OR PATCH

3 Michael Jordan	1500.00	2300.00
4 Kirk Hinrich	100.00	200.00
7 Steve Nash	60.00	150.00
15 Kobe Bryant	400.00	700.00
37 Ray Allen	75.00	150.00
43 Udonis Haslem	30.00	80.00
44 Mo Williams	20.00	50.00
45 Keith Bogans	12.00	30.00
46 Travis Hansen	12.00	30.00
47 Jason Kapono	12.00	30.00
48 Zaur Pachulia	12.00	30.00
49 Zarko Cabarkapa	12.00	30.00
50 Kyle Korver	15.00	40.00
51 Luke Walton	12.00	30.00
52 Maciej Lampe	12.00	30.00
53 Josh Howard	12.00	30.00
54 Leandro Barbosa	25.00	60.00
55 Kendrick Perkins	20.00	50.00
56 Ndudi Ebi	12.00	30.00
57 Jerome Beasley	12.00	30.00
58 Brian Cook	12.00	30.00
59 Travis Outlaw	15.00	40.00
60 Zoran Planinic	12.00	30.00
61 Boris Diaw	15.00	40.00
62 Steve Blake	20.00	50.00
63 Aleksandar Pavlovic	12.00	30.00
64 David West	20.00	50.00
65 Mike Sweetney	12.00	30.00
66 Troy Bell	12.00	30.00
67 Reece Gaines	12.00	30.00
68 Luke Ridnour	25.00	60.00
69 Marcus Banks	12.00	30.00
70 Dahntay Jones	12.00	30.00
71 Mickael Pietrus	12.00	30.00
72 Chris Kaman	25.00	60.00
73 Jarvis Hayes	12.00	30.00
74 Dwyane Wade	600.00	1200.00
75 Chris Bosh	250.00	500.00
76 Carmelo Anthony	300.00	600.00
77 Darko Milicic	50.00	120.00
78 LeBron James	2500.00	4000.00

2003-04 Exquisite Collection Jersey Parallel

Randomly seeded, this 38-card set is a partial parallel of the first 42 base cards. Each card contains a jersey swatch and is sequentially numbered to 25. Upon issue, cards 4, 20, 38 and 39 were not released.

*JERSEY: .5X TO 1.2X BASE HI

UNPRICED AU PATCH PRINT RUN ONE SET

UNPRICED PATCH PRINT RUN 10 SETS

3J Michael Jordan	700.00	1200.00
35J Tim Duncan	40.00	100.00
36J Manu Ginobili	40.00	100.00

2003-04 Exquisite Collection Rookie Patch Parallel

Randomly seeded, this 36-card set parallels the base rookies enhanced with a premium patch swatch and sequential numbering to the player's jersey number.

MOST NOT PRICED DUE TO SCARCITY

43 Udonis Haslem/40	100.00	250.00
44 Mo Williams/25	150.00	300.00
47 Jason Kapono/24	25.00	60.00
48 Zaur Pachulia/27	25.00	60.00
50 Kyle Korver/26	150.00	300.00
55 Kendrick Perkins/43	100.00	200.00
56 Ndudi Ebi/44	25.00	60.00
57 Jerome Beasley/24	25.00	60.00
59 Travis Outlaw/25	30.00	80.00
61 Boris Diaw/32	100.00	200.00
64 David West/30	150.00	300.00
65 Mike Sweetney/50	25.00	60.00
67 Reece Gaines/22	30.00	80.00
70 Dahntay Jones/30	60.00	120.00
72 Chris Kaman/35	75.00	150.00
73 Jarvis Hayes/24	50.00	120.00
76 Carmelo Anthony/15	2500.00	4000.00
77 Darko Milicic/31	100.00	250.00
78 LeBron James/23	10000.00	14000.00

2003-04 Exquisite Collection Emblems of Endorsement

Randomly seeded, this 12-card set has white borders along the top and bottom of the card, a centered black background with a full-color player action photo, two emblem swatches and authentic player autographs. Each card is sequentially numbered to 15.

CA Carmelo Anthony	700.00	1200.00
GP Gary Payton	200.00	400.00
KB Kobe Bryant	750.00	1500.00
KG Kevin Garnett	400.00	800.00
LB Larry Bird	300.00	600.00
LJ LeBron James	2500.00	4000.00
MJ Michael Jordan	2500.00	4000.00
RJ Richard Jefferson	100.00	200.00
RM Reggie Miller	175.00	350.00
SM Stephon Marbury	100.00	200.00
TM Tracy McGrady	200.00	400.00
YM Yao Ming	200.00	400.00

2003-04 Exquisite Collection Extra Exquisite

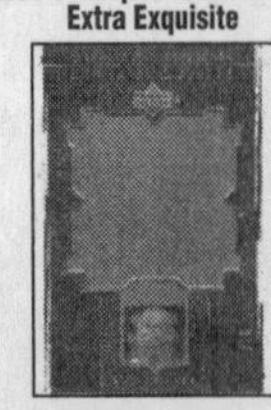

Randomly inserted in packs, this 42-card set places an oversized jersey swatch towards the top of the card and a small head-shot photo on the bottom of the card. Each card is sequentially numbered to 75.

*DUAL: .6X TO 1.5X BASE HI

DUAL PRINT RUN 25 SER.#'d SETS

AI Allen Iverson	75.00	200.00
AK Andrei Kirilenko	15.00	40.00
AM Alonzo Mourning	30.00	80.00
AS Amare Stoudemire	30.00	80.00
BD Baron Davis	15.00	40.00
CA Carmelo Anthony	50.00	100.00
CB Chris Bosh	30.00	80.00
CW Chris Webber	25.00	60.00
DN Dirk Nowitzki	30.00	80.00
DR David Robinson	40.00	100.00
DW Dwyane Wade	175.00	350.00
GP Gary Payton	15.00	40.00
IT Isiah Thomas	20.00	50.00
JE Julius Erving	30.00	80.00
JH Jarvis Hayes	15.00	40.00
JK Jason Kidd	25.00	60.00
JO Jermaine O'Neal	15.00	40.00
JR Jason Richardson	15.00	40.00
JS John Stockton	40.00	100.00
KA Kareem Abdul-Jabbar	30.00	80.00
KB Kobe Bryant	250.00	600.00
KB1 Kobe Bryant	250.00	600.00
KG Kevin Garnett	30.00	80.00
LB Larry Bird	50.00	120.00
LJ LeBron James	250.00	500.00
LJ1 LeBron James	250.00	500.00
MA Magic Johnson	40.00	100.00
MJ Michael Jordan	150.00	400.00
MJ1 Michael Jordan	150.00	400.00
PG Pau Gasol	15.00	40.00
PP Paul Pierce	25.00	60.00
RA Ray Allen	20.00	50.00
SF Steve Francis	20.00	50.00
SH Shawn Marion	20.00	50.00
SM Stephon Marbury	15.00	40.00
SN Steve Nash	30.00	80.00
SO Shaquille O'Neal	50.00	120.00
TD Tim Duncan	40.00	100.00
TM Tracy McGrady	30.00	80.00
WA Ben Wallace	15.00	40.00
WC Wilt Chamberlain	125.00	250.00
YM Yao Ming	25.00	60.00

2003-04 Exquisite Collection Limited Logos

This 30-card set is randomly seeded in packs and places a large logo swatch in the middle of the card with a a small head-shot of the featured player on the top and an authentic autograph on the bottom. Each card is sequentially numbered to 75.

AJ Antawn Jamison	80.00	160.00
AM Andre Miller	80.00	160.00
AS Amare Stoudemire	200.00	400.00
BD Baron Davis	100.00	200.00
CA1 Carmelo Anthony	500.00	1000.00
CA2 Carmelo Anthony Throwback	500.00	1000.00
CM Corey Maggette	80.00	160.00
DA David Robinson	250.00	500.00
DM Darko Milicic	80.00	160.00
DR Dennis Rodman	400.00	700.00
DY Dwyane Wade	2000.00	2800.00
GA Gilbert Arenas	100.00	200.00
GP Gary Payton	100.00	200.00
JK Jason Kidd	250.00	450.00
JM John Stockton	250.00	500.00
KB Kobe Bryant	3000.00	5000.00
KG Kevin Garnett	300.00	600.00
LB Larry Bird	300.00	600.00
LJ LeBron James	3000.00	5000.00
MA Magic Johnson	400.00	700.00
MJ Michael Jordan	5500.00	8500.00
PE Patrick Ewing	500.00	800.00
PP Paul Pierce	175.00	350.00
PS Peja Stojakovic	125.00	250.00
SA Shareef Abdur-Rahim	80.00	160.00
SC Sam Cassell	80.00	160.00
SM Shawn Marion	80.00	160.00
ST Stephon Marbury	100.00	200.00
TM Tracy McGrady	200.00	350.00
ZO Alonzo Mourning	250.00	450.00

2003-04 Exquisite Collection Noble Nameplates

Randomly inserted, this 30-card set places a full-color action photo on the right side of the card and a swatch of the player's jersey nameplate and autograph on the left. Each card is sequentially numbered to 25.

AH Al Harrington	50.00	125.00
AJ Antawn Jamison	40.00	100.00
AK Andrei Kirilenko	100.00	200.00
AS Amare Stoudemire	150.00	300.00
BD Baron Davis	75.00	150.00
CA Carmelo Anthony	600.00	1000.00
CB Chris Bosh	400.00	700.00
CM Corey Maggette	40.00	100.00
DM Darko Milicic	50.00	125.00
DY Dwyane Wade	1700.00	2500.00
GA Gilbert Arenas	100.00	200.00
GP Gary Payton	150.00	300.00
GR Glenn Robinson	40.00	100.00
IT Isiah Thomas	100.00	200.00
JK Jason Kidd	100.00	200.00
KB Kobe Bryant	2000.00	3000.00
KG Kevin Garnett	300.00	600.00
LJ LeBron James	2500.00	4000.00
MJ Michael Jordan	3000.00	6000.00
PE Patrick Ewing	400.00	700.00
PP Paul Pierce	100.00	200.00
PS Peja Stojakovic	60.00	150.00
RJ Richard Jefferson	40.00	100.00
RM Reggie Miller	200.00	400.00
SA Shareef Abdur-Rahim	40.00	100.00
SM Shawn Marion	40.00	100.00
ST Stephon Marbury	75.00	150.00
TM Tracy McGrady	200.00	400.00
TP Tony Parker	100.00	200.00
ZO Alonzo Mourning	175.00	350.00

2003-04 Exquisite Collection Number Piece Autographs

Randomly inserted, this 29-card set features full-color player action photos along with a jersey swatch in the shape of the player's jersey number. Each card is numbered to that number and showcases an authentic player autograph.

SOME UNPRICED DUE TO SCARCITY

AJ Antawn Jamison/33	40.00	100.00
AK Andrei Kirilenko/47	40.00	100.00
AM Alonzo Mourning/33	175.00	350.00
AS Amare Stoudemire/32	125.00	250.00
CA Carmelo Anthony/15	600.00	1000.00
DA David Robinson/50	200.00	350.00
DM Darius Miles/23	40.00	100.00
DR Dennis Rodman/91	150.00	325.00
GP Gary Payton/20	125.00	250.00
KG Kevin Garnett/21	300.00	550.00
LB Larry Bird/33	250.00	500.00
LJ LeBron James/23	3000.00	5000.00
MA Magic Johnson/32	300.00	600.00
MJ Michael Jordan/23	4000.00	6500.00
PE Patrick Ewing/33	300.00	550.00
PP Paul Pierce/34	75.00	150.00
RJ Richard Jefferson/24	40.00	100.00
RM Reggie Miller/31	500.00	800.00
SM Shawn Marion/31	60.00	150.00

2003-04 Exquisite Collection Patches Autographs

Randomly inserted, this 41-card set places a full color player photo on the left, a swatch of jersey patch in the middle and an authentic autograph on the right. Each card is sequentially numbered to 100.

AK Andrei Kirilenko	25.00	60.00
AM Antonio McDyess	30.00	80.00
AS Amare Stoudemire	75.00	150.00
BD Baron Davis	30.00	80.00
BR Bill Russell	250.00	450.00
CA Carmelo Anthony	300.00	600.00
CB Chris Bosh	200.00	400.00
CM Corey Maggette	25.00	60.00
DA David Robinson	75.00	150.00
DM Darius Miles	25.00	60.00
DR Dennis Rodman	150.00	300.00
EG Manu Ginobili	125.00	225.00
GA Gilbert Arenas	50.00	120.00
GP Gary Payton	75.00	150.00
GR Glenn Robinson	25.00	60.00
JE Julius Erving	150.00	300.00
JK Jason Kidd	50.00	125.00
JS John Stockton	100.00	250.00
JY Jerry Stackhouse	30.00	80.00
KB Kobe Bryant	600.00	1000.00
KG Kevin Garnett	125.00	250.00
LB Larry Bird	125.00	250.00
LJ LeBron James	1500.00	2500.00
LO Lamar Odom	30.00	80.00
MA Magic Johnson	150.00	300.00
MB Mike Bibby	25.00	60.00
MJ Michael Jordan	2000.00	3000.00
PE Patrick Ewing	300.00	600.00
PP Paul Pierce	50.00	120.00
PS Peja Stojakovic	75.00	150.00
RH Richard Hamilton	30.00	80.00
RJ Richard Jefferson	25.00	60.00
RM Reggie Miller	200.00	400.00
SA Shareef Abdur-Rahim	25.00	60.00
SC Sam Cassell	25.00	60.00
SH Shawn Marion	25.00	60.00
ST Stephon Marbury	40.00	100.00
TM Tracy McGrady	75.00	150.00
TP Tony Parker	50.00	120.00
YM Yao Ming	60.00	150.00
ZR Zach Randolph	30.00	80.00

2003-04 Exquisite Collection Scripted Swatches

Randomly inserted, this 12-card set utilizes a horizontal design with a small player head-shot along the top and a large swatch of autographed jersey patch in the middle. Each card is sequentially numbered to 25.

AS Amare Stoudemire	175.00	350.00
CA Carmelo Anthony	500.00	800.00
CM Corey Maggette	50.00	120.00
JK Jason Kidd	250.00	500.00
JS John Stockton	300.00	500.00
KG Kevin Garnett	400.00	700.00
LJ LeBron James	2500.00	4000.00
MJ Michael Jordan	2500.00	5000.00
PE Patrick Ewing	500.00	800.00
RM Reggie Miller	300.00	600.00
TM Tracy McGrady	250.00	500.00
YM Yao Ming	300.00	600.00

2004-05 Exquisite Collection

Released in June 2005, the second installation of Exquisite consists of a 90-card set with 42 veteran players and 48 rookie cards, most of which are autograph, memorabilia or both cards. Every card in the set is thick stock and all cards are numbered to either 225 or 99. Exquisite was packaged in one-pack maple wood boxes where packs contained five cards and carried a SRP of $500.

UNPRICED BLACK PRINT RUN ONE SET

1 Al Harrington	3.00	8.00
2 Paul Pierce	5.00	12.00
3 Emeka Okafor RC	8.00	20.00
4 Michael Jordan	100.00	200.00
5 LeBron James	50.00	125.00
6 Dirk Nowitzki	8.00	20.00
7 Carmelo Anthony	8.00	20.00
8 Kenyon Martin	4.00	10.00
9 Richard Hamilton	3.00	8.00
10 Ben Wallace	4.00	10.00
11 Jason Richardson	4.00	10.00
12 Yao Ming	8.00	20.00
13 Tracy McGrady	5.00	12.00
14 Reggie Miller	4.00	10.00
15 Corey Maggette	3.00	8.00
16 Kobe Bryant	50.00	125.00
17 Lamar Odom	4.00	10.00
18 Pau Gasol	4.00	10.00
19 Dwyane Wade	15.00	40.00
20 Shaquille O'Neal	12.00	30.00
21 Michael Redd	4.00	10.00
22 Kevin Garnett	8.00	20.00
23 Vince Carter	6.00	15.00
24 Jason Kidd	6.00	15.00
25 Baron Davis	4.00	10.00
26 Jamaal Magloire	2.50	6.00
27 Stephon Marbury	3.00	8.00
28 Steve Francis	4.00	10.00
29 Allen Iverson	6.00	15.00
30 Amare Stoudemire	5.00	12.00
31 Shawn Marion	4.00	10.00
32 Shareef Abdur-Rahim	3.00	8.00
33 Peja Stojakovic	4.00	10.00
34 Mike Bibby	4.00	10.00
35 Tim Duncan	6.00	15.00
36 Tony Parker	4.00	10.00
37 Ray Allen	4.00	10.00
38 Chris Bosh	4.00	10.00
39 Andrei Kirilenko	3.00	8.00
40 Carlos Boozer	4.00	10.00
41 Gilbert Arenas	4.00	10.00
42 Antawn Jamison	4.00	10.00
43 Andre Emmett JSY AU RC	10.00	25.00
44 Jameer Nelson JSY AU RC	20.00	50.00
45 Shaun Livingston JSY AU RC	12.00	30.00
46 Delonte West JSY AU RC	15.00	40.00
47 Trevor Ariza AU RC	10.00	25.00
48 Tony Allen JSY AU RC	20.00	50.00
49 Luke Jackson JSY AU RC	10.00	25.00
50 Dorell Wright JSY AU RC	30.00	80.00
51 Nenad Krstic JSY AU RC	10.00	25.00
52 Al Jefferson JSY RC	100.00	200.00
53 J.R. Smith JSY AU RC	50.00	120.00
54 Rafael Araujo JSY AU RC	10.00	25.00
55 Andris Biedrins JSY AU RC	20.00	50.00
56 Josh Smith JSY AU RC	75.00	150.00
57 Ha Seung-Jin JSY AU RC	10.00	25.00
58 Bernard Robinson JSY AU RC	10.00	25.00
59 Kevin Martin JSY AU RC	40.00	100.00
60 David Harrison JSY AU RC	20.00	50.00
61 Kris Humphries JSY AU RC	15.00	40.00
62 Anderson Varejao JSY AU RC	30.00	80.00
63 Jackson Vroman JSY AU RC	10.00	25.00
64 Sebastian Telfair JSY AU RC	10.00	25.00
65 Chris Duhon JSY AU RC	10.00	25.00
66 Kirk Snyder JSY AU RC	10.00	25.00
67 Andres Nocioni AU RC	8.00	20.00
68 Antonio Burks AU RC	8.00	20.00
69 Beno Udrih AU RC	8.00	20.00
70 D.J. Mbenga AU RC	8.00	20.00
71 Lionel Chalmers JSY AU RC	10.00	25.00
72 Robert Swift AU RC	8.00	20.00
73 Sasha Vujacic JSY AU RC	12.00	30.00
74 Donta Smith AU RC	8.00	20.00
75 Peter John Ramos AU RC	8.00	20.00
76 Justin Reed AU RC	8.00	20.00
77 Pape Sow AU RC	8.00	20.00
78 Pavel Podkolzin AU RC	8.00	20.00
79 Viktor Khryapa AU RC	8.00	20.00
80 John Edwards AU RC	8.00	20.00
81 Royal Ivey AU RC	8.00	20.00
82 Damien Wilkins AU RC	8.00	20.00
83 Erik Daniels AU RC	8.00	20.00
84 Luis Flores AU RC	8.00	20.00
85 Andre Iguodala JSY AU RC	150.00	300.00
86 Josh Childress JSY AU RC	25.00	60.00
87 Devin Harris JSY AU RC	60.00	150.00
88 Ben Gordon JSY AU RC	50.00	120.00
89 Luol Deng JSY AU RC	100.00	200.00
90 Dwight Howard JSY AU RC	1800.00	2600.00

2004-05 Exquisite Collection Jersey Parallel

Seeded randomly in packs, this 38-card set parallels the base set veterans enhanced with jersey swatches and sequential numbering to 25. A Patch parallel serially numbered to 10 and a Patch Autograph parallel serially numbered one of one were also produced and inserted.

*JSY PARALLEL: 1.25X TO 3X BASE HI

7 Carmelo Anthony	30.00	80.00
16 Kobe Bryant	100.00	250.00
20 Shaquille O'Neal	30.00	80
37 Ray Allen	15.00	40
38 Chris Bosh	15.00	40

2004-05 Exquisite Collectio

Platinum

Randomly seeded in packs, this 90-card set paralle the base set and is sequentially numbered to 25. A Black version was also issued and those cards are numbered one of one.

*1-42 PLATINUM: 2X TO 5X BASE HI

3 Emeka Okafor	75.00	15
19 Dwyane Wade	100.00	25
43 Andre Emmett	15.00	4
44 Jameer Nelson	20.00	5
45 Shaun Livingston	15.00	4
46 Delonte West	20.00	5
47 Trevor Ariza	15.00	4
48 Tony Allen	25.00	6
49 Luke Jackson	15.00	4
50 Dorell Wright	25.00	6
51 Nenad Krstic	15.00	4
52 Al Jefferson	40.00	10
53 J.R. Smith	20.00	5
54 Rafael Araujo	15.00	4
55 Andris Biedrins	20.00	5
56 Josh Smith	30.00	8
57 Ha Seung-Jin	15.00	4
58 Bernard Robinson	15.00	4
59 Kevin Martin	40.00	10
60 David Harrison	15.00	4
61 Kris Humphries	15.00	4
62 Anderson Varejao	20.00	5
63 Jackson Vroman	15.00	4
64 Sebastian Telfair	15.00	4
65 Chris Duhon	15.00	4
66 Kirk Snyder	15.00	4
67 Andres Nocioni	15.00	4
68 Antonio Burks	15.00	4
69 Beno Udrih	15.00	4
70 D.J. Mbenga	15.00	4
71 Lionel Chalmers	15.00	4
72 Robert Swift	15.00	4
73 Sasha Vujacic	15.00	4
74 Donta Smith	15.00	4
75 Peter John Ramos	15.00	4
76 Justin Reed	15.00	4
77 Pape Sow	15.00	4
78 Pavel Podkolzin	15.00	4
79 Viktor Khryapa	15.00	4
80 John Edwards	15.00	4
81 Royal Ivey	15.00	4
82 Damien Wilkins	15.00	4
83 Erik Daniels	15.00	4
84 Luis Flores	15.00	4
85 Andre Iguodala	50.00	12
86 Josh Childress	15.00	4
87 Devin Harris	30.00	8
88 Ben Gordon	30.00	8
89 Luol Deng	50.00	12
90 Dwight Howard	175.00	35

2004-05 Exquisite Collectio

Rookie Parallel

Numbered to each players jersey number, this 48 set parallels the rookie portion of the base set enhanced with gold foil highlights.

SOME NOT PRICED DUE TO SCARCITY

43 Andre Emmett JSY AU/14	50.00	12
44 Jameer Nelson JSY AU/14	400.00	70
45 Shaun Livingston JSY AU/14	50.00	12
47 Trevor Ariza AU/21	20.00	5
48 Tony Allen JSY AU/42	30.00	8
49 Luke Jackson JSY AU/33	20.00	5
53 J.R. Smith JSY/23	250.00	50
54 Rafael Araujo JSY AU/55	20.00	5
55 Andris Biedrins JSY AU/15	150.00	3
58 Bernard Robinson JSY/21	20.00	5
59 Kevin Martin JSY AU/23	175.00	3
61 Kris Humphries JSY AU/43	50.00	1
62 Anderson Varejao JSY AU/17	125.00	3
64 Sebastian Telfair JSY AU/31	40.00	1
65 Chris Duhon JSY AU/21	40.00	1
69 Beno Udrih AU/14	40.00	1
70 D.J. Mbenga AU/28	20.00	5
72 Robert Swift AU/31	20.00	5
73 Sasha Vujacic JSY AU/18	50.00	1
74 Donta Smith AU/15	20.00	5
75 Peter John Ramos AU/34	20.00	5
78 Pavel Podkolzin AU/24	20.00	5
79 Viktor Khryapa AU/38	20.00	5
80 John Edwards AU/54	20.00	5
81 Royal Ivey AU/36	20.00	5
83 Erik Daniels AU/15	20.00	5
87 Devin Harris JSY AU/34	100.00	2

2004-05 Exquisite Collecti

Dual Signature Shots

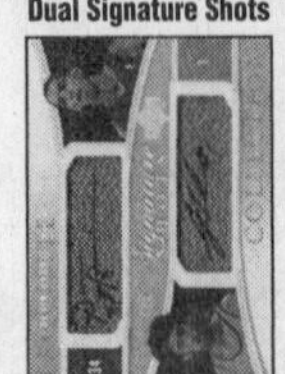

Inserted randomly in packs, this seven card set i horzontally designed with two small head shots players and an autographed basketball swatch. E card is sequentially numbered to 25. A version t also contains jersey patch swatches was also in and those cards are serially numbered to five.

UNPRICED PATCH PRINT RUN FIVE SETS

GD Ben Gordon Luol Deng	75.00
HC Devin Harris Josh Childress	40.00
HN Dwight Howard Jameer Nelson	100.00
IS Andre Iguodala J.R. Smith	50.00
KB Andrei Kirilenko Carlos Boozer	40.00
LT Shaun Livingston Sebastian Telfair	25.00

2004-05 Exquisite Collection Enshrinements Autographs

Randomly seeded in packs, this 42-card set has gold borders on the left and right side of the card, colored borders along the top and bottom of the card to match the player's team colors, a portrait photo, autograph and sequential numbering to 25.

ENAS1 Amare Stoudemire Purple 75.00 150.00
ENAS2 Amare Stoudemire Orange 75.00 150.00
ENBG Ben Gordon 75.00 150.00
ENBR1 Bill Russell Posed 125.00 250.00
ENBR2 Bill Russell Dunk 125.00 250.00
ENBW Ben Wallace 40.00 100.00
ENCA1 Carmelo Anthony Dribble 80.00 160.00
ENCA2 Carmelo Anthony Dunk 80.00 160.00
ENDH Dwight Howard 175.00 350.00
ENDH2 Dwight Howard 175.00 350.00
ENDR David Robinson 125.00 250.00
ENHO Hakeem Olajuwon 75.00 150.00
ENIT Isiah Thomas 40.00 100.00
ENJE1 Julius Erving Red 75.00 150.00
ENJE2 Julius Erving White 75.00 150.00
ENJK Jason Kidd 50.00 120.00
ENJS Josh Smith 40.00 100.00
ENJS1 John Stockton Black 100.00 200.00
ENJS2 John Stockton White 100.00 200.00
ENKB1 Kobe Bryant Yellow 350.00 600.00
ENKB2 Kobe Bryant Purple 350.00 600.00
ENKG Kevin Garnett 100.00 200.00
ENLB1 Larry Bird Green 100.00 200.00
ENLB2 Larry Bird White 100.00 200.00
ENLD Luol Deng 50.00 125.00
ENLJ1 LeBron James Red 300.00 600.00
ENLJ2 LeBron James White 300.00 600.00
ENMA1 Magic Johnson 100.00 200.00
ENMA2 Magic Johnson 100.00 200.00
ENMJ1 Michael Jordan Red 700.00 1000.00
ENMJ2 Michael Jordan White 700.00 1000.00
ENPP Paul Pierce 50.00 120.00
ENRA Ray Allen 50.00 120.00
ENRO Dennis Rodman 100.00 200.00
SN Steve Nash 100.00 200.00
SP Scottie Pippen Straight 400.00 550.00
SP2 Scottie Pippen Head Right 400.00 550.00
ST Stephon Marbury 50.00 120.00
TM1 Tracy McGrady Red 50.00 120.00
TM2 Tracy McGrady White 50.00 120.00
YM1 Yao Ming Red 50.00 125.00
YM2 Yao Ming White 50.00 125.00

2004-05 Exquisite Collection Extra Exquisite Jerseys

rted randomly into packs, this 42-card set is rontally designed, places player photos to the left large jersey swatch and is sequentially numbered 5. An Autographs version sequentially numbered to and a Dual player version sequentially numbered were also produced and inserted.

RICED DUAL PRINT RUN 10 SETS
RICED AUTO PRINT RUN 5 SETS
en Iverson 30.00 80.00
ndrei Kirilenko 10.00 25.00
ndre Iguodala 20.00 50.00
mare Stoudemire 15.00 40.00
aron Davis 12.00 30.00
en Gordon 15.00 40.00
en Wallace 12.00 30.00
armelo Anthony 25.00 60.00
hris Bosh 12.00 30.00
evin Harris 20.00 50.00
wight Howard 40.00 100.00
rk Nowitzki 20.00 50.00
vid Robinson 40.00 80.00
h Thomas 12.00 30.00
ius Erving 25.00 60.00
son Kidd 20.00 50.00
sh Smith 20.00 50.00
n Stockton 40.00 80.00
obe Bryant Purple 60.00 150.00
obe Bryant White 60.00 150.00
vin Garnett 25.00 60.00
ry Bird 40.00 100.00
l Deng 20.00 50.00
Bron James Red 80.00 200.00
Bron James White 80.00 200.00
gic Johnson 30.00 80.00
nu Ginobili 25.00 60.00
ichael Jordan Red 250.00 500.00
ichael Jordan White 250.00 500.00
l Pierce 15.00 40.00
Allen 15.00 40.00
gie Miller 30.00 80.00
nis Rodman 40.00 100.00
e Francis 12.00 30.00
n Livingston 12.00 30.00
e Nash 15.00 40.00
quille O'Neal 30.00 80.00
tie Pippen 75.00 150.00
hon Marbury 10.00 25.00
Duncan 20.00 50.00
y McGrady 15.00 40.00
Ming 25.00 60.00

2004-05 Exquisite Collection Limited Logos

Serially numbered to 50 and inserted randomly, this 42-card set contains an oversized swatch from the player's jersey logos and an autograph.

AK Andrei Kirilenko 75.00 150.00
AS Amare Stoudemire 150.00 250.00
BD Baron Davis 50.00 120.00
BG Ben Gordon 50.00 120.00
BW Ben Wallace 50.00 120.00
CA Carmelo Anthony 200.00 400.00
CB Carlos Boozer 50.00 120.00
CM Corey Maggette 50.00 120.00
DH1 Dwight Howard Blue 250.00 500.00
DH2 Dwight Howard White 250.00 500.00
DR David Robinson 200.00 400.00
GA Gilbert Arenas 75.00 150.00
HO Hakeem Olajuwon 150.00 300.00
IT Isiah Thomas 100.00 200.00
JK Jason Kidd 125.00 250.00
JS John Stockton 200.00 400.00
JW Jason Williams 150.00 300.00
KB1 Kobe Bryant Purple 2000.00 3000.00
KB2 Kobe Bryant Yellow 2000.00 3000.00
KG1 Kevin Garnett Black 150.00 300.00
KG2 Kevin Garnett Blue 150.00 300.00
KH Kirk Hinrich 50.00 120.00
LB Larry Bird 200.00 400.00
LD Luol Deng 60.00 150.00
LJ1 LeBron James Red 900.00 1500.00
LJ2 LeBron James White 900.00 1500.00
LO Lamar Odom 50.00 120.00
MA Magic Johnson 250.00 500.00
MJ Michael Jordan 2500.00 4500.00
MR Michael Redd 50.00 120.00
PG Pau Gasol 75.00 150.00
PP Paul Pierce 75.00 150.00
PS Peja Stojakovic 100.00 200.00
RA Ray Allen 250.00 500.00
RJ Richard Jefferson 50.00 120.00
RO Dennis Rodman 150.00 275.00
SM Shawn Marion 50.00 120.00
SN Steve Nash 250.00 450.00
ST Stephon Marbury 50.00 120.00
TM Tracy McGrady 100.00 200.00
TP Tony Parker 75.00 200.00
YM Yao Ming 100.00 200.00

2004-05 Exquisite Collection Number Pieces Autographs

Randomly inserted in packs and limited in number to the featured players jersey number, this 42-card set showcases autographs and swatches from the player's jersey number.

SOME UNPRICED DUE TO SCARCITY
AK Andrei Kirilenko/47 20.00 50.00
AS Amare Stoudemire/32 50.00 125.00
CA Carmelo Anthony/15 200.00 350.00
CM Corey Maggette/50 20.00 50.00
DE Devin Harris/34 50.00 120.00
DR David Robinson/50 100.00 200.00
HO Hakeem Olajuwon/34 60.00 120.00
KG Kevin Garnett/21 100.00 200.00
LB Larry Bird/33 250.00 350.00
LJ LeBron James/23 700.00 1200.00
MA Magic Johnson/34 150.00 300.00
MJ Michael Jordan/23 1200.00 1600.00
PG Pau Gasol/16 75.00 150.00
PP Paul Pierce/34 125.00 250.00
PS Peja Stojakovic/16 60.00 150.00
RA Ray Allen/34 100.00 200.00
RJ Richard Jefferson/24 20.00 50.00
RO Dennis Rodman/91 100.00 200.00
SM Shawn Marion/31 20.00 50.00
SP Scottie Pippen/33 350.00 500.00

2004-05 Exquisite Collection Patches Autographs

This 42-card set was randomly inserted in packs and places a jersey patch swatch in the middle of the card between a player photo and an autograph. Each card is serially numbered to 100.

AJ Antawn Jamison/100 20.00 50.00
AK Andrei Kirilenko/100 20.00 50.00
AS Amare Stoudemire/100 40.00 100.00
BD Baron Davis/100 25.00 60.00
BG Ben Gordon/100 20.00 50.00
BR Bill Russell/75 200.00 350.00
BW Ben Wallace/100 20.00 50.00
CA Carmelo Anthony/100 60.00 120.00
CB Carlos Boozer/100 20.00 50.00
DE Devin Harris/100 30.00 80.00
DH Dwight Howard/100 150.00 300.00
DR David Robinson/100 40.00 100.00
GP Gary Payton/100 50.00 125.00
HO Hakeem Olajuwon/50 50.00 120.00
IT Isiah Thomas/100 40.00 100.00
JE Julius Erving/50 125.00 250.00
JK Jason Kidd/100 40.00 100.00
JS John Stockton/100 75.00 150.00
KB Kobe Bryant/100 400.00 700.00
KG Kevin Garnett/100 75.00 150.00
KH Kirk Hinrich/100 20.00 50.00
LB Larry Bird/100 100.00 200.00
LD Luol Deng/100 25.00 60.00
LJ LeBron James/100 400.00 700.00
MA Magic Johnson/100 100.00 200.00
MB Mike Bibby/100 20.00 50.00
MJ Michael Jordan/100 1500.00 2500.00
MR Michael Redd/100 20.00 50.00
PG Pau Gasol/100 20.00 50.00
PP Paul Pierce/100 30.00 80.00
PS Peja Stojakovic/100 20.00 50.00
RA Ray Allen/100 125.00 225.00
RH Richard Hamilton/100 20.00 50.00
RJ Richard Jefferson/100 20.00 50.00
RO Dennis Rodman/100 100.00 200.00
SA Shareef Abdur-Rahim/100 20.00 50.00
SM Shawn Marion/100 20.00 50.00
SP Scottie Pippen/100 400.00 700.00
ST Stephon Marbury/100 25.00 60.00
TM Tracy McGrady/100 50.00 125.00
TP Tony Parker/100 25.00 60.00
YM Yao Ming/100 60.00 150.00

2004-05 Exquisite Collection Signature Shots Patches

Randomly seeded and serially numbered to 100, this 14-card set is horizontally designed and places a color player photo on the right, and a jersey patch swatch on the left above an autographed swatch of basketball.

AI Andre Iguodala 30.00 80.00
AK Andrei Kirilenko 20.00 50.00
BG Ben Gordon 25.00 60.00
BM Brad Miller 15.00 40.00
CB Carlos Boozer 15.00 40.00
DE Devin Harris 20.00 50.00
DH Dwight Howard 75.00 200.00
JC Josh Childress 15.00 40.00
JN Jameer Nelson 20.00 50.00
JR J.R. Smith 25.00 60.00
LD Luol Deng 30.00 80.00
SL Shaun Livingston 15.00 40.00
SM Shawn Marion 15.00 40.00
ST Sebastian Telfair 15.00 40.00

2005-06 Exquisite Collection

Released in July, Exquisite Collection is Upper Deck's most expensive product of the year. The base set pictures veterans on cards 1-42, rookie autograph jerseys serially numbered to 99 on cards 43-48, rookie jersey autographs serially numbered to 225 on cards 49-82 and rookie autographs serially numbered to 225 on cards 85-95. Exquisite was packaged in carved wood boxes that contain five cards and carried a suggested retail price of $500.

UNPRICED RAINBOW PRINT RUN ONE SET
1 Joe Johnson 4.00 10.00
2 Paul Pierce 5.00 12.00
3 Emeka Okafor 4.00 10.00
4 Ben Gordon 4.00 10.00
5 Michael Jordan 125.00 300.00
6 LeBron James 40.00 100.00
7 Dirk Nowitzki 8.00 20.00
8 Carmelo Anthony 8.00 20.00
9 Kenyon Martin 4.00 10.00
10 Chauncey Billups 4.00 10.00
11 Ben Wallace 4.00 10.00
12 Jason Richardson 4.00 10.00
13 Tracy McGrady 5.00 12.00
14 Yao Ming 5.00 12.00
15 Jermaine O'Neal 4.00 10.00
16 Elton Brand 4.00 10.00
17 Kobe Bryant 50.00 125.00
18 Pau Gasol 4.00 10.00
19 Shaquille O'Neal 12.00 30.00
20 Dwyane Wade 25.00 60.00
21 Michael Redd 4.00 10.00
22 Kevin Garnett 8.00 20.00
23 Vince Carter 8.00 20.00
24 Jason Kidd 6.00 15.00
25 J.R. Smith 4.00 10.00
26 Stephon Marbury 3.00 8.00
27 Quentin Richardson 3.00 8.00
28 Steve Francis 4.00 10.00
29 Dwight Howard 8.00 20.00
30 Allen Iverson 8.00 20.00
31 Chris Webber 4.00 10.00
32 Steve Nash 5.00 12.00
33 Amare Stoudemire 4.00 10.00
34 Zach Randolph 3.00 8.00
35 Mike Bibby 4.00 10.00
36 Peja Stojakovic 4.00 10.00
37 Tim Duncan 6.00 15.00
38 Tony Parker 4.00 10.00
39 Ray Allen 4.00 10.00
40 Chris Bosh 4.00 10.00
41 Andrei Kirilenko 3.00 8.00
42 Gilbert Arenas 4.00 10.00
43 Andrew Bogut JSY AU/99 RC 150.00 300.00
44 Marvin Williams JSY AU/99 RC 60.00 120.00
45 Deron Williams JSY AU/99 RC 400.00 750.00
46 Chris Paul JSY AU/99 RC 1200.00 2000.00
47 Raymond Felton JSY AU RC/99 60.00 150.00
48 Channing Frye JSY AU/99 RC 40.00 100.00
49 Martell Webster JSY AU RC 15.00 40.00
50 Charlie Villanueva JSY AU RC 15.00 40.00
51 Ike Diogu JSY AU RC 10.00 25.00
52 Andrew Bynum JSY AU RC 200.00 400.00
53 Sean May JSY AU RC 10.00 25.00
54 Rashad McCants JSY AU RC 25.00 50.00
55 Antoine Wright JSY AU RC 10.00 25.00
56 Joey Graham JSY AU RC 10.00 25.00
57 Danny Granger JSY AU RC 50.00 120.00
58 Gerald Green JSY AU RC 40.00 100.00
59 Hakim Warrick JSY AU RC 15.00 40.00
60 Julius Hodge JSY AU RC 10.00 25.00
61 Nate Robinson JSY AU RC 20.00 50.00
62 Jarrett Jack JSY AU RC 12.00 30.00
63 Francisco Garcia JSY AU RC 12.00 30.00
64 Luther Head JSY AU RC 10.00 25.00
65 Johan Petro JSY AU RC 10.00 25.00
66 Jason Maxiell JSY AU RC 10.00 25.00
67 Linas Kleiza JSY AU RC 10.00 25.00
68 Wayne Simien JSY AU RC 10.00 25.00
69 David Lee JSY AU RC 40.00 100.00
70 Salim Stoudamire JSY AU RC 10.00 25.00
71 Daniel Ewing JSY AU RC 10.00 25.00
72 Brandon Bass JSY AU RC 25.00 60.00
73 C.J. Miles JSY AU RC 20.00 50.00
74 Ersan Ilyasova JSY AU RC 30.00 80.00
75 Travis Diener JSY AU RC 10.00 25.00
76 Monta Ellis JSY AU RC 125.00 250.00
77 Chris Taft JSY AU RC 10.00 25.00
78 Martynas Andriuskevicius JSY AU RC10.00 25.00
79 Louis Williams JSY AU RC 40.00 70.00
80 Andray Blatche JSY AU RC 25.00 60.00
81 Ryan Gomes JSY AU RC 10.00 25.00
82 Sarunas Jasikevicius JSY AU RC 10.00 25.00
83 Yaroslav Korolev AU RC 6.00 15.00
85 Von Wafer AU RC 6.00 15.00
86 Orien Greene AU RC 6.00 15.00
87 Robert Whaley AU RC 6.00 15.00
88 Dijon Thompson AU RC 6.00 15.00
89 Bracey Wright AU RC 6.00 15.00
90 Amir Johnson AU RC 10.00 25.00
91 Ronny Turiaf AU RC 25.00 50.00
92 James Singleton AU RC 6.00 15.00
93 Alex Acker AU RC 6.00 15.00
94 Chuck Hayes AU RC 6.00 15.00
95 Lawrence Roberts AU RC 6.00 15.00
96 Stephen Graham AU RC 6.00 15.00

2005-06 Exquisite Collection Gold

Seeded in packs randomly, this 96-card set parallels the base set enhanced with gold backgrounds and gold foil and is serially numbered to 25. Rookie players do not have jersey swatches or autographs.

*1-42 GOLD: 1.25X TO 3X BASE HI
26 Stephon Marbury 12.00 30.00
43 Andrew Bogut 60.00 120.00
44 Marvin Williams 20.00 50.00
45 Deron Williams 100.00 175.00
46 Chris Paul 250.00 450.00
47 Raymond Felton 25.00 60.00
48 Channing Frye 20.00 50.00
49 Martell Webster 15.00 40.00
50 Charlie Villanueva 20.00 50.00
51 Ike Diogu 15.00 40.00
52 Andrew Bynum 50.00 125.00
53 Sean May 15.00 40.00
54 Rashad McCants 15.00 40.00
55 Antoine Wright 15.00 40.00
56 Joey Graham 15.00 40.00
57 Danny Granger 30.00 80.00
58 Gerald Green 20.00 50.00
59 Hakim Warrick 25.00 60.00
60 Julius Hodge 15.00 40.00
61 Nate Robinson 20.00 50.00
62 Jarrett Jack 15.00 40.00
63 Francisco Garcia 20.00 50.00
64 Luther Head 15.00 40.00
65 Johan Petro 15.00 40.00
66 Jason Maxiell 15.00 40.00
67 Linas Kleiza 15.00 40.00
68 Wayne Simien 15.00 40.00
69 David Lee 25.00 60.00
70 Salim Stoudamire 15.00 40.00
71 Daniel Ewing 15.00 40.00
72 Brandon Bass 20.00 50.00
73 C.J. Miles 20.00 50.00
74 Ersan Ilyasova 20.00 50.00
75 Travis Diener 15.00 40.00
76 Monta Ellis 60.00 150.00
77 Chris Taft 15.00 40.00
78 Martynas Andriuskevicius 15.00 40.00
79 Louis Williams 25.00 60.00
80 Andray Blatche 20.00 50.00
81 Ryan Gomes 15.00 40.00
82 Sarunas Jasikevicius 25.00 60.00
83 Yaroslav Korolev 15.00 40.00
84 Jose Calderon 15.00 40.00
85 Von Wafer 15.00 40.00
86 Orien Greene 15.00 40.00
87 Robert Whaley 15.00 40.00
88 Dijon Thompson 15.00 40.00
89 Bracey Wright 15.00 40.00
90 Amir Johnson 15.00 40.00
91 Ronny Turiaf 15.00 40.00
92 James Singleton 15.00 40.00
93 Alex Acker 15.00 40.00
94 Chuck Hayes 15.00 40.00
95 Lawrence Roberts 15.00 40.00
96 Stephen Graham 15.00 40.00

2005-06 Exquisite Collection Jerseys

Randomly seeded in packs, this 40-card set parallels the veteran player portion of the set enhanced with jersey swatches and serial numbering to 25.

*JERSEY: 1.25X TO 3X BASE HI
UNPRICED DUAL PRINT RUN 10 SETS
UNPRICED DUAL AUTO PRINT RUN 5 SETS
UNPRICED PATCH PRINT RUN 10 SETS
UNPRICED PATCH QUAD PRINT RUN 3 SETS
UNPRICED PATCH TRIPLE PRINT RUN 10 SETS

2005-06 Exquisite Collection Rookie Parallel

Randomly seeded in packs, this 53-card set parallels the rookie portion of the set enhanced with gold foil highlights and sequential numbering to the featured player's jersey number.

SOME UNPRICED DUE TO SCARCITY
44AP Marvin Williams JSY AU/24 50.00 120.00
47AP Raymond Felton JSY AU/20 100.00 200.00
50AP Charlie Villanueva JSY AU/31 30.00 80.00
52AP Andrew Bynum JSY AU/17 900.00 1500.00
53AP Sean May JSY AU/42 25.00 60.00
55AP Antoine Wright JSY AU/21 40.00 100.00
56AP Joey Graham JSY AU/14 25.00 60.00
57AP Danny Granger JSY AU/33 250.00 500.00
59AP Hakim Warrick JSY AU/21 150.00 300.00
60AP Julius Hodge JSY AU/32 25.00 60.00
63AP Francisco Garcia JSY AU/32 60.00 150.00
65AP Johan Petro JSY AU/27 25.00 60.00
66AP Jason Maxiell JSY AU/54 30.00 80.00
67AP Linas Kleiza JSY AU/43 25.00 60.00
68AP Wayne Simien JSY AU/25 25.00 60.00
69AP David Lee JSY AU/42 125.00 250.00
70AP Salim Stoudamire JSY AU/20 25.00 60.00
72AP Brandon Bass JSY AU/33 60.00 120.00
73AP C.J. Miles JSY AU/34 60.00 120.00
74AP Ersan Ilyasova JSY AU/23 30.00 80.00
75AP Travis Diener JSY AU/34 25.00 60.00
77AP Chris Taft JSY AU/21 25.00 60.00
78AP Andriuskevicius JSY AU/15 40.00 100.00
79AP Louis Williams JSY AU/23 125.00 250.00
80AP Andray Blatche JSY AU/32 75.00 200.00
85AP Von Wafer AU/23 25.00 60.00
86AP Orien Greene AU/100 25.00 60.00
87AP Robert Whaley AU/21 25.00 60.00
90AP Amir Johnson AU/25 60.00 120.00
91AP Ronny Turiaf AU/21 100.00 200.00
92AP James Singleton AU/15 25.00 60.00
94AP Chuck Hayes AU/44 25.00 60.00
95AP Lawrence Roberts AU/44 25.00 60.00

2005-06 Exquisite Collection Autographs Patches

Randomly seeded in packs, this 42-card set features color player photography, a centered swatch of jersey patch, and autograph and sequential numbering to 100.

APAB Andrew Bogut 50.00 100.00
APAN Andrew Bynum 100.00 175.00
APAW Antoine Wright 12.50 30.00
APCA Carmelo Anthony 50.00 120.00
APCB Chris Bosh 40.00 80.00
APCF Channing Frye 20.00 50.00
APCH Chauncey Billups 20.00 50.00
APCP Chris Paul 150.00 300.00
APCV Charlie Villanueva 12.50 30.00
APDE Dennis Rodman 50.00 120.00
APDG Danny Granger 30.00 80.00
APDH Dwight Howard 60.00 120.00
APDL David Lee 20.00 50.00
APDR David Robinson 60.00 150.00
APDW Deron Williams 60.00 120.00
APEB Elton Brand 12.50 30.00
APHW Hakim Warrick 15.00 40.00
APID Ike Diogu 12.50 30.00
APJJ Jarrett Jack 12.50 30.00
APJK Jason Kidd 30.00 80.00
APJR J.R. Smith 12.50 30.00
APJS John Stockton 75.00 200.00
APKG Kevin Garnett 75.00 150.00
APLB Larry Bird 100.00 200.00
APLH Larry Hughes 12.50 30.00
APLJ LeBron James 300.00 600.00
APLO Lamar Odom 25.00 60.00
APMA Magic Johnson 175.00 325.00
APMB Mike Bibby 12.50 30.00
APMJ Michael Jordan 500.00 1000.00
APMR Martell Webster 12.50 30.00
APMW Marvin Williams 20.00 50.00
APNR Nate Robinson 15.00 40.00
APPS Peja Stojakovic 15.00 40.00
APRF Raymond Felton 15.00 40.00
APSJ Sarunas Jasikevicius 20.00 50.00
APSM Sean May 12.50 30.00
APSP Scottie Pippen 150.00 300.00
APST Stephon Marbury 15.00 40.00
APTM Tracy McGrady 30.00 80.00
APTP Tayshaun Prince 15.00 40.00
APVC Vince Carter 30.00 80.00

2005-06 Exquisite Collection Emblems of Endorsements

Seeded randomly in packs, this 40-card set is horizontally designed with a player image between two patch swatches from jersey emblems and an autograph along the bottom. Each card is serially numbered to 15.

EMAB Andrew Bogut 150.00 300.00
EMAI Andre Iguodala 50.00 120.00
EMAJ Antawn Jamison 50.00 120.00
EMBW Bill Walton 175.00 350.00
EMCA Carmelo Anthony 150.00 300.00
EMCB Chauncey Billups 50.00 120.00
EMCH Chris Bosh 175.00 350.00
EMCM Corey Maggette 50.00 120.00
EMCP Chris Paul 400.00 700.00
EMDH Dwight Howard 150.00 325.00
EMDR David Robinson 175.00 350.00
EMEB Elton Brand 50.00 120.00
EMEO Emeka Okafor 50.00 120.00
EMHO Hakeem Olajuwon 100.00 200.00
EMJE Julius Erving 175.00 350.00
EMJS John Stockton 200.00 350.00
EMKG Kevin Garnett 200.00 400.00
EMKH Kirk Hinrich 100.00 200.00
EMLH Larry Hughes 50.00 120.00
EMLJ LeBron James 1200.00 2000.00
EMLO Lamar Odom 50.00 120.00
EMMJ Michael Jordan 3000.00 6000.00
EMMW Marvin Williams 60.00 150.00
EMPG Pau Gasol 75.00 150.00
EMPP Paul Pierce 50.00 120.00
EMPS Peja Stojakovic 60.00 150.00
EMRA Ron Artest 50.00 120.00
EMRH Richard Hamilton 50.00 120.00
EMRJ Richard Jefferson 50.00 120.00
EMSA Shareef Abdur-Rahim 50.00 120.00
EMSM Stephon Marbury 50.00 120.00
EMSN Steve Nash 200.00 400.00
EMSP Scottie Pippen 300.00 500.00
EMST Sebastian Telfair 50.00 120.00
EMTM Tracy McGrady 150.00 300.00
EMTP Tayshaun Prince 50.00 120.00
EMVC Vince Carter 150.00 300.00
EMYM Yao Ming 150.00 300.00

2005-06 Exquisite Collection Enshrinements

Seeded randomly in packs, this 41-card set places a full color portrait-style photo of players in between a foil design set to appear as a hall of fame plaque with an authentic player autograph. Each card is serially numbered to 25.

EEAB Andrew Bogut 40.00 100.00
EEAI Andre Iguodala 15.00 40.00
EEAJ Antawn Jamison 15.00 40.00
EEBD Baron Davis 15.00 40.00
EEBR Bill Russell 100.00 200.00
EECA Carmelo Anthony 40.00 80.00
EECB Chauncey Billups 20.00 50.00
EECF Channing Frye 20.00 50.00
EECH Chris Bosh 50.00 100.00
EECP Chris Paul 250.00 450.00
EEDE Dennis Rodman 50.00 120.00
EEDH Dwight Howard 50.00 100.00
EEDR David Robinson 75.00 150.00
EEDW Deron Williams 50.00 120.00
EEEB Elton Brand 15.00 40.00
EEEO Emeka Okafor 15.00 40.00
EEGG George Gervin 30.00 60.00
EEHO Hakeem Olajuwon 40.00 70.00
EEJE Julius Erving 75.00 150.00
EEJK Jason Kidd 40.00 80.00
EEJS John Stockton 75.00 150.00
EEKA Kareem Abdul-Jabbar 75.00 150.00
EEKG Kevin Garnett 75.00 150.00
EELB Larry Bird 100.00 200.00
EELJ LeBron James 300.00 600.00
EELO Lamar Odom 20.00 50.00
EEMA Magic Johnson 75.00 150.00
EEMJ Michael Jordan 900.00 1500.00
EEMW Marvin Williams 25.00 60.00
EEPP Paul Pierce 25.00 50.00
EERA Ron Artest 20.00 50.00
EESA Shareef Abdur-Rahim 15.00 40.00
EESM Stephon Marbury 15.00 40.00
EESN Steve Nash 50.00 120.00
EESP Scottie Pippen 125.00 250.00
EETM Tracy McGrady 40.00 80.00
EEVC Vince Carter 40.00 100.00
EEYM Yao Ming 40.00 80.00
EELJ2 LeBron James 250.00 500.00
EEMJ2 Michael Jordan 500.00 1000.00

2005-06 Exquisite Collection Extra Exquisite

Found randomly in packs, this horizontally designed card places a player photo on the left side of the card and a large swatch of jersey that covers roughly 75 percent of the card front. Each is serially numbered to 25.

UNPRICED DUAL PRINT RUN 10 SETS
UNPRICED AUTO PRINT RUN 5 SETS
EXAB Andrew Bogut 15.00 40.00
EXBR Bill Russell 50.00 100.00
EXBW Ben Wallace 10.00 25.00
EXCA Carmelo Anthony 20.00 50.00
EXCB Chris Bosh 20.00 40.00
EXCF Channing Frye 12.00 30.00
EXCP Chris Paul 40.00 100.00
EXCV Charlie Villanueva 12.00 30.00
EXDN Dirk Nowitzki 15.00 40.00
EXDR David Robinson 30.00 60.00
EXDW Deron Williams 25.00 60.00
EXEB Elton Brand 10.00 25.00
EXEO Emeka Okafor 10.00 25.00
EXIT Isiah Thomas 10.00 25.00
EXJO Jermaine O'Neal 10.00 25.00
EXJS John Stockton 25.00 50.00
EXKA Kareem Abdul-Jabbar 20.00 50.00
EXKB Kobe Bryant 50.00 100.00
EXKG Kevin Garnett 30.00 60.00
EXLB Larry Bird 40.00 100.00
EXLJ LeBron James 100.00 200.00
EXMA Magic Johnson 25.00 60.00
EXMG Manu Ginobili 15.00 30.00
EXMJ Michael Jordan 200.00 400.00
EXMW Marvin Williams 12.00 30.00
EXPS Peja Stojakovic 10.00 25.00
EXRA Ray Allen 15.00 30.00
EXRF Raymond Felton 15.00 40.00
EXRJ Richard Jefferson 10.00 25.00
EXRO Ron Artest 10.00 25.00
EXSO Shaquille O'Neal 30.00 60.00
EXSP Scottie Pippen 40.00 100.00
EXTD Tim Duncan 25.00 60.00
EXTM Tracy McGrady 12.00 30.00
EXVC Vince Carter 20.00 40.00
EXWC Wilt Chamberlain 60.00 120.00
EXYM Yao Ming 12.00 30.00
EXLJ2 LeBron James 100.00 200.00
EXLJ3 LeBron James 100.00 200.00
EXMJ2 Michael Jordan 200.00 400.00
EXMJ3 Michael Jordan 200.00 400.00
EXMW2 Marvin Williams 12.00 30.00

2005-06 Exquisite Collection Limited Logos

Randomly inserted, this 41-card set places a small head-shot photo on the top, a large patch swatche in the midde, team colored borders and an autograph on the bottom. Cards are limited to 50 serially numbered copies except the Bill Russell, which is numbered to 50.

LLAB Andrew Bogut 60.00 150.00
LLAJ Antawn Jamison 25.00 60.00
LLAL Al Jefferson 25.00 60.00
LLAN Andrew Bynum 150.00 300.00
LLBG Ben Gordon 40.00 100.00
LLBR Bill Russell/28 350.00 550.00
LLCA Carmelo Anthony 125.00 250.00
LLCB Chauncey Billups 30.00 80.00
LLCF Channing Frye 40.00 100.00
LLCH Chris Bosh 75.00 150.00
LLCP Chris Paul 400.00 700.00
LLCV Charlie Villanueva 25.00 60.00
LLDE Dennis Rodman 200.00 400.00
LLDH Dwight Howard 150.00 300.00
LLDR David Robinson 100.00 200.00
LLDW Deron Williams 200.00 350.00
LLEB Elton Brand 25.00 60.00
LLID Ike Diogu 25.00 60.00
LLJE Julius Erving 200.00 350.00
LLJK Jason Kidd 100.00 200.00
LLKG Kevin Garnett 125.00 250.00
LLLB Larry Bird 150.00 300.00
LLLH Larry Hughes 25.00 60.00
LLLJ LeBron James 1000.00 1800.00
LLMA Magic Johnson 200.00 400.00
LLMJ Michael Jordan 1700.00 2500.00
LLNR Nate Robinson 40.00 100.00
LLPP Paul Pierce 50.00 125.00
LLRA Ron Artest 30.00 80.00
LLRF Raymond Felton 30.00 80.00
LLRM Rashad McCants 25.00 60.00
LLSA Shareef Abdur-Rahim 30.00 80.00
LLSM Sean May 25.00 60.00
LLSN Steve Nash 100.00 225.00
LLSP Scottie Pippen 400.00 700.00
LLTC Tyson Chandler 25.00 60.00
LLTM Tracy McGrady 50.00 120.00
LLTP Tayshaun Prince 30.00 80.00
LLVC Vince Carter 100.00 250.00
LLYM Yao Ming 100.00 200.00
LLMW2 Marvin Williams 40.00 100.00

2005-06 Exquisite Collection Noble Nameplates

Limited to 25 serially numbered copies, this 57-card set places player photos on the right side of the card, a logo swatch and an autograph on the left side of the card.

NNAB Andrew Bogut 75.00 150.00
NNAJ Antawn Jamison 25.00 60.00
NNAN Andrew Bynum 200.00 400.00
NNBK Bernard King 25.00 60.00
NNBR Bill Russell 200.00 400.00
NNCA Carmelo Anthony 75.00 150.00
NNCB Carlos Boozer 25.00 60.00
NNCF Channing Frye 40.00 100.00
NNCH Chauncey Billups 25.00 60.00
NNCM Corey Maggette 25.00 60.00
NNCP Chris Paul 400.00 800.00
NNCS Chris Bosh 60.00 150.00
NNCV Charlie Villanueva 30.00 80.00
NNDA David Robinson 80.00 200.00
NNDG Danny Granger 75.00 150.00
NNDH Dwight Howard 100.00 200.00
NNDL David Lee 25.00 60.00
NNDR Dennis Rodman 125.00 250.00
NNEB Elton Brand 25.00 60.00
NNEO Emeka Okafor 25.00 60.00
NNGG Gerald Green 40.00 100.00
NNHO Hakeem Olajuwon 75.00 150.00
NNHW Hakim Warrick 30.00 80.00
NNID Ike Diogu 25.00 60.00
NNJE Julius Erving 125.00 250.00
NNJJ Joe Johnson 25.00 60.00
NNJK Jason Kidd 60.00 120.00
NNJN Jameer Nelson 25.00 60.00
NNJP Johan Petro 25.00 60.00
NNJR J.R. Smith 25.00 60.00
NNJS John Stockton 100.00 200.00
NNKA Kareem Abdul-Jabbar 100.00 200.00
NNLB Larry Bird 150.00 300.00
NNLJ LeBron James 500.00 1000.00
NNMB Mike Bibby 25.00 60.00
NNMJ Magic Johnson 100.00 200.00
NNMR Michael Redd 25.00 60.00
NNMW Marvin Williams 30.00 80.00
NNNR Nate Robinson 30.00 80.00
NNPP Paul Pierce 40.00 80.00
NNPS Peja Stojakovic 25.00 60.00
NNRA Ron Artest 40.00 100.00
NNRF Raymond Felton 40.00 80.00
NNRH Richard Hamilton 25.00 60.00
NNRJ Richard Jefferson 25.00 60.00
NNRM Rashad McCants 25.00 60.00
NNSA Shareef Abdur-Rahim 25.00 60.00
NNSC Speedy Claxton 25.00 60.00
NNSE Sean May 25.00 60.00
NNSF Stephon Marbury 25.00 60.00
NNSN Steve Nash 125.00 250.00
NNSP Scottie Pippen 250.00 400.00
NNST Sebastian Telfair 25.00 60.00
NNTM Tracy McGrady 80.00 200.00

NNTP Tayshaun Prince 40.00 80.00
NNVC Vince Carter 125.00 250.00
NNWF Walt Frazier 50.00 100.00

2005-06 Exquisite Collection Numbers

Serially numbered to featured player's jersey number, this set places player photos on the left, jersey swatches in the shape of the player's number and an autograph on the right.

STATED PRINT RUN ONE TO 91 SETS
SOME NOT PRICED DUE TO SCARCITY
ENCA Carmelo Anthony/15 250.00 400.00
ENDR Dennis Rodman/91 75.00 200.00
ENEB Elton Brand/42 20.00 50.00
ENEO Emeka Okafor/50 20.00 50.00
ENHO Hakeem Olajuwon/34 75.00 150.00
ENKG Kevin Garnett/21 175.00 350.00
ENLB Larry Bird/33 150.00 300.00
ENLJ LeBron James/23 900.00 1500.00
ENMA Magic Johnson/32 150.00 300.00
ENMJ Michael Jordan/23 1700.00 2500.00
ENMW Marvin Williams/24 40.00 100.00
ENPS Peja Stojakovic/16 50.00 100.00
ENSN Steve Nash/13 200.00 400.00
ENVC Vince Carter/15 200.00 400.00

2005-06 Exquisite Collection Numbers Dual

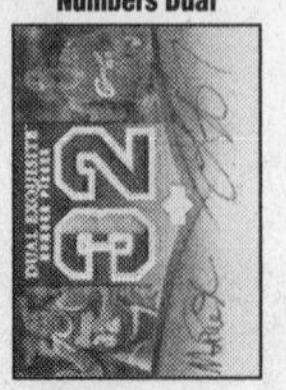

Serially numbered to featured players' jersey numbers, this set places player photos on each side and centered jersey swatches in the shape of the players' jersey number along with two autographs.

STATED PRINT RUN 12 TO 50 SETS
DNAB Kareem Abdul-Jabbar/33 250.00 500.00
Larry Bird
DNAC Carmelo Anthony/15 450.00 700.00
Vince Carter
DNBM Elton Brand/42 30.00 80.00
Sean May
DNHS Kirk Hinrich/12 100.00 200.00
John Stockton
DNJH Magic Johnson/32 150.00 300.00
Larry Hughes
DNJJ Michael Jordan/23 2000.00 3000.00
LeBron James
DNJW Richard Jefferson/24 40.00 100.00
Marvin Williams
DNOR Emeka Okafor/50 50.00 125.00
David Robinson
DNPR Tayshaun Prince/22 80.00 160.00
Michael Redd
DNSJ J.R. Smith/23 300.00 600.00
LeBron James
DNWG Hakim Warrick/21 175.00 350.00
Kevin Garnett

2005-06 Exquisite Collection Patches Quad

Inserted in packs randomly, this 14-card set places four players along with four swatches of jersey on each card front. Cards are limited to three serially numbered copies.

2005-06 Exquisite Collection Scripted Swatches

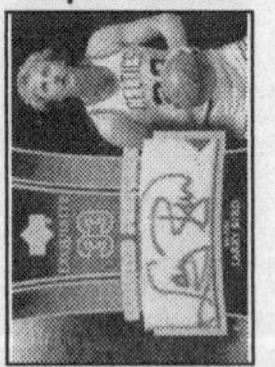

Randomly seeded in packs, this 29-card set is horizontally designed with player photos on the right side and an autographed jersey patch swatch on the left. Each card is serially numbered to either 3 or 25 copies.

UNPRICED DUAL PRINT RUN 5 SETS
SSAB Andrew Bogut/25 75.00 150.00
SSCA Carmelo Anthony/25 100.00 200.00
SSCB Chauncey Billups/25 25.00 60.00
SSCF Channing Frye/25 40.00 100.00
SSCH Chris Bosh/25 75.00 150.00
SSCP Chris Paul/25 250.00 500.00
SSCV Charlie Villanueva/25 40.00 100.00
SSDE Dennis Rodman/25 100.00 200.00
SSDH Dwight Howard/25 75.00 150.00
SSDM Desmond Mason/25 25.00 60.00
SSDR David Robinson/25 125.00 250.00
SSDW Deron Williams/25 75.00 150.00
SSEB Elton Brand/25 25.00 60.00
SSJK Jason Kidd/25 75.00 150.00
SSJS John Stockton/25 150.00 300.00
SSKA Kareem Abdul-Jabbar/25 175.00 350.00
SSKG Kevin Garnett/25 150.00 300.00
SSLB Larry Bird/25 200.00 400.00
SSLJ LeBron James/25 500.00 1000.00
SSMA Magic Johnson/25 175.00 350.00
SSMJ Michael Jordan/25 1200.00 1700.00
SSMW Marvin Williams/25 40.00 100.00
SSPP Paul Pierce/25 40.00 80.00
SSPS Peja Stojakovic/25 40.00 80.00
SSSN Steve Nash/25 200.00 350.00
SSTM Tracy McGrady/25 100.00 250.00
SSVC Vince Carter/25 80.00 200.00
SSYM Yao Ming/25 60.00 150.00

2006-07 Exquisite Collection

Released in early August 2007, Exquisite Collection features a 85-card set where cards 1-42 showcase veterans and #4 Adam Morrison's rookie and #31 J.J. Reidick's rookie serially numbered to 225, cards 43-48 showcase rookie autograph patches serially numbered to 99, cards 49-79 showcase rookie autograph patches serially numbered to 225 and cards 80-42 showcase rookie autographs serially numbered to 225. Also inserted in the product were special uncut sheet redemption cards and 24 serially numbered packs autographed by Kobe Bryant. Exquisite Collection originally carried a suggested retail price of $500 for a five-card wooden carved pack.

UNPRICED BLACK PRINT RUN ONE SET
UNPRICED BLACK RNBW PRINT RUN ONE SET
1 Joe Johnson 4.00 10.00
2 Paul Pierce 5.00 12.00
3 Emeka Okafor 4.00 10.00
4 Adam Morrison RC 5.00 12.00
5 Michael Jordan 75.00 200.00
6 Kirk Hinrich 4.00 10.00
7 LeBron James 30.00 80.00
8 Dirk Nowitzki 6.00 15.00
9 Carmelo Anthony 5.00 12.00
10 Allen Iverson 5.00 12.00
11 Chauncey Billups 4.00 10.00
12 Richard Hamilton 3.00 8.00
13 Baron Davis 4.00 10.00
14 Yao Ming 5.00 12.00
15 Tracy McGrady 5.00 12.00
16 Jermaine O'Neal 4.00 10.00
17 Elton Brand 4.00 10.00
18 Kobe Bryant 40.00 100.00
19 Lamar Odom 4.00 10.00
20 Pau Gasol 4.00 10.00
21 Dwyane Wade 15.00 40.00
22 Shaquille O'Neal 8.00 20.00
23 Michael Redd 4.00 10.00
24 Kevin Garnett 8.00 20.00
25 Vince Carter 5.00 12.00
26 Jason Kidd 6.00 15.00
27 Chris Paul 8.00 20.00
28 Peja Stojakovic 4.00 10.00
29 Stephon Marbury 3.00 8.00
30 Dwight Howard 6.00 15.00
31 J.J. Redick RC 10.00 25.00
32 Andre Iguodala 4.00 10.00
33 Steve Nash 6.00 15.00
34 Amare Stoudemire 6.00 15.00
35 Jarrett Jack 3.00 8.00
36 Mike Bibby 4.00 10.00
37 Tim Duncan 6.00 15.00
38 Tony Parker 4.00 10.00
39 Ray Allen 4.00 10.00
40 Chris Bosh 4.00 10.00
41 Deron Williams 6.00 15.00
42 Antawn Jamison 4.00 10.00
43 Andrea Bargnani JSY AU/99 RC 100.00 175.00
44 LaMarcus Aldridge JSY AU/99 RC 175.00 350.00
45 Tyrus Thomas JSY AU/99 RC 40.00 100.00
46 Brandon Roy JSY AU/99 RC 200.00 400.00
47 Rudy Gay JSY AU/99 RC 125.00 250.00
48 Shelden Williams JSY AU/99 RC 12.00 30.00
49 Randy Foye JSY AU RC 15.00 40.00
50 Patrick O'Bryant JSY AU RC 8.00 20.00
51 Saer Sene JSY AU RC 8.00 20.00
52 Hilton Armstrong JSY AU RC 8.00 20.00
53 Thabo Sefolosha JSY AU RC 20.00 50.00
54 Ronnie Brewer JSY AU RC 15.00 40.00
55 Cedric Simmons JSY AU RC 8.00 20.00
56 Rodney Carney JSY AU RC 8.00 20.00
57 Shawne Williams JSY AU RC 8.00 20.00
58 Quincy Douby JSY AU RC 8.00 20.00
59 Renaldo Balkman JSY AU RC 8.00 20.00
60 Rajon Rondo JSY AU RC 200.00 350.00
61 Marcus Williams JSY AU RC 8.00 20.00
62 Josh Boone JSY AU RC 8.00 20.00
63 Allan Ray JSY AU RC 8.00 20.00
64 Shannon Brown JSY AU RC 20.00 50.00
65 Jordan Farmar JSY AU RC 12.50 30.00
66 Dee Brown JSY AU RC 8.00 20.00
67 Maurice Ager JSY AU RC 8.00 20.00
68 Mardy Collins JSY AU RC 8.00 20.00
69 James White JSY AU RC 8.00 20.00
70 Steve Novak JSY AU RC 10.00 25.00
71 Solomon Jones JSY AU RC 8.00 20.00
72 Paul Davis JSY AU RC 8.00 20.00
73 P.J. Tucker JSY AU RC 8.00 20.00
74 Craig Smith JSY AU RC 8.00 20.00
75 Bobby Jones JSY AU RC 8.00 20.00
76 David Noel JSY AU RC 8.00 20.00
77 Jorge Garbajosa JSY AU RC 8.00 20.00
78 Daniel Gibson JSY AU RC 10.00 25.00
79 Sergio Rodriguez AU RC 8.00 20.00
80 Paul Millsap AU RC 15.00 40.00
81 Will Blalock AU RC 8.00 20.00
82 Hassan Adams AU RC 8.00 20.00
83 Kyle Lowry AU RC 30.00 80.00
84 James Augustine AU RC 8.00 20.00

2006-07 Exquisite Collection Gold

*1-42 GOLD: 1.5X TO 4X BASE HI
GOLD PRINT RUN 25 SER.#'d SETS
5 Michael Jordan 300.00 600.00
31 J.J. Redick 30.00 80.00
43 Andrea Bargnani 25.00 60.00
44 LaMarcus Aldridge 40.00 100.00
45 Tyrus Thomas 20.00 50.00
46 Brandon Roy 40.00 100.00
47 Rudy Gay 25.00 60.00
48 Shelden Williams 15.00 40.00
49 Randy Foye 20.00 50.00
50 Patrick O'Bryant 15.00 40.00
51 Saer Sene 15.00 40.00
52 Hilton Armstrong 15.00 40.00
53 Thabo Sefolosha 20.00 50.00
54 Ronnie Brewer 20.00 50.00
55 Cedric Simmons 15.00 40.00
56 Rodney Carney 15.00 40.00
57 Shawne Williams 15.00 40.00
58 Quincy Douby 15.00 40.00
59 Renaldo Balkman 15.00 40.00
60 Rajon Rondo 75.00 200.00
61 Marcus Williams 15.00 40.00
62 Josh Boone 15.00 40.00
63 Allan Ray 15.00 40.00
64 Shannon Brown 25.00 60.00
66 Dee Brown 15.00 40.00
67 Maurice Ager 15.00 40.00
68 Mardy Collins 15.00 40.00
69 James White 15.00 40.00
70 Steve Novak 15.00 40.00
71 Solomon Jones 15.00 40.00
72 Paul Davis 15.00 40.00
73 P.J. Tucker 15.00 40.00
74 Craig Smith 15.00 40.00
75 Bobby Jones 15.00 40.00
76 David Noel 15.00 40.00
77 Jorge Garbajosa 15.00 40.00
78 Daniel Gibson 20.00 50.00
79 Sergio Rodriguez 15.00 40.00
80 Paul Millsap 25.00 60.00
81 Will Blalock 15.00 40.00
82 Hassan Adams 15.00 40.00
83 Kyle Lowry 20.00 50.00
84 James Augustine 15.00 40.00

2006-07 Exquisite Collection Jerseys

*JERSEYS: 1.25X TO 3X BASE HI
JSY PRINT RUN 25 SER.#'d SETS
UNPRICED PATCH PRINT RUN 10 SETS
5J Michael Jordan 250.00 500.00
31J J.J. Redick 15.00 40.00
39J Ray Allen 15.00 40.00

2006-07 Exquisite Collection Rookie Parallel

SOME NOT PRICED DUE TO SCARCITY
44 LaMarcus Aldridge JSY AU/12 250.00 500.00
45 Tyrus Thomas JSY AU/24 80.00 200.00
47 Rudy Gay JSY AU/22 300.00 600.00
48 Shelden Williams JSY AU/33 25.00 60.00
50 Patrick O'Bryant JSY AU/26 25.00 60.00
51 Saer Sene JSY AU/18 40.00 100.00
52 Hilton Armstrong JSY AU/12 40.00 100.00
55 Cedric Simmons JSY AU/22 25.00 60.00
56 Rodney Carney JSY AU/25 25.00 60.00
59 Renaldo Balkman JSY AU/32 25.00 60.00
66 Dee Brown JSY AU/11 25.00 60.00
67 Maurice Ager JSY AU/13 60.00 150.00
68 Mardy Collins JSY AU/25 25.00 60.00
69 James White JSY AU/33 25.00 60.00
70 Steve Novak JSY AU/20 25.00 60.00
71 Solomon Jones JSY AU/44 25.00 60.00
72 Paul Davis JSY AU/40 25.00 60.00
75 Bobby Jones JSY AU/11 75.00 150.00
76 David Noel JSY AU/34 25.00 60.00
77 Jorge Garbajosa JSY AU/15 125.00 250.00
79 Sergio Rodriguez AU/11 30.00 80.00
80 Paul Millsap AU/24 100.00 200.00
83 Kyle Lowry AU/12 25.00 60.00
84 James Augustine AU/40 25.00 60.00

2006-07 Exquisite Collection Autographs Patches

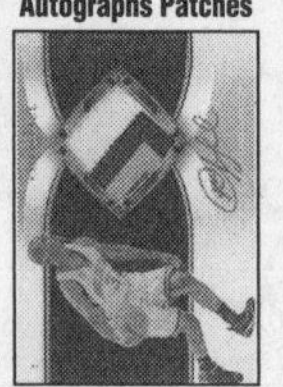

PRINT RUN 100 SER.#'d SETS
APAB Andrea Bargnani 25.00 60.00
APBG Ben Gordon 15.00 40.00
APBJ Bobby Jones 12.50 30.00
APBO Chris Bosh 30.00 60.00
APBR Brandon Roy 75.00 200.00
APCA Carmelo Anthony 60.00 150.00
APCB Chauncey Billups 20.00 50.00
APCP Chris Paul 75.00 200.00
APCS Craig Smith 12.50 30.00
APDA Baron Davis 12.50 30.00
APDG Daniel Gibson 12.50 30.00
APDN David Noel 12.50 30.00
APDR Dennis Rodman 50.00 125.00
APEO Emeka Okafor 12.50 30.00
APHO Hakeem Olajuwon 50.00 120.00
APJE Julius Erving 125.00 250.00
APJG Jorge Garbajosa 12.50 30.00
APJO Jermaine O'Neal 12.50 30.00
APJS J.R. Smith 15.00 40.00
APKB Kobe Bryant 500.00 1000.00
APLA LaMarcus Aldridge 50.00 125.00
APLB Larry Bird 100.00 200.00
APLJ LeBron James 500.00 1000.00
APMA Magic Johnson 100.00 250.00
APMJ Michael Jordan 1000.00 1600.00
APMW Marcus Williams 12.50 30.00
APPD Paul Davis 12.50 30.00
APRB Renaldo Balkman 12.50 30.00
APRC Rodney Carney 12.50 30.00
APRF Randy Foye 15.00 40.00
APRG Rudy Gay 40.00 100.00
APRJ Richard Jefferson 12.50 30.00
APRO Ronnie Brewer 25.00 50.00
APSB Shannon Brown 20.00 50.00
APSH Shawne Williams 12.50 30.00
APSW Shelden Williams 12.50 30.00
APTF T.J. Ford 12.50 30.00
APTT Tyrus Thomas 20.00 50.00
APVC Vince Carter 40.00 100.00
APWI Marvin Williams 12.50 30.00

2006-07 Exquisite Collection Emblems of Endorsements

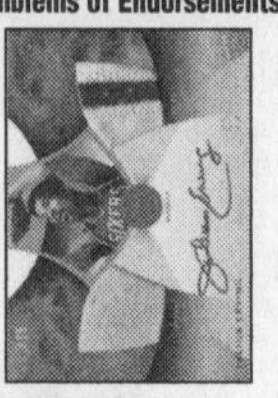

PRINT RUN 15 SER.#'d SETS
EMAB Andrea Bargnani 40.00 100.00
EMAI Andre Iguodala 40.00 100.00
EMAJ Antawn Jamison 20.00 50.00
EMAM Alonzo Mourning 125.00 250.00
EMBI Chauncey Billups 40.00 100.00
EMBR Brandon Roy 75.00 200.00
EMCA Carmelo Anthony 100.00 200.00
EMCB Chris Bosh 50.00 120.00
EMCD Clyde Drexler 75.00 150.00
EMCP Chris Paul 125.00 250.00
EMDR Dennis Rodman 75.00 150.00
EMDW Deron Williams 75.00 200.00
EMFE Raymond Felton 20.00 50.00
EMHO Hakeem Olajuwon 50.00 120.00
EMJE Julius Erving 125.00 250.00
EMJH Jeff Hornacek 40.00 100.00
EMJK Jason Kidd 100.00 250.00
EMJO Jermaine O'Neal 25.00 60.00
EMJS John Stockton 100.00 200.00
EMKA Kareem Abdul-Jabbar 75.00 150.00
EMKB Kobe Bryant 900.00 1500.00
EMLA LaMarcus Aldridge 75.00 150.00
EMLB Larry Bird 100.00 200.00
EMLJ LeBron James 900.00 1500.00
EMMA Magic Johnson 100.00 200.00
EMMJ Michael Jordan 2000.00 3000.00
EMMW Marcus Williams 20.00 50.00
EMPP Paul Pierce 75.00 150.00
EMPS Peja Stojakovic 40.00 100.00
EMRC Rodney Carney 20.00 50.00
EMRF Randy Foye 20.00 50.00
EMRG Rudy Gay 50.00 125.00
EMRJ Richard Jefferson 20.00 50.00
EMRO David Robinson 100.00 200.00
EMSL Shaun Livingston 20.00 50.00
EMSN Steve Nash 80.00 200.00
EMTM Tracy McGrady 60.00 150.00
EMTS Thabo Sefolosha 25.00 60.00
EMTT Tyrus Thomas 40.00 100.00
EMVC Vince Carter 75.00 200.00

2006-07 Exquisite Collection Enshrinements

PRINT RUN 25 SER.#'d SETS
UNPRICED DUAL PRINT RUN 10 SETS
EXAB Andrea Bargnani 25.00 60.00
EXBI Chauncey Billups 15.00 40.00
EXBR Bill Russell 80.00 200.00
EXCA Carmelo Anthony 40.00 80.00
EXCB Chris Bosh 30.00 80.00
EXCP Chris Paul 50.00 120.00
EXDA David Robinson 50.00 120.00
EXDR Dennis Rodman 60.00 150.00
EXHO Hakeem Olajuwon 30.00 80.00
EXJE Julius Erving 60.00 120.00
EXJK Jason Kidd 30.00 80.00
EXJO Jermaine O'Neal 15.00 40.00
EXJS John Stockton 60.00 150.00
EXJW James Worthy 40.00 100.00
EXKA Kareem Abdul-Jabbar 60.00 120.00
EXKB Kobe Bryant 200.00 400.00
EXKH Kirk Hinrich 15.00 40.00
EXLA LaMarcus Aldridge 30.00 80.00
EXLB Larry Bird 60.00 150.00
EXLJ LeBron James 175.00 350.00
EXLJ2 LeBron James 175.00 350.00
EXMA Magic Johnson 60.00 150.00
EXMJ Michael Jordan 400.00 800.00
EXMJ2 Michael Jordan 400.00 800.00
EXMW Marcus Williams 15.00 40.00
EXPP Paul Pierce 20.00 50.00
EXPR Tayshaun Prince 15.00 40.00
EXRB Renaldo Balkman 15.00 40.00
EXRC Rodney Carney 15.00 40.00
EXRF Randy Foye 15.00 40.00
EXRG Rudy Gay 30.00 80.00
EXRH Richard Hamilton 15.00 40.00
EXRI Pat Riley 30.00 80.00
EXRO Brandon Roy 40.00 100.00
EXSN Steve Nash 50.00 120.00
EXTF T.J. Ford 15.00 40.00
EXTM Tracy McGrady 25.00 60.00
EXTP Tony Parker 20.00 50.00
EXTT Tyrus Thomas 25.00 60.00
EXVC Vince Carter 30.00 60.00
EXWJ John Wooden 200.00 400.00
EXYM Yao Ming 30.00 80.00

2006-07 Exquisite Collection Extra Exquisite

PRINT RUN 25 SER.#'d SETS
UNPRICED JSY/PATCH PRINT RUN 10 SETS
AUTO PRINT RUN TEN SETS
UNPRICED J/P AUTO PRINT RUN 5 SETS
EEAB Andrea Bargnani 12.00 30.00
EEAI Allen Iverson 20.00 50.00
EEAM Alonzo Mourning 25.00 60.00
EEAR Ron Artest 10.00 25.00
EEAS Amare Stoudemire 8.00 20.00
EEBG Ben Gordon 8.00 20.00
EEBK Bernard King 8.00 20.00
EEBO Carlos Boozer 8.00 20.00
EEBR Brandon Roy 20.00 50.00
EEBW Ben Wallace 8.00 20.00
EECA Carmelo Anthony 15.00 40.00
EECB Chris Bosh 10.00 25.00
EECD Clyde Drexler 15.00 40.00
EECM Chris Mullin 10.00 25.00
EECP Chris Paul 15.00 40.00
EEDH Dwight Howard 12.00 30.00
EEDN Dirk Nowitzki 15.00 40.00
EEDR Dennis Rodman 20.00 50.00
EEEB Elton Brand 8.00 20.00
EEEM Earl Monroe 15.00 40.00
EEEO Emeka Okafor 8.00 20.00
EEGH Grant Hill 30.00 60.00
EEHO Hakeem Olajuwon 15.00 30.00
EEIA Andre Iguodala 8.00 20.00
EEIT Isiah Thomas 10.00 25.00
EEJE Julius Erving 15.00 40.00
EEJG Jorge Garbajosa 8.00 20.00
EEJO Jermaine O'Neal 8.00 20.00
EEJR J.J. Redick 10.00 25.00
EEJS John Stockton 12.00 30.00
EEJT Jason Terry 6.00 15.00
EEJW Jerry West 25.00 50.00
EEKA Kareem Abdul-Jabbar 20.00 40.00
EEKM Karl Malone 15.00 40.00
EELA LaMarcus Aldridge 20.00 50.00
EELJ LeBron James 40.00 100.00
EELJ2 LeBron James 40.00 100.00
EEMA Magic Johnson 20.00 50.00
EEMG Manu Ginobili 15.00 30.00
EEMJ Michael Jordan 150.00 300.00
EEMJ2 Michael Jordan 150.00 300.00
EEOR Oscar Robertson 15.00 40.00
EEPM Pete Maravich 150.00 225.00
EEPP Paul Pierce 10.00 25.00
EEPR Pat Riley 12.50 30.00
EERA Ray Allen 10.00 25.00
EERB Bill Russell 25.00 60.00
EERF Randy Foye 10.00 25.00
EERG Rudy Gay 12.00 30.00
EERI Jason Richardson 8.00 20.00
EERO David Robinson 30.00 80.00
EERR Rajon Rondo 30.00 80.00
EESM Shawn Marion 8.00 20.00
EESO Shaquille O'Neal 30.00 60.00
EETM Tracy McGrady 15.00 40.00
EETP Tony Parker 10.00 25.00
EETT Tyrus Thomas 10.00 25.00
EEVC Vince Carter 15.00 40.00
EEWC Wilt Chamberlain 40.00 80.00
EEYM Yao Ming 20.00 40.00

2006-07 Exquisite Collection Limited Logos

PRINT RUN 50 SER.#'d SETS
LLAB Andrea Bargnani 50.00 120.00
LLBG Ben Gordon 25.00 60.00
LLBI Chauncey Billups 25.00 60.00
LLBR Ronnie Brewer 25.00 60.00
LLCA Carmelo Anthony 100.00 200.00
LLCB Chris Bosh 60.00 150.00
LLCD Clyde Drexler 200.00 400.00
LLCP Chris Paul 150.00 300.00
LLCS Craig Smith 15.00 40.00
LLDA Baron Davis 20.00 50.00
LLDE Dennis Rodman 80.00 200.00
LLDG Daniel Gibson 20.00 50.00
LLDN David Noel 15.00 40.00
LLDR David Robinson 150.00 300.00
LLEO Emeka Okafor 15.00 40.00
LLHO Hakeem Olajuwon 60.00 150.00
LLJE Julius Erving 175.00 350.00
LLJF Jordan Farmar 30.00 80.00
LLJO Jermaine O'Neal 40.00 100.00
LLJS J.R. Smith 25.00 60.00
LLKB Kobe Bryant 1000.00 1600.00
LLLA LaMarcus Aldridge 100.00 250.00
LLLB Larry Bird 125.00 250.00
LLLJ LeBron James 700.00 1300.00
LLMA Magic Johnson 125.00 250.00
LLMJ Michael Jordan 3000.00 4500.00
LLMW Marcus Williams 15.00 40.00
LLRB Renaldo Balkman 15.00 40.00
LLRC Rodney Carney 15.00 40.00
LLRF Randy Foye 30.00 80.00
LLRG Rudy Gay 100.00 175.00
LLRJ Richard Jefferson 25.00 60.00
LLRO Brandon Roy 100.00 250.00
LLSN Steve Nash 100.00 200.00
LLST John Stockton 150.00 300.00
LLSW Shawne Williams 15.00 40.00
LLTT Tyrus Thomas 25.00 60.00
LLVC Vince Carter 60.00 150.00
LLWI Shelden Williams 15.00 40.00
LLWM Marvin Williams 30.00 80.00

2006-07 Exquisite Collection Noble Nameplates

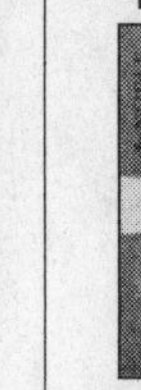

PRINT RUN 25 SER.#'d SETS
NNAB Andrea Bargnani 30.00 80.00
NNAJ Al Jefferson 15.00 40.00
NNAM Alonzo Mourning 75.00 200.00
NNBD Baron Davis 40.00 100.00
NNBG Ben Gordon 25.00 60.00
NNBO Chris Bosh 50.00 100.00
NNBR Brandon Roy 75.00 200.00
NNCA Carmelo Anthony 80.00 160.00
NNCB Chauncey Billups 25.00 60.00
NNCD Clyde Drexler 50.00 120.00
NNCP Chris Paul 75.00 150.00
NNCS Craig Smith 15.00 40.00
NNDE Dennis Rodman 75.00 150.00
NNDG Danny Granger 15.00 40.00
NNDI Boris Diaw 15.00 40.00
NNDN David Noel 15.00 40.00
NNDR David Robinson 75.00 150.00
NNEO Emeka Okafor 15.00 40.00
NNFE Raymond Felton 15.00 40.00
NNGD Daniel Gibson 20.00 50.00
NNGG Gerald Green 15.00 40.00
NNHO Hakeem Olajuwon 60.00 120.00
NNHW Hakim Warrick 15.00 40.00
NNJB Josh Boone 15.00 40.00
NNJE Julius Erving 100.00 200.00
NNJG Jorge Garbajosa 15.00 40.00
NNJK Jason Kidd 50.00 120.00
NNJO Jermaine O'Neal 30.00 60.00
NNJS J.R. Smith 25.00 60.00
NNJW Jerry West 150.00 300.00
NNKA Kareem Abdul-Jabbar 75.00 150.00
NNKB Kobe Bryant 400.00 700.00
NNKL Kyle Lowry 15.00 40.00
NNLA LaMarcus Aldridge 50.00 120.00
NNLB Larry Bird 100.00 200.00
NNLJ LeBron James 400.00 700.00
NNMA Magic Johnson 75.00 150.00
NNMB Mike Bibby 15.00 40.00
NNMJ Michael Jordan 1500.00 2500.00
NNMW Marcus Williams 15.00 40.00
NNPP Paul Pierce 40.00 100.00
NNPS Peja Stojakovic 30.00 80.00
NNQD Quincy Douby 15.00 40.00
NNRB Renaldo Balkman 15.00 40.00
NNRC Rodney Carney 15.00 40.00
NNRF Randy Foye 15.00 40.00
NNRG Rudy Gay 40.00 100.00
NNRH Richard Hamilton 25.00 60.00
NNRJ Richard Jefferson 15.00 40.00
NNRO Ronnie Brewer 15.00 40.00
NNSB Shannon Brown 25.00 60.00
NNSI Cedric Simmons 15.00 40.00
NNSN Steve Nash 100.00 200.00
NNST John Stockton 80.00 200.00
NNSW Shelden Williams 15.00 40.00
NNTM Tracy McGrady 60.00 150.00
NNTP Tayshaun Prince 15.00 40.00
NNTT Tyrus Thomas 20.00 50.00
NNVC Vince Carter 60.00 150.00
NNYM Yao Ming 60.00 150.00

2006-07 Exquisite Collection Numbers

PRINT RUNS LISTED IN CHECKLIST
SOME NOT PRICED DUE TO SCARCITY
ENAH Al Harrington/32 20.00 50.00
ENAM Alonzo Mourning/33 75.00 200.00
ENCA Carmelo Anthony/15 125.00 250.00
ENCD Clyde Drexler/22 75.00 150.00
ENCM Corey Maggette/50 15.00 40.00
ENDG Danny Granger/33 30.00 80.00
ENDN David Noel/34 15.00 40.00
ENDR David Robinson/50 60.00 150.00
ENEO Emeka Okafor/50 15.00 40.00
ENHO Hakeem Olajuwon/34 100.00 200.00
ENHW Hakim Warrick/21 25.00 60.00
ENKA Kareem Abdul-Jabbar/33 100.00 200.00
ENKB Kobe Bryant/24 500.00 800.00
ENLA LaMarcus Aldridge/12 150.00 300.00
ENLB Larry Bird/33 125.00 250.00
ENLH Larry Hughes/32 15.00 40.00
ENLJ LeBron James/23 400.00 800.00
ENMA Magic Johnson/32 125.00 250.00
ENMJ Michael Jordan/23 1000.00 1700.00
ENPO Patrick O'Bryant/26 15.00 40.00
ENPP Paul Pierce/34 50.00 125.00
ENPS Peja Stojakovic/16 50.00 120.00
ENRC Rodney Carney/25 20.00 50.00
ENRE Renaldo Balkman/32 15.00 40.00
ENRG Rudy Gay/22 50.00 120.00
ENRH Richard Hamilton/32 30.00 80.00
ENRJ Richard Jefferson/24 25.00 60.00
ENRO Dennis Rodman/91 75.00 150.00
ENSH Shelden Williams/33 15.00 40.00
ENSI Cedric Simmons/22 15.00 40.00
ENSL Shaun Livingston/14 30.00 60.00
ENTP Tayshaun Prince/22 25.00 60.00
ENTT Tyrus Thomas/24 100.00 200.00
ENVC Vince Carter/15 125.00 250.00
ENWI Marvin Williams/24 15.00 40.00
ENYM Yao Ming/11 125.00 250.00

2006-07 Exquisite Collection Numbers Dual

PRINT RUNS LISTED IN CHECKLIST
SOME NOT PRICED DUE TO SCARCITY
DENAA LaMarcus Aldridge 75.00 150.00
Hilton Armstrong/12
DENAC Carmelo Anthony 125.00 250.00
Vince Carter/15
DENAW Kareem Abdul-Jabbar 60.00 150.00
Shelden Williams/33
DENBG Larry Bird 100.00 200.00
Danny Granger/33
DENBH Renaldo Balkman 15.00 40.00
Larry Hughes/32
DENBJ Kobe Bryant 300.00 550.00
Richard Jefferson/24
DENBT Kobe Bryant 300.00 600.00
Tyrus Thomas/24
DENCC Rodney Carney 15.00 40.00
Mardy Collins/25
DENDG Clyde Drexler 75.00 150.00
Rudy Gay/22
DENJH Magic Johnson 100.00 200.00
Richard Hamilton/32
DENJJ Michael Jordan 1500.00 2500.00
LeBron James/23
DENOP Hakeem Olajuwon 60.00 150.00
Paul Pierce/34
DENOR Emeka Okafor 40.00 100.00
David Robinson/50
DENPG Tayshaun Prince 60.00 120.00
Rudy Gay/22
DENTW Tyrus Thomas 60.00 150.0
Marvin Williams/24

2006-07 Exquisite Collection Scripted Swatches

PRINT RUN 25 SER.#'d SETS
UNPRICED DUAL PRINT RUN FIVE SETS
SSAB Andrea Bargnani 40.00 100.
SSAD Adrian Dantley 25.00 60.
SSAH Al Harrington 15.00 40.
SSAJ Antawn Jamison 15.00 40.
SSBD Baron Davis 30.00 80.
SSBG Ben Gordon 25.00 60.
SSBO Chris Bosh 60.00 120
SSBR Brandon Roy 100.00 250
SSCA Carmelo Anthony 125.00 225
SSCB Chauncey Billups 20.00 50
SSCD Clyde Drexler 60.00 150
SSCM Corey Maggette 15.00 40
SSCP Chris Paul 100.00 225
SSCS Cedric Simmons 15.00 40
SSDB Dee Brown 15.00 40
SSDE Dennis Rodman 125.00 225
SSDG Danny Granger 30.00 80
SSDR David Robinson 100.00 200
SSDW Deron Williams 60.00 150
SSER Julius Erving 125.00 250
SSFE Raymond Felton 25.00 60
SSGG Gerald Green 15.00 40
SSGI Daniel Gibson 30.00 80
SSHA Hilton Armstrong 15.00 40
SSHO Hakeem Olajuwon 50.00 120
SSHW Hakim Warrick 15.00 4
SSJB Josh Boone 15.00 4
SSJE Richard Jefferson 15.00 4
SSJK Jason Kidd 50.00 12
SSJM Magic Johnson 60.00 15
SSJO Jermaine O'Neal 25.00 6
SSJS John Stockton 100.00 20
SSJW Jerry West 125.00 25
SSKA Kareem Abdul-Jabbar 100.00 20
SSKB Kobe Bryant 400.00 70
SSKH Kirk Hinrich 15.00 4
SSKL Kyle Lowry 25.00 6
SSLA LaMarcus Aldridge 75.00 15
SSLB Larry Bird 100.00 20
SSLJ LeBron James 300.00 6
SSLR Luke Ridnour 15.00
SSMA Marcus Williams 15.00
SSMB Mike Bibby 15.00
SSMC Mardy Collins 15.00
SSMJ Michael Jordan 1000.00 15
SSMP Morris Peterson 15.00
SSMW Martell Webster 15.00
SSPS Peja Stojakovic 30.00
SSPT Tony Parker 50.00
SSRB Renaldo Balkman 15.00
SSRC Rodney Carney 15.00
SSRF Randy Foye 15.00
SSRG Rudy Gay 100.00
SSRH Richard Hamilton 25.00
SSRO Ronnie Brewer 20.00
SSSB Shannon Brown 25.00
SSSM Craig Smith 15.00
SSSN Steve Nash 150.00
SSST Sebastian Telfair 15.00
SSSW Shelden Williams 15.00
SSTM Tracy McGrady 75.00
SSTP Tayshaun Prince 25.00
SSTT Tyrus Thomas 50.00
SSVC Vince Carter 60.00
SSWI Shawne Williams 15.00
SSYM Yao Ming 60.00

07-08 Exquisite Collection

ed in late July 2008, Exquisite Collection boasts card set where cards 1-60 feature veterans ntially numbered to 225, cards 61-93 feature players with both premium patch swatches and aphs sequentially numbered to 225, cards 94-97 rookie players with both premium patch es and autographs sequentially numbered to 99, 98-106 feature rookie players with autographs ntially numbered to 99 and cards 107-112 rookie players sequentially numbered to 99. card is printed on an extra-thick card stock, and autograph in the product is signed directly on Exquisite Collection is packaged in five card and carried an initial suggested retail price of

CED BLACK PRINT RUN ONE SET
on James 40.00 100.00
Ming 4.00 10.00
Bryant 40.00 100.00
ane Wade 12.00 30.00
McGrady 3.00 8.00
Iverson 4.00 10.00
uille O'Neal 6.00 15.00
n Garnett 6.00 15.00
e Nash 4.00 10.00
ight Howard 5.00 12.00
bert Arenas 3.00 8.00
ce Carter 4.00 10.00
Duncan 5.00 12.00
rmelo Anthony 4.00 10.00
k Nowitzki 4.00 10.00
are Stoudemire 3.00 8.00
ris Bosh 3.00 8.00
maine O'Neal 3.00 8.00
on Kidd 3.00 8.00
n Wallace 3.00 8.00
ul Pierce 4.00 10.00
awn Marion 3.00 8.00
chael Jordan 75.00 200.00
nu Ginobili 3.00 8.00
ny Parker 3.00 8.00
uncey Billups 3.00 8.00
is Paul 6.00 15.00
dre Iguodala 3.00 8.00
phon Marbury 2.50 6.00
Allen 3.00 8.00
mar Odom 3.00 8.00
on Terry 2.50 6.00
h Howard 2.50 6.00
ron Butler 3.00 8.00
eka Okafor 3.00 8.00
rcus Camby 2.00 5.00
Gasol 3.00 8.00
rlos Boozer 3.00 8.00
on Davis 3.00 8.00
chael Redd 3.00 8.00
Gordon 3.00 8.00
hard Hamilton 2.50 6.00
drew Bogut 3.00 8.00
son Chandler 2.50 6.00
y Curry 2.00 5.00
ry Hughes 2.50 6.00
Marcus Aldridge 4.00 10.00
drea Bargnani 4.00 10.00
ke Bibby 3.00 8.00
n Brand 3.00 8.00
Harrington 2.50 6.00
Jefferson 3.00 8.00
Johnson 3.00 8.00
shard Lewis 2.50 6.00
vin Martin 3.00 8.00
dre Miller 2.50 6.00
ndon Roy 4.00 10.00
rald Wallace 3.00 8.00
sheed Wallace 3.00 8.00
ron Williams 5.00 12.00
on Afflalo JSY AU RC 25.00 60.00
rris Almond JSY AU RC 10.00 25.00
ian Wright JSY AU RC 10.00 25.00
on Brooks JSY AU RC 12.00 30.00
bert Hill JSY AU RC 10.00 25.00
son Chandler JSY AU RC 30.00 60.00
equan Cook JSY AU RC 12.00 30.00
aris Crittenton JSY AU RC 10.00 25.00
mareo Davidson JSY AU RC 10.00 25.00
n Davis JSY AU RC 20.00 50.00
ed Dudley JSY AU RC 10.00 25.00
rey Brewer JSY AU RC 12.00 30.00
on Gray JSY AU RC 10.00 25.00
rean Green JSY AU RC 10.00 25.00
k Fazekas JSY AU RC 10.00 25.00
encer Hawes JSY AU RC 15.00 40.00
Horford JSY AU RC 50.00 120.00
Green JSY AU RC 30.00 80.00
l Landry JSY AU RC 10.00 25.00
ke Conley Jr. JSY AU RC 25.00 60.00
e Law JSY AU RC 10.00 25.00
minic McGuire JSY AU RC 10.00 25.00
sh McRoberts JSY AU RC 10.00 25.00
metris Nichols JSY AU RC 10.00 25.00
kim Noah JSY AU RC 50.00 125.00
be Pruitt JSY AU RC 10.00 25.00
is Richard JSY AU RC 10.00 25.00
on Smith JSY AU RC 10.00 25.00
. Strawberry JSY AU RC 10.00 25.00
dney Stuckey JSY AU RC 30.00 80.00
n Williams JSY AU RC 10.00 25.00
Thornton JSY AU RC 15.00 40.00
ndo Tucker JSY AU RC 10.00 25.00
rin Durant JSY AU/99 RC 3000.00 4500.00
rco Belinelli JSY AU/99 RC 30.00 80.00
s Scola JSY AU/99 RC 30.00 80.00
uis Amundson JSY AU/99 RC 15.00 40.00
. Watson AU RC 10.00 25.00
eikh Samb AU RC 10.00 25.00
an Navarro AU RC 10.00 25.00
mesOn Curry AU RC 10.00 25.00
amon Sessions AU RC 50.00 125.00
ario West AU RC 10.00 25.00
oby Karl AU RC 10.00 25.00

105 Oleksiy Pecherov AU RC 10.00 25.00
106 Jamario Moon AU RC 10.00 25.00
107 Kyrylo Fesenko RC 10.00 25.00
108 Yi Jianlian RC 15.00 40.00
109 Brandan Wright RC 10.00 25.00
110 Thaddeus Young RC 12.00 30.00
111 Nick Young RC 15.00 40.00
112 Greg Oden RC 30.00 80.00

2007-08 Exquisite Collection Gold

*1-60 GOLD: 2.5X TO 6X BASE HI
PRINT RUN 25 SER.#'d SETS
61 Arron Afflalo 25.00 60.00
62 Morris Almond 20.00 50.00
63 Julian Wright 20.00 50.00
64 Aaron Brooks 20.00 50.00
65 Herbert Hill 20.00 50.00
66 Wilson Chandler 30.00 80.00
67 Daequan Cook 20.00 50.00
68 Javaris Crittenton 20.00 50.00
69 Jermareo Davidson 20.00 50.00
70 Glen Davis 30.00 80.00
71 Jared Dudley 20.00 50.00
72 Corey Brewer 25.00 60.00
73 Aaron Gray 20.00 50.00
74 Taurean Green 20.00 50.00
75 Nick Fazekas 20.00 50.00
76 Spencer Hawes 20.00 50.00
77 Al Horford 25.00 60.00
78 Jeff Green 25.00 60.00
79 Carl Landry 20.00 50.00
80 Mike Conley Jr. 30.00 80.00
81 Acie Law 20.00 50.00
82 Dominic McGuire 20.00 50.00
83 Josh McRoberts 20.00 50.00
84 Demetris Nichols 20.00 50.00
85 Joakim Noah 75.00 200.00
86 Gabe Pruitt 20.00 50.00
87 Chris Richard 20.00 50.00
88 Jason Smith 20.00 50.00
89 D.J. Strawberry 20.00 50.00
90 Rodney Stuckey 30.00 80.00
91 Sean Williams 20.00 50.00
92 Al Thornton 20.00 50.00
93 Alando Tucker 20.00 50.00
94 Kevin Durant 700.00 1200.00
95 Marco Belinelli 20.00 50.00
96 Luis Scola 30.00 80.00
97 Louis Amundson 20.00 50.00
98 C.J. Watson 20.00 50.00
99 Cheikh Samb 20.00 50.00
100 Juan Navarro 20.00 50.00
101 JamesOn Curry 20.00 50.00
102 Ramon Sessions 30.00 80.00
103 Mario West 20.00 50.00
104 Coby Karl 20.00 50.00
105 Oleksiy Pecherov 20.00 50.00
106 Jamario Moon 20.00 50.00
107 Kyrylo Fesenko 20.00 50.00
108 Yi Jianlian 30.00 80.00
109 Brandan Wright 20.00 50.00
110 Thaddeus Young 25.00 60.00
111 Nick Young 30.00 80.00
112 Greg Oden 25.00 60.00

2007-08 Exquisite Collection Autographs Patches

PRINT RUN 35 SER.#'d SETS
EAAH Al Horford 75.00 150.00
EAAI Andre Iguodala 15.00 40.00
EAAJ Al Jefferson 15.00 40.00
EAAM Alonzo Mourning 75.00 150.00
EABG Ben Gordon 15.00 40.00
EABI Chauncey Billups 25.00 60.00
EABO Carlos Boozer 15.00 40.00
EABR Brandon Roy 30.00 60.00
EACA Carmelo Anthony 75.00 150.00
EACB Corey Brewer 15.00 40.00
EACD Clyde Drexler 60.00 120.00
EACH Chris Bosh 30.00 60.00
EACM Corey Maggette 15.00 40.00
EACP Chris Paul 100.00 200.00
EADG Daniel Gibson 15.00 40.00
EADR David Robinson 75.00 150.00
EAEO Emeka Okafor 15.00 40.00
EAHO Hakeem Olajuwon 30.00 60.00
EAJG Jeff Green 30.00 80.00
EAJK Jason Kidd 40.00 80.00
EAJN Joakim Noah 40.00 100.00
EAJO Magic Johnson 125.00 250.00
EAJS John Stockton 60.00 150.00
EAJW Julian Wright 20.00 50.00
EAKA Kelenna Azubuike 15.00 40.00
EAKD Kevin Durant 3000.00 4500.00
EAKG Kevin Garnett 125.00 250.00
EALB Larry Bird 75.00 150.00
EALH Larry Hughes 20.00 50.00
EALJ LeBron James 300.00 600.00
EAMB Mike Bibby 15.00 40.00
EAMC Mike Conley Jr. 40.00 100.00
EAPP Paul Pierce 40.00 100.00
EARA Ray Allen 75.00 150.00
EARF Raymond Felton 15.00 40.00
EARJ Richard Jefferson 15.00 40.00
EASB Shannon Brown 15.00 40.00
EASL Shaun Livingston 15.00 40.00
EATC Tyson Chandler 15.00 40.00
EATP Tayshaun Prince 15.00 40.00
EAVC Vince Carter 30.00 80.00

2007-08 Exquisite Collection Boxes

VALUES LISTED FOR AUTO EMPTY BOX
AH Al Horford/15 125.00 250.00
JJ Michael Jordan 500.00 1000.00
LeBron James/23
KB Kobe Bryant/24 400.00 600.00
KD Kevin Durant/35 400.00 800.00
LJ LeBron James/23 300.00 550.00
MJ Michael Jordan/23 500.00 700.00
SN Steve Nash/13 75.00 150.00
YM Yao Ming/11 75.00 150.00

2007-08 Exquisite Collection Draft Picks Reservation

A-F PRINT RUN 99 SER.#'d SETS
G-L PRINT RUN 199 SER.#'d SETS
DPA O.J. Mayo/99 300.00 600.00
Michael Beasley
Derrick Rose
DPB O.J. Mayo/99 60.00 150.00
Michael Beasley
Eric Gordon
DPC O.J. Mayo/99 40.00 100.00
Eric Gordon
Jerryd Bayless
DPD D.J. Augustin/99 175.00 350.00
Derrick Rose
Russell Westbrook
DPE Michael Beasley/99 50.00 120.00
Kevin Love
Joe Alexander
DPF Derrick Rose/99 125.00 250.00
Eric Gordon
Jerryd Bayless
DPG Brook Lopez/199 15.00 40.00
Jason Thompson
Joe Alexander
DPH Danilo Gallinari/199 100.00 250.00
Kevin Love
Russell Westbrook
DPI Brandon Rush/199 40.00 100.00
Danilo Gallinari
Russell Westbrook
DPJ D.J. Augustin/199 15.00 40.00
Brandon Rush
Jerryd Bayless
DPK Jason Thompson/199 15.00 40.00
Marreese Speights
Joe Alexander
DPL Roy Hibbert/199 25.00 50.00
Brook Lopez
Robin Lopez

2007-08 Exquisite Collection Enshrinements

PRINT RUN 25 SER.#'d SETS
ENAE Alex English 20.00 40.00
ENAR Arnie Risen 20.00 40.00
ENBL Bill Laimbeer 20.00 40.00
ENBR Bill Russell 75.00 200.00
ENBS Bill Sharman 20.00 40.00
ENBW Bill Walton 20.00 40.00
ENCD Clyde Drexler 40.00 80.00
ENCH Connie Hawkins 30.00 60.00
ENDR David Robinson 60.00 150.00
ENDT David Thompson 20.00 40.00
ENDW Dominique Wilkins 30.00 60.00
ENEB Elgin Baylor 40.00 80.00
ENGE George Gervin 25.00 60.00
ENGG Gail Goodrich 25.00 50.00
ENHO Hakeem Olajuwon 25.00 50.00
ENJE Julius Erving 50.00 120.00
ENJH John Havlicek 30.00 80.00
ENJK Jason Kidd 30.00 80.00
ENJL Jerry Lucas 25.00 60.00
ENJO Michael Jordan 400.00 700.00
ENJS John Stockton 75.00 150.00
ENJW James Worthy 40.00 80.00
ENKA Kareem Abdul-Jabbar 50.00 100.00
ENKB Kobe Bryant 200.00 400.00
ENKG Kevin Garnett 75.00 150.00
ENLA Bob Lanier 20.00 40.00
ENLB Larry Bird 50.00 125.00
ENLJ LeBron James 150.00 300.00
ENMJ Magic Johnson 50.00 100.00
ENMM Moses Malone 30.00 60.00
ENPP Paul Pierce 25.00 50.00
ENPR Pat Riley 20.00 40.00
ENRB Rick Barry 20.00 40.00
ENRO Dennis Rodman 40.00 80.00
ENRP Robert Parish 20.00 40.00
ENSK Steve Kerr 20.00 40.00
ENSN Steve Nash 40.00 100.00
ENTM Tracy McGrady 30.00 80.00
ENTP Tony Parker 20.00 40.00
ENVC Vince Carter 30.00 60.00
ENWE Jerry West 60.00 120.00
ENWF Walt Frazier 20.00 40.00
ENWU Wes Unseld 20.00 40.00

2007-08 Exquisite Collection Exclusives Autographs

STATED PRINT RUN 5 TO 35 SER.#'d SETS
SOME UNPRICED DUE TO SCARCITY
AH Al Horford/15 25.00 60.00
JG Jeff Green/22 25.00 60.00
JW Julian Wright/32 25.00 60.00
KB Kobe Bryant/24 250.00 500.00
KD Kevin Durant/35 400.00 800.00
LJ LeBron James/23 250.00 500.00
MJ Michael Jordan/23 400.00 800.00
SN Steve Nash/13 100.00 200.00
YM Yao Ming/11 30.00 80.00

2007-08 Exquisite Collection Exclusives Autographs Patches

STATED PRINT RUN 5 TO 35 SER.#'d SETS
SOME UNPRICED DUE TO SCARCITY
AH Al Horford/15 50.00 120.00
JN Joakim Noah/13 75.00 150.00
KB Kobe Bryant/24 400.00 700.00
KD Kevin Durant/35 600.00 1200.00
LJ LeBron James/23 300.00 600.00
MJ Michael Jordan/23 900.00 1500.00
SN Steve Nash/13 150.00 300.00
YM Yao Ming/11 50.00 120.00

2007-08 Exquisite Collection Exclusives Autographs Dual

STATED PRINT RUN 23 SER.#'d SETS
AMJLJ Michael Jordan 600.00 1000.00
LeBron James

2007-08 Exquisite Collection Exclusives Autographs Patches Dual

STATED PRINT RUN 23 SER.#'d SETS
PMJLJ Michael Jordan 800.00 1200.00
LeBron James

2007-08 Exquisite Collection Exclusives Memorabilia

STATED PRINT RUN 5 TO 35 SER.#'d SETS
SOME UNPRICED DUE TO SCARCITY
MAH Al Horford/15 12.50 30.00
MJN Joakim Noah/13 25.00 60.00
MJW Julian Wright/32 10.00 25.00
MKB Kobe Bryant/24 40.00 80.00
MKD Kevin Durant/35 60.00 150.00
MLJ LeBron James/23 50.00 100.00
MMJ Michael Jordan/23 100.00 200.00
MSN Steve Nash/13 20.00 50.00
MYM Yao Ming/11 15.00 40.00

2007-08 Exquisite Collection Exclusives Memorabilia Dual

STATED PRINT RUN 23 SER.#'d SETS
MMJLJ Michael Jordan 100.00 225.00
LeBron James

2007-08 Exquisite Collection Extra Quad Jerseys

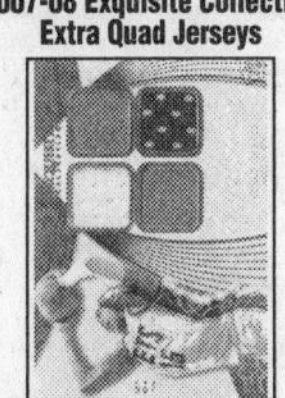

PRINT RUN 25 SER.#'d SETS
UNPRICED AUTO PRINT RUN 10 SETS
UNPRICED PATCH AUTO PRINT RUN 3 SETS
EQAD Adrian Dantley 5.00 12.00
EQAH Al Harrington 5.00 12.00
EQAI Andre Iguodala 5.00 12.00
EQAJ Al Jefferson 5.00 12.00
EQAM Alonzo Mourning 20.00 40.00
EQBD Baron Davis 5.00 12.00
EQBG Ben Gordon 5.00 12.00
EQBK Bernard King 5.00 12.00
EQBL Bill Laimbeer 5.00 12.00
EQBR Brandon Roy 6.00 15.00
EQCA Carmelo Anthony 8.00 20.00
EQCB Chris Bosh 8.00 20.00
EQCD Clyde Drexler 15.00 30.00
EQCM Corey Maggette 5.00 12.00
EQCP Chris Paul 10.00 25.00
EQDH Dwight Howard 10.00 25.00
EQDR David Robinson 15.00 30.00
EQDW Deron Williams 8.00 20.00
EQEO Emeka Okafor 5.00 12.00
EQFE Raymond Felton 5.00 12.00
EQGG George Gervin 5.00 12.00
EQHO Hakeem Olajuwon 8.00 20.00
EQJA Antawn Jamison 5.00 12.00
EQJE Julius Erving 15.00 40.00
EQJK Jason Kidd 6.00 15.00
EQJO Jermaine O'Neal 5.00 12.00
EQJS John Stockton 8.00 20.00
EQJW Jerry West 15.00 40.00
EQKA Kareem Abdul-Jabbar 8.00 20.00
EQKB Kobe Bryant 40.00 100.00
EQKG Kevin Garnett 15.00 30.00
EQKH Kirk Hinrich 5.00 12.00
EQLA LaMarcus Aldridge 5.00 12.00
EQLB Leandro Barbosa 5.00 12.00
EQLH Larry Hughes 5.00 12.00
EQLJ LeBron James 40.00 100.00
EQMA Magic Johnson 15.00 40.00
EQMB Mike Bibby 5.00 12.00
EQME Mark Eaton 5.00 12.00
EQMJ Michael Jordan 75.00 200.00
EQMM Moses Malone 5.00 12.00
EQMR Micheal Ray Richardson 5.00 12.00
EQMU Chris Mullin 5.00 12.00
EQPP Paul Pierce 8.00 20.00
EQPR Tayshaun Prince 5.00 12.00
EQRF Randy Foye 5.00 12.00
EQRG Rudy Gay 5.00 12.00
EQRJ Richard Jefferson 5.00 12.00
EQRO Dennis Rodman 8.00 20.00
EQRT Reggie Theus 5.00 12.00
EQSB Shannon Brown 5.00 12.00
EQSM Shawn Marion 5.00 12.00
EQSN Steve Nash 6.00 15.00
EQTC Tom Chambers 5.00 12.00
EQTM Tracy McGrady 6.00 15.00
EQTP Tony Parker 6.00 15.00
EQTT Tyrus Thomas 5.00 12.00
EQVC Vince Carter 10.00 25.00
EQWO James Worthy 10.00 25.00
EQYM Yao Ming 6.00 15.00

2007-08 Exquisite Collection Finalists Autographs Dual

PRINT RUN 25 SER.#'d SETS
FABG Rick Barry 30.00 60.00
Hal Greer
FABK Kobe Bryant 200.00 350.00
Jason Kidd
FABS Kobe Bryant 200.00 400.00
John Stockton
FACD Tom Chambers 50.00 100.00
Clyde Drexler
FAEJ Julius Erving 200.00 350.00
Kareem Abdul-Jabbar
FAEW Julius Erving 60.00 120.00
Bill Walton
FAFJ Derek Fisher 30.00 60.00
Richard Jefferson
FAGC Horace Grant 30.00 60.00
Tom Chambers
FAGL Horace Grant 30.00 60.00
Bill Laimbeer
FAHA John Havlicek 100.00 200.00
Kareem Abdul-Jabbar
FAJB Magic Johnson 250.00 450.00
Larry Bird
FAJP Tony Parker 150.00 300.00
LeBron James
FAJR Michael Jordan 300.00 600.00
Dennis Rodman
FALA Bill Laimbeer 75.00 150.00
Kareem Abdul-Jabbar
FANP Steve Nash 50.00 120.00
Tony Parker
FAOP Hakeem Olajuwon 40.00 80.00
Robert Parish
FAOR Hakeem Olajuwon 75.00 150.00
David Robinson
FAPJ Tayshaun Prince 175.00 350.00
LeBron James
FAPW Tony Parker 30.00 60.00
Deron Williams
FAWE James Worthy 50.00 100.00
Julius Erving

2007-08 Exquisite Collection Inscriptions

PRINT RUN 25 SER.#'d SETS
IAAD Adrian Dantley 2-Time Scoring 25.00 60.00
IAAM Alonzo Mourning ZO 100.00 200.00
IABD Baron Davis BDiddy 60.00 120.00
IABI Larry Bird None 75.00 200.00
IABL Bill Laimbeer Bad Boys 50.00 100.00
IABR Brandon Roy ROY 60.00 120.00
IACP Chris Paul 40.00 100.00
IADA Brad Daugherty No 1 Pick 20.00 50.00
IADG Daniel Gibson None 15.00 40.00
IADH Dwight Howard Superman 125.00 250.00
IADR David Robinson Admiral 75.00 200.00
IADT David Thompson Skywalker 25.00 50.00
IADW Dominique Wilkins 50.00 100.00
IAGG George Gervin None 25.00 60.00
IAGO Gail Goodrich None 25.00 60.00
IAHO Hakeem Olajuwon 75.00 150.00
IAJK Jason Kidd 6 Time All-NBA 75.00 200.00
IAJW James Worthy 50.00 125.00
IAKA Kareem Abdul-Jabbar None 60.00 150.00
IAKB Kobe Bryant Black Mamba 1800.00 3000.00
IAKG Kevin Garnett Big Ticket 350.00 600.00
IALB Leandro Barbosa #10 15.00 40.00
IALJ LeBron James Chosen One 500.00 1000.00
IAMC Michael Cooper 25.00 60.00
IAMJ Magic Johnson 5 Rings 125.00 250.00
IAMP Morris Peterson MoPete 15.00 40.00
IAPR Tayshaun Prince Palace Prince 30.00 80.00
IARO Dennis Rodman The Worm 125.00 250.00
IARP Robert Parish 60.00 120.00
IASM Sidney Moncrief Squid 20.00 50.00
IASN Steve Nash None 50.00 125.00
IASP Sam Perkins Big Smooth 40.00 80.00
IATM Tracy McGrady Mac Man 50.00 125.00
IATP Tony Parker 30.00 80.00
IAVC Vince Carter VC 100.00 200.00
IAWA Slick Watts 25.00 50.00
IAWE Jerry West Mr. Clutch 100.00 250.00
IAWF Walt Frazier 30.00 80.00

2007-08 Exquisite Collection Jerseys

PRINT RUN 25 SER.#'d SETS
UNPRICED PATCH PRINT RUN 10 SETS
UNPRICED PATCH AUTO PRINT RUN ONE SET
1 LeBron James 60.00 150.00
2 Yao Ming 15.00 40.00
3 Kobe Bryant 75.00 200.00
4 Dwyane Wade 30.00 80.00
5 Tracy McGrady 12.00 30.00
6 Allen Iverson 15.00 40.00
7 Shaquille O'Neal 25.00 60.00
8 Kevin Garnett 25.00 60.00
9 Steve Nash 15.00 40.00
10 Dwight Howard 20.00 50.00
11 Gilbert Arenas 12.00 30.00
12 Vince Carter 15.00 40.00
13 Tim Duncan 20.00 50.00
14 Carmelo Anthony 15.00 40.00
15 Dirk Nowitzki 15.00 40.00
16 Amare Stoudemire 12.00 30.00
17 Chris Bosh 12.00 30.00
18 Jermaine O'Neal 12.00 30.00
19 Jason Kidd 12.00 30.00
20 Ben Wallace 12.00 30.00
21 Paul Pierce 15.00 40.00
22 Shawn Marion 12.00 30.00
23 Michael Jordan 150.00 400.00
24 Manu Ginobili 12.00 30.00
25 Tony Parker 12.00 30.00
26 Chauncey Billups 12.00 30.00
27 Chris Paul 25.00 60.00
28 Andre Iguodala 12.00 30.00
29 Stephon Marbury 10.00 25.00
30 Ray Allen 15.00 40.00
31 Lamar Odom 12.00 30.00
32 Jason Terry 10.00 25.00
33 Josh Howard 10.00 25.00
34 Caron Butler 12.00 30.00
35 Emeka Okafor 12.00 30.00
36 Marcus Camby 8.00 20.00
37 Pau Gasol 12.00 30.00
38 Carlos Boozer 12.00 30.00
39 Baron Davis 12.00 30.00
40 Michael Redd 12.00 30.00
41 Ben Gordon 12.00 30.00
42 Richard Hamilton 10.00 25.00
43 Andrew Bogut 12.00 30.00
44 Tyson Chandler 10.00 25.00
45 Eddy Curry 8.00 20.00
46 Larry Hughes 10.00 25.00
47 LaMarcus Aldridge 15.00 40.00
48 Andrea Bargnani 15.00 40.00
49 Mike Bibby 12.00 30.00
50 Elton Brand 12.00 30.00
51 Al Harrington 10.00 25.00
52 Al Jefferson 12.00 30.00
53 Joe Johnson 12.00 30.00
54 Rashard Lewis 10.00 25.00
55 Kevin Martin 12.00 30.00
56 Andre Miller 10.00 25.00
57 Brandon Roy 15.00 40.00
58 Gerald Wallace 12.00 30.00
59 Rasheed Wallace 12.00 30.00
60 Deron Williams 20.00 50.00

2007-08 Exquisite Collection Limited Logos

PRINT RUN 50 SER.#'d SETS
LLAB Andrew Bogut 40.00 100.00
LLAI Andre Iguodala 30.00 80.00
LLAJ Al Jefferson 25.00 60.00
LLAL Al Horford 40.00 100.00
LLAM Alonzo Mourning 75.00 200.00
LLBD Baron Davis 25.00 60.00
LLBG Ben Gordon 25.00 60.00
LLBO Chris Bosh 50.00 120.00
LLBR Brandon Roy 60.00 150.00
LLCA Carmelo Anthony 75.00 200.00
LLCB Carlos Boozer 25.00 60.00
LLCP Chris Paul 100.00 200.00
LLDH Dwight Howard 100.00 175.00
LLDW Deron Williams 50.00 120.00
LLGG George Gervin 40.00 80.00
LLHA Al Harrington 25.00 60.00
LLJA Antawn Jamison 25.00 60.00
LLJK Jason Kidd 50.00 120.00
LLKB Kobe Bryant 1000.00 2000.00
LLKD Kevin Durant 2000.00 3000.00
LLKG Kevin Garnett 200.00 400.00
LLKH Kirk Hinrich 25.00 60.00
LLLA LaMarcus Aldridge 40.00 100.00
LLLH Larry Hughes 25.00 60.00
LLLJ LeBron James 500.00 800.00
LLMB Mike Bibby 25.00 60.00
LLNA Nate Archibald 50.00 120.00
LLPA Tony Parker 75.00 200.00
LLPP Paul Pierce 60.00 120.00
LLRF Randy Foye 25.00 60.00
LLRG Rudy Gay 40.00 80.00
LLRJ Richard Jefferson 25.00 60.00
LLRL Rashard Lewis 25.00 60.00
LLSB Shannon Brown 25.00 60.00
LLSL Shaun Livingston 25.00 60.00
LLSW Shelden Williams 25.00 60.00
LLTJ T.J. Ford 25.00 60.00
LLTM Tracy McGrady 60.00 150.00
LLTP Tayshaun Prince 25.00 60.00
LLVC Vince Carter 60.00 150.00
LLYM Yao Ming 75.00 150.00

2007-08 Exquisite Collection Noble Nameplates

PRINT RUN 25 SER.#'d SETS
NPAB Andrew Bogut 40.00 80.00
NPAH Al Harrington 15.00 40.00
NPAI Andre Iguodala 15.00 40.00
NPAJ Al Jefferson 15.00 40.00
NPAL Al Horford 40.00 100.00
NPAM Alonzo Mourning 75.00 150.00
NPAS Amare Stoudemire 60.00 120.00
NPBD Baron Davis 20.00 50.00
NPBG Ben Gordon 25.00 50.00
NPBO Chris Bosh 40.00 100.00
NPBR Brandon Roy 60.00 120.00
NPBY Andrew Bynum 50.00 120.00
NPCA Carmelo Anthony 40.00 100.00
NPCB Carlos Boozer 20.00 50.00
NPCO Corey Brewer 15.00 40.00
NPCP Chris Paul 100.00 200.00
NPDG Daniel Gibson 15.00 40.00
NPDH Dwight Howard 60.00 150.00
NPDI Boris Diaw 15.00 40.00
NPDR David Robinson 60.00 120.00
NPDW Deron Williams 50.00 100.00
NPEC Eddy Curry 15.00 40.00
NPEO Emeka Okafor 15.00 40.00
NPGG George Gervin 30.00 60.00
NPGR Darrell Griffith 15.00 40.00
NPJA Antawn Jamison 15.00 40.00
NPJO Jermaine O'Neal 15.00 40.00
NPKB Kobe Bryant 400.00 750.00
NPKD Kevin Durant 400.00 800.00
NPKG Kevin Garnett 100.00 200.00
NPKH Kirk Hinrich 20.00 50.00
NPKK Jason Kidd 25.00 50.00
NPLA LaMarcus Aldridge 30.00 80.00
NPLH Larry Hughes 15.00 40.00
NPLJ LeBron James 300.00 600.00
NPMB Mike Bibby 15.00 40.00
NPMM Moses Malone 30.00 60.00
NPMP Morris Peterson 15.00 40.00
NPPA Tony Parker 25.00 60.00
NPRF Raymond Felton 15.00 40.00
NPRG Rudy Gay 20.00 50.00
NPRJ Richard Jefferson 15.00 40.00
NPRO Dennis Rodman 75.00 150.00
NPSB Shane Battier 15.00 40.00
NPSH Shannon Brown 15.00 40.00
NPSL Shaun Livingston 15.00 40.00
NPSN Steve Nash 75.00 200.00
NPSS Stromile Swift 15.00 40.00
NPSW Shelden Williams 15.00 40.00
NPTJ T.J. Ford 15.00 40.00
NPTM Tracy McGrady 50.00 100.00
NPTP Tayshaun Prince 15.00 40.00
NPTT Tyrus Thomas 15.00 40.00
NPVC Vince Carter 75.00 150.00
NPYM Yao Ming 60.00 150.00

2007-08 Exquisite Collection Numbers

STATED PRINT RUN ONE TO 50 SER.#'d SETS
SOME UNPRICED DUE TO SCARCITY
ENAH Al Horford/15 50.00 120.00
ENAJ Al Jefferson/25 25.00 60.00
ENAM Alonzo Mourning/33 175.00 350.00
ENAT Alando Tucker/29 20.00 50.00
ENCA Carmelo Anthony/15 100.00 200.00
ENCB Corey Brewer/11 30.00 80.00
ENCD Clyde Drexler/22 60.00 120.00
ENCM Corey Maggette/50 20.00 50.00
ENDC Daequan Cook/14 20.00 50.00
ENDG Danny Granger/33 25.00 60.00
ENDH Dwight Howard/12 150.00 300.00
ENDR David Robinson/50 50.00 120.00
ENHO Hakeem Olajuwon/34 60.00 150.00
ENJG Jeff Green/22 50.00 120.00
ENJN Joakim Noah/13 100.00 225.00
ENJO Magic Johnson/32 125.00 250.00
ENJS Jason Smith/14 20.00 50.00
ENJW Jerry West/44 100.00 225.00
ENKA Kareem Abdul-Jabbar/33 125.00 250.00
ENKB Kobe Bryant/24 500.00 800.00
ENKD Kevin Durant/35 900.00 1500.00
ENKH Kirk Hinrich/12 40.00 100.00
ENLA LaMarcus Aldridge/12 60.00 150.00
ENLB Larry Bird/33 125.00 250.00
ENLJ LeBron James/23- 400.00 700.00
ENMA Morris Almond/22 20.00 50.00
ENMB Marco Belinelli/18 30.00 80.00
ENMJ Michael Jordan/23 1000.00 1800.00
ENMM Moses Malone/24 40.00 80.00
ENMR Micheal Ray Richardson/20 20.00 50.00
ENPP Paul Pierce/34 50.00 120.00
ENRA Ray Allen/20 60.00 120.00

ENRF Raymond Felton/20 20.00 50.00
ENRG Rudy Gay/22 25.00 60.00
ENRJ Richard Jefferson/24 20.00 50.00
ENRT Reggie Theus/24 20.00 50.00
ENSH Spencer Hawes/31 25.00 60.00
ENSN Steve Nash/13 125.00 250.00
ENSW Sean Williams/51 20.00 50.00
ENTC Tom Chambers/24 20.00 50.00
ENTH Al Thornton/12 30.00 80.00
ENTP Tayshaun Prince/22 25.00 60.00
ENTT Tyrus Thomas/24 40.00 100.00
ENVC Vince Carter/15 125.00 250.00
ENVD Vlade Divac/13 60.00 150.00
ENWC Wilson Chandler/21 40.00 100.00
ENWO James Worthy/42 60.00 120.00
ENWR Julian Wright/32 20.00 50.00
ENYM Yao Ming/11 125.00 250.00

2007-08 Exquisite Collection Numbers Dual

STATED PRINT RUN ONE TO 44 SER.#'d SETS
SOME UNPRICED DUE TO SCARCITY
AH Carmelo Anthony/15 80.00 160.00
Al Horford
BA Larry Bird/33 150.00 300.00
Kareem Abdul-Jabbar
BM Kobe Bryant/24 200.00 400.00
Moses Malone
CH Vince Carter/15 100.00 200.00
Al Horford
DH Kevin Durant/35 250.00 500.00
Herbert Hill
FC T.J. Ford/11 50.00 100.00
Mike Conley Jr.
GD Darrell Griffith/35 250.00 500.00
Kevin Durant
GG Rudy Gay/22 60.00 120.00
Jeff Green
HA Dwight Howard/12 100.00 200.00
LaMarcus Aldridge
HS Kirk Hinrich/12 100.00 200.00
John Stockton
JJ Michael Jordan/23 1000.00 1500.00
LeBron James
JT Richard Jefferson/24 30.00 80.00
Tyrus Thomas
MD Yao Ming/11 100.00 200.00
Glen Davis
NN Steve Nash/13 100.00 200.00
Joakim Noah
NP Joakim Noah/13 30.00 80.00
Gabe Pruitt
OP Hakeem Olajuwon/34 50.00 100.00
Paul Pierce
PD Tayshaun Prince/22 100.00 200.00
Clyde Drexler
RW Julian Wright/32 30.00 80.00
Chris Richard
SC Jason Smith/14 30.00 80.00
Daequan Cook
TH Dwight Howard/12 75.00 150.00
Al Thornton
WG Jerry West/44 75.00 150.00
George Gervin

2007-08 Exquisite Collection Rookie Parallel

SOME UNPRICED DUE TO SCARCITY
62 Morris Almond JSY AU/22 20.00 50.00
63 Julian Wright JSY AU/22 20.00 50.00
64 Aaron Brooks JSY AU/10 75.00 150.00
66 Wilson Chandler JSY AU 60.00 120.00
67 Daequan Cook JSY AU/14 40.00 100.00
69 Jermareo Davidson JSY AU/23 20.00 50.00
70 Glen Davis JSY AU/11 75.00 150.00
72 Corey Brewer JSY AU/22 25.00 60.00
73 Aaron Gray JSY AU/34 20.00 50.00
74 Taurean Green JSY AU 20.00 50.00
76 Spencer Hawes JSY AU/31 40.00 100.00
77 Al Horford JSY AU/35 125.00 250.00
78 Jeff Green JSY AU/22 75.00 150.00
79 Carl Landry JSY AU/10 75.00 150.00
80 Mike Conley Jr. JSY AU/11 50.00 120.00
81 Acie Law JSY AU 30.00 80.00
82 Dominic McGuire JSY AU 20.00 50.00
84 Demetris Nichols JSY AU/35 20.00 50.00
85 Joakim Noah JSY AU/13 250.00 400.00
86 Gabe Pruitt JSY AU/13 20.00 50.00
87 Chris Richard JSY AU/32 20.00 50.00
88 Jason Smith JSY AU/14 20.00 50.00
91 Sean Williams JSY AU/51 20.00 50.00
92 Al Thornton JSY AU/12 60.00 150.00
93 Alando Tucker JSY AU/29 20.00 50.00
94 Kevin Durant JSY AU/35 4000.00 6500.00
95 Marco Belinelli JSY AU/18 40.00 100.00
96 Luis Scola JSY AU 150.00 300.00
97 Louis Amundson JSY AU/20 20.00 50.00
98 C.J. Watson AU/23 20.00 50.00
99 Cheikh Samb AU/35 20.00 50.00
104 Coby Karl AU/11 20.00 50.00
105 Oleksiy Pecherov AU/14 20.00 50.00
106 Jamario Moon AU/33 20.00 50.00
107 Kyrylo Fesenko/44 20.00 50.00
109 Brandan Wright/32 20.00 50.00
110 Thaddeus Young/21 25.00 60.00
112 Greg Oden/52 40.00 100.00

2007-08 Exquisite Collection Scripted Swatches

PRINT RUN 15 SER.#'d SETS
UNPRICED DUAL PRINT RUN 5 SETS
SSAB Andrew Bogut 25.00 60.00
SSAH Al Harrington 15.00 40.00
SSAI Andre Iguodala 25.00 60.00
SSAJ Al Jefferson 25.00 60.00
SSAM Alonzo Mourning 125.00 250.00
SSBG Ben Gordon 25.00 60.00
SSBI Chauncey Billups 30.00 60.00
SSBO Chris Bosh 40.00 80.00
SSBR Brandon Roy 50.00 100.00
SSCA Carmelo Anthony 80.00 160.00
SSCK Chris Kaman 15.00 40.00
SSCM Chris Mullin 40.00 80.00
SSCO Corey Maggette 25.00 50.00
SSCP Chris Paul 100.00 200.00
SSDG Daniel Gibson 15.00 40.00
SSDH Dwight Howard 60.00 120.00
SSDI Boris Diaw 15.00 40.00
SSDM Desmond Mason 15.00 40.00
SSDR David Robinson 75.00 150.00
SSDW Deron Williams 50.00 120.00
SSEC Eddy Curry 15.00 40.00
SSEO Emeka Okafor 15.00 40.00
SSFE Raymond Felton 15.00 40.00
SSGG George Gervin 40.00 80.00
SSJA Antawn Jamison 15.00 40.00
SSJF Jordan Farmar 15.00 40.00
SSJH John Havlicek 50.00 100.00
SSJK Jason Kidd 60.00 120.00
SSJO Jermaine O'Neal 25.00 50.00
SSJS John Stockton 75.00 150.00
SSKB Kobe Bryant 500.00 900.00
SSKG Kevin Garnett 150.00 300.00
SSKH Kirk Hinrich 25.00 60.00
SSLA LaMarcus Aldridge 30.00 80.00
SSLB Larry Bird 75.00 150.00
SSLH Larry Hughes 15.00 40.00
SSLJ LeBron James 250.00 500.00
SSMA Donyell Marshall 15.00 40.00
SSMB Mike Bibby 15.00 40.00
SSMI Michael Jordan 1000.00 1800.00
SSMJ Magic Johnson 75.00 150.00
SSMM Moses Malone 40.00 80.00
SSMP Morris Peterson 15.00 40.00
SSPA Tony Parker 40.00 80.00
SSPP Paul Pierce 40.00 80.00
SSPR Mark Price 75.00 150.00
SSRC Rodney Carney 15.00 40.00
SSRF Randy Foye 15.00 40.00
SSRG Rudy Gay 40.00 80.00
SSRH Richard Hamilton 20.00 50.00
SSRJ Richard Jefferson 15.00 40.00
SSRL Rashard Lewis 30.00 80.00
SSRO Dennis Rodman 100.00 200.00
SSSB Shane Battier 15.00 40.00
SSSH Shannon Brown 20.00 50.00
SSSL Shaun Livingston 15.00 40.00
SSSN Steve Nash 125.00 250.00
SSSW Shelden Williams 15.00 40.00
SSTJ T.J. Ford 15.00 40.00
SSTM Tracy McGrady 50.00 100.00
SSTP Tayshaun Prince 25.00 60.00
SSTT Tyrus Thomas 20.00 50.00
SSVC Vince Carter 60.00 120.00
SSYM Yao Ming 50.00 100.00

2007-08 Exquisite Collection Uncut Sheet Redemptions

COMMON EXCH (1-22) 200.00 300.00
NO ODDS GIVEN

2008-09 Exquisite Collection

1-60 PRINT RUN 125 SER.#'d SETS
STATED PRINT RUN 55 TO 225 SER.#'d SETS
UNPRICED BLACK PRINT RUN ONE SET
UNPRICED PRESS PLATE PRINT RUN ONE SET
1 Kevin Garnett 10.00 25.00
2 LeBron James 50.00 120.00
3 Dwight Howard 10.00 25.00
4 Kobe Bryant 50.00 120.00
5 Carmelo Anthony 6.00 15.00
6 Tim Duncan 8.00 20.00
7 Yao Ming 6.00 15.00
8 Dwyane Wade 20.00 50.00
9 Dirk Nowitzki 6.00 15.00
10 Jason Kidd 5.00 12.00
11 Allen Iverson 6.00 15.00
12 Tracy McGrady 5.00 12.00
13 Steve Nash 5.00 12.00
14 Ray Allen 5.00 12.00
15 Amare Stoudemire 5.00 12.00
16 Vince Carter 6.00 15.00
17 Shaquille O'Neal 10.00 25.00
18 Chris Bosh 5.00 12.00
19 Gilbert Arenas 5.00 12.00
20 Chauncey Billups 5.00 12.00
21 Paul Pierce 6.00 15.00
22 Chris Paul 8.00 20.00
23 Michael Jordan 100.00 250.00
24 Carlos Boozer 5.00 12.00
25 Manu Ginobili 5.00 12.00
26 Shawn Marion 5.00 12.00
27 Tony Parker 5.00 12.00
28 Baron Davis 5.00 12.00
29 Kevin Durant 30.00 80.00
30 Josh Howard 4.00 10.00
31 Marcus Camby 3.00 8.00
32 Michael Redd 5.00 12.00
33 Caron Butler 5.00 12.00
34 Richard Hamilton 4.00 10.00
35 Andrea Bargnani 4.00 10.00
36 Tyson Chandler 4.00 10.00
37 Andrew Bogut 5.00 12.00
38 Joe Johnson 5.00 12.00
39 T.J. Ford 3.00 8.00
40 Rashard Lewis 4.00 10.00
41 Pau Gasol 5.00 12.00
42 David Lee 4.00 10.00
43 Andre Iguodala 5.00 12.00
44 Greg Oden 5.00 12.00
45 Corey Maggette 4.00 10.00
46 Andrew Bynum 6.00 15.00
47 Mo Williams 4.00 10.00
48 Elton Brand 5.00 12.00
49 Ben Gordon 5.00 12.00
50 Danny Granger 5.00 12.00
51 Richard Jefferson 5.00 12.00
52 Al Horford 5.00 12.00
53 Gerald Wallace 5.00 12.00
54 Rudy Gay 5.00 12.00
55 Deron Williams 5.00 12.00
56 Corey Brewer 4.00 10.00
57 Monta Ellis 5.00 12.00
58 Kevin Martin 5.00 12.00
59 Luol Deng 5.00 12.00
60 Brandon Roy 5.00 12.00
61 Kevin Love JSY AU RC 500.00 800.00
62 Joe Alexander JSY AU RC 12.00 30.00
63 D.J. Augustin JSY AU RC 20.00 50.00
64 Brook Lopez JSY AU RC 75.00 150.00
65 Jason Thompson JSY AU RC 15.00 40.00
66 Brandon Rush JSY AU RC 20.00 50.00
67 Anthony Randolph JSY AU RC 40.00 100.00
68 Robin Lopez JSY AU RC 12.00 30.00
69 Marreese Speights JSY AU RC 15.00 40.00
70 Roy Hibbert JSY AU RC 40.00 100.00
71 Javale McGee JSY AU RC 40.00 100.00
72 J.J. Hickson JSY AU RC 25.00 60.00
73 Ryan Anderson JSY AU RC 30.00 60.00
74 Courtney Lee JSY AU RC 40.00 80.00
75 Kosta Koufos JSY AU RC 12.00 30.00
76 George Hill JSY AU RC 30.00 80.00
77 Darrell Arthur JSY AU RC 20.00 50.00
78 Donte Greene JSY AU RC 12.00 30.00
79 D.J. White JSY AU/55 RC 30.00 60.00
80 J.R. Giddens JSY AU RC 12.00 30.00
81 Walter Sharpe JSY AU RC 12.00 30.00
82 Joey Dorsey JSY AU RC 12.00 30.00
83 Mario Chalmers JSY AU RC 40.00 70.00
84 DeAndre Jordan JSY AU RC 50.00 125.00
85 Kyle Weaver JSY AU RC 12.00 30.00
86 Sonny Weems JSY AU RC 12.00 30.00
87 Chris Douglas-Roberts JSY AU RC12.00 30.00
88 Rudy Fernandez JSY AU RC 40.00 80.00
89 Marc Gasol JSY AU/150 RC 50.00 120.00
90 O.J. Mayo JSY AU/99 RC 150.00 300.00
91 Michael Beasley JSY AU/99 RC 125.00 250.00
92 Derrick Rose JSY AU/99 RC 2500.00 3800.00
93 Russell Westbrook JSY AU RC 600.00 1100.00
94 Eric Gordon JSY AU RC 175.00 350.00
95 Nicolas Batum AU/99 RC 75.00 150.00
96 Mike Taylor AU/99 RC 10.00 25.00
97 Alexis Ajinca AU/99 RC 10.00 25.00
98 Luc Mbah A Moute AU/99 RC 10.00 25.00
99 Sean Singletary AU/99 RC 10.00 25.00
100 Danilo Gallinari AU/99 RC 75.00 150.00
NNO Uncut Sheet EXCH 100.00 200.00

2008-09 Exquisite Collection Gold

*1-50 GOLD: 1X TO 2.5X BASE HI
1-50 PRINT RUN 50 SER.#'d SETS
51-100 PRINT RUN 25 SER.#'d SETS
8 Dwyane Wade 75.00 150.00
14 Ray Allen 15.00 40.00
23 Michael Jordan 200.00 500.00
29 Kevin Durant 125.00 225.00
61 Kevin Love 150.00 300.00
62 Joe Alexander 15.00 40.00
63 D.J. Augustin 15.00 40.00
64 Brook Lopez 25.00 60.00
65 Jason Thompson 15.00 40.00
66 Brandon Rush 15.00 40.00
67 Anthony Randolph 20.00 50.00
68 Robin Lopez 15.00 40.00
69 Marreese Speights 15.00 40.00
70 Roy Hibbert 25.00 60.00
71 JaVale McGee 25.00 60.00
72 J.J. Hickson 20.00 50.00
73 Ryan Anderson 25.00 60.00
74 Courtney Lee 30.00 80.00
75 Kosta Koufos 15.00 40.00
76 George Hill 25.00 60.00
77 Darrell Arthur 15.00 40.00
78 Donte Greene 15.00 40.00
79 D.J. White 15.00 40.00
80 J.R. Giddens 15.00 40.00
81 Walter Sharpe 15.00 40.00
82 Joey Dorsey 15.00 40.00
83 Mario Chalmers 25.00 60.00
84 DeAndre Jordan 30.00 80.00
85 Kyle Weaver 15.00 40.00
86 Sonny Weems 15.00 40.00
87 Chris Douglas-Roberts 15.00 40.00
88 Rudy Fernandez 30.00 80.00
89 Marc Gasol 40.00 100.00
90 O.J. Mayo 25.00 60.00
91 Michael Beasley 25.00 60.00
92 Derrick Rose 400.00 700.00
93 Russell Westbrook 200.00 400.00
94 Eric Gordon 50.00 125.00
95 Nicolas Batum 25.00 60.00
96 Mike Taylor 15.00 40.00
97 Alexis Ajinca 15.00 40.00
98 Luc Mbah A Moute 15.00 40.00
99 Sean Singletary 15.00 40.00
100 Danilo Gallinari 25.00 60.00

2008-09 Exquisite Collection Autographs

STATED PRINT RUN 23 TO 35 SER.#'d SETS
AUTOAD Adrian Dantley/35 10.00 25.00
AUTOAG Artis Gilmore/35 10.00 25.00
AUTOAH Al Horford/35 8.00 20.00
AUTOAM Alonzo Mourning/35 50.00 120.00
AUTOBB Bobby Brown/35 6.00 15.00
AUTOBL Bill Laimbeer/35 10.00 25.00
AUTOBO Bob Lanier/35 10.00 25.00
AUTOBW Bill Walton/35 12.50 30.00
AUTOCB Carlos Boozer/35 10.00 25.00
AUTOCL Clyde Drexler/35 30.00 80.00
AUTODC Daequan Cook/35 10.00 25.00
AUTODE Derrick Rose/35 400.00 600.00
AUTODF Derek Fisher/35 15.00 30.00
AUTODH Dwight Howard/35 40.00 100.00
AUTODO Dominique Wilkins/35 20.00 50.00
AUTODW Deron Williams/35 25.00 50.00
AUTOEG Eric Gordon/35 40.00 100.00
AUTOFE Rudy Fernandez/35 15.00 30.00
AUTOGG George Gervin/35 15.00 40.00
AUTOGW Gerald Wallace/35 6.00 15.00
AUTOJB Jose Barea/35 30.00 80.00
AUTOJH John Havlicek/35 30.00 80.00
AUTOKB Kobe Bryant/24 200.00 400.00
AUTOKD Kevin Durant/35 150.00 300.00
AUTOKG Kevin Garnett/35 50.00 120.00
AUTOLJ LeBron James/23 200.00 400.00
AUTOLO Lamar Odom/35 20.00 50.00
AUTOMB Michael Beasley/35 25.00 60.00
AUTOMC Mike Conley Jr./35 10.00 25.00
AUTOMG Marc Gasol/35 20.00 40.00
AUTOOM O.J. Mayo/35 25.00 60.00
AUTOOR Oscar Robertson/35 75.00 150.00
AUTORD Dennis Rodman/35 40.00 100.00
AUTORF Randy Foye/35 6.00 15.00
AUTORO Brandon Roy/35 25.00 60.00
AUTORP Robert Parish/35 10.00 25.00
AUTORS Rodney Stuckey/35 10.00 25.00
AUTORW Russell Westbrook/35 100.00 250.00
AUTOSI Jack Sikma/35 10.00 25.00
AUTOSM Sidney Moncrief/35 8.00 20.00
AUTOWF Walt Frazier/35 8.00 20.00

2008-09 Exquisite Collection Big Jersey Autographs

STATED PRINT RUN 10 SER.#'d SETS
SOME UNPRICED DUE TO SCARCITY
BIGBD Baron Davis 40.00 100.00
BIGDH Dwight Howard 125.00 250.00
BIGKB Kobe Bryant 600.00 1000.00
BIGKD Kevin Durant 250.00 500.00
BIGKG Kevin Garnett 150.00 300.00
BIGLJ LeBron James 300.00 600.00
BIGRS Rodney Stuckey 40.00 100.00
BIGSN Steve Nash 100.00 200.00

2008-09 Exquisite Collection Emblems of Endorsement

STATED PRINT RUN ONE TO 10 SER.#'d SETS
SOME UNPRICED DUE TO SCARCITY
EEAH Al Horford/10 50.00 100.00
EECP Chris Paul/10 450.00 800.00
EEDE Derrick Rose White/10 1400.00 2100.00
EEDR Derrick Rose Red/10 1400.00 2100.00
EEDW Deron Williams/10 150.00 300.00
EEGH George Hill/10 100.00 200.00
EEJB Jerryd Bayless/10 125.00 250.00
EEJG Jeff Green/10 100.00 200.00
EEJK Jason Kidd/10 150.00 300.00
EEJS John Stockton/10 150.00 300.00
EEJW Jerry West/10 100.00 200.00
EEKB Kobe Bryant/10 2000.00 4000.00
EEKD Kevin Durant/10 250.00 500.00
EEKG Kevin Garnett/10 400.00 750.00
EEMC Mike Conley Jr./10 50.00 100.00
EEMJ Michael Jordan/10 5000.00 8000.00
EEOJ O.J. Mayo/10 150.00 300.00
EEOM O.J. Mayo/10 150.00 300.00
EEPP Paul Pierce/10 125.00 250.00
EERF Rudy Fernandez/10 125.00 250.00
EERO David Robinson/10 125.00 250.00
EERS Rodney Stuckey/10 60.00 120.00
EESW Sonny Weems/10 50.00 100.00
EEVC Vince Carter/10 250.00 500.00

2008-09 Exquisite Collection Enshrinements

PRINT RUN 23 TO 25 SER.#'d SETS
ENBR Bill Russell/25 60.00 150.00
ENCP Chris Paul/25 50.00 100.00
ENDR David Robinson/25 40.00 80.00
ENDW Dominique Wilkins/25 25.00 50.00
ENHO Hakeem Olajuwon/25 25.00 60.00
ENIT Isiah Thomas/25 20.00 40.00
ENJE Julius Erving/25 50.00 125.00
ENJO Magic Johnson/25 50.00 125.00
ENJS John Stockton/25 50.00 125.00
ENJW Jerry West/25 75.00 150.00
ENKA Kareem Abdul-Jabbar/25 50.00 100.00
ENKB Kobe Bryant/24 300.00 500.00
ENKG Kevin Garnett/25 60.00 120.00
ENLB Larry Bird/25 60.00 150.00
ENLJ LeBron James/23 300.00 500.00
ENMJ Michael Jordan/23 1200.00 1800.00
ENOR Oscar Robertson/25 125.00 225.00
ENRP Robert Parish/25 20.00 40.00
ENVC Vince Carter/25 30.00 80.00
ENWF Walt Frazier/25 20.00 40.00

2008-09 Exquisite Collection Enshrinements Dual

STATED PRINT RUN 23 TO 25 SER.#'d SETS
ENDBA Kareem Abdul-Jabbar 50.00 100.00
Bob McAdoo
ENDBJ Kobe Bryant 500.00 800.00
LeBron James
ENDBP Kobe Bryant 250.00 500.00
Paul Pierce
ENDCK Michael Cooper 40.00 80.00
Mitch Kupchak
ENDCW Vince Carter 40.00 80.00
Dominique Wilkins
ENDGA George Gervin 25.00 60.00
Adrian Dantley
ENDJB Magic Johnson 125.00 250.00
Larry Bird
ENDJJ Michael Jordan/23 1000.00 1800.00
LeBron James/23
ENDJR Michael Jordan 700.00 1200.00
Dennis Rodman
ENDKM Michael Jordan 1200.00 2000.00
Kobe Bryant
ENDMG Alonzo Mourning 100.00 200.00
Kevin Garnett
ENDMM Yao Ming 40.00 100.00
Tracy McGrady
ENDNK Jason Kidd 60.00 120.00
Steve Nash
ENDOR Hakeem Olajuwon 60.00 120.00
David Robinson
ENDRH John Havlicek 100.00 200.00
Bill Russell
ENDRJ Oscar Robertson 250.00 450.00
LeBron James
ENDSH Amare Stoudemire 50.00 100.00
Dwight Howard
ENDTP Isiah Thomas 75.00 150.00
Chris Paul
ENDWG Jerry West 50.00 125.00
Gail Goodrich
ENDWS John Stockton 60.00 120.00
Deron Williams

2008-09 Exquisite Collection Flawless Autographs

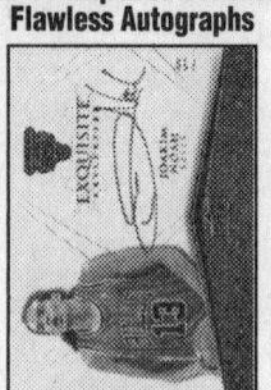

STATED PRINT RUN 23 TO 50 SER.#'d SETS
FLAWAB Andrew Bynum/50 20.00 50.00
FLAWAH Al Horford/50 15.00 40.00
FLAWAM Alonzo Mourning/25 60.00 120.00
FLAWBD Baron Davis/50 25.00 50.00
FLAWBR Bill Russell/25 75.00 150.00
FLAWCD Clyde Drexler/25 30.00 60.00
FLAWCP Chris Paul/25 50.00 120.00
FLAWDF Derek Fisher/47 15.00 40.00
FLAWDW Deron Williams/25 25.00 60.00
FLAWIT Isiah Thomas/25 40.00 100.00
FLAWJE Julius Erving/25 50.00 100.00
FLAWJN Joakim Noah/50 25.00 60.00
FLAWJW Jerry West/25 50.00 125.00
FLAWKA Kareem Abdul-Jabbar/25 60.00 150.00
FLAWKB Kobe Bryant/24 250.00 400.00
FLAWKD Kevin Durant/50 100.00 200.00
FLAWKG Kevin Garnett/50 50.00 100.00
FLAWLJ LeBron James/23 200.00 350.00
FLAWMC Michael Cooper/50 15.00 40.00
FLAWMJ Michael Jordan/23 700.00 1200.00
FLAWMK Mitch Kupchak/25 25.00 60.00
FLAWOR Oscar Robertson/25 75.00 150.00
FLAWPP Paul Pierce/50 30.00 80.00
FLAWRO Brandon Roy/50 20.00 50.00
FLAWRP Robert Parish/50 15.00 40.00
FLAWRS Rodney Stuckey/50 15.00 40.00
FLAWTM Tracy McGrady/50 25.00 60.00
FLAWVC Vince Carter/50 35.00 65.00

2008-09 Exquisite Collection Inscriptions

STATED PRINT RUN 20 TO 50 SER.#'d SETS
SCRIPTAD Adrian Dantley/25 12.50 30.00
SCRIPTAH Al Horford/50 8.00 20.00
SCRIPTAI Andre Iguodala/25 10.00 25.00
SCRIPTAM Alonzo Mourning #33/2575.00 150.00
SCRIPTAS Amare Stoudemire #1/25 25.00 60.00
SCRIPTBD Baron Davis/50 12.00 30.00
SCRIPTBL Bill Laimbeer/50 10.00 25.00
SCRIPTBM Bob McAdoo/50 15.00 40.00
SCRIPTBR Brandon Roy #7/50 20.00 50.00
SCRIPTCB Chauncey Billups/50 20.00 40.00
SCRIPTCP Chris Paul CP3/25 75.00 200.00
SCRIPTDC Daequan Cook/50 8.00 20.00
SCRIPTDG Darrell Griffith/25 15.00 30.00
Dr. Dunkenstein
SCRIPTDH Dwight Howard/50 50.00 100.00
SCRIPTDR Dennis Rodman/25 75.00 200.00
The Worm
SCRIPTDW Dominique Wilkins/25 60.00 150.00
SCRIPTGG George Gervin/50 15.00 40.00
SCRIPTGW Gerald Wallace/50 8.00 20.00
SCRIPTHA Hilton Armstrong #12/50 8.00 20.00
SCRIPTHO Hakeem Olajuwon #34/2520.00 40.00
SCRIPTJG Jeff Green/50 10.00 25.00
SCRIPTJK Jason Kidd/50 80.00 160.00
Mr. Triple Double
SCRIPTJS Jack Sikma 7 Time AS/5010.00 25.00
SCRIPTJW Jerry West/25 75.00 150.00
SCRIPTKB Kobe Bryant/24 500.00 800.00
SCRIPTKD Kevin Durant/50 125.00 250.00
SCRIPTKG Kevin Garnett/50 60.00 150.00
SCRIPTMC Mike Conley Jr./50 8.00 20.00
Money Mike
SCRIPTMW Marvin Williams #24/50 8.00 20.00
SCRIPTOR Oscar Robertson/25 100.00 200.00
SCRIPTPA Tony Parker/50 25.00 50.00
SCRIPTPP Paul Pierce The Truth/50 80.00 160.00
World's Greatest
SCRIPTRP Robert Parish/50 15.00 40.00
SCRIPTSM Sidney Moncrief/20 8.00 20.00
SCRIPTSN Steve Nash/50 40.00 80.00
SCRIPTTM Tracy McGrady/50 25.00 50.00
SCRIPTTP Tayshaun Prince/25 20.00 50.00
Palace Prince
SCRIPTVC Vince Carter Sanity/50 60.00 150.00
SCRIPTYM Yao Ming/50 40.00 100.00

2008-09 Exquisite Collection Inscriptions Dual

STATED PRINT RUN 10 SER.#'d SETS
SOME UNPRICED DUE TO SCARCITY
DINBK Bill Russell 200.00 350.00
Kevin Garnett
DINBW Carlos Boozer 100.00 200.00
Deron Williams
DINCH Dwight Howard 60.00 120.00
Tyson Chandler
DINCM Tracy McGrady 100.00 200.00
Vince Carter
DINDG Kevin Durant 100.00 200.00
Jeff Green
DINGR George Gervin 100.00 200.00
David Robinson
DINHN Kirk Hinrich 50.00 100.00
Joakim Noah
DINJW LeBron James 150.00 300.00
Mo Williams
DINKB Jason Kidd 100.00 200.00
Jose Barea
DINKM Kobe Bryant 1200.00 2000.00
Michael Jordan
DINNK Jason Kidd 100.00 200.00
Steve Nash
DINNS Steve Nash 100.00 200.00
Amare Stoudemire
DINPG Kevin Garnett 150.00 300.00
Paul Pierce
DINRD Kevin Durant 100.00 200.00
Brandon Roy
DINSP Rodney Stuckey 50.00 100.00
Tayshaun Prince
DINWP Deron Williams 200.00 350.00
Chris Paul

2008-09 Exquisite Collection Jerseys

*JERSEY: 1X TO 2.5X BASE HI
STATED PRINT RUN 35 SER.#'d SETS
2 LeBron James 100.00 250.00

2008-09 Exquisite Collection Limited Logos

STATED PRINT RUN 23 TO 25 SER.#'d SETS
LLAH Al Horford/25 25.00 50.00
LLAI Andre Iguodala/25 40.00 100.00
LLBD Baron Davis/25 40.00 100.00
LLCP Chris Paul/25 125.00 250.00
LLDH Dwight Howard/25 200.00 400.00
LLDL David Lee/25 25.00 50.00
LLDR Derrick Rose/25 750.00 1500.00
LLDW David West/25 25.00 50.00
LLEG Eric Gordon/25 100.00 200.00
LLGH George Hill/25 50.00 100.00
LLJG Jeff Green/25 40.00 80.00
LLJK Jason Kidd/25 75.00 150.00
LLJR J.R. Giddens/25 25.00 50.00
LLJS John Stockton/25 75.00 150.00
LLKB Kobe Bryant/24 900.00 1500.00
LLKG Kevin Garnett/25 250.00 450.00
LLKL Kevin Love/25 175.00 350.00
LLLJ LeBron James/23 600.00 1100.00
LLMB Michael Beasley/25 100.00 175.00
LLMJ Michael Jordan/23 3000.00 4500.00
LLPP Paul Pierce/25 200.00 400.00
LLRF Rudy Fernandez/25 75.00 150.00
LLRJ Richard Jefferson/25 25.00 50.00
LLRP Robert Parish/25 25.00 60.00
LLRS Rodney Stuckey/25 30.00 60.00
LLSB Shane Battier/25 25.00 50.00
LLSN Steve Nash/24 200.00 400.00
LLTC Tom Chambers/25 30.00 80.00
LLVC Vince Carter/25 200.00 400.00
LLVD Vlade Divac/25 100.00 200.00
LLWI Deron Williams/25 100.00 200.00

2008-09 Exquisite Collection Limited Throwback Logo Autographs

STATED PRINT RUN 22 TO 25 SER.#'d SETS
LTAR Anthony Randolph/25 75.00
LTBL Brook Lopez/25 50.00
LTBR Brandon Rush/22 20.00
LTCD Chris Douglas-Roberts/25 15.00
LTCL Courtney Lee/25 40.00
LTDA Darrell Arthur/25 15.00
LTDG Donte Greene/25 15.00
LTDJ D.J. Augustin/25 20.00
LTDR Derrick Rose/25 700.00
LTEG Eric Gordon/25 75.00
LTGH George Hill/25 60.00
LTJA Joe Alexander/25 15.00
LTJB Jerryd Bayless/25 30.00
LTJD Joey Dorsey/25 15.00
LTJG J.R. Giddens/25 15.00
LTJH J.J. Hickson/25 50.00
LTJM Javale McGee/25 60.00
LTJT Jason Thompson/25 30.00
LTKK Kosta Koufos/25 15.00
LTKL Kevin Love/25 150.00
LTMB Michael Beasley/25 60.00
LTMC Mario Chalmers/25 40.00
LTMS Marreese Speights/25 15.00
LTOM O.J. Mayo/25 60.00
LTRA Ryan Anderson/25 25.00
LTRL Robin Lopez/25 15.00
LTSW Sonny Weems/25 15.00
LTWS Walter Sharpe/25 15.00

2008-09 Exquisite Collection Noble Nameplates

STATED PRINT RUN 5 TO 25 SER.#'d SETS
SOME UNPRICED DUE TO SCARCITY
NAAH Al Horford/25 15.00
NAAJ Al Jefferson/25 20.00
NAAL Joe Alexander/25 15.00
NAAM Alonzo Mourning/25 100.00
NAAR Anthony Randolph/25 75.00
NAAT Al Thornton/25 15.00
NABA Jose Barea/25 75.00
NABD Baron Davis/25 30.00
NABG Ben Gordon/25 30.00
NABI Mike Bibby/25 15.00
NABR Corey Brewer/25 15.00
NACB Chauncey Billups/25 40.00
NACP Chris Paul/25 125.00
NADA D.J. Augustin/25 30.00
NADH Dwight Howard/25 50.00
NADR Derrick Rose/25 700.00
NADW David West/25 20.00
NAEG Eric Gordon/25 75.00
NAFE Raymond Felton/10 15.00
NAFG Francisco Garcia/25 15.00
NAGH George Hill/25 40.00
NAGP Gabe Pruitt/25 15.00
NAHA Al Harrington/18 15.00
NAJB Jerryd Bayless/25 40.00
NAJG Jeff Green/25 30.00
NAJJ J.J. Hickson/25 25.00
NAJK Jason Kidd/25 75.00
NAJM Jamario Moon/25 15.00
NAJO Jermaine O'Neal/25 15.00
NAJT Jason Thompson/25 30.00
NAKB Kobe Bryant/24 2000.00
NAKD Kevin Durant/25 200.00
NAKG Kevin Garnett/25 150.00
NAKL Kevin Love/25 150.00
NAKW Kyle Weaver/25 15.00
NALJ LeBron James/23 600.00
NAMB Michael Beasley/25 60.00
NAMC Mario Chalmers/14 50.00
NAMI Mike Conley Jr./25 25.00
NAMJ Michael Jordan/18 3000.00
NAMP Morris Peterson/25 15.00
NAOM O.J. Mayo/25 60.00
NAPP Paul Pierce/25 100.00
NARA Ray Allen/25 100.00
NARF Rudy Fernandez/25 25.00
NARJ Richard Jefferson/25 15.00
NARS Rodney Stuckey/20 25.00
NARY Ryan Anderson/25 25.00
NASB Shane Battier/20 15.00
NASH Spencer Hawes/25 15.00
NATC Tyson Chandler/25 30.00
NATM Tracy McGrady/25 150.00
NATP Tayshaun Prince/25 15.00
NAWI Deron Williams/25 50.00

2008-09 Exquisite Collection Patches

*PATCHES: 2X TO 5X BASE HI
PATCH PRINT RUN 10 SER.#'d SETS
UNPRICED AUTO PATCH PRINT RUN ONE SET
2 LeBron James 200.00

2008-09 Exquisite Collection Player Box Autographs

STATED PRINT RUN 5 TO 34 SER.#'d SETS
SOME UNPRICED DUE TO SCARCITY

PBAHO Hakeem Olajuwon/34	25.00	60.00
PBAJO Magic Johnson/32	50.00	100.00
PBAJS John Stockton/12	60.00	120.00
PBAKB Kobe Bryant/24	250.00	500.00
PBALB Larry Bird/33	60.00	120.00
PBALJ LeBron James/23	250.00	500.00
PBAMB Michael Beasley/30	30.00	80.00
PBAMJ Michael Jordan/23	1200.00	2000.00
PBAOM O.J. Mayo/32	30.00	80.00

2008-09 Exquisite Collection Player Box Base

STATED PRINT RUN 5 TO 34 SER.#'d SETS
SOME UNPRICED DUE TO SCARCITY

PBHO Hakeem Olajuwon/34	8.00	20.00
PBJO Magic Johnson/32	15.00	40.00
PBJS John Stockton/12	10.00	25.00
PBKB Kobe Bryant/24	40.00	100.00
PBLB Larry Bird/33	15.00	30.00
PBLJ LeBron James/23	30.00	80.00
PBMB Michael Beasley/30	6.00	15.00
PBMJ Michael Jordan/23	100.00	200.00
PBOM O.J. Mayo/32	6.00	15.00

2008-09 Exquisite Collection Player Box Memorabilia

TATED PRINT RUN 5 TO 34 SER.#'d SETS
OME UNPRICED DUE TO SCARCITY

BMHO Hakeem Olajuwon/34	10.00	25.00
BMJO Magic Johnson/32	25.00	60.00
BMJS John Stockton/12	20.00	40.00
BMKB Kobe Bryant/24	75.00	150.00
BMLB Larry Bird/33	20.00	40.00
BMMB Michael Beasley/30	10.00	25.00
BMMJ Michael Jordan/23	200.00	400.00
MOM O.J. Mayo/32	10.00	25.00

2008-09 Exquisite Collection layer Box Patches Autographs

MDR Derrick Rose/50	400.00	750.00
MHO Hakeem Olajuwon/34	75.00	200.00
MJO Magic Johnson/32	100.00	200.00
MJS John Stockton/12	100.00	200.00
MLB Larry Bird/33	100.00	200.00
MLJ LeBron James/23	300.00	600.00
MMB Michael Beasley/30	40.00	100.00
MMJ Michael Jordan/23	1200.00	2000.00
MOM O.J. Mayo/32	60.00	150.00

2008-09 Exquisite Collection Prime

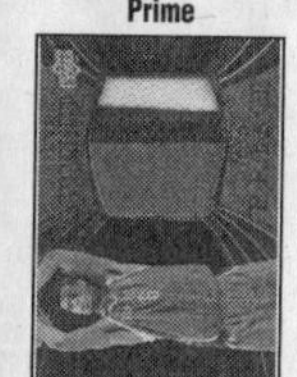

ED PRINT RUN 35 TO 50 SER.#'d SETS

AB Andrew Bynum	15.00	40.00
AI Allen Iverson	40.00	100.00
AM Adam Morrison	12.00	30.00
AN Andrew Bogut	25.00	50.00
AT Al Thornton	12.00	30.00
BC Carlos Boozer	12.00	30.00
BD Baron Davis	12.00	30.00
E Marco Belinelli	12.00	30.00
L Brook Lopez	15.00	40.00
O Chris Bosh	20.00	50.00
U Caron Butler	20.00	40.00
Y Michael Beasley	20.00	50.00
B Chauncey Billups	12.00	30.00
M Corey Maggette	12.00	30.00
O Corey Brewer	12.00	30.00
P Chris Paul	50.00	120.00
A D.J. Augustin	12.00	30.00
E Derrick Rose	150.00	300.00
H Dwight Howard/39	40.00	100.00
N Dirk Nowitzki	50.00	120.00
R Derrick Rose	150.00	300.00
B Elton Brand	12.00	30.00
G Eric Gordon	30.00	80.00
H Grant Hill	50.00	100.00
George Hill	20.00	50.00
A Joe Alexander	12.00	30.00
Jerryd Bayless	12.00	30.00
Jason Kidd	25.00	60.00
PRMJT Jason Thompson	12.00	30.00
PRMKD Kevin Durant	150.00	300.00
PRMKG Kevin Garnett	50.00	125.00
PRMKL Kevin Love	50.00	125.00
PRMKM Kevin Martin	12.00	30.00
PRMLJ LeBron James	150.00	325.00
PRMMA Stephon Marbury	25.00	50.00
PRMMB Mike Bibby	12.00	30.00
PRMMG Manu Ginobili	25.00	60.00
PRMMI Michael Beasley	20.00	50.00
PRMMS Marreese Speights	12.00	30.00
PRMOJ O.J. Mayo	20.00	50.00
PRMOM O.J. Mayo/35	20.00	50.00
PRMPA Tony Parker	12.00	30.00
PRMPG Pau Gasol	20.00	50.00
PRMPP Paul Pierce	25.00	60.00
PRMRF Rudy Fernandez	15.00	40.00
PRMRJ Richard Jefferson	12.00	30.00
PRMRL Rashard Lewis	10.00	25.00
PRMRO Brandon Roy/43	20.00	40.00
PRMRW Rasheed Wallace	15.00	40.00
PRMSB Shane Battier/45	12.00	30.00
PRMSM Shawn Marion	12.00	30.00
PRMSO Shaquille O'Neal	30.00	80.00
PRMTC Tyson Chandler	12.00	30.00
PRMTD Tim Duncan	30.00	80.00
PRMTP Tayshaun Prince	12.00	30.00
PRMTS Thabo Sefolosha	12.00	30.00
PRMWI Deron Williams/40	20.00	50.00
PRMZR Zach Randolph	12.00	30.00

2008-09 Exquisite Collection Rookie Parallel

STATED PRINT RUN ONE TO 44 SER.#'d SETS
SOME UNPRICED DUE TO SCARCITY

61 Kevin Love JSY AU/42	900.00	1500.00
62 Joe Alexander JSY AU/11	100.00	200.00
63 D.J. Augustin JSY AU/14	100.00	200.00
64 Brook Lopez JSY AU/11	250.00	400.00
65 Jason Thompson JSY AU/34	60.00	120.00
66 Brandon Rush JSY AU/25	40.00	100.00
68 Robin Lopez JSY AU/15	75.00	150.00
69 Marreese Speights JSY AU/16	75.00	150.00
71 Javale McGee JSY AU/34	100.00	200.00
72 J.J. Hickson JSY AU/21	125.00	250.00
73 Ryan Anderson JSY AU/20	40.00	100.00
74 Courtney Lee JSY AU/11	100.00	200.00
75 Kosta Koufos JSY AU/41	20.00	50.00
78 Donte Greene JSY AU/10	50.00	100.00
81 Walter Sharpe JSY AU/42	20.00	50.00
82 Joey Dorsey JSY AU/15	20.00	50.00
85 Kyle Weaver JSY AU/20	20.00	50.00
86 Sonny Weems JSY AU/13	40.00	100.00
89 Marc Gasol JSY AU/33	60.00	120.00
90 O.J. Mayo JSY AU/32	250.00	500.00
91 Michael Beasley JSY AU/30	200.00	400.00
95 Nicolas Batum AU/12	150.00	300.00
97 Alexis Ajinca AU/21	20.00	50.00
98 Luc Mbah A Moute AU/12	20.00	50.00
99 Sean Singletary AU/44	20.00	50.00
100 Danilo Gallinari AU/44	100.00	200.00

2008-09 Exquisite Collection Scripted Swatches

STATED PRINT RUN 12 TO 25 SER.#'d SETS

SCRPAB Andrew Bynum/25	50.00	125.00
SCRPAD Adrian Dantley/12	40.00	80.00
SCRPAH Al Horford/25	15.00	40.00
SCRPAL Al Jefferson/25	15.00	40.00
SCRPAR Anthony Randolph/25	40.00	100.00
SCRPAS Amare Stoudemire/25	50.00	100.00
SCRPBE Michael Beasley/25	40.00	100.00
SCRPBI Chauncey Billups/25	25.00	60.00
SCRPBL Brook Lopez/25	50.00	100.00
SCRPBR Brandon Roy/25	50.00	120.00
SCRPBY Michael Beasley/25	30.00	80.00
SCRPCL Courtney Lee/25	60.00	120.00
SCRPCM Corey Maggette/25	15.00	40.00
SCRPCP Chris Paul/25	125.00	250.00
SCRPDA Darrell Arthur/25	15.00	40.00
SCRPDE Derrick Rose White/25	900.00	1500.00
SCRPDH Dwight Howard/25	100.00	200.00
SCRPDJ D.J. Augustin/25	40.00	80.00
SCRPDL David Lee/25	15.00	40.00
SCRPDO DeAndre Jordan/25	30.00	80.00
SCRPDR Derrick Rose Red/25	900.00	1500.00
SCRPEG Eric Gordon Ball Right/25	75.00	150.00
SCRPGG George Gervin/25	15.00	40.00
SCRPGO Eric Gordon Ball Left/25	75.00	150.00
SCRPGR Danny Granger/25	40.00	80.00
SCRPHA Hilton Armstrong/25	15.00	40.00
SCRPHI George Hill/25	40.00	100.00
SCRPHR Al Harrington/25	15.00	40.00
SCRPID Ike Diogu/25	15.00	40.00
SCRPJB Jose Barea/25	40.00	100.00
SCRPJD Joey Dorsey/25	15.00	40.00
SCRPJK Jason Kidd/25	50.00	100.00
SCRPJO Jermaine O'Neal/25	15.00	40.00
SCRPJR J.R. Smith/25	15.00	40.00
SCRPJT Jason Thompson/25	40.00	80.00
SCRPKB Kobe Bryant/24	500.00	850.00
SCRPKD Kevin Durant/25	150.00	300.00
SCRPKG Kevin Garnett/25	150.00	300.00
SCRPKL Kevin Love/25	150.00	300.00
SCRPLB Larry Bird/25	100.00	200.00
SCRPLH Larry Hughes No Auto/25	15.00	40.00
SCRPLJ LeBron James/23	350.00	600.00
SCRPMA Desmond Mason/25	15.00	40.00
SCRPMC Mario Chalmers/21	50.00	100.00
SCRPMJ Michael Jordan/16	1200.00	2000.00
SCRPOJ O.J. Mayo Blue/25	60.00	150.00
SCRPOM O.J. Mayo White/25	60.00	150.00
SCRPRA Ryan Anderson/25	20.00	50.00
SCRPRF Rudy Fernandez/25	100.00	200.00
SCRPRJ Richard Jefferson/25	15.00	40.00
SCRPRO David Robinson/25	75.00	150.00
SCRPRS Ramon Sessions/25	20.00	50.00
SCRPRW Russell Westbrook/25	200.00	350.00
SCRPSB Shane Battier/25	30.00	80.00
SCRPSN Steve Nash/25	60.00	120.00
SCRPST John Stockton/25	100.00	200.00
SCRPVC Vince Carter/25	60.00	150.00
SCRPVD Vlade Divac/25	40.00	80.00

2008-09 Exquisite Collection Triple Patches

STATED PRINT RUN 10 SER.#'d SETS
SOME UNPRICED DUE TO SCARCITY

ETPAI Allen Iverson	75.00	150.00
ETPAS Amare Stoudemire	25.00	50.00
ETPCA Carmelo Anthony	40.00	80.00
ETPDH Dwight Howard	60.00	120.00
ETPDN Dirk Nowitzki	50.00	100.00
ETPDR Derrick Rose	200.00	400.00
ETPGA Gilbert Arenas	25.00	50.00
ETPJK Jason Kidd	25.00	50.00
ETPKB Kobe Bryant	150.00	300.00
ETPKM Kevin Martin	25.00	50.00
ETPLJ LeBron James	125.00	250.00
ETPLW Luke Walton	25.00	50.00
ETPMB Michael Beasley	40.00	100.00
ETPOM O.J. Mayo	40.00	100.00
ETPRA Ray Allen	25.00	60.00
ETPSN Steve Nash	40.00	80.00
ETPTD Tim Duncan	50.00	120.00
ETPVC Vince Carter	40.00	80.00

2009-10 Exquisite Collection

1-42 PRINT RUN 199 SER.#'d SETS
43-79 PRINT RUN 225 SER.#'d SETS
UNPRICED BLACK PRINT RUN ONE SET

1 Dwight Howard	20.00	50.00
2 LeBron James	80.00	200.00
3 Kobe Bryant	80.00	200.00
4 Dwyane Wade	40.00	100.00
5 Yao Ming	15.00	40.00
6 Tim Duncan	20.00	50.00
7 Kevin Garnett	25.00	60.00
8 Allen Iverson	20.00	50.00
9 Yi Jianlian	10.00	25.00
11 Chris Paul	20.00	50.00
12 Shaquille O'Neal	25.00	60.00
13 Carmelo Anthony	20.00	50.00
14 Vince Carter	15.00	40.00
15 Dirk Nowitzki	20.00	50.00
16 Chris Bosh	12.00	30.00
17 Manu Ginobili	12.00	30.00
18 Pau Gasol	12.00	30.00
19 Ray Allen	12.00	30.00
20 Paul Pierce	15.00	40.00
21 Jamal Crawford	20.00	50.00
22 Steve Nash	12.00	30.00
23 Michael Jordan	175.00	350.00
24 Gilbert Arenas	12.00	30.00
25 Luke Ridnour	10.00	25.00
26 Derrick Rose	100.00	225.00
27 Jose Calderon	10.00	25.00
28 Brandon Roy	12.00	30.00
29 Joe Johnson	12.00	30.00
30 Danny Granger	12.00	30.00
31 Greg Oden	10.00	25.00
32 Al Jefferson	12.00	30.00
33 Kevin Durant	100.00	175.00
34 Andre Iguodala	12.00	30.00
35 David Lee	10.00	25.00
36 Kevin Martin	12.00	30.00
37 O.J. Mayo	12.00	30.00
38 Zach Randolph	10.00	25.00
39 Gerald Wallace	12.00	30.00
40 Russell Westbrook	30.00	80.00
41 Deron Williams	12.00	30.00
42 Mo Williams	10.00	25.00
43 Blake Griffin RC	400.00	800.00
44 Ricky Rubio AU RC	300.00	600.00
45 James Harden AU RC	125.00	225.00
46 Tyreke Evans RC	60.00	120.00
47 Brandon Jennings RC	40.00	100.00
48 James Johnson AU RC	10.00	25.00
49 Earl Clark AU RC	10.00	25.00
50 Chase Budinger AU RC	10.00	25.00
51 DeJuan Blair RC	15.00	40.00
52 B.J. Mullens AU RC	10.00	25.00
53 Darren Collison AU RC	30.00	80.00
54 Tyler Hansbrough RC	20.00	50.00
55 Sam Young AU RC	10.00	25.00
56 Marcus Thornton AU RC	40.00	100.00
57 Jeff Teague AU RC	20.00	50.00
58 Jonny Flynn AU RC	12.00	30.00
59 Terrence Williams RC	10.00	25.00
60 Gerald Henderson AU RC	20.00	50.00
61 Hasheem Thabeet RC	10.00	25.00
62 Ty Lawson AU RC	50.00	125.00
63 Eric Maynor AU RC	10.00	25.00
64 Stephen Curry AU RC	100.00	200.00
65 DeMar DeRozan RC	30.00	80.00
66 Patrick Mills RC	20.00	50.00
67 Jordan Hill RC	10.00	25.00
68 Derrick Brown AU RC	10.00	25.00
69 Wayne Ellington AU RC	10.00	25.00
70 DaJuan Summers AU RC	10.00	25.00
71 Eric Maynor AU RC	12.50	30.00
72 Stephen Curry AU	100.00	200.00
73 Ricky Rubio AU	300.00	600.00
74 James Harden AU	125.00	225.00
75 James Johnson AU	10.00	25.00
76 Sam Young AU	10.00	25.00
77 Gerald Henderson AU	20.00	50.00
78 B.J. Mullens AU	10.00	25.00
79 Jonny Flynn AU	12.00	30.00

2009-10 Exquisite Collection Rookie Parallel

STATED PRINT RUN ONE TO 50 SETS
SOME UNPRICED DUE TO SCARCITY

43 Blake Griffin/23	1500.00	2300.00
46 Tyreke Evans/12	600.00	1000.00
48 James Johnson AU/23	30.00	80.00
50 Chase Budinger AU/34	30.00	80.00
51 DeJuan Blair/45	40.00	100.00
52 B.J. Mullens AU/32	30.00	80.00
54 Tyler Hansbrough/50	75.00	150.00
55 Sam Young AU/23	30.00	80.00
60 Gerald Henderson AU/15	50.00	125.00
61 Hasheem Thabeet/34	30.00	80.00
64 Stephen Curry AU/30	250.00	500.00
66 Patrick Mills/13	40.00	100.00
67 Jordan Hill/43	30.00	80.00
69 Wayne Ellington AU/22	30.00	80.00
72 Stephen Curry AU/31	250.00	500.00
75 James Johnson AU/23	30.00	80.00
76 Sam Young AU/23	30.00	80.00
77 Gerald Henderson AU/15	50.00	125.00
78 B.J. Mullens AU/32	30.00	80.00

2009-10 Exquisite Collection Autographs Patches

STATED PRINT RUN 50 SER.#'d SETS

PAA Arron Afflalo	12.00	30.00
PAB Andrew Bynum	50.00	125.00
PAJ Al Jefferson	15.00	40.00
PAM Alonzo Mourning	100.00	175.00
PAS Amare Stoudemire	40.00	100.00
PAZ Kelenna Azubuike	12.00	30.00
PBD Baron Davis	25.00	60.00
PBI Mike Bibby	25.00	60.00
PBL Bill Laimbeer	15.00	40.00
PBM Brad Miller	20.00	40.00
PBR Brandon Roy	40.00	80.00
PCD Clyde Drexler	40.00	100.00
PCH Tyson Chandler	20.00	50.00
PCO Corey Brewer	12.00	30.00
PCP Chris Paul	40.00	80.00
PDG Danny Granger	25.00	60.00
PDH Dwight Howard	75.00	200.00
PDM Desmond Mason	12.00	30.00
PDO Donyell Marshall	12.00	30.00
PDR David Robinson	60.00	150.00
PDW David West	12.00	30.00
PER Julius Erving	100.00	225.00
PGR Darrell Griffith	12.00	30.00
PJB Jerryd Bayless	12.00	30.00
PJE Jeff Green	25.00	60.00
PJF Jordan Farmar	12.00	30.00
PJG J.R. Giddens	12.00	30.00
PJK Jason Kidd	40.00	80.00
PJM Jamario Moon	12.00	30.00
PJN Joakim Noah	40.00	100.00
PJO Jermaine O'Neal	30.00	60.00
PJS J.R. Smith	20.00	50.00
PJW Jerry West	100.00	225.00
PKA Kareem Abdul-Jabbar	125.00	250.00
PKG Kevin Garnett	75.00	150.00
PKL Kevin Love	75.00	150.00
PLA LaMarcus Aldridge	30.00	80.00
PLB Larry Bird	75.00	200.00
PLH Larry Hughes	25.00	50.00
PLJ LeBron James	350.00	650.00
PLO Lamar Odom	25.00	60.00
PLW Luke Walton	20.00	40.00
PMA Magic Johnson	50.00	100.00
PMC Mike Conley Jr.	12.00	30.00
PMJ Michael Jordan	1000.00	2000.00
PMP Mark Price	75.00	150.00
PMW Mo Williams	20.00	40.00
POM O.J. Mayo	40.00	80.00
PPP Paul Pierce	50.00	120.00
PQR Quentin Richardson	12.00	30.00
PRF Randy Foye	15.00	40.00
PRJ Richard Jefferson	12.00	30.00
PRO Derrick Rose	250.00	500.00
PRP Robert Parish	30.00	80.00
PSA Stacey Augmon	12.00	30.00
PSH Spencer Hawes	12.00	30.00
PSN Steve Nash	100.00	200.00
PST John Stockton	50.00	120.00
PTC Tom Chambers	15.00	40.00
PTM Tracy McGrady	60.00	150.00
PTP Tayshaun Prince	15.00	40.00
PVC Vince Carter	50.00	120.00
PVD Vlade Divac	25.00	50.00
PWI Deron Williams	30.00	80.00
PYM Yao Ming	50.00	120.00

2009-10 Exquisite Collection Extra Exquisite Jerseys

PRINT RUN 50 SER.#'d SETS
*GOLD: .6X TO 1.5X BASE HI
GOLD PRINT RUN 25 SER.#'d SETS

XAB Andrew Bynum	10.00	25.00
XAI Allen Iverson	12.50	30.00
XAR Ron Artest	8.00	20.00
XAS Amare Stoudemire	8.00	20.00
XAT Al Thornton	6.00	15.00
XBW Brandan Wright	5.00	12.00
XBY Marcus Camby	5.00	12.00
XCA Carmelo Anthony	10.00	25.00
XCB Chris Bosh	8.00	20.00
XCM Chris Mullin/15	10.00	25.00
XDH Devin Harris	8.00	20.00
XDN Dirk Nowitzki	15.00	40.00
XDR Derrick Rose	50.00	125.00
XEB Elton Brand	8.00	20.00
XEG Eric Gordon	8.00	20.00
XGH Grant Hill	20.00	50.00
XHO Josh Howard	6.00	15.00
XIG Andre Iguodala	8.00	20.00
XJC Jose Calderon	6.00	15.00
XJR Jason Richardson	8.00	20.00
XJS Josh Smith	8.00	20.00
XJT Jason Terry	6.00	15.00
XKB Kobe Bryant	50.00	125.00
XKE Kevin Martin	8.00	20.00
XKG Kevin Garnett	15.00	40.00
XKM Karl Malone	10.00	25.00
XLB Leandro Barbosa	6.00	15.00
XLJ LeBron James	50.00	125.00
XLS Luis Scola	6.00	15.00
XLW Luke Walton	5.00	12.00
XMA Kenyon Martin	8.00	20.00
XME Monta Ellis	8.00	20.00
XMG Manu Ginobili	12.00	30.00
XMJ Michael Jordan	200.00	400.00
XMR Michael Redd	8.00	20.00
XOM O.J. Mayo	8.00	20.00
XPE Patrick Ewing	20.00	50.00
XPG Pau Gasol	15.00	30.00
XPP Paul Pierce	12.00	30.00
XPS Peja Stojakovic	15.00	30.00
XRA Ray Allen	12.00	30.00
XRG Rudy Gay	8.00	20.00
XRH Richard Hamilton	6.00	15.00
XRR Rajon Rondo	15.00	40.00
XRW Rasheed Wallace	8.00	20.00
XSM Shawn Marion	8.00	20.00
XSO Shaquille O'Neal	20.00	50.00
XSP Scottie Pippen	30.00	80.00
XST Sebastian Telfair	5.00	12.00
XSV Sasha Vujacic	5.00	12.00
XTD Tim Duncan	20.00	50.00
XTO Travis Outlaw	6.00	15.00
XTY Thaddeus Young	5.00	12.00
XYI Yi Jianlian	6.00	15.00
XZR Zach Randolph	6.00	15.00

2009-10 Exquisite Collection Extra Exquisite Patches

PRINT RUN 15 SER.#'d SETS

XAI Allen Iverson	100.00	200.00
XAR Ron Artest	30.00	80.00
XAS Amare Stoudemire	30.00	80.00
XAT Al Thornton	25.00	60.00
XBW Brandan Wright	20.00	50.00
XBY Marcus Camby	20.00	50.00
XCA Carmelo Anthony	100.00	200.00
XCB Chris Bosh	60.00	150.00
XCM Chris Mullin	30.00	80.00
XDH Devin Harris	30.00	80.00
XDN Dirk Nowitzki	60.00	150.00
XDR Derrick Rose	150.00	300.00
XEB Elton Brand	30.00	80.00
XEG Eric Gordon	30.00	80.00
XGH Grant Hill	100.00	200.00
XHO Josh Howard	25.00	60.00
XIG Andre Iguodala	30.00	80.00
XJC Jose Calderon	25.00	60.00
XJH Jeff Hornacek	50.00	100.00
XJR Jason Richardson	30.00	80.00
XJS Josh Smith	30.00	80.00
XJT Jason Terry	25.00	60.00
XKB Kobe Bryant	400.00	700.00
XKE Kevin Martin	30.00	80.00
XKG Kevin Garnett	60.00	150.00
XKM Karl Malone	40.00	100.00
XLB Leandro Barbosa	25.00	60.00
XLJ LeBron James	400.00	700.00
XLS Luis Scola	25.00	60.00
XLW Luke Walton	20.00	50.00
XMA Kenyon Martin	30.00	80.00
XMC Kevin McHale	30.00	80.00
XME Monta Ellis	40.00	100.00
XMG Manu Ginobili	30.00	80.00
XMJ Michael Jordan	500.00	1000.00
XMR Michael Redd	30.00	80.00
XNA Nate Archibald	30.00	80.00
XOM O.J. Mayo	40.00	100.00
XOR Oscar Robertson	30.00	80.00
XPE Patrick Ewing	100.00	200.00
XPG Pau Gasol	30.00	80.00
XPP Paul Pierce	40.00	100.00
XPS Peja Stojakovic	30.00	80.00
XRA Ray Allen	50.00	100.00
XRG Rudy Gay	30.00	80.00
XRH Richard Hamilton	25.00	60.00
XRR Rajon Rondo	50.00	100.00
XRW Rasheed Wallace	50.00	100.00
XSM Shawn Marion	50.00	100.00
XSO Shaquille O'Neal	100.00	200.00
XSP Scottie Pippen	125.00	250.00
XST Sebastian Telfair	20.00	50.00
XSV Sasha Vujacic	20.00	50.00
XTD Tim Duncan	125.00	250.00
XTO Travis Outlaw	25.00	60.00
XTY Thaddeus Young	20.00	50.00
XYI Yi Jianlian	30.00	80.00
XZR Zach Randolph	25.00	60.00

2009-10 Exquisite Collection Jerseys

*JERSEYS: .6X TO 1.5X BASE HI
JERSEY PRINT RUN 25 SER.#'d SETS
UNPRICED PATCH PRINT RUN 10 SETS
UNPRICED PATCH AU PRINT RUN ONE SET

2 LeBron James	80.00	200.00
3 Kobe Bryant	80.00	200.00
4 Dwyane Wade	40.00	100.00
15 Dirk Nowitzki	30.00	80.00
23 Michael Jordan	150.00	400.00
26 Derrick Rose	125.00	300.00
33 Kevin Durant	80.00	200.00
40 Russell Westbrook	50.00	125.00

2009-10 Exquisite Collection Limited Logos

STATED PRINT RUN 7 TO 25 SER.#'d SETS
SOME UNPRICED DUE TO SCARCITY

LAB Andrew Bynum/13	175.00	350.00
LAS Amare Stoudemire/15	125.00	250.00
LDH Dwight Howard/20	200.00	400.00
LDW David West/17	30.00	80.00
LJB Jerryd Bayless/20	40.00	100.00
LJE Julius Erving/20	175.00	350.00
LJF Jordan Farmar/20	50.00	120.00
LJG Jeff Green/20	50.00	100.00
LJK Jason Kidd/12	125.00	250.00
LJN Joakim Noah/18	60.00	150.00
LJO Jermaine O'Neal/14	50.00	125.00
LKL Kevin Love/14	250.00	500.00
LLB Larry Bird/16	200.00	400.00
LLJ LeBron James/16	700.00	1200.00
LLO Lamar Odom/15	75.00	150.00
LLW Luke Walton/13	50.00	125.00
LMJ Magic Johnson/16	250.00	500.00
LMW Mo Williams/18	30.00	80.00
LQR Quentin Richardson/17	30.00	80.00
LRA Ray Allen/18	200.00	400.00
LRO Derrick Rose/16	300.00	600.00
LSN Steve Nash/19	200.00	400.00
LTM Tracy McGrady/13	125.00	250.00
LTP Tayshaun Prince/14	30.00	80.00
LVC Vince Carter/25	125.00	250.00
LWI Deron Williams/18	125.00	250.00
LYM Yao Ming/11	150.00	300.00

2009-10 Exquisite Collection Noble Nameplates

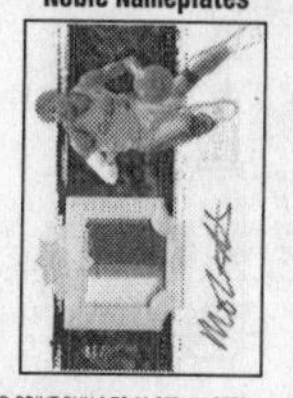

STATED PRINT RUN 3 TO 33 SER.#'d SETS
SOME UNPRICED DUE TO SCARCITY

NAB Andrew Bynum/15	60.00	120.00
NBD Baron Davis/19	25.00	60.00
NBL Bill Laimbeer/15	25.00	60.00
NBR Brandon Roy/15	75.00	200.00
NCP Chris Paul/15	125.00	225.00
NDH Dwight Howard/18	150.00	300.00
NDM Desmond Mason/25	25.00	60.00
NDR David Robinson/15	125.00	225.00
NJB Jerryd Bayless/20	25.00	60.00
NJE Julius Erving/17	125.00	250.00
NJF Jordan Farmar/26	25.00	60.00
NJG Jeff Green/12	25.00	60.00
NJK Jason Kidd/12	75.00	150.00
NJO Jermaine O'Neal/15	25.00	60.00
NJS J.R. Smith/21	25.00	60.00
NKL Kevin Love/12	100.00	200.00
NLA LaMarcus Aldridge/15	50.00	125.00
NLB Larry Bird/12	125.00	250.00
NLH Larry Hughes/18	25.00	60.00
NLJ LeBron James/18	600.00	1200.00
NLO Lamar Odom/16	30.00	80.00
NMI Michael Jordan/15	1200.00	2000.00
NMJ Magic Johnson/31	125.00	250.00
NMW Mo Williams/28	25.00	60.00
NPP Paul Pierce/15	75.00	150.00
NQR Quentin Richardson/33	25.00	60.00
NRA Ray Allen/18	200.00	300.00
NRO Derrick Rose/20	500.00	800.00
NRP Robert Parish/15	25.00	60.00
NSA Stacey Augmon/15	25.00	60.00
NSN Steve Nash/16	75.00	150.00
NST John Stockton/15	100.00	200.00
NTC Tom Chambers/15	25.00	60.00
NTM Tracy McGrady/20	50.00	100.00
NTP Tayshaun Prince/12	25.00	60.00
NVC Vince Carter/19	125.00	250.00
NWI Deron Williams/26	50.00	120.00

2009-10 Exquisite Collection Numbers

STATED PRINT RUN ONE TO 50 SER.#'d SETS
SOME UNPRICED DUE TO SCARCITY

ADJJ Michael Jordan/23 LeBron James	1500.00	2500.00
EDMA Alonzo Mourning/33 Kareem Abdul-Jabbar	150.00	275.00
EDRS John Stockton/12 Pat Riley	125.00	250.00
NPAB Andrew Bynum/17	100.00	200.00
NPAM Alonzo Mourning/33	125.00	250.00
NPBL Bill Laimbeer/40	25.00	60.00
NPBW Bill Walton/32	25.00	60.00
NPDE Dennis Rodman/50	75.00	150.00
NPDH Dwight Howard/12	200.00	400.00
NPDR David Robinson/50	75.00	150.00
NPDW David West/30	25.00	60.00
NPEO Emeka Okafor/50	25.00	60.00
NPGG George Gervin/44	30.00	80.00
NPJG Jeff Green/22	40.00	100.00
NPJN Joakim Noah/13	60.00	150.00
NPJW Jerry West/44	100.00	200.00
NPKA Kareem Abdul-Jabbar/33	125.00	250.00
NPKL Kevin Love/42	100.00	200.00
NPLJ LeBron James/23	500.00	900.00
NPMJ Michael Jordan/23	1500.00	2200.00
NPMP Mark Price/25	50.00	100.00
NPOM O.J. Mayo/32	60.00	120.00
NPPR Pat Riley/12	75.00	150.00
NPSN Steve Nash/13	150.00	300.00
NPST John Stockton/12	125.00	250.00
NPTC Tom Chambers/24	25.00	60.00
NPVC Vince Carter/15	125.00	225.00
NPVD Vlade Divac/21	25.00	60.00
NPYM Yao Ming/11	100.00	200.00

2009-10 Exquisite Collection Rookie Patch Flashback

STATED PRINT RUN 25 SER.#'d SETS

78A Michael Jordan/23	6000.00	8000.00
78C Bill Russell/19	1000.00	1500.00
78D Julius Erving/25	400.00	800.00
78E Larry Bird/25	300.00	600.00
78F Magic Johnson/25	350.00	700.00
78G Kareem Abdul-Jabbar/25	300.00	600.00
78H Kevin Garnett/25	300.00	550.00
78J Peyton Manning/25	400.00	700.00
78K John Elway/25	300.00	600.00
78L Jerry Rice/25	350.00	650.00
78O Adrian Peterson/25	400.00	800.00
78P Wayne Gretzky/25	750.00	1500.00
78Q Mario Lemieux/25	300.00	600.00
78R Steve Yzerman/25	200.00	400.00
78S Sidney Crosby/25	1200.00	2000.00
78T Patrick Roy/25	250.00	600.00
78U Gordie Howe/25	250.00	500.00

1991 Farley's Fruit Snacks Jordan

This set of four packages of fruit snacks was sponsored by Farley's Candy Co. of Chicago, Illinois. The packages measure 4 1/2" by 2 3/4", and each front features a different three-color (red, orange, and brown) drawing of Jordan and a different set of four answers. The complete list of questions appear on the outside of the box. On the packages, the answers are consecutively numbered (1-4; 5-8; 9-12; 13-16), and the set is checklisted below accordingly.

COMPLETE SET (4)	6.00	15.00
COMMON CARD (1-4)	2.00	5.00

2009-10 Fathead Tradeables

1 LeBron James	5.00	12.00
2 Kobe Bryant	5.00	12.00
3 Dwight Howard	1.50	4.00
4 Kevin Garnett	2.00	5.00
5 Chauncey Billups	1.00	2.50
6 Al Jefferson	1.00	2.50
7 Greg Oden	.75	2.00
8 Deron Williams	1.00	2.50
9 Mo Williams	.75	2.00
10 Yao Ming	1.25	3.00
11 Chris Paul	1.50	4.00
12 Steve Nash	1.00	2.50
13 Antawn Jamison	1.00	2.50
14 Manu Ginobili	1.00	2.50
15 Ray Allen	1.00	2.50
16 Baron Davis	1.00	2.50
17 Elton Brand	1.00	2.50
18 Joe Johnson	1.00	2.50
19 Kevin Durant	3.00	8.00
20 Tony Parker	1.00	2.50
21 Ben Gordon	1.00	2.50
22 Gerald Wallace	1.00	2.50
23 Michael Redd	1.00	2.50
24 Pau Gasol	1.00	2.50
25 Brandon Roy	1.00	2.50
26 Gilbert Arenas	1.00	2.50
27 Jason Kidd	1.00	2.50
28 Paul Pierce	1.25	3.00
29 Richard Hamilton	.75	2.00
30 Amare Stoudemire	1.00	2.50
31 Kevin Martin	1.00	2.50
32 Dwyane Wade	2.00	5.00
33 Vince Carter	1.25	3.00
34 Derrick Rose	3.00	8.00
35 Blake Griffin	6.00	15.00
36 Josh Smith	1.00	2.50
37 Shaquille O'Neal	2.00	5.00
38 Carmelo Anthony	1.25	3.00
39 David Lee	.75	2.00
40 Russell Westbrook	1.50	4.00
41 Tayshaun Prince	1.00	2.50
42 Andre Iguodala	1.00	2.50
43 Danny Granger	1.00	2.50
44 Tracy McGrady	1.00	2.50
45 Monta Ellis	1.00	2.50
46 O.J. Mayo	1.00	2.50
47 Dirk Nowitzki	1.25	3.00
48 Devin Harris	1.00	2.50
49 Chris Bosh	1.00	2.50
50 Tim Duncan	1.50	4.00

2010-11 Fathead Tradeables

1 Kobe Bryant	5.00	12.00
2 Rajon Rondo	1.25	3.00
3 Kevin Durant	3.00	8.00
4 Dwyane Wade	2.00	5.00
5 Dwight Howard	1.50	4.00
6 Derrick Rose	3.00	8.00
7 Dirk Nowitzki	1.25	3.00
8 Antawn Jamison	1.00	2.50
9 Andre Iguodala	1.00	2.50
10 Carmelo Anthony	1.25	3.00
11 Brandon Jennings	1.00	2.50
12 Chauncey Billups	1.00	2.50
13 Stephen Curry	1.25	3.00
14 Mo Williams	.75	2.00

15 Evan Turner 2.00 5.00
16 Devin Harris 1.00 2.50
17 Kevin Garnett 2.00 5.00
18 Jason Kidd 1.00 2.50
19 Brandon Roy 1.00 2.50
20 Kevin Martin 1.00 2.50
21 Chris Paul 1.50 4.00
22 Rudy Gay 1.00 2.50
23 Vince Carter 1.25 3.00
24 Aaron Brooks .60 1.50
25 Jason Richardson 1.00 2.50
26 Danny Granger 1.00 2.50
27 LaMarcus Aldridge 1.00 2.50
28 Joe Johnson 1.00 2.50
29 Manu Ginobili 1.00 2.50
30 Deron Williams 1.00 2.50
31 Ray Allen 1.00 2.50
32 Michael Beasley 1.00 2.50
33 Eric Gordon 1.00 2.50
34 Pau Gasol 1.00 2.50
35 Paul Pierce 1.25 3.00
36 Chris Bosh 1.00 2.50
37 Monta Ellis 1.00 2.50
38 J.J. Hickson .75 2.00
39 Andrea Bargnani .75 2.00
40 Steve Nash 1.00 2.50
41 Joakim Noah 1.00 2.50
42 Tyreke Evans 1.25 3.00
43 Tim Duncan 1.50 4.00
44 Shaquille O'Neal 2.00 5.00
45 David West 1.00 2.50
46 Russell Westbrook 1.25 3.00
47 Amare Stoudemire 1.00 2.50
48 Richard Hamilton .75 2.00
49 John Wall 4.00 10.00
50 Gerald Wallace 1.00 2.50

1993 Fax Pax World of Sport

The 1993 Fax Pax World of Sport set was issued in Great Britain and contains 40 standard size cards. This multisport set spotlights notable sports figures from around the world, who are the best in their respective sports. An Olympic subset of seven cards (28-34) is included. The full-bleed fronts feature color action and posed photos with a red-edged white stripe intersecting the photo across the bottom. Within the white stripe is displayed the athlete's name and his country's flag. The horizontal, white backs carry the athlete's name and sport at the top followed by biographical information. Career summary and statistics are printed within a gray box, edged in red.

COMPLETE SET (40) 10.00 20.00
5 Charles Barkley BK .40 1.00
6 Patrick Ewing BK .20 .50
7 Michael Jordan BK 2.00 5.00
8 Shaquille O'Neal BK 1.25 3.00
32 Toni Kukoc BK .10 .30

1993 FCA 50

This 50-card standard-size set was sponsored by Fellowship of Christian Athletes. The color player photos on the fronts are accented on three sides by a thin pink stripe; the card face itself shades from blue to white as one moves toward the bottom. The FCA logo, featuring a cross with two olive branches, is superimposed in the upper left corner, while the player's name is printed beneath the picture and his sport in the pink stripe on the left. On a blue background, the backs carry a close-up photo, biography, and the player's testimony.

COMPLETE SET (50) 10.00 20.00
11 Tanya Crevier BK .20 .50
37 Rob Pelinka BK .20 .50
39 Brent Price BK .20 .50
50 Kay Yow CO BK .20 .50

1993-94 Finest

The premier edition of the 1993-94 Finest basketball set (produced by Topps) contains 220 standard-size cards. The set is comprised of 180 player cards and a 40-card subset of ten of the best players in each of the four divisions as follows: Atlantic (90-99), Central (100-109), Midwest (110-119), and Pacific (120-129). These subset cards are commonly referred to as "brick" cards due to their brick wall background design. The seven-card packs (24 per box) included six player cards plus one subset card and had a suggested retail price of 3.99. Topps also issued a 14-card jumbo pack for 7.99, which included 11 regulars, two subsets, and a jumbo-only Main Attraction chase card. Packs hit the market upon release well above the aforementioned prices. The rainbow colored metallic front features a color action cutout on a metallic marble background. The white bordered back features a color player cutout on the left inset in a marble textured background. Rookie Cards of note include Vin Baker, Anfernee Hardaway, Jamal Mashburn and Chris Webber.

COMPLETE SET (220) 30.00 80.00
1 Michael Jordan 8.00 20.00
2 Larry Bird 1.00 2.50
3 Shaquille O'Neal 2.00 5.00
4 Benoit Benjamin .08 .25
5 Ricky Pierce .08 .25
6 Ken Norman .08 .25
7 Victor Alexander .08 .25
8 Mark Jackson .15 .40
9 Mark West .08 .25
10 Don MacLean .08 .25
11 Reggie Miller .30 .75
12 Sarunas Marciulionis .08 .25
13 Craig Ehlo .08 .25
14 Toni Kukoc RC 1.50 4.00
15 Glen Rice .15 .40
16 Otis Thorpe .15 .40
17 Reggie Williams .08 .25
18 Charles Smith .08 .25
19 Micheal Williams .08 .25
20 Tom Chambers .08 .25
21 David Robinson .60 1.50
22 Jamal Mashburn RC 2.00 5.00
23 Clifford Robinson .15 .40
24 Acie Earl RC .08 .25
25 Danny Ferry .08 .25
26 Bobby Hurley RC .15 .40
27 Eddie Johnson .08 .25
28 Detlef Schrempf .15 .40
29 Mike Brown .08 .25
30 Latrell Sprewell 1.00 2.50
31 Derek Harper .15 .40
32 Stacey Augmon .08 .25
33 Pooh Richardson .08 .25
34 Larry Krystkowiak .08 .25
35 Pervis Ellison .08 .25
36 Jeff Malone .08 .25
37 Sean Elliott .15 .40
38 John Paxson .08 .25
39 Robert Parish .15 .40
40 Mark Aguirre .08 .25
41 Danny Ainge .15 .40
42 Brian Shaw .08 .25
43 LaPhonso Ellis .08 .25
44 Carl Herrera .08 .25
45 Terry Cummings .08 .25
46 Chris Dudley .08 .25
47 Anthony Mason .15 .40
48 Chris Morris .08 .25
49 Todd Day .08 .25
50 Nick Van Exel RC 2.50 6.00
51 Larry Nance .08 .25
52 Derrick McKey .08 .25
53 Muggsy Bogues .15 .40
54 Andrew Lang .08 .25
55 Chuck Person .08 .25
56 Michael Adams .08 .25
57 Spud Webb .08 .25
58 Scott Skiles .08 .25
59 A.C. Green .15 .40
60 Terry Mills .08 .25
61 Xavier McDaniel .08 .25
62 B.J. Armstrong .08 .25
63 Donald Hodge .08 .25
64 Gary Grant .08 .25
65 Billy Owens .08 .25
66 Greg Anthony .08 .25
67 Jay Humphries .08 .25
68 Lionel Simmons .08 .25
69 Dana Barros .08 .25
70 Steve Smith .30 .75
71 Ervin Johnson RC .15 .40
72 Sleepy Floyd .08 .25
73 Blue Edwards .08 .25
74 Clyde Drexler .30 .75
75 Elden Campbell .08 .25
76 Hakeem Olajuwon .60 1.50
77 Clarence Weatherspoon .08 .25
78 Kevin Willis .08 .25
79 Isaiah Rider RC 1.50 4.00
80 Derrick Coleman .15 .40
81 Nick Anderson .15 .40
82 Bryant Stith .08 .25
83 Johnny Newman .08 .25
84 Calbert Cheaney RC .60 1.50
85 Oliver Miller .08 .25
86 Loy Vaught .08 .25
87 Isiah Thomas .30 .75
88 Dee Brown .08 .25
89 Horace Grant .15 .40
90 Patrick Ewing AF .15 .40
91 Clarence Weatherspoon AF .08 .25
92 Rony Seikaly AF .08 .25
93 Dino Radja AF .08 .25
94 Kenny Anderson AF .08 .25
95 John Starks AF .08 .25
96 Tom Gugliotta AF .15 .40
97 Steve Smith AF .15 .40
98 Derrick Coleman AF .08 .25
99 Shaquille O'Neal AF 1.00 2.50
100 Brad Daugherty CF .08 .25
101 Horace Grant CF .08 .25
102 Dominique Wilkins CF .15 .40
103 Joe Dumars CF .15 .40
104 Alonzo Mourning CF .30 .75
105 Scottie Pippen CF .75 2.00
106 Reggie Miller CF .15 .40
107 Mark Price CF .08 .25
108 Ken Norman CF .08 .25
109 Larry Johnson CF .15 .40
110 Jamal Mashburn MF .30 .75
111 Christian Laettner MF .15 .40
112 Karl Malone MF .30 .75
113 Dennis Rodman MF .30 .75
114 Mahmoud Abdul-Rauf MF .08 .25
115 Hakeem Olajuwon MF .30 .75
116 Jim Jackson MF .08 .25
117 John Stockton MF .15 .40
118 David Robinson MF .30 .75
119 Dikembe Mutombo MF .15 .40
120 Vlade Divac PF .08 .25
121 Dan Majerle PF .08 .25
122 Chris Mullin PF .15 .40
123 Shawn Kemp PF .30 .75
124 Danny Manning PF .08 .25
125 Charles Barkley PF .30 .75
126 Mitch Richmond PF .15 .40
127 Tim Hardaway PF .15 .40
128 Detlef Schrempf PF .08 .25
129 Clyde Drexler PF .15 .40
130 Christian Laettner .15 .40
131 Rodney Rogers RC .75 2.00
132 Rik Smits .15 .40
133 Chris Mills RC .75 2.00
134 Corie Blount RC .08 .25
135 Mookie Blaylock .15 .40
136 Jim Jackson .15 .40
137 Tom Gugliotta .30 .75
138 Dennis Scott .08 .25
139 Vin Baker RC 1.50 4.00
140 Gary Payton .60 1.50
141 Sedale Threatt .08 .25
142 Orlando Woolridge .08 .25
143 Avery Johnson .08 .25
144 Charles Oakley .15 .40
145 Harvey Grant .08 .25
146 Bimbo Coles .08 .25
147 Vernon Maxwell .08 .25
148 Danny Manning .15 .40
149 Hersey Hawkins .15 .40
150 Kevin Gamble .08 .25
151 Johnny Dawkins .08 .25
152 Olden Polynice .08 .25
153 Kevin Edwards .08 .25
154 Willie Anderson .08 .25
155 Wayman Tisdale .08 .25
156 Popeye Jones RC .08 .25
157 Dan Majerle .15 .40
158 Rex Chapman .08 .25
159 Shawn Kemp UER .60 1.50
(Misnumbered 136)
160 Eric Murdock .08 .25
161 Randy White .08 .25
162 Larry Johnson .30 .75
163 Dominique Wilkins .30 .75
164 Dikembe Mutombo .30 .75
165 Patrick Ewing .30 .75
166 Jerome Kersey .08 .25
167 Dale Davis .08 .25
168 Ron Harper .15 .40
169 Sam Cassell RC 2.50 6.00
170 Bill Cartwright .08 .25
171 John Williams .08 .25
172 Dino Radja RC .08 .25
173 Dennis Rodman 1.00 2.50
174 Kenny Anderson .15 .40
175 Robert Horry .15 .40
176 Chris Mullin .30 .75
177 John Salley .08 .25
178 Scott Burrell RC .60 1.50
179 Mitch Richmond .30 .75
180 Lee Mayberry .08 .25
181 James Worthy .30 .75
182 Rick Fox .08 .25
183 Kevin Johnson .15 .40
184 Lindsey Hunter RC .75 2.00
185 Marlon Maxey .08 .25
186 Sam Perkins .15 .40
187 Kevin Duckworth .08 .25
188 Jeff Hornacek .15 .40
189 Anfernee Hardaway RC 5.00 12.00
190 Rex Walters RC .08 .25
191 Mahmoud Abdul-Rauf .08 .25
192 Terry Dehere RC .08 .25
193 Brad Daugherty .08 .25
194 John Starks .15 .40
195 Rod Strickland .15 .40
196 Luther Wright RC .08 .25
197 Vlade Divac .15 .40
198 Tim Hardaway .30 .75
199 Joe Dumars .30 .75
200 Charles Barkley .60 1.50
201 Alonzo Mourning .60 1.50
202 Doug West .08 .25
203 Anthony Avent .08 .25
204 Lloyd Daniels .08 .25
205 Mark Price .15 .40
206 Rumeal Robinson .08 .25
207 Kendall Gill .15 .40
208 Scottie Pippen 1.25 3.00
209 Kenny Smith .08 .25
210 Walt Williams .08 .25
211 Hubert Davis .08 .25
212 Chris Webber RC 8.00 20.00
213 Rony Seikaly .08 .25
214 Sam Bowie .08 .25
215 Karl Malone .60 1.50
216 Malik Sealy .08 .25
217 Dale Ellis .08 .25
218 Harold Miner .08 .25
219 John Stockton .30 .75
220 Shawn Bradley RC .75 2.00

1993-94 Finest Refractors

This set of Refractor cards parallels that of the 220-card Finest set. Information provided by Topps indicated the cards were randomly inserted at a rate of one in every nine seven-card packs and one in approximately four 14-card jumbo packs. However, widespread evidence indicates the cards are easier to obtain. In addition, a good amount of the cards were included in retail "re-packs" at chains like Wal-Mart and Sams. The only difference in design to the basic cards is refracting foil that creates a glossy shine to the card fronts when held under light. Cards with an asterisk next to their listing signify that it is currently perceived to be in shorter supply. To ascertain values on individual cards, please refer to the multiplier in the header below, coupled with the value of the base card.

SP (10/28/35/40/47/49/53) 2.00 5.00
SP (56/57/107/190/204/218) 2.00 5.00
SP (33/36/41/78/89) 3.00 8.00
SP (91/116/128/142/147) 3.00 8.00
SP (155/180/211/217) 3.00 8.00
SP (7/12/48/64/66/170/182) 10.00 25.00
*STARS: 5X TO 12X HI COLUMN
*RCs: 2X TO 5X HI
2 Larry Bird 15.00 40.00
14 Toni Kukoc 8.00 20.00
50 Nick Van Exel ! 10.00 25.00
76 Hakeem Olajuwon 10.00 25.00
79 Isaiah Rider 6.00 15.00
84 Calbert Cheaney SP 6.00 15.00
90 Patrick Ewing AF 2.50 6.00
115 Hakeem Olajuwon MF 5.00 12.00
123 Shawn Kemp PF 5.00 12.00
125 Charles Barkley PF 5.00 12.00
129 Clyde Drexler PF 4.00 10.00
133 Chris Mills SP 6.00 15.00
169 Sam Cassell 8.00 20.00

1993-94 Finest Main Attraction

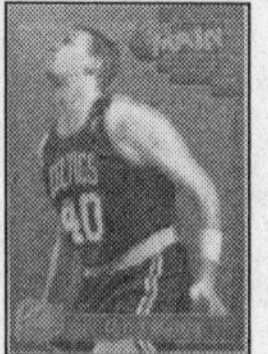

Distributed one per 14-card jumbo pack, a player from each of the 27 NBA teams is represented in this standard size set. The rainbow colored metallic front features a semi-embossed color action cutout on textured metallic background. The brick textured bordered back features a color action shot with a gold border. Player's statistics and profile appear below the photo. The cards are numbered on the back "X of 27."

COMPLETE SET (27) 25.00 50.00
1 Dominique Wilkins .60 1.50
2 Dino Radja .20 .50
3 Larry Johnson .60 1.50
4 Scottie Pippen 2.50 6.00
5 Mark Price .20 .50
6 Jamal Mashburn 1.25 3.00
7 Mahmoud Abdul-Rauf .20 .50
8 Joe Dumars .60 1.50
9 Chris Webber 5.00 12.00
10 Hakeem Olajuwon 1.25 3.00
11 Reggie Miller .60 1.50
12 Danny Manning .30 .75
13 Doug Christie .30 .75
14 Steve Smith .60 1.50
15 Eric Murdock .20 .50
16 Isaiah Rider 1.25 3.00
17 Derrick Coleman .30 .75
18 Patrick Ewing .60 1.50
19 Shaquille O'Neal 4.00 10.00
20 Shawn Bradley 1.50 4.00
21 Charles Barkley 1.25 3.00
22 Clyde Drexler .60 1.50
23 Mitch Richmond .60 1.50
24 David Robinson 1.25 3.00
25 Shawn Kemp 1.25 3.00
26 Karl Malone 1.25 3.00
27 Tom Gugliotta .60 1.50

1994-95 Finest

This 331-card standard size set was issued in two series of 165 and 166 cards each. Cards were distributed in seven-card packs carrying a suggested retail price of $5.00 each. Metallic silver fronts feature a color player photo against a prismatic background. The backs have a small photo, stats, bio and a "Finest Moment '93-94". The backs have blue borders with the player's name and position at the top. Topical subsets featured are City Legend-NYC (1-10), City Legend-Balt/DC (51-55), City Legend-Detroit (101-105), City Legend-Chicago (106-110), City Legend/LA (151-155), Finest's ACC's Best (201-209), Finest's Big East's Best (226-234), Finest's Big Ten's Best (250-259), and Finest's SEC's Best (275-284). Each card features a protective coating on front that was designed to protect the card from problems that may arise from handling. The coating can be removed by carefully peeling it from the card. Values provided below are for unpeeled cards. Peeled cards generally trade for about ten to twenty-five percent less. Rookie Cards of note include Grant Hill, Juwan Howard, Eddie Jones, Jason Kidd and Glenn Robinson.

COMPLETE SET (1-331) 90.00 220.00
COMPLETE SERIES 1 (165) 40.00 100.00
COMPLETE SERIES 2 (166) 50.00 120.00
1 Chris Mullin CY .30 .75
2 Anthony Mason CY .20 .50
3 John Salley CY .20 .50
4 Jamal Mashburn CY .30 .75
5 Mark Jackson CY .20 .50
6 Mario Elie CY .20 .50
7 Kenny Anderson CY .25 .60
8 Rod Strickland CY .30 .75
9 Kenny Smith CY .25 .60
10 Olden Polynice CY .20 .50
11 Derek Harper .50 1.25
12 Danny Ainge .60 1.50
13 Dino Radja .50 1.25
14 Eric Murdock .40 1.00
15 Sean Rooks .40 1.00
16 Dell Curry .40 1.00
17 Victor Alexander .40 1.00
18 Rodney Rogers .40 1.00
19 John Salley .40 1.00
20 Brad Daugherty .50 1.25
21 Elmore Spencer .40 1.00
22 Mitch Richmond .60 1.50
23 Rex Walters .40 1.00
24 Antonio Davis .40 1.00
25 B.J. Armstrong .40 1.00
26 Andrew Lang .40 1.00
27 Carl Herrera .40 1.00
28 Kevin Edwards .40 1.00
29 Micheal Williams .40 1.00
30 Clyde Drexler .75 2.00
31 Dana Barros .40 1.00
32 Shaquille O'Neal 4.00 10.00
33 Patrick Ewing .75 2.00
34 Charles Barkley 1.00 2.50
35 J.R. Reid .40 1.00
36 Lindsey Hunter .40 1.00
37 Jeff Malone .40 1.00
38 Rik Smits .50 1.25
39 Brian Williams .40 1.00
40 Shawn Kemp .60 1.50
41 Terry Porter .40 1.00
42 James Worthy .75 2.00
43 Rex Chapman .40 1.00
44 Stanley Roberts .40 1.00
45 Chris Smith .40 1.00
46 Dee Brown .40 1.00
47 Chris Gatling .40 1.00
48 Donald Hodge .40 1.00
49 Bimbo Coles .40 1.00
50 Derrick Coleman .50 1.25
51 Muggsy Bogues CY .25 .60
52 Reggie Williams CY .20 .50
53 David Wingate CY .20 .50
54 Sam Cassell CY .30 .75
55 Sherman Douglas CY .20 .50
56 Keith Jennings .40 1.00
57 Kenny Gattison .40 1.00
58 Brent Price .40 1.00
59 Luc Longley .40 1.00
60 Jamal Mashburn .60 1.50
61 Doug West .40 1.00
62 Walt Williams .40 1.00
63 Tracy Murray .40 1.00
64 Robert Pack .40 1.00
65 Johnny Dawkins .40 1.00
66 Vin Baker .60 1.50
67 Sam Cassell .60 1.50
68 Dale Davis .40 1.00
69 Terrell Brandon .40 1.00
70 Billy Owens .40 1.00
71 Ervin Johnson .40 1.00
72 Allan Houston .60 1.50
73 Craig Ehlo .40 1.00
74 Loy Vaught .40 1.00
75 Scottie Pippen 2.00 5.00
76 Sam Bowie .40 1.00
77 Anthony Mason .40 1.00
78 Felton Spencer .40 1.00
79 P.J. Brown .40 1.00
80 Christian Laettner .50 1.25
81 Todd Day .40 1.00
82 Sean Elliott .60 1.50
83 Grant Long .40 1.00
84 Xavier McDaniel .40 1.00
85 David Benoit .40 1.00
86 Larry Stewart .40 1.00
87 Donald Royal .40 1.00
88 Duane Causwell .40 1.00
89 Vlade Divac .60 1.50
90 Derrick McKey .40 1.00
91 Kevin Johnson .60 1.50
92 LaPhonso Ellis .40 1.00
93 Jerome Kersey .40 1.00
94 Muggsy Bogues .50 1.25
95 Tom Gugliotta .40 1.00
96 Jeff Hornacek .50 1.25
97 Kevin Willis .40 1.00
98 Chris Mills .40 1.00
99 Sam Perkins .40 1.00
100 Alonzo Mourning .75 2.00
101 Derrick Coleman CY .25 .60
102 Glen Rice CY .30 .75
103 Kevin Willis CY .20 .50
104 Chris Webber CY .75 2.00
105 Terry Mills CY .20 .50
106 Tim Hardaway CY .30 .75
107 Nick Anderson CY .20 .50
108 Terry Cummings CY .30 .75
109 Hersey Hawkins CY .20 .50
110 Ken Norman CY .20 .50
111 Nick Anderson .40 1.00
112 Tim Perry .40 1.00
113 Terry Dehere .40 1.00
114 Chris Morris .40 1.00
115 John Williams .40 1.00
116 Jon Barry .40 1.00
117 Rony Seikaly .50 1.25
118 Detlef Schrempf .60 1.50
119 Terry Cummings .60 1.50
120 Chris Webber 1.50 4.00
121 David Wingate .40 1.00
122 Popeye Jones .40 1.00
123 Sherman Douglas .40 1.00
124 Greg Anthony .40 1.00
125 Mookie Blaylock .40 1.00
126 Don MacLean .40 1.00
127 Lionel Simmons .40 1.00
128 Scott Brooks .40 1.00
129 Jeff Turner .40 1.00
130 Bryant Stith .40 1.00
131 Shawn Bradley .40 1.00
132 Byron Scott .50 1.25
133 Doug Christie .40 1.00
134 Dennis Rodman 2.00 5.00
135 Dan Majerle .60 1.50
136 Gary Grant .40 1.00
137 Bryon Russell .40 1.00
138 Will Perdue .40 1.00
139 Gheorghe Muresan .40 1.00
140 Kendall Gill .40 1.00
141 Isaiah Rider .60 1.50
142 Terry Mills .40 1.00
143 Willie Anderson .40 1.00
144 Hubert Davis .40 1.00
145 Lucious Harris .40 1.00
146 Spud Webb .60 1.50
147 Glen Rice .60 1.50
148 Dennis Scott .40 1.00
149 Robert Horry .60 1.50
150 John Stockton .75 2.00
151 Stacey Augmon CY .25 .60
152 Chris Mills CY .20 .50
153 Elden Campbell CY .20 .50
154 Jay Humphries CY .20 .50
155 Reggie Miller CY .40 1.00
156 George Lynch .40 1.00
157 Tyrone Hill .40 1.00
158 Lee Mayberry .40 1.00
159 Jon Koncak .40 1.00
160 Joe Dumars .60 1.50
161 Vernon Maxwell .40 1.00
162 Joe Kleine .40 1.00
163 Acie Earl .40 1.00
164 Steve Kerr .50 1.25
165 Rod Strickland .40 1.00
166 Glenn Robinson RC 1.50 4.00
167 Anfernee Hardaway 1.25 3.00
168 Latrell Sprewell .60 1.50
169 Sergei Bazarevich RC .75 2.00
170 Hakeem Olajuwon .60 1.50
171 Nick Van Exel .50 1.25
172 Buck Williams .30 .75
173 Antoine Carr .40 1.00
174 Corie Blount .40 1.00
175 Dominique Wilkins .60 1.50
176 Yinka Dare RC .75 2.00
177 Byron Houston .30 .75
178 LaSalle Thompson .30 .75
179 Doug Smith .30 .75
180 David Robinson .75 2.00
181 Eric Piatkowski RC 1.00 2.50
182 Scott Skiles .30 .75
183 Scott Burrell .30 .75
184 Mark West .30 .75
185 Billy Owens .30 .75
186 Brian Grant RC 1.25 3.00
187 Scott Williams .30 .75
188 Gerald Madkins .30 .75
189 Reggie Williams .30 .75
190 Danny Manning .40 1.00
191 Mike Brown .30 .75
192 Charles Smith .30 .75
193 Elden Campbell .30 .75
194 Ricky Pierce .30 .75
195 Karl Malone .60 1.50
196 Brooks Thompson RC .75 2.00
197 Alaa Abdelnaby .30 .75
198 Tyrone Corbin .30 .75
199 Johnny Newman .30 .75
200 Grant Hill CB 2.00 5.00
201 Kenny Anderson CB .30 .75
202 Olden Polynice CB .15 .40
203 Horace Grant CB .30 .75
204 Muggsy Bogues CB .20 .50
205 Mark Price CB .25 .60
206 Tom Gugliotta CB .15 .40
207 Christian Laettner CB .20 .50
208 Eric Montross CB .20 .50
209 Sam Cassell CB .25 .60
210 Charles Oakley .40 1.00
211 Harold Ellis .30 .75
212 Nate McMillan .30 .75
213 Chuck Person .40 1.00
214 Harold Miner .30 .75
215 Clarence Weatherspoon .30 .75
216 Robert Parish .50 1.25
217 Michael Cage .30 .75
218 Kenny Smith .40 1.00
219 Larry Krystkowiak .30 .75
220 Dikembe Mutombo .50 1.25
221 Wayman Tisdale .30 .75
222 Kevin Duckworth .30 .75
223 Vern Fleming .30 .75
224 Eric Mobley RC .75 2.00
225 Patrick Ewing CB .25 .60
226 Clifford Robinson CB .15 .40
227 Eric Murdock CB .15 .40
228 Derrick Coleman CB .15 .40
229 Otis Thorpe CB .15 .40
230 Alonzo Mourning CB .30 .75
231 Donyell Marshall CB .40 1.00
232 Dikembe Mutombo CB .25 .60
233 Rony Seikaly CB .20 .50
234 Chris Mullin CB .25 .60
235 Reggie Miller .60 1.50
236 Benoit Benjamin .30 .75
237 Sean Rooks .30 .75
238 Terry Davis .30 .75
239 Anthony Avent .30 .75
240 Grant Hill RC 8.00 20.00
241 Randy Woods .30 .75
242 Tom Chambers .50 1.25
243 Michael Adams .30 .75
244 Monty Williams RC .75 2.00
245 Chris Mullin .50 1.25
246 Bill Wennington .30 .75
247 Mark Jackson .50 1.25
248 Blue Edwards .30 .75
249 Jalen Rose RC 2.50 6.00
250 Glenn Robinson CB .75 2.00
251 Kevin Willis CB .15 .40
252 B.J. Armstrong CB .15 .40
253 Jim Jackson CB .15 .40
254 Steve Smith CB .20 .50
255 Chris Webber CB .60 1.50
256 Glen Rice CB .25 .60
257 Derek Harper CB .20 .50
258 Jalen Rose CB 1.00 2.50
259 Juwan Howard CB .60 1.50
260 Kenny Anderson .40 1.00
261 Calbert Cheaney .30 .75
262 Bill Cartwright .40 1.00
263 Mario Elie .30 .75
264 Chris Dudley .30 .75
265 Jim Jackson .30 .75
266 Antonio Harvey .30 .75
267 Bill Curley RC .75 2.00
268 Moses Malone .50 1.25
269 A.C. Green .50 1.25
270 Larry Johnson .50 1.25
271 Marty Conlon .30 .75
272 Greg Graham .30 .75
273 Eric Montross RC .75 2.00
274 Stacey King .30 .75
275 Charles Barkley CB .40 1.00
276 Chris Morris CB .15 .40
277 Robert Horry CB .25 .60
278 Dominique Wilkins CB .30 .75
279 Latrell Sprewell CB .30 .75
280 Shaquille O'Neal CB 1.25 3.00
281 Wesley Person CB .40 1.00
282 Mahmoud Abdul-Rauf CB .15 .40
283 Jamal Mashburn CB .25 .60
284 Dale Ellis CB .15 .40
285 Gary Payton .50 1.25
286 Jason Kidd RC 6.00 15.00
287 Ken Norman .30 .75
288 Juwan Howard RC 1.25 3.00
289 Lamond Murray RC .75 2.00
290 Clifford Robinson .30 .75
291 Frank Brickowski .30 .75
292 Adam Keefe .30 .75
293 Ron Harper .40 1.00
294 Tom Hammonds .30 .75
295 Otis Thorpe .30 .75
296 Rick Mahorn .30 .75
297 Alton Lister .30 .75
298 Vinny Del Negro .30 .75
299 Danny Ferry .30 .75
300 John Starks .40 1.00
301 Duane Ferrell .30 .75
302 Hersey Hawkins .30 .75
303 Khalid Reeves RC .75 2.00
304 Anthony Peeler .30 .75
305 Tim Hardaway .50 1.25
306 Rick Fox .30 .75
307 Jay Humphries .30 .75
308 Brian Shaw .30 .75
309 Danny Schayes .30 .75
310 Stacey Augmon .40 1.00
311 Oliver Miller .30 .75
312 Pooh Richardson .30 .75
313 Donyell Marshall RC .75 2.00
314 Aaron McKie RC .75 2.00
315 Mark Price .50 1.25
316 B.J. Tyler RC .75 2.00
317 Olden Polynice .30 .75
318 Avery Johnson .40 1.00
319 Derek Strong .30 .75
320 Toni Kukoc .60 1.50
321 Charlie Ward RC .75 2.00
322 Wesley Person RC .75 2.00
323 Eddie Jones RC 3.00 8.00
324 Horace Grant .40 1.00
325 Mahmoud Abdul-Rauf .30 .75
326 Sharone Wright RC .75 2.00
327 Kevin Gamble .30 .75
328 Sarunas Marciulionis .30 .75
329 Harvey Grant .30 .75
330 Bobby Hurley .50 1.25
331 Michael Jordan 8.00 20.00

1994-95 Finest Refractors

Parallel to the basic set, Refractors were randomly inserted in first and second packs at a rate of one in 12. Refractors are distinguished from the basic cards by their rainbow-like appearance that refracts more light. Just like regular issue Finest cards, each Refractor comes with a protective coating designed to protect the card from wear and tear. Values provided below are for unpeeled cards. Peeled cards trade for about twenty-five to fifty percent less. The set is condition sensitive. The cards marked with an asterisk are perceived to be more scarce than the other singles. To ascertain values on individual cards not listed please refer to the multiplier lines.

*SER.1 STARS: 2.5X TO 6X BASE CARD HI
*SER.1 SUBSETS: 5X TO 12X BASE HI
*SER.2 STARS: 3X TO 8X BASE HI
*SER.2 SUBSETS: 6X TO 15X BASE HI
*RCs: 3X TO 8X BASE HI
22 Mitch Richmond 8.00 20.00
30 Clyde Drexler 8.00 20.00
33 Patrick Ewing 8.00 20.00
34 Charles Barkley 12.00 30.00
40 Shawn Kemp 15.00 40.00
42 James Worthy 15.00 40.00
75 Scottie Pippen 25.00 60.00
100 Alonzo Mourning 10.00 25.00
102 Glen Rice CY SP 30.00 80.00
104 Chris Webber CY SP 20.00 40.00
106 Tim Hardaway CY SP 20.00 50.00
120 Chris Webber SP 40.00 80.00
134 Dennis Rodman 20.00 50.00
150 John Stockton SP 15.00 40.00
155 Reggie Miller CY SP 15.00 30.00
160 Joe Dumars 8.00
165 Glenn Robinson 25.00
167 Anfernee Hardaway 20.00
168 Latrell Sprewell 8.00
170 Hakeem Olajuwon 10.00
171 Nick Van Exel 8.00
175 Dominique Wilkins 8.00
180 David Robinson 12.00
195 Karl Malone 10.00
200 Grant Hill CB 20.00
230 Alonzo Mourning CB 10.00
235 Reggie Miller 8.00
245 Chris Mullin 8.00
255 Chris Webber CB 10.00
275 Charles Barkley CB 10.00
285 Gary Payton 8.00
320 Toni Kukoc 12.00
331 Michael Jordan 100.00 2

1994-95 Finest Cornerstor

Randomly inserted in second series packs at a r
one in every 24, cards from this 15-card standar
set highlight players who are foundations of thei
respective teams. The fronts have a color-action
set against a multi-colored background. The bac
have a color-photo and player information. Valu
provided below are for unpeeled cards. Peeled ca
generally trade for ten to twenty-five percent less

COMPLETE SET (15) 40.00
CS1 Shaquille O'Neal 10.00
CS2 Alonzo Mourning 3.00
CS3 Patrick Ewing 3.00
CS4 Karl Malone 3.00
CS5 Kenny Anderson 2.00
CS6 Latrell Sprewell 3.00
CS7 Dikembe Mutombo 2.50
CS8 Charles Barkley 4.00
CS9 John Stockton 3.00
CS10 Reggie Miller 3.00
CS11 Jamal Mashburn 2.50
CS12 Anfernee Hardaway 6.00
CS13 Jim Jackson 1.50
CS14 David Robinson 4.00
CS15 Hakeem Olajuwon 3.00

1994-95 Finest Cornerstor Refractors Test

This 15-card set is a parallel to the regular Corne
insert. The cards feature the "classic" regular ref
technology. These cards are considered test issu
since they were never intended to be released to
public. It is unknown how they made their way ir
market as these cards were not inserted into pac

CS1 Shaquille O'Neal 125.00
CS2 Alonzo Mourning 60.00
CS3 Patrick Ewing 60.00
CS4 Karl Malone 60.00
CS5 Kenny Anderson 60.00
CS6 Latrell Sprewell 60.00
CS7 Dikembe Mutombo 50.00
CS8 Charles Barkley 80.00 2
CS9 John Stockton 60.00
CS10 Reggie Miller 60.00
CS11 Jamal Mashburn 50.00
CS12 Anfernee Hardaway 80.00
CS13 Jim Jackson 30.00
CS14 David Robinson 80.00
CS15 Hakeem Olajuwon 60.00

1994-95 Finest Iron Mer

Randomly inserted in first series packs at a rate
in 24, cards from this 10-card standard-size set
spotlight players who played at least 3,000 minu
during the 1993-94 NBA season. These transpar
cards have a front design much like the basic Fi
cards with "Iron Man" at the top. The only desig
element on back is a small stat box at the botton
Unlike most other 1994-95 Finest cards, Iron Me
inserts have no protective coating.

COMPLETE SET (10) 15.00
1 Shaquille O'Neal 6.00
2 Kenny Anderson 1.50
3 Jim Jackson 1.25
4 Clarence Weatherspoon 1.25
5 Karl Malone 2.50
6 Dan Majerle 2.00
7 Anfernee Hardaway 3.00
8 David Robinson 3.00
9 Latrell Sprewell 2.50
10 Hakeem Olajuwon 2.50

1994-95 Finest Lottery Pri

Randomly inserted in second series packs at a r
one in six, cards from this 22-card standard-siz
showcase lottery picks who went on to become
players. The fronts have a color-action photo wi
background having a large basketball surrounde
variety of colors and stars. The backs have a col
photo and player information with the words "L
Prize" set against a basketball. Values provided
are for unpeeled cards. Peeled cards generally tr
ten to twenty-five percent less.

COMPLETE SET (22) 12.00
LP1 Patrick Ewing 1.00
LP2 Chris Mullin 1.00
LP3 David Robinson 1.50
LP4 Scottie Pippen 2.00
LP5 Kevin Johnson 1.00
LP6 Danny Manning .75
LP7 Mitch Richmond 1.00
LP8 Derrick Coleman .75
LP9 Gary Payton 1.00
LP10 Mahmoud Abdul-Rauf .60
LP11 Larry Johnson 1.00
LP12 Kenny Anderson 1.00
LP13 Dikembe Mutombo 1.00
LP14 Stacey Augmon .75
LP15 Shaquille O'Neal 2.50
LP16 Alonzo Mourning 1.25
LP17 Clarence Weatherspoon .60
LP18 Robert Horry 1.00
LP19 Chris Webber 1.50
LP20 Anfernee Hardaway 1.50
LP21 Jamal Mashburn 1.00
LP22 Vin Baker 1.00

94-95 Finest Lottery Prize Refractors Test

-card set is a parallel to the regular Lottery sert. The cards feature the "classic" regular technology. These cards are considered test ince they were never intended to be released to ic. It is unknown how they made their way into ket as these cards were not inserted into packs.

rick Ewing	40.00	100.00
is Mullin	30.00	80.00
id Robinson	50.00	125.00
ttie Pippen	60.00	150.00
in Johnson	30.00	80.00
ny Manning	25.00	60.00
ch Richmond	30.00	80.00
rick Coleman	25.00	60.00
y Payton	30.00	80.00
ahmoud Abdul-Rauf	20.00	50.00
rry Johnson	30.00	80.00
nny Anderson	25.00	60.00
kembe Mutombo	30.00	80.00
acey Augmon	25.00	60.00
aquille O'Neal	80.00	200.00
onzo Mourning	40.00	100.00
arence Weatherspoon	20.00	50.00
bert Horry	30.00	80.00
hris Webber	50.00	125.00
fernee Hardaway	50.00	125.00
mal Mashburn	30.00	80.00
n Baker	30.00	80.00

4-95 Finest Marathon Men

ly inserted into first series packs at a rate of 2, cards from this 12-card standard-size set t players who played in all 82 games during 3-94 NBA season. These transparent cards design on front that is similar to the basic issue words "Marathon Man" at the top. The back s a small stat box at the bottom. Unlike most 994-95 Finest cards, Marathon Men inserts protective coatings.

ETE SET (20)	20.00	50.00
Sprewell	3.00	8.00
Payton	2.00	5.00
Anderson	1.50	4.00
ackson	1.25	3.00
ey Hunter	1.25	3.00
Strickland	1.25	3.00
y Hawkins	1.25	3.00
Wilkins	1.25	3.00
rmstrong	1.25	3.00
rnee Hardaway	5.00	12.00
ey Augmon	1.50	4.00
Murdock	1.25	3.00
ence Weatherspoon	1.25	3.00
Malone	2.50	6.00
rles Oakley	1.50	4.00
Fox	1.25	3.00
Thorpe	1.25	3.00
mbe Mutombo	2.00	5.00
Brown	1.25	3.00
Green	2.00	5.00

994-95 Finest Rack Pack

nly inserted in second series packs at a rate of every 72, cards from this seven-card standard- spotlight a selection of top performers from the BA draft class. The fronts have a color-action with a basketball hoop and lights in the ound. The words "Rack Pack" appear at the top l-foil. The backs have player information inside nputer monitor. Like many of the Finest cards, ards also came with a protective covering. The isted below are for peeled cards. Peeled cards lly trade for ten to twenty-five percent less.

ETE SET (7)	15.00	40.00
ant Hill	8.00	20.00
esley Person	1.50	4.00
wan Howard	2.50	6.00
mond Murray	1.50	4.00
enn Robinson	3.00	8.00
nyell Marshall	1.50	4.00
son Kidd	8.00	20.00

994-95 Finest Rack Pack Refractors Test

even-card set is a parallel to the regular Rack nsert. The cards feature the "classic" regular r technology. These cards are considered test since they were never intended to be released to blic. It is unknown how they made their way into rket as these cards were not inserted into packs.

rant Hill	80.00	200.00
esley Person	15.00	40.00
iwan Howard	25.00	60.00
amond Murray	15.00	40.00
lenn Robinson	30.00	80.00
onyell Marshall	15.00	40.00
ason Kidd	80.00	200.00

1995-96 Finest

95-96 Topps Finest set was issued in two te series of 140 and 111 standard-size cards. for both series were issued in six-card packs ested retail price of $5.00). Each pack contained sic cards and one Mystery insert card. Basic cards feature blue-bordered metallic fronts and t action shots set against a swirling court round. The Rookie subset cards (111-139) orange-bordered cards. Magic Johnson's card was added very late in the production schedule nlike other player cards features a red border on front instead of blue. The checklist card (#111) has an uncorrected error - it should have been numbered 140 as the last card in the first series. Also, card #251, originally scheduled to be a checklist for the second series set, was never printed. Each card features an opaque coating that can be carefully peeled off designed to protect the card front from problems that may arise from handling. Values provided below are for unpeeled cards. Peeled cards generally trade for ten to twenty-five percent less. Noteworthy Rookie Cards include Michael Finley, Kevin Garnett, Joe Smith, Jerry Stackhouse and Damon Stoudamire.

COMPLETE SET (251)	90.00	180.00
COMPLETE SERIES 1 (140)	75.00	150.00
COMPLETE SERIES 2 (111)	15.00	30.00
1 Hakeem Olajuwon	1.00	2.50
2 Stacey Augmon	.60	1.50
3 John Starks	.60	1.50
4 Sharone Wright	.50	1.25
5 Jason Kidd	1.25	3.00
6 Lamond Murray	.50	1.25
7 Kenny Anderson	.60	1.50
8 James Robinson	.50	1.25
9 Wesley Person	.50	1.25
10 Latrell Sprewell	.75	2.00
11 Sean Elliott	.75	2.00
12 Greg Anthony	.50	1.25
13 Kendall Gill	.50	1.25
14 Mark Jackson	.75	2.00
15 John Stockton	1.00	2.50
16 Steve Smith	.60	1.50
17 Bobby Hurley	.75	2.00
18 Ervin Johnson	.50	1.25
19 Elden Campbell	.50	1.25
20 Vin Baker	.60	1.50
21 Micheal Williams	.50	1.25
22 Steve Kerr	.60	1.50
23 Kevin Duckworth	.50	1.25
24 Willie Anderson	.50	1.25
25 Joe Dumars	.75	2.00
26 Dale Ellis	.50	1.25
27 Bimbo Coles	.50	1.25
28 Nick Anderson	.50	1.25
29 Dee Brown	.50	1.25
30 Tyrone Hill	.50	1.25
31 Reggie Miller	1.00	2.50
32 Shaquille O'Neal	2.00	5.00
33 Brian Grant	.60	1.50
34 Charles Barkley	1.25	3.00
35 Cedric Ceballos	.50	1.25
36 Rex Walters	.50	1.25
37 Kenny Smith	.60	1.50
38 Popeye Jones	.50	1.25
39 Harvey Grant	.50	1.25
40 Gary Payton	.75	2.00
41 John Williams	.50	1.25
42 Sherman Douglas	.50	1.25
43 Oliver Miller	.50	1.25
44 Kevin Willis	.50	1.25
45 Isaiah Rider	.75	2.00
46 Gheorghe Muresan	.50	1.25
47 Blue Edwards	.50	1.25
48 Jeff Hornacek	.60	1.50
49 J.R. Reid	.50	1.25
50 Glenn Robinson	.75	2.00
51 Dell Curry	.50	1.25
52 Greg Graham	.50	1.25
53 Ron Harper	.60	1.50
54 Derek Harper	.60	1.50
55 Dikembe Mutombo	.75	2.00
56 Terry Mills	.50	1.25
57 Victor Alexander	.50	1.25
58 Malik Sealy	.50	1.25
59 Vincent Askew	.50	1.25
60 Mitch Richmond	.75	2.00
61 Duane Ferrell	.50	1.25
62 Dickey Simpkins	.50	1.25
63 Pooh Richardson	.50	1.25
64 Khalid Reeves	.50	1.25
65 Dino Radja	.60	1.50
66 Lee Mayberry	.50	1.25
67 Kenny Gattison	.50	1.25
68 Joe Kleine	.50	1.25
69 Tony Dumas	.50	1.25
70 Nick Van Exel	.75	2.00
71 Armon Gilliam	.50	1.25
72 Craig Ehlo	.50	1.25
73 Adam Keefe	.50	1.25
74 Chris Dudley	.50	1.25
75 Clyde Drexler	1.00	2.50
76 Jeff Turner	.50	1.25
77 Calbert Cheaney	.50	1.25
78 Vinny Del Negro	.50	1.25
79 Tim Perry	.50	1.25
80 Tim Hardaway	.75	2.00
81 B.J. Armstrong	.50	1.25
82 Muggsy Bogues	.60	1.50
83 Mark Macon	.50	1.25
84 Doug West	.50	1.25
85 Jalen Rose	1.00	2.50
86 Chris Mills	.50	1.25
87 Charles Oakley	.60	1.50
88 Andrew Lang	.50	1.25
89 Olden Polynice	.50	1.25
90 Sam Cassell	.75	2.00
91 Todd Day	.50	1.25
92 P.J. Brown	.50	1.25
93 Benoit Benjamin	.50	1.25
94 Sam Perkins	.50	1.25
95 Eddie Jones	1.00	2.50
96 Robert Parish	.75	2.00
97 Avery Johnson	.60	1.50
98 Lindsey Hunter	.50	1.25
99 Billy Owens	.50	1.25
100 Shawn Bradley	.50	1.25
101 Dale Davis	.50	1.25
102 Terry Dehere	.50	1.25
103 A.C. Green	.75	2.00
104 Christian Laettner	.60	1.50
105 Horace Grant	.60	1.50
106 Rony Seikaly	.60	1.50
107 Reggie Williams	.50	1.25
108 Toni Kukoc	.75	2.00
109 Terrell Brandon	.50	1.25
110 Clifford Robinson	.50	1.25
111 Joe Smith RC	1.50	4.00
112 Antonio McDyess RC	3.00	8.00
113 Jerry Stackhouse RC	4.00	10.00
114 Rasheed Wallace RC	4.00	10.00
115 Kevin Garnett RC	17.50	35.00
116 Bryant Reeves RC	.75	2.00
117 Damon Stoudamire RC	2.00	5.00
118 Shawn Respert RC	.75	2.00
119 Ed O'Bannon RC	.75	2.00
120 Kurt Thomas RC	.75	2.00
121 Gary Trent RC	.75	2.00
122 Cherokee Parks RC	.75	2.00
123 Corliss Williamson RC	.75	2.00
124 Eric Williams RC	.75	2.00
125 Brent Barry RC	1.25	3.00
126 Alan Henderson RC	.75	2.00
127 Bob Sura RC	.75	2.00
128 Theo Ratliff RC	1.50	4.00
129 Randolph Childress RC	.75	2.00
130 Jason Caffey RC	.75	2.00
131 Michael Finley RC	4.00	10.00
132 George Zidek RC	.75	2.00
133 Travis Best RC	.75	2.00
134 Loren Meyer RC	.75	2.00
135 David Vaughn RC	.75	2.00
136 Sherrell Ford RC	.75	2.00
137 Mario Bennett RC	.75	2.00
138 Greg Ostertag RC	.75	2.00
139 Cory Alexander RC	.75	2.00
140 Checklist (1-110) UER misnumbered #111	.50	1.25
141 Chucky Brown	.50	1.25
142 Eric Mobley	.50	1.25
143 Tom Hammonds	.50	1.25
144 Chris Webber	1.00	2.50
145 Carlos Rogers	.50	1.25
146 Chuck Person	.60	1.50
147 Brian Williams	.50	1.25
148 Kevin Gamble	.50	1.25
149 Dennis Rodman	1.50	4.00
150 Pervis Ellison	.50	1.25
151 Jayson Williams	.50	1.25
152 Buck Williams	.50	1.25
153 Allan Houston	.60	1.50
154 Tom Gugliotta	.50	1.25
155 Charles Smith	.50	1.25
156 Chris Gatling	.50	1.25
157 Darrin Hancock	.50	1.25
158 Blue Edwards	.50	1.25
159 Shawn Kemp	.75	2.00
160 Michael Cage	.50	1.25
161 Sedale Threatt	.50	1.25
162 Byron Scott	.60	1.50
163 Elliot Perry	.50	1.25
164 Jim Jackson	.50	1.25
165 Wayman Tisdale	.50	1.25
166 Vernon Maxwell	.50	1.25
167 Brian Shaw	.50	1.25
168 Haywoode Workman	.50	1.25
169 Mookie Blaylock	.50	1.25
170 Donald Royal	.50	1.25
171 Lorenzo Williams	.50	1.25
172 Eric Piatkowski UER Name spelled Paitkowski on back	.60	1.50
173 Sarunas Marciulionis	.50	1.25
174 Otis Thorpe	.50	1.25
175 Rex Chapman	.50	1.25
176 Felton Spencer	.50	1.25
177 John Salley	.50	1.25
178 Pete Chilcutt	.50	1.25
179 Scottie Pippen	1.25	3.00
180 Robert Pack	.50	1.25
181 Dana Barros	.50	1.25
182 Mahmoud Abdul-Rauf	.50	1.25
183 Eric Murdock	.50	1.25
184 Anthony Mason	.50	1.25
185 Will Perdue	.50	1.25
186 Jeff Malone	.50	1.25
187 Anthony Peeler	.50	1.25
188 Chris Childs	.50	1.25
189 Glen Rice	.75	2.00
190 Grant Hill	1.25	3.00
191 Michael Smith	.50	1.25
192 Sean Rooks	.50	1.25
193 Clifford Rozier	.50	1.25
194 Rik Smits	.60	1.50
195 Spud Webb	.75	2.00
196 Aaron McKie	.50	1.25
197 Nate McMillan	.50	1.25
198 Bobby Phills	.50	1.25
199 Dennis Scott	.50	1.25
200 Mark West	.50	1.25
201 George McCloud	.50	1.25
202 B.J. Tyler	.50	1.25
203 Lionel Simmons	.50	1.25
204 Loy Vaught	.50	1.25
205 Kevin Edwards	.50	1.25
206 Eric Montross	.50	1.25
207 Kenny Gattison	.50	1.25
208 Mario Elie	.50	1.25
209 Karl Malone	1.00	2.50
210 Ken Norman	.50	1.25
211 Antonio Davis	.50	1.25
212 Doc Rivers	.60	1.50
213 Hubert Davis	.50	1.25
214 Jamal Mashburn	.75	2.00
215 Donyell Marshall	.50	1.25
216 Sasha Danilovic RC	.75	2.00
217 Danny Manning	.60	1.50
218 Scott Burrell	.50	1.25
219 Vlade Divac	.75	2.00
220 Marty Conlon	.50	1.25
221 Clarence Weatherspoon	.50	1.25
222 Terry Porter	.50	1.25
223 Luc Longley	.50	1.25
224 Juwan Howard	.75	2.00
225 Danny Ferry	.50	1.25
226 Rod Strickland	.50	1.25
227 Bryant Stith	.50	1.25
228 Derrick McKey	.50	1.25
229 Michael Jordan	6.00	15.00
230 Jamie Watson	.50	1.25
231 Rick Fox	.50	1.25
232 Scott Williams	.50	1.25
233 Larry Johnson	.75	2.00
234 Anfernee Hardaway	1.25	3.00
235 Hersey Hawkins	.50	1.25
236 Robert Horry	.60	1.50
237 Kevin Johnson	.75	2.00
238 Rodney Rogers	.50	1.25
239 Detlef Schrempf	.75	2.00
240 Derrick Coleman	.60	1.50
241 Walt Williams	.50	1.25
242 LaPhonso Ellis	.50	1.25
243 Patrick Ewing	1.00	2.50
244 Grant Long	.50	1.25
245 David Robinson	1.25	3.00
246 Chris Mullin	.75	2.00
247 Alonzo Mourning	1.00	2.50
248 Dan Majerle	.75	2.00
249 Johnny Newman	.50	1.25
250 Chris Morris	.50	1.25
252 Magic Johnson	2.00	5.00

1995-96 Finest Refractors

Parallel to cards 1-110, 141-250 and 252, Refractors were randomly inserted into first and second series packs at a rate of one in 12. For the first time ever, Topps decided to randomly seed entire 24-pack boxes full of Refractors into their cases. The insertion ratio of these Refractor "Hot Boxes" is one in every 450 boxes. None of the regular issue first series Rookie Cards (111-139) were given parallel Refractor cards, thus the first series is complete at 110 cards. In addition, card #251 does not exist, thus the second series set is complete at 111 cards. The Magic Johnson card (#252) was inserted into one in every 216 packs, making it approximately six time easier to pull than other second series Refractors. Refractors are distinguished from the basic cards by their rainbow-like appearance that refracts more light. Just like regular issue cards, each Refractor comes with a protective coating to protect the card from wear and tear. To ascertain values on individual cards, please refer to the multiplier in the header below, coupled with the value of the base card.

*REF: 3X TO 8X HI COLUMN

229 Michael Jordan	100.00	250.00
252 Magic Johnson 6P	8.00	20.00

1995-96 Finest Dish and Swish

Randomly inserted into first series packs at a rate of one in 24, cards from this dual-sided, 29-card standard-size set feature combinations of two key players from each NBA team. Each side features one of the two players in game action, with the words "Dish" or "Swish" along the bottom. Values provided below are for unpeeled cards. Peeled cards generally trade for ten to twenty-five percent less. The set is sequenced in alphabetical order by team.

COMPLETE SET (29)	60.00	120.00
DS1 Mookie Blaylock Steve Smith	1.50	4.00
DS2 Sherman Douglas Dino Radja	1.50	4.00
DS3 Muggsy Bogues Larry Johnson	2.00	5.00
DS4 Scottie Pippen Michael Jordan	15.00	40.00
DS5 Mark Price Chris Mills	2.00	5.00
DS6 Jason Kidd Jamal Mashburn	3.00	8.00
DS7 Mahmoud Abdul-Rauf Dikembe Mutombo	2.00	5.00
DS8 Grant Hill Joe Dumars	4.00	10.00
DS9 Tim Hardaway Chris Mullin	3.00	8.00
DS10 Clyde Drexler Hakeem Olajuwon	4.00	10.00
DS11 Mark Jackson Reggie Miller	3.00	8.00
DS12 Pooh Richardson Lamond Murray	1.25	3.00
DS13 Nick Van Exel Cedric Ceballos	2.00	5.00
DS14 Glen Rice Khalid Reeves	2.00	5.00
DS15 Glenn Robinson Eric Murdock	2.00	5.00
DS16 Tom Gugliotta Christian Laettner	2.00	5.00
DS17 Kenny Anderson Derrick Coleman	1.50	4.00
DS18 Patrick Ewing Derek Harper	2.50	6.00
DS19 Anfernee Hardaway Shaquille O'Neal	6.00	15.00
DS20 Dana Barros Clarence Weatherspoon	1.25	3.00
DS21 Kevin Johnson Charles Barkley	3.00	8.00
DS22 Rod Strickland Clifford Robinson	1.25	3.00
DS23 Mitch Richmond Walt Williams	2.00	5.00
DS24 Avery Johnson David Robinson	3.00	8.00
DS25 Gary Payton Shawn Kemp	3.00	8.00
DS26 B.J.Armstrong Oliver Miller	1.25	3.00
DS27 John Stockton Karl Malone	4.00	10.00
DS28 Greg Anthony Byron Scott	1.50	4.00
DS29 Juwan Howard Chris Webber	4.00	10.00

1995-96 Finest Hot Stuff

Randomly inserted into first series packs at a rate of one in nine, cards from this 15-card standard-size set highlight some of the NBA's top stars in slam-dunk action. Orange-bordered fronts feature game action shots. The words "Hot Stuff" run down the left hand side of the card front. Values provided below are for unpeeled cards. Peeled cards generally trade for ten to twenty-five percent less.

COMPLETE SET (15)	12.50	30.00
HS1 Michael Jordan	8.00	20.00
HS2 Grant Hill	1.50	4.00
HS3 Clyde Drexler	1.25	3.00
HS4 Anfernee Hardaway	1.50	4.00
HS5 Sean Elliott	1.00	2.50
HS6 Latrell Sprewell	1.00	2.50
HS7 Larry Johnson	1.00	2.50
HS8 Eddie Jones	1.25	3.00
HS9 Karl Malone	1.25	3.00
HS10 John Starks	.75	2.00
HS11 Scottie Pippen	1.50	4.00
HS12 Shawn Kemp	1.00	2.50
HS13 Chris Webber	1.25	3.00
HS14 Isaiah Rider	1.00	2.50
HS15 Robert Horry	.75	2.00

1995-96 Finest Mystery

Inserted at a rate of one in every first and second series pack, cards from this 44-piece standard-size set were 1.25 times easier to pull than regular issue cards. The set contains a selection of some of the NBA's top stars and rookies. The first twenty-two cards, issued exclusively in first series packs, were designed in three different parallel styles (Bordered, Borderless and Borderless Refractors). The last twenty-two cards, issued exclusively in second series packs, were also designed in three different parallel styles (Bronze, Silver and Gold). Collectors had to peel off a dark protective coating to find out what version of the card they had obtained. The first series Mystery cards feature a radically different design to the second series. Each first series Bordered card front features a bronze outline, framing a cut-out action shot of the player against a metallic basketball background. The second series Bronze cards feature a mosaic-style, tiled border with bronze-colored features, framing a cut-out action shot of the player. The prices listed below are for the more common Bordered and Bronze cards. Values provided below are for peeled cards.

COMPLETE SET (44)	20.00	45.00
COMP.BORDER.SER.1 (22)	12.50	30.00
COMP.BRONZE SER.2 (22)	7.50	15.00

*BDLS./SILVER: 1.5X TO 4X HI COLUMN
*SILVER RCs: 1.25X TO 3X HI
BDLS: SER.1 STATED ODDS 1:24
SILVER: SER.2 STATED ODDS 1:24

M1 Michael Jordan	5.00	12.00
M2 Grant Hill	1.00	2.50
M3 Anfernee Hardaway	1.00	2.50
M4 Shawn Kemp	.60	1.50
M5 Kenny Anderson	.50	1.25
M6 Charles Barkley	1.00	2.50
M7 Latrell Sprewell	.60	1.50
M8 Chris Webber	.75	2.00
M9 Jason Kidd	1.00	2.50
M10 Glenn Robinson	.60	1.50
M11 David Robinson	1.00	2.50
M12 Karl Malone	.75	2.00
M13 Larry Johnson	.60	1.50
M14 Reggie Miller	.75	2.00
M15 Scottie Pippen	1.00	2.50
M16 Patrick Ewing	.75	2.00
M17 Mitch Richmond	.60	1.50
M18 Glen Rice	.60	1.50
M19 Jamal Mashburn	.60	1.50
M20 Juwan Howard	.60	1.50
M21 Hakeem Olajuwon	.75	2.00
M22 Shaquille O'Neal	1.50	4.00
M23 Alonzo Mourning	.60	1.50
M24 Dennis Rodman	1.00	2.50
M25 Joe Dumars	.50	1.25
M26 Tim Hardaway	.50	1.25
M27 Clyde Drexler	.60	1.50
M28 Jerry Stackhouse	1.50	4.00
M29 John Stockton	.60	1.50
M30 Derrick Coleman	.40	1.00
M31 Michael Finley	1.50	4.00
M32 Glen Rice	.50	1.25
M33 Mahmoud Abdul-Rauf	.30	.75
M34 Anthony Mason	.30	.75
M35 Nick Van Exel	.50	1.25
M36 Vin Baker	.40	1.00
M37 Horace Grant	.40	1.00
M38 John Starks	.40	1.00
M39 Clarence Weatherspoon	.30	.75
M40 Kevin Johnson	.50	1.25
M41 Joe Smith	1.00	2.50
M42 Dikembe Mutombo	.50	1.25
M43 Damon Stoudamire	1.25	3.00
M44 Antonio McDyess	1.25	3.00

1995-96 Finest Mystery Borderless Refractors/Gold

Randomly inserted into first and second series hobby packs at a rate of one in 96 and retail at one in 80, cards from this 44-card set parallel the more common Mystery Bordered/Bronze issue. Unlike the first series bordered cards, Borderless Refractor card fronts feature an action cutout against a full-bleed, prismatic, metallic basketball background. The second series Gold cards differ from the common second series Bronze cards with their brighter Gold framed front borders. Also, the words "gold" run in small repetitive type diagonally across the background of each card front. The more common Bronze cards have the word "bronze" running across the card fronts. Values provided below are for peeled cards.

*BDLS.REF: 8X TO 20X VALUE
*GOLD STARS: 6X TO 15X VALUE
*GOLD RCs: 4X TO 10X VALUE

M7 Latrell Sprewell	15.00	40.00

1995-96 Finest Rack Pack

Randomly inserted into packs at a rate of one in 72, cards from this 7-card set features a selection of top rookies from the 1995-96 campaign. Card fronts feature a colorful "swirl-like" background with a player photo and the set name "Rack Pack" underneath the photo. Card backs feature biographical information, a headshot and a brief commentary. Values below are for unpeeled cards. Peeled cards generally trade for ten to twenty-five percent less.

COMPLETE SET (7)	20.00	50.00
RP1 Jerry Stackhouse	6.00	15.00
RP2 Brent Barry	3.00	8.00
RP3 Damon Stoudamire	5.00	12.00
RP4 Joe Smith	4.00	10.00
RP5 Michael Finley	6.00	15.00
RP6 Antonio McDyess	5.00	12.00
RP7 Rasheed Wallace	6.00	15.00

1995-96 Finest Rack Pack Refractors Test

This seven-card set is a parallel to the regular Rack Pack insert. The cards feature the "classic" regular refractor technology. These cards are considered test issues since they were never intended to be released to the public. It is unknown how they made their way into the market as these cards were not inserted into packs.

RP1 Jerry Stackhouse	50.00	125.00
RP2 Brent Barry	25.00	60.00
RP3 Damon Stoudamire	40.00	100.00
RP4 Joe Smith	30.00	80.00
RP5 Michael Finley	50.00	125.00
RP6 Antonio McDyess	40.00	100.00
RP7 Rasheed Wallace	50.00	125.00

1995-96 Finest Veteran/Rookie

Randomly inserted in second series packs at a rate of one in 24, this 29-card set features rookie/veteran duos from a selection of NBA teams. The cards are dual-sided with each player getting a full photo on a separate side. Prices provided below are for unpeeled cards. Peeled cards generally trade for about ten to twenty-five percent less.

COMPLETE SET (29)	125.00	250.00
RV1 Joe Smith Latrell Sprewell	4.00	10.00
RV2 Antonio McDyess Dikembe Mutombo	5.00	12.00
RV3 Jerry Stackhouse Clarence Weatherspoon	5.00	12.00
RV4 Rasheed Wallace Chris Webber	8.00	20.00
RV5 Kevin Garnett Tim Gugliotta	12.00	30.00
RV6 Bryant Reeves Greg Anthony	3.00	8.00
RV7 Damon Stoudamire Willie Anderson	4.00	10.00
RV8 Shawn Respert Vin Baker	2.00	5.00
RV9 Ed O'Bannon Armon Gilliam	2.00	5.00
RV10 Kurt Thomas Alonzo Mourning	4.00	10.00
RV11 Gary Trent Rod Strickland	2.50	6.00
RV12 Cherokee Parks Jamal Mashburn	2.00	5.00
RV13 Corliss Williamson Mitch Richmond	3.00	8.00
RV14 Eric Williams Dino Radja	2.00	5.00
RV15 Brent Barry Loy Vaught	2.50	6.00
RV16 Alan Henderson Mookie Blaylock	2.50	6.00
RV17 Bob Sura Terrell Brandon	2.50	6.00
RV18 Theo Ratliff Grant Hill	5.00	12.00
RV19 Randolph Childress Rod Strickland	2.00	5.00
RV20 Jason Caffey Michael Jordan	15.00	40.00
RV21 Michael Finley Kevin Johnson	6.00	15.00
RV22 George Zidek Larry Johnson	2.50	6.00
RV23 Travis Best Reggie Miller	4.00	10.00
RV24 Loren Meyer Jason Kidd	4.00	10.00
RV25 David Vaughn Shaquille O'Neal	10.00	25.00
RV26 Sherell Ford Shawn Kemp	2.50	6.00
RV27 Mario Bennett Charles Barkley	4.00	10.00
RV28 Greg Ostertag Karl Malone	4.00	10.00
RV29 Cory Alexander David Robinson	4.00	10.00

1996-97 Finest

The 1996-97 Finest set was issued in two series totaling 291 cards. The 6-card packs retail for $5.00 each. The series one set is divided into 3-tiers of collectiblilty with cards B1-B100 defined as "common" cards, S101-S127 defined as "uncommon" and inserted at a rate of 1:4 packs and G128-G146 defined as "rare" and inserted at a rate of 1:24 packs. Each card is also arranged into individually designed theme sets - Gladiators, Maestros, Apprentices and Sterling. The series two set is also divided into 3-tiers of collectiblility with cards B147-B246 defined as "common", S247-S273 defined as "uncommon" and inserted at a rate of 1:4 packs and G274-G291 defined as "rare" and inserted at a rate of 1:24 packs. Each card is also arranged into individually designed theme sets - Mainstays, Sterling, Heirs and Foundations. Prices below are for unpeeled cards. Peeled cards generally trade for ten to twenty-five percent less. Card numbers 7 and 134 do not exist. The Christian Laettner bronze, Patrick Ewing gold and Jeff Hornacek gold were all numbered 136. Card number 269 (Kobe Bryant gold) is considered part of the gold set, while card number 289 (Shaquille O'Neal silver) is considered part of the silver set, though they are both out of "set" order. The set is condition sensitive.

COMPLETE SET (291)	300.00	600.00
COMPLETE SERIES 1 (146)	150.00	350.00
COMPLETE SERIES 2 (145)	150.00	300.00
COMP.BRONZE SET (200)	70.00	140.00
COMP.BRONZE SER.1 (100)	50.00	100.00
COMP.BRONZE SER.2 (100)	20.00	40.00
1 Scottie Pippen B	.60	1.50
2 Tim Legler B	.25	.60
3 Rex Walters B	.25	.60
4 Calbert Cheaney B	.25	.60
5 Dennis Rodman B	.75	2.00
6 Tyrone Hill B	.25	.60
7 Christian Laettner B UER Should be card number 7	.30	.75
8 Dell Curry B	.25	.60
9 Olden Polynice B	.25	.60
10 John Wallace B RC	.75	2.00
11 Martin Muursepp B RC	.75	2.00
12 Chuck Person B	.30	.75
13 Grant Hill B	.60	1.50
14 Shawn Kemp B	.40	1.00
15 B.J. Armstrong B	.25	.60
16 Gary Trent B	.25	.60
17 Scott Williams B	.25	.60
18 Dino Radja B	.30	.75
19 Roy Rogers B RC	.75	2.00
20 Tony Delk B RC	.75	2.00
21 Clifford Robinson B	.25	.60
22 Ray Allen B RC	3.00	8.00
23 Clyde Drexler B	.50	1.25
24 Elliot Perry B	.25	.60
25 Gary Payton B	.40	1.00
26 Dale Davis B	.25	.60
27 Horace Grant B	.30	.75
28 Brian Evans B RC	.75	2.00
29 Joe Smith B	.30	.75
30 Reggie Miller B	.50	1.25
31 Jermaine O'Neal B RC	2.00	5.00
32 Avery Johnson B	.30	.75
33 Ed O'Bannon B	.25	.60
34 Cedric Ceballos B	.25	.60
35 Jamal Mashburn B	.30	.75
36 Micheal Williams B	.25	.60
37 Detlef Schrempf B	.40	1.00
38 Damon Stoudamire B	.40	1.00
39 Jason Kidd B	.60	1.50
40 Tom Gugliotta B	.25	.60
41 Arvydas Sabonis B	.30	.75
42 Samaki Walker B RC	.75	2.00
43 Derek Fisher B RC	1.50	4.00
44 Patrick Ewing B	.50	1.25
45 Bryant Reeves B	.25	.60
46 Mookie Blaylock B	.25	.60
47 George Zidek B	.25	.60
48 Jerry Stackhouse B	.50	1.25
49 Vin Baker B	.30	.75
50 Michael Jordan B	3.00	8.00
51 Terrell Brandon B	.25	.60
52 Karl Malone B	.50	1.25
53 Lorenzen Wright B RC	.75	2.00
54 Shareef Abdur-Rahim B RC	1.50	4.00
55 Kurt Thomas B	.25	.60
56 Glen Rice B	.40	1.00
57 Shawn Bradley B	.25	.60
58 Todd Fuller B RC	.75	2.00
59 Dale Ellis B	.25	.60
60 David Robinson B	.60	1.50
61 Doug Christie B	.25	.60
62 Stephon Marbury B RC	2.00	5.00
63 Hakeem Olajuwon B	.50	1.25
64 Lindsey Hunter B	.25	.60
65 Anfernee Hardaway B	.60	1.50
66 Kevin Garnett B	1.00	2.50
67 Kendall Gill B	.25	.60
68 Sean Elliott B	.40	1.00
69 Allen Iverson B RC	4.00	10.00
70 Erick Dampier B RC	.75	2.00
71 Jerome Williams B RC	.75	2.00
72 Charles Jones B	.25	.60
73 Danny Manning B	.30	.75
74 Kobe Bryant B RC	15.00	40.00
75 Steve Nash B RC	4.00	10.00
76 Sam Perkins B	.25	.60
77 Horace Grant B	.30	.75
78 Alonzo Mourning B	.50	1.25
79 Kerry Kittles B RC	.75	2.00
80 LaPhonso Ellis B	.25	.60
81 Michael Finley B	.50	1.25
82 Marcus Camby B RC	1.25	3.00
83 Antonio McDyess B	.40	1.00
84 Antoine Walker B RC	1.50	4.00
85 Juwan Howard B	.30	.75
86 Bryon Russell B	.25	.60
87 Walter McCarty B RC	.75	2.00
88 Priest Lauderdale B RC	.75	2.00
89 Clarence Weatherspoon B	.25	.60
90 John Stockton B	.50	1.25
91 Mitch Richmond B	.40	1.00
92 Dontae' Jones B RC	.75	2.00
93 Michael Smith B	.25	.60
94 Brent Barry B	.30	.75
95 Chris Mills B	.25	.60
96 Dee Brown B	.25	.60
97 Terry Dehere B	.25	.60
98 Danny Ferry B	.25	.60
99 Gheorghe Muresan B	.25	.60
100 Checklist B	.25	.60
101 Jim Jackson S	.60	1.50
102 Cedric Ceballos S	.60	1.50
103 Glen Rice S	1.00	2.50
104 Tom Gugliotta S	.60	1.50
105 Mario Elie S	.60	1.50
106 Nick Anderson S	.60	1.50
107 Glenn Robinson S	1.00	2.50
108 Terrell Brandon S	.60	1.50
109 Tim Hardaway S	1.00	2.50
110 John Stockton S	1.25	3.00
111 Brent Barry S	.75	2.00
112 Mookie Blaylock S	.60	1.50
113 Tyus Edney S	.60	1.50
114 Gary Payton S	1.00	2.50
115 Joe Smith S	.75	2.00
116 Karl Malone S	1.25	3.00
117 Dino Radja S	.75	2.00
118 Alonzo Mourning S	1.25	3.00
119 Bryant Stith S	.60	1.50
120 Derrick McKey S	.60	1.50
121 Clyde Drexler S	1.25	3.00
122 Michael Finley S	1.25	3.00
123 Sean Elliott S	1.00	2.50
124 Hakeem Olajuwon S	1.25	3.00
125 Joe Dumars S	1.00	2.50
126 Shawn Bradley S	.60	1.50
127 Michael Jordan S	10.00	25.00
128 Latrell Sprewell G	3.00	8.00
129 Anfernee Hardaway G	5.00	12.00
130 Grant Hill G	5.00	12.00
131 Damon Stoudamire G	3.00	8.00
132 David Robinson G	5.00	12.00
133 Scottie Pippen G	5.00	12.00
135 Jason Kidd G	5.00	12.00
136A Jeff Hornacek G	2.50	6.00
136B Patrick Ewing G UER Should be card number 134	4.00	10.00
137 Jerry Stackhouse G	4.00	10.00
138 Kevin Garnett G	8.00	20.00
139 Mitch Richmond G	3.00	8.00
140 Juwan Howard G	2.50	6.00
141 Reggie Miller G	4.00	10.00
142 Christian Laettner G	2.50	6.00
143 Vin Baker G	2.50	6.00
144 Shawn Kemp G	3.00	8.00
145 Dennis Rodman G	6.00	15.00
146 Shaquille O'Neal G	8.00	20.00
147 Mookie Blaylock B	.25	.60
148 Derek Harper B	.30	.75
149 Gerald Wilkins B	.25	.60
150 Adam Keefe B	.25	.60
151 Billy Owens B	.25	.60
152 Terrell Brandon B	.25	.60
153 Antonio Davis B	.25	.60
154 Muggsy Bogues B	.30	.75
155 Cherokee Parks B	.25	.60
156 Rasheed Wallace B	.50	1.25
157 Lee Mayberry B	.25	.60
158 Craig Ehlo B	.25	.60
159 Todd Fuller B	.40	1.00
160 Charles Barkley B	.60	1.50
161 Glenn Robinson B	.40	1.00
162 Charles Oakley B	.30	.75
163 Chris Webber B	.50	1.25
164 Frank Brickowski B	.25	.60
165 Mark Jackson B	.40	1.00
166 Jayson Williams B	.25	.60
167 Clarence Weatherspoon B	.25	.60

168 Toni Kukoc B .40 1.00
169 Alan Henderson B .25 .60
170 Tony Delk B .40 1.00
171 Jamal Mashburn B .30 .75
172 Vinny Del Negro B .25 .60
173 Greg Ostertag B .25 .60
174 Shawn Bradley B .25 .60
175 Gheorghe Muresan B .25 .60
176 Brent Price B .25 .60
177 Rick Fox B .25 .60
178 Stacey Augmon B .30 .75
179 P.J. Brown B .25 .60
180 Jim Jackson B .25 .60
181 Hersey Hawkins B .25 .60
182 Danny Manning B .30 .75
183 Dennis Scott B .25 .60
184 Tom Gugliotta B .25 .60
185 Tyrone Hill B .25 .60
186 Malik Sealy B .25 .60
187 John Starks B .30 .75
188 Mark Price B .40 1.00
189 Elden Campbell B .25 .60
190 Mahmoud Abdul-Rauf B .25 .60
191 Will Perdue B .25 .60
192 Nate McMillan B .25 .60
193 Robert Horry B .30 .75
194 Dino Radja B .30 .75
195 Loy Vaught B .25 .60
196 Dikembe Mutombo B .40 1.00
197 Eric Montross B .25 .60
198 Sasha Danilovic B .25 .60
199 Kenny Anderson B .30 .75
200 Sean Elliott B .40 1.00
201 Mark West B .25 .60
202 Vlade Divac B .40 1.00
203 Joe Dumars B .40 1.00
204 Allan Houston B .30 .75
205 Kevin Garnett B 1.00 2.50
206 Rod Strickland B .25 .60
207 Robert Parish B .40 1.00
208 Jalen Rose B .30 .75
209 Armon Gilliam B .25 .60
210 Kerry Kittles B .40 1.00
211 Derrick Coleman B .30 .75
212 Greg Anthony B .25 .60
213 Joe Smith B .30 .75
214 Steve Smith B .30 .75
215 Tim Hardaway B .40 1.00
216 Tyus Edney B .25 .60
217 Steve Nash B 2.00 5.00
218 Anthony Mason B .25 .60
219 Otis Thorpe B .25 .60
220 Eddie Jones B .40 1.00
221 Rik Smits B .30 .75
222 Isaiah Rider B .30 .75
223 Bobby Phills B .25 .60
224 Antoine Walker B .75 2.00
225 Rod Strickland B .25 .60
226 Hubert Davis B .25 .60
227 Eric Williams B .25 .60
228 Danny Manning B .30 .75
229 Dominique Wilkins B .50 1.25
230 Brian Shaw B .25 .60
231 Larry Johnson B .40 1.00
232 Kevin Willis B .25 .60
233 Bryant Stith B .25 .60
234 Blue Edwards B .25 .60
235 Robert Pack B .25 .60
236 Brian Grant B .30 .75
237 Latrell Sprewell B .40 1.00
238 Glen Rice B .40 1.00
239 Jerome Williams B .40 1.00
240 Allen Iverson B 2.00 5.00
241 Popeye Jones B .25 .60
242 Clifford Robinson B .25 .60
243 Shaquille O'Neal B 1.00 2.50
244 Vitaly Potapenko B RC .75 2.00
245 Ervin Johnson B .25 .60
246 Checklist .25 .60
247 Scottie Pippen S 1.50 4.00
248 Jason Kidd S 1.50 4.00
249 Antonio McDyess S 1.00 2.50
250 Latrell Sprewell S 1.00 2.50
251 Lorenzen Wright S .60 1.50
252 Ray Allen S 2.50 6.00
253 Stephon Marbury S 1.50 4.00
254 Patrick Ewing S 1.25 3.00
255 Anfernee Hardaway S 1.50 4.00
256 Kenny Anderson S .75 2.00
257 David Robinson S 1.50 4.00
258 Marcus Camby S 1.00 2.50
259 Shareef Abdur-Rahim S 1.25 3.00
260 Dennis Rodman S 2.00 5.00
261 Juwan Howard S .75 2.00
262 Damon Stoudamire S 1.00 2.50
263 Shawn Kemp S 1.00 2.50
264 Mitch Richmond S 1.00 2.50
265 Jerry Stackhouse S 1.25 3.00
266 Horace Grant S .75 2.00
267 Kerry Kittles S .60 1.50
268 Vin Baker S .75 2.00
269 Kobe Bryant G 60.00 150.00
270 Reggie Miller S 1.25 3.00
271 Grant Hill S 1.50 4.00
272 Oliver Miller S .60 1.50
273 Chris Webber S 1.25 3.00
274 Dikembe Mutombo G 3.00 8.00
275 Antonio McDyess G 3.00 8.00
276 Clyde Drexler G 4.00 10.00
277 Brent Barry G 2.50 6.00
278 Tim Hardaway G 3.00 8.00
279 Glenn Robinson G 3.00 8.00
280 Allen Iverson G 10.00 25.00
281 Hakeem Olajuwon G 4.00 10.00
282 Marcus Camby G 3.00 8.00
283 John Stockton G 4.00 10.00
284 Shareef Abdur-Rahim G 4.00 10.00
285 Karl Malone G 4.00 10.00
286 Gary Payton G 3.00 8.00
287 Stephon Marbury G 5.00 12.00
288 Alonzo Mourning G 4.00 10.00
289 Shaquille O'Neal S 2.50 6.00
290 Charles Barkley G 5.00 12.00
291 Michael Jordan G 25.00 60.00

1996-97 Finest Refractors

This 291-card set parallels the basic set using the Finest refractive technology. This set is also divided into a 3-tier model of collectiblity using the same common, uncommon and rare themes. A Refractor comon card replaces a common card 1:12 packs and uses the classic Refractor foil. A Refractor uncommon card replaces a common card 1:48 packs and uses a mosaic Refractor foil pattern. A Refractor rare card replaces a common card 1:288 packs and uses a hyper-plaid Refractor foil pattern. Prices below are for unpeeled cards. Peeled cards generally trade for ten to twenty-five percent less. Card numbers 7 and 134 do not exist. The Christian Laettner bronze, Patrick Ewing gold and Jeff Hornacek gold were all numbered 136. Card number 269 (Kobe Bryant gold) is considered part of the gold set, while card number 289 (Shaquille O'Neal silver) is considered part of the silver set, though they are both out of "set" order. The set is condition sensitive.
*BRONZE STARS: 5X TO 12X BASIC CARDS
*BRONZE RCs: 2.5X TO 6X HI
*SILVER STARS: 2X TO 5X BASIC CARDS
*SILVER RCs: 1.25X TO 3X BASIC CARDS
*GOLD STARS/RCs: 1.25X TO 3X BASIC CARDS
74 Kobe Bryant B 175.00 350.00
290 Charles Barkley G 20.00 50.00
291 Michael Jordan G 250.00 500.00

1997-98 Finest Promos

COMPLETE SET (6) 2.50 6.00
27 Chris Webber .60 1.50
45 Vin Baker .50 1.25
57 Allen Iverson 1.25 3.00
67 Eddie Jones .60 1.50
68 Joe Smith .50 1.25
80 Gary Payton .60 1.50

1997-98 Finest

The complete set of Finest contained 326 total cards with the series one set containing 173 cards and the series two set containing 153. Both series were released in six card packs that carried a suggested retail price of $5. Like last year, the set is divided into three tiers: bronze, silver and gold. The bronze, or common, cards are the basic and encompass cards 1-120 and 174-273. The silver, or uncommon, cards were inserted at a rate of one in four packs and encompass cards 121-153 and cards 274-306. The gold, or rare, cards were inserted at a rate of one in 24 and encompass cards 154-173 and cards 307-326. Prices listed below are for unpeeled cards. Peeled cards generally trade for 75% of the listed prices. Please note that card "P68" was given out to dealers and members of the hobby press as a promotional card.
COMPLETE SET (326) 300.00 600.00
COMPLETE SERIES 1 (173) 150.00 300.00
COMPLETE SERIES 2 (153) 150.00 300.00
1 Scottie Pippen B .50 1.25
2 Tim Hardaway B .30 .75
3 Bo Outlaw B .20 .50
4 Rik Smits B .25 .60
5 Dale Ellis B .20 .50
6 Clyde Drexler B .40 1.00
7 Steve Smith B .25 .60
8 Nick Anderson B .20 .50
9 Juwan Howard B .25 .60
10 Cedric Ceballos B .20 .50
11 Shawn Bradley B .20 .50
12 Loy Vaught B .20 .50
13 Todd Day B .20 .50
14 Glen Rice B .30 .75
15 Bryant Stith B .20 .50
16 Bob Sura B .20 .50
17 Derrick McKey B .20 .50
18 Ray Allen B .40 1.00
19 Stephon Marbury B .40 1.00
20 David Robinson B .50 1.25
21 Anthony Peeler B .20 .50
22 Isaiah Rider B .20 .50
23 Mookie Blaylock B .20 .50
24 Damon Stoudamire B .30 .75
25 Rod Strickland B .20 .50
26 Glenn Robinson B .25 .60
27 Chris Webber B .30 .75
28 Christian Laettner B .25 .60
29 Joe Dumars B .30 .75
30 Mark Price B .30 .75
31 Jamal Mashburn B .25 .60
32 Danny Manning B .25 .60
33 John Stockton B .40 1.00
34 Detlef Schrempf B .30 .75
35 Tyus Edney B .20 .50
36 Chris Childs B .20 .50
37 Dana Barros B .20 .50
38 Bobby Phills B .20 .50
39 Michael Jordan B 2.50 6.00
40 Grant Hill B .50 1.25
41 Brent Barry B .25 .60
42 Rony Seikaly B .25 .60
43 Shareef Abdur-Rahim B .30 .75
44 Dominique Wilkins B .40 1.00
45 Vin Baker B .25 .60
46 Kendall Gill B .20 .50
47 Muggsy Bogues B .25 .60
48 Hakeem Olajuwon B .40 1.00
49 Reggie Miller B .40 1.00
50 Shaquille O'Neal B .75 2.00
51 Antonio McDyess B .25 .60
52 Michael Finley B .30 .75
53 Jerry Stackhouse B .30 .75
54 Brian Grant B .20 .50
55 Greg Anthony B .20 .50
56 Patrick Ewing B .40 1.00
57 Allen Iverson B .60 1.50
58 Rasheed Wallace B .30 .75
59 Shawn Kemp B .30 .75
60 Bryant Reeves B .20 .50
61 Kevin Garnett B .60 1.50
62 Allan Houston B .25 .60
63 Stacey Augmon B .25 .60
64 Rick Fox B .20 .50
65 Derek Harper B .25 .60
66 Lindsey Hunter B .20 .50
67 Eddie Jones B .30 .75
68 Joe Smith B .25 .60
69 Alonzo Mourning B .40 1.00
70 LaPhonso Ellis B .20 .50
71 Tyrone Hill B .20 .50
72 Charles Barkley B .50 1.25
73 Malik Sealy B .20 .50
74 Shandon Anderson B .20 .50
75 Arvydas Sabonis B .25 .60
76 Tom Gugliotta B .20 .50
77 Anfernee Hardaway B .50 1.25
78 Sean Elliott B .30 .75
79 Marcus Camby B .30 .75
80 Gary Payton B .30 .75
81 Kerry Kittles B .20 .50
82 Dikembe Mutombo B .30 .75
83 Antoine Walker B .30 .75
84 Terrell Brandon B .20 .50
85 Otis Thorpe B .20 .50
86 Mark Jackson B .30 .75
87 A.C. Green B .30 .75
88 John Starks B .25 .60
89 Kenny Anderson B .25 .60
90 Karl Malone B .40 1.00
91 Mitch Richmond B .30 .75
92 Derrick Coleman B .25 .60
93 Horace Grant B .25 .60
94 John Williams B .20 .50
95 Jason Kidd B .50 1.25
96 Mahmoud Abdul-Rauf B .20 .50
97 Walt Williams B .20 .50
98 Anthony Mason B .20 .50
99 Latrell Sprewell B .30 .75
100 Checklist .20 .50
101 Tim Duncan B RC 3.00 8.00
102 Keith Van Horn B RC 1.00 2.50
103 Chauncey Billups B RC 2.00 5.00
104 Antonio Daniels B RC .50 1.25
105 Tony Battie B RC .60 1.50
106 Tim Thomas B RC 1.00 2.50
107 Tracy McGrady B RC 2.50 6.00
108 Adonal Foyle B RC .50 1.25
109 Maurice Taylor B RC .50 1.25
110 Austin Croshere B RC .50 1.25
111 Bobby Jackson B RC .60 1.50
112 Olivier Saint-Jean B RC .50 1.25
113 John Thomas B RC .50 1.25
114 Derek Anderson B RC .50 1.25
115 Brevin Knight B RC .50 1.25
116 Charles Smith B RC .50 1.25
117 Johnny Taylor B RC .50 1.25
118 Jacque Vaughn B RC .50 1.25
119 Anthony Parker B RC .50 1.25
120 Paul Grant B RC .50 1.25
121 Stephon Marbury S 1.25 3.00
122 Terrell Brandon S .60 1.50
123 Dikembe Mutombo S 1.00 2.50
124 Patrick Ewing S 1.25 3.00
125 Scottie Pippen S 1.50 4.00
126 Antoine Walker S 1.00 2.50
127 Karl Malone S 1.25 3.00
128 Sean Elliott S 1.00 2.50
129 Chris Webber S 1.00 2.50
130 Shawn Kemp S 1.00 2.50
131 Hakeem Olajuwon S 1.25 3.00
132 Tim Hardaway S 1.00 2.50
133 Glen Rice S 1.00 2.50
134 Vin Baker S .75 2.00
135 Jim Jackson S .60 1.50
136 Kevin Garnett S 2.00 5.00
137 Kobe Bryant S 6.00 15.00
138 Damon Stoudamire S 1.00 2.50
139 Larry Johnson S 1.00 2.50
140 Latrell Sprewell S 1.00 2.50
141 Lorenzen Wright S .60 1.50
142 Toni Kukoc S 1.00 2.50
143 Allen Iverson S 2.00 5.00
144 Elden Campbell S .60 1.50
145 Tom Gugliotta S .60 1.50
146 David Robinson S 1.50 4.00
147 Jayson Williams S .60 1.50
148 Shaquille O'Neal S 2.50 6.00
149 Grant Hill S 1.50 4.00
150 Reggie Miller S 1.25 3.00
151 Clyde Drexler S 1.25 3.00
152 Ray Allen S 1.25 3.00
153 Eddie Jones S 1.00 2.50
154 Michael Jordan G 30.00 80.00
155 Dominique Wilkins G 5.00 12.00
156 Charles Barkley G 6.00 15.00
157 Jerry Stackhouse G 4.00 10.00
158 Juwan Howard G 3.00 8.00
159 Marcus Camby G 4.00 10.00
160 Christian Laettner G 3.00 8.00
161 Anthony Mason G 2.50 6.00
162 Joe Smith G 3.00 8.00
163 Kerry Kittles G 2.50 6.00
164 Mitch Richmond G 4.00 10.00
165 Shareef Abdur-Rahim G 4.00 10.00
166 Alonzo Mourning G 5.00 12.00
167 Dennis Rodman G 8.00 20.00
168 Antonio McDyess G 3.00 8.00
169 Shawn Bradley G 2.50 6.00
170 Anfernee Hardaway G 6.00 15.00
171 Jason Kidd G 6.00 15.00
172 Gary Payton G 4.00 10.00
173 John Stockton G 5.00 12.00
174 Allan Houston B .25 .60
175 Bob Sura B .20 .50
176 Clyde Drexler B .40 1.00
177 Glenn Robinson B .25 .60
178 Joe Smith B .25 .60
179 Larry Johnson B .30 .75
180 Mitch Richmond B .30 .75
181 Rony Seikaly B .25 .60
182 Tyrone Hill B .20 .50
183 Allen Iverson B .60 1.50
184 Brent Barry B .25 .60
185 Damon Stoudamire B .30 .75
186 Grant Hill B .50 1.25
187 John Stockton B .40 1.00
188 Latrell Sprewell B .30 .75
189 Mookie Blaylock B .20 .50
190 Samaki Walker B .20 .50
191 Vin Baker B .25 .60
192 Alonzo Mourning B .40 1.00
193 Brevin Knight B .30 .75
194 Danny Manning B .25 .60
195 Hakeem Olajuwon B .40 1.00
196 Johnny Taylor B .30 .75
197 Lorenzen Wright B .20 .50
198 Olden Polynice B .20 .50
199 Scottie Pippen B .50 1.25
200 Lindsey Hunter B .20 .50
201 Anfernee Hardaway B .50 1.25
202 Greg Anthony B .20 .50
203 David Robinson B .50 1.25
204 Horace Grant B .25 .60
205 Calbert Cheaney B .20 .50
206 Loy Vaught B .20 .50
207 Tariq Abdul-Wahad B .30 .75
208 Sean Elliott B .30 .75
209 Rodney Rogers B .20 .50
210 Anthony Mason B .20 .50
211 Bryant Reeves B .20 .50
212 David Wesley B .20 .50
213 Isaiah Rider B .20 .50
214 Karl Malone B .40 1.00
215 Mahmoud Abdul-Rauf B .20 .50
216 Patrick Ewing B .40 1.00
217 Shaquille O'Neal B .75 2.00
218 Antoine Walker B .30 .75
219 Charles Barkley B .50 1.25
220 Dennis Rodman B .60 1.50
221 Jamal Mashburn B .25 .60
222 Kendall Gill B .20 .50
223 Malik Sealy B .20 .50
224 Rasheed Wallace B .30 .75
225 Shareef Abdur-Rahim B .30 .75
226 Antonio Daniels B .30 .75
227 Charles Oakley B .25 .60
228 Derek Anderson B .30 .75
229 Jason Kidd B .50 1.25
230 Kenny Anderson B .25 .60
231 Marcus Camby B .30 .75
232 Ray Allen B .40 1.00
233 Shawn Bradley B .20 .50
234 Antonio McDyess B .25 .60
235 Chauncey Billups B 1.25 3.00
236 Detlef Schrempf B .30 .75
237 Jayson Williams B .20 .50
238 Kerry Kittles B .20 .50
239 Jalen Rose B .25 .60
240 Reggie Miller B .40 1.00
241 Shawn Kemp B .30 .75
242 Arvydas Sabonis B .25 .60
243 Tom Gugliotta B .20 .50
244 Dikembe Mutombo B .30 .75
245 Jeff Hornacek B .25 .60
246 Kevin Garnett B .60 1.50
247 Matt Maloney B .20 .50
248 Rex Chapman B .20 .50
249 Stephon Marbury B .40 1.00
250 Austin Croshere B .30 .75
251 Chris Childs B .20 .50
252 Eddie Jones B .30 .75
253 Jerry Stackhouse B .30 .75
254 Kevin Johnson B .30 .75
255 Maurice Taylor B .30 .75
256 Chris Mullin B .30 .75
257 Terrell Brandon B .20 .50
258 Avery Johnson B .25 .60
259 Chris Webber B .30 .75
260 Gary Payton B .30 .75
261 Jim Jackson B .20 .50
262 Kobe Bryant B 1.50 4.00
263 Michael Finley B .30 .75
264 Rod Strickland B .20 .50
265 Tim Hardaway B .30 .75
266 B.J. Armstrong B .20 .50
267 Christian Laettner B .25 .60
268 Glen Rice B .30 .75
269 Joe Dumars B .30 .75
270 LaPhonso Ellis B .20 .50
271 Michael Jordan B 2.50 6.00
272 Ron Mercer B RC .60 1.50
273 Checklist B .20 .50
274 Anfernee Hardaway S 1.50 4.00
275 Dennis Rodman S 2.00 5.00
276 Gary Payton S 1.00 2.50
277 Jamal Mashburn S .75 2.00
278 Shareef Abdur-Rahim S 1.00 2.50
279 Steve Smith S .75 2.00
280 Tony Battie S .75 2.00
281 Alonzo Mourning S 1.25 3.00
282 Bobby Jackson S .75 2.00
283 Christian Laettner S .75 2.00
284 Jerry Stackhouse S 1.00 2.50
285 Terrell Brandon S .60 1.50
286 Chauncey Billups S 2.50 6.00
287 Michael Jordan S 8.00 20.00
288 Glenn Robinson S .75 2.00
289 Jason Kidd S 1.50 4.00
290 Joe Smith S .75 2.00
291 Michael Finley S 1.00 2.50
292 Rod Strickland S .60 1.50
293 Ron Mercer S .75 2.00
294 Tracy McGrady S 3.00 8.00
295 Adonal Foyle S .60 1.50
296 Marcus Camby S 1.00 2.50
297 John Stockton S 1.25 3.00
298 Kerry Kittles S .60 1.50
299 Mitch Richmond S 1.00 2.50
300 Shawn Bradley S .60 1.50
301 Anthony Mason S .60 1.50
302 Antonio Daniels S .60 1.50
303 Antonio McDyess S .75 2.00
304 Charles Barkley S 1.50 4.00
305 Keith Van Horn S 1.25 3.00
306 Tim Duncan S 4.00 10.00
307 Dikembe Mutombo G 4.00 10.00
308 Grant Hill G 6.00 15.00
309 Shaquille O'Neal G 10.00 25.00
310 Keith Van Horn G 5.00 12.00
311 Shawn Kemp G 4.00 10.00
312 Antoine Walker G 4.00 10.00
313 Hakeem Olajuwon G 5.00 12.00
314 Vin Baker G 3.00 8.00
315 Patrick Ewing G 5.00 12.00
316 Tracy McGrady G 12.00 30.00
317 Glen Rice G 4.00 10.00
318 Reggie Miller G 5.00 12.00
319 Kevin Garnett G 8.00 20.00
320 Allen Iverson G 8.00 20.00
321 Karl Malone G 5.00 12.00
322 Scottie Pippen G 6.00 15.00
323 Kobe Bryant G 20.00 50.00
324 Stephon Marbury G 5.00 12.00
325 Tim Duncan G 15.00 40.00
326 Chris Webber G 4.00 10.00

1997-98 Finest Embossed

The 106-card embossed semi-parallel is made up of only the silver and gold cards from both series of the basic set. The first 33 cards from both series, or silver, were just embossed and were randomly inserted into packs at a rate of one in 16. The last 20 cards from both series, or gold, were both embossed and die cut. The were randomly inserted at a rate of one in 96. Prices below refer to unpeeled cards. Peeled cards generally trade at about 75% of the listed value. To ascertain values of individual cards, please refer to the multiplier listed below coupled with the value of the base card.
*SILVER: .5X TO 1.25X BASE HI
*SILVER RCs: .4X TO 1X BASE HI
*GOLD STARS: .6X TO 1.5X BASE HI
*GOLD RCs: .5X TO 1.25X BASE HI
154 Michael Jordan G 100.00 175.00

1997-98 Finest Embossed Refractors

This 106-card set parallels the basic series one and two Embossed sets. The first 33 silver embossed refractors from both sets were randomly inserted into packs at a rate of one in 192. These cards are serially numbered to 263 on the card back. The remaining 20 gold embossed die cut refractors from both sets were randomly inserted at a rate of one in 1,152 packs. These cards are serially numbered to 74 on the card back. To ascertain values on individual cards, please refer to the multiplier in the header below, coupled with the value of the base card.
*SILVER STARS/RCs: 4X TO 10X BASE HI
*GOLD STARS/RCs: 8X TO 20X BASE HI
137 Kobe Bryant S 125.00 250.00
154 Michael Jordan G 5000.00 7500.00
156 Charles Barkley G 250.00 500.00
167 Dennis Rodman G 500.00 1000.00
170 Anfernee Hardaway G 200.00 400.00
287 Michael Jordan S 200.00 400.00
308 Grant Hill G 200.00 400.00
309 Shaquille O'Neal G 300.00 600.00
313 Hakeem Olajuwon G 150.00 300.00
318 Reggie Miller G 175.00 350.00
322 Scottie Pippen G 300.00 600.00
323 Kobe Bryant G 1000.00 2000.00
326 Chris Webber G 150.00 300.00

1997-98 Finest Refractors

Randomly inserted into both series packs, this set parallels all three tiers of the basic set. The bronze refractors were inserted at a rate of one in 12. The silver refractors were inserted at a rate of one in 48 and were serially numbered to 1,090 sets. The gold refractors were inserted at a rate of one in 288 and were serially numbered to 289 sets. To ascertain values on individual cards, please refer to the multiplier in the header below, coupled with the value of the base card.
*BRONZE STARS: 4X TO 10X BASIC CARDS
*SILVER: 2X TO 5X BASIC CARDS
*GOLD STARS/RCs: 1.5X TO 4X BASIC CARDS
1 Scottie Pippen B 6.00 15.00
39 Michael Jordan B 30.00 80.00
101 Tim Duncan B 40.00 70.00
154 Michael Jordan G 400.00 700.00
287 Michael Jordan S 100.00 200.00
323 Kobe Bryant G 100.00 250.00

1998-99 Finest Promos

COMPLETE SET (6) 2.50 6.00
PP1 Dikembe Mutombo .75 2.00
PP2 Antoine Walker .75 2.00
PP3 Reggie Miller 1.00 2.50
PP4 John Stockton 1.00 2.50
PP5 Eddie Jones .75 2.00
PP6 Gary Payton .75 2.00

1998-99 Finest

The 1998-99 Finest set was released in two series with each containing 125 cards for a total of 250. This year's edition featured a thicker 29-point stock and a base set organized by position, with each position identified by a different graphic. Each pack contained six cards with a suggested retail price of $5.
COMPLETE SET (250) 50.00 100.00
COMPLETE SERIES 1 (125) 15.00 30.00
COMPLETE SERIES 2 (125) 25.00 60.00
1 Chris Mills .20 .50
2 Matt Maloney .20 .50
3 Sam Mitchell .20 .50
4 Corliss Williamson .20 .50
5 Bryant Reeves .20 .50
6 Juwan Howard .25 .60
7 Eddie Jones .30 .75
8 Ray Allen .40 1.00
9 Larry Johnson .30 .75
10 Travis Best .20 .50
11 Isaiah Rider .20 .50
12 Hakeem Olajuwon .40 1.00
13 Gary Trent .20 .50
14 Kevin Garnett .60 1.50
15 Dikembe Mutombo .30 .75
16 Brevin Knight .20 .50
17 Keith Van Horn .30 .75
18 Theo Ratliff .25 .60
19 Tim Hardaway .30 .75
20 Blue Edwards .20 .50
21 David Wesley .20 .50
22 Jaren Jackson .20 .50
23 Nick Anderson .20 .50
24 Rodney Rogers .20 .50
25 Antonio Davis .20 .50
26 Clarence Weatherspoon .20 .50
27 Kelvin Cato .20 .50
28 Tracy McGrady .50 1.25
29 Mookie Blaylock .20 .50
30 Ron Harper .25 .60
31 Allan Houston .25 .60
32 Brian Williams .20 .50
33 John Stockton .40 1.00
34 Hersey Hawkins .20 .50
35 Donyell Marshall .20 .50
36 Mark Strickland .20 .50
37 Rod Strickland .20 .50
38 Cedric Ceballos .20 .50
39 Danny Fortson .20 .50
40 Shaquille O'Neal .75 2.00
41 Kendall Gill .20 .50
42 Allen Iverson .60 1.50
43 Travis Knight .20 .50
44 Cedric Henderson .20 .50
45 Steve Kerr .25 .60
46 Antonio McDyess .25 .60
47 Darrick Martin .20 .50
48 Shandon Anderson .20 .50
49 Shareef Abdur-Rahim .30 .75
50 Antoine Carr .20 .50
51 Jason Kidd .50 1.25
52 Calbert Cheaney .20 .50
53 Antoine Walker .30 .75
54 Greg Anthony .20 .50
55 Jeff Hornacek .25 .60
56 Reggie Miller .40 1.00
57 Lawrence Funderburke .20 .50
58 Derek Strong .20 .50
59 Robert Horry .25 .60
60 Shawn Bradley .20 .50
61 Matt Bullard .20 .50
62 Terrell Brandon .20 .50
63 Dan Majerle .30 .75
64 Jim Jackson .20 .50
65 Anthony Peeler .20 .50
66 Bo Outlaw .20 .50
67 Khalid Reeves .20 .50
68 Toni Kukoc .30 .75
69 Mario Elie .20 .50
70 Derek Anderson .20 .50
71 Jalen Rose .25 .60
72 Tyrone Corbin .20 .50
73 Anthony Mason .20 .50
74 Lamond Murray .20 .50
75 Tom Gugliotta .20 .50
76 Arvydas Sabonis .25 .60
77 Brian Shaw .20 .50
78 Rick Fox .20 .50
79 Danny Manning .25 .60
80 Lindsey Hunter .20 .50
81 Michael Jordan 2.50 6.00
82 LaPhonso Ellis .20 .50
83 David Robinson .50 1.25
84 Christian Laettner .25 .60
85 Armon Gilliam .20 .50
86 Sherman Douglas .20 .50
87 Charlie Ward .20 .50
88 Shawn Kemp .30 .75
89 Gary Payton .30 .75
90 Doug Christie .20 .50
91 Voshon Lenard .20 .50
92 Detlef Schrempf .30 .75
93 Walter McCarty .20 .50
94 Sam Cassell .25 .60
95 Jerry Stackhouse .30 .75
96 Billy Owens .20 .50
97 Matt Geiger .20 .50
98 Avery Johnson .25 .60
99 Bobby Jackson .25 .60
100 Rex Chapman .20 .50
101 Andrew DeClercq .20 .50
102 Vlade Divac .30 .75
103 Erick Strickland .20 .50
104 Dean Garrett .20 .50
105 Grant Long .20 .50
106 Adonal Foyle .20 .50
107 Isaac Austin .20 .50
108 Michael Curry .20 .50
109 Darrell Armstrong .20 .50
110 Aaron McKie .20 .50
111 Stacey Augmon .25 .60
112 Anthony Johnson .20 .50
113 Vinny Del Negro .20 .50
114 Reggie Slater .20 .50
115 Lee Mayberry .20 .50
116 Tracy Murray .20 .50
117 Scottie Pippen .50 1.25
118 Sam Perkins .20 .50
119 Derek Fisher .30 .75
120 Mark Bryant .20 .50
121 Dale Davis .20 .50
122 B.J. Armstrong .20 .50
123 Charles Barkley .50 1.25
124 Horace Grant .25 .60
125 Checklist .20 .50
126 Alonzo Mourning .40 1.00
127 Kerry Kittles .20 .50
128 Eldridge Recasner .20 .50
129 Dell Curry .20 .50
130 Jamal Mashburn .25 .60
131 Eric Piatkowski .25 .60
132 Othella Harrington .20 .50
133 Pete Chilcutt .20 .50
134 Dennis Rodman .60 1.50
135 Patrick Ewing .40 1.00
136 Danny Schayes .20 .50
137 John Williams .20 .50
138 Joe Smith .25 .60
139 Tariq Abdul-Wahad .20 .50
140 Vin Baker .25 .60
141 Elden Campbell .20 .50
142 Chris Carr .20 .50
143 John Starks .25 .60
144 Felton Spencer .20 .50
145 Mark Jackson .30 .75
146 Dana Barros .20 .50
147 Eric Williams .20 .50
148 Wesley Person .20 .50
149 Joe Dumars .30 .75
150 Steve Smith .25 .60
151 Randy Brown .20 .50
152 A.C. Green .30 .75
153 Dee Brown .20 .50
154 Brian Grant .20 .50
155 Tim Thomas .30 .75
156 Howard Eisley .20 .50
157 Malik Sealy .20 .50
158 Maurice Taylor .20 .50
159 Tyrone Hill .20 .50
160 Chris Gatling .20 .50
161 Rodrick Rhodes .20 .50
162 Muggsy Bogues .25 .60
163 Kenny Anderson .25 .60
164 Zydrunas Ilgauskas .30 .75
165 Grant Hill .50 1.25
166 Lorenzen Wright .20 .50
167 Tony Battie .25 .60
168 Bobby Phills .20 .50
169 Michael Finley .30 .75
170 Anfernee Hardaway .50 1.25
171 Terry Porter .20 .50
172 P.J. Brown .20 .50
173 Clifford Robinson .20 .50
174 Olden Polynice .20 .50
175 Kobe Bryant 1.50 4.00
176 Sean Elliott .30 .75
177 Latrell Sprewell .30 .75
178 Rik Smits .25 .60
179 Darrell Armstrong .20 .50
180 Stephon Marbury .40 1.00
181 Brent Price .20 .50
182 Danny Fortson .20 .50
183 Vitaly Potapenko .20 .50
184 Anthony Parker .20 .50
185 Glenn Robinson .25 .60
186 Erick Dampier .20 .50
187 George McCloud .20 .50
188 Rasheed Wallace .30 .75
189 Aaron Williams .20 .50
190 Tim Duncan .60 1.50
191 Chauncey Billups .40 1.00
192 Jim McIlvaine .20 .50
193 Chris Mullin .30 .75
194 George Lynch .20 .50
195 Damon Stoudamire .30 .75
196 Bryon Russell .20 .50
197 Luc Longley .20 .50
198 Ron Mercer .25 .60
199 Alan Henderson .20 .50
200 Jayson Williams .20 .50
201 Ben Wallace .30 .75
202 Elliot Perry .20 .50
203 Walt Williams .20 .50
204 Cherokee Parks .20 .50
205 Brent Barry .25 .60
206 Hubert Davis .20 .50
207 Terry Davis .20
208 Loy Vaught .20
209 Adam Keefe .20
210 Karl Malone .40
211 Chuck Person .25
212 Chris Childs .20
213 Rony Seikaly .30
214 Ervin Johnson .20
215 Derrick McKey .20
216 Jerome Williams .20
217 Glen Rice .30
218 Steve Nash .50
219 Nick Van Exel .25
220 Chris Webber .30
221 Marcus Camby .25
222 Antonio Daniels .20
223 Mitch Richmond .30
224 Otis Thorpe .20
225 Charles Oakley .25
226 Michael Olowokandi RC .75
227 Mike Bibby RC 1.50
228 Raef LaFrentz RC .75
229 Antawn Jamison RC 1.50
230 Vince Carter RC 3.00
231 Robert Traylor RC .60
232 Jason Williams RC 1.50
233 Larry Hughes RC 1.25
234 Dirk Nowitzki RC 6.00
235 Paul Pierce RC 3.00
236 Bonzi Wells RC .60
237 Michael Doleac RC .60
238 Keon Clark RC .60
239 Michael Dickerson RC .60
240 Matt Harpring RC .75
241 Bryce Drew RC .60
242 Pat Garrity RC .60
243 Roshown McLeod RC .60
244 Ricky Davis RC 1.00
245 Brian Skinner RC .60
246 Tyronn Lue RC .60
247 Felipe Lopez RC .60
248 Sam Jacobson RC .60
249 Corey Benjamin RC .60
250 Nazr Mohammed RC .60

1998-99 Finest No Protect

Randomly inserted into both series packs at a ra one in four, this 250-card set parallels the base The cards do not feature the "peel" associated w Finest brand. The card backs are also metallic, differentiate. To determine card values, please re the multiplier below, coupled with the value of th card.
*STARS: 1.5X TO 4X BASE CARD HI
*RCs: .6X TO 1.5X BASE HI
234 Dirk Nowitzki 10.00

1998-99 Finest No Protect Refractors

Randomly inserted into both series packs at one this 250-card set parallels the No Protector inse cards feature the Finest Refractor technology. To ascertain values for these cards, please refer to t multiplier in the header below, coupled with the of the base card.
*STARS: 6X TO 15X BASE CARD HI
*RCs: 2.5X TO 6X BASE HI
81 Michael Jordan 50.00
230 Vince Carter 25.00
234 Dirk Nowitzki 30.00

1998-99 Finest Refracto

Randomly inserted in both series packs at a rate in 12, this 250-card set parallels the basic set. T cards feature the Finest Refractor technology. Ca backs also have the word "Refractor" to help differentiate the cards. To determine values for th Refractors, please refer to the multiplier in the he coupled with the value of the base card.
*REF.STARS: 3X TO 8X BASE CARD HI
*REF.RCs: 1.5X TO 4X BASE
81 Michael Jordan 40.00
230 Vince Carter 25.00

1998-99 Finest Arena Sta

Randomly inserted in series two packs at one in this 20-card set features player's who are home favorites. The cards feature a semi-holographic background with stars and basketballs. The card are numbered with an "AS" prefix.
COMPLETE SET (20) 40.00
AS1 Shaquille O'Neal 4.00
AS2 Stephon Marbury 2.00
AS3 Allen Iverson 3.00
AS4 John Stockton 2.00
AS5 Kobe Bryant 12.00
AS6 Alonzo Mourning 2.00
AS7 Damon Stoudamire 1.50
AS8 Scottie Pippen 2.50
AS9 Tim Hardaway 1.50
AS10 Karl Malone 2.00
AS11 Tim Duncan 3.00
AS12 Gary Payton 1.50
AS13 Antoine Walker 1.50
AS14 Keith Van Horn 1.50
AS15 Juwan Howard 1.25
AS16 David Robinson 2.50
AS17 Michael Finley 1.50
AS18 Shareef Abdur-Rahim 1.50
AS19 Michael Jordan 20.00
AS20 Vin Baker 1.25

1998-99 Finest Centurion

mly inserted into series one packs at a rate of
91, this 20-card set features players who will
e game into the year 2000. The cards are serial
ered to 500. Card backs are numbered with a "C"

3X TO 8X HI COLUMN
PRINT RUN 75 SERIAL #'d SETS
ant Hill 10.00 25.00
m Thomas 6.00 15.00
die Jones 6.00 15.00
ichael Finley 6.00 15.00
aquille O'Neal 15.00 40.00
be Bryant 40.00 100.00
ith Van Horn 6.00 15.00
m Duncan 12.00 30.00
toine Walker 6.00 15.00
Shareef Abdur-Rahim 6.00 15.00
Stephon Marbury 8.00 20.00
Kevin Garnett 12.00 30.00
Ray Allen 8.00 20.00
Kerry Kittles 4.00 10.00
Allen Iverson 12.00 30.00
Damon Stoudamire 6.00 15.00
Brevin Knight 4.00 10.00
Bryant Reeves 4.00 10.00
Ron Mercer 5.00 12.00
Zydrunas Ilgauskas 6.00 15.00

998-99 Finest Court Control

omly inserted into series two packs at one in 76,
0-card set features players who control the court
ine, to baseline. The cards are serially numbered
0. Card backs contain a "CC" prefix.
1.25X TO 3X HI COLUMN
PRINT RUN 150 SERIAL #'d SETS
Shareef Abdur-Rahim 3.00 8.00
Keith Van Horn 3.00 8.00
Tim Duncan 6.00 15.00
Antoine Walker 3.00 8.00
Stephon Marbury 4.00 10.00
Kevin Garnett 6.00 15.00
Grant Hill 5.00 12.00
Michael Finley 3.00 8.00
Ron Mercer 2.50 6.00
Damon Stoudamire 3.00 8.00
Michael Olowokandi 2.00 5.00
Mike Bibby 4.00 10.00
Antawn Jamison 4.00 10.00
Vince Carter 8.00 20.00
Jason Williams 4.00 10.00
Larry Hughes 3.00 8.00
Paul Pierce 8.00 20.00
Michael Dickerson 1.50 4.00
Bryce Drew 1.50 4.00
Felipe Lopez 1.50 4.00

1998-99 Finest Hardwood Honors

omly inserted in series one packs at a rate of one
, this 20-card set features players that captured
e of the league's most coveted awards last season
their outstanding play. Card backs feature a "H"
x.
PLETE SET (20) 75.00 150.00
ichael Jordan 40.00 100.00
haquille O'Neal 6.00 15.00
arl Malone 3.00 8.00
ddie Jones 2.50 6.00
ikembe Mutombo 2.50 6.00
Vesley Person 1.50 4.00
len Rice 2.50 6.00
avid Robinson 4.00 10.00
ik Smits 2.00 5.00
Steve Smith 2.00 5.00
Allen Iverson 5.00 12.00
Jayson Williams 1.50 4.00
Nick Anderson 1.50 4.00
Tim Duncan 5.00 12.00
Jason Kidd 4.00 10.00
Alonzo Mourning 3.00 8.00
Sam Cassell 2.00 5.00
Alan Henderson 1.50 4.00
Gary Payton 2.50 6.00
Scottie Pippen 4.00 10.00

998-99 Finest Mystery Finest

omly inserted in series one packs at a rate of one
, and series two packs at 1:36, this 40-card set
res superstars of the NBA, each showcased with
of two players on the back. Card backs carry a "M"
x.
.75X TO 2X HI COLUMN
SER.1 STATED ODDS 1:133 H/R
SER.2 STATED ODDS 1:144 H/R
Michael Jordan 20.00 50.00
be Bryant
Kobe Bryant 10.00 25.00
aquille O'Neal

M3 Shaquille O'Neal 6.00 15.00
David Robinson
M4 David Robinson 3.00 8.00
Tim Duncan
M5 Tim Duncan 2.00 5.00
Keith Van Horn
M6 Keith Van Horn 2.00 5.00
Scottie Pippen
M7 Scottie Pippen 4.00 10.00
Shareef Abdur-Rahim
M8 Shareef Abdur-Rahim 2.50 6.00
Grant Hill
M9 Grant Hill 6.00 15.00
Kevin Garnett
M10 Kevin Garnett 4.00 10.00
Stephon Marbury
M11 Stephon Marbury 1.50 4.00
Gary Payton
M12 Gary Payton 1.50 4.00
Vin Baker
M13 Vin Baker 1.50 4.00
Karl Malone
M14 Karl Malone 3.00 8.00
Shawn Kemp
M15 Shawn Kemp 1.50 4.00
Tim Thomas
M16 Tim Thomas 1.50 4.00
Antoine Walker
M17 Antoine Walker 1.25 3.00
Ron Mercer
M18 Ron Mercer 1.25 3.00
Kerry Kittles
M19 Kerry Kittles 1.25 3.00
Eddie Jones
M20 Eddie Jones 12.50 30.00
Michael Jordan
M21 Alonzo Mourning 4.00 10.00
Scottie Pippen
M22 Scottie Pippen 4.00 10.00
Antoine Walker
M23 Antoine Walker 1.25 3.00
Shareef Abdur-Rahim
M24 Shareef Abdur-Rahim 4.00 10.00
Kevin Garnett
M25 Kevin Garnett 2.50 6.00
Keith Van Horn
M26 Keith Van Horn 1.25 3.00
Tim Thomas
M27 Tim Thomas 2.00 5.00
Grant Hill
M28 Grant Hill 4.00 10.00
Anfernee Hardaway
M29 Anfernee Hardaway 2.50 6.00
Kerry Kittles
M30 Kerry Kittles 1.25 3.00
Jayson Williams
M31 Jayson Williams 1.50 4.00
Karl Malone
M32 Karl Malone 2.50 6.00
John Stockton
M33 John Stockton 2.00 5.00
Gary Payton
M34 Gary Payton 1.50 4.00
Ron Mercer
M35 Ron Mercer 1.50 4.00
Stephon Marbury
M36 Stephon Marbury 3.00 8.00
Allen Iverson
M37 Allen Iverson 6.00 15.00
Kobe Bryant
M38 Kobe Bryant 6.00 15.00
Tim Duncan
M39 Tim Duncan 5.00 12.00
Shaquille O'Neal
M40 Shaquille O'Neal 5.00 12.00
Alonzo Mourning

1998-99 Finest Oversized

Randomly inserted in series one boxes at one in three, and series two boxes at one per box, this 14-card set features 3 1/2" by 5" oversized Finest cards.
COMPLETE SET (14) 12.50 30.00
COMPLETE SERIES 1 (7) 10.00 20.00
COMPLETE SERIES 2 (7) 5.00 12.00
*REF: .75X TO 2X HI COLUMN
REF: SER.1/2 STATED ODDS 1:12 BOXES
1 Kevin Garnett 2.50 6.00
2 Keith Van Horn 1.25 3.00
3 Shaquille O'Neal 3.00 8.00
4 Shareef Abdur-Rahim 1.25 3.00
5 Antoine Walker 1.25 3.00
6 Gary Payton 1.25 3.00
7 Scottie Pippen 2.00 5.00
8 Alonzo Mourning .75 2.00
9 Kerry Kittles .40 1.00
10 Kobe Bryant 3.00 8.00
11 Stephon Marbury .75 2.00
12 Tim Duncan 1.25 3.00
13 Ron Mercer .50 1.25
14 Karl Malone .75 2.00

1999-00 Finest Promos

COMPLETE SET (6) 2.50 6.00
PP1 Reggie Miller .60 1.50
PP2 Corliss Williamson .40 1.00
PP3 Tom Gugliotta .40 1.00
PP4 Tracy McGrady 1.00 2.50
PP5 Anfernee Hardaway 1.00 2.50
PP6 Tim Duncan 1.25 3.00

1999-00 Finest

Both series of Finest was released as a 133 card sets, totalling 266 cards. Series one contained 100 veterans and three subsets: Gems, Rookies and Sensations. The subset cards were inserted one per pack. Series two contained 91 veterans and four subsets: Gold Medal Contenders, Catalyts, Edge and Rookies. The series two rookies were serially numbered to 2000 and inserted at one in 14 packs. Each pack contained five cards that carried a suggested retail price of $4.99 per pack.
COMPLETE SET (266) 100.00 210.00
COMPLETE SERIES 1 (133) 25.00 60.00
COMPLETE SERIES 2 (133) 75.00 150.00
COMP.SERIES 2 w/o RC (118) 15.00 40.00
1 Shareef Abdur-Rahim .30 .75
2 Kevin Willis .25 .60
3 Sean Elliott .40 1.00
4 Vlade Divac .40 1.00
5 Tom Gugliotta .25 .60
6 Matt Harpring .30 .75
7 Kerry Kittles .25 .60
8 Joe Smith .30 .75
9 Jamal Mashburn .30 .75
10 Tyrone Nesby RC .60 1.50
11 Alan Henderson .25 .60
12 Vitaly Potapenko .25 .60
13 Dickey Simpkins .25 .60
14 Michael Finley .40 1.00
15 Lindsey Hunter .25 .60
16 Antawn Jamison .40 1.00
17 Reggie Miller .40 1.00
18 Maurice Taylor .25 .60
19 Clarence Weatherspoon .25 .60
20 Sam Mitchell .25 .60
21 Latrell Sprewell .40 1.00
22 Michael Doleac .25 .60
23 Rex Chapman .25 .60
24 Peja Stojakovic .40 1.00
25 Vladimir Stepania .25 .60
26 Tracy McGrady .60 1.50
27 Cherokee Parks .25 .60
28 LaPhonso Ellis .25 .60
29 Hakeem Olajuwon .50 1.25
30 Adonal Foyle .25 .60
31 Bryant Stith .25 .60
32 Andrew DeClercq .25 .60
33 Toni Kukoc .40 1.00
34 Kenny Anderson .30 .75
35 Mike Bibby .40 1.00
36 Glen Rice .40 1.00
37 Avery Johnson .30 .75
38 Arvydas Sabonis .30 .75
39 Kornel David RC .60 1.50
40 Hubert Davis .25 .60
41 Grant Hill .50 1.25
42 Donyell Marshall .25 .60
43 Jalen Rose .30 .75
44 Derrick Coleman .30 .75
45 P.J. Brown .25 .60
46 Vin Baker .40 1.00
47 Clifford Robinson .25 .60
48 Allan Houston .30 .75
49 Kendall Gill .25 .60
50 Matt Geiger .25 .60
51 Larry Hughes .30 .75
52 Corliss Williamson .25 .60
53 Darrell Armstrong .25 .60
54 Bobby Jackson .30 .75
55 Bryon Russell .25 .60
56 Juwan Howard .30 .75
57 Dikembe Mutombo .40 1.00
58 Eddie Jones .40 1.00
59 Randy Brown .25 .60
60 Dirk Nowitzki .75 2.00
61 Jerome Williams .25 .60
62 Scottie Pippen .60 1.50
63 Dale Davis .25 .60
64 Kobe Bryant 2.00 5.00
65 Robert Traylor .25 .60
66 Tim Hardaway .40 1.00
67 Michael Olowokandi .25 .60
68 Walter McCarty .25 .60
69 Damon Stoudamire .40 1.00
70 Othella Harrington .25 .60
71 Chauncey Billups .40 1.00
72 John Starks .40 1.00
73 Ricky Davis .40 1.00
74 Glenn Robinson .30 .75
75 Dean Garrett .25 .60
76 Chris Childs .25 .60
77 Shawn Kemp .40 1.00
78 Allen Iverson .75 2.00
79 Brian Grant .25 .60
80 David Robinson .60 1.50
81 Tracy Murray .25 .60
82 Howard Eisley .25 .60
83 Doug Christie .30 .75
84 Gary Payton .40 1.00
85 John Stockton .50 1.25
86 Rod Strickland .25 .60
87 Tyrone Corbin .25 .60
88 Antonio Daniels .25 .60
89 Dee Brown .25 .60
90 Antoine Walker .40 1.00
91 Theo Ratliff .30 .75
92 Larry Johnson .40 1.00
93 Stephon Marbury .30 .75
94 Brevin Knight .25 .60
95 Antonio McDyess .30 .75
96 Bison Dele .25 .60
97 Cuttino Mobley .30 .75
98 Haywoode Workman .25 .60
99 J.R. Reid .25 .60
100 Travis Best .25 .60
101 Chris Webber GEM .60 1.50
102 Grant Hill GEM .75 2.00
103 Kevin Garnett GEM 1.25 3.00
104 Jason Kidd GEM 1.00 2.50
105 Gary Payton GEM .60 1.50
106 Shaquille O'Neal GEM 1.50 4.00
107 Alonzo Mourning GEM .75 2.00
108 Karl Malone GEM .75 2.00
109 John Stockton GEM .75 2.00
110 Elton Brand RC 1.50 4.00
111 Baron Davis RC 2.00 5.00
112 Aleksandar Radojevic RC .60 1.50
113 Cal Bowdler RC .60 1.50
114 Jumaine Jones RC .60 1.50
115 Jason Terry RC 1.50 4.00
116 Trajan Langdon RC .60 1.50
117 Dion Glover RC .60 1.50
118 Jeff Foster RC .60 1.50
119 Lamar Odom RC 2.00 5.00
120 Wally Szczerbiak RC 1.25 3.00
121 Shawn Marion RC 1.50 4.00
122 Kenny Thomas RC .60 1.50
123 Devean George RC .60 1.50
124 Scott Padgett RC .60 1.50
125 Tim Duncan SEN 1.25 3.00
126 Jason Williams SEN .75 2.00
127 Paul Pierce SEN 1.00 2.50
128 Kobe Bryant SEN 3.00 8.00
129 Keith Van Horn SEN .50 1.25
130 Vince Carter SEN 1.25 3.00
131 Matt Harpring SEN .50 1.25
132 Antawn Jamison SEN .60 1.50
133 Tracy McGrady SEN 1.00 2.50
134 Tim Duncan .75 2.00
135 Tariq Abdul-Wahad .25 .60
136 Luc Longley .25 .60
137 Steve Smith .25 .60
138 Alonzo Mourning .50 1.25
139 Kevin Garnett .75 2.00
140 Christian Laettner .30 .75
141 Rik Smits .40 1.00
142 Cedric Henderson .25 .60
143 Jim Jackson .30 .75
144 Dan Majerle .40 1.00
145 Bryant Reeves .25 .60
146 Antonio Davis .25 .60
147 Michael Smith .25 .60
148 Charlie Ward .25 .60
149 Chris Mullin .40 1.00
150 Danny Manning .25 .60
151 Eric Williams .25 .60
152 Hersey Hawkins .25 .60
153 Isaiah Rider .25 .60
154 Shandon Anderson .25 .60
155 Jason Kidd .60 1.50
156 Chris Whitney .25 .60
157 Brent Barry .30 .75
158 Patrick Ewing .50 1.25
159 George Lynch .25 .60
160 Dickey Simpkins .25 .60
161 Derek Anderson .25 .60
162 Ron Mercer .30 .75
163 David Wesley .25 .60
164 Mookie Blaylock .25 .60
165 Terrell Brandon .25 .60
166 Detlef Schrempf .30 .75
167 Olden Polynice .25 .60
168 Jayson Williams .25 .60
169 Eric Piatkowski .30 .75
170 A.C. Green .40 1.00
171 Chris Mills .25 .60
172 Chris Webber .40 1.00
173 Jeff Hornacek .30 .75
174 Calbert Cheaney .25 .60
175 Wesley Person .25 .60
176 Corey Benjamin .25 .60
177 Loy Vaught .25 .60
178 Keith Closs .25 .60
179 Bo Outlaw .25 .60
180 Mitch Richmond .40 1.00
181 Charles Oakley .30 .75
182 Felipe Lopez .25 .60
183 Eric Snow .30 .75
184 Paul Pierce .60 1.50
185 Elden Campbell .25 .60
186 Shaquille O'Neal 1.00 2.50
187 Charles Barkley .60 1.50
188 Mark Jackson .40 1.00
189 Scott Burrell .25 .60
190 Anfernee Hardaway .60 1.50
191 Samaki Walker .25 .60
192 Karl Malone .50 1.25
193 Jermaine O'Neal .40 1.00
194 Mario Elie .25 .60
195 Malik Sealy .25 .60
196 Voshon Lenard .25 .60
197 Chris Gatling .25 .60
198 Walt Williams .25 .60
199 Nick Van Exel .30 .75
200 Bimbo Coles .25 .60
201 John Wallace .25 .60
202 Anthony Mason .25 .60
203 Steve Nash .60 1.50
204 Erick Dampier .25 .60
205 Cedric Ceballos .25 .60
206 Derek Fisher .40 1.00
207 Marcus Camby .30 .75
208 Tyrone Hill .25 .60
209 Nick Anderson .25 .60
210 Sam Cassell .30 .75
211 Raef LaFrentz .30 .75
212 Ruben Patterson .25 .60
213 Rick Fox .25 .60
214 Jason Williams .50 1.25
215 Vince Carter .75 2.00
216 Michael Dickerson .25 .60
217 Steve Kerr .30 .75
218 Rasheed Wallace .40 1.00
219 Keith Van Horn .30 .75
220 Bob Sura .25 .60
221 Ray Allen .40 1.00
222 Jerry Stackhouse .40 1.00
223 Shawn Bradley .25 .60
224 Horace Grant .30 .75
225 Tim Duncan USA 1.25 3.00
226 Kevin Garnett USA 1.25 3.00
227 Jason Kidd USA 1.00 2.50
228 Steve Smith USA .40 1.00
229 Allan Houston USA .50 1.25
230 Tom Gugliotta USA .40 1.00
231 Gary Payton USA .60 1.50
232 Tim Hardaway USA .60 1.50
233 Vin Baker USA .60 1.50
234 Karl Malone CAT .75 2.00
235 Vince Carter CAT 1.25 3.00
236 Jason Williams CAT .75 2.00
237 Alonzo Mourning CAT .75 2.00
238 Anfernee Hardaway CAT 1.00 2.50
239 Mitch Richmond CAT .60 1.50
240 Steve Smith CAT .40 1.00
241 Charles Barkley CAT 1.00 2.50
242 Ron Mercer CAT .50 1.25
243 Shaquille O'Neal EDGE 1.50 4.00
244 Jason Kidd EDGE 1.00 2.50
245 Kevin Garnett EDGE 1.25 3.00
246 Tim Duncan EDGE 1.25 3.00
247 Ray Allen EDGE .60 1.50
248 Chris Webber EDGE .60 1.50
249 Jerry Stackhouse EDGE .60 1.50
250 Keith Van Horn EDGE .50 1.25
251 Patrick Ewing EDGE .75 2.00
252 Steve Francis RC 6.00 15.00
253 Jonathan Bender RC 2.50 6.00
254 Richard Hamilton RC 6.00 15.00
255 Andre Miller RC 6.00 15.00
256 Corey Maggette RC 5.00 12.00
257 William Avery RC 2.50 6.00
258 Ron Artest RC 6.00 15.00
259 James Posey RC 2.50 6.00
260 Quincy Lewis RC 2.50 6.00
261 Tim James RC 2.50 6.00
262 Vonteego Cummings RC 2.50 6.00
263 Anthony Carter RC 2.50 6.00
264 Mirsad Turkcan RC 2.50 6.00
265 Adrian Griffin RC 2.50 6.00
266 Ryan Robertson RC 2.50 6.00

1999-00 Finest Refractors

Randomly inserted in both series packs at one in 12 and series two rookies at one in 138, this 266-card set parallels the base set using Topps Refractor technology. To ascertain values on individual cards, please refer to the mutliplier in the header, coupled with the value of the base card.
*STARS: 2.5X TO 6X BASE CARD HI
*SUBSETS: 1.5X TO 4X HI
*SER.1 RCs: 1.25X TO 3X HI
*SER.2 RCs: .5X TO 1.25X HI

1999-00 Finest Refractors Gold

Randomly inserted in series one packs at one in 62 and series two packs at one in 31, this 266-card set parallels the base set. The cards feature a gold refractive background on a die cut card. The cards are also serially numbered to 100. To ascertain values on individual cards, please refer to the multiplier in the header, coupled with the value of the base card.
*STARS: 8X TO 20X BASE CARD HI
*SER.1 RCs: 4X TO 10X BASE HI
*SER.2 RCs: 1X TO 2.5X BASE HI
*SUBSETS: 5X TO 12X BASE HI

1999-00 Finest 24-Karat Touch

Randomly inserted in series two packs at one in 30, this 10-card set focuses on the top shooters in the NBA. The cards feature gold texture on the front. Card backs carry a "KT" prefix.
COMPLETE SET (10) 8.00 20.00
*REF: 2X TO 5X HI COLUMN
REF: SER.2 STATED ODDS 1:300, 1:150 HTA
KT1 Reggie Miller 1.50 4.00
KT2 Keith Van Horn 1.25 3.00
KT3 Allan Houston 1.25 3.00
KT4 Patrick Ewing 2.00 5.00
KT5 Anfernee Hardaway 2.50 6.00
KT6 Steve Smith 1.00 2.50
KT7 Glen Rice 1.50 4.00
KT8 Ray Allen 1.50 4.00
KT9 Charles Barkley 2.50 6.00
KT10 Mitch Richmond 1.50 4.00

1999-00 Finest Box Office Draws

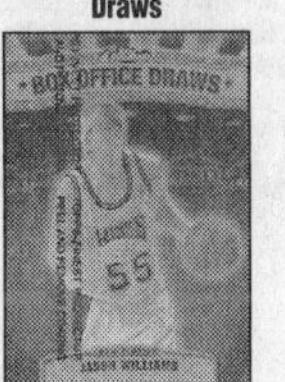

Randomly inserted in series two packs at one in 30, this 10-card set features marquee players who are loved by their fans around the world. Card backs carry a "BOD" prefix.
COMPLETE SET (10) 12.00 30.00
*REF: 2X TO 5X HI COLUMN
REF: SER.2 STATED ODDS 1:300, 1:150 HTA
BOD1 Shaquille O'Neal 4.00 10.00
BOD2 Patrick Ewing 2.00 5.00
BOD3 Karl Malone 2.00 5.00
BOD4 Jason Williams 2.00 5.00
BOD5 Charles Barkley 2.50 6.00
BOD6 Tim Duncan 3.00 8.00
BOD7 Kevin Garnett 3.00 8.00
BOD8 Alonzo Mourning 2.00 5.00
BOD9 Mitch Richmond 1.50 4.00
BOD10 Elton Brand 4.00 10.00

1999-00 Finest Double Double

Randomly inserted in series two packs at one in 20, this 15-card set features players who are most apt to put up a double-double in any game. Card backs carry a "D" prefix.
COMPLETE SET (15) 20.00 50.00
*REF: 2X TO 5X HI COLUMN
REF: SER.2 STATED ODDS 1:200, 1:100 HTA
D1 Jason Kidd 2.50 6.00
D2 Kobe Bryant 8.00 20.00
D3 Antoine Walker 1.50 4.00
D4 Chris Webber 1.50 4.00
D5 Anfernee Hardaway 2.50 6.00
D6 Shawn Kemp 1.50 4.00
D7 Tim Duncan 3.00 8.00
D8 Antonio McDyess 1.25 3.00
D9 Grant Hill 2.00 5.00
D10 Karl Malone 2.00 5.00
D11 Shaquille O'Neal 4.00 10.00
D12 Allen Iverson 3.00 8.00
D13 Jayson Williams 1.00 2.50
D14 Keith Van Horn 1.25 3.00
D15 Gary Payton 1.50 4.00

1999-00 Finest Double Feature Right Refractors

Randomly inserted in series one packs at one in 26, this 14-card set features some of the stars of the NBA paired up using a "split screen". This set is also refered to as Non-Refractor/Refractor. Card backs carry a "DF" prefix.
COMPLETE SET (14) 15.00 30.00
RIGHT/LEFT VARIATIONS EQUAL VALUE
*DUAL REF: 1X TO 2.5X BASE HI
DUAL REFRACTOR SER.1 ODDS 1:78, 1:36 HTA
DF1 Hakeem Olajuwon 1.50 4.00
Scottie Pippen
DF2 Paul Pierce 1.50 4.00
Antoine Walker
DF3 Shareef Abdur-Rahim 1.00 2.50
Mike Bibby
DF4 Alonzo Mourning 1.25 3.00
Tim Hardaway
DF5 Glenn Robinson 1.00 2.50
Ray Allen
DF6 Kevin Garnett 2.00 5.00
Joe Smith
DF7 Keith Van Horn .75 2.00
Stephon Marbury
DF8 Chris Webber 1.25 3.00
Jason Williams
DF9 Tim Duncan 2.00 5.00
David Robinson
DF10 Gary Payton 1.00 2.50
Vin Baker
DF11 Karl Malone 1.25 3.00
John Stockton
DF12 Jason Kidd 1.50 4.00
Tom Gugliotta
DF13 Mitch Richmond 1.00 2.50
Juwan Howard
DF14 Kobe Bryant 5.00 12.00
Shaquille O'Neal

1999-00 Finest Dunk Masters

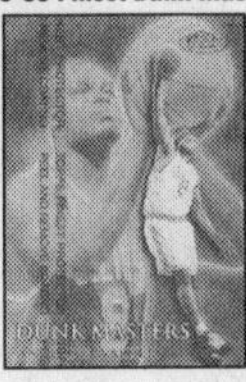

Randomly inserted in series one packs at one in 73, this 15-card set features some of the best dunkers in the league. The cards are serially numbered to 750. Card backs carry a "DM" prefix.
*REFRACTORS: 1.5X TO 4X HI COLUMN
REF: SER.1 ODDS 1:364, 1:168 HTA
REF: PRINT RUN 150 SERIAL #'d SETS
DM1 Kobe Bryant 25.00 60.00
DM2 Shaquille O'Neal 8.00 20.00
DM3 Chris Webber 3.00 8.00
DM4 Antonio McDyess 2.50 6.00
DM5 Michael Finley 3.00 8.00
DM6 Shawn Kemp 3.00 8.00
DM7 Tracy McGrady 5.00 12.00
DM8 Antoine Walker 3.00 8.00
DM9 Alonzo Mourning 4.00 10.00
DM10 Ray Allen 3.00 8.00
DM11 Kevin Garnett 6.00 15.00
DM12 Allen Iverson 6.00 15.00
DM13 Vince Carter 6.00 15.00
DM14 Tim Duncan 6.00 15.00
DM15 Scottie Pippen 6.00 15.00

1999-00 Finest Future's Finest

Randomly inserted in series one packs at one in 73, this 15-card set focuses on rookies from the 1999 draft class. The cards are serially numbered to 750. Card backs carry a "FF" prefix.
REF: 1.25X TO 3X HI COLUMN
REF: SER. ODDS 1:364, 1:168 HTA
REF: PRINT RUN 150 SERIAL #'d SETS
FF1 Elton Brand 3.00 8.00
FF2 Steve Francis 3.00 8.00
FF3 Baron Davis 4.00 10.00
FF4 Lamar Odom 4.00 10.00
FF5 Jonathan Bender 1.25 3.00
FF6 Wally Szczerbiak 2.50 6.00
FF7 Richard Hamilton 3.00 8.00
FF8 Andre Miller 3.00 8.00
FF9 Shawn Marion 3.00 8.00
FF10 Jason Terry 3.00 8.00
FF11 Trajan Langdon 1.25 3.00
FF12 Aleksandar Radojevic 1.25 3.00
FF13 Corey Maggette 2.50 6.00
FF14 William Avery 1.25 3.00
FF15 Cal Bowdler 1.25 3.00

1999-00 Finest Heirs to Air

Randomly inserted in series two packs at one in 36, this 10-card set features the top gravity-defiers in the NBA. Card backs carry a "HA" prefix.
COMPLETE SET (10) 15.00 40.00
SER.2 STATED ODDS 1:36, 1:16 HTA
HA1 Michael Finley 2.00 5.00
HA2 Brent Barry 1.50 4.00
HA3 Corey Maggette 4.00 10.00
HA4 Ron Mercer 1.50 4.00
HA5 Eddie Jones 2.00 5.00
HA6 Tracy McGrady 3.00 8.00
HA7 Vince Carter 4.00 10.00
HA8 Jerry Stackhouse 2.00 5.00
HA9 Ray Allen 2.00 5.00
HA10 Kobe Bryant 10.00 25.00

1999-00 Finest Leading Indicators

Randomly inserted in series one packs at one in 30, this 10-card set features the top producing players printed on thermal ink technology. By touching various points on the card, one could reveal each player's statistics from the 98-99 season. Card backs carry a "L" prefix.
COMPLETE SET (10) 10.00 25.00
L1 Stephon Marbury 1.00 2.50
L2 Paul Pierce 2.00 5.00
L3 Jason Kidd 2.00 5.00
L4 Gary Payton 1.25 3.00
L5 Keith Van Horn 1.00 2.50
L6 Reggie Miller 1.25 3.00
L7 Jason Williams 1.50 4.00
L8 Vince Carter 2.50 6.00
L9 Ray Allen 1.25 3.00
L10 Kobe Bryant 6.00 15.00

1999-00 Finest New Millennium

Randomly inserted in series one packs at one in 55, this 10-card set focuses on young player who have already proven they can carry the torch into the millennium. The cards are serially numbered to 1500. Card backs carry a "NM" prefix.
*REF: 1.25X TO 3X HI COLUMN
REF: SER.1 ODDS 1:273, 1:126 HTA
REF: PRINT RUN 300 SERIAL #'d SETS
NM1 Jason Williams 2.00 5.00
NM2 Vince Carter 3.00 8.00
NM3 Paul Pierce 2.50 6.00
NM4 Mike Bibby 1.50 4.00
NM5 Elton Brand 2.50 6.00
NM6 Steve Francis 2.50 6.00
NM7 Baron Davis 3.00 8.00
NM8 Lamar Odom 3.00 8.00
NM9 Jonathan Bender 1.00 2.50
NM10 Wally Szczerbiak 2.00 5.00

1999-00 Finest Next Generation

Randomly inserted in series two packs at one in 20, this 15-card set features young players that will lead the NBA in the next millennium. Card backs carry a "NG" prefix.
*REF: 1.5X TO 4X HI COLUMN
REF: SER.2 STATED ODDS 1:200, 1:100 HTA
NG1 Steve Francis 1.25 3.00
NG2 Jonathan Bender .50 1.25
NG3 Richard Hamilton 1.25 3.00
NG4 Andre Miller 1.25 3.00
NG5 Corey Maggette 1.00 2.50
NG6 William Avery .50 1.25
NG7 Ron Artest 1.25 3.00
NG8 Wally Szczerbiak 1.00 2.50
NG9 Quincy Lewis .50 1.25
NG10 Devean George .50 1.25
NG11 Vonteego Cummings .50 1.25
NG12 Lamar Odom 1.50 4.00
NG13 Shawn Marion 1.25 3.00
NG14 Elton Brand 1.25 3.00
NG15 Baron Davis 1.50 4.00

1999-00 Finest Producers

Randomly inserted in series one packs at one in 22, this 10-card set features the top producers from the 1998-99 season. Card backs carry a "FP" prefix.
COMPLETE SET (10) 8.00 20.00
*REFRACTORS: 1.25X TO 3X HI COLUMN
REF: SER.1 ODDS 1:109, 1:50 HTA
FP1 Shaquille O'Neal 2.50 6.00
FP2 Chris Webber 1.00 2.50
FP3 Karl Malone 1.25 3.00
FP4 Allen Iverson 2.00 5.00
FP5 Kevin Garnett 2.00 5.00
FP6 Jason Kidd 1.50 4.00
FP7 Grant Hill 1.25 3.00
FP8 Shareef Abdur-Rahim .75 2.00
FP9 Gary Payton 1.00 2.50
FP10 Charles Barkley 1.50 4.00

1999-00 Finest Salute

Randomly inserted in series one packs at one in 108 and series two at one in 100, this two card set features Rookie of the Year Vince Carter, NBA Finals MVP Tim Duncan and Scoring leader Allen Iverson on one card and the top six rookies from the Draft on the other. The cards carry a "FS" prefix. In addition to the regular card, a refractor version was inserted at one in 5,305 for series one and one in 4,616 for series two and a gold refractor version at one in 16,992 for series one and one in 8,539 for series two. Both gold refractor versions were serially numbered to 50. The set is considered complete with all six cards.
FS1 Vince Carter 1.50 4.00
Tim Duncan
Allen Iverson
FS1 Vince Carter 10.00 25.00
Tim Duncan
Allen Iverson
Refractor

FS1 Vince Carter 50.00 100.00
Tim Duncan
Allen Iverson
Gold Refractor
FS2 Draft Picks 1.50 4.00
Elton Brand
Steve Francis
Baron Davis
Lamar Odom
Jonathan Bender
Wally Szczerbiak
FS2 Draft Picks REF 25.00 60.00
Elton Brand
Steve Francis
Baron Davis
Lamar Odom
Jonathan Bender
Wally Szczerbiak
FS2 Draft Picks GR 100.00 200.00
Elton Brand
Steve Francis
Baron Davis
Lamar Odom
Jonathan Bender
Wally Szczerbiak

1999-00 Finest Team Finest Blue

Randomly inserted in series one packs at one in 55 and series two packs at one in 28, this set focuses on the top stars in the NBA. The cards are serially numbered to 1500. Card backs carry a "TF" prefix.

COMPLETE SET (20) 25.00 65.00
COMPLETE SERIES 1 (10) 10.00 25.00
COMPLETE SERIES 2 (10) 15.00 40.00
*BLUE REF: 1.5X TO 4X BASIC BLUE
BLUE REF: SER.1 ODDS 1:546, 1:252 HTA
BLUE REF: SER.2 ODDS 1:276, 1:127 HTA
BLUE REF: PRINT RUN 150 SERIAL #'d SETS
*RED: .75X TO 2X BASIC BLUE
RED: SER.1 STATED ODDS 1:18 HTA
RED: SER.2 STATED ODDS 1:9 HTA
RED: PRINT RUN 500 SERIAL #'d SETS
*GOLD: 1X TO 2.5X BASIC BLUE
GOLD: SER.1 STATED ODDS 1:35 HTA
GOLD: SER.2 STATED ODDS 1:18 HTA
GOLD: PRINT RUN 250 SERIAL #'d SETS
TF1 Shareef Abdur-Rahim 1.25 3.00
TF2 Stephon Marbury 1.25 3.00
TF3 Shawn Kemp 1.50 4.00
TF4 Allen Iverson 3.00 8.00
TF5 Antoine Walker 1.50 4.00
TF6 Hakeem Olajuwon 2.00 5.00
TF7 Tim Duncan 3.00 8.00
TF8 Karl Malone 2.00 5.00
TF9 Grant Hill 2.00 5.00
TF10 Keith Van Horn 1.25 3.00
TF11 Alonzo Mourning 2.00 5.00
TF12 Jason Kidd 2.50 6.00
TF13 Chris Webber 1.50 4.00
TF14 Shaquille O'Neal 4.00 10.00
TF15 Gary Payton 1.50 4.00
TF16 Kevin Garnett 3.00 8.00
TF17 Antonio McDyess 1.25 3.00
TF18 Kobe Bryant 8.00 20.00
TF19 Scottie Pippen 2.50 6.00
TF20 Vince Carter 3.00 8.00

1999-00 Finest Team Finest Gold Refractors

Randomly inserted in series one HTA packs at one in 352 and series two at one in 180, this 20-card set parallels the Finest Blue insert. The cards are serially numbered to 25. Card backs carry a "TF" prefix. To ascertain values on individual cards, please refer to the multiplier in the header, coupled with the value of the base insert.

*REFRACTORS: 5X TO 12X HI COLUMN
TF14 Shaquille O'Neal 60.00 150.00
TF18 Kobe Bryant 200.00 350.00

1999-00 Finest Team Finest Red Refractors

Randomly inserted in series one HTA packs at one in 175 and series two at one in 89, this 20-card set parallels the Finest Blue insert. The cards are serially numbered to 50. Card backs carry a "TF" prefix. To ascertain values on individual cards, please refer to the multiplier in the header, coupled with the value of the base insert.

*REFRACTORS: 3X TO 8X HI COLUMN
TF18 Kobe Bryant 100.00 250.00

2000-01 Finest

The 2000-01 Finest set was released in late November, in just one series. Each pack contained five cards and carried a suggested retail price of $5.00. The series one set was comprised of the following: 125 veterans, 25 rookies (serially numbered to 1599), 13 Off the Meter subset cards (inserted at one in eight) and 10 Gems subset cards (inserted at one in 24 packs).

COMPLETE SET (173) 125.00 250.00
COMPLETE SET w/o SP (125) 15.00 40.00
1 Shaquille O'Neal 1.00 2.50
2 P.J. Brown .25 .60
3 Joe Smith .30 .75
4 Kendall Gill .25 .60
5 Corey Maggette .30 .75
6 Marcus Camby .30 .75
7 Toni Kukoc .30 .75
8 Kobe Bryant 2.00 5.00
9 David Robinson .60 1.50
10 Ruben Patterson .25 .60
11 Allen Iverson .75 2.00
12 Glenn Robinson .30 .75
13 Anthony Carter .25 .60
14 Jonathan Bender .25 .60
15 Vince Carter .75 2.00
16 Jerry Stackhouse .30 .75
17 Raef LaFrentz .25 .60
18 Dikembe Mutombo .40 1.00
19 Baron Davis .40 1.00
20 Kenny Anderson .30 .75
21 Corey Benjamin .25 .60
22 Andre Miller .30 .75
23 Cedric Ceballos .25 .60
24 Christian Laettner .25 .60
25 Shandon Anderson .25 .60
26 Rik Smits .25 .60
27 Michael Olowokandi .25 .60
28 Sam Cassell .30 .75
29 Tom Gugliotta .25 .60
30 Jason Williams .40 1.00
31 Avery Johnson .30 .75
32 Karl Malone .50 1.25
33 Grant Hill .50 1.25
34 Paul Pierce .50 1.25
35 Antonio Davis .25 .60
36 Nick Anderson .25 .60
37 Alan Henderson .25 .60
38 Eddie Jones .40 1.00
39 Ron Artest .40 1.00
40 Brevin Knight .25 .60
41 Keon Clark .25 .60
42 Elton Brand .40 1.00
43 Reggie Miller .40 1.00
44 Steve Francis .40 1.00
45 Derek Anderson .25 .60
46 Alonzo Mourning .50 1.25
47 Terrell Brandon .25 .60
48 Larry Johnson .40 1.00
49 Keith Van Horn .30 .75
50 Jason Kidd .60 1.50
51 Scottie Pippen .60 1.50
52 Gary Payton .40 1.00
53 Robert Pack .25 .60
54 Adrian Griffin .25 .60
55 Jim Jackson .25 .60
56 Lamond Murray .25 .60
57 Larry Hughes .30 .75
58 Dirk Nowitzki .60 1.50
59 Vonteego Cummings .25 .60
60 Jalen Rose .30 .75
61 Arvydas Sabonis .30 .75
62 Kerry Kittles .25 .60
63 Kevin Garnett .75 2.00
64 Latrell Sprewell .30 .75
65 Shawn Marion .40 1.00
66 Darrell Armstrong .25 .60
67 Ron Mercer .25 .60
68 Damon Stoudamire .30 .75
69 Tracy McGrady .60 1.50
70 Theo Ratliff .25 .60
71 Lamar Odom .40 1.00
72 Charlie Ward .25 .60
73 John Amaechi .25 .60
74 Quincy Lewis .25 .60
75 Othella Harrington .25 .60
76 Doug Christie .25 .60
77 Richard Hamilton .30 .75
78 Donyell Marshall .25 .60
79 Vlade Divac .30 .75
80 Clifford Robinson .25 .60
81 Sean Elliott .30 .75
82 Rashard Lewis .40 1.00
83 Wally Szczerbiak .30 .75
84 Dale Davis .25 .60
85 Kelvin Cato .25 .60
86 Cuttino Mobley .30 .75
87 Travis Best .25 .60
88 Robert Horry .30 .75
89 Maurice Taylor .25 .60
90 Jamal Mashburn .30 .75
91 Tim Thomas .25 .60
92 Stephon Marbury .30 .75
93 Patrick Ewing .50 1.25
94 Eric Snow .25 .60
95 Anfernee Hardaway .60 1.50
96 Steve Smith .30 .75
97 Chris Webber .40 1.00
98 Rodney Rogers .25 .60
99 John Stockton .50 1.25
100 Tim Duncan .75 2.00
101 Ray Allen .40 1.00
102 Glen Rice .30 .75
103 Bryon Russell .25 .60
104 Tim Hardaway .40 1.00
105 Allan Houston .30 .75
106 Rasheed Wallace .40 1.00
107 Vin Baker .30 .75
108 Michael Dickerson .25 .60
109 Juwan Howard .30 .75
110 Hakeem Olajuwon .50 1.25
111 Shareef Abdur-Rahim .30 .75
112 Rod Strickland .30 .75
113 Hersey Hawkins .25 .60
114 Jason Terry .40 1.00
115 Anthony Mason .25 .60
116 Mike Bibby .40 1.00
117 Shawn Kemp .40 1.00
118 Derrick Coleman .30 .75
119 Antoine Walker .30 .75
120 Antawn Jamison .40 1.00
121 Michael Finley .40 1.00
122 Antonio McDyess .30 .75
123 Nick Van Exel .30 .75
124 Mitch Richmond .30 .75
125 Lindsey Hunter .25 .60
126 Kenyon Martin RC 5.00 12.00
127 Stromile Swift RC 2.00 5.00
128 Darius Miles RC 2.00 5.00
129 Marcus Fizer RC 2.00 5.00
130 Mike Miller RC 4.00 10.00
131 DerMarr Johnson RC 2.00 5.00
132 Chris Mihm RC 2.00 5.00
133 Jamal Crawford RC 3.00 8.00
134 Joel Przybilla RC 2.00 5.00
135 Keyon Dooling RC 2.00 5.00
136 Jerome Moiso RC 2.00 5.00
137 Etan Thomas RC 2.00 5.00
138 Courtney Alexander RC 2.00 5.00
139 Mateen Cleaves RC 2.00 5.00
140 Jason Collier RC 2.00 5.00
141 Desmond Mason RC 2.50 6.00
142 Quentin Richardson RC 3.00 8.00
143 Jamaal Magloire RC 2.00 5.00
144 Speedy Claxton RC 2.00 5.00
145 Morris Peterson RC 2.00 5.00
146 Donnell Harvey RC 2.00 5.00
147 DeShawn Stevenson RC 2.50 6.00
148 Mamadou N'Diaye RC 2.00 5.00
149 Erick Barkley RC 2.00 5.00
150 Mark Madsen RC 2.00 5.00
151 Allen Iverson 1.00 2.50
Stephon Marbury OTM
152 Vince Carter 2.50 6.00
Kobe Bryant OTM
153 Kevin Garnett 1.00 2.50
Shareef Abdur-Rahim OTM
154 Tracy McGrady .75 2.00
Scottie Pippen OTM
155 Tim Duncan 1.00 2.50
Elton Brand OTM
156 Steve Francis .50 1.25
Gary Payton OTM
157 Chris Webber .60 1.50
Karl Malone OTM
158 Alonzo Mourning .60 1.50
Patrick Ewing OTM
159 Latrell Sprewell .50 1.25
Eddie Jones OTM
160 Jason Kidd .75 2.00
John Stockton OTM
161 Reggie Miller .50 1.25
Allan Houston OTM
162 Rasheed Wallace .50 1.25
Antoine Walker OTM
163 Jerry Stackhouse .40 1.00
Jalen Rose OTM
164 Shaquille O'Neal GEM 2.50 6.00
165 Kobe Bryant GEM 5.00 12.00
166 Vince Carter GEM 2.00 5.00
167 Kevin Garnett GEM 2.00 5.00
168 Jason Williams GEM 1.00 2.50
169 Tracy McGrady GEM 1.50 4.00
170 Steve Francis GEM 1.00 2.50
171 Tim Duncan GEM 2.00 5.00
172 Elton Brand GEM 1.00 2.50
173 Grant Hill GEM 1.25 3.00

2000-01 Finest Gold Refractors

Randomly inserted in packs, this 173-card set parallels the base set. The cards feature gold refractive foil. The cards were serially numbered to 100. To ascertain values on individual cards, please refer to the multiplier in the header, coupled with the value of the base card.

*STARS: 10X TO 25X BASE CARD HI
*OTM: 8X TO 20X BASE HI
*GEMS: 4X TO 10X BASE HI
*RCs: 1X TO 2.5X BASE HI
RCs: STATED ODDS 1:336 H, 1:93 HTA
GEM: STATED ODDS 1:840 H, 1:233 HTA
OTM: STATED ODDS 1:323 H, 1:90 HTA
8 Kobe Bryant 100.00 225.00
43 Reggie Miller 12.00 30.00
64 Latrell Sprewell 10.00 25.00
152 Vince Carter 100.00 225.00
Kobe Bryant OTM
164 Shaquille O'Neal GEM 30.00 80.00
165 Kobe Bryant GEM 100.00 225.00

2000-01 Finest Man to Man

Randomly inserted in packs at one in 27 (one in 12 for HTA), this 10-card set focuses on comparisons between Tim Duncan and Elton Brand. They are each featured on five variations comparing five elements of the game (Dunking, Rebounding, Shooting, Blocking and Posting Up).

COMPLETE SET (10) 7.50 15.00
1A Tim Duncan DUNK 1.50 4.00
1B Elton Brand DUNK .75 2.00
2A Tim Duncan REB 1.50 4.00
2B Elton Brand REB .75 2.00
3A Tim Duncan SH 1.50 4.00
3B Elton Brand SH .75 2.00
4A Tim Duncan BLK 1.50 4.00
4B Elton Brand BLK .75 2.00
5A Tim Duncan PU 1.50 4.00
5B Elton Brand PU .75 2.00

2000-01 Finest Moments

Randomly inserted in packs at one in 14 (one in six HTA), this 21-card set features peak moments from NBA history, as well as from the 1999-2000 season. A special Vince Carter moments card was also produced that was serially numbered to 1000. That card is priced at the end of the set and is not included in the set price. Card backs carry a "FM" prefix.

COMPLETE SET (21) 12.50 25.00
*REF: .75X TO 2X HI COLUMN
REF: STATED ODDS 1:24 H, 1:11 HTA
FMAC Anthony Carter .50 1.25
FMAH Allan Houston .60 1.50
FMAI Allen Iverson 1.50 4.00
FMEB Elton Brand .75 2.00
FMGP Gary Payton .75 2.00
FMGR Glen Rice .60 1.50
FMJK Jason Kidd 1.25 3.00
FMJR Jalen Rose .60 1.50
FMJS John Starks .50 1.25
FMKM Karl Malone 1.00 2.50
FMLH Larry Hughes .60 1.50
FMLJ Larry Johnson .75 2.00
FMMC Mateen Cleaves .75 2.00
FMMJ Magic Johnson 2.00 5.00
FMSE Sean Elliott .60 1.50
FMSF Steve Francis .75 2.00
FMSO Shaquille O'Neal 2.00 5.00
FMTD Tim Duncan 1.50 4.00
FMTH Tim Hardaway .75 2.00
FMTK Toni Kukoc .60 1.50
FMTM Tracy McGrady 1.25 3.00
NNO Vince Carter/1000 8.00 20.00

2000-01 Finest Moments Refractors Autographs

Randomly inserted in packs at one in 112 (one in 51 HTA), this 18-card set is a parallel the the Moments insert. Each card features the player's autograph and the Topps "Certified Autograph" logo. Card backs carry a "FM" prefix.

GROUP A ODDS 1:258 H, 1:117 HTA
GROUP B ODDS 1:2026 H, 1:921 HTA
GROUP C ODDS 1:355 H, 1:161 HTA
GROUP D ODDS 1:253 H, 1:115 HTA
FMAH Allan Houston A 8.00 20.00
FMEB Elton Brand A 15.00 40.00
FMEJ Eddie Jones A 50.00 120.00
FMGP Gary Payton A 20.00 50.00
FMGR Glen Rice A 8.00 20.00
FMJR Jalen Rose A 15.00 30.00
FMJS John Starks D 40.00 100.00
FMLH Larry Hughes A 15.00 30.00
FMLJ Larry Johnson A 125.00 250.00
FMMC Mateen Cleaves D 10.00 25.00
FMMJ Magic Johnson C 50.00 120.00
FMMR Mitch Richmond C 15.00 40.00
FMSE Sean Elliott D 25.00 60.00
FMSF Steve Francis B 12.50 30.00
FMSO Shaquille O'Neal C 100.00 250.00
FMSO2 Shaquille O'Neal 100.00 250.00
FMTD Tim Duncan A 175.00 350.00
FMTM Tracy McGrady D 20.00 50.00

2000-01 Finest Moments Relics

Randomly inserted in packs at one in 59 (one in 27 for HTA), this 10-card set features swatches of game-worn jerseys from the 2000 USA Mens' Basketball Team. Each card features the Topps "Genuine Issue" sticker. Card backs carry a "FMR" prefix. Special Vince Carter and Kevin Garnett cards were produced also. These are sequentially numbered to 1000.

GROUP A 1:617 H, 1:280 HTA
GROUP B 1:127 H, 1:58 HTA
GROUP C 1:236 H, 1:107 HTA
GROUP D 1:430 H, 1:195 HTA
GROUP E 1:411 H, 1:187 HTA
GROUP F 1:394 H, 1:179 HTA
FMR1 Vin Baker D 5.00 12.00
FMR2 Antonio McDyess F 5.00 12.00
FMR3 Jason Kidd B 10.00 25.00
FMR4 Tim Hardaway B 5.00 12.00
FMR5 Allan Houston B 5.00 12.00
FMR6 Steve Smith C 5.00 12.00
FMR7 Alonzo Mourning E 5.00 12.00
FMR8 Gary Payton A 5.00 12.00
FMR9 Ray Allen B 5.00 12.00
FMR10 Shareef Abdur-Rahim C 5.00 12.00
FMR11 Vince Carter/1000 12.00 30.00
FMR12 Kevin Garnett/1000 8.00 20.00

2000-01 Finest Showmen

Randomly inserted in packs at one in 18 (one in eight HTA), this 10-card set features some of the flashiest players in the NBA. Card backs carry a "S" prefix.

COMPLETE SET (10) 4.00 10.00
S1 Chris Webber .60 1.50
S2 Elton Brand .60 1.50
S3 Tim Duncan 1.25 3.00
S4 Shareef Abdur-Rahim .50 1.25
S5 Jason Williams .60 1.50
S6 Grant Hill .75 2.00
S7 Lamar Odom .60 1.50
S8 Larry Hughes .50 1.25
S9 Michael Finley .60 1.50
S10 Latrell Sprewell .50 1.25

2000-01 Finest Title Quest

Randomly inserted in packs at one in 60 (one in 27 HTA), this 10-card set focuses on players who guided their teams into the playoffs last year. The cards feature Dufex technology. Card backs carry an "APT" prefix.

COMPLETE SET (10) 12.50 30.00
APT1 Reggie Miller 1.50 4.00
APT2 Alonzo Mourning 2.00 5.00
APT3 Allen Iverson 3.00 8.00
APT4 Latrell Sprewell 1.25 3.00
APT5 Jalen Rose 1.25 3.00
APT6 Scottie Pippen 2.50 6.00
APT7 Shaquille O'Neal 4.00 10.00
APT8 Kobe Bryant 10.00 25.00
APT9 Chris Webber 1.50 4.00
APT10 Rasheed Wallace 1.50 4.00

2000-01 Finest World's Finest

Randomly inserted in packs at one in 40 (one in 18 HTA), this 15-card set features players who have played for past USA teams. Card backs carry a "WF" prefix.

COMPLETE SET (15) 25.00 60.00
WF1 Tim Duncan 4.00 10.00
WF2 Vince Carter 4.00 10.00
WF3 Grant Hill 2.50 6.00
WF4 Kevin Garnett 4.00 10.00
WF5 Scottie Pippen 3.00 8.00
WF6 Karl Malone 2.50 6.00
WF7 Patrick Ewing 2.50 6.00
WF8 Tim Hardaway 2.00 5.00
WF9 Anfernee Hardaway 3.00 8.00
WF10 Reggie Miller 2.00 5.00
WF11 John Stockton 2.50 6.00
WF12 Ray Allen 2.00 5.00
WF13 Hakeem Olajuwon 2.50 6.00
WF14 David Robinson 3.00 8.00
WF15 Steve Smith 1.50 4.00

2002-03 Finest

Released in July 2003, Finest was issued as a 177-card set where base cards fall into several different formats where all cards were printed on foil-board. Card numbers 1-100 compose the base set, card numbers 101-120 feature rookie autographs and are serially numbered to 999, card numbers 121-156 showcase veteran players with a swatch of a jersey and are also sequentially numbered to 999, and card numbers 157-177 utilized the same format as the other rookies-autographed and numbered to 999. Please note that not all RC's had signed cards, and those / players are noted with an asterisk. Finest was packaged with three mini-boxes per box. Each mini-box contained six packs of five cards per pack and carried a suggested retail price of $40 per mini box. Ten un-numbered Draft Pick redemption cards were randomly inserted in packs for Draft Pick #1 through Draft Pick #10.

1 Dirk Nowitzki .60 1.50
2 Jason Terry .30 .75
3 Marcus Camby .30 .75
4 Joe Johnson .40 1.00
5 Shawn Marion .40 1.00
6 Andrei Kirilenko .40 1.00
7 Jamal Mashburn .30 .75
8 Andre Miller .30 .75
9 Jason Williams .30 .75
10 Tony Delk .25 .60
11 Tyson Chandler .30 .75
12 Jason Richardson .40 1.00
13 Derek Fisher .30 .75
14 Troy Hudson .25 .60
15 Kerry Kittles .25 .60
16 Peja Stojakovic .40 1.00
17 Kurt Thomas .25 .60
18 Jamaal Tinsley .25 .60
19 Matt Harpring .30 .75
20 Kenny Thomas .25 .60
21 Kwame Brown .25 .60
22 Antonio Davis .25 .60
23 David Robinson .60 1.50
24 Keith Van Horn .30 .75
25 Howard Eisley .25 .60
26 Jalen Rose .30 .75
27 Chauncey Billups .40 1.00
28 Corey Maggette .30 .75
29 Pau Gasol .50 1.25
30 Desmond Mason .30 .75
31 Brian Grant .25 .60
32 Eddie Griffin .25 .60
33 Voshon Lenard .25 .60
34 Al Harrington .30 .75
35 Calbert Cheaney .25 .60
36 Malik Rose .25 .60
37 Bonzi Wells .25 .60
38 Pat Garrity .25 .60
39 P.J. Brown .25 .60
40 Ray Allen .40 1.00
41 Karl Malone .50 1.25
42 Steve Nash .50 1.25
43 Antawn Jamison .40 1.00
44 Ron Artest .40 1.00
45 Shane Battier .40 1.00
46 Gary Payton .40 1.00
47 Kobe Bryant 2.00 5.00
48 Lucious Harris .25 .60
49 Richard Hamilton .30 .75
50 Darius Miles .25 .60
51 Marcus Fizer .25 .60
52 Antoine Walker .30 .75
53 Juwan Howard .30 .75
54 Eddie Jones .30 .75
55 Kenyon Martin .40 1.00
56 Derek Anderson .25 .60
57 Stephen Jackson .30 .75
58 Vince Carter .60 1.50
59 Larry Hughes .30 .75
60 Doug Christie .25 .60
61 Derrick Coleman .30 .75
62 Michael Finley .40 1.00
63 Wally Szczerbiak .30 .75
64 David Wesley .25 .60
65 Brad Miller .40 1.00
66 Clifford Robinson .25 .60
67 Shandon Anderson .25 .60
68 Stephon Marbury .30 .75
69 Bobby Jackson .25 .60
70 Brent Barry .25 .60
71 Ruben Patterson .25 .60
72 Rashard Lewis .40 1.00
73 Tony Battie .25 .60
74 Ben Wallace .40 1.00
75 Theo Ratliff .25 .60
76 Ricky Davis .30 .75
77 Nick Van Exel .30 .75
78 Mike Miller .40 1.00
79 Sam Cassell .30 .75
80 Malik Allen .25 .60
81 Mike Bibby .40 1.00
82 Scottie Pippen .60 1.50
83 Dikembe Mutombo .40 1.00
84 Latrell Sprewell .30 .75
85 Predrag Drobnjak .25 .60
86 Joe Smith .30 .75
87 Aaron Mckie .25 .60
88 Jamaal Magloire .25 .60
89 Keon Clark .25 .60
90 Eric Williams .25 .60
91 Raef Lafrentz .25 .60
92 Troy Murphy .40 1.00
93 Rick Fox .30 .75
94 Michael Redd .40 1.00
95 Radoslav Nesterovic .25 .60
96 Donyell Marshall .25 .60
97 Elton Brand .40 1.00
98 Robert Horry .30 .75
99 Zydrunas Ilgauskas .30 .75
100 Michael Jordan 3.00 8.00
101 Juaquin Hawkins AU RC 4.00 10.00
102 Dan Dickau AU RC 4.00 10.00
104 John Salmons AU RC 5.00 12.00
105 Tamar Slay AU RC 4.00 10.00
106 Melvin Ely AU RC 4.00 10.00
107 Jared Jeffries AU RC 4.00 10.00
108 Junior Harrington AU RC 4.00 10.00
110 Qyntel Woods AU RC 4.00 10.00
111 Ryan Humphrey AU RC 4.00 10.00
112 J.R. Bremer AU RC 4.00 10.00
113 Antoine Rigadeau AU RC 4.00 10.00
114 Jay Williams RC 2.50 6.00
115 Pat Burke AU RC 4.00 10.00
116 Smush Parker AU RC 4.00 10.00
117 Juan Dixon AU RC 5.00 12.00
118 Vincent Yarbrough AU RC 4.00 10.00
120 Rasual Butler AU RC 4.00 10.00
121 Baron Davis JSY 4.00 10.00
122 Shareef Abdur-Rahim JSY 3.00 8.00
123 Gilbert Arenas JSY 4.00 10.00
124 Travis Best JSY 2.50 6.00
125 Vlade Divac JSY 3.00 8.00
126 Tim Duncan JSY 8.00 20.00
127 Jason Kidd JSY 6.00 15.00
128 Kevin Garnett JSY 8.00 20.00
129 Anfernee Hardaway JSY 6.00 15.00
130 Allen Iverson JSY 6.00 15.00
131 Cuttino Mobley JSY 3.00 8.00
132 Steve Francis JSY 4.00 10.00
133 Jermaine O'Neal JSY 4.00 10.00
134 Lamar Odom JSY 4.00 10.00
135 Michael Olowokandi JSY 2.50 6.00
136 Paul Pierce JSY 5.00 12.00
137 Reggie Miller JSY 4.00 10.00
138 Chris Webber JSY 4.00 10.00
139 Richard Jefferson JSY 4.00 10.00
140 Allan Houston JSY 3.00 8.00
141 Glenn Robinson JSY 3.00 8.00
142 Jerome Williams JSY 2.50 6.00
143 John Stockton JSY 5.00 12.00
144 Rasheed Wallace JSY 4.00 10.00
145 Eric Snow JSY 2.50 6.00
146 Tracy McGrady JSY 6.00 15.00
147 Shaquille O'Neal JSY 10.00 25.00
148 Jerry Stackhouse JSY 3.00 8.00
149 Morris Peterson JSY 2.50 6.00
150 Darrell Armstrong JSY 2.50 6.00
151 Tony Parker JSY 5.00 12.00
152 Vladimir Radmanovic JSY 2.50 6.00
153 Anthony Mason JSY 2.50 6.00
154 Charles Oakley JSY 3.00 8.00
155 Grant Hill JSY 5.00 12.00
156 Vin Baker JSY 3.00 8.00
157 Chris Jefferies AU RC 4.00 10.00
158 Drew Gooden AU RC 6.00 15.00
159 Casey Jacobsen AU RC 4.00 10.00
160 Kareem Rush AU RC 4.00 10.00
161 Bostjan Nachbar AU RC 4.00 10.00
162 Tayshaun Prince AU RC 5.00 12.00
163 Manu Ginobili RC 10.00 25.00
164 Gordan Giricek AU RC 4.00 10.00
165 Raul Lopez AU RC 4.00 10.00
166 Dan Gadzuric AU RC 4.00 10.00
167 Marko Jaric AU 4.00 10.00
168 Lonny Baxter AU RC 4.00 10.00
169 Yao Ming AU RC 20.00 50.00
170 Mike Dunleavy AU RC 5.00 12.00
171 Caron Butler AU RC 6.00 15.00
172 Nene Hilario AU RC 5.00 12.00
173 Amare Stoudemire AU RC 15.00 40.00
174 Nikoloz Tskitishvili AU RC 4.00 10.00
175 Fred Jones AU RC 4.00 10.00
176 DaJuan Wagner AU RC 4.00 10.00
177 Carlos Boozer AU RC 8.00 20.00
178 LeBron James XRC 75.00 150.00
179 Darko Milicic XRC 5.00 12.00
180 Carmelo Anthony XRC 12.00 30.00
181 Chris Bosh XRC 10.00 25.00
182 Dwyane Wade XRC 20.00 50.00
183 Chris Kaman XRC 6.00 15.00
184 Kirk Hinrich XRC 6.00 15.00
185 T.J. Ford XRC 6.00 15.00
186 Mike Sweetney XRC 5.00 12.00
187 Jarvis Hayes XRC 5.00 12.00

2002-03 Finest Refractors

Randomly seeded in packs, this 177-card set parallels the base set enhanced with the rainbow holofoil refractor effect. Each card is sequentially numbered to 250.

*1-100 STARS: 2.5X TO 6X BASE CARD HI
*101-120 AU RCs: .6X TO 1.5X BASE CARD HI
*121-156 JSY: .6X TO 1.5X BASE CARD HI
*157-177 AU RCs: .6X TO 1.5X BASE CARD HI
*XRC: 1X TO 2.5X BASE CARD HI
100 Michael Jordan 40.00 100.00
163 Manu Ginobili AU 30.00 80.00
169 Yao Ming AU 40.00 100.00
173 Amare Stoudemire AU 30.00 80.00
178 LeBron James 300.00 500.00

2002-03 Finest Refractors G

Randomly seeded in packs, this 177-card set pa the base set enhanced with the rainbow holofoil refractor effect and gold backgrounds. Each card sequentially numbered to 25.

*GOLD 1-100: 20X TO 50X BASE HI
*GOLD AU RC 101-120: 2X TO 5X HI
*GOLD JSY 121-156: 2X TO 5X HI
*GOLD AU RC 157-177: 2X TO 5X HI
*GOLD XRC 178-187: 2.5X TO 6X HI
100 Michael Jordan 200.00 5
162 Tayshaun Prince AU 30.00
163 Manu Ginobili AU 75.00 2
173 Amare Stoudemire AU 125.00 2

2003-04 Finest

Released in late June 2004, Finest features a 185 base set divided up into 100 veteran base cards, veteran jersey cards numbered to 999, 42 rookie numbered to 999 and 13 draft pick redemption ca All of the cards are printed on holographic foil bo and several of the rookie cards implement jerseys autographs, both or none. The packaging include large boxes that contained three mini-boxes of si packs each. Packs contained five cards and each box carried a suggested retail price of $40.

COMP.SET w/o SP's (100) 15.00
UNPRICED X-FRACTOR PRINT RUN ONE SET
1 Zach Randolph .40
2 Keith Van Horn .30
3 Steve Francis .40
4 Al Harrington .30
5 Jason Kidd .60
6 Jamaal Tinsley .25
7 Lamar Odom .40
8 Antoine Walker .40
9 Tony Parker .40
10 Jamal Mashburn .30
11 Desmond Mason .30
12 Carlos Arroyo .30
13 Chris Andersen .60
14 Chris Wilcox .25
15 Vince Carter .60
16 Peja Stojakovic .40
17 Qyntel Woods .25
18 Mike Dunleavy .30
19 Sam Cassell .30
20 Allan Houston .30
21 Speedy Claxton .25
22 Rafer Alston .25
23 Michael Finley .40
24 Richard Jefferson .40
25 Larry Hughes .30
26 Pau Gasol .40
27 Maurice Taylor .25
28 Donyell Marshall .25
29 Darrell Armstrong .25
30 Latrell Sprewell .30
31 Reggie Miller .40
32 Stephon Marbury .30
33 Antawn Jamison .40
34 DerMarr Johnson .25
35 Shareef Abdur-Rahim .30
36 Tony Battie .25
37 Kwame Brown .25
38 Fred Jones .30
39 Jamal Crawford .30
40 Kurt Thomas .25
41 Eric Snow .25
42 Andre Miller .30
43 Ray Allen .40
44 Caron Butler .40
45 Corliss Williamson .25
46 Kenny Thomas .25
47 Jason Terry .30
48 Ronald Murray .25
49 Richard Hamilton .30
50 Elton Brand .40
51 Ron Artest .40
52 Jerome Williams .25
53 Ricky Davis .30
54 Brent Barry .25
55 Dikembe Mutombo .40
56 Earl Boykins .25
57 Brad Miller .40
58 Shane Battier .30
59 Tyson Chandler .30
60 Kelvin Cato .25
61 Shawn Marion .40
62 Bobby Jackson .25
63 Corey Maggette .30
64 Antonio McDyess .30
65 Drew Gooden .30
66 Mike Miller .40
67 Darius Miles .25
68 Stephen Jackson .30
69 Cuttino Mobley .30
70 Gary Payton .40
71 Toni Kukoc .40
72 Eddie Jones .30
73 Gilbert Arenas .40
74 Matt Harpring .30
75 Marko Jaric .25
76 Bonzi Wells .25
77 Nick Van Exel .30
78 Quentin Richardson .30
79 Rasho Nesterovic .25
80 Steve Nash .50
81 Morris Peterson .25
82 Nikoloz Tskitishvili .25
83 Damon Stoudamire .30
84 Bruce Bowen .25
85 Brian Grant .25
86 Jalen Rose .30
87 Jerry Stackhouse .30
88 Kobe Bryant 2.00
89 Eddy Curry .30
90 Tim Thomas .25
91 Erick Dampier .25
92 Jason Williams .30
93 Troy Murphy .40
94 Kerry Kittles .25
95 Zydrunas Ilgauskas .30
96 Theo Ratliff .25

iel Dalembert .25 .60
AcInnis .25 .60
n Howard .30 .75
Johnson .40 1.00
Pierce JSY 3.00 8.00
Wallace JSY 2.50 6.00
Ming JSY 5.00 12.00
naine O'Neal JSY 2.50 6.00
hard Lewis JSY 2.50 6.00
Malone JSY 3.00 8.00
n Iverson JSY 4.00 10.00
e Bibby JSY 2.50 6.00
heed Wallace JSY 2.50 6.00
e JSY 2.00 5.00
cy McGrady JSY 3.00 8.00
rei Kirilenko JSY 2.50 6.00
nu Ginobili JSY 3.00 8.00
yon Martin JSY 2.50 6.00
are Stoudemire JSY 4.00 10.00
on Davis JSY 2.50 6.00
hael Olowokandi JSY 2.00 5.00
los Boozer JSY 2.50 6.00
on Richardson JSY 2.50 6.00
k Nowitzki JSY 4.00 10.00
auncey Billups JSY 2.50 6.00
ris Webber JSY 2.50 6.00
nn Robinson JSY/807 2.00 5.00
in Garnett JSY 5.00 12.00
chael Redd JSY 2.50 6.00
vid Wesley JSY 2.00 5.00
shaun Prince JSY 2.50 6.00
naal Magloire JSY 2.00 5.00
n Duncan JSY 4.00 10.00
aquille O'Neal JSY 6.00 15.00
ko Milicic RC 2.50 6.00
ris Kaman RC 3.00 8.00
Bron James RC 100.00 200.00
hie Frahm RC 2.50 6.00
ve Blake RC 3.00 8.00
za Pachulia RC 2.50 6.00
th Bogans RC 2.50 6.00
k Hinrich AU RC 5.00 12.00
vis Hayes RC 2.50 6.00
ko Cabarkapa AU RC 4.00 10.00
ran Planinic AU RC 4.00 10.00
onis Haslem RC 3.00 8.00
vid West RC 3.00 8.00
ris Diaw AU RC 5.00 12.00
an Cook AU RC 4.00 10.00
udi Ebi AU RC 4.00 10.00
sh Howard AU RC 4.00 10.00
son Kapono AU RC 4.00 10.00
ke Walton AU RC 4.00 10.00
vis Hansen AU RC 4.00 10.00
llie Green AU RC 4.00 10.00
aurice Williams AU RC 6.00 15.00
ancisco Elson AU RC 4.00 10.00
e Korver AU RC 5.00 12.00
arquis Daniels AU RC 4.00 10.00
ris Bosh AU RC 15.00 40.00
wyane Wade AU RC 60.00 120.00
eksandar Pavlovic AU RC 4.00 10.00
ke Sweetney AU RC 4.00 10.00
arcus Banks AU RC 4.00 10.00
ke Ridnour AU RC 5.00 12.00
rmelo Anthony AU RC 40.00 80.00
ckael Pietrus AU RC 4.00 10.00
ece Gaines AU RC 4.00 10.00
ndrick Perkins AU RC 6.00 15.00
oy Bell AU RC 4.00 10.00
andro Barbosa AU RC 5.00 12.00
hntay Jones AU RC 4.00 10.00
. Ford AU RC 5.00 12.00
ck Collison AU RC 4.00 10.00
eron Smith AU RC 4.00 10.00
wight Howard XRC 15.00 40.00
neka Okafor XRC 8.00 20.00
n Gordon XRC 6.00 15.00
aun Livingston XRC 5.00 12.00
evin Harris XRC 8.00 20.00
sh Childress XRC 5.00 12.00
ol Deng XRC 8.00 20.00
afael Araujo XRC 5.00 12.00
dre Iguodala XRC 8.00 20.00
ke Jackson XRC 5.00 12.00
ndris Biedrins XRC 6.00 15.00
bert Swift XRC 5.00 12.00
bastian Telfair XRC 5.00 12.00

2003-04 Finest Refractors

d in packs, this 185-card set parallels the base nanced with Topps' rainbow holofoil refractor Cards are easily distinguishable on the back the card number by the word "Refractor." Several base cards are enhanced with jersey swatches ch card is sequentially numbered to 250. Gold tors numbered to 25 and X-Fractors serially ered one of one were also issued.
) REF.SINGLES: 2.5X TO 6X BASE HI
43 REF.SINGLES: .75X TO 2X BASE HI
.75X TO 2X BASE HI
n Kidd JSY 5.00 12.00
aul Pierce JSY 4.00 10.00
ao Ming JSY 6.00 15.00
arl Malone JSY 4.00 10.00
len Iverson JSY 5.00 12.00
acy McGrady JSY 4.00 10.00
nare Stoudemire JSY 5.00 12.00
irk Nowitzki JSY 5.00 12.00
evin Garnett JSY 6.00 15.00
m Duncan JSY 5.00 12.00
haquille O'Neal JSY 8.00 20.00
hris Kaman JSY 4.00 10.00
aza Pachulia JSY 3.00 8.00
irk Hinrich JSY AU 8.00 20.00
oris Diaw JSY AU 8.00 20.00
uke Walton AU 5.00 12.00
yle Korver AU 6.00 15.00
hris Bosh JSY AU 25.00 60.00
wyane Wade JSY AU 175.00 350.00
uke Ridnour JSY AU 8.00 20.00
armelo Anthony JSY AU 60.00 150.00
lickael Pietrus JSY AU 6.00 15.00
endrick Perkins JSY AU 10.00 25.00
eandro Barbosa JSY AU 8.00 20.00
.J. Ford JSY AU 8.00 20.00

03-04 Finest Refractors Gold

omly seeded in packs, this set parallels the base nhanced with a gold refractor effect and sequential ering to 25.
D 1-100: 12X TO 30X BASE HI
D JSY 101-130: 2X TO 5X BASE HI
D RC 131-143: 2.5X TO 6X BASE HI
D AU RC 144-172: 1.5X TO 4X BASE HI
D XRC 173-185: 1.25X TO 3X BASE HI
T RUN 25 SER.#'d SETS
hris Bosh AU 175.00 350.00
158 Dwyane Wade AU 300.00 600.00
163 Carmelo Anthony AU 250.00 450.00

2004-05 Finest

Released at the end of June, Finest boasts a 220-card set divided up as follows: cards 1-100 feature veteran players, cards 101-130 feature jersey cards sequentially numbered to 299, cards 131-150 features retired players sequentially numbered to 400, cards 151-160 feature rookie player cards sequentially numbered to 400, cards 161-190 feature autographed RC cards sequentially numbered to 299, and cards 191-220 were originally issued as draft pick redemption cards sequentially numbered to 599. The cards are redeemable for the coinciding draft pick where card 191 is the first and picks go on from there. All cards are printed on foil board with a white background, a black strip along the bottom and silver highlights around the player's picture. Finest was released in boxes that contained three mini-boxes and an incased uncirculated refractor blue card. Mini-boxes contained six packs each (18 total per box) and the SRP was $40 per mini-box.

COMP.SET w/o SP's (100) 15.00 40.00
UNPRICED WHITE PRINT RUN ONE SET
1 Richard Hamilton .30 .75
2 Mike Dunleavy .30 .75
3 Jamaal Tinsley .25 .60
4 Corey Maggette .30 .75
5 Zach Randolph .30 .75
6 Desmond Mason .30 .75
7 Marc Jackson .25 .60
8 Kobe Bryant 2.00 5.00
9 Mike Bibby .40 1.00
10 Vince Carter .60 1.50
11 Bonzi Wells .25 .60
12 Ricky Davis .30 .75
13 Steve Nash .50 1.25
14 Rashard Lewis .40 1.00
15 Eddy Curry .30 .75
16 Carlos Boozer .40 1.00
17 Brad Miller .40 1.00
18 Kurt Thomas .25 .60
19 Shareef Abdur-Rahim .30 .75
20 Grant Hill .50 1.25
21 Jason Hart .25 .60
22 Larry Hughes .30 .75
23 Lebron James 2.50 6.00
24 Udonis Haslem .30 .75
25 David Wesley .25 .60
26 Kenny Thomas .25 .60
27 Marcus Camby .30 .75
28 Michael Redd .40 1.00
29 Rasho Nesterovic .25 .60
30 Keith Van Horn .30 .75
31 Reggie Miller .40 1.00
32 Stephon Marbury .30 .75
33 Donyell Marshall .25 .60
34 Jermaine O'Neal .40 1.00
35 Antoine Walker .40 1.00
36 Rasheed Wallace .40 1.00
37 Antonio Daniels .25 .60
38 Damon Jones .25 .60
39 Caron Butler .40 1.00
40 Shawn Marion .40 1.00
41 Lee Nailon .25 .60
42 Damon Stoudamire .30 .75
43 Bob Sura .25 .60
44 Mehmet Okur .30 .75
45 Shane Battier .30 .75
46 Michael Finley .40 1.00
47 Doug Christie .25 .60
48 Eddie Jones .30 .75
49 Speedy Claxton .25 .60
50 Wally Szczerbiak .30 .75
51 Primoz Brezec .25 .60
52 Marko Jaric .25 .60
53 Antonio McDyess .30 .75
54 Jeff Mcinnis .25 .60
55 Tony Parker .40 1.00
56 Rafer Alston .25 .60
57 Troy Murphy .30 .75
58 Chris Mihm .25 .60
59 Jarvis Hayes .25 .60
60 Marquis Daniels .25 .60
61 Jamal Crawford .30 .75
62 Morris Peterson .25 .60
63 Luke Ridnour .30 .75
64 Mike Miller .40 1.00
65 Carlos Arroyo .30 .75
66 Gary Payton .40 1.00
67 Joe Johnson .40 1.00
68 Latrell Sprewell .30 .75
69 Allan Houston .30 .75
70 Earl Boykins .25 .60
71 Brendan Haywood .25 .60
72 Baron Davis .40 1.00
73 Fred Jones .25 .60
74 Joe Smith .30 .75
75 Jalen Rose .30 .75
76 Eddie Griffin .25 .60
77 Lamar Odom .40 1.00
78 Theo Ratliff .25 .60
79 Gordan Giricek .25 .60
80 Maurice Williams .30 .75
81 Tayshaun Prince .40 1.00
82 Kyle Korver .30 .75
83 Andre Miller .30 .75
84 Chris Wilcox .25 .60
85 Alonzo Mourning .50 1.25
86 Gilbert Arenas .40 1.00
87 Zydrunas Ilgauskas .30 .75
88 Jamaal Magloire .25 .60
89 Jason Williams .30 .75
90 Chucky Atkins .25 .60
91 Jeff Foster .25 .60
92 Kareem Rush .25 .60
93 Sam Cassell .30 .75
94 Josh Howard .40 1.00
95 Tyronn Lue .25 .60
96 Vladimir Radmanovic .25 .60
97 Chauncey Billups .40 1.00
98 Brent Barry .25 .60
99 Paul Pierce .50 1.25
100 Dwyane Wade 1.25 3.00
101 Al Harrington JSY 2.00 5.00
102 Antawn Jamison JSY 2.50 6.00
103 Kirk Hinrich JSY 2.50 6.00
104 Tim Duncan JSY 4.00 10.00
105 Gerald Wallace JSY 2.50 6.00
106 Dirk Nowitzki JSY 4.00 10.00
107 Chris Webber JSY 2.50 6.00
108 Jason Kidd JSY 4.00 10.00
109 Carmelo Anthony JSY 5.00 12.00
110 Tracy McGrady JSY 3.00 8.00
111 Elton Brand JSY 2.50 6.00
112 Pau Gasol JSY 2.50 6.00
113 Jason Richardson JSY 2.50 6.00
114 Chris Bosh JSY 2.50 6.00
115 Kevin Garnett JSY 5.00 12.00
116 Steve Francis JSY 2.50 6.00
117 Richard Jefferson JSY 2.50 6.00
118 Baron Davis JSY 2.50 6.00
119 Manu Ginobili JSY 3.00 8.00
120 Shaquille O'Neal JSY 6.00 15.00
121 Amare Stoudemire JSY 3.00 8.00
122 Yao Ming JSY 5.00 12.00
123 Kenyon Martin JSY 2.50 6.00
124 Allen Iverson JSY 4.00 10.00
125 Peja Stojakovic JSY 2.50 6.00
126 Drew Gooden JSY 2.00 5.00
127 Ray Allen JSY 2.50 6.00
128 Ben Wallace JSY 2.50 6.00
129 Andrei Kirilenko JSY 2.00 5.00
130 Quentin Richardson JSY 2.00 5.00
131 Larry Bird 6.00 15.00
132 George Gervin 2.00 5.00
133 Walt Frazier 2.00 5.00
134 Oscar Robertson 2.00 5.00
135 Elgin Baylor 2.00 5.00
136 Moses Malone 2.00 5.00
137 Pete Maravich 12.00 30.00
138 Bob Cousy 3.00 8.00
139 Earl Monroe 2.00 5.00
140 Kareem Abdul-Jabbar 3.00 8.00
141 Isiah Thomas 2.00 5.00
142 Kevin McHale 2.50 6.00
143 Bill Walton 2.00 5.00
144 John Havlicek 2.00 5.00
145 Rick Barry 2.00 5.00
146 Wilt Chamberlain 4.00 10.00
147 Bill Russell 3.00 8.00
148 Willis Reed 2.00 5.00
149 Julius Erving 4.00 10.00
150 Drazen Petrovic 3.00 8.00
151 Andre Iguodala RC 3.00 8.00
152 Luke Jackson RC 2.00 5.00
153 Kirk Snyder RC 2.00 5.00
154 Kevin Martin RC 2.50 6.00
155 Antonio Burks RC 2.00 5.00
156 Robert Swift RC 2.00 5.00
157 Dorell Wright RC 3.00 8.00
158 David Harrison RC 2.00 5.00
159 Dwight Howard RC 6.00 15.00
160 Al Jefferson RC 3.00 8.00
161 Justin Reed AU RC 5.00 12.00
162 Shaun Livingston AU RC 5.00 12.00
163 Luol Deng AU RC 8.00 20.00
164 Josh Smith AU RC 8.00 20.00
165 Jameer Nelson AU RC 6.00 15.00
166 Pavel Podkolzin AU RC 5.00 12.00
167 Emeka Okafor AU RC 8.00 20.00
168 Kris Humphries AU RC 5.00 12.00
169 J.R. Smith AU RC 6.00 15.00
170 Sebastian Telfair AU RC 5.00 12.00
171 Sasha Vujacic AU RC 5.00 12.00
172 Tony Allen AU RC 6.00 15.00
173 Romain Sato AU RC 5.00 12.00
174 Ben Gordon AU RC 6.00 15.00
175 Devin Harris AU RC 8.00 20.00
176 Josh Childress AU RC 5.00 12.00
177 Andre Barrett AU RC 5.00 12.00
178 Jackson Vroman AU RC 5.00 12.00
179 Lionel Chalmers AU RC 5.00 12.00
180 Delonte West AU RC 6.00 15.00
181 Nenad Krstic AU RC 5.00 12.00
182 Donta Smith AU RC 5.00 12.00
183 Chris Duhon AU RC 5.00 12.00
184 Peter John Ramos AU RC 5.00 12.00
185 Bernard Robinson AU RC 5.00 12.00
186 Beno Udrih AU RC 5.00 12.00
187 Andris Biedrins AU RC 6.00 15.00
188 Trevor Ariza AU RC 5.00 12.00
189 Rafael Araujo AU RC 5.00 12.00
190 Andres Nocioni AU RC 5.00 12.00
191 Andrew Bogut XRC 5.00 12.00
192 Marvin Williams XRC 4.00 10.00
193 Deron Williams XRC 8.00 20.00
194 Chris Paul XRC 12.00 30.00
195 Raymond Felton XRC 5.00 12.00
196 Martell Webster XRC 3.00 8.00
197 Charlie Villanueva XRC 4.00 10.00
198 Channing Frye XRC 4.00 10.00
199 Ike Diogu XRC 3.00 8.00
200 Andrew Bynum XRC 10.00 25.00
201 Salim Stoudamire XRC 3.00 8.00
202 Yaroslav Korolev XRC 3.00 8.00
203 Sean May XRC 3.00 8.00
204 Rashad McCants XRC 3.00 8.00
205 Antoine Wright XRC 3.00 8.00
206 Joey Graham XRC 3.00 8.00
207 Danny Granger XRC 6.00 15.00
208 Gerald Green XRC 4.00 10.00
209 Hakim Warrick XRC 4.00 10.00
210 Julius Hodge XRC 3.00 8.00
211 Nate Robinson XRC 4.00 10.00
212 Jarrett Jack XRC 3.00 8.00
213 Francisco Garcia XRC 4.00 10.00
214 Luther Head XRC 3.00 8.00
215 Daniel Ewing XRC 3.00 8.00
216 Jason Maxiell XRC 3.00 8.00
217 Linas Kleiza XRC 3.00 8.00
218 Brandon Bass XRC 4.00 10.00
219 Wayne Simien XRC 3.00 8.00
220 David Lee XRC 5.00 12.00

2004-05 Finest Refractors

Randomly inserted in packs, this 220-card set parallels the base set enhanced with Topps' rainbow holofoil refractor effect. Cards are numbered as follows: 1-100 serially numbered to 249, 101-130 are serially numbered to 179, 131-160 are serially numbered to 249, 161-190 are serially numbered to 179, and 191-220 are serially numbered to 359.
*1-100 REFRACTORS: 1.25X TO 3X BASE HI
*101-220 REFRACTORS: .5X TO 1.25X BASE HI
8 Kobe Bryant 12.00 30.00
23 LeBron James 12.00 30.00

2004-05 Finest Refractors Black

Randomly seeded in packs, this 220-card set parallels the base set enhanced with Topps' rainbow holofoil refractor effect, black background and print runs break down as follows: 1-100 serially numbered to 29, 101-130 are serially numbered to 19, 131-160 are serially numbered to 29, 161-190 are serially numbered to 19, and 191-220 are serially numbered to 39.
*1-100 REF.BLACK: 8X TO 20X BASE HI
*101-220 REF.BLACK: 1.5X TO 4X BASE HI
8 Kobe Bryant 50.00 125.00
23 LeBron James 60.00 150.00

2004-05 Finest Refractors Blue

Randomly inserted as uncirculated box toppers, this 220-card set parallels the base set enhanced with Topps' rainbow holofoil refractor effect, blue background and sequential numbering to 50.
*1-100 REF.BLUE: 4X TO 10X BASE HI
*101-220 REF.BLUE: .75X TO 2X BASE HI
8 Kobe Bryant 30.00 80.00
23 LeBron James 40.00 100.00
100 Dwyane Wade 15.00 40.00
159 Dwight Howard 15.00 40.00

2004-05 Finest Refractors Gold

Randomly seeded in packs, this 220-card set parallels the base set enhanced with Topps' rainbow holofoil refractor effect, gold background and print runs break down as follows: 1-100 serially numbered to 15, 101-130 are serially numbered to 12, 131-160 are serially numbered to 15, 161-190 are serially numbered to 12, and 191-220 are serially numbered to 25.
*1-100 REF.GOLD: 10X TO 25X BASE HI
*101-190 REF.GOLD: 2X TO 5X BASE HI
*191-220 REF.GOLD: 2.5X TO 6X BASE HI
8 Kobe Bryant 60.00 150.00
23 LeBron James 75.00 200.00

2004-05 Finest Refractors Green

Randomly seeded in packs, this 220-card set parallels the base set enhanced with Topps' rainbow holofoil refractor effect, green background and print runs break down as follows: 1-100 serially numbered to 49, 101-130 are serially numbered to 29, 131-160 are serially numbered to 49, 161-190 are serially numbered to 29, and 191-220 are serially numbered to 59.
*1-100 REF.GREEN: 4X TO 10X BASE HI
*101-220 REF.GREEN: .75X TO 2X BASE HI
8 Kobe Bryant 30.00 80.00
23 LeBron James 40.00 100.00
159 Dwight Howard 15.00 40.00

2004-05 Finest Refractors Red

Randomly seeded in packs, this 220-card set parallels the base set enhanced with Topps' rainbow holofoil refractor effect, red background and print runs break down as follows: 1-100 serially numbered to 149, 101-130 are serially numbered to 79, 131-160 are serially numbered to 149, 161-190 are serially numbered to 79, and 191-220 are serially numbered to 159.
*1-100 REF.RED: 1.5X TO 4X BASE HI
*101-220 REF.RED: .6X TO 1.5X BASE HI
8 Kobe Bryant 12.00 30.00
23 LeBron James 12.00 30.00
159 Dwight Howard 12.00 30.00

2004-05 Finest X-Fractors

Randomly inserted in packs, this 220-card set parallels the base set enhanced with Topps' rainbow holofoil refractor effect and a cross-hatched pattern. Cards are numbered as follows: 1-100 serially numbered to 199, 101-130 are serially numbered to 129, 131-160 are serially numbered to 199, 161-190 are serially numbered to 129, and 191-220 are serially numbered to 259.
*1-100 X-FRAC: 1.5X TO 4X BASE HI
*101-220 X-FRAC: .5X TO 1.25X BASE HI
8 Kobe Bryant 10.00 25.00
23 LeBron James 12.00 30.00

2004-05 Finest X-Fractors Black

Randomly seeded in packs, this 220-card set parallels the base set enhanced with Topps' rainbow holofoil refractor effect, black background where cards 1-190 are serially numbered to nine and cards 191-220 are serially numbered to 19.
1-190 NOT PRICED DUE TO SCARCITY
*191-220 X-FRAC.BLACK: 2.5X TO 6X BASE HI

2004-05 Finest X-Fractors Blue

Randomly inserted as uncirculated box toppers, this 220-card set parallels the base set enhanced with Topps' rainbow holofoil refractor effect, blue background and sequential numbering to 25.
*1-100 X-FRAC BLUE: 10X TO 25X BASE HI
*101-160 X-FRAC.BLUE: 1.5X TO 4X BASE HI
*161-190 X-FRAC BLUE: 1.25X TO 3X BASE HI
*191-220 X-FRAC BLUE: 2.5X TO 6X BASE HI

2004-05 Finest X-Fractors Green

Randomly seeded in packs, this 220-card set parallels the base set enhanced with Topps' rainbow holofoil refractor effect, black background and print runs break down as follows: 1-100 serially numbered to 19, 101-130 are serially numbered to 15, 131-160 are serially numbered to 19, 161-190 are serially numbered to 15, and 191-220 are serially numbered to 30.
*1-100 X-FRAC GREEN: 8X TO 20X BASE HI
*101-190 X-FRAC.GREEN: 1.5X TO 4X BASE HI
*191-220 X-FRAC.GREEN: 2X TO 5X BASE HI
8 Kobe Bryant 75.00 200.00
23 LeBron James 75.00 200.00

2004-05 Finest X-Fractors Red

Randomly seeded in packs, this 220-card set parallels the base set enhanced with Topps' rainbow holofoil refractor effect, black background and print runs break down as follows: 1-100 serially numbered to 99, 101-130 are serially numbered to 59, 131-160 are serially numbered to 99, 161-190 are serially numbered to 59, and 191-220 are serially numbered to 119.
*1-100 X-FRAC RED: 2.5X TO 6X BASE HI
*101-220 X-FRAC.RED: .6X TO 1.5X BASE HI
8 Kobe Bryant 15.00 40.00
23 LeBron James 20.00 50.00
100 Dwyane Wade 10.00 25.00

2004-05 Finest Far East Fabrics

Randomly seeded in packs, this 24-card set is horizontally designed and features a red background along the top and bottom, player photos on the left and a square jersey swatch on the right surrounded by Chinese words. Refractor parallels were issued for this set where base refractors are serially numbered to 50, X-Fractors are serially numbered to 10, and Super Fractors are one of ones.
*REFRACTORS: .6X TO 1.5X BASE HI
BJ Bobby Jackson 2.50 6.00
BM Brad Miller 4.00 10.00
BN Bostjan Nachbar 2.50 6.00
CW Chris Webber 4.00 10.00
DC Doug Christie 2.50 6.00
DM Dikembe Mutombo 5.00 12.00
DS Darius Songaila 2.50 6.00
ED Erik Daniels 4.00 10.00
GO Greg Ostertag 2.50 6.00
JH Juwan Howard 3.00 8.00
JJ Jim Jackson 2.50 6.00
KM Kevin Martin 5.00 12.00
MB Matt Barnes 2.50 6.00
ME Maurice Evans 4.00 10.00
MT Maurice Taylor 2.50 6.00
PS Peja Stojakovic 4.00 10.00
RB Ryan Bowen 2.50 6.00
RG Reece Gaines 2.50 6.00
SP Scott Padgett 2.50 6.00
TL Tyronn Lue 2.50 6.00
TM Tracy McGrady 5.00 12.00
YM Yao Ming 8.00 20.00
CWA Charlie Ward 2.50 6.00
MBI Mike Bibby 4.00 10.00

2004-05 Finest Moments Autographs

Randomly seeded, this 13-card set is borderless and showcases NBA legends on the top half of the card and a sticker autograph on the bottom half. Each card is sequentially numbered to 50. Several refractor parallels were produced with Topps' rainbow holofoil refractor effect. Refractors are sequentially numbered to 20, X-Fractors are sequentially numbered to seven and Super Fractors are one of ones.
*REFRACTORS: .6X TO 1.5X BASE HI
BW Bill Walton 15.00 40.00
CD Clyde Drexler 25.00 60.00
DB Dave Bing 30.00 80.00
DC Dave Cowens 12.50 30.00
DS Detlef Schrempf 15.00 40.00
EB Elgin Baylor 15.00 40.00
EM Earl Monroe 15.00 40.00
GG George Gervin 12.50 30.00
ME Mark Eaton 12.50 30.00
MM Moses Malone 12.50 30.00
RB Rick Barry 12.50 30.00
RP Robert Parish 15.00 40.00

2004-05 Finest Perfect Pairs Autographs

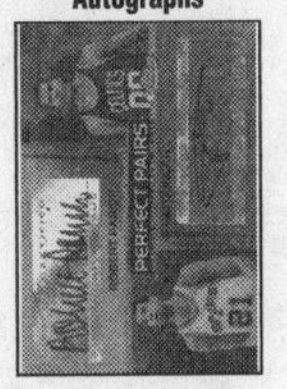

Randomly inserted in packs, this 15-card set pairs a two players on each card with their autographed stickers. Some pair a legend and a current player, and others players of the same position. Each card is limited to 50 copies. Refractor parallel versions of this set were issued too: Refractors are serially numbered to 20, X-Fractors are serially numbered to seven and Super Fractors are numbered one of one.
*REFRACTORS: .5X TO 1.25X BASE HI
AG Carmelo Anthony / George Gervin 30.00 60.00
DB Luol Deng / Elgin Baylor 15.00 40.00
DP Tim Duncan / Robert Parish 60.00 150.00
GB Ben Gordon / Dave Bing 25.00 60.00
HB Richard Hamilton / Rick Barry 15.00 40.00
MD Tracy McGrady / Clyde Drexler 30.00 60.00
MM Stephon Marbury / Earl Monroe 15.00 40.00
OD Shaquille O'Neal / Tim Duncan 150.00 300.00
OH Emeka Okafor / Spencer Haywood 15.00 40.00
OL Jermaine O'Neal / Bob Lanier 15.00 40.00
SC Amare Stoudemire / Dave Cowens 40.00 80.00
SS Peja Stojakovic / Detlef Schrempf 20.00 50.00
WE Ben Wallace / Mark Eaton 15.00 40.00
OHA Lamar Odom / Connie Hawkins 15.00 40.00

2005-06 Finest

Released in June 2005, this 169-card set features veteran players on cards 1-100, celebrities serially numbered to 599 on cards 101-105, rookies serially numbered to 599 on cards 106-125, rookie autographs serially numbered to 349 on cards 126-139 and Draft Pick redemptions for cards 140-169. Finest contains the first live redemption cards for the new 2006-07 rookie class. Base cards are printed on all foil with a basketball-looking background on the top and full color player photos on the bottom. Finest was packaged in a box that contains two six-pack mini boxes. Upon release, mini boxes carried a $40 SRP.
COMP.SET w/o SP's (100) 15.00 40.00
UNPRICED SUPERFR.PRINT RUN ONE SET
UNPRICED WHITE PRINT RUN ONE SET
UNPRICED WHITE X-FR PRINT RUN ONE SET
1 Shaquille O'Neal .75 2.00
2 Eddy Curry .30 .75
3 Ben Wallace .40 1.00
4 Wally Szczerbiak .30 .75
5 Richard Jefferson .40 1.00
6 Josh Howard .40 1.00
7 Grant Hill .50 1.25
8 Desmond Mason .25 .60
9 Corey Maggette .30 .75
10 Caron Butler .40 1.00
11 Andrei Kirilenko .30 .75
12 Al Harrington .30 .75
13 Tony Parker .40 1.00
14 Stephon Marbury .30 .75
15 Rafer Alston .25 .60
16 Marquis Daniels .25 .60
17 Luke Ridnour .30 .75
18 Kirk Hinrich .40 1.00
19 Jason Kidd .60 1.50
20 Morris Peterson .25 .60
21 Yao Ming .50 1.25
22 Nenad Krstic .25 .60
23 Mehmet Okur .25 .60
24 Shareef Abdur-Rahim .30 .75
25 Rashard Lewis .40 1.00
26 Luol Deng .40 1.00
27 Elton Brand .40 1.00
28 Dirk Nowitzki .60 1.50
29 Bobby Simmons .25 .60
30 Antawn Jamison .40 1.00
31 Tracy McGrady .50 1.25
32 Steve Francis .40 1.00
33 Kobe Bryant 2.00 5.00
34 Jason Richardson .40 1.00
35 J.R. Smith .40 1.00
36 Tayshaun Prince .40 1.00
37 Chauncey Billups .40 1.00
38 Allen Iverson .60 1.50
39 Ricky Davis .30 .75
40 Josh Smith .40 1.00
41 Brad Miller .40 1.00
42 Zach Randolph .30 .75
43 Troy Murphy .30 .75
44 Shawn Marion .40 1.00
45 Pau Gasol .40 1.00
46 Lamar Odom .40 1.00
47 Drew Gooden .30 .75
48 Darius Miles .25 .60
49 Chris Bosh .40 1.00
50 Antoine Walker .30 .75
51 Amare Stoudemire .40 1.00
52 Rasheed Wallace .40 1.00
53 Emeka Okafor .40 1.00
54 Steve Nash .50 1.25
55 Sam Cassell .40 1.00
56 Michael Finley .40 1.00
57 Manu Ginobili .40 1.00
58 Mike Dunleavy .30 .75
59 Jason Terry .30 .75
60 Jalen Rose .40 1.00
61 Ron Artest .40 1.00
62 Marcus Camby .30 .75
63 Udonis Haslem .30 .75
64 Kenyon Martin .40 1.00
65 Gerald Wallace .40 1.00
66 David West .40 1.00
67 Samuel Dalembert .25 .60
68 Jermaine O'Neal .40 1.00
69 Dwight Howard .75 2.00
70 T.J. Ford .30 .75
71 Smush Parker .25 .60
72 Sebastian Telfair .30 .75
73 Ray Allen .40 1.00
74 Michael Redd .40 1.00
75 Larry Hughes .30 .75
76 Jamaal Tinsley .25 .60
77 Chris Duhon .25 .60
78 Baron Davis .40 1.00
79 Andre Iguodala .40 1.00
80 Paul Pierce .50 1.25
81 Zydrunas Ilgauskas .30 .75
82 Tim Duncan .60 1.50
83 Shane Battier .30 .75
84 Peja Stojakovic .40 1.00
85 LeBron James 2.00 5.00
86 Kevin Garnett .75 2.00
87 Chris Webber .40 1.00
88 Carmelo Anthony .75 2.00
89 Vince Carter .60 1.50
90 Stephen Jackson .30 .75
91 Richard Hamilton .30 .75
92 Mike Bibby .40 1.00
93 Marko Jaric .25 .60
94 Jamal Crawford .30 .75
95 Gilbert Arenas .40 1.00
96 Dwyane Wade 1.00 2.50
97 Delonte West .30 .75
98 Ben Gordon .40 1.00
99 Andre Miller .30 .75
100 Joe Johnson .40 1.00
101 Jay-Z 2.50 6.00
102 Shannon Elizabeth 2.50 6.00
103 Jenny McCarthy 2.50 6.00
104 Carmen Electra 2.50 6.00
105 Christie Brinkley 2.50 6.00
106 Chris Paul RC 6.00 15.00
107 Channing Frye RC 2.00 5.00
108 Ike Diogu RC 1.50 4.00
109 Marvin Williams RC 2.00 5.00
110 Rashad McCants RC 1.50 4.00
111 Luther Head RC 1.50 4.00
112 Gerald Green RC 2.00 5.00
113 Salim Stoudamire RC 1.50 4.00
114 Jose Calderon RC 1.50 4.00
115 Andrew Bynum RC 5.00 12.00
116 Wayne Simien RC 1.50 4.00
117 Chris Taft RC 1.50 4.00
118 Ryan Gomes RC 1.50 4.00
119 Martell Webster RC 1.50 4.00
120 Johan Petro RC 1.50 4.00
121 Antoine Wright RC 1.50 4.00
122 Jarrett Jack RC 1.50 4.00
123 Daniel Ewing RC 1.50 4.00
124 Joey Graham RC 1.50 4.00
125 Nate Robinson RC 2.00 5.00
126 Andrew Bogut AU RC 8.00 20.00
127 Raymond Felton AU RC 8.00 20.00
128 Francisco Garcia AU RC 6.00 15.00
129 Danny Granger AU RC 10.00 25.00
130 Orien Greene AU RC 5.00 12.00
131 Sarunas Jasikevicius AU RC 5.00 12.00
132 Linas Kleiza AU RC 5.00 12.00
133 David Lee AU RC 8.00 20.00
134 Sean May AU RC 5.00 12.00
135 Fabricio Oberto AU RC 5.00 12.00
136 Charlie Villanueva AU RC 6.00 15.00
137 Hakim Warrick AU RC 6.00 15.00
138 James Singleton AU RC 5.00 12.00
139 Deron Williams AU RC 12.00 30.00
140 Andrea Bargnani XRC 5.00 12.00
141 LaMarcus Aldridge XRC 8.00 20.00
142 Adam Morrison XRC 4.00 10.00
143 Tyrus Thomas XRC 4.00 10.00
144 Shelden Williams XRC 3.00 8.00
145 Brandon Roy XRC 8.00 20.00
146 Randy Foye XRC 4.00 10.00
147 Rudy Gay XRC 5.00 12.00
148 Patrick O'Bryant XRC 3.00 8.00
149 Saer Sene XRC 3.00 8.00
150 J.J. Redick XRC 4.00 10.00
151 Hilton Armstrong XRC 3.00 8.00
152 Thabo Sefolosha XRC 4.00 10.00
153 Ronnie Brewer XRC 4.00 10.00
154 Cedric Simmons XRC 3.00 8.00
155 Rodney Carney XRC 3.00 8.00
156 Shawne Williams XRC 3.00 8.00
157 Craig Smith XRC 3.00 8.00
158 Quincy Douby XRC 3.00 8.00
159 Renaldo Balkman XRC 3.00 8.00
160 Rajon Rondo XRC 12.00 30.00
161 Marcus Williams XRC 3.00 8.00
162 Josh Boone XRC 3.00 8.00
163 Kyle Lowry XRC 4.00 10.00
164 Shannon Brown XRC 5.00 12.00
165 Jordan Farmar XRC 3.00 8.00
166 Sergio Rodriguez XRC 3.00 8.00
167 Maurice Ager XRC 3.00 8.00
168 Mardy Collins XRC 3.00 8.00
169 Paul Millsap XRC 5.00 12.00

2005-06 Finest Refractors

*1-100: 1X TO 2.5X BASE HI
*101-125: .5X TO 1.25X BASE HI
*126-139: SAME VALUE AS BASE
*140-169: .5X TO 1.25X BASE HI
1-100 REF.PRINT RUN 349 SER.#'d SETS
101-125 REF.RC PRINT RUN 249 SER.#'d SETS
126-139 REF.AU RC PRINT RUN 229 SER.#'d SETS
33 Kobe Bryant 8.00 20.00
85 LeBron James 8.00 20.00
106 Chris Paul 10.00 25.00
139 Deron Williams AU 15.00 40.00

2005-06 Finest Refractors Black

*1-100: 6X TO 15X BASE HI
*101-125: 3X TO 8X BASE HI
*126-169: 1.5X TO 4X BASE HI
STATED PRINT RUN 19 SER.#'d SETS
33 Kobe Bryant 50.00 125.00
85 LeBron James 50.00 125.00

2005-06 Finest Refractors Gold

*1-100: 5X TO 12X BASE HI
*101-125: 1.5X TO 4X BASE HI
*126-169: 1.25X TO 3X BASE HI
1-125 PRINT RUN 39 SER.#'d SETS
126-139 AU PRINT RUN 59 SER.#'d SETS
33 Kobe Bryant 40.00 100.00
85 LeBron James 40.00 100.00

2005-06 Finest Refractors Green

*1-100: 3X TO 8X BASE HI
*101-125: .75X TO 2X BASE HI
*126-139: .6X TO 1.5X BASE HI
*140-169: .75X TO 2X BASE HI
1-125 PRINT RUN 89 SER.#'d SETS
126-139 AU PRINT RUN 99 SER.#'d SETS
139 Deron Williams AU 25.00 60.00

2005-06 Finest Refractors Red

*1-100: 2.5X TO 6X BASE HI
*101-125: .6X TO 1.5X BASE HI
*126-139: .5X TO 1.25X BASE HI
*140-169: .6X TO 1.5X BASE HI
1-125 PRINT RUN 169 SER.#'d SETS
126-139 AU PRINT RUN 199 SER.#'d SETS
33 Kobe Bryant 15.00 40.00
85 LeBron James 15.00 40.00
139 Deron Williams AU 20.00 50.00

2005-06 Finest X-Fractors

*1-100: 2X TO 5X BASE HI
*101-125: .6X TO 1.5X BASE HI
*126-139: .5X TO 1.25X BASE HI
*140-169: .6X TO 1.5X BASE HI
1-100 PRINT RUN 229 SER.#'d SETS
101-125 PRINT RUN 199 SER.#'d SETS
126-139 PRINT RUN 169 SER.#'d SETS
33 Kobe Bryant 12.00 30.00
106 Chris Paul 15.00 40.00

2005-06 Finest X-Fractors Gold

*1-100: 6X TO 15X BASE HI
*101-125: 2X TO 5X BASE HI
*126-139: 1X TO 2.5X BASE HI
*140-169: 1.25X TO 3X BASE HI
1-125 PRINT RUN 29 SER.#'d SETS
126-139 PRINT RUN 39 SER.#'d SETS
106 Chris Paul 40.00 100.00

2005-06 Finest X-Fractors Green

*1-100: 3X TO 8X BASE HI
*101-125: 1X TO 2.5X BASE HI
*126-139: .6X TO 1.5X BASE HI
*140-169: .75X TO 2X BASE HI

1-125 PRINT RUN 69 SER.#'d SETS
126-139 PRINT RUN 79 SER.#'d SETS
33 Kobe Bryant 20.00 50.00
106 Chris Paul 20.00 50.00

2005-06 Finest X-Fractors Red

*1-100: 2.5X TO 6X BASE HI
*101-125: .75X TO 2X BASE HI
*126-139: .5X TO 1.25X BASE HI
*140-169: .6X TO 1.5X BASE HI
1-125 PRINT RUN 169 SER.#'d SETS
126-169 PRINT RUN 149 SER.#'d SETS
33 Kobe Bryant 15.00 40.00

2005-06 Finest Boxloaders Celebrity Moments

Inserted as box toppers, this five-card set is serially numbered to 399 and features gold foil cards sealed in Topps uncirculated cases.
AUTO'S NOT PRICED DUE TO SCARCITY
CB1 Christie Brinkley 2.50 6.00
CE1 Carmen Electra 2.50 6.00
JM1 Jenny McCarthy 2.50 6.00
JZ1 Jay-Z 2.50 6.00
SE1 Shannon Elizabeth 2.50 6.00

2005-06 Finest Boxloaders Iverson Moments

COMMON CARD (AI1-AI20) 2.50 6.00
PRINT RUN 399 SER.#'d SETS
UNPRICED AUTO PRINT RUN 3 SETS

2005-06 Finest Boxloaders Wade Moments

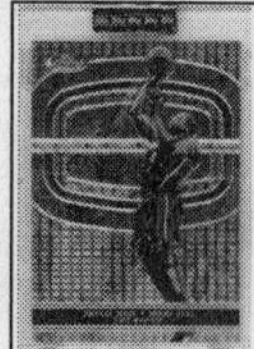

COMMON CARD (DW1-DW20) 4.00 10.00
PRINT RUN 399 SER.#'d SETS
UNPRICED AUTO PRINT RUN 5 SETS

2005-06 Finest Dress for Success Relics

*REFRACTORS: .6X TO 1.5X BASE HI
REFRACTOR PRINT RUN 29 SER.#'d SETS
UNPRICED X-FRACTOR PRINT RUN 9 SETS
UNPRICED SUPERFR.PRINT RUN ONE SET
UNPRICED AUTO PRINT RUN 5 SETS
AB Andrew Bogut 6.00 15.00
CV Charlie Villanueva 5.00 12.00
DW Dwyane Wade 10.00 25.00
FO Fabricio Oberto 4.00 10.00
JG Joey Graham 4.00 10.00
OG Orien Greene 4.00 10.00

2005-06 Finest Fact

*REFRACTORS: .6X TO 1.5X BASE HI
REFRACTOR PRINT RUN 199 SER.#'d SETS
*X-FRACTORS: .75X TO 2X BASE HI
X-FRACTOR PRINT RUN 99 SER.#'d SETS
UNPRICED PLATE PRINT RUN ONE SET
UNPRICED SUPERFR.PRINT RUN ONE SET
FF1 Shawn Marion 1.00 2.50
FF2 Joey Graham 1.00 2.50
FF3 Rasheed Wallace 1.00 2.50
FF4 Rashard Lewis 1.00 2.50
FF5 Pau Gasol 1.00 2.50
FF6 Josh Smith 1.00 2.50
FF7 Josh Howard 1.00 2.50
FF8 Sean May 1.00 2.50
FF9 Hakim Warrick 1.25 3.00
FF10 Elton Brand 1.00 2.50
FF11 Antawn Jamison 1.00 2.50
FF12 Tracy McGrady 1.25 3.00
FF13 Sarunas Jasikevicius 1.00 2.50
FF14 Rashad McCants 1.00 2.50
FF15 Orien Greene 1.00 2.50
FF16 Michael Redd 1.00 2.50
FF17 Gilbert Arenas 1.00 2.50
FF18 Gerald Green 1.25 3.00
FF19 Dwyane Wade 2.50 6.00
FF20 Allen Iverson 1.50 4.00
FF21 Shaquille O'Neal 2.00 5.00
FF22 Chris Paul 4.00 10.00
FF23 LeBron James 5.00 12.00
FF24 Dirk Nowitzki 1.50 4.00
FF25 Tim Duncan 1.50 4.00

2005-06 Finest Fact Autographs

*REFRACTORS: .6X TO 1.5X BASE AU HI
REF.PRINT RUN 15 TO 25 SETS
UNPRICED SUPERFR.PRINT RUN ONE SET
UNPRICED X-FR.PRINT RUN 4 TO 9 SETS
AI Allen Iverson 40.00 100.00
CB Christie Brinkley 50.00 100.00
CE Carmen Electra 50.00 100.00
DW Dwyane Wade 60.00 120.00
EO Emeka Okafor 10.00 25.00
JM Jenny McCarthy 50.00 100.00
JZ Jay-Z 50.00 120.00
SE Shannon Elizabeth 50.00 100.00
SO Shaquille O'Neal 40.00 80.00
VC Vince Carter 20.00 40.00

2005-06 Finest Fact Relics

PRINT RUN 1629 SER.#'d SETS
*REFRACTORS: .6X TO 1.5X BASE HI
REFRACTOR PRINT RUN 199 SER.#'d SETS
*X-FRACTORS: .75X TO 2X BASE HI
X-FRAC.PRINT RUN 49 SER.#'d SETS
UNPRICED AUTO PRINT RUN 5 SETS
UNPRICED PLATE PRINT RUN ONE SET
UNPRICED SUPERFR.PRINT RUN ONE SET
AI Allen Iverson 4.00 10.00
AJ Antawn Jamison 2.50 6.00
CP Chris Paul 5.00 12.00
DW Dwyane Wade 6.00 15.00
EB Elton Brand 2.50 6.00
HW Hakim Warrick 3.00 8.00
JG Joey Graham 2.50 6.00
JH Josh Howard 2.50 6.00
JS Josh Smith 2.50 6.00
OG Orien Greene 2.50 6.00
RL Rashard Lewis 2.50 6.00
RM Rashad McCants 2.50 6.00
RW Rasheed Wallace 2.50 6.00
SJ Sarunas Jasikevicius 2.50 6.00
SM Sean May 2.50 6.00
TM Tracy McGrady 3.00 8.00

2005-06 Finest Patchworks

*REFRACTORS: .6X TO 1.5X BASE HI
REFRACTOR PRINT RUN 29 SER.#'d SETS
UNPRICED SUPERFR.PRINT RUN ONE SET
UNPRICED X-FRAC PRINT RUN 9 SETS
AI Allen Iverson 10.00 25.00
AS Amare Stoudemire 6.00 15.00
DW Dwyane Wade 15.00 40.00
KB Kobe Bryant 20.00 50.00
KG Kevin Garnett 12.00 30.00
RA Ray Allen 6.00 15.00
SN Steve Nash 8.00 20.00
SO Shaquille O'Neal 12.00 30.00
TD Tim Duncan 10.00 25.00
TM Tracy McGrady 8.00 20.00
VC Vince Carter 10.00 25.00
YM Yao Ming 8.00 20.00

2006-07 Finest

Issued in mid June 2007, Finest is the first 2006-07 product to include redemption cards for the incoming 2007-08 rookie class highlighted by Greg Oden and Kevin Durant. The 131-card set utilizes an all foil-board card stock where cards 1-40 picture veteran players, 41-50 picture retired NBA legends, 51-100 picture rookies and 101-130 are draft pick exchange redemption cards. The base card design features red highlights along the top and bottom of the card for veterans and legends and white highlights for rookies. Draft Exchange cards feature the draft pick number on the front and redemption information on the back. The format for packing includes three mini boxes per box where each mini box contains six packs of five cards each. Finest carried an original suggested retail price of $50.00 per six-pack mini box.
COMP.SET w/o SPs (100) 20.00 40.00
XRC PRINT RUN 539 SER.#'d SETS
UNPRICED SUPERFR.PRINT RUN ONE SET
UNPRICED WHITE X-FRAC.PRINT RUN ONE SET
1 Carmelo Anthony .60 1.50
2 Ben Wallace .50 1.25
3 Baron Davis .50 1.25
4 Jermaine O'Neal .50 1.25
5 Dwyane Wade 1.25 3.00
6 Vince Carter .60 1.50
7 Dwight Howard .75 2.00
8 Steve Nash .60 1.50
9 Tim Duncan .75 2.00
10 Gilbert Arenas .50 1.25
11 Gerald Wallace .50 1.25
12 Dirk Nowitzki .75 2.00
13 Chauncey Billups .50 1.25
14 Yao Ming .60 1.50
15 Pau Gasol .50 1.25
16 Kevin Garnett 1.00 2.50
17 Chris Paul 1.00 2.50
18 Amare Stoudemire .50 1.25
19 Tony Parker .50 1.25
20 Andrei Kirilenko .40 1.00
21 Paul Pierce .60 1.50
22 LeBron James 2.50 6.00
23 Richard Hamilton .40 1.00
24 Tracy McGrady .60 1.50
25 Kobe Bryant 2.50 6.00
26 Michael Redd .50 1.25
27 Stephon Marbury .40 1.00
28 Andre Iguodala .50 1.25
29 Mike Bibby .50 1.25
30 Chris Bosh .50 1.25
31 Joe Johnson .50 1.25
32 Kirk Hinrich .50 1.25
33 Josh Howard .40 1.00
34 Jason Richardson .50 1.25
35 Elton Brand .50 1.25
36 Shaquille O'Neal 1.00 2.50
37 Jason Kidd .75 2.00
38 Allen Iverson .60 1.50
39 Zach Randolph .40 1.00
40 Ray Allen .50 1.25
41 Larry Bird 1.50 4.00
42 Isiah Thomas .50 1.25
43 Dominique Wilkins .60 1.50
44 Willis Reed .50 1.25
45 Robert Parish .50 1.25
46 Chris Mullin .50 1.25
47 Karl Malone .60 1.50
48 Calvin Murphy .50 1.25
49 Xavier McDaniel .50 1.25
50 Nate Archibald .50 1.25
51 Steve Novak RC 1.25 3.00
52 Shannon Brown RC 2.00 5.00
53 Sergio Rodriguez RC 1.25 3.00
54 Saer Sene RC 1.25 3.00
55 Ryan Hollins RC 1.25 3.00
56 Ronnie Brewer RC 1.50 4.00
57 Mile Ilic RC 1.25 3.00
58 Kyle Lowry RC 1.50 4.00
59 Hilton Armstrong RC 1.25 3.00
60 Craig Smith RC 1.25 3.00
61 Will Blalock RC 1.25 3.00
62 Thabo Sefolosha RC 1.50 4.00
63 Rodney Carney RC 1.25 3.00
64 Quincy Douby RC 1.25 3.00
65 P.J. Tucker RC 1.25 3.00
66 Josh Boone RC 1.25 3.00
67 Jordan Farmar RC 1.25 3.00
68 Damir Markota RC 1.25 3.00
69 Cedric Simmons RC 1.25 3.00
70 Allan Ray RC 1.25 3.00
71 Rudy Gay RC 2.00 5.00
72 Rajon Rondo RC 5.00 12.00
73 Patrick O'Bryant RC 1.25 3.00
74 Marcus Williams RC 1.25 3.00
75 Marcus Vinicius RC 1.25 3.00
76 James White RC 1.25 3.00
77 Dee Brown RC 1.25 3.00
78 David Noel RC 1.25 3.00
79 Daniel Gibson RC 1.50 4.00
80 Bobby Jones RC 1.25 3.00
81 Tyrus Thomas RC 1.50 4.00
82 Shelden Williams RC 1.25 3.00
83 Pops Mensah-Bonsu RC 1.25 3.00
84 Paul Davis RC 1.25 3.00
85 Mardy Collins RC 1.25 3.00
86 James Augustine RC 1.25 3.00
87 Hassan Adams RC 1.25 3.00
88 Chris Quinn RC 1.25 3.00
89 Brandon Roy RC 3.00 8.00
90 Andrea Bargnani RC 2.00 5.00
91 Solomon Jones RC 1.25 3.00
92 Shawne Williams RC 1.25 3.00
93 Renaldo Balkman RC 1.25 3.00
94 Randy Foye RC 1.50 4.00
95 Maurice Ager RC 1.25 3.00
96 LaMarcus Aldridge RC 3.00 8.00
97 Jorge Garbajosa RC 1.25 3.00
98 J.J. Redick RC 1.50 4.00
99 Alexander Johnson RC 1.25 3.00
100 Adam Morrison RC 1.50 4.00
101 Greg Oden XRC 4.00 10.00
102 Kevin Durant XRC 40.00 100.00
103 Al Horford XRC 4.00 10.00
104 Mike Conley Jr. XRC 4.00 10.00
105 Jeff Green XRC 4.00 10.00
106 Yi Jianlian XRC 5.00 12.00
107 Corey Brewer XRC 4.00 10.00
108 Brandan Wright XRC 3.00 8.00
109 Joakim Noah XRC 8.00 20.00
110 Spencer Hawes XRC 3.00 8.00
111 Acie Law XRC 3.00 8.00
112 Thaddeus Young XRC 4.00 10.00
113 Julian Wright XRC 3.00 8.00
114 Al Thornton XRC 3.00 8.00
115 Rodney Stuckey XRC 5.00 12.00
116 Nick Young XRC 5.00 12.00
117 Sean Williams XRC 3.00 8.00
118 Marco Belinelli XRC 3.00 8.00
119 Javaris Crittenton XRC 3.00 8.00
120 Jason Smith XRC 3.00 8.00
121 Daequan Cook XRC 3.00 8.00
122 Jared Dudley XRC 3.00 8.00
123 Wilson Chandler XRC 5.00 12.00
124 Carl Landry XRC 3.00 8.00
125 Morris Almond XRC 3.00 8.00
126 Aaron Brooks XRC 3.00 8.00
127 Arron Afflalo XRC 4.00 10.00
128 Gabe Pruitt XRC 3.00 8.00
129 Alando Tucker XRC 3.00 8.00
130 Marcus Williams XRC 3.00 8.00
NNO Rookie Autograph EXCH 75.00 175.00

2006-07 Finest Refractors

*1-50 REF: .75X TO 2X BASE HI
*51-100 REF: .5X TO 1.5X BASE HI
*101-130 XRC REF: .5X TO 1.25X BASE HI
REFRACTOR ODDS 1:6

2006-07 Finest Refractors Black

*1-50 REF.BLACK: 2.5X TO 6X BASE HI
*51-100 REF.BLACK: 1X TO 2.5X BASE HI
*101-130 REF.BLACK: 1X TO 2.5X BASE HI
PRINT RUN 99 SER.#'d SETS
72 Rajon Rondo 15.00 40.00

2006-07 Finest Refractors Blue

*1-50 REF.BLUE: 1X TO 2.5X BASE HI
*51-100 REF.BLUE: .75X TO 2X BASE HI
*101-130 REF.BLUE: .6X TO 1.5X BASE HI
REF.BLUE PRINT RUN 299 SER.#'d SETS
22 LeBron James 8.00 20.00
25 Kobe Bryant 8.00 20.00

2006-07 Finest Refractors Gold

*1-50 GOLD.REF: 6X TO 15X BASE HI
*51-100 GOLD.REF: 1.5X TO 4X BASE HI
*101-130 GOLD REF: 1.5X TO 4X BASE HI
PRINT RUN 50 SER.#'d SETS
22 LeBron James 50.00 125.00
25 Kobe Bryant 50.00 125.00
72 Rajon Rondo 25.00 60.00
98 J.J. Redick 10.00 25.00
101 Greg Oden 20.00 50.00
102 Kevin Durant 350.00 650.00

2006-07 Finest Refractors Green

*1-50 REF.GREEN: 1.25X TO 3X BASE HI
*51-100 REF.GREEN: .75X TO 2X BASE HI
*101-130 REF.GREEN: .75X TO 2X BASE HI
PRINT RUN 199 SER.#'d SETS
22 LeBron James 10.00 25.00
25 Kobe Bryant 10.00 25.00

2006-07 Finest Refractors Silver

*SILVER: .6X TO 1.5X BASE HI
STATED PRINT RUN 319 SER.#'d SETS

2006-07 Finest X-Fractors

*1-50 X-FRAC: 5X TO 12X BASE HI
*51-100 X-FRAC: 2X TO 5X BASE HI
*101-130 X-FRAC: 2X TO 5X BASE HI
X-FRAC.PRINT RUN 25 SER.#'d SETS
101 Greg Oden 50.00 120.00
102 Kevin Durant 300.00 600.00

2006-07 Finest Moments

COMPLETE SET (2) 4.00 10.00
ONE PER BOX AS TOPPER
*REFRACTORS: .75X TO 2X BASE HI
REFRACTORS 1:3 BOXES
AM Adam Morrison 1.25 3.00
LB Larry Bird 3.00 8.00

2006-07 Finest Moments Relics Autographs X-Fractors

AM Adam Morrison/50 20.00 40.00
LB Larry Bird/25 100.00 200.00

2006-07 Finest Moments Relics Refractors

AM Adam Morrison/499 5.00 12.00
LB Larry Bird/299 15.00 40.00

2006-07 Finest Rookie Autographs Refractors

GROUP A ODDS 1:456, GROUP B 1:150
GROUP C 1:66, GROUP D 1:48
GROUP E 1:36, GROUP F 1:36
GROUP G 1:144, GROUP H 1:24
*X-FRACTORS: .75X TO 2X BASE HI
X-FRACTOR PRINT RUN 25 SER.#'d SETS
UNPRICED SUPERFR.PRINT RUN ONE SET
51 Steve Novak D 4.00 10.00
52 Shannon Brown C 6.00 15.00
53 Sergio Rodriguez H 4.00 10.00
54 Saer Sene H 4.00 10.00
55 Ryan Hollins E 4.00 10.00
56 Ronnie Brewer D 5.00 12.00
57 Mile Ilic E 4.00 10.00
58 Kyle Lowry F 5.00 12.00
59 Hilton Armstrong D 4.00 10.00
60 Craig Smith F 4.00 10.00
61 Will Blalock H 4.00 10.00
62 Thabo Sefolosha D 6.00 15.00
63 Rodney Carney C 4.00 10.00
64 Quincy Douby C 4.00 10.00
66 Josh Boone D 4.00 10.00
67 Jordan Farmar E 4.00 10.00
68 Damir Markota E 4.00 10.00
69 Cedric Simmons B 4.00 10.00
70 Allan Ray E 4.00 10.00
72 Rajon Rondo E 30.00 60.00
73 Patrick O'Bryant C 4.00 10.00
74 Marcus Williams A 4.00 10.00
75 Marcus Vinicius G 4.00 10.00
76 James White E 4.00 10.00
77 Dee Brown F 4.00 10.00
80 Bobby Jones B 4.00 10.00
82 Shelden Williams C 4.00 10.00
83 Pops Mensah-Bonsu H 4.00 10.00
84 Paul Davis B 4.00 10.00
85 Mardy Collins D 4.00 10.00
87 Hassan Adams D 4.00 10.00
90 Andrea Bargnani A 6.00 15.00
91 Solomon Jones C 4.00 10.00
92 Shawne Williams F 4.00 10.00
93 Renaldo Balkman F 4.00 10.00
94 Randy Foye B 5.00 12.00
95 Maurice Ager C 4.00 10.00
97 Jorge Garbajosa H 4.00 10.00
98 J.J. Redick F 6.00 15.00
100 Adam Morrison H 5.00 12.00

2007-08 Finest

Released in June 2008, Finest boasts a 130-card all-foil base set where cards 1-40 feature base veteran players, cards 41-50 feature retired NBA legends, cards 51-100 feature rookies and cards 101-130 feature draft pick redemption cards for the newly drafted 2008-09 NBA rookie class. These exchange cards are the first ones issued for the 2005-06 class. Finest was packaged in boxes which were broken down into three mini-boxes per containing six packs of five cards each (one autograph card per mini-box). The original suggested retail price of the six-pack mini boxes was $40.
COMP.SET w/o DRAFT (100) 25.00 50.00
UNPRICED SUPERFRACTOR PRINT RUN ONE SET
UNPRICED WHITE X-FR.PRINT RUN ONE SET
1 Gilbert Arenas .50 1.25
2 Ray Allen .50 1.25
3 Dwyane Wade 1.25 3.00
4 Dirk Nowitzki .60 1.50
5 Manu Ginobili .50 1.25
6 Eddy Curry .30 .75
7 Jermaine O'Neal .50 1.25
8 Carlos Boozer .50 1.25
9 Tony Parker .50 1.25
10 Jason Kidd .50 1.25
11 Chris Bosh .50 1.25
12 Al Jefferson .50 1.25
13 Steve Nash .60 1.50
14 Chris Paul 1.00 2.50
15 Carmelo Anthony .60 1.50
16 Pau Gasol .50 1.25
17 Joe Johnson .50 1.25
18 Chauncey Billups .50 1.25
19 Andre Iguodala .50 1.25
20 Yao Ming .60 1.50
21 Tim Duncan .75 2.00
22 Michael Redd .50 1.25
23 Allen Iverson .60 1.50
24 Kobe Bryant 2.50 6.00
25 Kevin Garnett 1.00 2.50
26 Brandon Roy .60 1.50
27 Luol Deng .50 1.25
28 Deron Williams .75 2.00
29 Amare Stoudemire .50 1.25
30 Vince Carter .60 1.50
31 Tracy McGrady .50 1.25
32 Shaquille O'Neal 1.00 2.50
33 Jason Richardson .50 1.25
34 Paul Pierce .60 1.50
35 Baron Davis .50 1.25
36 Dwight Howard .75 2.00
37 Josh Howard .40 1.00
38 Kevin Martin .50 1.25
39 Ben Gordon .50 1.25
40 LeBron James 2.50 6.00
41 Isiah Thomas .50 1.25
42 Dominique Wilkins .60 1.50
43 Magic Johnson 1.25 3.00
44 Bill Russell .75 2.00
45 David Robinson .75 2.00
46 John Stockton .75 2.00
47 Jerry West .60 1.50
48 Moses Malone .50 1.25
49 Dennis Rodman .75 2.00
50 Larry Bird 1.50 4.00
51 Al Horford RC 1.25 3.00
52 Ramon Sessions RC 1.50 4.00
53 JamesOn Curry RC 1.00 2.50
54 Arron Afflalo RC 1.25 3.00
55 Carl Landry RC 1.00 2.50
56 Glen Davis RC 1.50 4.00
57 Jermareo Davidson RC 1.00 2.50
58 Nick Fazekas RC 1.00 2.50
59 Taurean Green RC 1.00 2.50
60 Cheikh Samb RC 1.00 2.50
61 Mike Conley Jr. RC 1.50 4.00
62 Chris Richard RC 1.00 2.50
63 Josh McRoberts RC 1.00 2.50
64 Alando Tucker RC 1.00 2.50
65 Brandan Wright RC 1.00 2.50
66 Jamario Moon RC 1.00 2.50
67 Jared Dudley RC 1.00 2.50
68 Dominic McGuire RC 1.00 2.50
69 Sean Williams RC 1.00 2.50
70 Mario West RC 1.00 2.50
71 Kevin Durant RC 12.00 30.00
72 Julian Wright RC 1.00 2.50
73 Yi Jianlian RC 1.50 4.00
74 Coby Karl RC 1.00 2.50
75 Aaron Brooks RC 1.00 2.50
76 Kyrylo Fesenko RC 1.00 2.50
77 Greg Oden RC 1.25 3.00
78 Juan Carlos Navarro RC 1.00 2.50
79 Nick Young RC 1.50 4.00
80 Thaddeus Young RC 1.25 3.00
81 Joakim Noah RC 2.50 6.00
82 Luis Scola RC 1.50 4.00
83 Aaron Gray RC 1.00 2.50
84 Herbert Hill RC 1.00 2.50
85 Al Thornton RC 1.00 2.50
86 D.J. Strawberry RC 1.00 2.50
87 Javaris Crittenton RC 1.00 2.50
88 Morris Almond RC 1.00 2.50
89 Spencer Hawes RC 1.00 2.50
90 C.J. Watson RC 1.00 2.50
91 Corey Brewer RC 1.25 3.00
92 Jeff Green RC 1.25 3.00
93 Marco Belinelli RC 1.00 2.50
94 Marcin Gortat RC 1.50 4.00
95 Acie Law RC 1.00 2.50
96 Daequan Cook RC 1.00 2.50
97 Gabe Pruitt RC 1.00 2.50
98 Jason Smith RC 1.00 2.50
99 Rodney Stuckey RC 1.50 4.00
100 Wilson Chandler RC 1.50 4.00
101 Derrick Rose XRC 40.00 100.00
102 Michael Beasley XRC 6.00 15.00
103 O.J. Mayo XRC 6.00 15.00
104 Russell Westbrook XRC 20.00 50.00
105 Kevin Love XRC 15.00 40.00
106 Danilo Gallinari XRC 6.00 15.00
107 Eric Gordon XRC 8.00 20.00
108 Joe Alexander XRC 4.00 10.00
109 D.J. Augustin XRC 4.00 10.00
110 Brook Lopez XRC 6.00 15.00
111 Jerryd Bayless XRC 4.00 10.00
112 Jason Thompson XRC 4.00 10.00
113 Brandon Rush XRC 4.00 10.00
114 Anthony Randolph XRC 5.00 12.00
115 Robin Lopez XRC 4.00 10.00
116 Marreese Speights XRC 4.00 10.00
117 Roy Hibbert XRC 6.00 15.00
118 JaVale McGee XRC 6.00 15.00
119 J.J. Hickson XRC 5.00 12.00
120 Alexis Ajinca XRC 4.00 10.00
121 Ryan Anderson XRC 6.00 15.00
122 Courtney Lee XRC 6.00 15.00
123 Kosta Koufos XRC 4.00 10.00
124 Walter Sharpe XRC 4.00 10.00
125 Nicolas Batum XRC 5.00 12.00
126 George Hill XRC 6.00 15.00
127 Darrell Arthur XRC 4.00 10.00
128 Donte Greene XRC 4.00 10.00
129 D.J. White XRC 4.00 10.00
130 J.R. Giddens XRC 4.00 10.00

2007-08 Finest Refractors

*1-100 REF: .6X TO 1.5X BASE HI
*101-130 REF: .5X TO 1.25X BASE HI
1-100 ODDS APPROX. 1:2
101-130 STATED ODDS 1:5

2007-08 Finest Refractors Black

*1-50 REF.BLACK: 3X TO 8X BASE HI
*51-100 REF.BLACK: 1.5X TO 4X BASE HI
*101-130 REF.BLACK: 1X TO 2.5X BASE HI
REF.BLACK PRINT RUN 75 SER.#'d SETS
71 Kevin Durant 75.00 200.00
101 Derrick Rose 200.00 400.00

2007-08 Finest Refractors Blue

*1-50 REF.BLUE: 1.25X TO 3X BASE HI
*51-100 REF.BLUE: .75X TO 2X BASE HI
*101-130 REF.BLUE: .6X TO 1.5X BASE HI
REF.BLUE PRINT RUN 199 SER.#'d SETS
71 Kevin Durant 40.00 100.00

2007-08 Finest Refractors Gold

*1-50 REF.GOLD: 10X TO 25X BASE HI
*51-100 REF.GOLD: 3X TO 8X BASE HI
*101-130 REF.GOLD: 1.25X TO 3X BASE HI
PRINT RUN 25 SER.#'d SETS
71 Kevin Durant 200.00 400.00
77 Greg Oden 20.00 50.00
101 Derrick Rose 200.00 400.00
104 Russell Westbrook 100.00 250.00

2007-08 Finest Refractors Green

*1-50 REF.GREEN: 2X TO 5X BASE HI
*51-100 REF.GREEN: 1.25X TO 3X BASE HI
*101-130 REF.GREEN: .75X TO 2X BASE HI
REF.GREEN PRINT RUN 149 SER.#'d SETS

2007-08 Finest Refractors Silver

*SILVER: .5X TO 1.25X BASE HI
STATED PRINT RUN 319 SER.#'d SETS
71 Kevin Durant 40.00 100.00

2007-08 Finest X-Fractors

*1-50 X-FRAC: 8X TO 20X BASE HI
*51-100 X-FRAC: 4X TO 10X BASE HI
*101-130 X-FRAC: 1.5X TO 4X BASE HI
STATED PRINT RUN 15 SER.#'d SETS
24 Kobe Bryant 75.00 200.00
40 LeBron James 75.00 200.00
71 Kevin Durant 400.00 800.00
77 Greg Oden 30.00 80.00
101 Derrick Rose 250.00 500.00
104 Russell Westbrook 100.00 250.00

2007-08 Finest Draft Picks Autographs Refractors

STATED ODDS 1:43
UNPRICED PLATE PRINT RUN ONE SET
UNPRICED SUPERFR.PRINT RUN ONE SET
UNPRICED X-FRACTOR PRINT RUN 10 SETS
102 Michael Beasley 25.00 60.00
103 O.J. Mayo 25.00 60.00
104 Russell Westbrook 75.00 200.00
105 Kevin Love 75.00 200.00
106 Danilo Gallinari 8.00 20.00
107 Eric Gordon 30.00 80.00
108 Joe Alexander 5.00 12.00
109 D.J. Augustin 5.00 12.00
110 Brook Lopez 8.00 20.00
111 Jerryd Bayless 5.00 12.00
112 Jason Thompson 5.00 12.00
113 Brandon Rush 5.00 12.00
114 Anthony Randolph 6.00 15.00
115 Robin Lopez 5.00 12.00
116 Marreese Speights 5.00 12.00
117 Roy Hibbert 8.00 20.00
118 JaVale McGee 8.00 20.00
119 J.J. Hickson 6.00 15.00
120 Alexis Ajinca 5.00 12.00
121 Ryan Anderson 8.00 20.00
122 Courtney Lee 8.00 20.00
123 Kosta Koufos 5.00 12.00
124 Walter Sharpe 5.00 12.00
125 Nicolas Batum 6.00 15.00
126 George Hill 8.00 20.00
127 Darrell Arthur 5.00 12.00
128 Donte Greene 5.00 12.00
129 D.J. White 5.00 12.00
130 J.R. Giddens 5.00 12.00

2007-08 Finest Redemption Autographs

These uniquely designed autographs were distributed via Topps Customer Service for other redemption cards that could not be fulfilled.
BG Ben Gordon 3.00 8.00
BR Brandon Roy 10.00 25.00

2007-08 Finest Rookie Autographs Refractors

GROUP A ODDS 1:31, GROUP B 1:12
GROUP C ODDS 1:4, GROUP D 1:3
GROUP E ODDS 1:3
UNPRICED SUPERFR.PRINT RUN ONE SET
UNPRICED X-FRAC.PRINT RUN 10 SETS
53 JamesOn Curry B 4.00
54 Arron Afflalo C 5.00
55 Carl Landry C 4.00
56 Glen Davis D 6.00
57 Jermareo Davidson E 4.00
58 Nick Fazekas D 4.00
59 Taurean Green B 4.00
63 Josh McRoberts B 4.00
64 Alando Tucker D 4.00
65 Brandan Wright A 4.00
66 Jamario Moon C 4.00
67 Jared Dudley D 4.00
68 Dominic McGuire B 4.00
69 Sean Williams D 4.00
70 Mario West E 4.00
73 Yi Jianlian A 6.00
74 Coby Karl C 4.00
75 Aaron Brooks D 4.00
77 Greg Oden A 20.00
78 Juan Carlos Navarro C 4.00
79 Nick Young A 8.00
80 Thaddeus Young A 5.00
83 Aaron Gray D 4.00
84 Herbert Hill E 4.00
85 Al Thornton C 4.00
86 D.J. Strawberry E 4.00
87 Javaris Crittenton B 4.00
88 Morris Almond C 4.00
89 Spencer Hawes C 4.00
93 Marco Belinelli A 4.00
94 Marcin Gortat C 8.00
95 Acie Law C 4.00
96 Daequan Cook B 4.00
97 Gabe Pruitt C 4.00
98 Jason Smith D 4.00
99 Rodney Stuckey C 6.00
100 Wilson Chandler D 6.00

2008-09 Finest Redempti[on] Autographs

These uniquely designed autographs were dist[ributed] via Topps Customer Service for other redempti[on cards] that could not be fulfilled.
DW Dwyane Wade 25.00

2001 Fire Fleer WNBA

This nine card perforated set was given out in P[ortland,] Oregon by Fleer at the Fire's game on 7/30/01 [and was] said to be given to the first 5000 fans.
COMPLETE SET (9) 10.00
1 Linda Hargrove .40
2 Sophia Witherspoon .40
3 Vanessa NyGaard .40
4 Sylvia Crawley .40
5 Portland Fire .40
6 Alisa Burras .40
7 Jackie Stiles 10.00
8 Stacey Thomas .40
9 Spot MASCOT .40

1991-93 5 Majeur

These French cards measures approximately 3 [by] 6" and are printed on thin glossy paper stock. T[he] pictures were perforated and issued in various i[ssues] of the French magazine "5 Majeur" between 19[91 and] 1993. The fronts of most cards feature color act[ion] player photos with white borders; however, man[y] border colors exist. All cards have the same bas[ic] format. The player's name is printed in block let[ters] at the top. The magazine name appears beneath [the] picture. The backs carry biographical informatio[n,] statistics, and a player profile in French. The ca[rds are] unnumbered and checklisted below in order by [the] magazine. The numbers coincide with the issue [number] where the cards were released. As you w[ill] notice this checklist is not complete, and we wil[l] continue to update it as more detailed informatio[n becomes] known.
COMPLETE SET 200.00
1 Kareem Abdul-Jabbar 5.00
2 Mahmoud Abdul-Rauf .75
3 Michael Adams .75
4 Mark Aguirre 1.25
5 Danny Ainge 1.50
6 Greg Anderson .75
7 Nick Anderson 1.00
8 B.J. Armstrong White 1.00
9 B.J. Armstrong Red 1.00
10 Stacey Augmon .75
11 Charles Barkley 76ers 4.00
12 Charles Barkley USA 3.00
13 Dana Barros .75
14 Larry Bird 6.00
15 Larry Bird USA 6.00
16 Mookie Blaylock 1.00
17 Muggsy Bogues 1.25
18 Manute Bol .75
19 Sam Bowie .75
20 Frank Brickowski .75
21 Scott Brooks .75
22 Dee Brown .75
23 Antoine Carr .75
24 Bill Cartwright 1.00
25 Terry Catledge .75
26 Wilt Chamberlain 5.00
27 Tom Chambers 1.25
28 Rex Chapman 1.25
29 Maurice Cheeks 1.25
30 Wayne Cooper .75
31 Tyrone Corbin .75
32 Terry Cummings 1.25
33 Lloyd Daniels .75
34 Brad Daugherty .75
35 Vinny Del Negro .75
36 Vlade Divac 1.50
37 James Donaldson .75
38 Clyde Drexler USA 4.00
39 Joe Dumars 2.00
40 Mark Eaton .75
41 Craig Ehlo .75
42 Sean Elliot 1.25
43 Dale Ellis .75
44 Patrick Ewing 2.50
45 Patrick Ewing USA 2.00

...nny Ferry .75 2.00
...m Fleming .75 2.00
...ndall Gill .75 2.00
...mon Gilliam .75 2.00
...race Grant 1.25 3.00
...C. Green 1.25 3.00
...fernee Hardaway 4.00 10.00
...m Hardaway 1.50 4.00
...rek Harper 1.25 3.00
...n Harper 1.25 3.00
...rsey Hawkins 1.25 3.00
...arl Herrera .75 2.00
...b Hill CO .75 2.00
...ff Hornacek 1.25 3.00
...bert Horry 1.25 3.00
...il Jackson CO 1.50 4.00
...vin Johnson 1.50 4.00
...agic Johnson USA 5.00 12.00
...nnie Johnson .75 2.00
...ichael Jordan White 20.00 40.00
...chael Jordan Red 12.50 30.00
...chael Jordan USA 15.00 40.00
...eorge Karl CO .75 2.00
...awn Kemp 1.50 4.00
...rome Kersey .75 2.00
...n Koncak .75 2.00
...ristian Laettner USA 1.50 4.00
...ll Laimbeer 1.25 3.00
...ndrew Lang .75 2.00
...iff Livingstone SP .75 2.00
...rant Long .75 2.00
...ohn Lucas CO .75 2.00
...eff Malone .75 2.00
...arl Malone 4.00 10.00
...arl Malone USA 3.00 8.00
...oses Malone 1.50 4.00
...arunas Marciulionis .75 2.00
...ernon Maxwell .75 2.00
...odney McCray .75 2.00
...avier McDaniel .75 2.00
...evin McHale 2.00 5.00
...ale McMillan .75 2.00
...eggie Miller 3.00 8.00
...hris Mullin 1.50 4.00
...hris Mullin USA 1.50 4.00
...racy Murray .75 2.00
...ikembe Mutombo 1.50 4.00
...arry Nance 1.25 3.00
...harles Oakley 1.00 2.50
...akeem Olajuwon 3.00 8.00
...haquille O'Neal 6.00 15.00
...illy Owens .75 2.00
...ohn Paxson White 1.25 3.00
...ohn Paxson Red 1.00 2.50
Gary Payton 2.50 6.00
Will Perdue .75 2.00
Sam Perkins 1.25 3.00
Drazen Petrovic 3.00 8.00
Ricky Pierce .75 2.00
Scottie Pippen White 3.00 8.00
Scottie Pippen Red 2.50 6.00
Scottie Pippen USA 3.00 8.00
Olden Polynice .75 2.00
Terry Porter 1.00 2.50
Paul Pressey .75 2.00
Mark Price 1.25 3.00
Kurt Rambis 1.25 3.00
J.R. Reid .75 2.00
Glen Rice 1.25 3.00
Pooh Richardson .75 2.00
Mitch Richmond 1.50 4.00
Fred Roberts .75 2.00
David Robinson 4.00 10.00
David Robinson USA 3.00 8.00
Rumeal Robinson .75 2.00
Dennis Rodman 2.00 5.00
Donald Royal .75 2.00
John Salley 1.00 2.50
Detlef Schrempf 1.25 3.00
Byron Scott Dribbling 1.25 3.00
Byron Scott Shooting 1.25 3.00
Dennis Scott .75 2.00
Rony Seikaly .75 2.00
Scott Skiles 1.25 3.00
Kenny Smith 1.25 3.00
John Starks 1.25 3.00
John Stockton 5.00 12.00
John Stockton USA 4.00 10.00
Rod Strickland .75 2.00
Isiah Thomas 2.50 6.00
Otis Thorpe .75 2.00
Sedale Threatt .75 2.00
Rudy Tomjanovich CO 1.00 2.50
Jeff Turner .75 2.00
Spud Webb 1.25 3.00
Dominique Wilkins White 3.00 8.00
Dominique Wilkins Red 1.50 4.00
Lenny Wilkens CO 1.25 3.00
Herb Williams .75 2.00
John Williams .75 2.00
Reggie Williams .75 2.00
Scott Williams .75 2.00
Kevin Willis White .75 2.00
Kevin Willis Red .75 2.00
David Wingate .75 2.00
Orlando Woolridge .75 2.00

1994-95 Flair

...s 326-card super-premium standard-size set (made ...Fleer) was issued in two series. The first series ...tains 175 cards while the second has 151 cards ...luding the late addition of Michael Jordan as card ...6). Cards were distributed in 10-card "hardpacks" ...turing a two-piece protective design wrapper), each ...a suggested retail price of $4.00. The cards have a ...yester laminate protective coating on both sides and ...made with extra thick 30 point stock. The front has ...color action photos blended. The back has one full ...or action photo with the player's statistics laid on ... Both sides have the player's name stamped in gold ...along with his team. The cards are numbered on ...back and checklisted below alphabetically within ...ns. The first series includes a "Dream Team II" ...set (159-172) commemorating the USA's team ...y at the 1994 World Championships in Toronto. Rookie Cards of note in this set include Grant Hill, Juwan Howard, Eddie Jones, Jason Kidd, and Glenn Robinson.

COMPLETE SET (326) 25.00 50.00
COMPLETE SERIES 1 (175) 7.50 15.00
COMPLETE SERIES 2 (151) 15.00 30.00
1 Stacey Augmon .25 .60
2 Mookie Blaylock .20 .50
3 Craig Ehlo .20 .50
4 Jon Koncak .20 .50
5 Andrew Lang .20 .50
6 Dee Brown .20 .50
7 Sherman Douglas .20 .50
8 Acie Earl .20 .50
9 Rick Fox .20 .50
10 Kevin Gamble .20 .50
11 Xavier McDaniel .20 .50
12 Dino Radja .25 .60
13 Tony Bennett .20 .50
14 Dell Curry .20 .50
15 Kenny Gattison .20 .50
16 Hersey Hawkins .20 .50
17 Larry Johnson .30 .75
18 Alonzo Mourning .40 1.00
19 David Wingate .20 .50
20 B.J. Armstrong .20 .50
21 Steve Kerr .25 .60
22 Toni Kukoc .40 1.00
23 Pete Myers .20 .50
24 Scottie Pippen .60 1.50
25 Bill Wennington .20 .50
26 Terrell Brandon .30 .75
27 Brad Daugherty .25 .60
28 Tyrone Hill .20 .50
29 Bobby Phills .20 .50
30 Mark Price .30 .75
31 Gerald Wilkins .20 .50
32 John Williams .20 .50
33 Lucious Harris .20 .50
34 Jim Jackson .20 .50
35 Jamal Mashburn .30 .75
36 Sean Rooks .20 .50
37 Doug Smith .20 .50
38 Mahmoud Abdul-Rauf .20 .50
39 LaPhonso Ellis .20 .50
40 Dikembe Mutombo .30 .75
41 Robert Pack .20 .50
42 Rodney Rogers .20 .50
43 Brian Williams .20 .50
44 Reggie Williams .20 .50
45 Joe Dumars .30 .75
46 Allan Houston .30 .75
47 Lindsey Hunter .20 .50
48 Terry Mills .20 .50
49 Victor Alexander .20 .50
50 Chris Gatling .20 .50
51 Billy Owens .20 .50
52 Latrell Sprewell .40 1.00
53 Chris Webber .50 1.25
54 Sam Cassell .30 .75
55 Carl Herrera .20 .50
56 Robert Horry .20 .50
57 Hakeem Olajuwon .40 1.00
58 Kenny Smith .25 .60
59 Otis Thorpe .20 .50
60 Antonio Davis .20 .50
61 Dale Davis .20 .50
62 Reggie Miller .40 1.00
63 Byron Scott .25 .60
64 Rik Smits .25 .60
65 Haywoode Workman .20 .50
66 Terry Dehere .20 .50
67 Harold Ellis .20 .50
68 Gary Grant .20 .50
69 Elmore Spencer .20 .50
70 Loy Vaught .20 .50
71 Elden Campbell .20 .50
72 Doug Christie .30 .75
73 Vlade Divac .30 .75
74 George Lynch .20 .50
75 Anthony Peeler .20 .50
76 Nick Van Exel .30 .75
77 James Worthy .40 1.00
78 Bimbo Coles .20 .50
79 Harold Miner .20 .50
80 John Salley .20 .50
81 Rony Seikaly .25 .60
82 Steve Smith .25 .60
83 Vin Baker .30 .75
84 Jon Barry .20 .50
85 Todd Day .20 .50
86 Lee Mayberry .20 .50
87 Eric Murdock .20 .50
88 Mike Brown .20 .50
89 Christian Laettner .25 .60
90 Isaiah Rider .30 .75
91 Doug West .20 .50
92 Micheal Williams .20 .50
93 Kenny Anderson .25 .60
94 Benoit Benjamin .20 .50
95 P.J. Brown .20 .50
96 Derrick Coleman .25 .60
97 Kevin Edwards .20 .50
98 Hubert Davis .20 .50
99 Patrick Ewing .40 1.00
100 Derek Harper .25 .60
101 Anthony Mason .20 .50
102 Charles Oakley .25 .60
103 Charles Smith .20 .50
104 John Starks .25 .60
105 Nick Anderson .20 .50
106 Anfernee Hardaway .50 1.25
107 Shaquille O'Neal .75 2.00
108 Dennis Scott .20 .50
109 Jeff Turner .20 .50
110 Dana Barros .20 .50
111 Shawn Bradley .20 .50
112 Jeff Malone .20 .50
113 Tim Perry .20 .50
114 Clarence Weatherspoon .20 .50
115 Danny Ainge .30 .75
116 Charles Barkley .50 1.25
117 A.C. Green .30 .75
118 Kevin Johnson .30 .75
119 Dan Majerle .30 .75
120 Clyde Drexler .40 1.00
121 Harvey Grant .20 .50
122 Jerome Kersey .20 .50
123 Clifford Robinson .30 .75
124 Rod Strickland .30 .75
125 Buck Williams .20 .50
126 Randy Brown .20 .50
127 Olden Polynice .20 .50
128 Mitch Richmond .30 .75
129 Lionel Simmons .20 .50
130 Spud Webb .30 .75
131 Walt Williams .20 .50
132 Willie Anderson .20 .50
133 Vinny Del Negro .20 .50
134 Sean Elliott .30 .75
135 Avery Johnson .25 .60
136 J.R. Reid .20 .50
137 David Robinson .50 1.25
138 Dennis Rodman .60 1.50
139 Kendall Gill .20 .50
140 Ervin Johnson .20 .50
141 Shawn Kemp .30 .75
142 Nate McMillan .20 .50
143 Gary Payton .30 .75
144 Sam Perkins .20 .50
145 David Benoit .20 .50
146 Jeff Hornacek .25 .60
147 Jay Humphries .20 .50
148 Karl Malone .40 1.00
149 Bryon Russell .20 .50
150 Felton Spencer .20 .50
151 John Stockton .40 1.00
152 Rex Chapman .20 .50
153 Calbert Cheaney .20 .50
154 Tom Gugliotta .20 .50
155 Don MacLean .20 .50
156 Gheorghe Muresan .20 .50
157 Doug Overton .20 .50
158 Brent Price .20 .50
159 Derrick Coleman USA .25 .60
160 Joe Dumars USA .30 .75
161 Tim Hardaway USA .30 .75
162 Kevin Johnson USA .30 .75
163 Larry Johnson USA .30 .75
164 Shawn Kemp USA .30 .75
165 Dan Majerle USA .30 .75
166 Reggie Miller USA .40 1.00
167 Alonzo Mourning USA .40 1.00
168 Shaquille O'Neal USA .75 2.00
169 Mark Price USA .30 .75
170 Steve Smith USA .25 .60
171 Isiah Thomas USA .30 .75
172 Dominique Wilkins USA .40 1.00
173 Checklist .20 .50
174 Checklist .20 .50
175 Checklist .20 .50
176 Tyrone Corbin .20 .50
177 Grant Long .20 .50
178 Ken Norman .20 .50
179 Steve Smith .25 .60
180 Blue Edwards .20 .50
181 Pervis Ellison .20 .50
182 Greg Minor RC .20 .50
183 Eric Montross RC .30 .75
184 Derek Strong .20 .50
185 David Wesley .20 .50
186 Dominique Wilkins .40 1.00
187 Michael Adams .20 .50
188 Muggsy Bogues .25 .60
189 Scott Burrell .20 .50
190 Darrin Hancock RC .30 .75
191 Robert Parish .30 .75
192 Jud Buechler .20 .50
193 Ron Harper .25 .60
194 Larry Krystkowiak .20 .50
195 Will Perdue .20 .50
196 Dickey Simpkins RC .30 .75
197 Michael Cage .20 .50
198 Tony Campbell .20 .50
199 Danny Ferry .20 .50
200 Chris Mills .20 .50
201 Popeye Jones .20 .50
202 Jason Kidd RC 1.50 4.00
203 Roy Tarpley .20 .50
204 Lorenzo Williams .20 .50
205 Dale Ellis .20 .50
206 Tom Hammonds .20 .50
207 Jalen Rose RC .75 2.00
208 Reggie Slater .20 .50
209 Bryant Stith .20 .50
210 Rafael Addison .20 .50
211 Bill Curley RC .30 .75
212 Johnny Dawkins .20 .50
213 Grant Hill RC 1.50 4.00
214 Mark Macon .20 .50
215 Oliver Miller .20 .50
216 Ivano Newbill .20 .50
217 Mark West .20 .50
218 Tom Gugliotta .20 .50
219 Tim Hardaway .30 .75
220 Keith Jennings .20 .50
221 Dwayne Morton .20 .50
222 Chris Mullin .30 .75
223 Ricky Pierce .20 .50
224 Carlos Rogers RC .30 .75
225 Clifford Rozier RC .30 .75
226 Rony Seikaly .25 .60
227 Tim Breaux .20 .50
228 Scott Brooks .20 .50
229 Mario Elie .20 .50
230 Vernon Maxwell .20 .50
231 Zan Tabak .20 .50
232 Mark Jackson .20 .50
233 Derrick McKey .20 .50
234 Tony Massenburg .20 .50
235 Lamond Murray RC .30 .75
236 Bo Outlaw .20 .50
237 Eric Piatkowski RC .40 1.00
238 Pooh Richardson .20 .50
239 Malik Sealy .20 .50
240 Cedric Ceballos .20 .50
241 Eddie Jones RC 1.00 2.50
242 Anthony Miller .30 .75
243 Tony Smith .20 .50
244 Sedale Threatt .20 .50
245 Ledell Eackles .20 .50
246 Kevin Gamble .20 .50
247 Matt Geiger .20 .50
248 Brad Lohaus .20 .50
249 Billy Owens .20 .50
250 Khalid Reeves RC .30 .75
251 Glen Rice .30 .75
252 Kevin Willis .20 .50
253 Marty Conlon .20 .50
254 Eric Mobley RC .20 .50
255 Johnny Newman .20 .50
256 Ed Pinckney .20 .50
257 Glenn Robinson RC .60 1.50
258 Pat Durham .20 .50
259 Howard Eisley .30 .75
260 Winston Garland .20 .50
261 Stacey King .20 .50
262 Donyell Marshall RC .30 .75
263 Sean Rooks .20 .50
264 Chris Smith .20 .50
265 Chris Childs RC .30 .75
266 Sleepy Floyd .20 .50
267 Armon Gilliam .20 .50
268 Sean Higgins .20 .50
269 Rex Walters .20 .50
270 Greg Anthony .20 .50
271 Charlie Ward RC .30 .75
272 Herb Williams .20 .50
273 Monty Williams RC .30 .75
274 Anthony Avent .20 .50
275 Anthony Bowie .20 .50
276 Horace Grant .25 .60
277 Donald Royal .20 .50
278 Brian Shaw .20 .50
279 Brooks Thompson RC .30 .75
280 Derrick Alston RC .30 .75
281 Willie Burton .20 .50
282 Greg Graham .20 .50
283 B.J. Tyler RC .30 .75
284 Scott Williams .20 .50
285 Sharone Wright RC .30 .75
286 Joe Kleine .20 .50
287 Danny Manning .25 .60
288 Elliot Perry .20 .50
289 Wesley Person RC .30 .75
290 Trevor Ruffin RC .30 .75
291 Wayman Tisdale .20 .50
292 Mark Bryant .20 .50
293 Chris Dudley .20 .50
294 Aaron McKie RC .50 1.25
295 Tracy Murray .20 .50
296 Terry Porter .20 .50
297 James Robinson .20 .50
298 Alaa Abdelnaby .20 .50
299 Duane Causwell .20 .50
300 Brian Grant RC .50 1.25
301 Bobby Hurley .20 .50
302 Michael Smith RC .30 .75
303 Terry Cummings .20 .50
304 Moses Malone .40 1.00
305 Julius Nwosu .20 .50
306 Chuck Person .25 .60
307 Doc Rivers .25 .60
308 Vincent Askew .20 .50
309 Sarunas Marciulionis .20 .50
310 Detlef Schrempf .30 .75
311 Dontonio Wingfield .30 .75
312 Antoine Carr .20 .50
313 Tom Chambers .20 .50
314 John Crotty .20 .50
315 Adam Keefe .20 .50
316 Jamie Watson RC .30 .75
317 Mitchell Butler .20 .50
318 Kevin Duckworth .20 .50
319 Juwan Howard RC .50 1.25
320 Jim McIlvaine RC .30 .75
321 Scott Skiles .30 .75
322 Anthony Tucker RC .30 .75
323 Chris Webber .50 1.25
324 Checklist .20 .50
325 Checklist .20 .50
326 Michael Jordan 4.00 10.00

1994-95 Flair Center Spotlight

Randomly inserted at a rate of one in every 25 first series packs, cards from this 6-card set features dominant centers. The fronts have a 100% etched-foil design with a full color action photo with three shadows of him in red, green and blue. The back also has a color photo with the red, green and blue shadowing on a white background along with player information. The cards are numbered on the back as "X of 6" and are sequenced in alphabetical order.

COMPLETE SET (6) 10.00 25.00
1 Patrick Ewing 2.00 5.00
2 Alonzo Mourning 2.00 5.00
3 Hakeem Olajuwon 2.00 5.00
4 Shaquille O'Neal 6.00 15.00
5 David Robinson 2.50 6.00
6 Chris Webber 4.00 10.00

1994-95 Flair Hot Numbers

Randomly inserted into first series packs at a rate of one in six, cards from this 20-card standard-size set feature a selection of players who consistently produce big statistics. The player's top statistical numbers are shown on the front of the card without identifying which category. While some numbers are obvious, like the player's points per game, other statistics are not, like steals and blocks, particularly for multi-talented players. The fronts also have full-color action photos with the team's colors used as the background along with the words "Hot Numbers". The backs also have a color picture with information on what type of player he is. The cards are numbered on the back as "X of 20" and are sequenced in alphabetical order.

COMPLETE SET (20) 15.00 40.00
1 Vin Baker 1.00 2.50
2 Sam Cassell 1.00 2.50
3 Patrick Ewing 1.25 3.00
4 Anfernee Hardaway 1.50 4.00
5 Robert Horry 1.00 2.50
6 Shawn Kemp 1.00 2.50
7 Toni Kukoc 1.25 3.00
8 Jamal Mashburn 1.00 2.50
9 Reggie Miller 1.25 3.00
10 Dikembe Mutombo 1.00 2.50
11 Hakeem Olajuwon 1.25 3.00
12 Shaquille O'Neal 2.50 6.00
13 Scottie Pippen 2.00 5.00
14 Isaiah Rider 1.00 2.50
15 David Robinson 1.50 4.00
16 Latrell Sprewell 1.25 3.00
17 John Starks .75 2.00
18 John Stockton 1.25 3.00
19 Nick Van Exel 1.00 2.50
20 Chris Webber 1.50 4.00

1994-95 Flair Playmakers

Randomly inserted into second series packs at a rate of one in four, cards from this 10-card standard-size set feature a selection of the best assist men in the NBA. The fronts have a full color action photo with a hardwood floor in the background. The back also has a color photo with player information set against a hardwood floor. The cards are numbered on the back as "X of 10" and are sequenced in alphabetical order.

COMPLETE SET (10) 3.00 8.00
1 Kenny Anderson .40 1.00
2 Mookie Blaylock .30 .75
3 Sam Cassell .50 1.25
4 Anfernee Hardaway .75 2.00
5 Robert Pack .30 .75
6 Scottie Pippen 1.00 2.50
7 Mark Price .50 1.25
8 Mitch Richmond .50 1.25
9 John Stockton .60 1.50
10 Nick Van Exel .50 1.25

1994-95 Flair Rejectors

Randomly inserted into second series packs at a rate of one in 25, cards from this six-card standard-size set feature a selection of top shot blockers in basketball. The fronts are 100% etched foil that have a full color action photo of the player. The background is three hands in red, green and blue seemingly up to reject a shot. The back also has a player photo along with information on him, such as his blocks per game. The background is nearly identical to the background on the front. The cards are numbered on the back as "X of 6" and are sequenced in alphabetical order.

COMPLETE SET (6) 12.00 30.00
1 Patrick Ewing 2.50 6.00
2 Alonzo Mourning 2.50 6.00
3 Dikembe Mutombo 2.00 5.00
4 Hakeem Olajuwon 2.50 6.00
5 Shaquille O'Neal 8.00 20.00
6 David Robinson 3.00 8.00

1994-95 Flair Scoring Power

Randomly inserted into first series packs at a rate of one in eight, cards from this 20-card standard-size set feature a selection of perennial NBA scoring leaders. The fronts emphasize the words scoring power as they are the size of the card laid out horizontally against a black background. There is a player photo in front of the words and another inside. The back also says "Scoring Power" across the entire card horizontally. There is also a player photo with information on him, namely about his scoring. The cards are numbered on the back as "X of 10" and are sequenced in alphabetical order.

COMPLETE SET (10) 8.00 20.00
1 Charles Barkley 1.50 4.00
2 Patrick Ewing 1.25 3.00
3 Karl Malone 1.25 3.00
4 Hakeem Olajuwon 1.25 3.00
5 Shaquille O'Neal 3.00 8.00
6 Scottie Pippen 2.00 5.00
7 Mitch Richmond 1.00 2.50
8 David Robinson 1.50 4.00
9 Latrell Sprewell 1.00 2.50
10 Dominique Wilkins 1.25 3.00

1994-95 Flair Wave of the Future

Randmly inserted into second series packs at a rate of one in seven, cards from this 10-card standard-size set feature a selection of top rookies from the 1994-95 season. Card fronts are laid out horizontally with three color photos of the player. The one in the middle has yellow glow surrounding it and the picture on the left is the same as the middle. The one on the left is a head shot of the color photo used on the back of the card. The back has player information including some college statistics. Both sides of the card have a wave in the background in the team's colors. The cards are numbered on the back as "X of 10" and are sequenced in alphabetical order.

COMPLETE SET (10) 8.00 20.00
1 Brian Grant 1.00 2.50
2 Grant Hill 3.00 8.00
3 Juwan Howard 1.00 2.50
4 Eddie Jones 2.00 5.00
5 Jason Kidd 3.00 8.00
6 Donyell Marshall .60 1.50
7 Eric Montross .60 1.50
8 Lamond Murray .60 1.50
9 Wesley Person .60 1.50
10 Glenn Robinson 1.25 3.00

1995-96 Flair

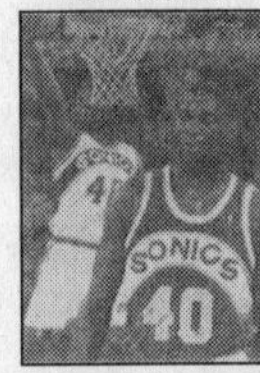

These 250-standard size cards comprise Fleer's premium1995-96 Flair set which was issued in two separate series of 150 and 100 cards respectively. Cards were issued in 9-card "hardpacks" (featuring a two-piece protective design wrapper) with a suggested retail price of $4.99. Player selection was restricted to recognized starters, top rookies and top players off the bench. Card fronts were upgraded from the previous year, each featuring 100% etched foil designs. Like the previous year, each card was printed on 30-point stock, giving the card twice the thickness of regular issue cards. First and second series cards are numbered alphabetically by team. Two subsets are included in the set: Rookies (199-228) and Style (229-248). Noteworthy Rookie Cards in this set include Michael Finley, Kevin Garnett, Antonio McDyess, Joe Smith, Jerry Stackhouse and Damon Stoudamire.

COMPLETE SET (250) 30.00 80.00
COMPLETE SERIES 1 (150) 15.00 40.00
COMPLETE SERIES 2 (100) 15.00 40.00
1 Stacey Augmon .40 1.00
2 Mookie Blaylock .30 .75
3 Grant Long .30 .75
4 Steve Smith .40 1.00
5 Dee Brown .30 .75
6 Sherman Douglas .30 .75
7 Eric Montross .30 .75
8 Dino Radja .40 1.00
9 David Wesley .30 .75
10 Muggsy Bogues .40 1.00
11 Scott Burrell .30 .75
12 Dell Curry .30 .75
13 Larry Johnson .50 1.25
14 Alonzo Mourning .60 1.50
15 Michael Jordan 4.00 10.00
16 Steve Kerr .40 1.00
17 Toni Kukoc .50 1.25
18 Scottie Pippen .75 2.00
19 Terrell Brandon .40 1.00
20 Tyrone Hill .30 .75
21 Chris Mills .30 .75
22 Bobby Phills .30 .75
23 Mark Price .50 1.25
24 John Williams .30 .75
25 Jim Jackson .30 .75
26 Popeye Jones .30 .75
27 Jason Kidd .75 2.00
28 Jamal Mashburn .50 1.25
29 Lorenzo Williams .30 .75
30 Mahmoud Abdul-Rauf .30 .75
31 Dikembe Mutombo .50 1.25
32 Robert Pack .30 .75
33 Jalen Rose .60 1.50
34 Bryant Stith .30 .75
35 Reggie Williams .30 .75
36 Joe Dumars .50 1.25
37 Grant Hill .75 2.00
38 Allan Houston .40 1.00
39 Lindsey Hunter .30 .75
40 Terry Mills .30 .75
41 Chris Gatling .30 .75
42 Tim Hardaway .50 1.25
43 Donyell Marshall .30 .75
44 Chris Mullin .50 1.25
45 Carlos Rogers .30 .75
46 Clifford Rozier .30 .75
47 Latrell Sprewell .50 1.25
48 Sam Cassell .50 1.25
49 Clyde Drexler .60 1.50
50 Mario Elie .30 .75
51 Robert Horry .40 1.00
52 Hakeem Olajuwon .60 1.50
53 Kenny Smith .30 .75
54 Antonio Davis .30 .75
55 Dale Davis .30 .75
56 Mark Jackson .50 1.25
57 Derrick McKey .30 .75
58 Reggie Miller .60 1.50
59 Rik Smits .40 1.00
60 Lamond Murray .30 .75
61 Pooh Richardson .30 .75
62 Malik Sealy .30 .75
63 Loy Vaught .30 .75
64 Elden Campbell .30 .75
65 Cedric Ceballos .30 .75
66 Vlade Divac .50 1.25
67 Eddie Jones .60 1.50
68 Nick Van Exel .50 1.25
69 Bimbo Coles .30 .75
70 Billy Owens .30 .75
71 Khalid Reeves .30 .75
72 Glen Rice .50 1.25
73 Kevin Willis .30 .75
74 Vin Baker .40 1.00
75 Todd Day .30 .75
76 Eric Murdock .30 .75
77 Glenn Robinson .50 1.25
78 Tom Gugliotta .30 .75
79 Christian Laettner .40 1.00
80 Isaiah Rider .50 1.25
81 Doug West .30 .75
82 Kenny Anderson .40 1.00
83 P.J. Brown .30 .75
84 Derrick Coleman .40 1.00
85 Armon Gilliam .30 .75
86 Chris Morris .30 .75
87 Hubert Davis .30 .75
88 Patrick Ewing .60 1.50
89 Derek Harper .40 1.00
90 Anthony Mason .40 1.00
91 Charles Oakley .40 1.00
92 Charles Smith .30 .75
93 John Starks .40 1.00
94 Nick Anderson .30 .75
95 Horace Grant .40 1.00
96 Anfernee Hardaway .75 2.00
97 Shaquille O'Neal 1.25 3.00
98 Dennis Scott .30 .75
99 Brian Shaw .30 .75
100 Dana Barros .30 .75
101 Shawn Bradley .30 .75
102 Clarence Weatherspoon .30 .75
103 Sharone Wright .30 .75
104 Charles Barkley .75 2.00
105 A.C. Green .50 1.25
106 Kevin Johnson .50 1.25
107 Dan Majerle .50 1.25
108 Danny Manning .40 1.00
109 Elliot Perry .30 .75
110 Wesley Person .30 .75
111 Terry Porter .30 .75
112 Clifford Robinson .30 .75
113 Rod Strickland .30 .75
114 Otis Thorpe .30 .75
115 Buck Williams .30 .75
116 Brian Grant .40 1.00
117 Bobby Hurley .50 1.25
118 Olden Polynice .30 .75
119 Mitch Richmond .50 1.25
120 Walt Williams .30 .75
121 Vinny Del Negro .30 .75
122 Sean Elliott .50 1.25
123 Avery Johnson .40 1.00
124 David Robinson .75 2.00
125 Dennis Rodman 1.00 2.50
126 Shawn Kemp .50 1.25
127 Nate McMillan .30 .75
128 Gary Payton .50 1.25
129 Sam Perkins .30 .75
130 Detlef Schrempf .50 1.25
131 B.J. Armstrong .30 .75
132 Jerome Kersey .30 .75
133 Oliver Miller .30 .75
134 John Salley .30 .75
135 David Benoit .30 .75
136 Antoine Carr .30 .75
137 Jeff Hornacek .40 1.00
138 Karl Malone .60 1.50
139 John Stockton .60 1.50
140 Greg Anthony .30 .75
141 Benoit Benjamin .30 .75
142 Blue Edwards .30 .75
143 Byron Scott .40 1.00
144 Calbert Cheaney .30 .75
145 Juwan Howard .50 1.25
146 Gheorghe Muresan .30 .75
147 Scott Skiles .30 .75
148 Chris Webber .60 1.50
149 Checklist .25 .60
150 Checklist .25 .60
151 Stacey Augmon .40 1.00
152 Mookie Blaylock .30 .75
153 Andrew Lang .30 .75
154 Steve Smith .40 1.00
155 Dana Barros .30 .75
156 Rick Fox .30 .75
157 Kendall Gill .30 .75
158 Khalid Reeves .30 .75
159 Glen Rice .50 1.25
160 Dennis Rodman 1.00 2.50
161 Dan Majerle .50 1.25
162 Tony Dumas .30 .75
163 Dale Ellis .30 .75
164 Otis Thorpe .30 .75
165 Rony Seikaly .40 1.00
166 Sam Cassell .50 1.25
167 Clyde Drexler .60 1.50
168 Robert Horry .40 1.00
169 Hakeem Olajuwon .60 1.50
170 Ricky Pierce .30 .75
171 Rodney Rogers .30 .75
172 Brian Williams .30 .75
173 Magic Johnson 1.25 3.00
174 Alonzo Mourning .60 1.50
175 Lee Mayberry .30 .75
176 Terry Porter .30 .75
177 Shawn Bradley .30 .75
178 Jayson Williams .30 .75
179 Gary Grant .30 .75
180 Jon Koncak .30 .75
181 Derrick Coleman .40 1.00
182 Vernon Maxwell .30 .75
183 John Williams .30 .75
184 Aaron McKie .30 .75
185 Michael Smith .30 .75
186 Chuck Person .40 1.00
187 Hersey Hawkins .30 .75
188 Shawn Kemp .50 1.25
189 Gary Payton .50 1.25
190 Detlef Schrempf .50 1.25
191 Chris Morris .30 .75
192 Robert Pack .30 .75
193 Willie Anderson EXP .15 .40
194 Oliver Miller EXP .15 .40
195 Alvin Robertson EXP .15 .40
196 Greg Anthony EXP .15 .40
197 Blue Edwards EXP .15 .40
198 Byron Scott EXP .20 .50
199 Cory Alexander RC .40 1.00
200 Brent Barry RC .60 1.50
201 Travis Best RC .40 1.00
202 Jason Caffey RC .40 1.00
203 Sasha Danilovic RC .40 1.00
204 Tyus Edney RC .40 1.00
205 Michael Finley RC 1.25 3.00
206 Kevin Garnett RC 3.00 8.00
207 Alan Henderson RC .40 1.00
208 Antonio McDyess RC 1.00 2.50
209 Loren Meyer RC .40 1.00
210 Lawrence Moten RC .40 1.00
211 Ed O'Bannon RC .40 1.00
212 Greg Ostertag RC .40 1.00
213 Cherokee Parks RC .40 1.00
214 Theo Ratliff RC .60 1.50
215 Bryant Reeves RC .40 1.00
216 Shawn Respert RC .40 1.00
217 Arvydas Sabonis RC .75 2.00
218 Joe Smith RC .75 2.00
219 Jerry Stackhouse RC 1.25 3.00
220 Damon Stoudamire RC 1.00 2.50
221 Bob Sura RC .40 1.00
222 Kurt Thomas RC .40 1.00
223 Gary Trent RC .40 1.00
224 David Vaughn RC .40 1.00
225 Rasheed Wallace RC 1.25 3.00
226 Eric Williams RC .40 1.00
227 Corliss Williamson RC .40 1.00
228 George Zidek RC .40 1.00
229 Vin Baker STY .20 .50
230 Charles Barkley STY .40 1.00
231 Patrick Ewing STY .30 .75
232 Anfernee Hardaway STY .40 1.00
233 Grant Hill STY .40 1.00

234 Larry Johnson STY .25 .60
235 Michael Jordan STY 2.00 5.00
236 Jason Kidd STY .40 1.00
237 Karl Malone STY .30 .75
238 Jamal Mashburn STY .25 .60
239 Reggie Miller STY .30 .75
240 Shaquille O'Neal STY .60 1.50
241 Scottie Pippen STY .40 1.00
242 Mitch Richmond STY .25 .60
243 Clifford Robinson STY .15 .40
244 David Robinson STY .40 1.00
245 Glenn Robinson STY .25 .60
246 John Stockton STY .30 .75
247 Nick Van Exel STY .25 .60
248 Chris Webber STY .30 .75
249 Checklist .25 .60
250 Checklist .25 .60

1995-96 Flair Anticipation

Randomly inserted in second series packs at a rate of one in 36, cards from this ten card standard-size set feature a collection of fan favorites. Borderless fronts have a full-color action raised cutouts and two ghosted images of the same shot in the player's team colors. Backs have a close-up color shot and a player profile. The set is sequenced in alphabetical order.

COMPLETE SET (10) 40.00 100.00
1 Grant Hill 5.00 12.00
2 Michael Jordan 20.00 50.00
3 Shawn Kemp 3.00 8.00
4 Jason Kidd 5.00 12.00
5 Alonzo Mourning 4.00 10.00
6 Hakeem Olajuwon 4.00 10.00
7 Shaquille O'Neal 10.00 25.00
8 Glenn Robinson 3.00 8.00
9 Joe Smith 3.00 8.00
10 Jerry Stackhouse 5.00 12.00

1995-96 Flair Center Spotlight

Randomly inserted in first series packs at a rate of one in 18, cards from this 6-card standard-size set feature a selection of the game's dominant centers. This was the second year in a row Flair included a Center Spotlight insert within their first series product. Each card is printed on clear plastic, with a full color action photo layered on top of a circular designed background. Backs are numbered on the left in gold foil and the player's blue silhouette serves as a background for biography and career highlights which are printed in white. The set is sequenced in alphabetical order.

COMPLETE SET (6) 8.00 20.00
1 Vlade Divac 1.50 4.00
2 Patrick Ewing 2.00 5.00
3 Alonzo Mourning 2.00 5.00
4 Hakeem Olajuwon 2.00 5.00
5 Shaquille O'Neal 4.00 10.00
6 David Robinson 2.50 6.00

1995-96 Flair Class of '95

Seeded in first series packs at the same rate as regular issue cards, these 15-cards were added to the first series Flair product just prior to release. Each card features one of the top rookies from the 1995 NBA draft in their new pro uniforms. Full color, cutout player action shots are placed against a glowing orange basketball backdrop. The set is sequenced in alphabetical order.

COMPLETE SET (15) 8.00 20.00
R1 Brent Barry .60 1.50
R2 Kevin Garnett 3.00 8.00
R3 Antonio McDyess 1.00 2.50
R4 Ed O'Bannon .40 1.00
R5 Cherokee Parks .40 1.00
R6 Bryant Reeves .40 1.00
R7 Shawn Respert .40 1.00
R8 Joe Smith .75 2.00
R9 Jerry Stackhouse 1.25 3.00
R10 Damon Stoudamire 1.00 2.50
R11 Kurt Thomas .40 1.00
R12 Gary Trent .40 1.00
R13 Rasheed Wallace 1.25 3.00
R14 Eric Williams .40 1.00
R15 Corliss Williamson .40 1.00

1995-96 Flair Hot Numbers

Randomly inserted in first series packs at rate of one in 36, cards from this 15-card standard-size set showcase the game's top players. Each card is given a three-dimensional effect by the addition of a special lenticular coating (a ribbed plastic material) on the front. The full color player photos are placed against a swirling background of numbers. The backs continue with the numbers motif that serve as a background for the full-color player cutout. Player's name and short biography are printed in white. The set is sequenced in alphabetical order.

COMPLETE SET (15) 200.00 350.00
1 Charles Barkley 12.00 30.00
2 Grant Hill 12.00 30.00
3 Eddie Jones 12.50 30.00
4 Michael Jordan 80.00 160.00
5 Shawn Kemp 10.00 25.00
6 Jason Kidd 12.00 30.00
7 Karl Malone 10.00 25.00
8 Alonzo Mourning 10.00 25.00
9 Dikembe Mutombo 8.00 20.00
10 Hakeem Olajuwon 10.00 25.00
11 Shaquille O'Neal 20.00 50.00
12 Glenn Robinson 8.00 20.00
13 Dennis Rodman 15.00 40.00
14 Latrell Sprewell 10.00 25.00
15 Chris Webber 10.00 25.00

1995-96 Flair New Heights

Randomly inserted in second series hobby packs only at a rate of one in 18, cards from this 10-card standard-size set feature some of the more popular players in the hobby. Borderless fronts have a full-color action cutout with a ghosted image trailing behind. Backs have player profile and biographies. The set is sequenced in alphabetical order.

COMPLETE SET (10) 20.00 50.00
1 Anfernee Hardaway 2.50 6.00
2 Grant Hill 2.50 6.00
3 Larry Johnson 1.50 4.00
4 Michael Jordan 12.00 30.00
5 Shawn Kemp 1.50 4.00
6 Karl Malone 2.00 5.00
7 Hakeem Olajuwon 2.00 5.00
8 David Robinson 2.50 6.00
9 Glenn Robinson 1.50 4.00
10 Chris Webber 2.00 5.00

1995-96 Flair Perimeter Power

Randomly inserted in first series packs at a rate of one in 12, cards from this 15-card set feature players that dominate play from the perimeter. Full-bleed team-color backgrounds include a player cutout with silver foil printing on the front. Backs are printed on a white background with another full-color action player shot.

COMPLETE SET (15) 6.00 15.00
1 Dana Barros .50 1.25
2 Clyde Drexler 1.00 2.50
3 Anfernee Hardaway 1.25 3.00
4 Tim Hardaway .75 2.00
5 Dan Majerle .75 2.00
6 Jamal Mashburn .75 2.00
7 Reggie Miller 1.00 2.50
8 Gary Payton .75 2.00
9 Scottie Pippen 1.25 3.00
10 Glen Rice .75 2.00
11 Mitch Richmond .75 2.00
12 Steve Smith .60 1.50
13 John Starks .60 1.50
14 John Stockton 1.00 2.50
15 Nick Van Exel .75 2.00

1995-96 Flair Play Makers

Randomly inserted in second series packs at a rate of one in 54 packs, this set of ten standard-size cards features a selection of some of the league's top playmakers. Fronts are printed in a 3-D lenticular format and feature the player in a full-color action shot. The background is a three-color chalkboard diagram. The diagram background continues on the back and a player profile appears in a screened box next to a full-color action player cutout. The set is sequenced in alphabetical order.

COMPLETE SET (10) 50.00 100.00
1 Clyde Drexler 8.00 20.00
2 Anfernee Hardaway 10.00 25.00
3 Jamal Mashburn 6.00 15.00
4 Reggie Miller 8.00 20.00
5 Gary Payton 6.00 15.00
6 Scottie Pippen 10.00 25.00
7 Mitch Richmond 6.00 15.00
8 David Robinson 10.00 25.00
9 Jerry Stackhouse 10.00 25.00
10 Nick Van Exel 6.00 15.00

1995-96 Flair Stackhouse's Scrapbook

Randomly inserted into one in every 24 second series packs, these two cards continue the cross-brand set of Fleer spokesperson Jerry Stackhouse. The two Flair cards represent the third of a four series, eight card set. Card fronts feature a a full-color action shot framed by a ghosted white border.

COMPLETE SET (2) 3.00 8.00
COMMON CARD (S5-S6) 2.00 5.00

1995-96 Flair Wave of the Future

The 10 cards in this standard-size set were randomly inserted at a rate of one in 12 second series packs and feature rookie NBA players with potential for greatness. A full-color player action cutout appears on the front with a watercolor backgound painted in a wave pattern. Backs continue with the wave pattern background and have another full-color action cutout. The cards are sequenced in alphabetical order.

COMPLETE SET (10) 8.00 20.00
1 Tyus Edney .50 1.25
2 Michael Finley 1.50 4.00
3 Kevin Garnett 4.00 10.00
4 Antonio McDyess 1.25 3.00
5 Ed O'Bannon .50 1.25
6 Arvydas Sabonis 1.00 2.50
7 Joe Smith 1.00 2.50
8 Jerry Stackhouse 1.50 4.00
9 Damon Stoudamire 1.25 3.00
10 Rasheed Wallace 1.50 4.00

1996-97 Flair Showcase Row 2

The 1996-97 Flair Showcase set was issued in one series totalling 270 cards and was deemed Hobby only for the first time. Each box contained 24 cards per box, five cards per pack with a suggested retail price of $4.99. The set does contain 270 cards, but is essentially a 90-card set with each player having three different front themes: Row 2 (Style), Row 1 (Grace) and Row 0 (Showcase). Each card also contains the following back themes: Showtime, Show Stoppers and Showpiece. By combining the two different themes, collectors can determine the different scarcity levels. For Row 2, or Style, using Style and Showtime (cards 1-30), the odds are 1.5 to one. Using Style and Showpiece (cards 31-60), the odds are one in 2. Using Style and Show Stoppers (cards 61-90), the odds are one in 1.5. A three-card promo strip of Jerry Stackhouse was released and is priced at the end of the set.

COMPLETE SET (90) 25.00 60.00
1 Anfernee Hardaway .75 2.00
2 Mitch Richmond .50 1.25
3 Allen Iverson RC 2.50 6.00
4 Charles Barkley .75 2.00
5 Juwan Howard .40 1.00
6 David Robinson .75 2.00
7 Gary Payton .50 1.25
8 Kerry Kittles RC .50 1.25
9 Dennis Rodman 1.00 2.50
10 Shaquille O'Neal 1.25 3.00
11 Stephon Marbury RC 1.25 3.00
12 John Stockton .60 1.50
13 Glenn Robinson .50 1.25
14 Hakeem Olajuwon .60 1.50
15 Jason Kidd .75 2.00
16 Jerry Stackhouse .60 1.50
17 Joe Smith .40 1.00
18 Reggie Miller .60 1.50
19 Grant Hill .75 2.00
20 Damon Stoudamire .50 1.25
21 Kevin Garnett 1.25 3.00
22 Clyde Drexler .60 1.50
23 Michael Jordan 4.00 10.00
24 Antonio McDyess .50 1.25
25 Chris Webber .60 1.50
26 Antoine Walker RC 1.00 2.50
27 Scottie Pippen .75 2.00
28 Karl Malone .60 1.50
29 Shareef Abdur-Rahim RC 1.00 2.50
30 Shawn Kemp .50 1.25
31 Kobe Bryant RC 8.00 20.00
32 Derrick Coleman .40 1.00
33 Alonzo Mourning .60 1.50
34 Anthony Mason .30 .75
35 Ray Allen RC 2.00 5.00
36 Arvydas Sabonis .40 1.00
37 Brian Grant .40 1.00
38 Bryant Reeves .30 .75
39 Christian Laettner .40 1.00
40 Tom Gugliotta .30 .75
41 Latrell Sprewell .50 1.25
42 Erick Dampier RC .50 1.25
43 Gheorghe Muresan .30 .75
44 Glen Rice .50 1.25
45 Patrick Ewing .60 1.50
46 Jim Jackson .30 .75
47 Michael Finley .60 1.50
48 Toni Kukoc .50 1.25
49 Marcus Camby RC .75 2.00
50 Kenny Anderson .40 1.00
51 Mark Price .50 1.25
52 Tim Hardaway .50 1.25
53 Mookie Blaylock .30 .75
54 Steve Smith .40 1.00
55 Terrell Brandon .30 .75
56 Lorenzen Wright RC .50 1.25
57 Sasha Danilovic .30 .75
58 Jeff Hornacek .40 1.00
59 Eddie Jones .50 1.25
60 Vin Baker .40 1.00
61 Chris Childs .30 .75
62 Clifford Robinson .30 .75
63 Anthony Peeler .30 .75
64 Dino Radja .40 1.00
65 Joe Dumars .50 1.25
66 Loy Vaught .30 .75
67 Rony Seikaly .40 1.00
68 Vitaly Potapenko RC .50 1.25
69 Chris Gatling .30 .75
70 Dale Ellis .30 .75
71 Allan Houston .40 1.00
72 Doug Christie .30 .75
73 LaPhonso Ellis .30 .75
74 Kendall Gill .30 .75
75 Rik Smits .40 1.00
76 Bobby Phills .30 .75
77 Malik Sealy .30 .75
78 Sean Elliott .50 1.25
79 Vlade Divac .50 1.25
80 David Wesley .30 .75
81 Dominique Wilkins .60 1.50
82 Danny Manning .40 1.00
83 Detlef Schrempf .50 1.25
84 Hersey Hawkins .30 .75
85 Lindsey Hunter .30 .75
86 Mahmoud Abdul-Rauf .30 .75
87 Shawn Bradley .30 .75
88 Horace Grant .40 1.00
89 Cedric Ceballos .30 .75
90 Jamal Mashburn .40 1.00
NNO Jerry Stackhouse Promo 3-card strip 2.00 5.00

1996-97 Flair Showcase Row 1

Row 1, or Grace was the middle tier of the Flair Showcase set. Each card contains one of the following back themes: Showtime, Show Stoppers and Showpiece. By combining the two different themes, collectors can determine the different scarcity levels. Using Grace and Show Stoppers (cards 1-30), the odds are one in 2.5. Using Grace and Showtime (cards 31-60), the odds are one in 2. Using Grace and Showpiece (cards 61-90), the odds are one in 3.5. To ascertain values of individual cards, please refer to the multiplier in the header, coupled with the value of the basic card.

*STARS: .75X TO 2X ROW 2
*RCs: .6X TO 1.5X ROW 2

1996-97 Flair Showcase Row 0

Row 0, or Showcase was the last tier of the Flair Showcase set. Each card contains one of the following back themes: Showtime, Show Stoppers and Showpiece. By combining the two different themes, collectors can determine the different scarcity levels. Using Showcase and Showpiece (cards 1-30), the odds are one in 24. Using Showcase and Show Stoppers (cards 31-60), the odds are one in 10. Finally, by using Showcase and Showtime (cards 61-90), the odds are one in 5. To ascertain values on individual cards, please refer to the multiplier in the header below, coupled with the value of the base card.

*STARS 1-30: 5X TO 12X ROW 2
*RCs 1-30: 2.5X TO 6X HI
*STARS 31-60: 3X TO 8X ROW 2
*RCs 31-60: 1.5X TO 4X ROW 2
*STARS/RCs 61-90: 1X TO 2.5X ROW 2
31 Kobe Bryant 50.00 120.00

1996-97 Flair Showcase Legacy Collection Row 2

Randomly inserted into packs at a rate of one in 30, this 90-card set parallels the regular set. A couple of differences: card fronts contain a different color holographic background as well as the "Legacy Collection" stamp. Card backs are numbered out of 150 - the first parallel set to be numbered as such. Unlike the basic set, which has several levels of collectibility, the parallel singles are all inserted at the same rate. Each player has three different cards. To ascertain values for individual cards, please refer to the multiplier in the header, coupled with the base card value.

*ROW 1/2 STARS: 12.5X TO 30X HI COLUMN
*ROW 1/2 RCs: 6X TO 15X HI
LEGACY: ROW 1 AND 2 SAME VALUE
1 Anfernee Hardaway 50.00 120.00
3 Allen Iverson 80.00 200.00
6 David Robinson 30.00 80.00
9 Dennis Rodman 60.00 150.00
10 Shaquille O'Neal 60.00 150.00
11 Stephon Marbury 25.00 60.00
14 Hakeem Olajuwon 30.00 80.00
15 Jason Kidd 40.00 100.00
18 Reggie Miller 30.00 80.00
19 Grant Hill 50.00 120.00
23 Michael Jordan 1500.00 2500.00
25 Chris Webber 25.00 60.00
27 Scottie Pippen 50.00 120.00
28 Karl Malone 25.00 60.00
30 Shawn Kemp 20.00 50.00
31 Kobe Bryant 1000.00 1800.00
35 Ray Allen 40.00 100.00
41 Latrell Sprewell 25.00 60.00

1996-97 Flair Showcase Legacy Collection Row 0

*STARS: 15X TO 40X HI
*RCs: 8X TO 20X HI
STATED PRINT RUN 150 SER.#'d SETS
1 Anfernee Hardaway 60.00 150.00
3 Allen Iverson 125.00 300.00
4 Charles Barkley 60.00 150.00
6 David Robinson 75.00 200.00
7 Gary Payton 30.00 80.00
9 Dennis Rodman 80.00 200.00
10 Shaquille O'Neal 125.00 300.00
11 Stephon Marbury 30.00 80.00
14 Hakeem Olajuwon 60.00 150.00
15 Jason Kidd 60.00 150.00
18 Reggie Miller 50.00 125.00
19 Grant Hill 60.00 150.00
23 Michael Jordan 1500.00 2500.00
25 Chris Webber 40.00 100.00
26 Antoine Walker 25.00 60.00
27 Scottie Pippen 125.00 300.00
28 Karl Malone 40.00 100.00
29 Shareef Abdur-Rahim 25.00 60.00
30 Shawn Kemp 40.00 100.00
31 Kobe Bryant 1200.00 2000.00
33 Alonzo Mourning 30.00 80.00
35 Ray Allen 75.00 150.00
41 Latrell Sprewell 60.00 150.00
49 Marcus Camby 30.00 80.00
71 Allan Houston 20.00 50.00
81 Dominique Wilkins 35.00 70.00

1996-97 Flair Showcase Class of '96

Randomly inserted in packs at a rate of one in five, this 20-card set features the top rookies from the class of 1996. Cards feature an embossed design.

COMPLETE SET (20) 20.00 50.00
1 Shareef Abdur-Rahim 1.50 4.00
2 Ray Allen 3.00 8.00
3 Shandon Anderson .75 2.00
4 Kobe Bryant 12.00 30.00
5 Marcus Camby 1.25 3.00
6 Erick Dampier .75 2.00
7 Derek Fisher 1.50 4.00
8 Todd Fuller .75 2.00
9 Othella Harrington .75 2.00
10 Allen Iverson 4.00 10.00
11 Kerry Kittles .75 2.00
12 Travis Knight .75 2.00
13 Matt Maloney .75 2.00
14 Stephon Marbury 2.00 5.00
15 Steve Nash 4.00 10.00
16 Jermaine O'Neal 2.00 5.00
17 Vitaly Potapenko .75 2.00
18 Roy Rogers .75 2.00
19 Antoine Walker 1.50 4.00
20 Lorenzen Wright .75 2.00

1996-97 Flair Showcase Hot Shots

Randomly inserted in packs at a rate of one in 90, this 20-card set features some of the best players in the NBA. Card fronts contain a photo of the player over a basketball surrounded by a die-cut flame. A small percentage of the press run contained errors to the names on the front of the cards.

COMPLETE SET (20) 700.00 1200.00
1 Michael Jordan 400.00 650.00
2 Kevin Garnett 30.00 80.00
3 Damon Stoudamire 12.00 30.00
4 Anfernee Hardaway 25.00 60.00
5 Shaquille O'Neal 30.00 80.00
6 Grant Hill 25.00 60.00
7 Dennis Rodman 40.00 80.00
8 Shawn Kemp 20.00 50.00
9 Scottie Pippen 40.00 70.00
10 Juwan Howard 10.00 25.00
11 Jason Kidd 20.00 50.00
12 Hakeem Olajuwon 15.00 40.00
13 Karl Malone 15.00 40.00
14 Joe Smith 10.00 25.00
15 David Robinson 20.00 50.00
16 Jerry Stackhouse 15.00 40.00
17 Antonio McDyess 12.00 30.00
18 Clyde Drexler 15.00 40.00
19 Gary Payton 15.00 40.00
20 Eddie Jones 12.00 30.00

1997-98 Flair Showcase Row 3

The 1997-98 Flair Showcase set was issued in one series totalling 80 cards. The 5-card packs retailed for $4.99 each. The Row 3 set was broken up into 4 levels with the following odds: Showtime (cards 1-20) at 1:0.9, Showstopper (cards 21-40) at 1:1.1, Showdown (cards 41-60) at 1:1.5 and Showpiece (cards 61-80) at 1:2. A four-card Grant Hill promo strip was also released and is priced at the bottom of the set.

COMPLETE SET (80) 15.00 40.00
1 Michael Jordan 4.00 10.00
2 Grant Hill .75 2.00
3 Allen Iverson 1.00 2.50
4 Kevin Garnett 1.00 2.50
5 Tim Duncan RC 2.50 6.00
6 Shawn Kemp .50 1.25
7 Shaquille O'Neal 1.25 3.00
8 Antoine Walker .50 1.25
9 Shareef Abdur-Rahim .50 1.25
10 Damon Stoudamire .50 1.25
11 Anfernee Hardaway .75 2.00
12 Keith Van Horn RC .75 2.00
13 Dennis Rodman 1.00 2.50
14 Ron Mercer RC .50 1.25
15 Stephon Marbury .60 1.50
16 Scottie Pippen .75 2.00
17 Kerry Kittles .30 .75
18 Kobe Bryant 2.50 6.00
19 Marcus Camby .50 1.25
20 Chauncey Billups RC 1.50 4.00
21 Tracy McGrady RC 2.00 5.00
22 Joe Smith .40 1.00
23 Brevin Knight RC .40 1.00
24 Danny Fortson RC .40 1.00
25 Tim Thomas RC .75 2.00
26 Gary Payton .50 1.25
27 David Robinson .75 2.00
28 Hakeem Olajuwon .60 1.50
29 Antonio Daniels RC .40 1.00
30 Antonio McDyess .40 1.00
31 Eddie Jones .50 1.25
32 Adonal Foyle RC .40 1.00
33 Glenn Robinson .40 1.00
34 Charles Barkley .75 2.00
35 Vin Baker .40 1.00
36 Jerry Stackhouse .50 1.25
37 Ray Allen .60 1.50
38 Derek Anderson RC .40 1.00
39 Isaac Austin .30 .75
40 Tony Battie RC .50 1.25
41 Tariq Abdul-Wahad RC .40 1.00
42 Dikembe Mutombo .50 1.25
43 Clyde Drexler .60 1.50
44 Chris Mullin .50 1.25
45 Tim Hardaway .50 1.25
46 Terrell Brandon .30 .75
47 John Stockton .60 1.50
48 Patrick Ewing .60 1.50
49 Horace Grant .40 1.00
50 Tom Gugliotta .30 .75
51 Mookie Blaylock .30 .75
52 Mitch Richmond .50 1.25
53 Anthony Mason .30 .75
54 Michael Finley .50 1.25
55 Jason Kidd .75 2.00
56 Karl Malone .60 1.50
57 Reggie Miller .60 1.50
58 Steve Smith .40 1.00
59 Glen Rice .50 1.25
60 Bryant Stith .30 .75
61 Loy Vaught .30 .75
62 Brian Grant .30 .75
63 Joe Dumars .50 1.25
64 Juwan Howard .40 1.00
65 Rik Smits .40 1.00
66 Alonzo Mourning .60 1.50
67 Allan Houston .40 1.00
68 Chris Webber .50 1.25
69 Kendall Gill .30 .75
70 Rony Seikaly .40 1.00
71 Kenny Anderson .40 1.00
72 John Wallace .30 .75
73 Bryant Reeves .30 .75
74 Brian Williams .30 .75
75 Larry Johnson .50 1.25
76 Shawn Bradley .30 .75
77 Kevin Johnson .50 1.25
78 Rod Strickland .30 .75
79 Rodney Rogers .30 .75
80 Rasheed Wallace .50 1.25
NNO Grant Hill PROMO 4-card strip 3.00 8.00

1997-98 Flair Showcase Row 2

The Row 2, or Style, parallels the basic set. The cards have four different combinations: Showstopper (cards 1-20) at 1:3, Showtime (cards 21-40) at 1:2.5, Showpiece (cards 41-60) at 1:4 and Showdown (cards 61-80) at 1:3.5. To ascertain values of individual cards, please refer to the multiplier listed below coupled with the value of the base card.

COMPLETE SET (80) 30.00 80.00
*STARS/RCs: .6X TO 1.5X ROW 3

1997-98 Flair Showcase Row 1

The Row 1, or Grace, parallels the basic set. The cards have four different combinations: Showdown (cards 1-20) at 1:16, Showpiece (cards 21-40) at 1:24, Showtime (cards 41-60) at 1:6 and Showstopper (cards 61-80) at 1:10. To ascertain values of individual cards, please refer to the multiplier listed below coupled with the value of the base card.

COMPLETE SET (80) 80.00 200.00
*STARS/RCs 1-20: 1.25X TO 3X ROW 3
*STARS/RCs 21-40: 1.5X TO 4X ROW 3
*STARS/RCs 41-60: .75X TO 2X ROW 3
*STARS 61-80: 1X TO 2.5X ROW 3

1997-98 Flair Showcase Row 0

The Row 0, or Showcase, parallels the basic set. The cards have four different combinations: Showpiece (cards 1-20) with serial numbering to 250, Showstopper (cards 21-40) with serial numbering to 500, Showdown (cards 41-60) with serial numbering to 1000 and Showtime (cards 61-80) with serial numbering to 2000. To ascertain values on individual cards, please refer to the multiplier in the header below, coupled with the value of the base card.

*STARS 1-20: 8X TO 20X ROW 3
*RCs 1-20: 5X TO 12X ROW 3
*STARS 21-40: 5X TO 12X ROW 3
*RCs 21-40: 4X TO 10X ROW 3
*STARS 41-60: 4X TO 10X ROW 3
*RCs 41-60: 3X TO 8X ROW 3
*STARS 61-80: 2X TO 5X ROW 3
1 Michael Jordan 250.00 500.00
5 Tim Duncan 40.00 100.00

1997-98 Flair Showcase Legacy Collection Row 3

Randomly inserted into packs, the Legacy Collection parallels all 80 basic cards and is serially numbered to 100. Each player has four different Legacy cards - Row 3, 2, 1, and 0. To ascertain values of individual cards, please refer to the multiplier in the header, coupled with the value of the base card.

*STARS: 15X TO 40X BASE CARD HI
*RCs: 8X TO 20X BASE HI
LEGACY: ALL ROWS SAME VALUE
1 Michael Jordan 1500.00 2300.00
5 Tim Duncan 125.00 225.00
11 Anfernee Hardaway 40.00 100.00
18 Kobe Bryant 400.00 1000.00
47 John Stockton 40.00 100.00
57 Reggie Miller 30.00 80.00
68 Chris Webber 30.00 80.00

1997-98 Flair Showcase Wave of the Future

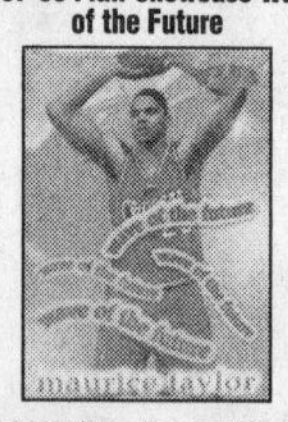

Randomly inserted into packs at one in 20, this 12-card set features some of the top rookies not to be included in the basic set. The cards are enclosed in plastic, which contains a liquid to simulate a water background within the card.

COMPLETE SET (12) 10.00 20.00
1 Corey Beck 1.25 3.00
2 Maurice Taylor 1.25 3.00
3 Chris Anstey 1.25 3.00
4 Keith Booth 1.25 3.00
5 Anthony Parker 1.25 3.00
6 Austin Croshere 1.25 3.00
7 Jacque Vaughn 1.25 3.00
8 God Shammgod 1.25 3.00
9 Bobby Jackson 1.50 4.00
10 Johnny Taylor 1.25 3.00
11 Ed Gray 1.25 3.00
12 Kelvin Cato 1.25 3.00

1998-99 Flair Showcase Row 3

This year's Flair Showcase was changed back to three levels, from four. The 90-card set was released in five-card packs which carried a suggested retail price of $4.99. The base Row 3 set, or Power, had a different insertion ratio for each set of 30 cards. Cards 1-30, or Power/Showtime were inserted one in 0.8; cards 31-60, or Power/Showdown were inserted one per pack and cards 61-90, or Power/Showpiece were inse[rted] one in 1.2.

COMPLETE SET (90) 20.00
1 Keith Van Horn .25
1A Keith Van Horn PROMO .40
2 Kobe Bryant 1.25
3 Tim Duncan .50
4 Kevin Garnett .50
5 Grant Hill .40
6 Allen Iverson .50
7 Shaquille O'Neal .60
8 Antoine Walker .25
9 Shareef Abdur-Rahim .25
10 Stephon Marbury .30
11 Ray Allen .30
12 Shawn Kemp .25
13 Tim Thomas .25
14 Scottie Pippen .40
15 Latrell Sprewell .25
16 Dirk Nowitzki RC 3.00
17 Antawn Jamison RC 1.25
18 Anfernee Hardaway .40
19 Larry Hughes RC 1.00
20 Robert Traylor RC .50
21 Kerry Kittles .15
22 Ron Mercer .20
23 Michael Olowokandi RC .60
24 Jason Kidd .40
25 Vince Carter RC 2.50
26 Charles Barkley .40
27 Antonio McDyess .20
28 Mike Bibby RC 1.25
29 Paul Pierce RC 2.50
30 Raef LaFrentz RC .60
31 Reggie Miller .30
32 Michael Finley .25
33 Eddie Jones .25
34 Tim Hardaway .25
35 Glenn Robinson .20
36 Brevin Knight .15
37 Gary Payton .25
38 David Robinson .40
39 Karl Malone .30
40 Derek Anderson .15
41 Patrick Ewing .30
42 Juwan Howard .20
43 Jayson Williams .15
44 Terrell Brandon .15
45 Hakeem Olajuwon .30
46 Isaac Austin .15
47 Glen Rice .25
48 Maurice Taylor .15
49 Damon Stoudamire .25
50 Brian Skinner RC .50
51 Nazr Mohammed RC .50
52 Tom Gugliotta .15
53 Al Harrington RC .75
54 Pat Garrity RC .50
55 Jason Williams RC 1.25
56 Tracy McGrady .40
57 Keon Clark RC .50
58 Vin Baker .20
59 Bonzi Wells RC .50
60 John Stockton .30
61 Isaiah Rider .15
62 Alonzo Mourning .30
63 Allan Houston .20
64 Dennis Rodman .50
65 Felipe Lopez RC .50
66 Joe Smith .20
67 Chris Webber .25
68 Mitch Richmond .25
69 Brent Barry .20
70 Mookie Blaylock .15
71 Donyell Marshall .15
72 Anthony Mason .15
73 Rod Strickland .15
74 Roshown McLeod RC .50
75 Matt Harpring RC .60
76 Detlef Schrempf .25
77 Michael Dickerson RC .50
78 Michael Doleac RC .50
79 John Starks .20
80 Ricky Davis RC .75
81 Steve Smith .20
82 Voshon Lenard .15
83 Toni Kukoc .25
84 Steve Nash .40
85 Vlade Divac .25
86 Rasheed Wallace .25
87 Bryon Russell .15
88 Antonio Daniels .15
89 Rik Smits .20
90 Joe Dumars .25

1998-99 Flair Showcase Row [2]

The parallel Row 2, or Passion, 90-card set was inserted at various levels, depending on the card theme. Cards 1-30, or Passion/Showdown was inserted at one in three; cards 31-60, or Passion/Showpiece was inserted at one in 1.3; an[d] cards 61-90, or Passion/Showtime was inserted a[t one] in two. To ascertain values for individual cards, pl[ease] refer to the multipliers in the header, coupled with [the] value of the base card.

COMPLETE SET (90) 60.00
*STARS: 1X TO 2.5X ROW 3
*RCs: .5X TO 1.25X ROW 3
1A K.Van Horn Promo .75

1998-99 Flair Showcase Row [1]

The parallel Row 1, or Showcase, 90-card set was inserted at various levels, depending on the card theme. Cards 1-30, or Showcase/Showpiece was inserted at one in 23 and serially numbered to 150[0]; cards 31-60, or Showcase/Showtime was inserted [at] one in 11 and serially numbered to 3000; and car[ds] 61-90, or Showcase/Showdown was inserted at o[ne in] 6 and serially numbered to 6000. To ascertain valu[es] for individual cards, please refer to the multipliers [in] the header, coupled with the value of the base car[d].

*1-30 STARS: 3X TO 8X ROW 3
*1-30 RCs: 2X TO 5X ROW 3
*31-60 STARS: 2.5X TO 6X ROW 3
*31-60 RCs: 1.5X TO 4X ROW 3
*61-90 STARS: 1.5X TO 4X ROW 3
*61-90 RCs: .75X TO 2X ROW 3
1A Keith Van Horn Promo 1.25

1998-99 Flair Showcase Lega[cy] Collection Row 3

Randomly inserted in packs, this 90-card set paral[lels] the base set. The cards feature blue foil stamping a[nd] are serially numbered to 99. To ascertain values o[n] individual cards, please refer to the multiplier in th[e] header, coupled with the value of the base card.

*STARS: 25X TO 60X VALUE
*RCs: 8X TO 20X VALUE
LEGACY: ALL ROWS EQUAL VALUE

Bryant 350.00 650.00
Garnett 40.00 100.00
Nowitzki 100.00 250.00
ernee Hardaway 40.00 100.00
e Carter 125.00 250.00
rles Barkley 30.00 80.00
on Williams 30.00 80.00
nis Rodman 125.00 225.00

98-99 Flair Showcase Class of '98

mly inserted into packs, this 15-card set features ar stars and sculpture embossing. The cards are numbered to 500.

LETE SET (15) 80.00 160.00
ael Olowokandi 4.00 10.00
Bibby 8.00 20.00
LaFrentz 4.00 10.00
wn Jamison 8.00 20.00
e Carter 20.00 50.00
rt Traylor 3.00 8.00
n Williams 8.00 20.00
y Hughes 6.00 15.00
Nowitzki 20.00 50.00
l Pierce 15.00 40.00
zi Wells 3.00 8.00
chael Doleac 3.00 8.00
chael Dickerson 3.00 8.00
Garrity 3.00 8.00
Harrington 5.00 12.00

1998-99 Flair Showcase takeit2.net

mly inserted in packs, this 15-card set features uter generated designs of some of the NBA's ball players. The cards are serially numbered to

ttie Pippen 10.00 25.00
Duncan 12.00 30.00
h Van Horn 6.00 15.00
nt Hill 10.00 25.00
e Bryant 30.00 80.00
oine Walker 6.00 15.00
in Garnett 12.00 30.00
n Iverson 15.00 40.00
reef Abdur-Rahim 6.00 15.00
fernee Hardaway 12.00 30.00
ephon Marbury 8.00 20.00
n Mercer 5.00 12.00
ichael Jordan 150.00 250.00
aquille O'Neal 15.00 40.00
hawn Kemp 6.00 15.00

1999-00 Flair Showcase

1999-00 Fleer Showcase product was released in 2000, and features a 130-card base set that is en into tiers as follows: 100 Base Veterans (1- and 30 Rookies (101-130) that are serial bered to 2000. Each pack contained 5 cards and ed a suggested retail price of $3.99.

PLETE SET (130) 75.00 150.00
PLETE SET w/o RC (100) 15.00 30.00
nce Carter .75 2.00
fernee Hardaway .60 1.50
ck Van Exel .30 .75
rry Kittles .25 .60
chael Doleac .25 .60
an Elliott .40 1.00
aquille O'Neal 1.00 2.50
ery Johnson .30 .75
an Grant .25 .60
erome Williams .25 .60
arry Hughes .30 .75
erry Stackhouse .40 1.00
lonzo Mourning .50 1.25
ntonio McDyess .30 .75
ason Kidd .60 1.50
ryon Russell .25 .60
akeem Olajuwon .50 1.25
uwan Howard .30 .75
aul Pierce .60 1.50
in Baker .40 1.00
arry Johnson .40 1.00
ary Trent .25 .60
ayson Williams .25 .60
im Hardaway .40 1.00
irk Nowitzki .75 2.00
amal Mashburn .30 .75
lenn Robinson .30 .75
hawn Bradley .25 .60
om Gugliotta .25 .60
ade Divac .40 1.00
avid Robinson .60 1.50
att Geiger .25 .60
rant Hill .50 1.25
aurice Taylor .25 .60
oni Kukoc .40 1.00
edric Ceballos .25 .60
37 Patrick Ewing .50 1.25
38 Ray Allen .40 1.00
39 Michael Finley .40 1.00
40 Robert Traylor .25 .60
41 Brevin Knight .25 .60
42 Marcus Camby .30 .75
43 Sam Cassell .30 .75
44 Antawn Jamison .40 1.00
45 Steve Smith .25 .60
46 Darrell Armstrong .25 .60
47 Mookie Blaylock .25 .60
48 Derek Anderson .25 .60
49 Hersey Hawkins .25 .60
50 Kobe Bryant 2.00 5.00
51 Shawn Kemp .40 1.00
52 Scottie Pippen .60 1.50
53 Chris Webber .40 1.00
54 Damon Stoudamire .40 1.00
55 Donyell Marshall .25 .60
56 Isaiah Rider .25 .60
57 Karl Malone .50 1.25
58 Kevin Garnett .75 2.00
59 Mario Elie .25 .60
60 Michael Dickerson .25 .60
61 Jahidi White .25 .60
62 Joe Smith .30 .75
63 Kenny Anderson .30 .75
64 Reggie Miller .40 1.00
65 Ruben Patterson .25 .60
66 Shareef Abdur-Rahim .30 .75
67 Allen Iverson .75 2.00
68 Glen Rice .40 1.00
69 Nick Anderson .25 .60
70 Rex Chapman .25 .60
71 Ron Mercer .30 .75
72 Tim Duncan .75 2.00
73 Al Harrington .40 1.00
74 Brent Barry .30 .75
75 Eddie Jones .40 1.00
76 Mike Bibby .40 1.00
77 Anthony Mason .25 .60
78 Michael Olowokandi .25 .60
79 Matt Harpring .30 .75
80 Stephon Marbury .30 .75
81 Tracy McGrady .60 1.50
82 Allan Houston .30 .75
83 Lindsey Hunter .25 .60
84 Tariq Abdul-Wahad .25 .60
85 Antoine Walker .40 1.00
86 Charles Barkley .60 1.50
87 Gary Payton .40 1.00
88 John Stockton .50 1.25
89 Mitch Richmond .40 1.00
90 Terrell Brandon .25 .60
91 Charles Oakley .30 .75
92 Bryant Reeves .25 .60
93 Dikembe Mutombo .40 1.00
94 Elden Campbell .25 .60
95 Jalen Rose .30 .75
96 Jason Williams .50 1.25
97 Keith Van Horn .30 .75
98 Latrell Sprewell .40 1.00
99 Raef LaFrentz .30 .75
100 Rasheed Wallace .40 1.00
101 Cal Bowdler RC 1.25 3.00
102 Dion Glover RC 1.25 3.00
103 Jason Terry RC 3.00 8.00
104 Adrian Griffin RC 1.25 3.00
105 Baron Davis RC 4.00 10.00
106 Michael Ruffin RC 1.25 3.00
107 Elton Brand RC 3.00 8.00
108 Ron Artest RC 3.00 8.00
109 Andre Miller RC 3.00 8.00
110 Trajan Langdon RC 1.25 3.00
111 James Posey RC 1.25 3.00
112 Vonteego Cummings RC 1.25 3.00
113 Kenny Thomas RC 1.25 3.00
114 Steve Francis RC 3.00 8.00
115 Jonathan Bender RC 1.25 3.00
116 Lamar Odom RC 4.00 10.00
117 Devean George RC 1.25 3.00
118 Tim James RC 1.25 3.00
119 Anthony Carter RC 1.25 3.00
120 Wally Szczerbiak RC 2.50 6.00
121 William Avery RC 1.25 3.00
122 Evan Eschmeyer RC 1.25 3.00
123 Corey Maggette RC 2.50 6.00
124 Jumaine Jones RC 1.25 3.00
125 Shawn Marion RC 3.00 8.00
126 Ryan Robertson RC 1.25 3.00
127 Aleksandar Radojevic RC 1.25 3.00
128 Quincy Lewis RC 1.25 3.00
129 Scott Padgett RC 1.25 3.00
130 Richard Hamilton RC 3.00 8.00
P1 Vince Carter PROMO 1.50 4.00

1999-00 Flair Showcase Legacy Collection

Randomly inserted in packs, this 130-card set parallels the base set. The cards were treated with a matte finish and serially numbered to 20. To ascertain values on individual cards, please refer to the multiplier in the header, coupled with the value of the base card.

*STARS: 30X TO 80X BASE CARD HI
*RCs: 4X TO 10X BASE HI
33 Grant Hill 50.00 125.00
35 Toni Kukoc 50.00 125.00
51 Shawn Kemp 50.00 125.00
52 Scottie Pippen 100.00 200.00

1999-00 Flair Showcase Ball of Fame

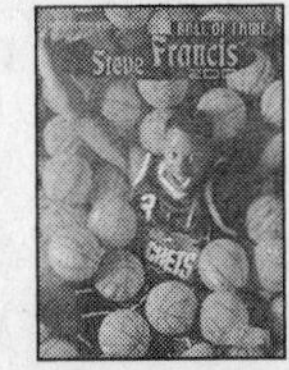

Randomly inserted in packs at one in five, this 15-card set featured rookies against a background of basketballs. Card backs carry a "BF" prefix.

COMPLETE SET (15) 15.00 40.00
BF1 Lamar Odom 3.00 8.00
BF2 Steve Francis 2.50 6.00
BF3 Elton Brand 2.50 6.00
BF4 Wally Szczerbiak 2.00 5.00
BF5 Shawn Marion 2.50 6.00
BF6 Jason Terry 2.50 6.00
BF7 Richard Hamilton 2.50 6.00
BF8 Andre Miller 2.50 6.00
BF9 Corey Maggette 2.00 5.00
BF10 Baron Davis 3.00 8.00
BF11 Vonteego Cummings 1.00 2.50
BF12 Kenny Thomas 1.00 2.50
BF13 Jumaine Jones 1.00 2.50
BF14 Trajan Langdon 1.00 2.50
BF15 Jonathan Bender 1.00 2.50

1999-00 Flair Showcase ConVINCEing

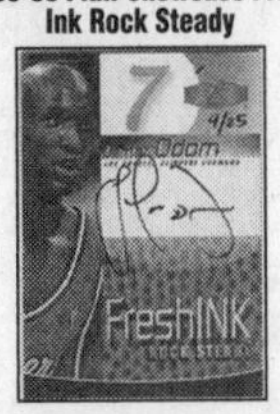

Randomly inserted in packs at one in 10, this 10-card set focused on Vince Carter and his on/off the court activities. Card backs carry a "C" prefix.

COMPLETE SET (10) 6.00 15.00
COMMON CARD (C1-C10) 1.25 3.00

1999-00 Flair Showcase Elevators

Randomly inserted in packs at one in 20, this 10-card set featured players who can soar above the others in the NBA. Card backs carry an "E" prefix.

COMPLETE SET (10) 10.00 25.00
E1 Vince Carter 1.50 4.00
E2 Lamar Odom 2.50 6.00
E3 Allen Iverson 1.50 4.00
E4 Kobe Bryant 6.00 15.00
E5 Grant Hill 1.00 2.50
E6 Eddie Jones .75 2.00
E7 Scottie Pippen 1.25 3.00
E8 Kevin Garnett 1.50 4.00
E9 Steve Francis 2.00 5.00
E10 Keith Van Horn .60 1.50

1999-00 Flair Showcase Feel the Game

Randomly inserted in packs at one in 120, this 15-card set featured a swatch of player-worn uniform. The cards are not numbered and listed below in alphabetical order.

1 William Avery 2.00 5.00
2 Vince Carter 10.00 25.00
3 Vonteego Cummings 2.00 5.00
4 Patrick Ewing 6.00 15.00
5 Brian Grant 3.00 8.00
6 Karl Malone 6.00 15.00
7 Shawn Marion 5.00 12.00
8 Alonzo Mourning 6.00 15.00
9 Lamar Odom 6.00 15.00
10 Shaquille O'Neal 12.00 30.00
11 Paul Pierce 8.00 20.00
12 David Robinson 8.00 20.00
13 Damon Stoudamire 5.00 12.00
14 Kenny Thomas 2.00 5.00
15 Antoine Walker 5.00 12.00

1999-00 Flair Showcase Fresh Ink

Randomly inserted in packs at one in 39, this 31-card set featured autographs of top NBA stars and rookies. The cards feature a congratulatory message on the back. The cards are not numbered and listed below in alphabetical order.

1 Tariq Abdul-Wahad 3.00 8.00
2 Ron Artest 8.00 20.00
3 William Avery 3.00 8.00
4 Tony Battie 3.00 8.00
5 Cal Bowdler 3.00 8.00
6 Vince Carter 15.00 40.00
7 Dion Glover 3.00 8.00
8 Chris Herren 4.00 10.00
9 Juwan Howard 4.00 10.00
10 Eddie Jones 5.00 12.00
11 Jumaine Jones 3.00 8.00
12 Brevin Knight 3.00 8.00
13 Toni Kukoc 12.00 30.00
14 Trajan Langdon 3.00 8.00
15 Quincy Lewis 3.00 8.00
16 Corey Maggette 6.00 15.00
17 Stephon Marbury 6.00 15.00
18 Tracy McGrady 15.00 30.00
19 Ron Mercer 4.00 10.00
20 Andre Miller 6.00 15.00
21 Lamar Odom 8.00 20.00
22 Hakeem Olajuwon 12.50 30.00
23 Scott Padgett 3.00 8.00
24 Scottie Pippen 75.00 200.00
25 James Posey 3.00 8.00
26 Aleksandar Radojevic 3.00 8.00
27 Glen Rice 5.00 12.00
28 Wally Szczerbiak 6.00 15.00
29 Jason Terry 6.00 15.00
30 Kenny Thomas 3.00 8.00
31 Jerome Williams 3.00 8.00

1999-00 Flair Showcase Fresh Ink Rock Steady

Randomly inserted in packs, this seven-card set is a semi-parallel of the Fresh Ink insert. The cards are serially numbered to 25. The cards are not numbered and listed below in alphabetical order.

1 Vince Carter 80.00 200.00
2 Chris Herren 12.00 30.00
3 Ron Mercer 20.00 50.00
4 Lamar Odom 60.00 150.00
5 Scottie Pippen 200.00 400.00
6 Aleksandar Radojevic 12.00 30.00
7 Kenny Thomas 12.00 30.00

1999-00 Flair Showcase Guaranteed Fresh

Randomly inserted in packs at one in 10, this 10-card set focuses on key players for each NBA team. Card backs carry a "GF" prefix.

COMPLETE SET (10) 6.00 15.00
GF1 Vince Carter 1.00 2.50
GF2 Shaquille O'Neal 1.25 3.00
GF3 Kevin Garnett 1.00 2.50
GF4 Kobe Bryant 2.50 6.00
GF5 Paul Pierce .75 2.00
GF6 Jason Williams .60 1.50
GF7 Stephon Marbury .40 1.00
GF8 Lamar Odom 1.50 4.00
GF9 Keith Van Horn .40 1.00
GF10 Wally Szczerbiak 1.00 2.50

1999-00 Flair Showcase License to Skill

Randomly inserted in packs at one in 20, this 10-card set featured players who lit-up the scoreboard. The cards are die cut. Card backs carry an "LS" prefix.

COMPLETE SET (10) 8.00 20.00
LS1 Vince Carter 1.50 4.00
LS2 Shaquille O'Neal 2.00 5.00
LS3 Tim Duncan 1.50 4.00
LS4 Keith Van Horn .60 1.50
LS5 Grant Hill 1.00 2.50
LS6 Allen Iverson 1.50 4.00
LS7 Antoine Walker .75 2.00
LS8 Scottie Pippen 1.25 3.00
LS9 Kobe Bryant 4.00 10.00
LS10 Lamar Odom 2.50 6.00

1999-00 Flair Showcase Next

Randomly inserted in packs at one in 2.5, this 20-card set focuses on younger players who will take the NBA into the millennium. Card backs carry an "N" prefix.

COMPLETE SET (20) 6.00 15.00
N1 Vince Carter .60 1.50
N2 James Posey .30 .75
N3 Jonathan Bender .30 .75
N4 Corey Maggette .60 1.50
N5 Devean George .30 .75
N6 Trajan Langdon .30 .75
N7 Shawn Marion .75 2.00
N8 William Avery .30 .75
N9 Adrian Griffin .30 .75
N10 Quincy Lewis .30 .75
N11 Kenny Thomas .30 .75
N12 Lamar Odom 1.00 2.50
N13 Dion Glover .30 .75
N14 Elton Brand .75 2.00
N15 Andre Miller .75 2.00
N16 Jason Terry .75 2.00
N17 Richard Hamilton .75 2.00
N18 Steve Francis .75 2.00
N19 Baron Davis 1.00 2.50
N20 Wally Szczerbiak .60 1.50

1999-00 Flair Showcase Rookie Showcase Firsts

Randomly inserted into packs, this 30-card insert set features some of the hottest rookies from 1999-00 season. There were only 500 serial-numbered sets of this insert produced.

COMPLETE SET (30) 75.00 150.00
*RC FIRSTS: .75X TO 2X BASE HI

2001-02 Flair

Released in late October 2001 as a 121 card set, Flair contains 90 regular cards, and 30 rookie cards numbered to 1500. Base cards feature white borders with player acton shots set against player portrait photos. Each box was issed with either a jumbo Sweet Shot memorabilia card or a jumbo Sweet Shot autograph card which is sealed in it's own wrapper. Flair was packaged in 20 pack boxes with each pack containing five cards.

COMP.SET w/o SP's (90) 12.50 30.00
1 Tracy McGrady .60 1.50
2 Derek Fisher .30 .75
3 Allen Iverson .75 2.00
4 Chris Webber .40 1.00
5 Jalen Rose .30 .75
6 Kenyon Martin .40 1.00
7 Jermaine O'Neal .40 1.00
8 Kobe Bryant 2.00 5.00
9 Bryon Russell .25 .60
10 Wally Szczerbiak .30 .75
11 Damon Stoudamire .30 .75
12 John Stockton .50 1.25
13 Glenn Robinson .30 .75
14 Steve Francis .40 1.00
15 Vince Carter .60 1.50
16 Peja Stojakovic .40 1.00
17 Rick Fox .30 .75
18 Allan Houston .30 .75
19 Danny Fortson .25 .60
20 Gary Payton .40 1.00
21 Darius Miles .25 .60
22 Kevin Garnett .75 2.00
23 Marcus Camby .30 .75
24 Desmond Mason .30 .75
25 Tim Duncan .75 2.00
26 Jamal Mashburn .30 .75
27 Andre Miller .30 .75
28 Antonio McDyess .30 .75
29 Morris Peterson .25 .60
30 Rasheed Wallace .40 1.00
31 Shawn Marion .40 1.00
32 Karl Malone .50 1.25
33 Grant Hill .50 1.25
34 Shaquille O'Neal 1.00 2.50
35 Hakeem Olajuwon .50 1.25
36 Corliss Williamson .25 .60
37 Paul Pierce .50 1.25
38 Antonio Davis .25 .60
39 Antonio Daniels .25 .60
40 Ray Allen .40 1.00
41 Dirk Nowitzki .60 1.50
42 Jerry Stackhouse .30 .75
43 Donyell Marshall .25 .60
44 Brian Grant .25 .60
45 Raef LaFrentz .25 .60
46 Corey Maggette .30 .75
47 Mike Miller .40 1.00
48 Jason Williams .30 .75
49 Jahidi White .25 .60
50 David Robinson .60 1.50
51 Shareef Abdur-Rahim .30 .75
52 Anfernee Hardaway .60 1.50
53 Baron Davis .40 1.00
54 DerMarr Johnson .25 .60
55 Dikembe Mutombo .40 1.00
56 David Wesley .25 .60
57 Chris Mihm .25 .60
58 Michael Finley .40 1.00
59 Eddie House .25 .60
60 Stromile Swift .25 .60
61 Courtney Alexander .25 .60
62 Ron Mercer .25 .60
63 Cuttino Mobley .30 .75
64 Tim Thomas .25 .60
65 Eddie Jones .30 .75
66 Lamar Odom .40 1.00
67 Terrell Brandon .25 .60
68 Rashard Lewis .40 1.00
69 Antoine Walker .30 .75
70 Latrell Sprewell .30 .75
71 Sam Cassell .30 .75
72 Mike Bibby .40 1.00
73 Speedy Claxton .25 .60
74 Steve Nash .60 1.50
75 Mark Jackson .30 .75
76 Ron Artest .40 1.00
77 Matt Harpring .30 .75
78 Wang Zhizhi .30 .75
79 Nazr Mohammed .25 .60
80 Jason Terry .40 1.00
81 Nick Van Exel .30 .75
82 Reggie Miller .40 1.00
83 Joe Smith .30 .75
84 Jason Kidd .60 1.50
85 Richard Hamilton .30 .75
86 Antawn Jamison .40 1.00
87 Alonzo Mourning .50 1.25
88 Stephon Marbury .30 .75
89 Scottie Pippen .60 1.50
90 Elton Brand .40 1.00
91 Kwame Brown RC 1.25 3.00
92 Eddie Griffin RC 1.25 3.00
93 Tyson Chandler RC 2.00 5.00
94 Omar Cook RC 1.25 3.00
95 Loren Woods RC 1.25 3.00
96 Alton Ford RC 1.25 3.00
97 Shane Battier RC 2.50 6.00
98 Joe Johnson RC 3.00 8.00
99 Rodney White RC 1.25 3.00
100 Pau Gasol RC 4.00 10.00
101 Zach Randolph RC 3.00 8.00
102 Vladimir Radmanovic RC 1.25 3.00
103 Brendan Haywood RC 1.50 4.00
104 Michael Bradley RC 1.25 3.00
105 Tony Parker RC 6.00 15.00
106 Jason Richardson RC 2.50 6.00
107 Gerald Wallace RC 2.00 5.00
108 Damone Brown RC 1.25 3.00
109 Richard Jefferson RC 2.50 6.00
110 Eddy Curry RC 2.00 5.00
111 DeSagana Diop RC 1.25 3.00
112 Brandon Armstrong RC 1.25 3.00
113 Troy Murphy RC 2.00 5.00
114 Kedrick Brown RC 1.25 3.00
115 Kirk Haston RC 1.25 3.00
116 Gilbert Arenas RC 2.00 5.00
117 Jeryl Sasser RC 1.25 3.00
118 Jamaal Tinsley RC 1.50 4.00
119 Terence Morris RC 1.25 3.00
120 Michael Wright RC 1.25 3.00
121 Michael Jordan 6.00 15.00

2001-02 Flair Courting Greatness

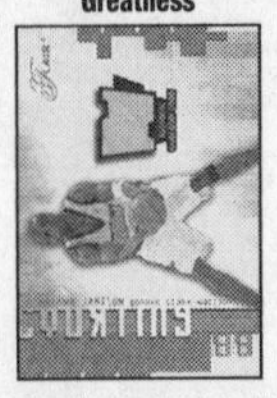

Randomly inserted in packs at the rate of one in 23, this 20-card set features top NBA player photos along with a swatch of a game used court. The cards are set up as a horizontal design, and the colors on the left and right borders match the featured player's team colors.

1 Vince Carter 6.00 15.00
2 Dirk Nowitzki 6.00 15.00
3 Allen Iverson 8.00 20.00
4 Tracy McGrady 6.00 15.00
5 Karl Malone 5.00 12.00
6 Antawn Jamison 4.00 10.00
7 Peja Stojakovic 4.00 10.00
8 Eddie Jones 3.00 8.00
9 Jason Williams 3.00 8.00
10 Hakeem Olajuwon 5.00 12.00
11 Antoine Walker 3.00 8.00
12 Jerry Stackhouse 3.00 8.00
13 Chris Webber 5.00 12.00
14 Latrell Sprewell 3.00 8.00
15 David Robinson 6.00 15.00
16 Stephon Marbury 3.00 8.00
17 Grant Hill 5.00 12.00
18 Shareef Abdur-Rahim 3.00 8.00
19 Jason Kidd 6.00 15.00
20 Scottie Pippen 6.00 15.00

2001-02 Flair Courting Greatness Ball and Court

Randomly inserted in packs, this 20-card set parallels the base Courting Greatness set enhanced with a swatch of a game used basketball and a piece of game used floor. Each card is serial numbered to 250.

1 Vince Carter 8.00 20.00
2 Dirk Nowitzki 8.00 20.00
3 Allen Iverson 10.00 25.00
4 Tracy McGrady 8.00 20.00
5 Karl Malone 6.00 15.00
6 Antawn Jamison 5.00 12.00
7 Peja Stojakovic 5.00 12.00
8 Eddie Jones 4.00 10.00
9 Jason Williams 4.00 10.00
10 Hakeem Olajuwon 8.00 20.00
11 Antoine Walker 4.00 10.00
12 Jerry Stackhouse 4.00 10.00
13 Chris Webber 8.00 20.00
14 Latrell Sprewell 4.00 10.00
15 David Robinson 8.00 20.00
16 Stephon Marbury 4.00 10.00
17 Grant Hill 6.00 15.00
18 Shareef Abdur-Rahim 4.00 10.00
19 Jason Kidd 8.00 20.00
20 Scottie Pippen 8.00 20.00

2001-02 Flair Hot Numbers

Randomly inserted in packs, this 20-card set features full color player action photos set against a gray and white face portrait. The jersey swatches are cut in the shape of a quarter of a circle, and each card is sequentially numbered to 100.

1 Darius Miles 5.00 12.00
2 Mike Miller 8.00 20.00
3 Tracy McGrady 12.00 30.00
4 Ray Allen 8.00 20.00
5 Baron Davis 8.00 20.00
6 Dikembe Mutombo 8.00 20.00
7 Kenyon Martin 8.00 20.00
8 Steve Francis 8.00 20.00
9 Patrick Ewing 12.00 30.00
10 Jason Kidd 12.00 30.00
11 Jerome Moiso 5.00 12.00
12 Richard Hamilton 6.00 15.00
13 Vince Carter 12.00 30.00
14 John Stockton 10.00 25.00
15 Mike Bibby 8.00 20.00
16 Reggie Miller 8.00 20.00
17 Jason Terry 8.00 20.00
18 Stephon Marbury 6.00 15.00
19 Chris Webber 8.00 20.00
20 Mitch Richmond 6.00 15.00

2001-02 Flair Jersey Heights

Randomly inserted in packs at the rate of one in 22, this 20-card set features full color player action photos set against a facial portrait of the featured player. Jersey swatches are in the shape of a quarter of a circle.

1 Darius Miles 2.50 6.00
2 Mike Miller 4.00 10.00
3 Tracy McGrady 6.00 15.00
4 Ray Allen 4.00 10.00
5 Baron Davis 4.00 10.00
6 Dikembe Mutombo 4.00 10.00
7 Kenyon Martin 4.00 10.00
8 Steve Francis 4.00 10.00
9 Patrick Ewing 5.00 12.00
10 Jason Kidd 6.00 15.00
11 Jerome Moiso 2.50 6.00
12 Richard Hamilton 3.00 8.00
13 Vince Carter 6.00 15.00
14 John Stockton 5.00 12.00
15 Mike Bibby 4.00 10.00
16 Reggie Miller 4.00 10.00
17 Jason Terry 4.00 10.00
18 Stephon Marbury 3.00 8.00
19 Chris Webber 4.00 10.00
20 Mitch Richmond 3.00 8.00

2001-02 Flair Sweet Shots

Randomly inserted as a jumbo box topper, this 33-card set features either a game used jersey or a player autograph from both veteran and rookie players. Autograph cards are all sequentially numbered-print runs are listed below.

1 Ray Allen JSY 5.00 12.00
2 Vince Carter JSY 8.00 20.00
3 Baron Davis JSY 5.00 12.00
4 Michael Dickerson JSY 3.00 8.00
5 Steve Francis JSY 5.00 12.00
6 Marc Jackson JSY 3.00 8.00
7 Antawn Jamison JSY 5.00 12.00
8 Rashard Lewis JSY 5.00 12.00
9 Karl Malone JSY 6.00 15.00
10 Shawn Marion JSY 5.00 12.00
11 Kenyon Martin JSY 5.00 12.00
12 Antonio McDyess JSY 4.00 10.00
13 Tracy McGrady JSY 8.00 20.00
14 Darius Miles JSY 3.00 8.00
15 Mike Miller JSY 5.00 12.00
16 Lamar Odom JSY 5.00 12.00
17 Gary Payton JSY 5.00 12.00
18 Morris Peterson JSY 3.00 8.00
19 David Robinson JSY 8.00 20.00
20 John Stockton JSY 6.00 15.00
21 Peja Stojakovic JSY 5.00 12.00
22 Jason Terry JSY 5.00 12.00
23 Antoine Walker JSY 4.00 10.00
24 Chris Webber JSY 5.00 12.00
25 Allen Iverson JSY 10.00 25.00
26 Kwame Brown AU/297 4.00 10.00
27 Eddy Curry AU/368 6.00 15.00
28 Michael Bradley AU/433 4.00 10.00
29 Brendan Haywood AU/345 5.00 12.00
30 Jason Collins AU/390 4.00 10.00
31 Richard Jefferson AU/330 8.00 20.00
32 Kedrick Brown AU/342 4.00 10.00
33 Vince Carter AU/245 20.00 50.00

2001-02 Flair Warming Up

Randomly inserted in packs at the rate of one in 27, this 20-card set features photos of players in their warm-up suits on the top half of the card, a black break in the middle of the card with the player's name and team name, and a swatch from a warm-up on the bottom of the card.

1 Jason Terry 3.00 8.00
2 Shareef Abdur-Rahim 2.50 6.00
3 Antoine Walker 2.50 6.00
4 Paul Pierce 4.00 10.00
5 Andre Miller 2.50 6.00
6 Steve Francis 3.00 8.00
7 Lamar Odom 3.00 8.00
8 Corey Maggette 2.50 6.00
9 Kenyon Martin 3.00 8.00
10 Grant Hill 4.00 10.00
11 Allen Iverson 6.00 15.00
12 Dikembe Mutombo 3.00 8.00
13 Stephon Marbury 2.50 6.00
14 Mike Bibby 3.00 8.00
15 Morris Peterson 2.00 5.00
16 Vince Carter 5.00 12.00
17 Karl Malone 4.00 10.00
18 John Stockton 4.00 10.00
19 Keith Van Horn 2.50 6.00
20 DerMarr Johnson 2.00 5.00

2001-02 Flair Warming Up Dual

Randomly inserted in packs at the rate of one in 80, this 10-card set parallels the design of the base Warming Up insert set featuring two players and two warm-up swatches.

1 Jason Terry 5.00 12.00
Shareef Abdur-Rahim
2 Antoine Walker 8.00 20.00
Paul Pierce
3 Andre Miller 5.00 12.00
Steve Francis
4 Lamar Odom 5.00 12.00
Corey Maggette
5 Kenyon Martin 5.00 12.00
Keith Van Horn
6 Allen Iverson 8.00 20.00
Dikembe Mutombo
7 Stephon Marbury 5.00 12.00
Mike Bibby
8 Morris Peterson 8.00 20.00
Vince Carter
9 Karl Malone 15.00 40.00
John Stockton
10 Grant Hill 6.00 15.00
DerMarr Johnson

2002-03 Flair

Released in mid-October 2002, this 120-card set features 90 base veteran cards and 30 Class of '02 cards sequentially numbered to 1750. Several of these Class of '02 cards were issued as Rookie Exchange cards. Flair's base design has metallic white ink around the outside, a gray-brown scale picture of the player in the background with a full color action photo superimposed on top. The Class of '02 cards, numbers 91-120, contain those words along the right side of the card and share the design of the base veteran cards. Every card contains bronze foil highlights. Flair was packaged in five card packs at an SRP of $5.99 with boxes containing 20 packs. Each box also contained a special box-topper pack which contained the over-sized sweet swatch cards which feature either a jersey or an autograph.

COMP.SET w/o SP's (90) 25.00 50.00
1 Tracy McGrady .60 1.50
2 Jamal Mashburn .30 .75
3 Allen Iverson .60 1.50
4 Alonzo Mourning .50 1.25
5 Joe Smith .30 .75
6 Wang Zhizhi .25 .60
7 Karl Malone .50 1.25
8 Keith Van Horn .30 .75
9 Joseph Forte .25 .60
10 Peja Stojakovic .40 1.00
11 Juwan Howard .30 .75
12 Brian Grant .25 .60
13 Glenn Robinson .30 .75
14 Antonio McDyess .30 .75
15 Vince Carter .60 1.50
16 Pau Gasol .50 1.25
17 Bonzi Wells .25 .60
18 Chucky Atkins .25 .60
19 Shane Battier .40 1.00
20 Steve Francis .40 1.00
21 Kevin Garnett .75 2.00
22 Antawn Jamison .40 1.00
23 Hedo Turkoglu .40 1.00
24 Kenyon Martin .40 1.00
25 Cuttino Mobley .30 .75
26 Steve Nash .50 1.25
27 Morris Peterson .25 .60
28 Jason Richardson .40 1.00
29 Antoine Walker .30 .75
30 Rasheed Wallace .40 1.00
31 Tim Duncan .75 2.00
32 Paul Pierce .50 1.25
33 Ben Wallace .40 1.00
34 Jason Kidd .60 1.50
35 Gary Payton .40 1.00
36 Mike Miller .40 1.00
37 Kobe Bryant 2.00 5.00
38 Baron Davis .40 1.00
39 Steve Smith .30 .75
40 Reggie Miller .40 1.00
41 Dirk Nowitzki .60 1.50
42 Rashard Lewis .40 1.00
43 Andre Miller .30 .75
44 David Wesley .25 .60
45 Ray Allen .40 1.00
46 Tyson Chandler .30 .75
47 Jamaal Tinsley .25 .60
48 Grant Hill .50 1.25
49 Richard Jefferson .40 1.00
50 Latrell Sprewell .30 .75
51 Jason Terry .30 .75
52 Alvin Williams .25 .60
53 Vin Baker .30 .75
54 Robert Horry .30 .75
55 Eddie Jones .30 .75
56 Andrei Kirilenko .40 1.00
57 Darius Miles .25 .60
58 Kedrick Brown .25 .60
59 Jermaine O'Neal .40 1.00
60 David Robinson .60 1.50
61 Jason Williams .30 .75
62 Wally Szczerbiak .30 .75
63 Mike Bibby .40 1.00
64 Shawn Marion .40 1.00
65 Shaquille O'Neal 1.00 2.50
66 Michael Redd .40 1.00
67 Chris Webber .40 1.00
68 Quentin Richardson .30 .75
69 Michael Jordan 3.00 8.00
70 Jamaal Magloire .25 .60
71 Radoslav Nesterovic .25 .60
72 Eddy Curry .30 .75
73 Michael Finley .40 1.00
74 Eddie Griffin .25 .60
75 Aaron McKie .25 .60
76 Tony Parker .50 1.25
77 Shareef Abdur-Rahim .30 .75
78 Jalen Rose .30 .75
79 Jerry Stackhouse .30 .75
80 Jumaine Jones .25 .60
81 Toni Kukoc .30 .75
82 Vladimir Radmanovic .25 .60
83 Zach Randolph .40 1.00
84 John Stockton .50 1.25
85 Mengke Bateer .25 .60
86 Dikembe Mutombo .40 1.00
87 Elton Brand .40 1.00
88 Allan Houston .30 .75
89 Joe Johnson .40 1.00
90 Kwame Brown .25 .60
91 Yao Ming RC 6.00 15.00
92 Jay Williams RC 2.50 6.00
93 Mike Dunleavy RC 2.50 6.00
94 Drew Gooden RC 3.00 8.00
95 DaJuan Wagner RC 2.00 5.00
96 Caron Butler RC 3.00 8.00
97 Jared Jeffries RC 2.00 5.00
98 Nene Hilario RC 2.50 6.00
99 Chris Wilcox RC 2.00 5.00
100 Nikoloz Tskitishvili RC 2.00 5.00
101 Kareem Rush RC 2.00 5.00
102 Curtis Borchardt RC 2.00 5.00
103 Qyntel Woods RC 2.00 5.00
104 Melvin Ely RC 2.00 5.00
105 Marcus Haislip RC 2.00 5.00
106 Carlos Boozer RC 4.00 10.00
107 Bostjan Nachbar RC 2.00 5.00
108 Amare Stoudemire RC 5.00 12.00
109 Frank Williams RC 2.00 5.00
110 Jiri Welsch RC 2.00 5.00
111 Fred Jones RC 2.00 5.00
112 Juan Dixon RC 2.50 6.00
113 Ryan Humphrey RC 2.00 5.00
114 Casey Jacobsen RC 2.00 5.00
115 Tayshaun Prince RC 2.50 6.00
116 Dan Dickau RC 2.00 5.00
117 Chris Jefferies RC 2.00 5.00
118 John Salmons RC 2.50 6.00
119 Manu Ginobili RC 5.00 12.00
120 Gordan Giricek RC 2.00 5.00

2002-03 Flair Row 1

Randomly inserted in packs, this 120-card set parallels the base Flair set with a foil shift from bronze to silver. Each card is numbered on the back to 150.
*ROW 1 STARS: 4X TO 10X BASE CARD HI
*ROW 1 RCs: .75X TO 2X BASE CARD HI

2002-03 Flair Row 2

Randomly inserted in packs, this 120-card set parallels the base Flair set with a fold background and gold foil highlights. Each card is numbered on the back to 25.
*ROW 2 STARS: 15X TO 40X BASE HI
*ROW 2 RCs: 3X TO 8X BASE HI

2002-03 Flair Court Kings

Randomly seeded in packs at the rate of one in four, this 25-card set uses a horizontal design with full color player action photos on one side and team logos on the other side. The background is a mix of gray and a wood-colored strip with the key and the three-point line drawn on it. All cards contain bronze foil highlights.

COMPLETE SET (25) 15.00 40.00
1 Kobe Bryant 3.00 8.00
2 Jerry Stackhouse .50 1.25
3 Steve Francis .60 1.50
4 Ray Allen .60 1.50
5 Kevin Garnett 1.25 3.00
6 Elton Brand .60 1.50
7 Jason Kidd 1.00 2.50
8 Mike Bibby .60 1.50
9 Allen Iverson 1.00 2.50
10 Tracy McGrady 1.00 2.50
11 Baron Davis .60 1.50
12 Tim Duncan 1.25 3.00
13 Latrell Sprewell .50 1.25
14 Paul Pierce .75 2.00
15 Vince Carter 1.00 2.50
16 Antawn Jamison .60 1.50
17 Eddie Jones .50 1.25
18 Darius Miles .40 1.00
19 Dirk Nowitzki 1.00 2.50
20 Karl Malone .75 2.00
21 Shaquille O'Neal 1.50 4.00
22 Michael Jordan 5.00 12.00
23 Antoine Walker .50 1.25
24 Kenyon Martin .60 1.50
25 Chris Webber .60 1.50

2002-03 Flair Court Kings Ball and Jersey

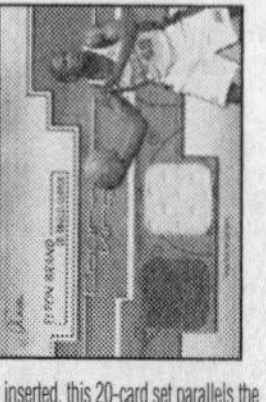

Randomly inserted, this 20-card set parallels the design of the base Court Kings insert enhanced with swatches of both jersey material and basketball. Each card is sequentially numbered to 100.

CKAI Allen Iverson 12.00 30.00
CKAJ Antawn Jamison 6.00 15.00
CKAW Antoine Walker 5.00 12.00
CKBD Baron Davis 6.00 15.00
CKCW Chris Webber 8.00 20.00
CKDM Darius Miles 4.00 10.00
CKDN Dirk Nowitzki 10.00 25.00
CKEB Elton Brand 6.00 15.00
CKEJ Eddie Jones 5.00 12.00
CKJK Jason Kidd 10.00 25.00
CKJS Jerry Stackhouse 5.00 12.00
CKKM Karl Malone 8.00 20.00
CKMB Mike Bibby 6.00 15.00
CKPP Paul Pierce 8.00 20.00
CKPS Peja Stojakovic 6.00 15.00
CKRA Ray Allen 6.00 15.00
CKSF Steve Francis 6.00 15.00
CKSM Stephon Marbury 5.00 12.00
CKTM Tracy McGrady 10.00 25.00
CKVC Vince Carter 10.00 25.00

2002-03 Flair Court Kings Game Used

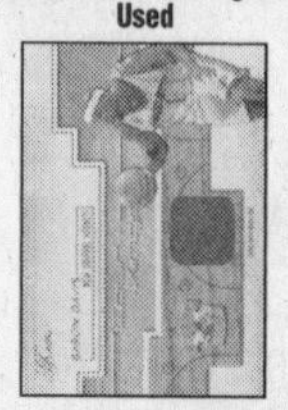

Randomly inserted in packs at the rate of one in 20, this 25-card set parallels the design of the base Court Kings insert. Each card contains a swatch of memorablila. Several players have different versions with different types of memorabilia; these are cataloged below.

CKAI Allen Iverson 5.00 12.00
CKAJ Antawn Jamison 3.00 8.00
CKAW Antoine Walker 2.50 6.00
CKBD Baron Davis 3.00 8.00
CKCW Chris Webber 3.00 8.00
CKDN Dirk Nowitzki 5.00 12.00
CKEB Elton Brand 3.00 8.00
CKEJ Eddie Jones 2.50 6.00
CKJK Jason Kidd 5.00 12.00
CKJS Jerry Stackhouse 2.50 6.00
CKLS Latrell Sprewell 2.50 6.00
CKMB Mike Bibby 3.00 8.00
CKPP Paul Pierce 4.00 10.00
CKRA Ray Allen 3.00 8.00
CKVC Vince Carter 5.00 12.00
CKDM1 Darius Miles WU 2.00 5.00
CKDM2 Darius Miles Shorts 2.00 5.00
CKKM1 Karl Malone WU 4.00 10.00
CKKM2 Karl Malone JSY 4.00 10.00
CKKM1 Kenyon Martin WU 3.00 8.00
CKKM2 Kenyon Martin JSY 3.00 8.00
CKSF1 Steve Francis WU 3.00 8.00
CKSF2 Steve Francis Shorts 3.00 8.00
CKTM1 Tracy McGrady Shorts 5.00 12.00
CKTM2 Tracy McGrady Shirt 5.00 12.00

2002-03 Flair Court Kings Game Used Dual

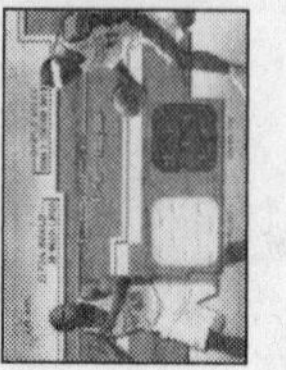

Randomly inserted in packs, this nine card set parallels the base Court Kings insert design, but features two players on each card and two swatches of jersey. Each card is sequentially numbered to 250.

BD/SF Baron Davis 10.00 25.00
Steve Francis
DN/KM Dirk Nowitzki 12.50 30.00
Karl Malone
EB/DM Elton Brand 10.00 25.00
Darius Miles
EJ/RA Eddie Jones 10.00 25.00
Ray Allen
JK/KM Jason Kidd 10.00 25.00
Kenyon Martin
JS/AI Jerry Stackhouse 12.50 30.00
Allen Iverson
MB/CW Mike Bibby 12.50 30.00
Chris Webber
PP/AW Paul Pierce 10.00 25.00
Antoine Walker
TM/VC Tracy McGrady 15.00 40.00
Vince Carter

2002-03 Flair Hot Numbers Patches

Randomly seeded in packs, this eight card set parallels the design of the New Heights insert enhanced with a swatch of the number patch off a jersey and the words "Hot Numbers" instead of "New Heights."

HNAI Allen Iverson 12.00 30.00
HNDM Darius Miles 5.00 12.00
HNDN Dirk Nowitzki 12.00 30.00
HNJK Jason Kidd 12.00 30.00
HNPG Pau Gasol 10.00 25.00
HNPP Paul Pierce 10.00 25.00
HNTM Tracy McGrady 12.00 30.00
HNVC Vince Carter 12.00 30.00

2002-03 Flair Jersey Heights

Inserted in packs at the rate of one in 16, this eight card set also parallels the design of the New Heights insert set. Each card contains a swatch from a game worn jersey, under which the words, "Jersey Heights" appear.

JHAI Allen Iverson 5.00 12.00
JHDM Darius Miles 2.00 5.00
JHDN Dirk Nowitzki 5.00 12.00
JHJK Jason Kidd 5.00 12.00
JHPG Pau Gasol 4.00 10.00
JHPP Paul Pierce 4.00 10.00
JHTM Tracy McGrady 5.00 12.00
JHVC Vince Carter 5.00 12.00

2002-03 Flair New Heights

Inserted in packs at the rate of one in ten, this 20-card set features a horizontal design with gray along the top and the bottom and a strip of cloudy sky through the middle. Color player photos appear on the right side and team logos appear on the left. Below the team logo, the words, "New Heights" appear. All cards have bronze foil highlights.

COMPLETE SET (20) 20.00 50.00
1 Tracy McGrady 1.50 4.00
2 Vince Carter 1.50 4.00
3 Jason Kidd 1.50 4.00
4 Tim Duncan 2.00 5.00
5 Dirk Nowitzki 1.50 4.00
6 Jamaal Tinsley .60 1.50
7 Kobe Bryant 5.00 12.00
8 Eddy Curry .75 2.00
9 Shane Battier 1.00 2.50
10 Peja Stojakovic 1.00 2.50
11 Michael Jordan 8.00 20.00
12 Darius Miles .60 1.50
13 Jason Richardson 1.00 2.50
14 Pau Gasol 1.25 3.00
15 Jerry Stackhouse .75 2.00
16 Shaquille O'Neal 2.50 6.00
17 Paul Pierce 1.25 3.00
18 Eddie Griffin .60 1.50
19 Kwame Brown .60 1.50
20 Allen Iverson 1.50 4.00

2002-03 Flair Sweet Swatch Autographs

Inserted in the one-per-box topper pack, these jumbo cards measure 5" X 7 3/4" and feature a large swatch of basketball-type material with bold player signatures. Each card is sequentially numbered-print runs listed below.
*GOLD: .75X TO 2X BASE HI
GOLD PRINT RUN 15 SER.#'d SETS

EC Eddy Curry/250 10.00 25.00
GR Glenn Robinson/400 10.00 25.00
JJ Joe Johnson/375 10.00 25.00
KB Kedrick Brown/75 10.00 25.00
MB Michael Bradley/75 10.00 25.00
SA Shareef Abdur-Rahim/500 10.00 25.00
VC Vince Carter/475 15.00 40.00
KBR Kwame Brown/200 10.00 25.00

2002-03 Flair Sweet Swatch Game Used

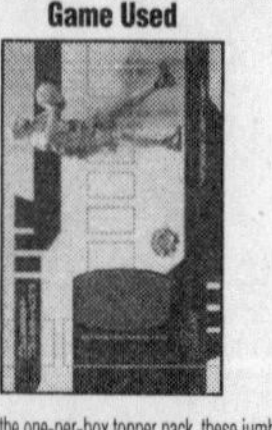

Inserted in the one-per-box topper pack, these jumbo cards measure 5" X 7 3/4" and feature a large swatch of game-worn memorabilia. Each card is sequentially numbered-print runs listed below.

SSAI Allen Iverson/975 8.00 20.00
SSDM Darius Miles/825 3.00 8.00
SSHT Hedo Turkoglu/650 5.00 12.00
SSJK Jason Kidd/800 8.00 20.00
SSJR Jason Richardson/625 5.00 12.00
SSJT Jamaal Tinsley/475 3.00 8.00
SSKM Kenyon Martin/900 5.00 12.00
SSMM Mike Miller/875 5.00 12.00
SSPG Pau Gasol/750 6.00 15.00
SSPP Paul Pierce/625 6.00 15.00
SSPS Peja Stojakovic/725 5.00 12.00
SSRA Ray Allen/850 5.00 12.00
SSSN Steve Nash/625 6.00 15.00
SSTM Tracy McGrady/850 8.00 20.00
SSTP Tony Parker/600 6.00 15.00
SSVC Vince Carter/975 8.00 20.00

2002-03 Flair Sweet Swatch Patches

Randomly inserted in the one-per-box topper packs, this 16-card set parallels the base Sweet Swatch Game Used insert set enhanced with large patch swatches from game-worn memorabilia. Each card is sequentially numbered-print runs listed below.
LOWER PRINT RUNS NOT PRICED

SSAI Allen Iverson/33 50.00 125.00
SSDM Darius Miles/26 20.00 50.00
SSJK Jason Kidd/33 40.00 100.00
SSJT Jamaal Tinsley/32 20.00 50.00
SSMM Mike Miller/31 30.00 80.00
SSPG Pau Gasol 40.00 100.00
SSPP Paul Pierce 40.00 100.00
SSRA Ray Allen/49 30.00 80.00
SSTP Tony Parker/32 40.00 100.00
SSVC Vince Carter/35 50.00 125.00

2002-03 Flair Wave of the Future

Randomly seeded in packs at the rate of one in 20, this 11-card set showcases this year's top rookies. Both the left and right side of the card have color strips to match the featured player's jersey colors. Player photos are on the left and team logos and the Draft NY 02 logo appears on the right. All cards contain bronze foil highlights.

COMPLETE SET (11) 15.00 40.00
1 Amare Stoudemire 4.00 10.00
2 Caron Butler 2.50 6.00
3 Chris Wilcox 1.50 4.00
4 DaJuan Wagner 1.50 4.00
5 Drew Gooden 2.50 6.00
6 Jared Jeffries 1.50 4.00
7 Jay Williams 2.00 5.00
8 Melvin Ely 1.50 4.00
9 Mike Dunleavy 2.00 5.00
10 Nene Hilario 2.00 5.00
11 Nikoloz Tskitishvili 1.50 4.00

2002-03 Flair Wave of the Future Jerseys

Randomly seeded in packs, this eight card set parallels the base Wave of the Future insert design enhanced with jersey swatches. Each card is sequentially numbered to 100. Patch versions were also inserted and are sequentially numbered to 50.
*PATCHES: .75X TO 2X HI

AS Amare Stoudemire 10.00 25.00
CB Caron Butler 6.00 15.00
CW Chris Wilcox 4.00 10.00
DG Drew Gooden 6.00 15.00
DW DaJuan Wagner 4.00 10.00
JJ Jared Jeffries 4.00 10.00
NH Nene Hilario 5.00 12.00
NT Nikoloz Tskitishvili 4.00 10.00

2003-04 Flair

Released in November 2003, Flair boasts a 120-card base set divided up into 90 veteran cards and 30 rookie cards sequentially numbered to 500. Base cards combine foreground action photos with background portrait photos and foil highlights. Flair was packaged in 20-pack boxes with packs containing five cards and carried a suggested retail price of $5.99.

COMP.SET w/o SP's (90) 15.00 40.00
UNPRICED ROW 2 PRINT RUN ONE SET
1 Jerry Stackhouse .25 .60
2 Eddie Griffin .20 .50
3 Jermaine O'Neal .30 .75
4 Kobe Bryant 1.50 4.00
5 Juwan Howard .25 .60
6 Alonzo Mourning .40 1.00
7 Kenny Thomas .20 .50
8 Chris Webber .30 .75
9 Radoslav Nesterovic .20 .50
10 Morris Peterson .20 .50
11 DeShawn Stevenson .20 .50
12 Steve Francis .30 .75
13 Andrei Kirilenko .30 .75
14 Kwame Brown .20 .50
15 Tim Duncan .50 1.25
16 Yao Ming .60 1.50
17 Jamaal Tinsley .20 .50
18 Shaquille O'Neal .75 2.00
19 Tracy McGrady .40 1.00
20 Dirk Nowitzki .50 1.25
21 Marcus Camby .25 .60
22 Elton Brand .30 .75
23 Latrell Sprewell .25 .60
24 Grant Hill .40 1.00
25 Shawn Marion .30 .75
26 Rasheed Wallace .30 .75
27 Ray Allen .30 .75
28 Antonio Davis .20 .50
29 Antoine Walker .30 .75
30 Ricky Davis .25 .60
31 Jason Kidd .50 1.25
32 Tony Parker .30 .75
33 Paul Pierce .40 1.00
34 Gary Payton .30 .75
35 Kenyon Martin .30 .75
36 Dale Davis .20 .50
37 Vladimir Radmanovic .20 .50
38 Matt Harpring .25 .60
39 Shareef Abdur-Rahim .25 .60
40 Antawn Jamison .30 .75
41 Eddie Jones .25 .60
42 Jamaal Magloire .20 .50
43 Jason Richardson .30 .75
44 Jonathan Bender .20 .50
45 Chris Wilcox .20 .50
46 Manu Ginobili .40 1.00
47 Chauncey Billups .30 .75
48 Jamal Mashburn .25 .60
49 Joe Smith .25 .60
50 Aaron McKie .20 .50
51 Theo Ratliff .20 .50
52 Eddy Curry .25 .60
53 Ron Artest .30 .75
54 Quentin Richardson .25 .60
55 Karl Malone .40 1.00
56 Pau Gasol .30 .75
57 Dan Dickau .20 .50
58 Darius Miles .20 .50
59 Ben Wallace .30 .75
60 Cuttino Mobley .25 .60
61 Lamar Odom .30 .75
62 Shane Battier .25 .60
63 Allan Houston .25 .60
64 Peja Stojakovic .30 .75
65 Dajuan Wagner .20 .50
66 Caron Butler .20 .50
67 Keith Van Horn .25 .60
68 Vincent Yarbrough .20 .50
69 Tim Thomas .20 .50
70 Troy Hudson .20 .50
71 Amare Stoudemire .50 1.25
72 Bobby Jackson .20 .50
73 Bonzi Wells .20 .50
74 Steve Nash .40 1.00
75 Gilbert Arenas .30 .75
76 Glenn Robinson .25 .60
77 Jalen Rose .25 .60
78 Michael Finley .30 .75
79 Nene .25 .60
80 Kevin Garnett .60 1.50
81 Richard Jefferson .30 .75
82 Baron Davis .30 .75
83 Mike Bibby .30 .75
84 Tyson Chandler .25 .60
85 Michael Redd .30 .75
86 Mike Dunleavy .25 .60
87 Drew Gooden .25 .60
88 Allen Iverson .50 1.25
89 Vince Carter .50 1.25
90 Larry Hughes .25 .60
91 Josh Howard RC 1.50 4.00
92 Maciej Lampe RC 1.50 4.00
93 Zarko Cabarkapa RC 1.50 4.00
94 LeBron James RC 30.00 80.00
95 Reece Gaines RC 1.50 4.00
96 Jarvis Hayes RC 1.50 4.00
97 Mickael Pietrus RC 1.50 4.00
98 T.J. Ford RC 2.00 5.00
99 Zoran Planinic RC 1.50 4.00
100 Luke Ridnour RC 2.00 5.00
101 Boris Diaw RC 2.00 5.00
102 Nick Collison RC 1.50 4.00
103 Travis Outlaw RC 2.00 5.00
104 Carmelo Anthony RC 5.00 12.00
105 Chris Kaman RC 2.00 5.00
106 Mike Sweetney RC 1.50 4.00
107 Kendrick Perkins RC 2.50 6.00
108 Jason Kapono RC 1.50 4.00
109 Troy Bell RC 1.50 4.00
110 Chris Bosh RC 3.00 8.00
111 Jerome Beasley RC 1.50 4.00
112 Darko Milicic RC 1.50 4.00
113 Dwyane Wade RC 8.00 20.00
114 David West RC 2.00 5.00
115 Kirk Hinrich RC 2.00 5.00
116 Dahntay Jones RC 1.50 4.00
117 Leandro Barbosa RC 2.00 5.00
118 Marcus Banks RC 1.50 4.00
119 Luke Walton RC 1.50 4.00
120 Ndudi Ebi RC 1.50 4.00

2003-04 Flair Rookie Jumbos

Inserted as a box-topper, these jumbo cards parallel the base rookie cards enhanced with sequential numbering to 400.

1 LeBron James 15.00 40.00
2 Darko Milicic 1.50 4.00
3 Carmelo Anthony 4.00 10.00
4 Chris Bosh 3.00 8.00
5 Dwyane Wade 8.00 20.00
6 Chris Kaman 2.00 5.00
7 Kirk Hinrich 2.00 5.00
8 T.J. Ford 2.00 5.00
9 Mike Sweetney 1.50 4.00
10 Jarvis Hayes 1.50 4.00
11 Mickael Pietrus 1.50 4.00
12 Nick Collison 1.50 4.00
13 Marcus Banks 1.50 4.00
14 Troy Bell 1.50 4.00
15 David West 2.00 5.00

2003-04 Flair Row 1

Randomly seeded in packs, this 120-card set parallels the base set enhanced with sequential numbering to 100. A Row 2 version exists as well and these cards are serially numbered one of one.
*1-90 ROW 1 SINGLES: 4X TO 10X BASE HI
*91-120 ROW 1 RCs: 1.25X TO 3X BASE HI

2003-04 Flair A Cut Abov

Randomly inserted in packs, this 20-card set fea full color player image in the foreground, a scale colored portrait in the background and a swatch game-worn memorabilia. Each card is sequential numbered to 500. A Final Cut version was also i and is sequentially numbered to 50.
*FINAL CUT: 1X TO 2.5X BASE HI

AH Allan Houston 2.00
AJ Antawn Jamison 2.50
BD Baron Davis 2.50
BW Bonzi Wells 2.00
CB Caron Butler 2.50
CW Chris Webber 2.50
DW Dajuan Wagner 2.00
GP Gary Payton 2.50
JK Jason Kidd 4.00
JR Jason Richardson 2.50
MG Manu Ginobili 3.00
PG Pau Gasol 2.50
PS Peja Stojakovic 2.50
RA Ron Artest 2.50
RD Ricky Davis 2.00
RM Reggie Miller 2.50
SA Shareef Abdur-Rahim 2.00
SN Steve Nash 3.00
TP Tayshaun Prince 2.50
VC Vince Carter 4.00
YM Yao Ming 5.00

2003-04 Flair Sweet Swatc

With backgrounds set to match the featured playe team color, this 20-card set places a rectangle sw of game-worn memorabilia centered vertically on left side of the card. Each card is sequentially numbered to 250. A Patch version sequentially numbered to 50 was also issued.
*PATCH: 1.25X TO 3X BASE HI

AH Allan Houston 2.00
AI Allen Iverson 4.00
AS Amare Stoudemire 4.00
CA Carmelo Anthony 6.00
CB Caron Butler 2.50
DG Drew Gooden 2.00
DJ Dahntay Jones 2.50
DN Dirk Nowitzki 4.00
DW Dwyane Wade 8.00
KG Kevin Garnett 5.00
LW Luke Walton 2.50
MB Marcus Banks 2.50
MS Mike Sweetney 2.50
PP Paul Pierce 3.00
SF Steve Francis 2.50
SN Steve Nash 3.00
TM Tracy McGrady 3.00
TO Travis Outlaw 3.00
TP Tony Parker 2.50
VC Vince Carter 4.00

2003-04 Flair Sweet Swatc Autographs

Randomly seeded in packs, this 23-card set parall the design of the Sweet Swatch insert enhanced w authentic player autographs. Each card is sequent numbered, and print runs are listed below. A Gold version sequentially numbered to 25 and a master version numbered one of one were also produced.

AS Amare Stoudemire/200 12.00
BC Brian Cook/150 5.00
CA Carmelo Anthony/271 25.00
CB Chris Bosh/100 15.00
DJ Dahntay Jones/200 5.00
DW Dwyane Wade/145 40.00
DW David West/200 6.00
JH Josh Howard 5.00
JK Jason Kapono/200 5.00
JO Jermaine O'Neal/20 20.00
KP Kendrick Perkins/100 8.00
LR Luke Ridnour/150 6.00
LW Luke Walton/200 5.00
MB Marcus Banks/120 5.00
ML Maciej Lampe/190 5.00
MP Mickael Pietrus/100 5.00
MS Mike Sweetney/100 5.00
PS Peja Stojakovic/15 15.00
TO Travis Outlaw/200 6.00
TP Tayshaun Prince/25 20.00

2003-04 Flair Sweet Swatch Autographs Gold

This parallel insert set is sequentially numbered t
*GOLD: .75X TO 2X BASE HI

CA Carmelo Anthony 100.00
JO Jermaine O'Neal 20.00
SF Steve Francis 20.00
TP Tayshaun Prince 20.00

)03-04 Flair Sweet Swatch Jumbos Away

d as a box-topper, this 20-card set utilizes the of the Sweet Swatch insert and places an ed swatch on the card front. Each card is tially numbered and print runs are listed below. ey Home version was also released and these are the same as the Away version-Patch versions lso issued and these cards are sequentially ered to 30.
E VERSION: .4X TO 1X BASE HI
H: 1.25X TO 3X BASE HI

an Houston/187	3.00	8.00
n Iverson/171	6.00	15.00
rmelo Anthony/125	10.00	25.00
ron Butler/201	4.00	10.00
ew Gooden/165	3.00	8.00
hntay Jones/144	4.00	10.00
rk Nowitzki/87	6.00	15.00
wyane Wade/116	15.00	40.00
vin Garnett/190	8.00	20.00
ike Walton/199	4.00	10.00
arcus Banks/135	4.00	10.00
ike Sweetney/173	4.00	10.00
ul Pierce/62	6.00	15.00
eve Francis/187	4.00	10.00
eve Nash/116	5.00	12.00
acy McGrady/183	5.00	12.00
avis Outlaw/165	5.00	12.00
ny Parker/125	4.00	10.00
nce Carter/139	6.00	15.00

)03-04 Flair Sweet Swatch Jumbos Double

mly seeded as a box-topper, this 10-card set es the Sweet Swatch design with two players and vatches of game-worn memorabilia. Each card is ntially numbered to 50.

cus Banks	15.00	40.00
Pierce		
y McGrady	12.50	30.00
v Gooden		
ane Wade	15.00	40.00
on Butler		
e Sweetney	10.00	25.00
n Houston		
are Stoudemire	15.00	40.00
in Garnett		
n Iverson	20.00	50.00
ce Carter		
ntay Jones	10.00	25.00
e Walton		
melo Anthony	15.00	40.00
vis Outlaw		
eve Francis	12.50	30.00
y Parker		

'003-04 Flair Sweet Swatch Jumbos Triple

omly inserted as a box-topper, this version of the t Swatch Jumbo set showcases three players with a swatch of game-worn memorabilia from Cards are sequentially numbered to 32. An raphed version sequentially numbered to three also issued.

melo Anthony	30.00	60.00
ris Bosh		
yane Wade		
maine O'Neal	12.50	30.00
a Stojakovic		
yshaun Prince		
vid West	12.50	30.00
an Cook		
vis Outlaw		
ke Ridnour	12.50	30.00
ckael Pietrus		
ke Sweetney		
sh Howard	12.50	30.00
ke Walton		
son Kapono		

2003-04 Flair Wave of the Future

Inserted in packs at the rate of one in 20, this 15-card set places rookeis from the 2003 NBA Draft in full-color in front of a water/wave background.

COMPLETE SET (15)	25.00	50.00
1 LeBron James	10.00	25.00
2 Darko Milicic	1.00	2.50
3 Carmelo Anthony	2.50	6.00
4 Chris Bosh	2.00	5.00
5 Dwyane Wade	4.00	10.00
6 Chris Kaman	1.25	3.00
7 Kirk Hinrich	1.25	3.00
8 T.J. Ford	1.25	3.00
9 Mike Sweetney	1.00	2.50
10 Jarvis Hayes	1.00	2.50
11 Mickael Pietrus	1.00	2.50
12 Nick Collison	1.00	2.50
13 Marcus Banks	1.00	2.50
14 Luke Ridnour	1.25	3.00
15 Reece Gaines	1.00	2.50

2003-04 Flair Wave of the Future Game Used

Inserted as a parallel set to the Wave of the Future insert, these cards are sequentially numbered to 250 and are enhanced with a swatch of game-used memorabilia. A Patch version sequentially numbered to 50 was also inserted.
*PATCH: .75X TO 2X BASE HI

CA Carmelo Anthony	6.00	15.00
CB Chris Bosh	5.00	12.00
CK Chris Kaman	3.00	8.00
DW David West	3.00	8.00
DW Dwyane Wade	10.00	25.00
JH Jarvis Hayes	2.50	6.00
LR Luke Ridnour	3.00	8.00
MB Marcus Banks	2.50	6.00
MP Mickael Pietrus	2.50	6.00
MS Mike Sweetney	2.50	6.00
RG Reece Gaines	2.50	6.00
TB Troy Bell	2.50	6.00

2003-04 Flair World Leaders

This 20-card horizontally designed set was inserted at the rate of one in 10. Full-color player photos appear on the right of this gold-colored card. A Game Used version was also inserted at the rate of one in 15.

COMPLETE SET (20)	15.00	30.00
1 Paul Pierce	1.00	2.50
2 Tim Duncan	1.25	3.00
3 Yao Ming	1.50	4.00
4 Shaquille O'Neal	2.00	5.00
5 Tracy McGrady	1.00	2.50
6 Dirk Nowitzki	1.25	3.00
7 Elton Brand	.75	2.00
8 Amare Stoudemire	1.25	3.00
9 Kevin Garnett	1.50	4.00
10 Allen Iverson	1.25	3.00
11 Vince Carter	1.25	3.00
12 Steve Francis	.75	2.00
13 Tony Parker	.75	2.00
14 Pau Gasol	.75	2.00
15 Ben Wallace	.75	2.00
16 Andrei Kirilenko	.75	2.00
17 Gilbert Arenas	.75	2.00
18 Jermaine O'Neal	.75	2.00
19 Chris Webber	.75	2.00
20 Drew Gooden	.60	1.50

2003-04 Flair World Leaders Game Used

Inserted at one in 15, this 20-card set parallels the base World Leaders set enhanced with a swatch of game-worn memorabilia.

AI Allen Iverson	4.00	10.00
AK Andrei Kirilenko	2.50	6.00
AS Amare Stoudemire	4.00	10.00
BW Ben Wallace	2.50	6.00
CR Chris Webber	2.50	6.00
DG Drew Gooden	2.00	5.00
DR Dirk Nowitzki	4.00	10.00
EB Elton Brand	2.50	6.00
GA Gilbert Arenas	2.50	6.00
JK Jason Kidd	4.00	10.00
KG Kevin Garnett	5.00	12.00
PG Pau Gasol	2.50	6.00
PP Paul Pierce	3.00	8.00
SF Steve Francis	2.50	6.00
SO Shaquille O'Neal	6.00	15.00
TD Tim Duncan	4.00	10.00
TM Tracy McGrady	3.00	8.00
TP Tony Parker	2.50	6.00
VC Vince Carter	4.00	10.00
YM Yao Ming	5.00	12.00

2004 Flair Significant Cuts

OVERALL AU ODDS 1:1 HOBBY
PRINT RUNS B/WN 1-200 COPIES PER
NO PRICING ON QTY OF 10 OR LESS

VC Vince Carter/200	20.00	40.00

2004-05 Flair

Issued in April 2005, Flair consists of a 90-card base set with 60 veteran players and 30 rookies sequentially numbered to 799. Base cards place full-color player action photography against a white background with a gold strip through the middle for veterans and a silver strip through the middle for rookies. Flair was offered in both Hobby and Retail formats where Hobby boxes contained a single pack of 12 cards and retail boxes contained 24 five-card packs.

COMP.SET w/o SP's (60)	30.00	70.00
UNPRICED ROW 2 PRINT RUN ONE SET		
1 Gilbert Arenas	.60	1.50
2 Richard Hamilton	.50	1.25
3 Stephon Marbury	.50	1.25
4 Tony Parker	.60	1.50
5 Michael Redd	.60	1.50
6 Latrell Sprewell	.50	1.25
7 Willie Green	.40	1.00
8 Joe Johnson	.60	1.50
9 Lamar Odom	.60	1.50
10 Tim Duncan	1.00	2.50
11 Ben Wallace	.60	1.50
12 Elton Brand	.60	1.50
13 Allen Iverson	1.00	2.50
14 Andrei Kirilenko	.50	1.25
15 Dirk Nowitzki	1.00	2.50
16 Paul Pierce	.75	2.00
17 Mike Dunleavy	.50	1.25
18 Zach Randolph	.50	1.25
19 David West	.60	1.50
20 Corey Maggette	.50	1.25
21 Dwyane Wade	2.00	5.00
22 Chris Bosh	.60	1.50
23 Michael Finley	.60	1.50
24 Kevin Garnett	1.25	3.00
25 Allan Houston	.50	1.25
26 Antawn Jamison	.60	1.50
27 Jermaine O'Neal	.60	1.50
28 Alonzo Mourning	.75	2.00
29 Gerald Wallace	.60	1.50
30 Jason Williams	.50	1.25
31 Tyronn Lue	.40	1.00
32 Pau Gasol	.60	1.50
33 Jason Kidd	1.00	2.50
34 Shareef Abdur-Rahim	.50	1.25
35 LeBron James	4.00	10.00
36 Shaquille O'Neal	1.50	4.00
37 Jason Richardson	.60	1.50
38 Rasheed Wallace	.60	1.50
39 Nene	.50	1.25
40 Tracy McGrady	.75	2.00
41 Luke Ridnour	.50	1.25
42 Peja Stojakovic	.60	1.50
43 Amare Stoudemire	.75	2.00
44 Carmelo Anthony	1.25	3.00
45 Steve Francis	.60	1.50
46 Antoine Walker	.60	1.50
47 Reggie Miller	.60	1.50
48 Mike Bibby	.60	1.50
49 Sam Cassell	.50	1.25
50 Richard Jefferson	.60	1.50
51 Jason Kapono	.40	1.00
52 Dajuan Wagner	.40	1.00
53 Kobe Bryant	3.00	8.00
54 Kenyon Martin	.60	1.50
55 T.J. Ford	.50	1.25
56 Ray Allen	.60	1.50
57 Vince Carter	1.00	2.50
58 Yao Ming	1.25	3.00
59 Baron Davis	.60	1.50
60 Joe Smith	.50	1.25
61 Luol Deng RC	2.50	6.00
62 J.R. Smith RC	2.00	5.00
63 Josh Childress RC	1.50	4.00
64 Shaun Livingston RC	1.50	4.00
65 Rafael Araujo RC	1.50	4.00
66 Devin Harris RC	2.50	6.00
67 Kevin Martin RC	2.00	5.00
68 Sasha Vujacic RC	1.50	4.00
69 Robert Swift RC	1.50	4.00
70 Andris Biedrins RC	2.00	5.00
71 Kirk Snyder RC	1.50	4.00
72 Jameer Nelson RC	2.00	5.00
73 Tony Allen RC	2.00	5.00
74 Chris Duhon RC	1.50	4.00
75 David Harrison RC	1.50	4.00
76 Andre Iguodala RC	2.50	6.00
77 Josh Smith RC	2.50	6.00
78 Andre Emmett RC	1.50	4.00
79 Luke Jackson RC	1.50	4.00
80 Dorell Wright RC	2.50	6.00
81 Ben Gordon RC	2.00	5.00
82 Dwight Howard RC	5.00	12.00
83 Kris Humphries RC	1.50	4.00
84 Al Jefferson RC	2.50	6.00
85 Jackson Vroman RC	1.50	4.00
86 Beno Udrih RC	1.50	4.00
87 Trevor Ariza RC	1.50	4.00
88 Sebastian Telfair RC	1.50	4.00
89 Emeka Okafor RC	2.50	6.00
90 Peter John Ramos RC	1.50	4.00

2004-05 Flair Row 1

Randomly inserted in packs, this 90-card set parallels the base set enhanced with bronze highlights and sequential numbering to 100. One of one Row 2 cards exist.
*1-60 ROW 1: 1X TO 2.5X BASE HI
*61-90 ROW 1 RCs: .5X TO 1.25X BASE HI

2004-05 Flair Courting Greatness Jerseys

Limited to 150 copies, this 28-card set places two players on each card with one jersey below the featured player on these cards. Patch parallels were also inserted that are sequentially numbered to 50 and logo one of one's exist for each individual player.
*PATCHES: .75X TO 2X BASE JSY HI

AI Allen Iverson	5.00	12.00
AJ Antawn Jamison	3.00	8.00
AS Amare Stoudemire	4.00	10.00
BW Ben Wallace	3.00	8.00
CB Chauncey Billups	3.00	8.00
DH Dwight Howard	8.00	20.00
DN Dirk Nowitzki	5.00	12.00
DW Dwyane Wade	10.00	25.00
GA Gilbert Arenas	3.00	8.00
GH Grant Hill	4.00	10.00
GP Gary Payton	3.00	8.00
IG Andre Iguodala	4.00	10.00
JK Jason Kidd	5.00	12.00
JR Jason Richardson	3.00	8.00
KG Kevin Garnett	6.00	15.00
LS Latrell Sprewell	2.50	6.00
MB Mike Bibby	3.00	8.00
MD Mike Dunleavy	2.50	6.00
MG Manu Ginobili	4.00	10.00
PP Paul Pierce	4.00	10.00
PS Peja Stojakovic	3.00	8.00
SN Steve Nash	4.00	10.00
TD Tim Duncan	5.00	12.00
TM Tracy McGrady	4.00	10.00
VC Vince Carter	5.00	12.00
HOW Josh Howard	3.00	8.00
SON Shaquille O'Neal	8.00	20.00
YAO Yao Ming	6.00	15.00

2004-05 Flair Courting Greatness Jerseys Retail

Randomly seeded in Retail packs at the rate of one in 48, this 28-card set parallels the design of the base Courting Greatness Jerseys with no sequential numbering.

2004-05 Flair Courting Greatness Jerseys Dual

Randomly seeded, this 14-card set parallels the design of the base Courting Greatness insert enhanced with two Jerseys and sequential numbering to 99. Dual Patch parallels were also issued and these are serially numbered to 15.
*PATCH: 1.25X TO 3X BASE HI
PATCH PRINT RUN 15 SER.#'d SETS

AIAI Andre Iguodala	5.00	12.00
Allen Iverson		
CBBW Chauncey Billups	5.00	12.00
Ben Wallace		
GAAJ Gilbert Arenas	5.00	12.00
Antawn Jamison		
GHDH Grant Hill	10.00	25.00
Dwight Howard		
GPPP Gary Payton	5.00	12.00
Paul Pierce		
JHDN Josh Howard	5.00	12.00
Dirk Nowitzki		
JKVC Jason Kidd	10.00	25.00
Vince Carter		
KGLS Kevin Garnett	6.00	15.00
Latrell Sprewell		
MDJR Mike Dunleavy	5.00	12.00
Jason Richardson		
PSMB Peja Stojakovic	5.00	12.00
Mike Bibby		
SNAS Steve Nash	6.00	15.00
Amare Stoudemire		
SODW Shaquille O'Neal	12.50	30.00
Dwyane Wade		
TDMG Tim Duncan	10.00	25.00
Manu Ginobili		
TMYM Tracy McGrady	10.00	25.00
Yao Ming		

2004-05 Flair Cuts and Glory Jerseys

Randomly inserted in packs, this eight card set features a horizontal design with a player photo on the right, a square jersey swatch in the top left and a signature in the middle. Background colors are set to match the player's team colors. All cards are serially numbered, print runs are listed in the checklist.
JSY/PATCH NOT PRICED DUE TO SCARCITY

BW Ben Wallace/75	20.00	50.00
JC Josh Childress/100	10.00	25.00
JS Jerry Stackhouse/50	10.00	25.00
PG Pau Gasol/100	15.00	30.00
PS Peja Stojakovic/75	15.00	30.00
RH Richard Hamilton/100	10.00	25.00
SM Stephon Marbury/55	12.50	30.00
TM Tracy McGrady/20	30.00	80.00

2004-05 Flair Cuts and Glory Patches

Randomly seeded, this eight card set parallels the design of the base Cuts and Glory Jerseys set enhanced with a patch swatch and sequential numbering to 50.

BW Ben Wallace	30.00	80.00
JC Josh Childress	15.00	40.00
PG Pau Gasol	20.00	50.00
PS Peja Stojakovic	15.00	40.00
RH Richard Hamilton	15.00	40.00
SM Stephon Marbury	20.00	50.00

2004-05 Flair Dynasty Foundations Jerseys

Randomly inserted in packs, this seven card set parallels the base Dynasty Foundations insert set enhanced with one swatch of game jersey and sequential numbering to 250.
*PATCHES: .75X TO 2X BASE HI
PATCH PRINT RUN 99 SER.#'d SETS

4 Carmelo Anthony JSY	6.00	15.00
Kenyon Martin		
Lafayette Lever		
Alex English		
Dan Issel		
9 David West	4.00	10.00
Baron Davis		
Jamal Mashburn		
Jamaal Magloire		
J.R. Smith JSY		
10 Julius Erving	6.00	15.00
Charles Barkley		
Bobby Jones		
Maurice Cheeks		
Allen Iverson JSY		
12 Clyde Drexler	4.00	10.00
Bill Walton		
Maurice Lucas		
Zach Randolph JSY		
Sebastian Telfair		
13 David Robinson	5.00	12.00
George Gervin		
Sean Elliott		
Tony Parker		
Tim Duncan JSY		
15 Alonzo Mourning	4.00	10.00
Chris Bosh JSY		
Jalen Rose		
Morris Peterson		
Rafer Alston		
17 Nate Archibald	3.00	8.00
Phil Ford		
Chris Webber		
Mike Bibby		
Peja Stojakovic JSY		

2004-05 Flair Dynasty Foundations Jerseys Dual

Randomly inserted in packs, this six card set parallels the base Dynasty Foundations insert set enhanced with two swatches of game jersey and sequential numbering to 150.

4 Carmelo Anthony JSY	6.00	15.00
Kenyon Martin JSY		
Lafayette Lever		
Alex English		
Dan Issel		
9 David West	6.00	15.00
Baron Davis JSY		
Jamal Mashburn		
Jamaal Magloire		
J.R. Smith JSY		
10 Julius Erving	15.00	40.00
Charles Barkley JSY		
Bobby Jones		
Maurice Cheeks		
Allen Iverson JSY		
12 Clyde Drexler	6.00	15.00
Bill Walton		
Maurice Lucas		
Zach Randolph JSY		
Sebastian Telfair JSY		
13 David Robinson JSY	10.00	25.00
George Gervin		
Sean Elliott		
Tony Parker		
Tim Duncan JSY		
17 Nate Archibald	6.00	15.00
Phil Ford		
Chris Webber JSY		
Mike Bibby		
Peja Stojakovic JSY		

2004-05 Flair Dynasty Foundations Patches Dual

Randomly inserted in packs, this six card set parallels the base Dynasty Foundations insert set enhanced with two swatches of game jersey patch and sequential numbering to 50.

4 Carmelo Anthony JSY	15.00	40.00
Kenyon Martin JSY		
Lafayette Lever		
Alex English		
Dan Issel		
9 David West	15.00	40.00
Baron Davis JSY		
Jamal Mashburn		
Jamaal Magloire		
J.R. Smith JSY		
10 Julius Erving	40.00	100.00
Charles Barkley JSY		
Bobby Jones		
Maurice Cheeks		
Allen Iverson JSY		
12 Clyde Drexler	15.00	40.00
Bill Walton		
Maurice Lucas		
Zach Randolph JSY		
Sebastian Telfair JSY		
17 Nate Archibald	15.00	40.00
Phil Ford		
Chris Webber JSY		
Mike Bibby		
Peja Stojakovic JSY		

2004-05 Flair Dynasty Foundations Jerseys Triple

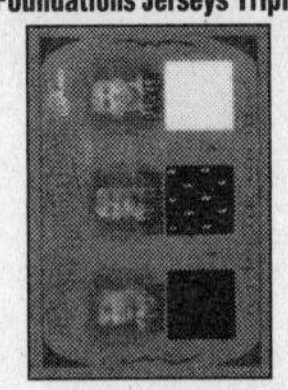

Randomly inserted in packs, this three card set parallels the base Dynasty Foundations insert set enhanced with three swatches of game jersey and sequential numbering to 99. A Quad Jerseys version numbered to 15 was also inserted along with a Triple Patches version that has patch swatches in the place of jerseys and is sequentially numbered to 25.
*PATCH TRIPLE: 1X TO 2.5X BASE HI

9 David West JSY	10.00	25.00
Baron Davis JSY		
Jamal Mashburn		
Jamaal Magloire		
J.R. Smith JSY		
13 David Robinson JSY	20.00	50.00
George Gervin		
Sean Elliott		
Tony Parker JSY		
Tim Duncan JSY		
17 Nate Archibald	10.00	25.00
Phil Ford		
Chris Webber JSY		
Mike Bibby JSY		
Peja Stojakovic JSY		

2004-05 Flair Head of the Class Jerseys

Randomly inserted in packs, this 10-card set features a horizontal design and three small black and white head shots of three players from the same year along the top of the card with three jersey swatches below. Each is sequentially numbered to the players' draft year.
STATED PRINT RUN 2 TO 99 SER.#'d SETS
SOME UNPRICED DUE TO SCARCITY
UNPRICED MASTERPIECE PRINT RUN ONE SET

BFD Elton Brand/99	6.00	15.00
Steve Francis		
Baron Davis		
DBM Tim Duncan/97	10.00	25.00
Chauncey Billups		
Tracy McGrady		
IMA Allen Iverson/96	10.00	25.00
Stephon Marbury		
Ray Allen		
NCJ Dirk Nowitzki/98	10.00	25.00
Vince Carter		
Antawn Jamison		
OMS Shaquille O'Neal/92	20.00	50.00
Alonzo Mourning		
Latrell Sprewell		
RPM David Robinson/87	30.00	60.00
Scottie Pippen		
Reggie Miller		
WHH Chris Webber/93	15.00	40.00
Anfernee Hardaway		
Allan Houston		

2004-05 Flair Head of the Class Patches

Randomly inserted in packs, this nine-card set parallels the base Head of the Class insert enhanced with patch swatches and sequential numbering to 33. A Masterpiece one of one was also produced.

BFD Elton Brand	25.00	60.00
Steve Francis		
Baron Davis		
DBM Tim Duncan	50.00	120.00
Chauncey Billups		
Tracy McGrady		
IMA Allen Iverson	50.00	120.00
Stephon Marbury		
Ray Allen		
NCJ Dirk Nowitzki	25.00	60.00
Vince Carter		
Antawn Jamison		
OMS Shaquille O'Neal	50.00	120.00
Alonzo Mourning		
Latrell Sprewell		
RPM David Robinson	100.00	225.00
Scottie Pippen		
Reggie Miller		
SMB Amare Stoudemire	25.00	60.00
Yao Ming		
Caron Butler		
SWG Jerry Stackhouse	25.00	60.00
Rasheed Wallace		
Kevin Garnett		
WHH Chris Webber	60.00	150.00
Anfernee Hardaway		
Allan Houston		

2004-05 Flair Significant Signings

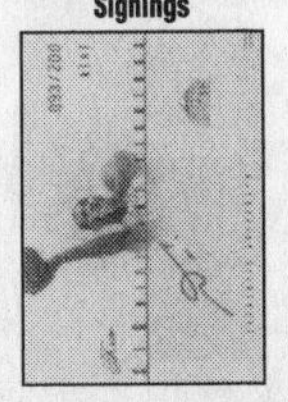

Randomly seeded in packs, this 21-card set features a tan background, centered player photos and a sticker autograph in the lower left hand corner. Each card is sequentially numbered to various quantities. Parallel version numbered to 50, 35, 25, and masterpiece one of one's were also issued.

N Nene/200	5.00	12.00
AJ Antawn Jamison/50	6.00	15.00
AS Amare Stoudemire/150	12.50	30.00
BG Ben Gordon/200	10.00	25.00
BM Brad Miller/150	5.00	12.00
CB Chauncey Billups/44	15.00	40.00
DH David Harrison/150	5.00	12.00
DW Dwyane Wade/75	40.00	100.00
DW David West/200	5.00	12.00
EB Elton Brand/75	6.00	15.00
JH Josh Howard/200	5.00	12.00
JS Josh Smith/200	8.00	20.00
JS2 J.R. Smith/250	10.00	25.00
KH Kris Humphries/200	5.00	12.00
KM Kenyon Martin/50	8.00	20.00
LO Lamar Odom/75	8.00	20.00
MB Mike Bibby/50	10.00	25.00
MG Manu Ginobili/75	15.00	40.00
MP Mickael Pietrus/200	5.00	12.00
RA Rafael Araujo/200	5.00	12.00
RJ Richard Jefferson/50	6.00	15.00

2004-05 Flair Significant Signings 50

Randomly inserted in packs, this 21-card set parallels the base Significant Signings set enhanced with sequential numbering to 50.

N Nene	6.00	15.00
AS Amare Stoudemire	15.00	40.00
DW Dwyane Wade	50.00	120.00
DW David West	6.00	15.00
JS Josh Smith	12.50	30.00
JS2 J.R. Smith	12.50	30.00
KH Kris Humphries	6.00	15.00

2004-05 Flair Significant Signings 35

Randomly inserted in packs, this 18-card set parallels the base Significant Signings set enhanced with sequential numbering to 35.

N Nene	8.00	20.00
BG Ben Gordon	15.00	40.00
BM Brad Miller	8.00	20.00
EB Elton Brand	10.00	25.00
JH Josh Howard	8.00	20.00
KM Kenyon Martin	12.50	30.00
LO Lamar Odom	12.50	30.00
MG Manu Ginobili	25.00	60.00
RA Rafael Araujo	8.00	20.00

2004-05 Flair Significant Signings 25

Randomly inserted in packs, this 19-card set parallels the base Significant Signings set enhanced with sequential numbering to 25.

AS Amare Stoudemire	25.00	60.00
DW Dwyane Wade	80.00	200.00
JH Josh Howard	10.00	25.00
MB Mike Bibby	15.00	40.00
MP Mickael Pietrus	10.00	25.00
RJ Richard Jefferson	12.50	30.00

2004-05 Flair Significant Signings Die Cuts

Randomly inserted in packs, this six card set parallels the base Significant Signings set enhanced with die cut edges and sequential numbering. The print runs are listed in the checklist.

AJ Al Jefferson/24	15.00	40.00
AS Amare Stoudemire/50	15.00	40.00
DW Dorell Wright/18	10.00	25.00
DW Dwyane Wade/20	80.00	200.00
JS Josh Smith/50	12.50	30.00
KH Kris Humphries/50	6.00	15.00

2004-05 Flair Significant Signings Jerseys

Randomly inserted in packs, this 18-card set parallels the base Significant Signings set enhanced with a jersey swatch and sequential numbering. Print runs for the cards we've found are listed in the checklist. A Jerseys 2 version was also inserted and is serially numbered to two, a Patch version with a patch swatch was inserted and is serially numbered to 10, and Patch one of one's were produced as well.

N Nene/25	10.00	25.00
AJ Antawn Jamison/15	15.00	40.00
AS Amare Stoudemire/25	25.00	60.00
DH David Harrison/25	10.00	25.00
DW Dwyane Wade/25	80.00	200.00
DW2 David West/25	10.00	25.00
EB Elton Brand/15	12.50	30.00
JH Josh Howard/25	10.00	25.00
JRS J.R. Smith/25	40.00	100.00
JS Josh Smith/25	40.00	100.00
KH Kris Humphries/25	10.00	25.00
KM Kenyon Martin/15	15.00	40.00
LJ Luke Jackson/50	10.00	25.00
LO Lamar Odom/25	15.00	40.00
MG Manu Ginobili/25	25.00	60.00
MP Mickael Pietrus/25	10.00	25.00
RJ Richard Jefferson/15	12.50	30.00

2003-04 Flair Final Edition

Released in late June 2004, Flair Final Edition was Fleer's final product issued for the 2003-04 season. The 90-card set is divided up into 65 base veteran cards and 25 rookie cards sequentially numbered to 799. The base cards show players in full color against a black and white background and have border colors set to match the team colors of the featured player. Flair Final Edition also included redemption cards for draft day materials including the team's logos, player's names and ping pong balls. Flair Final Edition was offered as both a Hobby and a Retail product with two distinctly different packagings. Retail were packed in four-card packs with 24 packs per box and carried a suggested retail price of $2.99; while hobby was

packaged as a single-pack box containing 12 cards and no suggested retail price was ever released.
COMP.SET w/o SP's (65) 12.50 30.00
UNPRICED ROW 2 PRINT RUN ONE SET
1 Allen Iverson .50 1.25
2 Juwan Howard .25 .60
3 Stephen Jackson .25 .60
4 Manu Ginobili .40 1.00
5 Steve Nash .40 1.00
6 Jason Terry .25 .60
7 Tayshaun Prince .30 .75
8 Stephon Marbury .25 .60
9 Eddie Jones .25 .60
10 Reggie Miller .30 .75
11 Baron Davis .30 .75
12 Donyell Marshall .20 .50
13 Mike Bibby .30 .75
14 Kobe Bryant 1.50 4.00
15 Jason Richardson .30 .75
16 Cuttino Mobley .25 .60
17 Andre Miller .25 .60
18 Corey Maggette .25 .60
19 Michael Finley .30 .75
20 Jason Kidd .50 1.25
21 Lamar Odom .30 .75
22 Tracy McGrady .40 1.00
23 Peja Stojakovic .30 .75
24 Richard Jefferson .30 .75
25 Rasheed Wallace .30 .75
26 Eddy Curry .25 .60
27 Ben Wallace .30 .75
28 Rashard Lewis .30 .75
29 Sam Cassell .25 .60
30 Anfernee Hardaway .50 1.25
31 Carlos Boozer .30 .75
32 Jamal Crawford .25 .60
33 Dirk Nowitzki .50 1.25
34 Steve Francis .30 .75
35 Chris Webber .30 .75
36 Elton Brand .30 .75
37 Michael Redd .30 .75
38 Jason Williams .25 .60
39 Nene .25 .60
40 Nick Van Exel .25 .60
41 Amare Stoudemire .50 1.25
42 Latrell Sprewell .25 .60
43 Tony Parker .30 .75
44 Keith Van Horn .25 .60
45 Pau Gasol .30 .75
46 Andrei Kirilenko .30 .75
47 Shareef Abdur-Rahim .25 .60
48 Tim Thomas .20 .50
49 Jerry Stackhouse .25 .60
50 Jermaine O'Neal .30 .75
51 Jamal Mashburn .25 .60
52 Matt Harpring .25 .60
53 Damon Stoudamire .25 .60
54 Zydrunas Ilgauskas .25 .60
55 Kevin Garnett .60 1.50
56 Tim Duncan .50 1.25
57 Yao Ming .60 1.50
58 Kenyon Martin .30 .75
59 Paul Pierce .40 1.00
60 Ron Artest .30 .75
61 Vince Carter .50 1.25
62 Shaquille O'Neal .75 2.00
63 Shawn Marion .30 .75
64 Gilbert Arenas .30 .75
65 Ray Allen .30 .75
66 Chris Bosh RC 4.00 10.00
67 Brian Cook RC 2.00 5.00
68 Luke Ridnour RC 2.50 6.00
69 Willie Green RC 2.00 5.00
70 Zarko Cabarkapa RC 2.00 5.00
71 Maurice Williams RC 3.00 8.00
72 Luke Walton RC 2.00 5.00
73 David West RC 2.50 6.00
74 Mickael Pietrus RC 2.00 5.00
75 LeBron James RC 25.00 60.00
76 Marcus Banks RC 2.00 5.00
77 Keith Bogans RC 2.00 5.00
78 Darko Milicic RC 2.00 5.00
79 Jarvis Hayes RC 2.00 5.00
80 Josh Howard RC 2.00 5.00
81 Chris Kaman RC 2.50 6.00
82 Mike Sweetney RC 2.00 5.00
83 Carmelo Anthony RC 5.00 12.00
84 Travis Outlaw RC 2.50 6.00
85 Kyle Korver RC 2.50 6.00
86 Boris Diaw RC 2.50 6.00
87 Dwyane Wade RC 8.00 20.00
88 Troy Bell RC 2.00 5.00
89 T.J. Ford RC 2.50 6.00
90 Kirk Hinrich RC 2.50 6.00

2003-04 Flair Final Edition Row 1

Randomly inserted in packs, this 90-card set parallels the base Flair Final Edition enhanced with sequential numbering to 100. A Row 2 parallel also exists, and these cards are numbered one of one.
*1-65 SINGLES: 2.5X TO 6X BASE CARD HI
*66-90 RC SINGLES: .75X TO 2X BASE HI

2003-04 Flair Final Edition Autograph Collection

Randomly seeded in packs, this 35-card set features a black border along the top, a brown-scale photo of the player and a cut signature along the bottom. Each card is sequentially numbered to 200 unless specifically noted below.
*AUTO 25: .75X TO 2X BASE HI
*AUTO 100: .5X TO 1.25X BASE HI
UNPRICED PARALLEL #'d TO 10 EXISTS
UNPRICED PARALLEL #'d TO ONE EXISTS
N Nene/200 5.00 12.00
AJ Antawn Jamison/200 5.00 12.00
AK Andrei Kirilenko/200 8.00 20.00
AS Amare Stoudemire/200 10.00 25.00
AW Antoine Walker/200 5.00 12.00
BD Baron Davis/200 6.00 15.00
BM Brad Miller/200 5.00 12.00
CM Corey Maggette/200 5.00 12.00
EG Manu Ginobili/200 15.00 40.00
FJ Fred Jones/200 5.00 12.00
GA Gilbert Arenas/200 6.00 15.00
GP Gary Payton/75 12.50 30.00
JD Juan Dixon/200 5.00 12.00
JJ Joe Johnson/200 6.00 15.00
JS Jerry Stackhouse/200 6.00 15.00
JW Jason Williams/200 12.50 30.00
KB Kwame Brown/200 5.00 12.00
LB Leandro Barbosa/200 5.00 12.00
LR Luke Ridnour/200 5.00 12.00
MP Mickael Pietrus/150 6.00 15.00
PP Paul Pierce/200 8.00 20.00
PS Peja Stojakovic/200 6.00 15.00
RH Richard Hamilton/200 6.00 15.00
RJ Richard Jefferson/200 5.00 12.00
RM Ronald Murray/200 5.00 12.00
SB Shane Battier/75 5.00 12.00
TP Tayshaun Prince/200 6.00 15.00
VC Vince Carter/100 12.50 30.00
WG Willie Green/200 5.00 12.00
CAB Carlos Boozer/200 5.00 12.00
CHB Chris Bosh/200 15.00 40.00
DAW Dajuan Wagner/200 5.00 12.00
DAW David West/150 6.00 15.00
DWW Dwyane Wade/200 30.00 80.00

2003-04 Flair Final Edition Courtside Cuts Jerseys 250

Randomly inserted in packs, this 20-card set feature white borders and full color player portrait-style photos with a centered swatch of jersey. Also released were versions sequentially numbered to 175, 125 and 75. Die Cut versions with rounded corners were also produced and versions are sequentially numbered to 25, 18, 13 and eight.
*JERSEY 175: .4X TO 1X BASE JSY HI
*JERSEY 125: .5X TO 1.25X BASE JSY HI
*JERSEY 75: .6X TO 1.5X BASE JSY HI
*JERSEY DC: 1X TO 2.5X BASE HI
*JERSEY GREEN: .4X TO 1X BASE HI
N Nene 2.00 5.00
AI Allen Iverson 4.00 10.00
BD Baron Davis 2.50 6.00
CA Carmelo Anthony 6.00 15.00
CK Chris Kaman 3.00 8.00
CM Cuttino Mobley 2.00 5.00
CW Chris Webber 2.50 6.00
EB Elton Brand 2.50 6.00
GA Gilbert Arenas 2.50 6.00
JS Jerry Stackhouse 2.00 5.00
LO Lamar Odom 2.50 6.00
MF Michael Finley 2.50 6.00
PS Peja Stojakovic 2.50 6.00
RM Reggie Miller 2.50 6.00
SN Steve Francis 2.50 6.00
SN Steve Nash 3.00 8.00
WG Willie Green 2.50 6.00
DAW David West 3.00 8.00
DWW Dwyane Wade 10.00 25.00
JON Jermaine O'Neal 2.50 6.00

2003-04 Flair Final Edition Courtside Cuts Patches

Randomly seeded in packs, this 20-card set parallels the Courtside Cuts set enahanced with premium swatches of patches. Each card is sequentially numbered to 50. A one of one version of this set was also produced along with Die-Cut versions, with rounded corners and versions numbered to five, three and one of one's. Dual versions were also inserted in packs and are sequentially numbered to 10.
*PATCH: 1.25X TO 3X BASE JSY HI

2003-04 Flair Final Edition Courtside Cuts Patches Gold

Randomly seeded in packs, this 15-card set is a parallel insert that is sequentially numbered. Print runs are listed below.
SOME NOT PRICED DUE TO SCARCITY
*DIE CUTS: .4X TO 1X BASE HI
N Nene/31 8.00 20.00
CA Carmelo Anthony/15 30.00 80.00
CK Chris Kaman/35 10.00 25.00
DW David West/30 12.00 30.00
EB Elton Brand/42 8.00 20.00
JS Jerry Stackhouse/42 6.00 15.00
RM Reggie Miller/31 15.00 40.00
WG Willie Green/33 8.00 20.00

2003-04 Flair Final Edition Courtside Cuts Patches Platinum

Randomly seeded in packs, this 15-card set is a parallel insert that is sequentially numbered. Print runs are listed below.
*DIE CUTS: .4X TO 1X BASE HI
N Nene/43 6.00 15.00
AI Allen Iverson/33 12.00 30.00
BD Baron Davis/41 8.00 20.00
CA Carmelo Anthony/43 20.00 50.00
CK Chris Kaman/28 10.00 25.00
CM Cuttino Mobley/45 6.00 15.00
CW Chris Webber/55 8.00 20.00
DW Dwyane Wade/42 30.00 80.00
DW David West/51 10.00 25.00
EB Elton Brand/28 8.00 20.00
GA Gilbert Arenas/25 8.00 20.00
JO Jermaine O'Neal/61 8.00 20.00
JS Jerry Stackhouse/25 12.50 30.00
LO Lamar Odom/42 8.00 20.00
MF Michael Finley/52 8.00 20.00
PS Peja Stojakovic/55 8.00 20.00
RM Reggie Miller/61 8.00 20.00
SF Steve Francis/45 8.00 20.00
SN Steve Nash/52 10.00 25.00
WG Willie Green/33 8.00 20.00

2003-04 Flair Final Edition Cuts and Glory Autographs

Inserted in packs randomly, this 17-card set features a full-color portrait style photo, a swatch of game worn memorabilia and a cut signature. Each card is sequentially numbered to 100. Several other versions of this set were issued and are numbered to 50, 15, three and one of one's.
*AUTO 50: .5X TO 1.25X BASE AUTO HI
CA Carmelo Anthony 30.00 80.00
CG Mike Bibby 10.00 25.00
DM Darius Miles 8.00 20.00
DR David Robinson 30.00 80.00
EC Eddy Curry 8.00 20.00
JK Jason Kidd 20.00 50.00
JO Jermaine O'Neal 10.00 25.00
KM Kenyon Martin 10.00 25.00
LO Lamar Odom 10.00 25.00
MB Marcus Banks 8.00 20.00
MS Mike Sweetney 8.00 20.00
RG Reece Gaines 8.00 20.00
RM Reggie Miller 30.00 80.00
TM Tracy McGrady 20.00 50.00
TP Tony Parker 10.00 25.00
VC Vince Carter 20.00 40.00
BEN Ben Wallace 20.00 50.00

2003-04 Flair Final Edition Hot Numbers Jerseys 250

Randomly inserted in packs, this 30-card set showcases a horizontal design with a full-color player image on the left, the player's jersey number in the middle and a swatch of jersey on the right. Several other versions were released numbered to 175, 125, 75 with Die Cut version numbered to 25, 18, 13, and eight.
*JERSEY 175: .4X TO 1X BASE HI
*JERSEY 125: .5X TO 1.25X BASE HI
*JERSEY 75: .6X TO 1.5X BASE HI
*DIE CUT: 1X TO 2.5X BASE HI
*GREEN: .4X TO 1X BASE HI
AI Allen Iverson 4.00 10.00
AS Amare Stoudemire 4.00 10.00
CA Carmelo Anthony 6.00 15.00
CB Chris Bosh 5.00 12.00
CM Corey Maggette 2.00 5.00
DN Dirk Nowitzki 4.00 10.00
DW Dwyane Wade 10.00 25.00
EB Elton Brand 2.50 6.00
JK Jason Kidd 4.00 10.00
JR Jason Richardson 2.50 6.00
KG Kevin Garnett 5.00 12.00
LS Latrell Sprewell 2.00 5.00
MB Mike Bibby 2.50 6.00
MF Michael Finley 2.50 6.00
MG Manu Ginobili 3.00 8.00
MR Michael Redd 2.50 6.00
PG Pau Gasol 2.50 6.00
PP Paul Pierce 3.00 8.00
RA Ray Allen 2.50 6.00
SF Steve Francis 2.50 6.00
TD Tim Duncan 4.00 10.00
TM Tracy McGrady 3.00 8.00
VC Vince Carter 4.00 10.00
JON Jermaine O'Neal 2.50 6.00
KAM Karl Malone 3.00 8.00
KEM Kenyon Martin 2.50 6.00
SHM Shawn Marion 2.50 6.00
SON Shaquille O'Neal 6.00 15.00
STM Stephon Marbury 2.00 5.00
YAO Yao Ming 5.00 12.00

2003-04 Flair Final Edition Hot Numbers Patches

Randomly inserted in packs, this 30-card set utilizes the same design as the Hot Numbers Jersey cards enhanced with premium patch swatches and sequential numbering to 50. A serially numbered one of one version was released along with die cut version numbered to five, three and one of one's.
*50 SINGLES: 1.25X TO 3X BASE JSY HI

2003-04 Flair Final Edition Hot Numbers Patches Gold

This set is a parallel insert and is sequentially numbered; print runs are listed below.
SOME UNPRICED DUE TO SCARCITY
AS Amare Stoudemire/32 15.00 40.00
CA Carmelo Anthony/15 25.00 60.00
CM Corey Maggette/50 10.00 25.00
DN Dirk Nowitzki/41 12.00 30.00
EB Elton Brand/42 8.00 20.00
KG Kevin Garnett/21 20.00 50.00
PG Pau Gasol/16 10.00 25.00
PP Paul Pierce/34 10.00 25.00
RA Ray Allen/34 8.00 20.00
TD Tim Duncan/21 15.00 40.00
SHM Shawn Marion/31 10.00 25.00
SON Shaquille O'Neal/34 20.00 50.00

2003-04 Flair Final Edition Hot Numbers Patches Platinum

This set is a parallel insert and is sequentially numbered; print runs are listed below.
AI Allen Iverson/33 12.00 30.00
AS Amare Stoudemire/29 12.00 30.00
CA Carmelo Anthony/43 20.00 50.00
CB Chris Bosh/33 15.00 40.00
CM Corey Maggette/28 6.00 15.00
DN Dirk Nowitzki/52 12.00 30.00
DW Dwyane Wade/42 30.00 80.00
EB Elton Brand/28 8.00 20.00
JK Jason Kidd/47 12.00 30.00
JR Jason Richardson/37 8.00 20.00
KG Kevin Garnett/58 15.00 40.00
LS Latrell Sprewell/58 10.00 25.00
MB Mike Bibby/55 8.00 20.00
MF Michael Finley/52 8.00 20.00
MG Manu Ginobili/57 10.00 25.00
MR Michael Redd/41 8.00 20.00
PG Pau Gasol/50 8.00 20.00
PP Paul Pierce/36 10.00 25.00
RA Ray Allen/37 8.00 20.00
SF Steve Francis/45 8.00 20.00
TD Tim Duncan/57 12.00 30.00
TM Tracy McGrady/21 10.00 25.00
VC Vince Carter/33 12.00 30.00
JON Jermaine O'Neal/61 8.00 20.00
KAM Karl Malone/56 10.00 25.00
KEM Kenyon Martin/47 8.00 20.00
SHM Shawn Marion/29 8.00 20.00
SON Shaquille O'Neal/56 20.00 50.00
STM Stephon Marbury/39 6.00 15.00
YAO Yao Ming/45 15.00 40.00

2003-04 Flair Final Edition Hot Numbers Retail

This non-memorabilia version of the Hot Numbers set was inserted in retail packs only. Each card is sequentially numbered to 500
1 Jason Kidd 2.50 6.00
2 Latrell Sprewell 1.25 3.00
3 Tracy McGrady 2.00 5.00
4 Carmelo Anthony 4.00 10.00
5 Manu Ginobili 2.00 5.00
6 Allen Iverson 2.50 6.00
7 Dirk Nowitzki 2.50 6.00
8 Pau Gasol 1.50 4.00
9 Ray Allen 1.50 4.00
10 Yao Ming 3.00 8.00
11 Michael Redd 1.50 4.00
12 Stephon Marbury 1.25 3.00
13 Amare Stoudemire 2.50 6.00
14 Vince Carter 2.50 6.00
15 Kevin Garnett 3.00 8.00
16 Kenyon Martin 1.50 4.00
17 Ben Wallace 1.50 4.00
18 Dwyane Wade 6.00 15.00
19 Zach Randolph 1.50 4.00
20 Paul Pierce 2.00 5.00
21 Jermaine O'Neal 1.50 4.00
22 Elton Brand 1.50 4.00
23 Steve Francis 1.50 4.00
24 Kirk Hinrich 2.00 5.00
25 Shaquille O'Neal 4.00 10.00
26 Mike Bibby 1.50 4.00
27 Shawn Marion 1.50 4.00
28 Michael Finley 1.50 4.00
29 Tim Duncan 2.50 6.00
30 LeBron James 15.00 40.00
31 Karl Malone 2.00 5.00
32 Chris Bosh 3.00 8.00
33 Kobe Bryant 8.00 20.00
34 Jason Richardson 1.50 4.00
35 Corey Maggette 1.25 3.00

2003-04 Flair Final Edition Hot Numbers Retail Gold

This set is a parallel insert and is sequentially numbered; print runs are listed below.
CARDS NUMBERED TO PLAYER JERSEY
MOST NOT PRICED DUE TO SCARCITY
8 Pau Gasol/16 10.00 25.00
30 LeBron James/23 150.00 300.00

2003-04 Flair Final Edition Power Game Jersey and Patch

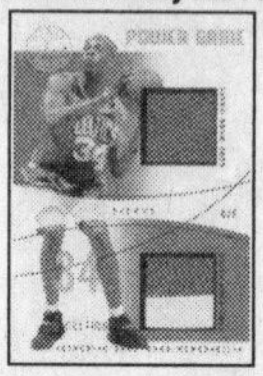

Randomly seeded, this 15-card set places full color player photos on the left side of the card and a swatch of both a game jersey and a game jersey patch on the right. Cards are sequentially numbered to 50 unless noted below. Also issued were one of ones and several die cut versions with rounded corners. The Die Cut versions are sequentially numbered to five, three and one of one's.
N Nene/50 6.00 15.00
AJ Antawn Jamison/50 8.00 20.00
AK Andrei Kirilenko/50 8.00 20.00
CW Chris Webber/75 8.00 20.00
DN Dirk Nowitzki/50 15.00 40.00
JH Jarvis Hayes/75 8.00 20.00
KG Kevin Garnett/50 15.00 40.00
KM Kenyon Martin/50 8.00 20.00
MS Mike Sweetney/50 8.00 20.00
PP Paul Pierce/75 10.00 25.00
RW Ben Wallace/50 8.00 20.00
TD Tim Duncan/50 12.00 30.00
VC Vince Carter/50 12.00 30.00
SON Shaquille O'Neal/50 20.00 50.00
YAO Yao Ming/75 15.00 40.00

2003-04 Flair Final Edition Power Game Jersey and Patch Gold

This set is a parallel insert and is sequentially numbered; print runs are listed below.
SOME UNPRICED DUE TO SCARCITY
AJ Antawn Jamison/33 10.00 25.00
AK Andrei Kirilenko/47 10.00 25.00
DN Dirk Nowitzki/41 15.00 40.00
JH Jarvis Hayes/24 10.00 25.00
KG Kevin Garnett/21 20.00 50.00
MS Mike Sweetney/50 10.00 25.00
PP Paul Pierce/34 12.00 30.00
TD Tim Duncan/21 15.00 40.00
VC Vince Carter/15 15.00 40.00
SON Shaquille O'Neal/34 25.00 60.00

2003-04 Flair Final Edition Power Game Jersey and Patch Platinum

This set is a parallel insert and is sequentially numbered; print runs are listed below.
N Nene/43 6.00 15.00
AJ Antawn Jamison/52 8.00 20.00
AK Andrei Kirilenko/42 8.00 20.00
CW Chris Webber/55 8.00 20.00
DN Dirk Nowitzki/52 12.00 30.00
JH Jarvis Hayes/25 8.00 20.00
KG Kevin Garnett/58 15.00 40.00
KM Kenyon Martin/47 8.00 20.00
MS Mike Sweetney/39 8.00 20.00
PP Paul Pierce/36 10.00 25.00
RW Ben Wallace/54 8.00 20.00
TD Tim Duncan/57 12.00 30.00
VC Vince Carter/33 12.00 30.00
SON Shaquille O'Neal/56 20.00 50.00
YAO Yao Ming/45 15.00 40.00

2003-04 Flair Final Edition Power Game Jerseys

Randomly seeded in packs, this 15-card set places a full-color player action photo on the left side of the card and a swatch of game jersey on the right. Each card is sequentially numbered to 250. Several other versions of this card were released including copies numbered to 175 and 125. Die Cut version sequentially numbered to 25, 18, 13 and eight were also produced.
*JERSEY 175: .4X TO 1X BASE HI
*JERSEY 125: .5X TO 1.25X BASE HI
*DIE CUT: 1X TO 2.5X BASE HI
N Nene 2.00 5.00
AJ Antawn Jamison 2.50 6.00
AK Andrei Kirilenko 2.50 6.00
CW Chris Webber 2.50 6.00
DN Dirk Nowitzki 4.00 10.00
JH Jarvis Hayes 2.50 6.00
KG Kevin Garnett 5.00 12.00
KM Kenyon Martin 2.50 6.00
MS Mike Sweetney 2.50 6.00
PP Paul Pierce 3.00 8.00
RW Ben Wallace 2.50 6.00
TD Tim Duncan 4.00 10.00
VC Vince Carter 4.00 10.00
SON Shaquille O'Neal 6.00 15.00
YAO Yao Ming 5.00 12.00

2003-04 Flair Final Edition Power Game Patches

Randomly inserted in packs, this set parallels the base Power Game Jerseys set enhanced with patches and sequential numbering to 75.
*75 PATCHES : 1.25X TO 3X BASE JSY HI

2003-04 Flair Final Edition SIGnificant Cuts

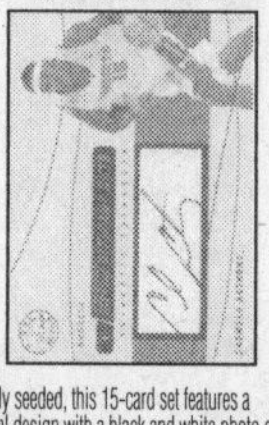

Randomly seeded, this 15-card set features a horizontal design with a black and white photo on the right side of the card and a cut signature on the left. Each card is sequentially numbered and print runs are listed below.
AJ Antawn Jamison/48 10.00 25.00
AK Andrei Kirilenko/76 15.00 40.00
BW Ben Wallace/50 12.00 30.00
CA Carmelo Anthony/50 30.00 80.00
DR David Robinson/50 50.00 120.00
DW Dwyane Wade/60 40.00 100.00
JK Jason Kidd/25 25.00 60.00
KM Kenyon Martin/60 10.00 25.00
MB Mike Bibby/50 10.00 25.00
PP Paul Pierce/60 20.00 50.00
RM Reggie Miller/49 60.00 120.00
SF Steve Francis/60 12.50 30.00
TM Tracy McGrady/50 30.00 80.00
TP Tony Parker/50 12.50 30.00
UH Udonis Haslem/76 10.00 25.00

1994 Flair USA

The 120 standard-size cards comprising this set pay tribute to the players of 1994 Team USA. Cards were distributed in 10-card packs (24 per box) with a suggested retail of $3.99. Each player has several cards highlighting various stages in his career. The cards are thicker than traditional basketball cards. The borderless fronts feature two blended color player photos. The player's name appears in gold-foil lettering near the bottom. The borderless backs carry a posed color photo with player information appearing in silver-foil lettering toward the bottom. The set concludes with a USA Basketball Women's Team Legends (113-118) subset and checklists (119-120). A wrapper offer gave collectors the chance to receive an additional 10 Flair USA cards (eight of Kevin Johnson and two team cards) by sending in $4 to Fleer by October 31, 1994.
COMPLETE SET (120) 12.00 30.00
1 Don Chaney CO .15 .40
2 Don Chaney CO .15 .40
3 Pete Gillen CO .15 .40
4 Pete Gillen CO .15 .40
5 Rick Majerus CO .15 .40
6 Rick Majerus CO .15 .40
7 Don Nelson CO .15 .40
8 Don Nelson CO .15 .40
9 Derrick Coleman .08 .25
10 Derrick Coleman .08 .25
11 Derrick Coleman .08 .25
12 Derrick Coleman .08 .25
13 Derrick Coleman .08 .25
14 Derrick Coleman .08 .25
15 Derrick Coleman .08 .25
16 Joe Dumars .15 .40
17 Joe Dumars .15 .40
18 Joe Dumars .15 .40
19 Joe Dumars .15 .40
20 Joe Dumars .15 .40
21 Joe Dumars .15 .40
22 Joe Dumars .15 .40
23 Joe Dumars .15 .40
24 Joe Dumars .15 .40
25 Tim Hardaway .10 .30
26 Tim Hardaway .10 .30
27 Tim Hardaway .10 .30
28 Tim Hardaway .10 .30
29 Tim Hardaway .10 .30
30 Tim Hardaway .10 .30
31 Tim Hardaway .10 .30
32 Tim Hardaway .10 .30
33 Larry Johnson .08 .25
34 Larry Johnson .08 .25
35 Larry Johnson .08 .25
36 Larry Johnson .08 .25
37 Larry Johnson .08 .25
38 Larry Johnson .08 .25
39 Larry Johnson .08 .25
40 Larry Johnson .08 .25
41 Shawn Kemp .15 .40
42 Shawn Kemp .15 .40
43 Shawn Kemp .15 .40
44 Shawn Kemp .15 .40
45 Shawn Kemp .15 .40
46 Shawn Kemp .15 .40
47 Shawn Kemp .15 .40
48 Shawn Kemp .15 .40
49 Dan Majerle .08 .25
50 Dan Majerle .08 .25
51 Dan Majerle .08 .25
52 Dan Majerle .08 .25
53 Dan Majerle .08 .25
54 Dan Majerle .08 .25
55 Dan Majerle .08 .25
56 Dan Majerle .08 .25
57 Reggie Miller .10 .30
58 Reggie Miller .10 .30
59 Reggie Miller .10 .30
60 Reggie Miller .10 .30
61 Reggie Miller .10 .30
62 Reggie Miller .10 .30
63 Reggie Miller .10 .30
64 Reggie Miller .10 .30
65 Alonzo Mourning .10 .30
66 Alonzo Mourning .10 .30
67 Alonzo Mourning .10 .30
68 Alonzo Mourning .10 .30
69 Alonzo Mourning .10 .30
70 Alonzo Mourning .10 .30
71 Alonzo Mourning .10 .30
72 Alonzo Mourning .10 .30
73 Shaquille O'Neal .60 1.50
74 Shaquille O'Neal .60 1.50
75 Shaquille O'Neal .60 1.50
76 Shaquille O'Neal .60 1.50
77 Shaquille O'Neal .60 1.50
78 Shaquille O'Neal .60 1.50
79 Shaquille O'Neal .60 1.50
80 Shaquille O'Neal .60 1.50
81 Mark Price .08 .25
82 Mark Price .08 .25
83 Mark Price .08 .25
84 Mark Price .08 .25
85 Mark Price .08 .25
86 Mark Price .08 .25
87 Mark Price .08 .25
88 Mark Price .08 .25
89 Steve Smith .08 .25
90 Steve Smith .08 .25
91 Steve Smith .08 .25
92 Steve Smith .08 .25
93 Steve Smith .08 .25
94 Steve Smith .08 .25
95 Steve Smith .08 .25
96 Steve Smith .08 .25
97 Isiah Thomas .10 .30
98 Isiah Thomas .10 .30
99 Isiah Thomas .10 .30
100 Isiah Thomas .10 .30
101 Isiah Thomas .10 .30
102 Isiah Thomas .10 .30
103 Isiah Thomas .10 .30
104 Isiah Thomas .10 .30
105 Dominique Wilkins .10 .30
106 Dominique Wilkins .10 .30
107 Dominique Wilkins .10 .30
108 Dominique Wilkins .10 .30
109 Dominique Wilkins .10 .30
110 Dominique Wilkins .10 .30
111 Dominique Wilkins .10 .30
112 Dominique Wilkins .10 .30
113 Carol Blazejowski .40 1.00
114 Teresa Edwards 1.50 4.00
115 Nancy Lieberman-Cline 1.50 4.00
116 Ann Meyers .75 2.00
117 Pat Summitt CO 6.00 15.00
118 Lynette Woodard .75 2.00
119 Checklist .10 .30
120 Checklist .10 .30

1994 Flair USA Kevin Johnson

This 10-card standard-size set was issued as a wrapper redemption offer. The collector sent in $4.00 to Fleer; the offer expired October 31, 1994. The final two cards are team checklist cards that picture on their fronts all the members of the U.S. Olympic basketball team. These reissued checklist cards include Johnson, who was added to the team later, in the team photo.
COMPLETE SET (10) 5.00 12.00
COMMON CARD (M1-M8) .50 1.25
119 Team Checklist 1.00 2.50
120 Team Checklist 1.00 2.50

1961-62 Fleer

The 1961-62 Fleer set was the company's only major basketball issue until the 1986-87 season. The cards were issued in five-cent wax packs with 24 packs in a box. The cards in the set measure the standard 2 1/2" by 3 1/2". Cards numbered 45 to 66 are action shots (designated IA) of players elsewhere in the set. Both the regular cards and the IA cards are numbered alphabetically within that particular subset. No known scarcities exist, although the set is quite popular since it contains the first mainstream basketball cards of many of the game's all-time greats including Elgin Baylor, Wilt Chamberlain, Oscar Robertson and Jerry West. Most cards are frequently found with centering problems
COMPLETE SET (66) 2800.00
1 Al Attles RC 40.00
2 Paul Arizin 25.00
3 Elgin Baylor RC 100.00
4 Walt Bellamy RC 30.00
5 Arlen Bockhorn 12.00
6 Bob Boozer RC 15.00
7 Carl Braun 15.00
8 Wilt Chamberlain RC 400.00
9 Larry Costello 10.00
10 Bob Cousy ! 80.00
11 Walter Dukes 10.00
12 Wayne Embry RC 20.00
13 Dave Gambee 10.00
14 Tom Gola 12.50
15 Sihugo Green RC 12.00
16 Hal Greer RC 40.00
17 Richie Guerin RC 20.00
18 Cliff Hagan 20.00
19 Tom Heinsohn 40.00
20 Bailey Howell RC 30.00
21 Rod Hundley 30.00
22 K.C. Jones RC 40.00
23 Sam Jones RC 40.00
24 Phil Jordan 12.00
25 John Kerr 20.00
26 Rudy LaRusso RC 20.00
27 George Lee 10.00
28 Bob Leonard 10.00
29 Clyde Lovellette 20.00
30 John McCarthy 10.00
31 Tom Meschery RC 15.00
32 Willie Naulls 15.00
33 Don Ohl RC 15.00
34 Bob Pettit 40.00
35 Frank Ramsey 15.00
36 Oscar Robertson RC 150.00
37 Guy Rodgers RC 15.00
38 Bill Russell ! 175.00
39 Dolph Schayes 25.00
40 Frank Selvy 12.00
41 Gene Shue 12.00
42 Jack Twyman 15.00
43 Jerry West RC 300.00
44 Len Wilkens UER RC/(Misspelled Wilkins 175.00 on card front)
45 Paul Arizin IA 15.00
46 Elgin Baylor IA 65.00
47 Wilt Chamberlain IA ! 200.00
48 Larry Costello IA 12.00
49 Bob Cousy IA 50.00
50 Walter Dukes IA 10.00
51 Tom Gola IA 15.00
52 Richie Guerin IA 12.00
53 Cliff Hagan IA 15.00
54 Tom Heinsohn IA 30.00
55 Bailey Howell IA 15.00
56 John Kerr IA 15.00
57 Rudy LaRusso IA 12.00
58 Clyde Lovellette IA 15.00
59 Bob Pettit IA 20.00
60 Frank Ramsey IA 15.00
61 Oscar Robertson IA ! 100.00
62 Bill Russell IA ! 100.00
63 Dolph Schayes IA 15.00
64 Gene Shue IA 12.00
65 Jack Twyman IA 15.00
66 Jerry West IA ! 150.00

1973-74 Fleer The Shots

This 21-card set was produced by artist R.G. Laug for Fleer. The cards measure approximately 2 1/2" 4". The cards were distributed in packs with one "Shots" card along with two team logo cloth patch and one stick of gum. The fronts feature an illustra of the shot depicted on the card. The illustration is color, although crudely drawn. The back has a discussion of the shot.
COMPLETE SET (21) 40.00
COMMON CARD (1-21) 1.50
21 The Good Shot 2.00

1974 Fleer Team Patches/Stickers

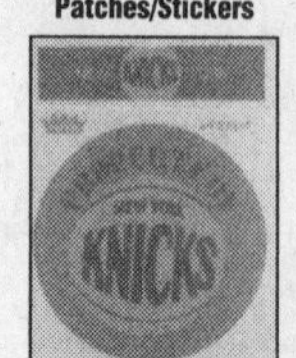

These cloth patches, each measuring 2 1/2" by 3 were sold in wax packs. There were two forms of distribution. One entailed packs including one pa one sticker, one Fleer "The Shots" card, and a stic gum. The other had two patches instead of a sticke The team name appears in a color bar across the t the patch. The team logo is printed inside a round-out area in the patch; the words "Property Of" are printed immediately above some of the logos and follow the curve of the logo. The backs are blank. stickers have the team name across the top and the team logo below. In addition to a NBA logo and st one cloth patch and one sticker were issued for ea NBA team. The patches are unnumbered and checklisted below in alphabetical order, with the N cloth patches listed first.
COMPLETE SET (38) 40.00
1 NBA Logo 1.00
2 Atlanta Hawks .75
3 Boston Celtics 1.00
4 Buffalo Braves 1.00
5 Chicago Bulls .75
6 Cleveland Cavaliers .75
7 Detroit Pistons .75
8 Golden State Warriors 1.00
9 Houston Rockets .75
10 Kansas City Kings .75

Angeles Lakers	1.00	2.50
aukee Bucks	.75	2.00
Orleans Jazz	1.00	2.50
York Knicks	1.00	2.50
adelphia 76ers	.75	2.00
enix Suns	.75	2.00
land Trail Blazers	.75	2.00
le Supersonics	.75	2.00
hington Bullets	.75	2.00
Logo	1.25	3.00
ta Hawks	1.00	2.50
on Celtics	1.25	3.00
alo Braves	1.25	3.00
ago Bulls	1.00	2.50
eland Cavaliers	1.00	2.50
oit Pistons	1.00	2.50
en State Warriors	1.00	2.50
ston Rockets	1.00	2.50
sas City Kings	1.25	3.00
Angeles Lakers	1.25	3.00
aukee Bucks	1.00	2.50
Orleans Jazz	1.25	3.00
York Knicks	1.25	3.00
adelphia 76ers	1.00	2.50
enix Suns	1.00	2.50
and Trail Blazers	1.00	2.50
tle Supersonics	1.00	2.50
hington Bullets	1.00	2.50

77-78 Fleer Team Stickers

easuring 2 1/2" by 3 3/16", this set features one or all twenty-two NBA teams. A color stripe the top carries the NBA logo and the words All Pro' Hi-Gloss Stickers." The sticker itself s of the team name and logo on a white und. Though all 22 NBA teams are represented set, there are 71 color variations in the set. The re blank. The team stickers are unnumbered ecklisted below in alphabetical order.

LETE SET (22)	7.50	15.00
ta Hawks	.30	.75
n Celtics	.40	1.00
o Braves	.40	1.00
go Bulls	.30	.75
land Cavaliers	.30	.75
er Nuggets	.30	.75
it Pistons	.30	.75
en State Warriors	.30	.75
ton Rockets	.30	.75
ana Pacers	.30	.75
sas City Kings	.40	1.00
Angeles Lakers	.40	1.00
vaukee Bucks	.30	.75
Jersey Nets	.30	.75
Orleans Jazz	.40	1.00
York Knicks	.40	1.00
adelphia 76ers	.30	.75
enix Suns	.30	.75
land Trail Blazers	.30	.75
Antonio Spurs	.30	.75
ttle Supersonics	.30	.75
hington Bullets	.30	.75

1986-87 Fleer

2-card standard-size set marks Fleer's return to ketball card industry after a 25-year hiatus. It arks what is considered to be the beginning of dern era of basketball cards. The cards were in 12-card wax packs (11 cards plus a sticker) ailed for 50 cents. Wax boxes consisted of 36 A stick of gum was also included in each pack. is checklisted alphabetically by the player's last Since only the Star Company had been issuing all cards nationally since 1983, most of the in this Fleer set already had cards which are ered Extended Rookie Cards. However, since er set was the first nationally distributed wax packs since the 1981-82 Topps issue, the players in the set are considered Rookie ncluding Michael Jordan. Other Rookie Cards, that had Star Company cards include Charles , Clyde Drexler, Patrick Ewing, Hakeem on, Isiah Thomas and Dominique Wilkins. Cards of those that did not previously appear in clude Joe Dumars, Karl Malone, Chris Mullin arles Oakley. Red, white and blue borders d a color photo that contains a Fleer "Premier" an upper corner. The card backs are printed in blue on white card stock. Several cards have " notations on them if the player was traded uent to the photo selection process. It's ant to note that some of the more expensive n this set (especially Michael Jordan) have been feited in the past few years. Checking key printing areas such as the "Fleer Premier" logo front and the players' association logo on the der eight or ten power magnification usually the legitimate from the counterfeits. The cards dition sensitive due to dark borders and g problems.

w/Stickers (143)	600.00	1100.00
LETE SET (132)	500.00	900.00
em Abdul-Jabbar	8.00	20.00
Adams	.75	2.00
Aguirre RC	1.50	4.00
y Ainge RC	4.00	10.00
Bagley RC	.75	2.00
Bailey RC	2.50	6.00
es Barkley RC	20.00	50.00
it Benjamin RC	1.00	2.50
Bird !	10.00	25.00
10 Otis Birdsong	.75	2.00
11 Rolando Blackman RC	1.25	3.00
12 Manute Bol RC	5.00	12.00
13 Sam Bowie RC	.75	2.00
14 Joe Barry Carroll	.75	2.00
15 Tom Chambers RC	2.00	5.00
16 Maurice Cheeks	.75	2.00
17 Michael Cooper	1.00	2.50
18 Wayne Cooper	.75	2.00
19 Pat Cummings	.75	2.00
20 Terry Cummings RC	2.50	6.00
21 Adrian Dantley	1.00	2.50
22 Brad Davis RC	.75	2.00
23 Walter Davis	.75	2.00
24 Darryl Dawkins	1.00	2.50
25 Larry Drew	.75	2.00
26 Clyde Drexler RC	20.00	40.00
27 Joe Dumars RC	10.00	25.00
28 Mark Eaton RC	.75	2.00
29 James Edwards	.75	2.00
30 Alex English	1.00	2.50
31 Julius Erving	6.00	15.00
32 Patrick Ewing RC	15.00	40.00
33 Vern Fleming RC	.75	2.00
34 Sleepy Floyd RC	.75	2.00
35 World B. Free	.75	2.00
36 George Gervin	1.50	4.00
37 Artis Gilmore	1.00	2.50
38 Mike Gminski	.75	2.00
39 Rickey Green	.75	2.00
40 Sidney Green	.75	2.00
41 David Greenwood	.75	2.00
42 Darrell Griffith	.75	2.00
43 Bill Hanzlik	.75	2.00
44 Derek Harper RC	3.00	8.00
45 Gerald Henderson	.75	2.00
46 Roy Hinson	.75	2.00
47 Craig Hodges RC	.75	2.00
48 Phil Hubbard	.75	2.00
49 Jay Humphries RC	.75	2.00
50 Dennis Johnson	2.50	6.00
51 Eddie Johnson RC	1.25	3.00
52 Frank Johnson RC	.75	2.00
53 Magic Johnson	10.00	25.00
54 Marques Johnson	.75	2.00
(Decimal point missing, rookie year scoring avg.)		
55 Steve Johnson UER	.75	2.00
(photo actually David Greenwood)		
56 Vinnie Johnson	.75	2.00
57 Michael Jordan RC	350.00	650.00
58 Clark Kellogg RC	.75	2.00
59 Albert King	.75	2.00
60 Bernard King	1.00	2.50
61 Bill Laimbeer	1.00	2.50
62 Allen Leavell	.75	2.00
63 Lafayette Lever RC	.75	2.00
64 Alton Lister	.75	2.00
65 Lewis Lloyd	.75	2.00
66 Maurice Lucas	.75	2.00
67 Jeff Malone RC	2.50	6.00
68 Karl Malone RC	15.00	40.00
69 Moses Malone	1.25	3.00
70 Cedric Maxwell	.75	2.00
71 Rodney McCray RC	.75	2.00
72 Xavier McDaniel RC	2.50	6.00
73 Kevin McHale	1.25	3.00
74 Mike Mitchell	.75	2.00
75 Sidney Moncrief	1.00	2.50
76 Johnny Moore	.75	2.00
77 Chris Mullin RC	10.00	25.00
78 Larry Nance RC	2.50	6.00
79 Calvin Natt	.75	2.00
80 Norm Nixon	.75	2.00
81 Charles Oakley RC	4.00	10.00
82 Hakeem Olajuwon RC	20.00	40.00
83 Louis Orr	.75	2.00
84 Robert Parish UER	1.25	3.00
(Misspelled Parrish on both sides)		
85 Jim Paxson	.75	2.00
86 Sam Perkins RC	2.50	6.00
87 Ricky Pierce RC	1.00	2.50
88 Paul Pressey RC	.75	2.00
89 Kurt Rambis RC	3.00	8.00
90 Robert Reid	.75	2.00
91 Doc Rivers RC	4.00	10.00
92 Alvin Robertson RC	.75	2.00
93 Cliff Robinson	.75	2.00
94 Tree Rollins	.75	2.00
95 Dan Roundfield	.75	2.00
96 Jeff Ruland	.75	2.00
97 Ralph Sampson RC	3.00	8.00
98 Danny Schayes RC	.75	2.00
99 Byron Scott RC	5.00	12.00
100 Purvis Short	.75	2.00
101 Jerry Sichting	.75	2.00
102 Jack Sikma	.75	2.00
103 Derek Smith	.75	2.00
104 Larry Smith	.75	2.00
105 Rory Sparrow	.75	2.00
106 Steve Stipanovich	.75	2.00
107 Terry Teagle	.75	2.00
108 Reggie Theus	1.00	2.50
109 Isiah Thomas RC	12.00	30.00
110 LaSalle Thompson RC	2.50	6.00
111 Mychal Thompson	.75	2.00
112 Sedale Threatt RC	.75	2.00
113 Wayman Tisdale RC	4.00	10.00
114 Andrew Toney	.75	2.00
115 Kelly Tripucka RC	.75	2.00
116 Mel Turpin	.75	2.00
117 Kiki Vandeweghe RC	1.00	2.50
118 Jay Vincent	.75	2.00
119 Bill Walton	1.50	4.00
(Missing decimal points on four lines of FG Percentage)		
120 Spud Webb RC	6.00	15.00
121 Dominique Wilkins RC	15.00	30.00
122 Gerald Wilkins RC	2.00	5.00
123 Buck Williams RC	2.50	6.00
124 Gus Williams	.75	2.00
125 Herb Williams RC	3.00	8.00
126 Kevin Willis RC	2.50	6.00
127 Randy Wittman	.75	2.00
128 Al Wood	.75	2.00
129 Mike Woodson	.75	2.00
130 Orlando Woolridge RC	3.00	8.00
131 James Worthy RC	8.00	20.00
132 Checklist 1-132	8.00	20.00

1986-87 Fleer Stickers

One of these eleven different standard-size stickers was inserted into each 1986-87 Fleer wax pack. The backs of the sticker cards are printed in blue and red on white card stock. The set numbering of the stickers is alphabetical by player's name. Based on the one-to-twelve proportion of stickers to regular cards in the wax packs, there are theoretically an equal number of sticker sets and regular sets. The cards are frequently found off-centered and most card backs are found with wax stains due to packaging.

COMPLETE SET (11)	75.00	150.00
1 Kareem Abdul-Jabbar	6.00	15.00
2 Larry Bird	5.00	12.00
3 Adrian Dantley	2.00	5.00
4 Alex English	2.00	5.00
5 Julius Erving	4.00	10.00
6 Patrick Ewing	5.00	12.00
7 Magic Johnson	6.00	15.00
8 Michael Jordan	50.00	125.00
9 Hakeem Olajuwon	6.00	15.00
10 Isiah Thomas	4.00	10.00
11 Dominique Wilkins	5.00	12.00

1987-88 Fleer

The 1987-88 Fleer basketball set contains 132 standard-size cards. The cards were issued in 12-card wax packs that retailed for 50 cents. A wax box consisted of 36 packs. A sticker card and stick of gum were included. The fronts are white with gray horizontal stripes. The backs are red, white and blue and show each player's complete NBA statistics. The cards are numbered in alphabetical order by last name. Rookie Cards include Brad Daugherty, A.C. Green, Chuck Person, Terry Porter, Detlef Schrempf and Hot Rod Williams. Other key Rookie Cards in this set, who had already had cards in previous Star sets, are Dale Ellis, John Paxson, and Otis Thorpe. The cards are frequently found off-centered.

COMPLETE w/Stickers (143)	100.00	200.00
COMPLETE SET (132)	60.00	150.00
1 Kareem Abdul-Jabbar !	3.00	8.00
2 Alvan Adams	.60	1.50
3 Mark Aguirre	.75	2.00
4 Danny Ainge	.75	2.00
5 John Bagley	.60	1.50
6 Thurl Bailey UER	.60	1.50
(reverse negative)		
7 Greg Ballard	.60	1.50
8 Gene Banks	.60	1.50
9 Charles Barkley	6.00	15.00
10 Benoit Benjamin	.60	1.50
11 Larry Bird !	8.00	20.00
12 Rolando Blackman	.60	1.50
13 Manute Bol	.60	1.50
14 Tony Brown	.60	1.50
15 Michael Cage RC	.60	1.50
16 Joe Barry Carroll	.60	1.50
17 Bill Cartwright	.75	2.00
18 Terry Catledge RC	.60	1.50
19 Tom Chambers	.60	1.50
20 Maurice Cheeks	.60	1.50
21 Michael Cooper	.75	2.00
22 Dave Corzine	.60	1.50
23 Terry Cummings	.75	2.00
24 Adrian Dantley	.60	1.50
25 Brad Daugherty RC	1.00	2.50
26 Walter Davis	.60	1.50
27 Johnny Dawkins RC	.60	1.50
28 James Donaldson	.60	1.50
29 Larry Drew	.60	1.50
30 Clyde Drexler	5.00	12.00
31 Joe Dumars	1.50	4.00
32 Mark Eaton	.60	1.50
33 Dale Ellis RC	1.00	2.50
34 Alex English	.75	2.00
35 Julius Erving	5.00	12.00
36 Mike Evans	.60	1.50
37 Patrick Ewing	4.00	10.00
38 Vern Fleming	.60	1.50
39 Sleepy Floyd	.60	1.50
40 Artis Gilmore	.75	2.00
41 Mike Gminski UER	.60	1.50
(reversed negative)		
42 A.C. Green RC	2.50	6.00
43 Rickey Green	.60	1.50
44 Sidney Green	.60	1.50
45 David Greenwood	.60	1.50
46 Darrell Griffith	.60	1.50
47 Bill Hanzlik	.60	1.50
48 Derek Harper	.75	2.00
49 Ron Harper RC	2.50	6.00
50 Gerald Henderson	.60	1.50
51 Roy Hinson	.60	1.50
52 Craig Hodges	.60	1.50
53 Phil Hubbard	.60	1.50
54 Dennis Johnson	.60	1.50
55 Eddie Johnson	.75	2.00
56 Magic Johnson	6.00	15.00
57 Steve Johnson	.60	1.50
58 Vinnie Johnson	.60	1.50
59 Michael Jordan !	30.00	80.00
60 Jerome Kersey RC	.60	1.50
61 Bill Laimbeer	.75	2.00
62 Lafayette Lever UER	.60	1.50
(Photo actually Otis Smith)		
63 Cliff Levingston RC	.60	1.50
64 Alton Lister	.60	1.50
65 John Long	.60	1.50
66 John Lucas	.60	1.50
67 Jeff Malone	.60	1.50
68 Karl Malone	6.00	15.00
69 Moses Malone	1.00	2.50
70 Cedric Maxwell	.60	1.50
71 Tim McCormick	.60	1.50
72 Rodney McCray	.60	1.50
73 Xavier McDaniel	.60	1.50
74 Kevin McHale	1.00	2.50
75 Nate McMillan RC	1.00	2.50
76 Sidney Moncrief	.60	1.50
77 Chris Mullin	1.50	4.00
78 Larry Nance	.75	2.00
79 Charles Oakley	1.00	2.50
80 Hakeem Olajuwon	6.00	15.00
81 Robert Parish UER	1.00	2.50
(Misspelled Parrish on both sides)		
82 Jim Paxson	.60	1.50
83 John Paxson RC	1.00	2.50
84 Sam Perkins	1.00	2.50
85 Chuck Person RC	1.00	2.50
86 Jim Petersen	.60	1.50
87 Ricky Pierce	.60	1.50
88 Ed Pinckney RC	.60	1.50
89 Terry Porter RC	1.00	2.50
(College Wisconsin, should be Wisconsin-Stevens Point)		
90 Paul Pressey	.60	1.50
91 Robert Reid	.60	1.50
92 Doc Rivers	1.00	2.50
93 Alvin Robertson	.60	1.50
94 Tree Rollins	.60	1.50
95 Ralph Sampson	.60	1.50
96 Mike Sanders	.60	1.50
97 Detlef Schrempf RC	4.00	10.00
98 Byron Scott	.75	2.00
99 Jerry Sichting	.60	1.50
100 Jack Sikma	.60	1.50
101 Larry Smith	.60	1.50
102 Rory Sparrow	.60	1.50
103 Steve Stipanovich	.60	1.50
104 Jon Sundvold	.60	1.50
105 Reggie Theus	.75	2.00
106 Isiah Thomas	2.50	6.00
107 LaSalle Thompson	.60	1.50
108 Mychal Thompson	.60	1.50
109 Otis Thorpe RC	2.00	5.00
110 Sedale Threatt	.60	1.50
111 Wayman Tisdale	.60	1.50
112 Kelly Tripucka	.60	1.50
113 Trent Tucker RC	.60	1.50
114 Terry Tyler	.60	1.50
115 Darnell Valentine	.60	1.50
116 Kiki Vandeweghe	.60	1.50
117 Darrell Walker RC	.60	1.50
118 Dominique Wilkins	2.00	5.00
119 Gerald Wilkins	.60	1.50
120 Buck Williams	.75	2.00
121 Herb Williams	.60	1.50
122 John Williams RC	.60	1.50
123 Hot Rod Williams RC	.75	2.00
124 Kevin Willis	.75	2.00
125 David Wingate RC	.60	1.50
126 Randy Wittman	.60	1.50
127 Leon Wood	.60	1.50
128 Mike Woodson	.60	1.50
129 Orlando Woolridge	.60	1.50
130 James Worthy	1.50	4.00
131 Danny Young RC	.60	1.50
132 Checklist 1-132	4.00	10.00

1987-88 Fleer Stickers

The 1987-88 Fleer Stickers is an 11-card standard-size set inserted one per wax pack. The fronts are red, white, blue and yellow. The backs are white and blue and contain career highlights. Based on the one-to-twelve proportion of stickers to regular cards in the wax packs, there are theoretically an equal number of sticker sets and regular sets. Virtually all cards from this set have wax-stained backs as a result of the packaging.

COMPLETE SET (11)	20.00	40.00
1 Magic Johnson	2.50	6.00
2 Michael Jordan	10.00	25.00
(In text, votes misspelled as voites)		
3 Hakeem Olajuwon UER	1.50	4.00
(Misspelled Olajuwan on card back)		
4 Larry Bird	2.50	6.00
5 Kevin McHale	.40	1.00
6 Charles Barkley	2.00	5.00
7 Dominique Wilkins	.60	1.50
8 Kareem Abdul-Jabbar	.60	1.50
9 Mark Aguirre	.40	1.00
10 Chuck Person	.40	1.00
11 Alex English	.40	1.00

1988-89 Fleer

The 1988-89 Fleer basketball set contains 132 standard-size cards. There are 119 regular cards, plus 12 All-Star cards and a checklist. This set was issued in wax packs of 12 cards, gum and a sticker. Wax boxes contained 36 wax packs. The outer borders are white and gray, while the inner borders correspond to the team colors. The backs are greenish and show full NBA statistics with limited biographical information. The set is ordered alphabetically by team with a few exceptions due to late trades. The only subset is All-Stars (120-131). Rookie Cards of note include Muggsy Bogues, Dell Curry, Horace Grant, Mark Jackson, Reggie Miller, Derrick McKey, Scottie Pippen, Mark Price and Dennis Rodman. There is also a Rookie Card of John Stockton who had previously only appeared in Star Company sets.

COMPLETE w/Stickers (143)	50.00	120.00
COMPLETE SET (132)	40.00	100.00
1 Antoine Carr RC	.30	.75
2 Cliff Levingston	.20	.50
3 Doc Rivers	.30	.75
4 Spud Webb	.30	.75
5 Dominique Wilkins	.60	1.50
6 Kevin Willis	.30	.75
7 Randy Wittman	.20	.50
8 Danny Ainge	.30	.75
9 Larry Bird	4.00	10.00
10 Dennis Johnson	.20	.50
11 Kevin McHale	.50	1.25
12 Robert Parish	.50	1.25
13 Muggsy Bogues RC	1.00	2.50
14 Dell Curry RC	.60	1.50
15 Dave Corzine	.20	.50
16 Horace Grant RC	2.00	5.00
17 Michael Jordan	10.00	25.00
18 Charles Oakley	.30	.75
19 John Paxson	.30	.75
20 Scottie Pippen UER RC	10.00	25.00
(Misspelled Pippin on card back)		
21 Brad Sellers RC	.20	.50
22 Brad Daugherty	.20	.50
23 Ron Harper	.30	.75
24 Larry Nance	.20	.50
25 Mark Price RC	.75	2.00
26 Hot Rod Williams	.20	.50
27 Mark Aguirre	.20	.50
28 Rolando Blackman	.20	.50
29 James Donaldson	.20	.50
30 Derek Harper	.30	.75
31 Sam Perkins	.30	.75
32 Roy Tarpley RC	.20	.50
33 Michael Adams RC	.20	.50
34 Alex English	.30	.75
35 Lafayette Lever	.20	.50
36 Blair Rasmussen RC	.20	.50
37 Danny Schayes	.20	.50
38 Jay Vincent	.20	.50
39 Adrian Dantley	.20	.50
40 Joe Dumars	.60	1.50
41 Vinnie Johnson	.20	.50
42 Bill Laimbeer	.30	.75
43 Dennis Rodman RC	6.00	15.00
44 John Salley RC	.30	.75
45 Isiah Thomas	.60	1.50
46 Winston Garland RC	.20	.50
47 Rod Higgins	.20	.50
48 Chris Mullin	.60	1.50
49 Ralph Sampson	.20	.50
50 Joe Barry Carroll	.20	.50
51 Sleepy Floyd	.20	.50
52 Rodney McCray	.20	.50
53 Hakeem Olajuwon	2.00	5.00
54 Purvis Short	.20	.50
55 Vern Fleming	.20	.50
56 John Long	.20	.50
57 Reggie Miller RC	6.00	15.00
58 Chuck Person	.20	.50
59 Steve Stipanovich	.20	.50
60 Wayman Tisdale	.20	.50
61 Benoit Benjamin	.20	.50
62 Michael Cage	.20	.50
63 Mike Woodson	.20	.50
64 Kareem Abdul-Jabbar	1.50	4.00
65 Michael Cooper	.20	.50
66 A.C. Green	.30	.75
67 Magic Johnson	4.00	10.00
68 Byron Scott	.30	.75
69 Mychal Thompson	.20	.50
70 James Worthy	.60	1.50
71 Duane Washington	.20	.50
72 Kevin Williams	.20	.50
73 Randy Breuer RC	.20	.50
74 Terry Cummings	.30	.75
75 Paul Pressey	.20	.50
76 Jack Sikma	.20	.50
77 John Bagley	.20	.50
78 Roy Hinson	.20	.50
79 Buck Williams	.30	.75
80 Patrick Ewing	1.25	3.00
81 Sidney Green	.20	.50
82 Mark Jackson RC	1.25	3.00
83 Kenny Walker RC	.20	.50
84 Gerald Wilkins	.20	.50
85 Charles Barkley	2.00	5.00
86 Maurice Cheeks	.20	.50
87 Mike Gminski	.20	.50
88 Cliff Robinson	.20	.50
89 Armon Gilliam RC	.60	1.50
90 Eddie Johnson	.20	.50
91 Mark West RC	.20	.50
92 Clyde Drexler	1.25	3.00
93 Kevin Duckworth RC	.20	.50
94 Steve Johnson	.20	.50
95 Jerome Kersey	.20	.50
96 Terry Porter	.20	.50
(College Wisconsin, should be Wisconsin-Stevens Point)		
97 Joe Kleine RC	.20	.50
98 Reggie Theus	.30	.75
99 Otis Thorpe	.30	.75
100 Kenny Smith RC	.60	1.50
(College NC State, should be North Carolina)		
101 Greg Anderson RC	.20	.50
102 Walter Berry RC	.20	.50
103 Frank Brickowski RC	.20	.50
104 Johnny Dawkins	.20	.50
105 Alvin Robertson	.20	.50
106 Tom Chambers	.20	.50
(Born 6/2/59, should be 6/21/59)		
107 Dale Ellis	.30	.75
108 Xavier McDaniel	.20	.50
109 Derrick McKey RC	.60	1.50
110 Nate McMillan UER	.20	.50
(Photo actually Kevin Williams)		
111 Thurl Bailey	.20	.50
112 Mark Eaton	.20	.50
113 Bobby Hansen RC	.20	.50
114 Karl Malone	2.00	5.00
115 John Stockton RC	8.00	20.00
116 Bernard King	.20	.50
117 Jeff Malone	.20	.50
118 Moses Malone	.60	1.50
119 John Williams	.20	.50
120 Michael Jordan AS	6.00	15.00
121 Mark Jackson AS	.60	1.50
122 Byron Scott AS	.20	.50
123 Magic Johnson AS	1.50	4.00
124 Larry Bird AS	2.00	5.00
125 Dominique Wilkins AS	.30	.75
126 Hakeem Olajuwon AS	.75	2.00
127 John Stockton AS	2.00	5.00
128 Alvin Robertson AS	.20	.50
129 Charles Barkley AS	.75	2.00
(Back says Buck Williams is member of Jets, should be Nets)		
130 Patrick Ewing AS	.60	1.50
131 Mark Eaton AS	.20	.50
132 Checklist 1-132	.20	.50

1988-89 Fleer Stickers

The 1988-89 Fleer Stickers is an 11-card standard-size set issued as a one per pack insert along with 12 cards from the regular 132-card set. The fronts are baby blue, red, and white. The backs are blue and pink and contain career highlights. The set is ordered alphabetically. Based on the one-to-twelve proportion of stickers to regular cards in the wax packs, there are theoretically an equal number of sticker sets and regular sets. Virtually all cards from this set have wax-stained backs as a result of the packaging.

COMPLETE SET (11)	10.00	20.00
1 Mark Aguirre	.15	.40
2 Larry Bird	2.00	5.00
3 Clyde Drexler	.50	1.25
4 Alex English	.15	.40
5 Patrick Ewing	.50	1.25
6 Magic Johnson	1.50	4.00
7 Michael Jordan	8.00	20.00
8 Karl Malone	.75	2.00
9 Kevin McHale	.15	.40
10 Isiah Thomas	.25	.60
11 Dominique Wilkins	.15	.40

1989-90 Fleer

The 1989-90 Fleer basketball set consists of 168 standard-size cards. The cards were distributed in 15-card wax packs (and one sticker) and in 36-card rack packs. Wax boxes contained 36 packs. The fronts feature color action player photos, with various color borders between white inner and outer borders. The player's name and position appear in the upper left corner, with the team logo superimposed over the upper right corner of the picture. The horizontally oriented backs have black lettering on red, pink, and white background and present career statistics, biographical information, and a performance index. The set is ordered alphabetically in team subsets (with a few exceptions due to late trades). The only subset is All-Star Game Combos (163-167). Rookie Cards of note in this set include Hersey Hawkins, Jeff Hornacek, Kevin Johnson, Reggie Lewis, Dan Majerle, Danny Manning, Mitch Richmond,, Rik Smits, and Rod Strickland. Cards from this set are frequently found off-center.

COMPLETE w/Stickers (179)	15.00	40.00
COMPLETE SET (168)	12.50	30.00
1 John Battle RC	.08	.20
2 Jon Koncak RC	.08	.20
3 Cliff Levingston	.08	.20
4 Moses Malone	.25	.60
5 Doc Rivers	.10	.30
6 Spud Webb UER	.10	.30
(Points per 48 minutes incorrect at 2.6)		
7 Dominique Wilkins	.25	.60
8 Larry Bird	1.25	3.00
9 Dennis Johnson	.08	.20
10 Reggie Lewis RC	.30	.75
11 Kevin McHale	.25	.60
12 Robert Parish	.10	.30
13 Ed Pinckney	.08	.20
14 Brian Shaw RC	.25	.60
15 Rex Chapman RC	.30	.75
16 Kurt Rambis	.08	.20
17 Robert Reid	.08	.20
18 Kelly Tripucka	.08	.20
19 Bill Cartwright UER	.08	.20
(First season 1978-80, should be 1979-80)		
20 Horace Grant	.10	.30
21 Michael Jordan	5.00	12.00
22 John Paxson	.08	.20
23 Scottie Pippen	2.00	5.00
24 Brad Sellers	.08	.20
25 Brad Daugherty	.10	.30
26 Craig Ehlo RC	.25	.60
27 Ron Harper	.10	.30
28 Larry Nance	.10	.30
29 Mark Price	.10	.30
30 Mike Sanders	.08	.20
31A Hot Rod Williams ERR	.40	1.00
31B Hot Rod Williams COR	.08	.20
32 Rolando Blackman UER	.08	.20
(Career blocks and points listed as 1961 and 2127, should be 196 and 12,127)		
33 Adrian Dantley	.08	.20
34 James Donaldson	.08	.20
35 Derek Harper	.10	.30
36 Sam Perkins	.10	.30
37 Herb Williams	.08	.20
38 Michael Adams	.08	.20
39 Walter Davis	.08	.20
40 Alex English	.25	.60
41 Lafayette Lever	.10	.30
42 Blair Rasmussen	.08	.20
43 Danny Schayes	.08	.20
44 Mark Aguirre	.08	.20
45 Joe Dumars	.20	.50
46 James Edwards	.08	.20
47 Vinnie Johnson	.10	.30
48 Bill Laimbeer	.10	.30
49 Dennis Rodman	1.25	3.00
50 Isiah Thomas	.25	.60
51 John Salley	.08	.20
52 Manute Bol	.10	.30
53 Winston Garland	.08	.20
54 Rod Higgins	.08	.20
55 Chris Mullin	.25	.60
56 Mitch Richmond RC	1.50	4.00
57 Terry Teagle	.08	.20
58 Derrick Chievous UER	.08	.20
(Stats correctly say 81 games in '88-89, text says 82)		
59 Sleepy Floyd	.08	.20
60 Tim McCormick	.08	.20
61 Hakeem Olajuwon	.50	1.25
62 Otis Thorpe	.10	.30
63 Mike Woodson	.08	.20
64 Vern Fleming	.08	.20
65 Reggie Miller	.75	2.00
66 Chuck Person	.10	.30
67 Detlef Schrempf	.10	.30
68 Rik Smits RC	.40	1.00
69 Benoit Benjamin	.08	.20
70 Gary Grant RC	.10	.30
71 Danny Manning RC	.40	1.00
72 Ken Norman RC	.08	.20
73 Charles Smith RC	.25	.60
74 Reggie Williams RC	.08	.20
75 Michael Cooper	.10	.30
76 A.C. Green	.10	.30
77 Magic Johnson	1.00	2.50
78 Byron Scott	.10	.30
79 Mychal Thompson	.08	.20
80 James Worthy	.25	.60
81 Kevin Edwards RC	.08	.20
82 Grant Long RC	.08	.20
83 Rony Seikaly RC	.25	.60
84 Rory Sparrow	.08	.20
85 Greg Anderson UER	.08	.20
(Stats show 1988-89 as 19888-89)		
86 Jay Humphries	.08	.20
87 Larry Krystkowiak RC	.10	.30
88 Ricky Pierce	.08	.20
89 Paul Pressey	.08	.20
90 Alvin Robertson	.08	.20
91 Jack Sikma	.08	.20
92 Steve Johnson	.08	.20
93 Rick Mahorn	.08	.20
94 David Rivers	.08	.20
95 Joe Barry Carroll	.08	.20
96 Lester Conner UER	.08	.20
(Garden State in stats, should be Golden State)		
97 Roy Hinson	.08	.20
98 Mike McGee	.08	.20
99 Chris Morris RC	.10	.30
100 Patrick Ewing	.30	.75
101 Mark Jackson	.10	.30
102 Johnny Newman RC	.25	.60
103 Charles Oakley	.10	.30
104 Rod Strickland RC	1.00	2.50
105 Trent Tucker	.08	.20
106 Kiki Vandeweghe	.08	.20
107A Gerald Wilkins	.08	.20
(U. of Tennessee)		
107B Gerald Wilkins	.08	.20
(U. of Tenn.)		
108 Terry Catledge	.08	.20
109 Dave Corzine	.08	.20
110 Scott Skiles RC	.25	.60
111 Reggie Theus	.10	.30
112 Ron Anderson RC	.08	.20
113 Charles Barkley	.50	1.25
114 Scott Brooks RC	.25	.60
115 Maurice Cheeks	.08	.20
116 Mike Gminski	.08	.20
117 Hersey Hawkins UER RC	.40	1.00
Born 9/29/65, should be 9/9/65)		
118 Christian Welp	.08	.20
119 Tom Chambers	.10	.30
120 Armon Gilliam	.08	.20
121 Jeff Hornacek RC	.40	1.00
122 Eddie Johnson	.10	.30
123 Kevin Johnson RC	.60	1.50
124 Dan Majerle RC	.40	1.00
125 Mark West	.08	.20
126 Richard Anderson	.08	.20
127 Mark Bryant RC	.08	.20
128 Clyde Drexler	.30	.75
129 Kevin Duckworth	.08	.20
130 Jerome Kersey	.08	.20
131 Terry Porter	.08	.20
132 Buck Williams	.10	.30
133 Danny Ainge	.10	.30
134 Ricky Berry	.08	.20
135 Rodney McCray	.08	.20
136 Jim Petersen	.08	.20
137 Harold Pressley	.08	.20
138 Kenny Smith	.08	.20
139 Wayman Tisdale	.08	.20
140 Willie Anderson RC	.08	.20
141 Frank Brickowski	.08	.20
142 Terry Cummings	.10	.30
143 Johnny Dawkins	.08	.20
144 Vernon Maxwell RC	.40	1.00
145 Michael Cage	.08	.20
146 Dale Ellis	.10	.30
147 Alton Lister	.08	.20
148 Xavier McDaniel UER	.08	.20
(All-Rookie team in 1985, not 1988)		
149 Derrick McKey	.08	.20
150 Nate McMillan	.10	.30
151 Thurl Bailey	.08	.20
152 Mark Eaton	.08	.20
153 Darrell Griffith	.08	.20
154 Eric Leckner	.08	.20
155 Karl Malone	.50	1.25
156 John Stockton	.75	2.00
157 Mark Alarie	.08	.20
158 Ledell Eackles RC	.08	.20
159 Bernard King	.10	.30
160 Jeff Malone	.08	.20
161 Darrell Walker	.08	.20
162A John Williams ERR	.20	.50
162B John Williams COR	.08	.20
163 Karl Malone AS John Stockton Mark Eaton	.40	1.00
164 Hakeem Olajuwon AS Clyde Drexler AS	.25	.60
165 Dominique Wilkins AS Moses Malone AS	.25	.60
166 Brad Daugherty AS Mark Price AS Larry Nance AS UER Bio says Nance had 204 blocks, should be 206)	.08	.20
167 Patrick Ewing AS Mark Jackson AS	.25	.60
168 Checklist 1-168	.08	.20

1989-90 Fleer Stickers

This set of 11 insert standard-size stickers features NBA All-Stars. One All-Star sticker was inserted in each 12-card wax pack. The front has a color action player photo. An aqua stripe with dark blue stars traverses the card top, and the same pattern reappears about halfway down the card face. The words "Fleer '89 All-Stars" appear at the top of the picture, with the player's name and position immediately below the picture. The back has a star pattern similar to the front. A career summary is printed in blue on a white background. Most card backs have problems with wax stains as a result of packaging.

COMPLETE SET (11) 5.00 12.00
1 Karl Malone .30 .75
2 Hakeem Olajuwon .30 .75
3 Michael Jordan 5.00 12.00
4 Charles Barkley .30 .75
5 Magic Johnson .60 1.50
6 Isiah Thomas .20 .50
7 Patrick Ewing .20 .50
8 Dale Ellis .08 .25
9 Chris Mullin .20 .50
10 Larry Bird .75 2.00
11 Tom Chambers .08 .25

1990-91 Fleer

The 1990-91 Fleer set contains 198 standard-size cards. The cards were available in 15-card wax packs, 23-card cello packs and 36-card rack packs. Wax boxes contained 36 wax packs. There were also 43 card pre-priced packs ($1.49) which containted Rookie Sensation inserts. The fronts feature a color action player photo, with a white inner border and a two-color (red on top and bottom, blue on sides) outer border on a white card face. The team logo is superimposed at the upper left corner of the picture, with the player's name and position appearing below the picture. The backs are printed in black, gray, and yellow, and present biographical and statistical information. The set is ordered alphabetically in team subsets (with a few exceptions due to late trades). The description, All-American, is properly capitalized on the back of cards 134 and 144, but is not capitalized on cards 20, 29, 51, 53, 59, 70, 119, 130, 178, and 192. Rookie Cards of note in the set include Nick Anderson, Mookie Blaylock, Vlade Divac, Sean Elliott, Tim Hardaway, Shawn Kemp, Glen Rice, and Clifford Robinson.

COMPLETE SET (198) 3.00 6.00
1 John Battle UER .02 .10
(Drafted in '84, should be '85)
2 Cliff Levingston .02 .10
3 Moses Malone .05 .15
4 Kenny Smith .02 .10
5 Spud Webb .02 .10
6 Dominique Wilkins .05 .15
7 Kevin Willis .02 .10
8 Larry Bird .25 .60
9 Dennis Johnson .02 .10
10 Joe Kleine .02 .10
11 Reggie Lewis .02 .10
12 Kevin McHale .02 .10
13 Robert Parish .02 .10
14 Jim Paxson .02 .10
15 Ed Pinckney .02 .10
16 Muggsy Bogues .02 .10
17 Rex Chapman .05 .15
18 Dell Curry .02 .10
19 Armon Gilliam .02 .10
20 J.R. Reid RC .02 .10
21 Kelly Tripucka .02 .10
22 B.J. Armstrong RC .02 .10
23A Bill Cartwright ERR
(No decimal points in FGP and FTP)
23B Bill Cartwright COR .02 .10
24 Horace Grant .02 .10
25 Craig Hodges .02 .10
26 Michael Jordan UER 1.50 4.00
(Led NBA in scoring 4 years, not 3)
27 Stacey King UER RC .02 .10
(Comma missing between progressed and Stacy)
28 John Paxson .02 .10
29 Will Perdue .02 .10
30 Scottie Pippen UER .25 .60
(Born AR, not AK)
31 Brad Daugherty .02 .10
32 Craig Ehlo .02 .10
33 Danny Ferry RC .02 .10
34 Steve Kerr .05 .15
35 Larry Nance .02 .10
36 Mark Price UER .02 .10
(Drafted by Cleveland, should be Dallas)
37 Hot Rod Williams .02 .10
38 Rolando Blackman .02 .10
39A Adrian Dantley ERR
(No decimal points in FGP and FTP)
39B Adrian Dantley COR .02 .10
40 Brad Davis .02 .10
41 James Donaldson UER .02 .10
(Text says in committed,& should be is committed)
42 Derek Harper .02 .10
43 Sam Perkins UER .02 .10
(First line of text should be intact)
44 Bill Wennington .02 .10
45 Herb Williams .02 .10
46 Michael Adams .02 .10
47 Walter Davis .02 .10
48 Alex English UER .02 .10
(Stats missing from '76-77 through '79-80)
49 Bill Hanzlik .02 .10
50 Lafayette Lever UER .02 .10
(Born AR, not AK)
51 Todd Lichti RC .02 .10
52 Blair Rasmussen .02 .10
53 Danny Schayes .02 .10
54 Mark Aguirre .02 .10
55 Joe Dumars .05 .15
56 James Edwards .02 .10
57 Vinnie Johnson .02 .10
58 Bill Laimbeer .02 .10
59 Dennis Rodman UER .15 .40
(College misspelled as coilege on back)
60 John Salley .02 .10
61 Isiah Thomas .05 .15
62 Manute Bol .02 .10
63 Tim Hardaway RC .40 1.00
64 Rod Higgins .02 .10
65 Sarunas Marciulionis RC .02 .10
66 Chris Mullin .05 .15
67 Mitch Richmond .07 .20
68 Terry Teagle .02 .10
69 Anthony Bowie UER RC .02 .10
(Seasons, not seeasons)
70 Sleepy Floyd .02 .10
71 Buck Johnson .02 .10
72 Vernon Maxwell .02 .10
73 Hakeem Olajuwon .08 .25
74 Otis Thorpe .02 .10
75 Mitchell Wiggins .02 .10
76 Vern Fleming .02 .10
77 George McCloud RC .05 .15
78 Reggie Miller .07 .20
79 Chuck Person .02 .10
80 Mike Sanders .02 .10
81 Detlef Schrempf .02 .10
82 Rik Smits .05 .15
83 LaSalle Thompson .02 .10
84 Benoit Benjamin .02 .10
85 Winston Garland .02 .10
86 Ron Harper .02 .10
87 Danny Manning .02 .10
88 Ken Norman .02 .10
89 Charles Smith .02 .10
90 Michael Cooper .02 .10
91 Vlade Divac RC .15 .40
92 A.C. Green .02 .10
93 Magic Johnson .20 .50
94 Byron Scott .02 .10
95 Mychal Thompson UER .02 .10
(Missing '78-79 stats from Portland)
96 Orlando Woolridge .02 .10
97 James Worthy .05 .15
98 Sherman Douglas RC .05 .15
99 Kevin Edwards .02 .10
100 Grant Long .02 .10
101 Glen Rice RC .25 .60
102 Rony Seikaly .40 1.00
Michael Jordan UER
103 Billy Thompson .02 .10
104 Jeff Grayer RC .02 .10
105 Jay Humphries .02 .10
106 Ricky Pierce .02 .10
107 Paul Pressey .02 .10
108 Fred Roberts .02 .10
109 Alvin Robertson .02 .10
110 Jack Sikma .02 .10
111 Randy Breuer .02 .10
112 Tony Campbell .02 .10
113 Tyrone Corbin .02 .10
114 Sam Mitchell UER RC .02 .10
(Mercer University, not Mercer College)
115 Tod Murphy UER .02 .10
(Born Long Beach, not Lakewood)
116 Pooh Richardson RC .02 .10
117 Mookie Blaylock RC .08 .25
118 Sam Bowie .02 .10
119 Lester Conner .02 .10
120 Dennis Hopson .02 .10
121 Chris Morris .02 .10
122 Charles Shackleford .02 .10
123 Purvis Short .02 .10
124 Maurice Cheeks .02 .10
125 Patrick Ewing .05 .15
126 Mark Jackson .02 .10
127A Johnny Newman ERR .15 .40
(Jr. misprinted as J. on card back)
127B Johnny Newman COR .02 .10
128 Charles Oakley .02 .10
129 Trent Tucker .02 .10
130 Kenny Walker .02 .10
131 Gerald Wilkins .02 .10
132 Nick Anderson RC .08 .25
133 Terry Catledge .02 .10
134 Sidney Green .02 .10
135 Otis Smith .02 .10
136 Reggie Theus .02 .10
137 Sam Vincent .02 .10
138 Ron Anderson .02 .10
139 Charles Barkley UER .08 .25
(FG Percentage .545.)
140 Scott Brooks UER .02 .10
('89-89 Philadelphia in wrong typeface)
141 Johnny Dawkins .02 .10
142 Mike Gminski .02 .10
143 Hersey Hawkins .02 .10
144 Rick Mahorn .02 .10
145 Derek Smith .02 .10
146 Tom Chambers .02 .10
147 Jeff Hornacek .02 .10
148 Eddie Johnson .02 .10
149 Kevin Johnson .05 .15
150A Dan Majerle ERR .30 .75
(Award in 1988; three-time selection)
150B Dan Majerle COR .05 .15
(Award in 1989; three-time selection)
151 Tim Perry .02 .10
152 Kurt Rambis .02 .10
153 Mark West .02 .10
154 Clyde Drexler .05 .15
155 Kevin Duckworth .02 .10
156 Byron Irvin .02 .10
157 Jerome Kersey .02 .10
158 Terry Porter .02 .10
159 Clifford Robinson RC .08 .25
160 Buck Williams .02 .10
161 Danny Young .02 .10
162 Danny Ainge .02 .10
163 Antoine Carr .02 .10
164 Pervis Ellison RC .02 .10
165 Rodney McCray .02 .10
166 Harold Pressley .02 .10
167 Wayman Tisdale .02 .10
168 Willie Anderson .02 .10
169 Frank Brickowski .02 .10
170 Terry Cummings .02 .10
171 Sean Elliott RC .10 .30
172 David Robinson .20 .50
173 Rod Strickland .05 .15
174 David Wingate .02 .10
175 Dana Barros RC .05 .15
176 Michael Cage UER .02 .10
(Born AR, not AK)
177 Dale Ellis .02 .10
178 Shawn Kemp RC .60 1.50
179 Xavier McDaniel .02 .10
180 Derrick McKey .02 .10
181 Nate McMillan .02 .10
182 Thurl Bailey .02 .10
183 Mike Brown .02 .10
184 Mark Eaton .02 .10
185 Blue Edwards RC .02 .10
186 Bobby Hansen .02 .10
187 Eric Leckner .02 .10
188 Karl Malone .08 .25
189 John Stockton .07 .20
190 Mark Alarie .02 .10
191 Ledell Eackles .02 .10
192A Harvey Grant .30 .75
(First name on card front in black)
192B Harvey Grant .02 .10
(First name on card front in white)
193 Tom Hammonds RC .02 .10
194 Bernard King .02 .10
195 Jeff Malone .02 .10
196 Darrell Walker .02 .10
197 Checklist 1-99 .02 .10
198 Checklist 100-198 .02 .10

1990-91 Fleer All-Stars

The 12-card All-Star insert standard-size set was randomly inserted in 1990-91 Fleer 12-card packs at a rate of one in five. The fronts feature a color action photo, framed by a basketball hoop and net on an aqua background. An orange stripe at the top represents the bottom of the backboard and has the words "Fleer '90 All-Stars." The player's name and position are given at the bottom between stars. The backs are printed in blue and pink with white borders and have career summaries.

COMPLETE SET (12) 9.00 18.00
1 Charles Barkley .30 .75
2 Larry Bird .75 2.00
3 Hakeem Olajuwon .30 .75
4 Magic Johnson .60 1.50
5 Michael Jordan 5.00 12.00
6 Isiah Thomas .20 .50
7 Karl Malone .30 .75
8 Tom Chambers .05 .15
9 John Stockton .25 .60
10 David Robinson .60 1.50
11 Clyde Drexler .20 .50
12 Patrick Ewing .20 .50

1990-91 Fleer Rookie Sensations

Randomly inserted in 23-card cello packs, the 1990-91 Fleer Rookie Sensations set consists of 10 standard-size cards. Cards were inserted at a rate of approximately one in five packs. The fronts feature color action player photos, with white and red borders on an aqua background. A basketball overlays the lower left corner of the picture, with the words "Rookie Sensation" in yellow lettering, and the player's name appearing in white lettering in the bottom red border. The backs are printed in black and red on gray background (with white borders) and present summaries of their college careers and rookie seasons. The key card is David Robinson's first insert.

COMPLETE SET (10) 6.00 15.00
1 David Robinson UER 3.00 8.00
(Text has 1988-90 season, should be 1989-90)
2 Sean Elliott UER .75 2.00
(Misspelled Elliot on card front)
3 Glen Rice 1.50 4.00
4 J.R. Reid .20 .50
5 Stacey King .10 .30
6 Pooh Richardson .20 .50
7 Nick Anderson .60 1.50
8 Tim Hardaway 2.50 6.00
9 Vlade Divac 1.00 2.50
10 Sherman Douglas .20 .50

1990-91 Fleer Update

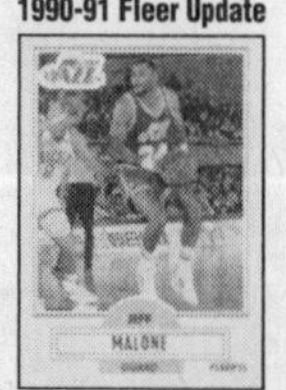

These cards are the same size and design as the regular issue yet were issued only in complete set form. Factory sets were distributed exclusively through hobby dealers. The set numbering is arranged alphabetically by team. The card numbers have a "U" prefix. Rookie Cards of note include Dee Brown, Elden Campbell, Cedric Ceballos, Derrick Coleman, Kendall Gill, Chris Jackson, Gary Payton, Drazen Petrovic, Dennis Scott and Loy Vaught. It's interesting to note that this is one of the first sets to actually get current year rookies pictured on trading cards.

COMP. FACT SET (100) 3.00 8.00
U1 Jon Koncak .01 .05
U2 Tim McCormick .01 .05
U3 Doc Rivers .05 .15
U4 Rumeal Robinson RC .01 .05
U5 Trevor Wilson .01 .05
U6 Dee Brown RC .10 .30
U7 Dave Popson .01 .05
U8 Kevin Gamble .01 .05
U9 Brian Shaw .10 .30
U10 Michael Smith .01 .05
U11 Kendall Gill RC .25 .60
U12 Johnny Newman .01 .05
U13 Steve Scheffler RC .01 .05
U14 Dennis Hopson .01 .05
U15 Cliff Levingston .01 .05
U16 Chucky Brown RC .01 .05
U17 John Morton .01 .05
U18 Gerald Paddio RC .01 .05
U19 Alex English .01 .05
U20 Fat Lever .01 .05
U21 Rodney McCray .01 .05
U22 Roy Tarpley .01 .05
U23 Randy White RC .01 .05
U24 Anthony Cook RC .01 .05
U25 Chris Jackson RC .10 .30
U26 Marcus Liberty RC .01 .05
U27 Orlando Woolridge .01 .05
U28 William Bedford RC .01 .05
U29 Lance Blanks RC .01 .05
U30 Scott Hastings .01 .05
U31 Tyrone Hill RC .05 .15
U32 Les Jepsen .01 .05
U33 Steve Johnson .01 .05
U34 Kevin Pritchard .01 .05
U35 Dave Jamerson RC .01 .05
U36 Kenny Smith .01 .05
U37 Greg Dreiling RC .01 .05
U38 Kenny Williams RC .01 .05
U39 Micheal Williams UER .05 .15
U40 Gary Grant .01 .05
U41 Bo Kimble RC .01 .05
U42 Loy Vaught RC .20 .50
U43 Elden Campbell RC .25 .60
U44 Sam Perkins .05 .15
U45 Tony Smith RC .01 .05
U46 Terry Teagle .01 .05
U47 Willie Burton RC .01 .05
U48 Bimbo Coles RC .10 .30
U49 Terry Davis RC .01 .05
U50 Alec Kessler RC .01 .05
U51 Greg Anderson .01 .05
U52 Frank Brickowski .01 .05
U53 Steve Henson RC .01 .05
U54 Brad Lohaus .01 .05
U55 Danny Schayes .01 .05
U56 Gerald Glass RC .01 .05
U57 Felton Spencer RC .05 .15
U58 Doug West RC .05 .15
U59 Jud Buechler RC .05 .15
U60 Derrick Coleman RC .25 .60
U61 Tate George RC .01 .05
U62 Reggie Theus .05 .15
U63 Greg Grant RC .01 .05
U64 Jerrod Mustaf RC .01 .05
U65 Eddie Lee Wilkins RC .01 .05
U66 Michael Ansley .01 .05
U67 Jerry Reynolds .01 .05
U68 Dennis Scott RC .15 .40
U69 Manute Bol .01 .05
U70 Armon Gilliam .01 .05
U71 Brian Oliver .01 .05
U72 Kenny Payne RC .01 .05
U73 Jayson Williams RC .40 1.00
U74 Kenny Battle RC .01 .05
U75 Cedric Ceballos RC .20 .50
U76 Negele Knight RC .01 .05
U77 Xavier McDaniel .01 .05
U78 Alaa Abdelnaby RC .01 .05
U79 Danny Ainge .05 .15
U80 Mark Bryant .01 .05
U81 Drazen Petrovic RC .10 .30
U82 Anthony Bonner RC .01 .05
U83 Duane Causwell RC .01 .05
U84 Bobby Hansen .01 .05
U85 Eric Leckner .01 .05
U86 Travis Mays RC .01 .05
U87 Lionel Simmons RC .05 .15
U88 Sidney Green .01 .05
U89 Tony Massenburg .01 .05
U90 Paul Pressey .01 .05
U91 Dwayne Schintzius RC .01 .05
U92 Gary Payton RC 2.50 6.00
U93 Olden Polynice .01 .05
U94 Jeff Malone .01 .05
U95 Walter Palmer .01 .05
U96 Delaney Rudd .01 .05
U97 Pervis Ellison .05 .15
U98 A.J. English RC .01 .05
U99 Greg Foster RC .05 .15
U100 Checklist 1-100 .01 .05

1991-92 Fleer

The complete 1991-92 Fleer basketball card set contains 400 standard-size cards. The set was distributed in two series of 240 and 160 cards, respectively. The cards were distributed in 12-card wax packs, 23-card cello packs and 36-card rack packs. Wax boxes contained 36 packs. The fronts feature color action player photos, bordered by a red stripe on the bottom, and gray and red stripes on the top. A 3/4" blue stripe checkered with black NBA logos runs the length of the card and serves as the left border of the picture. The team logo, player's name, and position are printed in white lettering in this stripe. The picture is bordered on the right side by a thin gray stripe and a thicker blue one. The backs present career summaries and are printed with black lettering on various pastel colors, superimposed over a wooden basketball floor background. The cards are numbered and checklisted below alphabetically according to teams within each series. Subsets include All-Stars (210-219), League Leaders (220-226), Slam Dunk (227-232), All Star Game Highlights (233-238) and Team Leaders (372-398). Rookie Cards of note include Kenny Anderson, Stacey Augmon, Terrell Brandon, Larry Johnson, Anthony Mason, Dikembe Mutombo, Steve Smith, and John Starks.

COMPLETE SET (400) 5.00 10.00
COMPLETE SERIES 1 (240) 2.50 5.00
COMPLETE SERIES 2 (160) 2.50 5.00
1 John Battle .02 .10
2 Jon Koncak .02 .10
3 Rumeal Robinson .02 .10
4 Spud Webb .02 .10
5 Bob Weiss CO .02 .10
6 Dominique Wilkins .05 .15
7 Kevin Willis .02 .10
8 Larry Bird .25 .60
9 Dee Brown .02 .10
10 Chris Ford CO .02 .10
11 Kevin Gamble .02 .10
12 Reggie Lewis .02 .10
13 Kevin McHale .02 .10
14 Robert Parish .02 .10
15 Ed Pinckney .02 .10
16 Brian Shaw .02 .10
17 Muggsy Bogues .02 .10
18 Rex Chapman .02 .10
19 Dell Curry .02 .10
20 Kendall Gill .02 .10
21 Eric Leckner .02 .10
22 Gene Littles CO .02 .10
23 Johnny Newman .02 .10
24 J.R. Reid .02 .10
25 B.J. Armstrong .02 .10
26 Bill Cartwright .02 .10
27 Horace Grant .02 .10
28 Phil Jackson CO .08 .25
29 Michael Jordan .75 2.00
30 Cliff Levingston .02 .10
31 John Paxson .02 .10
32 Will Perdue .02 .10
33 Scottie Pippen .20 .50
34 Brad Daugherty .02 .10
35 Craig Ehlo .02 .10
36 Danny Ferry .02 .10
37 Larry Nance .02 .10
38 Mark Price .02 .10
39 Darnell Valentine .02 .10
40 Hot Rod Williams .02 .10
41 Lenny Wilkens CO .02 .10
42 Richie Adubato CO .02 .10
43 Rolando Blackman .02 .10
44 James Donaldson .02 .10
45 Derek Harper .02 .10
46 Rodney McCray .02 .10
47 Randy White .02 .10
48 Herb Williams .02 .10
49 Chris Jackson .02 .10
50 Marcus Liberty .02 .10
51 Todd Lichti .02 .10
52 Blair Rasmussen .02 .10
53 Paul Westhead CO .02 .10
54 Reggie Williams .02 .10
55 Joe Wolf .02 .10
56 Orlando Woolridge .02 .10
57 Mark Aguirre .02 .10
58 Chuck Daly CO .02 .10
59 Joe Dumars .05 .15
60 James Edwards .02 .10
61 Vinnie Johnson .02 .10
62 Bill Laimbeer .02 .10
63 Dennis Rodman .10 .30
64 Isiah Thomas .05 .15
65 Tim Hardaway .08 .25
66 Rod Higgins .02 .10
67 Tyrone Hill .02 .10
68 Sarunas Marciulionis .02 .10
69 Chris Mullin .05 .15
70 Don Nelson CO .02 .10
71 Mitch Richmond .05 .15
72 Tom Tolbert .02 .10
73 Don Chaney CO .02 .10
74 Eric (Sleepy) Floyd .02 .10
75 Buck Johnson .02 .10
76 Vernon Maxwell .02 .10
77 Hakeem Olajuwon .08 .25
78 Kenny Smith .02 .10
79 Larry Smith .02 .10
80 Otis Thorpe .02 .10
81 Vern Fleming .02 .10
82 Bob Hill CO RC .02 .10
83 Reggie Miller .05 .15
84 Chuck Person .02 .10
85 Detlef Schrempf .02 .10
86 Rik Smits .02 .10
87 LaSalle Thompson .02 .10
88 Micheal Williams .02 .10
89 Gary Grant .02 .10
90 Ron Harper .02 .10
91 Bo Kimble .02 .10
92 Danny Manning .02 .10
93 Ken Norman .02 .10
94 Olden Polynice .02 .10
95 Mike Schuler CO .02 .10
96 Charles Smith .02 .10
97 Vlade Divac .02 .10
98 Mike Dunleavy CO .02 .10
99 A.C. Green .02 .10
100 Magic Johnson .20 .50
101 Sam Perkins .02 .10
102 Byron Scott .02 .10
103 Terry Teagle .02 .10
104 James Worthy .05 .15
105 Willie Burton .02 .10
106 Bimbo Coles .02 .10
107 Sherman Douglas .02 .10
108 Kevin Edwards .02 .10
109 Grant Long .02 .10
110 Kevin Loughery CO .02 .10
111 Glen Rice .05 .15
112 Rony Seikaly .02 .10
113 Frank Brickowski .02 .10
114 Dale Ellis .02 .10
115 Del Harris CO .02 .10
116 Jay Humphries .02 .10
117 Fred Roberts .02 .10
118 Alvin Robertson .02 .10
119 Danny Schayes .02 .10
120 Jack Sikma .02 .10
121 Tony Campbell .02 .10
122 Tyrone Corbin .02 .10
123 Sam Mitchell .02 .10
124 Tod Murphy .02 .10
125 Pooh Richardson .02 .10
126 Jimmy Rodgers CO .02 .10
127 Felton Spencer .02 .10
128 Mookie Blaylock .02 .10
129 Sam Bowie .02 .10
130 Derrick Coleman .02 .10
131 Chris Dudley .02 .10
132 Bill Fitch CO .02 .10
133 Chris Morris .02 .10
134 Drazen Petrovic .02 .10
135 Maurice Cheeks .02 .10
136 Patrick Ewing .05 .15
137 Mark Jackson .02 .10
138 Charles Oakley .02 .10
139 Pat Riley CO .02 .10
140 Trent Tucker .02 .10
141 Kiki Vandeweghe .02 .10
142 Gerald Wilkins .02 .10
143 Nick Anderson .02 .10
144 Terry Catledge .02 .10
145 Matt Guokas CO .02 .10
146 Jerry Reynolds .02 .10
147 Dennis Scott .02 .10
148 Scott Skiles .02 .10
149 Otis Smith .02 .10
150 Ron Anderson .02 .10
151 Charles Barkley .08 .25
152 Johnny Dawkins .02 .10
153 Armon Gilliam .02 .10
154 Hersey Hawkins .02 .10
155 Jim Lynam CO .02 .10
156 Rick Mahorn .02 .10
157 Brian Oliver .02 .10
158 Tom Chambers .02 .10
159 Cotton Fitzsimmons CO .02 .10
160 Jeff Hornacek .02 .10
161 Kevin Johnson .05 .15
162 Negele Knight .02 .10
163 Dan Majerle .02 .10
164 Xavier McDaniel .02 .10
165 Mark West .02 .10
166 Rick Adelman CO .02 .10
167 Danny Ainge .02 .10
168 Clyde Drexler .05 .15
169 Kevin Duckworth .02 .10
170 Jerome Kersey .02 .10
171 Terry Porter .02 .10
172 Clifford Robinson .02 .10
173 Buck Williams .02 .10
174 Antoine Carr .02 .10
175 Duane Causwell .02 .10
176 Jim Les RC .02 .10
177 Travis Mays .02 .10
178 Dick Motta CO .02 .10
179 Lionel Simmons .02 .10
180 Rory Sparrow .02 .10
181 Wayman Tisdale .02 .10
182 Willie Anderson .02 .10
183 Larry Brown CO .02 .10
184 Terry Cummings .02 .10
185 Sean Elliott .02 .10
186 Paul Pressey .02 .10
187 David Robinson .10 .30
188 Rod Strickland .05 .15
189 Benoit Benjamin .02 .10
190 Eddie Johnson .02 .10
191 K.C. Jones CO .02 .10
192 Shawn Kemp .15 .40
193 Derrick McKey .02 .10
194 Gary Payton .15 .40
195 Ricky Pierce .02 .10
196 Sedale Threatt .02 .10
197 Thurl Bailey .02 .10
198 Mark Eaton .02 .10
199 Blue Edwards .02 .10
200 Jeff Malone .02 .10
201 Karl Malone .08 .25
202 Jerry Sloan CO .02 .10
203 John Stockton .05 .15
204 Ledell Eackles .02 .10
205 Pervis Ellison .02 .10
206 A.J. English .02 .10
207 Harvey Grant .02 .10
208 Bernard King .02 .10
209 Wes Unseld CO .02 .10
210 Kevin Johnson AS .02 .10
211 Michael Jordan AS .40 1.00
212 Dominique Wilkins AS .02 .10
213 Charles Barkley AS .05 .15
214 Hakeem Olajuwon AS .05 .15
215 Patrick Ewing AS .02 .10
216 Tim Hardaway AS .05 .15
217 John Stockton AS .02 .10
218 Chris Mullin AS .02 .10
219 Karl Malone AS .05 .15
220 Michael Jordan LL .40 1.00
221 John Stockton LL .02 .10
222 Alvin Robertson LL .02 .10
223 Hakeem Olajuwon LL .05 .15
224 Buck Williams LL .02 .10
225 David Robinson LL .05 .15
226 Reggie Miller LL .02 .10
227 Blue Edwards SD .02 .10
228 Dee Brown SD .02 .10
229 Rex Chapman SD .02 .10
230 Kenny Smith SD .02 .10
231 Shawn Kemp SD .05 .15
232 Kendall Gill SD .02 .10
233 Michael Jordan .25 .60
'91 All Star Game
Enemies - A Love Story
(East Bench Scene)
234 Clyde Drexler ASG .05 .15
Kevin McHale ASG
235 Alvin Robertson ASG .02 .10
236 Patrick Ewing ASG .02 .10
Karl Malone ASG
237 Michael Jordan .25 .60
Magic Johnson
David Robinson
Patrick Ewing
238 Michael Jordan ASG .40 1.00
239 Checklist 1-120 .02 .10
240 Checklist 121-240 .02 .10
241 Stacey Augmon RC .05 .15
242 Maurice Cheeks .02 .10
243 Paul Graham RC .02 .10
244 Rodney Monroe RC .02 .10
245 Blair Rasmussen .02 .10
246 Alexander Volkov .02 .10
247 John Bagley .02 .10
248 Rick Fox RC .05 .15
249 Rickey Green .02 .10
250 Joe Kleine .02 .10
251 Stojko Vrankovic .02 .10
252 Allan Bristow CO .02 .10
253 Kenny Gattison .02 .10
254 Mike Gminski .02 .10
255 Larry Johnson RC .25 .60
256 Bobby Hansen .02
257 Craig Hodges .02
258 Stacey King .02
259 Scott Williams RC .02
260 John Battle .02
261 Winston Bennett .02
262 Terrell Brandon RC .20
263 Henry James .02
264 Steve Kerr .02
265 Jimmy Oliver RC .02
266 Brad Davis .02
267 Terry Davis .02
268 Donald Hodge RC .02
269 Mike Iuzzolino RC .02
270 Fat Lever .02
271 Doug Smith RC .02
272 Greg Anderson .02
273 Kevin Brooks RC .02
274 Walter Davis .02
275 Winston Garland .02
276 Mark Macon RC .02
277 Dikembe Mutombo RC .25
(Fleer '91 on front)
277B Dikembe Mutombo RC .25
(Fleer '91-92 on front)
278 William Bedford .02
279 Lance Blanks .02
280 John Salley .02
281 Charles Thomas RC .02
282 Darrell Walker .02
283 Orlando Woolridge .02
284 Victor Alexander RC .02
285 Vincent Askew RC .02
286 Mario Elie RC .05
287 Alton Lister .02
288 Billy Owens RC .05
289 Matt Bullard RC .02
290 Carl Herrera RC .02
291 Tree Rollins .02
292 John Turner .02
293 Dale Davis UER RC .05
(Photo on back actually Sean Green)
294 Sean Green RC .02
295 Kenny Williams .02
296 James Edwards .02
297 LeRon Ellis RC .02
298 Doc Rivers .02
299 Loy Vaught .02
300 Elden Campbell .02
301 Jack Haley .02
302 Keith Owens .02
303 Tony Smith .02
304 Sedale Threatt .02
305 Keith Askins RC .02
306 Alec Kessler .02
307 John Morton .02
308 Alan Ogg .02
309 Steve Smith RC .25
310 Lester Conner .02
311 Jeff Grayer .02
312 Frank Hamblen CO .02
313 Steve Henson .02
314 Larry Krystkowiak .02
315 Moses Malone .05
316 Thurl Bailey .02
317 Randy Breuer .02
318 Scott Brooks .02
319 Gerald Glass .02
320 Luc Longley RC .05
321 Doug West .02
322 Kenny Anderson RC .10
323 Tate George .02
324 Terry Mills RC .05
325 Greg Anthony RC .05
326 Anthony Mason RC .10
327 Tim McCormick .02
328 Xavier McDaniel .02
329 Brian Quinnett .02
330 John Starks RC .05
331 Stanley Roberts RC .02
332 Jeff Turner .02
333 Sam Vincent .02
334 Brian Williams RC .05
335 Manute Bol .02
336 Kenny Payne .02
337 Charles Shackleford .02
338 Jayson Williams .05
339 Cedric Ceballos .02
340 Andrew Lang .02
341 Jerrod Mustaf .02
342 Tim Perry .02
343 Kurt Rambis .02
344 Alaa Abdelnaby .02
345 Robert Pack RC .02
346 Danny Young .02
347 Anthony Bonner .02
348 Pete Chilcutt RC .02
349 Rex Hughes CO .02
350 Mitch Richmond .05
351 Dwayne Schintzius .02
352 Spud Webb .02
353 Antoine Carr .02
354 Sidney Green .02
355 Vinnie Johnson .02
356 Greg Sutton RC .02
357 Dana Barros .02
358 Michael Cage .02
359 Marty Conlon RC .02
360 Rich King RC .02
361 Nate McMillan .02
362 David Benoit RC .02
363 Mike Brown .02
364 Tyrone Corbin .02
365 Eric Murdock RC .02
366 Delaney Rudd .02
367 Michael Adams .02
368 Tom Hammonds .02
369 Larry Stewart RC .02
370 Andre Turner .02
371 David Wingate .02
372 Dominique Wilkins TL .02
373 Larry Bird TL .10
374 Rex Chapman TL .02
375 Michael Jordan TL .40
376 Brad Daugherty TL .02
377 Derek Harper TL .02
378 Dikembe Mutombo TL .05
379 Joe Dumars TL .02
380 Chris Mullin TL .02
381 Hakeem Olajuwon TL .05
382 Chuck Person TL .02
383 Charles Smith TL .02
384 James Worthy TL .02
385 Glen Rice TL .02

vin Robertson TL .02 .10
ony Campbell TL .02 .10
errick Coleman TL .02 .10
atrick Ewing TL .02 .10
cott Skiles TL .02 .10
harles Barkley TL .05 .15
evin Johnson TL .02 .10
lyde Drexler TL .02 .10
onel Simmons TL .02 .10
avid Robinson TL .05 .15
icky Pierce TL .02 .10
ohn Stockton TL .02 .10
ichael Adams TL .02 .10
hecklist .02 .10
hecklist .02 .10
Michael Jordan 3-D 600.00 1000.00
oper Redemption

1991-92 Fleer Dikembe Mutombo

2-card standard-size set was randomly inserted 1-92 Fleer second series 12-card wax packs at a approximately one in six. The set highlights the plishments of then Denver Nuggets' rookie be Mutombo. The front borders are dark red and ered with miniature black NBA logos. The ound of the color action photo is ghosted so that tured player stands out, and the color of the g on the front is mustard. On a pink round, the back has a color close-up photo and a ary of the player's performance. Mutombo aphed over 2,000 of these cards which were also nly inserted into packs. Those cards inserted in feature embossed Fleer logos for authenticity.

LETE SET (12) 2.00 5.00
ION MUTOMBO (1-12) .20 .50
ION AUTOGRAPH (AU) 12.50 30.00

1991-92 Fleer Pro-Visions

x-card standard-size set showcases outstanding layers. The set was distributed as a random in 1991-92 Fleer first series 12-card plastic-acks at a rate of approximately one per six The fronts feature a color player portrait by artist Terry Smith. The portrait is bordered on all y white, with the player's name in red lettering the picture. The backs present biographical ation and career summary in black lettering on a background (with white borders).

LETE SET (6) 1.50 4.00
d Robinson .20 .50
ael Jordan 1.25 3.00
les Barkley .15 .40
ck Ewing .08 .25
Malone .15 .40
ic Johnson .30 .75

1991-92 Fleer Rookie Sensations

)-card standard-size set showcases outstanding s from the 1990-91 season. The set was uted as a random insert in 1991-92 Fleer 23-ello packs at a rate of approximately two in every packs. The card fronts feature a color player inside a basketball rim and net. The picture is ed in magenta on all sides. The words "Rookie ions" appear above the picture, and player ation is given below the picture. An orange ball with the words "Fleer '91" appears in the eft corner on both sides of the card. The back magenta border and includes highlights of the 's rookie season.

LETE SET (10) 3.00 8.00
el Simmons .20 .50
nis Scott .30 .75
ck Coleman .60 1.50
all Gill .60 1.50
s Mays .20 .50
n Spencer .20 .50
e Burton .20 .50
s Jackson .20 .50
Payton 2.50 6.00
e Brown .20 .50

1991-92 Fleer Schoolyard

This six-card standard-size set of "Schoolyard Stars" was inserted one per 1991-92 Fleer 36-card rack packs. The card front features color action player photos. The photos are bordered on the left and bottom by a black stripe and a broken pink stripe. Yellow stripes traverse the card top and bottom, and the background is a gray cement-colored design. The back has a similar layout and presents a basketball tip in black lettering on white.

COMPLETE SET (6) 4.00 8.00
1 Chris Mullin .60 1.50
2 Isiah Thomas .60 1.50
3 Kevin McHale .60 1.50
4 Kevin Johnson .60 1.50
5 Karl Malone 2.50 6.00
6 Alvin Robertson .30 .75

1991-92 Fleer Dominique Wilkins

Cards from this 12-card insert standard-size set were randomly inserted in 1991-92 Fleer second series 12-card wax packs at a rate of approximately one per six. The set highlights the career of superstar Dominique Wilkins. The front borders are dark red and checkered with miniature black NBA logos. The background of the color action photo is ghosted so that the featured player stands out, and the color of the lettering on the front is mustard. On a pink background, the back has a color close-up photo and a summary of the player's performance. Wilkins personally autographed over 2,000 of these cards which were also randomly inserted in packs. Those cards inserted in packs feature embossed Fleer logos for authenticity.

COMPLETE SET (12) 1.50 4.00
COMMON WILKINS (1-12) .20 .50
COMMON AUTOGRAPH (AU) 30.00 60.00

1991-92 Fleer Mutombo/Wilkins Promo

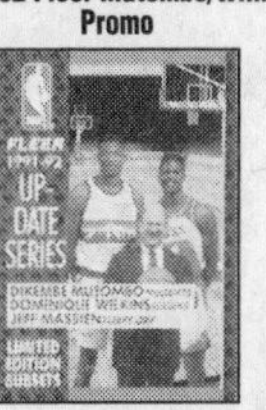

The Dikembe Mutombo/Dominique Wilkins Commemorative Card was issued to announce the introduction of the 1991-92 Fleer NBA set featuring Dikembe Mutombo and Dominique Wilkins. The card measures the standard size and displays a posed color photo of Dikembe Mutombo and Dominique Wilkins with Jeff Massien, Vice President of Fleercorp. The card is unnumbered. The card was issued to the Fleer dealer network and to various media.

1 Dikembe Mutombo 5.00 12.00
Dominique Wilkins
With Jeff Massien Fleer VP

1991-92 Fleer Tony's Pizza

These standard-size cards were issued in three-card plastic packs in specially marked boxes of Tony's Frozen Pizza during March and April. Reportedly the promotion went so well that regular cards were inserted when the special S-prefix numbered cards ran out. The cards feature glossy color player action shots with red, gray, and blue borders on their fronts. The player's name, position, and team logo appear in white lettering in the broad blue left margin, which has a pattern of small black NBA logos within it. The back of each card displays a head shot and another action photo at the top, with a brief player biography beneath, and a blue-and white-banded stat panel toward the bottom, all superimposed upon a wooden basketball floor pattern. These 120 cards are the same as the regular-issue cards and are numbered on the back with an "S- prefix.

COMPLETE SET (120) 120.00 300.00
1 Terry Teagle .60 1.50
2 Karl Malone 5.00 12.00
3 Patrick Ewing 3.00 8.00
4 Alvin Robertson .60 1.50
5 Scott Skiles .75 2.00
6 Frank Brickowski .60 1.50
7 Mookie Blaylock .75 2.00
8 Ricky Pierce .60 1.50
9 Gary Payton 3.00 8.00
10 Dennis Scott .75 2.00
11 Derrick McKey .60 1.50
12 Mark West .60 1.50
13 Mark Jackson 1.50 4.00
14 Glen Rice 2.00 5.00
15 Charles Barkley 5.00 12.00
16 David Robinson 4.00 10.00
17 Sam Bowie .75 2.00
18 Ron Harper 1.25 3.00
19 Reggie Miller 4.00 10.00
20 Lionel Simmons .60 1.50
21 Jerome Kersey .75 2.00
22 Rod Strickland .60 1.50
23 Charles Oakley .60 1.50
24 Rony Seikaly .60 1.50
25 Johnny Dawkins .60 1.50
26 Fred Roberts .60 1.50
27 Derrick Coleman .75 2.00
28 Bo Kimble .60 1.50
29 Chuck Person .60 1.50
30 Kiki Vandeweghe 1.25 3.00
31 Jeff Malone .60 1.50
32 Vlade Divac 1.25 3.00
33 Michael Jordan 20.00 50.00
34 Gerald Wilkins .75 2.00
35 Sarunas Marciulionis .75 2.00
36 Pooh Richardson .60 1.50
37 Hakeem Olajuwon 4.00 9.00
38 Rodney McCray .60 1.50
39 Larry Nance .75 2.00
40 Wayman Tisdale .60 1.50
41 Tom Chambers .75 2.00
42 A.C. Green 1.00 2.50
43 Bernard King .75 2.00
44 Reggie Williams .60 1.50
45 Chris Mullin 1.50 4.00
46 Bill Laimbeer 1.25 3.00
47 Kenny Smith .75 2.00
48 Harvey Grant .60 1.50
49 Mark Price 1.00 2.50
50 Olden Polynice .60 1.50
51 Isiah Thomas 3.00 8.00
52 Magic Johnson 5.00 12.00
53 John Paxson .75 2.00
54 Muggsy Bogues 1.25 3.00
55 Mitch Richmond 2.50 6.00
56 Dennis Rodman 3.00 8.00
57 Otis Thorpe .75 2.00
58 Larry Bird 8.00 20.00
59 Hot Rod Williams .60 1.50
60 Hersey Hawkins .75 2.00
61 Brian Shaw .75 2.00
62 Detlef Schrempf .75 2.00
63 Danny Manning .75 2.00
64 Thurl Bailey .60 1.50
65 Benoit Benjamin .60 1.50
66 Nick Anderson .75 2.00
67 Rex Chapman .75 2.00
68 Danny Ainge 1.25 3.00
69 Dee Brown .60 1.50
70 Chris Dudley .60 1.50
71 Kevin McHale 1.50 4.00
72 Dell Curry .60 1.50
73 Ken Norman .60 1.50
74 Mark Eaton .60 1.50
75 Shawn Kemp 2.50 6.00
76 Bill Cartwright .75 2.00
77 Terry Cummings .75 2.00
78 Clyde Drexler 4.00 10.00
79 Kevin Johnson 1.25 3.00
80 Dale Ellis .75 2.00
81 Tod Murphy .60 1.50
82 Brad Daugherty .60 1.50
83 Charles Smith .60 1.50
84 Horace Grant 1.25 3.00
85 Vernon Maxwell .60 1.50
86 Todd Lichti .60 1.50
87 Sean Elliott 1.25 3.00
88 Kevin Duckworth .60 1.50
89 Dan Majerle 1.25 3.00
90 James Worthy 1.50 4.00
91 Mark Aguirre .75 2.00
92 Kevin Willis .75 2.00
93 Reggie Lewis .75 2.00
94 Rumeal Robinson .60 1.50
95 Terry Porter .75 2.00
96 Rolando Blackman .75 2.00
97 Tony Campbell .60 1.50
98 Sam Perkins 1.25 3.00
99 Willie Burton .60 1.50
100 Joe Dumars 1.50 4.00
101 Felton Spencer .60 1.50
102 Danny Ferry .60 1.50
103 James Donaldson .60 1.50
104 Craig Ehlo .75 2.00
105 Clifford Robinson 1.00 2.50
106 Pervis Ellison .60 1.50
107 Tyrone Corbin .60 1.50
108 Byron Scott 1.25 3.00
109 Sherman Douglas .60 1.50
110 Tim Hardaway 2.00 5.00
111 Kendall Gill .75 2.00
112 J.R. Reid .60 1.50
113 Robert Parish 1.25 3.00
114 Dominique Wilkins 3.00 8.00
115 Buck Williams .75 2.00
116 Scottie Pippen 4.00 10.00
117 Sam Mitchell .60 1.50
118 John Stockton 6.00 15.00
119 Derek Harper .75 2.00
120 Chris Jackson .60 1.50

1991-92 Fleer Wheaties Sheets

These Fleer regular issue (gray back) cards were issued nine cards per collector sheet on the back of Wheaties cereal boxes. Eight different collector sheets were produced, and we have checklisted the cards below by boxes. These eight different nine-card gray-back sample sheets were offered on the back of more than four million Wheaties cereal boxes from February to April, 1992. The sheets included regular cards as well as insert and special cards; the non-regular cards are indicated below, e.g., All-Stars (AS), League Leaders (LL), Pro Visions (PV), Rookie Sensations (RS), Schoolyard (SY), and Slam Dunk (SD).

COMPLETE SET (8) 40.00 100.00
1 Terry Cummings 6.00 15.00
Felton Spencer RS
Mookie Blaylock
Joe Dumars
Charles Barkley PV
Rex Chapman
Reggie Miller LL
Horace Grant
Shawn Kemp
2 Chris Jackson RS 4.00 10.00
Sam Perkins
Sean Elliott
Tim Hardaway
Karl Malone PV
J.R. Reid
Wayman Tisdale
Chris Mullin SY
Rolando Blackman
3 Alvin Robertson 3.00 8.00
Robert Parish
Mark Aguirre
Tyrone Hill
Patrick Ewing PV
Brad Daugherty
Lionel Simmons RS
Terry Porter
Bimbo Coles
4 Blue Edwards SD 3.00 8.00
Bill Cartwright
Rony Seikaly
Vernon Maxwell
David Robinson PV
Sam Bowie
Hersey Hawkins
A.C. Green
Dee Brown RS
5 B.J. Armstrong 3.00 8.00
Jay Humphries
Isiah Thomas SY
Reggie Lewis
Kevin Johnson AS
Pooh Richardson
Dennis Scott RS
Kevin Duckworth
Otis Thorpe
6 Byron Scott 15.00 40.00
Kevin McHale SY
Muggsy Bogues
Detlef Schrempf
Michael Jordan PV
Willie Anderson
Johnny Dawkins
Kendall Gill RS
Glen Rice
7 Charles Smith 8.00 20.00
Derrick Coleman RS
Dennis Rodman
Gerald Wilkins
Hakeem Olajuwon AS
James Worthy
Tom Chambers
Buck Williams LL
Larry Bird
8 Kenny Smith SD 8.00 20.00
Scottie Pippen
Clyde Drexler
John Stockton
Dominique Wilkins AS
Derek Harper
Brian Shaw
Mark Price
Willie Burton RS

1992-93 Fleer

The complete 1992-93 Fleer basketball set contains 444 standard-size cards. The set was distributed in two series of 264 and 180 cards, respectively. First series cards were distributed in 17-card plastic-wrap packs, 32-card cello packs, and 42-card rack packs. Second series cards were distributed in 15-card plastic-wrap packs and 32-card cello packs. The fronts display color action player photos, enclosed by metallic bronze borders and accented on the right by two pebble-grain colored stripes. On a tan pebble-grain background, the horizontally oriented backs have a color close-up photo in the shape of the lane under the basket. Biography, career statistics, and player profile are included on the backs. The cards are numbered on the back and checklisted below alphabetically according to teams. Subsets include League Leaders (238-245), Award Winners (246-249), Pro-Visions (250-255), Schoolyard Stars (256-264) and Slam Dunk (265-300). The Slam Dunk subset is divided into five categories: Power, Grace, Champions, Little Big Men, and Great Defenders. Randomly inserted throughout the packs were more than 3,000 (Slam Dunk subset) cards signed by former NBA players Darryl Dawkins and Kenny Walker as well as by current NBA star Shawn Kemp. According to Fleer's advertising material, odds of finding a signed Slam Dunk card are one in 5,000 packs. Rookie Cards of note include Tom Gugliotta, Robert Horry, Christian Laettner, Alonzo Mourning, Shaquille O'Neal, Latrell Sprewell and Clarence Weatherspoon. A second series mail-in offer featuring an "All-Star Slam Dunk Team" card and an issue of Inside Stuff was available (expiring 6/30/93) in return for ten second series wrappers plus a dollar.

COMPLETE SET (444) 15.00 30.00
COMPLETE SERIES 1 (264) 7.50 15.00
COMPLETE SERIES 2 (180) 7.50 15.00
1 Stacey Augmon .02 .10
2 Duane Ferrell .02 .10
3 Paul Graham .02 .10
4A Jon Koncak .02 .10
(Shooting pose on back)
4B Jon Koncak .02 .10
(No ball visible
in photo on back)
5 Blair Rasmussen .02 .10
6 Rumeal Robinson .02 .10
7 Bob Weiss CO .02 .10
8 Dominique Wilkins .08 .25
9 Kevin Willis .02 .10
10 John Bagley .02 .10
11 Larry Bird .40 1.00
12 Dee Brown .02 .10
13 Chris Ford CO .02 .10
14 Rick Fox .02 .10
15 Kevin Gamble .02 .10
16 Reggie Lewis .02 .10
17 Kevin McHale .08 .25
18 Robert Parish .02 .10
19 Ed Pinckney .02 .10
20 Muggsy Bogues .02 .10
21 Allan Bristow CO .02 .10
22 Dell Curry .02 .10
23 Kenny Gattison .02 .10
24 Kendall Gill .02 .10
25 Larry Johnson .10 .30
26 Johnny Newman .02 .10
27 J.R. Reid .02 .10
28 B.J. Armstrong .02 .10
29 Bill Cartwright .02 .10
30 Horace Grant .02 .10
31 Phil Jackson CO .02 .10
32 Michael Jordan 1.25 3.00
33 Stacey King .02 .10
34 Cliff Levingston .02 .10
35 John Paxson .02 .10
36 Scottie Pippen .30 .75
37 Scott Williams .02 .10
38 John Battle .02 .10
39 Terrell Brandon .08 .25
40 Brad Daugherty .02 .10
41 Craig Ehlo .02 .10
42 Larry Nance .02 .10
43 Mark Price .02 .10
44 Mike Sanders .02 .10
45 Lenny Wilkens CO .02 .10
46 John Hot Rod Williams .02 .10
47 Richie Adubato CO .02 .10
48 Terry Davis .02 .10
49 Derek Harper .02 .10
50 Donald Hodge .02 .10
51 Mike Iuzzolino .02 .10
52 Rodney McCray .02 .10
53 Doug Smith .02 .10
54 Greg Anderson .02 .10
55 Winston Garland .02 .10
56 Dan Issel CO .02 .10
57 Chris Jackson .02 .10
58 Marcus Liberty .02 .10
59 Mark Macon .02 .10
60 Dikembe Mutombo .10 .30
61 Reggie Williams .02 .10
62 Mark Aguirre .02 .10
63 Joe Dumars .08 .25
64 Bill Laimbeer .02 .10
65 Olden Polynice .02 .10
66 Dennis Rodman .20 .50
67 Ron Rothstein CO .02 .10
68 John Salley .02 .10
69 Isiah Thomas .08 .25
70 Darrell Walker .02 .10
71 Orlando Woolridge .02 .10
72 Victor Alexander .02 .10
73 Mario Elie .02 .10
74 Tim Hardaway .10 .30
75 Tyrone Hill .02 .10
76 Sarunas Marciulionis .02 .10
77 Chris Mullin .08 .25
78 Don Nelson CO .02 .10
79 Billy Owens .02 .10
80 Sleepy Floyd UER .02 .10
(Went past 4000 assist mark; not 2000)
81 Avery Johnson .02 .10
82 Buck Johnson .02 .10
83 Vernon Maxwell .02 .10
84 Hakeem Olajuwon .15 .40
85 Kenny Smith .02 .10
86 Otis Thorpe .02 .10
87 Rudy Tomjanovich CO .02 .10
88 Dale Davis .02 .10
89 Vern Fleming .02 .10
90 Bob Hill CO .02 .10
91 Reggie Miller .08 .25
92 Chuck Person .02 .10
93 Detlef Schrempf .02 .10
94 Rik Smits .02 .10
95 LaSalle Thompson .02 .10
96 Micheal Williams .02 .10
97 Larry Brown CO .02 .10
98 James Edwards .02 .10
99 Gary Grant .02 .10
100 Ron Harper .02 .10
101 Danny Manning .02 .10
102 Ken Norman .02 .10
103 Doc Rivers .02 .10
104 Charles Smith .02 .10
105 Loy Vaught .02 .10
106 Elden Campbell .02 .10
107 Vlade Divac .02 .10
108 A.C. Green .02 .10
109 Sam Perkins .02 .10
110 Randy Pfund CO RC .02 .10
111 Byron Scott .02 .10
112 Terry Teagle .02 .10
113 Sedale Threatt .02 .10
114 James Worthy .08 .25
115 Willie Burton .02 .10
116 Bimbo Coles .02 .10
117 Kevin Edwards .02 .10
118 Grant Long .02 .10
119 Kevin Loughery CO .02 .10
120 Glen Rice .08 .25
121 Rony Seikaly .02 .10
122 Brian Shaw .02 .10
123 Steve Smith .10 .30
124 Frank Brickowski .02 .10
125 Mike Dunleavy CO .02 .10
126 Blue Edwards .02 .10
127 Moses Malone .08 .25
128 Eric Murdock .02 .10
129 Fred Roberts .02 .10
130 Alvin Robertson .02 .10
131 Thurl Bailey .02 .10
132 Tony Campbell .02 .10
133 Gerald Glass .02 .10
134 Luc Longley .02 .10
135 Sam Mitchell .02 .10
136 Pooh Richardson .02 .10
137 Jimmy Rodgers CO .02 .10
138 Felton Spencer .02 .10
139 Doug West .02 .10
140 Kenny Anderson .08 .25
141 Mookie Blaylock .02 .10
142 Sam Bowie .02 .10
143 Derrick Coleman .02 .10
144 Chuck Daly CO .02 .10
145 Terry Mills .02 .10
146 Chris Morris .02 .10
147 Drazen Petrovic .02 .10
148 Greg Anthony .02 .10
149 Rolando Blackman .02 .10
150 Patrick Ewing .08 .25
151 Mark Jackson .02 .10
152 Anthony Mason .08 .25
153 Xavier McDaniel .02 .10
154 Charles Oakley .02 .10
155 Pat Riley CO .02 .10
156 John Starks .02 .10
157 Gerald Wilkins .02 .10
158 Nick Anderson .02 .10
159 Anthony Bowie .02 .10
160 Terry Catledge .02 .10
161 Matt Guokas CO .02 .10
162 Stanley Roberts .02 .10
163 Dennis Scott .02 .10
164 Scott Skiles .02 .10
165 Brian Williams .02 .10
166 Ron Anderson .02 .10
167 Manute Bol .02 .10
168 Johnny Dawkins .02 .10
169 Armon Gilliam .02 .10
170 Hersey Hawkins .02 .10
171 Jeff Hornacek .02 .10
172 Andrew Lang .02 .10
173 Doug Moe CO .02 .10
174 Tim Perry .02 .10
175 Jeff Ruland .02 .10
176 Charles Shackleford .02 .10
177 Danny Ainge .02 .10
178 Charles Barkley .15 .40
179 Cedric Ceballos .02 .10
180 Tom Chambers .02 .10
181 Kevin Johnson .08 .25
182 Dan Majerle .02 .10
183 Mark West UER .02 .10
(Needs 33 blocks to reach 1000; not 31)
184 Paul Westphal CO .02 .10
185 Rick Adelman CO .02 .10
186 Clyde Drexler .08 .25
187 Kevin Duckworth .02 .10
188 Jerome Kersey .02 .10
189 Robert Pack .02 .10
190 Terry Porter .02 .10
191 Clifford Robinson .02 .10
192 Rod Strickland .08 .25
193 Buck Williams .02 .10
194 Anthony Bonner .02 .10
195 Duane Causwell .02 .10
196 Mitch Richmond .08 .25
197 Garry St. Jean CO RC .02 .10
198 Lionel Simmons .02 .10
199 Wayman Tisdale .02 .10
200 Spud Webb .02 .10
201 Willie Anderson .02 .10
202 Antoine Carr .02 .10
203 Terry Cummings .02 .10
204 Sean Elliott .02 .10
205 Dale Ellis .02 .10
206 Vinnie Johnson .02 .10
207 David Robinson .15 .40
208 Jerry Tarkanian CO RC .08 .25
209 Benoit Benjamin .02 .10
210 Michael Cage .02 .10
211 Eddie Johnson .02 .10
212 George Karl CO .02 .10
213 Shawn Kemp .20 .50
214 Derrick McKey .02 .10
215 Nate McMillan .02 .10
216 Gary Payton .20 .50
217 Ricky Pierce .02 .10
218 David Benoit .02 .10
219 Mike Brown .02 .10
220 Tyrone Corbin .02 .10
221 Mark Eaton .02 .10
222 Jay Humphries .02 .10
223 Larry Krystkowiak .02 .10
224 Jeff Malone .02 .10
225 Karl Malone .15 .40
226 Jerry Sloan CO .02 .10
227 John Stockton .08 .25
228 Michael Adams .02 .10
229 Rex Chapman .02 .10
230 Ledell Eackles .02 .10
231 Pervis Ellison .02 .10
232 A.J. English .02 .10
233 Harvey Grant .02 .10
234 LaBradford Smith .02 .10
235 Larry Stewart .02 .10
236 Wes Unseld CO .02 .10
237 David Wingate .02 .10
238 Michael Jordan LL .60 1.50
239 Dennis Rodman LL .08 .25
240 John Stockton LL .02 .10
241 Buck Williams LL .02 .10
242 Mark Price LL .02 .10
243 Dana Barros LL .02 .10
244 David Robinson LL .08 .25
245 Chris Mullin LL .02 .10
246 Michael Jordan MVP .60 1.50
247 Larry Johnson ROY UER .08 .25
(Scoring average was 19.2, not 19.7)
248 David Robinson POY .08 .25
249 Detlef Schrempf SM .02 .10
250 Clyde Drexler PV .02 .10
251 Tim Hardaway PV .08 .25
252 Kevin Johnson PV .02 .10
253 Larry Johnson PV UER .08 .25
(Scoring average was 19.2& not 19.7)
254 Scottie Pippen PV .15 .40
255 Isiah Thomas PV .02 .10
256 Larry Bird SY .20 .50
257 Brad Daugherty SY .02 .10
258 Kevin Johnson SY .02 .10
259 Larry Johnson SY .08 .25
260 Scottie Pippen SY .15 .40
261 Dennis Rodman SY .08 .25
262 Checklist 1 .02 .10
263 Checklist 2 .02 .10
264 Checklist 3 .02 .10
265 Charles Barkley SD .08 .25
266 Shawn Kemp SD .08 .25
267 Dan Majerle SD .02 .10
268 Karl Malone SD .08 .25
269 Buck Williams SD .02 .10
270 Clyde Drexler SD .02 .10
271 Sean Elliott SD .02 .10
272 Ron Harper SD .02 .10
273 Michael Jordan SD .60 1.50
274 James Worthy SD .02 .10
275 Cedric Ceballos SD .02 .10
276 Larry Nance SD .02 .10
277 Kenny Walker SD .02 .10
278 Spud Webb SD .02 .10
279 Dominique Wilkins SD .02 .10
280 Terrell Brandon SD .02 .10
281 Dee Brown SD .02 .10
282 Kevin Johnson SD .02 .10
283 Doc Rivers SD .02 .10
284 Byron Scott SD .02 .10
285 Manute Bol SD .02 .10
286 Dikembe Mutombo SD .08 .25
287 Robert Parish SD .02 .10
288 David Robinson SD .08 .25
289 Dennis Rodman SD .08 .25
290 Blue Edwards SD .02 .10
291 Patrick Ewing SD .02 .10
292 Larry Johnson SD .08 .25
293 Jerome Kersey SD .02 .10
294 Hakeem Olajuwon SD .08 .25
295 Stacey Augmon SD .02 .10
296 Derrick Coleman SD .02 .10
297 Kendall Gill SD .02 .10
298 Shaquille O'Neal SD 1.25 3.00
299 Scottie Pippen SD .15 .40
300 Darryl Dawkins SD .02 .10
301 Mookie Blaylock .02 .10
302 Adam Keefe RC .02 .10
303 Travis Mays .02 .10
304 Morlon Wiley .02 .10
305 Sherman Douglas .02 .10
306 Joe Kleine .02 .10
307 Xavier McDaniel .02 .10
308 Tony Bennett RC .02 .10
309 Tom Hammonds .02 .10
310 Kevin Lynch .02 .10
311 Alonzo Mourning RC .60 1.50
312 David Wingate .02 .10
313 Rodney McCray .02 .10
314 Will Perdue .02 .10
315 Trent Tucker .02 .10
316 Corey Williams RC .02 .10
317 Danny Ferry .02 .10
318 Jay Guidinger RC .02 .10
319 Jerome Lane .02 .10
320 Gerald Wilkins .02 .10
321 Steve Bardo RC .02 .10
322 Walter Bond RC .02 .10
323 Brian Howard RC .02 .10
324 Tracy Moore RC .02 .10
325 Sean Rooks RC .02 .10
326 Randy White .02 .10
327 Kevin Brooks .02 .10
328 LaPhonso Ellis RC .08 .25
329 Scott Hastings .02 .10
330 Todd Lichti .02 .10
331 Robert Pack .02 .10
332 Bryant Stith RC .02 .10
333 Gerald Glass .02 .10
334 Terry Mills .02 .10
335 Isaiah Morris RC .02 .10
336 Mark Randall .02 .10
337 Danny Young .02 .10
338 Chris Gatling .02 .10
339 Jeff Grayer .02 .10
340 Byron Houston RC .02 .10
341 Keith Jennings RC .02 .10
342 Alton Lister .02 .10
343 Latrell Sprewell RC .75 2.00
344 Scott Brooks .02 .10
345 Matt Bullard .02 .10
346 Carl Herrera .02 .10
347 Robert Horry RC .08 .25
348 Tree Rollins .02 .10
349 Greg Dreiling .02 .10
350 George McCloud .02 .10
351 Sam Mitchell .02 .10
352 Pooh Richardson .02 .10
353 Malik Sealy RC .02 .10
354 Kenny Williams .02 .10
355 Jaren Jackson RC .02 .10
356 Mark Jackson .02 .10
357 Stanley Roberts .02 .10
358 Elmore Spencer RC .02 .10
359 Kiki Vandeweghe .02 .10
360 John S. Williams .02 .10
361 Randy Woods RC .02 .10
362 Duane Cooper RC .02 .10
363 James Edwards .02 .10
364 Anthony Peeler RC .02 .10
365 Tony Smith .02 .10
366 Keith Askins .02 .10
367 Matt Geiger RC .02 .10
368 Alec Kessler .02 .10
369 Harold Miner RC .02 .10
370 John Salley .02 .10
371 Anthony Avent RC .02 .10
372 Todd Day RC .02 .10
373 Blue Edwards .02 .10
374 Brad Lohaus .02 .10
375 Lee Mayberry RC .02 .10
376 Eric Murdock .02 .10
377 Danny Schayes .02 .10
378 Lance Blanks .02 .10
379 Christian Laettner RC .20 .50
380 Bob McCann RC .02 .10
381 Chuck Person .02 .10
382 Brad Sellers .02 .10
383 Chris Smith RC .02 .10
384 Micheal Williams .02 .10
385 Rafael Addison .02 .10
386 Chucky Brown .02 .10
387 Chris Dudley .02 .10
388 Tate George .02 .10
389 Rick Mahorn .02 .10
390 Rumeal Robinson .02 .10
391 Jayson Williams .02 .10
392 Eric Anderson RC .02 .10
393 Rolando Blackman .02 .10
394 Tony Campbell .02 .10
395 Hubert Davis RC .02 .10
396 Doc Rivers .02 .10
397 Charles Smith .02 .10
398 Herb Williams .02 .10
399 Litterial Green RC .02 .10
400 Greg Kite .02 .10
401 Shaquille O'Neal RC 2.50 6.00
402 Jerry Reynolds .02 .10
403 Jeff Turner .02 .10
404 Greg Grant .02 .10
405 Jeff Hornacek .02 .10
406 Andrew Lang .02 .10
407 Kenny Payne .02 .10
408 Tim Perry .02 .10
409 C.Weatherspoon RC .08 .25
410 Danny Ainge .02 .10
411 Charles Barkley .15 .40
412 Negele Knight .02 .10
413 Oliver Miller RC .02 .10
414 Jerrod Mustaf .02 .10
415 Mark Bryant .02 .10
416 Mario Elie .02 .10
417 Dave Johnson RC .02 .10
418 Tracy Murray RC .02 .10
419 Reggie Smith RC .02 .10
420 Rod Strickland .08 .25
421 Randy Brown .02 .10
422 Pete Chilcutt .02 .10

423 Jim Les .02 .10
424 Walt Williams RC .08 .25
425 Lloyd Daniels RC .02 .10
426 Vinny Del Negro .02 .10
427 Dale Ellis .02 .10
428 Sidney Green .02 .10
429 Avery Johnson .02 .10
430 Dana Barros .02 .10
431 Rich King .02 .10
432 Isaac Austin RC .02 .10
433 John Crotty RC .02 .10
434 Stephen Howard RC .02 .10
435 Jay Humphries .02 .10
436 Larry Krystkowiak .02 .10
437 Tom Gugliotta RC .30 .75
438 Buck Johnson .02 .10
439 Charles Jones .02 .10
440 Don MacLean RC .02 .10
441 Doug Overton .02 .10
442 Brent Price RC .02 .10
443 Checklist 1 .02 .10
444 Checklist 2 .02 .10
SD266 Shawn Kemp AU 40.00 100.00
SD277 Kenny Walker AU 15.00 40.00
SD300 Darryl Dawkins AU 12.50 30.00
NNO Slam Dunk Wrapper Exchange 1.25 3.00

1992-93 Fleer All-Stars

This 24-card standard-size set was randomly inserted in first series 17-card packs and features outstanding players from the Eastern (1-12) and Western (13-24) Conference. According to Fleer's advertising materials, the odds of pulling an All-Star insert are approximately one per nine packs. The horizontal fronts display two color images of the featured player against a gradated silver-blue background. The cards are bordered by a darker silver-blue, and the player's name is gold-foil stamped at the lower right corner. The Orlando All-Star Weekend logo is in the upper right and the team logo in the lower left corner. The backs are white with silver-blue borders and present career highlights, the player's name, and the Orlando All-Star Weekend logo. The cards are numbered on the back in alphabetical order.

COMPLETE SET (24) 40.00 100.00
1 Michael Adams .40 1.00
2 Charles Barkley 2.50 6.00
3 Brad Daugherty .40 1.00
4 Joe Dumars 1.50 4.00
5 Patrick Ewing 1.50 4.00
6 Michael Jordan ! 12.00 30.00
7 Reggie Lewis 1.00 2.50
8 Scottie Pippen 5.00 12.00
9 Mark Price .40 1.00
10 Dennis Rodman 3.00 8.00
11 Isiah Thomas 1.50 4.00
12 Kevin Willis .40 1.00
13 Clyde Drexler 1.50 4.00
14 Tim Hardaway 2.00 5.00
15 Jeff Hornacek 1.00 2.50
16 Dan Majerle 1.00 2.50
17 Karl Malone 2.50 6.00
18 Chris Mullin 1.50 4.00
19 Dikembe Mutombo 1.50 4.00
20 Hakeem Olajuwon 2.50 6.00
21 David Robinson 2.50 6.00
22 John Stockton 1.50 4.00
23 Otis Thorpe 1.00 2.50
24 James Worthy 1.50 4.00

1992-93 Fleer Larry Johnson Promo

This Larry Johnson Commemorative Card was issued to announce the introduction of the 1992-93 Fleer NBA set featuring Larry Johnson. The standard-size card features a posed color photo of Larry Johnson with Paul Mullan, chairman and CEO of Fleercorp. The card has a gold metallic border and Larry Johnson's name is printed vertically in white lettering on blue and blue-green wedge-shaped stripes that have a pebble-grain texture. Paul Mullan's name is superimposed on the picture. A '92 Commemorative Card logo is in the lower right corner. The back has a beige pebble-grain background and displays information about the 1992-93 Fleer NBA set and the 1992-93 Fleer Larry Johnson NBA Rookie of the Year 12-card subset. The card is unnumbered.

NNO Larry Johnson 4.00 10.00
(With Paul Mullan, CEO of Fleer)

1992-93 Fleer Larry Johnson

Larry Johnson, the 1991-92 NBA Rookie of the Year, is featured in this 15-card signature series. The first 12 cards were available as random inserts in all forms of Fleer's first series packaging. The odds of pulling a Larry Johnson insert from a 17-card pack were one in 18, from a 32-card cello pack were one in 13 and from a 42-card rack pack were one in six. In addition, Larry personally autographed more than 2,000 of these cards, which were randomly inserted in the wax packs. These cards feature embossed Fleer logos on front for authenticity. According to Fleer's advertising materials, the odds of finding a signed Larry Johnson were approximately one in 15,000 packs. Collectors were also able to receive three additional Johnson cards and the premiere edition of NBA Inside Stuff magazine by sending in ten wrappers and 1.00 in a mail-in offer expiring 6/30/93. These standard-size cards feature color player photos framed by thin orange and blue borders on a silver-blue card face. The player's name and the words "NBA Rookie of the Year" are gold foil-stamped at the top. The backs feature an orange panel that summarizes Johnson's game and demeanor. His name and "NBA Rookie of the Year" appear at the top in a lighter orange.

COMMON L.JOHNSON (1-12) .50 1.25
COMMON AUTOGRAPH (AU) 20.00 50.00
COMMON SEND-OFF (13-15) 1.50 4.00

1992-93 Fleer Rookie Sensations

Randomly inserted in first series 32-card cello packs, this set features 12 of the top rookies from the 1991-92 season. According to information released by Fleer, the odds of pulling a Rookie Sensation is approximately one per five packs. Measuring the standard size, the cards feature the player in action against a computer generated team emblem on a gradated purple background. The words "Rookie Sensations" and the player's name are gold foil-stamped at the bottom. The backs display career highlights on a mint-green face with a purple border. The cards are numbered on the back in alphabetical order.

COMPLETE SET (12) 8.00 20.00
1 Greg Anthony .40 1.00
2 Stacey Augmon .75 2.00
3 Terrell Brandon 2.00 5.00
4 Rick Fox .75 2.00
5 Larry Johnson 2.50 6.00
6 Mark Macon .40 1.00
7 Dikembe Mutombo 2.50 6.00
8 Billy Owens .75 2.00
9 Stanley Roberts .40 1.00
10 Doug Smith .40 1.00
11 Steve Smith 2.50 6.00
12 Larry Stewart .40 1.00

1992-93 Fleer Sharpshooters

Randomly inserted in second series 15-card plastic-wrap packs, these 18 standard-size cards feature some of the NBA's best shooters. According to Fleer's advertising materials, the odds of finding a Sharpshooter card are approximately one in three packs. The color action photos on the fronts are odd-shaped, overlaying a purple geometric shape and resting on a silver card face. The "Sharp Shooter" logo is gold-foil stamped at the upper left corner, while the player's name is gold-foil stamped below the picture. On a wheat-colored panel inside blue borders, the backs present a player profile.

COMPLETE SET (18) 10.00 20.00
1 Reggie Miller 1.50 4.00
2 Dana Barros .30 .75
3 Jeff Hornacek .60 1.50
4 Drazen Petrovic .30 .75
5 Glen Rice 1.50 4.00
6 Terry Porter .30 .75
7 Mark Price .30 .75
8 Michael Adams .30 .75
9 Hersey Hawkins .60 1.50
10 Chuck Person .30 .75
11 John Stockton 1.50 4.00
12 Dale Ellis .30 .75
13 Clyde Drexler 1.50 4.00
14 Mitch Richmond 1.50 4.00
15 Craig Ehlo .30 .75
16 Dell Curry .30 .75
17 Chris Mullin 1.50 4.00
18 Rolando Blackman .30 .75

1992-93 Fleer Team Leaders

The 1992-93 Fleer Team Leaders were inserted into five of every six first series 42-card rack packs. A Larry Johnson Signature Series insert card replaced a Team Leader in every sixth rack pack. These 27 standard size cards feature a key member of each NBA team. The color action photos on the front are surrounded by thick dark blue borders, covered by a slick UV coating and stamped with gold foil printing. Because of the dark borders, these cards are condition sensitive. The full-color card backs include a player head shot accompanied by written text summarizing the player's career. The cards are numbered on the back in alphabetical order by team. A low production run of rack packs has contributed largely to the popularity of this set.

COMPLETE SET (27) 125.00 225.00
1 Dominique Wilkins 5.00 12.00
2 Reggie Lewis 2.00 5.00
3 Larry Johnson 5.00 12.00
4 Michael Jordan ! 50.00 125.00
5 Mark Price 1.00 2.50
6 Terry Davis 1.00 2.50
7 Dikembe Mutombo 5.00 12.00
8 Isiah Thomas 5.00 12.00
9 Chris Mullin 5.00 12.00
10 Hakeem Olajuwon 8.00 20.00
11 Reggie Miller 5.00 12.00
12 Danny Manning 2.00 5.00
13 James Worthy 5.00 12.00
14 Glen Rice 5.00 12.00
15 Alvin Robertson 1.00 2.50
16 Tony Campbell 1.00 2.50
17 Derrick Coleman 2.00 5.00
18 Patrick Ewing 5.00 12.00
19 Scott Skiles 1.00 2.50
20 Hersey Hawkins 2.00 5.00
21 Kevin Johnson 5.00 12.00
22 Clyde Drexler 5.00 12.00
23 Mitch Richmond 5.00 12.00
24 David Robinson 8.00 20.00
25 Ricky Pierce 1.00 2.50
26 Karl Malone 8.00 20.00
27 Pervis Ellison 1.00 2.50

1992-93 Fleer Total D

The 1992-93 Fleer Total D cards were randomly inserted into second series 32-card cello packs. According to Fleer's advertising materials, the odds of pulling a Total D card were approximately one per five packs. These 15 standard size cards feature some of the NBA's top defensive players. Card fronts feature colorized players against a black border, covered with a slick UV coating and gold stamped lettering. Because of these black borders, the cards are condition sensitive. The full-color card backs feature small player head shots accompanied by text describing the player's defensive abilities.

COMPLETE SET (15) 30.00 60.00
1 David Robinson 2.00 5.00
2 Dennis Rodman 3.00 8.00
3 Scottie Pippen 6.00 15.00
4 Joe Dumars 1.25 3.00
5 Michael Jordan ! 20.00 50.00
6 John Stockton 1.25 3.00
7 Patrick Ewing 1.25 3.00
8 Micheal Williams .60 1.50
9 Larry Nance .60 1.50
10 Buck Williams .75 2.00
11 Alvin Robertson .60 1.50
12 Dikembe Mutombo 1.25 3.00
13 Mookie Blaylock .75 2.00
14 Hakeem Olajuwon 2.00 5.00
15 Rony Seikaly .60 1.50

1992-93 Fleer Drake's

Sponsored by Drake's Bakery, four cards protected by a cello pack were inserted in selected Drake bakery products. The 54 cards in this set measure the standard size. The card design is identical to the 1992-93 Fleer regular issue, with color action player photos bordered in bronze; the only difference is in the card number. A basketball textured design in team colors runs down the right edge of the picture and carries the player's name. The horizontal backs display a player photo in an arch-shaped design that is team colored. Biographical information, statistics, and career highlights round out the back. The background has the texture and color of a basketball. The cards are numbered on the back and checklisted below alphabetically according to teams.

COMPLETE SET (55) 30.00 80.00
1 Dominique Wilkins 1.00 2.50
2 Mookie Blaylock .20 .50
3 Reggie Lewis .40 1.00
4 Dee Brown .25 .60
5 Alonzo Mourning 2.50 6.00
6 Larry Johnson .75 2.00
7 Michael Jordan 12.00 30.00
8 Scottie Pippen 2.00 5.00
9 Mark Price .40 1.00
10 Brad Daugherty .20 .50
11 Derek Harper .40 1.00
12 Sean Rooks .08 .25
13 Dikembe Mutombo .75 2.00
14 Chris Jackson .08 .25
15 Isiah Thomas .75 2.00
16 Joe Dumars .75 2.00
17 Chris Mullin .60 1.50
18 Tim Hardaway .60 1.50
19 Hakeem Olajuwon 1.25 3.00
20 Kenny Smith .20 .50
21 Reggie Miller 1.25 3.00
22 Detlef Schrempf .25 .60
23 Danny Manning .30 .75
24 Mark Jackson .40 1.00
25 Sedale Threatt .08 .25
26 James Worthy .50 1.25
27 Glen Rice .40 1.00
28 Rony Seikaly .08 .25
29 Blue Edwards .08 .25
30 Eric Murdock .08 .25
31 Christian Laettner 2.00 5.00
32 Micheal Williams .08 .25
33 Drazen Petrovic 2.00 5.00
34 Derrick Coleman .20 .50
35 Patrick Ewing 1.25 3.00
36 John Starks .40 1.00
37 Shaquille O'Neal 6.00 15.00
38 Scott Skiles .30 .75
39 Jeff Hornacek .40 1.00
40 Clarence Weatherspoon .40 1.00
41 Charles Barkley 1.50 4.00
42 Dan Majerle .50 1.25
43 Clyde Drexler 1.25 3.00
44 Terry Porter .20 .50
45 Mitch Richmond .60 1.50
46 Lionel Simmons .08 .25
47 David Robinson 1.50 4.00
48 Sean Elliott .50 1.25
49 Shawn Kemp 1.00 2.50
50 Gary Payton 1.50 4.00
51 John Stockton 2.00 5.00
52 Karl Malone 1.50 4.00
53 Pervis Ellison .08 .25
54 Tom Gugliotta 1.00 2.50
NNO Checklist Card .08 .25

1992-93 Fleer NBA Rising Stars Magazine Sheet

Inserted as a sheet in the NBA's Rising Stars Magazine, this 8-card sheet features perforated cards utilizing the same design as the 1992-93 base Fleer product. The cards are not numbered and are listed in order from top left to bottom right.

NNO Lionel Simmons .30 .75
NNO Kenny Anderson .30 .75
NNO Complete Sheet 5.00 12.00
NNO Clarence Weatherspoon .30 .75
NNO Cliff Robinson .30 .75
NNO Blue Edwards .30 .75
NNO Gary Payton .50 1.25
NNO Kendall Gill .30 .75
NNO Shaquille O'Neal 3.00 8.00

1992-93 Fleer Spalding Schoolyard Stars

These five standard-size promo cards were produced by Fleer for Spalding, and they were packaged in a cello pack and distributed with the purchase of a specially marked Spalding basketball. The packs are marked "For promotional use only, not for resale." The fronts feature color action player photos with black shadow borders on a gold card face. The player's name is in the upper left corner. The words "NBA Schoolyard Stars" are printed in white and yellow along the left edge of the picture. The backs have a basketball color and texture design with a pale blue shadow-bordered panel. The panel discusses an aspect of the player's game and concludes with several schoolyard tips. The cards are unnumbered and checklisted below in alphabetical order.

COMPLETE SET (5) 1.00 2.50
1 Larry Bird .60 1.50
2 Kevin Johnson .15 .40
3 Larry Johnson .25 .60
4 Scottie Pippen .40 1.00
5 Title Card .02 .10

1992-93 Fleer Team Night Sheets

Each of these 1992-93 Fleer Sheets is perforated and features slots for 12 standard-size player cards. Though some of the sheets show 12 players, others show 10 or 11, with the other slots filled by advertisement cards. Each of these sheets was given away in connection with a promotion. The Bulls sheet was available at Shell gas stations in the Chicago area; the sheets were sold for 99 cents with an eight-gallon minimum purchase. The Mavs sheet was handed out to all attendees of a late season Mavericks-Timberwolves game; the sheet featured one of the first Jim Jackson pro cards due to his late signing. The Magic sheet was promoted by Gooding's, a supermarket chain in central Florida; its owner, a season ticket holder, sponsored the giveaway of these sheets to the first 15,000 individuals at the Fan Appeal game (the last game of the year). The fronts of all the sheets feature color action player photos, enclosed by metallic bronze borders and accented on the right by two team color-coded pebble-grain stripes. On a tan pebble-grain background, the horizontal back carries on its left side a color close-up framed by an arch. On the right side are the player's name and position on two team color-coded stripes, followed below by biography, statistics, and career highlights. The cards differ from their regular issue counterparts in that they are unnumbered. They are checklisted below in alphabetical order, with any ad cards listed at the end.

COMPLETE SET (9) 25.00 60.00
1 John Bagley 2.50 6.00
Dee Brown
Sherman Douglas
Rick Fox
Kevin Gamble
Joe Kleine
Reggie Lewis
Xavier McDaniel
Kevin McHale
Robert Parish
Ed Pinckney
UNO Pizzeria (Ad card)
2 Tony Bennett 3.00 8.00
Muggsy Bogues
Dell Curry
Kenny Gattison
Kendall Gill
Mike Gminski
Hugo (Mascot)
Larry Johnson
Alonzo Mourning
Johnny Newman
David Wingate
Belk (Ad Card)
3 B.J. Armstrong 6.00 15.00
Bill Cartwright
Horace Grant
Michael Jordan
Stacey King
Rodney McCray
John Paxson
Will Perdue
Scottie Pippen
Trent Tucker
Corey Williams
Scott Williams
4 Walter Bond 2.50 6.00
Dexter Cambridge
Terry Davis
Derek Harper
Donald Hodge
Mike Iuzzolino
Jim Jackson
Sean Rooks
Doug Smith
Randy White
Morlon Wiley
Lay's Potato Chips/(Ad card)
5 Dale Davis 2.50 6.00
Vern Fleming
Bob Hill CO
George McCloud
Reggie Miller
Sam Mitchell
Pooh Richardson
Detlef Schrempf
Malik Sealy
Rik Smits
LaSalle Thompson
Pacers Gift Shop/(Ad card)
6 Elden Campbell 2.50 6.00
Duane Cooper
Vlade Divac
James Edwards
A.C. Green
Anthony Peeler
Sam Perkins
Byron Scott
Sedale Threatt
James Worthy
Toyota (Two ad cards)
7 Keith Askins 2.50 6.00
Willie Burton
Bimbo Coles
Kevin Edwards
Alec Kessler
Grant Long
Harold Miner
Glen Rice
John Salley
Rony Seikaly
Brian Shaw
Steve Smith
8 Anthony Avent 2.50 6.00
Frank Brickowski
Todd Day
Mike Dunleavy CO
Blue Edwards
Brad Lohaus
Moses Malone
Lee Mayberry
Eric Murdock
Fred Roberts
Alvin Robertson
Dan Schayes
9 Nick Anderson 10.00 25.00
Anthony Bowie
Terry Catledge
Steve Kerr
Greg Kite
Shaquille O'Neal
Jerry Reynolds
Dennis Scott
Scott Skiles
Jeff Turner
Brian Williams
Gooding's (Ad card)

1992-93 Fleer Tony's Pizza

These 108 standard-size cards came three to each pack (or two cards along with a coupon card) inserted into packages of Tony's frozen pizza. In design, all these cards are identical to 1992-93 Fleer regular issue cards; 72 of them derive from the first series and the 36 Slam Dunk cards derive from the second series. The Slam Dunk cards are harder to find as they were not inserted into the two-card packs that contained the coupon card. The fronts feature gold-bordered color player action photos, with the player's name and position displayed in team color-coded strips along the right edge that have the dimpled look of a basketball. The team logo appears at the bottom right. The simulated basketball texture continues on the horizontal reverse, but in tan. A color player action picture graces the left side, and a stat table is shown on the right. The player's name and position appear in team color-coded bars at the top. A brief biography and the team logo appear beneath and to the right, respectively, of the bars. Unlike the regular issue cards, these cards are unnumbered and thus checklisted below in alphabetical order within type.

COMPLETE SET (108) 25.00 60.00
1 Michael Adams .08 .25
2 Kenny Anderson .20 .50
3 Willie Anderson .08 .25
4 Greg Anthony .08 .25
5 B.J. Armstrong .08 .25
6 Thurl Bailey .08 .25
7 Benoit Benjamin .08 .25
8 Muggsy Bogues .20 .50
9 Sam Bowie .08 .25
10 Frank Brickowski .08 .25
11 Michael Cage .08 .25
12 Antoine Carr .08 .25
13 Duane Causwell .08 .25
14 Rex Chapman .20 .50
15 Tyrone Corbin .08 .25
16 Brad Daugherty .08 .25
17 Terry Davis .08 .25
18 Johnny Dawkins .08 .25
19 Vlade Divac .20 .50
20 Joe Dumars .40 1.00
21 Craig Ehlo .08 .25
22 Pervis Ellison .08 .25
23 Duane Ferrell .08 .25
24 Vern Fleming .08 .25
25 Winston Garland .08 .25
26 Horace Grant .30 .75
27 Tim Hardaway .60 1.50
28 Derek Harper .20 .50
29 Hersey Hawkins .20 .50
30 Chris Jackson .08 .25
31 Reggie Lewis .20 .50
32 Jeff Malone .08 .25
33 Moses Malone .30 .75
34 Danny Manning .20 .50
35 Sarunas Marciulionis .08 .25
36 Vernon Maxwell .08 .25
37 Kevin McHale .40 1.00
38 Reggie Miller 1.25 3.00
39 Chris Mullin .40 1.00
40 Ken Norman .08 .25
41 Charles Oakley .20 .50
42 Billy Owens .08 .25
43 Drazen Petrovic .75 2.00
44 Ricky Pierce .08 .25
45 J.R. Reid .08 .25
46 Glen Rice .40 1.00
47 Mitch Richmond .50 1.25
48 Alvin Robertson .08 .25
49 Clifford Robinson .20 .50
50 Rumeal Robinson .08 .25
51 Detlef Schrempf .20 .50
52 Dennis Scott .08 .25
53 Rony Seikaly .08 .25
54 Charles Shackleford .08 .25
55 Brian Shaw .08 .25
56 Scott Skiles .20 .50
57 Doug Smith .08 .25
58 Kenny Smith .20 .50
59 Steve Smith .40 1.00
60 Felton Spencer .08 .25
61 John Stockton 1.25 3.00
62 Isiah Thomas .60 1.50
63 Otis Thorpe .20 .50
64 Sedale Threatt .08 .25
65 Wayman Tisdale .08 .25
66 Loy Vaught .08 .25
67 Doug West .08 .25
68 Brian Williams .08 .25
69 Micheal Williams .08 .25
70 Reggie Williams .08 .25
71 Scott Williams .08 .25
72 Orlando Woolridge .08 .25
73 Stacey Augmon SD .40 1.00
74 Charles Barkley SD 1.50 4.00
75 Manute Bol SD .40 1.00
76 Terrell Brandon SD .40 1.00
77 Dee Brown SD .40 1.00
78 Cedric Ceballos SD .40 1.00
79 Derrick Coleman SD .40 1.00
80 Darryl Dawkins SD .40 1.00
81 Clyde Drexler SD 1.50 4.00
82 Blue Edwards SD .40 1.00
83 Sean Elliott SD .50 1.25
84 Patrick Ewing SD 1.25 3.00
85 Kendall Gill SD .50 1.25
86 Ron Harper SD .50 1.25
87 Kevin Johnson SD .50 1.25
88 Larry Johnson SD .60 1.50
89 Michael Jordan SD 6.00 15.00
90 Shawn Kemp SD .60 1.50
91 Jerome Kersey SD .40 1.00
92 Dan Majerle SD .50 1.25
93 Karl Malone SD 1.50 4.00
94 Dikembe Mutombo SD .60 1.50
95 Larry Nance SD .50 1.25
96 Hakeem Olajuwon SD 1.00 2.50
97 Shaquille O'Neal SD 6.00 15.00
98 Robert Parish SD .50 1.25
99 Scottie Pippen SD 1.25 3.00
100 Doc Rivers SD .50 1.25
101 David Robinson SD 1.50 4.00
102 Dennis Rodman SD 1.00 2.50
103 Byron Scott SD .50 1.25
104 Kenny Walker SD .40 1.00
105 Spud Webb SD .50 1.25
106 Dominique Wilkins SD 1.25 3.00
107 Buck Williams SD .50 1.25
108 James Worthy SD .60 1.50
XX Coupon Card .20 .50

1993-94 Fleer

The 1993-94 Fleer basketball card set contains 400 standard-size cards. The set was issued in two series consisting of 240 and 160 cards. Cards were primarily distributed in 15-card wax packs (1.29 suggested retail) and 21-card cello packs (1.99). Unlike the first series packs, all second series packs contained an insert card. There are 36 packs per wax box. The fronts are UV-coated and feature color action player photos and are enclosed by white borders. The player's name appears in the lower left and is superimposed over a colorful florescent background. The backs feature full-color printing and bold graphics combining the player's picture, name, and complete statistics. With the exception of card numbers 131, 174, and 216, the cards are numbered and checklisted below alphabetically in team order. Subsets are NBA League Leaders (221-228), NBA Award Winners (229-232), Pro-Visions (223-237), and checklists (238-240). Players traded since the first series are pictured with their new team in a 160-card second series (241-400) offering. Rookie Cards of note include Vin Baker, Anfernee Hardaway, Jamal Mashburn, Nick Van Exel and Chris Webber.

COMPLETE SET (400) 10.00 20.00
COMPLETE SERIES 1 (240) 5.00 10.00
COMPLETE SERIES 2 (160) 5.00 10.00
1 Stacey Augmon .01 .05
2 Mookie Blaylock .02 .10
3 Duane Ferrell .01
4 Paul Graham .01
5 Adam Keefe .01
6 Jon Koncak .01
7 Dominique Wilkins .08
8 Kevin Willis .01
9 Alaa Abdelnaby .01
10 Dee Brown .01
11 Sherman Douglas .01
12 Rick Fox .01
13 Kevin Gamble .01
14 Reggie Lewis .02
15 Xavier McDaniel .01
16 Robert Parish .02
17 Muggsy Bogues .02
18 Dell Curry .01
19 Kenny Gattison .01
20 Kendall Gill .02
21 Larry Johnson .08
22 Alonzo Mourning .15
23 Johnny Newman .01
24 David Wingate .01
25 B.J. Armstrong .01
26 Bill Cartwright .01
27 Horace Grant .02
28 Michael Jordan 1.25
29 Stacey King .01
30 John Paxson .01
31 Will Perdue .01
32 Scottie Pippen .30
33 Scott Williams .01
34 Terrell Brandon .02
35 Brad Daugherty .01
36 Craig Ehlo .01
37 Danny Ferry .01
38 Larry Nance .01
39 Mark Price .01
40 Mike Sanders .01
41 Gerald Wilkins .01
42 John Williams .01
43 Terry Davis .01
44 Derek Harper .02
45 Mike Iuzzolino .01
46 Jim Jackson .02
47 Sean Rooks .01
48 Doug Smith .01
49 Randy White .01
50 Mahmoud Abdul-Rauf .01
51 LaPhonso Ellis .01
52 Marcus Liberty .01
53 Mark Macon .01
54 Dikembe Mutombo .08
55 Robert Pack .01
56 Bryant Stith .01
57 Reggie Williams .01
58 Mark Aguirre .01
59 Joe Dumars .08
60 Bill Laimbeer .01
61 Terry Mills .01
62 Olden Polynice .01
63 Alvin Robertson .01
64 Dennis Rodman .20
65 Isiah Thomas .08
66 Victor Alexander .01
67 Tim Hardaway .08
68 Tyrone Hill .01
69 Byron Houston .01
70 Sarunas Marciulionis .01
71 Chris Mullin .08
72 Billy Owens .01
73 Latrell Sprewell .25
74 Scott Brooks .01
75 Matt Bullard .01
76 Carl Herrera .01
77 Robert Horry .02
78 Vernon Maxwell .01
79 Hakeem Olajuwon .15
80 Kenny Smith .01
81 Otis Thorpe .02
82 Dale Davis .01
83 Vern Fleming .01
84 George McCloud .01
85 Reggie Miller .08
86 Sam Mitchell .01
87 Pooh Richardson .01
88 Detlef Schrempf .02
89 Rik Smits .02
90 Gary Grant .01
91 Ron Harper .02
92 Mark Jackson .02
93 Danny Manning .02
94 Ken Norman .01
95 Stanley Roberts .01
96 Loy Vaught .01
97 John Williams .01
98 Elden Campbell .01
99 Doug Christie .02
100 Duane Cooper .01
101 Vlade Divac .02
102 A.C. Green .02
103 Anthony Peeler .01
104 Sedale Threatt .01
105 James Worthy .08
106 Bimbo Coles .01
107 Grant Long .01
108 Harold Miner .01
109 Glen Rice .02
110 John Salley .01
111 Rony Seikaly .01
112 Brian Shaw .01
113 Steve Smith .08
114 Anthony Avent .01
115 Jon Barry .01
116 Frank Brickowski .01
117 Todd Day .01
118 Blue Edwards .01
119 Brad Lohaus .01
120 Lee Mayberry .01
121 Eric Murdock .01
122 Thurl Bailey .01
123 Christian Laettner .02
124 Luc Longley .02
125 Chuck Person .01
126 Felton Spencer .01
127 Doug West .01
128 Micheal Williams .01
129 Rafael Addison .01
130 Kenny Anderson .02
131 Sam Bowie .01
132 Chucky Brown .01

errick Coleman .02 .10
hris Dudley .01 .05
ris Morris .01 .05
meal Robinson .01 .05
eg Anthony .01 .05
lando Blackman .01 .05
ny Campbell .01 .05
bert Davis .01 .05
trick Ewing .08 .25
thony Mason .02 .10
harles Oakley .02 .10
oc Rivers .02 .10
harles Smith .01 .05
hn Starks .02 .10
ck Anderson .02 .10
thony Bowie .01 .05
aquille O'Neal .50 1.25
nald Royal .01 .05
ennis Scott .01 .05
ott Skiles .01 .05
m Tolbert .01 .05
ff Turner .01 .05
n Anderson .01 .05
hnny Dawkins .01 .05
ersey Hawkins .02 .10
ff Hornacek .02 .10
drew Lang .01 .05
m Perry .01 .05
arence Weatherspoon .01 .05
nny Ainge .02 .10
harles Barkley .15 .40
dric Ceballos .02 .10
m Chambers .01 .05
chard Dumas .01 .05
vin Johnson .02 .10
egele Knight .01 .05
an Majerle .02 .10
iver Miller .01 .05
ark West .01 .05
ark Bryant .01 .05
yde Drexler .08 .25
evin Duckworth .01 .05
ario Elie .01 .05
rome Kersey .01 .05
rry Porter .01 .05
ifford Robinson .02 .10
d Strickland .02 .10
ck Williams .01 .05
thony Bonner .01 .05
uane Causwell .01 .05
itch Richmond .08 .25
onel Simmons .01 .05
ayman Tisdale .01 .05
oud Webb .02 .10
alt Williams .01 .05
toine Carr .01 .05
rry Cummings .01 .05
oyd Daniels .01 .05
nny Del Negro .01 .05
an Elliott .02 .10
ale Ellis .01 .05
ery Johnson .01 .05
R. Reid .01 .05
avid Robinson .15 .40
ichael Cage .01 .05
die Johnson .01 .05
awn Kemp .15 .40
errick McKey .01 .05
ete McMillan .01 .05
ry Payton .15 .40
m Perkins .02 .10
cky Pierce .01 .05
avid Benoit .01 .05
rone Corbin .01 .05
ark Eaton .01 .05
y Humphries .01 .05
rry Krystkowiak .01 .05
ff Malone .01 .05
rl Malone .15 .40
hn Stockton .08 .25
ichael Adams .01 .05
x Chapman .01 .05
rvis Ellison .01 .05
rvey Grant .01 .05
m Gugliotta .08 .25
ck Johnson .01 .05
Bradford Smith .01 .05
rry Stewart .01 .05
J. Armstrong LL .01 .05
edric Ceballos LL .01 .05
rry Johnson LL .02 .10
ichael Jordan LL .60 1.50
keem Olajuwon LL .08 .25
ark Price LL .01 .05
nnis Rodman LL .08 .25
hn Stockton LL .02 .10
harles Barkley AW .08 .25
keem Olajuwon AW .08 .25
aquille O'Neal AW .20 .50
ifford Robinson AW .01 .05
awn Kemp PV .08 .25
onzo Mourning PV .08 .25
keem Olajuwon PV .08 .25
hn Stockton PV .02 .10
ominique Wilkins PV .02 .10
ecklist 1-85 .01 .05
ecklist 86-165 .01 .05
ecklist 166-240 UER .01 .05
listed as Cliff Robinson;
ld be Dominique Wilkins)
ug Edwards RC .01 .05
aig Ehlo .01 .05
drew Lang .01 .05
nis Whatley .01 .05
ris Corchiani .01 .05
ie Earl RC .01 .05
mmy Oliver .01 .05
Pinckney .01 .05
no Radja RC .01 .05
att Wenstrom RC .01 .05
ny Bennett .01 .05
ott Burrell RC .08 .25
Ron Ellis .01 .05
rsey Hawkins .02 .10
die Johnson .01 .05
orie Blount RC .01 .05
Jo English RC .01 .05
ve Johnson .01 .05
eve Kerr .02 .10
ni Kukoc RC .40 1.00
te Myers .01 .05
l Wennington .01 .05
hn Battle .01 .05
rone Hill .01 .05
rald Madkins RC .01 .05
ris Mills RC .08 .25
bby Phills .01 .05
g Dreiling .01 .05

269 Lucious Harris RC .01 .05
270 Donald Hodge .01 .05
271 Popeye Jones RC .01 .05
272 Tim Legler RC .01 .05
273 Fat Lever .01 .05
274 Jamal Mashburn RC .25 .60
275 Darren Morningstar RC .01 .05
276 Tom Hammonds .01 .05
277 Darnell Mee RC .01 .05
278 Rodney Rogers RC .08 .25
279 Brian Williams .01 .05
280 Greg Anderson .01 .05
281 Sean Elliott .02 .10
282 Allan Houston RC .40 1.00
283 Lindsey Hunter RC .08 .25
284 Marcus Liberty .01 .05
285 Mark Macon .01 .05
286 David Wood .01 .05
287 Jud Buechler .01 .05
288 Chris Gatling .01 .05
289 Josh Grant RC .01 .05
290 Jeff Grayer .01 .05
291 Avery Johnson .01 .05
292 Chris Webber RC 1.00 2.50
293 Sam Cassell RC .40 1.00
294 Mario Elie .01 .05
295 Richard Petruska RC .01 .05
296 Eric Riley RC .01 .05
297 Antonio Davis RC .10 .30
298 Scott Haskin RC .01 .05
299 Derrick McKey .01 .05
300 Byron Scott .02 .10
301 Malik Sealy .01 .05
302 LaSalle Thompson .01 .05
303 Kenny Williams .01 .05
304 Haywoode Workman .01 .05
305 Mark Aguirre .01 .05
306 Terry Dehere RC .01 .05
307 Bob Martin RC .01 .05
308 Elmore Spencer .01 .05
309 Tom Tolbert .01 .05
310 Randy Woods .01 .05
311 Sam Bowie .01 .05
312 James Edwards .01 .05
313 Antonio Harvey RC .01 .05
314 George Lynch RC .01 .05
315 Tony Smith .01 .05
316 Nick Van Exel RC .30 .75
317 Manute Bol .01 .05
318 Willie Burton .01 .05
319 Matt Geiger .01 .05
320 Alec Kessler .01 .05
321 Vin Baker RC .25 .60
322 Ken Norman .01 .05
323 Danny Schayes .01 .05
324 Derek Strong RC .01 .05
325 Mike Brown .01 .05
326 Brian Davis RC .01 .05
327 Tellis Frank .01 .05
328 Marlon Maxey .01 .05
329 Isaiah Rider RC .20 .50
330 Chris Smith .01 .05
331 Benoit Benjamin .01 .05
332 P.J. Brown RC .08 .25
333 Kevin Edwards .01 .05
334 Armon Gilliam .01 .05
335 Rick Mahorn .01 .05
336 Dwayne Schintzius .01 .05
337 Rex Walters RC .01 .05
338 David Wesley RC .08 .25
339 Jayson Williams .02 .10
340 Anthony Bonner .01 .05
341 Herb Williams .01 .05
342 Litterial Green .01 .05
343 Anfernee Hardaway RC .75 2.00
344 Greg Kite .01 .05
345 Larry Krystkowiak .01 .05
346 Todd Lichti .01 .05
347 Keith Tower RC .01 .05
348 Dana Barros .01 .05
349 Shawn Bradley RC .08 .25
350 Michael Curry RC .01 .05
351 Greg Graham RC .01 .05
352 Warren Kidd RC .01 .05
353 Moses Malone .08 .25
354 Orlando Woolridge .01 .05
355 Duane Cooper .01 .05
356 Joe Courtney RC .01 .05
357 A.C. Green .02 .10
358 Frank Johnson .01 .05
359 Joe Kleine .01 .05
360 Malcolm Mackey RC .01 .05
361 Jerrod Mustaf .01 .05
362 Chris Dudley .01 .05
363 Harvey Grant .01 .05
364 Tracy Murray .01 .05
365 James Robinson RC .01 .05
366 Reggie Smith .01 .05
367 Kevin Thompson RC .01 .05
368 Randy Breuer .01 .05
369 Randy Brown .01 .05
370 Evers Burns RC .01 .05
371 Pete Chilcutt .01 .05
372 Bobby Hurley RC .02 .10
373 Jim Les .01 .05
374 Mike Peplowski RC .01 .05
375 Willie Anderson .01 .05
376 Sleepy Floyd .01 .05
377 Negele Knight .01 .05
378 Dennis Rodman .20 .50
379 Chris Whitney RC .01 .05
380 Vincent Askew .01 .05
381 Kendall Gill .02 .10
382 Ervin Johnson RC .02 .10
383 Chris King RC .01 .05
384 Rich King .01 .05
385 Steve Scheffler .01 .05
386 Detlef Schrempf .02 .10
387 Tom Chambers .01 .05
388 John Crotty .01 .05
389 Bryon Russell RC .08 .25
390 Felton Spencer .01 .05
391 Luther Wright RC .01 .05
392 Mitchell Butler RC .01 .05
393 Calbert Cheaney RC .02 .10
394 Kevin Duckworth .01 .05
395 Don MacLean .01 .05
396 Gheorghe Muresan RC .08 .25
397 Doug Overton .01 .05
398 Brent Price .01 .05
399 Checklist .01 .05
400 Checklist .01 .05

1993-94 Fleer All-Stars

Randomly inserted in 1993-94 Fleer first series 15-card packs, this 24-card standard-size set features 12 players from the Eastern Conference (1-12) and the Western Conference (13-24) that participated in the 1992-93 All-Star Game in Salt Lake City. According to wrapper information, All-Stars are randomly inserted into one of every 10 packs. The fronts are UV-coated and feature color action player photos enclosed by purple borders. The NBA All-Star logo appears in the lower left or right corner. The player's name is stamped in gold foil and appears at the bottom. The backs are also UV-coated and feature a full-color shot of the player along with a statistical performance sketch from the previous year. Each division's All-Stars are in alphabetical order.

COMPLETE SET (24) 30.00 80.00
1 Brad Daugherty .20 .50
2 Joe Dumars 1.00 2.50
3 Patrick Ewing 1.00 2.50
4 Larry Johnson 1.00 2.50
5 Michael Jordan 10.00 25.00
6 Larry Nance .20 .50
7 Shaquille O'Neal 5.00 12.00
8 Scottie Pippen UER 3.00 8.00
(Name spelled Pipen on front)
9 Mark Price .20 .50
10 Detlef Schrempf .40 1.00
11 Isiah Thomas 1.00 2.50
12 Dominique Wilkins 1.00 2.50
13 Charles Barkley 1.50 4.00
14 Clyde Drexler 1.00 2.50
15 Sean Elliott .40 1.00
16 Tim Hardaway 1.00 2.50
17 Shawn Kemp 1.50 4.00
18 Dan Majerle .40 1.00
19 Karl Malone 1.50 4.00
20 Danny Manning .40 1.00
21 Hakeem Olajuwon 1.50 4.00
22 Terry Porter .20 .50
23 David Robinson 1.50 4.00
24 John Stockton 1.00 2.50

1993-94 Fleer Clyde Drexler

Randomly inserted in all 1993-94 Fleer first series packs at an approximate rate of one in six, this 12-card standard-size set captures the greatest moments in Drexler's career. Drexler autographed more than 2,000 of his cards. These cards are embossed with Fleer logos for authenticity. Odds of getting a signed card were approximately 1 in 7,000 packs. The collector could acquire three additional cards and an issue of NBA Inside Stuff magazine through a mail-in for ten wrappers plus 1.50. The offer expired June 10, 1994. An additional card (No. 16) was offered free to collectors who subscribed to NBA Inside Stuff magazine. Since 12 cards were issued through packs, a 12-card set is considered complete. All 16 cards have the same basic design with the front featuring a unique two photo design, one color, and the other red-screened, serving as the background. The player's name as well as the Fleer logo appear at the top of the card in gold foil. The bottom of the card carries the words "Career Highlights," also stamped in gold foil. The back of the cards carry information about Drexler, with another red-screened photo again as the background. The cards are numbered on the back.The first twelve cards are numbered "X of 12" and the last four cards are simply numbered 13, 14, 15 and 16.

COMPLETE SET (12) 2.50 5.00
COMMON DREXLER (1-12) .20 .50
COMMON AUTOGRAPH (AU) 20.00 50.00
COMMON SEND-OFF (13-15) .75 2.00

1993-94 Fleer First Year Phenoms

These 10 standard-size cards feature top rookies from the 1993-94 season. Cards were randomly inserted in 1993-94 Fleer second-series 15-card wax and 21-card jumbo packs. The insertion rate was approximately one in four wax packs and one in three cello packs. The yellow-bordered fronts feature color player action cutouts superposed upon purple, yellow, and black florescent basketball court designs. The player's name appears vertically in gold foil near one corner, and the gold-foil set logo appears at the bottom left. The horizontal back sports a similar florescent design. A color player close-up cutout appears on one side; his name, team, and career highlights appear on the other. The cards are numbered on the back as "X of 10" and sequenced in alphabetical order.

COMPLETE SET (10) 4.00 8.00
1 Shawn Bradley .10 .30
2 Anfernee Hardaway 1.00 2.50
3 Lindsey Hunter .10 .30
4 Bobby Hurley .05 .15
5 Toni Kukoc .50 1.25
6 Jamal Mashburn .30 .75
7 Dino Radja .05 .15
8 Isaiah Rider .25 .60
9 Nick Van Exel .40 1.00
10 Chris Webber 1.25 3.00

1993-94 Fleer Internationals

This 12-card insert standard-size set features NBA players born outside the United States. The cards were randomly inserted in first series 15-card packs at a rate of one in 10. The fronts are UV-coated and feature a color player photo superimposed over a map of his country of origin. The player's name appears at the top of the card and is gold foil stamped. The backs are also UV-coated and feature a color shot of the player along with a brief biographical sketch. The set is sequenced in alphabetical order.

COMPLETE SET (12) 2.00 4.00
1 Alaa Abdelnaby .08 .25
2 Vlade Divac .25 .60
3 Patrick Ewing .50 1.25
4 Carl Herrera .08 .25
5 Luc Longley .25 .60
6 Sarunas Marciulionis .08 .25
7 Dikembe Mutombo .50 1.25
8 Rumeal Robinson .08 .25
9 Detlef Schrempf .25 .60
10 Rony Seikaly .08 .25
11 Rik Smits .25 .60
12 Dominique Wilkins .50 1.25

1993-94 Fleer Living Legends

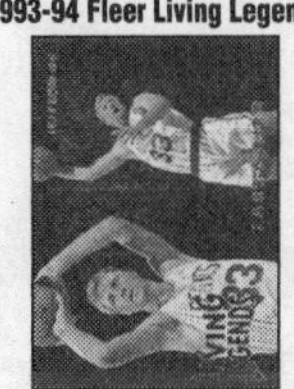

These six standard-size cards honoring veteran superstars were randomly inserted in 1993-94 Fleer second series 15-card (ratio of one in 37) and 21-card (one in 24) packs. The horizontal fronts feature color player action cutouts superimposed upon a borderless metallic motion-streaked background. The player's name and the set's logo appear at the bottom in gold foil. The horizontal back carries a color player close-up cutout on one side; his name, team, and career highlights appear on the other. The cards are numbered on the back as "X of 6" and are sequenced in alphabetical order

COMPLETE SET (6) 12.00 30.00
1 Charles Barkley 1.25 3.00
2 Larry Bird 2.50 6.00
3 Patrick Ewing .75 2.00
4 Michael Jordan 12.00 30.00
5 Hakeem Olajuwon 1.00 2.50
6 Dominique Wilkins .75 2.00

1993-94 Fleer Lottery Exchange

This 11-card standard-size set features the top players from the 1993 NBA Draft. Card fronts resemble that of the basic Fleer issue with the exception of a notation of what number pick the player was. Backs have a photo and statistics. The set could be obtained in exchange for the Draft Exchange card that was randomly inserted (one in 180) in first series packs. The expiration date was April 1, 1994. The cards are numbered on the back in draft order.

COMPLETE SET (11) 8.00 20.00
1 Chris Webber 4.00 10.00
2 Shawn Bradley .30 .75
3 Anfernee Hardaway 2.50 6.00
4 Jamal Mashburn .75 2.00
5 Isaiah Rider .60 1.50
6 Calbert Cheaney .10 .30
7 Bobby Hurley .10 .30
8 Vin Baker .75 2.00
9 Rodney Rogers .30 .75
10 Lindsey Hunter .30 .75
11 Allan Houston 1.25 3.00
NNO Expired Exchange Card .20 .50

1993-94 Fleer NBA Superstars

These 20 standard-size cards featuring NBA stars were randomly inserted in 1993-94 Fleer second-series 15-card packs. The fronts feature color player action cutouts superimposed upon multiple color action shots on the right side and the player's name in team color-coded vertical block lettering on the left. The set's title appears vertically along the left edge in gold foil. The horizontal back carries a color player close-up cutout on one side; his name, team, and career highlights appear on the other. The cards are numbered on the back as "X of 20" and are sequenced in alphabetical order.

COMPLETE SET (20) 7.50 15.00
1 Mahmoud Abdul-Rauf .05 .15
2 Charles Barkley .50 1.25
3 Derrick Coleman .10 .30
4 Clyde Drexler .30 .75
5 Joe Dumars .30 .75
6 Patrick Ewing .30 .75
7 Michael Jordan 4.00 10.00
8 Shawn Kemp .50 1.25
9 Christian Laettner .30 .75
10 Karl Malone .50 1.25
11 Danny Manning .15 .40
12 Reggie Miller .30 .75
13 Alonzo Mourning .50 1.25
14 Chris Mullin .40 1.00
15 Hakeem Olajuwon .50 1.25
16 Shaquille O'Neal 1.50 4.00
17 Mark Price .05 .15
18 Mitch Richmond .30 .75
19 David Robinson .50 1.25
20 Dominique Wilkins .30 .75

1993-94 Fleer Rookie Sensations

Randomly inserted in 29-card series one jumbo packs, these 24 standard-size UV-coated cards feature top rookies from the 1992-93 season. Odds of finding a Rookie Sensations card are approximately one in every five packs. The cards feature color player action photos on the fronts within silver-colored borders. Each player photo is superimposed upon a card design that has a basketball "earth" at the card bottom radiating "spotlight" beams that shade from yellow to magenta on a sky blue background. The player's name and the Rookie Sensations logo, both stamped in gold foil, appear in the lower left. Bordered in silver, the backs feature color close-ups of the players in the lower right or left. Blue "sky" and two intersecting yellow-to-magenta "spotlight" beams form the background. The player's name appears in silver-colored lettering at the top of the card above the player's NBA rookie-year highlights. The set is sequenced in alphabetical order.

COMPLETE SET (24) 25.00 50.00
1 Anthony Avent .30 .75
2 Doug Christie .60 1.50
3 Lloyd Daniels .30 .75
4 Hubert Davis .30 .75
5 Todd Day .30 .75
6 Richard Dumas .30 .75
7 LaPhonso Ellis .30 .75
8 Tom Gugliotta 1.50 4.00
9 Robert Horry .60 1.50
10 Byron Houston .30 .75
11 Jim Jackson UER .60 1.50
(Text on back states he played
in Big East; he played in Big Ten)
12 Adam Keefe .30 .75
13 Christian Laettner .60 1.50
14 Lee Mayberry .30 .75
15 Oliver Miller .30 .75
16 Harold Miner .30 .75
17 Alonzo Mourning 2.50 6.00
18 Shaquille O'Neal 10.00 25.00
19 Anthony Peeler .30 .75
20 Sean Rooks .30 .75
21 Latrell Sprewell 4.00 10.00
22 Bryant Stith .30 .75
23 Clarence Weatherspoon .30 .75
24 Walt Williams .30 .75

1993-94 Fleer Sharpshooters

These 10 standard-size cards were randomly inserted in 1993-94 Fleer second-series 15-card packs. The fronts feature color player action cutouts superposed upon color-screened action shots. The player's name appears at the upper right in gold foil. The set's logo appears at the bottom left. The black horizontal back carries a color player close-up cutout on one side; his name, card title, and career highlights appear on the other. The cards are numbered on the back as "X of 10" and are sequenced in alphabetical order.

COMPLETE SET (10) 10.00 25.00
1 Tom Gugliotta .75 2.00
2 Jim Jackson .30 .75
3 Michael Jordan 8.00 20.00
4 Dan Majerle .30 .75
5 Mark Price .15 .40
6 Glen Rice .30 .75
7 Mitch Richmond .75 2.00
8 Latrell Sprewell 2.00 5.00
9 John Starks .30 .75
10 Dominique Wilkins .75 2.00

1993-94 Fleer Towers of Power

These 30 standard-size cards were randomly inserted in 1993-94 Fleer second series 21-card jumbo packs at an approximate rate of two in every three packs. The fronts feature color player action cutouts superposed upon borderless backgrounds of city skylines. The player's name appears in gold foil in a lower corner. The gold-foil set logo appears in an upper corner. The back has the same borderless skyline background photo as the front and carries a color player cutout on one side, and his career highlights on the other. The cards are numbered on the back as "X of 30" and sequenced in alphabetical order.

COMPLETE SET (30) 25.00 60.00
1 Charles Barkley 2.00 5.00
2 Shawn Bradley .60 1.50
3 Derrick Coleman .60 1.50
4 Brad Daugherty .25 .60
5 Dale Davis .25 .60
6 Vlade Divac .60 1.50
7 Patrick Ewing 1.25 3.00
8 Horace Grant .60 1.50
9 Tom Gugliotta 1.25 3.00
10 Larry Johnson 1.25 3.00
11 Shawn Kemp 2.00 5.00
12 Christian Laettner .60 1.50
13 Karl Malone 2.00 5.00
14 Danny Manning .60 1.50
15 Jamal Mashburn 2.00 5.00
16 Oliver Miller .25 .60
17 Alonzo Mourning 2.00 5.00
18 Dikembe Mutombo 1.25 3.00
19 Ken Norman .25 .60
20 Hakeem Olajuwon 2.00 5.00
21 Shaquille O'Neal 6.00 15.00
22 Robert Parish .60 1.50
23 Olden Polynice .25 .60
24 Clifford Robinson .60 1.50
25 David Robinson 2.00 5.00
26 Dennis Rodman 2.50 6.00
27 Rony Seikaly .25 .60
28 Wayman Tisdale .25 .60
29 Chris Webber 8.00 20.00
30 Dominique Wilkins 1.25 3.00

1994-95 Fleer

The 390 cards comprising Fleer's '94-95 base-brand standard-size set were distributed in two separate series of 240 and 150 cards each. Cards were distributed in 15-card packs (SRP $1.29), 21-card magazine cello packs (SRP $1.99) and 23-card retail jumbo packs (SRP $2.27). The cards feature color player action shots on their white-bordered fronts. The player's name, team, and position appear in team-colored lettering set on an irregular team-colored foil patch at the lower left. The black-bordered back carries a color player action shot on the left side, with the player's name, biography, team logo, and statistics displayed on a team-colored background on the right. The cards are numbered on the back and grouped alphabetically within teams. Unlike previous years, there were no subset cards featured in this set. Each pack contained at least one insert card. One in every 72 packs (Hot Packs) contained only inserts. Rookie Cards of note in this set include Grant Hill, Juwan Howard, Eddie Jones, Jason Kidd and Glenn Robinson.

COMPLETE SET (390) 12.00 24.00
COMPLETE SERIES 1 (240) 6.00 12.00
COMPLETE SERIES 2 (150) 6.00 12.00
1 Stacey Augmon .12 .30
2 Mookie Blaylock .10 .25
3 Craig Ehlo .10 .25
4 Duane Ferrell .10 .25
5 Adam Keefe .10 .25
6 Jon Koncak .10 .25
7 Andrew Lang .10 .25
8 Danny Manning .12 .30
9 Kevin Willis .10 .25
10 Dee Brown .10 .25
11 Sherman Douglas .10 .25
12 Acie Earl .10 .25
13 Rick Fox .10 .25
14 Kevin Gamble .10 .25
15 Xavier McDaniel .10 .25
16 Robert Parish .15 .40
17 Ed Pinckney .10 .25
18 Dino Radja .12 .30
19 Muggsy Bogues .12 .30
20 Frank Brickowski .10 .25
21 Scott Burrell .10 .25
22 Dell Curry .10 .25
23 Kenny Gattison .10 .25
24 Hersey Hawkins .10 .25
25 Eddie Johnson .10 .25
26 Larry Johnson .15 .40
27 Alonzo Mourning .20 .50
28 David Wingate .10 .25
29 B.J. Armstrong .10 .25
30 Horace Grant .12 .30
31 Steve Kerr .12 .30
32 Toni Kukoc .20 .50
33 Luc Longley .10 .25
34 Pete Myers .10 .25
35 Scottie Pippen .30 .75
36 Bill Wennington .10 .25
37 Scott Williams .10 .25
38 Terrell Brandon .10 .25
39 Brad Daugherty .12 .30
40 Tyrone Hill .10 .25
41 Chris Mills .10 .25
42 Larry Nance .15 .40
43 Bobby Phills .10 .25
44 Mark Price .15 .40
45 Gerald Wilkins .10 .25
46 John Williams .10 .25
47 Lucious Harris .10 .25
48 Donald Hodge .10 .25
49 Jim Jackson .10 .25
50 Popeye Jones .10 .25
51 Tim Legler .10 .25
52 Fat Lever .10 .25
53 Jamal Mashburn .15 .40
54 Sean Rooks .10 .25
55 Doug Smith .10 .25
56 Mahmoud Abdul-Rauf .10 .25
57 LaPhonso Ellis .10 .25
58 Dikembe Mutombo .15 .40
59 Robert Pack .10 .25
60 Rodney Rogers .10 .25
61 Bryant Stith .10 .25
62 Brian Williams .10 .25
63 Reggie Williams .10 .25
64 Greg Anderson .10 .25
65 Joe Dumars .15 .40
66 Sean Elliott .15 .40
67 Allan Houston .15 .40
68 Lindsey Hunter .10 .25
69 Terry Mills .10 .25
70 Victor Alexander .10 .25
71 Chris Gatling .10 .25
72 Tim Hardaway .15 .40
73 Keith Jennings .10 .25
74 Avery Johnson .12 .30
75 Chris Mullin .15 .40
76 Billy Owens .10 .25
77 Latrell Sprewell .20 .50
78 Chris Webber .25 .60
79 Scott Brooks .10 .25
80 Sam Cassell .15 .40
81 Mario Elie .10 .25
82 Carl Herrera .10 .25
83 Robert Horry .15 .40
84 Vernon Maxwell .10 .25
85 Hakeem Olajuwon .20 .50
86 Kenny Smith .12 .30
87 Otis Thorpe .10 .25
88 Antonio Davis .10 .25
89 Dale Davis .10 .25
90 Vern Fleming .10 .25
91 Derrick McKey .10 .25
92 Reggie Miller .20 .50
93 Pooh Richardson .10 .25
94 Byron Scott .12 .30
95 Rik Smits .12 .30
96 Haywoode Workman .10 .25
97 Terry Dehere .10 .25
98 Harold Ellis .10 .25
99 Gary Grant .10 .25
100 Ron Harper .12 .30
101 Mark Jackson .15 .40
102 Stanley Roberts .10 .25
103 Elmore Spencer .10 .25
104 Loy Vaught .10 .25
105 Dominique Wilkins .20 .50
106 Elden Campbell .10 .25
107 Doug Christie .10 .25
108 Vlade Divac .15 .40
109 George Lynch .10 .25
110 Anthony Peeler .10 .25
111 Tony Smith .10 .25
112 Sedale Threatt .10 .25
113 Nick Van Exel .15 .40
114 James Worthy .20 .50
115 Bimbo Coles .10 .25
116 Grant Long .10 .25
117 Harold Miner .10 .25
118 Glen Rice .15 .40
119 John Salley .10 .25
120 Rony Seikaly .12 .30
121 Brian Shaw .10 .25
122 Steve Smith .12 .30
123 Vin Baker .15 .40
124 Jon Barry .10 .25
125 Todd Day .10 .25
126 Blue Edwards .10 .25
127 Lee Mayberry .10 .25
128 Eric Murdock .10 .25
129 Ken Norman .10 .25
130 Derek Strong .10 .25
131 Thurl Bailey .10 .25
132 Stacey King .10 .25
133 Christian Laettner .12 .30
134 Chuck Person .12 .30
135 Isaiah Rider .15 .40
136 Chris Smith .10 .25
137 Doug West .10 .25
138 Micheal Williams .10 .25
139 Kenny Anderson .12 .30
140 Benoit Benjamin .10 .25
141 P.J. Brown .10 .25
142 Derrick Coleman .12 .30
143 Kevin Edwards .10 .25
144 Armon Gilliam .10 .25
145 Chris Morris .10 .25
146 Johnny Newman .10 .25
147 Greg Anthony .10 .25
148 Anthony Bonner .10 .25
149 Hubert Davis .10 .25
150 Patrick Ewing .20 .50
151 Derek Harper .12 .30
152 Anthony Mason .10 .25
153 Charles Oakley .12 .30
154 Doc Rivers .12 .30
155 Charles Smith .10 .25
156 John Starks .12 .30
157 Nick Anderson .10 .25
158 Anthony Avent .10 .25
159 Anfernee Hardaway .25 .60
160 Shaquille O'Neal .40 1.00
161 Donald Royal .10 .25
162 Dennis Scott .10 .25
163 Scott Skiles .10 .25
164 Jeff Turner .10 .25
165 Dana Barros .10 .25
166 Shawn Bradley .10 .25
167 Greg Graham .10 .25
168 Eric Leckner .10 .25
169 Jeff Malone .10 .25
170 Moses Malone .15 .40
171 Tim Perry .10 .25
172 Clarence Weatherspoon .10 .25
173 Orlando Woolridge .10 .25
174 Danny Ainge .15 .40
175 Charles Barkley .25 .60
176 Cedric Ceballos .10 .25
177 A.C. Green .15 .40
178 Kevin Johnson .15 .40
179 Joe Kleine .10 .25
180 Dan Majerle .15 .40
181 Oliver Miller .10 .25
182 Mark West .10 .25
183 Clyde Drexler .20 .50
184 Harvey Grant .10 .25
185 Jerome Kersey .10 .25
186 Tracy Murray .10 .25
187 Terry Porter .10 .25
188 Clifford Robinson .10 .25
189 James Robinson .10 .25
190 Rod Strickland .10 .25
191 Buck Williams .10 .25
192 Duane Causwell .10 .25
193 Bobby Hurley .15 .40
194 Olden Polynice .10 .25
195 Mitch Richmond .15 .40

196 Lionel Simmons .10 .25
197 Wayman Tisdale .10 .25
198 Spud Webb .15 .40
199 Walt Williams .10 .25
200 Trevor Wilson .10 .25
201 Willie Anderson .10 .25
202 Antoine Carr .10 .25
203 Terry Cummings .15 .40
204 Vinny Del Negro .10 .25
205 Dale Ellis .10 .25
206 Negele Knight .10 .25
207 J.R. Reid .10 .25
208 David Robinson .25 .60
209 Dennis Rodman .30 .75
210 Vincent Askew .10 .25
211 Michael Cage .10 .25
212 Kendall Gill .10 .25
213 Shawn Kemp .15 .40
214 Nate McMillan .10 .25
215 Gary Payton .15 .40
216 Sam Perkins .10 .25
217 Ricky Pierce .10 .25
218 Detlef Schrempf .15 .40
219 David Benoit .10 .25
220 Tom Chambers .15 .40
221 Tyrone Corbin .10 .25
222 Jeff Hornacek .12 .30
223 Jay Humphries .10 .25
224 Karl Malone .20 .50
225 Bryon Russell .10 .25
226 Felton Spencer .10 .25
227 John Stockton .20 .50
228 Michael Adams .10 .25
229 Rex Chapman .10 .25
230 Calbert Cheaney .10 .25
231 Kevin Duckworth .10 .25
232 Pervis Ellison .10 .25
233 Tom Gugliotta .10 .25
234 Don MacLean .10 .25
235 Gheorghe Muresan .10 .25
236 Brent Price .10 .25
237 Toronto Raptors Logo .10 .25
238 Checklist .10 .25
239 Checklist .10 .25
240 Checklist .10 .25
241 Sergei Bazarevich RC .15 .40
242 Tyrone Corbin .10 .25
243 Grant Long .10 .25
244 Ken Norman .10 .25
245 Steve Smith .12 .30
246 Fred Vinson .10 .25
247 Blue Edwards .10 .25
248 Greg Minor RC .15 .40
249 Eric Montross RC .15 .40
250 Derek Strong .10 .25
251 David Wesley .10 .25
252 Dominique Wilkins .20 .50
253 Michael Adams .10 .25
254 Tony Bennett .10 .25
255 Darrin Hancock RC .15 .40
256 Robert Parish .15 .40
257 Corie Blount .10 .25
258 Jud Buechler .10 .25
259 Greg Foster .10 .25
260 Ron Harper .12 .30
261 Larry Krystkowiak .10 .25
262 Will Perdue .10 .25
263 Dickey Simpkins RC .15 .40
264 Michael Cage .10 .25
265 Tony Campbell .10 .25
266 Terry Davis .10 .25
267 Tony Dumas RC .15 .40
268 Jason Kidd RC .75 2.00
269 Roy Tarpley .10 .25
270 Morlon Wiley .10 .25
271 Lorenzo Williams .10 .25
272 Dale Ellis .10 .25
273 Tom Hammonds .10 .25
274 Cliff Levingston .10 .25
275 Darnell Mee .10 .25
276 Jalen Rose RC .40 1.00
277 Reggie Slater .10 .25
278 Bill Curley RC .15 .40
279 Johnny Dawkins .10 .25
280 Grant Hill RC .75 2.00
281 Eric Leckner .10 .25
282 Mark Macon .10 .25
283 Oliver Miller .10 .25
284 Mark West .10 .25
285 Manute Bol .10 .25
286 Tom Gugliotta .10 .25
287 Ricky Pierce .10 .25
288 Carlos Rogers RC .15 .40
289 Clifford Rozier RC .15 .40
290 Rony Seikaly .12 .30
291 Tim Breaux .10 .25
292 Chris Jent .10 .25
293 Eric Riley .10 .25
294 Zan Tabak .10 .25
295 Duane Ferrell .10 .25
296 Mark Jackson .15 .40
297 John Williams .10 .25
298 Matt Fish .10 .25
299 Tony Massenburg .10 .25
300 Lamond Murray RC .15 .40
301 Bo Outlaw RC .15 .40
302 Eric Piatkowski RC .20 .50
303 Pooh Richardson .10 .25
304 Randy Woods .10 .25
305 Sam Bowie .10 .25
306 Cedric Ceballos .10 .25
307 Antonio Harvey .10 .25
308 Eddie Jones RC .50 1.25
309 Anthony Miller RC .15 .40
310 Ledell Eackles .10 .25
311 Kevin Gamble .10 .25
312 Brad Lohaus .10 .25
313 Billy Owens .10 .25
314 Khalid Reeves RC .15 .40
315 Kevin Willis .10 .25
316 Marty Conlon .10 .25
317 Eric Mobley RC .15 .40
318 Johnny Newman .10 .25
319 Ed Pinckney .10 .25
320 Glenn Robinson RC .30 .75
321 Mike Brown .10 .25
322 Pat Durham .10 .25
323 Howard Eisley RC .15 .40
324 Andres Guibert .10 .25
325 Donyell Marshall RC .15 .40
326 Sean Rooks .10 .25
327 Yinka Dare RC .15 .40
328 Sleepy Floyd .10 .25
329 Sean Higgins .10 .25
330 Rick Mahorn .10 .25
331 Rex Walters .10 .25
332 Jayson Williams .10 .25
333 Charlie Ward RC .15 .40
334 Herb Williams .10 .25
335 Monty Williams RC .15 .40
336 Anthony Bowie .10 .25
337 Horace Grant .12 .30
338 Geert Hammink .10 .25
339 Tree Rollins .10 .25
340 Brian Shaw .10 .25
341 Brooks Thompson RC .15 .40
342 Derrick Alston RC .15 .40
343 Willie Burton .10 .25
344 Jaren Jackson .10 .25
345 B.J. Tyler RC .15 .40
346 Scott Williams .10 .25
347 Sharone Wright RC .15 .40
348 Antonio Lang RC .15 .40
349 Danny Manning .12 .30
350 Elliot Perry .10 .25
351 Wesley Person RC .15 .40
352 Trevor Ruffin .15 .40
353 Danny Schayes .10 .25
354 Aaron Swinson RC .15 .40
355 Wayman Tisdale .10 .25
356 Mark Bryant .10 .25
357 Chris Dudley .10 .25
358 James Edwards .10 .25
359 Aaron McKie RC .15 .40
360 Alaa Abdelnaby .10 .25
361 Frank Brickowski .10 .25
362 Randy Brown .10 .25
363 Brian Grant RC .25 .60
364 Michael Smith RC .15 .40
365 Henry Turner .10 .25
366 Sean Elliott .15 .40
367 Avery Johnson .12 .30
368 Moses Malone .15 .40
369 Julius Nwosu .10 .25
370 Chuck Person .12 .30
371 Chris Whitney .10 .25
372 Bill Cartwright .12 .30
373 Byron Houston .10 .25
374 Ervin Johnson .10 .25
375 Sarunas Marciulionis .10 .25
376 Antoine Carr .10 .25
377 John Crotty .10 .25
378 Adam Keefe .10 .25
379 Jamie Watson RC .15 .40
380 Mitchell Butler .10 .25
381 Juwan Howard RC .25 .60
382 Jim McIlvaine RC .15 .40
383 Doug Overton .10 .25
384 Scott Skiles .10 .25
385 Larry Stewart .10 .25
386 Kenny Walker .10 .25
387 Chris Webber .25 .60
388 Vancouver Grizzlies .10 .25
389 Checklist .10 .25
390 Checklist .10 .25

1994-95 Fleer All-Defensive

Randomly inserted in all first-series packs at a rate of one in nine, these 10 standard-size cards feature first and second All-NBA Defensive teams. Card fronts are borderless with color player action shots that have been faded to black-and-white. The player's name and first or second team designation appear in silver-foil lettering near the bottom. On a color-screened background, the back carries a color player cutout on one side and career highlights on the other. The cards are numbered on the back as "X of 10" and are sequenced in alphabetical order.

COMPLETE SET (10) 2.50 6.00
1 Mookie Blaylock .25 .60
2 Charles Oakley .30 .75
3 Hakeem Olajuwon .50 1.25
4 Gary Payton .40 1.00
5 Scottie Pippen .75 2.00
6 Horace Grant .30 .75
7 Nate McMillan .25 .60
8 David Robinson .60 1.50
9 Dennis Rodman .75 2.00
10 Latrell Sprewell .50 1.25

1994-95 Fleer All-Stars

Randomly inserted in 15-card first-series packs at a rate of one in two, these 26 standard-size cards feature borderless fronts with color player action shots and backgrounds that fade to black-and-white. The player's name and first or second team designation appear in silver-foil lettering near the bottom. On a color-screened background, the back carries a color player cutout on one side and career highlights on the other.

COMPLETE SET (26) 10.00 25.00
1 Kenny Anderson .50 1.25
2 B.J. Armstrong .40 1.00
3 Mookie Blaylock .40 1.00
4 Derrick Coleman .50 1.25
5 Patrick Ewing .75 2.00
6 Horace Grant .50 1.25
7 Alonzo Mourning .75 2.00
8 Charles Oakley .50 1.25
9 Shaquille O'Neal 1.50 4.00
10 Scottie Pippen 1.25 3.00
11 Mark Price .60 1.50
12 John Starks .50 1.25
13 Dominique Wilkins .75 2.00
14 Charles Barkley 1.00 2.50
15 Clyde Drexler .75 2.00
16 Kevin Johnson .60 1.50
17 Shawn Kemp .60 1.50
18 Karl Malone .75 2.00
19 Danny Manning .50 1.25
20 Hakeem Olajuwon .75 2.00
21 Gary Payton .60 1.50
22 Mitch Richmond .60 1.50
23 Clifford Robinson .40 1.00
24 David Robinson 1.00 2.50
25 Latrell Sprewell .75 2.00
26 John Stockton .75 2.00

1994-95 Fleer Award Winners

These four standard-size cards were random inserts in all first series packs at an approximate rate of one in 22. The set highlights four NBA award winners from the 1993-94 season. The horizontal fronts feature multiple player images. The player's name and his award appear at the bottom in gold-foil lettering. The horizontal back carries a color player close-up on one side and career highlights on the other. The cards are numbered "X of 4" and are sequenced in alphabetical order.

COMPLETE SET (4) 1.25 3.00
1 Dell Curry .30 .75
2 Don MacLean .30 .75
3 Hakeem Olajuwon .60 1.50
4 Chris Webber .75 2.00

1994-95 Fleer Career Achievement

Randomly inserted in all first series packs at rate of one in 37, these six standard-size cards feature veteran NBA superstars. The fronts feature color player cutouts on their borderless metallic fronts. The player's name appears in gold-foil lettering in a lower corner. The back carries a color player close-up in a lower corner, with career highlights appearing above and alongside. The cards are numbered on the back as "X of 6" and are sequenced in alphabetical order.

COMPLETE SET (6) 6.00 15.00
1 Patrick Ewing 2.00 5.00
2 Karl Malone 2.00 5.00
3 Hakeem Olajuwon 2.00 5.00
4 Robert Parish 1.50 4.00
5 Scottie Pippen 3.00 8.00
6 Dominique Wilkins 2.00 5.00

1994-95 Fleer First Year Phenoms

Randomly inserted into all second series packs at a rate of one in five, cards from this 10-card standard-size set feature a selection of the top rookies from 1994. These borderless cards feature a full color, cut-out player photo bursting forth from the center of the card, against a multi-imaged, shaded photo background. Card backs feature brief text on each player. The set is sequenced in alphabetical order.

COMPLETE SET (10) 4.00 10.00
1 Grant Hill 1.50 4.00
2 Jason Kidd 1.50 4.00
3 Donyell Marshall .30 .75
4 Eric Montross .30 .75
5 Lamond Murray .30 .75
6 Wesley Person .30 .75
7 Khalid Reeves .30 .75
8 Glenn Robinson .60 1.50
9 Jalen Rose .75 2.00
10 Sharone Wright .30 .75

1994-95 Fleer League Leaders

Randomly inserted in all first series Fleer packs at an approximate rate of one in 11, these eight standard-size cards showcase league statistical leaders from the 1993-94 season. Card fronts feature a horizontal design with color player cutouts set on hardwood backgrounds. The player's name and the category in which he led the NBA appear in gold-foil lettering at the bottom. On a hardwood background, the horizontal back carries a color player close-up on one side and career highlights on the other. The cards are numbered on the back as "X of 8" and are sequenced in alphabetical order.

COMPLETE SET (8) 2.00 5.00
1 Mahmoud Abdul-Rauf .25 .60
2 Nate McMillan .25 .60
3 Tracy Murray .25 .60
4 Dikembe Mutombo .40 1.00
5 Shaquille O'Neal 1.00 2.50
6 David Robinson .60 1.50
7 Dennis Rodman .75 2.00
8 John Stockton .50 1.25

1994-95 Fleer Lottery Exchange

This 11-card standard-size set was available exclusively by redeeming the Fleer Lottery Exchange card, which was randomly inserted into all first series packs at a rate of one in 175. The expiration date for the redemption was April 1st, 1995. Card design is very similar to the basic issue Fleer cards except for the Lottery Pick logo on front.

COMPLETE SET (11) 6.00 15.00
1 Glenn Robinson .75 2.00
2 Jason Kidd 2.00 5.00
3 Grant Hill 2.00 5.00
4 Donyell Marshall .40 1.00
5 Juwan Howard .60 1.50
6 Sharone Wright .40 1.00
7 Lamond Murray .40 1.00
8 Brian Grant .60 1.50
9 Eric Montross .40 1.00
10 Eddie Jones 1.25 3.00
11 Carlos Rogers .40 1.00
NNO Expired Exch.Card .40 1.00

1994-95 Fleer Pro-Visions

Randomly inserted in all first-series packs at a rate of one in five, these nine standard-size cards highlight some top NBA stars. Borderless fronts feature color paintings of the players on fanciful backgrounds. The player's name appears in gold-foil lettering in a lower corner. The back carries career highlights on a colorful ghosted abstract background.

COMPLETE SET (9) 1.25 3.00
1 Jamal Mashburn .25 .60
2 John Starks .20 .50
3 Toni Kukoc .30 .75
4 Derrick Coleman .20 .50
5 Chris Webber .40 1.00
6 Dennis Rodman .50 1.25
7 Gary Payton .25 .60
8 Anfernee Hardaway .40 1.00
9 Dan Majerle .25 .60

1994-95 Fleer Rookie Sensations

Randomly inserted at a rate of one in three first-series 21-card cello packs, these 25 standard-size cards feature a selection of the top rookies from the 1993-94 season. Card fronts feature color player action cutouts "breaking out" of borderless multicolored backgrounds. The player's name appears in gold-foil lettering in a lower corner. The back carries another color player action cutout on one side, and career highlights within a colored panel on the other. The cards are numbered on the back as "X of 25" and are sequenced in alphabetical order.

COMPLETE SET (25) 10.00 25.00
1 Vin Baker 1.00 2.50
2 Shawn Bradley .60 1.50
3 P.J. Brown .60 1.50
4 Sam Cassell 1.00 2.50
5 Calbert Cheaney .60 1.50
6 Antonio Davis .60 1.50
7 Acie Earl .60 1.50
8 Harold Ellis .60 1.50
9 Anfernee Hardaway 1.50 4.00
10 Allan Houston 1.00 2.50
11 Lindsey Hunter .60 1.50
12 Bobby Hurley 1.00 2.50
13 Popeye Jones .60 1.50
14 Toni Kukoc 1.25 3.00
15 George Lynch .60 1.50
16 Jamal Mashburn 1.00 2.50
17 Chris Mills .60 1.50
18 Gheorghe Muresan .60 1.50
19 Dino Radja .75 2.00
20 Isaiah Rider 1.00 2.50
21 James Robinson .60 1.50
22 Rodney Rogers .60 1.50
23 Bryon Russell .60 1.50
24 Nick Van Exel 1.00 2.50
25 Chris Webber 1.50 4.00

1994-95 Fleer Sharpshooters

Randomly inserted exclusively into second series retail packs at a rate of one in seven, cards from this 10-card standard-size set feature a selection of the NBA's best long-distance shooters. Card fronts feature color player photos cut out against a neon basketball background overlapped by a basketball net. The set is sequenced in alphabetical order.

COMPLETE SET (10) 5.00 12.00
1 Dell Curry .60 1.50
2 Joe Dumars 1.00 2.50
3 Dale Ellis .60 1.50
4 Dan Majerle 1.00 2.50
5 Reggie Miller 1.25 3.00
6 Mark Price 1.00 2.50
7 Glen Rice 1.00 2.50
8 Mitch Richmond 1.00 2.50
9 Dennis Scott .60 1.50
10 Latrell Sprewell 1.25 3.00

1994-95 Fleer Superstars

Randomly inserted into all second series packs at a rate of one in 37, cards from this six-card set feature a selection of veteran NBA stars with true Hall of Fame potential. Card fronts feature psychedelic, etched-foil backgrounds against a full color, cut out player photo. The set is sequenced in alphabetical order.

COMPLETE SET (6) 6.00 15.00
1 Charles Barkley 2.50 6.00
2 Patrick Ewing 2.00 5.00
3 Hakeem Olajuwon 2.00 5.00
4 Robert Parish 1.50 4.00
5 Scottie Pippen 3.00 8.00
6 Dominique Wilkins 2.00 5.00

1994-95 Fleer Team Leaders

Randomly inserted into all second series packs at a rate of one in three, cards from this nine-card standard-size set each feature three key players from an NBA team. Horizontal card fronts feature three full color, cut out player photos against a computer-enhanced graphic background. The backs have a head shot of all three players and infomation on them. The cards are numbered "X of 9." There are two variations of card #3. The error version lists Joe Dumars as a Houston Rocket. The corrected version lists him as a Detroit Piston. It appears that equal quantities of both versions exist.

COMPLETE SET (9) 1.25 3.00
1 Mookie Blaylock .25 .60
Dominique Wilkins
Alonzo Mourning
2 Scottie Pippen .40 1.00
Mark Price
Jamal Mashburn
3 Dikembe Mutombo ERR .25 .60
Joe Dumars
Latrell Sprewell
Card has Dumars with Rockets
3A Dikembe Mutombo COR .25 .60
Joe Dumars
Latrell Sprewell
4 Hakeem Olajuwon .25 .60
Reggie Miller
Loy Vaught
5 Vlade Divac .20 .50
Glen Rice
Vin Baker
6 Isaiah Rider .25 .60
Kenny Anderson
Patrick Ewing
7 Shaquille O'Neal .50 1.25
Clarence Weatherspoon
Charles Barkley
8 Rod Strickland .30 .75
Mitch Richmond
David Robinson
9 Shawn Kemp .25 .60
John Stockton
Rex Chapman

1994-95 Fleer Total D

Randomly inserted exclusively into second series hobby packs at a rate of one in seven, cards from this 10-card standard-size set feature a selection of the NBA's top defensive players. The fronts are laid out horizontally with a color photo and the player's name and team is in gold-foil at the bottom. "Total D" is in the background many times with a variety of colors set behind that. The backs have a head shot and information and why the player is so good defensively with a similar background to the front. The cards are numbered "X of 10" and are sequenced in alphabetical order.

COMPLETE SET (10) 3.00 8.00
1 Mookie Blaylock .40 1.00
2 Nate McMillan .40 1.00
3 Dikembe Mutombo .60 1.50
4 Charles Oakley .50 1.25
5 Hakeem Olajuwon .75 2.00
6 Gary Payton .60 1.50
7 Scottie Pippen 1.25 3.00
8 David Robinson 1.00 2.50
9 Latrell Sprewell .75 2.00
10 John Stockton .75 2.00

1994-95 Fleer Towers of Power

Randomly inserted exclusively into second series 21-card retail packs at a rate of one in five, cards from this 10-card standard-size set feature a selection of the top centers and power forwards in the NBA. The fronts have a color-action photo surrounded by a yellow glow with a tower in the background. The words "Tower of Power" are at the bottom in gold-foil. The backs are the same except for a different photo and player information at the bottom. The cards are numbered "X of 10" and are sequenced in alphabetical order.

COMPLETE SET (10) 8.00 20.00
1 Charles Barkley 1.50 4.00
2 Patrick Ewing 1.25 3.00
3 Shawn Kemp 1.00 2.50
4 Karl Malone 1.25 3.00
5 Alonzo Mourning 1.25 3.00
6 Dikembe Mutombo 1.00 2.50
7 Hakeem Olajuwon 1.25 3.00
8 Shaquille O'Neal 4.00 10.00
9 David Robinson 1.50 4.00
10 Chris Webber 1.50 4.00

1994-95 Fleer Triple Threats

Randomly inserted in all first-series packs at an approximate rate of one in nine, these 10 standard-size cards spotlight some top NBA stars. Card fronts feature borderless fronts with multiple color player action cutouts on black backgrounds highlighted by colorful basketball court designs. The player's name appears in gold-foil lettering in a lower corner. This background design continues on the back, which carries a color player cutout on one side and career highlights in a ghosted strip on the other. The cards are numbered on the back as "X of 10" and are sequenced in alphabetical order.

COMPLETE SET (10) 2.00 5.00
1 Mookie Blaylock .20 .50
2 Patrick Ewing .40 1.00
3 Shawn Kemp .30 .75
4 Karl Malone .40 1.00
5 Reggie Miller .40 1.00
6 Hakeem Olajuwon .40 1.00
7 Shaquille O'Neal .75 2.00
8 Scottie Pippen .60 1.50
9 David Robinson .50 1.25
10 Latrell Sprewell .40 1.00

1994-95 Fleer Young Lions

Randomly inserted into all second series packs at a rate of one in five, cards from this 6-card standard-size set feature a selection of popular players with three years or less of NBA experience. Fronts feature a player photo on the left and a lion photo on the right. In the bottom right corner there is gold-foil stamping of a lion, the term "Young Lion" and the player's name. The back has a brief biography and another player photo. The card is numbered in the lower right as "X" of 6. The set is sequenced in alphabetical order.

COMPLETE SET (6) 2.00 5.00
1 Vin Baker .40 1.00
2 Anfernee Hardaway .60 1.50
3 Larry Johnson .40 1.00
4 Alonzo Mourning .50 1.25
5 Shaquille O'Neal 1.00 2.50
6 Chris Webber .60 1.50

1995-96 Fleer

The 1995-96 Fleer set was issued in two separate series of 200 and 150 cards, respectively, for a total of 350. Cards were distributed in 11-card hobby and retail packs (SRP $1.49) and 17-card retail pre-priced packs (SRP $2.29). Each pack contains at least two insert cards. Special Hot Packs, containing a selection of only insert cards, were randomly seeded into one in every 72 packs. The borderless fronts feature four different background designs (one for each division) against a cut-out color player action shot. The backs have a color-action photo and the same picture set against a pixeled background, along with statistics. The cards are grouped alphabetically within teams. The set concludes with the following topical subsets: Rookies (280-319) and Firm Foundations (320-348). Rookie Cards of note in this set include Michael Finley, Kevin Garnett, Antonio McDyess, Joe Smith, Jerry Stackhouse and Damon Stoudamire.

COMPLETE SET (350) 20.00 40.00
COMPLETE SERIES 1 (200) 10.00 20.00
COMPLETE SERIES 2 (150) 10.00 20.00
1 Stacey Augmon .12 .30
2 Mookie Blaylock .10 .25
3 Craig Ehlo .10 .25
4 Andrew Lang .10 .25
5 Grant Long .10 .25
6 Ken Norman .10 .25
7 Steve Smith .12 .30
8 Dee Brown .10 .25
9 Sherman Douglas .10 .25
10 Eric Montross .10 .25
11 Dino Radja .12 .30
12 David Wesley .10 .25
13 Dominique Wilkins .20 .50
14 Muggsy Bogues .12 .30
15 Scott Burrell .10 .25
16 Dell Curry .10 .25
17 Hersey Hawkins .10 .25
18 Larry Johnson .15 .40
19 Alonzo Mourning .20 .50
20 Robert Parish .15 .40
21 B.J. Armstrong .10
22 Michael Jordan 1.25
23 Steve Kerr .12
24 Toni Kukoc .15
25 Will Perdue .10
26 Scottie Pippen .25
27 Terrell Brandon .10
28 Tyrone Hill .10
29 Chris Mills .10
30 Bobby Phills .10
31 Mark Price .15
32 John Williams .10
33 Lucious Harris .10
34 Jim Jackson .10
35 Popeye Jones .10
36 Jason Kidd .25
37 Jamal Mashburn .15
38 George McCloud .10
39 Roy Tarpley .10
40 Lorenzo Williams .10
41 Mahmoud Abdul-Rauf .10
42 Dale Ellis .10
43 LaPhonso Ellis .10
44 Dikembe Mutombo .15
45 Robert Pack .10
46 Rodney Rogers .10
47 Jalen Rose .20
48 Bryant Stith .10
49 Reggie Williams .10
50 Joe Dumars .15
51 Grant Hill .25
52 Allan Houston .12
53 Lindsey Hunter .10
54 Oliver Miller .10
55 Terry Mills .10
56 Mark West .10
57 Chris Gatling .10
58 Tim Hardaway .15
59 Donyell Marshall .10
60 Chris Mullin .15
61 Carlos Rogers .10
62 Clifford Rozier .10
63 Rony Seikaly .12
64 Latrell Sprewell .15
65 Sam Cassell .15
66 Clyde Drexler .20
67 Mario Elie .10
68 Carl Herrera .10
69 Robert Horry .12
70 Vernon Maxwell .10
71 Hakeem Olajuwon .20
72 Kenny Smith .12
73 Dale Davis .10
74 Mark Jackson .15
75 Derrick McKey .10
76 Reggie Miller .20
77 Sam Mitchell .10
78 Byron Scott .12
79 Rik Smits .12
80 Terry Dehere .10
81 Tony Massenburg .10
82 Lamond Murray .10
83 Pooh Richardson .10
84 Malik Sealy .10
85 Loy Vaught .10
86 Elden Campbell .10
87 Cedric Ceballos .10
88 Vlade Divac .15
89 Eddie Jones .20
90 Anthony Peeler .10
91 Sedale Threatt .10
92 Nick Van Exel .15
93 Bimbo Coles .10
94 Matt Geiger .10
95 Billy Owens .10
96 Khalid Reeves .10
97 Glen Rice .15
98 John Salley .10
99 Kevin Willis .10
100 Vin Baker .12
101 Marty Conlon .10
102 Todd Day .10
103 Lee Mayberry .10
104 Eric Murdock .10
105 Glenn Robinson .15
106 Winston Garland .10
107 Tom Gugliotta .10
108 Christian Laettner .12
109 Isaiah Rider .15
110 Sean Rooks .10
111 Doug West .10
112 Kenny Anderson .12
113 Benoit Benjamin .10
114 P.J. Brown .10
115 Derrick Coleman .12
116 Armon Gilliam .10
117 Chris Morris .10
118 Rex Walters .10
119 Hubert Davis .10
120 Patrick Ewing .20
121 Derek Harper .12
122 Anthony Mason .10
123 Charles Oakley .12
124 Charles Smith .10
125 John Starks .12
126 Nick Anderson .10
127 Anthony Bowie .10
128 Horace Grant .12
129 Anfernee Hardaway .25
130 Shaquille O'Neal .40
131 Donald Royal .10
132 Dennis Scott .10
133 Brian Shaw .10
134 Derrick Alston .10
135 Dana Barros .10
136 Shawn Bradley .10
137 Willie Burton .10
138 Clarence Weatherspoon .10
139 Scott Williams .10
140 Sharone Wright .10
141 Danny Ainge .15
142 Charles Barkley .25
143 A.C. Green .15
144 Kevin Johnson .15
145 Dan Majerle .15
146 Danny Manning .12
147 Elliot Perry .10
148 Wesley Person .10
149 Wayman Tisdale .10
150 Chris Dudley .10
151 Jerome Kersey .10
152 Aaron McKie .10
153 Terry Porter .10
154 Clifford Robinson .10
155 James Robinson .10
156 Rod Strickland .10
157 Otis Thorpe .10
158 Buck Williams .10

an Grant .12 .30
bby Hurley .15 .40
den Polynice .10 .25
tch Richmond .15 .40
chael Smith .10 .25
ud Webb .15 .40
alt Williams .10 .25
rry Cummings .15 .40
nny Del Negro .10 .25
an Elliott .15 .40
ery Johnson .12 .30
uck Person .12 .30
R. Reid .10 .25
c Rivers .12 .30
vid Robinson .25 .60
nnis Rodman .30 .75
ncent Askew .10 .25
ndall Gill .10 .25
awn Kemp .15 .40
runas Marciulionis .10 .25
te McMillan .10 .25
ry Payton .15 .40
m Perkins .10 .25
tlef Schrempf .15 .40
vid Benoit .10 .25
toine Carr .10 .25
e Edwards .10 .25
f Hornacek .12 .30
am Keefe .10 .25
rl Malone .20 .50
ton Spencer .10 .25
hn Stockton .20 .50
x Chapman .10 .25
lbert Cheaney .10 .25
wan Howard .15 .40
n MacLean .10 .25
eorghe Muresan .10 .25
ott Skiles .10 .25
ris Webber .20 .50
ecklist .10 .25
ecklist .10 .25
ecklist .10 .25
acey Augmon .12 .30
ookie Blaylock .10 .25
ant Long .10 .25
n Norman .10 .25
eve Smith .12 .30
ud Webb .15 .40
na Barros .10 .25
ck Fox .10 .25
ndall Gill .10 .25
alid Reeves .10 .25
en Rice .15 .40
c Longley .10 .25
ennis Rodman .30 .75
n Majerle .15 .40
ny Dumas .10 .25
m Hammonds .10 .25
more Spencer .10 .25
s Thorpe .10 .25
. Armstrong .10 .25
m Cassell .15 .40
de Drexler .20 .50
ario Elie .10 .25
bert Horry .12 .30
keem Olajuwon .20 .50
nny Smith .12 .30
tonio Davis .10 .25
die Johnson .10 .25
ky Pierce .10 .25
c Piatkowski .12 .30
dney Rogers .10 .25
an Williams .10 .25
rie Blount .10 .25
orge Lynch .10 .25
vin Gamble .10 .25
onzo Mourning .20 .50
c Mobley .10 .25
ry Porter .10 .25
cheal Williams .10 .25
vin Edwards .10 .25
n Fleming .10 .25
arlie Ward .10 .25
n Koncak .10 .25
chard Dumas .10 .25
f Malone .10 .25
rnon Maxwell .10 .25
hn Williams .10 .25
rvey Grant .10 .25
ntonio Wingfield .10 .25
one Corbin .10 .25
unas Marciulionis .10 .25
l Perdue .10 .25
sey Hawkins .10 .25
n Johnson .10 .25
awn Kemp .15 .40
ry Payton .15 .40
n Perkins .10 .25
tlef Schrempf .15 .40
ris Morris .10 .25
bert Pack .10 .25
llie Anderson ET .10 .25
nmy King ET .10 .25
ver Miller ET .10 .25
cy Murray ET .10 .25
Pinckney ET .10 .25
in Robertson ET .10 .25
los Rogers ET .10 .25
n Salley ET .10 .25
non Stoudamire ET .25 .60
Tabak ET .10 .25
raf Amaya ET .10 .25
g Anthony ET .10 .25
oit Benjamin ET .10 .25
e Edwards ET .10 .25
ny Gattison ET .10 .25
onio Harvey ET .10 .25
ris King ET .10 .25
wrence Moten ET .10 .25
ant Reeves ET .10 .25
on Scott ET .12 .30
y Alexander RC .15 .40
ome Allen RC .15 .40
nt Barry RC .25 .60
rio Bennett RC .15 .40
vis Best RC .15 .40
ior Burrough RC .15 .40
on Caffey RC .15 .40
dolph Childress RC .15 .40
ha Danilovic RC .15 .40
k Davis RC .15 .40
s Edney RC .15 .40
hael Finley RC .50 1.25
rrell Ford RC .15 .40
n Garnett RC 1.25 3.00
Henderson RC .15 .40
kie King RC .15 .40
ny King RC .15 .40

297 Donny Marshall RC .15 .40
298 Antonio McDyess RC .40 1.00
299 Loren Meyer RC .15 .40
300 Lawrence Moten RC .15 .40
301 Ed O'Bannon RC .15 .40
302 Greg Ostertag RC .15 .40
303 Cherokee Parks RC .15 .40
304 Theo Ratliff RC .25 .60
305 Bryant Reeves RC .15 .40
306 Shawn Respert RC .15 .40
307 Lou Roe RC .15 .40
308 Arvydas Sabonis RC .30 .75
309 Joe Smith RC .30 .75
310 Jerry Stackhouse RC .50 1.25
311 Damon Stoudamire RC .40 1.00
312 Bob Sura RC .15 .40
313 Kurt Thomas RC .15 .40
314 Gary Trent RC .15 .40
315 David Vaughn RC .15 .40
316 Rasheed Wallace RC .50 1.25
317 Eric Williams RC .15 .40
318 Corliss Williamson RC .15 .40
319 George Zidek RC .15 .40
320 Mookie Blaylock FF .10 .25
321 Dino Radja FF .12 .30
322 Larry Johnson FF .15 .40
323 Michael Jordan FF 1.25 3.00
324 Tyrone Hill FF .10 .25
325 Jason Kidd FF .25 .60
326 Dikembe Mutombo FF .15 .40
327 Grant Hill FF .25 .60
328 Joe Smith FF .20 .50
329 Hakeem Olajuwon FF .20 .50
330 Reggie Miller FF .20 .50
331 Loy Vaught FF .10 .25
332 Nick Van Exel FF .15 .40
333 Alonzo Mourning FF .20 .50
334 Glenn Robinson FF .15 .40
335 Kevin Garnett FF .75 2.00
336 Kenny Anderson FF .12 .30
337 Patrick Ewing FF .20 .50
338 Shaquille O'Neal FF .40 1.00
339 Jerry Stackhouse FF .30 .75
340 Charles Barkley FF .25 .60
341 Clifford Robinson FF .10 .25
342 Mitch Richmond FF .15 .40
343 David Robinson FF .25 .60
344 Shawn Kemp FF .15 .40
345 Damon Stoudamire FF .25 .60
346 Karl Malone FF .20 .50
347 Bryant Reeves FF .10 .25
348 Chris Webber FF .20 .50
349 Checklist (201-319) .10 .25
350 Checklist (320-350/ins.) .10 .25

1995-96 Fleer All-Stars

Randomly inserted in all first series packs at an approximate rate of one in three, these thirteen dual-player, double-sided standard-size cards feature members of the 1994-95 Eastern and Western Conference All-Star squads. Only All-Star MVP Mitch Richmond is given his own card. Both sides have a full-color action photo taken at the All-Star game with the West having a purple background and the East a green background. The bottoms have the Phoenix All-Star Weekend insignia with the player's name and conference in gold-foil. The cards are numbered "X of 13."

COMPLETE SET (13) 2.00 5.00
1 Grant Hill .40 1.00
Charles Barkley
2 Scottie Pippen .40 1.00
Shawn Kemp
3 Shaquille O'Neal .60 1.50
Hakeem Olajuwon
4 Anfernee Hardaway .40 1.00
Dan Majerle
5 Reggie Miller .30 .75
Latrell Sprewell
6 Vin Baker .20 .50
Cedric Ceballos
7 Tyrone Hill .30 .75
Karl Malone
8 Larry Johnson .25 .60
Detlef Schrempf
9 Patrick Ewing .40 1.00
David Robinson
10 Alonzo Mourning .30 .75
Dikembe Mutombo
11 Dana Barros .25 .60
Gary Payton
12 Joe Dumars .30 .75
John Stockton
13 Mitch Richmond AS MVP .25 .60

1995-96 Fleer Class Encounters

Randomly inserted in all second series packs at a rate of one in two, this 40-card standard-size set highlights the first 20 players of the 1995 draft and 20 of the most sucessful players from the 1994 draft. Full-bleed fronts have gold foil printing and one full-color action shot as the main background. Three head shots of the original appear in increasing size on the right side. Horizontal backs have a white-bordered, off-center head shot with a player profile printed in black type on a red background. Each group of cards is sequenced in alphabetical order.

COMPLETE SET (40) 8.00 20.00
1 Derrick Alston .25 .60
2 Brian Grant .30 .75
3 Grant Hill .60 1.50
4 Juwan Howard .40 1.00
5 Eddie Jones .50 1.25
6 Jason Kidd .60 1.50
7 Donyell Marshall .25 .60
8 Anthony Miller .25 .60
9 Eric Mobley .25 .60
10 Eric Montross .25 .60
11 Lamond Murray .25 .60
12 Wesley Person .25 .60
13 Eric Piatkowski .30 .75
14 Khalid Reeves .25 .60
15 Glenn Robinson .40 1.00
16 Carlos Rogers .25 .60
17 Jalen Rose .50 1.25
18 Clifford Rozier .25 .60
19 Michael Smith .25 .60
20 Sharone Wright .25 .60
21 Brent Barry .50 1.25
22 Jason Caffey .30 .75
23 Randolph Childress .30 .75
24 Kevin Garnett 2.50 6.00
25 Alan Henderson .30 .75
26 Antonio McDyess .75 2.00
27 Ed O'Bannon .30 .75
28 Cherokee Parks .30 .75
29 Theo Ratliff .50 1.25
30 Bryant Reeves .30 .75
31 Shawn Respert .30 .75
32 Joe Smith .60 1.50
33 Jerry Stackhouse 1.00 2.50
34 Damon Stoudamire .75 2.00
35 Bob Sura .30 .75
36 Kurt Thomas .30 .75
37 Gary Trent .30 .75
38 Rasheed Wallace 1.00 2.50
39 Eric Williams .30 .75
40 Corliss Williamson .30 .75

1995-96 Fleer Double Doubles

Randomly inserted in all first series packs at an approximate rate of one in three, these 12 cards feature players who averaged double figures per game in two statistical categories during the 1994-95 season. Full-bleed fronts features the player in two, split-shot color action photos separated by the words "Double Double" which are printed in the player's team colors. The player is again featured in full-color on the back with a career synopsis and '94-95 stats printed in black type. The set is sequenced in alphabetical order.

COMPLETE SET (12) 1.50 4.00
1 Vin Baker .25 .60
2 Vlade Divac .30 .75
3 Patrick Ewing .40 1.00
4 Tyrone Hill .20 .50
5 Popeye Jones .20 .50
6 Shawn Kemp .30 .75
7 Karl Malone .40 1.00
8 Dikembe Mutombo .30 .75
9 Hakeem Olajuwon .40 1.00
10 Shaquille O'Neal .75 2.00
11 David Robinson .50 1.25
12 John Stockton .40 1.00

1995-96 Fleer End to End

Randomly inserted in all second series packs at a rate of one in four, cards from this 20-card set focus on the NBA's leaders at both ends of the court. Borderless, horizontal fronts are split between two panels, one having a blue background with "End to End" in repeating print, and the other with a full-color action player shot. A player cutout is placed in the middle of the two panels. Horizontal backs have a full-color action cutout and a player profile.

COMPLETE SET (20) 8.00 20.00
1 Mookie Blaylock .30 .75
2 Vlade Divac .50 1.25
3 Clyde Drexler .60 1.50
4 Patrick Ewing .60 1.50
5 Horace Grant .40 1.00
6 Anfernee Hardaway .75 2.00
7 Grant Hill .75 2.00
8 Eddie Jones .60 1.50
9 Michael Jordan 4.00 10.00
10 Jason Kidd .75 2.00
11 Alonzo Mourning .60 1.50
12 Dikembe Mutombo .50 1.25
13 Hakeem Olajuwon .60 1.50
14 Shaquille O'Neal 1.25 3.00
15 Gary Payton .50 1.25
16 Scottie Pippen .75 2.00
17 David Robinson .75 2.00
18 Latrell Sprewell .50 1.25
19 John Stockton .60 1.50
20 Rod Strickland .30 .75

1995-96 Fleer Flair Hardwood Leaders

Issued one per pack in all first series packs, these 27 super-premium, double-thick Flair style standard-size cards feature each team's statistical leader or award winner from the 1994-95 season. The fronts have a color action photo with the key as the background. The backs have a color photo with a hardwood background and player information. The entire 27-card set was also issued as a commemorative sheet most notably distributed as a wrapper redemption at the San Antonio All-Star Jam Session show. The set is sequenced in alphabetical order by team.

COMPLETE SET (27) 7.50 15.00
1 Mookie Blaylock .25 .60
2 Dominique Wilkins .50 1.25
3 Alonzo Mourning .50 1.25
4 Michael Jordan 3.00 8.00
5 Mark Price .40 1.00
6 Jim Jackson .25 .60
7 Dikembe Mutombo .40 1.00
8 Grant Hill .60 1.50
9 Tim Hardaway .40 1.00
10 Hakeem Olajuwon .50 1.25
11 Reggie Miller .50 1.25
12 Loy Vaught .25 .60
13 Cedric Ceballos .25 .60
14 Glen Rice .40 1.00
15 Glenn Robinson .40 1.00
16 Christian Laettner .30 .75
17 Derrick Coleman .30 .75
18 Patrick Ewing .50 1.25
19 Shaquille O'Neal 1.00 2.50
20 Dana Barros .25 .60
21 Charles Barkley .60 1.50
22 Clifford Robinson .25 .60
23 Mitch Richmond .40 1.00
24 David Robinson .60 1.50
25 Gary Payton .40 1.00
26 Karl Malone .50 1.25
27 Chris Webber .50 1.25
NNO Uncut Sheet 8.00 20.00

1995-96 Fleer Franchise Futures

Randomly inserted into all first series packs at an approximate rate of one in 37, these nine etched-foil standard-size cards feature a selection of the game's hottest young stars. The fronts have a full-color action photo with a huge basketball and fire underneath it in the background. The backs have a color photo with a similar yet less snazzy version of the front background. The set is sequenced in alphabetical order.

COMPLETE SET (9) 12.50 30.00
1 Vin Baker 1.50 4.00
2 Anfernee Hardaway 3.00 8.00
3 Jim Jackson 1.25 3.00
4 Jamal Mashburn 2.00 5.00
5 Alonzo Mourning 2.50 6.00
6 Dikembe Mutombo 2.00 5.00
7 Shaquille O'Neal 5.00 12.00
8 Nick Van Exel 2.00 5.00
9 Chris Webber 2.50 6.00

1995-96 Fleer Rookie Phenoms

The 10 cards in this set were randomly inserted in second series hobby packs only at a rate of one in 24 and highlight the play of the NBA's best rookies. Borderless fronts are gold and silver foil finished with a full-color action cutout. Backs carry an extreme vertical color shot on the left and a player profile on the right.

COMPLETE SET (10) 12.50 30.00
HP CARDS: .1X TO .3X HI COLUMN
HP: SER.2 STATED ODDS 1:72 HOBBY
1 Kevin Garnett 6.00 15.00
2 Antonio McDyess 2.00 5.00
3 Ed O'Bannon .75 2.00
4 Bryant Reeves .75 2.00
5 Shawn Respert .75 2.00
6 Joe Smith 1.50 4.00
7 Jerry Stackhouse 2.50 6.00
8 Damon Stoudamire 2.00 5.00
9 Gary Trent .75 2.00
10 Rasheed Wallace 2.50 6.00

1995-96 Fleer Rookie Sensations

Randomly inserted exclusively into first series 17-card retail pre-priced packs at an approximate rate of one in five, these 15 cards spotlight the top rookies from the 1994-95 season. The fronts have a full-color action photo with the words "Rookie Sensation" in gold-foil around a basketball. The backs have a full-color photo with player information at the bottom in a yellow haze.

COMPLETE SET (15) 10.00 25.00
1 Brian Grant 1.25 3.00
2 Grant Hill 2.50 6.00
3 Juwan Howard 1.50 4.00
4 Eddie Jones 2.00 5.00
5 Jason Kidd 2.50 6.00
6 Donyell Marshall 1.00 2.50
7 Eric Montross 1.00 2.50
8 Lamond Murray 1.00 2.50
9 Wesley Person 1.00 2.50
10 Khalid Reeves 1.00 2.50
11 Glenn Robinson 1.50 4.00
12 Jalen Rose 2.00 5.00
13 Clifford Rozier 1.00 2.50
14 Michael Smith 1.00 2.50
15 Sharone Wright 1.00 2.50

1995-96 Fleer Stackhouse's Scrapbook

Randomly inserted into all second series packs at a rate one in every 24, these two cards represent the first part of a multi-series, eight-card, cross-brand set devoted to Fleer spokesperson Jerry Stackhouse.

COMPLETE SET (2) 1.50 4.00
COMMON CARD (S1-S2) 1.00 2.50

1995-96 Fleer Total D

Randomly inserted into first series 11-card hobby and retail packs at an approximate rate of one in five, these 12 standard-size cards feature a selection of the NBA's top defenders. The fronts have a color-action photo with the player's name and "Total D" on the side in gold-foil. The horizontal backs are split between a color action player photo on the left and a player profile printed in white and set against a gradated color background on the right. The set is sequenced in alphabetical order.

COMPLETE SET (12) 5.00 12.00
1 Mookie Blaylock .25 .60
2 Patrick Ewing .50 1.25
3 Michael Jordan 3.00 8.00
4 Alonzo Mourning .50 1.25
5 Dikembe Mutombo .40 1.00
6 Hakeem Olajuwon .50 1.25
7 Shaquille O'Neal 1.00 2.50
8 Gary Payton .40 1.00
9 Scottie Pippen .60 1.50
10 David Robinson .60 1.50
11 Dennis Rodman .75 2.00
12 John Stockton .50 1.25

1995-96 Fleer Total O

Randomly inserted in second series retail packs only at a rate of one in 12, cards from this 10-card standard-size set spotlight the NBA's offensive talent. Borderless fronts capture the player in a full-color action cutout with two red foil rings surrounding the image. All are on a backdrop of a basketball in the hands of a shooter and "Total O" is printed in silver foil on the ball. Backs are split between a full-color action player shot and a colored rock background containing a player profile printed in white type.

COMPLETE SET (10) 12.50 30.00
HP CARDS: .25X TO .6X HI COLUMN
HP: SER.2 STATED ODDS 1:72 RETAIL
1 Grant Hill 1.50 4.00
2 Michael Jordan 8.00 20.00
3 Jamal Mashburn 1.00 2.50
4 Reggie Miller 1.25 3.00
5 Hakeem Olajuwon 1.25 3.00
6 Shaquille O'Neal 2.50 6.00
7 Mitch Richmond 1.00 2.50
8 David Robinson 1.50 4.00
9 Glenn Robinson 1.00 2.50
10 Jerry Stackhouse 1.50 4.00

1995-96 Fleer Towers of Power

The big "Earth Shakers" of the NBA are represented in this 10-card set. Cards were randomly inserted into one in every 54 second series packs. Borderless fronts have etched copper foil designs and a full-color action player cutout. Backs are a three-tone color screen with a one-color action shot near the top right. A player profile appears in black type on the bottom half.

COMPLETE SET (10) 40.00 75.00
1 Shawn Kemp 4.00 10.00
2 Karl Malone 5.00 12.00
3 Antonio McDyess 5.00 12.00
4 Alonzo Mourning 5.00 12.00
5 Hakeem Olajuwon 5.00 12.00
6 Shaquille O'Neal 10.00 25.00
7 David Robinson 6.00 15.00
8 Glenn Robinson 4.00 10.00
9 Joe Smith 4.00 10.00
10 Chris Webber 5.00 12.00

1996 Fleer French Kellogg's Frosties

Produced by Fleer, these 30-cards are very similar to the Pop-Up cards that were produced for the 1995-96 Jam Session American issue, except these are mini versions. These cards were inserted into boxes of Kellogg's Frosties in France. The cards are not numbered and are checklisted below in alphabetical order.

COMPLETE SET (30) 40.00 100.00
1 Kenny Anderson 2.50 6.00
2 Mookie Blaylock 2.00 5.00
3 Muggsy Bogues 2.50 6.00
4 Sam Cassell 2.50 6.00
5 Clyde Drexler 4.00 10.00
6 Brian Grant 2.50 6.00
7 Horace Grant 2.50 6.00
8 Tim Hardaway 3.00 8.00
9 Grant Hill 5.00 12.00
10 Kevin Johnson 3.00 8.00
11 Jim Jackson 2.00 5.00
12 Jason Kidd 5.00 12.00
13 Christian Laettner 2.50 6.00
14 Dan Majerle 3.00 8.00
15 Vernon Maxwell 2.00 5.00
16 Oliver Miller 2.00 5.00
17 Eric Montross 2.00 5.00
18 Gheorghe Muresan 2.00 5.00
19 Lamond Murray 2.00 5.00
20 Dikembe Mutombo 3.00 8.00
21 Charles Oakley 2.50 6.00
22 Hakeem Olajuwon 4.00 10.00
23 Scottie Pippen 5.00 12.00
24 Glen Rice 3.00 8.00
25 Clifford Robinson 2.00 5.00
26 Glenn Robinson 3.00 8.00
27 Byron Scott 2.50 6.00
28 Rik Smits 2.50 6.00
29 John Stockton 4.00 10.00
30 Tony the Tiger .75 2.00

1996 Fleer/Mountain Dew Stackhouse

This five-card standard-sized set was inserted in the Philadelphia area as a premium for purchasing Mountain Dew soda. The cards have the same design as the regular issues, but have a Moutain Dew logo on the back of each card.

COMPLETE SET (5) 3.00 8.00
COMMON CARD (1-5) .75 2.00

1996-97 Fleer

The 1996-97 Fleer set was issued in two series totalling 300 cards. Both series had 150 cards issued in 11-card packs carrying a suggested retail price of $1.49 each. Card fronts contain a full-bleed photo with the player's last name in ghosted white letters and their first name in gold foil laid over it. The player's team name is also in gold foil under the player's first name. Card backs are horizontal with the team colors setting the background along with a basketball and the team logo. A photo of the player is provided along with statistical and biographical information. Cards are sequenced alphabetically within team order. The only subset is Hardwood Leaders (120-148). No Rookie Cards are featured in the first series. Card #83 (Jerry Stackhouse) was also used for promotional purposes.

COMPLETE SET (300) 17.50 35.00
COMPLETE SERIES 1 (150) 7.50 15.00
COMPLETE SERIES 2 (150) 10.00 20.00
1 Stacey Augmon .12 .30
2 Mookie Blaylock .10 .25
3 Christian Laettner .12 .30
4 Grant Long .10 .25
5 Steve Smith .12 .30
6 Rick Fox .10 .25
7 Dino Radja .12 .30
8 Eric Williams .10 .25
9 Kenny Anderson .12 .30
10 Dell Curry .10 .25
11 Larry Johnson .15 .40
12 Glen Rice .15 .40
13 Michael Jordan 1.25 3.00
14 Toni Kukoc .15 .40
15 Scottie Pippen .25 .60
16 Dennis Rodman .30 .75
17 Terrell Brandon .10 .25
18 Chris Mills .10 .25
19 Bobby Phills .10 .25
20 Bob Sura .10 .25
21 Jim Jackson .10 .25
22 Jason Kidd .25 .60
23 Jamal Mashburn .12 .30
24 George McCloud .10 .25
25 Mahmoud Abdul-Rauf .10 .25
26 Antonio McDyess .15 .40
27 Dikembe Mutombo .15 .40
28 Jalen Rose .12 .30
29 Bryant Stith .10 .25
30 Joe Dumars .15 .40
31 Grant Hill .25 .60
32 Allan Houston .12 .30
33 Theo Ratliff .10 .25
34 Otis Thorpe .10 .25
35 Chris Mullin .15 .40
36 Joe Smith .12 .30
37 Latrell Sprewell .15 .40
38 Kevin Willis .10 .25
39 Sam Cassell .12 .30
40 Clyde Drexler .20 .50
41 Robert Horry .12 .30
42 Hakeem Olajuwon .20 .50
43 Dale Davis .10 .25
44 Mark Jackson .15 .40
45 Derrick McKey .10 .25
46 Reggie Miller .20 .50
47 Rik Smits .12 .30
48 Brent Barry .12 .30
49 Malik Sealy .10 .25
50 Loy Vaught .10 .25
51 Brian Williams .10 .25
52 Elden Campbell .10 .25
53 Cedric Ceballos .10 .25
54 Vlade Divac .15 .40
55 Eddie Jones .15 .40
56 Nick Van Exel .15 .40
57 Tim Hardaway .15 .40
58 Alonzo Mourning .20 .50
59 Kurt Thomas .10 .25
60 Walt Williams .10 .25
61 Vin Baker .12 .30
62 Sherman Douglas .10 .25
63 Glenn Robinson .15 .40
64 Kevin Garnett .40 1.00
65 Tom Gugliotta .10 .25
66 Isaiah Rider .12 .30
67 Shawn Bradley .10 .25
68 Chris Childs .10 .25
69 Armon Gilliam .10 .25
70 Ed O'Bannon .10 .25
71 Patrick Ewing .20 .50
72 Derek Harper .12 .30
73 Anthony Mason .10 .25
74 Charles Oakley .12 .30
75 John Starks .12 .30
76 Nick Anderson .10 .25
77 Horace Grant .12 .30
78 Anfernee Hardaway .25 .60
79 Shaquille O'Neal .40 1.00
80 Dennis Scott .10 .25
81 Derrick Coleman .12 .30
82 Vernon Maxwell .10 .25
83 Jerry Stackhouse .20 .50
84 Clarence Weatherspoon .10 .25
85 Charles Barkley .25 .60
86 Michael Finley .20 .50
87 Kevin Johnson .15 .40
88 Wesley Person .10 .25
89 Clifford Robinson .10 .25
90 Arvydas Sabonis .12 .30
91 Rod Strickland .10 .25
92 Gary Trent .10 .25
93 Tyus Edney .10 .25
94 Brian Grant .12 .30
95 Billy Owens .10 .25
96 Mitch Richmond .15 .40
97 Vinny Del Negro .10 .25
98 Sean Elliott .15 .40
99 Avery Johnson .12 .30
100 David Robinson .25 .60
101 Hersey Hawkins .10 .25
102 Shawn Kemp .15 .40
103 Gary Payton .15 .40
104 Detlef Schrempf .15 .40
105 Oliver Miller .10 .25
106 Tracy Murray .10 .25
107 Damon Stoudamire .15 .40
108 Sharone Wright .10 .25
109 Jeff Hornacek .12 .30
110 Karl Malone .20 .50
111 John Stockton .20 .50
112 Greg Anthony .10 .25
113 Bryant Reeves .10 .25
114 Byron Scott .12 .30
115 Calbert Cheaney .10 .25
116 Juwan Howard .12 .30
117 Gheorghe Muresan .10 .25
118 Rasheed Wallace .20 .50
119 Chris Webber .20 .50
120 Mookie Blaylock HL .10 .25
121 Dino Radja HL .12 .30
122 Larry Johnson HL .15 .40
123 Michael Jordan HL 1.25 3.00
124 Terrell Brandon HL .10 .25
125 Jason Kidd HL .25 .60
126 Antonio McDyess HL .15 .40
127 Grant Hill HL .25 .60
128 Latrell Sprewell HL .15 .40
129 Hakeem Olajuwon HL .20 .50
130 Reggie Miller HL .20 .50
131 Loy Vaught HL .10 .25
132 Cedric Ceballos HL .10 .25
133 Alonzo Mourning HL .20 .50
134 Vin Baker HL .12 .30
135 Isaiah Rider HL .12 .30
136 Armon Gilliam HL .10 .25
137 Patrick Ewing HL .20 .50
138 Shaquille O'Neal HL .40 1.00
139 Jerry Stackhouse HL .20 .50
140 Charles Barkley HL .25 .60
141 Clifford Robinson HL .10 .25
142 Mitch Richmond HL .15 .40
143 David Robinson HL .25 .60
144 Shawn Kemp HL .15 .40
145 Damon Stoudamire HL .15 .40
146 Karl Malone HL .20 .50
147 Bryant Reeves HL .10 .25
148 Juwan Howard HL .12 .30
149 Checklist .10 .25
150 Checklist .10 .25
151 Alan Henderson .10 .25
152 Priest Lauderdale RC .15 .40
153 Dikembe Mutombo .15 .40
154 Dana Barros .10 .25
155 Todd Day .10 .25
156 Brett Szabo RC .15 .40
157 Antoine Walker RC .30 .75
158 Scott Burrell .10 .25
159 Tony Delk RC .15 .40
160 Vlade Divac .15 .40
161 Matt Geiger .10 .25
162 Anthony Mason .10 .25
163 Malik Rose RC .20 .50
164 Ron Harper .12 .30
165 Steve Kerr .12 .30
166 Luc Longley .10 .25
167 Danny Ferry .10 .25
168 Tyrone Hill .10 .25
169 Vitaly Potapenko RC .15 .40
170 Tony Dumas .10 .25
171 Chris Gatling .10 .25
172 Oliver Miller .10 .25
173 Eric Montross .10 .25
174 Samaki Walker RC .15 .40
175 Darvin Ham RC .15 .40
176 Mark Jackson .15 .40
177 Ervin Johnson .10 .25
178 Stacey Augmon .12 .30
179 Joe Dumars .15 .40
180 Grant Hill .25 .60
181 Grant Long .10 .25
182 Terry Mills .10 .25
183 Otis Thorpe .10 .25
184 Jerome Williams RC .15 .40
185 B.J. Armstrong .10 .25
186 Todd Fuller RC .15 .40
187 Ray Owes RC .15 .40
188 Mark Price .15 .40
189 Felton Spencer .10 .25
190 Charles Barkley .25 .60
191 Mario Elie .10 .25
192 Othella Harrington RC .15 .40
193 Matt Maloney RC .15 .40
194 Brent Price .10 .25
195 Kevin Willis .10 .25
196 Travis Best .10 .25
197 Erick Dampier RC .15 .40
198 Antonio Davis .10 .25
199 Jalen Rose .12 .30
200 Pooh Richardson .10 .25
201 Rodney Rogers .10 .25
202 Lorenzen Wright RC .15 .40
203 Kobe Bryant RC 3.00 8.00
204 Derek Fisher RC .30 .75
205 Travis Knight RC .15 .40
206 Shaquille O'Neal .40 1.00
207 Byron Scott .12 .30
208 P.J. Brown .10 .25
209 Sasha Danilovic .10 .25
210 Dan Majerle .15 .40
211 Martin Muursepp RC .15 .40
212 Ray Allen RC .60 1.50
213 Armon Gilliam .10 .25
214 Andrew Lang .10 .25
215 Moochie Norris RC .15 .40
216 Kevin Garnett .40 1.00
217 Tom Gugliotta .10 .25
218 Shane Heal RC .15 .40
219 Stephon Marbury RC .40 1.00
220 Stojko Vrankovic .10 .25

221 Kerry Kittles RC	.15	.40
222 Robert Pack	.10	.25
223 Jayson Williams	.10	.25
224 Allan Houston	.12	.30
225 Larry Johnson	.15	.40
226 Dontae' Jones RC	.15	.40
227 Walter McCarty RC	.15	.40
228 John Wallace RC	.15	.40
229 Charlie Ward	.10	.25
230 Brian Evans RC	.15	.40
231 Amal McCaskill RC	.15	.40
232 Brian Shaw	.10	.25
233 Mark Davis	.10	.25
234 Lucious Harris	.10	.25
235 Allen Iverson RC	.75	2.00
236 Sam Cassell	.12	.30
237 Robert Horry	.12	.30
238 Danny Manning	.12	.30
239 Steve Nash RC	.75	2.00
240 Kenny Anderson	.12	.30
241 Aleksandar Djordjevic RC	.15	.40
242 Jermaine O'Neal RC	.40	1.00
243 Isaiah Rider	.12	.30
244 Rasheed Wallace	.20	.50
245 Mahmoud Abdul-Rauf	.10	.25
246 Michael Smith	.10	.25
247 Corliss Williamson	.10	.25
248 Vernon Maxwell	.10	.25
249 Charles Smith	.10	.25
250 Dominique Wilkins	.20	.50
251 Craig Ehlo	.10	.25
252 Jim McIlvaine	.10	.25
253 Sam Perkins	.10	.25
254 Marcus Camby RC	.25	.60
255 Popeye Jones	.10	.25
256 Donald Whiteside RC	.15	.40
257 Walt Williams	.10	.25
258 Jeff Hornacek	.12	.30
259 Karl Malone	.20	.50
260 Bryon Russell	.10	.25
261 John Stockton	.20	.50
262 Shareef Abdur-Rahim RC	.30	.75
263 Anthony Peeler	.10	.25
264 Roy Rogers RC	.15	.40
265 Tim Legler	.10	.25
266 Tracy Murray	.10	.25
267 Rod Strickland	.10	.25
268 Ben Wallace RC	.75	2.00
269 Kevin Garnett CB	.40	1.00
270 Allan Houston CB	.12	.30
271 Eddie Jones CB	.15	.40
272 Jamal Mashburn CB	.12	.30
273 Antonio McDyess CB	.15	.40
274 Glenn Robinson CB	.15	.40
275 Joe Smith CB	.12	.30
276 Steve Smith CB	.12	.30
277 Jerry Stackhouse CB	.20	.50
278 Damon Stoudamire CB	.15	.40
279 Hakeem Olajuwon AS	.20	.50
280 Charles Barkley AS	.25	.60
281 Patrick Ewing AS	.20	.50
282 Michael Jordan AS	1.25	3.00
283 Clyde Drexler AS	.20	.50
284 Karl Malone AS	.20	.50
285 John Stockton AS	.20	.50
286 David Robinson AS	.25	.60
287 Scottie Pippen AS	.25	.60
288 Shawn Kemp AS	.15	.40
289 Shaquille O'Neal AS	.40	1.00
290 Mitch Richmond AS	.15	.40
291 Reggie Miller AS	.20	.50
292 Alonzo Mourning AS	.20	.50
293 Gary Payton AS	.15	.40
294 Anfernee Hardaway AS	.25	.60
295 Grant Hill AS	.25	.60
296 Dennis Rodman AS	.30	.75
297 Juwan Howard AS	.12	.30
298 Jason Kidd AS	.25	.60
299 Checklist	.10	.25
300 Checklist	.10	.25

1996-97 Fleer Decade of Excellence

Randomly inserted exclusively into both series hobby packs at a rate of one in 72, this 20-card set features reprints from the popular 1986-87 debut Fleer set. Card fronts are designated with the card name "Fleer Decade of Excellence 1986-1996" in gold foil to distinguish the card from the original issue. Card backs are identical to the 1986-87 release, but with a "1996" copyright.

COMPLETE SET (20)	50.00	110.00
COMPLETE SERIES 1 (10)	25.00	60.00
COMPLETE SERIES 2 (10)	25.00	50.00
1 Clyde Drexler	4.00	10.00
2 Joe Dumars	3.00	8.00
3 Derek Harper	2.50	6.00
4 Michael Jordan	12.00	30.00
5 Karl Malone	6.00	15.00
6 Chris Mullin	3.00	8.00
7 Charles Oakley	2.50	6.00
8 Sam Perkins	2.00	5.00
9 Ricky Pierce	2.00	5.00
10 Buck Williams	2.00	5.00
11 Charles Barkley	8.00	20.00
12 Patrick Ewing	4.00	10.00
13 Eddie Johnson	2.00	5.00
14 Hakeem Olajuwon	6.00	15.00
15 Robert Parish	3.00	8.00
16 Byron Scott	2.50	6.00
17 Wayman Tisdale	2.00	5.00
18 Gerald Wilkins	2.00	5.00
19 Herb Williams	2.00	5.00
20 Kevin Willis	2.00	5.00

1996-97 Fleer Franchise Futures

Randomly inserted exclusively into first series hobby packs at a rate of one in 54, this 10-card set features young stars that may be the future of their respecive teams. Card fronts feature an embossed photo with the card name "Franchise Future" running along the left side of the card in silver foil. The player's name is also treated with silver foil at the bottom of the card. Card backs feature a brief commentary on the player and are numbered "X of 10".

COMPLETE SET (10)	6.00	15.00
1 Kevin Garnett	2.50	6.00
2 Anfernee Hardaway	1.50	4.00
3 Grant Hill	1.50	4.00
4 Juwan Howard	.75	2.00
5 Jason Kidd	1.50	4.00
6 Antonio McDyess	1.00	2.50
7 Glenn Robinson	1.00	2.50
8 Joe Smith	.75	2.00
9 Jerry Stackhouse	1.25	3.00
10 Damon Stoudamire	1.00	2.50

1996-97 Fleer Game Breakers

Randomly inserted exclusively into first series retail packs at a rate of one in 48, this 15-card set features some of the top duos from the NBA. The card fronts are made of plastic and feature color action shots of both players represented. Both player's last names are in gold foil at the bottom under the Game Breakers card name. Card backs feature a background of the team's colors with a brief commentary on each individual player and are numbered "X of 15".

COMPLETE SET (15)	75.00	150.00
1 Michael Jordan Scottie Pippen	30.00	80.00
2 Jim Jackson Jason Kidd	6.00	15.00
3 Grant Hill Allan Houston	6.00	15.00
4 Joe Smith Latrell Sprewell	4.00	10.00
5 Clyde Drexler Hakeem Olajuwon	5.00	12.00
6 Cedric Ceballos Nick Van Exel	4.00	10.00
7 Tim Hardaway Alonzo Mourning	5.00	12.00
8 Vin Baker Glenn Robinson	4.00	10.00
9 Kevin Garnett Isaiah Rider	10.00	25.00
10 Anfernee Hardaway Shaquille O'Neal	12.50	30.00
11 Jerry Stackhouse Clarence Weatherspoon	5.00	12.00
12 Charles Barkley Michael Finley	6.00	15.00
13 Sean Elliott David Robinson	6.00	15.00
14 Shawn Kemp Gary Payton	8.00	20.00
15 Karl Malone John Stockton	5.00	12.00

1996-97 Fleer Lucky 13

Randomly inserted into all first series packs at a rate of one in 30, this 13-card set features cards that are redeemable for the top 13 player's selected in the 1996 NBA Draft. Card fronts contain a colorful background with a number from 1-13. Whatever card number is on the front corresponds to the rookie selected at that spot in the 1996 NBA draft and can be redeemed for a special card featuring that player. The expiration date for this redemption is April 1, 1997. Cards are numbered on the back as "X of 13".

COMPLETE SET (13)	25.00	60.00
1 Allen Iverson	6.00	15.00
2 Marcus Camby	2.00	5.00
3 Shareef Abdur-Rahim	2.50	6.00
4 Stephon Marbury	3.00	8.00
5 Ray Allen	5.00	12.00
6 Antoine Walker	2.50	6.00
7 Lorenzen Wright	1.25	3.00
8 Kerry Kittles	1.25	3.00
9 Samaki Walker	1.25	3.00
10 Erick Dampier	1.25	3.00
11 Todd Fuller	1.25	3.00
12 Vitaly Potapenko	1.25	3.00
13 Kobe Bryant	12.00	30.00
NNO Expired Trade Cards	.10	.30

1996-97 Fleer Rookie Rewind

Randomly inserted in all first series packs at a rate of one in 24, this 15-card set takes a look back at the top rookies from the 1995-96 class. Card fronts contain team colors in the background with both the card name "Rookie Rewind" and the player's last name treated in gold foil. Card backs contain another player shot and a brief commentary. Card backs are numbered as "X of 15".

COMPLETE SET (15)	10.00	25.00
1 Brent Barry	1.00	2.50
2 Tyus Edney	.75	2.00
3 Michael Finley	1.50	4.00
4 Kevin Garnett	3.00	8.00
5 Antonio McDyess	1.25	3.00
6 Bryant Reeves	.75	2.00
7 Arvydas Sabonis	1.00	2.50
8 Joe Smith	1.00	2.50
9 Jerry Stackhouse	1.25	3.00
10 Damon Stoudamire	1.25	3.00
11 Bob Sura	.75	2.00
12 Kurt Thomas	.75	2.00
13 Gary Trent	.75	2.00
14 Rasheed Wallace	1.50	4.00
15 Eric Williams	.75	2.00

1996-97 Fleer Rookie Sensations

Randomly inserted into all second series packs at a rate of one in 90, this 15-card set features etched-foil and embossing and focuses on the top rookies from the 1996-97 season.

COMPLETE SET (15)	75.00	150.00
1 Shareef Abdur-Rahim	4.00	10.00
2 Ray Allen	8.00	20.00
3 Kobe Bryant	30.00	80.00
4 Marcus Camby	3.00	8.00
5 Erick Dampier	2.00	5.00
6 Tony Delk	2.00	5.00
7 Allen Iverson	10.00	25.00
8 Kerry Kittles	2.00	5.00
9 Stephon Marbury	6.00	15.00
10 Steve Nash	10.00	25.00
11 Roy Rogers	2.00	5.00
12 Antoine Walker	4.00	10.00
13 Samaki Walker	2.00	5.00
14 John Wallace	2.00	5.00
15 Lorenzen Wright	2.00	5.00

1996-97 Fleer Stackhouse's All-Fleer

Randomly inserted in first series nine-card packs at a rate of one in 12 and one per special first series retail pack, this 12-card set features some of the top player's in the NBA as seen through Fleer Spokesman Jerry Stackhouse's eyes. Card fronts contain team colors in the background and have both the card name and the player's name running vertical in gold foil. Card backs contain a brief statistical summary and are numbered as "X of 12".

COMPLETE SET (12)	6.00	15.00
1 Charles Barkley	.75	2.00
2 Anfernee Hardaway	.75	2.00
3 Grant Hill	.75	2.00
4 Michael Jordan	4.00	10.00
5 Shawn Kemp	.50	1.25
6 Jason Kidd	.75	2.00
7 Karl Malone	.60	1.50
8 Hakeem Olajuwon	.60	1.50
9 Shaquille O'Neal	1.25	3.00
10 Gary Payton	.50	1.25
11 Scottie Pippen	.75	2.00
12 David Robinson	.75	2.00

1996-97 Fleer Stackhouse's Scrapbook

Randomly inserted into all first series packs at a rate of one in 24, cards from this two-card set highlight moments from Stackhouse's rookie year. In addition, they are the last installment to the cross-brand insert from all of the 1995-96 Fleer products.

COMPLETE SET (2)	1.50	4.00
COMMON STACK. (S9-S10)	1.00	2.50

1996-97 Fleer Swing Shift

Randomly inserted into all second series packs at a rate of one in 6, this 15-card set focuses on players who can not only play well from the outside, but who can also post up down low. Card fronts feature a "shattered" glass colored background.

COMPLETE SET (15)	5.00	12.00
1 Ray Allen	1.00	2.50
2 Charles Barkley	.60	1.50
3 Michael Finley	.60	1.50
4 Anfernee Hardaway	.75	2.00
5 Grant Hill	.75	2.00
6 Jim Jackson	.30	.75
7 Eddie Jones	.25	.60
8 Kerry Kittles	.60	1.50
9 Reggie Miller	.60	1.50
10 Gary Payton	.50	1.25
11 Scottie Pippen	.75	2.00
12 Mitch Richmond	.50	1.25
13 Steve Smith	.40	1.00
14 Latrell Sprewell	.50	1.25
15 Jerry Stackhouse	.60	1.50

1996-97 Fleer Thrill Seekers

Randomly inserted into second series hobby packs only at a rate of one in 240, this 15-card set uses Lenticular technology and showcases NBA players who know how to "thrill" NBA fans.

COMPLETE SET (15)	800.00	1300.00
1 Shareef Abdur-Rahim	15.00	40.00
2 Charles Barkley	40.00	100.00
3 Anfernee Hardaway	40.00	100.00
4 Grant Hill	40.00	100.00
5 Allen Iverson	40.00	100.00
6 Michael Jordan	350.00	650.00
7 Shawn Kemp	30.00	80.00
8 Jason Kidd	30.00	80.00
9 Stephon Marbury	20.00	50.00
10 Antonio McDyess	20.00	50.00
11 Reggie Miller	30.00	80.00
12 Alonzo Mourning	50.00	120.00
13 Shaquille O'Neal	50.00	125.00
14 David Robinson	30.00	80.00
15 Damon Stoudamire	20.00	50.00

1996-97 Fleer Total O

Randomly inserted into second series retail packs only at a rate of one in 44, this 10-card set features NBA players known for their offensive ability. Cards are printed on clear plastic stock and card fronts feature half of a colorful basketball in the background.

COMPLETE SET (10)	40.00	80.00
1 Anfernee Hardaway	5.00	12.00
2 Grant Hill	5.00	12.00
3 Juwan Howard	2.50	6.00
4 Michael Jordan	25.00	60.00
5 Shawn Kemp	3.00	8.00
6 Karl Malone	4.00	10.00
7 Alonzo Mourning	4.00	10.00
8 Hakeem Olajuwon	4.00	10.00
9 Shaquille O'Neal	8.00	20.00
10 Jerry Stackhouse	4.00	10.00

1996-97 Fleer Towers of Power

Randomly inserted into all second series packs at a rate of one in 30, this 10-card set focuses on the dominent men of the NBA. Card fronts feature etched foil.

COMPLETE SET (10)	15.00	30.00
1 Shareef Abdur-Rahim	1.50	4.00
2 Marcus Camby	1.25	3.00
3 Patrick Ewing	2.00	5.00
4 Kevin Garnett	4.00	10.00
5 Shawn Kemp	1.50	4.00
6 Hakeem Olajuwon	2.00	5.00
7 Shaquille O'Neal	4.00	10.00
8 David Robinson	2.50	6.00
9 Dennis Rodman	3.00	8.00
10 Joe Smith	1.25	3.00

1997-98 Fleer

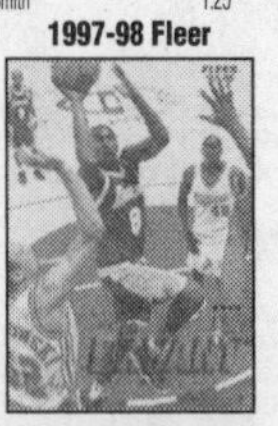

This 350-card set was released in two series with 10-card packs that carried a suggested retail price of $1.49 and $1.59. The cards carry a Textured Legend matte finish that makes the cards idea for autographs. The cards feature full-bleed action photos with the player's name appearing in gold foil block type at the bottom. The player's team and position are in gold foil script below the name. The backs carry career statistics.

COMPLETE SET (350)	20.00	40.00
COMPLETE SERIES 1 (200)	10.00	20.00
COMPLETE SERIES 2 (150)	10.00	20.00
1 Anfernee Hardaway	.25	.60
2 Mitch Richmond	.15	.40
3 Allen Iverson	.30	.75
4 Chris Webber	.15	.40
5 Sasha Danilovic	.10	.25
6 Avery Johnson	.12	.30
7 Kenny Anderson	.12	.30
8 Antoine Walker	.15	.40
9 Nick Van Exel	.12	.30
10 Mookie Blaylock	.10	.25
11 Wesley Person	.10	.25
12 Vlade Divac	.15	.40
13 Glenn Robinson	.12	.30
14 Chris Mills	.10	.25
15 Latrell Sprewell	.15	.40
16 Jayson Williams	.10	.25
17 Travis Best	.10	.25
18 Charlie Ward	.10	.25
19 Theo Ratliff	.12	.30
20 Gary Payton	.15	.40
21 Marcus Camby	.15	.40
22 Clyde Drexler	.20	.50
23 Michael Jordan	1.25	3.00
24 Antonio McDyess	.12	.30
25 Stephon Marbury	.20	.50
26 Isaac Austin	.10	.25
27 Shareef Abdur-Rahim	.15	.40
28 Malik Sealy	.10	.25
29 Arvydas Sabonis	.12	.30
30 Kerry Kittles	.10	.25
31 Reggie Miller	.20	.50
32 Karl Malone	.20	.50
33 Grant Hill	.25	.60
34 Hakeem Olajuwon	.20	.50
35 Danny Ferry	.10	.25
36 Dominique Wilkins	.20	.50
37 Armon Gilliam	.10	.25
38 Danny Manning	.12	.30
39 Larry Johnson	.15	.40
40 Dino Radja	.12	.30
41 Jason Caffey	.10	.25
42 Jerry Stackhouse	.15	.40
43 Alonzo Mourning	.20	.50
44 Shawn Bradley	.10	.25
45 Bo Outlaw	.10	.25
46 Bryon Russell	.10	.25
47 Doug West	.10	.25
48 Lawrence Moten	.10	.25
49 Dale Ellis	.10	.25
50 Kobe Bryant	.75	2.00
51 Carlos Rogers	.10	.25
52 Todd Fuller	.10	.25
53 Tyus Edney	.10	.25
54 Horace Grant	.12	.30
55 Dikembe Mutombo	.15	.40
56 Jim McIlvaine	.10	.25
57 Harvey Grant	.10	.25
58 Dean Garrett	.10	.25
59 Samaki Walker	.10	.25
60 Johnny Newman	.10	.25
61 Antonio Davis	.10	.25
62 Jamal Mashburn	.12	.30
63 Muggsy Bogues	.12	.30
64 Rod Strickland	.10	.25
65 Craig Ehlo	.10	.25
66 Rex Walters	.10	.25
67 Bob Sura	.10	.25
68 Travis Knight	.10	.25
69 Toni Kukoc	.15	.40
70 Antoine Carr	.10	.25
71 Mario Elie	.10	.25
72 Popeye Jones	.10	.25
73 David Wesley	.10	.25
74 John Wallace	.10	.25
75 Calbert Cheaney	.10	.25
76 Grant Long	.10	.25
77 Will Perdue	.10	.25
78 Rasheed Wallace	.15	.40
79 Chris Gatling	.10	.25
80 Corliss Williamson	.10	.25
81 B.J. Armstrong	.10	.25
82 Brian Shaw	.10	.25
83 Darrick Martin	.10	.25
84 Vinny Del Negro	.10	.25
85 Tony Delk	.10	.25
86 Greg Anthony	.10	.25
87 Mark Davis	.10	.25
88 Anthony Goldwire	.10	.25
89 Rex Chapman	.10	.25
90 Stojko Vrankovic	.10	.25
91 Dennis Rodman	.30	.75
92 Detlef Schrempf	.15	.40
93 Henry James	.10	.25
94 Tracy Murray	.10	.25
95 Voshon Lenard	.10	.25
96 Sharone Wright	.10	.25
97 Ed O'Bannon	.10	.25
98 Gerald Wilkins	.10	.25
99 Kevin Willis	.10	.25
100 Shaquille O'Neal	.40	1.00
101 Jim Jackson	.10	.25
102 Mark Price	.15	.40
103 Patrick Ewing	.20	.50
104 Lorenzen Wright	.10	.25
105 Tyrone Hill	.10	.25
106 Ray Allen	.20	.50
107 Jermaine O'Neal	.20	.50
108 Anthony Mason	.10	.25
109 Mahmoud Abdul-Rauf	.10	.25
110 Terry Mills	.10	.25
111 Gheorghe Muresan	.10	.25
112 Mark Jackson	.15	.40
113 Greg Ostertag	.10	.25
114 Kevin Johnson	.15	.40
115 Anthony Peeler	.10	.25
116 Rony Seikaly	.12	.30
117 Keith Askins	.10	.25
118 Todd Day	.10	.25
119 Chris Childs	.10	.25
120 Chris Carr	.10	.25
121 Erick Strickland RC	.15	.40
122 Elden Campbell	.10	.25
123 Elliot Perry	.10	.25
124 Pooh Richardson	.10	.25
125 Juwan Howard	.12	.30
126 Ervin Johnson	.10	.25
127 Eric Montross	.10	.25
128 Otis Thorpe	.10	.25
129 Hersey Hawkins	.10	.25
130 Bimbo Coles	.10	.25
131 Olden Polynice	.10	.25
132 Christian Laettner	.12	.30
133 Sean Elliott	.15	.40
134 Othella Harrington	.10	.25
135 Erick Dampier	.10	.25
136 Vitaly Potapenko	.10	.25
137 Doug Christie	.10	.25
138 Luc Longley	.10	.25
139 Clarence Weatherspoon	.10	.25
140 Gary Trent	.10	.25
141 Shandon Anderson	.10	.25
142 Sam Perkins	.10	.25
143 Derek Harper	.12	.30
144 Robert Horry	.12	.30
145 Roy Rogers	.10	.25
146 John Starks	.12	.30
147 Tyrone Corbin	.10	.25
148 Andrew Lang	.10	.25
149 Derek Strong	.10	.25
150 Joe Smith	.12	.30
151 Ron Harper	.12	.30
152 Sam Cassell	.12	.30
153 Brent Barry	.12	.30
154 LaPhonso Ellis	.10	.25
155 Matt Geiger	.10	.25
156 Steve Nash	.30	.75
157 Michael Smith	.10	.25
158 Eric Williams	.10	.25
159 Tom Gugliotta	.10	.25
160 Monty Williams	.10	.25
161 Lindsey Hunter	.10	.25
162 Oliver Miller	.10	.25
163 Brent Price	.10	.25
164 Derrick McKey	.10	.25
165 Robert Pack	.10	.25
166 Derrick Coleman	.12	.30
167 Isaiah Rider	.10	.25
168 Dan Majerle	.15	.40
169 Jeff Hornacek	.12	.30
170 Terrell Brandon	.10	.25
171 Nate McMillan	.10	.25
172 Cedric Ceballos	.10	.25
173 Derek Fisher	.15	.40
174 Rodney Rogers	.10	.25
175 Blue Edwards	.10	.25
176 Brooks Thompson	.10	.25
177 Sherman Douglas	.10	.25
178 Sam Mitchell	.10	.25
179 Charles Oakley	.12	.30
180 Greg Minor	.10	.25
181 Chris Mullin	.15	.40
182 P.J. Brown	.10	.25
183 Stacey Augmon	.12	.30
184 Don MacLean	.10	.25
185 Aaron McKie	.10	.25
186 Dale Davis	.10	.25
187 Vernon Maxwell	.10	.25
188 Dell Curry	.10	.25
189 Kendall Gill	.10	.25
190 Billy Owens	.10	.25
191 Steve Kerr	.12	.30
192 Matt Maloney	.10	.25
193 Dennis Scott	.10	.25
194 A.C. Green	.15	.40
195 George McCloud	.10	.25
196 Walt Williams	.10	.25
197 Eldridge Recasner	.10	.25
198 Checklist (Hawks/Bucks)	.10	.25
199 Checklist (T'wolves/Wizards)	.10	.25
200 Checklist (inserts)	.10	.25
201 Tim Duncan RC	1.00	2.50
202 Tim Thomas RC	.30	.75
203 Clifford Rozier	.10	.25
204 Bryant Reeves	.10	.25
205 Glen Rice	.15	.40
206 Darrell Armstrong	.10	.25
207 Juwan Howard	.12	.30
208 John Stockton	.20	.50
209 Antonio McDyess	.12	.30
210 James Cotton RC	.15	.40
211 Brian Grant	.10	.25
212 Chris Whitney	.10	.25
213 Antonio Davis	.10	.25
214 Kendall Gill	.10	.25
215 Adonal Foyle RC	.15	.40
216 Dean Garrett	.10	.25
217 Dennis Scott	.10	.25
218 Zydrunas Ilgauskas	.15	.40
219 Antonio Daniels RC	.15	.40
220 Derek Harper	.12	.30
221 Travis Knight	.10	.25
222 Bobby Hurley	.15	.40
223 Greg Anderson	.10	.25
224 Rod Strickland	.10	.25
225 David Benoit	.10	.25
226 Tracy McGrady RC	.75	2.00
227 Brian Williams	.10	.25
228 James Robinson	.10	.25
229 Randy Brown	.10	.25
230 Greg Foster	.10	.25
231 Reggie Miller	.20	.50
232 Eric Montross	.10	.25
233 Malik Rose	.10	.25
234 Charles Barkley	.25	.60
235 Tony Battie RC	.20	.50
236 Terry Mills	.10	.25
237 Jerald Honeycutt RC	.15	.40
238 Bubba Wells RC	.15	.40
239 John Wallace	.10	.25
240 Jason Kidd	.25	.60
241 Mark Price	.15	.40
242 Ron Mercer RC	.20	.50
243 Derrick Coleman	.12	.30
244 Fred Hoiberg	.10	.25
245 Wesley Person	.10	.25
246 Eddie Jones	.15	.40
247 Allan Houston	.12	.30
248 Keith Van Horn RC	.30	.75
249 Johnny Newman	.10	.25
250 Kevin Garnett	.30	.75
251 Latrell Sprewell	.15	.40
252 Tracy Murray	.10	.25
253 Charles O'Bannon RC	.15	.40
254 Lamond Murray	.10	.25
255 Jerry Stackhouse	.15	.40
256 Rik Smits	.12	.30
257 Alan Henderson	.10	.25
258 Tariq Abdul-Wahad RC	.15	.40
259 Nick Anderson	.10	.25
260 Calbert Cheaney	.10	.25
261 Scottie Pippen	.25	.60
262 Rodrick Rhodes RC	.15	.40
263 Derek Anderson RC	.15	.40
264 Dana Barros	.10	.25
265 Todd Day	.10	.25
266 Michael Finley	.15	.40
267 Kevin Edwards	.10	.25
268 Terrell Brandon	.10	.25
269 Bobby Phills	.10	.25
270 Kelvin Cato RC	.15	.40
271 Vin Baker	.12	.30
272 Eric Washington RC	.15	.40
273 Jim Jackson	.10	.25
274 Joe Dumars	.15	.40
275 David Robinson	.25	.60
276 Jayson Williams	.10	.25
277 Travis Best	.10	.25
278 Kurt Thomas	.10	.25
279 Otis Thorpe	.10	.25
280 Damon Stoudamire	.15	.40
281 John Williams	.10	.25
282 Loy Vaught	.10	.25
283 Bo Outlaw	.10	.25
284 Todd Fuller	.10	.25
285 Terry Dehere	.10	.25
286 Clarence Weatherspoon	.10	.25
287 Danny Fortson RC	.15	.40
288 Howard Eisley	.10	.25
289 Steve Smith	.12	.30
290 Chris Webber	.15	.40
291 Shawn Kemp	.15	.40
292 Sam Cassell	.12	.30
293 Rick Fox	.10	
294 Walter McCarty	.10	
295 Mark Jackson	.15	
296 Chris Mills	.10	
297 Jacque Vaughn RC	.15	
298 Shawn Respert	.10	
299 Scott Burrell	.10	
300 Allen Iverson	.30	
301 Charles Smith RC	.15	
302 Ervin Johnson	.10	
303 Hubert Davis	.10	
304 Eddie Johnson	.10	
305 Erick Dampier	.10	
306 Eric Williams	.10	
307 Anthony Johnson RC	.15	
308 David Wesley	.10	
309 Eric Piatkowski	.12	
310 Austin Croshere RC	.15	
311 Malik Sealy	.10	
312 George McCloud	.10	
313 Anthony Parker RC	.15	
314 Cedric Henderson RC	.15	
315 John Thomas RC	.15	
316 Cory Alexander	.10	
317 Johnny Taylor RC	.15	
318 Chris Mullin	.15	
319 J.R. Reid	.10	
320 George Lynch	.10	
321 Lawrence Funderburke RC	.15	
322 God Shammgod RC	.15	
323 Bobby Jackson RC	.20	
324 Khalid Reeves	.10	
325 Zan Tabak	.10	
326 Chris Gatling	.10	
327 Alvin Williams RC	.15	
328 Scot Pollard RC	.15	
329 Kerry Kittles	.10	
330 Tim Hardaway	.15	
331 Maurice Taylor RC	.15	
332 Keith Booth RC	.15	
333 Chris Morris	.10	
334 Bryant Stith	.10	
335 Terry Cummings	.15	
336 Ed Gray RC	.15	
337 Eric Snow	.10	
338 Clifford Robinson	.10	
339 Chris Dudley	.10	
340 Chauncey Billups RC	.60	
341 Paul Grant RC	.15	
342 Tyrone Hill	.10	
343 Joe Smith	.12	
344 Sean Rooks	.10	
345 Harvey Grant	.10	
346 Dale Davis	.10	
347 Brevin Knight RC	.15	
348 Serge Zwikker RC	.15	
349 Checklist (Hawks/Kings)	.10	
350 Checklist (Spurs/Wizards/Inserts)	.10	

1997-98 Fleer Crystal Collection

This set is a hobby only parallel to the 345 basic from the first series (excluding the checklists fro series). These cards were randomly inserted into at a rate of 1:2 and feature a glossy card stock w coating and silver foil rather than the matte finis ascertain values for individual cards, refer to the multiplier in the header coupled with the regular value.

*STARS: 1.5X TO 4X BASE CARD HI

*RCs: 1.25X TO 3X BASE HI

23 Michael Jordan	6.00

1997-98 Fleer Tiffany Collection

This hobby only set is a parallel to the 345 basic (excluding checklists) from both series. These c were randomly inserted into packs at a rate of 1: feature a glossy card stock with holographic foil than the matte finish. To ascertain values on ind cards, please refer to the multiplier in the header below, coupled with the value of the base card.

*STARS: 10X TO 25X BASE CARD HI

*RCs: 5X TO 12X BASE HI

23 Michael Jordan	50.00

1997-98 Fleer Decade of Excellence

Randomly inserted in series one hobby packs o rate of one in 36, this 12-card set showcases pl that have been in the NBA for 10 or more years photos from the 1987-88 season and graphic de showcasing the 1987-88 Fleer basketball desig

*RARE TRAD: 1.5X TO 4X HI COLUMN

RARE TRAD: SER.1 STATED ODDS 1:360 HOB

1 Charles Barkley	5.00
2 Clyde Drexler	4.00
3 Patrick Ewing	4.00
4 Kevin Johnson	3.00
5 Michael Jordan	15.00
6 Karl Malone	4.00
7 Reggie Miller	4.00
8 Hakeem Olajuwon	4.00
9 Scottie Pippen	5.00
10 Dennis Rodman	6.00
11 John Stockton	4.00
12 Dominique Wilkins	4.00

1997-98 Fleer Flair Hardwood Leaders

Randomly inserted in all series one packs at a r one in six, this 29-card set features the heavier

ated with the Flair brand. One player or "leader" ach team is depicted in the set.

'LETE SET (29)	15.00	40.00
stian Laettner	.50	1.25
ine Walker	.60	1.50
Rice	.60	1.50
nael Jordan	5.00	12.00
ll Brandon	.40	1.00
nael Finley	.60	1.50
nio McDyess	.50	1.25
t Hill	1.00	2.50
ll Sprewell	.60	1.50
keem Olajuwon	.75	2.00
ggie Miller	.75	2.00
Vaught	.40	1.00
aquille O'Neal	1.50	4.00
nzo Mourning	.75	2.00
Baker	.50	1.25
vin Garnett	1.25	3.00
ry Kittles	.40	1.00
rick Ewing	.75	2.00
ernee Hardaway	1.00	2.50
ry Stackhouse	.60	1.50
on Kidd	1.00	2.50
nny Anderson	.50	1.25
ch Richmond	.60	1.50
vid Robinson	1.00	2.50
awn Kemp	.60	1.50
mon Stoudamire	.60	1.50
Malone	.75	2.00
areef Abdur-Rahim	.60	1.50
ris Webber	.60	1.50

1997-98 Fleer Franchise Futures

nly inserted in series one retail packs only at a one in 36, this 10-card set focuses on players to three years experience who are their team's The cards feature a die cut design with a full foil front.

LETE SET (10)	8.00	20.00
eef Abdur-Rahim	1.00	2.50
Allen	1.25	3.00
Bryant	8.00	20.00
Garnett	2.00	5.00
Hill	1.50	4.00
n Howard	.75	2.00
Iverson	2.00	5.00
Kittles	.60	1.50
Smith	.75	2.00
non Stoudamire	1.00	2.50

97-98 Fleer Game Breakers

nly inserted in all series one packs at a rate of 288, this 12-card dual player set features some NBA's best duos. Card fronts carry etched-foil.

ael Jordan	50.00	125.00
is Rodman		
Dumars	10.00	25.00
Hill		
Smith	6.00	15.00
ll Sprewell		
es Barkley	10.00	25.00
em Olajuwon		
Jones	15.00	40.00
uille O'Neal		
Garnett	12.50	30.00
on Marbury		
Anderson	8.00	20.00
nee Hardaway		
Iverson	10.00	25.00
Stackhouse		
n Kemp	10.00	25.00
Payton		
cus Camby	6.00	15.00
n Stoudamire		
Malone	8.00	20.00
Stockton		
n Howard	8.00	20.00
Webber		

97-98 Fleer Goudey Greats

nly inserted into series two packs at a rate of our, this 15-card set features some of today's in the Goudey card style from yesteryear e with commentary from NBA Hall of Famer ny" Archibald.

ETE SET (15)	4.00	10.00
llen	.50	1.25
Drexler	.50	1.25
k Ewing	.50	1.25
nee Hardaway	.60	1.50
Hill	.60	1.50
on Marbury	.50	1.25
o Mourning	.50	1.25
ille O'Neal	1.00	2.50

9 Gary Payton	.40	1.00
10 Scottie Pippen	.60	1.50
11 David Robinson	.60	1.50
12 Joe Smith	.30	.75
13 John Stockton	.50	1.25
14 Damon Stoudamire	.40	1.00
15 Antoine Walker	.40	1.00

1997-98 Fleer Key Ingredients

Randomly inserted in series one retail packs only at a rate of one in two, this 15-card set features players who are the "key" to their teams' success..

COMPLETE SET (15)	2.50	6.00
*GOLD: 2.5X TO 6X KEY INGRED. HI		
GOLD: SER.1 STATED ODDS 1:18 HOB/RET		
1 Charles Barkley	.40	1.00
2 Marcus Camby	.25	.60
3 Anfernee Hardaway	.40	1.00
4 Juwan Howard	.20	.50
5 Shawn Kemp	.25	.60
6 Karl Malone	.30	.75
7 Stephon Marbury	.30	.75
8 Alonzo Mourning	.30	.75
9 Shaquille O'Neal	.60	1.50
10 Scottie Pippen	.40	1.00
11 Mitch Richmond	.25	.60
12 David Robinson	.40	1.00
13 Joe Smith	.20	.50
14 Jerry Stackhouse	.25	.60
15 Antoine Walker	.25	.60

1997-98 Fleer Million Dollar Moments

These cards were inserted one per pack in all 1997-98 Fleer basketball products. The set contains 50 cards. If a collector put together the complete set, they could win the Grand Prize of $1,000,000. The game ended on August 31, 1998. Cards numbered 46-50 originally were the tougher cards to pull, but were available at the more common level after the game ended.

COMPLETE SET (50)	2.50	6.00
1 Checklist (1-50)	.05	.15
2 Mark Jackson	.10	.25
3 Charles Barkley	.15	.40
4 Terrell Brandon	.05	.15
5 Wayman Tisdale	.05	.15
6 Clyde Drexler	.12	.30
7 Patrick Ewing	.12	.30
8 Kevin Garnett	.20	.50
9 Tom Gugliotta	.05	.15
10 Anfernee Hardaway	.15	.40
11 Tim Hardaway	.10	.25
12 Grant Hill	.15	.40
13 Allen Iverson	.20	.50
14 Shawn Kemp	.10	.25
15 Jason Kidd	.15	.40
16 Charles Oakley	.07	.20
17 Karl Malone	.12	.30
18 Alonzo Mourning	.12	.30
19 Shaquille O'Neal	.25	.60
20 Hakeem Olajuwon	.12	.30
21 Chris Webber	.10	.25
22 Scottie Pippen	.15	.40
23 Glen Rice	.10	.25
24 Mitch Richmond	.10	.25
25 David Robinson	.15	.40
26 Dennis Rodman	.20	.50
27 Jerry Stackhouse	.10	.25
28 John Stockton	.12	.30
29 Mookie Blaylock	.05	.15
30 Muggsy Bogues	.07	.20
31 Kobe Bryant	.50	1.25
32 Rex Chapman	.05	.15
33 Joe Dumars	.10	.25
34 Dale Ellis	.05	.15
35 Horace Grant	.07	.20
36 Jeff Hornacek	.07	.20
37 Damon Stoudamire	.10	.25
38 Kevin Johnson	.10	.25
39 Larry Johnson	.10	.25
40 Toni Kukoc	.10	.25
41 Danny Manning	.07	.20
42 Stephon Marbury	.12	.30
43 Reggie Miller	.12	.30
44 Chris Mullin	.10	.25
45 Dikembe Mutombo	.10	.25
46 Gary Payton	.10	.25
47 Christian Laettner	.07	.20
48 Glenn Robinson	.07	.20
49 Nick Van Exel	.07	.20
50 Marcus Camby	.10	.25

1997-98 Fleer Rookie Rewind

Randomly inserted in all series one packs at a rate of one in four, this 10-card set takes a look back at some of the best rookies from the 1996-97 season.

COMPLETE SET (10)	5.00	12.00
1 Shareef Abdur-Rahim	.60	1.50
2 Ray Allen	.75	2.00
3 Kobe Bryant	3.00	8.00
4 Marcus Camby	.60	1.50
5 Allen Iverson	1.25	3.00
6 Kerry Kittles	.40	1.00
7 Matt Maloney	.40	1.00
8 Stephon Marbury	.75	2.00
9 Roy Rogers	.40	1.00
10 Antoine Walker	.60	1.50

1997-98 Fleer Rookie Sensations

Randomly inserted into series two packs at a rate of one in eight, this 10-card set features color photos of some of the top rookies from the 1997 class.

COMPLETE SET (10)	4.00	10.00
1 Derek Anderson	.30	.75
2 Tony Battie	.40	1.00
3 Chauncey Billups	1.25	3.00
4 Austin Croshere	.30	.75
5 Antonio Daniels	.30	.75
6 Tim Duncan	2.00	5.00
7 Tracy McGrady	1.50	4.00
8 Ron Mercer	.40	1.00
9 Tim Thomas	.60	1.50
10 Keith Van Horn	.60	1.50

1997-98 Fleer Soaring Stars

Randomly inserted into series two retail packs at a rate of 1:2, this 20-card set showcases players who make headlines for their teams.

COMPLETE SET (20)	6.00	15.00
*HIGH STARS: 1.5X TO 4X SOARING HI		
HIGH FLY: SER.2 STATED ODDS 1:24 H/R		
1 Shareef Abdur-Rahim	.40	1.00
2 Ray Allen	.50	1.25
3 Charles Barkley	.60	1.50
4 Kobe Bryant	2.00	5.00
5 Marcus Camby	.40	1.00
6 Kevin Garnett	.75	2.00
7 Tim Hardaway	.40	1.00
8 Eddie Jones	.40	1.00
9 Michael Jordan	3.00	8.00
10 Shawn Kemp	.40	1.00
11 Jason Kidd	.60	1.50
12 Kerry Kittles	.25	.60
13 Karl Malone	.50	1.25
14 Antonio McDyess	.30	.75
15 Glen Rice	.40	1.00
16 Mitch Richmond	.40	1.00
17 Latrell Sprewell	.40	1.00
18 Jerry Stackhouse	.40	1.00
19 Antoine Walker	.40	1.00
20 Chris Webber	.40	1.00

1997-98 Fleer Thrill Seekers

Randomly inserted into series two packs at a rate of one in 288, this 10-card set highlights some of the NBA's ultimate crowd pleasers. The cards feature matte finish frames and 100% etched silver holofoil background and spot UV coating.

1 Shareef Abdur-Rahim	6.00	15.00
2 Kobe Bryant	40.00	100.00
3 Tim Duncan	20.00	50.00
4 Anfernee Hardaway	10.00	25.00
5 Grant Hill	12.00	30.00
6 Allen Iverson	12.00	30.00
7 Michael Jordan	100.00	200.00
8 Stephon Marbury	8.00	20.00
9 Dennis Rodman	15.00	40.00
10 Joe Smith	5.00	12.00

1997-98 Fleer Total O

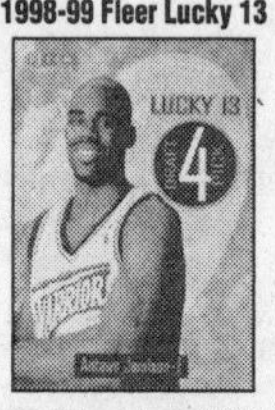

Randomly inserted into series two retail packs only at a rate of one in 18, this 10-card set focuses on key offensive players.

COMPLETE SET (10)	12.00	30.00
1 Anfernee Hardaway	1.50	4.00
2 Grant Hill	1.50	4.00
3 Juwan Howard	.75	2.00
4 Allen Iverson	2.00	5.00
5 Michael Jordan	8.00	20.00
6 Karl Malone	1.25	3.00
7 Stephon Marbury	1.25	3.00
8 Hakeem Olajuwon	1.25	3.00
9 Shaquille O'Neal	2.50	6.00
10 Damon Stoudamire	1.00	2.50

1997-98 Fleer Towers of Power

Randomly inserted into series two packs at a rate of one in 18, this 12-card set features some of the NBA's most dominate big men. Cards feature a die cut design.

COMPLETE SET (12)	12.00	30.00
1 Shareef Abdur-Rahim	1.25	3.00
2 Marcus Camby	1.25	3.00
3 Patrick Ewing	1.50	4.00
4 Kevin Garnett	2.50	6.00
5 Shawn Kemp	1.25	3.00
6 Karl Malone	1.50	4.00
7 Hakeem Olajuwon	1.50	4.00
8 Shaquille O'Neal	3.00	8.00
9 Dennis Rodman	2.50	6.00
10 Joe Smith	1.00	2.50
11 Antoine Walker	1.25	3.00
12 Chris Webber	1.25	3.00

1997-98 Fleer Zone

Randomly inserted into series two hobby packs only at a rate of one in 36, this 15-card set focuses on players known for getting into a "zone" during a game. Card design includes silver rainbow holofoil and a 100% etched foil background.

1 Shareef Abdur-Rahim	2.00	5.00
2 Kobe Bryant	10.00	25.00
3 Marcus Camby	2.00	5.00
4 Tim Duncan	6.00	15.00
5 Kevin Garnett	4.00	10.00
6 Anfernee Hardaway	3.00	8.00
7 Grant Hill	3.00	8.00
8 Juwan Howard	1.50	4.00
9 Allen Iverson	4.00	10.00
10 Michael Jordan	20.00	50.00
11 Hakeem Olajuwon	2.50	6.00
12 Gary Payton	2.00	5.00
13 Scottie Pippen	3.00	8.00
14 Glen Rice	2.00	5.00
15 Keith Van Horn	2.00	5.00

1998-99 Fleer

The 1998-99 Fleer set, which is also known as Fleer Tradition, was issued in one series with a total of 150 cards. The packs were issued with 10 cards per pack carrying a suggested retail price of $1.59. The set contains the topical subset: Plus Factor (133-147).

COMPLETE SET (150)	10.00	20.00
1 Kobe Bryant	.75	2.00
2 Corliss Williamson	.10	.25
3 Allen Iverson	.30	.75
4 Michael Finley	.15	.40
5 Juwan Howard	.12	.30
6 Marcus Camby	.12	.30
7 Toni Kukoc	.15	.40
8 Antoine Walker	.15	.40
9 Stephon Marbury	.20	.50
10 Tim Hardaway	.15	.40
11 Zydrunas Ilgauskas	.15	.40
12 John Stockton	.20	.50
13 Glenn Robinson	.12	.30
14 Isaiah Rider	.10	.25
15 Danny Fortson	.10	.25
16 Donyell Marshall	.10	.25
17 Chris Mullin	.15	.40
18 Shareef Abdur-Rahim	.15	.40
19 Bobby Phills	.10	.25
20 Gary Payton	.15	.40
21 Derrick Coleman	.12	.30
22 Larry Johnson	.15	.40
23 Michael Jordan	1.25	3.00
24 Danny Manning	.12	.30
25 Nick Anderson	.10	.25
26 Chris Gatling	.10	.25
27 Steve Smith	.12	.30
28 Chris Whitney	.10	.25
29 Terrell Brandon	.10	.25
30 Rasheed Wallace	.15	.40
31 Reggie Miller	.20	.50
32 Karl Malone	.20	.50
33 Grant Hill	.25	.60
34 Hakeem Olajuwon	.20	.50
35 Erick Dampier	.10	.25
36 Vin Baker	.12	.30
37 Tim Thomas	.15	.40
38 Mark Price	.15	.40
39 Shawn Bradley	.10	.25
40 Calbert Cheaney	.10	.25
41 Glen Rice	.15	.40
42 Kevin Willis	.10	.25
43 Chris Carr	.10	.25
44 Keith Van Horn	.15	.40
45 Jamal Mashburn	.12	.30
46 Eddie Jones	.15	.40
47 Brevin Knight	.10	.25
48 Olden Polynice	.10	.25
49 Bobby Jackson	.12	.30
50 David Robinson	.25	.60
51 Patrick Ewing	.20	.50
52 Samaki Walker	.10	.25
53 Antonio Daniels	.10	.25
54 Rodney Rogers	.10	.25
55 Dikembe Mutombo	.15	.40
56 Tracy McGrady	.25	.60
57 Walt Williams	.10	.25
58 Walter McCarty	.10	.25
59 Detlef Schrempf	.15	.40
60 Ervin Johnson	.10	.25
61 Michael Smith	.10	.25
62 Clifford Robinson	.10	.25
63 Brian Williams	.10	.25
64 Shandon Anderson	.10	.25
65 P.J. Brown	.10	.25
66 Scottie Pippen	.25	.60
67 Anthony Peeler	.10	.25
68 Tony Delk	.10	.25
69 David Wesley	.10	.25
70 John Starks	.12	.30
71 Nick Van Exel	.12	.30
72 Kerry Kittles	.10	.25
73 Tony Battie	.12	.30
74 Lamond Murray	.10	.25
75 Anfernee Hardaway	.25	.60
76 Jalen Rose	.12	.30
77 Derek Anderson	.10	.25
78 Avery Johnson	.12	.30
79 Michael Stewart	.10	.25
80 Brian Shaw	.10	.25
81 Chauncey Billups	.20	.50
82 Kenny Anderson	.12	.30
83 Bryon Russell	.10	.25
84 Jason Kidd	.25	.60
85 Tyrone Hill	.10	.25
86 Jim McIlvaine	.10	.25
87 Brian Grant	.10	.25
88 Bryant Stith	.10	.25
89 Brent Price	.10	.25
90 John Wallace	.10	.25
91 Dennis Rodman	.30	.75
92 Alonzo Mourning	.20	.50
93 Bimbo Coles	.10	.25
94 Chris Anstey	.10	.25
95 Lindsey Hunter	.10	.25
96 Ed Gray	.10	.25
97 Chris Mills	.10	.25
98 Rick Fox	.10	.25
99 Lorenzen Wright	.10	.25
100 Kevin Garnett	.30	.75
101 Shawn Kemp	.15	.40
102 Mark Jackson	.15	.40
103 Sam Cassell	.12	.30
104 Monty Williams	.10	.25
105 Ron Mercer	.12	.30
106 Bryant Reeves	.10	.25
107 Tracy Murray	.10	.25
108 Ray Allen	.20	.50
109 Maurice Taylor	.10	.25
110 Jerome Williams	.10	.25
111 Horace Grant	.12	.30
112 Tariq Abdul-Wahad	.10	.25
113 Travis Knight	.10	.25
114 Kendall Gill	.10	.25
115 Aaron McKie	.10	.25
116 Dean Garrett	.10	.25
117 Jeff Hornacek	.12	.30
118 Todd Fuller	.10	.25
119 Arvydas Sabonis	.12	.30
120 Voshon Lenard	.10	.25
121 Steve Nash	.25	.60
122 Cedric Henderson	.10	.25
123 Rodrick Rhodes	.10	.25
124 Mookie Blaylock	.10	.25
125 Hersey Hawkins	.10	.25
126 Doug Christie	.10	.25
127 Eric Piatkowski	.12	.30
128 Sean Elliott	.15	.40
129 Anthony Mason	.10	.25
130 Allan Houston	.12	.30
131 Antonio Davis	.10	.25
132 Hubert Davis	.10	.25
133 Rod Strickland PF	.10	.25
134 Jason Kidd PF	.25	.60
135 Mark Jackson PF	.15	.40
136 Marcus Camby PF	.12	.30
137 Dikembe Mutombo PF	.15	.40
138 Shawn Bradley PF	.10	.25
139 Dennis Rodman PF	.30	.75
140 Jayson Williams PF	.10	.25
141 Tim Duncan PF	.30	.75
142 Michael Jordan PF	1.25	3.00
143 Shaquille O'Neal PF	.40	1.00
144 Karl Malone PF	.20	.50
145 Mookie Blaylock PF	.10	.25
146 Brevin Knight PF	.10	.25
147 Doug Christie PF	.10	.25
148 Checklist	.10	.25
149 Checklist	.10	.25
150 Checklist	.10	.25
S44 Keith Van Horn SAMPLE	.75	2.00

1998-99 Fleer Vintage '61

Inserted one per hobby pack, this 147-card set parallels the basic set. The card design uses the 1961-62 Fleer basketball card design. To ascertain values on individual cards, please refer to the mulitplier in the header, coupled with the value of the base card.

COMPLETE SET (147)	40.00	70.00
*STARS: 1.5X TO 4X BASE CARD HI		

1998-99 Fleer Classic '61

Inserted into hobby packs only, this 147-card set parallels the Vintage '61 insert. The cards carry the same design, but are serially numbered to 61.

*STARS: 80X TO 200X BASE CARD HI		
1 Kobe Bryant	250.00	500.00
12 John Stockton	50.00	120.00
23 Michael Jordan	2000.00	3000.00
66 Scottie Pippen	60.00	150.00
142 Michael Jordan PF	500.00	1000.00

1998-99 Fleer Electrifying

Randomly inserted in packs at a rate of one in 72, this 10-card set features player's who consistently have electrifying performances. The card fronts feature a gold patterened full-foil background with embossed "electricity".

COMPLETE SET (10)	40.00	100.00
1 Kobe Bryant	20.00	50.00
2 Kevin Garnett	6.00	15.00
3 Anfernee Hardaway	5.00	12.00
4 Grant Hill	5.00	12.00
5 Allen Iverson	6.00	15.00
6 Michael Jordan	40.00	100.00
7 Shawn Kemp	3.00	8.00
8 Stephon Marbury	4.00	10.00
9 Gary Payton	3.00	8.00
10 Dennis Rodman	6.00	15.00

1998-99 Fleer Great Expectations

Randomly inserted in packs at a rate of one in 20, this 10-card set features players that represent the future of the NBA. The card fronts are bordered in gold holofoil with a matte finish background.

COMPLETE SET (10)	8.00	20.00
1 Shareef Abdur-Rahim	.75	2.00
2 Ray Allen	1.00	2.50
3 Kobe Bryant	4.00	10.00
4 Tim Duncan	1.50	4.00
5 Kevin Garnett	1.50	4.00
6 Grant Hill	1.25	3.00
7 Allen Iverson	1.50	4.00
8 Stephon Marbury	1.00	2.50
9 Keith Van Horn	.75	2.00
10 Antoine Walker	.75	2.00

1998-99 Fleer Lucky 13

Randomly inserted in packs at a rate of 1:96, this 13-card set features cards that were redeemable for corresponding draft picks. The expiration was June 1, 1999.

1 Michael Olowokandi	8.00	20.00
2 Mike Bibby	15.00	40.00
3 Raef LaFrentz	8.00	20.00
4 Antawn Jamison	15.00	40.00
5 Vince Carter	30.00	80.00
6 Robert Traylor	6.00	15.00
7 Jason Williams	15.00	40.00
8 Larry Hughes	12.00	30.00
9 Dirk Nowitzki	50.00	120.00
10 Paul Pierce	30.00	80.00
11 Bonzi Wells	6.00	15.00
12 Michael Doleac	6.00	15.00
13 Keon Clark	6.00	15.00
NNO Expired Trade Cards	.20	.50

1998-99 Fleer Playmakers Theatre

Randomly inserted into packs, this 15-card set features players that have a great impact on the game. The cards feature die cut, sculptured curtains against gold holofoil. The card backs feature commentary that recaps some of the player's greatest moments and sequential numbering to 100.

1 Shareef Abdur-Rahim	60.00	150.00
2 Ray Allen	80.00	200.00
3 Kobe Bryant	1000.00	1800.00
4 Tim Duncan	125.00	300.00
5 Kevin Garnett	125.00	300.00
6 Anfernee Hardaway	100.00	250.00
7 Grant Hill	125.00	300.00
8 Allen Iverson	125.00	300.00
9 Michael Jordan	3500.00	5000.00
10 Karl Malone	125.00	300.00
11 Stephon Marbury	80.00	200.00
12 Shaquille O'Neal	200.00	500.00
13 Scottie Pippen	100.00	250.00
14 Keith Van Horn	60.00	150.00
15 Antoine Walker	60.00	150.00

1998-99 Fleer Rookie Rewind

Randomly inserted in packs at one in 36, this 10-card set featues the players named by the NBA to the 1997-98 NBA All-Rookie Team. The card fronts feature silver hologoil accents and embossing.

COMPLETE SET (10)	6.00	15.00
1 Derek Anderson	.75	2.00
2 Tim Duncan	2.50	6.00
3 Cedric Henderson	.75	2.00
4 Zydrunas Ilgauskas	1.25	3.00
5 Bobby Jackson	1.00	2.50
6 Brevin Knight	.75	2.00
7 Ron Mercer	1.00	2.50
8 Maurice Taylor	.75	2.00
9 Tim Thomas	1.25	3.00
10 Keith Van Horn	1.25	3.00

1998-99 Fleer Timeless Memories

Randomly inserted into packs at a rate of one in 12, this 10-card set features players that make the moments great. Card fronts feature the player's face in a watch face with clouds swirling below.

COMPLETE SET (10)	4.00	10.00
1 Shareef Abdur-Rahim	.60	1.50
2 Ray Allen	.75	2.00
3 Vin Baker	.50	1.25
4 Anfernee Hardaway	1.00	2.50
5 Tim Hardaway	.60	1.50
6 Shaquille O'Neal	1.50	4.00
7 Scottie Pippen	1.00	2.50
8 David Robinson	1.00	2.50
9 Dennis Rodman	1.25	3.00
10 Antoine Walker	.60	1.50

1999-00 Fleer

This product, also known as Fleer Tradition, was released as a 220-card set. The 10-card packs carried a suggested retail price of $1.59. Each card contains full UV coating, foil stamping and complete statistics. Cards feature one of three foil colors: blue for Eastern Conference players, red for Western Conference players and gold for rookies. Three numbereless checklist cards were also available and inserted one in six packs.

COMPLETE SET (220)	20.00	40.00
1 Vince Carter	.40	1.00
2 Kobe Bryant	1.00	2.50
3 Keith Van Horn	.15	.40
4 Tim Duncan	.40	1.00
5 Grant Hill	.25	.60
6 Kevin Garnett	.40	1.00
7 Anfernee Hardaway	.30	.75
8 Jason Williams	.25	.60
9 Paul Pierce	.30	.75
10 Mookie Blaylock	.12	.30
11 Shawn Bradley	.12	.30
12 Kenny Anderson	.15	.40
13 Chauncey Billups	.20	.50
14 Elden Campbell	.12	.30
15 Jason Caffey	.12	.30
16 Brent Barry	.15	.40
17 Charles Barkley	.30	.75
18 Derek Anderson	.12	.30
19 Darrick Martin	.12	.30
20 Bison Dele	.12	.30
21 Rick Fox	.12	.30
22 Antonio Davis	.12	.30
23 Terrell Brandon	.12	.30
24 P.J. Brown	.12	.30
25 Toby Bailey	.12	.30
26 Ray Allen	.20	.50
27 Brian Grant	.12	.30
28 Scott Burrell	.12	.30
29 Tariq Abdul-Wahad	.12	.30
30 Marcus Camby	.15	.40
31 John Stockton	.25	.60
32 Nick Anderson	.12	.30
33 Antonio Daniels	.12	.30
34 Matt Geiger	.12	.30
35 Vin Baker	.20	.50
36 Dee Brown	.12	.30
37 Shandon Anderson	.12	.30
38 Calbert Cheaney	.12	.30
39 Shareef Abdur-Rahim	.15	.40
40 LaPhonso Ellis	.12	.30
41 Cedric Ceballos	.12	.30
42 Tony Battie	.15	.40
43 Keon Clark	.12	.30
44 Derrick Coleman	.15	.40
45 Erick Dampier	.12	.30
46 Corey Benjamin	.12	.30
47 Michael Dickerson	.12	.30
48 Cedric Henderson	.12	.30
49 Lamond Murray	.12	.30
50 Horace Grant	.15	.40
51 Shaquille O'Neal	.50	1.25
52 Dale Davis	.12	.30
53 Dean Garrett	.12	.30
54 Tim Hardaway	.20	.50
55 Gerald Brown RC	.20	.50
56 Sam Cassell	.15	.40
57 Jim Jackson	.15	.40
58 Kendall Gill	.12	.30
59 Eric Williams	.12	.30
60 Chris Childs	.12	.30
61 Vlade Divac	.20	.50
62 Darrell Armstrong	.12	.30
63 Mario Elie	.12	.30
64 Tyrone Hill	.12	.30
65 Dale Ellis	.12	.30
66 Doug Christie	.15	.40
67 Howard Eisley	.12	.30
68 Juwan Howard	.15	.40
69 Mike Bibby	.20	.50
70 Alan Henderson	.12	.30
71 Michael Finley	.20	.50
72 Dana Barros	.12	.30
73 Danny Fortson	.12	.30
74 Ricky Davis	.20	.50
75 Adonal Foyle	.12	.30
76 Cory Carr	.12	.30
77 Bryce Drew	.12	.30
78 Shawn Kemp	.20	.50
79 Tyrone Nesby RC	.20	.50
80 Lindsey Hunter	.12	.30
81 Ruben Patterson	.12	.30
82 Al Harrington	.20	.50

83 Bobby Jackson .15 .40
84 Dan Majerle .20 .50
85 Rex Chapman .12 .30
86 Dell Curry .12 .30
87 Walt Williams .12 .30
88 Kerry Kittles .12 .30
89 Isaiah Rider .12 .30
90 Patrick Ewing .25 .60
91 Lawrence Funderburke .12 .30
92 Isaac Austin .12 .30
93 Sean Elliott .20 .50
94 Larry Hughes .15 .40
95 Hersey Hawkins .12 .30
96 Tracy McGrady .30 .75
97 Jeff Hornacek .15 .40
98 Randell Jackson .12 .30
99 J.R. Henderson .12 .30
100 Roshown McLeod .12 .30
101 Steve Nash .30 .75
102 Ron Mercer .15 .40
103 Raef LaFrentz .15 .40
104 Eddie Jones .20 .50
105 Antawn Jamison .20 .50
106 Kornel David RC .20 .50
107 Othella Harrington .12 .30
108 Brevin Knight .12 .30
109 Michael Olowokandi .12 .30
110 Christian Laettner .15 .40
111 J.R. Reid .12 .30
112 Reggie Miller .20 .50
113 Andrae Patterson .12 .30
114 Jamal Mashburn .15 .40
115 Glenn Robinson .15 .40
116 Pat Garrity .12 .30
117 Stephon Marbury .15 .40
118 Arvydas Sabonis .15 .40
119 Allan Houston .15 .40
120 Peja Stojakovic .20 .50
121 Michael Doleac .12 .30
122 Avery Johnson .15 .40
123 Allen Iverson .40 1.00
124 Rashard Lewis .20 .50
125 Charles Oakley .15 .40
126 Karl Malone .25 .60
127 Tracy Murray .12 .30
128 Felipe Lopez .12 .30
129 Dikembe Mutombo .20 .50
130 Dirk Nowitzki .40 1.00
131 Vitaly Potapenko .12 .30
132 Antonio McDyess .15 .40
133 Anthony Mason .12 .30
134 Donyell Marshall .12 .30
135 Ron Harper .12 .30
136 Cuttino Mobley .15 .40
137 Wesley Person .12 .30
138 Rodney Rogers .12 .30
139 Jerry Stackhouse .20 .50
140 Glen Rice .20 .50
141 Chris Mullin .20 .50
142 Anthony Peeler .12 .30
143 Alonzo Mourning .25 .60
144 Tom Gugliotta .12 .30
145 Tim Thomas .15 .40
146 Damon Stoudamire .20 .50
147 Jayson Williams .12 .30
148 Larry Johnson .20 .50
149 Chris Webber .20 .50
150 Matt Harpring .15 .40
151 David Robinson .30 .75
152 George Lynch .12 .30
153 Gary Payton .20 .50
154 John Wallace .12 .30
155 Greg Ostertag .12 .30
156 Mitch Richmond .20 .50
157 Cherokee Parks .12 .30
158 Steve Smith .12 .30
159 Gary Trent .12 .30
160 Antoine Walker .20 .50
161 Johnny Taylor .12 .30
162 Brad Miller .20 .50
163 Chris Mills .12 .30
164 Charles Jones .12 .30
165 Hakeem Olajuwon .25 .60
166 Bob Sura .12 .30
167 Brian Skinner .12 .30
168 Korleone Young .12 .30
169 Tyronn Lue .12 .30
170 Jalen Rose .15 .40
171 Joe Smith .15 .40
172 Clarence Weatherspoon .12 .30
173 Jason Kidd .30 .75
174 Robert Traylor .12 .30
175 Rasheed Wallace .20 .50
176 Latrell Sprewell .20 .50
177 Corliss Williamson .12 .30
178 Bo Outlaw .12 .30
179 Malik Rose .12 .30
180 Nazr Mohammed .12 .30
181 Olden Polynice .12 .30
182 Kevin Willis .12 .30
183 Bryon Russell .12 .30
184 Bryant Reeves .12 .30
185 Rod Strickland .12 .30
186 Samaki Walker .12 .30
187 Nick Van Exel .15 .40
188 David Wesley .12 .30
189 John Starks .20 .50
190 Toni Kukoc .20 .50
191 Scottie Pippen .30 .75
192 Zydrunas Ilgauskas .15 .40
193 Maurice Taylor .12 .30
194 Rik Smits .20 .50
195 Clifford Robinson .12 .30
196 Bonzi Wells .12 .30
197 Charlie Ward .12 .30
198 Detlef Schrempf .15 .40
199 Theo Ratliff .15 .40
200 Rodrick Rhodes .12 .30
201 Ron Artest RC .50 1.25
202 William Avery RC .20 .50
203 Elton Brand RC .50 1.25
204 Baron Davis RC .60 1.50
205 Jumaine Jones RC .20 .50
206 Andre Miller RC .50 1.25
207 Lee Nailon RC .20 .50
208 James Posey RC .20 .50
209 Jason Terry RC .50 1.25
210 Kenny Thomas RC .20 .50
211 Steve Francis RC .50 1.25
212 Wally Szczerbiak RC .40 1.00
213 Richard Hamilton RC .50 1.25
214 Jonathan Bender RC .20 .50
215 Shawn Marion RC .50 1.25
216 Aleksandar Radojevic RC .20 .50
217 Tim James RC .20 .50
218 Trajan Langdon RC .20 .50
219 Lamar Odom RC .60 1.50
220 Corey Maggette RC .60 1.50
NNO Checklist #2 .12 .30
NNO Checklist #1 .12 .30
NNO Checklist #3 .12 .30

1999-00 Fleer Roundball Collection

Inserted one per retail pack only, this 220-card set parallels the base set. To ascertain values on individual cards, please refer to the multiplier in the header, coupled with the value of the base card.
*ROUND: 1X TO 2.5X BASE CARD HI

1999-00 Fleer Supreme Court Collection

Randomly inserted in series one hobby packs only, this 220-card set parallels the base set. The cards are stamped with green holofoil on the card front. The cards are also serially numbered to 20. To ascertain values on individual cards, please refer to the multiplier in the header, coupled with the value of the base card.
*STARS: 50X TO 125X BASE CARD HI
*RCs: 20X TO 50X BASE HI

1999-00 Fleer Fresh Ink

Randomly inserted in Fleer packs, this set features autographs from NBA players. The cards feature a congratulatory message on the back. Each card was serially numbered to 400. The cards are not numbered and listed below in alphabetical order.

1 Corey Benjamin 4.00 10.00
2 Mike Bibby 6.00 15.00
3 Michael Dickerson 4.00 10.00
4 Michael Doleac 4.00 10.00
5 Bryce Drew 4.00 10.00
6 Pat Garrity 4.00 10.00
7 Matt Harpring 4.00 10.00
8 Larry Hughes 6.00 15.00
9 Antawn Jamison 6.00 15.00
10 Raef LaFrentz 4.00 10.00
11 Felipe Lopez 4.00 10.00
12 Jelani McCoy 4.00 10.00
13 Brad Miller 6.00 15.00
14 Michael Olowokandi 4.00 10.00
15 Robert Traylor 4.00 10.00

1999-00 Fleer Game Breakers

Randomly inserted in series one packs, this 15-card set features NBA stars who can break a game wide open. The cards are die cut and serially numbered to 100.

1 Shareef Abdur-Rahim 12.00 30.00
2 Kobe Bryant 150.00 300.00
3 Vince Carter 30.00 80.00
4 Tim Duncan 30.00 80.00
5 Kevin Garnett 30.00 80.00
6 Anfernee Hardaway 25.00 60.00
7 Grant Hill 20.00 50.00
8 Allen Iverson 30.00 80.00
9 Shawn Kemp 20.00 50.00
10 Stephon Marbury 12.00 30.00
11 Ron Mercer 12.00 30.00
12 Shaquille O'Neal 40.00 100.00
13 Keith Van Horn 12.00 30.00
14 Antoine Walker 15.00 40.00
15 Jason Williams 20.00 50.00

1999-00 Fleer Masters of the Hardwood

Randomly inserted in series one packs at one in 18, this 15-card set showcases highly skilled player's who have mastered their position. Card fronts feature a silhouetted player against a simulated wood background.

COMPLETE SET (15) 15.00 30.00
1 Shareef Abdur-Rahim .75 2.00
2 Mike Bibby 1.00 2.50
3 Kobe Bryant 5.00 12.00
4 Tim Duncan 2.00 5.00
5 Kevin Garnett 2.00 5.00
6 Anfernee Hardaway 1.50 4.00
7 Grant Hill 1.25 3.00
8 Allen Iverson 2.00 5.00
9 Karl Malone 1.25 3.00
10 Stephon Marbury .75 2.00
11 Tracy McGrady 1.50 4.00
12 Ron Mercer .75 2.00
13 Scottie Pippen 1.50 4.00
14 Antoine Walker 1.00 2.50
15 Jason Williams 1.25 3.00

1999-00 Fleer Net Effect

Randomly inserted in series one packs at one in 96, this 10-card set features players who have a great effect on the game. The die cut cards are printed on opaque plastic stock and silhouettes the player's image against his team's primary color.

COMPLETE SET (10) 20.00 50.00
1 Kobe Bryant 10.00 25.00
2 Vince Carter 4.00 10.00
3 Tim Duncan 4.00 10.00
4 Kevin Garnett 4.00 10.00
5 Grant Hill 2.50 6.00
6 Allen Iverson 4.00 10.00
7 Shaquille O'Neal 5.00 12.00
8 Paul Pierce 3.00 8.00
9 Scottie Pippen 3.00 8.00
10 Keith Van Horn 1.50 4.00

1999-00 Fleer Rookie Sensations

Randomly inserted in series one packs at one in six, this 20-card set profiles players from the 98-99 rookie class. The player's image appears on a full gold foil stamped card.

COMPLETE SET (20) 6.00 15.00
1 Mike Bibby .60 1.50
2 Vince Carter 1.25 3.00
3 Ricky Davis .60 1.50
4 Michael Dickerson .40 1.00
5 Michael Doleac .40 1.00
6 Matt Harpring .50 1.25
7 Larry Hughes .50 1.25
8 Randell Jackson .40 1.00
9 Antawn Jamison .60 1.50
10 Raef LaFrentz .50 1.25
11 Felipe Lopez .40 1.00
12 Roshown McLeod .40 1.00
13 Brad Miller .60 1.50
14 Cuttino Mobley .50 1.25
15 Dirk Nowitzki 1.25 3.00
16 Michael Olowokandi .40 1.00
17 Paul Pierce 1.00 2.50
18 Peja Stojakovic .60 1.50
19 Robert Traylor .40 1.00
20 Jason Williams .75 2.00

2000-01 Fleer

The 2000-01 Fleer product, which is also known as Fleer Tradition, was released in January 2001, and featured a 300-card base set that was broken into tiers as follows: Base Veterans (1-226) Rookies (227-271) and Team Checklists (272-300). Each pack contained 10 cards and carried a suggested retail price of $2.99. Four versions were available of the NNO Vince Carter Old School Raptor card. Retail versions were not serial numbered, and the other versions include a sticker, one serial numbered to 1986, and an autograph numbered out of 15.

1 Lamar Odom .20 .50
2 Christian Laettner .12 .30
3 Michael Olowokandi .12 .30
4 Anthony Carter .12 .30
5 Steve Francis .20 .50
6 Darvin Ham .12 .30
7 Mitch Richmond .15 .40
8 Corliss Williamson .12 .30
9 Jason Terry .20 .50
10 Brian Grant .12 .30
11 Peja Stojakovic .20 .50
12 Rick Fox .15 .40
13 Tyrone Hill .12 .30
14 Chauncey Billups .20 .50
15 Otis Thorpe .15 .40
16 Richard Hamilton .15 .40
17 Ervin Johnson .12 .30
18 Jim Jackson .12 .30
19 Theo Ratliff .12 .30
20 Doug Christie .12 .30
21 Jalen Rose .15 .40
22 John Wallace .12 .30
23 Ruben Patterson .12 .30
24 Steve Nash .30 .75
25 Toni Kukoc .15 .40
26 Anthony Peeler .12 .30
27 Ray Allen .20 .50
28 Adonal Foyle .12 .30
29 Chris Whitney .12 .30
30 Nick Van Exel .15 .40
31 Sean Elliott .15 .40
32 Erick Strickland .12 .30
33 Jerry Stackhouse .15 .40
34 Antawn Jamison .20 .50
35 Grant Hill .25 .60
36 Antonio Daniels .12 .30
37 Karl Malone .25 .60
38 Keith Van Horn .15 .40
39 Ron Harper .15 .40
40 Stephon Marbury .15 .40
41 Bryon Russell .12 .30
42 Corey Maggette .15 .40
43 Hersey Hawkins .12 .30
44 Vince Carter .40 1.00
45 Paul Pierce .25 .60
46 Mikki Moore RC .20 .50
47 Othella Harrington .12 .30
48 Erick Dampier .12 .30
49 Jerome Williams .12 .30
50 Nick Anderson .12 .30
51 Tim Hardaway .20 .50
52 Allan Houston .15 .40
53 Tyrone Nesby .20 .50
54 Brevin Knight .12 .30
55 Chris Mills .12 .30
56 Ron Artest .20 .50
57 Walt Williams .12 .30
58 Duane Causwell .12 .30
59 Bonzi Wells .12 .30
60 Rasheed Wallace .20 .50
61 Dikembe Mutombo .20 .50
62 Jahidi White .12 .30
63 Chris Webber .20 .50
64 Tony Battie .12 .30
65 Mahmoud Abdul-Rauf .12 .30
66 Monty Williams .12 .30
67 Charlie Ward .12 .30
68 David Robinson .30 .75
69 Eric Snow .12 .30
70 Jermaine O'Neal .20 .50
71 Kurt Thomas .12 .30
72 James Posey .12 .30
73 Travis Best .12 .30
74 Jonathan Bender .12 .30
75 John Stockton .25 .60
76 Jacque Vaughn .12 .30
77 Ron Mercer .12 .30
78 Shawn Marion .20 .50
79 Larry Johnson .20 .50
80 Maurice Taylor .12 .30
81 Clifford Robinson .12 .30
82 Scot Pollard .12 .30
83 Patrick Ewing .25 .60
84 Terrell Brandon .12 .30
85 Horace Grant .15 .40
86 Vin Baker .15 .40
87 Al Harrington .15 .40
88 Larry Hughes .15 .40
89 David Wesley .12 .30
90 Wally Szczerbiak .15 .40
91 Charles Oakley .15 .40
92 Tim Thomas .12 .30
93 Mookie Blaylock .15 .40
94 Jamal Mashburn .15 .40
95 Roshown McLeod .12 .30
96 John Starks .12 .30
97 Rodney Rogers .12 .30
98 Juwan Howard .15 .40
99 Isaiah Rider .15 .40
100 Rashard Lewis .20 .50
101 Dion Glover .12 .30
102 Johnny Newman .12 .30
103 Avery Johnson .15 .40
104 Darrell Armstrong .12 .30
105 Eric Williams .12 .30
106 Gary Payton .20 .50
107 Antonio Davis .12 .30
108 Dirk Nowitzki .30 .75
109 Trajan Langdon .12 .30
110 Michael Dickerson .12 .30
111 Joe Smith .15 .40
112 Rod Strickland .15 .40
113 Shawn Kemp .20 .50
114 Voshon Lenard .12 .30
115 Marcus Camby .15 .40
116 Matt Harpring .15 .40
117 Isaac Austin .12 .30
118 Malik Rose .12 .30
119 Pat Garrity .12 .30
120 Kenny Thomas .12 .30
121 LaPhonso Ellis .15 .40
122 Danny Fortson .12 .30
123 Elton Brand .20 .50
124 Jason Williams .20 .50
125 Kobe Bryant 1.00 2.50
126 Tariq Abdul-Wahad .12 .30
127 Tracy McGrady .30 .75
128 Matt Geiger .12 .30
129 Antoine Walker .15 .40
130 Michael Finley .20 .50
131 Andre Miller .15 .40
132 Robert Horry .15 .40
133 Donyell Marshall .12 .30
134 Shareef Abdur-Rahim .15 .40
135 Vonteego Cummings .12 .30
136 Anthony Mason .12 .30
137 Mike Bibby .20 .50
138 Raef LaFrentz .12 .30
139 Glen Rice .15 .40
140 Chris Gatling .12 .30
141 Latrell Sprewell .15 .40
142 Austin Croshere .12 .30
143 Kenny Anderson .15 .40
144 Elden Campbell .12 .30
145 Jason Kidd .30 .75
146 Michael Doleac .12 .30
147 Muggsy Bogues .15 .40
148 Tim Duncan .40 1.00
149 Samaki Walker .12 .30
150 Gary Trent .12 .30
151 Kevin Garnett .40 1.00
152 Allen Iverson .40 1.00
153 Anfernee Hardaway .30 .75
154 Robert Traylor .12 .30
155 Scottie Pippen .30 .75
156 Shaquille O'Neal .50 1.25
157 Vlade Divac .15 .40
158 Lucious Harris .12 .30
159 Keon Clark .12 .30
160 Bo Outlaw .12 .30
161 P.J. Brown .12 .30
162 Derrick Coleman .15 .40
163 Mark Jackson .15 .40
164 Lamond Murray .12 .30
165 Dan Majerle .15 .40
166 Eddie Jones .20 .50
167 Cedric Ceballos .12 .30
168 Kendall Gill .12 .30
169 Tom Gugliotta .12 .30
170 Jeff McInnis .12 .30
171 Steve Smith .15 .40
172 Kevin Willis .12 .30
173 Lindsey Hunter .12 .30
174 Derek Anderson .12 .30
175 Shandon Anderson .12 .30
176 Adrian Griffin .12 .30
177 Baron Davis .20 .50
178 Radoslav Nesterovic .12 .30
179 Glenn Robinson .15 .40
180 Sam Cassell .15 .40
181 Chucky Atkins .12 .30
182 Arvydas Sabonis .15 .40
183 Damon Stoudamire .15 .40
184 Antonio McDyess .15 .40
185 Derek Fisher .20 .50
186 Bryant Reeves .12 .30
187 Hakeem Olajuwon .25 .60
188 Kerry Kittles .12 .30
189 Alan Henderson .12 .30
190 Sam Perkins .12 .30
191 Felipe Lopez .12 .30
192 Tracy Murray .12 .30
193 Shammond Williams .12 .30
194 Vitaly Potapenko .12 .30
195 John Amaechi .12 .30
196 Quincy Lewis .12 .30
197 Reggie Miller .20 .50
198 Cuttino Mobley .15 .40
199 Rex Chapman .12 .30
200 Dale Davis .12 .30
201 Andrew DeClercq .12 .30
202 Kelvin Cato .12 .30
203 Jon Barry .12 .30
204 Greg Anthony .12 .30
205 Brent Barry .12 .30
206 Derrick McKey .12 .30
207 Vince Carter UH .40 1.00
208 David Robinson UH .30 .75
209 Eric Snow UH .12 .30
210 Ray Allen UH .20 .50
211 Lamar Odom UH .20 .50
212 Dikembe Mutombo UH .20 .50
213 Brevin Knight UH .12 .30
214 Vin Baker UH .15 .40
215 Antoine Walker UH .15 .40
216 Mitch Richmond UH .15 .40
217 Elton Brand UH .20 .50
218 Jerome Williams UH .12 .30
219 Keith Van Horn UH .15 .40
220 Nick Van Exel UH .15 .40
221 Shaquille O'Neal UH .25 .60
222 Allan Houston UH .15 .40
223 Shareef Abdur-Rahim UH .15 .40
224 Karl Malone UH .25 .60
225 Terrell Brandon UH .12 .30
226 Eddie Jones UH .20 .50
227 Stromile Swift RC .25 .60
228 Dalibor Bagaric RC .25 .60
229 Erick Barkley RC .25 .60
230 Mike Miller RC .50 1.25
231 Kenyon Martin RC .60 1.50
232 Michael Redd RC .60 1.50
233 Darius Miles RC .25 .60
234 Chris Mihm RC .25 .60
235 Brian Cardinal RC .25 .60
236 Khalid El-Amin RC .25 .60
237 Hanno Mottola RC .25 .60
238 Jamaal Magloire RC .25 .60
239 Courtney Alexander RC .25 .60
240 Mamadou N'Diaye RC .25 .60
241 Chris Porter RC .25 .60
242 Quentin Richardson RC .40 1.00
243 Eddie House RC .25 .60
244 Joel Przybilla RC .25 .60
245 Soumaila Samake RC .25 .60
246 Speedy Claxton RC .25 .60
247 Desmond Mason RC .30 .75
248 Mike Smith RC .25 .60
249 Lavor Postell RC .25 .60
250 Ruben Garces RC .25 .60
251 DeShawn Stevenson RC .30 .75
252 Hedo Turkoglu RC .50 1.25
253 Keyon Dooling RC .25 .60
254 Dan Langhi RC .25 .60
255 Mateen Cleaves RC .25 .60
256 Donnell Harvey RC .25 .60
257 DerMarr Johnson RC .25 .60
258 Jason Collier RC .25 .60
259 Jake Voskuhl RC .25 .60
260 Mark Madsen RC .25 .60
261 Pepe Sanchez RC .25 .60
262 Morris Peterson RC .25 .60
263 Daniel Santiago RC .40 1.00
264 Etan Thomas RC .25 .60
265 A.J. Guyton RC .25 .60
266 Marcus Fizer RC .25 .60
267 Jamal Crawford RC .40 1.00
268 Jerome Moiso RC .25 .60
269 Olumide Oyedeji RC .25 .60
270 Paul McPherson RC .25 .60
271 Eduardo Najera RC .25 .60
272 Gary Trent .05 .15
Steve Nash
Christian Laettner
Michael Finley
Dirk Nowitzki
273 Antonio McDyess .05 .15
Raef LaFrentz
Tariq Abdul-Wahad
Nick Van Exel
James Posey
274 Steve Francis .10 .30
Maurice Taylor
Shandon Anderson
Walt Williams
Hakeem Olajuwon
275 Terrell Brandon .10 .30
Kevin Garnett
Wally Szczerbiak
Radoslav Nesterovic
Chauncey Billups
276 Sean Elliott .10 .30
Avery Johnson
David Robinson
Tim Duncan
Derek Anderson
277 Olden Polynice .10 .30
John Stockton
Karl Malone
Bryon Russell
John Starks
278 Othella Harrington .10 .30
Mike Bibby
Michael Dickerson
Bryant Reeves
Shareef Abdur-Rahim
279 Mookie Blaylock .10 .30
Erick Dampier
Danny Fortson
Larry Hughes
Antawn Jamison
280 Keyon Dooling .10 .30
Quentin Richardson
Darius Miles
Michael Olowokandi
Lamar Odom
281 Ron Harper .20 .50
Isaiah Rider
Kobe Bryant
Shaquille O'Neal
Robert Horry
282 Anfernee Hardaway .10 .30
Tom Gugliotta
Jason Kidd
Rodney Rogers
Clifford Robinson
283 Scottie Pippen .10 .30
Damon Stoudamire
Steve Smith
Arvydas Sabonis
Rasheed Wallace
284 Nick Anderson .10 .30
Peja Stojakovic
Vlade Divac
Jason Williams
Chris Webber
285 Gary Payton .10 .30
Desmond Mason
Patrick Ewing
Vin Baker
Rashard Lewis
286 Vitaly Potapenko .05 .15
Kenny Anderson
Adrian Grffin
Antoine Walker
Paul Pierce
287 Anthony Mason .05 .15
Eddie Jones
Tim Hardaway
Brian Grant
Dan Majerle
288 Kendall Gil .10 .30
Stephon Marbury
Kenyon Martin
Jim McIlvaine
Keith Van Horn
289 Latrell Sprewell .10 .30
Glen Rice
Marcus Camby
Larry Johnson
Allan Houston
290 Tracy McGrady .20 .50
John Amaechi
Darrell Armstrong
Grant Hill
Charles Outlaw
291 Tyrone Hill .10 .30
Theo Ratliff
Allen Iverson
Eric Snow
Toni Kukoc
292 Jahidi White .05 .15
Mike Smith
Mitch Richmond
Juwan Howard
Rod Strickland
293 DerMarr Johnson .05 .15
Jason Terry
Jim Jackson
Alan Henderson
Dikembe Mutombo
294 Elden Campbell .05 .15
David Wesley
P.J. Brown
Jamal Mashburn
Derrick Coleman
295 Ron Mercer .10 .30
Jamal Crawford
Elton Brand
Marcus Fizer
Dragan Tarlac
296 Brevin Knight .05 .15
Robert Traylor
Andre Miller
Chris Mihm
Lamond Murray
297 Chucky Atkins .05 .15
Jerry Stackhouse
Cedric Ceballos
Jerome Williams
John Wallace
298 Jermaine O'Neal .10 .30
Jalen Rose
Austin Croshere
Jonathan Bender
Reggie Miller
299 Tim Thomas .05 .15
Ervin Johnson
Sam Casell
Ray Allen
Glenn Robinson
300 Vince Carter .20 .50
Corliss Williamson
Morris Peterson
Mark Jackson
Antonio Davis
NNO Vince Carter OSR Sticker 2.00 5.00
NNO Vince Carter OSR/1986 8.00 20.00
NNO Vince Carter OSR AU/15 20.00 50.00

2000-01 Fleer Stickers

Randomly inserted into packs at one in 36, this 100-card insert set features stickers of different players throughout the 2000-01 Fleer base set.
*STARS: 3X TO 8X BASE HI
*RCs: 2X TO 5X BASE HI
*CL: 8X TO 20X BASE HI

2000-01 Fleer Autographics

Randomly inserted in 2000-01 Fleer products, this insert features autographed cards from some of the hottest players in the NBA. Please note that the cards are listed below in alphabetical order. Gold and silver versions were also issued and numbered to 50 and 250 respectively.
FOCUS STATED ODDS 1:48
GAME TIME STATED ODDS 1:287
GENUINE STATED ODDS 1:23
GLOSSY STATED ODDS 1:96 RETAIL
HOOPS STATED ODDS 1:72
MYSTIQUE STATED ODDS 1:48
PREMIUM STATED ODDS 1:288
ULTRA STATED ODDS 1:48
*GOLD: 1.25X TO 3X BASE AUTO HI
*SILVER: .5X TO 1.25X BASE AUTO HI

1 Darrell Armstrong 3.00 8.00
2 Ron Artest 8.00 20.00
3 Chucky Atkins 3.00 8.00
4 Travis Best 3.00 8.00
5 Mike Bibby 5.00 12.00
6 Muggsy Bogues 5.00 12.00
7 P.J. Brown 3.00 8.00
8 Elden Campbell 3.00 8.00
9 Vince Carter 12.50 30.00
10 Jason Collier 3.00 8.00
11 Baron Davis 6.00 15.00
12 Andrew DeClercq 3.00 8.00
13 Michael Dickerson 3.00 8.00
14 Vlade Divac 8.00 20.00
15 Michael Doleac 3.00 8.00
16 Dion Glover 3.00 8.00
17 Brian Grant 4.00 10.00
18 Adrian Griffin 3.00 8.00
19 Tom Gugliotta 3.00 8.00
20 Richard Hamilton 5.00 12.00
21 Al Harrington 3.00 8.00
22 Othella Harrington 3.00 8.00
23 Jason Hart 3.00 8.00
24 Allen Iverson 50.00 120.00
25 Antawn Jamison 5.00 12.00
26 Brevin Knight 3.00 8.00
27 Toni Kukoc 8.00 20.00
28 Raef LaFrentz 4.00
29 Dan Langhi 3.00
30 Voshon Lenard 3.00
31 Quincy Lewis 3.00
32 George Lynch 3.00
33 Corey Maggette 3.00
34 Stephon Marbury 6.00
35 Shawn Marion 6.00
36 Donyell Marshall 5.00
37 Jamal Mashburn 6.00
38 Tracy McGrady 15.00
39 Ron Mercer 4.00
40 Andre Miller 5.00
41 Reggie Miller 50.00
42 Alonzo Mourning 25.00
43 Dirk Nowitzki 50.00
44 Lamar Odom 6.00
45 Hakeem Olajuwon 12.50
46 Jermaine O'Neal 5.00
47 Ruben Patterson 3.00
48 Scot Pollard 3.00
49 Theo Ratliff 5.00
50 Michael Redd 5.00
51 Eddie Robinson 3.00
52 Glenn Robinson 5.00
53 Steve Smith 5.00
54 Jerry Stackhouse 5.00
55 Jason Terry 4.00
56 Kenny Thomas 3.00
57 Keith Van Horn 6.00
58 Antoine Walker 8.00
59 Shareef Abdur-Rahim 4.00
60 Howard Eisley 3.00

2000-01 Fleer Vince Carte Rookie Remnants

This three-card insert was randomly inserted into 2000-01 Fleer products. The set includes a Vince Carter floor card (numbered to 100), a Vince Cart floor/jersey card (numbered to 15), and finally an autographed Vince Carter floor/jersey card (numb 1/1).
NNO Vince Carter FLR/100 12.50

2000-01 Fleer Courting Hist

Randomly inserted into packs at one in 18, this 1 card insert set features players that look to put themselves into the record books in the very nea future. Card backs carry a "CH" prefix.

COMPLETE SET (10) 6.00
CH1 Vince Carter 1.00
CH2 Shaquille O'Neal 1.25
CH3 Grant Hill .60
CH4 Kobe Bryant 2.50
CH5 Tim Duncan 1.00
CH6 Jason Kidd .75
CH7 Kevin Garnett 1.00
CH8 Allen Iverson 1.00
CH9 Steve Francis .50
CH10 Elton Brand .50

2000-01 Fleer Feel the Gar

Randomly inserted in multiple releases, this set features swatches of game-used jerseys from to veterans and rookies in the NBA. The cards are numbered on the back and listed in alphabetica Gold and silver versions were also issued and numbered to 50 and 250 respectively.
EX STATED ODDS 1:72
FOCUS STATED ODDS 1:48
FUTURES STATED ODDS 1:331
MYSTIQUE STATED ODDS 1:72
PREMIUM STATED ODDS 1:56
SHOWCASE STATED ODDS 1:72
ULTRA STATED ODDS 1:48
*GOLD: 1.25X TO 3X BASE HI
*SILVER: .5X TO 1.25X BASE HI

1 Shareef Abdur-Rahim White 2.50
1B Shareef Abdur-Rahim Blue 2.50
2 Mike Bibby 3.00
3 Terrell Brandon 2.00
4 Vince Carter 6.00
5 Sam Cassell 2.50
6 Baron Davis 3.00
7 Michael Finley 3.00
8 Steve Francis 3.00
9 Robert Horry 2.50
10 Allan Houston 2.50
11 Allen Iverson 6.00
12 Eddie Jones 3.00
13 Jason Kidd 5.00
14 Quincy Lewis 2.00
15 Tyronn Lue 2.00
16 George Lynch 2.00
17 Corey Maggette 2.50
18 Karl Malone 4.00
19 Stephon Marbury 2.50
20 Shawn Marion 3.00
21 Tracy McGrady 5.00
22 Reggie Miller 3.00
23 Alonzo Mourning 4.00
24 Lamar Odom 3.00
25 Hakeem Olajuwon 4.00
26 Michael Olowokandi 2.00
27 Shaquille O'Neal Purple 8.00
27B Shaquille O'Neal Yellow 8.00
28 Scott Padgett 2.00
29 Gary Payton 3.00
30 Glenn Robinson 2.50
31 Joe Smith 2.50
32 John Stockton 4.00
33 Jason Terry 3.00

n Van Horn 2.50 6.00
ine Walker 2.50 6.00
s Webber 3.00 8.00
n Williams 3.00 8.00
d Robinson SP 12.50 30.00

2000-01 Fleer Genuine Coverage Nostalgic

ly inserted into packs at 1:144 Hobby, and etail, this 16-card insert features game-jersey s from up and coming prospects. Card backs numbered and are listed below in alphabetical r convenience.

ney Alexander 2.00 5.00
Barkley 2.00 5.00
y Claxton 2.00 5.00
n Cleaves 2.00 5.00
ll Harvey 2.00 5.00
rr Johnson 2.00 5.00
Madsen 2.00 5.00
n Martin 5.00 12.00
nd Mason 2.50 6.00
Miller 4.00 10.00
ne Moiso 2.00 5.00
Przybilla 2.00 5.00
awn Stevenson 2.50 6.00
nile Swift 2.00 5.00
Thomas 2.00 5.00
Turkoglu 4.00 10.00

2000-01 Fleer Hardcourt Classics

ly inserted into packs at one in 9, this 15-card t features players that will go down in history of the best to ever play the game. Card backs HC" prefix.

ETE SET (15) 7.50 15.00
ce Carter .75 2.00
l Malone .50 1.25
e Bryant 2.00 5.00
Duncan .75 2.00
ar Odom .40 1.00
on Williams .40 1.00
in Garnett .75 2.00
on Kidd .60 1.50
quille O'Neal 1.00 2.50
hris Webber .40 1.00
en Iverson .75 2.00
cottie Pippen .60 1.50
ant Hill .50 1.25
on Brand .40 1.00
acy McGrady .60 1.50

00-01 Fleer Rookie Retro

y inserted into packs at one in 36, this 20- t set features rookies on a retro designed d backs carry a "RR" prefix.

ETE SET (20) 8.00 20.00
ris Peterson .50 1.25
Marr Johnson .50 1.25
me Moiso .50 1.25
us Miles .50 1.25
us Fizer .50 1.25
Turkoglu 1.00 2.50
en Cleaves .50 1.25
yon Martin 1.25 3.00
aal Magloire .50 1.25
yon Dooling .50 1.25
Shawn Stevenson .60 1.50
entin Richardson .75 2.00
urtney Alexander .50 1.25
rk Madsen .50 1.25
e Miller 1.00 2.50
smond Mason .60 1.50
omile Swift .50 1.25
eedy Claxton .50 1.25
n Thomas .50 1.25
is Mihm .50 1.25

00-01 Fleer Season Pass

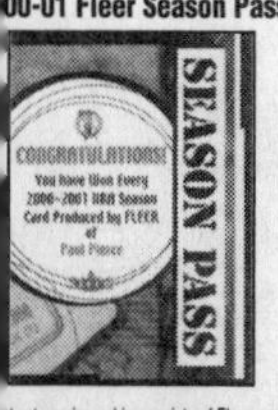

t set was issued in a variety of Fleer products ut the 2000-01 season. Individuals that e of these cards were able to redeem the card 2000-01 Fleer card of the depicted player ption of one of one masterpiece cards).

Please note that the exchange deadline for these cards was 12/01/01.

2000-01 Fleer Sharpshooters

Randomly inserted into packs at one in 6, this 20-card insert set features players that can flat out shoot the basketball. Card backs carry a "SS" prefix.

COMPLETE SET (20) 7.50 15.00
SS1 Vince Carter .75 2.00
SS2 Wally Szczerbiak .30 .75
SS3 Kobe Bryant 2.00 5.00
SS4 Eddie Jones .40 1.00
SS5 John Stockton .50 1.25
SS6 Ray Allen .40 1.00
SS7 Tracy McGrady .60 1.50
SS8 Shareef Abdur-Rahim .30 .75
SS9 Antoine Walker .30 .75
SS10 Tim Duncan .75 2.00
SS11 Larry Hughes .30 .75
SS12 Gary Payton .40 1.00
SS13 Dirk Nowitzki .60 1.50
SS14 Grant Hill .50 1.25
SS15 Scottie Pippen .60 1.50
SS16 Chris Webber .40 1.00
SS17 Stephon Marbury .30 .75
SS18 Anfernee Hardaway .60 1.50
SS19 Reggie Miller .40 1.00
SS20 Steve Francis .40 1.00

2006-07 Fleer

Released in early February 2007, Fleer boasts a 251-card base set with veteran players pictured on cards 1-200 and rookies pictured on cards 201-251. Veteran cards showcase full-color player images on a basic white-bordered card design while rookie cards feature a slighly different design that includes a silver border. Also found in boxes are redemption cards for buyback autographs signed on an original Fleer card from 1986-87, 1987-88 or 1988-89. Though no odds were released for these buyback autographs, each box does contain an original Fleer card from one of the aforementioned years. Packaging for Fleer includes both Hobby and Retail formats where each contains 36 ten-card packs. The original suggested retail price for Fleer was $1.59 per pack.

COMPLETE SET (250) 30.00 70.00
COMP.SET w/o RC's (200) 10.00 25.00
1 Josh Childress .20 .50
2 Al Harrington .20 .50
3 Joe Johnson .25 .60
4 Tyronn Lue .15 .40
5 Josh Smith .25 .60
6 Salim Stoudamire .15 .40
7 Marvin Williams .25 .60
8 Tony Allen .15 .40
9 Dan Dickau .15 .40
10 Al Jefferson .25 .60
11 Michael Olowokandi .15 .40
12 Paul Pierce .30 .75
13 Wally Szczerbiak .20 .50
14 Gerald Green .20 .50
15 Raymond Felton .30 .75
16 Brevin Knight .15 .40
17 Sean May .15 .40
18 Emeka Okafor .25 .60
19 Othella Harrington .15 .40
20 Gerald Wallace .25 .60
21 Tyson Chandler .20 .50
22 Luol Deng .25 .60
23 Chris Duhon .15 .40
24 Ben Gordon .25 .60
25 Kirk Hinrich .25 .60
26 Mike Sweetney .15 .40
27 Michael Jordan 2.00 5.00
28 Drew Gooden .20 .50
29 Larry Hughes .20 .50
30 Zydrunas Ilgauskas .20 .50
31 Damon Jones .15 .40
32 LeBron James 1.25 3.00
33 Donyell Marshall .15 .40
34 Anderson Varejao .20 .50
35 Erick Dampier .15 .40
36 Marquis Daniels .15 .40
37 Devin Harris .25 .60
38 Josh Howard .20 .50
39 Dirk Nowitzki .40 1.00
40 Jerry Stackhouse .20 .50
41 Jason Terry .20 .50
42 Carmelo Anthony .30 .75
43 Marcus Camby .20 .50
44 Reggie Evans .15 .40
45 Kenyon Martin .25 .60
46 Andre Miller .20 .50
47 Eduardo Najera .15 .40
48 Nene .20 .50
49 Chauncey Billups .25 .60
50 Richard Hamilton .20 .50
51 Jason Maxiell .15 .40
52 Antonio McDyess .20 .50
53 Tayshaun Prince .25 .60
54 Ben Wallace .25 .60
55 Rasheed Wallace .25 .60
56 Baron Davis .25 .60
57 Ike Diogu .15 .40
58 Mike Dunleavy .20 .50
59 Derek Fisher .20 .50
60 Adonal Foyle .15 .40
61 Troy Murphy .15 .40
62 Jason Richardson .25 .60
63 Rafer Alston .15 .40
64 Chuck Hayes .15 .40
65 Luther Head .20 .50
66 Juwan Howard .20 .50
67 Tracy McGrady .30 .75
68 Stromile Swift .15 .40
69 Yao Ming .30 .75
70 Austin Croshere .15 .40
71 Danny Granger .25 .60
72 Sarunas Jasikevicius .20 .50
73 Stephen Jackson .20 .50
74 Jermaine O'Neal .25 .60
75 Peja Stojakovic .25 .60
76 Jamaal Tinsley .15 .40
77 Elton Brand .25 .60
78 Sam Cassell .25 .60
79 Chris Kaman .20 .50
80 Yaroslav Korolev .15 .40
81 Shaun Livingston .15 .40
82 Corey Maggette .20 .50
83 Cuttino Mobley .20 .50
84 Kwame Brown .15 .40
85 Kobe Bryant 1.25 3.00
86 Andrew Bynum .40 1.00
87 Devean George .15 .40
88 Lamar Odom .25 .60
89 Ronny Turiaf .20 .50
90 Luke Walton .15 .40
91 Shane Battier .20 .50
92 Pau Gasol .25 .60
93 Bobby Jackson .15 .40
94 Mike Miller .25 .60
95 Lawrence Roberts .15 .40
96 Damon Stoudamire .20 .50
97 Hakim Warrick .20 .50
98 Alonzo Mourning .30 .75
99 Shaquille O'Neal .50 1.25
100 Gary Payton .25 .60
101 Wayne Simien .15 .40
102 Dwyane Wade .60 1.50
103 Antoine Walker .20 .50
104 Jason Williams .20 .50
105 Andrew Bogut .25 .60
106 T.J. Ford .20 .50
107 Jamaal Magloire .15 .40
108 Michael Redd .25 .60
109 Bobby Simmons .15 .40
110 Maurice Williams .20 .50
111 Mark Blount .15 .40
112 Ricky Davis .20 .50
113 Kevin Garnett .50 1.25
114 Eddie Griffin .15 .40
115 Troy Hudson .15 .40
116 Rashad McCants .15 .40
117 Vince Carter .30 .75
118 Jason Collins .15 .40
119 Richard Jefferson .25 .60
120 Jason Kidd .40 1.00
121 Nenad Krstic .15 .40
122 Jeff McInnis .15 .40
123 Antoine Wright .15 .40
124 Brandon Bass .15 .40
125 David West .25 .60
126 Desmond Mason .15 .40
127 Chris Paul .50 1.25
128 J.R. Smith .25 .60
129 Kirk Snyder .15 .40
130 Jamal Crawford .20 .50
131 Steve Francis .25 .60
132 Channing Frye .20 .50
133 Stephon Marbury .20 .50
134 Quentin Richardson .20 .50
135 Nate Robinson .25 .60
136 Jalen Rose .20 .50
137 Carlos Arroyo .20 .50
138 Keyon Dooling .15 .40
139 Grant Hill .30 .75
140 Dwight Howard .40 1.00
141 Darko Milicic .15 .40
142 Jameer Nelson .20 .50
143 DeShawn Stevenson .15 .40
144 Samuel Dalembert .15 .40
145 Steven Hunter .15 .40
146 Andre Iguodala .25 .60
147 Allen Iverson .30 .75
148 Kyle Korver .20 .50
149 Chris Webber .25 .60
150 Leandro Barbosa .20 .50
151 Raja Bell .20 .50
152 Boris Diaw .20 .50
153 Shawn Marion .25 .60
154 Steve Nash .30 .75
155 Amare Stoudemire .25 .60
156 Kurt Thomas .15 .40
157 Steve Blake .15 .40
158 Juan Dixon .15 .40
159 Joel Przybilla .15 .40
160 Zach Randolph .20 .50
161 Travis Outlaw .20 .50
162 Sebastian Telfair .15 .40
163 Martell Webster .20 .50
164 Shareef Abdur-Rahim .20 .50
165 Ron Artest .25 .60
166 Mike Bibby .25 .60
167 Francisco Garcia .20 .50
168 Brad Miller .25 .60
169 Kenny Thomas .15 .40
170 Bonzi Wells .15 .40
171 Bruce Bowen .15 .40
172 Tim Duncan .40 1.00
173 Michael Finley .25 .60
174 Manu Ginobili .25 .60
175 Tony Parker .25 .60
176 Ray Allen .25 .60
177 Danny Fortson .15 .40
178 Rashard Lewis .25 .60
179 Luke Ridnour .20 .50
180 Robert Swift .15 .40
181 Chris Wilcox .15 .40
182 Chris Bosh .25 .60
183 Jose Calderon .20 .50
184 Joey Graham .15 .40
185 Pape Sow .15 .40
186 Charlie Villanueva .25 .60
187 Morris Peterson .15 .40
188 Carlos Boozer .25 .60
189 Gordan Giricek .15 .40
190 Kris Humphries .15 .40
191 Andrei Kirilenko .20 .50
192 Mehmet Okur .15 .40
193 Deron Williams .40 1.00
194 Gilbert Arenas .25 .60
195 Andray Blatche .15 .40
196 Caron Butler .25 .60
197 Brendan Haywood .15 .40
198 Antawn Jamison .25 .60
199 Etan Thomas .15 .40
200 Antonio Daniels .15 .40
201 Tyrus Thomas RC .75 2.00
202 Adam Morrison RC .75 2.00
203 LaMarcus Aldridge RC 1.50 4.00
204 Rudy Gay RC 1.00 2.50
205 Andrea Bargnani RC 1.00 2.50
206 Rodney Carney RC RC .60 1.50
207 Alexander Johnson RC .60 1.50
208 Brandon Roy RC 1.50 4.00
209 Patrick O'Bryant RC .60 1.50
210 Randy Foye RC .75 2.00
211 Ronnie Brewer RC .75 2.00
212 Mardy Collins RC .60 1.50
213 Shelden Williams RC .60 1.50
214 J.J. Redick RC .75 2.00
215 Hilton Armstrong RC .60 1.50
216 Marcus Williams RC .60 1.50
217 Rajon Rondo RC 2.50 6.00
218 Cedric Simmons RC .60 1.50
219 Bobby Jones RC .60 1.50
220 Jordan Farmar RC .60 1.50
221 Maurice Ager RC .60 1.50
222 David Noel RC .60 1.50
223 James White RC .60 1.50
224 Leon Powe RC .60 1.50
225 Paul Millsap RC 1.00 2.50
226 Josh Boone RC .60 1.50
227 Kevin Pittsnogle RC .60 1.50
228 Daniel Gibson RC .75 2.00
229 Hassan Adams RC .60 1.50
230 Kyle Lowry RC .75 2.00
231 Renaldo Balkman RC .60 1.50
232 Dee Brown RC .60 1.50
233 Shawne Williams RC .60 1.50
234 P.J. Tucker RC .60 1.50
235 Craig Smith RC .60 1.50
236 Paul Davis RC .60 1.50
237 Pops Mensah-Bonsu RC .60 1.50
238 Denham Brown RC .60 1.50
239 Ryan Hollins RC .60 1.50
240 Allan Ray RC .60 1.50
241 Saer Sene RC .60 1.50
242 Shannon Brown RC 1.00 2.50
243 Thabo Sefolosha RC .75 2.00
244 Quincy Douby RC .60 1.50
245 Solomon Jones RC .60 1.50
246 Damir Markota RC .60 1.50
247 Steve Novak RC .60 1.50
248 Will Blalock RC .60 1.50
249 Tarence Kinsey RC .60 1.50
250 Vassilis Spanoulis RC .60 1.50
NNO Michael Jordan .40 1.00

2006-07 Fleer Glossy Parallel

*GLOSSY: .75X TO 2X BASE HI
GLOSSY RANDOM INSERTS IN PACKS
27 Michael Jordan 5.00 12.00

2006-07 Fleer 1986-87 20th Anniversary

APPROXIMATE ODDS 1:2
1 Nene 1.00 2.50
2 Andrea Bargnani 2.00 5.00
3 Maurice Ager 1.25 3.00
4 Allen Iverson 1.50 4.00
5 Antawn Jamison 1.25 3.00
6 Andrei Kirilenko 1.00 2.50
7 Adam Morrison 1.50 4.00
8 Amare Stoudemire 1.25 3.00
9 Shane Battier 1.00 2.50
10 Baron Davis 1.25 3.00
11 Ben Gordon 1.25 3.00
12 Chauncey Billups 1.25 3.00
13 Steve Blake .75 2.00
14 Brad Miller 1.25 3.00
15 Andrew Bogut 1.25 3.00
16 Brandon Roy 3.00 8.00
17 Bobby Simmons .75 2.00
18 Ben Wallace 1.25 3.00
19 Andrew Bynum 2.00 5.00
20 Carmelo Anthony 1.50 4.00
21 Chris Bosh 1.25 3.00
22 Channing Frye 1.00 2.50
23 Josh Childress 1.00 2.50
24 Chris Kaman 1.00 2.50
25 Cuttino Mobley 1.00 2.50
26 Chris Paul 2.50 6.00
27 Cedric Simmons 1.25 3.00
28 Charlie Villanueva 1.25 3.00
29 Dwight Howard 2.00 5.00
30 Boris Diaw 1.00 2.50
31 Dirk Nowitzki 2.00 5.00
32 Mike Dunleavy 1.00 2.50
33 Dwyane Wade 3.00 8.00
34 Elton Brand 1.25 3.00
35 Eddy Curry 1.00 2.50
36 Fred Jones .75 2.00
37 Randy Foye 1.50 4.00
38 Gilbert Arenas 1.25 3.00
39 Gerald Green 1.00 2.50
40 Grant Hill 1.50 4.00
41 Hilton Armstrong 1.25 3.00
42 Hedo Turkoglu 1.25 3.00
43 Larry Hughes 1.00 2.50
44 Hakim Warrick 1.00 2.50
45 Andre Iguodala 1.25 3.00
46 Josh Boone 1.25 3.00
47 Jamal Crawford 1.00 2.50
48 Al Jefferson 1.25 3.00
49 Jordan Farmar 1.25 3.00
50 Josh Howard 1.00 2.50
51 Joe Johnson 1.25 3.00
52 Jason Kidd 2.00 5.00
53 Jermaine O'Neal 1.25 3.00
54 Jason Richardson 1.25 3.00
55 Jerry Stackhouse 1.00 2.50
56 Jason Terry 1.00 2.50
57 Michael Jordan 20.00 50.00
58 Kobe Bryant 6.00 15.00
59 Kevin Garnett 2.50 6.00
60 Kirk Hinrich 1.25 3.00
61 Kyle Korver 1.00 2.50
62 Kyle Lowry 1.50 4.00
63 Kenyon Martin 1.25 3.00
64 Kevin Pittsnogle 1.25 3.00
65 Kirk Snyder .75 2.00
66 Kurt Thomas .75 2.00
67 LaMarcus Aldridge 3.00 8.00
68 Luol Deng 1.25 3.00
69 Rashard Lewis 1.25 3.00
70 Luther Head 1.00 2.50
71 LeBron James 8.00 20.00
72 Lamar Odom 1.25 3.00
73 Luke Ridnour 1.00 2.50
74 Luke Walton .75 2.00
75 Shawn Marion 1.25 3.00
76 Mike Bibby 1.25 3.00
77 Mardy Collins 1.25 3.00
78 Marquis Daniels .75 2.00
79 Manu Ginobili 1.25 3.00
80 Andre Miller 1.00 2.50
81 Jason Williams 1.00 2.50
82 Mehmet Okur .75 2.00
83 Morris Peterson .75 2.00
84 Michael Redd 1.25 3.00
85 Troy Murphy .75 2.00
86 Marcus Williams 1.25 3.00
87 Nate Robinson 1.25 3.00
88 Tony Parker 1.25 3.00
89 Pau Gasol 1.25 3.00
90 Patrick O'Bryant 1.25 3.00
91 Paul Pierce 1.50 4.00
92 Peja Stojakovic 1.25 3.00
93 P.J. Tucker 1.25 3.00
94 Quincy Douby 1.25 3.00
95 Ray Allen 1.25 3.00
96 Ronnie Brewer 1.50 4.00
97 Rodney Carney 1.25 3.00
98 Ricky Davis 1.00 2.50
99 J.J. Redick 1.50 4.00
100 Raymond Felton 1.50 4.00
101 Rudy Gay 2.00 5.00
102 Richard Hamilton 1.00 2.50
103 Richard Jefferson 1.25 3.00
104 Raef LaFrentz .75 2.00
105 Rashad McCants .75 2.00
106 Jalen Rose 1.00 2.50
107 Rajon Rondo 5.00 12.00
108 Rasheed Wallace 1.25 3.00
109 Shannon Brown 2.00 5.00
110 Sam Cassell 1.25 3.00
111 Samuel Dalembert .75 2.00
112 Steve Francis 1.25 3.00
113 Sean May .75 2.00
114 Steve Nash 1.50 4.00
115 Shaquille O'Neal 2.50 6.00
116 Saer Sene 1.25 3.00
117 Stephon Marbury 1.00 2.50
118 Shelden Williams 1.25 3.00
119 Tyson Chandler 1.00 2.50
120 Tim Duncan 2.00 5.00
121 Tracy McGrady 1.50 4.00
122 Tayshaun Prince 1.25 3.00
123 Thabo Sefolosha 1.50 4.00
124 Tyrus Thomas 1.50 4.00
125 Udonis Haslem 1.00 2.50
126 Vince Carter 1.50 4.00
127 Bonzi Wells .75 2.00
128 Deron Williams 2.00 5.00
129 Marvin Williams 1.25 3.00
130 Wally Szczerbiak 1.00 2.50
131 Yao Ming 1.50 4.00
132 Zach Randolph 1.00 2.50

2006-07 Fleer 1986-87 Michael Jordan Buyback Autographs

57 Michael Jordan/23 6000.00 10000.00

2006-07 Fleer Autographics

RANDOM INSERTS IN PACKS
AA Alex Acker 5.00 12.00
AB Andrea Bargnani 12.50 30.00
AI Andre Iguodala 8.00 20.00
BB Brent Barry 6.00 15.00
BJ Bobby Jones 5.00 12.00
BO Andrew Bogut SP 10.00 25.00
BS Bobby Simmons 5.00 12.00
CK Chris Kaman SP 6.00 15.00
CP Chris Paul SP 30.00 80.00
CS Cedric Simmons 5.00 12.00
CT Chris Taft 5.00 12.00
DH Dwight Howard SP 15.00 40.00
DN David Noel 5.00 12.00
DW Deron Williams 10.00 25.00
HA Hilton Armstrong 5.00 12.00
JF Jordan Farmar 8.00 20.00
KA Kareem Abdul-Jabbar SP 50.00 100.00
KL Kyle Lowry 6.00 15.00
LA LaMarcus Aldridge 12.50 30.00
LJ LeBron James SP 100.00 200.00
MA Maurice Ager 5.00 12.00
MC Mardy Collins 5.00 12.00
MW Marcus Williams 5.00 12.00
PM Paul Millsap 8.00 20.00
PS Peja Stojakovic 5.00 12.00
RB Ronnie Brewer 6.00 15.00
RG Rudy Gay 12.50 30.00
RO Brandon Roy 20.00 50.00
RR Rajon Rondo 25.00 60.00
SS Saer Sene 5.00 12.00
TT Tyrus Thomas 12.50 30.00

2006-07 Fleer Autographics Michael Jordan Autographics

COMMON CARD 350.00 650.00
RANDOM INSERTS IN PACKS

2006-07 Fleer Jordan's Greatest Moments

COMPLETE SET (10) 20.00 50.00
COMMON CARD 4.00 10.00
RANDOM INSERTS IN PACKS
UNPRICED AUTO PRINT RUN ONE SET

2006-07 Fleer Jordan's Platinum Influence

COMPLETE SET (20) 8.00 20.00
APPROXIMATE ODDS 1:3
AH A.J. Hawk 1.00 2.50
BA Renaldo Balkman 1.00 2.50
BU Reggie Bush 2.50 6.00
HA Hilton Armstrong 1.00 2.50
JR J.J. Redick 1.25 3.00
LA LaMarcus Aldridge 2.50 6.00
ML Matt Leinart 1.00 2.50
MW Marcus Williams 1.00 2.50
PO Patrick O'Bryant 1.00 2.50
QD Quincy Douby 1.00 2.50
RB Ronnie Brewer 1.25 3.00
RC Rodney Carney 1.00 2.50
RF Randy Foye 1.25 3.00
RG Rudy Gay 1.50 4.00
SH Santonio Holmes 1.00 2.50
SW Shelden Williams 1.00 2.50
TT Tyrus Thomas 1.25 3.00
VD Vernon Davis 1.00 2.50
VY Vince Young 2.00 5.00
WI Mario Williams 1.00 2.50

2006-07 Fleer Michael Jordan Missing Links

COMMON CARD 25.00 60.00
RANDOM INSERTS IN PACKS

2006-07 Fleer Rookie Sensations

COMPLETE SET (10) 6.00 15.00
APPROXIMATE ODDS 1:5
AB Andrea Bargnani 1.00 2.50
AM Adam Morrison .75 2.00
BR Brandon Roy 1.50 4.00
JM Shelden Williams .60 1.50
LA LaMarcus Aldridge 1.50 4.00
PO Patrick O'Bryant .60 1.50
RC Rodney Carney .60 1.50
RF Randy Foye .75 2.00
RG Rudy Gay 1.00 2.50
TT Tyrus Thomas .75 2.00

2006-07 Fleer Team Leaders

COMPLETE SET (20) 5.00 12.00
APPROXIMATE ODDS 1:2
AI Allen Iverson .50 1.25
BD Baron Davis .40 1.00
CB Chauncey Billups .40 1.00
DN Dirk Nowitzki .60 1.50
DW Dwyane Wade 1.00 2.50
EO Emeka Okafor .40 1.00
GA Gilbert Arenas .40 1.00
JK Jason Kidd .60 1.50
KB Kobe Bryant 2.00 5.00
KG Kevin Garnett .75 2.00
LJ LeBron James 2.00 5.00
MB Mike Bibby .40 1.00
MJ Michael Jordan 3.00 8.00
PP Paul Pierce .50 1.25
RA Ray Allen .40 1.00
SC Sam Cassell .40 1.00
SN Steve Nash .50 1.25
SO Shaquille O'Neal .75 2.00
TD Tim Duncan .60 1.50
TM Tracy McGrady .50 1.25

2006-07 Fleer Throwbacks

APPROXIMATE ODDS ONE PER BOX
BA Renaldo Balkman 2.50 6.00
BJ Bobby Jones 2.50 6.00
CS Craig Smith 2.50 6.00
DB Dee Brown 2.50 6.00
HA Hilton Armstrong 2.50 6.00
JB Josh Boone 2.50 6.00
JF Jordan Farmar 2.50 6.00
JR J.J. Redick 3.00 8.00
JW James White 2.50 6.00
KL Kyle Lowry 3.00 8.00
KP Kevin Pittsnogle 2.50 6.00
LA LaMarcus Aldridge 6.00 15.00
MA Maurice Ager 2.50 6.00
MC Mardy Collins 2.50 6.00
MW Marcus Williams 2.50 6.00
PD Paul Davis 2.50 6.00
PO Patrick O'Bryant 2.50 6.00
PT P.J. Tucker 2.50 6.00
RB Ronnie Brewer 3.00 8.00
RC Rodney Carney 2.50 6.00
RF Randy Foye 3.00 8.00
RG Rudy Gay 4.00 10.00
RR Rajon Rondo 6.00 15.00
SB Shannon Brown 4.00 10.00
SI Cedric Simmons 2.50 6.00
SJ Solomon Jones 2.50 6.00
SN Steve Novak 2.50 6.00
SW Shelden Williams 2.50 6.00
TT Tyrus Thomas 3.00 8.00
WI Shawne Williams 2.50 6.00

2006-07 Fleer Walmart Rookie Exclusive

*WALMART: .6X TO 1.5X BASE HI
UNPRICED AUTO PRINT RUN ONE SET

2007-08 Fleer

This 235-card set was released in January, 2008. The set was issued into the hobby in 15 card packs, which came 16 packs to a box and 12 boxes to a case where packs carried an intial suggested retail price of $3.99. Cards numbered 1-200 feature veterans while cards numbered 201-235 feature NBA rookies.

COMPLETE SET (235) 30.00 60.00
ONE JORDAN RELIC PER RETAIL SET
1 Chauncey Billups .20 .50
2 Amir Johnson .12 .30
3 Richard Hamilton .15 .40
4 Jason Maxiell .12 .30
5 Tayshaun Prince .20 .50
6 Rasheed Wallace .20 .50
7 Antonio McDyess .15 .40
8 Daniel Gibson .20 .50
9 Larry Hughes .15 .40
10 Zydrunas Ilgauskas .15 .40
11 Devin Brown .12 .30
12 LeBron James 1.00 2.50
13 Donyell Marshall .12 .30
14 Eric Snow .12 .30
15 Andrea Bargnani .25 .60
16 Chris Bosh .20 .50
17 T.J. Ford .15 .40
18 Jorge Garbajosa .15 .40
19 Radoslav Nesterovic .12 .30
20 Jose Calderon .15 .40
21 James Posey .12 .30
22 Alonzo Mourning .25 .60
23 Shaquille O'Neal .40 1.00
24 Dwyane Wade .50 1.25
25 Antoine Walker .15 .40
26 Jason Williams .15 .40
27 Udonis Haslem .15 .40
28 Luol Deng .20 .50
29 Ben Gordon .20 .50
30 Kirk Hinrich .20 .50
31 Ben Wallace .20 .50
32 Tyrus Thomas .20 .50
33 Thabo Sefolosha .20 .50
34 Chris Duhon .12 .30
35 Vince Carter .25 .60
36 Jason Collins .12 .30
37 Richard Jefferson .20 .50
38 Jason Kidd .20 .50
39 Nenad Krstic .12 .30
40 Marcus Williams .12 .30
41 Josh Boone .12 .30
42 Gilbert Arenas .20 .50
43 Caron Butler .20 .50
44 Antawn Jamison .20 .50
45 Brendan Haywood .12 .30
46 Antonio Daniels .12 .30
47 Etan Thomas .12 .30
48 Trevor Ariza .12 .30
49 Dwight Howard .30 .75
50 Rashard Lewis .15 .40
51 Jameer Nelson .15 .40
52 J.J. Redick .20 .50
53 Hedo Turkoglu .20 .50
54 Carlos Arroyo .15 .40
55 Ike Diogu .12 .30
56 Mike Dunleavy .15 .40
57 Jeff Foster .12 .30
58 Jermaine O'Neal .20 .50
59 Jamaal Tinsley .12 .30
60 Shawne Williams .12 .30
61 Rodney Carney .12 .30
62 Andre Iguodala .20 .50
63 Kyle Korver .15 .40
64 Andre Miller .15 .40
65 Willie Green .12 .30
66 Samuel Dalembert .12 .30
67 Raymond Felton .25 .60
68 Sean May .12 .30
69 Adam Morrison .20 .50
70 Emeka Okafor .20 .50
71 Jason Richardson .20 .50
72 Gerald Wallace .20 .50
73 Ryan Hollins .12 .30
74 David Lee .15 .40
75 Jamal Crawford UER .15 .40
New Jersey Knicks on back
76 Eddy Curry .12 .30
77 Stephon Marbury .15 .40
78 Zach Randolph .15 .40

79 Nate Robinson	.20	.50
80 Quentin Richardson	.15	.40
81 Josh Childress	.15	.40
82 Joe Johnson	.20	.50
83 Tyronn Lue	.12	.30
84 Josh Smith	.20	.50
85 Marvin Williams	.20	.50
86 Shelden Williams	.12	.30
87 Salim Stoudamire	.12	.30
88 Andrew Bogut	.20	.50
89 Bobby Simmons	.12	.30
90 David Noel	.12	.30
91 Michael Redd	.20	.50
92 Charlie Villanueva	.20	.50
93 Desmond Mason	.12	.30
94 Ray Allen	.20	.50
95 Rajon Rondo	.30	.75
96 Al Jefferson	.20	.50
97 Paul Pierce	.25	.60
98 Leon Powe	.12	.30
99 Tony Allen	.12	.30
100 Pau Gasol	.20	.50
101 Rudy Gay	.20	.50
102 Darko Milicic	.12	.30
103 Damon Stoudamire	.15	.40
104 Hakim Warrick	.15	.40
105 Mike Miller	.20	.50
106 Johan Petro	.12	.30
107 Wally Szczerbiak	.15	.40
108 Delonte West	.15	.40
109 Luke Ridnour	.15	.40
110 Chris Wilcox	.12	.30
111 Nick Collison	.12	.30
112 LaMarcus Aldridge	.25	.60
113 Channing Frye	.15	.40
114 Jarrett Jack	.15	.40
115 Brandon Roy	.25	.60
116 Martell Webster	.15	.40
117 Sergio Rodriguez	.12	.30
118 James Jones	.12	.30
119 Shareef Abdur-Rahim	.15	.40
120 Ron Artest	.20	.50
121 Mike Bibby	.20	.50
122 Francisco Garcia	.15	.40
123 Kevin Martin	.20	.50
124 Brad Miller	.15	.40
125 Mikki Moore	.12	.30
126 Ricky Davis	.15	.40
127 Randy Foye	.20	.50
128 Kevin Garnett	.40	1.00
129 Juwan Howard	.15	.40
130 Marko Jaric	.12	.30
131 Rashad McCants	.12	.30
132 Craig Smith	.12	.30
133 Hilton Armstrong	.12	.30
134 Tyson Chandler	.15	.40
135 Bobby Jackson	.12	.30
136 Chris Paul	.40	1.00
137 Rasual Butler	.12	.30
138 Peja Stojakovic	.20	.50
139 Morris Peterson	.12	.30
140 Elton Brand	.20	.50
141 Sam Cassell	.20	.50
142 Paul Davis	.12	.30
143 Corey Maggette	.15	.40
144 Cuttino Mobley	.15	.40
145 Chris Kaman	.15	.40
146 Baron Davis	.20	.50
147 Monta Ellis	.20	.50
148 Al Harrington	.15	.40
149 Stephen Jackson	.15	.40
150 Matt Barnes	.12	.30
151 Andris Biedrins	.12	.30
152 Kwame Brown	.12	.30
153 Kobe Bryant	1.00	2.50
154 Andrew Bynum	.25	.60
155 Jordan Farmar	.12	.30
156 Lamar Odom	.20	.50
157 Luke Walton	.12	.30
158 Maurice Evans	.12	.30
159 Carmelo Anthony	.25	.60
160 Marcus Camby	.12	.30
161 Allen Iverson	.25	.60
162 Kenyon Martin	.20	.50
163 Nene	.15	.40
164 J.R. Smith	.20	.50
165 Yakhouba Diawara	.12	.30
166 Shane Battier	.15	.40
167 Luther Head	.15	.40
168 Tracy McGrady	.20	.50
169 Yao Ming	.25	.60
170 Rafer Alston	.12	.30
171 Bonzi Wells	.12	.30
172 Steve Novak	.12	.30
173 Carlos Boozer	.20	.50
174 Ronnie Brewer	.15	.40
175 Andrei Kirilenko	.15	.40
176 Paul Millsap	.15	.40
177 Mehmet Okur	.12	.30
178 Deron Williams	.30	.75
179 Jarron Collins	.12	.30
180 Tim Duncan	.30	.75
181 Tony Parker	.20	.50
182 Manu Ginobili	.20	.50
183 Bruce Bowen	.12	.30
184 Brent Barry	.12	.30
185 Robert Horry	.15	.40
186 Michael Finley	.20	.50
187 Leandro Barbosa	.15	.40
188 Grant Hill	.25	.60
189 Shawn Marion	.20	.50
190 Steve Nash	.25	.60
191 Amare Stoudemire	.20	.50
192 Boris Diaw	.15	.40
193 Raja Bell	.15	.40
194 Maurice Ager	.12	.30
195 Devean George	.12	.30
196 Devin Harris	.20	.50
197 Josh Howard	.15	.40
198 Dirk Nowitzki	.25	.60
199 Jerry Stackhouse	.15	.40
200 Jason Terry	.15	.40
201 Arron Afflalo RC	.60	1.50
202 Morris Almond RC	.50	1.25
203 Marco Belinelli RC	.50	1.25
204 Corey Brewer RC	.60	1.50
205 Wilson Chandler RC	.75	2.00
206 Mike Conley Jr. RC	.75	2.00
207 Daequan Cook RC	.50	1.25
208 Javaris Crittenton RC	.50	1.25
209 Jermareo Davidson RC	.50	1.25
210 Glen Davis RC	.75	2.00
211 Jared Dudley RC	.50	1.25
212 Kevin Durant RC	5.00	12.00
213 Nick Fazekas RC	.50	1.25
214 Jeff Green RC	.60	1.50
215 Taurean Green RC	.50	1.25
216 Spencer Hawes RC	.50	1.25
217 Al Horford RC	.60	1.50
218 Aaron Brooks RC	.50	1.25
219 Carl Landry RC	.50	1.25
220 Acie Law RC	.50	1.25
221 Josh McRoberts RC	.50	1.25
222 Joakim Noah RC	1.25	3.00
223 Greg Oden RC	.60	1.50
224 Gabe Pruitt RC	.50	1.25
225 Jason Smith RC	.50	1.25
226 Rodney Stuckey RC	.75	2.00
227 Al Thornton RC	.50	1.25
228 Alando Tucker RC	.50	1.25
229 Sean Williams RC	.50	1.25
230 Yi Jianlian RC	.75	2.00
231 Brandan Wright RC	.50	1.25
232 Julian Wright RC	.50	1.25
233 Nick Young RC	.75	2.00
234 Thaddeus Young RC	.60	1.50
235 Chris Richard RC	.50	1.25
RCF Michael Jordan Floor	12.00	30.00
COAF M.Jordan Floor AU/23	1000.00	2000.00
RCPJ Michael Jordan JSY White	25.00	60.00
RCWU M.Jordan JSY Black/250	60.00	120.00

2007-08 Fleer Glossy

*GLOSSY: .75X TO 2X BASE HI
RANDOM INSERTS IN PACKS

2007-08 Fleer 1961-62

*1961-62 SINGLES: 1X TO 2.5X BASE HI
RANDOM INSERTS IN PACKS

2007-08 Fleer 1986-87 Rookies

*1986-87 RCs: .6X TO 1.5X BASE HI
APPROXIMATELY ONE PER PACK
*1986-87 RC GLOSSY: .75X TO 2X BASE HI
GLOSSY RANDOM INSERTS IN PACKS

2007-08 Fleer 1987-88

*1987-88: .6X TO 1.5X BASE HI
APPROXIMATELY ONE PER PACK

R71 Michael Jordan	6.00	15.00

2007-08 Fleer Decades of Excellence

COMPLETE SET (20)	25.00	50.00
RANDOM INSERTS IN PACKS		
*GLOSSY: .6X TO 1.5X BASE HI		
GLOSSY RANDOM INSERTS IN PACKS		
1 Larry Bird	3.00	8.00
2 Magic Johnson	2.50	6.00
3 Michael Jordan	8.00	20.00
4 Bill Laimbeer	1.00	2.50
5 David Robinson	1.50	4.00
6 Grant Hill	1.25	3.00
7 Hakeem Olajuwon	1.25	3.00
8 Robert Parish	1.00	2.50
9 John Stockton	1.50	4.00
10 Michael Jordan	8.00	20.00
11 Dennis Rodman	1.50	4.00
12 Shaquille O'Neal	2.00	5.00
13 LeBron James	5.00	12.00
14 Chauncey Billups	1.00	2.50
15 Kobe Bryant	5.00	12.00
16 Steve Nash	1.25	3.00
17 Dwyane Wade	2.50	6.00
18 Allen Iverson	1.25	3.00
19 Baron Davis	1.00	2.50
20 Tim Duncan	1.50	4.00

2007-08 Fleer Feel The Game

APPROXIMATE ODDS ONE PER BOX		
FGAB Andrea Bargnani	3.00	8.00
FGAI Allen Iverson	3.00	8.00
FGAJ Antawn Jamison	2.50	6.00
FGAM Alonzo Mourning	3.00	8.00
FGAS Amare Stoudemire	2.50	6.00
FGBO Carlos Boozer	2.50	6.00
FGBW Ben Wallace	2.50	6.00
FGCA Carmelo Anthony	3.00	8.00
FGCB Chauncey Billups	2.50	6.00
FGCH Chris Bosh	2.50	6.00
FGDH Dwight Howard	4.00	10.00
FGDN Dirk Nowitzki	3.00	8.00
FGDR David Robinson	4.00	10.00
FGEB Elton Brand	2.50	6.00
FGGH Grant Hill	4.00	10.00
FGHO Hakeem Olajuwon	3.00	8.00
FGJJ Joe Johnson	2.50	6.00
FGJK Jason Kidd	2.50	6.00
FGJO Michael Jordan	20.00	40.00
FGKB Kobe Bryant	6.00	15.00
FGKG Kevin Garnett	5.00	12.00
FGLB Larry Bird	8.00	20.00
FGLJ LeBron James	6.00	15.00
FGMJ Magic Johnson	6.00	15.00
FGMR Michael Redd	2.50	6.00
FGO' Jermaine O'Neal	2.50	6.00
FGPG Pau Gasol	2.50	6.00
FGPP Paul Pierce	3.00	8.00
FGPS Peja Stojakovic	2.50	6.00
FGRA Ray Allen	2.50	6.00
FGRH Richard Hamilton	2.00	5.00
FGRO Dennis Rodman	4.00	10.00
FGRW Rasheed Wallace	2.50	6.00
FGSM Stephon Marbury	2.00	5.00
FGSO Shaquille O'Neal	5.00	12.00
FGTD Tim Duncan	4.00	10.00
FGTM Tracy McGrady	2.50	6.00
FGTP Tony Parker	2.50	6.00
FGVC Vince Carter	3.00	8.00
FGYM Yao Ming	3.00	8.00

2007-08 Fleer Michael Jordan Missing Links

COMMON CARD	25.00	60.00
RANDOM INSERTS IN PACKS		

2007-08 Fleer NBA Classics

APPROXIMATELY ONE PER BOX		
TTAA Arron Afflalo	3.00	8.00
TTAB Aaron Brooks	2.50	6.00
TTAG Aaron Gray	2.50	6.00
TTAH Al Horford	3.00	8.00
TTAL Acie Law	2.50	6.00
TTAT Al Thornton	2.50	6.00
TTCB Corey Brewer	3.00	8.00
TTCL Carl Landry	2.50	6.00
TTCR Chris Richard	2.50	6.00
TTDM Dominic McGuire	2.50	6.00
TTDU Jared Dudley	2.50	6.00
TTGD Glen Davis	4.00	10.00
TTGP Gabe Pruitt	2.50	6.00
TTHA Adam Haluska	2.50	6.00
TTHH Herbert Hill	2.50	6.00
TTJC Javaris Crittenton	2.50	6.00
TTJD Jermareo Davidson	2.50	6.00
TTJG Jeff Green	3.00	8.00
TTJN Joakim Noah	6.00	15.00
TTJS Jason Smith	2.50	6.00
TTJW Julian Wright	2.50	6.00
TTKD Kevin Durant	10.00	25.00
TTMA Morris Almond	2.50	6.00
TTMC Mike Conley Jr.	4.00	10.00
TTNF Nick Fazekas	2.50	6.00
TTNY Nick Young	4.00	10.00
TTRS Rodney Stuckey	4.00	10.00
TTSH Spencer Hawes	2.50	6.00
TTSW Sean Williams	2.50	6.00
TTTG Taurean Green	2.50	6.00
TTTU Alando Tucker	2.50	6.00
TTTY Thaddeus Young	3.00	8.00
TTWC Wilson Chandler	4.00	10.00

2007-08 Fleer Rookie Sensations

COMPLETE SET (15)	12.50	25.00
RANDOM INSERTS IN PACKS		
*GLOSSY: .6X TO 1.5X BASE HI		
GLOSSY RANDOM INSERTS IN PACKS		
RS1 Greg Oden	1.00	2.50
RS2 Kevin Durant	6.00	15.00
RS3 Al Horford	1.00	2.50
RS4 Mike Conley Jr.	1.25	3.00
RS5 Jeff Green	1.00	2.50
RS6 Thaddeus Young	1.00	2.50
RS7 Corey Brewer	1.00	2.50
RS8 Brandan Wright	.75	2.00
RS9 Joakim Noah	2.00	5.00
RS10 Spencer Hawes	.75	2.00
RS11 Acie Law	.75	2.00
RS12 Julian Wright	.75	2.00
RS13 Al Thornton	.75	2.00
RS14 Rodney Stuckey	1.25	3.00
RS15 Nick Young	1.25	3.00

2008-09 Fleer

This set was released on January 6, 2009. The base set consists of 247 cards. Cards 1-200 feature veterans, and cards 201-247 feature rookie players.

COMPLETE SET (247)	20.00	50.00
ROOKIE STATED ODDS 1:1		
TRI-CARD STATED ODDS 1:3		
1 Ray Allen	.20	.50
2 Kevin Garnett	.40	1.00
3 Paul Pierce	.25	.60
4 Glen Davis	.15	.40
5 Rajon Rondo	.25	.60
6 Leon Powe	.12	.30
7 James Posey	.12	.30
8 Chauncey Billups	.20	.50
9 Richard Hamilton	.15	.40
10 Jason Maxiell	.12	.30
11 Tayshaun Prince	.20	.50
12 Rasheed Wallace	.20	.50
13 Rodney Stuckey	.25	.60
14 Antonio McDyess	.15	.40
15 Keith Bogans	.12	.30
16 Maurice Evans	.12	.30
17 Dwight Howard	.40	1.00
18 Rashard Lewis	.15	.40
19 Jameer Nelson	.15	.40
20 Hedo Turkoglu	.20	.50
21 Anthony Johnson	.12	.30
22 Ben Wallace	.20	.50
23 LeBron James	1.00	2.50
24 Zydrunas Ilgauskas	.15	.40
25 Delonte West	.15	.40
26 Anderson Varejao	.15	.40
27 Daniel Gibson	.20	.50
28 Mo Williams	.15	.40
29 Gilbert Arenas	.20	.50
30 Caron Butler	.20	.50
31 Brendan Haywood	.12	.30
32 Antawn Jamison	.20	.50
33 DeShawn Stevenson	.12	.30
34 Nick Young	.15	.40
35 Antonio Daniels	.12	.30
36 Andrea Bargnani	.15	.40
37 Chris Bosh	.20	.50
38 Jose Calderon	.15	.40
39 Jermaine O'Neal	.20	.50
40 Anthony Parker	.12	.30
41 Jamario Moon	.12	.30
42 Elton Brand	.20	.50
43 Samuel Dalembert	.12	.30
44 Willie Green	.12	.30
45 Andre Iguodala	.20	.50
46 Andre Miller	.15	.40
47 Louis Williams	.15	.40
48 Thaddeus Young	.15	.40
49 Mike Bibby	.15	.40
50 Zaza Pachulia	.12	.30
51 Al Horford	.20	.50
52 Joe Johnson	.20	.50
53 Josh Smith	.20	.50
54 Marvin Williams	.20	.50
55 Acie Law	.15	.40
56 Danny Granger	.20	.50
57 T.J. Ford	.12	.30
58 Mike Dunleavy	.15	.40
59 Jamaal Tinsley	.12	.30
60 Troy Murphy	.12	.30
61 Jeff Foster	.12	.30
62 Vince Carter	.25	.60
63 Yi Jianlian	.20	.50
64 Sean Williams	.15	.40
65 Devin Harris	.20	.50
66 Keyon Dooling	.12	.30
67 Josh Boone	.12	.30
68 Michael Jordan	1.50	4.00
69 Luol Deng	.20	.50
70 Ben Gordon	.20	.50
71 Joakim Noah	.20	.50
72 Kirk Hinrich	.20	.50
73 Andres Nocioni	.12	.30
74 Larry Hughes	.15	.40
75 Gerald Wallace	.20	.50
76 Emeka Okafor	.20	.50
77 Jason Richardson	.20	.50
78 Raymond Felton	.15	.40
79 Adam Morrison	.20	.50
80 Jared Dudley	.15	.40
81 Nazr Mohammed	.12	.30
82 Andrew Bogut	.20	.50
83 Charlie Villanueva	.20	.50
84 Michael Redd	.20	.50
85 Ramon Sessions	.15	.40
86 Richard Jefferson	.20	.50
87 Charlie Bell	.12	.30
88 Jamal Crawford	.15	.40
89 Eddy Curry	.12	.30
90 Stephon Marbury	.15	.40
91 Zach Randolph	.15	.40
92 Quentin Richardson	.15	.40
93 Nate Robinson	.20	.50
94 David Lee	.15	.40
95 Dwyane Wade	.40	1.00
96 Daequan Cook	.12	.30
97 Shawn Marion	.20	.50
98 Alonzo Mourning	.25	.60
99 Udonis Haslem	.15	.40
100 Dorell Wright	.12	.30
101 Kobe Bryant	1.00	2.50
102 Andrew Bynum	.25	.60
103 Jordan Farmar	.12	.30
104 Pau Gasol	.20	.50
105 Lamar Odom	.20	.50
106 Luke Walton	.12	.30
107 Sasha Vujacic	.12	.30
108 Tyson Chandler	.15	.40
109 Chris Paul	.30	.75
110 Hilton Armstrong	.12	.30
111 Peja Stojakovic	.20	.50
112 Rasual Butler	.12	.30
113 Julian Wright	.15	.40
114 Morris Peterson	.12	.30
115 Tony Parker	.20	.50
116 Tim Duncan	.30	.75
117 Manu Ginobili	.20	.50
118 Michael Finley	.20	.50
119 Kurt Thomas	.12	.30
120 Bruce Bowen	.12	.30
121 Fabricio Oberto	.12	.30
122 Mehmet Okur	.12	.30
123 Deron Williams	.20	.50
124 Carlos Boozer	.20	.50
125 Kyle Korver	.15	.40
126 Andrei Kirilenko	.15	.40
127 Paul Millsap	.15	.40
128 Ronnie Brewer	.15	.40
129 Shane Battier	.15	.40
130 Tracy McGrady	.20	.50
131 Yao Ming	.25	.60
132 Luis Scola	.15	.40
133 Luther Head	.12	.30
134 Carl Landry	.12	.30
135 Ron Artest	.20	.50
136 Grant Hill	.25	.60
137 Amare Stoudemire	.20	.50
138 Steve Nash	.20	.50
139 Shaquille O'Neal	.40	1.00
140 Leandro Barbosa	.15	.40
141 Boris Diaw	.12	.30
142 Raja Bell	.15	.40
143 Dirk Nowitzki	.25	.60
144 Jason Kidd	.20	.50
145 Josh Howard	.15	.40
146 Jerry Stackhouse	.15	.40
147 Jason Terry	.15	.40
148 Brandon Bass	.12	.30
149 Erick Dampier	.12	.30
150 Carmelo Anthony	.25	.60
151 Nene	.15	.40
152 Allen Iverson	.25	.60
153 Kenyon Martin	.20	.50
154 J.R. Smith	.20	.50
155 Linas Kleiza	.12	.30
156 Corey Maggette	.15	.40
157 Monta Ellis	.20	.50
158 Stephen Jackson	.15	.40
159 Al Harrington	.15	.40
160 Andris Biedrins	.12	.30
161 Kelenna Azubuike	.12	.30
162 C.J. Watson	.12	.30
163 LaMarcus Aldridge	.20	.50
164 Travis Outlaw	.15	.40
165 Greg Oden	.20	.50
166 Brandon Roy	.20	.50
167 Martell Webster	.15	.40
168 Steve Blake	.12	.30
169 Bobby Brown	.12	.30
170 Beno Udrih	.12	.30
171 Kevin Martin	.20	.50
172 Francisco Garcia	.15	.40
173 Brad Miller	.15	.40
174 John Salmons	.20	.50
175 Mikki Moore	.12	.30
176 Baron Davis	.20	.50
177 Chris Kaman	.15	.40
178 Shaun Livingston	.12	.30
179 Marcus Camby	.12	.30
180 Al Thornton	.15	.40
181 Cuttino Mobley	.15	.40
182 Ricky Davis	.15	.40
183 Corey Brewer	.15	.40
184 Randy Foye	.20	.50
185 Al Jefferson	.20	.50
186 Rashad McCants	.12	.30
187 Mike Miller	.20	.50
188 Sebastian Telfair	.12	.30
189 Mike Conley Jr.	.15	.40
190 Rudy Gay	.20	.50
191 Kyle Lowry	.20	.50
192 Hakim Warrick	.15	.40
193 Marko Jaric	.12	.30
194 Javaris Crittenton	.12	.30
195 Kevin Durant	.75	2.00
196 Jeff Green	.15	.40
197 Chris Wilcox	.12	.30
198 Damien Wilkins	.12	.30
199 Earl Watson	.12	.30
200 Desmond Mason	.12	.30
201 Derrick Rose RC	6.00	15.00
202 Michael Beasley RC	.75	2.00
203 O.J. Mayo RC	.75	2.00
204 Russell Westbrook RC	3.00	8.00
205 Kevin Love RC	2.00	5.00
206 Danilo Gallinari RC	.75	2.00
207 Eric Gordon RC	1.25	3.00
208 Joe Alexander RC	.50	1.25
209 D.J. Augustin RC	.50	1.25
210 Brook Lopez RC	.75	2.00
211 Jerryd Bayless RC	.50	1.25
212 Jason Thompson RC	.50	1.25
213 Brandon Rush RC	.50	1.25
214 Anthony Randolph RC	.60	1.50
215 Robin Lopez RC	.50	1.25
216 Marreese Speights RC	.50	1.25
217 Roy Hibbert RC	.75	2.00
218 Javale McGee RC	.75	2.00
219 J.J. Hickson RC	.60	1.50
220 Alexis Ajinca RC	.50	1.25
221 Ryan Anderson RC	.75	2.00
222 Courtney Lee RC	.75	2.00
223 Kosta Koufos RC	.50	1.25
224 George Hill RC	.75	2.00
225 Darrell Arthur RC	.50	1.25
226 Donte Greene RC	.50	1.25
227 D.J. White RC	.50	1.25
228 J.R. Giddens RC	.50	1.25
229 Walter Sharpe RC	.50	1.25
230 Joey Dorsey RC	.50	1.25
231 Mario Chalmers RC	.75	2.00
232 Kyle Weaver RC	.50	1.25
233 Sonny Weems RC	.50	1.25
234 Chris Douglas-Roberts RC	.50	1.25
235 Rudy Fernandez RC	.60	1.50
236 Derrick Rose Michael Beasley O.J. Mayo	4.00	10.00
237 Russell Westbrook Kevin Love Danilo Gallinari	2.50	6.00
238 Eric Gordon Joe Alexander D.J. Augustin	2.50	6.00
239 Brook Lopez Jerryd Bayless Jason Thompson	2.50	6.00
240 Brandon Rush Anthony Randolph Robin Lopez	1.50	4.00
241 Marreese Speights Roy Hibbert Javale McGee	2.00	5.00
242 J.J. Hickson Alexis Ajinca Ryan Anderson	1.50	4.00
243 Courtney Lee Kosta Koufos George Hill	1.50	4.00
244 Darrell Arthur Donte Greene D.J. White	1.50	4.00
245 J.R. Giddens Walter Sharpe Joey Dorsey	1.50	4.00
246 Mario Chalmers DeAndre Jordan Kyle Weaver	2.00	5.00
247 Sonny Weems Chris Douglas-Roberts Rudy Fernandez	1.50	4.00

2008-09 Fleer Glossy

*GLOSSY: .6X TO 1.5X BASE HI
RANDOM INSERTS IN PACKS

2008-09 Fleer 1986-87 Rookies

COMPLETE SET (30)	15.00	40.00
STATED ODDS 1:2		
*GLOSSY: .6X TO 1.5X BASE HI		
GLOSSY: RANDOM INSERTS IN PACKS		
86R163 Derrick Rose	8.00	20.00
86R164 Michael Beasley	1.50	4.00
86R165 O.J. Mayo	1.50	4.00
86R166 Russell Westbrook	5.00	12.00
86R167 Kevin Love	4.00	10.00
86R168 Eric Gordon	2.50	6.00
86R169 Joe Alexander	1.00	2.50
86R170 D.J. Augustin	1.00	2.50
86R171 Brook Lopez	1.50	4.00
86R172 Jerryd Bayless	1.00	2.50
86R173 Jason Thompson	1.00	2.50
86R174 Brandon Rush	1.00	2.50
86R175 Anthony Randolph	1.25	3.00
86R176 Robin Lopez	1.00	2.50
86R177 Marreese Speights	1.00	2.50
86R178 Roy Hibbert	1.50	4.00
86R179 Javale McGee	1.50	4.00
86R180 J.J. Hickson	1.25	3.00
86R181 Ryan Anderson	1.50	4.00
86R182 Courtney Lee	1.50	4.00
86R183 Kosta Koufos	1.00	2.50
86R184 George Hill	1.50	4.00
86R185 Darrell Arthur	1.00	2.50
86R186 Donte Greene	1.00	2.50
86R187 D.J. White	1.00	2.50
86R188 J.R. Giddens	1.00	2.50
86R189 Joey Dorsey	1.00	2.50
86R190 Sonny Weems	1.00	2.50
86R191 Chris Douglas-Roberts	1.00	2.50
86R192 Rudy Fernandez	1.25	3.00

2008-09 Fleer 1988-89

COMPLETE SET (132)	30.00	60.00
*88-89: .75X TO 2X BASE HI		
APPROXIMATE ODDS 1:3		

2008-09 Fleer All-Star Sensations

COMPLETE SET (26)	15.00	30.00
AS1 Allen Iverson	.60	1.50
AS2 David Robinson	.75	2.00
AS3 Dirk Nowitzki	.60	1.50
AS4 Dominique Wilkins	.60	1.50
AS5 Dwight Howard	1.00	2.50
AS6 Grant Hill	.60	1.50
AS7 Jason Kidd	.50	1.25
AS8 Jason Richardson	.50	1.25
AS9 John Stockton	.75	2.00
AS10 Josh Smith	.50	1.25
AS11 Julius Erving	1.00	2.50
AS12 Kevin Garnett	1.00	2.50
AS13 Kobe Bryant	2.50	6.00
AS14 Larry Bird	1.50	4.00
AS15 LeBron James	2.50	6.00
AS16 Magic Johnson	1.25	3.00
AS17 Michael Jordan	4.00	10.00
AS18 Ray Allen	.50	1.25
AS19 Rolando Blackman	.50	1.25
AS20 Shaquille O'Neal	1.00	2.50
AS21 Spud Webb	.50	1.25
AS22 Tim Duncan	.75	2.00
AS23 Tom Chambers	.50	1.25
AS24 Tracy McGrady	.50	1.25
AS25 Vince Carter	.60	1.50
AS26 Yao Ming	.60	1.50

2008-09 Fleer Feel the Game

RANDOM INSERTS IN PACKS		
FGCA Carmelo Anthony	3.00	8.00
FGDH Dwight Howard	5.00	12.00
FGGA Gilbert Arenas	2.50	6.00
FGKB Kobe Bryant	10.00	25.00
FGKG Kevin Garnett	5.00	12.00
FGLJ LeBron James	10.00	25.00
FGMJ Michael Jordan	20.00	50.00
FGSN Steve Nash	2.50	6.00
FGSO Shaquille O'Neal	5.00	12.00
FGYM Yao Ming	3.00	8.00

2008-09 Fleer First Year Phenoms

COMPLETE SET (10)	10.00	25.00
PH1 Derrick Rose	8.00	20.00
PH2 Michael Beasley	1.50	4.00
PH3 O.J. Mayo	1.50	4.00
PH4 Russell Westbrook	5.00	12.00
PH5 Kevin Love	4.00	10.00
PH6 Danilo Gallinari	1.50	4.00
PH7 Eric Gordon	2.50	6.00
PH8 Joe Alexander	1.00	2.50
PH9 D.J. Augustin	1.00	2.50
PH10 Brook Lopez	1.50	4.00

2008-09 Fleer Genuine Coverage

APPROXIMATE ODDS 1:10		
GCAI Andre Iguodala	2.50	6.00
GCAK Andrei Kirilenko	2.00	5.00
GCAS Amare Stoudemire	2.50	6.00
GCBO Chris Bosh	2.50	6.00
GCCA Carmelo Anthony	3.00	8.00
GCCB Chauncey Billups	2.50	6.00
GCCM Corey Maggette	2.00	5.00
GCDH Dwight Howard	5.00	12.00
GCDN Dirk Nowitzki	3.00	8.00
GCEB Elton Brand	2.50	6.00
GCGA Gilbert Arenas	2.50	6.00
GCJK Jason Kidd	2.50	6.00
GCJO Jermaine O'Neal	2.50	6.00
GCKB Kobe Bryant	10.00	25.00
GCKG Kevin Garnett	5.00	12.00
GCLJ LeBron James	10.00	25.00
GCRA Ray Allen	2.50	6.00
GCRH Richard Hamilton	2.00	5.00
GCRW Rasheed Wallace	2.50	6.00
GCSM Shawn Marion	2.50	6.00
GCSO Shaquille O'Neal	5.00	12.00
GCTD Tim Duncan	4.00	10.00
GCTM Tracy McGrady	2.50	6.00
GCVC Vince Carter	3.00	8.00
GCYM Yao Ming	3.00	8.00

2008-09 Fleer Living Legacies

COMPLETE SET (12)	15.00	30.00
LL1 Bill Russell	1.50	4.00
LL2 Bill Walton	1.00	2.50
LL3 Clyde Drexler	1.25	3.00
LL4 Dominique Wilkins	1.25	3.00
LL5 Hakeem Olajuwon	1.25	3.00
LL6 James Worthy	1.00	2.50
LL7 Julius Erving	2.00	5.00
LL8 Larry Bird	3.00	8.00
LL9 Magic Johnson	2.50	6.00
LL10 Michael Jordan	8.00	20.00
LL11 Oscar Robertson	1.00	2.50
LL12 Robert Parish	1.00	2.50

2008-09 Fleer Michael Jordan Retrospective

COMPLETE SET (23)	15.00	40.00
*GLOSSY: .6X TO 1.5X BASE HI		
RANDOM INSERTS IN PACKS		

2008-09 Fleer NBA Classic

APPROXIMATE ODDS 1:10	
NBAAR Anthony Randolph	2.50
NBABL Brook Lopez	3.00
NBABR Brandon Rush	2.00
NBACD Chris Douglas-Roberts	2.00
NBACL Courtney Lee	3.00
NBADA D.J. Augustin	2.00
NBADG Donte Greene	2.00
NBADJ DeAndre Jordan	4.00
NBADR Derrick Rose	12.00
NBAEG Eric Gordon	5.00
NBAGH George Hill	3.00
NBAJA Joe Alexander	2.00
NBAJB Jerryd Bayless	2.00
NBAJH J.J. Hickson	2.50
NBAJM Javale McGee	3.00
NBAJT Jason Thompson	2.00
NBAKK Kosta Koufos	2.00
NBAKL Kevin Love	6.00
NBAKW Kyle Weaver	2.00
NBAMB Michael Beasley	3.00
NBAMC Mario Chalmers	3.00
NBAMS Marreese Speights	2.00
NBAOM O.J. Mayo	3.00
NBAPE Patrick Ewing Jr	2.00
NBARA Ryan Anderson	3.00
NBARH Roy Hibbert	3.00
NBARL Robin Lopez	2.00
NBASW Sonny Weems	2.00
NBAWS Walter Sharpe	2.00

2008-09 Fleer Sharp Shoot

COMPLETE SET (20)	20.00
SS1 Anthony Parker	.75
SS2 B.J. Armstrong	1.25
SS3 Ben Gordon	1.25
SS4 Chauncey Billups	1.25
SS5 Daniel Gibson	1.25
SS6 Jason Kapono	.75
SS7 John Stockton	2.00
SS8 Kenny Smith	1.25
SS9 Kevin Martin	1.25
SS10 Larry Bird	4.00
SS11 Leandro Barbosa	1.00
SS12 Manu Ginobili	1.25
SS13 Mark Price	2.00
SS14 Michael Redd	1.25
SS15 Mike Miller	1.25
SS16 Peja Stojakovic	1.25
SS17 Rashard Lewis	1.00
SS18 Ray Allen	1.25
SS19 Steve Kerr	1.25
SS20 Steve Nash	1.25

2008-09 Fleer Signature Approval

APPROXIMATE ODDS 1:15	
SAAA Alexis Ajinca	5.00
SAAB Aaron Brooks	3.00
SAAM Alonzo Mourning	40.00
SAAN Carmelo Anthony	25.00
SAAT Al Thornton	8.00
SABB Bobby Brown	3.00
SABE Marco Belinelli	3.00
SABI Mike Bibby	5.00
SACA ML Carr	6.00
SACB Corey Brewer	3.00
SACH Maurice Cheeks	5.00
SACL Carl Landry	3.00
SACR Chris Richard	3.00
SACS Cheikh Samb	3.00
SADA D.J. Augustin	8.00
SADG Danilo Gallinari	8.00
SADH Dwight Howard	15.00
SADI Boris Diaw	4.00
SADJ Darnell Jackson	10.00
SADR Derrick Rose	75.00
SADS D.J. Strawberry	3.00
SAGD Glen Davis	6.00
SAJA Antawn Jamison	6.00
SAJG Jeff Green	4.00
SAJN Joakim Noah	6.00
SAKB Kobe Bryant	100.00
SAKD Kevin Durant	75.00
SAKG Kevin Garnett	40.00
SALM Luc Richard Mbah A Moute	5.00
SALO Lamar Odom	6.00
SALS Luis Scola	3.00
SAMA Morris Almond	4.00
SAMB Michael Beasley	25.00
SAMC Mike Conley Jr.	8.00
SAMJ Michael Jordan	300.00
SAOM O.J. Mayo	15.00
SAPO Patrick O'Bryant	3.00
SARH Richard Hendrix	3.00
SARM Rick Mahorn	8.00
SARS Ramon Sessions	4.00
SARW Russell Westbrook	40.00
SAST Rodney Stuckey	8.00
SASW Sean Williams	3.00
SAVC Vince Carter	15.00
SAWC Wilson Chandler	3.00
SAWH Walter Herrmann	3.00

002 Fleer All-Star NBA Jam Session

buted by Fleer at the 2002 NBA All-Star Jam
on show in Philadelphia, this card was available
Fleer show booth. Cards feature a full color
of Eric Snow set against a background with the
can flag along the top, the NBA Jam-Session
n the lower right-hand corner and the words,
NBA All-Star Jam Session Presented by Fleer-
sman" along the bottom
Snow .60 1.50

004 Fleer Authentic Player Autographs

D FOR UNFUFILLED EXCH
S FROM 2002-2004
en Gordon JSY/100 15.00 40.00
en Gordon/100 12.50 30.00
en Gordon/75 15.00 40.00
en Gordon/50 20.00 50.00
n Wallace/100 10.00 25.00
avid West/59 6.00 15.00
Dwyane Wade JSY/100 30.00 60.00
Dwyane Wade JSY/25 50.00 100.00
son Kidd/300 15.00 40.00
rry Stackhouse/126 5.00 12.00
rry Stackhouse/100 6.00 15.00
rry Stackhouse/50 10.00 25.00
arcus Banks/75 10.00 25.00
ebastian Telfair/250 6.00 15.00
ebastian Telfair/75 8.00 20.00
ebastian Telfair/50 10.00 25.00
ince Carter/300 15.00 40.00
ince Carter/150 20.00 40.00

005 Fleer Authentic Player Autographs

en Gordon/300 6.00 15.00
en Gordon/150 8.00 20.00
en Gordon/100 10.00 25.00
en Gordon/75 12.50 30.00
rew Gooden/300 5.00 12.00
rew Gooden/150 6.00 15.00
yane Wade/50 30.00 80.00
on Kidd/225 12.50 30.00
yshaun Prince/50 8.00 20.00
yshaun Prince/300 5.00 12.00
Ben Gordon JSY/100 8.00 20.00

2001-02 Fleer Authentix

ed in mid December 2001, this 135-card base
tains standard size cards. The cards have a
borders and a ticket style themed background.
action photos are set where poses are facing the
either in a jump shot pose or an "attacking the
ose. Authentix set contains 100 veteran players
rookie players. The rookie cards feature an
ded team replica ticket numbered to 1,250.
tix was packaged in 24 pack boxes where packs
ned five cards.

.SET w/o SP'S 12.50 30.00
e Carter .50 1.25
ll Brandon .20 .50
LaFrentz .20 .50
os Tsakalidis .20 .50
Brand .30 .75
d Robinson .50 1.25
ar Odom .30 .75
Hughes .25 .60
Payton .30 .75
Fox .25 .60
al Mashburn .25 .60
an Grant .20 .50
id Wesley .20 .50
e Smith .25 .60
ey Maggette .25 .60
hael Jordan 4.00 10.00
ly Szczerbiak .25 .60
oine Walker .25 .60
cus Camby .25 .60
heed Wallace .30 .75
vis Best .20 .50
o Ratliff .20 .50
honso Ellis .25 .60
Nowitzki .50 1.25
Thomas .20 .50
e Francis .30 .75
Duncan .60 1.50
ie House .20 .50
Mercer .20 .50
n Houston .25 .60
an Langdon .20 .50
Malone .40 1.00
n Robinson .25 .60
g Zhizhi .25 .60
n Kidd .50 1.25
rice Taylor .20 .50
s Webber .30 .75
38 Michael Dickerson .20 .50
39 Paul Pierce .40 1.00
40 Bonzi Wells .20 .50
41 Antawn Jamison .30 .75
42 Rashard Lewis .30 .75
43 Reggie Miller .30 .75
44 Patrick Ewing .40 1.00
45 Marcus Fizer .20 .50
46 Aaron McKie .20 .50
47 Marc Jackson .20 .50
48 Desmond Mason .25 .60
49 Jermaine O'Neal .30 .75
50 DeShawn Stevenson .20 .50
51 John Stockton .40 1.00
52 Tim Thomas .20 .50
53 Andre Miller .25 .60
54 Jumaine Jones .20 .50
55 Nick Van Exel .25 .60
56 Damon Stoudamire .25 .60
57 Stephon Marbury .25 .60
58 Clifford Robinson .20 .50
59 Hedo Turkoglu .30 .75
60 Kobe Bryant 1.50 4.00
61 Richard Hamilton .25 .60
62 Stromile Swift .20 .50
63 Chris Mihm .20 .50
64 Tracy McGrady .50 1.25
65 Jalen Rose .25 .60
66 Morris Peterson .20 .50
67 Alonzo Mourning .40 1.00
68 Courtney Alexander .20 .50
69 Michael Finley .30 .75
70 Shawn Marion .30 .75
71 Darius Miles .20 .50
72 Antonio Davis .20 .50
73 Ray Allen .30 .75
74 Shareef Abdur-Rahim .25 .60
75 Kevin Garnett .60 1.50
76 Latrell Sprewell .25 .60
77 Antonio McDyess .25 .60
78 Derek Anderson .20 .50
79 Derek Fisher .25 .60
80 Jason Terry .30 .75
81 Eddie Jones .25 .60
82 Hakeem Olajuwon .40 1.00
83 Toni Kukoc .25 .60
84 Sam Cassell .25 .60
85 Jamal Crawford .25 .60
86 Allen Iverson .60 1.50
87 Steve Nash .50 1.25
88 Dikembe Mutombo .30 .75
89 Shaquille O'Neal .75 2.00
90 Jerome Moiso .20 .50
91 Kenyon Martin .30 .75
92 Chucky Atkins .20 .50
93 Grant Hill .40 1.00
94 Jerry Stackhouse .25 .60
95 Jason Williams .25 .60
96 Baron Davis .30 .75
97 Mike Miller .30 .75
98 Joe Smith .25 .60
99 Peja Stojakovic .30 .75
100 Cuttino Mobley .25 .60
101 Kwame Brown RC 1.25 3.00
102 Jason Collins RC 1.25 3.00
103 Willie Solomon RC 1.25 3.00
104 Brendan Haywood RC 1.50 4.00
105 Jeff Trepagnier RC 1.25 3.00
106 Eddie Griffin RC 1.25 3.00
107 Joseph Forte RC 1.25 3.00
108 Rodney White RC 1.25 3.00
109 Jeryl Sasser RC 1.25 3.00
110 Samuel Dalembert RC 1.50 4.00
111 Shane Battier RC 2.50 6.00
112 Tony Parker RC 5.00 12.00
113 DeSagana Diop RC 1.25 3.00
114 Steven Hunter RC 1.25 3.00
115 Trenton Hassell RC 1.25 3.00
116 Michael Bradley RC 1.25 3.00
117 Brian Scalabrine RC 1.25 3.00
118 Troy Murphy RC 2.00 5.00
119 Brandon Armstrong RC 1.25 3.00
120 Pau Gasol RC 4.00 10.00
121 Gerald Wallace RC 2.00 5.00
122 Jason Richardson RC 2.50 6.00
123 Joe Johnson RC 3.00 8.00
124 Loren Woods RC 1.25 3.00
125 Vladimir Radmanovic RC 1.25 3.00
126 Jamaal Tinsley RC 1.50 4.00
127 Omar Cook RC 1.25 3.00
128 Kedrick Brown RC 1.25 3.00
129 Terence Morris RC 1.25 3.00
130 Richard Jefferson RC 2.50 6.00
131 Gilbert Arenas RC 2.00 5.00
132 Tyson Chandler RC 2.00 5.00
133 Kirk Haston RC 1.25 3.00
134 Eddy Curry RC 2.00 5.00
135 Zach Randolph RC 3.00 8.00

2001-02 Fleer Authentix Front Row Parallel

Randomly inserted in packs, this 135-card set parallels the base Fleer Authentix set enhanced with sequential numbering to 100 on the card back.
*FRONT STARS: 5X TO 12X BASE CARD HI
*FRONT RCs: 1.5X TO 4X BASE CARD HI

2001-02 Fleer Authentix Second Row Parallel

Randomly inserted in packs, this 135-card set parallels the base Fleer Authentix set enhanced with sequential numbering to 200 on the card back.
*SEC.ROW STARS: 3X TO 8X BASE CARD HI
*SEC.ROW RCs: 1X TO 2.5X BASE CARD HI

2001-02 Fleer Authentix Autograph Authentix

Randomly inserted in packs at a rate of one in 639, this insert set was horizontally designed with full colo player action photos. The player's team number is found in the upper left-hand corner, and basketball design is found in the lower left-hand corner. The center of the card features a ticket stub design with the player's autograph written across it. The right-hand side of the card has a perforated edge indicating it is the "ripped version".
1 Kwame Brown 10.00 25.00
2 Eddy Curry 12.00 30.00
3 Vince Carter 15.00 40.00

2001-02 Fleer Authentix Autograph Authentix UnRipped

Randomly inserted in packs, this set parallels the Autograph Authentix Ripped insert set. The right-hand side of the card does not have a perforated edge indicating it is the "unripped version". The cards are serially numbered out of 25.
1 Kwame Brown 15.00 40.00
2 Eddy Curry 25.00 60.00
3 Vince Carter 30.00 80.00

2001-02 Fleer Authentix Autographed Jersey Authentix

This one of one set features Vince Carter along with a swatch of his jersey and a his autograph. Originally issued as a redemption card, this is also the ripped verson with a perforated right edge.
UNRIPPED SER.#'d TO 1 EXISTS
1 Vince Carter 40.00 100.00

2001-02 Fleer Authentix Courtside Classics

Inserted one in every 22 packs, this 15-card set features some of the great players of the NBA. The standard size cards are horizontally designed with a black & white player photo in the foreground and fans sitting courtside in the background.
COMPLETE SET (15) 25.00 50.00
1 Steve Francis 1.00 2.50
2 Mike Miller 1.00 2.50
3 Kenyon Martin 1.00 2.50
4 Vince Carter 1.50 4.00
5 Alonzo Mourning 1.25 3.00
6 Anfernee Hardaway 1.50 4.00
7 Dikembe Mutombo 1.00 2.50
8 Chris Webber 1.00 2.50
9 Glenn Robinson .75 2.00
10 Jerry Stackhouse .75 2.00
11 Kobe Bryant 5.00 12.00
12 Kevin Garnett 2.00 5.00
13 Tim Duncan 2.00 5.00
14 Shaquille O'Neal 2.50 6.00
15 Michael Jordan 8.00 20.00

2001-02 Fleer Authentix Courtside Classics Memorabilia

Inserted one in every 74 packs, this 15-card set parallels the base Courtside Classics insert set enhanced with a swatch of the featured player's game worn jersey and a swatch of an arena seat.
*MULT PAR: 1X TO 2.5X BASE HI
MULT PAR PRINT RUN 150 SER.#'d SETS
AH Anfernee Hardaway 8.00 20.00
AM Alonzo Mourning 8.00 20.00
CW Chris Webber 5.00 12.00
DM Dikembe Mutombo 5.00 12.00
GR Glenn Robinson 4.00 10.00
JS Jerry Stackhouse 4.00 10.00
KM Kenyon Martin 5.00 12.00
MM Mike Miller 5.00 12.00
SF Steve Francis 5.00 12.00
VC Vince Carter 8.00 20.00

2001-02 Fleer Authentix Jersey Authentix Ripped

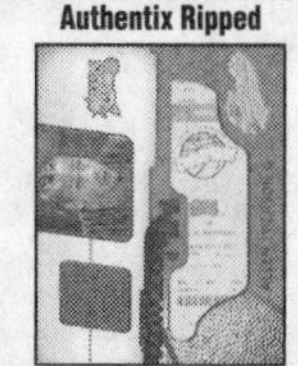

Inserted one in every 33 packs, this 15-card set features a replica team ticket and a piece of a game used jersey. The "ripped" version has a perforated right-hand side. An Unripped verions numbered to 50 was also issued.
*UNRIPPED: 1.5X TO 3X RIPPED JSY
1 Allen Iverson 8.00 20.00
2 Darius Miles 2.50 6.00
3 Tracy McGrady 6.00 15.00
4 Glenn Robinson 3.00 8.00
5 Rashard Lewis 4.00 10.00
6 Elton Brand 4.00 10.00
7 Andre Miller 3.00 8.00
8 Jason Terry 4.00 10.00
9 Vince Carter 6.00 15.00
10 Karl Malone 5.00 12.00
11 David Robinson 6.00 15.00
12 Lamar Odom 4.00 10.00
13 Antoine Walker 3.00 8.00
14 Shareef Abdur-Rahim 3.00 8.00
15 Jamal Mashburn 3.00 8.00

2001-02 Fleer Authentix Sweet Selections

Inserted one in every eleven packs, this 15-card set features 15 rookies where the words "Sweet Selections" appear vertically along the left hand side of the card. The background is white, and full color player photos are set against a gray scale portrait photo of the featured player.
COMPLETE SET (15) 12.50 30.00
1 Kwame Brown .75 2.00
2 Tyson Chandler 1.25 3.00
3 Pau Gasol 2.50 6.00
4 Eddy Curry 1.25 3.00
5 Jason Richardson 1.50 4.00
6 Shane Battier 1.50 4.00
7 Eddie Griffin .75 2.00
8 DeSagana Diop .75 2.00
9 Rodney White .75 2.00
10 Joe Johnson 2.00 5.00
11 Kedrick Brown .75 2.00
12 Vladimir Radmanovic .75 2.00
13 Richard Jefferson 1.50 4.00
14 Troy Murphy 1.25 3.00
15 Steven Hunter .75 2.00

2002-03 Fleer Authentix

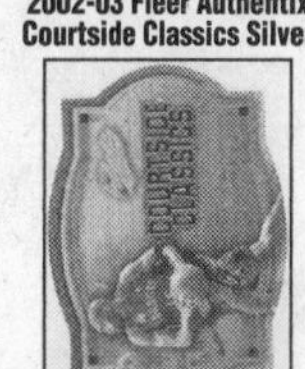

Issued in late October 2002, Fleer Authentix boasts a 135-card base set divided up into 100 veteran cards and 35 Rookie Authentix cards sequentially numbered to 1250. Base cards feature a full-color player action photo and an embedded mini-ticket. Authentix was released in five card packs that carried a suggested retail price of $3.99 with 24 packs per box.
COMPLETE SET (135) 125.00 250.00
COMP.SET w/o SP's (100) 15.00 40.00
1 Vince Carter .50 1.25
2 Bobby Jackson .20 .50
3 Cuttino Mobley .25 .60
4 John Stockton .40 1.00
5 Jamal Mashburn .25 .60
6 Ben Wallace .30 .75
7 Tim Duncan .60 1.50
8 Richard Jefferson .30 .75
9 Clifford Robinson .20 .50
10 Gary Payton .30 .75
11 Terrell Brandon .20 .50
12 Michael Finley .30 .75
13 Rasheed Wallace .30 .75
14 Jason Williams .25 .60
15 Andre Miller .25 .60
16 Shawn Marion .30 .75
17 Kobe Bryant 1.50 4.00
18 Jason Terry .25 .60
19 Latrell Sprewell .25 .60
20 Jerry Stackhouse .25 .60
21 Tony Parker .40 1.00
22 Ray Allen .30 .75
23 Dirk Nowitzki .50 1.25
24 Chris Webber .30 .75
25 Rick Fox .25 .60
26 Jermaine O'Neal .30 .75
27 Karl Malone .40 1.00
28 Allan Houston .25 .60
29 Jason Richardson .30 .75
30 Morris Peterson .20 .50
31 Kevin Garnett .60 1.50
32 Antawn Jamison .30 .75
33 Rashard Lewis .30 .75
34 Jason Kidd .50 1.25
35 Joe Smith .25 .60
36 David Robinson .50 1.25
37 Brian Grant .20 .50
38 Lamond Murray .20 .50
39 Damon Stoudamire .25 .60
40 Shane Battier .30 .75
41 Eddy Curry .25 .60
42 Dikembe Mutombo .30 .75
43 Jamaal Tinsley .20 .50
44 Courtney Alexander .20 .50
45 Wally Szczerbiak .25 .60
46 Antonio McDyess .25 .60
47 Mike Bibby .30 .75
48 Alonzo Mourning .40 1.00
49 Tyson Chandler .25 .60
50 Stephon Marbury .25 .60
51 Sam Cassell .25 .60
52 Steve Nash .40 1.00
53 Bonzi Wells .20 .50
54 Pau Gasol .40 1.00
55 Rodney Rogers .20 .50
56 Allen Iverson .50 1.25
57 Derek Fisher .25 .60
58 Travis Best .20 .50
59 Aaron McKie .20 .50
60 Darius Miles .20 .50
61 Richard Hamilton .25 .60
62 Marcus Camby .25 .60
63 Eddie Griffin .20 .50
64 Antonio Davis .20 .50
65 David Wesley .20 .50
66 Stromile Swift .20 .50
67 Brent Barry .20 .50
68 Glenn Robinson .25 .60
69 Antoine Walker .25 .60
70 Tracy McGrady .50 1.25
71 Steve Smith .25 .60
72 Michael Jordan 2.50 6.00
73 Mike Miller .30 .75
74 DeShawn Stevenson .20 .50
75 Raef LaFrentz .20 .50
76 Al Harrington .25 .60
77 Vlade Divac .25 .60
78 Eddie Jones .25 .60
79 Wesley Person .20 .50
80 Kenny Anderson .25 .60
81 Elton Brand .30 .75
82 Jalen Rose .25 .60
83 Joe Johnson .30 .75
84 Shaquille O'Neal .75 2.00
85 Paul Pierce .40 1.00
86 Grant Hill .40 1.00
87 Steve Francis .30 .75
88 Keon Clark .20 .50
89 Baron Davis .30 .75
90 Tim Thomas .20 .50
91 Shareef Abdur-Rahim .25 .60
92 Kenyon Martin .30 .75
93 Juwan Howard .25 .60
94 Peja Stojakovic .30 .75
95 Lamar Odom .30 .75
96 Toni Kukoc .25 .60
97 Darrell Armstrong .20 .50
98 Reggie Miller .30 .75
99 Andrei Kirilenko .30 .75
100 Keith Van Horn .25 .60
101 Yao Ming RC 6.00 15.00
102 Jay Williams RC 2.50 6.00
103 Mike Dunleavy RC 2.50 6.00
104 Drew Gooden RC 3.00 8.00
105 Nikoloz Tskitishvili RC 2.00 5.00
106 Caron Butler RC 3.00 8.00
107 Chris Wilcox RC 2.00 5.00
108 DaJuan Wagner RC 2.00 5.00
109 Nene Hilario RC 2.50 6.00
110 Qyntel Woods RC 2.00 5.00
111 Jared Jeffries RC 2.00 5.00
112 Tamar Slay RC 2.00 5.00
113 Marcus Haislip RC 2.00 5.00
114 Kareem Rush RC 2.00 5.00
115 Bostjan Nachbar RC 2.00 5.00
116 Melvin Ely RC 2.00 5.00
117 Jiri Welsch RC 2.00 5.00
118 Amare Stoudemire RC 5.00 12.00
119 Frank Williams RC 2.00 5.00
120 Rasual Butler RC 2.00 5.00
121 Dan Dickau RC 2.00 5.00
122 Carlos Boozer RC 4.00 10.00
123 Roger Mason RC 2.00 5.00
124 Corsley Edwards RC 2.00 5.00
125 Robert Archibald RC 2.00 5.00
126 John Salmons RC 2.50 6.00
127 Rod Grizzard RC 2.00 5.00
128 Dan Gadzuric RC 2.00 5.00
129 Sam Clancy RC 2.00 5.00
130 Fred Jones RC 2.00 5.00
131 Casey Jacobsen RC 2.00 5.00
132 Ryan Humphrey RC 2.00 5.00
133 Vincent Yarbrough RC 2.00 5.00
134 Juan Dixon RC 2.50 6.00
135 Tayshaun Prince RC 2.50 6.00

2002-03 Fleer Authentix Balcony

Randomly seeded in packs, this 135-card set parallels the base set without the embedded ticket and is enhanced with a blue strip towards the bottom of the card in which the word, "Balcony" appears. Each card is sequentially numbered to 250 in gold ink on the back.
*BALCONY STARS: 3X TO 8X BASE CARD HI
*BALCONY RCs: .6X TO 1.5X BASE CARD HI

2002-03 Fleer Authentix Club

Randomly seeded in packs, this 135-card set parallels the base set without the embedded ticket and is enhanced with a bronze strip towards the bottom of the card in which the word, "Club" appears. Each card is sequentially numbered to 100 in silver ink on the back.

*CLUB STARS: 5X TO 12X BASE CARD HI
*CLUB RCs: 1.25X TO 3X BASE CARD HI

2002-03 Fleer Authentix Standing Room Only

Randomly seeded in packs, this 135-card set parallels the base set without the embedded ticket and is enhanced with a gold strip towards the bottom of the card in which the words, "Standing Room Only" appear. Each card is sequentially numbered to 25 in gold ink on the back.
*SRO STARS: 20X TO 50X BASE HI
*SRO RCs: 3X TO 8X BASE HI

2002-03 Fleer Authentix Autographed Authentix

Randomly inserted in packs at the rate of one in 586, this four card set looks very similar to the base cards and contains an authentic player autograph.
1 Vince Carter 15.00 40.00

2002-03 Fleer Authentix Courtside Classics Silver

Randomly inserted in packs, this 15-card set features an oval die cut design with four corners protruding out of the oval as if it was overlayed with a rectangle. Full color player action photos appear on top of a wood grain and gray scale photo background.
COMPLETE SET (15) 25.00 60.00
*GOLD: .3X TO .8X BASE HI
GOLD RANDOM INSERTS IN RETAIL PACKS
1 Vince Carter 2.00 5.00
2 Tim Duncan 2.50 6.00
3 Ray Allen 1.25 3.00
4 Tony Parker 1.50 4.00
5 Michael Jordan 10.00 25.00
6 Chris Webber 1.25 3.00
7 Shaquille O'Neal 3.00 8.00
8 Kobe Bryant 6.00 15.00
9 Jason Kidd 2.00 5.00
10 Dirk Nowitzki 2.00 5.00
11 Shane Battier 1.25 3.00
12 Kevin Garnett 2.50 6.00
13 Jason Richardson 1.25 3.00
14 Karl Malone 1.50 4.00
15 Pau Gasol 1.50 4.00

2002-03 Fleer Authentix Draft Day Ticket

Randomly inserted in packs, this 10-card set features a horizontal design with player photos on the top and an embedded ticket from the 2002 NBA draft. Yao Ming is the only one in the set sequentially numbered to 100.
1 Yao Ming/100 15.00 40.00
2 Drew Gooden 6.00 15.00
3 Amare Stoudemire 10.00 25.00
4 Caron Butler 6.00 15.00
5 Chris Wilcox 4.00 10.00
6 DaJuan Wagner 4.00 10.00
7 Dan Dickau 4.00 10.00
8 Qyntel Woods 4.00 10.00

2002-03 Fleer Authentix Hometown Heroes Silver

Randomly inserted in packs, this 20-card set showcases a horizontal design with full color player action photos set against the back-drop of their team's home city. Each card is sequentially numbered to 500.
COMPLETE SET (20) 25.00 60.00
*GOLD: .25X TO .6X BASE HI
GOLD RANDOM INSERTS IN RETAIL PACKS
1 Vince Carter 2.50 6.00
2 Tim Duncan 3.00 8.00
3 Kobe Bryant 8.00 20.00
4 Chris Wilcox 1.50 4.00
5 Jay Williams 2.00 5.00
6 Dirk Nowitzki 2.50 6.00
7 Jared Jeffries 1.50 4.00
8 Kevin Garnett 3.00 8.00
9 Drew Gooden 2.50 6.00
10 Shane Battier 1.50 4.00
11 Juan Dixon 2.00 5.00
12 Allen Iverson 2.50 6.00
13 Jason Richardson 1.50 4.00
14 Mike Dunleavy 2.00 5.00
15 Tracy McGrady 2.50 6.00
16 Michael Jordan 12.00 30.00
17 Shaquille O'Neal 4.00 10.00
18 Paul Pierce 2.00 5.00
19 Steve Francis 1.50 4.00
20 Baron Davis 1.50 4.00

2002-03 Fleer Authentix Jersey Authentix

Randomly seeded in packs at the rate of one in 17, this 30-card set features a full color player photo at the top right and a jersey swatch at the top left. The bottom of the card has an embedded ticket below which the edge is jagged as if a stub has been torn off. All cards have red foil highlights. An Unripped version was also issued and is sequentially numbered to 50.
*UNRIPPED: .75X TO 2X BASE HI
1 Shareef Abdur-Rahim 2.50 6.00
2 Antoine Walker 2.50 6.00
3 Paul Pierce 4.00 10.00
4 Eddy Curry SP 2.50 6.00
5 Glenn Robinson 2.50 6.00
6 Vince Carter SP 5.00 12.00
7 Steve Francis 3.00 8.00
8 Reggie Miller 3.00 8.00
9 Darius Miles 2.00 5.00
10 Elton Brand 3.00 8.00
11 Lamar Odom 3.00 8.00
12 Stromile Swift 2.00 5.00
13 Ray Allen SP 3.00 8.00
14 Jason Kidd 5.00 12.00
15 Richard Jefferson 3.00 8.00
16 Kenyon Martin 3.00 8.00
17 Keith Van Horn 2.50 6.00
18 Baron Davis 3.00 8.00
19 Mike Miller 3.00 8.00
20 Grant Hill 4.00 10.00
21 Tracy McGrady 5.00 12.00
22 Allen Iverson 5.00 12.00
23 Dikembe Mutombo 3.00 8.00
24 Shawn Marion 3.00 8.00
25 Stephon Marbury 2.50 6.00
26 Chris Webber 3.00 8.00
27 Gary Payton 3.00 8.00
28 John Stockton 4.00 10.00
29 Karl Malone 4.00 10.00
30 Richard Hamilton 2.50 6.00

2002-03 Fleer Authentix Jersey Authentix All Star Tickets

This 13-card set is a semi-parallel to the regular Jersey Authentix insert set. The cards differ by featuring silver foil (instead of red), the words "All Star" above the ticket window and an All Star ticket in the ticket area. Announced print runs are listed below.
DM Dikembe Mutombo/71* 6.00 15.00

2002-03 Fleer Authentix Jersey Authentix Game of the Week

Randomly inserted in packs at the rate of one in 53, this 15-card set utilizes the set design from the base Jersey Authentix insert with two swatches of jersey along the top. The two featured players appear behind the jersey swatch. Card bottoms are jagged as if a ticket stub had been torn off.
1 Jason Kidd 8.00 20.00
Allen Iverson
2 Stephon Marbury 6.00 15.00
John Stockton
3 Shareef Abdur-Rahim 5.00 12.00
Darius Miles
4 Baron Davis 6.00 15.00
Reggie Miller
5 Richard Hamilton 5.00 12.00
Richard Jefferson
6 Karl Malone 8.00 20.00
Elton Brand
7 Vince Carter 10.00 25.00
Paul Pierce
8 Ray Allen 6.00 15.00
Steve Francis
9 Kenyon Martin 5.00 12.00
Lamar Odom
10 Antoine Walker 8.00 20.00
Chris Webber
11 Eddy Curry 5.00 12.00
Glenn Robinson
12 Grant Hill 6.00 15.00
Gary Payton
13 Tracy McGrady 6.00 15.00
Shawn Marion
14 Mike Miller 5.00 12.00
Keith Van Horn
15 Stromile Swift 5.00 12.00
Dikembe Mutombo

2002-03 Fleer Authentix Ticket for Four

Randomly inserted in packs, this 10-card set features a dual-sided design with two players and their jerseys on each side. Cards have white borders with a line right down the middle of each side and two separate colors- one for each of the players. Sequential numbering to 200 appears on the card back right in the middle.
1 Vince Carter 20.00 50.00
Baron Davis
Steve Francis
Allen Iverson
2 Vince Carter 15.00 40.00
Richard Jefferson
Tracy McGrady
Darius Miles
3 Vince Carter 15.00 40.00
Kevin Garnett
Karl Malone
Dirk Nowitzki
4 Vince Carter 20.00 50.00
Tyson Chandler
Paul Pierce
Chris Webber
5 Shane Battier 15.00 40.00
Shawn Marion
Mike Bibby
Vince Carter
6 Vince Carter 15.00 40.00
Jason Kidd
Jamaal Tinsley
Antoine Walker
7 Ray Allen 25.00 60.00
Vince Carter
Stephon Marbury
Cuttino Mobley
8 Vince Carter 15.00 40.00
Mike Miller
Quentin Richardson
Stromile Swift
9 Elton Brand 15.00 40.00
Vince Carter
Kenyon Martin
Morris Peterson
10 Shareef Abdur Rahim 15.00 40.00
Vince Carter
John Stockton
Keith Van Horn

2002-03 Fleer Authentix Tip-Off Ticket

Randomly seeded, this five card set parallels the design of the base Draft Day Tickets where each card is sequentially numbered to 15.
1 Yao Ming 40.00 100.00
2 Amare Stoudemire 30.00 80.00
3 Caron Butler 20.00 50.00
4 Chris Wilcox 12.00 30.00
5 Qyntel Woods 12.00 30.00

2003-04 Fleer Authentix

Issued in October 2003, Authentix boasts a 130-card set divided up into 100 veteran players and 30 rookies sequentially numbered to 1250. Authentix base cards place players in action on a background set to look like a ticket. Authentix was packaged in 24-pack boxes where packs contained five cards and carried a suggested retail price of $3.99.
COMP.SET w/o SP's (1-100) 15.00 40.00
1 Vince Carter .50 1.25
2 David Wesley .20 .50
3 Eddie Griffin .20 .50
4 Andrei Kirilenko .30 .75
5 Kerry Kittles .20 .50
6 Tayshaun Prince .30 .75

7 Tim Duncan .50 1.25
8 Troy Hudson .20 .50
9 Ben Wallace .30 .75
10 Manu Ginobili .40 1.00
11 Gary Payton .30 .75
12 Dajuan Wagner .20 .50
13 Stephon Marbury .25 .60
14 Shane Battier .25 .60
15 Zydrunas Ilgauskas .25 .60
16 Eric Snow .20 .50
17 Andre Miller .25 .60
18 Shareef Abdur-Rahim .25 .60
19 Kurt Thomas .20 .50
20 Vincent Yarbrough .20 .50
21 Mike Bibby .30 .75
22 Desmond Mason .25 .60
23 Steve Nash .40 1.00
24 Rasheed Wallace .30 .75
25 Kobe Bryant 1.50 4.00
26 Cuttino Mobley .25 .60
27 Matt Harpring .25 .60
28 Jamal Mashburn .25 .60
29 Mike Dunleavy .25 .60
30 Antonio Davis .20 .50
31 Michael Redd .30 .75
32 Richard Hamilton .25 .60
33 Predrag Drobnjak .20 .50
34 Kevin Garnett .60 1.50
35 Nene .25 .60
36 Bobby Jackson .20 .50
37 Jason Williams .25 .60
38 Ricky Davis .25 .60
39 Shawn Marion .30 .75
40 Kareem Rush .20 .50
41 Eddy Curry .25 .60
42 Gordan Giricek .20 .50
43 Brad Miller .30 .75
44 Kwame Brown .20 .50
45 Sam Cassell .25 .60
46 Juwan Howard .25 .60
47 Peja Stojakovic .30 .75
48 Brian Grant .20 .50
49 Al Harrington .25 .60
50 Allen Iverson .50 1.25
51 Caron Butler .30 .75
52 Dirk Nowitzki .50 1.25
53 Zach Randolph .30 .75
54 Pau Gasol .30 .75
55 Tony Delk .20 .50
56 Grant Hill .40 1.00
57 Shaquille O'Neal .75 2.00
58 Tyson Chandler .25 .60
59 Tracy McGrady .40 1.00
60 Ron Artest .30 .75
61 Jerry Stackhouse .25 .60
62 Jamaal Magloire .20 .50
63 Jason Richardson .30 .75
64 Morris Peterson .20 .50
65 Richard Jefferson .30 .75
66 Kenny Thomas .20 .50
67 Tony Parker .30 .75
68 Eddie Jones .25 .60
69 Paul Pierce .40 1.00
70 Drew Gooden .25 .60
71 Jermaine O'Neal .30 .75
72 Juan Dixon .20 .50
73 Baron Davis .30 .75
74 Antawn Jamison .30 .75
75 Rashard Lewis .30 .75
76 Nick Van Exel .25 .60
77 Bonzi Wells .20 .50
78 Speedy Claxton .20 .50
79 Carlos Boozer .30 .75
80 Amare Stoudemire .50 1.25
81 Elton Brand .30 .75
82 Jalen Rose .25 .60
83 Keith Van Horn .25 .60
84 Corey Maggette .25 .60
85 Antoine Walker .30 .75
86 Latrell Sprewell .25 .60
87 Yao Ming .60 1.50
88 Glenn Robinson .25 .60
89 Jason Kidd .50 1.25
90 Gilbert Arenas .30 .75
91 Ray Allen .30 .75
92 Wally Szczerbiak .25 .60
93 Michael Finley .30 .75
94 Chris Webber .30 .75
95 Reggie Miller .30 .75
96 Jason Terry .25 .60
97 Allan Houston .25 .60
98 Steve Francis .30 .75
99 Karl Malone .40 1.00
100 Kenyon Martin .30 .75
101 Carmelo Anthony RC 4.00 10.00
102 Troy Bell RC 1.50 4.00
103 T.J. Ford RC 2.00 5.00
104 LeBron James RC 20.00 50.00
105 Travis Outlaw RC 2.00 5.00
106 Mike Sweetney RC 1.50 4.00
107 Aleksandar Pavlovic RC 1.50 4.00
108 Dahntay Jones RC 1.50 4.00
109 Chris Bosh RC 3.00 8.00
110 Boris Diaw RC 2.00 5.00
111 Jarvis Hayes RC 1.50 4.00
112 Brian Cook RC 1.50 4.00
113 Luke Ridnour RC 2.00 5.00
114 David West RC 2.00 5.00
115 Zoran Planinic RC 1.50 4.00
116 Zarko Cabarkapa RC 1.50 4.00
117 Marcus Banks RC 1.50 4.00
118 Kirk Hinrich RC 2.00 5.00
119 Darko Milicic RC 1.50 4.00
120 Sofoklis Schortsanitis RC 1.50 4.00
121 Ndudi Ebi RC 1.50 4.00
122 Kendrick Perkins RC 2.50 6.00
123 Leandro Barbosa RC 2.00 5.00
124 Nick Collison RC 1.50 4.00
125 Reece Gaines RC 1.50 4.00
126 Chris Kaman RC 2.00 5.00
127 Mickael Pietrus RC 1.50 4.00
128 Dwyane Wade RC 6.00 15.00
129 Josh Howard RC 1.50 4.00
130 Carlos Delfino RC 2.00 5.00

2003-04 Fleer Authentix Balcony

Randomly inserted in packs, this 130-card set parallels the base set enhanced with the word "Balcony" on the card front and sequential numbering to 250.
*1-100 STARS: 2.5X TO 6X BASE HI
*101-130 RC's: .75X TO 2X BASE HI

2003-04 Fleer Authentix Club Box

Randomly inserted in packs, this 130-card set parallels the base set enhanced with the word "Club Box" on the card front and sequential numbering to 100.
*1-100 STARS: 4X TO 10X BASE HI
*101-130 RC's: 1.25X TO 3X BASE HI
25 Kobe Bryant 20.00 50.00

2003-04 Fleer Authentix Rookie Tickets

This four-panel rookie tickets were randomly inserted in packs. The mini tickets can be torn and switched into any rookie card from the product.
*TICKETS: .4X TO 1X BASE HI
ANNOUNCED PRINT RUN 250 SETS
104 LeBron James 25.00 50.00

2003-04 Fleer Authentix Standing Room Only

Seeded in packs randomly, this 130-card set parallels the base set enhanced with the words "Standing Room Only" on the card front and sequential numbering to 25.
*1-100 STARS: 8X TO 20X BASE HI
*101-130 RCs: 3X TO 8X BASE HI

2003-04 Fleer Authentix Autographs

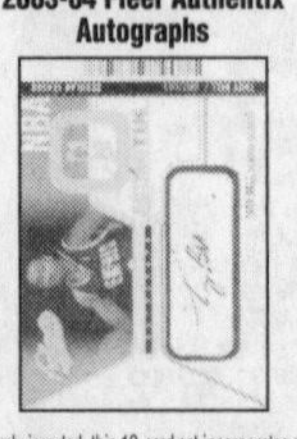

Randomly inserted, this 12-card set incorporates a horizontal design with a color player photo on the top and a cut signature on the bottom. The background is similar to that of the base cards, set to look like a ticket. Print runs are listed below.
AAAS Amare Stoudemire/225 12.50 30.00
AABW Ben Wallace/225 10.00 25.00
AACA Carmelo Anthony/350 25.00 60.00
AACB Chris Bosh/325 12.50 30.00
AADW Dwyane Wade/325 30.00 80.00
AAJH Josh Howard/225 5.00 12.00
AAKM Kenyon Martin/225 5.00 12.00
AAMS Mike Sweetney/325 5.00 12.00
AATB Troy Bell/225 5.00 12.00
AATP2 Tayshaun Prince/225 5.00 12.00

2003-04 Fleer Authentix Autographs All-Star

Inserted in packs, this 13-card set parallels the base Autographs set enhanced with sequential numbering to 150. A Playoff version was also inserted and is sequentially numbered to 50.
*PLAYOFF: .5X TO 1.25X ALL STAR HI
AAAM Alonzo Mourning 25.00 60.00
AAAS Amare Stoudemire 15.00 40.00
AABW Ben Wallace 12.00 30.00
AACA Carmelo Anthony 30.00 80.00
AACB Chris Bosh 15.00 40.00
AADW Dwyane Wade 40.00 100.00
AAJH Josh Howard 6.00 15.00
AAKM Kenyon Martin 6.00 15.00
AAMG Manu Ginobili 10.00 25.00
AAMS Mike Sweetney 6.00 15.00
AATB Troy Bell 6.00 15.00
AATP Tony Parker 8.00 20.00
AATP2 Tayshaun Prince 6.00 15.00

2003-04 Fleer Authentix Courtside Classics

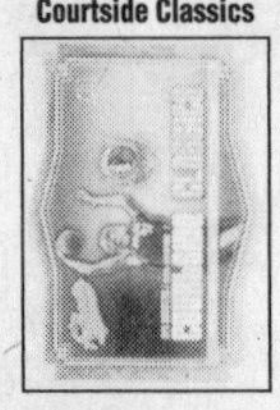

Seeded in packs at the rate of one in 12, this 10-card set features a die-cut design with a frame around the edges. Full color player action photos are set against a colored background.
COMPLETE SET (10) 8.00 20.00
1 Kevin Garnett 1.50 4.00
2 Vince Carter 1.25 3.00
3 Allen Iverson 1.25 3.00
4 Yao Ming 1.50 4.00
5 Tracy McGrady 1.00 2.50
6 Amare Stoudemire 1.25 3.00
7 Jason Richardson .75 2.00
8 Dirk Nowitzki 1.25 3.00
9 Jason Kidd 1.25 3.00
10 Tony Parker .75 2.00

2003-04 Fleer Authentix Courtside Classics Game-Used

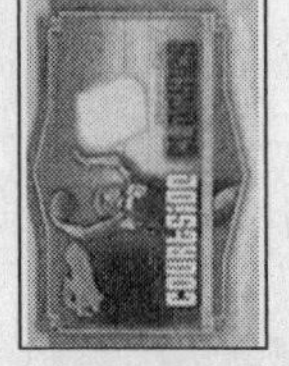

Inserted at one in 37, this 10-card set parallels the base Courtside Classics insert set enhanced with a swatch of game-worn memorabilia.
1 Kevin Garnett 5.00 12.00
2 Vince Carter 4.00 10.00
3 Allen Iverson 4.00 10.00
4 Yao Ming 5.00 12.00
5 Tracy McGrady 3.00 8.00
6 Amare Stoudemire 4.00 10.00
7 Jason Richardson 2.50 6.00
8 Dirk Nowitzki 4.00 10.00
9 Jason Kidd 4.00 10.00
10 Tony Parker 2.50 6.00

2003-04 Fleer Authentix Draft Day Ticket

This 10-card set is sequentially numbered to 400 and randomly seeded in packs. Each card features player photo and a swatch of a ticket from the 2003 NBA draft. A Gold version sequentially numbered to 10 was also issued.
1 Carmelo Anthony 6.00 15.00
2 Mike Sweetney 2.50 6.00
3 Chris Bosh 5.00 12.00
4 Dwyane Wade 10.00 25.00
5 Chris Kaman 3.00 8.00
6 Kirk Hinrich 3.00 8.00
7 T.J. Ford 3.00 8.00
8 Darko Milicic 2.50 6.00
9 Jarvis Hayes 2.50 6.00
10 Nick Collison 2.50 6.00

2003-04 Fleer Authentix Jersey Authentix

Inserted at the rate of one in 37, this 25-card set places a ticket replica towards the bottom of the horizontal design and a swatch of game-worn jersey and player photo towards the top. An All-Star version sequentially numbered to 80, and All-Star Unripped one of one and an Unripped version sequentially numbered to 50 were also produced.
*AS SINGLES: .75X TO 2X BASE JSY HI
*RIPPED: 1X TO 2.5X BASE JSY HI
JAN Nene 2.50 6.00
JAAI Allen Iverson 4.00 10.00
JAAS Amare Stoudemire 4.00 10.00
JABW Bonzi Wells 2.00 5.00
JABW Ben Wallace 2.50 6.00
JACB Carlos Boozer 2.50 6.00
JADN Dirk Nowitzki 4.00 10.00
JADW DaJuan Wagner 2.00 5.00
JAEC Eddy Curry 2.00 5.00
JAJK Jason Kidd 4.00 10.00
JAJO Jermaine O'Neal 2.50 6.00
JAJR Jason Richardson 2.50 6.00
JAKG Kevin Garnett 5.00 12.00
JAKM Kenyon Martin 2.50 6.00
JAKM Karl Malone 3.00 8.00
JALS Latrell Sprewell 2.00 5.00
JAPG Pau Gasol 2.50 6.00
JAPP Paul Pierce 3.00 8.00
JARM Reggie Miller 2.50 6.00
JASF Steve Francis 2.50 6.00
JASN Steve Nash 3.00 8.00
JATM Tracy McGrady 3.00 8.00
JATP Tayshaun Prince 2.50 6.00
JAVC Vince Carter 4.00 10.00
JAYM Yao Ming 5.00 12.00

2003-04 Fleer Authentix Jersey Authentix Autographs

Randomly inserted in packs, this 11-card set parallels the design from the Jersey Authentix set and is enhanced by a cut signature embedded towards the bottom of the horizontal design where the base version has the ticket replica. An All-Star version sequentially numbered to 50 was also produced along with a Playoff version sequentially numbered to 25.
*AS AUTO: .5X TO 1.25X BASE HI
*PLAYOFF AUTO: .6X TO 1.5X BASE HI
AJAAM Alonzo Mourning 30.00 80.00
AJAAS Amare Stoudemire 15.00 40.00
AJABW Ben Wallace 20.00 50.00
AJACA Carmelo Anthony 30.00 80.00
AJACB Chris Bosh 15.00 40.00
AJADW Dwyane Wade 50.00 120.00
AJAKM Kenyon Martin 10.00 25.00
AJAMS Mike Sweetney 10.00 25.00
AJATP2 Tayshaun Prince 10.00 25.00

2003-04 Fleer Authentix Jersey Authentix Game of the Week

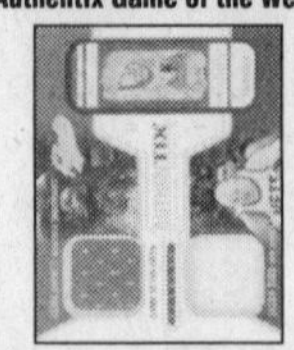

Inserted at the rate of one in 20, this 10-card set pairs two players along with two jersey swatches, one from each player, and a mini replica ticket towards the bottom of the card. An Ripped version sequentially numbered to 50 was also issued in packs.
*RIPPED: 1X TO 2.5X BASE JSY HI
1 Tracy McGrady 6.00 15.00
Ben Wallace
2 Yao Ming 8.00 20.00
Amare Stoudemire
3 Kevin Garnett 8.00 20.00
Jason Kidd
4 Kenyon Martin 8.00 20.00
Vince Carter
5 Dirk Nowitzki 6.00 15.00
Pau Gasol
6 Steve Francis 6.00 15.00
Allen Iverson
7 Steve Nash 5.00 12.00
Jason Richardson
8 Nene 5.00 12.00
Karl Malone
9 Tayshaun Prince 5.00 12.00
Paul Pierce
10 Carlos Boozer 5.00 12.00
Eddy Curry

2003-04 Fleer Authentix Ticket for Four

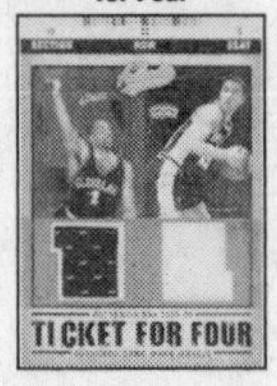

Inserted in packs randomly, this 10-card set places four players and four jerseys on each card; two on the front and two on the back. Cards are sequentially numbered to 100.
BGMM Carlos Boozer 15.00 40.00
Manu Ginobili
Stephon Marbury
Andre Miller
BHMB Mike Bibby 15.00 40.00
Richard Hamilton
Shawn Marion
Kwame Brown
JGDR Richard Jefferson 15.00 40.00
Drew Gooden
Baron Davis
Glenn Robinson
KPCW Jason Kidd 20.00 50.00
Tony Parker
Vince Carter
Chris Webber
MFIW Tracy McGrady 25.00 50.00
Steve Francis
Allen Iverson
Chris Webber
NGMN Nene 15.00 40.00
Pau Gasol
Reggie Miller
Steve Nash
OPMW Jermaine O'Neal 15.00 40.00
Tayshaun Prince
Karl Malone
Ben Wallace
PRGW Paul Pierce 25.00 50.00
Jason Richardson
Kevin Garnett
Bonzi Wells
SBCS Peja Stojakovic 15.00 40.00
Caron Butler
Tyson Chandler
Jerry Stackhouse
WMSC DaJuan Wagner 15.00 40.00
Yao Ming
Latrell Sprewell
Eddy Curry

2003-04 Fleer Authentix Ticket Studs

Inserted at one in six, this 15-card set is designed as a ticket to a game. Each has a full-color player action photo along with a section number, row number and seat number.
COMPLETE SET (15) 15.00 40.00
1 LeBron James 6.00 15.00
2 Vince Carter 1.00 2.50
3 Mike Sweetney .60 1.50
4 Chris Webber .60 1.50
5 Chris Bosh 1.25 3.00
6 Kobe Bryant 3.00 8.00
7 Dwyane Wade 2.50 6.00
8 Shaquille O'Neal 1.50 4.00
9 T.J. Ford .75 2.00
10 Kenyon Martin .60 1.50
11 Paul Pierce .75 2.00
12 Carmelo Anthony 1.50 4.00
13 Tim Duncan 1.00 2.50
14 Pau Gasol .60 1.50
15 Steve Francis .60 1.50

2004-05 Fleer Authentix

Released in November 2004, Fleer Authentix is a 138-card set consisting of 99 veterans (cards 1-100, card 55 not released) and 39 rookies (card 101 not released). Two tiers of rookies were issued: cards 101-129 are sequentially numbered to 750 and cards 130-140 feature a rookie player along with a cut signature of a member of the organization that drafted him. Cards 130-140 are sequentially numbered to 200. All cards feature tan borders, a full-color player action photo along the top and a ticket-themed bottom containing the player's name, position and team. Authentix was issued for both Hobby and Retail, with boxes containing 24 packs of five cards each.
COMPLETE SET (137)
COMP.SET w/o SP's (100) 15.00 40.00
UNPRICED PARALLEL PRINT RUN 10 SETS
1 Allen Iverson .50 1.25
2 Allan Houston .25 .60
3 Jermaine O'Neal .30 .75
4 Andrei Kirilenko .25 .60
5 Baron Davis .30 .75
6 Rasheed Wallace .30 .75
7 Manu Ginobili .40 1.00
8 Kenyon Martin .30 .75
9 Richard Hamilton .25 .60
10 Tony Parker .30 .75
11 Keith Van Horn .25 .60
12 Steve Nash .40 1.00
13 Darius Miles .20 .50
14 Jason Williams .25 .60
15 Carlos Boozer .30 .75
16 Amare Stoudemire .40 1.00
17 Kobe Bryant 1.50 4.00
18 Jason Terry .25 .60
19 Stephon Marbury .25 .60
20 Ben Wallace .30 .75
21 Tim Duncan .50 1.25
22 Michael Redd .30 .75
23 Antoine Walker .30 .75
24 Shareef Abdur-Rahim .25 .60
25 Luke Walton .20 .50
26 Reggie Miller .30 .75
27 Antawn Jamison .30 .75
28 Anfernee Hardaway .75 2.00
29 Yao Ming .60 1.50
30 Chris Bosh .30 .75
31 Latrell Sprewell .25 .60
32 Mike Dunleavy .25 .60
33 Luke Ridnour .25 .60
34 Kevin Garnett .60 1.50
35 Darko Milicic .20 .50
36 Bobby Jackson .20 .50
37 Caron Butler .30 .75
38 Dirk Nowitzki .50 1.25
39 Joe Johnson .30 .75
40 Pau Gasol .30 .75
41 Kirk Hinrich .30 .75
42 Willie Green .20 .50
43 Jamaal Tinsley .20 .50
44 Jarvis Hayes .20 .50
45 Sam Cassell .25 .60
46 Nene .25 .60
47 Mike Bibby .30 .75
48 Lamar Odom .30 .75
49 LeBron James 2.00 5.00
50 Marquis Daniels .20 .50
51 T.J. Ford .25 .60
52 Michael Finley .30 .75
53 Zach Randolph .25 .60
54 Bonzi Wells .20 .50
56 Stephen Jackson .25 .60
57 Gary Payton .30 .75
58 Jason Kapono .20 .50
59 Glenn Robinson .25 .60
60 Elton Brand .30 .75
61 Jerry Stackhouse .25 .60
62 Jamaal Magloire .20 .50
63 Tracy McGrady .40 1.00
64 Jalen Rose .25 .60
65 Kerry Kittles .20 .50
66 Nick Van Exel .25 .60
67 Rashard Lewis .30 .75
68 Desmond Mason .25 .60
69 Gerald Wallace .30 .75
70 Drew Gooden .25 .60
71 Corey Maggette .25 .60
72 Gilbert Arenas .30 .75
73 Tim Thomas .20 .50
74 Jason Richardson .30 .75
75 Ray Allen .30 .75
76 Carmelo Anthony .60 1.50
77 Peja Stojakovic .30 .75
78 Dwyane Wade 1.00 2.50
79 Dajuan Wagner .20 .50
80 Shawn Marion .30 .75
81 Shaquille O'Neal .75 2.00
82 Eddy Curry .25 .60
83 Samuel Dalembert .20 .50
84 Karl Malone .40 1.00
85 Ricky Davis .25 .60
86 Steve Francis .30 .75
87 Juwan Howard .25 .60
88 Carlos Arroyo .25 .60
89 Jamal Mashburn .30 .75
90 Mickael Pietrus .25 .60
91 Vince Carter .50 1.25
92 Jason Kidd .50 1.25
93 Andre Miller .25 .60
94 Chris Webber .30 .75
95 Chris Kaman .30 .75
96 Paul Pierce .40 1.00
97 Cuttino Mobley .25 .60
98 Ron Artest .30 .75
99 Matt Harpring .25 .60
100 Richard Jefferson .30 .75
102 Albert Miralles RC 1.50 4.00
103 Chris Duhon RC 1.50 4.00
104 Ha Seung-Jin RC 1.50 4.00
105 Antonio Burks RC 1.50 4.00
106 Andre Emmett RC 1.50 4.00
107 Donta Smith RC 1.50 4.00
108 Lionel Chalmers RC 1.50 4.00
109 Rickey Paulding RC 1.50 4.00
110 Jackson Vroman RC 1.50 4.00
111 Anderson Varejao RC 2.00 5.00
112 Beno Udrih RC 1.50 4.00
113 Sasha Vujacic RC 1.50 4.00
114 Kevin Martin RC 2.00 5.00
115 Tony Allen RC 2.00 5.00
116 Delonte West RC 2.00 5.00
117 Sergei Monia RC 1.50 4.00
118 Romain Sato RC 1.50 4.00
119 Jameer Nelson RC 2.00 5.00
120 Josh Smith RC 2.50 6.00
121 Kirk Snyder RC 1.50 4.00
122 Robert Swift RC 1.50 4.00
123 Andre Iguodala RC 2.50 6.00
124 Rafael Araujo RC 1.50 4.00
125 Luol Deng RC 2.50 6.00
126 Josh Childress RC 1.50 4.00
127 Ben Gordon RC 2.00 5.00
128 Emeka Okafor RC 2.50 6.00
129 Dwight Howard RC 5.00 12.00
130 David Harrison RC 30.00 75.00
Larry Bird AU
131 Shaun Livingston RC 10.00 25.00
Elgin Baylor AU
132 Devin Harris RC 15.00 30.00
Don Nelson AU
133 Luke Jackson RC 6.00 15.00
Paul Silas AU
134 Andris Biedrins RC 15.00 40.00
Chris Mullin AU
135 Sebastian Telfair RC 6.00 15.00
Maurice Cheeks AU
136 Kris Humphries RC 12.50 30.00
Jerry Sloan AU
137 Al Jefferson RC 12.50 30.00
Danny Ainge AU
138 J.R. Smith RC 15.00 40.00
Byron Scott RC
139 Dorrell Wright RC 10.00 25.00
Pat Riley AU
140 Trevor Ariza RC 8.00 20.00
Isiah Thomas AU

2004-05 Fleer Authentix Parallel 100

Randomly inserted in packs, this 138-card set parallels the base Fleer Authentix set and is sequentially numbered to 100.
*1-100: 2.5X TO 6X BASE CARD HI
*101-129: 1X TO 2.5X BASE CARD HI
CARDS 55 & 101 NOT ISSUED
132 Devin Harris 6.00 15.00
134 Andris Biedrins 5.00 12.00
137 Al Jefferson 6.00 15.00
138 J.R. Smith 5.00 12.00
139 Dorell Wright 6.00 15.00
140 Trevor Ariza 4.00 10.00

2004-05 Fleer Authentix Parallel 75

Randomly inserted in packs, this 138-card set parallels the base Fleer Authentix set and is sequentially numbered to 75.
*1-100: 3X TO 8X BASE CARD HI
*101-129: 1.25X TO 3X BASE CARD HI
CARDS 55 & 101 NOT ISSUED
132 Devin Harris 8.00 20.00
134 Andris Biedrins 6.00 15.00
137 Al Jefferson 8.00 20.00
138 J.R. Smith 6.00 15.00
139 Dorell Wright 8.00 20.00
140 Trevor Ariza 5.00 12.00

2004-05 Fleer Authentix Parallel 50

Randomly inserted in packs, this 138-card set parallels the base Fleer Authentix set and is sequentially numbered to 50.
*1-100: 4X TO 10X BASE CARD HI
*101-129: 1.5X TO 4X BASE CARD HI
CARDS 55 & 101 NOT ISSUED
132 Devin Harris 10.00 25.00
134 Andris Biedrins 8.00 20.00
137 Al Jefferson 10.00 25.00
138 J.R. Smith 8.00 20.00
139 Dorell Wright 10.00 25.00
140 Trevor Ariza 6.00 15.00

2004-05 Fleer Authentix Parallel 25

Randomly inserted in packs, this 138-card set parallels the base Fleer Authentix set and is sequentially numbered to 25.
*1-100: 6X TO 15X BASE HI
*101-129: 2X TO 5X BASE HI
CARDS 55 & 101 NOT ISSUED
132 Devin Harris 12.00 30.00
134 Andris Biedrins 10.00 25.00
137 Al Jefferson 12.00 30.00
138 J.R. Smith 10.00 25.00
139 Dorell Wright 12.00 30.00
140 Trevor Ariza 8.00 20.00

2004-05 Fleer Authentix Autographs

Limited to 50 serially numbered copies, this 28-card set features a ticket-style theme along the top of the card with a player photo and a cut signature along the bottom. Several parallel versions were issued for this set and are serially numbered to 25, 15, five and one of one.
*AUTO 25: .6X TO 1.5X BASE HI
BG Ben Gordon 8.00 20.00
CD Carlos Delfino 6.00 15.00
DH Devin Harris 10.00 25.00
DW Delonte West 8.00 20.00
GA Gilbert Arenas 6.00 15.00
HS Ha Seung-Jin 6.00 15.00
JC Josh Childress 6.00 15.00
JH Josh Howard 6.00 15.00
JS Josh Smith 10.00 25.00
KB Kwame Brown 6.00 15.00
KH Kris Humphries 6.00 15.00
KS Kirk Snyder 6.00 15.00
LD Luol Deng 10.00 25.00
LJ Luke Jackson 6.00 15.00
LO Lamar Odom 10.00
MB Marcus Banks 6.00
PP Paul Pierce 10.00
PS Peja Stojakovic 10.00
RH Richard Hamilton 10.00
RS Robert Swift 6.00
SL Shaun Livingston 6.00
SM Shawn Marion 8.00
ST Sebastian Telfair 6.00
VC Vince Carter 15.00
YT Yuta Tabuse 40.00

2004-05 Fleer Authentix Autographs Jerseys

Randomly inserted, this 25-card set parallels the design of the Autographs enahnced with a square swatch of game worn jersey centered towards the the cards and sequential numbering to 50. Sever different parallel sets numbered to 25, 15, five ar of one.
*AUTO 25: .6X TO 1.5X BASE HI
AS Amare Stoudemire 15.00
BD Baron Davis 10.00
CA Carmelo Anthony 20.00
CB Chris Bosh 12.50
CW Dwyane Wade 40.00
GA Gilbert Arenas 10.00
HS Ha Seung-Jin 8.00
JC Josh Childress 8.00
JK Jason Kidd 15.00
JO Jermaine O'Neal 10.00
KB Kwame Brown 8.00
KM Kenyon Martin 10.00
LO Lamar Odom 12.50
PP Paul Pierce 12.50
PS Peja Stojakovic 15.00
RG Reece Gaines 8.00
RH Richard Hamilton 12.50
SA Shareef Abdur-Rahim 8.00
SF Steve Francis 8.00
SM Shawn Marion 10.00
TO Travis Outlaw 8.00
VC Vince Carter 15.00
YT Yuta Tabuse 50.00
ZR Zach Randolph 8.00

2004-05 Fleer Authentix Autographs Patches

Randomly inserted, this 24-card set parallels the Autographs set enhanced with a swatch of patch the top of the card and sequential numbering to Four parallel versions of this set were also relea sequentially numbered to 15, 10, five and one o
AS Amare Stoudemire 30.00
BD Baron Davis 20.00
CA Carmelo Anthony 40.00
DW Dwyane Wade 80.00
GA Gilbert Arenas 15.00
JK Jason Kidd 30.00
JO Jermaine O'Neal 20.00
KB Kwame Brown 15.00
KM Kenyon Martin 20.00
LO Lamar Odom 25.00
RG Reece Gaines 15.00
SA Shareef Abdur-Rahim 15.00
SF Steve Francis 15.00
SM Shawn Marion 20.00
SN Steve Nash 75.00
TO Travis Outlaw 15.00
VC Vince Carter 25.00
ZR Zach Randolph 15.00

2004-05 Fleer Authentix D Night Flashbacks

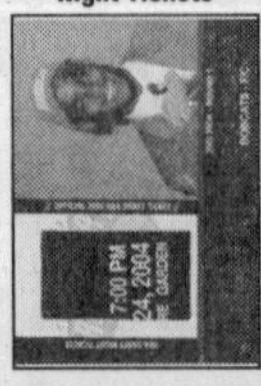

Inseted in packs at one in 248 Hobby and one in Retail, this six cards set features players from th 2003-04 NBA Draft. The cards are horizontally designed with black borders along the left and edges, and have a white background where pla photos are on the right and a mock-ticket from is on the left.
COMPLETE SET (6) 12.00
CA Carmelo Anthony 3.00
CB Chris Bosh 1.50
DM Darko Milicic 1.00
DW Dwyane Wade 5.00
KH Kirk Hinrich 1.50
LJ LeBron James 10.00

2004-05 Fleer Authentix D Night Tickets

Inserted in packs at the rate of one in 240 Hobb one in 480 Retail, this 10-card set features the Draft Class. The design is almost identical to th Night Flashbacks set mentioned above, but co actual swatch of ticket from the draft event on th
COMPLETE SET (10) 25.00

Jefferson 4.00 10.00
en Gordon 3.00 8.00
evin Harris 4.00 10.00
wight Howard 8.00 20.00
neka Okafor 4.00 10.00
osh Childress 2.50 6.00
uol Deng 4.00 10.00
uke Jackson 2.50 6.00
haun Livingston 2.50 6.00
ebastian Telfair 2.50 6.00

004-05 Fleer Authentix Game of the Week Jerseys

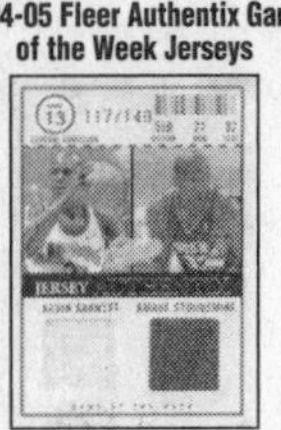

omly seeded in packs, this 20-card set parallels esign utilized by all of the aforementioned graph and memorabilia insert sets, but features players along the top and two swatches of jersey g the bottom. Each card is sequentially numbered, checklist for print runs. A Patch version enhanced wo game worn patches and sequentially bered to 10 was also inserted.

Carmelo Anthony/120 12.50 30.00
cy McGrady
Carmelo Anthony/60 25.00 60.00
yane Wade
Vince Carter/180 10.00 25.00
nyon Martin
Vince Carter/100 10.00 25.00
cy McGrady
im Duncan/110 10.00 25.00
vin Garnett
evin Garnett/140 6.00 15.00
are Stoudemire
len Iverson/90 10.00 25.00
ve Francis
Stephon Marbury/80 6.00 15.00
son Kidd
Kenyon Martin/50 6.00 15.00
are Stoudemire
teve Nash/170 6.00 15.00
chael Finley
Shaquille O'Neal/130 15.00 40.00
n Duncan
aul Pierce/190 6.00 15.00
son Richardson
Michael Redd/150 6.00 15.00
y Allen
Zach Randolph/200 6.00 15.00
n Wallace
Peja Stojakovic/40 15.00 40.00
k Nowitzki
Dwyane Wade/160 10.00 25.00
k Hinrich
Ben Wallace/30 8.00 20.00
maine O'Neal
Chris Webber/70 6.00 15.00
sheed Wallace

2004-05 Fleer Authentix Hot Tickets

ted in packs at the rate of one in 24 Hobby and n 48 Retail, this 10-card set has tan backgrounds e the outside of the card is framed and the inside res a lighter-colored oval. Inside the oval is a portrait-style shot of the player along the top, set e and player name in foil to match the player's color in the middle and team logo on the bottom.

PLETE SET (10) 8.00 20.00
len Iverson .75 2.00
Carmelo Anthony 1.00 2.50
obe Bryant 2.50 6.00
evin Garnett 1.00 2.50
eBron James 3.00 8.00
haquille O'Neal 1.25 3.00
im Duncan .75 2.00
racy McGrady .60 1.50
ince Carter .75 2.00
ao Ming 1.00 2.50

2004-05 Fleer Authentix Hot Tickets Jerseys

omly seeded, this 10-card set parallels the base ickets set but places a square swatch of jersey e the team logo is on the base. Each card is entially numbered to 450.

en Iverson 4.00 10.00
armelo Anthony 5.00 12.00
evin Garnett 5.00 12.00
haquille O'Neal 6.00 15.00
m Duncan 4.00 10.00
acy McGrady 3.00 8.00
nce Carter 4.00 10.00
ao Ming 5.00 12.00

2004-05 Fleer Authentix Jerseys

Randomly inserted in packs, this 35-card set parallels the design of all previously described autographed an memorabilia sets, but places a square swatch of jersey in the bottom center of the card--each is serially numbered to 175. Four parallel versions of the Jerseys set were issued and fie Patch parallels were issued. The Jerseys parallels are sequentially numbered to 150, 75, 25 and 10. Patch parallels are sequentially numbered to 50, 25, 15 and five.

*JERSEY 150: .4X TO 1X BASE HI
*JERSEY 75: .5X TO 1.25X BASE HI
*JERSEY 25: .75X TO 2X BASE HI
*PATCH: .75X TO 2X BASE JSY HI
*PATCH 25: 1.25X TO 3X BASE HI
1 Allen Iverson 4.00 10.00
2 Tim Duncan 4.00 10.00
3 Carmelo Anthony 5.00 12.00
4 Kevin Garnett 5.00 12.00
5 Vince Carter 4.00 10.00
6 Paul Pierce 3.00 8.00
7 Dwyane Wade 8.00 20.00
8 Yao Ming 5.00 12.00
9 Shaquille O'Neal 6.00 15.00
10 Jason Kidd 4.00 10.00
11 Dirk Nowitzki 4.00 10.00
12 Steve Francis 2.50 6.00
13 Tracy McGrady 3.00 8.00
14 Amare Stoudemire 3.00 8.00
15 Stephon Marbury 2.00 5.00
16 Kenyon Martin 2.50 6.00
17 Michael Finley 2.50 6.00
18 Steve Nash 3.00 8.00
19 Jason Richardson 2.50 6.00
20 Chris Webber 2.50 6.00
21 Karl Malone 3.00 8.00
22 Jermaine O'Neal 2.50 6.00
23 Tony Parker 2.50 6.00
24 Peja Stojakovic 2.50 6.00
25 Reggie Miller 2.50 6.00
26 Michael Redd 2.50 6.00
27 Rasheed Wallace 2.50 6.00
28 Ray Allen 2.50 6.00
29 Kirk Hinrich 2.50 6.00
30 Latrell Sprewell 2.00 5.00
31 Baron Davis 2.50 6.00
32 Ben Wallace 2.50 6.00
33 Shawn Marion 2.50 6.00
34 Lamar Odom 2.50 6.00
35 Zach Randolph 2.00 5.00

2004-05 Fleer Authentix Showstoppers

Inserted in packs at the rate of one in eight Hobby and one in 12 Retail, this 15-card set is horizontally designed with a green and black background, yellow lettering, a lighted sign that relembles the "Welcome to Las Vegas Sign" and places a player image on the right side of the card.

COMPLETE SET (15) 6.00 15.00
AI Allen Iverson .50 1.25
AS Amare Stoudemire .40 1.00
CA Carmelo Anthony .60 1.50
DN Dirk Nowitzki .50 1.25
DW Dwyane Wade 1.00 2.50
JK Jason Kidd .50 1.25
KB Kobe Bryant 1.50 4.00
KG Kevin Garnett .60 1.50
LJ LeBron James 2.00 5.00
MB Mike Bibby .30 .75
PP Paul Pierce .40 1.00
SO Shaquille O'Neal .75 2.00
TD Tim Duncan .50 1.25
VC Vince Carter .50 1.25
YM Yao Ming .60 1.50

2004-05 Fleer Authentix Tip-Off Trios

Randomly inserted in packs, this 15-card set features three player head shots on the left, top to bottom and three swatches of jersey to the right. Each card is sequentially numbered to 75. Two parallel versions were printed for this set and are numbered to 25 and five.

*TRIO 25: 1X TO 2.5X BASE HI
DM Dirk Nowitzki 10.00 25.00
Michael Finley
Jason Terry
DN Carmelo Anthony 10.00 25.00
Nene
Andre Miller
DP Ben Wallace 10.00 25.00
Rasheed Wallace
Richard Hamilton
HR Tracy McGrady 10.00 25.00
Yao Ming
Juwan Howard
IP Reggie Miller 10.00 25.00
Jermaine O'Neal
Ron Artest
LL Lamar Odom 10.00 25.00
Karl Malone
Luke Walton
MB T.J. Ford 10.00 25.00
Desmond Mason
Michael Redd
MH Eddie Jones 25.00 60.00
Shaquille O'Neal
Dwyane Wade
MT Kevin Garnett 12.50 30.00
Sam Cassell
Latrell Sprewell
NH Baron Davis 10.00 25.00
Jamal Mashburn
Jamaal Magloire
NK Allan Houston 10.00 25.00
Stephon Marbury
Jamal Crawford
OM Grant Hill 12.50 30.00
Steve Francis
Dwight Howard
PS Steve Nash 10.00 25.00
Shawn Marion
Amare Stoudemire
SK Chris Webber 10.00 25.00
Mike Bibby
Peja Stojakovic
SS Tim Duncan 15.00 40.00
Smanu Ginoili
Tony Parker

2002 Fleer Authentix WNBA

Released in the summer of 2002, this 120-card set is divided up into 100 veteran players and 20 rookie cards. Veteran cards place players on a ticket backdrop with an embedded ticket swatch in the card. Rookie cards are sequentially numbered to 2002.

COMPLETE SET (120) 75.00 150.00
COMPLETE SET w/o RC's (100) 12.50 30.00
1 Jackie Stiles .75 2.00
2 Taj McWilliams-Franklin .20 .50
3 Allison Feaster .25 .60
4 Sheryl Swoopes 1.25 3.00
5 Edwina Brown .25 .60
6 DeLisha Milton .20 .50
7 Tonya Edwards .20 .50
8 Svetlana Abrosimova .20 .50
9 Alicia Thompson .20 .50
10 Kristen Rasmussen .20 .50
11 Marie Ferdinand .20 .50
12 Coco Miller .20 .50
13 Tari Phillips .20 .50
14 Kristin Folkl .30 .75
15 Annie Burgess RC .20 .50
16 Elaine Powell .20 .50
17 Jamie Redd .20 .50
18 Sophia Witherspoon .30 .75
19 Shannon Johnson .20 .50
20 Amanda Lassiter .20 .50
21 Dawn Staley .50 1.25
22 Dominique Canty .30 .75
23 Jessie Hicks .20 .50
24 Mwadi Mabika .20 .50
25 Georgia Schweitzer .20 .50
26 Lauren Jackson 1.00 2.50
27 Natalie Williams .40 1.00
28 Tynesha Lewis .20 .50
29 Rushia Brown .20 .50
30 Tamicha Jackson .20 .50
31 Chasity Melvin .20 .50
32 Chamique Holdsclaw 1.25 3.00
33 Michelle Marciniak .30 .75
34 Lynn Pride .20 .50
35 Tammy Sutton-Brown .20 .50
36 Sandy Brondello .50 1.25
37 Semeka Randall .20 .50
38 Tammy Jackson .20 .50
39 Ukari Figgs .20 .50
40 Ruthie Bolton .60 1.50
41 Lisa Harrison .30 .75
42 Kate Starbird .30 .75
43 Katie Douglas .30 .75
44 Coquese Washington .20 .50
45 Sheri Sam .20 .50
46 Vickie Johnson .30 .75
47 Latasha Byears .30 .75
48 Erin Buescher .20 .50
49 Ann Wauters .25 .60
50 Kedra Holland-Corn .20 .50
51 Astou Ndiaye-Diatta .30 .75
52 Kara Wolters .25 .60
53 Tully Bevilaqua .20 .50
54 Simone Edwards RC .20 .50
55 Vicky Bullett .30 .75
56 Nykesha Sales .30 .75
57 Crystal Robinson .20 .50
58 Tina Thompson .60 1.50
59 Lisa Leslie 1.00 2.50
60 Deanna Nolan .20 .50
61 Jennifer Gillom .50 1.25
62 Nadine Malcolm RC .20 .50
63 Merlakia Jones .30 .75
64 Rebecca Lobo .60 1.50
65 Tamecka Dixon .30 .75
66 Yolanda Griffith .60 1.50
67 Teresa Weatherspoon .75 2.00
68 Penny Taylor .30 .75
69 Brooke Wyckoff .40 1.00
70 Murriel Page .25 .60
71 Adrienne Goodson .20 .50
72 Camille Cooper .20 .50
73 Kamila Vodichkova .20 .50
74 Jennifer Azzi .60 1.50
75 Katie Smith .60 1.50
76 Kristen Veal .20 .50
77 Tamika Catchings .50 1.25
78 Clarisse Machanguana .20 .50
79 Wendy Palmer .50 1.25
80 Ticha Penicheiro .50 1.25
81 Becky Hammon 1.00 2.50
82 Jennifer Rizzotti .50 1.25
83 Helen Luz .20 .50
84 Adrain Williams .20 .50
85 Tamika Whitmore .20 .50
86 Sylvia Crawley .20 .50
87 Edna Campbell .25 .60
88 Sonja Henning .20 .50
89 Vedrana Grgin .20 .50
90 Tracy Reid .30 .75
91 Betty Lennox .50 1.25
92 Andrea Stinson .40 1.00
93 Tangela Smith .20 .50
94 Margo Dydek .30 .75
95 Nikki McCray .50 1.25
96 Sue Wicks .30 .75
97 Olympia Scott-Richardson .20 .50
98 Ruth Riley .30 .75
99 Janeth Arcain .20 .50
100 Rita Williams .25 .60
101 Sue Bird RC 25.00 60.00
102 Swin Cash RC 6.00 15.00
103 Stacey Dales-Schuman RC 4.00 10.00
104 Asjha Jones RC 4.00 10.00
105 Nikki Teasley RC 2.50 6.00
106 Tamika Williams RC 4.00 10.00
107 Sheila Lambert RC 2.50 6.00
108 Lindsey Yamasaki RC 2.50 6.00
109 Shaunzinski Gortman RC 2.50 6.00
110 Michelle Snow RC 4.00 10.00
111 Danielle Crockrom RC 3.00 8.00
112 Hamchetou Maiga RC 2.50 6.00
113 Tawana McDonald RC 2.50 6.00
114 LaNeishea Caufield RC 2.50 6.00
115 Tamara Moore RC 2.50 6.00
116 Rosalind Ross RC 2.50 6.00
117 Zuzi Klimesova RC 2.50 6.00
118 Lenae Williams RC 2.50 6.00
119 Iziane Castro-Marques RC 2.50 6.00
120 Ayana Walker RC 3.00 8.00

2002 Fleer Authentix WNBA Front Row

Randomly seeded in packs, this 120-card set parallels the base set enhanced with sequential numbering to 100 on the card back.

*STARS 1-100: 5X TO 12X BASE CARD HI
*RCs 101-120: .75X TO 2X BASE CARD HI

2002 Fleer Authentix WNBA Autographed Authentix

Randomly inserted in packs, this set features three different Jackie Stiles autograph cards. The cards are sequentially numbered to 90, 49, and one.

1A Jackie Stiles AU/90 75.00 150.00
Unripped
1B Jackie Stiles JSY AU/49 100.00 200.00
Ripped

2002 Fleer Authentix WNBA Courtside Classics

Randomly inserted in packs at the rate of one in 22, this 10-card set features the WNBA's brightest stars.

COMPLETE SET (10) 10.00 25.00
1 Jackie Stiles 2.50 6.00
2 Sheri Sam .60 1.50
3 Betty Lennox 1.50 4.00
4 Teresa Weatherspoon 2.50 6.00
5 Katie Douglas 1.00 2.50
6 DeLisha Milton .60 1.50
7 Lauren Jackson 3.00 8.00
8 Murriel Page .75 2.00
9 Kedra Holland-Corn .60 1.50
10 Tina Thompson 2.00 5.00

2002 Fleer Authentix WNBA Memorabilia Authentix Ripped

Inserted in packs at the rate of one in eight, this 13-card set places a swatch of game worn memorabilia in the middle and the bottom edge of the card is jagged is if it has been ripped like a ticket stub.

*UNRIPPED: 3X TO 8X HI
UNRIPPED PRINT RUN 50 SER.#'d SETS
1 Jackie Stiles 5.00 12.00
2 Jennifer Gillom 3.00 8.00
3 Dawn Staley 3.00 8.00
4 Nikki McCray 3.00 8.00
5 Nykesha Sales 2.00 5.00
6 Becky Hammon 6.00 15.00
7 Sheryl Swoopes 6.00 15.00
8 Yolanda Griffith 4.00 10.00
9 Sue Bird 10.00 25.00
10 Lisa Leslie 6.00 15.00
11 Ruthie Bolton 4.00 10.00
12 Natalie Williams 2.50 6.00
13 Chamique Holdsclaw 6.00 15.00

2002 Fleer Authentix WNBA The Ticket

Inserted in packs, this 16-card set places a swatch of a ticket to a WBNA game next to the featured player. Each card is sequentially numbered.

1 Jackie Stiles/500 8.00 20.00
2 Lauren Jackson/575 10.00 25.00
3 Andrea Stinson/320 4.00 10.00
4 Jennifer Rizzotti/500 5.00 12.00
5 Ruth Riley/565 3.00 8.00
6 Deanna Nolan/310 3.00 8.00
7 Tamika Catchings/330 8.00 20.00
8 Sheryl Swoopes/600 8.00 20.00
9 Katie Smith/475 6.00 15.00
10 Becky Hammon/390 10.00 25.00
11 Nykesha Sales/375 3.00 8.00
12 Lisa Harrison/475 3.00 8.00
13 Yolanda Griffith/160 12.00 30.00
14 Natalie Williams/495 4.00 10.00
15 Chamique Holdsclaw/410 8.00 20.00
16 Lisa Leslie/450 8.00 20.00

2000-01 Fleer Authority

The 2000-01 Fleer Authority product was released in late February, 2001 and featured a 141-card base set that was broken into tiers as follows: Base Veterans (1-110), and Rookies (111-141) that were serial numbered to 650 and inserted at 1:16 packs.

COMPLETE SET (141) 80.00 160.00
COMP.SET w/o SP's (110) 10.00 25.00
1 Dikembe Mutombo .30 .75
2 Cuttino Mobley .25 .60
3 Brian Grant .20 .50
4 Grant Hill .40 1.00
5 Jim Jackson .20 .50
6 Derek Anderson .20 .50
7 Jerry Stackhouse .25 .60
8 Eddie Jones .30 .75
9 Tracy McGrady .50 1.25
10 Vin Baker .25 .60
11 Jason Terry .30 .75
12 Jerome Williams .20 .50
13 Tim Hardaway .30 .75
14 Darrell Armstrong .20 .50
15 Rashard Lewis .30 .75
16 Kenny Anderson .25 .60
17 Larry Hughes .25 .60
18 Anthony Mason .20 .50
19 Allen Iverson .60 1.50
20 Gary Payton .30 .75
21 Antoine Walker .25 .60
22 Antawn Jamison .30 .75
23 Glenn Robinson .25 .60
24 Toni Kukoc .25 .60
25 Ruben Patterson .20 .50
26 Paul Pierce .40 1.00
27 Mookie Blaylock .25 .60
28 Ray Allen .30 .75
29 Theo Ratliff .20 .50
30 Vince Carter .60 1.50
31 Jamal Mashburn .25 .60
32 Steve Francis .30 .75
33 Sam Cassell .25 .60
34 Jason Kidd .50 1.25
35 Mark Jackson .25 .60
36 Baron Davis .30 .75
37 Hakeem Olajuwon .40 1.00
38 Darvin Ham .20 .50
39 Anfernee Hardaway .50 1.25
40 Antonio Davis .20 .50
41 Derrick Coleman .25 .60
42 Maurice Taylor .20 .50
43 Kevin Garnett .60 1.50
44 Tom Gugliotta .20 .50
45 Karl Malone .40 1.00
46 Elton Brand .30 .75
47 Jonathan Bender .20 .50
48 Terrell Brandon .20 .50
49 Clifford Robinson .20 .50
50 John Stockton .40 1.00
51 Ron Artest .30 .75
52 Reggie Miller .30 .75
53 Joe Smith .25 .60
54 Shawn Kemp .30 .75
55 Bryon Russell .20 .50
56 Andre Miller .25 .60
57 Austin Croshere .20 .50
58 Wally Szczerbiak .25 .60
59 Scottie Pippen .50 1.25
60 Donyell Marshall .20 .50
61 Brevin Knight .20 .50
62 Travis Best .20 .50
63 Chauncey Billups .30 .75
64 Rasheed Wallace .30 .75
65 Shareef Abdur-Rahim .25 .60
66 Trajan Langdon .20 .50
67 Jalen Rose .25 .60
68 Stephon Marbury .25 .60
69 Steve Smith .25 .60
70 Mike Bibby .30 .75
71 Lamond Murray .20 .50
72 Lamar Odom .30 .75
73 Keith Van Horn .25 .60
74 Chris Webber .30 .75
75 Michael Dickerson .20 .50
76 Dirk Nowitzki .50 1.25
77 Corey Maggette .25 .60
78 Kerry Kittles .20 .50
79 Jason Williams .30 .75
80 Mitch Richmond .25 .60
81 Michael Finley .30 .75
82 Shaquille O'Neal .75 2.00
83 Allan Houston .25 .60
84 Peja Stojakovic .30 .75
85 Juwan Howard .25 .60
86 Nick Van Exel .25 .60
87 Kobe Bryant 1.50 4.00
88 Latrell Sprewell .25 .60
89 Tim Duncan .60 1.50
90 Richard Hamilton .25 .60
91 Antonio McDyess .25 .60
92 Glen Rice .25 .60
93 Larry Johnson .30 .75
94 David Robinson .50 1.25
95 Rod Strickland .25 .60
96 Raef LaFrentz .20 .50
97 Ron Harper .25 .60
98 Patrick Ewing .40 1.00
99 Sean Elliot .25 .60
100 Tariq Abdul-Wahad .20 .50
101 Chucky Atkins .20 .50
102 Marcus Camby .25 .60
103 Corliss Williamson .20 .50
104 Rodney Rogers .20 .50
105 Othella Harrington .20 .50
106 Alan Henderson .20 .50
107 David Wesley .20 .50
108 Michael Doleac .20 .50
109 Doug Christie .20 .50
110 Vitaly Potapenko .20 .50
111 DerMarr Johnson RC 1.50 4.00
112 Jamal Crawford RC 2.50 6.00
113 Morris Peterson RC 1.50 4.00
114 Erick Barkley RC 1.50 4.00
115 Kenyon Martin RC 4.00 10.00
116 Joel Przybilla RC 1.50 4.00
117 Speedy Claxton RC 1.50 4.00
118 Hedo Turkoglu RC 3.00 8.00
119 Etan Thomas RC 1.50 4.00
120 Eddie House RC 1.50 4.00
121 Marcus Fizer RC 1.50 4.00
122 Quentin Richardson RC 2.50 6.00
123 Donnell Harvey RC 1.50 4.00
124 DeShawn Stevenson RC 2.00 5.00
125 Chris Mihm RC 1.50 4.00
126 Courtney Alexander RC 1.50 4.00
127 Keyon Dooling RC 1.50 4.00
128 Jerome Moiso RC 1.50 4.00
129 Stephen Jackson RC 2.50 6.00
130 Chris Porter RC 1.50 4.00
131 Stromile Swift RC 1.50 4.00
132 Desmond Mason RC 2.00 5.00
133 Jason Collier RC 1.50 4.00
134 Mark Madsen RC 1.50 4.00
135 Mamadou N'Diaye RC 1.50 4.00
136 Darius Miles RC 1.50 4.00
137 Mateen Cleaves RC 1.50 4.00
138 Jamaal Magloire RC 1.50 4.00
139 Khalid El-Amin RC 1.50 4.00
140 Mike Miller RC 3.00 8.00
141 Marc Jackson RC 1.50 4.00

2000-01 Fleer Authority Rookies 1250

Upon release, these cards were available in graded form only. Since that time, a limited number of cards have found their way outside of their BGS slab cases.

*RC 1250: .2X TO .5X BASE RC

2000-01 Fleer Authority Prominence 125/75

Randomly inserted in packs, this 141-card set parallels the base Fleer Authority set enhanced with a gold background shift from the base silver/gray, and the word "Prominence" appears in rainbow holofoil above the player picture. Veteran players are sequentially numbered to 125, while rookies are numbered to 75.

*STARS 1-110: 8X TO 20X BASE HI
*ROOKIES 111-141: .6X TO 1.5X BASE HI

2000-01 Fleer Authority Prominence 75/25

Upon release, these cards were available in graded form only. Since that time, a limited number of cards have found their way outside of their BGS slab cases. Due to limited market activity, and the fact that the majority of the cards still remain encased in their BGS holders, these cards are checklisted, but unpriced. Veteran players are sequentially numbered to 75, while rookies are numbered to 25.

*STARS 1-110: 10X TO 25X BASE HI
*ROOKIES 111-141: 1.25X TO 3X BASE HI

2000-01 Fleer Authority Autographics SSD

The Fleer Authority Autographics SSD set is comprised of regular 2000-01 Fleer Autographics cards, but are enhanced with an embossed Fleer stamp of authority. Upon release, these cards were available in graded form only. Since that time, a limited number of cards have found their way outside of their BGS slab cases.

2000-01 Fleer Authority Autographics SSD Gold

The Fleer Authority Autographics SSD Gold set, sequentially numbered to 50, is comprised of regular 2000-01 Fleer Autographics Gold cards, but are enhanced with an embossed Fleer stamp of authority. Upon release, these cards were available in graded form only. Since that time, a limited number of cards have found their way outside of their BGS slab cases.

SEE 2000-01 FLEER AUTO GOLD FOR PRICES

2000-01 Fleer Authority Autographics SSD Silver

The Fleer Authority Autographics SSD Silver set, sequentially numbered to 250, is comprised of regular 2000-01 Fleer Autographics Silver cards, but are enhanced with an embossed Fleer stamp of authority. Upon release, these cards were available in graded form only. Since that time, a limited number of cards have found their way outside of their BGS slab cases.

SEE 2000-01 FLEER AUTO SILVER FOR PRICES

2000-01 Fleer Authority Vince Carter Rookie Remnants

This three-card insert was randomly inserted into 2000-01 Fleer products. The set includes a Vince Carter floor card (numbered to 100), a Vince Carter floor/jersey card (numbered to 15), and finally an autographed Vince Carter floor/jersey card (numbered 1 of 1).

VCRR1 Vince Carter FLR/100 12.50 30.00

2000-01 Fleer Authority Feel the Game

Randomly inserted in multiple releases, this set features swatches of game-used jerseys from top veterans and rookies in the NBA. The cards were inserted at one in 56 for Fleer Premium, 1:72 for Fleer Mystique, 1:48 Fleer Focus, and 1:48 for Ultra. The cards are not numbered on the back and listed in alphabetical order.

2000-01 Fleer Authority Figures

Randomly inserted in packs at the rate of one in 16, this 15-card set features a veteran player portrait style photo on the top half of the card, and a young star in action on the lower right hand side. Each card is sequentially numbered to 1250.

COMPLETE SET (15) 10.00 25.00
*FIGURES 499: .6X TO 1.5X HI
AF1 Courtney Alexander .60 1.50
Michael Finley
AF2 Mark Madsen 3.00 8.00
Kobe Bryant
AF3 DerMarr Johnson .60 1.50
Dikembe Mutombo
AF4 Mateen Cleaves .60 1.50
Jerry Stackhouse
AF5 Kenyon Martin 1.50 4.00
Keith Van Horn
AF6 Morris Peterson 1.25 3.00
Vince Carter
AF7 Darius Miles .60 1.50
Lamar Odom
AF8 Desmond Mason .75 2.00
Gary Payton
AF9 Stromile Swift .60 1.50
Shareef Abdur-Rahim
AF10 Speedy Claxton 1.25 3.00
Allen Iverson
AF11 DeShawn Stevenson .75 2.00
Karl Malone
AF12 Marcus Fizer .60 1.50
Elton Brand
AF13 Hedo Turkoglu 1.25 3.00
Chris Webber
AF14 Jason Collier .60 1.50
Steve Francis
AF15 Mike Miller 1.25 3.00
Grant Hill

2000-01 Fleer Authority Rookie Reflections

Authority Rookie Reflections and Fleer Feel the Game were inserted in packs at the combined ration of one in 16. This 22-card set features a horizontal card design with player action photos on the left side of the card, a swatch of game worn memorabilia in the center, and a portrait style photograph on the right.

RR1 Vince Carter 6.00 15.00
RR2 Grant Hill 4.00 10.00
RR3 Keyon Dooling 3.00 8.00
RR4 Jason Kidd 5.00 12.00
RR5 Chris Mihm 3.00 8.00
RR6 Darius Miles 3.00 8.00
RR7 Mike Miller 6.00 15.00
RR8 Quentin Richardson 5.00 12.00
RR9 Hanno Mottola 3.00 8.00
RR10 Allen Iverson 6.00 15.00
RR11 Desmond Mason 4.00 10.00
RR12 Andre Miller 2.50 6.00
RR13 Tracy McGrady 5.00 12.00
RR14 Shawn Marion 3.00 8.00
RR15 John Stockton 4.00 10.00
RR16 Lamar Odom 3.00 8.00
RR17 Vince Carter 8.00 20.00
Darius Miles
RR18 Grant Hill 4.00 10.00
Desmond Mason
RR19 Jason Kidd 5.00 12.00
Quentin Richardson
RR20 Allen Iverson 6.00 15.00
Keyon Dooling
RR21 Tracy McGrady 6.00 15.00
Mike Miller
RR22 Andre Miller 3.00 8.00
Chris Mihm

2000-01 Fleer Authority Seal of Approval

Upon release, these cards were available in graded form only. SInce that time, a limited number of cards have found their way outside of their BGS slab cases.

COMPLETE SET (15) 30.00 60.00
SA1 Kobe Bryant 12.00 30.00
SA2 Tim Duncan 4.00 10.00
SA3 Jason Kidd 3.00 8.00
SA4 Lamar Odom 2.00 5.00
SA5 Kevin Garnett 4.00 10.00
SA6 Elton Brand 2.00 5.00
SA7 Steve Francis 2.00 5.00
SA8 Stromile Swift 2.00 5.00
SA9 Kenyon Martin 5.00 12.00
SA10 Tracy McGrady 3.00 8.00
SA11 Allen Iverson 4.00 10.00
SA12 Grant Hill 2.50 6.00
SA13 Marcus Fizer 2.00 5.00
SA14 Shaquille O'Neal 5.00 12.00
SA15 Vince Carter 4.00 10.00

2000-01 Fleer Authority With Authority

Randomly seeded in packs at the rate of one in 16, this 20-card set features the game's most dominating names set against a background that fades to white along the edges. The upper left hand corner of the card is cut and rounded. Each card is sequentially numbered to 999.

*WA 299: .5X TO 1.25X HI
WA1 Dirk Nowitzki 1.50 4.00
WA2 Larry Hughes .75 2.00
WA3 Eddie Jones 1.00 2.50
WA4 Chris Webber 1.00 2.50
WA5 Grant Hill 1.25 3.00
WA6 Scottie Pippen 1.50 4.00
WA7 Shareef Abdur-Rahim .75 2.00
WA8 Kevin Garnett 2.00 5.00
WA9 Allen Iverson 2.00 5.00
WA10 Karl Malone 1.25 3.00
WA11 Kobe Bryant 5.00 12.00
WA12 Tim Duncan 2.00 5.00
WA13 Stephon Marbury .75 2.00
WA14 Shaquille O'Neal 2.50 6.00
WA15 Vince Carter. 2.00 5.00
WA16 Tracy McGrady 1.50 4.00
WA17 Gary Payton 1.00 2.50
WA18 Steve Francis 1.00 2.50
WA19 Elton Brand 1.00 2.50
WA20 Ray Allen 1.00 2.50

2003-04 Fleer Avant

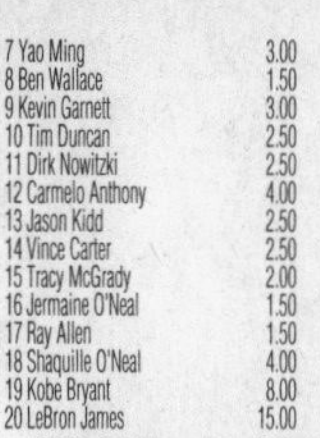

Released in late January 2004, this 90-card set is divided up into 56 veteran player cards, eight team USA cards sequentially numbered to 699 (cards 57-64) and 25 rookie players sequentially numbered to 699. Base cards are framed with a thick cardboard border and have painting-like pictures for the cards themselves. Avant was packaged in 18-pack boxes where packs contained four cards and carried a suggested retail price of $7.99.

COMP.SET w/o SP's 15.00 40.00
1 Ben Wallace .60 1.50
2 Glenn Robinson .50 1.25
3 Pau Gasol .60 1.50
4 Keon Clark .40 1.00
5 Kobe Bryant 3.00 8.00
6 Morris Peterson .40 1.00
7 Steve Francis .60 1.50
8 Amare Stoudemire 1.00 2.50
9 Mike Dunleavy Jr. .50 1.25
10 Kevin Garnett 1.25 3.00
11 Yao Ming 1.25 3.00
12 Stephon Marbury .50 1.25
13 Jason Richardson .60 1.50
14 Rasheed Wallace .60 1.50
15 Tayshaun Prince .60 1.50
16 Steve Nash .75 2.00
17 Jamal Mashburn .50 1.25
18 Reggie Miller .60 1.50
19 Chris Webber .60 1.50
20 Andre Miller .50 1.25
21 Peja Stojakovic .60 1.50
22 Nene .50 1.25
23 Manu Ginobili .75 2.00
24 Bonzi Wells .40 1.00
25 Lamar Odom .60 1.50
26 Kwame Brown .40 1.00
27 Caron Butler .60 1.50
28 Gilbert Arenas .60 1.50
29 Dirk Nowitzki 1.00 2.50
30 Allan Houston .50 1.25
31 Michael Finley .60 1.50
32 Drew Gooden .50 1.25
33 Shareef Abdur-Rahim .50 1.25
34 Michael Redd .60 1.50
35 Jerry Stackhouse .50 1.25
36 Scottie Pippen 1.00 2.50
37 Latrell Sprewell .50 1.25
38 Ron Artest .60 1.50
39 Derrick Coleman .50 1.25
40 Eddy Curry .50 1.25
41 Wally Szczerbiak .50 1.25
42 Dajuan Wagner .40 1.00
43 Baron Davis .60 1.50
44 Karl Malone .75 2.00
45 Andrei Kirilenko .60 1.50
46 Paul Pierce .75 2.00
47 Desmond Mason .50 1.25
48 Shaquille O'Neal 1.50 4.00
49 Rashard Lewis .60 1.50
50 Ricky Davis .50 1.25
51 Kerry Kittles .40 1.00
52 Quentin Richardson .50 1.25
53 Tony Parker .60 1.50
54 Elton Brand .60 1.50
55 Richard Jefferson .60 1.50
56 Kenyon Martin .60 1.50
57 Ray Allen 1.50 4.00
58 Mike Bibby 1.50 4.00
59 Tim Duncan 2.50 6.00
60 Allen Iverson 2.50 6.00
61 Jason Kidd 2.50 6.00
62 Tracy McGrady 2.00 5.00
63 Jermaine O'Neal 1.50 4.00
64 Larry Brown 3.00 8.00
65 LeBron James RC 25.00 60.00
66 Darko Milicic RC 2.00 5.00
67 Carmelo Anthony RC 5.00 12.00
68 Chris Bosh RC 4.00 10.00
69 Dwyane Wade RC 8.00 20.00
70 Chris Kaman RC 2.50 6.00
71 Kirk Hinrich RC 2.50 6.00
72 T.J. Ford RC 2.50 6.00
73 Mike Sweetney RC 2.00 5.00
74 Jarvis Hayes RC 2.00 5.00
75 Mickael Pietrus RC 2.00 5.00
76 Travis Hansen RC 2.00 5.00
77 Marcus Banks RC 2.00 5.00
78 Luke Ridnour RC 2.50 6.00
79 Reece Gaines RC 2.00 5.00
80 Troy Bell RC 2.00 5.00
81 Zarko Cabarkapa RC 2.00 5.00
82 David West RC 2.50 6.00
83 Aleksandar Pavlovic RC 2.00 5.00
84 Dahntay Jones RC 2.00 5.00
85 Boris Diaw RC 2.50 6.00
86 Zoran Planinic RC 2.00 5.00
87 Travis Outlaw RC 2.50 6.00
88 Brian Cook RC 2.00 5.00
89 Maciej Lampe RC 2.00 5.00
90 Nick Collison RC 2.00 5.00

2003-04 Fleer Avant Black and White

Inserted in packs, this 90-card set parallels the base set enhanced with black border and art-quality black and white photos. Each card is sequentially numbered to 199.

*1-56 SINGLES: 1X TO 2.5X BASE HI
*57-64 USA SINGLES: .5X TO 1.25X BASE HI
*65-90 RC SINGLES: .5X TO 1.25X BASE HI
69 Dwyane Wade 12.00 30.00

2003-04 Fleer Avant Candid Collection

Randomly seeded, this 20-card set utilizes a horizontal format with close-up portrait style photos of players striking familiar non-playing court poses with white borders. Each card is sequentially numbered to 199.

1 Allen Iverson 2.50 6.00
2 Steve Francis 1.50 4.00
3 Amare Stoudemire 2.50 6.00
4 Chris Webber 1.50 4.00
5 Paul Pierce 2.00 5.00
6 Caron Butler 1.50 4.00
7 Yao Ming 3.00 8.00
8 Ben Wallace 1.50 4.00
9 Kevin Garnett 3.00 8.00
10 Tim Duncan 2.50 6.00
11 Dirk Nowitzki 2.50 6.00
12 Carmelo Anthony 4.00 10.00
13 Jason Kidd 2.50 6.00
14 Vince Carter 2.50 6.00
15 Tracy McGrady 2.00 5.00
16 Jermaine O'Neal 1.50 4.00
17 Ray Allen 1.50 4.00
18 Shaquille O'Neal 4.00 10.00
19 Kobe Bryant 8.00 20.00
20 LeBron James 15.00 40.00

2003-04 Fleer Avant Candid Collection Memorabilia

Randomly inserted, this 10-card set parallels the design of the base Candid Collection insert enhanced with a swatch of game worn memorabilia. Each card is sequentially numbered to 250.

AI Allen Iverson 4.00 10.00
AS Amare Stoudemire 4.00 10.00
BW Ben Wallace 2.50 6.00
DN Dirk Nowitzki 4.00 10.00
JK Jason Kidd 4.00 10.00
KG Kevin Garnett 5.00 12.00
SF Steve Francis 2.50 6.00
TD Tim Duncan 4.00 10.00
TM Tracy McGrady 3.00 8.00
YM Yao Ming 5.00 12.00

2003-04 Fleer Avant Materials

Inserted in packs at the overall ratio of one in six packs for all memorabilia cards, this 45-card set parallels the look of the base Avant cards enhanced with a square swatch of game worn memorabilia. Several different versions of this set were issued, a Blue foil version numbered to 400, a Gold foil version numbered to 75 and a Patch version sequentially numbered to 25.

*BLUE: .4X TO 1X BASE HI
*GOLD: .6X TO 1.5X BASE HI
*PATCH: 1.5X TO 4X BASE HI
BC Brian Cook 2.50 6.00
BD Baron Davis 2.50 6.00
BW Ben Wallace 2.50 6.00
CA Carmelo Anthony 6.00 15.00
CB Chris Bosh 5.00 12.00
CK Chris Kaman 3.00 8.00
DG Drew Gooden 2.50 6.00
DJ Dahntay Jones 2.50 6.00
DW1 Dajuan Wagner 2.00 5.00
DW2 David West 3.00 8.00
DW3 Dwyane Wade 10.00 25.00
JH Jarvis Hayes 2.50 6.00
JK Jason Kidd 4.00 10.00
JO Jermaine O'Neal 2.50 6.00
JR Jason Richardson 2.50 6.00
KG Kevin Garnett 5.00 12.00
LR Luke Ridnour 3.00 8.00
MB1 Marcus Banks 2.50 6.00
MB2 Mike Bibby 2.50 6.00
MD Mike Dunleavy 2.00 5.00
MS Mike Sweetney 2.00 5.00
PG Pau Gasol 2.50 6.00
RA Ray Allen 2.50 6.00
RG Reece Gaines 2.50 6.00
SA Shareef Abdur-Rahim 2.00 5.00
SF Steve Francis 2.50 6.00
SM Stephon Marbury 2.00 5.00
SO Shaquille O'Neal 6.00 15.00
TB Troy Bell 2.50 6.00
TH Travis Hansen 2.50 6.00
TM Tracy McGrady 3.00 8.00
TO Travis Outlaw 3.00 8.00
TP1 Tayshaun Prince 2.50 6.00
WS Wally Szczerbiak 2.00 5.00
YM Yao Ming 5.00 12.00

2003-04 Fleer Avant Stars and Stripes

Randomly seeded in packs, this eight-card set features players on the original 2004 USA Dream Team roster. The cards are set to look like the American flag with a player photo on the left and the Dream Team jersey number in a red star on the right. Each card is sequentially numbered to 204.

1 Ray Allen 4.00 10.00
2 Mike Bibby 4.00 10.00
3 Larry Brown 4.00 10.00
4 Tim Duncan 6.00 15.00
5 Allen Iverson 6.00 15.00
6 Jason Kidd 6.00 15.00
7 Tracy McGrady 5.00 12.00
8 Jermaine O'Neal 4.00 10.00

2003-04 Fleer Avant Stars and Stripes Jerseys

Randomly seeded, this seven card set parallels the base Stars and Stripes set enhanced with a swatch from a Team USA jersey and sequential numbering to 500. A Red version and a patch version were also produced. Red version have red foil highlights and sequential numbering to 100 and patch version feature a swatch of game-worn patch and are numbered to each player's USA jersey number.

*RED SINGLES: .5X TO 1.25X BASE JSY HI
RED PRINT RUN 100 SER.#'d SETS
UNPRICED PATCH PRINT RUN TO USA JSY #
AI Allen Iverson 8.00 20.00
JK Jason Kidd 8.00 20.00
JO Jermaine O'Neal 5.00 12.00
MB Mike Bibby 5.00 12.00
RA Ray Allen 5.00 12.00
TD Tim Duncan 8.00 20.00
TM Tracy McGrady 6.00 15.00

2003-04 Fleer Avant Work of Heart

Inserted randomly, this 15-card set places two-tone brown-scale photos on a card with white borders. Each card is sequentially numbered to 299.

1 Yao Ming 3.00 8.00
2 Allen Iverson 2.50 6.00
3 Jason Kidd 2.50 6.00
4 Tim Duncan 2.50 6.00
5 Vince Carter 2.50 6.00
6 Ben Wallace 1.50 4.00
7 Dirk Nowitzki 2.50 6.00
8 Carmelo Anthony 4.00 10.00
9 Tracy McGrady 2.00 5.00
10 Shaquille O'Neal 4.00 10.00
11 LeBron James 15.00 40.00
12 Kobe Bryant 8.00 20.00
13 Paul Pierce 2.00 5.00
14 Chris Webber 1.50 4.00
15 Kevin Garnett 3.00 8.00

2003-04 Fleer Avant Work of Heart Jerseys

Sequentially numbered to 300, this 10-card set parallels the base Work of Heart set enhanced with jersey swatches.

AI Allen Iverson 4.00 10.00
BW Ben Wallace 2.50 6.00
CA Carmelo Anthony 6.00 15.00
DN Dirk Nowitzki 4.00 10.00
JK Jason Kidd 4.00 10.00
KG Kevin Garnett 5.00 12.00
TD Tim Duncan 4.00 10.00
TM Tracy McGrady 3.00 8.00
VC Vince Carter 4.00 10.00
YM Yao Ming 5.00 12.00

2002-03 Fleer Box Score

Released in early February 2003, this 240-card set features 135 base cards, 15 Rookie cards sequentially numbered to 1999, 30 Rising Star rookie cards, 30 All-Star cards, and 30 Around the World cards. Base cards feature full-color player action photography set against a white and silver background with white and silver borders. Rookie card numbers 136-150 utilize the same base card design enhanced with gold backgrounds and borders in place of the silver and Rising Star rookie cards, numbers 151-180, do the same with a shift to bronze. All-Star cards, numbers 181-210, place full color action photography on a yellow star with solid pastel colored backgrounds, and Around the World cards, numbers 211-240, place players on a globe with the Around the World logo along the top of the card which utilizes different nation's flags. Fleer Box Score was packaged in 18-pack boxes where packs contained seven cards and carried an SRP of $4.99. Each box also included a smaller supplemental box which contained a complete set of one of the subsets-Rising Stars, All-Stars, Around the World or Classic Miniatures (parallel base set design-30 cards). Supplemental boxes all included one memorabilia card. Supplemental boxes were available as well containing a seal with a serial number out of 100.

COMP.SET w/o SP's (135) 12.50 30.00
1 Kwame Brown .25 .60
2 Eddy Curry .30 .75
3 Allen Iverson .60 1.50
4 Elton Brand .40 1.00
5 Jason Kidd .60 1.50
6 Kedrick Brown .25 .60
7 Elden Campbell .25 .60
8 Jason Richardson .40 1.00
9 Shawn Marion .40 1.00
10 John Stockton .50 1.25
11 Theo Ratliff .25 .60
12 Marcus Fizer .25 .60
13 Tony Parker .50 1.25
14 Michael Redd .40 1.00
15 Vince Carter .60 1.50
16 Aaron McKie .25 .60
17 Michael Finley .40 1.00
18 Rashard Lewis .40 1.00
19 Steve Nash .50 1.25
20 Reggie Miller .40 1.00
21 Tim Duncan .75 2.00
22 Marcus Camby .30 .75
23 Michael Jordan 3.00 8.00
24 Donnell Harvey .25 .60
25 Michael Dickerson .25 .60
26 James Posey .30 .75
27 Vin Baker .30 .75
28 Antonio McDyess .30 .75
29 Mike Miller .40 1.00
30 Karl Malone .50 1.25
31 Corliss Williamson .25 .60
32 Derek Anderson .25 .60
33 Scottie Pippen .60 1.50
34 Paul Pierce .50 1.25
35 Steve Francis .40 1.00
36 Terrell Brandon .25 .60
37 Cuttino Mobley .30 .75
38 Ron Artest .40 1.00
39 Jonathan Bender .25 .60
40 Ron Mercer .25 .60
41 Dirk Nowitzki .60 1.50
42 Jermaine O'Neal .40 1.00
43 Ray Allen .40 1.00
44 Jason Terry .30 .75
45 Pau Gasol .50 1.25
46 Lamar Odom .40 1.00
47 P.J. Brown .25 .60
48 Kurt Thomas .25 .60
49 Grant Hill .50 1.25
50 David Robinson .60 1.50
51 Rasheed Wallace .40 1.00
52 Antawn Jamison .40 1.00
53 Juwan Howard .30 .75
54 Andre Miller .30 .75
55 Kenyon Martin .40 1.00
56 Jason Williams .30 .75
57 Travis Best .25 .60
58 Brian Grant .25 .60
59 Keith Van Horn .40 1.00
60 Alonzo Mourning .50 1.25
61 Rod Strickland .30 .75
62 Jamaal Tinsley .40 1.00
63 Sam Cassell .30 .75
64 Jalen Rose .30 .75
65 Tim Thomas .25 .60
66 Eddie Griffin .25 .60
67 Kevin Garnett .75 2.00
68 Darrell Armstrong .25 .60
69 Joe Smith .25 .60
70 Wally Szczerbiak .30 .75
71 Richard Jefferson .40 1.00
72 Chauncey Billups .40 1.00
73 Kerry Kittles .25 .60
74 Stromile Swift .25 .60
75 Dikembe Mutombo .40 1.00
76 Courtney Alexander .25 .60
77 Tony Delk .25 .60
78 Baron Davis .40 1.00
79 Ricky Davis .30 .75
80 Vlade Divac .30 .75
81 Allan Houston .30 .75
82 Richard Hamilton .30 .75
83 Moochie Norris .25 .60
84 Quentin Richardson .30 .75
85 Charlie Ward .25 .60
86 Troy Hudson .25 .60
87 Pat Garrity .25 .60
88 Kobe Bryant 2.00 5.00
89 Tracy McGrady .60 1.50
90 Clifford Robinson .25 .60
91 Glenn Robinson .30 .75
92 Todd MacCulloch .25 .60
93 Lamond Murray .25 .60
94 Eric Snow .25 .60
95 Eddie Jones .30 .75
96 Tom Gugliotta .25 .60
97 Anfernee Hardaway .60 1.50
98 Stephon Marbury .30 .75
99 Antoine Walker .30 .75
100 Gilbert Arenas .40 1.00
101 Ruben Patterson .25 .60
102 Shane Battier .40 1.00
103 David Wesley .25 .60
104 Damon Stoudamire .30 .75
105 Shaquille O'Neal 1.00 2.50
106 Bonzi Wells .25 .60
107 Mike Bibby .40 1.00
108 Jamal Mashburn .30 .75
109 Peja Stojakovic .40 1.00
110 Latrell Sprewell .30 .75
111 Chris Webber .40 1.00
112 Alvin Williams .25 .60
113 Trenton Hassell .25 .60
114 Derek Fisher .30 .75
115 Malik Rose .25 .60
116 Kenny Anderson .30 .75
117 Zydrunas Ilgauskas .30 .75
118 Raef LaFrentz .25 .60
119 Gary Payton .40 1.00
120 Vladimir Radmanovic .25 .60
121 Darius Miles .25 .60
122 Antonio Davis .25 .60
123 Larry Hughes .30 .75
124 Maurice Taylor .25 .60
125 Morris Peterson .25 .60
126 Nick Van Exel .30 .75
127 Ira Newble .25 .60
128 Eric Williams .25 .60
129 Andrei Kirilenko .40 1.00
130 Ben Wallace .40 1.00
131 Tyson Chandler .40 1.00
132 Desmond Mason .30 .75
133 Shareef Abdur-Rahim .30 .75
134 Danny Fortson .25 .60
135 Jerry Stackhouse .30 .75
136 Yao Ming RC 5.00 12.00
137 Juan Dixon RC 2.00 5.00
138 Caron Butler RC 2.50 6.00
139 Drew Gooden RC 2.50 6.00
140 DaJuan Wagner RC 1.50 4.00
141 Jared Jeffries RC 1.50 4.00
142 Pat Burke RC 1.50 4.00
143 Kareem Rush RC 1.50 4.00
144 Ryan Humphrey RC 1.50 4.00
145 Manu Ginobili RC 4.00 10.00
146 Predrag Savovic RC 1.50 4.00
147 Marcus Haislip RC 1.50 4.00
148 John Salmons RC 2.00 5.00
149 Fred Jones RC 1.50 4.00
150 Roger Mason RC 1.50 4.00
151 Jay Williams RS RC 1.25 3.00
152 Mike Dunleavy RS RC 1.25 3.00
153 Carlos Boozer RS RC 2.00 5.00
154 Dan Dickau RS RC 1.00 2.50
155 Tayshaun Prince RS RC 1.25 3.00
156 Nene Hilario RS RC 1.25 3.00
157 Amare Stoudemire RS RC 2.50 6.00
158 Frank Williams RS RC 1.00 2.50
159 Chris Wilcox RS RC 1.00 2.50
160 Robert Archibald RS RC 1.00 2.50
161 Lonny Baxter RS RC 1.00 2.50
162 Curtis Borchardt RS RC 1.00 2.50
163 Sam Clancy RS RC 1.00 2.50
164 Melvin Ely RS RC 1.00 2.50
165 Dan Gadzuric RS RC 1.00 2.50
166 Smush Parker RS RC 1.00 2.50
167 Chris Jefferies RS RC 1.00 2.50
168 Nikoloz Tskitishvili RS RC 1.00 2.50
169 Casey Jacobsen RS RC 1.00 2.50
170 Ronald Murray RS RC 1.00 2.50
171 Gordan Giricek RS RC 1.00 2.50
172 Rasual Butler RS RC 1.00 2.50
173 Jannero Pargo RS RC 1.00 2.50
174 Bostjan Nachbar RS RC 1.00 2.50
175 Jiri Welsch RS RC 1.00 2.50
176 Qyntel Woods RS RC 1.00 2.50
177 Vincent Yarbrough RS RC 1.00 2.50
178 Raul Lopez RS RC 1.00 2.50
179 Mehmet Okur RS RC 1.00 2.50
180 Reggie Evans RS RC 1.00 2.50
181 Karl Malone AS .50 1.25
182 Michael Jordan AS 3.00 8.00
183 Glen Rice AS .30 .75
184 John Stockton AS .50 1.25
185 David Robinson AS .60 1.50
186 Shaquille O'Neal AS 1.00 2.50
187 Dikembe Mutombo AS .40 1.00
188 Gary Payton AS .40 1.00
189 Alonzo Mourning AS .50 1.25
190 Scottie Pippen AS .60 1.50
191 Grant Hill AS .50 1.25
192 Vin Baker AS .30 .75
193 Kevin Garnett AS .75 2.00
194 Jason Kidd AS .60 1.50
195 Reggie Miller AS .40 1.00
196 Ray Allen AS .40 1.00
197 Kobe Bryant AS 2.00 5.00
198 Tim Duncan AS .75 2.00
199 Chris Webber AS .40 1.00
200 Anfernee Hardaway AS .60 1.50
201 Latrell Sprewell AS .30 .75
202 Vince Carter AS .60 1.50
203 Allen Iverson AS .60 1.50
204 Eddie Jones AS .30 .75
205 Antoine Walker AS .30 .75
206 Michael Finley AS .40 1.00
207 Tracy McGrady AS .60 1.50
208 Jerry Stackhouse AS .30 .75
209 Glenn Robinson AS .30 .75
210 Allan Houston AS .30 .75
211 Baron Davis AW .40 1.00
212 Tony Parker AW .50 1.25
213 Rick Fox AW .30 .75
214 Steve Nash AW .50 1.25
215 Jamaal Magloire AW .25 .60
216 Wang Zhizhi AW .25 .60
217 Mengke Bateer AW .25 .60
218 Dirk Nowitzki AW .60 1.50
219 Jake Tsakalidis AW .25 .60
220 Adonal Foyle AW .25 .60
221 Marko Jaric AW .40 1.00
222 Arvydas Sabonis AW .30 .75
223 Eduardo Najera AW .30 .75
224 Michael Olowokandi AW .25 .60
225 Darius Miles AW .25 .60
226 Andrei Kirilenko AW .40 1.00
227 Mamadou N'Diaye AW .25 .60
228 DeSagana Diop AW .25 .60
229 Rasho Nesterovic AW .25 .60
230 Pau Gasol AW .50 1.25
231 Vladimir Radmanovic AW .25 .60
232 Hedo Turkoglu AW .40 1.00
233 Tim Duncan AW .75 2.00
234 Peja Stojakovic AW .40 1.00
235 Toni Kukoc AW .30 .75
236 Zeljko Rebraca AW .25 .60
237 Vlade Divac AW .30 .75
238 Dikembe Mutombo AW .40 1.00
239 Shareef Abdur-Rahim AW .30 .75
240 Jason Richardson AW .40 1.00

2002-03 Fleer Box Score First Edition

Randomly inserted in packs, this 240-card set parallels the base set enhanced with a 1st edition banner on the card front and sequential numbering to 100 on the back.

*STARS 1-135: 3X TO 8X BASE CARD HI
*RCs 136-150: 1.25X TO 3X BASE CARD HI
*RCs 151-180: 2X TO 5X BASE HI
*AS 181-210: 3X TO 8X BASE HI
*AW 211-240: 3X TO 8X BASE HI

2002-03 Fleer Box Score All-Stars Roster Game-Used

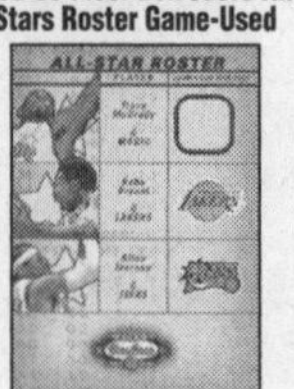

Randomly inserted at the rate of one per All-Stars supplemental box, this 10-card set utilizes the same design as the All-Stars subset cards enhanced with a swatch of game-used memorabilia.

ASR1 Karl Malone WU 4.00 10.00
Tim Duncan
Chris Webber
ASR2 Gary Payton Jsy 4.00 10.00
Jason Kidd
John Stockton
ASR3 Grant Hill Jsy 4.00 10.00
Michael Finley
Ray Allen
ASR4 Kevin Garnett Jsy 6.00 15.00
Shaquille O'Neal
Tim Duncan
ASR5 Jason Kidd Jsy 5.00 12.00
Allen Iverson
Tracy McGrady
ASR6 Vince Carter Jsy 8.00 20.00
Michael Jordan
Kobe Bryant
ASR7 Allen Iverson Jsy 6.00 15.00
Michael Jordan
Kobe Bryant
ASR8 Tracy McGrady Jsy 5.00 12.00
Kobe Bryant
Allen Iverson
ASR9 Jerry Stackhouse Jsy 4.00 10.00
Michael Jordan
Vince Carter
ASR10 Eddie Jones Jsy 4.00 10.00
Antoine Walker
Latrell Sprewell

2002-03 Fleer Box Score Around the World Memorabilia

Randomly inserted at the rate of one per Around the World supplemental box, this 10-card set utilizes the same design as the Around the World subset cards enhanced with a swatch of game-used memorabilia.

ATWM1 Tony Parker 4.00 10.00
ATWM2 Steve Nash JSY 4.00 10.00
ATWM3 Wang Zhizhi JSY 2.00 5.00
ATWM4 Dirk Nowitzki JSY 5.00 12.00
ATWM5 Michael Olowokandi JSY 2.00 5.00
ATWM6 Andrei Kirilenko Shirt 3.00 8.00
ATWM7 Pau Gasol Jacket 4.00 10.00
ATWM8 Hedo Turkoglu Pants 3.00 8.00
ATWM9 Peja Stojakovic Pants 3.00 8.00
ATWM10 Dikembe Mutombo Jacket 3.00 8.00

2002-03 Fleer Box Score Box Score Debuts

Randomly seeded in packs, this 15-card set includes a small photo of the featured player along the top, and placed in the middle of the cut-out borders is a piece of newsprint containing the player's debut game statistics. Each card is sequentially numbered to 2002.

BSD1 Yao Ming 4.00 10.00
BSD2 Juan Dixon 1.50 4.00
BSD3 Caron Butler 2.00 5.00
BSD4 Drew Gooden 2.00 5.00
BSD5 DaJuan Wagner 1.25 3.00
BSD6 Jared Jeffries 1.25 3.00
BSD7 Manu Ginobili 3.00 8.00
BSD8 Kareem Rush 1.25 3.00
BSD9 Jay Williams 1.50 4.00
BSD10 Mike Dunleavy 1.50 4.00
BSD11 Chris Wilcox 1.25 3.00
BSD12 Dan Dickau 1.25 3.00
BSD13 Tayshaun Prince 1.50 4.00
BSD14 Nene Hilario 1.50 4.00
BSD15 Amare Stoudemire 3.00 8.00

2002-03 Fleer Box Score Classic Miniatures

Randomly inserted in boxes as a Supplemental box, this 30-card set uses the base design on card that measure 2 1/2" X 3 1/4".

COMP.SEALED SET (31) 15.00 40.00
*1ST EDITION: 1.5X TO 4X MINIATURE HI
1ST EDITION PRINT RUN 100 SETS
CM1 Glenn Robinson .50 1.25
CM2 Paul Pierce .75 2.00
CM3 Jalen Rose .50 1.25
CM4 Darius Miles .40 1.00
CM5 Dirk Nowitzki 1.00 2.50
CM6 Jason Richardson .60 1.50
CM7 Antawn Jamison .60 1.50
CM8 Steve Francis .60 1.50
CM9 Reggie Miller .60 1.50
CM10 Jermaine O'Neal .60 1.50
CM11 Elton Brand .60 1.50
CM12 Kobe Bryant 3.00 8.00
CM13 Shaquille O'Neal 1.50 4.00
CM14 Pau Gasol .75 2.00
CM15 Ray Allen .60 1.50
CM16 Kevin Garnett 1.25 3.00
CM17 Jason Kidd 1.00 2.50
CM18 Baron Davis .60 1.50
CM19 Grant Hill .75 2.00
CM20 Tracy McGrady 1.00 2.50
CM21 Allen Iverson 1.00 2.50
CM22 Shawn Marion .60 1.50
CM23 Mike Bibby .60 1.50
CM24 Chris Webber .60 1.50
CM25 Tim Duncan 1.25 3.00
CM26 David Robinson 1.00 2.50
CM27 Gary Payton .60 1.50
CM28 Vince Carter 1.00 2.50
CM29 John Stockton .75 2.00
CM30 Michael Jordan 5.00 12.00

2002-03 Fleer Box Score Classic Miniatures Game-Used

Randomly inserted at the rate of one per Classic Miniatures supplemental box, this 10-card set utilizes the same design as the Classic Miniatures subset cards enhanced with a swatch of game-used memorabilia.

CMGU1 Elton Brand JSY 3.00
CMGU2 Steve Francis JSY 3.00
CMGU3 Jason Kidd JSY 5.00
CMGU4 Jermaine O'Neal JSY 3.00
CMGU5 Antawn Jamison Jacket 3.00
CMGU6 Mike Bibby JSY 3.00
CMGU7 Grant Hill JSY 4.00
CMGU8 Dirk Nowitzki JSY 5.00
CMGU9 Paul Pierce JSY 4.00
CMGU10 Allen Iverson JSY 5.00

2002-03 Fleer Box Score Di[sh] and Swish

Randomly inserted in packs at the rate of one in [...] this 20-card set showcases full-color player acti[on] photography set against a blacked-out true live background with the word "DISH" or "SWISH" in l[...] letters along the top and red foil highlights.

COMPLETE SET (20) 10.00
DS1 Jason Terry .60
DS2 Shareef Abdur-Rahim .60
DS3 Andre Miller .60
DS4 Elton Brand .75
DS5 Tracy McGrady 1.25
DS6 Grant Hill 1.00
DS7 Allen Iverson 1.25
DS8 Keith Van Horn .60
DS9 Mike Bibby .75
DS10 Chris Webber .75
DS11 Jason Kidd 1.25
DS12 Kenyon Martin .75
DS13 Steve Nash 1.00
DS14 Dirk Nowitzki 1.25
DS15 John Stockton 1.00
DS16 Karl Malone 1.00
DS17 Paul Pierce 1.00
DS18 Antoine Walker .60
DS19 Shane Battier .75
DS20 Pau Gasol 1.00

2002-03 Fleer Box Score Di[sh] and Swish Dual

Randomly seeded in packs at the rate of one in 1[...] this 10-card set utilizes the same design as the b[ase] Dish and Swish cards in a two-sided format wher[e] "dish" player appears on one side and the "swish["]player on the other.

COMPLETE SET (10) 20.00
DSD1 Jason Terry 2.00
Shareef Abdur-Rahim
DSD2 Andre Miller 2.50
Elton Brand
DSD3 Tracy McGrady 4.00
Grant Hill
DSD4 Allen Iverson 4.00
Keith Van Horn
DSD5 Mike Bibby 2.50
Chris Webber
DSD6 Jason Kidd 4.00
Kenyon Martin
DSD7 Steve Nash 4.00
Dirk Nowitzki
DSD8 John Stockton 3.00
Karl Malone
DSD9 Paul Pierce 3.00
Antoine Walker
DSD10 Shane Battier 3.00
Pau Gasol

2002-03 Fleer Box Score Di[sh] and Swish Memorabilia

Randomly inserted in packs at the rate of one in [...] this 20-card set replicates the design on the base [Dish] and Swish set enhanced with a swatch of game u[sed] memorabilia. Several different materials were use[d] are cataloged below.

DSM1 Jason Terry JSY 2.50
DSM2 Shareef Abdur-Rahim Jacket 2.50
DSM3 Andre Miller Shorts 2.50
DSM4 Elton Brand Shorts 3.00
DSM5 Tracy McGrady Jacket 5.00
DSM6 Grant Hill Pants 4.00
DSM7 Allen Iverson Shorts 5.00
DSM8 Keith Van Horn Pants 2.50
DSM9 Mike Bibby Jacket 3.00
DSM10 Chris Webber Pants 3.00
DSM11 Jason Kidd JSY 5.00
DSM12 Kenyon Martin Shorts 3.00
DSM13 Steve Nash JSY 4.00
DSM14 Dirk Nowitzki JSY 5.00
DSM15 John Stockton Pants 4.00
DSM16 Karl Malone Jacket 4.00
DSM17 Paul Pierce JSY 4.00
DSM18 Antoine Walker JSY 2.50
DSM19 Shane Battier JSY 3.00
DSM20 Pau Gasol JSY 4.00

2002-03 Fleer Box Score Freshman Orientation

Randomly inserted at one per Rising Stars supplemental box, this 10-card set has a horizontal design with a full color player action photo on the right and a swatch of game used memorabilia on the left against a white background.

Card	Lo	Hi
F01 Amare Stoudemire Shirt	8.00	20.00
F02 Lonny Baxter Shirt	3.00	8.00
F05 Yao Ming JSY	10.00	25.00
F06 Gordan Giricek Shirt	3.00	8.00
F07 Caron Butler Shorts	5.00	12.00
F08 Drew Gooden Shirt	5.00	12.00
F09 DaJuan Wagner Shirt	3.00	8.00
F010 Jared Jeffries Shirt	3.00	8.00

2002-03 Fleer Box Score Press Clippings

Randomly inserted at the rate of one in 18, this 15-card set features a horizontal design with a full color player action photo on one side and a montage of newspaper articles on the other. There are no true borders on these cards, however, outside coloring matches the featured player's team colors. Each card is enhanced with silver foil highlights.

Card	Lo	Hi
COMPLETE SET (15)	12.50	30.00
PC1 Vince Carter	1.25	3.00
PC2 Jason Richardson	.75	2.00
PC3 Stephon Marbury	.60	1.50
PC4 Steve Francis	.75	2.00
PC5 Ray Allen	.75	2.00
PC6 Peja Stojakovic	.75	2.00
PC7 Baron Davis	.75	2.00
PC8 Reggie Miller	.75	2.00
PC9 Darius Miles	.50	1.25
PC10 Kevin Garnett	1.50	4.00
PC11 Tim Duncan	1.50	4.00
PC12 Michael Jordan	8.00	20.00
PC13 Shaquille O'Neal	2.00	5.00
PC14 Latrell Sprewell	.60	1.50
PC15 Kobe Bryant	4.00	10.00

2002-03 Fleer Box Score Press Clippings Memorabilia

andomly seeded in packs at the rate of one in 12, this)-card set paralells the base Press Clippings insert nhanced with a swatch of game used memorabilia. atch versions were also issued and cards are quentially numbered to 50.
ATCH: 1.5X TO 4X BASE HI
TCH PRINT RUN 50 SER.#'d SETS

Card	Lo	Hi
M1 Vince Carter JSY	5.00	12.00
M2 Jason Richardson Jacket	3.00	8.00
M3 Stephon Marbury JSY	2.50	6.00
M4 Steve Francis JSY	3.00	8.00
M6 Peja Stojakovic JSY	3.00	8.00
M7 Baron Davis Shirt	3.00	8.00
M8 Reggie Miller Shorts	3.00	8.00
M9 Darius Miles JSY	2.00	5.00
M10 Kevin Garnett JSY	6.00	15.00

1998-99 Fleer Brilliants

debut 125-card set of Fleer Brilliants was released single series in five-card packs with a suggested il price of $4.99. Card fronts feature a silver rored styrene card with a background swirl pattern. d backs are horizontal with vitals and last year's stics. The rookie cards were slightly shortprinted, rted at a rate of one in two packs.

Card	Lo	Hi
MPLETE SET (125)	25.00	60.00
MPLETE SET w/o SP (100)	15.00	30.00
m Duncan	.60	1.50
kembe Mutombo	.30	.75
eve Nash	.50	1.25
arles Barkley	.50	1.25
die Jones	.30	.75
y Allen	.40	1.00
ephon Marbury	.40	1.00
fernee Hardaway	.50	1.25
ry Payton	.30	.75
on Mercer	.25	.60
ick Van Exel	.25	.60
rent Barry	.25	.60
llan Houston	.25	.60
very Johnson	.25	.60
areef Abdur-Rahim	.30	.75
od Strickland	.20	.50
in Baker	.25	.60
atrick Ewing	.40	1.00
aurice Taylor	.20	.50
awn Kemp	.30	.75
ichael Finley	.30	.75
eggie Miller	.40	1.00
e Smith	.25	.60
ni Kukoc	.30	.75
ue Edwards	.20	.50
e Dumars	.30	.75
m Gugliotta	.20	.50
rrell Brandon	.20	.50
ck Dampier	.20	.50
tonio McDyess	.25	.60
nyell Marshall	.20	.50
f Hornacek	.25	.60
vid Wesley	.20	.50
rek Anderson	.20	.50
n Harper	.25	.60
hn Starks	.25	.60
nny Anderson	.25	.60
thony Mason	.20	.50
evin Knight	.20	.50
toine Walker	.30	.75
okie Blaylock	.20	.50
42 LaPhonso Ellis	.20	.50
43 Tim Hardaway	.30	.75
44 Jim Jackson	.20	.50
45 Matt Maloney	.20	.50
46 Lamond Murray	.20	.50
47 Voshon Lenard	.20	.50
48 Isaiah Rider	.20	.50
49 Tracy Murray	.20	.50
50 Grant Hill	.50	1.25
51 Vlade Divac	.30	.75
52 Glenn Robinson	.25	.60
53 Tony Battie	.25	.60
54 Bobby Jackson	.25	.60
55 Jayson Williams	.20	.50
56 Doug Christie	.20	.50
57 Glen Rice	.30	.75
58 Tim Thomas	.30	.75
59 Lindsey Hunter	.20	.50
60 Scottie Pippen	.50	1.25
61 Marcus Camby	.25	.60
61B Keith Van Horn Promo	.60	1.50
62 Clifford Robinson	.20	.50
63 John Wallace	.20	.50
64 Larry Johnson	.30	.75
65 Bryon Russell	.20	.50
66 Isaac Austin	.20	.50
67 Sam Cassell	.25	.60
68 Allen Iverson	.60	1.50
69 Chauncey Billups	.40	1.00
70 Kobe Bryant	1.50	4.00
71 Kevin Willis	.20	.50
72 Jason Kidd	.50	1.25
73 Chris Webber	.30	.75
74 Rasheed Wallace	.30	.75
75 Karl Malone	.40	1.00
76 Shawn Bradley	.20	.50
77 Kerry Kittles	.20	.50
78 Mitch Richmond	.30	.75
79 Antonio Daniels	.20	.50
80 Kevin Garnett	.60	1.50
81 Nick Anderson	.20	.50
82 David Robinson	.50	1.25
83 Jamal Mashburn	.25	.60
84 Rodney Rogers	.20	.50
85 Michael Stewart	.20	.50
86 Rik Smits	.25	.60
87 Billy Owens	.20	.50
88 Damon Stoudamire	.30	.75
89 Theo Ratliff	.25	.60
90 Keith Van Horn	.30	.75
91 Hakeem Olajuwon	.40	1.00
92 Alonzo Mourning	.40	1.00
93 Steve Smith	.25	.60
94 Mark Jackson	.30	.75
95 Cedric Ceballos	.20	.50
96 Bryant Reeves	.20	.50
97 Juwan Howard	.25	.60
98 Detlef Schrempf	.30	.75
99 John Stockton	.40	1.00
100 Shaquille O'Neal	.75	2.00
101 Michael Olowokandi RC	.75	2.00
102 Mike Bibby RC	1.50	4.00
103 Raef LaFrentz RC	.75	2.00
104 Antawn Jamison RC	1.50	4.00
105 Vince Carter RC	3.00	8.00
106 Robert Traylor RC	.60	1.50
107 Jason Williams RC	1.50	4.00
108 Larry Hughes RC	1.25	3.00
109 Dirk Nowitzki RC	4.00	10.00
110 Paul Pierce RC	3.00	8.00
111 Bonzi Wells RC	.60	1.50
112 Michael Doleac RC	.60	1.50
113 Keon Clark RC	.60	1.50
114 Michael Dickerson RC	.60	1.50
115 Matt Harpring RC	.75	2.00
116 Bryce Drew RC	.60	1.50
117 Pat Garrity RC	.60	1.50
118 Roshown McLeod RC	.60	1.50
119 Ricky Davis RC	1.00	2.50
120 Rashard Lewis RC	1.50	4.00
121 Tyronn Lue RC	.60	1.50
122 Al Harrington RC	1.00	2.50
123 Corey Benjamin RC	.60	1.50
124 Felipe Lopez RC	.60	1.50
125 Korleone Young RC	.60	1.50

1998-99 Fleer Brilliants 24-Karat Gold

Randomly inserted in packs, this 125-card set parallels the base set. The cards feature a rainbow-holographic gold foil, rather than the standard silver. The cards are serially numbered to 24. To ascertain values on individual cards, please refer to the multiplier in the header, coupled with the value of the base card.
*STARS: 40X TO 100X BASE CARD HI
*RCs: 10X TO 25X BASE HI

Card	Lo	Hi
1 Tim Duncan	100.00	250.00
4 Charles Barkley	75.00	200.00
8 Anfernee Hardaway	60.00	150.00
20 Shawn Kemp	50.00	125.00
50 Grant Hill	60.00	150.00
60 Scottie Pippen	100.00	250.00
70 Kobe Bryant	250.00	600.00
80 Kevin Garnett	125.00	300.00
92 Alonzo Mourning	75.00	150.00
100 Shaquille O'Neal	100.00	250.00
105 Vince Carter	150.00	300.00
109 Dirk Nowitzki	150.00	300.00

1998-99 Fleer Brilliants Blue

Randomly inserted in packs at a rate of one in three for veterans and one in six for rookies, this 125-card set parallels the base set. The cards feature a blue background, rather than the standard silver. To ascertain values on individual cards, please refer to the multiplier in the header, coupled with the value of the base card.

Card	Lo	Hi
COMPLETE SET (125)	40.00	100.00

*STARS: .75X TO 2X BASE CARD HI
*RCs: .5X TO 1.25X BASE

1998-99 Fleer Brilliants Gold

Randomly inserted in packs, this 125-card set parallels the base set. The cards feature a gold background, rather than the standard silver. The cards are serially numbered to 99 on the back. To ascertain values on individual cards, please refer to the multiplier in the header, coupled with the value of the base card.
*STARS: 15X TO 40X BASE CARD HI
*RCs: 5X TO 12X BASE HI

Card	Lo	Hi
105 Vince Carter	60.00	150.00
109 Dirk Nowitzki	60.00	150.00

1998-99 Fleer Brilliants Illuminators

Randomly inserted in packs at one in ten, this 15-card set features young superstars who light up the scoreboard. The cards are printed on thick styrene with highly reflective mirrored foil.

Card	Lo	Hi
COMPLETE SET (15)	15.00	40.00
1 Michael Olowokandi	1.00	2.50
2 Mike Bibby	2.00	5.00
3 Antawn Jamison	2.00	5.00
4 Vince Carter	4.00	10.00
5 Robert Traylor	.75	2.00
6 Larry Hughes	1.50	4.00
7 Paul Pierce	4.00	10.00
8 Raef LaFrentz	1.00	2.50
9 Dirk Nowitzki	5.00	12.00
10 Corey Benjamin	.75	2.00
11 Michael Dickerson	.75	2.00
12 Roshown McLeod	.75	2.00
13 Ricky Davis	1.25	3.00
14 Tyronn Lue	.75	2.00
15 Al Harrington	1.25	3.00

1998-99 Fleer Brilliants Shining Stars

Randomly inserted in packs at one in 20, this 15-card set features some of the NBA's top veterans. The cards are printed on two-sided mirrored foil.

Card	Lo	Hi
COMPLETE SET (15)	20.00	50.00

*PULSARS: 4X TO 10X HI COLUMN
PULSARS: STATED ODDS 1:400

Card	Lo	Hi
1 Tim Thomas	1.25	3.00
2 Antoine Walker	1.25	3.00
3 Tim Duncan	2.50	6.00
4 Keith Van Horn	1.25	3.00
5 Grant Hill	2.00	5.00
6 Shaquille O'Neal	3.00	8.00
7 Kevin Garnett	2.50	6.00
8 Allen Iverson	2.50	6.00
9 Shareef Abdur-Rahim	1.25	3.00
10 Shawn Kemp	1.25	3.00
11 Anfernee Hardaway	2.00	5.00
12 Scottie Pippen	2.00	5.00
13 Stephon Marbury	1.50	4.00
14 Kobe Bryant	6.00	15.00
15 Ron Mercer	1.00	2.50

1994-95 Fleer European

This 270-card standard-size set was issued by Fleer for the French, Italian, German and Spanish markets. The cards were distributed in 8-card packs (30 packs per box). The set closely parallels the American 1994-95 Fleer issue. Unlike other U.S.-based foreign issues, these cards contain no foreign text but the wrapper and box are multi-lingual. A selection of cards share common numbers with the American versions, making them almost impossible to separately identify (for example card #1 Stacey Augmon). In these cases, the only difference can be found in the tiny trademark print on the card backs. European cards all say "1995 Fleer Corp." and American versions all say "1994 Fleer Corp.". The card fronts feature color player action shots surrounded by white borders. The player's name, team and position appear in team color-coded lettering set on an irregular team color-coded foil patch at the lower left. The black-bordered back carries a color player action shot on the left side, with the player's name, biography, team logo, and statistics displayed on the right. The cards are numbered on the back and grouped alphabetically according to teams.

Card	Lo	Hi
COMPLETE SET (270)	15.00	40.00
1 Stacey Augmon	.15	.40
2 Sergei Bazarevich	.20	.50
3 Mookie Blaylock	.12	.30
4 Tyrone Corbin	.12	.30
5 Craig Ehlo	.12	.30
6 Andrew Lang	.12	.30
7 Grant Long	.12	.30
8 Ken Norman	.12	.30
9 Steve Smith	.15	.40
10 Dee Brown	.12	.30
11 Sherman Douglas	.12	.30
12 Acie Earl	.12	.30
13 Blue Edwards	.12	.30
14 Rick Fox	.12	.30
15 Xavier McDaniel	.12	.30
16 Greg Minor	.20	.50
17 Eric Montross	.20	.50
18 Dino Radja	.15	.40
19 Dominique Wilkins	.25	.60
20 Michael Adams	.12	.30
21 Muggsy Bogues	.15	.40
22 Scott Burrell	.12	.30
23 Dell Curry	.12	.30
24 Kenny Gattison	.12	.30
25 Hersey Hawkins	.12	.30
26 Larry Johnson	.20	.50
27 Alonzo Mourning	.25	.60
28 Robert Parish	.20	.50
29 David Wingate	.12	.30
30 B.J. Armstrong	.12	.30
31 Corie Blount	.12	.30
32 Steve Kerr	.15	.40
33 Larry Krystkowiak	.12	.30
34 Toni Kukoc	.25	.60
35 Luc Longley	.12	.30
36 Will Perdue	.12	.30
37 Scottie Pippen	.40	1.00
38 Dickey Simpkins	.20	.50
39 Terrell Brandon	.12	.30
40 Brad Daugherty	.15	.40
41 Tyrone Hill	.12	.30
42 Chris Mills	.12	.30
43 Bobby Phills	.12	.30
44 Mark Price	.20	.50
45 Gerald Wilkins	.12	.30
46 John Williams	.12	.30
47 Tony Dumas	.20	.50
48 Jim Jackson	.12	.30
49 Popeye Jones	.12	.30
50 Jason Kidd	1.00	2.50
51 Jamal Mashburn	.20	.50
52 Doug Smith	.12	.30
53 Roy Tarpley	.12	.30
54 Mahmoud Abdul-Rauf	.12	.30
55 Dale Ellis	.12	.30
56 LaPhonso Ellis	.12	.30
57 Dikembe Mutombo	.20	.50
58 Robert Pack	.12	.30
59 Rodney Rogers	.12	.30
60 Jalen Rose	.50	1.25
61 Bryant Stith	.12	.30
62 Brian Williams	.12	.30
63 Reggie Williams	.12	.30
64 Bill Curley	.20	.50
65 Johnny Dawkins	.12	.30
66 Joe Dumars	.20	.50
67 Grant Hill	1.00	2.50
68 Allan Houston	.20	.50
69 Lindsey Hunter	.12	.30
70 Oliver Miller	.12	.30
71 Terry Mills	.12	.30
72 Mark West	.12	.30
73 Victor Alexander	.12	.30
74 Manute Bol	.12	.30
75 Chris Gatling	.12	.30
76 Tim Hardaway	.20	.50
77 Chris Mullin	.20	.50
78 Ricky Pierce	.12	.30
79 Clifford Rozier	.20	.50
80 Rony Seikaly	.15	.40
81 Latrell Sprewell	.25	.60
82 Chris Webber	.30	.75
83 Scott Brooks	.12	.30
84 Sam Cassell	.20	.50
85 Mario Elie	.12	.30
86 Carl Herrera	.12	.30
87 Robert Horry	.20	.50
88 Vernon Maxwell	.12	.30
89 Hakeem Olajuwon	.25	.60
90 Kenny Smith	.15	.40
91 Otis Thorpe	.12	.30
92 Antonio Davis	.12	.30
93 Dale Davis	.12	.30
94 Vern Fleming	.12	.30
95 Mark Jackson	.20	.50
96 Derrick McKey	.12	.30
97 Reggie Miller	.25	.60
98 Byron Scott	.15	.40
99 Rik Smits	.15	.40
100 John Williams	.12	.30
101 Haywoode Workman	.12	.30
102 Terry Dehere	.12	.30
103 Gary Grant	.12	.30
104 Lamond Murray	.20	.50
105 Eric Piatkowski	.25	.60
106 Pooh Richardson	.12	.30
107 Malik Sealy	.12	.30
108 Elmore Spencer	.12	.30
109 Loy Vaught	.12	.30
110 Elden Campbell	.12	.30
111 Cedric Ceballos	.12	.30
112 Vlade Divac	.20	.50
113 Eddie Jones	.60	1.50
114 George Lynch	.12	.30
115 Anthony Peeler	.12	.30
116 Tony Smith	.12	.30
117 Sedale Threatt	.12	.30
118 Nick Van Exel	.20	.50
119 Bimbo Coles	.12	.30
120 Kevin Gamble	.12	.30
121 Harold Miner	.12	.30
122 Billy Owens	.12	.30
123 Khalid Reeves	.20	.50
124 Glen Rice	.20	.50
125 John Salley	.12	.30
126 Kevin Willis	.12	.30
127 Vin Baker	.20	.50
128 Jon Barry	.12	.30
129 Todd Day	.12	.30
130 Lee Mayberry	.12	.30
131 Eric Mobley	.20	.50
132 Eric Murdock	.12	.30
133 Johnny Newman	.12	.30
134 Glenn Robinson	.40	1.00
135 Mike Brown	.12	.30
136 Stacey King	.12	.30
137 Christian Laettner	.15	.40
138 Donyell Marshall	.20	.50
139 Isaiah Rider	.20	.50
140 Sean Rooks	.12	.30
141 Doug West	.12	.30
142 Micheal Williams	.12	.30
143 Kenny Anderson	.15	.40
144 Benoit Benjamin	.12	.30
145 P.J. Brown	.12	.30
146 Derrick Coleman	.15	.40
147 Yinka Dare	.20	.50
148 Kevin Edwards	.12	.30
149 Sleepy Floyd	.12	.30
150 Armon Gilliam	.12	.30
151 Chris Morris	.12	.30
152 Greg Anthony	.12	.30
153 Hubert Davis	.12	.30
154 Patrick Ewing	.25	.60
155 Derek Harper	.15	.40
156 Anthony Mason	.15	.40
157 Charles Oakley	.15	.40
158 Doc Rivers	.15	.40
159 Charles Smith	.12	.30
160 John Starks	.15	.40
161 Charlie Ward	.20	.50
162 Monty Williams	.20	.50
163 Nick Anderson	.12	.30
164 Anthony Avent	.12	.30
165 Horace Grant	.15	.40
166 Anfernee Hardaway	.30	.75
167 Shaquille O'Neal	.50	1.25
168 Donald Royal	.12	.30
169 Dennis Scott	.12	.30
170 Brooks Thompson	.20	.50
171 Jeff Turner	.12	.30
172 Dana Barros	.12	.30
173 Shawn Bradley	.12	.30
174 Jeff Malone	.12	.30
175 Tim Perry	.12	.30
176 B.J. Tyler	.20	.50
177 Clarence Weatherspoon	.12	.30
178 Sharone Wright	.20	.50
179 Danny Ainge	.20	.50
180 Charles Barkley	.30	.75
181 A.C. Green	.20	.50
182 Kevin Johnson	.20	.50
183 Joe Kleine	.12	.30
184 Dan Majerle	.20	.50
185 Danny Manning	.15	.40
186 Wesley Person	.20	.50
187 Wayman Tisdale	.12	.30
188 Clyde Drexler	.25	.60
189 Harvey Grant	.12	.30
190 Jerome Kersey	.12	.30
191 Aaron McKie	.20	.50
192 Tracy Murray	.12	.30
193 Terry Porter	.12	.30
194 Clifford Robinson	.12	.30
195 Rod Strickland	.12	.30
196 Buck Williams	.12	.30
197 Brian Grant	.30	.75
198 Bobby Hurley	.20	.50
199 Olden Polynice	.12	.30
200 Mitch Richmond	.20	.50
201 Lionel Simmons	.12	.30
202 Spud Webb	.20	.50
203 Walt Williams	.12	.30
204 Trevor Wilson	.12	.30
205 Willie Anderson	.12	.30
206 Terry Cummings	.20	.50
207 Vinny Del Negro	.12	.30
208 Sean Elliott	.20	.50
209 Avery Johnson	.15	.40
210 Moses Malone	.20	.50
211 J.R. Reid	.12	.30
212 David Robinson	.30	.75
213 Dennis Rodman	.40	1.00
214 Bill Cartwright	.15	.40
215 Kendall Gill	.12	.30
216 Ervin Johnson	.12	.30
217 Shawn Kemp	.20	.50
218 Sarunas Marciulionis	.12	.30
219 Nate McMillan	.12	.30
220 Gary Payton	.20	.50
221 Sam Perkins	.12	.30
222 Detlef Schrempf	.20	.50
223 David Benoit	.12	.30
224 Jeff Hornacek	.15	.40
225 Jay Humphries	.12	.30
226 Karl Malone	.25	.60
227 Bryon Russell	.12	.30
228 Felton Spencer	.12	.30
229 John Stockton	.25	.60
230 Mitchell Butler	.12	.30
231 Rex Chapman	.12	.30
232 Calbert Cheaney	.12	.30
233 Kevin Duckworth	.12	.30
234 Tom Gugliotta	.12	.30
235 Don MacLean	.12	.30
236 Gheorghe Muresan	.12	.30
237 Scott Skiles	.12	.30
238 Atlanta Hawks	.12	.30
239 Boston Celtics	.12	.30
240 Charlotte Hornets	.12	.30
241 Chicago Bulls	.12	.30
242 Cleveland Cavaliers	.12	.30
243 Dallas Mavericks	.12	.30
244 Denver Nuggets	.12	.30
245 Detroit Pistons	.12	.30
246 Golden State Warriors	.12	.30
247 Houston Rockets	.12	.30
248 Indiana Pacers	.12	.30
249 Los Angeles Clippers	.12	.30
250 Los Angeles Lakers	.12	.30
251 Miami Heat	.12	.30
252 Milwaukee Bucks	.12	.30
253 Minnesota Timberwolves	.12	.30
254 New Jersey Nets	.12	.30
255 New York Knicks	.12	.30
256 Orlando Magic	.12	.30
257 Philadelphia 76ers	.12	.30
258 Phoenix Suns	.12	.30
259 Portland Trail Blazers	.12	.30
260 Sacramento Kings	.12	.30
261 San Antonio Spurs	.12	.30
262 Seattle Supersonics	.12	.30
263 Utah Jazz	.12	.30
264 Washington Bullets	.12	.30
265 Toronto Raptors	.12	.30
266 Vancouver Grizzlies	.12	.30
267 NBA Logo	.12	.30
268 Checklist 1-103	.12	.30
269 Checklist 104-204	.12	.30
270 Checklist 205-270	.12	.30
(Checklist Insert Sets)		

1994-95 Fleer European All-Defensive

Randomly inserted in Fleer European packs at an approximate rate of one in six, these five standard-size, double-sided cards feature first and second team All-NBA Defensive teams. The cards are borderless with color player action shots that have been faded to black and white. The player's name and first or second team designation appear in silver foil lettering near the bottom. The cards are unnumbered and checklisted below in alphabetical order.

Card	Lo	Hi
COMPLETE SET (5)	1.25	3.00
1 Mookie Blaylock	.60	1.50
Scottie Pippen		
2 Horace Grant	.30	.75
Gary Payton		
3 Nate McMillan	.60	1.50
Dennis Rodman		
4 Charles Oakley	.50	1.25
David Robinson		
5 Hakeem Olajuwon	.40	1.00
Latrell Sprewell		

1994-95 Fleer European Award Winners

Randomly inserted in Fleer European packs at an approximate rate of one in twelve, these two standard-size, double-sided cards highlight four NBA award winners from the 1993-94 season. The cards feature multiple player images. The player's name and his award appear at the bottom in gold- foil lettering. The cards are unnumbered and checklisted below in alphabetical order.

Card	Lo	Hi
COMPLETE SET (2)	.60	1.50
1 Dell Curry	.60	1.50
Chris Webber		
2 Don MacLean	.50	1.25
Hakeem Olajuwon		

1994-95 Fleer European Career Achievement Awards

Randomly inserted in Fleer European packs at an approximate rate of one in twelve, these two standard-size, double-sided cards highlight four NBA veteran superstars. The borderless cards feature color player action cutouts against a larger facial background shot. Unlike their American counterparts, the backgrounds of these cards are not foil-coated. The player's name appears in gold-foil lettering in a lower corner. The cards are unnumbered and checklisted below in alphabetical order.

Card	Lo	Hi
COMPLETE SET (2)	1.50	4.00
1 Patrick Ewing	1.00	2.50
Karl Malone		
2 Hakeem Olajuwon	1.50	4.00
Scottie Pippen		

1994-95 Fleer European League Leaders

Randomly inserted in Fleer European packs at an approximate rate of one in five, these four standard-size, double-sided cards showcase eight NBA statistical leaders from the 1993-94 season. The cards feature a horizontal design with color player cutouts set on hardwood backgrounds. The player's name and the category in which he led the NBA appear in gold-foil lettering at the bottom. The cards are unnumbered and checklisted below in alphabetical order.

Card	Lo	Hi
COMPLETE SET (4)	1.25	3.00
1 Mahmoud Abdul-Rauf	.60	1.50
Dennis Rodman		
2 Tracy Murray	.30	.75
Dikembe Mutombo		
3 Shaquille O'Neal	.75	2.00
David Robinson		
4 John Stockton	.40	1.00
Nate McMillan		

1994-95 Fleer European Triple Threats

Randomly inserted in Fleer European packs at an approximate rate of one in five, these five standard-size, double-sided cards highlight ten multi-dimensional NBA stars. The cards are borderless with multiple color player action cutouts on black backgrounds highlighted by colorful basketball court designs. The player's name appears in gold- foil lettering in a lower corner. The cards are unnumbered and checklisted below in alphabetical order.

Card	Lo	Hi
COMPLETE SET (5)	2.00	5.00
1 Mookie Blaylock	.60	1.50
Reggie Miller		
2 Patrick Ewing	1.25	3.00
Shaquille O'Neal		
3 Shawn Kemp	.75	2.00
David Robinson		
4 Karl Malone	.60	1.50
Latrell Sprewell		
5 Hakeem Olajuwon	1.00	2.50
Scottie Pippen		

1995-96 Fleer European

Card	Lo	Hi
COMPLETE SET (499)	20.00	50.00
1 Stacey Augmon	.12	.30
2 Mookie Blaylock	.10	.25
3 Craig Ehlo	.10	.25
4 Andrew Lang	.10	.25
5 Grant Long	.10	.25
6 Ken Norman	.10	.25
7 Steve Smith	.12	.30
8 Dee Brown	.10	.25
9 Sherman Douglas	.10	.25
10 Eric Montross	.10	.25
11 Dino Radja	.12	.30
12 David Wesley	.10	.25
13 Dominique Wilkins	.20	.50
14 Muggsy Bogues	.12	.30
15 Scott Burrell	.10	.25
16 Dell Curry	.10	.25
17 Hersey Hawkins	.10	.25
18 Larry Johnson	.15	.40
19 Alonzo Mourning	.20	.50
20 Robert Parish	.15	.40
21 B.J. Armstrong	.10	.25
22 Michael Jordan	1.25	3.00
23 Steve Kerr	.12	.30
24 Toni Kukoc	.15	.40
25 Will Perdue	.10	.25
26 Scottie Pippen	.25	.60
27 Terrell Brandon	.10	.25
28 Tyrone Hill	.10	.25
29 Chris Mills	.10	.25
30 Bobby Phills	.10	.25
31 Mark Price	.15	.40
32 John Williams	.10	.25
33 Lucious Harris	.10	.25
34 Jim Jackson	.10	.25
35 Popeye Jones	.10	.25
36 Jason Kidd	.25	.60
37 Jamal Mashburn	.15	.40
38 George McCloud	.10	.25
39 Roy Tarpley	.10	.25
40 Lorenzo Williams	.10	.25
41 Mahmoud Abdul-Rauf	.10	.25
42 Dale Ellis	.10	.25
43 LaPhonso Ellis	.10	.25
44 Dikembe Mutombo	.15	.40
45 Robert Pack	.10	.25
46 Rodney Rogers	.10	.25
47 Jalen Rose	.20	.50
48 Bryant Stith	.10	.25
49 Reggie Williams	.10	.25
50 Joe Dumars	.15	.40
51 Grant Hill	.25	.60
52 Allan Houston	.12	.30
53 Lindsey Hunter	.10	.25
54 Oliver Miller	.10	.25
55 Terry Mills	.10	.25
56 Mark West	.10	.25
57 Chris Gatling	.10	.25
58 Tim Hardaway	.15	.40
59 Donyell Marshall	.10	.25
60 Chris Mullin	.15	.40
61 Carlos Rogers	.10	.25
62 Clifford Rozier	.10	.25
63 Rony Seikaly	.12	.30
64 Latrell Sprewell	.15	.40
65 Sam Cassell	.15	.40
66 Clyde Drexler	.20	.50
67 Mario Elie	.10	.25
68 Carl Herrera	.10	.25
69 Robert Horry	.12	.30
70 Vernon Maxwell	.10	.25
71 Hakeem Olajuwon	.20	.50
72 Kenny Smith	.12	.30
73 Dale Davis	.10	.25
74 Mark Jackson	.15	.40
75 Derrick McKey	.10	.25
76 Reggie Miller	.20	.50
77 Sam Mitchell	.10	.25
78 Byron Scott	.12	.30
79 Rik Smits	.12	.30
80 Terry Dehere	.10	.25
81 Tony Massenburg	.10	.25
82 Lamond Murray	.10	.25
83 Pooh Richardson	.10	.25
84 Malik Sealy	.10	.25
85 Loy Vaught	.10	.25
86 Elden Campbell	.10	.25
87 Cedric Ceballos	.10	.25
88 Vlade Divac	.15	.40
89 Eddie Jones	.20	.50
90 Anthony Peeler	.10	.25
91 Sedale Threatt	.10	.25
92 Nick Van Exel	.15	.40
93 Bimbo Coles	.10	.25
94 Matt Geiger	.10	.25
95 Billy Owens	.10	.25
96 Khalid Reeves	.10	.25
97 Glen Rice	.15	.40
98 John Salley	.10	.25
99 Kevin Willis	.10	.25
100 Vin Baker	.12	.30
101 Marty Conlon	.10	.25
102 Todd Day	.10	.25
103 Lee Mayberry	.10	.25
104 Eric Murdock	.10	.25
105 Glenn Robinson	.15	.40
106 Winston Garland	.10	.25
107 Tom Gugliotta	.10	.25
108 Christian Laettner	.12	.30
109 Isaiah Rider	.15	.40
110 Sean Rooks	.10	.25
111 Doug West	.10	.25
112 Kenny Anderson	.12	.30
113 Benoit Benjamin	.10	.25
114 P.J. Brown	.10	.25
115 Derrick Coleman	.12	.30
116 Armon Gilliam	.10	.25
117 Chris Morris	.10	.25
118 Rex Walters	.10	.25
119 Hubert Davis	.10	.25
120 Patrick Ewing	.20	.50
121 Derek Harper	.12	.30
122 Anthony Mason	.10	.25
123 Charles Oakley	.12	.30
124 Charles Smith	.10	.25
125 John Starks	.12	.30
126 Nick Anderson	.10	.25
127 Anthony Bowie	.10	.25
128 Horace Grant	.12	.30
129 Anfernee Hardaway	.25	.60
130 Shaquille O'Neal	.40	1.00
131 Donald Royal	.10	.25
132 Dennis Scott	.10	.25
133 Brian Shaw	.10	.25
134 Derrick Alston	.10	.25
135 Dana Barros	.10	.25
136 Shawn Bradley	.10	.25
137 Willie Burton	.10	.25
138 Clarence Weatherspoon	.10	.25
139 Scott Williams	.10	.25
140 Sharone Wright	.10	.25
141 Danny Ainge	.15	.40
142 Charles Barkley	.25	.60
143 A.C. Green	.15	.40
144 Kevin Johnson	.15	.40
145 Dan Majerle	.15	.40
146 Danny Manning	.12	.30
147 Elliot Perry	.10	.25
148 Wesley Person	.10	.25
149 Wayman Tisdale	.10	.25
150 Chris Dudley	.10	.25
151 Jerome Kersey	.10	.25
152 Aaron McKie	.10	.25
153 Terry Porter	.10	.25
154 Clifford Robinson	.10	.25
155 James Robinson	.10	.25
156 Rod Strickland	.10	.25
157 Otis Thorpe	.10	.25
158 Buck Williams	.10	.25
159 Brian Grant	.12	.30
160 Bobby Hurley	.15	.40
161 Olden Polynice	.10	.25
162 Mitch Richmond	.15	.40
163 Michael Smith	.10	.25
164 Spud Webb	.15	.40
165 Walt Williams	.10	.25
166 Terry Cummings	.15	.40
167 Vinny Del Negro	.10	.25
168 Sean Elliott	.15	.40
169 Avery Johnson	.12	.30
170 Chuck Person	.12	.30
171 J.R. Reid	.10	.25
172 Doc Rivers	.12	.30
173 David Robinson	.25	.60
174 Dennis Rodman	.30	.75
175 Vincent Askew	.10	.25
176 Kendall Gill	.10	.25
177 Shawn Kemp	.15	.40
178 Sarunas Marciulionis	.10	.25
179 Nate McMillan	.10	.25
180 Gary Payton	.15	.40
181 Sam Perkins	.10	.25
182 Detlef Schrempf	.15	.40
183 David Benoit	.10	.25
184 Antoine Carr	.10	.25
185 Blue Edwards	.10	.25
186 Jeff Hornacek	.12	.30
187 Adam Keefe	.10	.25
188 Karl Malone	.20	.50
189 Felton Spencer	.10	.25
190 John Stockton	.20	.50
191 Rex Chapman	.10	.25
192 Calbert Cheaney	.10	.25
193 Juwan Howard	.15	.40
194 Don MacLean	.10	.25
195 Gheorghe Muresan	.10	.25
196 Scott Skiles	.10	.25
197 Chris Webber	.20	.50
198 Mookie Blaylock TD	.10	.25
199 Patrick Ewing TD	.20	.50
200 Michael Jordan TD	1.25	3.00
201 Alonzo Mourning TD	.20	.50
202 Dikembe Mutombo TD	.15	.40
203 Hakeem Olajuwon TD	.20	.50
204 Shaquille O'Neal TD	.40	1.00
205 Gary Payton TD	.15	.40
206 Scottie Pippen TD	.25	.60
207 David Robinson TD	.25	.60
208 Dennis Rodman TD	.30	.75
209 John Stockton TD	.20	.50
210 Brian Grant RS	.12	.30
211 Grant Hill RS	.25	.60
212 Juwan Howard RS	.15	.40
213 Eddie Jones RS	.20	.50
214 Jason Kidd RS	.25	.60
215 Donyell Marshall RS	.10	.25
216 Eric Montross RS	.10	.25
217 Lamond Murray RS	.10	.25
218 Wesley Person RS	.10	.25
219 Khalid Reeves RS	.10	.25

220 Glenn Robinson RS .15 .40
221 Jalen Rose RS .20 .50
222 Clifford Rozier RS .10 .25
223 Michael Smith RS .10 .25
224 Sharone Wright RS .10 .25
225 Grant Hill .25 .60
Charles Barkley AS
226 Scottie Pippen .25 .60
Shawn Kemp AS
227 Shaquille O'Neal .40 1.00
Hakeem Olajuwon AS
228 Anfernee Hardaway .25 .60
Dan Majerle AS
229 Reggie Miller .20 .50
Latrell Sprewell AS
230 Vin Baker .12 .30
Cedric Ceballos AS
231 Tyrone Hill .20 .50
Karl Malone AS
232 Larry Johnson .15 .40
Detlef Schrempf AS
233 Patrick Ewing .25 .60
David Robinson AS
234 Alonzo Mourning .20 .50
Dikembe Mutombo AS
235 Dana Barros .15 .40
Gary Payton AS
236 Joe Dumars .20 .50
John Stockton AS
237 Mitch Richmond MVP .15 .40
238 Atlanta Hawks Logo .10 .25
239 Boston Celtics Logo .10 .25
240 Charlotte Hornets Logo .10 .25
241 Chicago Bulls Logo .10 .25
242 Cleveland Cavaliers Logo .10 .25
243 Dallas Mavericks Logo .10 .25
244 Denver Nuggets Logo .10 .25
245 Detroit Pistons Logo .10 .25
246 Golden State Warriors Logo .10 .25
247 Houston Rockets Logo .10 .25
248 Indiana Pacers Logo .10 .25
249 Los Angeles Clippers Logo .10 .25
250 Los Angeles Lakers Logo .10 .25
251 Miami Heat Logo .10 .25
252 Milwaukee Bucks Logo .10 .25
253 Minnesota Timberwolves Logo .10 .25
254 New Jersey Nets Logo .10 .25
255 New York Knicks Logo .10 .25
256 Orlando Magic Logo .10 .25
257 Philadelphia 76ers Logo .10 .25
258 Phoenix Suns Logo .10 .25
259 Portland Trail Blazers Logo .10 .25
260 Sacramento Kings Logo .10 .25
261 San Antonio Spurs Logo .10 .25
262 Seattle Supersonics Logo .10 .25
263 Toronto Raptors Logo .10 .25
264 Utah Jazz Logo .10 .25
265 Vancouver Grizzlies Logo .10 .25
266 Washington Bullets Logo .10 .25
267 NBA Logo .10 .25
268 Checklist #1 .10 .25
269 Checklist #2 .10 .25
270 Checklist #3 .10 .25
271 Stacey Augmon .12 .30
272 Mookie Blaylock .10 .25
273 Grant Long .10 .25
274 Ken Norman .10 .25
275 Steve Smith .12 .30
276 Spud Webb .15 .40
277 Dana Barros .10 .25
278 Rick Fox .10 .25
279 Kendall Gill .10 .25
280 Khalid Reeves .10 .25
281 Glen Rice .15 .40
282 Luc Longley .10 .25
283 Dennis Rodman .30 .75
284 Dan Majerle .15 .40
285 Tony Dumas .10 .25
286 Elmore Spencer .10 .25
287 Otis Thorpe .10 .25
288 B.J. Armstrong .10 .25
289 Sam Cassell .15 .40
290 Clyde Drexler .20 .50
291 Mario Elie .10 .25
292 Robert Horry .12 .30
293 Hakeem Olajuwon .20 .50
294 Kenny Smith .12 .30
295 Antonio Davis .10 .25
296 Eddie Johnson .10 .25
297 Ricky Pierce .10 .25
298 Eric Piatkowski .12 .30
299 Rodney Rogers .10 .25
300 Brian Williams .10 .25
301 Corie Blount .10 .25
302 George Lynch .10 .25
303 Kevin Gamble .10 .25
304 Alonzo Mourning .20 .50
305 Eric Mobley .10 .25
306 Terry Porter .10 .25
307 Micheal Williams .10 .25
308 Kevin Edwards .10 .25
309 Vern Fleming .10 .25
310 Charlie Ward .10 .25
311 Jon Koncak .10 .25
312 Richard Dumas .10 .25
313 Jeff Malone .10 .25
314 Vernon Maxwell .10 .25
315 John Williams .10 .25
316 Harvey Grant .10 .25
317 Dontonio Wingfield .10 .25
318 Tyrone Corbin .10 .25
319 Sarunas Marciulionis .10 .25
320 Will Perdue .10 .25
321 Hersey Hawkins .10 .25
322 Ervin Johnson .10 .25
323 Shawn Kemp .15 .40
324 Gary Payton .15 .40
325 Sam Perkins .10 .25
326 Detlef Schrempf .15 .40
327 Chris Morris .10 .25
328 Robert Pack .10 .25
329 Willie Anderson ET .10 .25
330 Jimmy King ET .10 .25
331 Oliver Miller ET .10 .25
332 Tracy Murray ET .10 .25
333 Ed Pinckney ET .10 .25
334 Alvin Robertson ET .10 .25
335 Carlos Rogers ET .10 .25
336 John Salley ET .10 .25
337 Damon Stoudamire ET .25 .60
338 Zan Tabak ET .10 .25
339 Ashraf Amaya ET .10 .25
340 Greg Anthony ET .10 .25
341 Benoit Benjamin ET .10 .25
342 Blue Edwards ET .10 .25
343 Kenny Gattison ET .10 .25
344 Antonio Harvey ET .10 .25
345 Chris King ET .10 .25
346 Lawrence Moten ET .10 .25
347 Bryant Reeves ET .10 .25
348 Byron Scott ET .12 .30
349 Cory Alexander .15 .40
350 Jerome Allen .15 .40
351 Brent Barry .25 .60
352 Mario Bennett .15 .40
353 Travis Best .15 .40
354 Junior Burrough .15 .40
355 Jason Caffey .15 .40
356 Randolph Childress .15 .40
357 Sasha Danilovic .15 .40
358 Mark Davis .15 .40
359 Tyus Edney .15 .40
360 Michael Finley .50 1.25
361 Sherrell Ford .15 .40
362 Kevin Garnett 1.25 3.00
363 Alan Henderson .15 .40
364 Frankie King .15 .40
365 Jimmy King .15 .40
366 Donny Marshall .15 .40
367 Antonio McDyess .40 1.00
368 Loren Meyer .15 .40
369 Lawrence Moten .15 .40
370 Ed O'Bannon .15 .40
371 Greg Ostertag .15 .40
372 Cherokee Parks .15 .40
373 Theo Ratliff .25 .60
374 Bryant Reeves .15 .40
375 Shawn Respert .15 .40
376 Lou Roe .15 .40
377 Arvydas Sabonis .30 .75
378 Joe Smith .30 .75
379 Jerry Stackhouse .50 1.25
380 Damon Stoudamire .40 1.00
381 Bob Sura .15 .40
382 Kurt Thomas .15 .40
383 Gary Trent .15 .40
384 David Vaughn .15 .40
385 Rasheed Wallace .50 1.25
386 Eric Williams .15 .40
387 Corliss Williamson .15 .40
388 George Zidek .15 .40
389 Checklist .10 .25
390 Checklist .10 .25
391 Mookie Blaylock FF .10 .25
392 Dino Radja FF .12 .30
393 Larry Johnson FF .15 .40
394 Michael Jordan FF 1.25 3.00
395 Tyrone Hill FF .10 .25
396 Jason Kidd FF .25 .60
397 Dikembe Mutombo FF .15 .40
398 Grant Hill FF .25 .60
399 Joe Smith FF .30 .75
400 Hakeem Olajuwon FF .20 .50
401 Reggie Miller FF .20 .50
402 Loy Vaught FF .10 .25
403 Nick Van Exel FF .15 .40
404 Alonzo Mourning FF .20 .50
405 Glenn Robinson FF .15 .40
406 Kevin Garnett FF 1.25 3.00
407 Kenny Anderson FF .12 .30
408 Patrick Ewing FF .20 .50
409 Shaquille O'Neal FF .40 1.00
410 Jerry Stackhouse FF .50 1.25
411 Charles Barkley FF .25 .60
412 Clifford Robinson FF .10 .25
413 Mitch Richmond FF .15 .40
414 David Robinson FF .25 .60
415 Shawn Kemp FF .15 .40
416 Damon Stoudamire FF .40 1.00
417 Karl Malone FF .20 .50
418 Bryant Reeves FF .15 .40
419 Chris Webber FF .20 .50
420 Shawn Kemp TP .15 .40
421 Karl Malone TP .20 .50
422 Antonio McDyess TP .40 1.00
423 Alonzo Mourning TP .20 .50
424 Hakeem Olajuwon TP .20 .50
425 Shaquille O'Neal TP .40 1.00
426 David Robinson TP .25 .60
427 Glenn Robinson TP .15 .40
428 Joe Smith TP .30 .75
429 Chris Webber TP .20 .50
430 Derrick Alston CE .10 .25
431 Brian Grant CE .12 .30
432 Grant Hill CE .25 .60
433 Juwan Howard CE .15 .40
434 Eddie Jones CE .20 .50
435 Jason Kidd CE .25 .60
436 Donyell Marshall CE .10 .25
437 Anthony Miller CE .10 .25
438 Eric Mobley CE .10 .25
439 Eric Montross CE .10 .25
440 Lamond Murray CE .10 .25
441 Wesley Person CE .10 .25
442 Eric Piatkowski CE .12 .30
443 Khalid Reeves CE .10 .25
444 Glenn Robinson CE .15 .40
445 Carlos Rogers CE .10 .25
446 Jalen Rose CE .20 .50
447 Clifford Rozier CE .10 .25
448 Michael Smith CE .10 .25
449 Sharone Wright CE .10 .25
450 Brent Barry CE .25 .60
451 Jason Caffey CE .15 .40
452 Randolph Childress CE .15 .40
453 Kevin Garnett CE 1.25 3.00
454 Alan Henderson CE .15 .40
455 Antonio McDyess CE .40 1.00
456 Ed O'Bannon CE .15 .40
457 Cherokee Parks CE .15 .40
458 Theo Ratliff CE .25 .60
459 Bryant Reeves CE .15 .40
460 Shawn Respert CE .15 .40
461 Joe Smith CE .30 .75
462 Jerry Stackhouse CE .50 1.25
463 Damon Stoudamire CE .40 1.00
464 Bob Sura CE .15 .40
465 Kurt Thomas CE .15 .40
466 Gary Trent CE .15 .40
467 Rasheed Wallace CE .50 1.25
468 Eric Williams CE .15 .40
469 Corliss Williamson CE .15 .40
470 Mookie Blaylock EE .10 .25
471 Vlade Divac EE .15 .40
472 Clyde Drexler EE .20 .50
473 Patrick Ewing EE .20 .50
474 Horace Grant EE .12 .30
475 Anfernee Hardaway EE .25 .60
476 Grant Hill EE .25 .60
477 Eddie Jones EE .20 .50
478 Michael Jordan EE 1.25 3.00
479 Jason Kidd EE .25 .60
480 Alonzo Mourning EE .20 .50
481 Dikembe Mutombo EE .15 .40
482 Hakeem Olajuwon EE .20 .50
483 Shaquille O'Neal EE .40 1.00
484 Gary Payton EE .15 .40
485 Scottie Pippen EE .25 .60
486 David Robinson EE .25 .60
487 Latrell Sprewell EE .15 .40
488 John Stockton EE .20 .50
489 Rod Strickland EE .10 .25
490 Kevin Garnett RP 1.25 3.00
491 Antonio McDyess RP .40 1.00
492 Ed O'Bannon RP .15 .40
493 Bryant Reeves RP .15 .40
494 Shawn Respert RP .15 .40
495 Joe Smith RP .30 .75
496 Jerry Stackhouse RP .50 1.25
497 Damon Stoudamire RP .40 1.00
498 Gary Trent RP .15 .40
499 Rasheed Wallace RP .50 1.25

1996-97 Fleer European

This 330-card standard-size set was issued by Fleer for the French, Spanish, Italian, Portugese, German, Japanese and Chinese markets. The cards were distributed in 8-card packs, in two series, with 36 packs per box. The set closely parallels the American 1996-97 Fleer issue. The series one set contains 150 cards, as does the series two. But, a 30-card translation set, featuring team logos, was inserted in both series one and series two packs. Thus, a separate set line has been established for that set and each series has 150 cards. Unlike other U.S.-based foreign issues, these cards contain no foreign text, but the wrapper and box are multilingual. A selection of cards share common numbers with the American version, making them almost impossible to separately identify. Everything is identical, even the trademark lines. Most of those cards are from series one. Series two, for the most part, contains different card numbers. The main difference in the sets is the European also contains a Team Logo Translation subset, which the American version does not have. The backs of these cards have the basic American descriptions translated into the various languages. The following inserts were also available: Rookie Rewind and Stackhouse's All-Fleer in series one and Swing Shift in series two. Because these inserts are identical to the regular American inserts, they are priced the same. Please refer to those American inserts for values. The cards were distributed by Panini.

COMPLETE SET (330) 40.00 100.00
COMPLETE SERIES 1 (150) 12.50 30.00
COMPLETE SERIES 2 (150) 25.00 60.00
COMP.TRANSLATION SET (30) 2.50 6.00
1 Stacey Augmon .20 .50
2 Mookie Blaylock .15 .40
3 Christian Laettner .20 .50
4 Grant Long .15 .40
5 Steve Smith .20 .50
6 Rick Fox .15 .40
7 Dino Radja .20 .50
8 Eric Williams .15 .40
9 Kenny Anderson .20 .50
10 Dell Curry .15 .40
11 Larry Johnson .25 .60
12 Glen Rice .25 .60
13 Michael Jordan 2.00 5.00
14 Toni Kukoc .25 .60
15 Scottie Pippen .40 1.00
16 Dennis Rodman .50 1.25
17 Terrell Brandon .15 .40
18 Chris Mills .15 .40
19 Bobby Phills .15 .40
20 Bob Sura .15 .40
21 Jim Jackson .15 .40
22 Jason Kidd .40 1.00
23 Jamal Mashburn .20 .50
24 George McCloud .15 .40
25 Mahmoud Abdul-Rauf .15 .40
26 Antonio McDyess .25 .60
27 Dikembe Mutombo .25 .60
28 Jalen Rose .20 .50
29 Bryant Stith .15 .40
30 Joe Dumars .25 .60
31 Grant Hill .40 1.00
32 Allan Houston .20 .50
33 Theo Ratliff .15 .40
34 Otis Thorpe .15 .40
35 Chris Mullin .25 .60
36 Joe Smith .20 .50
37 Latrell Sprewell .25 .60
38 Kevin Willis .15 .40
39 Sam Cassell .20 .50
40 Clyde Drexler .30 .75
41 Robert Horry .20 .50
42 Hakeem Olajuwon .30 .75
43 Dale Davis .15 .40
44 Mark Jackson .25 .60
45 Derrick McKey .15 .40
46 Reggie Miller .30 .75
47 Rik Smits .20 .50
48 Brent Barry .20 .50
49 Malik Sealy .15 .40
50 Loy Vaught .15 .40
51 Brian Williams .15 .40
52 Elden Campbell .15 .40
53 Cedric Ceballos .15 .40
54 Vlade Divac .25 .60
55 Eddie Jones .25 .60
56 Nick Van Exel .25 .60
57 Tim Hardaway .25 .60
58 Alonzo Mourning .30 .75
59 Kurt Thomas .15 .40
60 Walt Williams .15 .40
61 Vin Baker .20 .50
62 Sherman Douglas .15 .40
63 Glenn Robinson .25 .60
64 Kevin Garnett .60 1.50
65 Tom Gugliotta .15 .40
66 Isaiah Rider .20 .50
67 Shawn Bradley .15 .40
68 Chris Childs .15 .40
69 Armon Gilliam .15 .40
70 Ed O'Bannon .15 .40
71 Patrick Ewing .30 .75
72 Derek Harper .20 .50
73 Anthony Mason .15 .40
74 Charles Oakley .20 .50
75 John Starks .20 .50
76 Nick Anderson .15 .40
77 Horace Grant .20 .50
78 Anfernee Hardaway .40 1.00
79 Shaquille O'Neal .60 1.50
80 Dennis Scott .15 .40
81 Derrick Coleman .20 .50
82 Vernon Maxwell .15 .40
83 Jerry Stackhouse .30 .75
84 Clarence Weatherspoon .15 .40
85 Charles Barkley .40 1.00
86 Michael Finley .30 .75
87 Kevin Johnson .25 .60
88 Wesley Person .15 .40
89 Clifford Robinson .15 .40
90 Arvydas Sabonis .20 .50
91 Rod Strickland .15 .40
92 Gary Trent .15 .40
93 Tyus Edney .15 .40
94 Brian Grant .20 .50
95 Billy Owens .15 .40
96 Mitch Richmond .25 .60
97 Vinny Del Negro .15 .40
98 Sean Elliott .25 .60
99 Avery Johnson .20 .50
100 David Robinson .40 1.00
101 Hersey Hawkins .15 .40
102 Shawn Kemp .25 .60
103 Gary Payton .25 .60
104 Detlef Schrempf .25 .60
105 Oliver Miller .15 .40
106 Tracy Murray .15 .40
107 Damon Stoudamire .25 .60
108 Sharone Wright .15 .40
109 Jeff Hornacek .20 .50
110 Karl Malone .30 .75
111 John Stockton .30 .75
112 Greg Anthony .15 .40
113 Bryant Reeves .15 .40
114 Byron Scott .20 .50
115 Calbert Cheaney .15 .40
116 Juwan Howard .20 .50
117 Gheorghe Muresan .15 .40
118 Rasheed Wallace .30 .75
119 Chris Webber .30 .75
120 Mookie Blaylock HL .15 .40
121 Dino Radja HL .20 .50
122 Larry Johnson HL .25 .60
123 Michael Jordan HL 2.00 5.00
124 Terrell Brandon HL .15 .40
125 Jason Kidd HL .40 1.00
126 Antonio McDyess HL .25 .60
127 Grant Hill HL .40 1.00
128 Latrell Sprewell HL .25 .60
129 Hakeem Olajuwon HL .30 .75
130 Reggie Miller HL .30 .75
131 Loy Vaught HL .15 .40
132 Cedric Ceballos HL .15 .40
133 Alonzo Mourning HL .30 .75
134 Vin Baker HL .20 .50
135 Isaiah Rider HL .20 .50
136 Armon Gilliam HL .15 .40
137 Patrick Ewing HL .30 .75
138 Shaquille O'Neal HL .60 1.50
139 Jerry Stackhouse HL .30 .75
140 Charles Barkley HL .40 1.00
141 Clifford Robinson HL .15 .40
142 Mitch Richmond HL .25 .60
143 David Robinson HL .40 1.00
144 Shawn Kemp HL .25 .60
145 Damon Stoudamire HL .25 .60
146 Karl Malone HL .30 .75
147 Bryant Reeves HL .15 .40
148 Juwan Howard HL .20 .50
149 Checklist .15 .40
150 Checklist .15 .40
151 Atlanta Hawks .20 .50
152 Boston Celtics .20 .50
153 Charlotte Hornets .20 .50
154 Chicago Bulls .20 .50
155 Cleveland Cavaliers .20 .50
156 Dallas Mavericks .20 .50
157 Denver Nuggets .20 .50
158 Detroit Pistons .20 .50
159 Golden State Warriors .20 .50
160 Houston Rockets .20 .50
161 Indiana Pacers .20 .50
162 Los Angeles Clippers .20 .50
163 Los Angeles Lakers .20 .50
164 Miami Heat .20 .50
165 Milwaukee Bucks .20 .50
166 Minnesota Timberwolves .20 .50
167 New Jersey Nets .20 .50
168 New York Knicks .20 .50
169 Orlando Magic .20 .50
170 Philadelphia 76ers .20 .50
171 Phoenix Suns .20 .50
172 Portland Trailblazers .20 .50
173 Sacramento Kings .20 .50
174 San Antonio Spurs .20 .50
175 Seattle Supersonics .20 .50
176 Toronto Raptors .20 .50
177 Utah Jazz .20 .50
178 Vancouver Grizzlies .20 .50
179 Washington Bullets .20 .50
180 NBA Logo .20 .50
181 Alan Henderson .15 .40
182 Priest Lauderdale .50 1.25
183 Dikembe Mutombo .25 .60
184 Dana Barros .15 .40
185 Todd Day .15 .40
186 Brett Szabo .50 1.25
187 Antoine Walker 1.00 2.50
188 Scott Burrell .15 .40
189 Tony Delk .50 1.25
190 Vlade Divac .25 .60
191 Matt Geiger .15 .40
192 Anthony Mason .15 .40
193 Malik Rose .60 1.50
194 Ron Harper .20 .50
195 Steve Kerr .20 .50
196 Luc Longley .15 .40
197 Danny Ferry .15 .40
198 Tyrone Hill .15 .40
199 Vitaly Potapenko .50 1.25
200 Tony Dumas .15 .40
201 Chris Gatling .15 .40
202 Oliver Miller .15 .40
203 Eric Montross .15 .40
204 Samaki Walker .50 1.25
205 Darvin Ham .50 1.25
206 Mark Jackson .25 .60
207 Ervin Johnson .15 .40
208 Stacey Augmon .20 .50
209 Joe Dumars .25 .60
210 Grant Hill .40 1.00
211 Grant Long .15 .40
212 Terry Mills .15 .40
213 Otis Thorpe .15 .40
214 Jerome Williams .50 1.25
215 B.J. Armstrong .15 .40
216 Todd Fuller .50 1.25
217 Ray Owes .50 1.25
218 Mark Price .25 .60
219 Felton Spencer .15 .40
220 Charles Barkley .40 1.00
221 Mario Elie .15 .40
222 Othella Harrington .50 1.25
223 Matt Maloney .50 1.25
224 Brent Price .15 .40
225 Kevin Willis .15 .40
226 Travis Best .15 .40
227 Erick Dampier .50 1.25
228 Antonio Davis .15 .40
229 Jalen Rose .20 .50
230 Pooh Richardson .15 .40
231 Rodney Rogers .15 .40
232 Lorenzen Wright .50 1.25
233 Kobe Bryant 10.00 25.00
234 Derek Fisher 1.00 2.50
235 Travis Knight .50 1.25
236 Shaquille O'Neal .60 1.50
237 Byron Scott .20 .50
238 P.J. Brown .15 .40
239 Sasha Danilovic .15 .40
240 Dan Majerle .25 .60
241 Martin Muursepp .50 1.25
242 Ray Allen 2.00 5.00
243 Armon Gilliam .15 .40
244 Andrew Lang .15 .40
245 Moochie Norris .50 1.25
246 Kevin Garnett .60 1.50
247 Tom Gugliotta .15 .40
248 Shane Heal .50 1.25
249 Stephon Marbury 1.25 3.00
250 Stojko Vrankovic .15 .40
251 Kerry Kittles .50 1.25
252 Robert Pack .15 .40
253 Jayson Williams .15 .40
254 Allan Houston .20 .50
255 Larry Johnson .25 .60
256 Dontae Jones .50 1.25
257 Walter McCarty .50 1.25
258 John Wallace .50 1.25
259 Charlie Ward .15 .40
260 Brian Evans .50 1.25
261 Amal McCaskill .50 1.25
262 Brian Shaw .15 .40
263 Mark Davis .15 .40
264 Lucious Harris .15 .40
265 Allen Iverson 2.50 6.00
266 Sam Cassell .20 .50
267 Robert Horry .20 .50
268 Danny Manning .20 .50
269 Steve Nash 2.50 6.00
270 Kenny Anderson .20 .50
271 Aleksandar Djordjevic .50 1.25
272 Jermaine O'Neal 1.25 3.00
273 Isaiah Rider .20 .50
274 Rasheed Wallace .30 .75
275 Mahmoud Abdul-Rauf .15 .40
276 Michael Smith .15 .40
277 Corliss Williamson .15 .40
278 Vernon Maxwell .15 .40
279 Charles Smith .15 .40
280 Dominique Wilkins .30 .75
281 Craig Ehlo .15 .40
282 Jim McIlvaine .15 .40
283 Sam Perkins .15 .40
284 Marcus Camby .75 2.00
285 Popeye Jones .15 .40
286 Donald Whiteside .50 1.25
287 Walt Williams .15 .40
288 Jeff Hornacek .20 .50
289 Karl Malone .30 .75
290 Bryon Russell .15 .40
291 John Stockton .30 .75
292 Shareef Abdur-Rahim 1.00 2.50
293 Anthony Peeler .15 .40
294 Roy Rogers .50 1.25
295 Tim Legler .15 .40
296 Tracy Murray .15 .40
297 Rod Strickland .15 .40
298 Ben Wallace 2.50 6.00
299 Kevin Garnett CB .60 1.50
300 Allan Houston CB .20 .50
301 Eddie Jones CB .25 .60
302 Jamal Mashburn CB .20 .50
303 Antonio McDyess CB .25 .60
304 Glenn Robinson CB .25 .60
305 Joe Smith CB .20 .50
306 Steve Smith CB .20 .50
307 Jerry Stackhouse CB .30 .75
308 Damon Stoudamire CB .25 .60
309 Hakeem Olajuwon AS .30 .75
310 Charles Barkley AS .40 1.00
311 Patrick Ewing AS .30 .75
312 Michael Jordan AS 2.00 5.00
313 Clyde Drexler AS .30 .75
314 Karl Malone AS .30 .75
315 John Stockton AS .30 .75
316 David Robinson AS .40 1.00
317 Scottie Pippen AS .40 1.00
318 Shawn Kemp AS .25 .60
319 Shaquille O'Neal AS .60 1.50
320 Mitch Richmond AS .25 .60
321 Reggie Miller AS .30 .75
322 Alonzo Mourning AS .30 .75
323 Gary Payton AS .25 .60
324 Anfernee Hardaway AS .40 1.00
325 Grant Hill AS .40 1.00
326 Dennis Rodman AS .50 1.25
327 Juwan Howard AS .20 .50
328 Jason Kidd AS .40 1.00
329 Checklist .15 .40
330 Checklist .15 .40

2001-02 Fleer Exclusive

Released in early January of 2002, this 149-card set features 120 veteran players on colorful card stock where the backgrounds match the pictured player's team colors, and each card front showcases two photos of the player. 29 rookie players were also included, and these cards have a gray background and, a photo of the rookie, and a swatch of a player worn jersey patch. The vast majority of rookie cards are multi-colored. These RC cards are not sequentially numbered, but print runs, provided by Fleer, are listed below. Exclusive was packed out in 24 pack boxes where each pack contained five cards.

COMPLETE SET (149) 150.00 300.00
COMP.SET w/o SP's (120) 15.00 40.00
1 Vince Carter .60 1.50
2 Tracy McGrady .60 1.50
3 Dikembe Mutombo .40 1.00
4 Kobe Bryant 2.00 5.00
5 Baron Davis .40 1.00
6 Alonzo Mourning .50 1.25
7 Allan Houston .30 .75
8 Paul Pierce .50 1.25
9 Jason Williams .30 .75
10 Marcus Camby .30 .75
11 Jason Terry .40 1.00
12 Anfernee Hardaway .60 1.50
13 Cuttino Mobley .30 .75
14 Kenyon Martin .40 1.00
15 Rashard Lewis .40 1.00
16 Darius Miles .25 .60
17 Jamal Mashburn .30 .75
18 Derek Fisher .30 .75
19 Sam Cassell .30 .75
20 Antonio McDyess .30 .75
21 John Stockton .50 1.25
22 Andre Miller .30 .75
23 Shawn Marion .40 1.00
24 Steve Nash .60 1.50
25 Kevin Garnett .75 2.00
26 Peja Stojakovic .40 1.00
27 Dirk Nowitzki .60 1.50
28 Chris Webber .40 1.00
29 Shaquille O'Neal 1.00 2.50
30 Stephon Marbury .30 .75
31 Eddie Jones .30 .75
32 Raef LaFrentz .25 .60
33 Wally Szczerbiak .30 .75
34 Richard Hamilton .30 .75
35 Michael Finley .40 1.00
36 Jason Kidd .60 1.50
37 Courtney Alexander .25 .60
38 Glenn Robinson .30 .75
39 Tim Duncan .75 2.00
40 Steve Francis .40 1.00
41 Stromile Swift .25 .60
42 Desmond Mason .30 .75
43 Shareef Abdur-Rahim .30 .75
44 Terrell Brandon .25 .60
45 Antawn Jamison .40 1.00
46 Latrell Sprewell .30 .75
47 Mateen Cleaves .25 .60
48 Karl Malone .50 1.25
49 Lamar Odom .40 1.00
50 Grant Hill .50 1.25
51 Reggie Miller .40 1.00
52 Ray Allen .40 1.00
53 David Robinson .60 1.50
54 Elton Brand .40 1.00
55 Jerry Stackhouse .30 .75
56 Brian Grant .25 .60
57 Hakeem Olajuwon .50 1.25
58 Jalen Rose .30 .75
59 Allen Iverson .75 2.00
60 Darrell Armstrong .25 .60
61 Joe Smith .30 .75
62 Anthony Mason .25 .60
63 Mike Bibby .40 1.00
64 Gary Payton .40 1.00
65 Glen Rice .30 .75
66 Shandon Anderson .25 .60
67 Antoine Walker .30 .75
68 Tim Thomas .25 .60
69 Patrick Ewing .50 1.25
70 Ben Wallace .40 1.00
71 Corey Maggette .30 .75
72 Larry Hughes .30 .75
73 Scottie Pippen .60 1.50
74 Michael Doleac .25 .60
75 Clifford Robinson .25 .60
76 Aaron McKie .25 .60
77 Marc Jackson .25 .60
78 Tom Gugliotta .25 .60
79 James Posey .25 .60
80 Moochie Norris .25 .60
81 Speedy Claxton .25 .60
82 Michael Redd .40 1.00
83 Rasheed Wallace .40 1.00
84 Juwan Howard .30 .75
85 Nick Van Exel .30 .75
86 Toni Kukoc .30 .75
87 Jamaal Magloire .25 .60
88 Jermaine O'Neal .40 1.00
89 Anthony Peeler .25 .60
90 Marcus Fizer .25 .60
91 Jumaine Jones .25 .60
92 Kendall Gill .25 .60
93 Antonio Daniels .25 .60
94 DerMarr Johnson .25 .60
95 Mitch Richmond .30 .75
96 Antonio Davis .25 .60
97 Ron Mercer .25 .60
98 Keyon Dooling .25 .60
99 Morris Peterson .25 .60
100 Derek Anderson .25 .60
101 Allen Iverson MO .75 2.00
102 Glenn Robinson MO .30 .75
103 Tim Duncan MO .75 2.00
104 Shaquille O'Neal MO 1.00 2.50
105 Vince Carter MO .60 1.50
106 Tracy McGrady MO .60 1.50
107 Jason Kidd MO .60 1.50
108 Karl Malone MO .50 1.25
109 Michael Jordan MO 6.00 15.00
110 Shareef Abdur-Rahim MO .30 .75
111 Grant Hill MO .50 1.25
112 Stephon Marbury MO .30 .75
113 Michael Finley MO .40 1.00
114 Antoine Walker MO .30 .75
115 Kobe Bryant MO 2.00 5.00
116 Dirk Nowitzki MO .60 1.50
117 Alonzo Mourning MO .50 1.25
118 John Stockton MO .50 1.25
119 Kevin Garnett MO .75 2.00
120 Eddie Jones MO .30 .75
121 Steven Hunter/500 RC 3.00 8.00
122 Tony Parker/500 RC 12.00 30.00
123 Zach Randolph/478 RC 8.00 20.00
124 Richard Jefferson/500 RC 6.00 15.00
125 Kedrick Brown/433 RC 3.00 8.00
126 Kwame Brown/472 RC 3.00 8.00
127 Brandon Armstrong/500 RC 3.00 8.00
128 Pau Gasol/474 RC 10.00 25.00
129 Troy Murphy/500 RC 5.00 12.00
130 Rodney White/500 RC 3.00 8.00
131 Jamaal Tinsley/500 RC 4.00 10.00
132 Jeryl Sasser/500 RC 3.00 8.00
133 Eddie Griffin/500 RC 3.00 8.00
134 Michael Bradley/476 RC 3.00 8.00
135 Vladimir Radmanovic/500 RC 3.00 8.00
136 Jason Richardson/388 RC 6.00 15.00
137 Shane Battier/500 RC 6.00 15.00
138 Joe Johnson/300 RC 8.00 20.00
139 Andrei Kirilenko/500 RC 8.00 20.00
140 Kirk Haston/500 RC 3.00 8.00
141 Jason Collins/500 RC 3.00 8.00
142 Tyson Chandler/500 RC 5.00 12.00
143 DeSagana Diop/499 RC 3.00 8.00
144 Gerald Wallace/467 RC 5.00 12.00
145 Joseph Forte/450 RC 3.00 8.00
146 Brendan Haywood/500 RC 4.00 10.00
147 Samuel Dalembert/360 RC 4.00 10.00
148 Eddy Curry/500 RC 5.00 12.00
149 Primoz Brezec/500 RC 3.00 8.00

2001-02 Fleer Exclusive Game Exclusives

Randomly inserted in packs, this 19-card set includes full color player action photos set against a white and gray backdrop and a swatch of a jersey in the lower left hand corner of the card front. Each card is sequentially numbered to 100.

*PATCH: 1.25X TO 3X HI
PATCH PRINT RUN 25 SER.#'d SETS
1 Vince Carter 8.00 20.00
2 Allen Iverson 10.00 25.00
3 Alonzo Mourning 6.00 15.00
4 Karl Malone 6.00 15.00
5 Darius Miles 3.00 8.00
6 Antonio McDyess 4.00 10.00
7 Ray Allen 5.00 12.00
8 Steve Francis 5.00 12.00
9 Lamar Odom 5.00 12.00
10 Kenyon Martin 5.00 12.00
11 Andre Miller 4.00 10.00
12 Rashard Lewis 5.00 12.00
13 Stromile Swift 3.00 8.00
14 Antonio Davis 3.00 8.00
15 Latrell Sprewell 4.00 10.00
16 Tracy McGrady 8.00 20.00
17 Jamal Mashburn 4.00 10.00
18 Dikembe Mutombo 5.00 12.0
19 Morris Peterson 3.00 8.0

2001-02 Fleer Exclusive Letter Perfect

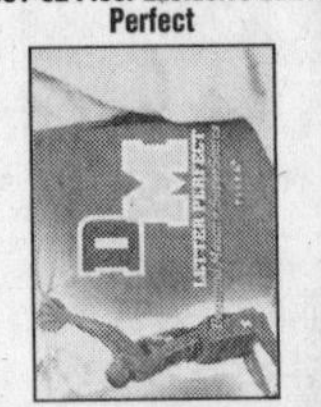

Randomly inserted in packs at the rate of one in 8, thi 25-card set has player action photos set against a colored background to match the featured players jersey colors. This horizontal card design places players on the left side of the card in action, and his initials on the right side. The right edge of the card is done in a different color and is slightly embossed.

COMPLETE SET (25) 10.00 25.
1 Vince Carter 1.00 2.5
2 Allen Iverson 1.25 3.
3 Alonzo Mourning .75 2.
4 Karl Malone .75 2.
5 Darius Miles .40 1.
7 Antonio McDyess .50 1.
8 Ray Allen .60 1.
9 Steve Francis .60 1.
10 Lamar Odom .60 1.
11 Kenyon Martin .60 1.
12 Andre Miller .50 1.
13 Rashard Lewis .60 1
14 Stromile Swift .40 1.
15 Antonio Davis .40 1
16 Latrell Sprewell .50 1.
17 Keith Van Horn .50 1
18 Tracy McGrady 1.00 2
19 Desmond Mason .50 1
20 Jason Terry .60 1
21 Jamal Mashburn .50 1
22 Paul Pierce .75 2
23 Morris Peterson .40
24 Baron Davis .60
25 Antoine Walker .50 1
6 Mike Miller .60 1

2001-02 Fleer Exclusive Lett Perfect JV

Randomly inserted in packs, this 24-card set para the base Letter Perfect insert set enhanced with a j appearing in the shape and in the place of one of letters in the player's initials. Each card is sequen numbered to 100. A Varsity version sequentially numbered to 25 was also issued.

*VARSITY: 1.25X TO 3X BASE HI
1 Vince Carter 8.00
2 Allen Iverson 10.00
3 Alonzo Mourning 8.00
4 Karl Malone 6.00
5 Darius Miles 3.00
6 Antonio McDyess 4.00
7 Ray Allen 5.00
8 Steve Francis 5.00
9 Lamar Odom 5.00
10 Kenyon Martin 5.00
11 Andre Miller 4.00
12 Rashard Lewis 5.00
13 Stromile Swift 3.00
14 Antonio Davis 3.00
15 Latrell Sprewell 4.00
16 Keith Van Horn 4.00
17 Tracy McGrady 8.00

mond Mason 4.00 10.00
on Terry 5.00 12.00
al Mashburn 4.00 10.00
l Pierce 6.00 15.00
ris Peterson 3.00 8.00
n Davis 5.00 12.00
ine Walker 4.00 10.00

01-02 Fleer Exclusive Team Fleer

ght card set features an array of jerseys, patches ographs. Abbreviations have been added below te which card contains the above mentioned ts. The odds on pulling card number one are at 96, and print runs have been added for the e set. The cards are set up horizontally with layer action photos set above a crown or crowns ding on how many players are on each card), the jersey versions, the crown is where the swatch is placed.

e Carter 6.00 15.00
+ Bird
e Carter JSY 12.50 30.00
+ Bird JSY/500
e Carter JSY/98 10.00 25.00
e Carter JSY Patch/15 20.00 50.00
e Carter JSY AU/100 20.00 50.00
Bird JSY/79 25.00 60.00
Bird JSY Patch/33 50.00 100.00
Bird JSY AU/100 100.00 200.00

2001-02 Fleer Exclusive Vinsanity Collection

mly inserted in packs at the rate of one in 70, e card set follows the career of Vince Carter. ard contains a swatch of some type of game-memorabilia where abbreviations of each item below. The cards are full color and have circular rabilia swatches. The #5, USA card, was initially l as a redemption.

e Carter UNC Shirt 8.00 20.00
e Carter Shirt 8.00 20.00
e Carter Warm 8.00 20.00
e Carter JSY 10.00 25.00
e Carter USA 10.00 25.00

2001-02 Fleer Exclusive sanity Collection Autographs

mly inserted in packs, this five card set parallels se Vinsanity Collection set enhanced with Vince Autographs. Each card is sequentially numbered

e Carter UNC Shirt 50.00 120.00
e Carter Shirt 50.00 120.00
e Carter Warm 50.00 120.00
e Carter JSY 60.00 150.00
e Carter USA JSY 60.00 150.00

1999-00 Fleer Focus

eer Focus set was released in one series, ning 150 cards. Each pack contained 10-cards suggested retail price of $2.99. The base set is up into 100 veterans and 50 rookies, with the s serially numbered to 3999. The first 999 cards n a portrait photo, while the remaining 3000 have an action photo.

PLETE SET (150) 75.00 150.00
PLETE SET w/o RC (100) 10.00 20.00
ernee Hardaway .50 1.25
ek Anderson .20 .50
son Williams .20 .50
Mercer .25 .60
y Stackhouse .30 .75
y Abdul-Wahad .20 .50
n Elliott .30 .75
lsey Hunter .20 .50
y Johnson .30 .75
eve Smith .25 .60
ef LaFrentz .25 .60
en Rose .25 .60
phon Marbury .25 .60
tlef Schrempf .25 .60
d Strickland .20 .50
ul Pierce .50 1.25
aurice Taylor .20 .50
llen Iverson .60 1.50
itch Richmond .30 .75
ry Trent .20 .50
ggie Miller .30 .75
erry Kittles .20 .50
asheed Wallace .30 .75
eve Nash .50 1.25
ottie Pippen .50 1.25
e Smith .25 .60
ason Williams .40 1.00
ichael Finley .30 .75
akeem Olajuwon .40 1.00
vin Garnett .60 1.50
errell Armstrong .20 .50
32 David Robinson .50 1.25
33 Anthony Mason .20 .50
34 Jamal Mashburn .25 .60
35 Gary Payton .30 .75
36 Bryon Russell .20 .50
37 Cedric Ceballos .20 .50
38 Michael Dickerson .25 .60
39 Robert Traylor .20 .50
40 Vin Baker .20 .50
41 Shawn Kemp .30 .75
42 Charles Barkley .50 1.25
43 Glenn Robinson .25 .60
44 Vince Carter .60 1.50
45 Zydrunas Ilgauskas .25 .60
46 Sam Cassell .25 .60
47 Tracy McGrady .50 1.25
48 Chris Mills .20 .50
49 Antawn Jamison .30 .75
50 Nick Anderson .20 .50
51 Avery Johnson .25 .60
52 Brent Barry .25 .60
53 Alonzo Mourning .40 1.00
54 Karl Malone .40 1.00
55 Toni Kukoc .30 .75
56 Ray Allen .30 .75
57 Charles Oakley .25 .60
58 Cuttino Mobley .25 .60
59 Kenny Anderson .25 .60
60 Tom Gugliotta .20 .50
61 Antoine Walker .30 .75
62 Kobe Bryant 1.50 4.00
63 Larry Hughes .25 .60
64 Vlade Divac .30 .75
65 Juwan Howard .25 .60
66 Isaiah Rider .20 .50
67 Antonio McDyess .25 .60
68 Rik Smits .30 .75
69 Keith Van Horn .25 .60
70 Doug Christie .25 .60
71 Elden Campbell .20 .50
72 Shaquille O'Neal .75 2.00
73 Matt Geiger .20 .50
74 Chris Webber .30 .75
75 Troy Hudson .30 .75
76 Eddie Jones .30 .75
77 Tim Hardaway .30 .75
78 Hersey Hawkins .20 .50
79 Shareef Abdur-Rahim .25 .60
80 Christian Laettner .25 .60
81 Latrell Sprewell .30 .75
82 Damon Stoudamire .30 .75
83 Jason Caffey .20 .50
84 Michael Olowokandi .20 .50
85 Horace Grant .25 .60
86 Grant Hill .40 1.00
87 Patrick Ewing .40 1.00
88 Clifford Robinson .20 .50
89 Ricky Davis .30 .75
90 Glen Rice .30 .75
91 Matt Harpring .25 .60
92 Mike Bibby .30 .75
93 Dikembe Mutombo .30 .75
94 Chris Mullin .30 .75
95 Marcus Camby .25 .60
96 Jason Kidd .50 1.25
97 John Starks .30 .75
98 Terrell Brandon .20 .50
99 Tim Duncan .60 1.50
100 John Stockton .40 1.00
101 Ron Artest RC 2.50 6.00
101A Ron Artest SP 4.00 10.00
102 William Avery RC 1.00 2.50
102A William Avery SP 1.50 4.00
103 Jonathan Bender RC 1.00 2.50
103A Jonathan Bender SP 1.50 4.00
104 Cal Bowdler RC 1.00 2.50
104A Cal Bowdler SP 1.50 4.00
105 Elton Brand RC 2.50 6.00
105A Elton Brand SP 4.00 10.00
106 Vonteego Cummings RC 1.00 2.50
106A Vonteego Cummings SP 1.50 4.00
107 Baron Davis RC 3.00 8.00
107A Baron Davis SP 5.00 12.00
108 Jeff Foster RC 1.00 2.50
108A Jeff Foster SP 1.50 4.00
109 Steve Francis RC 2.50 6.00
109A Steve Francis SP 4.00 10.00
110 Devean George RC 1.00 2.50
110A Devean George SP 1.50 4.00
111 Dion Glover RC 1.00 2.50
111A Dion Glover SP 1.50 4.00
112 Richard Hamilton RC 2.50 6.00
112A Richard Hamilton SP 4.00 10.00
113 Tim James RC 1.00 2.50
113A Tim James SP 1.50 4.00
114 Trajan Langdon RC 1.00 2.50
114A Trajan Langdon SP 1.50 4.00
115 Quincy Lewis RC 1.00 2.50
115A Quincy Lewis SP 1.50 4.00
116 Corey Maggette RC 2.00 5.00
116A Corey Maggette SP 3.00 8.00
117 Shawn Marion RC 2.50 6.00
117A Shawn Marion SP 4.00 10.00
118 Andre Miller RC 2.50 6.00
118A Andre Miller SP 4.00 10.00
119 Lamar Odom RC 3.00 8.00
119A Lamar Odom SP 5.00 12.00
120 Scott Padgett RC 1.00 2.50
120A Scott Padgett SP 1.50 4.00
121 James Posey RC 1.00 2.50
121A James Posey SP 1.50 4.00
122 Aleksandar Radojevic RC 1.00 2.50
122A Aleksandar Radojevic SP 1.50 4.00
123 Wally Szczerbiak RC 2.00 5.00
123A Wally Szczerbiak SP 3.00 8.00
124 Jason Terry RC 2.50 6.00
124A Jason Terry SP 4.00 10.00
125 Kenny Thomas RC 1.00 2.50
125A Kenny Thomas SP 1.50 4.00
126 Jumaine Jones RC 1.00 2.50
126A Jumaine Jones SP 1.50 4.00
127 Rick Hughes RC 1.00 2.50
127A Rick Hughes SP 1.50 4.00
128 John Celestand RC 1.00 2.50
128A John Celestand SP 1.50 4.00
129 Adrian Griffin RC 1.00 2.50
129A Adrian Griffin SP 1.50 4.00
130 Michael Ruffin RC 1.00 2.50
130A Michael Ruffin SP 1.50 4.00
131 Chris Herren RC 1.00 2.50
131A Chris Herren SP 1.50 4.00
132 Evan Eschmeyer RC 1.00 2.50
132A Evan Eschmeyer SP 1.50 4.00
133 Tim Young RC 1.00 2.50
133A Tim Young SP 1.50 4.00
134 Obinna Ekezie RC 1.00 2.50
134A Obinna Ekezie SP 1.50 4.00
135 Laron Profit RC 1.00 2.50
135A Laron Profit SP 1.50 4.00
136 A.J. Bramlett RC 1.00 2.50
136A A.J. Bramlett SP 1.50 4.00
137 Eddie Robinson RC 1.00 2.50
137A Eddie Robinson SP 1.50 4.00
138 Ryan Bowen RC 1.00 2.50
138A Ryan Bowen SP 1.50 4.00
139 Chucky Atkins RC 1.00 2.50
139A Chucky Atkins SP 1.50 4.00
140 Ryan Robertson RC 1.00 2.50
140A Ryan Robertson SP 1.50 4.00
141 Derrick Dial RC 1.00 2.50
141A Derrick Dial SP 1.50 4.00
142 Todd MacCulloch RC 1.00 2.50
142A Todd MacCulloch SP 1.50 4.00
143 DeMarco Johnson RC 1.00 2.50
143A DeMarco Johnson SP 1.50 4.00
144 Anthony Carter RC 1.00 2.50
144A Anthony Carter SP 1.50 4.00
145 Lazaro Borrell RC 1.00 2.50
145A Lazaro Borrell SP 1.50 4.00
146 Rafer Alston RC 1.25 3.00
146A Rafer Alston SP 2.00 5.00
147 Nikita Morgunov RC 1.00 2.50
147A Nikita Morgunov SP 1.50 4.00
148 Rodney Buford RC 1.00 2.50
148A Rodney Buford SP 1.50 4.00
149 Milt Palacio RC 1.00 2.50
149A Milt Palacio SP 1.50 4.00
150 Jermaine Jackson RC 1.00 2.50
150A Jermaine Jackson SP 1.50 4.00

1999-00 Fleer Focus Masterpiece Mania

Randomly inserted in packs, this 150-card set parallels the base set. The cards feature green, rather than gold foil. Each card is serially numbered to 300. To ascertain values on individual cards, please refer to the multiplier in the header, coupled with the value of the base card.

*STARS: 4X TO 10X BASE CARD HI
*RCs: .6X TO 1.5X BASE HI

1999-00 Fleer Focus Feel the Game

Randomly inserted in packs at one in 288, this 10-card set features pieces of player-worn jerseys.

1 Vince Carter 10.00 25.00
2 Kevin Garnett 10.00 25.00
3 Paul Pierce 8.00 20.00
4 Grant Hill 8.00 20.00
5 Tim Hardaway 5.00 12.00
6 Jayson Williams 3.00 8.00
7 Bryon Russell 3.00 8.00
8 Bryant Reeves 3.00 8.00
9 Keith Van Horn 4.00 10.00
10 Vin Baker 5.00 12.00

1999-00 Fleer Focus Focus Pocus

Randomly inserted in packs at one in 20, this 10-card set features players who are "magic" on the court. The cards feature silver and patterned holo-foil. Card backs carry a "FP" prefix.

FP1 Vince Carter 2.00 5.00
FP2 Tim Duncan 2.00 5.00
FP3 Shaquille O'Neal 2.50 6.00
FP4 Paul Pierce 1.50 4.00
FP5 Kobe Bryant 5.00 12.00
FP6 Kevin Garnett 2.00 5.00
FP7 Keith Van Horn .75 2.00
FP8 Jason Williams 1.25 3.00
FP9 Grant Hill 1.25 3.00
FP10 Allen Iverson 2.00 5.00

1999-00 Fleer Focus Fresh Ink

Randomly inserted in packs at one in 96, this 27-card set features autographs of top NBA stars and rookies. The cards are not numbered on the back and listed below in alphabetical order.

1 Charles Barkley 400.00 800.00
2 Vince Carter 15.00 40.00
3 Obinna Ekezie 3.00 8.00
4 Jeff Foster 3.00 8.00
5 Devean George 3.00 8.00
6 Tim Hardaway 10.00 25.00
7 Matt Harpring 3.00 8.00
8 Al Harrington 3.00 8.00
9 Juwan Howard 5.00 12.00
10 Eddie Jones 6.00 15.00
11 Shawn Kemp 30.00 80.00
12 Brevin Knight 3.00 8.00
13 Trajan Langdon 3.00 8.00
14 Stephon Marbury 6.00 15.00
15 Shawn Marion 6.00 15.00
16 Tracy McGrady 12.50 30.00
17 Roshown McLeod 3.00 8.00
18 Brad Miller 6.00 15.00
19 Alonzo Mourning 35.00 70.00
20 Shaquille O'Neal 50.00 120.00
21 Scott Padgett 3.00 8.00
22 Michael Ruffin 3.00 8.00
23 Damon Stoudamire 5.00 12.00
24 Wally Szczerbiak 6.00 15.00
25 Jason Terry 5.00 12.00
26 Keith Van Horn 5.00 12.00
27 Chris Webber 100.00 225.00

1999-00 Fleer Focus Ray of Light

Randomly inserted in packs at one in 20, this 15-card set features the top rookies from the 1999 NBA Draft Class. Each card features "light pen" signature art. Card backs carry a "RL" prefix.

COMPLETE SET (15) 8.00 20.00
RL1 Andre Miller 1.25 3.00
RL2 Baron Davis 1.50 4.00
RL3 Corey Maggette 1.00 2.50
RL4 Dion Glover .50 1.25
RL5 Elton Brand 1.25 3.00
RL6 Jason Terry 1.25 3.00
RL7 Jonathan Bender .50 1.25
RL8 Lamar Odom 1.50 4.00
RL9 Richard Hamilton 1.25 3.00
RL10 Shawn Marion 1.25 3.00
RL11 Steve Francis 1.25 3.00
RL12 Tim James .50 1.25
RL13 Trajan Langdon .50 1.25
RL14 Wally Szczerbiak 1.00 2.50
RL15 William Avery .50 1.25

1999-00 Fleer Focus Sean Elliott Night

This card was released by Fleer and given out to fans on the night of April 17, 2000 to help welcome Sean Elliott back into the lineup. The card is sequentially numbered to 30,000.

1 Sean Elliott .75 2.00

1999-00 Fleer Focus Soar Subjects

Randomly inserted in packs at one in six, this 15-card set highlights NBA stars who play with style and grace. Card backs carry a "SS" prefix.

COMPLETE SET (15) 6.00 15.00
*VIVID: 12X TO 30X HI COLUMN
VIVID: PRINT RUN 50 SERIAL #'d SETS
SS1 Allen Iverson 1.00 2.50
SS2 Anfernee Hardaway .75 2.00
SS3 Paul Pierce .75 2.00
SS4 Antoine Walker .50 1.25
SS5 Grant Hill .60 1.50
SS6 Keith Van Horn .60 1.50
SS7 Kevin Garnett 1.00 2.50
SS8 Kobe Bryant 2.50 6.00
SS9 Larry Hughes .40 1.00
SS10 Jason Williams .60 1.50
SS11 Scottie Pippen .75 2.00
SS12 Shaquille O'Neal 1.25 3.00
SS13 Vince Carter 1.00 2.50
SS14 Stephon Marbury .40 1.00
SS15 Tim Duncan 1.00 2.50

1999-00 Fleer Focus Toni Kukoc Night

This card was released by Fleer, and given to fans to welcome Toni Kukoc to his new team. The card is sequentially numbered to 30,000.

1 Toni Kukoc 2.00 5.00

2000-01 Fleer Focus

The 2000-01 Fleer Focus product was released in mid-December, 2001 and features a 236-card base set. The base set is broken into tiers as follows: 180 Veterans (1-180), 36 Rookies (181-216), and (20) 20/20 Subset cards. Each pack contained 10-card, and carried a $1.99 SRP.

COMPLETE SET w/o RC (200) 15.00 40.00
1 Vince Carter .60 1.50
2 Shawn Marion .30 .75
3 Muggsy Bogues .25 .60
4 Dikembe Mutombo .30 .75
5 Stephon Marbury .25 .60
6 Michael Dickerson .20 .50
7 Andre Miller .25 .60
8 Toni Kukoc .25 .60
9 Nick Van Exel .25 .60
10 Aaron Williams .20 .50
11 Derrick Coleman .25 .60
12 Wally Szczerbiak .25 .60
13 Rodney Rogers .20 .50
14 Tom Gugliotta .20 .50
15 Vonteego Cummings .20 .50
16 Cedric Ceballos .20 .50
17 Malik Rose .20 .50
18 Shawn Bradley .20 .50
19 Shandon Anderson .20 .50
20 Jacque Vaughn .20 .50
21 Jamie Feick .20 .50
22 Shawn Kemp .30 .75
23 Monty Williams .20 .50
24 Allan Houston .25 .60
25 Chauncey Billups .30 .75
26 Vlade Divac .25 .60
27 Othella Harrington .20 .50
28 Dale Davis .20 .50
29 Charlie Ward .20 .50
30 Hakeem Olajuwon .40 1.00
31 Ray Allen .30 .75
32 Lamar Odom .30 .75
33 Shaquille O'Neal .75 2.00
34 Chris Childs .20 .50
35 Nick Anderson .20 .50
36 Keon Clark .20 .50
37 Danny Fortson .20 .50
38 Sam Mitchell .20 .50
39 Travis Best .20 .50
40 Chris Webber .30 .75
41 Brent Barry .20 .50
42 Scottie Pippen .50 1.25
43 Reggie Miller .30 .75
44 Bryant Reeves .20 .50
45 Bobby Jackson .20 .50
46 Antonio McDyess .25 .60
47 Elden Campbell .20 .50
48 Kenny Anderson .25 .60
49 Christian Laettner .20 .50
50 Darrell Armstrong .20 .50
51 Vinny Del Negro .20 .50
52 Quincy Lewis .20 .50
53 Peja Stojakovic .30 .75
54 Matt Geiger .20 .50
55 Larry Hughes .25 .60
56 Tracy McGrady .50 1.25
57 Tim Hardaway .30 .75
58 Brevin Knight .20 .50
59 Michael Finley .30 .75
60 Jason Kidd .50 1.25
61 Matt Harpring .25 .60
62 Antawn Jamison .30 .75
63 Wesley Person .20 .50
64 Antonio Davis .20 .50
65 Roshown McLeod .20 .50
66 Anthony Peeler .20 .50
67 Grant Hill .40 1.00
68 Michael Olowokandi .20 .50
69 Kerry Kittles .20 .50
70 Elton Brand .30 .75
71 Tariq Abdul-Wahad .20 .50
72 Aaron McKie .25 .60
73 Andrew DeClercq .20 .50
74 Anfernee Hardaway .50 1.25
75 Bimbo Coles .20 .50
76 Terrell Brandon .20 .50
77 Jalen Rose .25 .60
78 Radoslav Nesterovic .25 .60
79 Howard Eisley .20 .50
80 Steve Smith .25 .60
81 Arvydas Sabonis .25 .60
82 Jim Jackson .20 .50
83 Corey Maggette .25 .60
84 James Posey .25 .60
85 LaPhonso Ellis .20 .50
86 Eric Snow .25 .60
87 Mikki Moore RC .30 .75
88 Baron Davis .30 .75
89 Jason Williams .25 .60
90 Mike Bibby .30 .75
91 Marcus Camby .25 .60
92 Bryon Russell .20 .50
93 Steve Francis .30 .75
94 Sam Cassell .25 .60
95 Rasheed Wallace .30 .75
96 Keith Van Horn .25 .60
97 Eddie Jones .30 .75
98 Corliss Williamson .25 .60
99 Ron Mercer .20 .50
100 Sean Elliott .25 .60
101 Shareef Abdur-Rahim .25 .60
102 Glen Rice .25 .60
103 Patrick Ewing .40 1.00
104 Adrian Griffin .20 .50
105 David Robinson .50 1.25
106 Isaac Austin .20 .50
107 Anthony Mason .20 .50
108 P.J. Brown .20 .50
109 Kendall Gill .20 .50
110 Tyrone Nesby .20 .50
111 Damon Stoudamire .25 .60
112 Latrell Sprewell .25 .60
113 Tim Duncan .60 1.50
114 Glenn Robinson .25 .60
115 John Wallace .20 .50
116 Erick Strickland .20 .50
117 Doug Christie .20 .50
118 Juwan Howard .25 .60
119 Tim Thomas .25 .60
120 Tyrone Hill .20 .50
121 Avery Johnson .20 .50
122 Jerome Williams .20 .50
123 Mitch Richmond .25 .60
124 Hersey Hawkins .20 .50
125 Donyell Marshall .25 .60
126 Derek Anderson .25 .60
127 Jamal Mashburn .25 .60
128 Richard Hamilton .25 .60
129 Alonzo Mourning .40 1.00
130 Kelvin Cato .20 .50
131 Lamond Murray .20 .50
132 Bo Outlaw .20 .50
133 Chris Carr .20 .50
134 Jonathan Bender .25 .60
135 Paul Pierce .40 1.00
136 Dan Majerle .25 .60
137 Ron Artest .30 .75
138 Jermaine O'Neal .30 .75
139 Chris Whitney .20 .50
140 Anthony Carter .20 .50
141 Gary Payton .30 .75
142 Kevin Garnett .60 1.50
143 Kevin Willis .20 .50
144 Charles Oakley .25 .60
145 Larry Johnson .30 .75
146 Bonzi Wells .20 .50
147 Clifford Robinson .20 .50
148 Chucky Atkins .20 .50
149 Brian Grant .20 .50
150 Voshon Lenard .20 .50
151 Antoine Walker .25 .60
152 Cuttino Mobley .25 .60
153 Robert Horry .25 .60
154 Tracy Murray .20 .50
155 Kobe Bryant 1.50 4.00
156 Joe Smith .25 .60
157 Jaren Jackson .20 .50
158 Scott Williams .20 .50
159 Allen Iverson .60 1.50
160 Rashard Lewis .30 .75
161 Chris Mills .20 .50
162 Karl Malone .40 1.00
163 John Amaechi .20 .50
164 Jason Terry .30 .75
165 Ruben Patterson .20 .50
166 Austin Croshere .20 .50
167 Maurice Taylor .20 .50
168 Rod Strickland .25 .60
169 Clarence Weatherspoon .20 .50
170 Lindsey Hunter .20 .50
171 David Wesley .20 .50
172 Jerry Stackhouse .25 .60
173 Scott Burrell .20 .50
174 John Stockton .40 1.00
175 Vitaly Potapenko .20 .50
176 Dirk Nowitzki .50 1.25
177 Vin Baker .25 .60
178 Rick Fox .25 .60
179 Mookie Blaylock .25 .60
180 Felipe Lopez .20 .50
181 Chris Mihm A RC .40 1.00
182 Mamadou N'Diaye A RC .40 1.00
183 Joel Przybilla A RC .40 1.00
184 Jamaal Magloire A RC .40 1.00
185 Iakovos Tsakalidis A RC .40 1.00
186 Etan Thomas A RC .40 1.00
187 Mark Madsen B RC .40 1.00
188 Hanno Mottola B RC .40 1.00
189 Donnell Harvey B RC .40 1.00
190 Jason Collier B RC .40 1.00
191 Eduardo Najera B RC .40 1.00
192 Jerome Moiso B RC .40 1.00
193 Mateen Cleaves C RC .60 1.50
194 Keyon Dooling C RC .60 1.50
195 Speedy Claxton C RC .60 1.50
196 Erick Barkley C RC .60 1.50
197 A.J. Guyton C RC .60 1.50
198 Jamal Crawford C RC 1.00 2.50
199 Dan Langhi D RC .40 1.00
200 Desmond Mason D RC .50 1.25
201 Chris Porter D RC .40 1.00
202 Corey Hightower D RC .40 1.00
203 Morris Peterson D RC .40 1.00
204 Hedo Turkoglu D RC .75 2.00
205 Courtney Alexander E RC .75 2.00
206 Quentin Richardson E RC 1.25 3.00
207 DeShawn Stevenson E RC 1.00 2.50
208 Michael Redd E RC 2.00 5.00
209 Chris Carrawell E RC .75 2.00
210 Mark Karcher E RC .75 2.00
211 Kenyon Martin F RC 3.00 8.00
212 Marcus Fizer F RC 1.25 3.00
213 Darius Miles F RC 1.25 3.00
214 Mike Miller F RC 2.50 6.00
215 DerMarr Johnson F RC 1.25 3.00
216 Stromile Swift F RC 1.25 3.00
217 Shaquille O'Neal 20 .50 1.25
218 Allen Iverson 20 .40 1.00
219 Grant Hill 20 .25 .60
220 Vince Carter 20 .40 1.00
221 Karl Malone 20 .25 .60
222 Chris Webber 20 .20 .50
223 Gary Payton 20 .20 .50
224 Jerry Stackhouse 20 .15 .40
225 Tim Duncan 20 .40 1.00
226 Kevin Garnett 20 .40 1.00
227 Michael Finley 20 .20 .50
228 Kobe Bryant 20 1.00 2.50
229 Stephon Marbury 20 .15 .40
230 Ray Allen 20 .20 .50
231 Alonzo Mourning 20 .25 .60
232 Glenn Robinson 20 .15 .40
233 Antoine Walker 20 .15 .40
234 Shareef Abdur-Rahim 20 .15 .40
235 Elton Brand 20 .20 .50
236 Eddie Jones 20 .20 .50

2000-01 Fleer Focus Draft Position

Randomly inserted in packs, this 216-card set is a partial parallel of the 2000-01 Fleer Focus base set. These cards are individually serial numbered to either 100, 200, or 300, and feature green foil stamping.

*100 STARS: 8X TO 20X BASE CARD HI
*200 STARS: 5X TO 12X BASE HI
*300 STARS: 4X TO 10X BASE HI
181 Chris Mihm/100 4.00 10.00
182 Mamadou N'Diaye/100 4.00 10.00
183 Joel Przybilla/100 4.00 10.00
184 Jamaal Magloire/100 4.00 10.00
185 Iakovos Tsakalidis/100 4.00 10.00
186 Etan Thomas/100 4.00 10.00
187 Mark Madsen/100 4.00 10.00
188 Hanno Mottola/200 2.50 6.00
189 Donnell Harvey/100 4.00 10.00
190 Jason Collier/100 4.00 10.00
191 Eduardo Najera/200 2.50 6.00
192 Jerome Moiso/100 4.00 10.00
193 Mateen Cleaves/100 4.00 10.00
194 Keyon Dooling/100 4.00 10.00
195 Speedy Claxton/100 4.00 10.00
196 Erick Barkley/100 4.00 10.00
197 A.J. Guyton/200 2.50 6.00
198 Jamal Crawford/100 6.00 15.00
199 Dan Langhi/200 2.50 6.00
200 Desmond Mason/100 5.00 12.00
201 Chris Porter/200 2.50 6.00
202 Corey Hightower/200 2.50 6.00
203 Morris Peterson/100 4.00 10.00
204 Hedo Turkoglu/100 8.00 20.00
205 Courtney Alexander/100 4.00 10.00
206 Quentin Richardson/100 6.00 15.00
207 DeShawn Stevenson/100 5.00 12.00
208 Michael Redd/100 6.00 15.00
209 Chris Carrawell/200 2.50 6.00
210 Mark Karcher/200 2.50 6.00
211 Kenyon Martin/100 10.00 25.00
212 Marcus Fizer/100 4.00 10.00
213 Darius Miles/100 4.00 10.00
214 Mike Miller/100 8.00 20.00
215 DerMarr Johnson/100 4.00 10.00
216 Stromile Swift/100 4.00 10.00

2000-01 Fleer Focus Arena Vision

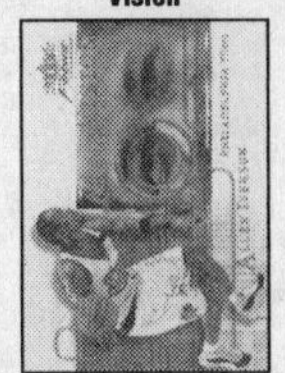

Randomly inserted in packs at one in 12, this 15-card set showcases the NBA's top players. Card backs carry a "AV" prefix.

COMPLETE SET (15) 8.00 20.00
AV1 Vince Carter 1.00 2.50
AV2 Eddie Jones .50 1.25
AV3 Tim Duncan 1.00 2.50
AV4 Kevin Garnett 1.00 2.50
AV5 Steve Francis .50 1.25
AV6 Jason Williams .50 1.25
AV7 Grant Hill .60 1.50
AV8 Elton Brand .50 1.25
AV9 Allen Iverson 1.00 2.50
AV10 Lamar Odom .50 1.25
AV11 Kobe Bryant 2.50 6.00
AV12 Jalen Rose .40 1.00
AV13 Paul Pierce .60 1.50
AV14 Shaquille O'Neal 1.25 3.00
AV15 Stephon Marbury .40 1.00

2000-01 Fleer Focus Vince Carter Rookie Remnants

This three-card insert was randomly inserted into 2000-01 Fleer products. The set includes a Vince Carter floor card (numbered to 100), a Vince Carter floor/jersey card (numbered to 15), and finally an autographed Vince Carter floor/jersey card (numbered 1 of 1).

NNO Vince Carter FLR/100 12.50 30.00

2000-01 Fleer Focus Planet Hardwood

Randomly inserted in packs at one in 24, this 10-card set showcases some of the best players to have every stepped onto the hardwood court. Card backs carry a "PH" prefix.

COMPLETE SET (10) 12.50 25.00
*VIP: 2.5X TO 6X VALUE
VIP: PRINT RUN 50 SERIAL #'d SETS
PH1 Vince Carter 1.50 4.00
PH2 Tim Duncan 1.50 4.00
PH3 Kevin Garnett 1.50 4.00
PH4 Kobe Bryant 4.00 10.00
PH5 Lamar Odom .75 2.00
PH6 Steve Francis .75 2.00
PH7 Shaquille O'Neal 2.00 5.00
PH8 Tracy McGrady 1.25 3.00
PH9 Grant Hill 1.00 2.50
PH10 Allen Iverson 1.50 4.00

2000-01 Fleer Focus Welcome to the NBA

Randomly inserted in packs at one in six, this 15-card set showcases the top rookies from the 1999-2000 season. Card backs carry a "WN" prefix.

COMPLETE SET (15) 3.00 8.00
*VIP: 5X TO 12X VALUE
VIP: PRINT RUN 50 SERIAL #'d SETS
WN1 Kenyon Martin .75 2.00
WN2 Stromile Swift .30 .75
WN3 Darius Miles .30 .75
WN4 Marcus Fizer .30 .75
WN5 Mike Miller .60 1.50
WN6 DerMarr Johnson .30 .75
WN7 Chris Mihm .30 .75
WN8 Jamal Crawford .50 1.25
WN9 Keyon Dooling .30 .75
WN10 Jerome Moiso .30 .75
WN11 Etan Thomas .30 .75
WN12 Courtney Alexander .30 .75
WN13 Mateen Cleaves .30 .75
WN14 Jason Collier .30 .75
WN15 Desmond Mason .40 1.00

2001-02 Fleer Focus

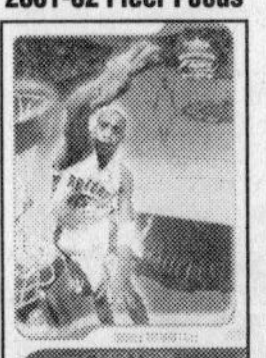

Released in March of 2002, Fleer Focus was a 130-card set broken down into 100 veteran player cards and 30 rookie cards sequentially numbered to 1850. Base cards showcase full colore player action photos with a white and gold border and the Fleer Focus logo in the upper left hand corner. A colored box, set to match team colors contains the player's name in gold ink. The rookie cards have the same design with a color shift from gold to silver on both the borders and the player names. A number box appears on the back of the card where RC's are sequentailly numbered to 1850. Five Ultra Update cards were also included in the pack-out, and these cards are listed under the base 2001-02 Ultra set. Fleer Focus was issued in 24 pack boxes where packs contained seven cards each.

COMP.SET w/o SP's (100) 10.00 25.00
1 Vince Carter .50 1.25
2 Steve Nash .50 1.25
3 Anthony Mason .20 .50
4 Avery Johnson .25 .60
5 Peja Stojakovic .30 .75
6 Shaquille O'Neal .75 2.00
7 Jason Kidd .50 1.25
8 Steve Smith .25 .60
9 Kobe Bryant 1.50 4.00
10 Eddie Robinson .20 .50
11 Allan Houston .25 .60
12 Larry Hughes .25 .60
13 Gary Payton .30 .75
14 Alonzo Mourning .40 1.00
15 Baron Davis .30 .75
16 Speedy Claxton .20 .50
17 Hakeem Olajuwon .40 1.00
18 Anthony Carter .20 .50
19 Raef LaFrentz .20 .50
20 Dikembe Mutombo .30 .75
21 Moochie Norris .20 .50
22 Karl Malone .40 1.00
23 Darrell Armstrong .20 .50
24 Allen Iverson .60 1.50
25 Danny Fortson .20 .50
26 Antonio Davis .20 .50
27 Eddie Jones .25 .60
28 Patrick Ewing .40 1.00
29 Stephon Marbury .25 .60
30 Cuttino Mobley .25 .60
31 Morris Peterson .20 .50
32 Glenn Robinson .25 .60
33 Paul Pierce .40 1.00
34 Shawn Marion .30 .75
35 Jermaine O'Neal .30 .75
36 Donyell Marshall .20 .50
37 Chauncey Billups .30 .75
38 Tracy McGrady .50 1.25
39 Vlade Divac .25 .60
40 Lamar Odom .30 .75
41 Chris Mihm .20 .50
42 Kenyon Martin .30 .75
43 Antonio McDyess .25 .60
44 Mike Bibby .30 .75
45 Darius Miles .20 .50
46 Wesley Person .20 .50
47 Mark Jackson .25 .60
48 Nick Van Exel .25 .60
49 Tim Duncan .60 1.50
50 Sam Cassell .25 .60
51 Jason Terry .30 .75
52 Bonzi Wells .20 .50
53 Al Harrington .25 .60
54 Richard Hamilton .25 .60
55 Wally Szczerbiak .25 .60
56 Toni Kukoc .25 .60
57 Rasheed Wallace .30 .75
58 Reggie Miller .30 .75
59 Courtney Alexander .20 .50
60 Terrell Brandon .20 .50
61 Dirk Nowitzki .50 1.25
62 Chris Webber .30 .75
63 Lindsey Hunter .20 .50
64 Andre Miller .25 .60
65 Clifford Robinson .20 .50
66 David Robinson .50 1.25
67 Stromile Swift .20 .50
68 Nazr Mohammed .20 .50
69 Kurt Thomas .20 .50
70 Corliss Williamson .20 .50
71 Rashard Lewis .30 .75
72 Lorenzen Wright .20 .50
73 David Wesley .20 .50
74 Derrick Coleman .25 .60
75 Jerry Stackhouse .25 .60
76 Antonio Daniels .20 .50
77 Mitch Richmond .25 .60
78 Ron Mercer .20 .50
79 Latrell Sprewell .25 .60
80 Antawn Jamison .30 .75
81 Desmond Mason .25 .60
82 Jason Williams .25 .60
83 Jamal Mashburn .25 .60
84 Grant Hill .40 1.00
85 Elton Brand .30 .75
86 Brian Grant .20 .50
87 Antoine Walker .25 .60
88 Anfernee Hardaway .50 1.25
89 Steve Francis .30 .75
90 John Stockton .40 1.00
91 Ray Allen .30 .75
92 Tim Hardaway .30 .75
93 Derek Anderson .20 .50
94 Jalen Rose .25 .60
95 Michael Jordan 5.00 12.00
96 Kevin Garnett .60 1.50
97 Shareef Abdur-Rahim .25 .60
98 Tony Delk .20 .50
99 Quentin Richardson .25 .60
100 Michael Finley .30 .75
101 Jamaal Tinsley RC 1.00 2.50
102 Zach Randolph RC 2.00 5.00
103 Kedrick Brown RC .75 2.00
104 Kirk Haston RC .75 2.00
105 Tyson Chandler RC 1.25 3.00
106 Shane Battier RC 1.50 4.00
107 Richard Jefferson RC 1.50 4.00
108 Gerald Wallace RC 1.25 3.00
109 DeSagana Diop RC .75 2.00
110 Ruben Boumtje-Boumtje RC .75 2.00
111 Rodney White RC .75 2.00
112 Eddie Griffin RC .75 2.00
113 Pau Gasol RC 2.50 6.00
114 Tony Parker RC 3.00 8.00
115 Kwame Brown RC .75 2.00
116 Vladimir Radmanovic RC .75 2.00
117 Troy Murphy RC 1.25 3.00
118 Loren Woods RC .75 2.00
119 Joe Johnson RC 2.00 5.00
120 Brandon Armstrong RC .75 2.00
121 Trenton Hassell RC .75 2.00
122 Andrei Kirilenko RC 2.00 5.00
123 Jason Richardson RC 1.50 4.00
124 Jason Collins RC .75 2.00
125 Jeryl Sasser RC .75 2.00
126 Michael Bradley RC .75 2.00
127 Eddy Curry RC 1.25 3.00
128 Joseph Forte RC .75 2.00
129 Brendan Haywood RC 1.00 2.50
130 Zeljko Rebraca RC .75 2.00

2001-02 Fleer Focus Numbers

Randomly inserted in packs, this 130-card parallel set is numbered based on the player's jersey number. Players will jersey numbers from 0-10 are numbered to 10, 11-20 are numbered to 20, etc. Each card features red foil accents on the card front.

*STARS/20: 15X TO 40X BASE CARD HI
*RCs/20: 6X TO 15X BASE CARD HI
*STARS/30:10X TO 25X BASE CARD HI
*RCs/30: 4X TO 10X BASE CARD HI
*STARS/40: 8X TO 20X BASE CARD HI
*RCs/40: 3X TO 8X BASE CARD HI
*STARS/50: 8X TO 20X BASE CARD HI
*RCs/50: 2.5X TO 6X BASE CARD HI
SOME NOT PRICED DUE TO SCARCITY

2001-02 Fleer Focus Materialistic Away

Randomly inserted in packs at the rate of one in 26, this 21-card set is a unique insert in which the center of the card is made of jersey material with a player likeness printed on it. Two images of the player appear on the felt, the left one is clearer while the second is blurry and appears to be a shadow. These cards have cardboard borders with the Fleer Focus logo appearing along the right side of the card, and the word "Away" and the player's name and team name centered along the bottom. A Home version was also issued and features a foil shift from silver to gold and is sequentially numbered to 50.

*HOME: 1.5X TO 4X AWAY HI
1 Kobe Bryant 12.00 30.00
2 Shaquille O'Neal 5.00 12.00
3 Kevin Garnett 4.00 10.00
4 Tim Duncan 4.00 10.00
5 Michael Jordan 25.00 60.00
6 Allen Iverson 4.00 10.00
7 Dirk Nowitzki 3.00 8.00
8 Kwame Brown 2.00 5.00
9 Tyson Chandler 3.00 8.00
10 Eddie Griffin 2.00 5.00
11 Shane Battier 4.00 10.00
12 Tracy McGrady 3.00 8.00
13 Steve Francis 2.00 5.00
14 Chris Webber 2.50 6.00
15 Vince Carter 3.00 8.00
15A Vince Carter AU 25.00 60.00
16 Jamaal Tinsley 2.50 6.00
17 Grant Hill 2.50 6.00
18 Jason Kidd 3.00 8.00
19 Karl Malone 2.50 6.00
20 Ray Allen 2.00 5.00
21 Pau Gasol 6.00 15.00

2001-02 Fleer Focus ROY Collection

Randomly seeded in packs at the rate of one in 22, this 15-card set revolves around NBA rookies of the year. The top of the card reveals what year the featured player won this honor in gold foil. A player action photo appear on the left side of this horizontal card design and a portrait photo on the right. Centered between these photos are the letters "ROY."

COMPLETE SET (15) 20.00 50.00
1 Vince Carter 2.00 5.00
2 Allen Iverson 2.50 6.00
3 Chris Webber 1.25 3.00
4 David Robinson 2.00 5.00
5 Steve Francis 1.25 3.00
6 Patrick Ewing 1.50 4.00
7 Damon Stoudamire 1.00 2.50
8 Jason Kidd 2.00 5.00
9 Mike Miller 1.25 3.00
10 Larry Bird 4.00 10.00
11 Grant Hill 1.50 4.00
12 Michael Jordan 10.00 25.00
13 Shaquille O'Neal 3.00 8.00
14 Elton Brand 1.25 3.00
15 Tim Duncan 2.50 6.00

2001-02 Fleer Focus ROY Collection Jerseys

Randomly inserted in packs at the rate of one in 55, this nine card set parallels the design of the base ROY collection enhanced with a swatch of a game worn jersey in place of the "O" in ROY. Two Vince Carter autographs were issued in this set, one is sequentially numbered to 15, which was originally released as an exchange card, and the other is sequentially numbered to 99. A Patch version was also issued sequentially numbered to 99.

COMPLETE SET (9) 40.00 100.00
*PATCHES: 1.25X TO 3X JERSEY HI
1 Vince Carter 6.00 15.00
1A Vince Carter AU/15 60.00 150.00
1B Vince Carter AU/99 25.00 50.00
2 Allen Iverson 8.00 20.00
3 Chris Webber 4.00 10.00
4 David Robinson 6.00 15.00
6 Patrick Ewing 5.00 12.00
8 Jason Kidd 6.00 15.00
9 Mike Miller 4.00 10.00
10 Larry Bird 12.00 30.00
11 Grant Hill 5.00 12.00

2001-02 Fleer Focus Trading Places

Randomly inserted in packs at the rate of one in 12, this 15-card set showcases two photos of a player that was either traded sometime durning the last season or during the off-season, or players in their college jerseys and their professional jerseys. The photo on the left is set against a black background, and the photo on the right against a white background. The player's name is centered between these two photos in silver ink.

COMPLETE SET (15) 15.00 30.00
1 Vince Carter 1.25 3.00
2 Patrick Ewing 1.00 2.50
3 Mike Bibby .75 2.00
4 Jason Kidd 1.25 3.00
5 Stephon Marbury .60 1.50
6 Corey Maggette .60 1.50
7 Elton Brand .75 2.00
8 Hakeem Olajuwon 1.00 2.50
9 Dikembe Mutombo .75 2.00
10 Eddie Jones .60 1.50
11 Michael Jordan 6.00 15.00
12 Grant Hill 1.00 2.50
13 Chris Webber .75 2.00
14 Shaquille O'Neal 2.00 5.00
15 Tracy McGrady 1.25 3.00

2001-02 Fleer Focus Trading Places Jerseys

Randomly inserted in packs at the rate of one in 51, this 10-card set parallels the base Trading Places set enhanced with a swatch of a player worn jersey. Shareef Abdur-Rahim has jersey versions only. A Patch parallel was also inserted with cards sequentially numbered to 50.

*PATCHES: 1.5X TO 4X JERSEYS HI
1 Vince Carter 6.00 15.00
2 Patrick Ewing 5.00 12.00
4 Jason Kidd 6.00 15.00
5 Stephon Marbury 3.00 8.00
6 Corey Maggette 3.00 8.00
7 Elton Brand 4.00 10.00
9 Dikembe Mutombo 4.00 10.00
10 Eddie Jones 3.00 8.00
13 Chris Webber 4.00 10.00
TPSA Shareef Abdur-Rahim 3.00 8.00

2003-04 Fleer Focus

Released in October 2003, Focus boasts a 160-card set divided up into 120 veteran players and 40 rookies sequentially numbered to 499. The design places players in full color against assorted single-color backgrounds which fade into white around the borders. Focus was packaged in 24-pack boxes where packs contained five cards and carried a suggested retail price of $2.99.

COMP.SET w/o SP's 12.50 30.00
1 Allan Houston .25 .60
2 Manu Ginobili .40 1.00
3 Allen Iverson .50 1.25
4 Kenyon Martin .30 .75
5 Rasho Nesterovic .20 .50
6 Tracy McGrady .40 1.00
7 Drew Gooden .25 .60
8 Tony Parker .30 .75
9 Troy Murphy .30 .75
10 Alonzo Mourning .40 1.00
11 Rasual Butler .20 .50
12 Alvin Williams .20 .50
13 Troy Hudson .20 .50
14 Gary Payton .30 .75
15 Tyson Chandler .25 .60
16 Ray Allen .30 .75
17 Amare Stoudemire .50 1.25
18 Chauncey Billups .30 .75
19 Gilbert Arenas .30 .75
20 Eddie Jones .25 .60
21 Vince Carter .50 1.25
22 Kobe Bryant 1.50 4.00
23 Reggie Miller .30 .75
24 Vincent Yarbrough .20 .50
25 Kevin Garnett .60 1.50
26 Andre Miller .25 .60
27 Glenn Robinson .25 .60
28 Kurt Thomas .20 .50
29 Vladimir Radmanovic .20 .50
30 Richard Jefferson .30 .75
31 Andrei Kirilenko .30 .75
32 Wally Szczerbiak .25 .60
33 Gordan Giricek .20 .50
34 Kwame Brown .20 .50
35 Yao Ming .60 1.50
36 Devean George .20 .50
37 Richard Hamilton .25 .60
38 Anfernee Hardaway .50 1.25
39 Grant Hill .40 1.00
40 Zach Randolph .30 .75
41 Dirk Nowitzki .50 1.25
42 Zydrunas Ilgauskas .25 .60
43 Antawn Jamison .30 .75
44 J.R. Bremer .20 .50
45 Latrell Sprewell .25 .60
46 Ron Artest .30 .75
47 Antoine Walker .30 .75
48 Eddy Curry .25 .60
49 Larry Hughes .25 .60
50 Jalen Rose .25 .60
51 Matt Harpring .25 .60
52 Sam Cassell .25 .60
53 Antonio McDyess .25 .60
54 Jamaal Tinsley .20 .50
55 Mehmet Okur .25 .60
56 Scottie Pippen .50 1.25
57 Antonio Davis .20 .50
58 Jamaal Magloire .20 .50
59 Michael Olowokandi .20 .50
60 Shane Battier .25 .60
61 Desmond Mason .25 .60
62 Baron Davis .30 .75
63 Jamal Mashburn .25 .60
64 Michael Redd .30 .75
65 Shaquille O'Neal .75 2.00
66 Ben Wallace .30 .75
67 Jason Terry .25 .60
68 Michael Finley .30 .75
69 Shareef Abdur-Rahim .25 .60
70 Bobby Jackson .20 .50
71 Jason Williams .25 .60
72 Mike Bibby .30 .75
73 Shawn Marion .30 .75
74 Ricky Davis .25 .60
75 Bonzi Wells .20 .50
76 Jason Kidd .50 1.25
77 Mike Miller .30 .75
78 Stephen Jackson .25 .60
79 Brad Miller .30 .75
80 Jason Richardson .30 .75
81 Mike Dunleavy Jr. .25 .60
82 Stephon Marbury .25 .60
83 Brian Grant .20 .50
84 Jay Williams .20 .50
85 Morris Peterson .20 .50
86 Steve Nash .40 1.00
87 Carlos Boozer .30 .75
88 Jermaine O'Neal .30 .75
89 Nene .25 .60
90 Eric Snow .20 .50
91 Steve Francis .30 .75
92 Caron Butler .30 .75
93 Jerry Stackhouse .25 .60
94 Nick Van Exel .25 .60
95 Tayshaun Prince .30 .75
96 Calbert Cheaney .20 .50
97 Pau Gasol .30 .75
98 Theo Ratliff .20 .50
99 Chris Webber .30 .75
100 Juan Dixon .20 .50
101 Paul Pierce .40 1.00
102 Tim Thomas .20 .50
103 Eddie Griffin .20 .50
104 Corey Maggette .25 .60
105 Juwan Howard .25 .60
106 Peja Stojakovic .30 .75
107 Tim Duncan .50 1.25
108 Keith Van Horn .25 .60
109 Cuttino Mobley .25 .60
110 Kareem Rush .20 .50
111 Predrag Drobnjak .20 .50
112 Tony Delk .20 .50
113 Dajuan Wagner .20 .50
114 Karl Malone .40 1.00
115 Rashard Lewis .30 .75
116 David Wesley .20 .50
117 Rasheed Wallace .30 .75
118 Derrick Coleman .25 .60
119 Donnell Harvey .20 .50
120 Elton Brand .30 .75
121 Carmelo Anthony RC 6.00 15.00
122 Keith Bogans RC 2.50 6.00
123 Leandro Barbosa RC 3.00 8.00
124 Troy Bell RC 2.50 6.00
125 Chris Bosh RC 5.00 12.00
126 Zarko Cabarkapa RC 2.50 6.00
127 Jason Kapono RC 2.50 6.00
128 Nick Collison RC 2.50 6.00
129 Boris Diaw-Riffiod RC 3.00 8.00
130 Marcus Banks RC 2.50 6.00
131 T.J. Ford RC 3.00 8.00
132 Reece Gaines RC 2.50 6.00
133 Travis Hansen RC 2.50 6.00
134 Jarvis Hayes RC 2.50 6.00
135 Kirk Hinrich RC 3.00 8.00
136 Josh Howard RC 2.50 6.00
137 LeBron James RC 25.00 60.00
138 Dahntay Jones RC 2.50 6.00
139 Chris Kaman RC 3.00 8.00
140 Maciej Lampe RC 2.50 6.00
141 Darko Milicic RC 2.50 6.00
142 Travis Outlaw RC 3.00 8.00
143 Mickael Pietrus RC 2.50 6.00
144 Rick Rickert RC 2.50 6.00
145 Luke Ridnour RC 3.00 8.00
146 Sofoklis Schortsanitis RC 2.50 6.00
147 Mike Sweetney RC 2.50 6.00
148 Dwyane Wade RC 10.00 25.00
149 Luke Walton RC 2.50 6.00
150 David West RC 3.00 8.00
151 Zoran Planinic RC 2.50 6.00
152 Ndudi Ebi RC 2.50 6.00
153 Aleksandar Pavlovic RC 2.50 6.00
154 Kendrick Perkins RC 4.00 10.00
155 Maurice Williams RC 4.00 10.00
156 Jerome Beasley RC 2.50 6.00
157 Slavko Vranes RC 2.50 6.00
158 Zaur Pachulia RC 2.50 6.00
159 Carlos Delfino RC 3.00 8.00
160 Brian Cook RC 2.50 6.00

2003-04 Fleer Focus Gold

Randomly inserted in packs, this 160-card set parallels the base Focus set enhanced with gold foil highlights and sequential numbering to 50.

*GOLD SINGLES: 5X TO 12X BASE HI
*GOLD RCs: 1.25X TO 3X BASE HI

2003-04 Fleer Focus Numbers Century

Randomly inserted in packs, this 160-card set parallels the base Focus set enhanced with sequential numbering to 100.

*SINGLES: 4X TO 10X BASE CARD HI
*RC's .6X TO 1.5X BASE CARD HI
137 LeBron James 60.00 150.00

2003-04 Fleer Focus Silver

Randomly inserted in packs, this 160-card set parallels the base Focus set enhanced with silver foil highlights and sequential numbering to 25.

*1-120 SILVER: 8X TO 20X BASE HI
*121-160 SILVER RCs: 1.5X TO 4X BASE HI

2003-04 Fleer Focus Auto Focus

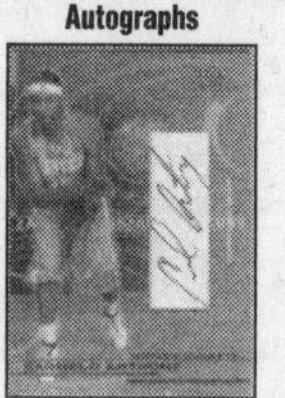

Inserted in packs, this 24-card set places player photos on the right side of the card where background colors are set to match the featured player's team colors and cards are sequentially numbered to 250.

1 Manu Ginobili 2.00 5.00
2 Eddy Curry 1.25 3.00
3 Tracy McGrady 2.00 5.00
4 Drew Gooden 1.25 3.00
5 Caron Butler 1.50 4.00
6 Amare Stoudemire 2.50 6.00
7 Tayshaun Prince 1.50 4.00
8 Vince Carter 2.50 6.00
9 Kevin Garnett 3.00 8.00
10 Dirk Nowitzki 2.50 6.00
11 Ben Wallace 1.50 4.00
12 Tony Parker 1.50 4.00
13 Steve Francis 1.50 4.00
14 Mike Bibby 1.50 4.00
15 Alonzo Mourning 2.00 5.00
16 Carmelo Anthony 4.00 10.00
17 Marcus Banks 1.50 4.00
18 Maciej Lampe 1.50 4.00
19 Mickael Pietrus 1.50 4.00
20 Luke Ridnour 2.00 5.00
21 Dwyane Wade 6.00 15.00
22 David West 2.00 5.00
23 Chris Bosh 3.00 8.00
24 Mike Sweetney 1.50 4.00
25 Troy Bell 1.50 4.00

2003-04 Fleer Focus Auto Focus Autographs

This 24-card set parallels the design of the base Auto Focus insert set enhanced with a vertial cut-signature on the left side of the card and sequential numbering to 100. Versions sequentially numbered to 50 and 25 were also issued.

*AUTO 50: .5X TO 1.25X BASE HI
1 Manu Ginobili 12.50 30.00
2 Eddy Curry 6.00 15.00
3 Steve Francis 6.00 15.00
4 Mike Bibby 12.50 30.00
5 Amare Stoudemire 12.50 30.00
6 Tayshaun Prince 8.00 20.00
7 Tracy McGrady 20.00 50.00
8 Alonzo Mourning 30.00 80.00
9 Ben Wallace 15.00 40.00
11 Carmelo Anthony 30.00 80.00
12 Marcus Banks 6.00 15.00
14 Mickael Pietrus 8.00 20.00
15 Luke Ridnour 8.00 20.00
16 Dwyane Wade 40.00 100.00
17 David West 8.00 20.00
18 Chris Bosh 20.00 50.00
19 Michael Sweetney 6.00 15.00
20 Troy Bell 6.00 15.00
22 Josh Howard 6.00 15.00
23 Leandro Barbosa 8.00 20.00

2003-04 Fleer Focus Autographs

This 24-card set parallels the design of the base Focus set enhanced with embedded cut signatures and sequential numbering to 100. Versions sequentially numbered to 50 and 25 were also produced.

*AUTO 50: .5X TO 1.25X BASE HI
*AUTO 25: .6X TO 1.5X BASE HI
4 Eddy Curry 6.00 15.00
10 Alonzo Mourning 30.00 80.00
17 Amare Stoudemire 12.00 30.00
91 Steve Francis 12.50 30.00
121 Carmelo Anthony 25.00 60.00
123 Leandro Barbosa 8.00 20.00
124 Troy Bell 6.00 15.00
125 Chris Bosh 12.00 30.00
130 Marcus Banks 6.00 15.00
143 Mickael Pietrus 8.00 20.00
145 Luke Ridnour 8.00 20.00
148 Dwyane Wade 40.00 100.00
150 David West 6.00 15.00
155 Mo Williams 8.00 20.00

2003-04 Fleer Focus Home and Aways

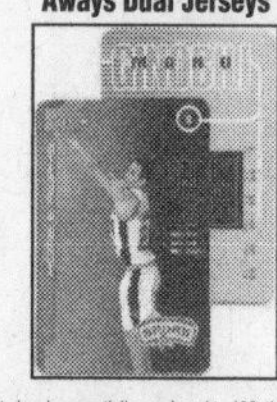

Randomly seeded and sequentially numbered to 500, this 15-card set features players with both home and away jerseys.

COMPLETE SET (15) 15.00 30.00
1 Kevin Garnett 2.50 6.00
2 Chris Webber 1.25 3.00
3 Allen Iverson 2.00 5.00
4 Scottie Pippen 2.00 5.00
5 Paul Pierce 1.50 4.00
6 Jason Kidd 2.00 5.00
7 Baron Davis 1.25 3.00
8 Steve Francis 1.25 3.00
9 Stephon Marbury 1.00 2.50
10 Antoine Walker 1.25 3.00
11 Vince Carter 2.00 5.00
12 Latrell Sprewell 1.00 2.50
13 Manu Ginobili 1.50 4.00
14 Caron Butler 1.25 3.00
15 Jason Richardson 1.25 3.00

2003-04 Fleer Focus Home and Aways Dual Jerseys

Inserted and sequentially numbered to 199, this 15-card set features swatches of players home and away jerseys with the home jersey in the shape of an "H" on one side and an away jersey in the shape of an "A" on the other.

HAAI Allen Iverson 8.00 20.00
HAAW Antoine Walker 5.00 12.00
HABD Baron Davis 5.00 12.00
HACB Caron Butler 5.00 12.00
HACW Chris Webber 5.00 12.00
HAJK Jason Kidd 8.00 20.00
HAJR Jason Richardson 5.00 12.00
HAKG Kevin Garnett 10.00 25.00
HALS Latrell Sprewell 4.00 10.00
HAMG Manu Ginobili 6.00 15.00
HAPP Paul Pierce 6.00 15.00
HASF Steve Francis 5.00 12.00
HASP Scottie Pippen 10.00 25.00
HAVC Vince Carter 8.00 20.00

2003-04 Fleer Focus NBA Shirtified

Randomly inserted in packs, this 25-card set places full-color player action photography on a solid colored background with his team logo in the lower left hand corner of the card. Each card is sequentiallly numbered to 750.

COMPLETE SET (25) 30.00 60.00
1 Tracy McGrady 1.50 4.00
2 Mike Bibby 1.25 3.00
3 Allen Iverson 2.00 5.00
4 Dirk Nowitzki 2.00 5.00
5 Paul Pierce 1.50 4.00
6 Antawn Jamison 1.25 3.00
7 Kenyon Martin 1.25 3.00
8 Shawn Marion 1.25 3.00
9 Rasheed Wallace 1.25 3.00
10 Caron Butler 1.25 3.00
11 Elton Brand 1.25 3.00
12 Eddy Curry 1.00 2.50
13 Michael Finley 1.25 3.00
14 Yao Ming 2.50 6.00
15 Vince Carter 2.00 5.00
16 Amare Stoudemire 2.00 5.00
17 Jermaine O'Neal 1.25 3.00
18 Peja Stojakovic 1.25 3.00
19 Karl Malone 1.50 4.00
20 Ben Wallace 1.25 3.00
21 Steve Francis 1.25 3.00
22 Baron Davis 1.25 3.00
23 Kobe Bryant 6.00 15.00
24 Shaquille O'Neal 3.00 8.00
25 Tim Duncan 2.00 5.00

2003-04 Fleer Focus NBA Shirtified Jerseys 250

Randomly seeded in packs, this 20-card set parallels the design of the base NBA Shirtified insert set enhanced with a swatch of jersey and sequential numbering to 250. Versions numbered to 150, 75, Numbers with swatches from the jersey number serially numbered to 99, Nameplates with swatches from the player's name numbered to 50 and NBA Logos numbered one of one.

*150 SINGLES: .5X TO 1.25X BASE HI
*75 SINGLES: .6X TO 1.5X BASE HI
*NAMEPLATES: 1.25X TO 3X BASE HI
*NUMBERS SINGLES: 1X TO 2.5X BASE HI
NSAI Allen Iverson 4.00 10.00
NSAJ Antawn Jamison 2.50 6.00
NSAS Amare Stoudemire 4.00 10.00
NSBW Ben Wallace 2.50 6.00
NSDN Dirk Nowitzki 4.00 10.00
NSEB Elton Brand 2.50 6.00
NSEC Eddy Curry 2.00
NSJO Jermaine O'Neal 2.50
NSKM Karl Malone 3.00
NSKM Kenyon Martin 2.50
NSLS Caron Butler 2.50
NSMB Mike Bibby 2.50
NSMF Michael Finley 2.50
NSPP Paul Pierce 3.00
NSPS Peja Stojakovic 2.50
NSRW Rasheed Wallace 2.50
NSSM Shawn Marion 2.50
NSTM Tracy McGrady 3.00
NSVC Vince Carter 4.00
NSYM Yao Ming 5.00

2003-04 Fleer Focus Tag Te

Randomly inserted in packs, this 15-card set pa
players with something in common. Ie: same tea
same rookie crop etc. One player appears on the
the other and both are set against a marble back
set to match the team color schemes of the play
Each card is sequentially numbered to 350.

1 Jason Kidd 1.50
Kenyon Martin
2 Mike Bibby 1.00
Peja Stojakovic
3 Tayshaun Prince 1.00
Ben Wallace
4 Allan Houston .75
Latrell Sprewell
5 Kevin Garnett 2.00
Troy Hudson
6 Steve Francis 2.00
Yao Ming
7 Steve Nash 1.50
Dirk Nowitzki
8 Paul Pierce 1.25
Antoine Walker
9 Tracy McGrady 1.25
Drew Gooden
10 Stephon Marbury 1.50
Amare Stoudemire
11 Darko Milicic 2.00
Chris Bosh
12 T.J. Ford 4.00
Dwyane Wade
13 LeBron James 10.00
Carmelo Anthony
14 Tim Duncan 1.50
Tony Parker
15 Kobe Bryant 6.00
Shaquille O'Neal

2003-04 Fleer Focus Tag Te Jerseys

Randomly inserted, this 10-card set parallels the
design of the base Tag Team set enhanced with t
swatches, one from each player, of game worn je
Each card is sequentially numbered to 250. A Ta
version numbered one of one was also inserted.

1 Jason Kidd 6.00
Kenyon Martin
2 Mike Bibby 5.00
Peja Stojakovic
3 Tayshaun Prince 5.00
Ben Wallace
4 Allan Houston 6.00
Latrell Sprewell
5 Kevin Garnett 8.00
Troy Hudson
6 Steve Francis 10.00
Yao Ming
7 Steve Nash 8.00
Dirk Nowitzki
9 Tracy McGrady 6.00
Drew Gooden
10 Stephon Marbury 6.00
Amare Stoudemire

1999-00 Fleer Force

Debuting in 1999-00, the Fleer Force set contain
235-cards with 200 veterans and 35 rookies. The
rookies were serially numbered to 1600. The car
base design is similar to the 99-00 Fleer Traditic
but the front carries a metallic look. Two special
Carter cards were also randomly inserted called
Carter. The first card features a swatch of "GI gea
worn by Carter. Those cards were inserted at one
300. The second is an autographed version of the
card, numbered to 15. Those cards are listed at t
of the base set.

COMPLETE SET (235) 75.00 1
COMPLETE SET w/o RC (200) 15.00
1 Vince Carter .60
2 Kobe Bryant 1.50
3 Keith Van Horn .25
4 Tim Duncan .60
5 Grant Hill .40

Garnett .60 1.50
ee Hardaway .50 1.25
Williams .40 1.00
ierce .50 1.25
kie Blaylock .20 .50
n Bradley .20 .50
y Anderson .25 .60
ncey Billups .30 .75
Campbell .20 .50
Caffey .20 .50
Barry .25 .60
es Barkley .50 1.25
Anderson .20 .50
ck Martin .20 .50
ael Curry .20 .50
Fox .20 .50
nio Davis .20 .50
ll Brandon .20 .50
Brown .20 .50
Bailey .20 .50
Allen .30 .75
Grant .20 .50
Burrell .20 .50
Abdul-Wahad .20 .50
us Camby .25 .60
Stockton .40 1.00
Anderson .20 .50
e Feick RC .30 .75
Geiger .20 .50
Baker .30 .75
Brown .20 .50
ndon Anderson .20 .50
on Maxwell .25 .60
eef Abdur-Rahim .25 .60
onso Ellis .20 .50
ric Ceballos .20 .50
Battie .25 .60
Clark .20 .50
ick Coleman .25 .60
Dampier .20 .50
y Benjamin .20 .50
ael Dickerson .20 .50
ic Henderson .20 .50
ond Murray .20 .50
me Williams .20 .50
quille O'Neal .75 2.00
Davis .20 .50
Garrett .20 .50
Hardaway .30 .75
nis Rodman .60 1.50
Cassell .25 .60
Jackson .25 .60
dall Gill .20 .50
Williams .20 .50
s Childs .20 .50
e Divac .30 .75
ell Armstrong .20 .50
io Elie .20 .50
n Jackson .20 .50
e Ellis .20 .50
g Christie .25 .60
ard Eisley .20 .50
an Howard .25 .60
e Bibby .30 .75
Henderson .20 .50
hael Finley .30 .75
a Barros .20 .50
Hudson .30 .75
y Davis .30 .75
Amaechi RC .30 .75
Strickland .20 .50
e Drew .20 .50
wn Kemp .30 .75
ne Nesby RC .30 .75
sey Hunter .20 .50
en Patterson .20 .50
Harrington .30 .75
by Jackson .25 .60
Majerle .30 .75
Chapman .20 .50
Curry .20 .50
ert Pack .20 .50
y Kittles .20 .50
ah Rider .20 .50
ick Ewing .40 1.00
rence Funderburke .20 .50
c Austin .20 .50
n Elliott .30 .75
y Hughes .25 .60
ani McCoy .20 .50
cy McGrady .50 1.25
Hornacek .25 .60
idi White .20 .50
any Manning .20 .50
shown McLeod .20 .50
eve Nash .50 1.25
n Mercer .25 .60
ef LaFrentz .25 .60
ddie Jones .30 .75
ntawn Jamison .30 .75
hucky Atkins RC .30 .75
thella Harrington .20 .50
revin Knight .20 .50
ichael Olowokandi .20 .50
hristian Laettner .25 .60
R. Reid .20 .50
eggie Miller .30 .75
azaro Borrell RC .30 .75
mal Mashburn .25 .60
enn Robinson .25 .60
at Garrity .20 .50
ephon Marbury .25 .60
vydas Sabonis .25 .60
lan Houston .25 .60
eja Stojakovic .30 .75
ichael Doleac .20 .50
very Johnson .25 .60
len Iverson .60 1.50
ashard Lewis .30 .75
harles Oakley .25 .60
arl Malone .40 1.00
acy Murray .20 .50
elipe Lopez .20 .50
ikembe Mutombo .30 .75
irk Nowitzki .60 1.50
italy Potapenko .20 .50
ntonio McDyess .25 .60
nthony Mason .20 .50
onyell Marshall .20 .50
ickey Simpkins .20 .50
uttino Mobley .25 .60
esley Person .20 .50
odney Rogers .20 .50

139 Jerry Stackhouse .30 .75
140 Glen Rice .30 .75
141 Chris Mullin .30 .75
142 Anthony Peeler .20 .50
143 Alonzo Mourning .40 1.00
144 Tom Gugliotta .20 .50
145 Tim Thomas .25 .60
146 Damon Stoudamire .30 .75
147 Jayson Williams .20 .50
148 Larry Johnson .30 .75
149 Chris Webber .30 .75
150 Matt Harpring .25 .60
151 David Robinson .50 1.25
152 George Lynch .20 .50
153 Gary Payton .30 .75
154 John Wallace .20 .50
155 Greg Ostertag .20 .50
156 Mitch Richmond .30 .75
157 Cherokee Parks .20 .50
158 Steve Smith .20 .50
159 Gary Trent .20 .50
160 Antoine Walker .30 .75
161 Chris Herren RC .30 .75
162 Ron Harper .20 .50
163 Chris Mills .20 .50
164 Fred Hoiberg .20 .50
165 Hakeem Olajuwon .40 1.00
166 Bob Sura .20 .50
167 Brian Skinner .20 .50
168 Loy Vaught .20 .50
169 A.C. Green .30 .75
170 Jalen Rose .25 .60
171 Joe Smith .25 .60
172 Clarence Weatherspoon .20 .50
173 Jason Kidd .50 1.25
174 Robert Traylor .20 .50
175 Rasheed Wallace .30 .75
176 Latrell Sprewell .30 .75
177 Corliss Williamson .20 .50
178 Bo Outlaw .20 .50
179 Malik Rose .20 .50
180 Nazr Mohammed .20 .50
181 Eric Murdock .20 .50
182 Kevin Willis .20 .50
183 Bryon Russell .20 .50
184 Bryant Reeves .20 .50
185 Rod Strickland .20 .50
186 Samaki Walker .20 .50
187 Nick Van Exel .25 .60
188 David Wesley .20 .50
189 John Starks .30 .75
190 Toni Kukoc .30 .75
191 Scottie Pippen .50 1.25
192 Johnny Newman .20 .50
193 Maurice Taylor .20 .50
194 Rik Smits .30 .75
195 Clifford Robinson .20 .50
196 Bonzi Wells .20 .50
197 Charlie Ward .20 .50
198 Detlef Schrempf .25 .60
199 Theo Ratliff .25 .60
200 Kelvin Cato .20 .50
201 Ron Artest RC 4.00 10.00
202 William Avery RC 1.50 4.00
203 Elton Brand RC 4.00 10.00
204 Baron Davis RC 5.00 12.00
205 Jumaine Jones RC 1.50 4.00
206 Andre Miller RC 4.00 10.00
207 Eddie Robinson RC 1.50 4.00
208 James Posey RC 1.50 4.00
209 Jason Terry RC 4.00 10.00
210 Kenny Thomas RC 1.50 4.00
211 Steve Francis RC 4.00 10.00
212 Wally Szczerbiak RC 3.00 8.00
213 Richard Hamilton RC 4.00 10.00
214 Jonathan Bender RC 1.50 4.00
215 Shawn Marion RC 4.00 10.00
216 Aleksandar Radojevic RC 1.50 4.00
217 Tim James RC 1.50 4.00
218 Trajan Langdon RC 1.50 4.00
219 Lamar Odom RC 5.00 12.00
220 Corey Maggette RC 3.00 8.00
221 Dion Glover RC 1.50 4.00
222 Cal Bowdler RC 1.50 4.00
223 Vonteego Cummings RC 1.50 4.00
224 Devean George RC 1.50 4.00
225 Anthony Carter RC 1.50 4.00
226 Laron Profit RC 1.50 4.00
227 Quincy Lewis RC 1.50 4.00
228 John Celestand RC 1.50 4.00
229 Obinna Ekezie RC 1.50 4.00
230 Scott Padgett RC 1.50 4.00
231 Michael Ruffin RC 1.50 4.00
232 Jeff Foster RC 1.50 4.00
233 Jermaine Jackson RC 1.50 4.00
234 Adrian Griffin RC 1.50 4.00
235 Todd MacCulloch RC 1.50 4.00
NNO Vince Carter 8.00 20.00
Sgt.Carter Jersey
NNO Vince Carter 40.00 80.00
Sgt.Carter AU/300

1999-00 Fleer Force Forcefield

Randomly inserted into packs, this 235-card set is a complete parallel of the 2000 Fleer Force base set. The set is broken into tiers as follows: 200 Base Veterans (1-200) 1:12, and 35 Rookies (201-235) that are serial numbered to 100. To ascertain values on individual cards, please refer to the multiplier in the header, coupled with the value of the base card.
*STARS: 1.25X TO 3X BASE CARD HI
*RCs: .75X TO 2X BASE HI

1999-00 Fleer Force Air Force One Five

Randomly inserted into packs at one in 24, this 15-card set highlights Vince Carter. Card backs carry an "AF" prefix.
COMPLETE SET (15) 10.00 25.00
COMMON CARD (AF1-AF15) 1.50 4.00
*FORCEFIELD: 2.5X TO 6X BASE HI
FF: PRINT RUN 150 SERIAL #'d SETS

1999-00 Fleer Force Attack Force

Randomly inserted in packs at one in six, this 20-card set focused on younger players in the league who will lead the attack in the next century. Card backs carry an "A" prefix.
COMPLETE SET (20) 8.00 20.00
*FF: .75X TO 2X BASE CARD HI
FF: STATED ODDS 1:24
A1 Vince Carter 1.00 2.50
A2 Lamar Odom 1.50 4.00
A3 Stephon Marbury .40 1.00
A4 Jason Terry 1.25 3.00
A5 Richard Hamilton 1.25 3.00
A6 Steve Francis 1.25 3.00
A7 Wally Szczerbiak 1.00 2.50
A8 Tracy McGrady .75 2.00
A9 Michael Finley .50 1.25
A10 Baron Davis 1.50 4.00
A11 Shawn Marion 1.25 3.00
A12 Jonathan Bender .50 1.25
A13 Elton Brand 1.25 3.00
A14 Shareef Abdur-Rahim .40 1.00
A15 Keith Van Horn .40 1.00
A16 Jerry Stackhouse .50 1.25
A17 Antonio McDyess .40 1.00
A18 Antoine Walker .50 1.25
A19 Steve Smith .30 .75
A20 Ron Artest 1.25 3.00

1999-00 Fleer Force Forceful

Randomly inserted in packs at one in 36, this 15-card set features impact players in the NBA. Card backs carry a "F" prefix.
COMPLETE SET (15) 20.00 50.00
*FF: .75X TO 2X BASE CARD HI
FF: STATED ODDS 1:144
F1 Vince Carter 2.50 6.00
F2 Lamar Odom 4.00 10.00
F3 Shaquille O'Neal 3.00 8.00
F4 Alonzo Mourning 1.50 4.00
F5 Kevin Garnett 2.50 6.00
F6 Tim Duncan 2.50 6.00
F7 Kobe Bryant 6.00 15.00
F8 Allen Iverson 2.50 6.00
F9 Jason Williams 1.50 4.00
F10 Paul Pierce 2.00 5.00
F11 Shareef Abdur-Rahim 1.00 2.50
F12 Stephon Marbury 1.00 2.50
F13 Grant Hill 1.50 4.00
F14 Keith Van Horn 1.00 2.50
F15 Karl Malone 1.50 4.00

1999-00 Fleer Force Mission Accomplished

Randomly inserted in packs at one in 12, this 15-card set features players who carry out the game plan night-in and night-out. Card backs carry a "MA" prefix.
COMPLETE SET (15) 10.00 25.00
*FF: .75X TO 2X BASE CARD HI
FF: STATED ODDS 1:48
MA1 Vince Carter 1.25 3.00
MA2 Lamar Odom 2.00 5.00
MA3 Allen Iverson 1.25 3.00
MA4 Tim Duncan 1.25 3.00
MA5 Charles Barkley 1.00 2.50
MA6 Jason Kidd 1.00 2.50
MA7 Steve Francis 1.50 4.00
MA8 Elton Brand 1.50 4.00
MA9 Kevin Garnett 1.25 3.00
MA10 Baron Davis 2.00 5.00
MA11 Paul Pierce 1.00 2.50
MA12 Scottie Pippen 1.00 2.50
MA13 Chris Webber .60 1.50
MA14 Anfernee Hardaway 1.00 2.50
MA15 David Robinson 1.00 2.50

1999-00 Fleer Force Operation Invasion

Randomly inserted in packs at one in 24, this 15-card set features the top players in the NBA that lead their team into battle. The cards feature on oval die cut design on the top and bottom. Card backs carry an "OI" prefix.
COMPLETE SET (15) 12.50 30.00
*FF: .75X TO 2X BASE CARD HI
FF: STATED ODDS 1:96
OI1 Vince Carter 2.00 5.00
OI2 Lamar Odom 3.00 8.00
OI3 Kobe Bryant 5.00 12.00
OI4 Tim Duncan 2.00 5.00
OI5 Paul Pierce 1.50 4.00
OI6 Kevin Garnett 2.00 5.00
OI7 Grant Hill 1.25 3.00
OI8 Allen Iverson 2.00 5.00
OI9 Jason Williams 1.25 3.00
OI10 Ron Mercer .75 2.00
OI11 Shaquille O'Neal 2.50 6.00
OI12 Keith Van Horn .75 2.00
OI13 Shareef Abdur-Rahim .75 2.00
OI14 Alonzo Mourning 1.25 3.00
OI15 Stephon Marbury .75 2.00

1999-00 Fleer Force Special Forces

Randomly inserted in packs at one in 12, this 15-card set features players who bring a special quality to the NBA. Card backs carry a "SF" prefix.
COMPLETE SET (15) 8.00 20.00
*FF: .75X TO 2X BASE CARD HI
FF: STATED ODDS 1:48
SF1 Vince Carter 1.25 3.00
SF2 Lamar Odom 2.00 5.00
SF3 Keith Van Horn .50 1.25
SF4 Stephon Marbury .50 1.25
SF5 Scottie Pippen 1.00 2.50
SF6 Ray Allen .60 1.50
SF7 Chris Webber .60 1.50
SF8 Jason Williams .75 2.00
SF9 Karl Malone .75 2.00
SF10 Patrick Ewing .75 2.00
SF11 Elton Brand 1.50 4.00
SF12 Grant Hill .75 2.00
SF13 Eddie Jones .60 1.50
SF14 Shaquille O'Neal 1.50 4.00
SF15 Kobe Bryant 3.00 8.00

2001-02 Fleer Force

Released in early February 2002, Fleer Force was a 180-card set divided up into 150 veteran player cards, which feature a white backdrop with player action photos set against an artist drawn portrait close-up of the player's face, and 30 rookie cards set up in a horizontal design with player portrait photos and gold foil stamping set against a basketball court style backdrop. The player photos appear along the left side of the card, and the player's number and the word "Rookie" appears on the right side. All of the cards in the set hava a colored strip set above the bottom border of the card containing the player's name, team, and position. The rookie cards have a number box in this strip on the right side of the card and are sequentially numbered to 999. The first 300 serially numbered rookie cards contain a postage stamp and a post office stamp of the city and date that the player made his league debut in. Force was packaged in 24 pack boxes where packs contained seven cards.
COMPLETE SET (180) 75.00 150.00
COMPLETE SET w/o SP's (150) 12.50 30.00
1 Vince Carter .50 1.25
2 Allan Houston .25 .60
3 Steve Francis .30 .75
4 Karl Malone .40 1.00
5 Joe Smith .25 .60
6 Raef LaFrentz .20 .50
7 David Robinson .50 1.25
8 Tim Thomas .20 .50
9 Antonio McDyess .25 .60
10 Steve Smith .25 .60
11 Eddie Jones .25 .60
12 Jumaine Jones .20 .50
13 Derek Anderson .20 .50
14 Shaquille O'Neal .75 2.00
15 Eddie Robinson .20 .50
16 Stephon Marbury .25 .60
17 Darius Miles .20 .50
18 Toni Kukoc .25 .60
19 Latrell Sprewell .25 .60
20 Wang Zhizhi .25 .60
21 Tim Duncan .60 1.50
22 Eddie House .20 .50
23 Chris Mihm .20 .50
24 Rasheed Wallace .30 .75
25 Kobe Bryant 1.50 4.00
26 Kenny Thomas .20 .50
27 John Stockton .40 1.00
28 Mike Bibby .30 .75
29 Larry Hughes .25 .60
30 Antonio Davis .20 .50
31 Ray Allen .30 .75
32 Corliss Williamson .20 .50
33 Desmond Mason .25 .60
34 Sam Cassell .25 .60
35 Dirk Nowitzki .50 1.25
36 Chris Webber .30 .75
37 Michael Dickerson .20 .50
38 Ron Mercer .20 .50
39 Iakovos Tsakalidis .20 .50
40 Derek Fisher .25 .60
41 Baron Davis .30 .75
42 Allen Iverson .60 1.50
43 Avery Johnson .25 .60
44 Courtney Alexander .20 .50
45 Alonzo Mourning .40 1.00
46 Steve Nash .50 1.25
47 Hedo Turkoglu .30 .75
48 Jason Williams .25 .60
49 David Wesley .20 .50
50 Dikembe Mutombo .30 .75
51 LaPhonso Ellis .25 .60
52 Trajan Langdon .20 .50
53 Damon Stoudamire .25 .60
54 Rick Fox .25 .60
55 Paul Pierce .40 1.00
56 Tracy McGrady .50 1.25
57 Lamar Odom .30 .75
58 Antoine Walker .25 .60
59 Mike Miller .30 .75
60 Jermaine O'Neal .30 .75
61 Michael Jordan 4.00 10.00
62 Jason Kidd .50 1.25
63 Marc Jackson .20 .50
64 Hakeem Olajuwon .40 1.00
65 Kevin Garnett .60 1.50
66 Nick Van Exel .25 .60
67 Rashard Lewis .30 .75
68 Brian Grant .20 .50
69 Keith Van Horn .25 .60
70 Grant Hill .40 1.00
71 Reggie Miller .30 .75
72 Richard Hamilton .25 .60
73 Marcus Camby .25 .60
74 Clifford Robinson .20 .50
75 Gary Payton .30 .75
76 Andre Miller .25 .60
77 Bonzi Wells .20 .50
78 Stromile Swift .20 .50
79 Marcus Fizer .20 .50
80 Shawn Marion .30 .75
81 Elton Brand .30 .75
82 Jamal Mashburn .25 .60
83 Aaron McKie .20 .50
84 Corey Maggette .25 .60
85 Jason Terry .30 .75
86 Anfernee Hardaway .50 1.25
87 Antawn Jamison .30 .75
88 Morris Peterson .20 .50
89 Wally Szczerbiak .25 .60
90 Jerry Stackhouse .25 .60
91 Shareef Abdur-Rahim .25 .60
92 Glenn Robinson .25 .60
93 Michael Finley .30 .75
94 Peja Stojakovic .30 .75
95 Jalen Rose .25 .60
96 Theo Ratliff .20 .50
97 Kurt Thomas .20 .50
98 Cuttino Mobley .25 .60
99 DeShawn Stevenson .20 .50
100 Terrell Brandon .20 .50
101 Kwame Brown RC 1.00 2.50
102 Tyson Chandler RC 1.50 4.00
103 Pau Gasol RC 3.00 8.00
104 Eddy Curry RC 1.50 4.00
105 Jason Richardson RC 2.00 5.00
106 Shane Battier RC 2.00 5.00
107 Eddie Griffin RC 1.00 2.50
108 DeSagana Diop RC 1.00 2.50
109 Rodney White RC 1.00 2.50
110 Joe Johnson RC 2.50 6.00
111 Kedrick Brown RC 1.00 2.50
112 Vladimir Radmanovic RC 1.00 2.50
113 Richard Jefferson RC 2.00 5.00
114 Troy Murphy RC 1.50 4.00
115 Steven Hunter RC 1.00 2.50
116 Kirk Haston RC 1.00 2.50
117 Michael Bradley RC 1.00 2.50
118 Jason Collins RC 1.00 2.50
119 Zach Randolph RC 2.50 6.00
120 Brendan Haywood RC 1.25 3.00
121 Joseph Forte RC 1.00 2.50
122 Jeryl Sasser RC 1.00 2.50
123 Brandon Armstrong RC 1.00 2.50
124 Andrei Kirilenko RC 2.50 6.00
125 Gerald Wallace RC 1.50 4.00
126 Samuel Dalembert RC 1.25 3.00
127 Jamaal Tinsley RC 1.25 3.00
128 Tony Parker RC 4.00 10.00
129 Loren Woods RC 1.00 2.50
130 Primoz Brezec RC 1.00 2.50
131 Dion Glover .20 .50
132 Moochie Norris .20 .50
133 Mark Jackson .25 .60
134 Bryon Russell .20 .50
135 Danny Fortson .20 .50
136 Kenyon Martin .30 .75
137 Alvin Williams .20 .50
138 Erick Dampier .20 .50
139 Clarence Weatherspoon .20 .50
140 Brent Barry .20 .50
141 Lamond Murray .20 .50
142 Lindsey Hunter .20 .50
143 Speedy Claxton .20 .50
144 James Posey .20 .50
145 Anthony Mason .20 .50
146 Mateen Cleaves .20 .50
147 Kenny Anderson .25 .60
148 Travis Best .20 .50
149 Patrick Ewing .40 1.00
150 Dana Barros .20 .50
151 Lorenzen Wright .20 .50
152 Rodney Rogers .20 .50
153 Brad Miller .30 .75
154 Anthony Peeler .20 .50
155 Antonio Daniels .20 .50
156 Tim Hardaway .30 .75
157 Quentin Richardson .25 .60
158 Darrell Armstrong .20 .50
159 Nazr Mohammad .20 .50
160 Todd MacCulloch .20 .50
161 Ruben Patterson .20 .50
162 Wesley Person .20 .50
163 Jeff McInnis .20 .50
164 Vin Baker .25 .60
165 George McCloud .20 .50
166 Chris Gatling .20 .50
167 Derrick Coleman .25 .60
168 Elden Campbell .20 .50
169 Glen Rice .25 .60
170 Donyell Marshall .20 .50
171 Juwan Howard .25 .60
172 Mitch Richmond .25 .60
173 Tom Gugliotta .20 .50
174 Chucky Atkins .20 .50
175 Michael Redd .30 .75
176 Malik Rose .20 .50
177 Lee Nailon .20 .50
178 Al Harrington .25 .60
179 Matt Harpring .25 .60
180 Tyronn Lue .20 .50

2001-02 Fleer Force Rookie Postmarks

Randomly inserted in packs, this 30-card semi-parallel set is comprised of the first 300 serially numbered copies of the base rookie cards. A full description of these cards appears in the paragraph for the base Fleer Force set.
*RC POSTMARKS: .75X TO 2X BASE RC HI

2001-02 Fleer Force Special Forces

Randomly seeded in packs, this 150-card set parallels the base Fleer Force set enhanced with sequential numbering in the colored bar that contains the player's name. Veteran cards, numbers 1-100 and 131-180 are sequentially numbered to 250, and Rookie cards, numbers 101-130 are sequentially numbered to 50.
*SF STARS: 4X TO 10X BASE CARD HI
*SF ROOKIES: 2.5X TO 6X BASE CARD HI
61 Michael Jordan 30.00 80.00

2001-02 Fleer Force Emblematic

Randomly seeded in packs, this 25-card die-cut horizontal set design contains two color photos of the featured player. The photo on the left is a full color action photo, and the photo on the right is a framed, in colors that match the player's team, portrait style photo. Card background have the team logo of the pictured player centered on a basketball court print, and the word "Emblem@tic" appears along the bottom third of the card and is enhanced with silver foil highlights. The bottom of the card is solid colored, again to match team colors, and the players name and team appears in silver foil. Each card is sequentaílly numbered to 399.
1 Vince Carter 4.00 10.00
2 Dikembe Mutombo 2.50 6.00
3 Tracy McGrady 4.00 10.00
4 Lamar Odom 2.50 6.00
5 Jason Kidd 4.00 10.00
6 Ray Allen 2.50 6.00
7 John Stockton 3.00 8.00
8 Paul Pierce 3.00 8.00
9 Baron Davis 2.50 6.00
10 Kenyon Martin 2.50 6.00
11 Richard Hamilton 2.00 5.00
12 Grant Hill 3.00 8.00
13 Morris Peterson 1.50 4.00
14 Shareef Abdur-Rahim 2.00 5.00
15 Peja Stojakovic 2.50 6.00
16 Gary Payton 2.50 6.00
17 Karl Malone 3.00 8.00
18 Keith Van Horn 2.00 5.00
19 Darius Miles 1.50 4.00
20 Allen Iverson 5.00 12.00
21 Michael Jordan 20.00 50.00
22 Kobe Bryant 12.00 30.00
23 Kevin Garnett 5.00 12.00
24 Shaquille O'Neal 6.00 15.00
25 Tim Duncan 5.00 12.00

2001-02 Fleer Force Emblematic Jerseys

Randomly seeded in packs, this 25-card set parallels the base Emblematic insert set enhanced with a swatch of a game-worn jersey. Each card is sequentially numbered to 50.
1 Vince Carter 15.00 40.00
2 Dikembe Mutombo 10.00 25.00
3 Tracy McGrady 15.00 40.00
4 Lamar Odom 10.00 25.00
5 Jason Kidd 15.00 40.00
6 Ray Allen 10.00 25.00
7 John Stockton 12.00 30.00
8 Paul Pierce 12.00 30.00
9 Baron Davis 10.00 25.00
10 Kenyon Martin 10.00 25.00
11 Richard Hamilton 8.00 20.00
12 Grant Hill 12.00 30.00
13 Morris Peterson 6.00 15.00
14 Shareef Abdur-Rahim 8.00 20.00
15 Peja Stojakovic 10.00 25.00
16 Gary Payton 10.00 25.00
17 Karl Malone 12.00 30.00
18 Keith Van Horn 8.00 20.00
19 Darius Miles 6.00 15.00
20 Allen Iverson 20.00 50.00

2001-02 Fleer Force Inside the Game

Randomly inserted in packs, this 20-card set features full color player action photos set against a basketball court background. The bottom third of the card is separated and the player's name, the words "inside the game," and the player's team name appear in silver foil. Each card is sequentially numbered to 699.
1 Karl Malone 2.00 5.00
2 Keith Van Horn 1.25 3.00
3 Darius Miles 1.00 2.50
4 John Stockton 2.00 5.00
5 Allen Iverson 3.00 8.00
6 Alonzo Mourning 2.00 5.00
7 Dikembe Mutombo 1.50 4.00
8 Tracy McGrady 2.50 6.00
9 Lamar Odom 1.50 4.00
10 Baron Davis 1.50 4.00
11 Michael Jordan 12.00 30.00
12 Kobe Bryant 8.00 20.00
13 Kevin Garnett 3.00 8.00
14 Shaquille O'Neal 4.00 10.00
15 Tim Duncan 3.00 8.00
16 Vince Carter 2.50 6.00
17 Steve Francis 1.50 4.00
18 Dirk Nowitzki 2.50 6.00
19 Chris Webber 1.50 4.00
20 Peja Stojakovic 1.50 4.00
NNO Vince Carter AU/275 15.00 40.00

2001-02 Fleer Force Inside the Game Jerseys

Randomly inserted in packs, this 15-card set parallels the design of the base Inside the Game insert set enhanced with a swatch of a game-worn jersey. Each card is sequentially numbered to 399. A Numbers version was released as well where each card is sequentially numbered to 99.
*NUMBERS: 1.25X TO 3X JSY HI
1 Karl Malone 4.00 10.00
2 Keith Van Horn 2.50 6.00
3 Darius Miles 2.00 5.00
4 John Stockton 4.00 10.00
5 Allen Iverson 6.00 15.00
6 Alonzo Mourning 4.00 10.00
7 Dikembe Mutombo 3.00 8.00
8 Tracy McGrady 5.00 12.00
9 Lamar Odom 3.00 8.00
10 Baron Davis 3.00 8.00
11 Vince Carter 5.00 12.00
12 Steve Francis 3.00 8.00
13 Dirk Nowitzki 5.00 12.00
14 Chris Webber 3.00 8.00
15 Peja Stojakovic 3.00 8.00

2001-02 Fleer Force True Colors Jerseys

Randomly inserted in packs, this 30-card set features full color player portrait photos set against their team's logo. The words "True Colors Game Worn Jersey" appear along the center of the card in silver foil, and the bottom of the card is white with a centered piece of a game worn jersey. The bottom of the card contains the words "1st Color" and the player's team in silver ink. Each card is sequentially numbered to 400. Versions with multiple colors were also issued. Four color cards are sequentially numbered to 50, three color cards are sequentially numbered to 100 and two color cards are sequentially numbered to 200.
*FOUR COLOR: 2X TO 5X ONE COLOR HI
*THREE COLOR: 1.25X TO 3X ONE COLOR HI
*TWO COLOR: .75X TO 2X ONE COLOR HI
1 Vince Carter 5.00 12.00
2 Kenyon Martin 3.00 8.00
3 Baron Davis 3.00 8.00
4 Tracy McGrady 5.00 12.00
5 Mike Miller 3.00 8.00
6 Aaron McKie 2.00 5.00
7 Darius Miles 2.00 5.00
8 Lamar Odom 3.00 8.00
9 Glenn Robinson 2.50 6.00
10 Karl Malone 4.00 10.00
11 John Stockton 4.00 10.00
12 Paul Pierce 4.00 10.00
13 Alonzo Mourning 4.00 10.00
14 Gary Payton 3.00 8.00
15 Stephon Marbury 2.50 6.00
16 Dikembe Mutombo 3.00 8.00
17 Shawn Marion 3.00 8.00
18 Richard Hamilton 2.50 6.00
19 Stromile Swift 2.00 5.00
20 Reggie Miller 3.00 8.00
21 Keith Van Horn 2.50 6.00
22 Steve Francis 3.00 8.00
23 Morris Peterson 2.00 5.00
24 Andre Miller 2.50 6.00
25 Quentin Richardson 2.50 6.00
26 Antonio McDyess 2.50 6.00
27 Anfernee Hardaway 5.00 12.00
28 Jason Williams 2.50 6.00
29 Grant Hill 4.00 10.00
30 Jason Terry 3.00 8.00

2000-01 Fleer Futures

The 2000-01 Fleer Futures product was released in Feb. 2001 and featured a 250-card base set broken into tiers as follows: Base Veterans (1-200), and Rookies

(201-250) (Please note that the even numbered rookies were inserted at 1:2, while the odd numbered rookies were inserted at 1:7). Card packs carried eight cards at the suggested retail price of $2.99.
COMPLETE SET (250) 40.00 80.00
COMPLETE SET w/o RCs (200) 10.00 25.00
1 Vince Carter .50 1.25
2 Dan Majerle .20 .50
3 George McCloud .15 .40
4 Radoslav Nesterovic .15 .40
5 Corey Maggette .20 .50
6 Derek Anderson .15 .40
7 Ray Allen .25 .60
8 Greg Ostertag .15 .40
9 Cedric Ceballos .15 .40
10 Danny Fortson .15 .40
11 Roshown McLeod .15 .40
12 Christian Laettner .15 .40
13 Avery Johnson .20 .50
14 Clarence Weatherspoon .15 .40
15 Michael Curry .15 .40
16 Chris Whitney .15 .40
17 Anthony Mason .15 .40
18 Antonio McDyess .20 .50
19 Vitaly Potapenko .15 .40
20 Shaquille O'Neal .60 1.50
21 David Robinson .40 1.00
22 Tyrone Hill .15 .40
23 Otis Thorpe .20 .50
24 Reggie Miller .25 .60
25 Kevin Garnett .50 1.25
26 Michael Dickerson .15 .40
27 John Amaechi .15 .40
28 Jason Kidd .40 1.00
29 Ron Artest .25 .60
30 Muggsy Bogues .20 .50
31 Antawn Jamison .25 .60
32 Brian Grant .15 .40
33 Stephon Marbury .20 .50
34 William Avery .15 .40
35 Paul Pierce .30 .75
36 Marcus Camby .20 .50
37 Kevin Willis .15 .40
38 Dikembe Mutombo .25 .60
39 Rashard Lewis .25 .60
40 Allan Houston .20 .50
41 Hakeem Olajuwon .30 .75
42 Rod Strickland .20 .50
43 Derrick Coleman .20 .50
44 Tariq Abdul-Wahad .15 .40
45 Terrell Brandon .15 .40
46 Michael Olowokandi .15 .40
47 Robert Horry .20 .50
48 Kelvin Cato .15 .40
49 Eric Williams .15 .40
50 Glen Rice .20 .50
51 Carlos Rogers .15 .40
52 Allen Iverson .50 1.25
53 P.J. Brown .15 .40
54 Jalen Rose .20 .50
55 Damon Stoudamire .20 .50
56 Damon Jones RC .25 .60
57 Darrell Armstrong .15 .40
58 Samaki Walker .15 .40
59 John Stockton .30 .75
60 Chucky Atkins .15 .40
61 Rasheed Wallace .25 .60
62 Jason Terry .25 .60
63 Aaron Williams .15 .40
64 Steve Nash .40 1.00
65 Antoine Walker .20 .50
66 Patrick Ewing .30 .75
67 Cuttino Mobley .20 .50
68 Aaron McKie .15 .40
69 Jamal Mashburn .20 .50
70 Scottie Pippen .40 1.00
71 Bryant Reeves .15 .40
72 Isaiah Rider .20 .50
73 Jaren Jackson .15 .40
74 Lindsey Hunter .15 .40
75 Jacque Vaughn .15 .40
76 Travis Best .15 .40
77 Vinny Del Negro .15 .40
78 Othella Harrington .15 .40
79 Michael Finley .25 .60
80 Brent Barry .15 .40
81 Brevin Knight .15 .40
82 Kurt Thomas .15 .40
83 Mark Jackson .20 .50
84 Richard Hamilton .20 .50
85 Anthony Carter .15 .40
86 Matt Harpring .20 .50
87 Bobby Jackson .15 .40
88 Jerome Williams .15 .40
89 Jahidi White .15 .40
90 Lorenzen Wright .15 .40
91 Kerry Kittles .15 .40
92 Anthony Peeler .15 .40
93 Kenny Anderson .20 .50
94 Latrell Sprewell .20 .50
95 Maurice Taylor .15 .40
96 Toni Kukoc .20 .50
97 Eddie Robinson .15 .40
98 Voshon Lenard .15 .40
99 Sam Mitchell .15 .40
100 Isaac Austin .15 .40
101 Michael Doleac .15 .40
102 Andre Miller .20 .50
103 Jason Williams .25 .60
104 Charles Oakley .20 .50
105 Mitch Richmond .20 .50
106 Bruce Bowen .15 .40
107 Keith Van Horn .20 .50
108 Wally Szczerbiak .20 .50
109 Tony Battie .15 .40
110 Larry Johnson .25 .60
111 Shandon Anderson .15 .40
112 Sam Cassell .20 .50
113 David Wesley .15 .40
114 James Posey .15 .40
115 Bonzi Wells .15 .40
116 Mike Bibby .25 .60
117 Andrew DeClercq .15 .40
118 Clifford Robinson .15 .40
119 Corliss Williamson .15 .40
120 Antonio Davis .15 .40
121 Eddie Jones .25 .60
122 Jamie Feick .15 .40
123 Anfernee Hardaway .40 1.00
124 Adrian Griffin .15 .40
125 Erick Strickland .15 .40
126 Doug Christie .15 .40
127 Scot Pollard .15 .40
128 Sam Perkins .15 .40
129 Raef LaFrentz .15 .40
130 Dale Davis .15 .40
131 Tyrone Nesby .25 .60
132 Rick Fox .20 .50
133 Tom Gugliotta .15 .40
134 Glenn Robinson .20 .50
135 Quincy Lewis .15 .40
136 Austin Croshere .15 .40
137 Shawn Kemp .25 .60
138 Lamar Odom .25 .60
139 Tim Duncan .50 1.25
140 Tim Thomas .15 .40
141 Bryon Russell .15 .40
142 Jermaine O'Neal .25 .60
143 Erick Dampier .15 .40
144 Shareef Abdur-Rahim .20 .50
145 Bo Outlaw .15 .40
146 Gary Payton .25 .60
147 Chris Gatling .15 .40
148 Vlade Divac .20 .50
149 Ben Wallace .25 .60
150 Larry Hughes .20 .50
151 Ron Mercer .15 .40
152 Karl Malone .30 .75
153 Jonathan Bender .15 .40
154 Mookie Blaylock .20 .50
155 Jim Jackson .15 .40
156 Chris Crawford .15 .40
157 Vin Baker .20 .50
158 Lamond Murray .15 .40
159 Charlie Ward .15 .40
160 Steve Francis .25 .60
161 Cherokee Parks .15 .40
162 Baron Davis .25 .60
163 Keon Clark .15 .40
164 Ruben Patterson .15 .40
165 Tracy McGrady .40 1.00
166 Antonio Daniels .15 .40
167 Scott Williams .15 .40
168 John Starks .15 .40
169 Jerry Stackhouse .20 .50
170 Vonteego Cummings .15 .40
171 LaPhonso Ellis .20 .50
172 Dirk Nowitzki .40 1.00
173 Horace Grant .20 .50
174 Wesley Person .15 .40
175 Peja Stojakovic .25 .60
176 Eric Snow .15 .40
177 Juwan Howard .20 .50
178 Tim Hardaway .25 .60
179 Kendall Gill .15 .40
180 Chauncey Billups .25 .60
181 Kobe Bryant 1.25 3.00
182 Sean Elliott .20 .50
183 Donyell Marshall .15 .40
184 Al Harrington .20 .50
185 Arvydas Sabonis .20 .50
186 Grant Hill .30 .75
187 Malik Rose .15 .40
188 Nazr Mohammed .15 .40
189 Elden Campbell .15 .40
190 Nick Van Exel .20 .50
191 Steve Smith .20 .50
192 Sean Rooks .15 .40
193 Monty Williams .15 .40
194 Elton Brand .25 .60
195 Chris Webber .25 .60
196 Mikki Moore RC .25 .60
197 Chris Mills .15 .40
198 Alan Henderson .15 .40
199 Shawn Bradley .15 .40
200 Shawn Marion .25 .60
201 Hedo Turkoglu RC 1.25 3.00
202 Iakovos Tsakalidis RC .25 .60
203 Kenyon Martin RC 1.50 4.00
204 Mamadou N'Diaye RC .25 .60
205 Stromile Swift RC .60 1.50
206 Pepe Sanchez RC .25 .60
207 Chris Mihm RC .60 1.50
208 Lavor Postell RC .25 .60
209 Marcus Fizer RC .60 1.50
210 Ruben Garces RC .25 .60
211 Courtney Alexander RC .60 1.50
212 A.J. Guyton RC .25 .60
213 Darius Miles RC .60 1.50
214 Ademola Okulaja RC .25 .60
215 Jerome Moiso RC .60 1.50
216 Khalid El-Amin RC .25 .60
217 Joel Przybilla RC .60 1.50
218 Mike Smith RC .25 .60
219 DerMarr Johnson RC .60 1.50
220 Soumaila Samake RC .25 .60
221 Mike Miller RC 1.25 3.00
222 Eddie House RC .25 .60
223 Quentin Richardson RC 1.00 2.50
224 Eduardo Najera RC .25 .60
225 Morris Peterson RC .60 1.50
226 Hanno Mottola RC .25 .60
227 Speedy Claxton RC .60 1.50
228 Ruben Wolkowyski RC .25 .60
229 Keyon Dooling RC .60 1.50
230 Olumide Oyedeji RC .25 .60
231 Mark Madsen RC .60 1.50
232 Mike Penberthy RC .25 .60
233 Mateen Cleaves RC .60 1.50
234 Brian Cardinal RC .25 .60
235 Etan Thomas RC .60 1.50
236 Garth Joseph RC .25 .60
237 Jason Collier RC .60 1.50
238 Paul McPherson RC .25 .60
239 Erick Barkley RC .60 1.50
240 Stephen Jackson RC .40 1.00
241 Desmond Mason RC .75 2.00
242 Jason Hart RC .25 .60
243 Jamal Crawford RC 1.00 2.50
244 Daniel Santiago RC .40 1.00
245 DeShawn Stevenson RC .75 2.00
246 Stanislav Medvedenko RC .25 .60
247 Donnell Harvey RC .60 1.50
248 Chris Porter RC .25 .60
249 Jamaal Magloire RC .60 1.50
250 Dalibor Bagaric RC .25 .60

2000-01 Fleer Futures Black Gold

Randomly inserted into hobby packs, this 50-card set is actually a parallel of all of the rookie cards found in the Fleer Futures base set. Each card has a black-foiled front and is serial numbered to 500.
*EVEN RCs: 2.5X TO 6X BASE CARD HI
*ODD RCs: 1X TO 2.5X BASE HI

2000-01 Fleer Futures Copper

Randomly inserted into packs, this 200-card set is actually a parallel of all of the veteran players found in the Fleer Futures base set. Each card has a copper-foiled front and is serial numbered to 750.
*STARS: 2.5X TO 6X BASE CARD HI

2000-01 Fleer Futures Gold

Randomly inserted into retail packs, this 50-card set is actually a parallel of all of the rookie cards found in the Fleer Futures base set. Each card has a gold-foiled front and is serial numbered to 500.
*EVEN RCs: 2.5X TO 6X BASE CARD HI
*ODD RCs: 1X TO 2.5X BASE HI

2000-01 Fleer Futures Autographics On Location

Randomly inserted into packs at one in 403, this 12-card insert features some of the hottest players in the league. Card backs carry a "AOL" prefix. Please note that there were only 240 produced for Vince Carter, Austin Croshere and Rashard Lewis. Lamar Odom and Jerry Stackhouse were redemptions that were not produced.
AOL1 Shareef Abdur-Rahim 10.00 25.00
AOL2 Travis Best 12.50 30.00
AOL3 Vince Carter/240 25.00 60.00
AOL4 Austin Croshere/240 10.00 25.00
AOL5 Baron Davis 20.00 50.00
AOL6 Rashard Lewis/240 20.00 50.00
AOL7 Dan Majerle 60.00 120.00
AOL8 Dirk Nowitzki 125.00 250.00
AOL10 Mitch Richmond 20.00 50.00
AOL11 Jalen Rose 10.00 25.00

2000-01 Fleer Futures Vince Carter Rookie Remnants

This three-card insert was randomly inserted into 2000-01 Fleer products. The set includes a Vince Carter floor card (numbered to 100), a Vince Carter floor/jersey card (numbered to 15), and finally an autographed Vince Carter floor/jersey card (numbered 1/1).
NNO Vince Carter FLR/100 12.50 30.00

2000-01 Fleer Futures Characteristics

Randomly inserted into packs at one in 28, this 10-card insert features some of the real "characters" in the NBA. Card backs carry a "C" prefix.
COMPLETE SET (10) 12.50 25.00
C1 Vince Carter 2.00 5.00
C2 Kobe Bryant 5.00 12.00
C3 Lamar Odom 1.00 2.50
C4 Kevin Garnett 2.00 5.00
C5 Allen Iverson 2.00 5.00
C6 Grant Hill 1.25 3.00
C7 Tim Duncan 2.00 5.00
C8 Steve Francis 1.00 2.50
C9 Jason Williams 1.00 2.50
C10 Shaquille O'Neal 2.50 6.00

2000-01 Fleer Futures Hot Commodities

Randomly inserted into packs at one in 28, this 10-card insert features some of the hottest players in the league. Card backs carry a "HC" prefix.
COMPLETE SET (10) 10.00 25.00
HC1 Vince Carter 1.50 4.00
HC2 Kobe Bryant 4.00 10.00
HC3 Kevin Garnett 1.50 4.00
HC4 Allen Iverson 1.50 4.00
HC5 Shaquille O'Neal 2.00 5.00
HC6 Steve Francis .75 2.00
HC7 Grant Hill 1.00 2.50
HC8 Tim Duncan 1.50 4.00
HC9 Lamar Odom .75 2.00
HC10 Tracy McGrady 1.25 3.00

2000-01 Fleer Futures Question Air

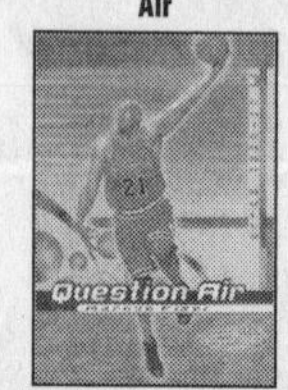

Randomly inserted into packs at one in 14, this 15-card insert features rookies that that hope to contribute in the NBA. Card backs carry a "QA" prefix.
COMPLETE SET (15) 3.00 8.00
QA1 Kenyon Martin .75 2.00
QA2 Stromile Swift .30 .75
QA3 Chris Mihm .30 .75
QA4 Marcus Fizer .30 .75
QA5 Courtney Alexander .30 .75
QA6 Darius Miles .30 .75
QA7 Jerome Moiso .30 .75
QA8 Desmond Mason .40 1.00
QA9 DerMarr Johnson .30 .75
QA10 Mike Miller .60 1.50
QA11 Quentin Richardson .50 1.25
QA12 Morris Peterson .30 .75
QA13 Etan Thomas .30 .75
QA14 Keyon Dooling .30 .75
QA15 Mateen Cleaves .30 .75

2000-01 Fleer Futures Rookie Game Jerseys

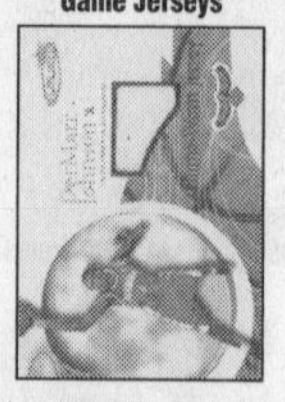

Randomly inserted into hobby packs, this 10-card insert features swatches of actual game-used jerseys from some of the hottest rookies in the league. Please note that this is a skip-numbered set.
*GJ: 1.5X TO 4X BASE HI 2.50 6.00

2000-01 Fleer Game Time

The 2000-01 Fleer Game Time product was released in late December 2001, and features a 120-card base set. The set is broken into tiers as follows: 90 Base Veterans (1-90), and 30 Rookies (91-120) (each rookie card is individually serial numbered to 2500). Each pack contained 5 cards, and carried a suggested retail price of $3.99.
COMPLETE SET w/o RC (90) 12.50 25.00
1 Vince Carter .60 1.50
2 Raef LaFrentz .20 .50
3 Kobe Bryant 1.50 4.00
4 Toni Kukoc .25 .60
5 Bonzi Wells .20 .50
6 Rashard Lewis .30 .75
7 Karl Malone .40 1.00
8 Juwan Howard .25 .60
9 Lindsey Hunter .20 .50
10 Alonzo Mourning .40 1.00
11 Larry Hughes .25 .60
12 Austin Croshere .20 .50
13 Charles Oakley .25 .60
14 Patrick Ewing .40 1.00
15 Vlade Divac .25 .60
16 Michael Finley .30 .75
17 Tim Hardaway .30 .75
18 Jason Kidd .50 1.25
19 Cal Bowdler .20 .50
20 Dirk Nowitzki .50 1.25
21 Terrell Brandon .20 .50
22 Allan Houston .25 .60
23 Theo Ratliff .20 .50
24 Chris Webber .30 .75
25 Shawn Kemp .30 .75
26 Jalen Rose .25 .60
27 Bryon Russell .20 .50
28 Jahidi White .20 .50
29 Trajan Langdon .20 .50
30 Baron Davis .30 .75
31 Cuttino Mobley .25 .60
32 Wally Szczerbiak .25 .60
33 Michael Dickerson .20 .50
34 Andre Miller .25 .60
35 Michael Olowokandi .20 .50
36 Ray Allen .30 .75
37 Latrell Sprewell .25 .60
38 Jason Williams .30 .75
39 Mikki Moore RC .30 .75
40 Shawn Marion .30 .75
41 Radoslav Nesterovic .20 .50
42 Ron Artest .30 .75
43 Vonteego Cummings .20 .50
44 Anfernee Hardaway .50 1.25
45 Jerome Williams .20 .50
46 John Stockton .40 1.00
47 Antawn Jamison .30 .75
48 Grant Hill .40 1.00
49 Elden Campbell .20 .50
50 Steve Francis .30 .75
51 Jamie Feick .20 .50
52 Gary Payton .30 .75
53 Elton Brand .30 .75
54 Eddie Jones .30 .75
55 Tom Gugliotta .20 .50
56 Richard Hamilton .25 .60
57 Dion Glover .20 .50
58 Shaquille O'Neal .75 2.00
59 Kevin Garnett .60 1.50
60 Paul Pierce .40 1.00
61 Brian Grant .20 .50
62 Tim Thomas .20 .50
63 Tracy McGrady .50 1.25
64 Jonathan Bender .20 .50
65 Adrian Griffin .20 .50
66 Lamar Odom .30 .75
67 Rasheed Wallace .30 .75
68 Mike Bibby .30 .75
69 Glenn Robinson .25 .60
70 Eddie Robinson .20 .50
71 Robert Horry .25 .60
72 Jerry Stackhouse .25 .60
73 Stephon Marbury .25 .60
74 Marcus Camby .25 .60
75 Scottie Pippen .50 1.25
76 David Robinson .50 1.25
77 Jason Terry .30 .75
78 Reggie Miller .30 .75
79 Larry Johnson .30 .75
80 Antonio Daniels .20 .50
81 Shareef Abdur-Rahim .25 .60
82 Ruben Patterson .20 .50
83 Nick Van Exel .25 .60
84 Keith Van Horn .25 .60
85 Antonio Davis .20 .50
86 Antoine Walker .25 .60
87 Allen Iverson .60 1.50
88 Antonio McDyess .25 .60
89 Tim Duncan .60 1.50
90 Hakeem Olajuwon .40 1.00
91 Jamaal Magloire RC .60 1.50
92 DerMarr Johnson RC .60 1.50
93 Jerome Moiso RC .60 1.50
94 Marcus Fizer RC .60 1.50
95 Jamal Crawford RC 1.00 2.50
96 Chris Mihm RC .60 1.50
97 Donnell Harvey RC .60 1.50
98 Courtney Alexander RC .60 1.50
99 Etan Thomas RC .60 1.50
100 Mamadou N'Diaye RC .60 1.50
101 Mateen Cleaves RC .60 1.50
102 Chris Porter RC .60 1.50
103 Jason Collier RC .60 1.50
104 Keyon Dooling RC .60 1.50
105 Darius Miles RC .60 1.50
106 Mark Madsen RC .60 1.50
107 Eddie House RC .60 1.50
108 Joel Przybilla RC .60 1.50
109 Kenyon Martin RC 1.50 4.00
110 Mike Miller RC 1.25 3.00
111 Speedy Claxton RC .60 1.50
112 Iakovos Tsakalidis RC .60 1.50
113 Erick Barkley RC .60 1.50
114 Hedo Turkoglu RC 1.25 3.00
115 Eduardo Najera RC .60 1.50
116 Desmond Mason RC .75 2.00
117 Morris Peterson RC .60 1.50
118 DeShawn Stevenson RC .75 2.00
119 Stromile Swift RC .60 1.50
120 Mike Smith RC .60 1.50

2000-01 Fleer Game Time Extra

Randomly inserted in packs at one in eight for veterans and serially numbered to 250 for rookies, this 120-card set parallels the base set. To ascertain values on individual cards, please refer to the multipliers in the header below, coupled with the value of the base card.
*STARS: 1.5X TO 4X BASE CARD HI
*RCs: 1X TO 2.5X BASE HI

2000-01 Fleer Game Time Attack the Rack

Randomly inserted into packs at one in four, this 20-card insert features players that are not afraid to attack the rack. Card backs carry an "AR" prefix.
COMPLETE SET (20) 7.50 15.00
AR1 Vince Carter .75 2.00
AR2 Lamar Odom .40 1.00
AR3 Kobe Bryant 2.00 5.00
AR4 Shareef Abdur-Rahim .30 .75
AR5 Allen Iverson .75 2.00
AR6 Jason Williams .40 1.00
AR7 Kevin Garnett .75 2.00
AR8 Tim Duncan .75 2.00
AR9 Latrell Sprewell .30 .75
AR10 Shaquille O'Neal 1.00 2.50
AR11 Jalen Rose .30 .75
AR12 Antawn Jamison .40 1.00
AR13 Paul Pierce .50 1.25
AR14 Grant Hill .50 1.25
AR15 Eddie Jones .40 1.00
AR16 Karl Malone .50 1.25
AR17 Elton Brand .40 1.00
AR18 Tracy McGrady .60 1.50
AR19 Michael Finley .40 1.00
AR20 Steve Francis .40 1.00

2000-01 Fleer Game Time Vince Carter Rookie Remnants

This three-card insert was randomly inserted into 2000-01 Fleer products. The set includes a Vince Carter floor card (numbered to 100), a Vince Carter floor/jersey card (numbered to 15), and finally an autographed Vince Carter floor/jersey card (numbered 1/1).
NNO Vince Carter FLR/100 12.50 30.00

2000-01 Fleer Game Time Change the Game

Randomly inserted into packs at one in 24, this 15-card insert features players that are changing the way people view the NBA. Card backs carry an "CG" prefix.
CG1 Vince Carter 2.00 5.00
CG2 Lamar Odom 1.00 2.50
CG3 Kobe Bryant 5.00 12.00
CG4 Allen Iverson 2.00 5.00
CG5 Jason Kidd 1.50 4.00
CG6 Grant Hill 1.25 3.00
CG7 Tim Duncan 2.00 5.00
CG8 Shaquille O'Neal 2.50 6.00
CG9 Kevin Garnett 2.00 5.00
CG10 Elton Brand 1.00 2.50
CG11 Stephon Marbury .75 2.00
CG12 Jason Williams 1.00 2.50
CG13 Keith Van Horn .75 2.00
CG14 Steve Francis 1.00 2.50
CG15 Gary Payton 1.00 2.50

2000-01 Fleer Game Time Uniformity

Randomly inserted into packs at one in 24, this 23-card insert features actual swatches from game-used jerseys. Please note that we have catalogued these cards below in alphabetical order for convenience. A special Vince Carter autographed jersey card was also released in this product, and are individually serial numbered to 150.
1 Shareef Abdur-Rahim 2.00 5.00
2 Mike Bibby 2.50 6.00
3 Vince Carter 5.00 12.00
4 Baron Davis 2.50 6.00
5 Sean Elliott 2.00 5.00
6 Allen Iverson 5.00 12.00
7 Toni Kukoc 2.00 5.00
8 Karl Malone 3.00 8.00
9 Stephon Marbury 2.00 5.00
10 Shawn Marion 2.50 6.00
11 Alonzo Mourning 3.00 8.00
12 Lamar Odom 2.50 6.00
13 Shaquille O'Neal Gold 6.00 15.00
14 Shaquille O'Neal Purple 6.00 15.00
15 Gary Payton 2.50 6.00
16 Scot Pollard 2.00 5.00
17 Jalen Rose 2.00 5.00
18 John Stockton 3.00 8.00
19 Wally Szczerbiak 2.00 5.00
20 Jason Terry 2.50 6.00
21 Keith Van Horn 2.00 5.00
22 Antoine Walker 2.00 5.00
23 David Wesley 1.50 4.00
GUVI Vince Carter AU/150 25.00 60.00

2000-01 Fleer Game Time Vince and the Revolution

Randomly inserted into packs, this 15-card insert features one of the NBA's most fascinating stars Vince Carter. Cards 1-5 were inserted into packs at one in nine, cards 6-10 were inserted at one in 24, and 11-15 were inserted at one in 144.
COMPLETE SET (15) 30.00 60.00
COMMON CARD (1-5) 1.00 2.50
COMMON CARD (6-10) 2.00 5.00
COMMON CARD (11-15) 5.00 12.00

2000-01 Fleer Genuine

The 2000-01 Fleer Genuine product was released in late December,2000 and features a 130-card base set. The base set consists of 100 Veterans (1-100), and 30 Rookies (101-130) that are individually serial numbered to 1500. Each pack contained 5 cards, and had a suggested retail price of $2.99.
COMPLETE SET w/o RC (100) 20.00 40.00
1 Vince Carter .75 2.00
2 Glenn Robinson .30 .75
3 Rasheed Wallace .40 1.00
4 Michael Dickerson .25 .60
5 Mikki Moore RC .40 1.00
6 Wally Szczerbiak .30 .75
7 Shawn Marion .40 1.00
8 Dan Majerle .30 .75
9 Trajan Langdon .25 .60
10 Chauncey Billups .40 1.00
11 Jason Kidd .60 1.50
12 Derrick Coleman .30 .75
13 Jason Terry .40 1.00
14 Eddie Jones .40 1.00
15 Scottie Pippen .60 1.50
16 Mike Bibby .40 1.00
17 Ron Mercer .25 .60
18 Hakeem Olajuwon .50 1.25
19 Patrick Ewing .50 1.25
20 Ruben Patterson .25 .60
21 Kenny Anderson .30 .75
22 Alonzo Mourning .50 1.25
23 Steve Smith .30 .75
24 Juwan Howard .30 .75
25 Antoine Walker .30 .75
26 Kobe Bryant 2.00 5.00
27 Chris Webber .40 1.00
28 Mitch Richmond .30 .75
29 Paul Pierce .50 1.25
30 Shaquille O'Neal 1.00 2.50
31 Jason Williams .40 1.00
32 Richard Hamilton .30 .75
33 Michael Finley .40 1.00
34 Jalen Rose .30 .75
35 Grant Hill .50 1.25
36 John Stockton .50 1.25
37 Vitaly Potapenko .25 .60
38 Glen Rice .30 .75
39 Vlade Divac .30 .75
40 Jahidi White .25 .60
41 Baron Davis .40
42 Michael Olowokandi .25
43 Tim Duncan .75
44 Rod Strickland .30
45 Jamal Mashburn .30
46 Lamar Odom .40
47 David Robinson .60
48 Travis Best .25
49 Raef LaFrentz .25
50 Keith Van Horn .30
51 Vonteego Cummings .25
52 Jerome Williams .25
53 Kevin Garnett .75
54 Anfernee Hardaway .60
55 Antonio McDyess .30
56 Reggie Miller .40
57 Tracy McGrady .60
58 Bryon Russell .25
59 Nick Van Exel .30
60 Allen Iverson .75
61 Karl Malone .50
62 David Wesley .25
63 Bob Sura .25
64 Stephon Marbury .30
65 Antonio Daniels .25
66 Shawn Kemp .40
67 Cuttino Mobley .30
68 Marcus Camby .30
69 Gary Payton .40
70 Dikembe Mutombo .40
71 Tim Hardaway .40
72 Bonzi Wells .25
73 Shareef Abdur-Rahim .30
74 Brevin Knight .25
75 Steve Francis .40
76 Allan Houston .30
77 Dion Glover .25
78 Dirk Nowitzki .60
79 Jonathan Bender .25
80 Darrell Armstrong .25
81 Antonio Davis .25
82 Jerry Stackhouse .30
83 Terrell Brandon .25
84 Tom Gugliotta .25
85 Sean Elliott .30
86 Elton Brand .40
87 Larry Hughes .30
88 Kerry Kittles .25
89 Vin Baker .30
90 Donyell Marshall .25
91 Tim Thomas .25
92 Toni Kukoc .30
93 Charles Oakley .30
94 Andre Miller .30
95 Austin Croshere .25
96 Latrell Sprewell .30
97 Mark Jackson .30
98 Antawn Jamison .40
99 Ray Allen .40
100 Theo Ratliff .25
101 Chris Mihm RC 1.50
102 Mateen Cleaves RC 1.50
103 Etan Thomas RC 1.50
104 Morris Peterson RC 1.50
105 Jamal Crawford RC 2.50
106 Darius Miles RC 1.50
107 Desmond Mason RC 2.00
108 Joel Przybilla RC 1.50
109 Mike Miller RC 3.00
110 Quentin Richardson RC 2.50
111 Jason Collier RC 1.50
112 Keyon Dooling RC 1.50
113 Courtney Alexander RC 1.50
114 Eddie House RC 1.50
115 DerMarr Johnson RC 1.50
116 Michael Redd RC 4.00
117 Mark Madsen RC 1.50
118 Stromile Swift RC 1.50
119 Mamadou N'Diaye RC 1.50
120 DeShawn Stevenson RC 2.00
121 Hedo Turkoglu RC 3.00
122 Stephen Jackson RC 2.50
123 Marcus Fizer RC 1.50
124 Khalid El-Amin RC 1.50
125 Speedy Claxton RC 1.50
126 Hanno Mottola RC 1.50
127 Jerome Moiso RC 1.50
128 Jamaal Magloire RC 1.50
129 Donnell Harvey RC 1.50
130 Kenyon Martin RC 4.00
NNO Vince Carter Main Man 15.00
NNO Vince Carter Main Man AU 200.00

2000-01 Fleer Genuine Formidable

Randomly inserted into packs at one in 23, this 15-card insert features some of the hottest players in the league. Card backs carry a "F" prefix.
COMPLETE SET (15) 20.00
F1 Vince Carter 2.00
F2 Lamar Odom 1.00
F3 Tracy McGrady 1.50
F4 Jason Williams 1.00
F5 Jason Kidd 1.50
F6 Chris Webber 1.00
F7 Elton Brand 1.00
F8 Steve Francis 1.00
F9 Grant Hill 1.25
F10 Shaquille O'Neal 2.50
F11 Allen Iverson 2.00
F12 Kobe Bryant 5.00
F13 Tim Duncan 2.00
F14 Kevin Garnett 2.00
F15 Latrell Sprewell .75

0-01 Fleer Genuine Genuine Coverage Plus

...nly inserted into packs, this 9-card set features ...es from actual game-worn jerseys. Card backs ... numbered, but are listed below in alphabetical ...r convenience.

...e Carter 10.00 25.00
...Malone 6.00 15.00
...n Marion 5.00 12.00
...r Odom 5.00 12.00
...uille O'Neal 12.00 30.00
...Pierce 6.00 15.00
...l Robinson 8.00 20.00
...ne Walker 4.00 10.00

0-01 Fleer Genuine Northern Flights

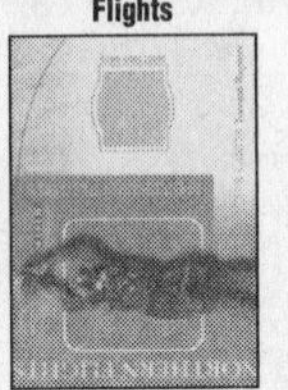

...nly inserted into packs at one in 22, this six-...sert features cards of high-flying Vince Carter. ...acks carry a "NF" prefix. Please note that there is ...n autographed Vince Carter card in this set that is ...bered but serial numbered to 150.

...PLETE SET (5) 25.00 60.00
...MON CARD (NF1-NF5) 6.00 15.00
...Vince Carter AU/150 20.00 50.00

0-01 Fleer Genuine Smooth Operators

...mly inserted into packs at one in 23, this 15-...nsert features players that are as smooth as ice ...court. Card backs carry a "SO" prefix.

...LETE SET (15) 15.00 30.00
Vince Carter 2.00 5.00
...amar Odom 1.00 2.50
Allen Iverson 2.00 5.00
Kobe Bryant 5.00 12.00
Kevin Garnett 2.00 5.00
Tim Duncan 2.00 5.00
Antawn Jamison 1.00 2.50
Michael Finley 1.00 2.50
Ray Allen 1.00 2.50
Paul Pierce 1.25 3.00
Karl Malone 1.25 3.00
Shaquille O'Neal 2.50 6.00
Elton Brand 1.00 2.50
Jason Williams 1.00 2.50
Jalen Rose .75 2.00

0-01 Fleer Genuine Yes Men

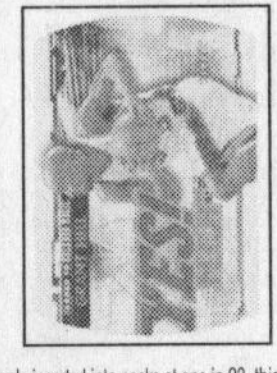

...omly inserted into packs at one in 23, this 10-...nsert features players that do what it takes to win. ...backs carry a "Y" prefix.

...PLETE SET (10) 8.00 20.00
...nce Carter 1.50 4.00
...amar Odom .75 2.00
...obe Bryant 4.00 10.00
...evin Garnett 1.50 4.00
...m Duncan 1.50 4.00
...ddie Jones .75 2.00
...llan Houston .60 1.50
...rant Hill 1.00 2.50
...ton Brand .75 2.00
...Steve Francis .75 2.00

2001-02 Fleer Genuine

...ased in mid October 2001, this 150-card base set ...ade up of holofoil card stock on standard size ...s. Each card is borderless, but has a drawn box ...ning a color action shot of the featured player. The ...er's team name runs down the left-side of the card ...the player's name runs horizontal across the bottom of the card. The set contains 120 veteran players and 30 rookies sequentially numbered to 1000 on the card back. Genuine was packaged in 24 pack boxes with each pack conatining five cards.

COMPLETE SET (150) 75.00 150.00
COMP.SET w/o SP's (120) 12.50 30.00
1 Larry Hughes .30 .75
2 Wally Szczerbiak .30 .75
3 Jahidi White .25 .60
4 Aaron McKie .25 .60
5 Antonio McDyess .30 .75
6 Tom Gugliotta .25 .60
7 Elton Brand .40 1.00
8 Lamar Odom .40 1.00
9 Chris Webber .40 1.00
10 Ron Artest .40 1.00
11 Gary Payton .40 1.00
12 Brian Grant .25 .60
13 Steve Nash .60 1.50
14 DerMarr Johnson .25 .60
15 Vince Carter .60 1.50
16 Kurt Thomas .25 .60
17 Cuttino Mobley .30 .75
18 Marc Jackson .25 .60
19 Stromile Swift .25 .60
20 Grant Hill .50 1.25
21 Raef LaFrentz .25 .60
22 Marcus Fizer .25 .60
23 Antonio Davis .25 .60
24 John Starks .25 .60
25 Trajan Langdon .25 .60
26 Jason Williams .30 .75
27 Toni Kukoc .30 .75
28 Morris Peterson .25 .60
29 Allen Iverson .75 2.00
30 Andre Miller .25 .60
31 Larry Johnson .40 1.00
32 Vitaly Potapenko .25 .60
33 Tim Thomas .25 .60
34 Eddie House .25 .60
35 Juwan Howard .30 .75
36 Joel Przybilla .25 .60
37 John Stockton .50 1.25
38 Michael Finley .40 1.00
39 Hedo Turkoglu .40 1.00
40 Keith Van Horn .40 1.00
41 Shawn Marion .40 1.00
42 Derek Fisher .30 .75
43 Terrell Brandon .25 .60
44 Jamal Mashburn .30 .75
45 Shareef Abdur-Rahim .30 .75
46 Brevin Knight .25 .60
47 Antoine Walker .30 .75
48 Mateen Cleaves .25 .60
49 Alonzo Mourning .50 1.25
50 Jermaine O'Neal .40 1.00
51 Kenyon Martin .40 1.00
52 Steve Smith .30 .75
53 Jerry Stackhouse .30 .75
54 Mike Bibby .40 1.00
55 Latrell Sprewell .30 .75
56 Iakovos Tsakalidis .25 .60
57 Sam Cassell .30 .75
58 Michael Dickerson .25 .60
59 Alan Henderson .25 .60
60 Allan Houston .30 .75
61 Patrick Ewing .50 1.25
62 Joe Smith .30 .75
63 Rick Fox .30 .75
64 Tracy McGrady .60 1.50
65 Scottie Pippen .60 1.50
66 Chauncey Billups .40 1.00
67 Voshon Lenard .25 .60
68 Jalen Rose .30 .75
69 Derrick Coleman .30 .75
70 Shaquille O'Neal 1.00 2.50
71 Anfernee Hardaway .60 1.50
72 Derek Anderson .25 .60
73 Travis Best .25 .60
74 Darius Miles .25 .60
75 Glenn Robinson .30 .75
76 Darrell Armstrong .25 .60
77 Dirk Nowitzki .60 1.50
78 Stephon Marbury .30 .75
79 Tyronn Lue .25 .60
80 Bonzi Wells .25 .60
81 Mike Miller .40 1.00
82 Tim Duncan .75 2.00
83 Tim Hardaway .40 1.00
84 Desmond Mason .30 .75
85 Ray Allen .40 1.00
86 Sean Elliott .25 .60
87 David Wesley .25 .60
88 Rasheed Wallace .40 1.00
89 Kevin Garnett .75 2.00
90 Dikembe Mutombo .40 1.00
91 Baron Davis .40 1.00
92 Donyell Marshall .25 .60
93 Eddie Jones .30 .75
94 Vin Baker .30 .75
95 Peja Stojakovic .40 1.00
96 Antawn Jamison .40 1.00
97 Maurice Taylor .25 .60
98 Courtney Alexander .25 .60
99 Steve Francis .40 1.00
100 Chris Mihm .25 .60
101 Kobe Bryant 2.00 5.00
102 Hakeem Olajuwon .50 1.25
103 Richard Hamilton .30 .75
104 Karl Malone .50 1.25
105 Chucky Atkins .25 .60
106 Eric Snow .25 .60
107 Ruben Patterson .25 .60
108 David Robinson .60 1.50
109 Bryon Russell .25 .60
110 Jason Terry .40 1.00
111 Jason Kidd .60 1.50
112 Charles Oakley .30 .75
113 Wang Zhizhi .30 .75
114 Quentin Richardson .30 .75
115 Clarence Weatherspoon .25 .60
116 Nick Van Exel .30 .75
117 Reggie Miller .40 1.00
118 Marcus Camby .30 .75
119 Corey Maggette .30 .75
120 Paul Pierce .50 1.25
121 Kwame Brown RC 1.25 3.00
122 Eddie Griffin RC 1.25 3.00
123 Eddy Curry RC 2.00 5.00
124 Jamaal Tinsley RC 1.50 4.00
125 Jason Richardson RC 2.50 6.00
126 Shane Battier RC 2.50 6.00
127 Troy Murphy RC 2.00 5.00
128 Richard Jefferson RC 2.50 6.00
129 DeSagana Diop RC 1.25 3.00
130 Tyson Chandler RC 2.00 5.00
131 Joe Johnson RC 3.00 8.00
132 Zach Randolph RC 3.00 8.00
133 Gerald Wallace RC 2.00 5.00
134 Loren Woods RC 1.25 3.00
135 Jason Collins RC 1.25 3.00
136 Rodney White RC 1.25 3.00
137 Jeryl Sasser RC 1.25 3.00
138 Kirk Haston RC 1.25 3.00
139 Pau Gasol RC 4.00 10.00
140 Kedrick Brown RC 1.25 3.00
141 Steven Hunter RC 1.25 3.00
142 Michael Bradley RC 1.25 3.00
143 Joseph Forte RC 1.25 3.00
144 Brandon Armstrong RC 1.25 3.00
145 Samuel Dalembert RC 1.50 4.00
146 Trenton Hassell RC 1.25 3.00
147 Gilbert Arenas RC 2.00 5.00
148 Omar Cook RC 1.25 3.00
149 Tony Parker RC 5.00 12.00
150 Terence Morris RC 1.25 3.00

2001-02 Fleer Genuine At Large

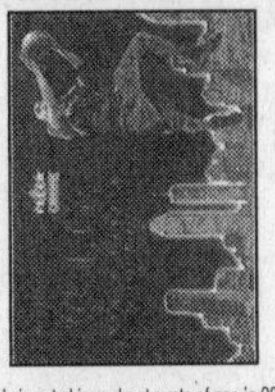

Randomly inserted in packs at a rate of one in 23, this 15-card insert set was designed horizontally on standard size cards. Each card background features a glowing city skyline of the player's corresponding team. The player stands in the forefront of the card outsizing the skyline.

COMPLETE SET (15) 20.00 40.00
AL1 Vince Carter 1.50 4.00
AL2 Dirk Nowitzki 1.50 4.00
AL3 Courtney Alexander .60 1.50
AL4 Jason Williams .75 2.00
AL5 Reggie Miller 1.00 2.50
AL6 Chris Webber 1.00 2.50
AL7 Elton Brand 1.00 2.50
AL8 Peja Stojakovic 1.00 2.50
AL9 Ray Allen 1.00 2.50
AL10 Shaquille O'Neal 2.50 6.00
AL11 Kevin Garnett 2.00 5.00
AL12 Kobe Bryant 5.00 12.00
AL13 Tim Duncan 2.00 5.00
AL14 Antawn Jamison 1.00 2.50
AL15 Latrell Sprewell .75 2.00

2001-02 Fleer Genuine Coverage Plus

Randomly inserted in packs at a rate of one in 24, this "Plus" insert set offers pieces of the featured player's game-worn jerseys. The cards have a horizontal design on standard size cards. White borders are present with an inside colored box highlighting the featured player. The player's name and team name run horizontal along the bottom edge and a circular swatch of a game worn uniform is placed in the lower left hand corner.

1 Shareef Abdur-Rahim 2.50 6.00
2 Darrell Armstrong 2.00 5.00
3 Mike Bibby 3.00 8.00
4 Vince Carter 5.00 12.00
5 Vince Carter Warm 5.00 12.00
6 Michael Dickerson 2.00 5.00
7 Patrick Ewing 4.00 10.00
8 Steve Francis 3.00 8.00
9 Richard Hamilton 2.50 6.00
10 Anfernee Hardaway 5.00 12.00
11 Grant Hill 4.00 10.00
12 DerMarr Johnson 2.00 5.00
13 Jason Kidd 5.00 12.00
14 Rashard Lewis 3.00 8.00
15 Corey Maggette 2.50 6.00
16 Stephon Marbury 2.50 6.00
17 Shawn Marion 3.00 8.00
18 Kenyon Martin 3.00 8.00
19 Tracy McGrady 5.00 12.00
20 Mike Miller 3.00 8.00
21 Lamar Odom 3.00 8.00
22 Quentin Richardson 2.50 6.00
23 Jerry Stackhouse 2.50 6.00
24 Keith Van Horn 2.50 6.00

2001-02 Fleer Genuine Final Cut

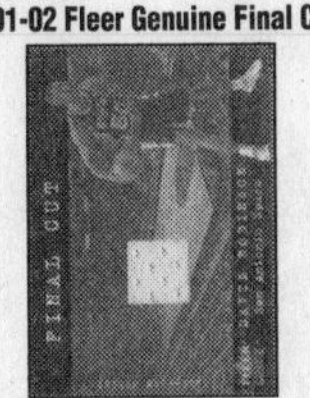

Randomly inserted in packs at a rate of one in 24, this 35-card insert set features square swatches of game-worn jerseys from the featured player. Full color player photos appear on the left while the top and bottom edge of this horizontal set design are black and contain the player's name and team. A black and white photo of a basketball arena appears in the background.

1 Shareef Abdur-Rahim 2.50 6.00
2 Vince Carter 5.00 12.00
3 Baron Davis 3.00 8.00
4 Sean Elliott 2.00 5.00
5 Patrick Ewing 4.00 10.00
6 Michael Finley 3.00 8.00
7 Anfernee Hardaway 5.00 12.00
8 Grant Hill 4.00 10.00
9 Allan Houston 2.50 6.00
10 Allen Iverson 6.00 15.00
11 Jason Kidd 5.00 12.00
12 Tyronn Lue 2.00 5.00
13 Karl Malone 4.00 10.00
14 Stephon Marbury 2.50 6.00
15 Shawn Marion 3.00 8.00
16 Kenyon Martin 3.00 8.00
17 Desmond Mason 2.50 6.00
18 Tracy McGrady 5.00 12.00
19 Mike Miller 3.00 8.00
20 Andre Miller 2.50 6.00
21 Alonzo Mourning 4.00 10.00
22 Lamar Odom 3.00 8.00
23 Gary Payton 3.00 8.00
24 Paul Pierce 4.00 10.00
25 Quentin Richardson 2.50 6.00
26 David Robinson 5.00 12.00
27 Glenn Robinson 2.50 6.00
28 John Stockton 4.00 10.00
29 Stromile Swift 2.00 5.00
30 Wally Szczerbiak 2.50 6.00
31 Jason Terry 3.00 8.00
32 Keith Van Horn 2.50 6.00
33 Antoine Walker 2.50 6.00
34 David Wesley 2.00 5.00
35 Jason Williams 2.50 6.00

2001-02 Fleer Genuine Names of the Game

Randomly inserted in packs at a rate of one in 26, this 15-card insert set pays homage to the various nicknames of NBA players and includes swatches of their game-worn jerseys. The standard size cards are horizontally designed with top and bottom borders. The player's name and team name are found in the center of the card with a color player photo on the left and the player's team logo on the right.

1 Shareef Abdur-Rahim 2.50 6.00
2 Vince Carter 5.00 12.00
3 Steve Francis 3.00 8.00
4 Anfernee Hardaway 5.00 12.00
5 Allen Iverson 6.00 15.00
6 Jason Kidd 5.00 12.00
7 Karl Malone 4.00 10.00
8 Tracy McGrady 5.00 12.00
9 Dikembe Mutombo 3.00 8.00
10 Hakeem Olajuwon 4.00 10.00
11 Gary Payton 3.00 8.00
12 Morris Peterson 2.00 5.00
13 David Robinson 5.00 12.00
14 Glenn Robinson 2.50 6.00
15 Chris Webber 3.00 8.00

2001-02 Fleer Genuine Names of the Game Autographs

Randomly inserted in packs, this five card set parallels the base Names of the Game insert enhanced with authentic player autographs. Each card is sequentially numbered to 100, and upon release, Shareef Abdur-Rahim was the only card not issued as an exchange.

1 Dikembe Mutombo 20.00 50.00
2 Hakeem Olajuwon 25.00 60.00
3 Shareef Abdur-Rahim 8.00 20.00
4 Vince Carter 25.00 60.00

2001-02 Fleer Genuine Skywalkers

Randomly inserted in packs at a rate of one in 23, this 15-card set has silver backgrounds with both a player action photo on the right and a portrait gray-scale photo on the left. The player's name and team name appear along the bottom in foil, and the word "Skywalkers" appears in blue.

COMPLETE SET (15) 15.00 30.00
SW1 Vince Carter 1.50 4.00
SW2 Lamar Odom 1.00 2.50
SW3 Shawn Marion 1.00 2.50
SW4 Kobe Bryant 5.00 12.00
SW5 Kevin Garnett 2.00 5.00
SW6 Tim Duncan 2.00 5.00
SW7 Antawn Jamison 1.00 2.50
SW8 Michael Finley 1.00 2.50
SW9 Ray Allen 1.00 2.50
SW10 Paul Pierce 1.25 3.00
SW11 Baron Davis 1.00 2.50
SW12 Antoine Walker .75 2.00
SW13 Desmond Mason .75 2.00
SW14 Jason Williams .75 2.00
SW15 Darius Miles .60 1.50

2001-02 Fleer Genuine Unstoppable

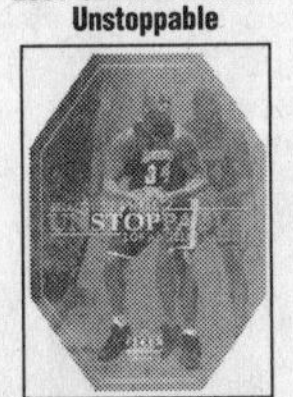

Randomly inserted in packs at the rate of one in 23, this 10-card die cut set appears as a "stretched" stopsign. The backgrounds are red and feature a full color player action photo as well as a gray scale "shadow" of the same picture in the background.

US1 Vince Carter 1.25 3.00
US2 Darius Miles .50 1.25
US3 Shaquille O'Neal 2.00 5.00
US4 Jerry Stackhouse .60 1.50
US5 Tim Duncan 1.50 4.00
US6 Eddie Jones .60 1.50
US7 Jason Kidd 1.25 3.00
US8 Glenn Robinson .60 1.50
US9 Elton Brand .75 2.00
US10 Dirk Nowitzki 1.25 3.00

2002-03 Fleer Genuine

Released in late August 2002, Fleer Genuine boasts a 135-card set comprised of 100 veteran players and 35 rookies sequentially numbered to 2002. The base cards have have "wooded" printed borders with a player photo set in the middle. The bottom edge of the card is solid colored and contains the player's name and team in foil. Upon initial release several of the rookies were available via redemption only. Fleer Genuine was packaged in 24-pack boxes where packs contained five cards and carried a suggested retail price of $2.99.

COMPLETE SET (135) 100.00 200.00
COMP.SET w/o SP's (100) 20.00 40.00
1 Shaquille O'Neal .75 2.00
2 Allen Iverson .50 1.25
3 Jerry Stackhouse .25 .60
4 Kobe Bryant 1.50 4.00
5 Jason Kidd .50 1.25
6 Andre Miller .25 .60
7 David Robinson .50 1.25
8 John Stockton .40 1.00
9 Glenn Robinson .25 .60
10 Chauncey Billups .30 .75
11 Chris Webber .30 .75
12 Antawn Jamison .30 .75
13 Sam Cassell .25 .60
14 Vlade Divac .25 .60
15 P.J. Brown .20 .50
16 Robert Horry .20 .50
17 Eric Snow .20 .50
18 Popeye Jones .20 .50
19 Paul Pierce .40 1.00
20 Eddie Griffin .20 .50
21 Marcus Camby .25 .60
22 Gary Payton .25 .60
23 Michael Jordan 2.50 6.00
24 Shareef Abdur-Rahim .25 .60
25 Anfernee Hardaway .50 1.25
26 Michael Finley .30 .75
27 Steve Nash .40 1.00
28 Shane Battier .30 .75
29 Stephon Marbury .25 .60
30 Dirk Nowitzki .50 1.25
31 Pau Gasol .40 1.00
32 Shawn Marion .20 .50
33 Rodney Rogers .20 .50
34 Steve Smith .25 .60
35 Darrell Armstrong .20 .50
36 Alvin Williams .20 .50
37 Nick Van Exel .25 .60
38 Jason Williams .25 .60
39 Ruben Patterson .20 .50
40 Juwan Howard .25 .60
41 Brian Grant .25 .60
42 Damon Stoudamire .25 .60
43 Antonio McDyess .25 .60
44 Eddie Jones .25 .60
45 Rasheed Wallace .30 .75
46 Larry Hughes .25 .60
47 Wally Szczerbiak .25 .60
48 Tony Parker .40 1.00
49 Ron Artest .30 .75
50 Kevin Garnett .60 1.50
51 Tim Duncan .60 1.50
52 Marcus Fizer .20 .50
53 Darius Miles .20 .50
54 Grant Hill .40 1.00
55 Andrei Kirilenko .30 .75
56 Jalen Rose .25 .60
57 Lamar Odom .25 .60
58 Tracy McGrady .50 1.25
59 Karl Malone .40 1.00
60 Jason Terry .25 .60
61 Steve Francis .30 .75
62 Kenyon Martin .25 .60
63 Brent Barry .20 .50
64 Antoine Walker .25 .60
65 Reggie Miller .30 .75
66 Allan Houston .25 .60
67 Vince Carter .50 1.25
68 Toni Kukoc .25 .60
69 Lamond Murray .20 .50
70 Jason Richardson .30 .75
71 Rick Fox .20 .50
72 Kerry Kittles .20 .50
73 Dikembe Mutombo .30 .75
74 Tyson Chandler .25 .60
75 Richard Hamilton .25 .60
76 Elden Campbell .20 .50
77 Jermaine O'Neal .30 .75
78 Mike Miller .30 .75
79 Morris Peterson .20 .50
80 Jamal Mashburn .20 .50
81 Elton Brand .30 .75
82 Kurt Thomas .20 .50
83 Antonio Davis .20 .50
84 Ben Wallace .30 .75
85 Anthony Mason .20 .50
86 Peja Stojakovic .30 .75
87 Kenny Anderson .25 .60
88 Cuttino Mobley .25 .60
89 Keith Van Horn .25 .60
90 Rashard Lewis .30 .75
91 Clifford Robinson .20 .50
92 Ray Allen .30 .75
93 Mike Bibby .30 .75
94 Baron Davis .30 .75
95 Jamaal Tinsley .25 .60
96 Latrell Sprewell .25 .60
97 Jon Barry .20 .50
98 Desmond Mason .25 .60
99 Alonzo Mourning .40 1.00
100 Bonzi Wells .20 .50
101 Jay Williams RC 2.00 5.00
102 Mike Dunleavy RC 2.00 5.00
103 Amare Stoudemire RC 4.00 10.00
104 Caron Butler RC 2.50 6.00
105 Jared Jeffries RC 1.50 4.00
106 Fred Jones RC 1.50 4.00
107 Bostjan Nachbar RC 1.50 4.00
108 Jiri Welsch RC 1.50 4.00
109 Juan Dixon RC 2.00 5.00
110 Curtis Borchardt RC 1.50 4.00
111 Kareem Rush RC 1.50 4.00
112 Qyntel Woods RC 1.50 4.00
113 Casey Jacobsen RC 1.50 4.00
114 Frank Williams RC 1.50 4.00
115 John Salmons RC 2.00 5.00
116 Dan Dickau RC 1.50 4.00
117 DaJuan Wagner RC 1.50 4.00
118 Drew Gooden RC 2.50 6.00
119 Nikoloz Tskitishvili RC 1.50 4.00
120 Yao Ming RC 5.00 12.00
121 Nene Hilario RC 2.00 5.00
122 Chris Wilcox RC 1.50 4.00
123 Melvin Ely RC 1.50 4.00
124 Marcus Haislip RC 1.50 4.00
125 Ryan Humphrey RC 1.50 4.00
126 Tayshaun Prince RC 2.00 5.00
127 Tito Maddox RC 1.50 4.00
128 Chris Jefferies RC 1.50 4.00
129 Manu Ginobili RC 4.00 10.00
130 Roger Mason RC 1.50 4.00
131 Robert Archibald RC 1.50 4.00
132 Vincent Yarbrough RC 1.50 4.00
133 Dan Gadzuric RC 1.50 4.00
134 Carlos Boozer RC 3.00 8.00
135 Rasual Butler RC 1.50 4.00

2002-03 Fleer Genuine Coverage

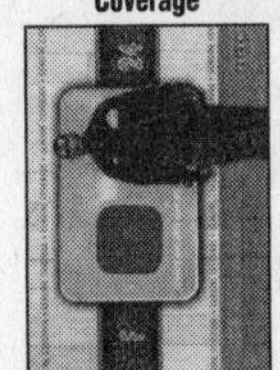

Randomly seeded in packs at the rate of one in 24, this 15-card set features a horizontal card design with printed "wood" borders along the top and bottom and a gray strip through the center. On this strip appears a player photo on the right and a rectangular swatch of memorabilia. Each card is enhanced with silver foil highlights. A gold version also packed out with the product where each card is sequentially numbered to 100.

*GOLD: .6X TO 1.5X HI
1 Vince Carter 5.00 12.00
2 Michael Dickerson 2.00 5.00
3 Keyon Dooling 2.00 5.00
4 Michael Finley 3.00 8.00
5 Tom Gugliotta 2.00 5.00
6 Richard Hamilton 2.50 6.00
7 Anfernee Hardaway 5.00 12.00
8 Grant Hill 4.00 10.00
9 DerMarr Johnson 2.00 5.00
10 Rashard Lewis 3.00 8.00
11 Antonio McDyess 2.50 6.00
12 Desmond Mason 2.50 6.00
13 Lamar Odom 3.00 8.00
14 Keith Van Horn 2.50 6.00
15 Antoine Walker 2.50 6.00

2002-03 Fleer Genuine Global Warning

Randomly inserted in pack at the rate of one in 12, this 10-card set showcases the top foreign players of the NBA. The bottom of the card background is a globe, the middle of the card contains silver foil highlights with the set name and player's name, above this appears the player's photo, and the top of the card fades to black.

COMPLETE SET (10) 5.00 12.00
1 Tim Duncan 1.25 3.00
2 Pau Gasol .75 2.00
3 Andrei Kirilenko .60 1.50
4 Patrick Ewing .75 2.00
5 Dikembe Mutombo .60 1.50
6 Steve Nash .75 2.00
7 Hakeem Olajuwon .75 2.00
8 Tony Parker .75 2.00
9 Dirk Nowitzki 1.00 2.50
10 Peja Stojakovic .60 1.50

2002-03 Fleer Genuine Global Warning Jersey

Randomly seeded in packs at the rate of one in 30, this six card set parallels the design of the base Global Warning insert set enhanced with a circular swatch of jersey at the bottom.

1 Pau Gasol 4.00 10.00
2 Andrei Kirilenko 3.00 8.00
3 Patrick Ewing 4.00 10.00
4 Dikembe Mutombo 3.00 8.00
5 Tony Parker 4.00 10.00
6 Peja Stojakovic 3.00 8.00

2002-03 Fleer Genuine Leaders

Randomly inserted in packs at the rate of one in 24, this 15-card set features a horizontal card design with an in-action player photo along the right of the card and an open space on the left. The background colors of the card are set to match the featured player's team colors.

COMPLETE SET (15) 15.00 40.00
1 Allen Iverson 1.50 4.00
2 Shaquille O'Neal 2.50 6.00
3 Paul Pierce 1.25 3.00
4 Tracy McGrady 1.50 4.00
5 Tim Duncan 2.00 5.00
6 Kobe Bryant 5.00 12.00
7 Vince Carter 1.50 4.00
8 Dirk Nowitzki 1.50 4.00
9 Michael Jordan 8.00 20.00
10 Steve Francis 1.00 2.50
11 Karl Malone 1.25 3.00
12 Elton Brand 1.00 2.50
13 Andre Miller .75 2.00
14 Jason Kidd 1.50 4.00
15 Baron Davis 1.00 2.50

2002-03 Fleer Genuine Leaders Jerseys

Randomly inserted in packs at the rate of one in 40, this 15-card set features a horizontal card design with an in-action player photo along the right of the card and a jersey swatch on the left. The top border of the card is in dark colors and the player's face appears just below. A Gold version sequentially numbered to 25 was inserted into packs as well.

*GOLD: 1.25X TO 3X HI
1 Allen Iverson 5.00 12.00
2 Paul Pierce 4.00 10.00
3 Tracy McGrady 5.00 12.00
4 Vince Carter 5.00 12.00
5 Steve Francis 3.00 8.00
6 Karl Malone 4.00 10.00
7 Elton Brand 3.00 8.00
8 Andre Miller 2.50 6.00
9 Jason Kidd 5.00 12.00
10 Baron Davis 3.00 8.00

2002-03 Fleer Genuine Names of the Game

Randomly inserted in packs at the rate of one in 12, this 15-card set features all white borders, a color player photo and silver foil highlights through the center of the card containing the set name and player's name.

COMPLETE SET (15) 10.00 25.00
1 Kobe Bryant 3.00 8.00
2 Ray Allen .60 1.50
3 Tracy McGrady 1.00 2.50
4 John Stockton .75 2.00
5 Paul Pierce .75 2.00
6 Allen Iverson 1.00 2.50
7 Michael Jordan 5.00 12.00
8 Vince Carter 1.00 2.50
9 Shaquille O'Neal 1.50 4.00
10 David Robinson 1.00 2.50
11 Kevin Garnett 1.25 3.00
12 Jason Kidd 1.00 2.50
13 Chris Webber .60 1.50
14 Ben Wallace .60 1.50
15 Shawn Marion .60 1.50

2002-03 Fleer Genuine Names of the Game Jerseys

Randomly inserted in packs at the rate of one in 30, this 10-card set parallels the design of the base Names of the Game insert set enhanced with a centered rectangular swatch of game worn memorabilia.

*GOLD: 1X TO 2.5X HI
GOLD: STATED PRINT RUN 50 SER.#'d SETS
1 Ray Allen 3.00 8.00
2 Tracy McGrady 5.00 12.00
3 John Stockton 4.00 10.00
4 Paul Pierce 4.00 10.00
5 Allen Iverson 5.00 12.00
6 Vince Carter 5.00 12.00
7 David Robinson 5.00 12.00

8 Jason Kidd 5.00 12.00
9 Chris Webber 3.00 8.00
10 Shawn Marion 3.00 8.00

2002-03 Fleer Genuine On the Up

Randomly inserted in packs at the rate of one in 12, this 15-card set features a die cut design in the shape of an arrow. The borders of the card are black, and the bottom contains silver foil highlights and the words, "On the Up" in white. Full color player action photos appear towards the top of the card in the middle of the arrow.

COMPLETE SET (15) 5.00 12.00
1 Pau Gasol .75 2.00
2 Jamaal Tinsley .40 1.00
3 Jason Richardson .60 1.50
4 Tony Parker .75 2.00
5 Shane Battier .60 1.50
6 Andrei Kirilenko .60 1.50
7 Kenyon Martin .60 1.50
8 Gilbert Arenas .60 1.50
9 Mike Miller .60 1.50
10 Darius Miles .40 1.00
11 Stromile Swift .40 1.00
12 Marcus Fizer .40 1.00
13 Iakovos Tsakalidis .40 1.00
14 Richard Jefferson .60 1.50
15 Speedy Claxton .40 1.00

2002-03 Fleer Genuine On the Up Jerseys

Randomly seeded in packs at the rate of one in 36, this eight card set parallels the base design of the On the Up insert set enhanced with a square swatch of game worn memorabilia.

1 Jason Richardson 3.00 8.00
2 Shane Battier 3.00 8.00
3 Kenyon Martin 3.00 8.00
4 Mike Miller 3.00 8.00
5 Darius Miles 2.00 5.00
6 Stromile Swift 2.00 5.00
7 Richard Jefferson 3.00 8.00
8 Speedy Claxton 2.00 5.00

2002-03 Fleer Genuine Prime Time Players

Randomly inserted in packs at the rate of one in 288, this 10-card set features a horizontal design with a light background. Player action photos appear on the left side of the card, and right below this photo, the player's number appears. The top right side of the card contains the words "Prime Time Players" in gold and the player's name and team name in the lower right hand corner.

COMPLETE SET (10) 40.00 100.00
1 Shaquille O'Neal 6.00 15.00
2 Allen Iverson 4.00 10.00
3 Vince Carter 4.00 10.00
4 Michael Jordan 25.00 60.00
5 Tracy McGrady 4.00 10.00
6 Tim Duncan 5.00 12.00
7 Kevin Garnett 5.00 12.00
8 Dirk Nowitzki 4.00 10.00
9 Paul Pierce 3.00 8.00
10 Kobe Bryant 12.00 30.00

2002-03 Fleer Genuine Prime Time Players Jerseys

Randomly seeded in packs at the rate of one in 300, this five card set parallels the design of the base Prime Time Players set enhanced with a square swatch of game used memorabilia.

1 Allen Iverson 6.00 15.00
2 Vince Carter 6.00 15.00
3 Tracy McGrady 6.00 15.00
4 Dirk Nowitzki 6.00 15.00
5 Paul Pierce 5.00 12.00

2003-04 Fleer Genuine Insider

Released in February 2004, Genuine Insider features a 140-card set divided up into 100 veteran player cards, 10 rookie cards sequentially numbered to 499 (cards 101-110), 20 rookie cards sequentially numbered to 799 (cards 111-130), and 10 mini rookie cards sequentially numbered to 350 (cards 131-140). The mini cards are found as inserts inside cards 101-110, hence the product name, Insider. Base cards feature colored background with the main focus being color to match the player's team colors. Genuine Insider was packaged in 24-pack boxes where packs contained five cards and carried a suggested retail price of $4.99.

COMP.SET w/o SP's (100) 12.50 30.00
1 Shareef Abdur-Rahim .25 .60
2 Andre Miller .25 .60
3 Reggie Miller .30 .75
4 Michael Redd .30 .75
5 Allan Houston .25 .60
6 Mike Bibby .30 .75
7 Kwame Brown .20 .50
8 Earl Boykins .20 .50
9 Ron Artest .30 .75
10 Eddie Jones .25 .60
11 Zach Randolph .30 .75
12 Derek Anderson .20 .50
13 Andrei Kirilenko .30 .75
14 Carlos Boozer .30 .75
15 Yao Ming .60 1.50
16 Pau Gasol .30 .75
17 Jamal Mashburn .25 .60
18 Shawn Marion .30 .75
19 Vince Carter .50 1.25
20 Eddy Curry .25 .60
21 Mike Dunleavy Jr. .25 .60
22 Kobe Bryant 1.50 4.00
23 Tim Thomas .20 .50
24 Drew Gooden .25 .60
25 Tim Duncan .50 1.25
26 Dajuan Wagner .20 .50
27 Speedy Claxton .20 .50
28 Karl Malone .40 1.00
29 Jason Kidd .50 1.25
30 Kenny Thomas .20 .50
31 Vladimir Radmanovic .20 .50
32 Tyson Chandler .25 .60
33 Jason Richardson .30 .75
34 Quentin Richardson .25 .60
35 Kerry Kittles .20 .50
36 Derrick Coleman .25 .60
37 Manu Ginobili .40 1.00
38 Paul Pierce .40 1.00
39 Ben Wallace .30 .75
40 Corey Maggette .25 .60
41 Sam Cassell .25 .60
42 Hedo Turkoglu .30 .75
43 Peja Stojakovic .30 .75
44 Gilbert Arenas .30 .75
45 Dirk Nowitzki .50 1.25
46 Al Harrington .25 .60
47 Caron Butler .30 .75
48 Baron Davis .30 .75
49 Rasheed Wallace .30 .75
50 Morris Peterson .20 .50
51 Steve Nash .40 1.00
52 Steve Francis .30 .75
53 Lamar Odom .30 .75
54 Jamaal Magloire .20 .50
55 Amare Stoudemire .50 1.25
56 Antonio Davis .20 .50
57 Dan Dickau .20 .50
58 Cuttino Mobley .25 .60
59 Jason Williams .25 .60
60 David Wesley .20 .50
61 Stephon Marbury .25 .60
62 Ray Allen .30 .75
63 Scottie Pippen .50 1.25
64 Nick Van Exel .25 .60
65 Shaquille O'Neal .75 2.00
66 Richard Jefferson .30 .75
67 Allen Iverson .50 1.25
68 Tony Parker .30 .75
69 Jason Terry .25 .60
70 Nenê .25 .60
71 Marko Jaric .20 .50
72 Troy Hudson .20 .50
73 Malik Rose .20 .50
74 Bobby Jackson .20 .50
75 Jerry Stackhouse .25 .60
76 Voshon Lenard .20 .50
77 Richard Hamilton .25 .60
78 Scot Pollard .20 .50
79 Latrell Sprewell .25 .60
80 Tracy McGrady .40 1.00
81 Chris Webber .30 .75
82 Raef LaFrentz .20 .50
83 Tayshaun Prince .30 .75
84 Elton Brand .30 .75
85 Kevin Garnett .60 1.50
86 Keon Clark .20 .50
87 Brad Miller .30 .75
88 Alvin Williams .20 .50
89 Michael Finley .30 .75
90 Jermaine O'Neal .30 .75
91 Desmond Mason .25 .60
92 Keith Van Horn .25 .60
93 Bonzi Wells .20 .50
94 Matt Harpring .25 .60
95 Darius Miles .20 .50
96 Eddie Griffin .20 .50
97 Shane Battier .25 .60
98 Kenyon Martin .30 .75
99 Glenn Robinson .25 .60
100 Rashard Lewis .30 .75
101 Carmelo Anthony RC 6.00 15.00
102 Troy Bell RC 2.50 6.00
103 T.J. Ford RC 3.00 8.00
104 LeBron James RC 30.00 80.00
105 Mike Sweetney RC 2.50 6.00
106 Chris Bosh RC 5.00 12.00
107 Jarvis Hayes RC 2.50 6.00
108 Darko Milicic RC 2.50 6.00
109 Chris Kaman RC 3.00 8.00
110 Dwyane Wade RC 10.00 25.00
111 Udonis Haslem RC 2.50 6.00
112 Josh Howard RC 2.00 5.00
113 Mickael Pietrus RC 2.00 5.00
114 Reece Gaines RC 2.00 5.00
115 Nick Collison RC 2.00 5.00
116 Leandrinho Barbosa RC 2.50 6.00
117 Kendrick Perkins RC 3.00 8.00
118 Ndudi Ebi RC 2.00 5.00
119 Willie Green RC 2.00 5.00
120 Kirk Hinrich RC 2.50 6.00
121 Marcus Banks RC 2.00 5.00
122 Zarko Cabarkapa RC 2.00 5.00
123 Zoran Planinic RC 2.00 5.00
124 David West RC 2.50 6.00
125 Luke Ridnour RC 2.50 6.00
126 Brian Cook RC 2.00 5.00
127 Boris Diaw RC 2.50 6.00
128 Dahntay Jones RC 2.00 5.00
129 Maciej Lampe RC 2.00 5.00
130 Travis Outlaw RC 2.50 6.00
131 Ben Handlogten MM RC 2.00 5.00
132 Jerome Beasley MM RC 2.00 5.00
133 Marquis Daniels MM RC 2.00 5.00
134 Luke Walton MM RC 2.00 5.00
135 Aleksandar Pavlovic MM RC 2.00 5.00
136 Matt Carroll MM RC 2.00 5.00
137 Curtis Borchardt MM 2.00 5.00
138 Jason Kapono MM RC 2.00 5.00
139 Steve Blake MM RC 2.50 6.00
140 Keith Bogans MM RC 2.00 5.00

2003-04 Fleer Genuine Insider Reflections

Randomly seeded in packs, this 140-card set parallels the base set enhanced with sequential numbering to 99 for cards 1-130 and sequential numbering to 148 for cards 131-140.

*1-100 REF: 4X TO 10X BASE HI
*101-110 RC REF: .6X TO 1.5X BASE HI
*111-130 RC REF: .75X TO 2X BASE HI
*131-140 RC REF: .75X TO 2X BASE HI

2003-04 Fleer Genuine Insider Genuine Article Insider

Inserted in packs, this 19-card set utilizes a horizontal design with full color player photos on the left and a swatch of game worn memorabilia on the right. Each card is sequentially numbered to 400.

*PATCH: 1.25X TO 3X BASE HI
PATCH PRINT RUN 50 SER.#'d SETS
1 Baron Davis 2.50 6.00
2 Nene 2.00 5.00
3 Mike Dunleavy 2.00 5.00
4 Tracy McGrady 3.00 8.00
5 Vince Carter 4.00 10.00
6 Allen Iverson 4.00 10.00
7 Jason Kidd 4.00 10.00
8 Shaquille O'Neal 6.00 15.00
9 Yao Ming 5.00 12.00
10 Steve Francis 2.50 6.00
11 Tyson Chandler 2.00 5.00
12 Amare Stoudemire 4.00 10.00
13 Kevin Garnett 5.00 12.00
14 Tim Duncan 4.00 10.00
15 Ben Wallace 2.50 6.00
16 Kenyon Martin 2.50 6.00
17 Peja Stojokovic 2.50 6.00
18 Mike Sweetney 2.50 6.00
19 Carmelo Anthony 6.00 15.00

2003-04 Fleer Genuine Insider Genuine Autograph Insider

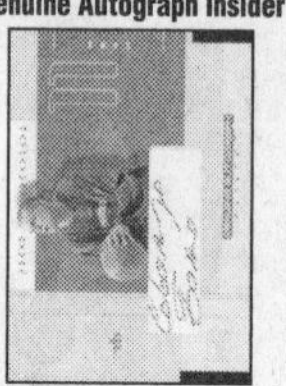

Inserted at one in 24, this 15-card set places full-color player photos in the middle of the horizontal design, team logo in the upper left hand corner and a centered cut signature below the player photo.

2 Carmelo Anthony 25.00 60.00
3 Dwyane Wade 30.00 80.00
5 Amare Stoudemire 8.00 20.00
6 Gilbert Arenas 8.00 20.00
7 Luke Ridnour 5.00 12.00
8 Dajuan Wagner 2.50 6.00
9 Tayshaun Prince 5.00 12.00
10 Earl Boykins 4.00 10.00
12 Maurice Williams 6.00 15.00
13 Travis Outlaw 5.00 12.00
14 Zarko Cabarkapa 4.00 10.00
15 Vince Carter 15.00 40.00

2003-04 Fleer Genuine Insider Scoring Threats

Seeded in packs at the rate of one in 20, this 10-card set places two player portrait photos, one on the top and one on the bottom in a one-color scale to match the player's team color.

COMPLETE SET (10) 8.00 20.00
1 Tracy McGrady 1.25 3.00
  Vince Carter
2 Allen Iverson 1.25 3.00
  Jason Kidd
3 Shaquille O'Neal 2.00 5.00
  Yao Ming
4 Steve Francis .75 2.00
  Jason Richardson
5 Amare Stoudemire 1.50 4.00
  Kevin Garnett
6 Paul Pierce 1.00 2.50
  Antoine Walker
7 Dirk Nowitzki 1.25 3.00
  Pau Gasol
8 Ray Allen .75 2.00
  Mike Bibby
9 Richard Jefferson .75 2.00
  Kenyon Martin
10 Tim Duncan 1.25 3.00
  Jermaine O'Neal

2003-04 Fleer Genuine Insider Scoring Threats Game Used

Inserted in packs at the rate of one in 48, this 10-card set parallels the design of the base Scoring Threats insert set enhanced with a swatch of memorabilia from one of the two players.

1 Tracy McGrady 4.00 10.00
  Vince Carter Jersey
2 Allen Iverson Jersey 4.00 10.00
  Jason Kidd
3 Shaquille O'Neal Jersey 6.00 15.00
  Yao Ming
4 Steve Francis Jersey 2.50 6.00
  Jason Richardson
5 Amare Stoudemire 5.00 12.00
  Kevin Garnett Jersey
6 Paul Pierce Jersey 3.00 8.00
  Antoine Walker
7 Dirk Nowitzki Jersey 4.00 10.00
  Pau Gasol
8 Ray Allen 2.50 6.00
  Mike Bibby Jersey
9 Richard Jefferson 2.50 6.00
  Kenyon Martin Jersey
10 Tim Duncan Jersey 4.00 10.00
  Jermaine O'Neal

2003-04 Fleer Genuine Insider Scoring Threats Game Used Dual

Sequentially numbered to 100, this seven cards set parallels the design of the Scoring Threats insert set enhanced with a swatch of jersey from each of the two players appearing on the card.

1 Tracy McGrady 10.00 25.00
  Vince Carter
2 Allen Iverson 8.00 20.00
  Jason Kidd
4 Amare Stoudemire 8.00 20.00
  Kevin Garnett
5 Dirk Nowitzki 8.00 20.00
  Pau Gasol
6 Tim Duncan 10.00 25.00
  Jermaine O'Neal

2003-04 Fleer Genuine Insider Team USA Insider

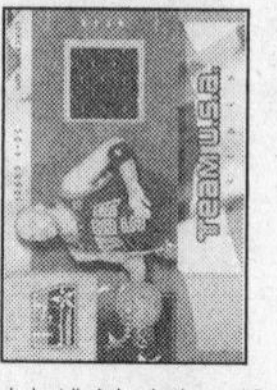

This set is horizontally designed and sequentially numbered to 325. The motif of the design is American flags with a player action photo in the middle, the Team USA and Genuine Insider logos to the left and a swatch of Team USA memorabilia on the right. Larry Brown's card does not include a swatch of memorabilia.

1 Ray Allen 5.00 12.00
2 Mike Bibby 5.00 12.00
3 Tim Duncan 8.00 20.00
4 Allen Iverson 8.00 20.00
5 Jason Kidd 8.00 20.00
6 Tracy McGrady 6.00 15.00
7 Jermaine O'Neal 5.00 12.00
8 Larry Brown 3.00 8.00

2003-04 Fleer Genuine Insider Tools of the Game

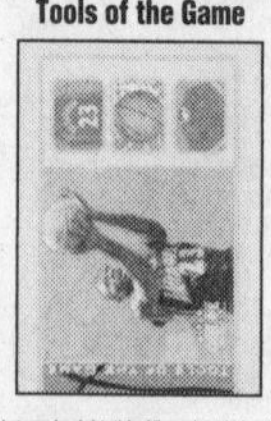

Inserted at one in eight, this 15-card set is horizontally designed and places a full-color player action photo in the middle and three small squares on the right side, stacked on top of eachother, with photos of the game's tool's such as ball, jerseys and warmups.

COMPLETE SET (15) 5.00 12.00
1 Amare Stoudemire .60 1.50
2 Shaquille O'Neal 1.00 2.50
3 Kevin Garnett .75 2.00
4 Vince Carter .60 1.50
5 Paul Pierce .50 1.25
6 Yao Ming .75 2.00
7 Jason Richardson .40 1.00
8 Chris Webber .40 1.00
9 Antoine Walker .40 1.00
10 Scottie Pippen .60 1.50
11 Elton Brand .40 1.00
12 Richard Jefferson .40 1.00
13 Steve Francis .40 1.00
14 Pau Gasol .40 1.00
15 Stephon Marbury .30 .75

2003-04 Fleer Genuine Insider Tools of the Game Game Used

Sequentially numbered to 199, this 15-card set parallels the design of the Tools of the Game set enhanced with a single swatch of memorabilia. Versions with Dual swatches (of which include, jerseys, balls, warmups etc.) are sequentially numbered to 99 and Triple swatch versions are sequentially numbered to 25.

*DUAL: .6X TO 1.5X BASE HI
*TRIPLE: 1.25X TO 3X BASE HI
1 Amare Stoudemire 4.00 10.00
2 Shaquille O'Neal 6.00 15.00
3 Kevin Garnett 5.00 12.00
4 Vince Carter 4.00 10.00
5 Paul Pierce 3.00 8.00
6 Yao Ming 5.00 12.00
7 Jason Richardson 2.50 6.00
8 Chris Webber 2.50 6.00
9 Antoine Walker 2.50 6.00
10 Scottie Pippen 6.00 15.00
11 Elton Brand 2.50 6.00
12 Richard Jefferson 2.50 6.00
13 Steve Francis 2.50 6.00
14 Pau Gasol 2.50 6.00
15 Stephon Marbury 2.00 5.00

2004-05 Fleer Genuine

Released in June, Genuine boasts a 135-card set divided up into 100 veteran players (cards 1-100) 10 retired players serially numbered to 500 (cards 101-110) and 25 rookies serially numbered to 500 (cards 111-135). Base cards have white borders with an oval-shaped area showcasing the player in action and is highlighted with the player's team colors. The cards also have embossed "dots" in on each of the sides. Buybacks were also inserted of original Fleer cards and are checklisted on our website at www.beckett.com. Genuine was released for both Hobby and Retail where Hobby boxes contained two mini-boxes of nine packs and Retal contained 24 packs. All packs contained five cards.

COMP.SET w/o SP's (100) 15.00 40.00
UNPRICED PARALLEL PRINT RUN 10 SETS
1 Rasheed Wallace .30 .75
2 Larry Hughes .25 .60
3 Allen Iverson .50 1.25
4 Josh Howard .30 .75
5 Bonzi Wells .20 .50
6 Jamaal Magloire .20 .50
7 Luke Ridnour .25 .60
8 Chauncey Billups .30 .75
9 Dwyane Wade 1.00 2.50
10 Amare Stoudemire .40 1.00
11 Earl Boykins .20 .50
12 Damon Jones .20 .50
13 Marquis Daniels .20 .50
14 Luke Walton .20 .50
15 Jamal Crawford .25 .60
16 Corliss Williamson .20 .50
17 Vince Carter .50 1.25
18 Antoine Walker .30 .75
19 Jason Richardson .30 .75
20 Jason Kidd .50 1.25
21 Peja Stojakovic .30 .75
22 Jeff McInnis .20 .50
23 Lamar Odom .30 .75
24 Allan Houston .25 .60
25 Jalen Rose .25 .60
26 LeBron James 2.00 5.00
27 Caron Butler .30 .75
28 Stephon Marbury .25 .60
29 Carlos Arroyo .25 .60
30 Zydrunas Ilgauskas .25 .60
31 Kobe Bryant 1.50 4.00
32 Steve Francis .30 .75
33 Carlos Boozer .30 .75
34 Primoz Brezec .20 .50
35 Reggie Miller .30 .75
36 Sam Cassell .25 .60
37 Ray Allen .30 .75
38 Drew Gooden .25 .60
39 Chris Wilcox .20 .50
40 Grant Hill .40 1.00
41 Andrei Kirilenko .25 .60
42 Kirk Hinrich .30 .75
43 Corey Maggette .25 .60
44 Cuttino Mobley .25 .60
45 Gilbert Arenas .30 .75
46 Tyson Chandler .25 .60
47 Elton Brand .30 .75
48 Samuel Dalembert .20 .50
49 Jarvis Hayes .20 .50
50 Ben Wallace .30 .75
51 Shawn Marion .30 .75
52 Michael Redd .30 .75
53 Richard Hamilton .25 .60
54 Desmond Mason .25 .60
55 Steve Nash .40 1.00
56 Antawn Jamison .30 .75
57 Kareem Rush .20 .50
58 Jermaine O'Neal .30 .75
59 Keith Van Horn .25 .60
60 Rashard Lewis .30 .75
61 Gerald Wallace .30 .75
62 Jamaal Tinsley .20 .50
63 Vladimir Radmanovic .20 .50
64 Predrag Drobnjak .20 .50
65 Mike Dunleavy .25 .60
66 Baron Davis .30 .75
67 Mike Bibby .30 .75
68 Ricky Davis .25 .60
69 Tracy McGrady .40 1.00
70 Richard Jefferson .30 .75
71 Chris Webber .30 .75
72 Michael Finley .30 .75
73 Pau Gasol .30 .75
74 David West .30 .75
75 Chris Bosh .30 .75
76 Gary Payton .30 .75
77 Yao Ming .60 1.50
78 Wally Szczerbiak .25 .60
79 Tim Duncan .50 1.25
80 Keith Bogans .20 .50
81 Stephen Jackson .25 .60
82 Kevin Garnett .60 1.50
83 Tony Parker .30 .75
84 Kenyon Martin .30 .75
85 Shaquille O'Neal .75 2.00
86 Shareef Abdur-Rahim .25 .60
87 Al Harrington .25 .60
88 Adonal Foyle .20 .50
89 Brian Scalabrine .20 .50
90 Brad Miller .30 .75
91 Carmelo Anthony .60 1.50
92 Udonis Haslem .25 .60
93 Zach Randolph .25 .60
94 Paul Pierce .40 1.00
95 Maurice Taylor .20 .50
96 Latrell Sprewell .25 .60
97 Manu Ginobili .40 1.00
98 Dirk Nowitzki .50 1.25
99 Jason Williams .25 .60
100 Nick Van Exel .25 .60
101 Charles Barkley 3.00 8.00
102 Jerry West 2.50 6.00
103 Magic Johnson 5.00 12.00
104 Kareem Abdul-Jabbar 3.00 8.00
105 Pete Maravich 12.00 30.00
106 Maurice Cheeks 2.00 5.00
107 Alex English 2.00 5.00
108 George Mikan 4.00 10.00
109 Wilt Chamberlain 4.00 10.00
110 Dominique Wilkins 2.50 6.00
111 Josh Childress RC 1.50 4.00
112 Josh Smith RC 2.50 6.00
113 Al Jefferson RC 2.50 6.00
114 Delonte West RC 2.00 5.00
115 Tony Allen RC 2.00 5.00
116 Emeka Okafor RC 2.50 6.00
117 Chris Duhon RC 1.50 4.00
118 Ben Gordon RC 2.00 5.00
119 Luol Deng RC 2.50 6.00
120 Andres Nocioni RC 1.50 4.00
121 David Harrison RC 1.50 4.00
122 Devin Harris RC 2.50 6.00
123 Shaun Livingston RC 1.50 4.00
124 Dorell Wright RC 2.50 6.00
125 J.R. Smith RC 2.00 5.00
126 Trevor Ariza RC 1.50 4.00
127 Dwight Howard RC 5.00 12.00
128 Jameer Nelson RC 2.00 5.00
129 Andre Iguodala RC 2.50 6.00
130 Sebastian Telfair RC 1.50 4.00
131 Kevin Martin RC 2.00 5.00
132 Ha Seung-Jin RC 1.50 4.00
133 Rafael Araujo RC 1.50 4.00
134 Kirk Snyder RC 1.50 4.00
135 Beno Udrih RC 1.50 4.00

2004-05 Fleer Genuine 100

Randomly inserted in packs, this 135-card set parallels the base set enhanced with silver highlights and sequential numbering to 100. A parallel version serially numbered to 10 was also issued with cards that contain bronze highlights.

*1-100: 2.5X TO 6X BASE HI
*101-110: 1.25X TO 3X BASE HI
*111-135: .5X TO 1.25X BASE HI
105 Pete Maravich 30.00 80.00

2004-05 Fleer Genuine Article

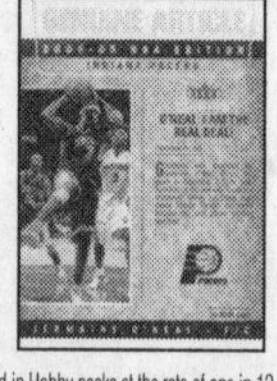

Inserted in Hobby packs at the rate of one in 12 and Retail at the rate of one in 15, this set is designed to look like a newspaper with a player photo on the left, text on the right and the set name along the top in silver foil.

COMPLETE SET (15) 10.00 25.00
1 Amare Stoudemire .75 2.00
2 LeBron James 4.00 10.00
3 Carmelo Anthony 1.25 3.00
4 Tracy McGrady .75 2.00
5 Jermaine O'Neal .60 1.50
6 Kobe Bryant 3.00 8.00
7 Pau Gasol .60 1.50
8 Shaquille O'Neal 1.50 4.00
9 Dwyane Wade 2.00 5.00
10 Michael Redd .60 1.50
11 Allen Iverson 1.00 2.50
12 Vince Carter 1.00 2.50
13 Chris Webber .60 1.50
14 Tony Parker .60 1.50
15 Andrei Kirilenko .50 1.25

2004-05 Fleer Genuine Article Autographs

Randomly seeded in packs, this eight card set features a similar, but horizontal design to the base Genuine Article set enhanced with sequential numbering, and autograph and silver foil highlights. Print runs range from 50 to 125.

AK Andrei Kirilenko/50 6.00 15.00
CA Carmelo Anthony/50 20.00 50.00
DW Dwyane Wade/50 40.00
JH Josh Howard/125 5.00
LJ Luke Jackson/125 5.00
LR Luke Ridnour/50 5.00
PG Pau Gasol/50 8.00
DWE David West 5.00

2004-05 Fleer Genuine Arti[cle] Autographs Gold

Randomly seeded, this eight card set parallels th[e] Genuine Article Autographs insert enhanced wit[h] foil highlights and sequential numbering ranging [from] 20 to 40.

*GOLD: .5X TO 1.25X BASE HI
DW Dwyane Wade/20 75.00

2004-05 Fleer Genuine Arti[cle] Autographs Patches

Randomly seeded, this eight card set parallels the Genuine Article Autographs insert enhanced with [a] swatch of game worn patch and sequential numb[ering] ranging from 10 to 40.

AK Andrei Kirilenko/30 12.50
CA Carmelo Anthony/20 50.00
JH Josh Howard/20 12.50
JO Jermaine O'Neal/20 15.00
LR Luke Ridnour/20 12.50
PG Pau Gasol/20 20.00
DWE David West/30 12.50
DWE1 David West/20 12.50

2004-05 Fleer Genuine Artic[le] Game Used

Randomly seeded in Hobby packs at the rate of o[ne in] 50 and Retail packs at the rate of one in 270, this card set parallels the design of the base Genuine Article set enhanced with a swatch of memorabili[a] the lower right hand corner and green foil highlig[hts]. Two parallel versions of the set were issued, one featuring red foil and sequential numbering to 14[9] another featuring a patch swatch and sequential numbering to 15.

*GAME USED 149: .5X TO 1.25X BASE GU HI
AI Allen Iverson 4.00
AK Andrei Kirilenko 2.00
AS Amare Stoudemire 3.00
CA Carmelo Anthony 5.00
DW Dwyane Wade 6.00
JO Jermaine O'Neal 2.50
PG Pau Gasol 2.50
SO Shaquille O'Neal 6.00
TM Tracy McGrady 3.00
VC Vince Carter 4.00

2004-05 Fleer Genuine At La[rge]

Inserted in Hobby packs at the rate of one in six an[d] Retail at the rate of one in eight, this 20-card set features cards with white borders along the top an[d] bottom and a starburst background colored to mat[ch] the featured player's jersey. In the spelling of the w[ord] large on the card, the @ symbol is used instead o[f] a.

COMPLETE SET (20) 10.00
1 Corey Maggette .40
2 Steve Francis .50
3 Jason Richardson .50
4 Dwyane Wade 1.50
5 Richard Jefferson .50
6 Ben Wallace .50
7 Carmelo Anthony 1.00
8 Kevin Garnett 1.00
9 Tim Duncan .75
10 Yao Ming 1.00
11 Vince Carter .75
12 Kobe Bryant 2.50
13 Ray Allen .50
14 Dirk Nowitzki .75
15 Shaquille O'Neal 1.25
16 Baron Davis .50
17 Jermaine O'Neal .50
18 Paul Pierce .60
19 LeBron James 3.00
20 Allen Iverson .75

2004-05 Fleer Genuine At La[rge] Autographs

ly inserted, this nine-card set features a similar
o the base At Large set but with a horizontal
hat utilizes a large blank white area towards the
e. Each card is serially numbered between 50

fferson/150	10.00	25.00
n Davis	6.00	15.00
Wallace/50	10.00	25.00
yane Wade/50	50.00	100.00
n Richardson	6.00	15.00
Smith/150	8.00	20.00
el Araujo/150	6.00	15.00
ard Jefferson/50	6.00	15.00
e Carter	15.00	40.00

4-05 Fleer Genuine At Large Autographs Gold

nly inserted, this nine card set parallels the base
e Autographs insert enhanced with gold foil and
umbering between 20 and 40.
: .5X TO 1.25X BASE HI

4-05 Fleer Genuine At Large Autographs Patches

nly inserted, this nine card set parallels the base
e Autographs insert enhanced with a patch
and serial numbering between 10 and 30.

efferson/30	25.00	60.00
Gordon/30	15.00	40.00
Wallace/30	20.00	50.00
yane Wade/20	75.00	150.00
n Richardson/20	12.50	30.00
Smith/30	15.00	40.00

4-05 Fleer Genuine At Large Game Used

nly seeded in Hobby packs at the rate of one in
Retail packs at the rate of one in 72, this 10-
et parallels the design of the base Genuine
set enhanced with a centered swatch of
abilia and green foil highlights. Two parallel
s of the set were issued, one featuring red foil
quential numbering to 199, and another
g a patch swatch and sequential numbering to

E USED 199: .5X TO 1.25X BASE GU HI
H: 1.25X TO 3X BASE HI

n Iverson	4.00	10.00
ron Davis	2.50	6.00
n Wallace	2.50	6.00
rmelo Anthony	5.00	12.00
wyane Wade	8.00	20.00
maine O'Neal	2.50	6.00
vin Garnett	5.00	12.00
ul Pierce	3.00	8.00
y Allen	2.50	6.00
hard Jefferson	2.50	6.00
eve Francis	2.50	6.00
aquille O'Neal	6.00	15.00
n Duncan	4.00	10.00
nce Carter	4.00	10.00
o Ming	5.00	12.00

4-05 Fleer Genuine Big Time

ed in Hobby packs at the rate of one in 99 and
at the rate of one in 125, this 15-card set places
r photo centered between silver and white
rs on the top of the card and a white bottom half
he insert name, team logo and Fleer logo.

PLETE SET (15)	25.00	60.00
yane Wade	5.00	12.00
ron James	10.00	25.00
be Bryant	8.00	20.00
aquille O'Neal	4.00	10.00
n Duncan	2.50	6.00
cy McGrady	2.00	5.00
hard Hamilton	1.25	3.00
vin Garnett	3.00	8.00
en Iverson	2.50	6.00
hris Webber	1.50	4.00
aul Pierce	2.00	5.00
o Ming	3.00	8.00
u Gasol	1.50	4.00
armelo Anthony	3.00	8.00
drei Kirilenko	1.25	3.00

04-05 Fleer Genuine Big Time Autographs

domly inserted, this 11-card set features a similar
gn to the base Big Time set but with a horizontal
gn that utilizes a large blank white area towards the
side. No odds were given. Gold versions
entially numbered between 25 and 50 were also
rted.
LD: .6X TO 1.5X BASE AU HI

Andris Biedrins	5.00	12.00
Andrei Kirilenko	4.00	10.00
Anderson Varejao	4.00	10.00
Ben Wallace	10.00	25.00
CD Carlos Delfino	4.00	10.00
DW Dorell Wright	8.00	20.00
KS Kirk Snyder	4.00	10.00
LC Lionel Chalmers	4.00	10.00
MP Mickael Pietrus	4.00	10.00
TA Tony Allen	5.00	12.00

2004-05 Fleer Genuine Big Time Autographs Patches

Randomly inserted, this nine card set parallels the base At Large Autographs insert enhanced with a patch swatch and serial numbering between 10 and 40.
SOME UNPRICED DUE TO SCARCITY

AB Andris Biedrins/40	10.00	25.00
AK Andrei Kirilenko/20	10.00	25.00
AV Anderson Varejao/40	12.50	30.00
CD Carlos Delfino/40	10.00	25.00
CD1 Carlos Delfino/20	12.50	30.00
DH David Harrison/40	10.00	25.00
DH1 David Harrison/20	12.50	30.00
KS Kirk Snyder/40	10.00	25.00
MP Mickael Pietrus/40	10.00	25.00
TA Tony Allen/20	12.50	30.00

2004-05 Fleer Genuine Big Time Game Used

Randomly seeded in Hobby packs at the rate of one in 60 and Retail packs at the rate of one in 308, this 10-card set parallels the design of the base Genuine Article set enhanced with a centered swatch of memorabilia and green foil highlights. Two parallel versions of the set were issued, one featuring red foil and sequential numbering to 49, and another featuring a patch swatch and sequential numbering to 10.
*GAME USED 49: .6X TO 1.5X BASE HI

AI Allen Iverson	4.00	10.00
AK Andrei Kirilenko	2.00	5.00
CA Carmelo Anthony	5.00	12.00
CW Chris Webber	2.50	6.00
DW Dwyane Wade	8.00	20.00
JO Jermaine O'Neal	2.50	6.00
KG Kevin Garnett	5.00	12.00
PG Pau Gasol	2.50	6.00
PP Paul Pierce	3.00	8.00
SO Shaquille O'Neal	6.00	15.00
TD Tim Duncan	4.00	10.00
TM Tracy McGrady	3.00	8.00
TP Tony Parker	2.50	6.00
YM Yao Ming	5.00	12.00
ZR Zach Randolph	2.00	5.00

2004-05 Fleer Genuine Buyback Autographs

Inserted in packs at the rate of one in 218, this set consists of the original cards.
STATED ODDS 1:218
SOME UNPRICED DUE TO SCARCITY

3B Clyde Drexler 88-9 Fleer	25.00	60.00
7B Magic Johnson 86-7 Fleer	50.00	120.00
8 Danny Ainge 88-9 Fleer	20.00	50.00
26 Clyde Drexler 86-7 Fleer	75.00	150.00
30 Clyde Drexler 87-8 Fleer	30.00	80.00
36 George Gervin 86-7 Fleer	12.50	30.00
68 Rik Smits 89-0 Fleer	15.00	40.00
119 Bill Walton 86-7 Fleer	15.00	40.00
133 Danny Ainge 89-0 Fleer	15.00	40.00
138 David Robinson 89-0 Hoops	40.00	100.00

2000-01 Fleer Glossy

The 2000-01 Fleer Glossy product was released in March, 2001 and featured a 245-card base set that was broken into tiers as follows: Base Veterans (1-200), and Rookies (201-245). Please note that the rookies were shortprinted as follows: Tier 1 201-210 serial numbered to 1000, Tier 2 211-235 serial numbered to 1500, and Tier 3 236-245 serial numbered to 1250. Also note that this was the first time that Fleer had ever released their "Glossy" brand in pack form. Card packs contained eight cards, and carried a suggested retail price of $2.99.

COMP.SET w/o SP's (200)	12.50	30.00
1 Lamar Odom	.30	.75
2 Christian Laettner	.20	.50
3 Michael Olowokandi	.20	.50
4 Anthony Carter	.20	.50
5 Steve Francis	.30	.75
6 Darvin Ham	.20	.50
7 Mitch Richmond	.25	.60
8 Corliss Williamson	.20	.50
9 Jason Terry	.30	.75
10 Brian Grant	.20	.50
11 Peja Stojakovic	.30	.75
12 Rick Fox	.25	.60
13 Tyrone Hill	.20	.50
14 Chauncey Billups	.30	.75
15 Otis Thorpe	.25	.60
16 Richard Hamilton	.25	.60
17 Ervin Johnson	.20	.50
18 Jim Jackson	.20	.50
19 Theo Ratliff	.20	.50
20 Doug Christie	.20	.50
21 Jalen Rose	.25	.60
22 John Wallace	.20	.50
23 Ruben Patterson	.20	.50
24 Steve Nash	.50	1.25
25 Toni Kukoc	.25	.60
26 Anthony Peeler	.20	.50
27 Ray Allen	.30	.75
28 Adonal Foyle	.20	.50
29 Chris Whitney	.20	.50
30 Nick Van Exel	.25	.60
31 Sean Elliott	.25	.60
32 Erick Strickland	.20	.50
33 Jerry Stackhouse	.25	.60
34 Antawn Jamison	.30	.75
35 Grant Hill	.40	1.00
36 Antonio Daniels	.20	.50
37 Karl Malone	.40	1.00
38 Keith Van Horn	.25	.60
39 Ron Harper	.25	.60
40 Stephon Marbury	.25	.60
41 Bryon Russell	.20	.50
42 Corey Maggette	.25	.60
43 Hersey Hawkins	.20	.50
44 Vince Carter	.60	1.50
45 Paul Pierce	.40	1.00
46 Mikki Moore RC	.30	.75
47 Othella Harrington	.20	.50
48 Erick Dampier	.20	.50
49 Jerome Williams	.20	.50
50 Nick Anderson	.20	.50
51 Tim Hardaway	.30	.75
52 Allan Houston	.25	.60
53 Tyrone Nesby	.30	.75
54 Brevin Knight	.20	.50
55 Chris Mills	.20	.50
56 Ron Artest	.30	.75
57 Walt Williams	.20	.50
58 Duane Causwell	.20	.50
59 Bonzi Wells	.20	.50
60 Rasheed Wallace	.30	.75
61 Dikembe Mutombo	.30	.75
62 Jahidi White	.20	.50
63 Chris Webber	.30	.75
64 Tony Battie	.20	.50
65 Mahmoud Abdul-Rauf	.20	.50
66 Monty Williams	.20	.50
67 Charlie Ward	.20	.50
68 David Robinson	.50	1.25
69 Eric Snow	.20	.50
70 Jermaine O'Neal	.30	.75
71 Kurt Thomas	.20	.50
72 James Posey	.20	.50
73 Travis Best	.20	.50
74 Jonathan Bender	.20	.50
75 John Stockton	.40	1.00
76 Jacque Vaughn	.20	.50
77 Ron Mercer	.20	.50
78 Shawn Marion	.30	.75
79 Larry Johnson	.30	.75
80 Maurice Taylor	.20	.50
81 Clifford Robinson	.20	.50
82 Scot Pollard	.20	.50
83 Patrick Ewing	.40	1.00
84 Terrell Brandon	.20	.50
85 Horace Grant	.25	.60
86 Vin Baker	.25	.60
87 Al Harrington	.25	.60
88 Larry Hughes	.25	.60
89 David Wesley	.20	.50
90 Wally Szczerbiak	.25	.60
91 Charles Oakley	.25	.60
92 Tim Thomas	.20	.50
93 Mookie Blaylock	.25	.60
94 Jamal Mashburn	.25	.60
95 Roshown McLeod	.20	.50
96 John Starks	.20	.50
97 Rodney Rogers	.20	.50
98 Juwan Howard	.25	.60
99 Isaiah Rider	.25	.60
100 Rashard Lewis	.30	.75
101 Dion Glover	.20	.50
102 Johnny Newman	.20	.50
103 Avery Johnson	.25	.60
104 Darrell Armstrong	.20	.50
105 Eric Williams	.20	.50
106 Gary Payton	.30	.75
107 Antonio Davis	.20	.50
108 Dirk Nowitzki	.50	1.25
109 Trajan Langdon	.20	.50
110 Michael Dickerson	.20	.50
111 Joe Smith	.25	.60
112 Rod Strickland	.25	.60
113 Shawn Kemp	.30	.75
114 Voshon Lenard	.20	.50
115 Marcus Camby	.25	.60
116 Matt Harpring	.25	.60
117 Isaac Austin	.20	.50
118 Malik Rose	.20	.50
119 Pat Garrity	.20	.50
120 Kenny Thomas	.20	.50
121 LaPhonso Ellis	.25	.60
122 Danny Fortson	.20	.50
123 Elton Brand	.30	.75
124 Jason Williams	.30	.75
125 Kobe Bryant	1.50	4.00
126 Tariq Abdul-Wahad	.20	.50
127 Tracy McGrady	.50	1.25
128 Matt Geiger	.20	.50
129 Antoine Walker	.25	.60
130 Michael Finley	.30	.75
131 Andre Miller	.25	.60
132 Robert Horry	.25	.60
133 Donyell Marshall	.20	.50
134 Shareef Abdur-Rahim	.25	.60
135 Vonteego Cummings	.20	.50
136 Anthony Mason	.20	.50
137 Mike Bibby	.30	.75
138 Raef LaFrentz	.20	.50
139 Glen Rice	.25	.60
140 Chris Gatling	.20	.50
141 Latrell Sprewell	.25	.60
142 Austin Croshere	.20	.50
143 Kenny Anderson	.25	.60
144 Elden Campbell	.20	.50
145 Jason Kidd	.50	1.25
146 Michael Doleac	.20	.50
147 Muggsy Bogues	.25	.60
148 Tim Duncan	.60	1.50
149 Samaki Walker	.20	.50
150 Gary Trent	.20	.50
151 Kevin Garnett	.60	1.50
152 Allen Iverson	.60	1.50
153 Anfernee Hardaway	.50	1.25
154 Robert Traylor	.20	.50
155 Scottie Pippen	.50	1.25
156 Shaquille O'Neal	.75	2.00
157 Vlade Divac	.25	.60
158 Lucious Harris	.20	.50
159 Keon Clark	.20	.50
160 Bo Outlaw	.20	.50
161 P.J. Brown	.20	.50
162 Derrick Coleman	.25	.60
163 Mark Jackson	.25	.60
164 Lamond Murray	.20	.50
165 Dan Majerle	.25	.60
166 Eddie Jones	.30	.75
167 Cedric Ceballos	.20	.50
168 Kendall Gill	.20	.50
169 Tom Gugliotta	.20	.50
170 Jeff McInnis	.20	.50
171 Steve Smith	.25	.60
172 Kevin Willis	.20	.50
173 Lindsey Hunter	.20	.50
174 Derek Anderson	.20	.50
175 Shandon Anderson	.20	.50
176 Adrian Griffin	.20	.50
177 Baron Davis	.30	.75
178 Radoslav Nesterovic	.20	.50
179 Glenn Robinson	.25	.60
180 Sam Cassell	.25	.60
181 Chucky Atkins	.20	.50
182 Arvydas Sabonis	.25	.60
183 Damon Stoudamire	.25	.60
184 Antonio McDyess	.25	.60
185 Derek Fisher	.30	.75
186 Bryant Reeves	.20	.50
187 Hakeem Olajuwon	.40	1.00
188 Kerry Kittles	.20	.50
189 Alan Henderson	.20	.50
190 Sam Perkins	.20	.50
191 Felipe Lopez	.20	.50
192 Tracy Murray	.20	.50
193 Shammond Williams	.20	.50
194 Vitaly Potapenko	.20	.50
195 John Amaechi	.20	.50
196 Quincy Lewis	.20	.50
197 Reggie Miller	.30	.75
198 Cuttino Mobley	.25	.60
199 Rex Chapman	.20	.50
200 Dale Davis	.20	.50
201 Stromile Swift RC	1.50	4.00
202 Stephen Jackson RC	2.50	6.00
203 Erick Barkley RC	1.50	4.00
204 Mike Miller RC	3.00	8.00
205 Kenyon Martin RC	4.00	10.00
206 Michael Redd RC	4.00	10.00
207 Darius Miles RC	1.50	4.00
208 Chris Mihm RC	1.50	4.00
209 Brian Cardinal RC	1.50	4.00
210 Khalid El-Amin RC	1.50	4.00
211 Hanno Mottola RC	1.25	3.00
212 Jamaal Magloire RC	1.25	3.00
213 Courtney Alexander RC	1.25	3.00
214 Mamadou N'Diaye RC	1.25	3.00
215 Chris Porter RC	1.25	3.00
216 Quentin Richardson RC	2.00	5.00
217 Eddie House RC	1.25	3.00
218 Joel Przybilla RC	1.25	3.00
219 Soumaila Samake RC	1.25	3.00
220 Speedy Claxton RC	1.25	3.00
221 Desmond Mason RC	1.50	4.00
222 Mike Smith RC	1.25	3.00
223 Lavor Postell RC	1.25	3.00
224 Pepe Sanchez RC	1.25	3.00
225 DeShawn Stevenson RC	1.50	4.00
226 Hedo Turkoglu RC	2.50	6.00
227 Keyon Dooling RC	1.25	3.00
228 Dan Langhi RC	1.25	3.00
229 Mateen Cleaves RC	1.25	3.00
230 Donnell Harvey RC	1.25	3.00
231 DerMarr Johnson RC	1.25	3.00
232 Jason Collier RC	1.25	3.00
233 Jake Voskuhl RC	1.25	3.00
234 Mark Madsen RC	1.25	3.00
235 Jabari Smith RC	1.25	3.00
236 Morris Peterson RC	1.25	3.00
237 Daniel Santiago RC	2.00	5.00
238 Etan Thomas RC	1.25	3.00
239 A.J. Guyton RC	1.25	3.00
240 Marcus Fizer RC	1.25	3.00
241 Jamal Crawford RC	2.00	5.00
242 Jerome Moiso RC	1.25	3.00
243 Olumide Oyedeji RC	1.25	3.00
244 Paul McPherson RC	1.25	3.00
245 Eduardo Najera RC	1.25	3.00
246 Marc Jackson AU RC	3.00	8.00
247 Mike Penberthy AU RC	3.00	8.00
248 Dragan Tarlac AU RC	3.00	8.00
249 Ruben Wolkowyski AU RC	3.00	8.00
250 Iakovos Tsakalidis AU RC	3.00	8.00
251 Ruben Garces AU RC	3.00	8.00

2000-01 Fleer Glossy Vince Carter Rookie Remnants

This three-card insert was randomly inserted into 2000-01 Fleer products. The set includes a Vince Carter floor card (numbered to 100), a Vince Carter floor/jersey card (numbered to 15), and finally an autographed Vince Carter floor/jersey card (numbered 1/1).

NNO Vince Carter FLR/100	12.50	30.00

2000-01 Fleer Glossy Class Acts

Randomly inserted into packs at one in 72, this 25-card insert features players that are class acts on and off the court. Card backs carry a "CA" prefix.

COMPLETE SET (25)	50.00	100.00
CA1 Hakeem Olajuwon	2.00	5.00
CA2 Karl Malone	2.00	5.00
CA3 Patrick Ewing	2.00	5.00
CA4 Ron Harper	1.25	3.00
CA5 David Robinson	2.50	6.00
CA6 Scottie Pippen	2.50	6.00
CA7 Mitch Richmond	1.25	3.00
CA8 Tim Hardaway	1.50	4.00
CA9 Gary Payton	1.50	4.00
CA10 Larry Johnson	1.50	4.00
CA11 Shaquille O'Neal	4.00	10.00
CA12 Allan Houston	1.25	3.00
CA13 Chris Webber	1.50	4.00
CA14 Jason Kidd	2.50	6.00
CA15 Grant Hill	2.00	5.00
CA16 Kevin Garnett	3.00	8.00
CA17 Allen Iverson	3.00	8.00
CA18 Kobe Bryant	8.00	20.00
CA19 Tracy McGrady	2.50	6.00
CA20 Tim Duncan	3.00	8.00
CA21 Dirk Nowitzki	2.50	6.00
CA22 Larry Hughes	1.25	3.00
CA23 Vince Carter	3.00	8.00
CA24 Elton Brand	1.50	4.00
CA25 Steve Francis	1.50	4.00

2000-01 Fleer Glossy Coach's Corner

Randomly inserted into packs at one in 108, this 7-card insert features autographed cards from some of the greatest modern-day coaches. The cards are listed below in alphabetical order for convenience.

1 Pat Riley	15.00	40.00
2 Doc Rivers	15.00	40.00
3 Paul Silas	10.00	25.00
4 Isiah Thomas	8.00	20.00
5 Rudy Tomjanovich	8.00	20.00
6 Jeff Van Gundy	10.00	25.00
7 Lenny Wilkens	10.00	25.00

2000-01 Fleer Glossy Game Breakers

Randomly inserted into packs at one in 24, this 10-card insert features players that are capable of breaking the game wide open. Card backs carry a "GB" prefix.

COMPLETE SET (10)	10.00	25.00
GB1 Allen Iverson	1.50	4.00
GB2 Elton Brand	.75	2.00
GB3 Grant Hill	1.00	2.50
GB4 Jason Kidd	1.25	3.00
GB5 Kevin Garnett	1.50	4.00
GB6 Kobe Bryant	4.00	10.00
GB7 Shaquille O'Neal	2.00	5.00
GB8 Steve Francis	.75	2.00
GB9 Tim Duncan	1.50	4.00
GB10 Vince Carter	1.50	4.00

2000-01 Fleer Glossy Hardwood Leaders

Randomly inserted into packs at one in 12, this 15-card insert features players that are the predominant leaders on the court. Card backs carry a "HL" prefix.

COMPLETE SET (15)	8.00	20.00
HL1 Allen Iverson	1.00	2.50
HL2 Jason Williams	.50	1.25
HL3 Vince Carter	1.00	2.50
HL4 Scottie Pippen	.75	2.00
HL5 Kevin Garnett	1.00	2.50
HL6 Karl Malone	.60	1.50
HL7 Grant Hill	.60	1.50
HL8 Jason Kidd	.75	2.00
HL9 Kobe Bryant	2.50	6.00
HL10 Elton Brand	.50	1.25
HL11 Shaquille O'Neal	1.25	3.00
HL12 Tim Duncan	1.00	2.50
HL13 Tracy McGrady	.75	2.00
HL14 Chris Webber	.50	1.25
HL15 Lamar Odom	.50	1.25

2000-01 Fleer Glossy Rookie Sensations

Randomly inserted into packs at one in 6, this 25-card insert features rookies that look to make a difference for their teams in years to come. Card backs carry a "RS" prefix.

COMPLETE SET (25)	6.00	15.00
RS1 Jamaal Magloire	.40	1.00
RS2 Etan Thomas	.40	1.00
RS3 Chris Mihm	.40	1.00
RS4 Joel Przybilla	.40	1.00
RS5 Mamadou N'Diaye	.40	1.00
RS6 Jason Collier	.40	1.00
RS7 DerMarr Johnson	.40	1.00
RS8 Jerome Moiso	.40	1.00
RS9 Darius Miles	.40	1.00
RS10 Marcus Fizer	.40	1.00
RS11 Kenyon Martin	1.00	2.50
RS12 Mark Madsen	.40	1.00
RS13 Mike Miller	.75	2.00
RS14 Desmond Mason	.50	1.25
RS15 Morris Peterson	.40	1.00
RS16 Hedo Turkoglu	.75	2.00
RS17 Mateen Cleaves	.40	1.00
RS18 Keyon Dooling	.40	1.00
RS19 DeShawn Stevenson	.50	1.25
RS20 Quentin Richardson	.60	1.50
RS21 Courtney Alexander	.40	1.00
RS22 Stromile Swift	.40	1.00
RS23 Stephen Jackson	.60	1.50
RS24 Erick Barkley	.40	1.00
RS25 Khalid El-Amin	.40	1.00

2000-01 Fleer Glossy Traditional Threads

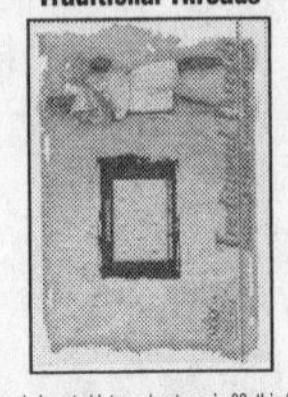

Randomly inserted into packs at one in 63, this 29-card insert features swatches from actual game-used jerseys. Please note that the cards have been listed below in alphabetical order for convenience.

1 Vince Carter	6.00	15.00
2 Baron Davis	3.00	8.00
3 Trajan Langdon	2.00	5.00
4 Grant Hill	4.00	10.00
5 Allen Iverson	6.00	15.00
6 Jason Kidd	5.00	12.00
7 Karl Malone	4.00	10.00
8 Stephon Marbury	2.50	6.00
9 Shawn Marion	3.00	8.00
10 Tracy McGrady	5.00	12.00
11 Andre Miller	2.50	6.00
12 Dikembe Mutombo	3.00	8.00
13 Lamar Odom	3.00	8.00
14 Shaquille O'Neal	10.00	25.00
15 Gary Payton	3.00	8.00
16 Jason Terry	3.00	8.00
17 John Stockton	4.00	10.00
18 Anfernee Hardaway	5.00	12.00
19 Jason Williams	3.00	8.00
20 Darius Miles	3.00	8.00
21 Chris Mihm	3.00	8.00
22 Desmond Mason	4.00	10.00
23 Keyon Dooling	3.00	8.00
24 DerMarr Johnson	3.00	8.00
25 Speedy Claxton	3.00	8.00
26 Kenyon Martin	8.00	20.00
27 Hanno Mottola	3.00	8.00
28 Mike Miller	6.00	15.00
29 Quentin Richardson	5.00	12.00

2000-01 Fleer Glossy Mutombo Arena

Limited to 25,000 copies, this special Dikembe Mutombo was given away in Philadelphia at a 76ers game sometime early in the 2000-01 NBA season.

1 Dikembe Mutombo	.50	1.25

2001 Fleer Hawaii Bobby Knight

Given away to participants by Fleer at the 2001 Kit Young Hawaii conference, this card features Bobby Knight, some information about him on the back, and a circular swatch of a game-worn coaching sweater.

NNO Bobby Knight	15.00	40.00

2006-07 Fleer Hot Prospects

Released in mid November 2006, Fleer Hot Prospects boasts a 112-card set which pictures veteran players on cards 1-60, rookie jersey sticker-autographs serially numbered to 150 on cards 61-70, rookie jersey sticker-autgraphs serially numbered to 250 on cards 71-89, rookie sticker-autographs on cards 90-103 serially numbered to either 500 or 150 (150 cards noted in checklist) and rookie cards serially numbered to 150 on cards 104-112. Base cards place full-color player auction photos on the middle with silver borders on the left and right and silver foil highlights. Hot Prospects boxes contain 15 pack of five cards each and carried an original per-pack suggested retail price of $9.99.

COMP.SET w/o SP's (60)	15.00	40.00
UNPRICED WHITE PRINT RUN 15 SETS		
1 Joe Johnson	.40	1.00
2 Marvin Williams	.40	1.00
3 Tony Allen	.25	.60
4 Paul Pierce	.50	1.25
5 Raymond Felton	.50	1.25
6 Emeka Okafor	.40	1.00
7 Ben Gordon	.40	1.00
8 Michael Jordan	3.00	8.00
9 Zydrunas Ilgauskas	.30	.75
10 LeBron James	2.00	5.00
11 Devin Harris	.40	1.00
12 Dirk Nowitzki	.60	1.50
13 Carmelo Anthony	.50	1.25
14 Nene	.30	.75
15 Chauncey Billups	.40	1.00
16 Ben Wallace	.40	1.00
17 Baron Davis	.40	1.00
18 Troy Murphy	.25	.60
19 Tracy McGrady	.50	1.25
20 Yao Ming	.50	1.25
21 Jermaine O'Neal	.40	1.00
22 Peja Stojakovic	.40	1.00
23 Corey Maggette	.30	.75
24 Sam Cassell	.40	1.00
25 Kobe Bryant	2.00	5.00
26 Lamar Odom	.40	1.00
27 Pau Gasol	.40	1.00
28 Hakim Warrick	.30	.75
29 Shaquille O'Neal	.75	2.00
30 Dwyane Wade	1.00	2.50
31 T.J. Ford	.30	.75
32 Michael Redd	.40	1.00
33 Kevin Garnett	.75	2.00
34 Troy Hudson	.25	.60
35 Vince Carter	.50	1.25
36 Jason Kidd	.60	1.50
37 Desmond Mason	.25	.60
38 Chris Paul	.75	2.00
39 Stephon Marbury	.30	.75
40 Nate Robinson	.40	1.00
41 Grant Hill	.50	1.25
42 Darko Milicic	.25	.60
43 Andre Iguodala	.40	1.00
44 Allen Iverson	.50	1.25
45 Steve Nash	.50	1.25
46 Amare Stoudemire	.40	1.00
47 Zach Randolph	.30	.75
48 Sebastian Telfair	.25	.60
49 Ron Artest	.40	1.00
50 Mike Bibby	.40	1.00
51 Tim Duncan	.60	1.50
52 Manu Ginobili	.40	1.00
53 Ray Allen	.40	1.00
54 Rashard Lewis	.40	1.00
55 Chris Bosh	.40	1.00
56 Charlie Villanueva	.40	1.00
57 Andrei Kirilenko	.30	.75
58 Deron Williams	.60	1.50
59 Gilbert Arenas	.40	1.00
60 Antawn Jamison	.40	1.00
61 Ronnie Brewer JSY AU RC	10.00	25.00
62 LaMarcus Aldridge JSY AU RC	20.00	50.00
63 Tyrus Thomas JSY AU RC	10.00	25.00
64 Shelden Williams JSY AU RC	8.00	20.00
65 Cedric Simmons JSY AU RC	8.00	20.00
66 Randy Foye JSY AU RC	10.00	25.00
67 Rudy Gay JSY AU RC	12.00	30.00
68 Patrick O'Bryant JSY AU RC	8.00	20.00
69 Rodney Carney JSY AU RC	8.00	20.00
70 Hilton Armstrong JSY AU RC	8.00	20.00
71 Denham Brown JSY AU RC	6.00	15.00
72 Dee Brown JSY AU RC	6.00	15.00
73 Allan Ray JSY AU RC	6.00	15.00
74 Shawne Williams JSY AU RC	6.00	15.00
75 Quincy Douby JSY AU RC	6.00	15.00
76 Renaldo Balkman JSY AU RC	6.00	15.00
77 Rajon Rondo JSY AU RC	30.00	80.00
78 Marcus Williams JSY AU RC	6.00	15.00
79 Josh Boone JSY AU RC	6.00	15.00
80 Kyle Lowry JSY AU RC	8.00	20.00
82 Jordan Farmar JSY AU RC	6.00	15.00
83 Maurice Ager JSY AU RC	6.00	15.00
84 Mardy Collins JSY AU RC	6.00	15.00
85 Shannon Brown JSY AU RC	10.00	25.00
86 James White JSY AU RC	6.00	15.00
87 Steve Novak JSY AU RC	6.00	15.00
88 Solomon Jones JSY AU RC	6.00	15.00
89 Paul Davis JSY AU RC	6.00	15.00
90 P.J. Tucker JSY AU RC	6.00	15.00
91 Craig Smith AU RC	5.00	12.00
92 Bobby Jones AU RC	5.00	12.00
93 David Noel AU RC	5.00	12.00
94 Andrea Bargnani AU/150 RC	12.00	30.00
95 James Augustine AU RC	5.00	12.00
96 Daniel Gibson AU RC	6.00	15.00
97 Brandon Roy AU/150 RC	20.00	50.00
98 Ryan Hollins AU RC	5.00	12.00
99 Hassan Adams AU RC	5.00	12.00
100 Pops Mensah-Bonsu AU RC	5.00	12.00
101 Will Blalock AU RC	5.00	12.00
102 Damir Markota AU RC	5.00	12.00
103 Saer Sene AU RC	5.00	12.00
104 Thabo Sefolosha AU RC	6.00	15.00
105 Leon Powe RC	2.50	6.00
106 J.J. Redick RC	3.00	8.00
107 Adam Morrison RC	3.00	8.00
108 Paul Millsap RC	4.00	10.00
109 J.R. Pinnock RC	2.50	6.00
110 Jorge Garbajosa RC	2.50	6.00
111 Vassilis Spanoulis RC	2.50	6.00
112 Yakhouba Diawara RC	2.50	6.00
113 Alexander Johnson RC	2.50	6.00

2006-07 Fleer Hot Prospects Red Hot

*1-60 RED: 2X TO 5X BASE HI
*61-70/94/97 RC RED: .6X TO 1.5X BASE HI
*71-113 RC RED: .75X TO 2X BASE HI

2006-07 Fleer Hot Prospects Alumni Ink

PRINT RUN 10 TO 25 SER.#'d SETS
UNPRICED RED PRINT RUN 10 SETS

AF Channing Frye/25 Hassan Adams	10.00	25.00
AW Carmelo Anthony/25 Hakim Warrick	20.00	50.00
BA Dee Brown/25 James Augustine	10.00	25.00
CJ Vince Carter/25 Antawn Jamison	25.00	60.00
DW Bill Walton/25 Baron Davis	12.00	30.00
EW Shelden Williams/25 Daniel Ewing	10.00	25.00
FH Ryan Hollins/25 Jordan Farmar	10.00	25.00
FL Kyle Lowry/25 Randy Foye	12.50	30.00
MG Donyell Marshall/25 Rudy Gay	10.00	25.00
OD Clyde Drexler/10 Hakeem Olajuwon	100.00	200.00
OG Emeka Okafor/25 Rudy Gay	10.00	25.00
PH Kirk Hinrich/25 Paul Pierce	25.00	60.00
PR Rajon Rondo/25 Tayshaun Prince	25.00	60.00

2006-07 Fleer Hot Prospects Double Team Memorabilia

PRINT RUN 50 SER.#'d SETS
*RED HOT: .75X TO 2X BASE HI
RED HOT PRINT RUN 25 SER.#'d SETS
UNPRICED PATCH PRINT RUN 10 SETS

AB Gilbert Arenas	4.00	10.00
Caron Butler		
AI Allen Iverson	6.00	15.00
Andre Iguodala		
AK Andrei Kirilenko	4.00	10.00
Rafael Araujo		
AL Ray Allen	4.00	10.00
Rashard Lewis		
BB Kobe Bryant	8.00	20.00
Kwame Brown		
BC Chris Bosh	4.00	10.00
Jose Calderon		
BK Ben Wallace	4.00	10.00
Kirk Hinrich		
BW Andrew Bogut	4.00	10.00
Marvin Williams		
CB Tyson Chandler	4.00	10.00
Kwame Brown		
CF Eddy Curry	4.00	10.00
Channing Frye		
CJ Vince Carter	5.00	12.00
Antawn Jamison		
CS Tyson Chandler	4.00	10.00
Peja Stojakovic		
CW Brian Cook	4.00	10.00
Luke Walton		
DG Tim Duncan	6.00	15.00
Manu Ginobili		
DI Samuel Dalembert	4.00	10.00
Andre Iguodala		
DJ Josh Howard	4.00	10.00
Devin Harris		
DK Samuel Dalembert	4.00	10.00
Kyle Korver		
FB Michael Finley	5.00	12.00
Bruce Bowen		
FM Raymond Felton	4.00	10.00
Sean May		
FR Steve Francis	4.00	10.00
Quentin Richardson		
GD Luol Deng	4.00	10.00
Ben Gordon		
HH Grant Hill	6.00	15.00
Dwight Howard		
HP Richard Hamilton	5.00	12.00
Tayshaun Prince		
IG Zydrunas Ilgauskas	4.00	10.00
Drew Gooden		
JD Marquis Daniels	4.00	10.00
Sarunas Jasikevicius		
JH Antawn Jamison	4.00	10.00
Brendan Haywood		
JI Allen Iverson	12.50	30.00
LeBron James		
KC Jason Kidd	6.00	15.00
Vince Carter		
KR Kevin Garnett	4.00	10.00
Ricky Davis		
KW Andrei Kirilenko	4.00	10.00
Deron Williams		
MD Jamaal Magloire	4.00	10.00
Juan Dixon		
MF Rashad McCants	4.00	10.00
Raymond Felton		
ML Corey Maggette	4.00	10.00
Shaun Livingston		
MM Tracy McGrady	5.00	12.00
Yao Ming		
MP Desmond Mason	6.00	15.00
Chris Paul		
MR Stephon Marbury	4.00	10.00
Nate Robinson		
MS Kenyon Martin	4.00	10.00
Stromile Swift		
NM Steve Nash	5.00	12.00
Shawn Marion		
OH Emeka Okafor	5.00	12.00
Dwight Howard		
PG Tony Parker	4.00	10.00
Manu Ginobili		
PS Paul Pierce	4.00	10.00
Wally Szczerbiak		
RJ Zach Randolph	4.00	10.00
Jarrett Jack		
RV Michael Redd	4.00	10.00
Charlie Villanueva		
TS Kurt Thomas	4.00	10.00
Amare Stoudemire		
WH Deron Williams	5.00	12.00
Luther Head		
WK Nenad Krstic	4.00	10.00
Antoine Wright		
WR Chris Wilcox	4.00	10.00
Luke Ridnour		
WS Antoine Walker	4.00	10.00
Wayne Simien		

2006-07 Fleer Hot Prospects Draft Day Postmarks Autographs

PRINT RUN 100 SER.#'d SETS

AB Andrea Bargnani	10.00	25.00
AD Hassan Adams	6.00	15.00
BA Renaldo Balkman	6.00	15.00
BJ Bobby Jones	6.00	15.00
BR Brandon Roy	25.00	60.00
CS Cedric Simmons	6.00	15.00
DB Denham Brown	6.00	15.00
DE Dee Brown	6.00	15.00
DN David Noel	6.00	15.00
HA Hilton Armstrong	6.00	15.00
JA James Augustine	6.00	15.00
JB Josh Boone	6.00	15.00
JF Jordan Farmar	6.00	15.00
JW James White	6.00	15.00
KL Kyle Lowry	8.00	20.00
LA LaMarcus Aldridge	25.00	60.00
MA Maurice Ager	6.00	15.00
MC Mardy Collins	6.00	15.00
MW Marcus Williams	6.00	15.00
PD Paul Davis	6.00	15.00
PO Patrick O'Bryant	6.00	15.00
PT P.J. Tucker	6.00	15.00
QD Quincy Douby	6.00	15.00
RB Ronnie Brewer	8.00	20.00
RC Rodney Carney	6.00	15.00
RF Randy Foye	8.00	20.00
RG Rudy Gay	20.00	40.00
RH Ryan Hollins	6.00	15.00
RR Rajon Rondo	60.00	150.00
SB Shannon Brown	10.00	25.00
SJ Solomon Jones	6.00	15.00
SM Craig Smith	6.00	15.00
SN Steve Novak	6.00	15.00
SS Saer Sene	6.00	15.00
SW Shelden Williams	6.00	15.00
TS Thabo Sefolosha	8.00	20.00
TT Tyrus Thomas	8.00	20.00
WI Shawne Williams	6.00	15.00

2006-07 Fleer Hot Prospects Draft Rewind

COMPLETE SET (60)	25.00	60.00
APPROXIMATE ODDS TWO PER BOX		
AB Andrew Bogut	1.00	2.50
AI Andre Iguodala	1.00	2.50
AJ Al Jefferson	1.00	2.50
AS Amare Stoudemire	1.00	2.50
BD Baron Davis	1.00	2.50
BG Ben Gordon	1.00	2.50
BM Brad Miller	1.00	2.50
BR Kobe Bryant	5.00	12.00
CA Carmelo Anthony	1.25	3.00
CB Chauncey Billups	1.00	2.50
CP Chris Paul	2.00	5.00
DG Drew Gooden	.75	2.00
DM Darko Milicic	.60	1.50
DN Dirk Nowitzki	1.50	4.00
DW Delonte West	.75	2.00
EB Elton Brand	1.00	2.50
EC Eddy Curry	.75	2.00
GA Gilbert Arenas	1.00	2.50
GD Devean George	.60	1.50
IV Allen Iverson	1.25	3.00
JA LeBron James	5.00	12.00
JC Jamal Crawford	.75	2.00
JD Juan Dixon	.60	1.50
JK Jason Kidd	1.50	4.00
JM Jamaal Magloire	.60	1.50
JO Jermaine O'Neal	1.00	2.50
JR Jason Richardson	1.00	2.50
JT Jason Terry	.75	2.00
KB Kwame Brown	.60	1.50
KG Kevin Garnett	2.00	5.00
KK Kyle Korver	.75	2.00
KM Kenyon Martin	1.00	2.50
LJ Luke Jackson	.60	1.50
LO Lamar Odom	1.00	2.50
LW Luke Walton	.60	1.50
MA Shawn Marion	1.00	2.50
MB Mike Bibby	1.00	2.50
MJ Michael Jordan	8.00	20.00
MM Mike Miller	1.00	2.50
MP Mickael Pietrus	.75	2.00
MS Mike Sweetney	.60	1.50
PG Pau Gasol	1.00	2.50
PS Peja Stojakovic	1.00	2.50
RA Ron Artest	1.00	2.50
RH Richard Hamilton	.75	2.00
SD Samuel Dalembert	.60	1.50
SF Steve Francis	1.00	2.50
SL Shaun Livingston	.60	1.50
SM Stephon Marbury	.75	2.00
SN Steve Nash	1.25	3.00
SO Shaquille O'Neal	2.00	5.00
TC Tyson Chandler	.75	2.00
TD Tim Duncan	1.50	4.00
TI Jamaal Tinsley	.60	1.50
TM Tracy McGrady	1.25	3.00
TP Tony Parker	1.00	2.50
VC Vince Carter	1.25	3.00
WA Dwyane Wade	2.50	6.00
WS Wally Szczerbiak	.75	2.00
YM Yao Ming	1.25	3.00
ZI Zydrunas Ilgauskas	.75	2.00

2006-07 Fleer Hot Prospects Draft Rewind Memorabilia

PRINT RUN 50 SER.#'d SETS
*RED HOT: .75X TO 2X BASE HI
RED HOT PRINT RUN 25 SER.#'d SETS
UNPRICED PATCH PRINT RUN 10 SETS

AI Andre Iguodala	3.00	8.00
AS Amare Stoudemire	3.00	8.00
BD Baron Davis	3.00	8.00
BG Ben Gordon	3.00	8.00
BR Kobe Bryant	10.00	25.00
CA Carmelo Anthony	4.00	10.00
DG Drew Gooden	2.50	6.00
DN Dirk Nowitzki	5.00	12.00
DW Delonte West	2.50	6.00
EB Elton Brand	3.00	8.00
EC Eddy Curry	2.50	6.00
GA Gilbert Arenas	3.00	8.00
GD Devean George	2.00	5.00
JA LeBron James	10.00	25.00
JC Jamal Crawford	2.50	6.00
JD Juan Dixon	2.50	6.00
JK Jason Kidd	5.00	12.00
JM Jamaal Magloire	2.00	5.00
JO Jermaine O'Neal	3.00	8.00
JR Jason Richardson	3.00	8.00
KB Kwame Brown	2.50	6.00
KG Kevin Garnett	6.00	15.00
KK Kyle Korver	2.50	6.00
KM Kenyon Martin	3.00	8.00
LJ Luke Jackson	2.50	6.00
LO Lamar Odom	3.00	8.00
LW Luke Walton	2.00	5.00
MA Shawn Marion	3.00	8.00
MB Mike Bibby	3.00	8.00
MP Mickael Pietrus	2.50	6.00
MS Mike Sweetney	2.50	6.00
PS Peja Stojakovic	3.00	8.00
RH Richard Hamilton	2.50	6.00
SD Samuel Dalembert	2.00	5.00
SF Steve Francis	3.00	8.00
SL Shaun Livingston	2.50	6.00
SM Stephon Marbury	2.50	6.00
SN Steve Nash	4.00	10.00
SO Shaquille O'Neal	6.00	15.00
TC Tyson Chandler	2.50	6.00
TD Tim Duncan	5.00	12.00
TI Jamaal Tinsley	2.00	5.00
TM Tracy McGrady	4.00	10.00
TP Tony Parker	3.00	8.00
VC Vince Carter	4.00	10.00
WS Wally Szczerbiak	2.50	6.00
YM Yao Ming	4.00	10.00
ZI Zydrunas Ilgauskas	2.50	6.00

2006-07 Fleer Hot Prospects Hot Materials Jerseys

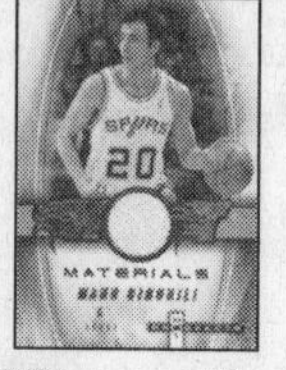

COMMON CARD	2.50	6.00
PRINT RUN 50 SER.#'d SETS		
*RED HOT: .75X TO 2X BASE HI		
RED HOT PRINT RUN 25 SER.#'d SETS		
UNPRICED PATCH PRINT RUN 10 SETS		
AB Andrew Bogut	3.00	8.00
AI Andre Iguodala	3.00	8.00
AS Amare Stoudemire	3.00	8.00
BA Andrea Bargnani	5.00	12.00
BD Baron Davis	3.00	8.00
BG Ben Gordon	3.00	8.00
BM Brad Miller	3.00	8.00
BR Brandon Roy	8.00	20.00
CB Chauncey Billups	3.00	8.00
CP Chris Paul	6.00	15.00
CW Chris Webber	3.00	8.00
DH Dwight Howard	5.00	12.00
DN Dirk Nowitzki	5.00	12.00
EB Elton Brand	3.00	8.00
EO Emeka Okafor	3.00	8.00
JK Jason Kidd	5.00	12.00
KB Kobe Bryant	10.00	25.00
KG Kevin Garnett	6.00	15.00
LA LaMarcus Aldridge	8.00	20.00
LJ LeBron James	10.00	25.00
LO Lamar Odom	3.00	8.00
MG Manu Ginobili	3.00	8.00
MW Marvin Williams	3.00	8.00
PG Pau Gasol	3.00	8.00
PP Paul Pierce	4.00	10.00
PS Peja Stojakovic	3.00	8.00
RB Ronnie Brewer	4.00	10.00
RF Randy Foye	4.00	10.00
RG Rudy Gay	5.00	12.00
RR Rajon Rondo	8.00	20.00
SF Steve Francis	3.00	8.00
SM Shawn Marion	3.00	8.00
SW Shelden Williams	3.00	8.00
TC Tyson Chandler	2.50	6.00
TT Tyrus Thomas	4.00	10.00
WI Chris Wilcox	2.50	6.00
WM Marcus Williams	3.00	8.00
WS Wally Szczerbiak	2.50	6.00
ZI Zydrunas Ilgauskas	2.50	6.00

2006-07 Fleer Hot Prospects Notable Newcomers

COMPLETE SET (20)	12.50	30.00
APPROXIMATE ODDS TWO PER BOX		
AB Andrea Bargnani	1.50	4.00
AD Hassan Adams	1.00	2.50
BJ Bobby Jones	1.00	2.50
BR Brandon Roy	2.50	6.00
CS Craig Smith	1.00	2.50
DN David Noel	1.00	2.50
HA Hilton Armstrong	1.00	2.50
JF Jordan Farmar	1.00	2.50
LA LaMarcus Aldridge	2.50	6.00
MC Mardy Collins	1.00	2.50
MW Marcus Williams	1.00	2.50
PO Patrick O'Bryant	1.00	2.50
QD Quincy Douby	1.00	2.50
RF Randy Foye	1.25	3.00
RG Rudy Gay	1.50	4.00
RH Ryan Hollins	1.00	2.50
RR Rajon Rondo	4.00	10.00
SN Steve Novak	1.00	2.50
SW Shelden Williams	1.00	2.50
TT Tyrus Thomas	1.25	3.00

2006-07 Fleer Hot Prospects Notable Notations

PRINT RUN 50 SER.#'d SETS
UNPRICED RED HOT PRINT RUN 10 SETS

AB Andrea Bargnani	8.00	20.00
BA Renaldo Balkman	5.00	12.00
BR Brandon Roy	12.00	30.00
CS Cedric Simmons	5.00	12.00
DB Denham Brown	5.00	12.00
DE Dee Brown	5.00	12.00
DN David Noel	5.00	12.00
JB Josh Boone	5.00	12.00
KP Kevin Pittsnogle	5.00	12.00
LA LaMarcus Aldridge	12.00	30.00
MA Maurice Ager	5.00	12.00
PD Paul Davis	5.00	12.00
QD Quincy Douby	5.00	12.00
RF Randy Foye	8.00	20.00
RG Rudy Gay	12.50	30.00
SB Shannon Brown	8.00	20.00
SC Craig Smith	5.00	12.00
TT Tyrus Thomas	6.00	15.00
WI Shawne Williams	5.00	12.00

2006-07 Fleer Hot Prospects Rookie Materials Letter Autographs

RANDOM INSERTS IN PACKS

AB Andrea Bargnani	25.00	50.00
BR Brandon Roy	30.00	80.00
CS Cedric Simmons	8.00	20.00
HA Hilton Armstrong	8.00	20.00
JB Josh Boone	8.00	20.00
JF Jordan Farmar	8.00	20.00
LA LaMarcus Aldridge	25.00	50.00
MC Mardy Collins	8.00	20.00
MW Marcus Williams	8.00	20.00
PO Patrick O'Bryant	8.00	20.00
QD Quincy Douby	8.00	20.00
RB Ronnie Brewer	10.00	25.00
RC Rodney Carney	8.00	20.00
RF Randy Foye	10.00	25.00
RG Rudy Gay	25.00	50.00
RR Rajon Rondo	40.00	100.00
SW Shelden Williams	8.00	20.00
TS Thabo Sefolosha	12.50	30.00
TT Tyrus Thomas	12.50	30.00
WI Shawne Williams	8.00	20.00

2006-07 Fleer Hot Prospects Sweet Selections Autographs

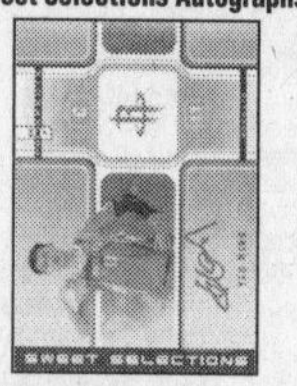

PRINT RUN 50 SER.#'d SETS

BR Brandon Roy	15.00	40.00
CA Carmelo Anthony	15.00	40.00
CB Carlos Boozer	5.00	12.00
CM Cuttino Mobley	5.00	12.00
CP Chris Paul	30.00	75.00
CS Cedric Simmons	5.00	12.00
DB Dee Brown	5.00	12.00
DE Denham Brown	5.00	12.00
DM Donyell Marshall	5.00	12.00
FR Randy Foye	5.00	12.00
HW Hakim Warrick	6.00	15.00
ID Ike Diogu	5.00	12.00
JA Antawn Jamison	5.00	12.00
JB Josh Boone	5.00	12.00
JC Josh Childress	5.00	12.00
JJ Joe Johnson	5.00	12.00
JR Jalen Rose	5.00	12.00
KA Kareem Abdul-Jabbar	40.00	80.00
KB Kwame Brown	5.00	12.00
KH Kirk Hinrich	10.00	25.00
KP Kevin Pittsnogle	5.00	12.00
LJ LeBron James	100.00	225.00
LR Luke Ridnour	5.00	12.00
MA Maurice Ager	5.00	12.00
MW Martell Webster	5.00	12.00
NR Nate Robinson	5.00	12.00
PO Patrick O'Bryant	5.00	12.00
PP Paul Pierce	6.00	15.00
RC Rodney Carney	5.00	12.00
RF Raymond Felton	6.00	15.00
RG Rudy Gay	8.00	20.00
RJ Richard Jefferson	5.00	12.00
RM Rashad McCants	5.00	12.00
SC Craig Smith	5.00	12.00
SN Steve Novak	5.00	12.00
SS Saer Sene	5.00	12.00
TF T.J. Ford	5.00	12.00
TP Tayshaun Prince	6.00	15.00
WS Shelden Williams	5.00	12.00
YM Yao Ming	15.00	40.00

2006-07 Fleer Hot Prospects Sweet Selections Autographs Jerseys

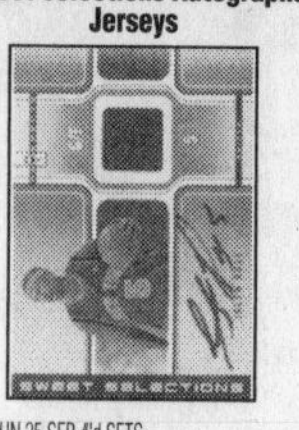

PRINT RUN 25 SER.#'d SETS
UNPRICED LOGO PRINT RUN ONE SET

CB Carlos Boozer	8.00	20.00
CP Chris Paul	30.00	80.00
CS Cedric Simmons	8.00	20.00
DE Denham Brown	8.00	20.00
DM Donyell Marshall	8.00	20.00
FR Randy Foye	10.00	25.00
HW Hakim Warrick	8.00	20.00
ID Ike Diogu	8.00	20.00
JA Antawn Jamison	10.00	25.00
JB Josh Boone	8.00	20.00
JC Josh Childress	8.00	20.00
JJ Joe Johnson	10.00	25.00
JR Jalen Rose	10.00	25.00
KA Kareem Abdul-Jabbar	75.00	150.00
KB Kwame Brown	8.00	20.00
KH Kirk Hinrich	15.00	40.00
LA LaMarcus Aldridge	20.00	50.00
LJ LeBron James	250.00	350.00
MA Maurice Ager	8.00	20.00
NR Nate Robinson	10.00	25.00
PP Paul Pierce	12.50	30.00
RC Rodney Carney	8.00	20.00
RF Raymond Felton	10.00	25.00
RG Rudy Gay	15.00	40.00
RJ Richard Jefferson	8.00	20.00
RM Rashad McCants	8.00	20.00
SC Craig Smith	8.00	20.00
SS Saer Sene	8.00	20.00
TP Tayshaun Prince	8.00	20.00
WS Shelden Williams	8.00	20.00
YM Yao Ming	25.00	60.00

2006-07 Fleer Hot Prospects We're #1

COMPLETE SET	6.00	15.00
APPROXIMATE ODDS ONE PER BOX		
AB Andrew Bogut	1.00	2.50
CW Chris Webber	1.00	2.50
DH Dwight Howard	1.50	4.00
EB Elton Brand	1.00	2.50
KB Kwame Brown	.60	1.50
KM Kenyon Martin	1.00	2.50
LJ LeBron James	5.00	12.00
SO Shaquille O'Neal	2.00	5.00
TD Tim Duncan	1.50	4.00
YM Yao Ming	1.25	3.00
AB2 Andrea Bargnani	1.50	4.00

2006-07 Fleer Hot Prospects We're #1 Memorabilia

PRINT RUN 50 SER.#'d SETS
*RED HOT: .75X TO 2X BASE HI
RED PRINT RUN 25 SER.#'d SETS
UNPRICED PATCH PRINT RUN 10 SETS

AB Andrew Bogut	3.00	8.00
CW Chris Webber	3.00	8.00
DH Dwight Howard	5.00	12.00
KB Kwame Brown	2.50	6.00
KM Kenyon Martin	3.00	8.00
LJ LeBron James	12.00	30.00
SO Shaquille O'Neal	6.00	15.00
TD Tim Duncan	5.00	12.00
YM Yao Ming	4.00	10.00

2007-08 Fleer Hot Prospects

This 133-card set was released in November, 2008. The set was issued into the hobby in five-card packs which came 18 packs to a box and packs carried an initial SRP of $6.99. Cards numbered 1-66 feature veterans while cards numbered 67-78 feature retired greats. All cards numbered 61-78 were issued to a stated print run of 399 serial numbered sets. Cards numbered 81-133 all feature 2007-08 NBA rookies and in that grouping cards numbered 85-93 were signed by the player and cards numbered 94-133 have both player-worn swatches as well as a signature. Cards numbered 79-84 were issued to a stated print run of 199 serial numbered sets, Cards numbered 85-93 were issued to a stated print run of 899 serial numbered sets while cards 94-121 were issued to a stated print run of 599 serial numbered sets and the set concludes with cards numbered 122-133 which were issued to a stated print run of 399 serial numbered sets.

COMP.SET w/o SP's (60)	10.00	25.00
UNPRICED BLUE PRINT RUN 10 SER.#'d SETS		
1 Kobe Bryant	1.50	4.00
2 Carmelo Anthony	.40	1.00
3 Gilbert Arenas	.30	.75
4 Dwyane Wade	.75	2.00
5 LeBron James	1.50	4.00
6 Michael Redd	.30	.75
7 Ray Allen	.30	.75
8 Allen Iverson	.40	1.00
9 Vince Carter	.40	1.00
10 Yao Ming	.40	1.00
11 Joe Johnson	.30	.75
12 Paul Pierce	.40	1.00
13 Tracy McGrady	.30	.75
14 Dirk Nowitzki	.40	1.00
15 Zach Randolph	.25	.60
16 Chris Bosh	.30	.75
17 Kevin Garnett	.60	1.50
18 Rashard Lewis	.25	.60
19 Ben Gordon	.30	.75
20 Carlos Boozer	.30	.75
21 Pau Gasol	.30	.75
22 Elton Brand	.30	.75
23 Michael Jordan	2.50	6.00
24 Amare Stoudemire	.30	.75
25 Kevin Martin	.30	.75
26 Baron Davis	.30	.75
27 Tim Duncan	.50	1.25
28 Richard Hamilton	.25	.60
29 Eddy Curry	.20	.50
30 Jermaine O'Neal	.30	.75
31 Caron Butler	.30	.75
32 Josh Howard	.25	.60
33 Ron Artest	.30	.75
34 Luol Deng	.30	.75
35 Steve Nash	.40	1.00
36 Tony Parker	.30	.75
37 David West	.30	.75
38 Andre Iguodala	.30	.75
39 Gerald Wallace	.30	.75
40 Jamal Crawford	.25	.60
41 Dwight Howard	.50	1.25
42 Mehmet Okur	.20	.50
43 Shawn Marion	.30	.75
44 Maurice Williams	.25	.60
45 Shaquille O'Neal	.60	1.50
46 Chris Paul	.60	1.50
47 Chauncey Billups	.30	.75
48 Brandon Roy	.40	1.00
49 Josh Smith	.30	.75
50 Deron Williams	.50	1.25
51 Jason Richardson	.30	.75
52 Al Jefferson	.30	.75
53 Lamar Odom	.30	.75
54 Raymond Felton	.40	1.00
55 Andre Miller	.25	.60
56 Jason Kidd	.30	.75
57 Zydrunas Ilgauskas	.25	.60
58 Andrea Bargnani	.40	1.00
59 Marcus Camby	.20	.50
60 Rudy Gay	.30	.75
61 LeBron James	4.00	10.00
62 Amare Stoudemire	.75	2.00
63 Vince Carter	1.00	2.50
64 Tim Duncan	1.25	3.00
65 Allen Iverson	1.00	2.50
66 Shaquille O'Neal	1.50	4.00
67 David Robinson	1.25	3.00
68 Michael Jordan	6.00	15.00
69 Darrell Griffith	.75	2.00
70 Larry Bird	2.50	6.00
71 Adrian Dantley	.75	2.00
72 Bob McAdoo	.75	2.00
73 Kareem Abdul-Jabbar	1.25	3.00
74 Wes Unseld	.75	2.00
75 Dave Bing	.75	2.00
76 Willis Reed	.75	2.00
77 Oscar Robertson	.75	2.00
78 Wilt Chamberlain	1.50	4.00
79 Greg Oden RC	5.00	12.00
80 Brandan Wright RC	4.00	10.00
81 Yi Jianlian RC	6.00	15.00
82 Nick Young RC	6.00	15.00
83 Thaddeus Young RC	5.00	12.00
84 Kyrylo Fesenko RC	4.00	10.00
85 Sun Yue AU RC	4.00	10.00
86 Brad Newley AU RC	4.00	10.00
87 Ramon Sessions AU RC	6.00	15.00
88 Sammy Mejia AU RC	4.00	10.00
89 JamesOn Curry AU RC	4.00	10.00
90 Renaldas Seibutis AU RC	4.00	10.00
91 Milovan Rakovic AU RC	4.00	10.00
92 Marco Belinelli AU RC	4.00	10.00
93 Darryl Watkins AU RC	4.00	10.00
94 Demetris Nichols JSY AU RC	6.00	15.00
95 Javaris Crittenton JSY AU RC	6.00	15.00
96 Jason Smith JSY AU RC	6.00	15.00
97 Daequan Cook JSY AU RC	6.00	15.00
98 Jared Dudley JSY AU RC	6.00	15.00
99 Wilson Chandler JSY AU RC	10.00	25.00
100 Morris Almond JSY AU RC	6.00	15.00
101 Aaron Brooks JSY AU RC	6.00	15.00
102 Arron Afflalo JSY AU RC	8.00	20.00
103 Alando Tucker JSY AU RC	6.00	15.00
104 Carl Landry JSY AU RC	6.00	15.00
105 Gabe Pruitt JSY AU RC	6.00	15.00
106 Marcus Williams JSY AU RC	6.00	15.00
107 Nick Fazekas JSY AU RC	6.00	15.00
108 Glen Davis JSY AU RC	10.00	25.00
109 Jermareo Davidson JSY AU RC	6.00	15.00
110 Josh McRoberts JSY AU RC	6.00	15.00
111 Herbert Hill JSY AU RC	6.00	15.00
112 Derrick Byars JSY AU RC	6.00	15.00
113 Adam Haluska JSY AU RC	6.00	15.00
114 Reyshawn Terry JSY AU RC	6.00	15.00
115 Jared Jordan JSY AU RC	6.00	15.00
116 Stephane Lasme JSY AU RC	6.00	15.00
117 Dominic McGuire JSY AU RC	6.00	15.00
118 Aaron Gray JSY AU RC	6.00	15.00
119 Taurean Green JSY AU RC	6.00	15.00
120 D.J. Strawberry JSY AU RC	6.00	15.00
121 Chris Richard JSY AU RC	6.00	15.00
122 Rodney Stuckey JSY AU RC	15.00	40.00
123 Kevin Durant JSY AU RC	250.00	450.00
124 Al Thornton JSY AU RC	10.00	25.00
125 Julian Wright JSY AU RC	10.00	25.00
126 Sean Williams JSY AU RC	10.00	25.00
127 Al Horford JSY AU RC	12.00	30.00
128 Mike Conley Jr.JSY AU RC	15.00	40.00
129 Jeff Green JSY AU RC	12.00	30.00
130 Corey Brewer JSY AU RC	12.00	30.00
131 Joakim Noah JSY AU RC	25.00	60.00
132 Spencer Hawes JSY AU RC	10.00	25.00
133 Acie Law JSY AU RC	10.00	25.00

2007-08 Fleer Hot Prospects Red

*1-60 RED: 5X TO 12X BASE HI
*61-78 RED: 1.5X TO 4X BASE HI
*79-84 RC RED: 1X TO 2.5X BASE HI
*85-93 RC RED: 1X TO 2.5X BASE HI
*94-121 RC RED: .6X TO 1.5X BASE HI
*122-133 RC RED: .5X TO 1.25X BASE HI
PRINT RUN 25 SER.#'d SETS

2007-08 Fleer Hot Prospect Autographics

APPROXIMATE ODDS ONE PER BOX
CARDS WITH F INSERTED IN FLEER

AA Arron Afflalo	5.00	1
AB Aaron Brooks F	4.00	1
AG Aaron Gray	4.00	1
AH Adam Haluska	4.00	1
AH2 Adam Haluska Blue	4.00	1
AH3 Al Horford Blue	6.00	1
AH4 Al Horford	6.00	1
AL Acie Law F	4.00	1
AT Al Thornton F	4.00	1
AT2 Al Thornton Blue F	4.00	1
AT3 Alando Tucker F	4.00	1
CA Carmelo Anthony Blue	15.00	4
CB Corey Brewer	5.00	1
CB2 Corey Brewer Blue	5.00	1
CL Carl Landry	4.00	1
CL2 Carl Landry Blue	4.00	1
CR Chris Richard	4.00	1
CR2 Chris Richard Blue	4.00	1
DB Derrick Byars	4.00	1
DB2 Derrick Byars Blue	4.00	1
DC Daequan Cook	4.00	1
DS D.J. Strawberry F	4.00	1
DS2 D.J. Strawberry Blue F	4.00	1
GD Glen Davis	8.00	2
GP Gabe Pruitt F	4.00	1
HH Herbert Hill F	4.00	1
JC Javaris Crittenton	4.00	1
JC2 Javaris Crittenton Blue	4.00	1
JD Jared Dudley	4.00	1
JD2 Jared Dudley Blue	4.00	1
JD3 Jermareo Davidson	4.00	1
JG Jeff Green	5.00	1
JG2 Jeff Green Blue	10.00	2
JM Josh McRoberts	4.00	1
JM2 Josh McRoberts Blue	4.00	1
JN Joakim Noah	10.00	2
JN2 Joakim Noah Blue	10.00	2
JS Jason Smith F	4.00	1
JW Julian Wright	4.00	1
KD Kevin Durant	125.00	25
KD2 Kevin Durant Blue	150.00	30
MA Morris Almond F	4.00	1
MB Marco Belinelli Blue F	4.00	1
MC Mike Conley Jr. F	6.00	1
MC2 Mike Conley Jr. Blue F	6.00	1
MW Marcus Williams	4.00	1
RS Rodney Stuckey	6.00	1
RS2 Rodney Stuckey Green	25.00	5
RT Reyshawn Terry	4.00	1
RT2 Reyshawn Terry Blue	4.00	1
SH Spencer Hawes	4.00	1
SH2 Spencer Hawes Blue F	4.00	1
SH3 Spencer Hawes Red F	4.00	1
SL Stephane Lasme	4.00	1
SM Craig Smith F	2.50	6
TG Taurean Green	4.00	1
TG2 Taurean Green Blue	4.00	1
WC Wilson Chandler	6.00	1

2007-08 Fleer Hot Prospects Class of

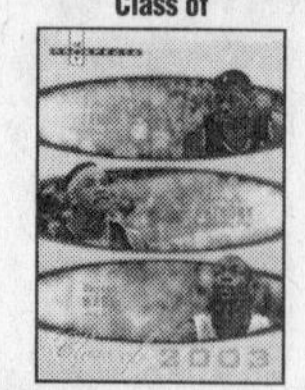

COMPLETE SET (15)	25.00	60
PRINT RUNS SAME AS CARD #		
1960 Oscar Robertson	2.50	6
Jerry West		
Lenny Wilkens		
1962 Dave DeBusschere	2.50	6.
Jerry Lucas		
John Havlicek		
1967 Walt Frazier	3.00	8.
Pat Riley		
Phil Jackson		
1970 Bob Lanier	5.00	12.
Pete Maravich		
Nate Archibald		
1972 Bob McAdoo	2.50	6
Paul Westphal		
Julius Erving		
1979 Magic Johnson	3.00	8.
Bill Cartwright		
Bill Laimbeer		
1984 Hakeem Olajuwon	6.00	15.
Michael Jordan		
John Stockton		
1992 Shaquille O'Neal	3.00	8.
Alonzo Mourning		
Robert Horry		
1996 Allen Iverson	4.00	10.
Kobe Bryant		
Steve Nash		
1997 Tim Duncan	3.00	8.
Chauncey Billups		
Tracy McGrady		
1998 Vince Carter	3.00	8.
Dirk Nowitzki		
Paul Pierce		
2001 Pau Gasol	2.50	6.
Tony Parker		
Gilbert Arenas		
2003 LeBron James	4.00	10.
Carmelo Anthony		
Dwyane Wade		
2007A Greg Oden	5.00	12.
Kevin Durant		
Michael Conley Jr.		
2007B Joakim Noah	4.00	10.
Al Horford		
Corey Brewer		

07-08 Fleer Hot Prospects Double Scribble

RUN 25 SER.#'d SETS
CED BLUE PRINT RUN ONE SET
CED RED PRINT RUN 10 SER.#'d SETS
larcus Aldridge 30.00 60.00
don Roy
ve Nash 125.00 225.00
Bryant
Ford 10.00 25.00
el Gibson
e Lowry 12.00 30.00
y Foye
niel Gibson 10.00 25.00
non Brown
n Gordon 20.00 50.00
n Rondo
us Thomas 50.00 100.00
ce Grant
vight Howard 15.00 40.00
es Augustine
ron James 600.00 1000.00
hael Jordan
ett Jack 20.00 40.00
Price
yshaun Prince 12.50 30.00
an Dantley
ardy Collins 10.00 25.00
ntin Richardson
e Brown 12.50 30.00
n Williams

007-08 Fleer Hot Prospects Draft Day Postmarks

RUN 50 SER.#'d SETS
ICED RED PRINT RUN 10 SER.#'d SETS
ron Afflalo 8.00 20.00
ron Brooks 6.00 15.00
ron Gray 6.00 15.00
Horford 15.00 40.00
ie Law 6.00 15.00
Thornton 6.00 15.00
orey Brewer 8.00 20.00
arl Landry 6.00 15.00
hris Richard 6.00 15.00
rmareo Davidson 6.00 15.00
errick Byars 6.00 15.00
aequan Cook 6.00 15.00
emetris Nichols 6.00 15.00
.J. Strawberry 6.00 15.00
len Davis 10.00 25.00
abe Pruitt 6.00 15.00
dam Haluska 6.00 15.00
varis Crittenton 6.00 15.00
mesOn Curry 6.00 15.00
red Dudley 6.00 15.00
ff Green 12.50 30.00
osh McRoberts 6.00 15.00
akim Noah 30.00 80.00
ulian Wright 8.00 20.00
evin Durant 200.00 400.00
Morris Almond 6.00 15.00
Mike Conley Jr. 12.50 30.00
Marcus Williams 6.00 15.00
ick Fazekas 6.00 15.00
amon Sessions 15.00 40.00
pencer Hawes 6.00 15.00
tephane Lasme 6.00 15.00
Sammy Mejia 6.00 15.00
Sean Williams 6.00 15.00
aurean Green 6.00 15.00
lando Tucker 6.00 15.00
Wilson Chandler 10.00 25.00
Kevin Durant 15.00 40.00
ersized Promo w
simile autograph

007-08 Fleer Hot Prospects Hot Materials

ROXIMATE ODDS ONE PER RETAIL BOX
D: .75X TO 2X BASE HI
PRINT RUN 25 SER.#'d SETS
Al Horford 3.00 8.00
Amare Stoudemire 2.50 6.00
Bill Laimbeer 2.50 6.00
Bill Russell 8.00 20.00
Corey Brewer 3.00 8.00
Clyde Drexler 3.00 8.00
Corey Maggette 2.00 5.00
Donyell Marshall 2.00 5.00
Dirk Nowitzki 3.00 8.00
Elton Brand 2.50 6.00
Grant Hill 5.00 12.00
Horace Grant 2.50 6.00
Julius Erving 5.00 12.00
ason Kidd 2.50 6.00
Joakim Noah 6.00 15.00
JO Jermaine O'Neal 2.50 6.00
JR Jason Richardson 2.50 6.00
JS John Stockton 4.00 10.00
JT Jamaal Tinsley 2.00 5.00
JW Julian Wright 2.50 6.00
KB Kobe Bryant 6.00 15.00
KD Kevin Durant 12.50 30.00
KG Kevin Garnett 5.00 12.00
LH Larry Hughes 2.00 5.00
LJ LeBron James 8.00 20.00
MC Mike Conley Jr. 4.00 10.00
MP Morris Peterson 1.50 4.00
N Nene 2.00 5.00
RA Ray Allen 2.50 6.00
RL Rashard Lewis 2.00 5.00
RW Rasheed Wallace 2.50 6.00
SM Shawn Marion 2.50 6.00
TC Tyson Chandler 2.00 5.00
TD Tim Duncan 4.00 10.00
TP Tony Parker 2.50 6.00
ZI Zydrunas Ilgauskas 2.00 5.00

2007-08 Fleer Hot Prospects NBA Game Issue

PRINT RUN 99 SER.#'d SETS
UNPRICED BLUE PRINT RUN ONE SET
*RED: .75X TO 2X BASE HI
RED PRINT RUN 25 SER.#'d SETS
AI Allen Iverson 5.00 12.00
BH Brendan Haywood 3.00 8.00
BL Bill Laimbeer 4.00 10.00
CA Carmelo Anthony 4.00 10.00
CD Clyde Drexler 5.00 12.00
DR David Robinson 8.00 20.00
EB Elton Brand 3.00 8.00
GH Grant Hill 8.00 20.00
HG Horace Grant 3.00 8.00
JE Julius Erving 5.00 12.00
JK Jason Kidd 3.00 8.00
JO Jermaine O'Neal 3.00 8.00
JS John Stockton 5.00 12.00
KB Kobe Bryant 10.00 25.00
KG Kevin Garnett 5.00 12.00
LJ LeBron James 10.00 25.00
MJ Michael Jordan 30.00 80.00
RA Ray Allen 3.00 8.00
RH Richard Hamilton 3.00 8.00
TD Tim Duncan 4.00 10.00

2007-08 Fleer Hot Prospects Notable Newcomers

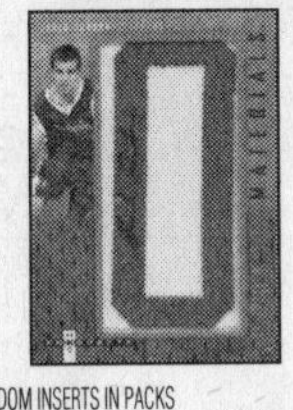

COMPLETE SET (20) 15.00 40.00
APPROXIMATELY TWO PER BOX
1 Kevin Durant 8.00 20.00
2 Joakim Noah 2.50 6.00
3 Al Horford 1.25 3.00
4 Corey Brewer 1.25 3.00
5 Julian Wright 1.00 2.50
6 Mike Conley Jr. 1.50 4.00
7 Jeff Green 1.25 3.00
8 Rodney Stuckey 1.50 4.00
9 Spencer Hawes 1.00 2.50
10 Acie Law 1.00 2.50
11 Al Thornton 1.00 2.50
12 Arron Afflalo 1.25 3.00
13 Marco Belinelli 1.00 2.50
14 Alando Tucker 1.00 2.50
15 Aaron Brooks 1.00 2.50
16 Javaris Crittenton 1.00 2.50
17 Wilson Chandler 1.50 4.00
18 Sun Yue 1.00 2.50
19 Taurean Green 1.00 2.50
20 D.J. Strawberry 1.00 2.50

2007-08 Fleer Hot Prospects Notable Notations

PRINT RUN 24 TO 50 SER.#'d SETS
UNPRICED BLUE PRINT RUN ONE SET
*RED: .5X TO 1.25X BASE HI
RED PRINT RUN 25 SER.#'d SETS
AM Alonzo Mourning/50 20.00 50.00
BD Baron Davis/50 6.00 15.00
BL Bill Laimbeer/50 10.00 25.00
DM Dan Majerle/50 15.00 40.00
DR Dennis Rodman/50 25.00 50.00
DT David Thompson/50 6.00 15.00
DW Slick Watts/50 6.00 15.00
HO Hakeem Olajuwon/50 15.00 40.00
JW Jamaal Wilkes/50 20.00 40.00
KB Kobe Bryant/24 100.00 175.00
LB Leandro Barbosa/50 6.00 15.00
LJ LeBron James/50 80.00 200.00
MP Morris Peterson/25 6.00 15.00
SM Sidney Moncrief/50 8.00 20.00
SP Sam Perkins/50 6.00 15.00
VC Vince Carter/48 20.00 40.00

2007-08 Fleer Hot Prospects Property of

STATED PRINT RUN 149 SER.#'d SETS
UNPRICED BLUE PRINT RUN ONE SET
*RED: .75X TO 2X BASE HI
RED PRINT RUN 25 SER.#'d SETS
AB Andrew Bogut 3.00 8.00
AK Andrei Kirilenko 2.50 6.00
AS Amare Stoudemire 3.00 8.00
BB Bruce Bowen 2.00 5.00
BR Elton Brand 3.00 8.00
CB Chauncey Billups 3.00 8.00
CF Channing Frye 2.50 6.00
CW Chris Wilcox 2.00 5.00
DB Devin Harris 3.00 8.00
DG Danny Granger 3.00 8.00
DH Dwight Howard 5.00 12.00
DM Desmond Mason 2.00 5.00
DN Dirk Nowitzki 4.00 10.00
DR David Robinson 5.00 12.00
DW Delonte West 2.50 6.00
EJ Eddie Jones 2.50 6.00
GW Gerald Wallace 3.00 8.00
JF Jordan Farmar 2.00 5.00
JM Jamaal Magloire 2.00 5.00
JR Jalen Rose 2.50 6.00
JT Jason Terry 2.50 6.00
KG Kevin Garnett 6.00 15.00
KH Kirk Hinrich 3.00 8.00
LD Luol Deng 3.00 8.00
LJ LeBron James 8.00 20.00
MD Mike Dunleavy 2.50 6.00
MG Manu Ginobili 3.00 8.00
MR Michael Redd 3.00 8.00
PG Pau Gasol 3.00 8.00
PP Paul Pierce 4.00 10.00
PS Peja Stojakovic 3.00 8.00
RA Ron Artest 3.00 8.00
RH Richard Hamilton 2.50 6.00
RJ Richard Jefferson 3.00 8.00
RL Rashard Lewis 2.50 6.00
SB Shane Battier 2.50 6.00
SF Steve Francis 3.00 8.00
SL Shaun Livingston 2.00 5.00
SM Shawn Marion 3.00 8.00
ZI Zydrunas Ilgauskas 2.50 6.00

2007-08 Fleer Hot Prospects Rookie Materials

RANDOM INSERTS IN PACKS
AA Arron Afflalo 10.00 25.00
AB Aaron Brooks 8.00 20.00
AG Aaron Gray 8.00 20.00
AH Adam Haluska 8.00 20.00
AL Acie Law 8.00 20.00
AT Al Thornton 8.00 20.00
CB Corey Brewer 10.00 25.00
CL Carl Landry 8.00 20.00
CR Chris Richard 8.00 20.00
DA Jermareo Davidson 8.00 20.00
DB Derrick Byars 8.00 20.00
GD Glen Davis 12.00 30.00
GP Gabe Pruitt 8.00 20.00
HO Al Horford 10.00 25.00
JA Javaris Crittenton 8.00 20.00
JD Jared Dudley 8.00 20.00
JG Jeff Green 10.00 25.00
JJ Jared Jordan 8.00 20.00
JM Josh McRoberts 8.00 20.00
JN Joakim Noah 20.00 50.00
JS Jason Smith 8.00 20.00
KD Kevin Durant 100.00 200.00
MA Morris Almond 8.00 20.00
MB Marco Belinelli 8.00 20.00
MC Mike Conley Jr. 12.00 30.00
MW Marcus Williams 8.00 20.00
NF Nick Fazekas 8.00 20.00
RS Rodney Stuckey 12.00 30.00
RT Reyshawn Terry 8.00 20.00
SH Spencer Hawes 8.00 20.00
SL Stephane Lasme 8.00 20.00
SW Sean Williams 8.00 20.00
TU Alando Tucker 8.00 20.00
WC Wilson Chandler 12.00 30.00

2007-08 Fleer Hot Prospects Rookie Photo Shoot Postmarks

STATED PRINT RUN 50 SER.#'d SETS
UNPRICED RED PRINT RUN 10 SETS
AA Arron Afflalo 8.00 20.00
AB Aaron Brooks 6.00 15.00
AG Aaron Gray 6.00 15.00
AH Al Horford 15.00 40.00
AL Acie Law 6.00 15.00
AT Al Thornton 6.00 15.00
CB Corey Brewer 8.00 20.00
CL Carl Landry 6.00 15.00
CR Chris Richard 6.00 15.00
DA Jermareo Davidson 6.00 15.00
DB Derrick Byars 6.00 15.00
DC Daequan Cook 6.00 15.00
DN Demetris Nichols 6.00 15.00
DS D.J. Strawberry 6.00 15.00
GD Glen Davis 10.00 25.00
GP Gabe Pruitt 6.00 15.00
HA Adam Haluska 6.00 15.00
JC Javaris Crittenton 6.00 15.00
JC JamesOn Curry 6.00 15.00
JD Jared Dudley 6.00 15.00
JG Jeff Green 12.50 30.00
JM Josh McRoberts 6.00 15.00
JN Joakim Noah 30.00 80.00
JW Julian Wright 8.00 20.00
KD Kevin Durant 200.00 400.00
MA Morris Almond 6.00 15.00
MC Mike Conley Jr. 12.50 30.00
MW Marcus Williams 6.00 15.00
NF Nick Fazekas 6.00 15.00
RS Ramon Sessions 15.00 40.00
SH Spencer Hawes 6.00 15.00
SL Stephane Lasme 6.00 15.00
SM Sammy Mejia 6.00 15.00
SW Sean Williams 6.00 15.00
TG Taurean Green 6.00 15.00
TU Alando Tucker 6.00 15.00
WC Wilson Chandler 10.00 25.00

2007-08 Fleer Hot Prospects Stat Tracker

COMPLETE SET (35) 20.00 40.00
APPROXIMATELY TWO PER BOX
1 A.C. Green .75 2.00
2 Adrian Dantley .75 2.00
3 Andre Miller .60 1.50
4 Andrea Bargnani 1.00 2.50
5 Antawn Jamison .75 2.00
6 Artis Gilmore .75 2.00
7 B.J. Armstrong .75 2.00
8 Baron Davis .75 2.00
9 Bill Laimbeer .75 2.00
10 Bill Russell 1.25 3.00
11 Bill Walton .75 2.00
12 Brandon Roy 1.00 2.50
13 Daniel Gibson .75 2.00
14 Dennis Rodman 1.25 3.00
15 Deron Williams 1.25 3.00
16 Donyell Marshall .50 1.25
17 Emeka Okafor .75 2.00
18 Hakeem Olajuwon 1.00 2.50
19 Jason Kidd .75 2.00
20 John Stockton 1.25 3.00
21 Kobe Bryant 4.00 10.00
22 Kobe Bryant 4.00 10.00
23 LeBron James 4.00 10.00
24 Magic Johnson 2.00 5.00
25 Mark Price .75 2.00
26 Michael Jordan 6.00 15.00
27 Michael Jordan 6.00 15.00
28 Paul Pierce 1.00 2.50
29 Robert Parish .75 2.00
30 Slick Watts .75 2.00
31 Steve Kerr .75 2.00
32 Steve Nash 1.00 2.50
33 Tom Chambers .75 2.00
34 Tyson Chandler .60 1.50
35 Vince Carter 1.00 2.50

2007-08 Fleer Hot Prospects Stat Tracker Jersey Autographs

PRINT RUN 23 TO 50 SER.#'d SETS
UNPRICED BLUE PRINT RUN ONE SET
*RED: .5X TO 1.25X BASE HI
RED PRINT RUN 25 SER.#'d SETS
2 Adrian Dantley/50 6.00 15.00
4 Andrea Bargnani/37 6.00 15.00
5 Antawn Jamison/50 6.00 15.00
8 Baron Davis/50 6.00 15.00
10 Bill Russell/50 75.00 150.00
11 Bill Walton/50 10.00 25.00
12 Brandon Roy/50 15.00 40.00
13 Daniel Gibson/50 6.00 15.00
14 Dennis Rodman/50 30.00 60.00
15 Deron Williams/50 15.00 30.00
16 Donyell Marshall/50 6.00 15.00
17 Emeka Okafor/50 6.00 15.00
18 Hakeem Olajuwon/50 20.00 50.00
19 Jason Kidd/50 15.00 30.00
20 John Stockton/50 35.00 75.00
22 Kobe Bryant/24 125.00 250.00
23 LeBron James/50 100.00 200.00
24 Magic Johnson/50 40.00 80.00
26 Michael Jordan/23 300.00 600.00
27 Michael Jordan/23 300.00 600.00
28 Paul Pierce/50 15.00 30.00
31 Steve Kerr/50 15.00 30.00
32 Steve Nash/50 35.00 75.00
33 Tom Chambers/50 10.00 25.00
34 Tyson Chandler/50 6.00 15.00
35 Vince Carter/50 20.00 40.00

2007-08 Fleer Hot Prospects Supreme Court

COMPLETE SET (30) 15.00 30.00
APPROXIMATELY TWO PER BOX
1 Shareef Abdur-Rahim .60 1.50
2 Leandro Barbosa .60 1.50
3 Rick Barry .75 2.00
4 Mike Bibby .75 2.00
5 Tom Chambers .75 2.00
6 Michael Cooper .75 2.00
7 Chuck Daly .75 2.00
8 Adrian Dantley .75 2.00
9 Brad Daugherty .75 2.00
10 Sean Elliott .75 2.00
11 Walt Frazier .75 2.00
12 A.C. Green .75 2.00
13 Connie Hawkins .75 2.00
14 Bobby Jackson .50 1.25
15 Antawn Jamison .75 2.00
16 Michael Jordan 6.00 15.00
17 Steve Kerr .75 2.00
18 Jason Kidd .75 2.00
19 Dan Majerle 1.00 2.50
20 Donyell Marshall .50 1.25
21 Chris Mihm .50 1.25
22 Andre Miller .60 1.50
23 Don Nelson .75 2.00
24 Robert Parish .75 2.00
25 Tony Parker .75 2.00
26 Mark Price .75 2.00
27 Tayshaun Prince .75 2.00
28 Glen Rice .75 2.00
29 Dennis Scott .75 2.00
30 Jerry Sloan .75 2.00

2007-08 Fleer Hot Prospects Supreme Court Autographs

PRINT RUN 15 TO 25 SER.#'d SETS
UNPRICED RED PRINT RUN 10 SER.#'d SETS
UNPRICED BLUE PRINT RUN ONE SET
AJ Antawn Jamison/25 6.00 15.00
AM Andre Miller/25 6.00 15.00
BJ Bobby Jackson/25 6.00 15.00
CH Connie Hawkins/25 15.00 30.00
JK Jason Kidd/25 15.00 30.00
LB Leandro Barbosa/25 6.00 15.00
MJ Michael Jordan/25 300.00 550.00
MP Mark Price/25 25.00 50.00
PR Tayshaun Prince/25 6.00 15.00
SA Shareef Abdur-Rahim/25 6.00 15.00
SK Steve Kerr/25 15.00 30.00
TC Tom Chambers/25 6.00 15.00
WF Walt Frazier/15 20.00 40.00

2002-03 Fleer Hot Shots

Issued in late January 2003, the 207-card Fleer Hot Shots set consisted of 100 base cards, 29 dual player give and go cards featuring a scorer and passer from each of the NBA's teams, 39 All-Star cards and 39 rookie cards. Base cards picture full color action player shots centered with a zoom-in portrait style photo on the right side. Rookie cards were designed horizontally and were available in several different formats: Shirt swatch RC cards were sequentially numbered to 200 while other versions are denoted with a material and a print run below. Several players that fall between numbers 169 and 207 do not have any material on the card, and card numbers 196-201 feature rookie players coupled with Vince Carter and a swatch of a VC jersey. Fleer Hot Shots was packaged in 20-pack boxes were packs contained eight cards and carried an SRP of $3.99.

COMP.SET w/o SP's (168) 15.00 40.00
1 Shareef Abdur-Rahim .25 .60
2 Kedrick Brown .20 .50
3 Trenton Hassell .20 .50
4 Raef LaFrentz .20 .50
5 Donnell Harvey .20 .50
6 Danny Fortson .20 .50
7 Maurice Taylor .20 .50
8 Wang Zhizhi .20 .50
9 Malik Allen .20 .50
10 Tim Thomas .20 .50
11 Jason Kidd .50 1.25
12 Jamaal Magloire .20 .50
13 Grant Hill .40 1.00
14 Anfernee Hardaway .50 1.25
15 Bonzi Wells .20 .50
16 Malik Rose .20 .50
17 Antonio Davis .20 .50
18 John Stockton .40 1.00
19 Theo Ratliff .20 .50
20 Paul Pierce .40 1.00
21 Jalen Rose .25 .60
22 Eduardo Najera .20 .50
23 Chauncey Billups .30 .75
24 Antawn Jamison .30 .75
25 Jonathan Bender .20 .50
26 Rick Fox .25 .60
27 Brian Grant .20 .50
28 Kevin Garnett .60 1.50
29 Kenyon Martin .30 .75
30 Allan Houston .25 .60
31 Tracy McGrady .50 1.25
32 Stephon Marbury .25 .60
33 Mike Bibby .30 .75
34 Predrag Drobnjak .20 .50
35 Lamond Murray .20 .50
36 Kwame Brown .20 .50
37 Glenn Robinson .25 .60
38 Antoine Walker .25 .60
39 Zydrunas Ilgauskas .25 .60
40 Clifford Robinson .20 .50
41 Dirk Nowitzki .50 1.25
42 Troy Murphy .30 .75
43 Al Harrington .25 .60
44 Shaquille O'Neal .75 2.00
45 Eddie House .20 .50
46 Troy Hudson .20 .50
47 Rodney Rogers .20 .50
48 Latrell Sprewell .25 .60
49 Allen Iverson .50 1.25
50 Derek Anderson .20 .50
51 Vlade Divac .25 .60
52 Rashard Lewis .30 .75
53 Morris Peterson .20 .50
54 Jerry Stackhouse .25 .60
55 Jason Terry .25 .60
56 Tyson Chandler .25 .60
57 Jumaine Jones .20 .50
58 Nick Van Exel .25 .60
59 Ben Wallace .30 .75
60 Jason Richardson .30 .75
61 Ron Mercer .20 .50
62 Shane Battier .30 .75
63 Eddie Jones .25 .60
64 Joe Smith .25 .60
65 Courtney Alexander .20 .50
66 Kurt Thomas .20 .50
67 Todd MacCulloch .20 .50
68 Ruben Patterson .20 .50
69 Tim Duncan .60 1.50
70 Gary Payton .30 .75
71 Jarron Collins .20 .50
72 Vin Baker .25 .60
73 Eddy Curry .25 .60
74 Michael Finley .30 .75
75 Marcus Camby .25 .60
76 Corliss Williamson .20 .50
77 Steve Francis .30 .75
78 Jermaine O'Neal .30 .75
79 Michael Dickerson .20 .50
80 Alonzo Mourning .40 1.00
81 Rod Strickland .25 .60
82 Elden Campbell .20 .50
83 Charlie Ward .20 .50
84 Aaron McKie .20 .50
85 Scottie Pippen .50 1.25
86 Tony Parker .40 1.00
87 Vladimir Radmanovic .20 .50
88 Matt Harpring .25 .60
89 Eddie Griffin .20 .50
90 Michael Olowokandi .20 .50
91 Stromile Swift .20 .50
92 Michael Redd .30 .75
93 Richard Jefferson .30 .75
94 Baron Davis .30 .75
95 Pat Garrity .20 .50
96 Tom Gugliotta .20 .50
97 Arvydas Sabonis .25 .60
98 David Robinson .50 1.25
99 Michael Bradley .20 .50
100 Karl Malone .40 1.00
101 Jason Terry .25 .60
Glenn Robinson
102 Tony Delk .40 1.00
Paul Pierce
103 Jalen Rose .25 .60
Marcus Fizer
104 Darius Miles .25 .60
Ricky Davis
105 Steve Nash .50 1.25
Dirk Nowitzki
106 Kenny Satterfield .25 .60
Juwan Howard
107 Richard Hamilton .30 .75
Ben Wallace
108 Gilbert Arenas .30 .75
Antawn Jamison
109 Moochie Norris .25 .60
Cuttino Mobley
110 Jamaal Tinsley .30 .75
Reggie Miller
111 Andre Miller .30 .75
Lamar Odom
112 Derek Fisher 1.50 4.00
Kobe Bryant
113 Jason Williams .30 .75
Shane Battier
114 Travis Best .25 .60
Eddie Jones
115 Sam Cassell .30 .75
Ray Allen
116 Terrell Brandon .25 .60
Wally Szczerbiak
117 Kerry Kittles .30 .75
Richard Jefferson
118 David Wesley .25 .60
Jamal Mashburn
119 Latrell Sprewell .25 .60
Antonio McDyess
120 Darrell Armstrong .30 .75
Mike Miller
121 Eric Snow .20 .50
Keith Van Horn
122 Stephon Marbury .30 .75
Shawn Marion
123 Damon Stoudamire .30 .75
Rasheed Wallace
124 Mike Bibby .30 .75
Chris Webber
125 Tony Parker .50 1.25
David Robinson
126 Kenny Anderson .30 .75
Rashard Lewis
127 Alvin Williams .50 1.25
Vince Carter
128 John Stockton .40 1.00
Karl Malone
129 Larry Hughes 2.50 6.00
Michael Jordan
130 Joe Johnson AS .30 .75
131 Andrei Kirilenko AS .30 .75
132 Brendan Haywood AS .20 .50
133 Zeljko Rebraca AS .20 .50
134 Quentin Richardson AS .25 .60
135 Chris Mihm AS .20 .50
136 Darius Miles AS .20 .50
137 Desmond Mason AS .25 .60
138 Hedo Turkoglu AS .30 .75
139 Jason Richardson AS .30 .75
140 Gerald Wallace AS .30 .75
141 Steve Francis AS .30 .75
142 Steve Nash AS .40 1.00
143 Peja Stojakovic AS .30 .75
144 Ray Allen AS .30 .75
145 Mike Miller AS .30 .75
146 Pau Gasol AS .40 1.00
147 Steve Smith AS .25 .60
148 Paul Pierce AS .40 1.00
149 Derek Fisher AS .25 .60
150 Cuttino Mobley AS .25 .60
151 Dikembe Mutombo AS .30 .75
152 Vince Carter AS .50 1.25
153 Antoine Walker AS .25 .60
154 Allen Iverson AS .50 1.25
155 Michael Jordan AS 2.50 6.00
156 Shaquille O'Neal AS .75 2.00
157 Tim Duncan AS .60 1.50
158 Kevin Garnett AS .60 1.50
159 Kobe Bryant AS 1.50 4.00
160 Shareef Abdur-Rahim AS .25 .60
161 Baron Davis AS .30 .75
162 Jason Kidd AS .50 1.25
163 Tracy McGrady AS .50 1.25
164 Jermaine O'Neal AS .30 .75
165 Elton Brand AS .30 .75
166 Gary Payton AS .30 .75
167 Wally Szczerbiak AS .25 .60
168 Chris Webber AS .30 .75
169 Yao Ming JSY/350 RC 12.00 30.00
170 Fred Jones/350 RC 4.00 10.00
171 Ryan Humphrey RC 4.00 10.00
172 Drew Gooden Hat/300 RC 6.00 15.00
173 Nikoloz Tskitishvili RC 4.00 10.00
174 Caron Butler Shorts/350 RC 6.00 15.00
175 Vincent Yarbrough RC 4.00 10.00
176 DaJuan Wagner RC 4.00 10.00
177 Nene Hilario RC 5.00 12.00
178 Qyntel Woods/350 RC 4.00 10.00
179 Jared Jeffries RC 4.00 10.00
180 Casey Jacobsen RC 4.00 10.00
181 Marcus Haislip Hat/300 RC 4.00 10.00
182 Kareem Rush/350 RC 4.00 10.00
183 Predrag Savovic RC 4.00 10.00
184 Melvin Ely RC 4.00 10.00
185 Amare Stoudemire RC 10.00 25.00
186 John Salmons RC 5.00 12.00
187 Chris Jefferies RC 4.00 10.00
188 Juan Dixon RC 5.00 12.00
189 Carlos Boozer RC 8.00 20.00
190 Roger Mason/350 RC 4.00 10.00
191 Ronald Murray/350 RC 4.00 10.00
192 Tayshaun Prince RC 5.00 12.00
193 Chris Wilcox/350 RC 4.00 10.00
194 Sam Clancy RC 4.00 10.00
195 Dan Gadzuric RC 4.00 10.00
196 Dan Dickau RC 4.00 10.00
Vince Carter JSY
197 Frank Williams RC 4.00 10.00
Vince Carter JSY
198 Mike Dunleavy RC 5.00 12.00
Vince Carter JSY/350
199 Jay Williams RC 5.00 12.00
Vince Carter JSY/350
200 Curtis Borchardt RC 4.00 10.00
Vince Carter JSY/350
201 Gordan Giricek RC 4.00 10.00
Vince Carter JSY/350
202 Pat Burke RC 2.50 6.00
203 Reggie Evans RC 2.50 6.00
204 Rasual Butler RC 2.50 6.00
205 Jiri Welsch RC 2.50 6.00
206 Mehmet Okur RC 2.50 6.00
207 Jannero Pargo RC 2.50 6.00

2002-03 Fleer Hot Shots Hot Hands

Randomly inserted in packs, this 207-card set parallels the base set enhanced with gold foil highlights. Card numbers 1-168 are sequentially numbered to 199 and rookie player cards, numbers 169-207, are sequentially numbered to 99. The rookie players cards do not contain a swatch of memorabilia.
*STARS: 3X TO 8X BASE CARD HI
*RCs 168-201: .5X TO 1.25X BASE CARD HI
*RCs 202-207: .75X TO 2X BASE HI

2002-03 Fleer Hot Shots Rookie Hats Off

Randomly inserted in packs, this 21-card set parallels the base RC cards enhanced with a swatch of draft day hat unless otherwise noted. The most common print run was 150, but the exceptions are listed with print runs below.
*HATS OFF: .4X TO 1X BASE RC HI

2002-03 Fleer Hot Shots All-Stars Triple Game-Used

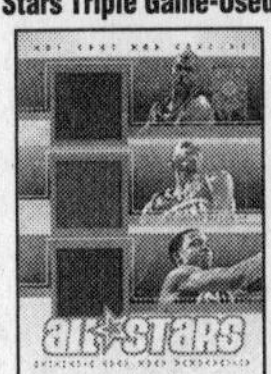

Randomly seeded in packs, this 10-card set features three players on each card front. A small head shot is present on the right side of the card while square swatches of game used memorabilia appear on the left. Each card is sequentially numbered to 25.
1 Vince Carter 50.00 120.00
Tracy McGrady
Allen Iverson
2 Jason Kidd 50.00 100.00
Paul Pierce
Baron Davis
3 Paul Pierce 20.00 50.00
Predrag Stojakovic
Ray Allen
4 Pau Gasol 20.00 50.00
Jason Richardson
Hidayet Turkoglu
5 Jermaine O'Neal 20.00 50.00
Dikembe Mutombo
Shareef Abdur-Rahim
6 Wally Szczerbiak 20.00 50.00
Mike Miller
Pau Gasol
7 Elton Brand 75.00 150.00
Kevin Garnett
Chris Webber
8 Darius Miles 20.00 50.00
Joe Johnson
Andrei Kirilenko
9 Gary Payton 40.00 100.00
Jason Kidd
Steve Nash
10 Jason Richardson 20.00 50.00
Desmond Mason
Steve Francis

2002-03 Fleer Hot Shots En Fuego

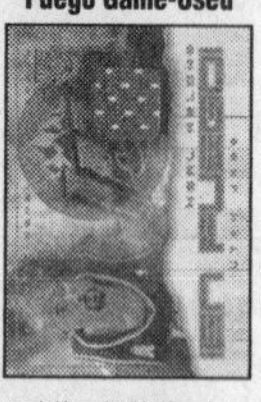

Seeded in packs at the rate of one in 12, this 12-card set showcases a horizontal design with player photos set against a fire background. All cards are highlighted with silver foil.

COMPLETE SET (12) 6.00 15.00
EF1 Elton Brand .60 1.50
EF2 Allen Iverson 1.00 2.50
EF3 Tracy McGrady 1.00 2.50
EF4 Jason Richardson .60 1.50
EF5 Vince Carter 1.00 2.50
EF6 Karl Malone .75 2.00
EF7 Stephon Marbury .50 1.25
EF8 Shareef Abdur-Rahim .50 1.25
EF9 Steve Francis .60 1.50
EF10 Kenyon Martin .60 1.50
EF11 Shaquille O'Neal 1.50 4.00
EF12 Tim Duncan 1.25 3.00

2002-03 Fleer Hot Shots En Fuego Game-Used

Randomly seeded in packs, this 10-card set parallels the base En Fuego insert set enhanced with bronze foil highlights and a square swatch of game used memorabilia. A Gold version was issued as well and is sequentially numbered to 50.

*GOLD: .5X TO 1.25X GAME USED HI
AI Allen Iverson 5.00 12.00
EB Elton Brand Shorts 3.00 8.00
JR Jason Richardson 3.00 8.00
KM Kenyon Martin Shorts 3.00 8.00
KM Karl Malone 4.00 10.00
SA Shareef Abdur-Rahim 2.50 6.00
SF Steve Francis 3.00 8.00
SM Stephon Marbury 2.50 6.00
TM Tracy McGrady 5.00 12.00
VC Vince Carter 5.00 12.00

2002-03 Fleer Hot Shots Give and Go Game-Used

Randomly inserted in packs, this 27-card set paralells the Give and Go cards from the base set enhanced with two swatches of game used memorabilia. Several different types of memorabilia were used, and they are cataloged below. Each card is sequentially numbered to 50.

101 Jason Terry Jkt 8.00 20.00
Glenn Robinson Jkt
102 Tony Delk JSY 10.00 25.00
Paul Pierce JSY
103 Jalen Rose JSY 8.00 20.00
Marcus Fizer Pants
104 Darius Miles JSY 8.00 20.00
Ricky Davis JSY
105 Steve Nash JSY 12.50 30.00
Dirk Nowitzki JSY
106 Kenny Satterfield JSY 8.00 20.00
Juwan Howard JSY
107 Richard Hamilton Shirt 8.00 20.00
Ben Wallace JSY
108 Gilbert Arenas Jkt 8.00 20.00
Antawn Jamison Pants
109 Moochie Norris JSY 8.00 20.00
Cuttino Mobley Jkt
110 Jamaal Tinsley JSY 10.00 25.00
Reggie Miller JSY
111 Andre Miller JSY 8.00 20.00
Lamar Odom Jkt
113 Jason Williams JSY 8.00 20.00
Shane Battier JSY
114 Travis Best JSY 8.00 20.00
Eddie Jones JSY
115 Sam Cassell Shirt 10.00 25.00
Ray Allen Shirt
116 Terrell Brandon JSY 8.00 20.00
Wally Szczerbiak JSY
117 Kerry Kittles Jkt 8.00 20.00
Richard Jefferson Shorts
118 David Wesley JSY 8.00 20.00
Jamal Mashburn JSY
119 Latrell Sprewell Shorts 8.00 20.00
Antonio McDyess JSY
120 Darrell Armstrong JSY 8.00 20.00
Mike Miller JSY
121 Eric Snow Jkt 8.00 20.00
Keith Van Horn Pants
122 Stephon Marbury JSY 8.00 20.00
Shawn Marion JSY
123 Damon Stoudamire Jkt 8.00 20.00
Rasheed Wallace Shirt
124 Mike Bibby JSY 10.00 25.00
Chris Webber JSY
125 Tony Parker JSY 12.50 30.00
David Robinson JSY
126 Kenny Anderson JSY 8.00 20.00
Rashard Lewis JSY
127 Alvin Williams Shirt 8.00 20.00
Vince Carter JSY
128 John Stockton JSY 12.50 30.00
Karl Malone Jkt

2002-03 Fleer Hot Shots Hot Numbers

Randomly inserted in packs at the rate of one in 20, this 20-card set utilizes a horizontal card design with a small player photo centered and a number statistic on the right side of the card. Each card is highlighted with silver foil.

COMPLETE SET (20) 15.00 40.00
HN1 Vince Carter 1.25 3.00
HN2 Gary Payton .75 2.00
HN3 Jason Kidd 1.25 3.00
HN4 Kevin Garnett 1.50 4.00
HN5 Pau Gasol 1.00 2.50
HN6 Darius Miles .50 1.25
HN7 Richard Jefferson .75 2.00
HN8 Corey Maggette .60 1.50
HN9 Kwame Brown .50 1.25
HN10 Antoine Walker .60 1.50
HN11 Shane Battier .75 2.00
HN12 Eddie Jones .60 1.50
HN13 Shawn Marion .75 2.00
HN14 Mike Bibby .75 2.00
HN15 Grant Hill 1.00 2.50
HN16 John Stockton 1.00 2.50
HN17 Lamar Odom .75 2.00
HN18 Keith Van Horn .60 1.50
HN19 Kobe Bryant 4.00 10.00
HN20 Michael Jordan 8.00 20.00

2002-03 Fleer Hot Shots Hot Numbers Game-Used

Randomly inserted in packs, this five card set parallels the base Hot Numbers set enhanced with a swatch of game used memorabilia and sequential numbering to 50.

DM Darius Miles 3.00 8.00
JK Jason Kidd 8.00 20.00
KB Kwame Brown 3.00 8.00
KG Kevin Garnett 10.00 25.00
VC Vince Carter 8.00 20.00

2002-03 Fleer Hot Shots Hot Shots Inserts

Randomly inserted in packs at the rate of one in eight, this 12-card set features top draft picks on a vertical card design with the words "Hot Shots" along the top where the word "hot" is printed in gold. Player portrat shots are placed in front of a red background where the top and bottom of the card are white.

COMPLETE SET (12) 10.00 25.00
1 Juan Dixon 1.00 2.50
2 Yao Ming 2.50 6.00
3 Caron Butler 1.25 3.00
4 Kareem Rush .75 2.00
5 Nene Hilario 1.00 2.50
6 Jay Williams 1.00 2.50
7 Jared Jeffries .75 2.00
8 Amare Stoudemire 2.00 5.00
9 Carlos Boozer 1.50 4.00
10 Drew Gooden 1.25 3.00
11 DaJuan Wagner .75 2.00
12 Mike Dunleavy 1.00 2.50

2002-03 Fleer Hot Shots Hot Shots Inserts Game-Used

Randomly seeded in packs, this 10-card set parallels the base Hot Shots insert card enhanced with a swatch of game used memorabilia. A Gold version sequentially numbered to 150 was also inserted in packs.

*GOLD: .75X TO 2X GAME USED HI
AS Amare Stoudemire 6.00 15.00
CB Caron Butler 4.00 10.00
CB Carlos Boozer 5.00 12.00
DG Drew Gooden 4.00 10.00
DW Dajuan Wagner 2.50 6.00
JD Juan Dixon 3.00 8.00
JJ Jared Jeffries 2.50 6.00
KR Kareem Rush 2.50 6.00
NH Nene Hilario 3.00 8.00
YM Yao Ming Jsy 8.00 20.00

2002-03 Fleer Hot Shots Net Burners

Randomly inserted in packs at the rate of one in 24, this 10-card set features a black border along the bottom and a white border along the top. Full color player photos are set against a burned net background, and cards are highlighted with silver foil.

COMPLETE SET (10) 8.00 20.00
NB1 Ray Allen 1.00 2.50
NB2 Peja Stojakovic 1.00 2.50
NB3 Reggie Miller 1.00 2.50
NB4 Dirk Nowitzki 1.50 4.00
NB5 Paul Pierce 1.25 3.00
NB6 Baron Davis 1.00 2.50
NB7 Steve Nash 1.25 3.00
NB8 Latrell Sprewell .75 2.00
NB9 Jermaine O'Neal 1.00 2.50
NB10 David Robinson 1.50 4.00

2002-03 Fleer Hot Shots Net Burners Game-Used

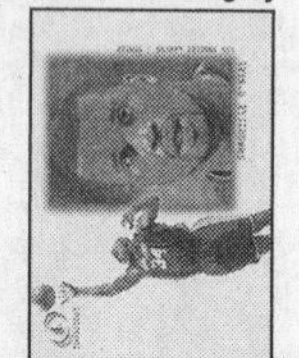

Seeded in packs, this five card set parallels the design of the base Net Burners insert enhanced with a swatch of game used memorabilia and sequential numbering to 100.

BW Ben Wallace JSY 5.00 12.00
CB Caron Butler Shorts 8.00 20.00
DN Dirk Nowitzki JSY 8.00 20.00
JS Jerry Stackhouse JSY 4.00 10.00
PP Paul Pierce JSY 6.00 15.00

2002-03 Fleer Hot Shots Net Burners Gold

Inserted in packs, this 10-card set parallels the base Net Burners insert set enhanced with gold foil highlights. Each card is sequentially numbered to 105.

1 Michael Finley 3.00 8.00
2 Ben Wallace 3.00 8.00
3 Jerry Stackhouse 2.50 6.00
4 Antawn Jamison 3.00 8.00
5 Jay Williams 4.00 10.00
6 Yao Ming 10.00 25.00
7 Drew Gooden 5.00 12.00
8 Amare Stoudemire 8.00 20.00
9 Caron Butler 5.00 12.00
10 Mike Dunleavy 4.00 10.00

2000-01 Fleer Legacy

The 2000-01 Fleer Legacy product released in June, 2001 and featured a 115-card base set that was broken into tiers as follows: 90 Base Veterans (1-90), and 25 Rookies; 12 of which include swatches of game-used jersey. Please note that each rookie card is serial numbered to 799. Each pack contained 5 cards, and a suggested retail price of $175 per box. Also note that this hobby exclusive product contained one Autographed Replica Jersey per box.

COMP.SET w/o SP's (90) 20.00 50.00
1 Vince Carter .75 2.00
2 Tim Duncan .75 2.00
3 Darrell Armstrong .25 .60
4 Chauncey Billups .40 1.00
5 Shawn Kemp .40 1.00
6 Stephon Marbury .30 .75
7 Dan Majerle .30 .75
8 Antawn Jamison .40 1.00
9 Hakeem Olajuwon .50 1.25
10 Kobe Bryant 2.00 5.00
11 Paul Pierce .50 1.25
12 Patrick Ewing .50 1.25
13 Steve Francis .40 1.00
14 Latrell Sprewell .30 .75
15 Andre Miller .30 .75
16 Gary Payton .40 1.00
17 Michael Finley .40 1.00
18 Brian Grant .25 .60
19 Scottie Pippen .60 1.50
20 Antonio Davis .25 .60
21 Jason Williams .40 1.00
22 Chris Gatling .25 .60
23 David Robinson .60 1.50
24 John Stockton .50 1.25
25 Matt Harpring .30 .75
26 Rashard Lewis .40 1.00
27 Dirk Nowitzki .60 1.50
28 Alan Henderson .25 .60
29 Rasheed Wallace .40 1.00
30 Ben Wallace .40 1.00
31 Chris Webber .40 1.00
32 Elton Brand .40 1.00
33 Anfernee Hardaway .60 1.50
34 Isaiah Rider .30 .75
35 Baron Davis .40 1.00
36 Eric Snow .25 .60
37 Tom Gugliotta .25 .60
38 Grant Hill .50 1.25
39 Lamar Odom .40 1.00
40 Kevin Garnett .75 2.00
41 Reggie Miller .40 1.00
42 Karl Malone .50 1.25
43 Ray Allen .40 1.00
44 Derek Anderson .25 .60
45 Glen Rice .30 .75
46 Antonio McDyess .30 .75
47 Eddie Jones .40 1.00
48 Mitch Richmond .30 .75
49 Mark Jackson .30 .75
50 Larry Johnson .40 1.00
51 Ron Mercer .25 .60
52 Jason Kidd .60 1.50
53 Voshon Lenard .25 .60
54 Rick Fox .30 .75
55 Rod Strickland .30 .75
56 Jalen Rose .30 .75
57 Tracy McGrady .60 1.50
58 Dikembe Mutombo .40 1.00
59 Richard Hamilton .30 .75
60 Jerry Stackhouse .30 .75
61 Peja Stojakovic .40 1.00
62 Sam Cassell .30 .75
63 Sean Elliott .30 .75
64 Keith Van Horn .30 .75
65 Mike Bibby .40 1.00
66 Larry Hughes .30 .75
67 Nick Van Exel .30 .75
68 Michael Dickerson .25 .60
69 Terrell Brandon .25 .60
70 Chucky Atkins .25 .60
71 John Starks .25 .60
72 Glenn Robinson .30 .75
73 Cuttino Mobley .30 .75
74 Shaquille O'Neal 1.00 2.50
75 Shareef Abdur-Rahim .30 .75
76 Danny Fortson .25 .60
77 Austin Croshere .25 .60
78 Jamal Mashburn .30 .75
79 Kenny Anderson .30 .75
80 Shawn Marion .40 1.00
81 Travis Best .25 .60
82 Derrick Coleman .30 .75
83 Toni Kukoc .30 .75
84 Allen Iverson .75 2.00
85 Allan Houston .30 .75
86 Antoine Walker .30 .75
87 Wally Szczerbiak .30 .75
88 Raef LaFrentz .25 .60
89 Tim Hardaway .40 1.00
90 Juwan Howard .30 .75
91 Kenyon Martin JSY RC 8.00 20.00
92 Stromile Swift RC 2.00 5.00
93 Darius Miles JSY RC 3.00 8.00
94 Mike Miller JSY RC 6.00 15.00
95 Marcus Fizer RC 2.00 5.00
96 Jerome Moiso JSY RC 3.00 8.00
97 DerMarr Johnson JSY RC 3.00 8.00
98 Quentin Richardson JSY RC 5.00 12.00
99 Morris Peterson JSY RC 3.00 8.00
100 Jamaal Magloire RC 2.00 5.00
101 Mateen Cleaves RC 2.00 5.00
102 Hedo Turkoglu RC 4.00 10.00
103 Chris Mihm JSY RC 3.00 8.00
104 Courtney Alexander RC 2.00 5.00
105 Joel Przybilla RC 2.00 5.00
106 Speedy Claxton JSY RC 3.00 8.00
107 Keyon Dooling JSY RC 3.00 8.00
108 Desmond Mason JSY RC 4.00 10.00
109 Jamal Crawford RC 3.00 8.00
110 DeShawn Stevenson RC 2.50 6.00
111 Stephen Jackson RC 3.00 8.00
112 Marc Jackson RC 2.00 5.00
113 Hanno Mottola JSY RC 3.00 8.00
114 Eduardo Najera RC 2.00 5.00
115 Wang Zhizhi RC 4.00 10.00
WUSA1 Vince Carter/600 30.00 80.00

2000-01 Fleer Legacy Ultimate Legacy

Randomly inserted into packs, this 115-card set is a complete parallel of the Fleer Legacy base set. Each card was produced with a gold-colored card front and is serial numbered to 175.

*STARS: 2.5X TO 6X BASE
*RCs: .6X TO 1.5X BASE
*JSY RCs: .4X TO 1X BASE

2000-01 Fleer Legacy Ball Of Fame

Randomly inserted into packs at one in 40, this 20-card set features a swatch of actual game-used basketball. Card backs carry a "BF" prefix.

BF1 Vince Carter 5.00 12.00
BF2 Kenyon Martin 6.00 15.00
BF3 Jason Williams 2.50 6.00
BF4 Ray Allen 2.50 6.00
BF5 Lamar Odom 2.50 6.00
BF6 Allen Iverson 5.00 12.00
BF7 Stephon Marbury 2.00 5.00
BF8 Tracy McGrady 4.00 10.00
BF9 Darius Miles 2.50 6.00
BF10 Steve Francis 2.50 6.00
BF11 Stromile Swift 2.50 6.00
BF12 Shawn Marion 2.50 6.00
BF13 Shawn Kemp 2.50 6.00
BF14 Larry Hughes 2.00 5.00
BF15 Baron Davis 2.50 6.00
BF16 Jalen Rose 2.00 5.00
BF17 Patrick Ewing 3.00 8.00
BF18 Karl Malone 3.00 8.00
BF19 Marcus Fizer 2.50 6.00
BF20 Wally Szczerbiak 2.00 5.00

2000-01 Fleer Legacy Floor Generals

Randomly inserted into packs at one in 18, this 20-card set features a swatch of actual game-used floor. Card backs carry an "FG" prefix.

FG1 Vince Carter 5.00 12.00
FG2 Allen Iverson 5.00 12.00
FG3 Chris Webber 2.50 6.00
FG4 Shaquille O'Neal 6.00 15.00
FG5 Reggie Miller 2.50 6.00
FG6 Tracy McGrady 4.00 10.00
FG7 David Robinson 4.00 10.00
FG8 Jason Kidd 4.00 10.00
FG9 Latrell Sprewell 2.00 5.00
FG10 Eddie Jones 2.50 6.00
FG11 Michael Finley 2.50 6.00
FG12 Jerry Stackhouse 2.00 5.00
FG13 Karl Malone 3.00 8.00
FG14 Anfernee Hardaway 4.00 10.00
FG15 Gary Payton 2.50 6.00
FG16 Shareef Abdur-Rahim 2.00 5.00
FG17 Tim Hardaway 2.50 6.00
FG18 Ray Allen 2.50 6.00
FG19 Stephon Marbury 2.00 5.00
FG20 John Stockton 3.00 8.00

2000-01 Fleer Legacy NBA Game Issue

Randomly inserted into packs at one in 15, this 30-card set features a swatch of actual game-used jersey. Card backs carry a "GI" prefix.

GI1 Vince Carter 5.00 12.00
GI2 Baron Davis 2.50 6.00
GI3 Trajan Langdon 2.00 5.00
GI4 Grant Hill 3.00 8.00
GI5 Allen Iverson 5.00 12.00
GI6 Jason Kidd 4.00 10.00
GI7 Karl Malone 3.00 8.00
GI8 Stephon Marbury 2.00 5.00
GI9 Shawn Marion 2.50 6.00
GI10 Tracy McGrady 4.00 10.00
GI11 Andre Miller 2.00 5.00
GI12 Dikembe Mutombo 2.50 6.00
GI13 Lamar Odom 2.50 6.00
GI14 Shaquille O'Neal 6.00 15.00
GI15 Gary Payton 2.50 6.00
GI16 Jason Terry 2.50 6.00
GI17 John Stockton 3.00 8.00
GI18 Patrick Ewing 3.00 8.00
GI19 Anfernee Hardaway 4.00 10.00
GI20 Jason Williams 2.50 6.00
GI21 Darius Miles 2.50 6.00
GI22 Chris Mihm 2.50 6.00
GI23 Desmond Mason 3.00 8.00
GI24 Keyon Dooling 2.50 6.00
GI25 DerMarr Johnson 2.50 6.00
GI26 Speedy Claxton 2.50 6.00
GI27 Kenyon Martin 6.00 15.00
GI28 Hanno Mottola 2.50 6.00
GI29 Mike Miller 5.00 12.00
GI30 Quentin Richardson 4.00 10.00

2000-01 Fleer Legacy Replica Jersey Autographs

Randomly inserted at one per box (box-topper), this 32-jersey set features autographed replica jerseys of some of the hottest players in the NBA. Please note that a few of the jerseys packed out as exchange cards, and must be redeemed to Fleer no longer than 6/01/02.

JERSEY ARJ29 DOES NOT EXIST
ARJ1 Alonzo Mourning Black/250 75.00 150.00
ARJ2 Antoine Walker Green/250 25.00 60.00
ARJ3 Courtney Alexander Blue/375 20.00 50.00
ARJ4 Darius Miles Red/300 20.00 50.00
ARJ5 DerMarr Johnson Red/400 20.00 50.00
ARJ6 Desmond Mason Red/350 20.00 50.00
ARJ7 Dikembe Mutombo Black/150 50.00 120.00
ARJ8 Eddie House Black/325 20.00 50.00
ARJ9 Eddie Jones Black/150 30.00 80.00
ARJ11 Jamal Crawford Black/400 20.00 50.00
ARJ12 Jason Terry Red/500 20.00 50.00
ARJ13 Keith Van Horn Black/100 25.00 60.00
ARJ14 Kenyon Martin Blue/300 25.00 60.00
ARJ14A Kenyon Martin Black/250 30.00 80.00
ARJ16 Larry Hughes Black/250 20.00 50.00
ARJ17 Marc Jackson Black/500 20.00 50.00
ARJ18 Marcus Camby Blue/400 25.00 60.00
ARJ19 Marcus Fizer Red/300 20.00 50.00
ARJ19A Marcus Fizer Black/100 25.00 60.00
ARJ20 Mateen Cleaves Blue/400 20.00 50.00
ARJ20A Mateen Cleaves Red/350 20.00 50.00
ARJ21 Mike Bibby Black/250 20.00 50.00
ARJ22 Paul Pierce Green/500 30.00 80.00
ARJ23 Peja Stojakovic Black/150 30.00 80.00
ARJ23A Peja Stojakovic Purple/150 30.00 80.00
ARJ24 Raef LaFrentz Black/400 20.00 50.00
ARJ25 Ron Artest Red/200 25.00 60.00
ARJ26 Shawn Marion Purple/400 25.00 60.00
ARJ28 Steve Francis Blue/400 20.00 50.00
ARJ30 Tom Gugliotta Purple/400 20.00 50.00
ARJ31 Vince Carter Black/750 50.00 120.00
ARJ31A Vince Carter White/250 75.00 150.00
ARJ32 Wally Szczerbiak Blue/400 20.00 50.00
ARJ32A Wally Szczerbiak Black/200 20.00 50.00

2001-02 Fleer Marquee

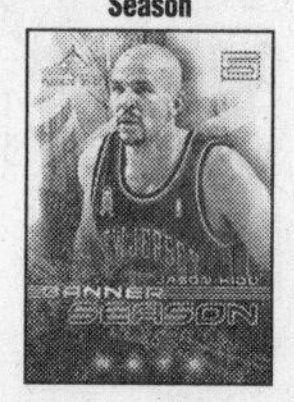

Released in early April 2002, Fleer Marquee breaks down into a 126-card set with 100 veteran player cards and 26 rookie cards. Card number 126, Mengke Bateer was a last minute addition to the set, so on press material, boxes and packs, Marquee is referred to as a 125-card set. The rookie breakdown is as follows: Card numbers 101-115 are sequentially numbered to 1500, card number 116-125 are sequentially numbered to 2500, and number 126 is sequentially numbered to 1500. Also included in packs was a limited Vince Carter NNO autographed card sequentially numbered to 113. Base cards feature an embossed gray-scale basketball texture along the bottom of the card with a silver foil Marquee logo in the left hand corner, and the player's name in the right. Full color action photos are centered with a solid white border and a fade to white edges on the left and right. Rookie cards are white on both the top and the bottom fading into the same embossed silver basketball texturing found on the veteran cards. Player action photos are set against an oval with runs directly through the center of the card. Each Hobby box contained a jumbo box-topper pack of one Feature Presentation card. See those sets for descriptions.

COMPLETE SET w/o SPs 12.50 30.00
1 DerMarr Johnson .20 .50
2 Darius Miles .20 .50
3 Michael Jordan 5.00 12.00
4 Speedy Claxton .20 .50
5 Stromile Swift .20 .50
6 Michael Finley .30 .75
7 Kurt Thomas .20 .50
8 Tim Duncan .60 1.50
9 Kenyon Martin .30 .75
10 Jermaine O'Neal .30 .75
11 Elton Brand .30 .75
12 Jamal Mashburn .25 .60
13 Jumaine Jones .20 .50
14 Stephon Marbury .25 .60
15 Eddie Jones .25 .60
16 Antonio McDyess .25 .60
17 Tim Thomas .20 .50
18 Gary Payton .30 .75
19 Latrell Sprewell .25 .60
20 Grant Hill .40 1.00
21 Jason Terry .30 .75
22 Marcus Fizer .20 .50
23 Anthony Mason .20 .50
24 Bonzi Wells .20 .50
25 Sam Cassell .25 .60
26 Jerry Stackhouse .25 .60
27 Hedo Turkoglu .30 .75
28 Morris Peterson .20 .50
29 John Stockton .40 1.00
30 Dikembe Mutombo .30 .75
31 Mitch Richmond .25 .60
32 Andre Miller .25 .60
33 Joe Smith .25 .60
34 Mike Bibby .30 .75
35 Wally Szczerbiak .25 .60
36 Steve Francis .30 .75
37 Nazr Mohammed .20 .50
38 Antoine Walker .25 .60
39 Courtney Alexander .20 .50
40 Shawn Marion .30 .75
41 Jason Williams .25 .60
42 Steve Nash .50 1.25
43 Antonio Davis .20 .50
44 Steve Smith .25 .60
45 Jason Kidd .50 1.25
46 Reggie Miller .30 .75
47 Quentin Richardson .25 .60
48 Baron Davis .30 .75
49 Juwan Howard .25 .60
50 Rasheed Wallace .30 .75
51 Brian Grant .20 .50
52 Nick Van Exel .25 .60
53 Donyell Marshall .20 .50
54 Vin Baker .25 .60
55 Allan Houston .25 .60
56 Mike Miller .30 .75
57 Shaquille O'Neal .75 2.00
58 Ron Mercer .20 .50
59 Lindsey Hunter .20 .50
60 Peja Stojakovic .30 .75
61 Ray Allen .30 .75
62 Antawn Jamison .30 .75
63 Theo Ratliff .20 .50
64 Vince Carter .50 1.25
65 DeShawn Stevenson .20 .50
66 Allen Iverson .60 1.50
67 Derek Fisher .25 .60
68 Dirk Nowitzki .50 1.25
69 Keith Van Horn .25 .60
70 David Robinson .50 1.25
71 Terrell Brandon .20 .50
72 Cuttino Mobley .25 .60
73 Shareef Abdur-Rahim .25 .60
74 Paul Pierce .40 1.00
75 Elden Campbell .20 .50
76 Anfernee Hardaway .50 1.25
77 Alonzo Mourning .40 1.00
78 Raef LaFrentz .20 .50
79 Richard Hamilton .25 .60
80 Rashard Lewis .30 .75
81 Marcus Camby .25 .60
82 Jalen Rose .25 .60
83 Lamar Odom .30 .75
84 David Wesley .20 .50
85 James Posey .20 .50
86 Derek Anderson .20 .50
87 Glenn Robinson .25 .60
88 Clifford Robinson .20 .50
89 Kerry Kittles .20 .50
90 Hakeem Olajuwon .40 1.00
91 Patrick Ewing .40 1.00
92 Tracy McGrady .50
93 Kobe Bryant 1.50
94 Chris Mihm .20
95 Lorenzen Wright .20
96 Chris Webber .30
97 Kevin Garnett .60
98 Larry Hughes .25
99 Keyon Dooling .20
100 Karl Malone .40
101 Joe Johnson RC 2.00
102 Tyson Chandler RC 1.25
103 Eddy Curry RC 1.25
104 Jason Richardson RC 1.50
105 Troy Murphy RC 1.25
106 Eddie Griffin RC .75
107 Jamaal Tinsley RC 1.00
108 Pau Gasol RC 2.50
109 Shane Battier RC 1.50
110 Richard Jefferson RC 1.50
111 Steven Hunter RC .75
112 Tony Parker RC 3.00
113 Vladimir Radmanovic RC .75
114 Andrei Kirilenko RC 2.00
115 Kwame Brown RC .75
116 Samuel Dalembert RC 1.00
Damone Brown RC
117 Joseph Forte RC .75
Kedrick Brown RC
118 Zach Randolph RC 2.00
Ruben Boumthe RC
119 Oscar Torres RC .75
Terence Morris RC
120 Alton Ford RC .75
Kenny Satterfield RC
121 Rodney White RC .75
Zelijko Rebraca RC
122 Trenton Hassell RC .75
Earl Watson RC
123 DeSagana Diop RC .75
Primoz Brezec RC
124 Ernest Brown RC 1.25
Gerald Wallace RC
125 Loren Woods RC 1.00
Bendan Haywood RC
126 Mengke Bateer RC .75
NNO Vince Carter AU/113 25.00

2001-02 Fleer Marquee Banner Season

Randomly inserted in packs at the rate of one in 20 this 20-card set places full color player photos aga an American flag and a fade to solid color bottom o the card where the color is set to match the featured player's unifor colors. The player's name and "Ban Season" appear in silver foil with the player's team name across the bottom in white.

COMPLETE SET (20) 30.00
1 Vince Carter 2.00
2 Shaquille O'Neal 3.00
3 Allen Iverson 2.50
4 Kevin Garnett 2.50
5 Dirk Nowitzki 2.00
6 Tim Duncan 2.50
7 Michael Jordan 10.00
8 Steve Francis 1.25
9 Grant Hill 1.50
10 Kobe Bryant 6.00
11 Kenyon Martin 1.25
12 Shareef Abdur-Rahim 1.00
13 Ray Allen 1.25
14 Tracy McGrady 2.00
15 Baron Davis 1.25
16 Chris Webber 1.25
17 Jason Kidd 2.00
18 Darius Miles .75
19 Paul Pierce 1.50
20 Karl Malone 1.50

2001-02 Fleer Marquee Banner Season Memorabilia

Randomly inserted in packs at the rate of one in 15, this 15-card set parallels the design from the base Banner Season set enhanced with a swatch of game used memorabilia.

AI Allen Iverson 6.00
BD Baron Davis 3.00
CW Chris Webber 3.00
DM Darius Miles 2.00
DN Dirk Nowitzki 5.00
GH Grant Hill 4.00
JK Jason Kidd 5.00
KM Kenyon Martin 3.00
MM Karl Malone 4.00
PP Paul Pierce 4.00
RA Ray Allen 3.00
SF Steve Francis 3.00
SR Shareef Abdur-Rahim 2.50
TM Tracy McGrady 5.00
VC Vince Carter 5.00

2001-02 Fleer Marquee Co-Stars

Randomly seeded in packs at the rate of one in 10, t 10-card set features a die cut design where the uppe right hand corner and the lower left hand corner are rounded. Veteran player portraits appear on the righ side of the card, and a rookie teammate action photo appears on the left. These two photos are split apart a strip down the middle that contains both player names and the words, "Co-Stars" in silver foil.

1 Michael Jordan 2.00
Kwame Brown

Francis 1.00 2.50
Griffin
McGrady 1.25 3.00
Hunter
Malone 1.25 3.00
i Kirilenko
e Miller 1.00 2.50
l Tinsley
Parker 2.50 6.00
Robinson
Battier 2.00 5.00
asol
Kidd 1.25 3.00
rd Jefferson
n Jamison 1.00 2.50
Richardson
Mercer 1.00 2.50
Curry

1-02 Fleer Marquee Feature Presentation Film

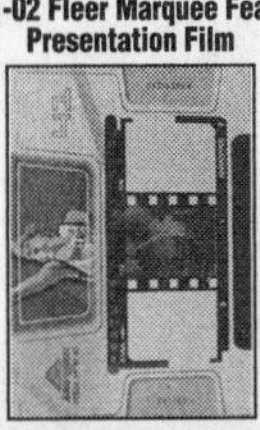

nly inserted as a box-topper, this jumbo card
s a player photo along the top, silver highlights
ingle-slide from an actual game film. Each card
entially numbered to 350. A Vince Carter
phed version was also inserted with this set,
sequentially numbered to 208.

e Carter 4.00 10.00
ce Carter AU/208 25.00 50.00
s Miles 1.50 4.00
n Kidd 4.00 10.00
Hill 3.00 8.00
Webber 2.50 6.00
Nowitzki 4.00 10.00
Iverson 5.00 12.00
McGrady 4.00 10.00
e Francis 2.50 6.00
Malone 3.00 8.00
in Garnett 5.00 12.00
e Bryant 12.00 30.00
Duncan 5.00 12.00
quille O'Neal 6.00 15.00

1-02 Fleer Marquee Feature Presentation Film/Jerseys

mly seeded as a box-topper, this 10-card set
ls the design of the base Feature Presentation
et enhanced with a large swatch of game used
abilia. Each card is sequentailly numbered to

JSY: 1X TO 2.5X BASE HI 4.00 10.00

1-02 Fleer Marquee Feature Presentation Triples

mly seeded as a box-topper, this 10-card set
ls the design of the base Feature Presentation
et enhanced with three different game film slides.
ard is sequentailly numbered to 100.

Hill 8.00 20.00

01-02 Fleer Marquee We're Number One

mly seeded in packs at the rate of one in 240,
-card set features die-cut cards in the shape of
mber one. The outside of the card is highlighted
lver ink, player photos are centered on top of a
rinted to look like a basketball, and the set name,
ee logo, and player's name appears centered on
ttom in silver hologfoil.

eem Olajuwon 3.00 8.00
d Robinson 4.00 10.00
quille O'Neal 6.00 15.00
s Webber 2.50 6.00
n Iverson 5.00 12.00
Duncan 5.00 12.00
n Brand 2.50 6.00
yon Martin 2.50 6.00
me Brown 2.50 6.00
nce Carter 4.00 10.00
ry Bird 8.00 20.00

01-02 Fleer Marquee We're Number One Memorabilia

mly inserted in packs at the rate of one in 32,
ght card set parallels the design of the We're
er One set enhanced with a swatch of game-used
rabilia.

eem Olajuwon 6.00 15.00
id Robinson 8.00 20.00
n Iverson 10.00 25.00
n Brand 5.00 12.00
yon Martin 5.00 12.00
me Brown 5.00 12.00
wame Brown AU/101 10.00 25.00
e Carter 8.00 20.00
nce Carter AU 25.00 60.00
y Bird 15.00 40.00
rry Bird AU 60.00 150.00

2001-02 Fleer Maximum

This 220 card set was issued in 15 card packs and released in March, 2002. The first 180 cards of the set featured veteran players while the final 40 cards of the set honored the leading NBA rookies. Those Rookie Cards had a stated print run of 1000 cards. A Vince Carter autograph card with a stated print run of 375 is noted at the end of these listings but is not considered part of the complete set.

COMPLETE SET (220) 75.00 150.00
COMP.SET w/o SP's (180) 12.50 30.00
1 Ray Allen .25 .60
2 Elton Brand .25 .60
3 Grant Hill .30 .75
4 Tracy McGrady .40 1.00
5 Chris Webber .25 .60
6 Latrell Sprewell .20 .50
7 Paul Pierce .30 .75
8 Jason Kidd .40 1.00
9 Shaquille O'Neal .60 1.50
10 Stephon Marbury .20 .50
11 Steve Francis .25 .60
12 Vince Carter .40 1.00
13 Allen Iverson .50 1.25
14 Kevin Garnett .50 1.25
15 Eddie Jones .20 .50
16 Antoine Walker .20 .50
17 Kobe Bryant 1.25 3.00
18 Avery Johnson .20 .50
19 Damon Stoudamire .20 .50
20 Kurt Thomas .15 .40
21 Aaron McKie .15 .40
22 Chris Whitney .15 .40
23 David Robinson .40 1.00
24 Erick Dampier .15 .40
25 Jumaine Jones .15 .40
26 Radoslav Nesterovic .15 .40
27 Robert Horry .20 .50
28 Ben Wallace .25 .60
29 Christian Laettner .15 .40
30 Eddie Robinson .15 .40
31 Alvin Williams .15 .40
32 Matt Harpring .20 .50
33 Terrell Brandon .15 .40
34 Tim Duncan .50 1.25
35 Bonzi Wells .15 .40
36 Clarence Weatherspoon .15 .40
37 George McCloud .15 .40
38 Jermaine O'Neal .25 .60
39 Al Harrington .20 .50
40 Antawn Jamison .25 .60
41 John Amaechi .15 .40
42 Rod Strickland .20 .50
43 Stacey Augmon .15 .40
44 Dion Glover .15 .40
45 Michael Dickerson .15 .40
46 Anfernee Hardaway .40 1.00
47 Rashard Lewis .25 .60
48 Shawn Bradley .15 .40
49 Todd MacCulloch .15 .40
50 Antonio McDyess .20 .50
51 Darrell Armstrong .15 .40
52 Jalen Rose .20 .50
53 Mike Bibby .25 .60
54 P.J. Brown .15 .40
55 Quincy Lewis .15 .40
56 Doug Christie .15 .40
57 Elden Campbell .15 .40
58 James Posey .15 .40
59 Karl Malone .30 .75
60 Patrick Ewing .30 .75
61 Sam Cassell .20 .50
62 Baron Davis .25 .60
63 Corey Maggette .20 .50
64 Donyell Marshall .15 .40
65 Ervin Johnson .15 .40
66 Horace Grant .20 .50
67 Nick Van Exel .20 .50
68 Vlade Divac .20 .50
69 Allan Houston .20 .50
70 Antonio Davis .15 .40
71 Dale Davis .15 .40
72 Eduardo Najera .15 .40
73 Kenny Anderson .20 .50
74 Kevin Willis .15 .40
75 LaPhonso Ellis .20 .50
76 Anthony Mason .15 .40
77 Greg Ostertag .15 .40
78 Jamal Mashburn .20 .50
79 Jeff McInnis .15 .40
80 Peja Stojakovic .25 .60
81 Scott Williams .15 .40
82 Bryon Russell .15 .40
83 Chucky Atkins .15 .40
84 Darius Miles .15 .40
85 David Wesley .15 .40
86 Hedo Turkoglu .25 .60
87 Mark Pope .15 .40
88 Dana Barros .15 .40
89 Glenn Robinson .20 .50
90 John Stockton .30 .75
91 Lamar Odom .25 .60
92 Mike Miller .25 .60
93 Ron Artest .25 .60
94 Adonal Foyle .15 .40
95 Andre Miller .20 .50
96 Eric Snow .15 .40
97 Stanislav Medvedenko .15 .40
98 Steve Smith .20 .50
99 Wally Szczerbiak .20 .50
100 Chris Mihm .15 .40
101 Danny Fortson .15 .40
102 Dikembe Mutombo .25 .60
103 Joe Smith .20 .50
104 Lindsey Hunter .15 .40
105 Malik Rose .15 .40
106 Austin Croshere .15 .40
107 Chris Gatling .15 .40
108 Hakeem Olajuwon .30 .75
109 Mark Jackson .20 .50
110 Milt Palacio .15 .40
111 Ruben Patterson .15 .40
112 Steve Nash .40 1.00
113 Brian Grant .15 .40
114 Dirk Nowitzki .40 1.00
115 Jeff Foster .15 .40
116 Morris Peterson .15 .40
117 Scottie Pippen .40 1.00
118 Lamond Murray .15 .40
119 Larry Hughes .20 .50
120 Shareef Abdur-Rahim .20 .50
121 Tony Delk .15 .40
122 Vin Baker .20 .50
123 Art Long .15 .40
124 Kenyon Martin .25 .60
125 Michael Finley .25 .60
126 Stromile Swift .15 .40
127 Toni Kukoc .20 .50
128 Alonzo Mourning .30 .75
129 Charlie Ward .15 .40
130 Eric Williams .15 .40
131 Jerome Williams .15 .40
132 Raef LaFrentz .15 .40
133 Rasheed Wallace .25 .60
134 Reggie Miller .25 .60
135 Cuttino Mobley .20 .50
136 Desmond Mason .20 .50
137 Jason Williams .20 .50
138 Keith Van Horn .20 .50
139 Nazr Mohammed .15 .40
140 Shawn Marion .25 .60
141 Tim Hardaway .25 .60
142 Anthony Carter .15 .40
143 Danny Manning .15 .40
144 Derek Anderson .15 .40
145 Jason Terry .25 .60
146 Kenny Thomas .15 .40
147 Othella Harrington .15 .40
148 Corliss Williamson .15 .40
149 Derek Fisher .20 .50
150 Ricky Davis .20 .50
151 Stephen Jackson .20 .50
152 Tryone Nesby .15 .40
153 Calvin Booth .15 .40
154 Emanual Davis .15 .40
155 Kerry Kittles .15 .40
156 Marc Jackson .15 .40
157 Samaki Walker .15 .40
158 Tom Gugliotta .15 .40
159 Wesley Person .15 .40
160 Antonio Daniels .15 .40
161 Charles Oakley .20 .50
162 Chauncey Billups .25 .60
163 Derrick Coleman .20 .50
164 Jerry Stackhouse .20 .50
165 Michael Jordan 4.00 10.00
166 Quentin Richardson .20 .50
167 Gary Payton .25 .60
168 Iakovos Tsakalidis .15 .40
169 Juwan Howard .20 .50
170 Lorenzen Wright .15 .40
171 Marcus Camby .20 .50
172 Maurice Taylor .15 .40
173 Jacque Vaughn .15 .40
174 Bruce Bowen .15 .40
175 Clifford Robinson .15 .40
176 Michael Olowokandi .15 .40
177 Richard Hamilton .20 .50
178 Ron Mercer .15 .40
179 Speedy Claxton .15 .40
180 Tim Thomas .15 .40
181 Joe Johnson HW RC 2.50 6.00
182 Pau Gasol HW RC 3.00 8.00
183 Kwame Brown HW RC 1.00 2.50
184 Zach Randolph HW RC 2.50 6.00
185 Jason Richardson HW RC 2.00 5.00
186 Jamaal Tinsley HW RC 1.25 3.00
187 Oscar Torres HW RC 1.00 2.50
188 Rodney White HW RC 1.00 2.50
189 Kedrick Brown HW RC 1.00 2.50
190 Tony Parker HW RC 4.00 10.00
191 Samuel Dalembert HW RC 1.25 3.00
192 Shane Battier HW RC 2.00 5.00
193 Loren Woods HW RC 1.00 2.50
194 Richard Jefferson HW RC 2.00 5.00
195 Jeff Trepagnier HW RC 1.00 2.50
196 Terence Morris HW RC 1.00 2.50
197 Eddie Griffin TC RC 1.00 2.50
198 Primoz Brezec TC RC 1.00 2.50
199 Vladimir Radmanovic TC RC 1.00 2.50
200 Gerald Wallace TC RC 1.50 4.00
201 Alton Ford TC RC 1.00 2.50
202 Steven Hunter TC RC 1.00 2.50
203 Michael Bradley TC RC 1.00 2.50
204 Brandon Armstrong TC RC 1.00 2.50
205 Jamaal Tinsley TC RC 1.25 3.00
206 Bobby Simmons TC RC 1.00 2.50
207 Zeljko Rebraca TC RC 1.00 2.50
208 Tony Parker TC RC 4.00 10.00
209 Troy Murphy TC RC 1.50 4.00
210 Kwame Brown TC RC 1.00 2.50
211 Andrei Kirilenko TC RC 2.50 6.00
212 Trenton Hassell TC RC 1.00 2.50
213 Pau Gasol TC RC 3.00 8.00
214 Tang Hamilton TC RC 1.00 2.50
215 Joseph Forte TC RC 1.00 2.50
216 Eddy Curry TC RC 1.50 4.00
217 DeSagana Diop TC RC 1.00 2.50
218 Joe Johnson TC RC 2.50 6.00
219 Tyson Chandler TC RC 1.50 4.00
220 Jason Collins TC RC 1.00 2.50
NNO Vince Carter AU/375 15.00 40.00

2001-02 Fleer Maximum Big Shots

Issued in packs at stated odds of one in eight, this 15 card set honors players who are known for not being afraid to take the final shot in a game.

COMPLETE SET (15) 8.00 20.00
1 Grant Hill .75 2.00
2 Ray Allen .60 1.50
3 Allen Iverson 1.25 3.00
4 Elton Brand .60 1.50
5 Baron Davis .60 1.50
6 Jason Terry .60 1.50
7 Mike Bibby .60 1.50
8 David Robinson 1.00 2.50
9 Paul Pierce .75 2.00
10 Dirk Nowitzki 1.00 2.50
11 Jerry Stackhouse .50 1.25
12 Shawn Marion .60 1.50
13 Tracy McGrady 1.00 2.50
14 Anfernee Hardaway 1.00 2.50
15 Vince Carter 1.00 2.50

2001-02 Fleer Maximum Big Shots Jerseys

Issued at stated odds of one in 20, this is a partial parallel to the Big Shots insert set. These cards have a swatch of game-used jersey on them.

1 Grant Hill 4.00 10.00
2 Allen Iverson 6.00 15.00
3 Elton Brand 3.00 8.00
4 Jason Terry 3.00 8.00
5 Mike Bibby 3.00 8.00
6 David Robinson 5.00 12.00
7 Paul Pierce 4.00 10.00
8 Shawn Marion 3.00 8.00
9 Tracy McGrady 5.00 12.00
10 Anfernee Hardaway 5.00 12.00
11 Vince Carter 5.00 12.00

2001-02 Fleer Maximum Floor Score

Issued at stated odds of one in eight, this 15-card set honors some of the NBA's leading scorers.

COMPLETE SET (15) 12.50 30.00
1 Jason Kidd 1.00 2.50
2 Lamar Odom .60 1.50
3 Baron Davis .60 1.50
4 Dirk Nowitzki 1.00 2.50
5 Ray Allen .60 1.50
6 Anfernee Hardaway 1.00 2.50
7 Latrell Sprewell .50 1.25
8 Chris Webber .60 1.50
9 Grant Hill .75 2.00
10 Vince Carter 1.00 2.50
11 Shaquille O'Neal 1.50 4.00
12 Michael Jordan 5.00 12.00
13 Kobe Bryant 3.00 8.00
14 Kevin Garnett 1.25 3.00
15 Tim Duncan 1.25 3.00

2001-02 Fleer Maximum Floor Score Court

Issued at stated odds of one in 40, these 10 cards form a partial parallel to the Floor Score insert set. These cards contain a piece of a floor used in an NBA game.

1 Jason Kidd 5.00 12.00
2 Lamar Odom 3.00 8.00
3 Baron Davis 3.00 8.00
4 Dirk Nowitzki 5.00 12.00
5 Ray Allen 3.00 8.00
6 Anfernee Hardaway 5.00 12.00
7 Latrell Sprewell 2.50 6.00
8 Chris Webber 3.00 8.00
9 Grant Hill 4.00 10.00
10 Vince Carter 5.00 12.00

2001-02 Fleer Maximum Performance

Randomly inserted into packs, these 10 cards feature players known for the full effort each night on the court. These cards were printed to a stated print run of 100 serial numbered sets.

1 Vince Carter 6.00 15.00
2 Tracy McGrady 6.00 15.00
3 Kobe Bryant 20.00 50.00
4 Michael Jordan 40.00 100.00
5 Shaquille O'Neal 10.00 25.00
6 Allen Iverson 8.00 20.00
7 Grant Hill 5.00 12.00
8 Kevin Garnett 8.00 20.00
9 Steve Francis 4.00 10.00
10 Tim Duncan 8.00 20.00

2001-02 Fleer Maximum Power

Issued at stated odds of one in 16, these 15 cards feature players known for their powerful perfomances on the court.

COMPLETE SET (15) 15.00 40.00
1 Kobe Bryant 5.00 12.00
2 Michael Jordan 8.00 20.00
3 Shaquille O'Neal 2.50 6.00
4 Kevin Garnett 2.00 5.00
5 Tim Duncan 2.00 5.00
6 Jason Kidd 1.50 4.00
7 Richard Hamilton .75 2.00
8 Vince Carter 1.50 4.00
9 Alonzo Mourning 1.25 3.00
10 John Stockton 1.25 3.00
11 Elton Brand 1.00 2.50
12 Steve Francis 1.00 2.50
13 Keith Van Horn .75 2.00
14 Stephon Marbury .75 2.00
15 Darius Miles .60 1.50

2001-02 Fleer Maximum Power Warm-Ups

Inserted at stated odds of one in 20, these 10 cards are a partial parallel to the Power insert set. These cards feature a swatch of the warm up uniforms worn by the featured player. A gold version was also produced with cards sequentially numbered to 25.

*GOLD: 2X TO 5X BASE HI
GOLD PRINT RUN 25 SER.#'d SETS
1 Jason Kidd 5.00 12.00
2 Richard Hamilton 2.50 6.00
3 Vince Carter 5.00 12.00
4 Alonzo Mourning 4.00 10.00
5 John Stockton 4.00 10.00
6 Elton Brand 3.00 8.00
7 Steve Francis 3.00 8.00
8 Keith Van Horn 2.50 6.00
9 Stephon Marbury 2.50 6.00
10 Darius Miles 2.00 5.00

2001-02 Fleer Maximum Two Point Shot Jersey/Floor

Randomly inserted into packs, these eight cards feature both a game-worn uniform swatch and a piece of a game-used floor. These cards have a stated print run of 25 serial numbered sets and are not priced due to market scarcity.

STATED PRINT RUN 25 SERIAL #'d SETS
1 Vince Carter 30.00 80.00
2 Elton Brand 20.00 50.00
3 Steve Francis 20.00 50.00
4 Jason Kidd 30.00 80.00
5 Allen Iverson 40.00 100.00
6 Tracy McGrady 30.00 80.00
7 Darius Miles 12.00 30.00
8 Paul Pierce 25.00 60.00

2007 Fleer Michael Jordan

COMPLETE SET (100) 15.00 40.00
COMMON CARD (1-100) .40 1.00

2007 Fleer Michael Jordan Award Winners

COMPLETE SET (20) 3.00 8.00
COMMON CARD .40 1.00

2007 Fleer Michael Jordan Playoff Highlights

COMPLETE SET (30) 6.00 15.00
COMMON CARD .40 1.00

2007 Fleer Michael Jordan Season Achievements

COMPLETE SET (50) 10.00 25.00
COMMON CARD .40 1.00

1999-00 Fleer Mystique

The 1999-00 Fleer Mystique product was released in April,2000 as a 150-card set. The set features 100 player cards, 40 rookie cards, and 10 superstar cards. The 40-card rookie subset is serial numbered to 2999, while the superstar subset is serial numbered to 2500. Each pack contained 5-cards and carried a suggested retail price of 4.99.

COMPLETE SET (150) 75.00 150.00
COMPLETE SET w/o SP (100) 15.00 30.00
UNPRICED MASTER PRINT RUN ONE SET
1 Allen Iverson .75 2.00
2 Grant Hill .50 1.25
3 Antawn Jamison .40 1.00
4 Glenn Robinson .30 .75
5 Kenny Anderson .30 .75
6 Dikembe Mutombo .40 1.00
7 Gary Trent .25 .60
8 Brevin Knight .25 .60
9 Chucky Brown .25 .60
10 Derek Anderson .25 .60
11 Ricky Davis .40 1.00
12 Chris Webber .40 1.00
13 Jalen Rose .30 .75
14 Antoine Walker .40 1.00
15 Michael Dickerson .25 .60
16 Tim Hardaway .40 1.00
17 Toni Kukoc .40 1.00
18 Raef LaFrentz .30 .75
19 Anthony Mason .25 .60
20 John Stockton .50 1.25
21 Hakeem Olajuwon .50 1.25
22 Shaquille O'Neal 1.00 2.50
23 Scottie Pippen .60 1.50
24 Maurice Taylor .25 .60
25 Tariq Abdul-Wahad .25 .60
26 Tracy McGrady .60 1.50
27 Joe Smith .30 .75
28 Rod Strickland .25 .60
29 Ruben Patterson .25 .60
30 Tom Gugliotta .25 .60
31 Ray Allen .40 1.00
32 Elden Campbell .25 .60
33 Lindsey Hunter .25 .60
34 Larry Johnson .40 1.00
35 Michael Olowokandi .25 .60
36 Mario Elie .25 .60
37 Anfernee Hardaway .60 1.50
38 Juwan Howard .30 .75
39 Karl Malone .50 1.25
40 Alonzo Mourning .50 1.25
41 Billy Owens .25 .60
42 Mitch Richmond .40 1.00
43 Darrell Armstrong .25 .60
44 Jason Williams .50 1.25
45 Mookie Blaylock .25 .60
46 Gary Payton .40 1.00
47 Brian Grant .25 .60
48 Paul Pierce .60 1.50
49 Michael Finley .40 1.00
50 Reggie Miller .40 1.00
51 Corliss Williamson .25 .60
52 Shandon Anderson .25 .60
53 Stephon Marbury .30 .75
54 Sam Cassell .30 .75
55 Bryon Russell .25 .60
56 Rasheed Wallace .40 1.00
57 Jayson Williams .25 .60
58 Damon Stoudamire .40 1.00
59 Terrell Brandon .25 .60
60 Loy Vaught .25 .60
61 Kobe Bryant 2.00 5.00
62 Vlade Divac .40 1.00
63 Derek Fisher .40 1.00
64 Isaiah Rider .25 .60
65 Eddie Jones .40 1.00
66 Kevin Garnett .75 2.00
67 David Robinson .60 1.50
68 Marcus Camby .30 .75
69 Glen Rice .40 1.00
70 Mike Bibby .40 1.00
71 Patrick Ewing .50 1.25
72 Robert Traylor .25 .60
73 Tim Duncan .75 2.00
74 Michael Doleac .25 .60
75 Steve Smith .25 .60
76 Allan Houston .30 .75
77 Jamal Mashburn .30 .75
78 Brent Barry .30 .75
79 Charles Barkley .60 1.50
80 Ron Mercer .30 .75
81 Jerry Stackhouse .40 1.00
82 Keith Van Horn .30 .75
83 Hersey Hawkins .25 .60
84 Avery Johnson .30 .75
85 Cedric Ceballos .25 .60
86 P.J. Brown .25 .60
87 Doug Christie .30 .75
88 Shawn Kemp .40 1.00
89 Dirk Nowitzki .75 2.00
90 Erick Dampier .25 .60
91 Antonio McDyess .30 .75
92 Mark Jackson .40 1.00
93 Clifford Robinson .25 .60
94 Vince Carter .75 2.00
95 Shareef Abdur-Rahim .30 .75
96 Vin Baker .40 1.00
97 Larry Hughes .30 .75
98 Jason Kidd .60 1.50
99 Kerry Kittles .25 .60
100 Latrell Sprewell .40 1.00
101 Lamar Odom RC 2.50 6.00
102 Elton Brand RC 2.00 5.00
103 Baron Davis RC 2.50 6.00
104 Jason Terry RC 2.00 5.00
105 Corey Maggette RC 1.50 4.00
106 Wally Szczerbiak RC 1.50 4.00
107 Richard Hamilton RC 2.00 5.00
108 Milt Palacio RC .75 2.00
109 Ron Artest RC 2.00 5.00
110 Eddie Robinson RC .75 2.00
111 Jumaine Jones RC .75 2.00
112 Andre Miller RC 2.00 5.00
113 Chucky Atkins RC .75 2.00
114 Kenny Thomas RC .75 2.00
115 Scott Padgett RC .75 2.00
116 Devean George RC .75 2.00
117 Tim Young RC .75 2.00
118 Tim James RC .75 2.00
119 Quincy Lewis RC .75 2.00
120 James Posey RC .75 2.00
121 Shawn Marion RC 2.00 5.00
122 Aleksandar Radojevic RC .75 2.00
123 Trajan Langdon RC .75 2.00
124 Laron Profit RC .75 2.00
125 Jonathan Bender RC .75 2.00
126 William Avery RC .75 2.00
127 Cal Bowdler RC .75 2.00
128 Dion Glover RC .75 2.00
129 Jeff Foster RC .75 2.00
130 Steve Francis RC 2.00 5.00
131 Adrian Griffin RC .75 2.00
132 Vonteego Cummings RC .75 2.00
133 Rafer Alston RC 1.00 2.50
134 Michael Ruffin RC .75 2.00
135 Chris Herren RC .75 2.00
136 Jermaine Jackson RC .75 2.00
137 Lazaro Borrell RC .75 2.00
138 Obinna Ekezie RC .75 2.00
139 Rick Hughes RC .75 2.00
140 Todd MacCulloch RC .75 2.00
141 Kobe Bryant STAR 6.00 15.00
142 Vince Carter STAR 2.50 6.00
143 Tim Duncan STAR 2.50 6.00
144 Kevin Garnett STAR 2.50 6.00
145 Allen Iverson STAR 2.50 6.00
146 Keith Van Horn STAR 1.00 2.50
147 Grant Hill STAR 1.50 4.00
148 Stephon Marbury STAR 1.00 2.50
149 Antoine Walker STAR 1.25 3.00
150 Shaquille O'Neal STAR 3.00 8.00

1999-00 Fleer Mystique Gold

Randomly inserted in packs at one in four, this insert parallels cards 1-100 of the Fleer Mystique base set. This set features gold-foil instead of the silver-foil found on the regular base set. To ascertain values on individual cards, please refer to the multiplier in the header, coupled with the value of the base card.

*GOLD: 1.25X TO 3X BASE CARD HI

1999-00 Fleer Mystique Feel the Game

Randomly inserted in packs at one in 120, this insert set features 11 superstars with swatches of their game-used jerseys. Card backs are not numbered, thus the cards are listed below alphabetically.

1 Vince Carter 10.00 25.00
2 Brian Grant 3.00 8.00
3 Raef LaFrentz 4.00 10.00
4 Karl Malone 6.00 15.00
5 Alonzo Mourning 6.00 15.00
6 Shaquille O'Neal 12.00 30.00
7 Gary Payton 5.00 12.00
8 David Robinson 8.00 20.00
9 Glenn Robinson 4.00 10.00
10 Joe Smith 4.00 10.00
11 John Stockton 6.00 15.00

1999-00 Fleer Mystique Fresh Ink

Randomly inserted in packs at one in 40, this insert set features autographed cards of 43 NBA players. The cards are not numbered and listed below alphabetically.

1 Ray Allen 10.00 25.00
2 Ron Artest 8.00 20.00
3 William Avery 3.00 8.00
4 Jonathan Bender 3.00 8.00
5 Mike Bibby 5.00 12.00
6 Cal Bowdler 3.00 8.00
7 Vince Carter 15.00 40.00
8 John Celestand 3.00 8.00
9 Vonteego Cummings 3.00 8.00
10 Baron Davis 8.00 20.00
11 Michael Dickerson 3.00 8.00
12 Michael Doleac 3.00 8.00
13 Evan Eschmeyer 3.00 8.00
14 Michael Finley 6.00 15.00
15 Steve Francis 8.00 20.00
16 Pat Garrity 3.00 8.00
17 Dion Glover 3.00 8.00
18 Brian Grant 3.00 8.00
19 Richard Hamilton 8.00 20.00
20 Tim Hardaway 8.00 20.00
21 Jumaine Jones 3.00 8.00
22 Shawn Kemp 40.00 100.00
23 Raef LaFrentz 3.00 8.00
24 Quincy Lewis 3.00 8.00
25 Stephon Marbury 5.00 12.00
26 Antonio McDyess 3.00 8.00
27 Andre Miller 4.00 10.00
28 Cuttino Mobley 3.00 8.00
29 Alonzo Mourning 25.00 60.00
30 Shaquille O'Neal 50.00 125.00
31 Lamar Odom 6.00 15.00
32 Hakeem Olajuwon 15.00 40.00
33 Michael Olowokandi 3.00 8.00
34 James Posey 3.00 8.00
35 Aleksandar Radojevic 3.00 8.00
36 Kenny Thomas 3.00 8.00
37 Robert Traylor 3.00 8.00
38 Keith Van Horn 5.00 12.00

1999-00 Fleer Mystique Point Perfect

Randomly inserted in packs, this 10-card insert features some of the NBA's top point guards. Each card was serial numbered to 1999. Card backs carry a "PP" prefix.

COMPLETE SET (10) 10.00 25.00
PP1 Mike Bibby 1.00 2.50
PP2 Stephon Marbury .75 2.00
PP3 Jason Williams 1.25 3.00
PP4 Jason Kidd 1.50 4.00
PP5 William Avery 1.00 2.50
PP6 Allen Iverson 2.00 5.00
PP7 Andre Miller 2.50 6.00
PP8 Baron Davis 3.00 8.00
PP9 Steve Francis 2.50 6.00
PP10 Jason Terry 2.50 6.00

1999-00 Fleer Mystique Raise the Roof

Randomly inserted in packs, this 10-card insert features some of the most electrifying players in the NBA. Each card was serial numbered to 100. Card backs carry an "RR" prefix.

RR1 Grant Hill 50.00 125.00
RR2 Keith Van Horn 25.00 60.00
RR3 Tim Duncan 100.00 200.00
RR4 Kobe Bryant 400.00 800.00
RR5 Vince Carter 60.00 150.00
RR6 Allen Iverson 60.00 150.00
RR7 Kevin Garnett 60.00 150.00
RR8 Shaquille O'Neal 80.00 200.00
RR9 Paul Pierce 50.00 125.00
RR10 Anfernee Hardaway 50.00 125.00

1999-00 Fleer Mystique Slamboree

Randomly inserted in packs, this insert set showcases 10-players that have turned slam dunks into an art form. Each card was serial numbered to 999. Card backs carry a "S" prefix.

COMPLETE SET (10) 12.50 30.00
S1 Antoine Walker 1.50 4.00
S2 Shareef Abdur-Rahim 1.25 3.00
S3 Antawn Jamison 1.50 4.00
S4 Tracy McGrady 2.50 6.00
S5 Larry Hughes 1.25 3.00
S6 Wally Szczerbiak 3.00 8.00
S7 Corey Maggette 3.00 8.00
S8 Lamar Odom 5.00 12.00
S9 Elton Brand 4.00 10.00
S10 Stephon Marbury 1.25 3.00

2000-01 Fleer Mystique

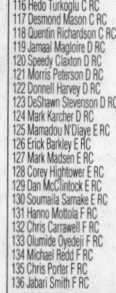

The 2000-01 Fleer Mystique product was released in October, 2000 and featured a 136-card base set that was broken into tiers as follows: Base Veterans (1-100), and Rookies (101-136) that were serial numbered as follows: 101-106 (numbered to 750), 107-112 (numbered to 1000), 113-118 (numbered to 2000), 119-124 (numbered to 3000), 125-130 (numbered to 4000), and 131-136 (numbered to 5000). Each pack contained five-cards and carried a suggested retail price of $4.99.

COMPLETE SET w/o RC (100) 15.00 30.00
1 Shaquille O'Neal .75 2.00
2 Gary Payton .30 .75
3 Nick Van Exel .25 .60
4 Alonzo Mourning .40 1.00
5 Shawn Marion .30 .75
6 Rod Strickland .25 .60
7 Mookie Blaylock .25 .60
8 Terrell Brandon .20 .50
9 Bryon Russell .20 .50
10 Jerry Stackhouse .25 .60
11 Glenn Robinson .25 .60
12 Rasheed Wallace .30 .75
13 Tracy McGrady .50 1.25
14 Raef LaFrentz .20 .50
15 P.J. Brown .20 .50
16 Anfernee Hardaway .50 1.25
17 Mike Bibby .30 .75
18 Elden Campbell .20 .50
19 Steve Francis .30 .75
20 Keith Van Horn .25 .60
21 Karl Malone .40 1.00
22 Dirk Nowitzki .50 1.25
23 Glen Rice .25 .60
24 Tom Gugliotta .20 .50
25 Avery Johnson .25 .60
26 Michael Finley .30 .75
27 Theo Ratliff .20 .50
28 Juwan Howard .25 .60
29 Anthony Carter .20 .50
30 Kobe Bryant 1.50 4.00
31 Toni Kukoc .25 .60
32 Jason Terry .30 .75
33 Elton Brand .30 .75
34 Reggie Miller .30 .75
35 Latrell Sprewell .25 .60
36 Adrian Griffin .20 .50
37 Cuttino Mobley .25 .60
38 Maurice Taylor .20 .50
39 Allen Iverson .60 1.50
40 Tim Duncan .60 1.50
41 Andre Miller .25 .60
42 Antonio Davis .20 .50
43 Howard Eisley .20 .50
44 Vlade Divac .25 .60
45 Brevin Knight .20 .50
46 Lamar Odom .30 .75
47 Ron Mercer .20 .50
48 Jason Williams .30 .75
49 Antawn Jamison .30 .75
50 Wally Szczerbiak .25 .60
51 Chris Webber .30 .75
52 Larry Hughes .25 .60
53 Kevin Garnett .60 1.50
54 Michael Dickerson .20 .50
55 Chucky Atkins .20 .50
56 Jalen Rose .25 .60
57 John Amaechi .20 .50
58 Shareef Abdur-Rahim .25 .60
59 Shawn Kemp .30 .75
60 Derek Anderson .20 .50
61 Darrell Armstrong .20 .50
62 Vin Baker .25 .60
63 Paul Pierce .40 1.00
64 Donyell Marshall .20 .50
65 Jamie Feick .20 .50
66 Travis Best .20 .50
67 Baron Davis .30 .75
68 Hakeem Olajuwon .40 1.00
69 Joe Smith .25 .60
70 Ruben Patterson .20 .50
71 Antonio McDyess .25 .60
72 Jamal Mashburn .25 .60
73 Jason Kidd .50 1.25
74 Eddie Jones .30 .75
75 Kenny Thomas .20 .50
76 Marcus Camby .25 .60
77 Doug Christie .20 .50
78 Ron Artest .30 .75
79 Mark Jackson .25 .60
80 Allan Houston .25 .60
81 John Stockton .40 1.00
82 Jerome Williams .20 .50
83 Tim Thomas .20 .50
84 Alan Henderson .20 .50
85 Antoine Walker .25 .60
86 Robert Horry .25 .60
87 Stephon Marbury .25 .60
88 David Robinson .50 1.25
89 Lindsey Hunter .20 .50
90 Richard Hamilton .25 .60
91 Damon Stoudamire .25 .60
92 Dikembe Mutombo .30 .75
93 Anthony Mason .20 .50
94 Austin Croshere .20 .50
95 Patrick Ewing .40 1.00
96 Mitch Richmond .25 .60
97 Grant Hill .40 1.00
98 Ray Allen .30 .75
99 Scottie Pippen .50 1.25
100 Vince Carter .60 1.50
101 Kenyon Martin A RC 6.00 15.00
102 Stromile Swift A RC 2.50 6.00
103 Darius Miles A RC 2.50 6.00
104 Marcus Fizer A RC 2.50 6.00
105 Mike Miller A RC 5.00 12.00
106 DerMarr Johnson A RC 2.50 6.00
107 Chris Mihm B RC 2.00 5.00
108 Jamal Crawford B RC 3.00 8.00
109 Joel Przybilla B RC 2.00 5.00
110 Keyon Dooling B RC 2.00 5.00
111 Jerome Moiso B RC 2.00 5.00
112 Etan Thomas B RC 2.00 5.00
113 Courtney Alexander C RC 1.50 4.00
114 Mateen Cleaves C RC 1.50 4.00
115 Jason Collier C RC 1.50 4.00
116 Hedo Turkoglu C RC 3.00 8.00
117 Desmond Mason C RC 2.00 5.00
118 Quentin Richardson C RC 2.50 6.00
119 Jamaal Magloire D RC 1.00 2.50
120 Speedy Claxton D RC 1.00 2.50
121 Morris Peterson D RC 1.00 2.50
122 Donnell Harvey D RC 1.00 2.50
123 DeShawn Stevenson D RC 1.25 3.00
124 Mark Karcher D RC 1.00 2.50
125 Mamadou N'Diaye E RC .60 1.50
126 Erick Barkley E RC .60 1.50
127 Mark Madsen E RC .60 1.50
128 Corey Hightower E RC .60 1.50
129 Dan McClintock E RC .60 1.50
130 Soumaila Samake E RC .60 1.50
131 Hanno Mottola F RC .50 1.25
132 Chris Carrawell F RC .50 1.25
133 Olumide Oyedeji F RC .50 1.25
134 Michael Redd F RC 1.25 3.00
135 Chris Porter F RC .50 1.25
136 Jabari Smith F RC .50 1.25

2000-01 Fleer Mystique Gold

Randomly inserted in packs at one in 20, this 136-card set parallels the base set. The cards feature a gold background. To ascertain values on individual cards, please refer to the multiplier in the header, coupled with the value of the base card.

COMPLETE SET (136) 125.00 250.00
*STARS: 1.5X TO 4X BASE CARD HI
*RCs: .2X TO .5X BASE HI

2000-01 Fleer Mystique Masterpiece

Randomly inserted in packs, this 136-card set parallels the base set. Please note that there was only one serial numbered set produced.

2000-01 Fleer Mystique Vince Carter Rookie Remnants

This three-card insert was randomly inserted into 2000-01 Fleer products. The set includes a Vince Carter floor card (numbered to 100), a Vince Carter floor/jersey card (numbered to 15), and finally an autographed Vince Carter floor/jersey card (numbered 1 of 1).

NNO Vince Carter FLR/100 12.50 30.00

2000-01 Fleer Mystique Dial 1

Randomly inserted in packs at one in 10, this 10-card set featurs players who can hit the long shots. Card backs carry a "DO" prefix.

COMPLETE SET (10) 3.00 8.00
DO1 Jason Kidd .75 2.00
DO2 Stephon Marbury .40 1.00
DO3 Allen Iverson 1.00 2.50
DO4 Jason Williams .50 1.25
DO5 Allan Houston .40 1.00
DO6 Eddie Jones .50 1.25
DO7 Ray Allen .50 1.25
DO8 Jalen Rose .40 1.00
DO9 Anfernee Hardaway .75 2.00
DO10 Vince Carter 1.00 2.50

2000-01 Fleer Mystique Film at Eleven

Randomly inserted in packs at one in 40, this 10-card set focuses on players who dominate the late night highlight reels. Card backs carry a "FE" prefix.

COMPLETE SET (10) 25.00 50.00
UNPRICED PARALLEL SERIAL #'d TO 11
FE1 Vince Carter 3.00 8.00
FE2 Kobe Bryant 8.00 20.00
FE3 Allen Iverson 3.00 8.00
FE4 Kevin Garnett 3.00 8.00
FE5 Tim Duncan 3.00 8.00
FE6 Steve Francis 1.50 4.00
FE7 Lamar Odom 1.50 4.00
FE8 Elton Brand 1.50 4.00
FE9 Tracy McGrady 2.50 6.00
FE10 Jason Williams 1.50 4.00

2000-01 Fleer Mystique Middle Men

Randomly inserted in packs at one in 10, this 10-card set focuses on players who are always in the "middle of the action" on the court. Card backs carry a "MM" prefix.

COMPLETE SET (10) 4.00 10.00
MM1 Shaquille O'Neal 1.25 3.00
MM2 Vince Carter 1.00 2.50
MM3 Paul Pierce .60 1.50
MM4 Tim Duncan 1.00 2.50
MM5 Grant Hill .60 1.50
MM6 David Robinson .75 2.00
MM7 Tracy McGrady .75 2.00
MM8 Jason Williams .50 1.25
MM9 Elton Brand .50 1.25
MM10 Lamar Odom .50 1.25

2000-01 Fleer Mystique NBAwesome

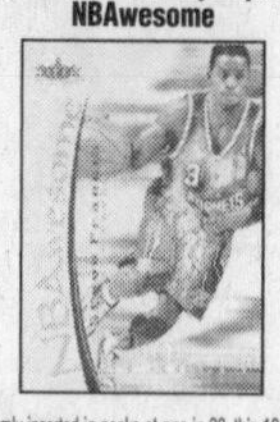

Randomly inserted in packs at one in 20, this 10-card set focuses on players who bring the fans out of their seats. Card backs carry a "NA" prefix.

COMPLETE SET (10) 12.50 25.00
NA1 Grant Hill 1.50 4.00
NA2 Steve Francis 1.25 3.00
NA3 Kobe Bryant 6.00 15.00
NA4 Elton Brand 1.25 3.00
NA5 Vince Carter 2.50 6.00
NA6 Lamar Odom 1.25 3.00
NA7 Kevin Garnett 2.50 6.00
NA8 Allen Iverson 2.50 6.00
NA9 Shareef Abdur-Rahim 1.00 2.50
NA10 Shaquille O'Neal 3.00 8.00

2000-01 Fleer Mystique Player of the Week

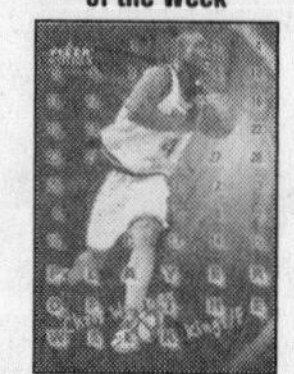

Randomly inserted in packs at one in five, this 15-card set features players who were voted as Player of the Week during the 1999-00 season. Card backs carry a "PW" prefix.

COMPLETE SET (15) 7.50 15.00
PW1 Sam Cassell .30 .75
PW2 Kevin Garnett .75 2.00
PW3 Vince Carter .75 2.00
PW4 Tim Duncan .75 2.00
PW5 Shaquille O'Neal 1.00 2.50
PW6 Alonzo Mourning .50 1.25
PW7 Jason Kidd .60 1.50
PW8 Chris Webber .40 1.00
PW9 Grant Hill .50 1.25
PW10 Steve Francis .40 1.00
PW11 Dikembe Mutombo .40 1.00
PW12 Michael Finley .40 1.00
PW13 Karl Malone .50 1.25
PW14 Jalen Rose .30 .75
PW15 Kobe Bryant 2.00 5.00

2003-04 Fleer Mystique

Released in January 2004, Mystique boasts a 120-card set comprised of 80 veteran player cards and 40 rookie cards sequentially numbered to 999. Base cards have a white and gray background that draws attention to the full-color player action photos and gold foil highlights. Mystique was packaged in 20-pack boxes where packs contained four cards and carried a suggested retail price of $5.99.

COMP.SET w/o SP's (80) 15.00 40.00
1 Eric Williams .20 .50
2 Dirk Nowitzki .50 1.25
3 Jason Richardson .30 .75
4 Corey Maggette .25 .60
5 Troy Hudson .20 .50
6 Tracy McGrady .40 1.00
7 Zach Randolph .30 .75
8 Bobby Jackson .20 .50
9 Dan Gadzuric .20 .50
10 Kevin Garnett .60 1.50
11 Manu Ginobili .40 1.00
12 Andrei Kirilenko .30 .75
13 Richard Hamilton .25 .60
14 Mike Bibby .30 .75
15 Vince Carter .50 1.25
16 Jermaine O'Neal .30 .75
17 Antoine Walker .30 .75
18 Jalen Rose .25 .60
19 Dajuan Wagner .20 .50
20 Nene .25 .60
21 Jamaal Tinsley .20 .50
22 Kobe Bryant 1.50 4.00
23 Shane Battier .25 .60
24 Allan Houston .25 .60
25 Jerry Stackhouse .25 .60
26 Eddie Jones .25 .60
27 Morris Peterson .20 .50
28 Richard Jefferson .30 .75
29 Tony Parker .30 .75
30 Glenn Robinson .25 .60
31 Ron Artest .30 .75
32 Marcus Haislip .20 .50
33 Drew Gooden .25 .60
34 Keith Van Horn .25 .60
35 Shareef Abdur-Rahim .25 .60
36 Michael Redd .30 .75
37 Stephon Marbury .25 .60
38 Tim Duncan .50 1.25
39 Eddie Griffin .20 .50
40 Kwame Brown .20 .50
41 Steve Francis .30 .75
42 Vladimir Radmanovic .20 .50
43 Kenyon Martin .30 .75
44 Eddy Curry .25 .60
45 Nikoloz Tskitishvili .20 .50
46 Shaquille O'Neal .75 2.00
47 Allen Iverson .50 1.25
48 Jason Kidd .50 1.25
49 Ben Wallace .30 .75
50 Caron Butler .30 .75
51 Dan Dickau .20 .50
52 Baron Davis .30 .75
53 Bruce Bowen .20 .50
54 Amare Stoudemire .50 1.25
55 Michael Finley .30 .75
56 Jamal Mashburn .25 .60
57 Pau Gasol .30 .75
58 Shawn Marion .30 .75
59 Rasheed Wallace .30 .75
60 Chris Webber .30 .75
61 Rodney White .20 .50
62 Tayshaun Prince .30 .75
63 Yao Ming .60 1.50
64 Latrell Sprewell .25 .60
65 Aaron McKie .20 .50
66 Bonzi Wells .20 .50
67 HedoTurkoglu .30 .75
68 Ray Allen .30 .75
69 Matt Harpring .25 .60
70 Paul Pierce .40 1.00
71 Darius Miles .20 .50
72 Chris Wilcox .20 .50
73 Steve Nash .40 1.00
74 Antawn Jamison .30 .75
75 Juan Dixon .20 .50
76 Peja Stojakovic .30 .75
77 Antonio Davis .20 .50
78 Kenny Thomas .20 .50
79 Elton Brand .30 .75
80 Gilbert Arenas .30 .75
81 Mickael Pietrus RC 2.00 5.00
82 Keith Bogans RC 2.00 5.00
83 Dahntay Jones RC 2.00 5.00
84 Darko Milicic RC 2.00 5.00
85 Torraye Braggs RC 2.00 5.00
86 Troy Bell RC 2.00 5.00
87 Maciej Lampe RC 2.00 5.00
88 Kendrick Perkins RC 3.00 8.00
89 Kirk Hinrich RC 2.50 6.00
90 Jason Kapono RC 2.00 5.00
91 Udonis Haslem RC 2.50 6.00
92 James Lang RC 2.00 5.00
93 Willie Green RC 2.00 5.00
94 Travis Outlaw RC 2.50 6.00
95 Nick Collison RC 2.00 5.00
96 Jarvis Hayes RC 2.00 5.00
97 Boris Diaw RC 2.50 6.00
98 Chris Bosh RC 4.00 10.00
99 LeBron James RC 25.00 60.00
100 Zarko Cabarkapa RC 2.00 5.00
101 Travis Hansen RC 2.00 5.00
102 James Jones RC 2.00 5.00
103 Aleksandar Pavlovic RC 2.00 5.00
104 Luke Walton RC 2.00 5.00
105 Maurice Williams RC 3.00 8.00
106 Linton Johnson RC 2.00 5.00
107 David West RC 2.50 6.00
108 Carmelo Anthony RC 5.00 12.00
109 T.J. Ford RC 2.50 6.00
110 Ndudi Ebi RC 2.00 5.00
111 Reece Gaines RC 2.00 5.00
112 Leandro Barbosa RC 2.50 6.00
113 Luke Ridnour RC 2.50 6.00
114 Brian Cook RC 2.00 5.00
115 Marcus Banks RC 2.00 5.00
116 Josh Howard RC 2.00 5.00
117 Chris Kaman RC 2.50 6.00
118 Zoran Planinic RC 2.00 5.00
119 Dwyane Wade RC 8.00 20.00
120 Mike Sweetney RC 2.00 5.00

2003-04 Fleer Mystique Die Cut

*81-120 DC SINGLES: .5X TO 1.25X BASE HI
DIE CUT PRINT RUN 600 SER.#'d SETS

2003-04 Fleer Mystique Gold

*1-80 SINGLES: 2.5X TO 6X BASE HI
1-80 PRINT RUN 150 SER.#'d SETS
*81-120 RCs: 1X TO 2.5X BASE HI
81-120 RC PRINT RUN 50 SER.#'d SETS
99 LeBron James 125.00 225.00

2003-04 Fleer Mystique Awe Pairs

Inserted in packs, this 20-card set pairs players from the same team on a horizontal card design that includes full color player portrait photos. Each card is squentially numbered to 500. Gold versions were also issued and are sequentially numbered to the total number of victories the featured players' total wins from the 2002-03 season..

*GOLD SINGLES/25-40: 1.5X TO 4X BASE HI
*GOLD SINGLES/40-60: 1.25X TO 3X HI COL.
GOLD #'d TO TEAM VICTORIES IN 2002-03
1 Shane Battier / Pau Gasol 1.00 2.50
2 Shawn Marion / Amare Stoudemire 1.50 4.00
3 Paul Pierce / Marcus Banks 1.25 3.00
4 Jalen Rose / Eddy Curry .75 2.00
5 DaJuan Wagner / LeBron James 6.00 15.00
6 Kevin Garnett / Troy Hudson 2.00 5.00
7 Tayshaun Prince / Ben Wallace 1.00 2.50
8 Nene / Carmelo Anthony 2.50 6.00
9 Kobe Bryant / Shaquille O'Neal 5.00 12.00
10 Drew Gooden / Tracy McGrady 1.25 3.00
11 Allen Iverson / Aaron McKie 1.50 4.00
12 Caron Butler / Dwyane Wade 4.00 10.00
13 Yao Ming / Steve Francis 2.00 5.00
14 Elton Brand / Chris Kaman 1.25 3.00
15 Allan Houston / Mike Sweetney 1.00 2.50
16 Peja Stojakovic / Chris Webber 1.00 2.50
17 Jermaine O'Neal / Ron Artest 1.00 2.50
18 Tim Duncan / Tony Parker 1.50 4.00
19 Vince Carter / Chris Bosh 2.00 5.00
20 Mike Dunleavy / Jason Richardson 1.00 2.50

2003-04 Fleer Mystique Awe Pairs Dual Jerseys

Randomly inserted in packs, this 17-card set parallels the design of the Awe Pairs set enhanced with a jersey swatch from each player and sequential numbering to 350. Several of the rookie players have Event Worn memorabilia on their cards rather than game worn memorabilia. Versions sequentially numbered to 250 and 35 were also produced.

*JSY/250 SINGLES: .5X TO 1.25X HI COL.
*JSY/35 SINGLES: 2X TO 5X HI COL.
AHMS Allan Houston / Mike Sweetney 4.00 10.00
AIAM Allen Iverson / Aaron McKie 5.00 12.00
CBDW Caron Butler / Dwyane Wade 8.00 20.00
DGTM Drew Gooden / Tracy McGrady 5.00 12.00
EBCK Elton Brand / Chris Kaman 4.00 10.00
JONRA Jermaine O'Neal / Ron Artest 4.00 10.00
JREC Jalen Rose / Eddy Curry 4.00 10.00
KGTH Kevin Garnett / Troy Hudson 5.00 12.00
MDJR Mike Dunleavy / Jason Richardson 4.00 10.00
PPMB Paul Pierce / Marcus Banks 4.00 10.00
PSCW Peja Stojakovic / Chris Webber 5.00 12.00
SBPG Shane Battier / Pau Gasol 4.00 10.00
SMAS Shawn Marion / Amare Stoudemire 5.00 12.00
TDTP Tim Duncan / Tony Parker 6.00 15.00
TPBW Tayshaun Prince / Ben Wallace 4.00 10.00
VCCB Vince Carter / Chris Bosh 6.00 15.00
YMSF Yao Ming / Steve Francis 6.00 15.00

2003-04 Fleer Mystique Ink Appeal

Randomly seeded in packs, this 10-card set utilizes a horizontal design with a player portrait centered towards the top of the card and a cut signature embedded in the bottom. Each card has red foil highlights and is sequentially numbered. Print runs are listed below. A sequentially numbered gold version was also issued, and these cards are not priced due to scarcity.

CA Carmelo Anthony/225 25.00 60.00
DW Dwyane Wade/150 50.00 120.00
JH Josh Howard/100 6.00 15.00
JK Jason Kapono/200 6.00 15.00
LR Luke Ridnour/100 8.00 20.00
MP Mickael Pietrus/150 6.00 15.00
VC Vince Carter/250 12.50 30.00
DWG Dajuan Wagner/125 6.00 15.00

2003-04 Fleer Mystique Ink Appeal Gold

This is a parallel insert set to Ink Appeal and cards are sequentially numbered below.

MOST NOT PRICED DUE TO SCARCITY
CA Carmelo Anthony/15 50.00 120.00
VC Vince Carter/15 20.00 50.00

2003-04 Fleer Mystique Rare Finds

Randomly inserted in packs, this 10-card set is horizontally designed, places three players across the card left to right and is sequentially numbered to 500.

COMPLETE SET (10) 12.50 30.00
1 Kobe Bryant / Kevin Garnett / Amare Stoudemire 3.00 8.00
2 Manu Ginobili / Peja Stojakovic / Andrei Kirilenko 2.00 5.00
3 Tony Parker / Steve Francis / Gary Payton 2.00 5.00
4 Kenyon Martin / Jason Kidd / Richard Jefferson 2.00 5.00
5 Dirk Nowitzki / Steve Nash / Michael Finley 2.00 5.00
6 Tracy McGrady / Allen Iverson / Pau Pierce 2.00 5.00
7 Tim Duncan / Yao Ming / Shaquille O'Neal 5.00 12.00
8 Vince Carter / Jerry Stackhouse / Antawn Jamison 2.00 5.00
9 Jalen Rose / Chris Webber / Juwan Howard 2.00 5.00
10 Richard Hamilton / Caron Butler / Ray Allen 2.00 5.00

2003-04 Fleer Mystique Rare Finds 50

This five-card set uses a similar design to the base rare finds set and cards are sequentially numbered to 50. A version numbered to 10 was also inserted in packs.

RARE/10 NOT PRICED DUE TO SCARCITY
AS Amare Stoudemire 12.50 30.00
CA Carmelo Anthony 25.00 60.00
DG Drew Gooden 5.00 12.00
TP Tayshaun Prince 5.00 12.00
VC Vince Carter 20.00 40.00

2003-04 Fleer Mystique Rare Finds Jerseys

Randomly seeded in packs, this 20-card set utilizes the same design as the Rare Finds 50 set enhanced with game worn jersey swatches and sequential numbering to 300. A version numbered to 30 was also inserted in packs.

*JERSEY 30: 1X TO 2.5X HI COL.
RFAI Allen Iverson 4.00 10.00
RFAS Amare Stoudemire 4.00 10.00
RFCB Caron Butler 2.50 6.00
RFCW Chris Webber 2.50 6.00
RFDN Dirk Nowitzki 4.00 10.00
RFJK Jason Kidd 4.00 10.00
RFJS Jerry Stackhouse 2.00 5.00
RFKG Kevin Garnett 5.00 12.00
RFMF Michael Finley 2.50 6.00
RFPP Paul Pierce 3.00 8.00
RFPS Peja Stojakovic 2.50 6.00
RFSN Steve Nash 3.00 8.00
RFSO Shaquille O'Neal 6.00 15.00
RFST Steve Francis 2.50 6.00
RFTD Tim Duncan 4.00 10.00
RFTM Tracy McGrady 3.00 8.00
RFTP Tony Parker 2.50 6.00
RFVC Vince Carter 4.00 10.00
RTKM Kenyon Martin 2.50 6.00
RTYM Yao Ming 5.00 12.00

2003-04 Fleer Mystique Rare Finds Jerseys Dual

Inserted in packs, this 15-card set parallels the design of the base Rare Finds insert set with two players enhanced with a jersey swatch from each player and sequential numbering to 250. A version numbered to 25 was issued as well.

*DUAL 25: 1.25X TO 3X BASE HI
CWJH Chris Webber / Juwan Howard 6.00 15.00
DNMF Dirk Nowitzki / Michael Finley 6.00 15.00
DNSN Dirk Nowitzki / Steve Nash 6.00 15.00
KGAS Kevin Garnett / Amare Stoudemire 6.00 15.00
KMJK Kenyon Martin / Jason Kidd 6.00 15.00
PSAK Peja Stojakovic / Andrei Kirilenko 6.00 1
SFGP Steve Francis / Gary Payton 6.00 1
TDSO Tim Duncan / Shaquille O'Neal 8.00 2
TDYM Tim Duncan / Yao Ming 8.00 2
TMAI Tracy McGrady / Allen Iverson 8.00 2
TMPP Tracy McGrady / Paul Pierce 8.00 2
TPSF Tony Parker / Steve Francis 6.00 1
VCAJ Vince Carter / Antawn Jamison 6.00 1
VCJS Vince Carter / Jerry Stackhouse 6.00 1
YMSO Yao Ming / Shaquille O'Neal 10.00 2

2003-04 Fleer Mystique Ra Finds Jerseys Triple

Randomly inserted in packs, this nine cards set parallels the design of the Rare Finds insert set enhanced with three players, three jersey swatches sequential numbering to 150. A version sequentia numbered to 15 was also produced and inserted i packs.

TRIPLE/15 NOT PRICED DUE TO SCARCITY
DSM Dirk Nowitzki / Steve Nash / Michael Finley 12.50 3
JCJ Jalen Rose / Chris Webber / Juwan Howard 10.00 2
KJR Kenyon Martin / Jason Kidd / Richard Jefferson 8.00 20
MPA Manu Ginobili / Peja Stojakovic / Andrei Kirkilenko 8.00 20
RCR Richard Hamilton / Caron Butler / Ray Allen 8.00 20
TAP Tracy McGrady / Allen Iverson / Paul Pierce 10.00 2
TSG Tony Parker / Steve Francis / Gary Payton 8.00 20
TYS Tim Duncan / Yao Ming / Shaquille O'Neal 12.50 30
VJA Vince Carter / Jerry Stackhouse / Antawn Jamison 8.00 20

2003-04 Fleer Mystique Secr Weapons

Randomly seeded and sequentially numbered to 50 this 15-card set places a line of color along the left side of the card and a full-color player action photo on a gray block background. Each card is sequentia numbered to 500. A Gold version sequentially numbered to the player's jersey number was also inserted.

COMPLETE SET (15) 30.00 75
*GOLD/30-50 SNGLS: .75X TO 2X HI COL.
1 LeBron James 20.00 50
2 Carmelo Anthony 4.00 10
3 Darko Milicic 1.50 4
4 Chris Kaman 2.00 5
5 Dwyane Wade 6.00 15
6 T.J. Ford 2.00 5
7 Chris Bosh 3.00 8
8 Kirk Hinrich 2.00 5
9 Mike Sweetney 1.50 4
10 Jarvis Hayes 1.50 4
11 Marcus Banks 1.50 4
12 Mickael Pietrus 1.50 4
13 Nick Collison 1.50 4
14 David West 2.00 5
15 Maciej Lampe 1.50 4

2003-04 Fleer Mystique Shini Stars

Seeded in packs randomly, this 15-card set places color player action photos on a card with stars appearing in the background and a line of color alo the left side to match the player's team color. Each is sequentially numbered to 500. A Gold version sequentially numbered to 75 was also inserted in packs.

*GOLD SINGLES: .75X TO 2X HI COL.
1 Antoine Walker 1.50 4.
2 Dirk Nowitzki 2.50 6.
3 Baron Davis 1.50 4
4 Peja Stojakovic 1.50 4
5 Ray Allen 1.50 4
6 Jason Kidd 2.50 6
7 Gilbert Arenas 1.50 4
8 Jason Richardson 1.50 4
9 Tim Duncan 2.50 6
10 Vince Carter 2.50 6
11 Shaquille O'Neal 4.00 10
12 Drew Gooden 1.25 3.
13 Pau Gasol 1.50 4.
14 Caron Butler 1.50 4.
15 Manu Ginobili 2.00 5.

3-04 Fleer Mystique Shining Stars Jerseys

mly seeded, this 14-card set parallels the design base Shining Stars insert set and is enhanced star-shaped jersey swatch in the lower right corner of the card. Each card is sequentially ered to 350. Other Jersey versions of this set ered to 250 and 75 were produced along with a up version numbered to 100. The warm-up ns were only available in Hobby and Retail blaster

EY/250: .4X TO 1X HI COL.
EY/75: .75X TO 2X HI COL.
M-UPS: .4X TO 1X HI COL.
Antoine Walker 2.50 6.00
Baron Davis 2.50 6.00
Caron Butler 2.50 6.00
Drew Gooden 2.00 5.00
Dirk Nowitzki 4.00 10.00
Jason Kidd 4.00 10.00
Jason Richardson 2.50 6.00
Manu Ginobili 3.00 8.00
Pau Gasol 2.50 6.00
Peja Stojakovic 2.50 6.00
Ray Allen 2.50 6.00
Shaquille O'Neal 6.00 15.00
Tim Duncan 4.00 10.00
Vince Carter 4.00 10.00

2003-04 Fleer Mystique Skyview

omly inserted in packs, this ten-card set is ned like the 1996-97 E-X basketball set with a r around the outside and full-color player photos st a cloudy sky background. Each card is entially numbered to 100. A Gold version where are sequentially numbered to between 30 and 58 lso issued.

PLETE SET (10) 40.00 80.00
D/30-50: 1X TO 2.5X HI COL.
D/50-60: .75X TO 2X HI COL.
Nowitzki 5.00 12.00
Ming 6.00 15.00
in Garnett 6.00 15.00
y McGrady 4.00 10.00
n Iverson 5.00 12.00
ve Francis 3.00 8.00
be Bryant 100.00 250.00
are Stoudemire 5.00 12.00
ris Webber 3.00 8.00
nce Carter 5.00 12.00

2003-04 Fleer Mystique Skyview Jerseys

ted in packs, this nine-card set parallels the look e base Skyview insert enhanced with a square ch of game worn jersey at the bottom of the card. card is sequentially numbered to 250. Two other ons of this card were also issued, one sequentially bered to 150 and another to 25.

SEY/150: .5X TO 1.25X BASE HI
SEY/25: 2X TO 5X BASE HI
Allen Iverson 5.00 12.00
S Amare Stoudemire 5.00 12.00
W Chris Webber 3.00 8.00
N Dirk Nowitzki 5.00 12.00
G Kevin Garnett 6.00 15.00
M Steve Francis 3.00 8.00
M Tracy McGrady 4.00 10.00
C Vince Carter 5.00 12.00
M Yao Ming 6.00 15.00

01-02 Fleer NBA All-Star Jam Session

n away at the NBA All-Star Game Show from uary 8th-10th, this single card set features adelphia home town hero, Eric Snow, the rseman. The card features both the Fleer and the Session logo and placed Eric Snow against an rican flag background.

Eric Snow .40 1.00

1997 Fleer NBA Jam Session Commemorative Sheet

ed at the 1997 NBA Jam Session in Cleveland, this gn a Card Commemorative Sheet was available ugh a wrapper exchange program at the Fleer h. The sheet features six of the cards from the n Faces insert in 1996-97 Fleer series one as gned by Shinto Imai and six of the cards from the Star subset in 1996-97 Fleer series two as gned by Krystin Penrod. Unfortunately, these cards not renumbered and could be cut and sold as mate inserts/cards from packs.

areef Abdur-Rahim FF 3.00 8.00
y Allen FF
be Bryant FF
arcus Camby FF
Kerry Kittles FF
Stephon Marbury FF
Charles Barkley AS
Patrick Ewing AS
John Stockton AS
Alonzo Mourning AS
Grant Hill AS
Jason Kidd AS

2000 Fleer NBA Jam Session Commemorative Sheet

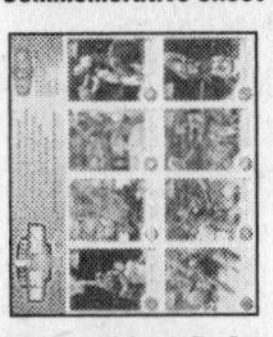

This sheet, featuring cards from the Fleer Focus set, was available at the 2000 NBA Jam Session in Oakland. The sheets were available via a wrapper exchange program at the Fleer/SkyBox booth.

NNO Vince Carter 4.00 10.00
Lamar Odom
Stephon Marbury
Keith Van Horn
Antawn Jamison
Allen Iverson
Grant Hill
Jason Williams

2003-04 Fleer Patchworks

Released in late March/early April 2004, this 120-card set is divided up into 90 veteran player cards and 30 rookie cards sequentially numbered to 799. Base cards feature a horizontal design with a black left side and a full color action photo right side. The player's team logo appears in the black on the left side. Fleer Patchworks was packaged in 18-pack boxes where packs contained five cards and carried a suggested retail price of $120 per box.

COMP.SET w/o SP's (90) 12.50 30.00
1 Shareef Abdur-Rahim .25 .60
2 Theo Ratliff .20 .50
3 Jason Terry .25 .60
4 Carlos Boozer .30 .75
5 Paul Pierce .40 1.00
6 Ricky Davis .25 .60
7 Tyson Chandler .25 .60
8 Jamal Crawford .25 .60
9 Eddy Curry .25 .60
10 Darius Miles .20 .50
11 Dajuan Wagner .20 .50
12 Michael Finley .30 .75
13 Steve Nash .40 1.00
14 Dirk Nowitzki .50 1.25
15 Earl Boykins .20 .50
16 Andre Miller .25 .60
17 Nene .25 .60
18 Richard Hamilton .25 .60
19 Tayshaun Prince .30 .75
20 Ben Wallace .30 .75
21 Mike Dunleavy .25 .60
22 Troy Murphy .30 .75
23 Jason Richardson .30 .75
24 Steve Francis .30 .75
25 Yao Ming .60 1.50
26 Cuttino Mobley .25 .60
27 Maurice Taylor .20 .50
28 Ron Artest .30 .75
29 Reggie Miller .30 .75
30 Jermaine O'Neal .30 .75
31 Jamaal Tinsley .20 .50
32 Elton Brand .30 .75
33 Marko Jaric .20 .50
34 Corey Maggette .25 .60
35 Kobe Bryant 1.50 4.00
36 Karl Malone .40 1.00
37 Shaquille O'Neal .75 2.00
38 Shane Battier .25 .60
39 Pau Gasol .30 .75
40 Jason Williams .25 .60
41 Caron Butler .30 .75
42 Lamar Odom .30 .75
43 Desmond Mason .25 .60
44 Michael Redd .30 .75
45 Tim Thomas .20 .50
46 Sam Cassell .25 .60
47 Kevin Garnett .60 1.50
48 Latrell Sprewell .25 .60
49 Wally Szczerbiak .25 .60
50 Richard Jefferson .30 .75
51 Jason Kidd .50 1.25
52 Kenyon Martin .30 .75
53 Baron Davis .30 .75
54 Jamal Mashburn .25 .60
55 Jamaal Magloire .20 .50
56 Allan Houston .25 .60
57 Stephon Marbury .25 .60
58 Kurt Thomas .20 .50
59 Drew Gooden .25 .60
60 Juwan Howard .25 .60
61 Tracy McGrady .40 1.00
62 Allen Iverson .50 1.25
63 Aaron McKie .20 .50
64 Glenn Robinson .25 .60
65 Kenny Thomas .20 .50
66 Shawn Marion .30 .75
67 Antonio McDyess .25 .60
68 Amare Stoudemire .50 1.25
69 Zach Randolph .30 .75
70 Damon Stoudamire .25 .60
71 Rasheed Wallace .30 .75
72 Qyntel Woods .20 .50
73 Mike Bibby .30 .75
74 Peja Stojakovic .30 .75
75 Chris Webber .30 .75
76 Tim Duncan .50 1.25
77 Manu Ginobili .40 1.00
78 Tony Parker .30 .75
79 Malik Rose .20 .50
80 Ray Allen .30 .75
81 Rashard Lewis .30 .75
82 Vladimir Radmanovic .20 .50
83 Vince Carter .50 1.25
84 Donyell Marshall .20 .50
85 Jalen Rose .25 .60
86 Matt Harpring .25 .60
87 Andrei Kirilenko .30 .75
88 Gilbert Arenas .30 .75
89 Larry Hughes .25 .60
90 Jerry Stackhouse .25 .60
91 Carmelo Anthony RC 3.00 8.00
92 Marcus Banks RC 1.25 3.00
93 Troy Bell RC 1.25 3.00
94 Chris Bosh RC 2.50 6.00
95 Zarko Cabarkapa RC 1.25 3.00
96 Nick Collison RC 1.25 3.00
97 Boris Diaw RC 1.50 4.00
98 Francisco Elson RC 1.25 3.00
99 T.J. Ford RC 1.50 4.00
100 Reece Gaines RC 1.25 3.00
101 Udonis Haslem RC 1.50 4.00
102 Jarvis Hayes RC 1.25 3.00
103 Kirk Hinrich RC 1.50 4.00
104 Josh Howard RC 1.25 3.00
105 LeBron James RC 20.00 40.00
106 Dahntay Jones RC 1.25 3.00
107 Chris Kaman RC 1.50 4.00
108 Jason Kapono RC 1.25 3.00
109 Raul Lopez 1.25 3.00
110 Darko Milicic RC 1.25 3.00
111 Zaur Pachulia RC 1.25 3.00
112 Mickael Pietrus RC 1.25 3.00
113 Zoran Planinic RC 1.25 3.00
114 Luke Ridnour RC 1.50 4.00
115 Darius Songaila .75 2.00
116 Mike Sweetney RC 1.25 3.00
117 Dwyane Wade RC 5.00 12.00
118 Luke Walton RC 1.25 3.00
119 David West RC 1.50 4.00
120 Maurice Williams RC 2.00 5.00

2003-04 Fleer Patchworks Ruby

This 120-card set parallels the base Fleer Patchworks set enhanced with red foil highlights and sequential numbering to 50.

*1-90 RUBY SINGLES: 5X TO 12X BASE HI
*91-120 RUBY RCs: 1.5X TO 4X BASE HI

2003-04 Fleer Patchworks By The Numbers

Inserted in Hobby packs at the rate of one in 24, Retail at one in 12 and Blasters at one in 24, this 15-card set is horizontally designed with a hardwood floor background. Player photos appear on the left while the player's jersey number appears on the right.

COMPLETE SET (15) 20.00 40.00
1 Carmelo Anthony 2.00 5.00
2 Steve Francis .75 2.00
3 Shaquille O'Neal 2.00 5.00
4 Kevin Garnett 1.50 4.00
5 Dwyane Wade 3.00 8.00
6 Tracy McGrady 1.00 2.50
7 Allen Iverson 1.25 3.00
8 Chris Webber .75 2.00
9 Tim Duncan 1.25 3.00
10 Dirk Nowitzki 1.25 3.00
11 Paul Pierce 1.00 2.50
12 LeBron James 8.00 20.00
13 Kobe Bryant 4.00 10.00
14 Jason Kidd 1.25 3.00
15 Vince Carter 1.25 3.00

2003-04 Fleer Patchworks By The Numbers Jerseys

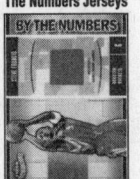

Randomly inserted at the rate of one in 300 Hobby and one in 77 Retail, this 12-card set parallels the design of the base By the Numbers insert set enhanced with jersey swatches in the shape of the featured player's jersey number. A patch version sequentially numbered to 100 was also inserted.

*PATCHES: .75X TO 2X BASE JSY HI
CA Carmelo Anthony 6.00 15.00
CW Chris Webber 3.00 8.00
DN Dirk Nowitzki 4.00 10.00
DW Dwyane Wade 10.00 25.00
JK Jason Kidd 4.00 10.00
KG Kevin Garnett 5.00 12.00
PP Paul Pierce 3.00 8.00
SF Steve Francis 2.50 6.00
TD Tim Duncan 4.00 10.00
TM Tracy McGrady 3.00 8.00
VC Vince Carter 4.00 10.00
SON Shaquille O'Neal 6.00 15.00

2003-04 Fleer Patchworks Courting Greatness

Randomly inserted in Hobby packs at the rate of one in 12, Retail at the rate of one in six and Blasters at the rate of one in 12, this 25-card set is also horizontally designed and the top and bottom of the card are framed by a basketball with the background designed to look like hard wood. Full color player photos appear to the left.

COMPLETE SET (24) 20.00 40.00
1 Dirk Nowitzki 1.00 2.50
2 Jarvis Hayes .60 1.50
3 Tony Parker .60 1.50
4 Drew Gooden .50 1.25
5 Yao Ming 1.25 3.00
6 Udonis Haslem .75 2.00
7 Zach Randolph .60 1.50
8 Carmelo Anthony 1.50 4.00
9 Kobe Bryant 3.00 8.00
10 Chris Bosh 1.25 3.00
11 Antawn Jamison .60 1.50
12 Ben Wallace .60 1.50
13 Manu Ginobili .75 2.00
14 Baron Davis .60 1.50
15 Vince Carter 1.00 2.50
16 Tayshaun Prince .60 1.50
17 Jermaine O'Neal .60 1.50
18 T.J. Ford .75 2.00
19 Josh Howard .60 1.50
20 Amare Stoudemire 1.00 2.50
21 Dwyane Wade 2.50 6.00
22 Michael Redd .60 1.50
23 LeBron James 6.00 15.00
24 Jason Richardson .60 1.50
25 Darko Milicic .60 1.50

2003-04 Fleer Patchworks Courting Greatness Jerseys

Randomly seeded, this 20-card set parallels the design of the base Courting Greatness insert set enhanced with a swatch of jersey on the left and sequential numbering to 350. A Patch version sequentially numbered to 150 was also inserted.

*PATCH: .75X TO 2X BASE JSY HI
AJ Antawn Jamison 2.50 6.00
AS Amare Stoudemire 4.00 10.00
BD Baron Davis 2.50 6.00
BW Ben Wallace 2.50 6.00
CA Carmelo Anthony 6.00 15.00
CB Chris Bosh 5.00 12.00
DG Drew Gooden 2.00 5.00
DN Dirk Nowitzki 4.00 10.00
DW Dwyane Wade 10.00 25.00
JH Jarvis Hayes 2.50 6.00
JH Josh Howard 2.50 6.00
JR Jason Richardson 2.50 6.00
MG Manu Ginobili 3.00 8.00
MR Michael Redd 2.50 6.00
TP Tony Parker 2.50 6.00
TP Tayshaun Prince 2.50 6.00
VC Vince Carter 4.00 10.00
YM Yao Ming 5.00 12.00
ZR Zach Randolph 2.50 6.00
JON Jermaine O'Neal 2.50 6.00

2003-04 Fleer Patchworks Jerseys

Randomly inserted in packs, this 20-card set features a split design with full color player action photos across the top and a tan bar on the bottom quarter of the card with a square swatch of jersey. Several multi-color versions were also inserted into packs: Dual color cards are sequentially numbered to 100 and Multicolor cards are sequentially numbered to 50.

*DUAL COLOR: .75X TO 2X BASE JSY HI
*MULITICOLOR: 1X TO 2.5X BASE JSY HI
N Nene 2.00 5.00
AI Allen Iverson 4.00 10.00
AK Andrei Kirilenko 2.50 6.00
AS Amare Stoudemire 4.00 10.00
DW Dajuan Wagner 2.00 5.00
GA Gilbert Arenas 2.50 6.00
GR Glenn Robinson 2.00 5.00
KG Kevin Garnett 5.00 12.00
KM Kenyon Martin 2.50 6.00
LR Luke Ridnour 3.00 8.00
MB Marcus Banks 2.50 6.00
MF Michael Finley 2.50 6.00
PS Peja Stojakovic 2.50 6.00
RH Richard Hamilton 2.00 5.00
RM Reggie Miller 2.50 6.00
SB Shane Battier 2.00 5.00
SN Steve Nash 3.00 8.00
TP Tony Parker 2.50 6.00
VC Vince Carter 4.00 10.00
YAO Yao Ming 5.00 12.00

2003-04 Fleer Patchworks Licensed Apparel

Randomly inserted in packs, this 20-card set features a horizontal design with a white background and the words "Licensed Apparel" appearing in purple. Each card has a jersey swatch and is sequentially numbered to 300. Several other versions of this set were issued: A Name version with swatches from the team's name is sequentially numbered to 150, a Number versions with swatches from jersey numbers is sequentially numbered to 100, a Name version with swatches from the player's name on the back of the jersey numbered to 50, a Tag version with swatches from the jersey tags sequentially numbered to 10 and an NBA logo from a jersey version is numbered one of one.

*NAME: 1.25X TO 3X BASE LIC.APP. HI
*NUMBER: 1X TO 2.5X BASE LIC.APP. HI
*TEAM NAME: .75X TO 2X BASE LIC.APP. HI
AH Allan Houston 2.00 5.00
BD Baron Davis 2.50 6.00
CW Chris Webber 2.50 6.00
EB Elton Brand 2.50 6.00
JR Jason Richardson 2.50 6.00
JS Jerry Stackhouse 2.00 5.00
KM Karl Malone 3.00 8.00
KM Kenyon Martin 2.50 6.00
LS Latrell Sprewell 2.00 5.00
MB Mike Bibby 2.50 6.00
MD Mike Dunleavy 2.00 5.00
MF Michael Finley 2.50 6.00
PG Pau Gasol 2.50 6.00
PP Paul Pierce 3.00 8.00
RA Ray Allen 3.00 8.00
SF Steve Francis 2.50 6.00
SM Stephon Marbury 2.00 5.00
TM Tracy McGrady 3.00 8.00
SAR Shareef Abdur-Rahim 2.00 5.00
SON Shaquille O'Neal 6.00 15.00

2003-04 Fleer Patchworks National Pastime

Randomly inserted in packs, this eight card set features players from the USA Olympic team. Cards are framed with gold borders and an arch towards the top of the card and are sequentially numbered to 250.

COMPLETE SET (8) 15.00 30.00
1 Jermaine O'Neal 1.50 4.00
2 Jason Kidd 2.50 6.00
3 Tracy McGrady 2.00 5.00
4 Allen Iverson 2.50 6.00
5 Mike Bibby 1.50 4.00
6 Tim Duncan 2.50 6.00
7 Ray Allen 1.50 4.00
8 Larry Brown 3.00 8.00

2003-04 Fleer Patchworks National Patchtime Jerseys NBA

Randomly seeded, this seven-card set parallels the design of the base National Patchtime set enhanced with a swatch of an NBA game jersey. Each card is sequentially numbered to 350. Several other versions of this set were issued: an NBA Patch version with premium swatches and sequential numbering to 100, a USA jersey version sequentially numbered to 200, a USA Patch version sequentially numbered to 75 and a USA/NBA Patch, which has two jersey swatches, sequentially numbered to 25.

*NBA PATCHES: 1.25X TO 3X BASE JSY HI
*USA JERSEY: .6X TO 1.5X BASE JSY HI
*USA PATCHES: 2X TO 5X BASE JSY HI
*USA/NBA PATCH: 3X TO 8X BASE HI
AI Allen Iverson 4.00 10.00
JK Jason Kidd 4.00 10.00
MB Mike Bibby 2.50 6.00
RA Ray Allen 2.50 6.00
TD Tim Duncan 4.00 10.00
TM Tracy McGrady 3.00 8.00
JON Jermaine O'Neal 2.50 6.00

2003-04 Fleer Patchworks Vince Carter Autographs

Inserted in packs at the overall odds of one in 216, this nine-card set features various combinations of Vince Carter jerseys, jersey colors and autographs. Each checklist description contains the color of the jersey Vince Carter is wearing in the picture, not the color of the jersey swatch on the card. Print runs are as follows: Jersey Autograph combos are sequentially numbered to 100, Jersey Patch Autographs are sequentially numbered to 150, Team Name Patch Autographs are sequentially numbered to 15 and NBA Logo Autographs are numbered one of one.

VC4 Vince Carter JSY AU White 15.00 40.00
VC5 Vince Carter JSY AU Purple 15.00 40.00
VC6 Vince Carter JSY AU Red 15.00 40.00
VC7 Vince Carter Patch AU White 20.00 50.00
VC8 Vince Carter Patch AU Purple 20.00 50.00
VC9 Vince Carter Patch AU Red 20.00 50.00

2001-02 Fleer Platinum

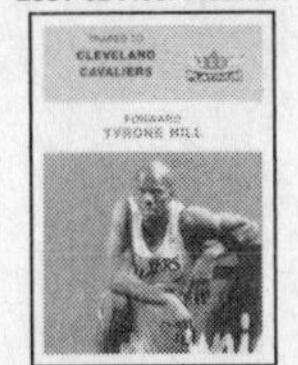

Released as a 250 card set, Fleer Platinum contains 200 regular cards, 30 rookies inserted at the rate of one in six hobby, one in three jumbo, and one in three rack pack, and 20 Highlight Film cards inserted at the same rate as the rookies.The base cards utilize the 1961-62 Fleer design where the top half of the card is in one bold color that contains the player's name, and the bottom half has a bold colored background which is overlayed by a black and white player photo. The rookie cards designed in the 1986-87 Fleer red, white and blue card stock. Highlight Film cards also use the base card stock except the bottom half has actual backgrounds behind the player action photos. Fleer Platinum was issued in late October of 2001, and was packed out in three different versions: hobby, jumbo and rack packs.

COMPLETE SET (250) 100.00 200.00
COMP.SET w/o SP's (200) 8.00 20.00
1 Tyrone Hill .15 .40
2 Sam Cassell .20 .50
3 Elton Brand .25 .60
4 Andre Miller .20 .50
5 Vitaly Potapenko .15 .40
6 Lamar Odom .25 .60
7 Mike Bibby .25 .60
8 Alan Henderson .15 .40
9 Dan Majerle .20 .50
10 Donyell Marshall .15 .40
11 Jason Williams .20 .50
12 Glen Rice .20 .50
13 Kobe Bryant 1.25 3.00
14 Pat Garrity .15 .40
15 Shawn Bradley .15 .40
16 Aaron Williams .15 .40
17 Antonio McDyess .20 .50
18 Jonathan Bender .15 .40
19 Ben Wallace .25 .60
20 Vince Carter .40 1.00
21 Maurice Taylor .15 .40
22 Antonio Daniels .15 .40
23 Rodney Rogers .15 .40
24 Patrick Ewing .30 .75
25 Chauncey Billups .25 .60
26 Steve Smith .20 .50
27 Antawn Jamison .25 .60
28 Mitch Richmond .20 .50
29 Jumaine Jones .15 .40
30 Glenn Robinson .20 .50
31 Ron Mercer .15 .40
32 Jelani McCoy .15 .40
33 Paul Pierce .30 .75
34 Jeff McInnis .15 .40
35 Michael Dickerson .15 .40
36 Toni Kukoc .20 .50
37 Anthony Mason .15 .40
38 Jamal Mashburn .20 .50
39 John Stockton .30 .75
40 Peja Stojakovic .25 .60
41 Charlie Ward .15 .40
42 Donnell Harvey .15 .40
43 Darrell Armstrong .15 .40
44 Michael Finley .25 .60
45 Kerry Kittles .15 .40
46 Voshon Lenard .15 .40
47 Reggie Miller .25 .60
48 Joe Smith .20 .50
49 Antonio Davis .15 .40
50 Hakeem Olajuwon .30 .75
51 David Robinson .40 1.00
52 Tony Delk .15 .40
53 Gary Payton .25 .60
54 Kevin Garnett .50 1.25
55 Arvydas Sabonis .20 .50
56 Larry Hughes .20 .50
57 Richard Hamilton .20 .50
58 Aaron McKie .15 .40
59 Tim Thomas .15 .40
60 Ron Artest .25 .60
61 Matt Harpring .20 .50
62 Kenny Anderson .20 .50
63 Quentin Richardson .20 .50
64 Damon Jones .15 .40
65 Theo Ratliff .15 .40
66 Brian Grant .15 .40
67 Eddie Robinson .15 .40
68 Karl Malone .30 .75
69 Bobby Jackson .15 .40
70 Larry Johnson .25 .60
71 Shareef Abdur-Rahim .20 .50
72 Grant Hill .30 .75
73 Eduardo Najera .15 .40
74 Keith Van Horn .20 .50
75 Nick Van Exel .20 .50
76 Jalen Rose .20 .50
77 Jerry Stackhouse .20 .50
78 Jerome Williams .15 .40
79 Cuttino Mobley .20 .50
80 Derek Anderson .15 .40
81 Anfernee Hardaway .40 1.00
82 Rashard Lewis .25 .60
83 Terrell Brandon .15 .40
84 Scottie Pippen .40 1.00
85 Danny Fortson .15 .40
86 Jahidi White .15 .40
87 Eric Snow .15 .40
88 Ervin Johnson .15 .40
89 Marcus Fizer .15 .40
90 Lamond Murray .15 .40
91 Antoine Walker .20 .50
92 Keyon Dooling .15 .40
93 Bryant Reeves .15 .40
94 Hanno Mottola .15 .40
95 Tim Hardaway .25 .60
96 David Wesley .15 .40
97 John Starks .15 .40
98 Hedo Turkoglu .25 .60
99 Allan Houston .20 .50
100 Rick Fox .20 .50
101 Bo Outlaw .15 .40
102 Juwan Howard .20 .50
103 Kendall Gill .15 .40
104 Raef LaFrentz .15 .40
105 Austin Croshere .15 .40
106 Chucky Atkins .15 .40
107 Morris Peterson .15 .40
108 Shandon Anderson .15 .40
109 Sean Elliott .15 .40
110 Tom Gugliotta .15 .40
111 Vin Baker .20 .50
112 Wally Szczerbiak .20 .50
113 Rasheed Wallace .25 .60
114 Vonteego Cummings .15 .40
115 Christian Laettner .15 .40
116 Dikembe Mutombo .25 .60
117 Lindsey Hunter .15 .40
118 Jamal Crawford .20 .50
119 Jim Jackson .15 .40
120 Bryant Stith .15 .40
121 Corey Maggette .20 .50
122 Mahmoud Abdul-Rauf .15 .40
123 Lorenzen Wright .15 .40
124 Alonzo Mourning .30 .75
125 Jamaal Magloire .15 .40
126 Bryon Russell .15 .40
127 Vlade Divac .20 .50
128 Marcus Camby .20 .50
129 Derek Fisher .20 .50
130 Mike Miller .25 .60
131 Steve Nash .40 1.00
132 Kenyon Martin .25 .60
133 James Posey .15 .40
134 Travis Best .15 .40
135 Corliss Williamson .15 .40
136 Alvin Williams .15 .40
137 Walt Williams .15 .40
138 Malik Rose .15 .40
139 Clifford Robinson .15 .40
140 Ruben Patterson .15 .40
141 LaPhonso Ellis .20 .50
142 Rod Strickland .20 .50
143 Marc Jackson .15 .40
144 Hubert Davis .15 .40
145 Speedy Claxton .15 .40
146 Scott Williams .15 .40
147 Tyronn Lue .15 .40
148 Chris Mihm .15 .40
149 George Lynch .15 .40
150 Michael Olowokandi .15 .40
151 Nazr Mohammed .15 .40
152 Eddie House .15 .40
153 Elden Campbell .15 .40
154 DeShawn Stevenson .15 .40
155 Doug Christie .15 .40
156 Kurt Thomas .15 .40
157 Robert Horry .20 .50
158 Radoslav Nesterovic .15 .40
159 Wang Zhizhi .20 .50
160 Stephen Jackson .20 .50
161 George McCloud .15 .40
162 Jermaine O'Neal .25 .60
163 Mateen Cleaves .15 .40
164 Charles Oakley .20 .50
165 Kenny Thomas .15 .40
166 Terry Porter .15 .40
167 Iakovos Tsakalidis .15 .40
168 Shammond Williams .15 .40
169 Anthony Peeler .15 .40
170 Damon Stoudamire .20 .50
171 Chris Porter .15 .40
172 Chris Whitney .15 .40
173 Raja Bell RC .30 .75
174 Darvin Ham .15 .40
175 A.J. Guyton .15 .40
176 Trajan Langdon .15 .40
177 Jerome Moiso .15 .40
178 Anthony Carter .15 .40
179 P.J. Brown .15 .40
180 Danny Manning .15 .40
181 Scot Pollard .15 .40
182 Mark Jackson .20 .50
183 Mark Madsen .15 .40
184 Michael Doleac .15 .40
185 Calvin Booth .15 .40
186 Kevin Willis .15 .40
187 Al Harrington .20 .50
188 Mikki Moore .15 .40
189 Keon Clark .15 .40
190 Moochie Norris .15 .40
191 Ron Harper .20 .50
192 Danny Ferry .15 .40
193 Jacque Vaughn .15 .40
194 Derrick Coleman .20 .50
195 Brent Barry .15 .40
196 Dion Glover .15 .40
197 Felipe Lopez .15 .40
198 Shawn Kemp .25 .60
199 Mookie Blaylock .20 .50
200 Bonzi Wells .15 .40
201 Vince Carter HL 1.50 4.00
202 Ray Allen HL 1.00 2.50
203 Darius Miles HL .60 1.50
204 Shaquille O'Neal HL 2.50 6.00
205 Stromile Swift HL .60 1.50
206 DerMarr Johnson HL .60 1.50
207 Eddie Jones HL .75 2.00
208 Chris Webber HL 1.00 2.50
209 Latrell Sprewell HL .75 2.00
210 Tracy McGrady HL 1.50 4.00
211 Dirk Nowitzki HL 1.50 4.00
212 Stephon Marbury HL .75 2.00
213 Steve Francis HL 1.00 2.50
214 Tim Duncan HL 2.00 5.00
215 Jason Kidd HL 1.50 4.00
216 Shawn Marion HL 1.00 2.50
217 Desmond Mason HL .75 2.00
218 Courtney Alexander HL .60 1.50
219 Baron Davis HL 1.00 2.50
220 Allen Iverson HL 2.00 5.00
221 Joe Johnson RC 2.50 6.00
222 Kedrick Brown RC 1.00 2.50
223 Joseph Forte RC 1.00 2.50
224 Kirk Haston RC 1.00 2.50
225 Tyson Chandler RC 1.50 4.00
226 Eddy Curry RC 1.50 4.00
227 DeSagana Diop RC 1.00 2.50
228 Jeff Trepagnier RC 1.00 2.50
229 Oscar Torres RC 1.00 2.50
230 Rodney White RC 1.00 2.50
231 Jason Richardson RC 2.00 5.00
232 Troy Murphy RC 1.50 4.00
233 Eddie Griffin RC 1.00 2.50
234 Jamaal Tinsley RC 1.25 3.00
235 Pau Gasol RC 3.00 8.00
236 Shane Battier RC 2.00 5.00
237 Richard Jefferson RC 2.00 5.00
238 Jason Collins RC 1.00 2.50
239 Brendan Haywood RC 1.25 3.00
240 Steven Hunter RC 1.00 2.50
241 Zach Randolph RC 2.50 6.00
242 Gerald Wallace RC 1.50 4.00
243 Tony Parker RC 4.00 10.00
244 Vladimir Radmanovic RC 1.00 2.50
245 Michael Bradley RC 1.00 2.50
246 Andrei Kirilenko RC 2.50 6.00
247 Kwame Brown RC 1.00 2.50
248 Alton Ford RC 1.00 2.50
249 Zeljko Rebraca RC 1.00 2.50
250 Trenton Hassell RC 1.00 2.50

2001-02 Fleer Platinum 15th Anniversary Reprints

Randomly inserted in hobby packs at the rate of one in 12, one six jumbo, and one in three in rack packs, this 25 card set reprints some of Fleer's most famous rookie cards in original Fleer card stock. Each card contains a Fleer Platinum logo stamp in one of the card's corners.

COMPLETE SET (25) 60.00 120.00
1 Michael Jordan 15.00 40.00
2 Karl Malone 2.50 6.00
3 Hakeem Olajuwon 2.50 6.00
4 Patrick Ewing 2.50 6.00
5 Reggie Miller 2.00 5.00
6 John Stockton 2.50 6.00
7 Scottie Pippen 3.00 8.00
8 David Robinson 3.00 8.00
9 Shaquille O'Neal 5.00 12.00
10 Alonzo Mourning 2.50 6.00
11 Chris Webber 2.00 5.00
12 Grant Hill 2.50 6.00
13 Jason Kidd 3.00 8.00
14 Eddie Jones 1.50 4.00

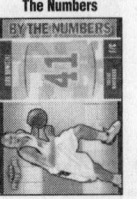

15 Kevin Garnett 4.00 10.00
16 Kobe Bryant 10.00 25.00
17 Allen Iverson 4.00 10.00
18 Shareef Abdur-Rahim 1.50 4.00
19 Tim Duncan 4.00 10.00
20 Tracy McGrady 3.00 8.00
21 Vince Carter 3.00 8.00
22 Dirk Nowitzki 3.00 8.00
23 Steve Francis 2.00 5.00
24 Darius Miles 1.25 3.00
25 Mike Miller 2.00 5.00

2001-02 Fleer Platinum Anniversary Edition

Randomly inserted in Hobby packs, this 250-card set parallels the base Fleer Platinum set. Cards are enhanced with sequential numbering and is divided up into two subsets. The 200 Anniversary Edition, card numbers 1-200, are sequentially numbered to 201, while the 50 Anniversary Edition, card numbers 201-250, are sequentially numbered to 21.
*ANNIV 1-200: 5X TO 12X BASE CARD HI
*ANNIV 201-250: 6X TO 15X HI
13 Kobe Bryant 20.00 50.00

2001-02 Fleer Platinum Classic Combinations

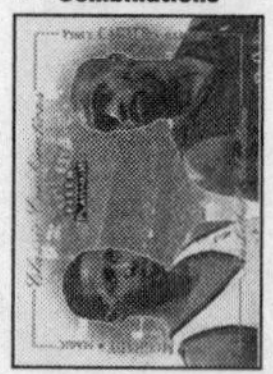

Randomly inserted in packs, this 15-card set features dual player cards sequentially numbered between 500 and 2000. Additionally, twelve cards contain dual game worn jersey swatches and are sequentially numbered to 100.
1 John Stockton/1000 Karl Malone 3.00 8.00
2 Allen Iverson/1000 Dikembo Mutombo 3.00 8.00
3 Jason Kidd/1000 Grant Hill 3.00 8.00
4 Steve Francis/1000 Elton Brand 3.00 8.00
5 Vince Carter/1000 Antawn Jamison 3.00 8.00
6 Hakeem Olajuwon/500 Patick Ewing 3.00 8.00
7 Vince Carter/500 Tracy McGrady 6.00 15.00
8 Kobe Bryant/500 Shaquille O'Neal 6.00 15.00
9 Tim Duncan/500 David Robinson 4.00 10.00
10 Kevin Garnett/500 Darius Miles 3.00 8.00
11 Dirk Nowitzki/2000 Michael Finley 3.00 8.00
12 Antoine Walker/2000 Paul Pierce 3.00 8.00
13 Ray Allen/2000 Glenn Robinson 3.00 8.00
14 Latrell Sprewell/2000 Allan Houston 3.00 8.00
15 Patrick Ewing/2000 Alonzo Mourning 3.00 8.00

2001-02 Fleer Platinum Classic Combinations Jerseys

Randomly inserted in packs, this 11 card set honors some of the best combinations currently in the NBA. This set honors either teammates past or present or players who attended the same college or even great rivalries. This set, which is a partial parallel to the Classic Combination insert set, features game worn jersey swatches on the card. These cards have a stated print run of 100 serial numbered sets.
1 John Stockton Karl Malone 12.00 30.00
2 Allen Iverson Dikembo Mutombo 10.00 25.00
3 Jason Kidd Grant Hill 10.00 25.00
4 Steve Francis Elton Brand 8.00 20.00
5 Vince Carter Antawn Jamison 12.00 30.00
6 Hakeem Olajuwon Patick Ewing 10.00 25.00
7 Vince Carter Tracy McGrady 15.00 40.00
11 Dirk Nowitzki Michael Finley 8.00 20.00
12 Antoine Walker Paul Pierce 8.00 20.00
13 Ray Allen Glenn Robinson 8.00 20.00
15 Patrick Ewing Alonzo Mourning 12.50 30.00

2001-02 Fleer Platinum Lucky 13

Randomly inserted in packs, these cards were issued as redemptions for the 13 "lottery" picks in the 2002 NBA draft. Upon redemption, a collector received a card of the player which had a stated print run of 500 serial numbered sets.
COMPLETE SET (13) 75.00 150.00
1 Kwame Brown 4.00 10.00
2 Tyson Chandler 6.00 15.00
3 Pau Gasol 12.00 30.00
4 Eddy Curry 6.00 15.00
5 Jason Richardson 8.00 20.00
6 Shane Battier 8.00 20.00
7 Eddie Griffin 4.00 10.00
8 DeSagana Diop 4.00 10.00
9 Rodney White 4.00 10.00
10 Joe Johnson 10.00 25.00
11 Kedrick Brown 4.00 10.00
12 Vladimir Radmanovic 4.00 10.00
13 Richard Jefferson 8.00 20.00

2001-02 Fleer Platinum Nameplates

Randomly inserted in Jumbo packs at the rate of one in 12, this 13-card set features top players on a license plate card stock of their respective team's home state. Each card contains both color action player photos and a swatch of a game worn jersey.
1 Alonzo Mourning/175 15.00 40.00
2 Hakeem Olajuwon/175 12.00 30.00
3 Allen Iverson/150 20.00 50.00
4 Stephon Marbury/100 8.00 20.00
5 Gary Payton/100 10.00 25.00
6 Glenn Robinson/50 8.00 20.00
7 Shareef Abdur-Rahim/250 8.00 20.00
8 Keith Van Horn/225 8.00 20.00
9 John Stockton/100 20.00 50.00
10 Antoine Walker/100 8.00 20.00
11 David Robinson/125 20.00 50.00
12 Michael Finley/175 10.00 25.00
13 Vince Carter/75 15.00 40.00

2001-02 Fleer Platinum National Patch Time

Inserted one in 24 packs, this 26-card set features cards with swatches of game-used pants and jersey. Each card has a color action player photo on the right, and a silver logo on the top left above a game used uniform swatch.
1 Tom Gugliotta 2.00 5.00
2 Shawn Marion 3.00 8.00
3 Darius Miles 2.00 5.00
4 Mike Miller 3.00 8.00
5 Jason Terry 3.00 8.00
6 Stromile Swift 2.00 5.00
7 Keith Van Horn 2.50 6.00
8 Ray Allen 3.00 8.00
9 Baron Davis 3.00 8.00
10 Shareef Abdur-Rahim 2.50 6.00
11 Stephon Marbury 2.50 6.00
12 Jason Kidd 5.00 12.00
13 Mike Bibby 3.00 8.00
14 Jerome Moiso 2.00 5.00
15 Richard Hamilton 2.50 6.00
16 Paul Pierce 4.00 10.00
17 Dikembe Mutombo 3.00 8.00
18 Gary Payton 3.00 8.00
19 Patrick Ewing 4.00 10.00
20 Vince Carter 5.00 12.00
21 Corey Maggette 2.50 6.00
22 Jacque Vaughn 2.00 5.00
23 Darrell Armstrong 2.00 5.00
24 Mitch Richmond 2.50 6.00
25 Allen Iverson 6.00 15.00
26 Desmond Mason 2.50 6.00

2001-02 Fleer Platinum Stadium Standouts

Randomly inserted at the rate of one in 18 hobby, one in six jumbo, and one in three rack pack, this set features 15 NBA player photos set in front of their home stadiums.
COMPLETE SET (15) 20.00 50.00
1 Vince Carter 2.00 5.00
2 Grant Hill 1.50 4.00
3 Kobe Bryant 6.00 15.00
4 Steve Francis 1.25 3.00
5 Tracy McGrady 2.00 5.00
6 Elton Brand 1.25 3.00
7 Kevin Garnett 2.50 6.00
8 Allen Iverson 2.50 6.00
9 Dirk Nowitzki 2.00 5.00
10 Shaquille O'Neal 3.00 8.00
11 Tim Duncan 2.50 6.00
12 Jason Kidd 2.00 5.00
13 Darius Miles .75 2.00
14 Chris Webber 1.25 3.00
15 Ray Allen 1.25 3.00

2002-03 Fleer Platinum

Released in late April 2003, Fleer Platinum boasts a 200-card set divided up into 160 base veteran cards and 40 rookie cards. Base cards feature a throw-back style base card with white borders, full color player action photography and the player's team logo in a circle in the lower right corner of the card. Platinum was packed in 19-pack boxes where the packs were divided up as follows: 14 wax packs with seven cards per pack, four jumbo packs with 20 cards per pack and one tri-pouch rack pack with 30 cards per pack. Each different pack set up had 10 rookies that were exclusive to that pack format and 10 rookies dispersed between all formats, card numbers 161-170. Cards 171-180 were only inseted in wax packs and were sequentially numbered to 750. Cards 181-190 were only inserted in jumbo packs and were sequentially numbered to 350, and cards 191-200 were only inserted in rack packs and were sequentially numbered to 250. Fleer Platinum Wax packs carried an SRP of $2.99.
COMP.SET w/o SP's (160) 15.00 40.00
1 Vince Carter .50 1.25
2 Lamar Odom .30 .75
3 Darrell Armstrong .20 .50
4 Kwame Brown .20 .50
5 Ron Artest .30 .75
6 Kurt Thomas .20 .50
7 Jerry Stackhouse .25 .60
8 Eddie Griffin .20 .50
9 David Wesley .20 .50
10 Morris Peterson .20 .50
11 Jon Barry .20 .50
12 Troy Hudson .20 .50
13 Kenny Anderson .25 .60
14 Corliss Williamson .20 .50
15 Kevin Garnett .60 1.50
16 Desmond Mason .25 .60
17 Lucious Harris .20 .50
18 Steve Smith .25 .60
19 Nick Van Exel .25 .60
20 Tyson Chandler .25 .60
21 Shane Battier .30 .75
22 Rasheed Wallace .30 .75
23 Donyell Marshall .20 .50
24 Anfernee Hardaway .50 1.25
25 Antoine Walker .25 .60
26 Kobe Bryant 1.50 4.00
27 Keith Van Horn .25 .60
28 Elton Brand .30 .75
29 Grant Hill .40 1.00
30 Elden Campbell .20 .50
31 John Stockton .40 1.00
32 Wally Szczerbiak .25 .60
33 Speedy Claxton .20 .50
34 Voshon Lenard .20 .50
35 Eddie Jones .25 .60
36 Bonzi Wells .20 .50
37 Jalen Rose .25 .60
38 Jason Williams .25 .60
39 Tom Gugliotta .20 .50
40 Juwan Howard .25 .60
41 Michael Redd .30 .75
42 David Robinson .50 1.25
43 Steve Nash .40 1.00
44 Vlade Divac .25 .60
45 Avery Johnson .25 .60
46 Scottie Pippen .50 1.25
47 Eric Williams .20 .50
48 Derek Fisher .25 .60
49 Tony Battie .20 .50
50 Rick Fox .25 .60
51 Theo Ratliff .20 .50
52 Corey Maggette .25 .60
53 Jermaine O'Neal .30 .75
54 Bryon Russell .20 .50
55 Steve Francis .30 .75
56 Jamal Mashburn .25 .60
57 Jerome Williams .20 .50
58 Gilbert Arenas .30 .75
59 Joe Smith .25 .60
60 Brent Barry .20 .50
61 Marcus Camby .25 .60
62 Toni Kukoc .25 .60
63 Tim Duncan .60 1.50
64 Ira Newble .20 .50
65 Brian Grant .20 .50
66 Jason Terry .25 .60
67 Andre Miller .25 .60
68 Mike Miller .30 .75
69 Troy Murphy .30 .75
70 P.J. Brown .20 .50
71 Jason Richardson .30 .75
72 Glenn Robinson .25 .60
73 Richard Jefferson .30 .75
74 Richard Hamilton .25 .60
75 Jason Kidd .50 1.25
76 Rashard Lewis .30 .75
77 Kenny Satterfield .20 .50
78 Terrell Brandon .20 .50
79 Dirk Nowitzki .50 1.25
80 Chris Webber .30 .75
81 Michael Finley .30 .75
82 Malik Allen .20 .50
83 Bobby Jackson .20 .50
84 Darius Miles .20 .50
85 Kendall Gill .20 .50
86 Damon Stoudamire .25 .60
87 Shammond Williams .20 .50
88 Stephon Marbury .25 .60
89 Shareef Abdur-Rahim .25 .60
90 Charlie Ward .20 .50
91 Michael Jordan 2.50 6.00
92 Jamaal Magloire .20 .50
93 Karl Malone .40 1.00
94 Kerry Kittles .20 .50
95 Lindsey Hunter .20 .50
96 Gary Payton .30 .75
97 Travis Best .20 .50
98 Derek Anderson .20 .50
99 Stromile Swift .20 .50
100 Shaquille O'Neal .75 2.00
101 Derrick Coleman .25 .60
102 DeShawn Stevenson .20 .50
103 Jamaal Tinsley .20 .50
104 Latrell Sprewell .25 .60
105 Larry Hughes .25 .60
106 Eddy Curry .25 .60
107 Shawn Marion .30 .75
108 Paul Pierce .40 1.00
109 Samaki Walker .20 .50
110 Allen Iverson .50 1.25
111 Michael Olowokandi .20 .50
112 Tracy McGrady .50 1.25
113 Shawn Bradley .20 .50
114 Reggie Miller .30 .75
115 Antonio McDyess .25 .60
116 Calbert Chaney .20 .50
117 Al Harrington .25 .60
118 Allan Houston .25 .60
119 Andrei Kirilenko .30 .75
120 Courtney Alexander .20 .50
121 Alvin Williams .20 .50
122 Antawn Jamison .30 .75
123 Dikembe Mutombo .30 .75
124 Tony Parker .40 1.00
125 Raef LaFrentz .20 .50
126 Ray Allen .30 .75
127 Peja Stojakovic .30 .75
128 Zydrunas Ilgauskas .25 .60
129 Gerald Wallace .30 .75
130 Ruben Patterson .20 .50
131 Pau Gasol .40 1.00
132 Joe Johnson .30 .75
133 Aaron McKie .20 .50
134 Walter McCarty .20 .50
135 Baron Davis .30 .75
136 Kenyon Martin .30 .75
137 Antonio Davis .20 .50
138 Ben Wallace .30 .75
139 Sam Cassell .25 .60
140 Mike Bibby .30 .75
141 Cuttino Mobley .25 .60
142 LaPhonso Ellis .25 .60
143 Shandon Anderson .20 .50
144 Hedo Turkoglu .30 .75
145 Matt Harpring .25 .60
146 Dion Glover .20 .50
147 Tony Delk .20 .50
148 Ricky Davis .25 .60
149 James Posey .20 .50
150 Chucky Atkins .20 .50
151 Danny Fortson .20 .50
152 Robert Horry .25 .60
153 Radoslav Nesterovic .20 .50
154 Pat Garrity .20 .50
155 Todd MacCulloch .20 .50
156 Eric Snow .20 .50
157 Malik Rose .20 .50
158 Vladimir Radmanovic .20 .50
159 Trenton Hassell .20 .50
160 Brad Miller .30 .75
161 Kareem Rush RC 1.25 3.00
162 Nikoloz Tskitishvili RC 1.25 3.00
163 Nene Hilario RC 1.50 4.00
164 Marcus Haislip RC 1.25 3.00
165 Jiri Welsch RC 1.25 3.00
166 Dan Dickau RC 1.25 3.00
167 Vincent Yarbrough RC 1.25 3.00
168 Tito Maddox RC 1.25 3.00
169 Mike Dunleavy RC 1.50 4.00
170 Chris Wilcox RC 1.25 3.00
171 Jared Jeffries RC 2.00 5.00
172 Bostjan Nachbar RC 2.00 5.00
173 Frank Williams RC 2.00 5.00
174 Reggie Evans RC 2.00 5.00
175 Casey Jacobsen RC 2.00 5.00
176 Tayshaun Prince RC 2.50 6.00
177 Mike Batiste RC 2.00 5.00
178 Drew Gooden RC 3.00 8.00
179 DaJuan Wagner RC 2.00 5.00
180 Tamar Slay RC 2.00 5.00
181 Melvin Ely RC 2.50 6.00
182 Rasual Butler RC 2.50 6.00
183 Dan Gadzuric RC 2.50 6.00
184 Ryan Humphrey RC 2.50 6.00
185 Gordan Giricek RC 2.50 6.00
186 Mehmet Okur RC 2.50 6.00
187 Jay Williams RC 3.00 8.00
188 Caron Butler RC 4.00 10.00
189 Qyntel Woods RC 2.50 6.00
190 Amare Stoudemire RC 6.00 15.00
191 Yao Ming RC 10.00 25.00
192 Carlos Boozer RC 6.00 15.00
193 John Salmons RC 4.00 10.00
194 Fred Jones RC 3.00 8.00
195 Juan Dixon RC 4.00 10.00
196 Manu Ginobili RC 8.00 20.00
197 Pat Burke RC 3.00 8.00
198 Smush Parker RC 3.00 8.00
199 Lonny Baxter RC 3.00 8.00
200 Ronald Murray RC 3.00 8.00

2002-03 Fleer Platinum Finish

Randomly inserted in packs, this 200-card set parallels the base Fleer Platinum set enhanced with a metallic silver finish around the borders. Each card is sequentially numbered to 100.
*STARS: 4X TO 10X BASE CARD HI
*161-170 RCs: 1.5X TO 4X BASE CARD HI
*171-180 RCs: 1X TO 2.5X BASE CARD HI
*181-190 RCs: .75X TO 2X BASE CARD HI
*191-200 RCs: .6X TO 1.5X BASE CARD HI

2002-03 Fleer Platinum Freshman Fabric

Randomly seeded in Rack packs at the rate of one in two, this 15-card set is designed horizontally with a close-up portrait photo of the player along the left side and a rather generous swatch of game used memorabilia on the right side.
AS Amare Stoudemire 6.00 15.00
CB Caron Butler 4.00 10.00
CB2 Carlos Boozer 5.00 12.00
CW Chris Wilcox 2.50 6.00
DD Dan Dickau 2.50 6.00
DG Drew Gooden 4.00 10.00
DW DaJuan Wagner 2.50 6.00
EG Manu Ginobili 6.00 15.00
JD Juan Dixon 3.00 8.00
KR Kareem Rush 2.50 6.00
NH Nene Hilario 3.00 8.00
NT Nikoloz Tskitishvili 2.50 6.00
QW Qyntel Woods 2.50 6.00
TP Tayshaun Prince 3.00 8.00
YM Yao Ming 8.00 20.00

2002-03 Fleer Platinum Guts and Glory

Randomly inserted in Rack packs at the rate of one in one, Jumbo packs at the rate of one in two, and Wax packs at the rate of one in four, this 10-card set places full-color player action photos on a green back-drop with white borders.
COMPLETE SET (10) 6.00 15.00
1GG Steve Nash 1.25 3.00
2GG Ben Wallace 1.00 2.50
3GG Antawn Jamison 1.00 2.50
4GG Elton Brand 1.00 2.50
5GG Kenyon Martin 1.00 2.50
6GG Rasheed Wallace 1.00 2.50
7GG Reggie Miller 1.00 2.50
8GG Andre Miller .75 2.00
9GG Vince Carter 1.50 4.00
10GG Richard Jefferson 1.00 2.50

2002-03 Fleer Platinum Inside the Playbook

Randomly seeded in packs, this 15-card set is die-cut in the shape of a note book with an embossed card front and small pictures of the featured player. Each card is sequentially numbered to 400.
1PB Paul Pierce 2.50 6.00
2PB Kobe Bryant 10.00 25.00
3PB Caron Butler 3.00 8.00
4PB Tracy McGrady 3.00 8.00
5PB Allen Iverson 3.00 8.00
6PB Tim Duncan 4.00 10.00
7PB Vince Carter 3.00 8.00
8PB Jay Williams 2.50 6.00
9PB Michael Jordan 15.00 40.00
10PB DaJuan Wagner 2.00 5.00
11PB Steve Nash 2.50 6.00
12PB Nene Hilario 2.50 6.00
13PB Ben Wallace 2.00 5.00
14PB Mike Dunleavy 2.50 6.00
15PB Yao Ming 6.00 15.00

2002-03 Fleer Platinum Inside the Playbook Game Used

Randomly inserted in packs, this nine card set parallels the base Playbook insert set enhanced with a swatch of game used memorabilia. Each card is sequentially numbered to 250.
AI Allen Iverson 5.00 12.00
BW Ben Wallace 3.00 8.00
CB Caron Butler 5.00 12.00
DW DaJuan Wagner 3.00 8.00
NH Nene Hilario 4.00 10.00
PP Paul Pierce 4.00 10.00
SN Steve Nash 4.00 10.00
TM Tracy McGrady 5.00 12.00
VC Vince Carter 5.00 12.00
YM Yao Ming 10.00 25.00

2002-03 Fleer Platinum Nameplates

Inserted randomly in Jumbo packs, this 30-card set showcases a horizontal design with a white background, a player photo on the right, a swatch of the name patch from the player's jersey and colored highlights to match the team colors. Each card has rounded corners and is sequentially numbered with print runs listed below.
AI Allen Iverson/485 12.50 30.00
AM Andre Miller/260 6.00 15.00
AS Amare Stoudemire/315 12.50 30.00
BD Baron Davis/110 15.00 40.00
BW Ben Wallace/145 20.00 50.00
CB Caron Butler/280 10.00 25.00
DG Drew Gooden/220 10.00 25.00
DM Darius Miles/115 10.00 25.00
DN Dirk Nowitzki/255 15.00 40.00
DR David Robinson/210 15.00 40.00
EB Elton Brand/225 6.00 15.00
JK Jason Kidd/300 15.00 40.00
JO Jermaine O'Neal/135 15.00 40.00
JS John Stockton/230 15.00 40.00
KB Kwame Brown/355 6.00 15.00
KG Kevin Garnett/400 15.00 40.00
KM Kenyon Martin/170 10.00 25.00
LS Latrell Sprewell/190 15.00 40.00
PG Pau Gasol/350 10.00 25.00
PP Paul Pierce/200 15.00 40.00
QW Qyntel Woods/325 6.00 15.00
RA Ray Allen/400 10.00 25.00
SF Steve Francis/385 8.00 20.00
SN Steve Nash/110 20.00 50.00
TC Tyson Chandler/355 6.00 15.00
TM Tracy McGrady/175 15.00 40.00
TP Tony Parker/115 15.00 40.00
VC Vince Carter/545 12.50 30.00
YM Yao Ming/290 15.00 30.00

2002-03 Fleer Platinum Portraits

Inserted randomly in Rack packs at one in four, Jumbo packs at one in eight and Wax packs at one in 14, this 15-card set features a close-up shot of the player with a dark colored border that matches team colors. All cards contain silver foil highlights.
COMPLETE SET (15) 20.00 50.00
1PP Vince Carter 2.00 5.00
2PP Jason Kidd 2.00 5.00
3PP Shane Battier 1.25 3.00
4PP Steve Francis 1.25 3.00
5PP Chris Webber 1.25 3.00
6PP Jason Richardson 1.25 3.00
7PP Richard Jefferson 1.25 3.00
8PP Dirk Nowitzki 2.00 5.00
9PP Kevin Garnett 2.50 6.00
10PP Baron Davis 1.25 3.00
11PP Darius Miles .75 2.00
12PP Tim Duncan 2.50 6.00
13PP Kobe Bryant 6.00 15.00
14PP Shaquille O'Neal 3.00 8.00
15PP Michael Jordan 10.00 25.00

2002-03 Fleer Platinum Portraits Game Worn Jerseys

Randomly inserted in Wax packs at the rate of on in 21, this nine card set parallels the base set design of the Portraits insert set enhanced with a swatch of game used memorabilia and gold foil highlights.
*PATCH: 1X TO 2.5X BASE HI
PATCH STATED PRINT RUN 100 SETS
BD Baron Davis 3.00 8.00
DN Dirk Nowitzki 5.00 12.00
JK Jason Kidd 5.00 12.00
JR Jason Richardson 3.00 8.00
KG Kevin Garnett 6.00 15.00
RJ Richard Jefferson 3.00 8.00
SB Shane Battier 3.00 8.00
SF Steve Francis 3.00 8.00
VC Vince Carter 5.00 12.00

2002-03 Fleer Platinum Vince Carter's All-Stars Game Used

Inserted randomly in Wax packs, this six card set pairs up Vince Carter with some of the NBA's top All-Stars on a throwback style card with a close up of Vince's face and a smaller full-body shot of the All-Star player. A swatch from each player is cut in the shap of a star and both are centered on the card horizontally. Each card is sequentially numbered to 250.
AI Vince Carter Allen Iverson 10.00 25.00
BW Vince Carter Ben Wallace 10.00 25.00
DN Vince Carter Dirk Nowitzki 10.00 25.00
JK Vince Carter Jason Kidd 10.00 25.00
KG Vince Carter Kevin Garnett 12.50 30.00
TM Vince Carter Tracy McGrady 10.00 25.00

2003-04 Fleer Platinum

Issued in March 2004, Platinum boasts a 200-card base set divided up as follows: 170 base veteran cards, where 1-141 share the same throwback design with a single color background and a sold color bar along the bottom, and cards 142-170 share an unsung heroes design that includes a close-up player portrait style shot and white borders. Cards 171-200 are rookies and utilize a design that resembles that of 1984 Fleer Baseball. Cards 171-180 are seeded at one in three for Wax, and one in two for Jumbo packs. Cards 181-190 were inserted in Wax packs only and are sequentially numbered to 750, and cards 191-200 were inserted in Jumbo packs only and are sequentially numbered to 500. Fleer Platinum was packaged in 20-pack boxes where 16 packs were Wax with seven cards per pack and a suggested retail price of $2.99 and four packs were Jumbo with 20 cards per pack and a suggested retail price of $4.99. Also included was one 2004 Ultra Hummer which sealed both a card and a die-cast GM Hummer with team logos to match the player on the card.
COMPLETE SET (200) 75.00 150.00
COMP.SET w/o SP's (170) 15.00 30.00
1 Shane Battier .20 .50
2 Brad Miller .25 .60
3 Jason Kidd .40 1.00
4 Nick Van Exel .20 .50
5 David Wesley .15 .40
6 Corey Maggette .20 .50
7 Juan Dixon .15 .40
8 Jamaal Tinsley .15 .40
9 Stromile Swift .15 .40
10 Dajuan Wagner .15 .40
11 Joe Smith .20 .50
12 Jermaine O'Neal .25 .60
13 Steve Nash .30 .75
14 Karl Malone .30 .75
15 Vince Carter .40 1.00
16 Antonio McDyess .20 .50
17 Tim Thomas .15 .40
18 Vladimir Radmanovic .15 .40
19 Scottie Pippen .40 1.00
20 Tracy McGrady .30
21 Darius Miles .15
22 Toni Kukoc .25
23 Antonio Davis .15
24 Jamal Crawford .20
25 Rasho Nesterovic .15
26 Carlos Boozer .25
27 Cuttino Mobley .20
28 Larry Hughes .20
29 Alvin Williams .15
30 Andre Miller .20
31 Amare Stoudemire .40
32 Eric Williams .15
33 Pau Gasol .25
34 Kenyon Martin .25
35 Elton Brand .25
36 Charlie Ward .15
37 Andrei Kirilenko .25
38 Aaron McKie .15
39 Maurice Taylor .15
40 Baron Davis .25
41 Dirk Nowitzki .40
42 Gary Payton .25
43 Grant Hill .30
44 Jalen Rose .20
45 Allan Houston .20
46 Erick Dampier .15
47 Brian Grant .15
48 Wally Szczerbiak .20
49 Greg Ostertag .15
50 Gilbert Arenas .25
51 Kenny Anderson .20
52 Juwan Howard .20
53 Jason Terry .20
54 Raef LaFrentz .15
55 Ricky Davis .20
56 Kobe Bryant 1.25
57 Chris Webber .25
58 P.J. Brown .15
59 Nene .20
60 Kenny Thomas .15
61 Mike Bibby .25
62 Chris Wilcox .15
63 Anfernee Hardaway .40
64 Drew Gooden .20
65 Rodney White .15
66 Shareef Abdur-Rahim .20
67 Quentin Richardson .20
68 Ben Wallace .25
69 Latrell Sprewell .20
70 Shaquille O'Neal .60
71 Vin Baker .15
72 Tony Parker .25
73 Stephen Jackson .20
74 Ray Allen .25
75 Eric Snow .15
76 Jason Richardson .25
77 Shammond Williams .15
78 Tayshaun Prince .25
79 Antawn Jamison .25
80 Derek Fisher .20
81 Jeff Foster .15
82 Kwame Brown .15
83 Yao Ming .50
84 Rasheed Wallace .25
85 Tyson Chandler .20
86 Mike Dunleavy .20
87 Alan Henderson .15
88 Rashard Lewis .25
89 Jamaal Magloire .15
90 Stephon Marbury .20
91 DeShawn Stevenson .15
92 Damon Stoudamire .20
93 Eddy Curry .20
94 Peja Stojakovic .25
95 Glenn Robinson .20
96 Mike Miller .25
97 Richard Hamilton .20
98 Kevin Garnett .50
99 Zach Randolph .25
100 Tony Delk .15
101 Clifford Robinson .15
102 Steve Francis .25
103 Curtis Borchardt .25
104 Jerry Stackhouse .20
105 Desmond Mason .20
106 Chauncey Billups .25
107 Sam Cassell .20
108 Michael Finley .25
109 Hedo Turkoglu .25
110 Ronald Murray .15
111 Allen Iverson .40
112 Richard Jefferson .25
113 Theo Ratliff .15
114 Ron Artest .25
115 Doug Christie .15
116 Lamar Odom .25
117 Lamond Murray .15
118 Bonzi Wells .15
119 Caron Butler .25
120 Marcus Camby .20
121 Manu Ginobili .30
122 Paul Pierce .30
123 Troy Hudson .15
124 Jim Jackson .15
125 Keith Van Horn .20
126 Reggie Miller .25
127 Tim Duncan .40
128 Shawn Marion .25
129 Eddie Jones .20
130 Matt Harpring .20
131 Elden Campbell .15
132 Marko Jaric .15
133 John Wallace .15
134 Erick Strickland .15
135 Voshon Lenard .15
136 Aaron Williams .15
137 Qyntel Woods .15
138 Kelvin Cato .15
139 Michael Curry .15
140 Vlade Divac .20
141 Jason Hart .15
142 Nazr Mohammed UH .15
143 Mike James UH .15
144 Jerome Williams UH .15
145 Zydrunas Ilgauskas UH .20
146 Antoine Walker UH .25
147 Earl Boykins UH .15
148 Mehmet Okur UH .20
149 Brian Cardinal UH .15
150 Bostjan Nachbar UH .15
151 Al Harrington UH .20
152 Eddie House UH .15
153 Devean George UH .15
154 Jason Williams UH .20
155 Rafer Alston UH .15
156 Michael Redd UH .25
157 Gary Trent UH .15

erry Kittles UH .15 .40
imal Mashburn UH .20 .50
urt Thomas UH .15 .40
yronn Lue UH .15 .40
errick Coleman UH .20 .50
oe Johnson UH .25 .60
ale Davis UH .15 .40
obby Jackson UH .15 .40
Aalik Rose UH .15 .40
rent Barry UH .15 .40
onyell Marshall UH .15 .40
arlos Arroyo UH .20 .50
an Thomas UH .15 .40
oran Planinic RC 1.00 2.50
ason Kapono RC 1.00 2.50
arko Cabarkapa RC 1.00 2.50
arko Milicic RC 1.00 2.50
leksandar Pavlovic RC 1.00 2.50
larcus Banks RC 1.00 2.50
Villie Green RC 1.00 2.50
donis Haslem RC 1.25 3.00
ick Collison RC 1.00 2.50
hris Kaman RC 1.25 3.00
.J. Ford RC 2.00 5.00
ravis Outlaw RC 2.00 5.00
eBron James RC 20.00 50.00
roy Bell RC 1.50 4.00
eece Gaines RC 1.50 4.00
avid West RC 2.00 5.00
irk Hinrich RC 2.00 5.00
hris Bosh RC 3.00 8.00
eandro Barbosa RC 2.00 5.00
wyane Wade RC 6.00 15.00
Mike Sweetney RC 2.00 5.00
arius Songaila 1.25 3.00
uke Ridnour RC 2.50 6.00
armelo Anthony RC 5.00 12.00
arvis Hayes RC 2.00 5.00
lickael Pietrus RC 2.00 5.00
ahntay Jones RC 2.00 5.00
osh Howard RC 2.00 5.00
laciej Lampe RC 2.00 5.00
uke Walton RC 2.00 5.00

03-04 Fleer Platinum Finish

omly seeded in packs, this 200-card set parallels ase Fleer Platinum set enhanced with sequential ering to 100.
0 SINGLES: 3X TO 8X BASE HI
-180 RCs: 1.25X TO 3X BASE HI
-190 RCs: 1X TO 2.5X BASE HI
-200 RCs: .75X TO 2X BASE HI
eBron James 100.00 250.00

2003-04 Fleer Platinum Big Signs

omly inserted in Wax at the rate of one in nine and o at the rate of one in eight, this 15-card set es a fold-out jumbo design with the player's in the middle of the opened card.
PLETE SET (15) 12.50 30.00
vin Garnett 1.25 3.00
en Iverson 1.00 2.50
aquille O'Neal 1.50 4.00
ko Milicic .60 1.50
be Bryant 3.00 8.00
Wallace .60 1.50
Bron James 6.00 15.00
yane Wade 2.50 6.00
Nowitzki 1.00 2.50
ron Davis .60 1.50
o Ming 1.25 3.00
rmelo Anthony 1.50 4.00
eja Stojakovic .60 1.50
rmaine O'Neal .60 1.50
nce Carter 1.00 2.50

2003-04 Fleer Platinum Big Signs Autographs

omly seeded in packs, this four card set is an graphed parallel of the big signs set where each s sequentially numbered to 50.
en Wallace 12.50 30.00
Dwyane Wade 50.00 120.00
ince Carter 15.00 40.00

2003-04 Fleer Platinum Inscribed

domly seeded, all of these cards are sequentially bered and feature a horizontal design with full- player portrait photos on the right and an edded cut signature on the left.
ne/188 4.00 10.00
ndrei Kirilenko/193 10.00 25.00
Ben Wallace/35 15.00 40.00
Carmelo Anthony/282 25.00 60.00
Carmelo Anthony 25.00 60.00
Chris Bosh/250 12.50 30.00
Drew Gooden/66 6.00 15.00
David Robinson/195 30.00 80.00
David West/250 5.00 12.00
Gilbert Arenas/315 8.00 20.00
Gilbert Arenas/32 15.00 40.00
yle Korver/87 15.00 30.00
areem Rush/248 4.00 10.00
eandro Barbosa/196 5.00 12.00
uke Ridnour/197 5.00 12.00
uke Walton/132 4.00 10.00
Marcus Banks/350 4.00 10.00
Manu Ginobili/198 12.50 30.00
Maciej Lampe/185 4.00 10.00
Mickael Pietrus/249 4.00 10.00
Mike Sweetney/264 4.00 10.00
yson Chandler/195 4.00 10.00
racy McGrady/99 20.00 50.00
ravis Outlaw/276 5.00 12.00
ayshaun Prince/185 6.00 15.00
Jdonis Haslem/195 5.00 12.00
Vince Carter/280 12.00 30.00
arko Cabarkapa/235 4.00 10.00
arko Cabarkapa/37 8.00 20.00
Caron Butler/365 5.00 12.00
Caron Butler/28 20.00 50.00

JHO Josh Howard/250 4.00 10.00
SHM Shawn Marion/101 8.00 20.00

2003-04 Fleer Platinum Locker Room Memorabilia

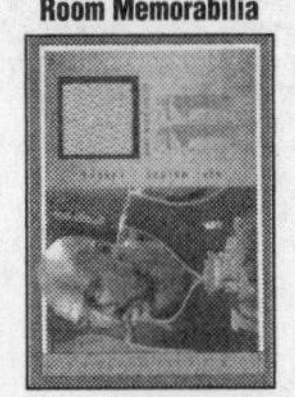

Randomly inserted in Hobby Wax packs at the rate of one in 24 and Retail at one in 96, this 25-card set features a horizontal design with player photos on the left and swatches of memorabilia on the right. A dual memorabilia version, where swatches are stacked on top of eachother was also inserted and is sequentially numbered to 50.
*DUAL SINGLES: 1.25X TO 3X BASE MEM.HI
N Nene 2.00 5.00
AK Andrei Kirilenko 2.50 6.00
BD Baron Davis 2.50 6.00
BW Ben Wallace 2.50 6.00
CB Caron Butler 2.50 6.00
EB Elton Brand 2.50 6.00
GR Glenn Robinson 2.00 5.00
JH Jarvis Hayes 2.50 6.00
JK Jason Kidd 4.00 10.00
JR Jason Richardson 2.50 6.00
KM Karl Malone 3.00 8.00
MD Mike Dunleavy 2.00 5.00
MF Michael Finley 2.50 6.00
MG Manu Ginobili 3.00 8.00
MR Michael Redd 2.50 6.00
PP Paul Pierce 3.00 8.00
PS Peja Stojakovic 2.50 6.00
RM Reggie Miller 2.50 6.00
SF Steve Francis 2.50 6.00
SM Stephon Marbury 2.00 5.00
SN Steve Nash 3.00 8.00
JON Jermaine O'Neal 2.50 6.00
SHM Shawn Marion 2.50 6.00
YAO Yao Ming 5.00 12.00
KMAR Kenyon Martin 2.50 6.00

2003-04 Fleer Platinum Nameplates

Randomly inserted in packs, this 30-card set is sequentially numbered and is set to look like a license plate with both a full-color player image and a premium swatch of memorabilia. A Dual player version was also produced and inserted and those cards are sequentially numbered to 25.
AH Allan Houston/450 5.00 12.00
AJ Antawn Jamison/145 6.00 15.00
BW Ben Wallace/90 8.00 20.00
CA Carmelo Anthony/380 12.00 30.00
CK Chris Kaman/465 6.00 15.00
CW Chris Webber/695 12.00 30.00
DW Dwyane Wade/465 20.00 50.00
DW Dajuan Wagner/585 4.00 10.00
GA Gilbert Arenas/235 6.00 15.00
JC Jamal Crawford/323 5.00 12.00
JH Jarvis Hayes/375 5.00 12.00
LR Luke Ridnour/710 6.00 15.00
LW Luke Walton/215 6.00 15.00
MB Mike Bibby/365 6.00 15.00
MD Mike Dunleavy/250 5.00 12.00
MG Manu Ginobili/195 8.00 20.00
MM Mike Miller/590 6.00 15.00
MP Mickael Pietrus/253 5.00 12.00
MR Michael Redd/725 6.00 15.00
RH Richard Hamilton/170 5.00 12.00
SB Shane Battier/715 5.00 12.00
SP Scottie Pippen/390 15.00 40.00
TD Tim Duncan/725 10.00 25.00
TO Travis Outlaw/590 6.00 15.00
TP Tayshaun Prince/455 6.00 15.00
VC Vince Carter/725 10.00 25.00
ZR Zach Randolph/210 6.00 15.00
SAR Shareef Abdur-Rahim/600 5.00 12.00

2003-04 Fleer Platinum Nameplates Dual

This set parallels the design of the Nameplates set but features two players and two swatches of memorabilia. Each card is sequentially numbered to 25.
GAJH Gilbert Arenas / Jarvis Hayes 25.00 60.00
GPLW Gary Payton / Luke Walton 25.00 60.00
MBCW Mike Bibby / Chris Webber 15.00 40.00
MDMP Mike Dunleavy / Mickeal Pietrus 20.00 50.00
SBMM Shane Battier / Mike Miller 15.00 40.00
TDMG Tim Duncanc / Manu Ginobili 30.00 80.00
TOZR Travis Outlaw / Zach Randolph 15.00 40.00

2003-04 Fleer Platinum NBA Scouting Report

Randomly seeded in packs, this 15-card set was designed to look like an open notebook where the outside is the texture of a basketball and the inside shows statistics and a small picture of the featured player. Each card is sequentially numbered to 400.
COMPLETE SET (15) 20.00 40.00
1 Shaquille O'Neal 2.50 6.00
2 Tracy McGrady 1.25 3.00
3 Tim Duncan 1.50 4.00
4 Jason Kidd 1.50 4.00
5 Amare Stoudemire 1.50 4.00
6 Kobe Bryant 5.00 12.00
7 Steve Francis 1.00 2.50
8 Kevin Garnett 2.00 5.00
9 Dirk Nowitzki 1.50 4.00
10 Jason Richardson 1.00 2.50
11 Darko Milicic 1.00 2.50
12 Jarvis Hayes 1.00 2.50
13 LeBron James 12.00 30.00
14 Chris Webber 1.00 2.50
15 Chris Bosh 2.00 5.00

2003-04 Fleer Platinum NBA Scouting Report Jerseys

Randomly inserted, this set parallels the design of the Scouting Report insert set enhanced with a jersey swatch and sequential numbering to 250.
AS Amare Stoudemire 4.00 10.00
CB Chris Bosh 5.00 12.00
DN Dirk Nowitzki 4.00 10.00
JH Jarvis Hayes 2.50 6.00
JK Jason Kidd 4.00 10.00
KG Kevin Garnett 5.00 12.00
SF Steve Francis 2.50 6.00
SO Shaquille O'Neal 6.00 15.00
TD Tim Duncan 4.00 10.00
TM Tracy McGrady 3.00 8.00

2003-04 Fleer Platinum Portraits

Randomly inserted in Hobby Wax packs at the rate of one in 18, Jumbo at one in four, and Retail at one in 14, this 15-card set features a bordered all-foil design with close-up player portrait style photos.
COMPLETE SET (15) 15.00 30.00
1 Pau Gasol 1.25 3.00
2 Yao Ming 2.50 6.00
3 Michael Finley 1.25 3.00
4 Tony Parker 1.25 3.00
5 Dwyane Wade 5.00 12.00
6 Darko Milicic 1.25 3.00
7 Tracy McGrady 1.50 4.00
8 Allen Iverson 2.00 5.00
9 Reggie Miller 1.25 3.00
10 Paul Pierce 1.50 4.00
11 Amare Stoudemire 2.00 5.00
12 Steve Nash 1.50 4.00
13 Caron Butler 1.25 3.00
14 Drew Gooden 1.00 2.50
15 Vince Carter 2.00 5.00

2003-04 Fleer Platinum Portraits Jerseys

Randomly seeded in Hobby Wax at the rate of one in 40 and Retail at one in 120, this 10-card set parallels the design of the base Portraits insert set enhanced with a square jersey swatch. A Patch version was also produced and is sequentially numbered to 100.
*PATCHES: .75X TO 2X BASE JSY HI
AI Allen Iverson 4.00 10.00
AS Amare Stoudemire 4.00 10.00
DW Dwyane Wade 10.00 25.00
MF Michael Finley 2.50 6.00
PG Pau Gasol 2.50 6.00
RM Reggie Miller 2.50 6.00
TM Tracy McGrady 3.00 8.00
TP Tony Parker 2.50 6.00
VC Vince Carter 4.00 10.00
YAO Yao Ming 5.00 12.00

2003-04 Fleer Platinum Showdown Series

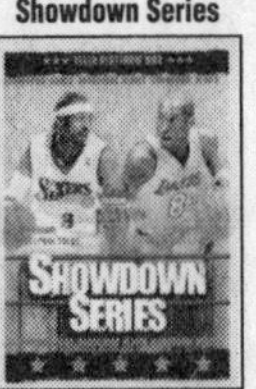

Inserted in Hobby Wax packs at the rate of one in 288 and Retail at one in 480, this 10-card set is designed in the format of a faded old boxing match poster with one player on the left and the other on the right.
1 Allen Iverson / Kobe Bryant 8.00 20.00
2 Jason Kidd / Tony Parker 4.00 10.00
3 Shaquille O'Neal / Tim Duncan 6.00 15.00
4 Paul Pierce / Antawn Walker 4.00 10.00
5 LeBron James / Carmelo Anthony 8.00 20.00
6 Jermaine O'Neal / Ben Wallace 4.00 10.00
7 Vince Carter / Tracy McGrady 5.00 12.00
8 Dirk Nowitzki / Chris Webber 5.00 12.00
9 Kevin Garnett / Amare Stoudemire 6.00 15.00
10 Nick Collison / Kirk Hinrich 4.00 10.00

2000-01 Fleer Premium

The 2000-01 Fleer Premium set was released in November, 2000. The 241-card base set features 200 veterans, and 41 Rookie cards. Please note that all rookies are serial numbered to 1999, and that the first 250 of cards 217-241 contain a ball swatch. Each pack contained eight cards, and carried a suggested retail price of $2.99.
COMPLETE SET w/o RC (200) 12.50 30.00
1 Vince Carter .60 1.50
2 Kobe Bryant 1.50 4.00
3 Jermaine Jackson .20 .50
4 Lamar Odom .30 .75
5 Robert Traylor .20 .50
6 Jason Kidd .50 1.25
7 Rashard Lewis .30 .75
8 Ron Artest .30 .75
9 Grant Hill .40 1.00
10 Kenny Thomas .20 .50
11 Anthony Carter .20 .50
12 Kerry Kittles .20 .50
13 Pat Garrity .20 .50
14 David Robinson .50 1.25
15 Bryant Reeves .20 .50
16 Fred Hoiberg .20 .50
17 Jerry Stackhouse .25 .60
18 Donyell Marshall .25 .60
19 Ron Harper .25 .60
20 Scott Burrell .20 .50
21 Ron Mercer .25 .60
22 Avery Johnson .25 .60
23 Jacque Vaughn .20 .50
24 Adrian Griffin .20 .50
25 Antonio McDyess .25 .60
26 Adonal Foyle .20 .50
27 Derek Fisher .30 .75
28 Terrell Brandon .25 .60
29 Matt Harpring .25 .60
30 Nazr Mohammed .20 .50
31 Tom Gugliotta .20 .50
32 Scott Padgett .20 .50
33 Detlef Schrempf .25 .60
34 Dirk Nowitzki .50 1.25
35 Mookie Blaylock .25 .60
36 James Posey .25 .60
37 Latrell Sprewell .25 .60
38 Michael Doleac .20 .50
39 Damon Stoudamire .25 .60
40 Tim Duncan .60 1.50
41 John Stockton .40 1.00
42 Danny Fortson .20 .50
43 Raef LaFrentz .20 .50
44 Steve Francis .30 .75
45 Travis Knight .20 .50
46 Kevin Garnett .60 1.50
47 Mitch Richmond .25 .60
48 Olden Polynice .20 .50
49 Derrick Coleman .25 .60
50 Ervin Johnson .20 .50
51 Shandon Anderson .20 .50
52 Jamal Mashburn .25 .60
53 Joe Smith .25 .60
54 Bo Outlaw .20 .50
55 Clifford Robinson .20 .50
56 Scottie Pippen .50 1.25
57 Chris Webber .30 .75
58 Doug Christie .20 .50
59 Michael Dickerson .20 .50
60 Anthony Mason .20 .50
61 Shawn Bradley .20 .50
62 Reggie Miller .30 .75
63 P.J. Brown .20 .50
64 Wally Szczerbiak .25 .60
65 Keon Clark .20 .50
66 Anthony Peeler .20 .50
67 Doug West .20 .50
68 Antoine Walker .25 .60
69 Trajan Langdon .20 .50
70 Mark Jackson .25 .60
71 Sam Cassell .25 .60
72 Kurt Thomas .20 .50
73 Ruben Patterson .20 .50
74 Alvin Williams .20 .50
75 Juwan Howard .25 .60
76 Baron Davis .30 .75
77 Otis Thorpe .25 .60
78 Austin Croshere .20 .50
79 Tony Delk .20 .50
80 William Avery .20 .50
81 Matt Geiger .20 .50
82 Richard Hamilton .25 .60
83 Ricky Davis .25 .60
84 Hubert Davis .20 .50
85 Jalen Rose .25 .60
86 Theo Ratliff .20 .50
87 Bobby Jackson .20 .50
88 Glenn Robinson .25 .60
89 Kendall Gill .20 .50
90 Laron Profit .20 .50
91 Brad Miller .30 .75
92 Cedric Ceballos .20 .50
93 Arvydas Sabonis .25 .60
94 Vitaly Potapenko .20 .50
95 Rod Strickland .25 .60
96 Erick Dampier .20 .50
97 Ryan Bowen .20 .50
98 Dale Davis .20 .50
99 Larry Johnson .30 .75
100 John Thomas .20 .50
101 Rodney Rogers .20 .50
102 Ray Allen .30 .75
103 Isaac Austin .20 .50
104 Radoslav Nesterovic .20 .50
105 Tariq Abdul-Wahad .20 .50
106 Jonathan Bender .20 .50
107 Tim Hardaway .30 .75
108 Jamie Feick .20 .50
109 Toni Kukoc .25 .60
110 Tyrone Corbin .20 .50
111 Aleksandar Radojevic .20 .50
112 Tony Battie .20 .50
113 Andre Miller .25 .60
114 Derek Anderson .20 .50
115 Tim Thomas .20 .50
116 Corey Maggette .25 .60
117 Rasheed Wallace .30 .75
118 Shammond Williams .20 .50
119 Charlie Ward .20 .50
120 Paul Pierce .40 1.00
121 Shawn Kemp .30 .75
122 Darrell Armstrong .20 .50
123 Fred Vinson .20 .50
124 Jim Jackson .20 .50
125 Steve Nash .50 1.25
126 Michael Stewart .20 .50
127 Maurice Taylor .20 .50
128 Michael Ruffin .20 .50
129 Vlade Divac .25 .60
130 LaPhonso Ellis .25 .60
131 Eddie Jones .30 .75
132 Hakeem Olajuwon .40 1.00
133 Rick Fox .25 .60
134 Patrick Ewing .40 1.00
135 Brian Grant .20 .50
136 Jaren Jackson .20 .50
137 Christian Laettner .20 .50
138 Greg Ostertag .20 .50
139 Anfernee Hardaway .50 1.25
140 Nick Van Exel .25 .60
141 Jason Caffey .20 .50
142 Michael Olowokandi .20 .50
143 Darvin Ham .20 .50
144 Calbert Cheaney .20 .50
145 Steve Smith .25 .60
146 Jason Williams .30 .75
147 Jelani McCoy .20 .50
148 Karl Malone .40 1.00
149 Dikembe Mutombo .30 .75
150 Wesley Person .20 .50
151 Kelvin Cato .20 .50
152 Alonzo Mourning .40 1.00
153 Terry Mills .20 .50
154 Allen Iverson .60 1.50
155 Bonzi Wells .20 .50
156 Antonio Daniels .20 .50
157 Shareef Abdur-Rahim .25 .60
158 Randy Brown .20 .50
159 Mike Bibby .30 .75
160 Travis Best .20 .50
161 Dan Majerle .25 .60
162 Aaron McKie .25 .60
163 Jason Terry .30 .75
164 Michael Finley .30 .75
165 Antonio Davis .20 .50
166 Lindsey Hunter .20 .50
167 Cuttino Mobley .25 .60
168 Glen Rice .25 .60
169 Stephon Marbury .25 .60
170 Sean Elliott .25 .60
171 Cedric Henderson .20 .50
172 Eric Snow .20 .50
173 Othella Harrington .20 .50
174 Vonteego Cummings .20 .50
175 John Amaechi .20 .50
176 Allan Houston .25 .60
177 Shawn Marion .30 .75
178 Scot Pollard .20 .50
179 Elton Brand .30 .75
180 Loy Vaught .20 .50
181 Larry Hughes .25 .60
182 Shaquille O'Neal .75 2.00
183 Keith Van Horn .25 .60
184 Terry Porter .25 .60
185 Quincy Lewis .20 .50
186 Alan Henderson .20 .50
187 Brevin Knight .20 .50
188 Walt Williams .20 .50
189 Clarence Weatherspoon .20 .50
190 Marcus Camby .25 .60
191 Corliss Williamson .20 .50
192 Gary Payton .30 .75
193 Felipe Lopez .20 .50
194 Elden Campbell .20 .50
195 Jerome Williams .20 .50
196 Antawn Jamison .30 .75
197 Gerard King .20 .50
198 Andrae Patterson .20 .50
199 Vin Baker .25 .60
200 Tracy McGrady .50 1.25
201 Chris Carrawell RC 1.25 3.00
202 Eduardo Najera RC 1.25 3.00
203 Olumide Oyedeji RC 1.25 3.00
204 Hanno Mottola RC 1.25 3.00
205 Dan McClintock RC 1.25 3.00
206 Jacquay Walls RC 1.25 3.00
207 Corey Hightower RC 1.25 3.00
208 Jamal Crawford RC 2.00 5.00
209 Soumaila Samake RC 1.25 3.00
210 Michael Redd RC 3.00 8.00
211 Jason Hart RC 1.25 3.00
212 Mark Karcher RC 1.25 3.00
213 Chris Porter RC 1.25 3.00
214 Eddie House RC 1.25 3.00
215 Jabari Smith RC 1.25 3.00
216 Dan Langhi RC 1.25 3.00
217 Desmond Mason RC 1.50 4.00
218 Darius Miles RC 1.50 4.00
219 Donnell Harvey RC 1.25 3.00
220 DeShawn Stevenson RC 1.50 4.00
221 Kenyon Martin RC 3.00 8.00
222 Joel Przybilla RC 1.25 3.00
223 Keyon Dooling RC 1.25 3.00
224 Speedy Claxton RC 1.25 3.00
225 Jerome Moiso RC 1.25 3.00
226 Hedo Turkoglu RC 2.50 6.00
227 Mark Madsen RC 1.25 3.00
228 Morris Peterson RC 1.25 3.00
229 Courtney Alexander RC 1.25 3.00
230 Etan Thomas RC 1.25 3.00
231 Mateen Cleaves RC 1.25 3.00
232 Stromile Swift RC 1.25 3.00
233 Marcus Fizer RC 1.25 3.00
234 Quentin Richardson RC 2.00 5.00
235 Jason Collier RC 1.25 3.00
236 Jamaal Magloire RC 1.25 3.00
237 Erick Barkley RC 1.25 3.00
238 DerMarr Johnson RC 1.25 3.00
239 Chris Mihm RC 1.25 3.00
240 Mamadou N'Diaye RC 1.25 3.00
241 Mike Miller RC 2.50 6.00

2000-01 Fleer Premium Rookie Game Balls

Randomly inserted into packs this 25-card insert features a swatch of actual game-used basketball. Please note that the first 250 of each RC numbered to 1999 contained a swatch of ball.
*GAME BALL: .6X TO 1.5X HI COLUMN

2000-01 Fleer Premium 10th Anni-VINCE-ry

Randomly inserted in packs at one in 24, this 10-card set celebrates the ten year anniversary of the Fleer/SkyBox Premium line. Each card features Vince Carter in the design for that particular year. Card backs carry an "AV" prefix.
COMPLETE SET (10) 20.00 40.00
COMMON CARD (AV1-AV10) 2.50 6.00

2000-01 Fleer Premium Vince Carter Rookie Remnants

This three-card insert was randomly inserted into 2000-01 Fleer products. The set includes a Vince Carter floor card (numbered to 100), a Vince Carter floor/jersey card (numbered to 15), and finally an autographed Vince Carter floor/jersey card (numbered 1/1).
NNO Vince Carter FLR/100 12.50 30.00

2000-01 Fleer Premium Name Game

Randomly inserted in packs at one in 24, this 15-card set features players who have become "household names". Card backs carry a "NG" prefix.
COMPLETE SET (15) 25.00 50.00
NG1 Vince Carter 2.50 6.00
NG2 Allen Iverson 2.50 6.00
NG3 Shaquille O'Neal 3.00 8.00
NG4 Jason Kidd 2.00 5.00
NG5 Jason Williams 1.25 3.00
NG6 Glenn Robinson 1.00 2.50
NG7 Karl Malone 1.50 4.00
NG8 Reggie Miller 1.25 3.00
NG9 Hakeem Olajuwon 1.50 4.00
NG10 Lamar Odom 1.25 3.00
NG11 Tim Duncan 2.50 6.00
NG12 Grant Hill 1.50 4.00
NG13 Kobe Bryant 6.00 15.00
NG14 Tracy McGrady 2.00 5.00
NG15 Kevin Garnett 2.50 6.00

2000-01 Fleer Premium Name Game Premium

Randomly inserted in packs, this 10-card set is a semi-parallel of the Name Game insert. The cards feature swatches of game-used uniform and were limited to just 50 of each.
NG1 Vince Carter 25.00 60.00
NG2 Allen Iverson 25.00 60.00
NG3 Shaquille O'Neal 30.00 80.00
NG4 Jason Kidd 20.00 50.00
NG5 Jason Williams 12.00 30.00
NG6 Glenn Robinson 10.00 25.00
NG7 Karl Malone 15.00 40.00
NG8 Reggie Miller 20.00 50.00
NG9 Hakeem Olajuwon 15.00 40.00
NG10 Lamar Odom 12.00 30.00

2000-01 Fleer Premium Skilled Artists

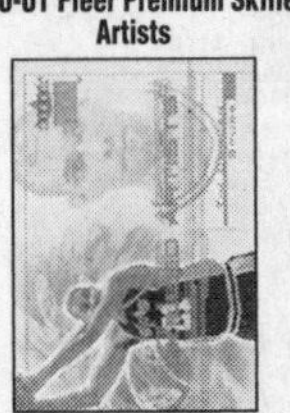

Randomly inserted in packs at one in 12, this 15-card set features players who use a combination of skill and creative direction to become quick strike artists. Card backs carry a "SA" prefix.
COMPLETE SET (15) 10.00 20.00
SA1 Vince Carter 1.25 3.00
SA2 Steve Francis .60 1.50
SA3 Paul Pierce .75 2.00
SA4 Gary Payton .60 1.50
SA5 Jason Williams .60 1.50
SA6 Larry Hughes .50 1.25
SA7 Tim Duncan 1.25 3.00
SA8 Kobe Bryant 3.00 8.00
SA9 Chris Webber .60 1.50
SA10 Tracy McGrady 1.00 2.50
SA11 Dirk Nowitzki 1.00 2.50
SA12 Elton Brand .60 1.50
SA13 Andre Miller .50 1.25
SA14 Ray Allen .60 1.50
SA15 Shareef Abdur-Rahim .50 1.25

2000-01 Fleer Premium Skilled Artists Premium

Randomly inserted in packs, this six-card set is a semi-parallel of the Skilled Artists insert. The cards feature a swatch of game-used jersey and were limited to just 100 cards.
SA1 Vince Carter 20.00 50.00
SA2 Steve Francis 10.00 25.00
SA3 Paul Pierce 12.00 30.00
SA4 Gary Payton 10.00 25.00
SA5 Jason Williams 10.00 25.00
SA6 Chris Webber 10.00 25.00

2000-01 Fleer Premium Skylines

Randomly inserted in packs at one in 144, this 10-card set features NBA players against the skyline of the city they play in. Card backs carry a "SL" prefix.
COMPLETE SET (10) 25.00 60.00
SL1 Vince Carter 4.00 10.00
SL2 Allen Iverson 4.00 10.00
SL3 Kobe Bryant 10.00 25.00
SL4 Latrell Sprewell 1.50 4.00
SL5 Elton Brand 2.00 5.00
SL6 Grant Hill 2.50 6.00
SL7 Steve Francis 2.00 5.00
SL8 Richard Hamilton 1.50 4.00
SL9 Gary Payton 2.00 5.00
SL10 David Robinson 3.00 8.00

2000-01 Fleer Premium Sole Train

Randomly inserted in packs at one in six, this 15-card set features players who carry their teams, night in and night out. Card backs carry a "ST" prefix.
COMPLETE SET (15) 4.00 10.00
ST1 Vince Carter .75 2.00
ST2 Marcus Camby .30 .75
ST3 Wally Szczerbiak .30 .75
ST4 Lamar Odom .40 1.00
ST5 Shaquille O'Neal 1.00 2.50
ST6 Antoine Walker .30 .75
ST7 Eddie Jones .40 1.00
ST8 Larry Hughes .30 .75
ST9 Baron Davis .40 1.00
ST10 Mike Bibby .40 1.00
ST11 Elton Brand .40 1.00
ST12 Kevin Garnett .75 2.00
ST13 Allen Iverson .75 2.00
ST14 Tim Duncan .75 2.00
ST15 Grant Hill .50 1.25

2000-01 Fleer Premium Sole Train Premium

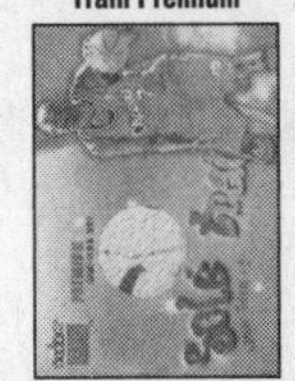

Randomly inserted in packs, this 10-card set is a semi-parallel to the Sole Train insert. The cards feature a swatch of game-used shoes and were limited to 50.
ST1 Vince Carter 15.00 40.00
ST2 Marcus Camby 6.00 15.00
ST3 Wally Szczerbiak 6.00 15.00
ST4 Lamar Odom 8.00 20.00
ST5 Shaquille O'Neal 40.00 100.00
ST6 Antoine Walker 6.00 15.00
ST7 Eddie Jones 8.00 20.00
ST8 Larry Hughes 6.00 15.00
ST9 Baron Davis 8.00 20.00
ST10 Mike Bibby 8.00 20.00

2001-02 Fleer Premium

Released in December 2001, This 185-card base set is standard size and contains 150 veterans as well as 35 rookies. The cards are borderless with a white background. A color action shot of the featured player graces the front of the card with his name running along the top of the card and his corresponding team name and position running down the right-hand side. The Rookie Cards (151-185) have a stated print run of 1500 sets.

COMPLETE SET (185) 100.00 200.00
COMP.SET w/o SP's (1-150) 15.00 40.00
1 Shareef Abdur-Rahim .25 .60
2 Charlie Ward .20 .50
3 Anfernee Hardaway .50 1.25
4 Robert Horry .25 .60
5 Michael Jordan 6.00 15.00
6 Trajan Langdon .20 .50
7 Dan Majerle .25 .60
8 Tracy McGrady .50 1.25
9 Alonzo Mourning .40 1.00
10 Gary Payton .30 .75
11 Erick Barkley .20 .50
12 Jerry Stackhouse .25 .60
13 Vince Carter .50 1.25
14 Speedy Claxton .20 .50
15 DerMarr Johnson .20 .50
16 Bryon Russell .20 .50
17 Derrick Coleman .25 .60
18 Kevin Willis .20 .50
19 Dirk Nowitzki .50 1.25
20 Derek Anderson .20 .50
21 Tim Hardaway .30 .75
22 Avery Johnson .25 .60
23 Quincy Lewis .20 .50
24 Shawn Marion .30 .75
25 Joe Smith .25 .60
26 Tim Thomas .20 .50
27 Bonzi Wells .20 .50
28 Ron Artest .30 .75
29 Elton Brand .30 .75
30 Mateen Cleaves .20 .50
31 Marcus Fizer .20 .50
32 Ervin Johnson .20 .50
33 Mark Madsen .20 .50
34 Andre Miller .25 .60
35 Nazr Mohammed .20 .50
36 Dikembe Mutombo .30 .75
37 Ben Wallace .30 .75
38 Scottie Pippen .50 1.25
39 Theo Ratliff .20 .50
40 Hedo Turkoglu .30 .75
41 Alvin Williams .20 .50
42 Corey Maggette .25 .60
43 Steve Francis .30 .75
44 Dean Garrett .20 .50
45 Wally Szczerbiak .25 .60
46 Brent Barry .20 .50
47 Vlade Divac .25 .60
48 LaPhonso Ellis .25 .60
49 Tyrone Hill .20 .50
50 Toni Kukoc .25 .60
51 George Lynch .20 .50
52 Antonio McDyess .25 .60
53 Paul Pierce .40 1.00
54 Mitch Richmond .25 .60
55 Latrell Sprewell .25 .60
56 Otis Thorpe .25 .60
57 Ray Allen .30 .75
58 Mike Bibby .30 .75
59 P.J. Brown .20 .50
60 Allan Houston .25 .60
61 Stephon Marbury .25 .60
62 Aaron McKie .20 .50
63 Reggie Miller .30 .75
64 Eduardo Najera .20 .50
65 Eddie Robinson .20 .50
66 John Stockton .40 1.00
67 Chris Webber .30 .75
68 Kenny Anderson .25 .60
69 Alan Henderson .20 .50
70 Dan Langhi .20 .50
71 Rashard Lewis .30 .75
72 Donyell Marshall .20 .50
73 Charles Oakley .25 .60
74 Stephen Jackson .25 .60
75 Clarence Weatherspoon .20 .50
76 David Wesley .20 .50
77 Kobe Bryant 1.50 4.00
78 Tom Gugliotta .20 .50
79 Darius Miles .20 .50
80 Cuttino Mobley .25 .60
81 Jason Terry .30 .75
82 Shandon Anderson .20 .50
83 Antonio Daniels .20 .50
84 Larry Hughes .25 .60
85 Raef LaFrentz .20 .50
86 Kenyon Martin .30 .75
87 Lamar Odom .30 .75
88 Jermaine O'Neal .30 .75
89 Glenn Robinson .25 .60
90 Damon Stoudamire .25 .60
91 Eddie House .20 .50
92 Antonio Davis .20 .50
93 Rick Fox .25 .60
94 Allen Iverson .60 1.50
95 Chris Mihm .20 .50
96 Hakeem Olajuwon .40 1.00
97 Clifford Robinson .20 .50
98 Derek Fisher .25 .60
99 Joel Przybilla .20 .50
100 Sean Rooks .20 .50
101 Jason Kidd .50 1.25
102 Antoine Walker .25 .60
103 Jason Williams .25 .60
104 Jamal Mashburn .25 .60
105 Courtney Alexander .20 .50
106 Vin Baker .25 .60
107 Chauncey Billups .30 .75
108 Marcus Camby .25 .60
109 Kevin Garnett .60 1.50
110 Juwan Howard .25 .60
111 Marc Jackson .20 .50
112 Karl Malone .40 1.00
113 Ricky Davis .25 .60
114 Desmond Mason .25 .60
115 Jerome Moiso .20 .50
116 Steve Nash .50 1.25
117 Quentin Richardson .25 .60
118 Peja Stojakovic .30 .75
119 Rasheed Wallace .30 .75
120 Travis Best .20 .50
121 Terrell Brandon .20 .50
122 Austin Croshere .20 .50
123 Tony Delk .20 .50
124 Anthony Mason .20 .50
125 Patrick Ewing .40 1.00
126 Brian Grant .20 .50
127 Bobby Jackson .20 .50
128 Eddie Jones .25 .60
129 Popeye Jones .20 .50
130 Brevin Knight .20 .50
131 Mike Miller .30 .75
132 Shaquille O'Neal .75 2.00
133 Morris Peterson .20 .50
134 Mookie Blaylock .25 .60
135 David Robinson .50 1.25
136 John Starks .20 .50
137 Stromile Swift .20 .50
138 Nick Van Exel .25 .60
139 Keith Van Horn .25 .60
140 Antawn Jamison .30 .75
141 Kurt Thomas .20 .50
142 Sam Cassell .25 .60
143 Tim Duncan .60 1.50
144 Baron Davis .30 .75
145 Jerome Williams .20 .50
146 Michael Finley .30 .75
147 Richard Hamilton .25 .60
148 Grant Hill .40 1.00
149 Jalen Rose .25 .60
150 Steve Smith .25 .60
151 Kwame Brown RC 1.25 3.00
152 Jeryl Sasser RC 1.25 3.00
153 Shane Battier RC 2.50 6.00
154 Gilbert Arenas RC 2.00 5.00
155 Jarron Collins RC 1.25 3.00
156 Jamaal Tinsley RC 1.50 4.00
157 Brandon Armstrong RC 1.25 3.00
158 Michael Bradley RC 1.25 3.00
159 Tyson Chandler RC 2.00 5.00
160 Joseph Forte RC 1.25 3.00
161 Brendan Haywood RC 1.50 4.00
162 Joe Johnson RC 3.00 8.00
163 Vladimir Radmanovic RC 1.25 3.00
164 Gerald Wallace RC 2.00 5.00
165 Steven Hunter RC 1.25 3.00
166 Richard Jefferson RC 2.50 6.00
167 DeSagana Diop RC 1.25 3.00
168 Terence Morris RC 1.25 3.00
169 Jason Richardson RC 2.50 6.00
170 Jeff Trepagnier RC 1.25 3.00
171 Kirk Haston RC 1.25 3.00
172 Eddy Curry RC 2.00 5.00
173 Eddie Griffin RC 1.25 3.00
174 Omar Cook RC 1.25 3.00
175 Pau Gasol RC 4.00 10.00
176 Troy Murphy RC 2.00 5.00
177 Trenton Hassell RC 1.25 3.00
178 Kedrick Brown RC 1.25 3.00
179 Zeljko Rebraca RC 1.25 3.00
180 Tony Parker RC 5.00 12.00
181 Rodney White RC 1.25 3.00
182 Jason Collins RC 1.25 3.00
183 Samuel Dalembert RC 1.50 4.00
184 Zach Randolph RC 3.00 8.00
185 Will Solomon RC 1.25 3.00

2001-02 Fleer Premium Star Rubies

Randomly inserted into packs, this is a parallel to the Fleer Premium set. The cards of the regular players have a stated print run of 100 serial numbered sets while the rookies have a stated print run of 50 serial numbered sets.

*RUBY STARS: 8X TO 20X BASE CARD HI
*RUBY RCs: 2X TO 5X BASE CARD HI
5 Michael Jordan 125.00 250.00
67 Chris Webber 8.00 20.00
77 Kobe Bryant 40.00 100.00

2001-02 Fleer Premium Commanding Respect

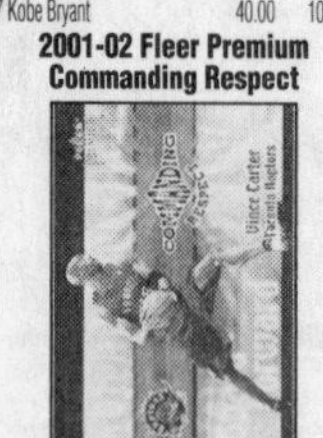

Inserted at stated odds of one in 20, this 25 card set features players whose mere presence on the court brings respect from their opponents.

COMPLETE SET (25) 30.00 60.00
1 Shaquille O'Neal 2.50 6.00
2 Tim Duncan 2.00 5.00
3 Marc Jackson .60 1.50
4 Kevin Garnett 2.00 5.00
5 Kobe Bryant 5.00 12.00
6 Chris Webber 1.00 2.50
7 Michael Jordan 8.00 20.00
8 Dirk Nowitzki 1.50 4.00
9 Ray Allen 1.00 2.50
10 Courtney Alexander .60 1.50
11 David Robinson 1.50 4.00
12 Darius Miles .60 1.50
13 Baron Davis 1.00 2.50
14 Tracy McGrady 1.50 4.00
15 Vince Carter 1.50 4.00
16 Antawn Jamison 1.00 2.50
17 Jerry Stackhouse .75 2.00
18 Allen Iverson 2.00 5.00
19 Jason Kidd 1.50 4.00
20 Antoine Walker .75 2.00
21 Karl Malone 1.25 3.00
22 Grant Hill 1.25 3.00
23 Rasheed Wallace 1.00 2.50
24 Anfernee Hardaway 1.50 4.00
25 Steve Francis 1.00 2.50

2001-02 Fleer Premium Commanding Respect Premium Patches

This is a partial parallel to the Commanding Respect insert set. These cards feature a game-worn patch from the featured players and are printed to a stated print run of 75 serial numbered sets.

AH Anfernee Hardaway 25.00 60.00
AI Allen Iverson 30.00 80.00
AW Antoine Walker 12.00 30.00
BD Baron Davis 15.00 40.00
CW Chris Webber 20.00 50.00
DM Darius Miles 10.00 25.00
GH Grant Hill 20.00 50.00
JK Jason Kidd 25.00 60.00
KM Karl Malone 20.00 50.00
MM Mike Miller 15.00 40.00
RA Ray Allen 15.00 40.00
RW Rasheed Wallace 15.00 40.00
SF Steve Francis 15.00 40.00
TM Tracy McGrady 25.00 60.00
VC Vince Carter 25.00 60.00

2001-02 Fleer Premium Rookie Revolution

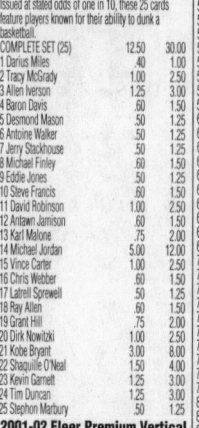

Inserted at stated odds at one in ten, this 10-card set features some of the highest selected draft picks of the 2002 NBA draft. These players were deemed to have the best chance of being long term NBA stars.

COMPLETE SET (10) 8.00 20.00
1 Kwame Brown .75 2.00
2 Eddy Curry 1.25 3.00
3 Tyson Chandler 1.25 3.00
4 Pau Gasol 2.50 6.00
5 Joe Johnson 2.00 5.00
6 Michael Bradley .75 2.00
7 Jason Richardson 1.50 4.00
8 DeSagana Diop .75 2.00
9 Troy Murphy 1.25 3.00
10 Jamaal Tinsley 1.00 2.50

2001-02 Fleer Premium Rookie Revolution Autographs

Issued as a partial parallel to the Rookie Revolution set, these four cards were randomly inserted into packs. Each of these cards had a stated print run of 50 serial numbered sets. Michael Bradley and Kwame Brown did not return their cards in time for inclusion in packs and these cards were issued as exchange cards.

NNO Michael Bradley 4.00 10.00
NNO Joe Johnson 15.00 40.00
NNO Eddy Curry 10.00 25.00
NNO Kwame Brown 6.00 15.00

2001-02 Fleer Premium Solid Performers

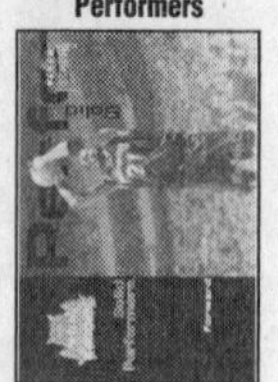

Inserted one in every 20 packs, this 30 card set features some of the NBA's most consistent performers.

COMPLETE SET (30) 30.00 80.00
1 Tracy McGrady 1.50 4.00
2 John Stockton 1.25 3.00
3 Dirk Nowitzki 1.50 4.00
4 Antawn Jamison 1.00 2.50
5 Scottie Pippen 1.50 4.00
6 Morris Peterson .60 1.50
7 Ray Allen 1.00 2.50
8 Antoine Walker .75 2.00
9 Anfernee Hardaway 1.50 4.00
10 Michael Jordan 8.00 20.00
11 Jerry Stackhouse .75 2.00
12 Karl Malone 1.25 3.00
13 Jason Kidd 1.50 4.00
14 Chris Webber 1.00 2.50
15 Vince Carter 1.50 4.00
16 Allen Iverson 2.00 5.00
17 Courtney Alexander .60 1.50
18 Darius Miles .60 1.50
19 Steve Francis 1.00 2.50
20 Grant Hill 1.25 3.00
21 Rasheed Wallace 1.00 2.50
22 Kenyon Martin 1.00 2.50
23 Shawn Marion 1.00 2.50
24 Elton Brand 1.00 2.50
25 Jason Terry 1.00 2.50
26 Kobe Bryant 5.00 12.00
27 Tim Duncan 2.00 5.00
28 Kevin Garnett 2.00 5.00
29 Reggie Miller 1.00 2.50
30 Shaquille O'Neal 2.50 6.00

2001-02 Fleer Premium Solid Performers Premium Jerseys

Issued at stated odds of one in 24, this 21 card set is a partial parallel to the Solid Performers insert set. These cards feature a game worn jersey swatch on them in addition to the player's photo and information.

AH Anfernee Hardaway 5.00 12.00
AI Allen Iverson 6.00 15.00
AW Antoine Walker 2.50 6.00
CW Chris Webber 3.00 8.00
DM Darius Miles 2.00 5.00
EB Elton Brand 3.00 8.00
GH Grant Hill 4.00 10.00
JK Jason Kidd 5.00 12.00
JS John Stockton 4.00 10.00
JS Jerry Stackhouse 2.50 6.00
JT Jason Terry 3.00 8.00
KM Karl Malone 4.00 10.00
MA Kenyon Martin 3.00 8.00
MM Mike Miller 3.00 8.00
MP Morris Peterson 2.00 5.00
RA Ray Allen 3.00 8.00
RW Rasheed Wallace 3.00 8.00
SF Steve Francis 3.00 8.00
SM Shawn Marion 3.00 8.00
TM Tracy McGrady 5.00 12.00
VC Vince Carter 5.00 12.00

2001-02 Fleer Premium Vertical Heights

Issued at stated odds of one in 10, these 25 cards feature players known for their ability to dunk a basketball.

COMPLETE SET (25) 12.50 30.00
1 Darius Miles .40 1.00
2 Tracy McGrady 1.00 2.50
3 Allen Iverson 1.25 3.00
4 Baron Davis .60 1.50
5 Desmond Mason .50 1.25
6 Antoine Walker .50 1.25
7 Jerry Stackhouse .50 1.25
8 Michael Finley .60 1.50
9 Eddie Jones .50 1.25
10 Steve Francis .60 1.50
11 David Robinson 1.00 2.50
12 Antawn Jamison .60 1.50
13 Karl Malone .75 2.00
14 Michael Jordan 5.00 12.00
15 Vince Carter 1.00 2.50
16 Chris Webber .60 1.50
17 Latrell Sprewell .50 1.25
18 Ray Allen .60 1.50
19 Grant Hill .75 2.00
20 Dirk Nowitzki 1.00 2.50
21 Kobe Bryant 3.00 8.00
22 Shaquille O'Neal 1.50 4.00
23 Kevin Garnett 1.25 3.00
24 Tim Duncan 1.25 3.00
25 Stephon Marbury .50 1.25

2001-02 Fleer Premium Vertical Heights Shoes

Randomly inserted in packs, these four cards are a partial parallel for the Vertical Heights insert set. These cards contain a piece of a game-worn shoe and have a stated print run of 100 serial numbered sets.

NNO Antoine Walker 8.00 20.00
NNO Vince Carter 15.00 40.00
NNO Jerry Stackhouse 8.00 20.00
NNO Lamar Odom 10.00 25.00

2002-03 Fleer Premium

Released in early October 2002, Fleer Premium consists of a 140-card set divided up into 15 All NBA Team cards, numbers 1-15, which have red white and blue trim across the bottom, 11 All Rookie Team cards, numbers 16-26, which have white backgrounds, 84 Veteran player cards, numbers 27-110, which have gold foil backgrounds, and 30 Rookies, numbers 111-140, which say "Premium Prospects" along the left side of the card and are sequentially numbered to 1500. All cards feature borders which are blue along the outside, then white inside, and have gold foil highlights. Premium was packaged in five card packs with a suggested retail price of $2.99 and boxes contained 24 packs.

COMP.SET w/o SP's (110) 15.00 40.00
1 Tracy McGrady .50 1.25
2 Tim Duncan .60 1.50
3 Shaquille O'Neal .75 2.00
4 Jason Kidd .50 1.25
5 Kobe Bryant 1.50 4.00
6 Kevin Garnett .60 1.50
7 Chris Webber .30 .75
8 Dirk Nowitzki .50 1.25
9 Gary Payton .30 .75
10 Allen Iverson .50 1.25
11 Ben Wallace .30 .75
12 Jermaine O'Neal .30 .75
13 Dikembe Mutombo .30 .75
14 Paul Pierce .40 1.00
15 Steve Nash .40 1.00
16 Pau Gasol .40 1.00
17 Jason Richardson .30 .75
18 Tony Parker .40 1.00
19 Andrei Kirilenko .30 .75
20 Shane Battier .30 .75
21 Jamaal Tinsley .20 .50
22 Richard Jefferson .30 .75
23 Joe Johnson .30 .75
24 Eddie Griffin .20 .50
25 Zeljko Rebraca .20 .50
26 Vladimir Radmanovic .20 .50
27 Damon Stoudamire .25 .60
28 Eddie Jones .25 .60
29 Tyson Chandler .25 .60
30 Karl Malone .40 1.00
31 David Wesley .20 .50
32 Steve Francis .30 .75
33 Hakeem Olajuwon .40 1.00
34 Baron Davis .30 .75
35 Antonio McDyess .25 .60
36 Mike Bibby .30 .75
37 Bonzi Wells .20 .50
38 Ray Allen .30 .75
39 Doug Christie .20 .50
40 Richard Hamilton .25 .60
41 Grant Hill .40 1.00
42 Elton Brand .30 .75
43 Gilbert Arenas .30 .75
44 Vlade Divac .25 .60
45 Sam Cassell .25 .60
46 Jalen Rose .25 .60
47 Peja Stojakovic .30 .75
48 Glenn Robinson .25 .60
49 Ricky Davis .25 .60
50 Antonio Daniels .20 .50
51 Tim Thomas .20 .50
52 Andre Miller .25 .60
53 Stephon Marbury .25 .60
54 Robert Horry .25 .60
55 Tony Delk .20 .50
56 David Robinson .50 1.25
57 Radoslav Nesterovic .20 .50
58 Lamond Murray .20 .50
59 Brent Barry .20 .50
60 Wally Szczerbiak .25 .60
61 Lee Nailon .20 .50
62 Rashard Lewis .30 .75
63 Kenyon Martin .30 .75
64 Michael Finley .30 .75
65 John Stockton .40 1.00
66 Allan Houston .25 .60
67 Terrell Brandon .20 .50
68 Donyell Marshall .20 .50
69 Marcus Camby .25 .60
70 Cuttino Mobley .25 .60
71 Shawn Marion .30 .75
72 Jason Williams .25 .60
73 Rodney Rogers .20 .50
74 Scottie Pippen .50 1.25
75 Brian Grant .20 .50
76 Clifford Robinson .20 .50
77 Antoine Walker .25 .60
78 Michael Dickerson .20 .50
79 Latrell Sprewell .25 .60
80 Ron Artest .30 .75
81 Shareef Abdur-Rahim .25 .60
82 Michael Jordan 2.50 6.00
83 Mike Miller .30 .75
84 Corey Maggette .25 .60
85 Antawn Jamison .30 .75
86 Rasheed Wallace .30 .75
87 Alonzo Mourning .40 1.00
88 Eddy Curry .25 .60
89 Derrick Coleman .25 .60
90 Joe Smith .25 .60
91 Darius Miles .20 .50
92 Nick Van Exel .25 .60
93 Derek Fisher .25 .60
94 Nazr Mohammed .20 .50
95 Morris Peterson .20 .50
96 Jamal Mashburn .25 .60
97 Jerry Stackhouse .25 .60
98 Kwame Brown .20 .50
99 Darrell Armstrong .20 .50
100 Reggie Miller .30 .75
101 Desmond Mason .25 .60
102 Antonio Davis .20 .50
103 Elden Campbell .20 .50
104 Voshon Lenard .20 .50
105 Eric Snow .20 .50
106 Lamar Odom .30 .75
107 Toni Kukoc .25 .60
108 Vince Carter .50 1.25
109 Keith Van Horn .25 .60
110 Juwan Howard .25 .60
111 Jay Williams RC 2.00 5.00
112 Yao Ming RC 5.00 12.00
113 Mike Dunleavy RC 2.00 5.00
114 Drew Gooden RC 2.50 6.00
115 Nikoloz Tskitishvili RC 1.50 4.00
116 DaJuan Wagner RC 1.50 4.00
117 Nene Hilario RC 2.00 5.00
118 Chris Wilcox RC 1.50 4.00
119 Amare Stoudemire RC 4.00 10.00
120 Caron Butler RC 2.50 6.00
121 Melvin Ely RC 1.50 4.00
122 Marcus Haislip RC 1.50 4.00
123 Jared Jeffries RC 1.50 4.00
124 Fred Jones RC 1.50 4.00
125 Bostjan Nachbar RC 1.50 4.00
126 Jiri Welsch RC 1.50 4.00
127 Juan Dixon RC 2.00 5.00
128 Curtis Borchardt RC 1.50 4.00
129 Ryan Humphrey RC 1.50 4.00
130 Kareem Rush RC 1.50 4.00
131 Qyntel Woods RC 1.50 4.00
132 Casey Jacobsen RC 1.50 4.00
133 Tayshaun Prince RC 2.00 5.00
134 Carlos Boozer RC 3.00 8.00
135 Frank Williams RC 1.50 4.00
136 John Salmons RC 2.00 5.00
137 Chris Jefferies RC 1.50 4.00
138 Dan Dickau RC 1.50 4.00
139 Manu Ginobili RC 4.00 10.00
140 Roger Mason RC 1.50 4.00

2002-03 Fleer Premium Emerald

Randomly inserted in packs, this 140-card set parallels the base Fleer Premium set enhanced with green foil highlights. Each card is sequentially numbered to 300.

*STARS: 2.5X TO 6X BASE CARD HI
*RCs: 1X TO 2.5X BASE CARD HI

2002-03 Fleer Premium Star Rubies

Randomly inserted in packs, this 140-card set parallels the base Fleer Premium set enhanced with red foil highlights. Each card is sequentially numbered to 100.

*STARS: 4X TO 10X BASE CARD HI
*RCs: 1.5X TO 4X BASE CARD HI
82 Michael Jordan 100.00 200.00

2002-03 Fleer Premium A Cut Above

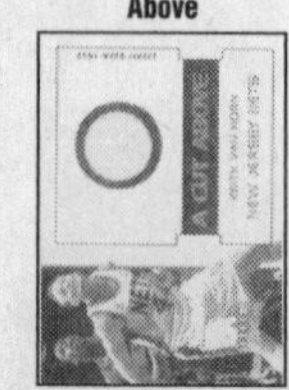

Randomly inserted in packs at the rate of one in 120, this ten card set features a horizontal design with full color player photos on the left and a white background with a circular swatch of game-used memorabilia on the right. Fleer confirmed Steve Francis and DerMarr Johnson as short prints and only 250 of each were produced. A Ruby version sequentially numbered to 100 was also included randomly in packs.

*RUBY: .75X TO 2X A CUT ABOVE HI
1 Keith Van Horn 2.50 6.00
2 Vince Carter 5.00 12.00
3 Steve Francis/250 3.00 8.00
4 Grant Hill 4.00 10.00
5 DerMarr Johnson/250 2.00 5.00
6 Jamal Mashburn 2.50 6.00
7 Lamar Odom 3.00 8.00
8 Quentin Richardson 2.50 6.00
9 Richard Hamilton 2.50 6.00
10 Jason Terry 2.50 6.00

2002-03 Fleer Premium Court Collection

Randomly inserted in packs at the rate of one in 175, this 10-card set features a horizontal design with a basketball court background, black and white player portrait photos on the left and a circular swatch of game used memorabilia on the right. Fleer confirmed Keyon Dooling as a short-print with only 250 cards made, and Wally Szczerbiak as a short-print with 125 cards made. A Ruby version was also inserted in packs and is sequentially numbered to 100.

*RUBY: .75X TO 2X COURT COLL.HI
1 Shareef Abdur-Rahim 2.50 6.00
2 Keyon Dooling/250 2.00 5.00
3 Rashard Lewis 3.00 8.00
4 Shawn Marion 3.00 8.00
5 Tracy McGrady 5.00 12.00
6 Alonzo Mourning 4.00 10.00
7 John Stockton 4.00 10.00
8 Wally Szczerbiak/125 2.50 6.00
9 Desmond Mason 2.50 6.00
10 Corey Maggette 2.50 6.00

2002-03 Fleer Premium Gear

Randomly seeded at one in 288, this nine card set is horizontally designed with full color player action photos on the left and a white right side with a circular swatch of game used memorabilia. The border between the color photo and the white side, as well as around the swatch of memorabilia, are shaped to look like a gear. Fleer confirmed Karl Malone and Morris Peterson as short-prints with 125 and 50 copies available respectively. A Ruby version was issued as well where cards are sequentially numbered to 100.

*RUBY: .75X TO 2X GEAR HI
1 Anfernee Hardaway 5.00 12.00
2 Vince Carter 5.00 12.00
3 Antawn Jamison 3.00 8.00
4 Karl Malone/125 4.00 10.00
5 Kenyon Martin 3.00 8.00
6 Andre Miller 2.50 6.00
7 Mike Miller 3.00 8.00
8 Dikembe Mutombo 3.00 8.00
9 Morris Peterson/50 2.00 5.00

2002-03 Fleer Premium Power

Randomly inserted in packs, this 10-card set feature full color player action photos set against a colored background to match the player's team color. The top 1/3 of the card is in white and all cards contain bronze foil highlights. Each card is sequentially numbered to 1000. A Ruby version was issued as well where the cards are sequentially numbered to 100.

1 Tim Duncan 2.50 6.00
2 Kobe Bryant 6.00 15.00
3 Ben Wallace 1.25 3.00
4 Michael Jordan 10.00 25.00
5 Shaquille O'Neal 3.00 8.00
6 Vince Carter 2.00 5.00
7 Kevin Garnett 2.50 6.00
8 Chris Webber 1.25 3.00
9 Karl Malone 1.50 4.00
10 Elton Brand 1.25 3.00

2002-03 Fleer Premium Power Ruby

Randomly inserted in packs, this 10-card set parallels the base Power insert set enhanced with red foil highlights. Each card is sequentially numbered to 100.

*RUBY: 1X TO 2.5X POWER HI
4 Michael Jordan 50.00 120.00

2002-03 Fleer Premium Prim Time

Randomly seeded in packs, this 15-card set feature full color player action photos set against a background that is colored to match the player's te colors on the top half and white on the bottom. Ca contain silver foil highlights and are sequentially numbered to 1500. A Ruby version was also issued packs and is sequentially numbered to 100.

COMPLETE SET (15) 10.00 25
*RUBY: 1.25X TO 3X PRIME TIME HI
1 Dirk Nowitzki 1.50 4
2 Vince Carter 1.50 4
3 Allen Iverson 1.50 4
4 Ray Allen 1.00 2
5 Darius Miles .60 1
6 Chris Webber 1.00 2
7 Elton Brand 1.00 2
8 Jason Kidd 1.50 4
9 Paul Pierce 1.25 3
10 Baron Davis 1.00 2
11 Stephon Marbury .75 2
12 Jerry Stackhouse .75 2
13 David Robinson 1.50 4
14 Gary Payton 1.00 2
15 Antoine Walker .75 2

2002-03 Fleer Premium Prim Time Game Used

Randomly inserted in packs at the rate of one in 75 this 14-card set parallels the design of the base Pri Time insert enhanced with a swatch of game used memorabilia. A Ruby version was inserted in packs is sequentially numbered to 100.

*RUBY: .75X TO 2X PT GAME USED HI
1 Vince Carter 5.00 12
2 Allen Iverson 5.00 12
3 Ray Allen 3.00 8
4 Darius Miles 2.00 5
5 Chris Webber 3.00 8
6 Elton Brand 3.00 8
7 Jason Kidd 5.00 12
8 Paul Pierce 4.00 10
9 Baron Davis 3.00 8
10 Stephon Marbury 2.50 6
11 Jerry Stackhouse 2.50 6
12 David Robinson 5.00 12
13 Gary Payton 3.00 8
14 Antoine Walker 2.50 6

2002-03 Fleer Premium Skylin

Randomly inserted in packs, this 20-card set has a horizontal card design with white borders on the top and the bottom and a strip in the middle showing th skyline of the featured player's team city. Full color player action shots are set in front on the right side the card. Each card is sequentially numbered to 250 A Ruby version was inserted into packs as well and cards are sequentially numbered to 100.

1 Michael Jordan 10.00 25
2 Shaquille O'Neal 3.00 8
3 Vince Carter 2.00 5
4 Kevin Garnett 2.50 6
5 Allen Iverson 2.00 5
6 Dirk Nowitzki 2.00 5
7 Darius Miles .75 2
8 Tracy McGrady 2.00 5
9 Chris Webber 1.25 3
10 Steve Francis 1.25 3
11 Jason Kidd 2.00 5
12 Stephon Marbury 1.00 2
13 Paul Pierce 1.50 4
14 Ray Allen 1.25 3
15 Kobe Bryant 6.00 15
16 Jay Williams 1.50 4
17 DaJuan Wagner 1.25 3
18 Yao Ming 4.00 10
19 Jared Jeffries 1.25 3
20 Amare Stoudemire 3.00 8

2002-03 Fleer Premium Skylin Ruby

Randomly inserted in packs, this 10-card set paralle the base Skylines insert set enhanced with red foil highlights. Each card is sequentially numbered to 1

*RUBY: 1X TO 2.5X SKYLINES HI
1 Michael Jordan 50.00 120

02-03 Fleer Premium Triple Threats

mly seeded, this 10-card set features full-color
action photos set against an one-color portrait
in the background. The words "3X Threats"
rs on the card front in silver foil, and each card is
ntially numbered to 250. A Ruby version was
ssued where cards are sequentially numbered to

n Iverson 4.00 10.00
y McGrady 4.00 10.00
e Francis 2.50 6.00
Allen 2.50 6.00
Duncan 5.00 12.00
e Bryant 12.00 30.00
hael Jordan 20.00 50.00
quille O'Neal 6.00 15.00
e Carter 4.00 10.00
vin Garnett 5.00 12.00

02-03 Fleer Premium Triple Threats Ruby

mly inserted in packs, this 10-card set parallels
se Triple Threats insert set enhanced with red foil
ghts. Each card is sequentially numbered to 100.
Y: .5X TO 1.25X TRIPLE THREATS HI
hael Jordan 50.00 120.00

2011-12 Fleer Retro

PLETE SET (83) 25.00 60.00
hael Jordan 3.00 8.00
ron James 2.00 5.00
Frazier .50 1.25
y Johnson .60 1.50
eem Olajuwon .60 1.50
dace Parker .75 2.00
istian Laettner .60 1.50
Greer .50 1.25
y West .60 1.50
nnis Rodman 1.00 2.50
fernee Hardaway 1.25 3.00
il Goodrich .50 1.25
orge Gervin .50 1.25
gin Baylor .50 1.25
l Walton .50 1.25
rry Bird 1.50 4.00
k Barry .50 1.25
mes Worthy .60 1.50
l Laimbeer .50 1.25
m Hardaway .50 1.25
vid Robinson .75 2.00
drian Dantley .50 1.25
onzo Mourning .60 1.50
agic Johnson 1.25 3.00
lius Erving 1.00 2.50
ark Jackson .50 1.25
l Cartwright .50 1.25
l Russell .75 2.00
J. Armstrong .50 1.25
b McAdoo .50 1.25
azzie Russell .50 1.25
ad Daugherty .50 1.25
yde Drexler .60 1.50
nny Manning .50 1.25
hn Havlicek .60 1.50
ant Hill .75 2.00
n Jackson .50 1.25
vid Thompson .50 1.25
dy Tomjanovich .50 1.25
ggie Theus .50 1.25
eddie Lewis .50 1.25
enny Smith .50 1.25
l Sharman .50 1.25
nnie Shelton .50 1.25
ni Kukoc .50 1.25
m Cassell .50 1.25
en Rice .50 1.25
rrell Griffith .50 1.25
eve Nash .50 1.25
ris Paul .75 2.00
istan Thompson RS 1.50 4.00
nas Valanciunas RS 1.25 3.00
smack Biyombo RS 1.00 2.50
mmer Fredette RS 2.00 5.00
ay Thompson RS 2.50 6.00
ec Burks RS 1.00 2.50
arkieff Morris RS 1.25 3.00
arcus Morris RS 1.00 2.50
whi Leonard RS 2.00 5.00
kola Vucevic RS .60 1.50
ris Singleton RS .60 1.50
bias Harris RS .75 2.00
cotty Hopson RS .60 1.50
olan Smith RS 1.00 2.50
ggie Jackson RS .75 2.00
arShon Brooks RS 2.00 5.00
Juan Johnson RS .75 2.00
orris Cole RS 1.50 4.00
ory Joseph RS .60 1.50
stin Harper RS .75 2.00
elvin Mack RS .75 2.00
ler Honeycutt RS .60 1.50
rdan Williams RS .75 2.00
handler Parsons RS 1.00 2.50
n Leuer RS .60 1.50
alcolm Lee RS .60 1.50
harles Jenkins RS .60 1.50
avis Leslie RS .60 1.50
eith Benson RS .60 1.50
osh Selby RS 1.00 2.50
Twaun Moore RS 1.00 2.50
emetri McCamey RS .60 1.50
urrell Summers RS .75 2.00

2011-12 Fleer Retro 1961-62

ED ODDS 1:100 PACKS
BACKGROUND VARIATIONS SAME VALUE
Bill Russell 10.00 25.00
David Robinson 10.00 25.00
Hakeem Olajuwon 8.00 20.00
ulius Erving 12.00 30.00
Magic Johnson 15.00 40.00
Jerry West 8.00 20.00
Larry Bird 20.00 50.00
eBron James 25.00 60.00
MJ1 Michael Jordan 60.00 150.00
WO1 James Worthy 8.00 20.00

2011-12 Fleer Retro 1961-62 Autographs

RANDOM INSERTS IN PACKS
ALL BACKGROUND VARIATIONS SAME VALUE
BR1 Bill Russell
DR1 David Robinson
HO1 Hakeem Olajuwon
JE1 Julius Erving
JO1 Magic Johnson 250.00 500.00
LB1 Larry Bird
LJ1 LeBron James 200.00 400.00
MJ1 Michael Jordan 750.00 1500.00
WO1 James Worthy

2011-12 Fleer Retro 1986-87

COMPLETE SET (15) 15.00 40.00
STATED ODDS 1:20 PACKS
AD Adrian Dantley 2.00 5.00
AM Alonzo Mourning 5.00 12.00
BW Bill Walton 2.00 5.00
CD Clyde Drexler 2.50 6.00
CP Chris Paul 3.00 8.00
DM Danny Manning 2.00 5.00
DR Dennis Rodman 4.00 10.00
EB Elgin Baylor 2.00 5.00
GG George Gervin 2.00 5.00
GH Grant Hill 2.50 6.00
GO Gail Goodrich 2.00 5.00
JH John Havlicek 2.50 6.00
LJ Larry Johnson 2.50 6.00
SN Steve Nash 2.00 5.00
WF Walt Frazier 2.00 5.00

2011-12 Fleer Retro 1986-87 Autographs

RANDOM INSERTS IN PACKS
AD Adrian Dantley 8.00 20.00
AM Alonzo Mourning
BW Bill Walton 25.00 60.00
CD Clyde Drexler 50.00 125.00
CP Chris Paul 75.00 150.00
DR Dennis Rodman 75.00 150.00
GG George Gervin
GH Grant Hill EXCH 150.00 300.00
GO Gail Goodrich
JH John Havlicek 30.00 80.00
LJ Larry Johnson 40.00 100.00

2011-12 Fleer Retro 1987-88

COMPLETE SET (20) 12.00 30.00
STATED ODDS 1:10 PACKS
AH Anfernee Hardaway 3.00 8.00
BA B.J. Armstrong 1.25 3.00
BL Bill Laimbeer 1.25 3.00
BM Bob McAdoo 1.25 3.00
BS Bill Sharman 1.25 3.00
CL Christian Laettner 1.50 4.00
CR Cazzie Russell 1.25 3.00
CW Chet Walker 1.25 3.00
DG Darrell Griffith 1.25 3.00
DT David Thompson 1.25 3.00
HG Hal Greer 1.25 3.00
JJ Jim Jackson 1.25 3.00
KS Kenny Smith 1.25 3.00
MJ Mark Jackson 1.25 3.00
PA Candace Parker 1.50 4.00
RB Rick Barry 1.25 3.00
RT Reggie Theus 1.25 3.00
SC Sam Cassell 1.25 3.00
TH Tim Hardaway 1.25 3.00
TO Rudy Tomjanovich 1.25 3.00

2011-12 Fleer Retro 1987-88 Autographs

RANDOM INSERTS IN PACKS
AH Anfernee Hardaway 125.00 225.00
BA B.J. Armstrong 12.00 30.00
BL Bill Laimbeer 12.00 30.00
BM Bob McAdoo 20.00 50.00
CL Christian Laettner 15.00 40.00
CR Cazzie Russell 10.00 25.00
CW Chet Walker 10.00 25.00
DT David Thompson 12.00 30.00
HG Hal Greer
JJ Jim Jackson 12.00 30.00
MJ Mark Jackson 10.00 25.00
PA Candace Parker 15.00 40.00
RT Reggie Theus 10.00 25.00
SC Sam Cassell
TH Tim Hardaway 15.00 40.00
TO Rudy Tomjanovich 10.00 25.00

2011-12 Fleer Retro 1988-89

COMPLETE SET (25) 15.00 40.00
STATED ODDS 1:5 PACKS
AB Alec Burks 1.25 3.00
BB Bismack Biyombo 1.25 3.00
BD Brad Daugherty 1.00 2.50
CJ Cory Joseph .75 2.00
CS Chris Singleton .75 2.00
FL Freddie Lewis 1.00 2.50
HA Tobias Harris 1.00 2.50
JF Jimmer Fredette 2.50 6.00
JH Justin Harper 1.00 2.50
JJ JaJuan Johnson 1.00 2.50
JV Jonas Valanciunas 1.50 4.00
KL Kawhi Leonard 2.50 6.00
KT Klay Thompson 3.00 8.00
LS Lonnie Shelton 1.00 2.50
MM Marcus Morris 1.25 3.00
MO Markieff Morris 1.50 4.00
MP MarShon Brooks 2.50 6.00
MR Micheal Ray Richardson 1.00 2.50
NS Nolan Smith 1.25 3.00
NV Nikola Vucevic .75 2.00
RH Robert Horry 1.25 3.00
RJ Reggie Jackson 1.00 2.50
TH Tyler Honeycutt .75 2.00
TK Toni Kukoc 1.00 2.50
TT Tristan Thompson 2.00 5.00

2011-12 Fleer Retro 1988-89 Autographs

RANDOM INSERTS IN PACKS
AB Alec Burks 12.00 30.00
BB Bismack Biyombo 12.00 30.00
CJ Cory Joseph 8.00 20.00
CS Chris Singleton 10.00 25.00
FL Freddie Lewis 6.00 15.00
HA Tobias Harris 12.00 30.00
JF Jimmer Fredette 30.00 80.00
JH Justin Harper
JJ JaJuan Johnson 10.00 25.00
JV Jonas Valanciunas 30.00 80.00
KL Kawhi Leonard 75.00 200.00
KT Klay Thompson 30.00 80.00
LS Lonnie Shelton 6.00 15.00
NS Nolan Smith 15.00 40.00
RH Robert Horry 15.00 40.00
RJ Reggie Jackson 10.00 25.00
TH Tyler Honeycutt 8.00 20.00
TT Tristan Thompson 30.00 80.00

2011-12 Fleer Retro A Cut Above

STATED ODDS 1:144 PACKS
1 Jimmer Fredette 12.00 30.00
2 Grant Hill 15.00 40.00
3 George Gervin 8.00 20.00
4 Alonzo Mourning 12.00 30.00
5 Hakeem Olajuwon 10.00 25.00
6 Clyde Drexler 12.00 30.00
7 Larry Bird 15.00 40.00
8 Julius Erving 15.00 40.00
9 Elgin Baylor 10.00 25.00
10 Magic Johnson 20.00 50.00
11 David Robinson 12.00 30.00
12 Michael Jordan 175.00 350.00
13 James Worthy 10.00 25.00
14 Tim Hardaway 8.00 20.00
15 John Havlicek 10.00 25.00
16 Bill Russell 12.00 30.00
17 Steve Nash 12.00 30.00
18 Anfernee Hardaway 20.00 50.00
19 Dennis Rodman 15.00 40.00
20 LeBron James 60.00 150.00
21 Walt Frazier 8.00 20.00
22 Bill Walton 8.00 20.00
23 Larry Johnson 10.00 25.00
24 Chris Paul 12.00 30.00
25 Jerry West 10.00 25.00

2011-12 Fleer Retro Autographics 1996-97

RANDOM INSERTS IN PACKS
AD Adrian Dantley 5.00 12.00
AJ Avery Johnson 6.00 15.00
AM Alonzo Mourning 75.00 150.00
BR Bill Russell 100.00 200.00
CC Cynthia Cooper 8.00 20.00
CD Clyde Drexler 30.00 80.00
CJ Cory Joseph 3.00 8.00
CR Cazzie Russell 4.00 10.00
CS Chris Singleton 3.00 8.00
CW Chet Walker 4.00 10.00
DA Dana Altman 3.00 8.00
DR David Robinson
DT David Thompson 8.00 20.00
GA Greg Anthony 8.00 20.00
GH Grant Hill EXCH
HG Hal Greer 5.00 12.00
HO Hakeem Olajuwon
JA LeBron James 300.00 600.00
JC Jim Calhoun 15.00 40.00
JD Jamie Dixon
JE Julius Erving 75.00 150.00
JF Jimmer Fredette 15.00 40.00
JH John Havlicek 25.00 60.00
JO Michael Jordan 600.00 1000.00
JS Jerry Sloan 8.00 20.00
JW James Worthy 25.00 60.00
LB Larry Bird 100.00 175.00
LJ Larry Johnson 20.00 50.00
LS Lonnie Shelton 3.00 8.00
MB Mike Brey 3.00 8.00
MF Mark Few 4.00 10.00
MJ Magic Johnson 50.00 125.00
PA Chris Paul 25.00 60.00
RH Robert Horry 8.00 20.00
RJ Reggie Jackson 4.00 10.00
RO Dennis Rodman 40.00 100.00
RT Reggie Theus 4.00 10.00
SA Steve Alford 5.00 12.00
SC Sam Cassell 4.00 10.00
TH Tim Hardaway 12.00 30.00
TM Thad Matta 12.00 30.00
TO Rudy Tomjanovich 4.00 10.00
TS Tubby Smith
WE Jerry West
WF Walt Frazier 10.00 25.00

2011-12 Fleer Retro Autographics 1997-98

RANDOM INSERTS IN PACKS
AM Alonzo Mourning 50.00 125.00
BB Bismack Biyombo 5.00 12.00
BD Billy Donovan
BM Bob McAdoo 12.00 30.00
BR Bo Ryan 8.00 20.00
BW Bruce Weber 4.00 10.00
CC Cynthia Cooper 8.00 20.00
CP Chris Paul 30.00 80.00
CR Cazzie Russell 4.00 10.00
DM Demetri McCamey 3.00 8.00
DR David Robinson 40.00 100.00
DS Durrell Summers 4.00 10.00
DT David Thompson 6.00 15.00
FL Freddie Lewis 3.00 8.00
HG Hal Greer 5.00 12.00
JB Jim Boeheim 15.00 40.00
JC Jeff Capel III 4.00 10.00
JE Julius Erving 50.00 125.00
JF Jimmer Fredette 15.00 40.00
JH Justin Harper 4.00 10.00
JJ JaJuan Johnson 4.00 10.00
JO Michael Jordan
JS Jack Sikma 6.00 15.00
JW James Worthy 25.00 60.00
LA Larry Johnson 25.00 60.00
LB Larry Bird 100.00 175.00
LJ LeBron James 300.00 600.00
LS Lonnie Shelton 3.00 8.00
MH Matt Howard 4.00 10.00
MJ Magic Johnson
MR Micheal Ray Richardson 3.00 8.00
NS Nolan Smith 5.00 12.00
RH Robert Horry 8.00 20.00
RO Dennis Rodman 50.00 125.00
RT Reggie Theus 4.00 10.00
RU Bill Russell 75.00 150.00
SC Sam Cassell 4.00 10.00
SF Steve Fisher 6.00 15.00
SL Jerry Sloan 10.00 25.00
TH Tobias Harris 4.00 10.00
TK Toni Kukoc 25.00 60.00
TO Rudy Tomjanovich 4.00 10.00
TP Terry Porter 6.00 15.00
TT Tristan Thompson 8.00 20.00
WF Walt Frazier 10.00 25.00

2011-12 Fleer Retro Autographics 1998-99

RANDOM INSERTS IN PACKS
AD Adrian Dantley 6.00 15.00
AH Anfernee Hardaway 75.00 150.00
AJ Avery Johnson 4.00 10.00
AM Alonzo Mourning 40.00 100.00
BB Bismack Biyombo 4.00 10.00
BH Bob Huggins 8.00 20.00
BM Bob McAdoo 12.00 30.00
BR Bill Russell
CC Cynthia Cooper 6.00 15.00
CP Chris Paul 30.00 80.00
CR Cazzie Russell 4.00 10.00
CW Chet Walker 3.00 8.00
DR David Robinson 40.00 100.00
DT David Thompson 8.00 20.00
GH Grant Hill EXCH 100.00 200.00
GW Gary Williams 10.00 25.00
HG Hal Greer 5.00 12.00
HO Ben Howland 2.50 6.00
JB John Beilein 4.00 10.00
JE Julius Erving EXCH 40.00 100.00
JF Jimmer Fredette 15.00 40.00
JH John Havlicek 25.00 60.00
JJ JaJuan Johnson 3.00 8.00
JO Magic Johnson 50.00 125.00
JS Jerry Sloan 6.00 15.00
JW James Worthy 25.00 60.00
LA Larry Johnson 15.00 40.00
LB Larry Bird
LJ LeBron James 300.00 600.00
LS Lonnie Shelton 2.50 6.00
MB MarShon Brooks 8.00 20.00
MH Matt Howard 3.00 8.00
MJ Michael Jordan 400.00 700.00
MM Markieff Morris 6.00 15.00
MP Matt Painter 5.00 12.00
OL Hakeem Olajuwon 25.00 60.00
PA Candace Parker 15.00 40.00
RH Robert Horry 8.00 20.00
RT Reggie Theus 3.00 8.00
SM Sean Miller 4.00 10.00
ST John Starks 20.00 50.00
TH Tyler Honeycutt 2.50 6.00
TK Toni Kukoc 12.00 30.00
TO Rudy Tomjanovich 4.00 10.00
WE Jerry West 30.00 80.00
WF Walt Frazier 10.00 25.00

2011-12 Fleer Retro Autographics 1999-00

RANDOM INSERTS IN PACKS
AD Adrian Dantley 5.00 12.00
AM Alonzo Mourning 30.00 80.00
BB Bismack Biyombo 4.00 10.00
BC Bobby Cremins 4.00 10.00
BM Bob McAdoo
BR Bill Russell 50.00 125.00
BS Bill Self 12.00 30.00
CC Cynthia Cooper 6.00 15.00
CD Clyde Drexler 25.00 60.00
CP Chris Paul 30.00 80.00
CR Cazzie Russell 3.00 8.00
CS Chris Singleton 2.50 6.00
CW Chet Walker 3.00 8.00
DM Demetri McCamey 2.50 6.00
DR David Robinson
DT David Thompson 6.00 15.00
FL Freddie Lewis 3.00 8.00
GG George Gervin 10.00 25.00
GH Grant Hill EXCH 100.00 200.00
HA John Havlicek
HD Homer Drew 4.00 10.00
HG Hal Greer 6.00 15.00
HO Hakeem Olajuwon 25.00 60.00
JE Julius Erving EXCH 40.00 100.00
JF Jimmer Fredette 15.00 40.00
JH Justin Harper 3.00 8.00
JO Magic Johnson
JS Jerry Sloan 6.00 15.00
JW Jay Wright 3.00 8.00
KB Keith Benson 2.50 6.00
LA Larry Johnson 30.00 80.00
LB Larry Bird 100.00 175.00
LJ LeBron James 300.00 600.00
LS Lonnie Shelton 2.50 6.00
MJ Michael Jordan
MM Mike Montgomery 4.00 10.00
RH Robert Horry 6.00 15.00
RM Rick Majerus 3.00 8.00
RT Rudy Tomjanovich 4.00 10.00
SG Seth Greenberg 4.00 10.00
SH Scotty Hopson 2.50 6.00
TH Tobias Harris 3.00 8.00
TI Tim Hardaway 15.00 40.00
TP Terry Porter 6.00 15.00
WF Walt Frazier 10.00 25.00
WO James Worthy 25.00 60.00

2011-12 Fleer Retro Autographs

RANDOM INSERTS IN PACKS
1 Michael Jordan
2 LeBron James 125.00 250.00
3 Walt Frazier 6.00 15.00
4 Larry Johnson 12.00 30.00
5 Hakeem Olajuwon 20.00 50.00
6 Candace Parker
8 Hal Greer 8.00 20.00
9 Jerry West
10 Dennis Rodman 30.00 80.00
11 Anfernee Hardaway 50.00 125.00
12 Gail Goodrich 20.00 50.00
13 George Gervin 10.00 25.00
14 Elgin Baylor
15 Bill Walton
16 Larry Bird 50.00 125.00
17 Rick Barry
18 James Worthy 15.00 40.00
19 Bill Laimbeer 5.00 12.00
20 Tim Hardaway 6.00 15.00
21 David Robinson 25.00 60.00
22 Adrian Dantley 4.00 10.00
23 Alonzo Mourning 25.00 60.00
24 Magic Johnson 40.00 100.00
25 Julius Erving 30.00 80.00
26 Mark Jackson 4.00 10.00
27 Bill Cartwright
28 Bill Russell 50.00 125.00
29 B.J. Armstrong 8.00 20.00
30 Bob McAdoo 10.00 25.00
31 Cazzie Russell 4.00 10.00
33 Clyde Drexler 25.00 60.00
34 Danny Manning 8.00 20.00
35 John Havlicek 10.00 25.00
36 Grant Hill 75.00 150.00
37 Jim Jackson 10.00 25.00
38 David Thompson 6.00 15.00
39 Rudy Tomjanovich 4.00 10.00
40 Reggie Theus 4.00 10.00
41 Freddie Lewis 4.00 10.00
42 Kenny Smith 8.00 20.00
43 Bill Sharman 8.00 20.00
44 Lonnie Shelton 4.00 10.00
45 Toni Kukoc 25.00 60.00
46 Sam Cassell 5.00 12.00
47 Glen Rice 8.00 20.00
48 Darrell Griffith 4.00 10.00
49 Steve Nash
50 Chris Paul 25.00 60.00
51 Tristan Thompson RS 6.00 15.00
52 Jonas Valanciunas RS 15.00 40.00
53 Bismack Biyombo RS 4.00 10.00
54 Jimmer Fredette RS 12.00 30.00
55 Klay Thompson RS 10.00 25.00
56 Alec Burks RS 4.00 10.00
57 Markieff Morris RS 6.00 15.00
58 Marcus Morris RS 4.00 10.00
59 Kawhi Leonard RS 12.00 30.00
60 Nikola Vucevic RS 2.50 6.00
61 Chris Singleton RS 2.50 6.00
62 Tobias Harris RS 3.00 8.00
63 Scotty Hopson RS 2.50 6.00
64 Nolan Smith RS 4.00 10.00
65 Reggie Jackson RS 3.00 8.00
66 MarShon Brooks RS 6.00 15.00
67 JaJuan Johnson RS 3.00 8.00
68 Norris Cole RS 6.00 15.00
69 Cory Joseph RS 2.50 6.00
70 Justin Harper RS 3.00 8.00
71 Shelvin Mack RS 3.00 8.00
72 Tyler Honeycutt RS 2.50 6.00
73 Jordan Williams RS 3.00 8.00
74 Chandler Parsons RS 4.00 10.00
75 Jon Leuer RS 2.50 6.00
76 Malcolm Lee RS 2.50 6.00
77 Charles Jenkins RS 2.50 6.00
78 Travis Leslie RS 2.50 6.00
79 Keith Benson RS 2.50 6.00
80 Josh Selby RS 4.00 10.00
81 E'Twaun Moore RS 4.00 10.00
82 Demetri McCamey RS 2.50 6.00
83 Durrell Summers RS 3.00 8.00

2011-12 Fleer Retro Big Men on Court

STATED ODDS 1:180 PACKS
1 Michael Jordan 175.00 350.00
2 LeBron James 60.00 150.00
3 Magic Johnson 25.00 60.00
4 Larry Bird 25.00 60.00
5 Bill Russell 12.00 30.00
6 Julius Erving 15.00 40.00
7 David Robinson 12.00 30.00
8 Hakeem Olajuwon 10.00 25.00
9 Alonzo Mourning 15.00 40.00
10 Anfernee Hardaway 20.00 50.00
11 Chris Paul 20.00 50.00
12 Grant Hill 25.00 60.00
13 Walt Frazier 8.00 20.00
14 James Worthy 10.00 25.00
15 Steve Nash 12.00 30.00

2011-12 Fleer Retro Competitive Advantage

STATED ODDS 1:144 PACKS
1 Michael Jordan 60.00 150.00
2 Magic Johnson 10.00 25.00
3 LeBron James 30.00 80.00
4 Larry Bird 15.00 40.00
5 Bill Russell 8.00 20.00
6 Julius Erving 8.00 20.00
7 David Robinson 8.00 20.00
8 Jimmer Fredette 8.00 20.00
9 Anfernee Hardaway 12.00 30.00
10 George Gervin 5.00 12.00
11 Hakeem Olajuwon 6.00 15.00
12 Jerry West 8.00 20.00
13 David Thompson 6.00 15.00
14 Larry Johnson 6.00 15.00
15 Grant Hill 8.00 20.00
16 Chris Paul 8.00 20.00
17 Steve Nash 6.00 15.00
18 Clyde Drexler 6.00 15.00
19 James Worthy 8.00 20.00
20 Alonzo Mourning 6.00 15.00

2011-12 Fleer Retro Flair Showcase

STATED PRINT RUN 150 SER.#'d SETS
1 Michael Jordan 250.00 500.00
2 LeBron James 80.00 200.00
3 Alonzo Mourning 8.00 20.00
4 Bill Russell 10.00 25.00
5 Chris Paul 8.00 20.00
6 Clyde Drexler 6.00 15.00
7 David Robinson 10.00 25.00
8 Grant Hill 20.00 50.00
9 Hakeem Olajuwon 8.00 20.00
10 James Worthy 6.00 15.00
11 Jerry West 8.00 20.00
12 John Havlicek 6.00 15.00
13 Julius Erving 10.00 25.00
14 Larry Bird 15.00 40.00
15 Larry Johnson 6.00 15.00
16 Magic Johnson 15.00 40.00
17 Steve Nash 10.00 25.00
18 Walt Frazier 5.00 12.00
19 Bob McAdoo 5.00 12.00
20 Adrian Dantley 5.00 12.00
21 Cazzie Russell 5.00 12.00
22 Christian Laettner 8.00 20.00
23 Danny Manning 5.00 12.00
24 Darrell Griffith 5.00 12.00
25 Dennis Rodman 12.00 30.00
26 Elgin Baylor 5.00 12.00
27 Gail Goodrich 5.00 12.00
28 George Gervin 5.00 12.00
29 Anfernee Hardaway 15.00 40.00
30 Jim Jackson 5.00 12.00
31 Candace Parker 8.00 20.00
32 Rick Barry 5.00 12.00
33 Tim Hardaway 5.00 12.00
34 David Thompson 5.00 12.00
35 Bill Walton 5.00 12.00
36 Glen Rice 5.00 12.00
37 Toni Kukoc 6.00 15.00
38 Micheal Ray Richardson 5.00 12.00
39 Chet Walker 5.00 12.00
40 Terry Porter 5.00 12.00
41 Kawhi Leonard 12.00 30.00
42 Jimmer Fredette 12.00 30.00
43 Bill Cartwright 5.00 12.00
44 Bill Laimbeer 5.00 12.00
45 Bobby Hurley 6.00 15.00
46 Brad Daugherty 5.00 12.00
47 Hal Greer 5.00 12.00
48 Reggie Theus 5.00 12.00
49 Robert Horry 6.00 15.00
50 Sam Cassell 5.00 12.00
51 Dominique Wilkins 6.00 15.00
52 Karl Malone 8.00 20.00
53 Chandler Parsons 6.00 15.00
54 MarShon Brooks 12.00 30.00
55 Jon Leuer 4.00 10.00
56 Alec Burks 6.00 15.00
57 Tristan Thompson 10.00 25.00
58 Markieff Morris 8.00 20.00
59 Norris Cole 6.00 15.00
60 Klay Thompson 15.00 40.00

2011-12 Fleer Retro Golden Touch

STATED ODDS 1:180 PACKS
1 Michael Jordan 125.00 250.00
2 LeBron James 60.00 150.00
3 Magic Johnson 15.00 40.00
4 Julius Erving 12.00 30.00
5 Hakeem Olajuwon 8.00 20.00
6 David Robinson 12.00 30.00
7 Steve Nash 10.00 25.00
8 Chris Paul 12.00 30.00
9 Larry Bird 20.00 50.00
10 Bill Russell 10.00 25.00
11 Jerry West 10.00 25.00
12 Grant Hill 20.00 50.00
13 James Worthy 8.00 20.00
14 Anfernee Hardaway 15.00 40.00
15 Jimmer Fredette 10.00 25.00

2011-12 Fleer Retro Intimidation Nation

STATED ODDS 1:180 PACKS
1 Grant Hill 25.00 60.00
2 George Gervin 8.00 20.00
3 Alonzo Mourning 12.00 30.00
4 Clyde Drexler 12.00 30.00
5 Hakeem Olajuwon 10.00 25.00
6 Larry Bird 25.00 60.00
7 Darrell Griffith 8.00 20.00
8 Julius Erving 15.00 40.00
9 Magic Johnson 20.00 50.00
10 David Robinson 12.00 30.00
11 David Thompson 8.00 20.00
12 Michael Jordan 175.00 350.00
13 James Worthy 10.00 25.00
14 Jim Jackson 8.00 20.00
15 Bill Russell
16 Steve Nash 10.00 25.00
17 Elgin Baylor 8.00 20.00
18 Dennis Rodman 15.00 40.00
19 Walt Frazier 8.00 20.00
20 LeBron James 60.00 150.00
21 Bill Walton 8.00 20.00
22 Larry Johnson 10.00 25.00
23 Tim Hardaway 8.00 20.00
24 Chris Paul 12.00 30.00
25 Jerry West 10.00 25.00
26 Danny Manning 8.00 20.00
27 Bob McAdoo 8.00 20.00
28 Adrian Dantley 8.00 20.00
29 John Havlicek 10.00 25.00
30 Reggie Theus 8.00 20.00
31 Chet Walker 8.00 20.00
32 Bill Laimbeer 8.00 20.00
33 Jimmer Fredette 10.00 25.00
34 Kawhi Leonard 10.00 25.00
35 Anfernee Hardaway 20.00 50.00

2011-12 Fleer Retro Jambalaya

STATED ODDS 1:360 PACKS
1 Michael Jordan 1000.00 1600.00
2 LeBron James 500.00 800.00
3 Bill Russell 125.00 300.00
4 Chris Paul 150.00 300.00
5 Grant Hill 100.00 200.00
6 Dominique Wilkins 50.00 125.00
7 David Robinson 60.00 150.00
8 Hakeem Olajuwon 50.00 125.00
9 James Worthy 60.00 150.00
10 Julius Erving 80.00 200.00
11 Larry Bird 125.00 300.00
12 Magic Johnson 200.00 400.00
13 Anfernee Hardaway 150.00 300.00
14 Dennis Rodman 80.00 200.00
15 Larry Johnson 80.00 200.00
16 Clyde Drexler 50.00 125.00
17 Alonzo Mourning 50.00 125.00
18 Walt Frazier 50.00 125.00
19 John Havlicek 50.00 125.00
20 Karl Malone 60.00 150.00
21 Jerry West 50.00 125.00

2011-12 Fleer Retro Metal Championship Hardware

STATED ODDS 1:90 PACKS
1 Michael Jordan 60.00 150.00
2 LeBron James 30.00 80.00
3 Magic Johnson 10.00 25.00
4 Bill Walton 5.00 12.00
5 Danny Manning 5.00 12.00
6 David Thompson 5.00 12.00
7 Larry Johnson 6.00 15.00
8 James Worthy 6.00 15.00
9 Grant Hill 15.00 40.00
10 Bill Russell 8.00 20.00
11 Christian Laettner 6.00 15.00
12 Glen Rice 5.00 12.00
13 Darrell Griffith 5.00 12.00
14 Gail Goodrich 5.00 12.00
15 John Havlicek 5.00 12.00

2011-12 Fleer Retro Noyz Boyz

STATED ODDS 1:144 PACKS
1 Bill Walton 8.00 20.00
2 Alonzo Mourning 12.00 30.00
3 Bill Russell 12.00 30.00
4 Chris Paul 12.00 30.00
5 Anfernee Hardaway 20.00 50.00
6 Clyde Drexler 12.00 30.00
7 David Robinson 15.00 40.00
8 David Thompson 8.00 20.00
9 Dennis Rodman 15.00 40.00
10 Grant Hill 20.00 50.00
11 Hakeem Olajuwon 10.00 25.00
12 James Worthy 10.00 25.00
13 Jerry West 10.00 25.00
14 Jim Jackson 8.00 20.00
15 Jimmer Fredette 12.00 30.00
16 Julius Erving 15.00 40.00
17 Kawhi Leonard 12.00 30.00
18 Larry Bird 20.00 50.00
19 Larry Johnson 10.00 25.00
20 LeBron James 60.00 150.00
21 Magic Johnson 20.00 50.00
22 Tim Hardaway 8.00 20.00
23 Michael Jordan 175.00 350.00
24 Steve Nash 12.00 30.00
25 Walt Frazier 8.00 20.00

2011-12 Fleer Retro Precious Metal Gems Red

STATED PRINT RUN 150 SER.#'d SETS
UNPRICED GREEN PRINT RUN 10 SETS
1 Michael Jordan 1800.00 3000.00
2 Mark Jackson 20.00 50.00
3 Hakeem Olajuwon 50.00 125.00
4 LeBron James 700.00 1300.00
5 Clyde Drexler 50.00 125.00
6 David Robinson 50.00 125.00
7 Christian Laettner 25.00 60.00
8 Jim Jackson 20.00 50.00
9 Adrian Dantley 20.00 50.00
10 Reggie Theus 20.00 50.00
11 John Havlicek 25.00 60.00
12 Dennis Rodman 60.00 150.00
13 Gail Goodrich 20.00 50.00
14 Danny Manning 20.00 50.00
15 Bob McAdoo 20.00 50.00
16 Walt Frazier 20.00 50.00
17 Bill Laimbeer 20.00 50.00
18 Hal Greer 20.00 50.00
19 Bill Cartwright 20.00 50.00
20 Rudy Tomjanovich 20.00 50.00
21 Bill Russell 60.00 150.00
22 Tim Hardaway 30.00 80.00
23 Cazzie Russell 20.00 50.00
24 David Thompson 20.00 50.00
25 Darrell Griffith 20.00 50.00
26 Rick Barry 20.00 50.00
27 George Gervin 25.00 60.00
28 Elgin Baylor 20.00 50.00
29 Alonzo Mourning 50.00 125.00
30 Bill Walton 20.00 50.00
31 Larry Johnson 40.00 100.00
32 Magic Johnson 100.00 200.00
33 Julius Erving 50.00 125.00
34 Jimmer Fredette 40.00 100.00
35 John Starks 25.00 60.00
36 Bill Sharman 20.00 50.00
37 Larry Bird 125.00 225.00
38 Grant Hill 100.00 200.00
39 Steve Nash 60.00 150.00
40 James Worthy 40.00 100.00

2011-12 Fleer Retro Precious Metal Gems Blue

*BLUE: .75X TO 2X BASE HI
STATED PRINT RUN 50 SER.#'d SETS
1 Michael Jordan 6000.00 10000.00
4 LeBron James 2000.00 3000.00
6 David Robinson 150.00 300.00
12 Dennis Rodman 200.00 350.00
21 Bill Russell 200.00 400.00
22 Tim Hardaway 125.00 250.00
28 Elgin Baylor 60.00 150.00
29 Alonzo Mourning 200.00 350.00
32 Magic Johnson 400.00 600.00
37 Larry Bird 300.00 550.00
38 Grant Hill 300.00 500.00
39 Steve Nash 200.00 400.00

2011-12 Fleer Retro Ultra Court Masters

STATED ODDS 1:90 PACKS
1 Michael Jordan 125.00 300.00
2 LeBron James 50.00 125.00
3 Larry Bird 25.00 60.00
4 Magic Johnson 12.00 30.00
5 Bill Russell 8.00 20.00
6 Julius Erving 10.00 25.00
7 David Robinson 10.00 25.00
8 Hakeem Olajuwon 6.00 15.00
9 Clyde Drexler 8.00 20.00
10 Grant Hill 15.00 40.00
11 Steve Nash 10.00 25.00
12 Chris Paul 8.00 20.00
13 Larry Johnson 6.00 15.00
14 Alonzo Mourning 10.00 25.00
15 James Worthy 10.00 25.00
16 David Thompson 5.00 12.00
17 Danny Manning 5.00 12.00
18 Jimmer Fredette 6.00 15.00
19 George Gervin 5.00 12.00
20 Anfernee Hardaway 20.00 50.00
21 Adrian Dantley 5.00 12.00
22 Walt Frazier 5.00 12.00
23 Bill Walton 5.00 12.00
24 Tim Hardaway 5.00 12.00
25 Jim Jackson 5.00 12.00

2011-12 Fleer Retro Ultra Stars

STATED ODDS 1:180 PACKS
1 Michael Jordan 100.00 200.00
2 LeBron James 50.00 125.00
3 Larry Bird 15.00 40.00
4 Magic Johnson 12.00 30.00
5 Bill Russell 8.00 20.00
6 Julius Erving 10.00 25.00
7 David Robinson 10.00 25.00
8 Hakeem Olajuwon 6.00 15.00
9 Jerry West 6.00 15.00
10 Grant Hill 15.00 40.00
11 Steve Nash 6.00 15.00
12 Chris Paul 10.00 25.00
13 Jimmer Fredette 6.00 15.00
14 John Havlicek 6.00 15.00
15 Alonzo Mourning 12.00 30.00
16 Clyde Drexler 8.00 20.00
17 Dennis Rodman 12.00 30.00
18 Larry Johnson 8.00 20.00
19 James Worthy 8.00 20.00
20 Tim Hardaway 5.00 12.00
21 Walt Frazier 5.00 12.00
22 Elgin Baylor 5.00 12.00
23 George Gervin 5.00 12.00
24 Anfernee Hardaway 15.00 40.00
25 Bill Walton 5.00 12.00

2001-02 Fleer Shoebox

This 180 card set was issued in February, 2002. In keeping with the name of the product, the packs were inserted into a "Converse All-Star" style shoe box. The first 150 cards of this set featured veterans while the last 30 cards feature some leading NBA rookies. Those Rookie Cards (151-180) had a stated print run of 2500 serial numbered sets.

COMP.SET w/o SP's (150) 10.00 25.00
1 Tariq Abdul-Wahad .20 .50
2 Glen Rice .25 .60
3 Derek Anderson .20 .50

4 Desmond Mason .25 .60
5 Al Harrington .25 .60
6 Mitch Richmond .25 .60
7 Felipe Lopez .20 .50
8 Andre Miller .25 .60
9 Jerry Stackhouse .25 .60
10 Jalen Rose .25 .60
11 Lindsey Hunter .20 .50
12 Tim Thomas .20 .50
13 Wally Szczerbiak .25 .60
14 Vince Carter .50 1.25
15 Nick Van Exel .25 .60
16 Jon Barry .20 .50
17 Aaron McKie .20 .50
18 Iakovos Tsakalidis .20 .50
19 Chris Webber .30 .75
20 Karl Malone .40 1.00
21 Shareef Abdur-Rahim .25 .60
22 Baron Davis .30 .75
23 Michael Doleac .20 .50
24 Jermaine O'Neal .30 .75
25 Elton Brand .30 .75
26 Glenn Robinson .25 .60
27 Tracy McGrady .50 1.25
28 Allen Iverson .60 1.50
29 Anfernee Hardaway .50 1.25
30 Scot Pollard .20 .50
31 David Robinson .50 1.25
32 John Stockton .40 1.00
33 Jason Williams .25 .60
34 Voshon Lenard .20 .50
35 Shaquille O'Neal .75 2.00
36 Grant Hill .40 1.00
37 Shawn Marion .30 .75
38 Vin Baker .25 .60
39 Raef LaFrentz .20 .50
40 Steve Francis .30 .75
41 Michael Dickerson .20 .50
42 Hedo Turkoglu .30 .75
43 Patrick Ewing .40 1.00
44 Dirk Nowitzki .50 1.25
45 Keyon Dooling .20 .50
46 Marcus Camby .25 .60
47 Bonzi Wells .20 .50
48 Tim Duncan .60 1.50
49 Jamaal Magloire .20 .50
50 Rick Fox .25 .60
51 Kendall Gill .20 .50
52 Michael Redd .30 .75
53 Keith Van Horn .25 .60
54 Eric Snow .20 .50
55 Theo Ratliff .20 .50
56 Clifford Robinson .20 .50
57 Moochie Norris .20 .50
58 Alonzo Mourning .40 1.00
59 Joe Smith .25 .60
60 Brent Barry .20 .50
61 Alvin Williams .20 .50
62 Antoine Walker .25 .60
63 Antonio McDyess .25 .60
64 Derek Fisher .25 .60
65 Ron Mercer .20 .50
66 Hakeem Olajuwon .40 1.00
67 Jamal Crawford .25 .60
68 Chris Mihm .20 .50
69 Ben Wallace .30 .75
70 Brian Grant .20 .50
71 Kevin Garnett .60 1.50
72 Shandon Anderson .20 .50
73 Shawn Bradley .20 .50
74 Danny Fortson .20 .50
75 Jeff McInnis .20 .50
76 LaPhonso Ellis .25 .60
77 Sam Cassell .25 .60
78 Rasheed Wallace .30 .75
79 Malik Rose .20 .50
80 Jahidi White .20 .50
81 Milt Palacio .20 .50
82 Tim Hardaway .30 .75
83 Antonio Daniels .20 .50
84 Tyronn Lue .20 .50
85 Cuttino Mobley .25 .60
86 DerMarr Johnson .20 .50
87 Lamond Murray .20 .50
88 Larry Hughes .25 .60
89 Reggie Miller .30 .75
90 Lorenzen Wright .20 .50
91 Eddie Jones .25 .60
92 Anthony Mason .20 .50
93 Todd MacCulloch .20 .50
94 Speedy Claxton .20 .50
95 Mateen Cleaves .20 .50
96 Gary Payton .30 .75
97 Morris Peterson .20 .50
98 Mike Miller .30 .75
99 Hanno Mottola .20 .50
100 Steve Nash .50 1.25
101 Stromile Swift .20 .50
102 Ray Allen .30 .75
103 Mark Jackson .25 .60
104 Stephon Marbury .25 .60
105 Mike Bibby .30 .75
106 Rashard Lewis .30 .75
107 Jason Kidd .50 1.25
108 P.J. Brown .20 .50
109 Kobe Bryant 1.50 4.00
110 Tom Gugliotta .20 .50
111 Richard Hamilton .25 .60
112 Antawn Jamison .30 .75
113 Lamar Odom .30 .75
114 Kurt Thomas .20 .50
115 Robert Horry .25 .60
116 Dikembe Mutombo .30 .75
117 Tony Delk .20 .50
118 Peja Stojakovic .30 .75
119 Donyell Marshall .20 .50
120 Paul Pierce .40 1.00
121 Michael Finley .30 .75
122 Quentin Richardson .25 .60
123 Kenyon Martin .30 .75
124 Allan Houston .25 .60
125 Scottie Pippen .50 1.25
126 Steve Smith .25 .60
127 Bryon Russell .20 .50
128 James Posey .20 .50
129 Terrell Brandon .20 .50
130 Toni Kukoc .25 .60
131 Stephen Jackson .25 .60
132 Marc Jackson .20 .50
133 Kelvin Cato .20 .50
134 Travis Best .20 .50
135 David Wesley .20 .50
136 Anthony Carter .20 .50
137 Michael Jordan 5.00 12.00
138 Darrell Armstrong .20 .50
139 Matt Harpring .25 .60
140 Antonio Davis .20 .50
141 Courtney Alexander .20 .50
142 Jamal Mashburn .25 .60
143 Jason Terry .30 .75
144 Marcus Fizer .20 .50
145 Juwan Howard .25 .60
146 Darius Miles .20 .50
147 Latrell Sprewell .25 .60
148 Damon Stoudamire .25 .60
149 John Starks .20 .50
150 Jumaine Jones .20 .50
151 Kedrick Brown RC .75 2.00
152 Trenton Hassell RC .75 2.00
153 Kwame Brown RC .75 2.00
154 Terence Morris RC .75 2.00
155 Richard Jefferson RC 1.50 4.00
156 Vladimir Radmanovic RC .75 2.00
157 Brandon Armstrong RC .75 2.00
158 Kirk Haston RC .75 2.00
159 Eddie Griffin RC .75 2.00
160 Steven Hunter RC .75 2.00
161 Troy Murphy RC 1.25 3.00
162 Andrei Kirilenko RC 2.00 5.00
163 Jeryl Sasser RC .75 2.00
164 Michael Bradley RC .75 2.00
165 Rodney White RC .75 2.00
166 Loren Woods RC .75 2.00
167 Zach Randolph RC 2.00 5.00
168 Joe Johnson RC 2.00 5.00
169 Eddy Curry RC 1.25 3.00
170 Jason Richardson RC 1.50 4.00
171 DeSagana Diop RC .75 2.00
172 Jamaal Tinsley RC 1.00 2.50
173 Pau Gasol RC 2.50 6.00
174 Jason Collins RC .75 2.00
175 Zeljko Rebraca RC .75 2.00
176 Shane Battier RC 1.50 4.00
177 Gerald Wallace RC 1.25 3.00
178 Joseph Forte RC .75 2.00
179 Tyson Chandler RC 1.25 3.00
180 Tony Parker RC 3.00 8.00

2001-02 Fleer Shoebox Footprints

Randomly inserted in packs, this is a parallel to the Fleer Shoebox set. These cards have a stated print run of 150 serial numbered sets.
*FOOT.STARS: 5X TO 12X BASE CARD HI
*FOOT.RCs: 2X TO 5X BASE CARD HI
137 Michael Jordan 40.00 100.00

2001-02 Fleer Shoebox NBA Flight School

Inserted at stated odds of one in 12 packs, this 20 cards insert sets honors some of the NBA's leading dunkers.
COMPLETE SET (20) 20.00 40.00
1 Richard Hamilton .60 1.50
2 Kobe Bryant 4.00 10.00
3 Michael Jordan 6.00 15.00
4 Desmond Mason .60 1.50
5 Antoine Walker .60 1.50
6 Baron Davis .75 2.00
7 Steve Francis .75 2.00
8 Elton Brand .75 2.00
9 Lamar Odom .75 2.00
10 Kevin Garnett 1.50 4.00
11 Latrell Sprewell .60 1.50
12 Tracy McGrady 1.25 3.00
13 Shawn Marion .75 2.00
14 Chris Webber .75 2.00
15 Vince Carter 1.25 3.00
16 Tim Duncan 1.50 4.00
17 Morris Peterson .50 1.25
18 Karl Malone 1.00 2.50
19 Jerry Stackhouse .60 1.50
20 Darius Miles .50 1.25

2001-02 Fleer Shoebox NBA Flight School Cadet

Inserted at stated odds of one in 63, this is a partial parallel to the Flight School insert set. These cards are differentiated from the standard insert by the game-worn jersey swatch. A Captain version of NBA Flight School was also issued. These cards are sequentially numbered to 75.
*CAPTAIN: 1.5X TO 4X CADET HI
1 Richard Hamilton 2.50 6.00
2 Desmond Mason 2.50 6.00
3 Antoine Walker 2.50 6.00
4 Baron Davis 3.00 8.00
5 Steve Francis 3.00 8.00
6 Elton Brand 3.00 8.00
7 Lamar Odom 3.00 8.00
8 Tracy McGrady 5.00 12.00
9 Shawn Marion 3.00 8.00
10 Chris Webber 3.00 8.00
11 Vince Carter 5.00 12.00
12 Morris Peterson 2.00 5.00
13 Karl Malone 4.00 10.00
14 Jerry Stackhouse 2.50 6.00
15 Darius Miles 2.00 5.00

2001-02 Fleer Shoebox Sole of the Game

Inserted at stated odds of one in 144, these 15 cards feature key NBA players including a Larry Bird tribute.
COMPLETE SET (15) 50.00 100.00
1 Karl Malone 2.50 6.00
2 Dirk Nowitzki 3.00 8.00
3 Ray Allen 2.00 5.00
4 Shaquille O'Neal 5.00 12.00
5 Antoine Walker 1.50 4.00
6 Grant Hill 2.50 6.00
7 Steve Francis 2.00 5.00
8 Kobe Bryant 10.00 25.00
9 Michael Jordan 20.00 50.00
10 Larry Bird 15.00 40.00
11 Darius Miles 1.25 3.00
12 Chris Webber 2.00 5.00
13 Allen Iverson 4.00 10.00
14 Rasheed Wallace 2.00 5.00
15 Vince Carter 3.00 8.00

2001-02 Fleer Shoebox Sole of the Game Ball

Randomly inserted in packs, this is a partial parallel to the Sole of the Game insert set. These cards have a stated print run of 300 serial numbered sets and contain a piece of basketball used in a game by the featured player.
1 Ray Allen 5.00 12.00
2 Vince Carter 8.00 20.00
3 Steve Francis 5.00 12.00
4 Grant Hill 6.00 15.00
5 Allen Iverson 10.00 25.00
6 Karl Malone 6.00 15.00
7 Darius Miles 3.00 8.00
8 Dirk Nowitzki 8.00 20.00
9 Antoine Walker 4.00 10.00
10 Rasheed Wallace 5.00 12.00
11 Chris Webber 6.00 15.00

2001-02 Fleer Shoebox Sole of the Game Jersey

Randomly inserted in packs, this is a partial parallel to the Sole of the Game insert set. These cards have a stated print run of 200 serial numbered sets and contain a game-worn jersey piece used in a game by the featured player. Some players uniforms were not available in time for inclusion in packs and they were issued as redemptions.
1 Ray Allen 4.00 10.00
2 Vince Carter 6.00 15.00
3 Steve Francis 4.00 10.00
4 Grant Hill 5.00 12.00
5 Allen Iverson 8.00 20.00
6 Karl Malone 5.00 12.00
7 Darius Miles 2.50 6.00
8 Dirk Nowitzki 6.00 15.00
9 Larry Bird 15.00 40.00
10 Antoine Walker 3.00 8.00
11 Rasheed Wallace 4.00 10.00

2001-02 Fleer Shoebox Sole of the Game Shoe

Randomly inserted in packs, this is a partial parallel to the Sole of the Game insert set. These cards have a stated print run of 100 serial numbered sets and contain a game-worn shoe piece used in a game by the featured player. Some players uniforms were not available in time for inclusion in packs and they were issued as redemptions.
1 Ray Allen 10.00 25.00
2 Larry Bird 60.00 120.00
3 Vince Carter 15.00 40.00
5 Grant Hill 12.00 30.00
6 Allen Iverson 20.00 50.00
7 Karl Malone 15.00 40.00
8 Darius Miles 6.00 15.00
9 Dirk Nowitzki 15.00 40.00
12 Rasheed Wallace 10.00 25.00
13 Chris Webber 10.00 25.00

2001-02 Fleer Shoebox Sole of the Game Triple

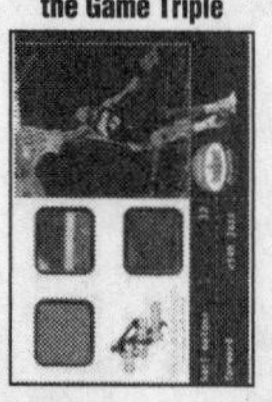

Randomly inserted in packs, this is a partial parallel to the Sole of the Game insert set. These cards have a stated print run of 50 serial numbered sets and contain a piece of basketball used in a game by the featured player. This 11 card set contains a piece of game-worn shoe, patch and basketball from the featured player.
1 Ray Allen 20.00 50.00
2 Vince Carter 30.00 80.00
3 Steve Francis 20.00 50.00
4 Grant Hill 25.00 60.00
5 Allen Iverson 40.00 100.00
6 Karl Malone 25.00 60.00
7 Darius Miles 12.00 30.00
8 Dirk Nowitzki 30.00 80.00

2001-02 Fleer Shoebox Tougher Than Leather

Inserted at stated odds of one in 36, these 20 cards feature players known for their physical play on the court.
COMPLETE SET (20) 25.00 50.00
1 Alonzo Mourning 1.50 4.00
2 Antonio McDyess 1.00 2.50
3 Paul Pierce 1.50 4.00
4 Peja Stojakovic 1.25 3.00
5 Dirk Nowitzki 2.00 5.00
6 Allen Iverson 2.50 6.00
7 Marcus Camby 1.00 2.50
8 Tracy McGrady 2.00 5.00
9 Kenyon Martin 1.25 3.00
10 Dikembe Mutombo 1.25 3.00
11 Rasheed Wallace 1.25 3.00
12 David Robinson 2.00 5.00
13 Shareef Abdur-Rahim 1.00 2.50
14 Glenn Robinson 1.00 2.50
15 Vince Carter 2.00 5.00
16 Antoine Walker 1.00 2.50
17 Trajan Langdon .75 2.00
18 Scottie Pippen 2.00 5.00
19 Eddie Jones 1.00 2.50
20 Lamar Odom 1.25 3.00

2001-02 Fleer Shoebox Tougher Than Leather Shoes

Randomly inserted into packs, this is a parallel of the "Tougher than Leather" insert set. These cards were printed to a stated print run of 100 serial numbered sets and each card contains a piece of game worn shoe. In addition Vince Carter signed a limited amount of cards for this insert set. Those cards, as well as Paul Pierce Shoe cards were issued as redemptions.
1 Alonzo Mourning 12.00 30.00
2 Antonio McDyess 8.00 20.00
3 Eddie Jones 8.00 20.00
5 Dirk Nowitzki 15.00 40.00
6 Marcus Camby 8.00 20.00
7 Tracy McGrady 15.00 40.00
8 Kenyon Martin 10.00 25.00
9 Dikembe Mutombo 10.00 25.00
10 Rasheed Wallace 10.00 25.00
11 David Robinson 15.00 40.00
12 Shareef Abdur-Rahim 8.00 20.00
13 Glenn Robinson 8.00 20.00
14 Vince Carter 15.00 40.00
14A Vince Carter AU 25.00 50.00
15 Antoine Walker 8.00 20.00
16 Allen Iverson 20.00 50.00
17 Scottie Pippen 15.00 40.00
18 Peja Stojakovic 10.00 25.00
19 Trajan Langdon 6.00 15.00
20 Lamar Odom 10.00 25.00

2000-01 Fleer Showcase

The 2000-01 Fleer Showcase product released in March, 2001 and featured a 121-card base set. The base set was broken into tiers as follows: Base Veterans (1-90) and Rookies (91-121) that were broken into three tiers. Tier 1 91-100 were serial numbered to 500, Tier 2 101-110 were serial numbered to 1500, and Tier 3 111-121 were serial numbered to 2000. Each pack contained five cards, and carried a suggested retail price of $4.99.
COMPLETE SET w/o RCs (90) 12.50 30.00
1 Vince Carter .75 2.00
2 Lamar Odom .40 1.00
3 Larry Hughes .30 .75
4 Brian Grant .25 .60
5 Bryon Russell .25 .60
6 Allan Houston .30 .75
7 Juwan Howard .30 .75
8 Cuttino Mobley .30 .75
9 Keith Van Horn .30 .75
10 Mike Bibby .40 1.00
11 Jerome Williams .25 .60
12 Ray Allen .40 1.00
13 Antonio Davis .25 .60
14 Adrian Griffin .25 .60
15 Dan Majerle .30 .75
16 Rasheed Wallace .40 1.00
17 Antonio McDyess .30 .75
18 Tim Thomas .25 .60
19 Theo Ratliff .25 .60
20 Charles Oakley .30 .75
21 Nick Van Exel .30 .75
22 Glenn Robinson .30 .75
23 Cal Bowdler .25 .60
24 Raef LaFrentz .25 .60
25 Terrell Brandon .25 .60
26 Allen Iverson .75 2.00
27 Patrick Ewing .50 1.25
28 Ron Artest .40 1.00
29 Michael Olowokandi .25 .60
30 Derek Anderson .25 .60
31 Dirk Nowitzki .60 1.50
32 Wally Szczerbiak .30 .75
33 Gary Payton .40 1.00
34 Michael Finley .40 1.00
35 Chauncey Billups .40 1.00
36 Jason Kidd .60 1.50
37 Rashard Lewis .40 1.00
38 Andre Miller .30 .75
39 Kevin Garnett .75 2.00
40 Tim Duncan .75 2.00
41 Jalen Rose .30 .75
42 Marcus Camby .30 .75
43 Richard Hamilton .30 .75
44 Austin Croshere .25 .60
45 Latrell Sprewell .30 .75
46 Shawn Marion .40 1.00
47 Jahidi White .25 .60
48 Elton Brand .40 1.00
49 Reggie Miller .40 1.00
50 David Robinson .60 1.50
51 Trajan Langdon .25 .60
52 Jonathan Bender .25 .60
53 Antonio Daniels .25 .60
54 Jason Terry .40 1.00
55 Eddie Jones .40 1.00
56 Mitch Richmond .30 .75
57 Antoine Walker .30 .75
58 Robert Horry .30 .75
59 Tracy McGrady .60 1.50
60 Scottie Pippen .60 1.50
61 Jerry Stackhouse .30 .75
62 Zydrunas Ilgauskas .30 .75
63 Toni Kukoc .30 .75
64 Karl Malone .50 1.25
65 Baron Davis .40 1.00
66 Shaquille O'Neal 1.00 2.50
67 Vlade Divac .30 .75
68 Eddie Robinson .25 .60
69 Dion Glover .25 .60
70 Jason Williams .40 1.00
71 Steve Francis .40 1.00
72 Glen Rice .30 .75
73 Clifford Robinson .25 .60
74 Shareef Abdur-Rahim .30 .75
75 Hakeem Olajuwon .50 1.25
76 Paul Pierce .50 1.25
77 Tim Hardaway .40 1.00
78 Darrell Armstrong .25 .60
79 Bonzi Wells .25 .60
80 Antawn Jamison .40 1.00
81 Stephon Marbury .30 .75
82 Tony Delk .25 .60
83 Michael Dickerson .25 .60
84 Jamal Mashburn .30 .75
85 Kobe Bryant 2.00 5.00
86 Grant Hill .50 1.25
87 Chris Webber .40 1.00
88 Vonteego Cummings .25 .60
89 Jamie Feick .25 .60
90 John Stockton .50 1.25
91 Kenyon Martin RC 8.00 20.00
92 Stromile Swift RC 3.00 8.00
93 Darius Miles RC 3.00 8.00
94 Marcus Fizer RC 3.00 8.00
95 Mike Miller RC 6.00 15.00
96 DerMarr Johnson RC 3.00 8.00
97 Chris Mihm RC 3.00 8.00
98 Jamal Crawford RC 5.00 12.00
99 Joel Przybilla RC 3.00 8.00
100 Keyon Dooling RC 3.00 8.00
101 Jerome Moiso RC 2.00 5.00
102 Etan Thomas RC 2.00 5.00
103 Courtney Alexander RC 2.00 5.00
104 Mateen Cleaves RC 2.00 5.00
105 Jason Collier RC 2.00 5.00
106 Hedo Turkoglu RC 4.00 10.00
107 Desmond Mason RC 2.50 6.00
108 Quentin Richardson RC 3.00 8.00
109 Jamaal Magloire RC 2.00 5.00
110 Speedy Claxton RC 2.00 5.00
111 Morris Peterson RC 1.50 4.00
112 Donnell Harvey RC 1.50 4.00
113 DeShawn Stevenson RC 2.00 5.00
114 Dalibor Bagaric RC 1.50 4.00
115 Mamadou N'Diaye RC 1.50 4.00
116 Erick Barkley RC 1.50 4.00
117 Mark Madsen RC 1.50 4.00
118 Chris Porter RC 1.50 4.00
119 Brian Cardinal RC 1.50 4.00
120 Iakovos Tsakalidis RC 1.50 4.00
121 Marc Jackson RC 3.00 8.00

2000-01 Fleer Showcase Legacy Collection

Randomly inserted into packs, this 121-card set is a complete parallel of the 2000-01 Fleer Showcase base set. Each card is clearly marked "Legacy Collection" and is serial numbered to only 50.
*STARS: 15X TO 40X BASE CARD HI
*RCs 91-100/121: .75X TO 2X BASE HI
*RCs 101-110: 1.25X TO 3X BASE HI
*RCs 111-120: 1.5X TO 4X BASE HI

2000-01 Fleer Showcase Masterpiece

Randomly inserted into packs, this 121-card set is a complete parallel of the 2000-01 Fleer Showcase base set. Each card is clearly marked "Masterpiece Collection" and is serial numbered to only 1.

2000-01 Fleer Showcase Avant Card

Randomly inserted in packs, each card in this 20-card set features an original piece of art (by Gerry Thomas) mounted in a card frame. Card backs carry a "AC" prefix. Please note that there wer only 201 of each card produced.
AC1 Vince Carter 12.00 30.00
AC2 Lamar Odom 6.00 15.00
AC3 Kobe Bryant 30.00 80.00
AC4 Kevin Garnett 12.00 30.00
AC5 Steve Francis 6.00 15.00
AC6 Jason Williams 6.00 15.00
AC7 Eddie Jones 6.00 15.00
AC8 Grant Hill 8.00 20.00
AC9 Elton Brand 6.00 15.00
AC10 Shaquille O'Neal 15.00 40.00
AC11 Allen Iverson 12.00 30.00
AC12 Tim Duncan 12.00 30.00
AC13 Jason Kidd 10.00 25.00
AC14 Kenyon Martin 12.00 30.00
AC15 Stromile Swift 5.00 12.00
AC16 Darius Miles 5.00 12.00
AC17 Marcus Fizer 5.00 12.00
AC18 Mike Miller 10.00 25.00
AC19 Jamal Crawford 8.00 20.00
AC20 Mateen Cleaves 5.00 12.00

2000-01 Fleer Showcase Vince Carter Rookie Remnants

This three-card insert was randomly inserted into 2000-01 Fleer products. The set includes a Vince Carter floor card (numbered to 100), a Vince Carter floor/jersey card (numbered to 15), and finally an autographed Vince Carter floor/jersey card (numbered 1/1).
NNO Vince Carter FLR/100 12.50 30.00

2000-01 Fleer Showcase ELEMENTary

Randomly inserted in packs at one in 48, this 10-card set compares your favorite NBA stars to elements on the periodical chart. Card backs carry an "E" prefix.
COMPLETE SET (10) 20.00 40.00
E1 Vince Carter 2.50 6.00
E2 Lamar Odom 1.25 3.00
E3 Kevin Garnett 2.50 6.00
E4 Steve Francis 1.25 3.00
E5 Grant Hill 1.50 4.00
E6 Eddie Jones 1.25 3.00
E7 Jason Williams 1.25 3.00
E8 Kobe Bryant 6.00 15.00
E9 Allen Iverson 2.50 6.00
E10 Shaquille O'Neal 3.00 8.00

2000-01 Fleer Showcase HIStory

Randomly inserted into packs at one in 24, this 10-card insert set tells the story of how ten players made it to the NBA. Card backs carry an "H" prefix.
COMPLETE SET (10) 12.50 25.00
H1 Vince Carter 1.50 4.00
H2 Lamar Odom .75 2.00
H3 Kobe Bryant 4.00 10.00
H4 Shaquille O'Neal 2.00 5.00
H5 Kevin Garnett 1.50 4.00
H6 Allen Iverson 1.50 4.00
H7 Steve Francis .75 2.00
H8 Eddie Jones .75 2.00
H9 Jason Williams .75 2.00
H10 Michael Finley .75 2.00

2000-01 Fleer Showcase In the Paint

Randomly inserted in packs at one in 110, this 26-card insert offers a piece of a hand-painted basketball from a top 2000-01 NBA rookie. Card backs carry an "P" prefix.
P1 Kenyon Martin 5.00 12.00
P2 Stromile Swift 2.00 5.00
P3 Darius Miles 2.00 5.00
P4 Marcus Fizer 2.00 5.00
P5 Mike Miller 4.00 10.00
P6 DerMarr Johnson 2.00 5.00
P7 Chris Mihm 2.00 5.00
P8 Joel Przybilla 2.00 5.00
P9 Keyon Dooling 2.00 5.00
P10 Jerome Moiso 2.00 5.00
P11 Etan Thomas 2.00 5.00
P12 Courtney Alexander 2.00 5.00
P13 Mateen Cleaves 2.00 5.00
P14 Jason Collier 2.00 5.00
P15 Hedo Turkoglu 4.00 10.00
P16 Desmond Mason 2.50 6.00
P17 Quentin Richardson 3.00 8.00
P18 Jamaal Magloire 2.00 5.00
P19 Speedy Claxton 2.00 5.00
P20 Morris Peterson 2.00 5.00
P21 Donnell Harvey 2.00 5.00
P22 DeShawn Stevenson 2.50 6.00
P23 Dalibor Bagaric 2.00 5.00
P24 Mamadou N'Diaye 2.00 5.00
P25 Erick Barkley 2.00 5.00
P26 Mark Madsen 2.00 5.00

2000-01 Fleer Showcase Showstoppers

Randomly inserted in packs at one in six, this 20-card set features players who are worth the price of admission themselves. Card backs carry a "S" prefix.
COMPLETE SET (20) 6.00 15.00
S1 Vince Carter 1.00 2.50
S2 Lamar Odom .50 1.25
S3 Tracy McGrady .75 2.00
S4 Karl Malone .60 1.50
S5 Scottie Pippen .75 2.00
S6 Antawn Jamison .50 1.25
S7 Chris Webber .50 1.25
S8 Allan Houston .40 1.00
S9 Baron Davis .50 1.25
S10 Rashard Lewis .50 1.25
S11 Jerry Stackhouse .40 1.00
S12 Ray Allen .50 1.25
S13 Keith Van Horn .40 1.00
S14 Tim Duncan 1.00 2.50
S15 Shareef Abdur-Rahim .40 1.00
S16 Jalen Rose .40 1.00
S17 Gary Payton .50 1.25
S18 Andre Miller .40 1.00
S19 Paul Pierce .60 1.50
S20 Antonio McDyess .40 1.00

2000-01 Fleer Showcase To Air is Human

Randomly inserted in packs at one in 12, this 15-card set features high-flyers that don't make mistakes when the game is on the line. Card backs carry a "TA" prefix.
COMPLETE SET (15) 6.00 15.00
TA1 Vince Carter 1.25 3.00
TA2 Lamar Odom .60 1.50
TA3 Grant Hill .75 2.00
TA4 Shareef Abdur-Rahim .50 1.25
TA5 Michael Finley .60
TA6 Larry Hughes .50
TA7 Latrell Sprewell .50
TA8 Tracy McGrady 1.00
TA9 Ray Allen .60
TA10 Desmond Mason .75
TA11 Kenyon Martin 1.50
TA12 Morris Peterson .60
TA13 Stromile Swift .60
TA14 DerMarr Johnson .60
TA15 Mike Miller 1.25

2001-02 Fleer Showcase

Issued in January, 2002 this 123 card set features a mix of rookie and veteran players. Cards numbered 91 featured special art cards of key superstars and printed to a stated print run of 500 serial numbered sets. In addition, the rookie cards were also broken down into several levels with cards 92 through 97 a having a stated print run of 500 serial numbered se Cards 98 through 112 have a stated print run of 10 serial numbered sets and cards 113-122 have a sta print run of 1500 serial numbered sets. Card 123, Wang ZhiZhi was also accorded the Avant treatmen and his card was issued to a stated print run 500 se numbered cards. In addition, Vince Carter signed 1 cards of his card number 87. That card is not considered part of the complete set.
COMPLETE SET (123) 150.00
COMP.SET w/o SP's (86) 20.00
UNPRICED MASTERPIECE PRINT RUN ONE SET
1 Grant Hill .50
2 Elton Brand .40
3 Sam Cassell .30
4 John Stockton .50
5 James Posey .25
6 Eddie Jones .30
7 Damon Stoudamire .30
8 Nick Van Exel .30
9 Brian Grant .25
10 Mike Miller .40
11 Steve Smith .30
12 Michael Finley .40
13 Peja Stojakovic .40
14 DerMarr Johnson .25
15 Reggie Miller .40
16 Quentin Richardson .30
17 Latrell Sprewell .30
18 Richard Hamilton .30
19 Michael Doleac .25
20 Derek Fisher .30
21 Marcus Camby .30
22 Stephon Marbury .30
23 Bryon Russell .25
24 Jumaine Jones .25
25 Anfernee Hardaway .60
26 P.J. Brown .25
27 Marc Jackson .25
28 Dikembe Mutombo .40
29 Andre Miller .30
30 Robert Horry .30
31 Tom Gugliotta .25
32 David Robinson .60
33 Ron Mercer .25
34 Shawn Marion .40
35 Ron Artest .40
36 Jason Williams .30
37 Scottie Pippen .60
38 Jerry Stackhouse .30
39 Stromile Swift .25
40 Rasheed Wallace .40
41 Alonzo Mourning .50
42 Eddie Robinson .25
43 Shareef Abdur-Rahim .30
44 Wally Szczerbiak .30
45 Antonio Davis .25
46 Glen Rice .30
47 Jason Kidd .60
48 Gary Payton .40
49 Steve Nash .60
50 Lamar Odom .40
51 Glenn Robinson .30
52 Mike Bibby .40
53 Hakeem Olajuwon .50
54 Theo Ratliff .25
55 Kenyon Martin .40
56 Jamal Mashburn .30
57 Larry Hughes .30
58 Speedy Claxton .25
59 Rashard Lewis .40
60 Raef LaFrentz .25
61 Antonio Daniels .25
62 Jason Terry .40
63 Jalen Rose .30
64 Terrell Brandon .25
65 Karl Malone .50
66 Antonio McDyess .30
67 Anthony Carter .25
68 Tim Hardaway .40
69 Antoine Walker .30
70 Cuttino Mobley .30
71 Allan Houston .30
72 Desmond Mason .30
73 Kurt Thomas .25
74 Juwan Howard .30
75 Tim Thomas .25
76 Tracy McGrady .60
77 Dirk Nowitzki .60
78 Tim Duncan .75
79 Chris Webber .40
80 Steve Francis .40
81 Paul Pierce .50
82 Darius Miles .25
83 Ray Allen .40
84 Baron Davis .40
85 Antawn Jamison .40
86 Michael Jordan 6.00
87 Vince Carter AVANT 4.00
87A Vince Carter AU/150 50.00
88 Kobe Bryant AVANT 12.00
89 Allen Iverson AVANT 5.00
90 Kevin Garnett AVANT 5.00

aquille O'Neal AVANT 6.00 15.00
ame Brown AVANT RC 5.00 12.00
die Griffin AVANT RC 5.00 12.00
dy Curry AVANT RC 8.00 20.00
ane Battier AVANT RC 10.00 25.00
e Johnson AVANT RC 12.00 30.00
son Chandler AVANT RC 8.00 20.00
son Richardson RC 2.50 6.00
ch Randolph RC 3.00 8.00
odney White RC 1.25 3.00
au Gasol RC 4.00 10.00
amaal Tinsley RC 1.50 4.00
roy Murphy RC 2.00 5.00
ichard Jefferson RC 2.50 6.00
eSagana Diop RC 1.25 3.00
oseph Forte RC 1.25 3.00
erald Wallace RC 2.00 5.00
oren Woods RC 1.25 3.00
ason Collins RC 1.25 3.00
eryl Sasser RC 1.25 3.00
eljko Rebraca RC 1.25 3.00
irk Haston RC 1.25 3.00
edrick Brown RC 1.25 3.00
teven Hunter RC 1.25 3.00
ichael Bradley RC 1.25 3.00
randon Armstrong RC 1.25 3.00
amuel Dalembert RC 1.50 4.00
rimoz Brezec RC 1.25 3.00
ndrei Kirilenko RC 3.00 8.00
ladimir Radmanovic RC 1.25 3.00
atko Varda RC 1.25 3.00
rendan Haywood RC 1.50 4.00
ang Zhizhi AVANT 2.00 5.00

01-02 Fleer Showcase Legacy

omly inserted in packs, this 123-card set
lels the base Fleer Showcase set where each card
stated print run of 50 serial numbered sets.
RS 1-86: 10X TO 25X BASE CARD HI
NT STARS: 1.5X TO 4X BASE CARD HI
NT RCs: .75X TO 2X BASE CARD HI
97-122: 3X TO 8X BASE CARD HI
ichael Jordan 250.00 500.00

01-02 Fleer Showcase Beasts of the East

omly inserted in packs at the rate of one in 26, 5-card set features the words "Beasts of the East" the top of the card with player action photos red on the card front with a swatch of game worn orabilia.

ce Carter 5.00 12.00
nce Carter AU/225 20.00 50.00
n Iverson 6.00 15.00
nzo Mourning 4.00 10.00
l Pierce 4.00 10.00
y McGrady 5.00 12.00
h Van Horn 2.50 6.00
oine Walker 2.50 6.00
hard Hamilton 2.50 6.00
dre Miller 2.50 6.00
kembe Mutombo 3.00 8.00
ike Miller 3.00 8.00
enyon Martin 3.00 8.00
ron Davis 3.00 8.00
y Allen 3.00 8.00

01-02 Fleer Showcase Best of the West

omly inserted in packs at the stated odds of one in is 15-card set features the words "Best of the along the top of the card with player action s centered on the card front with a swatch of worn memorabilia.

ell Brandon 2.00 5.00
Malone 4.00 10.00
ar Odom 3.00 8.00
ius Miles 2.00 5.00
id Robinson 5.00 12.00
is Webber 3.00 8.00
y Payton 3.00 8.00
ve Francis 3.00 8.00
mond Mason 2.50 6.00
ton Brand 3.00 8.00
awn Marion 3.00 8.00
hn Stockton 4.00 10.00
tawn Jamison 3.00 8.00
tonio McDyess 2.50 6.00
son Williams 2.50 6.00

001-02 Fleer Showcase Rival Revival

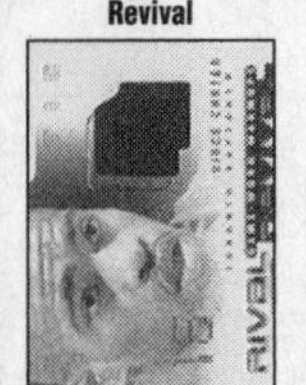

omly inserted in packs, this five card set features BA rivals with player photos and a game jersery h from each. Cards have a stated print run of 100 numbered sets.

ce Carter 10.00 25.00
cy McGrady
ce Carter 8.00 20.00
awn Jamison
ce Carter 12.50 30.00
en Iverson
id Robinson 10.00 25.00
embe Mutombo
ius Miles 8.00 20.00
yon Martin

2002-03 Fleer Showcase

Released in mid December 2002, Fleer Showcase consists of a 148-card set divided up as follows: 100 Row 3 Veteran Cards, numbers 1-100, 12 Row 2 Veteran Avant Cards, numbers 101-112, six Row 0 Veteran Avant Cards sequentially numbered to 1000, numbers 113-118, six Row 0 Rookie Avant Cards sequentially numbered to 500, numbers 119-124, and 24 Row 1 Rookie Cards sequentially numbered to 1500, card numbers 125-148. Base Row 3 and Row 1 cards have an embossed picture frame border with color's set to match the featured player's team colors with the team name, player name, and Fleer Showcase logo in bronze foil. Backgrounds are white with one-color minimalist portrait shots of players and full color action photos are set in front. Row 2 Avant cards have the embossed border and an embedded metallic photo that takes up the entire card front. Row 2 Avant Cards are highlighted with silver foil. Row 1 Avant Cards feature the same embossed border, but are cut with a glossy metallic photo of the player embedded on the left half of the card only and are highlighted with blue foil. Showcase was packaged in five card packs which carried a suggested retail price of $4.99, and boxes contained 24 packs.

COMP.SET w/o SP's (100) 12.50 30.00
UNPRICED MASTERPIECE PRINT RUN ONE SET
1 Michael Jordan 3.00 8.00
2 Shareef Abdur-Rahim .30 .75
3 Jalen Rose .30 .75
4 Antonio McDyess .30 .75
5 Malik Rose .25 .60
6 Juwan Howard .30 .75
7 Jason Williams .30 .75
8 Darrell Armstrong .25 .60
9 Karl Malone .50 1.25
10 Jason Terry .30 .75
11 David Wesley .25 .60
12 David Robinson .60 1.50
13 Gary Payton .40 1.00
14 Quentin Richardson .30 .75
15 Allan Houston .30 .75
16 Alvin Williams .25 .60
17 Jamal Mashburn .30 .75
18 Theo Ratliff .25 .60
19 Tyson Chandler .30 .75
20 Gilbert Arenas .40 1.00
21 Dikembe Mutombo .40 1.00
22 Calbert Cheaney .25 .60
23 Rodney Rogers .25 .60
24 Shane Battier .40 1.00
25 Mike Miller .40 1.00
26 John Stockton .50 1.25
27 Mengke Bateer .25 .60
28 Andre Miller .30 .75
29 Sam Cassell .30 .75
30 Anfernee Hardaway .60 1.50
31 Keith Van Horn .30 .75
32 Tony Battie .25 .60
33 Derek Fisher .30 .75
34 Grant Hill .50 1.25
35 Andrei Kirilenko .40 1.00
36 Toni Kukoc .30 .75
37 Jerry Stackhouse .30 .75
38 Latrell Sprewell .30 .75
39 Morris Peterson .25 .60
40 Darius Miles .30 .75
41 Eddie Jones .30 .75
42 Stephon Marbury .30 .75
43 Brent Barry .25 .60
44 DeShawn Stevenson .25 .60
45 Brian Grant .25 .60
46 Derrick Coleman .30 .75
47 Richard Hamilton .30 .75
48 Jason Richardson .40 1.00
49 Kerry Kittles .25 .60
50 Desmond Mason .30 .75
51 Stromile Swift .25 .60
52 Richard Jefferson .40 1.00
53 Vladimir Radmanovic .25 .60
54 Lamond Murray .25 .60
55 Troy Murphy .40 1.00
56 Kenyon Martin .40 1.00
57 Vlade Divac .30 .75
58 Chris Mihm .25 .60
59 Eddie Griffin .25 .60
60 Marc Jackson .25 .60
61 Peja Stojakovic .40 1.00
62 Vin Baker .30 .75
63 Cuttino Mobley .30 .75
64 Joe Smith .30 .75
65 Damon Stoudamire .30 .75
66 Eddy Curry .30 .75
67 Alonzo Mourning .50 1.25
68 Aaron McKie .25 .60
69 Kwame Brown .25 .60
70 Raef LaFrentz .25 .60
71 Jermaine O'Neal .40 1.00
72 Terrell Brandon .25 .60
73 Bonzi Wells .25 .60
74 Steve Nash .50 1.25
75 Jamaal Tinsley .25 .60
76 Wally Szczerbiak .30 .75
77 Scottie Pippen .60 1.50
78 Michael Finley .40 1.00
79 Reggie Miller .40 1.00
80 Glenn Robinson .30 .75
81 Rasheed Wallace .40 1.00
82 Antoine Walker .30 .75
83 Robert Horry .30 .75
84 Kurt Thomas .25 .60
85 Antonio Davis .25 .60
86 Nick Van Exel .30 .75
87 Al Harrington .30 .75
88 Tony Delk .25 .60
89 Joe Johnson .40 1.00
90 Chauncey Billups .40 1.00
91 P.J. Brown .25 .60
92 Tony Parker .50 1.25
93 Antawn Jamison .40 1.00
94 Courtney Alexander .25 .60
95 Kenny Anderson .30 .75
96 Clifford Robinson .25 .60
97 Lamar Odom .40 1.00
98 Anthony Carter .25 .60
99 Shawn Marion .40 1.00
100 Hedo Turkoglu .40 1.00
101 Paul Pierce AVANT 1.25 3.00
102 Dirk Nowitzki AVANT 1.50 4.00
103 Ben Wallace AVANT 1.00 2.50
104 Steve Francis AVANT 1.00 2.50
105 Pau Gasol AVANT 1.25 3.00
106 Ray Allen AVANT 1.00 2.50
107 Kevin Garnett AVANT 2.00 5.00
108 Jason Kidd AVANT 1.50 4.00
109 Baron Davis AVANT 1.00 2.50
110 Mike Bibby AVANT 1.00 2.50
111 Chris Webber AVANT 1.00 2.50
112 Tim Duncan AVANT 2.00 5.00
113 Kobe Bryant AVANT 8.00 20.00
114 Shaquille O'Neal AVANT 4.00 10.00
115 Tracy McGrady AVANT 2.50 6.00
116 Allen Iverson AVANT 2.50 6.00
117 Vince Carter AVANT 2.50 6.00
118 Elton Brand AVANT 1.50 4.00
119 Jay Williams AVANT RC 3.00 8.00
120 Yao Ming AVANT RC 8.00 20.00
121 Mike Dunleavy AVANT RC 3.00 8.00
122 DaJuan Wagner AVANT RC 2.50 6.00
123 Caron Butler AVANT RC 4.00 10.00
124 Drew Gooden AVANT RC 4.00 10.00
125 Manu Ginobili RC 5.00 12.00
126 Mehmet Okur RC 2.00 5.00
127 Nene Hilario RC 2.50 6.00
128 Nikoloz Tskitishvili RC 2.00 5.00
129 Tayshaun Prince RC 2.50 6.00
130 Bostjan Nachbar RC 2.00 5.00
131 Fred Jones RC 2.00 5.00
132 Melvin Ely RC 2.00 5.00
133 Chris Wilcox RC 2.00 5.00
134 Kareem Rush RC 2.00 5.00
135 Marcus Haislip RC 2.00 5.00
136 Frank Williams RC 2.00 5.00
137 Ryan Humphrey RC 2.00 5.00
138 John Salmons RC 2.50 6.00
139 Casey Jacobsen RC 2.00 5.00
140 Amare Stoudemire RC 5.00 12.00
141 Qyntel Woods RC 2.00 5.00
142 Chris Jefferies RC 2.00 5.00
143 Juan Dixon RC 2.50 6.00
144 Jared Jeffries RC 2.00 5.00
145 Lonny Baxter RC 2.00 5.00
146 Dan Dickau RC 2.00 5.00
147 Carlos Boozer RC 4.00 10.00
148 Vincent Yarbrough RC 2.00 5.00

2002-03 Fleer Showcase Legacy

Randomly inserted in packs, this 148-card set parallels the base Fleer Showcase set enhanced with gold foil and sequential numbering. Cards are serially numbered as follows: 1-100 are numbered to 100, 101-124 are numbered to 50, and 125-148 are numbered to 100.

*1-100 STARS: 5X TO 12X BASE CARD HI
*101-112 AVANT: 3X TO 8X BASE AVANT HI
*113-118 AVANT: 2X TO 5X BASE HI
*119-124 AVANT RCs: 1.5X TO 4X BASE HI
*125-148 RCs: 1.25X TO 3X BASE CARD HI

2002-03 Fleer Showcase Avant Card Materials

Randomly seeded in packs, this eight card set parallels the base Avant Card design enhanced with a swatch of jersey on the right side of the card. Each card is sequentially numbered to 202.

ACM1 Tracy McGrady 8.00 20.00
ACM2 Allen Iverson 8.00 20.00
ACM3 Vince Carter 8.00 20.00
ACM4 Elton Brand 5.00 12.00
ACM5 Yao Ming 15.00 40.00
ACM6 DaJuan Wagner 5.00 12.00
ACM7 Caron Butler 8.00 20.00
ACM8 Drew Gooden 8.00 20.00

2002-03 Fleer Showcase Avant Card SRO

Randomly seeded in packs, this 12-card set parallels the base Avant Card design enhanced with a full metallic gold background. Each card is sequentially numbered to 50, and the letters, "SRO" appear on the back of the card below the number rather than Row 2 or Row 0.

*SRO: 1.5X TO 4X BASE HI 6.00 15.00

2002-03 Fleer Showcase Basketball's Best

Randomly inserted in packs at the rate of one in eight, this 30-card set features a horizontal design where the background contains a colored wood effect towards the bottom, full color player action photos appear on the left, and the player's team logo appears in the upper right of the card. All cards have gray borders and silver foil highlights.

COMPLETE SET (30) 15.00 40.00
BB1 Vince Carter 1.00 2.50
BB2 Allen Iverson 1.00 2.50
BB3 Jason Kidd 1.00 2.50
BB4 Tracy McGrady 1.00 2.50
BB5 Ben Wallace .60 1.50
BB6 Baron Davis .60 1.50
BB7 Paul Pierce .75 2.00
BB8 Andre Miller .50 1.25
BB9 Jermaine O'Neal .60 1.50
BB10 Kevin Garnett 1.25 3.00
BB11 Pau Gasol .75 2.00
BB12 Dirk Nowitzki 1.00 2.50
BB13 Jason Terry .50 1.25
BB14 Tony Parker .75 2.00
BB15 Kobe Bryant 3.00 8.00
BB16 Mike Bibby .60 1.50
BB17 Steve Nash .75 2.00
BB18 Michael Jordan 5.00 12.00
BB19 Mike Miller .60 1.50
BB20 Kenyon Martin .60 1.50
BB21 Shareef Abdur-Rahim .50 1.25
BB22 Elton Brand .60 1.50
BB23 Grant Hill .60 1.50
BB24 Lamar Odom .75 2.00
BB25 Corey Maggette .50 1.25
BB26 Richard Jefferson .60 1.50
BB27 Keith Van Horn .50 1.25
BB28 Quentin Richardson .50 1.25
BB29 Andrei Kirilenko .60 1.50
BB30 Darius Miles .40 1.00

2002-03 Fleer Showcase Basketball's Best Memorabilia

Inserted in packs at the rate of one in 10, this 23-card set parallels the design of the base Basketball's Best insert but is enhanced with a swatch of game used memorabilia in the place of the team logo.

*GOLD: .75X TO 2X HI
GOLD: STATED PRINT RUN 100 SER.#'d SETS
BBM1 Vince Carter JSY 5.00 12.00
BBM2 Allen Iverson JSY 5.00 12.00
BBM3 Jason Kidd JSY 5.00 12.00
BBM4 Tracy McGrady Short 5.00 12.00
BBM5 Ben Wallace JSY 3.00 8.00
BBM6 Paul Pierce JSY 4.00 10.00
BBM7 Andre Miller JSY 2.50 6.00
BBM8 Jermaine O'Neal JSY 3.00 8.00
BBM9 Kevin Garnett JSY 6.00 15.00
BBM10 Jason Terry JSY 2.50 6.00
BBM11 Steve Nash JSY 4.00 10.00
BBM12 Mike Miller Short 3.00 8.00
BBM13 Kenyon Martin WU 3.00 8.00
BBM14 Shareef Abdur-Rahim Short 2.50 6.00
BBM15 Elton Brand WU 3.00 8.00
BBM16 Grant Hill Short 4.00 10.00
BBM17 Lamar Odom WU 3.00 8.00
BBM18 Corey Maggette WU 2.50 6.00
BBM19 Richard Jefferson WU 3.00 8.00
BBM20 Keith Van Horn WU 2.50 6.00
BBM21 Quentin Richardson JSY 2.50 6.00
BBM22 Andrei Kirilenko JSY 3.00 8.00
BBM23 Darius Miles Short 2.00 5.00
BAS1 Vince Carter AU/400 25.00 50.00

2002-03 Fleer Showcase Vince Carter Legacy Collection

Randomly inserted in packs, this 15-card set highlights the career of Vince Carter. Each card has brown borders, red banners along the top and bottom of the card, silver foil highlights, and sequential numbering to 1000.

COMPLETE SET (15) 20.00 50.00
COMMON CARD (VCL1-VCL15) 2.50 6.00

2002-03 Fleer Showcase Vince Carter Legacy Collection Game-Worn

Randomly seeded in packs at the rate of one in 48, this three card set utilizes the same design but is enhanced with a piece of game memorabilia.

VCG1 Vince Carter Warm 8.00 20.00
VCG2 Vince Carter JSY 10.00 25.00

2003-04 Fleer Showcase

Released in August 2003, this 130-card set is divided up into 90 veteran player cards, 10 veteran shortprints (cards 91-100) where no odds were ever given, but appear to be approximately five times tougher than regular base cards and 30 rookies sequentially numbered to 1000. Base cards feature a background black and white portrait photo with a full-color action photo in the foreground and the player's number in the lower right corner. Showcase was packaged in 16-pack boxes of five cards each and carried a suggested retail price of $5.49.

COMP.SET w/o SP's (100) 15.00 40.00
UNPRICED MASTERPIECE PRINT RUN ONE SET
1 Jason Richardson .50 1.25
2 Andrei Kirilenko .50 1.25
3 Steve Francis .50 1.25
4 Shareef Abdur-Rahim .50 1.25
5 Ben Wallace .50 1.25
6 Predrag Drobnjak .30 .75
7 Jalen Rose .40 1.00
8 Rashard Lewis .50 1.25
9 Darius Miles .30 .75
10 Bobby Jackson .30 .75
11 Steve Nash .60 1.50
12 Gilbert Arenas .50 1.25
13 Aaron McKie .30 .75
14 Reggie Miller .50 1.25
15 Elton Brand .50 1.25
16 Allan Houston .40 1.00
17 Pau Gasol .50 1.25
18 Jamaal Magloire .30 .75
19 Eddie Jones .40 1.00
20 Richard Jefferson .50 1.25
21 Wally Szczerbiak .40 1.00
22 Antonio McDyess .40 1.00
23 Michael Redd .50 1.25
24 Grant Hill .60 1.50
25 Jason Williams .40 1.00
26 Rasheed Wallace .50 1.25
27 Andre Miller .40 1.00
28 Peja Stojakovic .50 1.25
29 Cuttino Mobley .40 1.00
30 David Robinson .75 2.00
31 Richard Hamilton .40 1.00
32 Morris Peterson .30 .75
33 Karl Malone .60 1.50
34 Zydrunas Ilgauskas .40 1.00
35 Jerry Stackhouse .40 1.00
36 Eddy Curry .40 1.00
37 Sam Cassell .40 1.00
38 Troy Hudson .30 .75
39 Jason Terry .40 1.00
40 Kenyon Martin .50 1.25
41 Bonzi Wells .30 .75
42 Donnell Harvey .30 .75
43 Tracy McGrady .60 1.50
44 Allen Iverson .75 2.00
45 Jermaine O'Neal .50 1.25
46 Larry Hughes .40 1.00
47 Scottie Pippen .75 2.00
48 Antonio Davis .30 .75
49 Chris Webber .50 1.25
50 Vladimir Radmanovic .30 .75
51 Glenn Robinson .40 1.00
52 Antoine Walker .50 1.25
53 Ricky Davis .40 1.00
54 Michael Finley .50 1.25
55 Nick Van Exel .40 1.00
56 Tayshaun Prince .50 1.25
57 Antawn Jamison .50 1.25
58 Jamal Mashburn .40 1.00
59 Jamaal Tinsley .30 .75
60 Kerry Kittles .30 .75
61 Derek Fisher .40 1.00
62 Radoslav Nesterovic .30 .75
63 Mike Miller .50 1.25
64 Gary Payton .50 1.25
65 Brian Grant .30 .75
66 Baron Davis .50 1.25
67 Shane Battier .40 1.00
68 Latrell Sprewell .40 1.00
69 Keith Van Horn .40 1.00
70 Eddie Griffin .30 .75
71 Stephon Marbury .40 1.00
72 Chauncey Billups .50 1.25
73 Shawn Marion .50 1.25
74 Juwan Howard .40 1.00
75 Mike Bibby .50 1.25
76 DaJuan Wagner .30 .75
77 Tony Parker .50 1.25
78 Tyson Chandler .40 1.00
79 Ray Allen .50 1.25
80 Matt Harpring .40 1.00
81 Kwame Brown .30 .75
82 Troy Murphy .50 1.25
83 Ron Artest .50 1.25
84 Corey Maggette .40 1.00
85 Tony Delk .30 .75
86 Jamal Crawford .40 1.00
87 Vince Carter .75 2.00
88 Kevin Garnett 1.00 2.50
89 Jason Kidd .75 2.00
90 Paul Pierce .60 1.50
91 Nene SP 1.00 2.50
92 Drew Gooden SP 1.00 2.50
93 Caron Butler SP 1.25 3.00
94 Manu Ginobili SP 1.50 4.00
95 Dirk Nowitzki SP 2.00 5.00
96 Yao Ming SP 2.50 6.00
97 Amare Stoudemire SP 2.00 5.00
98 Kobe Bryant SP 6.00 15.00
99 Tim Duncan SP 2.00 5.00
100 Shaquille O'Neal SP 3.00 8.00
101 T.J. Ford RC 2.50 6.00
102 Chris Bosh RC 4.00 10.00
103 Boris Diaw RC 2.50 6.00
104 Luke Ridnour RC 2.50 6.00
105 Zoran Planinic RC 2.00 5.00
106 Josh Howard RC 2.00 5.00
107 Darko Milicic RC 2.00 5.00
108 Dahntay Jones RC 2.00 5.00
109 Mike Sweetney RC 2.00 5.00
110 Kirk Hinrich RC 2.50 6.00
111 Marcus Banks RC 2.00 5.00
112 Travis Outlaw RC 2.50 6.00
113 Brian Cook RC 2.00 5.00
114 Mario Austin RC 2.00 5.00
115 Dwyane Wade RC 8.00 20.00
116 Chris Kaman RC 2.50 6.00
117 Zarko Cabarkapa RC 2.00 5.00
118 Ndudi Ebi RC 2.00 5.00
119 Mickael Pietrus RC 2.00 5.00
120 Carmelo Anthony RC 5.00 12.00
121 Kendrick Perkins RC 3.00 8.00
122 Troy Bell RC 2.00 5.00
123 Maciej Lampe RC 2.00 5.00
124 Carlos Delfino RC 2.50 6.00
125 Leandro Barbosa RC 2.50 6.00
126 Sofoklis Schortsanitis RC 2.00 5.00
127 Reece Gaines RC 2.00 5.00
128 Nick Collison RC 2.00 5.00
129 David West RC 2.50 6.00
130 LeBron James RC 30.00 60.00

2003-04 Fleer Showcase Legacy

Randomly inserted in packs, this 130-card set parallels the base Fleer Showcase set enhanced with sequential numbering to 125.

*LEGACY SINGLES: 2.5X TO 6X BASE HI
*LEGACY SPs: 1.25X TO 3X BASE HI
*LEGACY RCs: 1.25X TO 3X BASE HI
98 Kobe Bryant 40.00 100.00

2003-04 Fleer Showcase Basketball's Best

Inserted in packs at the rate of one in 24, this 10-card set features a horizontal design with colored borders along the top and bottom and a white midde. Player black and white portraits appear on the left and a full color player action photo is centered.

COMPLETE SET (10) 8.00 20.00
1 Shaquille O'Neal 2.50 6.00
2 Amare Stoudemire 1.50 4.00
3 Jermaine O'Neal 1.00 2.50
4 Tim Duncan 1.50 4.00
5 Jason Richardson 1.00 2.50
6 Steve Francis 1.00 2.50
7 Ben Wallace 1.00 2.50
8 Chris Webber 1.00 2.50
9 DaJuan Wagner .60 1.50
10 Yao Ming 2.00 5.00

2003-04 Fleer Showcase Basketball's Best Memorabilia

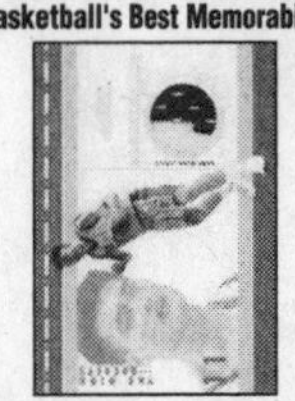

Randomly seeded, this 25-card set parallels the design of the Basketball's Best insert enhanced with a circular swatch of jersey on the right side of the card. A gold version was also inserted and these cards are sequentially numbered to 50.

*GOLD: 1.25X TO 3X BEST MEM.HI
1 Yao Ming 5.00 12.00
2 Steve Francis 2.50 6.00
3 Amare Stoudemire 4.00 10.00
4 Elton Brand 2.50 6.00
5 Paul Pierce 3.00 8.00
6 Tracy McGrady 3.00 8.00
7 Allen Iverson 4.00 10.00
8 Dirk Nowitzki 4.00 10.00
9 Antawn Jamison 2.50 6.00
10 Drew Gooden 2.00 5.00
11 DaJuan Wagner 2.00 5.00
12 David Robinson 4.00 10.00
13 Jermaine O'Neal 2.50 6.00
14 Stephon Marbury 2.00 5.00
15 Kevin Garnett 5.00 12.00
16 Jason Kidd 4.00 10.00
17 Vince Carter 4.00 10.00
18 Karl Malone 3.00 8.00
19 Tony Parker 2.50 6.00
20 Peja Stojakovic 2.50 6.00
21 Reggie Miller 2.50 6.00
22 Jason Richardson 2.50 6.00
23 Ray Allen 2.50 6.00
24 Jerry Stackhouse 2.00 5.00
25 Latrell Sprewell 2.00 5.00

2003-04 Fleer Showcase Hot Hands

Inserted at the rate of one in 288, this 10-card set places a full-color player action photo against the backdrop of a player's hands around an NBA basketball.

COMPLETE SET (10) 20.00 40.00
1 Tracy McGrady 3.00 8.00
2 Kobe Bryant 12.00 30.00
3 Allen Iverson 4.00 10.00
4 Dirk Nowitzki 4.00 10.00
5 Jason Kidd 4.00 10.00
6 Vince Carter 4.00 10.00
7 Steve Francis 2.50 6.00
8 Paul Pierce 3.00 8.00
9 Jason Richardson 2.50 6.00
10 Amare Stoudemire 4.00 10.00

2003-04 Fleer Showcase Hot Hands Game-Used

Randomly seeded, this 15-card set parallels the design of the base Hot Hands insert set enhanced with a swatch of game used memorabilia and sequential numbering to 375.

1 Tracy McGrady 4.00 10.00
2 Allen Iverson 5.00 12.00
3 Dirk Nowitzki 5.00 12.00
4 Jason Kidd 5.00 12.00
5 Vince Carter 5.00 12.00
6 Jerry Stackhouse 2.50 6.00
7 Paul Pierce 4.00 10.00
8 Stephon Marbury 2.50 6.00
9 Steve Francis 3.00 8.00
10 Peja Stojakovic 3.00 8.00
11 Caron Butler 3.00 8.00
12 Reggie Miller 3.00 8.00
13 Jason Richardson 3.00 8.00
14 Ray Allen 3.00 8.00
15 Amare Stoudemire 5.00 12.00

2003-04 Fleer Showcase Sweet Sigs

Randomly seeded and sequentially numbered, this 18-card set features a horizontal design with a small player portrait style photo in the upper right hand corner of the card and a centered embedded cut signature.

SGAM Amare Stoudemire/300 15.00 40.00
SGBC Brian Cook/800 4.00 10.00
SGCA Carmelo Anthony/400 25.00 50.00
SGEC Eddy Curry/540 4.00 10.00
SGJO Jermaine O'Neal/760 6.00 15.00
SGKB Kwame Brown/390 4.00 10.00
SGKM Kenyon Martin/690 6.00 15.00
SGMG Manu Ginobili/555 10.00 25.00
SGMP Mickael Pietrus/800 4.00 10.00
SGMS Mike Sweetney/800 4.00 10.00
SGPS Peja Stojakovic/760 6.00 15.00
SGSA Shareef Abdur-Rahim/760 4.00 10.00
SGSF Steve Francis/760 6.00 15.00
SGTB Troy Bell/800 4.00 10.00
SGTJ Dahntay Jones/800 4.00 10.00
SGTM Tracy McGrady/380 12.50 30.00
SGTP Tayshaun Prince/760 5.00 12.00

2003-04 Fleer Showcase Sweet Stitch

Inserted in packs at the rate of one in 12, this 10-card set features a centered full-color player portrait style photo framed by an NBA Basketball background.

COMPLETE SET (10) 6.00 15.00
1 Yao Ming 1.25 3.00
2 Kevin Garnett 1.25 3.00
3 Kobe Bryant 3.00 8.00
4 Elton Brand .60 1.50
5 DaJuan Wagner .40 1.00
6 Karl Malone .75 2.00
7 Antawn Jamison .60 1.50
8 Stephon Marbury .50 1.25
9 Michael Finley .60 1.50
10 Drew Gooden .50 1.25
11 David Robinson 1.00 2.50

2003-04 Fleer Showcase Sweet Stitch Game-Used

Inserted in packs randomly at the rate of one in 13, this 10-card set parallels the design of the base Sweet Stitch insert set enhanced with a skinny rectangular jersey swatch below the picture. A patch version was also inserted and is sequentially numbered to 50.

*PATCHES: 1.25X TO 3X GAME USE HI
1 Yao Ming 5.00 12.00
2 Kevin Garnett 5.00 12.00
4 Elton Brand 2.50 6.00
5 DaJuan Wagner 2.00 5.00
6 Karl Malone 3.00 8.00
7 Antawn Jamison 2.50 6.00
8 Stephon Marbury 2.00 5.00
9 Michael Finley 2.50 6.00
10 Drew Gooden 2.00 5.00

2004-05 Fleer Showcase

Released in August 2004, Fleer Showcase's base set consists of 120 cards, where cards 1-90 feature veteran players anc cards 91-120 feature rookies that are randomly numbered to either 199, 499 or 699. Base cards are printed on foil board and feature a head-shot photo of the player in the background and a full-color action photo in the foreground. Flair was packaged in both Hobby and Retail formats with Hobby boxes containing 16 packs of five cards each and retail containing 24 packs of four cards each.

COMP.SET w/o SP's (90) 15.00 40.00
UNPRICED MASTERPIECE PRINT RUN ONE SET
1 Kirk Hinrich .30 .75
2 Shaquille O'Neal .75 2.00
3 Allen Iverson .50 1.25
4 Carlos Arroyo .25 .60
5 Darko Milicic .20 .50
6 Sam Cassell .25 .60
7 Peja Stojakovic .30 .75
8 Ben Wallace .30 .75
9 T.J. Ford .25 .60
10 Chris Webber .30 .75
11 LeBron James 2.00 5.00
12 Karl Malone .40 1.00
13 Glenn Robinson .25 .60
14 Jarvis Hayes .20 .50
15 Bob Sura .20 .50
16 Yao Ming .60 1.50
17 Baron Davis .30 .75

18 Rashard Lewis .30 .75
19 Carlos Boozer .30 .75
20 Pau Gasol .30 .75
21 Tim Duncan .50 1.25
22 Gilbert Arenas .30 .75
23 Dajuan Wagner .20 .50
24 Bonzi Wells .20 .50
25 Dirk Nowitzki .50 1.25
26 Jason Williams .25 .60
27 Amare Stoudemire .40 1.00
28 Gerald Wallace .30 .75
29 Corey Maggette .25 .60
30 Tim Thomas .20 .50
31 Andrei Kirilenko .25 .60
32 Steve Nash .40 1.00
33 Caron Butler .30 .75
34 Shawn Marion .30 .75
35 Michael Finley .30 .75
36 Dwyane Wade 1.00 2.50
37 Joe Johnson .30 .75
38 Carmelo Anthony .60 1.50
39 Lamar Odom .30 .75
40 Darius Miles .20 .50
41 Mike Dunleavy .25 .60
42 Jason Kidd .50 1.25
43 Manu Ginobili .40 1.00
44 Jason Richardson .30 .75
45 Latrell Sprewell .25 .60
46 Willie Green .20 .50
47 Theron Smith .20 .50
48 Elton Brand .30 .75
49 Tracy McGrady .40 1.00
50 Matt Harpring .25 .60
51 Eddy Curry .25 .60
52 Chris Kaman .30 .75
53 Drew Gooden .25 .60
54 Stephen Jackson .25 .60
55 Mickael Pietrus .25 .60
56 Kenyon Martin .30 .75
57 Tony Parker .30 .75
58 Paul Pierce .40 1.00
59 Cuttino Mobley .25 .60
60 Jamal Mashburn .30 .75
61 Luke Ridnour .25 .60
62 Jamal Crawford .25 .60
63 Kobe Bryant 1.50 4.00
64 Keith Bogans .20 .50
65 Jerry Stackhouse .25 .60
66 Ricky Davis .25 .60
67 Jermaine O'Neal .30 .75
68 Jamaal Magloire .20 .50
69 Vince Carter .50 1.25
70 Jason Kapono .20 .50
71 Ron Artest .30 .75
72 Allan Houston .25 .60
73 Chris Bosh .30 .75
74 Rasheed Wallace .30 .75
75 Kevin Garnett .60 1.50
76 Mike Bibby .30 .75
77 Jason Terry .25 .60
78 Steve Francis .30 .75
79 Richard Jefferson .30 .75
80 Ray Allen .30 .75
81 Andre Miller .25 .60
82 Desmond Mason .25 .60
83 Zach Randolph .25 .60
84 Marcus Banks .20 .50
85 Reggie Miller .30 .75
86 Stephon Marbury .25 .60
87 Jalen Rose .25 .60
88 Nene .25 .60
89 Michael Redd .30 .75
90 Shareef Abdur-Rahim .25 .60
91 Emeka Okafor/199 RC 8.00 20.00
92 Jameer Nelson/199 RC 6.00 15.00
93 Dwight Howard/199 RC 15.00 40.00
94 Josh Smith/199 RC 8.00 20.00
95 Pavel Podkolzine/699 RC 2.00 5.00
96 Shaun Livingston/199 RC 5.00 12.00
97 Andre Iguodala/199 RC 8.00 20.00
98 Luol Deng/199 RC 8.00 20.00
99 Delonte West/699 RC 2.50 6.00
100 Andris Biedrins/699 RC 2.50 6.00
101 Sasha Vujacic/499 RC 2.50 6.00
102 Kris Humphries/499 RC 2.50 6.00
103 Ben Gordon/199 RC 6.00 15.00
104 Robert Swift/499 RC 2.50 6.00
105 Al Jefferson/499 RC 4.00 10.00
106 Sergei Monia/499 RC 2.50 6.00
107 Devin Harris/499 RC 4.00 10.00
108 Luke Jackson/499 RC 2.50 6.00
109 Anderson Varejao/499 RC 3.00 8.00
110 Sebastian Telfair/199 RC 5.00 12.00
111 Josh Childress/199 RC 5.00 12.00
112 J.R. Smith/499 RC 3.00 8.00
113 Viktor Khryapa/699 RC 2.00 5.00
114 Rafael Araujo/499 RC 2.50 6.00
115 Dorell Wright/499 RC 4.00 10.00
116 Ha Seung-Jin/699 RC 2.00 5.00
117 Tony Allen/699 RC 2.50 6.00
118 Kirk Snyder/699 RC 2.00 5.00
119 Chris Duhon/699 RC 2.00 5.00
120 Beno Udrih/699 RC 2.00 5.00

2004-05 Fleer Showcase Legacy

Randomly seeded in packs, this 120-card set parallels the base Fleer Showcase set enhanced with gold foil highlights and sequential numbering to 125. A Masterpiece one of one parallel was also produced.
*LEGACY SINGLES: 4X TO 10X BASE HI
*RC/199: .3X TO .75X BASE CARD HI
*RC/499: .6X TO 1.5X BASE CARD HI
*RC/699: .75X TO 2X BASE CARD HI
11 LeBron James 30.00 80.00
63 Kobe Bryant 30.00 60.00

2004-05 Fleer Showcase Feature Film

Inserted in packs, this 15-card set is horizontally designed with a white background on the left and a film cell of the player on the right. Each card is sequentially numbered to 50. Two patch parallels were also issued for this set. Both feature premium jersey patch swatches with one serially numbered to 25 and the other numbered to 10.
1 Allen Iverson 12.00 30.00
2 Kobe Bryant 40.00 100.00
3 Vince Carter 12.00 30.00
4 Kevin Garnett 15.00 40.00
5 LeBron James 50.00 125.00
6 Carmelo Anthony 15.00 40.00
7 Tracy McGrady 10.00 25.00
8 Shaquille O'Neal 20.00 50.00
9 Tim Duncan 12.00 30.00
10 Yao Ming 15.00 40.00
11 Jason Kidd 12.00 30.00
12 Karl Malone 10.00 25.00
13 Amare Stoudemire 10.00 25.00
14 Chris Bosh 8.00 20.00
15 Ray Allen 8.00 20.00

2004-05 Fleer Showcase Hot Hands

Seeded in Hobby packs at the rate of one in 192 and Retail at the rate of one in 480, this 15-card set is die cut in the shape of a flame where full-color player action photos are centered.
*PATCH: .6X TO 1.5X BASE HI
PATCH PRINT RUN 50 SER.#'d SETS
UNPRICED PATCH PAR.PRINT RUN 15 SETS
1 Yao Ming 20.00 50.00
2 Shaquille O'Neal 25.00 60.00
3 LeBron James 60.00 150.00
4 Carmelo Anthony 20.00 50.00
5 Dwyane Wade 30.00 80.00
6 Vince Carter 15.00 40.00
7 Kobe Bryant 50.00 125.00
8 Tim Duncan 15.00 40.00
9 Baron Davis 10.00 25.00
10 Manu Ginobili 12.00 30.00
11 Ron Artest 10.00 25.00
12 Ben Wallace 10.00 25.00
13 Andrei Kirilenko 8.00 20.00
14 Mike Bibby 10.00 25.00
15 Allen Iverson 15.00 40.00

2004-05 Fleer Showcase Playmakers

Inserted in packs at the rate of one in four for Hobby and one in eight for Retail, this 20-card set features a gray background, colors to match the player's team along the bottom and lower left and right sides and an action photo.
COMPLETE SET (20) 10.00 25.00
1 Jermaine O'Neal .50 1.25
2 Gary Payton .50 1.25
3 Kenyon Martin .50 1.25
4 Tony Parker .50 1.25
5 Chris Bosh .50 1.25
6 Dwyane Wade 1.50 4.00
7 Ben Wallace .50 1.25
8 Jason Kidd .75 2.00
9 Tracy McGrady .60 1.50
10 Kevin Garnett 1.00 2.50
11 Kobe Bryant 2.50 6.00
12 LeBron James 3.00 8.00
13 Paul Pierce .60 1.50
14 Stephon Marbury .40 1.00
15 Manu Ginobili .60 1.50
16 Amare Stoudemire .60 1.50
17 Reggie Miller .50 1.25
18 Dirk Nowitzki .75 2.00
19 Jason Richardson .50 1.25
20 Steve Francis .50 1.25

2004-05 Fleer Showcase Playmakers Jerseys

Inserted in Hobby packs at the rate of one in 96 and Retail packs at the rate of one in 26, this 18-card set parallels the Playmakers set enhanced with a jersey swatch in the lower left hand corner. Four parallel sets were issued, a Jersey version featuring silver foil and sequential numbering to 300, a Jersey version featuring gold foil and sequential numbering to 100 and a Jeresy version featuring a name plate swatch and sequential numbering to 50. There is also a one of one masterpiece.
*JERSEY 300: .5X TO 1.25X BASE JSY HI
*JERSEY 100: .6X TO 1.5X BASE JSY HI
AS Amare Stoudemire 3.00 8.00
BW Ben Wallace 2.50 6.00
CB Chris Bosh 2.50 6.00
DN Dirk Nowitzki 4.00 10.00
DW Dwyane Wade 8.00 20.00
GP Gary Payton 2.50 6.00
JK Jason Kidd 4.00 10.00
JO Jermaine O'Neal 2.50 6.00
JR Jason Richardson 2.50 6.00
KG Kevin Garnett 5.00 12.00
KM Kenyon Martin 2.50 6.00
MG Manu Ginobili 3.00 8.00
PP Paul Pierce 3.00 8.00
RM Reggie Miller 2.50 6.00
SF Steve Francis 2.50 6.00
SM Stephon Marbury 2.00 5.00
TM Tracy McGrady 3.00 8.00
TP Tony Parker 2.50 6.00

2004-05 Fleer Showcase Playmakers Jerseys Nameplates

Randomly inserted in packs, this 18-card set parallels the base Playmakers Jerseys set enhanced with a swatch of jersey from the player's name plate and sequential numbering to 50.
*NAMEPLATE: 1X TO 2.5X BASE JSY HI
RM Reggie Miller 10.00 25.00

2004-05 Fleer Showcase Playmakers Jerseys Numbers

Randomly inserted in packs, this 18-card set parallels the base Playmakers Jerseys but is sequentially numbered to the featured player's jersey number.
SOME NOT PRICED DUE TO SCARCITY
AS Amare Stoudemire/32 15.00 40.00
DN Dirk Nowitzki/41 10.00 25.00
GP Gary Payton/20 10.00 25.00
JR Jason Richardson/23 10.00 25.00
MG Manu Ginobili/20 10.00 25.00
PP Paul Pierce/34 10.00 25.00
RM Reggie Miller/31 12.50 30.00

2004-05 Fleer Showcase Playmakers Jerseys Win Total

Randomly inserted in packs, this 18-card set parallels the base Playmakers Jerseys but is sequentially numbered to the teams win total from the previous season.
AS Amare Stoudemire/29 6.00 15.00
BW Ben Wallace/54 5.00 12.00
CB Chris Bosh/33 5.00 12.00
DN Dirk Nowitzki/52 8.00 20.00
DW Dwyane Wade/42 15.00 40.00
GP Gary Payton/56 5.00 12.00
JK Jason Kidd/47 8.00 20.00
JO Jermaine O'Neal/61 5.00 12.00
JR Jason Richardson/37 5.00 12.00
KG Kevin Garnett/58 10.00 25.00
KM Kenyon Martin/47 5.00 12.00
MG Manu Ginobili/57 6.00 15.00
PP Paul Pierce/36 6.00 15.00
RM Reggie Miller/61 5.00 12.00
SF Steve Francis/45 5.00 12.00
SM Stephon Marbury/39 4.00 10.00
TM Tracy McGrady/21 6.00 15.00
TP Tony Parker/57 5.00 12.00

2004-05 Fleer Showcase Signatures

Randomly inserted, this set is horizontally designed with a player photo on the left above a cut signature. Silver foil lines run along a strip through the middle of the card, and these are sequentially numbered to 150 unless noted in the checklist. A Blue foil parallel was also issued, in which cards are sequentially numbered to either 75 or 99.
*BLUE: .5X TO 1.25X BASE SIG HI
AM Andre Miller/150 4.00 10.00
AV Anderson Varejao/150 5.00 12.00
BG Ben Gordon/150 10.00 25.00
CA Carmelo Anthony/150 15.00 40.00
CB Carlos Boozer/150 4.00 10.00
CD Chris Duhon/150 4.00 10.00
CD Carlos Delfino/150 4.00 10.00
CM Corey Maggette/150 4.00 10.00
DH Devin Harris/150 6.00 15.00
DM Darius Miles/150 4.00 10.00
DW Dwyane Wade/150 30.00 80.00
DW2 Dorell Wright/150 6.00 15.00
DW3 David West/150 4.00 10.00
GP Gary Payton/112 10.00 25.00
HS Ha Seung-Jin/150 4.00 10.00
JC Josh Childress/150 4.00 10.00
JH Josh Howard/150 4.00 10.00
JK Jason Kidd/150 10.00 25.00
JN Jameer Nelson/150 8.00 20.00
JO Jermaine O'Neal/150 6.00 15.00
JS Jerry Stackhouse/150 4.00 10.00
JS Josh Smith/150 12.50 30.00
KB Kwame Brown/150 4.00 10.00
KH Kris Humphries/150 4.00 10.00
KS Kirk Snyder/150 4.00 10.00
LD Luol Deng/150 8.00 20.00
LJ Luke Jackson/150 4.00 10.00
LO Lamar Odom/150 5.00 12.00
MB Mike Bibby/150 5.00 12.00
PP Pavel Podkolzine/150 4.00 10.00
PS Peja Stojakovic/100 8.00 20.00
RA Rafael Araujo/150 4.00 10.00
SL Shaun Livingston/150 4.00 10.00
SM Shawn Marion/150 6.00 15.00
ST Sebastian Telfair/150 4.00 10.00
TB Troy Bell/150 4.00 10.00
TP Tony Parker/71 6.00 15.00
VC Vince Carter/150 10.00 25.00
CBO Chris Bosh/150 6.00 15.00
DJW Dajuan Wagner/150 4.00 10.00
JRS J.R. Smith/150 10.00 25.00

2004-05 Fleer Showcase Signatures Jerseys

PRINT RUNS LISTED BELOW
SOME UNPRICED DUE TO SCARCITY
UNPRICED PATCH PRINT RUN ONE SET
AS Amare Stoudemire/32 20.00 50.00
CA Carmelo Anthony/15 40.00 100.00
DM Darius Miles/23 10.00 25.00
GP Gary Payton/20 25.00 60.00
JS Jerry Stackhouse/42 10.00 25.00
SM Shawn Marion/31 12.50 30.00

2004-05 Fleer Showcase Supreme Showcase

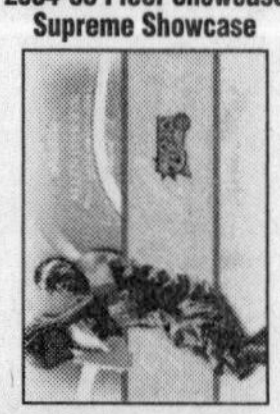

Inserted in Hobby packs at the rate of one in 16 and Retail packs at the rate of one in 24, this 24-card set utilizes a design similar to that of the Signatures set.
COMPLETE SET (20) 10.00 25.00
1 Carmelo Anthony 1.25 3.00
2 Yao Ming 1.25 3.00
3 Carlos Boozer .60 1.50
4 Vince Carter 1.00 2.50
5 Dwyane Wade 2.00 5.00
6 Dirk Nowitzki 1.00 2.50
7 Josh Howard .60 1.50
8 Steve Francis .60 1.50
9 Paul Pierce .75 2.00
10 Amare Stoudemire .75 2.00
11 Peja Stojakovic .60 1.50
12 Shaquille O'Neal 1.50 4.00
13 Tim Duncan 1.00 2.50
14 Kevin Garnett 1.25 3.00
15 Stephon Marbury .50 1.25
16 Tracy McGrady .75 2.00
17 Allen Iverson 1.00 2.50
18 Ray Allen .60 1.50
19 Ben Wallace .60 1.50
20 Jason Kidd 1.00 2.50

2004-05 Fleer Showcase Supreme Showcase Jerseys

Randomly inserted in packs, this 20-card set parallels the base Supreme Showcase set enhanced with a swatch of jersey and sequential numbering to 300. Several different parallel versions were produced for this set: Jerseys numbered to 100, All-Star numbered to 45, All-Star patches numbered to 10 and master piece one of ones.
*JERSEY 100: .5X TO 1.25X BASE JSY HI
*JERSEY ALL-STAR: .6X TO 1.5X BASE JSY HI
*JERSEY POINTS: .6X TO 1.5X BASE HI
POINTS PRINT RUN 19 TO 62 SETS
AI Allen Iverson 4.00 10.00
AS Amare Stoudemire 3.00 8.00
BW Ben Wallace 2.50 6.00
CA Carmelo Anthony 5.00 12.00
CB Carlos Boozer 2.50 6.00
DN Dirk Nowitzki 4.00 10.00
DW Dwyane Wade 8.00 20.00
JH Josh Howard 2.50 6.00
JK Jason Kidd 4.00 10.00
KG Kevin Garnett 5.00 12.00
PP Paul Pierce 3.00 8.00
PS Peja Stojakovic 2.50 6.00
RA Ray Allen 2.50 6.00
SF Steve Francis 2.50 6.00
SM Stephon Marbury 2.00 5.00
SO Shaquille O'Neal 6.00 15.00
TD Tim Duncan 4.00 10.00
TM Tracy McGrady 3.00 8.00
VC Vince Carter 4.00 10.00
YM Yao Ming 5.00 12.00

2004-05 Fleer Showcase Supreme Showcase Jerseys Numbers

Randomly inserted in packs, this 20-card set parallels the base Supreme Showcase Jerseys set enhanced with sequential numbering to the player's jersey number.
*NUMBER PATCH: 1X TO 2.5X BASE HI
SOME NOT PRICED DUE TO SCARCITY
AS Amare Stoudemire/32 8.00 20.00
DN Dirk Nowitzki/41 10.00 25.00
KG Kevin Garnett/21 12.00 30.00
PP Paul Pierce/34 8.00 20.00
RA Ray Allen/34 10.00 25.00
SO Shaquille O'Neal/32 15.00 40.00
VC Vince Carter/15 10.00 25.00

1996-97 Fleer Sprite

This 40-card set was issued as a dual promotion for Fleer/SkyBox and Sprite available exclusively through 7-Eleven convenience stores. For a limited time, with each purchase of Sprite customers received a free pack containing 3 cards from the set along with a checklist (with Grant Hill on the front) and a $.25 coupon on any Fleer or SkyBox product. Randomly inserted was a 10-card Hill tribute set that is listed after the base set. The cards are identical to the 1996-97 Fleer design, except the gold foil text is in yellow and the numbering is different on the back. Notable first year cards of Allen Iverson, Kobe Bryant, Stephon Marbury, Antoine Walker, Shareef Abdur-Rahim and Kerry Kittles.
COMPLETE SET (40) 15.00 40.00
1 Dikembe Mutombo .50 1.25
2 Steve Smith .40 1.00
3 Antoine Walker 1.25 3.00
4 Anthony Mason .30 .75
5 Toni Kukoc .50 1.25
6 Terrell Brandon .30 .75
7 Jim Jackson .30 .75
8 Jason Kidd .75 2.00
9 Oliver Miller .30 .75
10 Antonio McDyess .50 1.25
11 Grant Hill .75 2.00
12 Joe Smith .40 1.00
13 Charles Barkley .75 2.00
14 Clyde Drexler .60 1.50
15 Reggie Miller .60 1.50
16 Brent Barry .40 1.00
17 Kobe Bryant 6.00 15.00
18 Nick Van Exel .50 1.25
19 Alonzo Mourning .60 1.50
20 Ray Allen 2.50 6.00
21 Vin Baker .40 1.00
22 Kevin Garnett 1.25 3.00
23 Stephon Marbury 1.50 4.00
24 Kerry Kittles .60 1.50
25 Patrick Ewing .60 1.50
26 Larry Johnson .50 1.25
27 Anfernee Hardaway .75 2.00
28 Allen Iverson 3.00 8.00
29 Arvydas Sabonis .40 1.00
30 Mitch Richmond .50 1.25
31 Vinny Del Negro .30 .75
32 Gary Payton .50 1.25
33 Detlef Schrempf .50 1.25
34 Marcus Camby 1.00 2.50
35 Damon Stoudamire .50 1.25
36 Karl Malone .60 1.50
37 John Stockton .60 1.50
38 Shareef Abdur-Rahim 1.25 3.00
39 Juwan Howard .40 1.00
40 Chris Webber .60 1.50
NNO Grant Hill Checklist .40 1.00

1996-97 Fleer Sprite Grant Hill

Randomly inserted into packs of Fleer Sprite, this 10-card set features action shots of Fleer/SkyBox Spokesman Grant Hill. The fronts dawn the Fleer/SkyBox logo in the upper-left corner and Sprite and NBA logos in the bottom-left. Card backs have "Grant Hill Special Issue" in yellow letters at the top followed by themed biographical information. The cards are numbered as "X of 10".
COMPLETE SET (10) 4.00 10.00
COMMON CARD (1-10) .60 1.50

1996-97 Fleer Sprite Australian

This 40 card set is very similar to the 96-97 Fleer Sprite issue. The cards were released with Sprite and other than numbering differences are the same as the American Fleer issue.
COMPLETE SET (40) 40.00 80.00
1 Kenny Anderson 1.25 3.00
2 Chris Mills 1.00 2.50
3 Antonio McDyess 1.50 4.00
4 Joe Smith 1.25 3.00
5 Vin Baker 1.25 3.00
6 Ed O'Bannon 1.00 2.50
7 Anfernee Hardaway 2.50 6.00
8 Kevin Johnson 1.50 4.00
9 Mitch Richmond 1.50 4.00
10 Detlef Schrempf 1.50 4.00
11 John Stockton 2.00 5.00
12 Glen Rice 1.50 4.00
13 Clyde Drexler 2.00 5.00
14 Vlade Divac 1.50 4.00
15 Derek Harper 1.25 3.00
16 Charles Barkley 2.50 6.00
17 Hersey Hawkins 1.00 2.50
18 Karl Malone 2.00 5.00
19 Chris Webber 2.00 5.00
20 Alonzo Mourning 2.00 5.00
21 Clarence Weatherspoon 1.00 2.50
22 Dino Radja 1.25 3.00
23 Scottie Pippen 2.50 6.00
24 Jason Kidd 2.50 6.00
25 Grant Hill 2.50 6.00
26 Sam Cassell 1.25 3.00
27 Brian Williams 1.00 2.50
28 Tom Gugliotta 1.00 2.50
29 John Starks 1.25 3.00
30 Clifford Robinson 1.00 2.50
31 David Robinson 2.50 6.00
32 Damon Stoudamire 1.50 4.00
33 Greg Anthony 1.00 2.50
34 Toni Kukoc 1.50 4.00
35 Christian Laettner 1.25 3.00
36 Rik Smits 1.25 3.00
37 Tim Hardaway 1.50 4.00
38 Nick Anderson 1.00 2.50
39 Sean Elliott 1.50 4.00
40 Juwan Howard 1.25 3.00

2004-05 Fleer Sweet Sigs

Released in October 2004, the Sweet Sigs base showcases veteran players on cards 1-75 and rookies on cards 76-100 which are sequentially numbered to 999. Base cards feature a centered action photo with tan borders and red highlights. Sweet Sigs also marks the first product with Shaquille O'Neal in a Miami Heat jersey. Sweet Sigs was packaged for bot Hobby and retail where both featured six cards per pack, but hobby boxes had 12 packs and retail boxes had 24.
COMP.SET w/o SP's (75) 15.00 40.00
1 Kirk Hinrich .30 .75
2 Ron Artest .30 .75
3 T.J. Ford .25 .60
4 Stephon Marbury .25 .60
5 Antawn Jamison .30 .75
6 Jason Richardson .30 .75
7 Dwyane Wade 1.00 2.50
8 Shawn Marion .30 .75
9 Jermaine O'Neal .30 .75
10 Ricky Davis .25 .60
11 Richard Hamilton .25 .60
12 Karl Malone .40 1.00
13 Jason Williams .25 .60
14 Lamar Odom .30 .75
15 Allan Houston .25 .60
16 Allen Iverson .50 1.25
17 Peja Stojakovic .30 .75
18 Jarvis Hayes .20 .50
19 Stephen Jackson .25 .60
20 Richard Jefferson .30 .75
21 Jahidi White .20 .50
22 Carmelo Anthony .60 1.50
23 Baron Davis .30 .75
24 Dajuan Wagner .20 .50
25 Nene .25 .60
26 Ben Wallace .30 .75
27 Latrell Sprewell .25 .60
28 Ray Allen .30 .75
29 Andrei Kirilenko .25 .60
30 Antoine Walker .30 .75
31 Marcus Banks .20 .50
32 Pau Gasol .30 .75
33 Tony Parker .30 .75
34 Vince Carter .50 1.25
35 Mike Bibby .30 .75
36 Jim Jackson .20 .50
37 Shaquille O'Neal .75 2.00
38 Bonzi Wells .20 .50
39 Paul Pierce .40 1.00
40 Jason Kapono .20 .50
41 Reggie Miller .30 .75
42 Drew Gooden .25 .60
43 Shareef Abdur-Rahim .25 .60
44 Chris Bosh .30 .75
45 Steve Nash .40 1.00
46 Elton Brand .30 .75
47 Kevin Garnett .60 1.50
48 Kenyon Martin .30 .75
49 Jamal Crawford .25 .60
50 Dirk Nowitzki .50 1.25
51 Yao Ming .60 1.50
52 Jamaal Magloire .20 .50
53 Tim Duncan .50 1.25
54 Gilbert Arenas .30 .75
55 Steve Francis .30 .75
56 Corey Maggette .25 .60
57 Caron Butler .30 .75
58 Michael Redd .30 .75
59 Kyle Korver .25 .60
60 Amare Stoudemire .40 1.00
61 Carlos Boozer .30 .75
62 Darko Milicic .20 .50
63 Kobe Bryant 1.50 4.00
64 Tracy McGrady .40 1.00
65 Zach Randolph .25 .60
66 Luke Ridnour .25 .60
67 Carlos Arroyo .25 .60
68 Michael Finley .30 .75
69 Mickael Pietrus .25 .60
70 Darius Miles .20 .50
71 Chris Webber .30 .75
72 Eddy Curry .25 .60
73 Jason Kidd .50 1.25
74 Manu Ginobili .40 1.00
75 LeBron James 2.00 5.00
76 Emeka Okafor RC 2.50 6.00
77 Rafael Araujo RC 1.50 4.00
78 Andre Iguodala RC 2.50 6.00
79 Kris Humphries RC 1.50 4.00
80 Kevin Martin RC 2.00 5.00
81 Delonte West RC 2.00 5.00
82 Pavel Podkolzine RC 1.50 4.00
83 Al Jefferson RC 2.50 6.00
84 Shaun Livingston RC 1.50 4.00
85 Luke Jackson RC 1.50 4.00
86 Dorell Wright RC 2.50 6.00
87 Andris Biedrins RC 2.00 5.00
88 Sasha Vujacic RC 1.50 4.00
89 Jameer Nelson RC 2.00 5.00
90 Dwight Howard RC 5.00 12.00
91 Robert Swift RC 1.50 4.00
92 Josh Childress RC 1.50 4.00
93 Luol Deng RC 2.50 6.00
94 J.R. Smith RC 2.00 5.00
95 Kirk Snyder RC 1.50 4.00
96 Josh Smith RC 2.50 6.00
97 Devin Harris RC 2.50 6.00
98 Viktor Khryapa RC 1.50 4.00
99 Ben Gordon RC 2.00 5.00
100 Sebastian Telfair RC 1.50 4.00

2004-05 Fleer Sweet Sigs Parallel

Randomly inserted in packs, this 100-card set parallels the base set enhanced with gold foil highlights and blue around the outside border. Each card is sequentially numbered to 99. A Position parallel set was also inserted and is numbered from one to five based on what position is played by the athlete.
*1-75 PAR.SINGLES: 2X TO 5X BASE HI
*76-100 PAR.RC's: 1X TO 2X BASE HI

2004-05 Fleer Sweet Sigs Autographs

Randomly seeded, this 51-card set is horizontally designed with white borders and a clouded sky background. A small oval with a player portrait photo above a signed swatch of basketball. Each card is individually numbered with print runs listed in the checklist. Masterpiece one of ones were inserted also.
N Nene/200 4.00 10.00
AB Andris Biedrins/200 5.00 12.00
AJ Al Jefferson/200 15.00 40.00
AS Amare Stoudemire/200 8.00 20.00
AW Antoine Walker/50 10.00 25.00
BG Ben Gordon/200 15.00 30.00
CA Carmelo Anthony/150 20.00 50.00
CB Chris Bosh/150 8.00 20.00
DH Devin Harris/200 6.00 15.00
DW Dwyane Wade/150 30.00 80.00
EB Elton Brand/100 6.00 15.00
EC Eddy Curry/200 4.00 10.00
GA Gilbert Arenas/150 4.00 10.00
GP Gary Payton/50 12.50 30.00
JC Josh Childress/200 4.00 10.00
JH Josh Howard/200 4.00 10.00
JK Jason Kidd/50 15.00 40.00
JN Jameer Nelson/200 8.00 20.00
JS Jerry Stackhouse/150 6.00 15.00
KS Kirk Snyder/200 4.00 10.00
LD Luol Deng/150 10.00 25.00
LJ Luke Jackson/200 4.00 10.00
LO Lamar Odom/150 6.00 15.00
MB Mike Bibby/150 10.00 25.00
MD Mike Dunleavy/200 4.00 10.00
MS Mike Sweetney/200 4.00 10.00
PP Paul Pierce/50 15.00 40.00
RJ Richard Jefferson/200 4.00 10.00
RS Robert Swift/140 4.00 10.00
SF Steve Francis/50 8.00 20.00
SL Shaun Livingston/200 4.00 10.00
SM Stephon Marbury/50 8.00 20.00
ST Sebastian Telfair/200 4.00 10.00
TM Tracy McGrady/50 15.00 40.00
VC Vince Carter/150 12.50
YT Yuta Tabuse/149 25.00
ZR Zach Randolph/200 4.00
CAB Caron Butler/200 4.00
DAV David West/150 4.00
DEL Delonte West/150 6.00
DOR Dorell Wright/150 6.00
HSJ Ha Seung-Jin/99 4.00
JAS Jason Richardson/200 4.00
JON Jermaine O'Neal/100 10.00
JOS Josh Smith/200 10.00
JRS J.R. Smith/200 10.00
KEY Kenyon Martin/200 6.00
PAV Pavel Podkolzine/200 4.00
RAF Rafael Araujo/200 4.00
TAY Tayshaun Prince/200 6.00
TJF T.J. Ford/150 4.00

2004-05 Fleer Sweet Sigs Autographs Draft Pick

Randomly inserted in packs, this 50-card set para[llels] the base Autographs set enhanced with sequential numbering to match the player's draft pick numbe[r].
MOST NOT PRICED DUE TO SCARCITY
AJ Al Jefferson/15 40.00
JH Josh Howard/29 10.00
ZR Zach Randolph/19 10.00
DEL Delonte West/24 15.00
DOR Dorell Wright/19 15.00
HSJ Ha Seung-Jin/46 10.00
JON Jermaine O'Neal/17 15.00
JOS Josh Smith/17 20.00
JRS J.R. Smith/18 25.00

2004-05 Fleer Sweet Sigs Autographs Draft Year

Randomly inserted in packs, this 50-card set para[llels] the base Autographs set enhanced with gold foil highlights and sequential numbering to match the player's draft year. Anything after 2000 is marked just a single number.
MOST NOT PRICED DUE TO SCARCITY
AW Antoine Walker/96 8.00
EB Elton Brand/99 8.00
GP Gary Payton/90 12.00
JK Jason Kidd/94 12.50
JS Jerry Stackhouse/95 8.00
LO Lamar Odom/99 8.00
MB Mike Bibby/98 12.50
PP Paul Pierce/98 12.50
SF Steve Francis/99 8.00
SM Stephon Marbury/96 8.00
TM Tracy McGrady/97 12.50
VC Vince Carter/98 15.00
JON Jermaine O'Neal/96 10.00

2004-05 Fleer Sweet Sigs Hardcourt Heroics

Randomly inserted in Hobby and Retail packs at th[e] rate of one in six, this 25-card set features a horiz[ontal] design with a basketball court in the background. Player photos appear on the right side and the ca[rd is] highlighted with red foil.
COMPLETE SET (25) 10.00
1 Vince Carter .60
2 Kevin Garnett .75
3 Carmelo Anthony .75
4 Ben Wallace .40
5 Steve Francis .40
6 Richard Hamilton .30
7 Paul Pierce .50
8 Kobe Bryant 2.00
9 Chris Webber .40
10 Jason Richardson .40
11 Stephon Marbury .30
12 Jermaine O'Neal .40
13 Shaquille O'Neal 1.00
14 Allen Iverson .60
15 Tony Parker .40
16 Dwyane Wade 1.25
17 Mike Bibby .40
18 Tracy McGrady .50
19 Pau Gasol .40
20 Dirk Nowitzki .60
21 Tim Duncan .60
22 Jason Kidd .60
23 Yao Ming .75
24 Amare Stoudemire .50
25 LeBron James 2.50

2004-05 Fleer Sweet Sigs Hardcourt Heroics Jerseys

Randomly inserted, this 20-card set parallels the Hardcourt Heroics set enhanced with a square sw[atch] of jersey in the lower left corner and silver foil highlights. Cards are sequentially numbered to va[rious] amounts.
AI Allen Iverson/250 4.00
BW Ben Wallace 2.50
CA Carmelo Anthony/184 5.00
DN Dirk Nowitzki/35 8.00
DW Dwyane Wade 8.00
JK Jason Kidd/215 4.00
JO Jermaine O'Neal/74 2.50
KG Kevin Garnett/223 5.00
MB Mike Bibby/55 2.50
PG Pau Gasol/110 2.50
PP Paul Pierce/250 3.00
SF Steve Francis/40 8.00
SM Stephon Marbury/175 2.00
SO Shaquille O'Neal/200 6.00
TD Tim Duncan/124 4.00

TM Tracy McGrady/235 3.00 8.00
VC Vince Carter 4.00 10.00
YM Yao Ming/35 10.00 25.00

2004-05 Fleer Sweet Sigs Hardcourt Heroics Jerseys Retail

Randomly inserted at one in 24 Retail packs, this 20-card set parallels the base Hardcourt Heroics set enhanced with a square swatch of jersey in the lower left corner and red foil highlights.
*RETAIL: .4X TO 1X BASE HI 2.00 5.00

2004-05 Fleer Sweet Sigs Hardcourt Heroics Jerseys Dual

Randomly inserted, this 20-card set parallels the base Hardcourt Heroics set enhanced with two players and two square swatches of jersey. Cards are numbered to varying amounts.
MOST NOT PRICED DUE TO SCARCITY
CP Vince Carter/29 20.00 50.00
Paul Pierce
FW Steve Francis/18 20.00 50.00
Dwyane Wade
GA Kevin Garnett/25 20.00 50.00
Carmelo Anthony
MK Stephon Marbury/22 20.00 50.00
Jason Kidd

2004-05 Fleer Sweet Sigs Hardcourt Heroics Jerseys Quad

Randomly inserted, this 20-card set parallels the base Hardcourt Heroics set enhanced with four players and four jerseys. Cards are numbered to varying amounts.
MOST NOT PRICED DUE TO SCARCITY
BPGA Mike Bibby/42 25.00 60.00
Tony Parker
Kevin Garnett
Carmelo Anthony
MCP Allen Iverson/28 40.00 100.00
Tracy McGrady
Vince Carter
Paul Pierce
NOG Chris Webber/33 40.00 80.00
Dirk Nowitzki
Jermaine O'Neal
Pau Gasol

2004-05 Fleer Sweet Sigs Hardcourt Heroics Patches

Randomly inserted, this 20-card set parallels the base Hardcourt Heroics set enhanced with a square swatch jersey patch in the lower left corner and gold foil highlights. Each card is sequentially numbered to 50.
*PATCH: 1.25X TO 3X BASE HI
UNPRICED MASTERPIECE PRINT RUN ONE SET
Allen Iverson 20.00 50.00
Yao Ming 15.00 40.00

2004-05 Fleer Sweet Sigs Hardcourt Heroics Patches Black

Randomly inserted, this 20-card set parallels the base Hardcourt Heroics set enhanced with a square swatch jersey patch in the lower left corner and black foil highlights. The cards are numbered to varying amounts

MOST NOT PRICED DUE TO SCARCITY
Ben Wallace/35 8.00 20.00
Carmelo Anthony/15 15.00 40.00
Dirk Nowitzki/34 12.00 30.00
Kevin Garnett/21 15.00 40.00
Tim Duncan/21 12.00 30.00
Tracy McGrady/32 10.00 25.00

2004-05 Fleer Sweet Sigs Sweet Stitches Jerseys

Randomly inserted in packs, this 30-card set places a player action photo on the right of the card and a faded basketball in the background on the left. In the lower hand corner of the card there is a circular swatch of jersey. The cards are numbered to varying amounts.
SOME NOT PRICED DUE TO SCARCITY
Nene/19 4.00 10.00
Allan Houston/123 2.00 5.00
Amare Stoudemire/159 3.00 8.00
Chris Bosh/175 2.50 6.00
Chris Webber/129 3.00 8.00
Dirk Nowitzki/115 4.00 10.00
Dwyane Wade/137 8.00 20.00
Eddy Curry/113 2.00 5.00
Gilbert Arenas/89 2.50 6.00
Jason Kidd/136 4.00 10.00
Jason Richardson/64 2.50 6.00
Jerry Stackhouse/114 2.00 5.00
Kevin Garnett/95 5.00 12.00
Karl Malone/113 3.00 8.00
Latrell Sprewell/26 10.00 25.00
Pau Gasol/174 2.50 6.00
Richard Hamilton/103 2.00 5.00
Richard Jefferson/143 2.50 6.00
Steve Francis/26 10.00 25.00
Stephon Marbury/101 2.00 5.00
Steve Nash/132 3.00 8.00
Shaquille O'Neal/151 6.00 15.00
Tim Duncan/163 4.00 10.00
Tracy McGrady/171 3.00 8.00
Yao Ming/152 5.00 12.00

2004-05 Fleer Sweet Sigs Sweet Stitches Jerseys Retail

Randomly inserted in Retail packs at the rate of one in ... this 30-card set parallels the base Sweet Stitches Jerseys set enhanced with red foil highlights.
Nene SP 2.00 5.00
Allan Houston 2.00 5.00
Amare Stoudemire SP 3.00 8.00
Ben Wallace 2.50 6.00
Carmelo Anthony SP 5.00 12.00
Chris Bosh SP 2.50 6.00
Corey Maggette 2.00 5.00
Chris Webber 2.50 6.00
Dirk Nowitzki 4.00 10.00
Dwyane Wade 8.00 20.00
Eddy Curry 2.00 5.00
Gilbert Arenas 2.50 6.00
Jason Kidd 4.00 10.00
JR Jason Richardson SP 2.50 6.00
JS Jerry Stackhouse 2.00 5.00
KG Kevin Garnett 5.00 12.00
KM Karl Malone SP 3.00 8.00
LS Latrell Sprewell 2.00 5.00
MG Manu Ginobili 3.00 8.00
PG Pau Gasol SP 2.50 6.00
RH Richard Hamilton 2.00 5.00
RJ Richard Jefferson 2.50 6.00
SF Steve Francis SP 2.50 6.00
SM Stephon Marbury 2.00 5.00
SN Steve Nash 3.00 8.00
SO Shaquille O'Neal 6.00 15.00
TD Tim Duncan 4.00 10.00
TM Tracy McGrady 3.00 8.00
VC Vince Carter SP 4.00 10.00
YM Yao Ming SP 5.00 12.00

2004-05 Fleer Sweet Sigs Sweet Stitches Patches

Randomly inserted in packs, this 30-card set parallels the base Sweet Stitches Jerseys set enhanced with a patch swatch, gold foil and sequential numbering to 50.
*PATCH: 1X TO 2.5X BASE HI
UNPRICED MASTERPIECE PRINT RUN ONE SET
N Nene 5.00 12.00
BW Ben Wallace 6.00 15.00
CA Carmelo Anthony 12.00 30.00
CM Corey Maggette 5.00 12.00
CW Chris Webber 10.00 25.00
LS Latrell Sprewell 5.00 12.00
MG Manu Ginobili 8.00 20.00
SF Steve Francis 6.00 15.00
VC Vince Carter 10.00 25.00

2004-05 Fleer Sweet Sigs Sweet Stitches Patches Black

Randomly inserted in packs, this 30-card set parallels the base Sweet Stitches Jerseys set enhanced with a patch swatch, black foil and all cards are sequentially numbered to varying amounts.
SOME NOT PRICED DUE TO SCARCITY
N Nene/40 5.00 12.00
AS Amare Stoudemire/17 10.00 25.00
BW Ben Wallace/42 6.00 15.00
CA Carmelo Anthony/44 12.00 30.00
CB Chris Bosh/19 8.00 20.00
DN Dirk Nowitzki/28 12.00 30.00
GA Gilbert Arenas/40 6.00 15.00
JK Jason Kidd/33 10.00 25.00
JR Jason Richardson/36 6.00 15.00
JS Jerry Stackhouse/28 6.00 15.00
KG Kevin Garnett/35 12.00 30.00
KM Karl Malone/23 10.00 25.00
LS Latrell Sprewell/38 5.00 12.00
MG Manu Ginobili/41 8.00 20.00
PG Pau Gasol/27 8.00 20.00
RH Richard Hamilton/18 6.00 15.00
RJ Richard Jefferson/43 6.00 15.00
SF Steve Francis/36 6.00 15.00
SM Stephon Marbury/39 5.00 12.00
SO Shaquille O'Neal/31 20.00 50.00
TD Tim Duncan/23 12.00 30.00
TM Tracy McGrady/26 10.00 25.00
VC Vince Carter/15 12.00 30.00

2004-05 Fleer Sweet Sigs Sweet Stitches Jerseys Quad

Randomly inserted and numbered to varying amounts, this 10-card set features four players and four swatches of jersey and resembles the design of the base Sweet Stitches Jerseys set.
PRINT RUNS LISTED BELOW
SOME NOT PRICED DUE TO SCARCITY
ANGS Carmelo Anthony/30 40.00 80.00
Nene
Kevin Garnett
Latrell Sprewell
BCAS Chris Bosh/33 25.00 60.00
Vince Carter
Gilbert Arenas
Jerry Stackhouse
MFDG Yao Ming/18 40.00 80.00
Steve Francis
Tim Duncan
Manu Ginobili
MODG Karl Malone/31 50.00 100.00
Shaquille O'Neal
Tim Duncan
Manu Ginobili
MSGA Tracy McGrady/25 20.00 50.00
Amare Stoudemire
Kevin Garnett
Carmelo Anthony

2004-05 Fleer Sweet Sigs Sweet Stroke

Inserted in both Hobby and Retail packs at the rate of one in 12, this 15-card set places players in shooting poses on a tan and brown bordered card with red lettering for the player's name.
COMPLETE SET (15) 8.00 20.00
1 Dwyane Wade 1.50 4.00
2 Allen Iverson .75 2.00
3 Peja Stojakovic .50 1.25
4 Tony Parker .50 1.25
5 Ray Allen .50 1.25
6 Reggie Miller .50 1.25
7 Kevin Garnett 1.00 2.50
8 Dirk Nowitzki .75 2.00
9 Tim Duncan .75 2.00
10 Kobe Bryant 2.50 6.00
11 Tracy McGrady .60 1.50
12 Michael Finley .50 1.25
13 LeBron James 3.00 8.00
14 Baron Davis .50 1.25
15 Steve Nash .60 1.50

2004-05 Fleer Sweet Sigs Sweet Stroke Jerseys

Randomly seeded, this 12-card set parallels the look of the base Sweet Stroke Jerseys set enhanced with a square swatch of jersey in the lower left corner. Cards are sequentially numbered to varying amounts.
AI Allen Iverson/143 4.00 10.00
BD Baron Davis/224 2.50 6.00
DW Dwyane Wade/250 6.00 15.00
KG Kevin Garnett/197 5.00 12.00
MF Michael Finley/21 6.00 15.00
PS Peja Stojakovic/216 2.50 6.00
RA Ray Allen/238 2.50 6.00
RM Reggie Miller/163 2.50 6.00
SN Steve Nash/15 8.00 20.00
TD Tim Duncan/99 4.00 10.00
TM Tracy McGrady/200 3.00 8.00
TP Tony Parker/112 2.50 6.00

2004-05 Fleer Sweet Sigs Sweet Stroke Jerseys Retail

Randomly inserted in Retail packs at the rate of one in 108, this 12-card set parallels the base Sweet Stroke Jerseys set enhanced with red foil highlights.
*RETAIL: .4X TO 1X BASE HI 2.00 5.00

2004-05 Fleer Sweet Sigs Sweet Stroke Jerseys Quad

Randomly inserted, this six card set utilizes the look of the Sweet Stroke insert but combines four players and four jerseys. The cards are sequentially numbered to varying amounts.
MIGD Tracy McGrady/35 40.00 100.00
Allen Iverson
Kevin Garnett
Baron Davis
WAMM Dwyane Wade/29 30.00 80.00
Tracy McGrady
Reggie Miller
Ray Allen
WIMB Dwyane Wade/35 30.00 80.00
Allen Iverson
Reggie Miller
Baron Davis

2004-05 Fleer Sweet Sigs Sweet Stroke Patches

Randomly inserted in packs, this 12-card set parallels the base Sweet Stroke Jerseys set enhanced with a patch swatch, gold foil and sequential numbering to 50.
*PATCH: 1X TO 2.5X BASE HI
UNPRICED MASTERPIECE PRINT RUN ONE SET
DW Dwyane Wade 20.00 50.00
RM Reggie Miller 12.50 30.00

2004-05 Fleer Sweet Sigs Sweet Stroke Patches Black

Randomly inserted in packs, this 12-card set parallels the base Sweet Stroke Jerseys set enhanced with two patch swatches, black foil and all cards are sequentially numbered to varying amounts.
SOME NOT PRICED DUE TO SCARCITY
AI Allen Iverson/37 12.00 30.00
BD Baron Davis/69 6.00 15.00
DW Dwyane Wade/19 25.00 60.00
KG Kevin Garnett/21 15.00 40.00
RA Ray Allen/59 6.00 15.00
RM Reggie Miller/31 12.50 30.00
TD Tim Duncan/32 12.00 30.00
TM Tracy McGrady/62 8.00 20.00
TP Tony Parker/29 8.00 20.00

2004-05 Fleer Throwbacks

Released in March 2005, Fleer Throwbacks boasts a 100-card set featuring 65 veteran player cards, 11 rookies serially numbered to 50 (cards 66-76) and 24 rookie jersey cards serially numbered to 499. Base cards have a colored border with black horizontal stripes and rookie jersey cards have a square swatch of jersey centered towards the bottom of the card. Both Hobby and Retal packs contain five cards and Hobby boxes contain 15 packs while Retail boxes have 24.
COMP.SET w/o RC's (65) 15.00 40.00
UNPRICED ONE OF ONE PARALLEL EXISTS
1 Baron Davis .30 .75
2 Willie Green .20 .50
3 Allen Iverson .50 1.25
4 Jason Williams .25 .60
5 Kevin Garnett .60 1.50
6 Jason Richardson .30 .75
7 Lamar Odom .30 .75
8 Ben Wallace .30 .75
9 Steve Nash .40 1.00
10 Kobe Bryant 1.50 4.00
11 Kenyon Martin .30 .75
12 Jermaine O'Neal .30 .75
13 Tracy McGrady .40 1.00
14 Darko Mililic .20 .50
15 Pau Gasol .30 .75
16 Darius Miles .20 .50
17 Ray Allen .30 .75
18 Michael Redd .30 .75
19 Chris Bosh .30 .75
20 Peja Stojakovic .30 .75
21 Tim Duncan .50 1.25
22 Corey Maggette .25 .60
23 LeBron James 2.00 5.00
24 Antoine Walker .30 .75
25 Stephon Marbury .25 .60
26 Carlos Boozer .30 .75
27 Jason Kapono .20 .50
28 Grant Hill .40 1.00
29 Mike Bibby .30 .75
30 Jamaal Magloire .20 .50
31 Rashard Lewis .30 .75
32 Jason Kidd .50 1.25
33 Al Harrington .25 .60
34 Steve Francis .30 .75
35 Kirk Hinrich .30 .75
36 Amare Stoudemire .40 1.00
37 Gilbert Arenas .30 .75
38 Allan Houston .25 .60
39 Eddy Curry .25 .60
40 Latrell Sprewell .25 .60
41 Mickael Pietrus .25 .60
42 Zach Randolph .25 .60
43 Shaquille O'Neal .75 2.00
44 Jason Terry .25 .60
45 Richard Hamilton .25 .60
46 Karl Malone .40 1.00
47 Elton Brand .30 .75
48 Richard Jefferson .30 .75
49 Andrei Kirilenko .25 .60
50 Reggie Miller .30 .75
51 Yao Ming .60 1.50
52 Gary Payton .30 .75
53 Dirk Nowitzki .50 1.25
54 Dwyane Wade 1.00 2.50
55 Carmelo Anthony .60 1.50
56 Tony Parker .30 .75
57 T.J. Ford .25 .60
58 Vince Carter .50 1.25
59 Paul Pierce .40 1.00
60 Drew Gooden .25 .60
61 Antawn Jamison .30 .75
62 Manu Ginobili .40 1.00
63 Chris Webber .30 .75
64 Shawn Marion .30 .75
65 Jerry Stackhouse .25 .60
66 Andris Biedrins RC 4.00 10.00
67 Robert Swift RC 3.00 8.00
68 Pavel Podkolzin RC 3.00 8.00
69 Kevin Martin RC 4.00 10.00
70 Beno Udrih RC 3.00 8.00
71 David Harrison RC 3.00 8.00
72 Victor Khryapa RC 3.00 8.00
73 Jackson Vroman RC 3.00 8.00
74 Emeka Okafor RC 5.00 12.00
75 Andre Emmett RC 3.00 8.00
76 Andres Nocioni RC 3.00 8.00
77 Dwight Howard JSY RC 8.00 20.00
78 Ben Gordon JSY RC 3.00 8.00
79 Shaun Livingston JSY RC 2.50 6.00
80 Devin Harris JSY RC 4.00 10.00
81 Josh Childress JSY RC 2.50 6.00
82 Luol Deng JSY RC 4.00 10.00
83 Rafael Araujo JSY RC 2.50 6.00
84 Andre Iguodala JSY RC 4.00 10.00
85 Luke Jackson JSY RC 2.50 6.00
86 Sebastian Telfair JSY RC 2.50 6.00
87 Kris Humphries JSY RC 2.50 6.00
88 Al Jefferson JSY RC 4.00 10.00
89 Kirk Snyder JSY RC 2.50 6.00
90 Josh Smith JSY RC 4.00 10.00
91 J.R. Smith JSY RC 3.00 8.00
92 Dorell Wright JSY RC 4.00 10.00
93 Jameer Nelson JSY RC 3.00 8.00
94 Chris Duhon JSY RC 2.50 6.00
95 Delonte West JSY RC 3.00 8.00
96 Tony Allen JSY RC 3.00 8.00
97 Anderson Varejao JSY RC 3.00 8.00
98 Lionel Chalmers JSY RC 2.50 6.00
99 Bernard Robinson JSY RC 2.50 6.00
100 Trevor Ariza JSY RC 2.50 6.00

2004-05 Fleer Throwbacks 100

Randomly inserted in packs, this 100-card set parallels the base Fleer Throwbacks set enhanced with sequential numbering to 100. Other parallels numbered to 50, 25 and one of ones were produced.
*1-65 SINGLES: 2X TO 5X BASE HI

2004-05 Fleer Throwbacks 50

Randomly inserted in packs, this 100-card set parallels the base Fleer Throwbacks set enhanced with sequential numbering to 50.
*1-65 SINGLES: 3X TO 8X BASE HI

2004-05 Fleer Throwbacks 25

Randomly inserted in packs, this 100-card set parallels the base Fleer Throwbacks set enhanced with sequential numbering to 25.
*1-65 SINGLES: 6X TO 15X BASE HI
*66-76 SINGLES: .75X TO 2X BASE
*77-100 SINGLES: 1X TO 2.5X BASE HI

2004-05 Fleer Throwbacks Defining Authentic

Inserted in Hobby packs at the rate of one in 15 and retail packs at the rate of one in 24, these cards place faded color action photos on a bordered card.
COMPLETE SET (22) 12.50 30.00
1 Shaquille O'Neal 1.50 4.00
2 Tim Duncan 1.00 2.50
3 Tracy McGrady .75 2.00
4 Vince Carter 1.00 2.50
5 Yao Ming 1.25 3.00
6 Allen Iverson 1.00 2.50
7 Amare Stoudemire .75 2.00
8 Carmelo Anthony 1.25 3.00
9 Jason Kidd 1.00 2.50
10 Jermaine O'Neal .60 1.50
11 Jason Richardson .60 1.50
12 Kevin Garnett 1.25 3.00
13 Paul Pierce .75 2.00
14 Peja Stojakovic .60 1.50
15 Dirk Nowitzki 1.00 2.50
16 Kenyon Martin .60 1.50
17 Dwyane Wade 2.00 5.00
18 Steve Francis .60 1.50
19 Kobe Bryant 3.00 8.00
20 LeBron James 4.00 10.00

2004-05 Fleer Throwbacks Defining Authentic Jerseys

Randomly inserted in packs, this 20-card set parallels the design of the base Defining Authentc set enhanced with a square swatch of jersey in the lower left hand corner. Several parallel versions of this set were issued and break down as follows: Jerseys 99 are sequentially numbered to 99, Jersey one of ones and Jersey/Patch cards sequentially numbered to 25,
*JERSEY 99: .5X TO 1.25X BASE HI
*JERSEY/PATCH: 1.25X TO 3X BASE HI
AI Allen Iverson 4.00 10.00
AS Amare Stoudemire 3.00 8.00
CA Carmelo Anthony 5.00 12.00
DN Dirk Nowitzki 4.00 10.00
DW Dwyane Wade 6.00 15.00
JK Jason Kidd 4.00 10.00
JO Jermaine O'Neal 2.50 6.00
JR Jason Richardson 2.50 6.00
KG Kevin Garnett 5.00 12.00
KM Kenyon Martin 2.50 6.00
PP Paul Pierce 3.00 8.00
PS Peja Stojakovic 2.50 6.00
SF Steve Francis 2.50 6.00
SM Stephon Marbury 2.00 5.00
SN Steve Nash 3.00 8.00
SO Shaquille O'Neal 6.00 15.00
TD Tim Duncan 4.00 10.00
TM Tracy McGrady 3.00 8.00
VC Vince Carter 4.00 10.00
YM Yao Ming 5.00 12.00

2004-05 Fleer Throwbacks Defining Authentic Jerseys Dual

Randomly inserted in packs, this 15-card set parallels the design of the base Defining Authentic Jerseys set with two players and two swatches of Jersey. Each card is sequentially numbered to 99. One of ones were also inserted in packs. Jersey and Patch cards were printed as well and two versions exist, one serially numbered to 25 and the other done in a one of one format.
1 Yao Ming 8.00 20.00
Tim Duncan
2 Tracy McGrady 8.00 20.00
Vince Carter
3 Stephon Marbury 8.00 20.00
Allen Iverson
4 Jason Kidd 8.00 20.00
Paul Pierce
5 Allen Iverson 10.00 25.00
Vince Carter
7 Dirk Nowitzki 8.00 20.00
Peja Stojakovic
8 Amaré Stoudemire 8.00 20.00
Steve Nash
9 Jason Kidd 6.00 15.00
Kenyon Martin
10 Tracy McGrady 6.00 15.00
Steve Francis
11 Shaquille O'Neal 15.00 40.00
Dwyane Wade
12 Carmelo Anthony 6.00 15.00
Kenyon Martin
13 Tracy McGrady 8.00 20.00
Yao Ming
14 Carmelo Anthony 10.00 25.00
Dwyane Wade
15 Shaquille O'Neal 8.00 20.00
Jermaine O'Neal

2004-05 Fleer Throwbacks Defining Authentic Jerseys and Patch Dual

Randomly inserted in packs, this 20-card set parallels the design of the base Defining Authentc set enhanced with two players, two square swatches of jersey and is sequentially numbered to 25.
UNPRICED ONE OF ONE's EXIST
AM Carmelo Anthony 25.00 60.00
Kenyon Martin
DG Tim Duncan 30.00 80.00
Kevin Garnett
KM Jason Kidd 25.00 60.00
Kenyon Martin
KP Jason Kidd 25.00 60.00
Paul Pierce
MC Tracy McGrady 30.00 80.00
Vince Carter
MD Yao Ming 25.00 60.00
Tim Duncan
MF Tracy McGrady 25.00 60.00
Steve Francis
MI Stephon Marbury 25.00 60.00
Allen Iverson
MM Tracy McGrady 25.00 60.00
Yao Ming
NS Dirk Nowitzki 30.00 80.00
Peja Stojakovic
OO Shaquille O'Neal 30.00 80.00
Jermaine O'Neal
OW Shaquille O'Neal 40.00 100.00
Dwyane Wade
SN Amaré Stoudemire 25.00 60.00
Steve Nash

2004-05 Fleer Throwbacks Defining Authentic Jerseys Autographs

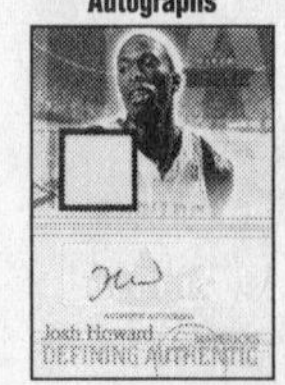

Randomly inserted in packs, this 30-card set parallels the design of the base Defining Authentc set enhanced with a square swatch of jersey and an autograph where cards are sequentially numbered to between 149 and 449.
UNPRICED PARALLEL PRINT RUN ONE SET
AJ Al Jefferson/149 10.00 25.00
BG Ben Gordon/249 8.00 20.00
CB Chauncey Billups/149 8.00 20.00
CD Chris Duhon/249 6.00 15.00
DH Devin Harris/149 10.00 25.00
DW2 Delonte West/149 8.00 20.00
EC Eddy Curry/249 6.00 15.00
GA Gilbert Arenas/199 6.00 15.00
JH Josh Howard/249 6.00 15.00
JS2 J.R. Smith/249 8.00 20.00
MD Marquis Daniels/249 6.00 15.00
NC Nick Collison/249 6.00 15.00
RA Rafael Araujo/449 6.00 15.00
TA Tony Allen/249 8.00 20.00
TF T.J. Ford/149 6.00 15.00
VC Vince Carter/249 15.00 40.00
YT Yuta Tabuse/449 12.00 30.00

2004-05 Fleer Throwbacks Defining Authentic Jerseys Autographs Numbers

Randomly inserted in packs, this 30-card set parallels the design of the base Defining Authentc set enhanced with a square swatch of jersey and an autograph where cards are numbered to the featured players jersey number.
MOST UNPRICED DUE TO SCARCITY
CA Carmelo Anthony/15 40.00 100.00
DH Devin Harris/34 15.00 40.00
JS Josh Smith/42 25.00 60.00
JS2 J.R. Smith/23 20.00 50.00
LJ Luke Jackson/33 12.50 30.00
RA Rafael Araujo/55 10.00 25.00

2004-05 Fleer Throwbacks Defining Authentic Jerseys Autographs Silver

Randomly inserted in packs, this 30-card set parallels the design of the base Defining Authentc set enhanced with a square swatch of jersey and an autograph and cards are numbered randomly. See checklist for print runs.
SOME NOT PRICED DUE TO SCARCITY
AJ Al Jefferson/50 20.00 50.00
BG Ben Gordon/50 15.00 40.00
CA Carmelo Anthony/50 25.00 60.00
CB Chauncey Billups/50 10.00 25.00
CD Chris Duhon/149 10.00 25.00
DH Devin Harris/50 15.00 40.00
DW Dwyane Wade/25 75.00 150.00
DW2 Delonte West/50 12.00 30.00
EC Eddy Curry/50 8.00 20.00
GA Gilbert Arenas/50 8.00 20.00
JH Josh Howard/149 8.00 20.00
JK Jason Kidd/25 20.00 50.00
JO Jermaine O'Neal/25 12.00 30.00
JR Jason Richardson/50
JS2 J.R. Smith/50 12.00 30.00
KM Kenyon Martin/25 20.00 50.00
LD Luol Deng/25 30.00 80.00
NC Nick Collison/149 8.00 20.00
RA Rafael Araujo/199 8.00 20.00
SL Shaun Livingston/50 10.00 25.00
SM Stephon Marbury/25 20.00 50.00
TA Tony Allen/199 12.00 30.00
TF T.J. Ford/50 8.00 20.00
VC Vince Carter/99 15.00 40.00
YT Yuta Tabuse/149 20.00 50.00

2004-05 Fleer Throwbacks Hardwood Classics

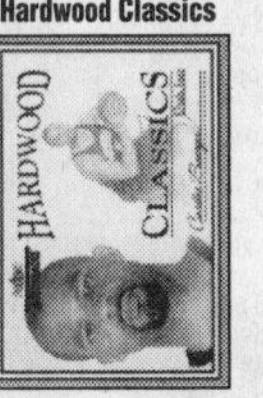

Randomly inserted in Hobby packs at the rate of one in 90 and Retail at the rate of one in 288, this 15-card set is horizontally designed with a white background and a full color player portrait head shot on the left and a black and white full body shot on the right.
COMPLETE SET (15) 15.00 40.00
1 Elton Brand 2.00 5.00
2 Lamar Odom 2.00 5.00
3 Carlos Boozer 2.00 5.00
4 Andrei Kirilenko 1.50 4.00
5 Zach Randolph 1.50 4.00
6 Darius Miles 1.25 3.00
7 Ben Wallace 2.00 5.00
8 Richard Hamilton 1.50 4.00
9 Pau Gasol 2.00 5.00
10 Chris Bosh 2.00 5.00
11 Baron Davis 2.00 5.00
12 Mike Bibby 2.00 5.00
13 Manu Ginobili 2.50 6.00
14 Tony Parker 2.00 5.00
15 Richard Jefferson 2.00 5.00

2004-05 Fleer Throwbacks Hardwood Classics Jerseys

Randomly inserted in packs, this 22-card set parallels the design of the base Hardwood Classics set enhanced with a swatch of jersey and sequential numbering to 99. A one of one version was also produced and inserted.
AK Andrei Kirilenko 2.50 6.00
BD Baron Davis 3.00 8.00
BW Ben Wallace 3.00 8.00
CB Carlos Boozer 3.00 8.00
CB Charles Barkley 40.00 100.00
CB Chris Bosh 3.00 8.00
DM Darius Miles 2.00 5.00
DR David Robinson 15.00 40.00
IT Isiah Thomas 8.00 20.00
KA Kareem Abdul-Jabbar 10.00 25.00
LB Larry Bird 40.00 80.00
LE Lamar Odom 3.00 8.00
MB Mike Bibby 3.00 8.00
MG Manu Ginobili 4.00 10.00
PE Patrick Ewing 15.00 40.00
PG Pau Gasol 3.00 8.00
RH Richard Hamilton 2.50 6.00
RJ Richard Jefferson 3.00 8.00
WF Walt Frazier 10.00 25.00
ZR Zach Randolph 2.50 6.00

2004-05 Fleer Throwbacks Hardwood Classics Jerseys and Patch

Randomly inserted in packs, this 22-card set parallels the design of the base Hardwood Classics set enhanced with two swatches of memorabilia and sequential numbering to the featured player's jersey number.
MOST NOT PRICED DUE TO SCARCITY
1 Elton Brand/42 8.00 20.00
4 Andrei Kirilenko/47 6.00 15.00
5 Zach Randolph/50 6.00 15.00
6 Darius Miles/23 6.00 15.00
8 Richard Hamilton/32 6.00 15.00
9 Pau Gasol/16 12.50 30.00
16 Kareem Abdul-Jabbar/33 25.00 60.00
17 Charles Barkley/34 75.00 150.00
18 David Robinson/50 20.00 50.00
21 Larry Bird/33 30.00 80.00
22 Patrick Ewing/33 25.00 60.00
23 Scottie Pippen/33 30.00 80.00

2004-05 Fleer Throwbacks Hardwood Classics Jerseys Dual

Randomly inserted in packs, this 22-card set parallels the design of the base Hardwood Classics set enhanced with two players and two swatches of jersey. Each card is serially numbered to 50. One of one Jerseys Dual cards were inserted along with Patches Dual serially numbered to 25.
*PATCH DUAL: .75X TO 2X BASE HI
BB Carlos Boozer 6.00 15.00
Elton Brand
BK Carlos Boozer 6.00 15.00
Andrei Kirilenko
BO Elton Brand 6.00 15.00
Lamar Odom
DB Baron Davis 6.00 15.00
Mike Bibby
GB Pau Gasol 8.00 20.00
Chris Bosh
GG Pau Gasol 8.00 20.00
Manu Ginobili
GP Manu Ginobili 8.00 20.00
Tony Parker
JH Richard Jefferson 6.00 15.00
Richard Hamilton
RM Zach Randolph 6.00 15.00
Darius Miles
WH Ben Wallace 8.00 20.00
Richard Hamilton

2004-05 Fleer Throwbacks Hardwood Classics Jerseys Autographs

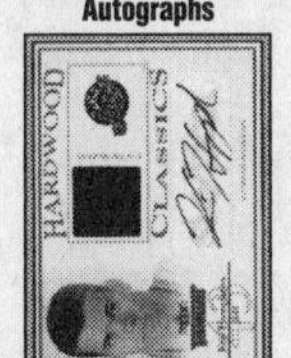

Randomly inserted in packs, this 22-card set parallels the design of the base Hardwood Classics set enhanced with both a jersey and an autograph. Cards were numbered to either 149 or 249.
UNPRICED ONE OF ONE's EXIST
AB Andris Biedrins/249 6.00 15.00
AK Andrei Kirilenko/249 10.00 25.00
DW Dorell Wright/149 10.00 25.00
GG George Gervin 10.00 25.00
JC Josh Childress/249 6.00 15.00
KH Kris Humphries/249 6.00 15.00

2004-05 Fleer Throwbacks Hardwood Classics Jerseys Autographs Numbers

Randomly inserted in packs, this 22-card set parallels the design of the base Hardwood Classics set enhanced with both a jersey and an autograph. Cards

were numbered to the featured player's jersey number.
SOME NOT PRICED DUE TO SCARCITY
AB Andris Biedrins/15 12.50 30.00
AK Andrei Kirilenko/47 25.00 60.00
BW2 Bill Walton/32 15.00 40.00
DM Darius Miles/23 10.00 25.00
EB Elton Brand/42 10.00 25.00
GG George Gervin/44 15.00 40.00
KH Kris Humphries/43 10.00 25.00
RH Richard Hamilton/32 15.00 40.00

2004-05 Fleer Throwbacks Hardwood Classics Jerseys Autographs Silver

Randomly inserted in packs, this 22-card set parallels the design of the base Hardwood Classics set enhanced with both a jersey and an autograph. Cards were numbered randomly, print runs are listed in the checklist.
AK Andrei Kirilenko/149 12.50 30.00
BS Byron Scott/249 8.00 20.00
BW Bill Walton/249 8.00 20.00
CB Carlos Boozer/50 8.00 20.00
CB2 Chris Bosh/25 25.00 60.00
DW Dorell Wright/50 12.50 30.00
GG George Gervin/200 15.00 40.00
JC Josh Childress/50 8.00 20.00
KH Kris Humphries/199 8.00 20.00
MC Maurice Cheeks/249 8.00 20.00
RH Richard Hamilton/149 10.00 25.00
ZR Zach Randolph/149 10.00 25.00

2004-05 Fleer Throwbacks Hardwood Classics Jerseys Redemption

Randomly inserted in Hobby packs at the rate of one in 667, this set consists of 20 different redemption cards for Mitchell and Ness throw back jerseys. Four different "Jersey of Your Choice" cards were also inserted where the obtainer gets to pick the jersey.
1 Dave Debusschere 20.00 50.00
2 Bill Russell 50.00 100.00
3 Bill Russell 50.00 100.00
4 George Gervin 40.00 100.00
5 Larry Bird 60.00 120.00
7 George Mikan 25.00 60.00
9 Magic Johnson 25.00 60.00
13 Bill Bradley 20.00 50.00
17 Jersey of Your Choice #1 100.00 200.00

2004-05 Fleer Throwbacks Nostalgia

Randomly inserted in packs, this 15-card set is horizontally designed with a player image in the center and color higlights to match team colors on the left and the right. Cards are all sequentially numbered to the year each player was drafted. A gold version was also produced and is numbered with only the last two digits of the year the player was drafted.
COMPLETE SET (15) 12.50 30.00
*GOLD/85-98: 1.5X TO 4X BASE HI
SOME GOLD UNPRICED DUE TO SCARCITY
1 Allen Iverson/1996 1.25 3.00
2 Kobe Bryant/1996 4.00 10.00
3 Shaquille O'Neal/1992 2.00 5.00
4 Karl Malone/1985 1.00 2.50
5 Kevin Garnett/1995 1.50 4.00
6 LeBron James/2003 5.00 12.00
7 Carmelo Anthony/2003 1.50 4.00
8 Dwyane Wade/2003 2.50 6.00
9 Baron Davis/1999 .75 2.00
10 Jason Kidd/1994 1.25 3.00
11 Tracy McGrady/1997 1.00 2.50
12 Paul Pierce/1998 1.00 2.50
13 Yao Ming/2002 1.50 4.00
14 Vince Carter/1998 1.25 3.00
15 Ben Wallace/1996 .75 2.00

2002-03 Fleer Tradition

Released in late December 2002, Fleer Tradition boasts a 300-card set divided up into 270 veteran players and 30 triple-player rookie cards. The base cards feature an old-school look on corrugated cardboard with white borders and framing around the photo in colors that match the player's team colors. Names and positions are in the upper left hand corner, and the team logo is in the upper right. The rookie card are set up like 1980-81 Topps in a horizontal tri-player format-except the perforations are printed on the card front. Tradition was packaged in nine card packs which carried a suggested retail price of $1.49, and boxes contained 40 packs. The PROMO card of Caron Butler listed at the end of the set was given away in Dallas at The American Airlines Center on November 30th to the first 12,000 fans through the gate.
COMPLETE SET (300) 30.00 80.00
1 Shareef Abdur-Rahim .20 .50
2 Dion Glover .15 .40
3 Theo Ratliff .15 .40
4 Nazr Mohammed .15 .40
5 Ira Newble .15 .40
6 Alan Henderson .15 .40
7 Vin Baker .20 .50
8 Tony Battie .15 .40
9 Eric Williams .15 .40
10 Shammond Williams .15 .40
11 Walter McCarty .15 .40
12 Bruno Sundov .15 .40
13 Donyell Marshall .15 .40
14 Marcus Fizer .15 .40
15 Eddie Robinson .15 .40
16 Trenton Hassell .15 .40
17 Ricky Davis .20 .50
18 Jumaine Jones .15 .40
19 Chris Mihm .15 .40
20 Zydrunas Ilgauskas .20 .50
21 Tyrone Hill .15 .40
22 Adrian Griffin .15 .40
23 Nick Van Exel .20 .50
24 Raef LaFrentz .15 .40
25 Eduardo Najera .15 .40
26 Shawn Bradley .15 .40
27 Evan Eschmeyer .15 .40
28 Walt Williams .15 .40
29 Raja Bell .20 .50
30 Marcus Camby .20 .50
31 Donnell Harvey .15 .40
32 Kenny Satterfield .15 .40
33 Rodney White .15 .40
34 Chris Whitney .15 .40
35 Clifford Robinson .15 .40
36 Zeljko Rebraca .15 .40
37 Corliss Williamson .15 .40
38 Chucky Atkins .15 .40
39 Jon Barry .15 .40
40 Michael Curry .15 .40
41 Erick Dampier .15 .40
42 Danny Fortson .15 .40
43 Adonal Foyle .15 .40
44 Troy Murphy .25 .60
45 Bob Sura .15 .40
46 Moochie Norris .15 .40
47 Kenny Thomas .15 .40
48 Terence Morris .15 .40
49 Glen Rice .20 .50
50 Maurice Taylor .15 .40
51 Erick Strickland .15 .40
52 Al Harrington .20 .50
53 Ron Artest .25 .60
54 Austin Croshere .15 .40
55 Ron Mercer .15 .40
56 Brad Miller .25 .60
57 Lamar Odom .25 .60
58 Keyon Dooling .15 .40
59 Corey Maggette .20 .50
60 Michael Olowokandi .15 .40
61 Stanislav Medvedenko .15 .40
62 Rick Fox .20 .50
63 Derek Fisher .20 .50
64 Samaki Walker .15 .40
65 Robert Horry .20 .50
66 Mark Madsen .15 .40
67 Wesley Person .15 .40
68 Michael Dickerson .15 .40
69 Lorenzen Wright .15 .40
70 Brevin Knight .15 .40
71 Travis Best .15 .40
72 Brian Grant .15 .40
73 Eddie Jones .20 .50
74 LaPhonso Ellis .20 .50
75 Anthony Carter .15 .40
76 Tim Thomas .15 .40
77 Toni Kukoc .20 .50
78 Anthony Mason .15 .40
79 Ervin Johnson .15 .40
80 Joel Przybilla .15 .40
81 Rod Strickland .20 .50
82 Terrell Brandon .15 .40
83 Anthony Peeler .15 .40
84 Joe Smith .20 .50
85 Gary Trent .15 .40
86 Rasho Nesterovic .15 .40
87 Loren Woods .15 .40
88 Felipe Lopez .15 .40
89 Dikembe Mutombo .25 .60
90 Rodney Rogers .15 .40
91 Jason Collins .15 .40
92 Kerry Kittles .15 .40
93 Lucious Harris .15 .40
94 Aaron Williams .15 .40
95 Jamal Mashburn .20 .50
96 David Wesley .15 .40
97 Elden Campbell .15 .40
98 Jerome Moiso .15 .40
99 P.J. Brown .15 .40
100 George Lynch .15 .40
101 Robert Traylor .15 .40
102 Antonio McDyess .20 .50
103 Kurt Thomas .15 .40
104 Clarence Weatherspoon .15 .40
105 Charlie Ward .15 .40
106 Lavor Postell .15 .40
107 Shandon Anderson .15 .40
108 Michael Doleac .15 .40
109 Othella Harrington .15 .40
110 Darrell Armstrong .15 .40
111 Steven Hunter .15 .40
112 Pat Garrity .15 .40
113 Horace Grant .20 .50
114 Jacque Vaughn .15 .40
115 Jeryl Sasser .15 .40
116 Todd MacCulloch .15 .40
117 Greg Buckner .15 .40
118 Eric Snow .15 .40
119 Samuel Dalembert .15 .40
120 Monty Williams .15 .40
121 Stephon Marbury .20 .50
122 Anfernee Hardaway .40 1.00
123 Tom Gugliotta .15 .40
124 Iakovos Tsakalidis .15 .40
125 Bo Outlaw .15 .40
126 Damon Stoudamire .20 .50
127 Jeff McInnis .15 .40
128 Derek Anderson .15 .40
129 Antonio Daniels .15 .40
130 Dale Davis .15 .40
131 Zach Randolph .25 .60
132 Bobby Jackson .15 .40
133 Chris Webber .25 .60
134 Vlade Divac .20 .50
135 Keon Clark .15 .40
136 Doug Christie .15 .40
137 Scot Pollard .15 .40
138 Mengke Bateer .15 .40
139 David Robinson .40 1.00
140 Steve Smith .20 .50
141 Malik Rose .15 .40
142 Speedy Claxton .15 .40
143 Danny Ferry .15 .40
144 Brent Barry .15 .40
145 Joseph Forte .15 .40
146 Vladimir Radmanovic .15 .40
147 Kenny Anderson .20 .50
148 Predrag Drobnjak .15 .40
149 Calvin Booth .15 .40
150 Ansu Sesay .15 .40
151 Voshon Lenard .15 .40
152 Lamond Murray .15 .40
153 Antonio Davis .15 .40
154 Lindsey Hunter .15 .40
155 Michael Bradley .15 .40
156 Jerome Williams .15 .40
157 Alvin Williams .15 .40
158 Mamadou N'Diaye .15 .40
159 Raul Lopez .25 .60
160 John Stockton .30 .75
161 Mark Jackson .20 .50
162 DeShawn Stevenson .15 .40
163 Calbert Cheaney .15 .40
164 Matt Harpring .20 .50
165 Jarron Collins .15 .40
166 Tyronn Lue .15 .40
167 Bryon Russell .15 .40
168 Larry Hughes .20 .50
169 Brendan Haywood .15 .40
170 Christian Laettner .15 .40
171 Glenn Robinson .20 .50
172 Tony Delk .15 .40
173 Antoine Walker .20 .50
174 Jalen Rose .20 .50
175 Jamal Crawford .20 .50
176 DeSagana Diop .15 .40
177 Michael Finley .25 .60
178 Dirk Nowitzki .40 1.00
179 Juwan Howard .20 .50
180 Chauncey Billups .25 .60
181 Richard Hamilton .20 .50
182 Antawn Jamison .25 .60
183 Steve Francis .25 .60
184 Eddie Griffin .15 .40
185 Jonathan Bender .15 .40
186 Reggie Miller .25 .60
187 Elton Brand .25 .60
188 Marco Jaric .25 .60
189 Kobe Bryant 1.25 3.00
190 Shaquille O'Neal .60 1.50
191 Jason Williams .20 .50
192 Stromile Swift .15 .40
193 Alonzo Mourning .30 .75
194 Malik Allen .15 .40
195 Sam Cassell .20 .50
196 Ray Allen .25 .60
197 Wally Szczerbiak .20 .50
197B Vince Carter Promo 1.00 2.50
198 Jason Kidd .40 1.00
199 Kenyon Martin .25 .60
200 Courtney Alexander .15 .40
201 Baron Davis .25 .60
202 Allan Houston .20 .50
203 Grant Hill .30 .75
204 Aaron McKie .15 .40
205 Keith Van Horn .20 .50
206 Shawn Marion .25 .60
207 Joe Johnson .25 .60
208 Scottie Pippen .40 1.00
209 Rasheed Wallace .25 .60
210 Peja Stojakovic .25 .60
211 Hedo Turkoglu .25 .60
212 Tony Parker .30 .75
213 Tim Duncan .50 1.25
214 Gary Payton .25 .60
215 Desmond Mason .20 .50
216 Vince Carter .40 1.00
217 Karl Malone .30 .75
218 Andrei Kirilenko .25 .60
219 Jerry Stackhouse .20 .50
220 Michael Jordan 2.00 5.00
221 DerMarr Johnson .15 .40
222 Kedrick Brown .15 .40
223 Eddy Curry .20 .50
224 Tyson Chandler .20 .50
225 Darius Miles .15 .40
226 Wang ZhiZhi .15 .40
227 James Posey .15 .40
228 Ben Wallace .25 .60
229 Jason Richardson .25 .60
230 Gilbert Arenas .25 .60
231 Eddie Griffin .15 .40
232 Jermaine O'Neal .25 .60
233 Quentin Richardson .20 .50
234 Devean George .15 .40
235 Shane Battier .25 .60
236 Pau Gasol .30 .75
237 Eddie House .15 .40
238 Michael Redd .25 .60
239 Troy Hudson .15 .40
240 Richard Jefferson .25 .60
241 Jamal Magloire .15 .40
242 Mike Miller .25 .60
243 Joe Johnson .25 .60
244 Ruben Patterson .15 .40
245 Gerald Wallace .25 .60
246 Tony Parker .30 .75
247 Rashard Lewis .25 .60
248 Morris Peterson .15 .40
249 Andrei Kirilenko .25 .60
250 Kwame Brown .15 .40
251 Jason Terry .20 .50
252 Paul Pierce .30 .75
253 Darius Miles .15 .40
254 Steve Nash .30 .75
255 Cuttino Mobley .20 .50
256 Jamaal Tinsley .15 .40
257 Andre Miller .20 .50
258 Shaquille O'Neal .60 1.50
259 Kobe Bryant 1.25 3.00
260 Kevin Garnett .50 1.25
261 Kenyon Martin .25 .60
262 Latrell Sprewell .20 .50
263 Tracy McGrady .40 1.00
264 Allen Iverson .40 1.00
265 Shawn Marion .25 .60
266 Bonzi Wells .15 .40
267 Mike Bibby .25 .60
268 Tim Duncan .50 1.25
269 Vince Carter .40 1.00
270 Michael Jordan 2.00 5.00
271 Yao Ming 1.50 4.00
Jay Williams
Mike Dunleavy
272 Manu Ginobili 1.50 4.00
Tayshaun Prince
Gordan Giricek
273 Jared Jeffries 1.00 2.50
Frank Williams
Jannero Pargo
274 Chris Wilcox 1.00 2.50
Juan Dixon
Lonny Baxter
275 DaJuan Wagner 1.00 2.50
Dan Dickau
Manu Ginobili
276 Melvin Ely 1.00 2.50
Chris Jefferies
Tito Maddox
277 Reggie Evans 1.00 2.50
J.R. Bremer
Frank Williams
278 Caron Butler 1.00 2.50
Marcus Haislip
Ryan Humphrey
279 Robert Archibald 1.00 2.50
Pat Burke
Nate Huffman
280 Drew Gooden 1.50 4.00
Amare Stoudemire
Qyntel Woods
281 Bostjan Nachbar 1.00 2.50
Jiri Welsch
Predrag Savovic
282 Curtis Borchardt 1.00 2.50
Casey Jacobsen
Dan Gadzuric
283 Sam Clancy 1.00 2.50
Mehmet Okur
Jamal Sampson
284 Tayshaun Prince 1.25 3.00
Kareem Rush
John Salmons
285 Yao Ming 1.50 4.00
Nikoloz Tskitishvili
Nene Hilario
286 DaJuan Wagner 1.00 2.50
Qyntel Woods
Tamar Slay
287 Melvin Ely 1.00 2.50
Macus Haislip
Fred Jones
288 Caron Butler 1.25 3.00
Manu Ginobili
Marcus Haislip
289 Roger Mason Jr. 1.00 2.50
Vincent Yarbrough
Dan Dickau
290 Ronald Murray 1.00 2.50
Chris Owens
Smush Parker
291 Rasual Butler 1.00 2.50
Jannero Pargo
Gordan Giricek
292 Drew Gooden 1.00 2.50
Nikoloz Tskitshvili
DaJuan Wagner
293 Nene Hilario 2.00 5.00
Chris Wilcox
Amare Stoudemire
294 Jay Williams 1.00 2.50
Ryan Humphrey
Qyntel Woods
295 Yao Ming 4.00 10.00
Amare Stoudemire
Kareem Rush
296 Nikoloz Tskitishvil 1.00 2.50
Caron Butler
Juan Dixon
297 Chris Wilcox 1.00 2.50
Fred Jones
Bostjan Nachbar
298 Mike Dunleavy 1.00 2.50
Nene Hilario
Casey Jacobsen
299 Jared Jeffries 1.00 2.50
Juan Dixon
Drew Gooden
300 Carlos Boozer 1.00 2.50
Jay Williams
Mike Dunleavy
PROMO Caron Butler PROMO 1.00 2.50

2002-03 Fleer Tradition Crystal

Randomly inserted in packs, this 300-card set parallels the base Fleer Tradition set enhanced with a silver glitter around the photo instead of the base card colors, and the card backs are sequentially numbered to 199 in silver foil.
*STARS: 3X TO 8X BASE CARD HI
*RCs: 1.25X TO 3X BASE CARD HI

2002-03 Fleer Tradition All-Stars

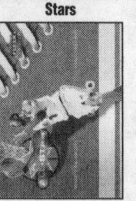

Randomly seeded in packs at the rate of one in 20, this 10-card set highlights NBA All-Stars on a horizontal card design with the layout of a pair of Converse All-Stars. The laces apper on the right side of the card, and the Fleer All-Star log appears on the left. A Sneak Edition version was also issued in packs where the card singles are sequentially numbered to 50.
COMPLETE SET (10) 8.00 20.00
*SNEAK ED: 4X TO 10X ALL-STARS HI
AS1 Vince Carter 1.00 2.50
AS2 Tim Duncan 1.25 3.00
AS3 Tracy McGrady 1.00 2.50
AS4 Michael Jordan 5.00 12.00
AS5 Shaquille O'Neal 1.50 4.00
AS6 Pau Gasol .75 2.00
AS7 Kevin Garnett 1.25 3.00
AS8 Kobe Bryant 3.00 8.00
AS9 Jason Richardson .60 1.50
AS10 Dirk Nowitzki 1.00 2.50

2002-03 Fleer Tradition Heads Up

Randomly seeded in packs at the rate of one in 10, this 10-card set has white borders, a colored border around the picture to match the player's team colors, and true life photos of the player's heads are oversized and mounted on a comically drawn smaller body.
COMPLETE SET (10) 4.00 10.00
HU1 Baron Davis .60 1.50
HU2 Jason Terry .50 1.25
HU3 Ben Wallace .60 1.50
HU4 Paul Pierce .75 2.00
HU5 Bonzi Wells .40 1.00
HU6 Allen Iverson 1.00 2.50
HU7 Vince Carter 1.00 2.50
HU8 Quentin Richardson .50 1.25
HU9 Eddy Curry .50 1.25
HU10 Darius Miles .40 1.00

2002-03 Fleer Tradition Heads Up Game-Used

Randomly inserted in packs, this 10-card set parallels the design of the base Heads Up insert enhanced with a square swatch of a game-worn headband. Print numbers were not officially released, but no player has more than 100 cards.
AI Allen Iverson 10.00 25.00
BW Bonzi Wells 4.00 10.00
BW Ben Wallace 6.00 15.00
DM Darius Miles 4.00 10.00
EC Eddy Curry 5.00 12.00
JT Jason Terry 5.00 12.00
PP Paul Pierce 8.00 20.00
QR Quentin Richardson 5.00 12.00

2002-03 Fleer Tradition Playground Rules

Inserted in packs at the rate of one in eight, this 30-card set features a horizontal design that places full color rookie player photos agains a brick wall on the right side and the words "Playground Rules" and the player's name in silver foil on the left.
COMPLETE SET (30) 15.00 40.00
PR1 Yao Ming 2.00 5.00
PR2 Fred Jones .60 1.50
PR3 Ryan Humphrey .60 1.50
PR4 Drew Gooden 1.00 2.50
PR5 Nikoloz Tskitshvili .60 1.50
PR6 Caron Butler 1.00 2.50
PR7 DaJuan Wagner .60 1.50
PR8 Nene Hilario .75 2.00
PR9 Qyntel Woods .60 1.50
PR10 Jared Jeffries .60 1.50
PR11 Casey Jacobsen .60 1.50
PR12 Marcus Haislip .60 1.50
PR13 Kareem Rush .60 1.50
PR14 Melvin Ely .60 1.50
PR15 Steve Logan .60 1.50
PR16 Amare Stoudemire 1.50 4.00
PR17 John Salmons .75 2.00
PR18 Chris Jefferies .60 1.50
PR19 Juan Dixon .75 2.00
PR20 Carlos Boozer 1.25 3.00
PR21 Roger Mason .60 1.50
PR22 Manu Ginobili 1.50 4.00
PR23 Tayshaun Prince .75 2.00
PR24 Chris Wilcox .60 1.50
PR25 Bostjan Nachbar .60 1.50
PR26 Jiri Welsch .60 1.50
PR27 Dan Dickau .60 1.50
PR28 Jay Williams .75 2.00
PR29 Mike Dunleavy .75 2.00
PR30 Frank Williams .60 1.50

2002-03 Fleer Tradition Road to the NBA

Randomly inserted in packs at the rate of one in 40, this 10-card set showcases a horizontal card design with player's centered over their team's logo and a background colored to match the player's team colors. A gray banner is arched across the top of the card containing the set name in yellow, and the contours of the card and the player's name appear in silver foil.
COMPLETE SET (10) 8.00 20.00
RTN1 Jerry Stackhouse .75 2.00
RTN2 Rasheed Wallace 1.00 2.50
RTN3 Allen Iverson 1.50 4.00
RTN4 Kevin Garnett 2.00 5.00
RTN5 Shawn Marion 1.00 2.50
RTN6 Chris Webber 1.00 2.50
RTN7 Glenn Robinson .75 2.00
RTN8 Antawn Jamison 1.00 2.50
RTN9 Dirk Nowitzki 1.50 4.00
RTN10 Vince Carter 1.50 4.00

2002-03 Fleer Tradition Road to the NBA Game-Used

Inserted in packs at the rate of one in 240, this 10-card set parallels the base Road to the NBA set enhanced with two swatches of game-use memorabilia from teams these guys have played on, including, college, high school, and foreign franchises.
RTN1 Jerry Stackhouse 4.00 10.00

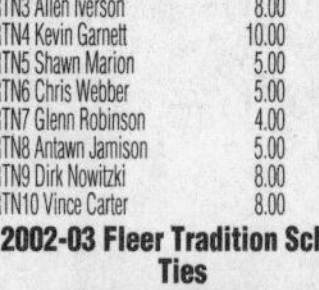

RTN3 Allen Iverson 8.00 20.00
RTN4 Kevin Garnett 10.00 25.00
RTN5 Shawn Marion 5.00 12.00
RTN6 Chris Webber 5.00 12.00
RTN7 Glenn Robinson 4.00 10.00
RTN8 Antawn Jamison 5.00 12.00
RTN9 Dirk Nowitzki 8.00 20.00
RTN10 Vince Carter 8.00 20.00

2002-03 Fleer Tradition School Ties

Inserted in packs at the rate of one in 20, this 10-card set places either two or three players on the same card who share the same college alma mater. The cards themselves are in the form of the old black and white bound note books where the top of the card has sharp corners (the spine) and the bottom of the card has rounded corners.
COMPLETE SET (10) 8.00 20.00
ST1 John Stockton 1.25 3.00
Dan Dickau
ST2 Antonio McDyess 1.25 3.00
Latrell Sprewell
ST3 Mike Miller 1.00 2.50
Jason Williams
ST4 Keith Van Horn 1.00 2.50
Andre Miller
ST5 Jason Kidd 1.25 3.00
Shareef Abdur-Rahim
ST6 Richard Jefferson 1.00 2.50
Jason Terry
Mike Bibby
ST7 Vince Carter 4.00 10.00
Michael Jordan
Jerry Stackhouse
ST8 Jalen Rose 2.50 6.00
Juwan Howard
Chris Webber
ST9 Dikembe Mutombo 1.25 3.00
Alonzo Mourning
Allen Iverson
ST10 Elton Brand 1.00 2.50
Grant Hill
Shane Battier

2002-03 Fleer Tradition School Ties Game-Used Dual or Triple

Randomly inserted in packs, this nine card set parallels the base School Ties enhanced with two or three swatches of memorabilia-one for each player where the jerseys and such were available. These swatches are circular shaped and appear below the player's picture. Each card is sequentially numbered to 100. Card number ST2 does not exist.
ST1 John Stockton JSY 10.00 25.00
Dan Dickau Shorts
ST3 Mike Miller Shorts 8.00 20.00
Jason Williams Jkt
ST4 Keith Van Horn Pants 8.00 20.00
Andre Miller Shorts
ST5 Jason Kidd Shorts 10.00 25.00
Shareef Abdur-Rahim JSY
ST6 Richard Jefferson Jkt 12.50 30.00
Jason Terry Jkt
Mike Bibby Pants
ST7 Vince Carter Jkt 10.00 25.00
Michael Jordan
Jerry Stackhouse Pants
ST9 Dikembe Mutombo Jkt 15.00 40.00
Alonzo Mourning JSY
Allen Iverson Shorts
ST10 Elton Brand Shorts 10.00 25.00
Grant Hill JSY
Shane Battier Jkt

2002-03 Fleer Tradition School Ties Game-Used Singles

Randomly inserted in packs at the rate of one in 23, this 21-card set parallels the base School Ties insert set enhanced with one circular swatch of game used memorabilia. Some of the pairs and or trio's have multiple variations. Also note, card number ST2 does not exist.
ST1A John Stockton JSY 4.00 10.00
Dan Dickau
ST1B John Stockton 3.00 8.00
Dan Dickau Shorts
ST3A Mike Miller Shorts 3.00 8.00
Jason Williams
ST3B Mike Miller 3.00 8.00
Jason Williams Jacket
ST4A Keith Van Horn Pants 3.00 8.00
Andre Miller
ST4B Keith Van Horn 3.00 8.00
Andre Miller Shorts
ST5A Jason Kidd Shorts 5.00 12.00
Shareef Abdul-Rahim
ST5B Jason Kidd 3.00
Shareef Abdul-Rahim JSY
ST6A Richard Jefferson Jkt 3.00
Jason Terry
Mike Bibby
ST6B Richard Jefferson 3.00
Jason Terry Jkt
Mike Bibby
ST6C Richard Jefferson 3.00
Jason Terry
Mike Bibby Pnts
ST7A Vince Carter Jacket 5.00
Michael Jordan
Jerry Stackhouse
ST7B Vince Carter 4.00
Michael Jordan
Jerry Stackhouse Pants
ST8A Jalen Rose JSY 3.00
Juwan Howard
Chris Webber
ST8B Jalen Rose 3.00
Juwan Howard
Chris Webber Pnts
ST9A Dekembe Mutombo Jkt 3.00
Alonzo Mourning
Allen Iverson
ST9B Dikembe Mutombo 4.00
Alonzo Mourning JSY
Allen Iverson
ST9C Dikembe Mutombo 5.00
Alonzo Mourning
Allen Iverson Short
ST10A Elton Brand Shorts 3.00
Grant Hill
Shane Battier
ST10B Elton Brand 3.00
Grant Hill JSY
Shane Battier
ST10C Elton Brand 3.00
Grant Hill
Shane Battier Jacket

2003-04 Fleer Tradition

Issued in late October/early September 2003, this card set is divided into 260 veteran players, inclu subset cards from numbers 221-260, 30 rookie c numbers 261-290 and inserted at the rate of one three, and 10 tri-cards featuring three rookie play each. Tradition was packaged in 36-pack boxes w packs contained 10 cards and carried a suggeste retail price of $1.49.
COMP.SET w/o RC's (260) 20.00
1 Shareef Abdur-Rahim .20
2 Vince Carter .40
3 Kevin Garnett .50
4 Bobby Jackson .15
5 Courtney Alexander .15
6 Tracy McGrady .30
7 Paul Pierce .30
8 Sam Cassell .20
9 Maurice Taylor .15
10 Pat Garrity .15
11 Casey Jacobsen .15
12 Malik Allen .15
13 Aaron McKie .15
14 Tyson Chandler .20
15 Scottie Pippen .40
16 Jason Terry .20
17 Pau Gasol .25
18 Antawn Jamison .25
19 Stanislav Medvedenko .15
20 Ray Allen .25
21 James Posey .15
22 Calbert Cheaney .15
23 Devean George .15
24 Tim Thomas .15
25 Marko Jaric .15
26 Ron Mercer .15
27 Rafer Alston .15
28 Tayshaun Prince .25
29 Doug Christie .15
30 Kendall Gill .15
31 Kurt Thomas .15
32 Richard Jefferson .25
33 Darius Miles .15
34 Kenny Anderson .20
35 Keon Clark .15
36 Vladimir Radmanovic .15
37 Kenny Thomas .15
38 Manu Ginobili .30
39 Jared Jeffries .15
40 Brad Miller .25
41 Derek Anderson .15
42 Zach Randolph .25
43 Speedy Claxton .15
44 Jamaal Tinsley .15
45 Gordan Giricek .15
46 Joe Johnson .25
47 Mike Miller .25
48 Shandon Anderson .15
49 Theo Ratliff .15
50 Derrick Coleman .20
51 Dion Glover .15
52 Nikoloz Tskitishvili .15
53 Jumaine Jones .15
54 Gilbert Arenas .25
55 Reggie Miller .25
56 Michael Redd .25
57 Jason Collins .15
58 Drew Gooden .20
59 Hedo Turkoglu .25
60 Eddie Jones .20
61 Andre Miller .20
62 Darrell Armstrong .15
63 Glen Rice .15
64 Jarron Collins .15
65 Nick Van Exel .20
66 Brian Grant .15
67 Shawn Kemp .25
68 Yao Ming .50
69 Ron Artest .25
70 Jamal Crawford .20

son Richardson .25 .60
die Griffin .15 .40
eith Van Horn .20 .50
son Kidd .40 1.00
ittino Mobley .20 .50
ent Barry .15 .40
ddy Curry .20 .50
entin Richardson .20 .50
ajuan Wagner .15 .40
m Gugliotta .15 .40
drei Kirilenko .25 .60
ane Battier .20 .50
onzo Mourning .30 .75
ifford Robinson .15 .40
ick Dampier .15 .40
itoine Walker .25 .60
arcus Haislip .15 .40
erry Kittles .15 .40
onny Baxter .15 .40
oy Murphy .25 .60
enn Robinson .20 .50
cky Davis .20 .50
chard Hamilton .20 .50
en Wallace .25 .60
oni Kukoc .25 .60
aja Bell .20 .50
kembe Mutombo .25 .60
die Robinson .15 .40
itonio Davis .15 .40
Anfernee Hardaway .40 1.00
Rasheed Wallace .25 .60
Christian Laettner .15 .40
Eduardo Najera .15 .40
Jonathan Bender .15 .40
Rodney Rogers .15 .40
Baron Davis .25 .60
Chris Webber .25 .60
Matt Harpring .20 .50
Raef LaFrentz .15 .40
Steve Nash .30 .75
Travis Best .15 .40
Tony Delk .15 .40
Malik Rose .15 .40
Al Harrington .20 .50
Bonzi Wells .15 .40
Voshon Lenard .15 .40
Radoslav Nesterovic .15 .40
Mike Bibby .25 .60
Dan Dickau .15 .40
Jalen Rose .20 .50
Lucious Harris .15 .40
David Wesley .15 .40
Rashard Lewis .25 .60
ra Newble .15 .40
Chauncey Billups .25 .60
Kareem Rush .15 .40
Michael Dickerson .15 .40
Walt Williams .15 .40
Donnell Harvey .15 .40
Tyronn Lue .15 .40
Carlos Boozer .25 .60
Moochie Norris .15 .40
John Salmons .25 .60
Vlade Divac .20 .50
Shammond Williams .15 .40
Brendan Haywood .15 .40
George Lynch .15 .40
Dirk Nowitzki .40 1.00
Bruce Bowen .15 .40
Brian Skinner .15 .40
Juan Dixon .15 .40
Eric Williams .15 .40
Grant Hill .30 .75
Corey Maggette .20 .50
Earl Boykins .15 .40
Lamar Odom .25 .60
Keyon Dooling .15 .40
Joe Smith .20 .50
Corliss Williamson .15 .40
Robert Horry .20 .50
Jamaal Magloire .15 .40
Mehmet Okur .20 .50
Elton Brand .25 .60
Steve Smith .15 .40
Predrag Drobnjak .15 .40
Allan Houston .20 .50
Jerome Williams .15 .40
Karl Malone .30 .75
Michael Olowokandi .15 .40
Terrell Brandon .15 .40
Eric Snow .15 .40
Tim Duncan .40 1.00
Juwan Howard .20 .50
Jason Williams .20 .50
Stephon Marbury .20 .50
J.R. Bremer .15 .40
Shaquille O'Neal .60 1.50
Mike Dunleavy .20 .50
Latrell Sprewell .20 .50
Troy Hudson .15 .40
Alvin Williams .15 .40
Shawn Marion .25 .60
Jermaine O'Neal .25 .60
P.J. Brown .15 .40
Howard Eisley .15 .40
Jerry Stackhouse .20 .50
Qyntel Woods .15 .40
Larry Hughes .20 .50
Donyell Marshall .15 .40
Greg Ostertag .15 .40
Kwame Brown .15 .40
Reggie Evans .15 .40
DeShawn Stevenson .15 .40
Lorenzen Wright .15 .40
Lindsey Hunter .15 .40
Kenyon Martin .25 .60
Kobe Bryant 1.25 3.00
Scott Padgett .15 .40
Michael Finley .25 .60
Peja Stojakovic .25 .60
Zydrunas Ilgauskas .20 .50
Vincent Yarbrough .15 .40
Jamal Mashburn .20 .50
Smush Parker .15 .40
Caron Butler .25 .60
Derek Fisher .20 .50
Damon Stoudamire .20 .50
Nene Hilario .20 .50
Allen Iverson .40 1.00
Anthony Mason .15 .40
Rasual Butler .15 .40
Tony Parker .25 .60
Marcus Fizer .15 .40
Amare Stoudemire .40 1.00
Marc Jackson .15 .40
206 Desmond Mason .20 .50
207 Marcus Camby .20 .50
208 Ruben Patterson .15 .40
209 Bob Sura .15 .40
210 Rick Fox .15 .40
211 Jim Jackson .15 .40
212 Walter McCarty .15 .40
213 Gary Payton .25 .60
214 Elden Campbell .15 .40
215 Steve Francis .25 .60
216 Stromile Swift .15 .40
217 Stephen Jackson .20 .50
218 Antonio McDyess .20 .50
219 Morris Peterson .15 .40
220 Wally Szczerbiak .20 .50
221 Tim Duncan AW .40 1.00
222 Amare Stoudemire AW .40 1.00
223 Bobby Jackson AW .15 .40
224 Ben Wallace AW .25 .60
225 Gilbert Arenas AW .25 .60
226 Tracy McGrady AW .30 .75
227 Kobe Bryant AW 1.25 3.00
228 Kevin Garnett AW .50 1.25
229 Shaquille O'Neal AW .60 1.50
230 Yao Ming AW .50 1.25
231 Stephon Marbury BS .20 .50
232 Ron Artest BS .25 .60
233 Troy Hudson BS .15 .40
234 Ray Allen BS .25 .60
235 Matt Harpring BS .20 .50
236 Jermaine O'Neal BS .25 .60
237 Jason Kidd BS .40 1.00
238 Jason Williams BS .20 .50
239 Zydrunas Ilgauskas BS .20 .50
240 Jamal Mashburn BS .20 .50
241 Yao Ming BS .50 1.25
242 Peja Stojakovic BS .25 .60
243 Tony Parker BS .25 .60
244 Caron Butler BS .25 .60
245 Amare Stoudemire BS .40 1.00
246 Troy Murphy BS .25 .60
247 Nene Hilario BS .20 .50
248 Allen Iverson BS .40 1.00
249 Kobe Bryant BS 1.25 3.00
250 Tim Duncan BS .40 1.00
251 Tracy McGrady BS .30 .75
252 Kevin Garnett BS .50 1.25
253 Drew Gooden BS .20 .50
254 Kenyon Martin BS .25 .60
255 Dirk Nowitzki BS .40 1.00
256 Paul Pierce BS .30 .75
257 Steve Francis BS .25 .60
258 Steve Nash BS .30 .75
259 Gary Payton BS .25 .60
260 Chris Webber BS .25 .60
261 LeBron James RC 6.00 15.00
262 Darko Milicic RC .60 1.50
263 Carmelo Anthony RC 1.50 4.00
264 Chris Bosh RC 1.25 3.00
265 Dwyane Wade RC 2.50 6.00
266 Chris Kaman RC .75 2.00
267 Kirk Hinrich RC .75 2.00
268 T.J. Ford RC .75 2.00
269 Mike Sweetney RC .60 1.50
270 Mickael Pietrus RC .60 1.50
271 Jarvis Hayes RC .60 1.50
272 Nick Collison RC .60 1.50
273 Marcus Banks RC .60 1.50
274 Luke Ridnour RC .75 2.00
275 Reece Gaines RC .60 1.50
276 Troy Bell RC .60 1.50
277 Zarko Cabarkapa RC .60 1.50
278 David West RC .75 2.00
279 Luke Walton RC .60 1.50
280 Dahntay Jones RC .60 1.50
281 Boris Diaw RC .75 2.00
282 Zoran Planinic RC .60 1.50
283 Travis Outlaw RC .75 2.00
284 Brian Cook RC .60 1.50
285 Jason Kapono RC .60 1.50
286 Ndudi Ebi RC .60 1.50
287 Kendrick Perkins RC 1.00 2.50
288 Leandro Barbosa RC .75 2.00
289 Josh Howard RC .60 1.50
290 Maciej Lampe RC .60 1.50
291 LeBron James RC 8.00 20.00
Darko Milicic RC
Carmelo Anthony RC
292 Mike Sweetney RC 1.50 4.00
Chris Bosh RC
Jarvis Hayes RC
293 Kirk Hinrich RC 1.25 3.00
Nick Collison RC
Chris Kaman RC
294 Mike Sweetney RC 1.25 3.00
David West RC
Brian Cook RC
295 Chris Kaman RC 1.50 4.00
Chris Bosh RC
Darko Milicic RC
296 T.J. Ford RC 2.50 6.00
Dwyane Ford RC
Kirk Hinrich RC
297 Mickael Pietrus RC 1.25 3.00
Dahntay Jones RC
Reece Gaines RC
298 T.J. Ford RC 1.25 3.00
Marcus Banks RC
Luke Ridnour RC
299 Mickael Pietrus RC 1.25 3.00
Zarko Cabarkapa RC
Jarvis Hayes RC
300 LeBron James RC 15.00 40.00
Carmelo Anthony RC
Dwyane Wade RC

2003-04 Fleer Tradition Crystal

Randomly inserted in packs, this 300-card set parallels the base Tradition set enhanced with sequential numbering to 175 for cards 1-260, 125 for cards 261-290 and 50 for cards 291-300.
*CRYSTAL SINGLES: 6X TO 15X BASE HI
*CRYSTAL RC's: 3X TO 8X BASE CARD HI
*CRYSTAL TRIPLE: 4X TO 10X BASE HI
261 LeBron James 75.00 150.00
300 LeBron James 125.00 225.00
Carmelo Anthony
Dwyane Wade

2003-04 Fleer Tradition Draft Day Rookie

Randomly seeded in packs, this 40-card set parallels the base set for card numbers 261-300 and is sequentially numbered to 375.
*261-290 DRAFT DAY: 1.5X TO 4X BASE HI
*291-300 DRAFT DAY: .75X TO 2X BASE HI
DRAFT DAY CARDS ARE #'s 261-300

2003-04 Fleer Tradition Heads Up

Inserted in packs at the rate of one in 12, this 10-card set features a horizontal design with a full color player photo on the right and white borders.
COMPLETE SET (10) 4.00 10.00
1 Kwame Brown .60 1.50
2 Scottie Pippen 1.50 4.00
3 Tim Thomas .60 1.50
4 Stephen Jackson .75 2.00
5 Allen Iverson 1.50 4.00
6 Richard Hamilton .75 2.00
7 Jermaine O'Neal 1.00 2.50
8 Elton Brand 1.00 2.50
9 Antoine Walker 1.00 2.50
10 Drew Gooden .75 2.00

2003-04 Fleer Tradition Heads Up Game Used

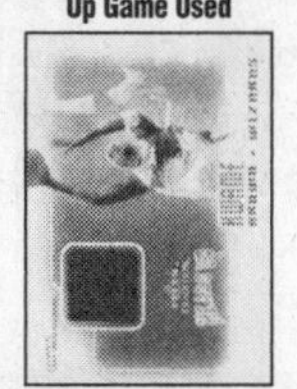

Randomly seeded, this 10-card set parallels the base Heads Up insert set enhanced with a swatch of game-worn headband on the left side of the card. Each card is sequentially numbered.
HUCA Carmelo Anthony/50 20.00 50.00
HUCB Chris Bosh/55 15.00 40.00
HUDW Dwyane Wade/65 30.00 80.00
HUKB Kwame Brown/40 8.00 20.00
HULR Luke Ridnour/55 10.00 25.00
HUMB Marcus Banks/50 8.00 20.00
HUMP Mickael Pietrus/50 8.00 20.00
HURG Reece Gaines/55 8.00 20.00
HUTB Troy Bell 8.00 20.00
HUTT Tim Thomas/60 8.00 20.00

2003-04 Fleer Tradition Milestones

Inserted at one in 144, this 10-card set features a horizontal design with a color player action photo on the right set against a black and white background. The left side has a solid color and a floating head portrait of the player.
COMPLETE SET (10) 15.00 40.00
1 Karl Malone 2.00 5.00
2 Kobe Bryant 8.00 20.00
3 Paul Pierce 2.00 5.00
4 Tracy McGrady 2.00 5.00
5 Kevin Garnett 3.00 8.00
6 Allen Iverson 2.50 6.00
7 Tim Duncan 2.50 6.00
8 Shaquille O'Neal 4.00 10.00
9 Vince Carter 2.50 6.00
10 Chris Webber 1.50 4.00

2003-04 Fleer Tradition Playground Rules

Inserted at one in six, this 20-card set places a color player action shot against a diagonally split background with the player's portrait showing in the top half.
COMPLETE SET (20) 15.00 30.00
1 LeBron James 8.00 20.00
2 Darko Milicic .75 2.00
3 Carmelo Anthony 2.00 5.00
4 Chris Bosh 1.50 4.00
5 Dwyane Wade 3.00 8.00
6 Chris Kaman 1.00 2.50
7 Kirk Hinrich 1.00 2.50
8 T.J. Ford 1.00 2.50
9 Mike Sweetney .75 2.00
10 Jarvis Hayes .75 2.00
11 Mickael Pietrus .75 2.00
12 Nick Collison .75 2.00
13 Marcus Banks .75 2.00
14 Luke Ridnour 1.00 2.50
15 Reece Gaines .75 2.00
16 Troy Bell .75 2.00
17 Zarko Cabarkapa .75 2.00
18 David West 1.00 2.50
19 Travis Outlaw 1.00 2.50
20 Dahntay Jones .75 2.00

2003-04 Fleer Tradition Rookie Hats Off

Randomly seeded and sequentially numbered to 180, this 12-card set places players and a swatch of the hat they wore on draft day on each card.
RHOCA Carmelo Anthony 12.00 30.00
RHOCB Chris Bosh 10.00 25.00
RHOCK Chris Kaman 6.00 15.00
RHODJ Dahntay Jones 5.00 12.00
RHODW Dwyane Wade 20.00 50.00
RHOJH Jarvis Hayes 5.00 12.00
RHOMJ Maciej Lampe 5.00 12.00
RHOMS Mike Sweetney 5.00 12.00
RHORG Reece Gaines 5.00 12.00
RHOSV Slavko Vranes 5.00 12.00
RHOZC Zarko Cabarkapa 5.00 12.00
RHOZP Zoran Planinic 5.00 12.00

2003-04 Fleer Tradition Throwback Threads

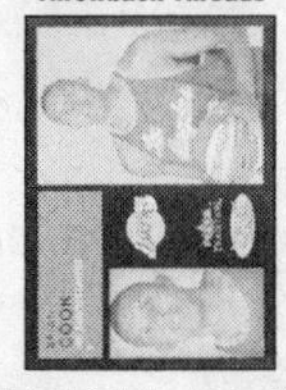

Inserted at one in 36, this 10-card set places full color player portrait photos on a card with black borders.
COMPLETE SET (10) 8.00 20.00
1 Carmelo Anthony 2.50 6.00
2 Luke Walton 1.00 2.50
3 Chris Kaman 1.25 3.00
4 Travis Outlaw 1.25 3.00
5 Kirk Hinrich 1.25 3.00
6 T.J. Ford 1.25 3.00
7 Brian Cook 1.00 2.50
8 Jarvis Hayes 1.00 2.50
9 Mickael Pietrus 1.00 2.50
10 Nick Collison 1.00 2.50

2003-04 Fleer Tradition Throwback Threads Event Worn

Randomly inserted, this 11-card set parallels the design of the base Thowback Threads insert enhanced with a swatch of from Mitchell and Ness throwback jerseys that were worn by the player at an event or photo shoot. No insert odds were given for this set, and these cards are not serial numbered.
*COMBO: 1.25X TO 3X BASE JSY HI
COMBO PRINT RUN 150 SETS
BC Brian Cook 2.50 6.00
CA Carmelo Anthony 6.00 15.00
CK Chris Kaman 3.00 8.00
DW David West 3.00 8.00
JH Jarvis Hayes 2.50 6.00
LR Luke Ridnour 3.00 8.00
LW Luke Walton 2.50 6.00
MB Marcus Banks 2.50 6.00
MP Mickael Pietrus 2.50 6.00
MS Mike Sweetney 2.50 6.00
TO Travis Outlaw 3.00 8.00

2003-04 Fleer Tradition Throwback Threads Dual Event Worn

Randomly inserted and sequentially numbered to 299, this five-card set parallels the design of the base Thowback Threads insert set enhanced with a horizontal design, a second player and two swatches from Mitchell and Ness throwback jerseys that were worn by the player at an event or photo shoot.
BCCK Brian Cook 6.00 15.00
Chris Kaman
CADW Carmelo Anthony 10.00 25.00
David West
LWTO Luke Walton 6.00 15.00
Travis Outlaw
MPJH Mickael Pietrus 6.00 15.00
Jarvis Hayes
MSMB Mike Sweetney 6.00 15.00
Marcus Banks

2004-05 Fleer Tradition

Released in December 2004, Tradition boasts a 268-card base set divided up as follows: cadrs 1-208 are veterans, cards 209-220 are Award Winners, cards 221-20 are inserted at one in four and feature rookies, and cards 251-268 are inserted at one in 18 and are rookie trios. Base cards have a red border and a tan background. Tradition was offered in both Hobby and Retail formats where both packs contain 10 cards, but Hobby is packaged in 36 pack boxes and Retail is packaged in 24 pack boxes.
COMP.SET w/o RC's (220) 20.00 50.00
1 Jonathan Bender .15 .40
2 Boris Diaw .20 .50
3 Eddie Robinson .15 .40
4 Jason Richardson .25 .60
5 Bonzi Wells .15 .40
6 Elden Campbell .15 .40
7 P.J. Brown .15 .40
8 Ray Allen .25 .60
9 Theron Smith .15 .40
10 Darko Milicic .15 .40
11 Bob Sura .15 .40
12 Sam Cassell .20 .50
13 Cuttino Mobley .20 .50
14 Andrei Kirilenko .20 .50
15 Raef LaFrentz .15 .40
16 Aleksandar Pavlovic .15 .40
17 Carmelo Anthony .50 1.25
18 Mickael Pietrus .20 .50
19 James Posey .15 .40
20 Nazr Mohammed .15 .40
21 Jalen Rose .20 .50
22 Jiri Welsch .15 .40
23 Drew Gooden .20 .50
24 Nene .20 .50
25 Troy Murphy .20 .50
26 Mike Miller .25 .60
27 T.J. Ford .20 .50
28 Allan Houston .20 .50
29 Donyell Marshall .15 .40
30 Chris Crawford .15 .40
31 Eric Snow .15 .40
32 Marcus Camby .20 .50
33 Devean George .15 .40
34 Eric Williams .15 .40
35 Kurt Thomas .15 .40
36 Rashard Lewis .25 .60
37 Alvin Williams .15 .40
38 David West .25 .60
39 Shawn Marion .25 .60
40 Mark Blount .15 .40
41 Dikembe Mutombo .25 .60
42 Stephen Jackson .20 .50
43 Rasual Butler .15 .40
44 Michael Redd .25 .60
45 Jason Kidd .40 1.00
46 Malik Rose .15 .40
47 Chris Bosh .25 .60
48 Antonio Daniels .15 .40
49 Doug Christie .15 .40
50 Stephon Marbury .20 .50
51 Gary Payton .25 .60
52 Michael Finley .25 .60
53 Ben Wallace .25 .60
54 Jason Williams .20 .50
55 Michael Olowokandi .15 .40
56 Steve Francis .25 .60
57 Chris Webber .25 .60
58 Tim Duncan .40 1.00
59 Carlos Arroyo .20 .50
60 Eddie House .15 .40
61 Mike Bibby .25 .60
62 Tony Parker .25 .60
63 Matt Harpring .20 .50
64 Richard Hamilton .20 .50
65 Corey Maggette .20 .50
66 Damon Jones .15 .40
67 Keith Bogans .15 .40
68 Willie Green .15 .40
69 Kirk Hinrich .25 .60
70 Jerry Stackhouse .20 .50
71 Chris Kaman .25 .60
72 Lamar Odom .25 .60
73 Dwyane Wade .75 2.00
74 Kevin Garnett .50 1.25
75 Allen Iverson .40 1.00
76 Theo Ratliff .15 .40
77 Shareef Abdur-Rahim .20 .50
78 Gilbert Arenas .25 .60
79 Jamal Sampson .15 .40
80 Josh Howard .25 .60
81 Latrell Sprewell .20 .50
82 Kyle Korver .20 .50
83 Brad Miller .25 .60
84 Rasho Nesterovic .15 .40
85 Larry Hughes .20 .50
86 Eddy Curry .20 .50
87 Rasheed Wallace .25 .60
88 Chris Wilcox .15 .40
89 Mark Madsen .15 .40
90 Kenny Thomas .15 .40
91 Zach Randolph .20 .50
92 Juan Dixon .15 .40
93 Tyson Chandler .20 .50
94 Stromile Swift .15 .40
95 Udonis Haslem .20 .50
96 Jason Collins .15 .40
97 Glenn Robinson .20 .50
98 Darius Miles .15 .40
99 Jared Jeffries .15 .40
100 Bobby Jackson .15 .40
101 Jahidi White .15 .40
102 Dirk Nowitzki .40 1.00
103 Wally Szczerbiak .20 .50
104 John Salmons .25 .60
105 Kwame Brown .15 .40
106 Jason Kapono .15 .40
107 Chauncey Billups .25 .60
108 Shane Battier .20 .50
109 Samuel Dalembert .15 .40
110 Manu Ginobili .30 .75
111 Anfernee Hardaway .60 1.50
112 Yao Ming .50 1.25
113 Eric Piatkowski .15 .40
114 Vlade Divac .20 .50
115 Ron Mercer .15 .40
116 Quentin Richardson .20 .50
117 Derek Anderson .15 .40
118 Jarvis Hayes .15 .40
119 Antonio Davis .15 .40
120 Erick Dampier .15 .40
121 Antonio McDyess .20 .50
122 Fred Jones .15 .40
123 Damon Stoudamire .20 .50
124 Jason Collier .15 .40
125 Frank Williams .15 .40
126 Kobe Bryant 1.25 3.00
127 Keith Van Horn .20 .50
128 Darrell Armstrong .15 .40
129 Steve Nash .30 .75
130 Nick Collison .15 .40
131 Ricky Davis .20 .50
132 Tracy McGrady .30 .75
133 Shaquille O'Neal .60 1.50
134 Desmond Mason .20 .50
135 Richard Jefferson .25 .60
136 Casey Jacobsen .15 .40
137 Ronald Murray .15 .40
138 Rafer Alston .15 .40
139 Tony Delk .15 .40
140 LeBron James 1.50 4.00
141 Earl Boykins .15 .40
142 Speedy Claxton .15 .40
143 Jamaal Tinsley .15 .40
144 Elton Brand .25 .60
145 Jamaal Magloire .15 .40
146 Jamal Crawford .20 .50
147 Peja Stojakovic .25 .60
148 Bruce Bowen .15 .40
149 Paul Pierce .30 .75
150 Jason Terry .20 .50
151 Kenyon Martin .25 .60
152 Maurice Taylor .15 .40
153 Toni Kukoc .20 .50
154 Aaron Williams .15 .40
155 Tony Battie .15 .40
156 Leandro Barbosa .25 .60
157 Carlos Boozer .25 .60
158 Brevin Knight .15 .40
159 Marquis Daniels .15 .40
160 Jim Jackson .15 .40
161 Caron Butler .25 .60
162 Troy Hudson .15 .40
163 DeShawn Stevenson .15 .40
164 Nick Van Exel .20 .50
165 Antawn Jamison .25 .60
166 Marcus Banks .15 .40
167 Derek Fisher .20 .50
168 Juwan Howard .20 .50
169 Reggie Miller .25 .60
170 Joe Smith .20 .50
171 Alonzo Mourning .30 .75
172 Mike Sweetney .15 .40
173 Mehmet Okur .20 .50
174 Brent Barry .15 .40
175 Al Harrington .20 .50
176 Dajuan Wagner .15 .40
177 Voshon Lenard .15 .40
178 Jermaine O'Neal .25 .60
179 Bobby Simmons .15 .40
180 Karl Malone .30 .75
181 Dan Gadzuric .15 .40
182 David Wesley .15 .40
183 Tim Thomas .15 .40
184 Amare Stoudemire .30 .75
185 Morris Peterson .15 .40
186 Fred Hoiberg .15 .40
187 Jeff McInnis .15 .40
188 Andre Miller .20 .50
189 Mike Dunleavy .20 .50
190 Ron Artest .25 .60
191 Kerry Kittles .15 .40
192 Baron Davis .25 .60
193 Vince Carter .40 1.00
194 Gerald Wallace .25 .60
195 Tayshaun Prince .25 .60
196 Marko Jaric .15 .40
197 Luke Walton .15 .40
198 Eddie Jones .20 .50
199 Hedo Turkoglu .25 .60
200 Joe Johnson .25 .60
201 Vladimir Radmanovic .15 .40
202 Gordan Giricek .15 .40
203 Antoine Walker .25 .60
204 Zydrunas Ilgauskas .20 .50
205 Clifford Robinson .15 .40
206 Pau Gasol .25 .60
207 Jamal Mashburn .25 .60
208 Luke Ridnour .20 .50
209 Kevin Garnett AW .60 1.50
210 LeBron James AW 2.00 5.00
211 Jason Kidd AW .50 1.25
212 Kobe Bryant AW 1.50 4.00
213 Shaquille O'Neal AW .75 2.00
214 Tim Duncan AW .50 1.25
215 Ron Artest AW .30 .75
216 Dwyane Wade AW 1.00 2.50
217 Kirk Hinrich AW .30 .75
218 Chris Bosh AW .30 .75
219 Carmelo Anthony AW .60 1.50
220 Antawn Jamison AW .30 .75
221 Dwight Howard RC 2.50 6.00
222 Emeka Okafor RC 1.25 3.00
223 Ben Gordon RC 1.00 2.50
224 Shaun Livingston RC .75 2.00
225 Devin Harris RC 1.25 3.00
226 Josh Childress RC .75 2.00
227 Luol Deng RC 1.25 3.00
228 Rafael Araujo RC .75 2.00
229 Andre Iguodala RC 1.25 3.00
230 Luke Jackson RC .75 2.00
231 Andris Biedrins RC 1.00 2.50
232 Robert Swift RC .75 2.00
233 Sebastian Telfair RC .75 2.00
234 Kris Humphries RC .75 2.00
235 Al Jefferson RC 1.25 3.00
236 Kirk Snyder RC .75 2.00
237 Josh Smith RC 1.25 3.00
238 J.R. Smith RC 1.00 2.50
239 Dorell Wright RC 1.25 3.00
240 Jameer Nelson RC 1.00 2.50
241 Pavel Podkolzine RC .75 2.00
242 Nenad Krstic RC .75 2.00
243 Andres Nocioni RC .75 2.00
244 Delonte West RC 1.00 2.50
245 Tony Allen RC 1.00 2.50
246 Kevin Martin RC 1.00 2.50
247 Sasha Vujacic RC .75 2.00
248 Beno Udrih RC .75 2.00
249 David Harrison RC .75 2.00
250 Anderson Varejao RC 1.00 2.50
251 Emeka Okafor 2.50 6.00
Ben Gordon
Dwight Howard
252 Dwight Howard 1.25 4.00
Jameer Nelson
Mario Kasun RC
253 Tony Allen 3.00 8.00
Al Jefferson
Delonte West
254 Luol Deng 2.50 6.00
Chris Duhon
Ben Gordon
255 Andres Nocioni 1.50 4.00
Kevin Martin
Sebastian Telfair
256 Josh Childress 1.50 4.00
Royal Ivey RC
Josh Smith
257 Devin Harris 1.25 4.00
Jameer Nelson
Sebastian Telfair
258 Lionel Chalmers RC 1.50 4.00
Antonio Burks RC
Andre Emmett RC
259 Luol Deng 1.50 4.00
Chris Duhon RC
Tim Pickett RC
260 Josh Childress 1.50 4.00
Luke Jackson
Andre Iguodala
261 Shaun Livingston 1.25 3.00
Dwight Howard
Robert Swift
262 Josh Smith 1.50 4.00
Al Jefferson
Sebastian Telfair
263 Shaun Livingston 1.25 3.00
Dorell Wright
J.R. Smith
264 Justin Reed 1.50 4.00
Jackson Vroman RC
Peter John Ramos RC
265 Pavel Podkolzine 1.50 4.00
Andris Biedrins
Nenad Krstic
266 Sasha Vujacic 3.00 8.00
Yuta Tabuse RC
Beno Udrih
267 Rafael Araujo 1.50 4.00
Kris Humphries
Kirk Snyder
268 Bernard Robinson RC 1.25 3.00
Pape Sow RC
Trevor Ariza

2004-05 Fleer Tradition Blue

Randomly inserted at approximately one per pack, this 268-card set parallels the base set enhanced with blue borders.
*BLUE: .5X TO 1.25X BASE HI

2004-05 Fleer Tradition Crystal

Randomly inserted in packs, this 268-card set parallels the base set enhanced with the word, crystal, in the upper right hand corner and cards 1-220 are sequentially numbered to 150, 221-250 are sequentially numbered to 75 and 251-268 are sequentially numbered to 25.
*CRYSTAL STARS: 2X TO 5X BASE HI
*CRYSTAL AW: 1.5X TO 4X BASE HI
*CRYSTAL RCs: 2X TO 5X BASE HI
*CRYSTAL TRIO: 3X TO 8X BASE HI

2004-05 Fleer Tradition Draft Day Rookies

Randomly seeded, this 48-card set parallels the rookie players only and is enhanced with yellow borders, a gold foil stamp on the front that reads, Draft Day Rookies and sequential numbering to 375.
*221-250 DRAFT: .75X TO 2X BASE HI
*251-268 DRAFT TRIO: .75X TO 2X BASE HI

2004-05 Fleer Tradition Green

Randomly seeded, this 268-card set parallels the base set enhanced with green borders. No stated odds were given for this parallel.
*GREEN: .6X TO 1.5X BASE HI

2004-05 Fleer Tradition Classic Combinations

Randomly inserted, this 20-card set is horizontally designed and pairs two players from the same team. Pictures on the card are in black and white and there are Red highlights along the bottom. Each card is serially numbered to 250.
1 Shaquille O'Neal 4.00 10.00
Dwyane Wade
2 Carmelo Anthony 2.50 6.00
Kenyon Martin
3 Kobe Bryant 4.00 10.00
Lamar Odom
4 Yao Ming 2.50 6.00
Tracy McGrady
5 Allan Houston 1.00 2.50
Stephon Marbury
6 Steve Francis 4.00 10.00
Dwight Howard
7 Kirk Hinrich 1.50 4.00
Ben Gordon
8 Elton Brand 1.25 3.00
Corey Maggette
9 Paul Pierce 1.50 4.00
Gary Payton
10 Allen Iverson 2.00 5.00
Andre Iguodala
11 LeBron James 4.00 10.00
Luke Jackson
12 Baron Davis 1.50 4.00
J.R. Smith
13 Dirk Nowitzki 2.00 5.00
Devin Harris
14 Andrei Kirilenko 1.25 3.00
Carlos Boozer
15 Ben Wallace 1.25 3.00
Rasheed Wallace
16 Reggie Miller 1.25 3.00
Jermaine O'Neal

17 Amaré Stoudemire 1.50 4.00
Steve Nash
18 Kevin Garnett 2.50 6.00
Latrell Sprewell
19 Jason Kidd 2.00 5.00
Richard Jefferson
20 Tim Duncan 2.00 5.00
Manu Ginobili

2004-05 Fleer Tradition Hardcourt Tributes

Inserted in both Hobby and Retail at one in six packs, this 20-card set places a close up photo on a silver background that is shaped like a shield.

COMPLETE SET (20) 12.50 30.00
1 Allen Iverson 1.00 2.50
2 Jason Kidd 1.00 2.50
3 Dwyane Wade 2.00 5.00
4 Kenyon Martin .60 1.50
5 Pau Gasol .60 1.50
6 Carmelo Anthony 1.25 3.00
7 Paul Pierce .75 2.00
8 Tracy McGrady .75 2.00
9 Shaquille O'Neal 1.50 4.00
10 Stephon Marbury .50 1.25
11 Steve Francis .60 1.50
12 Yao Ming 1.25 3.00
13 Peja Stojakovic .60 1.50
14 Kevin Garnett 1.25 3.00
15 Tim Duncan 1.00 2.50
16 Dirk Nowitzki 1.00 2.50
17 Vince Carter 1.00 2.50
18 Jason Richardson .60 1.50
19 Kobe Bryant 3.00 8.00
20 LeBron James 4.00 10.00

2004-05 Fleer Tradition Hardcourt Tributes Jerseys

Inserted in Hobby packs at the rate of one in 102 and Retail at the rate of one in 192, this 20-card set utilizes the design of the base Hardcourt Tributes set enhanced with a square swatch of jersey.

*PATCHES: 1X TO 2.5X BASE HI
1 Allen Iverson 4.00 10.00
2 Jason Kidd 4.00 10.00
3 Dwyane Wade 8.00 20.00
4 Kenyon Martin 2.50 6.00
5 Pau Gasol 2.50 6.00
6 Carmelo Anthony 5.00 12.00
7 Paul Pierce 3.00 8.00
8 Tracy McGrady 3.00 8.00
9 Shaquille O'Neal 6.00 15.00
10 Stephon Marbury 2.00 5.00
11 Steve Francis 2.50 6.00
12 Yao Ming 5.00 12.00
13 Peja Stojakovic 2.50 6.00
14 Kevin Garnett 5.00 12.00
15 Tim Duncan 4.00 10.00
16 Dirk Nowitzki 4.00 10.00
17 Vince Carter 4.00 10.00
18 Jason Richardson 2.50 6.00
19 Amare Stoudemire 3.00 8.00
20 Ben Wallace 2.50 6.00

2004-05 Fleer Tradition Rookie Hats Off

Randomly seeded, this 15-card set features a horizontal design with a black border along the top, a yellow border along the bottom and a green background. Player portrait photos in their Draft Day Hats appear on the right and a swatch of the hat from the picture appears in the upper left. Each card is sequentially numbered to 100.

1 Dwight Howard 20.00 50.00
2 Ben Gordon 8.00 20.00
3 Shaun Livingston 6.00 15.00
4 Devin Harris 10.00 25.00
5 Josh Childress 6.00 15.00
6 Luol Deng 10.00 25.00
7 Rafael Araujo 6.00 15.00
8 Andre Iguodala 10.00 25.00
9 Andris Biedrins 8.00 20.00
10 Kirk Snyder 6.00 15.00
11 Josh Smith 10.00 25.00
12 Jameer Nelson 8.00 20.00
13 Pavel Podkolzine 6.00 15.00
15 Beno Udrih 6.00 15.00

2004-05 Fleer Tradition Rookie Throwback Threads Jerseys

Inserted in Hobby packs at one in 112 and Retail at one in 240, this 24-card set parallels the look of the Rookie Hats Off insert but has a blue background and a swatch of jersey. Several other versions of this set were issued: Ball swatches are inserted one in 216 Hobby and one in 480 Retail, Headband swatches are inserted one in 612 Hobby and one in 960 Retail, Jersey and Ball swatches are serially numbered to 50 and Jersey and Headband swatches are serially numbered to 25.

*BALL: .5X TO 1.25X BASE HI
*HEADBAND: 1.25X TO 3X BASE HI
*JERSEY/BALL: 1.5X TO 4X BASE HI
*JSY/HEADBAND: 2X TO 5X BASE HI
1 Dwight Howard 8.00 20.00
2 Ben Gordon 3.00 8.00
3 Shaun Livingston 2.50 6.00
4 Devin Harris 4.00 10.00
5 Josh Childress 2.50 6.00
6 Luol Deng 4.00 10.00
7 Andre Iguodala 4.00 10.00
8 Rafael Araujo 2.50 6.00
9 Luke Jackson 2.50 6.00
10 Sebastian Telfair 2.50 6.00
11 Kris Humphries 2.50 6.00
12 Al Jefferson 4.00 10.00
13 Kirk Snyder 2.50 6.00
14 Josh Smith 4.00 10.00
15 J.R. Smith 3.00 8.00
16 Dorell Wright 4.00 10.00
17 Jameer Nelson 3.00 8.00
18 Delonte West 3.00 8.00
19 Tony Allen 3.00 8.00
20 Anderson Varejao 3.00 8.00
21 Lionel Chalmers 2.50 6.00
22 Chris Duhon 2.50 6.00
23 Bernard Robinson 2.50 6.00
24 Trevor Ariza 2.50 6.00

2004-05 Fleer Tradition Rookie Throwback Threads Dual

Inserted randomly, this 12-card set parallels the look of the Rookie Hats Off set but with a red background, sequential numbering to 100, two players, one on each side and two jerseys in the center of the card.

*PATCHES: .6X TO 1.5X BASE HI
1 Ben Gordon 6.00 15.00
Luol Deng
2 Dwight Howard 8.00 20.00
Jameer Nelson
3 Josh Childress 6.00 15.00
Josh Smith
4 Al Jefferson 5.00 12.00
Tony Allen
5 Shaun Livingston 5.00 12.00
Lionel Chalmers
6 Andre Iguodala 8.00 20.00
Trevor Ariza
7 Kris Humphries 5.00 12.00
Kirk Snyder
8 Devin Harris 6.00 15.00
Chris Duhon
10 Anderson Varejao 5.00 12.00
Bernard Robinson
11 Rafael Araujo 5.00 12.00
Luke Jackson
12 Jameer Nelson 5.00 12.00
Delonte West

2004-05 Fleer Tradition Signing Day

Inserted in Retail packs at the rate of one in 24, this 15-card set has white borders and a tan background and player photos are set against their new team logo. A Chrome parallel was inserted also and is sequentially numbered to 50.

COMPLETE SET (15) 10.00 25.00
*CHROME: 1.25X TO 3X BASE HI
1 Dwight Howard 2.50 6.00
2 Emeka Okafor 1.25 3.00
3 Ben Gordon 1.00 2.50
4 Shaun Livingston .75 2.00
5 Devin Harris 1.25 3.00
6 Josh Childress .75 2.00
7 Luol Deng 1.25 3.00
8 Andre Iguodala 1.25 3.00
9 Luke Jackson .75 2.00
10 Andris Biedrins 1.00 2.50
11 Robert Swift .75 2.00
12 Sebastian Telfair .75 2.00
13 Josh Smith 1.25 3.00
14 J.R. Smith 1.00 2.50
15 Jameer Nelson 1.00 2.50

2004-05 Fleer Tradition USA Basketball

Randomly inserted, this 13-card set features members of the USA basketball team on a card that is heavy with red white and blue and is serially numbered to 99.

1 LeBron James 25.00 60.00
2 Carmelo Anthony 6.00 15.00
3 Tim Duncan 5.00 12.00
4 Shawn Marion 3.00 8.00
5 Allen Iverson 5.00 12.00
6 Dwyane Wade 10.00 25.00
7 Amare Stoudemire 4.00 10.00
8 Richard Jefferson 3.00 8.00
9 Stephon Marbury 2.50 6.00
10 Carlos Boozer 3.00 8.00
11 Lamar Odom 3.00 8.00
12 Emeka Okafor 5.00 12.00
13 Larry Brown 4.00 10.00

2000-01 Fleer Triple Crown

The 2000-01 Fleer Triple Crown product was released in March, 2001 and featured a 241-card base set that was broken into tiers as follows: Rookies (1-40, 241), and Base Veterans (41-240). Please note that cards 1-40 and 241 were short-printed at the rate of one in four packs. Each pack contained 10 cards, and carried a suggested retail price of $1.99.

COMPLETE SET w/o RC (200) 12.50 25.00
1 Quentin Richardson RC .60 1.50
2 Khalid El-Amin RC .40 1.00
3 Courtney Alexander RC .40 1.00
4 Mike Penberthy RC .40 1.00
5 DerMarr Johnson RC .40 1.00
6 A.J. Guyton RC .40 1.00
7 Erick Barkley RC .40 1.00
8 Jamal Crawford RC .60 1.50
9 Hedo Turkoglu RC .75 2.00
10 Michael Redd RC 1.00 2.50
11 Stromile Swift RC .40 1.00
12 Eddie House RC .40 1.00
13 Keyon Dooling RC .40 1.00
14 Lavor Postell RC .40 1.00
15 Mateen Cleaves RC .40 1.00
16 Morris Peterson RC .40 1.00
17 DeShawn Stevenson RC .50 1.25
18 Darius Miles RC .40 1.00
19 Hanno Mottola RC .40 1.00
20 Jerome Moiso RC .40 1.00
21 Desmond Mason RC .50 1.25
22 Jason Collier RC .40 1.00
23 Ruben Wolkowyski RC .40 1.00
24 Eduardo Najera RC .40 1.00
25 Kenyon Martin RC 1.00 2.50
26 Marcus Fizer RC .40 1.00
27 Etan Thomas RC .40 1.00
28 Mark Madsen RC .40 1.00
29 Pepe Sanchez RC .40 1.00
30 Brian Cardinal RC .40 1.00
31 Chris Porter RC .40 1.00
32 Dan Langhi RC .40 1.00
33 Mike Miller RC .75 2.00
34 Chris Mihm RC .40 1.00
35 Mamadou N'Diaye RC .40 1.00
36 Dragan Tarlac RC .40 1.00
37 Iakovos Tsakalidis RC .40 1.00
38 Stephen Jackson RC .60 1.50
39 Jamaal Magloire RC .40 1.00
40 Joel Przybilla RC .40 1.00
41 Adrian Griffin .15 .40
42 Allan Houston .20 .50
43 Mahmoud Abdul-Rauf .15 .40
44 Avery Johnson .20 .50
45 Damon Stoudamire .20 .50
46 Jim Jackson .15 .40
47 Jason Williams .25 .60
48 Jason Kidd .40 1.00
49 Ray Allen .25 .60
50 Baron Davis .25 .60
51 Mark Jackson .20 .50
52 Darrick Martin .15 .40
53 Derek Fisher .25 .60
54 Anthony Peeler .15 .40
55 Vince Carter .50 1.25
56 Tim Hardaway .25 .60
57 Richard Hamilton .20 .50
58 Malik Rose .15 .40
59 Antonio Daniels .15 .40
60 Lindsey Hunter .15 .40
61 William Avery .15 .40
62 Reggie Miller .25 .60
63 Shareef Abdur-Rahim .20 .50
64 Travis Best .15 .40
65 John Stockton .30 .75
66 Kenny Anderson .20 .50
67 Trajan Langdon .15 .40
68 Sam Cassell .20 .50
69 Chucky Atkins .15 .40
70 Laron Profit .15 .40
71 Andre Miller .20 .50
72 Erick Strickland .15 .40
73 Ron Artest .25 .60
74 Kobe Bryant 1.25 3.00
75 Ricky Davis .20 .50
76 Allen Iverson .50 1.25
77 Steve Smith .20 .50
78 Alvin Williams .15 .40
79 Randy Brown .15 .40
80 Michael Dickerson .15 .40
81 Tyronn Lue .15 .40
82 Bonzi Wells .15 .40
83 Felipe Lopez .15 .40
84 Steve Francis .25 .60
85 Jaren Jackson .15 .40
86 Anthony Carter .15 .40
87 Mitch Richmond .20 .50
88 Sherman Douglas .15 .40
89 Cuttino Mobley .20 .50
90 Mario Elie .15 .40
91 Tariq Abdul-Wahad .15 .40
92 Ron Mercer .15 .40
93 Jalen Rose .20 .50
94 Mike Bibby .25 .60
95 Voshon Lenard .15 .40
96 Derek Anderson .15 .40
97 Kendall Gill .15 .40
98 Muggsy Bogues .20 .50
99 Eddie Jones .25 .60
100 Larry Hughes .20 .50
101 Latrell Sprewell .20 .50
102 Stephon Marbury .20 .50
103 Eric Piatkowski .15 .40
104 Brevin Knight .15 .40
105 Isaiah Rider .20 .50
106 Wesley Person .15 .40
107 Nick Van Exel .20 .50
108 Dell Curry .15 .40
109 Tony Delk .15 .40
110 Glen Rice .20 .50
111 Bobby Jackson .15 .40
112 Kerry Kittles .15 .40
113 John Starks .15 .40
114 Gary Payton .25 .60
115 Mookie Blaylock .20 .50
116 David Wesley .15 .40
117 Rod Strickland .20 .50
118 Terrell Brandon .15 .40
119 Steve Nash .40 1.00
120 Moochie Norris .15 .40
121 Eric Snow .15 .40
122 Chauncey Billups .25 .60
123 Darrell Armstrong .15 .40
124 Ron Harper .20 .50
125 Dion Glover .15 .40
126 Vin Baker .20 .50
127 Terry Mills .15 .40
128 Joe Smith .20 .50
129 Kurt Thomas .15 .40
130 Dirk Nowitzki .40 1.00
131 Sean Elliott .20 .50
132 Jerome Williams .15 .40
133 Larry Johnson .25 .60
134 LaPhonso Ellis .20 .50
135 Pat Garrity .15 .40
136 Lawrence Funderburke .15 .40
137 Elton Brand .25 .60
138 Rashard Lewis .25 .60
139 Shawn Kemp .25 .60
140 Elden Campbell .15 .40
141 Christian Laettner .15 .40
142 Al Harrington .20 .50
143 Billy Owens .15 .40
144 Wally Szczerbiak .20 .50
145 Jonathan Bender .15 .40
146 Karl Malone .30 .75
147 Andrew DeClercq .15 .40
148 Danny Manning .15 .40
149 Antoine Walker .20 .50
150 Jason Caffey .15 .40
151 P.J. Brown .15 .40
152 Matt Harpring .20 .50
153 Mark Strickland .15 .40
154 Theo Ratliff .15 .40
155 Ruben Patterson .15 .40
156 Tom Gugliotta .15 .40
157 Derrick Coleman .20 .50
158 Lorenzen Wright .15 .40
159 Tracy McGrady .40 1.00
160 Quincy Lewis .15 .40
161 Tony Battie .15 .40
162 Keith Van Horn .20 .50
163 Paul Pierce .30 .75
164 Glenn Robinson .20 .50
165 John Wallace .15 .40
166 Popeye Jones .15 .40
167 Kevin Garnett .50 1.25
168 Donyell Marshall .15 .40
169 Michael Finley .25 .60
170 Nick Anderson .15 .40
171 Danny Fortson .15 .40
172 Keon Clark .15 .40
173 Juwan Howard .20 .50
174 Brian Grant .15 .40
175 Marcus Camby .20 .50
176 Scottie Pippen .40 1.00
177 Shawn Marion .25 .60
178 Lamar Odom .25 .60
179 Charles Oakley .20 .50
180 Tim James .15 .40
181 Eric Williams .15 .40
182 Tim Duncan .50 1.25
183 Andrae Patterson .15 .40
184 Toni Kukoc .20 .50
185 Chris Mullin .25 .60
186 Alan Henderson .15 .40
187 Maurice Taylor .15 .40
188 Chris Webber .25 .60
189 Jamal Mashburn .20 .50
190 Rodney Rogers .15 .40
191 Loy Vaught .15 .40
192 Carlos Rogers .15 .40
193 Grant Hill .30 .75
194 George Lynch .15 .40
195 Antonio McDyess .20 .50
196 Tim Thomas .15 .40
197 Roshown McLeod .15 .40
198 Antawn Jamison .25 .60
199 Clifford Robinson .15 .40
200 Corey Maggette .20 .50
201 Horace Grant .20 .50
202 David Benoit .15 .40
203 Cedric Ceballos .15 .40
204 Antonio Davis .15 .40
205 Lamond Murray .15 .40
206 Jerry Stackhouse .20 .50
207 Jermaine O'Neal .25 .60
208 Anthony Mason .15 .40
209 Cedric Henderson .15 .40
210 Corliss Williamson .15 .40
211 Austin Croshere .15 .40
212 Radoslav Nesterovic .15 .40
213 Hakeem Olajuwon .30 .75
214 Nazr Mohammed .15 .40
215 David Robinson .40 1.00
216 Jeff McInnis .15 .40
217 Brad Miller .25 .60
218 Evan Eschmeyer .15 .40
219 Jelani McCoy .15 .40
220 Sean Rooks .15 .40
221 Dikembe Mutombo .25 .60
222 Othella Harrington .15 .40
223 John Amaechi .15 .40
224 Erick Dampier .15 .40
225 Calvin Booth .15 .40
226 Adonal Foyle .15 .40
227 Michael Doleac .15 .40
228 Michael Olowokandi .15 .40
229 Matt Geiger .15 .40
230 Vlade Divac .20 .50
231 Bryant Reeves .15 .40
232 Shaquille O'Neal .60 1.50
233 Todd Fuller .15 .40
234 Arvydas Sabonis .20 .50
235 Jim McIlvaine .15 .40
236 Isaac Austin .15 .40
237 Raef LaFrentz .15 .40
238 Rasheed Wallace .25 .60
239 Kelvin Cato .15 .40
240 Patrick Ewing .30 .75
241 Marc Jackson RC .40 1.00

2000-01 Fleer Triple Crown Vince Carter Rookie Remnants

This three-card insert was randomly inserted into 2000-01 Fleer products. The set includes a Vince Carter floor card (numbered to 100), a Vince Carter floor/jersey card (numbered to 15), and finally an autographed Vince Carter floor/jersey card (numbered 1/1).

NNO Vince Carter FLR/100 12.50 30.00

2000-01 Fleer Triple Crown Crown Jewels

Randomly inserted in packs at one in 84, this 15-card set highlights the marquee players that the fans say is well worth the admission price. Card backs carry a "CJ" prefix.

COMPLETE SET (15) 40.00 100.00
CJ1 Kevin Garnett 4.00 10.00
CJ2 Lamar Odom 2.00 5.00
CJ3 Allen Iverson 4.00 10.00
CJ4 Marcus Fizer 2.00 5.00
CJ5 Shaquille O'Neal 5.00 12.00
CJ6 Steve Francis 2.00 5.00
CJ7 Paul Pierce 2.50 6.00
CJ8 Elton Brand 2.00 5.00
CJ9 Chris Webber 2.00 5.00
CJ10 Tim Duncan 4.00 10.00
CJ11 Kobe Bryant 10.00 25.00
CJ12 Grant Hill 2.50 6.00
CJ13 Kenyon Martin 5.00 12.00
CJ14 Darius Miles 2.00 5.00
CJ15 Vince Carter 4.00 10.00

2000-01 Fleer Triple Crown Heir Force 01

Randomly inserted into packs at one in 10, this 15-card set features players that are so popular, they could almost hitch a ride on Air Force One. Card backs carry a "HF" prefix.

COMPLETE SET (15) 10.00 20.00
HF1 Kenyon Martin 1.50 4.00
HF2 Stromile Swift .60 1.50
HF3 Darius Miles .60 1.50
HF4 Courtney Alexander .60 1.50
HF5 Marcus Fizer .60 1.50
HF6 Keyon Dooling .60 1.50
HF7 Steve Francis .60 1.50
HF8 Elton Brand .60 1.50
HF9 Lamar Odom .60 1.50
HF10 Wally Szczerbiak .50 1.25
HF11 Vince Carter 1.25 3.00
HF12 Antawn Jamison .60 1.50
HF13 Jason Williams .60 1.50
HF14 Tim Duncan 1.25 3.00
HF15 Kobe Bryant 3.00 8.00

2000-01 Fleer Triple Crown Scoring Kings

Randomly inserted in packs, this 10-card set features the NBA's top scorers. Card backs carry a "SK" prefix. Please note that there were only 100 serial numbered sets produced.

SK1 Vince Carter 12.00 30.00
SK2 Shaquille O'Neal 15.00 40.00
SK3 Allen Iverson 12.00 30.00
SK4 Grant Hill 8.00 20.00
SK5 Chris Webber 6.00 15.00
SK6 Glenn Robinson 5.00 12.00
SK7 Lamar Odom 6.00 15.00
SK8 Gary Payton 6.00 15.00
SK9 Eddie Jones 6.00 15.00
SK10 Latrell Sprewell 5.00 12.00

2000-01 Fleer Triple Crown Scoring Menace

Randomly inserted in packs at one in 24, this 10-card set highlights players that can score with the best of them. Card backs carry a "SM" prefix.

COMPLETE SET (10) 7.50 15.00
SM1 Vince Carter 1.50 4.00
SM2 Shaquille O'Neal 2.00 5.00
SM3 Allen Iverson 1.50 4.00
SM4 Grant Hill 1.00 2.50
SM5 Chris Webber .75 2.00
SM6 Glenn Robinson .60 1.50
SM7 Lamar Odom .75 2.00
SM8 Gary Payton .75 2.00
SM9 Eddie Jones .75 2.00
SM10 Latrell Sprewell .60 1.50

2000-01 Fleer Triple Crown Shoot Arounds

Randomly inserted in packs at one in 72, each card in this 16-card set contains a swatch of pre-game warm-ups that the players actually wore. Cards are listed below in alphabetical order for convenience.

1 Vince Carter 6.00 15.00
2 Keyon Dooling 3.00 8.00
3 Grant Hill 4.00 10.00
4 Allen Iverson 6.00 15.00
5 Jason Kidd 5.00 12.00
6 Shawn Marion 3.00 8.00
7 Tracy McGrady 5.00 12.00
8 Chris Mihm 3.00 8.00
9 Darius Miles 3.00 8.00
10 Andre Miller 2.50 6.00
11 Mike Miller 6.00 15.00
12 Hanno Mottola 3.00 8.00
13 Lamar Odom 3.00 8.00
14 Quentin Richardson 5.00 12.00
15 John Stockton 4.00 10.00

2000-01 Fleer Triple Crown Triple Threats

Randomly inserted in packs at one in 5, this 15-card set highlights players that can shoot, pass, and rebound. Card backs carry a "TT" prefix.

COMPLETE SET (15) 4.00 10.00
TT1 Vince Carter .75 2.00
TT2 Jason Kidd .60 1.50
TT3 Gary Payton .40 1.00
TT4 Scottie Pippen .60 1.50
TT5 Hakeem Olajuwon .50 1.25
TT6 Kevin Garnett .75 2.00
TT7 Steve Francis .40 1.00
TT8 Antoine Walker .30 .75
TT9 Andre Miller .30 .75
TT10 Chris Webber .40 1.00
TT11 Lamar Odom .40 1.00
TT12 Tim Duncan .75 2.00
TT13 Grant Hill .50 1.25
TT14 David Robinson .60 1.50
TT15 Michael Finley .40 1.00

2000 Fleer Tuff Stuff Vince Carter

This card was released by Tuff Stuff in conjunction with Fleer magazine. The card features a facsimile autograph of superstar Vince Carter. The back of the card states that "This card contains a facsimile signature of Toronto Raptors star Vince Carter".

NNO Vince Carter 1.25 3.00

1996 Fleer USA

The 1996 Fleer USA set was issued in one series totalling 52 cards. The 3-card packs retailed for $4.99 each during the summer of 1996. Each pack contained two super-premium and one lenticular card which resulted in the super-premium cards being triple-printed. The set contains the topical subsets: In the Beginning (1-10), By the Numbers (11-20), Defining Moment (21-30), Masters of the Game (31-40), Around the World (41-50). Each Around the World, In the Beginning and Defining Moments card features the lenticular technology with rotating images of the earth, pulsating player images and a USA/5-ring logo that changes color. Each By the Numbers and Masters of the Game card features super-premium UV-coating, foil-stamping and printing on thick, 20-point stock.

COMPLETE SET (52) 20.00 50.00
1 Anfernee Hardaway IB 1.00 2.50
2 Grant Hill IB 1.00 2.50
3 Karl Malone IB .75 2.00
4 Reggie Miller IB .75 2.00
5 Hakeem Olajuwon IB .75 2.00
6 Shaquille O'Neal IB 1.50 4.00
7 Scottie Pippen IB 1.00 2.50
8 David Robinson IB 1.00 2.50
9 Glenn Robinson IB .60 1.50
10 John Stockton IB .75 2.00
11 Anfernee Hardaway BN .50 1.25
12 Grant Hill BN .50 1.25
13 Karl Malone BN .40 1.00
14 Reggie Miller BN .40 1.00
15 Hakeem Olajuwon BN .40 1.00
16 Shaquille O'Neal BN .75 2.00
17 Scottie Pippen BN .50 1.25
18 David Robinson BN .50 1.25
19 Glenn Robinson BN .30 .75
20 John Stockton BN .40 1.00
21 Anfernee Hardaway DM 1.00 2.50
22 Grant Hill DM 1.00 2.50
23 Karl Malone DM .75 2.00
24 Reggie Miller DM .75 2.00
25 Hakeem Olajuwon DM .75 2.00
26 Shaquille O'Neal DM 1.50 4.00
27 Scottie Pippen DM 1.00 2.50
28 David Robinson DM 1.00 2.50
29 Glenn Robinson DM .60 1.50
30 John Stockton DM .75 2.00
31 Anfernee Hardaway MAS .50
32 Grant Hill MAS .50
33 Karl Malone MAS .40
34 Reggie Miller MAS .40
35 Hakeem Olajuwon MAS .40
36 Shaquille O'Neal MAS .75
37 Scottie Pippen MAS .50
38 David Robinson MAS .50
39 Glenn Robinson MAS .30
40 John Stockton MAS .40
41 Anfernee Hardaway AW 1.00
42 Grant Hill AW 1.00
43 Karl Malone AW .75
44 Reggie Miller AW .75
45 Hakeem Olajuwon AW .75
46 Shaquille O'Neal AW 1.50
47 Scottie Pippen AW 1.00
48 David Robinson AW 1.00
49 Glenn Robinson AW .60
50 John Stockton AW .75
51 Team USA CL 51/52 1.25
52 Team USA CL 1.25

1996 Fleer USA Heroes

Randomly inserted exclusively into hobby packs a rate of one in 18, this 10-card set features the 10 original members of the 1996 USAB men's baske team in a special die-cut design with the top left c card clipped as the player is silhouetted across th American flag and extended out beyond the natur border of the card.

COMPLETE SET (10) 40.00
1 Anfernee Hardaway 8.00
2 Grant Hill 8.00
3 Karl Malone 6.00
4 Reggie Miller 6.00
5 Hakeem Olajuwon 6.00
6 Shaquille O'Neal 12.00
7 Scottie Pippen 8.00
8 David Robinson 8.00
9 Glenn Robinson 5.00
10 John Stockton 6.00

1996 Fleer USA Wrapper Exchange

Collectors were offered the chance to receive this special 12-card exchange set by sending in 15 wrappers (along with $3.00 for postage and hand The 12 cards consisted of three lenticular, two su premium and one Heroes insert of both Charles Barkley and Mitch Richmond.

COMPLETE SET (12) 4.00
M1 Charles Barkley ITB 1.00
M2 Mitch Richmond ITB .60
M3 Charles Barkley BTN .50
M4 Mitch Richmond BTN .30
M5 Charles Barkley ATW 1.00
M6 Mitch Richmond ATW .60
M7 Charles Barkley MAS .50
M8 Mitch Richmond MAS .30
M9 Charles Barkley DM 1.00
M10 Mitch Richmond DM .60
M11 Charles Barkley Heroes 1.50
M12 Mitch Richmond Heroes 1.00

2001 Fleer Viva Vince Cart

Given away at a Vince Carter basketball camp in this card was originally printed unautographed, h that is how it is cataloged. Vince Carter did sign several, possibly the majority for camp givaways, is uncertain as to how many he did in fact sign, a representative was present to certify the autograp The front features bright colors and the words, " Vince Carter," while the back, in spanish, is a che of basketball fundamental skills.

1 Vince Carter 1.50

2001 Fleer WNBA

The 2001 Fleer WNBA product was released in J 2001 and featured a 165-card base set. Each pac contained ten cards, and carried a suggested ret price of $1.49.

COMP.SET w/o RC (165) 10.00
1 Lisa Leslie .75
2 Andrea Stinson .30
3 Tammy Jackson .15
4 Nicky McCrimmon RC .20
5 Vickie Johnson .25
6 Maria Stepanova .15
7 Michelle Edwards .30
8 Tausha Mills .15
9 Edwina Brown .20
10 Jurgita Streimikyte .15
11 Keitha Dickerson RC .20
12 Taj McWilliams-Franklin .15
13 DeMya Walker .15
14 Adrienne Goodson .15
15 Eva Nemcova .25
16 Danielle McCulley RC .20
17 Shannon Johnson .15
18 Margo Dydek .25
19 Mery Andrade .15
20 Marlies Askamp .15
21 Adrain Williams .15
22 Sonja Henning .15
23 Astou Ndiaye-Diatta .25
24 Latasha Byears .25
25 Kate Paye RC .20
26 Yolanda Griffith .50
27 Kate Starbird .25
28 Jennifer Rizzotti .40
29 Umeki Webb .15
30 Tari Phillips .15
31 Tully Bevilaqua RC .30
32 Murriel Page .20
33 Tricia Bader Binford .15
34 Sheryl Swoopes 1.00
35 Debbie Black .25
36 Teresa Weatherspoon .60
37 Alisa Burras .15
38 Stacey Lovelace RC .50
39 Helen Darling .20
40 Tina Thompson .50

atrina Colleton .15 .40
amika Whitmore .15 .40
ylvia Crawley .15 .40
amie Redd RC .20 .50
racy Reid .25 .60
aneth Arcain .15 .40
tacy Frese RC .30 .75
race Daley .15 .40
ridget Pettis .15 .40
aty Steding .15 .40
eth Cunningham .15 .40
icki Hall RC .20 .50
maya Valdemoro .20 .50
ilena Flores .15 .40
ue Wicks .25 .60
ichelle Marciniak .25 .60
racy Henderson .15 .40
isha Ford .15 .40
annon Roland .15 .40
anessa Nygaard RC .20 .50
ollyanna Johns RC .20 .50
ordana Grubin .15 .40
hantia Owens .15 .40
intia Dos Santos .15 .40
ynn Pride .15 .40
obin Threatt RC .20 .50
laudia Maria das Neves RC .20 .50
hantel Tremitiere .15 .40
etty Lennox .50 1.25
uthie Bolton-Holifield .50 1.25
orie Hlede .25 .60
ominique Canty .25 .60
icia Thompson .15 .40
ristin Folkl .25 .60
aine Powell .15 .40
indy Blodgett .25 .60
harlotte Smith .15 .40
Iwadi Mabika .15 .40
arina Ferragut RC .30 .75
randy Reed .25 .60
uacy Barnes .15 .40
hamique Holdsclaw 1.00 2.50
awn Staley .40 1.00
ekeshia Henderson RC .20 .50
ronda Mapp .20 .50
ecky Hammon 1.00 2.50
dna Campbell .20 .50
ikki McCray .40 1.00
nna DeForge .15 .40
ta Williams .20 .50
ndrea Lloyd Curry .15 .40
ykesha Sales .25 .60
tacy Clinesmith RC .30 .75
aTonya Johnson .15 .40
arkita Aldridge .15 .40
halonda Enis .15 .40
endy Palmer .40 1.00
emecka Dixon .25 .60
atie Smith .50 1.25
Tonya Edwards .15 .40
ady Hardmon .15 .40
Dalma Ivanyi .15 .40
Tiffany Travis RC .30 .75
Tiffani Johnson RC .20 .50
DeLisha Milton .15 .40
Rebecca Lobo .50 1.25
Michele Timms .50 1.25
Andrea Garner RC .20 .50
Andrea Nagy .25 .60
Summer Erb .15 .40
Ukari Figgs .15 .40
Jennifer Gillom .40 1.00
Kedra Holland-Corn .15 .40
Natalie Williams .30 .75
Clarisse Machanguana .15 .40
E.C. Hill RC .20 .50
Lisa Harrison .25 .60
Angela Smith .15 .40
Vicky Bullett .25 .60
Ann Wauters .20 .50
Marla Brumfield RC .20 .50
Carla McGhee .15 .40
Sophia Witherspoon .25 .60
Tamicha Jackson .15 .40
Kara Wolters .20 .50
Maylana Martin .20 .50
Tiffany McCain RC .30 .75
Naomi Mulitauaopele .15 .40
Chasity Melvin .15 .40
Stephanie McCarty .30 .75
Sheri Sam .15 .40
Adrienne Johnson .25 .60
Jennifer Azzi .50 1.25
Allison Feaster .20 .50
Elena Tornikidou RC .20 .50
Sonja Tate .15 .40
Michelle Brogan RC .20 .50
Ticha Penicheiro .40 1.00
Keisha Anderson .15 .40
Merlakia Jones .25 .60
Monica Maxwell .15 .40
Kristen Rasmussen RC .30 .75
Stacey Thomas .15 .40
Kamila Vodichkova .15 .40
Angie Braziel .25 .60
Olympia Scott-Richardson .15 .40
Vedrana Grgin RC .20 .50
Shanele Stires .15 .40
Coquese Washington .15 .40
Crystal Robinson .15 .40
Texlan Quinney .15 .40
Michelle Cleary RC .20 .50
La'Keshia Frett .15 .40
Jessie Hicks .15 .40
Katrina Hibbert .15 .40
Cass Bauer .25 .60
Jessica Bibby .15 .40
Shea Mahoney RC .20 .50
Charmin Smith .25 .60
Oksana Zakaluzhnaya .15 .40
Tonya Washington .20 .50
Tushia Brown .15 .40
Amy Herrig RC .20 .50
Tara Williams .20 .50
Sandy Brondello .40 1.00
Tammy Sutton-Brown RC 5.00 12.00
Kelly Miller RC 5.00 12.00
Penny Taylor RC 6.00 15.00
Kelly Santos RC 5.00 12.00
Deanna Nolan RC 5.00 12.00
Le Kingi RC 5.00 12.00
Amanda Lassiter RC 5.00 12.00
Tisha Stafford-Odom RC 5.00 12.00
Ernesha Lewis RC 5.00 12.00
Tamika Catchings RC 10.00 25.00
176 Kelly Schumacher RC 5.00 12.00
177 Niele Ivey RC 5.00 12.00
178 Nicole Levandusky RC 5.00 12.00
179 Wendy Willits RC 5.00 12.00
180 Ruth Riley RC 6.00 15.00
181 Levys Torres RC 5.00 12.00
182 Janell Burse RC 5.00 12.00
183 Svetlana Abrosimova RC 5.00 12.00
184 Erin Buescher RC 5.00 12.00
185 Georgia Schweitzer RC 5.00 12.00
186 Camille Cooper RC 5.00 12.00
187 Brooke Wyckoff RC 8.00 20.00
188 Jaclyn Johnson RC 5.00 12.00
189 Tawona Alehaleem RC 5.00 12.00
190 Katie Douglas RC 8.00 20.00
191 Jaynetta Saunders RC 5.00 12.00
192 Kristen Veal RC 5.00 12.00
193 Jenny Mowe RC 5.00 12.00
194 Jackie Stiles RC 15.00 40.00
195 LaQuanda Barksdale RC 5.00 12.00
196 Lauren Jackson RC 20.00 50.00
197 Semeka Randall RC 5.00 12.00
198 Michaela Pavlickova RC 5.00 12.00
199 Marie Ferdinand RC 5.00 12.00
200 Shea Ralph RC 5.00 12.00
201 Cara Consuegra RC 5.00 12.00
202 Tamara Stocks RC 5.00 12.00
203 Coco Miller RC 5.00 12.00
204 Helen Luz RC 5.00 12.00

2001 Fleer WNBA Autographics

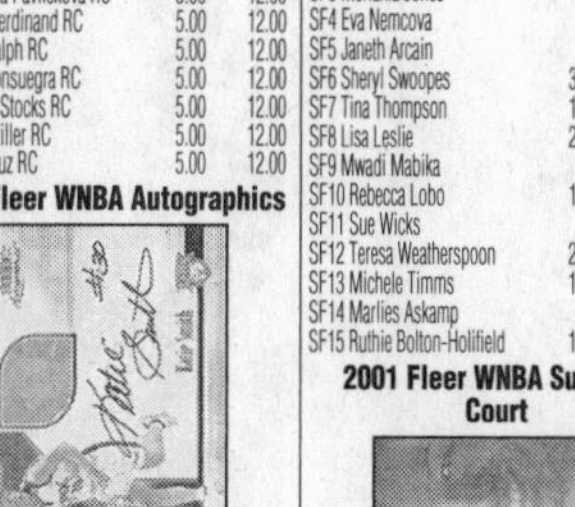

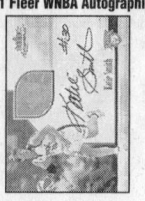

Randomly inserted into packs at one in 144, this insert set features autographs of the WNBA hottest players. Please note that the cards have been listed below in alphabetical order for convenience.

COMPLETE SET (6) 60.00 120.00
PLUS UNPRICED DUE TO SCARCITY
1 Jennifer Azzi 15.00 40.00
2 Betty Lennox 15.00 40.00
3 Lisa Leslie 15.00 40.00
4 Katie Smith 15.00 40.00
6 Sheryl Swoopes 15.00 40.00
5 Natalie Williams 15.00 40.00

2001 Fleer WNBA Autographics Extra

Randomly inserted into packs, this insert set is actually a complete parallel of the Autographics insert set. Each of these cards are serial numbered to 50. Please note that the cards have been listed below in alphabetical order for convenience.

*EXTRA: .6X TO 1.5X AUTOGRAPHICS HI

2001 Fleer WNBA Award Winners

Randomly inserted into packs at one in 30, this 10-card set focuses on some of the more prolific players from the 2000 WNBA season. Card backs carry an "AW" prefix.

COMPLETE SET (10) 10.00 25.00
AW1 Sheryl Swoopes 4.00 10.00
AW2 Natalie Williams 1.25 3.00
AW3 Lisa Leslie 3.00 8.00
AW4 Ticha Penicheiro 1.50 4.00
AW5 Tina Thompson 2.00 5.00
AW6 Katie Smith 2.00 5.00
AW7 Yolanda Griffith 2.00 5.00
AW8 Teresa Weatherspoon 2.50 6.00
AW9 Betty Lennox 2.00 5.00
AW10 Tari Phillips .60 1.50

2001 Fleer WNBA Global Game

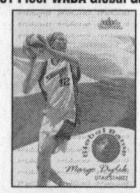

Randomly inserted into packs at one in 6, this 20-card insert set focuses on players that would dominate the game no matter what part of the world they were playing in. Card backs carry a "GG" prefix.

COMPLETE SET (20) 8.00 20.00
GG1 Janeth Arcain .40 1.00
GG2 Marlies Askamp .40 1.00
GG3 Mery Andrade .40 1.00
GG4 Tully Bevilaqua .60 1.50
GG5 Margo Dydek .60 1.50
GG6 Gordana Grubin .40 1.00
GG7 Mwadi Mabika .40 1.00
GG8 Andrea Nagy .60 1.50
GG9 Astou Ndiaye-Diatta .60 1.50
GG10 Eva Nemcova .60 1.50
GG11 Ticha Penicheiro 1.00 2.50
GG12 Maria Stepanova .40 1.00
GG13 Michele Timms 1.25 3.00
GG14 Kamila Vodichkova .40 1.00
GG15 Ann Wauters .50 1.25
GG16 Yolanda Griffith 1.25 3.00
GG17 Chamique Holdsclaw 2.50 6.00
GG18 Katie Smith 1.25 3.00
GG19 Nikki McCray 1.00 2.50
GG20 Natalie Williams .75 2.00

2001 Fleer WNBA Starting Five

Randomly inserted into packs at one in 12, this 15-card insert set focuses on players that you can find in the starting lineup almost every night. Card backs carry a "SF" prefix.

COMPLETE SET (15) 12.50 30.00
SF1 Vicky Bullett .75 2.00
SF2 Andrea Stinson 1.00 2.50
SF3 Merlakia Jones .75 2.00
SF4 Eva Nemcova .75 2.00
SF5 Janeth Arcain .50 1.25
SF6 Sheryl Swoopes 3.00 8.00
SF7 Tina Thompson 1.50 4.00
SF8 Lisa Leslie 2.50 6.00
SF9 Mwadi Mabika .50 1.25
SF10 Rebecca Lobo 1.50 4.00
SF11 Sue Wicks .75 2.00
SF12 Teresa Weatherspoon 2.00 5.00
SF13 Michele Timms 1.50 4.00
SF14 Marlies Askamp .50 1.25
SF15 Ruthie Bolton-Holifield 1.50 4.00

2001 Fleer WNBA Supreme Court

Randomly inserted into packs at one in 18, this 10-card insert set focuses on players that dominate the court. Card backs carry a "SC" prefix.

COMPLETE SET (10) 12.50 30.00
SC1 Chamique Holdsclaw 3.00 8.00
SC2 Natalie Williams 1.00 2.50
SC3 Betty Lennox 1.50 4.00
SC4 Yolanda Griffith 1.50 4.00
SC5 Sheryl Swoopes 3.00 8.00
SC6 Tina Thompson 1.50 4.00
SC7 Lisa Leslie 2.50 6.00
SC8 Jennifer Gillom 1.25 3.00
SC9 Ticha Penicheiro 1.25 3.00
SC10 Michele Timms 1.50 4.00

2001 Fleer Hersey WNBA

COMPLETE SET (12) 6.00 15.00
1 Chamique Holdsclaw 2.00 5.00
2 Sonja Henning .30 .75
3 Wendy Palmer .60 1.50
4 Brandy Reed .30 .75
5 Teresa Weatherspoon 1.00 2.50
6 Shannon Johnson .30 .75
7 Natalie Williams .60 1.50
8 Sophia Witherspoon .30 .75
9 Lisa Leslie 1.25 3.00
10 Katie Smith 1.00 2.50
11 Andrea Stinson .60 1.50
12 Kara Wolters .30 .75

1996-97 Fleer/SkyBox Jerry Stackhouse Sample

This unique sample two-card set features Jerry Stackhouse on the left card against a colorful red, blue and black background with the player's name running vertically along the bottom in white letters. The back of the card is not numbered and featues some biographical information on Stackhouse. The right portion of the card is a survey form that if completed by June 15, 1997 and sent it with three wrappers from any Fleer or SkyBox basketball card product, could be sent in for a limited edition Grant Hill jumbo card. Both cards are not-numbered and priced below. The Hill jumbo card is not considered a part of the set.

1 Jerry Stackhouse 1.25 3.00
2 Grant Hill Jumbo 4.00 10.00

1999 Fleer/SkyBox Dunkography

This one oversized card was sent to dealers commemorating the signing of both Vince Carter and Lamar Odom as company spokesmen. The card front features both Carter and Odom dunking against a "sky" background. The card is serially numbered to 3000 on the front. The NNO card back carries player information.

NNO Vince Carter 8.00 20.00
Lamar Odom

1971-72 Floridians McDonald's

This ten-card set of ABA Miami Floridians was sponsored by McDonald's. The cards measure approximately 2 1/2" by 4", including a 1/2" tear-off tab at the bottom. The bottom tab admitted one 14-or-under child to the game with each regular price adult ticket. Prices below refer to cards with tabs intact. The fronts feature color action player photos with rounded corners and black borders. The backs have player information, rules governing the free youth tickets, and an offer to receive an ABA basketball in exchange for a set of ten different Floridian tickets. The cards are unnumbered and are checklisted below in alphabetical order.

COMPLETE SET (10) 300.00 600.00
1 Warren Armstrong 40.00 80.00
2 Mack Calvin 50.00 100.00
3 Ron Franz 30.00 60.00
4 Ira Harge 30.00 60.00
5 Larry Jones 30.00 60.00
6 Willie Long 30.00 60.00
7 Sam Robinson 30.00 60.00
8 Al Tucker 30.00 60.00
9 George Tinsley 30.00 60.00
10 Lonnie Wright 30.00 60.00

1991 Foot Locker Slam Fest

This 30-card standard-size set was issued by Foot Locker in three ten-card series to commemorate the "Foot Locker Slam Fest" dunk contest televised during halftimes of NBC college basketball games through March 10, 1991. Each set contained two Domino's Pizza coupons and a 5.00 discount coupon on any purchase of 50.00 or more at Foot Locker. The set was released in substantial quantity after the promotional coupons expired. The fronts feature both posed and action photos enclosed in an arch like double red borders. The card top carries a blue border with "Foot Locker" in blue print on a white background. Beneath the photo appears "Limited Edition" and the player's name. The backs present career highlights, card series, and numbers placed within an arch of double red borders. The player's name and team name appear in black lettering at the bottom. The cards are numbered on the back; the card numbering below adds the number 10 to each card number in the second series and 20 to each card number in the third series.

COMPLETE SET (30) 2.00 5.00
11 Wilt Chamberlain BK 1.20 3.00
12 Cal Ramsey BK .02 .05
14 John Havlicek BK .40 1.00
15 Calvin Murphy BK .04 .10
16 Nate Thurmond BK .10 .25
17 John Havlicek BK .40 1.00
21 Jerry Lucas BK .10 .25
23 Elvin Hayes BK .10 .25
26 Earl Monroe BK .10 .25
29 Wilt Chamberlain BK .40 1.00
and Company

1985 Fournier Ases del Baloncesto

This set of 33 playing cards was produced in Spain. It is a card game similar to "Go Fish" and features mostly Spanish players who played in the Spanish Basketball League in 1985. Jimmy Wright and David Russell are two Americans included in this set. The cards came in a cardboard box, measure the standard size and have rounded corners. The fronts have color action player photos with the player's name and position, team name, the player's height and age beneath. The backs carry an orange and white pattern. Players from following teams are included in this set: Real Madrid C.F., Licor 43 Santa Coloma, Caja De Alava, Estudiantes Caja Postal, Forum Valladolid, R.C.D. Espanol-Juver, Cai Zaragoza, Breogan Caixa Galicia, Ron Negrita Juventud, and F.C. Barcelona.

COMPLETE SET (33) 30.00 80.00
1a Juan A. Corbalan 1.25 3.00
1b Fernando Martin 1.25 3.00
1c Fernando Romay 1.25 3.00
1d Lopez Iturriaga 1.25 3.00
2a Jordi Freixanet 1.25 3.00
2b Joaquin Costa 1.25 3.00
2c Miguel Angel Pou 1.25 3.00
2d Inaki Garayalde 1.25 3.00
3a Pedro Rodriguez 1.25 3.00
3b David Russell 4.00 10.00
3c Fco. Javier Lafuente 1.25 3.00
3d Alberto Ortega 1.25 3.00
4a Oscar Pena 1.25 3.00
4b Jose A. Alonso 1.25 3.00
4c Joaquin Salvo 1.25 3.00
4d Albert Illa 1.25 3.00
5a Francisco J. Zapata 1.25 3.00
5b Claude Riley 1.25 3.00
5c Jose Luis Diaz 1.25 3.00
5d Herminio San Epifanio 1.25 3.00
6a Manuel Sanchez 1.25 3.00
6b Jimmy Wright 2.50 6.00
6c Suso Fernandez 1.25 3.00
6d Pepe Collins 1.25 3.00
7a Jose Maria Margall 1.25 3.00
7b Jordi Villacampa 1.25 3.00
7c Jose A. Montero 1.25 3.00
7d Andres Jimenez 1.25 3.00
8a J.A. San Epifanio 1.25 3.00
8b Chico Sibilio 1.25 3.00
8c Ignacio Solozabal 1.25 3.00
8d Arturo S. Seara 1.25 3.00
NNO Title Card 2.00 5.00

1988 Fournier NBA Estrellas

This 33-card set was produced in Spain by Fournier and showcases many of the NBA hottest stars. The cards were distributed exclusively in cello-wrapped factory-sealed complete sets. The cards measure approximately 2 1/8" by 3 7/16" and have rounded corners. The fronts feature borderless high glossy action player photos; in the white stripe below the picture, player statistics are given. The entire area of the card backs displays the NBA logo in red, white, and blue (indicating that the set was licensed by the NBA for distribution in Spain). The cards are numbered on the front in the upper left corner. The card backs were written in Spanish. The set features Danny Manning's first professional card in addition to an early Muggsy Bogues issue.

COMPLETE SET (33) 12.50 30.00
1 Larry Bird 1.50 4.00
2 Robert Parish .30 .75
3 Kevin McHale .60 1.50
4 Magic Johnson 1.25 3.00
5 Kareem Abdul-Jabbar .75 2.00
6 Byron Scott .40 1.00
7 Isiah Thomas .60 1.50
8 Adrian Dantley .20 .50
9 Dominique Wilkins .60 1.50
10 Spud Webb .20 .50
11 Clyde Drexler .60 1.50
12 Terry Porter .20 .50
13 Mark Aguirre .20 .50
14 Muggsy Bogues .40 1.00
15 Patrick Ewing .75 2.00
16 Karl Malone 1.00 2.50
17 Charles Barkley 1.25 3.00
18 Ron Harper .40 1.00
19 Alex English .40 1.00
20 Xavier McDaniel .20 .50
21 Jeff Malone .20 .50
22 Michael Jordan 6.00 15.00
23 Hakeem Olajuwon 1.00 2.50
24 Ralph Sampson .20 .50
25 Buck Williams .20 .50
26 Chuck Person .20 .50
27 Alvin Robertson .20 .50
28 Tom Chambers .20 .50
29 Paul Pressey .20 .50
30 Danny Manning .60 1.50
31 LaSalle Thompson .20 .50
32 John Stockton 1.25 3.00
NNO Michael Jordan Rules 4.00 10.00

1988 Fournier NBA Estrellas Stickers

This ten-sticker set was produced in Spain by Fournier as a random insert with its regular set as only a portion of the sets contained a sticker insert. The stickers measure approximately 1" by 1 1/4" and picture the player from the chest up. The stickers come in a sealed pouch which is semi-transparent. The easiest stickers to find are Larry Bird, Magic Johnson, and Michael Jordan. The stickers are unnumbered and are listed below in alphabetical order.

COMPLETE SET (10) 300.00 500.00
1 Kareem Abdul-Jabbar 30.00 80.00
2 Mark Aguirre 20.00 50.00
3 Larry Bird DP 10.00 25.00
4 Magic Johnson DP 8.00 20.00
5 Michael Jordan DP 30.00 75.00
6 Moses Malone 25.00 60.00
7 Kevin McHale 25.00 60.00
8 Robert Parish 25.00 60.00
9 Isiah Thomas 25.00 60.00
10 James Worthy 25.00 60.00

1963 Gad Fun Cards

This set of 1963 Fun Cards were issued by a sports illustrator by the name of Gad from Minneapolis, Minnesota. The cards are printed on cardboard stock paper. The borderless fronts have black and white line drawings. A fun sport's fact or player career statistic is depicted in the drawing. The backs of the first six cards display numbers used to play the game explained on card number 6. The other backs carry a cartoon with a joke or riddle. Copyright information is listed on the lower portion of the card.

COMPLETE SET (84) 37.50 75.00
76 Buffalo Germans .25 .50
Basketball Squad

1998 GE David Robinson Phone Cards

Produced by General Electric, this 5-card set features different action shots of David Robinson on five different prepaid units of phone time. The units available were 30, 60, 75, 90 and 120. Callers could also use the phone card to listen to different messages from Robinson - or even leave him a message. The different units were priced as follows: 30 at $9.90, 60 at $19.80, 75 at $24.75, 90 at $29.70 and 120 at $39.60. The phone cards expire six months from first use or by June 30th, 1999. Prices below reflect cards with phone time intact. Used cards are priced at 20% of the listed value. The cards below are not numbered and listed alphabetically.

COMPLETE SET (5) 40.00 100.00
1 David Robinson 30 units 4.00 10.00
2 David Robinson 60 units 8.00 20.00
3 David Robinson 75 units 10.00 25.00
4 David Robinson 90 units 12.50 30.00
5 David Robinson 120 units 15.00 40.00

1971-72 Globetrotters Cocoa Puffs 28

This 1971-72 Harlem Globetrotters set was produced for Cocoa Puffs cereal by Fleer and contains 28 standard size cards. The cards were issued inside specially marked cereal boxes with four consecutively numbered cards per box. The card fronts have full color pictures with facsimile autographs. The card backs are subtitled "Cocoa Puffs presents the magicians of basketball and have black printing on gray card stock and feature biographical sketches and other interesting information about the Globetrotters. The cards are numbered on back X of 28.

COMPLETE SET (28) 90.00 180.00
1 Geese Ausbie and Curly Neal 7.50 15.00
2 Neal and Meadowlark 5.00 10.00
3 Meadowlark is Safe 3.00 8.00
4 Meadowlark Lemon Curly Neal and Geese Ausbie 3.00 8.00
5 Mel Davis and Bill Meggett 2.00 5.00
6 Geese Ausbie Meadowlark Lemon and Curly Neal 3.00 8.00
7 Geese Ausbie Meadowlark Lemon and Curly Neal 3.00 8.00
8 Mel Davis and Curly Neal 2.50 6.00
9 Meadowlark Lemon Curly Neal and Geese Ausbie 3.00 8.00
10 Curly Neal Meadowlark Lemon and Mel Davis 3.00 8.00
11 Football Routine 2.00 5.00
12 1970-71 Highlights 2.00 5.00
13 Pabs Robertson 2.00 5.00
14 Bobby Joe Mason 2.00 5.00
15 Pabs Robertson 2.00 5.00
16 Clarence Smith 2.00 5.00
17 Clarence Smith 2.00 5.00
18 Hubert (Geese) Ausbie 2.50 6.00
19 Hubert(Geese) Ausbie (Two balls) 2.50 6.00
20 Bobby Hunter 2.00 5.00
21 Bobby Hunter (One leg up) 2.00 5.00
22 Meadowlark Lemon (Three balls) 3.00 8.00
23 Meadowlark Lemon 3.00 8.00
24 Freddie (Curly) Neal 3.00 8.00
25 Freddie (Curly) Neal (Three paint brushes) 3.00 8.00
26 Meadowlark Lemon (Palming two balls) 3.00 8.00
27 Mel Davis (Leaning over with ball) 2.00 5.00
28 Freddie Curly Neal 7.50 15.00

1971-72 Globetrotters 84

The 1971-72 Harlem Globetrotters set was produced by Fleer and sold in wax packs. The set contains 84 standard size cards. The card fronts have full color pictures. The card backs have black printing on gray card stock and feature biographical sketches and other interesting information about the Globetrotters. The cards are numbered on back "X" of 84. A Globetrotter Emblem sticker was inserted in each wax pack.

COMPLETE SET (85) 75.00 150.00
1 Bob Showboat Hall 5.00 12.00
2 Bob Showboat Hall (kicking ball) .75 2.00
3 Bob Showboat Hall (passing behind back) .75 2.00
4 Pabs Robertson .75 2.00
5 Pabs Robertson .75 2.00
6 Pabs Robertson .75 2.00
7 Pabs Robertson .75 2.00
8 Pabs Robertson .75 2.00
9 Meadowlark Lemon (kicking behind back) 2.50 6.00
10 Meadowlark Lemon (rolling ball on arm) 2.50 6.00
11 Meadowlark Lemon (palming two balls) 2.50 6.00
12 Meadowlark Lemon (ball on neck) 2.50 6.00
13 Meadowlark Lemon (three balls) 2.50 6.00
14 Meadowlark Lemon (three balls in front) 2.50 6.00
15 Meadowlark Lemon (three balls) 2.50 6.00
16 Meadowlark Lemon (dribbling two balls) 2.50 6.00
17 Meadowlark Lemon (with cap) 2.50 6.00
18 Curley Neal Meadowlark Lemon and Mel Davis 2.50 6.00
19 Football Play (Meadowlark centering) 2.50 6.00
20 Meadowlark Lemon (hooking) 2.50 6.00
21 Hubert Geese Ausbie (balls between legs) 1.00 2.50
22 Hubert Geese Ausbie (ball under arm) 1.00 2.50
23 Hubert Geese Ausbie (ball on finger) 1.00 2.50
24 Hubert Geese Ausbie (ball behind back) 1.00 2.50
25 Hubert Geese Ausbie (no ball) 1.00 2.50
26 Geese Ausbie and {Curly Neal with confetti) 2.00 5.00
27 Freddie Curly Neal (artist) 2.50 6.00
28 Freddie Curly Neal (sitting on ball) 2.50 6.00
29 Freddie Curly Neal (two balls on head) 2.50 6.00
30 Mel Davis and Freddie Curly Neal 1.50 4.00
31 Freddie Curly Neall (smiling) 2.50 6.00
32 Freddie CurlyNeal (looking to side) 2.50 6.00
33 Mel Davis (looking down) .75 2.00
34 Mel Davis (ready to shoot) .75 2.00
35 Mel Davis (ball in hand) .75 2.00
36 Mel Davis (ball over head) .75 2.00
37 Mel Davis and Bill Meggett (leap frog) .75 2.00
38 Mel Davis (ball on knee) .75 2.00
39 Bobby Joe Mason (ball under arm) .75 2.00
40 Bobby Joe Mason (ball between legs) .75 2.00
41 Bobby Joe Mason (passing behind back) .75 2.00
42 Bobby Joe Mason and {Frank Stephens .75 2.00
43 Bobby Joe Mason (ball to side) .75 2.00
44 Bobby Joe Mason (ready to shoot) .75 2.00
45 Clarence Smith (three balls between legs) .75 2.00
46 Clarence Smith (on bike) .75 2.00
47 Clarence Smith (ball at ear) .75 2.00
48 Clarence Smith (dribbling on side) .75 2.00
49 Jerry Venable .75 2.00
50 Frank Stephens (hands in front) .75 2.00
51 Frank Stephens (ball on finger) .75 2.00
52 Frank Stephens (waiting for ball) .75 2.00
53 Frank Stephens (ball in hand) .75 2.00
54 Theodis Ray Lee (ball on hip) .75 2.00
55 Theodis Ray Lee (ball between knees) .75 2.00
56 Jerry Venable (palming ball) .75 2.00
57 Doug Himes (ball in air) .75 2.00
58 Doug Himes (ball behind back) .75 2.00
59 Bill Meggett (dribbling two balls) .75 2.00
60 Bill Meggett (ready to shoot) .75 2.00
61 Vincent White (ball on hip) .75 2.00
62 Vincent White (kicking ball) .75 2.00
63 Pablo and Showboat .75 2.00
64 Meadowlark Lemon Curly Neal and Geese Ausbie balls behind back) 2.50 6.00
65 Curley Neal Quarterback 2.50 6.00
66 Ausbie, Meadowlark, and Neal (looking at ball) 2.50 6.00
67 Curly Neal Meadowlark Lemon 2.50 6.00
68 Football Routine 1.00 2.50
69 Meadowlark To Neal To Ausbie 2.50 6.00
70 Meadowlark Is Safe At The Plate 2.50 6.00
71 1970-71 Highlights (baseball act) 1.00 2.50
72 1970-71 Highlights (Lemon and Neal) 2.50 6.00
73 Bobby Hunter (ball on hip) .75 2.00
74 Bobby Hunter (ball in hand) .75 2.00
75 Bobby Hunter (ball on shoulder) .75 2.00
76 Bobby Hunter (ball in air) .75 2.00
77 Bobby Hunter (passing between legs) .75 2.00
78 Jackie Jackson (ball on hip) 1.00 2.50
79 Jackie Jackson (ball behind back) 1.00 2.50
80 Jackie Jackson (ball in air) 1.00 2.50
81 Jackie Jackson/ ball on finger) 1.00 2.50
82 The Globetrotters 1.00 2.50
83 The Globetrotters 1.00 2.50
84 Dallas Thornton 2.50 6.00
NNO Globetrotter Official Peel-off Team Emblem Sticker 1.50 4.00

1971-72 Globetrotters Phoenix Candy

This eight-card set was issued as unnumbered cards on the back panels of Phoenix Candy boxes. The cards measure approximately 4 7/8" by 2 1/2" whereas the box measures approximately 3 1/4" by 6 1/2". The year of issue is assumed from the 71 over 72 inside a "clock face" on the box flap. Complete boxes are valued at 1.5 times the prices listed below.

Card	Low	High
COMPLETE SET (8)	175.00	350.00
1 J.C. Gipson	20.00	40.00
2 Bob Showboat Hall	20.00	40.00
3 Leon Hillard	20.00	40.00
4 Meadowlark Lemon	50.00	100.00
5 Freddie(Curly) Neal	40.00	80.00
6 Pablo Robertson	20.00	40.00
7 National Unit	25.00	50.00
(Team picture)		
8 International Unit	25.00	50.00
(Team picture)		

1974 Globetrotters Wonder Bread

Six of the twenty-five cards in this set depict Harlem Globetrotters. All cards were randomly inserted inside loaves of Wonder Bread and feature Hanna-Barbera TV cartoon show characters. The fronts feature a multi-color Globetrotter cartoon. The backs carry a lesson in how to do a magic trick. The cards are numbered on the back "X in a series of 25."

Card	Low	High
COMPLETE SET (6)	25.00	50.00
3 Curley Neal	7.50	15.00
B.J. Mason		
4 Curley Neal	7.50	15.00
Geese Ausbie		
5 J.C. Gipson	2.50	6.00
14 Pablo Robertson	2.50	6.00
16 Meadowlark and Granny	5.00	10.00
20 J.C. Gipson and Granny	2.50	6.00

1980 Globetrotters

This six photo set features black and white glossy 8" x10" s. The photo backs are blank, and the set is not numbered, therefore appear alphabetically.

Card	Low	High
COMPLETE SET (6)	10.00	20.00
1 Geese Ausbie	1.50	4.00
2 Geese Ausbie	2.00	5.00
Curly Neal		
Nate Branch		
3 Nate Branch	1.25	3.00
4 Billy Ray Hobley	1.25	3.00
5 Curly Neal	2.50	6.00
6 Dallas Thornton	1.50	4.00
Fred Neal		
Hubert Ausbie		
Nate Branch		
General Lee Holman		
Billy Ray Hobley		
Robert Paige		
Lionel Garrett		
Reggie Franklin		
Eddie Fields		

1985 Globetrotters

Issued on the back of the 1985 Harlem Globetrotters yearbook, this 11-card set features color fronts with white borders. Card backs feature the player's name in a red bar with their vitals listed in a light blue bar. The cards were not perforated. The cards are numbered below by the player's jersey number.

Card	Low	High
COMPLETE SET (11)	8.00	20.00
12 Billy Ray Hobley	.75	2.00
14 Larry Rivers	.75	2.00
15 Clyde Austin	.75	2.00
17 Ovie Dotson	.75	2.00
18 Jimmy Blacklock	.75	2.00
22 Fred Neal	2.50	6.00
26 Osborne Lockhart	.75	2.00
29 Harold Hubbard	.75	2.00
30 Robert Paige	.75	2.00
35 Hubert Ausbie	1.25	3.00
41 Sweet Lou Dunbar	1.25	3.00

1992 Globetrotters Promos

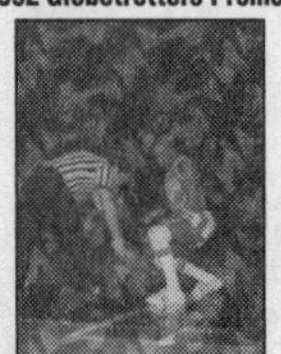

Produced by Comic Images, this six-card promo set previews the design of the 1992 Globetrotters 90 set. The cards measure the standard size. In contrast to the regular set, the front of each card is enhanced by a mosaic of silver metallic geometric shapes that reflect light when the card is tilted. The white backs display "Trotters' Trivia" printed in blue with the team name in large red block letters above. All the text is enclosed in a blue rectangle with blue stars running down each side.

Card	Low	High
COMPLETE SET (6)	6.00	15.00
P1 All-Time Greats	1.25	3.00
Sixty-Fifth Anniversary		
P2 Globetrotting	1.50	4.00
Fred (Curly) Neal		
Alan Alda		
P3 Famous Feats	1.50	4.00
Fred (Curly) Neal		
P4 Media Darlings	2.00	5.00
Mickey Mouse		
Fred (Curly) Neal		
P5 Honoraries	1.25	3.00
Team Photo		
P6 First City	2.00	5.00
Goldie Hawn		

1992 Globetrotters

Produced by Comic Images to celebrate the Harlem Globetrotters' Sixty-Fifth Anniversary, this 90-card standard-size set features black-and-white and color photos of Harlem Globetrotters from the inception of the team to the present. The white backs display "Trotters' Trivia" printed in blue with the team name in large red block letters above. All of the text is enclosed in a blue rectangle with blue stars running down each side.

Card	Low	High
COMPLETE SET (90)	5.00	12.00
1 Abe Saperstein	.20	.50
2 In The Beginning	.08	.25
3 Hinckley, Illinois	.08	.25
4 What's In A Name	.08	.25
5 Uniforms	.08	.25
6 International Competition	.08	.25
7 A Tie	.08	.25
8 Hard Times	.08	.25
9 Black and White	.08	.25
10 Courting Success	.08	.25
11 First Tournament	.08	.25
12 World Champions	.08	.25
13 Tricks and Treats	.20	.50
Lynette Woodard)		
14 Individual Talents	.08	.25
15 For The Boys	.08	.25
16 Globetrotting	.08	.25
17 The Big Screen	.08	.25
18 The Small Screen	.08	.25
19 Goodwill Ambassadors	.08	.25
20 Leaving Their Mark	.08	.25
21 Traveling Troubles	.08	.25
22 Have Court Will Travel	.08	.25
23 The NBA	.08	.25
24 Magic Powers	.08	.25
25 Almost Perfect	.08	.25
26 The End Of An Era	.08	.25
27 Celluloid Heroes	.08	.25
28 Star Power	.08	.25
29 Sweet Georgia Brown	.08	.25
30 The Year Of The Woman	.20	.50
Lynette Woodard		
31 Quotable Curly	.20	.50
Fred (Curly) Neal		
32 Honorary Globie Speaks	.08	.25
33 Whoopi For The Trotters	.20	.50
34 Globie Recollections	.08	.25
35 A B'Ball Oscar	.20	.50
Bob Hope		
36 Singing Their Praises	8.00	.25
37 Hurray For Hollywood	.08	.25
Geese Ausbie		
38 The Early Signs	.08	.25
39 Fast Forward	.08	.25
40 A Losing Streak	.08	.25
41 Pioneering Prankster	.08	.25
42 Changing Of The Guard	.08	.25
43 Breaking In	.08	.25
44 Trickster In Training	.20	.50
Meadowlark Lemon		
45 Wearing Many Hats	.08	.25
46 Beating The Odds	.08	.25
Boid Buie		
47 Double Take	.08	.25
Lance CudJoe		
Lawrence CudJoe		
48 Sweetwater	.08	.25
49 Founding Father	.08	.25
50 Fanciful First	.08	.25
Inman Jackson		
51 Ernest Aughburns	.08	.25
52 Clyde Austin	.08	.25
53 J.B. Brown	.08	.25
54 Michael Douglas	.08	.25
55 Sherwin Durham	.08	.25
56 Billy Ray Hobley	.20	.50
57 Curley Johnson	.08	.25
58 Jolette Law	.08	.25
59 Derick Polk	.08	.25
60 James(Twiggy) Sanders	.08	.25
61 Donald(Clyde) Sinclair	.08	.25
62 Antoine Scott	.08	.25
63 Sweet Lou Dunbar	.08	.25
64 Osbourne Lockhart	.08	.25
65 Lifelong Dream	.20	.50
Lynette Woodard		
66 A Real Show-Off	.08	.25
Clyde Austin		
67 Competition	.08	.25
Jimmy Blacklock		
68 A Blend Of Old And New	.08	.25
Ovie Dotson		
69 Globie Spirit	.08	.25
Harold Hubbard		
70 Carrying The Torch	.20	.50
Curly Neal		
71 Geese Ausbie	.08	.25
72 Fred(Curly) Neal	.20	.50
73 Go, Curly, Go	.20	.50
74 Larry(Gator) Rivers	.08	.25
75 Off Season	.08	.25
76 Sore Losers	.08	.25
Washington Generals		
(Team photo)		
77 Ovie Dotson	.08	.25
78 Come On In	.08	.25
79 Practice Makes Perfect	.08	.25
80 Trotters' 1st Trip	.08	.25
81 Winningest Team	.08	.25
82 City Slickers	.08	.25
83 You Win Some...	.08	.25
84 From Russia, With Love	.08	.25
85 Hold Your Fire	.08	.25
86 What A Crowd	.08	.25
87 Destined For Greatness	.08	.25
88 A Fantastic First	.08	.25
89 A Higher Calling	.20	.50
Gerald Ford		
NNO Checklist Card	.08	.25

1996 Globetrotters Real Action

Issued by Real Action; these 10 cards feature members of the Harlem Globetrotters. These cards, although they measure the standard size, are folded out and "pop-outs" of the featured players can be removed from the card. This set was also sponsored by Denny's. Since these cards are unnumbered, we have sequenced them in alphabetical order.

Card	Low	High
COMPLETE SET (11)	8.00	20.00
1 Arnold Bernard	1.25	3.00
2 Rodney English	1.50	4.00
3 Paul Gaffney	1.25	3.00
4 Barry Hardy	1.25	3.00
5 Curley Johnson	1.50	4.00
6 Reggie Perkins	1.25	3.00
7 Reggie Phillips	1.25	3.00
8 Trazel Silvers	1.25	3.00
9 Clyde Sinclair	1.25	3.00
10 Wun Versher	1.25	3.00
XX Display Card	.25	.60

2001 Greats of the Game

Released in September 2001, this 100-card base set offers a crisp, classic design on standard size cards. The cards stand out with a white background and spotlights on former collegiate players wearing their prospective team jerseys. The Fleer logo is found in the upper right-hand corner. The player's name and college team name run horizontal under the player's photo. The base set contains one subset: Queens of the Court that pays homage to some of the greatest lady hoopsters of all time. Greats of the Game was packaged in 24 pack boxes with each pack containing five cards.

Card	Low	High
COMPLETE SET (84)	20.00	50.00
1 Adolph Rupp	.40	1.00
2 Alonzo Mourning	.50	1.25
3 Antawn Jamison	.40	1.00
4 Antoine Walker	.30	.75
5 Bill Walton	.40	1.00
6 Bob Cousy	.60	1.50
7 Bob Lanier	.40	1.00
8 Bobby Cremins	.25	.60
9 Bobby Hurley	.40	1.00
10 Bobby Knight	.50	1.25
11 Cazzie Russell	.40	1.00
12 Charlie Ward	.25	.60
13 Christian Laettner	.75	2.00
14 Clyde Drexler	.50	1.25
15 Danny Ainge	.40	1.00
16 Danny Ferry	.75	2.00
17 Danny Manning	.75	2.00
18 Darrell Griffith	.40	1.00
19 Dave Cowens	.40	1.00
20 David Robinson	.60	1.50
21 David Thompson	.40	1.00
22 Dean Smith	.40	1.00
23 Don Haskins	.40	1.00
24 Eddie Jones	.30	.75
25 Elvin Hayes	.40	1.00
26 Gene Keady	.30	.75
27 George Mikan	.75	2.00
28 Glen Rice	.30	.75
29 Hakeem Olajuwon	.50	1.25
30 Isiah Thomas	.40	1.00
31 Jalen Rose	.30	.75
32 Jamal Mashburn	.30	.75
33 James Worthy	.50	1.25
34 Jerry Stackhouse	.30	.75
35 Jerry Lucas	.40	1.00
36 Jerry Tarkanian	.40	1.00
37 Jerry West	.50	1.25
38 Jim Valvano	.60	1.50
39 Joe Smith	.30	.75
40 John Thompson	.30	.75
41 John Havlicek	.50	1.25
42 John Wooden	.50	1.25
43 John Lucas	.25	.60
44 Kareem Abdul-Jabbar	.60	1.50
45 Keith Van Horn	.30	.75
46 Kent Benson	.40	1.00
47 Kerry Kittles	.25	.60
48 Lamar Odom	.40	1.00
49 Larry Bird	1.25	3.00
50 Larry Johnson	.40	1.00
51 Lefty Driesell	.75	2.00
52 Lenny Wilkens	.40	1.00
53 Lou Carnesecca	.25	.60
54 Marques Johnson	.40	1.00
55 Mateen Cleaves	.60	1.50
56 Mike Bibby	.40	1.00
57 Mike Krzyzewski	.60	1.50
58 Mychal Thompson	.30	.75
59 Nate Archibald	.40	1.00
60 Pat Riley	.50	1.25
61 Paul Arizin	.40	1.00
62 Pete Maravich	1.25	3.00
63 Phil Ford	.40	1.00
64 Ralph Sampson	.30	.75
65 Ray Meyer	.40	1.00
66 Rick Pitino	.60	1.50
67 Rick Barry	.40	1.00
68 Rollie Massimino	.25	.60
69 Sam Jones	.40	1.00
70 Sidney Moncrief	.40	1.00
71 Spud Webb	.40	1.00
72 Steve Alford	.40	1.00
73 Vince Carter	.60	1.50
74 Walt Frazier	.40	1.00
75 Wilt Chamberlain	.75	2.00
76 Carol Blazejowski QC	1.00	2.50
77 Cynthia Cooper QC	1.00	2.50
78 Chamique Holdsclaw QC	1.00	2.50
79 Lisa Leslie QC	1.00	2.50
80 Nancy Lieberman QC	1.00	2.50
81 Rebecca Lobo QC	1.00	2.50
82 Cheryl Miller QC	1.00	2.50
83 Sheryl Swoopes QC	1.00	2.50
84 Marcus Camby	.30	.75

2001 Greats of the Game All-American Collection

Randomly inserted in packs at a rate of one in six, this 14-card insert set features some of the greatest All-Americans to play the game. The standard size cards are horizontally designed. The player's photo is set in the center of the card with logos surrounding him in three of the four corners of the card. The All-American logo is found in the lower left-hand corner, the Fleer logo is found in the upper left-hand corner, and the player's college team logo is found in the upper right-hand corner. The fourth corner contains the player's college position and that is found in the lower right-hand corner.

Card	Low	High
COMPLETE SET (14)	8.00	20.00
AAC1 Hakeem Olajuwon	.75	2.00
AAC2 Vince Carter	1.00	2.50
AAC3 James Worthy	.75	2.00
AAC4 David Thompson	.60	1.50
AAC5 Paul Arizin	.60	1.50
AAC6 George Mikan	1.25	3.00
AAC7 Bob Cousy	1.00	2.50
AAC8 Steve Alford	.60	1.50
AAC9 Kent Benson	.60	1.50
AAC10 Isiah Thomas	.60	1.50
AAC11 Wilt Chamberlain	1.25	3.00
AAC12 Marques Johnson	.60	1.50
AAC13 Bill Walton	.60	1.50
AAC14 Jerry West	.75	2.00

2001 Greats of the Game All-American Collection Autographs

Randomly seeded, this 14-card set parallels the base All-American Collection insert set enhanced with authentic player autographs. Each card is sequentially numbered to the featured player's rookie season. Print runs listed below.

Card	Low	High
AAC1 Hakeem Olajuwon/84	40.00	80.00
AAC2 Vince Carter/98	40.00	80.00
AAC3 James Worthy/82	60.00	120.00
AAC4 David Thompson/77	20.00	50.00
AAC5 Paul Arizin/50	20.00	50.00
AAC6 George Mikan/46	150.00	300.00
AAC7 Bob Cousy/50	30.00	60.00
AAC8 Steve Alford/87	30.00	60.00
AAC9 Kent Benson/77	20.00	50.00
AAC12 Marques Johnson/77	20.00	50.00
AAC13 Bill Walton/74	30.00	80.00

2001 Greats of the Game Autographs

Randomly inserted in packs at the rate of one in 12, this 67-card set utilizes the base set design enhanced with authentic player autographs. There were several short printed cards issued with this set, and those appear below with print runs after the player name.

Card	Low	High
1 Kareem Abdul-Jabbar	30.00	80.00
2 Danny Ainge	8.00	20.00
3 Steve Alford	8.00	20.00
4 Nate Archibald	8.00	20.00
5 Paul Arizin	15.00	30.00
6 Rick Barry	8.00	20.00
7 Kent Benson	8.00	20.00
8 Mike Bibby	8.00	20.00
9 Larry Bird/200	150.00	300.00
10 Carol Blazejowski	10.00	25.00
11 Vince Carter	30.00	60.00
12 Mateen Cleaves	8.00	20.00
13 Cynthia Cooper	15.00	30.00
14 Bob Cousy	20.00	50.00
15 Dave Cowens	8.00	20.00
16 Clyde Drexler	10.00	25.00
17 Danny Ferry	8.00	20.00
18 Phil Ford	8.00	20.00
19 Walt Frazier	8.00	20.00
20 Darrell Griffith	8.00	20.00
21 John Havlicek/200	20.00	50.00
22 Elvin Hayes	8.00	20.00
23 Chamique Holdsclaw	15.00	40.00
24 Bobby Hurley	10.00	25.00
25 Antawn Jamison	8.00	20.00
26 Larry Johnson	15.00	40.00
27 Marques Johnson	8.00	20.00
28 Eddie Jones	8.00	20.00
29 Sam Jones	15.00	40.00
30 Kerry Kittles	8.00	20.00
31 Bobby Knight	30.00	60.00
32 Christian Laettner	25.00	60.00
33 Bob Lanier	8.00	20.00
34 Lisa Leslie	8.00	20.00
35 Nancy Lieberman-Cline	8.00	20.00
36 Jerry Lucas	8.00	20.00
37 John Lucas	8.00	20.00
38 Danny Manning	8.00	20.00
39 Jamal Mashburn	8.00	20.00
40 George Mikan/300	125.00	225.00
41 Cheryl Miller	15.00	40.00
42 Sidney Moncrief	8.00	20.00
43 Alonzo Mourning	12.50	30.00
45 Hakeem Olajuwon	15.00	40.00
46 Rick Pitino	15.00	40.00
47 Glen Rice	8.00	20.00
48 Pat Riley/150	40.00	80.00
49 David Robinson	50.00	100.00
50 Jalen Rose	10.00	25.00
51 Cazzie Russell	8.00	20.00
52 Ralph Sampson	8.00	20.00
53 Joe Smith	8.00	20.00
54 Jerry Stackhouse	8.00	20.00
55 Sheryl Swoopes	15.00	30.00
56 Isiah Thomas/219	15.00	30.00
57 David Thompson	8.00	20.00
58 Mychal Thompson	8.00	20.00
59 Keith Van Horn	8.00	20.00
60 Antoine Walker	8.00	20.00
61 Bill Walton	10.00	25.00
62 Charlie Ward	8.00	20.00
63 Spud Webb	8.00	20.00
64 Jerry West	20.00	50.00
65 Lenny Wilkens	8.00	20.00
66 John Wooden/300	75.00	150.00
67 James Worthy	30.00	60.00

2001 Greats of the Game Coach's Corner

Randomly inserted in packs at a rate of one in 10, this 16-card insert set features some of the most successful college coaches. The standard size cards include a color photo of the coach, his name, and the team he coached. The team's logo can also be found in the lower right-hand corner.

Card	Low	High
COMPLETE SET (16)	15.00	40.00
CC1 Lou Carnesecca	1.00	2.50
CC2 Bobby Cremins	1.00	2.50
CC3 Lefty Driesell	3.00	8.00
CC4 Don Haskins	1.00	2.50
CC5 Mike Krzyzewski	3.00	8.00
CC6 Rollie Massimino	1.00	2.50
CC7 Ray Meyer	1.00	2.50
CC8 Rick Pitino	2.50	6.00
CC9 Adolph Rupp	2.50	6.00
CC10 Dean Smith	2.50	6.00
CC11 Jerry Tarkanian	1.00	2.50
CC12 John Thompson	1.00	2.50
CC13 Bobby Knight	1.00	2.50
CC14 John Wooden	2.00	5.00
CC15 Jim Valvano	2.00	5.00
CC16 Gene Keady	1.00	2.50

2001 Greats of the Game Coach's Corner Autographs

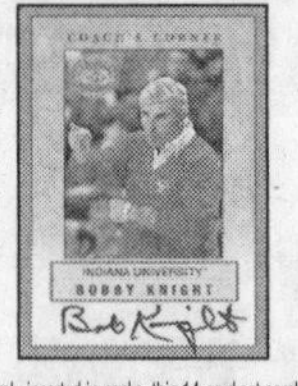

Randomly inserted in packs, this 14-card set parallels the base Coach's Corner set design enhanced with authentic coach autographs. Some of the deceased coaches do not appear in this set.

Card	Low	High
CC2 Bobby Cremins	15.00	40.00
CC3 Lefty Driesell	25.00	60.00
CC4 Don Haskins	15.00	40.00
CC5 Mike Krzyzewski	225.00	325.00
CC6 Rollie Massimino	15.00	40.00
CC7 Ray Meyer	15.00	40.00
CC8 Rick Pitino	20.00	50.00
CC10 Dean Smith	50.00	100.00
CC11 Jerry Tarkanian	20.00	50.00
CC12 John Thompson	50.00	120.00
CC13 Bobby Knight	40.00	100.00
CC14 John Wooden	100.00	200.00

2001 Greats of the Game Feel the Game Classics

Randomly inserted in packs at a rate of one in 24, this 25-card insert set offers circular game-used swatches from some of the legendary names in collegiate basketball history. Vince Carter and Bobby Knight have several different versions, and the type of memorabilia on the card has be added after the player name in the listings below.

Card	Low	High
1 Rick Barry	4.00	10.00
2 Larry Bird	12.00	30.00
3 Lou Carnasecca	4.00	10.00
4 Vince Carter JSY R	6.00	15.00
5 Vince Carter Shorts R	6.00	15.00
6 Vince Carter WU	6.00	15.00
7 Vince Carter Shirt	6.00	15.00
8 Vince Carter JSY H	6.00	15.00
9 Vince Carter Shorts H	6.00	15.00
10 Vince Carter	8.00	20.00
JSY-Short R/150		
11 Vince Carter	8.00	20.00
JSY-Short H/150		
12 Vince Carter	8.00	20.00
Warm-Shirt/200		
13 Vince Carter	15.00	40.00
JSY-Short-Shirt R/50		
14 Vince Carter	15.00	40.00
JSY-Short-Shirt H/50		
15 Vince Carter	12.00	30.00
JSY-Short-WU H/75		
16 Vince Carter	12.00	30.00
JSY-Short-WU R/75		
17 Vince Carter	20.00	50.00
JSY-Short-Shirt-WU H/15		
18 Vince Carter	20.00	50.00
JSY-Short-Shit-WU R/15		
20 Larry Johnson	4.00	10.00
21 Bobby Knight Ball	15.00	30.00
22 Bobby Knight Shirt	15.00	30.00
23 Pete Maravich	30.00	80.00
24 Isaiah Rider	4.00	10.00
25 Bill Walton	4.00	10.00

2001 Greats of the Game Feel the Game Hardwood Classics

Randomly inserted in packs at a rate of one 24, this 20-card insert set offers circular swatches of a game floor set next to player photos.

Card	Low	High
1 Steve Alford	5.00	12.00
2 Marcus Camby	5.00	12.00
4 Mateen Cleaves	5.00	12.00
6 Phil Ford SP	15.00	30.00
7 Antawn Jamison	5.00	12.00
8 Larry Johnson	5.00	12.00
9 Gene Keady	5.00	12.00
10 Bobby Knight	8.00	20.00
11 Mike Krzyzewski	10.00	25.00
13 Danny Manning	5.00	12.00
14 Glen Rice	5.00	12.00
15 Glenn Robinson	5.00	12.00
16 Jalen Rose	5.00	12.00
18 Sheryl Swoopes	6.00	15.00
19 Antoine Walker	5.00	12.00
20 Charlie Ward	5.00	12.00

2001 Greats of the Game Player of the Year

This 10-card insert set was randomly inserted in packs at a rate of one in 24. The standard size cards feature Player of the Year winners. The cards have a heading reading, "Player of the Year". There is an action shot of the featured player in the foreground of the card with a pencil sketching of him in the background.

Card	Low	High
COMPLETE SET (10)	15.00	40.00
POY1 Christian Laettner	5.00	12.00
POY2 Elvin Hayes	1.50	4.00
POY3 Larry Bird	6.00	15.00
POY4 Joe Smith	1.50	4.00
POY5 Cazzie Russell	1.50	4.00
POY6 Antawn Jamison	1.50	4.00
POY7 Danny Manning	2.50	6.00
POY8 David Robinson	1.50	4.00
POY9 Jerry Lucas	1.50	4.00
POY10 Kareem Abdul-Jabbar	2.50	6.00

2001 Greats of the Game Player of the Year Autographs

Randomly inserted in packs, this 10-card set parallels the Player of the Year insert set enhanced with player autographs and sequential numbering to the year each player was named player of the year. Print runs are listed below.

Card	Low	High
POY1 Christian Laettner/91	30.00	80.00
POY2 Elvin Hayes/68	20.00	50.00
POY3 Larry Bird/79	100.00	200.00
POY4 Joe Smith/95	12.50	30.00
POY5 Cazzie Russell/66	30.00	80.00
POY6 Antawn Jamison/98	12.50	30.00
POY7 Danny Manning/88	12.50	30.00
POY8 David Robinson/87	40.00	100.00
POY10 Kareem Abdul-Jabbar/69	60.00	150.00

2005-06 Greats of the Game

Released in June 2005, Greats of the game features retired players and veterans on cards 1-91, coaches on cards 92-100, autographed rookies serially numbered to 99 on cards 101-152 and rookies serially numbered to 99 on cards 153-169. Base veteran and retired player cards have brown borders while the rookies have silver borders. Greats was packaged in 15-pack boxes of five cards each and carried an initial SRP of $9.99.

Card	Price
COMP.SET w/o SP's (100)	25.00
1 Earl Monroe	.60
2 World Free	.60
3 James Worthy	.60
4 Bob McAdoo	.60
5 Connie Hawkins	.60
6 John Starks	.60
7 Byron Scott	.60
8 Brad Daugherty	.60
9 Chris Ford	.60
10 Jamaal Wilkes	.60
11 Julius Erving	1.25
12 Joe Carroll	.60
13 Bill Laimbeer	.60
14 Bill Walton	.60
15 Brian Winters	.60
16 David Robinson	1.00
17 Horace Grant	.60
18 Bob Pettit	.60
19 Dan Roundfield	.60
20 Kenny Walker	.60
21 Kenny Smith	.60
22 Thurl Bailey	.60
23 Cedric Maxwell	.60
24 Joe Dumars	.60
25 Adrian Dantley	.60
26 Dale Ellis	.60
27 John Stockton	1.25
28 Bob Lanier	.60
29 Bernard King	.60
30 Jerry Lucas	.60
31 Bill Russell	1.25
32 Hal Greer	.60
33 Billy Cunningham	.60
34 Jack Sikma	.60
35 Michael Cooper	.60
36 David Thompson	.60
37 Kareem Abdul-Jabbar	1.00
38 Bill Sharman	.60
39 George Gervin	.60
40 Kiki Vandeweghe	.60
41 Calvin Murphy	.60
42 Darryl Dawkins	.60
43 Vern Mikkelsen	.60
44 Dee Brown	.60
45 Dennis Rodman	1.00
46 Bobby Jones	.60
47 Hakeem Olajuwon	.75
48 Alvin Robertson	.60
49 Dennis Johnson	.75
50 Clyde Drexler	.75
51 Anthony Mason	.60
52 Larry Bird	2.00
53 LeBron James	3.00
54 Magic Johnson	1.50
55 Manute Bol	.60
56 Mookie Blaylock	.60
57 Mark Eaton	.60
58 Kevin McHale	.75
59 Maurice Cheeks	.60
60 Maurice Lucas	.60
61 Michael Jordan	5.00
62 Michael Ray Richardson	.60
63 B.J. Armstrong	.60
64 ML Carr	.60
65 Muggsy Bogues	.60
66 Nate Archibald	.60
67 Glen Rice	.60
68 Nate Thurmond	.60
69 Norm Nixon	.60
70 Bob Love	.60
71 Paul Arizin	.60
72 Ralph Sampson	.60
73 Rolando Blackman	.60
74 Reggie Theus	.60
75 Mitch Richmond	.60
76 Robert Parish	.60
77 Paul Westphal	.60
78 Sam Perkins	.60
79 Scottie Pippen	1.00
80 Sean Elliott	.60
81 Spud Webb	.60
82 Steve Kerr	.60
83 Tom Chambers	.60
84 Walt Bellamy	.60
85 Walt Frazier	.60
86 Jeff Hornacek	.60
87 Danny Manning	.60
88 Wes Unseld	.60
89 Geoff Petrie	.60
90 Xavier McDaniel	.60
91 Chris Mullin	.60
92 Buck Williams CC	.60
93 Dave Bing CC	.60
94 John Havlicek CC	.60
95 Karl Malone CC	.75
96 Artis Gilmore CC	.60
97 Doug Moe CC	.60
98 Doug Collins CC	.60
99 Chuck Daly CC	.60
100 Bob Knight CC	.75
101 Alex Acker AU RC	8.00
102 Amir Johnson AU RC	8.00
103 Andray Blatche AU RC	10.00
104 Andrew Bogut AU RC	20.00
105 Andrew Bynum AU RC	100.00
106 Antoine Wright AU RC	8.00
107 Yaroslav Korolev AU RC	8.00
108 Bracey Wright AU RC	8.00
109 Brandon Bass AU RC	10.00
110 C.J. Miles AU RC	10.00
111 Channing Frye AU RC	10.00
112 Charlie Villanueva AU RC	10.00
113 Chris Paul AU RC	150.00
114 Chris Taft AU RC	8.00
115 Chuck Hayes AU RC	8.00
116 Daniel Ewing AU RC	8.00
117 Danny Granger AU RC	25.00
118 David Lee AU RC	30.00
119 Deron Williams AU RC	100.00
120 Dijon Thompson AU RC	8.00
121 Ersan Ilyasova AU RC	10.00
122 Francisco Garcia AU RC	10.00
123 Gerald Green AU RC	10.00
124 Hakim Warrick AU RC	10.00
125 Ike Diogu AU RC	8.00
126 Jarrett Jack AU RC	8.00
127 Jason Maxiell AU RC	8.00
128 Joey Graham AU RC	8.00
129 Johan Petro AU RC	8.00
130 Julius Hodge AU RC	8.00
131 Lawrence Roberts AU RC	8.00
132 Linas Kleiza AU RC	8.00
133 Louis Williams AU RC	12.00
134 Luther Head AU RC	8.00
135 Martell Webster AU RC	8.00
136 M.Andriuskevicius AU RC	8.00
137 Marvin Williams AU RC	10.00

onta Ellis AU RC 60.00 150.00
ate Robinson AU RC 10.00 25.00
rien Greene AU RC 8.00 20.00
ashad McCants AU RC 8.00 20.00
aymond Felton AU RC 15.00 40.00
obert Whaley AU RC 8.00 20.00
onny Turiaf AU RC 20.00 50.00
yan Gomes AU RC 8.00 20.00
alim Stoudamire AU RC 8.00 20.00
arunas Jasikevicius AU RC 8.00 20.00
ean May AU RC 8.00 20.00
tephen Graham AU RC 8.00 20.00
ravis Diener AU RC 8.00 20.00
on Wafer AU RC 8.00 20.00
ayne Simien AU RC 8.00 20.00
havlik Randolph RC 3.00 8.00
lan Anderson RC 3.00 8.00
ndre Owens RC 3.00 8.00
nthony Roberson RC 3.00 8.00
rvydas Macijauskas RC 3.00 8.00
oniface N'Dong RC 3.00 8.00
evin Green RC 3.00 8.00
onell Taylor RC 3.00 8.00
arl Barron RC 3.00 8.00
steban Batista RC 3.00 8.00
abricio Oberto RC 3.00 8.00
awle Marshall RC 3.00 8.00
ames Singleton RC 3.00 8.00
ose Calderon RC 3.00 8.00
osh Powell RC 3.00 8.00
evin Burleson RC 3.00 8.00
onnie Price RC 3.00 8.00

005-06 Greats of the Game Autographs

mly seeded in packs, this 68-card set is ntally designed with player images on the left, on the right and player autographs along the n on a "hardwood" background. Though the are not serially numbered, Upper Deck did se some announce print runs. See checklist for s.

ICED GOLD PRINT RUN 10 SETS
Adrian Dantley 8.00 20.00
Alvin Robertson 8.00 20.00
B.J. Armstrong 8.00 20.00
Brad Daugherty 8.00 20.00
Bobby Jones 12.50 30.00
Bernard King/248* 8.00 20.00
Bill Laimbeer 20.00 50.00
Bob McAdoo 15.00 40.00
Muggsy Bogues/185* 10.00 25.00
Bob Pettit 12.50 30.00
Bill Russell/30* 200.00 400.00
Byron Scott/250* 10.00 25.00
Bill Walton/250* 12.50 30.00
Clyde Drexler/109* 25.00 50.00
Chris Ford 8.00 20.00
Connie Hawkins 12.50 30.00
Michael Cooper 8.00 20.00
Chuck Daly/84* 20.00 50.00
Dee Brown 8.00 20.00
Doug Collins 8.00 20.00
Darryl Dawkins 8.00 20.00
Dale Ellis 8.00 20.00
Dennis Johnson/236* 15.00 40.00
Doug Moe 8.00 20.00
David Robinson/62* 75.00 200.00
David Thompson 8.00 20.00
Walt Frazier/63* 12.50 30.00
George Gervin/250* 10.00 25.00
Hal Greer 8.00 20.00
Hakeem Olajuwon/62* 50.00 100.00
Julius Erving/30* 75.00 150.00
Jeff Hornacek 8.00 20.00
John Starks/250* 12.00 30.00
Jamaal Wilkes 8.00 20.00
Kareem Abdul-Jabbar/30* 150.00 300.00
Kiki Vandeweghe 8.00 20.00
Kenny Walker 8.00 20.00
Larry Bird/40* 75.00 150.00
LeBron James/30* 200.00 450.00
Magic Johnson/40* 60.00 120.00
Maurice Cheeks 8.00 20.00
Mark Eaton 8.00 20.00
Maurice Lucas 8.00 20.00
Michael Ray Richardson 8.00 20.00
Cedric Maxwell/250* 10.00 25.00
Nate Archibald/250* 10.00 25.00
Norm Nixon 8.00 20.00
Nate Thurmond 10.00 25.00
Paul Arizin 15.00 40.00
Paul Westphal/87* 10.00 25.00
Dennis Rodman/112* 50.00 120.00
Dan Roundfield 8.00 20.00
Ralph Sampson/230* 12.50 30.00
Reggie Theus 8.00 20.00
Sean Elliott/184* 15.00 40.00
Bill Sharman 10.00 25.00
Jack Sikma 8.00 20.00
Steve Kerr 8.00 20.00
Sam Perkins/184* 8.00 20.00
John Stockton/40* 60.00 120.00
Spud Webb/234* 10.00 25.00
Tom Chambers 8.00 20.00
Vern Mikkelsen 20.00 50.00
Walt Bellamy/248* 10.00 25.00
World Free 8.00 20.00
Brian Winters 8.00 20.00
Wes Unseld 8.00 20.00
Xavier McDaniel 8.00 20.00

005-06 Greats of the Game Gold

mly seeded in packs, this 169-card set parallels se Greats of the Game set enhanced with gold ghts and sequential numbering to 99 for cards 1- d sequential numbering to 25 for cards 101-

GOLD: 1.25X TO 3X BASE HI
52 GOLD AU: .75X TO 2X BASE HI
69 GOLD: .75X TO 2X BASE HI

2005-06 Greats of the Game Great Cuts

Limited to three serially numbered copies per card, this set places cut signatures of some of the NBA's greatest players on each card.

2009-10 Greats of the Game

COMPLETE SET (163) 30.00 60.00
1 Mark Jackson .30 .75
2 Freddie Lewis .30 .75
3 Brad Daugherty .30 .75
4 John Stockton .50 1.25
5 Shareef Abdur-Rahim .25 .60
6 Michael Jordan 2.50 6.00
7 Larry Johnson .30 .75
8 B.J. Armstrong .30 .75
9 Hakeem Olajuwon .40 1.00
10 Sam Perkins .30 .75
11 Steve Kerr .30 .75
12 Julius Erving .60 1.50
13 John Havlicek .30 .75
14 Clyde Lovellette .30 .75
15 Danny Manning .30 .75
16 Isiah Thomas .30 .75
17 Kevin Pittsnogle .20 .50
18 Clyde Drexler .40 1.00
19 Bill Cartwright .30 .75
20 Jerry West .40 1.00
21 Darrell Walker .30 .75
22 Pat Riley .30 .75
23 Cazzie Russell .30 .75
24 Lionel Hollins .30 .75
25 George Karl .30 .75
26 Terry Porter .30 .75
27 Jack Sikma .30 .75
28 Adrian Dantley .30 .75
29 Billy Donovan .40 1.00
30 Micheal Ray Richardson .30 .75
31 Hal Greer .30 .75
32 Terry Cummings .30 .75
33 Rick Mahorn .30 .75
34 Larry Nance .30 .75
35 Oscar Robertson .30 .75
36 James Harden RC 1.00 2.50
37 Horace Grant .30 .75
38 Steve Alford .30 .75
39 Magic Johnson .75 2.00
40 LeBron James 1.50 4.00
41 Yao Ming .40 1.00
42 Larry Bird 1.00 2.50
43 Tito Horford .30 .75
44 Ricky Rubio RC 1.50 4.00
45 George Gervin .30 .75
46 Gail Goodrich .30 .75
47 Chet Walker .30 .75
48 Vlade Divac .30 .75
49 Thurl Bailey .30 .75
50 Dominique Wilkins .40 1.00
51 Bob Lanier .30 .75
52 Bill Sharman .30 .75
53 Don Nelson .30 .75
54 Ron Harper .30 .75
55 Bernard King .30 .75
56 Robert Parish .30 .75
57 Elgin Baylor .30 .75
58 Dave Cowens .30 .75
59 Dennis Rodman .50 1.25
60 Rod Hundley .30 .75
61 Bill Walton .30 .75
62 David Thompson .40 1.00
63 Bill Laimbeer .30 .75
64 Bob McAdoo .30 .75
65 Kareem Abdul-Jabbar .50 1.25
66 Bill Russell .50 1.25
67 Alonzo Mourning .40 1.00
68 Jerry Sloan .30 .75
69 Avery Johnson .30 .75
70 Bobby Hurley .40 1.00
71 Moses Malone .30 .75
72 Chris Mullin .30 .75
73 Derrick Rose 1.00 2.50
74 Stacey Augmon .30 .75
75 Darrell Griffith .30 .75
76 Danny Ferry .50 1.25
77 Michael Cooper .30 .75
78 Brandon Roy .30 .75
79 Bob Pettit .30 .75
80 David Robinson .50 1.25
81 Sam Cassell .30 .75
82 Glen Rice .30 .75
83 Calbert Cheaney .30 .75
84 Christian Laettner .50 1.25
85 Mateen Cleaves .20 .50
86 Derrick Rose GD 2.00 5.00
87 Yao Ming GD .75 2.00
88 Brandon Roy GD .60 1.50
89 LeBron James GD 3.00 8.00
90 James Harden GD 2.00 5.00
91 Michael Jordan GD 5.00 12.00
92 Michael Cooper GD .60 1.50
93 Moses Malone GD .60 1.50
94 Kevin Pittsnogle GD .40 1.00
95 Chris Mullin GD .60 1.50
96 Alonzo Mourning GD .75 2.00
97 Horace Grant GD .60 1.50
98 Larry Nance GD .60 1.50
99 Larry Bird GD 2.00 5.00
100 Julius Erving GD 1.25 3.00
101 Tito Horford GD .60 1.50
102 George Gervin GD .60 1.50
103 Red Hundley GD .60 1.50
104 Mateen Cleaves GD .40 1.00
105 Calbert Cheaney GD .60 1.50
106 Brandon Roy BMC .75 2.00
107 Calbert Cheaney BMC .75 2.00
108 Bill Cartwright BMC .75 2.00
109 Danny Ferry BMC 1.25 3.00
110 Danny Manning BMC .75 2.00
111 Darrell Walker BMC .75 2.00
112 Bill Laimbeer BMC .75 2.00
113 LeBron James BMC 4.00 10.00
114 Derrick Rose BMC 2.50 6.00
115 Hakeem Olajuwon BMC 1.00 2.50
116 Horace Grant BMC .75 2.00
117 James Harden BMC 2.50 6.00
118 Bill Russell BMC 1.25 3.00
119 Larry Bird BMC 2.50 6.00
120 Larry Johnson BMC .75 2.00
121 Michael Jordan BMC 6.00 15.00
122 Bill Walton BMC .75 2.00
123 Shareef Abdur-Rahim BMC .60 1.50
124 Sam Perkins BMC .75 2.00
125 Jerry West 1.25 3.00
Kevin Pittsnogle
126 Bill Walton 1.50 4.00
Kareem Abdul-Jabbar
127 Larry Johnson 1.00 2.50
Staceygmon
128 Dave Cowens 1.00 2.50
Sam Cassell
129 David Thompson 1.25 3.00
Thurl Bailey
130 Magic Johnson 2.50 6.00
Mateen Cleaves
131 Bill Cartwright 1.50 4.00
Bill Russell
132 Bobby Hurley 1.50 4.00
Danny Ferry
133 Horace Grant 1.00 2.50
Larry Nance
134 Christian Laettner 1.50 4.00
Danny Ferry
135 Freddie Lewis 1.00 2.50
Lionel Hollins
136 Cazzie Russell 1.00 2.50
Glen Rice
137 B.J. Armstrong 1.00 2.50
Don Nelson
138 Adriant Dantley 1.00 2.50
Bill Laimbeer
139 Chris Mullin 1.00 2.50
Mark Jackson
140 Bob McAdoo 1.00 2.50
George Karl
141 Clyde Lovellette 1.00 2.50
Danny Manning
142 Clyde Drexler 1.25 3.00
Hakeem Olajuwon
143 Dave Cowens OS .75 2.00
144 Bernard King OS .75 2.00
145 Mark Jackson OS .75 2.00
146 Danny Ferry OS 1.25 3.00
147 Darrell Griffith OS .75 2.00
148 Cazzie Russell OS .75 2.00
149 George Karl OS .75 2.00
150 Sam Perkins OS .75 2.00
151 Julius Erving OS 1.50 4.00
152 Larry Bird OS 2.50 6.00
153 Isiah Thomas OS .75 2.00
154 Michael Jordan OS 6.00 15.00
155 Freddie Lewis OS .75 2.00
156 John Stockton OS 1.25 3.00
157 Pat Riley OS .75 2.00
158 Jack Sikma OS .75 2.00
159 Oscar Robertson OS .75 2.00
160 Chris Mullin OS .75 2.00
161 George Gervin OS .75 2.00
162 Bill Walton OS .75 2.00
163 Kareem Abdul-Jabbar OS 1.25 3.00

2009-10 Greats of the Game 199

*GREATS 199 1-85: 1.5X TO 4X BASE HI
*GREATS 199 86-105: .75X TO 2X BASE HI
*GREATS 199 106-124: .6X TO 1.5X BASE HI
*GREATS 199 125-142: .75X TO 2X BASE HI
*GREATS 199 143-163: .6X TO 1.5X BASE HI
STATED PRINT RUN 199 SER.#'d SETS

2009-10 Greats of the Game 50

*GREATS 50 1-85: 4X TO 10X BASE HI
*GREATS 50 86-105: 2X TO 5X BASE HI
*GREATS 50 106-124: 1.5X TO 4X BASE HI
*GREATS 50 125-142: 1.5X TO 4X BASE HI
*GREATS 50 143-163: 1.5X TO 4X BASE HI
PRINT RUN 50 SER.#'d SETS

2009-10 Greats of the Game Autographs

STATED ODDS 1:8
86-163 UNPRICED PRINT RUN 10 SETS
1 Mark Jackson 5.00 12.00
2 Freddie Lewis 4.00 10.00
4 John Stockton 50.00 120.00
5 Shareef Abdur-Rahim 4.00 10.00
6 Michael Jordan 350.00 550.00
8 B.J. Armstrong 5.00 12.00
10 Sam Perkins SP 20.00 50.00
11 Steve Kerr 4.00 10.00
12 Julius Erving SP 40.00 80.00
13 John Havlicek 20.00 40.00
15 Danny Manning 8.00 20.00
17 Kevin Pittsnogle 4.00 10.00
19 Bill Cartwright 8.00 20.00
20 Jerry West 20.00 50.00
21 Darrell Walker 4.00 10.00
22 Pat Riley 15.00 40.00
25 George Karl SP 40.00 80.00
26 Terry Porter 6.00 15.00
27 Jack Sikma 4.00 10.00
28 Adrian Dantley 4.00 10.00
29 Bill Donovan 15.00 30.00
30 Michael Ray Richardson 4.00 10.00
31 Hal Greer 5.00 12.00
32 Terry Cummings 5.00 12.00
33 Rick Mahorn 5.00 12.00
34 Larry Nance 6.00 15.00
35 Oscar Robertson 60.00 120.00
36 James Harden 12.00 30.00
37 Horace Grant 15.00 30.00
38 Steve Alford 5.00 12.00
39 Magic Johnson SP 100.00 200.00
40 LeBron James 125.00 250.00
41 Yao Ming 15.00 30.00
42 Larry Bird 40.00 100.00
43 Tito Horford 4.00 10.00
44 Ricky Rubio 40.00 100.00
45 George Gervin 15.00 30.00
46 Gail Goodrich 10.00 25.00
47 Chet Walker 8.00 20.00
48 Vlade Divac 6.00 15.00
49 Thurl Bailey 5.00 12.00
50 Dominique Wilkins 15.00 30.00
51 Bob Lanier 8.00 20.00
52 Bill Sharman 20.00 40.00
53 Don Nelson 10.00 25.00
54 Ron Harper 8.00 20.00
55 Bernard King 5.00 12.00
57 Elgin Baylor 12.50 30.00
59 Dennis Rodman 20.00 50.00
60 Rod Hundley 10.00 25.00
61 Bill Walton 10.00 25.00
62 David Thompson 6.00 15.00
63 Bill Laimbeer 6.00 15.00
64 Bob McAdoo 15.00 40.00
66 Bill Russell SP 75.00 150.00
67 Alonzo Mourning 25.00 50.00
68 Jerry Sloan 8.00 20.00
69 Avery Johnson 4.00 10.00
70 Bobby Hurley 6.00 15.00
71 Moses Malone 15.00 40.00
72 Chris Mullin 15.00 40.00
73 Derrick Rose 40.00 80.00
75 Darrell Griffith 4.00 10.00
76 Danny Ferry 4.00 10.00
77 Michael Cooper 4.00 10.00
78 Brandon Roy 8.00 20.00
79 Bob Pettit SP 40.00 100.00
81 Sam Cassell 5.00 12.00
82 Glen Rice 8.00 20.00
83 Calbert Cheaney 4.00 10.00
84 Christian Laettner 10.00 25.00
85 Mateen Cleaves 4.00 10.00

2009-10 Greats of the Game Memorable Monikers

STATED PRINT RUN 15 SER.#'d SETS
UNPRICED DUAL PRINT RUN 5 SER.#'d SETS
MBD Billy Donovan 15.00 30.00
MBL Bill Laimbeer 10.00 25.00
MBR Brandon Roy 10.00 25.00
MCW Chet Walker 15.00 30.00
MGG George Gervin 10.00 25.00
MHA Ron Harper 25.00 50.00
MHU Rod Hundley 15.00 30.00
MJA LeBron James 200.00 400.00
MJE Julius Erving 40.00 100.00
MMR Micheal Ray Richardson 10.00 25.00
MSC Sam Cassell 15.00 30.00
MYM Yao Ming 30.00 80.00

2009-10 Greats of the Game Old School Swatches

STATED ODDS 1:16 PACKS
OS1 Adrian Dantley 2.50 6.00
OS2 Magic Johnson 6.00 15.00
OS3 Alonzo Mourning 3.00 8.00
OS4 Larry Bird 8.00 20.00
OS5 Bernard King 2.50 6.00
OS6 Bill Laimbeer 2.50 6.00
OS7 Bill Russell 8.00 20.00
OS8 Bill Walton 2.50 6.00
OS9 Michael Jordan 20.00 50.00
OS10 Walt Frazier 2.50 6.00
OS11 Clyde Drexler 3.00 8.00
OS12 Stacey Augmon 3.00 8.00
OS14 David Robinson 4.00 10.00
OS15 Dennis Rodman 4.00 10.00
OS16 George Gervin 2.50 6.00
OS17 Hakeem Olajuwon 3.00 8.00
OS18 Horace Grant 2.50 6.00
OS19 Isiah Thomas 3.00 8.00
OS20 LeBron James 8.00 20.00
OS21 Micheal Ray Richardson 2.50 6.00
OS22 Steve Francis 2.50 6.00
OS23 Michael Cooper 2.50 6.00
OS24 Jerry West 6.00 15.00
OS25 John Stockton 4.00 10.00
OS26 James Worthy SP 5.00 12.00
OS27 Julius Erving 6.00 15.00
OS28 Kareem Abdul-Jabbar 6.00 15.00
OS29 Vlade Divac 2.50 6.00
OS30 Steve Kerr 2.50 6.00
OS31 Moses Malone 2.50 6.00
OS32 Rick Fox 2.50 6.00
OS33 Oscar Robertson 5.00 12.00
OS34 Pat Riley 4.00 10.00
OS35 Robert Parish 2.50 6.00
OS36 Sam Cassell 2.50 6.00

1995-96 Grizzlies/Topps

Produced by the Topps Company, this 9-card set commemorated the Vancover Grizzlies inaugural season. Card fronts are identical to the 1995-96 Topps regular issue, but each contains a special expansion gold-foil logo. Cards were originally supposed to be renumbered 10-18, but the numbers on the backs were identical to that of the basic set.

COMPLETE SET (9) 3.00 8.00
10 Byron Scott UER .50 1.25
Numbered 175
11 Blue Edwards UER .40 1.00
Numbered 177
12 Antonio Harvey UER .40 1.00
Numbered 236
13 Kenny Gattison UER .40 1.00
Numbered 180
14 Gerald Wilkins UER .40 1.00
Numbered 174
15 Greg Anthony UER .40 1.00
Numbered 178
16 Lawrence Moten UER .40 1.00
Numbered 231
17 Bryant Reeves UER 1.25 3.00
Numbered 202
18 Checklist .40 1.00

2001-02 Grizzlies Topps

Released by Topps, this nine-card set features a horizontal design with the Grizzlies logo in the background and was given away during the 2001-02 season.

COMPLETE SET (9) 1.50 4.00
VG1 Shareef Abdur-Rahim .40 1.00
VG3 Michael Dickerson .30 .75
VG4 Othella Harrington .30 .75
VG5 Bryant Reeves .30 .75
VG6 Damon Jones .30 .75
VG7 Isaac Austin .30 .75
VG8 Stromile Swift .30 .75
VG9 Tony Massenburg .30 .75
VG10 Grant Long .30 .75

2009-10 Hall of Fame

COMPLETE SET (149) 75.00 150.00
PRINT RUN 599 SER.#'d SETS
UNPRICED MARBLE PRINT RUN ONE SET
1 Kareem Abdul-Jabbar 2.50 6.00
2 Nate Archibald 1.50 4.00
3 Paul Arizin 1.50 4.00
4 Rick Barry 1.50 4.00
5 Elgin Baylor 1.50 4.00
6 John Beckman 1.50 4.00
7 Walt Bellamy 1.50 4.00
8 Dave Bing 1.50 4.00
9 Larry Bird 5.00 12.00
10 Carol Blazejowski 1.50 4.00
11 Al Cervi 1.50 4.00
12 Wilt Chamberlain 3.00 8.00
13 Cynthia Cooper 2.00 5.00
14 Bob Cousy 2.50 6.00
15 Dave Cowens 1.50 4.00
16 Billy Cunningham 1.50 4.00
17 Adrian Dantley 1.50 4.00
18 Bob Davies 1.50 4.00
19 Dave DeBusschere 1.50 4.00
20 Anne Donovan 1.50 4.00
21 Clyde Drexler 2.00 5.00
22 Joe Dumars 1.50 4.00
23 Alex English 1.50 4.00
24 Patrick Ewing 2.00 5.00
25 Walt Frazier 1.50 4.00
26 Joe Fulks 2.00 5.00
27 Harry Gallatin 1.50 4.00
28 Pop Gates 2.00 5.00
29 George Gervin 1.50 4.00
30 Tom Gola 1.50 4.00
31 Gail Goodrich 1.50 4.00
32 Hal Greer 1.50 4.00
33 Cliff Hagan 1.50 4.00
34 John Havlicek 1.50 4.00
35 Connie Hawkins 1.50 4.00
36 Elvin Hayes 1.50 4.00
37 Tom Heinsohn 1.50 4.00
38 Bailey Howell 1.50 4.00
39 Dan Issel 1.50 4.00
40 Buddy Jeannette 1.50 4.00
41 Dennis Johnson 1.50 4.00
42 Magic Johnson 4.00 10.00
43 Neil Johnston 1.50 4.00
44 K.C. Jones 1.50 4.00
45 Sam Jones 2.00 5.00
46 Bob Lanier 1.50 4.00
47 Nancy Lieberman 2.00 5.00
48 Clyde Lovellette 1.50 4.00
49 Jerry Lucas 1.50 4.00
50 Pete Maravich 5.00 12.00
51 Bob McAdoo 1.50 4.00
52 Kevin McHale 1.50 4.00
53 Ed Macauley 1.50 4.00
54 Karl Malone 2.00 5.00
55 Moses Malone 1.50 4.00
56 Slater Martin 1.50 4.00
57 Ann Meyers 1.50 4.00
58 George Mikan 3.00 8.00
59 Vern Mikkelsen 1.50 4.00
60 Cheryl Miller 1.50 4.00
61 Earl Monroe 1.50 4.00
62 Calvin Murphy 1.50 4.00
63 Hakeem Olajuwon 2.00 5.00
64 James Naismith 1.50 4.00
65 Robert Parish 1.50 4.00
66 Drazen Petrovic 3.00 8.00
67 Bob Pettit 1.50 4.00
68 Andy Phillip 2.00 5.00
69 Jim Pollard 2.00 5.00
70 Scottie Pippen 3.00 8.00
71 Frank Ramsey 1.50 4.00
72 Willis Reed 1.50 4.00
73 Arnie Risen 1.50 4.00
74 Oscar Robertson 1.50 4.00
75 David Robinson 2.50 6.00
76 Bill Russell 2.50 6.00
77 Dolph Schayes 1.50 4.00
78 Bill Sharman 1.50 4.00
79 John Stockton 2.50 6.00
80 Maurice Stokes 1.50 4.00
81 Isiah Thomas 1.50 4.00
82 David Thompson 2.00 5.00
83 Nate Thurmond 1.50 4.00
84 Jack Twyman 1.50 4.00
85 Wes Unseld 1.50 4.00
86 Bill Walton 1.50 4.00
87 Bobby Wanzer 1.50 4.00
88 Jerry West 2.00 5.00
89 Lenny Wilkens 1.50 4.00
90 Dominique Wilkins 2.00 5.00
91 Lynette Woodard 1.50 4.00
92 John Wooden 2.00 5.00
93 James Worthy 2.00 5.00
94 George Yardley 1.50 4.00
95 Phog Allen 1.50 4.00
96 Red Auerbach 2.00 5.00
97 Jim Boeheim 1.50 4.00
98 Larry Brown 1.50 4.00
99 Lou Carnesecca 1.50 4.00
100 Jody Conradt 2.00 5.00
101 Denny Crum 1.50 4.00
102 Chuck Daly 1.50 4.00
103 Ed Diddle 1.50 4.00
104 Clarence Gaines 1.50 4.00
105 Alex Hannum 1.50 4.00
106 Red Holzman 1.50 4.00
107 Hank Iba 1.50 4.00
108 Phil Jackson 2.00 5.00
109 Bob Knight 2.00 5.00
110 Mike Krzyzewski 2.00 5.00
111 John Kundla 1.50 4.00
112 Al McGuire 1.50 4.00
113 Ray Meyer 1.50 4.00
114 Jack Ramsay 1.50 4.00
116 Adolph Rupp 1.50 4.00
117 Jerry Sloan 1.50 4.00
118 Dean Smith 2.00 5.00
119 C. Vivian Stringer 1.50 4.00
120 Pat Summitt 1.50 4.00
121 John Thompson 1.50 4.00
122 Roy Williams 1.50 4.00
123 Meadowlark Lemon 1.50 4.00
124 Wilt Chamberlain 3.00 8.00
125 Lenny Wilkens 1.50 4.00
126 Marques Haynes 1.50 4.00
127 Oscar Robertson 1.50 4.00
128 Abe Saperstein 2.00 5.00
129 Harry Flournoy 1.50 4.00
130 Nevil Shed 1.50 4.00
131 David Lattin 2.00 5.00
132 Willie Worsley 1.50 4.00
133 Orsten Artis 1.50 4.00
134 Willie Cager 2.00 5.00
135 Don Haskins 2.00 5.00
136 Hubie Brown 1.50 4.00
137 Walter Brown 1.50 4.00
138 Jerry Colangelo 2.00 5.00
139 Chick Hearn 1.50 4.00
140 Pete Newell 1.50 4.00
141 Amos Alonzo Stagg 1.50 4.00
142 Chuck Taylor 1.50 4.00
143 Dick Vitale 2.00 5.00
144 Larry O'Brien 1.50 4.00
145 Nat Holman 2.00 5.00
146 Paul Endacott 1.50 4.00
147 Bud Foster 1.50 4.00
148 1960 USA Oly BK Team 2.00 5.00
149 1992 USA Oly BK Team 3.00 8.00
150 Bob Kurland 1.50 4.00

2009-10 Hall of Fame Black Border

*BLACK: .6X TO 1.5X BASE HI
BLACK PRINT RUN 199 SER.#'d SETS

2009-10 Hall of Fame Dream Team

COMPLETE SET (9) 25.00 50.00
PRINT RUN 349 SER.#'d SETS
*BLACK: .5X TO 1.25X BASE HI
BLACK PRINT RUN 199 SER.#'d SETS
UNPRICED MARBLE PRINT RUN ONE SET
1 Larry Bird 10.00 25.00
2 Magic Johnson 8.00 20.00
3 Clyde Drexler 4.00 10.00
4 Karl Malone 4.00 10.00
5 David Robinson 5.00 12.00
6 John Stockton 5.00 12.00
7 Patrick Ewing 4.00 10.00
8 Chris Mullin 3.00 8.00
9 Scottie Pippen 6.00 15.00

2009-10 Hall of Fame Dream Team Game Threads

STATED PRINT RUN 500 TO 1075 SETS
1 Larry Bird/975 10.00 25.00
2 Magic Johnson/750 12.00 30.00
3 Clyde Drexler/650 8.00 20.00
4 Karl Malone/1075 6.00 15.00
5 David Robinson/900 8.00 20.00
6 John Stockton/500 8.00 20.00
7 Patrick Ewing/975 8.00 20.00
8 Chris Mullin/600 6.00 15.00
9 Scottie Pippen/875 8.00 20.00

2009-10 Hall of Fame Dream Team Game Threads Prime

STATED PRINT RUN 99 SER.#'d SETS
1 Larry Bird 40.00 100.00
2 Magic Johnson 30.00 80.00
3 Clyde Drexler 30.00 80.00
4 Karl Malone 30.00 80.00
5 David Robinson 30.00 80.00
6 John Stockton 30.00 80.00
7 Patrick Ewing 30.00 80.00
8 Chris Mullin 30.00 80.00
9 Scottie Pippen 40.00 100.00

2009-10 Hall of Fame Dream Team Marks of Fame

STATED PRINT RUN 44 TO 49 SER.#'d SETS
1 Larry Bird/49 250.00 450.00
2 Magic Johnson/44 200.00 400.00
3 Clyde Drexler/49 200.00 350.00
6 John Stockton/49 200.00 350.00
8 Chris Mullin/49 125.00 250.00
9 Scottie Pippen/49 350.00 600.00

2009-10 Hall of Fame Famed Cuts

STATED PRINT RUN ONE TO 20 SER.#'d SETS
MOST NOT PRICED DUE TO SCARCITY
2 Clarence Gaines/20 60.00 150.00

2009-10 Hall of Fame Famed Fabrics

STATED PRINT RUN 20 TO 599 SER.#'d SETS
UNPRICED PRIME PRINT RUN 10 SETS
1 Alex English/325 3.00 8.00
2 Tom Heinsohn/99 3.00 8.00
3 Bob Lanier/399 3.00 8.00
4 Clyde Drexler/599 4.00 10.00
5 Larry Bird/20 25.00 50.00
6 Dave Cowens/149 5.00 12.00
7 Dominique Wilkins/549 4.00 10.00
9 Hakeem Olajuwon/399 4.00 10.00
10 Isiah Thomas/325 3.00 8.00
11 Joe Dumars/250 3.00 8.00
12 Dennis Johnson/325 4.00 10.00
13 Karl Malone/599 4.00 10.00
14 Kevin McHale/399 4.00 10.00
15 Magic Johnson/250 6.00 15.00
16 Patrick Ewing/599 4.00 10.00
17 John Stockton/99 6.00 15.00
18 George Mikan/99 12.00 30.00
19 Dan Issel/99 3.00 8.00
20 Robert Parish/549 3.00 8.00
21 Kareem Abdul-Jabbar/99 6.00 15.00
22 Scottie Pippen/599 6.00 15.00

2009-10 Hall of Fame Famed Signatures

STATED PRINT RUN 10 TO 899 SER.#'d SETS
1 Kareem Abdul-Jabbar/50 75.00 150.00
2 Nate Archibald/499 8.00 20.00
3 Rick Barry/489 8.00 20.00
4 Elgin Baylor/199 15.00 40.00
6 Carol Blazejowski/899 6.00 15.00
7 Cynthia Cooper/499 10.00 25.00
9 Dave Cowens/499 10.00 25.00
10 Adrian Dantley/499 6.00 15.00
11 Anne Donovan/899 6.00 15.00
12 Joe Dumars/399 8.00 20.00
13 Alex English/499 6.00 15.00
14 Walt Frazier/394 10.00 25.00
15 Harry Gallatin/699 6.00 15.00
16 George Gervin/398 8.00 20.00
17 Tom Gola/899 10.00 25.00
18 Gail Goodrich/499 6.00 15.00
19 Hal Greer/499 8.00 20.00
20 Cliff Hagan/499 6.00 15.00
21 John Havlicek/199 15.00 40.00
22 Connie Hawkins/599 10.00 25.00
23 Elvin Hayes/364 6.00 15.00
24 Bailey Howell/599 6.00 15.00
25 K.C. Jones/399 8.00 20.00
27 Bob Lanier/499 8.00 20.00
28 Nancy Lieberman/496 6.00 15.00
29 Bob McAdoo/391 8.00 20.00
30 Kevin McHale/100 40.00 100.00
33 Ann Meyers/499 8.00 20.00
35 Cheryl Miller/499 10.00 25.00
36 Earl Monroe/399 10.00 25.00
37 Hakeem Olajuwon/299 20.00 50.00
38 Robert Parish/499 10.00 25.00
39 Willis Reed/499 10.00 25.00
40 Oscar Robertson/99 50.00 120.00
42 Bill Russell/99 75.00 150.00
43 Bill Sharman/499 8.00 20.00
44 Isiah Thomas/499 10.00 25.00
45 David Thompson/599 6.00 15.00
46 Nate Thurmond/499 10.00 25.00
47 Wes Unseld/492 8.00 20.00
48 Bill Walton/249 10.00 25.00
49 Lenny Wilkens/499 6.00 15.00
50 Dominique Wilkins/199 15.00 40.00
51 James Worthy/249 30.00 80.00
58 Pat Summitt/599 60.00 120.00
60 Harry Flournoy/899 6.00 15.00
61 Nevil Shed/899 6.00 15.00
62 David Lattin/890 6.00 15.00
63 Orsten Artis/899 6.00 15.00
64 Willie Cager/899 6.00 15.00
65 Willie Worsley/850 6.00 15.00

2009-10 Hall of Fame High Class

COMPLETE SET (5) 10.00 25.00
STATED PRINT RUN 399 SER.#'d SETS
*BLACK: .6X TO 1.5X BASE HI
BLACK PRINT RUN 199 SER.#'d SETS
UNPRICED MARBLE PRINT RUN ONE SET
1 George Mikan 3.00 8.00
2 Bill Russell 2.50 6.00
3 Jerry West 2.00 5.00
4 Pete Maravich 5.00 12.00
5 Magic Johnson 4.00 10.00

2009-10 Hall of Fame High Praise

COMPLETE SET (9) 15.00 30.00
STATED PRINT RUN 399 SER.#'d SETS
1 Kareem Abdul-Jabbar 2.50 6.00
2 Oscar Robertson 1.50 4.00
3 Gail Goodrich 1.50 4.00
4 Bill Walton 1.50 4.00
5 Dominique Wilkins 2.00 5.00
6 Phil Jackson 2.00 5.00
7 David Robinson 2.50 6.00
8 Larry Bird 5.00 12.00
9 Wilt Chamberlain 3.00 8.00

2009-10 Hall of Fame Monikers

STATED PRINT RUN 10 TO 299 SER.#'d SETS
SOME UNPRICED DUE TO SCARCITY
1 Larry Bird/10
2 Walt Frazier/99 15.00 40.00
3 Nancy Lieberman/198 8.00 20.00
4 Dominique Wilkins/25 25.00 60.00
5 Bob Cousy/25 100.00 200.00
6 Elvin Hayes/99 15.00 40.00
7 George Gervin/199 15.00 40.00
8 Nate Archibald/299 8.00 20.00
9 Harry Gallatin/299 10.00 25.00
10 Connie Hawkins/199 12.00 30.00
11 Earl Monroe/199 15.00 40.00
12 Robert Parish/149 8.00 20.00
13 Jerry West/25 60.00 150.00
14 Hakeem Olajuwon/49 25.00 60.00
15 Oscar Robertson/25 100.00 225.00
16 John Havlicek/49 100.00 175.00
17 Nate Thurmond/199 12.50 30.00
18 Carol Blazejowski/299 8.00 20.00
19 Cynthia Cooper/294 8.00 20.00
20 Adrian Dantley/199 8.00 20.00
22 Clyde Drexler/99 25.00 60.00
23 Calvin Murphy/299 8.00 20.00
24 David Thompson/149 8.00 20.00
25 Isiah Thomas/99 12.50 30.00

2009-10 Hall of Fame Scoring Legends

COMPLETE SET (20) 20.00 40.00
STATED PRINT RUN 399 SER.#'d SETS
*BLACK: .6X TO 1.5X BASE HI
BLACK PRINT RUN 199 SER.#'d SETS
UNPRICED MARBLE PRINT RUN ONE SET
1 Kareem Abdul-Jabbar 2.50 6.00
2 Moses Malone 1.50 4.00
3 Dan Issel 1.50 4.00
4 Elvin Hayes 1.50 4.00
5 Oscar Robertson 1.50 4.00
6 Dominique Wilkins 2.00 5.00
7 George Gervin 1.50 4.00
8 John Havlicek 1.50 4.00
9 Rick Barry 1.50 4.00
10 Jerry West 2.00 5.00
11 Magic Johnson 4.00 10.00
12 Isiah Thomas 1.50 4.00
13 Lenny Wilkens 1.50 4.00
14 Bob Cousy 2.50 6.00
15 Nate Archibald 1.50 4.00
16 Bill Russell 2.50 6.00
17 Robert Parish 1.50 4.00
18 Nate Thurmond 1.50 4.00
19 Walt Bellamy 1.50 4.00
20 Wes Unseld 1.50 4.00

2009-10 Hall of Fame Scoring Legends Game Threads

STATED PRINT RUN 25 TO 249 SER.#'d SETS
1 Kareem Abdul-Jabbar/249 6.00 15.00
3 Dan Issel/249 3.00 8.00
6 Dominique Wilkins/249 4.00 10.00
8 John Havlicek/25 10.00 25.00
9 Rick Barry/49 3.00 8.00
11 Magic Johnson/249 6.00 15.00
12 Isiah Thomas/199 3.00 8.00
17 Robert Parish/249 3.00 8.00

2009-10 Hall of Fame Scoring Legends Game Threads Prime

STATED PRINT RUN 25 SER.#'d SETS
1 Kareem Abdul-Jabbar 8.00 20.00
3 Dan Issel 6.00 15.00
6 Dominique Wilkins 6.00 15.00
8 John Havlicek 12.00 30.00
9 Rick Barry 6.00 15.00
11 Magic Johnson 15.00 40.00
12 Isiah Thomas 15.00 40.00
17 Robert Parish 8.00 20.00

1968-74 Hall of Fame Bookmarks

These bookmarks commemorate individuals who were elected to the Basketball Hall of Fame. The cards were probably issued year after year (with additions) by the Hall of Fame book store. They measure approximately 2 7/16" by 6 3/8". The top of the front has a blue-tinted 2 1/8" by 2 5/16 "mug shot" of the individual on paper stock. In blue lettering the individual's name and a brief biography are printed below the picture. The backs are blank and the cards are unnumbered. The last seven cards listed below were inducted in 1969 (47-48), 1970 (49-51), 1972 (52), and 1974 (53); there are some slight style and size differences in these later issue cards compared to the first 46 cards in the set.

COMPLETE SET (53)	100.00	200.00
1 Forrest C. Allen	.60	1.50
2 Arnold J. Auerbach	1.25	3.00
3 Clair F. Bee	.60	1.50
4 Bernhard Borgmann	.20	.50
5 Walter A. Brown	.20	.50
6 John W. Bunn	.20	.50
7 Howard G. Cann	.20	.50
8 H. Clifford Carlson	.20	.50
9 Everett S. Dean	.20	.50
10 Forrest S. DeBernardi	.20	.50
11 Henry G. Dehnert	.20	.50
12 Harold E. Foster	.20	.50
13 Amory T. Gill	.20	.50
14 Victor A. Hanson	.20	.50
15 Edward J. Hickox	.20	.50
16 Paul D. Hinkle	.20	.50
17 Howard A. Hobson	.20	.50
18 Nat Holman	.75	2.00
19 Charles D. Hyatt	.20	.50
20 Henry P. Iba	.60	1.50
21 Edward S. Irish	.25	.60
22 Alvin F. Julian	.20	.50
23 Matthew P. Kennedy	.20	.50
24 Robert A. Kurland	.40	1.00
25 Ward L. Lambert	.60	1.50
26 Joe Lapchick	.40	1.00
27 Kenneth D. Loeffler	.20	.50
28 Angelo Luisetti	.50	1.25
29 Ed Macauley	.50	1.25
30 Branch McCracken	.25	.60
31 George Mikan	2.00	5.00
32 William G. Mokray	.20	.50
33 Charles C. Murphy	.60	1.50
34 James Naismith	1.25	3.00
35 Andy Phillip	.40	1.00
36 John S. Roosma	.20	.50
37 Adolph F. Rupp	1.50	4.00
38 John D. Russell	.20	.50
39 Arthur A. Schabinger	.20	.50
40 Amos Alonzo Stagg	1.25	3.00
41 Charles H. Taylor	.20	.50
42 John A. Thompson	.20	.50
43 David Tobey	.20	.50
44 Oswald Tower	.20	.50
45 David H. Walsh	.20	.50
46 John R. Wooden	2.00	5.00
47 Bernard Carnevale	6.00	15.00
48 Bob Davies	8.00	20.00
49 Bob Cousy	15.00	40.00
50 Bob Pettit	12.50	30.00
51 Abraham M. Saperstein	10.00	25.00
52 Adolph Schayes	10.00	25.00
53 Bill Russell	20.00	50.00

2005 Hardwood Heroes NBA Medallions

Created by Activa Promotions, this 30-card set features NBA stars on Medallion coins. The cards were distributed via both 7-11 stores and USA Today. The coins were available, one per day, from April 25, 2005 through June 3, 2005. There was also a color collectors album available to house the medallions.

COMPLETE SET (30)	25.00	60.00
1 Ray Allen	1.25	3.00
2 Carmelo Anthony	2.00	5.00
3 Elton Brand	1.25	3.00
4 Kobe Bryant	5.00	12.00
5 Vince Carter	1.50	4.00
6 Tim Duncan	1.50	4.00
7 Steve Francis	1.25	3.00
8 Kevin Garnett	2.00	5.00
9 Pau Gasol	1.25	3.00
10 Kirk Hinrich	1.25	3.00
11 Allen Iverson	1.50	4.00
12 LeBron James	5.00	12.00
13 Antawn Jamison	1.25	3.00
14 Jason Kidd	1.50	4.00
15 Andrei Kirilenko	1.25	3.00
16 Stephon Marbury	1.25	3.00
17 Tracy McGrady	1.50	4.00
18 Yao Ming	1.50	4.00
19 Steve Nash	1.50	4.00
20 Dirk Nowitzki	1.50	4.00
21 Jermaine O'Neal	1.25	3.00
22 Shaquille O'Neal	2.00	5.00
23 Emeka Okafor	1.25	3.00
24 Tony Parker	1.25	3.00
25 Paul Pierce	1.50	4.00
26 Jason Richardson	1.25	3.00
27 Peja Stojakovic	1.25	3.00
28 Amare Stoudemire	1.50	4.00
29 Dwyane Wade	3.00	8.00
30 Ben Wallace	1.25	3.00

1959-60 Hawks Busch Bavarian

These black and white photo-like cards were sponsored by Busch Bavarian Beer and feature members of the St. Louis Hawks. The cards are blank backed and measure approximately 4" by 5". The cards show a facsimile autograph of the player on a drop-out background. The set is dated by the fact that 1959-60 was John McCarthy's first year with the St. Louis Hawks.

COMPLETE SET (5)	400.00	800.00
1 Sihugo Green	100.00	200.00
2 Cliff Hagan	125.00	250.00
3 Clyde Lovellette	125.00	250.00
4 John McCarthy	75.00	150.00
5 Bob Pettit	250.00	450.00

1978-79 Hawks Coke/WPLO

This rather unattractive 14-card set was sponsored by V-103/WPLO radio and Coca-Cola, and they were given out at 7-Eleven stores. The cards are printed on thin cardboard stock and measure approximately 3 by 4 1/4". The fronts feature a black and white pen and ink drawing of the player's head, with the Hawks' and Coke logos in the lower corners in red. The back has a career summary and the sponsor's "V-103 Disco Stereo" at the bottom. The cards are unnumbered and are checklisted below in alphabetical order.

COMPLETE SET (14)	25.00	50.00
1 Hubie Brown CO	5.00	12.00
2 Charlie Criss	2.00	5.00
3 John Drew	2.00	5.00
4 Mike Fratello CO	3.00	8.00
5 Jack Givens	3.00	8.00
6 Steve Hawes	1.25	3.00
7 Armond Hill	1.50	4.00
8 Eddie Johnson	2.00	5.00
9 Frank Layden CO	3.00	8.00
10 Butch Lee	1.25	3.00
11 Tom McMillen	2.50	6.00
12 Tree Rollins	2.50	6.00
13 Dan Roundfield	1.50	4.00
14 Rick Wilson	1.25	3.00

1961 Hawks Essex Meats

The 1961 Essex Meats set contains 13 standard-size cards featuring the St. Louis Hawks. The fronts picture a posed black and white photo of the player with his name at the bottom of the card in bold-faced type. The backs of this white-stock card feature the player's name, brief physical data and biographical information. The cards are unnumbered and give no indication of the producer on the card. The cards were distributed by Bonnie Brands. The catalog designation for the set is F175. There is reportedly an additional card in the set, Sihugo Green.

COMPLETE SET (13)	150.00	275.00
1 Barney Cable	6.00	15.00
2 Al Ferrari	6.00	15.00
3 Larry Foust	6.00	15.00
4 Cliff Hagan	25.00	45.00
5 Vern Hatton	10.00	20.00
6 Cleo Hill	6.00	15.00
7 Fred LaCour	6.00	15.00
8 Fuzzy Levane CO	8.00	20.00
9 Clyde Lovellette	25.00	45.00
10 John McCarthy	6.00	15.00
11 Shellie McMillon	6.00	15.00
12 Bob Pettit	45.00	90.00
13 Bobby Sims	6.00	15.00

1979-80 Hawks Majik Market

The 1979-80 Majik Market/Coca-Cola Atlanta Hawks set contains 15 cards on thin white stock. Cards are approximately 3" by 4 1/4". The fronts of the cards include a crude, black line drawing of the player, the player's name and, in red, a Coke logo and a stylized Hawks logo. The backs contain biographical data and a summary of the player's activity during the 1978-79 season. The Majik Market logo and the call letters V-103/WPLO are printed in red on the back of the cards. Most collectors consider the set quite unattractive and poorly produced. The cards are unnumbered and are checklisted below in alphabetical order.

COMPLETE SET (15)	25.00	50.00
1 Hubie Brown CO	3.00	8.00
2 John Brown	1.25	3.00
3 Charlie Criss	2.00	5.00
4 John Drew	2.00	5.00
5 Mike Fratello ACO	2.50	6.00
6 Jack Givens	2.50	6.00
7 Steve Hawes	1.50	4.00
8 Armond Hill	1.50	4.00
9 Eddie Johnson	2.00	5.00
10 Jimmy McElroy	1.25	3.00
11 Tom McMillen	2.50	6.00
12 Sam Pellom	1.25	3.00
13 Tree Rollins	2.50	6.00
14 Dan Roundfield	2.00	5.00
15 Brendan Suhr ACO	1.50	4.00

1986-87 Hawks Pizza Hut

The 1986-87 Atlanta Hawks Team Photo Night (January 30, 1987) set was sponsored by Pizza Hut. This photo album was distributed to fans attending the Atlanta Hawks home game. It consists of three sheets, each measuring approximately 8 1/4" by 11" and joined together to form one continuous sheet. The first sheet features a team photo of the Hawks. While the second sheet presents two rows of five cards each, the third sheet presents eight additional player cards, with the remaining two slots filled in by Pizza Hut coupons. After perforation, the cards measure approximately 2 1/4" by 3 3/4". The card front features a color player portrait, with a red border on white card stock. The player's name and position are given below the picture, along with the team and Pizza Hut logos. The backs present career statistics in a horizontal format. The cards are unnumbered and checklisted below in the order they appear in the album, with coaching staff listed first and then the players in alphabetical order.

COMPLETE SET (18)	15.00	40.00
1 Mike Fratello CO	1.25	3.00
2 Willis Reed ACO	1.50	4.00
3 Brendan Suhr ACO	.40	1.00
4 Brian Hill ACO	1.00	2.50
5 Joe O'Toole TR	.40	1.00
6 John Battle	.60	1.50
7 Antoine Carr	1.00	2.50
8 Scott Hastings	.75	2.00
9 Jon Koncak	.75	2.00
10 Cliff Levingston	.75	2.00
11 Mike McGee	.75	2.00
12 Doc Rivers	2.50	6.00
13 Tree Rollins	.75	2.00
14 Spud Webb	2.00	5.00
15 Dominique Wilkins	8.00	20.00
16 Gus Williams	.75	2.00
17 Kevin Willis	2.50	6.00
18 Randy Wittman	1.25	3.00

1987-88 Hawks Pizza Hut

The 1987-88 Atlanta Hawks Team Photo Night set was sponsored by Pizza Hut. This photo album was distributed to fans attending the Atlanta Hawks home game on March 11, 1988. The set consists of three sheets, each measuring approximately 8 1/4" by 11" and joined together to form one continuous sheet. The first sheet features a team photo of the Hawks. While the second sheet presents two rows of five cards each, the third sheet presents seven additional player cards, with the remaining three slots filled in by Pizza Hut coupons. After perforation, the cards measure approximately 2 3/16" by 3 3/4". The card front features a color action player photo, with a red border on white card stock. The player's name and position are given below the picture, along with the team and Pizza Hut logos. The back presents career statistics in a horizontal format. The cards are unnumbered and are checklisted below in the order they appear in the album.

COMPLETE SET (17)	20.00	50.00
1 Mike Fratello CO	1.50	4.00
2 Brendan Suhr ASST	.75	2.00
3 Brian Hill ASST	1.00	2.50
4 Don Chaney ASST	.75	2.00
5 Joe O'Toole TR	.40	1.00
6 John Battle	.60	1.50
7 Antoine Carr	1.00	2.50
8 Scott Hastings	.75	2.00
9 Jon Koncak	.75	2.00
10 Cliff Levingston	1.00	2.50
11 Doc Rivers	2.50	6.00
12 Tree Rollins	1.00	2.50
13 Chris Washburn	.75	2.00
14 Spud Webb	2.00	5.00
15 Dominique Wilkins	8.00	20.00
16 Kevin Willis	2.00	5.00
17 Randy Wittman	1.25	3.00

1968-69 Hawks Team Issue

Measuring 8" by 10", this seven photo set was released during the 1968-69 Atlanta Hawks. Each photo features a posed shot with the player's name in the lower left-hand corner and the team name in the lower right. Each photo is in black and white with blank backs. The photos are not numbered and listed below in alphabetical order.

COMPLETE SET (7)	20.00	40.00
1 Zelmo Beaty	5.00	10.00
2 Joe Caldwell	3.00	8.00
3 Jim Davis	2.50	6.00
4 Dennis Hamilton	2.50	6.00
5 Skip Harlicka	2.50	6.00
6 George Lehmann	3.00	8.00
7 Don Ohl	2.50	6.00

1969-70 Hawks Team Issue

This 10-photo team issue set was released to the press for the Atlanta Hawks' 1969-70 season. The photos measure 8" x 10", are black and white and are blank-backed. All that appears on the photo is a player close-up or action shot set against a white background and the player's name and "Atlanta Hawks" at the bottom. The photos are checklisted below in alphabetical order.

COMPLETE SET (10)	30.00	60.00
1 Butch Beard	3.00	8.00
2 Bill Bridges	2.50	6.00
3 Joe Caldwell	2.50	6.00
4 Jim Davis	2.00	5.00
5 Gary Gregor	2.00	5.00
6 Richie Guerin CO	2.50	6.00
7 Walt Hazzard	5.00	10.00
8 Lou Hudson	6.00	12.00
9 Don Ohl	2.50	6.00
10 Grady O'Malley	2.00	5.00

1972-73 Hawks Team Issue

Measuring 8" by 10", this 9-photo set features members of the 1972-73 Atlanta Hawks. Half of the set features a two-shot front and the other half features one large posed shot. All of the photos are in black and white. The backs are blank and not numbered, thus, listed below in alphabetical order.

COMPLETE SET (9)	17.50	35.00
1 Don Adams	1.50	4.00
2 Walt Bellamy	3.00	8.00
3 Bob Christian	1.25	3.00
4 Herm Gilliam	1.25	3.00
5 Jeff Halliburton	1.25	3.00
6 Lou Hudson	3.00	8.00
7 Tom Payne	1.50	4.00
8 George Trapp	1.25	3.00
9 Jim Washington	1.25	3.00

1977-78 Hawks Team Issue

These 12 photos, which are black and white glossies and measure 8" by 10" feature members of the 1977-78 Atlanta Hawks. Since these photos are unnumbered, we have sequenced them in alphabetical order.

COMPLETE SET (12)	12.50	25.00
1 Hubie Brown HEAD CO	1.50	4.00
2 John Brown	.75	2.00
3 Charles Criss	1.00	2.50
4 John Drew	1.00	2.50
5 Steve Hawes	.75	2.00
6 Armond Hill	1.00	2.50
7 Eddie Johnson	.75	2.00
8 Ollie Johnson	.75	2.00
9 Tom McMillen	1.50	4.00
10 Tony Robertson	.75	2.00
11 Wayne Rollins	1.00	2.50
12 Mike Fratello ACO	1.50	4.00
Frank Layden ACO		

1978-79 Hawks Team Issue

This 4 1/2" x 6" set was produced for the Atlanta Hawks during the 1978-79 season. The set features 11 full-colored cards of the team's players.

COMPLETE SET (11)	20.00	50.00
1 John Drew	2.50	6.00
2 Eddie Johnson	2.50	6.00
3 Dan Roundfield	3.00	8.00
4 Tree Rollins	3.00	8.00
5 Butch Lee	3.00	8.00
6 Jack Givens	3.00	8.00
7 Tom McMillen	3.00	8.00
8 Armond Hill	2.00	5.00
9 Steve Hawes	2.00	5.00
10 Charlie Criss	2.00	5.00
11 Rick Wilson	2.00	5.00

1993-94 Heat Bookmarks

Measuring 2 1/2" by 8", these four bookmarks were sponsored by the Miami Herald. The color action photo on the top portion is framed by a black inner border and a orangish-yellow outer border. The remainder of the front has biography, a "Join the Winning Team! Read" slogan, as well as team and sponsor logos. In black print on a white background, the back carries ten "Heat Tips For Reading With Children." The bookmarks are unnumbered and checklisted below in alphabetical order.

COMPLETE SET (4)	1.60	4.00
1 Grant Long	.40	1.00
2 Harold Miner	.40	1.00
3 Rony Seikaly	.40	1.00
4 Steve Smith	.75	2.00

2001-02 Hawks Topps

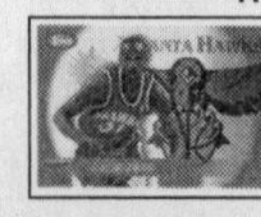

Released by Topps, this set features a horizontal design with the Atlanta Hawks logo in the background. Our information on this set is incomplete. If you have further information about this product, please contact us at basketballmag@beckett.com.

COMPLETE SET (11)	2.00	5.00
AH2 Hanno Mottola	.30	.75
AH4 Alan Henderson	.30	.75
AH6 Anthony Johnson	.30	.75
AH7 Chris Crawford	.30	.75
AH9 Roshown McLeod	.30	.75
AH10 DerMarr Johnson	.30	.75
AH11 Cal Bowdler	.30	.75
AH12 Lorenzen Wright	.30	.75
AH13 Dion Glover	.30	.75
AH14 Jason Terry	.50	1.25
NNO Atlanta Hawks	.25	.60

1989-90 Heat Publix

This 15-card set was distributed in Publix stores in the greater Miami area. The cards measure approximately 2" by 3 1/2" and feature members of the Miami Heat. The fronts feature a color action player photo, with the player's name and position in the stripe below the picture. The back has biographical and statistical information. The cards are unnumbered and are checklisted below in alphabetical order. The set features early cards of Glen Rice and Rony Seikaly among others.

COMPLETE SET (15)	40.00	100.00
1 Terry Davis	2.00	5.00
2 Sherman Douglas	6.00	15.00
3 Kevin Edwards	3.00	8.00
4 Tony Fiorentino CO	2.00	5.00
5 Tellis Frank	2.00	5.00
6 Scott Haffner	2.00	5.00
7 Grant Long	6.00	15.00
8 Heat Mascot	1.50	4.00
9 Glen Rice	15.00	40.00
10 Ron Rothstein CO	5.00	12.00
11 Rony Seikaly	6.00	15.00
12 Rory Sparrow	2.50	6.00
13 Jon Sundvold	2.50	6.00
14 Billy Thompson	3.00	7.00
15 Dave Wohl CO	3.00	8.00

1990-91 Heat Publix

This 16-card set was sponsored by Domino's Pizza, Dixie, and Bumble Bee Tuna and features members of the Miami Heat. The cards were issued in a sheet that contains 16 player cards and four manufacturers' coupons; after perforation, the cards and coupons alike measure the standard size (2 1/2" by 3 1/2"). The front features a color action player photo on a black background. The team logo appears in the upper right corner, while the player's name appears in white lettering below the picture. The back has biographical and statistical information. The cards are unnumbered and are checklisted below as they are listed on the panel, in alphabetical order with coaches at the end.

COMPLETE SET (16)	8.00	20.00
1 Keith Askins	.60	1.50
2 Willie Burton	.60	1.50
3 Bimbo Coles	.75	2.00
4 Terry Davis	.40	1.00
5 Sherman Douglas	.75	2.00
6 Kevin Edwards	.75	2.00
7 Alec Kessler	.40	1.00
8 Grant Long	1.25	3.00
9 Alan Ogg	.40	1.00
10 Glen Rice	3.00	8.00
11 Rony Seikaly	1.25	3.00
12 Jon Sundvold	.40	1.00
13 Billy Thompson	.75	2.00
14 Ron Rothstein CO	1.25	3.00
15 Dave Wohl CO	1.25	3.00
16 Tony Fiorentino CO	.40	1.00

2008-09 Heat Upper Deck

COMPLETE SET (14)	2.50	6.00
1 Dwyane Wade	.60	1.50
2 Shawn Marion	.30	.75
3 Udonis Haslem	.25	.60
4 Yakhouba Diawara	.20	.50
5 Dorell Wright	.20	.50
6 Daequan Cook	.20	.50
7 Chris Quinn	.20	.50
8 Mark Blount	.20	.50
9 Marcus Banks	.20	.50
10 Alonzo Mourning	.40	1.00
11 Michael Beasley	.50	1.25
12 Mario Chalmers	.50	1.25
13 Erik Spoelstra CO	.20	.50
14 Glen Rice	.30	.75

1910 Helmar Premiums

These premiums were drawn by reknowned artist Hamilton King who originally illustrated advertistments for Coca Cola around 1900. These images are known as the "Women in Athletic Costumes" series. Smokers could redeem coupons for these lithographs either on card stock, on satin or on bookbinding leather. There was also a gift slip which checklisted all the premiums available from the tobacco company, which also listed the number of coupons required for each specific type of premium.

COMPLETE SET	2500.00	5000.00
1 Card Stock	200.00	400.00
2 Individual Satin	400.00	800.00
3 Leather	1000.00	2000.00
4 Satin Pillow Top	1500.00	3000.00
Eight Women shown including Basketball Girl		

1997 Highland Mint Legends Mint-Cards

Highland Mint produced its own brand of professional basketball Mint-Cards, known as Hardcourt Legends. Each card contained 4.25 Troy Ounces of .999 silver, bronze, or 24K gold-plated .999 silver. The initial suggested retail price was $50 for bronze, $235 for silver, and $500 or $650 for gold. The cards were packaged in a lucite display case in an album. The enclosed certificate of authenticity carries the serial number. The cards are checklisted below alphabetically; the mintage figures for each card are also listed.

COMPLETE SET (7)	400.00	800.00
1 Kareem Abdul-Jabbar 95	150.00	225.00
S/1000		
2 Kareem Abdul-Jabbar 95	20.00	35.00
B/5000		
3 Larry Bird 95	250.00	450.00
G/500		
4 Larry Bird 95	150.00	225.00
S/1000		
5 Larry Bird 95	20.00	35.00
B/5000		
6 Jerry West 95	150.00	225.00
S/500		
7 Jerry West 95	20.00	35.00
B/2500		

1997 Highland Mint Magnum Series Medallions

Measuring 2 1/2" in diameter and encased in a 6" by 5" velvet box, these larger medallions feature Bulls' megastar Michael Jordan. The relief on these medallions are 10 times greater than the regular medallions. The silver version include 4 Troy Ounces of .999 silver.

COMPLETE SET (2)	100.00	200.00
1 Michael Jordan	175.00	250.00
Silver 750		
2 Michael Jordan	15.00	30.00
Bronze 3000		

1997 Highland Mint Mini Mint-Cards

These mini Mint-Cards are not replicas but feature Highland Mint's own design. They are one-quarter scale of regular Mint-Cards. The high relief on the fronts is four times greater than that used on regular Mint-Cards. The backs display text and statistics. Each card is individually-numbered, includes a certificate of authenticity, and is packaged in a leather display box. Mini Mint-Cards were issued as a matching set with the cards displayed side by side. Both cards carry the same serial number. The mintage is given below with reference to silver and bronze versions. The suggested retail price was $150.00 for the silver, and $65.00 for the bronze.

COMPLETE SET (4)	100.00	250.00
1 Grant Hill	40.00	100.00
Jason Kidd		
Silver 1000		
2 Grant Hill	15.00	30.00
Jason Kidd		
Bronze 5000		
3 Michael Jordan	75.00	150.00
Michael Jordan		
Silver 1000		
4 Michael Jordan	20.00	50.00
Michael Jordan		
Bronze 5000		

1997 Highland Mint Mint-Cards Fleer/Hoops/UD

These Highland Mint cards are metal replicas of already issued Fleer, Hoops and Upper Deck cards. All these standard size replicas contain 4.25 Troy Ounces of .999 silver, bronze, or 24K gold plated .999 silver metal. Suggested retail are 50.00 for bronze and 235.00 for silver. Each card includes a certificate of authenticity, and is packaged in a numbered album and a three-piece Lucite display. The cards are checklisted below alphabetically; the final mintage figures for each card are also listed.

COMPLETE SET (19)	1200.00	2000.00
1 Charles Barkley 86-87	150.00	200.00
S/1000		
2 Charles Barkley 86-87	12.50	30.00
B/5000		
3 Anfernee Hardaway 93-94UD	150.00	200.00
S/500		
4 Anfernee Hardaway 93-94UD	12.50	30.00
B/2500		
5 Anfernee Hardaway 93-94UDSE	150.00	200.00
S/500		
6 Anfernee Hardaway 93-94UDSE	10.00	25.00
B/2500		
7 Magic Johnson 90-91	150.00	200.00
S/1000		
8 Magic Johnson 90-91	20.00	35.00
B/5000		
9 Michael Jordan 91-92	250.00	450.00
G/500		
10 Michael Jordan 91-92	175.00	250.00
S/1000		
11 Michael Jordan 91-92	20.00	50.00
B/5000		
12 Hakeem Olajuwon 86-87	150.00	200.00
S/250		
13 Hakeem Olajuwon 86-87	10.00	25.00
B/1500		
14 David Robinson 89-90	150.00	200.00
S/1000		
15 David Robinson 89-90	20.00	35.00
B/5000		
16 Jerry Stackhouse 95-96	150.00	200.00
S/500		
17 Jerry Stackhouse 95-96	10.00	25.00
B/2500		
18 Damon Stoudamire 95-96	150.00	200.00
S/500		
19 Damon Stoudamire 95-96	10.00	25.00
B/2500		

1997 Highland Mint Mint-Coins

These medallions feature the player's likeness, name, uniform number, and signature on one side, with career statistics on the reverse side. Each includes one Troy Ounce of .999 silver, bronze, or 24K gold plated .999 silver metal. The medallions are checklisted below alphabetically.

COMPLETE SET (31)	900.00	1500.00
1 Larry Bird	30.00	50.00
Silver 7500		
2 Chicago Bulls 70 Wins	30.00	50.00
Silver 2500		
3 Chicago Bulls Division	30.00	50.00
Silver 1000		
4 Chicago Bulls Conference	30.00	50.00
Silver 5000		
5 Chicago Bulls Finals	30.00	50.00
Silver 7500		
6 Chicago Bulls Finals	35.00	60.00
Gold Signature 1500		
7 Chicago Bulls	30.00	50.00
Seattle SuperSonics		
Conference Silver 500		
8 Kevin Garnett	30.00	50.00
Silver 7500		
9 Anfernee Hardaway	30.00	50.00
Gold Signature 1500		
10 Anfernee Hardaway	30.00	50.00
Silver 7500		
11 Anfernee Hardaway	2.50	
Bronze 25000		
12 Allen Iverson	30.00	5
Silver 3000		
13 Larry Johnson	30.00	5
Silver 7500		
14 Michael Jordan	400.00	80
Gold 100		
15 Michael Jordan	30.00	5
Gold Signature 1000		
16 Michael Jordan	30.00	5
Silver 7500		
17 Michael Jordan	5.00	1
Bronze 25000		
18 Shawn Kemp	30.00	5
Silver 7500		
19 Orlando Magic	30.00	5
Silver 5000		
20 Orlando Magic Div.	30.00	5
Silver 1000		
21 Scottie Pippen	30.00	5
Silver 7500		
22 Mitch Richmond	30.00	5
Gold Signature 1000		
23 Dennis Rodman	30.00	5
Red hair		
Silver 7500		
24 Dennis Rodman	2.50	
Green hair		
Bronze 12500		
25 Dennis Rodman	2.50	
Yellow hair		
Bronze 12500		
26 Dennis Rodman 3-coin set	20.00	4
Bronze 2500		
27 San Antonio Spurs Div.	30.00	5
Silver 1000		
28 Seattle Supersonics Div.	30.00	5
Silver 1000		
29 Seattle Supersonics Conf.	30.00	5
Silver 5000		
30 John Stockton	30.00	5
Silver 7500		
31 Nick Van Exel	30.00	5
Silver 7500		

1997 Highland Mint Sandbla Mint-Cards

These Highland Mint cards are metal replicas of already issued Pinnacle cards. All these standard replicas contain approximately 4.25 ounces of .9 silver or bronze metal and feature a "sandblast" background that accents the shiny surface of the player's likeness. Suggested retail are 60.00 for b and 250.00 for silver. Each card includes a certifi of authenticity, and is packaged in a numbered al and a three-piece Lucite display. The cards are checklisted below alphabetically; the final mintage figures for each card are also listed.

COMPLETE SET (2)	100.00	1
1 Grant Hill 96	150.00	2
S/500		
2 Grant Hill 96	15.00	3
B/2500		

2001 Highland Mint Shaqui O'Neal Promo

This card was given out to members of the hobby media to promote the upcoming Highland Mint products for the 2000-01 NBA Season. This card unnumbered and contains a swatch of jersey use the 1999-00 NBA Finals. The actual card is stabb a very thick plastic holder.

NNO Shaquille O'Neal Jsy	30.00	

1994-95 Hoop Magazine/Mother's Cookie

Sponsored by Mother's Cookies, Hoop Magazine featured 8 1/2" by 11" cards of NBA stars. At participating arenas, fans who purchased a Hoop program also received one of 27 different jumbo One star from each NBA team is represented in th The fronts display color action player photos ins black border. The player's name appears in the t wider black border, and the team logo is overprin the picture. In red and purple print, the back carri advertisement for Mother's Cookies. The photos numbered "No. X/27" on the front in the lower rig corner.

COMPLETE SET (27)	40.00	1
1 Mookie Blaylock	1.25	
2 Dee Brown	1.25	
3 Alonzo Mourning	2.50	
4 B.J. Armstrong	1.25	
5 Mark Price	2.00	
6 Jason Kidd	5.00	
7 Dikembe Mutombo	2.00	
8 Joe Dumars	2.00	
9 Latrell Sprewell	2.50	
10 Hakeem Olajuwon	4.00	
11 Reggie Miller	4.00	
12 Loy Vaught	1.25	
13 Vlade Divac	2.00	
14 Glen Rice	2.00	
15 Vin Baker	2.00	
16 Isaiah Rider	2.00	
17 Kenny Anderson	1.50	
18 Patrick Ewing	4.00	
19 Shaquille O'Neal	5.00	
20 Clarence Weatherspoon	1.25	
21 Charles Barkley	4.00	
22 Clyde Drexler	5.00	
23 Mitch Richmond	2.00	
24 David Robinson	4.00	
25 Gary Payton	2.00	
26 John Stockton	4.00	
27 Calbert Cheaney	1.25	

1995-96 Hoop Magazine/Mother's Cookies

sored by Mother's Cookies, Hoop Magazine
ed 8 1/2" by 11" cards of NBA stars. At
ipating arenas, fans who purchased a Hoop game
am also received one of 29 jumbo cards. One star
each NBA team is represented in the set. The
feature glossy color player photos framed by
borders. The player's name appears in either the
bottom borders in team color-coded lettering;
am logo is overprinted on the picture. In red and
e print, the backs carry a Mother's Cookies
tisement. The jumbo cards are numbered "x/29"
e front at the lower right corner.

PLETE SET (29) 80.00 200.00
g Ehlo 1.50 4.00
e Montross 1.50 4.00
ry Johnson 2.50 6.00
hael Jordan 50.00 120.00
rell Brandon 1.50 4.00
Jackson 1.50 4.00
nmoud Abdul-Rauf 1.50 4.00
n Houston 2.00 5.00
Hardaway 2.50 6.00
yde Drexler 3.00 8.00
k Smits 2.00 5.00
mond Murray 1.50 4.00
ade Divac 2.50 6.00
en Rice 2.50 6.00
enn Robinson 2.50 6.00
nn Gugliotta 1.50 4.00
O'Bannon 1.25 3.00
trick Ewing 3.00 8.00
nfernee Hardaway 4.00 10.00
rry Stackhouse 4.00 10.00
evin Johnson 2.50 6.00
d Strickland 1.50 4.00
itch Richmond 2.50 6.00
wery Johnson 2.00 5.00
etlef Schrempf 2.50 6.00
amon Stoudamire 3.00 8.00
rl Malone 3.00 8.00
eg Anthony 1.50 4.00
wan Howard 2.50 6.00

1995-96 Hoop Magazine/Mother's Cookies Award Winners

from this over-sized set were distributed in
s of Hoop magazine and sold at selected arenas
ghout the nation during the 1995-96 campaign.
card represents a different Award Winner from the
95 campaign.

PLETE SET (7) 10.00 25.00
id Robinson 4.00 10.00
on Kidd 4.00 10.00
nt Hill 4.00 10.00
a Barros 1.50 4.00
hony Mason 1.50 4.00
Harris CO 1.25 3.00
embe Mutombo 2.50 6.00

1989-90 Hoops

989-90 Hoops set contains 352 standard-size
. The cards were issued in two series of 300 and
rds. Hoops' initial venture in the basketball
et helped spark the basketball card boom of 1989-
he cards were issued in 15-card packs. The fronts
e color action player photos, bordered by a
tball lane in one of the team's colors. On a white
ace the player's name appears in black lettering
the picture. The backs have head shots of the
rs, biographical information and statistics printed
pale yellow background with white borders. The
are numbered on the back. The key Rookie Card
s set is David Robinson (138). This is his lone
e Card. Beware of Robinson counterfeits which
stinguishable primarily by comparison to a real
or under magnification. Other Rookie Cards of
nclude Hersey Hawkins, Jeff Hornacek, Kevin
son, Steve Kerr, Reggie Lewis, Dan Majerle,
y Manning, Mitch Richmond, Rik Smits and Rod
kland. The second series features the premier
of the expansion teams (Minnesota and
do), traded players, a special NBA Championship
of the Detroit Pistons and a Robinson In Action
card. Since the original Detroit Pistons World
ps card (No. 353A) was so difficult for collectors
d in packs, Hoops produced another edition
3) of the card that was available direct from the
any free of charge. If a collector wished to acquire
r more from the company, additional copies were
ble for 35 cents per card. The set is considered
ete with the less difficult version. The short
(SP below) in the first series are those cards
were dropped to make room for the new second
cards on the printing sheet.

COMPLETE SET (352) 12.50 25.00
COMPLETE SERIES 1 (300) 10.00 20.00
COMPLETE SERIES 2 (52) 2.50 5.00
1 Joe Dumars .08 .25
2 Tree Rollins .02 .10
3 Kenny Walker .02 .10
4 Mychal Thompson .02 .10
5 Alvin Robertson SP .08 .25
6 Vinny Del Negro RC .08 .25
7 Greg Anderson SP .08 .25
8 Rod Strickland RC .30 .75
9 Ed Pinckney .02 .10
10 Dale Ellis .02 .10
11 Chuck Daly CO RC .08 .25
12 Eric Leckner .02 .10
13 Charles Davis .02 .10
14 Cotton Fitzsimmons CO .02 .10
(No NBA logo on back in bottom right)
15 Byron Scott .02 .10
16 Derrick Chievous .02 .10
17 Reggie Lewis RC .10 .30
18 Jim Paxson .02 .10
19 Tony Campbell RC .02 .10
20 Rolando Blackman .02 .10
21 Michael Jordan AS .60 1.50
22 Cliff Levingston .02 .10
23 Roy Tarpley .02 .10
24 Harold Pressley UER .02 .10
(Cinderella misspelled as cindarella)
25 Larry Nance .02 .10
26 Chris Morris RC .02 .10
27 Bob Hansen UER .02 .10
(Drafted in '84, should say '83)
28 Mark Price AS .02 .10
29 Reggie Miller .25 .60
30 Karl Malone .15 .40
31 Sidney Lowe SP .08 .25
32 Ron Anderson .02 .10
33 Mike Gminski .02 .10
34 Scott Brooks RC .08 .25
35 Kevin Johnson RC .20 .50
36 Mark Bryant RC .02 .10
37 Rik Smits RC .10 .30
38 Tim Perry RC .02 .10
39 Ralph Sampson .02 .10
40 Danny Manning UER RC .10 .30
(Missing 1988 in draft info)
41 Kevin Edwards RC .02 .10
42 Paul Mokeski .02 .10
43 Dale Ellis AS .02 .10
44 Walter Berry .02 .10
45 Chuck Person .02 .10
46 Rick Mahorn SP .08 .25
47 Joe Kleine .02 .10
48 Brad Daugherty AS .02 .10
49 Mike Woodson .02 .10
50 Brad Daugherty .02 .10
51 Shelton Jones SP .08 .25
52 Michael Adams .02 .10
53 Wes Unseld CO .02 .10
54 Rex Chapman RC .08 .25
55 Kelly Tripucka .02 .10
56 Rickey Green .02 .10
57 Frank Johnson SP .08 .25
58 Johnny Newman RC .02 .10
59 Billy Thompson .02 .10
60 Stu Jackson CO .02 .10
61 Walter Davis .02 .10
62 Brian Shaw SP UER RC .10 .30
(Gary Grant led rookies in assists, not Shaw)
63 Gerald Wilkins .02 .10
64 Armon Gilliam .02 .10
65 Maurice Cheeks SP .10 .30
66 Jack Sikma .02 .10
67 Harvey Grant RC .08 .25
68 Jim Lynam CO .02 .10
69 Clyde Drexler AS .02 .10
70 Xavier McDaniel .02 .10
71 Danny Young .02 .10
72 Fennis Dembo .02 .10
73 Mark Acres SP .08 .25
74 Brad Lohaus SP RC .08 .25
75 Manute Bol .02 .10
76 Purvis Short .02 .10
77 Allen Leavell .02 .10
78 Johnny Dawkins SP .08 .25
79 Paul Pressey .02 .10
80 Patrick Ewing .08 .25
81 Bill Wennington RC .15 .40
82 Danny Schayes .02 .10
83 Derek Smith .02 .10
84 Moses Malone AS .02 .10
85 Jeff Malone .02 .10
86 Otis Smith SP RC .08 .25
87 Trent Tucker .02 .10
88 Robert Reid .02 .10
89 John Paxson .02 .10
90 Chris Mullin .08 .25
91 Tom Garrick .02 .10
92 Willis Reed CO SP UER .10 .30
(Gambling, should be Grambling)
93 Dave Corzine SP .08 .25
94 Mark Alarie .02 .10
95 Mark Aguirre .02 .10
96 Charles Barkley AS .07 .20
97 Sidney Green SP .08 .25
98 Kevin Willis .02 .10
99 Dave Hoppen .02 .10
100 Terry Cummings SP .10 .30
101 Dwayne Washington SP .08 .25
102 Larry Brown CO .02 .10
103 Kevin Duckworth .02 .10
104 Uwe Blab SP .08 .25
105 Terry Porter .02 .10
106 Craig Ehlo RC .08 .25
107 Don Casey CO .02 .10
108 Pat Riley CO .08 .25
109 John Salley .02 .10
110 Charles Barkley .15 .40
111 Sam Bowie SP .10 .30
112 Earl Cureton .02 .10
113 Craig Hodges UER .02 .10
(3-pointing shooting)
114 Benoit Benjamin .02 .10
115A Spud Webb ERR SP .08 .25
(Signed 9/27/85)
115B Spud Webb COR .02 .10
(Second series; signed 9/26/85)
116 Karl Malone AS .08 .25
117 Sleepy Floyd .02 .10
118 Hot Rod Williams .02 .10
119 Michael Holton .02 .10
120 Alex English .02 .10
121 Dennis Johnson .02 .10
122 Wayne Cooper SP .08 .25
123A Don Chaney CO .02 .10
(Line next to NBA coaching record)
123B Don Chaney CO .02 .10
(No line)
124 A.C. Green .02 .10
125 Adrian Dantley .02 .10
126 Del Harris CO .08 .25
127 Dick Harter CO .02 .10
128 Reggie Williams RC .02 .10
129 Bill Hanzlik .02 .10
130 Dominique Wilkins .08 .25
131 Herb Williams .02 .10
132 Steve Johnson SP .08 .25
133 Alex English AS .02 .10
134 Darrell Walker .02 .10
135 Bill Laimbeer .02 .10
136 Fred Roberts RC .02 .10
137 Hersey Hawkins RC .15 .40
138 David Robinson SP RC 5.00 12.00
139 Brad Sellers SP .08 .25
140 John Stockton .25 .60
141 Grant Long RC .02 .10
142 Marc Iavaroni SP .08 .25
143 Steve Alford SP RC .10 .30
144 Jeff Lamp SP .08 .25
145 Buck Williams SP UER .10 .30
(Won ROY in '81, should say '82)
146 Mark Jackson AS .02 .10
147 Jim Petersen .02 .10
148 Steve Stipanovich SP .10 .30
149 Sam Vincent SP RC .10 .30
150 Larry Bird .40 1.00
151 Jon Koncak RC .02 .10
152 Olden Polynice RC .08 .25
153 Randy Breuer .02 .10
154 John Battle RC .02 .10
155 Mark Eaton .02 .10
156 Kevin McHale AS UER .02 .10
(No TM on Celtics logo on back)
157 Jerry Sichting SP .08 .25
158 Pat Cummings SP .08 .25
159 Patrick Ewing AS .02 .10
160 Mark Price .02 .10
161 Jerry Reynolds CO .02 .10
162 Ken Norman RC .08 .25
163 John Bagley SP UER .08 .25
(Picked in '83, should say '82)
164 Christian Welp SP .08 .25
165 Reggie Theus SP .10 .30
166 Magic Johnson AS .15 .40
167 John Long UER .02 .10
(Picked in '79, should say '78)
168 Larry Smith SP .08 .25
169 Charles Shackleford RC .02 .10
170 Tom Chambers .02 .10
171A John MacLeod CO SP .08 .25
ERR (NBA logo in wrong place)
171B John MacLeod CO .02 .10
COR (Second series)
172 Ron Rothstein CO .02 .10
173 Joe Wolf .02 .10
174 Mark Eaton AS .02 .10
175 Jon Sundvold .02 .10
176 Scott Hastings SP .08 .25
177 Isiah Thomas AS .02 .10
178 Hakeem Olajuwon AS .08 .25
179 Mike Fratello CO .02 .10
180 Hakeem Olajuwon .15 .40
181 Randolph Keys .02 .10
182 Richard Anderson UER .02 .10
(Trail Blazers on front should be all caps)
183 Dan Majerle RC .20 .50
184 Derek Harper .02 .10
185 Robert Parish .02 .10
186 Ricky Berry SP .08 .25
187 Michael Cooper .02 .10
188 Vinnie Johnson .02 .10
189 James Donaldson .02 .10
190 Clyde Drexler UER .08 .25
(4th pick, should be 14th)
191 Jay Vincent SP .08 .25
192 Nate McMillan .02 .10
193 Kevin Duckworth AS .02 .10
194 Ledell Eackles RC .02 .10
195 Eddie Johnson .02 .10
196 Terry Teagle .02 .10
197 Tom Chambers AS .02 .10
198 Joe Barry Carroll .02 .10
199 Dennis Hopson RC .02 .10
200 Michael Jordan 1.25 3.00
201 Jerome Lane RC .02 .10
202 Greg Kite RC .02 .10
203 David Rivers SP .08 .25
204 Sylvester Gray .02 .10
205 Ron Harper .02 .10
206 Frank Brickowski .02 .10
207 Rory Sparrow .02 .10
208 Gerald Henderson .02 .10
209 Rod Higgins UER .02 .10
('85-86 stats should also include San Antonio and Seattle)
210 James Worthy .08 .25
211 Dennis Rodman .40 1.00
212 Ricky Pierce .02 .10
213 Charles Oakley .02 .10
214 Steve Colter .02 .10
215 Danny Ainge .02 .10
216 Lenny Wilkens CO UER .02 .10
(No NBA logo on back in bottom right)
217 Larry Nance AS .02 .10
218 Muggsy Bogues .02 .10
219 James Worthy AS .02 .10
220 Lafayette Lever .02 .10
221 Quintin Dailey SP .08 .25
222 Lester Conner .02 .10
223 Jose Ortiz .02 .10
224 Micheal Williams SP UER RC .10 .30
(Misspelled Michael on card)
225 Wayman Tisdale .02 .10
226 Mike Sanders SP .08 .25
227 Jim Farmer SP .08 .25
228 Mark West .02 .10
229 Jeff Hornacek RC .10 .30
230 Chris Mullin AS .02 .10
231 Vern Fleming .02 .10
232 Kenny Smith .02 .10
233 Derrick McKey .02 .10
234 Dominique Wilkins AS .02 .10
235 Willie Anderson RC .02 .10
236 Keith Lee SP .08 .25
237 Buck Johnson RC .02 .10
238 Randy Wittman .02 .10
239 Terry Catledge SP .08 .25
240 Bernard King .02 .10
241 Darrell Griffith .02 .10
242 Horace Grant .02 .10
243 Rony Seikaly RC .10 .30
244 Scottie Pippen .60 1.50
245 Michael Cage UER .02 .10
(Picked in '85, should say '84)
246 Kurt Rambis .02 .10
247 Morlon Wiley SP RC .08 .25
248 Ronnie Grandison .02 .10
249 Scott Skiles SP RC .15 .40
250 Isiah Thomas .08 .25
251 Thurl Bailey .02 .10
252 Doc Rivers .02 .10
253 Stuart Gray SP .08 .25
254 John Williams .02 .10
255 Bill Cartwright .02 .10
256 Terry Cummings AS .02 .10
257 Rodney McCray .02 .10
258 Larry Krystkowiak RC .02 .10
259 Will Perdue RC .15 .40
260 Mitch Richmond RC .50 1.25
261 Blair Rasmussen .02 .10
262 Charles Smith RC .08 .25
263 Tyrone Corbin SP RC .08 .25
264 Kelvin Upshaw .02 .10
265 Otis Thorpe .02 .10
266 Phil Jackson CO .08 .25
267 Jerry Sloan CO .08 .25
268 John Shasky .02 .10
269A Bernie Bickerstaff CO SP .08 .25
ERR (Born 2/11/44)
269B Bernie Bickerstaff CO .02 .10
COR (Second series; Born 11/2/43)
270 Magic Johnson .30 .75
271 Vernon Maxwell RC .08 .25
272 Tim McCormick .02 .10
273 Don Nelson CO .02 .10
274 Gary Grant RC .02 .10
275 Sidney Moncrief SP .08 .25
276 Roy Hinson .02 .10
277 Jimmy Rodgers CO .02 .10
278 Antoine Carr .02 .10
279A Orlando Woolridge SP .08 .25
ERR (No Trademark)
279B Orlando Woolridge .02 .10
COR (Second series)
280 Kevin McHale .08 .25
281 LaSalle Thompson .02 .10
282 Detlef Schrempf .08 .25
283 Doug Moe CO .02 .10
284A James Edwards .02 .10
(Small black line next to card number)
284B James Edwards .02 .10
(No small black line)
285 Jerome Kersey .02 .10
286 Sam Perkins .02 .10
287 Sedale Threatt .02 .10
288 Tim Kempton SP .08 .25
289 Mark McNamara .02 .10
290 Moses Malone .08 .25
291 Rick Adelman CO UER .02 .10
(Chemekata misspelled as Chemketa)
292 Dick Versace CO .02 .10
293 Alton Lister SP .08 .25
294 Winston Garland .02 .10
295 Kiki Vandeweghe .02 .10
296 Brad Davis .02 .10
297 John Stockton AS .08 .25
298 Jay Humphries .02 .10
299 Dell Curry .02 .10
300 Mark Jackson .02 .10
301 Morlon Wiley .02 .10
302 Reggie Theus .02 .10
303 Otis Smith .02 .10
304 Tod Murphy RC .02 .10
305 Sidney Green .02 .10
306 Shelton Jones .02 .10
307 Mark Acres .02 .10
308 Terry Catledge .02 .10
309 Larry Smith .02 .10
310 David Robinson IA .75 2.00
311 Johnny Dawkins .02 .10
312 Terry Cummings .02 .10
313 Sidney Lowe .02 .10
314 Bill Musselman CO .02 .10
315 Buck Williams UER .02 .10
(Won ROY in '81, should say '82)
316 Mel Turpin .02 .10
317 Scott Hastings .02 .10
318 Scott Skiles .02 .10
319 Tyrone Corbin .02 .10
320 Maurice Cheeks .02 .10
321 Matt Guokas CO .02 .10
322 Jeff Turner .02 .10
323 David Wingate .02 .10
324 Steve Johnson .02 .10
325 Alton Lister .02 .10
326 Ken Bannister .02 .10
327 Bill Fitch CO UER .02 .10
(Copyright missing on bottom of back)
328 Sam Vincent .02 .10
329 Larry Drew .02 .10
330 Rick Mahorn .02 .10
331 Christian Welp .02 .10
332 Brad Lohaus .02 .10
333 Frank Johnson .02 .10
334 Jim Farmer .02 .10
335 Wayne Cooper .02 .10
336 Mike Brown RC .02 .10
337 Sam Bowie .02 .10
338 Kevin Gamble RC .02 .10
339 Jerry Ice Reynolds RC .02 .10
340 Mike Sanders .02 .10
341 Bill Jones UER .02 .10
(Center on front, should be F)
342 Greg Anderson .02 .10
343 Dave Corzine .02 .10
344 Micheal Williams UER .02 .10
(Misspelled Michael on card)
345 Jay Vincent .02 .10
346 David Rivers .02 .10
347 Caldwell Jones UER .02 .10
(He was not starting center on '83 Sixers)
348 Brad Sellers .02 .10
349 Scott Roth .02 .10
350 Alvin Robertson .02 .10
351 Steve Kerr RC .25 .60
352 Stuart Gray .02 .10
353A Pistons Champions SP 1.50 4.00
353B Pistons Champions UER .20 .50
(George Blaha misspelled Blahha)

1989-90 Hoops Checklists

Hoops made available two different checklists to collectors, primarily by phone request. The checklists are not actually cards but are more like folded four-panel booklets, although when folded they do measure 2 1/2" by 3 1/2". The production on these was rather limited.

COMPLETE SET (2) 1.60 4.00
COMMON CARD (1-2) .80 2.00

1990-91 Hoops

The complete 1990-91 Hoops basketball set contains 440 standard-size cards. The set was distributed in two series of 336 and 104 cards, respectively. The cards were issued in 15-card plastic-wrap packs which came 36 to a box. On the front the color action player photo appears in the shape of a basketball lane, bordered by gold on the All-Star cards (1-26) and by silver on the regular issues (27-331, 336). The player's name and the stripe below the picture are printed in one of the team's colors. The team logo at the lower right corner rounds out the card face. The back of the regular issue has a color head shot and biographical information as well as college and pro statistics, framed by a basketball lane. The set is arranged alphabetically according to teams. Subsets are Coaches (305-331/343-354), NBA Finals (337-342), Team Checklists (355-381), Inside Stuff (382-385), Stay in School (386-387), Don't Foul Out (388-389), Lottery Selections (390-400), and Updates (401-438). Some of the All-Star cards (card numbers 2, 6, and 8) can be found with or without a printing mistake, i.e., no T in the trademark logo on the card back. A few of the cards (card numbers 14, 66, 144, and 279) refer to the player as "all America" rather than "All America". The following cards can be found with or without a black line under the card number, height, and birthplace: 20, 23, 24, 29, and 87. Rookie Cards of note included in the set are Nick Anderson, Mookie Blaylock, Derrick Coleman, Vlade Divac, Sean Elliott, Kendall Gill, Tim Hardaway, Chris Jackson, Shawn Kemp, Gary Payton, Drazen Petrovic, Glen Rice, Clifford Robinson and Dennis Scott. The short prints (SP below) in the first series are those cards which were dropped to make room for the new second series cards on the printing sheet.

COMPLETE SET (440) 7.50 15.00
COMPLETE SERIES 1 (336) 5.00 10.00
COMPLETE SERIES 2 (104) 2.50 5.00
1 Charles Barkley AS SP .08 .25
2 Larry Bird AS SP .25 .60
3 Joe Dumars AS SP .05 .15
4 Patrick Ewing AS SP UER .08 .25
(A-S blocks listed as 1, should be 5)
5 Michael Jordan AS SP UER .75 2.00
(Won Slam Dunk in '87 and '88, not '86 and '88)
6 Kevin McHale AS SP .02 .10
7 Reggie Miller AS SP .05 .15
8 Robert Parish AS SP .02 .10
9 Scottie Pippen AS SP .25 .60
10 Dennis Rodman AS SP .15 .40
11 Isiah Thomas AS SP .05 .15
12 Dominique Wilkins AS SP .05 .15
13A All-Star Checklist SP .08 .25
ERR (No card number)
13B All-Star Checklist SP .02 .10
COR (Card number on back)
14 Rolando Blackman AS SP .02 .10
15 Tom Chambers AS SP .02 .10
16 Clyde Drexler AS SP .05 .15
17 A.C. Green AS SP .02 .10
18 Magic Johnson AS SP .20 .50
19 Kevin Johnson AS SP .05 .15
20 Lafayette Lever AS SP .02 .10
21 Karl Malone AS SP .08 .25
22 Chris Mullin AS SP .05 .15
23 Hakeem Olajuwon AS SP .08 .25
24 David Robinson AS SP .20 .50
25 John Stockton AS SP .07 .20
26 James Worthy AS SP .05 .15
27 John Battle .02 .10
28 Jon Koncak .02 .10
29 Cliff Levingston SP .02 .10
30 John Long SP .02 .10
31 Moses Malone .05 .15
32 Doc Rivers .05 .15
33 Kenny Smith SP .02 .10
34 Alexander Volkov .02 .10
35 Spud Webb .05 .15
36 Dominique Wilkins .05 .15
37 Kevin Willis .02 .10
38 John Bagley .02 .10
39 Larry Bird .25 .60
40 Kevin Gamble .02 .10
41 Dennis Johnson SP .02 .10
42 Joe Kleine .02 .10
43 Reggie Lewis .02 .10
44 Kevin McHale .05 .15
45 Robert Parish .05 .15
46 Jim Paxson SP .02 .10
47 Ed Pinckney .02 .10
48 Brian Shaw .05 .15
49 Richard Anderson SP .02 .10
50 Muggsy Bogues .05 .15
51 Rex Chapman .05 .15
52 Dell Curry .02 .10
53 Kenny Gattison RC .02 .10
54 Armon Gilliam .02 .10
55 Dave Hoppen .02 .10
56 Randolph Keys .02 .10
57 J.R. Reid RC .02 .10
58 Robert Reid SP .02 .10
59 Kelly Tripucka .02 .10
60 B.J. Armstrong RC .05 .15
61 Bill Cartwright .02 .10
62 Charles Davis SP .02 .10
63 Horace Grant .05 .15
64 Craig Hodges .02 .10
65 Michael Jordan .75 2.00
66 Stacey King RC .02 .10
67 John Paxson .02 .10
68 Will Perdue .02 .10
69 Scottie Pippen .25 .60
70 Winston Bennett .02 .10
71 Chucky Brown RC .02 .10
72 Derrick Chievous .02 .10
73 Brad Daugherty .02 .10
74 Craig Ehlo .02 .10
75 Steve Kerr .05 .15
76 Paul Mokeski SP .02 .10
77 John Morton .02 .10
78 Larry Nance .02 .10
79 Mark Price .02 .10
80 Hot Rod Williams .02 .10
81 Steve Alford .02 .10
82 Rolando Blackman .02 .10
83 Adrian Dantley SP .02 .10
84 Brad Davis .02 .10
85 James Donaldson .02 .10
86 Derek Harper .02 .10
87 Sam Perkins SP .02 .10
88 Roy Tarpley .02 .10
89 Bill Wennington SP .02 .10
90 Herb Williams .02 .10
91 Michael Adams .02 .10
92 Joe Barry Carroll SP .02 .10
93 Walter Davis UER .02 .10
(Born NC, not PA)
94 Alex English SP .02 .10
95 Bill Hanzlik .02 .10
96 Jerome Lane .02 .10
97 Lafayette Lever SP .02 .10
98 Todd Lichti RC .02 .10
99 Blair Rasmussen .02 .10
100 Danny Schayes SP .02 .10
101 Mark Aguirre .02 .10
102 William Bedford RC .02 .10
103 Joe Dumars .05 .15
104 James Edwards .02 .10
105 Scott Hastings .02 .10
106 Gerald Henderson SP .02 .10
107 Vinnie Johnson .02 .10
108 Bill Laimbeer .02 .10
109 Dennis Rodman .15 .40
110 John Salley .02 .10
111 Isiah Thomas UER .05 .15
(No position listed on the card)
112 Manute Bol SP .02 .10
113 Tim Hardaway RC .40 1.00
114 Rod Higgins .02 .10
115 Sarunas Marciulionis RC .02 .10
116 Chris Mullin UER .05 .15
(Born Brooklyn, NY not New York, NY)
117 Jim Petersen .02 .10
118 Mitch Richmond .07 .20
119 Mike Smrek .02 .10
120 Terry Teagle SP .02 .10
121 Tom Tolbert RC .02 .10
122 Christian Welp SP .02 .10
123 Byron Dinkins SP .02 .10
124 Eric (Sleepy) Floyd .02 .10
125 Buck Johnson .02 .10
126 Vernon Maxwell .02 .10
127 Hakeem Olajuwon .08 .25
128 Larry Smith .02 .10
129 Otis Thorpe .02 .10
130 Mitchell Wiggins SP .02 .10
131 Mike Woodson .02 .10
132 Greg Dreiling RC .02 .10
133 Vern Fleming .02 .10
134 Rickey Green SP .02 .10
135 Reggie Miller .07 .20
136 Chuck Person .02 .10
137 Mike Sanders .02 .10
138 Detlef Schrempf .02 .10
139 Rik Smits .05 .15
140 LaSalle Thompson .02 .10
141 Randy Wittman .02 .10
142 Benoit Benjamin .02 .10
143 Winston Garland .02 .10
144 Tom Garrick .02 .10
145 Gary Grant .02 .10
146 Ron Harper .02 .10
147 Danny Manning .02 .10
148 Jeff Martin .02 .10
149 Ken Norman .02 .10
150 David Rivers SP .02 .10
151 Charles Smith .02 .10
152 Joe Wolf SP .02 .10
153 Michael Cooper SP .02 .10
154 Vlade Divac UER RC .15 .40
(Height 6'11, should be 7'1)
155 Larry Drew .02 .10
156 A.C. Green .05 .15
157 Magic Johnson .20 .50
158 Mark McNamara SP .02 .10
159 Byron Scott .02 .10
160 Mychal Thompson .02 .10
161 Jay Vincent SP .02 .10
162 Orlando Woolridge SP .02 .10
163 James Worthy .05 .15
164 Sherman Douglas RC .05 .15
165 Kevin Edwards .02 .10
166 Tellis Frank SP .02 .10
167 Grant Long .02 .10
168 Glen Rice RC .25 .60
169A Rony Seikaly Athens .02 .10
169B Rony Seikaly Beirut .02 .10
170 Rory Sparrow SP .02 .10
171A Jon Sundvold .02 .10
(First series)
171B Billy Thompson .02 .10
(Second series)
172A Billy Thompson .02 .10
(First series)
172B Jon Sundvold .02 .10
(Second series)
173 Greg Anderson .02 .10
174 Jeff Grayer RC .02 .10
175 Jay Humphries .02 .10
176 Frank Kornet .02 .10
177 Larry Krystkowiak .02 .10
178 Brad Lohaus .02 .10
179 Ricky Pierce .02 .10
180 Paul Pressey SP .02 .10
181 Fred Roberts .02 .10
182 Alvin Robertson .02 .10
183 Jack Sikma .02 .10
184 Randy Breuer .02 .10
185 Tony Campbell .02 .10
186 Tyrone Corbin .02 .10
187 Sidney Lowe SP .02 .10
188 Sam Mitchell RC .02 .10
189 Tod Murphy .02 .10
190 Pooh Richardson RC .02 .10
191 Scott Roth SP .02 .10
192 Brad Sellers SP .02 .10
193 Mookie Blaylock RC .08 .25
194 Sam Bowie .02 .10
195 Lester Conner .02 .10
196 Derrick Gervin .02 .10
197 Jack Haley RC .02 .10
198 Roy Hinson .02 .10
199 Dennis Hopson SP .02 .10
200 Chris Morris .02 .10
201 Purvis Short SP .02 .10
202 Maurice Cheeks .02 .10
203 Patrick Ewing .05 .15
204 Stuart Gray .02 .10
205 Mark Jackson .02 .10
206 Johnny Newman SP .02 .10
207 Charles Oakley .02 .10
208 Trent Tucker .02 .10
209 Kiki Vandeweghe .02 .10
210 Kenny Walker .02 .10
211 Eddie Lee Wilkins .02 .10
212 Gerald Wilkins .02 .10
213 Mark Acres .02 .10
214 Nick Anderson RC .08 .25
215 Michael Ansley UER .02 .10
(Ranked first, not third)
216 Terry Catledge .02 .10
217 Dave Corzine SP .02 .10
218 Sidney Green SP .02 .10
219 Jerry Reynolds .02 .10
220 Scott Skiles .02 .10
221 Otis Smith .02 .10
222 Reggie Theus SP .02 .10
223A Sam Vincent 1.50 4.00
(Shows Michael Jordan)
223B Sam Vincent .02 .10
(Second series and shows Sam dribbling)
224 Ron Anderson .02 .10
225 Charles Barkley .08 .25
226 Scott Brooks SP UER .02 .10
(Born French Camp, not Lathron, Cal.)
227 Johnny Dawkins .02 .10
228 Mike Gminski .02 .10
229 Hersey Hawkins .02 .10
230 Rick Mahorn .02 .10
231 Derek Smith SP .02 .10
232 Bob Thornton .02 .10
233 Kenny Battle RC .02 .10
234A Tom Chambers .02 .10
(First series; Forward on front)
234B Tom Chambers .02 .10
(Second series; Guard on front)
235 Greg Grant SP RC .02 .10
236 Jeff Hornacek .02 .10
237 Eddie Johnson .02 .10
238A Kevin Johnson .05 .15
(First series; Guard on front)
238B Kevin Johnson .05 .15
(Second series; Forward on front)
239 Dan Majerle .05 .15
240 Tim Perry .02 .10
241 Kurt Rambis .02 .10
242 Mark West .02 .10
243 Mark Bryant .02 .10
244 Wayne Cooper .02 .10
245 Clyde Drexler .05 .15
246 Kevin Duckworth .02 .10
247 Jerome Kersey .02 .10
248 Drazen Petrovic RC .02 .10
249A Terry Porter ERR .20 .50
(No NBA symbol on back)
249B Terry Porter COR .02 .10
250 Clifford Robinson RC .08 .25
251 Buck Williams .02 .10
252 Danny Young .02 .10
253 Danny Ainge SP UER .02 .10
(Middle name Ray misspelled as Rae on back)
254 Randy Allen SP .02 .10
255 Antoine Carr .02 .10
256 Vinny Del Negro SP .02 .10
257 Pervis Ellison SP RC .02 .10
258 Greg Kite SP .02 .10
259 Rodney McCray SP .02 .10
260 Harold Pressley SP .02 .10
261 Ralph Sampson .02 .10
262 Wayman Tisdale .02 .10
263 Willie Anderson .02 .10
264 Uwe Blab SP .02 .10
265 Frank Brickowski SP .02 .10
266 Terry Cummings .02 .10
267 Sean Elliott RC .10 .30
268 Caldwell Jones SP .02 .10
269 Johnny Moore SP .02 .10
270 David Robinson .20 .50
271 Rod Strickland .05 .15
272 Reggie Williams .02 .10
273 David Wingate SP .02 .10
274 Dana Barros UER RC .05 .15
(Born April, not March)
275 Michael Cage UER .02 .10
(Drafted '84, not '85)
276 Quintin Dailey .02 .10
277 Dale Ellis .02 .10
278 Steve Johnson SP .02 .10
279 Shawn Kemp RC .60 1.50
280 Xavier McDaniel .02 .10
281 Derrick McKey .02 .10
282 Nate McMillan .02 .10
283 Olden Polynice .02 .10
284 Sedale Threatt .02 .10
285 Thurl Bailey .02 .10
286 Mike Brown .02 .10
287 Mark Eaton UER .02 .10
(72nd pick, not 82nd)
288 Blue Edwards RC .02 .10
289 Darrell Griffith .02 .10
290 Bobby Hansen SP .02 .10
291 Eric Leckner SP .02 .10
292 Karl Malone .08 .25
293 Delaney Rudd .02 .10
294 John Stockton .07 .20
295 Mark Alarie .02 .10
296 Ledell Eackles SP .02 .10
297 Harvey Grant .02 .10
298A Tom Hammonds RC .02 .10
(No rookie logo on front)
298B Tom Hammonds RC .02 .10
(Rookie logo on front)
299 Charles Jones .02 .10
300 Bernard King .02 .10
301 Jeff Malone SP .02 .10
302 Mel Turpin SP .02 .10
303 Darrell Walker .02 .10
304 John Williams .02 .10
305 Bob Weiss CO .02 .10
306 Chris Ford CO .02 .10
307 Gene Littles CO .02 .10
308 Phil Jackson CO .05 .15
309 Lenny Wilkens CO .02 .10
310 Richie Adubato CO .02 .10
311 Doug Moe CO SP .02 .10
312 Chuck Daly CO .02 .10
313 Don Nelson CO .02 .10
314 Don Chaney CO .02 .10
315 Dick Versace CO .02 .10
316 Mike Schuler CO .02 .10
317 Pat Riley CO SP .05 .15
318 Ron Rothstein CO .02 .10
319 Del Harris CO .02 .10
320 Bill Musselman CO .02 .10
321 Bill Fitch CO .02 .10
322 Stu Jackson CO .02 .10

323 Matt Guokas CO .02 .10
324 Jim Lynam CO .02 .10
325 Cotton Fitzsimmons CO .02 .10
326 Rick Adelman CO .02 .10
327 Dick Motta CO .02 .10
328 Larry Brown CO .02 .10
329 K.C. Jones CO .02 .10
330 Jerry Sloan CO .02 .10
331 Wes Unseld CO .02 .10
332 Checklist 1 SP .02 .10
333 Checklist 2 SP .02 .10
334 Checklist 3 SP .02 .10
335 Checklist 4 SP .02 .10
336 Danny Ferry SP RC .08 .25
337 Pistons Celebrate .05 .15
Dennis Rodman
338 Buck Williams FIN .05 .15
Dennis Rodman
339 Joe Dumars FIN .05 .15
340 Jerome Kersey FIN .02 .10
Isiah Thomas
341A Vinnie Johnson FIN ERR .02 .10
No headline on back
341B Vinnie Johnson COR .02 .10
342 Pistons Celebrate UER .02 .10
James Edwards Player named as Sidney Green is really David Greenwood
343 K.C. Jones CO .02 .10
344 Wes Unseld CO .02 .10
345 Don Nelson CO .02 .10
346 Bob Weiss CO .02 .10
347 Chris Ford CO .02 .10
348 Phil Jackson CO .05 .15
349 Lenny Wilkens CO .02 .10
350 Don Chaney CO .02 .10
351 Mike Dunleavy CO .02 .10
352 Matt Guokas CO .02 .10
353 Rick Adelman CO .02 .10
354 Jerry Sloan CO .02 .10
355 Dominique Wilkins TC .02 .10
356 Larry Bird TC .10 .30
357 Rex Chapman TC .02 .10
358 Michael Jordan TC .40 1.00
359 Mark Price TC .02 .10
360 Rolando Blackman TC .02 .10
361 Michael Adams TC UER .02 .10
(Westhead should be card 422, not 440)
362 Joe Dumars TC UER .02 .10
(Gerald Henderson's name and number not listed)
363 Chris Mullin TC .02 .10
364 Hakeem Olajuwon TC .05 .15
365 Reggie Miller TC .05 .15
366 Danny Manning TC .02 .10
367 Magic Johnson TC UER .08 .25
(Dunleavy listed as 439, should be 351)
368 Rony Seikaly TC .02 .10
369 Alvin Robertson TC .02 .10
370 Pooh Richardson TC .02 .10
371 Chris Morris TC .02 .10
372 Patrick Ewing TC .02 .10
373 Nick Anderson TC .05 .15
374 Charles Barkley TC .05 .15
375 Kevin Johnson TC .02 .10
376 Clyde Drexler TC .02 .10
377 Wayman Tisdale TC .02 .10
378 David Robinson TC .08 .25
(Basketball fully visible)
378B David Robinson TC .10 .30
(Basketball partially visible)
379 Xavier McDaniel TC .02 .10
380 Karl Malone TC .05 .15
381 Bernard King TC .02 .10
382 Michael Jordan .40 1.00
Playground
383 Karl Malone Lights .05 .15
384 European Imports .02 .10
(Vlade Divac
Sarunas Marciulionis)
385 Super Streaks .40 1.00
Stay In School
(Magic Johnson and Michael Jordan)
386 Johnny Newman .02 .10
(Stay in School)
387 Dell Curry .02 .10
(Stay in School)
388 Patrick Ewing .02 .10
(Don't Foul Out)
389 Isiah Thomas .02 .10
(Don't Foul Out)
390 Derrick Coleman LS RC .10 .30
391 Gary Payton LS RC .60 1.50
392 Chris Jackson LS RC .02 .10
393 Dennis Scott LS RC .07 .20
394 Kendall Gill LS RC .10 .30
395 Felton Spencer LS RC .02 .10
396 Lionel Simmons LS RC .02 .10
397 Bo Kimble LS RC .02 .10
398 Willie Burton LS RC .02 .10
399 Rumeal Robinson LS RC .02 .10
400 Tyrone Hill LS RC .02 .10
401 Tim McCormick U .02 .10
402 Sidney Moncrief U .02 .10
403 Johnny Newman U .02 .10
404 Dennis Hopson U .02 .10
405 Cliff Levingston U .02 .10
406A Danny Ferry U ERR .10 .30
(No position on front of card)
406B Danny Ferry U COR .05 .15
407 Alex English U .02 .10
408 Lafayette Lever U .02 .10
409 Rodney McCray U .02 .10
410 Mike Dunleavy U CO .02 .10
411 Orlando Woolridge U .02 .10
412 Joe Wolf U .02 .10
413 Tree Rollins U .02 .10
414 Kenny Smith U .02 .10
415 Sam Perkins U .02 .10
416 Terry Teagle U .02 .10
417 Frank Brickowski U .02 .10
418 Danny Schayes U .02 .10
419 Scott Brooks U .02 .10
420 Reggie Theus U .02 .10
421 Greg Grant U .02 .10
422 Paul Westhead U CO .02 .10
423 Greg Kite U .02 .10
424 Manute Bol U .02 .10
425 Rickey Green U .02 .10
426 Ed Nealy U .02 .10
427 Danny Ainge U .02 .10
428 Bobby Hansen U .02 .10
429 Eric Leckner U .02 .10
430 Rory Sparrow U .02 .10
431 Bill Wennington U .02 .10
432 Paul Pressey U .02 .10
433 David Greenwood U .02 .10
434 Mark McNamara U .02 .10
435 Sidney Green U .02 .10
436 Dave Corzine U .02 .10
437 Jeff Malone U .02 .10
438 Pervis Ellison U .02 .10
439 Checklist 5 .02 .10
440 Checklist 6 .02 .10
NNO David Robinson and .50 1.25
All-Rookie Team/(No stats on back)
NNO David Robinson and 2.50 6.00
All-Rookie Team/(Stats on back)

1991-92 Hoops Prototypes

This ten-card set measures the standard size. The fronts features color action player photos, with differing color borders in one of the team's colors. The player's name appears above the picture, and the team logo overlays the lower left corner of the picture. In a horizontal format the back has a head shot of the player, biographical information, and college and pro statistics. The words "Prototype" are written in block lettering across the back.

COMPLETE SET (10) 12.00 30.00
3 Sidney Moncrief 1.25 3.00
9 Larry Bird 6.00 15.00
18 Muggsy Bogues 1.50 4.00
120 Alvin Robertson 1.25 3.00
135 Chris Dudley 1.25 3.00
142 Charles Oakley 1.50 4.00
150 Jerry Reynolds 1.25 3.00
159 Armon Gilliam 1.25 3.00
204 Sedale Threatt 1.25 3.00
210 Jeff Malone 1.25 3.00

1991-92 Hoops Prototypes 00

This ten-card set measures the standard size (2 1/2" by 3 1/2"). The fronts features color action player photos, with differing color borders in one of the team's colors. The player's name appears above the picture, and the team logo overlays the lower left corner of the picture. In a horizontal format the back has a head shot of the player, biographical information, and college and pro statistics. The words "Prototype" are written in block lettering across the back. The cards are numbered on the back as 001, 002, etc.

COMPLETE SET (10) 60.00 150.00
1 Clyde Drexler 6.00 15.00
2 Patrick Ewing 6.00 15.00
3 Magic Johnson 8.00 20.00
4 Michael Jordan 20.00 50.00
4B Michael Jordan Metal 150.00 300.00
5 Karl Malone 10.00 25.00
6 Hakeem Olajuwon 6.00 15.00
7 Charles Barkley AS 6.00 15.00
8 Magic Johnson AS 8.00 20.00
9 Karl Malone AS 10.00 25.00
10 Dominique Wilkins AS 4.00 10.00

1991-92 Hoops

The complete 1991-92 Hoops basketball set contains 590 standard-size cards. The set was released in two series of 330 and 260 cards, respectively. For the first time, second series packs contained only second series cards. The fronts feature color action player photos, with different color borders on a white card face. The player's name is printed in black lettering in the upper left corner, and the team logo is superimposed over the lower left corner of the picture. In a horizontal format the backs have color head shots and biographical information on the left side, while the right side presents college and pro statistics. The cards are numbered on the back and checklisted below alphabetically within team order. Subsets are Coaches (221-247), All-Stars East (248-260), All-Stars West (261-273), Teams (274-300), Centennial Card honoring James Naismith (301), Inside Stuff (302-305), League Leaders (306-313), Milestones (314-318), NBA yearbook (319-324), Public Service messages (325-327/544/545), Supreme Court (449-502), Art Cards (503-529), Active Leaders (530-537), NBA Hoops Tribune (538-543), Draft Picks (546-556), USA Basketball 1976 (557), USA Basketball 1984 (558-564), USA Basketball 1988 (565-574) and USA Basketball 1992 (575-588). Rookie Cards of note include Kenny Anderson, Stacey Augmon, Terrell Brandon, Larry Johnson, Anthony Mason, Dikembe Mutombo, Steve Smith, and John Starks. A short-printed Naismith card, numbered CC1, was inserted into wax packs. It features a colorized photo of Dr. Naismith standing between two peach baskets like those used in the first basketball game. The back narrates the invention of the game of basketball. An unnumbered Centennial card featuring the Centennial logo was also available via a mail-in offer. Second series packs featured a randomly inserted Gold Foil USA Basketball logo card. A special individually numbered (out of 10,000) "Head of the Class" (showing the top six draft picks from 1991) card was made available to the first 10,000 fans requesting one along with three wrappers from each series of 1991-92 Hoops cards. The card is numbered "of 10,000" and features tiny pictures of the top six players selected in the 1991 NBA draft.

COMPLETE SET (590) 12.50 25.00
COMPLETE SERIES 1 (330) 5.00 10.00
COMPLETE SERIES 2 (260) 7.50 15.00
1 John Battle .02 .10
2 Moses Malone UER .08 .25
(119 rebounds 1982-83, should be 1194)
3 Sidney Moncrief .02 .10
4 Doc Rivers .02 .10
5 Rumeal Robinson UER .02 .10
(Back says 11th pick in 1990, should be 10th)
6 Spud Webb .02 .10
7 Dominique Wilkins .08 .25
8 Kevin Willis .02 .10
9 Larry Bird .40 1.00
10 Dee Brown .02 .10
11 Kevin Gamble .02 .10
12 Joe Kleine .02 .10
13 Reggie Lewis .02 .10
14 Kevin McHale .02 .10
15 Robert Parish .02 .10
16 Ed Pinckney .02 .10
17 Brian Shaw .02 .10
18 Muggsy Bogues .02 .10
19 Rex Chapman .02 .10
20 Dell Curry .02 .10
21 Kendall Gill .02 .10
22 Mike Gminski .02 .10
23 Johnny Newman .02 .10
24 J.R. Reid .02 .10
25 Kelly Tripucka .02 .10
26 B.J. Armstrong UER .02 .10
(B.J. on front, Benjamin Roy on back)
27 Bill Cartwright .02 .10
28 Horace Grant .02 .10
29 Craig Hodges .02 .10
30 Michael Jordan 1.25 3.00
31 Stacey King .02 .10
32 Cliff Levingston .02 .10
33 John Paxson .02 .10
34 Scottie Pippen .30 .75
35 Chucky Brown .02 .10
36 Brad Daugherty .02 .10
37 Craig Ehlo .02 .10
38 Danny Ferry .02 .10
39 Larry Nance .02 .10
40 Mark Price .02 .10
41 Darnell Valentine .02 .10
42 Hot Rod Williams .02 .10
43 Rolando Blackman .02 .10
44 Brad Davis .02 .10
45 James Donaldson .02 .10
46 Derek Harper .02 .10
47 Fat Lever .02 .10
48 Rodney McCray .02 .10
49 Roy Tarpley .02 .10
50 Herb Williams .02 .10
51 Michael Adams .02 .10
52 Chris Jackson UER .02 .10
(Born in Mississippi, not Michigan)
53 Jerome Lane .02 .10
54 Todd Lichti .02 .10
55 Blair Rasmussen .02 .10
56 Reggie Williams .02 .10
57 Joe Wolf .02 .10
58 Orlando Woolridge .02 .10
59 Mark Aguirre .02 .10
60 Joe Dumars .08 .25
61 James Edwards .02 .10
62 Vinnie Johnson .02 .10
63 Bill Laimbeer .02 .10
64 Dennis Rodman .20 .50
65 John Salley .02 .10
66 Isiah Thomas .08 .25
67 Tim Hardaway .15 .40
68 Rod Higgins .02 .10
69 Tyrone Hill .02 .10
70 Alton Lister .02 .10
71 Sarunas Marciulionis .02 .10
72 Chris Mullin .08 .25
73 Mitch Richmond .08 .25
74 Tom Tolbert .02 .10
75 Eric(Sleepy) Floyd .02 .10
76 Buck Johnson .02 .10
77 Vernon Maxwell .02 .10
78 Hakeem Olajuwon .15 .40
79 Kenny Smith .02 .10
80 Larry Smith .02 .10
81 Otis Thorpe .02 .10
82 David Wood RC .02 .10
83 Vern Fleming .02 .10
84 Reggie Miller .08 .25
85 Chuck Person .02 .10
86 Mike Sanders .02 .10
87 Detlef Schrempf .02 .10
88 Rik Smits .02 .10
89 LaSalle Thompson .02 .10
90 Micheal Williams .02 .10
91 Winston Garland .02 .10
92 Gary Grant .02 .10
93 Ron Harper .02 .10
94 Danny Manning .02 .10
95 Jeff Martin .02 .10
96 Ken Norman .02 .10
97 Olden Polynice .02 .10
98 Charles Smith .02 .10
99 Vlade Divac .02 .10
100 A.C. Green .02 .10
101 Magic Johnson .30 .75
102 Sam Perkins .02 .10
103 Byron Scott .02 .10
104 Terry Teagle .02 .10
105 Mychal Thompson .02 .10
106 James Worthy .08 .25
107 Willie Burton .02 .10
108 Bimbo Coles .02 .10
109 Terry Davis .02 .10
110 Sherman Douglas .02 .10
111 Kevin Edwards .02 .10
112 Alec Kessler .02 .10
113 Glen Rice .08 .25
114 Rony Seikaly .02 .10
115 Frank Brickowski .02 .10
116 Dale Ellis .02 .10
117 Jay Humphries .02 .10
118 Brad Lohaus .02 .10
119 Fred Roberts .02 .10
120 Alvin Robertson .02 .10
121 Danny Schayes .02 .10
122 Jack Sikma .02 .10
123 Randy Breuer .02 .10
124 Tony Campbell .02 .10
125 Tyrone Corbin .02 .10
126 Gerald Glass .02 .10
127 Sam Mitchell .02 .10
128 Tod Murphy .02 .10
129 Pooh Richardson .02 .10
130 Felton Spencer .02 .10
131 Mookie Blaylock .02 .10
132 Sam Bowie .02 .10
133 Jud Buechler .02 .10
134 Derrick Coleman .02 .10
135 Chris Dudley .02 .10
136 Chris Morris .02 .10
137 Drazen Petrovic .02 .10
138 Reggie Theus .02 .10
139 Maurice Cheeks .02 .10
140 Patrick Ewing .08 .25
141 Mark Jackson .02 .10
142 Charles Oakley .02 .10
143 Trent Tucker .02 .10
144 Kiki Vandeweghe .02 .10
145 Kenny Walker .02 .10
146 Gerald Wilkins .02 .10
147 Nick Anderson .02 .10
148 Michael Ansley .02 .10
149 Terry Catledge .02 .10
150 Jerry Reynolds .02 .10
151 Dennis Scott .02 .10
152 Scott Skiles .02 .10
153 Otis Smith .02 .10
154 Sam Vincent .02 .10
155 Ron Anderson .02 .10
156 Charles Barkley .15 .40
157 Manute Bol .02 .10
158 Johnny Dawkins .02 .10
159 Armon Gilliam .02 .10
160 Rickey Green .02 .10
161 Hersey Hawkins .02 .10
162 Rick Mahorn .02 .10
163 Tom Chambers .02 .10
164 Jeff Hornacek .02 .10
165 Kevin Johnson .08 .25
166 Andrew Lang .02 .10
167 Dan Majerle .02 .10
168 Xavier McDaniel .02 .10
169 Kurt Rambis .02 .10
170 Mark West .02 .10
171 Danny Ainge .02 .10
172 Mark Bryant .02 .10
173 Walter Davis .02 .10
174 Clyde Drexler .08 .25
175 Kevin Duckworth .02 .10
176 Jerome Kersey .02 .10
177 Terry Porter .02 .10
178 Clifford Robinson .02 .10
179 Buck Williams .02 .10
180 Anthony Bonner .02 .10
181 Antoine Carr .02 .10
182 Duane Causwell .02 .10
183 Bobby Hansen .02 .10
184 Travis Mays .02 .10
185 Lionel Simmons .02 .10
186 Rory Sparrow .02 .10
187 Wayman Tisdale .02 .10
188 Willie Anderson .02 .10
189 Terry Cummings .02 .10
190 Sean Elliott .02 .10
191 Sidney Green .02 .10
192 David Greenwood .02 .10
193 Paul Pressey .02 .10
194 David Robinson .20 .50
195 Dwayne Schintzius .02 .10
196 Rod Strickland .08 .25
197 Benoit Benjamin .02 .10
198 Michael Cage .02 .10
199 Eddie Johnson .02 .10
200 Shawn Kemp .25 .60
201 Derrick McKey .02 .10
202 Gary Payton .25 .60
203 Ricky Pierce .02 .10
204 Sedale Threatt .02 .10
205 Thurl Bailey .02 .10
206 Mike Brown .02 .10
207 Mark Eaton .02 .10
208 Blue Edwards UER .02 .10
(Forward/guard on front, guard on back)
209 Darrell Griffith .02 .10
210 Jeff Malone .02 .10
211 Karl Malone .15 .40
212 John Stockton .08 .25
213 Ledell Eackles .02 .10
214 Pervis Ellison .02 .10
215 A.J. English .02 .10
216 Harvey Grant .02 .10
(Shown boxing out twin brother Horace)
217 Charles Jones .02 .10
218 Bernard King .02 .10
219 Darrell Walker .02 .10
220 John Williams .02 .10
221 Bob Weiss CO .02 .10
222 Chris Ford CO .02 .10
223 Gene Littles CO .02 .10
224 Phil Jackson CO .08 .25
225 Lenny Wilkens CO .02 .10
226 Richie Adubato CO .02 .10
227 Paul Westhead CO .02 .10
228 Chuck Daly CO .02 .10
229 Don Nelson CO .02 .10
230 Don Chaney CO .02 .10
231 Bob Hill CO UER RC .02 .10
(Coached under Ted Owens, not Ted Owen)
232 Mike Schuler CO .02 .10
233 Mike Dunleavy CO .02 .10
234 Kevin Loughery CO .02 .10
235 Del Harris CO .02 .10
236 Jimmy Rodgers CO .02 .10
237 Bill Fitch CO .02 .10
238 Pat Riley CO .02 .10
239 Matt Guokas CO .02 .10
240 Jim Lynam CO .02 .10
241 Cotton Fitzsimmons CO .02 .10
242 Rick Adelman CO .02 .10
243 Dick Motta CO .02 .10
244 Larry Brown CO .02 .10
245 K.C. Jones CO .02 .10
246 Jerry Sloan CO .02 .10
247 Wes Unseld CO .02 .10
248 Charles Barkley AS .08 .25
249 Brad Daugherty AS .02 .10
250 Joe Dumars AS .02 .10
251 Patrick Ewing AS .02 .10
252 Hersey Hawkins AS .02 .10
253 Michael Jordan AS .60 1.50
254 Bernard King AS .02 .10
255 Kevin McHale AS .02 .10
256 Robert Parish AS .02 .10
257 Ricky Pierce AS .02 .10
258 Alvin Robertson AS .02 .10
259 Dominique Wilkins AS .02 .10
260 Chris Ford CO AS .02 .10
261 Tom Chambers AS .02 .10
262 Clyde Drexler AS .02 .10
263 Kevin Duckworth AS .02 .10
264 Tim Hardaway AS .08 .25
265 Kevin Johnson AS .02 .10
266 Magic Johnson AS .15 .40
267 Karl Malone AS .08 .25
268 Chris Mullin AS .02 .10
269 Terry Porter AS .02 .10
270 David Robinson AS .08 .25
271 John Stockton AS .02 .10
272 James Worthy AS .02 .10
273 Rick Adelman CO AS .02 .10
274 Atlanta Hawks TC UER .02 .10
(Actually began as Tri-Cities Blackhawks)
275 Boston Celtics TC UER .02 .10
(No NBA Hoops logo on card front)
276 Charlotte Hornets TC .02 .10
277 Chicago Bulls TC .02 .10
278 Cleveland Cavaliers TC .02 .10
279 Dallas Mavericks TC .02 .10
280 Denver Nuggets TC .02 .10
281 Detroit Pistons TC UER .02 .10
(Pistons not NBA Finalists until 1988
Ft. Wayne Pistons in Finals in 1955 and 1956)
282 Golden State Warriors TC .02 .10
283 Houston Rockets TC .02 .10
284 Indiana Pacers TC .02 .10
285 Los Angeles Clippers TC .02 .10
286 Los Angeles Lakers TC .02 .10
287 Miami Heat TC .02 .10
288 Milwaukee Bucks TC .02 .10
289 Minnesota Timberwolves TC .02 .10
290 New Jersey Nets TC .02 .10
291 New York Knicks TC UER .02 .10
(Golden State not mentioned as an active charter member of NBA)
292 Orlando Magic TC .02 .10
293 Philadelphia 76ers TC .02 .10
294 Phoenix Suns TC .02 .10
295 Portland Trail Blazers TC .02 .10
296 Sacramento Kings TC .02 .10
297 San Antonio Spurs TC .02 .10
298 Seattle Supersonics TC .02 .10
299 Utah Jazz TC .02 .10
300 Washington Bullets TC .02 .10
301 James Naismith .02 .10
Centennial Card
302 Kevin Johnson IS .02 .10
303 Reggie Miller IS .02 .10
304 Hakeem Olajuwon IS .08 .25
305 Robert Parish IS .02 .10
306 Scoring Leaders .40 1.00
Michael Jordan
Karl Malone
307 3-Point FG Percent .02 .10
League Leaders
Jim Les
Trent Tucker
308 Free Throw Percent .02 .10
League Leaders
Reggie Miller
Jeff Malone
309 Blocks League Leaders .08 .25
Hakeem Olajuwon
David Robinson
310 Steals League Leaders .02 .10
Alvin Robertson
John Stockton
311 Rebounds LL UER .20 .50
David Robinson
Dennis Rodman
(Robinson credited as playing for Houston)
312 Assists League Leaders .02 .10
John Stockton
Magic Johnson
313 Field Goal Percent .02 .10
League Leaders
Buck Williams
Robert Parish
314 Larry Bird UER .20 .50
Milestone
(Should be card 315 to fit Milestone sequence)
315 Alex English .02 .10
Moses Malone
Milestone UER
(Should be card 314 and be a League Leader card)
316 Magic Johnson MS .15 .40
317 Michael Jordan MS .60 1.50
318 Moses Malone MS .02 .10
319 Larry Bird YB .20 .50
320 Maurice Cheeks YB .02 .10
321 Magic Johnson YB .15 .40
322 Bernard King YB .02 .10
323 Moses Malone YB .02 .10
324 Robert Parish YB .02 .10
325 All-Star Jam .02 .10
Jammin' With Will Smith
(Stay in School)
326 All-Star Jam .02 .10
Jammin' With The Boys and Will Smith
(Stay in School)
327 David Robinson .08 .25
Leave Alcohol Out
328 Checklist 1 .02 .10
329 Checklist 2 UER .02 .10
(Card front is from 330)
330 Checklist 3 UER .02 .10
(Card front is from 329; card 327 listed operation, should be celebration)
331 Maurice Cheeks .02 .10
332 Duane Ferrell .02 .10
333 Jon Koncak .02 .10
334 Gary Leonard .02 .10
335 Travis Mays .02 .10
336 Blair Rasmussen .02 .10
337 Alexander Volkov .02 .10
338 John Bagley .02 .10
339 Rickey Green UER .02 .10
(Ricky on front)
340 Derek Smith .02 .10
341 Stojko Vrankovic .02 .10
342 Anthony Frederick RC .02 .10
343 Kenny Gattison .02 .10
344 Eric Leckner .02 .10
345 Will Perdue .02 .10
346 Scott Williams RC .02 .10
347 John Battle .02 .10
348 Winston Bennett .02 .10
349 Henry James .02 .10
350 Steve Kerr .02 .10
351 John Morton .02 .10
352 Terry Davis .02 .10
353 Randy White .02 .10
354 Greg Anderson .02 .10
355 Anthony Cook .02 .10
356 Walter Davis .02 .10
357 Winston Garland .02 .10
358 Scott Hastings .02 .10
359 Marcus Liberty .02 .10
360 William Bedford .02 .10
361 Lance Blanks .02 .10
362 Brad Sellers .02 .10
363 Darrell Walker .02 .10
364 Orlando Woolridge .02 .10
365 Vincent Askew RC .02 .10
366 Mario Elie RC .08 .25
367 Jim Petersen .02 .10
368 Matt Bullard RC .02 .10
369 Gerald Henderson .02 .10
370 Dave Jamerson .02 .10
371 Tree Rollins .02 .10
372 Greg Dreiling .02 .10
373 George McCloud .02 .10
374 Kenny Williams .02 .10
375 Randy Wittman .02 .10
376 Tony Brown .02 .10
377 Lanard Copeland .02 .10
378 James Edwards .02 .10
379 Bo Kimble .02 .10
380 Doc Rivers .02 .10
381 Loy Vaught .02 .10
382 Elden Campbell .08 .25
383 Jack Haley .02 .10
384 Tony Smith .02 .10
385 Sedale Threatt .02 .10
386 Keith Askins RC .02 .10
387 Grant Long .02 .10
388 Alan Ogg .02 .10
389 Jon Sundvold .02 .10
390 Lester Conner .02 .10
391 Jeff Grayer .02 .10
392 Steve Henson .02 .10
393 Larry Krystkowiak .02 .10
394 Moses Malone .08 .25
395 Scott Brooks .02 .10
396 Tellis Frank .02 .10
397 Doug West .02 .10
398 Rafael Addison RC .02 .10
399 Dave Feitl RC .02 .10
400 Tate George .02 .10
401 Terry Mills RC .08 .25
402 Tim McCormick .02 .10
403 Xavier McDaniel .02 .10
404 Anthony Mason RC .20 .50
405 Brian Quinnett .02 .10
406 John Starks RC .08 .25
407 Mark Acres .02 .10
408 Greg Kite .02 .10
409 Jeff Turner .02 .10
410 Morlon Wiley .02 .10
411 Dave Hoppen .02 .10
412 Brian Oliver .02 .10
413 Kenny Payne .02 .10
414 Charles Shackleford .02 .10
415 Mitchell Wiggins .02 .10
416 Jayson Williams .08 .25
417 Cedric Ceballos .02 .10
418 Negele Knight .02 .10
419 Andrew Lang .02 .10
420 Jerrod Mustaf .02 .10
421 Ed Nealy .02 .10
422 Tim Perry .02 .10
423 Alaa Abdelnaby .02 .10
424 Wayne Cooper .02 .10
425 Danny Young .02 .10
426 Dennis Hopson .02 .10
427 Les Jepsen .02 .10
428 Jim Les RC .02 .10
429 Mitch Richmond .08 .25
430 Dwayne Schintzius .02 .10
431 Spud Webb .02 .10
432 Jud Buechler .02 .10
433 Antoine Carr .02 .10
434 Tom Garrick .02 .10
435 Sean Higgins RC .02 .10
436 Avery Johnson .02 .10
437 Tony Massenburg .02 .10
438 Dana Barros .02 .10
439 Quintin Dailey .02 .10
440 Bart Kofoed RC .02 .10
441 Nate McMillan .02 .10
442 Delaney Rudd .02 .10
443 Michael Adams .02 .10
444 Mark Alarie .02 .10
445 Greg Foster .02 .10
446 Tom Hammonds .02 .10
447 Andre Turner .02 .10
448 David Wingate .02 .10
449 Dominique Wilkins SC .02 .10
450 Kevin Willis SC .02 .10
451 Larry Bird SC .20 .50
452 Robert Parish SC .02 .10
453 Rex Chapman SC .02 .10
454 Kendall Gill SC .02 .10
455 Michael Jordan SC .60 1.50
456 Scottie Pippen SC .15 .40
457 Brad Daugherty SC .02 .10
458 Larry Nance SC .02 .10
459 Rolando Blackman SC .02 .10
460 Derek Harper SC .02 .10
461 Chris Jackson SC .02 .10
462 Todd Lichti SC .02 .10
463 Joe Dumars SC .02 .10
464 Isiah Thomas SC .02 .10
465 Tim Hardaway SC .08 .25
466 Chris Mullin SC .02 .10
467 Hakeem Olajuwon SC .08 .25
468 Otis Thorpe SC .02 .10
469 Reggie Miller SC .02 .10
470 Detlef Schrempf SC .02 .10
471 Ron Harper SC .02 .10
472 Charles Smith SC .02 .10
473 Magic Johnson SC .15 .40
474 James Worthy SC .02 .10
475 Sherman Douglas SC .02 .10
476 Rony Seikaly SC .02 .10
477 Jay Humphries SC .02 .10
478 Alvin Robertson SC .02 .10
479 Tyrone Corbin SC .02 .10
480 Pooh Richardson SC .02 .10
481 Sam Bowie SC .02 .10
482 Derrick Coleman SC .02 .10
483 Patrick Ewing SC .02 .10
484 Charles Oakley SC .02 .10
485 Dennis Scott SC .02 .10
486 Scott Skiles SC .02 .10
487 Charles Barkley SC .08 .25
488 Hersey Hawkins SC .02 .10
489 Tom Chambers SC .02 .10
490 Kevin Johnson SC .02 .10
491 Clyde Drexler SC .02 .10
492 Terry Porter SC .02 .10
493 Lionel Simmons SC .02 .10
494 Wayman Tisdale SC .02 .10
495 Terry Cummings SC .02 .10
496 David Robinson SC .08 .25
497 Shawn Kemp SC .08 .25
498 Ricky Pierce SC .02 .10
499 Reggie Miller SC .02 .10
500 John Stockton SC .02 .10
501 Harvey Grant SC .02 .10
502 Bernard King SC .02
503 Travis Mays Art .02
504 Kevin McHale Art .02
505 Muggsy Bogues Art .02
506 Scottie Pippen Art .15
507 Brad Daugherty Art .02
508 Derek Harper Art .02
509 Chris Jackson Art .02
510 Isiah Thomas Art .02
511 Tim Hardaway Art .08
512 Otis Thorpe Art .02
513 Chuck Person Art .02
514 Ron Harper Art .02
515 James Worthy Art .02
516 Sherman Douglas Art .02
517 Dale Ellis Art .02
518 Tony Campbell Art .02
519 Derrick Coleman Art .02
520 Gerald Wilkins Art .02
521 Scott Skiles Art .02
522 Manute Bol Art .02
523 Tom Chambers Art .02
524 Terry Porter Art .02
525 Lionel Simmons Art .02
526 Sean Elliott Art .02
527 Shawn Kemp Art .08
528 John Stockton Art .02
529 Harvey Grant Art .02
530 Michael Adams AL .02
531 Charles Barkley AL .08
532 Larry Bird AL .20
533 Maurice Cheeks AL .02
534 Mark Eaton AL .02
535 Magic Johnson AL .15
536 Michael Jordan AL .60
537 Moses Malone AL .02
538 Sam Perkins FIN .02
539 Scottie Pippen FIN .08
James Worthy
540 Vlade Divac FIN .02
541 John Paxson FIN .02
542 Michael Jordan FIN .60
543 Michael Jordan FIN .60
544 Otis Smith SIS .02
545 Jeff Turner SIS .02
546 Larry Johnson RC .40
547 Kenny Anderson RC .20
548 Billy Owens RC .08
549 Dikembe Mutombo RC .40
550 Steve Smith RC .40
551 Doug Smith RC .02
552 Luc Longley RC .08
553 Mark Macon RC .02
554 Stacey Augmon RC .08
555 Brian Williams RC .08
556 Terrell Brandon RC .30
557 Walter Davis USA .02
558 Vern Fleming USA .02
559 Joe Kleine USA .02
560 Jon Koncak USA .02
561 Sam Perkins USA .02
562 Alvin Robertson USA .02
563 Wayman Tisdale USA .02
564 Jeff Turner USA .02
565 Willie Anderson USA .02
566 Stacey Augmon USA .08
567 Bimbo Coles USA .02
568 Jeff Grayer USA .02
569 Hersey Hawkins USA .02
570 Dan Majerle USA .02
571 Danny Manning USA .02
572 J.R. Reid USA .02
573 Mitch Richmond USA .20
574 Charles Smith USA .02
575 Charles Barkley USA .30
576 Larry Bird USA .75
577 Patrick Ewing USA .20
578 Magic Johnson USA .60
579 Michael Jordan USA 3.00
580 Karl Malone USA .30
581 Chris Mullin USA .08
582 Scottie Pippen USA .60
583 David Robinson USA .40
584 John Stockton USA .20
585 Chuck Daly CO USA .02
586 Lenny Wilkens CO USA .02
587 P.J.Carlesimo CO USA RC .02
588 Mike Krzyzewski CO USA RC .15
589 Checklist Card 1 .02
590 Checklist Card 2 .02
CC1 Naismith Special .40
XX Head of the Class 10.00
Kenny Anderson
Larry Johnson
Dikembe Mutombo
Billy Owens
Doug Smith
Steve Smith
NNO Centennial Card .20
(Sendaway)
NNO Team USA SP .40
Title Card

1991-92 Hoops All-Star MV

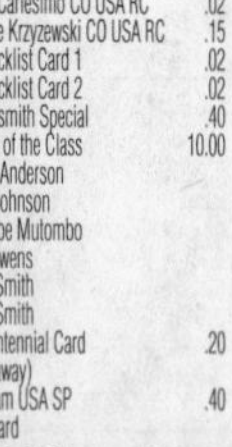

This six-card standard-size insert set commemo the most valuable player of the NBA All-Star gam from 1986 to 1991. Two cards were inserted in e second series rack pack. On a white card face, th features non-action color photos framed by eithe blue (7, 9, 12) or red (8, 10, 11) border. The top border is jagged and displays the player's name the year the award was received appears in a col box in the lower left corner. The backs have the s design and feature a color action photo from the Star game. The cards are numbered on the back Roman numerals.

COMPLETE SET (6) 10.00
7 Isiah Thomas .50
8 Tom Chambers .08
9 Michael Jordan 6.00
10 Karl Malone .75
11 Magic Johnson 1.50
12 Charles Barkley .75

1991-92 Hoops Slam Dunk

six-card standard size insert set of "Slam Dunk
npions" features the winners of the All-Star
end slam dunk competition from 1984 to 1991.
cards were issued two per first series 47-card rack
The front has a color photo of the player dunking
all, with royal blue borders on a white card face.
player's name appears in orange lettering in a
e stripe above the picture, and the year the player
is given in a "Slam Dunk Champion" emblem
aying the lower left corner of the picture. The
n of the back is similar to the front, only with an
ded caption on a yellow-green background. A
ng of a basketball entering a rim appears at the
left corner. The cards are numbered on the back
oman numerals.

PLETE SET (6) 7.50 15.00
ry Nance .20 .50
minique Wilkins .50 1.25
d Webb .20 .50
chael Jordan 8.00 20.00
ny Walker .08 .25
Brown .08 .25

1992-93 Hoops Prototypes

isting of four standard-size cards in a cello pack,
dvance-run card pack was issued to preview the
n of the forthcoming Hoops regular series issue.
ional packs could be obtained through a mail-in
for 1.00 for postage and handling, with a limit of
back per address while supplies lasted. Card
ber 1 carries an advertisement for 1992-93 Hoops
s I; card numbers 2-4 are identical to their regular
counterparts (card numbers 153, 309, and 229
ectively), except that these prototype cards are
mbered. After the advertisement card, the cards
sted below in alphabetical order by player's last
.

PLETE SET (4) .80 2.00
92-93 Series I .08 .25
vertisement)
rick Ewing .20 .50
gic Johnson .40 1.00
n Stockton .20 .50

1992-93 Hoops

complete 1992-93 Hoops basketball set contains
standard-size cards. The set was released in two
s of 350 and 140 cards, respectively. Both series
s contained 12 cards each with a suggested retail
of 79 cents each. Reported production quantities
20,000 20-box wax cases of the first series and
ximately 14,000 20-box wax cases of the second
s. The basic card fronts display color action player
s surrounded by white borders. A color stripe
ting one of the team's colors cuts across the
re and the player's name is printed vertically in a
parent stripe bordering the left side of the picture.
horizontally oriented backs carry a color head shot,
aphy, career highlights, and complete statistics
ege and pro). The cards are checklisted below
betically according to teams. Subsets include
hes (239-265), Team cards (266-292), NBA All-
East (293-305), NBA All-Stars West (306-319),
e Leaders (320-327), Magic Moments (328-
NBA Inside Stuff (332-333), NBA Stay in School
-335), Basketball Tournament of the Americas
-347) and Trivia (481-485). Rookie cards,
ered throughout the set, have a gold rather than a
ted white stripe. The team logo appears in the
left corner and intersects a team color-coded
that contains the player's position. The
ontal backs show a white background and include
stics (collegiate and pro), biographies, and career
maries. A close-up photo is at the upper left.
ie Cards of note include Tom Gugliotta, Robert
, Christian Laettner, Alonzo Mourning, Shaquille
al, Bobby Phills, Latrell Sprewell and Clarence
herspoon. A Magic Johnson "Commemorative
" and a Patrick Ewing "Ultimate Game" card were
omly inserted in first series foil packs. One-
sand of each were autographed. The odds of
ng an autographed card were one in 14,400 packs.
randomly inserted into second series foil packs
a Patrick Ewing Art card (reported odds were one
21 packs), a Chicago Bulls Championship card
rted odds were one per 32 packs) and a John
kton "Ultimate Game" card (reported odds were
per 92 packs). Stockton autographed 1,633 of
e cards (reported odds were one per 5,732 packs).
randomly inserted into first series packs was a
Basketball Team card. A Barcelona Plastic card
also randomly inserted in first series packs at a
f approximately one per 720 packs. This card is
d and listed with the 1992 Skybox USA set where
s originally available.

PLETE SET (490) 17.50 35.00
PLETE SERIES 1 (350) 7.50 15.00
PLETE SERIES 2 (140) 10.00 20.00
cey Augmon .02 .10
urice Cheeks .02 .10
ane Ferrell .02 .10
ul Graham .02 .10
Koncak .02 .10
ir Rasmussen .02 .10
meal Robinson .02 .10
minique Wilkins .08 .25
in Willis .02 .10
rry Bird .40 1.00
e Brown .02 .10
erman Douglas .02 .10
13 Rick Fox .02 .10
14 Kevin Gamble .02 .10
15 Reggie Lewis .02 .10
16 Kevin McHale .08 .25
17 Robert Parish .02 .10
18 Ed Pinckney UER .02 .10
(Wrong trade info,
Kleine to Sacramento
and Lohaus to Boston)
19 Muggsy Bogues .02 .10
20 Dell Curry .02 .10
21 Kenny Gattison .02 .10
22 Kendall Gill .02 .10
23 Mike Gminski .02 .10
24 Larry Johnson .10 .30
25 Johnny Newman .02 .10
26 J.R. Reid .02 .10
27 B.J. Armstrong .02 .10
28 Bill Cartwright .02 .10
29 Horace Grant .02 .10
30 Michael Jordan 1.25 3.00
31 Stacey King .02 .10
32 John Paxson .02 .10
33 Will Perdue .02 .10
34 Scottie Pippen .30 .75
35 Scott Williams .02 .10
36 John Battle .02 .10
37 Terrell Brandon .08 .25
38 Brad Daugherty .02 .10
39 Craig Ehlo .02 .10
40 Danny Ferry .02 .10
41 Henry James .02 .10
42 Larry Nance .02 .10
43 Mark Price .02 .10
44 Hot Rod Williams .02 .10
45 Rolando Blackman .02 .10
46 Terry Davis .02 .10
47 Derek Harper .02 .10
48 Mike Iuzzolino .02 .10
49 Fat Lever .02 .10
50 Rodney McCray .02 .10
51 Doug Smith .02 .10
52 Randy White .02 .10
53 Herb Williams .02 .10
54 Greg Anderson .02 .10
55 Winston Garland .02 .10
56 Chris Jackson .02 .10
57 Marcus Liberty .02 .10
58 Todd Lichti .02 .10
59 Mark Macon .02 .10
60 Dikembe Mutombo .10 .30
61 Reggie Williams .02 .10
62 Mark Aguirre .02 .10
63 William Bedford .02 .10
64 Joe Dumars .08 .25
65 Bill Laimbeer .02 .10
66 Dennis Rodman .20 .50
67 John Salley .02 .10
68 Isiah Thomas .08 .25
69 Darrell Walker .02 .10
70 Orlando Woolridge .02 .10
71 Victor Alexander .02 .10
72 Mario Elie .02 .10
73 Chris Gatling .02 .10
74 Tim Hardaway .10 .30
75 Tyrone Hill .02 .10
76 Alton Lister .02 .10
77 Sarunas Marciulionis .02 .10
78 Chris Mullin .08 .25
79 Billy Owens .02 .10
80 Matt Bullard .02 .10
81 Sleepy Floyd .02 .10
82 Avery Johnson .02 .10
83 Buck Johnson .02 .10
84 Vernon Maxwell .02 .10
85 Hakeem Olajuwon .15 .40
86 Kenny Smith .02 .10
87 Larry Smith .02 .10
88 Otis Thorpe .02 .10
89 Dale Davis .02 .10
90 Vern Fleming .02 .10
91 George McCloud .02 .10
92 Reggie Miller .08 .25
93 Chuck Person .02 .10
94 Detlef Schrempf .02 .10
95 Rik Smits .02 .10
96 LaSalle Thompson .02 .10
97 Micheal Williams .02 .10
98 James Edwards .02 .10
99 Gary Grant .02 .10
100 Ron Harper .02 .10
101 Danny Manning .02 .10
102 Ken Norman .02 .10
103 Olden Polynice .02 .10
104 Doc Rivers .02 .10
105 Charles Smith .02 .10
106 Loy Vaught .02 .10
107 Elden Campbell .02 .10
108 Vlade Divac .02 .10
109 A.C. Green .02 .10
110 Sam Perkins .02 .10
111 Byron Scott .02 .10
112 Tony Smith .02 .10
113 Terry Teagle .02 .10
114 Sedale Threatt .02 .10
115 James Worthy .08 .25
116 Willie Burton .02 .10
117 Bimbo Coles .02 .10
118 Kevin Edwards .02 .10
119 Alec Kessler .02 .10
120 Grant Long .02 .10
121 Glen Rice .08 .25
122 Rony Seikaly .02 .10
123 Brian Shaw .02 .10
124 Steve Smith .10 .30
125 Frank Brickowski .02 .10
126 Dale Ellis .02 .10
127 Jeff Grayer .02 .10
128 Jay Humphries .02 .10
129 Larry Krystkowiak .02 .10
130 Moses Malone .08 .25
131 Fred Roberts .02 .10
132 Alvin Robertson .02 .10
133 Danny Schayes .02 .10
134 Thurl Bailey .02 .10
135 Scott Brooks .02 .10
136 Tony Campbell .02 .10
137 Gerald Glass .02 .10
138 Luc Longley .02 .10
139 Sam Mitchell .02 .10
140 Pooh Richardson .02 .10
141 Felton Spencer .02 .10
142 Doug West .02 .10
143 Rafael Addison .02 .10
144 Kenny Anderson .08 .25
145 Mookie Blaylock .02 .10
146 Sam Bowie .02 .10
147 Derrick Coleman .02 .10
148 Chris Dudley .02 .10
149 Terry Mills .02 .10
150 Chris Morris .02 .10
151 Drazen Petrovic .02 .10
152 Greg Anthony .02 .10
153 Patrick Ewing .08 .25
154 Mark Jackson .02 .10
155 Anthony Mason .08 .25
156 Xavier McDaniel .02 .10
157 Charles Oakley .02 .10
158 John Starks .02 .10
159 Gerald Wilkins .02 .10
160 Nick Anderson .02 .10
161 Terry Catledge .02 .10
162 Jerry Reynolds .02 .10
163 Stanley Roberts .02 .10
164 Dennis Scott .02 .10
165 Scott Skiles .02 .10
166 Jeff Turner .02 .10
167 Sam Vincent .02 .10
168 Brian Williams .02 .10
169 Ron Anderson .02 .10
170 Charles Barkley .15 .40
171 Manute Bol .02 .10
172 Johnny Dawkins .02 .10
173 Armon Gilliam .02 .10
174 Hersey Hawkins .02 .10
175 Brian Oliver .02 .10
176 Charles Shackleford .02 .10
177 Jayson Williams .02 .10
178 Cedric Ceballos .02 .10
179 Tom Chambers .02 .10
180 Jeff Hornacek .02 .10
181 Kevin Johnson .08 .25
182 Negele Knight .02 .10
183 Andrew Lang .02 .10
184 Dan Majerle .02 .10
185 Tim Perry .02 .10
186 Mark West .02 .10
187 Alaa Abdelnaby .02 .10
188 Danny Ainge .02 .10
189 Clyde Drexler .08 .25
190 Kevin Duckworth .02 .10
191 Jerome Kersey .02 .10
192 Robert Pack .02 .10
193 Terry Porter .02 .10
194 Clifford Robinson .02 .10
195 Buck Williams .02 .10
196 Anthony Bonner .02 .10
197 Duane Causwell .02 .10
198 Pete Chilcutt .02 .10
199 Dennis Hopson .02 .10
200 Mitch Richmond .08 .25
201 Lionel Simmons .02 .10
202 Wayman Tisdale .02 .10
203 Spud Webb .02 .10
204 Willie Anderson .02 .10
205 Antoine Carr .02 .10
206 Terry Cummings .02 .10
207 Sean Elliott .02 .10
208 Sidney Green .02 .10
209 David Robinson .15 .40
210 Rod Strickland .08 .25
211 Greg Sutton .02 .10
212 Dana Barros .02 .10
213 Benoit Benjamin .02 .10
214 Michael Cage .02 .10
215 Eddie Johnson .02 .10
216 Shawn Kemp .20 .50
217 Derrick McKey .02 .10
218 Nate McMillan .02 .10
219 Gary Payton .20 .50
220 Ricky Pierce .02 .10
221 David Benoit .02 .10
222 Mike Brown .02 .10
223 Tyrone Corbin .02 .10
224 Mark Eaton .02 .10
225 Blue Edwards .02 .10
226 Jeff Malone .02 .10
227 Karl Malone .15 .40
228 Eric Murdock .02 .10
229 John Stockton .08 .25
230 Michael Adams .02 .10
231 Rex Chapman .02 .10
232 Ledell Eackles .02 .10
233 Pervis Ellison .02 .10
234 A.J. English .02 .10
235 Harvey Grant .02 .10
236 Charles Jones .02 .10
237 LaBradford Smith .02 .10
238 Larry Stewart .02 .10
239 Bob Weiss CO .02 .10
240 Chris Ford CO .02 .10
241 Allan Bristow CO .02 .10
242 Phil Jackson CO .02 .10
243 Lenny Wilkens CO .02 .10
244 Richie Adubato CO .02 .10
245 Dan Issel CO .02 .10
246 Ron Rothstein CO .02 .10
247 Don Nelson CO .02 .10
248 Rudy Tomjanovich CO .02 .10
249 Bob Hill CO .02 .10
250 Larry Brown CO .02 .10
251 Randy Pfund CO RC .02 .10
252 Kevin Loughery CO .02 .10
253 Mike Dunleavy CO .02 .10
254 Jimmy Rodgers CO .02 .10
255 Chuck Daly CO .02 .10
256 Pat Riley CO .02 .10
257 Matt Guokas CO .02 .10
258 Doug Moe CO .02 .10
259 Paul Westphal CO .02 .10
260 Rick Adelman CO .02 .10
261 Garry St. Jean CO RC .02 .10
262 Jerry Tarkanian CO RC .02 .10
263 George Karl CO .02 .10
264 Jerry Sloan CO .02 .10
265 Wes Unseld CO .02 .10
266 Atlanta Hawks TC .02 .10
267 Boston Celtics TC .02 .10
268 Charlotte Hornets TC .02 .10
269 Chicago Bulls TC .02 .10
270 Cleveland Cavaliers TC .02 .10
271 Dallas Mavericks TC .02 .10
272 Denver Nuggets TC .02 .10
273 Detroit Pistons TC .02 .10
274 Golden State Warriors TC .02 .10
275 Houston Rockets TC .02 .10
276 Indiana Pacers TC .02 .10
277 Los Angeles Clippers TC .02 .10
278 Los Angeles Lakers TC .02 .10
279 Miami Heat TC .02 .10
280 Milwaukee Bucks TC .02 .10
281 Minnesota Timberwolves TC .02 .10
282 New Jersey Nets TC .02 .10
283 New York Knicks TC .02 .10
284 Orlando Magic TC .02 .10
285 Philadelphia 76ers TC .02 .10
286 Phoenix Suns TC .02 .10
287 Portland Trail Blazers TC .02 .10
288 Sacramento Kings TC .02 .10
289 San Antonio Spurs TC .02 .10
290 Seattle Supersonics TC .02 .10
291 Utah Jazz TC .02 .10
292 Washington Bullets TC .02 .10
293 Michael Adams AS .02 .10
294 Charles Barkley AS .08 .25
295 Brad Daugherty AS .02 .10
296 Joe Dumars AS .02 .10
297 Patrick Ewing AS .02 .10
298 Michael Jordan AS .60 1.50
299 Reggie Lewis AS .02 .10
300 Scottie Pippen AS .15 .40
301 Mark Price AS .02 .10
302 Dennis Rodman AS .08 .25
303 Isiah Thomas AS .02 .10
304 Kevin Willis AS .02 .10
305 Phil Jackson CO AS .02 .10
306 Clyde Drexler AS .02 .10
307 Tim Hardaway AS .08 .25
308 Jeff Hornacek AS .02 .10
309 Magic Johnson AS .15 .40
310 Dan Majerle AS .02 .10
311 Karl Malone AS .08 .25
312 Chris Mullin AS .02 .10
313 Dikembe Mutombo AS .08 .25
314 Hakeem Olajuwon AS .08 .25
315 David Robinson AS .08 .25
316 John Stockton AS .02 .10
317 Otis Thorpe AS .02 .10
318 James Worthy AS .02 .10
319 Don Nelson CO AS .02 .10
320 Scoring League Leaders .40 1.00
Michael Jordan
Karl Malone
321 Three-Point Field .02 .10
Goal Percent
League Leaders
Dana Barros
Drazen Petrovic
322 Free Throw Percent .10 .30
League Leaders
Mark Price
Larry Bird
323 Blocks League Leaders .08 .25
David Robinson
Hakeem Olajuwon
324 Steals League Leaders .08 .25
John Stockton
Micheal Williams
325 Rebounds League .08 .25
Leaders
Dennis Rodman
Kevin Willis
326 Assists League Leaders .08 .25
John Stockton
Kevin Johnson
327 Field Goal Percent .02 .10
League Leaders
Buck Williams
Otis Thorpe
328 Magic Moments 1980 .08 .25
329 Magic Moments 1985 .08 .25
330 Magic Moments 87 and 88 .08 .25
331 Magic Numbers .08 .25
332 Drazen Petrovic IS .02 .10
333 Patrick Ewing IS .02 .10
334 David Robinson STAY .08 .25
335 Kevin Johnson STAY .02 .10
336 Charles Barkley USA .08 .25
337 Larry Bird USA .20 .50
338 Clyde Drexler USA .02 .10
339 Patrick Ewing USA .02 .10
340 Magic Johnson USA .15 .40
341 Michael Jordan USA .60 1.50
342 Christian Laettner USA RC .20 .50
343 Karl Malone USA .08 .25
344 Chris Mullin USA .02 .10
345 Scottie Pippen USA .15 .40
346 David Robinson USA .08 .25
347 John Stockton USA .02 .10
348 Checklist 1 .02 .10
349 Checklist 2 .02 .10
350 Checklist 3 .02 .10
351 Mookie Blaylock .07 .20
352 Adam Keefe RC .02 .10
353 Travis Mays .02 .10
354 Morlon Wiley .02 .10
355 Joe Kleine .02 .10
356 Bart Kofoed .02 .10
357 Xavier McDaniel .02 .10
358 Tony Bennett RC .02 .10
359 Tom Hammonds .02 .10
360 Kevin Lynch .02 .10
361 Alonzo Mourning RC 1.00 2.50
362 Rodney McCray .02 .10
363 Trent Tucker .02 .10
364 Corey Williams RC .02 .10
365 Steve Kerr .07 .20
366 Jerome Lane .02 .10
367 Bobby Phills RC .15 .40
368 Mike Sanders .02 .10
369 Gerald Wilkins .02 .10
370 Donald Hodge .02 .10
371 Brian Howard RC .02 .10
372 Tracy Moore RC .02 .10
373 Sean Rooks RC .02 .10
374 Kevin Brooks .02 .10
375 LaPhonso Ellis RC .15 .40
376 Scott Hastings .02 .10
377 Robert Pack .02 .10
378 Bryant Stith RC .07 .20
379 Robert Werdann RC .02 .10
380 Lance Blanks .02 .10
381 Terry Mills .02 .10
382 Isaiah Morris RC .02 .10
383 Olden Polynice .02 .10
384 Brad Sellers .02 .10
385 Jud Buechler .02 .10
386 Jeff Grayer .02 .10
387 Byron Houston RC .02 .10
388 Keith Jennings RC .02 .10
389 Latrell Sprewell RC 1.25 3.00
390 Scott Brooks .02 .10
391 Carl Herrera .02 .10
392 Robert Horry RC .15 .40
393 Tree Rollins .02 .10
394 Kennard Winchester .02 .10
395 Greg Dreiling .02 .10
396 Sean Green .02 .10
397 Sam Mitchell .02 .10
398 Pooh Richardson .02 .10
399 Malik Sealy RC .07 .20
400 Kenny Williams .02 .10
401 Jaren Jackson RC .07 .20
402 Mark Jackson .07 .20
403 Stanley Roberts .02 .10
404 Elmore Spencer RC .02 .10
405 Kiki Vandeweghe .02 .10
406 John Williams .02 .10
407 Randy Woods RC .02 .10
408 Alex Blackwell RC .02 .10
409 Duane Cooper RC .02 .10
410 Anthony Peeler RC .07 .20
411 Keith Askins .02 .10
412 Matt Geiger RC .07 .20
413 Harold Miner RC .07 .20
414 John Salley .02 .10
415 Alaa Abdelnaby .02 .10
416 Todd Day RC .07 .20
417 Blue Edwards .02 .10
418 Brad Lohaus .02 .10
419 Lee Mayberry RC .02 .10
420 Eric Murdock .02 .10
421 Christian Laettner .30 .75
422 Bob McCann RC .02 .10
423 Chuck Person .02 .10
424 Chris Smith RC .02 .10
425 Gundars Vetra RC .02 .10
426 Micheal Williams .02 .10
427 Chucky Brown .02 .10
428 Tate George .02 .10
429 Rick Mahorn .02 .10
430 Rumeal Robinson .02 .10
431 Jayson Williams .07 .20
432 Eric Anderson RC .02 .10
433 Rolando Blackman .02 .10
434 Tony Campbell .02 .10
435 Hubert Davis RC .07 .20
436 Bo Kimble .02 .10
437 Doc Rivers .07 .20
438 Charles Smith .02 .10
439 Anthony Bowie .02 .10
440 Litterial Green RC .02 .10
441 Greg Kite .02 .10
442 Shaquille O'Neal RC 4.00 10.00
443 Donald Royal .02 .10
444 Greg Grant .02 .10
445 Jeff Hornacek .07 .20
446 Andrew Lang .02 .10
447 Kenny Payne .02 .10
448 Tim Perry .02 .10
449 C.Weatherspoon RC .15 .40
450 Danny Ainge .07 .20
451 Charles Barkley .25 .60
452 Tim Kempton .02 .10
453 Oliver Miller RC .07 .20
454 Mark Bryant .02 .10
455 Mario Elie .07 .20
456 Dave Jamerson RC .02 .10
457 Tracy Murray RC .07 .20
458 Rod Strickland .15 .40
459 Vincent Askew .02 .10
460 Randy Brown .02 .10
461 Marty Conlon .02 .10
462 Jim Les .02 .10
463 Walt Williams RC .15 .40
464 William Bedford .02 .10
465 Lloyd Daniels RC .02 .10
466 Vinny Del Negro .02 .10
467 Dale Ellis .02 .10
468 Larry Smith .02 .10
469 David Wood .02 .10
470 Rich King .02 .10
471 Isaac Austin RC .07 .20
472 John Crotty RC .02 .10
473 Stephen Howard RC .02 .10
474 Jay Humphries .02 .10
475 Larry Krystkowiak .02 .10
476 Tom Gugliotta RC .50 1.25
477 Buck Johnson .02 .10
478 Don MacLean RC .02 .10
479 Doug Overton .02 .10
480 Brent Price RC .07 .20
481 David Robinson TRV .15 .40
482 Magic Johnson TRV .25 .60
483 John Stockton TRV .07 .20
484 Patrick Ewing TRV .07 .20
485 Answer Card TRIV .15 .40
Magic Johnson
David Robinson
Patrick Ewing
John Stockton
486 John Stockton STAY .07 .20
487 Ahmad Rashad .07 .20
Willow Bay
Inside Stuff
488 Rookie Checklist .02 .10
489 Checklist 1 .02 .10
490 Checklist 2 .02 .10
AC1 Patrick Ewing Art .20 .50
SU1 John Stockton Game AU 100.00 200.00
SU1 John Stockton Game .60 1.50
His Ultimate Game
TR1 NBA Championship 1.25 3.00
Michael Jordan
Clyde Drexler
NNO Magic Johnson Comm .40 1.00
NNO Magic Johnson Comm AU 75.00 150.00
NNO Patrick Ewing Game .20 .50
His Ultimate Game
NNO Patrick Ewing Game AU 80.00 160.00

1992-93 Hoops Draft Redemption

A "Lottery Exchange Card" randomly inserted (reportedly at a rate of one per 360 packs) in 1992-93 Hoops first series 12-card foil packs entitled the collector to receive this NBA Draft Redemption Lottery Exchange set. It consists of ten standard size cards of the top 1992 NBA Draft Picks. The first eleven players drafted are represented, with the exception of Jim Jackson, the late-signing fourth pick. Insert sets began to be mailed out during the week of January 4, 1993, and the redemption period expired on March 31, 1993. According to SkyBox International media releases a total of 25,876 sets were released to the public; 24,461 Lottery Exchange cards were redeemed. An additional 415 sets were claimed through a second chance drawing (selected from 149,166 mail-in entries). Finally, 1,000 more sets were released for public relations and promotional use. A reserve of 1,000 sets were held for replacement of damaged sets and 500 sets were kept for SkyBox International archives. In the color photos on the fronts, the players appear in dress attire in front of a gray studio background, except for cards C and J. The player's name is printed in white in a hardwood floor border design at the bottom of the card. A NBA Draft icon overlaps the border and the photo. A one inch tall hardwood design number at the upper left corner indicates the order the players were drafted. The horizontal backs display white backgrounds with a similar hardwood stripe containing the player's name across the top. A shadowed close-up photo is displayed next to college statistics and a player profile. The cards are lettered on the back. Sets still in the factory-sealed bags are valued at a premium of up to 20 percent above the complete set price below.

COMPLETE SET (10) 25.00 60.00
A Shaquille O'Neal 15.00 40.00
B Alonzo Mourning 4.00 10.00
C Christian Laettner 1.50 4.00
D LaPhonso Ellis 1.25 3.00
E Tom Gugliotta 2.50 6.00
F Walt Williams .75 2.00
G Todd Day .75 2.00
H Clarence Weatherspoon .75 2.00
I Adam Keefe .75 2.00
J Robert Horry 1.25 3.00
NNO Draft Redemption Card .40 1.00
(Stamped)
NNO Draft Redemption Card 1.25 3.00
(Unstamped)

1992-93 Hoops Magic's All-Rookies

This 10-card standard size set was randomly inserted into Hoops second series 12-card foil packs. They were inserted at a rate of one in 30 packs. The set features Magic Johnson's selections of the top rookies from the 1992-93 season. The cards show color action player photos and have a gold foil stripe containing the player's name down the left edge and a thinner stripe across the bottom printed with the city's name. The Magic's All-Rookie Team logo appears in the lower left corner. The backs display a small close-up picture of Magic Johnson in a yellow Los Angeles Lakers' warm-up jacket. A yellow stripe down the left edge contains the set name (Magic's All-Rookie Team) and the card number. The white background is printed in black with Magic's evaluation of the player.

COMPLETE SET (10) 40.00 70.00
1 Shaquille O'Neal 15.00 40.00
2 Alonzo Mourning 6.00 15.00
3 Christian Laettner 2.00 5.00
4 LaPhonso Ellis 1.25 3.00
5 Tom Gugliotta 1.50 4.00
6 Walt Williams 1.25 3.00
7 Todd Day 1.25 3.00
8 Clarence Weatherspoon 1.25 3.00
9 Robert Horry 2.00 5.00
10 Harold Miner 1.25 3.00

1992-93 Hoops More Magic Moments

Randomly inserted (at a reported rate of one card per 195 packs) into 1992-93 Hoops second series 12-card packs, this three-card standard-size set commemorates Magic Johnson's return to training camp and pre-season game action. Each card features a color player photo bordered in white. Team color-coded bars and lettering accent the picture on the left edge and below, and a team color-coded star overwritten with the words "More Magic" appears at the lower left corner. Over ghosted photos similar or identical to the front photos, the backs summarize Magic's return, his performance in his first game, his performance in his last game, and his decision to retire again. The cards are numbered on the back with an "M" prefix.

COMPLETE SET (3) 45.00 70.00
COMMON MAGIC (M1-M3) 15.00 25.00

1992-93 Hoops Supreme Court

This 10-card, standard-size set was randomly inserted (at a reported rate of one card per 11 packs) in Hoops second series 12-card foil packs and features color action player photos on the front. A gold foil stripe frames the pictures which are surrounded by a hardwood floor design. The player's name is printed in gold foil down the left side. A gray and burnt-orange logo printed with the words "Supreme Court 1992-93" appears in the lower left corner. A purple stripe containing the phrase "The Fan's Choice" runs across the bottom of the picture. Hoops promoted The Supreme Court Sweepstakes, which offered fans the opportunity to select the ten players who appeared in this subset. The backs are white with black print. A small color player photo with rounded corners is displayed next to a personal profile. The cards are numbered on the back with an "SC" prefix.

COMPLETE SET (10) 15.00 30.00
SC1 Michael Jordan 6.00 15.00
SC2 Scottie Pippen 2.00 5.00
SC3 David Robinson 1.00 2.50
SC4 Patrick Ewing .60 1.50
SC5 Clyde Drexler .60 1.50
SC6 Karl Malone 1.00 2.50
SC7 Charles Barkley 1.00 2.50
SC8 John Stockton .60 1.50
SC9 Chris Mullin .60 1.50
SC10 Magic Johnson 1.00 2.50

1993-94 Hoops Promo Panel

Hoops issued this nine-card sheet to promote the 1993-94 Hoops regular issue. The standard-size cards were issued on a perforated sheet. The fronts feature full-bleed glossy color player photos. Each player's name and team logo appear in team-colors along a ghosted band at the bottom. The back presents a color head shot of the player with a team-color shadow box border at the top right corner. The player's name and a short biography are printed on a hardwood floor design at the top. Below, the player's college and NBA statistics, displayed in separate tables on a white background, round out the card. The individual cards on the sheet are unnumbered and checklisted below in alphabetical order.

NNO Hoops panel 2.00 5.00
Joe Dumars
Patrick Ewing
Tim Hardaway
Dan Majerle
Jeff Malone
Xavier McDaniel
Reggie Miller
David Robinson

1993-94 Hoops Prototypes

Distributed beginning in July 1993 to promote the September 1993 release of its 300-card first series, these standard-size (2 1/2" by 3 1/2") promo cards feature full-bleed glossy color player photos on the fronts. Each player's name and team logo appear in team colors along a ghosted band at the bottom. The back presents a color head shot of the player in a small rectangle bordered with a team color in the top right corner; alongside is his jersey number and position within a team-colored bar. The player's name and a short biography are printed on a hardwood floor design at the top. Below, the player's college and NBA stats, displayed in separate tables on a white background, round out the card. The cards are unnumbered and checklisted below in alphabetical order.

COMPLETE SET (7) 1.20 3.00
1 Jim Jackson .15 .40
2 Larry Johnson .15 .40
3 Karl Malone .50 1.25
4 Harold Miner .02 .10
5 Dikembe Mutombo .15 .40
6 Shaquille O'Neal .75 2.00
7 Cover Card .02 .10

1993-94 Hoops

This 421-card standard-size set was issued in separate series of 300 and 121 cards. Cards were distributed in 13-card foil (12 basic cards plus one gold card) and 26-card jumbo (24 basic and two gold cards) packs. Cards feature full-bleed glossy color player photos on the fronts. Each player's name and team logo appear in team colors along a ghosted band at the bottom. The back presents a color head shot of the player in a small rectangle bordered with a team color in the top right corner. Alongside is his jersey number and position within a team-colored bar. The player's name and a short biography are printed on a hardwood floor design at the top. Below, the player's college and NBA stats, displayed in separate tables on a white background, round out the card. The cards are numbered on the back and listed alphabetically within team order. Subsets are Coaches (230-256), All-Stars (257-282), League Leaders (283-290), Boys and Girls Club (291), Hoops Tribune (292-297), and Checklists (298-300/419-420). Rookie Cards of note include Vin Baker, Anfernee Hardaway, Jamal Mashburn, Nick Van Exel and Chris Webber.

COMPLETE SET (421) 10.00 20.00
COMPLETE SERIES 1 (300) 6.00 12.00
COMPLETE SERIES 2 (121) 4.00 8.00
BEWARE COUNTERFEIT BIRD/MAGIC AU
1 Stacey Augmon .01 .05
2 Mookie Blaylock .02 .10
3 Duane Ferrell .01 .05
4 Paul Graham .01 .05
5 Adam Keefe .01 .05
6 Blair Rasmussen .01 .05
7 Dominique Wilkins .08 .25
8 Kevin Willis .01 .05
9 Alaa Abdelnaby .01 .05
10 Dee Brown .01 .05
11 Sherman Douglas .01 .05
12 Rick Fox .01 .05
13 Kevin Gamble .01 .05
14 Joe Kleine .01 .05
15 Xavier McDaniel .01 .05
16 Robert Parish .02 .10
17 Tony Bennett .01 .05
18 Muggsy Bogues .02 .10
19 Dell Curry .01 .05
20 Kenny Gattison .01 .05
21 Kendall Gill .02 .10

22 Larry Johnson .08 .25
23 Alonzo Mourning .15 .40
24 Johnny Newman .01 .05
25 B.J. Armstrong .01 .05
26 Bill Cartwright .01 .05
27 Horace Grant .02 .10
28 Michael Jordan 1.25 3.00
29 Stacey King .01 .05
30 John Paxson .01 .05
31 Will Perdue .01 .05
32 Scottie Pippen .30 .75
33 Scott Williams .01 .05
34 Moses Malone .08 .25
35 John Battle .01 .05
36 Terrell Brandon .02 .10
37 Brad Daugherty .01 .05
38 Craig Ehlo .01 .05
39 Danny Ferry .01 .05
40 Larry Nance .01 .05
41 Mark Price .01 .05
42 Gerald Wilkins .01 .05
43 John Williams .01 .05
44 Terry Davis .01 .05
45 Derek Harper .02 .10
46 Donald Hodge .01 .05
47 Mike Iuzzolino .01 .05
48 Jim Jackson .02 .10
49 Sean Rooks .01 .05
50 Doug Smith .01 .05
51 Randy White .01 .05
52 Mahmoud Abdul-Rauf .01 .05
53 LaPhonso Ellis .01 .05
54 Marcus Liberty .01 .05
55 Mark Macon .01 .05
56 Dikembe Mutombo .08 .25
57 Robert Pack .01 .05
58 Bryant Stith .01 .05
59 Reggie Williams .01 .05
60 Mark Aguirre .01 .05
61 Joe Dumars .08 .25
62 Bill Laimbeer .01 .05
63 Terry Mills .01 .05
64 Olden Polynice .01 .05
65 Alvin Robertson .01 .05
66 Dennis Rodman .20 .50
67 Isiah Thomas .08 .25
68 Victor Alexander .01 .05
69 Tim Hardaway .08 .25
70 Tyrone Hill .01 .05
71 Byron Houston .01 .05
72 Sarunas Marciulionis .01 .05
73 Chris Mullin .08 .25
74 Billy Owens .01 .05
75 Latrell Sprewell .25 .60
76 Scott Brooks .01 .05
77 Matt Bullard .01 .05
78 Carl Herrera .01 .05
79 Robert Horry .02 .10
80 Vernon Maxwell .01 .05
81 Hakeem Olajuwon .15 .40
82 Kenny Smith .01 .05
83 Otis Thorpe .02 .10
84 Dale Davis .01 .05
85 Vern Fleming .01 .05
86 George McCloud .01 .05
87 Reggie Miller .08 .25
88 Sam Mitchell .01 .05
89 Pooh Richardson .01 .05
90 Detlef Schrempf .02 .10
91 Malik Sealy .01 .05
92 Rik Smits .02 .10
93 Gary Grant .01 .05
94 Ron Harper .02 .10
95 Mark Jackson .02 .10
96 Danny Manning .02 .10
97 Ken Norman .01 .05
98 Stanley Roberts .01 .05
99 Elmore Spencer .01 .05
100 Loy Vaught .01 .05
101 John Williams .01 .05
102 Randy Woods .01 .05
103 Benoit Benjamin .01 .05
104 Elden Campbell .01 .05
105 Doug Christie UER .02 .10
(Has uniform number on front and 35 on back)
106 Vlade Divac .02 .10
107 Anthony Peeler .01 .05
108 Tony Smith .01 .05
109 Sedale Threatt .01 .05
110 James Worthy .08 .25
111 Bimbo Coles .01 .05
112 Grant Long .01 .05
113 Harold Miner .01 .05
114 Glen Rice .02 .10
115 John Salley .01 .05
116 Rony Seikaly .01 .05
117 Brian Shaw .01 .05
118 Steve Smith .08 .25
119 Anthony Avent .01 .05
120 Jon Barry .01 .05
121 Frank Brickowski .01 .05
122 Todd Day .01 .05
123 Blue Edwards .01 .05
124 Brad Lohaus .01 .05
125 Lee Mayberry .01 .05
126 Eric Murdock .01 .05
127 Derek Strong RC .01 .05
128 Thurl Bailey .01 .05
129 Christian Laettner .02 .10
130 Luc Longley .02 .10
131 Marlon Maxey .01 .05
132 Chuck Person .01 .05
133 Chris Smith .01 .05
134 Doug West .01 .05
135 Micheal Williams .01 .05
136 Rafael Addison .01 .05
137 Kenny Anderson .02 .10
138 Sam Bowie .01 .05
139 Chucky Brown .01 .05
140 Derrick Coleman .02 .10
141 Chris Morris .01 .05
142 Rumeal Robinson .01 .05
143 Greg Anthony .01 .05
144 Rolando Blackman .01 .05
145 Hubert Davis .01 .05
146 Patrick Ewing .08 .25
147 Anthony Mason .02 .10
148 Charles Oakley .02 .10
149 Doc Rivers .02 .10
150 Charles Smith .01 .05
151 John Starks .02 .10
152 Nick Anderson .02 .10
153 Anthony Bowie .01 .05
154 Litterial Green .01 .05
155 Shaquille O'Neal .50 1.25
156 Donald Royal .01 .05
157 Dennis Scott .01 .05
158 Scott Skiles .01 .05
159 Tom Tolbert .01 .05
160 Jeff Turner .01 .05
161 Ron Anderson .01 .05
162 Johnny Dawkins .01 .05
163 Hersey Hawkins .02 .10
164 Jeff Hornacek .02 .10
165 Andrew Lang .01 .05
166 Tim Perry .01 .05
167 Clarence Weatherspoon .01 .05
168 Danny Ainge .02 .10
169 Charles Barkley .15 .40
170 Cedric Ceballos .02 .10
171 Richard Dumas .01 .05
172 Kevin Johnson .02 .10
173 Dan Majerle .02 .10
174 Oliver Miller .01 .05
175 Mark West .01 .05
176 Clyde Drexler .08 .25
177 Kevin Duckworth .01 .05
178 Mario Elie .01 .05
179 Dave Johnson .01 .05
180 Jerome Kersey .01 .05
181 Tracy Murray .01 .05
182 Terry Porter .01 .05
183 Clifford Robinson .02 .10
184 Rod Strickland .02 .10
185 Buck Williams .01 .05
186 Anthony Bonner .01 .05
187 Randy Brown .01 .05
188 Duane Causwell .01 .05
189 Pete Chilcutt .01 .05
190 Mitch Richmond .08 .25
191 Lionel Simmons .01 .05
192 Wayman Tisdale .01 .05
193 Spud Webb .02 .10
194 Walt Williams .01 .05
195 Willie Anderson .01 .05
196 Antoine Carr .01 .05
197 Terry Cummings .01 .05
198 Lloyd Daniels .01 .05
199 Sean Elliott .02 .10
200 Dale Ellis .01 .05
201 Avery Johnson .01 .05
202 J.R. Reid .01 .05
203 David Robinson .15 .40
204 Dana Barros .01 .05
205 Michael Cage .01 .05
206 Eddie Johnson .01 .05
207 Shawn Kemp .15 .40
208 Derrick McKey .01 .05
209 Nate McMillan .01 .05
210 Gary Payton .15 .40
211 Sam Perkins .02 .10
212 Ricky Pierce .01 .05
213 David Benoit .01 .05
214 Tyrone Corbin .01 .05
215 Mark Eaton .01 .05
216 Jay Humphries .01 .05
217 Jeff Malone .01 .05
218 Karl Malone .15 .40
219 John Stockton .08 .25
220 Michael Adams .01 .05
221 Rex Chapman .01 .05
222 Pervis Ellison .01 .05
223 Harvey Grant .01 .05
224 Tom Gugliotta .08 .25
225 Don MacLean .01 .05
226 Doug Overton .01 .05
227 Brent Price .01 .05
228 LaBradford Smith .01 .05
229 Larry Stewart .01 .05
230 Lenny Wilkens CO .02 .10
231 Chris Ford CO .01 .05
232 Allan Bristow CO .01 .05
233 Phil Jackson CO .02 .10
234 Mike Fratello CO .02 .10
235 Quinn Buckner CO .01 .05
236 Dan Issel CO .01 .05
237 Don Chaney CO .01 .05
238 Don Nelson CO .02 .10
239 Rudy Tomjanovich CO .02 .10
240 Larry Brown CO .02 .10
241 Bob Weiss CO .01 .05
242 Randy Pfund CO .01 .05
243 Kevin Loughery CO .01 .05
244 Mike Dunleavy CO .01 .05
245 Sidney Lowe CO .01 .05
246 Chuck Daly CO .02 .10
247 Pat Riley CO .02 .10
248 Brian Hill CO .01 .05
249 Fred Carter CO .01 .05
250 Paul Westphal CO .01 .05
251 Rick Adelman CO .01 .05
252 Garry St. Jean CO .01 .05
253 John Lucas CO .01 .05
254 George Karl CO .02 .10
255 Jerry Sloan CO .02 .10
256 Wes Unseld CO .02 .10
257 Michael Jordan AS .60 1.50
258 Isiah Thomas AS .02 .10
259 Scottie Pippen AS .15 .40
260 Larry Johnson AS .02 .10
261 Dominique Wilkins AS .02 .10
262 Joe Dumars AS .02 .10
263 Mark Price AS .01 .05
264 Shaquille O'Neal AS .20 .50
265 Patrick Ewing AS .02 .10
266 Larry Nance AS .01 .05
267 Detlef Schrempf AS .01 .05
268 Brad Daugherty AS .01 .05
269 Charles Barkley AS .08 .25
270 Clyde Drexler AS .02 .10
271 Sean Elliott AS .01 .05
272 Tim Hardaway AS .02 .10
273 Shawn Kemp AS .08 .25
274 Dan Majerle AS .01 .05
275 Karl Malone AS .08 .25
276 Danny Manning AS .01 .05
277 Hakeem Olajuwon AS .08 .25
278 Terry Porter AS .01 .05
279 David Robinson AS .08 .25
280 John Stockton AS .02 .10
281 East Team Photo .01 .05
282 West Team Photo .01 .05
283 Michael Jordan .40 1.00
Dominique Wilkins
Karl Malone LL
284 Dennis Rodman .20 .50
Shaquille O'Neal
Dikembe Mutombo LL
285 Cedric Ceballos .01 .05
Brad Daugherty
Dale Davis LL
286 John Stockton .02 .10
Tim Hardaway
Scott Skiles LL
287 Mark Price .01 .05
Mahmoud Abdul-Rauf
Eddie Johnson LL
288 B.J. Armstrong .01 .05
Chris Mullin
Kenny Smith LL
289 Michael Jordan .40 1.00
Mookie Blaylock
John Stockton LL
290 Hakeem Olajuwon .15 .40
Shaquille O'Neal
Dikembe Mutombo LL
291 Boys and Girls Club .02 .10
David Robinson
292 B.J. Armstrong TRIB .01 .05
293 Scottie Pippen TRIB .15 .40
294 Kevin Johnson TRIB .01 .05
295 Charles Barkley TRIB .08 .25
296 Richard Dumas TRIB .01 .05
297 Horace Grant TRIB .08 .25
298 David Robinson CL .01 .05
299 David Robinson CL .01 .05
300 David Robinson CL .01 .05
301 Craig Ehlo .01 .05
302 Jon Koncak .01 .05
303 Andrew Lang .01 .05
304 Chris Corchiani .01 .05
305 Acie Earl RC .01 .05
306 Dino Radja RC .01 .05
307 Scott Burrell RC .08 .25
308 Hersey Hawkins .02 .10
309 Eddie Johnson .01 .05
310 David Wingate .01 .05
311 Corie Blount RC .01 .05
312 Steve Kerr .02 .10
313 Toni Kukoc RC .40 1.00
314 Pete Myers .01 .05
315 Jay Guidinger .01 .05
316 Tyrone Hill .01 .05
317 Gerald Madkins RC .01 .05
318 Chris Mills RC .08 .25
319 Bobby Phills .01 .05
320 Lucious Harris RC .01 .05
321 Popeye Jones RC .01 .05
322 Fat Lever .01 .05
323 Jamal Mashburn RC .25 .60
324 Darren Morningstar RC .01 .05
(See also 334)
325 Kevin Brooks .01 .05
326 Tom Hammonds .01 .05
327 Darnell Mee RC .01 .05
328 Rodney Rogers RC .08 .25
329 Brian Williams .01 .05
330 Greg Anderson .01 .05
331 Sean Elliott .02 .10
332 Allan Houston RC .40 1.00
333 Lindsey Hunter RC .08 .25
334 David Wood UER .01 .05
(Card misnumbered 324)
335 Jud Buechler .01 .05
336 Chris Gatling .01 .05
337 Josh Grant RC .01 .05
338 Jeff Grayer .01 .05
339 Keith Jennings .01 .05
340 Avery Johnson .01 .05
341 Chris Webber RC 1.00 2.50
342 Sam Cassell RC .40 1.00
343 Mario Elie .01 .05
344 Eric Riley RC .01 .05
345 Antonio Davis RC .10 .30
346 Scott Haskin RC .01 .05
347 Gerald Paddio .01 .05
348 LaSalle Thompson .01 .05
349 Ken Williams .01 .05
350 Mark Aguirre .01 .05
351 Terry Dehere RC .01 .05
352 Henry James .01 .05
353 Sam Bowie .01 .05
354 George Lynch RC .01 .05
355 Kurt Rambis .01 .05
356 Nick Van Exel RC .30 .75
357 Trevor Wilson .01 .05
358 Keith Askins .01 .05
359 Manute Bol .01 .05
360 Willie Burton .01 .05
361 Matt Geiger .01 .05
362 Alec Kessler .01 .05
363 Vin Baker RC .25 .60
364 Ken Norman .01 .05
365 Danny Schayes .01 .05
366 Mike Brown .01 .05
367 Isaiah Rider RC .20 .50
368 Benoit Benjamin .01 .05
369 P.J. Brown RC .08 .25
370 Kevin Edwards .01 .05
371 Armon Gilliam .01 .05
372 Rick Mahorn .01 .05
373 Dwayne Schintzius .01 .05
374 Rex Walters RC .01 .05
375 Jayson Williams .02 .10
376 Eric Anderson .01 .05
377 Anthony Bonner .01 .05
378 Tony Campbell .01 .05
379 Herb Williams .01 .05
380 Anfernee Hardaway RC .75 2.00
381 Greg Kite .01 .05
382 Larry Krystkowiak .01 .05
383 Todd Lichti .01 .05
384 Dana Barros .01 .05
385 Shawn Bradley RC .08 .25
386 Greg Graham RC .01 .05
387 Warren Kidd RC .01 .05
388 Eric Leckner .01 .05
389 Moses Malone .08 .25
390 A.C. Green .02 .10
391 Frank Johnson .01 .05
392 Joe Kleine .01 .05
393 Malcolm Mackey RC .01 .05
394 Jerrod Mustaf .01 .05
395 Mark Bryant .01 .05
396 Chris Dudley .01 .05
397 Harvey Grant .01 .05
398 James Robinson RC .01 .05
399 Reggie Smith .01 .05
400 Randy Brown .01 .05
401 Bobby Hurley RC .02 .10
402 Jim Les .01 .05
403 Vinny Del Negro .01 .05
404 Sleepy Floyd .01 .05
405 Dennis Rodman .20 .50
406 Chris Whitney RC .01 .05
407 Vincent Askew .01 .05
408 Kendall Gill .02 .10
409 Ervin Johnson RC .02 .10
410 Rich King .01 .05
411 Detlef Schrempf .02 .10
412 Tom Chambers .01 .05
413 John Crotty .01 .05
414 Felton Spencer .01 .05
415 Luther Wright RC .01 .05
416 Calbert Cheaney RC .02 .10
417 Kevin Duckworth .01 .05
418 Gheorghe Muresan RC .08 .25
419 David Robinson CL .01 .05
420 David Robinson CL .01 .05
421 David Robinson CL .01 .05
DR1 David Robinson .15 .40
Commemorative 1989
Rookie Card
MB1 Magic Johnson .20 .50
Larry Bird
Commemorative
MB1A Magic Johnson AU 75.00 200.00
Larry Bird AU
NNO David Robinson Comm AU 40.00 100.00
NNO David Robinson 4.00 10.00
Expired Voucher
NNO Magic Johnson 15.00 30.00
Larry Bird
Expired Voucher

1993-94 Hoops Fifth Anniversary Gold

Inserted one per 13-card pack and two per 26-card jumbo pack, this 423-card set parallels the regular 1993-94 Hoops issue. The only differences are the Fifth Anniversary embossed gold-foil seal, gold-foil stripes highlighting the player's name on the front and UV coating. The cards are numbered on the back. Please refer to the multiplier below (coupled with the corresponding regular issue cards) to ascertain value.

COMPLETE SET (423) 30.00 60.00
COMPLETE SERIES 1 (301) 17.50 35.00
COMPLETE SERIES 2 (122) 12.50 25.00
*STARS: 1.25X TO 2.5X BASE CARD HI
*RCs: 1X TO 2X BASE HI

1993-94 Hoops Admiral's Choice

Randomly inserted in second series 13-card foil and 26-card jumbo packs at a rate of one in 12, this five-card standard-size set features David Robinson's selection of the best starting five players in the game today. The cards have borderless fronts with color player photos. The player's name appears in gold-foil lettering at the top. The white back features a color player photo on the left with the player profile on the right. The cards are numbered on the back with an "AC" prefix.

COMPLETE SET (5) 1.50 3.00
AC1 Shawn Kemp .20 .50
AC2 Derrick Coleman .05 .15
AC3 Kenny Anderson .05 .15
AC4 Shaquille O'Neal .60 1.50
AC5 Chris Webber 1.25 3.00

1993-94 Hoops David's Best

Inserted into one in every ten first series 1993-94 Hoops 13-card foil packs, these UV-coated cards feature color action photos of David Robinson against featured opponents. The "David's Best" logo runs across the bottom of the card in "golden crystal-foil" lettering. The back of the cards present Robinson's stat line from the selected game and a brief synopsis of the highlights. The cards are numbered on the back with a "DB" prefix.

COMPLETE SET (5) 1.00 2.50
COMMON CARD (DB1-DB5) .30 .75

1993-94 Hoops Draft Redemption

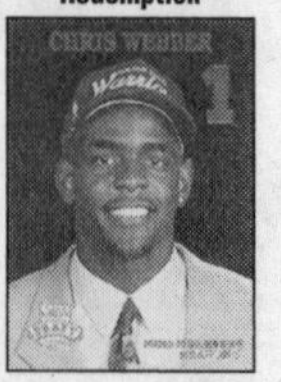

For the second consecutive year, a redemption card was randomly inserted into series one packs at a rate of one in 360. The card could be sent in for this 11-card standard-size set by March 31, 1994. The cards feature a full-color head photo on the front. The player's name appears centered at the top in gold foil. The player's draft number also appears in gold foil at the upper right. The horizontal back features a color player head shot on the left, with player statistics and biography alongside on the right. The cards are numbered on the back with an "LP" prefix and sequenced in draft lottery order.

COMPLETE SET (11) 15.00 40.00
LP1 Chris Webber 6.00 15.00
LP2 Shawn Bradley .60 1.50
LP3 Anfernee Hardaway 5.00 12.00
LP4 Jamal Mashburn 1.50 4.00
LP5 Isaiah Rider 1.25 3.00
LP6 Calbert Cheaney .25 .60
LP7 Bobby Hurley .25 .60
LP8 Vin Baker 1.50 4.00
LP9 Rodney Rogers .60 1.50
LP10 Lindsey Hunter .60 1.50
LP11 Allan Houston 2.50 6.00
NNO Redeemed Draft Card .08 .25
NNO Unredeemed Draft Card .60 1.50

1993-94 Hoops Face to Face

Randomly inserted in first series 13-card foil packs at a rate of one in 20, these 12 standard-size cards feature a standout rookie from 1992-93 on one side and a veteran All-Star with similar skills on the other. The full-bleed glossy color player action photos on both sides are reproduced over metallic-type backgrounds. On both sides, the Face to Face logo and the player's name appears at the bottom. The cards are numbered on the second side with an "FTF" prefix.

COMPLETE SET (12) 15.00 30.00
1 Shaquille O'Neal 2.50 6.00
David Robinson
2 Alonzo Mourning 1.25 3.00
Patrick Ewing
3 Christian Laettner 1.00 2.50
Shawn Kemp
4 Jim Jackson .75 2.00
Clyde Drexler
5 LaPhonso Ellis .50 1.25
Larry Johnson
6 Clarence Weatherspoon 1.00 2.50
Charles Barkley
7 Tom Gugliotta 1.25 3.00
Karl Malone
8 Walt Williams 1.50 4.00
Magic Johnson
9 Robert Horry 1.25 3.00
Scottie Pippen
10 Harold Miner 5.00 12.00
Michael Jordan
11 Todd Day .75 2.00
Chris Mullin
12 Richard Dumas .30 .75
Dominique Wilkins

1993-94 Hoops Magic's All-Rookies

Randomly inserted in second-series 13-card foil and 26-card jumbo packs at a rate of one in 30, this 10-card standard size set features Magic Johnson's projected All-Rookie team for 1993-94. The borderless front features a full-color action shot with the player's name in a gold-foil strip at the bottom. The borderless back features an italicized player profile written by Magic Johnson set against a ghosted background photo of Magic.

COMPLETE SET (10) 20.00 40.00
1 Chris Webber 6.00 15.00
2 Shawn Bradley .60 1.50
3 Anfernee Hardaway 5.00 12.00
4 Jamal Mashburn 1.50 4.00
5 Isaiah Rider 1.25 3.00
6 Calbert Cheaney .25 .60
7 Bobby Hurley .25 .60
8 Vin Baker 1.50 4.00
9 Lindsey Hunter .60 1.50
10 Toni Kukoc 2.50 6.00

1993-94 Hoops Scoops

Randomly inserted in second series 13-card foil packs, this 28-card set measures the standard size. Photos feature unique above the rim photography of a star player from each of the 27 NBA teams. Cards are either horizontal or vertical. The player's name, his team's name, and logo appear in a black bar under the photo, while the NBA Hoops Scoops logo appears in the upper right or left corner. On a white background, the backs carry trivia questions about the teams. The cards are numbered on the back with an "HS" prefix. These cards are as plentiful as the regular issue cards.

COMPLETE SET (28) .50 1.00
*GOLD CARDS:2.5X TO X VALUE
HS1 Dominique Wilkins .08 .25
HS2 Robert Parish .02 .10
HS3 Alonzo Mourning .08 .25
HS4 Scottie Pippen .08 .25
HS5 Larry Nance .01 .05
HS6 Derek Harper .02 .10
HS7 Reggie Williams .01 .05
HS8 Bill Laimbeer .01 .05
HS9 Tim Hardaway .08 .25
HS10 Hakeem Olajuwon UER .08 .25
(Robert Horry is featured player)
HS11 LaSalle Thompson .01 .05
HS12 Danny Manning .02 .10
HS13 James Worthy .08 .25
HS14 Grant Long .01 .05
HS15 Blue Edwards .01 .05
HS16 Christian Laettner .02 .10
HS17 Derrick Coleman .02 .10
HS18 Patrick Ewing .08 .25
HS19 Nick Anderson .01 .05
HS20 Clarence Weatherspoon .01 .05
HS21 Charles Barkley .08 .25
HS22 Clifford Robinson .01 .05
HS23 Lionel Simmons .01 .05
HS24 David Robinson .08 .25
HS25 Shawn Kemp .08 .25
HS26 Karl Malone .08 .25
HS27 Rex Chapman .01 .05
HS28 Answer Card .01 .05

1993-94 Hoops Supreme Court

Randomly inserted into second series 13-card foil and 26-card jumbo packs, this 11-card standard-size set reflects the All-NBA team as chosen by media members that report on the hobby. Card fronts feature full-color action player photos set against a wood grain vertical bar with the player's name centered at the top in silver-foil lettering. The backs carry color player action shots along the left side and player statistics along the right side. The cards are numbered on the back with an "SC" prefix.

COMPLETE SET (11) 4.00 10.00
SC1 Charles Barkley .30 .75
SC2 David Robinson .30 .75
SC3 Patrick Ewing .20 .50
SC4 Shaquille O'Neal 1.00 2.50
SC5 Larry Johnson .20 .50
SC6 Karl Malone .30 .75
SC7 Alonzo Mourning .30 .75
SC8 John Stockton .20 .50
SC9 Hakeem Olajuwon UER .30 .75
(Name spelled Olajwon on front)
SC10 Scottie Pippen .60 1.50
SC11 Michael Jordan 2.50 6.00

1994-95 Hoops Preview

This standard-size card previews the design of the 1994-95 Hoops regular series. The front features a full-bleed color action player photo. A team color-coded stripe cuts across the bottom of the picture and carries the player's name, position, and Hoops logo. The back has a color headshot, biography, statistics (collegiate and pro), and player profile. The card is unnumbered.

NNO David Robinson .75 2.00

1994-95 Hoops Promo Sheet

Measuring 7" by 10 1/2", this promo sheet was issued to preview the second series of the 1994-95 Hoops set. The perforated sheet consists of six cards, with an advertisement on a strip attached to the left edge. The cards are identical their regular issue counterparts except that the card numbers have been omitted. Cards are priced individually due to the large number of sheets that were seperated.

COMPLETE SET (6) 1.00 2.50
1 Jason Kidd 1.00 2.50
2 Donyell Marshall .20 .50
3 Eric Montross .20 .50
Rodney Rogers
4 Alonzo Mourning .25 .60
5 John Starks .15 .40
6 Dennis Rodman .40 1.00

1994-95 Hoops

The 450 standard-size cards comprising the '94-95 Hoops set were distributed in two separate series of 300 and 150 cards each. Cards were issued in 12-card hobby and retail packs (suggested retail price first series $0.99, second series $1.19) and 24-card retail jumbo packs. All second series packs contained at least one insert card (12-card packs had one insert and 24-card jumbo packs had two). Cards feature borderless color player action shots on the front. The player's name, position, and team name appear in white lettering within a team colored stripe near the bottom. The white back carries a color player head shot at the upper left, with the player's name and brief biography appearing alongside to the right. Statistics and career highlights follow below. The cards are numbered on the back and grouped alphabetically within teams. Subsets include All-Stars (224-251), League Leaders (252-258), Award Winners (259-265), Tribune (266-273), Coaches (274-295/383-388), Team Cards (391-420), Top This (421-430) and Gold Mine (431-450). A special Shaquille O'Neal Press Sheet (featuring 100 of his previously issued Hoops and SkyBox cards in an uncut poster-size format) was available by sending in thirty-two first series wrappers along with a check or money order for $1.50. As a special bonus 100 Press Sheets were autographed by O'Neal and randomly mailed out to collectors who responded to the promotion, which expired on March 1st, 1995. A special Grant Hill Commemorative card was available by sending in two second series wrappers along with a check or money order for $3.00 before the June 15th expiration date. Rookie Cards of note include Grant Hill, Juwan Howard, Eddie Jones, Jason Kidd and Glenn Robinson.

COMPLETE SET (450) 12.00 24.00
COMPLETE SERIES 1 (300) 6.00 12.00
COMPLETE SERIES 2 (150) 6.00 12.00
1 Stacey Augmon .12 .30
2 Mookie Blaylock .10 .25
3 Doug Edwards .10 .25
4 Craig Ehlo .10
5 Jon Koncak .10
6 Danny Manning .12
7 Kevin Willis .10
8 Dee Brown .10
9 Sherman Douglas .10
10 Acie Earl .10
11 Kevin Gamble .10
12 Xavier McDaniel .10
13 Robert Parish .15
14 Dino Radja .12
15 Tony Bennett .10
16 Muggsy Bogues .12
17 Scott Burrell .10
18 Dell Curry .10
19 Hersey Hawkins .10
20 Eddie Johnson .10
21 Larry Johnson .15
22 Alonzo Mourning .20
23 B.J. Armstrong .10
24 Corie Blount .10
25 Bill Cartwright .12
26 Horace Grant .12
27 Toni Kukoc .20
28 Luc Longley .10
29 Pete Myers .10
30 Scottie Pippen .30
31 Scott Williams .10
32 Terrell Brandon .10
33 Brad Daugherty .12
34 Tyrone Hill .10
35 Chris Mills .10
36 Larry Nance .15
37 Bobby Phills .10
38 Mark Price .15
39 Gerald Wilkins .10
40 John Williams .10
41 Terry Davis .10
42 Lucious Harris .10
43 Jim Jackson .10
44 Popeye Jones .10
45 Tim Legler .10
46 Jamal Mashburn .15
47 Sean Rooks .10
48 Mahmoud Abdul-Rauf .10
49 LaPhonso Ellis .10
50 Dikembe Mutombo .15
51 Robert Pack .10
52 Rodney Rogers .10
53 Bryant Stith .10
54 Brian Williams .10
55 Reggie Williams .10
56 Greg Anderson .10
57 Joe Dumars .15
58 Sean Elliott .15
59 Allan Houston .15
60 Lindsey Hunter .10
61 Mark Macon .10
62 Terry Mills .10
63 Victor Alexander .10
64 Chris Gatling .10
65 Tim Hardaway .15
66 Avery Johnson .12
67 Sarunas Marciulionis .10
68 Chris Mullin .15
69 Billy Owens .10
70 Latrell Sprewell .20
71 Chris Webber .25
72 Matt Bullard .10
73 Sam Cassell .15
74 Mario Elie .10
75 Carl Herrera .10
76 Robert Horry .15
77 Vernon Maxwell .10
78 Hakeem Olajuwon .20
79 Kenny Smith .12
80 Otis Thorpe .10
81 Antonio Davis .10
82 Dale Davis .10
83 Vern Fleming .10
84 Scott Haskin .10
85 Derrick McKey .10
86 Reggie Miller .20
87 Byron Scott .12
88 Rik Smits .12
89 Haywoode Workman .10
90 Terry Dehere .10
91 Harold Ellis .10
92 Gary Grant .10
93 Ron Harper .12
94 Mark Jackson .15
95 Stanley Roberts .10
96 Loy Vaught .10
97 Dominique Wilkins .20
98 Elden Campbell .10
99 Doug Christie .10
100 Vlade Divac .15
101 Reggie Jordan .10
102 George Lynch .10
103 Anthony Peeler .10
104 Sedale Threatt .10
105 Nick Van Exel .15
106 James Worthy .20
107 Bimbo Coles .10
108 Matt Geiger .10
109 Grant Long .10
110 Harold Miner .10
111 Glen Rice .15
112 John Salley .10
113 Rony Seikaly .12
114 Brian Shaw .10
115 Steve Smith .12
116 Vin Baker .15
117 Jon Barry .10
118 Todd Day .10
119 Lee Mayberry .10
120 Eric Murdock .10
121 Ken Norman .10
122 Mike Brown .10
123 Stacey King .10
124 Christian Laettner .12
125 Chuck Person .12
126 Isaiah Rider .15
127 Chris Smith .10
128 Doug West .10
129 Micheal Williams .10
130 Kenny Anderson .12
131 Benoit Benjamin .10
132 P.J. Brown .10
133 Derrick Coleman .12
134 Kevin Edwards .10
135 Armon Gilliam .10
136 Chris Morris .10
137 Rex Walters .10
138 David Wesley .10
139 Greg Anthony .10
140 Anthony Bonner .10
141 Hubert Davis .10

Card	Low	High
atrick Ewing	.20	.50
erek Harper	.12	.30
nthony Mason	.10	.25
harles Oakley	.12	.30
harles Smith	.10	.25
ohn Starks	.12	.30
ick Anderson	.10	.25
nthony Avent	.10	.25
nthony Bowie	.10	.25
nfernee Hardaway	.25	.60
haquille O'Neal	.40	1.00
onald Royal	.10	.25
ennis Scott	.10	.25
cott Skiles	.10	.25
eff Turner	.10	.25
ana Barros	.10	.25
hawn Bradley	.10	.25
reg Graham	.10	.25
arren Kidd	.10	.25
ric Leckner	.10	.25
eff Malone	.10	.25
im Perry	.10	.25
larence Weatherspoon	.10	.25
anny Ainge	.15	.40
harles Barkley	.25	.60
edric Ceballos	.10	.25
.C. Green	.15	.40
evin Johnson	.15	.40
alcolm Mackey	.10	.25
an Majerle	.15	.40
liver Miller	.10	.25
ark West	.10	.25
lyde Drexler	.20	.50
hris Dudley	.10	.25
arvey Grant	.10	.25
racy Murray	.10	.25
erry Porter	.10	.25
lifford Robinson	.10	.25
ames Robinson	.10	.25
od Strickland	.10	.25
uck Williams	.10	.25
uane Causwell	.10	.25
obby Hurley	.15	.40
lden Polynice	.10	.25
itch Richmond	.15	.40
ionel Simmons	.10	.25
ayman Tisdale	.10	.25
pud Webb	.15	.40
alt Williams	.10	.25
illie Anderson	.10	.25
loyd Daniels	.10	.25
inny Del Negro	.10	.25
ale Ellis	.10	.25
.R. Reid	.10	.25
avid Robinson	.25	.60
ennis Rodman	.30	.75
endall Gill	.10	.25
rvin Johnson	.10	.25
hawn Kemp	.15	.40
hris King	.10	.25
ate McMillan	.10	.25
ary Payton	.15	.40
am Perkins	.10	.25
icky Pierce	.10	.25
etlef Schrempf	.15	.40
avid Benoit	.10	.25
om Chambers	.15	.40
yrone Corbin	.10	.25
eff Hornacek	.12	.30
arl Malone	.20	.50
ryon Russell	.10	.25
elton Spencer	.10	.25
ohn Stockton	.20	.50
uther Wright	.10	.25
ichael Adams	.10	.25
itchell Butler	.10	.25
ex Chapman	.10	.25
albert Cheaney	.10	.25
ervis Ellison	.10	.25
om Gugliotta	.10	.25
on MacLean	.10	.25
heorghe Muresan	.10	.25
enny Anderson AS	.12	.30
.J. Armstrong AS	.10	.25
ookie Blaylock AS	.10	.25
errick Coleman AS	.12	.30
atrick Ewing AS	.20	.50
orace Grant AS	.12	.30
lonzo Mourning AS	.20	.50
haquille O'Neal AS	.40	1.00
harles Oakley AS	.12	.30
cottie Pippen AS	.30	.75
ark Price AS	.15	.40
ohn Starks AS	.12	.30
ominique Wilkins AS	.20	.50
ast Team	.10	.25
harles Barkley AS	.25	.60
lyde Drexler AS	.20	.50
evin Johnson AS	.15	.40
hawn Kemp AS	.15	.40
arl Malone AS	.20	.50
anny Manning AS	.12	.30
akeem Olajuwon AS	.20	.50
ary Payton AS	.15	.40
itch Richmond AS	.15	.40
lifford Robinson AS	.10	.25
avid Robinson AS	.25	.60
atrell Sprewell AS	.20	.50
ohn Stockton AS	.20	.50
est Team	.10	.25
racy Murray LL Armstrong gie Miller	.10	.25
ohn Stockton LL ggsy Bogues okie Blaylock	.10	.25
ikembe Mutombo LL keem Olajuwon id Robinson	.15	.40
ahmoud Abdul-Rauf LL gie Miller ky Pierce	.10	.25
ennis Rodman LL quille O'Neal in Willis	.15	.40
avid Robinson LL quille O'Neal keem Olajuwon	.15	.40
ate McMillan LL ttie Pippen okie Blaylock	.15	.40
hris Webber AW	.25	.60
akeem Olajuwon AW	.20	.50
akeem Olajuwon AW	.20	.50
ell Curry AW	.10	.25
cottie Pippen AW	.30	.75
nfernee Hardaway AW	.25	.60
on MacLean AW	.10	.25
266 Hakeem Olajuwon FIN	.20	.50
267 Derek Harper FIN	.12	.30
268 Sam Cassell FIN	.15	.40
269 Hakeem Olajuwon TRIB	.20	.50
270 Patrick Ewing FIN Hakeem Olajuwon	.15	.40
271 Carl Herrera FIN	.10	.25
272 Vernon Maxwell FIN	.10	.25
273 Hakeem Olajuwon FIN	.20	.50
274 Lenny Wilkens CO	.15	.40
275 Chris Ford CO	.10	.25
276 Allan Bristow CO	.10	.25
277 Phil Jackson CO	.15	.40
278 Mike Fratello CO	.15	.40
279 Dick Motta CO	.10	.25
280 Dan Issel CO	.15	.40
281 Don Chaney CO	.10	.25
282 Don Nelson CO	.15	.40
283 Rudy Tomjanovich CO	.15	.40
284 Larry Brown CO	.15	.40
285 Del Harris CO UER (Back refers to Ralph Sampson and Akeem Olajuwon as part of '80-'81 Rockets)	.10	.25
286 Kevin Loughery CO	.10	.25
287 Mike Dunleavy CO	.10	.25
288 Sidney Lowe CO	.10	.25
289 Pat Riley CO	.15	.40
290 Brian Hill CO	.10	.25
291 John Lucas CO	.10	.25
292 Paul Westphal CO	.10	.25
293 Garry St. Jean CO	.10	.25
294 George Karl CO	.15	.40
295 Jerry Sloan CO	.15	.40
296 Magic Johnson COMM	.40	1.00
297 Denzel Washington SPEC	.15	.40
298 Checklist	.10	.25
299 Checklist	.10	.25
300 Checklist	.10	.25
301 Sergei Bazarevich RC	.15	.40
302 Tyrone Corbin	.10	.25
303 Grant Long	.10	.25
304 Ken Norman	.10	.25
305 Steve Smith	.12	.30
306 Blue Edwards	.10	.25
307 Greg Minor RC	.15	.40
308 Eric Montross RC	.15	.40
309 Dominique Wilkins	.20	.50
310 Michael Adams	.10	.25
311 Darrin Hancock RC	.15	.40
312 Robert Parish	.15	.40
313 Ron Harper	.12	.30
314 Dickey Simpkins RC	.15	.40
315 Michael Cage	.10	.25
316 Tony Dumas RC	.15	.40
317 Jason Kidd RC	.75	2.00
318 Roy Tarpley	.10	.25
319 Dale Ellis	.10	.25
320 Jalen Rose RC	.40	1.00
321 Bill Curley RC	.15	.40
322 Grant Hill RC	.75	2.00
323 Oliver Miller	.10	.25
324 Mark West	.10	.25
325 Tom Gugliotta	.10	.25
326 Ricky Pierce	.10	.25
327 Carlos Rogers RC	.15	.40
328 Clifford Rozier RC	.15	.40
329 Rony Seikaly	.12	.30
330 Tim Breaux	.10	.25
331 Duane Ferrell	.10	.25
332 Mark Jackson	.15	.40
333 Lamond Murray RC	.15	.40
334 Bo Outlaw RC	.15	.40
335 Eric Piatkowski RC	.20	.50
336 Pooh Richardson	.10	.25
337 Malik Sealy	.10	.25
338 Cedric Ceballos	.10	.25
339 Eddie Jones RC	.50	1.25
340 Anthony Miller RC	.15	.40
341 Kevin Gamble	.10	.25
342 Brad Lohaus	.10	.25
343 Billy Owens	.10	.25
344 Khalid Reeves RC	.15	.40
345 Kevin Willis	.10	.25
346 Eric Mobley RC	.15	.40
347 Johnny Newman	.10	.25
348 Ed Pinckney	.10	.25
349 Glenn Robinson RC	.30	.75
350 Howard Eisley RC	.15	.40
351 Donyell Marshall RC	.15	.40
352 Yinka Dare RC	.15	.40
353 Charlie Ward RC	.15	.40
354 Monty Williams RC	.15	.40
355 Horace Grant	.12	.30
356 Brian Shaw	.10	.25
357 Brooks Thompson RC	.15	.40
358 Derrick Alston RC	.15	.40
359 B.J.Tyler RC	.15	.40
360 Scott Williams	.10	.25
361 Sharone Wright RC	.15	.40
362 Antonio Lang RC	.15	.40
363 Danny Manning	.12	.30
364 Wesley Person RC	.15	.40
365 Wayman Tisdale	.10	.25
366 Trevor Ruffin RC	.15	.40
367 Aaron McKie RC	.15	.40
368 Brian Grant RC	.25	.60
369 Michael Smith RC	.15	.40
370 Sean Elliott	.15	.40
371 Avery Johnson	.12	.30
372 Chuck Person	.12	.30
373 Bill Cartwright	.12	.30
374 Sarunas Marciulionis	.10	.25
375 Dontonio Wingfield RC	.15	.40
376 Antoine Carr	.10	.25
377 Jamie Watson RC	.15	.40
378 Juwan Howard RC	.25	.60
379 Jim McIlvaine RC	.15	.40
380 Scott Skiles	.10	.25
381 Anthony Tucker RC	.15	.40
382 Chris Webber	.25	.60
383 Bill Fitch CO	.15	.40
384 Bill Blair CO	.10	.25
385 Butch Beard CO	.10	.25
386 P.J. Carlesimo CO	.10	.25
387 Bob Hill CO	.10	.25
388 Jim Lynam CO	.10	.25
389 Checklist 4	.10	.25
390 Checklist 5	.10	.25
391 Atlanta Hawks TC	.10	.25
392 Boston Celtics TC	.10	.25
393 Charlotte Hornets TC	.10	.25
394 Chicago Bulls TC	.10	.25
395 Cleveland Cavaliers TC	.10	.25
396 Dallas Mavericks TC	.10	.25
397 Denver Nuggets TC	.10	.25
398 Detroit Pistons TC	.10	.25
399 Golden State Warriors TC	.10	.25
400 Houston Rockets TC	.10	.25
401 Indiana Pacers TC	.10	.25
402 Los Angeles Clippers TC	.10	.25
403 Los Angeles Lakers TC	.10	.25
404 Miami Heat TC	.10	.25
405 Milwaukee Bucks TC	.10	.25
406 Minnesota Timberwolves TC	.10	.25
407 New Jersey Nets TC	.10	.25
408 New York Knicks TC	.10	.25
409 Orlando Magic TC	.10	.25
410 Philadelphia 76ers TC	.10	.25
411 Phoenix Suns TC	.10	.25
412 Portland Trail Blazers TC	.10	.25
413 Sacramento Kings TC	.10	.25
414 San Antonio Spurs TC	.10	.25
415 Seattle Supersonics TC	.10	.25
416 Utah Jazz TC	.10	.25
417 Washington Bullets TC	.10	.25
418 Toronto Raptors TC	.10	.25
419 Vancouver Grizzlies TC	.10	.25
420 NBA Logo Card	.10	.25
421 Glenn Robinson TOP Chris Webber	.15	.40
422 Jason Kidd TOP Shawn Bradley	.40	1.00
423 Grant Hill TOP Anfernee Hardaway	.40	1.00
424 Donyell Marshall TOP Jamal Mashburn	.10	.25
425 Juwan Howard TOP Isaiah Rider	.12	.30
426 Sharone Wright TOP Calbert Cheaney	.10	.25
427 Lamond Murray TOP Bobby Hurley	.10	.25
428 Brian Grant TOP Vin Baker	.12	.30
429 Eric Montross TOP Rodney Rogers	.10	.25
430 Eddie Jones TOP Lindsey Hunter	.25	.60
431 Craig Ehlo GM	.10	.25
432 Dino Radja GM	.12	.30
433 Toni Kukoc GM	.20	.50
434 Mark Price GM	.15	.40
435 Latrell Sprewell GM	.20	.50
436 Sam Cassell GM	.15	.40
437 Vernon Maxwell GM	.10	.25
438 Haywoode Workman GM	.10	.25
439 Harold Ellis GM	.10	.25
440 Cedric Ceballos GM	.10	.25
441 Vlade Divac GM	.15	.40
442 Nick Van Exel GM	.15	.40
443 John Starks GM	.12	.30
444 Scott Williams GM	.10	.25
445 Clifford Robinson GM	.10	.25
446 Spud Webb GM	.15	.40
447 Avery Johnson GM	.12	.30
448 Dennis Rodman GM	.30	.75
449 Sarunas Marciulionis GM	.10	.25
450 Nate McMillan GM	.10	.25
PR1 Grant Hill PROMO	4.00	10.00
NNO Grant Hill Wrapper Exch.	1.50	4.00
NNO Shaquille O'Neal Sheet Wrapper Exchange Autograph	200.00	400.00
NNO Shaquille O'Neal Sheet Wrap.Exch.	15.00	30.00

1994-95 Hoops Big Numbers

Randomly inserted in first series hobby and retail foil packs at a rate of one in 30, this 12 standard-size set features color player action cutouts on their black horizontal and borderless fronts. The player's name and a number representing his Big Number accomplishment appear in silver-foil lettering offset to one side. The white horizontal back carries a color player head shot at the right, with a description of his Big Number accomplishment appearing alonside. The cards are numbered on the back with a "BN" prefix.

Card	Low	High
COMPLETE SET (12)	15.00	40.00
*RAINBOW CARDS: EQUAL VALUE TO SILVER		
ONE RAINBOW PER SER.1 RETAIL PACK		
BN1 David Robinson	2.00	5.00
BN2 Jamal Mashburn	1.25	3.00
BN3 Hakeem Olajuwon	1.50	4.00
BN4 Patrick Ewing	1.50	4.00
BN5 Shaquille O'Neal	3.00	8.00
BN6 Latrell Sprewell	1.50	4.00
BN7 Chris Webber	2.00	5.00
BN8 Anfernee Hardaway	2.00	5.00
BN9 Scottie Pippen	2.50	6.00
BN10 Isaiah Rider	1.25	3.00
BN11 Alonzo Mourning	1.50	4.00
BN12 Charles Barkley	2.00	5.00

1994-95 Hoops Draft Redemption

For the third straight year, a redemption card was randomly inserted into first series packs at a rate of one in 360. The card could be sent in for this 11-card standard size set on or before the June 15th, 1995 deadline. The cards feature a full-color player photo cut out against a computer-generated background with a big number (corresponding to the player's draft selection) zooming out of the side. This set is sequenced in draft order.

Card	Low	High
COMPLETE SET (11)	8.00	20.00
1 Glenn Robinson	1.00	2.50
2 Jason Kidd	2.50	6.00
3 Grant Hill	2.50	6.00
4 Donyell Marshall	.50	1.25
5 Juwan Howard	.75	2.00
6 Sharone Wright	.50	1.25
7 Lamond Murray	.50	1.25
8 Brian Grant	.75	2.00
9 Eric Montross	.50	1.25
10 Eddie Jones	1.50	4.00
11 Carlos Rogers	.50	1.25
NNO Expired Exch.Card	.40	1.00

1994-95 Hoops Magic's All-Rookies

Randomly inserted into all second series packs (12-card hobby and retail packs at a rate of one in twelve, 24-card retail jumbo packs at an approximate rate of slightly greater than one per pack), cards from this 12-card standard-size set feature a selection of top rookies from the 1994-95 season. The fronts have a color action photo with different color backgrounds for each card with designs in them. The word "Magic's" is in the upper right corner and "All-Rookie" is three-dimensonally encompassing the player. The backs have a picture of Magic Johnson holding the card showing the front. On the left side it says "Magic's All-Rookie Team" and the their is player commentary at the bottom.

Card	Low	High
COMPLETE SET (10)	5.00	12.00
*FOIL CARDS: 1.25X TO 3X HI COLUMN		
FOIL SER.2 STATED ODDS 1:36		
*JUMBO CARDS: .75X TO 2X HI COLUMN		
JUMBO ONE PER SER.2 HOBBY BOX		
AR1 Glenn Robinson	.60	1.50
AR2 Jason Kidd	1.50	4.00
AR3 Grant Hill	1.50	4.00
AR4 Donyell Marshall	.30	.75
AR5 Juwan Howard	.50	1.25
AR6 Sharone Wright	.30	.75
AR7 Brian Grant	.50	1.25
AR8 Eddie Jones	1.00	2.50
AR9 Jalen Rose	.75	2.00
AR10 Wesley Person	.30	.75

1994-95 Hoops Power Ratings

Inserted one per pack into all second series packs, cards from this 54-card standard-size set feature a selection of the top players in the NBA. Cards feature a photo of the player silhouetted over flame-thrower graphics. Backs present a second photo and colorful bar chart of the players stats in seven key categories. Two players per team were included in this set.

Card	Low	High
COMPLETE SET (54)	3.00	8.00
PR1 Mookie Blaylock	.12	.30
PR2 Stacey Augmon	.15	.40
PR3 Dino Radja	.15	.40
PR4 Dominique Wilkins	.25	.60
PR5 Larry Johnson	.20	.50
PR6 Alonzo Mourning	.25	.60
PR7 Toni Kukoc	.25	.60
PR8 Scottie Pippen	.40	1.00
PR9 John Williams	.12	.30
PR10 Mark Price	.20	.50
PR11 Jim Jackson	.12	.30
PR12 Jamal Mashburn	.20	.50
PR13 Dale Ellis	.12	.30
PR14 LaPhonso Ellis	.12	.30
PR15 Joe Dumars	.20	.50
PR16 Lindsey Hunter	.12	.30
PR17 Latrell Sprewell	.25	.60
PR18 Chris Mullin	.20	.50
PR19 Vernon Maxwell	.12	.30
PR20 Hakeem Olajuwon	.25	.60
PR21 Mark Jackson	.20	.50
PR22 Reggie Miller	.25	.60
PR23 Pooh Richardson	.12	.30
PR24 Loy Vaught	.12	.30
PR25 Vlade Divac	.20	.50
PR26 Nick Van Exel	.20	.50
PR27 Glen Rice	.20	.50
PR28 Billy Owens	.12	.30
PR29 Vin Baker	.20	.50
PR30 Eric Murdock	.12	.30
PR31 Christian Laettner	.15	.40
PR32 Isaiah Rider	.20	.50
PR33 Kenny Anderson	.15	.40
PR34 Derrick Coleman	.15	.40
PR35 Patrick Ewing	.25	.60
PR36 John Starks	.15	.40
PR37 Nick Anderson	.12	.30
PR38 Anfernee Hardaway	.30	.75
PR39 Shawn Bradley	.12	.30
PR40 Clarence Weatherspoon	.12	.30
PR41 Charles Barkley	.30	.75
PR42 Kevin Johnson	.20	.50
PR43 Clyde Drexler	.25	.60
PR44 Clifford Robinson	.12	.30
PR45 Mitch Richmond	.20	.50
PR46 Olden Polynice	.12	.30
PR47 Sean Elliott	.20	.50
PR48 Chuck Person	.15	.40
PR49 Shawn Kemp	.20	.50
PR50 Gary Payton	.20	.50
PR51 Jeff Hornacek	.15	.40
PR52 Karl Malone	.25	.60
PR53 Rex Chapman	.12	.30
PR54 Don MacLean	.12	.30

1994-95 Hoops Predators

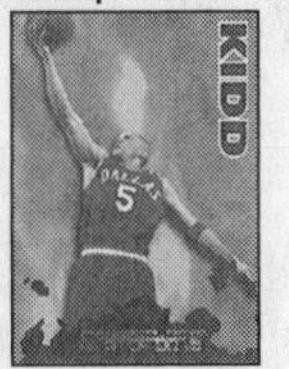

Randomly inserted into all secönd series packs (one in every twelve 12-card packs and two per 24-card jumbo pack), cards from this 8-card standard-size set feature eight league leaders from the 1993-94 season. Design is very similar to the Power Ratings inserts. The set is sequenced in alphabetical order. There was also a Jumbo card of the David Robinson Predator inserted into Series 2 Sam's boxes. That card is listed below at the end of the set.

Card	Low	High
COMPLETE SET (8)	1.25	3.00
P1 Mahmoud Abdul-Rauf	.20	.50
P2 Dikembe Mutombo	.30	.75
P3 Shaquille O'Neal	.75	2.00
P4 Tracy Murray	.20	.50
P5 David Robinson	.50	1.25
P6 Dennis Rodman	.60	1.50
P7 Nate McMillan	.20	.50
P8 John Stockton	.40	1.00
NNO David Robinson Jumbo	.40	1.00

1994-95 Hoops Supreme Court

Randomly inserted in first series hobby and retail packs at a rate of one in four, the 50 standard-size parallel cards comprising the '94-95 Hoops Supreme Court set feature a selection of the top stars within the basic issue first series Hoops set. Unlike the regular issue cards, each Supreme Court insert features a special embossed gold-foil logo on the card front. The cards are also numbered on the back with an "SC" prefix.player head shot at the upper left, with the player's name and brief biography appearing alongside to the right. Statistics and career highlights follow below. The cards are numbered on the back with an "SC" prefix.

Card	Low	High
COMPLETE SET (50)	8.00	20.00
SC1 Mookie Blaylock	.15	.40
SC2 Danny Manning	.20	.50
SC3 Dino Radja	.20	.50
SC4 Larry Johnson	.25	.60
SC5 Alonzo Mourning	.30	.75
SC6 B.J. Armstrong	.15	.40
SC7 Horace Grant	.20	.50
SC8 Toni Kukoc	.30	.75
SC9 Brad Daugherty	.20	.50
SC10 Mark Price	.25	.60
SC11 Jim Jackson	.15	.40
SC12 Jamal Mashburn	.25	.60
SC13 Dikembe Mutombo	.25	.60
SC14 Joe Dumars	.25	.60
SC15 Lindsey Hunter	.15	.40
SC16 Tim Hardaway	.25	.60
SC17 Chris Mullin	.25	.60
SC18 Sam Cassell	.25	.60
SC19 Hakeem Olajuwon	.30	.75
SC20 Reggie Miller	.30	.75
SC21 Dominique Wilkins	.30	.75
SC22 Nick Van Exel	.25	.60
SC23 Harold Miner	.15	.40
SC24 Steve Smith	.20	.50
SC25 Vin Baker	.25	.60
SC26 Christian Laettner	.20	.50
SC27 Isaiah Rider	.25	.60
SC28 Kenny Anderson	.20	.50
SC29 Derrick Coleman	.20	.50
SC30 Patrick Ewing	.30	.75
SC31 John Starks	.20	.50
SC32 Anfernee Hardaway	.40	1.00
SC33 Shaquille O'Neal	.60	1.50
SC34 Shawn Bradley	.15	.40
SC35 Clarence Weatherspoon	.15	.40
SC36 Charles Barkley	.40	1.00
SC37 Kevin Johnson	.25	.60
SC38 Oliver Miller	.15	.40
SC39 Clyde Drexler	.30	.75
SC40 Clifford Robinson	.15	.40
SC41 Mitch Richmond	.25	.60
SC42 Bobby Hurley	.25	.60
SC43 David Robinson	.40	1.00
SC44 Dennis Rodman	.50	1.25
SC45 Gary Payton	.25	.60
SC46 Shawn Kemp	.25	.60
SC47 John Stockton	.30	.75
SC48 Karl Malone	.30	.75
SC49 Calbert Cheaney	.15	.40
SC50 Tom Gugliotta	.15	.40

1995-96 Hoops National Promos

A cello pack containing these standard-size promo cards was given away at the SkyBox booth during the 16th National Sports Collectors Convention in St. Louis. The set consists of two regular issue cards (2, 6) and four subset cards (1, 3-5). They are identical to their regular issue counterparts except for the absence of numbering. The cards are checklisted below in alphabetical order.

Card	Low	High
COMPLETE SET (7)	1.25	3.00
1 Kenny Anderson	.25	.60
2 Vin Baker	.25	.60
3 A.C. Green	.30	.75
4 Jason Kidd	.50	1.25
5 Glen Rice	.30	.75
6 Rony Seikaly	.25	.60
7 Title Card	.20	.50

1995-96 Hoops Promo Sheet 1

Measuring 7" by 10 1/2", this promo sheet was issued to preview the first series of the 1995-96 Hoops set. The perforated sheet consists of six cards, with an advertisement on a strip attached to the left edge. The cards are identical their regular issue counterparts except that the card numbers have been omitted. With the exception of the Majerle card, the rest of the cards are from insert sets. The cards are priced individually due to the high number of sheets torn apart.

Card	Low	High
COMPLETE SET (6)	1.25	3.00
1 Eddie Jones	.50	1.25
2 Detlef Schrempf	.40	1.00
3 Dan Majerle	.40	1.00
4 Juwan Howard	.40	1.00
5 Larry Johnson	.40	1.00
6 Scott Burrell	.25	.60

1995-96 Hoops Promo Sheet 2

Measuring 7" by 10 1/2", this promo sheet was issued to preview the second series of the 1995-96 Hoops set. The perforated sheet consists of six cards, with an advertisement on a strip attached to the left edge. The cards are identical their regular issue counterparts except that the card numbers have been omitted. The cards are priced individually due to the high number of sheets torn apart.

Card	Low	High
COMPLETE SET (6)	2.00	5.00
1 Anfernee Hardaway	.60	1.50
2 John Stockton	.50	1.25
3 Antonio McDyess	1.00	2.50
4 Charles Barkley	.60	1.50
5 John Salley	.25	.60
6 Glenn Robinson	.40	1.00

1995-96 Hoops

The 1995-96 Hoops basketball set was issued in two series of 250 and 150 standard-size cards respectively for a total of 400. Series one cards were issued in 12-card hobby and retail packs (SRP $1.29) and 20-card retail jumbo packs (SRP $1.99). Series two cards were issued in 8-card hobby and retail packs for $.99 each. Fronts have a full-color action photo with the player's name in gold foil surrounded by his team's color. The backs have a color photo with pro and college career statistics. Cards are grouped alphabetically within teams. The following subsets are featured: Coaches (171-197), Sizzlin' Sophs (198-207), Milestones (208-217), Buzzer Beaters (218-227), Pipeline (228-232), Class Acts (233-242), Triple Threats (243-247), Player/Coach Updates (291-333), Coaches (334-337), Expansion Teams (338-357), Earthshakers (358-372), Rock/House (373-387) and Wicked Dishes (388-397). A special Grant Hill Tribute card, featuring a clear acetate center, was randomly inserted into one in every 360 series one packs. All insert cards feature 3-D technology. A pair of Grant Hill 3-D glasses was available by sending in two first series wrappers and a check or money order for $3.50. In addition, a limited edition Grant Hill Commemorative Co-Rookie of the Year card was available by sending in a check or money order for $9.95 plus two series one wrappers. Both promotions were detailed on first series wrappers and both expired December 31, 1995. Rookie Cards of note in this set include Michael Finley, Kevin Garnett, Antonio McDyess, Joe Smith, Jerry Stackhouse and Damon Stoudamire.

Card	Low	High
COMPLETE SET (400)	17.50	35.00
COMPLETE SERIES 1 (250)	10.00	20.00
COMPLETE SERIES 2 (150)	7.50	15.00
1 Stacey Augmon	.12	.30
2 Mookie Blaylock	.10	.25
3 Craig Ehlo	.10	.25
4 Andrew Lang	.10	.25
5 Grant Long	.10	.25
6 Ken Norman	.10	.25
7 Steve Smith	.12	.30
8 Dee Brown	.10	.25
9 Sherman Douglas	.10	.25
10 Pervis Ellison	.10	.25
11 Eric Montross	.10	.25
12 Dino Radja	.12	.30
13 Dominique Wilkins	.20	.50
14 Muggsy Bogues	.12	.30
15 Scott Burrell	.10	.25
16 Dell Curry	.10	.25
17 Hersey Hawkins	.10	.25
18 Larry Johnson	.15	.40
19 Alonzo Mourning	.20	.50
20 B.J. Armstrong	.10	.25
21 Michael Jordan	1.25	3.00
22 Toni Kukoc	.15	.40
23 Will Perdue	.10	.25
24 Scottie Pippen	.25	.60
25 Dickey Simpkins	.10	.25
26 Terrell Brandon	.10	.25
27 Tyrone Hill	.10	.25
28 Chris Mills	.10	.25
29 Bobby Phills	.10	.25
30 Mark Price	.15	.40
31 John Williams	.10	.25
32 Tony Dumas	.10	.25
33 Jim Jackson	.10	.25
34 Popeye Jones	.10	.25
35 Jason Kidd	.25	.60
36 Jamal Mashburn	.15	.40
37 Roy Tarpley	.10	.25
38 Mahmoud Abdul-Rauf	.10	.25
39 LaPhonso Ellis	.10	.25
40 Dikembe Mutombo	.15	.40
41 Robert Pack	.10	.25
42 Rodney Rogers	.10	.25
43 Jalen Rose	.20	.50
44 Bryant Stith	.10	.25
45 Joe Dumars	.15	.40
46 Grant Hill	.25	.60
47 Allan Houston	.12	.30
48 Lindsey Hunter	.10	.25
49 Oliver Miller	.10	.25
50 Terry Mills	.10	.25
51 Chris Gatling	.10	.25
52 Tim Hardaway	.15	.40
53 Donyell Marshall	.10	.25
54 Chris Mullin	.15	.40
55 Carlos Rogers	.10	.25
56 Clifford Rozier	.10	.25
57 Rony Seikaly	.12	.30
58 Latrell Sprewell	.15	.40
59 Sam Cassell	.15	.40
60 Clyde Drexler	.20	.50
61 Robert Horry	.12	.30
62 Vernon Maxwell	.10	.25
63 Hakeem Olajuwon	.20	.50
64 Kenny Smith	.12	.30
65 Dale Davis	.10	.25
66 Mark Jackson	.15	.40
67 Derrick McKey	.10	.25
68 Reggie Miller	.20	.50
69 Byron Scott	.12	.30
70 Rik Smits	.12	.30
71 Terry Dehere	.10	.25
72 Lamond Murray	.10	.25
73 Eric Piatkowski	.12	.30
74 Pooh Richardson	.10	.25
75 Malik Sealy	.10	.25
76 Loy Vaught	.10	.25
77 Elden Campbell	.10	.25
78 Cedric Ceballos	.10	.25
79 Vlade Divac	.15	.40
80 Eddie Jones	.20	.50
81 Sedale Threatt	.10	.25
82 Nick Van Exel	.15	.40
83 Bimbo Coles	.10	.25
84 Harold Miner	.10	.25
85 Billy Owens	.10	.25
86 Khalid Reeves	.10	.25
87 Glen Rice	.15	.40
88 Kevin Willis	.10	.25
89 Vin Baker	.12	.30
90 Marty Conlon	.10	.25
91 Todd Day	.10	.25
92 Eric Mobley	.10	.25
93 Eric Murdock	.10	.25
94 Glenn Robinson	.15	.40
95 Winston Garland	.10	.25
96 Tom Gugliotta	.10	.25
97 Christian Laettner	.12	.30
98 Isaiah Rider	.15	.40
99 Sean Rooks	.10	.25
100 Doug West	.10	.25
101 Kenny Anderson	.12	.30
102 Benoit Benjamin	.10	.25
103 Derrick Coleman	.12	.30
104 Kevin Edwards	.10	.25
105 Armon Gilliam	.10	.25
106 Chris Morris	.10	.25
107 Patrick Ewing	.20	.50
108 Derek Harper	.12	.30
109 Anthony Mason	.10	.25
110 Charles Oakley	.12	.30
111 Charles Smith	.10	.25
112 John Starks	.12	.30
113 Monty Williams	.10	.25
114 Nick Anderson	.10	.25
115 Horace Grant	.12	.30
116 Anfernee Hardaway	.25	.60
117 Shaquille O'Neal	.40	1.00
118 Dennis Scott	.10	.25
119 Brian Shaw	.10	.25
120 Dana Barros	.10	.25
121 Shawn Bradley	.10	.25
122 Willie Burton	.10	.25
123 Jeff Malone	.10	.25
124 Clarence Weatherspoon	.10	.25
125 Sharone Wright	.10	.25
126 Charles Barkley	.25	.60
127 A.C. Green	.15	.40
128 Kevin Johnson	.15	.40
129 Dan Majerle	.15	.40
130 Danny Manning	.12	.30
131 Elliot Perry	.10	.25
132 Wesley Person	.10	.25
133 Chris Dudley	.10	.25
134 Clifford Robinson	.10	.25
135 James Robinson	.10	.25
136 Rod Strickland	.10	.25
137 Otis Thorpe	.10	.25
138 Buck Williams	.10	.25
139 Brian Grant	.12	.30
140 Olden Polynice	.10	.25
141 Mitch Richmond	.15	.40
142 Michael Smith	.10	.25
143 Spud Webb	.15	.40
144 Walt Williams	.10	.25
145 Vinny Del Negro	.10	.25
146 Sean Elliott	.15	.40
147 Avery Johnson	.12	.30
148 Chuck Person	.12	.30
149 David Robinson	.25	.60
150 Dennis Rodman	.30	.75
151 Kendall Gill	.10	.25
152 Ervin Johnson	.10	.25
153 Shawn Kemp	.15	.40
154 Nate McMillan	.10	.25
155 Gary Payton	.15	.40
156 Detlef Schrempf	.15	.40
157 Dontonio Wingfield	.10	.25
158 David Benoit	.10	.25
159 Jeff Hornacek	.12	.30
160 Karl Malone	.20	.50
161 Felton Spencer	.10	.25
162 John Stockton	.20	.50
163 Jamie Watson	.10	.25
164 Rex Chapman	.10	.25
165 Calbert Cheaney	.10	.25
166 Juwan Howard	.15	.40
167 Don MacLean	.10	.25
168 Gheorghe Muresan	.10	.25
169 Scott Skiles	.10	.25
170 Chris Webber	.20	.50
171 Lenny Wilkens CO	.12	.30
172 Allan Bristow CO	.10	.25
173 Phil Jackson CO	.15	.40
174 Mike Fratello CO	.10	.30
175 Dick Motta CO	.10	.25
176 Bernie Bickerstaff CO	.10	.25
177 Doug Collins CO	.10	.25
178 Rick Adelman CO	.10	.25
179 Rudy Tomjanovich CO	.12	.30
180 Larry Brown CO	.12	.30
181 Bill Fitch CO	.10	.25
182 Del Harris CO	.10	.25
183 Mike Dunleavy CO	.10	.25
184 Bill Blair CO	.10	.25
185 Butch Beard CO	.10	.25
186 Pat Riley CO	.15	.40
187 Brian Hill CO	.10	.25

Card		
188 John Lucas CO	.12	.30
189 Paul Westphal CO	.10	.25
190 P.J. Carlesimo CO	.10	.25
191 Garry St. Jean CO	.10	.25
192 Bob Hill CO	.10	.25
193 George Karl CO	.12	.30
194 Brendan Malone CO	.10	.25
195 Jerry Sloan CO	.12	.30
196 Kevin Pritchard CO	.10	.25
197 Jim Lynam CO	.10	.25
198 Brian Grant SS	.12	.30
199 Grant Hill SS	.25	.60
200 Juwan Howard SS	.15	.40
201 Eddie Jones SS	.20	.50
202 Jason Kidd SS	.25	.60
203 Donyell Marshall SS	.10	.25
204 Eric Montross SS	.10	.25
205 Glenn Robinson SS	.15	.40
206 Jalen Rose SS	.20	.50
207 Sharone Wright SS	.10	.25
208 Dana Barros MS	.10	.25
209 Joe Dumars MS	.15	.40
210 A.C. Green MS	.15	.40
211 Grant Hill MS	.25	.60
212 Karl Malone MS	.20	.50
213 Reggie Miller MS	.20	.50
214 Glen Rice MS	.15	.40
215 John Stockton MS	.20	.50
216 Lenny Wilkens MS	.12	.30
217 Dominique Wilkins MS	.20	.50
218 Kenny Anderson BB	.12	.30
219 Mookie Blaylock BB	.10	.25
220 Larry Johnson BB	.15	.40
221 Shawn Kemp BB	.15	.40
222 Toni Kukoc BB	.15	.40
223 Jamal Mashburn BB	.15	.40
224 Glen Rice BB	.15	.40
225 Mitch Richmond BB	.15	.40
226 Latrell Sprewell BB	.15	.40
227 Rod Strickland BB	.10	.25
228 Michael Adams PL Darrick Martin	.10	.25
229 Craig Ehlo PL Jerome Harmon	.10	.25
230 Mario Elie PL George McCloud	.10	.25
231 Anthony Mason PL Chucky Brown	.10	.25
232 John Starks PL Tim Legler	.12	.30
233 Muggsy Bogues CA	.12	.30
234 Joe Dumars CA	.15	.40
235 LaPhonso Ellis CA	.10	.25
236 Patrick Ewing CA	.20	.50
237 Grant Hill CA	.25	.60
238 Kevin Johnson CA	.15	.40
239 Dan Majerle CA	.15	.40
240 Karl Malone CA	.20	.50
241 Hakeem Olajuwon CA	.20	.50
242 David Robinson CA	.25	.60
243 Dana Barros TT	.10	.25
244 Scott Burrell TT	.10	.25
245 Reggie Miller TT	.20	.50
246 Glen Rice TT	.15	.40
247 John Stockton TT	.20	.50
248 Checklist #1	.10	.25
249 Checklist #2	.10	.25
250 Checklist #3	.10	.25
251 Alan Henderson RC	.15	.40
252 Junior Burrough RC	.15	.40
253 Eric Williams RC	.15	.40
254 George Zidek RC	.15	.40
255 Jason Caffey RC	.15	.40
256 Donny Marshall RC	.15	.40
257 Bob Sura RC	.15	.40
258 Loren Meyer RC	.15	.40
259 Cherokee Parks RC	.15	.40
260 Antonio McDyess RC	.40	1.00
261 Theo Ratliff RC	.25	.60
262 Lou Roe RC	.15	.40
263 Andrew DeClercq RC	.15	.40
264 Joe Smith RC	.30	.75
265 Travis Best RC	.15	.40
266 Brent Barry RC	.25	.60
267 Frankie King RC	.15	.40
268 Sasha Danilovic RC	.15	.40
269 Kurt Thomas RC	.15	.40
270 Shawn Respert RC	.15	.40
271 Jerome Allen RC	.15	.40
272 Kevin Garnett RC	1.25	3.00
273 Ed O'Bannon RC	.15	.40
274 David Vaughn RC	.15	.40
275 Jerry Stackhouse RC	.50	1.25
276 Mario Bennett RC	.15	.40
277 Michael Finley RC	.50	1.25
278 Randolph Childress RC	.15	.40
279 Arvydas Sabonis RC	.30	.75
280 Gary Trent RC	.15	.40
281 Tyus Edney RC	.15	.40
282 Corliss Williamson RC	.15	.40
283 Cory Alexander RC	.15	.40
284 Sherrell Ford RC	.15	.40
285 Jimmy King RC	.15	.40
286 Damon Stoudamire RC	.40	1.00
287 Greg Ostertag RC	.15	.40
288 Lawrence Moten RC	.15	.40
289 Bryant Reeves RC	.15	.40
290 Rasheed Wallace RC	.50	1.25
291 Spud Webb	.15	.40
292 Dana Barros	.10	.25
293 Rick Fox	.10	.25
294 Kendall Gill	.10	.25
295 Khalid Reeves	.10	.25
296 Glen Rice	.15	.40
297 Luc Longley	.10	.25
298 Dennis Rodman	.30	.75
299 Dan Majerle	.15	.40
300 Lorenzo Williams	.10	.25
301 Dale Ellis	.10	.25
302 Reggie Williams	.10	.25
303 Otis Thorpe	.10	.25
304 B.J. Armstrong	.10	.25
305 Pete Chilcutt	.10	.25
306 Mario Elie	.10	.25
307 Antonio Davis	.10	.25
308 Ricky Pierce	.10	.25
309 Rodney Rogers	.10	.25
310 Brian Williams	.10	.25
311 Corie Blount	.10	.25
312 George Lynch	.10	.25
313 Alonzo Mourning	.20	.50
314 Lee Mayberry	.10	.25
315 Terry Porter	.10	.25
316 P.J. Brown	.10	.25
317 Hubert Davis	.10	.25
318 Charlie Ward	.10	.25
319 Jon Koncak	.10	.25
320 Derrick Coleman	.12	.30
321 Richard Dumas	.10	.25
322 Vernon Maxwell	.10	.25
323 Wayman Tisdale	.10	.25
324 Dontonio Wingfield	.10	.25
325 Tyrone Corbin	.10	.25
326 Bobby Hurley	.15	.40
327 Will Perdue	.10	.25
328 J.R. Reid	.10	.25
329 Hersey Hawkins	.10	.25
330 Sam Perkins	.10	.25
331 Adam Keefe	.10	.25
332 Chris Morris	.10	.25
333 Robert Pack	.10	.25
334 M.L. Carr CO	.10	.25
335 Pat Riley CO	.15	.40
336 Don Nelson CO	.12	.30
337 Brian Winters CO	.10	.25
338 Willie Anderson ET	.10	.25
339 Acie Earl ET	.10	.25
340 Jimmy King ET	.10	.25
341 Oliver Miller ET	.10	.25
342 Tracy Murray ET	.10	.25
343 Ed Pinckney ET	.10	.25
344 Alvin Robertson ET	.10	.25
345 Carlos Rogers ET	.10	.25
346 John Salley ET	.10	.25
347 Damon Stoudamire ET	.25	.60
348 Zan Tabak ET	.10	.25
349 Greg Anthony ET	.10	.25
350 Blue Edwards ET	.10	.25
351 Kenny Gattison ET	.10	.25
352 Antonio Harvey ET	.10	.25
353 Chris King ET	.10	.25
354 Darrick Martin ET	.10	.25
355 Lawrence Moten ET	.10	.25
356 Bryant Reeves ET	.10	.25
357 Byron Scott ET	.12	.30
358 Michael Jordan ES	1.25	3.00
359 Dikembe Mutombo ES	.15	.40
360 Grant Hill ES	.25	.60
361 Robert Horry ES	.12	.30
362 Alonzo Mourning ES	.20	.50
363 Vin Baker ES	.12	.30
364 Isaiah Rider ES	.15	.40
365 Charles Oakley ES	.12	.30
366 Shaquille O'Neal ES	.40	1.00
367 Jerry Stackhouse ES	.30	.75
368 Clarence Weatherspoon ES	.10	.25
369 Charles Barkley ES	.25	.60
370 Sean Elliott ES	.15	.40
371 Shawn Kemp ES	.15	.40
372 Chris Webber ES	.20	.50
373 Spud Webb RH	.15	.40
374 Muggsy Bogues RH	.12	.30
375 Toni Kukoc RH	.15	.40
376 Dennis Rodman RH	.30	.75
377 Jamal Mashburn RH	.15	.40
378 Jalen Rose RH	.20	.50
379 Clyde Drexler RH	.20	.50
380 Mark Jackson RH	.15	.40
381 Cedric Ceballos RH	.10	.25
382 Nick Van Exel RH	.15	.40
383 John Starks RH	.12	.30
384 Vernon Maxwell RH	.10	.25
385 Shawn Kemp RH	.15	.40
386 Gary Payton RH	.15	.40
387 Karl Malone RH	.20	.50
388 Mookie Blaylock WD	.10	.25
389 Muggsy Bogues WD	.12	.30
390 Jason Kidd WD	.25	.60
391 Tim Hardaway WD	.15	.40
392 Nick Van Exel WD	.15	.40
393 Kenny Anderson WD	.12	.30
394 Anfernee Hardaway WD	.25	.60
395 Rod Strickland WD	.10	.25
396 Avery Johnson WD	.12	.30
397 John Stockton WD	.20	.50
398 Grant Hill SPEC	.25	.60
399 Checklist (251-367)	.10	.25
400 Checklist (368-400/Ins.)	.10	.25
NNO Grant Hill Co-ROY Exchange	5.00	12.00
NNO Grant Hill Sweepstakes	.30	.75
NNO Grant Hill Tribute	10.00	25.00

1995-96 Hoops Block Party

Randomly inserted into all first series packs at an approximate rate of one in two packs, these 25 standard-size cards highlight the top shot-blockers in the NBA. The fronts have a full-color action photo with a multi-colored, computer-generated background and the words "Block Party" at the top in gold-foil. The backs have a color photo on the left side with a similar background to the front with player information and statistics on the right.

Card		
COMPLETE SET (25)	3.00	8.00
1 Oliver Miller	.20	.50
2 Dennis Rodman	.60	1.50
3 Scottie Pippen	.50	1.25
4 Dikembe Mutombo	.30	.75
5 Vlade Divac	.30	.75
6 Brian Grant	.25	.60
7 Alonzo Mourning	.40	1.00
8 Hakeem Olajuwon	.40	1.00
9 Patrick Ewing	.40	1.00
10 Shawn Kemp	.30	.75
11 Vin Baker	.25	.60
12 Horace Grant	.25	.60
13 Dale Davis	.20	.50
14 Juwan Howard	.30	.75
15 Eddie Jones	.40	1.00
16 Eric Montross	.20	.50
17 Tyrone Hill	.20	.50
18 Tom Gugliotta	.20	.50
19 Shawn Bradley	.20	.50
20 Dan Majerle	.30	.75
21 Loy Vaught	.20	.50
22 Donyell Marshall	.20	.50
23 Chris Webber	.40	1.00
24 Derrick Coleman	.25	.60
25 Walt Williams	.20	.50

1995-96 Hoops Grant Hill Dunks/Slams

Cards D1-D5 were randomly inserted exclusively into one in every 36 first series 12-card hobby packs, while cards S1-S5 were randomly inserted exclusively into one in every 36 first series retail 12-card packs. All cards are foil-coated, featuring an assortion of Grant Hill dunking and slamming photos. The fronts each carry an oversized letter, so that cards D1-D5 spell out "DUNK!!!," and cards S1-S5 spell out "SLAM!". All cards are designed to be viewed through special Grant Hill 3-D glasses which were available through an on-wrapper offer.

Card		
COMPLETE SET (10)	10.00	20.00
COMPLETE DUNKS SET (5)	5.00	12.00
COMPLETE SLAMS SET (5)	5.00	12.00
COMMON DUNK/SLAM (D1-D5)	1.50	4.00

1995-96 Hoops Grant's All-Rookies

Randomly inserted in all second series packs at a rate of one in 64, this 10-card standard-size set continues the tradition of the Magic's All-Rookies sets featured in earlier Hoops products. New spokesperson Grant Hill replaces Magic Johnson, picking 10 players who may follow in his own footsteps. Hill is pictured alongside the featured rookie on the horizontal fronts. The left side of the card contains a silver hologram strip with "Top 10" cut out to give the card a 3-D look when viewed with the Grant Hill 3-D glasses. Backs carry another full color cutout shot of the player set against the borderless color background. The "Top 10" logo is once again placed on the back. The player's name is printed across the top in gold and a player profile is printed in white. The set is sequenced in alphabetical order by team.

Card		
COMPLETE SET (10)	20.00	50.00
AR1 Cherokee Parks	1.25	3.00
AR2 Antonio McDyess	3.00	8.00
AR3 Theo Ratliff	2.00	5.00
AR4 Joe Smith	2.50	6.00
AR5 Shawn Respert	1.25	3.00
AR6 Kevin Garnett	10.00	25.00
AR7 Ed O'Bannon	1.25	3.00
AR8 Jerry Stackhouse	4.00	10.00
AR9 Damon Stoudamire	3.00	8.00
AR10 Rasheed Wallace	4.00	10.00

1995-96 Hoops HoopStars

Randomly inserted in all second series packs at a rate of one in 16, this 12-card standard-size set presents top players on multi-colored cards featuring color foils for the HoopStars logo and player name. The set is sequenced in alphabetical order by team.

Card		
COMPLETE SET (12)	6.00	15.00
HS1 Scottie Pippen	1.25	3.00
HS2 Jim Jackson	.50	1.25
HS3 Antonio McDyess	1.00	2.50
HS4 Clyde Drexler	1.00	2.50
HS5 Alonzo Mourning	1.00	2.50
HS6 Glenn Robinson	.75	2.00
HS7 Patrick Ewing	1.00	2.50
HS8 Anfernee Hardaway	1.25	3.00
HS9 Shawn Kemp	.75	2.00
HS10 Karl Malone	1.00	2.50
HS11 Juwan Howard	.75	2.00
HS12 Rasheed Wallace	1.25	3.00

1995-96 Hoops Hot List

Randomly inserted in second series hobby packs only at a rate of one in 32, this 10-card standard-size set features full-bleed fronts with a full-color player cutout set against a blue foil background. Player's name is printed vertically in copper foil on a purple foil strip. HOT is printed diagonally across the front. Backs feature a full-color action shot with the player's stats printed below the photo. The set is sequenced in alphabetical order by team.

Card		
COMPLETE SET (10)	15.00	40.00
1 Michael Jordan	10.00	25.00
2 Jason Kidd	2.00	5.00
3 Jamal Mashburn	1.25	3.00
4 Grant Hill	2.00	5.00
5 Joe Smith	1.25	3.00
6 Hakeem Olajuwon	1.50	4.00
7 Glenn Robinson	1.25	3.00
8 Shaquille O'Neal	4.00	10.00
9 Jerry Stackhouse	2.00	5.00
10 David Robinson	2.00	5.00

1995-96 Hoops Number Crunchers

Randomly inserted into all first series packs at an approximate rate of one in two packs, these 25 standard-size cards highlight players that attained notable statistical achievements during the 1994-95 season. The fronts have a color-action photo with the player's number in a multi-color background and the word "Crunchers" spelled out on a tic-tac-toe board in the lower left corner in gold-foil. The backs have a color-action photo with a huge multi-colored ball in the background along with player information and statistics.

Card		
COMPLETE SET (25)	4.00	10.00
1 Michael Jordan	2.00	5.00
2 Shaquille O'Neal	.60	1.50
3 Grant Hill	.40	1.00
4 Detlef Schrempf	.25	.60
5 Kenny Anderson	.20	.50
6 Anfernee Hardaway	.40	1.00
7 Latrell Sprewell	.25	.60
8 Jamal Mashburn	.25	.60
9 Nick Van Exel	.25	.60
10 Charles Barkley	.40	1.00
11 Mitch Richmond	.25	.60
12 David Robinson	.40	1.00
13 Gary Payton	.25	.60
14 Rod Strickland	.15	.40
15 Glenn Robinson	.25	.60
16 Reggie Miller	.30	.75
17 Karl Malone	.30	.75
18 Jim Jackson	.15	.40
19 Clyde Drexler	.30	.75
20 Glen Rice	.25	.60
21 Isaiah Rider	.25	.60
22 Cedric Ceballos	.15	.40
23 John Stockton	.30	.75
24 Jason Kidd	.40	1.00
25 Mookie Blaylock	.15	.40

1995-96 Hoops Power Palette

Randomly inserted in second series retail packs only at a rate of one in 32, this 10-card set is a parallel version of the Hoops SkyView insert. Unlike the acetate-centered SkyView cards, the more common Power Palette's feature metallic foil backgrounds.

Card		
COMPLETE SET (10)	20.00	50.00
1 Michael Jordan	10.00	25.00
2 Jason Kidd	2.00	5.00
3 Grant Hill	2.00	5.00
4 Joe Smith	1.25	3.00
5 Hakeem Olajuwon	1.50	4.00
6 Glenn Robinson	1.25	3.00
7 Anfernee Hardaway	2.00	5.00
8 Shaquille O'Neal	3.00	8.00
9 Jerry Stackhouse	2.00	5.00
10 Charles Barkley	2.00	5.00

1995-96 Hoops SkyView

Randomly inserted in all second series packs at a rate of one in 480, cards from this 10-card standard-size set are extra-thick and replace two basic issue cards in the pack. The front of the card presents a die-cut action photo over a multi-color plastic acetate window. The set is sequenced in alphabetical order by team.

Card		
COMPLETE SET (10)	125.00	250.00
SV1 Michael Jordan	100.00	200.00
SV2 Jason Kidd	10.00	25.00
SV3 Grant Hill	10.00	25.00
SV4 Joe Smith	5.00	12.00
SV5 Hakeem Olajuwon	8.00	20.00
SV6 Glenn Robinson	6.00	15.00
SV7 Anfernee Hardaway	10.00	25.00
SV8 Shaquille O'Neal	15.00	40.00
SV9 Jerry Stackhouse	8.00	20.00
SV10 Charles Barkley	10.00	25.00

1995-96 Hoops Slamland

Inserted into all second series packs at a rate of one per pack, cards from this 50-card standard-size set showcase top stars printed over one of five different animated "Slamland" backgrounds. The card fronts feature the player's name, area of expertise and a distinctive foil-stamped Slamland designation. The set is sequenced in alphabetical order by team.

Card		
COMPLETE SET (50)	3.00	8.00
SL1 Stacey Augmon	.12	.30
SL2 Steve Smith	.12	.30
SL3 Eric Montross	.10	.25
SL4 Dino Radja	.12	.30
SL5 Dell Curry	.10	.25
SL6 Larry Johnson	.15	.40
SL7 Scottie Pippen	.25	.60
SL8 Dennis Rodman	.30	.75
SL9 Tyrone Hill	.10	.25
SL10 Jim Jackson	.10	.25
SL11 Jamal Mashburn	.15	.40
SL12 Dikembe Mutombo	.15	.40
SL13 Joe Dumars	.15	.40
SL14 Grant Hill	.25	.60
SL15 Allan Houston	.12	.30
SL16 Donyell Marshall	.10	.25
SL17 Latrell Sprewell	.15	.40
SL18 Sam Cassell	.15	.40
SL19 Hakeem Olajuwon	.20	.50
SL20 Reggie Miller	.20	.50
SL21 Loy Vaught	.10	.25
SL22 Vlade Divac	.15	.40
SL23 Eddie Jones	.20	.50
SL24 Alonzo Mourning	.20	.50
SL25 Kevin Willis	.10	.25
SL26 Vin Baker	.12	.30
SL27 Glenn Robinson	.15	.40
SL28 Tom Gugliotta	.10	.25
SL29 Kenny Anderson	.12	.30
SL30 Derrick Coleman	.12	.30
SL31 Patrick Ewing	.20	.50
SL32 John Starks	.12	.30
SL33 Dennis Scott	.10	.25
SL34 Jerry Stackhouse	.50	1.25
SL35 Charles Barkley	.25	.60
SL36 Kevin Johnson	.15	.40
SL37 Danny Manning	.12	.30
SL38 Clifford Robinson	.10	.25
SL39 Brian Grant	.12	.30
SL40 Mitch Richmond	.15	.40
SL41 Walt Williams	.10	.25
SL42 David Robinson	.25	.60
SL43 Gary Payton	.15	.40
SL44 Detlef Schrempf	.15	.40
SL45 Damon Stoudamire	.40	1.00
SL46 Karl Malone	.20	.50
SL47 John Stockton	.20	.50
SL48 Bryant Reeves	.15	.40
SL49 Juwan Howard	.15	.40
SL50 Chris Webber	.20	.50

1995-96 Hoops Top Ten

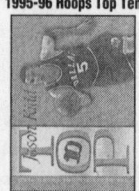

Randomly inserted into all first series packs at an approximate rate of one in 12, these 10 standard-size cards feature a selection of former lottery picks that are on their way to or have already attained great success in the NBA. The fronts are laid out horizontally with a color-action photo and a wide strip down the left side that reads "Top" with 10 in the middle of the O. The background on each card is different and has a multi-colored cloudy look. The backs have the same background as the front with a color-action photo and player information at the top.

Card		
COMPLETE SET (10)	10.00	25.00
AR1 Shaquille O'Neal	2.00	5.00
AR2 Grant Hill	1.25	3.00
AR3 Chris Webber	1.00	2.50
AR4 Jamal Mashburn	.75	2.00
AR5 Anfernee Hardaway	1.25	3.00
AR6 Alonzo Mourning	1.00	2.50
AR7 Michael Jordan	6.00	15.00
AR8 Charles Barkley	1.25	3.00
AR9 Glenn Robinson	.75	2.00
AR10 Jason Kidd	1.25	3.00

1996-97 Hoops

The 1996-97 Hoops set was issued in two series. The first series had a total of 200 cards, while the second series contained 150. Both series had 9-card packs that carried a suggested retail price of $1.29 each. Card fronts contain a full bleed action shot with the player's name written in gold foil diagonally across the bottom right. Card backs have a small photo of the player in the top left corner with complete college and pro statistics as well as biographical information. The cards are grouped alphabetically within team order. Some Rookie Cards that were included in the second series were Shareef Abdur-Rahim, Kobe Bryant, Marcus Camby, Allen Iverson, Stephon Marbury and Antoine Walker. Also, a Grant Hill Z-Force Preview card was randomly inserted into series one packs at a rate of one in 360 packs. It previewed the inaugural edition of SkyBox Z-Force. A non-numbered two-card promo sheet was also issued which featured a regular issue Grant Hill card and a HIPnotized Jerry Stackhouse.

Card		
COMPLETE SET (350)	17.50	35.00
COMPLETE SERIES 1 (200)	7.50	15.00
COMPLETE SERIES 2 (150)	10.00	20.00
1 Stacey Augmon	.12	.30
2 Mookie Blaylock	.10	.25
3 Alan Henderson	.10	.25
4 Christian Laettner	.12	.30
5 Grant Long	.10	.25
6 Steve Smith	.12	.30
7 Dana Barros	.10	.25
8 Todd Day	.10	.25
9 Rick Fox	.10	.25
10 Eric Montross	.10	.25
11 Dino Radja	.12	.30
12 Eric Williams	.10	.25
13 Kenny Anderson	.12	.30
14 Scott Burrell	.10	.25
15 Dell Curry	.10	.25
16 Matt Geiger	.10	.25
17 Larry Johnson	.15	.40
18 Glen Rice	.15	.40
19 Ron Harper	.12	.30
20 Michael Jordan	1.25	3.00
21 Steve Kerr	.12	.30
22 Toni Kukoc	.15	.40
23 Luc Longley	.10	.25
24 Scottie Pippen	.25	.60
25 Dennis Rodman	.30	.75
26 Terrell Brandon	.10	.25
27 Danny Ferry	.10	.25
28 Tyrone Hill	.10	.25
29 Chris Mills	.10	.25
30 Bobby Phills	.10	.25
31 Bob Sura	.10	.25
32 Tony Dumas	.10	.25
33 Jim Jackson	.10	.25
34 Popeye Jones	.10	.25
35 Jason Kidd	.25	.60
36 Jamal Mashburn	.12	.30
37 George McCloud	.10	.25
38 Cherokee Parks	.10	.25
39 Mahmoud Abdul-Rauf	.10	.25
40 LaPhonso Ellis	.10	.25
41 Antonio McDyess	.15	.40
42 Dikembe Mutombo	.15	.40
43 Jalen Rose	.12	.30
44 Bryant Stith	.10	.25
45 Joe Dumars	.15	.40
46 Grant Hill	.25	.60
47 Allan Houston	.12	.30
48 Lindsey Hunter	.10	.25
49 Terry Mills	.10	.25
50 Theo Ratliff	.10	.25
51 Otis Thorpe	.10	.25
52 B.J. Armstrong	.10	.25
53 Donyell Marshall	.10	.25
54 Chris Mullin	.15	.40
55 Joe Smith	.12	.30
56 Rony Seikaly	.12	.30
57 Latrell Sprewell	.15	.40
58 Mark Bryant	.10	.25
59 Sam Cassell	.12	.30
60 Clyde Drexler	.20	.50
61 Mario Elie	.10	.25
62 Robert Horry	.12	.30
63 Hakeem Olajuwon	.20	.50
64 Travis Best	.10	.25
65 Antonio Davis	.10	.25
66 Mark Jackson	.15	.40
67 Derrick McKey	.10	.25
68 Reggie Miller	.20	.50
69 Rik Smits	.12	.30
70 Brent Barry	.12	.30
71 Terry Dehere	.10	.25
72 Pooh Richardson	.10	.25
73 Rodney Rogers	.10	.25
74 Loy Vaught	.10	.25
75 Brian Williams	.10	.25
76 Elden Campbell	.10	.25
77 Cedric Ceballos	.10	.25
78 Vlade Divac	.15	.40
79 Eddie Jones	.15	.40
80 Anthony Peeler	.10	.25
81 Nick Van Exel	.15	.40
82 Sasha Danilovic	.10	.25
83 Tim Hardaway	.15	.40
84 Alonzo Mourning	.20	.50
85 Kurt Thomas	.10	.25
86 Walt Williams	.10	.25
87 Vin Baker	.12	.30
88 Sherman Douglas	.10	.25
89 Johnny Newman	.10	.25
90 Shawn Respert	.10	.25
91 Glenn Robinson	.15	.40
92 Kevin Garnett	.40	1.00
93 Tom Gugliotta	.10	.25
94 Andrew Lang	.10	.25
95 Sam Mitchell	.10	.25
96 Isaiah Rider	.12	.30
97 Shawn Bradley	.10	.25
98 P.J. Brown	.10	.25
99 Chris Childs	.10	.25
100 Armon Gilliam	.10	.25
101 Ed O'Bannon	.10	.25
102 Jayson Williams	.10	.25
103 Hubert Davis	.10	.25
104 Patrick Ewing	.20	.50
105 Anthony Mason	.10	.25
106 Charles Oakley	.12	.30
107 John Starks	.12	.30
108 Charlie Ward	.10	.25
109 Nick Anderson	.10	.25
110 Horace Grant	.12	.30
111 Anfernee Hardaway	.25	.60
112 Shaquille O'Neal	.40	1.00
113 Dennis Scott	.10	.25
114 Brian Shaw	.10	.25
115 Derrick Coleman	.12	.30
116 Vernon Maxwell	.10	.25
117 Trevor Ruffin	.10	.25
118 Jerry Stackhouse	.20	.50
119 Clarence Weatherspoon	.10	.25
120 Charles Barkley	.25	.60
121 Michael Finley	.20	.50
122 A.C. Green	.15	.40
123 Kevin Johnson	.15	.40
124 Danny Manning	.12	.30
125 Wesley Person	.10	.25
126 John Williams	.10	.25
127 Harvey Grant	.10	.25
128 Aaron McKie	.10	.25
129 Clifford Robinson	.10	.25
130 Arvydas Sabonis	.12	.30
131 Rod Strickland	.10	.25
132 Gary Trent	.10	.25
133 Tyus Edney	.10	.25
134 Brian Grant	.12	.30
135 Billy Owens	.10	.25
136 Olden Polynice	.10	.25
137 Mitch Richmond	.15	.40
138 Corliss Williamson	.10	.25
139 Vinny Del Negro	.10	.25
140 Sean Elliott	.15	.40
141 Avery Johnson	.12	.30
142 Chuck Person	.12	.30
143 David Robinson	.25	.60
144 Charles Smith	.10	.25
145 Sherrell Ford	.10	.25
146 Hersey Hawkins	.10	.25
147 Shawn Kemp	.15	.40
148 Nate McMillan	.10	.25
149 Gary Payton	.15	.40
150 Detlef Schrempf	.15	.40
151 Oliver Miller	.10	.25
152 Tracy Murray	.10	.25
153 Carlos Rogers	.10	.25
154 Damon Stoudamire	.15	.40
155 Zan Tabak	.10	.25
156 Sharone Wright	.10	.25
157 Antoine Carr	.10	.25
158 Jeff Hornacek	.12	.30
159 Adam Keefe	.10	.25
160 Karl Malone	.20	.50
161 Chris Morris	.10	.25
162 John Stockton	.20	.50
163 Greg Anthony	.10	.25
164 Blue Edwards	.10	.25
165 Chris King	.10	.25
166 Lawrence Moten	.10	.25
167 Bryant Reeves	.10	.25
168 Byron Scott	.12	.30
169 Calbert Cheaney	.10	.25
170 Juwan Howard	.12	.30
171 Tim Legler	.10	.25
172 Gheorghe Muresan	.10	.25
173 Rasheed Wallace	.20	.50
174 Chris Webber	.20	.50
175 Steve Smith BF	.12	.30
176 Michael Jordan BF	1.25	3.00
177 Scottie Pippen BF	.25	.60
178 Dennis Rodman BF	.30	
179 Allan Houston BF	.12	
180 Hakeem Olajuwon BF	.20	
181 Patrick Ewing BF	.20	
182 Anfernee Hardaway BF	.25	
183 Shaquille O'Neal BF	.40	
184 Charles Barkley BF	.25	
185 Arvydas Sabonis BF	.12	
186 David Robinson BF	.25	
187 Shawn Kemp BF	.15	
188 Gary Payton BF	.15	
189 Karl Malone BF	.20	
190 Kenny Anderson PLA	.12	
191 Toni Kukoc PLA	.15	
192 Brent Barry PLA	.12	
193 Cedric Ceballos PLA	.10	
194 Shawn Bradley PLA	.10	
195 Charles Oakley PLA	.12	
196 Dennis Scott PLA	.10	
197 Clifford Robinson PLA	.10	
198 Mitch Richmond PLA	.15	
199 Checklist	.10	
200 Checklist	.10	
201 Dikembe Mutombo	.15	
202 Dee Brown	.10	
203 David Wesley	.10	
204 Vlade Divac	.15	
205 Anthony Mason	.10	
206 Chris Gatling	.10	
207 Eric Montross	.10	
208 Ervin Johnson	.10	
209 Stacey Augmon	.12	
210 Joe Dumars	.15	
211 Grant Hill	.25	
212 Charles Barkley	.25	
213 Jalen Rose	.12	
214 Lamond Murray	.10	
215 Shaquille O'Neal	.40	
216 P.J. Brown	.15	
217 Dan Majerle	.15	
218 Armon Gilliam	.10	
219 Andrew Lang	.10	
220 Kevin Garnett	.40	
221 Tom Gugliotta	.10	
222 Cherokee Parks	.10	
223 Doug West	.10	
224 Kendall Gill	.10	
225 Robert Pack	.10	
226 Allan Houston	.12	
227 Larry Johnson	.15	
228 Rony Seikaly	.12	
229 Gerald Wilkins	.10	
230 Michael Cage	.10	
231 Lucious Harris	.10	
232 Sam Cassell	.12	
233 Robert Horry	.12	
234 Kenny Anderson	.12	
235 Isaiah Rider	.12	
236 Rasheed Wallace	.20	
237 Mahmoud Abdul-Rauf	.10	
238 Vernon Maxwell	.10	
239 Dominique Wilkins	.20	
240 Jim McIlvaine	.10	
241 Hubert Davis	.10	
242 Popeye Jones	.10	
243 Walt Williams	.10	
244 Karl Malone	.20	
245 John Stockton	.20	
246 Anthony Peeler	.10	
247 Tracy Murray	.10	
248 Rod Strickland	.10	
249 Lenny Wilkens CO	.15	
250 M.L. Carr CO	.15	
251 Dave Cowens CO	.15	
252 Phil Jackson CO	.15	
253 Mike Fratello CO	.15	
254 Jim Cleamons CO	.15	
255 Dick Motta CO	.15	
256 Doug Collins CO	.15	
257 Rick Adelman CO	.15	
258 Rudy Tomjanovich CO	.15	
259 Larry Brown CO	.15	
260 Bill Fitch CO	.15	
261 Del Harris CO	.15	
262 Pat Riley CO	.15	
263 Chris Ford CO	.15	
264 Flip Saunders CO	.15	
265 John Calipari CO	.15	
266 Jeff Van Gundy CO	.15	
267 Brian Hill CO	.15	
268 Johnny Davis CO	.15	
269 Danny Ainge CO	.15	
270 P.J. Carlesimo CO	.15	
271 Garry St. Jean CO	.15	
272 Bob Hill CO	.15	
273 George Karl CO	.15	
274 Darrell Walker CO	.15	
275 Jerry Sloan CO	.15	
276 Brian Winters CO	.15	
277 Jim Lynam CO	.15	
278 Shareef Abdur-Rahim RC	.30	
279 Ray Allen RC	.60	
280 Shandon Anderson RC	.15	
281 Kobe Bryant RC	4.00	
282 Marcus Camby RC	.25	
283 Erick Dampier RC	.15	
284 Emanual Davis RC	.15	
285 Tony Delk RC	.15	
286 Brian Evans RC	.15	
287 Derek Fisher RC	.30	
288 Todd Fuller RC	.15	
289 Dean Garrett RC	.15	
290 Reggie Geary RC	.15	
291 Darvin Ham RC	.15	
292 Othella Harrington RC	.15	
293 Shane Heal RC	.15	
294 Mark Hendrickson RC	.15	
295 Allen Iverson RC	.75	
296 Dontae' Jones RC	.15	
297 Kerry Kittles RC	.15	
298 Priest Lauderdale RC	.15	
299 Matt Maloney RC	.15	
300 Stephon Marbury RC	.40	
301 Walter McCarty RC	.15	
302 Jeff McInnis RC	.15	
303 Martin Muursepp RC	.15	
304 Steve Nash RC	.75	
305 Moochie Norris RC	.15	
306 Jermaine O'Neal RC	.40	
307 Vitaly Potapenko RC	.15	
308 Virginius Praskevicius RC	.15	
309 Roy Rogers RC	.15	
310 Malik Rose RC	.20	
311 James Scott RC	.15	
312 Antoine Walker RC	.30	
313 Samaki Walker RC	.15	
314 Ben Wallace RC	.75	
315 John Wallace RC	.15	

Jerome Williams RC .15 .40
Lorenzen Wright RC .15 .40
Charles Barkley ST .25 .60
Derrick Coleman ST .12 .30
Michael Finley ST .20 .50
Stephon Marbury ST .20 .50
Reggie Miller ST .20 .50
Alonzo Mourning ST .20 .50
Shaquille O'Neal ST .40 1.00
Gary Payton ST .15 .40
Dennis Rodman ST .30 .75
Damon Stoudamire ST .15 .40
Vin Baker CBG .12 .30
Clyde Drexler CBG .20 .50
Patrick Ewing CBG .20 .50
Anfernee Hardaway CBG .25 .60
Grant Hill CBG .25 .60
Juwan Howard CBG .12 .30
Larry Johnson CBG .15 .40
Michael Jordan CBG 1.25 3.00
Shawn Kemp CBG .15 .40
Jason Kidd CBG .25 .60
Karl Malone CBG .20 .50
Reggie Miller CBG .20 .50
Hakeem Olajuwon CBG .20 .50
Scottie Pippen CBG .25 .60
Mitch Richmond CBG .15 .40
David Robinson CBG UER .25 .60
ck David Robinison
Dennis Rodman CBG .30 .75
Joe Smith CBG .12 .30
Jerry Stackhouse CBG .20 .50
John Stockton CBG .20 .50
Jerry Stackhouse BG .20 .50
Checklist (201-350/inserts) .10 .25
Checklist (inserts) .10 .25
Grant Hill 1.00 2.50
rry Stackhouse PROMO
) Grant Hill 4.00 10.00
Force Preview

1996-97 Hoops Silver

rted at a rate of two per special retail box and one special retail pack, this set is a semi-parallel of the -card basic set even though the actual number of s in the Silver set is 98. Card fronts are identical to regular issue except they have the player's name in r foil rather than gold. To ascertain values on vidual cards, please refer to the multiplier in the er, coupled with the value of the base card.

MPLETE SET (98) 25.00 50.00
ER: 1.5X TO 4X BASE CARD HI

1996-97 Hoops Fly With

domly inserted in series two retail packs only at a of one in 24, this 10-card set focuses on the high- g acrobats of ten NBA players. Cards feature clear tic stock and a cloud background on the fronts.

MPLETE SET (10) 10.00 25.00
harles Barkley 2.50 6.00
wan Howard 1.25 3.00
son Kidd 2.50 6.00
onzo Mourning 2.00 5.00
ry Payton 1.50 4.00
vid Robinson 2.50 6.00
nnis Rodman 3.00 8.00
e Smith 1.25 3.00
rry Stackhouse 2.00 5.00
amon Stoudamire 1.50 4.00

1996-97 Hoops Grant's All-Rookies

domly inserted in all series two packs at a rate of e in 360, this 11-card set features the SkyView nology as Grant Hill selects his picks for the best kies from the 1996-97 class. Despite no serial bering, the stated print run for the set was 996 of h card.

MPLETE SET (11) 150.00 300.00
hareef Abdur-Rahim 8.00 20.00
ay Allen 15.00 40.00
obe Bryant 80.00 200.00
arcus Camby 6.00 15.00
rant Hill 12.00 30.00
llen Iverson 20.00 50.00
erry Kittles 4.00 10.00
tephon Marbury 10.00 25.00
ntoine Walker 8.00 20.00
Samaki Walker 4.00 10.00
orenzen Wright 4.00 10.00

1996-97 Hoops Head to Head

domly inserted at a rate of one in 24 packs, this 10- d set features dual-player cards of either teammates young players. Card fronts contain action photos of h players and the logo "Head to Head" in gold foil at bottom of the card. In addition, the logo and both of player's first names are treated with a diamond-like ment. Card backs are divided into four quadrants two of them featuring action shots and the other featuring a brief commentary on each player. Card ks are numbered with a "HH" prefix.

MPLETE SET (10) 10.00 25.00
1 Larry Johnson .75 2.00
len Rice
2 Michael Jordan 6.00 15.00
cottie Pippen
3 Jason Kidd 1.25 3.00
rant Hill
4 Clyde Drexler 1.00 2.50
akeem Olajuwon
5 Vin Baker .75 2.00
lenn Robinson
6 Anfernee Hardaway 2.00 5.00
haquille O'Neal
7 Antonio McDyess 1.00 2.50
rry Stackhouse
8 Sean Elliott 1.25 3.00
avid Robinson
9 Joe Smith .75 2.00
amon Stoudamire
0 Karl Malone 1.00 2.50
hn Stockton

1996-97 Hoops HIPnotized

Randomly inserted at a rate of one in four packs, this 20-card set features some of the top players in the game. Card fronts are full bleed action shots with a swirling background. The logo "HIPnotized" and the player's last name are in gold foil. Card backs are horizontal with statistical and biographical information as well as a having a brief commentary next to the photo. Cards are numbered with a "H" prefix.

COMPLETE SET (20) 5.00 12.00
H1 Steve Smith .40 1.00
H2 Dana Barros .30 .75
H3 Larry Johnson .50 1.25
H4 Dennis Rodman 1.00 2.50
H5 Terrell Brandon .30 .75
H6 Jason Kidd .75 2.00
H7 Grant Hill .75 2.00
H8 Clyde Drexler .60 1.50
H9 Reggie Miller .60 1.50
H10 Alonzo Mourning .60 1.50
H11 Glenn Robinson .50 1.25
H12 Patrick Ewing .60 1.50
H13 Shaquille O'Neal 1.25 3.00
H14 Jerry Stackhouse .60 1.50
H15 Charles Barkley .75 2.00
H16 Clifford Robinson .30 .75
H17 Mitch Richmond .50 1.25
H18 David Robinson .75 2.00
H19 Gary Payton .50 1.25
H20 Juwan Howard .40 1.00

1996-97 Hoops Hot List

Randomly inserted in series two hobby packs only at a rate of one in 48, this 20-card set features a flamed front on clear plastic stock.

COMPLETE SET (20) 75.00 150.00
1 Vin Baker 2.00 5.00
2 Patrick Ewing 3.00 8.00
3 Michael Finley 3.00 8.00
4 Kevin Garnett 6.00 15.00
5 Anfernee Hardaway 4.00 10.00
6 Grant Hill 4.00 10.00
7 Allan Houston 2.00 5.00
8 Michael Jordan 25.00 60.00
9 Shawn Kemp 2.50 6.00
10 Christian Laettner 2.00 5.00
11 Karl Malone 3.00 8.00
12 Antonio McDyess 2.50 6.00
13 Reggie Miller 3.00 8.00
14 Hakeem Olajuwon 3.00 8.00
15 Shaquille O'Neal 8.00 20.00
16 Scottie Pippen 4.00 10.00
17 Mitch Richmond 2.50 6.00
18 Isaiah Rider 2.00 5.00
19 Rod Strickland 1.50 4.00
20 Chris Webber 3.00 8.00

1996-97 Hoops Rookie Headliners

Randomly inserted at a rate of one in 72 hobby packs, this 10-card set focuses on some of the best rookies from the 1995-96 class. Card fronts are designed similar to a game ticket with both the left and right borders in gold foil. The action shot of the player is located between the two borders and the player's last name is in gold foil on top of the photo. Card backs have a shot of the player in the middle of the card against a light gold background along with a brief commentary on the player. The player's rookie statistics are located along the left border. Card backs are numbered as "X of 10".

COMPLETE SET (10) 15.00 40.00
1 Antonio McDyess 2.50 6.00
2 Joe Smith 2.00 5.00
3 Brent Barry 2.00 5.00
4 Kevin Garnett 6.00 15.00
5 Jerry Stackhouse 3.00 8.00
6 Michael Finley 3.00 8.00
7 Arvydas Sabonis 2.00 5.00
8 Tyus Edney 1.50 4.00
9 Damon Stoudamire 2.50 6.00
10 Bryant Reeves 1.50 4.00

1996-97 Hoops Rookies

Randomly inserted in all series two packs at one in six, this 30-card set focuses on the season's best first year players. Card fronts carry a gold foiled background.

COMPLETE SET (30) 20.00 40.00
1 Shareef Abdur-Rahim 1.25 3.00
2 Ray Allen 2.50 6.00
3 Kobe Bryant 8.00 20.00
4 Marcus Camby 1.00 2.50
5 Erick Dampier .60 1.50
6 Emanual Davis .60 1.50
7 Tony Delk .60 1.50
8 Brian Evans .60 1.50
9 Derek Fisher 1.25 3.00
10 Todd Fuller .60 1.50
11 Othella Harrington .60 1.50
12 Allen Iverson 3.00 8.00
13 Dontae' Jones .60 1.50
14 Kerry Kittles .60 1.50
15 Priest Lauderdale .60 1.50
16 Matt Maloney .60 1.50
17 Stephon Marbury 1.50 4.00
18 Walter McCarty .60 1.50
19 Jeff McInnis .60 1.50
20 Martin Muursepp .60 1.50
21 Steve Nash 3.00 8.00
22 Moochie Norris .60 1.50
23 Jermaine O'Neal 1.50 4.00
24 Vitaly Potapenko .60 1.50
25 Roy Rogers .60 1.50
26 Antoine Walker 1.25 3.00
27 Samaki Walker .60 1.50
28 John Wallace .60 1.50
29 Jerome Williams .60 1.50
30 Lorenzen Wright .60 1.50

1996-97 Hoops Starting Five

Randomly inserted in all series two packs at one in 12, this 29-card set features each team's starting five. Card fronts feature a full shot of the team's primary player with the other four starters in gold boxes at the bottom of the card.

COMPLETE SET (29) 15.00 30.00
1 Mookie Blaylock .60 1.50
Christian Laettner
Dikembe Mutombo
Ken Norman
Steve Smith
Atlanta Hawks
2 Dana Barros .50 1.25
Dee Brown
Todd Day
Rick Fox
Dino Radja
Boston Celtics
3 Tyrone Bogues .60 1.50
Dell Curry
Vlade Divac
Anthony Mason
Glen Rice
Charlotte Hornets
4 Michael Jordan 5.00 12.00
Toni Kukoc
Luc Longley
Scottie Pippen
Dennis Rodman
Chicago Bulls
5 Terrell Brandon .60 1.50
Tyrone Hill
Chris Mills
Bobby Phills
Vitaly Potapenko
Cleveland Cavaliers
6 Chris Gatling 1.00 2.50
Jim Jackson
Jason Kidd
Jamal Mashburn
Oliver Miller
Dallas Mavericks
7 LaPhonso Ellis .60 1.50
Mark Jackson
Ervin Johnson
Antonio McDyess
Bryant Stith
Denver Nuggets
8 Stacey Augmon 1.00 2.50
Joe Dumars
Grant Hill
Lindsey Hunter
Otis Thorpe
Detroit Pistons
9 Chris Mullin .60 1.50
Mark Price
Felton Spencer
Joe Smith
Latrell Sprewell
Golden State Warriors
10 Charles Barkley 1.00 2.50
Clyde Drexler
Hakeem Olajuwon
Brent Price
Kevin Willis
Houston Rockets
11 Dale Davis .75 2.00
Duane Ferrell
Reggie Miller
Jalen Rose
Rik Smits
Indiana Pacers
12 Terry Dehere .40 1.00
Bo Outlaw
Pooh Richardson
Rodney Rogers
Loy Vaught
Los Angeles Clippers
13 Elden Campbell 1.50 4.00
Cedric Ceballos
Eddie Jones
Shaquille O'Neal
Nick Van Exel
Los Angeles Lakers
14 P.J. Brown .75 2.00
Tim Hardaway
Dan Majerle
Alonzo Mourning
Kurt Thomas
Miami Heat
15 Ray Allen 1.25 3.00
Vin Baker
Sherman Douglas
Andrew Lang
Glenn Robinson
Milwaukee Bucks
16 Kevin Garnett .75 2.00
Tom Gugliotta
Stephon Marbury
Cherokee Parks
James Robinson
Minnesota Timberwolves
17 Shawn Bradley .40 1.00
Kendall Gill
Ed O'Bannon
Khalid Reeves
Jayson Williams
New Jersey Nets
18 Patrick Ewing .75 2.00
Allan Houston
Larry Johnson
Charles Oakley
John Starks
New York Knicks
19 Nick Anderson 1.00 2.50
Horace Grant
Anfernee Hardaway
Dennis Scott
Rony Seikaly
Orlando Magic
20 Michael Cage 1.50 4.00
Derrick Coleman
Allen Iverson
Jerry Stackhouse
Clarence Weatherspoon
Philadelphia 76ers
21 Sam Cassell .75 2.00
Michael Finley
Robert Horry
Kevin Johnson
Danny Manning
Phoenix Suns
22 Kenny Anderson .75 2.00
Isaiah Rider
Clifford Robinson
Arvydas Sabonis
Rasheed Wallace
Portland Trail Blazers
23 Mahmoud Abdul-Rauf .60 1.50
Brian Grant
Billy Owens
Olden Polynice
Mitch Richmond
Sacramento Kings
24 Avery Johnson 1.00 2.50
Vernon Maxwell
David Robinson
Charles Smith
Dominique Wilkins
San Antonio Spurs
25 Hersey Hawkins .60 1.50
Shawn Kemp
Gary Payton
Sam Perkins
Detlef Schrempf
Seattle Supersonics
26 Marcus Camby 1.00 2.50
Hubert Davis
Popeye Jones
Damon Stoudamire
Walt Williams
Toronto Raptors
27 Jeff Hornacek .75 2.00
Adam Keefe
Karl Malone
Greg Ostertag
John Stockton
Utah Jazz
28 Shareef Abdur-Rahim .60 1.50
George Lynch
Lee Mayberry
Anthony Peeler
Bryant Reeves
Vancouver Grizzlies
29 Calbert Cheaney .75 2.00
Juwan Howard
Gheorghe Muresan
Rod Strickland
Chris Webber
Washington Bullets

1996-97 Hoops Superfeats

Randomly inserted at a rate of one in 36 retail packs, this 10-card set features players who had super "feats" during the 1995-96 NBA season. Card fronts feature a colorful background with a full color action shot of the player on top. The player's name and the logo "Superfeats" are treated with gold foil. Card backs feature another action shot of the player and a brief commentary on the extraordinary achievements the player had the previous season. Card backs are also numbered as "X of 10".

COMPLETE SET (10) 20.00 50.00
1 Michael Jordan 15.00 40.00
2 Jason Kidd 3.00 8.00
3 Grant Hill 3.00 8.00
4 Hakeem Olajuwon 2.50 6.00
5 Alonzo Mourning 2.50 6.00
6 Anthony Mason 1.25 3.00
7 Anfernee Hardaway 3.00 8.00
8 Jerry Stackhouse 2.50 6.00
9 Shawn Kemp 2.00 5.00
10 Damon Stoudamire 2.00 5.00

1997-98 Hoops

The 1997-98 Hoops set was released in two series, with each 165-card series distributed in 10-card packs with a suggested retail price of $.99. Card fronts feature color player images on computer graphic treatment backgrounds. The set includes the League Leaders subset (1-8) and two checklist cards (164-165). The backs carry player information and statistics. A Grant Hill promo card was issued to preview the product. It is priced below.

COMPLETE SET (330) 15.00 40.00
COMPLETE SERIES 1 (165) 6.00 15.00
COMPLETE SERIES 2 (165) 10.00 25.00
1 Michael Jordan LL .60 1.50
2 Dennis Rodman LL .15 .40
3 Mark Jackson LL .07 .20
4 Shawn Bradley LL .05 .15
5 Glen Rice LL .07 .20
6 Mookie Blaylock LL .05 .15
7 Gheorghe Muresan LL .05 .15
8 Mark Price LL .07 .20
9 Tyrone Corbin .10 .25
10 Christian Laettner .12 .30
11 Priest Lauderdale .10 .25
12 Dikembe Mutombo .15 .40
13 Steve Smith .12 .30
14 Todd Day .10 .25
15 Rick Fox .10 .25
16 Brett Szabo .10 .25
17 Antoine Walker .15 .40
18 David Wesley .10 .25
19 Muggsy Bogues .12 .30
20 Dell Curry .10 .25
21 Tony Delk .10 .25
22 Anthony Mason .12 .30
23 Glen Rice .15 .40
24 Malik Rose .10 .25
25 Steve Kerr .12 .30
26 Toni Kukoc .15 .40
27 Luc Longley .10 .25
28 Robert Parish .15 .40
29 Scottie Pippen .25 .60
30 Dennis Rodman .30 .75
31 Terrell Brandon .12 .30
32 Danny Ferry .10 .25
33 Tyrone Hill .10 .25
34 Bobby Phills .10 .25
35 Vitaly Potapenko .10 .25
36 Shawn Bradley .10 .25
37 Sasha Danilovic .10 .25
38 Derek Harper .12 .30
39 Martin Muursepp .10 .25
40 Robert Pack .10 .25
41 Khalid Reeves .10 .25
42 Vincent Askew .10 .25
43 Dale Ellis .10 .25
44 LaPhonso Ellis .10 .25
45 Antonio McDyess .12 .30
46 Bryant Stith .10 .25
47 Joe Dumars .15 .40
48 Grant Hill .25 .60
49 Lindsey Hunter .10 .25
50 Aaron McKie .10 .25
51 Theo Ratliff .12 .30
52 Scott Burrell .10 .25
53 Todd Fuller .10 .25
54 Chris Mullin .15 .40
55 Mark Price .15 .40
56 Joe Smith .12 .30
57 Latrell Sprewell .15 .40
58 Clyde Drexler .20 .50
59 Mario Elie .10 .25
60 Othella Harrington .10 .25
61 Matt Maloney .10 .25
62 Hakeem Olajuwon .20 .50
63 Kevin Willis .10 .25
64 Travis Best .10 .25
65 Erick Dampier .10 .25
66 Antonio Davis .10 .25
67 Dale Davis .10 .25
68 Mark Jackson .15 .40
69 Reggie Miller .20 .50
70 Brent Barry .12 .30
71 Darrick Martin .10 .25
72 Bo Outlaw .10 .25
73 Loy Vaught .10 .25
74 Lorenzen Wright .10 .25
75 Kobe Bryant .75 2.00
76 Derek Fisher .15 .40
77 Robert Horry .12 .30
78 Eddie Jones .15 .40
79 Travis Knight .10 .25
80 George McCloud .10 .25
81 Shaquille O'Neal .40 1.00
82 P.J. Brown .10 .25
83 Tim Hardaway .15 .40
84 Voshon Lenard .10 .25
85 Jamal Mashburn .12 .30
86 Alonzo Mourning .15 .40
87 Ray Allen .20 .50
88 Vin Baker .12 .30
89 Sherman Douglas .10 .25
90 Armon Gilliam .10 .25
91 Glenn Robinson .12 .30
92 Kevin Garnett .30 .75
93 Dean Garrett .10 .25
94 Tom Gugliotta .10 .25
95 Stephon Marbury .20 .50
96 Doug West .10 .25
97 Chris Gatling .10 .25
98 Kendall Gill .10 .25
99 Kerry Kittles .10 .25
100 Jayson Williams .10 .25
101 Chris Childs .10 .25
102 Patrick Ewing .20 .50
103 Allan Houston .12 .30
104 Larry Johnson .12 .30
105 Charles Oakley .12 .30
106 John Starks .10 .25
107 John Wallace .10 .25
108 Nick Anderson .10 .25
109 Horace Grant .12 .30
110 Anfernee Hardaway .25 .60
111 Rony Seikaly .12 .30
112 Derek Strong .10 .25
113 Derrick Coleman .12 .30
114 Allen Iverson .30 .75
115 Doug Overton .10 .25
116 Jerry Stackhouse .15 .40
117 Rex Walters .10 .25
118 Cedric Ceballos .10 .25
119 Kevin Johnson .15 .40
120 Jason Kidd .25 .60
121 Steve Nash .30 .75
122 Wesley Person .10 .25
123 Kenny Anderson .12 .30
124 Jermaine O'Neal .20 .50
125 Isaiah Rider .12 .30
126 Arvydas Sabonis .12 .30
127 Gary Trent .10 .25
128 Tyus Edney .10 .25
129 Brian Grant .10 .25
130 Olden Polynice .10 .25
131 Mitch Richmond .15 .40
132 Corliss Williamson .10 .25
133 Vinny Del Negro .10 .25
134 Sean Elliott .10 .25
135 Avery Johnson .10 .25
136 Will Perdue .10 .25
137 Dominique Wilkins .20 .50
138 Craig Ehlo .10 .25
139 Hersey Hawkins .12 .30
140 Shawn Kemp .15 .40
141 Jim McIlvaine .10 .25
142 Sam Perkins .10 .25
143 Detlef Schrempf .12 .30
144 Marcus Camby .15 .40
145 Doug Christie .12 .30
146 Popeye Jones .10 .25
147 Damon Stoudamire .12 .30
148 Walt Williams .10 .25
149 Jeff Hornacek .12 .30
150 Karl Malone .20 .50
151 Greg Ostertag .10 .25
152 Bryon Russell .10 .25
153 John Stockton .20 .50
154 Shareef Abdur-Rahim .15 .40
155 Greg Anthony .10 .25
156 Anthony Peeler .10 .25
157 Bryant Reeves .10 .25
158 Roy Rogers .10 .25
159 Calbert Cheaney .10 .25
160 Juwan Howard .12 .30
161 Gheorghe Muresan .10 .25
162 Rod Strickland .10 .25
163 Chris Webber .15 .40
164 Checklist .10 .25
165 Checklist .10 .25
166 Tim Duncan RC 1.00 2.50
167 Chauncey Billups RC .60 1.50
168 Keith Van Horn RC .30 .75
169 Tracy McGrady RC .75 2.00
170 John Thomas RC .10 .25
171 Tim Thomas RC .30 .75
172 Ron Mercer RC .20 .50
173 Scot Pollard RC .10 .25
174 Jason Lawson RC .10 .25
175 Keith Booth RC .10 .25
176 Adonal Foyle RC .10 .25
177 Bubba Wells RC .10 .25
178 Derek Anderson RC .15 .40
179 Rodrick Rhodes RC .10 .25
180 Kelvin Cato RC .10 .25
181 Serge Zwikker RC .10 .25
182 Ed Gray RC .10 .25
183 Brevin Knight RC .15 .40
184 Alvin Williams RC .15 .40
185 Paul Grant RC .10 .25
186 Austin Croshere RC .25 .60
187 Chris Crawford RC .10 .25
188 Anthony Johnson RC .10 .25
189 James Cotton RC .10 .25
190 James Collins RC .10 .25
191 Tony Battie RC .20 .50
192 Tariq Abdul-Wahad RC .15 .40
193 Danny Fortson RC .15 .40
194 Maurice Taylor RC .15 .40
195 Bobby Jackson RC .20 .50
196 Charles Smith RC .15 .40
197 Johnny Taylor RC .15 .40
198 Jerald Honeycutt RC .15 .40
199 Marko Milic RC .15 .40
200 Anthony Parker RC .15 .40
201 Jacque Vaughn RC .15 .40
202 Antonio Daniels RC .15 .40
203 Charles O'Bannon RC .15 .40
204 God Shammgod RC .15 .40
205 Kebu Stewart RC .15 .40
206 Mookie Blaylock .10 .25
207 Chucky Brown .10 .25
208 Alan Henderson .10 .25
209 Dana Barros .10 .25
210 Tyus Edney .10 .25
211 Travis Knight .10 .25
212 Walter McCarty .10 .25
213 Vlade Divac .15 .40
214 Matt Geiger .10 .25
215 Bobby Phills .10 .25
216 J.R. Reid .10 .25
217 David Wesley .10 .25
218 Scott Burrell .10 .25
219 Ron Harper .12 .30
220 Michael Jordan 1.25 3.00
221 Bill Wennington .10 .25
222 Mitchell Butler .10 .25
223 Zydrunas Ilgauskas .15 .40
224 Shawn Kemp .15 .40
225 Wesley Person .10 .25
226 Shawnelle Scott RC .15 .40
227 Bob Sura .10 .25
228 Hubert Davis .10 .25
229 Michael Finley .15 .40
230 Dennis Scott .10 .25
231 Erick Strickland RC .15 .40
232 Samaki Walker .10 .25
233 Dean Garrett .10 .25
234 Priest Lauderdale .10 .25
235 Eric Williams .10 .25
236 Grant Long .10 .25
237 Malik Sealy .10 .25
238 Brian Williams .10 .25
239 Muggsy Bogues .12 .30
240 Bimbo Coles .10 .25
241 Brian Shaw .10 .25
242 Joe Smith .12 .30
243 Latrell Sprewell .15 .40
244 Charles Barkley .25 .60
245 Emanual Davis .10 .25
246 Brent Price .10 .25
247 Reggie Miller .20 .50
248 Chris Mullin .15 .40
249 Jalen Rose .12 .30
250 Rik Smits .12 .30
251 Mark West .10 .25
252 Lamond Murray .10 .25
253 Pooh Richardson .10 .25
254 Rodney Rogers .10 .25
255 Stojko Vrankovic .10 .25
256 Jon Barry .10 .25
257 Corie Blount .10 .25
258 Elden Campbell .10 .25
259 Rick Fox .10 .25
260 Nick Van Exel .12 .30
261 Isaac Austin .10 .25
262 Dan Majerle .15 .40
263 Terry Mills .10 .25
264 Mark Strickland RC .15 .40
265 Terrell Brandon .10 .25
266 Tyrone Hill .10 .25
267 Ervin Johnson .10 .25
268 Andrew Lang .10 .25
269 Elliot Perry .10 .25
270 Chris Carr .10 .25
271 Reggie Jordan .10 .25
272 Sam Mitchell .10 .25
273 Stanley Roberts .10 .25
274 Michael Cage .10 .25
275 Sam Cassell .12 .30
276 Lucious Harris .10 .25
277 Kerry Kittles .15 .40
278 Don MacLean .10 .25
279 Chris Dudley .10 .25
280 Chris Mills .10 .25
281 Charlie Ward .10 .25
282 Buck Williams .10 .25
283 Herb Williams .10 .25
284 Derek Harper .12 .30
285 Mark Price .15 .40
286 Gerald Wilkins .10 .25
287 Allen Iverson .30 .75
288 Jim Jackson .10 .25
289 Eric Montross .10 .25
290 Jerry Stackhouse .15 .40
291 Clarence Weatherspoon .10 .25
292 Tom Chambers .10 .25
293 Rex Chapman .10 .25
294 Danny Manning .12 .30
295 Antonio McDyess .12 .30
296 Clifford Robinson .10 .25
297 Stacey Augmon .10 .25
298 Brian Grant .10 .25
299 Rasheed Wallace .15 .40
300 Mahmoud Abdul-Rauf .10 .25
301 Terry Dehere .10 .25
302 Billy Owens .10 .25
303 Michael Smith .10 .25
304 Cory Alexander .10 .25
305 Chuck Person .12 .30
306 David Robinson .25 .60
307 Charles Smith .10 .25
308 Monty Williams .10 .25
309 Vin Baker .12 .30
310 Jerome Kersey .10 .25
311 Nate McMillan .10 .25
312 Gary Payton .15 .40
313 Eric Snow .10 .25
314 Carlos Rogers .10 .25
315 Zan Tabak .10 .25
316 John Wallace .10 .25
317 Sharone Wright .10 .25
318 Shandon Anderson .10 .25
319 Antoine Carr .10 .25
320 Howard Eisley .10 .25
321 Chris Morris .10 .25
322 Pete Chilcutt .10 .25
323 George Lynch .10 .25
324 Chris Robinson .15 .40
325 Otis Thorpe .10 .25
326 Harvey Grant .10 .25
327 Darvin Ham .10 .25
328 Juwan Howard .12 .30
329 Ben Wallace .20 .50
330 Chris Webber .15 .40
NNO Grant Hill Promo .60 1.50

1997-98 Hoops Chairman of the Boards

Randomly inserted into series two packs at a rate of one in 9, this 10-card set focuses on some of the players considered the best rebounders in the NBA. The card fronts carry 100% etched silver foil. Card backs carry a "CB" prefix.

COMPLETE SET (10) 6.00 15.00
CB1 Shaquille O'Neal 2.00 5.00
CB2 Dikembe Mutombo .75 2.00
CB3 Dennis Rodman 1.50 4.00
CB4 Patrick Ewing 1.00 2.50
CB5 Charles Barkley 1.25 3.00
CB6 Karl Malone 1.00 2.50
CB7 Rasheed Wallace .75 2.00
CB8 Chris Webber .75 2.00
CB9 Tim Duncan 1.50 4.00
CB10 Kevin Garnett 1.50 4.00

1997-98 Hoops Chill with Hill

Randomly inserted in series one packs at a rate of one in 10, this 10-card set features candid photos of Grant Hill on foil backgrounds which present a photographic essay in a day in his life.

COMPLETE SET (10) 4.00 10.00
COMMON HILL (1-10) .60 1.50

1997-98 Hoops Dish N Swish

Randomly inserted in series one retail packs only at a rate of one in 18, this 10-card set features the top point guards in the league who are adept at both passing and shooting.

COMPLETE SET (10) 15.00 40.00
DS1 Mookie Blaylock .75 2.00
DS2 Terrell Brandon .75 2.00
DS3 Anfernee Hardaway 2.00 5.00
DS4 Allen Iverson 2.50 6.00
DS5 Michael Jordan 12.50 30.00
DS6 Jason Kidd 2.00 5.00
DS7 Stephon Marbury 1.50 4.00
DS8 Gary Payton 1.25 3.00
DS9 John Stockton 1.50 4.00
DS10 Damon Stoudamire 1.25 3.00

1997-98 Hoops Frequent Flyer Club

Randomly inserted in series one hobby packs only at a rate of one in 36, this 20-card set features color photos of players with great dunking ability on a cloud background. The horizontal cards are printed on a special foil-stamped card with rounded corners. Card backs are numbered with a "FF" prefix.

*UPGRADE: 1.5X TO 4X BASE FREQ FLYER
UPGRADE: SER.1 STATED ODDS 1:360 HOB
FF1 Christian Laettner 1.50 4.00
FF2 Antoine Walker 2.00 5.00
FF3 Glen Rice 2.00 5.00
FF4 Michael Jordan 15.00 40.00
FF5 Dennis Rodman 4.00 10.00
FF6 Grant Hill 3.00 8.00
FF7 Latrell Sprewell 2.00 5.00
FF8 Charles Barkley 3.00 8.00
FF9 Kobe Bryant 10.00 25.00
FF10 Shaquille O'Neal 5.00 12.00
FF11 Ray Allen 2.50 6.00
FF12 Kevin Garnett 4.00 10.00
FF13 Kerry Kittles 1.25 3.00
FF14 Anfernee Hardaway 3.00 8.00
FF15 Jerry Stackhouse 2.00 5.00
FF16 Cedric Ceballos 1.25 3.00
FF17 Shawn Kemp 2.00 5.00
FF18 Marcus Camby 2.00 5.00
FF19 Juwan Howard 1.50 4.00
FF20 Chris Webber 2.00 5.00

1997-98 Hoops Great Shots

Inserted one per series two pack, this 30-card set features some of the best NBA players on mini-posters that measure 5"x7".

COMPLETE SET (30) 2.50 6.00
1 Dikembe Mutombo .10 .25
2 Antoine Walker .10 .25
3 Glen Rice .10 .25
4 Dennis Rodman .20 .50
5 Derek Anderson .10 .25
Brevin Knight
6 Michael Finley .10 .25
7 Danny Fortson .12 .30
Tony Battie
Bobby Jackson
8 Grant Hill .15 .40
9 Joe Smith .07 .20
10 Charles Barkley .15 .40

11 Reggie Miller .12 .30
12 Lamond Murray .05 .15
13 Kobe Bryant .50 1.25
14 Alonzo Mourning .12 .30
15 Ray Allen .12 .30
16 Kevin Garnett .20 .50
17 Stephon Marbury .15 .40
18 Kerry Kittles .05 .15
19 Patrick Ewing .12 .30
20 Anfernee Hardaway .15 .40
21 Allen Iverson .20 .50
22 Jason Kidd .15 .40
23 Rasheed Wallace .10 .25
24 Mitch Richmond .10 .25
25 David Robinson .15 .40
26 Gary Payton .10 .25
27 Damon Stoudamire .10 .25
28 John Stockton .12 .30
29 Shareef Abdur-Rahim .10 .25
30 Chris Webber .10 .25

1997-98 Hoops High Voltage

Randomly inserted in series two hobby packs at a rate of one in 36, this 20-card set features fan favorites who can electrify a crowd. Card fronts carry a holofoil background. Card backs are numbered with a "HV" prefix.
HV1 Kobe Bryant 10.00 25.00
HV2 Eddie Jones 2.00 5.00
HV3 Ray Allen 2.50 6.00
HV4 Anfernee Hardaway 3.00 8.00
HV5 Grant Hill 3.00 8.00
HV6 Shareef Abdur-Rahim 2.00 5.00
HV7 Marcus Camby 2.00 5.00
HV8 Allen Iverson 4.00 10.00
HV9 Kerry Kittles 1.25 3.00
HV10 Kevin Garnett 4.00 10.00
HV11 Stephon Marbury 2.50 6.00
HV12 Chris Webber 2.00 5.00
HV13 Antoine Walker 2.00 5.00
HV14 Michael Jordan 35.00 70.00
HV15 Tim Duncan 6.00 15.00
HV16 Dennis Rodman 4.00 10.00
HV17 Scottie Pippen 3.00 8.00
HV18 Shawn Kemp 2.00 5.00
HV19 Hakeem Olajuwon 2.50 6.00
HV20 Karl Malone 2.50 6.00

1997-98 Hoops High Voltage 500

This 20-card parallel set was randomly inserted into hobby packs of series two Hoops. These cards, as opposed to the base High Voltage insert, are serially numbered to 500 and feature a "Light Fantastic" background. Card backs are numbered with a "HV" prefix. To ascertain values on individual cards, please refer to the multiplier in the header below, coupled with the value of the base card.
*STARS: 4X TO 10X HI COLUMN
HV2 Eddie Jones 25.00 60.00
HV14 Michael Jordan 600.00 1200.00
HV16 Dennis Rodman 50.00 120.00
HV17 Scottie Pippen 40.00 100.00

1997-98 Hoops HOOPerstars

Randomly inserted in series one packs at a rate of one in 288, this 10-card die cut set features the best and brightest NBA stars on etched foil backgrounds. Card backs are numbered with a "H" prefix.
COMPLETE SET (10) 75.00 150.00
H1 Michael Jordan 75.00 150.00
H2 Grant Hill 8.00 20.00
H3 Shaquille O'Neal 12.00 30.00
H4 Ray Allen 6.00 15.00
H5 Stephon Marbury 6.00 15.00
H6 Anfernee Hardaway 8.00 20.00
H7 Allen Iverson 10.00 25.00
H8 Shawn Kemp 5.00 12.00
H9 Marcus Camby 5.00 12.00
H10 Shareef Abdur-Rahim 5.00 12.00

1997-98 Hoops 911

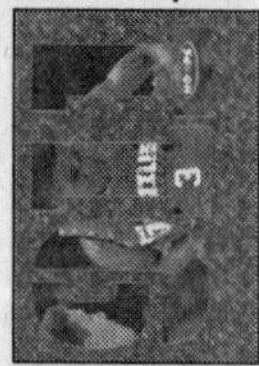

Randomly inserted in series two packs at a rate of one in 288, this 10-card set features a two-piece card with some of the NBA's best "emergency" players. The card is contained in a lazer-cut sleeve. Card backs are numbered with a "N" prefix.
COMPLETE SET (10) 125.00 225.00
N1 Michael Jordan 100.00 200.00
N2 Grant Hill 10.00 25.00
N3 Shawn Kemp 6.00 15.00
N4 Stephon Marbury 8.00 20.00
N5 Damon Stoudamire 6.00 15.00
N6 Shaquille O'Neal 15.00 40.00
N7 Shareef Abdur-Rahim 6.00 15.00
N8 Allen Iverson 12.00 30.00
N9 Antoine Walker 6.00 15.00
N10 Anfernee Hardaway 10.00 25.00

1997-98 Hoops Rock the House

Randomly inserted in series two retail packs at a rate of one in 18, this 10-card set features some of the NBA's most crowd pleasing players. Card backs are numbered with a "RH" prefix.
COMPLETE SET (10) 15.00 40.00
RH1 Anfernee Hardaway 2.00 5.00
RH2 Stephon Marbury 1.50 4.00
RH3 Grant Hill 2.00 5.00
RH4 Shaquille O'Neal 3.00 8.00
RH5 Kerry Kittles .75 2.00
RH6 Michael Jordan 10.00 25.00
RH7 Ray Allen 1.50 4.00
RH8 Damon Stoudamire 1.25 3.00
RH9 Kevin Garnett 2.50 6.00
RH10 Shawn Kemp 1.25 3.00

1997-98 Hoops Rookie Headliners

Randomly inserted in series one packs at a rate of one in 48, this 10-card set showcases the top rookies from the 1996-97 season with silhouetted action shots and a portrait shot on foil with a newspaper print background. Card backs are numbered with a "RH" prefix.
COMPLETE SET (10) 15.00 30.00
RH1 Antoine Walker 1.50 4.00
RH2 Matt Maloney 1.00 2.50
RH3 Kobe Bryant 8.00 20.00
RH4 Ray Allen 2.00 5.00
RH5 Stephon Marbury 2.00 5.00
RH6 Kerry Kittles 1.00 2.50
RH7 John Wallace 1.00 2.50
RH8 Allen Iverson 3.00 8.00
RH9 Marcus Camby 1.50 4.00
RH10 Shareef Abdur-Rahim 1.50 4.00

1997-98 Hoops Talkin' Hoops

Inserted one in every series one pack, this 30-card set features color player photos of top NBA players with a commentary on the player by NBC personality Bill Walton. Card backs are numbered with a "TH" prefix.
COMPLETE SET (30) 4.00 10.00
TH1 Christian Laettner .15 .40
TH2 Antoine Walker .20 .50
TH3 Glen Rice .20 .50
TH4 Dennis Rodman .40 1.00
TH5 Scottie Pippen .30 .75
TH6 Terrell Brandon .12 .30
TH7 Michael Finley .20 .50
TH8 Grant Hill .30 .75
TH9 Joe Smith .15 .40
TH10 Charles Barkley .30 .75
TH11 Hakeem Olajuwon .25 .60
TH12 Reggie Miller .25 .60
TH13 Loy Vaught .12 .30
TH14 Shaquille O'Neal .50 1.25
TH15 Kobe Bryant 1.00 2.50
TH16 Kevin Garnett .40 1.00
TH17 Tom Gugliotta .12 .30
TH18 Kerry Kittles .12 .30
TH19 John Wallace .12 .30
TH20 Patrick Ewing .25 .60
TH21 Jerry Stackhouse .25 .60
TH22 David Robinson .30 .75
TH23 Gary Payton .30 .75
TH24 Shawn Kemp .20 .50
TH25 Damon Stoudamire .20 .50
TH26 John Stockton .25 .60
TH27 Karl Malone .25 .60
TH28 Shareef Abdur-Rahim .20 .50
TH29 Juwan Howard .15 .40
TH30 Chris Webber .20 .50

1997-98 Hoops Top of the World

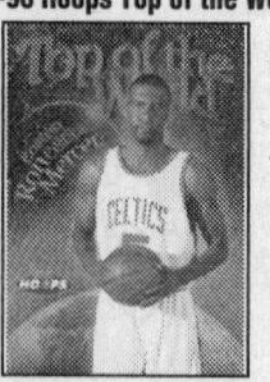

Randomly inserted in series two packs at a rate of one in 48, this 15-card set features 15 of the top rookies from the 1997 draft class. Card backs are numbered with a "TW" prefix.
COMPLETE SET (15) 12.00 30.00
TW1 Tim Duncan 5.00 12.00
TW2 Tim Thomas 1.50 4.00
TW3 Tony Battie 1.00 2.50
TW4 Keith Van Horn 1.50 4.00
TW5 Antonio Daniels .75 2.00
TW6 Derek Anderson .75 2.00
TW7 Chauncey Billups 3.00 8.00
TW8 Tracy McGrady 4.00 10.00
TW9 Danny Fortson .75 2.00
TW10 Austin Croshere .75 2.00
TW11 Tariq Abdul-Wahad .75 2.00
TW12 Adonal Foyle .75 2.00
TW13 Rodrick Rhodes .75 2.00
TW14 Ron Mercer 1.00 2.50
TW15 Charles Smith .75 2.00

1998-99 Hoops Promo Sheet

This promo sheet was distributed to dealers and hobby contacts to promote the 98/9 Hoops Basketball product. The sheet features 6 promo cards that carry a "Sample" designation on the back of each card.
1 Grant Hill .60 1.50
2 Kevin Garnett .75 2.00
3 Tim Duncan .75 2.00
4 Allen Iverson .75 2.00
5 Keith Van Horn .40 1.00
6 Shaquille O'Neal 1.00 2.50

1998-99 Hoops

The 1998-99 Hoops set consists of 167 standard size cards. The 12-card packs retail for a suggested price of $1.29. The fronts carry color action photos of NBA players in the foreground with an enlarged version of the photo in the background. The backs provide current statistics as well as what the featured player likes to do when he's not on the court. The set contains the subset Steppin' Out (156-165).
COMPLETE SET (167) 10.00 20.00
1 Kobe Bryant .75 2.00
2 Glenn Robinson .12 .30
3 Derek Anderson .10 .25
4 Terry Dehere .10 .25
5 Jalen Rose .12 .30
6 Zydrunas Ilgauskas .15 .40
7 Scott Williams .10 .25
8 Toni Kukoc .15 .40
9 John Stockton .20 .50
10 Kevin Garnett .30 .75
11 Jerome Williams .10 .25
12 Anthony Mason .10 .25
13 Harvey Grant .10 .25
14 Mookie Blaylock .10 .25
15 Tyrone Hill .10 .25
16 Dale Davis .10 .25
17 Eric Washington .10 .25
18 Aaron McKie .10 .25
19 Jermaine O'Neal .15 .40
20 Anfernee Hardaway .25 .60
21 Derrick Coleman .12 .30
22 Allan Houston .12 .30
23 Michael Jordan 1.25 3.00
24 Jason Kidd .25 .60
25 Tyrone Corbin .10 .25
26 Jacque Vaughn .10 .25
27 Bobby Jackson .12 .30
28 Chris Anstey .10 .25
29 Brent Barry .12 .30
30 Shareef Abdur-Rahim .15 .40
31 Jeff Hornacek .12 .30
32 Ed Gray .10 .25
33 Grant Hill .25 .60
34 Steve Smith .12 .30
35 Rony Seikaly .15 .40
36 Mark Jackson .15 .40
37 Shawn Bradley .10 .25
38 Corie Blount .10 .25
39 Erick Dampier .10 .25
40 Kerry Kittles .10 .25
41 David Wesley .10 .25
42 Horace Grant .12 .30
43 Bobby Hurley .15 .40
44 Tariq Abdul-Wahad .10 .25
45 Brian Williams .10 .25
46 Ray Allen .20 .50
47 Kenny Anderson .12 .30
48 Rodrick Rhodes .10 .25
49 Greg Foster .10 .25
50 Tim Duncan .30 .75
51 Steve Nash .25 .60
52 Kelvin Cato .10 .25
53 Donyell Marshall .10 .25
54 Marcus Camby .12 .30
55 Kevin Willis .10 .25
56 Michael Finley .15 .40
57 Muggsy Bogues .12 .30
58 Mark Price .15 .40
59 Larry Johnson .15 .40
60 Karl Malone .20 .50
61 Greg Ostertag .10 .25
62 Sean Elliott .15 .40
63 Johnny Taylor .10 .25
64 Howard Eisley .10 .25
65 Chris Childs .10 .25
66 Walt Williams .10 .25
67 Tracy Murray .10 .25
68 Patrick Ewing .20 .50
69 Olden Polynice .10 .25
70 Allen Iverson .30 .75
71 David Robinson .25 .60
72 Calbert Cheaney .10 .25
73 Lamond Murray .10 .25
74 Scot Pollard .10 .25
75 Alonzo Mourning .20 .50
76 Tracy McGrady .25 .60
77 Jim McIlvaine .10 .25
78 Bob Sura .10 .25
79 Anthony Peeler .10 .25
80 Keith Van Horn .15 .40
81 Maurice Taylor .10 .25
82 Charles Smith .10 .25
83 Dikembe Mutombo .15 .40
84 Nick Anderson .10 .25
85 Austin Croshere .10 .25
86 Armon Gilliam .10 .25
87 Eddie Jones .15 .40
88 Glen Rice .15 .40
89 Sam Cassell .12 .30
90 Stephon Marbury .20 .50
91 Elliot Perry UER .10 .25
Back spelled Elliott
92 Jamal Mashburn .12 .30
93 Adonal Foyle .10 .25
94 Avery Johnson .12 .30
95 Micheal Williams .10 .25
96 Danny Fortson .10 .25
97 Brevin Knight .10 .25
98 Ron Harper .12 .30
99 Chauncey Billups .20 .50
100 Shaquille O'Neal .40 1.00
101 Brent Price .10 .25
102 Tim Thomas .15 .40
103 Khalid Reeves .10 .25
104 Chris Gatling .10 .25
105 Terry Cummings .15 .40
106 Vin Baker .12 .30
107 Bryant Reeves .10 .25
108 John Starks .12 .30
109 Juwan Howard .12 .30
110 Antoine Walker .15 .40
111 Rodney Rogers .10 .25
112 Nick Van Exel .12 .30
113 Chris Whitney .10 .25
114 Bobby Phills .10 .25
115 Travis Knight .10 .25
116 Robert Horry .12 .30
117 Erick Strickland .10 .25
118 Dontae Jones .10 .25
119 Tony Battie .12 .30
120 Lindsey Hunter .10 .25
121 Reggie Miller .20 .50
122 John Wallace .10 .25
123 Ron Mercer .12 .30
124 Antonio Daniels .10 .25
125 Paul Grant .10 .25
126 Voshon Lenard .10 .25
127 Shawn Kemp .15 .40
128 Antonio Davis .10 .25
129 Hakeem Olajuwon .20 .50
130 Danny Manning .12 .30
131 Bimbo Coles .10 .25
132 Tim Hardaway .15 .40
133 Lorenzo Williams .10 .25
134 Dan Majerle .15 .40
135 Bryant Stith .10 .25
136 Randy Brown .10 .25
137 Hubert Davis .10 .25
138 Gary Payton .15 .40
139 Rasheed Wallace .15 .40
140 Chris Robinson .10 .25
141 Doug Christie .10 .25
142 Brian Grant .10 .25
143 Isaiah Rider .10 .25
144 Kendall Gill .10 .25
145 Lorenzen Wright .10 .25
146 Ervin Johnson .10 .25
147 Monty Williams .10 .25
148 Keith Closs .10 .25
149 Tony Delk .10 .25
150 Hersey Hawkins .10 .25
151 Dean Garrett .10 .25
152 Cedric Henderson .10 .25
153 Detlef Schrempf .15 .40
154 Dana Barros .10 .25
155 Dee Brown .10 .25
156 Jayson Williams SO .10 .25
157 Charles Barkley SO .25 .60
158 Damon Stoudamire SO .15 .40
159 Scottie Pippen SO .25 .60
160 Joe Smith SO .12 .30
161 Antonio McDyess SO .12 .30
162 Jerry Stackhouse SO .15 .40
163 Dennis Rodman SO .30 .75
164 Shaquille O'Neal SO .40 1.00
165 Grant Hill SO .25 .60
166 Checklist .10 .25
167 Checklist .10 .25

1998-99 Hoops Starting Five

The 1998-99 Hoops Starting Five set consists of 165 cards and is a parallel to the 1998-99 Hoops base set. The cards are randomly inserted in packs and are serially numbered to five.

1998-99 Hoops Bams

The 1998-99 Hoops Bams set consists of 10 cards and is an insert to the 1998-99 Hoops base set. The cards are randomly inserted in packs and each card is serially numbered to 250. The fronts feature ten of the game's most fearsome dunkers and is silver holo foil-stamped..
1 Michael Jordan 1000.00 1700.00
2 Kobe Bryant 175.00 350.00
3 Allen Iverson 50.00 125.00
4 Shaquille O'Neal 60.00 150.00
5 Tim Duncan 50.00 125.00
6 Shareef Abdur-Rahim 25.00 60.00
7 Keith Van Horn 25.00 60.00
8 Grant Hill 60.00 150.00
9 Anfernee Hardaway 60.00 150.00
10 Kevin Garnett 60.00 150.00

1998-99 Hoops Slam Bams

The 1998-99 Hoops Slam Bams set consists of 10 cards and is a hobby only insert parallel to the 1998-99 Hoops Bams insert set. The cards are randomly inserted in packs and are serially numbered to 100.
*STARS: 1.25X TO 3X BAMS INSERT
1 Michael Jordan 2000.00 3200.00
2 Kobe Bryant 1000.00 2000.00
3 Allen Iverson 200.00 500.00

1998-99 Hoops Freshman Flashback

The 1998-99 Hoops Freshman Flashback set consists of 10 cards and is an insert to the 1998-99 Hoops base set. The cards are randomly inserted in packs and are serially numbered to 1,000. The fronts feature black and white head and shoulder photos of the top 1997-98 rookies.
COMPLETE SET (10) 40.00 80.00
1 Tim Duncan 12.00 30.00
2 Keith Van Horn 6.00 15.00
3 Tim Thomas 6.00 15.00
4 Antonio Daniels 4.00 10.00
5 Brevin Knight 4.00 10.00
6 Danny Fortson 4.00 10.00
7 Maurice Taylor 4.00 10.00
8 Chauncey Billups 8.00 20.00
9 Bobby Jackson 5.00 12.00
10 Derek Anderson 4.00 10.00

1998-99 Hoops Prime Twine

The 1998-99 Hoops Prime Twine set consists of 10 cards and is an insert to the 1998-99 Hoops base set. The cards are randomly inserted in packs and are serially numbered to 500. The fronts feature color action photos of an NBA player in the foreground going up for the uniquely designed basket in the background. Each card is die-cut on the outside and gold foil-stamped on the inside.
1 Dennis Rodman 50.00 125.00
2 Allen Iverson 50.00 125.00
3 Karl Malone 25.00 60.00
4 Antonio McDyess 15.00 40.00
5 Damon Stoudamire 20.00 50.00
6 Eddie Jones 20.00 50.00
7 Scottie Pippen 30.00 80.00
8 Shawn Kemp 25.00 60.00
9 Antoine Walker 20.00 50.00
10 Stephon Marbury 25.00 60.00

1998-99 Hoops Pump Up The Jam

The 1998-99 Hoops Pump Up The Jam set consists of 10 cards and is an insert to the 1998-99 Hoops base set. The cards are randomly inserted in packs at a rate of one in 4. The fronts carry a color action photo of the featured player in the foreground with a shoulder and head shot of the player in the background. The card is designed to resemble a movie poster with the player's credits written along the bottom of the card.
COMPLETE SET (10) 4.00 10.00
1 Stephon Marbury .40 1.00
2 Allen Iverson .60 1.50
3 Grant Hill .50 1.25
4 Kobe Bryant 1.50 4.00
5 Michael Jordan 2.50 6.00
6 Antoine Walker .30 .75
7 Shareef Abdur-Rahim .30 .75
8 Shawn Kemp .30 .75
9 Anfernee Hardaway .50 1.25
10 Antonio McDyess .25 .60

1998-99 Hoops Rejectors

The 1998-99 Hoops Rejectors set consists of 10 cards and is an insert to the 1998-99 Hoops base set. The cards are randomly inserted in packs and serially numbered to 2,500. The fronts feature color action photos printed on gold foil-stamped cards. Running along the left side of the card are four smaller individual color photos of the featured player.
COMPLETE SET (10) 30.00 60.00
1 Dikembe Mutombo 2.50 6.00
2 Marcus Camby 2.00 5.00
3 Shaquille O'Neal 8.00 20.00
4 Tim Duncan 5.00 12.00
5 Shawn Bradley 1.50 4.00
6 Chris Webber 2.50 6.00
7 Patrick Ewing 3.00 8.00
8 Kevin Garnett 5.00 12.00
9 David Robinson 4.00 10.00
10 Michael Stewart 1.50 4.00

1998-99 Hoops Shout Outs

The 1998-99 Hoops Shout Outs set consists of 30 cards and is an insert to the 1998-99 Hoops base set. The cards are inserted one per pack. The fronts feature full color photos of the players expressing themselves against a white background.
COMPLETE SET (30) 4.00 10.00
1 Shareef Abdur-Rahim .15 .40
2 Chauncey Billups .20 .50
3 Terrell Brandon UER .10 .25
Back spelled Terrrell
4 Patrick Ewing .20 .50
5 Michael Finley .15 .40
6 Adonal Foyle .10 .25
7 Kevin Garnett .30 .75
8 Anfernee Hardaway .25 .60
9 Tim Hardaway .15 .40
10 Grant Hill .25 .60
11 Tim Thomas .15 .40
12 Bobby Jackson .12 .30
13 Michael Jordan 1.25 3.00
14 Shawn Kemp .15 .40
15 Jason Kidd .25 .60
16 Karl Malone .20 .50
17 Stephon Marbury .20 .50
18 Anthony Mason .10 .25
19 Reggie Miller .20 .50
20 Dikembe Mutombo .15 .40
21 Kobe Bryant .75 2.00
22 Hakeem Olajuwon .20 .50
23 Gary Payton .15 .40
24 Michael Stewart .10 .25
25 David Robinson .25 .60
26 Maurice Taylor .10 .25
27 Keith Van Horn .15 .40
28 Antoine Walker .15 .40
29 Rasheed Wallace .15 .40
30 Juwan Howard .12 .30

1999-00 Hoops

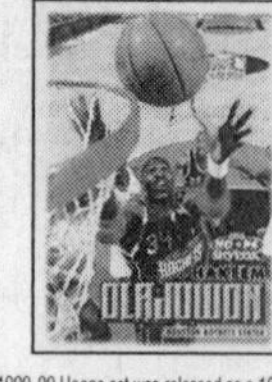

The 1999-00 Hoops set was released as a 185-card set that featured 117 player cards, 48 sophomore sensation cards and 20 rookie cards. There was only one series offered. Each pack contained 12-cards and carried a suggested retail price of $1.29.
COMPLETE SET (185) 15.00 30.00
1 Paul Pierce .30 .75
2 Ray Allen .20 .50
3 Jason Williams .25 .60
4 Sean Elliott .20 .50
5 Al Harrington .20 .50
6 Bobby Phills .12 .30
7 Tyronn Lue .12 .30
8 James Cotton .12 .30
9 Anthony Peeler .12 .30
10 LaPhonso Ellis .12 .30
11 Voshon Lenard .12 .30
12 Kornel David RC .20 .50
13 Michael Finley .20 .50
14 Danny Fortson .12 .30
15 Antawn Jamison .20 .50
16 Reggie Miller .20 .50
17 Shaquille O'Neal .50 1.25
18 P.J. Brown .12 .30
19 Roshown McLeod .12 .30
20 Larry Johnson .20 .50
21 Rashard Lewis .20 .50
22 Tracy McGrady .30 .75
23 Peja Stojakovic .20 .50
24 Tracy Murray .12 .30
25 Gary Payton .20 .50
26 Ricky Davis .20 .50
27 Kobe Bryant 1.00 2.50
28 Avery Johnson .15 .40
29 Kevin Garnett .40 1.00
30 Charles Jones .12 .30
31 Brevin Knight .12 .30
32 Lindsey Hunter .12 .30
33 Felipe Lopez .12 .30
34 Rik Smits .20 .50
35 Maurice Taylor .12 .30
36 Corey Benjamin .12 .30
37 Ervin Johnson .12 .30
38 Steve Smith .12 .30
39 Austin Croshere .12 .30
40 Matt Geiger .12 .30
41 Tom Gugliotta .12 .30
42 Radoslav Nesterovic RC .20 .50
43 Juwan Howard .15 .40
44 Keon Clark .12 .30
45 Latrell Sprewell .20 .50
46 George Lynch .12 .30
47 Greg Ostertag .12 .30
48 J.R. Henderson .12 .30
49 Kerry Kittles .12 .30
50 Matt Harpring .15 .40
51 Duane Causwell .12 .30
52 Andrae Patterson .12 .30
53 Jerry Stackhouse .20 .50
54 Adonal Foyle .12 .30
55 Bryce Drew .12 .30
56 Chris Childs .12 .30
57 Charles Smith .12 .30
58 Rony Seikaly .20 .50
59 Chauncey Billups .20 .50
60 Grant Hill .25 .60
61 Marlon Garnett RC .20 .50
62 Tim Hardaway .20 .50
63 Vlade Divac .20 .50
64 Chris Gatling .12 .30
65 Glenn Robinson .15 .40
66 Michael Olowokandi .12 .30
67 Elliot Perry .12 .30
68 Howard Eisley .12 .30
69 Glen Rice .20 .50
70 Marcus Camby .15 .40
71 Theo Ratliff .15 .40
72 Brian Skinner .12 .30
73 Kenny Anderson .15 .40
74 Jamal Mashburn .15 .40
75 Vladimir Stepania .12 .30
76 Jayson Williams .12 .30
77 Brian Grant .12 .30
78 Raef LaFrentz .15 .40
79 John Starks .20 .50
80 Mike Bibby .20 .50
81 Stephon Marbury .15 .40
82 Armon Gilliam .12 .30
83 Sam Jacobson .12 .30
84 Derrick Coleman .15 .40
85 Allan Houston .15 .40
86 Miles Simon .12 .30
87 Allen Iverson .40 1.00
88 Derek Anderson .12 .30
89 Chris Anstey .12 .30
90 Larry Hughes .15 .40
91 Vitaly Potapenko .12 .30
92 Cherokee Parks .12 .30
93 Donyell Marshall .12 .30
94 Danny Manning .12 .30
95 Bryon Russell .12 .30
96 Randell Jackson .12 .30
97 Antoine Walker .20 .50
98 Dirk Nowitzki .40 1.00
99 Karl Malone .25 .60
100 Vince Carter .40 1.00
101 Eddie Jones .20 .50
102 Bryant Stith .12 .30
103 Korleone Young .12 .30
104 Tim Duncan .40 1
105 Jerome Kersey .12
106 Bonzi Wells .12
107 Wesley Person .12
108 Steve Nash .30
109 Tyrone Nesby RC .20
110 Doug Christie .15
111 David Robinson .30
112 Ruben Patterson .12
113 Dikembe Mutombo .20
114 Ron Mercer .15
115 Elden Campbell .12
116 Kevin Willis .12
117 Hakeem Olajuwon .25
118 Shawn Kemp .20
119 Eric Montross .12
120 Shareef Abdur-Rahim .15
121 Bob Sura .12
122 James Robinson .12
123 Shawn Bradley .12
124 Robert Traylor .12
125 Dean Garrett .12
126 Keith Van Horn .15
127 Patrick Ewing .25
128 Isaac Austin .12
129 Jason Kidd .30
130 Isaiah Rider .12
131 Jerome James RC .20
132 John Stockton .25
133 Jason Caffey .12
134 Bryant Reeves .12
135 Michael Dickerson .12
136 Chris Mullin .20
137 Rasheed Wallace .20
138 Cuttino Mobley .15
139 Antonio McDyess .15
140 Chris Webber .20
141 Jelani McCoy .12
142 Damon Stoudamire .20
143 Gerald Brown .20
144 Cory Carr .12
145 Brent Barry .15
146 Alan Henderson .12
147 Nazr Mohammed .12
148 Bison Dele .12
149 Scottie Pippen .30
150 Michael Doleac .12
151 Nick Anderson .12
152 Alonzo Mourning .25
153 Jahidi White .12
154 Jalen Rose .15
155 Brad Miller .20
156 Andrew DeClercq .12
157 Erick Strickland .12
158 Toni Kukoc .20
159 Pat Garrity .12
160 Bobby Jackson .15
161 Steve Kerr .15
162 Toby Bailey .12
163 Charles Oakley .15
164 Rod Strickland .12
165 Rodrick Rhodes .12
166 Ron Artest RC .50 1.
167 William Avery RC .20
168 Elton Brand RC .50 1.
169 Baron Davis RC .60 1.
170 John Celestand RC .20
171 Jumaine Jones RC .20
172 Andre Miller RC .50 1.
173 Lee Nailon RC .20
174 James Posey RC .20
175 Jason Terry RC .50 1.
176 Kenny Thomas RC .20
177 Steve Francis RC .50 1.
178 Wally Szczerbiak RC .40 1.
179 Richard Hamilton RC .50 1.
180 Jonathan Bender RC .20
181 Shawn Marion RC .50 1.
182 Aleksandar Radojevic RC .20
183 Tim James RC .20
184 Trajan Langdon RC .20
185 Corey Maggette RC .40 1.

1999-00 Hoops Build Your Own Card

Randomly inserted in packs at one in four, this 10-ca[rd] set features an opportunity for collectors to build the[ir] own insert set. Collectors had the opportunity to se[lect] from three different fronts and three different backs f[or] each of the ten players.
COMPLETE SET (10) 8.00 20.
1 Tim Duncan 1.50 4.
2 Keith Van Horn .60 1.
3 Vince Carter 1.50 4.
4 Grant Hill 1.00 2.
5 Shaquille O'Neal 2.00 5.
6 Kevin Garnett 1.50 4.
7 Allen Iverson 1.50 4.
8 Jason Williams 1.00 2.
9 Kobe Bryant 4.00 10.
10 Paul Pierce 1.25 3.

1999-00 Hoops Build Your Own Card Redemptions

These redemption cards were available by sending i[n] the original player redemption along with $10 and collectors could "make" their own Hoops card, havi[ng] the ability to choose from any combination of three different fronts and three different backs per player - thus, each player has nine different redemption card[s] available. Each of the cards were serially numbered out of 250.
1a Tim Duncan 40.00 100.
Ball F/Body B
1b Tim Duncan 40.00 100.
Ball F/Head B
1c Tim Duncan 40.00 100.
Ball F/Horizonal B
1d Tim Duncan 40.00 100.
No Ball F/Body B
1e Tim Duncan 40.00 100.
No Ball F/Head B
1f Tim Duncan 40.00 100.
No Ball F/Horizontal B
1g Tim Duncan 40.00 100.
Shoot F/Body B
1h Tim Duncan 40.00 100.
Shoot F/Head B
1i Tim Duncan 40.00 100.
Shoot F/Horizontal B
2a Keith Van Horn 15.00 40.
Ball F/Body B
2b Keith Van Horn 15.00 40.
Ball F/Head B
2c Keith Van Horn 15.00 40.
Ball F/Horizontal B
2d Keith Van Horn 15.00 40.
No Ball F/Body B
2e Keith Van Horn 15.00 40.
No Ball F/Head B

th Van Horn 15.00 40.00
Ball F/Horizontal B
ith Van Horn 15.00 40.00
ot F/Body B
ith Van Horn 15.00 40.00
ot F/Head B
ith Van Horn 15.00 40.00
ot F/Horizontal B
nce Carter 40.00 100.00
F/Body B
nce Carter 40.00 100.00
F/Head B
nce Carter 40.00 100.00
F/Horizonal B
nce Carter 40.00 100.00
Ball F/Body B
nce Carter 40.00 100.00
Ball F/Head B
nce Carter 40.00 100.00
Ball F/Horizontal B
nce Carter 40.00 100.00
oot F/Body B
nce Carter 40.00 100.00
oot F/Head B
nce Carter 40.00 100.00
oot F/Horizontal B
rant Hill 60.00 150.00
l F/Body B
rant Hill 60.00 150.00
F/Head B
ant Hill 60.00 150.00
F/Horizonal B
ant Hill 60.00 150.00
Ball F/Body B
ant Hill 60.00 150.00
Ball F/Head B
ant Hill 60.00 150.00
Ball F/Horizontal B
rant Hill 60.00 150.00
oot F/Body B
rant Hill 60.00 150.00
oot F/Head B
ant Hill 60.00 150.00
oot F/Horizontal B
haquille O'Neal 50.00 125.00
l F/Body B
haquille O'Neal 50.00 125.00
ll F/Head B
haquille O'Neal 50.00 125.00
ll F/Horizonal B
haquille O'Neal 50.00 125.00
Ball F/Body B
haquille O'Neal 50.00 125.00
Ball F/Head B
haquille O'Neal 50.00 125.00
Ball F/Horizontal B
haquille O'Neal 50.00 125.00
oot F/Body B
haquille O'Neal 50.00 125.00
oot F/Head B
haquille O'Neal 50.00 125.00
oot F/Horizontal B
evin Garnett 40.00 100.00
ll F/Body B
evin Garnett 40.00 100.00
ll F/Head B
evin Garnett 40.00 100.00
ll F/Horizonal B
evin Garnett 40.00 100.00
Ball F/Body B
evin Garnett 40.00 100.00
Ball F/Head B
evin Garnett 40.00 100.00
Ball F/Horizontal B
evin Garnett 40.00 100.00
oot F/Body B
evin Garnett 40.00 100.00
oot F/Head B
evin Garnett 40.00 100.00
oot F/Horizontal B
llen Iverson 40.00 100.00
ll F/Body B
llen Iverson 40.00 100.00
ll F/Head B
llen Iverson 40.00 100.00
ll F/Horizonal B
llen Iverson 40.00 100.00
Ball F/Body B
llen Iverson 40.00 100.00
Ball F/Head B
llen Iverson 40.00 100.00
o Ball F/Horizontal B
llen Iverson 40.00 100.00
oot F/Body B
llen Iverson 40.00 100.00
oot F/Head B
llen Iverson 40.00 100.00
oot F/Horizontal B
ason Williams 30.00 80.00
ll F/Body B
ason Williams 30.00 80.00
ll F/Head B
ason Williams 30.00 80.00
ll F/Horizonal B
ason Williams 30.00 80.00
o Ball F/Body B
ason Williams 30.00 80.00
o Ball F/Head B
ason Williams 30.00 80.00
o Ball F/Horizontal B
ason Williams 30.00 80.00
oot F/Body B
ason Williams 30.00 80.00
oot F/Head B
ason Williams 30.00 80.00
oot F/Horizontal B
Kobe Bryant 100.00 250.00
all F/Body B
Kobe Bryant 100.00 250.00
all F/Head B
Kobe Bryant 100.00 250.00
all F/Horizonal B
Kobe Bryant 100.00 250.00
o Ball F/Body B
Kobe Bryant 100.00 250.00
o Ball F/Head B
obe Bryant 100.00 250.00
o Ball F/Horizontal B
Kobe Bryant 100.00 250.00
oot F/Body B
Kobe Bryant 100.00 250.00
oot F/Head B
obe Bryant 100.00 250.00
oot F/Horizontal B
Paul Pierce 30.00 80.00
ll F/Body B

10b Paul Pierce 30.00 80.00
Ball F/Head B
10c Paul Pierce 30.00 80.00
Ball F/Horizonal B
10d Paul Pierce 30.00 80.00
No Ball F/Body B
10e Paul Pierce 30.00 80.00
No Ball F/Head B
10f Paul Pierce 30.00 80.00
No Ball F/Horizontal B
10g Paul Pierce 30.00 80.00
Shoot F/Body B
10h Paul Pierce 30.00 80.00
Shoot F/Head B
10i Paul Pierce 30.00 80.00
Shoot F/Horizontal B

1999-00 Hoops Calling Card

Randomly inserted in packs at one in eight, this 15-card set features signature moves from some of the best in the NBA. Card backs carry a "CC" prefix.

COMPLETE SET (15) 5.00 12.00
CC1 Kobe Bryant 2.50 6.00
CC2 Kevin Garnett 1.00 2.50
CC3 Tim Hardaway .50 1.25
CC4 Grant Hill .60 1.50
CC5 Allen Iverson 1.00 2.50
CC6 Karl Malone .60 1.50
CC7 Shawn Kemp .50 1.25
CC8 Stephon Marbury .40 1.00
CC9 Shaquille O'Neal 1.25 3.00
CC10 Hakeem Olajuwon .60 1.50
CC11 Ray Allen .50 1.25
CC12 Damon Stoudamire .50 1.25
CC13 Jason Williams .60 1.50
CC14 Keith Van Horn .40 1.00
CC15 Dikembe Mutombo .50 1.25

1999-00 Hoops Dunk Mob

Randomly inserted in packs at one in 144, this 10-card set highlights some of the league's best dunkers on a silver holo-foil stamped card. Card backs carry a "DM" prefix.

COMPLETE SET (10) 25.00 60.00
DM1 Shaquille O'Neal 10.00 25.00
DM2 Stephon Marbury 3.00 8.00
DM3 Paul Pierce 6.00 15.00
DM4 Antawn Jamison 4.00 10.00
DM5 Michael Olowokandi 2.50 6.00
DM6 Scottie Pippen 6.00 15.00
DM7 Antonio McDyess 3.00 8.00
DM8 Vince Carter 8.00 20.00
DM9 Ron Mercer 3.00 8.00
DM10 Shawn Kemp 4.00 10.00

1999-00 Hoops Name Plates

Randomly inserted in packs at one in four, this 10-card set features a die cut and embossed card modeled after vanity license plates featuring NBA players that have prominent nicknames. Card backs carry a "NP" prefix.

COMPLETE SET (10) 2.00 5.00
NP1 Shareef Abdur-Rahim .20 .50
NP2 Allen Iverson .50 1.25
NP3 Karl Malone .30 .75
NP4 Gary Payton .25 .60
NP5 Hakeem Olajuwon .30 .75
NP6 Glenn Robinson .20 .50
NP7 Kevin Garnett .50 1.25
NP8 Anfernee Hardaway .40 1.00
NP9 David Robinson .40 1.00
NP10 Shaquille O'Neal .60 1.50

1999-00 Hoops Pure Players

Randomly inserted in packs, this 10-card set features a profile of top NBA players on silver plastic stock with orange foil type. The cards are serially numbered to 500. Card backs carry a "PP" prefix.

COMPLETE SET (10) 100.00 200.00
*100 STARS: 1.5X TO 4X HI COLUMN
100: PRINT RUN 100 SERIAL #'d SETS
PP1 Tim Duncan 15.00 40.00
PP2 Keith Van Horn 6.00 15.00
PP3 Stephon Marbury 6.00 15.00
PP4 Grant Hill 15.00 40.00
PP5 Kobe Bryant 40.00 100.00
PP6 Kevin Garnett 15.00 40.00
PP7 Allen Iverson 15.00 40.00
PP8 Antoine Walker 8.00 20.00
PP9 Shareef Abdur-Rahim 6.00 15.00
PP10 Anfernee Hardaway 12.00 30.00

1999-00 Hoops Y2K Corps

Randomly inserted in packs at one in 16, this 10-card set features the top rookies from last year. The cards are set against an embossed and silver foil-stamped backing. Card backs carry a "BB" prefix.

COMPLETE SET (10) 3.00 8.00
BB1 Michael Olowokandi .40 1.00
BB2 Mike Bibby .60 1.50
BB3 Jason Williams .75 2.00
BB4 Dirk Nowitzki 1.25 3.00
BB5 Vince Carter 1.25 3.00
BB6 Robert Traylor .40 1.00
BB7 Larry Hughes .50 1.25
BB8 Paul Pierce 1.00 2.50
BB9 Matt Harpring .50 1.25
BB10 Michael Dickerson .40 1.00

2004-05 Hoops

Released in April, 2005, this is the return of Hoops, a brand that has been on hiatus since 1999-00. The 197-card set divides into 165 veteran cards, seven Hoops History cards serially numbered to 1989 (card numbers 166-175) and 25 rookie cards serially numbered to 1750 (card numbers 176-200). Base cards are borderless and feature a strip along the bottom with the player's information. Hoops was packaged in 24-pack boxes of five cards each. Upon release, packs carried a SRP of $1.99.

COMP.SET w/o SP's (165) 15.00 40.00
CARDS 168-170 NOT RELEASED
1 Dwyane Wade .75 2.00
2 Vince Carter .40 1.00
3 Luke Walton .15 .40
4 Alonzo Mourning .30 .75
5 Antoine Walker .25 .60
6 Jerry Stackhouse .20 .50
7 Chris Wilcox .15 .40
8 Udonis Haslem .20 .50
9 Michael Redd .25 .60
10 Darius Miles .15 .40
11 Jarvis Hayes .15 .40
12 Kirk Hinrich .25 .60
13 Tayshaun Prince .25 .60
14 Caron Butler .25 .60
15 Sam Cassell .20 .50
16 Kurt Thomas .15 .40
17 Bruce Bowen .15 .40
18 Jared Jeffries .15 .40
19 Keith Bogans .15 .40
20 Chauncey Billups .25 .60
21 Lamar Odom .25 .60
22 Fred Hoiberg .15 .40
23 Cuttino Mobley .20 .50
24 Manu Ginobili .30 .75
25 Juan Dixon .15 .40
26 Predrag Drobnjak .15 .40
27 Nene .20 .50
28 Elton Brand .25 .60
29 Rasual Butler .15 .40
30 Nick Van Exel .20 .50
31 Carlos Arroyo .20 .50
32 Zydrunas Ilgauskas .20 .50
33 Troy Murphy .20 .50
34 Jason Williams .20 .50
35 Jason Kidd .40 1.00
36 Samuel Dalembert .15 .40
37 Vladimir Radmanovic .15 .40
38 Kenny Anderson .20 .50
39 Kenyon Martin .25 .60
40 Jamaal Tinsley .15 .40
41 Damon Jones .15 .40
42 Shareef Abdur-Rahim .20 .50
43 Ricky Davis .20 .50
44 Earl Boykins .15 .40
45 Austin Croshere .15 .40
46 Keith Van Horn .20 .50
47 Theo Ratliff .15 .40
48 Mehmet Okur .20 .50
49 Paul Pierce .30 .75
50 Marcus Camby .20 .50
51 Stephen Jackson .20 .50
52 Maurice Williams .20 .50
53 Brad Miller .25 .60
54 Carlos Boozer .25 .60
55 Dirk Nowitzki .40 1.00
56 Dikembe Mutombo .25 .60
57 James Posey .15 .40
58 Baron Davis .25 .60
59 Shawn Marion .25 .60
60 Ronald Murray .15 .40
61 Gary Payton .25 .60
62 Andre Miller .20 .50
63 Reggie Miller .25 .60
64 Zaza Pachulia .15 .40
65 Bobby Jackson .15 .40
66 Peja Stojakovic .25 .60
67 Jiri Welsch .15 .40
68 Darko Milicic .15 .40
69 Ron Artest .25 .60
70 T.J. Ford .20 .50
71 Andrei Kirilenko .20 .50
72 Jason Kapono .15 .40
73 Jermaine O'Neal .25 .60
74 Desmond Mason .20 .50
75 Chris Webber .25 .60
76 Morris Peterson .15 .40
77 Ben Wallace .25 .60
78 Antonio Davis .15 .40
79 Slava Medvedenko .15 .40
80 Brian Scalabrine .15 .40
81 Jamal Crawford .20 .50
82 Josh Howard .25 .60
83 Tyson Chandler .20 .50
84 Rasheed Wallace .25 .60
85 Chris Mihm .15 .40
86 Latrell Sprewell .20 .50
87 Mike Sweetney .15 .40
88 Robert Horry .20 .50
89 Michael Finley .25 .60
90 Bostjan Nachbar .15 .40
91 Allan Houston .20 .50
92 Joe Johnson .25 .60
93 Jalen Rose .20 .50
94 Marquis Daniels .15 .40
95 Tyronn Lue .15 .40
96 Stephon Marbury .20 .50
97 Quentin Richardson .20 .50
98 Chris Bosh .25 .60
99 Dajuan Wagner .15 .40
100 Derek Fisher .20 .50
101 Devean George .15 .40
102 Zoran Planinic .15 .40
103 Corliss Williamson .15 .40
104 Brent Barry .15 .40
105 Drew Gooden .20 .50
106 Clifford Robinson .15 .40
107 Shane Battier .20 .50
108 P.J. Brown .15 .40
109 Willie Green .15 .40
110 Nick Collison .15 .40
111 Al Harrington .20 .50
112 Carmelo Anthony .50 1.25
113 Corey Maggette .20 .50
114 Eddie Jones .20 .50
115 Zach Randolph .20 .50
116 Raja Bell .20 .50
117 Jeff McInnis .15 .40
118 Yao Ming .50 1.25
119 Brian Cardinal .15 .40
120 Jamaal Magloire .15 .40
121 Kyle Korver .20 .50
122 Luke Ridnour .20 .50
123 Jason Terry .20 .50
124 Maurice Taylor .15 .40
125 Bonzi Wells .15 .40
126 David West .25 .60
127 Amare Stoudemire .30 .75
128 Ray Allen .25 .60
129 Eddy Curry .20 .50
130 Richard Hamilton .20 .50
131 Kobe Bryant 1.25 3.00
132 Kevin Garnett .50 1.25
133 Steve Francis .25 .60
134 Tim Duncan .40 1.00
135 Larry Hughes .20 .50
136 LeBron James 1.50 4.00
137 Adonal Foyle .15 .40
138 Pau Gasol .25 .60
139 Richard Jefferson .25 .60
140 Allen Iverson .40 1.00
141 Antonio Daniels .15 .40
142 Eric Williams .15 .40
143 Primoz Brezec .15 .40
144 Jason Richardson .25 .60
145 Chris Kaman .25 .60
146 Troy Hudson .15 .40
147 Hedo Turkoglu .25 .60
148 Tony Parker .25 .60
149 Gilbert Arenas .25 .60
150 Eric Snow .15 .40
151 Tracy McGrady .30 .75
152 Stromile Swift .15 .40
153 Dan Dickau .15 .40
154 Steve Nash .30 .75
155 Rashard Lewis .25 .60
156 Gerald Wallace .25 .60
157 Mike Dunleavy .20 .50
158 Bobby Simmons .15 .40
159 Wally Szczerbiak .20 .50
160 Grant Hill .30 .75
161 Mike Bibby .25 .60
162 Antawn Jamison .25 .60
163 Antonio McDyess .20 .50
164 Shaquille O'Neal .60 1.50
165 Rafer Alston .15 .40
166 Charles Barkley HH 4.00 10.00
167 David Robinson HH 4.00 10.00
171 Larry Bird HH 8.00 20.00
172 Scottie Pippen HH 4.00 10.00
173 Isiah Thomas HH 2.50 6.00
174 Kevin McHale HH 3.00 8.00
175 Dominique Wilkins HH 3.00 8.00
176 Josh Childress RC 1.25 3.00
177 Josh Smith RC 2.00 5.00
178 Al Jefferson RC 2.00 5.00
179 Delonte West RC 1.50 4.00
180 Tony Allen RC 1.50 4.00
181 Emeka Okafor RC 2.00 5.00
182 Bernard Robinson RC 1.25 3.00
183 Ben Gordon RC 1.50 4.00
184 Luol Deng RC 2.00 5.00
185 Andres Nocioni RC 1.25 3.00
186 Luke Jackson RC 1.25 3.00
187 Devin Harris RC 2.00 5.00
188 Andris Biedrins RC 1.50 4.00
189 Shaun Livingston RC 1.25 3.00
190 Dorell Wright RC 2.00 5.00
191 J.R. Smith RC 1.50 4.00
192 Trevor Ariza RC 1.25 3.00
193 Dwight Howard RC 4.00 10.00
194 Jameer Nelson RC 1.50 4.00
195 Andre Iguodala RC 2.00 5.00
196 Sebastian Telfair RC 1.25 3.00
197 Kevin Martin RC 1.50 4.00
198 David Harrison RC 1.25 3.00
199 Rafael Araujo RC 1.25 3.00
200 Kirk Snyder RC 1.25 3.00

2004-05 Hoops 100

Randomly inserted in packs, this 197-card set parallels the base Hoops set enhanced with a foil card front and sequential numbering to 100.

*1-165 SINGLES: 3X TO 8X BASE HI
*166-175 HH: .6X TO 1.5X BASE HI
*176-200 RC's: .75X TO 2X BASE HI

2004-05 Hoops Autographs

Randomly seeded, this 25-card set parallels the look of the base Hoops set enhanced with a cut signature. Each card is serially numbered to 75. A parallel version of this set serially numbered to 25 was also inserted.

*AUTO 25: .6X TO 1.5X BASE HI
AB Andris Biedrins 6.00 15.00
BG Ben Gordon 6.00 15.00
CB2 Carlos Boozer 5.00 12.00
DH David Harrison 5.00 12.00
DW David West 6.00 15.00
KK Kyle Korver 10.00 25.00
LD Luol Deng 8.00 20.00
LJ Luke Jackson 5.00 12.00
LR Luke Ridnour 5.00 12.00
MD Marquis Daniels 5.00 12.00
PS Peja Stojakovic 12.00 30.00
RH Richard Hamilton 10.00 25.00
SB Shane Battier 5.00 12.00

2004-05 Hoops Great Shots

Randomly inserted at the rage of one in 72 packs, this 10-card set utilizes a horizontal design where player images appear on the right against a black and red colored background.

COMPLETE SET (10) 10.00 25.00
1 Kobe Bryant 4.00 10.00
2 LeBron James 5.00 12.00
3 Carmelo Anthony 1.50 4.00
4 Ben Wallace .75 2.00
5 Tim Duncan 1.25 3.00
6 Kevin Garnett 1.50 4.00
7 Jason Kidd 1.25 3.00
8 Yao Ming 1.50 4.00
9 Amare Stoudemire 1.00 2.50
10 Dwyane Wade 2.50 6.00

2004-05 Hoops Great Shots Jerseys

Randomly inserted in packs, this eight-card set parallels the base Great Shots insert enhanced with a square swatch of jersey on the left side of the card. The background is blue, as is the border around the jersey. A Green version containing a small green foil emblem was issued for some players, and a patch version sequentially numbered to 25 was also inserted.

*GREEN: .4X TO 1X BASE JSY HI
*PATCH: 1X TO 2.5X BASE HI
AS Amare Stoudemire 3.00 8.00
BW Ben Wallace 2.50 6.00
CA Carmelo Anthony 5.00 12.00
DW Dwyane Wade 8.00 20.00
JK Jason Kidd 4.00 10.00
KG Kevin Garnett 5.00 12.00
TD Tim Duncan 4.00 10.00
YM Yao Ming 5.00 12.00

2004-05 Hoops Hot List

Inserted in packs at one in 10, this 15-card set features a tan wood-looking background with player images on the right and the words Hot List on the left. The "o" from hot list is on fire.

COMPLETE SET (15) 8.00 20.00
1 Dwyane Wade 1.50 4.00
2 LeBron James 3.00 8.00
3 Kobe Bryant 2.50 6.00
4 Shaquille O'Neal 1.25 3.00
5 Michael Redd .50 1.25
6 Tracy McGrady .60 1.50
7 Richard Hamilton .40 1.00
8 Tony Parker .50 1.25
9 Allen Iverson .75 2.00
10 Chris Webber .50 1.25
11 Paul Pierce .60 1.50
12 Jermaine O'Neal .50 1.25
13 Pau Gasol .50 1.25
14 Zach Randolph .40 1.00
15 Andrei Kirilenko .40 1.00

2004-05 Hoops Hot List Jerseys

Randomly inserted in packs at the rate of one in 144, this 13-card set parallels the base Hot List set enhanced with a swatch of jersey in the letter "o" from the words, Hot List.

UNPRICED PATCH PRINT RUN 10 SETS
AI Allen Iverson 4.00 10.00
AK Andrei Kirilenko 2.00 5.00
CW Chris Webber 2.50 6.00
DW Dwyane Wade 8.00 20.00
JO Jermaine O'Neal 2.50 6.00
MR Michael Redd 2.50 6.00
RH Richard Hamilton 2.00 5.00
SO Shaquille O'Neal 6.00 15.00
TM Tracy McGrady 3.00 8.00
ZR Zach Randolph 2.00 5.00

2004-05 Hoops Nameplates

Randomly inserted in packs, this 30-card set is horizontally designed with a player photo on the left side of the card and a square swatch from the name plate on the back of the player's jersey. Cards are all sequentially numbered. An autographed version also serially numbered to 25 were also produced.

PLATES 25 NOT PRICED DUE TO SCARCITY
UNPRICED AU PRINT RUN 25 SETS
AS Amare Stoudemire/43 8.00 20.00
CA Carmelo Anthony/48 12.00 30.00
CK Chris Kaman/40 6.00 15.00
KG Kevin Garnett/48 12.00 30.00
LD Luol Deng/26 12.00 30.00
MD Mike Dunleavy/48 5.00 12.00
MG Manu Ginobili/49 8.00 20.00
MS Mike Sweetney/47 5.00 12.00
RJ Richard Jefferson/50 6.00 15.00
SC Sam Cassell/28 6.00 15.00
VC Vince Carter/45 10.00 25.00

2004-05 Hoops Nameplates Dual

Randomly inserted in packs, this 15-card set parallels the design of the Nameplates insert with two players and two swatches of name plate. Each card is sequentially numbered to 25.

BD Carlos Boozer 15.00 40.00
Luol Deng
DN Baron Davis 10.00 25.00
Jameer Nelson
IG Allen Iverson 30.00 80.00
Kevin Garnett
JM Richard Jefferson 10.00 25.00
Kenyon Martin
KL Chris Kaman 10.00 25.00
Shaun Livingston
MS Darko Milicic 10.00 25.00
Peja Stojakovic

2004-05 Hoops Nameplates Triple

Randomly inserted in packs, this 15-card set parallels the design of the Nameplates insert with three players and three swatches of name plate. Each card is sequentially numbered to 13.

GCS Kevin Garnett 30.00 80.00
Sam Cassell
Latrell Sprewell
KSD Chris Kaman 12.50 30.00
Peja Stojakovic
Mike Dunleavy

2004-05 Hoops Supreme Court

Inserted in packs at one in eight, this 20-card set centers player photos on a brown background with the words, Supreme Court, appearing along the top.

COMPLETE SET (20) 12.50 30.00
1 Kobe Bryant 2.50 6.00
2 LeBron James 3.00 8.00
3 Shaquille O'Neal 1.25 3.00
4 Ben Wallace .50 1.25
5 Yao Ming 1.00 2.50
6 Vince Carter .75 2.00
7 Tim Duncan .75 2.00
8 Kevin Garnett 1.00 2.50
9 Carmelo Anthony 1.00 2.50
10 Richard Jefferson .50 1.25
11 Dwyane Wade 1.50 4.00
12 Steve Francis .50 1.25
13 Dirk Nowitzki .75 2.00
14 Allen Iverson .75 2.00
15 Jermaine O'Neal .50 1.25
16 Corey Maggette .40 1.00
17 Paul Pierce .60 1.50
18 Baron Davis .50 1.25
19 Ray Allen .50 1.25
20 Jason Richardson .50 1.25

2004-05 Hoops Supreme Court Jerseys

Randomly inserted in packs, this 18-card set parallels the base Supreme Court insert enhanced with a swatch of jersey on the right side of the card. A Green version containing a small green foil emblem was issued for some players, and a patch version sequentially numbered to 25 was also inserted.

*GREEN: .4X TO 1X BASE JSY HI
*PATCH: 1X TO 2.5X BASE HI
AI Allen Iverson 4.00 10.00
BW Ben Wallace 2.50 6.00
CA Carmelo Anthony 5.00 12.00
CM Corey Maggette 2.00 5.00
DN Dirk Nowitzki 4.00 10.00
DW Dwyane Wade 8.00 20.00
JR Jason Richardson 2.50 6.00
KG Kevin Garnett 5.00 12.00
PP Paul Pierce 3.00 8.00
RA Ray Allen 2.50 6.00
RJ Richard Jefferson 2.50 6.00
SO Shaquille O'Neal 6.00 15.00
TD Tim Duncan 4.00 10.00
VC Vince Carter 4.00 10.00
YM Yao Ming 5.00 12.00

2005-06 Hoops

Issued in February 2007, this 184-card set features veteran players on cards 1-142 and rookie players on cards 143-184. The base design is borderless with full color player images and a color bar across the bottom in team colors featuring the player's name and team logo. Hoops was packaged in 24-pack boxes where packs contain five cards and carried an initial SRP of $1.99.

COMPLETE SET (184) 20.00 50.00
1 Josh Childress .20 .50
2 Al Harrington .20 .50
3 Josh Smith .25 .60
4 Tony Delk .15 .40
5 Joe Johnson .25 .60
6 Al Jefferson .25 .60
7 Paul Pierce .30 .75
8 Ricky Davis .20 .50
9 Tony Allen .15 .40
10 Dan Dickau .15 .40
11 Keith Bogans .15 .40
12 Emeka Okafor .25 .60
13 Kareem Rush .15 .40
14 Gerald Wallace .25 .60
15 Primoz Brezec .15 .40
16 Ben Gordon .25 .60
17 Luol Deng .25 .60
18 Kirk Hinrich .25 .60
19 Chris Duhon .15 .40
20 Michael Jordan 2.00 5.00
21 LeBron James 1.25 3.00
22 Larry Hughes .20 .50
23 Donyell Marshall .15 .40
24 Drew Gooden .20 .50
25 Zydrunas Ilgauskas .20 .50
26 Erick Dampier .15 .40
27 Jason Terry .20 .50
28 Josh Howard .25 .60
29 Dirk Nowitzki .40 1.00
30 Jerry Stackhouse .20 .50
31 Carmelo Anthony .50 1.25
32 Marcus Camby .20 .50
33 Nene .20 .50
34 Kenyon Martin .25 .60
35 Chauncey Billups .25 .60
36 Richard Hamilton .20 .50
37 Ben Wallace .25 .60
38 Rasheed Wallace .25 .60
39 Tayshaun Prince .25 .60
40 Baron Davis .25 .60
41 Mike Dunleavy .20 .50
42 Mickael Pietrus .20 .50
43 Jason Richardson .25 .60
44 Tracy McGrady .30 .75
45 Yao Ming .30 .75
46 Stromile Swift .15 .40
47 Bob Sura .15 .40
48 Jermaine O'Neal .25 .60
49 Ron Artest .25 .60
50 Fred Jones .15 .40
51 Stephen Jackson .20 .50
52 Corey Maggette .20 .50
53 Elton Brand .25 .60
54 Shaun Livingston .15 .40
55 Chris Wilcox .15 .40
56 Chris Kaman .25 .60
57 Kobe Bryant 1.25 3.00
58 Lamar Odom .25 .60
59 Kwame Brown .15 .40
60 Luke Walton .15 .40
61 Devean George .15 .40
62 Pau Gasol .25 .60
63 Shane Battier .20 .50
64 Bobby Jackson .15 .40
65 Eddie Jones .20 .50
66 Lorenzen Wright .15 .40
67 Shaquille O'Neal .50 1.25
68 Dwyane Wade .60 1.50
69 Antoine Walker .20 .50
70 Jason Williams .20 .50
71 James Posey .15 .40
72 T.J. Ford .20 .50
73 Dan Gadzuric .15 .40
74 Desmond Mason .15 .40
75 Michael Redd .25 .60
76 Kevin Garnett .50 1.25
77 Sam Cassell .25 .60
78 Eddie Griffin .15 .40
79 Wally Szczerbiak .20 .50
80 Michael Olowokandi .15 .40
81 Jeff McInnis .15 .40
82 Vince Carter .40 1.00
83 Jason Kidd .40 1.00
84 Richard Jefferson .25 .60
85 Clifford Robinson .15 .40
86 P.J. Brown .15 .40
87 Jamaal Magloire .15 .40
88 J.R. Smith .25 .60
89 Speedy Claxton .15 .40
90 Jamal Crawford .20 .50
91 Stephon Marbury .20 .50
92 Quentin Richardson .20 .50
93 Mike Sweetney .15 .40
94 Malik Rose .15 .40
95 Steve Francis .25 .60
96 Dwight Howard .50 1.25

97 Keyon Dooling	.15	.40
98 Grant Hill	.30	.75
99 Jameer Nelson	.20	.50
100 Allen Iverson	.40	1.00
101 Samuel Dalembert	.15	.40
102 Chris Webber	.25	.60
103 Andre Iguodala	.25	.60
104 Kyle Korver	.20	.50
105 Steve Nash	.30	.75
106 Shawn Marion	.25	.60
107 Amare Stoudemire	.25	.60
108 Kurt Thomas	.15	.40
109 Darius Miles	.15	.40
110 Zach Randolph	.20	.50
111 Sebastian Telfair	.20	.50
112 Ruben Patterson	.15	.40
113 Joel Przybilla	.15	.40
114 Mike Bibby	.25	.60
115 Peja Stojakovic	.25	.60
116 Brad Miller	.25	.60
117 Bonzi Wells	.15	.40
118 Tim Duncan	.40	1.00
119 Manu Ginobili	.25	.60
120 Tony Parker	.25	.60
121 Robert Horry	.20	.50
122 Bruce Bowen	.15	.40
123 Ray Allen	.25	.60
124 Rashard Lewis	.25	.60
125 Vladimir Radmanovic	.15	.40
126 Luke Ridnour	.20	.50
127 Reggie Evans	.15	.40
128 Chris Bosh	.25	.60
129 Morris Peterson	.15	.40
130 Rafer Alston	.15	.40
131 Rafael Araujo	.15	.40
132 Jalen Rose	.25	.60
133 Carlos Boozer	.25	.60
134 Gordan Giricek	.15	.40
135 Matt Harpring	.20	.50
136 Andrei Kirilenko	.20	.50
137 Mehmet Okur	.15	.40
138 Gilbert Arenas	.25	.60
139 Antawn Jamison	.25	.60
140 Caron Butler	.25	.60
141 Antonio Daniels	.15	.40
142 Brendan Haywood	.15	.40
143 Sarunas Jasikevicius RC	.75	2.00
144 Ryan Gomes RC	.75	2.00
145 Andray Blatche RC	1.00	2.50
146 Bracey Wright RC	.75	2.00
147 Louis Williams RC	1.25	3.00
148 Martynas Andriuskevicius RC	.75	2.00
149 Chris Taft RC	.75	2.00
150 Monta Ellis RC	1.50	4.00
151 Travis Diener RC	.75	2.00
152 Ersan Ilyasova RC	1.00	2.50
153 Yaroslav Korolev RC	.75	2.00
154 C.J. Miles RC	1.00	2.50
155 Brandon Bass RC	1.00	2.50
156 Daniel Ewing RC	.75	2.00
157 Salim Stoudamire RC	.75	2.00
158 David Lee RC	1.25	3.00
159 Wayne Simien RC	.75	2.00
160 Linas Kleiza RC	.75	2.00
161 Jason Maxiell RC	.75	2.00
162 Johan Petro RC	.75	2.00
163 Luther Head RC	.75	2.00
164 Francisco Garcia RC	1.00	2.50
165 Jarrett Jack RC	.75	2.00
166 Nate Robinson RC	1.00	2.50
167 Julius Hodge RC	.75	2.00
168 Hakim Warrick RC	1.00	2.50
169 Gerald Green RC	1.00	2.50
170 Danny Granger RC	1.50	4.00
171 Joey Graham RC	.75	2.00
172 Antoine Wright RC	.75	2.00
173 Rashad McCants RC	.75	2.00
174 Sean May RC	.75	2.00
175 Andrew Bynum RC	2.50	6.00
176 Ike Diogu RC	.75	2.00
177 Channing Frye RC	1.00	2.50
178 Charlie Villanueva RC	1.00	2.50
179 Martell Webster RC	.75	2.00
180 Raymond Felton RC	1.25	3.00
181 Chris Paul RC	3.00	8.00
182 Deron Williams RC	2.00	5.00
183 Marvin Williams RC	1.00	2.50
184 Andrew Bogut RC	1.25	3.00

2005-06 Hoops Genuine Coverage

Randomly inserted in packs, this 41-card set features full color player photos and swatches of memorabilia. SP information was provided by Upper Deck.

GCAH Al Harrington	2.00	5.00
GCAK Andrei Kirilenko	2.00	5.00
GCAM Antonio McDyess	2.00	5.00
GCAS Amare Stoudemire SP	2.50	6.00
GCBD Baron Davis	2.50	6.00
GCCA Caron Butler	2.50	6.00
GCCB Carlos Boozer	2.50	6.00
GCCM Corey Maggette	2.00	5.00
GCCW Chris Webber	2.50	6.00
GCDA Darko Milicic	2.00	5.00
GCDF Derek Fisher	2.00	5.00
GCDG Devean George	2.00	5.00
GCDM Darius Miles	2.00	5.00
GCDN Dirk Nowitzki	4.00	10.00
GCDW David Wesley	2.00	5.00
GCJJ Joe Johnson	2.50	6.00
GCJT Jason Terry	2.00	5.00
GCKB Kwame Brown	2.00	5.00
GCKG Kevin Garnett SP	5.00	12.00
GCKT Kurt Thomas	2.00	5.00
GCLJ LeBron James SP	10.00	25.00
GCME Carmelo Anthony	5.00	12.00
GCMG Manu Ginobili	2.50	6.00
GCNE Nene	2.00	5.00
GCNK Nenad Krstic	2.00	5.00
GCQR Quentin Richardson	2.00	5.00
GCRA Rafael Araujo	2.00	5.00
GCRL Rashard Lewis	2.50	6.00
GCRW Rasheed Wallace	2.50	6.00
GCSA Shareef Abdur-Rahim	2.00	5.00
GCSB Shane Battier	2.00	5.00
GCSC Sam Cassell	2.50	6.00
GCSD Samuel Dalembert	2.00	5.00
GCSF Steve Francis	2.50	6.00
GCSM Shawn Marion	2.50	6.00
GCSS Stromile Swift	2.00	5.00
GCTC Tyson Chandler	2.00	5.00
GCTD Tim Duncan	4.00	10.00
GCTM Tracy McGrady	3.00	8.00
GCUH Udonis Haslem	2.00	5.00
GCWS Wally Szczerbiak	2.00	5.00

2005-06 Hoops HoopScripts

Inserted at approximately one per box, this 33-card set is horizontally designed with a player photo on the left, his jersey number on the right and an autograph sticker over the number.

HSAA Alex Acker	4.00	10.00
HSAB Andray Blatche	5.00	12.00
HSAJ Amir Johnson	4.00	10.00
HSBB Brandon Bass	5.00	12.00
HSBW Bracey Wright	4.00	10.00
HSCM C.J. Miles	5.00	12.00
HSDH Dwight Howard SP	12.50	30.00
HSDL David Lee	6.00	15.00
HSDT Dijon Thompson	4.00	10.00
HSEI Ersan Ilyasova	5.00	12.00
HSFG Francisco Garcia	5.00	12.00
HSGG Gerald Green	5.00	12.00
HSID Ike Diogu	4.00	10.00
HSJG Joey Graham	4.00	10.00
HSJH Julius Hodge	4.00	10.00
HSJJ Jarrett Jack	4.00	10.00
HSJM Jason Maxiell	4.00	10.00
HSJP Johan Petro	4.00	10.00
HSJS James Singleton	4.00	10.00
HSLH Luther Head	4.00	10.00
HSLJ LeBron James SP	100.00	200.00
HSLK Linas Kleiza	4.00	10.00
HSLR Lawrence Roberts	4.00	10.00
HSLW Louis Williams	6.00	15.00
HSMA Martynas Andriuskevicius	4.00	10.00
HSMW Martell Webster	4.00	10.00
HSNR Nate Robinson	5.00	12.00
HSOG Orien Greene	4.00	10.00
HSRF Raymond Felton	6.00	15.00
HSRG Ryan Gomes	4.00	10.00
HSRM Rashad McCants	4.00	10.00
HSRW Robert Whaley	4.00	10.00
HSVW Von Wafer	4.00	10.00

2005-06 Hoops LBJ Profiles

Inserted at approximately eight per box, this 30-card set showcases highlights from LeBron James' career. Cards are horizontally designed with a red area containing text on the left and an action photo on the right.

COMPLETE SET (30)	12.50	30.00
COMMON CARD (LBJ1-LBJ30)	.75	2.00

2005-06 Hoops MJ Profiles

Inserted at approximately eight per box, this 30-card set showcases highlights from Michael Jordan's career. Cards are horizontally designed with a red area containing text on the left and an action photo on the right.

COMPLETE SET (30)	15.00	40.00
COMMON CARD (MJ1-MJ30)	1.25	3.00

2011-12 Hoops

COMPLETE SET (278)	25.00	60.00
UNPRICED AP BLACK PRINT RUN ONE SET		
1 Jamal Crawford	.25	.60
2 Kirk Hinrich	.30	.75
3 Al Horford	.25	.60
4 Joe Johnson	.30	.75
5 Marvin Williams	.25	.60
6 Josh Smith	.30	.75
7 Ray Allen	.30	.75
8 Brandon Bass	.20	.50
9 Glen Davis	.25	.60
10 Kevin Garnett	.60	1.50
11 Jeff Green	.25	.60
12 Jermaine O'Neal	.30	.75
13 Troy Murphy	.20	.50
14 Paul Pierce	.40	1.00
15 Rajon Rondo	.40	1.00
16 D.J. Augustin	.20	.50
17 Kwame Brown	.20	.50
18 DeSagana Diop	.20	.50
19 Eduardo Najera	.20	.50
20 Tyrus Thomas	.25	.60
21 Omer Asik	.25	.60
22 Carlos Boozer	.30	.75
23 Ronnie Brewer	.25	.60
24 Rasual Butler	.20	.50
25 Luol Deng	.30	.75
26 Kyle Korver	.25	.60
27 Joakim Noah	.30	.75
28 Derrick Rose	1.00	2.50
29 Baron Davis	.30	.75
30 Semih Erden	.20	.50
31 Daniel Gibson	.25	.60
32 Luke Harangody	.25	.60
33 Antawn Jamison	.30	.75
34 Anderson Varejao	.25	.60
35 J.J. Barea	.30	.75
36 Rodrigue Beaubois	.25	.60
37 Caron Butler	.25	.60
38 Brian Cardinal	.20	.50
39 Tyson Chandler	.25	.60
40 Rudy Fernandez	.25	.60
41 Dominique Jones	.20	.50
42 Jason Kidd	.30	.75
43 Ian Mahinmi	.20	.50
44 Shawn Marion	.30	.75
45 Dirk Nowitzki	.40	1.00
46 DeShawn Stevenson	.20	.50
47 Chris Andersen	.30	.75
48 Danilo Gallinari	.30	.75
49 Nene	.25	.60
50 Ty Lawson	.30	.75
51 Corey Brewer	.20	.50
52 Andre Miller	.25	.60
53 Timofey Mozgov	.20	.50
54 Austin Daye	.20	.50
55 Ben Gordon	.30	.75
56 Richard Hamilton	.25	.60
57 Jonas Jerebko	.20	.50
58 Tracy McGrady	.30	.75
59 Tayshaun Prince	.30	.75
60 DaJuan Summers	.20	.50
61 Charlie Villanueva	.25	.60
62 Ben Wallace	.30	.75
63 Terrico White	.20	.50
64 Stephen Curry	.30	.75
65 Monta Ellis	.30	.75
66 David Lee	.25	.60
67 Jeremy Lin	1.25	3.00
68 Andris Biedrins	.20	.50
69 Ekpe Udoh	.20	.50
70 Chase Budinger	.20	.50
71 Goran Dragic	.30	.75
72 Jordan Hill	.20	.50
73 Kevin Martin	.30	.75
74 Patrick Patterson	.25	.60
75 Luis Scola	.25	.60
76 Hasheem Thabeet	.20	.50
77 Darren Collison	.30	.75
78 Mike Dunleavy Jr.	.20	.50
79 T.J. Ford	.20	.50
80 Danny Granger	.30	.75
81 Tyler Hansbrough	.30	.75
82 George Hill	.25	.60
83 Josh McRoberts	.20	.50
84 Brandon Rush	.20	.50
85 Lance Stephenson	.20	.50
86 Al-Farouq Aminu	.20	.50
87 Ike Diogu	.20	.50
88 Randy Foye	.20	.50
89 Eric Gordon	.30	.75
90 Blake Griffin	.60	1.50
91 DeAndre Jordan	.30	.75
92 Chris Kaman	.25	.60
93 Ryan Gomes	.20	.50
94 Mo Williams	.25	.60
95 Metta World Peace	.30	.75
96 Matt Barnes	.20	.50
97 Steve Blake	.20	.50
98 Kobe Bryant	1.25	3.00
99 Andrew Bynum	.40	1.00
100 Derrick Caracter	.20	.50
101 Derek Fisher	.25	.60
102 Pau Gasol	.30	.75
103 Lamar Odom	.30	.75
104 Darrell Arthur	.20	.50
105 Shane Battier	.25	.60
106 Marc Gasol	.30	.75
107 Rudy Gay	.30	.75
108 O.J. Mayo	.30	.75
109 Zach Randolph	.25	.60
110 Ishmael Smith	.20	.50
111 Greivis Vasquez	.25	.60
112 Sam Young	.20	.50
113 Joel Anthony	.20	.50
114 Mike Bibby	.25	.60
115 Chris Bosh	.30	.75
116 Mario Chalmers	.30	.75
117 Juwan Howard	.25	.60
118 Udonis Haslem	.25	.60
119 LeBron James	1.25	3.00
120 Mike Miller	.30	.75
121 Dexter Pittman	.20	.50
122 Dwyane Wade	.60	1.50
123 Jon Brockman	.20	.50
124 Carlos Delfino	.20	.50
125 Drew Gooden	.25	.60
126 Ersan Ilyasova	.25	.60
127 Stephen Jackson	.25	.60
128 Brandon Jennings	.30	.75
129 Luc Mbah a Moute	.20	.50
130 Larry Sanders	.20	.50
131 Beno Udrih	.20	.50
132 Andrew Bogut	.30	.75
133 Michael Beasley	.30	.75
134 Wayne Ellington	.20	.50
135 Lazar Hayward	.20	.50
136 Kevin Love	.40	1.00
137 Darko Milicic	.20	.50
138 Brad Miller	.25	.60
139 Nikola Pekovic	.30	.75
140 Luke Ridnour	.25	.60
141 Ricky Rubio	.75	2.00
142 Martell Webster	.25	.60
143 Jordan Farmar	.20	.50
144 Sundiata Gaines	.20	.50
145 Anthony Morrow	.20	.50
146 Damion James	.20	.50
147 Brook Lopez	.30	.75
148 Brandan Wright	.20	.50
149 Kris Humphries	.20	.50
150 Johan Petro	.20	.50
151 Deron Williams	.30	.75
152 Trevor Ariza	.20	.50
153 Carl Landry	.20	.50
154 David West	.30	.75
155 Jason Smith	.20	.50
156 Jarrett Jack	.25	.60
157 Emeka Okafor	.30	.75
158 Chris Paul	.50	1.25
159 Quincy Pondexter	.20	.50
160 Carmelo Anthony	.40	1.00
161 Chauncey Billups	.30	.75
162 Derrick Brown	.20	.50
163 Anthony Carter	.20	.50
164 Landry Fields	.30	.75
165 Toney Douglas	.20	.50
166 Amare Stoudemire	.30	.75
167 Jerome Jordan RC	.30	.75
168 Cole Aldrich	.20	.50
169 Nick Collison	.20	.50
170 Kevin Durant	1.00	2.50
171 James Harden	.40	1.00
172 Serge Ibaka	.30	.75
173 B.J. Mullens	.20	.50
174 Eric Maynor	.20	.50
175 Russell Westbrook	.40	1.00
176 Ryan Anderson	.25	.60
177 Chris Duhon	.20	.50
178 Dwight Howard	.50	1.25
179 Jameer Nelson	.25	.60
180 J.J. Redick	.30	.75
181 Jason Richardson	.30	.75
182 Hedo Turkoglu	.30	.75
183 Craig Brackins	.20	.50
184 Elton Brand	.30	.75
185 Andre Iguodala	.30	.75
186 Jason Kapono	.20	.50
187 Jodie Meeks	.25	.60
188 Evan Turner	.30	.75
189 Louis Williams	.25	.60
190 Thaddeus Young	.20	.50
191 Michael Redd	.30	.75
192 Vince Carter	.40	1.00
193 Channing Frye	.25	.60
194 Grant Hill	.40	1.00
195 Marcin Gortat	.30	.75
196 Steve Nash	.30	.75
197 Hakim Warrick	.25	.60
198 LaMarcus Aldridge	.30	.75
199 Marcus Camby	.20	.50
200 Raymond Felton	.25	.60
201 Wesley Matthews	.30	.75
202 Greg Oden	.25	.60
203 Armon Johnson	.20	.50
204 Gerald Wallace	.30	.75
205 Elliot Williams	.20	.50
206 DeMarcus Cousins	.40	1.00
207 Samuel Dalembert	.20	.50
208 Tyreke Evans	.30	.75
209 Francisco Garcia	.25	.60
210 Donte Greene	.20	.50
211 Jason Thompson	.20	.50
212 Marcus Thornton	.30	.75
213 Hassan Whiteside	.20	.50
214 DeJuan Blair	.25	.60
215 Da'Sean Butler	.20	.50
216 Tim Duncan	.50	1.25
217 Manu Ginobili	.30	.75
218 Richard Jefferson	.30	.75
219 Matt Bonner	.20	.50
220 Gary Neal	.30	.75
221 Tony Parker	.30	.75
222 Tiago Splitter	.25	.60
223 Solomon Alabi	.20	.50
224 Leandro Barbosa	.25	.60
225 Andrea Bargnani	.25	.60
226 Jose Calderon	.25	.60
227 Ed Davis	.25	.60
228 DeMar DeRozan	.30	.75
229 Amir Johnson	.20	.50
230 Raja Bell	.25	.60
231 C.J. Miles	.20	.50
232 Jeremy Evans	.20	.50
233 Derrick Favors	.30	.75
234 Devin Harris	.30	.75
235 Gordon Hayward	.30	.75
236 Al Jefferson	.30	.75
237 Earl Watson	.20	.50
238 Paul Millsap	.25	.60
239 Mehmet Okur	.20	.50
240 Andray Blatche	.20	.50
241 Trevor Booker	.20	.50
242 Jordan Crawford	.30	.75
243 Josh Howard	.25	.60
244 Ronny Turiaf	.20	.50
245 Rashard Lewis	.25	.60
246 JaVale McGee	.25	.60
247 John Wall	.50	1.25
248 Derrick Rose	1.00	2.50
249 Dwyane Wade	.60	1.50
250 LeBron James	1.25	3.00
251 Chris Bosh	.30	.75
252 Amare Stoudemire	.30	.75
253 Dwight Howard	.50	1.25
254 Kevin Garnett	.60	1.50
255 Paul Pierce	.40	1.00
256 Rajon Rondo	.40	1.00
257 Ray Allen	.30	.75
258 Kobe Bryant	1.25	3.00
259 Chris Paul	.50	1.25
260 Carmelo Anthony	.40	1.00
261 Dirk Nowitzki	.40	1.00
262 Kevin Durant	1.00	2.50
263 Tim Duncan	.50	1.25
264 Blake Griffin	.60	1.50
265 Pau Gasol	.30	.75
266 Deron Williams	.30	.75
267 Manu Ginobili	.30	.75
268 Kobe Bryant	1.25	3.00
269 Blake Griffin	.60	1.50
270 Kevin Durant	1.00	2.50
271 Dirk Nowitzki	.40	1.00
272 LeBron James	1.25	3.00
273 Derrick Rose	1.00	2.50
274 Chris Paul	.50	1.25
275 Paul Pierce	.40	1.00
276 Carmelo Anthony	.40	1.00
277 Kevin Love	.40	1.00
278 Kobe Bryant	1.25	3.00
279 Dallas Mavericks SP	8.00	20.00
BG1 Blake Griffin Blake Superior	50.00	120.00
KB1 Kobe Bryant Black Mamba	60.00	150.00

2011-12 Hoops Artist's Proofs

*ARTIST PROOF: 2.5X TO 6X BASE HI
RANDOM INSERTS IN PACKS

67 Jeremy Lin	10.00	25.00

2011-12 Hoops Glossy

*GLOSSY: 1.5X TO 4X BASE HI
RANDOM INSERTS IN PACKS

2011-12 Hoops 89-90 Buyback Autographs

RANDOM INSERTS IN PACKS

70 Xavier McDaniel	20.00	50.00
120 Alex English	15.00	40.00
125 Adrian Dantley	20.00	50.00
310 David Robinson	125.00	225.00
311 Dale Ellis		

2011-12 Hoops A Night to Remember

COMPLETE SET (20)	12.00	30.00
RANDOM INSERTS IN PACKS		
1 Wilt Chamberlain	1.25	3.00
2 Dwight Howard	1.00	2.50
3 Magic Johnson	1.50	4.00
4 Kobe Bryant	2.50	6.00
5 Bill Russell	1.00	2.50
6 Magic Johnson	1.50	4.00
7 Wilt Chamberlain	1.25	3.00
8 Wilt Chamberlain	1.25	3.00
9 Ray Allen	.60	1.50
10 Elgin Baylor	.60	1.50
11 John Stockton	1.00	2.50
12 Hakeem Olajuwon	.75	2.00
13 Dwyane Wade	1.25	3.00
14 Ray Allen	.60	1.50
15 Bob Cousy	1.00	2.50
16 Scott Skiles	.60	1.50
17 Mark Eaton	.60	1.50
18 Rick Barry	.60	1.50
19 Jason Terry	.50	1.25
20 Vince Carter	.75	2.00

2011-12 Hoops Action Photos

COMPLETE SET (25)	10.00	25.00
RANDOM INSERTS IN PACKS		
1 Derrick Rose	1.50	4.00
2 JaVale McGee	.40	1.00
3 Paul Pierce	.60	1.50
4 LeBron James	2.00	5.00
5 Dwight Howard	.75	2.00
6 Carmelo Anthony	.60	1.50
7 Gary Neal	.50	1.25
8 Dirk Nowitzki	.60	1.50
9 Kevin Love	.60	1.50
10 Al Horford	.40	1.00
11 Amare Stoudemire	.50	1.25
12 Steve Nash	.50	1.25
13 John Wall	.75	2.00
14 Chris Paul	.75	2.00
15 Kevin Durant	1.50	4.00
16 Pau Gasol	.50	1.25
17 Tyson Chandler	.40	1.00
18 Rajon Rondo	.60	1.50
19 Nene	.40	1.00
20 Deron Williams	.50	1.25
21 Blake Griffin	1.00	2.50
22 Stephen Curry	.50	1.25
23 Marc Gasol	.50	1.25
24 Kobe Bryant	2.00	5.00
25 Dwyane Wade	1.00	2.50

2011-12 Hoops Autographs

RANDOM INSERTS IN PACKS
SOME SP's UNPRICED DUE TO SCARCITY

4 Joe Johnson SP	6.00	15.00
11 Jeff Green SP	6.00	15.00
16 D.J. Augustin SP	5.00	12.00
18 DeSagana Diop	2.50	6.00
21 Omer Asik SP	8.00	20.00
22 Carlos Boozer SP	10.00	25.00
23 Ronnie Brewer SP	25.00	60.00
25 Luol Deng SP	20.00	50.00
27 Joakim Noah SP	10.00	25.00
28 Derrick Rose SP	125.00	250.00
30 Semih Erden	2.50	6.00
31 Daniel Gibson SP	15.00	40.00
32 Luke Harangody	2.50	6.00
33 Antawn Jamison SP	5.00	12.00
34 Anderson Varejao	2.50	6.00
35 J.J. Barea	8.00	20.00
36 Rodrigue Beaubois	2.50	6.00
37 Caron Butler SP	20.00	50.00
41 Dominique Jones	2.50	6.00
43 Ian Mahinmi	3.00	8.00
45 Dirk Nowitzki SP	75.00	200.00
47 Chris Andersen SP	15.00	40.00
48 Danilo Gallinari SP	5.00	12.00
53 Timofey Mozgov SP	5.00	12.00
54 Austin Daye SP	5.00	12.00
55 Ben Gordon SP	5.00	12.00
56 Richard Hamilton SP	15.00	40.00
57 Jonas Jerebko SP	5.00	12.00
58 Tracy McGrady SP	40.00	100.00
60 DaJuan Summers	2.50	6.00
61 Charlie Villanueva SP	5.00	12.00
63 Terrico White	2.50	6.00
64 Stephen Curry SP	20.00	50.00
65 Monta Ellis SP	12.00	30.00
66 David Lee SP	5.00	12.00
67 Jeremy Lin	50.00	125.00
69 Ekpe Udoh SP	5.00	12.00
70 Chase Budinger SP	6.00	15.00
71 Goran Dragic SP	8.00	20.00
72 Jordan Hill	2.50	6.00
73 Kevin Martin SP	10.00	25.00
74 Patrick Patterson	4.00	10.00
75 Luis Scola SP	5.00	12.00
76 Hasheem Thabeet	2.50	6.00
78 Mike Dunleavy Jr. SP	5.00	12.00
79 T.J. Ford SP	5.00	12.00
80 Danny Granger SP	12.00	30.00
81 Tyler Hansbrough SP	5.00	12.00
82 George Hill SP	8.00	20.00
85 Lance Stephenson	2.50	6.00
88 Randy Foye	2.50	6.00
90 Blake Griffin SP	80.00	200.00
92 Chris Kaman SP	5.00	12.00
93 Ryan Gomes SP	15.00	40.00
94 Mo Williams SP	5.00	12.00
98 Kobe Bryant SP	125.00	250.00
99 Andrew Bynum SP	12.00	30.00
100 Derrick Caracter	2.50	6.00
101 Derek Fisher SP	8.00	20.00
103 Lamar Odom SP	10.00	25.00
105 Shane Battier SP	6.00	15.00
107 Rudy Gay SP	60.00	150.00
108 O.J. Mayo SP	6.00	15.00
109 Zach Randolph SP	8.00	20.00
110 Ishmael Smith	2.50	6.00
111 Greivis Vasquez	2.50	6.00
112 Sam Young	2.50	6.00
114 Mike Bibby SP	5.00	12.00
115 Chris Bosh SP	25.00	60.00
121 Dexter Pittman SP	5.00	12.00
123 Jon Brockman	2.50	6.00
127 Stephen Jackson SP	40.00	80.00
130 Larry Sanders	2.50	6.00
131 Beno Udrih SP	20.00	50.00
132 Andrew Bogut SP	6.00	15.00
133 Michael Beasley SP	8.00	20.00
134 Wayne Ellington	2.50	6.00
135 Lazar Hayward SP	6.00	15.00
136 Kevin Love SP	40.00	100.00
137 Darko Milicic SP	6.00	15.00
139 Nikola Pekovic	8.00	20.00
140 Luke Ridnour SP	5.00	12.00
144 Sundiata Gaines SP	5.00	12.00
146 Damion James SP	5.00	12.00
147 Brook Lopez SP	15.00	40.00
149 Kris Humphries	4.00	10.00
151 Deron Williams SP	20.00	50.00
152 Trevor Ariza SP	5.00	12.00
153 Carl Landry	2.50	6.00
157 Emeka Okafor SP	5.00	12.00
158 Chris Paul SP	100.00	200.00
159 Quincy Pondexter SP	5.00	12.00
160 Carmelo Anthony SP	75.00	150.00
162 Derrick Brown SP	5.00	12.00
164 Landry Fields SP	6.00	15.00
165 Toney Douglas SP	5.00	12.00
167 Jerome Jordan	2.50	6.00
168 Cole Aldrich	2.50	6.00
170 Kevin Durant SP	125.00	250.00
173 B.J. Mullens	2.50	6.00
175 Russell Westbrook SP	20.00	50.00
179 Jameer Nelson SP	5.00	12.00
180 J.J. Redick	5.00	12.00
182 Hedo Turkoglu SP	5.00	12.00
183 Craig Brackins SP	5.00	12.00
187 Jodie Meeks	3.00	8.00
189 Louis Williams SP	5.00	12.00
192 Vince Carter SP	25.00	60.00
193 Channing Frye SP	5.00	12.00
194 Grant Hill SP	75.00	150.00
196 Steve Nash SP	40.00	100.00
197 Hakim Warrick SP	5.00	12.00
198 LaMarcus Aldridge SP	10.00	25.00
199 Marcus Camby SP	8.00	20.00
200 Raymond Felton SP	8.00	20.00
201 Wesley Matthews SP	5.00	12.00
203 Armon Johnson	2.50	6.00
204 Gerald Wallace SP	6.00	15.00
205 Elliot Williams	2.50	6.00
206 DeMarcus Cousins SP	12.00	30.00
207 Samuel Dalembert	2.50	6.00
208 Tyreke Evans SP	20.00	50.00
210 Donte Greene	2.50	6.00
213 Hassan Whiteside	2.50	6.00
214 DeJuan Blair SP	8.00	20.00
215 Da'Sean Butler	2.50	6.00
220 Gary Neal SP	8.00	20.00
221 Tony Parker SP	15.00	40.00
222 Tiago Splitter SP	8.00	20.00
223 Solomon Alabi	2.50	6.00
225 Andrea Bargnani SP	20.00	50.00
226 Jose Calderon	2.50	6.00
227 Ed Davis	2.50	6.00
228 DeMar DeRozan SP	5.00	12.00
229 Amir Johnson	2.50	6.00
232 Jeremy Evans	3.00	8.00
233 Derrick Favors SP	5.00	12.00
234 Devin Harris SP	15.00	40.00
235 Gordon Hayward SP	12.00	30.00
236 Al Jefferson SP	5.00	12.00
238 Paul Millsap	2.50	6.00
241 Trevor Booker SP	5.00	12.00
242 Jordan Crawford SP	100.00	175.00
243 Josh Howard SP	5.00	12.00
246 JaVale McGee SP	10.00	25.00
248 Derrick Rose SP	125.00	250.00
251 Chris Bosh SP	25.00	60.00
258 Kobe Bryant SP	100.00	225.00
259 Chris Paul SP	60.00	150.00
261 Dirk Nowitzki SP	75.00	200.00
262 Kevin Durant SP	125.00	250.00
264 Blake Griffin SP	80.00	200.00
266 Deron Williams SP	20.00	50.00
268 Kobe Bryant SP	125.00	250.00
269 Blake Griffin SP	80.00	200.00
270 Kevin Durant SP	125.00	25
271 Dirk Nowitzki SP	75.00	20
273 Derrick Rose SP	125.00	25
274 Chris Paul SP	100.00	20
277 Kevin Love SP	40.00	10
278 Kobe Bryant SP	125.00	25

2011-12 Hoops BIGS

COMPLETE SET (15)	12.00	3
RANDOM INSERTS IN RETAIL PACKS		
1 Dwight Howard	2.00	
2 Tim Duncan	2.00	
3 Andrew Bynum	1.50	
4 Al Jefferson	1.25	
5 Tyson Chandler	1.00	
6 Kevin Love	1.50	
7 Zach Randolph	1.00	
8 Andrew Bogut	1.25	
9 Nene	1.00	
10 Brook Lopez	1.25	
11 Joakim Noah	1.25	
12 Amare Stoudemire	1.25	
13 Andrea Bargnani	1.00	
14 Al Horford	1.00	
15 Samuel Dalembert	.75	

2011-12 Hoops Courtside

COMPLETE SET (15)	10.00	25
RANDOM INSERTS IN PACKS		
1 Kobe Bryant	2.00	5
2 LeBron James	2.00	5
3 Chris Paul	.75	2
4 Dwight Howard	.75	2
5 Kevin Durant	1.50	4
6 Blake Griffin	1.00	2
7 Carmelo Anthony	.60	1
8 Kevin Love	.60	1
9 Steve Nash	.50	1
10 Dwyane Wade	1.00	2
11 Dirk Nowitzki	.60	1
12 Derrick Rose	1.50	4
13 Tony Parker	.50	1
14 Deron Williams	.50	1
15 Paul Pierce	.60	1.

2011-12 Hoops Dreams

COMPLETE SET (9)	4.00	10.
RANDOM INSERTS IN PACKS		
1 John Wall	.75	2.
2 DeMarcus Cousins	.60	1.
3 James Harden	.60	1.
4 Blake Griffin	1.00	2.
5 Landry Fields	.50	1
6 Stephen Curry	.50	1
7 Jordan Crawford	.50	1
8 Tyreke Evans	.50	1
9 Darren Collison	.50	1

2011-12 Hoops Hall of Fame Heroes

COMPLETE SET (20)	12.00	30.
RANDOM INSERTS IN PACKS		
1 Bill Russell	1.00	2.
2 Jerry West	.75	2.
3 Oscar Robertson	.75	2.
4 Walt Bellamy	.60	1.
5 Nate Thurmond	.60	1.
6 Elgin Baylor	.60	1.
7 John Havlicek	.75	2.
8 Willis Reed	.60	1.
9 Magic Johnson	1.50	4.
10 Bob Lanier	.60	1.
11 Wilt Chamberlain	1.25	3.
12 Larry Bird	2.00	5.
13 Karl Malone	.75	2.
14 David Robinson	1.00	2.
15 Rick Barry	.60	1.
16 Dolph Schayes	.60	1.
17 Bill Walton	.60	1.
18 George Gervin	.60	1.
19 John Stockton	1.00	2.
20 Pete Maravich	2.00	5.

11-12 Hoops Private Signings

ED PRINT RUN 49 TO 299 SETS		
Jefferson	12.00	30.00
auncey Billups	20.00	50.00
h Randolph	15.00	40.00
nar Odom	40.00	80.00
is Williams	12.00	30.00
ly Gay	15.00	40.00
e Calderon	12.00	30.00
orge Hill	12.00	30.00
phen Jackson	15.00	40.00
e Johnson	15.00	40.00
arcus Camby	15.00	40.00

2011-12 Hoops Slam Dunk Winners

PLETE SET (15)	8.00	20.00
DOM INSERTS IN PACKS		
rry Nance	.60	1.50
minique Wilkins	.75	2.00
ud Webb	.60	1.50
nny Walker	.60	1.50
minique Wilkins	.75	2.00
dric Ceballos	.60	1.50
ent Barry	.40	1.00
be Bryant	2.50	6.00
nce Carter	.75	2.00
ason Richardson	.60	1.50
osh Smith	.60	1.50
Nate Robinson	.60	1.50
Dwight Howard	1.00	2.50
Nate Robinson	.60	1.50
Blake Griffin	1.25	3.00

2012-13 Hoops

PLETE SET (300)	25.00	60.00
PRICED AP BLACK PRINT RUN ONE SET		
ery Bradley	.30	.75
andon Bass	.20	.50
vin Garnett	.60	1.50
ul Pierce	.40	1.00
jon Rondo	.40	1.00
y Allen	.30	.75
oc Rivers CO	.30	.75
eron Williams	.30	.75
rook Lopez	.30	.75
Kris Humphries	.20	.50
Anthony Morrow	.20	.50
Jordan Farmar	.20	.50
Gerald Wallace	.30	.75
Avery Johnson CO	.30	.75
Amare Stoudemire	.30	.75
Carmelo Anthony	.40	1.00
Landry Fields	.30	.75
Tyson Chandler	.25	.60
Jeremy Lin	.75	2.00
Steve Novak	.20	.50
Mike Woodson CO	.30	.75
Andre Iguodala	.30	.75
Jodie Meeks	.25	.60
Jrue Holiday	.30	.75
Louis Williams	.25	.60
Elton Brand	.30	.75
Evan Turner	.30	.75
Spencer Hawes	.20	.50
Doug Collins CO	.30	.75
Andrea Bargnani	.25	.60
DeMar DeRozan	.30	.75
Gary Forbes	.20	.50
Jose Calderon	.25	.60
Linas Kleiza	.20	.50
Ed Davis	.25	.60
Dwane Casey CO	.30	.75
Dirk Nowitzki	.40	1.00
Rodrigue Beaubois	.25	.60
Shawn Marion	.30	.75
Jason Kidd	.30	.75
Jason Terry	.25	.60
Vince Carter	.40	1.00
Ian Mahinmi	.20	.50
Rick Carlisle CO	.30	.75
Kyle Lowry	.25	.60
Kevin Martin	.30	.75
Luis Scola	.25	.60
Chase Budinger	.20	.50
Patrick Patterson	.25	.60
Goran Dragic	.30	.75
Kevin McHale CO	.30	.75
Marc Gasol	.30	.75
Mike Conley	.25	.60
O.J. Mayo	.30	.75
Rudy Gay	.30	.75
Zach Randolph	.25	.60
Lester Hudson	.20	.50
Dante Cunningham	.20	.50
Lionel Hollins CO	.30	.75
Emeka Okafor	.30	.75
Carl Landry	.20	.50
Chris Kaman	.25	.60
Eric Gordon	.30	.75
Greivis Vasquez	.25	.60
Trevor Ariza	.20	.50
Monty Williams CO	.30	.75
DeJuan Blair	.25	.60
Boris Diaw	.25	.60
Manu Ginobili	.30	.75
Tim Duncan	.50	1.25
Tony Parker	.30	.75
Danny Green	.30	.75
73 Gregg Popovich CO	.30	.75
74 Carlos Boozer	.30	.75
75 Derrick Rose	1.00	2.50
76 Joakim Noah	.30	.75
77 Luol Deng	.30	.75
78 Richard Hamilton	.25	.60
79 Taj Gibson	.25	.60
80 Ronnie Brewer	.25	.60
81 Tom Thibodeau CO	.30	.75
82 Alonzo Gee	.25	.60
83 Anderson Varejao	.25	.60
84 Antawn Jamison	.30	.75
85 Daniel Gibson	.25	.60
86 Byron Scott CO	.30	.75
87 Ben Gordon	.30	.75
88 Greg Monroe	.30	.75
89 Rodney Stuckey	.30	.75
90 Tayshaun Prince	.30	.75
91 Jonas Jerebko	.20	.50
92 Lawrence Frank CO	.30	.75
93 Danny Granger	.30	.75
94 David West	.30	.75
95 Paul George	.30	.75
96 Roy Hibbert	.25	.60
97 Darren Collison	.30	.75
98 George Hill	.25	.60
99 A.J. Price	.20	.50
100 Frank Vogel CO	.30	.75
101 Brandon Jennings	.30	.75
102 Drew Gooden	.25	.60
103 Monta Ellis	.30	.75
104 Ersan Ilyasova	.25	.60
105 Mike Dunleavy	.20	.50
106 Luc Mbah a Moute	.20	.50
107 Scott Skiles CO	.30	.75
108 Arron Afflalo	.20	.50
109 Danilo Gallinari	.30	.75
110 Ty Lawson	.30	.75
111 Wilson Chandler	.25	.60
112 JaVale McGee	.25	.60
113 Andre Miller	.25	.60
114 Timofey Mozgov	.20	.50
115 George Karl CO	.30	.75
116 Kevin Love	.40	1.00
117 Luke Ridnour	.25	.60
118 Michael Beasley	.30	.75
119 Nikola Pekovic	.30	.75
120 Ricky Rubio	.75	2.00
121 Wesley Johnson	.25	.60
122 J.J. Barea	.30	.75
123 Rick Adelman CO	.30	.75
124 LaMarcus Aldridge	.30	.75
125 Nicolas Batum	.30	.75
126 Wesley Matthews	.30	.75
127 Jonny Flynn	.20	.50
128 J.J. Hickson	.25	.60
129 Jamal Crawford	.25	.60
130 Raymond Felton	.25	.60
131 Kaleb Canales CO	.30	.75
132 Derek Fisher	.25	.60
133 James Harden	.40	1.00
134 Kendrick Perkins	.25	.60
135 Kevin Durant	1.00	2.50
136 Russell Westbrook	.40	1.00
137 Serge Ibaka	.30	.75
138 Daequan Cook	.20	.50
139 Nick Collison	.20	.50
140 Scott Brooks CO	.30	.75
141 Al Jefferson	.30	.75
142 DeMarre Carroll	.20	.50
143 Gordon Hayward	.30	.75
144 Paul Millsap	.25	.60
145 Derrick Favors	.30	.75
146 Josh Howard	.25	.60
147 Tyrone Corbin CO	.30	.75
148 Al Horford	.25	.60
149 Jeff Teague	.25	.60
150 Joe Johnson	.30	.75
151 Josh Smith	.30	.75
152 Tracy McGrady	.30	.75
153 Marvin Williams	.25	.60
154 Zaza Pachulia	.20	.50
155 Larry Drew CO	.30	.75
156 LeBron James	1.25	3.00
157 Dwyane Wade	.60	1.50
158 Chris Bosh	.30	.75
159 Mario Chalmers	.30	.75
160 Joel Anthony	.20	.50
161 Udonis Haslem	.25	.60
162 Shane Battier	.25	.60
163 Erik Spoelstra CO	.30	.75
164 Dwight Howard	.50	1.25
165 Hedo Turkoglu	.30	.75
166 J.J. Redick	.30	.75
167 Jameer Nelson	.25	.60
168 Jason Richardson	.30	.75
169 Ryan Anderson	.25	.60
170 Glen Davis	.25	.60
171 Chris Duhon	.20	.50
172 John Wall	.50	1.25
173 Trevor Booker	.20	.50
174 Jordan Crawford	.30	.75
175 Nene	.25	.60
176 Kevin Seraphin	.25	.60
177 Rashard Lewis	.25	.60
178 Randy Wittman CO	.30	.75
179 Andrew Bogut	.30	.75
180 Stephen Curry	.30	.75
181 David Lee	.25	.60
182 Dorell Wright	.20	.50
183 Nate Robinson	.30	.75
184 Brandon Rush	.20	.50
185 Richard Jefferson	.30	.75
186 Mark Jackson CO	.30	.75
187 Blake Griffin	.60	1.50
188 Chauncey Billups	.30	.75
189 Chris Paul	.50	1.25
190 Mo Williams	.25	.60
191 Nick Young	.25	.60
192 Eric Bledsoe	.30	.75
193 DeAndre Jordan	.30	.75
194 Caron Butler	.25	.60
195 Vinny Del Negro CO	.30	.75
196 Ramon Sessions	.25	.60
197 Andrew Bynum	.40	1.00
198 Kobe Bryant	1.25	3.00
199 Metta World Peace	.30	.75
200 Pau Gasol	.30	.75
201 Matt Barnes	.20	.50
202 Devin Ebanks	.25	.60
203 Mike Brown CO	.30	.75
204 Shannon Brown	.30	.75
205 Marcin Gortat	.30	.75
206 Grant Hill	.40	1.00
207 Robin Lopez	.20	.50
208 Steve Nash	.30	.75
209 Channing Frye	.25	.60
210 Alvin Gentry CO	.30	.75
211 Marcus Thornton	.30	.75
212 DeMarcus Cousins	.40	1.00
213 Tyreke Evans	.30	.75
214 Terrence Williams	.20	.50
215 Jason Thompson	.20	.50
216 John Salmons	.30	.75
217 Keith Smart CO	.30	.75
218 Gerald Henderson	.20	.50
219 Corey Maggette	.25	.60
220 D.J. Augustin	.20	.50
221 Byron Mullens	.20	.50
222 Mike Dunlap CO	.30	.75
223 Kyrie Irving RC	4.00	10.00
224 Derrick Williams RC	2.00	5.00
225 Enes Kanter RC	1.25	3.00
226 Tristan Thompson RC	1.25	3.00
227 Jan Vesely RC	.75	2.00
228 Bismack Biyombo RC	.75	2.00
229 Brandon Knight RC	2.00	5.00
230 Kemba Walker RC	1.25	3.00
231 Jimmer Fredette RC	1.50	4.00
232 Klay Thompson RC	2.00	5.00
233 Alec Burks RC	.75	2.00
234 Markieff Morris RC	1.00	2.50
235 Marcus Morris RC	.75	2.00
236 Kawhi Leonard RC	1.50	4.00
237 Nikola Vucevic RC	.50	1.25
238 Iman Shumpert RC	1.50	4.00
239 Chris Singleton RC	.50	1.25
240 Tobias Harris RC	.60	1.50
241 Nolan Smith RC	.75	2.00
242 Kenneth Faried RC	1.50	4.00
243 Reggie Jackson RC	.60	1.50
244 MarShon Brooks RC	1.50	4.00
245 Jordan Hamilton RC	.50	1.25
246 JaJuan Johnson RC	.60	1.50
247 Norris Cole RC	1.25	3.00
248 Cory Joseph RC	.50	1.25
249 Jimmy Butler RC	1.00	2.50
250 Isaiah Thomas RC	1.25	3.00
251 Charles Jenkins RC	.50	1.25
252 Chandler Parsons RC	.75	2.00
253 Lavoy Allen RC	.60	1.50
254 Jeremy Tyler RC	.50	1.25
255 Jon Leuer RC	.50	1.25
256 Jeremy Pargo RC	.50	1.25
257 Greg Stiemsma RC	.75	2.00
258 Andrew Goudelock RC	.60	1.50
259 Josh Harrellson RC	1.00	2.50
260 Elliot Williams	.20	.50
261 Vernon Macklin RC	.50	1.25
262 Mickell Gladness RC	.50	1.25
263 Jordan Williams RC	.60	1.50
264 Terrel Harris RC	.50	1.25
265 Josh Selby RC	.75	2.00
266 DeAndre Liggins RC	1.00	2.50
267 Jerome Jordan	.20	.50
268 Derrick Byars	.20	.50
269 Tyler Honeycutt RC	.50	1.25
270 Justin Harper RC	.60	1.50
271 Shelvin Mack RC	.60	1.50
272 Trey Thompkins RC	.50	1.25
273 Julyan Stone RC	.50	1.25
274 Walker Russell RC	.50	1.25
275 Anthony Davis RC	4.00	10.00
276 Michael Kidd-Gilchrist RC	2.00	5.00
277 Bradley Beal RC	1.50	4.00
278 Dion Waiters RC	1.50	4.00
279 Thomas Robinson RC	1.50	4.00
280 Damian Lillard RC	2.00	5.00
281 Harrison Barnes RC	1.50	4.00
282 Terrence Ross RC	1.00	2.50
283 Andre Drummond RC	1.00	2.50
284 Austin Rivers RC	1.50	4.00
285 Meyers Leonard RC	.75	2.00
286 Jeremy Lamb RC	1.00	2.50
287 John Henson RC	.75	2.00
288 Moe Harkless RC	.60	1.50
289 Tyler Zeller RC	1.00	2.50
290 Evan Fournier RC	.60	1.50
291 Perry Jones III RC	1.25	3.00
292 Bernard James RC	.50	1.25
293 Quincy Acy RC	.60	1.50
294 Quincy Miller RC	.60	1.50
295 2012 West All-Stars	.40	1.00
296 2012 East All-Stars	.40	1.00
297 Serge Ibaka	.30	.75
298 Rajon Rondo	.40	1.00
299 Chris Paul	.50	1.25
300 Dwight Howard	.50	1.25
KD1 Kevin Durant Durantula	60.00	150.00
MH1 Miami Heat SP	10.00	25.00

2012-13 Hoops Artist's Proofs

*VETS: 2X TO 5X BASE HI		
*RCs: 1X TO 2.5X BASE HI		
RANDOM INSERTS IN PACKS		
223 Kyrie Irving	15.00	40.00
275 Anthony Davis	15.00	40.00
295 2012 West All-Stars	2.50	6.00
296 2012 East All-Stars	2.50	6.00

2012-13 Hoops Glossy

*VETS: 1.5X TO 4X BASE HI		
*RCs: .5X TO 1.25X BASE HI		
RANDOM INSERTS IN PACKS		
223 Kyrie Irving	8.00	20.00
275 Anthony Davis	6.00	15.00

2012-13 Hoops 89-90 Buyback Autographs

RANDOM INSERTS IN PACKS		
39 Ralph Sampson	20.00	50.00
108 Pat Riley		
138 David Robinson		
178 Hakeem Olajuwon AS	50.00	125.00
180 Hakeem Olajuwon		
183 Dan Majerle	35.00	70.00
244 Scottie Pippen		
271 Vernon Maxwell	25.00	60.00

2012-13 Hoops Action Photos

COMPLETE SET (20)	8.00	20.00
RANDOM INSERTS IN PACKS		
1 Kobe Bryant	2.00	5.00
2 Kevin Durant	1.50	4.00
3 LeBron James	2.00	5.00
4 Dwyane Wade	1.00	2.50
5 Kevin Love	.60	1.50
6 Dwight Howard	.75	2.00
7 Derrick Rose	1.50	4.00
8 Chris Paul	.75	2.00
9 Dirk Nowitzki	.60	1.50
10 Russell Westbrook	.60	1.50
11 Carmelo Anthony	.60	1.50
12 Amare Stoudemire	.50	1.25
13 Paul Pierce	.60	1.50
14 Blake Griffin	1.00	2.50
15 LaMarcus Aldridge	.50	1.25
16 Rajon Rondo	.60	1.50
17 Serge Ibaka	.50	1.25
18 Andrew Bynum	.60	1.50
19 James Harden	.60	1.50
20 Chris Bosh	.50	1.25

2012-13 Hoops Autographs

RANDOM INSERTS IN PACKS		
1 Avery Bradley SP	10.00	25.00
2 Brandon Bass	6.00	15.00
7 Doc Rivers CO	15.00	40.00
9 Brook Lopez SP	15.00	40.00
14 Avery Johnson CO	6.00	15.00
15 Amare Stoudemire SP		
17 Landry Fields	4.00	10.00
19 Jeremy Lin SP		
20 Steve Novak	5.00	12.00
24 Jrue Holiday SP	10.00	25.00
27 Evan Turner SP		
30 Andrea Bargnani SP	20.00	50.00
32 Gary Forbes	2.50	6.00
33 Jose Calderon	6.00	15.00
37 Dirk Nowitzki SP		
40 Jason Kidd SP		
42 Vince Carter SP	40.00	80.00
44 Rick Carlisle CO SP	15.00	40.00
45 Kyle Lowry	2.50	6.00
46 Kevin Martin SP	10.00	25.00
47 Luis Scola	4.00	10.00
48 Chase Budinger	2.50	6.00
49 Patrick Patterson	3.00	8.00
50 Goran Dragic	5.00	12.00
51 Kevin McHale CO SP	30.00	80.00
53 Mike Conley	4.00	10.00
56 Zach Randolph SP	20.00	50.00
57 Lester Hudson	2.50	6.00
58 Dante Cunningham	2.50	6.00
60 Emeka Okafor SP	25.00	60.00
63 Eric Gordon SP	5.00	12.00
67 DeJuan Blair	5.00	12.00
68 Boris Diaw	4.00	10.00
72 Danny Green	4.00	10.00
76 Joakim Noah SP		
78 Richard Hamilton SP		
79 Taj Gibson	5.00	12.00
80 Ronnie Brewer		
84 Antawn Jamison SP	8.00	20.00
85 Daniel Gibson	2.50	6.00
86 Byron Scott CO SP	5.00	12.00
87 Ben Gordon SP		
88 Greg Monroe	5.00	12.00
90 Tayshaun Prince SP	5.00	12.00
95 Paul George SP		
96 Roy Hibbert SP		
98 George Hill	5.00	12.00
99 A.J. Price	2.50	6.00
103 Monta Ellis SP		
104 Ersan Ilyasova	3.00	8.00
108 Arron Afflalo	4.00	10.00
109 Danilo Gallinari SP		
111 Wilson Chandler	3.00	8.00
113 Andre Miller	8.00	20.00
116 Kevin Love SP		
117 Luke Ridnour		
120 Ricky Rubio SP	75.00	150.00
121 Wesley Johnson SP	6.00	15.00
127 Jonny Flynn	3.00	8.00
129 Jamal Crawford	5.00	12.00
134 Kendrick Perkins	5.00	12.00
135 Kevin Durant SP		
136 Russell Westbrook SP		
142 DeMarre Carroll	2.50	6.00
143 Gordon Hayward SP		
144 Paul Millsap	2.50	6.00
145 Derrick Favors SP	30.00	80.00
146 Josh Howard SP	8.00	20.00
148 Al Horford SP	10.00	25.00
149 Jeff Teague	4.00	10.00
161 Udonis Haslem	4.00	10.00
162 Shane Battier SP	25.00	60.00
166 J.J. Redick SP		
173 Trevor Booker	2.50	6.00
174 Jordan Crawford SP	12.00	30.00
176 Kevin Seraphin	3.00	8.00
179 Andrew Bogut SP	20.00	50.00
180 Stephen Curry SP	20.00	50.00
187 Blake Griffin SP	75.00	150.00
188 Chauncey Billups SP	25.00	60.00
189 Chris Paul SP EXCH	40.00	100.00
190 Mo Williams SP	20.00	50.00
192 Eric Bledsoe	6.00	15.00
198 Kobe Bryant SP	100.00	200.00
200 Pau Gasol SP		
202 Devin Ebanks SP	5.00	12.00
205 Marcin Gortat	10.00	25.00
207 Robin Lopez	2.50	6.00
208 Steve Nash SP	40.00	100.00
209 Channing Frye SP	5.00	12.00
211 Marcus Thornton SP		
212 DeMarcus Cousins SP	25.00	60.00
214 Terrence Williams	6.00	15.00
218 Gerald Henderson	3.00	8.00
223 Kyrie Irving	200.00	350.00
224 Derrick Williams	15.00	40.00
225 Enes Kanter	8.00	20.00
226 Tristan Thompson	8.00	20.00
227 Jan Vesely	6.00	15.00
228 Bismack Biyombo	5.00	12.00
229 Brandon Knight	20.00	50.00
230 Kemba Walker	15.00	40.00
231 Jimmer Fredette	10.00	25.00
232 Klay Thompson EXCH	15.00	40.00
233 Alec Burks	5.00	12.00
234 Markieff Morris	6.00	15.00
235 Marcus Morris	5.00	12.00
236 Kawhi Leonard	12.00	30.00
238 Iman Shumpert	20.00	50.00
239 Chris Singleton	3.00	8.00
240 Tobias Harris	4.00	10.00
241 Nolan Smith	5.00	12.00
242 Kenneth Faried	10.00	25.00
243 Reggie Jackson	4.00	10.00
244 MarShon Brooks	10.00	25.00
245 Jordan Hamilton	3.00	8.00
246 JaJuan Johnson	4.00	10.00
247 Norris Cole	8.00	20.00
248 Cory Joseph	3.00	8.00
249 Jimmy Butler	6.00	15.00
250 Isaiah Thomas	8.00	20.00
251 Charles Jenkins	3.00	8.00
252 Chandler Parsons	5.00	12.00
253 Lavoy Allen	4.00	10.00
254 Jeremy Tyler	3.00	8.00
255 Jon Leuer	3.00	8.00
257 Greg Stiemsma	5.00	12.00
258 Andrew Goudelock	4.00	10.00
259 Josh Harrellson	6.00	15.00
261 Vernon Macklin	3.00	8.00
263 Jordan Williams	4.00	10.00
265 Josh Selby	5.00	12.00
266 DeAndre Liggins	6.00	15.00
268 Derrick Byars	2.50	6.00
269 Tyler Honeycutt	3.00	8.00
271 Shelvin Mack	4.00	10.00
272 Trey Thompkins	3.00	8.00
275 Anthony Davis	125.00	250.00
276 Michael Kidd-Gilchrist	40.00	100.00
277 Bradley Beal	20.00	50.00
278 Dion Waiters EXCH	12.00	30.00
279 Thomas Robinson	25.00	60.00
281 Harrison Barnes	40.00	100.00
282 Terrence Ross	8.00	20.00
283 Andre Drummond	20.00	50.00
284 Austin Rivers	30.00	80.00
285 Meyers Leonard	8.00	20.00
286 Jeremy Lamb	15.00	40.00
287 John Henson	10.00	25.00
288 Moe Harkless	6.00	15.00
289 Tyler Zeller	6.00	15.00
290 Evan Fournier	5.00	12.00
291 Perry Jones III	12.00	30.00
292 Bernard James	3.00	8.00
293 Quincy Acy	4.00	10.00
294 Quincy Miller	4.00	10.00
298 Rajon Rondo SP		
299 Chris Paul SP EXCH	40.00	100.00

2012-13 Hoops Board Members

COMPLETE SET (20)	6.00	15.00
RANDOM INSERTS IN PACKS		
1 Kevin Love	.60	1.50
2 Dwight Howard	.75	2.00
3 Andrew Bynum	.60	1.50
4 Kris Humphries	.30	.75
5 Blake Griffin	1.00	2.50
6 DeMarcus Cousins	.60	1.50
7 Pau Gasol	.50	1.25
8 Marc Gasol	.50	1.25
9 Marcin Gortat	.50	1.25
10 Tyson Chandler	.40	1.00
11 Joakim Noah	.50	1.25
12 Greg Monroe	.50	1.25
13 Josh Smith	.50	1.25
14 Al Jefferson	.50	1.25
15 David Lee	.40	1.00
16 Tim Duncan	.75	2.00
17 Kevin Durant	1.50	4.00
18 LeBron James	2.00	5.00
19 DeAndre Jordan	.50	1.25
20 LaMarcus Aldridge	.50	1.25

2012-13 Hoops Courtside

COMPLETE SET (20)	8.00	20.00
RANDOM INSERTS IN PACKS		
1 Chris Paul	.75	2.00
2 Tony Parker	.50	1.25
3 Antawn Jamison	.50	1.25
4 Derrick Rose	1.50	4.00
5 Rajon Rondo	.60	1.50
6 Dwyane Wade	1.00	2.50
7 John Wall	.75	2.00
8 Steve Nash	.50	1.25
9 David Lee	.40	1.00
10 Ricky Rubio	1.25	3.00
11 Kevin Love	.60	1.50
12 Russell Westbrook	.60	1.50
13 Deron Williams	.50	1.25
14 LeBron James	2.00	5.00
15 Kobe Bryant	2.00	5.00
16 Kevin Durant	1.50	4.00
17 Blake Griffin	1.00	2.50
18 LaMarcus Aldridge	.50	1.25
19 Dwight Howard	.75	2.00
20 Dirk Nowitzki	.60	1.50

2012-13 Hoops Draft Night

COMPLETE SET (20)	15.00	40.00
RANDOM INSERTS IN PACKS		
1 Anthony Davis	6.00	15.00
2 Michael Kidd-Gilchrist	3.00	8.00
3 Bradley Beal	2.50	6.00
4 Dion Waiters	2.50	6.00
5 Thomas Robinson	2.50	6.00
6 Damian Lillard	3.00	8.00
7 Harrison Barnes	2.50	6.00
8 Terrence Ross	1.50	4.00
9 Andre Drummond	1.50	4.00
10 Austin Rivers	2.50	6.00
11 Meyers Leonard	1.25	3.00
12 Jeremy Lamb	1.50	4.00
13 John Henson	1.25	3.00
14 Moe Harkless	1.00	2.50
15 Tyler Zeller	1.50	4.00
16 Evan Fournier	1.00	2.50
17 Perry Jones III	2.00	5.00
18 Bernard James	.75	2.00
19 Quincy Acy	1.00	2.50
20 Quincy Miller	1.00	2.50

2012-13 Hoops Draft Night Autographs

RANDOM INSERTS IN PACKS		
1 Anthony Davis	200.00	350.00
2 Michael Kidd-Gilchrist	50.00	125.00
3 Bradley Beal		
4 Dion Waiters EXCH	20.00	50.00
5 Thomas Robinson	40.00	100.00
7 Harrison Barnes	40.00	100.00
8 Terrence Ross	12.00	30.00
9 Andre Drummond	25.00	60.00
10 Austin Rivers	40.00	100.00
11 Meyers Leonard	12.00	30.00
12 Jeremy Lamb	25.00	60.00
13 John Henson	10.00	25.00
14 Moe Harkless	8.00	20.00
15 Tyler Zeller	12.00	30.00
16 Evan Fournier	8.00	20.00
17 Perry Jones III	15.00	40.00
18 Bernard James	6.00	15.00
19 Quincy Acy	8.00	20.00
20 Quincy Miller	8.00	20.00

2012-13 Hoops Franchise Greats

COMPLETE SET (20)	40.00	100.00
RANDOM INSERTS IN PACKS		
1 Magic Johnson	5.00	12.00
2 Kareem Abdul-Jabbar	3.00	8.00
3 Shaquille O'Neal	4.00	10.00
4 Wilt Chamberlain	4.00	10.00
5 Larry Bird	6.00	15.00
6 John Havlicek	2.50	6.00
7 Bill Russell	3.00	8.00
8 Patrick Ewing	2.50	6.00
9 Julius Erving	4.00	10.00
10 Scottie Pippen	4.00	10.00
11 John Stockton	3.00	8.00
12 Karl Malone	2.50	6.00
13 Dominique Wilkins	2.50	6.00
14 Isiah Thomas	2.00	5.00
15 Hakeem Olajuwon	2.50	6.00
16 Kobe Bryant	8.00	20.00
17 Dirk Nowitzki	2.50	6.00
18 Paul Pierce	2.50	6.00
19 Tim Duncan	3.00	8.00
20 Kevin Durant	6.00	15.00

2012-13 Hoops Kobe's All-Rookie Team

RANDOM INSERTS IN PACKS		
1 Isaiah Thomas	10.00	25.00
2 Kyrie Irving	30.00	80.00
3 Derrick Williams	15.00	40.00
4 Kemba Walker	10.00	25.00
5 Jimmer Fredette	12.00	30.00
6 Markieff Morris	8.00	20.00
7 Kenneth Faried	12.00	30.00
8 Brandon Knight	15.00	40.00
9 Kawhi Leonard	12.00	30.00
10 MarShon Brooks	12.00	30.00
11 Klay Thompson	15.00	40.00
12 Iman Shumpert	12.00	30.00
13 Chandler Parsons	6.00	15.00
14 Bismack Biyombo	6.00	15.00
15 Tristan Thompson	10.00	25.00
16 Ricky Rubio	15.00	40.00
17 Norris Cole	10.00	25.00
18 Alec Burks	6.00	15.00
19 Gustavo Ayon	5.00	12.00
20 Nikola Vucevic	4.00	10.00
21 Ivan Johnson	5.00	12.00
22 Enes Kanter	10.00	25.00
23 Lavoy Allen	5.00	12.00
24 Greg Stiemsma	6.00	15.00
25 Josh Harrellson	8.00	20.00
26 Darius Morris	5.00	12.00
27 Daniel Orton	6.00	15.00
28 E'Twaun Moore	6.00	15.00
29 Andrew Goudelock	5.00	12.00
30 Tobias Harris	5.00	12.00

2012-13 Hoops Rookie Impact

COMPLETE SET (28)	12.00	30.00
RANDOM INSERTS IN PACKS		
1 Kyrie Irving	3.00	8.00
2 Brandon Knight	1.50	4.00
3 MarShon Brooks	1.25	3.00
4 Klay Thompson	1.50	4.00
5 Kemba Walker	1.00	2.50
6 Isaiah Thomas	1.00	2.50
7 Kenneth Faried	1.25	3.00
8 Chandler Parsons	.60	1.50
9 Iman Shumpert	1.25	3.00
10 Derrick Williams	1.50	4.00
11 Tristan Thompson	1.00	2.50
12 Kawhi Leonard	1.25	3.00
13 Jimmer Fredette	1.25	3.00
14 Markieff Morris	.75	2.00
15 Alec Burks	.60	1.50
16 Norris Cole	1.00	2.50
17 Josh Harrellson	.75	2.00
18 Gustavo Ayon	.50	1.25
19 Charles Jenkins	.40	1.00
20 Bismack Biyombo	.60	1.50
21 Jan Vesely	.60	1.50
22 Jimmy Butler	.75	2.00
23 Enes Kanter	1.00	2.50
24 Jeremy Tyler	.40	1.00
25 Ricky Rubio	1.25	3.00
26 Tobias Harris	.50	1.25
27 Andrew Goudelock	.50	1.25
28 Lavoy Allen	.50	1.25

2012-13 Hoops Rookie Impact Autographs

RANDOM INSERTS IN PACKS		
1 Kyrie Irving	200.00	400.00
2 Brandon Knight	20.00	50.00
3 MarShon Brooks	12.00	30.00
4 Klay Thompson	15.00	40.00
5 Kemba Walker	15.00	40.00
6 Isaiah Thomas	10.00	25.00
7 Kenneth Faried	12.00	30.00
8 Chandler Parsons	6.00	15.00
9 Iman Shumpert	20.00	50.00
10 Derrick Williams	15.00	40.00
11 Tristan Thompson	10.00	25.00
12 Kawhi Leonard	15.00	40.00
13 Jimmer Fredette	12.00	30.00
14 Markieff Morris	8.00	20.00
15 Alec Burks	6.00	15.00
16 Norris Cole	15.00	40.00
17 Josh Harrellson	8.00	20.00
18 Gustavo Ayon EXCH	5.00	12.00
19 Charles Jenkins	4.00	10.00
20 Bismack Biyombo	6.00	15.00
21 Jan Vesely	6.00	15.00
22 Jimmy Butler	10.00	25.00
23 Enes Kanter	10.00	25.00
24 Jeremy Tyler	4.00	10.00
26 Tobias Harris	5.00	12.00
27 Andrew Goudelock	8.00	20.00
28 Lavoy Allen	8.00	20.00

2012-13 Hoops Spark Plugs

COMPLETE SET (20)	4.00	10.00
RANDOM INSERTS IN PACKS		
1 James Harden	.60	1.50
2 Jason Terry	.40	1.00
3 Manu Ginobili	.50	1.25
4 Joakim Noah	.50	1.25
5 Tyson Chandler	.40	1.00
6 Anderson Varejao	.40	1.00
7 Steve Novak	.30	.75
8 Chase Budinger	.30	.75
9 Shane Battier	.40	1.00
10 Mo Williams	.40	1.00
11 Al Harrington	.40	1.00
12 Lou Williams	.40	1.00
13 J.R. Smith	.50	1.25
14 Glen Davis	.40	1.00
15 Tyler Hansbrough	.50	1.25
16 Thaddeus Young	.30	.75
17 O.J. Mayo	.50	1.25
18 George Hill	.40	1.00
19 Jamal Crawford	.40	1.00
20 Avery Bradley	.50	1.25

1990 Hoops 100 Superstars

This 100-card standard-size set is a partial remake of the 1989-90 Hoops set. The pictures used are the same. This set was primarily sold through the Sears catalog. The backs have a head shot in the same format as the front, as well as biographical and statistical information (only up through the 1988-89 season) on a pale yellow background. However, they differ from the Hoops issue in the yellow coloring on the card fronts and a new card numbering system. The cards are numbered on the back and arranged alphabetically according to teams as follows: Atlanta Hawks (1-4), Boston Celtics (5-8), Charlotte Hornets (9-11), Chicago Bulls (12-15), Cleveland Cavaliers (16-19), Dallas Mavericks (20-23), Denver Nuggets (24-26), Detroit Pistons (27-30), Golden State Warriors (31-34), Houston Rockets (35-38), Indiana Pacers (39-42), Los Angeles Clippers (43-46), Los Angeles Lakers (47-50), Miami Heat (51-53), Milwaukee Bucks (54-57), Minnesota Timberwolves (58-60), New Jersey Nets (61-63), New York Knicks (64-67), Orlando Magic (68-70), Philadelphia 76ers (71-74), Phoenix Suns (75-78), Portland Trail Blazers (79-82), Sacramento Kings (83-85), San Antonio Spurs (86-88), Seattle Supersonics (89-92), Utah Jazz (93-96), and Washington Bullets (97-100).

COMP.FACT SET (100)	6.00	15.00
1 Doc Rivers	.20	.50
2 Dominique Wilkins	.40	1.00
3 Spud Webb	.20	.50
4 Moses Malone	.20	.50
5 Reggie Lewis	.20	.50
6 Larry Bird	.75	2.00
7 Kevin McHale	.40	1.00
8 Robert Parish	.20	.50
9 Muggsy Bogues	.30	.75
10 Rex Chapman	.20	.50
11 Kelly Tripucka	.07	.10
12 Michael Jordan	2.00	5.00
13 Scottie Pippen	.75	2.00
14 John Paxson	.15	.40
15 Bill Cartwright	.15	.40
16 Mark Price	.30	.75
17 Larry Nance	.20	.50
18 Hot Rod Williams	.07	.10
19 Brad Daugherty	.07	.20
20 Derek Harper	.20	.50
21 Rolando Blackman	.20	.50
22 Sam Perkins	.20	.50
23 James Donaldson	.07	.10
24 Michael Adams	.07	.10
25 Lafayette Lever	.07	.10
26 Alex English	.20	.50
27 Isiah Thomas	.40	1.00
28 Joe Dumars	.40	1.00
29 Bill Laimbeer	.30	.75
30 Dennis Rodman	.50	1.25
31 Mitch Richmond	.60	1.50
32 Chris Mullin	.30	.75
33 Manute Bol	.20	.50
34 Rod Higgins	.07	.10
35 Sleepy Floyd	.07	.10
36 Otis Thorpe	.07	.20
37 Buck Johnson	.07	.10
38 Hakeem Olajuwon	.40	1.00
39 Vern Fleming	.07	.10
40 Reggie Miller	.40	1.00
41 Chuck Person	.07	.20
42 Rik Smits	.30	.75
43 Benoit Benjamin	.07	.10
44 Charles Smith	.08	.25
45 Gary Grant	.07	.10
46 Danny Manning	.50	1.25
47 Magic Johnson	.60	1.50
48 Byron Scott	.20	.50
49 A.C. Green	.20	.50
50 James Worthy	.30	.75
51 Kevin Edwards	.07	.10
52 Rory Sparrow	.07	.10
53 Rony Seikaly	.07	.20
54 Jay Humphries	.07	.10
55 Alvin Robertson	.07	.20
56 Ricky Pierce	.07	.20
57 Jack Sikma	.07	.20
58 Tyrone Corbin	.07	.10
59 Sidney Lowe	.07	.10
60 Steve Johnson	.07	.10
61 Dennis Hopson	.07	.10
62 Chris Morris	.07	.20
63 Roy Hinson	.07	.10
64 Mark Jackson	.30	.75
65 Gerald Wilkins	.07	.10
66 Charles Oakley	.07	.20
67 Patrick Ewing	.40	1.00
68 Reggie Theus	.20	.50
69 Sam Vincent	.07	.10
70 Terry Catledge	.07	.10
71 Hersey Hawkins	.30	.75
72 Johnny Dawkins	.07	.10
73 Charles Barkley	.40	1.00
74 Mike Gminski	.07	.20
75 Kevin Johnson	.40	1.00
76 Jeff Hornacek	.40	1.00
77 Tom Chambers	.20	.50
78 Eddie Johnson	.07	.20
79 Terry Porter	.20	.50
80 Clyde Drexler	.40	1.00
81 Jerome Kersey	.07	.10
82 Kevin Duckworth	.07	.10
83 Danny Ainge	.30	.75
84 Rodney McCray	.07	.10
85 Wayman Tisdale	.20	.50
86 Willie Anderson	.07	.20
87 Terry Cummings	.15	.40
88 David Robinson	.75	2.00
89 Dale Ellis	.07	.20
90 Derrick McKey	.07	.20
91 Xavier McDaniel	.07	.10
92 Michael Cage	.07	.10
93 John Stockton	.60	1.50
94 Karl Malone	.60	1.50
95 Thurl Bailey	.07	.10
96 Mark Eaton	.07	.20
97 Jeff Malone	.07	.10

98 Darrell Walker	.07	.10
99 Bernard King	.20	.50
100 John Williams	.07	.20

1991 Hoops 100 Superstars

This 100-card set is a partial remake of the 1990-91 Hoops set, and it was primarily sold through the Sears catalog. The standard-size cards use the same pictures. The backs have a color headshot, with biographical and statistical information (only up through the 1989-90 season) in a basketball lane format. However, these cards differ from the regular Hoops issue in the gold coloring on the card fronts and a new numbering system. The players are arranged alphabetically within teams, and the teams are arranged alphabetically as follows: Atlanta Hawks (1-4), Boston Celtics (5-9), Charlotte Hornets (10-11), Chicago Bulls (12-16), Cleveland Cavaliers (17-19), Dallas Mavericks (20-24), Denver Nuggets (25-26), Detroit Pistons (27-31), Golden State Warriors (32-34), Houston Rockets (35-38), Indiana Pacers (39-41), Los Angeles Clippers (42-45), Los Angeles Lakers (46-51), Miami Heat (52-54), Milwaukee Bucks (55-57), Minnesota Timberwolves (58-60), New Jersey Nets (61-63), New York Knicks (64-67), Orlando Magic (68-70), Philadelphia 76ers (71-74), Phoenix Suns (75-79), Portland Trail Blazers (80-83), Sacramento Kings (84-85), San Antonio Spurs (86-90), Seattle Supersonics (91-93), Utah Jazz (94-97), and Washington Bullets (98-100).

COMP.FACT SET (100)	35.00	65.00
1 Moses Malone	.40	1.00
2 Doc Rivers	.40	1.00
3 Spud Webb	.25	.60
4 Dominique Wilkins	1.25	3.00
5 Larry Bird	2.50	6.00
6 Reggie Lewis	.40	1.00
7 Kevin McHale	.50	1.25
8 Robert Parish	.40	1.00
9 Brian Shaw	.25	.60
10 Muggsy Bogues	.40	1.00
11 Johnny Newman	.15	.40
12 Horace Grant	.40	1.00
13 Michael Jordan	8.00	20.00
14 Scottie Pippen	2.00	5.00
15 Brad Daugherty	.15	.40
16 Craig Ehlo	.15	.40
17 Larry Nance	.40	1.00
18 Mark Price	.60	1.50
19 Hot Rod Williams	.15	.40
20 Rolando Blackman	.40	1.00
21 James Donaldson	.15	.40
22 Derek Harper	.40	1.00
23 Fat Lever	.15	.40
24 Roy Tarpley	.15	.40
25 Michael Adams	.15	.40
26 Orlando Woolridge	.15	.40
27 Joe Dumars	.75	2.00
28 Bill Laimbeer	.75	2.00
29 Vinnie Johnson	.40	1.00
30 Dennis Rodman	1.25	3.00
31 Isiah Thomas	1.25	3.00
32 Chris Mullin	.75	2.00
33 Tim Hardaway	.75	2.00
34 Mitch Richmond	.75	2.00
35 Sleepy Floyd	.15	.40
36 Hakeem Olajuwon	1.00	2.50
37 Kenny Smith	.40	1.00
38 Otis Thorpe	.25	.60
39 Reggie Miller	1.25	3.00
40 Chuck Person	.15	.40
41 Detlef Schrempf	.30	.75
42 Danny Manning	.30	.75
43 Ken Norman	.15	.40
44 Ron Harper	.40	1.00
45 Charles Smith	.15	.40
46 Vlade Divac	.40	1.00
47 A.C. Green	.40	1.00
48 Magic Johnson	2.00	5.00
49 Byron Scott	.60	1.50
50 James Worthy	.75	2.00
51 Sam Perkins	.30	.75
52 Rony Seikaly	.40	1.00
53 Sherman Douglas	.15	.40
54 Glen Rice	.75	2.00
55 Jay Humphries	.15	.40
56 Alvin Robertson	.15	.40
57 Jack Sikma	.15	.40
58 Tony Campbell	.15	.40
59 Tyrone Corbin	.15	.40
60 Pooh Richardson	.15	.40
61 Roy Hinson	.15	.40
62 Chris Morris	.15	.40
63 Reggie Theus	.30	.75
64 Maurice Cheeks	.30	.75
65 Patrick Ewing	1.00	2.50
66 Mark Jackson	.40	1.00
67 Charles Oakley	.25	.60
68 Nick Anderson	.25	.60
69 Terry Catledge	.15	.40
70 Scott Skiles	.30	.75
71 Charles Barkley	1.50	4.00
72 Johnny Dawkins	.25	.60
73 Hersey Hawkins	.25	.60
74 Rick Mahorn	.15	.40
75 Tom Chambers	.25	.60
76 Jeff Hornacek	.40	1.00
77 Kevin Johnson	.40	1.00
78 Dan Majerle	.40	1.00
79 Mark West	.15	.40
80 Clyde Drexler	1.25	3.00
81 Terry Porter	.20	.50
82 Jerome Kersey	.15	.40
83 Buck Williams	.30	.75
84 Antoine Carr	.15	.40
85 Wayman Tisdale	.15	.40
86 Willie Anderson	.15	.40
87 Terry Cummings	.25	.60
88 Paul Pressey	.15	.40
89 David Robinson	2.00	5.00
90 Rod Strickland	.25	.60
91 Michael Cage	.15	.40
92 Shawn Kemp	.75	2.00
93 Derrick McKey	.15	.40
94 Thurl Bailey	.15	.40
95 Jeff Malone	.15	.40
96 Karl Malone	1.50	4.00
97 John Stockton	2.00	5.00
98 Harvey Grant	.15	.40
99 Bernard King	.30	.75
100 Darrell Walker	.15	.40

1992 Hoops 100 Superstars

This 100-card standard-size set is a partial remake of the 1991-92 Hoops set, and it was primarily sold through the Sears catalog. It is by far the toughest of the Hoops 100 Superstars sets issued between 1990 and 1992. The cards feature color action player photos framed by team color-coded borders against a copper card face. The player's name appears in the copper margin at the top. The horizontal backs are white and display a small player picture framed in the team's primary color. Biographical information appears below the photo. The player's college statistics and NBA record are included along with career highlights. The cards are numbered on the back, grouped alphabetically within teams, and checklisted below according to teams as follows: Atlanta Hawks (1-3), Boston Celtics (4-8), Charlotte Hornets (9-12), Chicago Bulls (13-16), Cleveland Cavaliers (17-20), Dallas Mavericks (21-23), Denver Nuggets (24-26), Detroit Pistons (27-30), Golden State Warriors (31-33), Houston Rockets (34-36), Indiana Pacers (37-39), Los Angeles Clippers (40-43), Los Angeles Lakers (44-49), Miami Heat (50-52), Milwaukee Bucks (53-56), Minnesota Timberwolves (57-60), New Jersey Nets (61-63), New York Knicks (64-68), Orlando Magic (69-71), Philadelphia 76ers (72-75), Phoenix Suns (76-78), Portland Trail Blazers (79-81), Sacramento Kings (82-85), San Antonio Spurs (86-89), Seattle Supersonics (90-92), Utah Jazz (93-96), and Washington Bullets (97-100).

COMP.FACT SET (100)	60.00	150.00
1 Rumeal Robinson	.25	.60
2 Dominique Wilkins	2.50	6.00
3 Kevin Willis	.50	1.25
4 Larry Bird	6.00	15.00
5 Dee Brown	.25	.60
6 Kevin Gamble	.25	.60
7 Kevin McHale	1.50	4.00
8 Robert Parish	1.00	2.50
9 Dell Curry	.25	.60
10 Muggsy Bogues	1.00	2.50
11 Kendall Gill	.50	1.25
12 Johnny Newman	.25	.60
13 Horace Grant	1.00	2.50
14 Michael Jordan	10.00	25.00
15 John Paxson	1.00	2.50
16 Scottie Pippen	4.00	10.00
17 Brad Daugherty	.25	.60
18 Larry Nance	.60	1.50
19 Mark Price	1.00	2.50
20 Hot Rod Williams	.25	.60
21 Rolando Blackman	.75	2.00
22 Derek Harper	.75	2.00
23 Rodney McCray	.25	.60
24 Chris Jackson	.25	.60
25 Todd Lichti	.25	.60
26 Orlando Woolridge	.25	.60
27 Joe Dumars	1.25	3.00
28 Bill Laimbeer	1.00	2.50
29 Dennis Rodman	3.00	8.00
30 Isiah Thomas	2.50	6.00
31 Tim Hardaway	1.50	4.00
32 Sarunas Marciulionis	.50	1.25
33 Chris Mullin	1.25	3.00
34 Hakeem Olajuwon	2.00	5.00
35 Kenny Smith	.50	1.25
36 Otis Thorpe	.50	1.25
37 Reggie Miller	2.00	5.00
38 Chuck Person	.25	.60
39 Detlef Schrempf	.50	1.25
40 Ron Harper	.75	2.00
41 Danny Manning	.75	2.00
42 Ken Norman	.25	.60
43 Charles Smith	.25	.60
44 Vlade Divac	.75	2.00
45 A.C. Green	.75	2.00
46 Magic Johnson	5.00	12.00
47 Sam Perkins	.75	2.00
48 Byron Scott	.75	2.00
49 James Worthy	1.50	4.00
50 Kevin Edwards	.25	.60
51 Glen Rice	1.00	2.50
52 Rony Seikaly	.25	.60
53 Dale Ellis	.25	.60
54 Jay Humphries	.25	.60
55 Moses Malone	.75	2.00
56 Alvin Robertson	.25	.60
57 Tony Campbell	.25	.60
58 Sam Mitchell	.25	.60
59 Pooh Richardson	.25	.60
60 Felton Spencer	.25	.60
61 Mookie Blaylock	.50	1.25
62 Sam Bowie	.50	1.25
63 Derrick Coleman	.50	1.25
64 Patrick Ewing	2.00	5.00
65 Xavier McDaniel	.25	.60
66 Charles Oakley	.50	1.25
67 Kiki Vandeweghe	.75	2.00
68 Gerald Wilkins	.40	1.00
69 Terry Catledge	.25	.60
70 Dennis Scott	.40	1.00
71 Scott Skiles	.50	1.25
72 Charles Barkley	4.00	10.00
73 Johnny Dawkins	.25	.60
74 Armon Gilliam	.25	.60
75 Hersey Hawkins	.50	1.25
76 Tom Chambers	.75	2.00
77 Jeff Hornacek	.75	2.00
78 Kevin Johnson	1.00	2.50
79 Clyde Drexler	2.50	6.00
80 Jerome Kersey	.50	1.25
81 Terry Porter	.40	1.00
82 Mitch Richmond	1.25	3.00
83 Lionel Simmons	.25	.60
84 Wayman Tisdale	.25	.60
85 Spud Webb	.75	2.00
86 Antoine Carr	.25	.60
87 Sean Elliott	1.00	2.50
88 David Robinson	4.00	10.00
89 Rod Strickland	.25	.60
90 Shawn Kemp	2.00	5.00
91 Gary Payton	2.00	5.00
92 Ricky Pierce	.25	.60
93 Blue Edwards	.25	.60
94 Jeff Malone	.25	.60
95 Karl Malone	5.00	12.00
96 John Stockton	6.00	15.00
97 Michael Adams	.25	.60
98 Pervis Ellison	.25	.60
99 Harvey Grant	.25	.60
100 Bernard King	.75	2.00

1990 Hoops Action Photos

These large action photos are taken from the NBA's official photo library and were primarily sold through retail outlets and toy stores. Original suggested retail price was $1.49 per card, but the photos did not sell well and were eventually closed out nationwide at around twenty-five cents each. The fronts feature an approximately 8" by 10" borderless color glossy player photo with biographical information, statistics, and career highlights on the back. The team logo, player's name, and NBA logo appear in different color stripes below each picture. Each photo is individually wrapped and is accompanied by an offer to order five-photo team sets for $7.50 each. The complete set includes a special "Superstar Set" (1-22) and five players from each of the NBA's 27 teams. These unnumbered photos are checklisted below alphabetically according to teams as follows: Atlanta (23-27), Boston (28-32), Charlotte (33-37), Chicago (38-42), Cleveland (43-47), Dallas (48-52), Denver (53-57), Detroit (58-62), Golden State (63-67), Houston (68-72), Indiana (73-77), LA. Clippers (78-82), L.A. Lakers (83-87), Miami (88-92), Milwaukee (93-97), Minnesota (98-102), New Jersey (103-107), New York (108-112), Orlando (113-117), Philadelphia (118-122), Phoenix (123-127), Portland (128-132), Sacramento (133-137), San Antonio (138-142), Seattle (143-147), Utah (148-152), and Washington (153-157).

COMPLETE SET (157)	30.00	75.00
1 Larry Bird	1.50	4.00
2 Charles Barkley	.75	2.00
3 Tom Chambers	.50	1.25
4 Clyde Drexler	.75	2.00
5 Joe Dumars	.50	1.25
6 Alex English	.50	1.25
7 Dale Ellis	.50	1.25
8 Patrick Ewing	.75	2.00
9 Mark Jackson	.50	1.25
10 Magic Johnson	1.25	3.00
11 Michael Jordan	3.00	8.00
12 Karl Malone	.75	2.00
13 Moses Malone	.50	1.25
14 Kevin McHale	.50	1.25
15 Chris Mullin	.50	1.25
16 Hakeem Olajuwon	.75	2.00
17 Mark Price	.50	1.25
18 David Robinson	1.25	3.00
19 John Stockton	.75	2.00
20 Isiah Thomas	.50	1.25
21 Dominique Wilkins	.50	1.25
22 James Worthy	.50	1.25
23 John Battle	.50	1.25
24 Moses Malone	.50	1.25
25 Doc Rivers	.50	1.25
26 Spud Webb	.50	1.25
27 Dominique Wilkins	.50	1.25
28 Dennis Johnson	.50	1.25
29 Reggie Lewis	.50	1.25
30 Larry Bird	1.50	4.00
31 Kevin McHale	.50	1.25
32 Robert Parish	.50	1.25
33 Muggsy Bogues	.50	1.25
34 Rex Chapman	.50	1.25
35 Kelly Tripucka	.50	1.25
36 Dell Curry	.50	1.25
37 J.R. Reid	.50	1.25
38 John Paxson	.50	1.25
39 Michael Jordan	3.00	8.00
40 Scottie Pippen	1.50	4.00
41 Stacey King	.50	1.25
42 Bill Cartwright	.50	1.25
43 Mark Price	.50	1.25
44 Craig Ehlo	.50	1.25
45 Larry Nance	.50	1.25
46 John Williams	.50	1.25
47 Brad Daugherty	.50	1.25
48 Derek Harper	.50	1.25
49 Rolando Blackman	.50	1.25
50 Sam Perkins	.50	1.25
51 Brad Davis	.50	1.25
52 James Donaldson	.50	1.25
53 Michael Adams	.50	1.25
54 Fat Lever	.50	1.25
55 Alex English	.50	1.25
56 Danny Schayes	.50	1.25
57 Blair Rasmussen	.50	1.25
58 Isiah Thomas	.50	1.25
59 Joe Dumars	.50	1.25
60 Bill Laimbeer	.50	1.25
61 John Salley	.50	1.25
62 Dennis Rodman	1.25	3.00
63 Mitch Richmond	.50	1.25
64 Tim Hardaway	1.25	3.00
65 Rod Higgins	.50	1.25
66 Chris Mullin	.50	1.25
67 Manute Bol	.50	1.25
68 John Lucas	.50	1.25
69 Mitchell Wiggins	.50	1.25
70 Otis Thorpe	.50	1.25
71 Buck Johnson	.50	1.25
72 Hakeem Olajuwon	.75	2.00
73 Vern Fleming	.50	1.25
74 Reggie Miller	.75	2.00
75 LaSalle Thompson	.50	1.25
76 Chuck Person	.50	1.25
77 Rik Smits	.50	1.25
78 Gary Grant	.50	1.25
79 Ron Harper	.50	1.25
80 Charles Smith	.50	1.25
81 Danny Manning	.50	1.25
82 Ken Norman	.50	1.25
83 Magic Johnson	1.25	3.00
84 Byron Scott	.50	1.25
85 A.C. Green	.50	1.25
86 James Worthy	.50	1.25
87 Michael Cooper	.50	1.25
88 Kevin Edwards	.50	1.25
89 Sherman Douglas	.50	1.25
90 Grant Long	.50	1.25
91 Rony Seikaly	.50	1.25
92 Rory Sparrow	.50	1.25
93 Jay Humphries	.50	1.25
94 Alvin Robertson	.50	1.25
95 Paul Pressey	.50	1.25
96 Ricky Pierce	.50	1.25
97 Jack Sikma	.50	1.25
98 Sidney Lowe	.50	1.25
99 Tony Campbell	.50	1.25
100 Tyrone Corbin	.50	1.25
101 Sam Mitchell	.50	1.25
102 Pooh Richardson	.50	1.25
103 Lester Conner	.50	1.25
104 Dennis Hopson	.50	1.25
105 Charles Shackleford	.50	1.25
106 Chris Morris	.50	1.25
107 Roy Hinson	.50	1.25
108 Mark Jackson	.50	1.25
109 Johnny Newman	.50	1.25
110 Gerald Wilkins	.50	1.25
111 Charles Oakley	.50	1.25
112 Patrick Ewing	.75	2.00
113 Reggie Theus	.50	1.25
114 Sam Vincent	.50	1.25
115 Terry Catledge	.50	1.25
116 Jerry Reynolds	.50	1.25
117 Dave Corzine	.50	1.25
118 Hersey Hawkins	.50	1.25
119 Johnny Dawkins	.50	1.25
120 Charles Barkley	.75	2.00
121 Rick Mahorn	.50	1.25
122 Mike Gminski	.50	1.25
123 Kevin Johnson	.50	1.25
124 Jeff Hornacek	.50	1.25
125 Tom Chambers	.50	1.25
126 Eddie Johnson	.50	1.25
127 Mark West	.50	1.25
128 Terry Porter	.50	1.25
129 Clyde Drexler	.75	2.00
130 Jerome Kersey	.50	1.25
131 Kevin Duckworth	.50	1.25
132 Mark Bryant	.50	1.25
133 Danny Ainge	.50	1.25
134 Kenny Smith	.50	1.25
135 Rodney McCray	.50	1.25
136 Wayman Tisdale	.50	1.25
137 Harold Pressley	.50	1.25
138 Maurice Cheeks	.50	1.25
139 Willie Anderson	.50	1.25
140 Terry Cummings	.50	1.25
141 Sean Elliott	.75	2.00
142 David Robinson	1.25	3.00
143 Dale Ellis	.50	1.25
144 Nate McMillan	.50	1.25
145 Derrick McKey	.50	1.25
146 Xavier McDaniel	.50	1.25
147 Michael Cage	.50	1.25
148 John Stockton	.75	2.00
149 Blue Edwards	.50	1.25
150 Karl Malone	.75	2.00
151 Thurl Bailey	.50	1.25
152 Mark Eaton	.50	1.25
153 Jeff Malone	.50	1.25
154 Darrell Walker	.50	1.25
155 Bernard King	.50	1.25
156 John Williams	.50	1.25
157 Charles Jones	.50	1.25

2011 Hoops All-Star Game

These cards were distributed via a wrapper redemption during the NBA All-Star Jam Session in Los Angeles in February 2011. The card fronts feature the All-Star logo.

COMPLETE SET (4)	10.00	20.00
AS-BG Blake Griffin	5.00	12.00
AS-JW John Wall	6.00	15.00
AS-KB Kobe Bryant	5.00	12.00
AS-KD Kevin Durant	2.00	5.00

1989-90 Hoops All-Star Panels

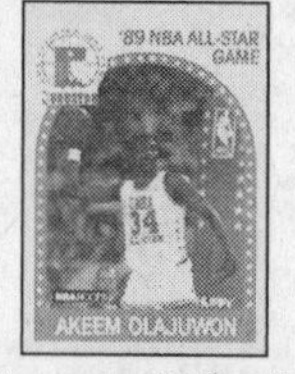

This 24-card set commemorates the February 1990 NBA All-Star Game and Weekend in Miami. It was issued in four panels of six cards each, with two cards per row inserted in the official All-Star Game program. The number listed adjacent to the player's name below is the panel number for reference although the panels themselves are not numbered. Reportedly 15,000 sets were produced. After perforation, the cards measure the standard size. The front features a color action player photo, enframed by a red arch with white stars on white card stock. Inside a thin red border the back has player statistics and career summary. The cards are numbered on the back with the same numbers as in the regular series, but the numbers are not consecutive. The cards are exactly identical to the regular issue All-Star cards and hence have the same values in the same shape. Keeping the insert intact is highly recommended.

COMPLETE SET (4)	10.00	25.00
1 Tom Chambers	3.00	8.00
Moses Malone		
Chris Mullin		
Larry Nance		
John Stockton		
Dominique Wilkins		
2 Brad Daugherty	3.00	8.00
Kevin Duckworth		
Alex English		
Mark Jackson		
Magic Johnson		
Isiah Thomas		
3 Terry Cummings	3.00	8.00
Dale Ellis		
Karl Malone		
Kevin McHale		
Hakeem Olajuwon		
Mark Price		
4 Charles Barkley	4.00	10.00
Clyde Drexler		
Mark Eaton		
Patrick Ewing		
Michael Jordan		
James Worthy		

1990-91 Hoops All-Star Panels

These five panels were issued one per All-Star program at the 1991 NBA All-Star game. Each perforated sheet consists of six standard-size cards, arranged in three rows with two cards per row. The color action player photos on the fronts were taken during the 1990 All-Star game in Miami on Feb. 11, 1990. These pictures have the typical Hoops "basketball lane" design and are gold-bordered. Cards picture All-Stars on the East squad are accented by a blue star and a blue stripe carrying a row ofwhite stars; likewise, cards picturing All-Stars on the West squad have a red star and stripe. On a white background with a gray star, the backs carry statistics and player profile. Neither the panels nor the cards are numbered. The cards are checklisted below according to panels, beginning in the upper left corner.

COMPLETE SET (5)	10.00	25.00
1 Michael Jordan	2.50	6.00
James Worthy		
Isiah Thomas		
A.C. Green		
Reggie Miller		
Hakeem Olajuwon		
2 Karl Malone	3.00	8.00
Magic Johnson		
Patrick Ewing		
David Robinson		
Michael Jordan		
Charles Barkley		
3 Kevin McHale	1.50	4.00
Fat Lever		
Joe Dumars		
Rolando Blackman		
Robert Parish		
Kevin Johnson		
4 Dominique Wilkins	2.50	6.00
David Robinson		
Dennis Rodman		
Chris Mullin		
Scottie Pippen		
Tom Chambers		
5 Patrick Ewing	3.00	8.00
Magic Johnson		
Larry Bird		
John Stockton		
Charles Barkley		
Clyde Drexler		

1989-90 Hoops Announcers

In 1989-90, Hoops issued cards for use as business cards to certain announcers (broadcasters). Reportedly between 200 and 1000 cards were printed of each announcer, and some of the announcers (e.g., Rick Barry) autographed their cards. It has been reported that Barry signed 100 of his cards for sale into the organized hobby. The standard-size cards have the same design as the regular issue, with a color photo in the shape of basketball lane. The back contains biographical information. For the TNT broadcasters the card face is silver, and the color stripe below the picture intersects a circular-shaped TNT Sports logo in the lower right corner. We have checklisted these unnumbered cards below in alphabetical order.

COMPLETE SET (7)	200.00	500.00
1 John Andarise	15.00	40.00
2 Rick Barry TNT	80.00	200.00
3 Skip Caray TNT	30.00	80.00
4 Jack Givens TNT	25.00	60.00
5 Steve Jones	25.00	60.00
6 Pat Lafferty	15.00	40.00
7 Craig Sager TNT	25.00	60.00

1990-91 Hoops Announcers

The 1990-91 edition of Hoops Announcer or Broadcaster cards feature 57 announcers from various radio and TV stations. The main radio announcer for each NBA team is represented, and the cards were given to announcers to serve as business cards. The standard-size cards feature a color shot of the announcer inside a basketball lane design. The card face is silver, and the color stripe below the picture intersects a circular-shaped logo with the TV or radio station call letters. The back has biographical information on the sportcaster and a TV or radio advertisement. The cards are unnumbered and checklisted below in alphabetical order. Production quantities for each card were reportedly 250 to 1000 per announcer.

COMPLETE SET (58)	900.00	1800.00
1 Marv Albert	15.00	40.00
2 Steve Albert	12.50	30.00
3 John Andarise	12.50	30.00
4 Jerry Baker	12.50	30.00
5 Jim Barnett	12.50	30.00
6 Jim Barniak	12.50	30.00
7 Rick Barry	60.00	150.00
8 Ron Boone	12.50	30.00
9 Mark Boyle	12.50	30.00
10 Hubie Brown	20.00	50.00
11 Kevin Calabro	12.50	30.00
12 Harry Caray III	12.50	30.00
13 Skip Caray	20.00	50.00
14 Doug Collins	20.00	50.00
15 Chet Coppock	12.50	30.00
16 Bob Costas	30.00	75.00
17 Jim Durham	12.50	30.00
18 Dick Enberg	20.00	50.00
19 Jim Foley	12.50	30.00
20 Mike Fratello	20.00	50.00
21 Gary Gerould	12.50	30.00
22 Jack Givens	15.00	40.00
23 Mike Gorman	12.50	30.00
24 Tom Hanneman	12.50	30.00
25 Kevin Harlan	12.50	30.00
26 Dick Harter	12.50	30.00
27 Fred Hickman	15.00	40.00
28 Steve Holman	12.50	30.00
29 Jay Howard	12.50	30.00
30 Jim Irwin	12.50	30.00
31 Dan Issel	50.00	120.00
32 Ernie Johnson Jr.	20.00	50.00
33 Steve Jones	15.00	40.00
34 Johnny (Red) Kerr	24.00	60.00
35 Jeff Kingery	12.50	30.00
36 Ralph Lawler	12.50	30.00
37 Joe McConnell	12.50	30.00
38 L. Allen McCoy	12.50	30.00
39 Jonathan Miller	12.50	30.00
40 Bob Neal	12.50	30.00
41 Glenn Ordway	12.50	30.00
42 M. John Proctor	12.50	30.00
43 Ed Randall	12.50	30.00
44 Mike Rice	12.50	30.00
45 Pat Riley	50.00	120.00
46 Andrew Rosenberg	12.50	30.00
47 Tommy Roy	12.50	30.00
48 Tim James Roye	12.50	30.00
49 Craig Sager (Play-by-play)	15.00	40.00
50 Craig Sager (Biography)	15.00	40.00
51 Bill Schonely	12.50	30.00
52 Charles Slowes	12.50	30.00
53 David Steele	12.50	30.00
54 Hannah Storm	20.00	50.00
55 Ron Thulin	12.50	30.00
56 Gerry Vaillancourt	12.50	30.00
57 Pete Van Wieren	12.50	30.00
58 William Worrell	12.50	30.00

1991 Hoops Larry Bird Video

This standard-size card was enclosed in cellophane and included as an insert with the "Larry Bird - Basketball Legend" VHS video tape. The front has a color photo of Bird shooting the basketball, with the Boston Garden parquet floor serving as the border on the front and back. The lower right corner of the picture is cut off to allow space for the team logo. The back has a color close-up photo, a street sign from the intersection of Main St. and Larry Bird Blvd., and career highlights within a drawing of Indiana's borders. The NBA Hoops logo appears on the card front. The card is unnumbered.

NNO Larry Bird	6.00	15.00

1990-91 Hoops CollectABooks

These card-size "books" measure approximately 2 1/2" by 3 3/8". The set was issued in four different boxes, with 12 different mini-books in each box. Each book consists of eight pages, including the front and back covers. The front cover features a borderless color player photo, with the player's above the picture in the team's color stripe. Pages 2 and 3 have a color "mug shot" of the player, biographical information, team logo, and career highlights. A color stripe runs across the bottom of each page, with the team name in white lettering. Pages 4 and 5 have a "personal story" about the player. Page 6 has career statistics (college and pro), while page 7 features a borderless color action photo. The top half of the back cover has another color player photo, with a player quote below the picture. An additional special collect-a-book chronicles the Detroit Piston's march to consecutive NBA World Championships. It was available free to consumers only through an offer on second series 1990-91 Hoops packs; fans could receive two booklets free, and additional booklets could be purchased for 50 cents each. The eight-page Pistons booklet features four color photos of the Pistons' top players, a three-page story recapping the team's 1989 and 1990 championship seasons, and playoff statistics for each player. The front cover shows several Piston players with the Larry O'Brien Trophy, while the back cover features Thomas and Dumars, MVP's of the 1989 and 1990 NBA Finals respectively.

COMPLETE SET (48)	6.00	15.00
1 Sam Bowie	.05	.15
2 Tom Chambers	.10	.30
3 Clyde Drexler	.40	1.00
4 Michael Jordan	2.00	5.00
5 Karl Malone	.60	1.50
6 Kevin McHale	.20	.50
7 Reggie Miller	.40	1.00
8 Mark Price	.20	.50
9 Mitch Richmond	.40	1.00
10 Doc Rivers	.10	.30
11 Rony Seikaly	.10	.30
12 Wayman Tisdale	.05	.15
13 Charles Barkley	.40	1.00
14 Terry Cummings	.10	.30
15 Patrick Ewing	.40	1.00
16 Terry Porter	.10	.30
17 Danny Manning	.10	.30
18 Larry Nance	.10	.30
19 Robert Parish	.10	.30
20 Chuck Person	.10	.30
21 Ricky Pierce	.05	.15
22 John Stockton	.60	1.50
23 Isiah Thomas	.20	.50
24 Spud Webb	.10	
25 Michael Adams	.05	
26 Muggsy Bogues	.10	
27 Joe Dumars	.20	
28 Hersey Hawkins	.10	
29 Magic Johnson	.50	
30 Bernard King	.10	
31 Chris Mullin	.20	
32 Charles Oakley	.10	
33 Alvin Robertson	.05	
34 David Robinson	.50	
35 Dominique Wilkins	.30	
36 Buck Williams	.10	
37 Larry Bird	.75	
38 Rolando Blackman	.05	
39 Mark Eaton	.10	
40 Kevin Johnson	.20	
41 J.R. Reid	.05	
42 Xavier McDaniel	.05	
43 Hakeem Olajuwon	.40	
44 Scottie Pippen	.60	
45 Pooh Richardson	.10	
46 Dennis Rodman	.50	
47 Charles Smith	.05	
48 James Worthy	.20	
XX Detroit Pistons	.20	

1999-00 Hoops Decade

The 1999-00 Hoops Decade set was released as a card set. There was only one series offered. Each contained 10 cards and carried a suggested retail of $1.49.

COMPLETE SET (180)	20.00
1 David Robinson	.30
2 Mookie Blaylock	.12
3 Jaren Jackson	.12
4 Andre Miller RC	.50
5 Michael Olowokandi	.12
6 Glenn Robinson	.15
7 Steve Smith	.12
8 Eric Snow	.15
9 Antoine Walker	.20
10 Nick Anderson	.12
11 Jonathan Bender RC	.20
12 Sean Elliott	.20
13 Danny Fortson	.12
14 Adonal Foyle	.12
15 Richard Hamilton RC	.50
16 Shawn Kemp	.20
17 Christian Laettner	.15
18 Rashard Lewis	.20
19 Danny Manning	.12
20 Mitch Richmond	.20
21 Shawn Bradley	.12
22 Tim Duncan	.40
23 Tim Hardaway	.20
24 Antawn Jamison	.20
25 Jeff Hornacek	.15
26 Jumaine Jones RC	.20
27 Corey Maggette RC	.40
28 Vitaly Potapenko	.12
29 Jerry Stackhouse	.20
30 Jason Terry RC	.50
31 Baron Davis RC	.60
32 Matt Harpring	.15
33 Glen Rice	.20
34 Vladimir Stepania	.12
35 Jayson Williams	.12
36 Wally Szczerbiak RC	.40
37 Michael Doleac	.12
38 Hersey Hawkins	.12
39 Allan Houston	.15
40 Hakeem Olajuwon	.25
41 Damon Stoudamire	.20
42 Jelani McCoy	.12
43 Aleksandar Radojevic RC	.20
44 Cal Bowdler RC	.20
45 Tyronn Lue	.12
46 Andrae Patterson	.12
47 Karl Malone	.25
48 Alonzo Mourning	.25
49 Vince Carter	.40
50 Darrell Armstrong	.12
51 Terrell Brandon	.12
52 John Celestand RC	.20
53 Grant Hill	.25
54 Stephon Marbury	.15
55 Tracy McGrady	.30
56 Reggie Miller	.20
57 Clifford Robinson	.12
58 Arvydas Sabonis	.15
59 William Avery RC	.20
60 Calbert Cheaney	.12
61 Jermaine Jackson RC	.20
62 Allen Iverson	.40
63 Larry Johnson	.20
64 Toni Kukoc	.20
65 Raef LaFrentz	.15
66 Isaiah Rider	.12
67 Jeff Foster RC	.20
68 Juwan Howard	.15
69 Kerry Kittles	.12
70 Brevin Knight	.12
71 Voshon Lenard	.12
72 Latrell Sprewell	.20
73 Maurice Taylor	.12
74 Chris Webber	.20
75 Jerome Williams	.12
76 Scott Padgett RC	.20
77 Vin Baker	.20
78 Chris Childs	.12
79 Erick Dampier	.12
80 Anfernee Hardaway	.30
81 Jamal Mashburn	.15
82 Todd Fuller	.12
83 Eric Piatkowski	.15
84 Gary Trent	.12
85 Kevin Garnett	.40
86 Chris Mullin	.20
87 Charles Oakley	.15
88 Detlef Schrempf	.15
89 Elton Brand RC	.50
90 Patrick Ewing	.25
91 Devean George RC	.20
92 Brian Grant	.12
93 Larry Hughes	.15

..n Majerle .20 .50
..awn Marion RC .50 1.25
..ttino Mobley .15 .40
..ul Pierce .30 .75
..ant Reeves .12 .30
..ith Van Horn .15 .40
Corliss Williamson .12 .30
Tariq Abdul-Wahad .12 .30
Brent Barry .15 .40
Elden Campbell .12 .30
Mark Jackson .20 .50
Lamond Murray .12 .30
Bryon Russell .12 .30
Jason Williams .25 .60
Ray Allen .20 .50
Ron Artest RC .50 1.25
Charles Barkley .30 .75
Cedric Ceballos .12 .30
Jason Kidd .30 .75
Donyell Marshall .12 .30
John Stockton .25 .60
Mike Bibby .20 .50
Ricky Davis .20 .50
Steve Francis RC .50 1.25
Tom Gugliotta .12 .30
Laron Profit RC .20 .50
Joe Smith .15 .40
Doug Christie .15 .40
Kenny Anderson .15 .40
Michael Dickerson .12 .30
Zydrunas Ilgauskas .15 .40
Bobby Jackson .15 .40
Quincy Lewis RC .20 .50
Shandon Anderson .12 .30
Bo Outlaw .12 .30
Scottie Pippen .30 .75
Rodney Rogers .12 .30
Rik Smits .20 .50
Chauncey Billups .20 .50
Chris Crawford .12 .30
Kornel David RC .20 .50
Tony Delk .12 .30
Kendall Gill .12 .30
Trajan Langdon RC .20 .50
Ron Mercer .15 .40
Othella Harrington .12 .30
Gheorghe Muresan .12 .30
Isaac Austin .12 .30
Dion Glover RC .20 .50
Avery Johnson .15 .40
Antonio McDyess .15 .40
Steve Nash .30 .75
Tyrone Nesby RC .20 .50
Shaquille O'Neal .50 1.25
James Posey RC .20 .50
Rod Strickland .12 .30
Kobe Bryant 1.00 2.50
Michael Finley .20 .50
Anthony Mason .12 .30
Dikembe Mutombo .20 .50
John Starks .20 .50
Kenny Thomas RC .20 .50
Matt Geiger .12 .30
Tim James RC .20 .50
Eddie Jones .20 .50
Lamar Odom RC .60 1.50
Nick Van Exel .15 .40
Sam Cassell .15 .40
Vonteego Cummings RC .20 .50
Lindsey Hunter .12 .30
Dirk Nowitzki .40 1.00
Gary Payton .20 .50
Shareef Abdur-Rahim .15 .40
Jalen Rose .15 .40
Robert Traylor .12 .30
Derek Anderson .12 .30
Corey Benjamin .12 .30
Marcus Camby .15 .40
Vlade Divac .20 .50
Mario Elie .12 .30
Felipe Lopez .12 .30
Rafer Alston RC .25 .60
Antonio Davis .12 .30
Howard Eisley .12 .30
Theo Ratliff .15 .40
Tim Thomas .15 .40
Rasheed Wallace .20 .50

999-00 Hoops Decade Hoopla

..domly inserted in packs at one in three, this 180 ..d set parallels the Hoops Decade set. The cards ..ure various colored foils. To ascertain values on ..vidual cards, please refer to the multiplier in the ..der, coupled with the values of the base set.
..OPLA: 1.25X TO 3X BASE CARD HI

999-00 Hoops Decade Hoopla Plus

..ndomly inserted in packs at a rate of one in thirty ..ks. This 180-card set parallels the Hoops Decade ..The cards feature a silver foiled background. To ..ertain values on individual cards, please refer to the ..ltiplier in the header, coupled with the value of the ..e set.
..US: 6X TO 15X BASE CARD HI

1999-00 Hoops Decade Draft Day Dominance

..ndomly inserted in packs at one in thirty-two, this 10 ..d set features a dominant player from each of the ..t 10 NBA Draft classes on a card design from the ..ops card of that year. Card backs carry a "DD" ..fix.
..MPLETE SET (10) 8.00 20.00
..RALLEL: .75X TO 2X HI COLUMN
..RALLEL: PRINT RUN 1989 SERIAL #'d SETS
1 David Robinson 1.50 4.00
2 Gary Payton 1.00 2.50
3 Dikembe Mutombo 1.00 2.50
4 Shaquille O'Neal 2.50 6.00
5 Anfernee Hardaway 1.50 4.00
6 Grant Hill 1.25 3.00
7 Antonio McDyess .75 2.00
8 Kobe Bryant 5.00 12.00
9 Keith Van Horn .75 2.00
10 Vince Carter 2.00 5.00

1999-00 Hoops Decade Genuine Coverage

Randomly inserted into packs at one in 893, this 10-card insert set features twelve different memorabilia cards featuring pieces of game-worn uniforms from each of the player's early days.
1 Shareef Abdur-Rahim 8.00 20.00
2 Ray Allen 10.00 25.00
3 Patrick Ewing 12.00 30.00
4 Grant Hill 15.00 40.00
5 Juwan Howard 8.00 20.00
6 Antonio McDyess 8.00 20.00
7 Hakeem Olajuwon 12.00 30.00
8 David Robinson 15.00 40.00
9 Keith Van Horn 8.00 20.00
10 Antoine Walker 10.00 25.00

1999-00 Hoops Decade New Style

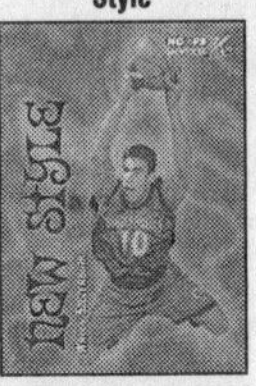

Randomly inserted in packs at one in eighteen, this 15-card insert set features 15 rookies who will blend their style of game into the NBA of the new millennium on 100% silver holofoil stmped cards. Card backs carry a "NS" prefix.
COMPLETE SET (15) 4.00 10.00
*PARALLEL: 1X TO 2.5X HI COLUMN
PARALLEL: PRINT RUN 1989 SERIAL #'d SETS
NS1 Steve Francis .75 2.00
NS2 Lamar Odom 1.00 2.50
NS3 Wally Szczerbiak .60 1.50
NS4 Elton Brand .75 2.00
NS5 Baron Davis 1.00 2.50
NS6 Corey Maggette .60 1.50
NS7 Trajan Langdon .30 .75
NS8 Cal Bowdler .30 .75
NS9 Richard Hamilton .75 2.00
NS10 Ron Artest .75 2.00
NS11 Jason Terry .75 2.00
NS12 Jonathan Bender .30 .75
NS13 Andre Miller .75 2.00
NS14 Shawn Marion .75 2.00
NS15 William Avery .30 .75

1999-00 Hoops Decade Retrospection Collection

Randomly inserted in packs at 1 in 108, this 10-card set features 10 players on a Skyview design from Hoops' past. Card backs carry a "RC" prefix.
COMPLETE SET (10) 30.00 80.00
RC1 Kevin Garnett 6.00 15.00
RC2 Kobe Bryant 30.00 80.00
RC3 Allen Iverson 6.00 15.00
RC4 Vince Carter 6.00 15.00
RC5 Jason Williams 4.00 10.00
RC6 Ron Mercer 2.50 6.00
RC7 Tim Duncan 6.00 15.00
RC8 Anfernee Hardaway 5.00 12.00
RC9 Scottie Pippen 5.00 12.00
RC10 Shaquille O'Neal 8.00 20.00

1999-00 Hoops Decade Up Tempo

Randomly inserted in packs at one in nine packs, this 15-card set features 15 players that can step up their game at any given moment on 100% silver holofoil stamped cards. Card backs carry a "UT" prefix.
COMPLETE SET (15) 6.00 15.00
*PARALLEL: 1.5X TO 4X HI COLUMN
PARALLEL: PRINT RUN 1989 SERIAL #'d SETS
UT1 Allen Iverson 1.00 2.50
UT2 Kevin Garnett 1.00 2.50
UT3 Shaquille O'Neal 1.25 3.00
UT4 Tim Duncan 1.00 2.50
UT5 Stephon Marbury .40 1.00
UT6 Keith Van Horn .40 1.00
UT7 Paul Pierce .75 2.00
UT8 Vince Carter 1.00 2.50
UT9 Antawn Jamison .50 1.25
UT10 Larry Hughes .60 1.50
UT11 Jason Williams .60 1.50
UT12 Antoine Walker .60 1.50
UT13 Grant Hill .60 1.50
UT14 Steve Francis 1.25 3.00
UT15 Lamar Odom 1.50 4.00

1993-94 Hoops Gold Medal Bread

These 49 standard-size cards were produced by Hoops for Gold Medal Bread, and were inserted in its products. The card design is nearly identical to the regular 1993-94 Hoops set. The fronts feature borderless glossy color player action shots, with the player's name and team logo appearing in team colors along a ghosted band at the bottom. The back presents a color head shot of the player in a small rectangle bordered with a team color at the upper right. Alongside is his jersey number and position within a team-colored bar. The player's name and a short biography are printed on a hardwood floor design at the top. Below, the player's college and NBA stats, displayed in separate tables on a white background, round out the card. The cards are unnumbered and checklisted below in alphabetical order.
COMPLETE SET (49) 40.00 100.00
1 B.J. Armstrong 1.00 2.50
2 Thurl Bailey 1.00 2.50
3 Rolando Blackman 1.25 3.00
4 Mookie Blaylock 1.25 3.00
5 Muggsy Bogues 1.25 3.00
6 Anthony Bowie 1.00 2.50
7 Chucky Brown 1.00 2.50
8 Dee Brown 1.00 2.50
9 Duane Causwell 1.00 2.50
10 Cedric Ceballos 1.25 3.00
11 Rex Chapman 1.25 3.00
12 Bimbo Coles 1.00 2.50
13 Tyrone Corbin 1.00 2.50
14 Terry Cummings 1.25 3.00
15 Todd Day 1.00 2.50
16 Joe Dumars 2.00 5.00
17 Mark Eaton 1.00 2.50
18 Vern Fleming 1.00 2.50
19 Kevin Gamble 1.00 2.50
20 Kendall Gill 1.25 3.00
21 Tom Gugliotta 3.00 8.00
22 Derek Harper 1.25 3.00
23 Ron Harper 1.50 4.00
24 Hersey Hawkins 1.25 3.00
25 Tyrone Hill 1.00 2.50
26 Adam Keefe 1.00 2.50
27 Shawn Kemp 3.00 8.00
28 Jerome Kersey 1.00 2.50
29 Stacey King 1.00 2.50
30 Luc Longley 1.25 3.00
31 Moses Malone 1.50 4.00
32 Anthony Mason 1.25 3.00
33 Vernon Maxwell 1.00 2.50
34 Xavier McDaniel 1.00 2.50
35 Oliver Miller 1.00 2.50
36 Sam Mitchell 1.00 2.50
37 Chris Morris 1.00 2.50
38 Dikembe Mutombo 2.00 5.00
39 Billy Owens 1.00 2.50
40 Robert Parish 1.50 4.00
41 Sam Perkins 1.25 3.00
42 Olden Polynice 1.00 2.50
43 Terry Porter 1.00 2.50
44 J.R. Reid 1.00 2.50
45 Rony Seikaly 1.00 2.50
46 Lionel Simmons 1.00 2.50
47 Scott Skiles 1.25 3.00
48 Sedale Threatt 1.00 2.50
49 Loy Vaught 1.00 2.50

2000-01 Hoops Hot Prospects

The 2000-01 Hoops Hot Prospects set was released in November,2000 as a 145-card set. The set features 120 Veterans (1-120), and 25 Rookies (121-145) each numbered to 1000. Each pack contained 5 cards, and carried a suggested retail price of $5.99.
COMPLETE SET w/o RC (120) 15.00 40.00
1 Vince Carter .75 2.00
2 Wesley Person .25 .60
3 Juwan Howard .30 .75
4 Rodney Rogers .25 .60
5 Tim Duncan .75 2.00
6 Rasheed Wallace .40 1.00
7 Anthony Peeler .25 .60
8 John Amaechi .25 .60
9 Tim Hardaway .30 .75
10 Mark Jackson .30 .75
11 Latrell Sprewell .30 .75
12 Kevin Garnett .75 2.00
13 Alonzo Mourning .50 1.25
14 Jerome Williams .25 .60
15 Anfernee Hardaway .60 1.50
16 Clifford Robinson .25 .60
17 Mike Bibby .40 1.00
18 Allen Iverson .75 2.00
19 Terrell Brandon .25 .60
20 Jerry Stackhouse .30 .75
21 Brian Grant .25 .60
22 Lamond Murray .25 .60
23 Nick Anderson .25 .60
24 Alan Henderson .25 .60
25 Bryon Russell .25 .60
26 Elton Brand .40 1.00
27 Antawn Jamison .40 1.00
28 Mitch Richmond .30 .75
29 Marcus Camby .30 .75
30 Raef LaFrentz .25 .60
31 Damon Stoudamire .25 .60
32 Vin Baker .30 .75
33 Allan Houston .30 .75
34 Doug Christie .25 .60
35 Stephon Marbury .30 .75
36 Tim Thomas .30 .75
37 Tracy McGrady .60 1.50
38 Shareef Abdur-Rahim .30 .75
39 Eddie Jones .40 1.00
40 Glenn Robinson .30 .75
41 Sam Cassell .30 .75
42 Dan Majerle .30 .75
43 Maurice Taylor .25 .60
44 Anthony Mason .25 .60
45 Dirk Nowitzki .60 1.50
46 Kobe Bryant 2.00 5.00
47 Kerry Kittles .25 .60
48 Derrick Coleman .30 .75
49 Cuttino Mobley .30 .75
50 Nick Van Exel .30 .75
51 LaPhonso Ellis .30 .75
52 Kendall Gill .25 .60
53 Hakeem Olajuwon .50 1.25
54 Rashard Lewis .40 1.00
55 Dale Davis .25 .60
56 Keith Van Horn .30 .75
57 Michael Finley .40 1.00
58 Othella Harrington .25 .60
59 Gary Payton .40 1.00
60 Michael Dickerson .25 .60
61 Voshon Lenard .25 .60
62 Patrick Ewing .50 1.25
63 Ron Mercer .25 .60
64 Kenny Anderson .30 .75
65 Shaquille O'Neal 1.00 2.50
66 Tariq Abdul-Wahad .25 .60
67 Antonio Davis .25 .60
68 Rick Fox .30 .75
69 Lamar Odom .40 1.00
70 Derek Anderson .25 .60
71 Vitaly Potapenko .25 .60
72 Karl Malone .50 1.25
73 Wally Szczerbiak .30 .75
74 Jason Williams .40 1.00
75 Steve Francis .40 1.00
76 John Starks .25 .60
77 Ron Artest .40 1.00
78 Grant Hill .50 1.25
79 Theo Ratliff .25 .60
80 Antonio McDyess .30 .75
81 Antoine Walker .30 .75
82 Sean Elliott .30 .75
83 Ruben Patterson .25 .60
84 Ray Allen .40 1.00
85 Tom Gugliotta .25 .60
86 Scottie Pippen .60 1.50
87 Jim Jackson .25 .60
88 Joe Smith .30 .75
89 Reggie Miller .40 1.00
90 Richard Hamilton .30 .75
91 Paul Pierce .50 1.25
92 Mookie Blaylock .25 .60
93 Glen Rice .30 .75
94 P.J. Brown .25 .60
95 Avery Johnson .25 .60
96 John Stockton .50 1.25
97 Tyrone Hill .25 .60
98 Tracy Murray .25 .60
99 Darrell Armstrong .25 .60
100 Steve Smith .30 .75
101 Shawn Kemp .40 1.00
102 Jalen Rose .30 .75
103 Vonteego Cummings .25 .60
104 Larry Hughes .30 .75
105 Charles Oakley .30 .75
106 Rod Strickland .30 .75
107 Christian Laettner .30 .75
108 Baron Davis .40 1.00
109 Jamal Mashburn .30 .75
110 Lindsey Hunter .25 .60
111 Toni Kukoc .30 .75
112 Austin Croshere .25 .60
113 Chris Webber .40 1.00
114 Vlade Divac .30 .75
115 Andre Miller .30 .75
116 Larry Johnson .40 1.00
117 Jason Kidd .60 1.50
118 David Robinson .60 1.50
119 Donyell Marshall .25 .60
120 Jason Terry .40 1.00
121 Kenyon Martin JSY RC 5.00 12.00
122 Stromile Swift JSY RC 2.00 5.00
123 Chris Mihm JSY RC 2.00 5.00
124 Marcus Fizer JSY RC 2.00 5.00
125 Courtney Alexander JSY RC 2.00 5.00
126 Darius Miles JSY RC 2.00 5.00
127 Jerome Moiso JSY RC 2.00 5.00
128 Joel Przybilla JSY RC 2.00 5.00
129 DerMarr Johnson JSY RC 2.00 5.00
130 Mike Miller JSY RC 4.00 10.00
131 Quentin Richardson JSY RC 3.00 8.00
132 Morris Peterson JSY RC 2.00 5.00
133 Speedy Claxton JSY RC 2.00 5.00
134 Keyon Dooling JSY RC 2.00 5.00
135 Mark Madsen JSY RC 2.00 5.00
136 Mateen Cleaves JSY RC 2.00 5.00
137 Etan Thomas JSY RC 2.00 5.00
138 Jason Collier JSY RC 2.00 5.00
139 Erick Barkley JSY RC 2.00 5.00
140 Desmond Mason JSY RC 2.50 6.00
141 Mamadou N'Diaye JSY RC 2.00 5.00
142 DeShawn Stevenson JSY RC 2.50 6.00
143 Donnell Harvey JSY RC 2.00 5.00
144 Jamaal Magloire JSY RC 2.00 5.00
145 Hedo Turkoglu JSY RC 4.00 10.00

2000-01 Hoops Hot Prospects A'la Carter

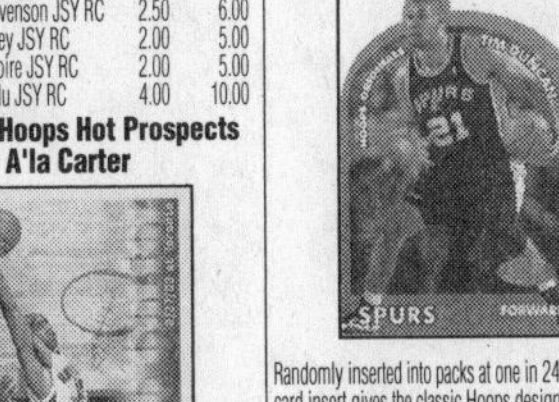

Randomly inserted into retail packs at one in five, this 20-card set features various cards of Vince Carter. Card backs carry an "AC" prefix.
COMPLETE SET (20) 12.00 30.00
COMMON CARD (AC1-AC20) .75 2.00

2000-01 Hoops Hot Prospects Vince Carter First In Flight

Some Vince Carter "special" cards were inserted into packs called First In Flight. The Game Jersey version was numbered to 250, the Shooting Shirt was numbered to 750 and the Warm-ups were numbered to 1000. All versions had autographed variations numbered to 15.
AU'S NOT PRICED DUE TO SCARCITY
1 Vince Carter Jersey/250 15.00 40.00
3 Vince Carter Shirt/750 12.50 30.00
5 Vince Carter Warm-Up/1000 10.00 25.00

2000-01 Hoops Hot Prospects Vince Carter Rookie Remnants

This three-card insert was randomly inserted into 2000-01 Fleer products. The set includes a Vince Carter floor card (numbered to 100), a Vince Carter floor/jersey card (numbered to 15), and finally an autographed Vince Carter floor/jersey card (numbered 1/1).
NNO Vince Carter FLR/100 12.50 30.00

2000-01 Hoops Hot Prospects Determined

Randomly inserted into packs at one in 12 packs, this 10-card insert features players that are determined to win. Card backs carry a "D" prefix.
COMPLETE SET (10) 5.00 12.00
D1 Vince Carter 1.00 2.50
D2 Lamar Odom .50 1.25
D3 Steve Francis .50 1.25
D4 Kobe Bryant 2.50 6.00
D5 Jason Williams .50 1.25
D6 Karl Malone .60 1.50
D7 Allen Iverson 1.00 2.50
D8 Elton Brand .50 1.25
D9 Tim Duncan 1.00 2.50
D10 Kevin Garnett 1.00 2.50

2000-01 Hoops Hot Prospects Genuine Coverage

Randomly inserted into packs at one in 96, this 17-card insert features game-worn sneaker cards of superstars such as Shaquille O'Neal, Lamar Odom, Eddie Jones and Vince Carter. Card backs carry a "GC" prefix.
GC1 Lamar Odom 4.00 10.00
GC2 Antoine Walker 3.00 8.00
GC3 Shaquille O'Neal 10.00 25.00
GC4 Darrell Armstrong 2.50 6.00
GC5 Larry Hughes 3.00 8.00
GC6 Marcus Camby 3.00 8.00
GC7 Nick Van Exel 3.00 8.00
GC8 Michael Dickerson 2.50 6.00
GC9 Baron Davis 4.00 10.00
GC10 Vince Carter 8.00 20.00
GC11 Mike Bibby 4.00 10.00
GC12 Wally Szczerbiak 3.00 8.00
GC13 Jerry Stackhouse 3.00 8.00
GC14 Eddie Jones 4.00 10.00
GC15 Shawn Kemp 5.00 12.00
GC16 Rick Fox 3.00 8.00
GC17 Jamal Mashburn 3.00 8.00

2000-01 Hoops Hot Prospects Originals

Randomly inserted into packs at one in 24, this 10-card insert gives the classic Hoops design a modern makeover as 10 NBA stars are portrayed on these brilliant die-cut cards. Card backs carry a "H" prefix.
COMPLETE SET (10) 10.00 25.00
H1 Vince Carter 1.50 4.00
H2 Tim Duncan 1.50 4.00
H3 Kevin Garnett 1.50 4.00
H4 Kobe Bryant 4.00 10.00
H5 Lamar Odom .75 2.00
H6 Steve Francis .75 2.00
H7 Shaquille O'Neal 2.00 5.00
H8 David Robinson 1.25 3.00
H9 Grant Hill 1.00 2.50
H10 Allen Iverson 1.50 4.00

2000-01 Hoops Hot Prospects Rookie Headliners

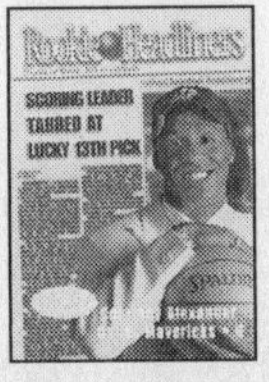

Randomly inserted into packs at one in eight, this 15-card insert features rookies that are sure to make headlines this upcoming season. Card backs carry a "RH" prefix.
COMPLETE SET (15) 3.00 8.00
RH1 Kenyon Martin .75 2.00
RH2 Stromile Swift .30 .75
RH3 Darius Miles .30 .75
RH4 Jerome Moiso .30 .75
RH5 Chris Mihm .30 .75
RH6 Marcus Fizer .30 .75
RH7 Courtney Alexander .30 .75
RH8 DerMarr Johnson .30 .75
RH9 Mike Miller .60 1.50
RH10 Quentin Richardson .50 1.25
RH11 Morris Peterson .30 .75
RH12 Keyon Dooling .30 .75
RH13 Mateen Cleaves .30 .75
RH14 Etan Thomas .30 .75
RH15 Jamal Crawford .50 1.25

2001-02 Hoops Hot Prospects

Released in late November 2001, this 108-card base set is standard size and borderless. The background is designed to resemble that of a hardwood court. The featured player's name is represented in the upper left-hand and right-hand corners. The featured player's name runs along the center bottom of the card with the Hoops logo just above it. The set contains 80 veterans and 28 rookies. The rookies contain a swatch of jersey and are sequentially numbered to 1000 unless noted in the set listing below by /300 which are numbered to 300.
COMP.SET w/o SP's (80) 15.00 40.00
1 Vince Carter .60 1.50
2 John Stockton .50 1.25
3 Steve Smith .30 .75
4 Kevin Garnett .75 2.00
5 Larry Hughes .30 .75
6 Ron Mercer .25 .60
7 Marcus Fizer .25 .60
8 Rashard Lewis .40 1.00
9 Mike Miller .40 1.00
10 Darius Miles .25 .60
11 Michael Finley .40 1.00
12 Marcus Camby .30 .75
13 Morris Peterson .25 .60
14 Shawn Marion .40 1.00
15 Alonzo Mourning .50 1.25
16 Jamal Mashburn .30 .75
17 Michael Jordan 6.00 15.00
18 Jason Williams .30 .75
19 Latrell Sprewell .30 .75
20 Reggie Miller .40 1.00
21 Glenn Robinson .30 .75
22 Steve Francis .40 1.00
23 Antoine Walker .30 .75
24 Stromile Swift .25 .60
25 Damon Stoudamire .30 .75
26 Allan Houston .30 .75
27 Kobe Bryant 2.00 5.00
28 Dirk Nowitzki .60 1.50
29 Iakovos Tsakalidis .25 .60
30 Gary Payton .40 1.00
31 Allen Iverson .75 2.00
32 Eddie Jones .30 .75
33 Mateen Cleaves .25 .60
34 Nick Van Exel .30 .75
35 Terrell Brandon .25 .60
36 Wally Szczerbiak .30 .75
37 Jalen Rose .30 .75
38 Elton Brand .40 1.00
39 DerMarr Johnson .25 .60
40 Peja Stojakovic .40 1.00
41 Jason Kidd .60 1.50
42 Sam Cassell .30 .75
43 Cuttino Mobley .30 .75
44 Toni Kukoc .30 .75
45 DeShawn Stevenson .25 .60
46 David Robinson .60 1.50
47 Grant Hill .50 1.25
48 Shaquille O'Neal 1.00 2.50
49 Andre Miller .30 .75
50 Corey Maggette .30 .75
51 Jason Terry .40 1.00
52 Aaron McKie .25 .60
53 Eddie House .25 .60
54 Steve Nash .60 1.50
55 Clifford Robinson .25 .60
56 Chris Webber .40 1.00
57 Kenyon Martin .40 1.00
58 Jermaine O'Neal .40 1.00
59 Baron Davis .40 1.00
60 Mitch Richmond .30 .75
61 Antawn Jamison .40 1.00
62 Paul Pierce .50 1.25
63 Shareef Abdur-Rahim .30 .75
64 Rasheed Wallace .40 1.00
65 Ray Allen .40 1.00
66 Lamar Odom .40 1.00
67 Chris Mihm .25 .60
68 Raef LaFrentz .25 .60
69 Patrick Ewing .50 1.25
70 Tracy McGrady .60 1.50
71 Derek Fisher .40 1.00
72 Jerry Stackhouse .30 .75
73 Antonio McDyess .30 .75
74 Karl Malone .50 1.25
75 Dikembe Mutombo .40 1.00
76 Hakeem Olajuwon .40 1.00
77 David Wesley .25 .60
78 Courtney Alexander .25 .60
79 Tim Duncan .75 2.00
80 Stephon Marbury .30 .75
81 Kwame Brown JSY RC 3.00 8.00
82 Tyson Chandler JSY RC 5.00 12.00
83 Pau Gasol JSY RC 10.00 25.00
84 Eddy Curry JSY RC 5.00 12.00
85 Jason Richardson JSY/300 RC 10.00 25.00
86 Shane Battier JSY RC 6.00 15.00
87 Eddie Griffin JSY/300 RC 5.00 12.00
88 DeSagana Diop JSY RC 3.00 8.00
89 Rodney White JSY RC 3.00 8.00
90 Joe Johnson JSY/300 RC 12.00 30.00
91 Kedrick Brown JSY/300 RC 5.00 12.00
92 Vladimir Radmanovic JSY RC 3.00 8.00
93 Richard Jefferson JSY RC 6.00 15.00
94 Troy Murphy JSY RC 5.00 12.00
95 Steven Hunter JSY RC 3.00 8.00
96 Kirk Haston JSY RC 3.00 8.00
97 Michael Bradley JSY RC 3.00 8.00
98 Jason Collins JSY RC 3.00 8.00
99 Zach Randolph JSY RC 8.00 20.00
100 Brendan Haywood JSY RC 4.00 10.00
101 Joseph Forte JSY RC 3.00 8.00
102 Jeryl Sasser JSY RC 3.00 8.00
103 Brandon Armstrong JSY/300 RC 5.00 12.00
104 Andrei Kirilenko JSY RC 8.00 20.00
105 Primos Brezec JSY RC 3.00 8.00
106 Samuel Dalembert JSY/300 RC 6.00 15.00
107 Jamaal Tinsley JSY RC 4.00 10.00
108 Tony Parker JSY RC 12.00 30.00

2001-02 Hoops Hot Prospects Rookie Autographs

Randomly inserted in packs, this five card set parallels the base version of the five featured rookies enhanced with authentic player autographs. Each card is sequentially numbered to 100.
81 Kwame Brown JSY AU 10.00 25.00
84 Eddy Curry JSY AU 15.00 40.00
90 Joe Johnson JSY AU 25.00 60.00
91 Kedrick Brown JSY AU 10.00 25.00
97 Michael Bradley JSY AU 10.00 25.00

2001-02 Hoops Hot Prospects Certified Cuts

Randomly inserted in packs at a rate of 1:44, this 11-card insert set features autographed cards of NBA players that look as though they have signed on the line of a personal check. The cards are horizontally designed, standard size, and borderless. A color head shot of the featured player sits above the signature with his corresponding team logo in the upper left-hand corner.
1 Kwame Brown 5.00 12.00
2 Eddy Curry 8.00 20.00
3 Kedrick Brown 5.00 12.00
4 Joe Johnson 12.00 30.00
5 Michael Bradley 5.00 12.00
6 Richard Jefferson 10.00 25.00
7 Brendan Haywood 6.00 15.00
8 Kirk Haston 5.00 12.00
9 Omar Cook 5.00 12.00
10 Vince Carter 20.00 50.00
11 Larry Bird 100.00 200.00

2001-02 Hoops Hot Prospects Hot Materials

This 43-card insert set is randomly inserted in packs at a rate of 1:7. The cards offer swatches of the featured player's game-used jerseys. The swatches set atop a jersey designed background with the player's team name and number standing out behind a color action shot of the player.
1 Vince Carter 5.00 12.00
2 Darius Miles 2.00 5.00
3 Stephon Marbury 2.50 6.00
4 John Stockton 4.00 10.00
5 Steve Francis 3.00 8.00
6 Tracy McGrady 5.00 12.00
7 Lamar Odom 3.00 8.00
8 Corey Maggette 2.50 6.00
9 Stromile Swift 2.00 5.00
10 Morris Peterson 2.00 5.00
11 Jason Kidd 5.00 12.00
12 Karl Malone 4.00 10.00
13 Baron Davis 3.00 8.00
14 Gary Payton 3.00 8.00
15 Paul Pierce 4.00 10.00
16 Desmond Mason 2.50 6.00
17 Dikembe Mutombo 3.00 8.00
18 Mike Miller 3.00 8.00
19 Craig Claxton 2.00 5.00
20 Antoine Walker 2.50 6.00
21 Allen Iverson 6.00 15.00
22 Reggie Miller 3.00 8.00
23 Chris Webber 3.00 8.00
24 Shawn Marion 3.00 8.00
25 Allan Houston 2.50 6.00
26 Kenyon Martin 3.00 8.00
27 Alonzo Mourning 4.00 10.00
28 Grant Hill 4.00 10.00
29 Kwame Brown 2.00 5.00
30 Tyson Chandler 3.00 8.00
31 Eddy Curry 3.00 8.00
32 Shane Battier 4.00 10.00
33 Eddie Griffin 2.00 5.00
34 Rodney White 2.00 5.00
35 Pau Gasol 6.00 15.00
36 Vladimir Radmanovic 2.00 5.00
37 Richard Jefferson 4.00 10.00
38 Steven Hunter 2.00 5.00
39 Kirk Haston 2.00 5.00
40 Michael Bradley 2.00 5.00
41 Jason Collins 2.00 5.00
42 Zach Randolph 5.00 12.00
43 Brendan Haywood 2.50 6.00

2001-02 Hoops Hot Prospects Hot Tandems

Serially #'d to 100, this 43-card insert set highlights dual players with swatches of their game-worn jerseys. The horizontally designed, standard size cards have each featured player, along with his team number, on the left-hand and right-hand sides of the card.

1 Vince Carter 10.00 25.00
Tracy McGrady
2 Kwame Brown 6.00 15.00
Eddy Curry
3 Karl Malone 6.00 15.00
John Stockton
4 DeSagana Diop 6.00 15.00
Stromile Swift
5 Shane Battier 6.00 15.00
Stromile Swift
6 Paul Pierce 8.00 20.00
Antoine Walker
7 Eddie Griffin 6.00 15.00
Jason Kidd
8 Rodney White 6.00 15.00
Steve Francis
9 Mike Miller 6.00 15.00
Michael Bradley
10 Tyson Chandler 8.00 20.00
Darius Miles
11 Stephon Marbury 10.00 25.00
Jason Kidd
12 Allen Iverson 10.00 25.00
Vince Carter
13 Allen Iverson 8.00 20.00
Darius Miles
14 Reggie Miller 8.00 20.00
Baron Davis
15 Chris Webber 8.00 20.00
Karl Malone
16 Alonzo Mourning 8.00 20.00
Dikembe Mutombo
17 Kenyon Martin 6.00 15.00
Lamar Odom
18 Allan Houston 6.00 15.00
Reggie Miller
19 Grant Hill 6.00 15.00
Tracy McGrady
20 Pau Gasol 10.00 25.00
Chris Webber
21 Dikembe Mutombo 6.00 15.00
Speedy Claxton
22 Grant Hill 10.00 25.00
Steve Francis
23 Gary Payton 6.00 15.00
Stephon Marbury
24 Vladimir Radmanovic 6.00 15.00
Desmond Mason
25 Shawn Marion 6.00 15.00
Desmond Mason
26 Richard Jefferson 6.00 15.00
Kenyon Martin
27 Kirk Haston 6.00 15.00
Baron Davis
28 Vince Carter 10.00 25.00
Morris Peterson
29 Vince Carter 10.00 25.00
Lamar Odom
30 Vince Carter 10.00 25.00
Darius Miles
31 Vince Carter 8.00 20.00
Kwame Brown
32 Vince Carter 10.00 25.00
Chris Webber
33 Allen Iverson 10.00 25.00
Jason Kidd
34 Eddie Griffin 6.00 15.00
Darius Miles
35 Eddy Curry 6.00 15.00
Eddie Griffin
36 Eddie Griffin 6.00 15.00
Kwame Brown
37 Allen Iverson 10.00 25.00
Speedy Claxton
38 Tyson Chandler 6.00 15.00
Eddy Curry
39 Tyson Chandler 6.00 15.00
Kwame Brown
40 Shane Battier 8.00 20.00
Tyson Chandler
41 Shane Battier 6.00 15.00
Kwame Brown
42 Grant Hill 10.00 25.00
Reggie Miller
43 Chris Webber 8.00 20.00
Darius Miles

2001-02 Hoops Hot Prospects Inside Vince Carter

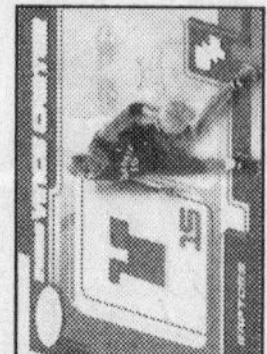

This special 10-card insert set has a different memorabilia items for each Vince Carter card. All cards are sequentially numbered. Autographed versions of each card were also inserted and sequentially numbered to 15.

1 Vince Carter JSY H/1000 6.00 15.00
2 Vince Carter JSY R/900 6.00 15.00
3 Vince Carter WARM/800 6.00 15.00
4 Vince Carter SHIRT/700 6.00 15.00
5 Vince Carter HS FLOOR/600 8.00 20.00
6 Vince Carter UNC JSY/500 10.00 25.00
7 Vince Carter BALL/400 8.00 20.00
8 Vince Carter USA JSY/300 10.00 25.00
9 Vince Carter FLOOR/200 10.00 25.00
10 Vince Carter SHOE/100 25.00 60.00

2001-02 Hoops Hot Prospects Inside Vince Carter Autographs

This special 10-card parallel insert set has a different autographed memorabilia item for each Vince Carter card. Each card is sequentially numbered to 15.

1 Vince Carter JSY H 75.00 150.00
2 Vince Carter JSY R 75.00 150.00
3 Vince Carter WARM 75.00 150.00
4 Vince Carter SHIRT 75.00 150.00
5 Vince Carter HS FLOOR 75.00 150.00
6 Vince Carter UNC JSY 100.00 200.00
7 Vince Carter BALL 100.00 200.00
8 Vince Carter USA JSY 75.00 150.00
9 Vince Carter FLOOR 75.00 150.00
10 Vince Carter SHOE 100.00 200.00

2002-03 Hoops Hot Prospects

Release in early November 2002, Hoops Hot Prospects showcases a 116-card set divided up into 80 veteran player cards, 29 Jersey Rookie cards sequentially numbered to 500, card numbers 81-108, six Rookie Cards sequentially numbered to 900, card numbers 109-114, and five Rookie Cards sequentially numbered to 1500, card numbers 115-120. Base cards have borders on all sides, solid colors appear along the top, the left, and the right side, while a basketball looking border is along the bottom. The card backgrounds are done in a one-color scale and appear metallic. Rookie Jersey cards have a close-up portrait style photo towards the top, and a square jersey swatch centered towards the bottom. Hoops was packaged in five-card packs where boxes contained 15 packs.

COMP.SET w/o SP's (80) 20.00 50.00
1 Vince Carter .60 1.50
2 Chris Webber .40 1.00
3 Latrell Sprewell .30 .75
4 Brian Grant .25 .60
5 Jerry Stackhouse .30 .75
6 Joe Smith .30 .75
7 Jason Terry .30 .75
8 Shawn Marion .40 1.00
9 Wally Szczerbiak .30 .75
10 Reggie Miller .40 1.00
11 Steve Nash .50 1.25
12 Karl Malone .50 1.25
13 Damon Stoudamire .30 .75
14 Jamal Mashburn .30 .75
15 Kobe Bryant 2.00 5.00
16 Paul Pierce .50 1.25
17 Tony Parker .50 1.25
18 Mike Miller .40 1.00
19 Sam Cassell .30 .75
20 Eddie Griffin .25 .60
21 Jason Williams .30 .75
22 Jason Richardson .40 1.00
23 Antoine Walker .30 .75
24 Tim Duncan .75 2.00
25 Baron Davis .40 1.00
26 Glenn Robinson .30 .75
27 Darius Miles .25 .60
28 Dirk Nowitzki .60 1.50
29 John Stockton .50 1.25
30 Allen Iverson .60 1.50
31 Richard Jefferson .40 1.00
32 Rick Fox .30 .75
33 Ben Wallace .40 1.00
34 Michael Jordan 3.00 8.00
35 Rasheed Wallace .40 1.00
36 Alonzo Mourning .50 1.25
37 Steve Francis .40 1.00
38 Jalen Rose .30 .75
39 Rashard Lewis .40 1.00
40 Tracy McGrady .60 1.50
41 David Wesley .25 .60
42 Pau Gasol .50 1.25
43 Antawn Jamison .40 1.00
44 Shareef Abdur-Rahim .30 .75
45 Mike Bibby .40 1.00
46 Dikembe Mutombo .40 1.00
47 Kevin Garnett .75 2.00
48 Elton Brand .40 1.00
49 Lamond Murray .25 .60
50 Morris Peterson .25 .60
51 Joe Johnson .40 1.00
52 Kenyon Martin .40 1.00
53 Shaquille O'Neal 1.00 2.50
54 Antonio McDyess .30 .75
55 Vin Baker .30 .75
56 Marcus Camby .30 .75
57 Ray Allen .40 1.00
58 Jermain O'Neal 1.00 2.50
59 Eddy Curry .30 .75
60 David Robinson .60 1.50
61 Clifford Robinson .25 .60
62 Rodney Rogers .25 .60
63 Peja Stojakovic .40 1.00
64 Allan Houston .30 .75
65 Shane Battier .40 1.00
66 Jamaal Tinsley .25 .60
67 Michael Finley .40 1.00
68 Kenny Anderson .30 .75
69 Stephon Marbury .30 .75
70 Terrell Brandon .25 .60
71 Lamar Odom .40 1.00
72 Raef LaFrentz .25 .60
73 Jamaal Magloire .25 .60
74 Bonzi Wells .25 .60
75 Jason Kidd .60 1.50
76 Cuttino Mobley .30 .75
77 Tyson Chandler .30 .75
78 Gary Payton .40 1.00
79 Grant Hill .50 1.25
80 Eddie Jones .30 .75
81 Yao Ming JSY RC 12.00 30.00
82 Fred Jones JSY RC 4.00 10.00
83 Ryan Humphrey JSY RC 4.00 10.00
84 Drew Gooden JSY RC 6.00 15.00
85 Nikoloz Tskitishvili JSY RC 4.00 10.00
86 Caron Butler JSY RC 6.00 15.00
87 Vincent Yarbrough JSY RC 4.00 10.00
88 DaJuan Wagner JSY RC 4.00 10.00
89 Nene Hilario JSY RC 5.00 12.00
90 Qyntel Woods JSY RC 4.00 10.00
91 Jared Jeffries JSY RC 4.00 10.00
92 Casey Jacobsen JSY RC 4.00 10.00
93 Marcus Haislip JSY RC 4.00 10.00
94 Kareem Rush JSY RC 4.00 10.00
95 Predrag Savovic JSY RC 4.00 10.00
96 Melvin Ely JSY RC 4.00 10.00
97 Steve Logan JSY RC 4.00 10.00
98 Amare Stoudemire JSY RC 10.00 25.00
99 John Salmons JSY RC 5.00 12.00
100 Chris Jefferies JSY RC 4.00 10.00
101 Juan Dixon JSY RC 5.00 12.00
102 Carlos Boozer JSY RC 8.00 20.00
103 Roger Mason JSY RC 4.00 10.00
104 Rod Grizzard JSY RC 4.00 10.00
105 Tayshaun Prince JSY RC 5.00 12.00
106 Chris Wilcox JSY RC 4.00 10.00
107 Sam Clancy JSY RC 4.00 10.00
108 Dan Gadzuric JSY RC 4.00 10.00
109 Dan Dickau/900 RC 2.00 5.00
110 Jay Williams/900 RC 2.50 6.00
111 Mike Dunleavy/900 RC 2.50 6.00
112 Robert Archibald/900 RC 2.00 5.00
113 Curtis Borchardt/900 RC 2.00 5.00
114 Bostjan Nachbar/900 RC 2.00 5.00
115 Jiri Welsch/1500 RC 2.00 5.00
116 Frank Williams/1500 RC 2.00 5.00
117 Rasual Butler/1500 RC 2.00 5.00
118 Tamar Slay/1500 RC 2.00 5.00
119 Ronald Murray/1500 RC 2.00 5.00
120 Corsley Edwards/1500 RC 2.00 5.00

2002-03 Hoops Hot Prospects Certified Cuts

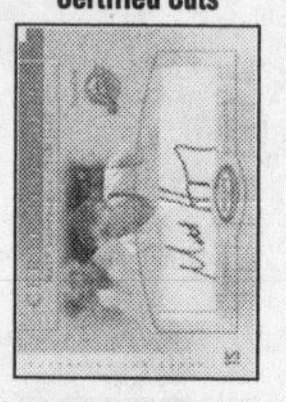

Seeded in packs at the rate of one in 142, this 16-card set uses a horizontal card design, contains embedded cut signatures, a small portrait photo of the player and the player's team logo.

1 Vince Carter 20.00 50.00
2 Shareef Abdur-Rahim 8.00 20.00
4 Kwame Brown 8.00 20.00
5 Joe Johnson 12.50 30.00
6 Michael Bradley 8.00 20.00
7 Eddy Curry 10.00 25.00
9 Cuttino Mobley 8.00 20.00
10 Matt Harpring 8.00 20.00
11 Brian Grant 8.00 20.00
12 Tracy McGrady 40.00 80.00
13 Antonio McDyess 10.00 25.00
14 Larry Hughes 10.00 25.00

2002-03 Hoops Hot Prospects Class Of

Randomly inserted in packs at the rate of one in 15, this 20-card set pairs players from the same draft year on this horizontally designed card. Each player is separated by white borders and a white line down the middle of the card, and every card has silver foil highlights.

STATED ODDS 1:15
1 Kenyon Martin 1.50 4.00
Darius Miles
2 Keith Van Horn 2.00 5.00
Tracy McGrady
3 Steve Francis 1.50 4.00
Baron Davis
4 Allen Iverson 2.00 5.00
Stephon Marbury
5 Jamaal Tinsley 1.50 4.00
Pau Gasol
6 Glenn Robinson 2.00 5.00
Jason Kidd
7 Hedo Turkoglu 1.50 4.00
Quentin Richardson
8 David Robinson 2.00 5.00
Reggie Miller
9 Dirk Nowitzki 3.00 8.00
Vince Carter
10 Ray Allen 1.50 4.00
Antoine Walker
11 Mike Miller 1.50 4.00
Speedy Claxton
12 Jared Jeffries 1.50 4.00
DaJuan Wagner
13 Jason Richardson 2.00 5.00
Tony Parker
14 Lamar Odom 1.50 4.00
Andrei Kirilenko
15 Wally Szczerbiak 1.50 4.00
Elton Brand
16 Amare Stoudemire 2.00 5.00
Drew Gooden
17 Shawn Marion 1.50 4.00
Jason Terry
18 Steve Nash 2.00 5.00
Peja Stojakovic
19 Paul Pierce 2.50 6.00
Vince Carter
20 Caron Butler 2.50 6.00
Yao Ming

2002-03 Hoops Hot Prospects Class Of Jerseys

Randomly seeded, this 20-card set parallels the base Class Of insert set enhanced with swatches of game used material. Each card is sequentially numbered to 375.

1 Kenyon Martin 5.00 12.00
Darius Miles
2 Keith Van Horn 8.00 20.00
Tracy McGrady
3 Steve Francis 6.00 15.00
Baron Davis
4 Allen Iverson 8.00 20.00
Stephon Marbury
5 Jamaal Tinsley 5.00 12.00
Pau Gasol
6 Glenn Robinson 6.00 15.00
Jason Kidd
7 Hedo Turkoglu 5.00 12.00
Quentin Richardson
8 David Robinson 10.00 25.00
Reggie Miller
9 Dirk Nowitzki 12.50 30.00
Vince Carter
10 Ray Allen 6.00 15.00
Antoine Walker
11 Mike Miller 5.00 12.00
Speedy Claxton
12 Jared Jeffries 5.00 12.00
DaJuan Wagner
13 Jason Richardson 6.00 15.00
Tony Parker
14 Lamar Odom 5.00 12.00
Andrei Kirilenko
15 Wally Szczerbiak 5.00 12.00
Elton Brand
16 Amare Stoudemire 6.00 15.00
Drew Gooden
17 Shawn Marion 5.00 12.00
Jason Terry
18 Steve Nash 5.00 12.00
Peja Stojakovic
19 Paul Pierce 10.00 25.00
Vince Carter
20 Caron Butler 8.00 20.00
Yao Ming

2002-03 Hoops Hot Prospects Hot Materials

Inserted in packs at the rate of one in eight, this 45-card set is horizontally designed and places full color player action photos on the left side of the card and a swatch of game worn memorabilia on the right side. The card background is set to match the featured player's jersey colors. A Red Hot Materials parallel set was also inserted where cards are sequentially numbered to 50.

*RED HOT: 1X TO 2.5X HOT MAT.HI
1 Vince Carter 5.00 12.00
2 Steve Francis 3.00 8.00
3 Hedo Turkoglu 3.00 8.00
4 Baron Davis 3.00 8.00
5 Dikembe Mutombo 3.00 8.00
6 Allen Iverson 5.00 12.00
7 Pau Gasol 4.00 10.00
8 Keith Van Horn 2.50 6.00
9 Lamar Odom 3.00 8.00
10 Jason Kidd 5.00 12.00
11 Paul Pierce 4.00 10.00
12 Speedy Claxton 2.00 5.00
13 Steve Nash 4.00 10.00
14 Alonzo Mourning 4.00 10.00
15 Elton Brand 3.00 8.00
16 Corey Maggette 2.50 6.00
17 Jason Richardson 3.00 8.00
18 Desmond Mason 2.50 6.00
19 Antoine Walker 2.50 6.00
20 Cuttino Mobley 2.50 6.00
21 Richard Jefferson 3.00 8.00
22 Darius Miles 2.00 5.00
23 Tracy McGrady 5.00 12.00
24 Peja Stojakovic 3.00 8.00
25 Gary Payton 3.00 8.00
26 Mike Miller 3.00 8.00
27 Tony Parker 4.00 10.00
28 Kenyon Martin 3.00 8.00
29 Yao Ming 10.00 25.00
30 Amare Stoudemire 8.00 20.00
32 Drew Gooden 5.00 12.00
33 Nikoloz Tskitishvili 3.00 8.00
34 Caron Butler 5.00 12.00
35 Fred Jones 3.00 8.00
36 DaJuan Wagner 3.00 8.00
37 Nene Hilario 4.00 10.00
38 Qyntel Woods 3.00 8.00
39 Jared Jeffries 3.00 8.00
40 Tayshaun Prince 4.00 10.00
41 Marcus Haislip 3.00 8.00
42 Kareem Rush 3.00 8.00
43 Ryan Humphrey 3.00 8.00
44 Melvin Ely 3.00 8.00
45 Carlos Boozer 6.00 15.00

2002-03 Hoops Hot Prospects Hot Tandems

Inserted in packs, this 43-card set parallels the design of the Hot Materials set, but instead places two players and two swatches of game used memorabilia on the card front. Each different side is colored to match the featured player's uniform colors, and cards are sequentially numbered to 100. A Red Hot Tandems parallel set was also inserted into packs where singles are sequentially numbered to 10.

ASTERISK NEVER INSERTED IN PACKS
1 Vince Carter 10.00 25.00
Steve Francis
2 Vince Carter 12.50 30.00
Yao Ming
3 Vince Carter 10.00 25.00
Tracy McGrady
4 Vince Carter 6.00 15.00
DaJuan Wagner
5 Vince Carter 10.00 25.00
Paul Pierce
6 Hedo Turkoglu 6.00 15.00
Peja Stojakovic
7 Tracy McGrady 10.00 25.00
Allen Iverson
8 Baron Davis 6.00 15.00
Cuttino Mobley
9 Dikembe Mutombo 6.00 15.00
Nene Hilario
10 Allen Iverson 8.00 20.00
Yao Ming
11 Pau Gasol 6.00 15.00
Ryan Humphrey
13 Lamar Odom 6.00 15.00
Darius Miles
14 Richard Jefferson 8.00 20.00
Jason Kidd
15 Cuttino Mobley 6.00 15.00
Steve Francis
16 Gary Payton 8.00 20.00
Tony Parker
17 Mike Miller 6.00 15.00
Kenyon Martin
18 Drew Gooden 6.00 15.00
Carlos Boozer
19 Melvin Ely 6.00 15.00
Marcus Haislip
20 Qyntel Woods 8.00 20.00
Amare Stoudemire
21 Caron Butler 6.00 15.00
Fred Jones
22 Jared Jeffries 6.00 15.00
Nene Hilario
23 Amare Stoudemire 8.00 20.00
Darius Miles
24 Richard Jefferson 6.00 15.00
Caron Butler
25 DaJuan Wagner 6.00 15.00
Kareem Rush
26 Tony Parker 8.00 20.00
Jason Kidd
27 Pau Gasol 8.00 20.00
Dirk Nowitzki
28 Baron Davis 6.00 15.00
Kareem Rush
29 Steve Nash 10.00 25.00
Dirk Nowitzki
30 Carlos Boozer 6.00 15.00
Elton Brand
31 Alonzo Mourning 8.00 20.00
Dikembe Mutombo
32 Melvin Ely 6.00 15.00
Elton Brand
34 Keith Van Horn 6.00 15.00
Kenyon Martin
35 Ryan Humphrey 6.00 15.00
Peja Stojakovic
36 Lamar Odom 6.00 15.00
Corey Maggette
37 Hedo Turkoglu 6.00 15.00
Nikoloz Tskitishvili
38 Jason Richardson 6.00 15.00
Paul Pierce
39 Jason Richardson 6.00 15.00
Drew Gooden
40 Marcus Haislip 6.00 15.00
Qyntel Woods
41 Fred Jones 6.00 15.00
Antoine Walker
42 Antoine Walker 6.00 15.00
Gary Payton
43 Mike Miller 6.00 15.00
Casey Jacobsen

2002-03 Hoops Hot Prospects Stat Tracker

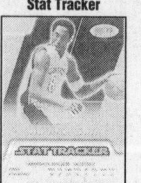

Randomly inserted in packs, this 10-card set showcases top players of the NBA in full color action with borders on the left and right set to match the featured player's team colors. Originally Fleer released that the print number was supposed to be 750, however, each player's card is sequentially numbered to a different number.

1 Vince Carter/57 6.00 15.00
2 Michael Jordan/60 40.00 100.00
3 Kobe Bryant/80 20.00 50.00
4 Shaquille O'Neal/67 10.00 25.00
5 Kevin Garnett/79 8.00 20.00
6 Allen Iverson 6.00 15.00
7 Tracy McGrady/74 6.00 15.00
8 Tim Duncan/82 8.00 20.00
10 Dirk Nowitzki/76 6.00 15.00

2002-03 Hoops Hot Prospects Supreme Court

Inserted in packs at the rate of one in seven, this 15-card set features top rookies on a horizontally designed card. Backgrounds are set to match the player's team colors and places a full color action photo on top of a close-up portrait shot on the left side and the team logo on the right.

COMPLETE SET (15) 12.50 30.00
1 Melvin Ely 1.00 2.50
2 Jay Williams 1.25 3.00
3 Mike Dunleavy 1.25 3.00
4 Drew Gooden 1.50 4.00
5 Nikoloz Tskitishvili 1.00 2.50
6 Caron Butler 1.50 4.00
7 Chris Wilcox 1.00 2.50
8 DaJuan Wagner 1.00 2.50
9 Nene Hilario 1.25 3.00
10 Qyntel Woods 1.00 2.50
11 Jared Jeffries 1.00 2.50
12 Juan Dixon 1.25 3.00
13 Amare Stoudemire 2.50 6.00
14 Kareem Rush 1.00 2.50
15 Bostjan Nachbar 1.00 2.50

2002-03 Hoops Hot Prospects Triple Patch

Randomly seeded in packs, this 15-card set places three players on a horizontally designed card. Each player appears with his own background color and a square swatch of a patch from game-used memorabilia. Each card is sequentially numbered to 75.

1 Jason Kidd 25.00 60.00
Steve Francis
Tracy McGrady
2 Allen Iverson 50.00 120.00
Vince Carter
Paul Pierce
3 Jason Richardson 15.00 40.00
Richard Jefferson
Darius Miles
4 Baron Davis 15.00 40.00
Pau Gasol
Lamar Odom
5 Steve Nash 25.00 60.00
Alonzo Mourning
Elton Brand
6 Antoine Walker 25.00 60.00
Peja Stojakovic
Gary Payton
7 Tony Parker 20.00 50.00
Kenyon Martin
Hedo Turkoglu
8 Dikembe Mutombo 15.00 40.00
Keith Van Horn
Speedy Claxton
9 Corey Maggette 15.00 40.00
Desmond Mason
Cuttino Mobley
10 Mike Miller 20.00 50.00
Yao Ming
DaJuan Wagner
11 Amare Stoudemire 20.00 50.00
Dan Dickau
Drew Gooden
12 Caron Butler 15.00 40.00
Qyntel Woods
Jared Jeffries
13 Kareem Rush 15.00 40.00
Melvin Ely
Nikoloz Tskitishvili
14 Fred Jones 15.00 40.00
Nene Hilario
Tayshaun Prince
15 Marcus Haislip 15.00 40.00
Ryan Humphrey
Carlos Boozer

2003-04 Hoops Hot Prospects

Released in December 2003, this 117-card set is comprised of 80 veteran player cards, six autographed rookie cards (numbers 81-87) sequentially numbered to 600, seven jersey rookie cards (numbers 88-94) sequentially numbered to 500, 17 autographed jersey rookie cards (numbers 95-111) sequentially numbered to 400, and six rookie cards sequentially numbered to 1000 (numbers 112-117). Hoops Hot Prospects was packaged in 15-pack boxes of five cards each and carried a suggested retail price of $7.99.

COMP.SET w/o SP's 15.00 40.00
UNPRICED WHITE HOT PRINT RUN ONE SET
1 Shareef Abdur-Rahim .30 .75
2 Mike Bibby .40 1.00
3 Allan Houston .30 .75
4 Pau Gasol .40 1.00
5 Tayshaun Prince .40 1.00
6 Darius Miles .25 .60
7 Ray Allen .40 1 (cut off)
8 Amare Stoudemire .60
9 Latrell Sprewell .30
10 Jamaal Tinsley .25
11 Nene .30
12 Matt Harpring .30
13 Bonzi Wells .25
14 Alonzo Mourning .50
15 Elton Brand .40
16 Paul Pierce .50
17 Tony Parker .40
18 Glenn Robinson .30
19 Marcus Haislip .25
20 Eddie Griffin .25
21 Jamaal Magloire .25
22 Gilbert Arenas .40 1 (cut off)
23 Antoine Walker .40 1 (cut off)
24 Manu Ginobili .50 1 (cut off)
25 Jamal Mashburn .30
26 Michael Redd .40 1 (cut off)
27 Ron Artest .40 1 (cut off)
28 Steve Nash .50 1 (cut off)
29 Andrei Kirilenko .40 1 (cut off)
30 Stephon Marbury .30
31 Richard Jefferson .40 1 (cut off)
32 Kobe Bryant 2.00 5 (cut off)
33 Cuttino Mobley .30
34 Juan Dixon .25
35 Rasheed Wallace .40 1 (cut off)
36 Eddie Jones .30
37 Steve Francis .40 1 (cut off)
38 Dajuan Wagner .25
39 Vladimir Radmanovic .25
40 Drew Gooden .30
41 Baron Davis .40 1 (cut off)
42 Mike Miller .40 1 (cut off)
43 Jason Richardson .40 1 (cut off)
44 Dan Dickau .25
45 Chris Webber .40 1 (cut off)
46 Kenny Thomas .25
47 Kevin Garnett .75 2 (cut off)
48 Reggie Miller .40 1 (cut off)
49 Dirk Nowitzki .60 1 (cut off)
50 Vince Carter .60 1 (cut off)
51 Zach Randolph .40 1 (cut off)
52 Jason Kidd .60 1 (cut off)
53 Shaquille O'Neal 1.00 2 (cut off)
54 Nikoloz Tskitishvili .25
55 Jerry Stackhouse .30
56 Tracy McGrady .50 1 (cut off)
57 Desmond Mason .30
58 Yao Ming .75 2. (cut off)
59 Jalen Rose .30
60 Tim Duncan .60 1 (cut off)
61 Ben Wallace .40 1. (cut off)
62 Mike Dunleavy .30
63 Peja Stojakovic .40 1 (cut off)
64 Keith Van Horn .30
65 Karl Malone .50 1 (cut off)
66 Jermaine O'Neal .40 1 (cut off)
67 Michael Finley .40 1 (cut off)
68 Morris Peterson .25
69 Shawn Marion .40 1 (cut off)
70 John Salmons .40 1. (cut off)
71 Chris Wilcox .25
72 Rodney White .25
73 Kwame Brown .25
74 Bobby Jackson .25
75 Kenyon Martin .40 1. (cut off)
76 Antawn Jamison .40 1. (cut off)
77 Eddy Curry .30
78 Bruce Bowen .25
79 Allen Iverson .60 1. (cut off)
80 Caron Butler .40 1. (cut off)
81 Boris Diaw AU RC 5.00 12. (cut off)
82 Quinton Ross AU RC 4.00 10. (cut off)
83 Matt Carroll AU RC 4.00 10. (cut off)
84 Travis Hansen AU RC 4.00 10. (cut off)
85 Zaur Pachulia AU RC 4.00 10. (cut off)
86 Zarko Cabarkapa AU RC 4.00 10. (cut off)
87 Maciej Lampe AU RC 4.00 10. (cut off)
88 Ndudi Ebi JSY RC 5.00 12. (cut off)
89 Jarvis Hayes JSY RC 5.00 12. (cut off)
90 Steve Blake JSY RC 6.00 15. (cut off)
91 Keith Bogans JSY RC 5.00 12. (cut off)
92 Reece Gaines JSY RC 5.00 12. (cut off)
93 Chris Kaman JSY RC 6.00 15. (cut off)
94 Slavko Vranes JSY RC 5.00 12. (cut off)
95 Carmelo Anthony JSY AU RC 75.00 150. (cut off)
96 Troy Bell JSY AU RC 6.00 15. (cut off)
97 Travis Outlaw JSY AU RC 8.00 20. (cut off)
98 Mike Sweetney JSY AU RC 6.00 15. (cut off)
99 Dahntay Jones JSY AU RC 6.00 15. (cut off)
100 Chris Bosh JSY AU RC 30.00 80. (cut off)
101 Brian Cook JSY AU RC 6.00 15. (cut off)
102 Luke Ridnour JSY AU RC 8.00 20. (cut off)
103 David West JSY AU RC 8.00 20. (cut off)
104 Marcus Banks JSY AU RC 6.00 15. (cut off)
105 Kendrick Perkins JSY AU RC 10.00 25. (cut off)
106 Leandro Barbosa JSY AU RC 8.00 20. (cut off)
107 Mickael Pietrus JSY AU RC 6.00 15. (cut off)
108 Dwyane Wade JSY AU RC 100.00 200. (cut off)
109 Josh Howard JSY AU RC 6.00 15. (cut off)
110 Jason Kapono JSY AU RC 6.00 15. (cut off)
111 Luke Walton JSY AU RC 6.00 15. (cut off)
112 LeBron James RC 20.00 50. (cut off)
113 T.J. Ford RC 2.50 6. (cut off)
114 Zoran Planinic RC 2.00 5. (cut off)
115 Darko Milicic RC 2.00 5. (cut off)
116 Kirk Hinrich RC 2.50 6. (cut off)
117 Nick Collison RC 2.00 5. (cut off)

2003-04 Hoops Hot Prospects Cream of the Crop

Inserted in packs at the rate of one in five, this 15-ca[rd] set features a horizontal design where the new rookie photo is centered and framed in tan.

COMPLETE SET (15) 15.00 40.0 (cut off)
1 LeBron James 8.00 20.0 (cut off)
2 Mike Sweetney .75 2.0 (cut off)
3 Chris Bosh 1.50 4.0 (cut off)
4 Darko Milicic .75 2.0 (cut off)
5 Nick Collison .75 2.0 (cut off)
6 Luke Ridnour 1.00 2. (cut off)
7 Kirk Hinrich 1.00 2. (cut off)

rnelo Anthony	2.00	5.00
is Kaman	1.00	2.50
ckael Pietrus	.75	2.00
rvis Hayes	.75	2.00
ece Gaines	.75	2.00
vyane Wade	3.00	8.00
arcus Banks	.75	2.00
J. Ford	1.00	2.50

003-04 Hoops Hot Prospects Hot Materials

omly inserted in packs, this 30-card set is ontally designed and has an all-black background. r images appear on the left in full color and a h of game worn memorabilia appears in the upper corner. Each card is sequentially numbered to Red and white versions were inserted also, where ards are sequentially numbered to 50 and white are one of one's.

SINGLES: .75X TO 2X HI COLUMN

rmelo Anthony	6.00	15.00
vyane Wade	10.00	25.00
ckael Pietrus	2.50	6.00
ke Sweetney	2.50	6.00
ris Bosh	5.00	12.00
ris Kaman	3.00	8.00
shaun Prince	2.50	6.00
are Stoudemire	4.00	10.00
ıl Pierce	3.00	8.00
ony Parker	2.50	6.00
anu Ginobili	3.00	8.00
teve Nash	3.00	8.00
teve Francis	2.50	6.00
ason Richardson	2.50	6.00
evin Garnett	5.00	12.00
irk Nowitzki	4.00	10.00
nce Carter	4.00	10.00
ason Kidd	4.00	10.00
acy McGrady	3.00	8.00
ao Ming	5.00	12.00
en Wallace	2.50	6.00
enyon Martin	2.50	6.00
llen Iverson	4.00	10.00
aron Butler	2.50	6.00
naquille O'Neal	6.00	15.00
aron Davis	2.50	6.00
rew Gooden	2.00	5.00
ichael Redd	2.50	6.00
onzi Wells	2.00	5.00
ike Dunleavy	2.00	5.00

003-04 Hoops Hot Prospects Hot Tandems

omly inserted in packs, this 25-card set utilizes lesign of the hot materials cards with pictures of players and two swatches of game worn orabilia. Each card is squentially numbered to Red and white versions of this set were also ted. Red cards are sequentially numbered to 10 white cards are numbered one of one.

rmelo Anthony vyane Wade	25.00	60.00
ckael Pietrus ke Sweetney	5.00	12.00
ris Bosh ris Kaman	8.00	20.00
nare Stoudemire o Ming	12.50	30.00
yshaun Prince n Wallace	5.00	12.00
son Richardson ke Dunleavy	5.00	12.00
vin Garnett rk Nowitzki	8.00	20.00
ichael Redd nzi Wells	5.00	12.00
ny Parker anu Ginobili	8.00	20.00
racy McGrady ew Gooden	6.00	15.00
aron Davis eve Francis	5.00	12.00
ince Carter en Iverson	10.00	25.00
Steve Nash son Kidd	8.00	20.00
Kenyon Martin aquille O'Neal	8.00	20.00
aul Pierce ron Butler	6.00	15.00
armelo Anthony acy McGrady	20.00	40.00
hris Bosh nce Carter	10.00	25.00
mare Stoudemire evin Garnett	8.00	20.00
ao Ming en Iverson	10.00	25.00
Dirk Nowitzki enyon Martin	6.00	15.00
Ben Wallace aquille O'Neal	15.00	30.00
ason Richardson ickael Pietrus	5.00	12.00
ony Parker eve Nash	6.00	15.00
ason Kidd aron Davis	6.00	15.00
ayshaun Prince ew Gooden	5.00	12.00

2003-04 Hoops Hot Prospects Player Graphs

Released originally as a replacement for autograph redemptions Fleer was unable to fulfill, many of these Vince Carter cards hit the secondary market after the summer 2005 Fleer auction following the company's bankruptcy and closing of business, leading us to believe most copies were not issued through the mail, but were purchased at that auction.

PN Nene	8.00	20.00
PVC Vince Carter	15.00	40.00

2003-04 Hoops Hot Prospects Sweet Selections

Randomly inserted at the rate of one in 15, this 10-card set pairs draft picks and which spot they were taken. The draft number appears on the bottom of this horizontally designed card and two player pictures appear above it one on the left and the other right.

COMPLETE SET (10)	10.00	25.00
1 Yao Ming Allen Iverson	2.50	6.00
2 Jason Richardson Ray Allen	1.50	4.00
3 Pau Gasol Baron Davis	1.50	4.00
4 Amare Stoudemire Shawn Marion	2.00	5.00
5 Shaquille O'Neal Tim Duncan	2.50	6.00
6 Tyson Chandler Steve Francis	1.50	4.00
7 Vince Carter Kevin Garnett	2.50	6.00
8 Jason Kidd Gary Payton	2.00	5.00
9 Darius Miles Shareef Abdur-Rahim	1.50	4.00
10 Dirk Nowitzki Tracy McGrady	2.00	5.00

2003-04 Hoops Hot Prospects Sweet Selections Game Used

Randomly seeded, this ten-card set parallels the base Sweet Selections set enhanced with swatches of game used material from each player and sequential numbering to 375.

1 Yao Ming Allen Iverson	8.00	20.00
2 Jason Richardson Ray Allen	4.00	10.00
3 Pau Gasol Baron Davis	4.00	10.00
4 Amare Stoudemire Shawn Marion	5.00	12.00
5 Shaquille O'Neal Tim Duncan	10.00	25.00
6 Tyson Chandler Steve Francis	4.00	10.00
7 Vince Carter Kevin Garnett	8.00	20.00
8 Jason Kidd Gary Payton	6.00	15.00
9 Darius Miles Shareef Abdur-Rahim	4.00	10.00
10 Dirk Nowitzki Tracy McGrady	6.00	15.00

2003-04 Hoops Hot Prospects Triple Patches

Randomly inserted in packs, this 15-card set utilizes the design of the hot materials set with three player photos along the top and three swatches of game-worn material patches along the bottom. Each card is sequentially numbered to 50. A white one of one version was also produced.

1 Carmelo Anthony Dwyane Wade Mickael Pietrus	50.00	120.00
2 Mike Sweetney Chris Bosh Chris Kaman	30.00	80.00
3 Amare Stoudemire Yao Ming Tayshaun Prince	30.00	80.00
4 Manu Ginobili Steve Nash Steve Francis	30.00	80.00
5 Kevin Garnett Dirk Nowitzki Vince Carter	30.00	80.00
6 Tracy McGrady Kenyon Martin Allen Iverson	40.00	100.00
7 Paul Pierce Tony Parker Jason Richardson	30.00	80.00
8 Ben Wallace Caron Butler Shaquille O'Neal	30.00	80.00
9 Bonzi Wells Mike Dunleavy Drew Gooden	25.00	60.00
10 Jason Kidd Baron Davis Michael Redd	30.00	80.00
11 Carmelo Anthony Vince Carter Tracy McGrady	40.00	100.00
12 Amare Stoudemire Kevin Garnett Dirk Nowitzki	30.00	80.00
13 Allen Iverson Paul Pierce Jason Richardson	30.00	80.00
14 Yao Ming Ben Wallace Chris Kaman	25.00	60.00
15 Steve Nash Steve Francis Jason Kidd	25.00	60.00

2003 Hoops Hot Prospects All-Star Game

Produced by Fleer for distribution at the 2003 NBA Jam Session All-Star Game show in Atlanta, this six card set features the top rookies of the 2002 NBA draft and utilize the same base design as 2002-03 Hoops Hot Prospects. Only 2500 total sets were produced and were available to collectors who purchased and opened five packs of Fleer Products at the Fleer show booth.

COMPLETE SET (6)	15.00	40.00
1 Yao Ming	8.00	20.00
2 Drew Gooden	2.50	6.00
3 Caron Butler	2.50	6.00
4 Amare Stoudemire	6.00	15.00
5 Nene Hilario	2.00	5.00
6 DaJuan Wagner	1.50	4.00

2004-05 Hoops Hot Prospects

Released in November 2004, Hoops Hot Prospects boasts a 110-card checklist divided up into 70 veteran players, 20 jersey autographed rookies serially numbered to either 150 or 350 (cards 71-90), 10 jersey rookies serially numbered to 350 (cards 91-100) and 10 rookie cards serially numbered to 1000 (cards 101-110). Base veteran cards feature white borders and foil backgrounds, while rookies have white borders and a player portrait photo towards the top. In the case of cards that have jerseys, the jersey is right below the photo, and in the case of cards that have autographs, the autograph is at the bottom of the card. Hoops was offered for both Hobby and Retail were all packs containted five cards, but Hobby was released with 15 packs per box and Retail with 24.

COMP.SET w/o SP's (70)	15.00	40.00
UNPRICED WHITE HOT PRINT RUN ONE SET		
1 Dwyane Wade	1.25	3.00
2 Chris Bosh	.40	1.00
3 Peja Stojakovic	.40	1.00
4 Darius Miles	.25	.60
5 Drew Gooden	.30	.75
6 Latrell Sprewell	.30	.75
7 Caron Butler	.40	1.00
8 Shaquille O'Neal	1.00	2.50
9 Reggie Miller	.40	1.00
10 Corey Maggette	.30	.75
11 Tracy McGrady	.50	1.25
12 Ben Wallace	.40	1.00
13 Steve Nash	.50	1.25
14 Paul Pierce	.50	1.25
15 Jarvis Hayes	.25	.60
16 Ray Allen	.40	1.00
17 Chris Webber	.40	1.00
18 Amare Stoudemire	.50	1.25
19 Pau Gasol	.40	1.00
20 Jermaine O'Neal	.40	1.00
21 Yao Ming	.75	2.00
22 Richard Hamilton	.30	.75
23 Kirk Hinrich	.40	1.00
24 Antoine Walker	.40	1.00
25 Carlos Arroyo	.30	.75
26 Luke Ridnour	.30	.75
27 Mike Bibby	.40	1.00
28 Tim Duncan	.60	1.50
29 Shareef Abdur-Rahim	.30	.75
30 Willie Green	.25	.60
31 Jamaal Magloire	.25	.60
32 Stephen Jackson	.30	.75
33 Karl Malone	.50	1.25
34 Elton Brand	.40	1.00
35 Jason Richardson	.40	1.00
36 Steve Francis	.40	1.00
37 Jason Kidd	.60	1.50
38 Kevin Garnett	.75	2.00
39 Jason Williams	.30	.75
40 Ron Artest	.40	1.00
41 Darko Milicic	.25	.60
42 Carmelo Anthony	.75	2.00
43 Carlos Boozer	.40	1.00
44 Michael Finley	.40	1.00
45 Marcus Fizer	.25	.60
46 Ricky Davis	.30	.75
47 Andrei Kirilenko	.30	.75
48 Tony Parker	.40	1.00
49 Shawn Marion	.40	1.00
50 Allan Houston	.30	.75
51 Kenyon Martin	.40	1.00
52 T.J. Ford	.30	.75
53 Nene	.30	.75
54 LeBron James	2.50	6.00
55 Eddy Curry	.30	.75
56 Jason Terry	.30	.75
57 Vince Carter	.60	1.50
58 Zach Randolph	.30	.75
59 Allen Iverson	.60	1.50
60 Stephon Marbury	.30	.75
61 Richard Jefferson	.40	1.00
62 Baron Davis	.40	1.00
63 Michael Redd	.40	1.00
64 Lamar Odom	.40	1.00
65 Kobe Bryant	2.00	5.00
66 Mickael Pietrus	.30	.75
67 Dirk Nowitzki	.60	1.50
68 Dajuan Wagner	.25	.60
69 Jason Kapono	.25	.60
70 Antawn Jamison	.40	1.00
71 Ben Gordon JSY AU/350 RC	8.00	20.00
72 Shaun Livingston JSY AU/350 RC	6.00	15.00
73 Devin Harris JSY AU/150 RC	10.00	25.00
74 Josh Childress JSY AU/150 RC	6.00	15.00
75 Luol Deng JSY AU/150 RC	12.00	30.00
76 Rafael Araujo JSY AU/350 RC	6.00	15.00
77 Luke Jackson JSY AU/150 RC	6.00	15.00
78 Andris Biedrins JSY AU RC	8.00	20.00
79 Yuta Tabuse JSY AU/350 RC	12.00	30.00
80 Sebastian Telfair JSY AU/350 RC	6.00	15.00
81 Kris Humphries JSY AU/350 RC	6.00	15.00
82 Kirk Snyder JSY AU/150 RC	6.00	15.00
83 Josh Smith JSY AU/150 RC	10.00	25.00
84 J.R. Smith JSY AU/350 RC	8.00	20.00
85 Dorell Wright JSY AU/350 RC	10.00	25.00
86 Jameer Nelson JSY AU/350 RC	8.00	20.00
87 Delonte West JSY AU/350 RC	8.00	20.00
88 Tony Allen JSY AU/350 RC	8.00	20.00
89 Seung-Jin JSY AU/350 RC	6.00	15.00
90 Al Jefferson JSY AU/150 RC	10.00	25.00
91 Dwight Howard JSY RC	15.00	40.00
92 Andre Iguodala JSY RC	8.00	20.00
93 Jackson Vroman JSY RC	5.00	12.00
94 Lionel Chalmers JSY RC	5.00	12.00
95 Kevin Martin JSY RC	6.00	15.00
96 Sasha Vujacic JSY RC	5.00	12.00
97 Andre Emmett JSY RC	5.00	12.00
98 David Harrison JSY RC	5.00	12.00
99 Anderson Varejao JSY RC	6.00	15.00
100 Chris Duhon JSY RC	5.00	12.00
101 Emeka Okafor RC	3.00	8.00
102 Viktor Khryapa RC	2.00	5.00
103 Peter John Ramos RC	2.00	5.00
104 Sergei Monia RC	2.00	5.00
105 Beno Udrih RC	2.00	5.00
106 Pavel Podkolzine RC	2.00	5.00
107 Trevor Ariza RC	2.00	5.00
108 Royal Ivey RC	2.00	5.00
109 Bernard Robinson RC	2.00	5.00
110 Robert Swift RC	2.00	5.00

2004-05 Hoops Hot Prospects Red Hot

Randomly inserted in packs, this 110-card set parallels the base Hoops Hot Prospects set enhanced with red foil highlights and sequential numbering to 50. A White Hot one of one version was also produced.

*1-70 RED: 2X TO 5X BASE HI
*71-90 RED: 1X TO 2.5X BASE HI
*91-100 RED: .6X TO 1.5X BASE HI
*101-110 RED: .75X TO 2X BASE HI

2004-05 Hoops Hot Prospects Alumni Ink

Randomly inserted in packs, this 10-card set features a hinged card that opens up on the inside with one player and his autograph on one side and another on the other. Both autographs are cut signatures and the cards are limited to 50 copies. Also released was a Red Hot set serially numbered to 10 and a White Hot set numbered one of one.

CJ Vince Carter Antawn Jamison	30.00	60.00
MB Stephon Marbury Chris Bosh	15.00	40.00
RR Zach Randolph Jason Richardson	15.00	40.00
WN Delonte West Jameer Nelson	25.00	50.00
WP Antawn Walker Tayshaun Prince	15.00	40.00

2004-05 Hoops Hot Prospects Double Team

Inserted in Hobby packs at the rate of one in 45 and Retail at the rate of one in 96, this 13-card set is horizontally designed and pictures the featured player on the left in his NBA uniform and on the right in his Team USA uniform.

COMPLETE SET (13)	12.50	30.00
AI Allen Iverson	1.25	3.00
AS Amare Stoudemire	1.00	2.50
CA Carmelo Anthony	1.50	4.00
CB Carlos Boozer	.75	2.00
DW Dwyane Wade	2.50	6.00
EO Emeka Okafor	1.25	3.00
LB Larry Brown	2.50	6.00
LJ LeBron James	5.00	12.00
LO Lamar Odom	.75	2.00
RJ Richard Jefferson	.75	2.00
SM Shawn Marion	.75	2.00
SM Stephon Marbury	.60	1.50
TD Tim Duncan	1.25	3.00

2004-05 Hoops Hot Prospects Double Team Jerseys

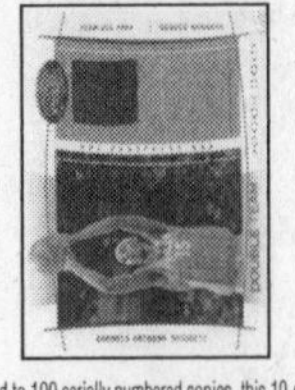

Limited to 100 serially numbered copies, this 10-card set parallels the look of the base Double Team insert but instead of having an image of the player in his Team USA jersey, it includes a swatch of NBA memorabilia and USA memorabilia. Eight parallel sets were issued as well, Red Hot serially numbered to 25, White Hot numbered one of one, Patches serially numbered to 50, Patch Red Hot serially numbered to 10, Patch White Hot numbered one of one, Patch Autographs serially numbered to 25, Patch Autographs Red Hot serially numbered to five and Patch Autographs White Hot numbered one of one.

*RED HOT: .6X TO 1.5X BASE HI
*PATCH SINGLES: 1.25X TO 3X BASE JSY HI

AI Allen Iverson	5.00	12.00
AS Amare Stoudemire	4.00	10.00
CA Carmelo Anthony	6.00	15.00
CB Carlos Boozer	3.00	8.00
DW Dwyane Wade	10.00	25.00
LO Lamar Odom	3.00	8.00
RJ Richard Jefferson	3.00	8.00
SM Shawn Marion	3.00	8.00
SM Stephon Marbury	3.00	8.00
TD Tim Duncan	5.00	12.00

2004-05 Hoops Hot Prospects Double Team Patches Autographs

Randomly inserted in packs, this 10-card set parallels the base Double Team Jerseys insert set enhanced with patch swatches, an autograph and sequential numbering to 25.

UNPRICED RED HOT PRINT RUN 5 SETS
UNPRICED WHITE HOT PRINT RUN ONE SET

CA Carmelo Anthony	100.00	200.00
RJ Richard Jefferson	15.00	40.00
SM Stephon Marbury	40.00	100.00

2004-05 Hoops Hot Prospects Draft Rewind

Inserted in both Hobby and Retail packs at the rate of one in five, this 30-card set is horizontally designed with player's likenesses featured on the left in scale color to match their team's main color and the team's logo in a white box on the right.

COMPLETE SET (30)	10.00	25.00
1 Dwyane Wade	1.25	3.00
2 Lamar Odom	.40	1.00
3 Peja Stojakovic	.40	1.00
4 Shaquille O'Neal	1.00	2.50
5 Reggie Miller	.40	1.00
6 Tracy McGrady	.50	1.25
7 Steve Nash	.50	1.25
8 Paul Pierce	.50	1.25
9 Ray Allen	.40	1.00
10 Dirk Nowitzki	.60	1.50
11 Amare Stoudemire	.50	1.25
12 Pau Gasol	.40	1.00
13 Jermaine O'Neal	.40	1.00
14 Yao Ming	.75	2.00
15 Kirk Hinrich	.40	1.00
16 Tim Duncan	.60	1.50
17 Karl Malone	.50	1.25
18 Mike Bibby	.40	1.00
19 Steve Francis	.40	1.00
20 Jason Kidd	.60	1.50
21 Kevin Garnett	.75	2.00
22 Darko Milicic	.25	.60
23 Carmelo Anthony	.75	2.00
24 Tony Parker	.40	1.00
25 Kenyon Martin	.40	1.00
26 LeBron James	2.50	6.00
27 Vince Carter	.60	1.50
28 Allen Iverson	.60	1.50
29 Stephon Marbury	.30	.75
30 Kobe Bryant	2.00	5.00

2004-05 Hoops Hot Prospects Draft Rewind Jerseys

Randomly seeded in packs, this 28-card set parallels the base Draft Rewind set enhanced with a swatch of jersey on the right side. Each card is sequentially numbered to a random amount. Two parallel sets were inserted as well: Red Hot which is sequentially numbered to 10 and White Hot which is done in one of one format.

AI Allen Iverson/101	5.00	12.00
AS Amare Stoudemire/109	4.00	10.00
CA Carmelo Anthony/103	6.00	15.00
DM Darko Milicic/102	2.00	5.00
DN Dirk Nowitzki/109	5.00	12.00
DW Dwyane Wade/105	10.00	25.00
JK Jason Kidd/102	5.00	12.00
JO Jermaine O'Neal/117	3.00	8.00
KG Kevin Garnett/105	6.00	15.00
KH Kirk Hinrich/107	3.00	8.00
KM Kenyon Martin/101	3.00	8.00
KM Karl Malone/103	4.00	10.00
LO Lamar Odom/104	3.00	8.00
MB Mike Bibby/102	3.00	8.00
PG Pau Gasol/103	3.00	8.00
PP Paul Pierce/110	4.00	10.00
PS Peja Stojakovic/114	3.00	8.00
RA Ray Allen/105	3.00	8.00
RM Reggie Miller/111	3.00	8.00
SF Steve Francis/102	3.00	8.00
SM Stephon Marbury/104	2.50	6.00
SN Steve Nash/115	4.00	10.00
SO Shaquille O'Neal/101	8.00	20.00
TD Tim Duncan/101	5.00	12.00
TM Tracy McGrady/109	4.00	10.00
TP Tony Parker/128	3.00	8.00
VC Vince Carter/105	5.00	12.00
YM Yao Ming/101	6.00	15.00

2004-05 Hoops Hot Prospects Draft Rewind Patches

Serially numbered to random amounts, this 27-card set parallels the Draft Rewind Jerseys set enhanced with patch swatches. Two parallel versions of this set were issued: Red Hot serially numbered to five and White Hot numbered one of one.

MOST NOT PRICED DUE TO SCARCITY

AS Amare Stoudemire/19	10.00	25.00
CA Carmelo Anthony/13	15.00	40.00
DN Dirk Nowitzki/19	12.00	30.00
DW Dwyane Wade/15	25.00	60.00
JO Jermaine O'Neal/27	8.00	20.00
LO Lamar Odom/14	8.00	20.00
PG Pau Gasol/13	8.00	20.00
PP Paul Pierce/20	10.00	25.00
PS Peja Stojakovic/24	8.00	20.00
SM Stephon Marbury/14	8.00	20.00
TM Tracy McGrady/19	10.00	25.00
TP Tony Parker/38	8.00	20.00
VC Vince Carter/15	12.00	30.00

2004-05 Hoops Hot Prospects Hot Materials

Serially numbered to 500, this 35-card set features white borders, player action photos, accent colors to match the player's team colors and a square swatch of jersey centered towards the bottom of the card. Two parallels versions were released for this set: Red Hot sequentially numbered to 50 and White Hot in a one of one format.

*RED SINGLES: .6X TO 1.5X BASE JSY HI

AI Allen Iverson	4.00	10.00
AS Amare Stoudemire	3.00	8.00
BD Baron Davis	2.50	6.00
BG Ben Gordon	3.00	8.00
BW Ben Wallace	2.50	6.00
CA Carmelo Anthony	5.00	12.00
CB Chris Bosh	2.50	6.00
DH Devin Harris	4.00	10.00
DH2 Dwight Howard	8.00	20.00
DM Darko Milicic	2.00	5.00
DN Dirk Nowitzki	4.00	10.00
DW Dwyane Wade	6.00	15.00
JC Josh Childress	2.50	6.00
JK Jason Kidd	4.00	10.00
JO Jermaine O'Neal	2.50	6.00
JR Jason Richardson	2.50	6.00
KG Kevin Garnett	5.00	12.00
KH Kirk Hinrich	2.50	6.00
LD Luol Deng	4.00	10.00
LO Lamar Odom	2.50	6.00
MB Mike Bibby	2.50	6.00
PG Pau Gasol	2.50	6.00
PP Paul Pierce	3.00	8.00
PS Peja Stojakovic	2.50	6.00
RA Ray Allen	2.50	6.00
RJ Richard Jefferson	2.50	6.00
SF Steve Francis	2.50	6.00
SL Shaun Livingston	2.50	6.00
SM Stephon Marbury	2.00	5.00
SM2 Shawn Marion	2.50	6.00
SO Shaquille O'Neal	6.00	15.00
TD Tim Duncan	4.00	10.00
TM Tracy McGrady	3.00	8.00
VC Vince Carter	4.00	10.00
YM Yao Ming	5.00	12.00

2004-05 Hoops Hot Prospects Notable Newcomers

Inserted in both Hobby and Retail packs at the rate of one in 15, this 15-card set places player portrait photos in the upper left hand corner of the card in blue, and a stripe across the middle of a mostly white background.

COMPLETE SET (15)	12.50	30.00
1 Dwight Howard	2.50	6.00
2 Emeka Okafor	1.25	3.00
3 Ben Gordon	1.00	2.50
4 Shaun Livingston	.75	2.00
5 Devin Harris	1.25	3.00
6 Josh Childress	.75	2.00
7 Luol Deng	1.25	3.00
8 Andre Iguodala	1.25	3.00
9 Luke Jackson	.75	2.00
10 Sebastian Telfair	.75	2.00
11 Kris Humphries	.75	2.00
12 Al Jefferson	1.25	3.00
13 LeBron James	5.00	12.00
14 Carmelo Anthony	1.50	4.00
15 Dwyane Wade	2.50	6.00

2004-05 Hoops Hot Prospects Notable Notations

Randomly seeded in packs, this nine-card set parallels the design of the Notable Notations insert set enhanced with a cut signature at the bottom of the the card and sequential numbering to 50.

AJ Al Jefferson	12.00	30.00
BG Ben Gordon	10.00	25.00
CA Carmelo Anthony	20.00	50.00
DH Devin Harris	12.00	30.00
JC Josh Childress	8.00	20.00
KH Kris Humphries	8.00	20.00
LJ Luke Jackson	8.00	20.00
SL Shaun Livingston	8.00	20.00
ST Sebastian Telfair	8.00	20.00

1991-92 Hoops McDonald's

Four-card cello packs, featuring three NBA cards and one Olympic team card, were distributed at participating McDonald's restaurants with the purchase of any Extra Value Meal, or for 49 cents with any other purchase. A specially marked instant winner card replaced a regular card in one in 20,000 packs, and the holder of this card received the complete 70-card "Superstar" set. After the termination of the promotion many of the excess remaining 70-card sets found their way into the hobby and are now much easier to find. The standard-size cards display color action photos enclosed by different color borders on a white card face. The horizontally oriented backs have a color head shot as well as biographical and statistical information. The set divides into three sections and is checklisted below as follows: player cards (1-50 listed alphabetically according to teams), USA Olympic basketball team (51-62), and Chicago Bulls (63-70 available only in the Chicago area).

COMPLETE SET (70)	10.00	25.00
COMPLETE NAT.SET (62)	6.00	15.00
COMPLETE BULLS SET (8)	2.40	6.00
1 Dominique Wilkins	.20	.50
2 Larry Bird	.50	1.25
3 Kevin McHale	.15	.40
4 Robert Parish	.15	.40
5 Michael Jordan	1.50	4.00
6 John Paxson	.05	.05
7 Scottie Pippen	.50	1.25
8 Brad Daugherty	.05	.05
9 Rolando Blackman	.05	.05
10 Derek Harper	.05	.15
11 Joe Dumars	.07	.20
12 Bill Laimbeer	.05	.15
13 Isiah Thomas	.07	.20
14 Tim Hardaway	.30	.75
15 Chris Mullin	.07	.20
16 Hakeem Olajuwon	.30	.75
17 Reggie Miller	.30	.75
18 Chuck Person	.05	.05
19 Charles Smith	.05	.05
20 Vlade Divac	.05	.15
21 James Worthy	.08	.25
22 Rony Seikaly	.05	.05
23 Alvin Robertson	.05	.05
24 Pooh Richardson	.05	.05
25 Derrick Coleman	.08	.25
26 Patrick Ewing	.30	.75
27 Xavier McDaniel	.05	.05
28 Dennis Scott	.05	.15
29 Scott Skiles	.05	.05
30 Charles Barkley	.30	.75
31 Hersey Hawkins	.05	.15
32 Tom Chambers	.05	.05
33 Kevin Johnson	.10	.30
34 Clyde Drexler	.30	.75
35 Terry Porter	.05	.05
36 Buck Williams	.05	.15
37 Mitch Richmond	.30	.75
38 Lionel Simmons	.05	.05
39 Terry Cummings	.05	.05
40 Sean Elliott	.05	.15
41 David Robinson	.30	.75
42 Shawn Kemp	.25	.60
43 Ricky Pierce	.05	.05
44 Karl Malone	.50	1.25
45 John Stockton	.50	1.25
46 Bernard King	.05	.15
47 Larry Johnson	.30	.75
48 Dikembe Mutombo	.40	1.00
49A Billy Owens ERR (Back photo actually Steve Smith)	.40	1.00
49B Billy Owens COR	.07	.20
50 Kenny Anderson	.05	.15
51 Charles Barkley USA	.40	1.00
52 Larry Bird USA	.60	1.50
53 Patrick Ewing USA	.40	1.00
54 Magic Johnson USA	.40	1.00
55 Michael Jordan USA	2.00	5.00
56 Karl Malone USA	.50	1.25
57 Chris Mullin USA	.20	.50
58 Scottie Pippen USA	.50	1.25
59 David Robinson USA	.40	1.00
60 John Stockton USA	.50	1.25
61 Chuck Daly CO USA	.40	1.00
62 USAB Team	.40	1.00
63 B.J. Armstrong	.30	.75
64 Bill Cartwright	.30	.75
65 Horace Grant	.40	1.00
66 Craig Hodges	.30	.75
67 Stacey King	.30	.75
68 Cliff Levingston	.30	.75
69 Will Perdue	.30	.75
70 Scott Williams	.30	.75

1994-95 Hoops NSCC Sheet

Given away at the National Sports Collectors Convention (August 2, 4-7, 1994), this promotional sheet measures approximately 7 1/2" by 12". After perforation, each card measures the standard size. The cards preview the design of the 1994-95 Hoops series. The fronts display full-bleed color action photos. A team color-coded stripe cuts across the bottom and carries the player's name, team logo, and position. The backs carry a color headshot, biography, statistics, and player profile. A mustard stripe beneath the last row of cards has a gold foil seal indicating the serial number and the production total (20,000). The individual cards

on the sheet are unnumbered and ordered below as they are arranged on the sheet.
NNO Hoops panel 2.00 5.00
Dino Radja
Scott Burrell
Anfernee Hardaway
Latrell Sprewell
Jim Jackson
Hakeem Olajuwon
Vin Baker
Gheorghe Muresan

1994-95 Hoops Schick

As part of a second quarter promotion by Schick Shaving Products Group, a division of the Warner-Lambert Co., this 30-card set features 29 of the NBA's top rookies. The checklist card, which completes the set, features Donyell Marshall shaving with the official NBA Tracer razor on its front. Three cards were available in each specially-marked package of Tracer 5 and 10 pack refills. The package also included a special mail-in offer card whereby the collector received the complete set by sending in three proofs-of-purchase plus 2.50 for postage and handling. The offer expired 12/31/95 or while supplies lasted. These cards have the same design as their regular issue counterparts, except that the word "Rookie" and the player's name on the fronts are in gold (rather than gold-foil) lettering. Also these cards are unnumbered and thus listed below in alphabetical order.

COMPLETE SET (30) 12.00 30.00
1 Sergei Bazarevich .60 1.50
2 Bill Curley .60 1.50
3 Tony Dumas .60 1.50
4 Brian Grant 1.00 2.50
5 Darrin Hancock .60 1.50
6 Grant Hill 3.00 8.00
7 Eddie Jones 2.00 5.00
8 Jason Kidd 3.00 8.00
9 Aaron McKie .60 1.50
10 Donyell Marshall .60 1.50
11 Anthony Miller .60 1.50
12 Greg Minor .60 1.50
13 Eric Mobley .60 1.50
14 Eric Montross .60 1.50
15 Lamond Murray .60 1.50
16 Eric Piatkowski .75 2.00
17 Wesley Person .60 1.50
18 Khalid Reeves .60 1.50
19 Glenn Robinson 1.25 3.00
20 Carlos Rogers .60 1.50
21 Jalen Rose 1.50 4.00
22 Clifford Rozier .60 1.50
23 Dickey Simpkins .60 1.50
24 Brooks Thompson .60 1.50
25 Anthony Tucker .60 1.50
26 B.J. Tyler .60 1.50
27 Charlie Ward .60 1.50
28 Monty Williams .60 1.50
29 Sharone Wright .60 1.50
30 Donyell Marshall CL .60 1.50
Shaving)

1993-94 Hoops Sheets

The fronts feature borderless glossy color player action shots, with the player's name and team logo appearing in team colors along a ghosted band at the bottom. The back presents a color head shot of the player in a small rectangle bordered with a team color at the upper right. Alongside is his jersey number and position within a team-colored bar. The player's name and a short biography are printed on a hardwood floor design at the top. Below, the player's college and NBA stats, displayed in separate tables on a white background, round out the card. The cards are unnumbered and checklisted below in alphabetical order.

COMPLETE SET (6) 12.00 30.00
1 B.J. Armstrong 4.00 10.00
Bill Cartwright
Horace Grant
Phil Jackson
Stacy King
John Paxson
Will Perdue
Scottie Pippen
Scott Williams
2 Greg Anderson 2.50 6.00
Don Chaney CO
Joe Dumars
Sean Elliott
Allan Houston
Lindsey Hunter
Terry Mills
Olden Polynice
Isiah Thomas
David Wood
3 Kenny Anderson 2.50 6.00
Derrick Coleman
Chris Morris
Chuck Daly CO
Rick Mahorn
Jayson Williams
Kevin Edwards
Armon Gilliam
Dwayne Schintzius
Chucky Brown
Benoit Benjamin
Rex Walters
4 Greg Anthony 2.50 6.00
Patrick Ewing
Charles Oakley
Charles Smith
John Starks
5 Danny Ainge 3.00 8.00
Charles Barkley
Cedric Ceballos
A.C. Green
Kevin Johnson
Dan Majerle
Oliver Miller
Mark West
Paul Westphal CO
6 Nick Anderson 4.00 10.00
Anthony Bowie
Shaquille O'Neal
Donald Royal
Scott Skiles
Jeff Turner

1994-95 Hoops Sheets

Distributed one per customer on game nights at various NBA arenas, these perforated sheets consist of standard-size cards and vary in size, depending on the number cards featured. On some sheets, one or more card slots have sponsors' advertisements rather than player cards. The fronts feature borderless glossy color player action shots, with the player's name and team logo appearing in a team color-coded bar at the bottom. The back presents a color head shot of the player, along with biography, statistics and profile. The cards are unnumbered and checklisted below in alphabetical order.

COMPLETE SET (18) 30.00 80.00
1 Stacey Augmon 2.50 6.00
Mookie Blaylock
Tyrone Corbin
Craig Ehlo
Jon Koncak
Andrew Lang
Ken Norman
Steve Smith
Lenny Wilkens CO
2 Michael Adams 2.50 6.00
Tony Bennett
Muggsy Bogues
Scott Burrell
Dell Curry
Kenny Gattison
Darrin Hancock
Hersey Hawkins
Larry Johnson
Alonzo Mourning
Robert Parish
David Wingate
3 Muggsy Bogues 2.50 6.00
Dell Curry
Hersey Hawkins
Larry Johnson
Alonzo Mourning
4 Michael Adams 2.50 6.00
Tony Bennett
Muggsy Bogues
Scott Burrell
Dell Curry
Kenny Gattison
Hersey Hawkins
Larry Johnson
Alonzo Mourning
Robert Parish
David Wingate
5 B.J. Armstrong 3.00 8.00
Corie Blount
Phil Jackson
Steve Kerr
Toni Kukoc
Luc Longley
Scottie Pippen
Bill Wennington
6 Terry Davis 3.00 8.00
Tony Dumas
Lucious Harris
Jim Jackson
Popeye Jones
Jason Kidd
Jamal Mashburn
Dick Motta CO
7 Mahmoud Abdul-Rauf 2.50 6.00
LaPhonso Ellis
Dan Issel CO
Dikembe Mutombo
Robert Pack
Rodney Rogers
Bryant Stith
Brian Williams
Reggie Williams
8 Don Chaney CO 5.00 12.00
Bill Curley
Joe Dumars
Grant Hill
Allan Houston
Lindsey Hunter
Mark Macon
Oliver Miller
Terry Mills
Mark West
9 Bill Blair CO 2.50 6.00
Mike Brown
Stacey King
Christian Laettner
Donyell Marshall
Isaiah Rider
Doug West
Michael Williams
10 Greg Anthony 3.00 8.00
Anthony Bonner
Hubert Davis
Patrick Ewing
Derek Harper
Anthony Mason
Charles Oakley
Charles Smith
John Starks
Herb Williams
11 Nick Anderson 5.00 12.00
Anthony Bowie
Horace Grant
Anfernee Hardaway
Shaquille O'Neal
Tree Rollins
Donald Royal
Dennis Scott
Brian Shaw
Brooks Thompson
Jeff Turner
12 Danny Ainge 4.00 10.00
Charles Barkley
A.C. Green
Kevin Johnson
Joe Kleine
Dan Majerle
Danny Manning
Elliot Perry
Wesley Person
Wayman Tisdale
13 P.J. Carlesimo CO 4.00 10.00
Clyde Drexler
Chris Dudley
Harvey Grant
Jerome Kersey
Tracy Murray
Terry Porter
Clifford Robinson
James Robinson
14 Vincent Askew 3.00 8.00
Bill Cartwright
Ervin Johnson
George Karl CO
Shawn Kemp
Sarunas Marciulionis
Nate McMillan
Gary Payton
Sam Perkins
Detlef Schrempf
Dontonio Wingfield
15 David Benoit 2.50 6.00
Tom Chambers
John Crotty
Jeff Hornacek
Karl Malone
Byron Russell
Jerry Sloan CO
Felton Spencer
John Stockton
16 Mitchell Butler 2.50 6.00
Rex Chapman
Calbert Cheaney
Don MacClean
Gheorghe Muresan
Scott Skiles
Chris Webber
Team Card
17 Mitchell Butler 4.00 10.00
Rex Chapman
Calbert Cheaney
Kevin Duckworth
Juwan Howard
Don MacLean
Jim McIlvaine
Gheorghe Muresan
Scott Skiles
Kenny Walker
Chris Webber
18 Mitchell Butler 4.00 10.00
Rex Chapman
Calbert Cheaney
Kevin Duckworth
Juwan Howard
Don MacLean
Jim McIlvaine
Gheorghe Muresan
Scott Skiles
Kenny Walker
Chris Webber

1995-96 Hoops Sheets

The fronts feature borderless glossy color player action shots, with the player's name and team logo along a "torn-out" band at the bottom. The back presents a a color action shot along the left border. The player's name and a short biography are printed against a white background. The cards are unnumbered and checklisted below in alphabetical order.

COMPLETE SET (13) 15.00 40.00
1 Lenny Wilkens CO 2.00 5.00
Stacey Augmon
Mookie Blaylock
Craig Ehlo
Alan Henderson
Andrew Lang
Grant Long
Ken Norman
Steve Smith
Spud Webb
2 Muggsy Bogues 2.00 5.00
Kendall Gill
Glen Rice
Scott Burrell
Larry Johnson
Dell Curry
George Zidek
Khalid Reeves
3 Phil Jackson CO 4.00 10.00
Jason Caffey
Michael Jordan
Toni Kukoc
Luc Longley
Scottie Pippen
Dennis Rodman
Dickey Simpkins
4 Grant Hill 2.50 6.00
Joe Dumars
Terry Mills
Allan Houston
Lindsey Hunter
Theo Ratliff
Otis Thorpe
Doug Collins CO
5 Sedale Threatt 2.50 6.00
Frankie King
Nick Van Exel
Vlade Divac
Cedric Ceballos
Eddie Jones
George Lynch
Elden Campbell
Corie Blount
Del Harris CO
6 Shawn Bradley 2.00 5.00
Kevin Edwards
Rick Mahorn
Kendall Gill
P.J. Brown
Butch Beard CO
Armon Gilliam
Ed O'Bannon
Chris Childs
Yinka Dare
Jayson Williams
7 Patrick Ewing 2.00 5.00
Charles Oakley
John Starks
Anthony Mason
Don Nelson CO
Derek Harper
Charles Smith
Herb Williams
Hubert Davis
8 Nick Anderson 2.50 6.00
Anthony Bowie
Horace Grant
Anfernee Hardaway
Jon Koncak
Shaquille O'Neal
Donald Royal
Dennis Scott
Brian Shaw
Jeff Turner
David Vaughn
9 Elliot Perry 2.00 5.00
A.C. Green
Wayman Tisdale
Mario Bennett
Charles Barkley
Danny Manning
Wesley Person
Michael Finley
Kevin Johnson
10 Clifford Robinson 2.00 5.00
Rod Strickland
Chris Dudley
Arvydas Sabonis
Buck Williams
James Robinson
P.J. Carlesimo CO
Randolph Childress
Gary Trent
Dontonio Wingfield
11 Mitch Richmond 2.00 5.00
Olden Polynice
Brian Grant
Michael Smith
Tyus Edney
Bobby Hurley
Corliss Williamson
Garry St. Jean CO
12 David Benoit 3.00 8.00
Jeff Hornacek
Karl Malone
Felton Spencer
John Stockton
Adam Keefe
Jerry Sloan CO
13 Mitchell Butler 2.50 6.00
Calbert Cheaney
Juwan Howard
Tim Legler
Jim McIlvaine
Gheorghe Muresan
Robert Pack
Brent Price
Mark Price
Rasheed Wallace
Chris Webber

1996-97 Hoops Sheets

Distributed one per customer on game nights at various NBA arenas, these perforated sheets consist of standard-size cards and vary in size, depending on the number cards featured. On some sheets, one or more card slots have sponsors' advertisements rather than player cards. The fronts feature borderless glossy color player action shots, with the player's name and team logo appearing at the bottom. The gold-foil is missing from these cards versus their regular Hoops cards. The back presents the player's biography, statistics and profile. The cards are unnumbered and checklisted below in alphabetical order. Currently, we only have the two sheets checklisted. More will be added as we get them checklisted.

COMPLETE SET (2) 8.00 20.00
1A Byron Scott 8.00 20.00
Nick Van Exel
Shaquille O'Neal
Del Harris
Derek Fisher
Kobe Bryant
Robert Horry
Sean Rooks
Eddie Jones
Jerome Kersey
Elden Campbell
1B Byron Scott LA .40 1.00
1C Nick Van Exel LA .40 1.00
1D Shaquille O'Neal LA .75 2.00
1E Del Harris LA .40 1.00
1F Derek Fisher LA .75 2.00
1G Robert Horry LA .40 1.00
1H Kobe Bryant LA 3.00 8.00
1I Sean Rooks LA .40 1.00
1J Eddie Jones LA .40 1.00
1K Jerome Kersey LA .40 1.00
1L Elden Campbell LA .40 1.00
2A Wesley Person 1.50 4.00
John Williams
Danny Manning
Kevin Johnson
2B Wesley Person SUNS .40 1.00
2C John Williams SUNS .40 1.00
2D Danny Manning SUNS .40 1.00
2E Kevin Johnson SUNS .40 1.00

2002-03 Hoops Stars

Released in early January 2003, Hoops Stars features a 200-card set divided up into 170 veteran cards and 30 rookie cards. Base cards feature a color player photo centered on a patterned background which is made to look like a basketball court on the right and combination of colors and true life background on the left. Each card is highlighted with silver foil. Hoops Stars was packaged in 20-pack boxes with 19 packs containing 10 cards and one Superstar pack containing five cards with different color foil versions of base and insert cards for a roster that consists of 25 different players. Hoops Stars packs carried an SRP of $2.99.

COMP.SET w/o RC's (170) 12.50 30.00
1 Tracy McGrady .50 1.25
2 Kevin Garnett .60 1.50
3 Allen Iverson .50 1.25
4 Keith Van Horn .25 .60
5 Kwame Brown .20 .50
6 Alan Henderson .20 .50
7 Kenny Anderson .25 .60
8 Antoine Walker .25 .60
9 Tony Delk .20 .50
10 Tony Battie .20 .50
11 Wally Szczerbiak .25 .60
12 Paul Pierce .40 1.00
13 Glenn Robinson .25 .60
14 Tim Thomas .20 .50
15 Vince Carter .50 1.25
16 Pau Gasol .40 1.00
17 Eddy Curry .25 .60
18 Darrell Armstrong .20 .50
19 Sam Cassell .25 .60
20 Darius Miles .20 .50
21 Jason Richardson .30 .75
22 Elton Brand .30 .75
23 Michael Jordan 2.50 6.00
24 Andre Miller .25 .60
25 Anfernee Hardaway .50 1.25
26 Steve Nash .40 1.00
27 Ron Artest .30 .75
28 Raef LaFrentz .20 .50
29 Troy Hudson .20 .50
30 Rasheed Wallace .30 .75
31 Ricky Davis .25 .60
32 Juwan Howard .25 .60
33 Steve Francis .30 .75
34 Shaquille O'Neal .75 2.00
35 James Posey .20 .50
36 DeShawn Stevenson .20 .50
37 Clifford Robinson .20 .50
38 Jerry Stackhouse .25 .60
39 Chauncey Billups .30 .75
40 Mike Bibby .30 .75
41 Dirk Nowitzki .50 1.25
42 Corliss Williamson .20 .50
43 Antawn Jamison .30 .75
44 Jamal Mashburn .25 .60
45 Danny Fortson .20 .50
46 Reggie Miller .30 .75
47 Scottie Pippen .50 1.25
48 Donnell Harvey .20 .50
49 Moochie Norris .20 .50
50 Corey Maggette .25 .60
51 Eddie Griffin .20 .50
52 Karl Malone .40 1.00
53 Maurice Taylor .20 .50
54 Al Harrington .25 .60
55 Kenyon Martin .30 .75
56 Nick Van Exel .25 .60
57 Jermaine O'Neal .30 .75
58 Anthony Mason .20 .50
59 Jamaal Tinsley .20 .50
60 Chris Mihm .20 .50
61 Lamar Odom .30 .75
62 Cuttino Mobley .25 .60
63 Michael Olowokandi .20 .50
64 Michael Finley .30 .75
65 Anthony Peeler .20 .50
66 Mengke Bateer .20 .50
67 Rick Fox .25 .60
68 Steve Smith .25 .60
69 Robert Horry .25 .60
70 Devean George .20 .50
71 Jason Williams .25 .60
72 Stromile Swift .20 .50
73 Marcus Fizer .20 .50
74 Michael Dickerson .20 .50
75 Shane Battier .30 .75
76 Larry Hughes .25 .60
77 Brian Skinner .20 .50
78 Eddie Jones .25 .60
79 Malik Allen .20 .50
80 Ray Allen .30 .75
81 Jumaine Jones .20 .50
82 Donyell Marshall .20 .50
83 Toni Kukoc .25 .60
84 Michael Redd .30 .75
85 Ron Mercer .20 .50
86 Terrell Brandon .20 .50
87 Latrell Sprewell .25 .60
88 Kobe Bryant 1.50 4.00
89 Kurt Thomas .20 .50
90 Rasho Nesterovic .20 .50
91 Shareef Abdur-Rahim .25 .60
92 Eduardo Najera .20 .50
93 Jamaal Magloire .20 .50
94 Antonio Davis .20 .50
95 Rodney Rogers .20 .50
96 Jason Collins .20 .50
97 Marcus Camby .25 .60
98 Joe Smith .25 .60
99 Richard Jefferson .30 .75
100 Gilbert Arenas .30 .75
101 Courtney Alexander .20 .50
102 David Wesley .20 .50
103 Baron Davis .30 .75
104 Elden Campbell .20 .50
105 Jason Kidd .50 1.25
106 P.J. Brown .20 .50
107 Rashard Lewis .30 .75
108 Alvin Williams .20 .50
109 Kerry Kittles .20 .50
110 Charlie Ward .20 .50
111 Kedrick Brown .20 .50
112 Shandon Anderson .20 .50
113 Grant Hill .40 1.00
114 Tyson Chandler .25 .60
115 Brent Barry .20 .50
116 Travis Best .20 .50
117 Mike Miller .30 .75
118 Aaron McKie .20 .50
119 Theo Ratliff .20 .50
120 Todd MacCulloch .20 .50
121 Trenton Hassell .20 .50
122 Vin Baker .25 .60
123 Dion Glover .20 .50
124 Stephon Marbury .25 .60
125 Ben Wallace .30 .75
126 Glen Rice .25 .60
127 Joe Johnson .30 .75
128 Chris Webber .30 .75
129 Damon Stoudamire .25 .60
130 Voshon Lenard .20 .50
131 Troy Murphy .30 .75
132 Desmond Mason .25 .60
133 Ruben Patterson .20 .50
134 John Stockton .40 1.00
135 Bobby Jackson .20 .50
136 Shawn Marion .30 .75
137 Jarron Collins .20 .50
138 Tom Gugliotta .20 .50
139 Doug Christie .20 .50
140 Zeljko Rebraca .20 .50
141 Tim Duncan .60 1.50
142 David Robinson .50 1.25
143 Tony Parker .40 1.00
144 Derek Fisher .25 .60
145 Speedy Claxton .20 .50
146 Eric Snow .20 .50
147 Gary Payton .30 .75
148 Pat Garrity .20 .50
149 Joseph Forte .20 .50
150 Derek Anderson .20 .50
151 Vladimir Radmanovic .20 .50
152 Samuel Dalembert .20 .50
153 Allan Houston .25 .60
154 Jalen Rose .25 .60
155 Dikembe Mutombo .30 .75
156 Jerome Williams .20 .50
157 Antonio McDyess .25 .60
158 Morris Peterson .20 .50
159 Bonzi Wells .20 .50
160 Hedo Turkoglu .30 .75
161 Gerald Wallace .30 .75
162 Andrei Kirilenko .30 .75
163 Matt Harpring .25 .60
164 Peja Stojakovic .30 .75
165 Zydrunas Ilgauskas .25 .60
166 Richard Hamilton .25 .60
167 Brian Grant .20 .50
168 Christian Laettner .20 .50
169 Jason Terry .25 .60
170 Alonzo Mourning .40 1.00
171 Yao Ming RC 3.00 8.00
172 Jay Williams RC 1.25 3.00
173 Mike Dunleavy RC 1.25 3.00
174 Chris Wilcox RC 1.00 2.50
175 Amare Stoudemire RC 2.50 6.00
176 Fred Jones RC 1.00 2.50
177 Caron Butler RC 1.50 4.00
178 Melvin Ely RC 1.00 2.50
179 Drew Gooden RC 1.50 4.00
180 DaJuan Wagner RC 1.00 2.50
181 Jared Jeffries RC 1.00 2.50
182 Nikoloz Tskitishvili RC 1.00 2.50
183 Nene Hilario RC 1.25 3.00
184 Dan Dickau RC 1.00 2.50
185 Marcus Haislip RC 1.00 2.50
186 Gordan Giricek RC 1.00 2.50
187 Jiri Welsch RC 1.00 2.50
188 Juan Dixon RC 1.25 3.00
189 Curtis Borchardt RC 1.00 2.50
190 Ryan Humphrey RC 1.00 2.50
191 Kareem Rush RC 1.00 2.50
192 Qyntel Woods RC 1.00 2.50
193 Casey Jacobsen RC 1.00 2.50
194 Tayshaun Prince RC 1.25 3.00
195 Frank Williams RC 1.00 2.50
196 Pat Burke RC 1.00 2.50
197 Chris Jefferies RC 1.00 2.50
198 Carlos Boozer RC 2.00 5.00
199 Manu Ginobili RC 2.50 6.00
200 Vincent Yarbrough RC 1.00 2.50

2002-03 Hoops Stars Five-Star

Randomly inserted in packs, this 200-card set parallels the base Hoops Stars set with a foil shift from the base silver to bronze. Each card is sequentially numbered to 299 on the card back.
*STARS: 2.5X TO 6X BASE CARD HI
*RCs: .6X TO 1.5X BASE CARD HI

2002-03 Hoops Stars Platinum

Randomly inserted in the one-per-box Superstars packs, this six card set utilizes the base set design enhanced with platinum foil higlights and sequential numbering to 100. This is a skip-numbered set and only the players from the Superstars roster who do not have jersey card versions are featured.
*STARS: 4X TO 10X BASE CARD HI
*RC's: 1.25X TO 3X BASE CARD HI
23 Michael Jordan 30.00 80.00
34 Shaquille O'Neal 8.00 20.00
88 Kobe Bryant 15.00 40.00
141 Tim Duncan 6.00 15.00
172 Jay Williams 4.00 10.00
173 Mike Dunleavy 4.00 10.00

2002-03 Hoops Stars Red

Randomly inserted in the one-per-box Superstars packs, this 25-card set utilizes the base set design where cards are enhanced with red foil highlights. This is a skip-numbered set and only the players from the Superstars roster are featured.
*STARS: 1.25X TO 3X BASE CARD HI
*RCs: .4X TO 1X BASE CARD HI
1 Tracy McGrady 1.50 4.00
2 Kevin Garnett 2.00 5.00
3 Allen Iverson 1.50 4.00
12 Paul Pierce 1.25 3.00
15 Vince Carter 1.50 4.00
16 Pau Gasol 1.25 3.00
20 Darius Miles .60 1.50
21 Jason Richardson 1.00 2.50
23 Michael Jordan 8.00 20.00
33 Steve Francis 1.00 2.50
34 Shaquille O'Neal 2.50 6.00
40 Mike Bibby 1.00 2
41 Dirk Nowitzki 1.50 4
52 Karl Malone 1.25 3
88 Kobe Bryant 5.00 12
103 Baron Davis 1.00 2
105 Jason Kidd 1.50 4
141 Tim Duncan 2.00 5
171 Yao Ming 3.00 8
172 Jay Williams 1.25 3
173 Mike Dunleavy 1.25 3
177 Caron Butler 1.50 4
179 Drew Gooden 1.50 4
180 DaJuan Wagner 1.00 2

2002-03 Hoops Stars Future Stars

Randomly inserted in packs at the rate of one in 10, this 15-card set uses a horizontal design with photo of top rookies on the left side of the card, a colored strip across the middle set to match the player's tea colors and silver foil highlights. A Blue version of th set was inserted into the box-topper Super Star pac

COMPLETE SET (15) 10.00 25
*BLUE: .6X TO 1.5X FUTURE STAR HI
FS1 Yao Ming 2.50 6
FS2 Jay Williams 1.00 2
FS3 Mike Dunleavy 1.00 2
FS4 Chris Wilcox .75 2
FS5 Amare Stoudemire 2.00 5
FS6 Fred Jones .75 2
FS7 Caron Butler 1.25 3
FS8 Melvin Ely .75 2
FS9 Drew Gooden 1.25 3
FS10 DaJuan Wagner .75 2
FS11 Jared Jeffries .75 2
FS12 Nikoloz Tskitishvili .75 2
FS13 Nene Hilario 1.00 2
FS14 Dan Dickau .75 2
FS15 Juan Dixon 1.00 2

2002-03 Hoops Stars Future Stars Game-Used

Randomly inserted in packs at the rate of one in 52, this 11-card set parallels the design of the base Futu Stars insert set enhanced with a swatch of game-use shoot shirt on the right side of the card.

FSGU1 Chris Wilcox 2.50 6.
FSGU2 Amare Stoudemire 6.00 15.
FSGU3 Fred Jones 2.50 6.
FSGU4 Caron Butler 4.00 10.
FSGU5 Melvin Ely 2.50 6.
FSGU6 Drew Gooden 4.00 10.
FSGU7 DaJuan Wagner 2.50 6.
FSGU8 Jared Jeffries 2.50 6.
FSGU9 Nene Hilario 3.00 8.
FSGU11 Juan Dixon 3.00 8.

2002-03 Hoops Stars Raising U

Randomly inserted in packs at the rate of one in five, this 25-card set places player photos on a blue strea background with sweeping color mixed in to match t player's team colors. Each card contains silver foil highlights. A Blue version of this set was inserted in the box-topper Super Star packs.

COMPLETE SET (25) 15.00 40.
*BLUE: .6X TO 1.5X RAISING UP HI
RU1 Jason Kidd 1.00 2.
RU2 Kevin Garnett 1.25 3.
RU3 Vince Carter 1.00 2.
RU4 Baron Davis .60 1.
RU5 Paul Pierce .75 2.
RU6 Dirk Nowitzki 1.00 2.
RU7 Shaquille O'Neal 1.50 4.
RU8 Michael Jordan 5.00 12.
RU9 Tim Duncan 1.25 3.
RU10 Allen Iverson 1.00 2.
RU11 Jason Richardson .60 1.
RU12 Pau Gasol .75 2.
RU13 Steve Francis .60 1.
RU14 Kobe Bryant 3.00 8.
RU15 Mike Bibby .60 1.
RU16 Grant Hill .75 2.
RU17 Tracy McGrady 1.00 2.
RU18 Karl Malone .75 2.
RU19 Darius Miles .40 1.
RU20 Jay Williams .75 2.
RU21 Mike Dunleavy .75 2.
RU22 Drew Gooden 1.00 2.
RU23 DaJuan Wagner .60 1.
RU24 Caron Butler 1.00 2.
RU25 Yao Ming 2.00 5.

2002-03 Hoops Stars Raising Up Game-Used

Randomly inserted in packs, this 15-card set parallels the design from the base Raising Up set enhanced with a swatch of game used memorabilia. Several different types of memorabilia were used and are notated below in the checklist. Each card is sequentially numbered to 250.

RUGU1 Jason Kidd Pants 5.00 12.00
RUGU2 Kevin Garnett Jacket 6.00 15.00
RUGU3 Vince Carter JSY 5.00 12.00
RUGU4 Paul Pierce Pants 4.00 10.00
RUGU5 Allen Iverson JSY 6.00 15.00
RUGU6 Pau Gasol Jacket 4.00 10.00
RUGU7 Steve Francis Shorts 3.00 8.00
RUGU8 Grant Hill JSY 4.00 10.00
RUGU9 Tracy McGrady JSY 5.00 12.00
RUGU10 Karl Malone Pants 4.00 10.00
RUGU11 Darius Miles JSY 2.00 5.00
RUGU12 Drew Gooden Shorts 5.00 12.00
RUGU13 DaJuan Wagner Shorts 3.00 8.00
RUGU14 Caron Butler Shorts 5.00 12.00
RUGU15 Yao Ming JSY 10.00 25.00

2002-03 Hoops Stars Rare Air

Randomly seeded in packs at the rate of one in 30, this 20-card set fatures full color action photos set against a background that looks like a clouded sky on the top and the top of the key towards the bottom. Each card is highlighted with silver foil. A Blue version of this set was inserted into the box-topper Super Star packs.

COMPLETE SET (20) 20.00 50.00
*BLUE: .6X TO 1.5X RARE AIR HI
RA1 Jason Kidd 2.00 5.00
RA2 Kevin Garnett 2.50 6.00
RA3 Vince Carter 2.00 5.00
RA4 Baron Davis 1.25 3.00
RA5 Paul Pierce 1.50 4.00
RA6 Dirk Nowitzki 2.00 5.00
RA7 Shaquille O'Neal 3.00 8.00
RA8 Michael Jordan 10.00 25.00
RA9 Tim Duncan 2.50 6.00
RA10 Allen Iverson 2.00 5.00
RA11 Jason Richardson 1.25 3.00
RA12 Pau Gasol 1.50 4.00
RA13 Steve Francis 1.25 3.00
RA14 Kobe Bryant 6.00 15.00
RA15 Mike Bibby 1.25 3.00
RA16 Grant Hill 1.50 4.00
RA17 Tracy McGrady 2.00 5.00
RA18 Karl Malone 1.50 4.00
RA19 Darius Miles .75 2.00
RA20 Latrell Sprewell 1.00 2.50

2002-03 Hoops Stars Rare Air Game-Used

Randomly inserted in packs at the rate of one in 52, this 10-card set parallels the design of the base Rare Air insert set enhanced with a swatch of game used memorabilia. Different types of memorabilia were used, as they are notated below with the checklist.

RAGU1 Jason Kidd Jacket 5.00 12.00
RAGU2 Kevin Garnett JSY 6.00 15.00
RAGU3 Vince Carter JSY 5.00 12.00
RAGU4 Paul Pierce Jacket 4.00 10.00
RAGU5 Dirk Nowitzki JSY 5.00 12.00
RAGU6 Allen Iverson Pants 5.00 12.00
RAGU7 Pau Gasol Pants 4.00 10.00
RAGU8 Grant Hill Pants 4.00 10.00
RAGU9 Tracy McGrady Pants 5.00 12.00
RAGU10 Karl Malone JSY 4.00 10.00

2002-03 Hoops Stars Star Gazing

Randomly inserted in packs at the rate of one in 20, this 25-card set showcases a horizontal design where a player photo appears on the left of the card and the right side of the card is die cut around a silver foil star in the upper right hand corner. Background start as basketball texture on the left and shift to colors that match the featured player's team colors on the right. A Blue version of this set was inserted into the box-topper Super Star packs.

COMPLETE SET (25) 20.00 50.00
*BLUE: .6X TO 1.5X STAR GAZE HI
SG1 Jason Kidd 1.50 4.00
SG2 Kevin Garnett 2.00 5.00
SG3 Vince Carter 1.50 4.00
SG4 Baron Davis 1.00 2.50
SG5 Paul Pierce 1.25 3.00
SG6 Dirk Nowitzki 1.50 4.00
SG7 Shaquille O'Neal 2.50 6.00
SG8 Michael Jordan 8.00 20.00
SG9 Tim Duncan 2.00 5.00
SG10 Allen Iverson 1.50 4.00
SG11 Jason Richardson 1.00 2.50
SG12 Pau Gasol 1.25 3.00
SG13 Steve Francis 1.00 2.50
SG14 Kobe Bryant 5.00 12.00
SG15 Mike Bibby 1.00 2.50
SG16 Grant Hill 1.25 3.00
SG17 Tracy McGrady 1.50 4.00
SG18 Karl Malone 1.25 3.00
SG19 Darius Miles .60 1.50
SG20 Jay Williams 1.25 3.00
SG21 Mike Dunleavy 1.25 3.00
SG22 Drew Gooden 1.50 4.00
SG23 DaJuan Wagner 1.00 2.50
SG24 Caron Butler 1.50 4.00
SG25 Yao Ming 3.00 8.00

2002-03 Hoops Stars Star Gazing Game-Used

Randomly seeded in packs, this 12-card set parallels the set design from the base Star Gazing insert enhanced with a swatch of game used memorabilia. Several different types of memorabilia were used and are notated below in the checklist. Each card is sequentially numbered to 50.

AI Allen Iverson JSY 10.00 25.00
CB Caron Butler JSY 10.00 25.00
DG Drew Gooden Shorts 10.00 25.00
DN Dirk Nowitzki JSY 10.00 25.00
DW DaJuan Wagner Shorts 6.00 15.00
JK Jason Kidd Shorts 10.00 25.00
KG Kevin Garnett JSY 12.00 30.00
MB Mike Bibby JSY 6.00 15.00
PG Pau Gasol Jacket 8.00 20.00
PP Paul Pierce JSY 8.00 20.00
TM Tracy McGrady JSY 10.00 25.00
VC Vince Carter JSY 10.00 25.00

2002-03 Hoops Stars Superstars Game-Used

Randomly inserted in the one-per-box Superstars pack, this 19-card set parallels the base set design enhanced with a swatch of game used memorabilia. Several different types of memorabilia were used and these are noted in the checklist below. Cards contain no foil highlights.

AI Allen Iverson JSY 5.00 12.00
BD Baron Davis Pants 3.00 8.00
CB Caron Butler Shirt 5.00 12.00
DG Drew Gooden Shirt 5.00 12.00
DM Darius Miles Jacket 2.00 5.00
DN Dirk Nowitzki JSY 5.00 12.00
DW DaJuan Wagner Shirt 3.00 8.00
GH Grant Hill Jacket 4.00 10.00
JK Jason Kidd Jacket 5.00 12.00
JR Jason Richardson Pants 3.00 8.00
KG Kevin Garnett JSY 6.00 15.00
KM Karl Malone Pants 4.00 10.00
MB Mike Bibby Jacket 3.00 8.00
PG Pau Gasol Jacket 4.00 10.00
PP Paul Pierce Jacket 4.00 10.00
SF Steve Francis JSY 3.00 8.00
TM Tracy McGrady Pants 5.00 12.00
VC Vince Carter JSY 5.00 12.00
YM Yao Ming JSY 10.00 25.00

1990-91 Hoops Team Night Sheets

These team sheets were given out during a series of "NBA HOOPS Nights," which took place primarily between February and April at NBA arenas across the country. Fans attending the game on those nights received a free perforated 12-card sheet featuring NBA Hoops cards of the hometown team's top players. On some sheets, a few of the card slots are sponsors' coupons or advertisements rather than player cards. It was reported that generally between 10,000 and 20,000 card sheets were given away during these promotions. Many of the teams distributed additional card sheets through locally sponsored in-store promotions. The only team not participating was the Sacramento Kings. The Lakers set was actually issued as three panels of three cards plus a Taco Bell game card; only the Teagle card differs from his regular Hoops Series I card, which showed him with the Golden State Warriors. As part of the fourth annual McDonald's Open, the Knicks sheet was distributed to 20,000 youngsters attending a special "Kids Clinic" held October 12, 1990 in Barcelona, Spain. The Knicks team sheet also comes in a second version; after Stuart Gray was traded, another 10,000 new sets were made without Gray but with the additions of Brian Quinnett and John Starks. The Timberwolves cards were issued in four two-card vertical panels with one Burger King coupon per panel. The Supersonics sheet also comes in four versions; one pair of versions (Coke or Combos) has Dale Ellis and Olden Polynice, but after they were traded, reportedly 10,000 new sets were produced which included instead Ricky Pierce and Benoit Benjamin. The Utah Jazz cards were never issued as a sheet but cut into individual cards. All of these 12-card perforated sheets feature standard-size individual cards. The fronts feature color action player photos within a free-throw lane border of silver. Below the picture on a team-color coded bar are the words "NBA Hoops" with the team logo appearing in the lower right corner. The player's name and position are printed in team colors on the upper left edge. The backs sport a similar free-throw lane border with a small head shot of the player located in the upper right portion. The player's biography, college and NBA statistics are provided in separate charts with a brief career summary listed at the bottom. Cards marked with an asterisk are different from their regular issue Hoops card. The cards are unnumbered and checklisted below in alphabetical order.

COMPLETE SET (26) 80.00 200.00
1 John Battle 2.50 6.00
Jon Koncak
Moses Malone
Tim McCormick
Sidney Moncrief
Doc Rivers
Rumeal Robinson
Spud Webb
Dominique Wilkins
Kevin Willis
2 Larry Bird 4.00 10.00
Chris Ford CO
Kevin Gamble
Joe Kleine
Reggie Lewis
Kevin McHale
Robert Parish
Ed Pinckney
Brian Shaw
3 Muggsy Bogues 2.50 6.00
Rex Chapman
Dell Curry
Kenny Gattison
Mike Gminski *
Randolph Keys
Gene Littles CO
Johnny Newman
Robert Reid
Kelly Tripucka
4 B.J. Armstrong 5.00 12.00
Bill Cartwright
Horace Grant
H.Grant
S.Pippen *
Dennis Hopson
Michael Jordan
Stacey King
Cliff Levingston
John Paxson
Will Perdue
Scottie Pippen
5 Winston Bennett 2.50 6.00
Chucky Brown
Brad Daugherty
Craig Ehlo
Danny Ferry
Steve Kerr
Larry Nance
Mark Price
Len Wilkens CO
Hot Rod Williams
6 Richie Adubato CO 2.50 6.00
Alex English
Rolando Blackman
Brad Davis
James Donaldson
Derek Harper
Fat Lever
Rodney McCray
Roy Tarpley
Randy White *
Herb Williams
7 Michael Adams 2.50 6.00
Walter Davis
Bill Hanzlik
Chris Jackson
Jerome Lane
Todd Lichti
Blair Rasmussen
Paul Westhead CO
Joe Wolf
Orlando Woolridge
8 Mark Aguirre 3.00 8.00
William Bedford
Chuck Daly CO
Joe Dumars
James Edwards
Scott Hastings
Vinnie Johnson
Bill Laimbeer
Dennis Rodman
John Salley
Isiah Thomas
9 Tim Hardaway 4.00 10.00
Rod Higgins
Tyrone Hill
Sarunas Marciulionis
Chris Mullin
Don Nelson CO
Jim Petersen
Mitch Richmond
Mike Smrek
Tom Tolbert
10 Don Chaney CO 4.00 10.00
Sleepy Floyd
Buck Johnson
Vernon Maxwell
Hakeem Olajuwon
Kenny Smith
Larry Smith
Otis Thorpe
11 Greg Dreiling * 2.50 6.00
Vern Fleming *
George McCloud *
Reggie Miller *
Chuck Person *
Mike Sanders *
Detlef Schrempf *
Rik Smits *
LaSalle Thompson *
Randy Wittman *
12 Benoit Benjamin 2.50 6.00
Winston Garland
Tom Garrick
Gary Grant
Ron Harper
Bo Kimble
Danny Manning
Jeff Martin
Ken Norman
Mike Schuler CO
Charles Smith
13 Vlade Divac S2 3.00 8.00
Mike Dunleavy CO S3
A.C. Green S2
Magic Johnson S3
Sam Perkins S2
Byron Scott S1
Terry Teagle S1 *
Mychal Thompson S3
James Worthy S1
14 Willie Burton 2.50 6.00
Sherman Douglas
Kevin Edwards
Grant Long
Glen Rice
Ron Rothstein CO
Rony Seikaly
Jon Sundvold
Billy Thompson
15 Greg Anderson 2.50 6.00
Frank Brickowski
Jeff Grayer
Del Harris CO
Jay Humphries
Frank Kornet
Brad Lohaus
Ricky Pierce
Fred Roberts
Alvin Robertson
Dan Schayes
Jack Sikma
16 Randy Breuer S3 2.50 6.00
Scott Brooks S4
Tony Campbell S3
Tyrone Corbin S4
Sam Mitchell S2
Tod Murphy S2
Bill Musselman CO S1
Pooh Richardson S1
17 Charles Chips 2.50 6.00
Mookie Blaylock
Sam Bowie
Derrick Coleman
Lester Conner
Bill Fitch CO
Derrick Gervin
Jack Haley
Roy Hinson
Chris Morris
Reggie Theus
18A Maurice Cheeks 10.00 25.00
Patrick Ewing
Stuart Gray
Mark Jackson
Charles Oakley
Trent Tucker
Kiki Vandeweghe
Kenny Walker
Eddie Lee Wilkins
Gerald Wilkins
18B Maurice Cheeks 5.00 12.00
Patrick Ewing
Mark Jackson
Charles Oakley
Brian Quinnett
John Starks
Trent Tucker
Kiki Vandeweghe
Kenny Walker
Eddie Lee Wilkins
Gerald Wilkins
19 Mark Acres 2.50 6.00
Nick Anderson
Michael Ansley
Terry Catledge
Matt Guokas CO
Greg Kite
Jerry Reynolds
Dennis Scott
Scott Skiles
Otis Smith
Sam Vincent
20 Ron Anderson 3.00 8.00
Charles Barkley
Manute Bol
Johnny Dawkins
Armon Gilliam *
Hersey Hawkins
Jim Lynam CO
Rick Mahorn
21 Ken Battle 8.00 20.00
Tom Chambers
Cotton Fitzsimmons CO
Jeff Hornacek
Kevin Johnson
Dan Majerle
Ed Nealy
Tim Perry
Kurt Rambis
Mark West
22 Rick Adelman CO 10.00 25.00
Danny Ainge
Mark Bryant
Wayne Cooper
Clyde Drexler
Kevin Duckworth
Jerome Kersey
Drazen Petrovic
Terry Porter
Cliff Robinson
Buck Williams
Danny Young
23 Willie Anderson 5.00 12.00
Larry Brown CO
Terry Cummings
Sean Elliott
David Greenwood
Paul Pressey
David Robinson
Rod Strickland
The Coyote (Mascot)
Brad Townsend
Buck Harvey/89-90 Midwest Div.Champs
24A Dana Barros 4.00 10.00
Michael Cage
Quintin Dailey
Dale Ellis
Eddie Johnson *
Shawn Kemp
Derrick McKey
Nate McMillan
Gary Payton
Olden Polynice
Sedale Threatt
24B Combos 4.00 10.00
Dana Barros
Michael Cage
Quintin Dailey
Dale Ellis
Eddie Johnson *
Shawn Kemp
Derrick McKey
Nate McMillan
Gary Payton
Olden Polynice
Sedale Threatt
24C Dana Barros 4.00 10.00
Benoit Benjamin
Michael Cage
Quintin Dailey
Eddie Johnson *
Shawn Kemp
Derrick McKey
Nate McMillan
Gary Payton
Ricky Pierce
Sedale Threatt
24D Dana Barros 4.00 10.00
Benoit Benjamin
Michael Cage
Quintin Dailey
Eddie Johnson *
Shawn Kemp
Derrick McKey
Nate McMillan
Gary Payton
Ricky Pierce
Sedale Threatt
25 Thurl Bailey 5.00 12.00
Mike Brown
Mark Eaton
Blue Edwards
Darrell Griffith
Jeff Malone
Karl Malone
Delaney Rudd
Jerry Sloan CO
John Stockton
26 Mark Alarie 2.50 6.00
Pervis Ellison
Harvey Grant
Tom Hammonds
Charles Jones
Bernard King
Wes Unseld CO
Darrell Walker
John Williams

1991-92 Hoops Team Night Sheets

These 12-card perforated sheets feature standard-size cards. On some sheets, a few of the card slots have sponsors' coupons or advertisements rather than player cards. The fronts feature color action player photos with team-color coded borders on a white card face. The player's name is printed in black lettering in the upper left corner, and the team logo is superimposed over the lower left corner of the picture. In a horizontal format the backs have color head shots and biographical information on the left side, while the right side presents college and pro statistics. The cards are unnumbered and checklisted below in alphabetical order.

COMPLETE SET (27) 60.00 150.00
1 Stacey Augmon 3.00 8.00
Maurice Cheeks
Jon Koncak
Blair Rasmussen
Rumeal Robinson
Alexander Volkov
Bob Weiss CO
Dominique Wilkins
Kevin Willis
2 John Bagley 4.00 10.00
Larry Bird
Dee Brown
Kevin Gamble
Joe Kleine
Reggie Lewis
Kevin McHale
Robert Parish
Ed Pinckney
3 Muggsy Bogues 3.00 8.00
Rex Chapman
Dell Curry
Kenny Gattison
Kendall Gill
Mike Gminski
Hugo (Mascot)
Larry Johnson
Eric Leckner
Johnny Newman
J.R. Reid
4A B.J. Armstrong 5.00 12.00
Bill Cartwright
Horace Grant
Bobby Hansen
Craig Hodges
Michael Jordan
Stacey King
Cliff Levingston
John Paxson
Will Perdue
Scottie Pippen
Scott Williams
4B B.J. Armstrong 5.00 12.00
Bill Cartwright
Horace Grant
Bobby Hansen
Craig Hodges
Michael Jordan
Stacey King
Cliff Levingston
John Paxson
Will Perdue
Scottie Pippen
Mark Randall
5 John Battle 3.00 8.00
Winston Bennett
Terrell Brandon
Brad Daugherty
Craig Ehlo
Danny Ferry
Henry James
Steve Kerr
Larry Nance
Mark Price
Lenny Wilkens CO
John Williams
6 Richie Adubato CO 2.50 6.00
Rolando Blackman
Brad Davis
Terry Davis
James Donaldson
Derek Harper
Fat Lever
Rodney McCray
Doug Smith
Randy White
Herb Williams
7 Cadillac Anderson 2.50 6.00
Walter Davis
Winston Garland
Chris Jackson
Marcus Liberty
Todd Lichti
Mark Macon
Dikembe Mutombo
Paul Westhead CO
Reggie Williams
8 Mark Aguirre 3.00 8.00
William Bedford
Chuck Daly CO
Joe Dumars
Bill Laimbeer
Dennis Rodman
John Salley
Brad Sellers
Isiah Thomas
Darrell Walker
Orlando Woolridge
9 Vincent Askew 2.50 6.00
Mario Elie
Tim Hardaway
Rod Higgins
Tyrone Hill
Alton Lister
Sarunas Marciulionis
Chris Mullin
Don Nelson CO
Jim Petersen
Tom Tolbert
10 Don Chaney CO 3.00 8.00
Eric Floyd
Dave Jamerson
Buck Johnson
Vernon Maxwell
Hakeem Olajuwon
Kenny Smith
Larry Smith
Otis Thorpe
11 Greg Dreiling 2.50 6.00
Vern Fleming
George McCloud
Reggie Miller
Chuck Person
Detlef Schrempf
Rik Smits
LaSalle Thompson
Micheal Williams
Randy Wittman
12 James Edwards 2.50 6.00
Gary Grant
Ron Harper
Bo Kimble
Danny Manning
Ken Norman
Olden Polynice
Doc Rivers
Mike Schuler CO
Charles Smith
Loy Vaught
13 Elden Campbell 2.50 6.00
Vlade Divac
A.C. Green
Jack Haley
Sam Perkins
Byron Scott
Tony Smith
Sedale Threatt
James Worthy
14 Keith Askins 2.50 6.00
Willie Burton
Bimbo Coles
Kevin Edwards
Alec Kessler
Grant Long
Glen Rice
Rony Seikaly
Brian Shaw
Steve Smith
15 Frank Brickowski 3.00 8.00
Dale Ellis
Jeff Grayer
Jay Humphries
Larry Krystkowiak
Brad Lohaus
Moses Malone
Fred Roberts
Alvin Robertson
Dan Schayes
Snickers USA Olympic
Team 1992 with
Steve Henson and
Lester Conner
16 Randy Breuer 2.50 6.00
Scott Brooks
Tony Campbell
Luc Longley
Sam Mitchell
Pooh Richardson
Felton Spencer
Doug West
17 Rafael Addison 2.50 6.00
Kenny Anderson
Mookie Blaylock
Sam Bowie
Derrick Coleman
Chris Dudley
Tate George
Terry Mills
Chris Morris
Drazen Petrovic
18 Greg Anthony 3.00 8.00
Anthony Mason
Patrick Ewing
Mark Jackson
Tim McCormick
Xavier McDaniel
Charles Oakley
Brian Quinnett
John Starks
Kiki Vandeweghe
Gerald Wilkins
19 Mark Acres 2.50 6.00
Nick Anderson
Terry Catledge
Greg Kite
Jerry Reynolds
Dennis Scott
Scott Skiles
Otis Smith
Jeff Turner
Sam Vincent
Brian Williams
20 Ron Anderson 2.50 6.00
Charles Barkley
Manute Bol
Johnny Dawkins
Armon Gilliam
Hersey Hawkins
Jim Lynam CO
Charles Shackleford
21 Cedric Ceballos 2.50 6.00
Tom Chambers
Cotton Fitzsimmons CO
Jeff Hornacek
Kevin Johnson
Negele Knight
Andrew Lang
Dan Majerle
Tim Perry
22 Alaa Abdelnaby 3.00 8.00
Danny Ainge
Mark Bryant
Wayne Cooper
Clyde Drexler
Kevin Duckworth
Jerome Kersey
Terry Porter
Cliff Robinson
Buck Williams
Danny Young
23 Anthony Bonner 2.50 6.00
Randy Brown
Duane Causwell
Pete Chilcutt
Dennis Hopson
Les Jepsen
Jim Les
Mitch Richmond
Dwayne Schintzius
Lionel Simmons
Wayman Tisdale
Spud Webb
24 Willie Anderson 3.00 8.00
Antoine Carr
Terry Cummings
Coby Dietrick and
with Dave Barnett ANN
Sean Elliott
Sidney Green
Paul Pressey
David Robinson
David Robinson (Portrait)
Rod Strickland
Greg Sutton
25 Dana Barros 3.00 8.00
Benoit Benjamin
Michael Cage
Marty Conlon
Eddie Johnson
Shawn Kemp
Rich King
Derrick McKey
Nate McMillan
Gary Payton
Ricky Pierce
26 David Benoit 4.00 10.00
Mike Brown
Tyrone Corbin
Mark Eaton
Blue Edwards
Jeff Malone
Karl Malone
Eric Murdock
Delaney Rudd
Jerry Sloan CO
John Stockton
27 Michael Adams 2.50 6.00
Mark Alarie
Ledell Eackles
Pervis Ellison
A.J. English
Greg Foster
Harvey Grant
Tom Hammonds
Charles Jones
Bernard King
Wes Unseld CO

1999 Hoops WNBA

Released for the first time by Fleer/SkyBox, this 110-card set was distributed in 10-card packs that carried a suggested retail price of $1.29. The set contained the following subsets: 7 Future Phenomenons, 8 League Leaders, 6 Postseason Rewind and 2 checklists.

COMPLETE SET (110) 6.00 15.00
1 Cynthia Cooper PR .60 1.50
2 Houston vs. Phoenix PR .20 .50
3 Houston vs. Phoenix PR .20 .50
4 Houston vs. Phoenix PR .20 .50
5 Houston vs. Charlotte PR .20 .50
6 Phoenix vs. Cleveland PR .20 .50
7 Cynthia Cooper LL .60 1.50
8 Lisa Leslie LL .50 1.25
9 Isabelle Fijalkowski LL .10 .25
10 Eva Nemcova LL .15 .40
11 Sandy Brondello LL .40 1.00
12 Ticha Penicheiro LL .50 1.25
13 Teresa Weatherspoon LL .40 1.00

14 Margo Dydek LL	.40	1.00
15 Andrea Kuklova	.20	.50
16 Christy Smith	.20	.50
17 Penny Moore	.30	.75
18 Octavia Blue RC	.20	.50
19 Vickie Johnson	.30	.75
20 Latasha Byears	.30	.75
21 Vicky Bullett	.30	.75
22 Franthea Price RC	.20	.50
23 Tina Thompson	.75	2.00
24 Teresa Weatherspoon	.75	2.00
25 Maria Stepanova RC	.20	.50
26 Merlakia Jones	.30	.75
27 Razija Mujanovic RC	.20	.50
28 Rhonda Mapp	.25	.60
29 Kristi Harrower RC	.30	.75
30 Penny Toler	.30	.75
31 Margo Dydek RC	.75	2.00
32 Kim Perrot	.60	1.50
33 Cindy Brown	.40	1.00
34 Eva Nemcova	.30	.75
35 Quacy Barnes	.20	.50
36 Tracy Reid RC	.40	1.00
37 Chantel Tremitiere	.20	.50
38 Lady Hardmon	.20	.50
39 Michelle Griffiths RC	.40	1.00
40 Sheryl Swoopes	1.25	3.00
41 Sandy Brondello RC	.75	2.00
42 Andrea Stinson	.40	1.00
43 Marlies Askamp RC	.30	.75
44 Rachael Sporn RC	.30	.75
45 Nikki McCray	.60	1.50
46 Andrea Congreaves	.20	.50
47 Toni Foster	.30	.75
48 Kim Williams	.20	.50
49 Carla Porter RC	.30	.75
50 Jamila Wideman	.30	.75
51 Isabelle Fijalkowski	.20	.50
52 Korie Hlede RC	.60	1.50
53 Tora Suber	.30	.75
54 Sue Wicks	.30	.75
55 Coquese Washington RC	.40	1.00
56 Sharon Manning	.20	.50
57 Tammy Jackson	.20	.50
58 Tangela Smith	.20	.50
59 Suzie McConnell-Serio	.50	1.25
60 Lisa Leslie	1.00	2.50
61 Wendy Palmer	.50	1.25
62 Adia Barnes RC	.30	.75
63 La'Shawn Brown RC	.20	.50
64 Janeth Arcain	.20	.50
65 Ruthie Bolton-Holifield	.60	1.50
66 Bridget Pettis	.20	.50
67 Pamela McGee	.30	.75
68 Rebecca Lobo	.60	1.50
69 Cindy Blodgett RC	.60	1.50
70 Rita Williams	.25	.60
71 Mwadi Mabika	.20	.50
72 Sophia Witherspoon	.30	.75
73 Janice Braxton	.20	.50
74 Cynthia Cooper	1.25	3.00
75 Tammi Reiss	.30	.75
76 Umeki Webb	.20	.50
77 Kym Hampton	.30	.75
78 LaTonya Johnson RC	.30	.75
79 Michele Timms	.60	1.50
80 Kisha Ford	.20	.50
81 Monica Lamb RC	.30	.75
82 Keri Chaconas RC	.20	.50
83 Elena Baranova	.50	1.25
84 Linda Burgess	.20	.50
85 Tamecka Dixon	.30	.75
86 Heidi Burge	.20	.50
87 Michelle Edwards	.40	1.00
88 Yolanda Moore RC	.20	.50
89 Ticha Penicheiro RC	1.00	2.50
90 Alessandra Santos de Oliveira RC	.30	.75
91 Rushia Brown	.20	.50
92 Lynette Woodard	.40	1.00
93 Katrina Colleton RC	.20	.50
94 Bridgette Gordon	.20	.50
95 Jennifer Gillom	.50	1.25
96 Murriel Page	.30	.75
97 Olympia Scott-Richardson	.20	.50
98 Adrienne Johnson RC	.60	1.50
99 Gergana Branzova FP RC	.20	.50
100 Allison Feaster FP RC	.50	1.25
101 Brandy Reed FP RC	.60	1.50
102 Katie Smith FP RC	.75	2.00
103 Natalie Williams FP RC	.60	1.50
104 Jennifer Azzi FP RC	.75	2.00
105 Chamique Holdsclaw FP RC	2.00	5.00
106 Dawn Staley FP RC	.75	2.00
107 Nykesha Sales FP RC	.60	1.50
108 Kristin Folkl FP RC	.50	1.25
109 Checklist	.20	.50
110 Checklist	.20	.50

1999 Hoops WNBA Autographics

Randomly inserted in packs at one in 144, this 14-card set features autographs from some of the top names in the WNBA. The cards feature black autographs only.
*BLUE CENTURY MARKS: 1.25X TO 3X HI
BLUE: PRINT RUN 50 SERIAL #'d SETS

1 Cynthia Cooper	30.00	80.00
2 Kristin Folkl	12.00	30.00
3 Bridgette Gordon	5.00	12.00
4 Lisa Leslie	25.00	60.00
5 Suzie McConnell-Serio	12.00	30.00
6 Nikki McCray	15.00	40.00
7 Nykesha Sales	10.00	25.00
8 Dawn Staley	12.00	30.00
9 Andrea Stinson	10.00	25.00
10 Sheryl Swoopes	30.00	80.00
11 Michele Timms	15.00	40.00
12 Penny Toler	8.00	20.00
13 Teresa Weatherspoon	20.00	50.00

1999 Hoops WNBA Award Winners

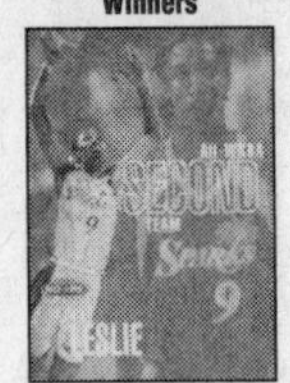

Randomly inserted in packs at one in 24, this 10-card set features All-WNBA First and Second team players on a matte silver and silver holographic foil stamped card.

COMPLETE SET (10)	20.00	50.00
1 Tina Thompson	4.00	10.00
2 Sheryl Swoopes	6.00	15.00
3 Jennifer Gillom	2.50	6.00
4 Cynthia Cooper	6.00	15.00
5 Suzie McConnell-Serio	2.50	6.00
6 Cindy Brown	2.00	5.00
7 Eva Nemcova	1.50	4.00
8 Lisa Leslie	5.00	12.00
9 Andrea Stinson	2.00	5.00
10 Teresa Weatherspoon	4.00	10.00

1999 Hoops WNBA Building Blocks

Randomly inserted in packs at one in four, this 8-card set features top WNBA stars. The cards are on a matte silver-foil.

COMPLETE SET (8)	3.00	8.00
1 Dawn Staley	1.00	2.50
2 Rebecca Lobo	.75	2.00
3 Tracy Reid	.50	1.25
4 Korie Hlede	.75	2.00
5 Ticha Penicheiro	1.25	3.00
6 Tammi Reiss	.40	1.00
7 Nikki McCray	.75	2.00
8 Jennifer Gillom	.60	1.50

1999 Hoops WNBA Talk of the Town

Randomly inserted in packs at one in 12, this 12-card set features a player from each WNBA team pictured against a cityscape of her team's city. The cards also feature gold-foil stamping.

COMPLETE SET (12)	10.00	25.00
1 Cynthia Cooper	3.00	8.00
2 Michele Timms	1.50	4.00
3 Suzie McConnell-Serio	1.25	3.00
4 Lisa Leslie	2.50	6.00
5 Andrea Stinson	1.00	2.50
6 Elena Baranova	1.25	3.00
7 Cindy Brown	1.00	2.50
8 Teresa Weatherspoon	2.00	5.00
9 Nikki McCray	1.50	4.00
10 Ruthie Bolton-Holifield	1.50	4.00
11 Nykesha Sales	1.50	4.00
12 Kristin Folkl	1.25	3.00

1992-93 Hornets Hive Five

The 1992-93 Hornets Hive Five set consists of five numbered Charlotte Hornets player cards with matching lapel pins, and six game cards. The five player cards were available through Fast Fare convenience stores and Crown gasoline stations in North Carolina, South Carolina, and Georgia. The game cards were distributed free to customers and consisted of five Charlotte Hornet Honeybee Cheerleaders and one mascot card (Hugo the Hornet). The player cards measure approximately 2 1/2" by 5 1/8". The fronts feature color action player photos with the set title, "The Hive Five", printed above the picture. On a border below the photo appears the player's name and team number. Below the border is the team logo and sponsors' logos. The back displays a player head shot with biography listed vertically along the left edge. The cards are numbered on the back. The six game cards measure approximately 2" by 4". The fronts carry a portrait of the cheerleaders bordered by the words "Charlotte Honey Bees" above and below with an outer border. The bottom section of the card contains three scratch-off basketball designs with the possiblity to win a prize by matching two prizes. Prizes include autographed player Hive Five set, a team jacket, a team jersey, a team hat, Dutchess Honey Bun, and popcorn. The game cards are unnumbered and listed below alphabetically.

COMPLETE SET (11)	6.00	15.00
1 Larry Johnson	1.50	4.00
2 Kendall Gill	1.25	3.00
3 Muggsy Bogues	1.25	3.00
4 Dell Curry	.75	2.00
5 Alonzo Mourning	3.00	8.00
NNO Hugo the Hornet	.20	.50
NNO Kim Bailey	.20	.50
NNO Paris Floyd	.20	.50
NNO Michelle Lee	.20	.50
NNO Angela Pooser	.20	.50
NNO Tara Wood	.20	.50

1992-93 Hornets Standups

Issued in four sets of three each, these stand-ups were given away, one set per customer, with a purchase at Charlotte area Burger King restaurants during the 1992-93 basketball season. The 12 stand-ups measure approximately 4" by 8 7/8" and feature color action cut-outs on purplish backgrounds. The player's facsimile autograph appears across the photo. The white back carries the player's name, biography, and statistics. The logos for Burger King, Coca-Cola, WJZY Radio, and the Hornets also appear on the front and back. The stand-ups are arranged below by set number, Set 1 (1-3), Set 2 (4-6), Set 3 (7-9), Set 4 (10-12), and listed alphabetically within each set.

COMPLETE SET (12)	20.00	50.00
1 Tony Bennett	1.50	4.00
2 Dell Curry	1.50	4.00
3 Alonzo Mourning	5.00	12.00
4 Muggsy Bogues	3.00	8.00
5 Mike Gminski	1.50	4.00
6 Johnny Newman	1.50	4.00
7 Kenny Gattison	1.50	4.00
8 Kendall Gill	2.50	6.00
9 David Wingate	1.50	4.00
10 Sidney Green	1.50	4.00
11 Larry Johnson	3.00	8.00
12 Kevin Lynch	1.50	4.00

2008-09 Hot Prospects

This set was released on October 14, 2008. The base set consists of 162 cards. Cards 1-110 feature veterans, with cards 91-110 serial numbered of 499. Cards 111-136 are rookie cards featuring jersey swatches and autographs, serial numbered of 399, and cards 137-142 are similar but serial numbered to 199. Cards 143-156 are autographed rookie cards serial numbered of 199, and cards 157-162 are basic rookie cards serial numbered of 199.

COMP.SET w/o SPs (90)	10.00	25.00
UNPRICED WHITE PRINT RUN ONE SET		
1 LaMarcus Aldridge	.40	1.00
2 Ray Allen	.40	1.00
3 Carmelo Anthony	.50	1.25
4 Gilbert Arenas	.40	1.00
5 Ron Artest	.40	1.00
6 Mike Bibby	.30	.75
7 Chauncey Billups	.40	1.00
8 Andrew Bogut	.40	1.00
9 Carlos Boozer	.40	1.00
10 Chris Bosh	.40	1.00
11 Elton Brand	.40	1.00
12 Corey Brewer	.30	.75
13 Kobe Bryant	2.00	5.00
14 Caron Butler	.40	1.00
15 Jose Calderon	.30	.75
16 Marcus Camby	.25	.60
17 Vince Carter	.50	1.25
18 Mike Conley Jr.	.30	.75
19 Daequan Cook	.25	.60
20 Jamal Crawford	.30	.75
21 Baron Davis	.40	1.00
22 Luol Deng	.40	1.00
23 Tim Duncan	.60	1.50
24 Mike Dunleavy	.30	.75
25 Kevin Durant	1.50	4.00
26 Francisco Garcia	.30	.75
27 Kevin Garnett	.75	2.00
28 Pau Gasol	.40	1.00
29 Rudy Gay	.40	1.00
30 Daniel Gibson	.40	1.00
31 Manu Ginobili	.40	1.00
32 Ben Gordon	.40	1.00
33 Danny Granger	.40	1.00
34 Jeff Green	.30	.75
35 Richard Hamilton	.30	.75
36 Al Harrington	.30	.75
37 Al Horford	.40	1.00
38 Dwight Howard	.75	2.00
39 Josh Howard	.30	.75
40 Andre Iguodala	.40	1.00
41 Allen Iverson	.50	1.25
42 Stephen Jackson	.30	.75
43 LeBron James	2.00	5.00
44 Antawn Jamison	.40	1.00
45 Al Jefferson	.40	1.00
46 Richard Jefferson	.40	1.00
47 Yi Jianlian	.40	1.00
48 Joe Johnson	.40	1.00
49 Chris Kaman	.30	.75
50 Jason Kidd	.40	1.00
51 Kyle Korver	.30	.75
52 Rashard Lewis	.30	.75
53 Corey Maggette	.30	.75
54 Stephon Marbury	.30	.75
55 Shawn Marion	.40	1.00
56 Kevin Martin	.40	1.00
57 Rashad McCants	.25	.60
58 Tracy McGrady	.40	1.00
59 Andre Miller	.30	.75
60 Yao Ming	.50	1.25
61 Jamario Moon	.25	.60
62 Steve Nash	.40	1.00
63 Joakim Noah	.40	1.00
64 Andres Nocioni	.25	.60
65 Dirk Nowitzki	.50	1.25
66 Jermaine O'Neal	.40	1.00
67 Shaquille O'Neal	.75	2.00
68 Greg Oden	.40	1.00
69 Emeka Okafor	.40	1.00
70 Tony Parker	.40	1.00
71 Chris Paul	.60	1.50
72 Paul Pierce	.50	1.25
73 Zach Randolph	.30	.75
74 Michael Redd	.40	1.00
75 Jason Richardson	.40	1.00
76 Brandon Roy	.40	1.00
77 Luis Scola	.30	.75
78 Peja Stojakovic	.40	1.00
79 Amare Stoudemire	.40	1.00
80 Hedo Turkoglu	.40	1.00
81 Dwyane Wade	.75	2.00
82 Ben Wallace	.40	1.00
83 Gerald Wallace	.40	1.00
84 Rasheed Wallace	.40	1.00
85 Luke Walton	.25	.60
86 David West	.40	1.00
87 Chris Wilcox	.25	.60
88 Deron Williams	.40	1.00
89 Sean Williams	.30	.75
90 Thaddeus Young	.30	.75
91 Ray Allen	.75	2.00
92 Carmelo Anthony	1.00	2.50
93 Chauncey Billups	.75	2.00
94 Kobe Bryant	4.00	10.00
95 Vince Carter	1.00	2.50
96 Baron Davis	.75	2.00
97 Tim Duncan	1.25	3.00
98 Kevin Garnett	1.50	4.00
99 Pau Gasol	.75	2.00
100 Dwight Howard	1.50	4.00
101 Allen Iverson	1.00	2.50
102 LeBron James	4.00	10.00
103 Michael Jordan	6.00	15.00
104 Tracy McGrady	.75	2.00
105 Yao Ming	1.00	2.50
106 Steve Nash	.75	2.00
107 Joakim Noah	.75	2.00
108 Dirk Nowitzki	1.00	2.50
109 Shaquille O'Neal	1.50	4.00
110 Dwyane Wade	1.50	4.00
111 Kyle Weaver JSY AU RC	6.00	15.00
112 Joe Alexander JSY AU RC	6.00	15.00
113 D.J. Augustin JSY AU RC	6.00	15.00
114 Brook Lopez JSY AU RC	12.00	30.00
115 Jerryd Bayless JSY AU RC	6.00	15.00
116 Jason Thompson JSY AU RC	6.00	15.00
117 Brandon Rush JSY AU RC	6.00	15.00
118 Anthony Randolph JSY AU RC	8.00	20.00
119 Robin Lopez JSY AU RC	6.00	15.00
120 Marreese Speights JSY AU RC	6.00	15.00
121 Roy Hibbert JSY AU RC	10.00	25.00
122 Javale McGee JSY AU RC	10.00	25.00
123 J.J. Hickson JSY AU RC	8.00	20.00
124 Ryan Anderson JSY AU RC	10.00	25.00
125 Courtney Lee JSY AU RC	10.00	25.00
126 Kosta Koufos JSY AU RC	6.00	15.00
127 George Hill JSY AU RC	10.00	25.00
128 Darrell Arthur JSY AU RC	6.00	15.00
129 Donte Greene JSY AU RC	6.00	15.00
130 Sonny Weems JSY AU RC	6.00	15.00
131 J.R. Giddens JSY AU RC	6.00	15.00
132 Walter Sharpe JSY AU RC	6.00	15.00
133 Joey Dorsey JSY AU RC	6.00	15.00
134 Mario Chalmers JSY AU RC	12.00	30.00
135 DeAndre Jordan JSY AU RC	12.00	30.00
136 Patrick Ewing Jr JSY AU RC	6.00	15.00
137 Derrick Rose JSY AU/199 RC	250.00	450.00
138 Michael Beasley JSY AU/199 RC	20.00	50.00
139 O.J. Mayo JSY AU/199 RC	20.00	50.00
140 Russell Westbrook JSY AU/199 RC	75.00	150.00
141 Kevin Love JSY AU/199 RC	75.00	150.00
142 Eric Gordon JSY AU/199 RC	30.00	80.00
143 Luc Richard Mbah A Moute AU RC	5.00	12.00
144 James Mays AU RC	5.00	12.00
145 Sonny Weems AU	5.00	12.00
146 Chris Douglas-Roberts AU RC	5.00	12.00
147 Deron Washington AU RC	5.00	12.00
148 David Padgett AU RC	5.00	12.00
149 Bill Walker AU RC	5.00	12.00
150 Malik Hairston AU RC	5.00	12.00
151 Richard Hendrix AU RC	5.00	12.00
152 DeVon Hardin AU RC	5.00	12.00
153 Darnell Jackson AU RC	5.00	12.00
154 Maarty Leunen AU RC	5.00	12.00
155 Mike Taylor AU RC	5.00	12.00
156 James Gist AU RC	5.00	12.00
157 Sean Singletary RC	5.00	12.00
158 Joe Crawford RC	5.00	12.00
159 Trent Plaisted RC	5.00	12.00
160 Shan Foster RC	5.00	12.00
161 Juan Palacios RC	5.00	12.00
162 Jaycee Carroll RC	5.00	12.00

2008-09 Hot Prospects Blue

*1-110 BLUE: .5X TO 1.25X BASE HI
RANDOM INSERTS IN PACKS

111 Kyle Weaver	1.50	4.00
112 Joe Alexander	1.50	4.00
113 D.J. Augustin	1.50	4.00
114 Brook Lopez	2.50	6.00
115 Jerryd Bayless	1.50	4.00
116 Jason Thompson	1.50	4.00
117 Brandon Rush	1.50	4.00
118 Anthony Randolph	2.00	5.00
119 Robin Lopez	1.50	4.00
120 Marreese Speights	1.50	4.00
121 Roy Hibbert	2.50	6.00
122 Javale McGee	2.50	6.00
123 J.J. Hickson	2.00	5.00
124 Ryan Anderson	2.50	6.00
125 Courtney Lee	2.50	6.00
126 Kosta Koufos	1.50	4.00
127 George Hill	2.50	6.00
128 Darrell Arthur	1.50	4.00
129 Donte Greene	1.50	4.00
130 Sonny Weems	1.50	4.00
131 J.R. Giddens	1.50	4.00
132 Walter Sharpe	1.50	4.00
133 Joey Dorsey	1.50	4.00
134 Mario Chalmers	2.50	6.00
135 DeAndre Jordan	3.00	8.00
136 Patrick Ewing Jr.	1.50	4.00
137 Derrick Rose	12.00	30.00
138 Michael Beasley	2.50	6.00
139 O.J. Mayo	2.50	6.00
140 Russell Westbrook	8.00	20.00
141 Kevin Love	6.00	15.00
142 Eric Gordon	4.00	10.00
143 Luc Richard Mbah A Moute	1.00	2.50
144 James Mays	1.00	2.50
145 Sonny Weems	1.00	2.50
146 Chris Douglas-Roberts	1.00	2.50
147 Deron Washington	1.00	2.50
148 David Padgett	1.00	2.50
149 Bill Walker	1.00	2.50
150 Malik Hairston	1.00	2.50
151 Richard Hendrix	1.00	2.50
152 DeVon Hardin	1.00	2.50
153 Darnell Jackson	1.00	2.50
154 Maarty Leunen	1.00	2.50
155 Mike Taylor	1.00	2.50
156 James Gist	1.00	2.50
157 Sean Singletary	1.00	2.50
158 Joe Crawford	1.00	2.50
159 Trent Plaisted	1.00	2.50
160 Shan Foster	1.00	2.50
161 Juan Palacios	1.00	2.50
162 Jaycee Carroll	1.00	2.50

2008-09 Hot Prospects Red

*1-90 RED: 3X TO 8X BASE HI
*91-110 RED: 1.5X TO 4X BASE HI
*111-162 RED: .75X TO 2X BASE HI
RED PRINT RUN 25 SER.#'d SETS

13 Kobe Bryant	20.00	50.00
103 Michael Jordan	40.00	100.00
137 Derrick Rose JSY AU	350.00	700.00

2008-09 Hot Prospects Alumni Mates

COMPLETE SET (20)	10.00	25.00
AM1 Gilbert Arenas / Richard Jefferson	1.50	4.00
AM2 Jason Kidd / Shareef Abdur-Rahim	1.50	4.00
AM3 Shane Battier / Carlos Boozer	1.50	4.00
AM4 Dan Majerle / Chris Kaman	1.50	4.00
AM5 Al Horford / Joakim Noah	1.50	4.00
AM6 Dikembe Mutombo / Alonzo Mourning	3.00	8.00
AM7 Walt Bellamy / Eric Gordon	1.50	4.00
AM8 Michael Beasley / Rolando Blackman	2.00	5.00
AM9 Shaquille O'Neal / Glen Davis	3.00	8.00
AM10 Derrick Rose / Shawne Williams	2.50	6.00
AM11 Jason Richardson / Zach Randolph	1.50	4.00
AM12 Vince Carter / Antawn Jamison	2.50	6.00
AM13 Adrian Dantley / Bill Laimbeer	1.50	4.00
AM14 Mike Conley Jr. / Greg Oden	1.50	4.00
AM15 Kevin Durant / LaMarcus Aldridge	2.00	5.00
AM16 Ray Allen / Richard Hamilton	1.50	4.00
AM17 Julius Erving / Marcus Camby	2.00	5.00
AM18 Kareem Abdul-Jabbar / Bill Walton	2.00	5.00
AM19 Bill Sharman / O.J. Mayo	1.50	4.00
AM20 David West / James Posey	1.50	4.00

2008-09 Hot Prospects Cream of the Crop

COMPLETE SET (30)	15.00	30.00
APPROXIMATE ODDS 1:6		
CC1 Brandon Roy	1.00	2.50
CC2 Chris Paul	1.50	4.00
CC3 LeBron James	5.00	12.00
CC4 Amare Stoudemire	1.00	2.50
CC5 Joe Johnson	1.00	2.50
CC6 Tony Parker	1.00	2.50
CC7 Gilbert Arenas	1.00	2.50
CC8 Michael Redd	1.00	2.50
CC9 Richard Hamilton	.75	2.00
CC10 Shawn Marion	1.00	2.50
CC11 Manu Ginobili	1.00	2.50
CC12 Dirk Nowitzki	1.25	3.00
CC13 Paul Pierce	1.25	3.00
CC14 Tracy McGrady	1.00	2.50
CC15 Kobe Bryant	5.00	12.00
CC16 Steve Nash	1.00	2.50
CC17 Rasheed Wallace	1.00	2.50
CC18 Larry Johnson	1.00	2.50
CC19 Detlef Schrempf	1.00	2.50
CC20 Vlade Divac	1.00	2.50
CC21 Mitch Richmond	1.00	2.50
CC22 Scottie Pippen	1.50	4.00
CC23 David Robinson	1.50	4.00
CC24 Chris Mullin	1.00	2.50
CC25 Karl Malone	1.25	3.00
CC26 Isiah Thomas	1.00	2.50
CC27 Kevin McHale	1.25	3.00
CC28 Larry Bird	3.00	8.00
CC29 Oscar Robertson	1.00	2.50
CC30 Wilt Chamberlain	2.00	5.00

2008-09 Hot Prospects Draft Day Postmarks

STATED PRINT RUN 50 SER#'d SETS

DDAA Alexis Ajinca	8.00	20.00
DDAD Darrell Arthur	8.00	20.00
DDAR Anthony Randolph	10.00	25.00
DDBL Brook Lopez	12.00	30.00
DDBR Brandon Rush	8.00	20.00
DDCD Chris Douglas-Roberts	8.00	20.00
DDDA D.J. Augustin	8.00	20.00
DDDG Danilo Gallinari	12.00	30.00
DDDR Derrick Rose	150.00	300.00
DDDW D.J. White	8.00	20.00
DDEG Eric Gordon	20.00	50.00
DDGR Donte Greene	8.00	20.00
DDJA Joe Alexander	8.00	20.00
DDJB Jerryd Bayless	8.00	20.00
DDJD Joey Dorsey	8.00	20.00
DDJG J.R. Giddens	8.00	20.00
DDJH J.J. Hickson	10.00	25.00
DDJM Javale McGee	12.00	30.00
DDJT Jason Thompson	8.00	20.00
DDKK Kosta Koufos	8.00	20.00
DDKL Kevin Love	30.00	80.00
DDLM Luc Richard Mbah A Moute	8.00	20.00
DDMB Michael Beasley	12.00	30.00
DDMC Mario Chalmers	15.00	40.00
DDOJ O.J. Mayo	20.00	50.00
DDPE Patrick Ewing Jr	8.00	20.00
DDRA Ryan Anderson	12.00	30.00
DDRH Roy Hibbert	12.00	30.00
DDRL Robin Lopez	8.00	20.00
DDRW Russell Westbrook	75.00	150.00

2008-09 Hot Prospects Hot Materials

COMBINED AU/MEM ODDS 1:9
*RED: .75X TO 2X BASE HI
RED PRINT RUN 25 SER.#'d SETS
UNPRICED PATCH PRINT RUN ONE SET

HMAB Andrew Bogut	2.50	6.00
HMAI Allen Iverson	3.00	8.00
HMAS Amare Stoudemire	2.50	6.00
HMBR Brandon Roy	2.50	6.00
HMCA Carmelo Anthony	3.00	8.00
HMCB Caron Butler	2.50	6.00
HMDG Danny Granger	2.50	6.00
HMDH Dwight Howard	5.00	12.00
HMDN Dirk Nowitzki	3.00	8.00
HMEO Emeka Okafor	2.50	6.00
HMJJ Joe Johnson	2.50	6.00
HMJK Jason Kidd	2.50	6.00
HMKB Kobe Bryant	8.00	20.00
HMKD Kevin Durant	10.00	25.00
HMKG Kevin Garnett	5.00	12.00
HMLJ LeBron James	8.00	20.00
HMMB Mike Bibby	2.00	5.00
HMPG Pau Gasol	2.50	6.00
HMRA Ray Allen	2.50	6.00
HMRH Richard Hamilton	2.00	5.00
HMRJ Richard Jefferson	2.50	6.00
HMRW Rasheed Wallace	2.50	6.00
HMSB Shane Battier	2.00	5.00
HMSM Shawn Marion	2.50	6.00
HMSN Steve Nash	2.50	6.00
HMSO Shaquille O'Neal	5.00	12.00
HMTD Tim Duncan	4.00	10.00
HMTP Tayshaun Prince	2.50	6.00
HMVC Vince Carter	3.00	8.00
HMYM Yao Ming	3.00	8.00

2008-09 Hot Prospects Hot Tandems

COMPLETE SET (20)	8.00	20.00
APPROXIMATE ODDS 1:6		
HT1 Larry Bird / Paul Pierce	2.00	5.00
HT2 Michael Jordan / Scottie Pippen	4.00	10.00
HT3 Allen Iverson / Carmelo Anthony	1.50	4.00
HT4 Isiah Thomas / Joe Dumars	1.25	3.00
HT5 Chauncey Billups / Richard Hamilton	1.25	3.00
HT6 Jason Kidd / Dirk Nowitzki	1.25	3.00
HT7 Tracy McGrady / Yao Ming	1.50	4.00
HT8 Clyde Drexler / Hakeem Olajuwon	2.00	5.00
HT9 Magic Johnson / Kobe Bryant	3.00	8.00
HT10 Michael Redd / Richard Jefferson	1.25	3.00
HT11 Chris Paul / David West	2.00	5.00
HT12 Patrick Ewing / Willis Reed	1.50	4.00
HT13 Phil Jackson / Bill Bradley	1.25	3.00
HT14 Julius Erving / Wilt Chamberlain	3.00	8.00
HT15 Steve Nash / Amare Stoudemire	2.00	5.00
HT16 Brandon Roy / Greg Oden	1.25	3.00
HT17 George Gervin / David Robinson	2.00	5.00
HT18 Kevin Durant / Jeff Green	1.50	4.00
HT19 John Stockton / Karl Malone	2.00	5.00
HT20 Gilbert Arenas / Antawn Jamison	1.25	3.00

2008-09 Hot Prospects NBA Game Issue Jerseys

PRINT RUN 149 SER.#'d SETS
*RED: .75X TO 2X BASE HI
RED PRINT RUN 25 SER.#'d SETS
UNPRICED PATCH PRINT RUN ONE SET

NBAAB Andrew Bynum	3.00	8.00
NBAAI Allen Iverson	3.00	8.00
NBAAS Amare Stoudemire	2.50	6.00
NBABA Andrea Bargnani	2.00	5.00
NBABD Baron Davis	2.50	6.00
NBABR Brandon Roy	2.50	6.00
NBABU Caron Butler	2.50	6.00
NBACA Carmelo Anthony	3.00	8.00
NBACB Carlos Boozer	2.50	6.00
NBADH Dwight Howard	5.00	12.00
NBADN Dirk Nowitzki	3.00	8.00
NBADW Deron Williams	2.50	6.00
NBAGA Gilbert Arenas	2.50	6.00
NBAJH Josh Howard	2.00	5.00
NBAJJ Joe Johnson	2.50	6.00
NBAJK Jason Kidd	2.50	6.00
NBAJR Jason Richardson	2.50	6.00
NBAKB Kobe Bryant	8.00	20.00
NBAKG Kevin Garnett	5.00	12.00
NBALJ LeBron James	8.00	20.00
NBAMB Mike Bibby	2.00	5.00
NBAMJ Michael Jordan	20.00	50.00
NBAPG Pau Gasol	2.50	6.00
NBARG Rudy Gay	2.50	6.00
NBASM Shawn Marion	2.50	6.00
NBASN Steve Nash	2.50	6.00
NBASO Shaquille O'Neal	6.00	15.00
NBATD Tim Duncan	4.00	10.00
NBATP Tony Parker	2.50	6.00
NBAYM Yao Ming	3.00	8.00

2008-09 Hot Prospects Numbers Game Autographs Jerseys

CARDS #'d TO PLAYER JSY #
SOME UNPRICED DUE TO SCARCITY
UNPRICED RED PRINT RUN 5 SETS
UNPRICED PATCH PRINT RUN ONE SET

NGAB Andrew Bynum/17	15.00	40.00
NGAH Al Horford/15	20.00	40.00
NGBW Bill Walton/32	10.00	25.00
NGCA Carmelo Anthony/15	20.00	40.00
NGCK Chris Kaman/35	6.00	15.00
NGDG Danny Granger/33	12.00	30.00
NGDH Dwight Howard/12	40.00	70.00
NGDM Desmond Mason/24	10.00	25.00
NGDR David Robinson/50	40.00	100.00
NGEO Emeka Okafor/50	6.00	15.00
NGJS John Stockton/12	75.00	150.00
NGKB Kobe Bryant/24	125.00	250.00
NGKD Kevin Durant/35	75.00	200.00
NGLJ LeBron James/23	125.00	250.00
NGMA Donyell Marshall/42	6.00	15.00
NGMG Corey Maggette/50	6.00	15.00
NGRF Raymond Felton/20	6.00	15.00
NGRJ Richard Jefferson/24	8.00	20.00
NGSB Shane Battier/31	6.00	15.00
NGTP Tayshaun Prince/22	8.00	20.00
NGTT Tyrus Thomas/24	8.00	20.00
NGVC Vince Carter/15	20.00	50.00
NGYM Yao Ming/11	30.00	80.00

2008-09 Hot Prospects Property of Jerseys

STATED PRINT RUN 199 SER.#'d SETS
*RED: .75X TO 2X BASE HI
RED PRINT RUN 25 SER.#'d SETS
UNPRICED PATCH PRINT RUN ONE SET

POAB Andrew Bogut	2.50	6.00
POAI Andre Iguodala	2.50	6.00
POAJ Antawn Jamison	2.50	6.00
POBO Chris Bosh	2.50	6.00
POBW Ben Wallace	2.50	6.00
POCB Chauncey Billups	2.50	6.00
POCK Chris Kaman	2.00	5.00
POCM Corey Maggette	2.00	5.00
POCP Chris Paul	4.00	10.00
PODG Daniel Gibson	2.50	6.00
PODW Dwyane Wade	5.00	12.00
POEB Elton Brand	2.50	6.00
POGR Danny Granger	2.50	6.00
POGW Gerald Wallace	2.50	6.00
POJC Jose Calderon	6.00	15.00
POJJ Joe Johnson	2.50	6.00
POJR Jason Richardson	2.50	6.00
POKD Kevin Durant	10.00	25.00
POKG Kevin Garnett	5.00	12.00
POKM Kevin Martin	2.50	6.00
POLJ LeBron James	8.00	20.00
POMB Mike Bibby	2.00	5.00
POMG Manu Ginobili	2.50	6.00
POPG Pau Gasol	2.50	6.00
PORJ Richard Jefferson	2.50	6.00
PORL Rashard Lewis	2.00	5.00
PORW Rasheed Wallace	2.50	6.00
POSB Shane Battier	2.00	5.00
POSM Shawn Marion	2.50	6.00
POWI Deron Williams	2.50	6.00

2008-09 Hot Prospects Rookie Materials Autographs Patches

COMBINED AU/MEM ODDS 1:9

RMAD Darrell Arthur	8.00	20.00
RMAR Anthony Randolph	20.00	40.00
RMBL Brook Lopez	12.00	30.00
RMBR Brandon Rush	8.00	20.00
RMBW Bill Walker	8.00	20.00
RMCD Chris Douglas-Roberts	8.00	20.00
RMDA Darnell Jackson	8.00	20.00

G Danilo Gallinari 12.00 30.00
JJ D.J. Augustin 8.00 20.00
R Derrick Rose 250.00 500.00
W D.J. White 8.00 20.00
G Eric Gordon 25.00 60.00
H George Hill 12.00 30.00
R Donte Greene 8.00 20.00
A Joe Alexander 8.00 20.00
B Jerryd Bayless 8.00 20.00
C Joe Crawford 8.00 20.00
D Joey Dorsey 8.00 20.00
G J.R. Giddens 8.00 20.00
H J.J. Hickson 10.00 25.00
M JaVale McGee 15.00 40.00
O DeAndre Jordan 15.00 40.00
T Jason Thompson 8.00 20.00
K Kosta Koufos 8.00 20.00
L Kevin Love 30.00 80.00
W Kyle Weaver 8.00 20.00
M Luc Richard Mbah A Moute 8.00 20.00
B Michael Beasley 20.00 50.00
C Mario Chalmers 15.00 40.00
H Malik Hairston 8.00 20.00
S Marreese Speights 8.00 20.00
M O.J. Mayo 30.00 80.00
E Patrick Ewing Jr 8.00 20.00
A Ryan Anderson 12.00 30.00
H Roy Hibbert 12.00 30.00
L Robin Lopez 8.00 20.00
S Sean Singletary 8.00 20.00
W Sonny Weems 8.00 20.00
A Deron Washington 8.00 20.00
S Walter Sharpe 8.00 20.00

08-09 Hot Prospects Supreme Court

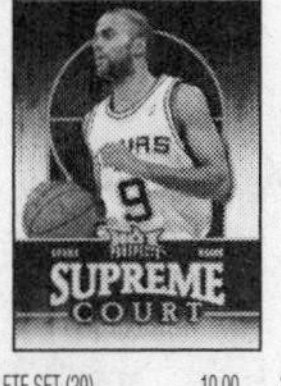

MPLETE SET (20) 10.00 25.00
ROXIMATE ODDS 1:6
Mike Bibby .60 1.50
Ray Allen .75 2.00
Michael Jordan 6.00 15.00
LeBron James 4.00 10.00
Jason Kidd .75 2.00
Chauncey Billups .75 2.00
Shane Battier .60 1.50
Tracy McGrady .75 2.00
Elton Brand .75 2.00
0 Kobe Bryant 4.00 10.00
1 Derek Fisher .60 1.50
2 Dwyane Wade 1.50 4.00
3 Dwight Howard 1.50 4.00
4 Andre Miller .60 1.50
5 Steve Nash .75 2.00
6 Greg Oden .75 2.00
7 Tony Parker .75 2.00
8 Jeff Green .60 1.50
9 Chris Bosh .75 2.00
0 Antawn Jamison .75 2.00

008-09 Hot Prospects Sweet Selections Autographs

TED PRINT RUN 25 SER.#'d SETS
RICED RED PRINT RUN FIVE SETS
RICED SPECTRUM PRINT RUN ONE SET
J Antawn Jamison 8.00 20.00
M Alonzo Mourning 30.00 80.00
W Bill Walton 15.00 30.00
B Chauncey Billups 8.00 20.00
P Chris Paul 20.00 50.00
G Darrell Griffith 8.00 20.00
H Dwight Howard 20.00 50.00
R David Robinson 30.00 80.00
T David Thompson 8.00 20.00
W Dominique Wilkins 25.00 50.00
O Hakeem Olajuwon 20.00 40.00
A LeBron James 100.00 200.00
K Jason Kidd 15.00 40.00
D Kevin Durant 75.00 150.00
J Larry Johnson 30.00 80.00
O Sidney Moncrief 8.00 20.00
R Micheal Ray Richardson 8.00 20.00
M Yao Ming 15.00 30.00

980-81 Hustle Chicago/La-Z-Boy Team Issue

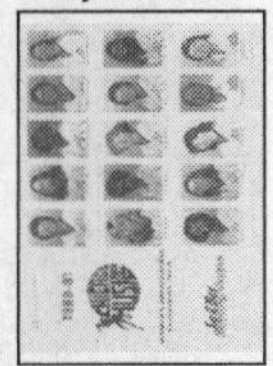

team-issued photo measures approximately 8 by 11" and feature black and white player portraits ne sheet. The player's name is listed below the o. The sheet contains portraits of the Chicago tle from the Women's Professional Basketball n Association. The backs contains a La-Z-Boy rtisement The photo is unnumbered.

Caldwell 12.50 25.00
Candler
Digitale
Easterling
Fincher
Geils
Gleason CO
Hodgson
Kiday
Matthews
Mayo
McWhorter
lissen
Steele TR
White

1972-73 Icee Bear

The 1972-73 Icee Bear set contains 20 player cards each measuring approximately 3" by 5". The cards are printed on thin stock. The fronts feature color facial pictures, and the backs show brief biographical information. The set may have been printed in 1973-74 or perhaps later as they were available in the Seattle area as late as summer 1974. The cards were reportedly distributed one card with each Icee Bear Slurpee purchased. There are four cards that are more difficult to find than the other 16; these four are listed as SP's in the checklist below.

COMPLETE SET (20) 100.00 175.00
1 Kareem Abdul-Jabbar 15.00 30.00
2 Dennis Awtrey 1.25 3.00
3 Tom Boerwinkle 2.00 5.00
4 Austin Carr SP 3.00 8.00
5 Wilt Chamberlain 20.00 40.00
6 Archie Clark SP 15.00 40.00
7 Dave DeBusschere 3.00 8.00
8 Walt Frazier SP 6.00 12.00
9 John Havlicek 7.50 15.00
10 Connie Hawkins 5.00 10.00
11 Bob Love 2.00 5.00
12 Jerry Lucas 4.00 10.00
13 Pete Maravich SP 35.00 65.00
14 Calvin Murphy 2.00 5.00
15 Oscar Robertson 10.00 20.00
16 Jerry Sloan 3.00 8.00
17 Wes Unseld 2.50 6.00
18 Dick Van Arsdale 1.25 3.00
19 Jerry West 15.00 30.00
20 Sidney Wicks 3.00 8.00

2000 IMAX Michael Jordan Postcards

These two postcards were given out at IMAX theatres and other participating stores. The set features two Michael Jordan postcards that are advertisements for two made for television movies.

COMPLETE SET (2) 4.00 10.00

1991 Impel U.S. Olympic Hall of Fame

Produced by Impel Marketing Inc., this 90-card set salutes members of the U.S. Olympic Hall of Fame. A portion of the proceeds from the sale of these cards supported the 1992 U.S. Olympic team. The cards were available in 15-card packs, and collectors could obtain a collector's album to display the set for $12.99 plus $3.00 postage and handling. Also the cards were packaged in sets of three, along with a "Medals and Millions" game piece, inside specially-marked multi-packs of Coca-Cola products in a promotion cosponsored by Coca-Cola U.S.A. and CBS. Six cards from the set (Beamon, Fleming, Jenner, Owens, Rudolph, and Spitz) were issued as prototypes in a cello pack; they are unnumbered and clearly marked as such on the backs in the upper right corner. The fronts display a mix of color and black-and-white photos inside a gold inner border. The outer border is light gray, and a red, white, and blue ribbon cuts across the middle of the card. The backs carry a closeup photo, career summary, and career highlights.

COMPLETE SET (90) 6.00 15.00
55 Bill Bradley .20 .50
56 Lucious Jackson .12 .30
57 1964 U.S. Basketball Team .12 .30
Soviet player
58 Bill Bradley .20 .50
59 1964 U.S. Basketball Team Photo .12 .30
60 Lucious Jackson .20 .50
Bill Bradley
61 Henry Iba CO .12 .30
74 Henry Iba .10 .25

1992 Impel U.S. Olympic Hopefuls

COMPLETE SET (110) 8.00 20.00
7 U.S. Olympic Baseball Team .20 .50
8 Charles Barkley BK .40 1.00
9 Larry Bird BK .75 2.00
10 Patrick Ewing BK .30 .75
11 Magic Johnson BK .60 1.50
12 Michael Jordan BK 2.00 5.00
13 Karl Malone BK .40 1.00
14 Chris Mullin BK .20 .50
15 Scottie Pippen BK .50 1.25
16 David Robinson BK .50 1.25
17 John Stockton BK .30 .75
18 U.S. Olympic Basketball Team .10 .25
19 Teresa Edwards BK .10 .25
20 Bridgette Gordon BK .10 .25
21 Andrea Lloyd BK .10 .25
22 Katrina McClain BK .10 .25

1994-95 Imprinted Pins

Produced by Imprinted Products Corporation, this 28-pin set includes the 27 current NBA teams as well as the two new expansion teams, the Toronto Raptors and Vancouver Grizzlies. The pins were packaged in a clam-shell design that allowed consumers to view the team pins.

COMPLETE SET (29) 20.00 50.00
1 Atlanta Hawks .75 2.00
2 Boston Celtics 1.25 3.00
3 Charlotte Hornets .75 2.00
4 Chicago Bulls 1.25 3.00
5 Cleveland Cavaliers .75 2.00
6 Dallas Mavericks .75 2.00
7 Denver Nuggets .75 2.00
8 Detroit Pistons .75 2.00
9 Golden State Warriors .75 2.00
10 Houston Rockets .75 2.00
11 Indiana Pacers .75 2.00
12 Los Angeles Clippers .75 2.00
13 Los Angeles Lakers 1.25 3.00
14 Miami Heat .75 2.00
15 Milwaukee Bucks .75 2.00
16 Minnesota Timberwolves .75 2.00
17 New Jersey Nets .75 2.00
18 New York Knicks 1.25 3.00
19 Orlando Magic 1.25 3.00
20 Philadelphia 76ers .75 2.00
21 Phoenix Suns .75 2.00
22 Portland Trail Blazers .75 2.00
23 Sacramento Kings .75 2.00
24 San Antonio Spurs .75 2.00
25 Seattle Supersonics .75 2.00
26 Toronto Raptors .75 2.00
27 Utah Jazz .75 2.00
28 Vancouver Grizzlies .75 2.00
29 Washington Bullets .75 2.00

2007-08 ITG Ultimate Memorabilia Cityscapes

STATED PRINT RUN 24 SERIAL #'d SETS
2 Ilya Kovalchuk 10.00 25.00
Dominique Wilkins

2011 In The Game Canadiana Mega Memorabilia Silver

MM37 Steve Nash L 10.00 20.00

2011 In The Game Canadiana Red

BLUE/50: .75X TO 2X BASIC RED
UNPRICED ONYX ANNOUNCED RUN 5
ANNOUNCED PRINT RUN 180 SETS
41 James Naismith .60 1.50

1950-70 J.D. McCarthy Postcards

This 15-postcard set was released by J.D. McCarthy in the 1950-70's. Each card was produced in black and white and measured 3.25x5.5. Please note that these postcards have blank backs, and are listed below in alphabetical order. This list may be far from complete and because of the wide disparity of years, please note no pricing is provided. Any further information on cards or pricing would be appreciated.

COMPLETE SET (15)
1 Rick Barry
2 Rick Barry
3 Dave Bing
4 Dave DeBusschere
5 Archie Dees
6 Terry Dischinger
7 Walter Dukes
8 Bailey Howell
9 Bob Lanier
10 Lloyd Love
11 Dick McGuire
12 Eddie Miles
13 Jackie Moreland
14 Gene Shue
15 John Tresvant

1993-94 Jam Session

This 240-card set was issued in 1993 by Fleer and features oversized cards measuring approximately 2 1/2" by 4 3/4". Cards were issued in 12-card packs (36 per box) with a suggested retail pack price of 1.59. One insert card is included in every pack. The full-bleed fronts feature glossy color action player photos. Across the bottom edge of the picture appears a team color-coded bar with the player's name, position and team. The NBA Jam Session logo is superposed on the lower right corner. The backs are divided in half vertically with the left side carrying a second action shot and on the right side a panel with a background that fades from green to white. On the panel appears biography, career highlights, statistics and team logo. The cards are numbered on the back and checklisted below alphabetically within and according to teams. Rookie Cards of note include Anfernee Hardaway, Jamal Mashburn and Chris Webber.

COMPLETE SET (240) 18.00 30.00
1 Stacey Augmon .05 .15
2 Mookie Blaylock .08 .25
3 Doug Edwards RC .05 .15
4 Duane Ferrell .05 .15
5 Paul Graham .05 .15
6 Adam Keefe .05 .15
7 Jon Koncak .05 .15
8 Dominique Wilkins .20 .50
9 Kevin Willis .05 .15
10 Alaa Abdelnaby .05 .15
11 Dee Brown .05 .15
12 Sherman Douglas .05 .15
13 Rick Fox .05 .15
14 Kevin Gamble .05 .15
15 Xavier McDaniel .05 .15
16 Robert Parish .08 .25
17 Muggsy Bogues .08 .25
18 Scott Burrell RC .20 .50
19 Dell Curry .05 .15
20 Kenny Gattison .05 .15
21 Hersey Hawkins .08 .25
22 Eddie Johnson .05 .15
23 Larry Johnson .20 .50
24 Alonzo Mourning .25 .60
25 Johnny Newman .05 .15
26 David Wingate .05 .15
27 B.J. Armstrong .05 .15
28 Corie Blount RC .05 .15
29 Bill Cartwright .05 .15
30 Horace Grant .08 .25
31 Stacey King .05 .15
32 John Paxson .05 .15
33 Michael Jordan 2.50 6.00
34 Scottie Pippen .60 1.50
35 Scott Williams .05 .15
36 Terrell Brandon .08 .25
37 Brad Daugherty .05 .15
38 Danny Ferry .05 .15
39 Tyrone Hill .05 .15
40 Chris Mills RC .20 .50
41 Larry Nance .05 .15
42 Mark Price .05 .15
43 Gerald Wilkins .05 .15
44 John Williams .05 .15
45 Terry Davis .05 .15
46 Derek Harper .08 .25
47 Donald Hodge .05 .15
48 Jim Jackson .08 .25
49 Jamal Mashburn RC .40 1.00
50 Sean Rooks .05 .15
51 Doug Smith .05 .15
52 Mahmoud Abdul-Rauf .05 .15
53 Kevin Brooks .05 .15
54 LaPhonso Ellis .05 .15
55 Mark Macon .05 .15
56 Dikembe Mutombo .08 .25
57 Rodney Rogers RC .20 .50
58 Bryant Stith .05 .15
59 Reggie Williams .05 .15
60 Joe Dumars .20 .50
61 Sean Elliott .08 .25
62 Bill Laimbeer .05 .15
63 Terry Mills .05 .15
64 Olden Polynice .05 .15
65 Alvin Robertson .05 .15
66 Isiah Thomas .20 .50
67 Victor Alexander .05 .15
68 Chris Gatling .05 .15
69 Tim Hardaway .20 .50
70 Byron Houston .05 .15
71 Sarunas Marciulionis .05 .15
72 Chris Mullin .20 .50
73 Billy Owens .05 .15
74 Latrell Sprewell .50 1.25
75 Chris Webber RC 2.00 5.00
76 Scott Brooks .05 .15
77 Matt Bullard .05 .15
78 Sam Cassell RC .50 1.25
79 Mario Elie .05 .15
80 Carl Herrera .05 .15
81 Robert Horry .08 .25
82 Vernon Maxwell .05 .15
83 Hakeem Olajuwon .30 .75
84 Kenny Smith .05 .15
85 Otis Thorpe .08 .25
86 Dale Davis .05 .15
87 Vern Fleming .05 .15
88 Scott Haskin RC .05 .15
89 Reggie Miller .20 .50
90 Sam Mitchell .05 .15
91 Pooh Richardson .05 .15
92 Detlef Schrempf .08 .25
93 Malik Sealy .05 .15
94 Rik Smits .08 .25
95 Terry Dehere RC .05 .15
96 Ron Harper .08 .25
97 Mark Jackson .08 .25
98 Danny Manning .08 .25
99 Stanley Roberts .05 .15
100 Loy Vaught .05 .15
101 John Williams .05 .15
102 Sam Bowie .05 .15
103 Elden Campbell .05 .15
104 Doug Christie .05 .15
105 Vlade Divac .08 .25
106 James Edwards .05 .15
107 George Lynch RC .05 .15
108 Anthony Peeler .05 .15
109 Sedale Threatt .05 .15
110 James Worthy .20 .50
111 Bimbo Coles .05 .15
112 Grant Long .05 .15
113 Harold Miner .05 .15
114 Glen Rice .08 .25
115 John Salley .05 .15
116 Rony Seikaly .05 .15
117 Brian Shaw .05 .15
118 Steve Smith .20 .50
119 Anthony Avent .05 .15
120 Vin Baker RC .50 1.25
121 Jon Barry .05 .15
122 Frank Brickowski .05 .15
123 Todd Day .05 .15
124 Blue Edwards .05 .15
125 Brad Lohaus .05 .15
126 Lee Mayberry .05 .15
127 Eric Murdock .05 .15
128 Ken Norman .05 .15
129 Thurl Bailey .05 .15
130 Mike Brown .05 .15
131 Christian Laettner .08 .25
132 Luc Longley .08 .25
133 Chuck Person .05 .15
134 Chris Smith .05 .15
135 Doug West .05 .15
136 Micheal Williams .05 .15
137 Kenny Anderson .08 .25
138 Benoit Benjamin .05 .15
139 Derrick Coleman .08 .25
140 Armon Gilliam .05 .15
141 Rick Mahorn .05 .15
142 Chris Morris .05 .15
143 Rumeal Robinson .05 .15
144 Rex Walters RC .05 .15
145 Greg Anthony .05 .15
146 Rolando Blackman .05 .15
147 Tony Campbell .05 .15
148 Hubert Davis .05 .15
149 Patrick Ewing .20 .50
150 Anthony Mason .08 .25
151 Charles Oakley .08 .25
152 Doc Rivers .08 .25
153 Charles Smith .05 .15
154 John Starks .08 .25
155 Herb Williams .05 .15
156 Nick Anderson .08 .25
157 Anthony Bowie .05 .15
158 Litterial Green .05 .15
159 Anfernee Hardaway RC 1.50 4.00
160 Shaquille O'Neal 1.00 2.50
161 Donald Royal .05 .15
162 Dennis Scott .05 .15
163 Scott Skiles .05 .15
164 Jeff Turner .05 .15
165 Dana Barros .05 .15
166 Shawn Bradley RC .20 .50
167 Johnny Dawkins .05 .15
168 Greg Graham RC .05 .15
169 Jeff Hornacek .08 .25
170 Moses Malone .20 .50
171 Tim Perry .05 .15
172 Clarence Weatherspoon .05 .15
173 Danny Ainge .08 .25
174 Charles Barkley .30 .75
175 Cedric Ceballos .08 .25
176 A.C. Green .08 .25
177 Frank Johnson .05 .15
178 Kevin Johnson .08 .25
179 Negele Knight .05 .15
180 Malcolm Mackey RC .05 .15
181 Dan Majerle .08 .25
182 Oliver Miller .05 .15
183 Mark West .05 .15
184 Clyde Drexler .20 .50
185 Chris Dudley .05 .15
186 Harvey Grant .05 .15
187 Jerome Kersey .05 .15
188 Terry Porter .05 .15
189 Clifford Robinson .08 .25
190 James Robinson RC .05 .15
191 Rod Strickland .08 .25
192 Buck Williams .05 .15
193 Randy Brown .05 .15
194 Duane Causwell .05 .15
195 Bobby Hurley RC .08 .25
196 Mitch Richmond .20 .50
197 Lionel Simmons .05 .15
198 Wayman Tisdale .05 .15
199 Spud Webb .08 .25
200 Walt Williams .05 .15
201 Willie Anderson .05 .15
202 Antoine Carr .05 .15
203 Terry Cummings .05 .15
204 Lloyd Daniels .05 .15
205 Vinny Del Negro .05 .15
206 Sleepy Floyd .05 .15
207 Avery Johnson .05 .15
208 J.R. Reid .05 .15
209 David Robinson .30 .75
210 Dennis Rodman .25 .60
211 Michael Cage .05 .15
212 Kendall Gill .08 .25
213 Ervin Johnson RC .08 .25
214 Shawn Kemp .20 .50
215 Derrick McKey .05 .15
216 Nate McMillan .05 .15
217 Gary Payton .30 .75
218 Sam Perkins .08 .25
219 Ricky Pierce .05 .15
220 Isaac Austin .05 .15
221 David Benoit .05 .15
222 Tom Chambers .05 .15
223 Tyrone Corbin .05 .15
224 Mark Eaton .05 .15
225 Jay Humphries .05 .15
226 Jeff Malone .05 .15
227 Karl Malone .50 1.25
228 John Stockton .30 .75
229 Luther Wright RC .05 .15
230 Michael Adams .05 .15
231 Calbert Cheaney RC .08 .25
232 Kevin Duckworth .05 .15
233 Pervis Ellison .05 .15
234 Tom Gugliotta .20 .50
235 Buck Johnson .05 .15
236 Doug Overton .05 .15
237 LaBradford Smith .05 .15
238 Larry Stewart .05 .15
239 Checklist .05 .15
240 Checklist .05 .15

1993-94 Jam Session Gamebreakers

Randomly inserted into 12-card packs at a rate of one in four, this eight-card 2 1/2" by 4 3/4" set features some of the NBA's top players. The borderless fronts feature color action cutouts on multicolored backgrounds highlighted by grid lines. The player's name appears in gold foil at the lower left. The back features a color player head shot with a screened background similar to the front. The player's name appears above the photo, career highlights appear below. The cards are numbered on the back as "X of 8."

COMPLETE SET (8) 2.00 4.00
1 Charles Barkley .50 1.25
2 Tim Hardaway .30 .75
3 Kevin Johnson .20 .50
4 Dan Majerle .20 .50
5 Scottie Pippen 1.00 2.50
6 Mark Price .08 .25
7 John Starks .20 .50
8 Dominique Wilkins .30 .75

1993-94 Jam Session Rookie Standouts

Randomly inserted in 12-card packs at a rate of one in four, this oversized (2 1/2" by 4 3/4") eight-card set features borderless fronts with full-color player action photos. The player's name appears in gold-foil lettering in the lower left corner. The back features a color player action head shot with the player's statistics below. The cards are numbered on the back as "X of 8."

COMPLETE SET (8) 10.00 20.00
1 Vin Baker 1.25 3.00
2 Shawn Bradley .50 1.25
3 Calbert Cheaney .30 .75
4 Anfernee Hardaway UER 4.00 10.00
Text states drafted after
senior year instead of junior
5 Bobby Hurley .20 .50
6 Jamal Mashburn 1.00 2.50
7 Rodney Rogers .30 .75
8 Chris Webber 5.00 12.00

1993-94 Jam Session Second Year Stars

Randomly inserted into Jam Session 12-card packs at a rate of one in four, this eight-card 2 1/2" by 4 3/4" set features some of the NBA's top second-year players. The borderless fronts feature a color action cutout on a rainbow-colored background. The player's name appears in gold foil in the lower right. The back features a color player head shot with screened rainbow background. The players name appears above the photo with a player profile displayed below. The cards are numbered on the back as "X of 8.

COMPLETE SET (8) 2.50 5.00
1 Tom Gugliotta .30 .75
2 Jim Jackson .15 .40
3 Christian Laettner .15 .40
4 Oliver Miller .08 .25
5 Harold Miner .08 .25
6 Alonzo Mourning .40 1.00
7 Shaquille O'Neal 1.50 4.00
8 Walt Williams .08 .25

1993-94 Jam Session Slam Dunk Heroes

Randomly inserted in 12-card Jam Session packs at a rate of one in four, this eight-card 2 1/2" by 4 3/4" set features some of the NBA's top slam dunkers. The borderless fronts feature color action cutouts on multicolored posterized background. The player's name appears vertically in gold foil near the bottom. The back features a color player head shot. The player's name appears above the photo, a player profile is displayed below. The cards are numbered on the back as "X of 8."

COMPLETE SET (8) 3.00 8.00
1 Patrick Ewing .25 .60
2 Larry Johnson .30 .75
3 Shawn Kemp .30 .75
4 Karl Malone .75 2.00
5 Alonzo Mourning .40 1.00
6 Hakeem Olajuwon .50 1.25
7 Shaquille O'Neal 1.50 4.00
8 David Robinson .50 1.25

1993-94 Jam Session Team Night Sheets

These perforated Jam Session sheets were apparently handed out on game nights at various NBA arenas. Some sheets consists of eight cards, arranged in two rows of four each; other sheets had a third row for a total of 12 cards. Other sheets are known to exist (e.g., Orlando); furthermore, some sheets have cards that were created for the team night sheets but were never issued in the basic set (e.g., Kukoc, Hardaway, and Van Exel). If separated, the cards measure 2 1/2" by 4 3/4". The cards have the same design as the regular 1993-94 Jam Session cards, except that they are unnumbered. The sheets are checklisted below in alphabetical order by team name.

COMPLETE SET (9) 12.00 30.00
1 Alaa Abdelnaby 2.00 5.00
Dee Brown
Sherman Douglas
Rick Fox
Kevin Gamble
Xavier McDaniel
Robert Parish 00
Sony (Ad card)
2 Quinn Buckner CO 2.50 6.00
Terry Davis
Lucious Harris
Donald Hodge
Jim Jackson
Popeye Jones
Tom Legler
Fat Lever
Jamal Mashburn
Sean Rooks
Doug Smith
Doritos (Ad Card)
3 B.J. Armstrong 2.50 6.00
Corie Blount
Bill Cartwright
Horace Grant
Phil Jackson CO
Stacey King
Toni Kukoc
John Paxson
Will Perdue
Scottie Pippen
Scott Williams
Rust-oleum (Ad Card)
4 Joe Dumars 2.00 5.00
Sean Elliott
Bill Laimbeer
Terry Mills
Olden Polynice
Isiah Thomas
Pistons Logo
LCI International (Ad card)
5 Larry Brown CO 2.00 5.00
Antonio Davis
Dale Davis
Vern Fleming
Scott Haskin
Derrick McKey
Reggie Miller
Sam Mitchell
Pooh Richardson
Malik Sealy
Rik Smits
Combos Snacks (Ad card)
6 Mark Aguirre 2.00 5.00
Terry Dehere
Gary Grant
Ron Harper
Mark Jackson
Danny Manning
Stanley Roberts
Elmore Spencer
Tom Tolbert
Loy Vaught
Bob Weiss CO
Snickers
Kudos (Ad card)
7 Sam Bowie 2.00 5.00
Elden Campbell
Doug Christie
Vlade Divac
James Edwards
George Lynch
Anthony Peeler
Tony Smith
Sedale Threatt
Nick Van Exel
Team Logo
8 Vin Baker 2.50 6.00
Jon Barry
Frank Brickowski
Todd Day
Blue Edwards
Brad Lohaus
Lee Mayberry
Eric Murdock
Ken Norman
Danny Schayes
Derek Strong
Usinger's (Ad card)
9 Greg Anthony 2.00 5.00
Rolando Blackman
Hubert Davis
Patrick Ewing
Derek Harper
Anthony Mason
Charles Oakley
Charles Smith
John Starks
Herb Williams
WIZ (Two ad cards)

1993-94 Jam Session Ticket Stubs

During the All-Star Weekend, these ticket stub cards were given only to the public. No cards were given out with stubs attached. Without the stubs attached, the cards measure approximately 2 1/2" by 4 3/4". One card was given out during each of the four days of the event: Thursday (Barkley), Friday (Pippen), Saturday (O'Neal), and Sunday (Drexler/Robinson). The fronts feature full-bleed color action player photos except at the bottom where the pictures are edged by a blue fading to red stripe. A Fleer "All Star NBA Jam Session" logo is printed at the lower left. On a white background, the backs contain text describing the conditions governing the use of this ticket. The cards are unnumbered and checklisted below in alphabetical order. Cards found with the stub still intact are valued at five times the values listed below.

COMPLETE SET (4) 6.00 15.00
1 Charles Barkley 1.50 4.00
2 Clyde Drexler 1.50 4.00
David Robinson
3 Shaquille O'Neal 4.00 10.00
4 Scottie Pippen 2.50 6.00

1994-95 Jam Session

The complete 1994-95 Jam Session set consists of 200 oversized (2 1/2" by 4 3/4") cards. The cards were issued in 12-card packs with 36 packs per box. Each pack has one card from one of the four insert sets. Suggested retail price was $1.59 per pack. Cello packs consisting of three player cards and a cover card were given away at McDonald's restaurants in the Phoenix area to promote the Jam Session featured at the NBA All-Star weekend. The fronts have full-bleed color action photos that are tightly cropped so the player takes up a larger percentage of the card than in most sets. The NBA Jam Session logo is superimposed on the lower right corner and the player's name and team is just above it in the teams color. The backs have color-action photos on the right side with statistics and information on the left that is set against the color of the player's team. The entire card is UV coated as are all the insert sets. The cards are numbered on the back and grouped alphabetically within teams. Rookie Cards of note in this set include Grant Hill, Eddie Jones and Jason Kidd.

COMPLETE SET (200) 10.00 25.00
1 Stacey Augmon .20 .50
2 Mookie Blaylock .15 .40
3 Tyrone Corbin .15 .40
4 Craig Ehlo .15 .40
5 Ken Norman .15 .40
6 Kevin Willis .15 .40
7 Dee Brown .15 .40
8 Sherman Douglas .15 .40
9 Acie Earl .15 .40
10 Blue Edwards .15 .40
11 Pervis Ellison .15 .40
12 Rick Fox .15 .40
13 Xavier McDaniel .15 .40
14 Eric Montross RC .25 .60
15 Dino Radja .20 .50
16 Dominique Wilkins .30 .75
17 Michael Adams .15 .40
18 Muggsy Bogues .20 .50
19 Dell Curry .15 .40
20 Kenny Gattison .15 .40
21 Hersey Hawkins .15 .40
22 Larry Johnson .25 .60
23 Alonzo Mourning .30 .75
24 Robert Parish .25 .60
25 B.J. Armstrong .15 .40
26 Ron Harper .20 .50
27 Steve Kerr .20 .50
28 Toni Kukoc .30 .75
29 Pete Myers .15 .40
30 Will Perdue .15 .40
31 Scottie Pippen .50 1.25
32 Terrell Brandon .15 .40
33 Michael Cage .15 .40
34 Brad Daugherty .20 .50
35 Chris Mills .15 .40
36 Bobby Phills .15 .40
37 Mark Price .25 .60
38 Gerald Wilkins .15 .40
39 John Williams .15 .40
40 Jim Jackson .15 .40
41 Jason Kidd RC 1.25 3.00
42 Jamal Mashburn .25 .60
43 Sean Rooks .15 .40
44 Doug Smith .15 .40
45 Mahmoud Abdul-Rauf .15 .40
46 LaPhonso Ellis .15 .40
47 Dikembe Mutombo .25 .60
48 Robert Pack .15 .40
49 Rodney Rogers .15 .40
50 Jalen Rose RC .60 1.50
51 Bryant Stith .15 .40
52 Reggie Williams .15 .40
53 Bill Curley RC .25 .60
54 Joe Dumars .25 .60
55 Grant Hill RC 1.25 3.00
56 Allan Houston .25 .60
57 Lindsey Hunter .15 .40
58 Oliver Miller .15 .40
59 Terry Mills .15 .40
60 Mark West .15 .40
61 Chris Gatling .15 .40
62 Tim Hardaway .25 .60
63 Chris Mullin .25 .60
64 Billy Owens .15 .40
65 Ricky Pierce .15 .40
66 Latrell Sprewell .30 .75
67 Chris Webber .40 1.00
68 Sam Cassell .25 .60
69 Mario Elie .15 .40
70 Carl Herrera .15 .40
71 Robert Horry .25 .60
72 Vernon Maxwell .15 .40
73 Hakeem Olajuwon .30 .75
74 Kenny Smith .20 .50
75 Otis Thorpe .15 .40
76 Antonio Davis .15 .40
77 Dale Davis .15 .40
78 Mark Jackson .25 .60
79 Derrick McKey .15 .40
80 Reggie Miller .30 .75
81 Byron Scott .20 .50
82 Rik Smits .20 .50
83 Haywoode Workman .15 .40
84 Gary Grant .15 .40
85 Pooh Richardson .15 .40
86 Stanley Roberts .15 .40
87 Elmore Spencer .15 .40
88 Loy Vaught .15 .40
89 Elden Campbell .15 .40
90 Cedric Ceballos .15 .40
91 Doug Christie .15 .40
92 Vlade Divac .25 .60
93 Eddie Jones RC .75 2.00
94 George Lynch .15 .40
95 Anthony Peeler .15 .40
96 Nick Van Exel .25 .60
97 James Worthy .30 .75
98 Grant Long .15 .40
99 Harold Miner .15 .40
100 Glen Rice .25 .60
101 John Salley .15 .40
102 Rony Seikaly .20 .50
103 Steve Smith .20 .50
104 Vin Baker .25 .60
105 Jon Barry .15 .40
106 Todd Day .15 .40
107 Lee Mayberry .15 .40
108 Eric Murdock .15 .40
109 Stacey King .15 .40
110 Christian Laettner .20 .50
111 Donyell Marshall RC .25 .60
112 Isaiah Rider .25 .60
113 Doug West .15 .40
114 Micheal Williams .15 .40
115 Kenny Anderson .20 .50
116 P.J. Brown .15 .40
117 Derrick Coleman .20 .50
118 Yinka Dare RC .25 .60
119 Kevin Edwards .15 .40
120 Armon Gilliam .15 .40
121 Chris Morris .15 .40
122 Anthony Bonner .15 .40
123 Hubert Davis .15 .40
124 Patrick Ewing .30 .75
125 Derek Harper .20 .50
126 Anthony Mason .15 .40
127 Charles Oakley .20 .50
128 Doc Rivers .20 .50
129 Charles Smith .15 .40
130 John Starks .20 .50
131 Charlie Ward RC .25 .60
132 Nick Anderson .15 .40
133 Anthony Bowie .15 .40
134 Horace Grant .20 .50
135 Anfernee Hardaway .40 1.00
136 Shaquille O'Neal .60 1.50
137 Dennis Scott .15 .40
138 Jeff Turner .15 .40
139 Dana Barros .15 .40
140 Shawn Bradley .15 .40
141 Johnny Dawkins .15 .40
142 Jeff Malone .15 .40
143 Tim Perry .15 .40
144 Clarence Weatherspoon .15 .40
145 Scott Williams .15 .40
146 Danny Ainge .25 .60
147 Charles Barkley .40 1.00
148 A.C. Green .25 .60
149 Kevin Johnson .25 .60
150 Joe Kleine .15 .40
151 Antonio Lang .25 .60
152 Dan Majerle .25 .60
153 Danny Manning .20 .50
154 Wayman Tisdale .15 .40
155 Clyde Drexler .30 .75
156 Harvey Grant .15 .40
157 Tracy Murray .15 .40
158 Terry Porter .15 .40
159 Clifford Robinson .15 .40
160 Rod Strickland .15 .40
161 Buck Williams .15 .40
162 Bobby Hurley .25 .60
163 Olden Polynice .15 .40
164 Mitch Richmond .25 .60
165 Lionel Simmons .15 .40
166 Spud Webb .25 .60
167 Walt Williams .15 .40
168 Willie Anderson .15 .40
169 Terry Cummings .25 .60
170 Vinny Del Negro .15 .40
171 Sean Elliott .25 .60
172 Avery Johnson .20 .50
173 Chuck Person .20 .50
174 J.R. Reid .15 .40
175 David Robinson .40 1.00
176 Dennis Rodman .50 1.25
177 Bill Cartwright .20 .50
178 Kendall Gill .15 .40
179 Shawn Kemp .25 .60
180 Nate McMillan .15 .40
181 Gary Payton .25 .60
182 Sam Perkins .15 .40
183 Detlef Schrempf .25 .60
184 David Benoit .15 .40
185 Jeff Hornacek .20 .50
186 Jay Humphries .15 .40
187 Karl Malone .30 .75
188 Bryon Russell .15 .40
189 Felton Spencer .15 .40
190 John Stockton .30 .75
191 Mitchell Butler .15 .40
192 Rex Chapman .15 .40
193 Calbert Cheaney .15 .40
194 Tom Gugliotta .15 .40
195 Don MacLean .15 .40
196 Gheorghe Muresan .15 .40
197 Scott Skiles .15 .40
198 Checklist .15 .40
199 Checklist .15 .40
200 Checklist .15 .40

1994-95 Jam Session Flashing Stars

This eight card oversized (2 1/2" by 4 3/4") set was randomly inserted in 12-card packs at a rate of approximately one in two. The set is composed of the flashiest players in the game like Anfernee Hardaway and Reggie Miller. The fronts have full-bleed color action photos similar to the regular set but the background has swirling colors. The player's name and words "Flashing Star" are in gold foil at the bottom. The NBA Jam Session logo is superimposed on the upper right corner. The backs have color action photos and information explaining why he is a "Flashing star." The cards are numbered on the back as "X of 8" and are sequenced in alphabetical order.

COMPLETE SET (8) 2.00 5.00
1 Anfernee Hardaway .75 2.00
2 Robert Horry .50 1.25
3 Dan Majerle .50 1.25
4 Reggie Miller .60 1.50
5 Mitch Richmond .50 1.25
6 Isaiah Rider .50 1.25
7 Latrell Sprewell .60 1.50
8 Dominique Wilkins .60 1.50

1994-95 Jam Session Gamebreakers

This eight card oversized (2 1/2" by 4 3/4") set was randomly inserted in 12-card packs at a rate of one in four. The set is composed of players who can take control of the game. The fronts have full-bleed color action photos similar to the regular set but the background is a basketball going through a net. The player image is also pushed out slightly which can also be seen from the back to give it a 3-D look. The NBA Jam Session logo is superimposed on the upper right corner. The backs have three layers to it. The background has two colors that are different on each card. A full-color action photo of the player is the middle layer. Up front is the player name in the middle and player information is a hazy white box underneath. The cards are numbered on the back as "X of 8" and are sequenced in alphabetical order.

COMPLETE SET (8) 3.00 8.00
1 Charles Barkley .75 2.00
2 Patrick Ewing .60 1.50
3 Karl Malone .60 1.50
4 Alonzo Mourning .60 1.50
5 Hakeem Olajuwon .60 1.50
6 Shaquille O'Neal 1.25 3.00
7 Scottie Pippen 1.00 2.50
8 David Robinson .75 2.00

1994-95 Jam Session Rookie Standouts

This 20-card oversized (2 1/2" by 4 3/4") set was available exclusively via mail. Information on obtaining the set was on the packs and you had to pay $3.95 to receive the set. The wrapper offer expired on June 30th, 1995. The set contains a selection of the top rookies from the 1994-95 season. The fronts have full-bleed color action photos on a painted background with a black and white action photo in the looming behind. The NBA Jam Session logo is superimposed on the upper left corner. The player's name and the "Rookie Standout" with a basketball under it are in gold foil at the bottom of the card. The backs have a full color action photo also on a painted background and information on the rookie particularly about his college career. The cards are numbered on the back as "X of 20" and are sequenced in alphabetical order.

COMPLETE SET (20) 5.00 12.00
1 Brian Grant .40 1.00
2 Grant Hill 1.25 3.00
3 Juwan Howard .40 1.00
4 Eddie Jones .75 2.00
5 Jason Kidd 1.25 3.00
6 Donyell Marshall .25 .60
7 Eric Montross .25 .60
8 Lamond Murray .25 .60
9 Wesley Person .25 .60
10 Khalid Reeves .25 .60
11 Glenn Robinson .50 1.25
12 Carlos Rogers .25 .60
13 Jalen Rose .60 1.50
14 Clifford Rozier .25 .60
15 Dickey Simpkins .25 .60
16 Michael Smith .25 .60
17 Anthony Tucker .25 .60
18 Charlie Ward .25 .60
19 Monty Williams .25 .60
20 Sharone Wright .25 .60

1994-95 Jam Session Second Year Stars

This eight card oversized (2 1/2" by 4 3/4") set was randomly inserted in 12-card packs at a rate of one in four. The set consists of the best rookies from the 93-94 crop. The fronts are laid out horizontally and have full-bleed color action photos. The player is surrounded by a glowing yellow. The background has a close-up of his face from the action shot and copies of the shot in television screens behind that. The bottom says the player's name and "Second Year Star" in gold foil. The backs are laid out vertically with a full color action photo also surrounded by a glowing yellow on the left with player information on the right. The background is the same player photo set in numerous television screens similar to the front. The cards are numbered on the back as "X of 8" and are sequenced in alphabetical order.

COMPLETE SET (8) 2.00 5.00
1 Vin Baker .50 1.25
2 Anfernee Hardaway .75 2.00
3 Lindsey Hunter .30 .75
4 Toni Kukoc .60 1.50
5 Jamal Mashburn .50 1.25
6 Dino Radja .40 1.00
7 Isaiah Rider .50 1.25
8 Chris Webber .75 2.00

1994-95 Jam Session Slam Dunk Heroes

Cards from this eight-card oversized (2 1/2" by 4 3/4") set were randomly inserted in packs at a rate of one in 36. The set is made up of players who jam with authority, namely centers and forwards. The cards have a 100% etched foil design. The fronts have a full color action photo with the player's name and the words "Slam Dunk Hero" boxing in a net are at the bottom in gold foil. The backs have a fuller color action photo on the left with player information on the right. The background on both the fronts and backs have a psychedelic look to it with basketballs floating about. The cards are numbered on the back as "X of 8" and are sequenced in alphabetical order.

COMPLETE SET (8) 25.00 60.00
1 Charles Barkley 5.00 12.00
2 Larry Johnson 3.00 8.00
3 Shawn Kemp 3.00 8.00
4 Jamal Mashburn 3.00 8.00
5 Dikembe Mutombo 3.00 8.00
6 Hakeem Olajuwon 4.00 10.00
7 Shaquille O'Neal 8.00 20.00
8 Chris Webber 5.00 12.00

1995-96 Jam Session

The 1995-96 NBA Jam Session regular card set was issued in one series of 118 cards with 2 checklist cards. Cards were distributed in eight card hobby and retail packs carrying a suggested retail price of $1.59. Forty of the cards are titled "Connection Collection" and feature two players that form a unique tandem. The 78 regular cards are full-bleed color player action photos with a strip at the top with the word "JAM" repeating. Backs include a full color action player shot with a screened strip containing the players biography, a short personality profile, a player rating and NBA career summary. The "Connection Collection" cards are borderless with one-color backgrounds and a full-color action player cutout. Backs of the Connection Collection cards feature an extreme vertical and skewed full-color action photo of the player with a player biography, career stats and a short player profile. Cards are grouped alphabetically by team name. There are no Rookie Cards in this set.

COMPLETE SET (120) 10.00 25.00
1 Stacey Augmon CC .20 .50
2 Mookie Blaylock .15 .40
3 Grant Long .15 .40
4 Steve Smith .20 .50
5 Dee Brown CC .15 .40
6 Sherman Douglas .15 .40
7 Eric Montross .15 .40
8 Dino Radja .20 .50
9 Muggsy Bogues CC .20 .50
10 Scott Burrell .15 .40
11 Larry Johnson CC .25 .60
12 Alonzo Mourning .30 .75
13 Michael Jordan CC 2.00 5.00
14 Steve Kerr .20 .50
15 Toni Kukoc CC .25 .60
16 Scottie Pippen .40 1.00
17 Terrell Brandon .15 .40
18 Tyrone Hill .15 .40
19 Mark Price CC .25 .60
20 John Williams .15 .40
21 Jim Jackson .15 .40
22 Popeye Jones CC .15 .40
23 Jason Kidd CC .40 1.00
24 Jamal Mashburn .25 .60
25 Mahmoud Abdul-Rauf .15 .40
26 Dikembe Mutombo CC .25 .60
27 Robert Pack CC .15 .40
28 Jalen Rose .30 .75
29 Joe Dumars CC .25 .60
30 Grant Hill CC .40 1.00
31 Allan Houston .20 .50
32 Terry Mills .15 .40
33 Chris Gatling .15 .40
34 Tim Hardaway CC .25 .60
35 Donyell Marshall .15 .40
36 Chris Mullin CC .25 .60
37 Latrell Sprewell .25 .60
38 Sam Cassell .25 .60
39 Clyde Drexler CC .30 .75
40 Robert Horry .20 .50
41 Hakeem Olajuwon CC .30 .75
42 Kenny Smith .20 .50
43 Dale Davis .15 .40
44 Mark Jackson .25 .60
45 Reggie Miller CC .30 .75
46 Rik Smits .20 .50
47 Lamond Murray .15 .40
48 Pooh Richardson CC .15 .40
49 Malik Sealy .15 .40
50 Loy Vaught .15 .40
51 Cedric Ceballos .15 .40
52 Vlade Divac .25 .60
53 Eddie Jones .30 .75
54 Nick Van Exel .25 .60
55 Billy Owens .15 .40
56 Khalid Reeves .15 .40
57 Glen Rice CC .25 .60
58 Kevin Willis .15 .40
59 Vin Baker .20 .50
60 Todd Day .15 .40
61 Eric Murdock .15 .40
62 Glenn Robinson CC .25 .60
63 Tom Gugliotta .15 .40
64 Christian Laettner CC .20 .50
65 Isaiah Rider CC .25 .60
66 Doug West .15 .40
67 Kenny Anderson .20 .50
68 P.J. Brown .15 .40
69 Derrick Coleman .20 .50
70 Armon Gilliam .15 .40
71 Patrick Ewing CC .30 .75
72 Derek Harper .20 .50
73 Charles Oakley .20 .50
74 John Starks CC .20 .50
75 Horace Grant CC .20 .50
76 Anfernee Hardaway CC .40 1.00
77 Shaquille O'Neal CC .60 1.50
78 Dennis Scott .15 .40
79 Dana Barros CC .15 .40
80 Shawn Bradley .15 .40
81 Clarence Weatherspoon .15 .40
82 Sharone Wright .15 .40
83 Charles Barkley CC .40 1.00
84 Kevin Johnson CC .25 .60
85 Dan Majerle CC .25 .60
86 Wesley Person CC .15 .40
87 Harvey Grant .15 .40
88 Clifford Robinson .15 .40
89 Rod Strickland .15 .40
90 Buck Williams .15 .40
91 Brian Grant .20 .50
92 Olden Polynice .15 .40
93 Mitch Richmond .25 .60
94 Walt Williams .15 .40
95 Sean Elliott .25 .60
96 Avery Johnson .20 .50
97 David Robinson CC .40 1.00
98 Dennis Rodman .50 1.25
99 Shawn Kemp CC .25 .60
100 Nate McMillan .15 .40
101 Gary Payton .25 .60
102 Detlef Schrempf .25 .60
103 Willie Anderson .15 .40
104 Jerome Kersey .15 .40
105 Oliver Miller .15 .40
106 Ed Pinckney CC .15 .40
107 David Benoit .15 .40
108 Jeff Hornacek CC .20 .50
109 Karl Malone CC .30 .75
110 John Stockton .30 .75
111 Greg Anthony .15 .40
112 Benoit Benjamin .15 .40
113 Blue Edwards .15 .40
114 Kenny Gattison .15 .40
115 Calbert Cheaney .15 .40
116 Juwan Howard .25 .60
117 Gheorghe Muresan CC .15 .40
118 Chris Webber CC .30 .75
119 Checklist .15 .40
120 Checklist .15 .40
NNO Grant Hill Foil Tribute 12.50 30.00

1995-96 Jam Session Die Cuts

This 120-card die cut set parallels the 1995-96 Jam Session set. One die cut card was inserted into each pack. These cards are identical to their regular issue counterparts except for the different die-cut styles at the top (or bottom) of the card; in addition, these die-cut cards can be distinguished by a "D" prefix before the card number. Please refer to the multipliers provided in the header to ascertain values.

COMPLETE SET (120) 25.00 60.00
*DIE CUTS: .75X TO 2X HI COLUMN

1995-96 Jam Session Fuel Injectors

Randomly inserted into all packs at a rate of one in 36, these nine cards feature hot stars of the '90s. Borderless fronts have two-toned backgrounds with the player in a full-color action cutout. The player's image has a fuzzy outline, giving it an electric look. A screened box contains the player's biography and a player profile. The player's career summary appears in black type near the bottom of the card. The set is sequenced in alphabetical order.

COMPLETE SET (9) 40.00 80.00
1 Grant Hill 6.00 15.00
2 Larry Johnson 4.00 10.00
3 Eddie Jones 5.00 12.00
4 Jason Kidd 6.00 15.00
5 Hakeem Olajuwon 5.00 12.00
6 Shaquille O'Neal 10.00 25.00
7 Scottie Pippen 6.00 15.00
8 Glenn Robinson 4.00 10.00
9 Latrell Sprewell 4.00 10.00

1995-96 Jam Session Pop-Ups

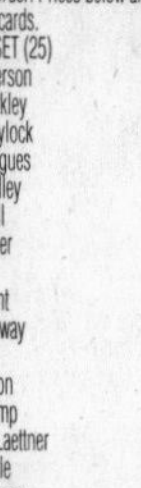

Seeded at a rate of one per pack these pop-up cards highlight the play of 25 NBA standouts. Fronts feature the player in full-color action with a crowd background printed with horizontal lines. The cards are perforated around the player's image so that it can be separated from the rest of the card, popped out and displayed standing. Card backs give instructions on how to assemble the card for display. The set is sequenced in alphabetical order. Prices below are for mint unperforated cards.

COMPLETE SET (25) 4.00 10.00
1 Kenny Anderson .25 .60
2 Charles Barkley .50 1.25
3 Mookie Blaylock .20 .50
4 Muggsy Bogues .25 .60
5 Shawn Bradley .20 .50
6 Sam Cassell .30 .75
7 Clyde Drexler .40 1.00
8 Brian Grant .25 .60
9 Horace Grant .25 .60
10 Tim Hardaway .30 .75
11 Grant Hill .50 1.25
12 Jim Jackson .20 .50
13 Shawn Kemp .30 .75
14 Christian Laettner .25 .60
15 Dan Majerle .30 .75
16 Eric Montross .20 .50
17 Alonzo Mourning .40 1.00
18 Gheorghe Muresan .20 .50
19 Lamond Murray .20 .50
20 Dikembe Mutombo .30 .75
21 Charles Oakley .25 .60
22 Scottie Pippen .50 1.25
23 Mark Price .30 .75
24 Glen Rice .30 .75
25 Clifford Robinson .20 .50

1995-96 Jam Session Pop-Ups Bonus

Randomly inserted exclusively in retail packs at a rate of one in 24, this five-card set features a selection of NBA stars. The card fronts are borderless with a full-color action shot set against a crowd background with horizontal fading lines. The player's image is perforated for pop-out assembly. The unnumbered backs include instruction for assembly of the cards. The set is sequenced in alphabetical order. Prices below refer to mint unperforated cards.

COMPLETE SET (5) 8.00 20.00
1 Patrick Ewing 3.00 8.00
2 Grant Hill 4.00 10.00
3 Glenn Robinson 2.50 6.00
4 Jason Kidd 4.00 10.00
5 Jerry Stackhouse 4.00 10.00

1995-96 Jam Session Rookies

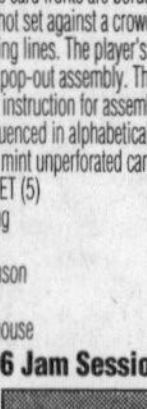

Randomly inserted in packs at a rate of one in six, cards from this 10-card set highlight the '95-96 freshman crop. Borderless fronts include a full-color player action cutout with stars winding around the player's image. "Rookie" is printed in a spiraling pattern and serves as the background. Numbered backs feature the player in a full-color cutout pose standing on a hovering star and the background continues with the spiraling pattern with the word "rookie". The player's last name appears over his head.

COMPLETE SET (10) 5.00 12.00
1 Joe Smith 1.00 2.50
2 Antonio McDyess 1.25 3.00
3 Jerry Stackhouse 1.50 4.00
4 Rasheed Wallace 1.50 4.00
5 Bryant Reeves .50 1.25
6 Shawn Respert .50 1.25
7 Cherokee Parks .50 1.25
8 Alan Henderson .50 1.25
9 George Zidek .50 1.25
10 Sherrell Ford .50 1.25

1995-96 Jam Session Show Stoppers

Randomly inserted exclusively in hobby packs at a rate of one in 48, this set of nine cards is the rarest of the '95-96 Jam Session collection and features some of the game's best players. The full-bleed, fronts show the player in a full-color cutout against a sparkling, etched blue-foil background The players name is stamped in gold foil at the bottom of the card in all caps. A digital image of the player serves as a background and a smaller full-color action player shot appears on the bottom half of the card. The player's biography and profile wrap around the color shot and his NBA totals appear at the bottom of the card. The set is sequenced in alphabetical order and is condition sensitive due to the etched foil edges.

COMPLETE SET (9) 125.00 250.00
1 Anfernee Hardaway 15.00 40.00
2 Grant Hill 15.00 40.00
3 Michael Jordan 60.00 150.00
4 Karl Malone 10.00 25.00
5 Jamal Mashburn 8.00 20.00
6 Reggie Miller 10.00 25.00
7 David Robinson 12.00 30.00
8 John Stockton 10.00 25.00
9 Chris Webber 10.00 25.00

1995 Jam Session Game Test Samples

Jam Session Test Samples was printed as a sample test card that comes from a never produced for distribution card set. The set's designer turned over his design and concept for this issue, and Fleer ran off a "test" batch of approximately 50-60 sets. The samples were returned to the designer. At this point in time, new management at Fleer decided against putting this set into production and distribution. Each card measures 2.50 x 4.75 inches.

COMPLETE SET (14) 350.00 650.00
P1 Michael Jordan 125.00 250.00
P2 Scottie Pippen 35.00 75.00
P3 Anfernee Hardaway 20.00 40.00
P4 Larry Johnson 15.00 30.00
P5 Shaquille O'Neal 40.00 80.00
P6 Alonzo Mourning 20.00 40.00
P7 Grant Hill 20.00 40.00
P8 John Stockton 50.00 100.00
P9 Karl Malone 40.00 80.00
P10 Kevin Johnson 15.00 30.00
P11 Charles Barkley 40.00 80.00
P12 David Robinson 40.00 80.00
P13 Shawn Kemp 20.00 40.00
P14 Jason Kidd 30.00 60.00

1992-93 Jazz Chevron

This set of cards and pins was sponsored by Chevron. Each card measures 2 1/2" by 5 1/4". The larger top portion presents a color action photo edged by thin team color-coded stripes and a gold section. The smaller bottom portion is white and carries the gold player pin and a Chevron advertisement. The backs display a color closeup photo, biography, checklist, and Chevron advertisement.

COMPLETE SET (5) 9.00 18.00
1 Tyrone Corbin .75 2.00
2 John Stockton 3.00 8.00
3 Jeff Malone .75 2.00
4 Tom Chambers 1.25 3.00
5 Karl Malone 3.00 8.00

1989 Jazz Old Home

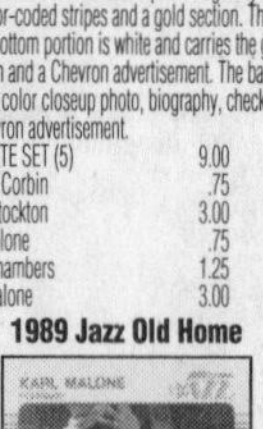

This 13-card standard-size set of Utah Jazz was sponsored by Old Home bread (and printed by Fleer), and the Old Home company logo appears on both sides of the card. The cards were distributed as an insert one per loaf of bread with a different card featured each week. The color action player photo on the front has rounded corners, and it is superimposed on a background of yellow, green, and purple stripes of varying width. The player's name and team logo appear above the picture, and the words "1989 Collector's Series" below. That statistics on the card backs are complete up through the 1987-88 season. The horizontally oriented backs are printed in pink and red and present biographical and statistical information

COMPLETE SET (13) 40.00 80.
1 Thurl Bailey 2.00 5.
2 Mike Brown 1.00 2.
3 Mark Eaton 2.00 5
4 Darrell Griffith 2.00 5
5 Bobby Hansen 1.50 4
6 Marc Iavaroni 1.50 4
7 Frank Layden CO 2.50 6
8 Eric Leckner 1.25 3
9 Jim Les 1.25 3
10 Karl Malone 12.50 30
11 Jose Ortiz 1.50 4
12 Scott Roth 1.25 3
13 John Stockton 15.00 40.

1993-94 Jazz Old Home

These 11 standard-size cards were produced by Ho for Metz Baking Co.'s Old Home Bread, and were inserted in its products. Twenty thousand cards of e player and coach were produced; 200,000 logo card were also printed up. One player card and one logo card were inserted per loaf. The card design is nearl identical to the regular 1993-94 Hoops set. The fror feature borderless glossy color player action shots, with the player's name and team logo appearing in team colors along a ghosted band at the bottom. Th back presents a color head shot of the player in a sr rectangle bordered with a team color at the upper ri Alongside is his jersey number and position within team-colored bar. The player's name and a short biography are printed on a hardwood floor design a the top. Below, the player's college and NBA stats, displayed in separate tables on a white background, round out the card. The cards are unnumbered and checklisted below in alphabetical order.

COMPLETE SET (11) 15.00 35
1 David Benoit .40 1
2 Tom Chambers 1.25 3.
3 Ty Corbin .40 1.
4 Mark Eaton .40 1.
5 Jay Humphries .40 1.
6 Jeff Malone .40 1.
7 Karl Malone 6.00 15.
8 Jerry Sloan CO 2.00 5.
9 Felton Spencer .40 1
10 John Stockton 6.00 15
11 Logo Card DP .40 1.

1988-89 Jazz Smokey

The 1988-89 Smokey Utah Jazz set contains eight 8 by 10" (approximately) cards featuring color action photos. The card backs feature a large fire safety cartoon and player information in the form of year-b year statistics for each NBA regular season and playoffs. The cards are unnumbered and are ordered below alphabetically. The set was sponsored by the Utah Department of State Lands and Forestry and U.S.D.A. Forest Service. The player's name, number and position are overprinted in white in the lower ri corner of each obverse.

COMPLETE SET (8) 45.00 85.
1 Thurl Bailey 3.00 8.
2 Mark Eaton 3.00 8.
3 Bobby Hansen 3.00 8.
4 Frank Layden CO 3.00 8.
5 Karl Malone 15.00 40.
6 Marc Iavaroni 4.00 10.
7 John Stockton 15.00 40.
8 Smokey Bear 1.25 3.

1990-91 Jazz Star

This 12-card set of Utah Jazz measures the standard size. The fronts feature color action shots, with purp borders that wash out in the middle of the card face. The horizontally oriented backs are printed in purple white and have various kinds of player information.

COMPLETE SET (12) 1.50 4.
1 Karl Malone 1.00 2.
2 John Stockton 1.00 2.
3 Mark Eaton .20
4 Blue Edwards .20
5 Thurl Bailey .20
6 Mike Brown .08
7 Jeff Malone .20
8 Andy Toolson .08
9 Darrell Griffith .20
10 Delaney Rudd .08
11 Walter Palmer .08
12 Jerry Sloan CO .20

1975-76 Jazz Team Issue

This 8"x10" set was produced for the New Orleans J during the 1975-76 season. The set features nine bl and white cards of the team's players.

COMPLETE SET (9) 12.50 25
1 Ron Behagen 1.25 3
2 Fred Boyd 1.25 3.
3 E.C. Coleman 1.25 3.

ron James	1.25	3.00
ch Kelley	1.25	3.00
n McElroy	1.25	3.00
uie Nelson	1.25	3.00
wd Stallworth	1.25	3.00
te Williams	1.25	3.00

1973-74 Jets Allentown CBA

crude eight-card set was produced by G.S. Gallery llentown, Pennsylvania, whose name and address listed at the bottom of each card. The cards feature mbers of the Allentown Jets of the CBA and sure approximately 2 5/8" by 4 1/4". Uncut sheets available as well. The card fronts are printed in k ink on light-blue construction-paper stock; the backs are blank. These sets were originally lable from the producer for less than 50 cents each uantity.

MPLETE SET (8)	15.00	30.00
ny Johnson	2.00	5.00
'ie McGuire	3.00	8.00
ank Card	2.00	5.00
orge Lehmann	2.50	6.00
nnis Bell	2.00	5.00
n Wilburn	2.00	5.00
orge Bruns	2.00	5.00
l Mast	2.50	6.00

963 Jewish Sports Champions

16 cards in this set, measuring roughly 2 2/3" x re cut out of an "Activity Funbook" entitled Jewish rts Champions. The set pays tribute to famous ish athletes from baseball, football, bull fighting to s. The cards have a green border with a yellow rground and a player close-up illustration. Cards are still attached carry a premium over those that been cut-out. The cards are unnumbered and d below in alphabetical order with an assigned t prefix (BB-baseball, BK- basketball, BX- boxing, football, OT- other).

MPLETE SET (16)	100.00	200.00
Nat Holman BK	12.50	25.00
Dolph Schayes BK	10.00	20.00

973 Jewish Sports Champions

16 cards in this set, measuring roughly 2 2/3" x re cut out of a sequel to the 1968 Activity book. This time, the cards come from a funbook led "More Jewish Sports Champions". There are variations to each card that are valued equally. One a pink border with a yellow background and blue on the player close-up illustration. The other has a background and black ink on the player tration. Cards that are still attached carry a nium over those that have been cut-out. The cards unnumbered and listed below in alphabetical order.

MPLETE SET (16)	65.00	125.00
nold (Red) Auerbach BK	15.00	30.00

1985-86 JMS Game

se standard size cards were issued by J.M.S. in t team sheets as part of a table top game and red nine players each from the Philadelphia 76ers), Boston Celtics (10-18), and Los Angeles Lakers 27). The front features a color action player photo, a blue border on red background. Player mation appears in a white capsule, and statistics given below the picture in a pink box. In a zontal format the back has a statistical breakdown by year and brief biographical information.

PLETE SET (27)	50.00	120.00
aurice Cheeks	2.00	5.00
osés Malone	2.50	6.00
obby Jones	2.00	5.00
arles Barkley	10.00	25.00
ius Erving	8.00	20.00
nt Richardson	.75	2.00
drew Toney	1.25	3.00
dale Threatt	.75	2.00
em Johnson	.75	2.00
ill Walton	3.00	8.00
anny Ainge	2.50	6.00
obert Parish	2.50	6.00
evin McHale	3.00	8.00
arry Bird	10.00	25.00
ennis Johnson	2.00	5.00
ay Williams	.75	2.00
cott Wedman	.75	2.00
reg Kite	.75	2.00
Michael Cooper	1.50	4.00
areem Abdul-Jabbar	5.00	12.00
amaal Wilkes	1.50	4.00
ob McAdoo	2.00	5.00
ames Worthy	3.00	8.00
agic Johnson	8.00	20.00
Michael McGee	.75	2.00
urt Rambis	1.50	4.00
yron Scott	2.00	5.00

1994-96 John Deere

a three year period, the John Deere tractor pany used professional athletes to promote their ucts and included cards of these athletes in their These five cards were issued in 1994 (Ryan and eck), 1995 (Jackson and Petty) and 1996 (Larry . For our cataloguing purposes we are sequencing cards in alphabetical order. Larry Bird signed e cards for this promotion but these cards are so traded that no pricing is available

PLETE SET (5)	15.00	40.00
1 Larry Bird	4.00	10.00
AU1 Larry Bird AU		

1957-58 Kahn's

The 1957-58 Kahn's Basketball set contains 11 black and white cards. Cards are approximately 3 3/16" by 3 15/16". The backs contain "How To" articles and instructional text. Only Cincinnati Royals players are depicted.

COMPLETE SET (11)	2000.00	3000.00
1 Richard Duckett	75.00	150.00
2 George King	75.00	150.00
3 Clyde Lovellette	300.00	550.00
4 Tom Marshall	75.00	150.00
5 Jim Paxson UER/(Misspelled Paxton)	150.00	275.00
6 Dave Piontek	75.00	150.00
7 Richard Regan	75.00	150.00
8 Dick Ricketts	175.00	275.00
9 Maurice Stokes	300.00	600.00
10 Jack Twyman	300.00	500.00
11 Bobby Wanzer	150.00	275.00

1958-59 Kahn's

The 1958-59 Kahn's Basketball set contains 10 black and white cards. Cards measure approximately 3 1/4" by 3 15/16". The backs feature a short narrative entitled "My Greatest Thrill in Basketball" allegedly written by the player depicted on the front. Only Cincinnati Royals players are depicted. The Sihugo Green card is supposedly a little tougher to find than the other cards in the set.

COMPLETE SET (10)	1000.00	1500.00
1 Arlen Bockhorn	60.00	125.00
2 Archie Dees	60.00	125.00
3 Sihugo Green	100.00	175.00
4 Vern Hatton	80.00	160.00
5 Tom Marshall	60.00	125.00
6 Jack Parr	80.00	160.00
7 Jim Palmer	60.00	125.00
Card lists him as George, his middle name		
8 Jim Palmer	60.00	125.00
9 Dave Piontek	60.00	125.00
10 Jack Twyman	200.00	325.00

1959-60 Kahn's

The 1959-60 Kahn's Basketball set features 10 black and white cards. Cards are approximately 3 1/4" by 4". The backs feature descriptive narratives allegedly written by the player depicted on the front. No statistics are featured on the backs. Only Cincinnati Royals players are depicted.

COMPLETE SET (10)	500.00	900.00
1 Arlen Bockhorn	50.00	100.00
2 Wayne Embry	75.00	150.00
3 Tom Marshall	50.00	100.00
4 Med Park	60.00	120.00
5 Dave Piontek	50.00	100.00
6 Hub Reed	50.00	100.00
7 Phil Rollins	50.00	100.00
8 Larry Staverman	50.00	100.00
9 Jack Twyman	100.00	225.00
10 Win Wilfong	50.00	100.00

1960-61 Kahn's

The 1960-61 Kahn's Basketball set features 12 black and white cards. Cards are approximately 3 1/4" by 3 15/16". The backs contain statistical season-by-season records up through the 1959-60 season, player vital statistics, and a short biography of the player's career. The key cards in the set are the first professional cards of Hall of Famers Oscar Robertson and Jerry West. The Lakers' Jerry West is the only non-Cincinnati Royals player depicted and his card does not have any statistical breakdown.

COMPLETE SET (12)	2000.00	3200.00
1 Arlen Bockhorn	30.00	60.00
2 Bob Boozer	45.00	90.00
3 Ralph E. Davis	25.00	60.00
4 Wayne Embry	50.00	100.00
5 Mike Farmer	25.00	60.00
6 Phil Jordan	30.00	60.00
7 Hub Reed	25.00	60.00
8 Oscar Robertson	700.00	1300.00
9 Larry Staverman	25.00	60.00
10 Jack Twyman	75.00	150.00
11 Jerry West	900.00	1500.00
12 Win Wilfong	25.00	60.00

1961-62 Kahn's

The 1961-62 Kahn's Basketball set consists of 13 black and white cards. Cards measure approximately 3 3/16" by 4 1/16". The Lakers' Jerry West is the only non-Cincinnati Royals player depicted and there is also a card of coach Charley Wolf. The backs of the cards are blank; this was the only year the Kahn's basketball cards were blank backed.

COMPLETE SET (13)	1100.00	1600.00
1 Arlen Bockhorn	20.00	50.00
2 Bob Boozer	35.00	75.00
3 Joe Buckhalter	25.00	50.00
4 Wayne Embry	30.00	60.00
5 Bob Nordmann	25.00	50.00
6 Hub Reed	25.00	50.00
7 Oscar Robertson	300.00	600.00
8 Adrian Smith	35.00	75.00
9 Jack Twyman	65.00	125.00
10 Bob Wiesenhahn	25.00	50.00
11 Jerry West	400.00	800.00
12 Charley Wolf CO	20.00	50.00
13 Dave Zeller	25.00	50.00

1962-63 Kahn's

The 1962-63 Kahn's Basketball set contains 11 black and white cards. Cards measure approximately 3 1/4" by 4 3/16". Jerry West of the Lakers is the only non-Cincinnati Royals player depicted and there is also a card of Royals' coach Charley Wolf. The backs feature a short biography of the player depicted on the front of the card. The Jerry West card has a picture with no border around it. Cards of Bockhorn, Boozer, Reed, and Twyman are oriented horizontally.

COMPLETE SET (11)	500.00	1000.00
1 Arlen Bockhorn HOR	15.00	40.00
2 Bob Boozer HOR	25.00	50.00
3 Wayne Embry	30.00	55.00
4 Tom Hawkins	30.00	65.00
5 Bud Olsen	15.00	40.00
6 Hub Reed HOR	15.00	40.00
7 Oscar Robertson	150.00	300.00
8 Adrian Smith	25.00	50.00
9 Jack Twyman HOR	40.00	80.00
10 Jerry West	200.00	400.00
11 Charley Wolf CO	15.00	40.00

1963-64 Kahn's

The 1963-64 Kahn's Basketball set contains 13 black and white cards. Cards measure approximately 3 1/4" by 4 3/16". This is the only Kahn's basketball set on which there is a distinctive white border on the fronts of the cards; in this respect the set is similar to the 1963 Kahn's baseball and football sets. A brief biography of the player is contained on the back of the card. Jerry West of the Lakers is the only non-Cincinnati Royals player depicted and there is also a card of coach Jack McMahon. The Jerry West card is identical to that of the previous year except set in smaller type and with the distinctive white border on the front. The cards of Bob Boozer and Jack Twyman are oriented horizontally.

COMPLETE SET (13)	400.00	800.00
1 Jay Arnette	15.00	30.00
2 Arlen Bockhorn	15.00	30.00
3 Bob Boozer HOR	20.00	45.00
4 Wayne Embry	20.00	45.00
5 Tom Hawkins	35.00	55.00
6 Jerry Lucas	60.00	120.00
7 Jack McMahon CO	15.00	30.00
8 Bud Olsen	15.00	30.00
9 Oscar Robertson	100.00	200.00
10 Adrian Smith	15.00	40.00
11 Tom Thacker	15.00	30.00
12 Jack Twyman HOR	30.00	65.00
13 Jerry West	125.00	250.00

1964-65 Kahn's

The 1964-65 Kahn's Basketball set contains 12 full-color subjects on 14 distinct cards. Cards measure approximately 3" by 3 5/8". These cards come in two types distinguishable by the color of the printing on the backs. Type I cards (1-3) have light maroon printing on the backs, while type II (4-12) have black printing on the backs. The fronts are completely devoid of any written material. There are two poses each of Jerry Lucas and Oscar Robertson.

COMPLETE SET (14)	325.00	650.00
1 Happy Hairston	35.00	70.00
2 Jack McMahon CO	15.00	40.00
3 George Wilson	15.00	30.00
4 Jay Arnette	15.00	30.00
5 Arlen Bockhorn	15.00	30.00
6 Wayne Embry	20.00	45.00
7 Tom Hawkins	20.00	50.00
8A Jerry Lucas (Windows open right thumb hidden)	40.00	80.00
8B Jerry Lucas No windows visible; right thumb barely visible)	40.00	80.00
9 Bud Olsen	15.00	30.00
10A Oscar Robertson Facing side	75.00	150.00
10B Oscar Robertson Facing front	75.00	150.00
11 Adrian Smith	15.00	40.00
12 Jack Twyman	30.00	60.00

1965-66 Kahn's

The 1965-66 Kahn's Basketball set contains four full-color cards featuring players of the Cincinnati Royals. Cards in this set measure approximately 3" by 3 9/16". This was the last of the Kahn's Basketball issues and the second in full color. The fronts are devoid of all written material, and the backs are printed in red ink. The "Compliments of Kahn's, The Wiener the World Awaited" slogan appears on the backs of the cards. The set is presumed complete with the following cards.

COMPLETE SET (4)	150.00	300.00
1 Wayne Embry	20.00	40.00
2 Jerry Lucas	40.00	80.00
3 Oscar Robertson	75.00	150.00
4 Jack Twyman	30.00	60.00

1971 Keds KedKards

This set is composed of crude artistic renditions of popular subjects from various sports from 1971 who were apparently celebrity endorsers of Keds shoes. The cards actually form a complete panel on the Keds tennis shoes box. The three different panels are actually different sizes; the Bing panel contains smaller cards. The smaller Bubba Smith shows him without beard and standing straight; the larger Bubba Smith shows him leaning over, with beard, and jersey number partially visible. The individual player card portions of the card panels measure approximately 2 15/16" by 2 3/4" and 2 5/16" by 2 3/16" respectively, although it should noted that there are slight size differences among the individual cards even on the same panel. The panel background is colored in black and yellow. On the Bench/Reed card (number 3 below) each player measures approximately 5 1/4" by 3 1/2". A facsimile autograph appears in the upper left corner of each player's drawing. The Bench/Reed was issued with the Keds Champion boys basketball shoe box, printed on the box top with a black broken line around the card to follow when cutting the card out.

COMPLETE SET (3)	112.50	225.00
1BK Dave Bing BK Clark Graebner/(Tennis) Bubba Smith FB Jim Maloney BB	30.00	60.00
2BK Willis Reed BK/ Stan Smith/(Tennis) Bubba Smith FB Johnny Bench BB	30.00	60.00
3BK Willis Reed BK Johnny Bench BB	30.00	60.00

1991-92 Kellogg's College Greats

The 1991-92 Kellogg's College Basketball Greats set contains 18 standard-size cards. The cards were inserted into boxes of Kellogg's Raisin Bran through the end of March, 1992. The complete set, including a special card holder, was also available for 2.99 with three proofs of purchase from any size box of Kellogg's Raisin Bran. The front design features a color action photo with the player in his college uniform. The pictures are bordered in different colors on different cards, and the words "College Basketball Greats" is written vertically along the left of each card. In a horizontal format, the back presents outstanding achievements of the player and his college statistics.

COMPLETE SET (18)	2.50	6.00
1 Kenny Anderson	.20	.50
2 Clyde Drexler	.20	.50
3 Wayman Tisdale	.08	.25
4 Horace Grant	.08	.25
5 Kevin Johnson	.08	.25
6 Karl Malone	.40	1.00
7 Larry Bird	.75	2.00
8 John Stockton	.40	1.00
9 Doug Smith	.08	.25
10 Mark Price	.08	.25
11 Hakeem Olajuwon	.30	.75
12 Charles Smith	.08	.25
13 Bernard King	.08	.25
14 Tim Hardaway	.20	.50
15 Spud Webb	.08	.25
16 Mark Macon	.08	.25
17 Scottie Pippen	.50	1.25
18 Gary Payton	.40	1.00
xx Album Holder	.60	1.50

1993 Kellogg's College Greats Postercards

This ten-card set was manufactured by Star Pics Inc. for Kellogg's. One of these postercards was inserted into specially marked boxes of Kellogg's Raisin Bran. The cards measure the standard size when folded, but the card front can be lifted up to reveal the postercard, a 2 1/2" by 7" full-length action shot of the player. The card fronts, when folded, display close-up color player photos with colorful graphic art backgrounds within white borders. The Kellogg's College Greats logo appears at the upper left. The players' names are printed in border stripes of various colors at the bottom. The backs are white and present player profiles. The words "Kellogg's Raisin Bran Presents" appear at the top. The inside (postercard) features full-length action shots against a graphic art background that is similar to the front. The players' names are printed on bottom border stripes of various colors. The cards are unnumbered and checklisted below in alphabetical order.

COMPLETE SET (10)	3.00	8.00
1 Kareem Abdul-Jabbar	1.00	2.50
2 Teresa Edwards	1.00	2.50
3 Christian Laettner	.30	.75
4 Danny Manning	.30	.75
5 Cheryl Miller	1.00	2.50
6 Harold Miner	.20	.50
7 Chris Mullin	.30	.75
8 Scottie Pippen	1.25	3.00
9 David Robinson	.75	2.00
10 Isiah Thomas	.30	.75

1998-99 Kellogg's NBA/WNBA

COMPLETE SET (56)	3.00	8.00
*SILVER: .4 TO 1X BASE HI		
1 Grant Hill	.15	.40
2 Dikembe Mutombo	.10	.25
3 Mookie Blaylock	.05	.15
4 Antoine Walker	.10	.25
5 Chauncey Billups	.12	.30
6 Glen Rice	.10	.25
7 Vlade Divac	.10	.25
8 Scott Burrell	.05	.15
9 Ron Harper	.07	.20
10 Luc Longley	.05	.15
11 Samaki Walker	.05	.15
12 Michael Finley	.10	.25
13 Tony Battie	.07	.20
14 Joe Dumars	.10	.25
15 Jerry Stackhouse	.10	.25
16 Joe Smith	.07	.20
17 Hakeem Olajuwon	.12	.30
18 Chris Mullin	.10	.25
19 Brent Barry	.07	.20
20 Eddie Jones	.10	.25
21 Kobe Bryant	.50	1.25
22 Tim Hardaway	.10	.25
23 Terrell Brandon	.05	.15
24 Keith Van Horn	.10	.25
25 Sam Cassell	.07	.20
26 Charlie Ward	.05	.15
27 Horace Grant	.07	.20
28 Jason Kidd	.15	.40
29 Antonio McDyess	.07	.20
30 Jermaine O'Neal	.10	.25
31 Mitch Richmond	.10	.25
32 David Robinson	.15	.40
33 Tim Duncan	.20	.50
34 Vin Baker	.07	.20
35 Marcus Camby	.07	.20
36 Damon Stoudamire	.10	.25
37 Karl Malone	.12	.30
38 John Stockton	.12	.30
39 Shareef Abdur-Rahim	.10	.25
40 Juwan Howard	.07	.20
41 Sheryl Swoopes	.20	.50
42 Cynthia Cooper	.20	.50
43 Vicky Bullett	.05	.15
44 Andrea Stinson	.05	.15
45 Michelle Edwards	.12	.30
46 Eva Nemcova	.05	.15
47 Lisa Leslie	.20	.50
48 Tamecka Dixon	.05	.15
49 Rebecca Lobo	.15	.40
50 Teresa Weatherspoon	.12	.30
51 Michele Timms	.10	.25
52 Bridget Pettis	.05	.15
53 Ruthie Bolton-Holifield	.10	.25
54 Bridgette Gordon	.05	.15
55 Tammi Reiss	.05	.15
56 Wendy Palmer	.05	.15

1948 Kellogg's Pep

These small cards measure approximately 1 7/16" by 1 5/8". The card front presents a black and white head-and-shoulders shot of the player, with a white border. The back has the player's name and a brief description of his accomplishments. The cards are unnumbered, but have been assigned numbers below using a sport (BB- baseball, FB- football, BK- basketball, OT- other) prefix. Other Movie Star Kellogg's Pep cards exist, but they are not listed below. The catalog designation for this set is F273-19. An album was also produced to house the set.

COMPLETE SET (20)	700.00	1400.00
BK1 George Mikan	225.00	450.00

1996 Kellogg's Raptors Stoudamire

These 3 3-D "motion" cards were issued in specially marked boxes of Canadian Kellogg's Frosted Flakes. One card was inserted per box, and only three different cards are known to exist. The box does not list a checklist, so information on any other cards would be appreciated.

COMPLETE SET (3)	4.00	10.00
COMMON CARD (1-3)	1.50	4.00

1992 Kellogg's Team USA Posters

Featuring members of the 1992 U.S. Olympic basketball team, this set of five posters was wrapped in a cello pack and placed between the two cereal boxes of a Kellogg's Raisin Bran jumbo pack. Each poster measures approximately 6 3/4" by 9 1/2" and is printed on glossy paper stock. Kellogg's was an official sponsor of the 1992 U.S. Olympic Team. Inside gold borders, the fronts feature color action cutouts set on a dark background with smoke arising from the hardwood floor. Across the top, the player's name appears in gold lettering, with his nickname in red-and-white lettering. The player's facsimile autograph appears in purple ink across each poster. The backs are blank. The posters were produced and designed by Costacos Brothers. The posters are unnumbered and checklisted below in alphabetical order.

COMPLETE SET (5)	10.00	25.00
1 Larry Bird Larry Legend	4.00	10.00
2 Karl Malone Mailman	3.00	8.00
3 Chris Mullin Court Warrior	2.00	5.00
4 David Robinson Admiral	3.00	8.00
5 John Stockton Playmaker	4.00	9.00

1988 Kenner Starting Lineup Cards

1 Kareem Abdul-Jabbar	2.00	5.00
2 Michael Adams	.75	2.00
3 Mark Aguirre	1.25	3.00
4 Danny Ainge	1.25	3.00
5 Thurl Bailey	4.00	10.00
6 Charles Barkley	2.50	6.00
7 Walter Berry	.75	2.00
8 Larry Bird	3.00	8.00
9 Rolando Blackman	1.50	4.00
10 Michael Cage	.75	2.00
11 Joe Barry Carroll	.75	2.00
12 Tom Chambers	.75	2.00
13 Maurice Cheeks	.75	2.00
14 Michael Cooper	2.00	5.00
15 Terry Cummings	.75	2.00
16 Adrian Dantley	2.00	5.00
17 Brad Daugherty	.75	2.00
18 Johnny Dawkins	.75	2.00
19 Clyde Drexler	1.50	4.00
20 Mark Eaton	4.00	10.00
21 Dale Ellis	1.25	3.00
22 Alex English	1.25	3.00
23 Patrick Ewing	1.50	4.00
24 Sleepy Floyd	1.25	3.00
25 Winston Garland	.75	2.00
26 Armon Gilliam	.75	2.00
27 Mike Gminski	.75	2.00
28 David Greenwood	.75	2.00
29 Derek Harper	1.25	3.00
30 Ron Harper	2.00	5.00
31 Rod Higgins	.75	2.00
32 Dennis Hopson	.75	2.00
33 Jeff Hornacek	1.25	3.00
34 Mark Jackson	1.00	2.50
35 Dennis Johnson	1.00	2.50
36 Eddie Johnson	.75	2.00
37 Magic Johnson	2.50	6.00
38 Steve Johnson	.75	2.00
39 Vinnie Johnson	1.50	4.00
40 Michael Jordan	8.00	20.00
41 Bernard King	.75	2.00
42 Bill Laimbeer	2.00	5.00
43 Lafayette Lever	.75	2.00
44 Jeff Malone	.75	2.00
45 Karl Malone	8.00	20.00
46 Moses Malone	2.00	5.00
47 Danny Manning	1.00	2.50
48 Rodney McCray	1.50	4.00
49 Xavier McDaniel	.75	2.00
50 Kevin McHale	1.00	2.50
51 Derrick McKey	.75	2.00
52 Reggie Miller	6.00	15.00
53 Sidney Moncrief	1.50	4.00
54 Chris Mullin	1.50	4.00
55 Hakeem Olajuwon	1.50	4.00
56 Robert Parish	2.00	5.00
57 John Paxon	.75	2.00
58 Sam Perkins	1.50	4.00
59 Chuck Person	.75	2.00
60 Scottie Pippen	4.00	10.00
61 Terry Porter	.75	2.00
62 Paul Pressey	.75	2.00
63 Mark Price	2.50	6.00
64 Doc Rivers	1.00	2.50
65 Alvin Robertson	.75	2.00
66 Cliff Robinson	.75	2.00
67 Ralph Sampson	.75	2.00
68 Danny Schayes	1.50	4.00
69 Jack Sikma	1.25	3.00
70 Kenny Smith	.75	2.00
71 Steve Stipanovich	1.25	3.00
72 John Stockton	8.00	20.00
73 Isiah Thomas	1.25	3.00
74 Lasalle Thompson	.75	2.00
75 Otis Thorpe	.75	2.00
76 Wayman Tisdale	.75	2.00
77 Kiki Vandeweghe	.75	2.00
78 Spud Webb	1.00	2.50
79 Dominique Wilkins	1.50	4.00
80 Gerald Wilkins	.75	2.00
81 Buck Williams	.75	2.00
82 John Williams	.75	2.00
83 Reggie Williams	.75	2.00
84 Kevin Willis	.75	2.00
85 James Worthy	1.50	4.00

1988 Kenner Starting Lineup Unissued Cards

This five-card set was released to hobby dealers in 1988 to promote Kenner's Starting Lineup figures. These cards are unnumbered and are listed below in alphabetical order.

COMPLETE SET (5)	20.00	50.00
1 Muggsy Bogues	6.00	15.00
2 Walter Davis	2.00	5.00
3 Charles Oakley	6.00	15.00
4 Reggie Theus	4.00	10.00
5 Orlando Woolridge	2.00	5.00

1989 Kenner Starting Lineup Cards

1 Rex Chapman	2.50	6.00
2 Dell Curry	2.50	6.00
3 Ron Harper	2.50	6.00
4 Larry Nance	2.50	6.00
5 Kelly Tripucka	2.50	6.00

1989 Kenner Starting Lineup Legends Collection Cards

1 Julius Erving	3.00	8.00
2 Wilt Chamberlain	2.50	6.00
3 John Havlicek	1.50	4.00
4 Oscar Robertson	2.00	5.00

1989 Kenner Starting Lineup One On One Cards

1 Charles Barkley	3.00	8.00
2 Larry Bird	5.00	12.00
3 Patrick Ewing	2.50	6.00
4 Magic Johnson	4.00	10.00
5 Michael Jordan	10.00	25.00
6 Kevin McHale	2.50	6.00
7 Isiah Thomas	2.50	6.00
8 Dominique Wilkins	2.50	6.00

1990 Kenner Starting Lineup Cards

1 Charles Barkley RY	2.00	5.00
1b Charles Barkley	2.00	5.00
2 Larry Bird RY	3.00	8.00
2b Larry Bird	3.00	8.00
3 Tom Chambers RY	.75	2.00
3b Tom Chambers	.75	2.00
4 Clyde Drexler RY	1.50	4.00
4b Clyde Drexler	1.50	4.00
5 Joe Dumars RY	1.25	3.00
5b Joe Dumars	1.25	3.00
6 Patrick Ewing RY	1.50	4.00
6b Patrick Ewing	1.50	4.00
7 Magic Johnson RY	2.50	6.00
7b Magic Johnson	2.50	6.00
8 Michael Jordan RY	8.00	20.00
8b Michael Jordan	8.00	20.00
9 Karl Malone RY	1.50	4.00
9b Karl Malone	1.50	4.00
10 Chris Mullin RY	1.25	3.00
10b Chris Mullin	1.25	3.00
11 David Robinson RY	2.00	5.00
11b David Robinson	2.00	5.00
12 Byron Scott RY	.75	2.00
12b Byron Scott	.75	2.00
13 John Stockton RY	1.50	4.00
13b John Stockton	1.50	4.00
14 Isiah Thomas RY	1.25	3.00
14b Isiah Thomas	1.25	3.00
15 Spud Webb RY	1.00	2.50
15b Spud Webb	1.00	2.50
16 Dominique Wilkins RY	1.25	3.00
16b Dominique Wilkins	1.25	3.00
17 James Worthy RY	1.25	3.00
17b James Worthy	1.25	3.00

1991 Kenner Starting Lineup Cards

1 Charles Barkley	1.50	4.00
2 Clyde Drexler	1.25	3.00
3 David Robinson	1.50	4.00
4 Dennis Rodman	2.00	5.00
5 Derrick Coleman	1.00	2.50
6 Dominique Wilkins	1.25	3.00
7 Isiah Thomas	1.00	2.50
8 Joe Dumars	1.00	2.50
9 Kevin Johnson	1.00	2.50
10 Larry Bird	2.50	6.00
11 Magic Johnson	2.00	5.00
12 Michael Jordan Dunk	4.00	10.00
13 Michael Jordan Dribbling	4.00	10.00
14 Patrick Ewing	1.25	3.00
15 Reggie Lewis	1.00	2.50
16 Spud Webb	1.00	2.50

1992 Kenner Starting Lineup Cards

1 Charles Barkley	1.50	4.00
2 Larry Bird	2.50	6.00
3 Manute Bol	.75	2.00
4 Dee Brown	.75	2.00
5 Derrick Coleman	.75	2.00
6 Vlade Divac	.75	2.00
7 Clyde Drexler	1.25	3.00
8 Joe Dumars	1.00	2.50
9 Patrick Ewing	1.25	3.00
10 Tim Hardaway	1.00	2.50
11 Kevin Johnson	1.00	2.50
12 Larry Johnson	1.25	3.00
13 Magic Johnson	2.00	5.00
14 Michael Jordan	4.00	10.00
15 Dan Majerle	.75	2.00
16 Karl Malone	1.25	3.00
17 Reggie Miller	1.25	3.00
18 Chris Mullin	1.00	2.50
19 Dikembe Mutombo	1.00	2.50
20 Hakeem Olajuwon	1.25	3.00
21 John Paxson	.75	2.00
22 Scottie Pippen	2.00	5.00
23 Mark Price	1.00	2.50
24 David Robinson	1.50	4.00
25 Dennis Rodman	2.00	5.00
26 John Stockton	1.25	3.00
27 Isiah Thomas	1.00	2.50

1993 Kenner Starting Lineup Cards
1 Kenny Anderson TSC 1.00 2.50
1b Kenny Anderson Topps .75 2.00
2 Stacey Augmon TSC 1.00 2.50
2b Stacey Augmon Topps .75 2.00
3 Charles Barkley TSC 2.00 5.00
3b Charles Barkley Topps 1.50 4.00
4 Brad Daugherty TSC 1.00 2.50
4b Brad Daugherty Topps .75 2.00
5 Todd Day TSC 1.00 2.50
5b Todd Day Topps .75 2.00
6 Clyde Drexler TSC 1.50 4.00
6b Clyde Drexler Topps 1.25 3.00
7 Sean Elliott TSC 1.25 3.00
7b Sean Elliott Topps 1.00 2.50
8 Patrick Ewing TSC 1.50 4.00
8b Patrick Ewing Topps 1.25 3.00
9 Horace Grant TSC 1.00 2.50
9b Horace Grant Topps .75 2.00
10 Tom Gugliotta TSC 1.00 2.50
10b Tom Gugliotta Topps .75 2.00
11 Tim Hardaway TSC 1.25 3.00
11b Tim Hardaway Topps 1.00 2.50
12 Larry Johnson TSC 1.25 3.00
12b Larry Johnson Topps 1.00 2.50
13 Michael Jordan TSC 5.00 12.00
13b Michael Jordan Topps 4.00 10.00
14 Shawn Kemp TSC 1.25 3.00
14b Shawn Kemp Topps 1.00 2.50
15 Christian Laettner TSC 1.25 3.00
15b Christian Laettner Topps 1.00 2.50
16 Dan Majerle TSC 1.00 2.50
16b Dan Majerle Topps .75 2.00
17 Karl Malone TSC 1.50 4.00
17b Karl Malone Topps 1.25 3.00
18 Alonzo Mourning TSC 2.00 5.00
18b Alonzo Mourning Topps 1.50 4.00
19 Dikembe Mutombo TSC 1.25 3.00
19b Dikembe Mutombo Topps 1.00 2.50
20 Shaquille O'Neal TSC 5.00 12.00
20b Shaquille O'Neal Topps 4.00 10.00
21 Scottie Pippen TSC 2.50 6.00
21b Scottie Pippen Topps 2.00 5.00
22 Terry Porter TSC 1.00 2.50
22b Terry Porter Topps .75 2.00
23 Mark Price TSC 1.25 3.00
23b Mark Price Topps 1.00 2.50
24 Glen Rice TSC 1.25 3.00
24b Glen Rice Topps 1.00 2.50
25 Mitch Richmond TSC 1.25 3.00
25b Mitch Richmond Topps 1.00 2.50
26 David Robinson TSC 2.00 5.00
26b David Robinson Topps 1.50 4.00
27 Detlef Schrempf TSC 1.25 3.00
27b Detlef Schrempf Topps 1.00 2.50
28 John Stockton TSC 1.50 4.00
28b John Stockton Topps 1.25 3.00
29 Dominique Wilkins TSC 1.50 4.00
29b Dominique Wilkins Topps 1.25 3.00

1994 Kenner Starting Lineup Cards
1 B.J. Armstrong .75 2.00
2 Stacey Augmon .75 2.00
3 Charles Barkley 1.50 4.00
4 Shawn Bradley 1.00 2.50
5 Calbert Cheaney 1.00 2.50
6 Derrick Coleman .75 2.00
7 Sean Elliott 1.00 2.50
8 LaPhonso Ellis 1.00 2.50
9 Patrick Ewing 1.25 3.00
10 Anfernee Hardaway 3.00 8.00
11 Jim Jackson 1.00 2.50
12 Larry Johnson 1.00 2.50
13 Shawn Kemp 1.00 2.50
14 Karl Malone 1.25 3.00
15 Jamal Mashburn 1.25 3.00
16 Harold Miner .75 2.00
17 Alonzo Mourning 1.25 3.00
18 Chris Mullin 1.00 2.50
19 Hakeem Olajuwon 1.25 3.00
20 Shaquille O'Neal 2.50 6.00
21 Scottie Pippen 2.00 5.00
22 David Robinson 1.50 4.00
23 Dennis Rodman 2.00 5.00
24 Latrell Sprewell 1.50 4.00
25 Chris Webber 2.50 6.00
26 Dominique Wilkins 1.25 3.00

1995 Kenner Starting Lineup Cards
1 Charles Barkley 1.50 4.00
2 Muggsy Bogues 1.00 2.50
3 Patrick Ewing 1.25 3.00
4 Horace Grant .75 2.00
5 Anfernee Hardaway 1.50 4.00
6 Grant Hill 3.00 8.00
7 Jeff Hornacek .75 2.00
8 Jim Jackson .75 2.00
9 Shawn Kemp 1.00 2.50
10 Jason Kidd 3.00 8.00
11 Toni Kukoc 1.25 3.00
12 Dan Majerle .75 2.00
13 Karl Malone 1.25 3.00
14 Reggie Miller 1.25 3.00
15 Eric Montross .75 2.00
16 Alonzo Mourning 1.25 3.00
17 Hakeem Olajuwon 1.25 3.00
18 Shaquille O'Neal 2.50 6.00
19 Robert Pack .75 2.00
20 Scottie Pippen 2.00 5.00
21 Mark Price 1.00 2.50
22 Cliff Robinson .75 2.00
23 David Robinson 1.50 4.00
24 Glenn Robinson 1.25 3.00
25 Steve Smith 1.00 2.50
26 Latrell Sprewell 1.00 2.50
27 John Starks 1.00 2.50
28 Nick Van Exel 1.00 2.50
29 Clarence Weatherspoon .75 2.00
30 Chris Webber 1.25 3.00
31 Dominique Wilkins 1.25 3.00

1995 Kenner Starting Lineup Timeless Legends Cards
1 Kareem Abdul-Jabbar 1.50 4.00
2 Wilt Chamberlain 2.00 5.00

1996 Kenner Starting Lineup Cards
1 Vin Baker 1.00 2.50
2 Charles Barkley 1.50 4.00
3 Clyde Drexler 1.25 3.00
4 Sean Elliott 1.00 2.50
5 Patrick Ewing 1.25 3.00
6 Kevin Garnett 4.00 10.00
7 Anfernee Hardaway 1.50 4.00
8 Grant Hill 1.50 4.00
9 Tyrone Hill .75 2.00
10 Juwan Howard 1.00 2.50
11 Larry Johnson 1.00 2.50
12 Eddie Jones 1.00 2.50
13 Jason Kidd 1.50 4.00
14 Karl Malone 1.25 3.00
15 Jamal Mashburn 1.00 2.50
16 Antonio McDyess 1.00 2.50
17 Reggie Miller 1.25 3.00
18 Alonzo Mourning 1.25 3.00
19 Hakeem Olajuwon 1.25 3.00
20 Shaquille O'Neal 2.50 6.00
21 Gary Payton 1.00 2.50
22 Scottie Pippen 2.00 5.00
23 Dino Radja .75 2.00
24 Bryant Reeves .75 2.00
25 Pooh Richardson .75 2.00
26 Mitch Richmond 1.00 2.50
27 Cliff Robinson .75 2.00
28 David Robinson 1.50 4.00
29 Glenn Robinson 1.00 2.50
30 Dennis Rodman 2.00 5.00
31 Joe Smith 1.00 2.50
32 Rik Smits .75 2.00
33 Jerry Stackhouse 1.25 3.00
34 Damon Stoudamire 1.25 3.00
NNO Grant Hill 1.50 4.00
Detroit Pistons Exclusive
NNO Grant Hill 1.50 4.00
Kmart Special

1996 Kenner Starting Lineup Extended Series Cards
1 Charles Barkley 1.50 4.00
2 Kobe Bryant 10.00 25.00
3 Grant Hill 1.50 4.00
4 Allen Iverson 4.00 10.00
5 Larry Johnson 1.00 2.50
6 Dikembe Mutombo 1.00 2.50
7 Shaquille O'Neal 2.50 6.00
8 Damon Stoudamire 1.00 2.50

1997 Kenner Starting Lineup Anaheim Convention Cards
1 Jason Kidd 1.50 4.00
w/Traded To Phoenix Line
2 Shaquille O'Neal 2.50 6.00

1997 Kenner Starting Lineup Atlanta Convention Cards
1 Christian Laettner 1.00 2.50
2 Glen Rice 1.00 2.50

1997 Kenner Starting Lineup Cards
1 Shareef Abdur-Rahim 1.25 3.00
2 Ray Allen 2.50 6.00
3 Kenny Anderson .75 2.00
4 Vin Baker .75 2.00
5 Charles Barkley 1.50 4.00
6 Terrell Brandon .75 2.00
7 Marcus Camby 1.25 3.00
8 Vlade Divac .75 2.00
9 Patrick Ewing 1.25 3.00
10 Michael Finley 1.00 2.50
11 Kevin Garnett 2.00 5.00
12 Horace Grant .75 2.00
14 Grant Hill 1.50 4.00
15 Allan Houston 1.00 2.50
16 Juwan Howard .75 2.00
17 Allen Iverson 1.50 4.00
18 Shawn Kemp 1.00 2.50
19 Jason Kidd 1.50 4.00
20 Kerry Kittles .75 2.00
21 Stephon Marbury 1.00 2.50
22 Reggie Miller 1.25 3.00
23 Alonzo Mourning 1.25 3.00
24 Hakeem Olajuwon 1.25 3.00
25 Shaquille O'Neal 2.50 6.00
26 Gary Payton 1.00 2.50
27 Scottie Pippen 2.00 5.00
28 Mitch Richmond 1.00 2.50
29 David Robinson 1.50 4.00
30 Dennis Rodman 2.00 5.00
31 Bill Russell Dunking 2.00 5.00
32 Bill Russell Dribbling 2.00 5.00
33 Steve Smith 1.00 2.50
34 Latrell Sprewell 1.00 2.50
35 John Stockton 1.25 3.00
36 Damon Stoudamire 1.00 2.50
37 Nick Van Exel .75 2.00
38 Loy Vaught .75 2.00
39 Antoine Walker 1.00 2.50
40 Chris Webber 1.25 3.00

1997 Kenner Starting Lineup Classic Doubles Cards
1 Kareem Abdul-Jabbar 1.50 4.00
2 Wilt Chamberlain 2.00 5.00
3 Joe Dumars 1.00 2.50
4 Patrick Ewing 1.25 3.00
5 Karl Malone 1.25 3.00
6 Kevin McHale 1.00 2.50
7 Hakeem Olajuwon 1.25 3.00
8 Willis Reed 1.00 2.50
9 John Stockton 1.25 3.00

1997 Kenner Starting Lineup Edison Convention Cards
1 Larry Johnson 1.00 2.50
2 Jerry Stackhouse 1.00 2.50

1997 Kenner Starting Lineup Timeless Legends Cards
1 Walt Frazier 1.00 2.50
2 Bill Walton 1.00 2.50

1998 Kenner Starting Lineup Cards
1 Vin Baker 1.00 2.50
2 Terrell Brandon .75 2.00
3 Kobe Bryant 4.00 10.00
4 Patrick Ewing 1.25 3.00
5 Kevin Garnett 1.50 4.00
6 Grant Hill 1.50 4.00
7 Allen Iverson 1.50 4.00
8 Magic Johnson 2.00 5.00
9 Shawn Kemp 1.00 2.50
10 Jason Kidd 1.25 3.00
11 Karl Malone 1.25 3.00
12 Stephon Marbury 1.00 2.50
13 Alonzo Mourning 1.25 3.00
14 Shaquille O'Neal 2.50 6.00
15 Dennis Rodman 2.00 5.00
16 Rik Smits .75 2.00

1985-86 Kings Big League
This skip-numbered standard-sized set was issued during the 1985-86 season by Big League Trading cards. Each card was produced with white borders, and the card backs carry a "A310" suffix.

COMPLETE SET (18) 10.00 25.00
2 Bill Jones .40 1.00
Frank Hamblen
3 Joe Axelson .40 1.00
9 Joe Meriweather .40 1.00
10 Eddie Nealy .40 1.00
11 Mark Olberding .40 1.00
13 LaSalle Thompson .40 1.00
16 Mike Woodson .40 1.00
17 Don Buse .75 2.00
18 Larry Drew .40 1.00
19 Rick Benner .40 1.00
Bob Whitsitt
Sondra Kasserman
22 Phil Johnson .40 1.00
23 Kings Team Photo .75 2.00
24 Sacramento Arena .40 1.00
25 Eddie Johnson .75 2.00
26 Mark McNamara .40 1.00
30 Reggie Theus 2.00 5.00
32 Otis Thorpe 2.00 5.00
33 Peter Verhoeven .40 1.00

1988-89 Kings Carl's Jr.
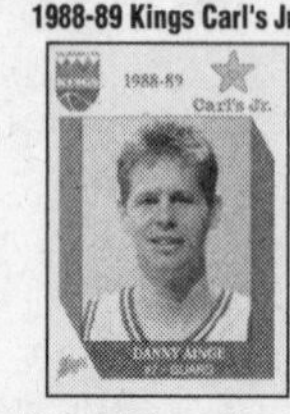

The 1988-89 Carl's Jr. Sacramento Kings set contains 12 cards each measuring approximately 2 1/2" by 3 1/2". There are 11 player cards and one coach card in this set. The cards were issued in three strips of four players plus a coupon for savings at Carl's Jr. restaurants before May 31, 1989. Since this set was issued in late spring of 1989, it includes comments and statistics about the 1988-89 season. The set was produced for Carl's Jr. by Sports Marketing Inc. of Redmond, Washington. The cards are unnumbered except for uniform number; they are ordered below by uniform number.

COMPLETE SET (12) 4.00 10.00
2 Michael Jackson .20 .50
7 Danny Ainge 1.50 4.00
15 Vinny Del Negro 1.25 3.00
21 Harold Pressley .20 .50
22 Rodney McCray .40 1.00
23 Wayman Tisdale .60 1.50
30 Kenny Smith 1.50 4.00
34 Ricky Berry .20 .50
43 Jim Petersen .20 .50
50 Ben Gillery .20 .50
54 Brad Lohaus .20 .50
NNO Jerry Reynolds CO .20 .50

1989-90 Kings Carl's Jr.

This 12-card set of Sacramento Kings was sponsored by Carl's Jr. restaurants and issued in three panels, each containing four player cards and one sponsor's coupon. The cards were given away at three different games in strips of four player cards each. After perforation, the player cards measure the standard size. The front features a color action player photo, with red, white, and blue borders on white card stock. The player's name is written between a thin blue stripe and the top border. The team and sponsors' logos overlay the lower corners of the picture, with the year, position, and uniform number below the picture. The back has two team logos in the upper corners, with biographical information and career summary. The cards are unnumbered and checklisted below by uniform number. The set includes an early professional card of Pervis Ellison, the first pick of the 1989 NBA draft. The player groups on the panels were as follows: Michael Jackson, Vinny Del Negro, Wayman Tisdale, and Pervis Ellison; Danny Ainge, Kenny Smith, Randy Allen, and Ralph Sampson; and Harold Pressley, Rodney McCray, Greg Kite, and Jerry Reynolds.

COMPLETE SET (12) 4.00 10.00
2 Michael Jackson .20 .50
7 Danny Ainge 1.25 3.00
15 Vinny Del Negro .60 1.50
21 Harold Pressley .20 .50
22 Rodney McCray .40 1.00
23 Wayman Tisdale .40 1.00
30 Kenny Smith 1.25 3.00
32 Greg Kite .20 .50
40 Randy Allen .20 .50
42 Pervis Ellison .60 1.50
50 Ralph Sampson .40 1.00
NNO Jerry Reynolds CO .20 .50

1973-74 Kings Linnett
Measuring 8 1/2" by 11", these nine charcoal drawings are facial portraits by noted sports artist Charles Linnett. The player's facsimile autograph is inscribed across the lower right corner. The backs are blank. Three portraits were included in each package, with a suggested retail price of 99 cents. The portraits are unnumbered and checklisted below in alphabetical order. The set is dated by the fact that 1973-74 was John Block's and Ken Durrett's last year with the Kings but Ron Behagen's and Jimmy Walker's first year with the team.

COMPLETE SET (9) 20.00 40.00
1 Nate Archibald 7.50 15.00
2 Ron Behagen 1.00 2.50
3 John Block 2.00 5.00
4 Mike D'Antoni 2.00 5.00
5 Ken Durrett 1.00 2.50
6 Sam Lacey 3.00 8.00
7 Larry McNeill 1.00 2.50
8 Jimmy Walker 3.00 8.00
9 Nate Williams 1.00 2.50

1990-91 Kings Safeway

This 12-card set of Sacramento Kings was sponsored by Safeway stores and issued in three panels, each containing four player cards and one sponsor's coupon. After perforation, the player cards measure the standard size. The front features a color action player photo, with red, white, and blue borders on white card stock. The player's name is written between a thin blue stripe and the top border. The team and sponsors' logos overlay the lower corners of the picture, with the year, position, and uniform number below the picture. The back has two team logos in the upper corners, with biographical information and career summary. The cards are unnumbered and are checklisted below in alphabetical order.

COMPLETE SET (12) 4.00 8.00
1 Anthony Bonner .30 .75
2 Antoine Carr .40 1.00
3 Duane Causwell .40 1.00
4 Steve Colter .30 .75
5 Bobby Hansen .40 1.00
6 Eric Leckner .30 .75
7 Travis Mays .30 .75
8 Dick Motta CO .40 1.00
9 Lionel Simmons .40 1.00
10 Rory Sparrow .30 .75
11 Wayman Tisdale .60 1.50
12 Bill Wennington .40 1.00

1985-86 Kings Smokey

This 15-card set features members of the Sacramento Kings of the NBA. The cards were originally distributed as a perforated sheet along with (and perforated to) a large team photo. The sheet was distributed to fans attending the Kings' Card Night home game. The cards are numbered on the back in the upper right corner. The cards measure approximately 4" by 5 1/2". The card backs contain a fire safety cartoon but minimal information about the player.

COMPLETE SET (16) 10.00 25.00
1 Smokey Emblem .75 2.00
2 Phil Johnson CO .75 2.00
3 Frank Hamblen ACO .75 2.00
Jerry Reynolds ACO
Bill Jones TR
4 Smokey Bear .75 2.00
5 Michael Adams 1.25 3.00
6 Larry Drew 1.00 2.50
7 Carl Henry 1.00 2.50
8 Eddie Johnson 2.00 5.00
9 Rich Kelley .75 2.00
10 Joe Kleine 1.25 3.00
11 Mark Olberding .75 2.00
12 Reggie Theus 2.50 6.00
13 LaSalle Thompson .75 2.00
14 Otis Thorpe 3.00 8.00
15 Terry Tyler .75 2.00
16 Mike Woodson 1.25 3.00

1986-87 Kings Smokey

This 15-card set features members of the Sacramento Kings of the NBA. The cards were originally distributed as a perforated sheet along with (and perforated to) a large team photo. The sheet was distributed to fans attending the Kings' Card Night home game. Since the cards are unnumbered, they are listed below in alphabetical order. The player's uniform number (given on both sides of the card) is also listed below. The cards measure approximately 2 3/8" by 3". The card backs contain a fire safety cartoon but minimal information about the player.

COMPLETE SET (15) 10.00 25.00
1 Don Buse ACO .75 2.00
2 Franklin Edwards 10 .75 2.00
3 Eddie Johnson 8 2.00 5.00
4 Bill Jones TR .75 2.00
5 Joe Kleine 35 1.00 2.50
6 Mark Olberding 53 .75 2.00
7 Harold Pressley 21 .75 2.00
8 Jerry Reynolds CO .75 2.00
9 Johnny Rogers 32 .75 2.00
10 Derek Smith 18 1.25 3.00
11 Reggie Theus 24 2.50 6.00
12 LaSalle Thompson 41 .75 2.00
13 Otis Thorpe 33 2.50 6.00
14 Terry Tyler 40 .75 2.00
15 Othell Wilson 2 .75 2.00

1975-76 Kings Team Issue

This oversized set was produced for the Kansas City Kings during the 1975-76 season. The set features 10 cards of the team's players and coaches

COMPLETE SET (10) 12.50 25.00
1 Bob Bigelow 1.25 3.00
2 Glenn Hansen 1.25 3.00
3 Ollie Johnson 1.25 3.00
4 Larry McNeill 1.25 3.00
5 Bill Robinzine 1.25 3.00
6 Jimmy Walker 1.50 4.00
7 Lee Winfield 1.25 3.00
8 Richard Washington 1.25 3.00
9 Dan Sparks ACO 1.25 3.00
10 Phil Johnson CO 1.25 3.00

1993-94 Knicks Alamo

Sponsored by Alamo, this 5-card set measures 3 1/2" by 5 1/2" and features the 1993- 94 New York Knicks. The fronts have borderless color action player photos. The backs have a postcard format and carry the player's name and position, the team's logo and address and the sponsor's logo. The cards are unnumbered and checklisted below in alphabetical order.

COMPLETE SET (5) 1.50 4.00
1 Greg Anthony .40 1.00
2 Anthony Mason .40 1.00
3 Charles Oakley .40 1.00
4 Pat Riley CO .75 2.00
5 John Starks .75 2.00

1988-89 Knicks Frito Lay

This 15-card set was sponsored by Frito Lay. The cards were issued in two sheets; after perforation, the cards measure approximately 2 1/2" by 3 1/2". The front design has color action player photos with white borders. The team logo appears in the lower left corner, with the player's name to the right in a yellow stripe. The horizontally oriented backs have blank print on a gray and white background and present biographical and statistical information. The cards are unnumbered and checklisted below in alphabetical order.

COMPLETE SET (15) 20.00 50.00
1 Greg Butler .40 1.00
2 Patrick Ewing 8.00 20.00
3 Sidney Green .40 1.00
4 Mark Jackson 4.00 10.00
5 Pete Myers .75 2.00
6 Johnny Newman .75 2.00
7 Charles Oakley 1.50 4.00
8 Rick Pitino CO 2.50 6.00
9 Rod Strickland 2.00 5.00
10 Trent Tucker .75 2.00
11 Kiki Vandeweghe 2.00 5.00
12 Kenny Walker .75 2.00
13 Eddie Lee Wilkins .40 1.00
14 Gerald Wilkins 1.25 3.00
15 Frito Lay .40 1.00
Manufacturer's Coupon

1984-85 Knicks Getty Photos
These player cards were printed four to a 7" by 9" panel. Though the panel is not actually perforated, black broken lines indicate where the cards could be cut. After cutting, the cards measure approximately 3 1/2" by 4". The front features a borderless color action photo on thin white cardboard stock. In one of the margins that runs alongside the card, a facsimile autograph is written running the length of the card. A one-inch strip at the bottom of each sheet presents the Knicks' and sponsor's logos. The back has the New York Knicks' logo and a sponsor advertisement that reads "Getty. The Proof is at the Pump." The cards are unnumbered and we have checklisted them below in alphabetical order. The set is dated by the fact that 1984-85 was James Bailey, Ken Bannister, Butch Carter, and Pat Cummings' first year with the Knicks.

COMPLETE SET (11) 20.00 50.00
1 James Bailey 1.25 3.00
2 Ken Bannister 1.25 3.00
3 Hubie Brown CO 4.00 9.00
4 Butch Carter 2.00 5.00
5 Pat Cummings 1.50 4.00
6 Ernie Grunfeld 3.00 8.00
7 Bernard King 5.00 12.00
8 Louis Orr 1.50 4.00
9 Rory Sparrow 2.00 5.00
10 Trent Tucker 2.00 5.00
11 Darrell Walker 3.00 8.00

1989-90 Knicks Marine Midland

This 14-card set of New York Knicks was sponsored by Marine Midland Bank. The cards were issued in one sheet with three rows of five cards each, and they measure the standard size after perforation. The 15th slot is filled by the sponsor's advertisement. The front features a color action photo of the player, with orange borders. The upper left corner of the picture is cut out to provide space for the uniform number. The team logo overlays the lower right corner of the picture, and a row of miniature blue triangles run beneath the bottom orange border. In a horizontal format the back is divided into two boxes and presents biographical (on blue) and statistical information. The cards are unnumbered and are checklisted below in alphabetical order.

COMPLETE SET (14) 15.00 40.00
1 Greg Butler .50 1.25
2 Patrick Ewing 6.00 15.00
3 Mark Jackson 2.50 6.00
4 Stu Jackson CO .75 2.00
5 Charles Oakley 1.50 4.00
6 Pete Myers .60 1.50
7 Johnny Newman .60 1.50
8 Brian Quinnett .50 1.25
9 Rod Strickland 1.25 3.00
10 Trent Tucker .60 1.50
11 Kiki Vandeweghe 1.50 4.00
12 Kenny Walker .75 2.00
13 Gerald Wilkins .75 2.00
14 Eddie Lee Wilkins .50 1.25

1970-71 Knicks Photos
This six card oversized set was released during the 1970-71 season, and features such Knick stars as Bill Bradley and Walt Frazier. Please note that these black and white cards measure 8"x10", and have blank backs.

COMPLETE SET (6) 75.00 150.00
1 Dick Barnett 5.00 10.00
2 Bill Bradley 20.00 40.00
3 Dave DeBusschere 15.00 30.00
4 Walt Frazier 20.00 40.00
5 Willis Reed 15.00 30.00
6 Danny Whelan TR 5.00 10.00

1962-63 Knicks Photos
This six card oversized glossy set was released during the 1962-63 season, and features such Knick stars as Willie Naulls. Please note that these black and white cards measure 8"x10", and have the player names stamped on back. Obviously, this checklist is incomplete and all additional information is welcome.

COMPLETE SET (6) 75.00 150.00
1 Dave Budd 10.00 20.00
2 Donnis Butcher 10.00 20.00
3 Knicks Team Photo 20.00 40.00
4 Whitey Martin 10.00 20.00
5 Willie Naulls 25.00 50.00
6 Unknown

1972-73 Knicks Photos

This two card oversized set was released during the 1972-73 season, and features such Knicks stars as Bill Bradley and Phil Jackson. Please note that these black and white cards measure 8"x10", and have blank backs.

COMPLETE SET (2) 12.50 25.00
1 Dick Barnett 7.50 15.00
Henry Bibby
Bill Bradley
Dave DeBusschere
Walt Frazier
John Gianelli
Phil Jackson
2 Jerry Lucas 5.00 10.00
Dean Meminger
Earl Monroe
Willis Reed
Tom Riker
Red Holzman CO

1970-71 Knicks Portraits
Each of these black and white illustrated portraits measure approximately 9" by 12". The player's name and facsimile autograph are also contained on the front. The backs are blank. The photos are unnumbered and listed below alphabetically.

COMPLETE SET (8) 75.00 150.00
1 Dick Barnett 5.00 10.00
2 Dave DeBusschere 12.50 25.00
3 Walt Frazier 20.00 40.00
4 Red Holzman CO 10.00 20.00
5 Willis Reed 15.00 30.00
6 Mike Riordan 5.00 10.00
7 Cazzie Russell 10.00 20.00
8 Dave Stallworth 5.00 10.00

1986-87 Knicks Tickets
These 24 tickets were issued throughout the 1986-87 N.Y. Knicks basketball season. These are the actual ticket stubs that one would use for admission into Madison Square Garden.

COMPLETE SET (24) 25.00 60.00
1 Dick McGuire 1.25 3.00
Joe Lapchick
Carl Braun
2 N.Y. Knicks Team Photo 1.50 4.00
3 Hubie Brown 1.50 4.00
4 Rory Sparrow .75 2.00
5 Dave Stallworth .75 2.00
6 Bill Bradley 3.00 8.00
7 Jerry Lucas 1.50 4.00
8 Trent Tucker .75 2
9 Walt Frazier 2.50 6
10 Willis Reed 2.00 5
11 Red Holzman CO 1.50 4
12 Mike Riordan .75 2
13 Harry Gallatin .75 2
14 Johnny Green .75 2
15 Kenny Walker .75 2
16 Bill Cartwright 1.25 3
17 Butch Beard .75 2
18 Dean Meminger .75 2
19 Mel Hutchins .75 2
20 Phil Jackson 2.50 6
21 Pat Cummings .75 2
22 Kenny Sears 1.25 3
23 Bernard King 1.50 4
24 Howard Komives .75 2

2008-09 Knicks Upper Deck
COMPLETE SET (14) 2.50 6
1 Jamal Crawford .25
2 Stephon Marbury .25
3 Zach Randolph .25
4 David Lee .25
5 Quentin Richardson .25
6 Nate Robinson .30
7 Eddy Curry .20
8 Wilson Chandler .25
9 Jared Jeffries .20
10 Mardy Collins .20
11 Chris Duhon .20
12 Danilo Gallinari .50 1
13 Mike D'Antoni CO .20
14 Patrick Ewing .40 1

2001-02 Lakers American Express

This six-card set was given away at the April 11, 20 Lakers game versus the Minnesota Timberwolves. These cards measure 5" by 7" and honor great play from the days when the lakers played in Minneapol The fronts feature a posed shot of the player while t back can be used as a postcard. Since these cards a unnumbered, we have sequenced them in alphabeti order.

COMPLETE SET (6) 6.00 15
1 John Kundla CO 1.25 3
2 Clyde Lovellette 1.25 3
3 Slater Martin 1.25 3
4 George Mikan 3.00 8
5 Vern Mikkelsen 1.25 3
6 Jim Pollard 1.25 3

1982-83 Lakers BASF

This 13-card set was produced by BASF audio and video tapes in a promotional tie-in with the Los Angeles Lakers. The cards were distributed by Big Ben's and The Wherehouse (both chain record and tape stores in southern California), one player per week, with the final card scheduled for distribution during the week of the NBA championship series. T cards measure approximately 5" by 7" and are unnumbered except for uniform number; they are li below in alphabetical order for convenience. This s can be distinguished from the other two years of BA Lakers sets in that it is the only year the set was als sponsored by Big Ben's and the only year there wer no facsimile autographs on the back. The set featur James Worthy's first professional card.

COMPLETE SET (13) 8.00 20
1 Kareem Abdul-Jabbar 2.00 5
2 Michael Cooper 1.00 2
3 Clay Johnson .60 1
4 Magic Johnson 2.50 6
5 Eddie Jordan .75 2
6 Mark Landsberger .60 1
7 Bob McAdoo 1.25 3
8 Mike McGee .40 1
9 Norm Nixon 1.00 2
10 Kurt Rambis 1.50 4
11 Jamaal Wilkes 1.00 2
12 James Worthy 3.00 8
13 Team Card 1.00 2
(Team roster on back)

1983-84 Lakers BASF
This 14-card set was produced by BASF audio and video tapes in a promotional tie-in with the Los Angeles Lakers. The cards measure approximately 5 by 7" and are unnumbered except for uniform numb they are listed below in alphabetical order for convenience. This set can be distinguished from th other two years of BASF Lakers sets in that it is the only year the set was referenced on the front of the as "Switch to BASF". The set features an early Byro Scott card.

COMPLETE SET (14) 10.00 25
1 Kareem Abdul-Jabbar 2.00 5
2 Michael Cooper 1.00 2

lvin Garrett .60 1.50
agic Johnson 2.50 6.00
tch Kupchak .75 2.00
b McAdoo 1.25 3.00
ke McGee .60 1.50
ven Nater .60 1.50
rt Rambis 1.25 3.00
yron Scott 1.50 4.00
arry Spriggs .40 1.00
amaal Wilkes .75 2.00
ames Worthy 1.50 4.00
eam Photo 1.25 3.00
am roster on back)

1984-85 Lakers BASF

12-card set was produced by BASF audio and tapes in a promotional tie-in with the Los eles Lakers. The cards measure approximately 5" and are unnumbered except for uniform number; are listed below in alphabetical order for venience.

PLETE SET (12) 12.00 30.00
reem Abdul-Jabbar 2.50 6.00
chael Cooper 1.25 3.00
gic Johnson 3.00 8.00
tch Kupchak 1.00 2.50
nnie Lester 1.25 3.00
b McAdoo 1.25 3.00
ke McGee .60 1.50
rt Rambis 1.25 3.00
ron Scott 1.25 3.00
arry Spriggs .75 2.00
Jamaal Wilkes 1.50 4.00
ames Worthy 2.00 5.00
eam Photo 2.00 5.00
am roster on back)

1960-61 Lakers Bell Brand

card measures approximately 6" by 3 1/2" and res Frank Selvy of the Los Angeles Lakers etball team. The card was inserted one per bag of Brand Potato Chips reportedly midway through the -61 season. The left half of the card features the r whereas the the right side features a 1961 Los les Lakers schedule. The reverse carries a Bell d ad along with a coupon offer of a free game with purchase of potato chips. The card is printed e ink on heavy white paper stock. The catalog gnation is F391-1.

Frank Selvy 400.00 700.00

1961-62 Lakers Bell Brand

nattractive cards within this ten-card set measure ximately 6" by 3 1/2" and feature members of the Angeles Lakers basketball team. The cards were ted one per bag of Bell Brand Potato Chips. Each r has two versions of his card, once in blue ink on stock and again in brown ink on cream-tinted . The blue-tint versions show a schedule starting October 27, whereas the brown-tint versions have edule starting with December 2. Some veteran ctors feel that the blue-tint versions are touygher d. The left half of the card features the player eas the right side features a Bell Brand ad. The se has the Los Angeles Lakers schedule behind ayer photo and the free ticket offer behind the ad. atalog designation is F391-2. The key cards in et are Elgin Baylor and Jerry West.

PLETE SET (10) 5000.00 8000.00
in Baylor 1500.00 2500.00
Felix 200.00 400.00
n Hawkins 300.00 600.00
d Hundley 400.00 800.00
ward Joliff 175.00 350.00
dy LaRusso 250.00 500.00
d Schaus CO 200.00 600.00
nk Selvy 250.00 450.00
ry West 2400.00 3000.00
ayne Yates 150.00 300.00

1992 Lakers Chevron Pins

apel pin set features five "Laker Legends" who d between 1957 and 1985. The gold-tone pins the team name and the years the player was with akers printed in purple at the top. A basketball makes up the largest portion of the pin with the 's image superimposed on the basketball. The 's name is at the bottom. The pins come attached 1/2" by 5 1/8" card that is divided into two ns. The top portion resembles a trading card, ying a color action player photo in a oval shape ed by thin purple lines. A white banner below the contains the team name. Above the picture, on the e-yellow background, is the word "Legend" in purple letters. The entire upper portion is ed by a purple border with ornate corner ng. The lower portion makes up only one-third of rd and displays the player's name and a purple e. Within this area is the lapel pin and the sor logo. The backs are white and are printed in with biographical information, statistics, career ghts, and a checklist for the other pins in the set. ards are unnumbered and checklisted below in betical order.

PLETE SET (5) 5.00 12.00
n Baylor 1.50 4.00
2 Gail Goodrich 1.00 2.50
3 Rod Hundley .75 2.00
4 Jerry West 2.00 5.00
5 Jamaal Wilkes .75 2.00

1974-75 Lakers Datsun

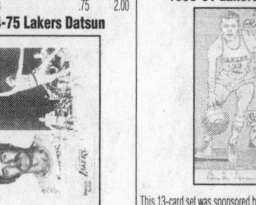

These 16 blank backed 8 1/4" x 10 1/4" black and white photos were issued during the 1975-75 season to Southern California Datsun dealers. The photos were given out to customers as a promotional offer as well as a Laker game as a complete set with an accompying envelope.

COMPLETE SET (16) 25.00 50.00
1 Bill Sharman CO 2.00 5.00
John Barnhill ACO
2 Pete Newell GM 1.25 3.00
Larry Creger
3 Chick Hearn ANN 3.00 8.00
Lynn Shackelford ANN
4 Lucius Allen 1.25 3.00
5 Zelmo Beaty 1.25 3.00
6 Corky Calhoun 1.25 3.00
7 Gail Goodrich 2.00 5.00
8 Happy Hairston 1.25 3.00
9 Connie Hawkins 2.00 5.00
10 Stu Lantz 1.25 3.00
11 Stan Love 1.25 3.00
12 Pat Riley 3.00 8.00
13 Cazzie Russell 1.50 4.00
14 Elmore Smith 1.25 3.00
15 Kermit Washington 1.25 3.00
16 Brian Winters 1.25 3.00

1985-86 Lakers Denny's Coins

This nine-coin silver-colored set was distributed by Denny's Restaurants. Each coin measures approximately 1 1/2 " in diameter. The fronts feature an embossed image of the player's head, with the team name, player's name, and jersey number circling the edge of the coin. The backs carry the sponsor logo. The coins are unnumbered and checklisted below in alphabetical order.

COMPLETE SET (9) 15.00 40.00
1 Kareem Abdul-Jabbar 4.00 10.00
2 Michael Cooper 1.25 3.00
3 Magic Johnson 6.00 15.00
4 Bob McAdoo 1.25 3.00
5 Mike McGee .60 1.50
6 Kurt Rambis 1.25 3.00
7 Byron Scott 1.25 3.00
8 Jamaal Wilkes 1.25 3.00
9 James Worthy 2.50 6.00

1993 Lakers Forum

This set features great sports and entertainment personalities who have appeared at the Great Western Forum in Los Angeles during the past 25 years. The set was sponsored by the Los Angeles Times and "Rebuild LA" and celebrates the 25th Anniversary of the Forum with 25,000 sets produced. The set includes one randomly inserted bonus card in each pack of an outstanding Laker basketball player. The bonus cards were numbered on the back with the prefix "BC". The bonus cards were randomly inserted; one could buy five regular sets and still not guarantee a complete insert set. Noted sports artist Terry Smith designed the set. Proceeds from the 12-card sets, originally priced at 25.00 each, were intended to benefit Los Angeles-area Boys and Girls Clubs. The sets were sold at the Forum's box office and concession stands during all Forum events. Sets could also be ordered through Ticketmaster outlets. The cards measure approximately 2 1/2" by 5". The black card fronts have an inner blue border on the left, right, and upper edges. Across the top is a 25th Anniversary design printed on the border with black points along the upper border edge. The name of the highlighted athlete is printed in white with the first name along the left edge and the last name appearing on the bottom edge. The horizontal backs carry a close-up posed shot on the left with a colored panel on the right giving career highlights and significant information pertaining to their appearances at the Great Western Forum.

COMPLETE SET (11) 4.00 10.00
1 Great Western Forum .10 .25
BC1 Elgin Baylor 5.00 12.00
BC2 Wilt Chamberlain 8.00 20.00
BC3 Jerry West 6.00 15.00
BC4 Kareem Abdul-Jabbar 6.00 15.00
BC5 Magic Johnson HOR 8.00 20.00

1972-73 Lakers Lunch Bags

Measuring 6" by 11", these five paper lunch bags were manufacturered by Mason Hamlin Ind. in 1972. The bags feature blue pencil drawings with the player's name and "Los Angeles" at the bottom of the bag. There are no backs. The bags are not numbered and listed below in alphabetical order.

COMPLETE SET (5) 25.00 50.00
1 Wilt Chamberlain 10.00 20.00
2 Happy Hairston 3.00 8.00
3 Gail Goodrich 5.00 10.00
4 Jim McMillian 2.50 6.00
5 Jerry West 6.00 12.00

1950-51 Lakers Scott's

This 13-card set was sponsored by Scott's Potato Chips as indicated by its logo appearing on the card face. The cards were printed on heavy stock. A complete set was redeemable for tickets to Minneapolis Lakers games and Minneapolis Lakers player photos. The cards measure approximately 2" by 4 1/2" and were distributed in potato chip and cheese potato boxes. The fronts have a cartoon-like drawing of the player in an action pose, with a facsimile autograph below the drawing. The cards are unnumbered and checklisted below in alphabetical order. The Bud Grant in the set also was active as a player in the CFL and later went on to fame as coach of the Minnesota Vikings.

COMPLETE SET (13) 14000.00 21000.00
1 Bobby Doll 300.00 600.00
2 Arnie Ferrin 400.00 800.00
3 Bud Grant 2000.00 2500.00
4 Bob Harrison 400.00 800.00
5 Joey Hutton 300.00 600.00
6 Tony Jaros 300.00 600.00
7 John Kundla CO 400.00 800.00
8 Slater Martin 900.00 1400.00
9 George Mikan 6000.00 12000.00
10 Vern Mikkelsen 1000.00 1600.00
11 Kevin O'Shea 300.00 600.00
12 Jim Pollard 1000.00 1600.00
13 Herm Schaeffer 300.00 600.00

1969-70 Lakers Tickets

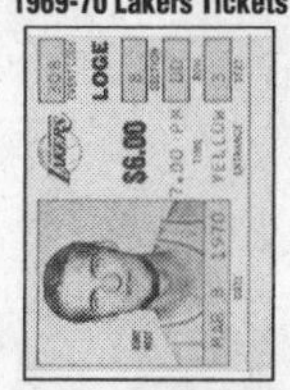

Issued as part of the regular admission tickets to Los Angeles Laker home games, there feature players from the Western Conference Champion Los Angeles Lakers. The tickets are not numbered and listed in alphabetical order below.

COMPLETE SET 40.00 80.00
1 Elgin Baylor 12.50 25.00
2 Wilt Chamberlain 15.00 30.00
3 Keith Erickson 5.00 10.00
4 Jerry West 15.00 30.00

2008-09 Lakers Upper Deck

COMPLETE SET (14) 2.50 6.00
1 Kobe Bryant 1.50 4.00
2 Lamar Odom .30 .75
3 Pau Gasol .30 .75
4 Andrew Bynum .40 1.00
5 Derek Fisher .25 .60
6 Luke Walton .20 .50
7 Vladimir Radmanovic .20 .50
8 Jordan Farmar .20 .50
9 Sasha Vujacic .20 .50
10 Trevor Ariza .20 .50
11 Chris Mihm .20 .50
12 Sun Yue .40 1.00
13 Phil Jackson CO .30 .75
14 Magic Johnson .75 2.00

1979-80 Lakers/Kings Alta-Dena

This eight-card set was sponsored by Alta-Dena Dairy, and its logo adorns the bottom of both sides of the card. The cards measure approximately 2 3/4" by 4" and feature color action player photos on the fronts. While the sides of the picture have no borders, green and red-orange stripes border the picture on its top and bottom. The player's name appears in black lettering in the top red-orange stripe. The team logo appears in the bottom red-orange stripe. The back has an offer for youngsters 14-and-under, who could present the complete eight-card set in the souvenir folder to the Forum Box Office and receive a half-price discount on certain tickets to any one of the Lakers and Kings games listed on the reverse of the card. The cards are unnumbered and are checklisted below in alphabetical order. This small set features Los Angeles Kings and Los Angeles Lakers as they were both owned by Jerry Buss. Cards 1-4 are Los Angeles Lakers (NBA) and Cards 5-8 are Los Angeles Kings (NHL). The set must have been planned and produced in the late summer of 1979 since Adrian Dantley was traded to Utah for Spencer Haywood on September 13

COMPLETE SET (8) 10.00 20.00
1 Adrian Dantley 1.25 3.00
2 Don Ford .40 1.00
3 Kareem Abdul-Jabbar 5.00 12.00
4 Norm Nixon .75 2.00

1999-00 Las Vegas Silver Bandits

COMPLETE SET (21) 2.50 6.00
1 Team CL .08 .25
2 Bandit MASCOT .08 .25
3 Silver Bandit Dancers .08 .25
4 Radio Crew .08 .25
5 Patrick Ballinger TR .08 .25
6 Isaac Burton .20 .50
7 Harold Ellis .40 1.00
8 Michael J. Frog .20 .50
9 Barry Hecker CO .40 1.00
10 J.R. Henderson .30 .75
11 Deeandre Hulett .20 .50
12 Michael Johnson .20 .50
13 Doug Lee .20 .50
14 Marcus Liberty .30 .75
15 Jeff Martin .30 .75
16 Tim Neverett ANN .20 .50
17 Eric Schraeder .20 .50
18 Rolland Todd CO .20 .50
19 Doug Swenson .20 .50
20 Mark Wade .20 .50
21 Rocky Walls .20 .50

2012-13 Leaf

COMPLETE SET (100) 15.00 40.00
AG1 Artis Gilmore .60 1.50
AM1 Arnett Moultrie .50 1.25
AN1 Andrew Nicholson .75 2.00
AY1 Alex Young .50 1.25
BB1 Bradley Beal 1.50 4.00
BHS Bob Hurley Sr. .60 1.50
BJ1 Bernard James .50 1.25
BR1 Bill Russell 1.00 2.50
CB1 Carol Blazejowski .60 1.50
CD1 Clyde Drexler .75 2.00
CH1 Cliff Hagan .60 1.50
CH2 Connie Hawkins .60 1.50
CM1 Chris Mullin .60 1.50
DC1 Dave Cowens .60 1.50
DC2 Dusan Cantekin .50 1.25
DG1 Draymond Green .50 1.25
DG2 Drew Gordon .50 1.25
DI1 Dan Issel .60 1.50
DJO Darius Johnson-Odom 1.00 2.50
DL1 Damian Lillard 2.00 5.00
DL2 Doron Lamb 1.25 3.00
DR1 Dennis Rodman 1.25 3.00
DS1 Dolph Schayes .60 1.50
DW1 Dominique Wilkins .75 2.00
DW2 Dion Waiters 1.50 4.00
EB1 Elgin Baylor .60 1.50
EH1 Elvin Hayes .60 1.50
EL1 Earl Lloyd .60 1.50
EU1 Edwin Ubiles .60 1.50
FA1 Furkan Aldemir .50 1.25
FE1 Festus Ezeli .60 1.50
FM1 Fab Melo 1.00 2.50
GG1 Gail Goodrich .60 1.50
GP1 Gary Payton .60 1.50
HG1 Hal Greer .60 1.50
HG2 Harry Gallatin .60 1.50
HP1 Herb Pope .50 1.25
IK1 Ilkan Karaman .50 1.25
JC1 Jae Crowder .60 1.50
JC2 Jared Cunningham .60 1.50
JC3 Jim Calhoun .60 1.50
JCB J'Covan Brown .50 1.25
JG1 Jorge Gutierrez .50 1.25
JJ1 John Jenkins .75 2.00
JK1 John Kundla .60 1.50
JL1 Jeremy Lamb 1.00 2.50
JS1 Jerry Sloan .60 1.50
JS2 John Shurna .50 1.25
JT1 Jordan Taylor .60 1.50
JT2 Jeffery Taylor .50 1.25
JW1 James Worthy .75 2.00
KE1 Kim English .60 1.50
KM1 Karl Malone .75 2.00
KM2 Kendall Marshall 1.00 2.50
KM3 Kevin Murphy .50 1.25
KM4 Khris Middleton .50 1.25
KOQ Kyle O'Quinn .50 1.25
MD1 Marcus Denmon .50 1.25
MH1 Marques Haynes .50 1.25
MH2 Moe Harkless .60 1.50
MJ1 Magic Johnson 1.50 4.00
ML1 Meyers Leonard .75 2.00
MM1 Moses Malone .60 1.50
MP1 Miles Plumlee .60 1.50
MS1 Mike Scott .50 1.25
MSB MarShon Brooks 1.50 4.00
MT1 Marquis Teague 1.00 2.50
NA1 Nate Archibald .60 1.50
NO1 Nnemkadi Ogwumike .60 1.50
NT1 Nate Thurmond .60 1.50
OC1 Olek Czyz .50 1.25
OJ1 Orlando Johnson .50 1.25
PJ3 Perry Jones III 1.25 3.00
RB1 Rick Barry .60 1.50
RH1 Robbie Hummel .60 1.50
RR1 Ricky Rubio 1.50 4.00
RS1 Robert Sacre .75 2.00
RW1 Royce White 1.00 2.50
SM1 Scott Machado .50 1.25
SP1 Scottie Pippen 1.25 3.00
TH1 Tu Holloway .50 1.25
TJ1 Terrence Jones 1.25 3.00
TP1 The Professor .50 1.25
TR1 Terrence Ross 1.00 2.50
TS1 Tornike Shengelia .50 1.25
TT1 Tristan Thompson 1.25 3.00
TT2 Tyshawn Taylor .60 1.50
TW1 Tony Wroten .60 1.50
TZ1 Tomislav Zubcic .50 1.25
TZ2 Tyler Zeller 1.00 2.50
WB1 Will Barton .60 1.50
WB2 William Buford .50 1.25
XG1 Xavier Gibson .50 1.25
YG1 Yancy Gates .50 1.25
CW11 Chet Walker .60 1.50

2012-13 Leaf Autographs

RANDOM INSERTS IN RETAIL PACKS
AG1 Artis Gilmore 3.00 8.00
AM1 Arnett Moultrie 2.50 6.00
AN1 Andrew Nicholson 4.00 10.00
AY1 Alex Young 2.50 6.00
BB1 Bradley Beal 8.00 20.00
BJ1 Bernard James 2.50 6.00
CH1 Cliff Hagan
CH2 Connie Hawkins 3.00 8.00
DC1 Dave Cowens 4.00 10.00
DG1 Draymond Green 2.50 6.00
DG2 Drew Gordon 2.50 6.00
DJO Darius Johnson-Odom 8.00 20.00
DL1 Damian Lillard
DL2 Doron Lamb 8.00 20.00
DR1 Dennis Rodman 12.00 30.00
DW1 Dominique Wilkins 10.00 25.00
DW2 Dion Waiters
EH1 Elvin Hayes
EU1 Edwin Ubiles 3.00 8.00
FE1 Festus Ezeli 3.00 8.00
FM1 Fab Melo 10.00 25.00
GG1 Gail Goodrich 3.00 8.00
GP1 Gary Payton
HG1 Hal Greer 3.00 8.00
HP1 Herb Pope 2.50 6.00
JC1 Jae Crowder 3.00 8.00
JC2 Jared Cunningham 3.00 8.00
JC3 Jim Calhoun 10.00 25.00
JCB J'Covan Brown 2.50 6.00
JG1 Jorge Gutierrez 2.50 6.00
JJ1 John Jenkins 6.00 15.00
JL1 Jeremy Lamb 6.00 15.00
JS2 John Shurna 2.50 6.00
JT1 Jordan Taylor 3.00 8.00
JT2 Jeffery Taylor 2.50 6.00
JW1 James Worthy 8.00 20.00
KE1 Kim English 3.00 8.00
KM2 Kendall Marshall 8.00 20.00
KM3 Kevin Murphy 2.50 6.00
KM4 Khris Middleton 2.50 6.00
KOQ Kyle O'Quinn 2.50 6.00
MD1 Marcus Denmon 2.50 6.00
MH2 Moe Harkless 3.00 8.00
ML1 Meyers Leonard 8.00 20.00
MP1 Miles Plumlee
MS1 Mike Scott 2.50 6.00
MT1 Marquis Teague
NA1 Nate Archibald 3.00 8.00
NO1 Nnemkadi Ogwumike 6.00 15.00
OC1 Olek Czyz 5.00 12.00
OJ1 Orlando Johnson 2.50 6.00
PJ3 Perry Jones III 6.00 15.00
RH1 Robbie Hummel 5.00 12.00
RS1 Robert Sacre 4.00 10.00
SM1 Scott Machado 2.50 6.00
TH1 Tu Holloway 2.50 6.00
TJ1 Terrence Jones
TR1 Terrence Ross 5.00 12.00
TS1 Tornike Shengelia 2.50 6.00
TT2 Tyshawn Taylor 3.00 8.00
TW1 Tony Wroten
TZ1 Tomislav Zubcic 2.50 6.00
TZ2 Tyler Zeller 10.00 25.00
WB1 Will Barton
WB2 William Buford 2.50 6.00
YG1 Yancy Gates 2.50 6.00

2011-12 Leaf Best of Basketball Autographs

ONE PER PACK
UNPRICED RED PRINT RUN 5 SETS
UNPRICED PLATE PRINT RUN ONE SET
AG1 Artis Gilmore 5.00 12.00
BH1 Bailey Howell 5.00 12.00
BH2 Bob Hurley Sr. 10.00 25.00
BR1 Bill Russell 40.00 100.00
CB1 Carol Blazejowski 5.00 12.00
CH1 Cliff Hagan 5.00 12.00
DI1 Dan Issel 5.00 12.00
DR1 Dennis Rodman 15.00 40.00
DS1 Dolph Schayes 5.00 12.00
EH1 Elvin Hayes 6.00 15.00
EL1 Earl Lloyd 10.00 25.00
HG1 Harry Gallatin 5.00 12.00
JK1 John Kundla 10.00 25.00
JS1 Jerry Sloan 8.00 20.00
MB1 MarShon Brooks 10.00 25.00
MG1 Marques Haynes 10.00 25.00
MJ1 Magic Johnson 30.00 80.00
ML1 Meadowlark Lemon 15.00 40.00
MM1 Moses Malone 8.00 20.00
NT1 Nate Thurmond 5.00 12.00
OR1 Oscar Robertson 25.00 60.00
RB1 Rick Barry 6.00 15.00
RR1 Ricky Rubio 30.00 80.00
TP1 The Professor 5.00 12.00
TT1 Tristan Thompson 8.00 20.00
SP1A Scottie Pippen 100.00 200.00

2011-12 Leaf Best of Basketball Autographs Green

*GREEN: .5X TO 1.25X HI COLUMN
STATED PRINT RUN 5 TO 25 SER.#'d SETS
SOME UNPRICED DUE TO SCARCITY
EL1 Earl Lloyd/25 15.00 40.00
MB1 MarShon Brooks/25 25.00 60.00
RR1 Ricky Rubio/25 50.00 125.00
TP1 The Professor/25 12.00 30.00
TT1 Tristan Thompson/25 15.00 40.00

2011 Leaf Legends of Sport

STATED PRINT RUN 6-50
NO PRICING ON CARDS #'d TO 12 OR LESS
BA7 Artis Gilmore/15 12.00 30.00
BA11 Bill Russell/20 50.00 120.00
BA28 Elvin Hayes/15 10.00 25.00
BA51 Meadowlark Lemon/50 20.00 50.00
BA57 Moses Malone/15 15.00 40.00
BA60 Oscar Robertson/15 40.00 80.00
BA69 Rick Barry/27 10.00 25.00

2011 Leaf Legends of Sport Award Winners Autographs Bronze

STATED PRINT RUN 10-50
AW1 Artis Gilmore/15 12.00 30.00
AW3 Bill Russell/20 60.00 120.00

2011 Leaf Legends of Sport Cut Signatures

IT3 Isiah Thomas 12.00 30.00

2011 Leaf Legends of Sport Moments of Greatness Autographs Bronze

STATED PRINT RUN 10-50
MG11 Elvin Hayes/15 10.00 25.00
MG29 Rick Barry/26 10.00 25.00

2011 Leaf Legends of Sport Numeration Autographs

STATED PRINT RUN 4-30
NO PRICING ON CARDS #'d TO 12 OR LESS

2011 Leaf Legends of Sport Perennial All-Stars Autographs

STATED PRINT RUN 5-24
NO PRICING ON CARDS #'d TO 13 OR LESS

2011 Leaf Muhammad Ali Fans of Ali Autographs Bronze

OVERALL NON-ALI AUTO ODDS TWO PER PACK
CARD FAU7 NOT ISSUED
FAU3 Magic Johnson 40.00 80.00
FAU10 Dennis Rodman 25.00 50.00

2011 Leaf Muhammad Ali Fans of Ali Autographs Gold

STATED PRINT RUN 5 SER. #'d SETS
UNPRICED DUE TO SCARCITY
CARD FAU7 NOT ISSUED

2011 Leaf Muhammad Ali Fans of Ali Autographs Silver

*SILVER: .6X TO 1.2X BRONZE
STATED PRINT RUN 25 SER. #'d SETS
CARD FAU7 NOT ISSUED

2011 Leaf Muhammad Ali Metal Fans of Ali Autographs

FAUM2 Dennis Rodman 20.00 40.00
FAUM9 Magic Johnson 25.00 50.00

2012 Leaf National Convention

AG1 Artis Gilmore .20 .50
CD1 Clyde Drexler .40 1.00
CH1 Cliff Hagan .20 .50
CH2 Connie Hawkins .25 .60
CM1 Chris Mullin .30 .75
DC1 Dave Cowens .20 .50
DR1 Dennis Rodman .75 2.00
DW1 Dominique Wilkins .40 1.00
EB1 Elgin Baylor .20 .50
EH1 Elvin Hayes .20 .50
GG1 Gail Goodrich .20 .50
GP1 Gary Payton .30 .75
HG1 Hal Greer .20 .50
JC3 Jim Calhoun .20 .50
JW1 James Worthy .40 1.00
MJ1 Magic Johnson .75 2.00
NA1 Nate Archibald .20 .50
SP1 Scottie Pippen .60 1.50

2012 Leaf National Convention VIP

COMPLETE SET (5) 5.00 12.00
VIP1 Bradley Beal 1.50 4.00

2012-13 Leaf Signature

UNPRICED BLUE PRINT RUN 5 TO 10 SETS
UNPRICED PLATE PRINT RUN ONE SET
UNPRICED PURPLE PRINT RUN ONE SET
UNPRICED RED PRINT RUN 5 SETS
AH1 Anfernee Hardaway
AM1 Arnett Moultrie 3.00 8.00
AN1 Andrew Nicholson 5.00 12.00
AY1 Alex Young 3.00 8.00
BB1 Bradley Beal 15.00 40.00
CD1 Clyde Drexler 15.00 40.00
DG1 Draymond Green 3.00 8.00
DG2 Drew Gordon 3.00 8.00
DL1 Damian Lillard 25.00 60.00
DL2 Doron Lamb 8.00 20.00
DR1 Dennis Rodman 15.00 40.00
DW1 Dominique Wilkins 12.00 30.00
DW2 Dion Waiters 10.00 25.00
EU1 Edwin Ubiles 4.00 10.00
FE1 Festus Ezeli 4.00 10.00
FM1 Fab Melo 6.00 15.00
HP1 Herb Pope 3.00 8.00
JC1 Jae Crowder 4.00 10.00
JC2 Jared Cunningham 4.00 10.00
JCB J'Covan Brown 3.00 8.00
JJ1 John Jenkins 5.00 12.00
JL1 Jeremy Lamb 6.00 15.00
JT2 Jeffery Taylor 3.00 8.00
KE1 Kim English 4.00 10.00
KM1 Karl Malone 40.00 100.00
KM2 Kendall Marshall 6.00 15.00
KM4 Khris Middleton 3.00 8.00
MD1 Marcus Denmon 3.00 8.00
MH1 Marques Haynes 6.00 15.00
MH2 Moe Harkless 4.00 10.00
ML1 Meyers Leonard 5.00 12.00
MS1 Mike Scott 3.00 8.00
MT1 Marquis Teague 8.00 20.00
NO1 Nnemkadi Ogwumike 3.00 8.00
OJ1 Orlando Johnson 3.00 8.00
PJ3 Perry Jones III 8.00 20.00
RS1 Robert Sacre 5.00 12.00
RW1 Royce White 6.00 15.00
SM1 Scott Machado 3.00 8.00
SP1 Scottie Pippen 75.00 150.00
TH1 Tu Holloway 3.00 8.00
TJ1 Terrence Jones 8.00 20.00
TR1 Terrence Ross 6.00 15.00
TT2 Tyshawn Taylor 4.00 10.00
TW1 Tony Wroten 4.00 10.00
TZ2 Tyler Zeller 8.00 20.00
WB1 Will Barton 4.00 10.00
XG1 Xavier Gibson 3.00 8.00
YG1 Yancy Gates 3.00 8.00

2012-13 Leaf Signature Gold

*GOLD: .6X TO 1.5X BASE HI
STATED PRINT RUN 10 TO 25 SETS
DW2 Dion Waiters 25.00 60.00
FM1 Fab Melo 12.00 30.00
JJ1 John Jenkins 10.00 25.00
NO1 Nnemkadi Ogwumike 8.00 20.00
PJ3 Perry Jones III 20.00 50.00
RW1 Royce White 15.00 40.00

2012-13 Leaf Signature Silver

*SILVER: .5X TO 1.25X BASE HI
STATED PRINT RUN 25 TO 99 SETS
DL1 Damian Lillard/99 40.00 100.00
JJ1 John Jenkins/50 10.00 25.00
TT2 Tyshawn Taylor/99 6.00 15.00

2012-13 Leaf Signature All-American Gold

*GOLD: .5X TO 1.25X SILVER
STATED PRINT RUN 25 SER.#'d SETS
NO1 Nnemkadi Ogwumike 8.00 20.00
TZ2 Tyler Zeller 15.00 40.00

2012-13 Leaf Signature All-American Silver

STATED PRINT RUN 75 TO 99 SER.#'d SETS
AM1 Arnett Moultrie/99 4.00 10.00
BB1 Bradley Beal/99 15.00 40.00
DL1 Damian Lillard/99 50.00 125.00
DL2 Doron Lamb/99 10.00 25.00
DW2 Dion Waiters/99 12.00 30.00
FM1 Fab Melo/99 8.00 20.00
JL1 Jeremy Lamb/99 8.00 20.00
JT2 Jeffery Taylor/99 4.00 10.00
KM2 Kendall Marshall/99 8.00 20.00
MH2 Moe Harkless/99 5.00 12.00
ML1 Meyers Leonard/99 8.00 20.00
NO1 Nnemkadi Ogwumike/99 4.00 10.00
PJ3 Perry Jones III/99
TJ1 Terrence Jones/99 10.00 25.00
TR1 Terrence Ross/99 8.00 20.00
TW1 Tony Wroten/99 5.00 12.00
TZ2 Tyler Zeller/75 10.00 25.00

2012-13 Leaf Signature Black and White

RANDOM INSERTS IN PACKS
UNPRICED BLUE PRINT RUN 3 SETS
UNPRICED GOLD PRINT RUN 5 SETS
UNPRICED PURPLE PRINT RUN ONE SET
UNPRICED RED PRINT RUN 2 SETS
UNPRICED SILVER PRINT RUN 10 SETS
BB1 Bradley Beal
CD1 Clyde Drexler
DL1 Damian Lillard 25.00 60.00
DL2 Doron Lamb 10.00 25.00
DR1 Dennis Rodman
DW1 Dominique Wilkins
KM1 Karl Malone 40.00 100.00
KM2 Kendall Marshall 8.00 20.00
NO1 Nnemkadi Ogwumike
PJ3 Perry Jones III
SP1 Scottie Pippen 100.00 200.00
TJ1 Terrence Jones 10.00 25.00

2012-13 Leaf Signature Droppin' Dimes Gold

*GOLD: .5X TO 1.25X SILVER
STATED PRINT RUN 25 SER.#'d SETS
DL1 Damian Lillard 50.00 125.00

2012-13 Leaf Signature Droppin' Dimes Silver

STATED PRINT RUN 49 TO 99 SETS
DL1 Damian Lillard/75 25.00 60.00
KM2 Kendall Marshall/99 10.00 25.00
MT1 Marquis Teague/99 10.00 25.00
SM1 Scott Machado/49 4.00 10.00
TT2 Tyshawn Taylor/99 5.00 12.00
TW1 Tony Wroten/99 5.00 12.00

2012-13 Leaf Signature Scottie Pippen Patch Autographs

STATED PRINT RUN ONE TO 99 SETS
SOME UNPRICED DUE TO SCARCITY
SP1 Scottie Pippen/99 150.00 300.00
SP2 Scottie Pippen Blue/25 250.00 400.00

2012-13 Leaf Signature So Money! Gold

*GOLD: .5X TO 1.25X SILVER
STATED PRINT RUN 25 SER.#'d SETS
NO1 Nnemkadi Ogwumike 8.00 20.00

2012-13 Leaf Signature So Money! Silver

STATED PRINT RUN 40 TO 99 SETS
BB1 Bradley Beal/99 15.00 40.00
DL1 Damian Lillard/99 40.00 100.00
DL2 Doron Lamb/99 10.00 25.00
JJ1 John Jenkins/99 8.00 20.00
JL1 Jeremy Lamb/99 8.00 20.00
KM1 Karl Malone/40 50.00 125.00
MH2 Moe Harkless/99 5.00 12.00
MT1 Marquis Teague/99 10.00 25.00
NO1 Nnemkadi Ogwumike/99 4.00 10.00
PJ3 Perry Jones III/75 10.00 25.00
TR1 Terrence Ross/99 8.00 20.00
TZ2 Tyler Zeller/75 10.00 25.00

2012-13 Leaf Signature Takin' it to the Hole Gold

*GOLD: .5X TO 1.25X SILVER
STATED PRINT RUN 25 SER.#'d SETS
DG1 Draymond Green 6.00 15.00
DL1 Damian Lillard 60.00 150.00
NO1 Nnemkadi Ogwumike 8.00 20.00

2012-13 Leaf Signature Takin' it to the Hole Silver

STATED PRINT RUN 99 SER.#'d SETS
AM1 Arnett Moultrie/99 4.00 10.00
AN1 Andrew Nicholson/99 6.00 15.00
BB1 Bradley Beal/99 15.00 40.00
DG1 Draymond Green/49 4.00 10.00
DL1 Damian Lillard/75 30.00 80.00
DW2 Dion Waiters/49 12.00 30.00
JT2 Jeffery Taylor/49 4.00 10.00
NO1 Nnemkadi Ogwumike/99 4.00 10.00
RW1 Royce White/99 8.00 20.00
TJ1 Terrence Jones/49 10.00 25.00
TR1 Terrence Ross/99 8.00 20.00
WB1 Will Barton/99 5.00 12.00

1992 Lime Rock Larry Bird

This three-card hologram set was produced by Lime Rock Productions and packaged in a black folder displaying a three-dimensional embossed etching of Larry Bird. According to Lime Rock, the production run was 10,000 cases or 250,000 sets, and 2,500 autographed cards were randomly inserted throughout the packaging process (one in every 100 sets). A numbered certificate of authenticity was included with each set. The cards measure the standard size and depict three stages in his career: 1) his passing skill at Indiana State; 2) his patented shooting style at Boston; and 3) posed in a red, white, and blue warm-up in anticipation of his participation in the Summer Olympic games in Barcelona. The backs have color photos and an extended caption summarizing Bird's career.

COMPLETE SET (3) 1.50 4.00
COMMON CARD (1-3) .60 1.50

2009-10 Limited

1-100 PRINT RUN 199 SER.#'d SETS
101-150 PRINT RUN 99 SER.#'d SETS
151-180 PRINT RUN 299 SER.#'d SETS
UNPRICED GOLD PRINT RUN 10 SETS
UNPRICED PLATINUM PRINT RUN ONE SET
1 Andre Iguodala 1.50 4.00
2 Elton Brand 1.50 4.00
3 Samuel Dalembert 1.00 2.50
4 Chris Duhon 1.00 2.50
5 David Lee 1.25 3.00
6 Wilson Chandler 1.25 3.00

7 Kevin Garnett 3.00 8.00
8 Paul Pierce 2.00 5.00
9 Rasheed Wallace 1.50 4.00
10 Ray Allen 1.50 4.00
11 Brook Lopez 1.50 4.00
12 Courtney Lee 1.25 3.00
13 Devin Harris 1.50 4.00
14 Andrea Bargnani 1.25 3.00
15 Chris Bosh 1.50 4.00
16 Hedo Turkoglu 1.50 4.00
17 Ben Wallace 1.50 4.00
18 Richard Hamilton 1.25 3.00
19 Rodney Stuckey 1.50 4.00
20 Tayshaun Prince 1.50 4.00
21 Derrick Rose 5.00 12.00
22 Luol Deng 1.50 4.00
23 Tyrus Thomas 1.25 3.00
24 Daniel Gibson 1.25 3.00
25 LeBron James 8.00 20.00
26 Mo Williams 1.25 3.00
27 Shaquille O'Neal 3.00 8.00
28 Danny Granger 1.50 4.00
29 Jeff Foster 1.00 2.50
30 T.J. Ford 1.00 2.50
31 Andrew Bogut 1.50 4.00
32 Kurt Thomas 1.00 2.50
33 Michael Redd 1.50 4.00
34 Dwight Howard 2.50 6.00
35 Jameer Nelson 1.25 3.00
36 Rashard Lewis 1.25 3.00
37 Vince Carter 2.00 5.00
38 Joe Johnson 1.50 4.00
39 Marvin Williams 1.25 3.00
40 Mike Bibby 1.25 3.00
41 Antawn Jamison 1.50 4.00
42 Caron Butler 1.50 4.00
43 Gilbert Arenas 1.50 4.00
44 Gerald Wallace 1.50 4.00
45 Raymond Felton 1.25 3.00
46 Tyson Chandler 1.25 3.00
47 Dwyane Wade 3.00 8.00
48 Jermaine O'Neal 1.50 4.00
49 Mario Chalmers 1.50 4.00
50 Michael Beasley 1.50 4.00
51 Aaron Brooks 1.00 2.50
52 Shane Battier 1.50 4.00
53 Trevor Ariza 1.00 2.50
54 O.J. Mayo 1.50 4.00
55 Rudy Gay 1.50 4.00
56 Zach Randolph 1.25 3.00
57 Chris Paul 2.50 6.00
58 David West 1.50 4.00
59 Emeka Okafor 1.50 4.00
60 James Posey 1.00 2.50
61 Dirk Nowitzki 2.00 5.00
62 Jason Kidd 1.50 4.00
63 Jason Terry 1.25 3.00
64 Josh Howard 1.25 3.00
65 Antonio McDyess 1.25 3.00
66 Tim Duncan 2.50 6.00
67 Tony Parker 1.50 4.00
68 Brandon Roy 1.50 4.00
69 Greg Oden 1.25 3.00
70 LaMarcus Aldridge 1.50 4.00
71 Rudy Fernandez 1.25 3.00
72 Corey Brewer 1.00 2.50
73 Kevin Love 2.50 6.00
74 Ramon Sessions 1.25 3.00
75 Andrei Kirilenko 1.25 3.00
76 Carlos Boozer 1.50 4.00
77 Deron Williams 1.50 4.00
78 Jeff Green 1.25 3.00
79 Kevin Durant 5.00 12.00
80 Russell Westbrook 2.50 6.00
81 Carmelo Anthony 2.00 5.00
82 Chauncey Billups 1.50 4.00
83 Kenyon Martin 1.50 4.00
84 Derek Fisher 1.25 3.00
85 Kobe Bryant 8.00 20.00
86 Lamar Odom 1.50 4.00
87 Pau Gasol 1.50 4.00
88 Ron Artest 1.50 4.00
89 Andris Biedrins 1.00 2.50
90 Anthony Randolph 1.25 3.00
91 Stephen Jackson 1.25 3.00
92 Amare Stoudemire 1.50 4.00
93 Channing Frye 1.25 3.00
94 Steve Nash 1.50 4.00
95 Baron Davis 1.50 4.00
96 Eric Gordon 1.50 4.00
97 Marcus Camby 1.00 2.50
98 Andres Nocioni 1.00 2.50
99 Kevin Martin 1.50 4.00
100 Spencer Hawes 1.25 3.00
101 Magic Johnson 5.00 12.00
102 Glen Rice 2.00 5.00
103 Wilt Chamberlain 4.00 10.00
104 World B. Free 2.00 5.00
105 Julius Erving 4.00 10.00
106 Alex English 2.00 5.00
107 Al Cervi 2.00 5.00
108 John Salley 2.00 5.00
109 Al Attles 2.00 5.00
110 Maurice Cheeks 2.00 5.00
111 Bob Cousy 3.00 8.00
112 Cazzie Russell 2.00 5.00
113 Dave Bing 2.00 5.00
114 Bob McAdoo 2.00 5.00
115 Albert King 2.00 5.00
116 Alonzo Mourning 2.50 6.00
117 Sleepy Floyd 2.00 5.00
118 John Havlicek 2.00 5.00
119 Gheorghe Muresan 2.00 5.00
120 Sidney Moncrief 2.00 5.00
121 Jamal Mashburn 2.00 5.00
122 Kevin McHale 2.00 5.00
123 Larry Bird 6.00 15.00
124 Vlade Divac 2.00 5.00
125 Sean Elliott 2.00 5.00
126 Chris Ford 2.00 5.00
127 Campy Russell 2.00 5.00
128 Muggsy Bogues 2.00 5.00
129 Elgin Baylor 2.00 5.00
130 Bill Walton 2.00 5.00
131 Rickey Green 2.00 5.00
132 Hal Greer 2.00 5.00
133 Norm Nixon 2.00 5.00
134 Jerry Sloan 2.00 5.00
135 David Robinson 3.00 8.00
136 Darryl Dawkins 2.00 5.00
137 Cliff Hagan 2.00 5.00
138 Clyde Drexler 2.50 6.00
139 Dikembe Mutombo 2.00 5.00
140 Jo Jo White 2.00 5.00
141 LaSalle Thompson 2.00 5.00
142 Michael Cooper 2.00 5.00
143 Shawn Bradley 2.00 5.00
144 Walt Frazier 2.00 5.00
145 Harry Gallatin 2.00 5.00
146 Connie Hawkins 2.00 5.00
147 Moses Malone 2.00 5.00
148 Walt Bellamy 2.00 5.00
149 Pete Maravich 15.00 30.00
150 Bill Russell 3.00 8.00
151 Blake Griffin JSY AU RC 100.00 200.00
152 Hasheem Thabeet JSY AU RC 6.00 15.00
153 James Harden JSY AU RC 20.00 50.00
154 Tyreke Evans JSY AU RC 15.00 40.00
155 Jonny Flynn JSY AU RC 6.00 15.00
156 Stephen Curry JSY AU RC 15.00 40.00
157 Jordan Hill JSY AU RC 6.00 15.00
158 Brandon Jennings JSY AU RC 12.00 30.00
159 Terrence Williams JSY AU RC 6.00 15.00
160 Gerald Henderson JSY AU RC 6.00 15.00
161 Tyler Hansbrough JSY AU RC 10.00 25.00
162 Earl Clark JSY AU RC 6.00 15.00
163 Austin Daye JSY AU RC 6.00 15.00
164 James Johnson JSY AU RC 6.00 15.00
165 Jrue Holiday JSY AU RC 12.00 30.00
166 Ty Lawson JSY AU RC 10.00 25.00
167 Jeff Teague JSY AU RC 8.00 20.00
168 Eric Maynor JSY AU RC 6.00 15.00
169 Darren Collison JSY AU RC 10.00 25.00
170 Omri Casspi JSY AU RC 6.00 15.00
171 B.J. Mullens JSY AU RC 6.00 15.00
172 Rodrigue Beaubois JSY AU RC 8.00 20.00
173 Taj Gibson JSY AU RC 8.00 20.00
174 DeMarre Carroll JSY AU RC 6.00 15.00
175 Wayne Ellington JSY AU RC 6.00 15.00
176 Toney Douglas JSY AU RC 6.00 15.00
177 DeJuan Blair JSY AU RC 8.00 20.00
178 Chase Budinger JSY AU RC 6.00 15.00
179 Sam Young JSY AU RC 6.00 15.00
180 Jodie Meeks JSY AU RC 8.00 20.00

2009-10 Limited Silver Spotlight

*1-100 SILVER: 1X TO 2.5X BASE HI
*101-150 SILVER: .75X TO 2X BASE HI
*151-180 SILVER: .75X TO 2X BASE HI
SILVER PRINT RUN 25 SER.#'d SETS
151 Blake Griffin JSY AU 250.00 500.00
153 James Harden JSY AU 40.00 100.00
154 Tyreke Evans JSY AU 40.00 100.00
156 Stephen Curry JSY AU 40.00 100.00

2009-10 Limited Banner Season

COMPLETE SET (20) 25.00 50.00
PRINT RUN 99 SER.#'d SETS
UNPRICED GOLD PRINT RUN 10 SER.#'d SETS
UNPRICED PLATINUM PRINT RUN ONE SET
*SILVER: .75X TO 2X BASE HI
SILVER PRINT RUN 25 SER.#'d SETS
1 Al Jefferson 1.50 4.00
2 Brandon Roy 1.50 4.00
3 Joe Johnson 1.50 4.00
4 Kevin Martin 1.50 4.00
5 Dirk Nowitzki 2.00 5.00
6 Danny Granger 1.50 4.00
7 Tony Parker 1.50 4.00
8 Kobe Bryant 8.00 20.00
9 Dwyane Wade 3.00 8.00
10 LeBron James 8.00 20.00
11 Stephen Jackson 1.25 3.00
12 Dwight Howard 2.50 6.00
13 Chris Paul 2.50 6.00
14 Carmelo Anthony 2.00 5.00
15 Deron Williams 1.50 4.00
16 Kevin Durant 5.00 12.00
17 Chris Bosh 1.50 4.00
18 Devin Harris 1.50 4.00
19 Paul Pierce 2.00 5.00
20 Michael Redd 1.50 4.00

2009-10 Limited Banner Season Materials

STATED PRINT RUN 5 TO 99 SER.#'d SETS
*PRIME: .75X TO 2X BASE HI
PRIME PRINT RUN ONE TO 25 SER.#'d SETS
1 Al Jefferson/99 3.00 8.00
2 Brandon Roy/99 3.00 8.00
3 Joe Johnson/99 3.00 8.00
5 Dirk Nowitzki/99 4.00 10.00
8 Kobe Bryant/99 8.00 20.00
9 Dwyane Wade/49 6.00 15.00
10 LeBron James/49 10.00 25.00
11 Stephen Jackson/99 2.50 6.00
12 Dwight Howard/99 5.00 12.00
13 Chris Paul/99 5.00 12.00
14 Carmelo Anthony/99 4.00 10.00
15 Deron Williams/49 3.00 8.00
17 Chris Bosh/99 3.00 8.00
19 Paul Pierce/49 4.00 10.00
20 Michael Redd/49 3.00 8.00

2009-10 Limited Banner Season Materials Signatures

STATED PRINT RUN 5 TO 49 SER.#'d SETS
SOME UNPRICED DUE TO SCARCITY
PRIME.SIG PRINT RUN ONE TO 10 SETS
PRIME.SIG UNPRICED DUE TO SCARCITY
8 Kobe Bryant/49 100.00 200.00

2009-10 Limited Decade Dominance

COMPLETE SET (20) 30.00 60.00
PRINT RUN 99 SER.#'d SETS
UNPRICED GOLD PRINT RUN 10 SER.#'d SETS
UNPRICED PLATINUM PRINT RUN ONE SET
*SILVER: .6X TO 1.5X BASE HI
SILVER PRINT RUN 25 SER.#'d SETS
UNPRICED MATERIAL PRINT RUN 10 SETS
UNPRICED PRIME PRINT RUN ONE TO 10 SETS
UNPRICED PRIME.SIG PRINT RUN 1 TO 5 SETS
1 Jerry West 2.50 6.00
2 Oscar Robertson 2.00 5.00
3 Wilt Chamberlain 4.00 10.00
4 Bill Russell 3.00 8.00
5 Bill Sharman 2.00 5.00
6 Bill Walton 2.00 5.00
7 Willis Reed 2.00 5.00
8 Walt Frazier 2.00 5.00
9 John Havlicek 2.00 5.00
10 Alex English 2.00 5.00
11 Elvin Hayes 2.00 5.00
12 Larry Bird 8.00 20.00
13 Magic Johnson 5.00 12.00
14 Isiah Thomas 2.00 5.00
15 Kareem Abdul-Jabbar 3.00 8.00
16 Dennis Rodman 3.00 8.00
17 Dell Curry 2.00 5.00
18 Kobe Bryant 8.00 20.00
19 LeBron James 8.00 20.00
20 Dirk Nowitzki 2.00 5.00

2009-10 Limited Decade Dominance Materials Signatures

STATED PRINT RUN 10 TO 49 SER.#'d SETS
SOME UNPRICED DUE TO SCARCITY
1 Jerry West/25 30.00 80.00
9 John Havlicek/25 30.00 60.00
10 Alex English/20 15.00 30.00
18 Kobe Bryant/49 100.00 200.00

2009-10 Limited Decade Dominance Signatures

STATED PRINT RUN 5 TO 49 SER.#'d SETS
SOME UNPRICED DUE TO SCARCITY
1 Jerry West/25 20.00 50.00
2 Oscar Robertson/49 25.00 60.00
5 Bill Sharman/49 8.00 20.00
6 Bill Walton/49 8.00 20.00
9 John Havlicek/49 15.00 30.00
10 Alex English/15 10.00 25.00
17 Dell Curry/49 8.00 20.00
18 Kobe Bryant/25 100.00 200.00
20 Dirk Nowitzki/25 40.00 100.00

2009-10 Limited Freshmen Jumbo

STATED PRINT RUN 99 SER.#'d SETS
UNPRICED PRIME PRINT RUN 10 SETS
*NUMBERS: .4X TO 1X JUMBO
NUMBERS PRINT RUN 99 SER.#'d SETS
UNPRICED NUMB.PRIME PRINT RUN 10 SETS
UNPRICED PRIME.SIG PRINT RUN 5 SETS
1 Blake Griffin 15.00 40.00
2 Hasheem Thabeet 2.50 6.00
3 James Harden 8.00 20.00
4 Tyreke Evans 6.00 15.00
5 DeMar DeRozan 4.00 10.00
6 Jonny Flynn 2.50 6.00
7 Stephen Curry 6.00 15.00
8 Jordan Hill 2.50 6.00
9 Brandon Jennings 5.00 12.00
10 Terrence Williams 2.50 6.00
11 Gerald Henderson 2.50 6.00
12 Tyler Hansbrough 4.00 10.00
13 Earl Clark 2.50 6.00
14 Austin Daye 2.50 6.00
15 James Johnson 2.50 6.00
16 Jrue Holiday 5.00 12.00
17 Ty Lawson 4.00 10.00
18 Jeff Teague 3.00 8.00
19 Eric Maynor 2.50 6.00
20 Darren Collison 4.00 10.00
21 Omri Casspi 2.50 6.00
22 B.J. Mullens 2.50 6.00
23 Rodrigue Beaubois 3.00 8.00
24 Taj Gibson 3.00 8.00
25 DeMarre Carroll 2.50 6.00
26 Wayne Ellington 2.50 6.00
27 Toney Douglas 2.50 6.00
28 DeJuan Blair 3.00 8.00
29 Chase Budinger 2.50 6.00
30 Sam Young 2.50 6.00

2009-10 Limited Freshmen Jumbo Jersey Numbers Signatures

STATED PRINT RUN 49 SER.#'d SETS
JUMBO SIGS: .4X TO 1X BASE HI
JUMBO SIGS PRINT RUN 49 SER.#'d SETS
1 Blake Griffin 125.00 250.00
2 Hasheem Thabeet 6.00 15.00
4 Tyreke Evans 25.00 60.00
6 Jonny Flynn 6.00 15.00
7 Stephen Curry 25.00 60.00
8 Jordan Hill 6.00 15.00
9 Brandon Jennings 12.00 30.00
10 Terrence Williams 6.00 15.00
11 Gerald Henderson 6.00 15.00
12 Tyler Hansbrough 10.00 25.00
13 Earl Clark 6.00 15.00
14 Austin Daye 6.00 15.00
15 James Johnson 6.00 15.00
16 Jrue Holiday 12.00 30.00
17 Ty Lawson 10.00 25.00
18 Jeff Teague 8.00 20.00
20 Darren Collison 10.00 25.00
21 Omri Casspi 6.00 15.00
22 B.J. Mullens 6.00 15.00
23 Rodrigue Beaubois 8.00 20.00
24 Taj Gibson 8.00 20.00
25 DeMarre Carroll 6.00 15.00
27 Toney Douglas 6.00 15.00
28 DeJuan Blair 8.00 20.00
29 Chase Budinger 6.00 15.00
30 Sam Young 6.00 15.00

2009-10 Limited Glass Cleaners

COMPLETE SET (20) 30.00 60.00
PRINT RUN 99 SER.#'d SETS
UNPRICED GOLD PRINT RUN 10 SER.#'d SETS
UNPRICED PLATINUM PRINT RUN ONE SET
*SILVER: .75X TO 2X BASE HI
SILVER PRINT RUN 25 SER.#'d SETS
1 Kareem Abdul-Jabbar 2.50 6.00
2 Shaquille O'Neal 3.00 8.00
3 Bill Russell 2.50 6.00
4 Dennis Rodman 2.50 6.00
5 Elvin Hayes 1.50 4.00
6 Kobe Bryant 8.00 20.00
7 Elton Brand 1.50 4.00
8 Dirk Nowitzki 2.00 5.00
9 Tim Duncan 2.50 6.00
10 Nate Thurmond 1.50 4.00
11 Hakeem Olajuwon 2.00 5.00
12 Wes Unseld 1.50 4.00
13 Jermaine O'Neal 1.50 4.00
14 Chris Bosh 1.50 4.00
15 Robert Parish 1.50 4.00
16 Artis Gilmore 1.50 4.00
17 David Robinson 2.50 6.00
18 Pau Gasol 1.50 4.00
19 Dikembe Mutombo 1.50 4.00
20 Moses Malone 1.50 4.00

2009-10 Limited Glass Cleaners Materials

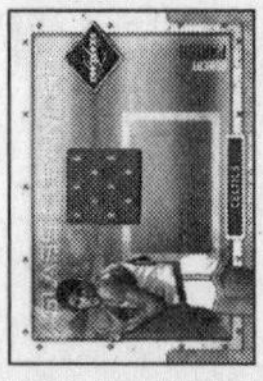

STATED PRINT RUN 49 TO 99 SER.#'d SETS
*PRIME: .75X TO 2X BASE HI
PRIME PRINT RUN ONE TO 25 SER.#'d SETS
1 Kareem Abdul-Jabbar/49 6.00 15.00
6 Kobe Bryant/99 10.00 25.00
7 Elton Brand/49 3.00 8.00
8 Dirk Nowitzki/99 4.00 10.00
9 Tim Duncan/99 5.00 12.00
11 Hakeem Olajuwon/99 5.00 12.00
13 Jermaine O'Neal/49 3.00 8.00
14 Chris Bosh/99 3.00 8.00
15 Robert Parish/99 4.00 10.00
18 Pau Gasol/99 3.00 8.00
20 Moses Malone/99 4.00 10.00

2009-10 Limited Glass Cleaners Materials Signatures

STATED PRINT RUN 10 TO 49 SER.#'d SETS
SOME UNPRICED DUE TO SCARCITY
UNPRICED PRIME.SIG PRINT RUN 1 TO 5 SETS
6 Kobe Bryant/49 100.00 200.00
15 Robert Parish/25 12.50 30.00

2009-10 Limited Glass Cleaners Signatures

STATED PRINT RUN 49 SER.#'d SETS
1 Kareem Abdul-Jabbar 40.00 80.00
3 Bill Russell 75.00 150.00
4 Dennis Rodman 30.00 80.00
5 Elvin Hayes 8.00 20.00
6 Kobe Bryant 100.00 200.00
7 Elton Brand 8.00 20.00
10 Nate Thurmond 10.00 25.00
12 Wes Unseld 8.00 20.00
13 Jermaine O'Neal 8.00 20.00
14 Chris Bosh 8.00 20.00
15 Robert Parish 10.00 25.00
16 Artis Gilmore 10.00 25.00
18 Pau Gasol 25.00 50.00

2009-10 Limited Jumbo Jersey Numbers Signatures

STATED PRINT RUN 10 TO 49 SER.#'d SETS
SOME UNPRICED DUE TO SCARCITY
NUM.PRIME SIG. PRINT RUN ONE TO 5 SETS
UNPRICED DUE TO SCARCITY
UNPRICED PRIME SIG.PRINT RUN 5 SETS
13 Andre Iguodala/49 6.00 15.00
14 Kobe Bryant/25 125.00 250.00
15 Carlos Boozer/25 6.00 15.00

2009-10 Limited Jumbo Signatures

PRINT RUN 10 TO 25 SER.#'d SETS
SOME UNPRICED DUE TO SCARCITY
14 Kobe Bryant/25 125.00 250.00
15 Carlos Boozer/25 6.00 15.00

2009-10 Limited Monikers Gold

STATED PRINT RUN ONE TO 25 SER.#'d SETS
SOME UNPRICED DUE TO SCARCITY
UNPRICED PLATINUM PRINT RUN ONE SET
13 Devin Harris/25 10.00 25.00
28 Danny Granger/25 6.00 15.00
40 Mike Bibby/25 8.00 20.00
50 Michael Beasley/25 10.00 25.00
52 Shane Battier/25 6.00 15.00
73 Kevin Love/25 15.00 40.00
76 Carlos Boozer/25 6.00 15.00
85 Kobe Bryant/25 125.00 225.00
107 Al Cervi/25 6.00 15.00
109 Al Attles/15 8.00 20.00
111 Bob Cousy/25 25.00 60.00
112 Cazzie Russell/25 8.00 20.00
114 Bob McAdoo/25 20.00 40.00
117 Sleepy Floyd/25 8.00 20.00
120 Sidney Moncrief/25 8.00 20.00
125 Sean Elliott/25 15.00 40.00
127 Campy Russell/25 8.00 20.00
130 Bill Walton/25 8.00 20.00
132 Hal Greer/25 6.00 15.00
138 Clyde Drexler/25 30.00 60.00
145 Harry Gallatin/25 6.00 15.00

2009-10 Limited Monikers Materials

STATED PRINT RUN 10 TO 25 SER.#'d SETS
SOME UNPRICED DUE TO SCARCITY
2 Andre Iguodala/25 8.00 20.00
7 Carlos Boozer/25 8.00 20.00
10 Chris Bosh/25 15.00 40.00
14 David Lee/25 8.00 20.00
15 Deron Williams/25 10.00 25.00
18 Elton Brand/25 8.00 20.00
20 Jason Kidd/25 15.00 30.00
21 Jermaine O'Neal/25 8.00 15.00
23 Kobe Bryant/25 125.00 225.00
25 Michael Beasley/25 15.00 30.00
26 Mike Bibby/25 10.00 25.00
27 Rajon Rondo/25 20.00 50.00
28 Ray Allen/25 30.00 60.00
32 Shane Battier/25 8.00 20.00
36 Alex English/20 15.00 30.00
37 Artis Gilmore/25 12.00 30.00
38 Dikembe Mutombo/25 30.00 75.00
40 Kareem Abdul-Jabbar/25 30.00 60.00
43 Larry Bird/25 40.00 100.00
47 Robert Parish/25 20.00 40.00
48 Dan Issel/25 10.00 25.00

2009-10 Limited Monikers Materials Prime

STATED PRINT RUN ONE TO 25 SER.#'d SETS
SOME UNPRICED DUE TO SCARCITY
37 Artis Gilmore/25 20.00 40.00
48 Dan Issel/25 15.00 30.00

2009-10 Limited Retired Numbers

COMPLETE SET (20) 25.00 50.00
STATED PRINT RUN 99 SER.#'d SETS
UNPRICED GOLD PRINT RUN 10 SER.#'d SETS
UNPRICED PLATINUM PRINT RUN ONE SET
*SILVER: .6X TO 1.5X BASE HI
SILVER PRINT RUN 25 SER.#'d SETS
1 Bill Russell 3.00 8.00
2 Larry Bird 6.00 15.00
3 Bob Love 2.00 5.00
4 Larry Nance 2.00 5.00
5 Alex English 2.00 5.00
6 Isiah Thomas 2.00 5.00
7 Rick Barry 2.00 5.00
8 Clyde Drexler 2.50 6.00
9 Magic Johnson 5.00 12.00
10 Kareem Abdul-Jabbar 3.00 8.00
11 Jerry West 2.50 6.00
12 Oscar Robertson 2.00 5.00
13 Willis Reed 2.00 5.00
14 Julius Erving 4.00 10.00
15 Bill Walton 2.00 5.00
16 Mitch Richmond 2.00 5.00
17 David Robinson 3.00 8.00
18 John Stockton 3.00 8.00
19 Elvin Hayes 2.00 5.00
20 Wes Unseld 2.00 5.00

2009-10 Limited Retired Numbers Materials

STATED PRINT RUN 99 SER.#'d SETS
UNPRICED PRIME PRINT RUN 10 SER.#'d SETS
UNPRICED PRIME.SIG PRINT RUN 5 SETS
2 Larry Bird 10.00 25.00
5 Alex English 4.00 10.00
6 Isiah Thomas 4.00 10.00
8 Clyde Drexler 5.00 12.00
9 Magic Johnson 8.00 20.00
10 Kareem Abdul-Jabbar 8.00 20.00
11 Jerry West 8.00 20.00
14 Julius Erving 8.00 20.00
16 Mitch Richmond 4.00 10.00
18 John Stockton 6.00 15.00

2009-10 Limited Retired Numbers Materials Signatures

STATED PRINT RUN 10 TO 49 SER.#'d SETS
SOME UNPRICED DUE TO SCARCITY
5 Alex English/25 10.00 25.00
8 Clyde Drexler/49 25.00 60.00
11 Jerry West/25 40.00 80.00

2009-10 Limited Retired Numbers Signatures

STATED PRINT RUN ONE TO 25 SER.#'d SETS
SOME UNPRICED DUE TO SCARCITY
5 Alex English/15 10.00 25.00
7 Rick Barry/25 10.00 25.00
8 Clyde Drexler/25 25.00 50.00
11 Jerry West/25 25.00 50.00
12 Oscar Robertson/25 30.00 80.00
13 Willis Reed/25 20.00 40.00
20 Wes Unseld/25 10.00 25.00

2009-10 Limited Team Trademarks

COMPLETE SET (20) 15.00 30.00
STATED PRINT RUN 99 SER.#'d SETS
UNPRICED GOLD PRINT RUN 10 SER.#'d SETS
UNPRICED PLATINUM PRINT RUN ONE SET
*SILVER: 1.25X TO 3X BASE HI
SILVER PRINT RUN 25 SER.#'d SETS
1 Tony Parker 1.00 2.50
2 Kobe Bryant 5.00 12.00
3 Dirk Nowitzki 1.25 3.00
4 Chris Bosh 1.00 2.50
5 Paul Pierce 1.25 3.00
6 Richard Hamilton .75 2
7 Yao Ming 1.25 3
8 Chris Paul 1.50 4
9 Dwight Howard 1.50 4
10 Amare Stoudemire 1.00 2
11 Brandon Roy 1.00 2
12 Kevin Love 1.50 4
13 Dwyane Wade 2.00 5
14 Gilbert Arenas 1.00 2
15 Deron Williams 1.00 2
16 Andre Iguodala 1.00 2
17 Devin Harris 1.00 2
18 Andrew Bogut 1.00 2
19 Carmelo Anthony 1.25 3
20 LeBron James 5.00 12

2009-10 Limited Team Trademarks Materials

STATED PRINT RUN 10 TO 99 SER.#'d SETS
*PRIME: .75X TO 2X BASE HI
PRIME PRINT RUN ONE TO 25 SETS
1 Tony Parker/10
2 Kobe Bryant/49 10.00 25
3 Dirk Nowitzki/99 4.00 10
4 Chris Bosh/99 3.00 8
5 Paul Pierce/49 4.00 10
6 Richard Hamilton/99 2.50 6
7 Yao Ming/99 4.00 10
8 Chris Paul/99 5.00 12
9 Dwight Howard/99 5.00 12
10 Amare Stoudemire/99 3.00 8
11 Brandon Roy/99 3.00 8
12 Kevin Love/49 5.00 12
13 Dwyane Wade/49 6.00 15
14 Gilbert Arenas/99 3.00 8
15 Deron Williams/49 3.00 8
16 Andre Iguodala/99 3.00 8
18 Andrew Bogut/99 3.00 8
19 Carmelo Anthony/99 4.00 10
20 LeBron James/49 10.00 25

2009-10 Limited Team Trademarks Materials Prime Signatures

STATED PRINT RUN ONE TO 25 SER.#'d SETS
SOME UNPRICED DUE TO SCARCITY
16 Andre Iguodala/25 8.00 20

2009-10 Limited Team Trademarks Materials Signatures

STATED PRINT RUN 5 TO 25 SER.#'d SETS
SOME UNPRICED DUE TO SCARCITY
2 Kobe Bryant/25 100.00 20
12 Kevin Love/25 15.00 4

2009-10 Limited Threads Pri

STATED PRINT RUN ONE TO 25 SER.#'d SETS
SOME UNPRICED DUE TO SCARCITY
UNPRICED THREADS PRINT RUN 10 SETS
1 Andre Iguodala/25 6.00 1
4 Chris Duhon/25 4.00 1
5 David Lee/25 5.00 1
7 Kevin Garnett/25 12.00 3
18 Richard Hamilton/25 5.00 1
25 LeBron James/25 25.00 5
29 Jeff Foster/25 4.00 1
36 Rashard Lewis/25 5.00 1
41 Antawn Jamison/25 6.00 1
44 Gerald Wallace/25 6.00 1
51 Aaron Brooks/25 4.00 1
58 David West/25 6.00 1
63 Jason Terry/25 5.00 1
64 Josh Howard/25 5.00 1
66 Tim Duncan/25 10.00 2
68 Brandon Roy/25 6.00 1
69 Greg Oden/25 5.00 1
70 LaMarcus Aldridge/25 6.00 1
73 Kevin Love/25 10.00 2
75 Andrei Kirilenko/25 5.00 1
76 Carlos Boozer/25 6.00 1
85 Kobe Bryant/25 25.00 5
98 Andres Nocioni/25 4.00 1
101 Magic Johnson/25 15.00 3
106 Alex English/25 6.00 1
122 Kevin McHale/25 8.00 2
138 Clyde Drexler/25 15.00 3
139 Dikembe Mutombo/25 15.00 3

2009-10 Limited Trios

COMPLETE SET (15) 25.00 5
STATED PRINT RUN 99 SER.#'d SETS
UNPRICED GOLD PRINT RUN 10 SETS
UNPRICED PLATINUM PRINT RUN ONE SET
*SILVER: .75X TO 2X BASE HI
SILVER PRINT RUN 25 SER.#'d SETS
1 Kobe Bryant 8.00 2
Dwyane Wade
LeBron James

ight Howard 3.00 8.00
te Robinson
aquille O'Neal
ris Paul 2.50 6.00
son Kidd
eve Nash
ake Griffin 10.00 25.00
sheem Thabeet
nes Harden
reke Evans 4.00 10.00
nny Flynn
ephen Curry
vin Garnett 3.00 8.00
ul Pierce
y Allen
rry Bird 5.00 12.00
vin McHale
bert Parish
n Artest 1.50 4.00
rlos Boozer
on Brand
agic Johnson 4.00 10.00
reem Abdul-Jabbar
ichael Cooper
anny Granger 1.50 4.00
mar Odom
ane Battier
ony Parker 1.50 4.00
ke Bibby
J. Ford
Walt Frazier 1.50 4.00
il Goodrich
nny Wilkens
ill Russell 2.50 6.00
illis Reed
lph Schayes
lvin Hayes 1.50 4.00
tis Gilmore
es Unseld
erry West 2.50 6.00
car Robertson
b Cousy

09-10 Limited Trios Materials

TED PRINT RUN 49 SER.#'d SETS
RICED PRIME PRINT RUN 10 SER.#'d SETS
be Bryant 20.00 50.00
vyane Wade
Bron James
ke Griffin 12.00 30.00
sheem Thabeet
nes Harden
eke Evans 15.00 40.00
nny Flynn
ephen Curry
vin Garnett 10.00 25.00
ul Pierce
y Allen
ry Bird 20.00 40.00
vin McHale
bert Parish

2009-10 Limited Trios Signatures

ED PRINT RUN 10 TO 49 SER.#'d SETS
ke Griffin/49 100.00 200.00
sheem Thabeet
nes Harden
reke Evans/49 50.00 120.00
nny Flynn
ephen Curry

2010-11 Limited

P.SET w/o RCs (150) 125.00 250.00
) STATED PRINT RUN 199 SETS
190 RC JSY AU PRINT RUN 249 SETS
RICED PLATINUM PRINT RUN ONE SET
H.EXPIRATION 5/3/2012
te Robinson 1.50 4.00
ul Pierce 2.00 5.00
on Rondo 2.00 5.00
aquille O'Neal 3.00 8.00
ook Lopez 1.50 4.00
vin Harris 1.50 4.00
vis Outlaw 1.25 3.00
are Stoudemire 1.50 4.00
nilo Gallinari 1.50 4.00
aymond Felton 1.25 3.00
oney Douglas 1.00 2.50
ndre Iguodala 1.50 4.00
ton Brand 1.50 4.00
ue Holiday 1.50 4.00
ouis Williams 1.25 3.00
ndrea Bargnani 1.25 3.00
eMar DeRozan 1.50 4.00
se Calderon 1.25 3.00
arlos Boozer 1.50 4.00
errick Rose 5.00 12.00
akim Noah 1.50 4.00
derson Varejao 1.25 3.00
tawn Jamison 1.50 4.00
o Williams 1.25 3.00
n Wallace 1.50 4.00
chard Hamilton 1.25 3.00
dney Stuckey 1.50 4.00
acy McGrady 1.50 4.00
nny Granger 1.50 4.00
J. Ford 1.00 2.50
ler Hansbrough 1.50 4.00
drew Bogut 1.50 4.00
andon Jennings 1.50 4.00
rey Maggette 1.25 3.00
35 Michael Redd 1.50 4.00
36 Al Horford 1.25 3.00
37 Joe Johnson 1.50 4.00
38 Josh Smith 1.50 4.00
39 Gerald Wallace 1.50 4.00
40 Stephen Jackson 1.25 3.00
41 Tyrus Thomas 1.25 3.00
42 Chris Bosh 1.50 4.00
43 Dwyane Wade 3.00 8.00
44 LeBron James 8.00 20.00
45 Mike Miller 1.50 4.00
46 Dwight Howard 2.50 6.00
47 J.J. Redick 1.50 4.00
48 Jason Williams 1.25 3.00
49 Rashard Lewis 1.25 3.00
50 JaVale McGee 1.25 3.00
51 Kirk Hinrich 1.50 4.00
52 Yi Jianlian 1.25 3.00
53 Caron Butler 1.50 4.00
54 Dirk Nowitzki 2.00 5.00
55 Jason Kidd 1.50 4.00
56 Tyson Chandler 1.25 3.00
57 Aaron Brooks 1.00 2.50
58 Kevin Martin 1.50 4.00
59 Shane Battier 1.25 3.00
60 Yao Ming 2.00 5.00
61 Marc Gasol 1.50 4.00
62 O.J. Mayo 1.50 4.00
63 Rudy Gay 1.50 4.00
64 Zach Randolph 1.25 3.00
65 Chris Paul 2.50 6.00
66 Marcus Thornton 1.50 4.00
67 Trevor Ariza 1.00 2.50
68 Manu Ginobili 1.50 4.00
69 Tim Duncan 2.50 6.00
70 Tony Parker 1.50 4.00
71 Carmelo Anthony 2.00 5.00
72 Chauncey Billups 1.50 4.00
73 Chris Andersen 1.50 4.00
74 Jonny Flynn 1.00 2.50
75 Kevin Love 2.00 5.00
76 Michael Beasley 1.50 4.00
77 Brandon Roy 1.50 4.00
78 LaMarcus Aldridge 1.50 4.00
79 Marcus Camby 1.00 2.50
80 James Harden 2.00 5.00
81 Kevin Durant 5.00 12.00
82 Russell Westbrook 2.00 5.00
83 Al Jefferson 1.50 4.00
84 Deron Williams 1.50 4.00
85 Raja Bell 1.25 3.00
86 David Lee 1.25 3.00
87 Monta Ellis 1.50 4.00
88 Stephen Curry 2.00 5.00
89 Baron Davis 1.50 4.00
90 Blake Griffin 4.00 10.00
91 Chris Kaman 1.25 3.00
92 Derek Fisher 1.25 3.00
93 Kobe Bryant 8.00 20.00
94 Pau Gasol 1.50 4.00
95 Grant Hill 2.00 5.00
96 Jason Richardson 1.50 4.00
97 Steve Nash 1.50 4.00
98 Carl Landry 1.00 2.50
99 Samuel Dalembert 1.00 2.50
100 Tyreke Evans 2.00 5.00
101 Alex English 1.50 4.00
102 Alvan Adams 1.50 4.00
103 Artis Gilmore 1.50 4.00
104 Bernard King 1.50 4.00
105 Bill Laimbeer 1.50 4.00
106 Bill Russell 2.50 6.00
107 Bill Sharman 1.50 4.00
108 Bill Walton 1.50 4.00
109 Bob Lanier 1.50 4.00
110 Bob McAdoo 1.50 4.00
111 Bob Pettit 1.50 4.00
112 Calvin Murphy 1.50 4.00
113 Cazzie Russell 1.50 4.00
114 Cedric Maxwell 1.50 4.00
115 Cliff Hagan 1.50 4.00
116 Connie Hawkins 1.50 4.00
117 Darrell Griffith 1.50 4.00
118 Dominique Wilkins 2.00 5.00
119 Elgin Baylor 1.50 4.00
120 Elvin Hayes 1.50 4.00
121 Gail Goodrich 1.50 4.00
122 Gary Payton 1.50 4.00
123 George Gervin 1.50 4.00
124 George Mikan 3.00 8.00
125 Hakeem Olajuwon 2.00 5.00
126 James Worthy 2.00 5.00
127 Jeff Hornacek 1.50 4.00
128 Jerry Lucas 1.50 4.00
129 Jerry Sloan 1.50 4.00
130 Jerry West 2.00 5.00
131 Kareem Abdul-Jabbar 2.50 6.00
132 Karl Malone 2.00 5.00
133 K.C. Jones 1.50 4.00
134 Kelly Tripucka 1.50 4.00
135 Larry Bird 5.00 12.00
136 Lenny Wilkens 1.50 4.00
137 Magic Johnson 4.00 10.00
138 Mark Aguirre 1.50 4.00
139 Nate Archibald 1.50 4.00
140 Nate Thurmond 1.50 4.00
141 Robert Parish 1.50 4.00
142 Walt Frazier 1.50 4.00
143 Wes Unseld 1.50 4.00
144 Willis Reed 1.50 4.00
145 Adrian Dantley 1.50 4.00
146 Bailey Howell 1.50 4.00
147 Chris Mullin 1.50 4.00
148 Clyde Drexler 2.00 5.00
149 Hal Greer 1.50 4.00
150 Harry Gallatin 1.50 4.00
151 Al-Farouq Aminu JSY AU RC 6.00 15.00
152 Andy Rautins JSY AU RC 6.00 15.00
153 Avery Bradley JSY AU RC 12.00 30.00
154 Cole Aldrich JSY AU RC 6.00 15.00
155 Craig Brackins JSY AU RC 6.00 15.00
156 Damion James JSY AU RC 6.00 15.00
157 Daniel Orton JSY AU RC 6.00 15.00
158 Da'Sean Butler JSY AU RC 6.00 15.00
159 DeMarcus Cousins JSY AU RC 20.00 50.00
160 Derrick Favors JSY AU RC 12.00 30.00
161 Devin Ebanks JSY AU RC 8.00 20.00
162 Dexter Pittman JSY AU RC 6.00 15.00
163 Dominique Jones JSY AU RC 6.00 15.00
164 Ed Davis JSY AU RC 8.00 20.00
165 Ekpe Udoh JSY AU RC 6.00 15.00
166 Elliot Williams JSY AU RC 6.00 15.00
167 Eric Bledsoe JSY AU RC 10.00 25.00
168 Evan Turner JSY AU RC 12.00 30.00
169 Gani Lawal JSY AU RC 6.00 15.00
170 Gordon Hayward JSY AU RC 12.00 30.00
171 Greg Monroe JSY AU RC 12.00 30.00
172 Greivis Vasquez JSY AU RC 12.00 30.00
173 Hassan Whiteside JSY AU RC 6.00 15.00
174 James Anderson JSY AU RC 6.00 15.00
175 John Wall JSY AU RC 50.00 125.00
176 Jordan Crawford JSY AU RC 10.00 25.00
177 Lance Stephenson JSY AU RC 6.00 15.00
178 Larry Sanders JSY AU RC 6.00 15.00
179 Lazar Hayward JSY AU RC 6.00 15.00
180 Luke Babbitt JSY AU RC 6.00 15.00
181 Luke Harangody JSY AU RC 6.00 15.00
182 Patrick Patterson JSY AU RC 10.00 25.00
183 Paul George JSY AU RC 15.00 40.00
184 Quincy Pondexter JSY AU RC 6.00 15.00
185 Terrico White JSY AU RC 6.00 15.00
186 Keith Gallon JSY AU RC 6.00 15.00
187 Trevor Booker JSY AU RC 6.00 15.00
188 Wesley Johnson JSY AU RC 10.00 25.00
189 Willie Warren JSY AU RC 6.00 15.00
190 Xavier Henry JSY AU RC 8.00 20.00

2010-11 Limited Gold Spotlight

*1-150 GOLD: .6X TO 1.5X BASE HI
1-150 PRINT RUN 49 SER.#'d SETS
151-190 PRINT RUN 10 SER.#'d SETS
151-190 NOT PRICED DUE TO SCARCITY

2010-11 Limited Silver Spotlight

*1-150 SILVER: .5X TO 1.25X BASE HI
1-150 PRINT RUN 149 SER.#'d SETS
*151-190 SILVER: .75X TO 2X BASE HI
151-190 PRINT RUN 25 SER.#'d SETS
159 DeMarcus Cousins JSY AU 60.00 150.00
160 Derrick Favors JSY AU 30.00 80.00
167 Eric Bledsoe JSY AU 25.00 60.00
175 John Wall JSY AU 250.00 500.00
176 Jordan Crawford JSY AU 25.00 60.00
183 Paul George JSY AU 40.00 100.00

2010-11 Limited Banner Season

COMPLETE SET (20) 20.00 50.00
STATED PRINT RUN 149 SER.#'d SETS
*GOLD: .75X TO 2X BASE HI
GOLD PRINT RUN 24 SER.#'d SETS
*SILVER: .6X TO 1.5X BASE HI
SILVER PRINT RUN 49 SER.#'d SETS
UNPRICED PLATINUM PRINT RUN ONE SET
1 Kevin Durant 4.00 10.00
2 LeBron James 6.00 15.00
3 Carmelo Anthony 1.50 4.00
4 Kobe Bryant 6.00 15.00
5 Dwyane Wade 2.50 6.00
6 Monta Ellis 1.25 3.00
7 Dirk Nowitzki 1.50 4.00
8 Danny Granger 1.25 3.00
9 Chris Bosh 1.25 3.00
10 Amare Stoudemire 1.25 3.00
11 Brandon Jennings 1.25 3.00
12 Joe Johnson 1.25 3.00
13 Derrick Rose 4.00 10.00
14 Zach Randolph 1.00 2.50
15 Kevin Martin 1.25 3.00
16 David Lee 1.00 2.50
17 Tyreke Evans 1.50 4.00
18 Brook Lopez 1.25 3.00
19 Deron Williams 1.25 3.00
20 Paul Pierce 1.50 4.00

2010-11 Limited Banner Season Materials

STATED PRINT RUN 25 TO 99 SER.#'d SETS
*PRIME: .75X TO 2X HI
PRIME: PRINT RUN 5 TO 25 SER.#'d SETS
1 Kevin Durant/99 10.00 25.00
2 LeBron James/49 8.00 20.00
3 Carmelo Anthony/99 4.00 10.00
4 Kobe Bryant/99 8.00 20.00
5 Dwyane Wade/99 6.00 15.00
7 Dirk Nowitzki/99 4.00 10.00
8 Danny Granger/25 3.00 8.00
9 Chris Bosh/49 3.00 8.00
10 Amare Stoudemire/99 3.00 8.00
11 Brandon Jennings/99 3.00 8.00
12 Joe Johnson/99 3.00 8.00
13 Derrick Rose/49 10.00 25.00
16 David Lee/49 2.50 6.00
17 Tyreke Evans/25 4.00 10.00
18 Brook Lopez/49 3.00 8.00
19 Deron Williams/99 3.00 8.00
20 Paul Pierce/99 4.00 10.00

2010-11 Limited Banner Season Materials Signatures

STATED PRINT RUN 5 TO 49 SER.#'d SETS
SOME UNPRICED DUE TO SCARCITY
PRIME SIG.PRINT RUN ONE TO 10 SETS
PRIME SIG.UNPRICED DUE TO SCARCITY
4 Kobe Bryant/25 100.00 200.00
11 Brandon Jennings/49 10.00 25.00

2010-11 Limited Decade Dominance

COMPLETE SET (20) 25.00 50.00
STATED PRINT RUN 149 SER.#'d SETS
*GOLD: 1X TO 2.5X BASE HI
GOLD PRINT RUN 24 SER.#'d SETS
*SILVER: .6X TO 1.5X BASE HI
SILVER PRINT RUN 49 SER.#'d SETS
UNPRICED PLATINUM PRINT RUN ONE SET
1 Bob Pettit 1.50 4.00
2 Elgin Baylor 1.50 4.00
3 Lenny Wilkens 1.50 4.00
4 Gail Goodrich 1.50 4.00
5 Earl Monroe 1.50 4.00
6 George Gervin 1.50 4.00
7 David Thompson 2.00 5.00
8 Sidney Moncrief 1.50 4.00
9 Hakeem Olajuwon 2.00 5.00
10 Bernard King 1.50 4.00
11 Isiah Thomas 1.50 4.00
12 Darryl Dawkins 1.50 4.00
13 Patrick Ewing 2.00 5.00
14 Scottie Pippen 3.00 8.00
15 Karl Malone 2.00 5.00
16 Clyde Drexler 2.00 5.00
17 John Stockton 2.50 6.00
18 Kobe Bryant 8.00 20.00
19 Tim Duncan 2.50 6.00
20 Dwyane Wade 3.00 8.00

2010-11 Limited Decade Dominance Materials

STATED PRINT RUN 99 SER.#'d SETS
MAT.PRIME PRINT RUN 5 TO 10 SER.#'d SETS
MAT.PRIME UNPRICED DUE TO SCARCITY
PRIME SIG.PRINT RUN ONE TO 5 SER.#'d SETS
PRIME SIG.UNPRICED DUE TO SCARCITY
9 Hakeem Olajuwon/99 4.00 10.00
10 Bernard King/99 3.00 8.00
13 Patrick Ewing/99 6.00 15.00
14 Scottie Pippen/99 8.00 20.00
15 Karl Malone/99 4.00 10.00
16 Clyde Drexler/99 4.00 10.00
17 John Stockton/99 5.00 12.00
18 Kobe Bryant/99 8.00 20.00
19 Tim Duncan/99 5.00 12.00
20 Dwyane Wade/99 6.00 15.00

2010-11 Limited Decade Dominance Materials Signatures

STATED PRINT RUN ONE TO 25 SER.#'d SETS
SOME UNPRICED DUE TO SCARCITY
9 Hakeem Olajuwon/25 20.00 50.00
14 Scottie Pippen/25 100.00 200.00
17 John Stockton/25 40.00 100.00
18 Kobe Bryant/25 100.00 200.00

2010-11 Limited Decade Dominance Signatures

STATED PRINT RUN 25 TO 99 SER.#'d SETS
1 Bob Pettit/99 EXCH 6.00 15.00
2 Elgin Baylor/99 EXCH 6.00 15.00
3 Lenny Wilkens/99 6.00 15.00
4 Gail Goodrich/99 6.00 15.00
5 Earl Monroe/99 10.00 25.00
6 George Gervin/99 8.00 20.00
7 David Thompson/99 6.00 15.00
8 Sidney Moncrief/99 6.00 15.00
9 Hakeem Olajuwon/99 20.00 50.00
10 Bernard King/99 6.00 15.00
11 Isiah Thomas/99 EXCH 8.00 20.00
12 Darryl Dawkins/99 6.00 15.00
14 Scottie Pippen/99 75.00 150.00
16 Clyde Drexler/99 15.00 40.00
17 John Stockton/99 35.00 70.00
18 Kobe Bryant/25 100.00 200.00

2010-11 Limited Freshmen Jumbo

STATED PRINT RUN 99 SER.#'d SETS
*NUMBERS: .4X TO 1X BASE HI
NUMBERS PRINT RUN 99 SER.#'d SETS
1 John Wall 10.00 25.00
2 Evan Turner 5.00 12.00
3 Derrick Favors 5.00 12.00
4 Wesley Johnson 4.00 10.00
5 DeMarcus Cousins 8.00 20.00
6 Ekpe Udoh 2.50 6.00
7 Greg Monroe 5.00 12.00
8 Al-Farouq Aminu 2.50 6.00
9 Gordon Hayward 5.00 12.00
10 Paul George 6.00 15.00
11 Cole Aldrich 2.50 6.00
12 Xavier Henry 3.00 8.00
13 Ed Davis 3.00 8.00
14 Patrick Patterson 4.00 10.00
15 Larry Sanders 2.50 6.00
16 Luke Babbitt 2.50 6.00
17 Kevin Seraphin 3.00 8.00
18 Eric Bledsoe 4.00 10.00
19 Avery Bradley 5.00 12.00
20 James Anderson 2.50 6.00
21 Craig Brackins 2.50 6.00
22 Elliot Williams 2.50 6.00
23 Trevor Booker 2.50 6.00
24 Damion James 2.50 6.00
25 Dominique Jones 2.50 6.00
26 Quincy Pondexter 2.50 6.00
27 Jordan Crawford 4.00 10.00
28 Greivis Vasquez 3.00 8.00
29 Daniel Orton 2.50 6.00
30 Lazar Hayward 2.50 6.00

2010-11 Limited Freshmen Jumbo Prime

*PRIME: 1X TO 2.5X BASE HI
STATED PRINT RUN 25 SER.#'d SETS
UNPRICED PRIME SIG.PRINT RUN 10 SETS
*NUMBERS: .4X TO 1X BASE HI
NUMBERS: PRINT RUN 10 TO 25 SETS
UNPRICED NUM.PR.SIG PRINT RUN 10 SETS
1 John Wall 25.00 60.00
2 Evan Turner 12.00 30.00
3 Derrick Favors 12.00 30.00
4 Wesley Johnson 10.00 25.00
5 DeMarcus Cousins 20.00 50.00
6 Ekpe Udoh 6.00 15.00
7 Greg Monroe 12.00 30.00
8 Al-Farouq Aminu 6.00 15.00
9 Gordon Hayward 12.00 30.00
10 Paul George 15.00 40.00
11 Cole Aldrich 6.00 15.00
12 Xavier Henry 8.00 20.00
13 Ed Davis 8.00 20.00
14 Patrick Patterson 10.00 25.00
15 Larry Sanders 6.00 15.00
16 Luke Babbitt 6.00 15.00
17 Kevin Seraphin 8.00 20.00
18 Eric Bledsoe 10.00 25.00
19 Avery Bradley 12.00 30.00
20 James Anderson 6.00 15.00
21 Craig Brackins 6.00 15.00
22 Elliot Williams 6.00 15.00
23 Trevor Booker 6.00 15.00
24 Damion James 6.00 15.00
25 Dominique Jones 6.00 15.00
26 Quincy Pondexter 6.00 15.00
27 Jordan Crawford 10.00 25.00
28 Greivis Vasquez 8.00 20.00
29 Daniel Orton 6.00 15.00
30 Lazar Hayward 6.00 15.00

2010-11 Limited Freshmen Jumbo Signatures

STATED PRINT RUN 99 SER.#'d SETS
*NUMBERS: .4X TO 1X BASE HI
NUMBERS PRINT RUN 99 SER.#'d SETS
1 John Wall 75.00 200.00
2 Evan Turner 12.00 30.00
3 Derrick Favors 12.00 30.00
4 Wesley Johnson 10.00 25.00
5 DeMarcus Cousins 20.00 50.00
6 Ekpe Udoh 6.00 15.00
7 Greg Monroe 12.00 30.00
8 Al-Farouq Aminu 6.00 15.00
9 Gordon Hayward 12.00 30.00
10 Paul George 15.00 40.00
11 Cole Aldrich 6.00 15.00
12 Xavier Henry 8.00 20.00
13 Ed Davis 8.00 20.00
14 Patrick Patterson 10.00 25.00
15 Larry Sanders 6.00 15.00
16 Luke Babbitt 6.00 15.00
17 Kevin Seraphin 8.00 20.00
18 Eric Bledsoe 10.00 25.00
19 Avery Bradley 12.00 30.00
20 James Anderson 6.00 15.00
21 Craig Brackins 6.00 15.00
22 Elliot Williams 6.00 15.00
23 Trevor Booker 6.00 15.00
24 Damion James 6.00 15.00
25 Dominique Jones 6.00 15.00
26 Quincy Pondexter 6.00 15.00
27 Jordan Crawford 10.00 25.00
28 Greivis Vasquez 8.00 20.00
29 Daniel Orton 6.00 15.00
30 Lazar Hayward 6.00 15.00

2010-11 Limited Glass Cleaners

COMPLETE SET (20) 20.00 40.00
STATED PRINT RUN 149 SER.#'d SETS
*GOLD: 1X TO 2.5X BASE HI
GOLD PRINT RUN 24 SER.#'d SETS
*SILVER: .6X TO 1.5X BASE HI
SILVER PRINT RUN 49 SER.#'d SETS
UNPRICED PLATINUM PRINT RUN ONE SET
1 Shaquille O'Neal 2.50 6.00
2 David Lee 1.00 2.50
3 Chris Bosh 1.25 3.00
4 Carlos Boozer 1.25 3.00
5 Kevin Love 1.50 4.00
6 Lamar Odom 1.25 3.00
7 Jason Kidd 1.25 3.00
8 Elgin Baylor 1.25 3.00
9 Oscar Robertson 1.50 4.00
10 Kevin McHale 1.25 3.00
11 Bill Walton 1.25 3.00
12 Troy Murphy .75 2.00
13 Dave Cowens 1.25 3.00
14 Mark Eaton 1.25 3.00
15 Alonzo Mourning 1.50 4.00
16 Elvin Hayes 1.25 3.00
17 Kareem Abdul-Jabbar 2.00 5.00
18 Bill Russell 2.00 5.00
19 Artis Gilmore 1.25 3.00
20 Kobe Bryant 6.00 15.00

2010-11 Limited Glass Cleaners Materials

STATED PRINT RUN 49 TO 99 SER.#'d SETS
2 David Lee/49 2.50 6.00
3 Chris Bosh/49 3.00 8.00
4 Carlos Boozer/49 3.00 8.00
5 Kevin Love/99 4.00 10.00
6 Lamar Odom/99 3.00 8.00
7 Jason Kidd/49 4.00 10.00
10 Kevin McHale/99 3.00 8.00
13 Dave Cowens/99 3.00 8.00
14 Mark Eaton/99 3.00 8.00
15 Alonzo Mourning/99 5.00 12.00
19 Artis Gilmore/99 3.00 8.00
20 Kobe Bryant/99 8.00 20.00

2010-11 Limited Glass Cleaners Materials Signatures

STATED PRINT RUN 5 TO 49 SER.#'d SETS
SOME UNPRICED DUE TO SCARCITY
PRIME SIG.PRINT RUN ONE TO FIVE SETS
PRIME SIG.UNPRICED DUE TO SCARCITY
5 Kevin Love/49 15.00 40.00
6 Lamar Odom/49 10.00 25.00
10 Kevin McHale/49 20.00 50.00
13 Dave Cowens/25 10.00 25.00
19 Artis Gilmore/49 10.00 25.00
20 Kobe Bryant/25 100.00 200.00

2010-11 Limited Glass Cleaners Signatures

STATED PRINT RUN 25 TO 99 SER.#'d SETS
2 David Lee/99 EXCH 5.00 12.00
3 Chris Bosh/49 12.50 30.00
4 Carlos Boozer/49 EXCH 6.00 15.00
5 Kevin Love/99 15.00 40.00
6 Lamar Odom/49 8.00 20.00
7 Jason Kidd/49 12.50 30.00
8 Elgin Baylor/49 EXCH 6.00 15.00
9 Oscar Robertson/49 50.00 120.00
10 Kevin McHale/49 20.00 50.00
11 Bill Walton/49 8.00 20.00
13 Dave Cowens/49 6.00 15.00
15 Alonzo Mourning/49 20.00 50.00
16 Elvin Hayes/49 5.00 12.00
17 Kareem Abdul-Jabbar/49 30.00 80.00
18 Bill Russell/25 50.00 120.00
19 Artis Gilmore/99 6.00 15.00
20 Kobe Bryant/25 100.00 200.00

2010-11 Limited Jumbo

STATED PRINT RUN 25 TO 99 SER.#'d SETS
*NUMBERS: .4X TO 1X BASE HI
NUMBERS PRINT RUN 25 TO 99 SETS
PRIME PRINT RUN 5 TO 10 SER.#'d SETS
PRIME UNPRICED DUE TO SCARCITY
NUMBERS PRIME PRINT RUN 5 TO 10 SETS
NUMBERS UNPRICED DUE TO SCARCITY
1 Chris Paul/99 5.00 12.00
2 Dwyane Wade/99 6.00 15.00
3 LeBron James/99 10.00 25.00
4 Kobe Bryant/99 10.00 25.00
5 Kevin Durant/99 10.00 25.00
6 Allen Iverson/49 4.00 10.00
7 Andrew Bogut/99 3.00 8.00
8 Ben Gordon/99 3.00 8.00
9 Carmelo Anthony/99 4.00 10.00
10 Chris Bosh/99 3.00 8.00
11 Deron Williams/99 3.00 8.00
12 Tyreke Evans/25 4.00 10.00
13 Dwight Howard/99 5.00 12.00
14 Tim Duncan/99 5.00 12.00
15 Kevin Garnett/99 6.00 15.00
16 Luol Deng/49 3.00 8.00
17 Gerald Wallace/99 3.00 8.00
18 Alex English/25 3.00 8.00
19 Dominique Wilkins/49 4.00 10.00
20 Patrick Ewing/99 6.00 15.00

2010-11 Limited Jumbo Jersey Numbers Signatures

STATED PRINT RUN 5 TO 25 SER.#'d SETS
SOME UNPRICED DUE TO SCARCITY
PRIME SIG.PRINT RUN ONE TO 5 SER.#'d SETS
PRIME SIG.UNPRICED DUE TO SCARCITY
4 Kobe Bryant/25 100.00 200.00
19 Dominique Wilkins/25 20.00 50.00

2010-11 Limited Jumbo Signatures

STATED PRINT RUN 5 TO 25 SER.#'d SETS
SOME UNPRICED DUE TO SCARCITY
PRIME SIG.PRINT RUN ONE TO 5 SER.#'d SETS
PRIME SIG.UNPRICED DUE TO SCARCITY
4 Kobe Bryant/25 100.00 200.00
19 Dominique Wilkins/25 20.00 50.00

2010-11 Limited Monikers Gold

STATED PRINT RUN 5 TO 99 SER.#'d SETS
SOME UNPRICED DUE TO SCARCITY
UNPRICED PLATINUM PRINT RUN ONE SET
6 Devin Harris/49 5.00 12.00
8 Amare Stoudemire/15 25.00 60.00
11 Toney Douglas/99 5.00 12.00
12 Andre Iguodala/99 5.00 12.00
14 Jrue Holiday/99 6.00 15.00
17 DeMar DeRozan/99 6.00 15.00
26 Richard Hamilton/99 6.00 15.00
31 Tyler Hansbrough/99 6.00 15.00
33 Brandon Jennings/25 15.00 40.00
57 Aaron Brooks/99 5.00 12.00
59 Shane Battier/99 5.00 12.00
66 Marcus Thornton/99 5.00 12.00
74 Jonny Flynn/99 5.00 12.00
77 Brandon Roy/49 8.00 20.00
80 James Harden/99 10.00 25.00
83 Al Jefferson/99 6.00 15.00
89 Baron Davis/49 6.00 15.00
90 Blake Griffin/99 75.00 150.00
93 Kobe Bryant/25 100.00 200.00
98 Carl Landry/99 5.00 12.00
100 Tyreke Evans/99 10.00 25.00
101 Alex English/25 6.00 15.00
102 Alvan Adams/49 6.00 15.00
103 Artis Gilmore/49 8.00 20.00
106 Bill Russell/25 50.00 120.00
109 Bob Lanier/49 5.00 12.00
110 Bob McAdoo/49 12.50 30.00
111 Bob Pettit/49 12.50 30.00
113 Cazzie Russell/49 6.00 15.00
115 Cliff Hagan/25 5.00 12.00
118 Dominique Wilkins/49 15.00 40.00
120 Elvin Hayes/49 5.00 12.00
121 Gail Goodrich/49 5.00 12.00
122 Gary Payton/25 20.00 50.00
123 George Gervin/25 6.00 15.00
125 Hakeem Olajuwon/25 15.00 40.00
127 Jeff Hornacek/25 8.00 20.00
133 K.C. Jones/25 10.00 25.00
135 Larry Bird/24 40.00 100.00
136 Lenny Wilkens/49 6.00 15.00
139 Nate Archibald/99 6.00 15.00
140 Nate Thurmond/99 5.00 12.00
141 Robert Parish/25 8.00 20.00
144 Willis Reed/49 6.00 15.00
145 Adrian Dantley/25 6.00 15.00
149 Hal Greer/99 5.00 12.00

2010-11 Limited Monikers Materials

STATED PRINT RUN 5 TO 99 SER.#'d SETS
SOME UNPRICED DUE TO SCARCITY
3 Brandon Jennings/49 10.00 25.00
4 Brandon Roy/49 8.00 20.00
5 Carlos Boozer/25 10.00 25.00
8 Chris Andersen/49 20.00 50.00
10 Chris Kaman/49 6.00 15.00
11 Chris Mullin/25 12.50 30.00
14 Danny Manning/25 12.00 30.00
16 Derek Fisher/49 12.50 30.00
17 Detlef Schrempf/99 10.00 25.00
19 Gary Payton/25 12.50 30.00
20 Glen Rice/99 6.00 15.00
21 Jalen Rose/25 10.00 25.00
23 Jeff Hornacek/25 8.00 20.00
24 Jermaine O'Neal/25 10.00 25.00
25 Joe Dumars/25 10.00 25.00
26 Kareem Abdul-Jabbar/25 50.00 120.00
27 Kelly Tripucka/99 6.00 15.00
28 Kevin Johnson/99 20.00 50.00
29 Kevin Love/99 15.00 40.00
30 Kobe Bryant/25 100.00 200.00
31 Lamar Odom/49 6.00 15.00
32 Larry Johnson/99 15.00 40.00
33 Magic Johnson/25 50.00 125.00
34 Maurice Cheeks/49 6.00 15.00
35 Michael Cage/99 6.00 15.00
36 Pau Gasol/25 15.00 40.00
37 Ray Allen/49 25.00 60.00
38 Robert Parish/25 10.00 25.00
39 Ron Artest/99 10.00 25.00
40 Russell Westbrook/99 15.00 40.00
41 Rudy Fernandez/99 EXCH 6.00 15.00
42 Sam Perkins/25 8.00 20.00
43 Scottie Pippen/25 100.00 200.00
44 Shane Battier/99 6.00 15.00
45 Shawn Bradley/99 6.00 15.00
46 Stephen Curry/99 12.50 30.00
47 Steve Nash/21 30.00 80.00
48 Tony Parker/25 12.50 30.00
49 Tyreke Evans/25 12.50 30.00
50 Vince Carter/25 20.00 50.00

2010-11 Limited Monikers Materials Prime

STATED PRINT RUN ONE TO 25 SER.#'d SETS
SOME UNPRICED DUE TO SCARCITY
4 Brandon Roy/25 15.00 40.00
17 Detlef Schrempf/25 20.00 50.00
20 Glen Rice/25 15.00 40.00
27 Kelly Tripucka/25 10.00 25.00
28 Kevin Johnson/25 50.00 120.00
29 Kevin Love/25 25.00 60.00
32 Larry Johnson/25 50.00 125.00
34 Maurice Cheeks/25 10.00 25.00
35 Michael Cage/25 10.00 25.00
37 Ray Allen/25 30.00 80.00
39 Ron Artest/25 20.00 50.00
40 Russell Westbrook/25 25.00 60.00
41 Rudy Fernandez/25 EXCH 10.00 25.00
44 Shane Battier/25 12.00 30.00
45 Shawn Bradley/25 10.00 25.00
46 Stephen Curry/25 20.00 50.00

2010-11 Limited Next Day Autographs

STATED PRINT RUN 90 TO 99 SER.#'d SETS
1 Ekpe Udoh/99 12.00 30.00
2 Gordon Hayward/99 25.00 60.00
3 Lance Stephenson/99 12.00 30.00
4 Trevor Booker/99 12.00 30.00
6 Paul George/99 60.00 150.00
7 Greg Monroe/90 30.00 80.00
8 Derrick Favors/99 30.00 80.00
9 Gani Lawal/93 12.00 30.00
10 Craig Brackins/99 12.00 30.00
11 Cole Aldrich/99 12.00 30.00
12 Xavier Henry/99 15.00 40.00
13 John Wall/99 200.00 400.00
14 DeMarcus Cousins/99 40.00 100.00
15 Patrick Patterson/99 20.00 50.00
16 Eric Bledsoe/99 20.00 50.00
17 Daniel Orton/99 12.00 30.00
18 Lazar Hayward/99 12.00 30.00
19 Hassan Whiteside/95 12.00 30.00
20 Greivis Vasquez/99 15.00 40.00
21 Elliot Williams/99 12.00 30.00
22 Luke Babbitt/99 12.00 30.00
23 Ed Davis/99 15.00 40.00
24 Luke Harangody/98 12.00 30.00
25 Evan Turner/99 25.00 60.00
26 Willie Warren/99 12.00 30.00
27 Keith Gallon/99 12.00 30.00
28 James Anderson/99 12.00 30.00
29 Dominique Jones/99 12.00 30.00
30 Wesley Johnson/99 20.00 50.00
31 Terrico White/96 12.00 30.00
32 Avery Bradley/99 25.00 60.00
33 Dexter Pittman/97 12.00 30.00
34 Damion James/99 12.00 30.00
35 Larry Sanders/99 12.00 30.00
36 Al-Farouq Aminu/99 12.00 30.00
37 Quincy Pondexter/97 12.00 30.00
38 Da'Sean Butler/99 12.00 30.00
39 Devin Ebanks/99 15.00 40.00
40 Jordan Crawford/99 20.00 50.00
41 Jeremy Lin/99 400.00 700.00

2010-11 Limited Retired Numbers

COMPLETE SET (20) 20.00 40.00
STATED PRINT RUN 149 SER.#'d SETS
*GOLD: 1X TO 2.5X BASE HI
GOLD PRINT RUN 24 SER.#'d SETS
*SILVER: .6X TO 1.5X BASE HI
SILVER PRINT RUN 49 SER.#'d SETS
UNPRICED PLATINUM PRINT RUN ONE SET
1 Bob Pettit 1.50 4.00
2 Mark Price 1.50 4.00
3 Rolando Blackman 1.50 4.00
4 Elgin Baylor 1.50 4.00
5 Nate Archibald 1.50 4.00
6 Darrell Griffith 1.50 4.00
7 Dan Issel 1.50 4.00
8 Al Attles 1.50 4.00
9 Sidney Moncrief 1.50 4.00
10 Earl Monroe 1.50 4.00
11 Mark Eaton 1.50 4.00
12 Tom Heinsohn 1.50 4.00
13 Hakeem Olajuwon 2.00 5.00
14 Gail Goodrich 1.50 4.00
15 George Gervin 1.50 4.00
16 Nate Thurmond 1.50 4.00
17 Joe Dumars 1.50 4.00
18 Calvin Murphy 1.50 4.00
19 Dave Cowens 1.50 4.00
20 Alvan Adams 1.50 4.00

2010-11 Limited Retired Numbers Materials

STATED PRINT RUN 99 SER.#'d SETS
PRIME PRINT RUN 5 TO 10 SER.#'d SETS
PRIME UNPRICED DUE TO SCARCITY
2 Mark Price 5.00 12.00
3 Rolando Blackman 3.00 8.00
6 Darrell Griffith 3.00 8.00
7 Dan Issel 3.00 8.00
11 Mark Eaton 3.00 8.00
13 Hakeem Olajuwon 4.00 10.00
17 Joe Dumars 3.00 8.00
19 Dave Cowens 3.00 8.00
20 Alvan Adams 3.00 8.00

2010-11 Limited Retired Numbers Materials Signatures

STATED PRINT RUN ONE TO 49 SER.#'d SETS
SOME UNPRICED DUE TO SCARCITY
PRIME SIG.PRINT RUN ONE TO 5 SER.#'d SETS
PRIME SIG.UNPRICED DUE TO SCARCITY
2 Mark Price/49 15.00 40.00
3 Rolando Blackman/49 8.00 20.00
7 Dan Issel/49 8.00 20.00
13 Hakeem Olajuwon/25 15.00 40.00
19 Dave Cowens/25 8.00 20.00
20 Alvan Adams/49 8.00 20.00

2010-11 Limited Retired Numbers Signatures

STATED PRINT RUN 49 TO 99 SER.#'d SETS
1 Bob Pettit/99 10.00 25.00
2 Mark Price/99 EXCH 10.00 25.00
3 Rolando Blackman/99 5.00 12.00
4 Elgin Baylor/99 EXCH 5.00 12.00
5 Nate Archibald/99 6.00 15.00
7 Dan Issel/99 8.00 20.00
8 Al Attles/39 EXCH 5.00 12.00
9 Sidney Moncrief/99 5.00 12.00
10 Earl Monroe/99 8.00 20.00
12 Tom Heinsohn/49 EXCH 10.00 25.00
13 Hakeem Olajuwon/99 15.00 40.00
14 Gail Goodrich/99 8.00 20.00
15 George Gervin/99 10.00 25.00
16 Nate Thurmond/99 5.00 12.00
17 Joe Dumars/99 10.00 25.00
18 Calvin Murphy/49 5.00 12.00
19 Dave Cowens/49 5.00 12.00
20 Alvan Adams/99 5.00 12.00

2010-11 Limited Team Trademarks

COMPLETE SET (20) 15.00 30.00
STATED PRINT RUN 149 SER.#'d SETS
*GOLD: 1.5X TO 4X BASE HI
GOLD PRINT RUN 24 SER.#'d SETS
*SILVER: 1X TO 2.5X BASE HI
SILVER PRINT RUN 49 SER.#'d SETS
UNPRICED PLATINUM PRINT RUN ONE SET
1 Al Jefferson .75 2.00
2 Brandon Jennings .75 2.00
3 Brook Lopez .75 2.00
4 David Lee .60 1.50
5 David West .75 2.00
6 Deron Williams .75 2.00
7 Derrick Rose 2.50 6.00
8 Elton Brand .75 2.00
9 Gerald Wallace .75 2.00
10 Jason Kidd .75 2.00
11 Joe Johnson .75 2.00
12 Kevin Durant 2.50 6.00
13 Kevin Martin .75 2.00
14 Kobe Bryant 4.00 10.00
15 LeBron James 4.00 10.00
16 Marc Gasol .75 2.00
17 Monta Ellis .75 2.00
18 Rajon Rondo 1.00 2.50
19 Steve Nash .75 2.00
20 Vince Carter 1.00 2.50

2010-11 Limited Team Trademarks Materials

STATED PRINT RUN 49 TO 99 SER.#'d SETS
1 Al Jefferson/49 3.00 8.00

2 Brandon Jennings/99 3.00 8.00
3 Brook Lopez/49 3.00 8.00
4 David Lee/49 2.50 6.00
5 David West/99 3.00 8.00
6 Deron Williams/99 3.00 8.00
7 Derrick Rose/49 10.00 25.00
8 Elton Brand/99 3.00 8.00
9 Gerald Wallace/99 3.00 8.00
10 Jason Kidd/49 3.00 8.00
11 Joe Johnson/99 3.00 8.00
12 Kevin Durant/99 8.00 20.00
14 Kobe Bryant/99 10.00 25.00
15 LeBron James/49 12.00 30.00
16 Marc Gasol/99 3.00 8.00
18 Rajon Rondo/99 4.00 10.00
19 Steve Nash/99 3.00 8.00
20 Vince Carter/99 4.00 10.00

2010-11 Limited Team Trademarks Materials Prime Signatures

STATED PRINT RUN ONE TO 25 SER.#'d SETS
SOME UNPRICED DUE TO SCARCITY
16 Marc Gasol/25 12.50 30.00

2010-11 Limited Team Trademarks Materials Signatures

STATED PRINT RUN 5 TO 49 SER.#'d SETS
SOME UNPRICED DUE TO SCARCITY
2 Brandon Jennings/49 12.50 30.00
14 Kobe Bryant/25 100.00 200.00
16 Marc Gasol/49 10.00 25.00
18 Rajon Rondo/49 15.00 40.00
19 Steve Nash/25 30.00 80.00
20 Vince Carter/25 20.00 50.00

2010-11 Limited Threads

STATED PRINT RUN 10 TO 199 SER.#'d SETS
SOME UNPRICED DUE TO SCARCITY
2 Paul Pierce/99 4.00 10.00
3 Rajon Rondo/199 4.00 10.00
5 Brook Lopez/99 3.00 8.00
6 Devin Harris/199 3.00 8.00
8 Amare Stoudemire/199 3.00 8.00
11 Toney Douglas/199 2.00 5.00
12 Andre Iguodala/199 3.00 8.00
13 Elton Brand/199 3.00 8.00
14 Jrue Holiday/199 3.00 8.00
16 Andrea Bargnani/199 2.50 6.00
17 DeMar DeRozan/199 3.00 8.00
18 Jose Calderon/199 2.50 6.00
19 Carlos Boozer/199 3.00 8.00
20 Derrick Rose/49 10.00 25.00
21 Joakim Noah/199 3.00 8.00
26 Richard Hamilton/199 2.50 6.00
27 Rodney Stuckey/199 3.00 8.00
29 Danny Granger/25 3.00 8.00
30 T.J. Ford/199 2.00 5.00
31 Tyler Hansbrough/199 3.00 8.00
32 Andrew Bogut/199 3.00 8.00
33 Brandon Jennings/199 3.00 8.00
35 Michael Redd/199 3.00 8.00
36 Al Horford/199 2.50 6.00
37 Joe Johnson/199 3.00 8.00
38 Josh Smith/199 3.00 8.00
39 Gerald Wallace/199 3.00 8.00
42 Chris Bosh/199 3.00 8.00
43 Dwyane Wade/199 6.00 15.00
44 LeBron James/99 10.00 25.00
46 Dwight Howard/199 5.00 12.00
47 J.J. Redick/199 3.00 8.00
48 Jason Williams/199 2.50 6.00
49 Rashard Lewis/199 2.50 6.00
53 Caron Butler/199 3.00 8.00
54 Dirk Nowitzki/199 4.00 10.00
55 Jason Kidd/49 3.00 8.00
59 Shane Battier/199 2.50 6.00
61 Marc Gasol/199 3.00 8.00
62 O.J. Mayo/199 3.00 8.00
63 Rudy Gay/199 3.00 8.00
65 Chris Paul/199 5.00 12.00
68 Manu Ginobili/199 3.00 8.00
69 Tim Duncan/99 5.00 12.00
70 Tony Parker/199 3.00 8.00
71 Carmelo Anthony/199 4.00 10.00
72 Chauncey Billups/199 3.00 8.00
73 Chris Andersen/199 3.00 8.00
74 Jonny Flynn/199 2.00 5.00
75 Kevin Love/199 4.00 10.00
77 Brandon Roy/199 3.00 8.00
78 LaMarcus Aldridge/199 3.00 8.00
79 Marcus Camby/199 2.00 5.00
80 James Harden/199 4.00 10.00
82 Russell Westbrook/199 4.00 10.00
83 Al Jefferson/199 3.00 8.00
84 Deron Williams/199 3.00 8.00
86 David Lee/99 2.50 6.00
88 Stephen Curry/199 4.00 10.00
89 Baron Davis/199 3.00 8.00
90 Blake Griffin/199 8.00 20.00
91 Chris Kaman/199 2.50 6.00
92 Derek Fisher/199 2.50 6.00
93 Kobe Bryant/199 8.00 20.00
94 Pau Gasol/199 3.00 8.00
95 Grant Hill/199 4.00 10.00
96 Jason Richardson/99 3.00 8.00
97 Steve Nash/199 3.00 8.00
101 Alex English/99 3.00 8.00
102 Alvan Adams/199 3.00 8.00
104 Bernard King/199 3.00 8.00
109 Bob Lanier/199 3.00 8.00
117 Darrell Griffith/199 3.00 8.00
118 Dominique Wilkins/99 4.00 10.00
124 George Mikan/99 12.00 30.00
125 Hakeem Olajuwon/199 4.00 10.00
127 Jeff Hornacek/99 3.00 8.00
132 Karl Malone/199 4.00 10.00
137 Magic Johnson/199 6.00 15.00
141 Robert Parish/199 3.00 8.00
147 Chris Mullin/199 3.00 8.00
148 Clyde Drexler/199 4.00 10.00

2010-11 Limited Threads Prime

*PRIME: .75X TO 2X BASE HI
STATED PRINT RUN 5 TO 25 SER.#'d SETS
SOME UNPRICED DUE TO SCARCITY
17 DeMar DeRozan/25 8.00 20.00
43 Dwyane Wade/25 15.00 40.00
48 Jason Williams/25 10.00 25.00
81 Kevin Durant/25 20.00 50.00
95 Grant Hill/25 12.50 30.00
97 Steve Nash/25 6.00 15.00
104 Bernard King/25 10.00 25.00
118 Dominique Wilkins/25 10.00 25.00
125 Hakeem Olajuwon/25 10.00 25.00
131 Kareem Abdul-Jabbar/25 12.50 30.00
132 Karl Malone/25 12.50 30.00
147 Chris Mullin/25 8.00 20.00

2010-11 Limited Trios

COMPLETE SET (10) 20.00 40.00
STATED PRINT RUN 149 SER.#'d SETS
*GOLD: .75X TO 2X BASE HI
GOLD PRINT RUN 24 SER.#'d SETS
*SILVER: .6X TO 1.5X BASE HI
SILVER PRINT RUN 99 SER.#'d SETS
UNPRICED PLATINUM PRINT RUN ONE SET
1 Kobe Bryant / Lamar Odom / Pau Gasol 4.00 10.00
2 Brandon Jennings / Stephen Curry / Tyreke Evans 2.50 6.00
3 Carmelo Anthony / Chauncey Billups / Chris Andersen 1.50 4.00
4 Allen Iverson / Jason Kidd / Steve Nash 3.00 8.00
5 Kevin Durant / Kobe Bryant / LeBron James 6.00 15.00
6 George Mikan / Pete Maravich / Wilt Chamberlain 5.00 12.00
7 Elgin Baylor / Walt Bellamy / Wes Unseld 1.50 4.00
8 Clyde Drexler / Isiah Thomas / John Stockton 5.00 12.00
9 Magic Johnson / Kareem Abdul-Jabbar / Larry Bird 6.00 15.00
10 Bill Russell / Jerry West / Oscar Robertson 4.00 10.00

2010-11 Limited Trios Materials

STATED PRINT RUN 49 SER.#'d SETS
UNPRICED PRIME PRINT RUN 5 TO 10 SETS
1 Kobe Bryant / Lamar Odom / Pau Gasol 10.00 25.00
2 Brandon Jennings / Stephen Curry / Tyreke Evans 6.00 15.00
3 Carmelo Anthony / Chauncey Billups / Chris Andersen 5.00 12.00
4 Allen Iverson / Jason Kidd / Steve Nash 8.00 20.00
5 Kevin Durant / Kobe Bryant / LeBron James 25.00 60.00
8 Clyde Drexler / Isiah Thomas / John Stockton 10.00 25.00

2010-11 Limited Trios Signatures

STATED PRINT RUN 5 TO 49 SER.#'d SETS
SOME UNPRICED DUE TO SCARCITY
1 Kobe Bryant/49 / Lamar Odom / Pau Gasol 125.00 250.00
2 Brandon Jennings/49 / Stephen Curry / Tyreke Evans 40.00 100.00

2011-12 Limited

STATED PRINT RUN 299 SER.#'d SETS
UNPRICED PLATINUM PRINT RUN ONE SET
1 Kobe Bryant 6.00 15.00
2 Metta World Peace 1.50 4.00
3 Pau Gasol 1.50 4.00
4 Andrew Bynum 2.00 5.00
5 Derek Fisher 1.25 3.00
6 Chris Bosh 1.50 4.00
7 Dwyane Wade 3.00 8.00
8 LeBron James 6.00 15.00
9 Mario Chalmers 1.50 4.00
10 Shane Battier 1.25 3.00
11 Dirk Nowitzki 2.00 5.00
12 Delonte West 1.00 2.50
13 Jason Kidd 1.50 4.00
14 Jason Terry 1.25 3.00
15 Lamar Odom 1.50 4.00
16 Vince Carter 2.00 5.00
17 Blake Griffin 3.00 8.00
18 Chauncey Billups 1.50 4.00
19 Chris Paul 2.50 6.00
20 Eric Bledsoe 1.50 4.00
21 Caron Butler 1.25 3.00
22 DeAndre Jordan 1.50 4.00
23 Grant Hill 2.00 5.00
24 Hakim Warrick 1.25 3.00
25 Steve Nash 1.50 4.00
26 Marcin Gortat 1.50 4.00
27 David Lee 1.25 3.00
28 Monta Ellis 1.50 4.00
29 Nate Robinson 1.50 4.00
30 Stephen Curry 1.50 4.00
31 James Harden 2.00 5.00
32 Kevin Durant 5.00 12.00
33 Russell Westbrook 2.00 5.00
34 Serge Ibaka 1.50 4.00
35 Nick Collison 1.00 2.50
36 Dwight Howard 2.50 6.00
37 J.J. Redick 1.50 4.00
38 Jason Richardson 1.50 4.00
39 Hedo Turkoglu 1.50 4.00
40 John Wall 2.50 6.00
41 Nick Young 1.25 3.00
42 Andray Blatche 1.00 2.50
43 Kevin Garnett 3.00 8.00
44 Paul Pierce 2.00 5.00
45 Rajon Rondo 2.00 5.00
46 Ray Allen 1.50 4.00
47 Brook Lopez 1.50 4.00
48 Deron Williams 1.50 4.00
49 Kris Humphries 1.00 2.50
50 Mehmet Okur 1.00 2.50
51 J.J. Barea 1.50 4.00
52 Kevin Love 2.00 5.00
53 Ricky Rubio 4.00 10.00
54 Michael Beasley 1.50 4.00
55 DeMarcus Cousins 2.00 5.00
56 Marcus Thornton 1.50 4.00
57 Francisco Garcia 1.25 3.00
58 Tyreke Evans 1.50 4.00
59 Emeka Okafor 1.50 4.00
60 Eric Gordon 1.50 4.00
61 Jarrett Jack 1.25 3.00
62 Chris Kaman 1.25 3.00
63 Jeff Teague 1.25 3.00
64 Joe Johnson 1.50 4.00
65 Josh Smith 1.50 4.00
66 Jerry Stackhouse 1.25 3.00
67 Tracy McGrady 1.50 4.00
68 Mike Conley 1.25 3.00
69 Rudy Gay 1.50 4.00
70 Marc Gasol 1.50 4.00
71 Zach Randolph 1.25 3.00
72 Danny Granger 1.50 4.00
73 Darren Collison 1.50 4.00
74 Roy Hibbert 1.25 3.00
75 George Hill 1.25 3.00
76 Tyler Hansbrough 1.50 4.00
77 Amare Stoudemire 1.50 4.00
78 Jeremy Lin 6.00 15.00
79 Carmelo Anthony 2.00 5.00
80 Tyson Chandler 1.25 3.00
81 LaMarcus Aldridge 1.50 4.00
82 Raymond Felton 1.25 3.00
83 Wesley Matthews 1.50 4.00
84 Andre Iguodala 1.50 4.00
85 Evan Turner 1.50 4.00
86 Jrue Holiday 1.50 4.00
87 Spencer Hawes 1.00 2.50
88 Al Jefferson 1.50 4.00
89 Gordon Hayward 1.50 4.00
90 Paul Millsap 1.25 3.00
91 Raja Bell 1.25 3.00
92 DeJuan Blair 1.25 3.00
93 Manu Ginobili 1.50 4.00
94 Tim Duncan 2.50 6.00
95 Tony Parker 1.50 4.00
96 Carlos Boozer 1.50 4.00
97 Derrick Rose 5.00 12.00
98 Joakim Noah 1.50 4.00
99 Luol Deng 1.50 4.00
100 Chris Andersen 1.50 4.00
101 Danilo Gallinari 1.50 4.00
102 Nene 1.25 3.00
103 Ty Lawson 1.50 4.00
104 Andrea Bargnani 1.25 3.00
105 DeMar DeRozan 1.50 4.00
106 Jose Calderon 1.25 3.00
107 Ed Davis 1.25 3.00
108 Anderson Varejao 1.25 3.00
109 Antawn Jamison 1.50 4.00
110 Daniel Gibson 1.25 3.00
111 Andrew Bogut 1.50 4.00
112 Brandon Jennings 1.50 4.00
113 Stephen Jackson 1.25 3.00
114 Ersan Ilyasova 1.25 3.00
115 Boris Diaw 1.25 3.00
116 D.J. Augustin 1.00 2.50
117 Tyrus Thomas 1.25 3.00
118 Chase Budinger 1.00 2.50
119 Kevin Martin 1.50 4.00
120 Kyle Lowry 1.25 3.00
121 Luis Scola 1.25 3.00
122 Ben Gordon 1.50 4.00
123 Greg Monroe 1.50 4.00
124 Rodney Stuckey 1.50 4.00
125 Tayshaun Prince 1.50 4.00
126 Jerry West 2.00 5.00
127 Pete Maravich 5.00 12.00
128 Scottie Pippen 3.00 8.00
129 Hakeem Olajuwon 2.00 5.00
130 Adrian Dantley 1.50 4.00
131 Tom Chambers 1.50 4.00
132 Larry Bird 5.00 12.00
133 Bernard King 1.50 4.00
134 Moses Malone 1.50 4.00
135 Robert Parish 1.50 4.00
136 Bill Cartwright 1.50 4.00
137 Rolando Blackman 1.50 4.00
138 Bob Lanier 1.50 4.00
139 Walt Frazier 1.50 4.00
140 Elvin Hayes 1.50 4.00
141 Elgin Baylor 1.50 4.00
142 Dave Cowens 1.50 4.00
143 Kareem Abdul-Jabbar 2.50 6.00
144 Nate Thurmond 1.50 4.00
145 Oscar Robertson 2.00 5.00
146 Bill Russell 2.50 6.00
147 Wilt Chamberlain 3.00 8.00
148 Karl Malone 2.00 5.00
149 Magic Johnson 4.00 10.00
150 Isiah Thomas 1.50 4.00
151 George Gervin 1.50 4.00
152 Dikembe Mutombo 1.50 4.00
153 Kevin Willis 1.50 4.00
154 Dennis Rodman 3.00 8.00
155 John Stockton 2.50 6.00
156 Gary Payton 1.50 4.00
157 Anfernee Hardaway 4.00 10.00
158 John Starks 1.50 4.00
159 Wes Unseld 1.50 4.00
160 Rick Mahorn 1.50 4.00
161 Charles Oakley 1.50 4.00
162 Spud Webb 1.50 4.00
163 Larry Johnson 2.00 5.00
164 Julius Erving 3.00 8.00
165 Joe Dumars 1.50 4.00
166 Shawn Kemp 6.00 15.00
167 Nick Van Exel 1.50 4.00
168 Mitch Richmond 1.50 4.00
169 Jeff Hornacek 1.50 4.00
170 David Robinson 2.50 6.00
171 Patrick Ewing 2.00 5.00
172 Clyde Drexler 2.00 5.00
173 Xavier McDaniel 1.50 4.00
174 Alonzo Mourning 2.00 5.00
175 Dominique Wilkins 2.00 5.00
176 James Worthy 2.00 5.00
177 Steve Kerr 1.50 4.00
178 Connie Hawkins 1.50 4.00
179 Darryl Dawkins 1.50 4.00
180 Mark Jackson 1.50 4.00
181 Kurt Rambis 1.50 4.00
182 Earl Monroe 1.50 4.00
183 Maurice Cheeks 1.50 4.00
184 Ernie DiGregorio 1.50 4.00
185 Detlef Schrempf 1.50 4.00
186 Bill Walton 1.50 4.00
187 Artis Gilmore 1.50 4.00
188 Nate Archibald 1.50 4.00
189 David Thompson 1.50 4.00
190 John Havlicek 2.00 5.00
191 Dan Majerle 1.50 4.00
192 Muggsy Bogues 1.50 4.00
193 Tim Hardaway 1.50 4.00
194 Jalen Rose 1.50 4.00
195 Shaquille O'Neal 3.00 8.00
196 Scott Brooks 1.50 4.00
197 Mike Dunleavy Sr. 1.50 4.00
198 Pat Riley 1.50 4.00
199 Kenny Smith 1.50 4.00
200 Alonzo Mourning 2.00 5.00

2011-12 Limited Gold Spotlight

*GOLD STARS: 1.5X TO 4X BASE HI
*GOLD LEGENDS: 1.25X TO 3X HI
STATED PRINT RUN 25 SER.#'d SETS
7 Dwyane Wade 15.00 40.00
8 LeBron James 30.00 80.00
23 Grant Hill 12.00 30.00
32 Kevin Durant 25.00 60.00
33 Russell Westbrook 10.00 25.00
46 Ray Allen 8.00 20.00
51 J.J. Barea 8.00 20.00
53 Ricky Rubio 15.00 40.00
78 Jeremy Lin 30.00 80.00
152 Dikembe Mutombo 8.00 20.00
163 Larry Johnson 8.00 20.00
166 Shawn Kemp 30.00 80.00
171 Patrick Ewing 12.00 30.00
174 Alonzo Mourning 15.00 40.00
195 Shaquille O'Neal 15.00 40.00
200 Alonzo Mourning 15.00 40.00

2011-12 Limited Silver Spotlight

*SILVER: .6X TO 1.5X BASE HI
STATED PRINT RUN 49 SER.#'d SETS
53 Ricky Rubio 6.00 15.00
154 Dennis Rodman 6.00 15.00
166 Shawn Kemp 20.00 50.00
174 Alonzo Mourning 8.00 20.00
195 Shaquille O'Neal 6.00 15.00
200 Alonzo Mourning 8.00 20.00

2011-12 Limited 2011 Draft Pick Redemptions Autographs

RANDOM INSERTS IN PACKS
XRCA TBD AU EXCH 25.00 60.00
XRCB TBD AU EXCH 10.00 25.00
XRCC TBD AU EXCH 10.00 25.00
XRCD TBD AU EXCH 10.00 25.00
XRCE TBD AU EXCH 10.00 25.00
XRCF TBD AU EXCH 10.00 25.00
XRCG TBD AU EXCH 10.00 25.00
XRCH TBD AU EXCH 10.00 25.00
XRCI TBD AU EXCH 10.00 25.00
XRCJ TBD AU EXCH 10.00 25.00
XRCK TBD AU EXCH 10.00 25.00
XRCL TBD AU EXCH 10.00 25.00
XRCM TBD AU EXCH 10.00 25.00
XRCN TBD AU EXCH 10.00 25.00
XRCO TBD AU EXCH 10.00 25.00
XRCP TBD AU EXCH 10.00 25.00
XRCQ TBD AU EXCH 10.00 25.00
XRCR TBD AU EXCH 10.00 25.00
XRCS TBD AU EXCH 10.00 25.00
XRCT TBD AU EXCH 10.00 25.00
XRCU TBD AU EXCH 10.00 25.00
XRCV TBD AU EXCH 10.00 25.00
XRCW TBD AU EXCH 10.00 25.00
XRCX TBD AU EXCH 10.00 25.00
XRCY TBD AU EXCH 10.00 25.00
XRCZ TBD AU EXCH 10.00 25.00
XRCAA TBD AU EXCH 10.00 25.00
XRCBB TBD AU EXCH 10.00 25.00
XRCCC TBD AU EXCH 10.00 25.00
XRCDD TBD AU EXCH 10.00 25.00
XRCEE TBD AU EXCH 10.00 25.00
XRCFF TBD AU EXCH 10.00 25.00
XRCGG TBD AU EXCH 10.00 25.00
XRCHH TBD AU EXCH 10.00 25.00
XRCII TBD AU EXCH 10.00 25.00

2011-12 Limited 2012 Draft Pick Redemptions

RANDOM INSERTS IN PACKS
1 Anthony Davis EXCH 100.00 200.00
2 Michael Kidd-Gilchrist EXCH 30.00 80.00
3 Bradley Beal EXCH 25.00 60.00
4 Dion Waiters EXCH 25.00 60.00
5 Thomas Robinson EXCH 25.00 60.00
6 Damian Lillard EXCH 30.00 80.00
7 Harrison Barnes EXCH 25.00 60.00
8 Terrence Ross EXCH 15.00 40.00
9 Andre Drummond EXCH 15.00 40.00
10 Austin Rivers EXCH 25.00 60.00
11 Meyers Leonard EXCH 12.00 30.00
12 Jeremy Lamb EXCH 15.00 40.00
13 Kendall Marshall EXCH 15.00 40.00
14 John Henson EXCH 12.00 30.00
15 Maurice Harkless EXCH 10.00 25.00
16 Royce White EXCH 15.00 40.00
17 Tyler Zeller EXCH 15.00 40.00
18 Terrence Jones EXCH 20.00 50.00
19 Andrew Nicholson EXCH 12.00 30.00
20 Evan Fournier EXCH 10.00 25.00

2011-12 Limited Decade Dominance Materials

STATED PRINT RUN 5 TO 99 SER.#'d SETS
SOME UNPRICED DUE TO SCARCITY
1 Larry Bird/99 10.00 25.00
2 Robert Parish/99 3.00 8.00
3 Artis Gilmore/99 3.00 8.00
4 Dennis Johnson/99 4.00 10.00
5 David Robinson/99 5.00 12.00
6 Alex English/99 3.00 8.00
8 James Worthy/49 5.00 12.00
9 Dennis Rodman/99 6.00 15.00
10 Kevin Johnson/99 3.00 8.00
11 Shaquille O'Neal/99 8.00 20.00
12 Patrick Ewing/99 8.00 20.00
13 Ray Allen/99 5.00 12.00
14 Karl Malone/99 4.00 10.00
15 Clyde Drexler/99 4.00 10.00
16 LeBron James/99 12.00 30.00
17 Dwyane Wade/99 6.00 15.00
18 Kevin Garnett/49 8.00 20.00
19 Tim Duncan/99 5.00 12.00
20 Allen Iverson/25 12.00 30.00

2011-12 Limited Decade Dominance Materials Prime

*PRIME: 1.25X TO 3X BASE HI
STATED PRINT RUN ONE TO 25 SETS
SOME UNPRICED DUE TO SCARCITY
11 Shaquille O'Neal/25 30.00 80.00
12 Patrick Ewing/25 40.00 100.00
18 Kevin Garnett/15 20.00 50.00

2011-12 Limited Decade Dominance Materials Signatures

STATED PRINT RUN 10 TO 49 SER.#'d SETS
SOME UNPRICED DUE TO SCARCITY
UNPRICED PRIME PRINT RUN 5 SETS
3 Robert Parish/49 10.00 25.00
4 Kevin McHale/49 20.00 50.00
5 Joe Dumars/49 10.00 25.00
6 Isiah Thomas/49 12.00 30.00
7 Spencer Haywood/49 6.00 15.00
9 Alex English/49 6.00 15.00
15 Kobe Bryant/49 125.00 225.00
20 Dikembe Mutombo/49 20.00 50.00

2011-12 Limited Decade Dominance Signatures

STATED PRINT RUN 10 TO 99 SER.#'d SETS
SOME UNPRICED DUE TO SCARCITY
1 Wes Unseld/99 6.00 15.00
2 Dave Cowens/99 6.00 15.00
3 Walt Frazier/99 10.00 25.00
4 John Havlicek/25 20.00 50.00
5 Bob McAdoo/99 12.00 30.00
6 Bob Dandridge/99 6.00 15.00
7 Nate Archibald/99 6.00 15.00
8 Bill Walton/99 8.00 20.00
10 George Gervin/99 10.00 25.00
11 Grant Hill/50 125.00 225.00
13 Hakeem Olajuwon/50 25.00 60.00
17 Kobe Bryant/99 100.00 200.00

2011-12 Limited Glass Cleaners Materials

STATED PRINT RUN 49 TO 99 SER.#'d SETS
1 Kobe Bryant/99 12.00 30.00
2 Blake Griffin/99 6.00 15.00
3 Kevin Durant/99 10.00 25.00
4 Joakim Noah/99 3.00 8.00
5 Kevin Love/99 4.00 10.00
6 Marc Gasol/99 3.00 8.00
7 LaMarcus Aldridge/99 3.00 8.00
8 Dwight Howard/99 5.00 12.00
9 Shaquille O'Neal/99 10.00 25.00
10 Moses Malone/49 3.00 8.00
11 Robert Parish/49 3.00 8.00
12 Dennis Rodman/99 8.00 20.00
13 Hakeem Olajuwon/60 4.00 10.00
14 Dikembe Mutombo/99 3.00 8.00
15 Yao Ming/99 4.00 10.00
16 Karl Malone/99 4.00 10.00
17 DeAndre Jordan/99 3.00 8.00
18 Amare Stoudemire/99 3.00 8.00
19 Tyson Chandler/99 2.50 6.00
20 LeBron James/99 12.00 30.00

2011-12 Limited Glass Cleaners Materials Prime

*PRIME: 1.25X TO 3X BASE HI
STATED PRINT RUN 5 TO 25 SER.#'d SETS
SOME UNPRICED DUE TO SCARCITY
14 Dikembe Mutombo/25 15.00 40.00

2011-12 Limited Glass Cleaners Materials Signatures

STATED PRINT RUN 25 TO 49 SER.#'d SETS
1 Kobe Bryant/49 100.00 200.00
2 Blake Griffin/49 50.00 125.00
3 Kevin Durant/49 EXCH 125.00 225.00
4 Joakim Noah/49 10.00 25.00
5 Kevin Love/49 15.00 40.00
6 Marc Gasol/49 EXCH 12.00 30.00
7 Marcin Gortat/49 12.00 30.00
8 Dirk Nowitzki/25 75.00 150.00
9 Serge Ibaka/49 EXCH 12.00 30.00
10 Anderson Varejao/49 EXCH 6.00 15.00
11 Robert Parish/25 12.00 30.00
12 Dennis Rodman/25 40.00 100.00
13 Hakeem Olajuwon/25 25.00 60.00
14 Dikembe Mutombo/25 30.00 80.00
15 Artis Gilmore/25 12.00 30.00
16 Nate Thurmond/25 20.00 50.00
17 David Robinson/25 40.00 100.00
18 DeMarcus Cousins/49 15.00 40.00
19 Josh Smith/49 6.00 15.00
20 Andrew Bynum/25 12.00 30.00

2011-12 Limited Glass Cleaners Materials Signatures Prime

STATED PRINT RUN 5 TO 25 SER.#'d SETS
SOME UNPRICED DUE TO SCARCITY
4 Joakim Noah/25 15.00 40.00
6 Marc Gasol/15 EXCH 20.00 50.00
7 Marcin Gortat/25 25.00 60.00
9 Serge Ibaka/25 EXCH 20.00 50.00
10 Anderson Varejao/25 EXCH 10.00 25.00
18 DeMarcus Cousins/25 25.00 60.00
19 Josh Smith/15 10.00 25.00
20 Andrew Bynum/15 20.00 50.00

2011-12 Limited Glass Cleaners Signatures

STATED PRINT RUN 25 TO 99 SER.#'d SETS
1 Kobe Bryant/50 125.00 250.00
2 Blake Griffin/25 100.00 200.00
3 Kevin Durant/25 125.00 225.00
4 Joakim Noah/49 12.00 30.00
5 Kevin Love/25 40.00 100.00
6 Marc Gasol/99 EXCH 15.00 40.00
7 Marcin Gortat/99 12.00 30.00
8 Kris Humphries/99 EXCH 6.00 15.00
9 Serge Ibaka/99 EXCH 12.00 30.00
10 Anderson Varejao/99 EXCH 6.00 15.00
11 Robert Parish/99 8.00 20.00
12 Dennis Rodman/25 100.00 175.00
13 Hakeem Olajuwon/25 30.00 80.00
14 Dikembe Mutombo/99 15.00 40.00
15 Artis Gilmore/99 8.00 20.00
16 Nate Thurmond/99 10.00 25.00
17 David Robinson/25 50.00 125.00
18 DeMarcus Cousins/99 20.00 50.00
19 Josh Smith/99 6.00 15.00
20 Andrew Bynum/49 20.00 50.00

2011-12 Limited Jumbo

STATED PRINT RUN 49 TO 99 SER.#'d SETS
UNPRICED PRIME PRINT RUN 5 TO 10 SETS
1 LeBron James/49 20.00 50.00
2 Dwyane Wade/49 8.00 20.00
3 Dwight Howard/49 6.00 15.00
4 Kevin Garnett/49 8.00 20.00
5 David Lee/99 3.00 8.00
6 Grant Hill/49 10.00 25.00
7 David West/99 4.00 10.00
8 Manu Ginobili/49 4.00 10.00
9 Jason Terry/49 3.00 8.00
10 O.J. Mayo/99 4.00 10.00
11 Ben Gordon/99 4.00 10.00
12 Joe Johnson/99 4.00 10.00
13 Jrue Holiday/99 4.00 10.00
14 Ryan Anderson/99 3.00 8.00
15 Nick Young/99 3.00 8.00
16 Mo Williams/49 3.00 8.00
17 Pau Gasol/99 4.00 10.00
18 DeMarcus Cousins/99 5.00 12.00
19 Luis Scola/99 3.00 8.00
20 Marcus Thornton/99 4.00 10.00
21 Emeka Okafor/99 4.00 10.00
22 Tim Duncan/49 6.00 15.00
23 Chris Andersen/99 4.00 10.00
24 Michael Beasley/99 4.00 10.00
25 Serge Ibaka/99 5.00 12.00
26 Gerald Wallace/99 4.00 10.00
27 Marcus Camby/99 2.50 6.00
28 Chauncey Billups/99 4.00 10.00
29 Tyson Chandler/99 3.00 8.00
30 Tyler Hansbrough/99 4.00 10.00

2011-12 Limited Jumbo Signatures

STATED PRINT RUN 10 TO 99 SER.#'d SETS
SOME UNPRICED DUE TO SCARCITY
1 Blake Griffin/15 75.00 150.00
2 Deron Williams/15
3 Stephen Curry/24 15.00 40.00
4 James Harden/24 EXCH 15.00 40.00
5 Kobe Bryant/24 125.00 225.00
7 Marcus Thornton/99 8.00 20.00
8 Eric Gordon/24 10.00 25.00
9 Ray Allen/15 EXCH 30.00 80.00
10 Jrue Holiday/49 12.00 30.00
11 Joakim Noah/24 10.00 25.00
12 Jeff Teague/99 6.00 15.00
13 Shane Battier/49 12.00 30.00
14 J.J. Redick/49 8.00 20.00
15 Nene/24 EXCH 10.00 25.00
16 Raymond Felton/24 6.00 15.00
17 Gordon Hayward/99 8.00 20.00
18 Rudy Gay/49 EXCH 8.00 20.00
19 DeMar DeRozan/24 EXCH 8.00 20.00
20 Serge Ibaka/99 EXCH 10.00 25.00

2011-12 Limited Jumbo Signatures Prime

STATED PRINT RUN 5 TO 15 SER.#'d SETS
SOME UNPRICED DUE TO SCARCITY
7 Marcus Thornton/15 20.00 50.00
11 Joakim Noah/15 25.00 60.00
13 Shane Battier/15 25.00 60.00
14 J.J. Redick/15 25.00 60.00
15 Nene/15 EXCH 20.00 50.00
16 Raymond Felton/15
17 Gordon Hayward/15 40.00 100.00

2011-12 Limited Jumbo Jersey Numbers

STATED PRINT RUN 49 TO 99 SER.#'d SETS
1 Dwight Howard/49 6.00 15.00
2 Carmelo Anthony/99 5.00 12.00
3 Boris Diaw/99 3.00 8.00
4 Shawn Marion/99 4.00 10.00
5 Vince Carter/99 5.00 12.00
6 LeBron James/49 20.00 50.00
7 Tim Duncan/99 6.00 15.00
8 Kevin Garnett/99 8.00 20.00
9 Dwyane Wade/99 8.00 20.00
10 DeAndre Jordan/99 4.00 10.00
11 Darren Collison/99 4.00 10.00
12 Danilo Gallinari/99 4.00 10.00
13 Pau Gasol/99 4.00 10.00
14 Nick Young/99 3.00 8.00
15 Devin Harris/99 4.00 10.00
16 Kyle Lowry/99 3.00 8.00
17 Metta World Peace/99 4.00 10.00
18 Mario Chalmers/99 4.00 10.00
19 LaMarcus Aldridge/99 4.00 10.00
20 Lamar Odom/99 4.00 10.00

2011-12 Limited Jumbo Jersey Numbers Prime

*PRIME: 1.5X TO 4X BASE HI
STATED PRINT RUN 14 TO 25 SER.#'d SETS
5 Vince Carter/15 25.00 60.00
7 Tim Duncan/15 50.00 125.00
17 Metta World Peace/15 20.00 50.00

2011-12 Limited Jumbo Jersey Numbers Signatures

STATED PRINT RUN 5 TO 99 SER.#'d SETS
SOME UNPRICED DUE TO SCARCITY
3 Andre Miller/99 6.00 15.00
4 Andrea Bargnani/49 8.00 20.00
5 James Harden/49 EXCH 15.00 40.00
6 Blake Griffin/25 75.00 150.00
7 Tyson Chandler/25 10.00 25.00
8 Tyreke Evans/25 20.00 50.00
10 Anderson Varejao/49 EXCH 6.00 15.00
11 Andrew Bogut/99 8.00 20.00
12 Greg Monroe/99 6.00 15.00
13 Paul George/99 15.00 40.00
14 Kevin Love/25 20.00 50.00
15 Ray Allen/15 EXCH
16 Trevor Booker/99 6.00 15.00
17 Wesley Matthews/99 6.00 15.00
18 Derrick Favors/49 10.00 25.00
19 Patrick Patterson/99 6.00 15.00
20 Marc Gasol/25 EXCH 15.00 40.00

2011-12 Limited Jumbo Jersey Numbers Signatures Prime

STATED PRINT RUN 5 TO 25 SER.#'d SETS
SOME UNPRICED DUE TO SCARCITY
3 Andre Miller/25 15.00 40.00
4 Andrea Bargnani/25 15.00 40.00
5 James Harden/25 EXCH 50.00 125.00
7 Tyson Chandler/25 15.00 40.00
8 Tyreke Evans/25 30.00 80.00
10 Anderson Varejao/25 EXCH 15.00 40.00
11 Andrew Bogut/25 25.00 60.00
12 Greg Monroe/25 30.00 80.00
16 Trevor Booker/25 15.00 40.00
17 Wesley Matthews/25 15.00 40.00
18 Derrick Favors/25 25.00 60.00
20 Marc Gasol/25 EXCH 30.00 80.00

2011-12 Limited Masterful Marks Signatures

STATED PRINT RUN 10 TO 50 SER.#'d SETS
SOME UNPRICED DUE TO SCARCITY
1 Adrian Dantley/50 4.00 10.00
2 Andre Iguodala/50 4.00 10.00
3 Andre Miller/50 4.00 10.00
4 Anfernee Hardaway/25 75.00 200.00
5 Arron Afflalo/50 4.00 10.00
6 Bill Walton/50 6.00 15.00
7 Blake Griffin/25 40.00 100.00
8 Brook Lopez/50 5.00 12.00
9 Carlos Boozer/50 8.00 20.00
10 Charlie Villanueva/50 4.00 10.00
11 Chase Budinger/50 4.00 10.00
12 Chris Andersen/25 30.00 80.00
13 Chris Paul/25 EXCH 40.00 100
14 Daniel Gibson/50 4.00 10
15 Danny Manning/50 5.00 12
16 Darren Collison/50 EXCH 5.00 12
17 DeAndre Jordan/50 EXCH 6.00 15
18 Derek Fisher/50 EXCH 6.00 15
19 Derrick Rose/25 EXCH
20 Gordon Hayward/50 4.00 10
21 Ian Mahinmi/50 EXCH 4.00 10
22 J.J. Barea/50 EXCH 10.00 25
23 Roy Hibbert/50 4.00 10
24 James Harden/50 EXCH 12.00 30
25 Jason Kidd/25 20.00 50
26 Jeremy Lin/50 60.00 150
27 Joe Johnson/25 EXCH 12.00 30
28 John Starks/50 15.00 40
29 Jordan Crawford/50 5.00 12
30 Jordan Farmar/50 EXCH 4.00 10
31 Jose Calderon/50 4.00 10
32 Kendrick Perkins/50 8.00 20
34 Kevin Martin/50 6.00 15
35 Kobe Bryant/50 100.00 200
36 LaMarcus Aldridge/50 10.00 25
37 Luol Deng/50 EXCH 8.00 20
38 Marcin Gortat/50 15.00 40
39 Michael Finley/50 15.00 40
40 Monta Ellis/50 8.00 20
41 Nene/50 EXCH 5.00 12
42 Pau Gasol/50 12.00 30
43 Deron Williams/50 15.00 40
44 Rajon Rondo/25
45 Richard Hamilton/25 10.00 25
46 Rodrigue Beaubois/50 8.00 20
47 Russell Westbrook/25 20.00 50
48 Serge Ibaka/50 EXCH 12.00 30
49 Stephen Curry/50 12.00 30
50 Zach Randolph/50 6.00 15

2011-12 Limited Monikers Materials

STATED PRINT RUN 10 TO 49 SER.#'d SETS
SOME UNPRICED DUE TO SCARCITY
UNPRICED PRIME PRINT RUN ONE TO 5 SETS
1 Kobe Bryant/25 125.00 225
4 Brandon Jennings/25 EXCH 12.00 30
5 Kevin Love/25 20.00 50
6 Russell Westbrook/49 20.00 50
7 Andre Iguodala/49 8.00 20
8 Greg Monroe/49 8.00 20
10 Tyson Chandler/49 8.00 20
11 Paul Millsap/49 8.00 20
12 Tony Parker/25 15.00 40
13 LaMarcus Aldridge/25 10.00 25
16 Marc Gasol/49 EXCH 12.00 30
17 Danny Granger/15
19 Danilo Gallinari/25 8.00 20
20 Andrea Bargnani/25 8.00 20

2011-12 Limited Potential Signatures

STATED PRINT RUN 25 TO 99 SER.#'d SETS
1 DeMar DeRozan/50 10.00
2 Greg Monroe/99 5.00
3 Chase Budinger/99 3.00
4 Jonas Jerebko/99 EXCH 3.00
5 Marco Belinelli/99 3.00
6 Ed Davis/99 EXCH 3.00
7 Eric Bledsoe/99 5.00
8 Al-Farouq Aminu/99 3.00
9 Landry Fields/99 6.00
10 James Harden/50 EXCH 12.00
11 Derrick Favors/50 EXCH 6.00
12 Evan Turner/25 8.00
13 Wesley Matthews/99 5.00
14 Timofey Mozgov/99 3.00
15 DeMarcus Cousins/50 12.00
16 Serge Ibaka/99 EXCH 10.00
17 Jeremy Lin/99 EXCH 50.00
18 D.J. Augustin/50 EXCH 3.00
19 Trevor Booker/99 3.00
20 Darren Collison/99 EXCH 4.00
21 Jrue Holiday/99 6.00
22 Tyreke Evans/25 12.00
23 John Wall/25 EXCH 30.00
24 Brandon Jennings/25
25 Eric Gordon/99 EXCH 8.00
26 Ekpe Udoh/99 EXCH 3.00
27 Tyler Hansbrough/50 4.00
28 Jordan Crawford/99 5.00
29 George Hill/99 5.00
30 JaVale McGee/99 EXCH 5.00
31 Paul George/99 10.00
32 Gordon Hayward/99 6.00
33 Tiago Splitter/99 EXCH 5.00
34 Gary Neal/99 EXCH 4.00
35 Ty Lawson/99 EXCH 10.00
36 Marcus Thornton/99 4.00
37 Blake Griffin/25 50.00
38 Russell Westbrook/50 20.00
39 Patrick Patterson/99 3.00
40 Austin Daye/99 EXCH 3.00
41 Marc Gasol/99 EXCH 8.00
42 Jason Thompson/99 EXCH 3.00
43 Greivis Vasquez/99 EXCH 6.00
44 Stephen Curry/99 8.00
45 DeJuan Blair/99 4.00
46 Gerald Henderson/99 3.00
47 Terrence Williams/99 4.00
48 Jodie Meeks/99 EXCH 4.00
49 Jeff Teague/99 3.00
50 Nikola Pekovic/99 EXCH 6.00

2011-12 Limited Retired Numbers Materials

STATED PRINT RUN 5 TO 99 SER.#'d SETS
SOME UNPRICED DUE TO SCARCITY
1 Magic Johnson/25 10.00
2 Kareem Abdul-Jabbar/99 6.00
5 Patrick Ewing/99 8.00
6 Hakeem Olajuwon/49 5.00
7 John Stockton/99 6.00
8 Alonzo Mourning/99 8.00
9 Chris Mullin/99 4.00
10 David Robinson/99 6.00
11 Mitch Richmond/99 4.00
12 Julius Erving/99 8.00
13 Alex English/99 4.00
14 Dennis Johnson/99 4.00
15 Kevin McHale/99 4.00
16 Larry Bird/49 12.00
17 Sam Jones/99 5.00
18 Bill Laimbeer/99 4.00
19 Darrell Griffith/99 4.00
20 Karl Malone/99 5.00

2011-12 Limited Retired Numbers Materials Prime

*PRIME: 1X TO 2.5X BASE HI
STATED PRINT RUN ONE TO 25 SER.#'d SETS

ME UNPRICED DUE TO SCARCITY
trick Ewing/25 30.00 80.00
onzo Mourning/25 40.00 100.00
ris Mullin/25 15.00 40.00
Mitch Richmond/25 25.00 60.00

2011-12 Limited Retired umbers Materials Signatures

TED PRINT RUN 5 TO 49 SER.#'d SETS
ME UNPRICED DUE TO SCARCITY
ris Mullin/49 12.00 30.00
yde Drexler/25 40.00 100.00
vin McHale/25 15.00 40.00
bert Parish/49 12.00 30.00
m Jones/25 12.00 30.00
ah Thomas/49 15.00 40.00
e Dumars/49 10.00 25.00
ominique Wilkins/25 EXCH 20.00 50.00
cottie Pippen/25 150.00 250.00
lagic Johnson/25 75.00 150.00
ames Worthy/25 60.00 150.00
ohn Stockton/25 50.00 125.00
lark Eaton/49 8.00 20.00
om Chambers/49 8.00 20.00
eorge Gervin/49 10.00 25.00
an Issel/49 8.00 20.00
lex English/49 8.00 20.00

2011-12 Limited Retired umbers Materials Signatures Prime

TED PRINT RUN ONE TO 25 SER.#'d SETS
E UNPRICED DUE TO SCARCITY
ris Mullin/15 30.00 80.00
e Dumars/25 20.00 50.00
ohn Stockton/15
lark Eaton/15 12.00 30.00
om Chambers/15 12.00 30.00
eorge Gervin/25 15.00 40.00
lark Price/15
an Issel/15 12.00 30.00
lex English/25 12.00 30.00

2011-12 Limited Retired Numbers Signatures

TED PRINT RUN 25 TO 99 SER.#'d SETS
ve Cowens/50 10.00 25.00
Walton/50 12.00 30.00
ry Porter/99 10.00 25.00
ando Blackman/99 10.00 25.00
e Dumars/50 10.00 25.00
b Love/99 10.00 25.00
orge McGinnis/99 10.00 25.00
Pettit/50 10.00 25.00
l Goodrich/50 10.00 25.00
ominique Wilkins/50 20.00 50.00
arl Monroe/25 15.00 40.00
alt Frazier/50 12.00 30.00
C. Jones/50 10.00 25.00
es Unseld/50 10.00 25.00
an Majerle/99 10.00 25.00
ff Hornacek/99 10.00 25.00
ade Divac/99 10.00 25.00
eorge Gervin/50 10.00 25.00
ean Elliott/99 10.00 25.00
enny Wilkens/50 10.00 25.00

2011-12 Limited Signatures

ED PRINT RUN 10 TO 99 SER.#'d SETS
E UNPRICED DUE TO SCARCITY
RICED PLATINUM PRINT RUN ONE SET
ke Griffin/15 50.00 125.00
on Rondo/25
on Williams/25
on Chandler/25 8.00 20.00
phen Jackson/49 EXCH 5.00 12.00
drea Bargnani/49 5.00 12.00
nta Ellis/49 8.00 20.00
be Bryant/49 100.00 175.00
is Paul/15 EXCH 50.00 125.00
reke Evans/25 15.00 40.00
rrick Rose/15 100.00 200.00
tawn Jamison/49 5.00 12.00
eve Nash/15 30.00 80.00
anny Granger/25 6.00 15.00
n Gordon/25 6.00 15.00
dre Iguodala/25 6.00 15.00
evin Martin/49 5.00 12.00
dy Gay/49 EXCH 6.00 15.00
c Gordon/49 8.00 20.00
ny Parker/25 10.00 25.00
sh Smith/49 EXCH 5.00 12.00
J. Augustin/49 EXCH 5.00 12.00
ris Bosh/15 EXCH 20.00 50.00
remy Lin/25 100.00 175.00
ne/49 EXCH 8.00 20.00
vin Love/25 15.00 40.00
Marcus Aldridge/49 10.00 25.00
Jefferson/25 EXCH 8.00 20.00
iley Howell/49 5.00 12.00
rryl Dawkins/99 5.00 12.00
te Archibald/49 5.00 12.00
edric Maxwell/99 5.00 12.00
ris Mullin/49 10.00 25.00
rt Rambis/99 8.00 20.00
bert Parish/25 8.00 20.00
orge Gervin/49 6.00 15.00
tlef Schrempf/99 8.00 20.00
nny Smith/49 5.00 12.00
l Walton/25 8.00 20.00
ah Thomas/25 10.00 25.00
ade Divac/99 8.00 20.00
m Chambers/49 5.00 12.00
vid Robinson/15 75.00 150.00
ff Hornacek/99 5.00 12.00
e Dumars/25 10.00 25.00
n Hardaway/99 8.00 20.00

2011-12 Limited Signatures Gold Spotlight

ED PRINT RUN 3 TO 24 SER.#'d SETS
E UNPRICED DUE TO SCARCITY
phen Jackson/24 EXCH 6.00 15.00
rea Bargnani/15 6.00 15.00
tawn Jamison/24 6.00 15.00
vin Martin/24 8.00 20.00
dy Gay/24 EXCH 8.00 20.00
iley Howell/24 8.00 20.00
rryl Dawkins/24 6.00 15.00
dric Maxwell/24 6.00 15.00
ris Mullin/24 15.00 40.00
rt Rambis/24 12.00 30.00
tlef Schrempf/24 20.00 50.00
de Divac/24 12.00 30.00
m Chambers/24 6.00 15.00
f Hornacek/24 6.00 15.00
n Hardaway/24 15.00 40.00

2011-12 Limited Signatures Silver Spotlight

STATED PRINT RUN 5 TO 49 SER.#'d SETS
SOME UNPRICED DUE TO SCARCITY
3 Deron Williams/15 12.00 30.00
5 Stephen Jackson/49 EXCH 5.00 12.00
6 Andrea Bargnani/49 5.00 12.00
7 Monta Ellis/25 10.00 25.00
8 Kobe Bryant/25 100.00 200.00
12 Antawn Jamison/49 5.00 12.00
18 Kevin Martin/49 5.00 12.00
19 Rudy Gay/49 EXCH 6.00 15.00
20 Eric Gordon/25 8.00 20.00
22 Josh Smith/25 8.00 20.00
23 D.J. Augustin/25 EXCH 5.00 12.00
25 Jeremy Lin/15 100.00 200.00
27 Nene/25 EXCH 8.00 20.00
30 LaMarcus Aldridge/25 12.00 30.00
32 Bailey Howell/49 5.00 12.00
33 Darryl Dawkins/49 5.00 12.00
34 Nate Archibald/25 6.00 15.00
35 Cedric Maxwell/49 5.00 12.00
36 Chris Mullin/49 12.00 30.00
37 Kurt Rambis/49 10.00 25.00
39 George Gervin/25 8.00 20.00
40 Detlef Schrempf/49 12.00 30.00
41 Kenny Smith/25 5.00 12.00
44 Vlade Divac/49 10.00 25.00
45 Tom Chambers/49 5.00 12.00
47 Jeff Hornacek/49 5.00 12.00
48 Joe Dumars/15 12.00 30.00
50 Tim Hardaway/49 10.00 25.00

2011-12 Limited Team Trademarks Materials

STATED PRINT RUN 75 TO 99 SER.#'d SETS
*PRIME: 1X TO 2.5X HI COLUMN
PRIME PRINT RUN 5 TO 25 SETS
SOME UNPRICED DUE TO SCARCITY
1 Kobe Bryant/75 12.00 30.00
2 Blake Griffin/99 6.00 15.00
3 Carlos Boozer/99 3.00 8.00
4 Rajon Rondo/99 4.00 10.00
5 Carmelo Anthony/99 4.00 10.00
6 Tyreke Evans/99 3.00 8.00
7 Dwyane Wade/99 6.00 15.00
8 Dirk Nowitzki/99 4.00 10.00
9 Danny Granger/99 3.00 8.00
10 David Lee/99 2.50 6.00
11 Tony Parker/99 3.00 8.00
12 Dwight Howard/99 5.00 12.00
13 Al Horford/99 2.50 6.00
14 Kevin Durant/99 10.00 25.00
15 LeBron James/99 12.00 30.00
16 Stephen Jackson/99 2.50 6.00
17 Paul Millsap/99 2.50 6.00
18 Kevin Love/99 4.00 10.00
19 Kevin Garnett/99 6.00 15.00
20 LaMarcus Aldridge/99 3.00 8.00

2011-12 Limited Team Trademarks Materials Signatures

STATED PRINT RUN 25 TO 99 SER.#'d SETS
1 Kobe Bryant/25 125.00 225.00
2 Rudy Gay/99 EXCH 10.00 25.00
3 Ty Lawson/99 EXCH 8.00 20.00
4 Roy Hibbert/99 6.00 15.00
5 James Harden/49 EXCH 12.00 30.00
6 Tyreke Evans/49 10.00 25.00
7 Deron Williams/49 12.00 30.00
8 Greg Monroe/99 6.00 15.00
9 Stephen Curry/49 12.00 30.00
10 Kevin Love/25 25.00 60.00
11 Serge Ibaka/99 EXCH 10.00 25.00
12 Kevin Durant/25 EXCH 125.00 225.00
13 LaMarcus Aldridge/49 10.00 25.00
14 Josh Smith/49 6.00 15.00
15 Blake Griffin/25 50.00 125.00
16 Brandon Jennings/25 EXCH 10.00 25.00
17 Andre Iguodala/49 8.00 20.00
18 DeMarcus Cousins/49 15.00 40.00
19 Kevin Martin/49 6.00 15.00
20 Gordon Hayward/99 8.00 20.00

2011-12 Limited Team Trademarks Materials Signatures Prime

STATED PRINT RUN 5 TO 25 SER.#'d SETS
SOME UNPRICED DUE TO SCARCITY
2 Rudy Gay/25 EXCH 15.00 40.00
3 Ty Lawson/25 20.00 50.00
4 Roy Hibbert/25 12.00 30.00
5 James Harden/25 EXCH 30.00 80.00
8 Greg Monroe/25 15.00 40.00
11 Serge Ibaka/25 EXCH 25.00 60.00
14 Josh Smith/25 12.00 30.00
17 Andre Iguodala/25 25.00 60.00
18 DeMarcus Cousins/25 30.00 80.00
19 Kevin Martin/25 12.00 30.00
20 Gordon Hayward/25 15.00 40.00

2011-12 Limited Team Trademarks Signatures

STATED PRINT RUN 10 TO 49 SER.#'d SETS
SOME UNPRICED DUE TO SCARCITY
2 Tyreke Evans/25 10.00 25.00
3 Luol Deng/49 8.00 20.00
4 Al Jefferson/25 8.00 20.00
8 Kobe Bryant/49 100.00 200.00
9 Monta Ellis/49 8.00 20.00
10 Kevin Love/15 25.00 60.00
11 Rajon Rondo/25 EXCH 20.00 50.00
12 Russell Westbrook/25 25.00 60.00
13 LaMarcus Aldridge/49 10.00 25.00
17 Eric Gordon/49 6.00 15.00
18 Danny Granger/25 8.00 20.00
19 Kevin Martin/49 6.00 15.00
20 Danilo Gallinari/49 EXCH 6.00 15.00

2011-12 Limited Threads

STATED PRINT RUN 49 TO 99 SER.#'d SETS
1 Derrick Rose/99 10.00 25.00
2 Ray Allen/99 5.00 12.00
3 Chris Paul/99 5.00 12.00
4 Dwight Howard/99 5.00 12.00
5 Jason Kidd/99 3.00 8.00
6 Deron Williams/99 3.00 8.00
7 Evan Turner/99 3.00 8.00
8 Kobe Bryant/99 12.00 30.00
9 Amare Stoudemire/99 3.00 8.00
10 Elton Brand/99 3.00 8.00
11 Jose Calderon/99 2.50 6.00
12 Stephen Curry/99 3.00 8.00
13 Steve Nash/99 3.00 8.00
14 Andrew Bynum/99 4.00 10.00
15 DeMarcus Cousins/99 4.00 10.00
16 Joakim Noah/99 3.00 8.00
17 Anderson Varejao/99 2.50 6.00
18 Greg Monroe/99 3.00 8.00
19 Tyler Hansbrough/99 3.00 8.00
20 Manu Ginobili/99 3.00 8.00
21 Tim Duncan/99 5.00 12.00
22 Luis Scola/99 2.50 6.00
23 LeBron James/99 12.00 30.00
24 Dwyane Wade/99 6.00 15.00
25 John Wall/99 5.00 12.00
26 Brandon Jennings/99 3.00 8.00
27 Joe Johnson/99 3.00 8.00
28 D.J. Augustin/99 2.00 5.00
29 Zach Randolph/99 2.50 6.00
30 Emeka Okafor/99 3.00 8.00
31 Jason Terry/99 2.50 6.00
32 Ricky Rubio/99 10.00 25.00
33 Ty Lawson/99 3.00 8.00
34 Paul Pierce/99 4.00 10.00
35 Kevin Durant/99 10.00 25.00
36 James Harden/99 4.00 10.00
37 Kevin Love/99 4.00 10.00
38 LaMarcus Aldridge/99 3.00 8.00
39 Tyreke Evans/99 3.00 8.00
40 Carlos Boozer/99 3.00 8.00
41 Dirk Nowitzki/99 4.00 10.00
42 Paul Millsap/99 2.50 6.00
43 Alonzo Mourning/99 8.00 20.00
44 Derrick Coleman/49 8.00 20.00
45 Clyde Drexler/99 4.00 10.00
46 Dennis Scott/99 3.00 8.00
47 Chuck Person/99 3.00 8.00
48 Glen Rice/99 3.00 8.00
49 Jalen Rose/99 3.00 8.00
50 Karl Malone/99 4.00 10.00

2011-12 Limited Threads Prime

*PRIME: 1X TO 2.5X BASE HI
STATED PRINT RUN 5 TO 25 SER.#'d SETS
SOME UNPRICED DUE TO SCARCITY
11 Jose Calderon/25 8.00 20.00
26 Brandon Jennings/25 10.00 25.00
32 Ricky Rubio/25 40.00 100.00
48 Glen Rice/25 10.00 25.00
49 Jalen Rose/25 12.00 30.00

2011-12 Limited Trios Materials

STATED PRINT RUN 25 TO 49 SER.#'d SETS
UNPRICED SIG PRINT RUN 5 TO 10 SETS
1 Derrick Rose/25 30.00 80.00
Kobe Bryant
Dwyane Wade
2 Blake Griffin/49 12.00 30.00
LaMarcus Aldridge
Kevin Love
3 Shawn Marion/49 10.00 25.00
Steve Nash
Amare Stoudemire
4 LeBron James/25 30.00 80.00
Dirk Nowitzki
Kevin Durant
5 Dwight Howard/49 8.00 20.00
Andrea Bargnani
Andrew Bogut
6 Kevin Garnett/49 10.00 25.00
Carmelo Anthony
Chris Bosh
7 Chris Paul/49 12.00 30.00
Rajon Rondo
Monta Ellis
8 Russell Westbrook/49 10.00 25.00
Deron Williams
Tony Parker
9 Grant Hill/25 20.00 50.00
Jason Kidd
Ray Allen
10 Alonzo Mourning/25 30.00 80.00
Glen Rice
Shaquille O'Neal

2011-12 Limited Trios Materials Prime

*PRIME: 1X TO 2.5X HI COLUMN
STATED PRINT RUN 5 TO 15 SER.#'d SETS
SOME UNPRICED DUE TO SCARCITY
1 Derrick Rose/15 60.00 150.00
Kobe Bryant
Dwyane Wade
5 Dwight Howard/15 30.00 80.00
Andrea Bargnani
Andrew Bogut
6 Kevin Garnett/15 30.00 80.00
Carmelo Anthony
Chris Bosh
10 Alonzo Mourning/15 60.00 150.00
Glen Rice
Shaquille O'Neal

2011-12 Limited Trophy Case Materials

STATED PRINT RUN 25 TO 99 SER.#'d SETS
1 Derrick Rose/75 10.00 25.00
2 Kobe Bryant/49 15.00 40.00
3 Steve Nash/75 3.00 8.00
4 David Robinson/75 5.00 12.00
5 Hakeem Olajuwon/49 4.00 10.00
6 Blake Griffin/75 6.00 15.00
7 Josh Smith/99 3.00 8.00
8 Vince Carter/99 4.00 10.00
9 Daequan Cook/99 2.00 5.00
10 Glen Rice/99 3.00 8.00
11 Jason Kidd/99 3.00 8.00
12 Deron Williams/99 3.00 8.00
13 Stephen Curry/99 3.00 8.00
14 Kevin Love/99 4.00 10.00
15 Danny Granger/99 3.00 8.00
16 Hedo Turkoglu/99 3.00 8.00
17 Monta Ellis/99 3.00 8.00
18 Tyreke Evans/99 3.00 8.00
19 Isiah Thomas/99 3.00 8.00
20 Tom Chambers/99 3.00 8.00
21 Zydrunas Ilgauskas/99 2.00 5.00
22 Andre Iguodala/99 3.00 8.00
23 David Lee/99 2.50 6.00
24 Daniel Gibson/99 2.50 6.00
25 Kevin Durant/49 10.00 25.00
26 John Wall/99 5.00 12.00
27 Rajon Rondo/99 5.00 12.00
28 Tony Parker/99 3.00 8.00
29 Derek Fisher/99 2.50 6.00
30 Robert Parish/49 3.00 8.00
31 Michael Cooper/99 3.00 8.00
32 Pau Gasol/99 3.00 8.00
33 Joe Dumars/75 3.00 8.00
34 Kevin McHale/75 3.00 8.00
35 Kareem Abdul-Jabbar/25 5.00 12.00
36 Dennis Rodman/75 8.00 20.00
37 Scottie Pippen/75 10.00 25.00
38 Allen Iverson/75 8.00 20.00
39 Eddie Jones/99 3.00 8.00
40 Manu Ginobili/99 3.00 8.00
41 Peja Stojakovic/99 3.00 8.00
42 Quentin Richardson/99 2.50 6.00
43 Dwight Howard/99 5.00 12.00
44 Nate Robinson/99 3.00 8.00
45 Karl Malone/99 5.00 12.00
46 Shaquille O'Neal/49 10.00 25.00
47 Allen Iverson/25 15.00 40.00
48 Kevin Garnett/49 6.00 15.00
49 Dirk Nowitzki/99 4.00 10.00
50 LeBron James/49 15.00 40.00

2011-12 Limited Trophy Case Materials Prime

*PRIME: 1.25X TO 3X BASE HI
STATED PRINT RUN ONE TO 25 SER.#'d SETS
SOME UNPRICED DUE TO SCARCITY
1 Derrick Rose/25 40.00 100.00
8 Vince Carter/25 15.00 40.00
21 Zydrunas Ilgauskas/25 12.00 30.00
27 Rajon Rondo/25 20.00 50.00
28 Tony Parker/25 12.00 30.00
29 Derek Fisher/25 10.00 25.00
38 Allen Iverson/15 30.00 80.00
39 Eddie Jones/25 15.00 40.00
46 Shaquille O'Neal/25 40.00 100.00
47 Allen Iverson/15 30.00 80.00
49 Dirk Nowitzki/25 15.00 40.00

2011-12 Limited Trophy Case Materials Signatures

STATED PRINT RUN 15 TO 49 SER.#'d SETS
1 Derrick Rose/25 EXCH 100.00 200.00
2 Kobe Bryant/25 125.00 225.00
3 Steve Nash/15 30.00 80.00
4 David Robinson/15 75.00 150.00
5 Hakeem Olajuwon/15 25.00 60.00
6 Blake Griffin/25 75.00 150.00
7 Josh Smith/49 6.00 15.00
8 Vince Carter/15 40.00 100.00
9 Daequan Cook/49 EXCH 6.00 15.00
10 Glen Rice/49 10.00 25.00
11 Jason Kidd/15 20.00 50.00
12 Deron Williams/15 12.00 30.00
13 Stephen Curry/49 10.00 25.00
14 Kevin Love/15 25.00 60.00
15 Danny Granger/15 6.00 15.00
16 Hedo Turkoglu/49 EXCH 8.00 20.00
17 Monta Ellis/49 8.00 20.00
18 Tyreke Evans/15 15.00 40.00
19 Isiah Thomas/25 12.00 30.00
20 Tom Chambers/25 6.00 15.00
21 Zydrunas Ilgauskas/49 8.00 20.00
22 Andre Iguodala/49 6.00 15.00
23 David Lee/49 6.00 15.00
24 Daniel Gibson/49 6.00 15.00
25 Kevin Durant/25 EXCH 125.00 250.00
26 John Wall/15 40.00 100.00
27 Rajon Rondo/15 EXCH
28 Tony Parker/15 25.00 60.00
29 Derek Fisher/49 EXCH 8.00 20.00
30 Robert Parish/25 10.00 25.00
31 Michael Cooper/49 12.00 30.00
32 Pau Gasol/15 15.00 40.00
33 Joe Dumars/25 12.00 30.00
34 Sam Jones/25 15.00 40.00
35 Bailey Howell/15 15.00 40.00
36 Earl Monroe/15 15.00 40.00
37 Amare Stoudemire/49 12.00 30.00
38 Clyde Drexler/25 20.00 50.00
39 Bill Laimbeer/25 10.00 25.00
40 Dennis Rodman/25 40.00 100.00
41 Ron Harper/49 12.00 30.00
42 Dominique Wilkins/25 EXCH 20.00 50.00
43 Dikembe Mutombo/25 25.00 60.00
44 Gary Payton/25 40.00 80.00
45 Mark Eaton/49 6.00 15.00
46 Chris Paul/25 EXCH 40.00 100.00
47 Tyreke Evans/25 12.00 30.00
48 Mitch Richmond/25 30.00 80.00
49 Larry Bird/25 50.00 125.00
50 Julius Erving/25 50.00 125.00

2011-12 Limited Trophy Case Materials Signatures Prime

STATED PRINT RUN ONE TO 25 SER.#'d SETS
SOME UNPRICED DUE TO SCARCITY
1 Derrick Rose/15 EXCH 175.00 350.00
2 Kobe Bryant/15 175.00 350.00
4 David Robinson/15 75.00 150.00
5 Hakeem Olajuwon/15 30.00 80.00
6 Blake Griffin/15 125.00 250.00
7 Josh Smith/25 10.00 25.00
9 Daequan Cook/25 EXCH 10.00 25.00
10 Glen Rice/25 20.00 50.00
11 Jason Kidd/25 30.00 80.00
13 Stephen Curry/25 25.00 60.00
16 Hedo Turkoglu/25 EXCH
19 Isiah Thomas/25 EXCH 15.00 40.00
20 Tom Chambers/15 12.00 30.00
21 Zydrunas Ilgauskas/25 15.00 40.00
22 Andre Iguodala/25 10.00 25.00
23 David Lee/25 10.00 25.00
24 Daniel Gibson/25 10.00 25.00
25 Kevin Durant/15 EXCH
26 John Wall/25 75.00 150.00
29 Derek Fisher/25 EXCH 15.00 40.00
30 Robert Parish/15 12.00 30.00
31 Michael Cooper/25 15.00 40.00
33 Joe Dumars/15 15.00 40.00
34 Sam Jones/15 30.00 80.00
37 Amare Stoudemire/25 20.00 50.00
38 Clyde Drexler/25 40.00 70.00
40 Dennis Rodman/15 75.00 200.00
41 Ron Harper/25 30.00 80.00
42 Dominique Wilkins/15 EXCH 25.00 60.00
43 Dikembe Mutombo/15 50.00 125.00
44 Gary Payton/25 50.00 100.00
45 Mark Eaton/25 10.00 25.00
46 Chris Paul/15 EXCH
47 Tyreke Evans/15 20.00 50.00
48 Mitch Richmond/25 40.00 100.00
50 Julius Erving/15 100.00 175.00

2011-12 Limited Trophy Case Signatures

STATED PRINT RUN 25 TO 49 SER.#'d SETS
1 Derrick Rose/25 EXCH 100.00 200.00
2 Kobe Bryant/25 100.00 200.00
3 Steve Nash/25 35.00 70.00
4 David Robinson/25 30.00 80.00
5 Hakeem Olajuwon/25 20.00 50.00
6 Blake Griffin/25 50.00 125.00
7 Josh Smith/49 6.00 15.00
8 Vince Carter/25 40.00 100.00
9 Daequan Cook/49 EXCH 6.00 15.00
10 Glen Rice/49 6.00 15.00
11 Jason Kidd/25 15.00 40.00
12 Deron Williams/25 12.00 30.00
13 Stephen Curry/49 10.00 25.00
14 Kevin Love/25 20.00 50.00
15 Danny Granger/25 6.00 15.00
16 Hedo Turkoglu/49 EXCH 6.00 15.00
17 Monta Ellis/49 6.00 15.00
18 Tyreke Evans/25 12.00 30.00
19 Isiah Thomas/49 EXCH 12.00 30.00
20 Tom Chambers/49 6.00 15.00
21 Zydrunas Ilgauskas/49 6.00 15.00
22 Andre Iguodala/25 6.00 15.00
23 David Lee/49 6.00 15.00
24 Daniel Gibson/49 6.00 15.00
25 Kevin Durant/25 EXCH 125.00 250.00
26 John Wall/25 40.00 100.00
27 Rajon Rondo/25 EXCH
28 Tony Parker/25 15.00 40.00
29 Derek Fisher/49 EXCH 8.00 20.00
30 Robert Parish/49 8.00 20.00
31 Michael Cooper/49 6.00 15.00
32 Pau Gasol/25 12.00 30.00
33 Joe Dumars/49 8.00 20.00
34 Anfernee Hardaway/25 50.00 125.00
35 Ralph Sampson/49 6.00 15.00
36 George Gervin/49 8.00 20.00
37 David Thompson/49 6.00 15.00
38 Lenny Wilkens/49 6.00 15.00
39 Hal Greer/49 6.00 15.00
40 Bill Sharman/49 8.00 20.00
41 Aaron Brooks/49 6.00 15.00
42 Dale Ellis/49 6.00 15.00
43 Mark Price/49 15.00 40.00
44 Jeff Hornacek/49 6.00 15.00
45 Bill Walton/49 8.00 20.00
46 Dave Cowens/49 6.00 15.00
47 Bob McAdoo/49 12.00 30.00
48 Mitch Richmond/49 30.00 80.00
49 Larry Bird/25 50.00 125.00
50 Julius Erving/25 50.00 125.00

1973-74 Linnett Portraits

Measuring 8 1/2" by 11", these 112 charcoal drawings are facial portraits by noted sports artist Charles Linnett. The player's facsimile autograph is inscribed across the lower right corner. The backs are blank. Three portraits of players from the same team were included in each clear plastic packet. A checklist was also included in each packet, with an offer to order individual player portraits for 50 cents each. Originally, the suggested retail price was 99 cents. In later issues, the price was raised to $1.19. The portraits are unnumbered and listed alphabetically according to teams as follows: Atlanta Hawks (1-10), Boston Celtics (11-22), Buffalo Braves (23-33), Capitol Bullets (34-36), Chicago Bulls (37-43), Cleveland Cavaliers (44-45), Detroit Pistons (46), Golden State Warriors (47-56), Houston Rockets (57-59), Kansas City-Omaha Kings (60-67), Los Angeles Lakers (68-76), Milwaukee Bucks (77-85), New York Knicks (86-96), Philadelphia 76ers (97), Phoenix Suns (98-105), Portland Trail Blazers (106-107), and Seattle Supersonics (108). This listing concludes with four Harlem Globetrotter portraits (109-112).

COMPLETE SET (112) 350.00 700.00
1 Walt Bellamy 2.50 6.00
2 Steve Bracey 2.00 5.00
3 John Brown 2.00 5.00
4 Bob Christian 2.00 5.00
5 Herm Gilliam 2.00 5.00
6 Lou Hudson 2.50 6.00
7 Dwight Jones 2.00 5.00
8 Pete Maravich 12.50 25.00
9 Dale Schlueter 2.00 5.00
10 Jim Washington 2.00 5.00
11 Don Chaney 2.50 6.00
12 Dave Cowens 5.00 10.00
13 Steve Downing 2.00 5.00
14 Hank Finkel 2.00 5.00
15 Phil Hankinson 2.00 5.00
16 John Havlicek 7.50 15.00
17 Steve Kuberski 2.00 5.00
18 Don Nelson 3.00 8.00
19 Paul Silas 2.50 6.00
20 Paul Westphal 5.00 10.00
21 Jo Jo White 2.50 6.00
22 Art Williams 2.00 5.00
23 Ken Charles 2.00 5.00
24 Ernie DiGregorio 3.00 8.00
(Wearing a turtle neck)
25 Ernie DiGregorio 3.00 8.00
(Wearing a t-shirt)
26 Garfield Heard 2.50 6.00
27 Bob Kauffman 2.00 5.00
28 Mike Macaluso 2.00 5.00
29 Bob McAdoo 6.00 12.00
30 Jim McMillian 2.50 6.00
31 Paul Ruffner 2.00 5.00
32 Randy Smith 2.50 6.00
33 Dave Wohl 2.00 5.00
34 Archie Clark 2.50 6.00
35 Elvin Hayes 6.00 12.00
36 Howard Porter 2.50 6.00
37 Dennis Awtrey 2.00 5.00
38 Tom Boerwinkle 2.50 6.00
39 Bob Love 2.50 6.00
40 Jerry Sloan 3.00 8.00
41 Norm Van Lier 2.50 6.00
42 Chet Walker 2.50 6.00
43 Bob Weiss 2.50 6.00
44 Austin Carr 2.50 6.00
45 Lenny Wilkens 3.00 8.00
46 Bob Lanier 5.00 10.00
47 Jim Barnett 2.00 5.00
48 Rick Barry 5.00 10.00
49 Butch Beard 2.50 6.00
50 Derrek Dickey 2.50 6.00
51 Charlie Johnson 2.00 5.00
52 Clyde Lee 2.00 5.00
53 Jeff Mullins 2.50 6.00
54 Clifford Ray 2.00 5.00
55 Cazzie Russell 2.50 6.00
56 Nate Thurmond 3.00 8.00
57 Kevin Kunnert 2.00 5.00
58 Calvin Murphy 3.00 8.00
59 Jimmy Walker 2.50 6.00
60 Nate Archibald 3.00 8.00
61 Ron Behagen 2.00 5.00
62 John Block 2.00 5.00
63 Mike D'Antoni 2.00 5.00
64 Ken Durrett 2.00 5.00
65 Sam Lacey 2.00 5.00
66 Larry McNeill 2.00 5.00
67 Nate Williams 2.00 5.00
68 Bill Bridges 2.00 5.00
69 Mel Counts 2.00 5.00
70 Keith Erickson 2.00 5.00
71 Gail Goodrich 3.00 8.00
72 Happy Hairston 2.50 6.00
73 Jim Price 2.00 5.00
74 Pat Riley 6.00 12.00
75 Elmore Smith 2.00 5.00
76 Jerry West 6.00 12.00
77 Kareem Abdul-Jabbar 10.00 20.00
78 Lucius Allen 2.00 5.00
79 Bob Dandridge 2.50 6.00
80 Mickey Davis 2.00 5.00
81 Terry Driscoll 2.00 5.00
82 Russell Lee 2.00 5.00
83 Jon McGlocklin 2.00 5.00
84 Curtis Perry 2.00 5.00
85 Oscar Robertson 5.00 10.00
86 Henry Bibby 2.50 6.00
87 Bill Bradley 6.00 12.00
88 Dave DeBusschere 3.00 8.00
89 Walt Frazier 5.00 10.00
90 John Gianelli 2.00 5.00
91 Phil Jackson 5.00 10.00
92 Jerry Lucas 3.00 8.00
93 Dean Meminger 2.00 5.00
94 Earl Monroe 3.00 8.00
95 Willis Reed 3.00 8.00
96 Harthorne Wingo 2.00 5.00
97 Tom Van Arsdale 2.50 6.00
98 Mike Bantom 2.00 5.00
99 Corky Calhoun 2.00 5.00
100 Lamar Green 2.00 5.00
101 Clem Haskins 2.00 5.00
102 Connie Hawkins 5.00 10.00
103 Charlie Scott 2.50 6.00
104 Dick Van Arsdale 2.50 6.00
105 Neal Walk 2.00 5.00
106 Geoff Petrie 2.50 6.00
107 Sidney Wicks 3.00 8.00
108 Spencer Haywood 3.00 8.00
109 Geese Ausbie 2.50 6.00
110 Marques Haynes 3.00 8.00
111 Meadowlark Lemon 3.00 8.00
112 Curly Neal 3.00 8.00

1991 Little Basketball Big Leaguers

This 45-card set was included in a book titled "Little Basketball Big Leaguers: Amazing Boyhood Stories of Today's Basketball Stars," published by Little Simon, a division of Simon and Schuster. The book devotes two pages to each player and includes a photograph from their childhood, along with a narrative of how they made it into professional basketball. The cards are located at the back of the book in nine-card perforated sheets that measure 7 1/2" by 10 1/2". If they were separated, the individual cards would measure the standard size (2 1/2" by 3 1/2"). The fronts carry black-and-white head shot of the players taken during childhood. The picture is edged above and below by gold-orange stripes carrying the player's name and the set title respectively. The backs are borderless and have the same gold-orange stripe above and below the data listed. The backs also contain biographical information and a brief career summary. The cards are unnumbered and checklisted below in alphabetical order.

COMPLETE SET (45) 10.00 25.00
1 Danny Ainge .20 .50
2 Charles Barkley .75 2.00
3 Larry Bird 2.00 5.00
4 Rolando Blackman .10 .30
5 Muggsy Bogues .20 .50
6 Sam Bowie .10 .30
7 Brad Daugherty .10 .30
8 Johnny Dawkins .10 .30
9 James Donaldson .10 .30
10 Kevin Duckworth .10 .30
11 Chris Dudley .10 .30
12 A.J. English .10 .30
13 Harvey Grant .20 .50
Horace Grant
14 Jeff Hornacek .20 .50
15 Chris Jackson .10 .30
16 Mark Jackson .20 .50
17 Magic Johnson 1.50 4.00
18 Kevin Johnson .30 .75
19 Michael Jordan 12.00 30.00
20 Greg Kite .10 .30
21 Reggie Lewis .20 .50
22 Kevin McHale .40 1.00
23 Reggie Miller .60 1.50
24 Johnny Newman .10 .30
25 Robert Parish .30 .75
26 John Paxson .10 .30
27 Chuck Person .10 .30
28 Terry Porter .10 .30
29 Mark Price .10 .30
30 J.R. Reid .10 .30
31 Glen Rice .60 1.50
32 Doc Rivers .20 .50
33 Fred Roberts .10 .30
34 Byron Scott .20 .50
35 Jack Sikma .10 .30
36 Kenny Smith .10 .30
37 John Stockton 1.00 2.50
38 Wayman Tisdale .10 .30
39 Kiki Vandeweghe .10 .30
40 Spud Webb .20 .50
41 Dominique Wilkins .40 1.00
42 John Williams .10 .30
43 David Wood .10 .30
44 Orlando Woolridge .10 .30
45 James Worthy .40 1.00

1997 Little Sun Tim Duncan

This commemorative envelope was produced for Tim Duncan's debut night (October 31, 1997) against the Denver Nuggets. Each envelope was produced in a hand-numbered edition of 200 and could be ordered for $12.50 direct from Little Sun. Each envelope is postmarked in Denver, Colorado and features a black-and-white photograph. The front text describes Duncan's debut performance, and inside the envelope is a "stuffer card", which contains that actual box score from the game.

1 Tim Duncan 5.00 12.00

1989-90 Magic Pepsi

This eight-card set of Orlando Magic was sponsored by Pepsi. The standard-size cards feature on the front a posed color player photo, without borders on the sides. While the player's name and team logo appears in the aqua stripe above the picture, the Pepsi logo and the words "89/90 Inaugural Season Collector's Card" appear in red stripe below the picture. Also an official sweepstakes entry sticker is attached to each card face. This sticker was to be peeled off and affixed to an official entry form available at participating stores. By collecting four stickers, one was entitled to enter the sweepstakes. The back presents 1988-89 statistics and career highlights, and is printed in black lettering on blue background, with a white stripe at the card bottom. The cards are unnumbered and are checklisted below in alphabetical order. The set features Nick Anderson's first professional card.

COMPLETE SET (8) 15.00 40.00
1 Nick Anderson 6.00 15.00
2 Michael Ansley 2.00 5.00
3 Terry Catledge 2.00 5.00
4 Dave Corzine 2.00 5.00
5 Sidney Green 2.00 5.00
6 Otis Smith 2.00 5.00
7 Sam Vincent 2.00 5.00
8 Stuff the Magic Dragon 2.50 6.00

2001-02 Magic Topps

Produced by Topps in conjunction with AT&T, this seven-card set features a horizontal design with the Magic logo in the background and was given away during the 2001-02 season.

COMPLETE SET (7) 1.25 3.00
OM2 Darrell Armstrong .30 .75
OM3 Michael Doleac .30 .75
OM4 Pat Garrity .30 .75
OM5 Andrew DeClercq .30 .75
OM8 Bo Outlaw .30 .75
OM9 Doc Rivers CO .40 1.00
OM10 John Amaechi .30 .75

2006-07 Magic Upper Deck

COMPLETE SET (15) 5.00 12.00
1 Trevor Ariza .40 1.00
2 Carlos Arroyo .40 1.00
3 James Augustine .40 1.00
4 Tony Battie .40 1.00
5 Keith Bogans .40 1.00
6 Travis Diener .40 1.00
7 Keyon Dooling .40 1.00
8 Pat Garrity .40 1.00
9 Grant Hill 1.00 2.50
10 Dwight Howard 2.00 5.00
11 Darko Milicic .40 1.00
12 Jameer Nelson .60 1.50
13 Bo Outlaw .40 1.00
14 J.J. Redick 1.00 2.50
15 Hedo Turkoglu .40 1.00

2007-08 Magic Upper Deck

COMPLETE SET (15) 5.00 12.00
1 Trevor Ariza .40 1.00
2 Carlos Arroyo .40 1.00
3 James Augustine .40 1.00
4 Tony Battie .40 1.00
5 Keith Bogans .40 1.00
6 Keyon Dooling .40 1.00
7 Pat Garrity .40 1.00
8 Dwight Howard 1.50 4.00
9 Rashard Lewis .60 1.50
10 Jameer Nelson .60 1.50
11 J.J. Redick .40 1.00
12 Hedo Turkoglu .40 1.00
13 Marcin Gortat .40 1.00
14 Adonal Foyle .40 1.00
15 Mascot .40 1.00

2008-09 Magic Upper Deck 20th Anniversary

COMPLETE SET (20) 8.00 20.00
1 Nick Anderson .50 1.25
2 Scott Skiles .50 1.25
3 Otis Smith .50 1.25
4 Anthony Bowie .50 1.25
5 Jeff Turner .50 1.25
6 Donald Royal .50 1.25
7 Shaquille O'Neal 1.50 4.00
8 Dennis Scott .50 1.25
9 Danny Schayes .50 1.25
10 Darrell Armstrong .50 1.25
11 Bo Outlaw .50 1.25
12 Mike Miller .50 1.25
13 Pat Garrity .50 1.25
14 Tracy McGrady 1.00 2.50
15 Grant Hill 1.00 2.50
16 Jameer Nelson .60 1.50
17 Hedo Turkoglu .50 1.25
18 Dwight Howard 1.50 4.00
19 Rashard Lewis .60 1.50
20 Courtney Lee .75 2.00

1989 Magnetables

This set of 35 magnets measure approximately 2" x 3". Reportedly, there are different production numbers for each magnet with more being produced for the bigger stars. The fronts contain color action shots. The player's team name resides at the top right corner and the player's name is towards the bottom. The company that produced the set, Phoenix, is printed at the bottom left along with an NBA copyright and the year 1989.

COMPLETE SET (35)	45.00	90.00
1 Mark Aguirre	1.00	2.50
2 Willie Anderson	.75	2.00
3 Charles Barkley	2.50	6.00
4 Larry Bird	3.00	8.00
5 Rolando Blackman	1.00	2.50
6 Tom Chambers	1.00	2.50
7 Clyde Drexler	2.00	5.00
8 Joe Dumars	1.25	3.00
9 Dale Ellis	.75	2.00
10 Alex English	1.00	2.50
11 Patrick Ewing	1.50	4.00
12 Roy Hinson	.75	2.00
13 Kevin Johnson	1.50	4.00
14 Magic Johnson	3.00	8.00
15 Vinnie Johnson	.75	2.00
16 Michael Jordan	8.00	20.00
17 Bernard King	1.00	2.50
18 Bill Laimbeer	1.00	2.50
19 Dan Majerle	1.50	4.00
20 Karl Malone	2.50	6.00
21 Moses Malone	1.25	3.00
22 Kevin McHale	1.50	4.00
23 Chris Mullin	1.25	3.00
24 Ken Norman	.75	2.00
25 Hakeem Olajuwon	2.00	5.00
26 Chuck Person	.75	2.00
27 Mark Price	1.00	2.50
28 Mitch Richmond	2.50	6.00
29 Dennis Rodman	2.00	5.00
30 Kenny Smith	.75	2.00
31 Jon Sundvold	.75	2.00
32 Isiah Thomas	1.50	4.00
33 Kelly Tripucka	.75	2.00
34 Dominique Wilkins	2.50	6.00
35 James Worthy	1.50	4.00

1987 Marketcom/Sports Illustrated

This 20-card white-bordered, multi-sport set measures approximately 3 1/16" by 4 14/16" and features color action photos of players in various sports produced by Marketcom. Cards #1-13 display Baseball players; cards #14-17, Basketball players; cards #18-10, Football players. The backs are blank. The set was issued to promote the Sports Illustrated sticker line. The cards are unnumbered and checklisted below alphabetically within each sport.

COMPLETE SET (20)	60.00	150.00
14 Larry Bird	6.00	15.00
15 Magic Johnson	6.00	15.00
16 Michael Jordan	16.00	40.00
17 Dominique Wilkins	2.00	5.00

1971 Mattel Mini-Records

This 18-disc set was designed to be played on a special Mattel mini-record player, which is not included in the complete set price. Each black plastic disc, approximately 2 1/2" in diameter, features a recording on one side and a color drawing of the player on the other. The picture appears on a paper disk that is glued onto the smooth unrecorded side of the mini-record. On the recorded side, the player's name and the set's subtitle appear in arcs stamped in the central portion of the mini-record. The hand-engraved player's name appears again along with a production number, copyright symbol, and the Mattel name and year of production in the ring between the central portion of the record and the grooves. The ivory discs are the ones which are double sided and are considered to be much tougher than the black discs. They are currently valued at 2X the regular records. They were also known as "Mattel Show 'N Tell". The discs are unnumbered and checklisted below in alphabetical order according to sport.

COMPLETE SET (18)	200.00	400.00
BK1 Lew Alcindor	8.00	20.00
BK2 Elgin Baylor	4.00	10.00
BK3 Wilt Chamberlain	8.00	20.00
BK4 Jerry Lucas	3.00	8.00
BK5 Pete Maravich	10.00	25.00
BK6 John Havlicek	4.00	10.00
BK7 Willis Reed	3.00	8.00
BK8 Oscar Robertson	4.00	10.00
BK9 Bill Russell SP	50.00	100.00
BK10 Jerry West	6.00	15.00

1994-95 Mavericks Bookmarks

This set of six bookmarks was jointly sponsored by HSE, Foot Locker, and KLIF 570 AM radio. Each bookmark was given away at a home game during the 1994-95 season. Just 5,000 of each were produced. The bookmarks measure 3" by 10" and have a high-gloss UV coating. A full-bleed purple-tinted action photo appears on the front. The player's name and number appear in green typewritten lettering. The player's signature and uniform number are inscribed across the lower portion of the bookmark. On a black background, the back has a color headshot and biography as well as "college capsule" and "personal capsule" features. The message "Don't Foul Out. Stay in School." completes the back. The bookmarks are numbered on the back.

COMPLETE SET (6)	5.00	12.00
1 Jim Jackson	1.25	3.00
2 Jamal Mashburn	1.25	3.00
3 Jason Kidd	2.50	6.00
4 Popeye Jones	.40	1.00
5 Tony Dumas	.40	1.00
6 Terry Davis	.40	1.00

1988-89 Mavericks Bud Light BLC

The 1988-89 Bud Light Dallas Mavericks set contains 14 standard-size cards comprised of 12 players and two coaches. This set was produced for distribution at the Mavericks "card night" promotion but may not have actually been used by the Mavericks. However the sets do exist within the hobby as the cards were not all destroyed. The set may have been rejected by the Mavericks because of the inclusion of Roy Tarpley and Mark Aguirre; however there is no indication that either the Tarpley or Aguirre cards is any harder to find than the others in the set. The set was produced for the Mavericks by Big League Cards of New Jersey. The set is unnumbered except for uniform numbers on the card backs.

COMPLETE SET (14)	10.00	25.00
12 Derek Harper	1.50	4.00
15 Brad Davis	.50	1.25
20 Morlon Wiley	.25	.60
22 Rolando Blackman	1.50	4.00
23 Bill Wennington	.50	1.50
24 Mark Aguirre	1.50	4.00
32 Detlef Schrempf	3.00	8.00
33 Uwe Blab	.25	.60
40 James Donaldson	.25	.60
41 Terry Tyler	.25	.60
42 Roy Tarpley	1.00	2.50
44 Sam Perkins	1.50	4.00
NNO Richie Adubato ACO Garfield Heard ACO	.50	1.25
NNO John MacLeod CO	.50	1.25

1988-89 Mavericks Bud Light Card Night

The 1988-89 Bud Light Dallas Mavericks set contains 13 standard-size cards comprised of 12 players and head coach John MacLeod. This set was produced for distribution at the Mavericks "card night' promotion and is apparently a rework of the set immediately above since Roy Tarpley and Mark Aguirre are not even in this set and many late season acquisitions are noted. It is not known what company produced these cards for the Mavericks and Bud Light. The set is unnumbered except for uniform numbers on the card backs.

COMPLETE SET (13)	6.00	15.00
4 Adrian Dantley	1.25	3.00
12 Derek Harper	1.25	3.00
15 Brad Davis	.40	1.00
20 Morlon Wiley	.20	.50
21 Anthony Jones	.20	.50
22 Rolando Blackman	1.25	3.00
23 Bill Wennington	.40	1.00
32 Herb Williams	.40	1.00
33 Uwe Blab	.20	.50
40 James Donaldson	.20	.50
41 Terry Tyler	.20	.50
44 Sam Perkins	1.25	3.00
NNO John MacLeod CO	.20	.50

1989-90 Mavericks Dr. Pepper

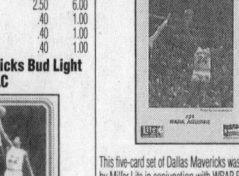

This 13-card standard size set was sponsored by Dr. Pepper and distributed at a Mavs home game. The fronts have color action shots surrounded by a white border. The top dawns two Dr. Pepper logos in each corner and the Mavs logo and the years 1989-1990. The players name along with team name appear at the bottom. The black and white backs have another Dr. Pepper logo, biographical player information and a small description of the player's career highlights. In addition, each card has the same anti-drug message at the bottom. The cards are unnumbered and listed below in alphabetical order.

COMPLETE SET (13)	8.00	20.00
1 Richie Adubato CO	.40	1.00
2 Steve Alford	1.25	3.00
3 Rolando Blackman	1.50	4.00
4 Adrian Dantley	1.50	4.00
5 Brad Davis	1.25	3.00
6 James Donaldson	.40	1.00
7 Derek Harper	1.50	4.00
8 Anthony Jones	.40	1.00
9 Sam Perkins	1.50	4.00
10 Roy Tarpley	.40	1.00
11 Bill Wennington	.40	1.00
12 Randy White	.40	1.00
13 Herb Williams	.60	1.50

1987-88 Mavericks Miller Lite

This five-card set of Dallas Mavericks was sponsored by Miller Lite in conjunction with WBAP Radio 820. These oversized cards measure approximately 4" by 6". The front features a borderless color action photo of the player on white card stock. The player's number and name are given below the picture in black lettering, and sponsors' logos in the lower corners complete the card face. The backs are blank. The cards are unnumbered and we have checklisted them below in alphabetical order.

COMPLETE SET (5)	6.00	15.00
1 Mark Aguirre	1.50	4.00
2 Rolando Blackman	1.50	4.00
3 James Donaldson	.75	2.00
4 Derek Harper	1.50	4.00
5 Sam Perkins	1.50	4.00

2010-11 Mavericks Panini NBA Champions

This 36-card set commemorates the 2010-11 NBA Champion Dallas Mavericks. Produced by Panini, this set was available through normal distribution channels, as well as through the companies website for an SRP of $20.

COMPLETE SET (36)	12.50	25.00
1 Dirk Nowitzki	1.00	2.50
2 Jason Kidd	.75	2.00
3 Jason Terry	.60	1.50
4 Tyson Chandler	.60	1.50
5 Shawn Marion	.75	2.00
6 J.J. Barea	.75	2.00
7 DeShawn Stevenson	.50	1.25
8 Brendan Haywood	.50	1.25
9 Brian Cardinal	.50	1.25
10 Caron Butler	.75	2.00
11 Peja Stojakovic	.75	2.00
12 Ian Mahinmi	.75	2.00
13 Corey Brewer	.50	1.25
14 Dominique Jones	.75	2.00
15 Rodrigue Beaubois	.60	1.50
16 Alexis Ajinca	.50	1.25
17 Sasha Pavlovic	.50	1.25
18 Steve Novak	.50	1.25
19 Rick Carlisle CO	.50	1.25
20 Playoff Win 1 Round 1, Game 1	.50	1.25
21 Playoff Win 2 Round 1, Game 2	.50	1.25
22 Playoff Win 3 Round 1, Game 5	.50	1.25
23 Playoff Win 4 Round 1, Game 6	.50	1.25
24 Playoff Win 5 Round 2, Game 1	.50	1.25
25 Playoff Win 6 Round 2, Game 2	.50	1.25
26 Playoff Win 7 Round 2, Game 3	.50	1.25
27 Playoff Win 8 Round 2, Game 4	.50	1.25
28 Playoff Win 9 Round 3, Game 1	.50	1.25
29 Playoff Win 10 Round 3, Game 3	.50	1.25
30 Playoff Win 11 Round 3, Game 4	.50	1.25
31 Playoff Win 12 Round 3, Game 5	.50	1.25
32 Playoff Win 13 Finals, Game 2	.50	1.25
33 Playoff Win 14 Finals, Game 4	.50	1.25
34 Playoff Win 15 Finals, Game 5	.50	1.25
35 Playoff Win 16 Finals, Game 6	.50	1.25
36 Dirk Nowitzki MVP	1.00	2.50

2000 Mavericks Rolando Blackman Retirement Sheet

This sheet was passed out at the March 11,2000 Mavericks game to honor all-time Maverick great, Rolando Blackman. The sheet features many different photos of Blackman, and his career statistics are on the back.

1 Rolando Blackman	1.25	3.00

1995-96 Mavericks Taco Bell

The Dallas Mavericks teamed together with Taco Bell Restaurants of Dallas/Fort Worth to issue four postcard-size (3 1/2" by 5") "Triple J" trading cards. Individual cards were cello-wrapped and available at all participating Taco Bell restaurants in the metroplex for 99 cents with any food purchase. Ten cents of every card sold was donated to the West Dallas Community School and the Boys and Girls Clubs of the Metroplex. The production run was 83,000 sets, with a different card being issued each week through February. Against a ghosted photo, the fronts display a caricature of one of the "Triple J Mavericks" by comic book illustrator Larry Webber. The player's name is stamped vertically in royal blue foil along one of the sides. The backs of all four cards can be combined to form a "Triple J" picture of all three players. Finally, a special "Triple" J ad card was distributed at the 1/27/96 Mavericks home game to kick off the promotion. Just 10,000 ad cards were produced; this card is listed below after the other cards.

COMPLETE SET (4)	2.00	5.00
1 Jim Jackson	.40	1.00
2 Jason Kidd (NBA Rookie of the Year)	1.25	3.00
3 Jason Kidd	1.25	3.00
4 Jamal Mashburn	.40	1.00
NNO Triple J Ad Card	2.50	6.00

1981-82 Mavericks Team Issue

This 5" x7" set was produced for the Dallas Mavericks during the 1981-82 season. The set features five black and white cards of the team's players and coaches.

COMPLETE SET (5)	8.00	20.00
1 Mark Aguirre	2.50	6.00
2 Brad Davis	2.00	5.00
3 Jim Spanarkel	1.50	4.00
4 Tom LaGarde	1.25	3.00
5 Oliver Mack	1.25	3.00

2001-02 Mavericks Topps

Produced by Topps in association with Minyard Food Stores and Sprite, this 15-card set was given away to the first 10,000 fans at the February 21, 2002 game against the Boston Celtics. The base cards feature white borders with gray and blue framing around full color player action photos.

COMPLETE SET (15)	5.00	12.00
DMAG Adrian Griffin	.40	1.00
DMDH Donnell Harvey	.40	1.00
DMDN Dirk Nowitzki	1.25	3.00
DMDAN Don Nelson CO	.40	1.00
DMDRM Danny Manning	.40	1.00
DMEE Evan Eschmeyer	.40	1.00
DMEN Eduardo Najera	.40	1.00
DMGB Greg Buckner	.40	1.00
DMJH Juwan Howard	.50	1.25
DMJN Johnny Newman	.40	1.00
DMMF Michael Finley	.60	1.50
DMSB Shawn Bradley	.40	1.00
DMSN Steve Nash	1.00	2.50
DMTH Tim Hardaway	.60	1.50
DMWZ Wang Zhizhi	.50	1.25

1990-91 McDonald's Jordan Joyner-Kersee

This 16-card set featuring Michael Jordan and Jackie Joyner-Kersee was sponsored by McDonald's restaurants as part of their "Sports Tips" series. The cards of each subject were issued on a 10 7/8" by 8 1/8" perforated sheet (two rows of four cards each) as a special insert in Sports Illustrated for Kids. The two sheets were attached connecting Michael Jordan and 1988 Olympic gold medalist Jackie Joyner-Kersee. After perforation, the cards measure the standard size (2 1/2" by 3 1/2"). The front has a color action photo of Jordan, with four different border stripes on each side of the picture: red above, green below, yellow with black dots on the left, and black , blue candy-stripe on the right. Jordan's autograph is inscribed on the red border, while the card title appears in the green border. The back has a hint on how to perform the move, a training tip, and a nutrition tip. A pink top border stripe and a green bottom border stripe frame this information. The Joyner-Kersee cards are styled similarly. The cards are numbered on both sides; the Joyner-Kersee cards are numbered below using a JK-prefix to distinguish from the similarly numbered Jordan cards.

COMPLETE SET (16)	8.00	20.00
COMMON MJ	1.00	2.50
COMMON JJK	.75	2.00

1993-94 McDonald's Lakers Magnets

This 3-card set was given out at participating McDonald's restaurants during the 1993-94 season. The set features three of the L.A. Lakers players on a relatively smaller magnetic card.

COMPLETE SET (3)	5.00	12.00
1 Nick Van Exel	4.00	10.00
2 Doug Christie	1.25	3.00
3 George Lynch	1.25	3.00

1995 McDonald's Looney Tunes All-Star Showdown Cups

This six-cup set was available in McDonald's in 1995 and features NBA Players teamed up with different Looney Tunes characters. The cups are not numbered and listed below in alphabetical order.

COMPLETE SET (6)	5.00	12.00
1 Larry Bird Sylvester	1.25	3.00
2 Charles Barkley Tasmanian Devil	1.25	3.00
3 Shawn Kemp Daffy Duck	.60	1.50
4 Michael Jordan Bugs Bunny	3.00	8.00
5 Larry Johnson Wile E. Coyote	.60	1.50
6 Reggie Miller Road Runner	1.25	3.00

1994 McDonald's Nothing But Net MVP Cups

This 6-cup set was sponsered by the NBA, Coke and McDonald's and features various MVP's from the past. Each cup contains dates of important games and a quote from the player about the game. The cups are numbered.

COMPLETE SET (6)	7.00	14.00
1 Michael Jordan	2.00	5.00
2 Julius Erving	1.25	3.00
3 Larry Bird	1.25	3.00
4 Moses Malone	.75	2.00
5 Charles Barkley	.75	2.00
6 Bill Walton	.75	2.00

1994 McDonald's Nothing But Net MVP Fry Boxes

This set of six MVPs was printed on boxes of McDonald's large fries and endorsed by the NBA. If cut, the cards would measure approximately 3" by 3 7/8". The fronts feature a color action player photo on a white background. The players' names are printed above their photos with the year they were voted MVP. The set title is superposed at the upper right and extends onto the box design. The information on the back is printed on the reverse side of the fries box. The data is not presented in a pie-shaped format. The player's name is printed on a team color-coded, arch-shaped bar at the top. The year (or years) the player was voted MVP is listed below, followed by the player's MVP stats. A head shot, biography and team logo round out the back. The cards are unnumbered and checklisted below in alphabetical order.

COMPLETE SET (6)	9.00	18.00
1 Charles Barkley 1993 MVP	1.50	4.00
2 Larry Bird 1984 MVP	1.50	4.00
3 Julius Erving 1981 MVP	1.50	4.00
4 Michael Jordan 1988, 1991, 1992 MVP	3.00	8.00
5 Moses Malone 1979, 1982, 1983 MVP	1.00	2.50
6 Bill Walton 1978 MVP	1.25	3.00

1992 McDonald's USA Dream Team Cups

This 10-cup set was available at McDonald's during the initial Dream Team Olympics. The cups feature career highlights of each Dream Team member and a facsimile autograph. Each of the cups are numbered. Two other cups were available via redemption (Clyde Drexler and Christian Laettner) and are not numbered. Those cups are not considered part of the set.

COMPLETE SET (10)	10.00	25.00
1 Charles Barkley	1.25	3.00
2 Larry Bird	1.50	4.00
3 Patrick Ewing	.75	2.00
4 Magic Johnson	1.50	4.00
5 Michael Jordan	4.00	10.00
6 Karl Malone	1.25	3.00
7 Chris Mullin	.75	2.00
8 Scottie Pippen	1.25	3.00
9 David Robinson	1.25	3.00
10 John Stockton	1.50	4.00
NNO Clyde Drexler	2.50	6.00
NNO Christian Laettner	1.50	4.00

1994 McDonald's USA Dream Team 2 Cups

Sponsered by the NBA, Coke and McDonald's, this 13-cup set features members from the USA Dream Team 2. Each cup features career highlights and carries a facsimile autograph. The cups are numbered.

COMPLETE SET (13)	6.00	15.00
1 Isiah Thomas	.60	1.50
2 Larry Johnson	.40	1.00
3 Shawn Kemp	.50	1.25
4 Dan Majerle	.60	1.50
5 Dominique Wilkins	.75	2.00
6 Derrick Coleman	.40	1.00
7 Alonzo Mourning	.75	2.00
8 Steve Smith	.60	1.50
9 Joe Dumars	.60	1.50
10 Mark Price	.60	1.50
11 Shaquille O'Neal	2.00	5.00
12 Reggie Miller	.75	2.00
13 Tim Hardaway	.60	1.50

1994 McDonald's USA Dream Team 2 Fry Boxes

This set of 11 Dream Teamers was printed on boxes of McDonald's large fries and endorsed by the NBA. The fronts feature a color player photo on a red, white and blue background. The players' names are printed above their photos inside one of the white stars. The set title is at the lower right. The information on the back is printed on the reverse side of the fries box. The back lists a schedule of games along with sponser logos for TNT, TBS and NBC. The cards are unnumbered and checklisted below in alphabetical order.

COMPLETE SET (11)	8.00	20.00
1 Derrick Coleman	.75	2.00
2 Joe Dumars	.75	2.00
3 Tim Hardaway	1.00	2.50
4 Larry Johnson	.75	2.00
5 Shawn Kemp	.75	2.00
6 Dan Majerle	.75	2.00
7 Reggie Miller	1.50	4.00
8 Alonzo Mourning	1.25	3.00
9 Steve Smith	.75	2.00
10 Isiah Thomas	1.25	3.00
11 Dominique Wilkins	1.50	4.00

1993 McDonald's/Footlocker Patrick Ewing

This 1 card set was released at participating McDonald's restaraunts during the 1993-94 season. This card is actually a game card that was good for discounts on Foot Locker prodcuts. Winners either got an autographed Patrick Ewing basketball, season tickets to see the New York Knicks play, 10% of their next purchase at Footlocker, or $50 off their next purchse at Footlocker.

1 Patrick Ewing	8.00	20.00

1995-96 Metal

The 1995-96 premiere issue of Metal basketball by Fleer/SkyBox consists of 220 standard-size cards issued in two separate series of 120 and 100 cards respectively. The eight-card packs carried a suggested retail price of $2.49 each. Borderless fronts feature the player in a full-color action cutout against a multicolored, hand engraved, metallic foil background. Backs picture the player in a full-color action shot with his team's logo printed at the bottom. The only subset is Nuts and Bolts (209-218). Rookie Cards of note include Michael Finley, Kevin Garnett, Antonio McDyess, Joe Smith, Jerry Stackhouse and Damon Stoudamire.

COMPLETE SET (220)	20.00	40.00
COMPLETE SERIES 1 (120)	10.00	20.00
COMPLETE SERIES 2 (100)	10.00	20.00
1 Stacey Augmon	.20	.50
2 Mookie Blaylock	.15	.40
3 Grant Long	.15	.40
4 Steve Smith	.20	.50
5 Dee Brown	.15	.40
6 Sherman Douglas	.15	.40
7 Eric Montross	.15	.40
8 Dino Radja	.20	.50
9 Muggsy Bogues	.20	.50
10 Scott Burrell	.15	.40
11 Larry Johnson	.25	.60
12 Alonzo Mourning	.30	.75
13 Michael Jordan	2.00	5.00
14 Toni Kukoc	.25	.60
15 Scottie Pippen	.40	1.00
16 Terrell Brandon	.15	.40
17 Tyrone Hill	.15	.40
18 Mark Price	.25	.60
19 John Williams	.15	.40
20 Jim Jackson	.15	.40
21 Popeye Jones	.15	.40
22 Jason Kidd	.40	1.00
23 Jamal Mashburn	.25	.60
24 Mahmoud Abdul-Rauf	.15	.40
25 Dikembe Mutombo	.25	.60
26 Robert Pack	.15	.40
27 Jalen Rose	.30	.75
28 Joe Dumars	.25	.60
29 Grant Hill	.40	1.00
30 Lindsey Hunter	.15	.40
31 Terry Mills	.15	.40
32 Tim Hardaway	.25	.60
33 Donyell Marshall	.15	.40
34 Chris Mullin	.25	.60
35 Clifford Rozier	.15	.40
36 Latrell Sprewell	.25	
37 Sam Cassell	.25	
38 Clyde Drexler	.30	
39 Robert Horry	.20	
40 Hakeem Olajuwon	.30	
41 Kenny Smith	.20	
42 Dale Davis	.15	
43 Mark Jackson	.25	
44 Derrick McKey	.15	
45 Reggie Miller	.30	
46 Rik Smits	.20	
47 Lamond Murray	.15	
48 Pooh Richardson	.15	
49 Malik Sealy	.15	
50 Loy Vaught	.15	
51 Elden Campbell	.15	
52 Cedric Ceballos	.15	
53 Vlade Divac	.25	
54 Eddie Jones	.30	
55 Nick Van Exel	.25	
56 Bimbo Coles	.15	
57 Billy Owens	.15	
58 Khalid Reeves	.15	
59 Glen Rice	.25	
60 Kevin Willis	.15	
61 Vin Baker	.20	
62 Todd Day	.15	
63 Eric Murdock	.15	
64 Glenn Robinson	.25	
65 Tom Gugliotta	.15	
66 Christian Laettner	.20	
67 Isaiah Rider	.25	
68 Kenny Anderson	.20	
69 P.J. Brown	.15	
70 Derrick Coleman	.20	
71 Patrick Ewing	.30	
72 Anthony Mason	.15	
73 Charles Oakley	.20	
74 John Starks	.20	
75 Nick Anderson	.15	
76 Horace Grant	.20	
77 Anfernee Hardaway	.40	
78 Shaquille O'Neal	.60	
79 Dennis Scott	.15	
80 Dana Barros	.15	
81 Shawn Bradley	.15	
82 Clarence Weatherspoon	.15	
83 Sharone Wright	.15	
84 Charles Barkley	.40	
85 Kevin Johnson	.25	
86 Dan Majerle	.25	
87 Danny Manning	.20	
88 Wesley Person	.15	
89 Clifford Robinson	.15	
90 Rod Strickland	.15	
91 Otis Thorpe	.15	
92 Buck Williams	.15	
93 Brian Grant	.20	
94 Olden Polynice	.15	
95 Mitch Richmond	.25	
96 Walt Williams	.15	
97 Sean Elliott	.25	
98 Avery Johnson	.20	
99 David Robinson	.40	
100 Dennis Rodman	.50	
101 Shawn Kemp	.25	
102 Nate McMillan	.15	
103 Gary Payton	.25	
104 Detlef Schrempf	.25	
105 B.J. Armstrong	.15	
106 Oliver Miller	.15	
107 John Salley	.15	
108 David Benoit	.15	
109 Jeff Hornacek	.20	
110 Karl Malone	.30	
111 John Stockton	.30	
112 Greg Anthony	.15	
113 Benoit Benjamin	.15	
114 Byron Scott	.20	
115 Calbert Cheaney	.15	
116 Juwan Howard	.25	
117 Gheorghe Muresan	.15	
118 Chris Webber	.30	
119 Checklist	.15	
120 Checklist	.15	
121 Stacey Augmon	.20	
122 Mookie Blaylock	.15	
123 Alan Henderson RC	.25	
124 Andrew Lang	.15	
125 Ken Norman	.15	
126 Steve Smith	.20	
127 Dana Barros	.15	
128 Rick Fox	.15	
129 Eric Williams RC	.25	
130 Kendall Gill	.15	
131 Khalid Reeves	.15	
132 Glen Rice	.25	
133 George Zidek RC	.25	
134 Dennis Rodman	.50	
135 Danny Ferry	.15	
136 Dan Majerle	.25	
137 Chris Mills	.15	
138 Bobby Phills	.15	
139 Bob Sura RC	.25	
140 Tony Dumas	.15	
141 Dale Ellis	.15	
142 Don MacLean	.15	
143 Antonio McDyess RC	.60	
144 Bryant Stith	.15	
145 Allan Houston	.20	
146 Theo Ratliff RC	.40	
147 Otis Thorpe	.15	
148 B.J. Armstrong	.15	
149 Rony Seikaly	.20	
150 Joe Smith RC	.50	
151 Sam Cassell	.25	
152 Clyde Drexler	.30	
153 Robert Horry	.20	
154 Hakeem Olajuwon	.30	
155 Antonio Davis	.15	
156 Ricky Pierce	.15	
157 Brent Barry RC	.40	
158 Terry Dehere	.15	
159 Rodney Rogers	.15	
160 Brian Williams	.15	
161 Magic Johnson	.60	
162 Sasha Danilovic RC	.25	
163 Alonzo Mourning	.30	
164 Kurt Thomas RC	.25	
165 Sherman Douglas	.15	
166 Shawn Respert RC	.25	
167 Kevin Garnett RC	2.00	
168 Terry Porter	.15	
169 Shawn Bradley	.15	
170 Kevin Edwards	.15	

d O'Bannon RC .25 .60
ayson Williams .15 .40
erek Harper .20 .50
harles Smith .15 .40
rian Shaw .15 .40
errick Coleman .20 .50
ernon Maxwell .15 .40
revor Ruffin .15 .40
erry Stackhouse RC .75 2.00
ichael Finley RC .75 2.00
.C. Green .25 .60
ohn Williams .15 .40
aron McKie .15 .40
rvydas Sabonis RC .50 1.25
ary Trent RC .25 .60
yus Edney RC .25 .60
arunas Marciulionis .15 .40
ichael Smith .15 .40
orliss Williamson RC .25 .60
inny Del Negro .15 .40
ersey Hawkins .15 .40
hawn Kemp .25 .60
ary Payton .25 .60
am Perkins .15 .40
etlef Schrempf .25 .60
illie Anderson .15 .40
liver Miller .15 .40
racy Murray .15 .40
lvin Robertson .15 .40
amon Stoudamire RC .60 1.50
hris Morris .15 .40
reg Anthony .15 .40
lue Edwards .15 .40
ic Murdock .15 .40
yant Reeves RC .25 .60
yron Scott .20 .50
obert Pack .15 .40
asheed Wallace RC .75 2.00
nfernee Hardaway NB .20 .50
rant Hill NB .20 .50
arry Johnson NB .12 .30
ichael Jordan NB 1.00 2.50
ason Kidd NB .20 .50
arl Malone NB .15 .40
haquille O'Neal NB .30 .75
cottie Pippen NB .20 .50
avid Robinson NB .20 .50
enn Robinson NB .12 .30
hecklist .15 .40
hecklist .15 .40

95-96 Metal Silver Spotlight

120 cards parallel the first series of Metal and eeded at a rate of one per first series pack. The d series was discontinued due to lack of collector se. These "Silver Spotlight" cards are identical egular cards with the exception of having etched lver foil backgrounds instead of the multi- d backgrounds of the basic cards. Please refer to ltiplier listed below for values on singles.

LETE SET (120) 30.00 60.00
S: 1.25X TO 3X BASE CARD HI

5-96 Metal Maximum Metal

mly inserted in all series one packs at a rate of 36, cards from this 10-card standard-size set ht some NBA impact players. These cards have etball-shaped die cut design and feature a full- layer action cutout on the front. The background ver foil diamond-plate basketball going through . Backs continue with the diamond plate ball and hoop background and also feature a or player cutout. The player's name and a player are printed on the back. The set is sequenced in etical order.

LETE SET (10) 20.00 50.00
es Barkley 2.50 6.00
ck Ewing 2.00 5.00
Hill 2.50 6.00
ael Jordan 12.00 30.00
n Kemp 1.50 4.00
Malone 2.00 5.00
em Olajuwon 2.00 5.00
uille O'Neal 4.00 10.00
Richmond 1.50 4.00
d Robinson 2.50 6.00

995-96 Metal Metal Force

nly inserted exclusively in second series retail at a rate of one in 54, cards from this 15-card set a selection of the NBA's top stars and rookies. ard is made of a clear plastic material and comes protective coating on front. Prices provided efer to unpeeled cards. Peeled cards generally r ten to twenty-five percent less.

ETE SET (15) 75.00 150.00
aker 3.00 8.00
es Barkley 6.00 15.00
c Ceballos 2.50 6.00
Hill 6.00 15.00
Johnson 4.00 10.00
: Johnson 10.00 25.00
n Kemp 4.00 10.00
Malone 5.00 12.00
l Mashburn 4.00 10.00
tie Pippen 8.00 20.00
n Robinson 4.00 10.00
nis Rodman 8.00 20.00
Smith 4.00 10.00
y Stackhouse 6.00 15.00
s Webber 5.00 12.00

95-96 Metal Molten Metal

nly inserted in all series one packs at a rate of 72, cards from this 10-card standard-size set a selection of up and coming NBA stars. The eature full-color action cutouts set against d multicolored laminated foil backgrounds. ess backs feature the player in a full-color cutout and a white box surrounding a player which is printed in white type. The set is ced in alphabetical order.

LETE SET (10) 40.00 100.00
ee Hardaway 8.00 20.00
Hill 8.00 20.00
t Horry 4.00 10.00
Jones 6.00 15.00
Kukoc 5.00 12.00
Mashburn 5.00 12.00
o Mourning 6.00 15.00
Robinson 5.00 12.00
l Sprewell 5.00 12.00
s Webber 6.00 15.00

1995-96 Metal Rookie Roll Call

Spotlighting the '95-96 rookie class, cards from this 10-card standard-size set were randomly inserted in both series one hobby and retail packs. Though these cards are considered inserts, they were distributed at the same rate as regular issue cards. The cards display hand-engraved, metalized foil designs and are numbered on the back. The set is sequenced in alphabetical order.

COMPLETE SET (10) 2.00 5.00
*SILV.SPOTLIGHT: 1X TO 2.5X HI COLUMN
RANDOM INSERTS IN ALL SER.1 PACKS
R1 Brent Barry .50 1.25
R2 Antonio McDyess .75 2.00
R3 Ed O'Bannon .30 .75
R4 Cherokee Parks .30 .75
R5 Bryant Reeves .30 .75
R6 Shawn Respert .30 .75
R7 Joe Smith .60 1.50
R8 Jerry Stackhouse 1.00 2.50
R9 Gary Trent .30 .75
R10 Rasheed Wallace 1.00 2.50

1995-96 Metal Scoring Magnets

Randomly inserted exclusively into second series hobby packs at a rate of one in 54, cards from this 8-card set feature a selection of the NBA's top scoring threats. Card fronts have embossed player shots with the card name "Scoring Magnet" in silver foil running vertical along both sides of the player. Card backs contain a brief commentary and are numbered as "X of 8".

COMPLETE SET (8) 30.00 80.00
1 Anfernee Hardaway 4.00 10.00
2 Grant Hill 4.00 10.00
3 Magic Johnson 6.00 15.00
4 Michael Jordan 15.00 40.00
5 Jason Kidd 4.00 10.00
6 Hakeem Olajuwon 3.00 8.00
7 Shaquille O'Neal 6.00 15.00
8 David Robinson 4.00 10.00

1995-96 Metal Slick Silver

Randomly inserted exclusively into first series hobby packs at a rate of one in seven, cards from this 10-card standard-size set highlight the league's premier point and shooting guards. The clear acetate cards feature the player in a full-color action shot with a ghost images on the front. Backs feature a player profile printed on the player's reverse silhouette. The set is sequenced in alphabetical order.

COMPLETE SET (10) 20.00 40.00
1 Kenny Anderson 1.25 3.00
2 Anfernee Hardaway 2.50 6.00
3 Michael Jordan 12.00 30.00
4 Jason Kidd 2.50 6.00
5 Reggie Miller 2.00 5.00
6 Gary Payton 1.50 4.00
7 Mitch Richmond 1.50 4.00
8 Latrell Sprewell 1.50 4.00
9 John Stockton 2.00 5.00
10 Nick Van Exel 1.50 4.00

1995-96 Metal Stackhouse's Scrapbook

Randomly inserted into one in every 24 second series packs, these two cards continue the eight-card, cross-brand set devoted Fleer spokesperson Jerry Stackhouse. Card #S7 often sells for a premium due to the appearance of Michael Jordan.

COMPLETE SET (2) 3.00 8.00
S7 Jerry Stackhouse 2.50 6.00
w/Michael Jordan
S8 Jerry Stackhouse 1.25 3.00

1995-96 Metal Steel Towers

Randomly inserted exclusively into series one retail and magazine packs at a rate of one in four, cards from this 10-card insert set focus on the leagues top big men. Full-bleed fronts have silver foil backgrounds and are stamped with skyscraper designs. Backs are two-toned according to player's team colors and feature a full-color action shot and a player profile printed next to it. Skyscraper designs also appear in the background on the backs. The set is sequenced in alphabetical order.

COMPLETE SET (10) 5.00 12.00
1 Shawn Bradley .60 1.50
2 Vlade Divac 1.00 2.50
3 Patrick Ewing 1.25 3.00
4 Alonzo Mourning 1.25 3.00
5 Dikembe Mutombo 1.00 2.50
6 Hakeem Olajuwon 1.25 3.00
7 Shaquille O'Neal 2.50 6.00
8 David Robinson 1.50 4.00
9 Rik Smits .75 2.00
10 Kevin Willis .60 1.50

1995-96 Metal Tempered Steel

Randomly inserted into all second series packs at a rate of one in 12, cards from this 12-card set feature a selection of top rookies from the 1995-96 season. Card fronts have a colorful foil-etched background with the the "Tempered Steel" logo written in cursive running along the left side. Card backs feature an action shot and a brief commentary next to it. Card backs are numbered as "X of 12".

COMPLETE SET (12) 15.00 30.00
1 Sasha Danilovic .75 2.00
2 Tyus Edney .75 2.00
3 Michael Finley 2.50 6.00
4 Kevin Garnett 6.00 15.00
5 Antonio McDyess 2.00 5.00
6 Bryant Reeves .75 2.00
7 Arvydas Sabonis 1.50 4.00
8 Joe Smith 1.50 4.00
9 Jerry Stackhouse 2.50 6.00
10 Damon Stoudamire 2.50 6.00
11 Rasheed Wallace 2.50 6.00
12 Eric Williams .75 2.00

1996-97 Metal

Produced by Fleer/SkyBox, the 1996 Metal set is comprised of 250 cards with eight-card packs carrying a suggested retail price of $2.49. Borderless fronts feature the player in a full-color action cutout against an etched color and silver foil background. The player's name is printed in silver foil and embossed along the right side of the card. Backs picture the player in a full-color action shot with his team's logo printed at the bottom against a "steel" background. The player's name and statistics run vertically along the right side of the card. The cards are grouped alphabetically within teams and checklisted below alphabetically according to team. The Series one Fresh Foundation subset contains the Rookie Cards of Stephon Marbury, Shareef Abdur-Rahim, Ray Allen, Kobe Bryant and Steve Nash. Card #73 (Jerry Stackhouse) was also used for promotional purposes.

COMPLETE SET (250) 25.00 45.00
COMPLETE SERIES 1 (150) 15.00 25.00
COMPLETE SERIES 2 (100) 10.00 20.00
1 Mookie Blaylock .15 .40
2 Christian Laettner .20 .50
3 Steve Smith .20 .50
4 Dana Barros .15 .40
5 Rick Fox .15 .40
6 Dino Radja .20 .50
7 Eric Williams .15 .40
8 Dell Curry .15 .40
9 Matt Geiger .15 .40
10 Glen Rice .25 .60
11 Michael Jordan 2.00 5.00
12 Toni Kukoc .25 .60
13 Luc Longley .15 .40
14 Scottie Pippen .40 1.00
15 Dennis Rodman .50 1.25
16 Terrell Brandon .15 .40
17 Danny Ferry .15 .40
18 Chris Mills .15 .40
19 Bobby Phills .15 .40
20 Bob Sura .15 .40
21 Jim Jackson .15 .40
22 Jason Kidd .40 1.00
23 Jamal Mashburn .20 .50
24 George McCloud .15 .40
25 LaPhonso Ellis .15 .40
26 Antonio McDyess .25 .60
27 Bryant Stith .15 .40
28 Joe Dumars .25 .60
29 Grant Hill .40 1.00
30 Theo Ratliff .15 .40
31 Otis Thorpe .15 .40
32 Chris Mullin .25 .60
33 Joe Smith .20 .50
34 Latrell Sprewell .25 .60
35 Sam Cassell .20 .50
36 Clyde Drexler .30 .75
37 Robert Horry .20 .50
38 Hakeem Olajuwon .30 .75
39 Antonio Davis .15 .40
40 Dale Davis .15 .40
41 Derrick McKey .15 .40
42 Reggie Miller .30 .75
43 Rik Smits .20 .50
44 Brent Barry .20 .50
45 Malik Sealy .15 .40
46 Loy Vaught .15 .40
47 Elden Campbell .15 .40
48 Cedric Ceballos .15 .40
49 Eddie Jones .25 .60
50 Nick Van Exel .25 .60
51 Sasha Danilovic .15 .40
52 Tim Hardaway .25 .60
53 Alonzo Mourning .30 .75
54 Kurt Thomas .15 .40
55 Vin Baker .20 .50
56 Sherman Douglas .15 .40
57 Glenn Robinson .25 .60
58 Kevin Garnett .60 1.50
59 Tom Gugliotta .15 .40
60 Doug West .15 .40
61 Shawn Bradley .15 .40
62 Ed O'Bannon .15 .40
63 Jayson Williams .15 .40
64 Patrick Ewing .30 .75
65 Charles Oakley .20 .50
66 John Starks .20 .50
67 Nick Anderson .15 .40
68 Horace Grant .20 .50
69 Anfernee Hardaway .40 1.00
70 Dennis Scott .15 .40
71 Brian Shaw .15 .40
72 Derrick Coleman .20 .50
73 Jerry Stackhouse .30 .75
74 Clarence Weatherspoon .15 .40
75 Charles Barkley .40 1.00
76 Michael Finley .30 .75
77 Kevin Johnson .20 .50
78 Wesley Person .15 .40
79 Aaron McKie .15 .40
80 Clifford Robinson .15 .40
81 Arvydas Sabonis .20 .50
82 Gary Trent .15 .40
83 Tyus Edney .15 .40
84 Brian Grant .20 .50
85 Billy Owens .15 .40
86 Olden Polynice .15 .40
87 Mitch Richmond .25 .60
88 Vinny Del Negro .15 .40
89 Sean Elliott .25 .60
90 Avery Johnson .20 .50
91 David Robinson .40 1.00
92 Hersey Hawkins .15 .40
93 Shawn Kemp .25 .60
94 Gary Payton .25 .60
95 Sam Perkins .15 .40
96 Detlef Schrempf .25 .60
97 Doug Christie .15 .40
98 Damon Stoudamire .25 .60
99 Sharone Wright .15 .40
100 Jeff Hornacek .20 .50
101 Karl Malone .30 .75
102 John Stockton .30 .75
103 Greg Anthony .15 .40
104 Blue Edwards .15 .40
105 Bryant Reeves .15 .40
106 Juwan Howard .20 .50
107 Gheorghe Muresan .15 .40
108 Chris Webber .30 .75
109 Kenny Anderson OTM .20 .50
110 Stacey Augmon OTM .20 .50
111 Chris Childs OTM .15 .40
112 Vlade Divac OTM .25 .60
113 Allan Houston OTM .20 .50
114 Mark Jackson OTM .25 .60
115 Larry Johnson OTM .25 .60
116 Grant Long OTM .15 .40
117 Anthony Mason OTM .15 .40
118 Dikembe Mutombo OTM .25 .60
119 Shaquille O'Neal OTM .60 1.50
120 Isaiah Rider OTM .20 .50
121 Rod Strickland OTM .15 .40
122 Rasheed Wallace OTM .30 .75
123 Jalen Rose OTM .25 .60
124 Anfernee Hardaway MET .40 1.00
125 Tim Hardaway MET .25 .60
126 Allan Houston MET .20 .50
127 Eddie Jones MET .25 .60
128 Michael Jordan MET 2.00 5.00
129 Reggie Miller MET .30 .75
130 Glen Rice MET .25 .60
131 Mitch Richmond MET .25 .60
132 Steve Smith MET .20 .50
133 John Stockton MET .30 .75
134 Stephon Marbury FF RC .60 1.50
135 Shareef Abdur-Rahim FF RC .50 1.25
136 Ray Allen FF RC 1.00 2.50
137 Kobe Bryant FF RC 5.00 12.00
138 Steve Nash FF RC 1.25 3.00
139 Grant Hill MS .40 1.00
140 Jason Kidd MS .40 1.00
141 Karl Malone MS .30 .75
142 Hakeem Olajuwon MS .30 .75
143 Shaquille O'Neal MS .60 1.50
144 Gary Payton MS .25 .60
145 Scottie Pippen MS .40 1.00
146 Jerry Stackhouse MS .30 .75
147 Damon Stoudamire MS .25 .60
148 Rod Strickland MS .15 .40
149 Checklist (1-102) .15 .40
150 Checklist (103-150/inserts) .15 .40
151 Tyrone Corbin .15 .40
152 Dikembe Mutombo .25 .60
153 Antoine Walker RC .50 1.25
154 David Wesley .15 .40
155 Vlade Divac .25 .60
156 Anthony Mason .15 .40
157 Ron Harper .20 .50
158 Steve Kerr .20 .50
159 Robert Parish .25 .60
160 Tyrone Hill .15 .40
161 Vitaly Potapenko RC .15 .40
162 Sam Cassell .20 .50
163 Chris Gatling .15 .40
164 Samaki Walker RC .25 .60
165 Dale Ellis .15 .40
166 Mark Jackson .20 .50
167 Ervin Johnson .15 .40
168 Grant Hill .40 1.00
169 Lindsey Hunter .15 .40
170 Todd Fuller RC .25 .60
171 Mark Price .25 .60
172 Charles Barkley .40 1.00
173 Othella Harrington RC .25 .60
174 Matt Maloney RC .25 .60
175 Kevin Willis .15 .40
176 Travis Best .15 .40
177 Erick Dampier RC .25 .60
178 Jalen Rose .20 .50
179 Rodney Rogers .15 .40
180 Lorenzen Wright RC .20 .50
181 Kobe Bryant 2.50 6.00
182 Robert Horry .20 .50
183 Shaquille O'Neal .60 1.50
184 P.J. Brown .15 .40
185 Dan Majerle .25 .60
186 Ray Allen .50 1.25
187 Armon Gilliam .15 .40
188 Andrew Lang .15 .40
189 Stephon Marbury .30 .75
190 Stojko Vrankovic .15 .40
191 Kendall Gill .15 .40
192 Kerry Kittles RC .25 .60
193 Robert Pack .15 .40
194 Chris Childs .15 .40
195 Allan Houston .20 .50
196 Larry Johnson .25 .60
197 John Wallace RC .25 .60
198 Rony Seikaly .20 .50
199 Gerald Wilkins .15 .40
200 Lucious Harris .15 .40
201 Allen Iverson RC 1.25 3.00
202 Cedric Ceballos .15 .40
203 Jason Kidd .40 1.00
204 Danny Manning .20 .50
205 Steve Nash .60 1.50
206 Kenny Anderson .20 .50
207 Isaiah Rider .20 .50
208 Rasheed Wallace .30 .75
209 Mahmoud Abdul-Rauf .15 .40
210 Corliss Williamson .15 .40
211 Vernon Maxwell .15 .40
212 Dominique Wilkins .30 .75
213 Craig Ehlo .15 .40
214 Jim McIlvaine .15 .40
215 Marcus Camby RC .40 1.00
216 Hubert Davis .15 .40
217 Walt Williams .15 .40
218 Shandon Anderson RC .25 .60
219 Bryon Russell .15 .40
220 Shareef Abdur-Rahim .25 .60
221 Roy Rogers RC .25 .60
222 Tracy Murray .15 .40
223 Rod Strickland .15 .40
224 Kevin Garnett MET .60 1.50
225 Karl Malone MET .30 .75
226 Alonzo Mourning MET .30 .75
227 Hakeem Olajuwon MET .30 .75
228 Gary Payton MET .25 .60
229 Scottie Pippen MET .40 1.00
230 David Robinson MET .40 1.00
231 Dennis Rodman MET .50 1.25
232 Latrell Sprewell MET .25 .60
233 Jerry Stackhouse MET .30 .75
234 Marcus Camby FF .20 .50
235 Todd Fuller FF .12 .30
236 Allen Iverson FF .60 1.50
237 Kerry Kittles FF .30 .75
238 Roy Rogers FF .12 .30
239 Anfernee Hardaway MS .40 1.00
240 Juwan Howard MS .20 .50
241 Michael Jordan MS 2.00 5.00
242 Shawn Kemp MS .25 .60
243 Gary Payton MS .25 .60
244 Mitch Richmond MS .25 .60
245 Glenn Robinson MS .25 .60
246 John Stockton MS .30 .75
247 Damon Stoudamire MS .25 .60
248 Chris Webber MS .30 .75
249 Checklist .15 .40
250 Checklist .15 .40

1996-97 Metal Precious Metal

Randomly inserted into hobby packs at a rate of one in 36, this 98-card set is a parallel of the Series two set only (minus the checklists). These cards differ from the basic set with the background of the card being completely silver. To ascertain values on individual cards, please refer to the multiplier in the header, coupled with the value of the base card.

*STARS: 12X TO 30X HI COLUMN
*ROOKIES: 6X TO 15X HI
*ROOKIE FF SUBSET: 12X TO 30X HI
181 Kobe Bryant 125.00 250.00

1996-97 Metal Cyber-Metal

Randomly inserted in all series two packs at a rate of one in 6, this 20-card set features NBA players as "Terminator-type" characters.

COMPLETE SET (20) 20.00 40.00
1 Shareef Abdur-Rahim 1.25 3.00
2 Ray Allen 2.50 6.00
3 Vin Baker .75 2.00
4 Charles Barkley 1.50 4.00
5 Kobe Bryant 8.00 20.00
6 Patrick Ewing 1.25 3.00
7 Jason Kidd 1.50 4.00
8 Karl Malone 1.25 3.00
9 Stephon Marbury 1.50 4.00
10 Reggie Miller 1.25 3.00
11 Alonzo Mourning 1.25 3.00
12 Hakeem Olajuwon 1.25 3.00
13 Gary Payton 1.00 2.50
14 Scottie Pippen 1.50 4.00
15 Mitch Richmond 1.00 2.50
16 David Robinson 1.50 4.00
17 Joe Smith .75 2.00
18 Latrell Sprewell 1.00 2.50
19 John Stockton 1.25 3.00
20 Chris Webber 1.25 3.00

1996-97 Metal Decade of Excellence

Randomly inserted in all first series packs at a rate of one in 100, this 10 card set features metalized foil replicas of the 1986-87 Fleer NBA cards. Card backs carry a "M" prefix.

COMPLETE SET (10) 15.00 40.00
M1 Clyde Drexler 2.50 6.00
M2 Joe Dumars 2.00 5.00
M3 Derek Harper 1.50 4.00
M4 Michael Jordan 15.00 40.00
M5 Karl Malone 2.50 6.00
M6 Chris Mullin 2.00 5.00
M7 Charles Oakley 1.50 4.00
M8 Sam Perkins 1.25 3.00
M9 Ricky Pierce 1.25 3.00
M10 Buck Williams 1.25 3.00

1996-97 Metal Freshly Forged

Randomly inserted in all series two packs at a rate of one in 24, this 15-card set focuses on younger players and features an original art illustrated background on each card.

COMPLETE SET (15) 25.00 60.00
1 Shareef Abdur-Rahim 1.50 4.00
2 Ray Allen 3.00 8.00
3 Kobe Bryant 8.00 20.00
4 Marcus Camby 1.25 3.00
5 Kevin Garnett 3.00 8.00
6 Anfernee Hardaway 2.00 5.00
7 Grant Hill 2.00 5.00
8 Allen Iverson 4.00 10.00
9 Jason Kidd 2.00 5.00
10 Stephon Marbury 2.00 5.00
11 Glenn Robinson 1.25 3.00
12 Joe Smith 1.00 2.50
13 Jerry Stackhouse 1.50 4.00
14 Damon Stoudamire 1.25 3.00
15 Antoine Walker 1.50 4.00

1996-97 Metal Maximum Metal

The first ten cards were randomly inserted in first series hobby packs only at a rate of one in 180. This 10-card set features embossed metalized cards of ten of the fan's favorite impact players. The fronts display color action player images with a metallic foil basketball in the background. The backs carry player information. The final ten cards were randomly inserted in second series retail packs only at a rate of one in 120. These cards feature the same design used in series one.

COMPLETE SET (20) 190.00 375.00
COMPLETE SERIES 1 (10) 150.00 300.00
COMPLETE SERIES 2 (10) 40.00 75.00
1 Charles Barkley 10.00 25.00
2 Anfernee Hardaway 10.00 25.00
3 Grant Hill 12.00 30.00
4 Michael Jordan 75.00 200.00
5 Jason Kidd 10.00 25.00
6 Karl Malone 8.00 20.00
7 Hakeem Olajuwon 8.00 20.00
8 Gary Payton 6.00 15.00
9 David Robinson 10.00 25.00
10 Damon Stoudamire 6.00 15.00
11 Juwan Howard 5.00 12.00
12 Shawn Kemp 8.00 20.00
13 Kerry Kittles 3.00 8.00
14 Stephon Marbury 8.00 20.00
15 Dennis Rodman 12.00 30.00
16 Joe Smith 5.00 12.00
17 Jerry Stackhouse 8.00 20.00
18 John Stockton 8.00 20.00
19 Antoine Walker 6.00 15.00
20 Chris Webber 10.00 25.00

1996-97 Metal Metal Edge

Randomly inserted in all first series packs at a rate of one in 36, this 15-card set features players known for their agressiveness in driving to the basket. The fronts display a color player photo a geometric metallic foil background. The backs carry player information.

COMPLETE SET (15) 35.00 70.00
1 Charles Barkley 4.00 10.00
2 Jamal Mashburn 2.00 5.00
3 Alonzo Mourning 3.00 8.00
4 Gary Payton 2.50 6.00
5 Scottie Pippen 4.00 10.00
6 Steve Smith 2.00 5.00
7 Latrell Sprewell 2.50 6.00
8 John Stockton 3.00 8.00
9 Nick Van Exel 2.50 6.00
10 Chris Webber 3.00 8.00
11 Stephon Marbury 3.00 8.00
12 Shareef Abdur-Rahim 2.50 6.00
13 Ray Allen 5.00 12.00
14 Antoine Walker 2.50 6.00
15 Kobe Bryant 12.00 30.00

1996-97 Metal Minted Metal

These redemption cards were randomly inserted into hobby packs of series two at one in 720 packs and were exchangeable for Highland Mint cards. The selected two players are the Fleer Spokesmen, Grant Hill and Jerry Stackhouse. The expiration date for the cards was March 1, 1998. Both players have the following redemptions available: All-Metal 14kt. gold, Gold-plated, Silver and Bronze cards. Both the Gold and the Solid Gold cards for each player are not priced below due to lack of market information.

COMP.BRONZE SET (2) 40.00 80.00
1 Grant Hill Bronze 15.00 30.00
2 Jerry Stackhouse Bronze 12.50 25.00
3 Grant Hill Silver 40.00 100.00
4 Jerry Stackhouse Silver 30.00 80.00

1996-97 Metal Molten Metal

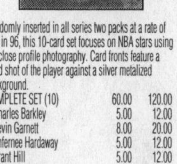

The first ten cards were randomly inserted in series one retail packs only at a rate of one in 180. This 10-card set features some of the hottest up and coming stars who have one to three years NBA experience. The fronts display color action player photos on a 3-D background. The backs carry player information. The final twenty cards were randomly inserted in series two hobby packs at a rate of one in 72. The second series cards feature embossed technology.

COMPLETE SET (30) 200.00 400.00
COMPLETE SERIES 1 (10) 75.00 150.00
COMPLETE SERIES 2 (20) 125.00 250.00
1 Michael Finley 12.00 30.00
2 Kevin Garnett 25.00 60.00
3 Anfernee Hardaway 15.00 40.00
4 Grant Hill 15.00 40.00
5 Juwan Howard 8.00 20.00
6 Jason Kidd 15.00 40.00
7 Antonio McDyess 10.00 25.00
8 Joe Smith 8.00 20.00
9 Jerry Stackhouse 12.00 30.00
10 Damon Stoudamire 10.00 25.00
11 Shareef Abdur-Rahim 5.00 12.00
12 Ray Allen 10.00 25.00
13 Charles Barkley 8.00 20.00
14 Terrell Brandon 3.00 8.00
15 Marcus Camby 4.00 10.00
16 Tom Gugliotta 3.00 8.00
17 Allen Iverson 12.00 30.00
18 Michael Jordan 50.00 125.00
19 Kerry Kittles 2.50 6.00
20 Karl Malone 6.00 15.00
21 Hakeem Olajuwon 6.00 15.00
22 Shaquille O'Neal 12.00 30.00
23 Gary Payton 5.00 12.00
24 Scottie Pippen 8.00 20.00
25 David Robinson 8.00 20.00
26 Glenn Robinson 5.00 12.00
27 Joe Smith 4.00 10.00
28 Latrell Sprewell 5.00 12.00
29 Antoine Walker 5.00 12.00
30 Chris Webber 5.00 12.00

1996-97 Metal Net-Rageous

Randomly inserted in all series two packs at a rate of one in 288, this 10-card set features some of the best players in the NBA against a die-cut background.

COMPLETE SET (10) 150.00 300.00
1 Kevin Garnett 15.00 40.00
2 Anfernee Hardaway 10.00 25.00
3 Grant Hill 10.00 25.00
4 Juwan Howard 5.00 12.00
5 Michael Jordan 100.00 225.00
6 Shawn Kemp 10.00 25.00
7 Shaquille O'Neal 15.00 40.00
8 Dennis Rodman 15.00 40.00
9 Jerry Stackhouse 8.00 20.00
10 Damon Stoudamire 6.00 15.00

1996-97 Metal Platinum Portraits

Randomly inserted in all series two packs at a rate of one in 96, this 10-card set focuses on NBA stars using up-close profile photography. Card fronts feature a head shot of the player against a silver metalized background.

COMPLETE SET (10) 60.00 120.00
1 Charles Barkley 5.00 12.00
2 Kevin Garnett 8.00 20.00
3 Anfernee Hardaway 5.00 12.00
4 Grant Hill 5.00 12.00
5 Michael Jordan 40.00 70.00
6 Shawn Kemp 3.00 8.00
7 Karl Malone 4.00 10.00
8 Shaquille O'Neal 8.00 20.00
9 Hakeem Olajuwon 4.00 10.00
10 Damon Stoudamire 3.00 8.00

1996-97 Metal Power Tools

Randomly inserted in all first series packs at a rate of one in 18, this 10-card set features color action player cutouts of power players on etched foil backgrounds of machine gears. The backs carry player information.

COMPLETE SET (10) 10.00 20.00
1 Vin Baker 1.25 3.00
2 Charles Barkley 2.50 6.00
3 Horace Grant 1.25 3.00
4 Juwan Howard 1.25 3.00
5 Larry Johnson 1.50 4.00
6 Shawn Kemp 1.50 4.00
7 Karl Malone 2.00 5.00
8 Antonio McDyess 1.50 4.00
9 Dennis Rodman 3.00 8.00
10 Joe Smith 1.25 3.00

1996-97 Metal Steel Slammin'

Randomly inserted in all first series packs at a rate of one in 72, this 10-card set features the NBA's top slam-dunkers performing their craft on a metal die-cut card. The fronts display a color action player image on a metallic background. The backs carry player information.

COMPLETE SET (10) 50.00 100.00
1 Brent Barry 2.50 6.00
2 Clyde Drexler 4.00 10.00
3 Michael Finley 4.00 10.00
4 Kevin Garnett 8.00 20.00
5 Eddie Jones 3.00 8.00
6 Michael Jordan 25.00 60.00
7 Shawn Kemp 3.00 8.00
8 Shaquille O'Neal 8.00 20.00
9 Joe Smith 2.50 6.00
10 Jerry Stackhouse 4.00 10.00

1999-00 Metal

The 1999-00 Metal product was released in April,2000 as a 180-card set. The set features 150 players and 30 rookie subset cards. The rookies are seeded at one in two packs. Each pack contained 10-cards and carried a suggested retail price of 1.99.

COMPLETE SET (180) 15.00 40.00
1 Vince Carter .40 1.00
2 Stephon Marbury .15 .40
3 David Robinson .30 .75
4 Ray Allen .20 .50
5 P.J. Brown .12 .30
6 Shawn Kemp .20 .50
7 Cedric Ceballos .12 .30
8 Dale Davis .12 .30
9 Rodney Rogers .12 .30
10 Chris Gatling .12 .30
11 Bryant Reeves .12 .30
12 Al Harrington .20 .50
13 Brent Barry .15 .40
14 Brevin Knight .12 .30
15 Radoslav Nesterovic RC .20 .50
16 Tom Gugliotta .12 .30
17 Charles Barkley .30 .75
18 Cuttino Mobley .15 .40
19 Corliss Williamson .12 .30
20 Hersey Hawkins .12 .30
21 Mike Bibby .20 .50
22 Pat Garrity .12 .30
23 Kelvin Cato .12 .30
24 Alan Henderson .12 .30
25 Alvin Williams .12 .30
26 Antonio McDyess .15 .40
27 Damon Stoudamire .20 .50
28 Kerry Kittles .12 .30
29 Michael Olowokandi .12 .30
30 Brent Price .12 .30
31 Fred Hoiberg .12 .30
32 Glenn Robinson .15 .40
33 Hakeem Olajuwon .25 .60
34 Monty Williams .12 .30
35 Terry Porter .12 .30
36 Allen Iverson .40 1.00
37 Juwan Howard .15 .40
38 Mario Elie .12 .30
39 Mookie Blaylock .12 .30
40 Sam Cassell .15 .40
41 Toni Kukoc .20 .50
42 Anthony Mason .12 .30
43 George Lynch .12 .30
44 John Starks .20 .50
45 Malik Rose .12 .30
46 Rod Strickland .12 .30
47 Tim Thomas .15 .40
48 Howard Eisley .12 .30
49 Kenny Anderson .15 .40
50 Kurt Thomas .12 .30
51 Lindsey Hunter .12 .30
52 Rick Fox .12 .30
53 Vlade Divac .20 .50
54 Avery Johnson .15 .40
55 Dale Ellis .12 .30
56 Donyell Marshall .12 .30
57 Elden Campbell .12 .30
58 Larry Hughes .15 .40
59 Mitch Richmond .20 .50
60 Chris Mills .12 .30
61 David Wesley .12 .30
62 Gary Payton .20 .50
63 Isaac Austin .12 .30
64 Robert Traylor .12 .30
65 Theo Ratliff .15 .40
66 Antawn Jamison .20 .50
67 Eddie Jones .20 .50
68 Kevin Garnett .40 1.00
69 Matt Geiger .12 .30
70 Vernon Maxwell .15 .40
71 Antonio Davis .12 .30
72 Dirk Nowitzki .40 1.00
73 Johnny Newman .12 .30
74 Maurice Taylor .12 .30
75 Steve Smith .12 .30
76 Derek Anderson .12 .30
77 Doug Christie .15 .40
78 Erick Strickland .12 .30
79 Keith Van Horn .15 .40
80 Luc Longley .12 .30
81 Alonzo Mourning .25 .60
82 Christian Laettner .15 .40
83 Jamal Mashburn .15 .40
84 Jon Barry .15 .40
85 Patrick Ewing .25 .60
86 Shareef Abdur-Rahim .15 .40
87 Vitaly Potapenko .12 .30
88 Darrell Armstrong .12 .30
89 Eric Williams .12 .30
90 Jerome Williams .12 .30
91 Nick Anderson .12 .30
92 Othella Harrington .12 .30
93 Tim Hardaway .20 .50
94 Eric Piatkowski .15 .40
95 Isaiah Rider .12 .30
96 Kendall Gill .12 .30
97 Rasheed Wallace .20 .50
98 Robert Pack .12 .30
99 Tracy McGrady .30 .75
100 Allan Houston .15 .40
101 Brian Grant .12 .30
102 Dikembe Mutombo .20 .50
103 Karl Malone .25 .60
104 Nick Van Exel .15 .40
105 Shaquille O'Neal .50 1.25
106 Chris Anstey .12 .30
107 Michael Dickerson .12 .30
108 Shandon Anderson .12 .30
109 Tariq Adbul-Wahad .12 .30
110 Tim Duncan .40 1.00
111 Voshon Lenard .12 .30
112 Bimbo Coles .12 .30
113 Detlef Schrempf .15 .40
114 John Stockton .25 .60
115 Kobe Bryant 1.00 2.50
116 Latrell Sprewell .20 .50
117 Raef LaFrentz .15 .40
118 Antoine Walker .20 .50
119 Bryon Russell .12 .30
120 Derek Fisher .20 .50
121 Jason Williams .25 .60
122 Jerry Stackhouse .20 .50
123 Larry Johnson .20 .50
124 Clifford Robinson .12 .30
125 Horace Grant .15 .40
126 Malik Sealy .12 .30
127 Michael Finley .20 .50
128 Rik Smits .20 .50
129 Dell Curry .12 .30
130 Jim Jackson .15 .40
131 Ron Mercer .15 .40
132 Scott Burrell .12 .30
133 Scottie Pippen .30 .75
134 Troy Hudson .20 .50
135 Anfernee Hardaway .30 .75
136 Anthony Peeler .12 .30
137 Jalen Rose .15 .40
138 Lamond Murray .12 .30
139 Ruben Patterson .12 .30
140 Chris Webber .20 .50
141 Glen Rice .20 .50
142 Grant Hill .25 .60
143 Jeff Hornacek .15 .40
144 Marcus Camby .15 .40
145 Paul Pierce .30 .75
146 Bob Sura .12 .30
147 Jason Kidd .30 .75
148 Reggie Miller .20 .50
149 Terrell Brandon .12 .30
150 Vin Baker .20 .50
151 Lamar Odom RC 1.00 2.50
152 Steve Francis RC .75 2.00
153 Elton Brand RC .75 2.00
154 Wally Szczerbiak RC .60 1.50
155 Adrian Griffin RC .30 .75
156 Andre Miller RC .75 2.00
157 Jason Terry RC .75 2.00
158 Richard Hamilton RC .75 2.00
159 Ron Artest RC .75 2.00
160 Shawn Marion RC .75 2.00
161 James Posey RC .30 .75
162 Greg Buckner RC .30 .75
163 Chucky Atkins RC .30 .75
164 Corey Maggette RC .60 1.50
165 Todd MacCulloch RC .30 .75
166 Baron Davis RC 1.00 2.50
167 Trajan Langdon RC .30 .75
168 Bruno Sundov RC .30 .75
169 Scott Padgett RC .30 .75
170 Vonteego Cummings RC .30 .75
171 Ryan Bowen RC .30 .75
172 Jonathan Bender RC .30 .75
173 Jermaine Jackson RC .30 .75
174 Devean George RC .30 .75
175 Chris Herren RC .30 .75
176 Rodney Buford RC .30 .75
177 Laron Profit RC .30 .75
178 Mirsad Turkcan RC .30 .75
179 Eddie Robinson RC .30 .75
180 Anthony Carter RC .30 .75

1999-00 Metal Emeralds

Randomly inserted in packs at one in four for veterans and one in eight for rookies, this 180-card set parallels the base set. The cards feature a green tint at the top. To ascertain values on individual cards, please refer to the multiplier in the header, coupled with the value of the base card.

*STARS: 2X TO 5X BASE CARD HI
*RCs: .5X TO 1.25X BASE HI

1999-00 Metal Vince Carter Scrapbook

Randomly inserted in packs at one in eight, this 10-card set focuses on Vince Carter, with action and casual shots. Card backs carry a "VC" prefix.

COMPLETE SET (10) 12.50 25.00
COMMON CARD (VC1-VC10) 1.50 4.00

1999-00 Metal Genuine Coverage

Randomly inserted in packs at one in 288, this six-card set features swatches of game-used jerseys. The cards are not numbered and listed below in alphabetical order.

1 Vince Carter 12.00 30.00
2 Karl Malone 8.00 20.00
3 Shaquille O'Neal 15.00 40.00
4 Paul Pierce 10.00 25.00
5 John Stockton 8.00 20.00
6 Antoine Walker 6.00 15.00

1999-00 Metal Heavy Metal

Randomly inserted in packs at one in 20, this 10-card set features NBA players against a black and silver background. Card backs carry a "HM" prefix.

COMPLETE SET (10) 8.00 20.00
HM1 Kobe Bryant 3.00 8.00
HM2 Vince Carter 1.25 3.00
HM3 Lamar Odom 2.00 5.00
HM4 Kevin Garnett 1.25 3.00
HM5 Shawn Kemp .60 1.50
HM6 Shareef Abdur-Rahim .50 1.25
HM7 Antonio McDyess .50 1.25
HM8 Tim Duncan 1.25 3.00
HM9 Keith Van Horn .50 1.25
HM10 Shaquille O'Neal 1.50 4.00

1999-00 Metal Platinum Portraits

Randomly inserted in packs at one in four, this 15-card set focuses on the top rookies from 1999. The cards feature an up close portrait shot of each player. Card backs carry a "PP" prefix.

COMPLETE SET (15) 6.00 15.00
PP1 Elton Brand 1.00 2.50
PP2 Lamar Odom 1.25 3.00
PP3 Steve Francis 1.00 2.50
PP4 Richard Hamilton 1.00 2.50
PP5 Baron Davis 1.25 3.00
PP6 Vonteego Cummings .40 1.00
PP7 Corey Maggette .75 2.00
PP8 James Posey .40 1.00
PP9 Shawn Marion 1.00 2.50
PP10 Wally Szczerbiak .75 2.00
PP11 Jason Terry 1.00 2.50
PP12 Andre Miller 1.00 2.50
PP13 Scott Padgett .40 1.00
PP14 Trajan Langdon .40 1.00
PP15 Jonathan Bender .40 1.00

1999-00 Metal Rivalries

Randomly inserted in packs at one in four, this 15-card set features some of the great rivalries in the NBA. Card backs carry a "R" prefix.

COMPLETE SET (15) 5.00 12.00
R1 Allen Iverson / Stephon Marbury .60 1.50
R2 Jason Kidd / Gary Payton .50 1.25
R3 Mike Bibby / Jason Williams .40 1.00
R4 Patrick Ewing / Alonzo Mourning .40 1.00
R5 Tim Duncan / Kevin Garnett .60 1.50
R6 Anfernee Hardaway / Kobe Bryant 1.50 4.00
R7 Charles Barkley / Karl Malone .50 1.25
R8 Antonio McDyess / Shareef Abdur-Rahim .25 .60
R9 Vince Carter / Grant Hill .60 1.50
R10 Antoine Walker / Keith Van Horn .30 .75
R11 Shawn Kemp / Elton Brand .75 2.00
R12 Shaquille O'Neal / David Robinson .75 2.00
R13 Raef LaFrentz / Dirk Nowitzki .60 1.50
R14 Steve Francis / John Stockton .75 2.00
R15 Lamar Odom / Scottie Pippen 1.00 2.50

1999-00 Metal Scoring Magnets

Randomly inserted at one in 20, this 10-card set features the top scoring players in the NBA. The cards feature die cutting on the right side. Card backs carry a "SM" prefix.

COMPLETE SET (10) 4.00 10.00
SM1 Grant Hill .75 2.00
SM2 Stephon Marbury .50 1.25
SM3 Allen Iverson 1.25 3.00
SM4 Ray Allen .60 1.50
SM5 Steve Francis 1.50 4.00
SM6 Ron Mercer .50 1.25
SM7 Paul Pierce 1.00 2.50
SM8 Latrell Sprewell .60 1.50
SM9 Glenn Robinson .50 1.25
SM10 Eddie Jones .60 1.50

1997-98 Metal Universe

The Metal Universe set was issued in only one series, containing 125 cards that came in nine card packs with a suggested retail price of $2.49. Card fronts contain an action shot of the player with some form of a "cartoon" scene surrouding the player. The player's name is against a silver bar running along the card bottom. Card back contain a photo and statistics.

COMPLETE SET (125) 10.00 25.00
1 Charles Barkley .40 1.00
2 Dell Curry .15 .40
3 Derek Fisher .25 .60
4 Derek Harper .20 .50
5 Avery Johnson .20 .50
6 Steve Smith .20 .50
7 Alonzo Mourning .30 .75
8 Rod Strickland .15 .40
9 Chris Mullin .25 .60
10 Rony Seikaly .20 .50
11 Vin Baker .20 .50
12 Austin Croshere RC .25 .60
13 Vinny Del Negro .15 .40
14 Sherman Douglas .15 .40
15 Priest Lauderdale .15 .40
16 Cedric Ceballos .15 .40
17 LaPhonso Ellis .15 .40
18 Luc Longley .15 .40
19 Brian Grant .15 .40
20 Allen Iverson .50 1.25
21 Anthony Mason .15 .40
22 Bryant Reeves .15 .40
23 Michael Jordan 2.50 6.00
24 Dale Ellis .15 .40
25 Terrell Brandon .15 .40
26 Patrick Ewing .30 .75
27 Allan Houston .20 .50
28 Damon Stoudamire .25 .60
29 Loy Vaught .15 .40
30 Walt Williams .15 .40
31 Shareef Abdur-Rahim .25 .60
32 Mario Elie .15 .40
33 Juwan Howard .20 .50
34 Tom Gugliotta .15 .40
35 Glen Rice .25 .60
36 Isaiah Rider .15 .40
37 Arvydas Sabonis .20 .50
38 Derrick Coleman .20 .50
39 Kevin Willis .15 .40
40 Kendall Gill .15 .40
41 John Wallace .15 .40
42 Tracy McGrady RC 1.25 3.00
43 Travis Best .15 .40
44 Malik Rose .15 .40
45 Anfernee Hardaway .40 1.00
46 Roy Rogers .15 .40
47 Kerry Kittles .15 .40
48 Matt Maloney .15 .40
49 Antonio McDyess .20 .50
50 Shaquille O'Neal .60 1.50
51 George McCloud .15 .40
52 Wesley Person .15 .40
53 Shawn Bradley .15 .40
54 Antonio Davis .15 .40
55 P.J. Brown .15 .40
56 Joe Dumars .25 .60
57 Horace Grant .20 .50
58 Steve Kerr .20 .50
59 Hakeem Olajuwon .30 .75
60 Tim Hardaway .25 .60
61 Toni Kukoc .25 .60
62 Ron Mercer RC .30 .75
63 Gary Payton .25 .60
64 Grant Hill .40 1.00
65 Detlef Schrempf .25 .60
66 Tim Duncan RC 1.50 4.00
67 Shawn Kemp .25 .60
68 Voshon Lenard .15 .40
69 Othella Harrington .15 .40
70 Hersey Hawkins .15 .40
71 Lindsey Hunter .15 .40
72 Antoine Walker .25 .60
73 Jamal Mashburn .20 .50
74 Kenny Anderson .20 .50
75 Todd Day .15 .40
76 Todd Fuller .15 .40
77 Jermaine O'Neal .30 .75
78 David Robinson .40 1.00
79 Erick Dampier .15 .40
80 Keith Van Horn RC .50 1.25
81 Kobe Bryant 1.25 3.00
82 Chris Childs .15 .40
83 Scottie Pippen .40 1.00
84 Marcus Camby .25 .60
85 Danny Ferry .15 .40
86 Jeff Hornacek .20 .50
87 Bo Outlaw .15 .40
88 Larry Johnson .25 .60
89 Tony Delk .15 .40
90 Stephon Marbury .30 .75
91 Robert Pack .15 .40
92 Chris Webber .25 .60
93 Clyde Drexler .30 .75
94 Eddie Jones .25 .60
95 Jerry Stackhouse .25 .60
96 Tyrone Hill .15 .40
97 Karl Malone .30 .75
98 Reggie Miller .30 .75
99 Bryon Russell .15 .40
100 Dale Davis .15 .40
101 Steve Nash .50 1.25
102 Vitaly Potapenko .15 .40
103 Nick Anderson .15 .40
104 Ray Allen .30 .75
105 Sean Elliott .25 .60
106 Dikembe Mutombo .25 .60
107 Dennis Rodman .50 1.25
108 Lorenzen Wright .15 .40
109 Kevin Garnett .50 1.25
110 Christian Laettner .20 .50
111 Mitch Richmond .25 .60
112 Joe Smith .20 .50
113 Jason Kidd .40 1.00
114 Glenn Robinson .20 .50
115 Mark Price .25 .60
116 Mark Jackson .25 .60
117 Bobby Phills .15 .40
118 John Starks .20 .50
119 John Stockton .30 .75
120 Mookie Blaylock .15 .40
121 Dean Garrett .15 .40
122 Olden Polynice .15 .40
123 Latrell Sprewell .25 .60
124 Checklist .15 .40
125 Checklist .15 .40

1997-98 Metal Universe Precious Metal Gems

Serially numbered to 100, this 123-card set is a parallel to the basic set. The card fronts feature a full color red background for 90% of the production run, while a full green color background accounts for the remaining 10%. To ascertain values of the green cards, please refer to the multiplier listed below coupled with the value of the red card.

*STARS: 100X TO 250X BASE CARD HI
*RCs: 50X TO 120X BASE HI

1 Charles Barkley 400.00 800.00
7 Alonzo Mourning 150.00 300.00
23 Michael Jordan 4000.00 6000.00
26 Patrick Ewing 150.00 300.00
50 Shaquille O'Neal 300.00 600.00
59 Hakeem Olajuwon 150.00 300.00
66 Tim Duncan 500.00 800.00
67 Shawn Kemp 100.00 200.00
78 David Robinson 200.00 400.00
81 Kobe Bryant 3000.00 5000.00
83 Scottie Pippen 200.00 400.00
92 Chris Webber 150.00 300.00
93 Clyde Drexler 125.00 250.00
97 Karl Malone 200.00 400.00
98 Reggie Miller 150.00 300.00
101 Steve Nash 250.00 450.00
107 Dennis Rodman 500.00 1000.00
109 Kevin Garnett 200.00 400.00
113 Jason Kidd 200.00 400.00
119 John Stockton 200.00 400.00

1997-98 Metal Universe Gold Universe

Randomly inserted in retail packs only at a rate of one in 120, this 10-card set features some of the shining stars of the NBA.

COMPLETE SET (10) 50.00 120.00
1 Damon Stoudamire 8.00 20.00
2 Shawn Kemp 8.00 20.00
3 John Stockton 10.00 25.00
4 Jerry Stackhouse 8.00 20.00
5 John Wallace 5.00 12.00
6 Juwan Howard 6.00 15.00
7 David Robinson 12.00 30.00
8 Gary Payton 8.00 20.00
9 Joe Smith 6.00 15.00
10 Charles Barkley 12.00 30.00

1997-98 Metal Universe Planet Metal

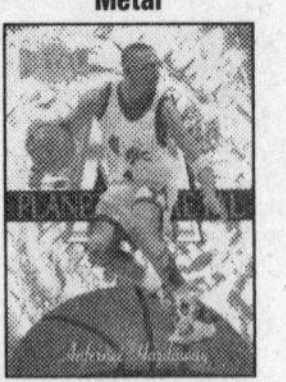

Randomly inserted in packs at a rate of one in 24, this 15-card set focuses on the NBA's best depicted as a universe. Card fronts feature a silver metallic background with a "swirling" planet in the background.

COMPLETE SET (15) 50.00 100.00
1 Michael Jordan 25.00 60.00
2 Allen Iverson 3.00 8.00
3 Kobe Bryant 10.00 25.00
4 Shaquille O'Neal 4.00 10.00
5 Stephon Marbury 2.00 5.00
6 Marcus Camby 1.50 4.00
7 Anfernee Hardaway 2.50 6.00
8 Kevin Garnett 3.00 8.00
9 Shareef Abdur-Rahim 1.50 4.00
10 Dennis Rodman 3.00 8.00
11 Grant Hill 2.50 6.00
12 Hakeem Olajuwon 2.00 5.00
13 David Robinson 2.50 6.00
14 Charles Barkley 2.50 6.00
15 Gary Payton 1.50 4.00

1997-98 Metal Universe Platinum Portraits

Randomly inserted in packs at a rate of one in 288, this 15-card set features NBA stars in a Hall of Fame plaque treatment. The cards feature a matrix-etching the form a picture of the player's face.

COMPLETE SET (15) 600.00 1000.00
1 Michael Jordan 400.00 750.00
2 Allen Iverson 25.00 60.00
3 Kobe Bryant 150.00 300.00
4 Shaquille O'Neal 30.00 80.00
5 Stephon Marbury 15.00 40.00
6 Marcus Camby 12.00 30.00
7 Anfernee Hardaway 20.00 50.00
8 Kevin Garnett 25.00 60.00
9 Shareef Abdur-Rahim 12.00 30.00
10 Dennis Rodman 40.00 80.00
11 Ray Allen 15.00 40.00
12 Grant Hill 25.00 60.00
13 Kerry Kittles 8.00 20.00
14 Antoine Walker 12.00 30.00
15 Scottie Pippen 20.00 50.00

1997-98 Metal Universe Reebok Chase Bronze

Inserted one per series one pack, this 15-card insert set features players who wear Reebok merchandise. Card backs carry one of three colors: bronze, gold or silver. The bronze is the base set and is priced below. To ascertain values of individual cards, please refer to the multiplier listed below coupled with the value of the base card.

COMPLETE SET (15) 2.00 5.00
*GOLD: 1.25X TO 3X BRONZE
*SILVER: .5X TO 1.25X BRONZE
5 Avery Johnson .20 .50
6 Steve Smith .20 .50
13 Vinny Del Negro .15 .40
16 Cedric Ceballos .15 .40
20 Allen Iverson .50 1.25
32 Mario Elie .15 .40
50 Shaquille O'Neal .60 1.50
67 Shawn Kemp .25 .60
68 Voshon Lenard .15 .40
74 Kenny Anderson .20 .50
91 Robert Pack .15 .40
93 Clyde Drexler .30 .75
96 Tyrone Hill .15 .40
114 Glenn Robinson .20 .50
116 Mark Jackson .25 .60

1997-98 Metal Universe Silver Slams

Randomly inserted in packs at one in 6, this 20-card set focuses on the young rising stars of the NBA. The cards feature black and white photos of the players against colorful foilboard. Odd numbers are printed on orange, even numbers are printed on purple.

COMPLETE SET (20) 6.00 15.00
1 Ray Allen .75 2.00
2 Kerry Kittles .40 1.00
3 Antoine Walker .60 1.50
4 Scottie Pippen 1.00 2.50
5 Damon Stoudamire .60 1.50
6 Shawn Kemp .60 1.50
7 Jerry Stackhouse .60 1.50
8 John Wallace .40 1.00
9 Juwan Howard .50 1.25
10 Gary Payton .60 1.50
11 Joe Smith .50 1.25
12 Terrell Brandon .40 1.00
13 Hakeem Olajuwon .75 2.00
14 Tom Gugliotta .40 1.00
15 Glen Rice .60 1.50
16 Charles Barkley 1.00 2.50
17 David Robinson 1.00 2.50
18 Patrick Ewing .75 2.00
19 Christian Laettner .50 1.25
20 Chris Webber .60 1.50

1997-98 Metal Universe Titanium

Randomly inserted in hobby packs only at a rate of one in 72, this 20-card set features some of the NBA's most explosive players on die cut cards. The cards are on clear plastic stock with the script in a light-blue foil.

COMPLETE SET (20) 400.00 700.00
1 Michael Jordan 100.00 225.00
2 Allen Iverson 20.00 50.00
3 Kobe Bryant 50.00 125.00
4 Shaquille O'Neal 25.00 60.00
5 Stephon Marbury 12.00 30.00
6 Marcus Camby 10.00 25.00
7 Anfernee Hardaway 40.00 100.00
Being Guarded by Michael Jordan
8 Kevin Garnett 20.00 50.00
9 Shareef Abdur-Rahim 10.00 25.00
10 Dennis Rodman 20.00 50.00
11 Ray Allen 12.00 30.00
12 Grant Hill 15.00 40.00
13 Kerry Kittles 6.00 15.00
14 Antoine Walker 10.00 25.00
15 Scottie Pippen 15.00 40.00
16 Damon Stoudamire 10.00 25.00
17 Shawn Kemp 12.00 30.00
18 Hakeem Olajuwon 12.00 30.00
19 Jerry Stackhouse 10.00 25.00
20 Juwan Howard 8.00 20.00

1998-99 Metal Universe

The 1998-99 Metal Universe set consists of 125 standard size cards. The 8-card packs retail for a suggested price of $2.69. The fronts feature full color game-action photos with brushed metal backgrounds and an embossed nameplate with the look of forged steel.

COMPLETE SET (125) 12.50 25.00
1 Michael Jordan 2.00
2 Mario Elie .15
3 Voshon Lenard .15
4 John Starks .20
5 Juwan Howard .20
6 Michael Finley .25
7 Bobby Jackson .20
8 Glenn Robinson .20
9 Antonio McDyess .20
10 Marcus Camby .20
11 Zydrunas Ilgauskas .25
12 LaPhonso Ellis .15
13 Terrell Brandon .15
14 Rex Chapman .15
15 Rod Strickland .15
16 Dennis Rodman .50
17 Clarence Weatherspoon .15
18 P.J. Brown .15
19 Anfernee Hardaway .40
20 Dikembe Mutombo .25
21 Gary Trent .15
22 Patrick Ewing .30
23 Sam Mack .15
24 Scottie Pippen .40
25 Shaquille O'Neal .60
26 Donyell Marshall .15
27 Bo Outlaw .15
28 Isaiah Rider .15
29 Detlef Schrempf .25
30 Mark Price .25
31 Jim Jackson .15
32 Eddie Jones .25
33 Allen Iverson .50
34 Corliss Williamson .15
35 Tim Duncan .50
36 Ron Harper .20
37 Tony Delk .15
38 Derek Fisher .25
39 Kendall Gill .15
40 Theo Ratliff .20
41 Kelvin Cato .15
42 Antoine Walker .25
43 Lamond Murray .15
44 Avery Johnson .20
45 John Stockton .30
46 David Wesley .15
47 Brian Williams .15
48 Elden Campbell .15
49 Sam Cassell .20
50 Grant Hill .40
51 Tracy McGrady .40
52 Glen Rice .25
53 Kobe Bryant 1.25
54 Cherokee Parks .15
55 John Wallace .15
56 Bobby Phills .15
57 Jerry Stackhouse .25
58 Lorenzen Wright .15
59 Stephon Marbury .30
60 Shandon Anderson .15
61 Jeff Hornacek .20
62 Joe Dumars .25
63 Tom Gugliotta .15
64 Johnny Newman .15
65 Kevin Garnett .50
66 Clifford Robinson .15
67 Dennis Scott .15
68 Anthony Mason .15
69 Rodney Rogers .15
70 Bryon Russell .15
71 Maurice Taylor .15
72 Mookie Blaylock .15
73 Shawn Bradley .15
74 Matt Maloney .15
75 Karl Malone .30
76 Larry Johnson .25
77 Calbert Cheaney .15
78 Steve Smith .20
79 Toni Kukoc .25
80 Reggie Miller .30
81 Jayson Williams .15
82 Gary Payton .25
83 George Lynch .15
84 Wesley Person .15
85 Charles Barkley .40
86 Tim Hardaway .25
87 Darrell Armstrong .15
88 Rasheed Wallace .25
89 Tariq Abdul-Wahad .15
90 Kenny Anderson .20
91 Chris Mullin .25
92 Keith Van Horn .25
93 Hersey Hawkins .15
94 Billy Owens .15
95 Ron Mercer .20
96 Rik Smits .20
97 David Robinson .40
98 Derek Anderson .15
99 Danny Fortson .15
100 Jason Kidd .40
101 Sean Elliott .25
102 Chauncey Billups .30
103 Tyrone Hill .15
104 Alan Henderson .15
105 Chris Anstey .15
106 Hakeem Olajuwon .30
107 Allan Houston .20
108 Bryant Reeves .15
109 Anthony Johnson .15
110 Shawn Kemp .25
111 Brevin Knight .15
112 A.C. Green .25
113 Ray Allen .30
114 Tim Thomas .25
115 Walter McCarty .15
116 Jalen Rose .20
117 Kerry Kittles .15
118 Vin Baker .20
119 Shareef Abdur-Rahim .25
120 Alonzo Mourning .30
121 Joe Smith .20
122 Tracy Murray .15
123 Damon Stoudamire .25
124 Checklist .15
125 Checklist .15
NNO Grant Hill SAMPLE .75

1998-99 Metal Universe Precious Metal Gems

The 1998-99 Metal Universe Precious Metal G consists of 123 cards and is a parallel to the 19 Metal Universe base set. The cards are serially numbered to 50 of each and were only releasec hobby boxes. To ascertain values on individua please refer to the multiplier in the header, cou

he value of the base card.
RS: 50X TO 120X BASE CARD HI
chael Jordan 6000.00 10000.00
cottie Pippen 80.00 200.00
haquille O'Neal 125.00 300.00
ddie Jones 75.00 150.00
len Iverson 200.00 400.00
m Duncan 80.00 200.00
obe Bryant 2000.00 3000.00
evin Garnett 100.00 250.00
harles Barkley 200.00 400.00

998-99 Metal Universe Grant Hill Blowup

oversized Metal Universe card features Grant Hill
Detroit Pistons. The card is listed as a "sample"
e back, and is serial numbered to 10,000.
nt Hill 1.50 4.00

98-99 Metal Universe Big Ups

998-99 Metal Universe Big Ups set consists of rds and is an insert to the 1998-99 Metal rse base set. The cards are randomly inserted in at a rate of one in 18. The fronts feature full color photos with a visual background of the planet . The Metal Universe logo sits in the upper left r.

PLETE SET (15) 8.00 20.00
phon Marbury 1.00 2.50
reef Abdur-Rahim .75 2.00
ttie Pippen 1.25 3.00
rcus Camby .60 1.50
Allen 1.00 2.50
n Iverson 1.50 4.00
ry Kittles .50 1.25
nis Rodman 1.50 4.00
non Stoudamire .75 2.00
toine Walker .75 2.00
fernee Hardaway 1.25 3.00
awn Kemp .75 2.00
wan Howard .60 1.50
ry Payton .75 2.00
m Duncan 1.50 4.00

1998-99 Metal Universe Linchpins

998-99 Metal Universe Linchpins set consists of rds and is an insert to the 1998-99 Metal rse base set. The cards are randomly inserted in at a rate of one in 360. The fronts feature color player photos silhouetted on a card with laser t pins in the background. The Metal Universe s located at the bottom center of the card.

PLETE SET (10) 500.00 800.00
quille O'Neal 30.00 80.00
e Bryant 125.00 225.00
in Garnett 25.00 60.00
nt Hill 20.00 50.00
wn Kemp 15.00 40.00
h Van Horn 12.00 30.00
oine Walker 12.00 30.00
hael Jordan 300.00 600.00
y Payton 12.00 30.00
n Duncan 25.00 60.00

1998-99 Metal Universe Neophytes

998-99 Metal Universe Neophytes set consists of ds and is an insert to the 1998-99 Metal rse base set. The cards are randomly inserted in at a rate of one in 6. The fronts feature full color action photos of the top young stars in the NBA The Metal Universe logo is found at the left n corner and the featured player's name lines the de of the gold- and silver-foiled stamped card.

PLETE SET (15) 2.50 6.00
nio Daniels .25 .60
by Jackson .30 .75
vin Knight .25 .60
uncey Billups .50 1.25
ny Fortson .25 .60
k Anderson .25 .60
que Vaughn .25 .60
h Van Horn .40 1.00
rice Taylor .25 .60
chael Stewart .25 .60
n Mercer .30 .75
n Thomas .40 1.00
n Duncan .75 2.00
acy McGrady .60 1.50
drunas Ilgauskas .40 1.00

1998-99 Metal Universe Planet Metal

The 1998-99 Metal Universe Planet Metal set consists of 15 cards and is an insert to the 1998-99 Metal Universe base set. The cards are randomly inserted in packs at a rate of one in 36. The fronts feature full color action photos on top of a uniquely designed space-age die-cut design of the planet Earth. The Metal Universe logo can be found in the lower right corner.

COMPLETE SET (15) 100.00 200.00
1 Michael Jordan 50.00 125.00
2 Antoine Walker 4.00 10.00
3 Scottie Pippen 6.00 15.00
4 Grant Hill 6.00 15.00
5 Dennis Rodman 8.00 20.00
6 Kobe Bryant 20.00 50.00
7 Kevin Garnett 8.00 20.00
8 Shaquille O'Neal 10.00 25.00
9 Stephon Marbury 5.00 12.00
10 Kerry Kittles 2.50 6.00
11 Anfernee Hardaway 6.00 15.00
12 Allen Iverson 8.00 20.00
13 Damon Stoudamire 4.00 10.00
14 Marcus Camby 3.00 8.00
15 Shareef Abdur-Rahim 4.00 10.00

1998-99 Metal Universe Two for Me, Zero for You

The 1998-99 Metal Universe Two For Me set consists of 15 cards and is an insert to the 1998-99 Metal Universe base set. The cards are randomly inserted in packs at a rate of one in 96. The fronts feature a color game-action photo of two NBA players. The right side of the card reads, "Two 4 Me". The Metal Universe logo sits in the upper left corner.

COMPLETE SET (15) 75.00 150.00
1 Kobe Bryant 15.00 40.00
2 Anfernee Hardaway 5.00 12.00
3 Allen Iverson 6.00 15.00
4 Michael Jordan 40.00 100.00
5 Stephon Marbury 4.00 10.00
6 Ron Mercer 2.50 6.00
7 Shareef Abdur-Rahim 3.00 8.00
8 Marcus Camby 2.50 6.00
9 Damon Stoudamire 3.00 8.00
10 Kevin Garnett 6.00 15.00
11 Grant Hill 5.00 12.00
12 Scottie Pippen 5.00 12.00
13 Keith Van Horn 3.00 8.00
14 Dennis Rodman 6.00 15.00
15 Shaquille O'Neal 8.00 20.00

1997-98 Metal Universe Championship Promo Sheet

Released as a six-card sheet, this offered a sneak peek at the basic set design. The sheet was not perforated, but could be cut into individual cards since the backs are numbered. The back of the sheet features information on the basic set and the inserts.

1 Grant Hill 1.25 3.00
Kobe Bryant
Allen Iverson
Keith Van Horn
Kevin Garnett
Tim Duncan

1997-98 Metal Universe Championship

The 1997-98 Metal Universe Championship set was issued in one series totalling 100 cards. The debut set was issued in eight-card packs which carried a suggested retail price of $2.69.

COMPLETE SET (100) 10.00 25.00
1 Shaquille O'Neal .60 1.50
2 Chris Mills .15 .40
3 Tariq Abdul-Wahad RC .25 .60
4 Adonal Foyle RC .25 .60
5 Kendall Gill .15 .40
6 Vin Baker .20 .50
7 Chauncey Billups RC 1.00 2.50
8 Bobby Jackson RC .30 .75
9 Keith Van Horn RC .50 1.25
10 Avery Johnson .20 .50
11 Juwan Howard .20 .50
12 Steve Smith .20 .50
13 Alonzo Mourning .30 .75
14 Anfernee Hardaway .40 1.00
15 Sean Elliott .25 .60
16 Danny Fortson RC .25 .60
17 John Stockton .30 .75
18 John Thomas RC .25 .60
19 Lorenzen Wright .15 .40
20 Mark Price .25 .60
21 Rasheed Wallace .25 .60
22 Ray Allen .30 .75
23 Michael Jordan 2.00 5.00
24 John Wallace .15 .40
25 Bryant Reeves .15 .40
26 Allen Iverson .50 1.25
27 Antoine Walker .25 .60
28 Terrell Brandon .15 .40
29 Damon Stoudamire .25 .60
30 Antonio Daniels RC .25 .60
31 Corey Beck .25 .60
32 Tyrone Hill .15 .40
33 Grant Hill .40 1.00
34 Tim Thomas RC .50 1.25
35 Clifford Robinson .15 .40
36 Tracy McGrady RC 1.25 3.00
37 Chris Webber .25 .60
38 Austin Croshere RC .25 .60
39 Reggie Miller .30 .75
40 Derek Anderson RC .25 .60
41 Kevin Garnett .50 1.25
42 Kevin Johnson .25 .60
43 Antonio McDyess .20 .50
44 Brevin Knight RC .25 .60
45 Charles Barkley .40 1.00
46 Tom Gugliotta .15 .40
47 Jason Kidd .40 1.00
48 Marcus Camby .25 .60
49 God Shammgod RC .25 .60
50 Wesley Person .15 .40
51 Clyde Drexler .30 .75
52 Paul Grant RC .25 .60
53 Rod Strickland .15 .40
54 Tony Delk .15 .40
55 Stephon Marbury .30 .75
56 Detlef Schrempf .25 .60
57 Joe Smith .20 .50
58 Sam Cassell .20 .50
59 Gary Payton .25 .60
60 Chris Crawford RC .25 .60
61 Hakeem Olajuwon .30 .75
62 Dennis Rodman .50 1.25
63 Eddie Jones .25 .60
64 Mitch Richmond .25 .60
65 David Wesley .15 .40
66 Tony Battie RC .30 .75
67 Isaac Austin .15 .40
68 Isaiah Rider .15 .40
69 Jacque Vaughn RC .25 .60
70 Tim Hardaway .25 .60
71 Darrell Armstrong .15 .40
72 Tim Duncan RC 1.50 4.00
73 Glen Rice .25 .60
74 Bubba Wells RC .25 .60
75 Maurice Taylor RC .25 .60
76 Kelvin Cato RC .25 .60
77 Shareef Abdur-Rahim .25 .60
78 Shawn Kemp .25 .60
79 Michael Finley .25 .60
80 Chris Mullin .25 .60
81 Ron Mercer RC .30 .75
82 Brian Williams .15 .40
83 Kerry Kittles .15 .40
84 David Robinson .40 1.00
85 Scottie Pippen .40 1.00
86 Kobe Bryant 1.25 3.00
87 Anthony Johnson RC .25 .60
88 Karl Malone .30 .75
89 Mookie Blaylock .15 .40
90 Joe Dumars .25 .60
91 Patrick Ewing .30 .75
92 Bobby Phills .15 .40
93 Dennis Scott .15 .40
94 Rodney Rogers .15 .40
95 Jim Jackson .15 .40
96 Kenny Anderson .20 .50
97 Jerry Stackhouse .25 .60
98 Larry Johnson .25 .60
99 Checklist .15 .40
100 Checklist .15 .40

1997-98 Metal Universe Championship Precious Metal Gems

Randomly inserted into packs, this 98-card set parallels the regular base set, minus the checklists. The cards are serially numbered to 50 on the back. To ascertain values on individual cards, please refer to the multiplier in the header below, coupled with the value of the base card.

*STARS: 75X TO 200X BASE CARD HI
*RCs: 40X TO 100X BASE HI
1 Shaquille O'Neal 400.00 700.00
13 Alonzo Mourning 75.00 200.00
14 Anfernee Hardaway 150.00 300.00
17 John Stockton 125.00 250.00
23 Michael Jordan 2500.00 4000.00
26 Allen Iverson 150.00 400.00
33 Grant Hill 150.00 300.00
36 Tracy McGrady 175.00 350.00
37 Chris Webber 125.00 225.00
39 Reggie Miller 125.00 250.00
41 Kevin Garnett 200.00 400.00
45 Charles Barkley 150.00 300.00
47 Jason Kidd 100.00 250.00
51 Clyde Drexler 125.00 225.00
61 Hakeem Olajuwon 150.00 300.00
62 Dennis Rodman 400.00 800.00
72 Tim Duncan 600.00 1000.00
78 Shawn Kemp 100.00 200.00
84 David Robinson 150.00 300.00
85 Scottie Pippen 200.00 400.00
86 Kobe Bryant 400.00 800.00
88 Karl Malone 200.00 400.00
91 Patrick Ewing 80.00 200.00

1997-98 Metal Universe Championship All-Millenium Team

Randomly inserted into packs at a rate of one in six, this 20-card set features top veterans and rising stars pictured against etched-foil fronts.

COMPLETE SET (20) 10.00 25.00
1 Stephon Marbury .60 1.50
2 Shareef Abdur-Rahim .50 1.25
3 Karl Malone .60 1.50
4 Scottie Pippen .75 2.00
5 Michael Jordan 4.00 10.00
6 Marcus Camby .50 1.25
7 Kobe Bryant 2.50 6.00
8 Allen Iverson 1.00 2.50
9 Kerry Kittles .30 .75
10 Ray Allen .60 1.50
11 Dennis Rodman 1.00 2.50
12 Damon Stoudamire .50 1.25
13 Antoine Walker .50 1.25
14 Anfernee Hardaway .75 2.00
15 Hakeem Olajuwon .60 1.50
16 Shawn Kemp .50 1.25
17 Antonio Daniels .50 1.25
18 Juwan Howard .40 1.00
19 Gary Payton .50 1.25
20 Tim Duncan 1.50 4.00

1997-98 Metal Universe Championship Championship Galaxy

Randomly inserted into packs at a rate of one in 192, this 15-card set pays tribute to players who currently wear NBA Championship rings and many young players who hope to obtain one in the future. The cards feature a foiled background with a double-etched player image surrounded by a "riveted" border.

COMPLETE SET (15) 300.00 500.00
1 Michael Jordan 150.00 300.00
2 Allen Iverson 15.00 40.00
3 Kobe Bryant 40.00 100.00
UER front Kobe, Bryant
4 Shaquille O'Neal 20.00 50.00
5 Stephon Marbury 10.00 25.00
6 Marcus Camby 8.00 20.00
7 Anfernee Hardaway 12.00 30.00
8 Kevin Garnett 15.00 40.00
9 Shareef Abdur-Rahim 8.00 20.00
10 Dennis Rodman 15.00 40.00
11 Grant Hill 12.00 30.00
12 Kerry Kittles 5.00 12.00
13 Antoine Walker 8.00 20.00
14 Scottie Pippen 12.00 30.00
15 Damon Stoudamire 8.00 20.00

1997-98 Metal Universe Championship Future Champions

Randomly inserted into packs at a rate of one in 18, this 15-card set focuses on rookie players. The cards appear three-dimensional with an action photo encased in a copper frame that is die cut at the bottom.

COMPLETE SET (15) 10.00 25.00
1 Tim Duncan 3.00 8.00
2 Tony Battie .60 1.50
3 Keith Van Horn 1.00 2.50
4 Antonio Daniels .50 1.25
5 Chauncey Billups 2.00 5.00
6 Ron Mercer .60 1.50
7 Tracy McGrady 2.50 6.00
8 Danny Fortson .50 1.25
9 Brevin Knight .50 1.25
10 Derek Anderson .50 1.25
11 Bobby Jackson .60 1.50
12 Jacque Vaughn .50 1.25
13 Tim Thomas 1.00 2.50
14 Austin Croshere .50 1.25
15 Kelvin Cato .50 1.25

1997-98 Metal Universe Championship Hardware

Randomly inserted into packs at a rate of one in 360, this 15-card set focuses on players who have a shot to one day take home an NBA honor, such as Scoring Champion, Rookie of the Year and MVP. The cards feature dual foils with an embossed background.

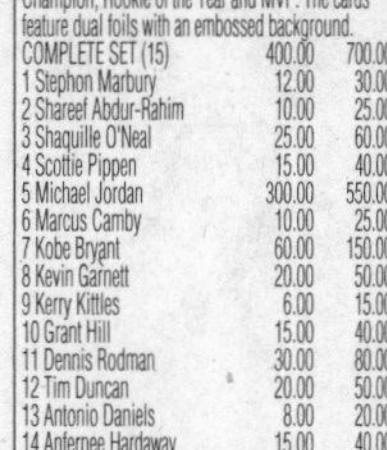

COMPLETE SET (15) 400.00 700.00
1 Stephon Marbury 12.00 30.00
2 Shareef Abdur-Rahim 10.00 25.00
3 Shaquille O'Neal 25.00 60.00
4 Scottie Pippen 15.00 40.00
5 Michael Jordan 300.00 550.00
6 Marcus Camby 10.00 25.00
7 Kobe Bryant 60.00 150.00
8 Kevin Garnett 20.00 50.00
9 Kerry Kittles 6.00 15.00
10 Grant Hill 15.00 40.00
11 Dennis Rodman 30.00 80.00
12 Tim Duncan 20.00 50.00
13 Antonio Daniels 8.00 20.00
14 Anfernee Hardaway 15.00 40.00
15 Allen Iverson 20.00 50.00

1997-98 Metal Universe Championship Trophy Case

Randomly inserted into packs at a rate of one in 96, this 10-card set features ten of the best players in the NBA presented on a 3-D sculptured embossed background.

COMPLETE SET (10) 25.00 60.00
1 Kevin Garnett 6.00 15.00
2 Grant Hill 5.00 12.00
3 Damon Stoudamire 3.00 8.00
4 Shaquille O'Neal 8.00 20.00
5 Ray Allen 4.00 10.00
6 Gary Payton 3.00 8.00
7 Shawn Kemp 3.00 8.00
8 Hakeem Olajuwon 4.00 10.00
9 John Stockton 4.00 10.00
10 Antoine Walker 3.00 8.00

1994 Metallic Impressions

Produced by Metallic Impressions for Classic, Inc., this 20-card standard-size set devotes four cards each to five of basketball's best centers. The set is titled "Centers of Attention," and production was limited to 12,500 hobby sets. Each set is accompanied by an individually numbered certificate of authenticity.

COMPLETE SET (20) 20.00 50.00
1 Hakeem Olajuwon 1.25 3.00
2 Hakeem Olajuwon 1.25 3.00
3 Hakeem Olajuwon 1.25 3.00
4 Hakeem Olajuwon 1.25 3.00
5 Patrick Ewing .75 2.00
6 Patrick Ewing .75 2.00
7 Patrick Ewing .75 2.00
8 Patrick Ewing .75 2.00
9 Alonzo Mourning .75 2.00
10 Alonzo Mourning .75 2.00
11 Alonzo Mourning .75 2.00
12 Alonzo Mourning .75 2.00
13 Dikembe Mutombo .60 1.50
14 Dikembe Mutombo .60 1.50
15 Dikembe Mutombo .60 1.50
16 Dikembe Mutombo .60 1.50
17 Shaquille O'Neal 4.00 10.00
18 Shaquille O'Neal 4.00 10.00
19 Shaquille O'Neal 4.00 10.00
20 Shaquille O'Neal 4.00 10.00

1997 Mexico Wonder Bread

Produced by Wonder Bread in Mexico, and having approval from the NBA, this 40-card set was inserted one per pack of Palitos De Pan tortilla snacks. The cards measure approximately 1 1/2" by 3" and are die cut, so they can stand. The card fronts feature the player's name at both the top and the bottom with the team logo in the upper right-hand corner. The card back features Spanish instructions on making the card stand.

COMPLETE SET (40) 100.00 200.00
1 Dikembe Mutombo 3.00 8.00
2 Mookie Blaylock 2.00 5.00
3 Dino Radja 2.50 6.00
4 Glen Rice 3.00 8.00
5 Toni Kukoc 3.00 8.00
6 Luc Longley 2.00 5.00
7 Terrell Brandon 2.00 5.00
8 A.C. Green 3.00 8.00
9 Antonio McDyess 2.50 6.00
10 Otis Thorpe 2.00 5.00
11 Joe Dumars 3.00 8.00
12 Chris Mullin 3.00 8.00
13 Hakeem Olajuwon 4.00 10.00
14 Charles Barkley 6.00 15.00
15 Rik Smits 2.50 6.00
16 Brent Barry 2.50 6.00
17 Eddie Jones 3.00 8.00
18 Elden Campbell 2.00 5.00
19 Alonzo Mourning 4.00 10.00
20 Tim Hardaway 3.00 8.00
21 Vin Baker 2.50 6.00
22 Tom Gugliotta 2.00 5.00
23 Kevin Garnett 6.00 15.00
24 Jayson Williams 2.00 5.00
25 Allan Houston 2.50 6.00
26 Anfernee Hardaway 5.00 12.00
27 Jerry Stackhouse 3.00 8.00
28 Allen Iverson 6.00 15.00
29 Cedric Ceballos 2.00 5.00
30 Arvydas Sabonis 2.50 6.00
31 Mitch Richmond 3.00 8.00
32 David Robinson 5.00 12.00
33 Avery Johnson 2.50 6.00
34 Gary Payton 3.00 8.00
35 Shawn Kemp 3.00 8.00
36 Damon Stoudamire 3.00 8.00
37 Marcus Camby 3.00 8.00
38 Karl Malone 4.00 10.00
39 Shareef Abdur-Rahim 3.00 8.00
40 Chris Webber 3.00 8.00

2005 Mid Mon Valley Hall of Fame

This set was released in 2005 by the Mid Mon Valley Sports Hall of Fame. Each card features a local sport legend printed on white card stock with a black and white artist's rendering of the featured subject on the front. The cover card proclaims the set as "Series 1 (2001-2005)" inductees.

COMPLETE SET (36) 10.00 20.00
151 Ashley Totedo Women's BK .30 .75
157 Gina Naccarato Women's BK .30 .75

2006 Mid Mon Valley Hall of Fame

This set was released in 2006 by the Mid Mon Valley Sports Hall of Fame. Each card features a local sport legend printed on white card stock with a black and white artist's rendering of the featured subject on the front. The cover card proclaims the set as "Series 2 (1997-2000/2006)" inductees.

COMPLETE SET (36) 10.00 20.00
95 Elmer Benyak BK .30 .75
97 Mouse Chacko BB BK .30 .75
105 Fran LaMendola CO BK .30 .75
114 Dick DiBiaso CO BK .30 .75
117 Don Asmonga CO BK .30 .75

1984-85 Miller Lite/NBA All-Star Charity Classic

This 6 card set was given out in conjunction with a charity half-court 3-on-3 game that was held during halftime of one of the 1984-85 Dallas Mavericks home games. The cards measure approximately 5" by 7" and feature black and white action shots of each player from his NBA career, and also feature sponsor logos from Spalding, Miller Lite, the Dallas Mavericks, and local radio station 98-KZEW. The black text on the backs contain information on the game and an appeal for fans to vote for the upcoming All-Star game in Indianapolis, which was held on February 10, 1985. The cards are unnumbered and are listed below in alphabetical order.

COMPLETE SET (6) 10.00 25.00
1 Connie Hawkins 2.50 6.00
2 Pete Maravich 8.00 20.00
3 Calvin Murphy 1.50 4.00
4 Nate Thurmond 1.50 4.00
5 Paul Westphal 1.50 4.00
6 Jo Jo White 1.50 4.00

1976-77 MSA Drinking Cups

This set of MSA (Michael Schacter Associates) Drinking Cups was released in 1976. According to our information, there are relatively few cups that have the MSA credit ONLY. The oval bands that surround the player photo are blue and maize and they are reportedly far rarer than the already rare MSA Circle K variety. This set features some of the top players in the game. Please note that these cups are not numbered and are listed below in alphabetical order.

1 Kareem Abdul-Jabbar 25.00 50.00
2 Alvan Adams 10.00 20.00
3 Nate Archibald 15.00 30.00
4 Dennis Awtrey 10.00 20.00
5 Rick Barry 15.00 30.00
6 Otis Birdsong 10.00 20.00
7 Mike Bratz 10.00 20.00
8 Allan Bristow 10.00 20.00
9 Fred Brown 10.00 20.00
10 Louis Dampier 10.00 20.00
11 Adrian Dantley 15.00 30.00
12 Walter Davis 10.00 20.00
13 John Drew 10.00 20.00
14 Julius Erving 25.00 50.00
15 Walt Frazier 15.00 30.00
16 George Gervin 20.00 40.00
17 Artis Gilmore 15.00 30.00
18 Bob Gross 10.00 20.00
19 John Havlicek 20.00 40.00
20 Elvin Hayes 20.00 40.00
21 Spencer Haywood 15.00 30.00
22 Garfield Heard 10.00 20.00
23 Lionel Hollins 10.00 20.00
24 Dan Issel 15.00 30.00
25 Marques Johnson 10.00 20.00
26 Bernard King 10.00 20.00
27 Billy Knight 10.00 20.00
28 Bob Lanier 15.00 30.00
29 Ron Lee 10.00 20.00
30 Maurice Lucas 10.00 20.00
31 Pete Maravich 30.00 60.00
32 Bob McAdoo 15.00 30.00
33 Earl Monroe 15.00 30.00
34 Calvin Murphy 15.00 30.00
35 Mark Olberding 10.00 20.00
36 Curtis Perry 10.00 20.00
37 Charlie Scott 10.00 20.00
38 Phil Smith 10.00 20.00
39 Ricky Sobers 10.00 20.00
40 David Thompson 15.00 30.00
41 Rudy Tomjanovich 15.00 30.00
42 Dave Twardzik 10.00 20.00
43 Norm Van Lier 10.00 20.00
44 Bill Walton 15.00 30.00
45 Marvin Webster 10.00 20.00
46 Paul Westphal 10.00 20.00

1911 Murad College Series T51

These colorful cigarette cards featured several colleges and a variety of sports and recreations of the day and were issued in packs of Murad Cigarettes. The cards measure approximately 2" by 3". Two variations of each of the first 50 cards were produced; one variation says "College Series" on back, the other, "2nd Series". The drawings on cards of the 2nd Series are slightly different from those of the College Series. There are 6 different series of 25 in the College Series and they are listed here in the order that they appear on the checklist on the cardbacks. There is also a larger version (5" x 8") that was available for the first 25 cards as a premium (catalog designation T6) offer that could be obtained in exchange for 15 Murad cigarette coupons; the offers expired June 30, 1911.

*2ND SERIES: .4X TO 1X COLLEGE SERIES
24 Williams College Basketball 40.00 80.00
35 Northwestern Basketball 40.00 80.00
120 Luther Basketball 40.00 80.00
150 Xavier Basketball 40.00 80.00

1911 Murad College Series Premiums T6

24 Williams College Basketball 300.00 500.00

1974 Nabisco Sugar Daddy

This set of 25 tiny (approximately 1 1/16" by 2 3/4") cards features athletes from a variety of popular pro sports. One card was included in specially marked Sugar Daddy and Sugar Mama candy bars. The cards were designed to be placed on a 18" by 24" poster, which could only be obtained through a mail-in offer direct from Nabisco. The set is referred to as "Pro Faces" as the cards show an enlarged head photo with a small caricature body. Cards 1-10 are football players, cards 11-16 and 22 are hockey players, and cards 17-21 and 23-25 are basketball players. Each card was produced in two printings. The first printing has a copyright date of 1973 printed on the backs (although the cards are thought to have been released in early 1974) and the second printing is missing a copyright date altogether.

COMPLETE SET (25) 75.00 150.00
17 Oscar Robertson 10.00 20.00
18 Spencer Haywood 2.50 5.00
19 Jo Jo White 2.50 5.00
20 Connie Hawkins 5.00 10.00
21 Nate Thurmond 2.50 6.00
23 Chet Walker 2.50 6.00
24 Calvin Murphy 2.50 5.00
25 Kareem Abdul-Jabbar 12.50 25.00

1975 Nabisco Sugar Daddy

This set of 25 tiny (approximately 1 1/16" by 2 3/4") cards features athletes from a variety of popular pro sports. One card was included in specially marked Sugar Daddy and Sugar Mama candy bars. The cards were designed to be placed on a 18" by 24" poster, which could only be obtained through a mail-in offer direct from Nabisco. The set is referred to as "Sugar Daddy All-Stars". As with the set of the previous year, the cards show an enlarged head photo with a small caricature body with a flag background of stars and stripes. This set is referred on the back as Series No. 2 and has a red, white, and blue background behind the picture on the front of the card. Cards 1-10 are pro football players and the remainder are pro basketball (17-21, 23-25) and hockey (11-16, 22) players.

COMPLETE SET (25) 75.00 150.00
17 Jerry Sloan 2.50 5.00
18 Spencer Haywood 2.50 5.00
19 Bob Lanier 3.00 8.00
20 Connie Hawkins 4.00 10.00
21 Geoff Petrie 1.50 4.00
23 Chet Walker 2.00 5.00
24 Bob McAdoo 3.00 8.00
25 Kareem Abdul-Jabbar 10.00 25.00

1976 Nabisco Sugar Daddy 1

This set of 25 tiny (approximately 1 1/16" by 2 3/4") cards features action scenes from a variety of popular sports from around the world. One card was included in specially marked Sugar Daddy and Sugar Mama candy bars. The set is referred to as "Sugar Daddy Sports World - Series 1" on the backs of the cards. The cards are in color with a relatively wide white border around the front of the cards.

COMPLETE SET (25) 40.00 80.00
11 Basketball 5.00 10.00

1976 Nabisco Sugar Daddy 2

This set of 25 tiny (approximately 1 1/16" by 2 3/4") cards features action scenes from a variety of popular sports from around the world. One card was included in specially marked Sugar Daddy and Sugar Mama candy bars. The set is referred to as "Sugar Daddy Sports World - Series 2" on the backs of the cards. The cards are in color with a relatively wide white border around the front of the cards.

COMPLETE SET (25) 40.00 80.00
13 Basketball 5.00 10.00

1997 Nabisco/Post Penny Hardaway Posters

These 11"x17" posters of Anfernee "Penny" Hardaway came exclusively in boxes of Post HoneyComb and Nabisco Frosted Shredded Wheat cereals. Posters one (green border) and two (orange border) were available in HoneyComb and posters three (red border) and four (blue border) were available in Frosted Shredded Wheat.

COMPLETE SET (4) 2.50 6.00
COMMON POSTER (1-4) .75 2.00

2004 National Trading Card Day

This 53-card set (49 basic cards plus four cover cards) was given out in five separate sealed packs (one from each of the following manufacturers: Donruss, Fleer, Press Pass, Topps and Upper Deck). One of the five packs was distributed at no cost to each patron that visited a participating sports card shop on April 3rd, 2004 as part of the National Trading Card Day promotion in an effort to increase awareness of collecting sports cards. The 50-card set is composed of 16 baseball, 9 basketball, 10 football, 4 golf, 5 hockey and 4 NASCAR cards. Of note, first year cards of NBA rookie stars LeBron James and Carmelo Anthony were included respectively within the UD and Fleer packs. An early Alex Rodriguez Yankees card was also highlighted within the Fleer pack.

F1-F9 ISSUED IN FLEER PACK
T1-T12 ISSUED IN TOPPS PACK
DP1-DP6 ISSUED IN DONRUSS PACK
PP1-PP7 ISSUED IN PRESS PASS PACK
UD1-UD15 ISSUED IN UPPER DECK PACK
F7 Vince Carter .30 .75
F8 Carmelo Anthony .40 1.00
F9 Yao Ming .30 .75
T9 Shaquille O'Neal .20 .50
T10 Kirk Hinrich .15 .40
T11 Tracy McGrady .30 .75
UD6 Kevin Garnett .30 .75
UD7 LeBron James .75 2.00
UD8 Michael Jordan 1.00 2.50

2001 NBA All-Star Game

This three card set was handed out at the 2001 NBA All-Star Game, and features cards of Vince Carter, Shaquille O'Neal, and Kobe Bryant. The Vince Carter card was produced by Fleer and pictures Carter dribbling a basketball in front of the White House. The Shaquille O'Neal card was produced by The Topps Company, and features Shaq on his basic Topps Heritage card from 2000-01 with a special "All-Star Game" stamp on the front. Finally, the Kobe Bryant card was produced by Upper Deck and features Kobe going up for a dunk. Please note that all of these cards have a special "2001 All-Star Game" stamp on the front.

COMPLETE SET (3)	5.00	12.00
1 Vince Carter Fleer	2.50	6.00
2 Shaquille O'Neal Topps	1.50	4.00
3 Kobe Bryant Upper Deck	3.00	8.00

1973-74 NBA Players Association

This set contains 40 full-color postcard format cards measuring approximately 3 3/8" by 5 5/8". The front features a borderless posed "action" shot of the player. The back has the player's name at the top, and the NBA Players Association logo. The cards are unnumbered and are checklisted below in alphabetical order. There are ten tougher cards which are marked as SP in the checklist below. The two toughest of these are Mike Newlin and Paul Silas. Walt Bellamy was listed on the checklist, but was never issued, having been replaced by Lou Hudson.

COMPLETE SET (40)	250.00	500.00
1 Lucius Allen	1.50	4.00
2 Dave Bing SP	8.00	20.00
3 Bill Bradley	4.00	10.00
4 Fred Carter SP	7.50	15.00
5 Austin Carr	1.50	4.00
6 Dave Cowens	5.00	10.00
7 Dave DeBusschere	5.00	10.00
8 Ernie DiGregorio	2.50	6.00
9 Gail Goodrich	5.00	10.00
10 Hal Greer	3.00	8.00
11 John Havlicek	7.50	15.00
12 Connie Hawkins	5.00	10.00
13 Spencer Haywood	2.00	5.00
14 Lou Hudson	2.00	5.00
15 Bob Kauffman	1.25	3.00
16 Bob Lanier	4.00	10.00
17 Bob Love	3.00	8.00
18 Jack Marin	2.00	5.00
19 Jim McMillian	2.00	5.00
20 Earl Monroe SP	12.50	25.00
21 Calvin Murphy	3.00	8.00
22 Mike Newlin SP	40.00	80.00
23 Geoff Petrie	2.50	6.00
24 Willis Reed SP	12.50	25.00
25 Rich Rinaldi	1.50	4.00
26 Mike Riordan SP	7.50	15.00
27 Oscar Robertson SP	20.00	40.00
28 Cazzie Russell	2.00	5.00
29 Paul Silas SP	40.00	80.00
30 Jerry Sloan	3.00	8.00
31 Elmore Smith	1.50	4.00
32 Dick Snyder	1.50	4.00
33 Nate Thurmond	3.00	8.00
34 Rudy Tomjanovich	4.00	10.00
35 Wes Unseld	5.00	10.00
36 Dick Van Arsdale SP	10.00	20.00
37 Tom Van Arsdale	1.50	4.00
38 Chet Walker SP	10.00	25.00
39 Jo Jo White	2.50	6.00
40 Len Wilkens	5.00	10.00

1973-74 NBA Players Association 8x10

These ten (approximately) 8" by 10" cards feature full-bleed color posed "action" player photos on the matte-finished fronts. The backs carry the NBA Players Association logo. The cards are unnumbered and checklisted below according to the order sheet. On an order sheet concerning the reprinting of the 1973-74 NBA Players Assn. set, these large photos are mentioned as individual mat finish 8" by 10" pictures.

COMPLETE SET (10)	75.00	150.00
A Dave DeBusschere	10.00	20.00
B John Havlicek	20.00	40.00
C Willis Reed	10.00	20.00
D Ernie DiGregorio	5.00	10.00
E Dave Cowens	10.00	20.00
F Oscar Robertson	20.00	40.00
G Bill Bradley	12.50	25.00
H Jo Jo White	5.00	10.00
I Nate Thurmond	7.50	15.00
J Gail Goodrich	10.00	20.00

2008-09 NBA Starting Five

This seven-card set was available through the Starting Five promotion from the NBA and manufactured by both Topps and Upper Deck. The regular cards from Topps feature the 2008-09 Topps Chrome design with an additional "Starting Five" logo on the card front. The regular cards from Upper Deck feature a new design, but also carry a Starting Five logo. Card backs from Upper Deck carry the player's initials, while the Topps cards are not numbered. In addition, autographs of Derrick Rose, Dwayne Wade, Magic Johnson and Michael Jordan were randomly inserted in packs.

DR Derrick Rose	8.00	20.00
Upper Deck		
LJ LeBron James	5.00	12.00
Black Jersey Upper Deck		
LJ LeBron James	5.00	12.00
White Jersey Upper Deck		
MJ Michael Jordan	8.00	20.00
Upper Deck		
NNO Magic Johnson	2.50	6.00
Topps		
NNO Magic Johnson Autograph	100.00	200.00
Topps		
NNO Greg Oden	1.00	2.50
Topps		
NNO Dwyane Wade	2.00	5.00
Topps		
NNO Dwyane Wade Autograph		
Topps		
AUDR Derrick Rose Autograph	200.00	400.00
Upper Deck		
AUMJ Michael Jordan Autograph	300.00	500.00
Upper Deck		

2010-11 NBA Starting Five

This six-card set was available through the Starting Five promotion from the NBA and manufactured by Panini. The regular cards feature the 2010-11 Donruss design with an additional "Starting Five" logo on the card front. Card backs carry the player's initials. In addition, an autograph of Derrick Favors and Wesley Johnson were randomly inserted which were on a Playoff Preferred card.

COMPLETE SET (6)	4.00	10.00
DF Derrick Favors AU	10.00	25.00
Playoff Preferred		
DH Dwight Howard	.60	1.50
DW Dwyane Wade	.75	2.00
JW John Wall	1.50	4.00
KB Kobe Bryant	2.00	5.00
KD Kevin Durant	1.25	3.00
LJ LeBron James	2.00	5.00
WJ Wesley Johnson AU	8.00	20.00
Playoff Preferred		

1971-72 NBA Stickers

This sticker sheet was released during the 1971-72 season, and features team logo stickers of 17 teams. This sheet measures 5.5x9.25 and was done in full color. Please note that this sticker sheet has a blank back.

1 Team Logos	2.00	5.00

1998 NBA Wrapper Rebound Shaquille O'Neal

This promotion was a joint effort between the NBA, Fleer/SkyBox, Topps and Upper Deck. Fans who collected series two wrappers of SkyBox Z-Force, Stadium Club, Ultra and Upper Deck could redeem those for a variety of Shaquille O'Neal collectibles. Collectors could redeem eight wrappers for a facsimile autographed poster, 40 wrappers for an exclusive four-card set featuring one card from each NBA partner, and 200 wrappers for an uncut basketball card sheet. There was also a grand prize of four tickets to an NBA game and O'Neal autographed merchandise. The promotion ran from January 15, 1998 through June 15, 1998. Listed below are the prices for the poster, four-card set and the uncut sheet. The complete set price is for the four-card set only.

COMPLETE SET (4)	12.00	30.00
1 Shaquille O'Neal Fleer	4.00	10.00
2 Shaquille O'Neal SkyBox	4.00	10.00
3 Shaquille O'Neal Topps	4.00	10.00
4 Shaquille O'Neal Upper Deck	4.00	10.00
NNO Shaquille O'Neal Poster	4.00	10.00
NNO Uncut NBA Sheet	15.00	40.00

2007 NBA Valentines

Released by Paper Magic Group in conjunction with the NBA, this set features six valentines measuring 2 1/2" x 4 1/4" an Allen Iverson valentine measuring 4 1/4" x 6 1/4" a tattoo sheet featuring five team logo tattos of all the represented teams (35 total) and a 15" x 19" poster with all seven players in the set placed horizontally next to each other. All these contents were packaged into a single box, and the box carried an initial suggested retail price of $2.99.

NNO Tim Duncan	.40	1.00
NNO Allen Iverson	.40	1.00
NNO LeBron James	.75	2.00
NNO Tim Duncan	.75	2.00
Allen Iverson		
LeBron James		
Tracy McGrady		
Steve Nash		
Dirk Nowitzki		
Dwyane Wade		
Poster		
NNO Dirk Nowitzki	.40	1.00
NNO Dwyane Wade	.60	1.50
NNO Tattoos	.20	.50
NNO Tracy McGrady	.40	1.00
NNO Steve Nash	.40	1.00

1969 NBAP Members

These rather unattractive cards, which definitely vary somewhat in size, measure approximately 2 3/4" by 4 1/2". The blank-backed cards feature borderless black-and-white photos and have light blue bottoms. These cards must not have been licensed by the NBA because the red, white and blue NBA logos have been airbrushed out. The cards may have been made from boxes of basketball shoes, possibly Converse. There may also be other cards in the set. Small and large versions of the logo card exist, both of which are almost square and are red, white, and blue. The cards are unumnbered and are listed below,in alphabetical order. With some recent discoveries, it is believed that this set was issued into the 1970's as there was a recently discovered Kareem Abdul-Jabbar card. However, with the inclusion of Bill Russell, it becomes obvious that this set was issued over a number of years as Russell retired after the 1968-69 season.

COMPLETE SET (20)	3500.00	5000.00
1 Kareem Abdul-Jabbar	300.00	600.00
2 Elgin Baylor	200.00	400.00
3 Zelmo Beaty	75.00	150.00
4 Bob Boozer	75.00	150.00
5 Bill Bradley	100.00	200.00
6 Wilt Chamberlain	400.00	700.00
7 John Havlicek	200.00	400.00
8 Don Kojis	75.00	150.00
9 Jerry Lucas	100.00	200.00
10 Eddie Miles	75.00	150.00
11 Jeff Mullins	75.00	150.00
12 Willis Reed	100.00	200.00
13 Oscar Robertson	250.00	500.00
14 Bill Russell	400.00	700.00
15 Wes Unseld	100.00	200.00
16 Dick Van Arsdale	75.00	150.00
17 Chet Walker	75.00	150.00
18 Jerry West	400.00	700.00
19 Len Wilkens	100.00	200.00
20 NBAP Logo	75.00	150.00

1984-85 Nets Getty

This 12-card set was produced by Getty and issued in four sheets, with three player cards per sheet. Getty Gas stations distributed the sheets to customers one per week. The sheets measure approximately 8" by 11". Although the sheets are not actually perforated, the black broken lines indicate that the cut cards measure 3 5/8" by 6 3/4". The front features a borderless color action shot, with the player's facsimile autograph below the picture. The player's name and number appear above the picture in block lettering. The New Jersey Nets and Getty logos appear at the bottom of each sheet. The cards are unnumbered and have been listed below in alphabetical order.

COMPLETE SET (12)	15.00	40.00
1 Stan Albeck CO	1.25	3.00
2 Otis Birdsong	2.00	5.00
3 Darwin Cook	1.25	3.00
4 Darryl Dawkins	4.00	10.00
5 Mike Gminski	2.00	5.00
6 Albert King	1.50	4.00
7 Mike O'Koren	1.50	4.00
8 Kelvin Ransey	1.25	3.00
9 M.Ray Richardson	1.50	4.00
10 Jeff Turner	2.00	5.00
11 Buck Williams	4.00	10.00
12 Duncan (Mascot)	1.25	3.00

1990-91 Nets Kayo/Breyers

This 14-card standard-size set of New Jersey Nets was sponsored by Kayo Cards and Breyers Ice Cream. The front features a color action player photo, with a thin red border. The left corner is cut out, and the word "Kayo" appears. The team logo overlays the left bottom corner of the picture, and the player's position and name are given below the picture in black and white lettering on red. The outer border is blue, which washes out as one moves toward the card bottom. The back has biographical information as well as college and pro statistics, enframed by a black border. As on the front, the red outer border washes out. The set features an early professional card of Derrick Coleman.

COMPLETE SET (14)	3.00	8.00
1 Mookie Blaylock	.75	2.00
2 Sam Bowie	.60	1.50
3 Jud Buechler	.40	1.00
4 Derrick Coleman	.75	2.00
5 Lester Conner	.30	.75
6 Chris Dudley	.40	1.00
7 Tate George	.30	.75
8 Derrick Gervin	.30	.75
9 Jack Haley	.30	.75
10 Kirk Lee	.30	.75
11 Chris Morris	.40	1.00
12 Reggie Theus	1.00	2.50
13 Bill Fitch CO	.30	.75
14 Nets Home Schedule	.30	.75

1986 Nets Lifebuoy/Star

The 1986 Star Lifebuoy New Jersey Nets set contains 14 cards, one for each of the 12 players, one for Head Coach Dave Wohl, and a checklist card. The set's basic design is identical to those of the Star Company's regular NBA sets. The front borders are royal blue, and the backs show each player's NBA statistics. The cards show a Star '86 logo in the upper right corner. The cards measure approximately 2 1/2" by 3 1/2". The cards are numbered in the upper left corner of the reverse; the numbering corresponds to alphabetical order by player.

COMPLETE SET (14)	5.00	12.00
1 Dave Wohl CO	.75	2.00
2 Otis Birdsong	.60	1.50
3 Bobby Cattage	.40	1.00
4 Darwin Cook	.40	1.00
5 Darryl Dawkins	1.50	4.00
6 Mike Gminski	.60	1.50
7 Mickey Johnson	.40	1.00
8 Albert King	.50	1.25
9 Mike O'Koren	.50	1.25
10 Kelvin Ransey	.40	1.00
11 Micheal Ray Richardson	.50	1.25
12 Jeff Turner	.75	2.00
13 Buck Williams	1.50	4.00
14 Title Card/	.40	1.00
Checklist on back)		

1971-72 Nets New York Team Issue

Each of these team-issued photos measure approximately 8" by 10" and feature black and white player portraits on two sheets. The player's name is listed below the photo. Each sheet contains either six or eight player portraits. The backs are blank. The photos are unnumbered and listed below alphabetically.

COMPLETE SET (2)	12.50	25.00
1 Jim Ard	7.50	15.00
Rick Barry		
Jeff Congdon		
Joe Depre		
Sonny Dove		
Jarrett Durham		
Manny Leaks		
Bill Melchionni		
2 Roy Boe PRES	5.00	10.00
Lou Carnesecca CO		
Billy Paultz		
John Roche		
Ollie Taylor		
Tom Washington		

2001-02 Nets Topps

Released by Topps, this 10-card set features a horizontal design with the Nets logo in the background and was given away during the 2001-02 season.

COMPLETE SET (10)	2.00	5.00
NN1 Stephon Marbury	.40	1.00
NN2 Keith Van Horn	.40	1.00
NN3 Kendall Gill	.30	.75
NN4 Jamie Feick	.30	.75
NN5 Stephen Jackson	.40	1.00
NN6 Byron Scott	.40	1.00
NN7 Johnny Newman	.30	.75
NN8 Aaron Williams	.30	.75
NN9 Lucious Harris	.30	.75
NN10 Kenyon Martin	.50	1.25

1974 New York News This Day in Sports

These cards are newspaper clippings of drawings by Hollreiser and are accompanied by textual description highlighting a player's unique sports feat. Cards are approximately 2" X 4 1/4". These are multisport cards and aranged in chronological order.

COMPLETE SET (40)	50.00	120.00
36 Wilt Chamberlain	2.00	4.00
Dec. 6, 1963		

1991 Nike Michael Jordan/Spike Lee

This six-card standard-size set was issued by Nike (in complete set form) to depict memorable Nike commercials starring Michael Jordan and Spike Lee. Nike had reportedly planned originally to produce an additional set of cards every three months featuring other world famous athletes in Nike commercials. The cards all have the same horizontally oriented front, with oval-shaped photos of Michael Jordan and Mars Blackmon (the character played by Spike Lee) and a Nike Trading Cards logo. A different quote appears at the top of each card front. The backs are either horizontally or vertically oriented and have either a black and white photo or a commercial advertisement. The cards are numbered on the front.

COMPLETE SET (6)	2.50	6.00
1 Earth/Mars 1988	.75	2.00
2 High Flying 1989	.60	1.50
3 Do You Know 1990	.60	1.50
4 Stay in School 1991	.60	1.50
5 Genie 1991	.60	1.50
With Little Richard		
6 Michael Jordan Flight	.75	2.00

1985 Nike

This oversized (slightly larger than 3x5 cards) multisport set was issued by Nike to promote athletic shoe sales. Although the set contains an attractive rookie-season card of Michael Jordan, the fairly plentiful supply has kept the market value quite affordable. Sets were distributed in shrinkwrapped form. The cards are unnumbered and are listed here in alphabetical order.

COMP.FACTORY SET (5)	50.00	125.00
COMPLETE SET (5)	30.00	75.00
2 Michael Jordan	20.00	50.00

1983-85 Nike Poster Cards

The cards in this set measure approximately 5" by 7" and were produced for use by retailers of Nike full-size posters as a promotional counter display. The cards are plastic coated and feature color pictures of players posed in unique settings. The hole at the top was designed so that dealers could attach the cards to the display with a soft plastic fastener provided by Nike. The borders are black. Originally, 27-cards were issued together and others were added later as new posters were created. The backs are plain white and carry the poster name, item number, and the player names (except on group photos). The cards are numbered only by the item number on back and have been listed below according to the final two digits of that number.

COMPLETE SET (43)	125.00	225.00
1 The Supreme Court	3.00	6.00
(Seventeen NBA players)		
2 Iceman	5.00	12.00
George Gervin		
6 Dr. Dunkenstein	1.25	3.00
Darrell Griffith		
19 Moses	3.00	8.00
Moses Malone		
20 Jam Session	2.00	5.00
24 NBA players with musical instruments)		
25 Silk	2.00	5.00
Jamaal Wilkes		
30 Board Room	2.00	5.00
(28 NBA players)		
33 Stormin' Norman	1.50	4.00
Norm Nixon		
34 Secretary of Defense	2.50	6.00
Bobby Jones		
35 Air Force I	5.00	10.00
Michael Cooper		
Calvin Natt		
Bobby Jones		
Jamaal Wilkes		
Moses Malone		
43 Sir Sid	3.00	8.00
Sidney Moncrief		
57 Air Force	10.00	25.00
Moses Malone		
Charles Barkley		
62 Manute Bol Growth Chart	2.00	5.00
5-in by 13-in		
68 Shirts and Skins	1.25	3.00

1993 Nike/Warner Michael Jordan

The Nike/Warner Michael Jordan set is comprised of 12 stickers, divided into two series of six stickers each. The first series is dubbed "Aerospace Jordan Trading Stickers," and includes six standard-size stickers. The second series dubbed "The Scream Team," also consists of six stickers. Each series of stickers was issued by Nike and features color pictures of Michael Jordan and characters from Warner Brothers cartoons. The Nike logo appears on each card. The peel-off backs are white. The stickers are unnumbered and checklisted below in alphabetical order according to description within each series: series one (1-6) and series two (7-12).

COMPLETE SET (12)	5.00	12.00
1 Martian	.40	1.00
(With basketball)		
2 Martian	.40	1.00
(The Best on Earth,		
The Best on Mars)		
3 Martian and his dog	.40	1.00
(Hanging from		
pulverized planetoid)		
4 Michael Jordan	.75	2.00
(Palming Martian		
by helmet crest)		
5 Michael Jordan	.75	2.00
(Riding in Bugs'		
flying saucer)		
6 Porky Pig	.40	1.00
(Piloting flying saucer)		
7 Aerospace	.75	2.00
(Michael Jordan slam		
dunking in space)		
8 J-J-Just Do It	.40	1.00
(Porky Pig in Nikes)		
9 Nice Shoes Indeed	.40	1.00
(Martian with his dog,		
holding a Nike)		
10 The Scream Team	.75	2.00
(Michael Jordan with Bugs)		
11 Warning:	.40	1.00
(Martian and		
warning message)		
12 What's Up Jock	.40	1.00
(Bugs slam dunking		
in space)		

1996 No Fear

This eight-card jumbo-sized set was issued through No Fear. It is a multi-sport set that features a posed color player shot on the front and a white back featuring a slogan by No Fear. The mode of distribution is unclear. The cards are not numbered and checklisted below in alphabetical order.

COMPLETE SET (8)	5.00	12.00
7 Chris Mills BK	.40	1.00

1977-78 Nuggets Iron-On

This six item iron-on set was sponsored by Pepsi-Cola, and was released during the 1977-78 season, and features some of the Denver Nugget players and coaches. The iron-ons measure 6 1/4"x11".

COMPLETE SET (6)	20.00	40.00
1 Dan Issel	5.00	10.00
2 Brian Taylor	2.00	5.00
3 Bobby Wilkerson	2.00	5.00
4 Bobby Jones	5.00	10.00
5 Larry Brown CO	3.00	8.00
6 David Thompson	5.00	10.00

1975-76 Nuggets Pepsi Cans

The 1975-76 Nuggets Pepsi Cans feature 15 players, coaches and front office personnel of the Denver Nuggets. The top of the panel that features the player contains the salutation "Congratulations Denver Nuggets", which contains below it a sketch of the player, as well as a facsimile signature and a short biography. These standard-sized aluminum cans then have below the player sketch "75-76 ABA Regular Season Champions". The cans contain no numbering other than jersey numbers, thus the set is listed alphabetically below. Cans opened from the bottom command up to a 25% premium over the prices below.

COMPLETE SET (15)	80.00	160.00
1 Byron Beck	5.00	10.00
2 Larry Brown CO	7.50	15.00
3 Jimmy Foster	3.00	8.00
4 Gus Gerard	3.00	8.00
5 George Irvine	3.00	8.00
6 Dan Issel	12.50	25.00
7 Bobby Jones	10.00	20.00
8 Doug Moe ACO	7.50	15.00
9 Carl Scheer GM	3.00	8.00
10 Ralph Simpson	5.00	10.00
11 Claude Terry	3.00	8.00
12 David Thompson	12.50	25.00
13 Monte Towe	5.00	10.00
14 Marvin Webster	3.00	8.00
15 Chuck Williams	3.00	8.00

1976-77 Nuggets Pepsi Cans

The 1976-77 Nuggets Pepsi Can Issue contains 17 standard-sized aluminum cans which portray players, coaches, and the team trainer. The cans state "Congratulations Denver Nuggets" and have a sketched drawing of the player with a facsimile signature and short biography next to the drawing. Below the drawing the can states "76-77 Midwest Division Champions" and has the NBA logo beside it. The cans contain no number except for players' uniform numbers--they are checklisted alphabetically below. Cans opened from the bottom command up to a 25% premium over the prices below.

COMPLETE SET (17)	60.00	120.00
1 Byron Beck	3.00	8.00
2 Larry Brown CO	5.00	10.00
3 Mack Calvin	3.00	8.00
4 Frank Hamblen ACO	2.00	5.00
5 George Irvine ACO	2.00	5.00
6 Dan Issel	10.00	20.00
7 Bobby Jones	7.50	15.00
8 Ted McClain	2.00	5.00
9 Jim Price	2.00	5.00
10 Carl Scheer GM	2.00	5.00
11 Paul Silas	3.00	8.00
12 Roland Taylor	2.00	5.00
13 David Thompson	10.00	20.00
14 Monte Towe	3.00	8.00
15 Bob Travaglini TR	2.00	5.00
16 Marvin Webster	2.00	5.00
17 Willie Wise	3.00	8.00

1982-83 Nuggets Police

This set contains 14 cards measuring 2 5/8" by 4 1/8" featuring the Denver Nuggets. Backs contain safety tips and are printed with black ink. The set was sponsored by Colorado National Banks, the Denver Nuggets, and the metropolitan area police Juvenile Crime Prevention Bureaus. The cards are unnumbered except for uniform number.

COMPLETE SET (14)	4.00	8.00
2 Alex English	1.25	3.00
7 Billy McKinney	.30	.75
21 Rob Williams	.30	.75
22 Glen Gondrezick	.30	.75
23 T.R. Dunn	.30	.75
24 Bill Hanzlik	.30	.75
25 Dave Robisch	.30	.75
43 James Ray	.30	.75
44 Dan Issel	1.00	2.50
53 Rich Kelley	.30	.75
55 Kiki Vandeweghe	.75	2.00
NNO Carl Scheer Pres/GM	.30	.75
NNO Doug Moe CO	.40	1.00
NNO Bill Ficke ACO	.30	.75
Bob Travaglini TR		

1983-84 Nuggets Police

This set contains 14 cards measuring 2 5/8" by 4 1/8" featuring the Denver Nuggets. Backs contain safety tips with black printing. The team name written vertically on the front is distinctive in that "Denver" is in red and "Nuggets" is in blue. The cards are unnumbered except for uniform number.

COMPLETE SET (14)	4.00	8.00
2 Alex English	1.00	2.50
5 Mike Evans	.30	.75
21 Rob Williams	.30	.75
23 T.R. Dunn	.30	.75
24 Bill Hanzlik	.30	.75
32 Howard Carter	.30	.75
33 Ken Dennard	.30	.75
34 Danny Schayes	.40	1.00
35 Richard Anderson	.30	.75
44 Dan Issel	.75	2.00
55 Kiki Vandeweghe	.50	1.25
NNO Carl Scheer Pres GM	.30	.75
NNO Bill Ficke ACO	.30	.75
NNO Doug Moe CO	.40	1.00

1985-86 Nuggets Police/Wendy's

The 1985-86 Wendy's Denver Nuggets set contains cards each measuring approximately 2 1/2" by 5". contest entry form tab is attached to each card (included in the dimensions above). The cards were distributed weekly. As part of the promotion a draw was held each week for two tickets to Denver Nugg home games and a free Wendy's meal. The set was also co-sponsored by Continental Airlines and Panasonic. The card fronts have color photos with and beige borders. The backs are black and white a have safety tips.

COMPLETE SET (12)	3.00
1 Alex English	.75
2 Mike Evans	.30
3 Bill Hanzlik	.30
4 Pete Williams	.30
5 Danny Schayes	.30
6 Wayne Cooper	.30
7 Blair Rasmussen	.30
8 Elston Turner	1.25
w/Michael Jordan	
9 Lafayette Lever	.40
10 T.R. Dunn	.30
11 Willie White	.30
12 Calvin Natt	.30

1988-89 Nuggets Police/Pep

This 12-card set was sponsored by Pepsi, Pizza H and The Children's Hospital of Denver. The cards measure approximately 2 5/8" by 4 1/8". The front features a borderless color action player photo. Th player's number and name appear in white lettering a purple stripe at the top of the card face, while tea and sponsor logos appear in the white stripe at the bottom. The back is printed in blue on white and presents a safety tip from the player. The English a Lever variation cards differ only in the safety tip fo on the back. The cards are unnumbered but they a numbered on the card front at the top by uniform number. The two Alex English cards and two Fat L cards are exactly the same except for the safety tip.

COMPLETE SET (12)	3.00
2A Alex English	.75
(If someone is hurt	
in an accident ...)	
2B Alex English	.75
(You should never	
run around ...)	
6 Walter Davis	.60
12A Fat Lever	.20
(Always wear a helmet	
when you're ...)	
12B Fat Lever	.20
(If you're ever in	
danger& the most ...)	
14 Michael Adams	.40
20 Elston Turner	.20
24 Bill Hanzlik	.20
34 Danny Schayes	.30
35 Jerome Lane	.20
41 Blair Rasmussen	.20
42 Wayne Cooper	.20

1988-89 Nuggets Portraits

Measuring 11" by 17", these posters featured six members of the 1988-89 Denver Nuggets. Each p features two black and white drawings of the play (one portrait, one in-action) with a facsimile autog The fronts also feature 7-11 coupons. The backs a blank. The posters are not numbered and listed be in alphabetical order.

COMPLETE SET (6)	9.00
1 Wayne Cooper	1.25
2 T.R. Dunn	1.25
3 Alex English	2.50
4 Fat Lever	1.50
5 Calvin Natt	1.25
6 Elston Turner	1.25
Mike Evans	
Bill Hanzlik	

1989-90 Nuggets Police/Pep

This 12-card set was sponsored by Pepsi, 7/Eleven, and The Children's Hospital of Denver. Beginning in early February, the cards were given out in 7/Eleven stores with Pepsi products. They measure approximately 2 5/8" by 4 1/8". The front features a borderless color action player photo. Two stripes descend from the top of the picture on the right. The longer of the two has alternating black and yellow diagonal sections. In the white stripe appears the player's name and number. The team logo and sponsors' logos appear in the white stripe at the bottom of the card face. The back is printed in lavender on white card stock and presents a safety tip from the player. The cards are unnumbered and checklisted below in alphabetical order.

COMPLETE SET (12) 3.00 8.00
1 Michael Adams .25 .60
2 Walter Davis .60 1.50
3 T.R. Dunn .20 .50
4 Alex English .75 2.00
5 Bill Hanzlik .20 .50
6 Eddie Hughes .20 .50
7 Tim Kempton .20 .50
8 Jerome Lane .20 .50
9 Lafayette Lever .30 .75
10 Todd Lichti .20 .50
11 Blair Rasmussen .20 .50
12 Danny Schayes .30 .75

2002-03 Nuggets Team Issue

Issued through the Denver Nuggets, this 11-card set features members of the 2002-03 Nuggets Squad. Each card boasts full color player action photography on the front of the card and a blank back. These cards measure 3.5" X 5" and are not numbered so they appear in alphabetical order.

COMPLETE SET (11) 6.00 15.00
1 Chris Anderson 1.25 3.00
2 Ryan Bowen .75 2.00
3 Marcus Camby 1.25 3.00
4 Junior Harrington .75 2.00
5 Donnell Harvey .75 2.00
6 Nene Hilario 1.00 2.50
7 Juwan Howard .75 2.00
8 Predrag Savovic .75 2.00
9 Nikoloz Tskitishvili .75 2.00
10 Rodney White .75 2.00
11 Vincent Yarbrough .75 2.00

1999 Omni CBA

Produced by Omni, this set features players of the Chinese Basketball Association. Our checklisting information is incomplete. If you have information regarding this set, please email us at basketballmag@beckett.com.

Wang ZhiZhi .30 .75
2 Yao Ming 1.50 4.00
6 Mengke Bateer .30 .75

1993-94 Oklahoma City Cavalry CBA

Issued by the Cavalry and sponsored by Lipton Teas, this 14-card set features color photos and a card stock that includes blue borders. The sets were either sold at Cavalry home games or given away as part of a promotional night.

COMPLETE SET (14) 1.50 4.00
COMMON CARD (1-14) .15 .40
Isaac Austin .30 .75
Mike Bell .15 .40
Henry Bibby CO .60 1.50
Mike Bell .15 .40
Terry Faggins .15 .40
Kermit Holmes .15 .40
Steffond Johnson .15 .40
Sebastian Neal .15 .40
Keith Owens .15 .40
Kelsey Weems .15 .40
Corey Williams .15 .40
Byron Wilson .15 .40
Cheerleaders .15 .40
Checklist .15 .40

1994 Hakeem Olajuwon Fan Club

Printed on thin card stock, these two standard- size cards were issued to members of the Hakeem the Dream Fan Club. The fronts feature full-bleed color photos, except on the right where a blue stripe carrying the player's name in red lettering edges the picture. The lower left corner has a yellow seal that reads "Most Valuable Player, 1993- 1994 NBA Season." On a black-and-white action cutout, the back of card number one presents "Awards," while that of card number two "1993-94 Statistics." The cards are unnumbered.

COMPLETE SET (2) 4.00 10.00
COMMON CARD (1-2) 2.00 5.00

1979 Open Pantry

This set is an unnumbered, 12-card issue featuring players from Milwaukee area professional sports teams five Brewers baseball (1-5), five Bucks basketball (6-10), and two Packers football (11-12). Cards are black and white with red trim and measure approximately 5" by 6". Cards were sponsored by Open Pantry, Lake to Lake, and MACC (Milwaukee Athletes against Childhood Cancer). The cards are unnumbered and hence are listed and numbered below alphabetically within sport.

COMPLETE SET (12) 12.50 25.00
6 Kent Benson 2.00 4.00
7 Junior Bridgeman 2.00 4.00
8 Quinn Buckner 2.50 5.00
9 Marques Johnson 3.00 6.00
10 Jon McGlocklin 2.00 4.00

1991-92 Outlaws Wichita GBA

This 11-card set features the 1991-92 Wichita Outlaws of the Global Basketball Assocation. The cards were produced by Rock's Dugout and printed on thick card stock. Both sides of the standard-size cards are horizontally oriented. Inside marbled burgundy borders, the fronts display a color close-up photo superimposed over a black and white action shot. The backs carry brief biographical information, career summary, and a Rock's Dugout advertisement. Five hundred hand-numbered and uncut sheets were also produced, although these sheets did not include the checklist card.

COMPLETE SET (11) 3.00 8.00
1 Rick Shore .40 1.00
2 Jeff Cummings .40 1.00
3 Brent Dabbs .50 1.25
4 Melvon Foster .50 1.25
5 Paul Guffrovich .40 1.00
6 Tyrone Powell .40 1.00
7 Omar Roland .40 1.00
8 Ricky Ross .40 1.00
9 Robert Spellman .40 1.00
10 Cody Walters .40 1.00
NNO Checklist Card .40 1.00

1971-72 Pacers Drinking Cups

This set of Pacers Drinking Cups consists of colorful portraits by distinguished artist Nicholas Volpe. The set features six clear plastic cups that has a paper portrait inserted between the layers of clear plastic. Please note that these cups are not numbered, and are listed below in alphabetical order.

COMPLETE SET (6) 50.00 100.00
1 Mel Daniels 12.50 25.00
2 Bill Keller 7.50 15.00
3 Art Becker 7.50 15.00
4 Bob Netolicky 10.00 20.00
5 Roger Brown 12.50 25.00
6 Rick Mount 10.00 20.00

1971-72 Pacers Marathon Oil

This set of Marathon Oil Pro Star Portraits consists of colorful portraits by distinguished artist Nicholas Volpe. The cards were part of a gas station promotion. Each portrait measures approximately 7 1/2" by 9 7/8" and features a painting of the player's face on a black background, with an action painting superimposed to the side. A facsimile autograph in white appears at the bottom of the portrait. At the bottom of each portrait is a postcard measuring 7 1/2" by 4" after perforation. While the back of the portrait has offers for a basketball photo album, autographed tumblers, and a poster, the postcard itself may be used to apply for a Marathon credit card. The portraits are unnumbered and checklisted below according to alphabetical order.

COMPLETE SET (12) 40.00 80.00
1 Warren Armstrong 2.50 6.00
2 John Barnhill 2.00 5.00
3 Art Becker 3.00 8.00
4 Roger Brown 3.00 8.00
5A Mel Daniels 5.00 12.00
Releasing ball from both hands
5B Mel Daniels 5.00 12.00
Releasing ball from right hand
6 Earle Higgins 2.00 5.00
7 Bill Keller 5.00 10.00
8 Bob Leonard CO 5.00 10.00
9 Freddie Lewis 3.00 8.00
10 Rick Mount 6.00 12.00
11 Bob Netolicky 3.00 8.00

1971-72 Pacers Team Issue

Each of these team-issued photos measure approximately 8" by 10" and feature black and white player portraits on sheets. Each sheet contains either seven or eight player portraits. The player's name is listed below the photo. The backs are blank. The photos are unnumbered and listed below alphabetically. George McGinnis is featured in his rookie year.

COMPLETE SET (2) 12.50 25.00
1 Roger Brown 7.50 15.00
Wayne Chapman
Mel Daniels
Earle Higgins
Darnell Hillman
Bill Keller
Freddie Lewis
George McGinnis
2 Bob Hooper ACO 5.00 10.00
Bob Leonard CO
Rick Mount
Bob Netolicky
Don Sidle
John Weissert GM
Marv Winkler

1988-89 Pacers Team Issue

The 12 cards in this set are black and white, blank backed and measure approximately 5" x 7". The cards are essentially press photos, but are printed on dull paper stock instead of photo quality. Not listed in the checklist is Julius Erving's appearance on John Long's card. In the card shown above, Erving demonstrates some sort of free jazz dance during his final hurrah in the league.

COMPLETE SET (12) 15.00 40.00
1 Greg Dreiling .75 2.00
2 Vern Fleming 2.00 5.00
3 Anthony Frederick .75 2.00
4 Stuart Gray .75 2.00
5 John Long 2.00 5.00
with Julius Erving
6 Reggie Miller 8.00 20.00
7 Chuck Person 2.50 6.00
8 Scott Skiles 2.50 6.00
9 Everette Stephens .75 2.00
10 Steve Stipanovich .75 2.00
11 Wayman Tisdale 2.50 6.00
12 Herb Williams 2.00 5.00

2009-10 Panini

COMPLETE SET (400) 50.00 120.00
1 Eddie House .10 .25
2 Glen Davis .12 .30
3 Kendrick Perkins .12 .30
4 Kevin Garnett .30 .75
5 Leon Powe .10 .25
6 Paul Pierce .20 .50
7 Rajon Rondo .20 .50
8 Rasheed Wallace .15 .40
9 Ray Allen .15 .40
10 Stephon Marbury .12 .30
11 Tony Allen .10 .25
12 Bobby Simmons .10 .25
13 Brook Lopez .15 .40
14 Chris Douglas-Roberts .10 .25
15 Courtney Lee .12 .30
16 Devin Harris .15 .40
17 Jarvis Hayes .10 .25
18 Josh Boone .10 .25
19 Keyon Dooling .10 .25
20 Rafer Alston .10 .25
21 Tony Battie .10 .25
22 Yi Jianlian .12 .30
23 Al Harrington .12 .30
24 Chris Duhon .10 .25
25 Danilo Gallinari .15 .40
26 Darko Milicic .10 .25
27 David Lee .12 .30
28 Jared Jeffries .10 .25
29 Larry Hughes .12 .30
30 Nate Robinson .15 .40
31 Wilson Chandler .12 .30
32 Andre Iguodala .15 .40
33 Donyell Marshall .10 .25
34 Elton Brand .15 .40
35 Jason Kapono .10 .25
36 Louis Williams .12 .30
37 Marreese Speights .12 .30
38 Samuel Dalembert .10 .25
39 Thaddeus Young .10 .25
40 Willie Green .10 .25
41 Andrea Bargnani .12 .30
42 Chris Bosh .15 .40
43 Hedo Turkoglu .15 .40
44 Joey Graham .10 .25
45 Jose Calderon .12 .30
46 Pops Mensah-Bonsu .10 .25
47 Quincy Douby .10 .25
48 Reggie Evans .10 .25
49 Devean George .10 .25
50 Antoine Wright .10 .25
51 Jarrett Jack .12 .30
52 Aaron Gray .10 .25
53 Brad Miller .12 .30
54 Derrick Rose .50 1.25
55 Joakim Noah .15 .40
56 John Salmons .15 .40
57 Kirk Hinrich .15 .40
58 Luol Deng .15 .40
59 Tyrus Thomas .12 .30
60 Anderson Varejao .12 .30
61 Daniel Gibson .12 .30
62 Delonte West .10 .25
63 Joe Smith .12 .30
64 LeBron James .75 2.00
65 Mo Williams .12 .30
66 Shaquille O'Neal .30 .75
67 Wally Szczerbiak .12 .30
68 Zydrunas Ilgauskas .10 .25
69 Anthony Parker .10 .25
70 Jamario Moon .10 .25
71 Allen Iverson .20 .50
72 Ben Gordon .15 .40
73 Charlie Villanueva .12 .30
74 Fabricio Oberto .10 .25
75 Jason Maxiell .10 .25
76 Kwame Brown .10 .25
77 Chris Wilcox .10 .25
78 Richard Hamilton .12 .30
79 Rodney Stuckey .15 .40
80 Tayshaun Prince .15 .40
81 Will Bynum .10 .25
82 Brandon Rush .12 .30
83 Danny Granger .15 .40
84 Jeff Foster .10 .25
85 Marquis Daniels .10 .25
86 Mike Dunleavy .10 .25
87 Rasho Nesterovic .10 .25
88 Roy Hibbert .15 .40
89 Stephen Graham .10 .25
90 T.J. Ford .10 .25
91 Travis Diener .10 .25
92 Troy Murphy .10 .25
93 Dahntay Jones .10 .25
94 Earl Watson .10 .25
95 Andrew Bogut .15 .40
96 Bruce Bowen .10 .25
97 Joe Alexander .10 .25
98 Keith Bogans .10 .25
99 Kurt Thomas .10 .25
100 Luc Mbah a Moute .10 .25
101 Luke Ridnour .12 .30
102 Michael Redd .15 .40
103 Ramon Sessions .12 .30
104 Al Horford .15 .40
105 Joe Johnson .15 .40
106 Josh Smith .15 .40
107 Marvin Williams .12 .30
108 Maurice Evans .10 .25
109 Mike Bibby .12 .30
110 Ronald Murray .10 .25
111 Solomon Jones .10 .25
112 Jamal Crawford .12 .30
113 Zaza Pachulia .10 .25
114 Boris Diaw .12 .30
115 D.J. Augustin .12 .30
116 DeSagana Diop .10 .25
117 Dontell Jefferson RC .15 .40
118 Gerald Wallace .15 .40
119 Juwan Howard .12 .30
120 Nazr Mohammed .10 .25
121 Raja Bell .12 .30
122 Raymond Felton .12 .30
123 Vladimir Radmanovic .10 .25
124 Tyson Chandler .12 .30
125 Chris Quinn .10 .25
126 Daequan Cook .10 .25
127 Dwyane Wade .30 .75
128 James Jones .15 .40
129 Jermaine O'Neal .15 .40
130 Luther Head .10 .25
131 Mario Chalmers .15 .40
132 Michael Beasley .15 .40
133 Udonis Haslem .12 .30
134 Anthony Johnson .10 .25
135 Dwight Howard .25 .60
136 J.J. Redick .15 .40
137 Jameer Nelson .12 .30
138 Mickael Pietrus .10 .25
139 Rashard Lewis .12 .30
140 Vince Carter .20 .50
141 Brandon Bass .10 .25
142 Matt Barnes .10 .25
143 Andray Blatche .10 .25
144 Antawn Jamison .15 .40
145 Brendan Haywood .10 .25
146 Caron Butler .15 .40
147 DeShawn Stevenson .10 .25
148 Gilbert Arenas .15 .40
149 Mike James .10 .25
150 Mike Miller .15 .40
151 Nick Young .12 .30
152 Randy Foye .10 .25
153 Tim Thomas .10 .25
154 Dirk Nowitzki .20 .50
155 Erick Dampier .10 .25
156 Gerald Green .12 .30
157 James Singleton .10 .25
158 Jason Kidd .15 .40
159 Jason Terry .12 .30
160 Greg Buckner .10 .25
161 Shawn Marion .15 .40
162 Jose Barea .20 .50
163 Josh Howard .12 .30
164 Aaron Brooks .10 .25
165 Brent Barry .10 .25
166 Carl Landry .10 .25
167 Dikembe Mutombo .15 .40
168 Luis Scola .12 .30
169 Shane Battier .15 .40
170 Tracy McGrady .15 .40
171 Trevor Ariza .10 .25
172 Von Wafer .10 .25
173 Yao Ming .20 .50
174 Darius Miles .10 .25
175 Darrell Arthur .12 .30
176 Hakim Warrick .12 .30
177 Marc Gasol .15 .40
178 Mike Conley Jr. .12 .30
179 O.J. Mayo .15 .40
180 Jerry Stackhouse .12 .30
181 Zach Randolph .12 .30
182 Rudy Gay .15 .40
183 Chris Paul .25 .60
184 Emeka Okafor .15 .40
185 David West .15 .40
186 Devin Brown .10 .25
187 James Posey .10 .25
188 Julian Wright .10 .25
189 Morris Peterson .10 .25
190 Peja Stojakovic .15 .40
191 Rasual Butler .10 .25
192 Drew Gooden .12 .30
193 Manu Ginobili .15 .40
194 Matt Bonner .10 .25
195 Michael Finley .15 .40
196 Richard Jefferson .15 .40
197 Roger Mason .10 .25
198 Tim Duncan .25 .60
199 Antonio McDyess .12 .30
200 Tony Parker .15 .40
201 Anthony Carter .10 .25
202 Carmelo Anthony .20 .50
203 Chauncey Billups .15 .40
204 Chris Andersen .25 .60
205 J.R. Smith .15 .40
206 Kenyon Martin .15 .40
207 Linas Kleiza .10 .25
208 Arron Afflalo .10 .25
209 Nene .12 .30
210 Al Jefferson .15 .40
211 Bobby Brown .10 .25
212 Corey Brewer .10 .25
213 Darius Songaila .10 .25
214 Kevin Love .25 .60
215 Rodney Carney .10 .25
216 Quentin Richardson .12 .30
217 Ryan Gomes .10 .25
218 Brandon Roy .15 .40
219 Greg Oden .12 .30
220 Jerryd Bayless .12 .30
221 Joel Przybilla .10 .25
222 LaMarcus Aldridge .15 .40
223 Nicolas Batum .15 .40
224 Rudy Fernandez .12 .30
225 Steve Blake .10 .25
226 Travis Outlaw .12 .30
227 Andre Miller .12 .30
228 D.J. White .10 .25
229 Desmond Mason .10 .25
230 Jeff Green .12 .30
231 Kevin Durant .50 1.25
232 Nenad Krstic .10 .25
233 Nick Collison .10 .25
234 Russell Westbrook .25 .60
235 Thabo Sefolosha .12 .30
236 Andrei Kirilenko .12 .30
237 C.J. Miles .10 .25
238 Carlos Boozer .15 .40
239 Deron Williams .15 .40
240 Kosta Koufos .10 .25
241 Kyle Korver .12 .30
242 Matt Harpring .12 .30
243 Mehmet Okur .10 .25
244 Paul Millsap .12 .30
245 Ronnie Brewer .12 .30
246 Andris Biedrins .10 .25
247 Anthony Morrow .10 .25
248 Anthony Randolph .12 .30
249 Brandan Wright .10 .25
250 C.J. Watson .10 .25
251 Corey Maggette .12 .30
252 Kelenna Azubuike .10 .25
253 Marco Belinelli .10 .25
254 Monta Ellis .15 .40
255 Acie Law .10 .25
256 Ronny Turiaf .10 .25
257 Stephen Jackson .12 .30
258 Al Thornton .12 .30
259 Baron Davis .15 .40
260 Chris Kaman .12 .30
261 Eric Gordon .15 .40
262 Fred Jones .10 .25
263 Marcus Camby .10 .25
264 Ricky Davis .12 .30
265 Steve Novak .10 .25
266 Sebastian Telfair .10 .25
267 Craig Smith .10 .25
268 Adam Morrison .12 .30
269 Andrew Bynum .20 .50
270 Derek Fisher .12 .30
271 Jordan Farmar .10 .25
272 Josh Powell .10 .25
273 Kobe Bryant .75 2.00
274 Lamar Odom .15 .40
275 Luke Walton .10 .25
276 Pau Gasol .15 .40
277 Ron Artest .15 .40
278 Sasha Vujacic .10 .25
279 Alando Tucker .10 .25
280 Sasha Pavlovic .10 .25
281 Amare Stoudemire .15 .40
282 Ben Wallace .15 .40
283 Goran Dragic RC .25 .60
284 Grant Hill .20 .50
285 Jared Dudley .10 .25
286 Jason Richardson .15 .40
287 Leandro Barbosa .12 .30
288 Channing Frye .12 .30
289 Steve Nash .15 .40
290 Andres Nocioni .10 .25
291 Beno Udrih .10 .25
292 Bobby Jackson .10 .25
293 Francisco Garcia .12 .30
294 Ike Diogu .10 .25
295 Jason Thompson .10 .25
296 Kevin Martin .15 .40
297 Rashad McCants .10 .25
298 Sergio Rodriguez .10 .25
299 Sean May .10 .25
300 Spencer Hawes .12 .30
301 Blake Griffin RC 5.00 12.00
302 Hasheem Thabeet RC .75 2.00
303 James Harden RC 2.50 6.00
304 Tyreke Evans RC 2.00 5.00
305 Hasheem Thabeet RC .75 2.00
306 Jonny Flynn RC .75 2.00
307 Stephen Curry RC 2.00 5.00
308 Jordan Hill RC .75 2.00
309 DeMar DeRozan RC 1.25 3.00
310 Brandon Jennings RC 1.50 4.00
311 Terrence Williams RC .75 2.00
312 Gerald Henderson RC .75 2.00
313 Tyler Hansbrough RC 1.25 3.00
314 Earl Clark RC .75 2.00
315 Austin Daye RC .75 2.00
316 James Johnson RC .75 2.00
317 Jrue Holiday RC 1.50 4.00
318 Ty Lawson RC 1.25 3.00
319 Jeff Teague RC 1.00 2.50
320 Eric Maynor RC .75 2.00
321 Darren Collison RC 1.25 3.00
322 Blake Griffin RC 5.00 12.00
323 Omri Casspi RC .75 2.00
324 B.J. Mullens RC .75 2.00
325 Rodrigue Beaubois RC 1.00 2.50
326 Taj Gibson RC 1.00 2.50
327 DeMarre Carroll RC .75 2.00
328 Wayne Ellington RC .75 2.00
329 Toney Douglas RC .75 2.00
330 Tyreke Evans RC 2.00 5.00
331 Jeff Pendergraph RC .75 2.00
332 Jermaine Taylor RC .75 2.00
333 Dante Cunningham RC .75 2.00
334 DaJuan Summers RC .75 2.00
335 Sam Young RC .75 2.00
336 DeJuan Blair RC 1.00 2.50
337 Jon Brockman RC .75 2.00
338 Derrick Brown RC .75 2.00
339 Jodie Meeks RC 1.00 2.50
340 Patrick Beverley RC .75 2.00
341 Marcus Thornton RC 1.25 3.00
342 Chase Budinger RC .75 2.00
343 Jack McClinton RC .75 2.00
344 Danny Green RC 1.25 3.00
345 Taylor Griffin RC .75 2.00
346 A.J. Price RC .75 2.00
347 Jonas Jerebko RC .75 2.00
348 Lester Hudson RC .75 2.00
349 Goran Suton RC .75 2.00
350 Ty Lawson RC 1.25 3.00
351 Blake Griffin RC 5.00 12.00
352 Hasheem Thabeet RC .75 2.00
353 James Harden RC 2.50 6.00
354 Tyreke Evans RC 2.00 5.00
355 Jordan Hill RC .75 2.00
356 Jonny Flynn RC .75 2.00
357 Stephen Curry RC 2.00 5.00
358 Jordan Hill RC .75 2.00
359 DeMar DeRozan RC 1.25 3.00
360 Brandon Jennings RC 1.50 4.00
361 Terrence Williams RC .75 2.00
362 Gerald Henderson RC .75 2.00
363 Tyler Hansbrough RC 1.25 3.00
364 Earl Clark RC .75 2.00
365 Austin Daye RC .75 2.00
366 James Johnson RC .75 2.00
367 Jrue Holiday RC 1.50 4.00
368 Ty Lawson RC 1.25 3.00
369 Jeff Teague RC 1.00 2.50
370 Eric Maynor RC .75 2.00
371 Darren Collison RC 1.25 3.00
372 Stephen Curry RC 2.00 5.00
373 Omri Casspi RC .75 2.00
374 B.J. Mullens RC .75 2.00
375 Rodrigue Beaubois RC 1.00 2.50
376 Taj Gibson RC 1.00 2.50
377 DeMarre Carroll RC .75 2.00
378 Wayne Ellington RC .75 2.00
379 Toney Douglas RC .75 2.00
380 Tyler Hansbrough RC 1.25 3.00
381 Jeff Pendergraph RC .75 2.00
382 Jermaine Taylor RC .75 2.00
383 Dante Cunningham RC .75 2.00
384 DaJuan Summers RC .75 2.00
385 Sam Young RC .75 2.00
386 DeJuan Blair RC 1.00 2.50
387 Jon Brockman RC .75 2.00
388 Derrick Brown RC .75 2.00
389 Jodie Meeks RC 1.00 2.50
390 Patrick Beverley RC .75 2.00
391 Marcus Thornton RC 1.25 3.00
392 Chase Budinger RC .75 2.00
393 Jack McClinton RC .75 2.00
394 Danny Green RC 1.25 3.00
395 Taylor Griffin RC .75 2.00
396 A.J. Price RC .75 2.00
397 Jonas Jerebko RC .75 2.00
398 Lester Hudson RC .75 2.00
399 Goran Suton RC .75 2.00
400 James Harden RC 2.50 6.00

2009-10 Panini Artists Proof

*AP 1-300: 1.25X TO 3X BASE HI
*AP 301-400: .75X TO 2X BASE HI
STATED PRINT RUN 199 SER.#'d SETS
301 Blake Griffin 12.50 30.00
322 Blake Griffin 12.50 30.00
351 Blake Griffin 12.50 30.00

2009-10 Panini Glossy

*GLOSSY: 1-300: .75X TO 2X BASE HI
*GLOSSY: 301-400: .6X TO 1.5X BASE HI
RANDOM INSERTS IN PACKS

2009-10 Panini All-Pro Team

COMPLETE SET (20) 8.00 20.00
RANDOM INSERTS IN PACKS
*AP: .75X TO 2X BASE HI
AP PRINT RUN 199 SER.#'d SETS
*GLOSSY: .6X TO 1.5X BASE HI
GLOSSY RANDOM INSERTS IN PACKS
1 LeBron James 2.50 6.00
2 Dirk Nowitzki .60 1.50
3 Dwight Howard .75 2.00
4 Kobe Bryant 2.50 6.00
5 Dwyane Wade 1.00 2.50
6 Tim Duncan .75 2.00
7 Paul Pierce .60 1.50
8 Yao Ming .60 1.50
9 Brandon Roy .50 1.25
10 Chris Paul .75 2.00
11 Carmelo Anthony .60 1.50
12 Pau Gasol .50 1.25
13 Shaquille O'Neal 1.00 2.50
14 Chauncey Billups .50 1.25
15 Tony Parker .50 1.25
16 Deron Williams .50 1.25
17 Kevin Garnett 1.00 2.50
18 Chris Bosh .50 1.25
19 Joe Johnson .50 1.25
20 Kevin Durant 1.50 4.00

2009-10 Panini Block Party

COMPLETE SET (10) 5.00 12.00
RANDOM INSERTS IN PACKS
*AP: 1X TO 2.5X BASE HI
AP PRINT RUN 199 SER.#'d SETS
*GLOSSY:.6X TO 1.5X BASE HI
GLOSSY RANDOM INSERTS IN PACKS
1 Dwight Howard 1.25 3.00
2 Chris Andersen 2.00 2.00
3 Jermaine O'Neal .75 2.00
4 Yao Ming 1.00 2.50
5 Chris Kaman .60 1.50
6 Joakim Noah .75 2.00
7 Kevin Garnett 1.50 4.00
8 Pau Gasol .75 2.00
9 Amare Stoudemire .75 2.00
10 Dikembe Mutombo .75 2.00

2009-10 Panini Decals

COMPLETE SET (31)
RANDOM INSERTS IN
1 Josh Smith [illegible]
2 Paul Pierce [illegible]
3 Gerald Wallace [illegible]
4 Derrick Rose [illegible]
5 LeBron James [illegible]
6 Dirk Nowitzki .75 [illegible]
7 Carmelo Anthony .75 2.00
8 Richard Hamilton .60 1.50
9 Stephen Jackson .60 1.50
10 Yao Ming .75 2.00
11 Danny Granger .60 1.50
12 Zach Randolph .60 1.50
13 Kobe Bryant 3.00 8.00
14 O.J. Mayo .60 1.50
15 Dwyane Wade 1.25 3.00
16 Michael Redd .60 1.50
17 Al Jefferson .60 1.50
18 Devin Harris .60 1.50
19 Chris Paul 1.00 2.50
20 Al Harrington .60 1.50
21 Kevin Durant 2.00 5.00
22 Dwight Howard 1.00 2.50
23 Andre Iguodala .60 1.50
24 Steve Nash .60 1.50
25 Brandon Roy .60 1.50
26 Kevin Martin .60 1.50
27 Tony Parker .60 1.50
28 Chris Bosh .60 1.50
29 Deron Williams .60 1.50
30 Gilbert Arenas .60 1.50
32 Blake Griffin 4.00 10.00

2009-10 Panini Future Stars

COMPLETE SET (20) 4.00 10.00
RANDOM INSERTS IN PACKS
*AP: 1.25X TO 3X BASE HI
AP PRINT RUN 199 SER.#'d SETS
*GLOSSY: .75X TO 2X BASE HI
GLOSSY RANDOM INSERTS IN PACKS
1 Al Thornton .40 1.00
2 Andrew Bynum .60 1.50
3 Charlie Villanueva .40 1.00
4 David Lee .40 1.00
5 J.J. Redick .50 1.25
6 Jarrett Jack .40 1.00
7 Jeff Green .40 1.00
8 Kelenna Azubuike .30 .75
9 LaMarcus Aldridge .50 1.25
10 Linas Kleiza .30 .75
11 Luis Scola .40 1.00
12 Monta Ellis .50 1.25
13 Nate Robinson .50 1.25
14 Nick Young .40 1.00
15 Paul Millsap .40 1.00
16 Rajon Rondo .60 1.50
17 Ronnie Brewer .40 1.00
18 Rudy Gay .50 1.25
19 Ryan Gomes .30 .75
20 Randy Foye .30 .75

2009-10 Panini Glow in the Dark Stickers

COMPLETE SET (30) 3.00 8.00
RANDOM INSERTS IN PACKS
1 Atlanta Hawks .20 .50
2 Boston Celtics .60 1.50
3 Charlotte Bobcats .20 .50
4 Chicago Bulls .40 1.00
5 Cleveland Cavaliers .40 1.00
6 Dallas Mavericks .20 .50
7 Denver Nuggets .20 .50
8 Detroit Pistons .30 .75
9 Golden State Warriors .20 .50
10 Houston Rockets .20 .50
11 Indiana Pacers .20 .50
12 Los Angeles Clippers .20 .50
13 Los Angeles Lakers .60 1.50
14 Memphis Grizzlies .20 .50
15 Miami Heat .20 .50
16 Milwaukee Bucks .20 .50
17 Minnesota Timberwolves .20 .50
18 New Jersey Nets .20 .50
19 New Orleans Hornets .20 .50
20 New York Knicks .40 1.00
21 Oklahoma City Thunder .20 .50
22 Orlando Magic .20 .50
23 Philadelphia 76ers .20 .50
24 Phoenix Suns .20 .50
25 Portland Trail Blazers .20 .50
26 Sacramento Kings .20 .50
27 San Antonio Spurs .30 .75
28 Toronto Raptors .20 .50
29 Utah Jazz .20 .50
30 Washington Wizards .20 .50

2009-10 Panini Headliners

COMPLETE SET (10) 6.00 15.00
RANDOM INSERTS IN PACKS
*AP: 1X TO 2.5X BASE HI
AP PRINT RUN 199 SER.#'d SETS
*GLOSSY: .6X TO 1.5X BASE HI
GLOSSY RANDOM INSERTS IN PACKS
1 Chauncey Billups .60 1.50
2 Nate Robinson .60 1.50
3 Jason Kidd .60 1.50
4 LeBron James 3.00 8.00
5 Derrick Rose 2.00 5.00
6 Dwight Howard 1.00 2.50

on James 3.00 8.00
obe Bryant 3.00 8.00
Pat Riley .60 1.50
10 Blake Griffin 4.00 10.00
8a Kobe Bryant AU/30 125.00 225.00

2009-10 Panini Inscriptions

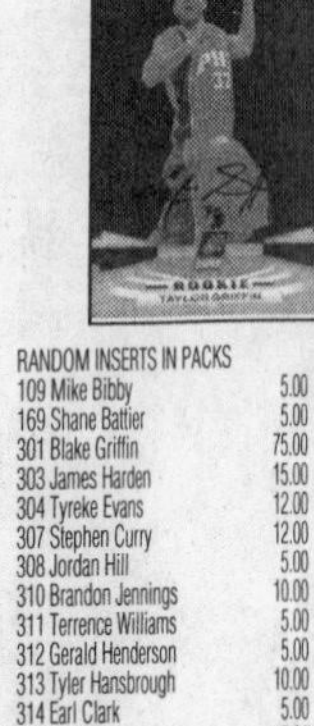

RANDOM INSERTS IN PACKS
109 Mike Bibby 5.00 12.00
169 Shane Battier 5.00 12.00
301 Blake Griffin 75.00 200.00
303 James Harden 15.00 40.00
304 Tyreke Evans 12.00 30.00
307 Stephen Curry 12.00 30.00
308 Jordan Hill 5.00 12.00
310 Brandon Jennings 10.00 25.00
311 Terrence Williams 5.00 12.00
312 Gerald Henderson 5.00 12.00
313 Tyler Hansbrough 10.00 25.00
314 Earl Clark 5.00 12.00
315 Austin Daye 5.00 12.00
316 James Johnson 5.00 12.00
317 Jrue Holiday 10.00 25.00
319 Jeff Teague 6.00 15.00
321 Darren Collison 8.00 20.00
322 Blake Griffin 75.00 200.00
323 Omri Casspi 5.00 12.00
324 B.J. Mullens 5.00 12.00
325 Rodrigue Beaubois 6.00 15.00
326 Taj Gibson 6.00 15.00
327 DeMarre Carroll 5.00 12.00
329 Toney Douglas 5.00 12.00
330 Tyreke Evans 12.00 30.00
331 Jeff Pendergraph 5.00 12.00
332 Jermaine Taylor 5.00 12.00
333 Dante Cunningham 5.00 12.00
334 DaJuan Summers 5.00 12.00
336 DeJuan Blair 6.00 15.00
337 Jon Brockman 5.00 12.00
338 Derrick Brown 5.00 12.00
339 Jodie Meeks 6.00 15.00
341 Marcus Thornton 8.00 20.00
342 Chase Budinger 5.00 12.00
343 Jack McClinton 5.00 12.00
344 Danny Green 8.00 20.00
345 Taylor Griffin 5.00 12.00
346 A.J. Price 5.00 12.00
348 Lester Hudson 5.00 12.00
349 Goran Suton 5.00 12.00
351 Blake Griffin 75.00 200.00
354 Tyreke Evans 12.00 30.00
355 Jordan Hill 5.00 12.00
357 Stephen Curry 12.00 30.00
358 Jordan Hill 5.00 12.00
360 Brandon Jennings 10.00 25.00
361 Terrence Williams 5.00 12.00
362 Gerald Henderson 5.00 12.00
363 Tyler Hansbrough 10.00 25.00
364 Earl Clark 5.00 12.00
365 Austin Daye 5.00 12.00
366 James Johnson 5.00 12.00
367 Jrue Holiday 10.00 25.00
369 Jeff Teague 6.00 15.00
371 Darren Collison 8.00 20.00
372 Stephen Curry 12.00 30.00
373 Omri Casspi 5.00 12.00
374 B.J. Mullens 5.00 12.00
375 Rodrigue Beaubois 6.00 15.00
376 Taj Gibson 6.00 15.00
377 DeMarre Carroll 5.00 12.00
379 Toney Douglas 5.00 12.00
380 Tyler Hansbrough 10.00 25.00
381 Jeff Pendergraph 5.00 12.00
382 Jermaine Taylor 5.00 12.00
383 Dante Cunningham 5.00 12.00
384 DaJuan Summers 5.00 12.00
386 DeJuan Blair 6.00 15.00
387 Jon Brockman 5.00 12.00
388 Derrick Brown 5.00 12.00
389 Jodie Meeks 6.00 15.00
391 Marcus Thornton 8.00 20.00
392 Chase Budinger 5.00 12.00
393 Jack McClinton 5.00 12.00
394 Danny Green 8.00 20.00
395 Taylor Griffin 5.00 12.00
396 A.J. Price 5.00 12.00
398 Lester Hudson 5.00 12.00
399 Goran Suton 5.00 12.00

2009-10 Panini Jam Masters

COMPLETE SET (10) 6.00 15.00
RANDOM INSERTS IN PACKS
*AP: 1X TO 2.5X BASE HI
AP PRINT RUN 199 SER.#'d SETS
*GLOSSY: .6X TO 1.5X BASE HI
GLOSSY RANDOM INSERTS IN PACKS
1 Tim Duncan 1.25 3.00
2 Shaquille O'Neal 1.50 4.00
3 Dwyane Wade 1.50 4.00
4 LeBron James 4.00 10.00
5 Kobe Bryant 4.00 10.00
6 Danny Granger .75 2.00
7 Nate Robinson .75 2.00
8 Chris Bosh .75 2.00
9 Kevin Durant 2.50 6.00
10 Chris Paul 1.25 3.00

2009-10 Panini Legends of the Game

COMPLETE SET (10) 4.00 10.00
RANDOM INSERTS IN PACKS
*AP: .75X TO 2X BASE HI
AP PRINT RUN 199 SER.#'d SETS
*GLOSSY: .6X TO 1.5X BASE HI
GLOSSY RANDOM INSERTS IN PACKS
1 Jerry West 1.25 3.00
2 John Havlicek 1.00 2.50
3 Bernard King 1.00 2.50
4 Glen Rice 1.00 2.50
5 Willis Reed 1.00 2.50
6 Detlef Schrempf 1.00 2.50
7 Dennis Rodman 1.50 4.00
8 Lenny Wilkens 1.00 2.50
9 Bob Cousy 1.50 4.00
10 Sleepy Floyd 1.00 2.50

2009-10 Panini Legends of the Game Signatures

RANDOM INSERTS IN PACKS
1 Jerry West 20.00 40.00
5 Willis Reed 8.00 20.00
8 Lenny Wilkens 6.00 15.00
10 Sleepy Floyd 6.00 15.00

2009-10 Panini Next Day Signatures

RANDOM INSERTS IN PACKS
2 B.J. Mullens 30.00 80.00
3 Blake Griffin 1200.00 2000.00
4 Brandon Jennings 100.00 200.00
5 Chase Budinger 30.00 80.00
6 DaJuan Summers 30.00 80.00
7 Darren Collison 50.00 125.00
8 DeJuan Blair 40.00 100.00
9 DeMarre Carroll 30.00 80.00
11 Eric Maynor 75.00 150.00
13 Hasheem Thabeet 30.00 80.00
14 James Harden 150.00 300.00
15 James Johnson 40.00 100.00
17 Jeff Teague 75.00 150.00
18 Jermaine Taylor 30.00 80.00
19 Jodie Meeks 75.00 150.00
20 Jonny Flynn 30.00 80.00
24 Rodrigue Beaubois 100.00 200.00
25 Sam Young 30.00 80.00
26 Stephen Curry 125.00 250.00
29 Terrence Williams 30.00 80.00
31 Ty Lawson 125.00 225.00
32 Tyler Hansbrough 100.00 200.00

2009-10 Panini The Franchise

COMPLETE SET (20) 10.00 25.00
RANDOM INSERTS IN PACKS
*AP: .75X TO 2X BASE HI
AP PRINT RUN 199 SER.#'d SETS
*GLOSSY: .6X TO 1.5X BASE HI
GLOSSY RANDOM INSERTS IN PACKS
1 Andre Iguodala .75 2.00
2 Carmelo Anthony 1.00 2.50
3 Chris Paul 1.25 3.00
4 Derrick Rose 2.50 6.00
5 Dirk Nowitzki 1.00 2.50
6 Dwight Howard 1.00 2.50
7 Dwyane Wade 1.50 4.00
8 Gerald Wallace .75 2.00
9 Josh Smith .75 2.00
10 Kevin Durant 2.50 6.00
11 Kevin Garnett 1.50 4.00
12 Kevin Martin .75 2.00
13 Kobe Bryant 4.00 10.00
14 LeBron James 4.00 10.00
15 Richard Hamilton .60 1.50
16 Rudy Gay .75 2.00
17 Stephen Jackson .60 1.50
18 Steve Nash .75 2.00
19 Tony Parker .75 2.00
20 Yao Ming 1.00 2.50

2010 Panini All-Star Game

These cards were distributed via a wrapper redemption during the NBA All-Star Jam Session in Dallas in February 2010. The card fronts feature the All-Star logo.
COMPLETE SET (14) 20.00 40.00
BG Blake Griffin 8.00 20.00
BJ Brandon Jennings 3.00 8.00
CP Chris Paul 1.00 2.50
DH Dwight Howard 1.00 2.50
DN Dirk Nowitzki 1.00 2.50
DW Dwyane Wade 1.25 3.00
KB Kobe Bryant 3.00 8.00
KD Kevin Durant 2.00 5.00
KG Kevin Garnett 1.00 2.50
LJ LeBron James 3.00 8.00
SN Steve Nash 1.00 2.50
TD Tim Duncan 1.00 2.50
TE Tyreke Evans 4.00 10.00
YM Yao Ming 1.00 2.50

2011 Panini Black Friday Autographs

Released in November 2011 as part of the Panini Black Friday promotion, these cards features autographs on some newly designed cards and/or previously issued items.
BJ Brandon Jennings Adrenalyn 10.00 25.00
KB Kobe Bryant Patch/30 100.00 200.00
OC Omri Casspi Adrenalyn 3.00 8.00

2010 Panini Century Sports Stamp Autographs

STATED PRINT RUN 5-100
NO PRICING ON QTY 25 OR LESS
12A Bill Walton/36 10.00 25.00
13A Bobby Wanzer/75 6.00 15.00
14A George Gervin/67 6.00 15.00
14B George Gervin/33 8.00 20.00
15A Kevin McHale/33 10.00 25.00
23A Al Cervi/65 6.00 15.00
23B Al Cervi/35 8.00 20.00
28A Elvin Hayes/30 10.00 25.00
29A Bailey Howell/50 10.00 25.00
30A Dan Issel/50 15.00 40.00
31A Clyde Lovellette/75 15.00 40.00
34A Arnie Risen/80 10.00 25.00
35A Dolph Schayes/75 8.00 20.00
36A David Thompson/75 10.00 25.00

2010 Panini Century Sports Stamp Materials

STATED PRINT RUN 1-250
NO PRICING ON QTY 25 OR LESS
2A O.J. Mayo/40 4.00 10.00
2B O.J. Mayo/40 29c 4.00 10.00
3A Derrick Rose/100 4c BK 8.00 20.00
3B Derrick Rose/250 29c 6.00 15.00
3C Derrick Rose/250 4c US Flag 6.00 15.00
4A Michael Beasley/250 4c 3.00 8.00
4B Michael Beasley/250 29c 3.00 8.00
11B Alex English/250 29c 3.00 8.00
17A Wes Unseld/125 4c 3.00 8.00
17B Wes Unseld/125 29c 3.00 8.00
27A Cliff Hagan/250 4c 3.00 8.00
27B Cliff Hagan/250 29c 3.00 8.00
28A Elvin Hayes/250 4c 3.00 8.00
28B Elvin Hayes/250 29c 3.00 8.00
29A Bailey Howell/150 4c 3.00 8.00
29B Bailey Howell/150 29c 3.00 8.00
30A Dan Issel/250 4c 3.00 8.00
30B Dan Issel/250 29c 3.00 8.00
32A Robert Parish/50 4c 5.00 12.00
32B Robert Parish/50 29c 5.00 12.00

2010 Panini Century Sports Stamp Materials Autographs

STATED PRINT RUN 2-50
NO PRICING ON QTY 25 OR LESS
27B Cliff Hagan/40 15.00 40.00

2012 Panini Father's Day

RANDOM INSERTS IN FATHER'S DAY PACKS
CRACKED ICE/25: 5X TO 12X BASE HI
1 Kobe Bryant 1.00 2.50
2 Blake Griffin .60 1.50
3 Kevin Durant .75 2.00
4 John Wall .50 1.25
5 Dirk Nowitzki 1.25 1.00
6 Derrick Rose .75 2.00

2012 Panini Father's Day Draft Day Hats

RANDOM INSERTS IN FATHERS DAY PACKS
1 DeMarcus Cousins 8.00 20.00
2 Cole Aldrich 4.00 10.00
3 Derrick Favors 6.00 15.00
4 Ekpe Udoh 4.00 10.00
5 Evan Turner 6.00 15.00
6 Gordon Hayward 6.00 15.00
7 Greg Monroe 6.00 15.00
8 Paul George 6.00 15.00
9 Wesley Johnson 5.00 12.00
10 Xavier Henry 5.00 12.00
BG Blake Griffin 12.00 30.00

2012 Panini Father's Day Elements

RANDOM INSERTS IN FATHERS DAY PACKS
CRACKED ICE/25: 5X TO 12X BASE HI
9 Kobe Bryant 1.00 2.50
10 Blake Griffin .60 1.50

2012 Panini Father's Day Kobe Bryant Shoes

RANDOM INSERTS IN FATHERS DAY PACKS
KB1 Kobe Bryant 40.00 70.00
KB2 Kobe Bryant 40.00 70.00

2012 Panini Father's Day Legends

RANDOM INSERTS IN FATHERS DAY PACKS
CRACKED ICE/25: 5X TO 12X BASE HI
3 Larry Bird .75 2.00
4 Magic Johnson .60 1.50

2012 Panini Father's Day NBA Finals Memorabilia

RANDOM INSERTS IN FATHERS DAY PACKS
1 Dirk Nowitzki 20.00 50.00
2 Jason Kidd 20.00 50.00
3 Jason Terry 20.00 50.00
4 LeBron James 50.00 120.00
5 Dwyane Wade 40.00 100.00
MVP Dirk Nowitzki 40.00 100.00
NNO Net Card 50.00 120.00

2012 Panini Father's Day Rookie of the Year Jerseys

RANDOM INSERTS IN FATHERS DAY PACKS
3 Blake Griffin 20.00 50.00

2012 Panini Father's Day Season Highlights

RANDOM INSERTS IN FATHERS DAY PACKS
CRACKED ICE/25: 5X TO 12X BASE HI
1 Kobe Bryant 1.00 2.50
2 Kevin Durant .75 2.00
3 Kevin Durant .75 2.00

2010-11 Panini Gold Standard

STATED PRINT RUN 299 SER.#'d SETS
EWING, MARAVICH, RODMAN HAVE VAR
ALL VAR STILL TOTAL JUST 299 CARDS
UNPRICED BLACK GOLD PRINT RUN ONE SET
EXCH EXPIRATION 1/14/2013
1 Kevin Durant 4.00 10.00
2 Kobe Bryant 6.00 15.00
3 Derrick Rose 4.00 10.00
4 Paul Pierce 1.50 4.00
5 Ty Lawson 1.25 3.00
6 Amare Stoudemire 1.25 3.00
7 Deron Williams 1.25 3.00
8 Blake Griffin 3.00 8.00
9 Kevin Love 1.50 4.00
10 Russell Westbrook 1.50 4.00
11 Monta Ellis 1.25 3.00
12 Tim Duncan 2.00 5.00
13 Steve Nash 1.50 4.00
14 Jrue Holiday 1.25 3.00
15 Kevin Martin 1.25 3.00
16 Dirk Nowitzki 1.50 4.00
17 Stephen Jackson 1.00 2.50
18 LeBron James 6.00 15.00
19 Eric Gordon 1.25 3.00
20 Tayshaun Prince 1.25 3.00
21 Derek Fisher 1.00 2.50
22 Vince Carter 1.50 4.00
23 Antawn Jamison 1.25 3.00
24 Tyreke Evans 1.50 4.00
25 Al Horford 1.00 2.50
26 Danny Granger 1.25 3.00
27 Marcus Camby .75 2.00
28 Rajon Rondo 1.50 4.00
29 Carmelo Anthony 1.50 4.00
30 Michael Beasley 1.25 3.00
31 Dwight Howard 2.00 5.00
32 Tony Parker 1.25 3.00
33 Chris Bosh 1.25 3.00
34 LaMarcus Aldridge 1.25 3.00
35 Stephen Curry 1.50 4.00
36 Brook Lopez 1.25 3.00
37 Tyson Chandler 1.00 2.50
38 Jason Richardson 1.25 3.00
39 Anderson Varejao 1.00 2.50
40 Andre Iguodala 1.25 3.00
41 Marc Gasol 1.25 3.00
42 Danilo Gallinari 1.25 3.00
43 Joe Johnson 1.25 3.00
44 DeMar DeRozan 1.25 3.00
45 Devin Harris 1.25 3.00
46 Andrei Kirilenko 1.00 2.50
47 Brandon Roy 1.25 3.00
48 Raymond Felton 1.00 2.50
49 Pau Gasol 1.25 3.00
50 Dwyane Wade 2.50 6.00
51 Aaron Brooks .75 2.00
52 Zach Randolph 1.00 2.50
53 Jason Terry 1.00 2.50
54 Charlie Villanueva 1.00 2.50
55 Jeff Green 1.00 2.50
56 Channing Frye 1.00 2.50
57 Al Thornton 1.00 2.50
58 Manu Ginobili 1.25 3.00
59 David West 1.25 3.00
60 Andrew Bogut 1.25 3.00
61 Jonny Flynn .75 2.00
62 David Lee 1.25 3.00
63 Tracy McGrady 1.25 3.00
64 Luol Deng 1.25 3.00
65 Elton Brand 1.25 3.00
66 Emeka Okafor 1.00 2.50
67 Kevin Garnett 2.50 6.00
68 Carl Landry .75 2.00
69 Jameer Nelson 1.00 2.50
70 Joakim Noah 1.25 3.00
71 Chris Kaman 1.00 2.50
72 Rudy Gay 1.25 3.00
73 Richard Jefferson 1.00 2.50
74 Andrea Bargnani 1.00 2.50
75 Jamal Crawford 1.00 2.50
76 Grant Hill 3.00 8.00
77 Lamar Odom 1.25 3.00
78 Paul Millsap 1.00 2.50
79 Luis Scola 1.00 2.50
80 J.R. Smith 1.25 3.00
81 Ray Allen 1.25 3.00
82 Tyler Hansbrough 1.25 3.00
83 Ben Wallace 1.25 3.00
84 J.J. Hickson 1.00 2.50
85 Al Jefferson 1.25 3.00
86 Jason Kidd 1.25 3.00
87 Luke Ridnour 1.00 2.50
88 Nene 1.00 2.50
89 Sasha Vujacic .75 2.00
90 Rashard Lewis 1.25 3.00
91 D.J. Augustin 1.00 2.50
92 Ron Artest 1.25 3.00
93 Yao Ming 1.50 4.00
94 Juwan Howard 1.00 2.50
95 Roy Hibbert 1.00 2.50
96 Carlos Boozer 1.25 3.00
97 Wilson Chandler 1.00 2.50
98 DeJuan Blair 1.00 2.50
99 Shaquille O'Neal 2.50 6.00
100 Chris Paul 2.00 5.00
101 Baron Davis 1.25 3.00
102 Leandro Barbosa 1.00 2.50
103 Josh Smith 1.25 3.00
104 John Salmons 1.25 3.00
105 Hedo Turkoglu 1.25 3.00
106 Ben Gordon 1.25 3.00
107 Gerald Henderson .75 2.00
108 Serge Ibaka 1.50 4.00
109 Shane Battier 1.00 2.50
110 Andrew Bynum 1.50 4.00
111 Chauncey Billups 1.25 3.00
112 Nick Young 1.00 2.50
113 Dorell Wright .75 2.00
114 Gilbert Arenas 1.25 3.00
115 Darko Milicic .75 2.00
116 Caron Butler 1.25 3.00
117 Zydrunas Ilgauskas .75 2.00
118 Trevor Ariza .75 2.00
119 Troy Murphy .75 2.00
120 J.J. Redick 1.25 3.00
121 Gerald Wallace 1.25 3.00
122 Samuel Dalembert .75 2.00
123 Shawn Marion 1.25 3.00
124 Rudy Fernandez 1.00 2.50
125 Brandon Jennings 1.25 3.00
126 JaVale McGee 1.00 2.50
127 O.J. Mayo 1.25 3.00
128 James Harden 1.50 4.00
129 Chris Andersen 1.25 3.00
130 Toney Douglas .75 2.00
131 Glen Davis 1.00 2.50
132 Richard Hamilton 1.00 2.50
133 George Hill 1.00 2.50
134 Louis Williams 1.00 2.50
135 Al Harrington 1.00 2.50
136 Anthony Morrow .75 2.00
137 Daniel Gibson 1.00 2.50
138 Wesley Matthews 1.25 3.00
139 Kris Humphries .75 2.00
140 Rodrigue Beaubois 1.00 2.50
141 A.J. Price .75 2.00
142 Chase Budinger .75 2.00
143 Donte Greene .75 2.00
144 Andre Miller 1.00 2.50
145 Ryan Gomes .75 2.00
146 Jodie Meeks 1.25 3.00
147 Kendrick Perkins 1.00 2.50
148 Taj Gibson 1.00 2.50
149 Boris Diaw 1.00 2.50
150 Derrick Brown .75 2.00
151 Jeff Teague 1.00 2.50
152 Wayne Ellington .75 2.00
153 Terrence Williams .75 2.00
154 Robin Lopez .75 2.00
155 Jermaine O'Neal 1.25 3.00
156 Austin Daye 1.25 3.00
157 J.J. Barea 1.25 3.00
158 Darren Collison 1.25 3.00
159 Goran Dragic 1.25 3.00
160 Beno Udrih .75 2.00
161 Earl Clark .75 2.00
162 Hakim Warrick 1.00 2.50
163 Sam Young 1.25 3.00
164 Ronnie Brewer 1.00 2.50
165 Omri Casspi .75 2.00
166 T.J. Ford .75 2.00
167 Chris Douglas-Roberts .75 2.00
168 Eric Maynor .75 2.00
169 James Johnson 1.25 3.00
170 Patrick Mills 1.00 2.50
171 Mark Jackson 1.50 4.00
172 Chris Webber 1.50 4.00
173 Derek Harper 1.50 4.00
174A Patrick Ewing Knicks 2.00 5.00
174B Patrick Ewing Magic SP
174C Patrick Ewing Sonics SP
175 Brad Daugherty 1.50 4.00
176 Kenny Anderson 1.50 4.00
177 Scott Skiles 1.50 4.00
178 Charles Oakley 1.50 4.00
179 Dan Majerle 1.50 4.00
180A Pete Maravich Hawks 5.00 12.00
180B Pete Maravich Celtics SP
180C Pete Maravich Jazz SP 6.00 15.00
181 Wilt Chamberlain 3.00 8.00
182 Horace Grant 1.50 4.00
183 Glen Rice 1.50 4.00
184 Shawn Kemp 2.50 6.00
185 Jo Jo White 1.50 4.00
186 Jalen Rose 1.50 4.00
187A Dennis Rodman Pistons 6.00 15.00
187B Dennis Rodman Bulls SP 6.00 15.00
187C Dennis Rodman Lakers SP 6.00 15.00
187D Dennis Rodman Mavericks SP
187E Dennis Rodman Spurs SP 6.00 15.00
188 Dave DeBusschere 1.50 4.00
189 Oscar Robertson 2.00 5.00
190 Bill Walton 1.50 4.00
191 Kareem Abdul-Jabbar 2.50 6.00
192 Larry Bird 5.00 12.00
193 Dan Issel 1.50 4.00
194 Doc Rivers 1.50 4.00
195 George McGinnis 1.50 4.00
196 Bill Russell 2.50 6.00
197 Christian Laettner 2.00 5.00
198 Dolph Schayes 1.50 4.00
199 M.L. Carr 1.50 4.00
200 Darryl Dawkins 1.50 4.00
201 David Thompson 2.00 5.00
202 Bob Lanier 1.50 4.00
203 Michael Cooper 1.50 4.00
204 Bernard King 1.50 4.00
205 Bailey Howell 1.50 4.00
206 Al Attles 1.50 4.00
207 Dikembe Mutombo 1.50 4.00
208 Bob McAdoo 1.50 4.00
209 Artis Gilmore 1.50 4.00
210 A.C. Green 1.50 4.00
211 Dominique Wilkins 2.00 5.00
212 Alonzo Mourning 2.00 5.00
213 John Wall AU RC 50.00 125.00
214 Evan Turner AU RC 12.00 30.00
215 Derrick Favors AU RC 12.00 30.00
216 Wesley Johnson AU RC 20.00 50.00
217 DeMarcus Cousins AU RC 20.00 50.00
218 Ekpe Udoh AU RC 6.00 15.00
219 Greg Monroe AU RC 12.00 30.00
220 Al-Farouq Aminu AU RC 6.00 15.00
221 Gordon Hayward AU RC 12.00 30.00
222 Paul George AU RC 15.00 40.00
223 Cole Aldrich AU RC 6.00 15.00
224 Xavier Henry AU RC 8.00 20.00
225 Ed Davis AU RC 8.00 20.00
226 Patrick Patterson AU RC 10.00 25.00
227 Larry Sanders AU RC 6.00 15.00
228 Luke Babbitt AU RC 6.00 15.00
229 Kevin Seraphin AU RC 8.00 20.00
230 Eric Bledsoe AU RC 10.00 25.00
231 Avery Bradley AU RC 12.00 30.00
232 James Anderson AU RC 6.00 15.00
233 Elliot Williams AU RC EXCH 6.00 15.00
234 Landry Fields AU RC 10.00 25.00
235 Greivis Vasquez AU RC 8.00 20.00
236 Dominique Jones AU RC 6.00 15.00
237 Gary Neal AU RC 10.00 25.00
238 Daniel Orton AU RC 6.00 15.00
239 Lazar Hayward AU RC 6.00 15.00
240 Devin Ebanks AU RC 8.00 20.00
241 Timofey Mozgov AU RC 6.00 15.00
242 Luke Harangody AU RC 6.00 15.00
243 Omer Asik AU RC 8.00 20.00
244 Eugene Jeter AU RC 6.00 15.00
245 Gary Forbes AU RC 6.00 15.00
246 Nikola Pekovic AU RC EXCH 10.00 25.00
247 Jordan Crawford AU RC 10.00 25.00

2010-11 Panini Gold Standard Platinum Gold

*STARS: 1.5X TO 4X BASE HI
*RETIRED: 1.25X TO 3X BASE HI
*ROOKIES: .75X TO 2X BASE HI
STATED PRINT RUN 25 SER.#'d SETS
76 Grant Hill 15.00 40.00
184 Shawn Kemp 30.00 80.00
212 Alonzo Mourning 12.00 30.00
213 John Wall AU 150.00 300.00
214 Evan Turner AU 30.00 80.00
215 Derrick Favors AU 30.00 80.00
217 DeMarcus Cousins AU 50.00 125.00
230 Eric Bledsoe AU 25.00 60.00

2010-11 Panini Gold Standard 24-Karat Kobe

COMMON CARD (1-15) 5.00 12.00
STATED PRINT RUN 299 SER.#'d SETS
UNPRICED GOLD RUSH PRINT RUN ONE SET

2010-11 Panini Gold Standard 24-Karat Kobe Materials Signatures

COMMON CARD 100.00 200.00
STATED PRINT RUN 49 SER.#'d SETS

2010-11 Panini Gold Standard 24-Karat Kobe Materials Signatures Prime

COMMON CARD 150.00 300.00
STATED PRINT RUN 24 SER.#'d SETS

2010-11 Panini Gold Standard 24-Karat Kobe Signatures

COMMON CARD 100.00 200.00
STATED PRINT RUN 49 SER.#'d SETS

2010-11 Panini Gold Standard Gold Bars

STATED PRINT RUN 299 SER.#'d SETS
UNPRICED GOLD RUSH PRINT RUN 10 SETS
1 Kevin Durant 5.00 12.00
2 Dwight Howard 2.50 6.00
3 Dwyane Wade 3.00 8.00
4 Kobe Bryant 8.00 20.00
5 LaMarcus Aldridge 1.50 4.00
6 Brandon Jennings 1.50 4.00
7 Kevin Garnett 3.00 8.00
8 Eric Gordon 1.50 4.00
9 Deron Williams 1.50 4.00
10 Kevin Love 2.00 5.00
11 Monta Ellis 1.50 4.00
12 Carmelo Anthony 1.50 4.00
13 Chris Paul 2.50 6.00
14 Kevin Martin 1.50 4.00
15 Derrick Rose 5.00 12.00

2010-11 Panini Gold Standard Gold Bars Materials

STATED PRINT RUN 199 SER.#'d SETS
1 Kevin Durant 8.00 20.00
2 Dwight Howard 5.00 12.00
3 Dwyane Wade 6.00 15.00
4 Kobe Bryant 10.00 25.00
5 LaMarcus Aldridge 3.00 8.00
6 Brandon Jennings 3.00 8.00
7 Kevin Garnett 6.00 15.00
8 Eric Gordon 3.00 8.00
10 Kevin Love 4.00 10.00
11 Monta Ellis 3.00 8.00
13 Chris Paul 5.00 12.00
15 Derrick Rose 10.00 25.00

2010-11 Panini Gold Standard Gold Bars Materials Prime

*PRIME: .75X TO 2X BASE HI
STATED PRINT RUN ONE TO 25 SER.#'d SETS
SOME UNPRICED DUE TO SCARCITY
1 Kevin Durant/25 20.00 50.00

2010-11 Panini Gold Standard Gold Bars Materials Signatures

STATED PRINT RUN 5 TO 49 SER.#'d SETS
SOME UNPRICED DUE TO SCARCITY
4 Kobe Bryant/24 100.00 200.00
5 LaMarcus Aldridge/49 8.00 20.00
8 Eric Gordon/49 10.00 25.00
10 Kevin Love/49 20.00 50.00

2010-11 Panini Gold Standard Gold Bars Materials Signatures Prime

STATED PRINT RUN ONE TO 25 SER.#'d SETS
SOME UNPRICED DUE TO SCARCITY
5 LaMarcus Aldridge/25 12.50 30.00
10 Kevin Love/25 25.00 60.00

2010-11 Panini Gold Standard Gold Bars Signatures

STATED PRINT RUN 5 TO 49 SER.#'d SETS
SOME UNPRICED DUE TO SCARCITY
4 Kobe Bryant/24 100.00 200.00
5 LaMarcus Aldridge/49 6.00 15.00
8 Eric Gordon/40 10.00 25.00
10 Kevin Love/25 15.00 40.00
14 Kevin Martin/49 6.00 15.00

2010-11 Panini Gold Standard Gold Crowns

STATED PRINT RUN 299 SER.#'d SETS
UNPRICED GOLD RUSH PRINT RUN 8 SETS
1 Kevin Durant 4.00 10.00
2 Dwight Howard 2.00 5.00
3 Stephen Curry 1.50 4.00
4 Amare Stoudemire 1.25 3.00
5 Rajon Rondo 1.50 4.00
6 Kevin Love 1.50 4.00
7 Andrew Bogut 1.25 3.00
8 Chris Paul 2.00 5.00
9 Steve Nash 1.25 3.00
10 Kobe Bryant 6.00 15.00
11 Serge Ibaka 1.50 4.00
12 Deron Williams 1.25 3.00
13 Luke Ridnour 1.00 2.50
14 Monta Ellis 1.25 3.00
15 LeBron James 6.00 15.00
16 JaVale McGee 1.00 2.50
17 Emeka Okafor 1.25 3.00
18 Chauncey Billups 1.25 3.00
19 Raymond Felton 1.00 2.50
20 Tyson Chandler 1.00 2.50
21 Russell Westbrook 1.50 4.00
22 Dwyane Wade 2.50 6.00
23 Tim Duncan 2.00 5.00
24 Jose Calderon 1.00 2.50
25 Pau Gasol 1.25 3.00

2010-11 Panini Gold Standard Gold Crowns Materials

STATED PRINT RUN 99 TO 249 SER.#'d SETS
1 Kevin Durant/249 10.00 25.00
2 Dwight Howard/249 6.00 15.00
3 Stephen Curry/99 5.00 12.00
4 Amare Stoudemire/249 4.00 10.00
5 Rajon Rondo/249 5.00 12.00
6 Kevin Love/249 5.00 12.00
7 Andrew Bogut/249 4.00 10.00
8 Chris Paul/249 6.00 15.00
9 Steve Nash/249 4.00 10.00
10 Kobe Bryant/249 10.00 25.00
11 Serge Ibaka/249 5.00 12.00
13 Luke Ridnour/249 3.00 8.00
14 Monta Ellis/249 4.00 10.00
15 LeBron James/249 10.00 25.00
16 JaVale McGee/249 3.00 8.00
17 Emeka Okafor/249 4.00 10.00
20 Tyson Chandler/249 3.00 8.00
21 Russell Westbrook/249 5.00 12.00
22 Dwyane Wade/249 8.00 20.00
23 Tim Duncan/249 6.00 15.00
24 Jose Calderon/249 3.00 8.00
25 Pau Gasol/249 4.00 10.00

2010-11 Panini Gold Standard Gold Crowns Materials Prime

*PRIME: .6X TO 1.5X BASE HI
STATED PRINT RUN ONE TO 25 SER.#'d SETS
SOME UNPRICED DUE TO SCARCITY
1 Kevin Durant/25 20.00 50.00
9 Steve Nash/25 8.00 20.00
15 LeBron James/25 25.00 60.00
22 Dwyane Wade/25 20.00 50.00

2010-11 Panini Gold Standard Gold Crowns Materials Signatures

STATED PRINT RUN 5 TO 199 SER.#'d SETS
SOME UNPRICED DUE TO SCARCITY
3 Stephen Curry/199 10.00 25.
5 Rajon Rondo/25 20.00 50.
6 Kevin Love/49 12.50 30.
7 Andrew Bogut/199 6.00 15.
10 Kobe Bryant/24 100.00 200.
11 Serge Ibaka/199 10.00 25.
13 Luke Ridnour/199 4.00 10.
16 JaVale McGee/199 5.00 12.
17 Emeka Okafor/25 5.00 12.
20 Tyson Chandler/199 5.00 12.

2010-11 Panini Gold Standard Gold Crowns Materials Signatures Prime

STATED PRINT RUN 3 TO 25 SER.#'d SETS
SOME UNPRICED DUE TO SCARCITY
3 Stephen Curry/25 15.00 40.
5 Rajon Rondo/25 25.00 60.
6 Kevin Love/25 20.00 50.
7 Andrew Bogut/25 12.50 30.
10 Kobe Bryant/24 150.00 300.
11 Serge Ibaka/25 20.00 50.
13 Luke Ridnour/25 8.00 20.
16 JaVale McGee/25 8.00 20.
17 Emeka Okafor/25 8.00 20.
20 Tyson Chandler/25 10.00 25.
21 Russell Westbrook/25 30.00 80.

2010-11 Panini Gold Standard Gold Crowns Signatures

STATED PRINT RUN 5 TO 69 SER.#'d SETS
SOME UNPRICED DUE TO SCARCITY
3 Stephen Curry/69 10.00 25
5 Rajon Rondo/25 15.00 40
6 Kevin Love/49 12.00 30
10 Kobe Bryant/49 100.00 200
11 Serge Ibaka/69 4.00 10
13 Luke Ridnour/69 4.00 10
16 JaVale McGee/69 4.00 10
17 Emeka Okafor/49 4.00 10
18 Chauncey Billups/25 6.00 15
19 Raymond Felton/69 4.00 10
20 Tyson Chandler/49 5.00 12

2010-11 Panini Gold Standard Gold Medalists

STATED PRINT RUN 299 SER.#'d SETS
UNPRICED GOLD RUSH PRINT RUN 10 SETS
1 Dwight Howard 2.50 6
2 Tayshaun Prince 1.50 4
3 Michael Redd 1.50 4
4 LeBron James 8.00 20
5 Dwyane Wade 3.00 8

6 Jason Kidd 1.50 4.00
7 Carlos Boozer 1.50 4.00
8 Chris Bosh 1.50 4.00
9 Chris Paul 2.50 6.00
10 Kevin Garnett 3.00 8.00
11 Larry Johnson 2.00 5.00
12 Mark Price 1.50 4.00
13 Shaquille O'Neal 3.00 8.00
14 Steve Smith 1.50 4.00
15 Dan Majerle 1.50 4.00
16 Dominique Wilkins 2.00 5.00
17 Joe Dumars 1.50 4.00
18 Kevin Johnson 1.50 4.00
19 Alonzo Mourning 3.00 8.00
20 David Robinson 3.00 8.00

2010-11 Panini Gold Standard Gold Medalists Materials

STATED PRINT RUN 299 SER.#'d SETS
1 Dwight Howard 6.00 15.00
2 Tayshaun Prince 4.00 10.00
3 Michael Redd 4.00 10.00
4 LeBron James 12.00 30.00
5 Dwyane Wade 8.00 20.00
6 Jason Kidd 4.00 10.00
7 Carlos Boozer 4.00 10.00
8 Chris Bosh 4.00 10.00
9 Chris Paul 6.00 15.00
10 Kevin Garnett 8.00 20.00
11 Larry Johnson 5.00 12.00
12 Mark Price 5.00 12.00
13 Shaquille O'Neal 8.00 20.00
14 Steve Smith 4.00 10.00
15 Dan Majerle 4.00 10.00
16 Dominique Wilkins 5.00 12.00
17 Joe Dumars 4.00 10.00
18 Kevin Johnson 4.00 10.00
19 Alonzo Mourning 5.00 12.00

2010-11 Panini Gold Standard Gold Medalists Materials Prime

*PRIME: 1X TO 2.5X BASE HI
STATED PRINT RUN 25 SER.#'d SETS
4 LeBron James 50.00 125.00
5 Dwyane Wade 40.00 100.00
6 Jason Kidd 20.00 50.00
8 Chris Bosh 12.50 30.00
11 Larry Johnson 30.00 80.00
13 Shaquille O'Neal 40.00 100.00
15 Dan Majerle 15.00 40.00
16 Dominique Wilkins 15.00 40.00
17 Joe Dumars 25.00 60.00
18 Kevin Johnson 20.00 50.00
19 Alonzo Mourning 30.00 80.00
20 David Robinson 30.00 80.00

2010-11 Panini Gold Standard Gold Medalists Materials Signatures

STATED PRINT RUN 10 TO 99 SER.#'d SETS
SOME UNPRICED DUE TO SCARCITY
Carlos Boozer/49 10.00 25.00
Larry Johnson/99 25.00 60.00
Mark Price/49 40.00 100.00
Steve Smith/99 10.00 25.00
Dan Majerle/49 15.00 40.00
Joe Dumars/25 25.00 60.00
Kevin Johnson/49 20.00 50.00

2010-11 Panini Gold Standard Gold Medalists Materials Signatures Prime

STATED PRINT RUN 5 TO 25 SER.#'d SETS
SOME UNPRICED DUE TO SCARCITY
Carlos Boozer/25 20.00 50.00
Larry Johnson/25 60.00 150.00
Mark Price/25 60.00 150.00
Steve Smith/25 30.00 80.00
Dan Majerle/25 20.00 50.00
Joe Dumars/25 30.00 80.00
Kevin Johnson/25 50.00 120.00

2010-11 Panini Gold Standard Gold Medalists Signatures

STATED PRINT RUN 10 TO 199 SER.#'d SETS
SOME UNPRICED DUE TO SCARCITY
Carlos Boozer/49 6.00 15.00
Mark Price/199 12.50 30.00
Steve Smith/49 10.00 25.00
Dan Majerle/199 10.00 25.00
Joe Dumars/25 20.00 50.00
Kevin Johnson/49 15.00 40.00

2010-11 Panini Gold Standard Gold Medalists Signatures Dual

STATED PRINT RUN 5 TO 50 SER.#'d SETS
SOME UNPRICED DUE TO SCARCITY
ron Davis/50 15.00 40.00
ussell Westbrook
uggsy Bogues/50 15.00 40.00
nny Flynn
alt Bellamy/50 10.00 25.00
son Chandler
ke Bibby/50 15.00 40.00
ephen Curry
ry West/25 125.00 250.00
be Bryant
vin Love/35 30.00 80.00
ce Carter
eron Williams/35 20.00 50.00
c Gordon
hris Mullin/50 30.00 80.00
ristian Laettner
ominique Wilkins/35 30.00 80.00
n Majerle
lyde Drexler/25 60.00 150.00
minique Wilkins
iah Thomas/50 25.00 60.00
n Elliott

2010-11 Panini Gold Standard Gold Mining

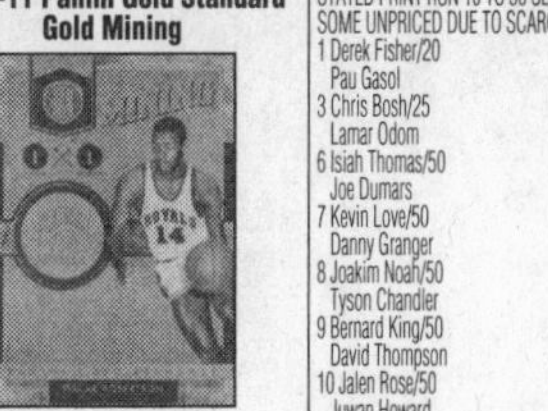

STATED PRINT RUN 299 SER.#'d SETS
UNPRICED GOLD RUSH PRINT RUN 8 SETS
1 Chris Paul 2.00 5.00
2 Bernard King 1.25 3.00
3 Derrick Rose 4.00 10.00
4 Blake Griffin 3.00 8.00
5 Magic Johnson 3.00 8.00
6 Tim Duncan 2.00 5.00
7 Kobe Bryant 6.00 15.00
8 Kareem Abdul-Jabbar 2.00 5.00
9 Stephen Curry 1.50 4.00
10 Dwyane Wade 2.50 6.00
11 Amare Stoudemire 1.25 3.00
12 Oscar Robertson 1.50 4.00
13 Chris Bosh 1.25 3.00
14 Dirk Nowitzki 1.50 4.00
15 Derek Fisher 1.00 2.50
16 Larry Bird 4.00 10.00
17 Kevin Love 1.50 4.00
18 Wilt Chamberlain 2.50 6.00
19 Kevin Durant 4.00 10.00
20 LeBron James 6.00 15.00

2010-11 Panini Gold Standard Gold Mining Materials

STATED PRINT RUN 49 TO 299 SER.#'d SETS
1 Chris Paul/299 5.00 12.00
2 Bernard King/299 3.00 8.00
4 Blake Griffin/299 8.00 20.00
5 Magic Johnson/99 10.00 25.00
6 Tim Duncan/299 5.00 12.00
7 Kobe Bryant/299 10.00 25.00
9 Stephen Curry/99 4.00 10.00
10 Dwyane Wade/299 6.00 15.00
11 Amare Stoudemire/299 3.00 8.00
13 Chris Bosh/299 3.00 8.00
14 Dirk Nowitzki/299 4.00 10.00
15 Derek Fisher/299 2.50 6.00
16 Larry Bird/49 10.00 25.00
17 Kevin Love/299 4.00 10.00
19 Kevin Durant/299 6.00 15.00
20 LeBron James/299 10.00 25.00

2010-11 Panini Gold Standard Gold Mining Materials Prime

*PRIME: .75X TO 2X BASE HI
STATED PRINT RUN ONE TO 25 SER.#'d SETS
SOME UNPRICED DUE TO SCARCITY
14 Dirk Nowitzki/25 12.00 30.00
15 Derek Fisher/25 8.00 20.00
19 Kevin Durant/25 20.00 50.00
20 LeBron James/25 25.00 60.00

2010-11 Panini Gold Standard Gold Mining Materials Signatures

STATED PRINT RUN 3 TO 49 SER.#'d SETS
SOME UNPRICED DUE TO SCARCITY
2 Bernard King/49 6.00 15.00
7 Kobe Bryant/24 100.00 200.00
9 Stephen Curry/49 10.00 25.00
15 Derek Fisher/49 10.00 25.00

2010-11 Panini Gold Standard Gold Mining Materials Signatures Prime

STATED PRINT RUN 3 TO 25 SER.#'d SETS
SOME UNPRICED DUE TO SCARCITY
2 Bernard King/25 15.00 40.00
7 Kobe Bryant/24 150.00 300.00
9 Stephen Curry/25 15.00 40.00
15 Derek Fisher/25 20.00 50.00

2010-11 Panini Gold Standard Gold Mining Signatures

STATED PRINT RUN 3 TO 99 SER.#'d SETS
SOME UNPRICED DUE TO SCARCITY
2 Bernard King/99 5.00 12.00
7 Kobe Bryant/24 100.00 200.00
9 Stephen Curry/99 10.00 25.00
15 Derek Fisher/99 10.00 25.00
17 Kevin Love/25 15.00 40.00

2010-11 Panini Gold Standard Gold Mining Signatures Dual

STATED PRINT RUN 10 TO 50 SER.#'d SETS
SOME UNPRICED DUE TO SCARCITY
1 Derek Fisher/20 20.00 50.00
Pau Gasol
3 Chris Bosh/25 25.00 60.00
Lamar Odom
6 Isiah Thomas/50 20.00 50.00
Joe Dumars
7 Kevin Love/50 15.00 40.00
Danny Granger
8 Joakim Noah/50 15.00 40.00
Tyson Chandler
9 Bernard King/50 12.50 30.00
David Thompson
10 Jalen Rose/50 12.50 30.00
Juwan Howard

2010-11 Panini Gold Standard Gold NBA Logos

STATED PRINT RUN 5 TO 199 SER.#'d SETS
SOME UNPRICED DUE TO SCARCITY
1 Al Attles/199 6.00 15.00
2 Alex English/199 6.00 15.00
5 Artis Gilmore/199 8.00 20.00
7 Bill Walton/99 10.00 25.00
10 Connie Hawkins/199 8.00 20.00
11 Dave Cowens/99 8.00 20.00
14 Dolph Schayes/99 8.00 20.00
16 Elvin Hayes/99 10.00 25.00
17 Gail Goodrich/99 10.00 25.00
19 George Gervin/99 10.00 25.00
20 Isiah Thomas/99 12.00 30.00
21 Jack Twyman/199 8.00 20.00
22 Jalen Rose/199 6.00 15.00
24 Jeff Hornacek/199 8.00 20.00
30 Kelly Tripucka/199 6.00 15.00
32 Kobe Bryant/99 100.00 200.00
34 Lenny Wilkens/99 8.00 20.00
36 Michael Beasley/25 12.00 30.00
38 Nate Archibald/99 8.00 20.00
41 Rick Barry/199 8.00 20.00
42 Robert Horry/199 10.00 25.00
43 Robert Parish/199 8.00 20.00
44 Rolando Blackman/199 6.00 15.00
45 Sam Perkins/199 8.00 20.00
47 Stephen Curry/199 12.00 30.00
49 Tyreke Evans/25 15.00 40.00
50 Walt Frazier/25 20.00 50.00

2010-11 Panini Gold Standard Gold Nuggets

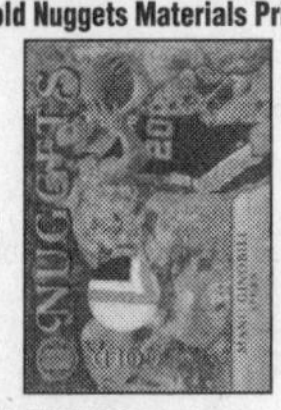

STATED PRINT RUN 299 SER.#'d SETS
UNPRICED GOLD RUSH PRINT RUN 10 SETS
1 LeBron James 6.00 15.00
2 Kobe Bryant 6.00 15.00
3 Blake Griffin 3.00 8.00
4 Kevin Durant 4.00 10.00
5 Paul Pierce 1.50 4.00
6 Dirk Nowitzki 1.50 4.00
7 Derrick Rose 4.00 10.00
8 Kevin Love 1.50 4.00
9 Tyreke Evans 1.50 4.00
10 Carmelo Anthony 1.50 4.00
11 Amare Stoudemire 1.25 3.00
12 Dwyane Wade 2.50 6.00
13 Deron Williams 1.25 3.00
14 LaMarcus Aldridge 1.25 3.00
15 Rajon Rondo 1.50 4.00
16 Russell Westbrook 1.50 4.00
17 Brandon Jennings 1.25 3.00
18 Eric Gordon 1.25 3.00
19 Pau Gasol 1.25 3.00
20 Steve Nash 1.25 3.00
21 Al Jefferson 1.25 3.00
22 D.J. Augustin 1.00 2.50
23 Raymond Felton 1.00 2.50
24 Kevin Garnett 2.50 6.00
25 Aaron Brooks .75 2.00
26 Chris Paul 2.00 5.00
27 Tim Duncan 2.00 5.00
28 Monta Ellis 1.25 3.00
29 Tracy McGrady 1.25 3.00
30 Dwight Howard 2.00 5.00
31 Andrea Bargnani 1.00 2.50
32 Antawn Jamison 1.25 3.00
33 Joe Johnson 1.25 3.00
34 Lamar Odom 1.25 3.00
35 Tyson Chandler 1.00 2.50
36 Andre Miller 1.00 2.50
37 Devin Harris 1.25 3.00
38 Roy Hibbert 1.00 2.50
39 Rudy Gay 1.25 3.00
40 David West 1.25 3.00
41 Kevin Martin 1.25 3.00
42 Jameer Nelson 1.00 2.50
43 Nene 1.00 2.50
44 Al Horford 1.00 2.50
45 Manu Ginobili 1.25 3.00
46 Shaquille O'Neal 2.50 6.00
47 Stephen Curry 1.50 4.00
48 Jeff Green 1.00 2.50
49 Joakim Noah 1.25 3.00
50 Jason Richardson 1.25 3.00

2010-11 Panini Gold Standard Gold Nuggets Materials

STATED PRINT RUN 49 TO 199 SER.#'d SETS
1 LeBron James/199 10.00 25.00
2 Kobe Bryant/199 10.00 25.00
3 Blake Griffin/199 8.00 20.00
4 Kevin Durant/199 10.00 25.00
5 Paul Pierce/199 4.00 10.00
6 Dirk Nowitzki/199 4.00 10.00
7 Derrick Rose/199 10.00 25.00
8 Kevin Love/199 4.00 10.00
9 Tyreke Evans/199 4.00 10.00
11 Amare Stoudemire/199 3.00 8.00
12 Dwyane Wade/199 6.00 15.00
14 LaMarcus Aldridge/199 3.00 8.00
15 Rajon Rondo/199 4.00 10.00
16 Russell Westbrook/199 4.00 10.00
17 Brandon Jennings/199 3.00 8.00
18 Eric Gordon/199 3.00 8.00
19 Pau Gasol/199 3.00 8.00
20 Steve Nash/199 3.00 8.00
21 Al Jefferson/199 3.00 8.00
22 D.J. Augustin/199 2.50 6.00
24 Kevin Garnett/199 6.00 15.00
26 Chris Paul/199 5.00 12.00
27 Tim Duncan/199 5.00 12.00
28 Monta Ellis/199 3.00 8.00
30 Dwight Howard/199 5.00 12.00
31 Andrea Bargnani/199 2.50 6.00
32 Antawn Jamison/199 3.00 8.00
33 Joe Johnson/199 3.00 8.00
34 Lamar Odom/199 3.00 8.00
35 Tyson Chandler/199 2.50 6.00
36 Andre Miller/199 2.50 6.00
39 Rudy Gay/49 3.00 8.00
40 David West/199 3.00 8.00
42 Jameer Nelson/199 2.50 6.00
43 Nene/199 2.50 6.00
44 Al Horford/199 2.50 6.00
45 Manu Ginobili/199 3.00 8.00
46 Shaquille O'Neal/199 6.00 15.00
47 Stephen Curry/99 4.00 10.00
49 Joakim Noah/75 4.00 10.00

2010-11 Panini Gold Standard Gold Nuggets Materials Prime

*PRIME: .75X TO 2X BASE HI
STATED PRINT RUN 10 TO 25 SER.#'d SETS
SOME UNPRICED DUE TO SCARCITY
1 LeBron James/25 25.00 60.00
4 Kevin Durant/25 25.00 60.00
6 Dirk Nowitzki/25 10.00 25.00
7 Derrick Rose/25 25.00 60.00
16 Russell Westbrook/25 10.00 25.00
19 Pau Gasol/25 8.00 20.00
20 Steve Nash/25 10.00 25.00
45 Manu Ginobili/25 12.00 30.00
46 Shaquille O'Neal/25 20.00 50.00
49 Joakim Noah/25 10.00 25.00

2010-11 Panini Gold Standard Gold Nuggets Materials Signatures

STATED PRINT RUN 3 TO 99 SER.#'d SETS
SOME UNPRICED DUE TO SCARCITY
2 Kobe Bryant/24 100.00 200.00
8 Kevin Love/25 15.00 40.00
9 Tyreke Evans/25 15.00 40.00
14 LaMarcus Aldridge/25 10.00 25.00
15 Rajon Rondo/25 15.00 40.00
16 Russell Westbrook/25 20.00 50.00
17 Brandon Jennings/25 12.50 30.00
21 Al Jefferson/25 6.00 15.00
22 D.J. Augustin/49 5.00 12.00
31 Andrea Bargnani/25 6.00 15.00
32 Antawn Jamison/25 6.00 15.00
33 Joe Johnson/25 8.00 20.00
36 Andre Miller/49 6.00 15.00
39 Rudy Gay/25 10.00 25.00
42 Jameer Nelson/49 5.00 12.00
44 Al Horford/25 5.00 12.00
47 Stephen Curry/99 10.00 25.00
49 Joakim Noah/25 12.50 30.00

2010-11 Panini Gold Standard Gold Nuggets Materials Signatures Prime

STATED PRINT RUN ONE TO 25 SER.#'d SETS
SOME UNPRICED DUE TO SCARCITY
2 Kobe Bryant/24 150.00 300.00
8 Kevin Love/15 25.00 60.00
14 LaMarcus Aldridge/15 12.50 30.00
15 Rajon Rondo/15 30.00 80.00
16 Russell Westbrook/25 25.00 60.00
21 Al Jefferson/25 8.00 20.00
22 D.J. Augustin/25 8.00 20.00
31 Andrea Bargnani/15 8.00 20.00
32 Antawn Jamison/15 10.00 25.00
33 Joe Johnson/15 12.50 30.00
35 Tyson Chandler/15 10.00 25.00
36 Andre Miller/25 10.00 25.00
42 Jameer Nelson/15 8.00 20.00
44 Al Horford/25 8.00 20.00
47 Stephen Curry/25 20.00 50.00

2010-11 Panini Gold Standard Gold Nuggets Signatures

STATED PRINT RUN ONE TO 99 SER.#'d SETS
SOME UNPRICED DUE TO SCARCITY
2 Kobe Bryant/24 100.00 200.00
8 Kevin Love/25 12.00 30.00
9 Tyreke Evans/25 15.00 40.00
17 Brandon Jennings/49 10.00 25.00
18 Eric Gordon/99 6.00 15.00
21 Al Jefferson/25 6.00 15.00
22 D.J. Augustin/99 4.00 10.00
23 Raymond Felton/49 4.00 10.00
25 Aaron Brooks/99 4.00 10.00
31 Andrea Bargnani/49 4.00 10.00
32 Antawn Jamison/49 5.00 12.00
33 Joe Johnson/25 6.00 15.00
35 Tyson Chandler/49 5.00 12.00
36 Andre Miller/99 5.00 12.00
37 Devin Harris/99 5.00 12.00
38 Roy Hibbert/99 4.00 10.00
39 Rudy Gay/49 8.00 20.00
42 Jameer Nelson/49 4.00 10.00
44 Al Horford/99 4.00 10.00
47 Stephen Curry/99 10.00 25.00
48 Jeff Green/99 5.00 12.00
49 Joakim Noah/25 12.50 30.00

2010-11 Panini Gold Standard Gold Records

STATED PRINT RUN 299 SER.#'d SETS
UNPRICED GOLD RUSH PRINT RUN 10 SETS
1 Ray Allen 1.50 4.00
2 John Stockton 2.50 6.00
3 Wilt Chamberlain 3.00 8.00
4 Hakeem Olajuwon 2.00 5.00
5 Steve Nash 1.50 4.00
6 Mark Eaton 1.50 4.00
7 John Stockton 2.50 6.00
8 Kareem Abdul-Jabbar 2.50 6.00
9 Wilt Chamberlain 3.00 8.00
10 Karl Malone 2.00 5.00
11 Robert Parish 1.50 4.00
12 John Stockton 2.50 6.00
13 Jerry West 2.00 5.00
14 Moses Malone 1.50 4.00
15 Kareem Abdul-Jabbar 2.50 6.00

2010-11 Panini Gold Standard Gold Records Materials

STATED PRINT RUN 49 TO 299 SER.#'d SETS
1 Ray Allen/299 3.00 8.00
2 John Stockton/49 6.00 15.00
5 Steve Nash/299 3.00 8.00
6 Mark Eaton/299 3.00 8.00
7 John Stockton/49 6.00 15.00
8 Kareem Abdul-Jabbar/99 5.00 12.00
10 Karl Malone/299 4.00 10.00
11 Robert Parish/299 3.00 8.00
12 John Stockton/49 6.00 15.00
14 Moses Malone/299 3.00 8.00

2010-11 Panini Gold Standard Gold Records Materials Prime

*PRIME: 1.25X TO 3X BASE HI
STATED PRINT RUN 10 TO 25 SER.#'d SETS
SOME UNPRICED DUE TO SCARCITY
4 Hakeem Olajuwon/25 12.00 30.00
5 Steve Nash/25 12.00 30.00
10 Karl Malone/25 12.00 30.00

2010-11 Panini Gold Standard Gold Records Materials Signatures

STATED PRINT RUN 2 TO 25 SER.#'d SETS
SOME UNPRICED DUE TO SCARCITY
6 Mark Eaton/25 8.00 20.00
11 Robert Parish/25 10.00 25.00

2010-11 Panini Gold Standard Gold Records Materials Signatures Prime

STATED PRINT RUN ONE TO 25 SER.#'d SETS
SOME UNPRICED DUE TO SCARCITY
6 Mark Eaton/25 15.00 40.00
11 Robert Parish/25 20.00 50.00

2010-11 Panini Gold Standard Gold Records Signatures

STATED PRINT RUN 5 TO 99 SER.#'d SETS
SOME UNPRICED DUE TO SCARCITY
6 Mark Eaton/99 6.00 15.00
11 Robert Parish/25 10.00 25.00

2010-11 Panini Gold Standard Gold Rings

STATED PRINT RUN 299 SER.#'d SETS
UNPRICED GOLD RUSH PRINT RUN 8 SETS
1 Magic Johnson 4.00 10.00
2 Tim Duncan 2.50 6.00
3 Rajon Rondo 2.00 5.00
4 Dwyane Wade 3.00 8.00
5 Kobe Bryant 8.00 20.00
6 Scottie Pippen 3.00 8.00
7 Alonzo Mourning 2.00 5.00
8 Isiah Thomas 1.50 4.00
9 Dennis Rodman 3.00 8.00
10 Pau Gasol 1.50 4.00
11 Ray Allen 1.50 4.00
12 Hakeem Olajuwon 2.00 5.00
13 Tony Parker 1.50 4.00
14 Bill Walton 1.50 4.00
15 Kareem Abdul-Jabbar 2.50 6.00
16 Richard Hamilton 1.25 3.00
17 Julius Erving 3.00 8.00
18 Elvin Hayes 1.50 4.00
19 Paul Pierce 2.00 5.00
20 Robert Horry 2.00 5.00

2010-11 Panini Gold Standard Gold Rings Materials

STATED PRINT RUN 49 TO 299 SER.#'d SETS
1 Magic Johnson/99 10.00 25.00
2 Tim Duncan/299 6.00 15.00
3 Rajon Rondo/299 5.00 12.00
4 Dwyane Wade/299 8.00 20.00
5 Kobe Bryant/299 10.00 25.00
6 Scottie Pippen/299 8.00 20.00
7 Alonzo Mourning/299 5.00 12.00
8 Isiah Thomas/199 4.00 10.00
9 Dennis Rodman/49 8.00 20.00
10 Pau Gasol/299 4.00 10.00
11 Ray Allen/299 4.00 10.00
12 Hakeem Olajuwon/299 5.00 12.00
13 Tony Parker/299 4.00 10.00
15 Kareem Abdul-Jabbar/99 6.00 15.00
16 Richard Hamilton/299 3.00 8.00
17 Julius Erving/149 8.00 20.00
19 Paul Pierce/299 5.00 12.00
20 Robert Horry/299 5.00 12.00

2010-11 Panini Gold Standard Gold Rings Materials Prime

*PRIME: .75X TO 2X BASE HI
STATED PRINT RUN 5 TO 25 SER.#'d SETS
SOME UNPRICED DUE TO SCARCITY
1 Magic Johnson/25 15.00 40.00
6 Scottie Pippen/25 40.00 100.00
7 Alonzo Mourning/25 30.00 80.00
12 Hakeem Olajuwon/25 12.00 30.00

2010-11 Panini Gold Standard Gold Rings Materials Signatures

STATED PRINT RUN 5 TO 49 SER.#'d SETS
SOME UNPRICED DUE TO SCARCITY
3 Rajon Rondo/49 15.00 40.00
5 Kobe Bryant/24 125.00 250.00
8 Isiah Thomas/49 12.50 30.00
9 Dennis Rodman/25 30.00 80.00
11 Ray Allen/25 30.00 60.00
12 Hakeem Olajuwon/25 25.00 60.00
13 Tony Parker/25 12.50 30.00
16 Richard Hamilton/49 6.00 15.00
20 Robert Horry/49 15.00 40.00

2010-11 Panini Gold Standard Gold Rings Materials Signatures Prime

STATED PRINT RUN 3 TO 25 SER.#'d SETS
SOME UNPRICED DUE TO SCARCITY
3 Rajon Rondo/25 25.00 60.00
5 Kobe Bryant/24 150.00 300.00
8 Isiah Thomas/25 20.00 50.00
13 Tony Parker/25 20.00 50.00
16 Richard Hamilton/25 8.00 20.00
20 Robert Horry/25 30.00 80.00

2010-11 Panini Gold Standard Gold Rings Signatures

STATED PRINT RUN 5 TO 69 SER.#'d SETS
SOME UNPRICED DUE TO SCARCITY
3 Rajon Rondo/49 15.00 40.00
5 Kobe Bryant/49 100.00 200.00
7 Alonzo Mourning/25 30.00 80.00
8 Isiah Thomas/49 EXCH 12.50 30.00
9 Dennis Rodman/25 30.00 80.00
12 Hakeem Olajuwon/25 20.00 50.00
13 Tony Parker/49 10.00 25.00
14 Bill Walton/49 10.00 25.00
16 Richard Hamilton/49 6.00 15.00
18 Elvin Hayes/49 6.00 15.00
20 Robert Horry/69 12.50 30.00

2010-11 Panini Gold Standard Gold Rings Signatures Dual

STATED PRINT RUN 10 TO 50 SER.#'d SETS
SOME UNPRICED DUE TO SCARCITY
1 Paul Pierce/20 30.00 80.00
Rajon Rondo
2 Isiah Thomas/50 12.50 30.00
Bill Laimbeer
3 Rajon Rondo/20 50.00 120.00
Ray Allen
5 Kobe Bryant/50 100.00 225.00
Pau Gasol
6 Kobe Bryant/25 125.00 250.00
Derek Fisher
7 Tony Parker/50 25.00 60.00
Robert Horry
8 Hakeem Olajuwon/20 50.00 120.00
Clyde Drexler
9 Chauncey Billups/50 12.50 30.00
Richard Hamilton
10 Gary Payton/20 40.00 100.00
Alonzo Mourning

2010-11 Panini Gold Standard Gold Stars

STATED PRINT RUN 299 SER.#'d SETS
UNPRICED GOLD RUSH PRINT RUN 8 SETS
1 Blake Griffin 3.00 8.00
2 Dwight Howard 2.00 5.00
3 Russell Westbrook 1.50 4.00
4 Lamar Odom 1.25 3.00
5 Jonny Flynn .75 2.00
6 Carlos Boozer 1.25 3.00
7 Raymond Felton 1.00 2.50
8 Ray Allen 1.25 3.00
9 Ben Gordon 1.25 3.00
10 Jameer Nelson 1.00 2.50
11 Dirk Nowitzki 1.50 4.00
12 Marc Gasol 1.25 3.00
13 Monta Ellis 1.25 3.00
14 Shane Battier 1.00 2.50
15 Andre Iguodala 1.25 3.00
16 Andrei Kirilenko 1.00 2.50
17 Nene 1.00 2.50
18 Steve Nash 1.25 3.00
19 Jordan Farmar .75 2.00
20 Andrea Bargnani 1.00 2.50
21 Kevin Durant 4.00 10.00
22 Tyson Chandler 1.00 2.50
23 Derrick Rose 4.00 10.00
24 Kobe Bryant 6.00 15.00
25 Amare Stoudemire 1.25 3.00

2010-11 Panini Gold Standard Gold Stars Materials

STATED PRINT RUN 99 SER.#'d SETS
1 Blake Griffin 8.00 20.00
2 Dwight Howard 5.00 12.00
3 Russell Westbrook 4.00 10.00
4 Lamar Odom 3.00 8.00
5 Jonny Flynn 2.00 5.00
8 Ray Allen 3.00 8.00
9 Ben Gordon 3.00 8.00
10 Jameer Nelson 2.50 6.00
11 Dirk Nowitzki 4.00 10.00
12 Marc Gasol 3.00 8.00
13 Monta Ellis 3.00 8.00
15 Andre Iguodala 3.00 8.00
16 Andrei Kirilenko 2.50 6.00
17 Nene 2.50 6.00
18 Steve Nash 3.00 8.00
20 Andrea Bargnani 2.50 6.00
21 Kevin Durant 8.00 20.00
22 Tyson Chandler 2.50 6.00
23 Derrick Rose 10.00 25.00
24 Kobe Bryant 10.00 25.00
25 Amare Stoudemire 3.00 8.00

2010-11 Panini Gold Standard Gold Stars Materials Prime

*PRIME: .75X TO 2X BASE HI
STATED PRINT RUN 2 TO 25 SER.#'d SETS
SOME UNPRICED DUE TO SCARCITY
11 Dirk Nowitzki/25 10.00 25.00
21 Kevin Durant/25 20.00 50.00

2010-11 Panini Gold Standard Gold Stars Materials Signatures

STATED PRINT RUN 5 TO 49 SER.#'d SETS
SOME UNPRICED DUE TO SCARCITY
3 Russell Westbrook/25 20.00 50.00
4 Lamar Odom/30 10.00 25.00
5 Jonny Flynn/35 5.00 12.00
9 Ben Gordon/49 5.00 12.00
10 Jameer Nelson/49 5.00 12.00
15 Andre Iguodala/49 6.00 15.00
16 Andrei Kirilenko/25 6.00 15.00
22 Tyson Chandler/20 8.00 20.00
24 Kobe Bryant/15 100.00 200.00

2010-11 Panini Gold Standard Gold Stars Materials Signatures Prime

STATED PRINT RUN 2 TO 25 SER.#'d SETS
SOME UNPRICED DUE TO SCARCITY
5 Jonny Flynn/20 8.00 20.00
9 Ben Gordon/25
10 Jameer Nelson/20
15 Andre Iguodala/20
22 Tyson Chandler/20

2010-11 Pani[…] Gold Stars Signa[…]

STATED PRINT RUN 5 TO 99 SER.#'d SETS
SOME UNPRICED DUE TO SCARCITY
4 Lamar Odom/25 10.00 25.00
5 Jonny Flynn/50 4.00 10.00
6 Carlos Boozer/99 6.00 15.00
7 Raymond Felton/99 4.00 10.00
8 Ray Allen/25 30.00 60.00
10 Jameer Nelson/99 4.00 10.00
14 Shane Battier/99 5.00 12.00
15 Andre Iguodala/99 4.00 10.00
16 Andrei Kirilenko/49 4.00 10.00
20 Andrea Bargnani/25 5.00 12.00
22 Tyson Chandler/49 5.00 12.00
24 Kobe Bryant/24 100.00 200.00

2010-11 Panini Gold Standard Gold Team Logos

STATED PRINT RUN 5 TO 199 SER.#'d SETS
SOME UNPRICED DUE TO SCARCITY
1 Aaron Brooks/199 6.00 15.00
2 Alvan Adams/199 6.00 15.00
4 Andre Iguodala/99 6.00 15.00
5 Andrew Bogut/199 8.00 20.00
6 Andrew Bynum/49 12.50 30.00
7 Baron Davis/49 8.00 20.00
8 Bernard King/199 8.00 20.00
9 Bill Laimbeer/199 8.00 20.00
10 Bill Walton/99 10.00 25.00
11 Billy Cunningham/99 25.00 60.00
13 Boris Diaw/199 6.00 15.00
14 Brandon Jennings/49 12.50 30.00
15 Brook Lopez/99 6.00 15.00
16 Carl Landry/199 6.00 15.00
17 Carlos Boozer/199 10.00 25.00
18 Channing Frye/199 6.00 15.00
20 Danilo Gallinari/199 6.00 15.00
21 David Lee/99 6.00 15.00
22 DeMar DeRozan/199 8.00 20.00
23 Derek Fisher/199 8.00 20.00
26 Elvin Hayes/199 8.00 20.00
27 Emeka Okafor/49 6.00 15.00
28 Eric Gordon/199 10.00 25.00
29 J.J. Barea/199 EXCH 12.50 30.00
30 Jalen Rose/199 6.00 15.00
31 Jeff Green/199 6.00 15.00
32 Joakim Noah/99 12.50 30.00
33 Juwan Howard/199 8.00 20.00
34 Kendrick Perkins/199 10.00 25.00
36 LaMarcus Aldridge/199 8.00 20.00
37 Michael Cooper/199 8.00 20.00
41 Raymond Felton/199 6.00 15.00
42 Russell Westbrook/199 20.00 50.00
43 Stephen Curry/199 10.00 25.00
44 Tony Parker/25 10.00 25.00
45 Tracy McGrady/25 25.00 60.00
47 Walter Berry/199 6.00 15.00
48 Zach Randolph/99 10.00 25.00
49 Tyson Chandler/199 6.00 15.00
50 Robin Lopez/199 6.00 15.00

2010-11 Panini Gold Standard Golden Age

STATED PRINT RUN 299 SER.#'d SETS
UNPRICED GOLD RUSH PRINT RUN 5 SETS
1 Magic Johnson 3.00 8.00
2 Tim Hardaway 1.25 3.00
3 David Robinson 2.00 5.00
4 Dikembe Mutombo 1.25 3.00
5 Jerry West 1.50 4.00
6 Tom Heinsohn 1.25 3.00
7 Dennis Rodman 2.00 5.00
8 Rick Barry 1.25 3.00
9 Bob Lanier 1.25 3.00
10 Oscar Robertson 1.50 4.00
11 Larry Bird 4.00 10.00
12 John Stockton 2.00 5.00
13 Julius Erving 2.50 6.00
14 Hakeem Olajuwon 1.50 4.00
15 David Thompson 1.50 4.00
16 Elvin Hayes 1.25 3.00
17 Walt Bellamy 1.25 3.00
18 Elgin Baylor 1.25 3.00
19 Darryl Dawkins 1.25 3.00
20 Bill Russell 2.00 5.00

2010-11 Panini Gold Standard Golden Age Materials

STATED PRINT RUN 49 TO 299 SER.#'d SETS
1 Magic Johnson/99 8.00 20.00
2 Tim Hardaway/299 3.00 8.00
4 Dikembe Mutombo/299 3.00 8.00
7 Dennis Rodman/99 6.00 15.00
9 Bob Lanier/99 3.00 8.00
11 Larry Bird/49 10.00 25.00
12 John Stockton/299 5.00 12.00
13 Julius Erving/149 6.00 15.00
14 Hakeem Olajuwon/299 4.00 10.00

2010-11 Panini Gold Standard Golden Age Materials Prime

*PRIME: .75X TO 2X BASE HI
STATED PRINT RUN 5 TO 25 SER.#'d SETS
SOME UNPRICED DUE TO SCARCITY
2 Tim Hardaway/25 12.00 30.00
4 Dikembe Mutombo/25 10.00 25.00
14 Hakeem Olajuwon/25 10.00 25.00

2010-11 Panini Gold Standard Golden Age Materials Signatures

STATED PRINT RUN 3 TO 49 SER.#'d SETS
SOME UNPRICED DUE TO SCARCITY
4 Dikembe Mutombo/49 15.00 40.00
9 Bob Lanier/25 10.00 25.00

2010-11 Panini Gold Standard Golden Age Materials Signatures Prime

STATED PRINT RUN ONE TO 25 SER.#'d SETS
SOME UNPRICED DUE TO SCARCITY

Dikembe Mutombo/25 30.00 80.00
6 Tom Heinsohn/25 25.00 60.00
8 Rick Barry/25 20.00 50.00
9 Bob Lanier/25 20.00 50.00

2010-11 Panini Gold Standard Golden Age Signatures

STATED PRINT RUN 2 TO 99 SER.#'d SETS
SOME UNPRICED DUE TO SCARCITY
2 Tim Hardaway/99 10.00 25.00
4 Dikembe Mutombo/99 15.00 40.00
6 Tom Heinsohn/99 10.00 25.00
8 Rick Barry/99 6.00 15.00
9 Bob Lanier/50 5.00 12.00
15 David Thompson/99 5.00 12.00
16 Elvin Hayes/75 6.00 15.00
17 Walt Bellamy/75 5.00 12.00
19 Darryl Dawkins/99 5.00 12.00

2010-11 Panini Gold Standard Golden Age Signatures Dual

STATED PRINT RUN 5 TO 50 SER.#'d SETS
SOME UNPRICED DUE TO SCARCITY
5 Darryl Dawkins/50 10.00 25.00
Maurice Cheeks
6 Darrell Griffith/50 10.00 25.00
Mark Eaton
8 Adrian Dantley/50 10.00 25.00
Rolando Blackman
10 Isiah Thomas/50 20.00 50.00
Joe Dumars

2010-11 Panini Gold Standard Golden Anniversary

STATED PRINT RUN 299 SER.#'d SETS
UNPRICED GOLD RUSH PRINT RUN 10 SETS
1 Kareem Abdul-Jabbar 2.00 5.00
2 Elgin Baylor 1.25 3.00
3 Rick Barry 1.25 3.00
4 Larry Bird 4.00 10.00
5 Sam Jones 1.25 3.00
6 Oscar Robertson 1.50 4.00
7 Bill Russell 2.00 5.00
8 Jerry West 1.50 4.00
9 Bill Walton 1.25 3.00
10 Lenny Wilkens 1.25 3.00
11 Scottie Pippen 2.50 6.00
12 David Robinson 2.00 5.00
13 Hakeem Olajuwon 1.50 4.00
14 Dolph Schayes 1.25 3.00
15 Julius Erving 2.50 6.00
16 Clyde Drexler 1.50 4.00
17 George Gervin 1.25 3.00
18 Dave Cowens 1.25 3.00
19 John Havlicek 1.50 4.00
20 Magic Johnson 3.00 8.00

2010-11 Panini Gold Standard Golden Anniversary Materials

STATED PRINT RUN 49 TO 299 SER.#'d SETS
1 Kareem Abdul-Jabbar/99 5.00 12.00
4 Larry Bird/49 10.00 25.00
11 Scottie Pippen/299 8.00 20.00
12 David Robinson/299 5.00 12.00
13 Hakeem Olajuwon/149 4.00 10.00
15 Julius Erving/149 6.00 15.00
16 Clyde Drexler/299 4.00 10.00
17 George Gervin/299 3.00 8.00
18 Dave Cowens/125 3.00 8.00
20 Magic Johnson/99 8.00 20.00

2010-11 Panini Gold Standard Golden Anniversary Materials Prime

*PRIME: .75X TO 2X BASE HI
STATED PRINT RUN ONE TO 25 SER.#'d SETS
SOME UNPRICED DUE TO SCARCITY
11 Scottie Pippen/25 60.00 150.00
13 Hakeem Olajuwon/25 10.00 25.00

2010-11 Panini Gold Standard Golden Anniversary Materials Signatures

STATED PRINT RUN 10 TO 49 SER.#'d SETS
SOME UNPRICED DUE TO SCARCITY
12 David Robinson/49 30.00 80.00
13 Hakeem Olajuwon/25 25.00 60.00
17 George Gervin/49 12.50 30.00

2010-11 Panini Gold Standard Golden Anniversary Materials Signatures Prime

STATED PRINT RUN 5 TO 25 SER.#'d SETS
SOME UNPRICED DUE TO SCARCITY
12 David Robinson/25 40.00 100.00
13 Hakeem Olajuwon/25 30.00 80.00
17 George Gervin/25 15.00 40.00

2010-11 Panini Gold Standard Golden Anniversary Signatures

STATED PRINT RUN 5 TO 49 SER.#'d SETS
SOME UNPRICED DUE TO SCARCITY
2 Elgin Baylor/25 15.00 40.00
3 Rick Barry/49 10.00 25.00
5 Sam Jones/49 12.00 30.00
6 Oscar Robertson/25 40.00 100.00
9 Bill Walton/49 10.00 25.00
10 Lenny Wilkens/49 8.00 20.00
12 David Robinson/25 30.00 80.00
14 Dolph Schayes/49 8.00 20.00
16 Clyde Drexler/25 25.00 60.00
17 George Gervin/30 10.00 25.00
18 Dave Cowens/49 8.00 20.00

2010-11 Panini Gold Standard Golden Anniversary Signatures Dual

STATED PRINT RUN 5 TO 50 SER.#'d SETS
SOME UNPRICED DUE TO SCARCITY
3 David Robinson/20 60.00 150.00
George Gervin
4 Walt Frazier/25 25.00 60.00
Earl Monroe
6 Hal Greer/50 12.50 30.00
Dolph Schayes
7 Dave Cowens/50 12.50 30.00
Robert Parish
8 Elvin Hayes/25 30.00 80.00
Hakeem Olajuwon
9 James Worthy/25 40.00 100.00
Elgin Baylor
10 Sidney Moncrief/25 50.00 125.00
Oscar Robertson
13 Walt Frazier/50 25.00 60.00
Willis Reed
15 Rick Barry/50 15.00 40.00
Nate Thurmond

2010-11 Panini Gold Standard Golden Threads

STATED PRINT RUN 299 SER.#'d SETS
1 Sam Jones 1.50 4.00
Rajon Rondo
2 Magic Johnson 8.00 20.00
Kobe Bryant
3 Julius Erving 2.50 6.00
Andre Iguodala
4 Dennis Rodman 2.00 5.00
DeJuan Blair
5 Rolando Blackman 1.25 3.00
Jason Kidd
6 Walt Frazier 1.25 3.00
Chauncey Billups
7 Scottie Pippen 5.00 12.00
Derrick Rose
8 Robert Parish 1.50 4.00
Paul Pierce
9 Alonzo Mourning 2.50 6.00
Chris Bosh
10 Willis Reed 1.25 3.00
Amare Stoudemire

2010-11 Panini Gold Standard Golden Threads Materials

STATED PRINT RUN 25 TO 299 SER.#'d SETS
2 Magic Johnson/299 12.00 30.00
Kobe Bryant
3 Julius Erving/99 6.00 15.00
Andre Iguodala
5 Rolando Blackman/25 5.00 12.00
Jason Kidd
8 Robert Parish/299 4.00 10.00
Paul Pierce
9 Alonzo Mourning/299 5.00 12.00
Chris Bosh

2010-11 Panini Gold Standard Golden Threads Materials Prime

*PRIME: 1X TO 2.5X BASE HI
STATED PRINT RUN 3 TO 25 SER.#'d SETS
SOME UNPRICED DUE TO SCARCITY
9 Alonzo Mourning/25 20.00 50.00
Chris Bosh

2010-11 Panini Gold Standard Golden Threads Signatures

STATED PRINT RUN 10 TO 25 SER.#'d SETS
SOME UNPRICED DUE TO SCARCITY
1 Sam Jones/25 20.00 50.00
Rajon Rondo
4 Dennis Rodman/25 50.00 120.00
DeJuan Blair
5 Rolando Blackman/25 20.00 50.00
Jason Kidd
6 Walt Frazier/25 20.00 50.00
Chauncey Billups
9 Alonzo Mourning/25 50.00 120.00
Chris Bosh

2010-11 Panini Gold Standard Signatures

STATED PRINT RUN 5 TO 299 SER.#'d SETS
SOME UNPRICED DUE TO SCARCITY
2 Kobe Bryant/75 75.00 150.00
5 Ty Lawson/299 6.00 15.00
9 Kevin Love/25 15.00 40.00
15 Kevin Martin/299 4.00 10.00
17 Stephen Jackson/299 4.00 10.00
19 Eric Gordon/299 5.00 12.00
23 Antawn Jamison/199 4.00 10.00
24 Tyreke Evans/25 12.50 30.00
25 Al Horford/99 5.00 12.00
26 Danny Granger/50 6.00 15.00
28 Rajon Rondo/49 12.50 30.00
30 Michael Beasley/25 10.00 25.00
32 Tony Parker/25 15.00 40.00
34 LaMarcus Aldridge/299 8.00 20.00
35 Stephen Curry/299 10.00 25.00
36 Brook Lopez/99 5.00 12.00
37 Tyson Chandler/199 6.00 15.00
40 Andre Iguodala/299 4.00 10.00
42 Danilo Gallinari/299 4.00 10.00
43 Joe Johnson/49 8.00 20.00
44 DeMar DeRozan/299 6.00 15.00
45 Devin Harris/299 4.00 10.00
46 Andrei Kirilenko/199 4.00 10.00
47 Brandon Roy/25 8.00 20.00
48 Raymond Felton/199 4.00 10.00
51 Aaron Brooks/299 4.00 10.00
52 Zach Randolph/49 6.00 15.00
54 Charlie Villanueva/49 4.00 10.00
55 Jeff Green/299 4.00 10.00
56 Channing Frye/220 4.00 10.00
57 Al Thornton/299 4.00 10.00
62 David Lee/199 5.00 12.00
66 Emeka Okafor/25 5.00 12.00
68 Carl Landry/299 4.00 10.00
69 Jameer Nelson/199 4.00 10.00
70 Joakim Noah/99 8.00 20.00
71 Chris Kaman/99 4.00 10.00
74 Andrea Bargnani/49 5.00 12.00
76 Grant Hill/25 125.00 250.00
77 Lamar Odom/25 10.00 25.00
80 J.R. Smith/299 4.00 10.00
82 Tyler Hansbrough/199 6.00 15.00
85 Al Jefferson/49 4.00 10.00
87 Luke Ridnour/199 4.00 10.00
91 D.J. Augustin/299 4.00 10.00
94 Juwan Howard/299 4.00 10.00
95 Roy Hibbert/299 4.00 10.00
98 DeJuan Blair/299 4.00 10.00
101 Baron Davis/49 5.00 12.00
103 Josh Smith/199 5.00 12.00
105 Hedo Turkoglu/299 4.00 10.00
106 Ben Gordon/49 5.00 12.00
107 Gerald Henderson/299 4.00 10.00
108 Serge Ibaka/299 8.00 20.00
109 Shane Battier/149 5.00 12.00
111 Chauncey Billups/23 12.50 30.00
115 Darko Milicic/299 4.00 10.00
116 Caron Butler/49 5.00 12.00
118 Trevor Ariza/49 5.00 12.00
120 J.J. Redick/299 4.00 10.00
121 Gerald Wallace/99 6.00 15.00
122 Samuel Dalembert/299 4.00 10.00
125 Brandon Jennings/149 10.00 25.00
126 JaVale McGee/299 4.00 10.00
128 James Harden/149 12.00 30.00
129 Chris Andersen/25 30.00 80.00
130 Toney Douglas/299 4.00 10.00
132 Richard Hamilton/49 6.00 15.00
133 George Hill/299 4.00 10.00
137 Daniel Gibson/299 4.00 10.00
138 Wesley Matthews/299 5.00 12.00
139 Kris Humphries/49 5.00 12.00
140 Rodrigue Beaubois/299 4.00 10.00
141 A.J. Price/299 4.00 10.00
142 Chase Budinger/299 4.00 10.00
143 Donte Greene/99 4.00 10.00
144 Andre Miller/199 5.00 12.00
145 Ryan Gomes/299 4.00 10.00
146 Jodie Meeks/299 4.00 10.00
147 Kendrick Perkins/99 6.00 15.00
148 Taj Gibson/199 5.00 12.00
149 Boris Diaw/199 4.00 10.00
150 Derrick Brown/299 4.00 10.00
151 Jeff Teague/299 4.00 10.00
152 Wayne Ellington/199 4.00 10.00
153 Terrence Williams/199 4.00 10.00
154 Robin Lopez/149 4.00 10.00
155 Jermaine O'Neal/25 10.00 25.00
156 Austin Daye/299 4.00 10.00
157 J.J. Barea/199 10.00 25.00
158 Darren Collison/299 4.00 10.00
159 Goran Dragic/149 8.00 20.00
160 Beno Udrih/149 4.00 10.00
161 Earl Clark/99 4.00 10.00
162 Hakim Warrick/149 4.00 10.00
163 Sam Young/99 5.00 12.00
164 Ronnie Brewer/199 4.00 10.00
165 Omri Casspi/299 4.00 10.00
166 T.J. Ford/199 4.00 10.00
167 Chris Douglas-Roberts/99 4.00 10.00
168 Eric Maynor/79 4.00 10.00
169 James Johnson/99 4.00 10.00
170 Patrick Mills/99 15.00 40.00
179 Dan Majerle/199 6.00 15.00
183 Glen Rice/299 6.00 15.00
186 Jalen Rose/299 5.00 12.00
190 Bill Walton/49 8.00 20.00
193 Dan Issel/49 5.00 12.00
194 Doc Rivers/49 10.00 25.00
195 George McGinnis/42 5.00 12.00
197 Christian Laettner/25 15.00 40.00
198 Dolph Schayes/49 8.00 20.00
199 M.L. Carr/99 5.00 12.00
200 Darryl Dawkins/99 5.00 12.00
201 David Thompson/99 4.00 10.00
202 Bob Lanier/49 5.00 12.00
204 Bernard King/99 4.00 10.00
205 Bailey Howell/99 8.00 20.00
206 Al Attles/99 4.00 10.00
207 Dikembe Mutombo/49 12.00 30.00
208 Bob McAdoo/99 10.00 25.00
209 Artis Gilmore/99 8.00 20.00
210 A.C. Green/99 8.00 20.00
211 Dominique Wilkins/99 10.00 25.00
212 Alonzo Mourning/99 15.00 40.00

2011-12 Panini Gold Standard

COMMON CARD (1-225) 1.25 3.00
STATED PRINT RUN 299 SER.#'d SETS
170/179/183/210/213/214 HAVE VAR
ALL VAR STILL TOTAL JUST 299 CARDS
UNPRICED BLACK GOLD PRINT RUN ONE SET
UNPRICED PLAT.GOLD PRINT RUN 10 SETS
UNPRICED BULLION PRINT RUN 1 TO 2 SETS
1 Paul Pierce 2.50 6.00
2 LaMarcus Aldridge 2.00 5.00
3 Al Jefferson 2.00 5.00
4 Pau Gasol 2.00 5.00
5 DeMarcus Cousins 2.50 6.00
6 Danilo Gallinari 2.00 5.00
7 Dwight Howard 3.00 8.00
8 Ty Lawson 2.00 5.00
9 Luke Ridnour 1.50 4.00
10 Emeka Okafor 2.00 5.00
11 Ray Allen 2.00 5.00
12 LeBron James 8.00 20.00
13 Eric Gordon 2.00 5.00
14 Nate Robinson 2.00 5.00
15 Kobe Bryant 8.00 20.00
16 Damion James 1.25 3.00
17 Kevin Garnett 4.00 10.00
18 DeJuan Blair 1.50 4.00
19 Jeremy Lin 8.00 20.00
20 Kris Humphries 1.25 3.00
21 Andre Iguodala 2.00 5.00
22 Andrea Bargnani 1.50 4.00
23 Evan Turner 2.00 5.00
24 Carmelo Anthony 2.50 6.00
25 DeAndre Jordan 2.00 5.00
26 Rajon Rondo 2.50 6.00
27 Kevin Durant 6.00 15.00
28 John Wall 3.00 8.00
29 Mo Williams 1.50 4.00
30 Marcin Gortat 2.00 5.00
31 Chauncey Billups 2.00 5.00
32 Tyson Chandler 1.50 4.00
33 Steve Nash 2.00 5.00
34 Caron Butler 1.50 4.00
35 Derek Fisher 1.50 4.00
36 Marcus Thornton 2.00 5.00
37 Jose Calderon 1.50 4.00
38 Zach Randolph 1.50 4.00
39 Grant Hill 3.00 8.00
40 Avery Bradley 2.00 5.00
41 Channing Frye 1.50 4.00
42 Matt Barnes 1.25 3.00
43 Jason Thompson 1.25 3.00
44 Chris Paul 3.00 8.00
45 Tyreke Evans 2.00 5.00
46 Carlos Boozer 2.00 5.00
47 Brandon Rush 1.25 3.00
48 Joakim Noah 2.00 5.00
49 Rudy Gay 2.00 5.00
50 Luol Deng 2.00 5.00
51 Amare Stoudemire 2.00 5.00
52 Taj Gibson 1.50 4.00
53 Anderson Varejao 1.50 4.00
54 Deron Williams 2.00 5.00
55 Antawn Jamison 2.00 5.00
56 Ramon Sessions 1.50 4.00
57 Rodney Stuckey 2.00 5.00
58 Chris Bosh 2.00 5.00
59 Trevor Booker 1.25 3.00
60 Ben Gordon 2.00 5.00
61 Tony Parker 2.00 5.00
62 Danny Granger 2.00 5.00
63 Jodie Meeks 1.50 4.00
64 George Hill 1.50 4.00
65 Ed Davis 1.50 4.00
66 Paul George 2.00 5.00
67 Landry Fields 2.00 5.00
68 Roy Hibbert 1.50 4.00
69 Russell Westbrook 2.50 6.00
70 Thabo Sefolosha 1.50 4.00
71 Darren Collison 2.00 5.00
72 Delonte West 1.25 3.00
73 Jerryd Bayless 1.25 3.00
74 Stephen Jackson 1.50 4.00
75 Dirk Nowitzki 2.50 6.00
76 Tim Duncan 3.00 8.00
77 Drew Gooden 1.50 4.00
78 Shawn Marion 2.00 5.00
79 Brook Lopez 2.00 5.00
80 Kevin Martin 2.00 5.00
81 Manu Ginobili 2.00 5.00
82 Marc Gasol 2.00 5.00
83 Al-Farouq Aminu 1.25 3.00
84 Gary Neal 2.00 5.00
85 Patrick Patterson 1.50 4.00
86 Mike Conley 1.50 4.00
87 Stephen Curry 2.00 5.00
88 Michael Beasley 2.00 5.00
89 Al Harrington 1.50 4.00
90 Larry Sanders 1.25 3.00
91 Ryan Anderson 1.50 4.00
92 Nicolas Batum 2.00 5.00
93 Dwyane Wade 4.00 10.00
94 Gerald Wallace 2.00 5.00
95 Monta Ellis 2.00 5.00
96 Jared Dudley 1.25 3.00
97 Jrue Holiday 2.00 5.00
98 Nick Young 1.50 4.00
99 Nene 1.50 4.00
100 Vince Carter 2.50 6.00
101 Elton Brand 2.00 5.00
102 Andrew Bynum 2.50 6.00
103 Greg Monroe 2.00 5.00
104 Tyler Hansbrough 2.00 5.00
105 Andrew Bogut 2.00 5.00
106 Jeff Teague 1.50 4.00
107 D.J. Augustin 1.25 3.00
108 Jason Terry 1.50 4.00
109 Austin Daye 1.25 3.00
110 Brandon Jennings 2.00 5.00
111 Gordon Hayward 2.00 5.00
112 Kyle Lowry 1.50 4.00
113 Jamal Crawford 1.50 4.00
114 Jason Richardson 2.00 5.00
115 James Harden 2.50 6.00
116 Boris Diaw 1.50 4.00
117 Chris Andersen 2.00 5.00
118 Kevin Love 2.50 6.00
119 Kirk Hinrich 2.00 5.00
120 Shane Battier 1.50 4.00
121 Ersan Ilyasova 1.50 4.00
122 Jason Kidd 2.00 5.00
123 Wesley Matthews 2.00 5.00
124 Serge Ibaka 2.00 5.00
125 Hedo Turkoglu 2.00 5.00
126 Paul Millsap 1.50 4.00
127 JaVale McGee 1.50 4.00
128 Timofey Mozgov 1.25 3.00
129 Nikola Pekovic 2.00 5.00
130 Luis Scola 1.50 4.00
131 Mario Chalmers 2.00 5.00
132 Jameer Nelson 1.50 4.00
133 Tayshaun Prince 2.00 5.00
134 Blake Griffin 4.00 10.00
135 Wesley Johnson 1.50 4.00
136 Derrick Favors 2.00 5.00
137 Kendrick Perkins 1.50 4.00
138 Chase Budinger 1.25 3.00
139 Devin Harris 2.00 5.00
140 Tiago Splitter 1.50 4.00
141 DeMar DeRozan 2.00 5.00
142 Derrick Rose 6.00 15.00
143 Josh Smith 2.00 5.00
144 Ricky Rubio 5.00 12.00
145 Jordan Crawford 2.00 5.00
146 J.J. Redick 2.00 5.00
147 Greivis Vasquez 1.50 4.00
148 Al Horford 1.50 4.00
149 Brandon Bass 1.25 3.00
150 Anthony Morrow 1.25 3.00
151 Baron Davis 2.00 5.00
152 Thaddeus Young 1.25 3.00
153 James Johnson 1.25 3.00
154 Ekpe Udoh 1.25 3.00
155 Metta World Peace 2.00 5.00
156 Michael Redd 2.00 5.00
157 John Salmons 2.00 5.00
158 Omri Casspi 1.25 3.00
159 Richard Hamilton 1.50 4.00
160 Alonzo Gee RC 2.50 6.00
161 J.J. Hickson 1.50 4.00
162 Rodrigue Beaubois 1.50 4.00
163 Marreese Speights 1.25 3.00
164 Xavier Henry 1.50 4.00
165 Reggie Williams 1.50 4.00
166 Raja Bell 1.50 4.00
167 Raymond Felton 1.50 4.00
168 Daequan Cook 1.25 3.00
169 David Lee 1.50 4.00
170A Tracy McGrady Hawks/149* 2.00 5.00
170B Tracy McGrady/11*
New York Knicks
170C Tracy McGrady/45* 12.00 30.00
Orlando Magic
170D Tracy McGrady/9*
Detroit Pistons
170E Tracy McGrady/30* 25.00 60.00
Toronto Raptors
170F Tracy McGrady/55* 4.00 10.00
Houston Rockets
171 Joel Anthony 1.25 3.00
172 Tyrus Thomas 1.50 4.00
173 Joe Johnson 2.00 5.00
174 Randy Foye 1.25 3.00
175 Gerald Henderson 1.25 3.00
176 Jack Sikma 2.00 5.00
177 Paul Silas 2.00 5.00
178 Harry Gallatin 2.00 5.00
179A Gary Payton Sonics/199* 4.00 10.00
179B Gary Payton/30* 25.00 60.00
Milwaukee Bucks
179C Gary Payton/25* 25.00 60.00
Boston Celtics
179D Gary Payton/25* 30.00 80.00
Miami Heat
179E Gary Payton/20* 25.00 60.00
Los Angeles Lakers
180 Detlef Schrempf 2.00 5.00
181 John Salley 2.00 5.00
182 Earl Monroe 2.00 5.00
183A Bill Walton Blazers/209* 4.00 10.00
183B Bill Walton/40* 20.00 50.00
Boston Celtics
183C Bill Walton/30* 12.00 30.00
Los Angeles Clippers
183D Bill Walton/20* 15.00 40.00
San Diego Clippers
184 Shawn Kemp 5.00 12.00
185 Wilt Chamberlain 4.00 10.00
186 Dan Issel 2.00 5.00
187 Jerry West 2.50 6.00
188 Bill Russell 3.00 8.00
189 Robert Parish 2.00 5.00
190 Maurice Cheeks 2.00 5.00
191 Allen Iverson 3.00 8.00
192 Anfernee Hardaway 5.00 12.00
193 Horace Grant 2.00 5.00
194 Walt Frazier 2.00 5.00
195 Yao Ming 2.50 6.00
196 Sean Elliott 2.00 5.00
197 Rod Strickland 2.00 5.00
198 Magic Johnson 5.00 12.00
199 Sam Jones 2.00 5.00
200 Tom Sanders 2.00 5.00
201 George Mikan 4.00 10.00
202 Steve Kerr 2.00 5.00
203 Walt Bellamy 2.00 5.00
204 Bruce Bowen 2.00 5.00
205 Larry Johnson 4.00 10.00
206 Cedric Ceballos 2.00 5.00
207 Vlade Divac 2.00 5.00
208 Rex Chapman 2.00 5.00
209 Karl Malone 2.50 6.00
210A Shaquille O'Neal Magic/79* 12.00 30.00
210B Shaquille O'Neal/50* 10.00 25.00
Cleveland Cavaliers
210C Shaquille O'Neal/20*
Boston Celtics
210D Shaquille O'Neal/40*
Miami Heat
210E Shaquille O'Neal/70* 12.00 30.00
Los Angeles Lakers
210F Shaquille O'Neal/40*
Phoenix Suns
211 John Starks 2.00 5.00
212 Zydrunas Ilgauskas 1.25 3.00
213A Robert Horry Rockets/129* 4.00 10.00
213B Robert Horry/60* 10.00 25.00
Los Angeles Lakers
213C Robert Horry/40* 12.00 30.00
San Antonio Spurs
213D Robert Horry/70* 4.00 10.00
Phoenix Suns
214A Dikembe Mutombo Nuggets/99*4.00 10.00
214B Dikembe Mutombo/30* 8.00 20.00
Philadelphia 76ers
214C Dikembe Mutombo/80* 6.00 15.00
Atlanta Hawks
214D Dikembe Mutombo/20*
New York Knicks
214E Dikembe Mutombo/10*
New Jersey Nets
214F Dikembe Mutombo/60* 8.00 20.00
Houston Rockets
215 Brad Davis 2.00 5.00
216 Jonny Flynn 1.25 3.00
217 Jamal Mashburn 2.00 5.00
218 Marvin Williams 1.50 4.00
219 John Lucas III 1.50 4.00
220 Nick Collison 1.25 3.00
221 J.J. Barea 2.00 5.00
222 Jonas Jerebko 1.25 3.00
223 Danny Green 2.00 5.00
224 Omer Asik 1.50 4.00
225 Dorell Wright 1.25 3.00

2011-12 Panini Gold Standard 14K Autographs

STATED PRINT RUN 25 TO 149 SER.#'d SETS
1 Allan Houston/149 8.00 20.00
2 Robert Parish/49 6.00 15.00
3 Adrian Dantley/149 5.00 12.00
4 Elgin Baylor/74 10.00 25.00
5 Ray Allen/49 EXCH 25.00 60.00
6 Clyde Drexler/49 20.00 50.00
7 Paul Pierce/49 15.00 40.00
8 Gary Payton/49 25.00 60.00
9 Larry Bird/49 40.00 100.00
10 Hal Greer/49 5.00 12.00
11 Walt Bellamy/49 6.00 15.00
12 Bob Pettit/49 10.00 25.00
13 Vince Carter/49 25.00 60.00
14 David Robinson/49 40.00 100.00
15 Mitch Richmond/149 10.00 25.00
16 Tom Chambers/149 5.00 12.00
17 John Stockton/25 50.00 125.00
18 Bernard King/149 5.00 12.00
19 Bob Lanier/49 6.00 15.00
20 Gail Goodrich/49 12.00 30.00
21 Dale Ellis/149 5.00 12.00
22 Scottie Pippen/49 EXCH 125.00 225.00
23 Isiah Thomas/49 12.00 30.00
24 Bob McAdoo/149 10.00 25.00
25 Antawn Jamison/149 5.00 12.00
26 Mark Aguirre/149 5.00 12.00
27 Dolph Schayes/49 5.00 12.00
28 Glen Rice/149 EXCH 6.00 15.00
29 Tracy McGrady/25 20.00 50.00
30 World B. Free/49 6.00 15.00
31 Calvin Murphy/49 5.00 12.00
32 Chris Mullin/149 10.00 25.00
33 Lenny Wilkens/49 5.00 12.00
34 Bailey Howell/49 10.00 25.00
35 Magic Johnson/49 40.00 100.00
36 Rolando Blackman/149 5.00 12.00
37 Earl Monroe/49 12.00 30.00
38 Kevin McHale/49 15.00 40.00
39 Michael Finley/149 6.00 15.00
41 Kevin Willis/149 5.00 12.00
42 Spencer Haywood/149 5.00 12.00
43 George McGinnis/149 5.00 12.00
44 Hersey Hawkins/149 5.00 12.00
45 Jason Kidd/25 20.00 50.00
46 Grant Hill/49 80.00 200.00
47 Nate Archibald/49 8.00 20.00
48 Joe Dumars/49 10.00 25.00
49 James Worthy/49 25.00 60.00
50 Billy Cunningham/49 15.00 40.00
51 Steve Nash/25 40.00 100.00
52 Juwan Howard/149 5.00 12.00
53 Rod Strickland/149 5.00 12.00
54 Kiki Vandeweghe/49 8.00 20.00
55 Jack Twyman/99 6.00 15.00
56 Detlef Schrempf/149 EXCH 8.00 20.00
57 Jeff Hornacek/49 6.00 15.00
58 Terry Porter/149 6.00 15.00
59 Walt Frazier/49 10.00 25.00
60 Tim Hardaway/149 8.00 20.00

2011-12 Panini Gold Standard 14K Memorabilia

STATED PRINT RUN 2 TO 149 SER.#'d SETS
SOME UNPRICED DUE TO SCARCITY
1 LeBron James/99 20.00 50.00
2 Chris Webber/99 10.00 25.00
3 Scottie Pippen/75 10.00 25.00
4 Chauncey Billups/49 5.00 12.00
5 Dennis Johnson/25 6.00 15.00
7 Shawn Marion/99 5.00 12.00
8 Elton Brand/99 5.00 12.00
9 Shawn Kemp/49 50.00 125.00
10 LeBron James/25 30.00 80.00
11 Vince Carter/99 8.00 20.00
12 Carmelo Anthony/149 6.00 15.00
13 Richard Hamilton/25 8.00 20.00
14 Rashard Lewis/99 4.00 10.00
15 Chauncey Billups/99 5.00 12.00
16 Mike Bibby/99 4.00 10.00
17 Jamaal Wilkes/25 15.00 40.00
18 Allan Houston/49 5.00 12.00
19 Dwyane Wade/149 12.00 30.00
21 Andre Miller/99 4.00 10.00
22 Alonzo Mourning/99 8.00 20.00
23 Pau Gasol/99 5.00 12.00
24 Joe Johnson/149 5.00 12.00
25 Eddie Jones/49 12.00 30.00
26 Paul Pierce/149 10.00 25.00
27 David Robinson/49 10.00 25.00
28 Ray Allen/99 6.00 15.00
29 Scottie Pippen/49 12.00 30.00
30 Tracy McGrady/35 5.00 12.00
31 Vince Carter/99 8.00 20.00
32 Tracy McGrady/99 5.00 12.00
33 Jason Terry/99 4.00 10.00
34 Steve Nash/49 5.00 12.00
35 Jason Kidd/49 5.00 12.00
36 Jason Richardson/99 5.00 12.00
37 Robert Parish/49 5.00 12.00
38 Clyde Drexler/49 8.00 20.00
40 Tom Chambers/49 5.00 12.00
41 Grant Hill/99 15.00 40.00
42 Kiki Vandeweghe/99 5.00 12.00
43 Chris Mullin/25 10.00 25.00
44 Mark Aguirre/49 5.00 12.00
45 Joe Dumars/25 5.00 12.00
46 Kevin Willis/49 5.00 12.00
47 Kevin McHale/49 5.00 12.00
48 Earl Monroe/25 30.00 80.00
49 Antawn Jamison/99 5.00 12.00
50 Isiah Thomas/25 8.00 20.00
51 John Stockton/49 12.00 30.00
52 Mitch Richmond/20 20.00 50.00
53 Larry Bird/25 25.00 60.00
55 James Worthy/25 10.00 25.00
57 Glen Rice/49 5.00 12.00

2011-12 Panini Gold Standard 14K Memorabilia Prime

STATED PRINT RUN ONE TO 25 SER.#'d SETS
SOME UNPRICED DUE TO SCARCITY
12 Carmelo Anthony/25 15.00 40.00
19 Dwyane Wade/25 75.00 150.00
26 Paul Pierce/25

2011-12 Panini Gold Standard 2011 Draft Pick Redemptions Autographs

RANDOM INSERTS IN PACKS
XRCA TBD AU EXCH 25.00 60.00
XRCB TBD AU EXCH 10.00 25.00
XRCC TBD AU EXCH 10.00 25.00
XRCD TBD AU EXCH 10.00 25.00
XRCE TBD AU EXCH 10.00 25.00
XRCF TBD AU EXCH 10.00 25.00
XRCG TBD AU EXCH 10.00 25.00
XRCH TBD AU EXCH 10.00 25.00
XRCI TBD AU EXCH 10.00 25.00
XRCJ TBD AU EXCH 10.00 25.00
XRCK TBD AU EXCH 10.00 25.00
XRCL TBD AU EXCH 10.00 25.00
XRCM TBD AU EXCH 10.00 25.00
XRCN TBD AU EXCH 10.00 25.00
XRCO TBD AU EXCH 10.00 25.00
XRCP TBD AU EXCH 10.00 25.00
XRCQ TBD AU EXCH 10.00 25.00
XRCR TBD AU EXCH 10.00 25.00
XRCS TBD AU EXCH 10.00 25.00
XRCT TBD AU EXCH 10.00 25.00
XRCU TBD AU EXCH 10.00 25.00
XRCV TBD AU EXCH 10.00 25.00
XRCW TBD AU EXCH 10.00 25.00
XRCX TBD AU EXCH 10.00 25.00
XRCY TBD AU EXCH 10.00 25.00
XRCZ TBD AU EXCH 10.00 25.00
XRCAA TBD AU EXCH 10.00 25.00
XRCBB TBD AU EXCH 10.00 25.00
XRCCC TBD AU EXCH 10.00 25.00
XRCDD TBD AU EXCH 10.00 25.00
XRCEE TBD AU EXCH 10.00 25.00
XRCFF TBD AU EXCH 10.00 25.00
XRCGG TBD AU EXCH 10.00 25.00
XRCHH TBD AU EXCH 10.00 25.00
XRCII TBD AU EXCH 10.00 25.00

2011-12 Panini Gold Standard 2012 Draft Pick Redemptions

RANDOM INSERTS IN PACKS
1 Anthony Davis EXCH 100.00 200.00
2 Michael Kidd-Gilchrist EXCH 25.00 60.00
3 Bradley Beal EXCH 20.00 50.00
4 Dion Waiters EXCH 20.00 50.00
5 Thomas Robinson EXCH 20.00 50.00
6 Damian Lillard EXCH 25.00 60.00
7 Harrison Barnes EXCH 20.00 50.00
8 Terrence Ross EXCH 12.00 30.00
9 Andre Drummond EXCH 12.00 30.00
10 Austin Rivers EXCH 20.00 50.00
11 Meyers Leonard EXCH 10.00 25.00
12 Jeremy Lamb EXCH 12.00 30.00
13 Kendall Marshall EXCH 12.00 30.00
14 John Henson EXCH 10.00 25.00
15 Maurice Harkless EXCH 8.00 20.00
16 Royce White EXCH 12.00 30.00
17 Tyler Zeller EXCH 12.00 30.00
18 Terrence Jones EXCH 15.00 40.00
19 Andrew Nicholson EXCH 10.00 25.00
20 Evan Fournier EXCH 8.00 20.00
21 Jared Sullinger EXCH 20.00 50.00
22 Fab Melo EXCH 12.00 30.00
23 John Jenkins EXCH 10.00 25.00
24 Jared Cunningham EXCH 8.00 20.00
25 Tony Wroten EXCH 8.00 20.00
26 Miles Plumlee EXCH 8.00 20.00
27 Arnett Moultrie EXCH 6.00 15.00
28 Perry Jones III EXCH 15.00 40.00
29 Marquis Teague EXCH 12.00 30.00
30 Festus Ezeli EXCH 8.00 20.00

2011-12 Panini Gold Standard 24K Autographs

STATED PRINT RUN 10 TO 149 SER.#'d SETS
SOME UNPRICED DUE TO SCARCITY
1 Kareem Abdul-Jabbar/25 50.00 125.00
2 Julius Erving/25 50.00 125.00
3 Hakeem Olajuwon/25 30.00 80.00
4 Kobe Bryant/49 100.00 200.00
5 Dan Issel/149 6.00 15.00
6 Elvin Hayes/49 6.00 15.00
7 Dirk Nowitzki/25 100.00 175.00
8 Oscar Robertson/25 40.00 100.00
9 Dominique Wilkins/25 15.00 40.00
10 George Gervin/149 10.00 25.00
11 John Havlicek/25 20.00 50.00
12 Alex English/149 6.00 15.00
13 Rick Barry/149 8.00 20.00
14 Jerry West/25 40.00 100.00
15 Shaquille O'Neal/20 100.00 175.00

2011-12 Panini Gold Standard 24K Memorabilia

STATED PRINT RUN 10 TO 149 SER.#'d SETS
SOME UNPRICED DUE TO SCARCITY
1 Kareem Abdul-Jabbar/49 12.00 30.00
2 Karl Malone/49 8.00 20.00
4 Kobe Bryant/149 25.00 60.00
5 Shaquille O'Neal/149 12.00 30.00
6 Moses Malone/49 6.00 15.00
7 Kevin Garnett/149 12.00 30.00
8 Hakeem Olajuwon/49 8.00 20.00
9 Dirk Nowitzki/149 8.00 20.00
10 Dominique Wilkins/149 8.00 20.00
11 George Gervin/149 6.00 15.00
12 Alex English/149 6.00 15.00
13 Jerry West/25 20.00 50.00
14 Patrick Ewing/149 8.00 20.00
15 Shaquille O'Neal/121 12.00 30.00
16 Allen Iverson/30 20.00 50.00

2011-12 Panini Gold Standard 24K Memorabilia Prime

*PRIME: 1X TO 2.5X BASE HI
STATED PRINT RUN 5 TO 25 SER.#'d SETS
SOME UNPRICED DUE TO SCARCITY
4 Kobe Bryant/25 175.00 350.0
14 Patrick Ewing/25 50.00 125.0

2011-12 Panini Gold Standard Black Gold Threads

STATED PRINT RUN 10 TO 149 SER.#'d SETS
SOME UNPRICED DUE TO SCARCITY
UNPRICED PRIME PRINT RUN 1 TO 5 SETS
1 Dirk Nowitzki/149 8.00 20.
2 Brandon Jennings/49 5.00 12.
3 Ricky Rubio/49 20.00 50.
4 Russell Westbrook/149 6.00 15.
5 Shawn Marion/49 5.00 12.
6 Shawn Kemp/49 30.00 80.
7 Stephen Curry/149 5.00 12.
8 Tim Duncan/49 8.00 20.
9 Toni Kukoc/49 8.00 20.
10 Tracy McGrady/49 5.00 12
11 Tyler Hansbrough/30 6.00 15
12 LeBron James/149 20.00 50
13 Dwight Howard/149 8.00 20
14 Drew Gooden/49 4.00 10
15 Dwyane Wade/149 10.00 25
16 Gary Payton/25 40.00 100
17 Jason Terry/25 6.00 15
18 Joakim Noah/25 6.00 15
19 Al Jefferson/149 5.00 12
20 Alonzo Mourning/49 40.00 100
21 Amare Stoudemire/49 5.00 12
22 Andre Iguodala/49 5.00 12
23 Andrew Bynum/149 6.00 15
24 Derrick Rose/149 15.00 40
25 Kobe Bryant/149 20.00 50
26 Kevin Garnett/49 10.00 25
27 Kevin Love/49 6.00 15
28 LaMarcus Aldridge/49 5.00 12
29 Manu Ginobili/49 5.00 12
30 Marc Gasol/49 5.00 12
31 Pau Gasol/49 6.00 15
32 Paul Pierce/149 8.00 20
33 Ben Gordon/49 5.00 12
34 Serge Ibaka/149 5.00 12
35 David Lee/49 4.00 10
36 DeMarcus Cousins/149 6.00 15
37 Andrew Bogut/49 5.00 12
38 Bill Cartwright/49 5.00 12
39 Blake Griffin/149 10.00 25
40 Brendan Haywood/149 3.00
41 Brook Lopez/149 5.00 1
42 Carlos Boozer/149 5.00 1
43 Carmelo Anthony/49 8.00 2
44 Chris Bosh/149 5.00 1
45 Chris Webber/49 12.00 3
46 Chuck Hayes/99 3.00
47 Courtney Lee/99 4.00 1
48 Darren Collison/49 5.00 1
49 Roy Hibbert/82 4.00 1
50 Derrick Favors/99 5.00 1
51 Danny Granger/99 5.00 1
52 Eddie Jones/49 10.00 2

van Turner/149 5.00 12.00
len Davis/99 4.00 10.00
rant Hill/99 15.00 40.00
reg Monroe/149 5.00 12.00
ames Harden/149 6.00 15.00
ason Kidd/99 6.00 15.00
aVale McGee/149 4.00 10.00
oe Dumars/25
ohn Wall/149 8.00 20.00
rue Holiday/149 5.00 12.00
ulius Erving/25 15.00 40.00
arl Malone/49 15.00 40.00
evin Durant/149 15.00 40.00
evin Willis/49 5.00 12.00
icolas Batum/149 5.00 12.00
uis Scola/99 4.00 10.00
uol Deng/99 5.00 12.00
yreke Evans/49 6.00 15.00
ince Carter/99 8.00 20.00
atrick Ewing/99 10.00 25.00
mri Casspi/49 3.00 8.00
ick Van Exel/49 10.00 25.00
loses Malone/25 8.00 20.00
lichael Beasley/49 5.00 12.00
lario Chalmers/49 5.00 12.00
ajon Rondo/49 8.00 20.00
osh Smith/99 5.00 12.00
udy Gay/99 5.00 12.00
andry Fields/149 5.00 12.00
iki Vandeweghe/99 5.00 12.00
evin Johnson/149 5.00 12.00
hris Paul/149 8.00 20.00
ndrea Bargnani/99 4.00 10.00
atrick Patterson/149 4.00 10.00
hris Kaman/99 4.00 10.00
lene/49 4.00 10.00
pencer Hawes/149 3.00 8.00
leepy Floyd/149 5.00 12.00
hawn Bradley/99 5.00 12.00
lex English/25 8.00 20.00
ill Laimbeer/49 5.00 12.00
chris Andersen/49 5.00 12.00
Danilo Gallinari/49 5.00 12.00
eMar DeRozan/149 5.00 12.00
'ao Ming/49 6.00 15.00
Tony Parker/49

2011-12 Panini Gold Standard Gold Rush

TED PRINT RUN 49 SER.#'d SETS
be Bryant 60.00 150.00
ul Pierce 20.00 50.00
Marcus Aldridge 15.00 40.00
ny Parker 40.00 70.00
reke Evans 15.00 40.00
ck Young 12.00 30.00
arc Gasol 15.00 40.00
sh Smith 15.00 40.00
evin Durant 50.00 125.00
Chris Bosh 15.00 40.00
mare Stoudemire 15.00 40.00
Kevin Martin 15.00 40.00
eBron James 60.00 150.00
ames Harden 20.00 50.00
Andrew Bogut 20.00 50.00
Al Jefferson 15.00 40.00
ason Terry 12.00 30.00
ason Kidd 25.00 60.00
Danny Granger 15.00 40.00
Dwyane Wade 50.00 125.00
y Lawson 15.00 40.00
lade Divac 15.00 40.00
ohn Starks 15.00 40.00
Gary Payton 25.00 60.00
Blake Griffin 30.00 80.00
Stephen Curry 15.00 40.00
Jordan Crawford 15.00 40.00
Gordon Hayward 15.00 40.00
Chris Paul 25.00 60.00
Pau Gasol 15.00 40.00
Brandon Jennings 15.00 40.00
Toni Kukoc 25.00 60.00
Landry Fields 15.00 40.00
Derrick Rose 50.00 125.00
Scottie Pippen 30.00 80.00
David Lee 12.00 30.00
Vince Carter 25.00 60.00
Shawn Marion 15.00 40.00
Andre Iguodala 15.00 40.00
Andre Miller 12.00 30.00
Jrue Holiday 15.00 40.00
Earl Monroe 15.00 40.00
David Robinson 25.00 60.00
Jerry West 20.00 50.00
Julius Erving 30.00 80.00
Wilt Chamberlain 30.00 80.00
Dwight Howard 25.00 60.00
George Mikan 30.00 80.00
Chris Mullin 15.00 40.00
Shaquille O'Neal 40.00 100.00

2011-12 Panini Gold Standard Gold Stars Materials

TED PRINT RUN 9 TO 149 SER.#'d SETS
ME UNPRICED DUE TO SCARCITY
evin Durant/149 10.00 25.00
cky Rubio/149 10.00 25.00
ajon Rondo/149 5.00 12.00
errick Rose/149 10.00 25.00
eBron James/149 12.00 30.00
ony Parker/149 3.00 8.00
eve Nash/149 4.00 10.00
irk Nowitzki/149 4.00 10.00
mare Stoudemire/149 3.00 8.00
Chris Paul/149 5.00 12.00
Dwight Howard/149 5.00 12.00
Dwyane Wade/149 6.00 15.00
Deron Williams/149 3.00 8.00
Andrea Bargnani/149 2.50 6.00
Tim Duncan/149 5.00 12.00
Carlos Boozer/149 3.00 8.00
Kevin Garnett/149 6.00 15.00
Kevin Love/149 4.00 10.00
LaMarcus Aldridge/149 3.00 8.00
Greg Monroe/149 3.00 8.00
Roy Hibbert/149 2.50 6.00
Russell Westbrook/149 5.00 12.00
Brandon Jennings/149 3.00 8.00
Kobe Bryant/149 12.00 30.00
Josh Smith/149 3.00 8.00
Monta Ellis/149 3.00 8.00
Chris Bosh/149 3.00 8.00
D.J. Augustin/40 2.50 6.00
Al Jefferson/149 3.00 8.00
Andrew Bynum/149 4.00 10.00
Ryan Anderson/149 2.50 6.00
Brook Lopez/149 3.00 8.00
Marcin Gortat/149 6.00 15.00
John Wall/149 5.00 12.00

35 Tyreke Evans/149 3.00 8.00
36 Kevin Martin/149 3.00 8.00
37 Carmelo Anthony/149 4.00 10.00
38 Paul Pierce/149 5.00 12.00
40 Marcus Thornton/149 3.00 8.00

2011-12 Panini Gold Standard Gold Stars Materials Prime

*PRIME: 1.25X TO 3X BASE HI
STATED PRINT RUN 3 TO 25 SER.#'d SETS
SOME UNPRICED DUE TO SCARCITY
1 Kevin Durant/25 40.00 100.00
2 Ricky Rubio/25 50.00 125.00
4 Derrick Rose/25 40.00 100.00
6 Tony Parker/25 12.00 30.00
12 Dwyane Wade/25 40.00 70.00
24 Kobe Bryant/15 50.00 125.00
27 Chris Bosh/25 12.00 30.00

2011-12 Panini Gold Standard Golden 50 Materials

STATED PRINT RUN 5 TO 149 SER.#'d SETS
SOME UNPRICED DUE TO SCARCITY
1 James Worthy/25 8.00 20.00
2 Robert Parish/99 6.00 15.00
3 Kevin McHale/99 5.00 12.00
4 Kareem Abdul-Jabbar/25 8.00 20.00
5 Karl Malone/99 6.00 15.00
6 Sam Jones/25 8.00 20.00
7 George Gervin/149 5.00 12.00
8 Patrick Ewing/149 6.00 15.00
9 Shaquille O'Neal/149 10.00 25.00
10 Earl Monroe/149 6.00 15.00
11 Scottie Pippen/149 10.00 25.00
12 Clyde Drexler/149 6.00 15.00
13 David Robinson/99 8.00 20.00
14 Julius Erving/25 12.00 30.00
15 John Stockton/99 8.00 20.00
16 Isiah Thomas/99 5.00 12.00
18 George Mikan/25 15.00 40.00
19 Hakeem Olajuwon/149 6.00 15.00
20 Julius Erving/25 12.00 30.00
21 Shaquille O'Neal/149 10.00 25.00
22 Shaquille O'Neal/57 12.00 30.00
23 Shaquille O'Neal/149 10.00 25.00
24 Scottie Pippen/149 10.00 25.00
25 Clyde Drexler/149 6.00 15.00

2011-12 Panini Gold Standard Golden 50 Materials Prime

*PRIME: 1X TO 2.5X BASE HI
STATED PRINT RUN ONE TO 25 SER.#'d SETS
SOME UNPRICED DUE TO SCARCITY
21 Shaquille O'Neal/21 25.00 60.00

2011-12 Panini Gold Standard Greatest Graphs

STATED PRINT RUN 10 TO 149 SER.#'d SETS
SOME UNPRICED DUE TO SCARCITY
1 John Havlicek/25 40.00 70.00
2 Kareem Abdul-Jabbar/25 75.00 150.00
3 Julius Erving/25 50.00 125.00
4 Lenny Wilkens/149 6.00 15.00
5 Nate Archibald/149 6.00 15.00
6 Rick Barry/25 12.00 30.00
7 Elgin Baylor/49 15.00 40.00
8 Larry Bird/25 50.00 125.00
9 Dave Cowens/149 8.00 20.00
10 Billy Cunningham/149 20.00 50.00
11 Clyde Drexler/25 35.00 70.00
12 Walt Frazier/149 10.00 25.00
13 Hal Greer/149 6.00 15.00
14 Elvin Hayes/149 6.00 15.00
15 Magic Johnson/25 100.00 200.00
16 Sam Jones/25 20.00 50.00
17 Bob Pettit/25 50.00 125.00
18 Kevin McHale/25 25.00 60.00
19 Earl Monroe/25 15.00 40.00
20 Hakeem Olajuwon/25 30.00 80.00
21 Robert Parish/149 8.00 20.00
22 Scottie Pippen/25 EXCH 175.00 350.00
23 Willis Reed/25 15.00 40.00
24 Oscar Robertson/25 50.00 125.00
25 David Robinson/25 50.00 125.00
27 Dolph Schayes/149 6.00 15.00
29 John Stockton/25 50.00 125.00
30 Isiah Thomas/149 EXCH 10.00 25.00
31 Nate Thurmond/149 6.00 15.00
32 Wes Unseld/149 6.00 15.00
33 Bill Walton/99 8.00 20.00
35 James Worthy/25 35.00 70.00

2011-12 Panini Gold Standard Hall of Gold Materials

STATED PRINT RUN 5 TO 149 SER.#'d SETS
SOME UNPRICED DUE TO SCARCITY
1 Dominique Wilkins/149 5.00 12.00
2 Dennis Rodman/149 8.00 20.00
3 Clyde Drexler/149 5.00 12.00
4 Joe Dumars/49 4.00 10.00
5 George Gervin/149 4.00 10.00
6 Alex English/149 4.00 10.00
8 Patrick Ewing/149 10.00 25.00
10 Artis Gilmore/25 4.00 10.00
11 David Robinson/149 6.00 15.00
13 James Worthy/25 8.00 20.00
15 Dan Issel/25 4.00 10.00
17 Karl Malone/149 5.00 12.00
18 Kevin McHale/99 4.00 10.00
21 Scottie Pippen/149 8.00 20.00
22 John Stockton/49 8.00 20.00
23 Isiah Thomas/49 4.00 10.00
24 Dennis Johnson/149 4.00 10.00
25 Chris Mullin/49 6.00 15.00

2011-12 Panini Gold Standard Hall of Gold Materials Prime

*PRIME: 1X TO 2.5X BASE HI
STATED PRINT RUN ONE TO 25 SER.#'d SETS
SOME UNPRICED DUE TO SCARCITY
21 Scottie Pippen/25 40.00 100.00

2011-12 Panini Gold Standard Marks of the Hall Autographs

STATED PRINT RUN 10 TO 149 SER.#'d SETS
SOME UNPRICED DUE TO SCARCITY
1 Pat Riley/25 75.00 150.00
2 Kareem Abdul-Jabbar/25 50.00 125.00
3 Nate Archibald/99 10.00 25.00
4 Bobby Wanzer/149 6.00 15.00
5 Elgin Baylor/24 40.00 70.00
7 Dolph Schayes/149 10.00 25.00
8 Bob Pettit/25 25.00 60.00
9 Arnie Risen/149 8.00 20.00
10 Robert Parish/149 8.00 20.00
11 Oscar Robertson/25 50.00 125.00
13 Hal Greer/149 6.00 15.00
14 Frank Ramsey/149 6.00 15.00
15 Willis Reed/25 25.00 60.00
16 John Havlicek/25 40.00 70.00
17 Chris Mullin/149 12.00 30.00
18 Bob McAdoo/149 10.00 25.00
20 Clyde Lovellette/149 8.00 20.00
21 Harry Gallatin/149 6.00 15.00
23 Dan Issel/149 8.00 20.00
26 James Worthy/25 30.00 80.00
27 Dominique Wilkins/25 30.00 80.00
28 Lenny Wilkens/149 6.00 15.00
29 Bill Walton/99 10.00 25.00
30 Wes Unseld/99 8.00 20.00
31 David Thompson/99 8.00 20.00
32 Isiah Thomas/149 EXCH 12.00 30.00
33 John Stockton/25 60.00 150.00
34 Scottie Pippen/25 150.00 300.00
35 Calvin Murphy/149 8.00 20.00
36 Earl Monroe/149 12.00 30.00
37 Bob Lanier/25 20.00 50.00
38 Sam Jones/25 40.00 100.00
39 K.C. Jones/25 25.00 60.00
40 George Gervin/149 10.00 25.00
41 Elvin Hayes/149 8.00 20.00
42 Gail Goodrich/149 6.00 15.00
43 Walt Frazier/99 15.00 40.00
45 Joe Dumars/149 8.00 20.00
46 Dave Cowens/99 12.00 30.00
47 Clyde Drexler/25 40.00 100.00
48 Alex English/99 8.00 20.00
49 Adrian Dantley/149 6.00 15.00
50 Artis Gilmore/25 15.00 40.00

2011-12 Panini Gold Standard Private Signings

RANDOM INSERTS IN PACKS
1 Oscar Robertson 50.00 125.00
2 John Wall 100.00 200.00
3 Elgin Baylor 25.00 60.00
4 Kareem Abdul-Jabbar 75.00 150.00
5 John Stockton 100.00 200.00
6 Magic Johnson 100.00 175.00
7 Kevin Durant 250.00 450.00
8 Julius Erving
9 Derrick Rose 150.00 250.00
10 David Robinson 50.00 125.00
11 Bill Russell 75.00 150.00
12 Jerry West 25.00 60.00
13 John Havlicek 30.00 80.00
14 Pat Riley 30.00 80.00
15 Grant Hill 150.00 300.00
16 Toni Kukoc 25.00 60.00

2011-12 Panini Gold Standard Signs of Gold

STATED PRINT RUN 10 TO 149 SER.#'d SETS
SOME UNPRICED DUE TO SCARCITY
1 Chris Paul/25 EXCH 40.00 100.00
4 Andrew Bynum/25 10.00 25.00
5 Russell Westbrook/49 EXCH 25.00 60.00
6 Ray Allen/25 EXCH
7 DeMarcus Cousins/49 15.00 40.00
8 Kobe Bryant/49 100.00 200.00
11 Artis Gilmore/49 6.00 15.00
12 Ronnie Brewer/149 4.00 10.00
14 Mike Bibby/49 6.00 15.00
15 Danny Granger/49 6.00 15.00
16 Al Jefferson/49 6.00 15.00
17 David Lee/149 EXCH 4.00 10.00
18 LaMarcus Aldridge/49 8.00 20.00
19 Jamal Crawford/149 8.00 20.00
20 Joe Johnson/25 10.00 25.00
21 Deron Williams/25 15.00 40.00
22 Jason Kidd/25 20.00 50.00
23 Luol Deng/49 8.00 20.00
24 Andrea Bargnani/49 8.00 20.00
25 Kevin Love/25 25.00 60.00
26 Glen Rice/149 EXCH 5.00 12.00
27 David Thompson/49 4.00 10.00
28 David Robinson/25 40.00 100.00
29 Paul George/149 10.00 25.00
30 Greg Monroe/149 5.00 12.00
31 Walt Frazier/49 8.00 20.00
33 Detlef Schrempf/149 EXCH 6.00 15.00
34 Stephen Curry/49 10.00 25.00
35 Tyreke Evans/49 10.00 25.00
36 Marcin Gortat/149 6.00 15.00
37 Kevin Martin/149 4.00 10.00
38 Michael Beasley/49 EXCH 5.00 12.00
39 Blake Griffin/25 50.00 125.00
40 Brandon Jennings/49 EXCH 10.00 25.00
41 Mike Conley/149 4.00 10.00
42 Chauncey Billups/25 10.00 25.00
43 Ty Lawson/149 EXCH 8.00 20.00
44 Tony Parker/25 20.00 50.00
45 O.J. Mayo/149 EXCH 6.00 15.00
46 Vince Carter/25 30.00 80.00
47 Clyde Drexler/25 25.00 60.00
48 Mo Williams/25 5.00 12.00
49 Jeff Teague/149 4.00 10.00
50 Dikembe Mutombo/49 15.00 40.00
51 James Harden/49 EXCH 12.00 30.00
52 Serge Ibaka/149 EXCH 8.00 20.00
53 Juwan Howard/149 5.00 12.00
54 Bernard King/149 4.00 10.00
55 Robert Parish/49 6.00 15.00
56 Mark Price/149 10.00 25.00
57 Danilo Gallinari/49 5.00 12.00
58 Jason Richardson/49 4.00 10.00
59 Andre Iguodala/49 8.00 20.00
60 Grant Hill/25 150.00 300.00
61 George Gervin/49 10.00 25.00
62 World B. Free/49 6.00 15.00
63 Metta World Peace/25 EXCH 10.00 25.00
64 Spencer Haywood/149 4.00 10.00
65 Gerald Wallace/49 6.00 15.00
66 Dave Cowens/49 6.00 15.00
67 Hal Greer/49 4.00 10.00
68 Delonte West/149 4.00 10.00
69 Shane Battier/49 10.00 25.00
70 Ben Gordon/25 4.00 10.00
71 Kyle Lowry/149 4.00 10.00
72 Ersan Ilyasova/149 6.00 15.00
73 Kris Humphries/149 EXCH 4.00 10.00
74 Chris Kaman/49 4.00 10.00
75 Trevor Ariza/49 EXCH 4.00 10.00
76 J.R. Smith/149 4.00 10.00
77 DeJuan Blair/149 EXCH 6.00 15.00
78 DeMar DeRozan/49 8.00 20.00
79 Gordon Hayward/149 6.00 15.00
80 Nick Young/149 6.00 15.00
81 D.J. Augustin/49 4.00 10.00
82 Richard Hamilton/25 12.00 30.00
83 Joakim Noah/49 12.00 30.00
84 Paul Westphal/49 5.00 12.00
85 Jose Calderon/149 5.00 12.00
86 Isiah Thomas/149 EXCH 10.00 25.00
87 Mitch Richmond/149 10.00 25.00
88 Alonzo Mourning/25 100.00 200.00
89 Xavier Henry/149 4.00 10.00
90 Marc Gasol/25 EXCH 12.00 30.00
91 Tayshaun Prince/49 5.00 12.00
93 Bill Walton/49 8.00 20.00
94 K.C. Jones/25 10.00 25.00
95 Elvin Hayes/25 8.00 20.00
96 Jalen Rose/149 5.00 12.00
97 Jamal Mashburn/149 6.00 15.00
98 James Worthy/49 20.00 50.00
99 Mark Aguirre/149 4.00 10.00
100 Muggsy Bogues/149 10.00 25.00

2011-12 Panini Gold Standard Superscribe Autographs

STATED PRINT RUN 25 TO 149 SER.#'d SETS
1 Stephen Curry/149 12.00 30.00
2 Brandon Jennings/49 EXCH 12.00 30.00
3 DeMar DeRozan/149 8.00 20.00
4 Antawn Jamison/149 5.00 12.00
5 Stephen Jackson/149 6.00 15.00
6 Luis Scola/149 EXCH 6.00 15.00
7 Kevin Love/25 30.00 80.00
8 Kyle Lowry/149 4.00 10.00
9 Ryan Anderson/149 4.00 10.00
10 Roy Hibbert/149 6.00 15.00
11 Tyson Chandler/99 10.00 25.00
12 Paul George/149 15.00 40.00
13 Gary Neal/149 EXCH 6.00 15.00
14 Evan Turner/25 20.00 50.00
15 David Thompson/149 4.00 10.00
16 Jameer Nelson/149 4.00 10.00
17 Channing Frye/149 4.00 10.00
18 Luke Ridnour/149 4.00 10.00
19 Chris Kaman/149 5.00 12.00
20 Jeff Teague/149 4.00 10.00
21 Rajon Rondo/49 EXCH 30.00 80.00
22 Gerald Wallace/49 8.00 20.00
23 Josh Smith/49 6.00 15.00
24 Kobe Bryant USA Inscription/149700.00 1300.00
25 Jrue Holiday/149 8.00 20.00
26 Wesley Matthews/149 6.00 15.00
27 Devin Harris/149 EXCH 6.00 15.00
28 Shane Battier/149 8.00 20.00
29 Russell Westbrook/49 40.00 70.00
30 Chase Budinger/149 4.00 10.00
31 DeJuan Blair/149 EXCH 5.00 12.00
32 Blake Griffin/49 50.00 125.00
33 Jodie Meeks/149 EXCH 6.00 15.00
34 Caron Butler/49 8.00 20.00
35 Kevin Durant/49 150.00 275.00
36 Landry Fields/149 8.00 20.00
37 Derek Fisher/149 8.00 20.00
38 Rudy Gay/149 EXCH 6.00 15.00
39 Nene/149 EXCH 6.00 15.00
40 Tyler Hansbrough/149 5.00 12.00
41 Ty Lawson/149 10.00 25.00
42 Kris Humphries/149 EXCH 4.00 10.00
43 Marcin Gortat/149 8.00 20.00
44 DeMarcus Cousins/149 15.00 40.00
45 Eric Gordon/149 8.00 20.00
46 Serge Ibaka/149 EXCH 10.00 25.00
47 Chris Andersen/49 30.00 80.00
48 DeAndre Jordan/149 10.00 25.00
49 Zach Randolph/49 8.00 20.00
50 J.R. Smith/149 4.00 10.00

2012-13 Panini Kobe Anthology

COMMON CARD (1-200) 2.50 6.00
RANDOM INSERTS IN 12-13 PANINI PRODUCTS

2012-13 Panini Kobe Anthology Gold

COMMON CARD (1-200) 12.00 30.00
STATED PRINT RUN 24 SER.#'d SETS
UNPRICED PLATINUM PRINT RUN 8 SETS

2012-13 Panini Kobe Anthology Memorabilia

COMMON CARD (1-50) 15.00 40.00
STATED PRINT RUN 24 SER.#'d SETS
UNPRICED PRIME PRINT RUN 8 SETS

2009 Panini National Convention

These cards were randomly inserted into silver packs that were available at the 2009 National in Cleveland and feature the design used in 2009-10 Prestige. There were also parallel versions available for the rookie players - these were Blue #'d xx/50; Red #'d xx/50 and Gold #'d xx/25.

*BLUE: .6X TO 1.5X BASE HI
*GOLD: .75X TO 2X BASE HI
*RED: .6X TO 1.5X BASE HI
BG Blake Griffin 10.00 25.00
BW Bill Walton OS .60 1.50
DR Derrick Rose 10.00 25.00
HT Hasheem Thabeet 2.00 5.00
KM Kevin McHale OS .60 1.50
LB Larry Bird OS 2.00 5.00
TH Tyler Hansbrough 3.00 8.00

2009 Panini National Convention Autographs

For the 2009 National Sports Collectors Convention, newly licensed Panini had two of their new spokesman sign at their booth for free. Earlier in the week, Panini gave away trade cards, which served to hold a place in the line for the cardholder, however, both Blake Griffin and Tyler Hansbrough signed many more autographs than just the 150 trade cards that were handed out on the floor.

BG Blake Griffin Fabric 125.00 300.00
HT Hasheem Thabeet Fabric 8.00 20.00
OM O.J. Mayo Fabric 15.00 40.00
TH Tyler Hansbrough Fabric 30.00 80.00
BG09 Blake Griffin 75.00 200.00
BG0925 Blake Griffin/25 125.00 300.00
BG0950 Blake Griffin/50 75.00 200.00
TH09 Tyler Hansbrough 20.00 50.00
TH0925 Tyler Hansbrough/25 30.00 80.00
TH0950 Tyler Hansbrough/50 25.00 60.00
NNO Blake Griffin Trade 4.00 10.00
NNO Tyler Hansbrough Trade 2.00 5.00

2011 Panini National Convention VIP

COMPLETE SET (6) 75.00 150.00
*RED: 1.25X TO 3X BASE HI
RED PRINT RUN 25 SER.#'d SETS
UNPRICED BLUE PRINT RUN 10 SETS
UNPRICED GREEN PRINT RUN 5 SETS
VIP 5 AND 6 DO NOT HAVE PARALLELS
VIP1 Kobe Bryant 2.50 6.00
VIP2 Blake Griffin 1.50 4.00
VIP3 John Wall 2.00 5.00
VIP4 Kevin Durant 2.00 5.00
VIP5 Kyrie Irving 50.00 125.00
VIP6 Derrick Williams 15.00 40.00

2012 Panini National Convention

1-20 CRACKED ICE/25: 5X TO 12X BASE HI
21-40 CRACKED ICE/25: 1.5X TO 4X BASE HI
UNPRICED PLATE ANNCD PRINT RUN 5 SETS
6 Kobe Bryant 1.00 2.50
7 Blake Griffin .50 1.25
8 Kevin Durant .75 2.00
20 Bill Russell .60 1.50
35 Kyrie Irving/499 8.00 20.00
36 Derrick Williams/499 2.50 6.00
37 Anthony Davis/499 8.00 20.00
38 Michael Kidd-Gilchrist/499 4.00 10.00
39 Thomas Robinson/499 3.00 8.00
40 Harrison Barnes/499 2.50 6.00

2012 Panini National Convention VIP

COMPLETE SET (6) 12.00 30.00
4 Kyrie Irving 4.00 10.00
5 Anthony Davis 4.00 10.00
6 Michael Kidd-Gilchrist 2.50 6.00

2011-12 Panini Past and Present

COMPLETE SET (200) 25.00 60.00
1 LaMarcus Aldridge .40 1.00
2 Ray Allen .40 1.00
3 Chris Andersen .40 1.00
4 Carmelo Anthony .50 1.25
5 Shane Battier .30 .75
6 Eric Bledsoe .40 1.00
7 Carlos Boozer .40 1.00
8 Chris Bosh .40 1.00
9 Elton Brand .40 1.00
10 Andrew Bynum .50 1.25
11 Vince Carter .50 1.25
12 Tyson Chandler .30 .75
13 Darren Collison .40 1.00
14 Mike Conley .30 .75
15 Stephen Curry .40 1.00
16 Baron Davis .40 1.00
17 Brandon Bass .25 .60
18 Luol Deng .40 1.00
19 DeMar DeRozan .40 1.00
20 Tim Duncan .60 1.50
21 Kevin Durant 1.25 3.00
22 Monta Ellis .40 1.00
23 Raymond Felton .30 .75
24 Derek Fisher .30 .75
25 Kevin Garnett .75 2.00
26 Marc Gasol .40 1.00
27 Pau Gasol .40 1.00
28 Manu Ginobili .40 1.00
29 Marcin Gortat .40 1.00
30 Danny Granger .40 1.00
31 Blake Griffin .75 2.00
32 James Harden .50 1.25
33 Devin Harris .40 1.00
34 Roy Hibbert .30 .75
35 George Hill .30 .75
36 Grant Hill .50 1.25
37 Dwight Howard .60 1.50
38 Serge Ibaka .40 1.00
39 Andre Iguodala .40 1.00
40 LeBron James 1.50 4.00
41 Al Jefferson .40 1.00
42 Brandon Jennings .40 1.00
43 Joe Johnson .40 1.00
44 DeAndre Jordan .40 1.00
45 Jason Kidd .40 1.00
46 Ty Lawson .40 1.00
47 Brook Lopez .40 1.00
48 Kevin Love .50 1.25
49 Shawn Marion .40 1.00
50 Wesley Matthews .40 1.00
51 Tracy McGrady .40 1.00
52 Greg Monroe .40 1.00
53 Steve Nash .40 1.00
54 Nene .30 .75
55 Joakim Noah .40 1.00
56 Dirk Nowitzki .50 1.25
57 Chris Paul .60 1.50
58 Tony Parker .40 1.00
59 Paul Pierce .50 1.25
60 Jason Richardson .40 1.00
61 Rajon Rondo .50 1.25
62 Ricky Rubio 1.00 2.50
63 Josh Smith .40 1.00
64 Tiago Splitter .30 .75
65 Amare Stoudemire .40 1.00
66 Jason Terry .30 .75
67 Hedo Turkoglu .40 1.00
68 Evan Turner .40 1.00
69 Ekpe Udoh .25 .60
70 Dwyane Wade .75 2.00
71 David West .40 1.00
72 Russell Westbrook .50 1.25
73 Deron Williams .40 1.00
74 Jeremy Lin 1.00 2.50
75 Thaddeus Young .25 .60
76 Elgin Baylor .40 1.00
77 Larry Bird 1.25 3.00
78 Julius Erving .75 2.00
79 Patrick Ewing .50 1.25
80 George Gervin .40 1.00
81 John Havlicek .50 1.25
82 Magic Johnson 1.00 2.50
83 Sam Jones .40 1.00
84 Karl Malone .50 1.25
85 Pete Maravich 1.25 3.00
86 George Mikan .75 2.00
87 Hakeem Olajuwon .50 1.25
88 Shaquille O'Neal .75 2.00
89 Scottie Pippen .75 2.00
90 Willis Reed .40 1.00
91 Oscar Robertson .50 1.25
92 David Robinson .60 1.50
93 Bill Russell .60 1.50
94 John Stockton .60 1.50
95 Isiah Thomas .40 1.00
96 David Thompson .40 1.00
97 Wes Unseld .40 1.00
98 Bill Walton .40 1.00
99 Jerry West .50 1.25
100 James Worthy .50 1.25
101 Carmelo Anthony .50 1.25
102 Ray Allen .40 1.00
103 Shane Battier .30 .75
104 Andrea Bargnani .30 .75
105 Michael Beasley .40 1.00
106 Chauncey Billups .40 1.00
107 Andrew Bogut .40 1.00
108 Carlos Boozer .40 1.00
109 Chris Bosh .40 1.00
110 Elton Brand .40 1.00
111 Kobe Bryant 1.50 4.00
112 Tyson Chandler .30 .75
113 DeMarcus Cousins .50 1.25
114 Stephen Curry .40 1.00
115 Baron Davis .40 1.00
116 Luol Deng .40 1.00
117 Tim Duncan .60 1.50
118 Kevin Durant 1.25 3.00
119 Monta Ellis .40 1.00
120 Tyreke Evans .40 1.00
121 Kevin Garnett .75 2.00
122 Pau Gasol .40 1.00
123 Rudy Gay .40 1.00
124 Eric Gordon .40 1.00
125 Danny Granger .40 1.00
126 Blake Griffin .75 2.00
127 Richard Hamilton .30 .75
128 Roy Hibbert .30 .75
129 Tyler Hansbrough .40 1.00
130 James Harden .50 1.25
131 Devin Harris .40 1.00
132 Grant Hill .50 1.25
133 Al Horford .30 .75
134 Dwight Howard .60 1.50
135 Serge Ibaka .40 1.00
136 Andre Iguodala .40 1.00
137 LeBron James 1.50 4.00
138 Stephen Jackson .30 .75
139 Al Jefferson .40 1.00
140 Joe Johnson .40 1.00
141 Jason Kidd .40 1.00
142 Ty Lawson .40 1.00
143 David Lee .30 .75
144 Brook Lopez .40 1.00
145 Kevin Love .50 1.25
146 Kyle Lowry .30 .75
147 Shawn Marion .40 1.00
148 Kevin Martin .40 1.00
149 Andre Miller .30 .75
150 Paul Millsap .30 .75
151 Steve Nash .40 1.00
152 Jameer Nelson .30 .75
153 Nene .30 .75
154 Joakim Noah .40 1.00
155 Dirk Nowitzki .50 1.25
156 Lamar Odom .40 1.00
157 Emeka Okafor .40 1.00
158 Chris Paul .60 1.50
159 Paul Pierce .50 1.25
160 Zach Randolph .30 .75
161 Rajon Rondo .50 1.25
162 Derrick Rose 1.25 3.00
163 Luis Scola .30 .75
164 Josh Smith .40 1.00
165 Amare Stoudemire .40 1.00
166 Rodney Stuckey .40 1.00
167 Jeff Teague .30 .75
168 Jason Terry .30 .75
169 Hedo Turkoglu .40 1.00
170 Dwyane Wade .75 2.00
171 John Wall .60 1.50
172 Gerald Wallace .40 1.00
173 Russell Westbrook .50 1.25
174 Deron Williams .40 1.00
175 Jeremy Lin 1.00 2.50
176 Nate Archibald .40 1.00
177 B.J. Armstrong .40 1.00
178 Elgin Baylor .40 1.00
179 Rick Barry .40 1.00
180 Walt Bellamy .40 1.00
181 Bill Cartwright .40 1.00
182 Tom Chambers .40 1.00
183 Bob Cousy .60 1.50
184 Dave DeBusschere .40 1.00
185 Walt Frazier .40 1.00
186 Harry Gallatin .40 1.00
187 Artis Gilmore .40 1.00
188 Phil Jackson .50 1.25
189 K.C. Jones .40 1.00
190 Mitch Kupchak .40 1.00
191 Clyde Lovellette .40 1.00
192 Jerry Lucas .40 1.00
193 Moses Malone .40 1.00
194 Gail Goodrich .40 1.00
195 Vern Mikkelsen .40 1.00
196 Bob Pettit .40 1.00
197 Robert Parish .40 1.00
198 Wes Unseld .40 1.00
199 Jo Jo White .40 1.00
200 Lenny Wilkens .40 1.00

2011-12 Panini Past and Present 2011 Draft Pick Redemptions Autographs

RANDOM INSERTS IN PACKS
XRCA TBD AU EXCH 25.00 60.00
XRCB TBD AU EXCH 10.00 25.00
XRCC TBD AU EXCH 10.00 25.00
XRCD TBD AU EXCH 10.00 25.00
XRCE TBD AU EXCH 10.00 25.00
XRCF TBD AU EXCH 10.00 25.00
XRCG TBD AU EXCH 10.00 25.00
XRCH TBD AU EXCH 10.00 25.00
XRCI TBD AU EXCH 10.00 25.00
XRCJ TBD AU EXCH 10.00 25.00
XRCK TBD AU EXCH 10.00 25.00
XRCL TBD AU EXCH 10.00 25.00
XRCM TBD AU EXCH 10.00 25.00
XRCN TBD AU EXCH 10.00 25.00
XRCO TBD AU EXCH 10.00 25.00
XRCP TBD AU EXCH 10.00 25.00
XRCQ TBD AU EXCH 10.00 25.00
XRCR TBD AU EXCH 10.00 25.00
XRCS TBD AU EXCH 10.00 25.00
XRCT TBD AU EXCH 10.00 25.00
XRCU TBD AU EXCH 10.00 25.00
XRCV TBD AU EXCH 10.00 25.00
XRCW TBD AU EXCH 10.00 25.00
XRCX TBD AU EXCH 10.00 25.00
XRCY TBD AU EXCH 10.00 25.00
XRCZ TBD AU EXCH 10.00 25.00
XRCAA TBD AU EXCH 10.00 25.00
XRCBB TBD AU EXCH 10.00 25.00
XRCCC TBD AU EXCH 10.00 25.00
XRCDD TBD AU EXCH 10.00 25.00
XRCEE TBD AU EXCH 10.00 25.00
XRCFF TBD AU EXCH 10.00 25.00
XRCGG TBD AU EXCH 10.00 25.00
XRCHH TBD AU EXCH 10.00 25.00
XRCII TBD AU EXCH 10.00 25.00

2011-12 Panini Past and Present 2012 Draft Pick Redemptions

RANDOM INSERTS IN PACKS
1 Anthony Davis EXCH 60.00 150.00
2 Michael Kidd-Gilchrist EXCH 20.00 50.00
3 Bradley Beal EXCH 15.00 40.00
4 Dion Waiters EXCH 15.00 40.00
5 Thomas Robinson EXCH 15.00 40.00
6 Damian Lillard EXCH 20.00 50.00
7 Harrison Barnes EXCH 15.00 40.00
8 Terrence Ross EXCH 10.00 25.00
9 Andre Drummond EXCH 10.00 25.00
10 Austin Rivers EXCH 15.00 40.00
11 Meyers Leonard EXCH 8.00 20.00
12 Jeremy Lamb EXCH 10.00 25.00
13 Kendall Marshall EXCH 10.00 25.00
14 John Henson EXCH 8.00 20.00
15 Maurice Harkless EXCH 6.00 15.00
16 Royce White EXCH 10.00 25.00
17 Tyler Zeller EXCH 10.00 25.00
18 Terrence Jones EXCH 12.00 30.00
19 Andrew Nicholson EXCH 8.00 20.00
20 Evan Fournier EXCH 6.00 15.00
21 Jared Sullinger EXCH 15.00 40.00
22 Fab Melo EXCH 10.00 25.00
23 John Jenkins EXCH 8.00 20.00
24 Jared Cunningham EXCH 6.00 15.00
25 Tony Wroten EXCH 6.00 15.00
NNO COMPLETE SET EXCH 200.00 400.00

2011-12 Panini Past and Present Autographs

RANDOM INSERTS IN PACKS
5 Shane Battier 15.00 40.00
6 Eric Bledsoe 8.00 20.00
14 Mike Conley 5.00 12.00
16 Baron Davis 6.00 15.00
31 Blake Griffin 60.00 120.00
32 James Harden 25.00 60.00
36 Grant Hill 100.00 200.00
38 Serge Ibaka EXCH 8.00 20.00
42 Brandon Jennings 12.00 30.00
47 Brook Lopez 5.00 12.00
48 Kevin Love 15.00 40.00
52 Greg Monroe 5.00 12.00
53 Steve Nash 30.00 80.00
56 Dirk Nowitzki 60.00 120.00
61 Rajon Rondo 20.00 50.00
65 Amare Stoudemire 12.00 30.00
68 Evan Turner 10.00 25.00
72 Russell Westbrook 25.00 60.00
74 Jeremy Lin 75.00 200.00
76 Elgin Baylor 12.00 30.00
80 George Gervin 10.00 25.00
83 Sam Jones 8.00 20.00
87 Hakeem Olajuwon 25.00 60.00
91 Oscar Robertson 40.00 100.00
96 David Thompson 5.00 12.00
97 Wes Unseld 10.00 25.00
98 Bill Walton 6.00 15.00
100 James Worthy 20.00 50.00
103 Shane Battier 15.00 40.00
107 Andrew Bogut 10.00 25.00
111 Kobe Bryant 100.00 200.00
113 DeMarcus Cousins 15.00 40.00
114 Stephen Curry 6.00 15.00
115 Baron Davis 6.00 15.00
126 Blake Griffin 60.00 120.00
127 Richard Hamilton 8.00 20.00
133 Al Horford 5.00 12.00
135 Serge Ibaka EXCH 8.00 20.00
144 Brook Lopez 5.00 12.00
145 Kevin Love 15.00 40.00
151 Steve Nash 30.00 80.00
155 Dirk Nowitzki 60.00 120.00
157 Emeka Okafor 5.00 12.00
158 Chris Paul EXCH 60.00 120.00
161 Rajon Rondo 20.00 50.00
162 Derrick Rose 100.00 200.00
163 Luis Scola 5.00 12.00
165 Amare Stoudemire 12.00 30.00
167 Jeff Teague 5.00 12.00
173 Russell Westbrook 25.00 60.00
175 Jeremy Lin 75.00 200.00
176 Nate Archibald 12.00 30.00
177 B.J. Armstrong 8.00 20.00
178 Elgin Baylor 12.00 30.00
179 Rick Barry 12.00 30.00
182 Tom Chambers 5.00 12.00
185 Walt Frazier 20.00 50.00
186 Harry Gallatin 5.00 12.00
187 Artis Gilmore 8.00 20.00
188 Phil Jackson 300.00 600.00
189 K.C. Jones 8.00 20.00
191 Clyde Lovellette 8.00 20.00
194 Gail Goodrich 8.00 20.00
196 Bob Pettit 8.00 20.00
197 Robert Parish 8.00 20.00
198 Wes Unseld 10.00 25.00
200 Lenny Wilkens 5.00 12.00

2011-12 Panini Past and Present Bread for Energy

COMPLETE SET (50) 25.00 60.00
RANDOM INSERTS IN PACKS
1 Carmelo Anthony 1.00 2.50
2 Leandro Barbosa .60 1.50
3 J.J. Barea .75 2.00
4 Andrea Bargnani .60 1.50
5 Andray Blatche .50 1.25
6 Ronnie Brewer .60 1.50
7 Carlos Boozer .75 2.00
8 Mario Chalmers .75 2.00
9 Darren Collison .75 2.00
10 Stephen Curry .75 2.00
11 DeMar DeRozan .75 2.00
12 Kevin Durant 2.50 6.00
13 Tyreke Evans .75 2.00
14 Raymond Felton .60 1.50
15 Landry Fields .75 2.00
16 Danilo Gallinari .75 2.00
17 Kevin Garnett 1.50 4.00
18 Marc Gasol .75 2.00
19 Pau Gasol .75 2.00
20 Taj Gibson .60 1.50
21 Manu Ginobili .75 2.00
22 Devin Harris .75 2.00
23 Gordon Hayward .75 2.00
24 Grant Hill 1.00 2.50
25 Jrue Holiday .75 2.00
26 Al Horford .60 1.50
27 Dwight Howard 1.25 3.00
28 Stephen Jackson .60 1.50
29 Amir Johnson .50 1.25
30 Carl Landry .50 1.25
31 David Lee .60 1.50
32 Rashard Lewis .60 1.50

33 Corey Maggette .60 1.50
34 Tracy McGrady .75 2.00
35 Joakim Noah .75 2.00
36 Lamar Odom .75 2.00
37 Mehmet Okur .50 1.25
38 Tony Parker .75 2.00
39 J.J. Redick .75 2.00
40 Luke Ridnour .60 1.50
41 Rajon Rondo 1.00 2.50
42 Derrick Rose 2.50 6.00
43 Jason Terry .60 1.50
44 Dwyane Wade 1.50 4.00
45 John Wall 1.25 3.00
46 Hakim Warrick .60 1.50
47 David West .75 2.00
48 Russell Westbrook 1.00 2.50
49 Deron Williams .75 2.00
50 Anderson Varejao .60 1.50

2011-12 Panini Past and Present Bread for Health

COMPLETE SET (50) 25.00 60.00
RANDOM INSERTS IN PACKS
1 LaMarcus Aldridge .75 2.00
2 Ray Allen .75 2.00
3 Chauncey Billups .75 2.00
4 Andrew Bogut .75 2.00
5 Chris Bosh .75 2.00
6 Elton Brand .75 2.00
7 Kobe Bryant 3.00 8.00
8 Chase Budinger .50 1.25
9 Andrew Bynum 1.00 2.50
10 Jose Calderon .60 1.50
11 Tyson Chandler .60 1.50
12 DeMarcus Cousins 1.00 2.50
13 Jamal Crawford .60 1.50
14 Luol Deng .75 2.00
15 Tim Duncan 1.25 3.00
16 Monta Ellis .75 2.00
17 Derek Fisher .60 1.50
18 Rudy Gay .75 2.00
19 Drew Gooden .60 1.50
20 Ben Gordon .75 2.00
21 Danny Granger .75 2.00
22 Blake Griffin 1.50 4.00
23 James Harden 1.00 2.50
24 Kris Humphries .50 1.25
25 Andre Iguodala .75 2.00
26 Chris Kaman .60 1.50
27 Jason Kidd .75 2.00
28 Jarrett Jack .60 1.50
29 LeBron James 3.00 8.00
30 Antawn Jamison .75 2.00
31 Al Jefferson .75 2.00
32 Brandon Jennings .75 2.00
33 Joe Johnson .75 2.00
34 Brook Lopez .75 2.00
35 Kevin Love 1.00 2.50
36 Kevin Martin .75 2.00
37 JaVale McGee .60 1.50
38 Andre Miller .60 1.50
39 Greg Monroe .75 2.00
40 Steve Nash .75 2.00
41 Gary Neal .75 2.00
42 Dirk Nowitzki 1.00 2.50
43 Paul Pierce 1.00 2.50
44 Tayshaun Prince .75 2.00
45 Zach Randolph .60 1.50
46 Brandon Rush .50 1.25
47 Amare Stoudemire .75 2.00
48 Rodney Stuckey .75 2.00
49 Evan Turner .75 2.00
50 D.J. White .50 1.25

2011-12 Panini Past and Present Bread for Life

COMPLETE SET (50) 75.00 150.00
RANDOM INSERTS IN PACKS
1 Elgin Baylor 1.50 4.00
2 Larry Bird 6.00 15.00
3 Wilt Chamberlain 5.00 12.00
4 Phil Chenier 1.50 4.00
5 Maurice Cheeks 1.50 4.00
6 Clyde Drexler 2.00 5.00
7 Dale Ellis 1.50 4.00
8 Sean Elliott 1.50 4.00
9 Julius Erving 3.00 8.00
10 Patrick Ewing 6.00 15.00
11 Harry Gallatin 1.50 4.00
12 A.C. Green 1.50 4.00
13 Anfernee Hardaway 4.00 10.00
14 Ron Harper 1.50 4.00
15 Hersey Hawkins 1.50 4.00
16 Robert Horry 2.00 5.00
17 Mark Jackson 1.50 4.00
18 Magic Johnson 6.00 15.00
19 Dave Cowens 1.50 4.00
20 Bill Laimbeer 1.50 4.00
21 Dan Majerle 1.50 4.00
22 Karl Malone 2.00 5.00
23 Pete Maravich 5.00 12.00
24 Bob McAdoo 1.50 4.00
25 George Mikan 3.00 8.00
26 Alonzo Mourning 6.00 15.00
27 Dikembe Mutombo 1.50 4.00
28 Charles Oakley 1.50 4.00
29 Hakeem Olajuwon 2.00 5.00
30 Shaquille O'Neal 3.00 8.00
31 Robert Parish 1.50 4.00
32 Gary Payton 1.50 4.00
33 Scottie Pippen 3.00 8.00
34 Sam Perkins 1.50 4.00
35 Terry Porter 1.50 4.00
36 Mark Price 1.50 4.00
37 Glen Rice 1.50 4.00
38 Arnie Risen 1.50 4.00
39 Dennis Rodman 3.00 8.00
40 Tree Rollins 1.50 4.00
41 Bill Russell 2.50 6.00
42 Jack Sikma 1.50 4.00
43 Kenny Smith 1.50 4.00
44 Dolph Schayes 1.50 4.00
45 Paul Silas 1.50 4.00
46 Isiah Thomas 1.50 4.00
47 Chet Walker 1.50 4.00
48 Dominique Wilkins 2.00 5.00
49 Lenny Wilkens 1.50 4.00
50 Kevin Willis 1.50 4.00

2011-12 Panini Past and Present Breakout

COMPLETE SET (30) 15.00 40.00
RANDOM INSERTS IN PACKS
1 Blake Griffin 1.50 4.00
2 John Wall 1.25 3.00
3 DeMarcus Cousins 1.00 2.50
4 Stephen Curry .75 2.00
5 Brandon Jennings .75 2.00
6 Taj Gibson .60 1.50
7 Tyler Hansbrough .75 2.00
8 Tyreke Evans .75 2.00
9 Brook Lopez .75 2.00
10 Eric Gordon .75 2.00
11 Andrew Bynum 1.00 2.50
12 Derrick Rose 2.50 6.00
13 Russell Westbrook 1.00 2.50
14 Kevin Love 1.00 2.50
15 DeJuan Blair .60 1.50
16 James Harden 1.00 2.50
17 Jrue Holiday .75 2.00
18 Wesley Matthews .75 2.00
19 Derrick Favors .75 2.00
20 Landry Fields .75 2.00
21 Greg Monroe .75 2.00
22 Jeremy Lin 2.00 5.00
23 Serge Ibaka .75 2.00
24 Eric Bledsoe .75 2.00
25 DeMar DeRozan .75 2.00
26 Gordon Hayward .75 2.00
27 Danilo Gallinari .75 2.00
28 Michael Beasley .75 2.00
29 O.J. Mayo .75 2.00
30 Ricky Rubio 2.00 5.00

2011-12 Panini Past and Present Breakout Autographs

RANDOM INSERTS IN PACKS
1 Blake Griffin 75.00 150.00
3 DeMarcus Cousins 12.00 30.00
4 Stephen Curry 8.00 20.00
6 Taj Gibson 8.00 20.00
8 Tyreke Evans 8.00 20.00
9 Brook Lopez 6.00 15.00
10 Eric Gordon 8.00 20.00
12 Derrick Rose EXCH 75.00 150.00
13 Russell Westbrook 20.00 50.00
14 Kevin Love 15.00 40.00
15 DeJuan Blair 5.00 12.00
16 James Harden EXCH 12.00 30.00
17 Jrue Holiday 5.00 12.00
18 Wesley Matthews 5.00 12.00
19 Derrick Favors 6.00 15.00
20 Landry Fields 5.00 12.00
21 Greg Monroe 5.00 12.00
22 Jeremy Lin 75.00 200.00
23 Serge Ibaka EXCH 10.00 25.00
24 Eric Bledsoe 8.00 20.00
25 DeMar DeRozan 10.00 25.00
26 Gordon Hayward 6.00 15.00
27 Danilo Gallinari 5.00 12.00
28 Michael Beasley 5.00 12.00

2011-12 Panini Past and Present Changing Times

COMPLETE SET (30) 20.00 50.00
RANDOM INSERTS IN PACKS
1 Bill Russell 1.25 3.00
2 Oscar Robertson 1.00 2.50
3 Dolph Schayes .75 2.00
4 Al Attles .75 2.00
5 Bob Cousy 1.25 3.00
6 Lenny Wilkens .75 2.00
7 Harry Gallatin .75 2.00
8 George Mikan 1.50 4.00
9 Clyde Lovellette .75 2.00
10 Julius Erving 1.50 4.00
11 George Gervin .75 2.00
12 Dan Issel .75 2.00
13 David Thompson .75 2.00
14 Artis Gilmore .75 2.00
15 Spencer Haywood .75 2.00
16 Connie Hawkins .75 2.00
17 Mel Daniels .75 2.00
18 Billy Cunningham .75 2.00
19 George McGinnis .75 2.00
20 Bobby Jones .75 2.00
21 Kobe Bryant 3.00 8.00
22 Blake Griffin 1.50 4.00
23 Kevin Durant 2.50 6.00
24 Chris Paul 1.25 3.00
25 LeBron James 3.00 8.00
26 Dirk Nowitzki 1.00 2.50
27 Derrick Rose 2.50 6.00
28 Kevin Love 1.00 2.50
29 Marc Gasol .75 2.00
30 Monta Ellis .75 2.00

2011-12 Panini Past and Present Elusive Ink Autographs

RANDOM INSERTS IN PACKS
AA Anthony Avent 4.00 10.00
AC Archie Clark 4.00 10.00
AH Allan Houston 10.00 25.00
AJ Avery Johnson 5.00 12.00
AM Anthony Mason 12.00 30.00
BA B.J. Armstrong 10.00 25.00
BB Brent Barry 5.00 12.00
BD Brad Davis 4.00 10.00
BE Bob Elliott 4.00 10.00
BG Brian Grant 4.00 10.00
BL Bob Love 5.00 12.00
BO Bo Outlaw 4.00 10.00
BR Bryant Reeves 4.00 10.00
BS Bob Sura 4.00 10.00
BW Bill Wennington 6.00 15.00
BW Buck Williams 4.00 10.00
CC Cedric Ceballos 12.00 30.00
CO Charles Oakley 6.00 15.00
DB Dee Brown 5.00 12.00
DC Dell Curry 4.00 10.00
DF Danny Ferry 4.00 10.00
DM Danny Manning 8.00 20.00
GM Gheorghe Muresan 8.00 20.00
HD Hubert Davis 4.00 10.00
HH Hersey Hawkins 4.00 10.00
JM Jamal Mashburn 12.00 30.00
JP John Paxson 8.00 20.00
JS John Salley 4.00 10.00
JS John Starks 10.00 25.00
KA Kenny Anderson 5.00 12.00
KK Kerry Kittles 4.00 10.00
KS Kenny Smith 8.00 20.00
KW Kevin Willis 4.00 10.00
LF Lawrence Funderburke 4.00 10.00
LL Luc Longley 10.00 25.00
LN Larry Nance 4.00 10.00
LS LaBradford Smith 4.00 10.00
LW Luther Wright 4.00 10.00
MA Mark Aguirre 5.00 12.00
MB Muggsy Bogues 6.00 15.00
ME Mario Elie 5.00 12.00
MF Michael Finley 5.00 12.00
MJ Major Jones 4.00 10.00
MR Marv Roberts 4.00 10.00
MW Morlon Wiley 4.00 10.00
NA Nick Anderson 8.00 20.00
OB Otis Birdsong 4.00 10.00
RB Ron Brewer 4.00 10.00
RC Rex Chapman 6.00 15.00
RM Rick Mahorn 6.00 15.00
RS Rod Strickland 4.00 10.00
RS Rory Sparrow 4.00 10.00
RT Reggie Theus 4.00 10.00
SA Stacey Augmon 4.00 10.00
SE Sean Elliott 6.00 15.00
SF Sleepy Floyd 4.00 10.00
SK Steve Kerr 8.00 20.00
SM Scooter McCray 4.00 10.00
SP Scot Pollard 4.00 10.00
TB Thurl Bailey 4.00 10.00
TG Tom Gugliotta 4.00 10.00
TH Tim Hardaway 6.00 15.00
VB Vin Baker 5.00 12.00
WB Willie Burton 4.00 10.00
VDN Vinny Del Negro EXCH 4.00 10.00

2011-12 Panini Past and Present Fireworks

COMPLETE SET (20) 25.00 60.00
RANDOM INSERTS IN PACKS
1 Kevin Durant 4.00 10.00
2 LeBron James 5.00 12.00
3 Kobe Bryant 5.00 12.00
4 Dwyane Wade 2.50 6.00
5 Dwight Howard 2.00 5.00
6 Blake Griffin 2.50 6.00
7 Dirk Nowitzki 1.50 4.00
8 Derrick Rose 4.00 10.00
9 Carmelo Anthony 1.50 4.00
10 Amare Stoudemire 1.25 3.00
11 Monta Ellis 1.25 3.00
12 Kevin Garnett 2.50 6.00
13 Kevin Love 1.50 4.00
14 John Wall 2.00 5.00
15 Russell Westbrook 1.50 4.00
16 Rajon Rondo 1.50 4.00
17 Josh Smith 1.25 3.00
18 Jeremy Lin 3.00 8.00
19 Chris Paul 2.00 5.00
20 Tyreke Evans 1.25 3.00

2011-12 Panini Past and Present Gamers Jerseys

RANDOM INSERTS IN PACKS
1 Amare Stoudemire 4.00 10.00
2 Al Jefferson 4.00 10.00
3 Allan Houston 4.00 10.00
4 Al Horford 3.00 8.00
5 Allen Iverson 12.00 30.00
6 Alonzo Mourning 15.00 40.00
7 Andre Iguodala 4.00 10.00
8 Avery Bradley 4.00 10.00
9 Darren Collison 4.00 10.00
10 Ben Wallace 4.00 10.00
11 Beno Udrih 2.50 6.00
12 Ed Davis 3.00 8.00
13 Blake Griffin 8.00 20.00
14 Bobby Jackson 4.00 10.00
15 Brandon Jennings 4.00 10.00
16 Brendan Haywood 2.50 6.00
17 Brook Lopez 4.00 10.00
18 Carlos Boozer 4.00 10.00
19 Grant Hill 8.00 20.00
20 Charles Oakley 4.00 10.00
21 Charlie Villanueva 3.00 8.00
22 Chris Andersen 5.00 12.00
23 Chris Bosh 4.00 10.00
24 Chris Webber 10.00 25.00
25 Cole Aldrich 2.50 6.00
26 Danny Granger 4.00 10.00
27 DeMar DeRozan 4.00 10.00
28 Damion James 2.50 6.00
29 Daniel Orton 2.50 6.00
30 Danny Manning 4.00 10.00
31 Patrick Ewing 12.00 30.00
32 Derrick Favors 4.00 10.00
33 Ekpe Udoh 2.50 6.00
34 Evan Turner 4.00 10.00
35 Greg Monroe 4.00 10.00
36 Hassan Whiteside 2.50 6.00
37 J.J. Redick 4.00 10.00
38 James Anderson 2.50 6.00
39 Jason Richardson 4.00 10.00
40 Jermaine O'Neal 4.00 10.00
41 Joe Johnson 4.00 10.00
42 John Wall 6.00 15.00
43 John Stockton 6.00 15.00
44 David Robinson 8.00 20.00
45 Kevin Durant 12.00 30.00
46 Kevin Garnett 8.00 20.00
47 Kevin Love 5.00 12.00
48 Gary Neal 4.00 10.00
49 Kobe Bryant 15.00 40.00
50 Lance Stephenson 2.50 6.00
51 Larry Johnson 8.00 20.00
52 Lazar Hayward 2.50 6.00
53 LeBron James 20.00 50.00
54 Landry Fields 4.00 10.00
55 Luke Walton 2.50 6.00
56 Manu Ginobili 4.00 10.00
57 Marcus Camby 2.50 6.00
58 Mario Chalmers 4.00 10.00
59 Marvin Williams 3.00 8.00
60 Mo Williams 3.00 8.00
61 Marc Gasol 4.00 10.00
62 Eric Bledsoe 4.00 10.00
63 Patrick Patterson 3.00 8.00
64 Paul George 4.00 10.00
65 Pau Gasol 4.00 10.00
66 Paul Pierce 8.00 20.00
67 Peja Stojakovic 6.00 15.00
68 Quincy Pondexter 2.50 6.00
69 Raja Bell 3.00 8.00
70 Rajon Rondo 5.00 12.00
71 Ray Allen 8.00 20.00
72 Hedo Turkoglu 4.00 10.00
73 Jeff Teague 3.00 8.00
74 Ramon Sessions 3.00 8.00
75 Reggie Miller 15.00 40.00
76 Robert Parish 4.00 10.00
77 Robin Lopez 2.50 6.00
78 Rodrigue Beaubois 3.00 8.00
79 Stephen Curry 4.00 10.00
80 Ron Harper 4.00 10.00
81 Roy Hibbert 3.00 8.00
82 Rudy Gay 4.00 10.00
83 Russell Westbrook 5.00 12.00
84 Steve Nash 4.00 10.00
85 LaMarcus Aldridge 4.00 10.00
86 Jalen Rose 4.00 10.00
87 Spencer Hawes 2.50 6.00
88 Andrew Bogut 4.00 10.00
89 Tim Duncan 6.00 15.00
90 Toney Douglas 2.50 6.00
91 Tony Parker 4.00 10.00
92 Trevor Booker 2.50 6.00
93 Ty Lawson 4.00 10.00
94 Tyrus Thomas 3.00 8.00
95 Udonis Haslem 3.00 8.00
96 Terrence Williams 2.50 6.00
97 Yao Ming 5.00 12.00
98 Zach Randolph 3.00 8.00
99 Jrue Holiday 4.00 10.00
100 Derrick Rose 12.00 30.00

2011-12 Panini Past and Present Gamers Jerseys Prime

*PRIME: 2.5X TO 6X BASE HI
STATED PRINT RUN ONE TO 25 SETS
SOME UNPRICED DUE TO SCARCITY
37 J.J. Redick/15 40.00 70.00

2011-12 Panini Past and Present Modern Marks Autographs

RANDOM INSERTS IN PACKS
1 Kobe Bryant 150.00 300.00
2 Blake Griffin 75.00 150.00
3 Kevin Durant 125.00 250.00
4 Derrick Rose EXCH 100.00 200.00
5 Chris Paul 75.00 150.00
6 Kevin Love 40.00 100.00
7 LaMarcus Aldridge 30.00 80.00
8 Stephen Curry 25.00 60.00
9 Marc Gasol
10 Andrew Bogut 25.00 60.00

2011-12 Panini Past and Present Raining 3's

COMPLETE SET (20) 20.00 50.00
RANDOM INSERTS IN PACKS
1 Dirk Nowitzki 1.25 3.00
2 Joe Johnson 1.00 2.50
3 Carmelo Anthony 1.25 3.00
4 Vince Carter 1.25 3.00
5 Paul Pierce 1.25 3.00
6 Kobe Bryant 4.00 10.00
7 Kevin Durant 3.00 8.00
8 Jason Terry .75 2.00
9 LeBron James 4.00 10.00
10 Jeremy Lin 2.50 6.00
11 Derrick Rose 3.00 8.00
12 Jason Richardson 1.00 2.50
13 Ray Allen 1.00 2.50
14 Steve Nash 1.00 2.50
15 Larry Bird 3.00 8.00
16 Robert Horry 1.25 3.00
17 Allen Iverson 1.25 3.00
18 Dan Majerle 1.00 2.50
19 Chris Mullin 1.00 2.50
20 John Stockton 1.50 4.00

2011-12 Panini Past and Present Variations

RANDOM INSERTS IN PACKS
1 Ray Allen 2.50 6.00
2 Carmelo Anthony 3.00 8.00
3 Chris Bosh 2.50 6.00
4 Kobe Bryant 10.00 25.00
5 Vince Carter 3.00 8.00
6 Baron Davis 2.50 6.00
7 Tim Duncan 4.00 10.00
8 Kevin Durant 8.00 20.00
9 Kevin Garnett 5.00 12.00
10 Blake Griffin 5.00 12.00
11 Grant Hill 6.00 15.00
12 Dwight Howard 4.00 10.00
13 LeBron James 10.00 25.00
14 DeAndre Jordan 2.50 6.00
15 Jason Kidd 2.50 6.00
16 Kevin Love 3.00 8.00
17 Steve Nash 4.00 10.00
18 Dirk Nowitzki 3.00 8.00
19 Chris Paul 4.00 10.00
20 Paul Pierce 3.00 8.00
21 Rajon Rondo 3.00 8.00
22 Amare Stoudemire 2.50 6.00
23 Dwyane Wade 5.00 12.00
24 Deron Williams 2.50 6.00
25 Metta World Peace 2.50 6.00
26 Larry Bird 8.00 20.00
27 Julius Erving 5.00 12.00
28 Patrick Ewing 6.00 15.00
29 George Gervin 2.50 6.00
30 Magic Johnson 12.00 30.00
31 Karl Malone 3.00 8.00
32 Pete Maravich 8.00 20.00
33 George Mikan 5.00 12.00
34 Shaquille O'Neal 5.00 12.00
35 Scottie Pippen 5.00 12.00
36 Oscar Robertson 3.00 8.00
37 David Robinson 4.00 10.00
38 Bill Russell 4.00 10.00
39 John Stockton 6.00 15.00
40 Isiah Thomas 2.50 6.00
41 David Thompson 2.50 6.00
42 Bill Walton 2.50 6.00
43 Jerry West 3.00 8.00
44 Bob Cousy 4.00 10.00
45 Dave DeBusschere 2.50 6.00
46 Artis Gilmore 2.50 6.00
47 Phil Jackson 3.00 8.00
48 Moses Malone 2.50 6.00
49 Robert Parish 2.50 6.00
50 Wes Unseld 2.50 6.00

2011-12 Panini Preferred

PS PRINT RUN 10 TO 99 SER.#'d SETS
PC PRINT RUN 15 TO 74 SER.#'d SETS
SL PRINT RUN 5 TO 99 SER.#'d SETS
CR PRINT RUN 24 TO 99 SER.#'d SETS
PS STANDS FOR PREFERRED SIGNATURES
PC STANDS FOR PANINIS CHOICE
SL STANDS FOR SILHOUETTE
CR STANDS FOR CROWN ROYALE
UNPRICED BLACK PRINT RUN ONE SET
1 Walt Bellamy PS/25 AU 5.00 12.00
2 Adrian Dantley PS/74 AU 4.00 10.00
3 Al Thornton PS/74 AU 4.00 10.00
4 Alex English PS/74 AU 4.00 10.00
5 Alonzo Mourning PS/25 AU 30.00 80.00
6 Andre Iguodala PS/25 AU 5.00 12.00
7 Andre Miller PS/49 AU 4.00 10.00
8 Andrea Bargnani PS/25 AU 6.00 15.00
9 Andrei Kirilenko PS/25 AU 6.00 15.00
10 Artis Gilmore PS/25 AU 8.00 20.00
11 Bailey Howell PS/74 AU 5.00 12.00
12 Bernard King PS/74 AU 6.00 15.00
13 Bill Cartwright PS/74 AU 6.00 15.00
14 Bill Laimbeer PS/74 AU 4.00 10.00
16 Bill Walton PS/25 AU 10.00 25.00
18 Bob Dandridge PS/74 AU 4.00 10.00
19 Bob McAdoo PS/74 AU 10.00 25.00
20 Brandon Jennings PS/25 AU 10.00 25.00
21 Byron Scott PS/49 AU 6.00 15.00
22 Calvin Murphy PS/25 AU 5.00 12.00
23 Campy Russell PS/74 AU 4.00 10.00
24 Cazzie Russell PS/74 AU 4.00 10.00
25 Cedric Maxwell PS/74 AU 4.00 10.00
26 Charles Oakley PS/74 AU 10.00 25.00
27 Chris Ford PS/74 AU 4.00 10.00
28 Chris Mullin PS/74 AU 10.00 25.00
30 Christian Laettner PS/25 AU 6.00 15.00
31 Clyde Lovellette PS/25 AU 8.00 20.00
32 Connie Hawkins PS/74 AU 8.00 20.00
33 Dan Issel PS/74 AU 5.00 12.00
34 Dan Majerle PS/74 AU 5.00 12.00
35 Darrell Griffith PS/74 AU 4.00 10.00
36 Darren Collison PS/74 AU 4.00 10.00
37 Darryl Dawkins PS/74 AU 5.00 12.00
38 Dave Cowens PS/49 AU 5.00 12.00
40 David Thompson PS/74 AU 4.00 10.00
41 DeMar DeRozan PS/25 AU 5.00 12.00
44 Detlef Schrempf PS/74 AU 8.00 20.00
45 Dikembe Mutombo PS/74 AU 15.00 40.00
46 Dirk Nowitzki PS/15 AU 100.00 175.00
47 Elgin Baylor PS/20 AU 15.00 40.00
48 Elvin Hayes PS/49 AU 5.00 12.00
49 Eric Gordon PS/49 AU 5.00 12.00
50 Frank Ramsey PS/74 AU 6.00 15.00
51 Gail Goodrich PS/25 AU 8.00 20.00
52 George Gervin PS/25 AU 10.00 25.00
53 George McGinnis PS/74 AU 4.00 10.00
54 Grant Hill PS/15 AU 100.00 200.00
55 Hakeem Olajuwon PS/15 AU 30.00 80.00
56 Isiah Thomas PS/25 AU 10.00 25.00
57 James Harden PS/25 AU 15.00 40.00
58 James Worthy PS/15 AU 25.00 60.00
59 Jeff Hornacek PS/74 AU 5.00 12.00
61 Jrue Holiday PS/49 AU 8.00 20.00
65 Kiki Vandeweghe PS/74 AU 4.00 10.00
66 Kobe Bryant PS/49 AU 100.00 200.00
68 Lenny Wilkens PS/25 AU 8.00 20.00
69 Luol Deng PS/25 AU 10.00 25.00
71 Mark Aguirre PS/74 AU 4.00 10.00
72 Mark Eaton PS/74 AU 4.00 10.00
73 Mark Price PS/74 AU 10.00 25.00
74 Maurice Cheeks PS/74 AU 4.00 10.00
75 Michael Cage PS/74 AU 4.00 10.00
76 Mitch Richmond PS/74 AU 10.00 25.00
77 Monta Ellis PS/49 AU 8.00 20.00
78 Nate Archibald PS/25 AU 8.00 20.00
79 Nate Thurmond PS/25 AU 8.00 20.00
82 Paul Westphal PS/74 AU 4.00 10.00
83 Ralph Sampson PS/74 AU 5.00 12.00
84 Robert Horry PS/49 AU 8.00 20.00
85 Robert Parish PS/25 AU 8.00 20.00
86 Rolando Blackman PS/74 AU 4.00 10.00
87 Sam Perkins PS/74 AU 4.00 10.00
88 Spencer Haywood PS/74 AU 4.00 10.00
89 Stephen Curry PS/49 AU 10.00 25.00
90 Stephen Jackson PS/74 AU 4.00 10.00
91 Steve Smith PS/74 AU 4.00 10.00
92 Tom Heinsohn PS/74 AU 10.00 25.00
93 Dominique Wilkins PS/25 AU 20.00 50.00
94 Toney Douglas PS/74 AU 4.00 10.00
95 Toni Kukoc PS/74 AU 10.00 25.00
96 Ty Lawson PS/49 AU 6.00 15.00
97 Walt Frazier PS/25 AU 10.00 25.00
98 Zach Randolph PS/25 AU 8.00 20.00
99 Xavier McDaniel PS/74 AU 4.00 10.00
100 World B. Free PS/25 AU 6.00 15.00
101 Walt Bellamy PC/25 AU 6.00 15.00
102 Adrian Dantley PC/74 AU 5.00 12.00
103 Al Thornton PC/74 AU EXCH 5.00 12.00
104 Alex English PC/74 AU 5.00 12.00
105 Alonzo Mourning PC/25 AU 50.00 120.00
106 Andre Iguodala PC/25 AU 6.00 15.00
107 Andre Miller PC/49 AU 5.00 12.00
108 Andrea Bargnani PC/25 AU 6.00 15.00
110 Artis Gilmore PC/25 AU 10.00 25.00
111 Bailey Howell PC/74 AU 6.00 15.00
112 Bernard King PC/74 AU 8.00 20.00
113 Bill Cartwright PC/74 AU 8.00 20.00
114 Bill Laimbeer PC/74 AU 6.00 15.00
115 Bill Russell PC/15 AU 75.00 150.00
116 Bill Walton PC/25 AU 10.00 25.00
117 Blake Griffin PC/25 AU 125.00 300.00
118 Bob Dandridge PC/74 AU 5.00 12.00
119 Bob McAdoo PC/74 AU 10.00 25.00
120 Brandon Jennings PC/25 AU 12.00 30.00
121 Byron Scott PC/74 AU 5.00 12.00
122 Calvin Murphy PC/25 AU 6.00 15.00
123 Campy Russell PC/74 AU 5.00 12.00
124 Cazzie Russell PC/74 AU 5.00 12.00
125 Cedric Maxwell PC/74 AU 5.00 12.00
126 Charles Oakley PC/74 AU 12.00 30.00
127 Chris Ford PC/74 AU 5.00 12.00
128 Chris Mullin PC/74 AU 10.00 25.00
129 Chris Paul PC/25 AU 50.00 125.00
130 Christian Laettner PC/25 AU 8.00 20.00
131 Clyde Lovellette PC/25 AU 8.00 20.00
132 Connie Hawkins PC/25 AU 8.00 20.00
133 Dan Issel PC/74 AU 5.00 12.00
134 Dan Majerle PC/74 AU 6.00 15.00
135 Darrell Griffith PC/74 AU 5.00 12.00
136 Darren Collison PC/74 AU 6.00 15.00
137 Darryl Dawkins PC/74 AU 5.00 12.00
138 Dave Cowens PC/25 AU 12.00 30.00
139 David Robinson PC/25 AU 60.00 150.00
140 David Thompson PC/74 AU 6.00 15.00
141 DeMar DeRozan PC/25 AU 10.00 25.00
142 Dennis Rodman PC/25 AU 40.00 100.00
143 Derrick Rose PC/20 AU 200.00 450.00
144 Detlef Schrempf PC/74 AU 8.00 20.00
145 Dikembe Mutombo PC/74 AU 15.00 40.00
146 Elgin Baylor PC/25 AU 15.00 40.00
147 Elvin Hayes PC/25 AU 6.00 15.00
148 Eric Gordon PC/25 AU 8.00 20.00
149 Frank Ramsey PC/74 AU 6.00 15.00
150 Gail Goodrich PC/25 AU 8.00 20.00
151 George Gervin PC/25 AU 15.00 40.00
152 George McGinnis PC/74 AU 5.00 12.00
153 Grant Hill PC/25 AU 100.00 200.00
154 Hakeem Olajuwon PC/25 AU 30.00 80.00
155 Isiah Thomas PC/25 AU 12.00 30.00
156 James Harden PC/25 AU 20.00 50.00
157 James Worthy PC/25 AU 25.00 60.00
158 Jeff Hornacek PC/74 AU 8.00 20.00
159 John Stockton PC/15 AU 50.00 125.00
160 Jrue Holiday PC/74 AU 8.00 20.00
161 Julius Erving PC/15 AU 50.00 125.00
162 Kareem Abdul-Jabbar PC/15 AU100.00 200.00
163 Kevin Durant PC/25 AU 175.00 350.00
164 Kiki Vandeweghe PC/74 AU EXCH5.00 12.00
165 Kobe Bryant PC/49 AU 150.00 300.00
166 Larry Bird PC/15 AU 100.00 175.00
167 Lenny Wilkens PC/25 AU 10.00 25.00
168 Luol Deng PC/25 AU 12.00 30.00
169 Magic Johnson PC/15 AU 75.00 150.00
170 Mark Aguirre PC/74 AU 5.00 12.00
171 Mark Eaton PC/74 AU 5.00 12.00
172 Mark Price PC/74 AU 12.00 30.00
173 Maurice Cheeks PC/74 AU 5.00 12.00
174 Michael Cage PC/74 AU 5.00 12.00
175 Mitch Richmond PC/74 AU 10.00 25.00
176 Monta Ellis PC/49 AU 10.00 25.00
177 Nate Archibald PC/25 AU 12.00 30.00
178 Nate Thurmond PC/25 AU 10.00 25.00
179 Oscar Robertson PC/25 AU 50.00 125.00
180 Pat Riley PC/25 AU 15.00 40.00
181 Paul Westphal PC/74 AU 5.00 12.00
182 Ralph Sampson PC/74 AU 6.00 15.00
183 Robert Horry PC/74 AU 8.00 20.00
184 Robert Parish PC/25 AU 10.00 25.00
185 Rolando Blackman PC/74 AU 5.00 12.00
186 Sam Perkins PC/74 AU 5.00 12.00
187 Spencer Haywood PC/74 AU 5.00 12.00
188 Stephen Curry PC/74 AU 12.00 30.00
189 Stephen Jackson PC/74 AU 5.00 12.00
190 Steve Nash PC/20 AU 30.00 80.00
191 Steve Smith PC/74 AU 5.00 12.00
192 Tom Heinsohn PC/74 AU 8.00 20.00
193 Dominique Wilkins PC/25 AU 15.00 40.00
194 Toney Douglas PC/74 AU 5.00 12.00
195 Toni Kukoc PC/49 AU 15.00 40.00
196 Ty Lawson PC/49 AU 8.00 20.00
197 Walt Frazier PC/25 AU 25.00 60.00
198 Zach Randolph PC/25 AU 10.00 25.00
199 Xavier McDaniel PC/74 AU 5.00 12.00
200 World B. Free PC/25 AU 10.00 25.00
201 Al Jefferson SL/25 JSY AU 10.00 25.00
202 Al Thornton SL/49 JSY AU EXCH10.00 25.00
203 Alex English SL/49 JSY AU 10.00 25.00
204 Alonzo Mourning SL/25 JSY AU50.00 125.00
205 Andre Iguodala SL/49 JSY AU 12.00 30.00
206 Andrea Bargnani SL/49 JSY AU 10.00 25.00
208 Artis Gilmore SL/25 JSY AU 20.00 50.00
210 Ben Gordon SL/25 JSY AU 12.00 30.00
211 Bernard King SL/24 JSY AU 15.00 40.00
212 Blake Griffin SL/25 JSY AU 175.00 325.00
213 Brandon Jennings SL/49 JSY AU15.00 40.00
214 Charles Oakley SL/99 JSY AU 20.00 50.00
215 Chris Paul SL/25 JSY AU 75.00 200.00
216 Clyde Drexler SL/25 JSY AU 60.00 150.00
217 Dan Issel SL/49 JSY AU 10.00 25.00
218 Darrell Griffith SL/49 JSY AU 10.00 25.00
220 DeMar DeRozan SL/49 JSY AU 15.00 40.00
223 Detlef Schrempf SL/99 JSY AU 12.00 30.00
224 Dikembe Mutombo SL/49 JSY AU25.00 60.00
226 Grant Hill SL/25 JSY AU 125.00 250.00
227 Hakeem Olajuwon SL/25 JSY AU75.00 150.00
228 Isiah Thomas SL/25 JSY AU 35.00 70.00
229 James Worthy SL/25 JSY AU 50.00 125.00
230 Jason Kidd SL/20 JSY AU 50.00 125.00
234 Kevin Love SL/25 JSY AU 100.00 200.00
235 Kiki Vandeweghe SL/99 JSY AU10.00 25.00
236 Kobe Bryant SL/49 JSY AU 250.00 400.00
237 Luol Deng SL/49 JSY AU 25.00 60.00
238 Mark Aguirre SL/49 JSY AU 10.00 25.00
239 Mark Eaton SL/99 JSY AU 10.00 25.00
240 Maurice Cheeks SL/49 JSY AU 10.00 25.00
241 Michael Cage SL/99 JSY AU 10.00 25.00
242 Mitch Richmond SL/25 JSY AU 40.00 80.00
243 Monta Ellis SL/49 JSY AU 20.00 50.00
246 Robert Parish SL/49 JSY AU 15.00 40.00
247 Stephen Curry SL/99 JSY AU 20.00 50.00
248 Dominique Wilkins SL/25 JSY AU30.00 80.00
249 Toni Kukoc SL/49 JSY AU 30.00 80.00
250 Ty Lawson SL/49 JSY AU 15.00 40.00
251 Artis Gilmore CR/25 AU 10.00 25.00
252 Bill Walton CR/25 AU 10.00 25.00
253 Dan Issel CR/25 AU 8.00 20.00
254 Darryl Dawkins CR/25 AU 6.00 15.00
255 Dave Cowens CR/25 AU 10.00 25.00
256 David Thompson CR/25 AU 8.00 20.00
257 Elgin Baylor CR/25 AU 15.00 40.00
258 George Gervin CR/25 AU 12.00 30.00
259 Oscar Robertson CR/25 AU 50.00 125.00
260 Walt Frazier CR/24 AU 20.00 50.00
261 Cole Aldrich CR/99 AU 3.00 8.00
262 Al-Farouq Aminu CR/99 AU 5.00 12.00
263 James Anderson CR/99 AU 3.00 8.00
264 Luke Babbitt CR/99 AU 3.00 8.00
265 Eric Bledsoe CR/99 AU 6.00 15.00
266 Trevor Booker CR/99 AU 3.00 8.00
267 Craig Brackins CR/99 AU 3.00 8.00
268 Avery Bradley CR/99 AU 10.00 25.00
269 DeMarcus Cousins CR/49 AU 20.00 50.00
270 Jordan Crawford CR/99 AU 6.00 15.00
271 Ed Davis CR/99 AU 3.00 8.00
272 Derrick Favors CR/49 AU 10.00 25.00
273 Landry Fields CR/99 AU 6.00 15.00
274 Paul George CR/99 AU 12.00 30.00
275 Luke Harangody CR/99 AU 3.00 8.00
276 Gordon Hayward CR/99 AU 8.00 20.00
277 Lazar Hayward CR/99 AU 3.00 8.00
278 Xavier Henry CR/99 AU 3.00 8.00
279 Wesley Johnson CR/49 AU 6.00 15.00
280 Greg Monroe CR/99 AU 8.00 20.00
281 Daniel Orton CR/99 AU 3.00 8.00
282 Patrick Patterson CR/99 AU 5.00 12.00
284 Gary Neal CR/99 AU 5.00 12.00
285 Devin Ebanks CR/99 AU 5.00 12.00
286 Evan Turner CR/49 AU 10.00 25.00
287 Ekpe Udoh CR/98 AU 3.00 8.00
288 Greivis Vasquez CR/99 AU 8.00 20.00
289 John Wall CR/49 AU 50.00 125.00
290 Elliot Williams CR/99 AU 3.00 8.00
291 Cole Aldrich PS/99 AU 4.00 10.00
292 Al-Farouq Aminu PS/99 AU 3.00 8.00
293 James Anderson PS/99 AU 3.00 8.00
294 Luke Babbitt PS/99 AU 3.00 8.00
295 Eric Bledsoe PS/99 AU 5.00 12.00
296 Trevor Booker PS/99 AU 3.00 8.00
297 Craig Brackins PS/99 AU 3.00 8.00
298 Avery Bradley PS/99 AU 8.00 20.00
299 DeMarcus Cousins PS/49 AU 15.00 40.00
300 Jordan Crawford PS/99 AU 4.00 10.00
301 Ed Davis PS/99 AU 3.00 8.00
302 Derrick Favors PS/49 AU 6.00 15.00
303 Landry Fields PS/99 AU 5.00 12.00
304 Paul George PS/99 AU 8.00 20.00
305 Luke Harangody PS/99 AU 3.00 8.00
306 Gordon Hayward PS/99 AU 6.00 15.00
307 Lazar Hayward PS/99 AU EXCH 3.00 8.00
308 Xavier Henry PS/99 AU 3.00 8.00
309 Wesley Johnson PS/49 AU 5.00 12.00
310 Greg Monroe PS/99 AU 6.00 15.00
311 Daniel Orton PS/99 AU 3.00 8.00
312 Patrick Patterson PS/99 AU 4.00 10.00
313 Andy Rautins PS/99 AU 3.00 8.00
314 Gary Neal PS/99 AU 3.00 8.00
315 Devin Ebanks PS/99 AU 4.00 10.00
316 Evan Turner PS/49 AU 6.00 15.00
317 Ekpe Udoh PS/99 AU 3.00 8.00
318 Greivis Vasquez PS/99 AU 6.00 15.00
319 John Wall PS/49 AU 30.00 80.00
320 Elliot Williams PS/99 AU 3.00 8.00
321 Cole Aldrich SL/99 JSY AU 6.00 15.00
322 Al-Farouq Aminu SL/99 JSY AU 6.00 15.00
323 James Anderson SL/99 JSY AU 8.00 20.00
324 Luke Babbitt SL/99 JSY AU 6.00 15.00
325 Eric Bledsoe SL/99 JSY AU 12.00 3
326 Trevor Booker SL/99 JSY AU 6.00 1
327 Craig Brackins SL/99 JSY AU 6.00 1
328 Avery Bradley SL/99 JSY AU 12.00 3
329 DeMarcus Cousins SL/49 JSY AU30.00 8
330 Jordan Crawford SL/99 JSY AU 10.00 2
331 Ed Davis SL/99 JSY AU 6.00 1
332 Derrick Favors SL/49 JSY AU 15.00 4
333 Landry Fields SL/99 JSY AU 12.00 3
334 Paul George SL/99 JSY AU 15.00 4
335 Luke Harangody SL/99 JSY AU 6.00 1
336 Gordon Hayward SL/99 JSY AU 15.00 4
337 Lazar Hayward SL/99 JSY AU 6.00 1
338 Xavier Henry SL/99 JSY AU 6.00 1
339 Wesley Johnson SL/49 JSY AU 8.00 2
340 Greg Monroe SL/99 JSY AU 15.00 4
341 Daniel Orton SL/99 JSY AU 6.00 1
342 Patrick Patterson SL/99 JSY AU 8.00 2
344 Gary Neal SL/99 JSY AU 10.00 2
345 Devin Ebanks SL/99 JSY AU 10.00 2
346 Evan Turner SL/49 JSY AU 35.00 7
347 Ekpe Udoh SL/99 JSY AU 6.00 1
348 Greivis Vasquez SL/99 JSY AU 12.00 3
349 John Wall SL/49 JSY AU 75.00 20
350 Elliot Williams SL/99 JSY AU 6.00 1

2011-12 Panini Preferred Bl

PS STATED PRINT RUN 5 TO 49 SETS
PC STATED PRINT RUN 6 TO 50 SER.#'d SETS
SOME UNPRICED DUE TO SCARCITY
32 Connie Hawkins PS/25 AU 10.00 2
82 Paul Westphal PS/25 AU 5.00 1
83 Ralph Sampson PS/25 AU 5.00 1
84 Robert Horry PS/25 AU 12.00 3
86 Rolando Blackman PS/25 AU 8.00 2
87 Sam Perkins PS/25 AU 5.00 1
88 Spencer Haywood PS/25 AU 5.00 1
90 Stephen Jackson PS/25 AU 5.00 1
91 Steve Smith PS/25 AU 5.00 1
92 Tom Heinsohn PS/25 AU 20.00 5
94 Toney Douglas PS/25 AU 5.00 1
95 Toni Kukoc PS/25 AU 20.00 5
99 Xavier McDaniel PS/25 AU 5.00 1
101 Walt Bellamy PC/15 AU 8.00 2
102 Adrian Dantley PC/50 AU 5.00 1
103 Al Thornton PC/50 AU EXCH 5.00 1
104 Alex English PC/50 AU 6.00 1
105 Alonzo Mourning PC/15 AU 75.00 15
106 Andre Iguodala PC/20 AU 6.00 1
107 Andre Miller PC/50 AU 5.00 1
108 Andrea Bargnani PC/20 AU 6.00 1
110 Artis Gilmore PC/20 AU 10.00 2
111 Bailey Howell PC/50 AU 6.00 1
112 Bernard King PC/50 AU 8.00 2
113 Bill Cartwright PC/50 AU 8.00 2
114 Bill Laimbeer PC/50 AU 8.00 2
116 Bill Walton PC/20 AU 10.00 2
118 Bob Dandridge PC/50 AU 5.00 1
119 Bob McAdoo PC/50 AU 10.00 2
120 Brandon Jennings PC/20 AU 15.00 4
121 Byron Scott PC/50 AU 5.00 1
122 Calvin Murphy PC/20 AU 8.00 2
123 Campy Russell PC/50 AU 5.00 1
124 Cazzie Russell PC/50 AU 5.00 1
125 Cedric Maxwell PC/50 AU 6.00 1
126 Charles Oakley PC/50 AU 12.00 3
127 Chris Ford PC/50 AU 5.00 1
128 Chris Mullin PC/50 AU 12.00 3
129 Chris Paul PC/15 AU 50.00 12
130 Christian Laettner PC/20 AU 10.00 2
131 Clyde Lovellette PC/20 AU 8.00 2
132 Connie Hawkins PC/35 AU 10.00 2
133 Dan Issel PC/50 AU 6.00 1
134 Dan Majerle PC/50 AU 8.00 2
135 Darrell Griffith PC/50 AU 5.00 1
136 Darren Collison PC/50 AU 6.00 1
137 Darryl Dawkins PC/50 AU 5.00 1
138 Dave Cowens PC/20 AU 12.00 3
139 David Robinson PC/15 AU 60.00 15
140 David Thompson PC/50 AU 6.00 1
141 DeMar DeRozan PC/15 AU 10.00 2
142 Dennis Rodman PC/25 AU 30.00 8
143 Derrick Rose PC/15 AU 300.00 50
144 Detlef Schrempf PC/50 AU 10.00 2
145 Dikembe Mutombo PC/50 AU 15.00 4
146 Elgin Baylor PC/20 AU 15.00 4
147 Elvin Hayes PC/20 AU 6.00 1
148 Eric Gordon PC/50 AU 8.00 2
149 Frank Ramsey PC/50 AU 8.00 2
150 Gail Goodrich PC/20 AU 8.00 2
151 George Gervin PC/20 AU 15.00 4
152 George McGinnis PC/50 AU 5.00 1
153 Grant Hill PC/15 AU 100.00 20
154 Hakeem Olajuwon PC/15 AU 30.00 8
155 Isiah Thomas PC/20 AU 20.00 5
156 James Harden PC/20 AU 25.00 6
157 James Worthy PC/15 AU 25.00 6
158 Jeff Hornacek PC/50 AU 10.00 2
160 Jrue Holiday PC/50 AU 10.00 2
164 Kiki Vandeweghe PC/50 AU EXCH5.00 1
165 Kobe Bryant PC/50 AU 175.00 35
167 Lenny Wilkens PC/20 AU 12.00 3
168 Luol Deng PC/20 AU 15.00 4
170 Mark Aguirre PC/50 AU 5.00 1
171 Mark Eaton PC/50 AU 5.00 1
172 Mark Price PC/50 AU 20.00 5
173 Maurice Cheeks PC/50 AU 5.00 1
174 Michael Cage PC/50 AU 5.00 1
175 Mitch Richmond PC/50 AU 12.00 3
176 Monta Ellis PC/25 AU 12.00 3
177 Nate Archibald PC/20 AU 10.00 2
178 Nate Thurmond PC/20 AU 10.00 2
179 Oscar Robertson PC/15 AU 50.00 12
180 Pat Riley PC/15 AU 15.00 4
181 Paul Westphal PC/35 AU 5.00 1
182 Ralph Sampson PC/35 AU 8.00 2
183 Robert Horry PC/35 AU 10.00 2
184 Robert Parish PC/20 AU 10.00 2
185 Rolando Blackman PC/35 AU 8.00 2
186 Sam Perkins PC/35 AU 5.00 1
187 Spencer Haywood PC/35 AU 5.00 1
188 Stephen Curry PC/35 AU 15.00 4
189 Stephen Jackson PC/35 AU 5.00 1
190 Steve Nash PC/15 AU 30.00 8
191 Steve Smith PC/35 AU 5.00 1
192 Tom Heinsohn PC/35 AU 10.00 2
193 Dominique Wilkins PC/20 AU 20.00 5
194 Toney Douglas PC/35 AU 5.00 1
195 Toni Kukoc PC/35 AU 20.00 5
196 Ty Lawson PC/35 AU 10.00 2
197 Walt Frazier PC/20 AU 20.00 5
198 Zach Randolph PC/20 AU 12.00 3
199 Xavier McDaniel PC/35 AU 8.00 2
200 World B. Free PC/20 AU 10.00 2
291 Cole Aldrich PS/49 AU 5.00 1
292 Al-Farouq Aminu PS/49 AU 4.00 1
293 James Anderson PS/49 AU 4.00 1
294 Luke Babbitt PS/49 AU 4.00 1
295 Eric Bledsoe PS/49 AU 6.00 1

296 Trevor Booker PS/49 AU 4.00 10.00
297 Craig Brackins PS/49 AU 4.00 10.00
298 Avery Bradley PS/49 AU 8.00 20.00
300 Jordan Crawford PS/49 AU 5.00 12.00
301 Ed Davis PS/49 AU 4.00 10.00
303 Landry Fields PS/49 AU 8.00 20.00
304 Paul George PS/49 AU 10.00 25.00
305 Luke Harangody PS/49 AU 4.00 10.00
306 Gordon Hayward PS/49 AU 8.00 20.00
307 Lazar Hayward PS/49 AU EXCH 4.00 10.00
308 Xavier Henry PS/49 AU 4.00 10.00
310 Greg Monroe PS/49 AU 8.00 20.00
311 Daniel Orton PS/49 AU 4.00 10.00
312 Patrick Patterson PS/49 AU 5.00 12.00
313 Andy Rautins PS/49 AU 4.00 10.00
314 Gary Neal PS/49 AU 5.00 12.00
315 Devin Ebanks PS/49 AU 5.00 12.00
317 Ekpe Udoh PS/49 AU 5.00 12.00
318 Greivis Vasquez PS/49 AU 8.00 20.00
320 Elliot Williams PS/49 AU 4.00 10.00

2011-12 Panini Preferred Emerald

PS STATED PRINT RUN 2 TO 75 SER.#'d SETS
PC STATED PRINT RUN 2 TO 5 SER.#'d SETS
SOME UNPRICED DUE TO SCARCITY
291 Cole Aldrich PS/75 AU 4.00 10.00
292 Al-Farouq Aminu PS/75 AU 3.00 8.00
293 James Anderson PS/75 AU 3.00 8.00
294 Luke Babbitt PS/75 AU 3.00 8.00
295 Eric Bledsoe PS/75 AU 5.00 12.00
296 Trevor Booker PS/75 AU 3.00 8.00
297 Craig Brackins PS/75 AU 3.00 8.00
298 Avery Bradley PS/75 AU 8.00 20.00
299 DeMarcus Cousins PS/25 AU 15.00 40.00
300 Jordan Crawford PS/75 AU 4.00 10.00
301 Ed Davis PS/75 AU 3.00 8.00
302 Derrick Favors PS/25 AU 8.00 20.00
303 Landry Fields PS/75 AU 8.00 20.00
304 Paul George PS/75 AU 10.00 25.00
305 Luke Harangody PS/75 AU 3.00 8.00
306 Gordon Hayward PS/75 AU 6.00 15.00
307 Lazar Hayward PS/75 AU EXCH 3.00 8.00
308 Xavier Henry PS/75 AU 3.00 8.00
309 Wesley Johnson PS/25 AU 8.00 20.00
310 Greg Monroe PS/75 AU 6.00 15.00
311 Daniel Orton PS/75 AU 3.00 8.00
312 Patrick Patterson PS/75 AU 4.00 10.00
313 Andy Rautins PS/75 AU 3.00 8.00
314 Gary Neal PS/75 AU 5.00 12.00
315 Devin Ebanks PS/75 AU 5.00 12.00
316 Evan Turner PS/25 AU 10.00 25.00
317 Ekpe Udoh PS/75 AU 3.00 8.00
318 Greivis Vasquez PS/75 AU 6.00 15.00
319 John Wall PS/25 AU 40.00 100.00
320 Elliot Williams PS/75 AU 3.00 8.00

2011-12 Panini Preferred Gold

PC STATED PRINT RUN 5 TO 10 SER.#'d SETS
CR STATED PRINT RUN 10 TO 25 SER.#'d SETS
SOME UNPRICED DUE TO SCARCITY
261 Cole Aldrich CR/25 AU 4.00 10.00
262 Al-Farouq Aminu CR/25 AU 8.00 20.00
263 James Anderson CR/25 AU 5.00 12.00
264 Luke Babbitt CR/25 AU 4.00 10.00
265 Eric Bledsoe CR/25 AU 10.00 25.00
266 Trevor Booker CR/25 AU 6.00 15.00
267 Craig Brackins CR/25 AU 4.00 10.00
268 Avery Bradley CR/25 AU 12.00 30.00
269 DeMarcus Cousins CR/25 AU 25.00 60.00
270 Jordan Crawford CR/25 AU 10.00 25.00
71 Ed Davis CR/25 AU 4.00 10.00
72 Derrick Favors CR/25 AU 12.00 30.00
73 Landry Fields CR/25 AU 8.00 20.00
74 Paul George CR/25 AU 15.00 40.00
75 Luke Harangody CR/25 AU 4.00 10.00
76 Gordon Hayward CR/25 AU 15.00 40.00
77 Lazar Hayward CR/25 AU 4.00 10.00
78 Xavier Henry CR/25 AU 4.00 10.00
79 Wesley Johnson CR/25 AU 8.00 20.00
80 Greg Monroe CR/25 AU 12.00 30.00
81 Daniel Orton CR/25 AU 4.00 10.00
82 Patrick Patterson CR/25 AU 8.00 20.00
84 Gary Neal CR/25 AU 8.00 20.00
85 Devin Ebanks CR/25 AU 8.00 20.00
86 Evan Turner CR/25 AU 20.00 50.00
87 Ekpe Udoh CR/25 AU 10.00 25.00
88 Greivis Vasquez CR/25 AU 15.00 40.00
89 John Wall CR/25 AU 60.00 150.00
90 Elliot Williams CR/25 AU 4.00 10.00

2011-12 Panini Preferred Silhouettes Prime

ATED PRINT RUN ONE TO 25 SER.#'d SETS
ME UNPRICED DUE TO SCARCITY
2 Al Thornton/15 EXCH 25.00 60.00
3 Alex English/25 60.00 150.00
5 Andre Iguodala/15 60.00 150.00
3 Brandon Jennings/25 40.00 100.00
4 Charles Oakley/25 50.00 125.00
8 Darrell Griffith/25 40.00 100.00
4 Dikembe Mutombo/25 125.00 225.00
5 Kiki Vandeweghe/25 40.00 100.00
7 Luol Deng/25 75.00 150.00
8 Mark Aguirre/25 40.00 100.00
9 Mark Eaton/15 25.00 60.00
0 Maurice Cheeks/25 75.00 150.00
1 Michael Cage/25 30.00 80.00
2 Mitch Richmond/25 75.00 200.00
3 Monta Ellis/15 100.00 175.00
7 Stephen Curry/25 100.00 200.00
9 Toni Kukoc/25 150.00 300.00
0 Ty Lawson/25 125.00 250.00
1 Cole Aldrich/25 25.00 60.00
2 Al-Farouq Aminu/25 50.00 125.00
3 James Anderson/25 25.00 60.00
5 Trevor Booker/25 40.00 100.00
9 DeMarcus Cousins/25 100.00 200.00
2 Derrick Favors/25 60.00 150.00
3 Landry Fields/25 50.00 125.00
6 Gordon Hayward/25 50.00 125.00
7 Lazar Hayward/24 30.00 80.00
8 Xavier Henry/20 25.00 60.00
0 Greg Monroe/25 100.00 200.00
1 Daniel Orton/25 25.00 60.00
4 Gary Neal/25 30.00 80.00

345 Devin Ebanks/25 50.00 125.00
346 Evan Turner/25 100.00 200.00
347 Ekpe Udoh/25 50.00 125.00
349 John Wall/25 175.00 350.00
350 Elliot Williams/25 30.00 80.00

2011-12 Panini Preferred Silver

STATED PRINT RUN 5 TO 25 SER.#'d SETS
SOME UNPRICED DUE TO SCARCITY
102 Adrian Dantley PC/25 AU 6.00 15.00
103 Al Thornton PC/25 AU EXCH 6.00 15.00
104 Alex English PC/25 AU 8.00 20.00
106 Andre Iguodala PC/15 AU 10.00 25.00
107 Andre Miller PC/20 AU 6.00 15.00
108 Andrea Bargnani PC/15 AU 10.00 25.00
110 Artis Gilmore PC/15 AU 10.00 25.00
111 Bailey Howell PC/25 AU 8.00 20.00
112 Bernard King PC/25 AU 10.00 25.00
113 Bill Cartwright PC/25 AU 10.00 25.00
114 Bill Laimbeer PC/25 AU 8.00 20.00
116 Bill Walton PC/15 AU 12.00 30.00
118 Bob Dandridge PC/25 AU 6.00 15.00
119 Bob McAdoo PC/25 AU 15.00 40.00
120 Brandon Jennings PC/15 AU 20.00 50.00
121 Byron Scott PC/25 AU 8.00 20.00
122 Calvin Murphy PC/15 AU 8.00 20.00
123 Campy Russell PC/25 AU 6.00 15.00
124 Cazzie Russell PC/25 AU 6.00 15.00
125 Cedric Maxwell PC/25 AU 6.00 15.00
126 Charles Oakley PC/25 AU 15.00 40.00
127 Chris Ford PC/25 AU 6.00 15.00
128 Chris Mullin PC/25 AU 20.00 50.00
130 Christian Laettner PC/15 AU 10.00 25.00
131 Clyde Lovellette PC/15 AU 10.00 25.00
132 Connie Hawkins PC/25 AU 10.00 25.00
133 Dan Issel PC/25 AU 6.00 15.00
134 Dan Majerle PC/25 AU 10.00 25.00
135 Darrell Griffith PC/25 AU 6.00 15.00
136 Darren Collison PC/25 AU 6.00 15.00
137 Darryl Dawkins PC/25 AU 6.00 15.00
138 Dave Cowens PC/15 AU 12.00 30.00
140 David Thompson PC/25 AU 6.00 15.00
141 DeMar DeRozan PC/20 AU 10.00 25.00
142 Dennis Rodman PC/15 AU 40.00 100.00
144 Detlef Schrempf PC/25 AU 15.00 40.00
145 Dikembe Mutombo PC/25 AU 20.00 50.00
146 Elgin Baylor PC/15 AU 15.00 40.00
147 Elvin Hayes PC/15 AU 10.00 25.00
148 Eric Gordon PC/15 AU 12.00 30.00
149 Frank Ramsey PC/25 AU 10.00 25.00
150 Gail Goodrich PC/15 AU 10.00 25.00
151 George Gervin PC/15 AU 15.00 40.00
152 George McGinnis PC/24 AU 6.00 15.00
155 Isiah Thomas PC/15 AU 30.00 80.00
156 James Harden PC/15 AU 25.00 60.00
158 Jeff Hornacek PC/25 AU 10.00 25.00
160 Jrue Holiday PC/25 AU 12.00 30.00
164 Kiki Vandeweghe PC/25 AU EXCH6.00 15.00
165 Kobe Bryant PC/15 AU 250.00 400.00
167 Lenny Wilkens PC/15 AU 12.00 30.00
168 Luol Deng PC/15 AU 20.00 50.00
170 Mark Aguirre PC/25 AU 6.00 15.00
171 Mark Eaton PC/25 AU 6.00 15.00
172 Mark Price PC/25 AU 30.00 80.00
173 Maurice Cheeks PC/25 AU 6.00 15.00
174 Michael Cage PC/25 AU 6.00 15.00
175 Mitch Richmond PC/25 AU 15.00 40.00
176 Monta Ellis PC/20 AU 15.00 40.00
177 Nate Archibald PC/17 AU 12.00 30.00
178 Nate Thurmond PC/15 AU 10.00 25.00
181 Paul Westphal PC/25 AU 6.00 15.00
182 Ralph Sampson PC/25 AU 10.00 25.00
183 Robert Horry PC/25 AU 15.00 40.00
184 Robert Parish PC/15 AU 10.00 25.00
185 Rolando Blackman PC/25 AU 8.00 20.00
186 Sam Perkins PC/25 AU 6.00 15.00
187 Spencer Haywood PC/25 AU 6.00 15.00
188 Stephen Curry PC/25 AU 20.00 50.00
189 Stephen Jackson PC/25 AU 6.00 15.00
191 Steve Smith PC/25 AU 6.00 15.00
192 Tom Heinsohn PC/25 AU 10.00 25.00
194 Toney Douglas PC/25 AU 6.00 15.00
195 Toni Kukoc PC/25 AU 25.00 60.00
196 Ty Lawson PC/25 AU 12.00 30.00
197 Walt Frazier PC/15 AU 25.00 60.00
198 Zach Randolph PC/15 AU 12.00 30.00
199 Xavier McDaniel PC/25 AU 8.00 20.00
200 World B. Free PC/15 AU 10.00 25.00

2011-12 Panini Preferred All-Star Memorabilia

STATED PRINT RUN 50 TO 199 SER.#'d SETS
1 Allen Iverson/99 20.00 50.00
Derrick Rose
Rajon Rondo
Jason Kidd
Chris Paul
Steve Nash
Tony Parker
2 Blake Griffin/199 25.00 60.00
Dwyane Wade
Kevin Durant
Carmelo Anthony
Dirk Nowitzki
LeBron James
Derrick Rose
3 Rashard Lewis/79 40.00 100.00
Xavier McDaniel
Detlef Schrempf
Gary Payton
Shawn Kemp
Ray Allen
Kevin Durant
4 LeBron James/199 20.00 50.00
David West
Dwyane Wade
Mo Williams
Josh Howard
Carmelo Anthony
Chris Kaman
5 Alonzo Mourning/50 30.00 80.00
Ray Allen
Kevin Garnett
Grant Hill
Larry Johnson
David Robinson
Anfernee Hardaway
6 Chris Mullin/50 30.00 80.00
John Stockton
Karl Malone
Scottie Pippen
Christian Laettner
Clyde Drexler
Larry Bird
7 Patrick Ewing/50 30.00 80.00
Larry Bird
Clyde Drexler
Chris Mullin
Magic Johnson
Karl Malone
John Stockton
8 Charles Oakley/199 20.00 50.00
Earl Monroe
Larry Johnson
Mark Jackson
Patrick Ewing
John Starks
Amare Stoudemire
9 Kobe Bryant/99 25.00 60.00
Jermaine O'Neal
Vince Carter
Paul Pierce
Kevin Garnett
Tracy McGrady
Allen Iverson
10 Kareem Abdul-Jabbar/50 30.00 80.00
Moses Malone
Shaquille O'Neal
Kobe Bryant
David Robinson
Hakeem Olajuwon
Karl Malone

2011-12 Panini Preferred All-Star Memorabilia Prime

STATED PRINT RUN 10 TO 25 SER.#'d SETS
SOME UNPRICED DUE TO SCARCITY
1 Allen Iverson/25 100.00 200.00
Derrick Rose
Rajon Rondo
Jason Kidd
Chris Paul
Steve Nash
Tony Parker
2 Blake Griffin/25 150.00 300.00
Dwyane Wade
Kevin Durant
Carmelo Anthony
Dirk Nowitzki
LeBron James
Derrick Rose
4 LeBron James/25 100.00 200.00
David West
Dwyane Wade
Mo Williams
Josh Howard
Carmelo Anthony
Chris Kaman
5 Alonzo Mourning/25 100.00 200.00
Ray Allen
Kevin Garnett
Grant Hill
Larry Johnson
David Robinson
Anfernee Hardaway
8 Charles Oakley/25 75.00 150.00
Earl Monroe
Larry Johnson
Mark Jackson
Patrick Ewing
John Starks
Amare Stoudemire
9 Kobe Bryant/25 75.00 150.00
Jermaine O'Neal
Vince Carter
Paul Pierce
Kevin Garnett
Tracy McGrady
Allen Iverson
10 Kareem Abdul-Jabbar/25 100.00 200.00
Moses Malone
Shaquille O'Neal
Kobe Bryant
David Robinson
Hakeem Olajuwon
Karl Malone

2011-12 Panini Preferred Assists Memorabilia

STATED PRINT RUN 50 TO 199 SER.#'d SETS
1 John Stockton/99 20.00 50.00
Isiah Thomas
Gary Payton
Mark Jackson
Magic Johnson
Jason Kidd
Steve Nash
2 Jason Kidd/199 20.00 50.00
Steve Nash
Tony Parker
Chris Paul
Dwyane Wade
Rajon Rondo
Derrick Rose
3 Kobe Bryant/50 30.00 80.00
Larry Bird
Rajon Rondo
Derek Fisher
Magic Johnson
Nick Van Exel
Gary Payton
4 Chauncey Billups/199 15.00 40.00
Stephen Curry
Russell Westbrook
Deron Williams
Andre Miller
Mo Williams
Derrick Rose
5 Derrick Rose/199 15.00 40.00
Chauncey Billups
Monta Ellis
Rajon Rondo
Russell Westbrook
Chris Paul
Stephen Curry
6 John Stockton/50 25.00 60.00
Mark Price
Isiah Thomas
Kevin Johnson
Magic Johnson
Mark Jackson
Larry Bird

2011-12 Panini Preferred Assists Memorabilia Prime

STATED PRINT RUN 5 TO 25 SER.#'d SETS
SOME UNPRICED DUE TO SCARCITY
1 John Stockton/25 100.00 200.00
Isiah Thomas
Gary Payton
Mark Jackson
Magic Johnson
Jason Kidd
Steve Nash
2 Jason Kidd/25 100.00 200.00
Steve Nash
Tony Parker
Chris Paul
Dwyane Wade
Rajon Rondo
Derrick Rose
4 Chauncey Billups/25 30.00 80.00
Stephen Curry
Russell Westbrook
Deron Williams
Andre Miller
Mo Williams
Derrick Rose
5 Derrick Rose/25 60.00 150.00
Chauncey Billups
Monta Ellis
Rajon Rondo
Russell Westbrook
Chris Paul
Stephen Curry

2011-12 Panini Preferred Centers Memorabilia

STATED PRINT RUN 99 TO 199 SER.#'d SETS
1 Andrea Bargnani/199 10.00 25.00
Marc Gasol
Anderson Varejao
Marcin Gortat
Andrew Bogut
Timofey Mozgov
2 Amare Stoudemire/199 10.00 25.00
Andrea Bargnani
Mehmet Okur
Pau Gasol
Kevin Love
Emeka Okafor
3 Emeka Okafor/199 10.00 25.00
Chris Andersen
Marcus Camby
Tyson Chandler
Dwight Howard
Greg Oden
4 Bill Cartwright/99 20.00 50.00
David Robinson
Hakeem Olajuwon
Dikembe Mutombo
Mark Eaton
Manute Bol

2011-12 Panini Preferred Centers Memorabilia Prime

STATED PRINT RUN 10 TO 25 SER.#'d SETS
SOME UNPRICED DUE TO SCARCITY
1 Andrea Bargnani/25 30.00 80.00
Marc Gasol
Anderson Varejao
Marcin Gortat
Andrew Bogut
Timofey Mozgov
2 Amare Stoudemire/25 30.00 80.00
Andrea Bargnani
Mehmet Okur
Pau Gasol
Kevin Love
Emeka Okafor
3 Emeka Okafor/25 40.00 100.00
Chris Andersen
Marcus Camby
Tyson Chandler
Dwight Howard
Greg Oden

2011-12 Panini Preferred Decades Memorabilia

STATED PRINT RUN 10 TO 199 SER.#'d SETS
SOME UNPRICED DUE TO SCARCITY
UNPRICED PRIME PRINT RUN 3 TO 10 SETS
2 Bill Laimbeer/25 20.00 50.00
Cedric Maxwell
Kevin McHale
James Worthy
Kiki Vandeweghe
Michael Cooper
Mark Aguirre
Dennis Johnson
3 Patrick Ewing/25 30.00 80.00
Magic Johnson
Mark Eaton
Kiki Vandeweghe
Isiah Thomas
Joe Dumars
Larry Bird
Danny Ainge
4 Alonzo Mourning/99 20.00 50.00
Dan Majerle
Chris Mullin
Dennis Rodman
Patrick Ewing
Mark Jackson
Mark Price
John Starks
5 Danny Manning/99 20.00 50.00
Mitch Richmond
Mark Jackson
Larry Johnson
Patrick Ewing
Ron Harper
Karl Malone
Dennis Scott
6 Allen Iverson/199 20.00 50.00
Alonzo Mourning
Ray Allen
Ben Wallace
Kevin Johnson
Shawn Kemp
Nick Van Exel
Larry Johnson
7 Kobe Bryant/199 25.00 60.00
Scottie Pippen
Anfernee Hardaway
Allen Iverson
Tracy McGrady
Paul Pierce
Vince Carter
Steve Nash
8 Carmelo Anthony/199 20.00 50.00
Manu Ginobili
Tony Parker
Pau Gasol
Dwight Howard
Joe Johnson
Yao Ming
LeBron James

2011-12 Panini Preferred Defense Memorabilia

STATED PRINT RUN 25 TO 199 SER.#'d SETS
UNPRICED PRIME PRINT RUN 3 TO 10 SETS
1 Patrick Ewing/50 30.00 80.00
Robert Parish
David Robinson
Manute Bol
Kareem Abdul-Jabbar
Dikembe Mutombo
Hakeem Olajuwon
2 Shaquille O'Neal/25 50.00 120.00
Kareem Abdul-Jabbar
Patrick Ewing
Wilt Chamberlain
David Robinson
Alonzo Mourning
Yao Ming
3 Josh Smith/199 10.00 25.00
Ben Wallace
Chris Andersen
Emeka Okafor
Tyrus Thomas
Tyson Chandler
Andrei Kirilenko
4 Julius Erving/25 25.00 60.00
Kevin McHale
Patrick Ewing
Spencer Haywood
Magic Johnson
Maurice Cheeks
John Stockton
5 Tayshaun Prince/199 10.00 25.00
Raja Bell
Rajon Rondo
Monta Ellis
Shane Battier
Ron Artest
Matt Barnes
6 Andre Miller/50 20.00 50.00
Tony Parker
Chris Paul
Jason Kidd
John Stockton
Isiah Thomas
Gary Payton

2011-12 Panini Preferred Forwards Memorabilia

STATED PRINT RUN 125 TO 199 SETS
1 Blake Griffin/125 20.00 50.00
Dirk Nowitzki
Tracy McGrady
Paul Pierce
Kevin Durant
Tim Duncan
Chris Bosh
2 Greg Monroe/199 10.00 25.00
Paul George
Larry Sanders
Patrick Patterson
Al-Farouq Aminu
Lazar Hayward
Landry Fields
3 Craig Brackins/199 10.00 25.00
Ed Davis
DeMarcus Cousins
Ekpe Udoh
Devin Ebanks
Damion James
Evan Turner
4 Joakim Noah/199 10.00 25.00
Andre Iguodala
LaMarcus Aldridge
Hedo Turkoglu
Lamar Odom
Luol Deng
Carmelo Anthony
5 Chris Mullin/125 10.00 25.00
Chuck Person
Derrick Coleman
Glen Rice
Dennis Scott
Kevin Willis
Larry Johnson
6 Karl Malone/125 15.00 40.00
Scottie Pippen
Kiki Vandeweghe
Derrick Coleman
Tom Chambers
Clyde Drexler
Dominique Wilkins

2011-12 Panini Preferred Forwards Memorabilia Prime

STATED PRINT RUN 15 TO 25 SER.#'d SETS
1 Blake Griffin/25 75.00 150.00
Dirk Nowitzki
Tracy McGrady
Paul Pierce
Kevin Durant
Tim Duncan
Chris Bosh
4 Joakim Noah/25 30.00 80.00
Andre Iguodala
LaMarcus Aldridge
Hedo Turkoglu
Lamar Odom
Luol Deng
Carmelo Anthony
5 Chris Mullin/15 75.00 150.00
Chuck Person
Derrick Coleman
Glen Rice
Dennis Scott
Kevin Willis
Larry Johnson
6 Karl Malone/25 125.00 250.00
Scottie Pippen
Kiki Vandeweghe
Derrick Coleman
Tom Chambers
Clyde Drexler
Dominique Wilkins

2011-12 Panini Preferred Inducted Memorabilia

STATED PRINT RUN 50 TO 99 SER.#'d SETS
UNPRICED PRIME PRINT RUN 3 SETS
1 Chris Mullin/99 25.00 60.00
Dominique Wilkins
Clyde Drexler
David Robinson
Isiah Thomas
John Stockton
Hakeem Olajuwon
Patrick Ewing
2 Larry Bird/50 50.00 120.00
Patrick Ewing
Karl Malone
Kareem Abdul-Jabbar
Wilt Chamberlain
David Robinson
Dominique Wilkins
Julius Erving
3 Julius Erving/50 40.00 100.00
Larry Bird
Moses Malone
Robert Parish
David Robinson
Kareem Abdul-Jabbar
Joe Dumars
Magic Johnson
4 Kevin McHale/99 20.00 50.00
Scottie Pippen
Joe Dumars
John Stockton
James Worthy
Karl Malone
Chris Mullin
Alex English

2011-12 Panini Preferred Legends Memorabilia

STATED PRINT RUN 50 TO 150 SER.#'d SETS
UNPRICED PRIME PRINT RUN 3 TO 10 SETS
1 George Mikan/50 50.00 120.00
Shaquille O'Neal
Kareem Abdul-Jabbar
Elgin Baylor
Magic Johnson
Wilt Chamberlain
2 Shaquille O'Neal/150 25.00 60.00
Patrick Ewing
Dikembe Mutombo
Hakeem Olajuwon
Kareem Abdul-Jabbar
David Robinson
3 Karl Malone/150 25.00 60.00
Dennis Rodman
Isiah Thomas
John Stockton
Patrick Ewing
Scottie Pippen
4 Larry Bird/50 40.00 100.00
Magic Johnson
Isiah Thomas
Kareem Abdul-Jabbar
Julius Erving
Clyde Drexler
5 Danny Ainge/50 30.00 80.00
Shaquille O'Neal
Robert Parish
Larry Bird
Kevin McHale
Sam Jones
6 Alex English/150 20.00 50.00
Patrick Ewing
Kevin McHale
Robert Parish
Moses Malone
Bernard King

2011-12 Panini Preferred Rebound Memorabilia

STATED PRINT RUN 199 SER.#'d SETS
1 Alonzo Mourning/199 20.00 50.00
Patrick Ewing
Karl Malone
Hakeem Olajuwon
David Robinson
Shaquille O'Neal
Dennis Rodman
2 Amare Stoudemire/199 20.00 50.00
Kevin Durant
Dwight Howard
Kevin Love
Dirk Nowitzki
Kevin Garnett
LeBron James
3 Carlos Boozer/199 10.00 25.00
Luol Deng
Zach Randolph
Al Jefferson
David Lee
Mehmet Okur
Chris Bosh
4 Samuel Dalembert/199 10.00 25.00
Andrew Bogut
Chris Kaman
Marcus Camby
Joakim Noah
Zydrunas Ilgauskas
Marc Gasol
5 Nene/199 10.00 25.00
Luol Deng
Anderson Varejao
Kevin Love
Tyson Chandler
Drew Gooden
Shawn Bradley
6 Brad Miller/199 10.00 25.00
Taj Gibson
LaMarcus Aldridge
Greg Oden
Paul Millsap
David West
Udonis Haslem

2011-12 Panini Preferred Rebound Memorabilia Prime

STATED PRINT RUN 10 TO 25 SER.#'d SETS
SOME UNPRICED DUE TO SCARCITY
1 Alonzo Mourning/25 100.00 200.00
Patrick Ewing
Karl Malone
Hakeem Olajuwon
David Robinson
Shaquille O'Neal
Dennis Rodman
2 Amare Stoudemire/25 125.00 225.00
Kevin Durant
Dwight Howard
Kevin Love
Dirk Nowitzki
Kevin Garnett
LeBron James
4 Samuel Dalembert/25 40.00 80.00
Andrew Bogut
Chris Kaman
Marcus Camby
Joakim Noah
Zydrunas Ilgauskas
Marc Gasol
5 Nene/25
Luol Deng
Anderson Varejao
Kevin Love
Tyson Chandler
Drew Gooden
Shawn Bradley
6 Brad Miller/25 30.00
Taj Gibson
LaMarcus Aldridge
Greg Oden
Paul Millsap
David West
Udonis Haslem

2011-12 Panini Preferred Rookies Memorabilia

STATED PRINT RUN 99 SER.#'d SETS
1 Jordan Crawford 12.00 30.00
John Wall
Evan Turner
Greg Monroe
DeMarcus Cousins
Landry Fields
2 John Wall 10.00 25.00
Andy Rautins
DeMarcus Cousins
Larry Sanders
Evan Turner
Derrick Favors
3 Eric Bledsoe 10.00 25.00
John Wall
Evan Turner
Ekpe Udoh
DeMarcus Cousins
Lazar Hayward
4 John Wall 10.00 25.00
Cole Aldrich
Ekpe Udoh
James Anderson
Jordan Crawford
Devin Ebanks
5 Craig Brackins 15.00 40.00
John Wall
Dexter Pittman
DeMarcus Cousins
Jeremy Lin
Gary Neal
6 John Wall 12.00 30.00
Dominique Jones
Ekpe Udoh
Quincy Pondexter
Gordon Hayward
Evan Turner
7 Wesley Johnson 10.00 25.00
John Wall
Gordon Hayward
Quincy Pondexter
Ekpe Udoh
Lance Stephenson
8 John Wall 12.00 30.00
Landry Fields
Ekpe Udoh
Quincy Pondexter
Gordon Hayward
Jordan Crawford

2011-12 Panini Preferred Rookies Memorabilia Prime

STATED PRINT RUN 25 SER.#'d SETS
1 Jordan Crawford 60.00 150.00
John Wall
Evan Turner
Greg Monroe
DeMarcus Cousins
Landry Fields
2 John Wall 40.00 100.00
Andy Rautins
DeMarcus Cousins
Larry Sanders
Evan Turner
Derrick Favors
3 Eric Bledsoe 40.00 100.00
John Wall
Evan Turner
Ekpe Udoh
DeMarcus Cousins
Lazar Hayward
4 John Wall 40.00 100.00
Cole Aldrich
Ekpe Udoh
James Anderson
Jordan Crawford
Devin Ebanks
5 Craig Brackins 60.00 150.00
John Wall
Dexter Pittman
DeMarcus Cousins
Jeremy Lin
Gary Neal
6 John Wall 40.00 100.00
Dominique Jones
Ekpe Udoh
Quincy Pondexter
Gordon Hayward
Evan Turner
7 Wesley Johnson 60.00 150.00
John Wall
Gordon Hayward
Quincy Pondexter
Ekpe Udoh
Lance Stephenson
8 John Wall 40.00 100.00
Landry Fields
Ekpe Udoh
Quincy Pondexter
Gordon Hayward
Jordan Crawford

2011-12 Panini Preferred Slam Dunk Memorabilia

STATED PRINT RUN 99 TO 199 SER.#'d SETS
1 Kobe Bryant/125 30.00 80.00
Shaquille O'Neal
Kevin Garnett
Tracy McGrady
Vince Carter
Grant Hill
David Robinson
Chris Webber
2 Scottie Pippen/125 30.00 80.00
Clyde Drexler
Grant Hill
Kevin Garnett
Shaquille O'Neal
Dominique Wilkins
Shawn Kemp
Larry Johnson
3 Julius Erving/99 30.00 80.00

...e Griffin
...ominique Wilkins
Kobe Bryant
LeBron James
Vince Carter
Dwyane Wade
Clyde Drexler
4 Blake Griffin/99 15.00 40.00
Andre Iguodala
Russell Westbrook
Thaddeus Young
JaVale McGee
Taj Gibson
DeMar DeRozan
Serge Ibaka
5 Yao Ming/125 20.00 50.00
Tim Duncan
LaMarcus Aldridge
Amare Stoudemire
Dwight Howard
Pau Gasol
Kevin Garnett
Shaquille O'Neal
6 Kevin Durant/125 40.00 100.00
Julius Erving
Kobe Bryant
Dominique Wilkins
LeBron James
Dwyane Wade
Vince Carter
Blake Griffin
7 Nate Robinson/199 15.00 40.00
Russell Westbrook
Tyson Chandler
Rudy Gay
Jason Richardson
Josh Smith
Chris Andersen
Carmelo Anthony
8 Julius Erving/99 25.00 60.00
Dominique Wilkins
Thaddeus Young
Clyde Drexler
Blake Griffin
Serge Ibaka
DeMar DeRozan
Larry Johnson

2011-12 Panini Preferred Slam Dunk Memorabilia Prime

STATED PRINT RUN 25 SER.#'d SETS
1 Kobe Bryant 100.00 200.00
Shaquille O'Neal
Kevin Garnett
Tracy McGrady
Vince Carter
Grant Hill
David Robinson
Chris Webber
2 Scottie Pippen 175.00 350.00
Clyde Drexler
Grant Hill
Kevin Garnett
Shaquille O'Neal
Dominique Wilkins
Shawn Kemp
Larry Johnson
3 Julius Erving 150.00 300.00
Blake Griffin
Dominique Wilkins
Kobe Bryant
LeBron James
Vince Carter
Dwyane Wade
Clyde Drexler
4 Blake Griffin 50.00 125.00
Andre Iguodala
Russell Westbrook
Thaddeus Young
JaVale McGee
Taj Gibson
DeMar DeRozan
Serge Ibaka
5 Yao Ming 100.00 200.00
Tim Duncan
LaMarcus Aldridge
Amare Stoudemire
Dwight Howard
Pau Gasol
Kevin Garnett
Shaquille O'Neal
6 Kevin Durant 200.00 400.00
Julius Erving
Kobe Bryant
Dominique Wilkins
LeBron James
Dwyane Wade
Vince Carter
Blake Griffin
7 Nate Robinson 50.00 125.00
Russell Westbrook
Tyson Chandler
Rudy Gay
Jason Richardson
Josh Smith
Chris Andersen
Carmelo Anthony
8 Julius Erving 75.00 200.00
Dominique Wilkins
Thaddeus Young
Clyde Drexler
Blake Griffin
Serge Ibaka
DeMar DeRozan
Larry Johnson

2009-10 Panini Season Update

COMPLETE SET (200) 25.00 50.00
UNPRICED PLATINUM PRINT RUN ONE SET
1 Kobe Bryant HL 1.25 3.00
2 Brandon Jennings HL .50 1.25
3 Ray Allen HL .40 1.00
Dirk Nowitzki HL
Tim Duncan HL
4 Kevin Durant HL .75 2.00
5 Rajon Rondo HL .30 .75
6 Ben Gordon HL .25 .60
7 Pau Gasol HL 1.25 3.00
Lamar Odom HL
Kobe Bryant HL
8 Jason Kidd HL .25 .60
9 Vince Carter HL .30 .75
10 NBA All-Star Game .25 .60
Attendance Record HL
11 Dwyane Wade HL .50 1.25
12 Karl Malone HL .50 1.25
Scottie Pippen HL
13 Kobe Bryant HL 1.25 3.00
14 Kevin Durant HL .75 2.00
15 Don Nelson HL .25 .60
16 Josh Smith HL .25 .60
17 Tyreke Evans HL .60 1.50
18 LeBron James HL 1.25 3.00
19 2010 NBA Lottery HL .25 .60
20 Los Angeles Lakers HL/16th Title 1.25 3.00
Kobe Bryant
Sasha Vujacic
Derek Fisher
Shannon Brown
Ron Artest
Jordan Farmar
Andrew Bynum
21 Rajon Rondo .30 .75
22 Paul Pierce .30 .75
23 Kevin Garnett .50 1.25
24 Rasheed Wallace .25 .60
25 Glen Davis .20 .50
26 Ray Allen .25 .60
27 Brook Lopez .25 .60
28 Devin Harris .25 .60
29 Courtney Lee .20 .50
30 Chris Douglas-Roberts .15 .40
31 Al Harrington .20 .50
32 David Lee .20 .50
33 Tracy McGrady .25 .60
34 Danilo Gallinari .25 .60
35 Amare Stoudemire SP 4.00 10.00
36 Andre Iguodala .25 .60
37 Louis Williams .20 .50
38 Allen Iverson .30 .75
39 Samuel Dalembert .15 .40
40 Elton Brand .25 .60
41 Thaddeus Young .15 .40
42 Chris Bosh .25 .60
43 Jarrett Jack .20 .50
44 Andrea Bargnani .20 .50
45 Hedo Turkoglu .25 .60
46 Jose Calderon .20 .50
47 Jason Kidd .25 .60
48 Dirk Nowitzki .30 .75
49 Caron Butler .20 .50
50 Jason Terry .20 .50
51 Shawn Marion .25 .60
52 Brendan Haywood .15 .40
53 Aaron Brooks .15 .40
54 Trevor Ariza .15 .40
55 Luis Scola .20 .50
56 Shane Battier .20 .50
57 Kevin Martin .25 .60
58 Zach Randolph .20 .50
59 Rudy Gay .25 .60
60 O.J. Mayo .25 .60
61 Marc Gasol .25 .60
62 Mike Conley Jr. .20 .50
63 Darrell Arthur .20 .50
64 David West .25 .60
65 Emeka Okafor .25 .60
66 Chris Paul .40 1.00
67 Peja Stojakovic .25 .60
68 Morris Peterson .15 .40
69 Tim Duncan .40 1.00
70 Manu Ginobili .25 .60
71 George Hill .25 .60
72 Tony Parker .25 .60
73 Richard Jefferson .25 .60
74 Antonio McDyess .20 .50
75 Joakim Noah .25 .60
76 Derrick Rose .75 2.00
77 Kirk Hinrich .25 .60
78 Luol Deng .25 .60
79 Carlos Boozer SP 6.00 15.00
80 Brad Miller .20 .50
81 Antawn Jamison .25 .60
82 LeBron James 1.25 3.00
83 Anderson Varejao .20 .50
84 Shaquille O'Neal .50 1.25
85 Mo Williams .20 .50
86 J.J. Hickson .20 .50
87 Ben Gordon .25 .60
88 Tayshaun Prince .25 .60
89 Richard Hamilton .20 .50
90 Ben Wallace .25 .60
91 Rodney Stuckey .20 .50
92 Jason Maxiell .15 .40
93 Danny Granger .25 .60
94 Roy Hibbert .20 .50
95 Mike Dunleavy .15 .40
96 Troy Murphy .15 .40
97 Dahntay Jones .15 .40
98 Brandon Rush .20 .50
99 Andrew Bogut .25 .60
100 John Salmons .20 .50
101 Luke Ridnour .20 .50
102 Carlos Delfino .15 .40
103 Michael Redd .25 .60
104 Carmelo Anthony .30 .75
105 Chris Andersen .40 1.00
106 J.R. Smith .20 .50
107 Nene .20 .50
108 Chauncey Billups .25 .60
109 Al Jefferson .25 .60
110 Kevin Love .40 1.00
111 Corey Brewer .15 .40
112 Ryan Gomes .15 .40
113 LaMarcus Aldridge .25 .60
114 Brandon Roy .25 .60
115 Rudy Fernandez .20 .50
116 Andre Miller .20 .50
117 Juwan Howard .20 .50
118 Nicolas Batum .25 .60
119 Kevin Durant .75 2.00
120 Russell Westbrook .40 1.00
121 Jeff Green .20 .50
122 Nenad Krstic .15 .40
123 Nick Collison .15 .40
124 Deron Williams .25 .60
125 Carlos Boozer .25 .60
126 Mehmet Okur .15 .40
127 Paul Millsap .20 .50
128 Andrei Kirilenko .20 .50
129 Monta Ellis .25 .60
130 Anthony Morrow .15 .40
131 Corey Maggette .20 .50
132 C.J. Watson .15 .40
133 Kobe Bryant 1.25 3.00
134 Pau Gasol .25 .60
135 Lamar Odom .25 .60
136 Andrew Bynum .30 .75
137 Ron Artest .25 .60
138 Derek Fisher .25 .60
139 Luke Walton .15 .40
140 Amare Stoudemire .25 .60
141 Steve Nash .25 .60
142 Jason Richardson .20 .50
143 Robin Lopez .15 .40
144 Grant Hill .30 .75
145 Channing Frye .20 .50
146 Spencer Hawes .20 .50
147 Beno Udrih .15 .40
148 Jason Thompson .15 .40
149 Carl Landry .15 .40
150 Donte Greene .15 .40
151 Andres Nocioni .15 .40
152 Josh Smith .25 .60
153 Jamal Crawford .20 .50
154 Al Horford .25 .60
155 Joe Johnson .25 .60
156 Mike Bibby .20 .50
157 Marvin Williams .20 .50
158 Gerald Wallace .25 .60
159 Stephen Jackson .20 .50
160 Raymond Felton .20 .50
161 Boris Diaw .20 .50
162 D.J. Augustin .20 .50
163 Michael Beasley .25 .60
164 Dwyane Wade .50 1.25
165 Jermaine O'Neal .25 .60
166 Udonis Haslem .20 .50
167 Chris Bosh SP 6.00 15.00
168 LeBron James 12.50 30.00
169 Dwight Howard .40 1.00
170 Vince Carter .30 .75
171 Rashard Lewis .20 .50
172 J.J. Redick .25 .60
173 Jameer Nelson .20 .50
174 Matt Barnes .15 .40
175 Al Thornton .20 .50
176 Josh Howard .20 .50
177 Randy Foye .15 .40
178 Mike Miller .25 .60
179 Andray Blatche .15 .40
180 Shaun Livingston .15 .40
181 LeBron James AS 1.25 3.00
182 Dwight Howard AS .40 1.00
183 Dwyane Wade AS .50 1.25
184 Chris Bosh AS .25 .60
185 Rajon Rondo AS .30 .75
186 Joe Johnson AS .25 .60
187 Paul Pierce AS .30 .75
188 Derrick Rose AS .75 2.00
189 Al Horford AS .25 .60
190 David Lee AS .20 .50
191 Carmelo Anthony AS .30 .75
192 Dirk Nowitzki AS .30 .75
193 Chauncey Billups AS .25 .60
194 Deron Williams AS .25 .60
195 Amare Stoudemire AS .25 .60
196 Pau Gasol AS .25 .60
197 Steve Nash AS .25 .60
198 Kevin Durant AS .75 2.00
199 Chris Kaman AS .20 .50
200 Tim Duncan AS .40 1.00

2009-10 Panini Season Update Gold

*GOLD: 5X TO 12X BASE HI
STATED PRINT RUN 24 SER.#'d SETS
35 Amare Stoudemire 3.00 8.00
79 Carlos Boozer 3.00 8.00
167 Chris Bosh 3.00 8.00
168 LeBron James 30.00 80.00

2009-10 Panini Season Update Silver

*SILVER: 2.5X TO 6X BASE HI
STATED PRINT RUN 99 SER.#'d SETS
35 Amare Stoudemire 1.50 4.00
79 Carlos Boozer 1.50 4.00
167 Chris Bosh 1.50 4.00
168 LeBron James 25.00 50.00

2009-10 Panini Season Update All-Star Patches

COMPLETE SET (5) 40.00 80.00
STATED PRINT RUN 499 SER.#'d SETS
1 Kobe Bryant 15.00 40.00
2 Dirk Nowitzki 8.00 20.00
3 Chris Bosh 8.00 20.00
4 LeBron James 15.00 40.00
5 Dwyane Wade 10.00 25.00

2009-10 Panini Season Update Christmas Cards Materials

PRINT RUN 499 SER.#'d SETS
*PRIME: .75X TO 2X BASE HI
PRIME PRINT RUN 25 SER.#'d SETS
1 Andre Miller 3.00 8.00
2 Amare Stoudemire 4.00 10.00
3 Anthony Carter 2.50 6.00
4 Arron Afflalo 2.50 6.00
5 Brandon Roy 4.00 10.00
6 Carlos Arroyo 3.00 8.00
7 Carmelo Anthony 5.00 12.00
8 Channing Frye 3.00 8.00
9 Chauncey Billups 4.00 10.00
10 Daequan Cook 2.50 6.00
11 Dorell Wright 2.50 6.00
12 Dwight Howard 6.00 15.00
13 Dwyane Wade 8.00 20.00
14 Earl Clark 4.00 10.00
15 Goran Dragic 6.00 15.00
16 J.J. Redick 4.00 10.00
17 J.R. Smith 4.00 10.00
18 Jameer Nelson 3.00 8.00
19 Jared Dudley 2.50 6.00
20 Jason Richardson 4.00 10.00
21 Jason Williams 3.00 8.00
22 Jeff Pendergraph 4.00 10.00
23 Jermaine O'Neal 4.00 10.00
24 Jerryd Bayless 3.00 8.00
25 Joel Anthony 4.00 10.00
26 LaMarcus Aldridge 4.00 10.00
27 Louis Amundson 2.50 6.00
28 Marcin Gortat 4.00 10.00
29 Mario Chalmers 4.00 10.00
30 Martell Webster 3.00 8.00
31 Matt Barnes 2.50 6.00
32 Michael Beasley 4.00 10.00
33 Mickael Pietrus 2.50 6.00
34 Quentin Richardson 3.00 8.00
35 Rashard Lewis 3.00 8.00
36 Robin Lopez 2.50 6.00
37 Ryan Anderson 4.00 10.00
38 Steve Nash 4.00 10.00
39 Ty Lawson 6.00 15.00
40 Udonis Haslem 3.00 8.00

2009-10 Panini Season Update Lakers Legacy

COMPLETE SET (10) 4.00 10.00
RANDOM INSERTS IN PACKS
1 Kobe Bryant 2.50 6.00
2 Derek Fisher .50 1.25
3 Nick Van Exel .60 1.50
4 Pau Gasol .60 1.50
5 Robert Horry .75 2.00
6 Kareem Abdul-Jabbar 1.00 2.50
7 Gary Payton .60 1.50
8 Luke Walton .40 1.00
9 Lamar Odom .60 1.50
10 Andrew Bynum .75 2.00

2009-10 Panini Season Update Lakers Legacy Jerseys

COMPLETE SET (10) 30.00 80.00
1 Kobe Bryant 8.00 20.00
2 Derek Fisher 4.00 10.00
3 Nick Van Exel 4.00 10.00
4 Pau Gasol 4.00 10.00
5 Robert Horry 4.00 10.00
6 Kareem Abdul-Jabbar 12.00 30.00
7 Gary Payton 4.00 10.00
8 Luke Walton 4.00 10.00
9 Lamar Odom 4.00 10.00
10 Andrew Bynum 4.00 10.00

2009-10 Panini Season Update Lakers Legacy Jerseys Prime

*PRIME: 1.25X TO 3X HI COLUMN
STATED PRINT RUN 10 TO 49 SER.#'d SETS
1 Kobe Bryant/49 20.00 50.00
6 Kareem Abdul-Jabbar/49 20.00 50.00
10 Andrew Bynum/15 15.00 40.00

2009-10 Panini Season Update Playoff Debuts

COMPLETE SET (19) 8.00 20.00
RANDOM INSERTS IN PACKS
*GOLD: 2X TO 5X BASE HI
GOLD PRINT RUN 24 SER.#'d SETS
UNPRICED PLATINUM PRINT RUN ONE SET
*SILVER: 1X TO 2.5X BASE HI
SILVER PRINT RUN 99 SER.#'d SETS
1 Kevin Durant 2.00 5.00
2 Brandon Jennings 1.25 3.00
3 Robin Lopez .40 1.00
4 D.J. Augustin .50 1.25
5 Wesley Matthews 1.00 2.50
6 Taj Gibson .75 2.00
7 Nate Robinson .60 1.50
8 Russell Westbrook 1.00 2.50
9 Adam Morrison .50 1.25
10 DeJuan Blair .75 2.00
11 Jeff Teague .75 2.00
12 Jeff Pendergraph .60 1.50
13 J.J. Hickson .50 1.25
14 Rodrigue Beaubois .75 2.00
15 Jeff Green .50 1.25
16 Raymond Felton .50 1.25
17 Jamal Crawford .50 1.25
18 Ty Lawson 1.00 2.50
19 Ryan Anderson .60 1.50

2009-10 Panini Season Update Rookie Challenge

COMPLETE SET (16) 15.00 30.00
RANDOM INSERTS IN PACKS
1 Stephen Curry 2.50 6.00
2 Tyreke Evans 2.50 6.00
3 Brandon Jennings 2.00 5.00
4 Anthony Morrow .60 1.50
5 Brook Lopez 1.00 2.50
6 Danilo Gallinari 1.00 2.50
7 DeJuan Blair 1.25 3.00
8 Eric Gordon 1.00 2.50
9 Jonas Jerebko 1.00 2.50
10 Jonny Flynn 1.00 2.50
11 Kevin Love 1.50 4.00
12 Marc Gasol 1.00 2.50
13 Michael Beasley 1.00 2.50
14 O.J. Mayo 1.00 2.50
15 Omri Casspi 1.00 2.50
16 Russell Westbrook 1.50 4.00

2009-10 Panini Season Update Rookie Challenge Jerseys

RANDOM INSERTS IN PACKS
PRIME PRINT RUN 5 TO 10 SER.#'d SETS
PRIME UNPRICED DUE TO SCARCITY
1 Stephen Curry 5.00 12.00
2 Tyreke Evans 5.00 12.00
3 Brandon Jennings 4.00 10.00
4 Anthony Morrow 2.00 5.00
5 Brook Lopez 3.00 8.00
6 Danilo Gallinari 3.00 8.00
7 DeJuan Blair 2.50 6.00
8 Eric Gordon 3.00 8.00
9 Jonas Jerebko 2.00 5.00
10 Jonny Flynn 2.00 5.00
11 Kevin Love 5.00 12.00
12 Marc Gasol 3.00 8.00
13 Michael Beasley 3.00 8.00
14 O.J. Mayo 3.00 8.00
15 Omri Casspi 2.00 5.00
16 Russell Westbrook 5.00 12.00

2009-10 Panini Season Update Rookie Challenge Jerseys Signatures

STATED PRINT RUN 25 SER.#'d SETS
UNPRICED PRIME PRINT RUN ONE TO 10 SETS
1 Stephen Curry 20.00 50.00
2 Tyreke Evans 20.00 50.00
3 Brandon Jennings 15.00 40.00
7 DeJuan Blair 10.00 25.00
9 Jonas Jerebko 8.00 20.00
10 Jonny Flynn 8.00 20.00
11 Kevin Love 15.00 40.00
13 Michael Beasley 10.00 25.00
15 Omri Casspi 8.00 20.00

2009-10 Panini Season Update Rookie Challenge Signatures

PRINT RUN 49 SER.#'d SETS
1 Stephen Curry 15.00 40.00
2 Tyreke Evans 15.00 40.00
3 Brandon Jennings 12.00 30.00
7 DeJuan Blair 8.00 20.00
9 Jonas Jerebko 6.00 15.00
10 Jonny Flynn 6.00 15.00
11 Kevin Love 10.00 25.00
13 Michael Beasley 8.00 20.00
15 Omri Casspi 6.00 15.00
16 Russell Westbrook 15.00 40.00

2009-10 Panini Season Update Rookie Duals Signatures

STATED PRINT RUN 49 TO 99 SER.#'d SETS
1 Blake Griffin/49 75.00 200.00
Brandon Jennings
2 Blake Griffin/49 100.00 250.00
Stephen Curry
3 Blake Griffin/49 100.00 250.00
Tyreke Evans
4 Tyreke Evans/49 30.00 80.00
Brandon Jennings
5 Tyreke Evans/49 40.00 100.00
Stephen Curry
6 Brandon Jennings/49 40.00 80.00
Stephen Curry
7 Stephen Curry/49 20.00 50.00
Darren Collison
8 Blake Griffin/49 75.00 150.00
Taylor Griffin
9 Taylor Griffin/99 8.00 20.00
Earl Clark
10 James Harden/99 25.00 60.00
Serge Ibaka
11 James Harden/99 12.00 30.00
Eric Maynor
12 Serge Ibaka/99 12.50 30.00
Eric Maynor
13 James Harden/99 10.00 25.00
B.J. Mullens
14 Serge Ibaka/99 10.00 25.00
B.J. Mullens
15 Wayne Ellington/99 8.00 20.00
Jonny Flynn
16 Jonny Flynn/99 6.00 15.00
Wayne Ellington
17 Ty Lawson/99 8.00 20.00
Jonny Flynn
18 Taj Gibson/99 12.50 30.00
Ty Lawson
19 Taj Gibson/99 15.00 30.00
James Johnson
20 James Johnson/99 6.00 15.00
Jeff Teague
21 Taj Gibson/99 8.00 20.00
Jeff Teague
22 Hasheem Thabeet/99 8.00 20.00
DeMarre Carroll
23 Hasheem Thabeet/99 6.00 15.00
Sam Young
24 DeMarre Carroll/99 6.00 15.00
Sam Young
25 DeMarre Carroll/99 8.00 20.00
DeMar DeRozan
26 A.J. Price/99 10.00 25.00
Tyler Hansbrough
27 DeMar DeRozan/99 10.00 25.00
Tyler Hansbrough
28 Stephen Curry/49 15.00 40.00
Jordan Hill
29 Jordan Hill/99 6.00 15.00
Terrence Williams
30 Terrence Williams/99 6.00 15.00
Gerald Henderson
31 James Harden/99 10.00 25.00
Terrence Williams
32 Jrue Holiday/99 8.00 20.00
Terrence Williams
33 Terrence Williams/99 6.00 15.00
Austin Daye
34 Jonny Flynn/99 6.00 15.00
Jordan Hill
35 James Harden/99 12.00 30.00
Jeff Teague
36 Darren Collison/99 8.00 20.00
Jeff Teague
37 Toney Douglas/99 6.00 15.00
Lester Hudson
38 Toney Douglas/99 6.00 15.00
Wayne Ellington
39 Tyler Hansbrough/99 10.00 25.00
B.J. Mullens
40 Tyler Hansbrough/99 8.00 20.00
Lester Hudson
41 Rodrigue Beaubois/49 25.00 60.00
Tyreke Evans
42 Stephen Curry/49 20.00 50.00
Rodrigue Beaubois
43 Rodrigue Beaubois/99 15.00 40.00
Omri Casspi
44 Tyreke Evans/49 25.00 60.00
Omri Casspi
45 Omri Casspi/99 6.00 15.00
Jeff Pendergraph
46 Jonas Jerebko/99 6.00 15.00
Austin Daye
47 Jonas Jerebko/99 6.00 15.00
DaJuan Summers
48 DaJuan Summers/99 6.00 15.00
Austin Daye
49 Omri Casspi/99 8.00 20.00
Jonas Jerebko
50 Darren Collison/99 12.50 30.00
Marcus Thornton
51 Marcus Thornton/99 6.00 15.00
Derrick Brown
52 Jrue Holiday/99 15.00 40.00
Jodie Meeks
53 Jeff Pendergraph/99 10.00 25.00
Patrick Mills
54 Omri Casspi/99 6.00 15.00
Jon Brockman
55 Tyreke Evans/49 20.00 50.00
Jon Brockman
56 Jon Brockman/99 6.00 15.00
Taylor Griffin
57 David Andersen/99 6.00 15.00
Jordan Hill
58 Jordan Hill/99 6.00 15.00
Chase Budinger
59 Jermaine Taylor/99 8.00 20.00
Chase Budinger
60 Jermaine Taylor/99 6.00 15.00
David Andersen
61 Jeff Pendergraph/99 6.00 15.00
Dante Cunningham
62 Dante Cunningham/99 12.00 30.00
Patrick Mills
63 Wesley Matthews/99 8.00 20.00
Sundiata Gaines
64 A.J. Price/99 6.00 15.00
Jodie Meeks
65 Brandon Jennings/49 15.00 40.00
Jodie Meeks
66 DeJuan Blair/99 8.00 20.00
DaJuan Summers
67 DeJuan Blair/99 6.00 15.00
Earl Clark
68 DeJuan Blair/99 6.00 15.00
James Johnson
69 DeMar DeRozan/99 10.00 25.00
DeJuan Blair
70 Hasheem Thabeet/99 10.00 25.00
Serge Ibaka
71 Wesley Matthews/99 8.00 20.00
Toney Douglas
72 Wayne Ellington/99 6.00 15.00
Lester Hudson
73 Lester Hudson/99 6.00 15.00
Sundiata Gaines
74 Jrue Holiday/99 8.00 20.00
Chase Budinger
75 Rodrigue Beaubois/99 25.00 50.00
DeMar DeRozan

2009-10 Panini Season Update Rookie Triples Signatures

STATED PRINT RUN 25 TO 49 SER.#'d SETS
1 Tyreke Evans/25 75.00 150.00
Stephen Curry
Brandon Jennings
2 James Harden/99 30.00 80.00
Eric Maynor
Serge Ibaka
3 Blake Griffin/25 100.00 200.00
DeJuan Blair
DeMar DeRozan
4 Darren Collison/49 15.00 40.00
Rodrigue Beaubois
Jonny Flynn
5 Jordan Hill/49 10.00 25.00
Chase Budinger
Jermaine Taylor
6 Taj Gibson/49 8.00 20.00
Ty Lawson
Terrence Williams
7 Tyler Hansbrough/49 10.00 25.00
A.J. Price
Gerald Henderson
8 Blake Griffin/25 75.00 150.00
Taylor Griffin
Earl Clark
9 Austin Daye/49 10.00 25.00
Jonas Jerebko
DaJuan Summers
10 Hasheem Thabeet/49 8.00 20.00
Sam Young
DeMarre Carroll
11 Tyreke Evans/25 30.00 60.00
Omri Casspi
Jon Brockman
12 Tyler Hansbrough/49 10.00 25.00
B.J. Mullens
Jodie Meeks
13 Darren Collison/49 8.00 20.00
Marcus Thornton
Derrick Brown
14 Jeff Pendergraph/49 12.00 30.00
Dante Cunningham
Patrick Mills
15 Stephen Curry/25 30.00 60.00
Jonny Flynn
Ty Lawson
16 Earl Clark/49 8.00 20.00
Austin Daye
James Johnson
17 Jrue Holiday/49 12.50 30.00
Jeff Teague
Rodrigue Beaubois
18 Toney Douglas/49 8.00 20.00
Lester Hudson
Jodie Meeks
19 DeJuan Blair/49 15.00 30.00
DeMar DeRozan
DeMarre Carroll
20 Wesley Matthews/49 10.00 25.00
Toney Douglas
Lester Hudson
21 Brandon Jennings/25 25.00 60.00
Darren Collison
Jonny Flynn
22 Terrence Williams/49 8.00 20.00
Gerald Henderson
Jeff Teague
23 Blake Griffin/25 100.00 200.00
Hasheem Thabeet
James Harden
24 Jonny Flynn/49 10.00 25.00
Earl Clark
Jrue Holiday
25 Tyler Hansbrough/49 25.00 60.00
Wayne Ellington
Ty Lawson

2009-10 Panini Season Update Signatures

STATED PRINT RUN ONE TO 100 SER.#'d SETS
SOME UNPRICED DUE TO SCARCITY
28 Darryl Dawkins/99 6.00 15.00
33 Mark Price/50 12.50 30.00
34 Mark Price/25 15.00 40.00
35 Robert Horry/50 25.00 60.00
37 Hakeem Olajuwon/50 15.00 40.00
38 Hakeem Olajuwon/25 25.00 50.00
39 Joe Dumars/50 8.00 20.00
40 Joe Dumars/25 10.00 25.00
41 Dominique Wilkins/50 15.00 30.00
42 Dominique Wilkins/25 15.00 40.00
44 Elgin Baylor/25 12.50 30.00
45 Sidney Moncrief/50 6.00 15.00
46 Sidney Moncrief/25 8.00 20.00

2010-11 Panini Season Update

COMPLETE SET (200) 15.00 40.00
EXCH EXPIRATION 1/20/2013
UNPRICED PLATINUM PRINT RUN ONE SET
1 Glen Davis .20 .50
2 Jeff Green .20 .50
3 Kevin Garnett .50 1.25
4 Paul Pierce .30 .75
5 Rajon Rondo .30 .75
6 Ray Allen .25 .60
7 Shaquille O'Neal .50 1.25
8 Anthony Morrow .15 .40
9 Brook Lopez .25 .60
10 Deron Williams .25 .60
11 Kris Humphries .15 .40
12 Sasha Vujacic .15 .40
13 Travis Outlaw .20 .50
14 Amare Stoudemire .25 .60
15 Carmelo Anthony .30 .75
16 Chauncey Billups .25 .60
17 Ronny Turiaf .15 .40
18 Shawne Williams .15 .40
19 Toney Douglas .15 .40
20 Andre Iguodala .25 .60
21 Andres Nocioni .15 .40
22 Elton Brand .25 .60
23 Jrue Holiday .25 .60
24 Louis Williams .20 .50
25 Spencer Hawes .20 .50
26 Thaddeus Young .15
27 Andrea Bargnani .20
28 DeMar DeRozan .25
29 Jose Calderon .20
30 Leandro Barbosa .20
31 Linas Kleiza .15
32 Sonny Weems .15
33 Carlos Boozer .25
34 Derrick Rose .75 2.0
35 Joakim Noah .25
36 Kyle Korver .20
37 Luol Deng .25
38 Ronnie Brewer .20
39 Taj Gibson .20
40 Anderson Varejao .20
41 Antawn Jamison .25
42 Daniel Gibson .20
43 J.J. Hickson .20
44 Baron Davis .25
45 Ramon Sessions .20
46 Austin Daye .15
47 Ben Gordon .25
48 Charlie Villanueva .20
49 Richard Hamilton .20

50 Rodney Stuckey .25 .60
51 Tayshaun Prince .25 .60
52 Tracy McGrady .25 .60
53 Danny Granger .25 .60
54 Darren Collison .25 .60
55 Jeff Foster .15 .40
56 Mike Dunleavy .15 .40
57 Roy Hibbert .20 .50
58 T.J. Ford .15 .40
59 Tyler Hansbrough .25 .60
60 Andrew Bogut .25 .60
61 Brandon Jennings .25 .60
62 Carlos Delfino .15 .40
63 Corey Maggette .20 .50
64 Drew Gooden .20 .50
65 Ersan Ilyasova .20 .50
66 John Salmons .25 .60
67 Luc Mbah a Moute .15 .40
68 Al Horford .20 .50
69 Jamal Crawford .20 .50
70 Jeff Teague .20 .50
71 Joe Johnson .25 .60
72 Josh Smith .25 .60
73 Marvin Williams .20 .50
74 Boris Diaw .20 .50
75 D.J. Augustin .20 .50
76 Gerald Henderson .15 .40
77 Stephen Jackson .20 .50
78 Tyrus Thomas .20 .50
79 Chris Bosh .25 .60
80 Dwyane Wade .50 1.25
81 Eddie House .15 .40
82 LeBron James 1.25 3.00
83 Mike Miller .25 .60
84 Mike Bibby .20 .50
85 Udonis Haslem .20 .50
86 Brandon Bass .15 .40
87 Dwight Howard .40 1.00
88 Gilbert Arenas .25 .60
89 Hedo Turkoglu .25 .60
90 J.J. Redick .25 .60
91 Jameer Nelson .20 .50
92 Jason Richardson .25 .60
93 Andray Blatche .15 .40
94 JaVale McGee .20 .50
95 Kirk Hinrich .25 .60
96 Nick Young .20 .50
97 Rashard Lewis .20 .50
98 Caron Butler .25 .60
99 Dirk Nowitzki .30 .75
100 Jason Kidd .25 .60
101 Jason Terry .20 .50
102 Peja Stojakovic .25 .60
103 Corey Brewer .15 .40
104 Shawn Marion .25 .60
105 Tyson Chandler .20 .50
106 Goran Dragic .25 .60
107 Kevin Martin .25 .60
108 Kyle Lowry .20 .50
109 Luis Scola .20 .50
110 Yao Ming .30 .75
111 Marc Gasol .25 .60
112 Shane Battier .20 .50
113 Mike Conley Jr. .20 .50
114 O.J. Mayo .25 .60
115 Rudy Gay .25 .60
116 Zach Randolph .20 .50
117 Chris Paul .40 1.00
118 David West .25 .60
119 Emeka Okafor .25 .60
120 Carl Landry .15 .40
121 Trevor Ariza .15 .40
122 DeJuan Blair .20 .50
123 George Hill .20 .50
124 Manu Ginobili .25 .60
125 Richard Jefferson .25 .60
126 Tim Duncan .40 1.00
127 Tony Parker .25 .60
128 Al Harrington .20 .50
129 Arron Afflalo .15 .40
130 Danilo Gallinari .25 .60
131 Raymond Felton .20 .50
132 Wilson Chandler .20 .50
133 Chris Andersen .25 .60
134 J.R. Smith .25 .60
135 Kenyon Martin .25 .60
136 Nene .20 .50
137 Anthony Randolph .20 .50
138 Darko Milicic .15 .40
139 Kevin Love .30 .75
140 Luke Ridnour .20 .50
141 Martell Webster .20 .50
142 Michael Beasley .25 .60
143 Andre Miller .20 .50
144 Gerald Wallace .25 .60
145 Brandon Roy .25 .60
146 LaMarcus Aldridge .25 .60
147 Nicolas Batum .25 .60
148 Rudy Fernandez .20 .50
149 Wesley Matthews .25 .60
150 James Harden .30 .75
151 Kendrick Perkins .20 .50
152 Kevin Durant .75 2.00
153 Russell Westbrook .30 .75
154 Serge Ibaka .30 .75
155 Al Jefferson .25 .60
156 Andrei Kirilenko .20 .50
157 C.J. Miles .15 .40
158 Devin Harris .25 .60
159 Paul Millsap .20 .50
160 Raja Bell .20 .50
161 Andris Biedrins .15 .40
162 Al Thornton .20 .50
163 David Lee .20 .50
164 Dorell Wright .15 .40
165 Monta Ellis .25 .60
166 Reggie Williams .30 .75
167 Stephen Curry .30 .75
168 Mo Williams .20 .50
169 Blake Griffin .60 1.50
170 Chris Kaman .20 .50
171 Eric Gordon .25 .60
172 Ryan Gomes .15 .40
173 Andrew Bynum .30 .75
174 Derek Fisher .20 .50
175 Kobe Bryant 1.25 3.00
176 Lamar Odom .25 .60
177 Pau Gasol .25 .60
178 Ron Artest .25 .60
179 Channing Frye .20 .50
180 Aaron Brooks .15 .40
181 Grant Hill .30 .75
182 Marcin Gortat .25 .60
183 Steve Nash .25 .60
184 Vince Carter .30 .75
185 Beno Udrih .15 .40
186 Marcus Thornton .25 .60
187 Francisco Garcia .20 .50
188 Omri Casspi .15 .40
189 Samuel Dalembert .15 .40
190 Tyreke Evans .30 .75
191 Blake Griffin .60 1.50
192 Ray Allen .25 .60
193 Kobe Bryant 1.25 3.00
194 Kevin Durant .75 2.00
195 Kevin Love .30 .75
196 George Karl .25 .60
197 Blake Griffin .60 1.50
198 Derrick Rose .75 2.00
199 Lamar Odom .25 .60
200 Kevin Love .30 .75

2010-11 Panini Season Update Gold

*GOLD: 5X TO 12X BASE HI
STATED PRINT RUN 24 SER.#'d SETS
181 Grant Hill 12.50 30.00

2010-11 Panini Season Update Silver

*SILVER: 2.5X TO 6X BASE HI
STATED PRINT RUN 99 SER.#'d SETS
181 Grant Hill 8.00 20.00

2010-11 Panini Season Update All-Stars

COMPLETE SET (25) 8.00 20.00
RANDOM INSERTS IN PACKS
1 Al Horford .30 .75
2 Amare Stoudemire .40 1.00
3 Carmelo Anthony .50 1.25
4 Chauncey Billups .40 1.00
5 Chris Bosh .40 1.00
6 Chris Kaman .30 .75
7 David Lee .30 .75
8 Deron Williams .40 1.00
9 Derrick Rose 1.25 3.00
10 Dirk Nowitzki .50 1.25
11 Dwight Howard .60 1.50
12 Gerald Wallace .40 1.00
13 Jason Kidd .40 1.00
14 Joe Johnson .40 1.00
15 Kevin Durant 1.25 3.00
16 Kevin Garnett .75 2.00
17 LeBron James 2.00 5.00
18 Pau Gasol .40 1.00
19 Paul Pierce .50 1.25
20 Rajon Rondo .50 1.25
21 Steve Nash .40 1.00
22 Tim Duncan .60 1.50
23 Zach Randolph .30 .75
24 Kobe Bryant 2.00 5.00
25 Chris Paul .60 1.50

2010-11 Panini Season Update All-Stars Materials

RANDOM INSERTS IN PACKS
UNPRICED PRIME PRINT RUN 10 SETS
1 Al Horford 2.00 5.00
2 Amare Stoudemire 2.50 6.00
3 Carmelo Anthony 3.00 8.00
4 Chauncey Billups 2.50 6.00
5 Chris Bosh 2.50 6.00
6 Chris Kaman 2.00 5.00
7 David Lee 2.00 5.00
8 Deron Williams 2.50 6.00
9 Derrick Rose 8.00 20.00
10 Dirk Nowitzki 3.00 8.00
11 Dwight Howard 4.00 10.00
12 Gerald Wallace 2.50 6.00
13 Jason Kidd 2.50 6.00
14 Joe Johnson 2.50 6.00
15 Kevin Durant 6.00 15.00
16 Kevin Garnett 5.00 12.00
17 LeBron James 10.00 25.00
18 Pau Gasol 2.50 6.00
19 Paul Pierce 3.00 8.00
20 Rajon Rondo 3.00 8.00
21 Steve Nash 2.50 6.00
22 Tim Duncan 4.00 10.00
23 Zach Randolph 2.00 5.00
24 Kobe Bryant 10.00 25.00
25 Chris Paul 4.00 10.00

2010-11 Panini Season Update Green Week Jerseys

STATED PRINT RUN 10 TO 799 SER.#'d SETS
SOME UNPRICED DUE TO SCARCITY
1 Andre Miller/10
2 Anthony Carter/799 2.00 5.00
3 Arron Afflalo/799 2.00 5.00
4 Brandon Bass/799 2.00 5.00
5 Brandon Roy/99 2.50 6.00
6 Caron Butler/25 2.50 6.00
7 Chauncey Billups/50 2.50 6.00
8 Chris Andersen/699 2.50 6.00
9 Dante Cunningham/799 2.00 5.00
10 Dirk Nowitzki/399 3.00 8.00
11 Dwight Howard/99 4.00 10.00
12 J.R. Smith/499 2.50 6.00
13 Jameer Nelson/449 2.00 5.00
14 Jason Terry/649 2.00 5.00
15 Juwan Howard/799 2.00 5.00
16 LaMarcus Aldridge/799 2.50 6.00
17 Marcin Gortat/749 5.00 12.00
18 Martell Webster/799 2.00 5.00
19 Mickael Pietrus/349 2.00 5.00
20 Nene/699 2.00 5.00
21 Nicolas Batum/799 2.50 6.00
22 Rashard Lewis/799 2.00 5.00
23 Rudy Fernandez/749 2.00 5.00
24 Ryan Anderson/799 2.00 5.00
25 Shawn Marion/799 2.50 6.00
26 Ty Lawson/799 2.50 6.00
27 Vince Carter/799 3.00 8.00
28 Erick Dampier/799 2.00 5.00
29 Matt Barnes/799 2.00 5.00
30 Jerryd Bayless/799 2.00 5.00

2010-11 Panini Season Update Green Week Jerseys Prime

*PRIME: 1X TO 2.5X BASE HI
STATED PRINT RUN ONE TO 49 SER.#'d SETS
SOME UNPRICED DUE TO SCARCITY
1 Andre Miller/49 5.00 12.00
8 Chris Andersen/29 8.00 20.00
20 Nene/15 6.00 15.00

2010-11 Panini Season Update Rookie Challenge

COMPLETE SET (15) 5.00 12.00
RANDOM INSERTS IN PACKS
1 DeMarcus Cousins 1.25 3.00
2 Derrick Favors .75 2.00
3 Eric Bledsoe .60 1.50
4 Gary Neal .60 1.50
5 Greg Monroe .75 2.00
6 Landry Fields .60 1.50
7 Wesley Johnson .60 1.50
8 Brandon Jennings .40 1.00
9 DeJuan Blair .30 .75
10 DeMar DeRozan .40 1.00
11 James Harden .50 1.25
12 Jrue Holiday .40 1.00
13 Serge Ibaka .50 1.25
14 Stephen Curry .50 1.25
15 Wesley Matthews .40 1.00

2010-11 Panini Season Update Rookie Challenge Materials

STATED PRINT RUN 799 SER.#'d SETS
UNPRICED PRIME PRINT RUN 5 SETS
1 DeMarcus Cousins 5.00 12.00
2 Derrick Favors 3.00 8.00
3 Eric Bledsoe 2.50 6.00
4 Gary Neal 2.50 6.00
5 Greg Monroe 3.00 8.00
6 Landry Fields 2.50 6.00
7 Wesley Johnson 2.50 6.00
8 Brandon Jennings 2.50 6.00
9 DeJuan Blair 2.00 5.00
10 DeMar DeRozan 2.50 6.00
11 James Harden 3.00 8.00
12 Jrue Holiday 2.50 6.00
13 Serge Ibaka 3.00 8.00
14 Stephen Curry 3.00 8.00
15 Wesley Matthews 2.50 6.00

2010-11 Panini Season Update Rookie Challenge Materials Signatures

STATED PRINT RUN 25 SER.#'d SETS
UNPRICED PRIME PRINT RUN 5 SETS
1 DeMarcus Cousins 25.00 60.00
2 Derrick Favors 15.00 40.00
3 Eric Bledsoe 12.00 30.00
4 Gary Neal 12.00 30.00
5 Greg Monroe 15.00 40.00
6 Landry Fields 12.00 30.00
7 Wesley Johnson 12.00 30.00
8 Brandon Jennings 12.50 30.00
9 DeJuan Blair 8.00 20.00
10 DeMar DeRozan 12.00 30.00
11 James Harden 20.00 50.00
12 Jrue Holiday 10.00 25.00
13 Serge Ibaka 10.00 25.00
14 Stephen Curry 25.00 60.00
15 Wesley Matthews 12.00 30.00

2010-11 Panini Season Update Rookie Challenge Signatures

STATED PRINT RUN 49 SER.#'d SETS
1 DeMarcus Cousins 15.00 40.00
2 Derrick Favors 10.00 25.00
3 Eric Bledsoe 8.00 20.00
4 Gary Neal 8.00 20.00
5 Greg Monroe 10.00 25.00
6 Landry Fields 8.00 20.00
7 Wesley Johnson 8.00 20.00
8 Brandon Jennings 8.00 20.00
9 DeJuan Blair 5.00 12.00
10 DeMar DeRozan 5.00 12.00
11 James Harden 10.00 25.00
12 Jrue Holiday 6.00 15.00
13 Serge Ibaka EXCH 6.00 15.00
14 Stephen Curry 10.00 25.00
15 Wesley Matthews 6.00 15.00

2010-11 Panini Season Update Rookie Duals Signatures

STATED PRINT RUN 10 TO 99 SER.#'d SETS
SOME UNPRICED DUE TO SCARCITY
UNPRICED TRIPLE PRINT RUN 10 SETS
4 Evan Turner 20.00 50.00
Derrick Favors
5 Evan Turner 25.00 60.00
DeMarcus Cousins
6 Evan Turner 15.00 40.00
Wesley Johnson
7 Derrick Favors 12.50 30.00
Wesley Johnson
8 Derrick Favors 15.00 40.00
DeMarcus Cousins
9 Wesley Johnson 20.00 50.00
DeMarcus Cousins
10 Wesley Johnson 8.00 20.00
Ekpe Udoh
12 DeMarcus Cousins 20.00 50.00
Greg Monroe
13 Ekpe Udoh 6.00 15.00
Greg Monroe
14 Ekpe Udoh 5.00 12.00
Al-Farouq Aminu
15 Greg Monroe 6.00 15.00
Al-Farouq Aminu
16 Greg Monroe 12.50 30.00
Gordon Hayward
17 Al-Farouq Aminu 8.00 20.00
Gordon Hayward
18 Al-Farouq Aminu 8.00 20.00
Paul George
19 Gordon Hayward 12.50 30.00
Paul George
20 Gordon Hayward 8.00 20.00
Cole Aldrich
21 Paul George 8.00 20.00
Cole Aldrich
22 Paul George 8.00 20.00
Xavier Henry
23 Cole Aldrich 6.00 15.00
Xavier Henry
24 Cole Aldrich 5.00 12.00
Ed Davis
25 Xavier Henry 6.00 15.00
Ed Davis
26 Xavier Henry 6.00 15.00
Patrick Patterson
27 Patrick Patterson 6.00 15.00
Ed Davis
28 Ed Davis 6.00 15.00
Larry Sanders
29 Patrick Patterson 6.00 15.00
Larry Sanders
30 Luke Babbitt 6.00 15.00
Elliot Williams
31 Luke Babbitt 6.00 15.00
Armon Johnson
32 Eric Bledsoe 6.00 15.00
Willie Warren
33 Eric Bledsoe 8.00 20.00
Daniel Orton
34 Eric Bledsoe 10.00 25.00
Patrick Patterson
35 Craig Brackins 10.00 25.00
Evan Turner
36 Trevor Booker 8.00 20.00
Jordan Crawford
37 Trevor Booker 8.00 20.00
Kevin Seraphin
38 Damion James 5.00 12.00
Dexter Pittman
39 Damion James 5.00 12.00
Avery Bradley
40 Avery Bradley 5.00 12.00
Luke Harangody
41 Avery Bradley 6.00 15.00
Semih Erden
42 Dominique Jones 5.00 12.00
Quincy Pondexter
43 Jordan Crawford 6.00 15.00
Kevin Seraphin
44 Greivis Vasquez 10.00 25.00
Xavier Henry
45 Greivis Vasquez 10.00 25.00
Daniel Orton
46 Daniel Orton 8.00 20.00
Lazar Hayward
47 Lazar Hayward 6.00 15.00
Wesley Johnson
48 Lazar Hayward 6.00 15.00
Nikola Pekovic
49 Hassan Whiteside 20.00 50.00
DeMarcus Cousins
50 Terrico White 8.00 20.00
Greg Monroe
51 Andy Rautins 10.00 25.00
Landry Fields
52 Andy Rautins 5.00 12.00
Timofey Mozgov
53 Landry Fields 8.00 20.00
Timofey Mozgov
54 Lance Stephenson 5.00 12.00
Paul George
55 Lance Stephenson 5.00 12.00
Dexter Pittman
56 Devin Ebanks 6.00 15.00
Derrick Caracter
57 Gani Lawal 5.00 12.00
Solomon Alabi
58 Jeremy Evans 10.00 25.00
Gordon Hayward
59 Gary Neal 10.00 25.00
Gary Forbes
60 Jeremy Lin 100.00 200.00
Omer Asik
61 Jeremy Lin 100.00 200.00
Ekpe Udoh
62 Willie Warren 6.00 15.00
Cole Aldrich
63 Willie Warren 5.00 12.00
Xavier Henry
64 James Anderson 10.00 25.00
Gary Neal
65 Omer Asik 5.00 12.00
Semih Erden
66 Dominique Jones 6.00 15.00
Jordan Crawford
67 Daniel Orton 5.00 12.00
Hassan Whiteside
68 Hassan Whiteside 5.00 12.00
Armon Johnson
69 Armon Johnson 5.00 12.00
Terrico White
70 Terrico White 5.00 12.00
Andy Rautins
71 Landry Fields 6.00 15.00
Lance Stephenson
72 Lance Stephenson 5.00 12.00
Devin Ebanks
73 Devin Ebanks 5.00 12.00
Gani Lawal
74 Solomon Alabi 5.00 12.00
Luke Harangody
75 Luke Harangody 5.00 12.00
Willie Warren

2010-11 Panini Season Update Signatures

STATED PRINT RUN 10 TO 299 SER.#'d SETS
SOME UNPRICED DUE TO SCARCITY
2 Jeff Green/199 6.00 15.00
9 Brook Lopez/99 4.00 10.00
11 Kris Humphries/299 3.00 8.00
19 Toney Douglas/299 3.00 8.00
24 Louis Williams/199 3.00 8.00
27 Andrea Bargnani/99 5.00 12.00
28 DeMar DeRozan/25 5.00 12.00
29 Jose Calderon/199 8.00 20.00
32 Sonny Weems/299 3.00 8.00
38 Ronnie Brewer/299 3.00 8.00
41 Antawn Jamison/99 4.00 10.00
42 Daniel Gibson/99 3.00 8.00
46 Austin Daye/299 3.00 8.00
48 Charlie Villanueva/99 3.00 8.00
56 Mike Dunleavy/99 3.00 8.00
57 Roy Hibbert/299 3.00 8.00
58 T.J. Ford/199 3.00 8.00
59 Tyler Hansbrough/99 5.00 12.00
70 Jeff Teague/299 3.00 8.00
72 Josh Smith/99 4.00 10.00
76 Gerald Henderson/299 3.00 8.00
77 Stephen Jackson/199 3.00 8.00
90 J.J. Redick/99 4.00 10.00
91 Jameer Nelson/25 3.00 8.00
94 JaVale McGee/299 3.00 8.00
106 Goran Dragic/99 6.00 15.00
112 Shane Battier/25 6.00 15.00
115 Rudy Gay/299 5.00 12.00
122 DeJuan Blair/299 3.00 8.00
123 George Hill/299 3.00 8.00
131 Raymond Felton/49 3.00 8.00
134 J.R. Smith/299 3.00 8.00
138 Darko Milicic/299 3.00 8.00
140 Luke Ridnour/299 3.00 8.00
143 Andre Miller/299 3.00 8.00
149 Wesley Matthews/299 4.00 10.00
150 James Harden/49 10.00 25.00
152 Kevin Durant/24 125.00 250.00
154 Serge Ibaka/299 EXCH 5.00 12.00
156 Andrei Kirilenko/99 3.00 8.00
158 Devin Harris/25 5.00 12.00
163 David Lee/25 5.00 12.00
165 Monta Ellis/299 6.00 15.00
167 Stephen Curry/99 10.00 25.00
169 Blake Griffin/15 75.00 150.00
171 Eric Gordon/299 5.00 12.00
172 Ryan Gomes/299 3.00 8.00
175 Kobe Bryant/49 100.00 200.00
180 Aaron Brooks/299 3.00 8.00
185 Beno Udrih/299 3.00 8.00
186 Marcus Thornton/299 5.00 12.00
188 Omri Casspi/299 3.00 8.00
189 Samuel Dalembert/299 3.00 8.00
190 Tyreke Evans/99 10.00 25.00
193 Kobe Bryant/49 100.00 200.00
194 Kevin Durant/24 125.00 250.00

2010-11 Panini Season Update Throwback Threads

STATED PRINT RUN 199 TO 799 SER.#'d SETS
1 Jermaine O'Neal/799 3.00 8.00
2 Dikembe Mutombo/299 3.00 8.00
3 Tracy McGrady/799 3.00 8.00
4 Larry Johnson/299 10.00 25.00
5 Stephen Jackson/499 2.50 6.00
6 Scottie Pippen/399 6.00 15.00
7 Raja Bell/799 2.50 6.00
8 Toni Kukoc/399 3.00 8.00
9 Marcin Gortat/499 5.00 12.00
10 Kelly Tripucka/299 3.00 8.00
11 Jason Kidd/499 3.00 8.00
12 Ron Harper/399 3.00 8.00
13 Amare Stoudemire/199 3.00 8.00
14 Chuck Person/299 3.00 8.00
15 Tyson Chandler/599 2.50 6.00
16 Xavier McDaniel/299 3.00 8.00
17 Raymond Felton/299 2.50 6.00
18 Moses Malone/299 3.00 8.00
19 Trevor Ariza/499 2.00 5.00
20 Tom Chambers/299 3.00 8.00

2010-11 Panini Season Update Throwback Threads Prime

*PRIME: 1X TO 2.5X BASE HI
STATED PRINT RUN 25 TO 49 SER.#'d SETS
9 Marcin Gortat/49 15.00 40.00
12 Ron Harper/49 10.00 25.00

1976 Panini Olympic Stickers

This 300-sticker set celebrate the 1976 Montreal Olympics as well as Olympic athletes from earlier games. Each sticker measures 1 15/16" by 2 11/16", and a collector's album was available for displaying the stickers. The white-bordered stickers have mostly color photos. The player's name appears at the bottom between icons representing the event and the country's flag. The first six stickers are designed to form a composite of Canada, the host country for the summer and winter olympic games. Then follows a subset of men (7-10) who played a role in organizing the olympic games. The next subset is arranged according to olympiad (numbered with Roman numerals) as follows: I. 1896 Athens (11-15); II. 1900 Paris (16-20); III. 1904 St. Louis (21-25); IV. 1908 London (26-30); V. 1912 Stockholm (30-35); VII. 1920 Antwerp (36-40); VIII. 1924 Paris (41-45); IX. 1928 Amsterdam (46-50); X. 1932 Los Angeles (51-55); XI. 1936 Berlin (56-60); XIV. 1948 London (61-65); XV. 1952 Helsinki (66-70); XVI. Melbourne (71-75); XVII. 1960 Rome (76-80); XVIII. 1964 Tokyo (81-85); XIX. 1968 Mexico (86-90); and XX. 1972 Munchen (91-95). After two Canadian stickers (96-97) appear athletes from various countries who participated in the XXI. olympiad (98-300).

COMPLETE SET (300) 50.00 100.00
162 U.S.A. Men's Basketball Team 2.00 4.00
163 S.S.S.R. Men's Basketball Team 2.00 4.00
164 Yugoslavia Men's Basketball Team .13 .25
165 Italy Men's Basketball Team/ .13 .25
166 Brazil Men's Basketball .13 .25
167 Cuba Men's Basketball Team .13 .25
168 Mexico Men's Basketball .13 .25
169 U.S.S.R. Women's BK Team .50 1.00
170 Czechoslovakia Women's BK Team .13 .25
171 Italy Women's Basketball .13 .25

1987 Panini Stickers

138 Magic Johnson
141 Michael Jordan 20.00 50.00

1990-91 Panini Stickers

This set of 180 basketball stickers was produced and distributed by Panini primarily through mass market retailers. The stickers measure 1 15/16" by 2 15/16" and are issued in sheets consisting of three rows of four stickers each. The sheets were included with the sticker album itself. The stickers feature color action photos of the players on a white background. The team name is given in a light blue stripe below the picture, with a basketball icon to the right. The player's name appears at the bottom of the sticker. The stickers are numbered on the back. Stickers 1-162 showcase NBA players according to their teams. The remaining 18 stickers are lettered A-R and feature 1990 NBA All-Stars (A-J); Jordan, Bird, and Olajuwon (K-M); and the 1990 NBA Finals (N-R).

COMPLETE SET (180) 12.00 30.00
1 Magic Johnson .40 1.00
2 Mychal Thompson .08 .25
3 Vlade Divac .15 .40
4 Byron Scott .08 .25
5 James Worthy .20 .50
6 A.C. Green .08 .25
7 Jerome Kersey .08 .25
8 Clyde Drexler .40 1.00
9 Buck Williams .08 .25
10 Kevin Duckworth .08 .25
11 Terry Porter .08 .25
12 Cliff Robinson .15 .40
13 Tom Chambers .08 .25
14 Dan Majerle .15 .40
15 Mark West .08 .25
16 Kevin Johnson .15 .40
17 Jeff Hornacek .15 .40
18 Kurt Rambis .08 .25
19 Nate McMillan .08 .25
20 Shawn Kemp .50 1.25
21 Dale Ellis .08 .25
22 Michael Cage .08 .25
23 Xavier McDaniel .08 .25
24 Derrick McKey .08 .25
25 Manute Bol .08 .25
26 Chris Mullin .20 .50
27 Terry Teagle .08 .25
28 Tim Hardaway .20 .50
29 Sarunas Marciulionis .08 .25
30 Mitch Richmond .40 1.00
31 Gary Grant .08 .25
32 Danny Manning .15 .40
33 Benoit Benjamin .08 .25
34 Ron Harper .15 .40
35 Ken Norman .08 .25
36 Charles Smith .08 .25
37 Harold Pressley .08 .25
38 Antoine Carr .08 .25
39 Danny Ainge .15 .40
40 Wayman Tisdale .08 .25
41 Ralph Sampson .08 .25
42 Vinny Del Negro .08 .25
43 David Robinson .50 1.25
44 Sean Elliott .20 .50
45 Terry Cummings .15 .40
46 Willie Anderson .08 .25
47 Rod Strickland .15 .40
48 Frank Brickowski .08 .25
49 Karl Malone .60 1.50
50 Darrell Griffith .08 .25
51 John Stockton .60 1.50
52 Blue Edwards .08 .25
53 Mark Eaton .08 .25
54 Thurl Bailey .08 .25
55 Rolando Blackman .08 .25
56 Sam Perkins .08 .25
57 James Donaldson .08 .25
58 Herb Williams .08 .25
59 Roy Tarpley .08 .25
60 Derek Harper .08 .25
61 Michael Adams .08 .25
62 Blair Rasmussen .08 .25
63 Jerome Lane .08 .25
64 Walter Davis .08 .25
65 Todd Lichti .08 .25
66 Joe Barry Carroll .08 .25
67 Vernon Maxwell .08 .25
68 Otis Thorpe .08 .25
69 Hakeem Olajuwon .40 1.00
70 Buck Johnson .08 .25
71 Eric (Sleepy) Floyd .08 .25
72 Mitchell Wiggins .08 .25
73 Tony Campbell .08 .25
74 Tod Murphy .08 .25
75 Tyrone Corbin .08 .25
76 Sam Mitchell .08 .25
77 Randy Breuer .08 .25
78 Pooh Richardson .08 .25
79 Rex Chapman .15 .40
80 Dell Curry .08 .25
81 Muggsy Bogues .15 .40
82 J.R. Reid .08 .25
83 Armon Gilliam .08 .25
84 Kelly Tripucka .08 .25
85 Dennis Rodman .50 1.25
86 Joe Dumars .20 .50
87 Isiah Thomas .20 .50
88 Bill Laimbeer .15 .40
89 Vinnie Johnson .08 .25
90 James Edwards .08 .25
91 Michael Jordan 1.50 4.00
92 Stacey King .08 .25
93 Scottie Pippen .60 1.50
94 John Paxson .08 .25
95 Horace Grant .08 .25
96 Craig Hodges .08 .25
97 Brad Lohaus .08 .25
98 Jack Sikma .08 .25
99 Ricky Pierce .08 .25
100 Greg Anderson .08 .25
101 Alvin Robertson .08 .25
102 Jay Humphries .08 .25
103 Mark Price .15 .40
104 Winston Bennett .08 .25
105 Brad Daugherty .08 .25
106 Craig Ehlo .08 .25
107 Larry Nance .08 .25
108 Hot Rod Williams .08 .25
109 Rik Smits .15 .40
110 Chuck Person .08 .25
111 Reggie Miller .40 1.00
112 LaSalle Thompson .08 .25
113 Detlef Schrempf .15 .40
114 Vern Fleming .08 .25
115 Moses Malone .15 .40
116 Doc Rivers .15 .40
117 Dominique Wilkins .25 .60
118 Spud Webb .15 .40
119 Kevin Willis .08 .25
120 Kenny Smith .08 .25
121 Otis Smith .08 .25
122 Sidney Green
123 Nick Anderson
124 Scott Skiles
125 Jerry Reynolds
126 Terry Catledge
127 Charles Barkley
128 Ron Anderson .08
129 Hersey Hawkins .08 .25
130 Mike Gminski .08 .25
131 Johnny Dawkins .08 .25
132 Rick Mahorn .08 .25
133 Michael Smith .08 .25
134 Reggie Lewis .08 .25
135 Larry Bird 1.00 2.50
136 Kevin McHale .20 .50
137 Joe Kleine .08 .25
138 Robert Parish .15 .40
139 Maurice Cheeks .08 .25
140 Patrick Ewing .40 1.00
141 Charles Oakley .15 .40
142 Gerald Wilkins .08 .25
143 Kenny Walker .15 .40
144 Mark Jackson .08 .25
145 Mark Alarie .08 .25
146 John Williams .08 .25
147 Darrell Walker .08 .25
148 Bernard King .08 .25
149 Harvey Grant .08 .25
150 Ledell Eackles .08 .25
151 Glen Rice .50 1.25
152 Kevin Edwards .08 .25
153 Tellis Frank .08 .25
154 Rony Seikaly .08 .25
155 Billy Thompson .08 .25
156 Sherman Douglas .08 .25
157 Roy Hinson .08 .25
158 Chris Morris .08 .25
159 Lester Conner .08 .25
160 Sam Bowie .08 .25
161 Purvis Short .08 .25
162 Mookie Blaylock .15 .40
A John Stockton AS .25 .60
B Magic Johnson AS .25 .60
C A.C. Green AS .08 .25
D Hakeem Olajuwon AS .25 .60
E James Worthy AS .15 .40
F Isiah Thomas AS .10 .30
G Michael Jordan AS .75 2.00
H Larry Bird AS .40 1.00
I Patrick Ewing AS .25 .60
J Charles Barkley AS .25 .60
K Michael Jordan .75 2.00
L Larry Bird .40 1.00
M Hakeem Olajuwon .25 .60
N NBA Finals .08 .25
O NBA Finals .08 .25
P NBA Finals .08 .25
Q NBA Finals .08 .25
R NBA Finals .08 .25
XX Panini Album .40 1.00

1991-92 Panini Stickers

This set of 192 basketball stickers was produced and distributed by Panini primarily through mass market retailers. Unlike the previous year's issue, these were distributed only in the usual Panini packet of six stickers with 100 packets (suggested retail price of 39 cents) per box. The stickers measure approximately 1 7/8" by 2 15/16". The fronts feature player action shots. The stickers are numbered on the back and checklisted below alphabetically according to teams within the divisions. The set closes with the All-Rookie Team (179-186) and All-NBA 1st Team (187-192).

COMPLETE SET (192) 10.00 25.00
1 NBA Official .07 .20
Licensed Product Logo
2 1991 NBA Finals Logo .07 .20
3 Chris Mullin .30 .75
4 Mitch Richmond .30 .75
5 Alton Lister .07 .20
6 Tim Hardaway .30 .75
7 Tom Tolbert .07 .20
8 Rod Higgins .07 .20
9 Charles Smith .07 .20
10 Ron Harper .20 .50
11 Olden Polynice .07 .20
12 Ken Norman .07 .20
13 Gary Grant .07 .20
14 Danny Manning .15 .40
15 Sam Perkins .08 .25
16 Vlade Divac .08 .25
17 James Worthy .30 .75
18 Magic Johnson .75 2.00
19 A.C. Green .20 .50
20 Byron Scott .20 .50
21 Kevin Johnson .15 .40
22 Mark West .07 .20
23 Dan Majerle .30 .75
24 Jeff Hornacek .30 .75
25 Xavier McDaniel .07 .20
26 Tom Chambers .20 .50
27 Terry Porter .07 .20
28 Kevin Duckworth .07 .20
29 Clyde Drexler .40 1.00
30 Jerome Kersey .07 .20
31 Buck Williams .15 .40
32 Danny Ainge .20 .50
33 Wayman Tisdale .07 .20
34 Antoine Carr .07 .20
35 Lionel Simmons .07 .20
36 Travis Mays .07 .20
37 Rory Sparrow .07 .20
38 Duane Causwell .07 .20
39 Benoit Benjamin .07 .20
40 Michael Cage .07 .20
41 Derrick McKey .07 .20
42 Shawn Kemp .30 .75
43 Gary Payton .60 1.50
44 Ricky Pierce .07 .20
45 Derek Harper .15 .40
46 James Donaldson .07 .20
47 Randy White .07 .20
48 Rodney McCray .07 .20
49 Alex English .20 .50
50 Rolando Blackman .15 .40

[illegible] Orlando Woolridge .07 .20
52 Todd Lichti .07 .20
53 Chris Jackson .07 .20
54 Blair Rasmussen .07 .20
55 Reggie Williams .07 .20
56 Marcus Liberty .07 .20
57 Hakeem Olajuwon .50 1.25
58 Kenny Smith .07 .20
59 Vernon Maxwell .07 .20
60 Otis Thorpe .08 .25
61 Buck Johnson .07 .20
62 Larry Smith .07 .20
63 Pooh Richardson .07 .20
64 Felton Spencer .07 .20
65 Tod Murphy .07 .20
66 Tyrone Corbin .07 .20
67 Tony Campbell .07 .20
68 Sam Mitchell .15 .40
69 Dennis Scott .08 .25
70 Nick Anderson .08 .25
71 Terry Catledge .07 .20
72 Scott Skiles .20 .50
73 Otis Smith .07 .20
74 Greg Kite .07 .20
75 Terry Cummings .15 .40
76 Rod Strickland .08 .25
77 David Robinson .60 1.50
78 Willie Anderson .07 .20
79 Sean Elliott .20 .50
80 Paul Pressey .07 .20
81 John Stockton .75 2.00
82 Jeff Malone .07 .20
83 Mark Eaton .07 .20
84 Thurl Bailey .07 .20
85 Karl Malone .75 2.00
86 Blue Edwards .07 .20
87 Kevin Johnson .15 .40
88 '91 Western Division .08 .25
89 NBA All-Star Weekend .07 .20
90 Magic Johnson AS .40 1.00
91 Karl Malone AS .40 1.00
92 David Robinson AS .30 .75
93 Chris Mullin AS .20 .50
94 Charles Barkley AS .30 .75
95 '91 Eastern Division .08 .25
96 Michael Jordan AS 1.00 2.50
97 Isiah Thomas AS .30 .75
98 Charles Barkley AS .40 1.00
99 Patrick Ewing AS .30 .75
100 Larry Bird AS .50 1.25
101 Dominique Wilkins .40 1.00
102 Kevin Willis .08 .25
103 John Battle .07 .20
104 Doc Rivers .20 .50
105 Spud Webb .08 .25
106 Moses Malone .15 .40
107 J.R. Reid .07 .20
108 Johnny Newman .07 .20
109 Rex Chapman .15 .40
110 Muggsy Bogues .20 .50
111 Mike Gminski .07 .20
112 Kendall Gill .15 .40
113 Scottie Pippen .60 1.50
114 Bill Cartwright .08 .25
115 John Paxson .08 .25
116 Michael Jordan 1.50 4.00
117 Horace Grant .15 .40
118 B.J. Armstrong .07 .20
119 Brad Daugherty .07 .20
120 Larry Nance .08 .25
121 Hot Rod Williams .07 .20
122 Craig Ehlo .07 .20
123 Darnell Valentine .07 .20
124 Danny Ferry .07 .20
125 Isiah Thomas .40 1.00
126 James Edwards .07 .20
127 Bill Laimbeer .20 .50
128 Vinnie Johnson .07 .20
129 Joe Dumars .30 .75
130 Dennis Rodman .40 1.00
131 Reggie Miller .40 1.00
132 Detlef Schrempf .08 .25
133 Chuck Person .07 .20
134 LaSalle Thompson .07 .20
135 Vern Fleming .07 .20
136 Rik Smits .08 .25
137 Dale Ellis .08 .25
138 Frank Brickowski .07 .20
139 Jay Humphries .07 .20
140 Jack Sikma .07 .20
141 Fred Roberts .07 .20
142 Alvin Robertson .07 .20
143 Robert Parish .20 .50
144 Kevin McHale .30 .75
145 Kevin Gamble .07 .20
146 Larry Bird .75 2.00
147 Reggie Lewis .15 .40
148 Brian Shaw .15 .40
149 Sherman Douglas .07 .20
150 Rony Seikaly .07 .20
151 Glen Rice .30 .75
152 Grant Long .07 .20
153 Billy Thompson .07 .20
154 Willie Burton .07 .20
155 Reggie Theus .08 .25
156 Sam Bowie .08 .25
157 Derrick Coleman .08 .25
158 Drazen Petrovic .60 1.50
159 Mookie Blaylock .08 .25
160 Chris Morris .07 .20
161 Gerald Wilkins .07 .20
162 Charles Oakley .08 .25
163 Patrick Ewing .40 1.00
164 Kiki Vandeweghe .20 .50
165 Maurice Cheeks .15 .40
166 John Starks .20 .50
167 Hersey Hawkins .08 .25
168 Rick Mahorn .07 .20
169 Charles Barkley .50 1.25
170 Rickey Green .07 .20
171 Ron Anderson .07 .20
172 Armon Gilliam .07 .20
173 Bernard King .15 .40
174 Ledell Eackles .07 .20
175 John Williams .07 .20
176 Darrell Walker .07 .20
177 Haywoode Workman .07 .20
178 Harvey Grant .07 .20
179 Derrick Coleman ART .07 .20
180 Dee Brown ART .07 .20
181 Lionel Simmons ART .07 .20
182 Felton Spencer ART .07 .20
183 Dennis Scott ART .07 .20
184 Gary Payton ART .40 1.00
185 Travis Mays ART .07 .20
186 Kendall Gill ART .08 .25
187 All-NBA 1st Team .08 .25
188 Charles Barkley AS .40 1.00
189 Patrick Ewing AS .30 .75
190 Michael Jordan AS 1.00 2.50
191 Karl Malone AS .50 1.25
192 Magic Johnson AS .50 1.25
XX Panini Album 1.25 3.00

1992-93 Panini Stickers

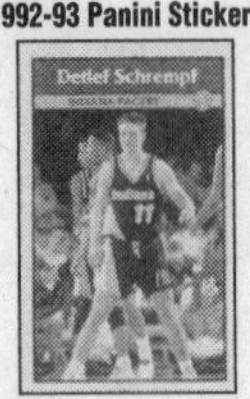

The 192 stickers in this set measure approximately 1 15/16" by 3" and were to be pasted in a 9" by 11" album. The fronts feature color action player photos with white borders. Two team color-coded bars at the top contain the player's name and team. The backs are white and carry the set name, sticker number, and manufacturer logo. Six players from each of the 27 NBA teams are featured. The stickers are numbered on the back and checklisted below according to special subsets and teams.

COMPLETE SET (192) 8.00 20.00
1 Shaquille O'Neal 2.50 6.00
2 Tracy Murray .07 .20
3 Robert Horry .40 1.00
4 Bryant Stith .07 .20
5 Randy Woods .07 .20
6 Adam Keefe .07 .20
7 Byron Houston .07 .20
8 Duane Cooper .07 .20
9 Western Playoffs .07 .20
(Action scene left)
10 Western Playoffs .07 .20
(Action scene right)
11 Clyde Drexler .40 1.00
12 Michael Jordan 1.50 4.00
13 Eastern Playoffs .07 .20
(Action scene left)
14 Eastern Playoffs .07 .20
(Action scene right)
15 Chicago Bulls Logo .07 .20
16 1992 NBA Finals .30 .75
(Action scene
upper left; Michael Jordan pictured)
17 1992 NBA Finals .30 .75
(Action scene
upper right; Michael Jordan pictured)
18 1992 NBA Finals .30 .75
(Action scene
lower left; Michael Jordan pictured)
19 1992 NBA Finals .30 .75
(Action scene
lower right; Michael Jordan pictured)
20 Michael Jordan MVP 1.50 4.00
21 Tim Hardaway .30 .75
22 Chris Mullin .30 .75
23 Billy Owens .07 .20
24 Sarunas Marciulionis .15 .40
25 Jeff Grayer .07 .20
26 Tyrone Hill .07 .20
27 Danny Manning .15 .40
28 Ron Harper .15 .40
29 Ken Norman .07 .20
30 Charles Smith .07 .20
31 Gary Grant .07 .20
32 Doc Rivers .15 .40
33 James Worthy .30 .75
34 Sam Perkins .15 .40
35 Byron Scott .15 .40
36 Sedale Threatt .07 .20
37 Elden Campbell .07 .20
38 A.C. Green .15 .40
39 Charles Barkley .40 1.00
40 Kevin Johnson .15 .40
41 Tom Chambers .15 .40
42 Dan Majerle .15 .40
43 Mark West .07 .20
44 Danny Ainge .15 .40
45 Buck Williams .15 .40
46 Clyde Drexler .40 1.00
47 Jerome Kersey .07 .20
48 Terry Porter .15 .40
49 Clifford Robinson .07 .20
50 Kevin Duckworth .07 .20
51 Mitch Richmond .25 .60
52 Lionel Simmons .07 .20
53 Wayman Tisdale .07 .20
54 Spud Webb .15 .40
55 Duane Causwell .07 .20
56 Jim Les .07 .20
57 Eddie Johnson .07 .20
58 Ricky Pierce .07 .20
59 Shawn Kemp .25 .60
60 Benoit Benjamin .07 .20
61 Gary Payton .40 1.00
62 Dana Barros .07 .20
63 Herb Williams .07 .20
64 Doug Smith .07 .20
65 Terry Davis .07 .20
66 Derek Harper .15 .40
67 Mike Iuzzolino .07 .20
68 Rodney McCray .07 .20
69 Greg Anderson .07 .20
70 Reggie Williams .07 .20
71 Dikembe Mutombo .30 .75
72 Mark Macon .07 .20
73 Winston Garland .07 .20
74 Chris Jackson .07 .20
75 Otis Thorpe .07 .20
76 Hakeem Olajuwon .40 1.00
77 Vernon Maxwell .07 .20
78 Kenny Smith .07 .20
79 Avery Johnson .15 .40
80 Sleepy Floyd .07 .20
81 Pooh Richardson .07 .20
82 Tony Campbell .07 .20
83 Thurl Bailey .07 .20
84 Doug West .07 .20
85 Gerald Glass .07 .20
86 Felton Spencer .07 .20
87 David Robinson .40 1.00
88 Terry Cummings .07 .20
89 Sidney Green .07 .20
90 Sean Elliott .15 .40
91 Willie Anderson .07 .20
92 Antoine Carr .07 .20
93 Clyde Drexler FF .25 .60
94 Patrick Ewing FF .20 .50
95 Magic Johnson FF .30 .75
96 Scottie Pippen FF .25 .60
97 John Stockton FF .30 .75
98 Tim Hardaway FF .08 .25
99 David Robinson FF .25 .60
100 Karl Malone FF .25 .60
101 Chris Mullin FF .15 .40
102 Michael Jordan FF 1.50 4.00
103 Mark Eaton .07 .20
104 Karl Malone .40 1.00
105 Jeff Malone .07 .20
106 John Stockton .50 1.25
107 David Benoit .07 .20
108 Jay Humphries .07 .20
109 Alvin Robertson .07 .20
110 Moses Malone .15 .40
111 Sam Vincent .07 .20
112 Frank Brickowski .07 .20
113 Fred Roberts .07 .20
114 Blue Edwards .07 .20
115 Stacey Augmon .07 .20
116 Rumeal Robinson .07 .20
117 Paul Graham .07 .20
118 Dominique Wilkins .40 1.00
119 Kevin Willis .07 .20
120 Duane Ferrell .07 .20
121 Tyrone Bogues .10 .30
122 Kendall Gill .07 .20
123 Dell Curry .07 .20
124 Larry Johnson .20 .50
125 Johnny Newman .07 .20
126 J.R. Reid .07 .20
127 Scottie Pippen .60 1.50
128 Michael Jordan 1.50 4.00
129 Bill Cartwright .08 .25
130 Horace Grant .15 .40
131 John Paxson .15 .40
132 B.J. Armstrong .07 .20
133 Mark Price .15 .40
134 Brad Daugherty .07 .20
135 Larry Nance .15 .40
136 Craig Ehlo .10 .30
137 Hot Rod Williams .07 .20
138 Terrell Brandon .08 .25
139 Joe Dumars .30 .75
140 Isiah Thomas .40 1.00
141 Dennis Rodman .40 1.00
142 Orlando Woolridge .07 .20
143 John Salley .15 .40
144 Bill Laimbeer .15 .40
145 Reggie Miller .40 1.00
146 Detlef Schrempf .15 .40
147 Chuck Person .07 .20
148 Micheal Williams .07 .20
149 Rik Smits .07 .20
150 Vern Fleming .07 .20
151 Lester Conner .07 .20
152 Nick Anderson .07 .20
153 Scott Skiles .10 .30
154 Terry Catledge .07 .20
155 Jerry Reynolds .07 .20
156 Dennis Scott .07 .20
157 Rick Fox .07 .20
158 Reggie Lewis .07 .20
159 Robert Parish .15 .40
160 Kevin Gamble .07 .20
161 Kevin McHale .20 .50
162 John Bagley .07 .20
163 Steve Smith .20 .50
164 Glen Rice .20 .50
165 Grant Long .07 .20
166 Rony Seikaly .07 .20
167 Bimbo Coles .07 .20
168 Willie Burton .07 .20
169 Derrick Coleman .07 .20
170 Drazen Petrovic .30 .75
171 Sam Bowie .07 .20
172 Chris Morris .07 .20
173 Mookie Blaylock .07 .20
174 Chris Dudley .07 .20
175 Patrick Ewing .30 .75
176 Mark Jackson .15 .40
177 Xavier McDaniel .07 .20
178 John Starks .10 .30
179 Charles Oakley .07 .20
180 Rolando Blackman .07 .20
181 Hersey Hawkins .07 .20
182 Johnny Dawkins .07 .20
183 Armon Gilliam .07 .20
184 Jeff Hornacek .15 .40
185 Tim Perry .07 .20
186 Andrew Lang .07 .20
187 Pervis Ellison .07 .20
188 Michael Adams .07 .20
189 Harvey Grant .07 .20
190 Ledell Eackles .07 .20
191 A.J. English .07 .20
192 David Wingate .07 .20
XX Panini Album .75 2.00

1993-94 Panini Stickers

The 253 stickers in this set measure approximately 2 3/8" by 3 3/8" and were to be pasted in a 9" by 11" album. On a team color-coded background with a black border, the fronts feature slightly tilted color action player photos framed by a thin white border. The team name appears above the photo, while the player's name is under the photo. The team logo is superimposed at the bottom right corner of the photo. The backs are white and carry the set name, sticker number, and manufacturer logo. The stickers are numbered on the back and checklisted below according to teams. In the middle of the album is a poster featuring the 1993 NBA Honor Roll (A-F).

COMPLETE SET (253) 8.00 20.00
1 John Paxson .07 .20
(top part of photo)
2 John Paxson .07 .20
(bottom part of photo)
3 Charles Barkley .20 .50
(top part of photo)
4 Charles Barkley .20 .50
(bottom part of photo)
5 Victor Alexander .07 .20
6 Chris Gatling .07 .20
7 Tim Hardaway .20 .50
8 Warriors Team Logo .07 .20
9 Tyrone Hill .07 .20
10 Sarunas Marciulionis .10 .30
11 Chris Mullin .20 .50
12 Billy Owens .07 .20
13 Latrell Sprewell .40 1.00
14 Gary Grant .07 .20
15 Ron Harper .20 .50
16 Mark Jackson .20 .50
17 Clippers Team Logo .07 .20
18 Danny Manning .08 .25
19 Ken Norman .07 .20
20 Stanley Roberts .07 .20
21 Loy Vaught .07 .20
22 John Williams .07 .20
23 Sam Bowie .08 .25
24 Elden Campbell .07 .20
25 Vlade Divac .20 .50
26 Lakers Team Logo .07 .20
27 A.C. Green .15 .40
28 Anthony Peeler .07 .20
29 Doug Christie .07 .20
30 Sedale Threatt .07 .20
31 James Worthy .30 .75
32 Danny Ainge .20 .50
33 Charles Barkley .40 1.00
34 Cedric Ceballos .08 .25
35 Suns Team Logo .07 .20
36 Tom Chambers .15 .40
37 Richard Dumas .07 .20
38 Kevin Johnson .15 .40
39 Dan Majerle .20 .50
40 Oliver Miller .07 .20
41 Clyde Drexler .40 1.00
42 Mario Elie .07 .20
43 Harvey Grant .07 .20
44 Trailblazers Team Logo .07 .20
45 Jerome Kersey .07 .20
46 Terry Porter .08 .25
47 Clifford Robinson .08 .25
48 Rod Strickland .07 .20
49 Buck Williams .15 .40
50 Anthony Bonner .07 .20
51 Duane Causwell .07 .20
52 Kurt Rambis .12 .30
53 Kings Team Logo .07 .20
54 Mitch Richmond .30 .75
55 Lionel Simmons .07 .20
56 Wayman Tisdale .07 .20
57 Spud Webb .15 .40
58 Walt Williams .07 .20
59 Dana Barros .07 .20
60 Eddie Johnson .07 .20
61 Shawn Kemp .25 .60
62 Supersonics Team Logo .07 .20
63 Derrick McKey .07 .20
64 Nate McMillan .15 .40
65 Gary Payton .40 1.00
66 Sam Perkins .15 .40
67 Ricky Pierce .07 .20
68 Terry Davis .07 .20
69 Derek Harper .15 .40
70 Donald Hodge .07 .20
71 Mavericks Team Logo .07 .20
72 Mike Iuzzolino .07 .20
73 Jim Jackson .15 .40
74 Sean Rooks .07 .20
75 Doug Smith .07 .20
76 Randy White .07 .20
77 LaPhonso Ellis .08 .25
78 Scott Hastings .07 .20
79 Mahmoud Abdul-Rauf .07 .20
80 Nuggets Team Logo .07 .20
81 Marcus Liberty .07 .20
82 Mark Macon .07 .20
83 Dikembe Mutombo .20 .50
84 Robert Pack .07 .20
85 Reggie Williams .07 .20
86 Scott Brooks .07 .20
87 Sleepy Floyd .07 .20
88 Carl Herrera .07 .20
89 Rockets Team Logo .07 .20
90 Robert Horry .20 .50
91 Vernon Maxwell .07 .20
92 Hakeem Olajuwon .40 1.00
93 Kenny Smith .08 .25
94 Otis Thorpe .08 .25
95 Thurl Bailey .07 .20
96 Chris Smith .07 .20
97 Mike Brown .07 .20
98 Timberwolves Team Logo .07 .20
99 Christian Laettner .20 .50
100 Luc Longley .08 .25
101 Chuck Person .07 .20
102 Doug West .07 .20
103 Micheal Williams .07 .20
104 Willie Anderson .07 .20
105 Antoine Carr .07 .20
106 Terry Cummings .08 .25
107 Spurs Team Logo .07 .20
108 Sean Elliott .15 .40
109 Dale Ellis .07 .20
110 Avery Johnson .15 .40
111 J.R. Reid .07 .20
112 David Robinson .40 1.00
113 David Benoit .07 .20
114 Tyrone Corbin .07 .20
115 Mark Eaton .07 .20
116 Jazz Team Logo .07 .20
117 Jay Humphries .07 .20
118 Jeff Malone .07 .20
119 Karl Malone .60 1.50
120 Felton Spencer .07 .20
121 John Stockton .60 1.50
122 Anthony Avent .07 .20
123 Frank Brickowski .07 .20
124 Todd Day .07 .20
125 Bucks Team Logo .07 .20
126 Blue Edwards .07 .20
127 Brad Lohaus .07 .20
128 Moses Malone .20 .50
129 Lee Mayberry .07 .20
130 Eric Murdock .07 .20
131 Stacey Augmon .07 .20
132 Mookie Blaylock .15 .40
133 Duane Ferrell .07 .20
134 Hawks Team Logo .07 .20
135 Steve Henson .07 .20
136 Adam Keefe .07 .20
137 Jon Koncak .07 .20
138 Dominique Wilkins .40 1.00
139 Kevin Willis .07 .20
140 Muggsy Bogues .15 .40
141 Dell Curry .07 .20
142 Kenny Gattison .07 .20
143 Hornets Team Logo .07 .20
144 Kendall Gill .08 .25
145 Larry Johnson .20 .50
146 Alonzo Mourning .30 .75
147 Johnny Newman .07 .20
148 David Wingate .07 .20
149 B.J. Armstrong .07 .20
150 Bill Cartwright .07 .20
151 Horace Grant .15 .40
152 Bulls Team Logo .07 .20
153 Stacey King .07 .20
154 John Paxson .15 .40
155 Will Perdue .07 .20
156 Scottie Pippen .60 1.50
157 Scott Williams .07 .20
158 Terrell Brandon .08 .25
159 Brad Daugherty .07 .20
160 Craig Ehlo .07 .20
161 Cavaliers Team Logo .07 .20
162 Danny Ferry .07 .20
163 Larry Nance .15 .40
164 Mark Price .20 .50
165 Gerald Wilkins .07 .20
166 Hot Rod Williams .07 .20
167 Mark Aguirre .25 .60
168 Joe Dumars .25 .60
169 Bill Laimbeer .15 .40
170 Pistons Team Logo .07 .20
171 Terry Mills .07 .20
172 Olden Polynice .07 .20
173 Alvin Robertson .07 .20
174 Dennis Rodman .30 .75
175 Isiah Thomas .30 .75
176 Dale Davis .08 .25
177 Vern Fleming .07 .20
178 Reggie Miller .40 1.00
179 Pacers Team Logo .07 .20
180 Pooh Richardson .07 .20
181 Detlef Schrempf .15 .40
182 Malik Sealy .15 .40
183 Rik Smits .08 .25
184 LaSalle Thompson .07 .20
185 Nick Anderson .08 .25
186 Anthony Bowie .07 .20
187 Shaquille O'Neal 1.25 3.00
188 Magic Team Logo .07 .20
189 Donald Royal .07 .20
190 Dennis Scott .07 .20
191 Scott Skiles .20 .50
192 Tom Tolbert .07 .20
193 Jeff Turner .07 .20
194 Alaa Abdelnaby .07 .20
195 Dee Brown .07 .20
196 Sherman Douglas .07 .20
197 Celtics Team Logo .07 .20
198 Rick Fox .15 .40
199 Kevin Gamble .07 .20
200 Xavier McDaniel .08 .25
201 Robert Parish .15 .40
202 Lorenzo Williams .07 .20
203 Bimbo Coles .07 .20
204 Matt Geiger .07 .20
205 Harold Miner .07 .20
206 Heat Team Logo .07 .20
207 Glen Rice .20 .50
208 John Salley .08 .25
209 Rony Seikaly .07 .20
210 Brian Shaw .07 .20
211 Steve Smith .20 .50
212 Rafael Addison .07 .20
213 Kenny Anderson .08 .25
214 Benoit Benjamin .07 .20
215 Nets Team Logo .07 .20
216 Derrick Coleman .08 .25
217 Chris Dudley .07 .20
218 Rick Mahorn .07 .20
219 Chris Morris .07 .20
220 Rumeal Robinson .07 .20
221 Greg Anthony .07 .20
222 Rolando Blackman .15 .40
223 Patrick Ewing .30 .75
224 Knicks Team Logo .07 .20
225 Anthony Mason .08 .25
226 Charles Oakley .08 .25
227 Doc Rivers .15 .40
228 Charles Smith .07 .20
229 John Starks .15 .40
230 Ron Anderson .07 .20
231 Johnny Dawkins .07 .20
232 Armon Gilliam .07 .20
233 76ers Team Logo .07 .20
234 Hersey Hawkins .08 .25
235 Jeff Hornacek .20 .50
236 Andrew Lang .07 .20
237 Tim Perry .07 .20
238 Clarence Weatherspoon .07 .20
239 Michael Adams .07 .20
240 Rex Chapman .15 .40
241 Kevin Duckworth .07 .20
242 Bullets Team Logo .07 .20
243 Pervis Ellison .07 .20
244 Tom Gugliotta .08 .25
245 Don MacLean .07 .20
246 Brent Price .07 .20
247 LaBradford Smith .07 .20
A Charles Barkley MVP .40 1.00
B Mahmoud Abdul-Rauf MIP .08 .25
C Shaquille O'Neal ROY 1.00 2.50
D Hakeem Olajuwon Def POY .40 1.00
E John Stockton CV .50 1.25
F Clifford Robinson SM .07 .20
XX Panini Album .75 2.00

1994-95 Panini Stickers

This 230-card sticker set was issued in the United States and most of Europe. Stickers came in 6-card packets and sold for about 49-cents each. In addition to the regularly numbered 220-cards, there is a 10-card 1994 NBA All-Rookie Team subset numbered A-J. Each sticker is slightly smaller than a standard-sized trading cards and each feature full color photos surrounded by a white border, except for the Future Star subset cards scattered throughout the set that feature foil borders.. The backs of each sticker contain a large number and licensing information.

COMPLETE SET (230) 25.00 60.00
1 Toronto Raptors .30 .75
2 Toronto Raptors .30 .75
3 Vancouver Grizzlies .30 .75
4 Vancouver Grizzlies .30 .75
5 Stacey Augmon .40 1.00
6 Mookie Blaylock .30 .75
7 Craig Ehlo .30 .75
8 Duane Ferrell .30 .75
9 Adam Keefe .30 .75
10 Andrew Lang .30 .75
11 Danny Manning .40 1.00
12 Kevin Willis .30 .75
13 Dee Brown .30 .75
14 Sherman Douglas .30 .75
15 Pervis Ellison .30 .75
16 Rick Fox .30 .75
17 Kevin Gamble .30 .75
18 Xavier McDaniel .30 .75
19 Dino Radja .40 1.00
20 Dominique Wilkins .60 1.50
21 Michael Adams .30 .75
22 Muggsy Bogues .40 1.00
23 Dell Curry .30 .75
24 Kenny Gattison .30 .75
25 Hersey Hawkins .30 .75
26 Larry Johnson .50 1.25
27 Alonzo Mourning .60 1.50
28 Robert Parish .50 1.25
29 B.J. Armstrong .30 .75
30 Steve Kerr .40 1.00
31 Toni Kukoc .60 1.50
32 Luc Longley .30 .75
33 Pete Myers .30 .75
34 Will Perdue .30 .75
35 Scottie Pippen 1.00 2.50
36 Bill Wennington .30 .75
37 Terrell Brandon .30 .75
38 Michael Cage .30 .75
39 Brad Daugherty .40 1.00
40 Tyrone Hill .30 .75
41 Chris Mills .30 .75
42 Mark Price .50 1.25
43 Gerald Wilkins .30 .75
44 John Williams .30 .75
45 Greg Anderson .30 .75
46 Joe Dumars .50 1.25
47 Allan Houston .50 1.25
48 Lindsey Hunter .30 .75
49 Eric Leckner .30 .75
50 Mark Macon .30 .75
51 Terry Mills .30 .75
52 Mark West .30 .75
53 Antonio Davis .30 .75
54 Dale Davis .30 .75
55 Mark Jackson .50 1.25
56 Derrick McKey .30 .75
57 Reggie Miller .60 1.50
58 Byron Scott .40 1.00
59 Rik Smits .40 1.00
60 Haywoode Workman .30 .75
61 Vernell Bimbo Coles .30 .75
62 Matt Geiger .30 .75
63 Grant Long .30 .75
64 Harold Miner .30 .75
65 Glen Rice .50 1.25
66 John Salley .30 .75
67 Rony Seikaly .40 1.00
68 Steve Smith .40 1.00
69 Vin Baker .50 1.25
70 Jon Barry .30 .75
71 Anthony Cook .30 .75
72 Todd Day .30 .75
73 Brad Lohaus .30 .75
74 Lee Mayberry .30 .75
75 Eric Murdock .30 .75
76 Ed Pinckney .30 .75
77 Kenny Anderson .40 1.00
78 Benoit Benjamin .30 .75
79 P.J. Brown .30 .75
80 Derrick Coleman .40 1.00
81 Kevin Edwards .30 .75
82 Armon Gilliam .30 .75
83 Chris Morris .30 .75
84 Rex Walters .30 .75
85 Greg Anthony .30 .75
86 Hubert Davis .30 .75
87 Patrick Ewing .60 1.50
88 Derek Harper .40 1.00
89 Anthony Mason .30 .75
90 Charles Oakley .40 1.00
91 Charles Smith .30 .75
92 John Starks .40 1.00
93 Nick Anderson .30 .75
94 Anthony Avent .30 .75
95 Horace Grant .40 1.00
96 Anfernee Hardaway .75 2.00
97 Shaquille O'Neal 1.25 3.00
98 Donald Royal .30 .75
99 Dennis Scott .30 .75
100 Jeff Turner .30 .75
101 Dana Barros .30 .75
102 Shawn Bradley .30 .75
103 Johnny Dawkins .30 .75
104 Jeff Malone .30 .75
105 Tim Perry .30 .75
106 Clarence Weatherspoon .30 .75
107 Scott Williams .30 .75
108 Orlando Woolridge .30 .75
109 Rex Chapman .30 .75
110 Calbert Cheaney .30 .75
111 Kevin Duckworth .30 .75
112 Tom Gugliotta .30 .75
113 Don MacLean .30 .75
114 Gheorghe Muresan .30 .75
115 Brent Price .30 .75
116 Scott Skiles .30 .75
117 Tony Campbell .30 .75
118 Lucious Harris .30 .75
119 Donald Hodge .30 .75
120 Jim Jackson .30 .75
121 Popeye Jones .30 .75
122 Jamal Mashburn .50 1.25
123 Sean Rooks .30 .75
124 Doug Smith .30 .75
125 Mahmoud Abdul-Rauf .30 .75
126 LaPhonso Ellis .30 .75
127 Dikembe Mutombo .50 1.25
128 Robert Pack .30 .75
129 Rodney Rogers .30 .75
130 Bryant Stith .30 .75
131 Brian Williams .30 .75
132 Reggie Williams .30 .75
133 Victor Alexander .30 .75
134 Chris Gatling .30 .75
135 Tim Hardaway .50 1.25
136 Keith Jennings .30 .75
137 Chris Mullin .50 1.25
138 Billy Owens .30 .75
139 Latrell Sprewell .60 1.50
140 Chris Webber .75 2.00
141 Sam Cassell .50 1.25
142 Mario Elie .30 .75
143 Carl Herrera .30 .75
144 Robert Horry .50 1.25
145 Vernon Maxwell .30 .75
146 Hakeem Olajuwon .60 1.50
147 Kenny Smith .40 1.00
148 Otis Thorpe .30 .75
149 Terry Dehere .30 .75
150 Harold Ellis .30 .75
151 Gary Grant .30 .75
152 Ron Harper .40 1.00
153 Pooh Richardson .30 .75
154 Malik Sealy .30 .75
155 Elmore Spencer .30 .75
156 Loy Vaught .30 .75
157 Elden Campbell .30 .75
158 Doug Christie .30 .75
159 Vlade Divac .50 1.25
160 Anthony Peeler .30 .75
161 Tony Smith .30 .75
162 Sedale Threatt .30 .75
163 Nick Van Exel .50 1.25
164 James Worthy .60 1.50
165 Thurl Bailey .30 .75
166 Mike Brown .30 .75
167 Stacey King .30 .75
168 Christian Laettner .40 1.00
169 Isaiah Rider .50 1.25
170 Chris Smith .30 .75
171 Doug West .30 .75
172 Micheal Williams .30 .75
173 Danny Ainge .50 1.25
174 Charles Barkley .75 2.00
175 Cedric Ceballos .30 .75
176 A.C. Green .50 1.25
177 Frank Johnson .30 .75
178 Kevin Johnson .50 1.25
179 Dan Majerle .50 1.25
180 Oliver Miller .30 .75
181 Mark Bryant .30 .75
182 Clyde Drexler .60 1.50
183 Harvey Grant .30 .75
184 Jerome Kersey .30 .75
185 Terry Porter .30 .75
186 Clifford Robinson .30 .75
187 Rod Strickland .30 .75
188 Buck Williams .30 .75
189 Randy Brown .30 .75
190 Olden Polynice .30 .75
191 Mitch Richmond .50 1.25
192 Lionel Simmons .30 .75
193 Andre Spencer .30 .75
194 Wayman Tisdale .30 .75
195 Spud Webb .50 1.25
196 Walt Williams .30 .75
197 Willie Anderson .30 .75
198 Vinny Del Negro .30 .75
199 Sean Elliott .50 1.25
200 Dale Ellis .30 .75
201 Avery Johnson .40 1.00
202 Chuck Person .40 1.00
203 David Robinson .75 2.00
204 Dennis Rodman 1.00 2.50
205 Kendall Gill .30 .75
206 Ervin Johnson .30 .75
207 Shawn Kemp .50 1.25
208 Sarunas Marciulionis .30 .75
209 Nate McMillan .30 .75
210 Gary Payton .50 1.25
211 Sam Perkins .30 .75
212 Detlef Schrempf .50 1.25
213 David Benoit .30 .75
214 Tyrone Corbin .30 .75
215 Jeff Hornacek .40 1.00
216 Jay Humphries .30 .75
217 Karl Malone .60 1.50
218 Felton Spencer .30 .75
219 John Stockton .60 1.50
220 Luther Wright .30 .75
A Chris Webber ART .75 2.00
B Anfernee Hardaway ART .75 2.00
C Vin Baker ART .50 1.25
D Jamal Mashburn ART .50 1.25
E Isaiah Rider ART .50 1.25
F Dino Radja ART .40 1.00
G Nick Van Exel ART .50 1.25
H Toni Kukoc ART .60 1.50
I Lindsey Hunter ART .30 .75
J Shawn Bradley ART .30 .75
XX Panini Album .40 1.00

1995-96 Panini Stickers

The 288 stickers in this set measure approximately 2 1/8" by 3" and were to be pasted in a 9" by 10 3/4" album. The fronts feature color action player photos with white borders. The player's name runs vertically down one side of the photo while the team name and logo appear in a bottom corner inside a basketball. The white backs carry the set name, sticker number, and manufacturer logo. The stickers are checklisted below according to teams. The set closes with NBA League Leaders (271-280) NBA Rookie Sensations (281-288).

COMPLETE SET (288) 15.00 40.00
1 Dee Brown .15 .40
2 Sherman Douglas .15 .40
3 Pervis Ellison .15 .40
4 Rick Fox .15 .40
5 Greg Minor .15 .40
6 Celtics Team Logo .15 .40
7 Eric Montross .15 .40
8 Dino Radja .20 .50
9 David Wesley .15 .40
10 Rex Chapman .15 .40
11 Bimbo Coles .15 .40
12 Kevin Gamble .15 .40
13 Matt Geiger .15 .40
14 Billy Owens .15 .40
15 Heat Team Logo .15 .40
16 Khalid Reeves .15 .40
17 Glen Rice .25 .60
18 Kevin Willis .15 .40
19 Kenny Anderson .20 .50
20 P.J. Brown .15 .40
21 Chris Childs .15 .40
22 Derrick Coleman .20 .50
23 Kevin Edwards .15 .40
24 Nets Team Logo .15 .40
25 Armon Gilliam .15 .40
26 Chris Morris .15 .40
27 Jayson Williams .15 .40
28 Anthony Bonner .15 .40
29 Hubert Davis .15 .40
30 Patrick Ewing .30 .75
31 Derek Harper .20 .50
32 Anthony Mason .15 .40
33 Knicks Team Logo .15 .40
34 Charles Oakley .20 .50
35 Charles Smith .15 .40
36 John Starks .20 .50
37 Nick Anderson .15 .40
38 Horace Grant .20 .50
39 Anfernee Hardaway .40 1.00
40 Shaquille O'Neal .60 1.50
41 Donald Royal .15 [illegible]
42 Magic Team Logo .15 [illegible]
43 Dennis Scott .15 [illegible]
44 Brian Shaw .15 [illegible]
45 Jeff Turner .15 [illegible]
46 Derrick Alston .15 [illegible]
47 Dana Barros .15 [illegible]
48 Shawn Bradley .15 [illegible]
49 Willie Burton .15 [illegible]
50 Jeff Malone .15 [illegible]
51 76ers Team Logo .15 [illegible]
52 Clarence Weatherspoon .15 [illegible]
53 Scott Williams .15 [illegible]
54 Sharone Wright .15 [illegible]
55 Mitchell Butler .15 [illegible]
56 Calbert Cheaney .15 [illegible]
57 Juwan Howard .25 [illegible]
58 Don MacLean .15 [illegible]
59 Gheorghe Muresan .15 [illegible]
60 Bullets Team Logo .15 [illegible]
61 Doug Overton .15 [illegible]
62 Scott Skiles .15 [illegible]
63 Chris Webber .30 [illegible]

64 Stacey Augmon	.20	.50
65 Mookie Blaylock	.15	.40
66 Craig Ehlo	.15	.40
67 Andrew Lang	.15	.40
68 Grant Long	.15	.40
69 Hawks Team Logo	.15	.40
70 Ken Norman	.15	.40
71 Steve Smith	.20	.50
72 Spud Webb	.25	.60
73 Tony Bennett	.15	.40
74 Muggsy Bogues	.20	.50
75 Scott Burrell	.15	.40
76 Dell Curry	.15	.40
77 Kendall Gill	.15	.40
78 Hornets Team Logo	.15	.40
79 Larry Johnson	.25	.60
80 Alonzo Mourning	.30	.75
81 Robert Parish	.25	.60
82 Ron Harper	.20	.50
83 Michael Jordan	2.00	5.00
84 Steve Kerr	.20	.50
85 Toni Kukoc	.25	.60
86 Luc Longley	.15	.40
87 Bulls Team Logo	.15	.40
88 Will Perdue	.15	.40
89 Scottie Pippen	.40	1.00
90 Bill Wennington	.15	.40
91 Terrell Brandon	.15	.40
92 Michael Cage	.15	.40
93 Danny Ferry	.15	.40
94 Tyrone Hill	.15	.40
95 Chris Mills	.15	.40
96 Cavaliers Team Logo	.15	.40
97 Bobby Phills	.15	.40
98 Mark Price	.25	.60
99 John Williams	.15	.40
100 Bill Curley	.15	.40
101 Joe Dumars	.25	.60
102 Grant Hill	.40	1.00
103 Allan Houston	.20	.50
104 Lindsey Hunter	.15	.40
105 Pistons Team Logo	.15	.40
106 Mark Macon	.15	.40
107 Terry Mills	.15	.40
108 Mark West	.15	.40
109 Antonio Davis	.15	.40
110 Dale Davis	.15	.40
111 Duane Ferrell	.15	.40
112 Mark Jackson	.25	.60
113 Derrick McKey	.15	.40
114 Pacers Team Logo	.15	.40
115 Reggie Miller	.30	.75
116 Rik Smits	.20	.50
117 Haywoode Workman	.15	.40
118 Vin Baker	.20	.50
119 Jon Barry	.15	.40
120 Marty Conlon	.15	.40
121 Todd Day	.15	.40
122 Lee Mayberry	.15	.40
123 Bucks Team Logo	.15	.40
124 Eric Mobley	.15	.40
125 Eric Murdock	.15	.40
126 Glenn Robinson	.25	.60
127 Willie Anderson	.15	.40
128 B.J. Armstrong	.15	.40
129 Acie Earl	.15	.40
130 Jerome Kersey	.15	.40
131 Tony Massenburg	.15	.40
132 Raptors Team Logo	.15	.40
133 Oliver Miller	.15	.40
134 John Salley	.15	.40
135 B.J. Tyler	.15	.40
136 Larry Johnson POW	.25	.60
137 Shawn Kemp POW	.25	.60
138 Karl Malone POW	.30	.75
139 Jamal Mashburn POW	.25	.60
140 Alonzo Mourning POW	.30	.75
141 Hakeem Olajuwon POW	.30	.75
142 Shaquille O'Neal POW	.60	1.50
143 David Robinson POW	.40	1.00
144 Chris Webber POW	.30	.75
145 Lucious Harris	.15	.40
146 Jim Jackson	.15	.40
147 Popeye Jones	.15	.40
148 Jason Kidd	.40	1.00
149 Jamal Mashburn	.25	.60
150 Mavericks Team Logo	.15	.40
151 George McCloud	.15	.40
152 Roy Tarpley	.15	.40
153 Lorenzo Williams	.15	.40
154 Mahmoud Abdul-Rauf	.15	.40
155 LaPhonso Ellis	.15	.40
156 Dikembe Mutombo	.25	.60
157 Robert Pack	.15	.40
158 Jalen Rose	.30	.75
159 Nuggets Team Logo	.15	.40
160 Bryant Stith	.15	.40
161 Brian Williams	.15	.40
162 Reggie Williams	.15	.40
163 Chucky Brown	.15	.40
164 Sam Cassell	.25	.60
165 Clyde Drexler	.30	.75
166 Mario Elie	.15	.40
167 Carl Herrera	.15	.40
168 Rockets Team Logo	.15	.40
169 Robert Horry	.20	.50
170 Hakeem Olajuwon	.30	.75
171 Kenny Smith	.20	.50
172 Tom Gugliotta	.15	.40
173 Christian Laettner	.20	.50
174 Darrick Martin	.15	.40
175 Isaiah Rider	.25	.60
176 Sean Rooks	.15	.40
177 Timberwolves Team Logo	.15	.40
178 Chris Smith	.15	.40
179 Doug West	.15	.40
180 Micheal Williams	.15	.40
181 Vinny Del Negro	.15	.40
182 Sean Elliott	.25	.60
183 Avery Johnson	.20	.50
184 Chuck Person	.20	.50
185 J.R. Reid	.15	.40
186 Spurs Team Logo	.15	.40
187 Doc Rivers	.20	.50
188 David Robinson	.40	1.00
189 Dennis Rodman	.50	1.25
190 David Benoit	.15	.40
191 Jeff Hornacek	.20	.50
192 Adam Keefe	.15	.40
193 Karl Malone	.30	.75
194 Bryon Russell	.15	.40
195 Jazz Team Logo	.15	.40
196 Felton Spencer	.15	.40
197 John Stockton	.30	.75
198 Jamie Watson	.15	.40
199 Greg Anthony	.15	.40
200 Benoit Benjamin	.15	.40
201 Blue Edwards	.15	.40
202 Doug Edwards	.15	.40
203 Kenny Gattison	.15	.40
204 Grizzlies Team Logo	.15	.40
205 Antonio Harvey	.15	.40
206 Byron Scott	.20	.50
207 Larry Stewart	.15	.40
208 Chris Gatling	.15	.40
209 Tim Hardaway	.25	.60
210 Donyell Marshall	.15	.40
211 Chris Mullin	.25	.60
212 Carlos Rogers	.15	.40
213 Warriors Team Logo	.15	.40
214 Clifford Rozier	.15	.40
215 Rony Seikaly	.20	.50
216 Latrell Sprewell	.25	.60
217 Terry Dehere	.15	.40
218 Harold Ellis	.15	.40
219 Lamond Murray	.15	.40
220 Bo Outlaw	.15	.40
221 Pooh Richardson	.15	.40
222 Clippers Team Logo	.15	.40
223 Rodney Rogers	.15	.40
224 Malik Sealy	.15	.40
225 Loy Vaught	.15	.40
226 Sam Bowie	.15	.40
227 Elden Campbell	.15	.40
228 Cedric Ceballos	.15	.40
229 Vlade Divac	.25	.60
230 Eddie Jones	.30	.75
231 Lakers Team Logo	.15	.40
232 Anthony Peeler	.15	.40
233 Sedale Threatt	.15	.40
234 Nick Van Exel	.25	.60
235 Charles Barkley	.40	1.00
236 A.C. Green	.25	.60
237 Kevin Johnson	.25	.60
238 Dan Majerle	.25	.60
239 Danny Manning	.20	.50
240 Suns Team Logo	.15	.40
241 Elliot Perry	.15	.40
242 Wesley Person	.15	.40
243 Wayman Tisdale	.15	.40
244 Chris Dudley	.15	.40
245 Harvey Grant	.15	.40
246 Aaron McKie	.15	.40
247 Terry Porter	.15	.40
248 Clifford Robinson	.15	.40
249 Trail Blazers Team Logo	.15	.40
250 Rod Strickland	.15	.40
251 Otis Thorpe	.15	.40
252 Buck Williams	.15	.40
253 Randy Brown	.15	.40
254 Brian Grant	.20	.50
255 Bobby Hurley	.25	.60
256 Olden Polynice	.15	.40
257 Mitch Richmond	.25	.60
258 Kings Team Logo	.15	.40
259 Lionel Simmons	.15	.40
260 Michael Smith	.15	.40
261 Walt Williams	.15	.40
262 Vincent Askew	.15	.40
263 Hersey Hawkins	.15	.40
264 Shawn Kemp	.25	.60
265 Sarunas Marciulionis	.15	.40
266 Nate McMillan	.15	.40
267 Supersonics Team Logo	.15	.40
268 Gary Payton	.25	.60
269 Sam Perkins	.15	.40
270 Detlef Schrempf	.25	.60
271 Chris Gatling LL	.15	.40
272 Popeye Jones LL	.15	.40
273 Steve Kerr LL	.20	.50
274 Karl Malone LL	.30	.75
275 Dikembe Mutombo LL	.25	.60
276 Shaquille O'Neal LL	.60	1.50
277 Scottie Pippen LL	.40	1.00
278 Dennis Rodman LL	.50	1.25
279 John Stockton LL	.30	.75
280 Spud Webb LL	.25	.60
281 Brian Grant ROO	.20	.50
282 Grant Hill ROO	.40	1.00
283 Juwan Howard ROO	.25	.60
284 Eddie Jones ROO	.30	.75
285 Jason Kidd ROO	.40	1.00
286 Eric Montross ROO	.15	.40
287 Wesley Person ROO	.15	.40
288 Glenn Robinson ROO	.25	.60
XX Panini Album	.75	2.00

2009-10 Panini Stickers

COMPLETE SET (384)	30.00	80.00
1 Boston Celtics Logo	.10	.25
2 Kevin Garnett	.30	.75
3 Paul Pierce	.20	.50
4 Rajon Rondo	.20	.50
5 Lester Hudson	.15	.40
6 Ray Allen	.15	.40
7 Kendrick Perkins	.12	.30
8 Eddie House	.10	.25
9 Glen Davis	.12	.30
10 Rasheed Wallace	.15	.40
11 Robert Parish	.15	.40
12 New Jersey Nets Logo	.10	.25
13 Devin Harris	.15	.40
14 Brook Lopez	.15	.40
15 Yi Jianlian	.12	.30
16 Terrence Williams	.15	.40
17 Bobby Simmons	.10	.25
18 New Jersey Nets Records	.10	.25
19 Jarvis Hayes	.10	.25
20 Tony Battie	.10	.25
21 Rafer Alston	.10	.25
22 Courtney Lee	.12	.30
23 New York Knicks Logo	.10	.25
24 Al Harrington	.12	.30
25 Danilo Gallinari	.15	.40
26 Chris Duhon	.10	.25
27 Jordan Hill	.15	.40
28 Wilson Chandler	.12	.30
29 Willis Reed	.15	.40
30 Nate Robinson	.15	.40
31 David Lee	.12	.30
32 Jared Jeffries	.10	.25
33 Darko Milicic	.10	.25
34 Philadelphia 76ers Logo	.10	.25
35 Andre Iguodala	.15	.40
36 Thaddeus Young	.10	.25
37 Samuel Dalembert	.10	.25
38 Jrue Holiday	.30	.75
39 Elton Brand	.15	.40
40 Billy Cunningham	.15	.40
41 Louis Williams	.12	.30
42 Willie Green	.10	.25
43 Jason Kapono	.10	.25
44 Primoz Brezec	.10	.25
45 Toronto Raptors Logo	.10	.25
46 Chris Bosh	.15	.40
47 Andrea Bargnani	.12	.30
48 Jose Calderon	.12	.30
49 DeMar DeRozan	.25	.60
50 Rasho Nesterovic	.10	.25
51 Toronto Raptors Records	.10	.25
52 Marco Belinelli	.10	.25
53 Jarrett Jack	.12	.30
54 Antoine Wright	.10	.25
55 Hedo Turkoglu	.15	.40
56 Chicago Bulls Logo	.10	.25
57 Derrick Rose	.50	1.25
58 Luol Deng	.15	.40
59 John Salmons	.15	.40
60 James Johnson	.15	.40
61 Brad Miller	.12	.30
62 Chicago Bulls Records	.10	.25
63 Joakim Noah	.15	.40
64 Tyrus Thomas	.12	.30
65 Jannero Pargo	.10	.25
66 Kirk Hinrich	.15	.40
67 Cleveland Cavaliers Logo	.10	.25
68 LeBron James	.75	2.00
69 Mo Williams	.12	.30
70 Delonte West	.10	.25
71 Danny Green	.25	.60
72 Daniel Gibson	.12	.30
73 Cleveland Cavaliers Records	.10	.25
74 Anthony Parker	.10	.25
75 Shaquille O'Neal	.30	.75
76 Anderson Varejao	.12	.30
77 Zydrunas Ilgauskas	.10	.25
78 Detroit Pistons Logo	.10	.25
79 Tayshaun Prince	.15	.40
80 Richard Hamilton	.12	.30
81 Rodney Stuckey	.15	.40
82 Austin Daye	.15	.40
83 Ben Gordon	.15	.40
84 Isiah Thomas	.15	.40
85 Will Bynum	.10	.25
86 Kwame Brown	.10	.25
87 Charlie Villanueva	.12	.30
88 Ben Wallace	.15	.40
89 Indiana Pacers Logo	.10	.25
90 Danny Granger	.15	.40
91 Mike Dunleavy	.10	.25
92 T.J. Ford	.10	.25
93 Tyler Hansbrough	.25	.60
94 Jeff Foster	.10	.25
95 Indiana Pacers Records	.10	.25
96 Earl Watson	.10	.25
97 Dahntay Jones	.10	.25
98 Troy Murphy	.10	.25
99 Brandon Rush	.12	.30
100 Milwaukee Bucks Logo	.10	.25
101 Andrew Bogut	.15	.40
102 Michael Redd	.15	.40
103 Francisco Elson	.10	.25
104 Brandon Jennings	.30	.75
105 Charlie Bell	.10	.25
106 Luke Ridnour	.12	.30
107 Luc Mbah A Moute	.10	.25
108 Hakim Warrick	.12	.30
109 Ersan Ilyasova	.12	.30
110 Oscar Robertson	.15	.40
111 Atlanta Hawks Logo	.10	.25
112 Joe Johnson	.15	.40
113 Josh Smith	.15	.40
114 Mike Bibby	.12	.30
115 Jeff Teague	.20	.50
116 Al Horford	.15	.40
117 Bob Pettit	.15	.40
118 Maurice Evans	.10	.25
119 Zaza Pachulia	.10	.25
120 Marvin Williams	.12	.30
121 Jamal Crawford	.12	.30
122 Charlotte Bobcats Logo	.10	.25
123 Boris Diaw	.12	.30
124 Gerald Wallace	.15	.40
125 Raja Bell	.12	.30
126 Gerald Henderson	.15	.40
127 DeSagana Diop	.10	.25
128 Charlotte Bobcats Records	.10	.25
129 D.J. Augustin	.12	.30
130 Vladimir Radmanovic	.10	.25
131 Tyson Chandler	.12	.30
132 Raymond Felton	.12	.30
133 Miami Heat Logo	.10	.25
134 Dwyane Wade	.30	.75
135 Mario Chalmers	.15	.40
136 Michael Beasley	.15	.40
137 Chris Quinn	.10	.25
138 Udonis Haslem	.12	.30
139 Miami Heat Records	.10	.25
140 Daequan Cook	.10	.25
141 Joel Anthony	.15	.40
142 Quentin Richardson	.12	.30
143 Jermaine O'Neal	.15	.40
144 Orlando Magic Logo	.10	.25
145 Dwight Howard	.25	.60
146 Rashard Lewis	.12	.30
147 Jameer Nelson	.12	.30
148 Mickael Pietrus	.10	.25
149 J.J. Redick	.15	.40
150 Orlando Magic Records	.10	.25
151 Anthony Johnson	.10	.25
152 Vince Carter	.20	.50
153 Ryan Anderson	.15	.40
154 Matt Barnes	.10	.25
155 Washington Wizards Logo	.10	.25
156 Antawn Jamison	.15	.40
157 Gilbert Arenas	.15	.40
158 Caron Butler	.15	.40
159 Nick Young	.12	.30
160 Andray Blatche	.10	.25
161 Elvin Hayes	.15	.40
162 Mike James	.10	.25
163 Mike Miller	.15	.40
164 Randy Foye	.10	.25
165 Fabricio Oberto	.10	.25
166 Andre Iguodala MIN	.15	.40
167 Joe Johnson MIN	.15	.40
168 O.J. Mayo MIN	.15	.40
169 Anthony Morrow 3PT	.10	.25
170 Jameer Nelson 3PT	.12	.30
171 Troy Murphy 3PT	.10	.25
172 Chris Paul STEAL	.25	.60
173 Dwyane Wade STEAL	.30	.75
174 Jason Kidd STEAL	.15	.40
175 David Lee DD	.12	.30
176 Dwight Howard DD	.25	.60
177 Chris Paul DD	.25	.60
178 Terry Cummings PTT	.15	.40
179 Blake Griffin PTT	1.00	2.50
180 Walt Frazier PTT	.15	.40
181 Jordan Hill PTT	.15	.40
182 Pau Gasol PTT	.15	.40
183 Marc Gasol PTT	.15	.40
184 Kevin Durant PTT	.50	1.25
185 James Harden PTT	.50	1.25
186 Mitch Richmond PTT	.15	.40
187 Omri Casspi PTT	.15	.40
188 Chris Mullin PTT	.15	.40
189 Stephen Curry PTT	.40	1.00
190 Alvan Adams PTT	.15	.40
191 Taylor Griffin PTT	.15	.40
192 Jose Calderon FT	.12	.30
193 Ray Allen FT	.15	.40
194 Steve Nash FT	.15	.40
195 Dwight Howard BL	.25	.60
196 Chris Andersen BL	.25	.60
197 Marcus Camby BL	.10	.25
198 Chris Paul AST	.25	.60
199 Deron Williams AST	.15	.40
200 Steve Nash AST	.15	.40
201 Dwight Howard REB	.25	.60
202 David Lee REB	.12	.30
203 Troy Murphy REB	.10	.25
204 Denver Nuggets Logo	.10	.25
205 Carmelo Anthony	.20	.50
206 Chauncey Billups	.15	.40
207 J.R. Smith	.15	.40
208 Ty Lawson	.25	.60
209 Nene	.12	.30
210 Denver Nuggets Records	.10	.25
211 Kenyon Martin	.15	.40
212 Arron Afflalo	.10	.25
213 Chris Andersen	.25	.60
214 Joey Graham	.10	.25
215 Minnesota Timberwolves Logo	.10	.25
216 Al Jefferson	.15	.40
217 Ryan Gomes	.10	.25
218 Kevin Love	.25	.60
219 Jonny Flynn UER	.15	.40
Last name incorrectly spelled Flinn		
220 Ryan Hollins	.10	.25
221 Minnesota Timberwolves Records	.10	.25
222 Damien Wilkins	.10	.25
223 Corey Brewer	.10	.25
224 Ramon Sessions	.12	.30
225 Sasha Pavlovic	.10	.25
226 Oklahoma City Thunder Logo	.10	.25
227 Kevin Durant	.50	1.25
228 Jeff Green	.12	.30
229 Russell Westbrook	.25	.60
230 James Harden	.50	1.25
231 Nenad Krstic	.10	.25
232 Oklahoma City Thunder Records	.10	.25
233 Thabo Sefolosha	.12	.30
234 Shaun Livingston	.10	.25
235 Kevin Ollie	.10	.25
236 Kyle Weaver	.10	.25
237 Portland Trail Blazers Logo	.10	.25
238 Brandon Roy	.15	.40
239 LaMarcus Aldridge	.15	.40
240 Travis Outlaw	.12	.30
241 Jeff Pendergraph	.15	.40
242 Steve Blake	.10	.25
243 Bill Walton	.15	.40
244 Rudy Fernandez	.12	.30
245 Greg Oden	.12	.30
246 Joel Przybilla	.10	.25
247 Andre Miller	.12	.30
248 Utah Jazz Logo	.10	.25
249 Deron Williams	.15	.40
250 Carlos Boozer	.15	.40
251 Mehmet Okur	.10	.25
252 Eric Maynor	.15	.40
253 Ronnie Brewer	.12	.30
254 Karl Malone	.20	.50
255 Andrei Kirilenko	.12	.30
256 C.J. Miles	.10	.25
257 Kyle Korver	.12	.30
258 Paul Millsap	.12	.30
259 Golden State Warriors Logo	.10	.25
260 Stephen Jackson	.12	.30
261 Monta Ellis	.15	.40
262 Corey Maggette	.12	.30
263 Stephen Curry	.40	1.00
264 Kelenna Azubuike	.10	.25
265 Rick Barry	.15	.40
266 Andris Biedrins	.10	.25
267 Anthony Morrow	.10	.25
268 Ronny Turiaf	.10	.25
269 C.J. Watson	.10	.25
270 Los Angeles Clippers Logo	.10	.25
271 Eric Gordon	.15	.40
272 Al Thornton	.12	.30
273 Chris Kaman	.12	.30
274 Blake Griffin	1.00	2.50
275 Marcus Camby	.10	.25
276 Los Angeles Clippers Records	.10	.25
277 Rasual Butler	.10	.25
278 Baron Davis	.15	.40
279 Sebastian Telfair	.10	.25
280 Craig Smith	.10	.25
281 Los Angeles Lakers Logo	.10	.25
282 Kobe Bryant	.75	2.00
283 Pau Gasol	.15	.40
284 Andrew Bynum	.20	.50
285 Adam Morrison	.12	.30
286 Lamar Odom	.15	.40
287 Kareem Abdul-Jabbar	.25	.60
288 Derek Fisher	.12	.30
289 Sasha Vujacic	.10	.25
290 Jordan Farmar	.10	.25
291 Ron Artest	.15	.40
292 Phoenix Suns Logo	.10	.25
293 Steve Nash	.15	.40
294 Jason Richardson	.15	.40
295 Amare Stoudemire	.15	.40
296 Earl Clark	.15	.40
297 Leandro Barbosa	.12	.30
298 Phoenix Suns Records	.10	.25
299 Channing Frye	.12	.30
300 Grant Hill	.20	.50
301 Jared Dudley	.10	.25
302 Goran Dragic	.25	.60
303 Sacramento Kings Logo	.10	.25
304 Kevin Martin	.15	.40
305 Andres Nocioni	.10	.25
306 Francisco Garcia	.12	.30
307 Tyreke Evans	.40	1.00
308 Spencer Hawes	.12	.30
309 Sacramento Kings Records	.10	.25
310 Jason Thompson	.10	.25
311 Beno Udrih	.10	.25
312 Sean May	.10	.25
313 Sergio Rodriguez	.10	.25
314 Dallas Mavericks Logo	.10	.25
315 Dirk Nowitzki	.20	.50
316 Jason Kidd	.15	.40
317 Josh Howard	.12	.30
318 Rodrigue Beaubois	.20	.50
319 Jason Terry	.12	.30
320 Dallas Mavericks Records	.10	.25
321 Jose Barea	.20	.50
322 Erick Dampier	.10	.25
323 Shawn Marion	.15	.40
324 Tim Thomas	.10	.25
325 Houston Rockets Logo	.10	.25
326 Yao Ming	.20	.50
327 Tracy McGrady	.15	.40
328 Luis Scola	.12	.30
329 Jermaine Taylor	.15	.40
330 Aaron Brooks	.10	.25
331 Clyde Drexler	.20	.50
332 Shane Battier	.15	.40
333 Carl Landry	.10	.25
334 Kyle Lowry	.12	.30
335 Trevor Ariza	.10	.25
336 Memphis Grizzlies Logo	.10	.25
337 O.J. Mayo	.15	.40
338 Rudy Gay	.15	.40
339 Marc Gasol	.15	.40
340 Hasheem Thabeet	.15	.40
341 Mike Conley Jr.	.12	.30
342 Memphis Grizzlies Records	.10	.25
343 Darrell Arthur	.12	.30
344 Marko Jaric	.10	.25
345 Zach Randolph	.12	.30
346 Steven Hunter	.10	.25
347 New Orleans Hornets Logo	.10	.25
348 Chris Paul	.25	.60
349 David West	.15	.40
350 Peja Stojakovic	.15	.40
351 Darren Collison	.25	.60
352 Ike Diogu	.10	.25
353 New Orleans Hornets Records	.10	.25
354 James Posey	.10	.25
355 Emeka Okafor	.15	.40
356 Hilton Armstrong	.10	.25
357 Devin Brown	.10	.25
358 San Antonio Spurs Logo	.10	.25
359 Tony Parker	.15	.40
360 Tim Duncan	.25	.60
361 Manu Ginobili	.15	.40
362 DeJuan Blair	.20	.50
363 Roger Mason	.10	.25
364 George Gervin	.15	.40
365 Matt Bonner	.10	.25
366 Michael Finley	.15	.40
367 Richard Jefferson	.15	.40
368 Antonio McDyess	.12	.30
369 Kobe Bryant PTS	.75	2.00
370 Dwyane Wade PTS	.30	.75
371 LeBron James PTS	.75	2.00
372 Shaquille O'Neal FG	.30	.75
373 Nene FG	.12	.30
374 Andris Biedrins FG	.10	.25
375 Dwyane Wade SCO	.30	.75
376 LeBron James SCO	.75	2.00
377 Kobe Bryant SCO	.75	2.00
378 LeBron James PRA	.75	2.00
379 Dwyane Wade PRA	.30	.75
380 Chris Paul PRA	.25	.60
381 LeBron James MVP	.75	2.00
382 Kobe Bryant FIN MVP	.75	2.00
383 Jason Terry 6th Man	.12	.30
384 Derrick Rose ROY	.50	1.25

2010-11 Panini Stickers

COMPLETE SET (378)	30.00	80.00
1 NBA Logo	.08	.30
2 2011 All-Star Game Logo	.08	.25
3 2011 Playoffs Logo	.08	.25
4 2011 Finals Logo	.08	.25
5 Western Conference Logo	.08	.25
6 Eastern Conference Logo	.08	.25
7 Boston Celtics Logo	.08	.25
8 Paul Pierce	.20	.50
9 Ray Allen	.15	.40
10 Shaquille O'Neal	.30	.75
11 Rajon Rondo	.20	.50
12 Rasheed Wallace	.15	.40
13 Jermaine O'Neal	.15	.40
14 Nate Robinson	.15	.40
15 Boston Celtics Leaders	.08	.25
16 Glen Davis	.12	.30
17 Kevin Garnett	.30	.75
18 New Jersey Nets Logo	.08	.25
19 Brook Lopez	.15	.40
20 Travis Outlaw	.12	.30
21 Jordan Farmar	.10	.25
22 Devin Harris	.15	.40
23 Anthony Morrow	.10	.25
24 Kris Humphries	.10	.25
25 Troy Murphy	.10	.25
26 Terrence Williams	.10	.25
27 Johan Petro	.10	.25
28 New York Knicks Logo	.08	.25
29 Amare Stoudemire	.15	.40
30 Danilo Gallinari	.15	.40
31 Kelenna Azubuike	.10	.25
32 Wilson Chandler	.12	.30
33 Bill Walker	.10	.25
34 Ronny Turiaf	.10	.25
35 Toney Douglas	.10	.25
36 Raymond Felton	.12	.30
37 Anthony Randolph	.12	.30
38 Philadelphia 76ers Logo	.08	.25
39 Andre Iguodala	.15	.40
40 Louis Williams	.12	.30
41 Thaddeus Young	.10	.25
42 Elton Brand	.15	.40
43 Jodie Meeks	.15	.40
44 Marreese Speights	.10	.25
45 Jrue Holiday	.15	.40
46 Spencer Hawes	.12	.30
47 Andres Nocioni	.10	.25
48 Toronto Raptors Logo	.08	.25
49 Andrea Bargnani	.12	.30
50 Leandro Barbosa	.12	.30
51 Amir Johnson	.10	.25
52 Jarrett Jack	.12	.30
53 Jose Calderon	.12	.30
54 DeMar DeRozan	.15	.40
55 Sonny Weems	.10	.25
56 Julian Wright	.10	.25
57 Marcus Banks	.10	.25
58 Chicago Bulls Logo	.08	.25
59 Derrick Rose	.50	1.25
60 Carlos Boozer	.15	.40
61 Luol Deng	.15	.40
62 Chicago Bulls Leaders	.08	.25
63 Joakim Noah	.15	.40
64 Ronnie Brewer	.12	.30
65 Flip Murray	.10	.25
66 Kyle Korver	.12	.30
67 Jannero Pargo	.10	.25
68 Taj Gibson	.12	.30
69 Cleveland Cavaliers Logo	.08	.25
70 Antawn Jamison	.15	.40
71 J.J. Hickson	.12	.30
72 Mo Williams	.12	.30
73 Jamario Moon	.10	.25
74 Anthony Parker	.10	.25
75 Ryan Hollins	.10	.25
76 Ramon Sessions	.12	.30
77 Cleveland Cavaliers Leaders	.08	.25
78 Daniel Gibson	.12	.30
79 Anderson Varejao	.12	.30
80 Detroit Pistons Logo	.08	.25
81 Richard Hamilton	.12	.30
82 Rodney Stuckey	.15	.40
83 Tayshaun Prince	.15	.40
84 Jonas Jerebko	.10	.25
85 Ben Gordon	.15	.40
86 Chris Wilcox	.10	.25
87 DaJuan Summers	.10	.25
88 Ben Wallace	.15	.40
89 Austin Daye	.10	.25
90 Indiana Pacers Logo	.08	.25
91 Danny Granger	.15	.40
92 Roy Hibbert	.12	.30
93 T.J. Ford	.10	.25
94 Darren Collison	.15	.40
95 Dahntay Jones	.10	.25
96 Brandon Rush	.12	.30
97 A.J. Price	.10	.25
98 Mike Dunleavy	.10	.25
99 Tyler Hansbrough	.15	.40
100 Milwaukee Bucks Logo	.08	.25
101 Brandon Jennings	.15	.40
102 Corey Maggette	.12	.30
103 Andrew Bogut	.15	.40
104 Carlos Delfino	.10	.25
105 John Salmons	.15	.40
106 Drew Gooden	.12	.30
107 Chris Douglas-Roberts	.10	.25
108 Milwaukee Bucks Leaders	.08	.25
109 Luc Mbah a Moute	.10	.25
110 Ersan Ilyasova	.12	.30
111 Atlanta Hawks Logo	.08	.25
112 Joe Johnson	.15	.40
113 Josh Smith	.15	.40
114 Mike Bibby	.12	.30
115 Jamal Crawford	.12	.30
116 Al Horford	.12	.30
117 Maurice Evans	.10	.25
118 Jeff Teague	.12	.30
119 Marvin Williams	.12	.30
120 Zaza Pachulia	.10	.25
121 Charlotte Bobcats Logo	.08	.25
122 Stephen Jackson	.12	.30
123 Gerald Wallace	.15	.40
124 Boris Diaw	.12	.30
125 Charlotte Bobcats Leaders	.08	.25
126 Nazr Mohammed	.10	.25
127 D.J. Augustin	.12	.30
128 Shaun Livingston	.10	.25
129 Erick Dampier	.10	.25
130 Tyrus Thomas	.12	.30
131 Gerald Henderson	.10	.25
132 Miami Heat Logo	.08	.25
133 Dwyane Wade	.30	.75
134 LeBron James	.75	2.00
135 Chris Bosh	.15	.40
136 Udonis Haslem	.12	.30
137 Zydrunas Ilgauskas	.10	.25
138 Mike Miller	.15	.40
139 Carlos Arroyo	.12	.30
140 Mario Chalmers	.15	.40
141 Joel Anthony	.10	.25
142 Orlando Magic Logo	.08	.25
143 Dwight Howard	.25	.60
144 Quentin Richardson	.12	.30
145 Vince Carter	.20	.50
146 Rashard Lewis	.12	.30
147 Jameer Nelson	.12	.30
148 Ryan Anderson	.12	.30
149 J.J. Redick	.15	.40
150 Orlando Magic Leaders	.08	.25
151 Marcin Gortat	.15	.40
152 Mickael Pietrus	.10	.25
153 Washington Wizards Logo	.08	.25
154 Gilbert Arenas	.15	.40
155 Yi Jianlian	.12	.30
156 Andray Blatche	.10	.25
157 Josh Howard	.12	.30
158 Al Thornton	.12	.30
159 Kirk Hinrich	.15	.40
160 Nick Young	.12	.30
161 Fabricio Oberto	.10	.25
162 JaVale McGee	.12	.30
163 Dallas Mavericks Logo	.08	.25
164 Dirk Nowitzki	.20	.50
165 Jason Kidd	.15	.40
166 Caron Butler	.15	.40
167 Jason Terry	.12	.30
168 DeShawn Stevenson	.10	.25
169 Shawn Marion	.15	.40
170 Brendan Haywood	.10	.25
171 Dallas Mavericks Leaders	.08	.25
172 Rodrigue Beaubois	.12	.30
173 Tyson Chandler	.12	.30
174 Houston Rockets Logo	.08	.25
175 Aaron Brooks	.10	.25
176 Kevin Martin	.15	.40
177 Yao Ming	.20	.50
178 Houston Rockets Leaders	.08	.25
179 Shane Battier	.12	.30
180 Kyle Lowry	.12	.30
181 Chase Budinger	.10	.25
182 Chuck Hayes	.10	.25
183 Brad Miller	.12	.30
184 Luis Scola	.12	.30
185 Memphis Grizzlies Logo	.08	.25
186 O.J. Mayo		
187 Mike Conley Jr.		
188 Rudy Gay		
189 Memphis Grizzlies Lo		
190 Zach Randolph		
191 Sam Young		
192 Hasheem Thabeet	.10	
193 Marc Gasol	.15	.40
194 Darrell Arthur	.10	.25
195 Hamed Haddadi	.10	.25
196 New Orleans Hornets Logo	.08	.25
197 Chris Paul	.25	.60
198 Peja Stojakovic	.15	.40
199 Trevor Ariza	.10	.25
200 Emeka Okafor	.15	.40
201 David West	.15	.40
202 Marcus Thornton	.15	.40
203 Aaron Gray	.10	.25
204 Darius Songaila	.10	.25
205 Marco Belinelli	.10	.25
206 San Antonio Spurs Logo	.08	.25
207 Tim Duncan	.25	.60
208 Manu Ginobili	.15	.40
209 Tony Parker	.15	.40
210 San Antonio Spurs Leaders	.08	.25
211 Richard Jefferson	.15	.40
212 DeJuan Blair	.12	.30
213 Matt Bonner	.10	.25
214 Tiago Splitter	.20	.50
215 Antonio McDyess	.12	.30
216 George Hill	.12	.30
217 Denver Nuggets Logo	.08	.25
218 Carmelo Anthony	.20	.50
219 Chauncey Billups	.15	.40
220 Chris Andersen	.15	.40
221 Arron Afflalo	.10	.25
222 Ty Lawson	.15	.40
223 Kenyon Martin	.15	.40
224 Al Harrington	.12	.30
225 Denver Nuggets Leaders	.08	.25
226 J.R. Smith	.15	.40
227 Nene	.12	.30
228 Minnesota Timberwolves Logo	.08	.25
229 Kevin Love	.20	.50
230 Sebastian Telfair	.10	.25
231 Corey Brewer	.10	.25
232 Jonny Flynn	.10	.25
233 Michael Beasley	.15	.40
234 Kosta Koufos	.10	.25
235 Luke Ridnour	.12	.30
236 Martell Webster	.12	.30
237 Darko Milicic	.10	.25
238 Oklahoma City Thunder Logo	.08	.25
239 Kevin Durant	.50	1.25
240 Russell Westbrook	.20	.50
241 Jeff Green	.12	.30
242 James Harden	.20	.50
243 Serge Ibaka	.20	.50
244 Nenad Krstic	.10	.25
245 Nick Collison	.10	.25
246 Oklahoma City Thunder Leaders	.08	.25
247 Eric Maynor	.10	.25
248 Thabo Sefolosha	.12	.30
249 Portland Trail Blazers Logo	.08	.25
250 LaMarcus Aldridge	.15	.40
251 Andre Miller	.12	.30
252 Jerryd Bayless	.10	.25
253 Dante Cunningham	.10	.25
254 Nicolas Batum	.15	.40
255 Marcus Camby	.10	.25
256 Brandon Roy	.15	.40
257 Greg Oden	.12	.30
258 Rudy Fernandez	.12	.30
259 Utah Jazz Logo	.08	.25
260 Deron Williams	.15	.40
261 Al Jefferson	.15	.40
262 Mehmet Okur	.10	.25
263 Utah Jazz Leaders	.08	.25
264 C.J. Miles	.10	.25
265 Andrei Kirilenko	.12	.30
266 Raja Bell	.12	.30
267 Sundiata Gaines	.10	.25
268 Paul Millsap	.12	.30
269 Ronnie Price	.10	.25
270 Golden State Warriors Logo	.08	.25
271 Monta Ellis	.15	.40
272 Stephen Curry	.20	.50
273 Andris Biedrins	.10	.25
274 Golden State Warriors Leaders	.08	.25
275 Dorell Wright	.10	.25
276 Reggie Williams	.20	.50
277 David Lee	.12	.30
278 Charlie Bell	.10	.25
279 Dan Gadzuric	.10	.25
280 Vladimir Radmanovic	.10	.25
281 Los Angeles Clippers Logo	.08	.25
282 Chris Kaman	.12	.30
283 Eric Gordon	.15	.40
284 Baron Davis	.15	.40
285 Rasual Butler	.10	.25
286 Craig Smith	.10	.25
287 Randy Foye	.10	.25
288 Ryan Gomes	.10	.25
289 Brian Cook	.10	.25
290 Blake Griffin	.40	1.00
291 Los Angeles Lakers Logo	.08	.25
292 Kobe Bryant	.75	2.00
293 Ron Artest	.15	.40
294 Pau Gasol	.15	.40
295 Los Angeles Lakers Leaders	.08	.25
296 Derek Fisher	.12	.30
297 Lamar Odom	.15	.40
298 Andrew Bynum	.20	.50
299 Steve Blake	.10	.25
300 Luke Walton	.10	.25
301 Sasha Vujacic	.10	.25
302 Phoenix Suns Logo	.08	.25
303 Steve Nash	.15	.40
304 Goran Dragic	.15	.40
305 Hedo Turkoglu	.15	.40
306 Phoenix Suns Leaders	.08	.25
307 Jared Dudley	.10	.25
308 Channing Frye	.12	.30
309 Grant Hill	.20	.50
310 Jason Richardson	.15	.40
311 Robin Lopez	.10	.25
312 Hakim Warrick	.12	.30
313 Sacramento Kings Logo	.08	.25
314 Tyreke Evans	.20	.50
315 Carl Landry	.10	.25
316 Beno Udrih	.10	.25
317 Jason Thompson	.10	.25
318 Omri Casspi	.10	.25
319 Donte Greene	.10	.25
320 Francisco Garcia	.12	.30
321 Antoine Wright	.10	.25
322 Samuel Dalembert	.10	.25
323 Kobe Bryant 2000	.75	2.00

Kobe Bryant 2000 .75 2.00
325 Kobe Bryant 2001 .75 2.00
326 Kobe Bryant 2001 .75 2.00
327 Kobe Bryant 2002 .75 2.00
328 Kobe Bryant 2002 .75 2.00
329 Kobe Bryant 2004 .75 2.00
330 Kobe Bryant 2008 .75 2.00
331 Kobe Bryant 2009 .75 2.00
332 Kobe Bryant 2009 .75 2.00
333 Kobe Bryant 2010 .75 2.00
334 Kobe Bryant 2010 .75 2.00
335 Kobe Bryant 2010 .75 2.00
336 NBA Europe 2010 .08 .25
337 NBA Europe 2010 .08 .25
338 NBA Europe 2010 .08 .25
339 NBA Europe 2010 .08 .25
340 NBA London 2011 .08 .25
341 Noche Latina 2010 .08 .25
342 Noche Latina 2010 .08 .25
343 NBA Mexico 2010 .08 .25
344 NBA China 2010 .08 .25
345 NBA China 2010 .08 .25
346 NBA China 2010 .08 .25
347 NBA without borders .08 .25
348 NBA without borders .08 .25
349 John Wall .60 1.50
350 Evan Turner .30 .75
351 Derrick Favors .30 .75
352 Wesley Johnson .25 .60
353 DeMarcus Cousins .50 1.25
354 Ekpe Udoh .15 .40
355 Greg Monroe .30 .75
356 Al-Farouq Aminu .15 .40
357 Gordon Hayward .30 .75
358 Paul George .40 1.00
359 Cole Aldrich .15 .40
360 Xavier Henry .20 .50
361 Ed Davis .20 .50
362 Patrick Patterson .25 .60
363 Larry Sanders .15 .40
364 Luke Babbitt .15 .40
365 Eric Bledsoe .25 .60
366 Avery Bradley .30 .75
367 James Anderson .15 .40
368 Craig Brackins .15 .40
369 Elliot Williams .15 .40
370 Trevor Booker .15 .40
371 Damion James .15 .40
372 Dominique Jones .15 .40
373 LeBron James MVP .75 2.00
374 Tyreke Evans ROY .20 .50
375 Jamal Crawford 6th Man .12 .30
376 Kobe Bryant FIN MVP .75 2.00
377 Dwyane Wade AS MVP .30 .75
378 Dwight Howard DEF POY .25 .60

1987-88 Panini Spanish Stickers

The 1987-88 Panini Spanish Supersport Sticker set consists of 161 stickers, each measuring approximately 2 1/8" by 3". The stickers were designed to be placed in an album measuring approximately 9 1/8" by 10 3/4". The sticker fronts display color photos of athletes from several countries and representing various sports. Among the sports represented are Basketball (1-42), Track and Field (43-84), Soccer (85-126), Motor Sports (127-140), Bicyling (141-147), and Tennis (148-161).

COMPLETE SET (161) 200.00 400.00
1 Larry Bird 15.00 40.00
2 Kareem Abdul-Jabbar 10.00 25.00
3 Earvin Magic Johnson 12.00 30.00
4 Michael Jordan 40.00 100.00
5 Isiah Thomas 6.00 15.00
6 Stephen Baeck .20 .50
7 Tony Balogun .20 .50
8 Alexandr Belostenni .20 .50
9 Karl Brown .20 .50
10 Fanis Christodoulou .20 .50
11 Danko Cvjeticanin .20 .50
12 Sandro Dell'Agnello .20 .50
13 Vlade Divac 3.00 8.00
14 Nikos Filippou .20 .50
15 Nikos Gallis 1.25 3.00
16 Valeri Goborov .20 .50
17 Andrea Gracis .20 .50
18 Henning Harnisch .20 .50
19 Colin Irish .20 .50
20 Pertram Koch .20 .50
21 Jens Kujawa .20 .50
22 Rimas Kurtinaitis .75 2.00
23 Bob McAdoo 4.00 10.00
24 Walter Magnifico 8.00 20.00
25 Sharunas Marchulenis 2.00 5.00
26 Sven Meyer .20 .50
27 Igor Miglinieks .20 .50
28 Jacques Monclar .20 .50
29 Frederic Monetti .20 .50
30 Stephane Ostrowski .75 2.00
31 Drazen Petrovic 6.00 15.00
32 Dino Radja 1.50 4.00
33 Zoran Radovic .40 1.00
34 Antonello Riva 1.25 3.00
35 Oscar Schmidt 6.00 15.00
36 Christian Soule .20 .50
37 Titt Sokk .20 .50
38 Francesco Vescovi .20 .50
39 Georges Vestris .20 .50
40 Alexander Volkov 1.25 3.00
41 Stojan Vrankovic 1.25 3.00
42 Panagiotis Yiannakis .20 .50

1988-89 Panini Stickers Spanish

The 1989 (covering the 1988-89 season) Panini Spanish basketball set consists of 292 stickers, each measuring approximately 2" by 2 5/8". The sticker album measures approximately 9" by 12". The fronts display color action player photos enclosed by white borders. The stickers are numbered on the back and arranged alphabetically according to teams within the Atlantic and Central Divisions of the Western Conference, and the Midwest and Pacific Divisions of the Eastern Conference. The set closes with several topical subsets: All Star Game (253-258), East All Stars (259-271), West All Stars (272-284), and 1989 Stars NBA (285-292).

COMPLETE SET (292) 250.00 500.00
1 NBA Official .40 1.00
2 NBA Official .40 1.00
3 Boston Celtics Logo .40 1.00
4 Jimmy Rodgers CO .40 1.00
5 Dennis Johnson 1.25 3.00
6 Brian Shaw .75 2.00
7 Danny Ainge 1.25 3.00
8 Larry Bird 12.50 30.00
9 Kevin McHale 3.00 8.00
10 Robert Parish 1.50 4.00
11 Robert Parish IA .75 2.00
12 Celtics Jersey .40 1.00
13 Charlotte Hornets .40 1.00
14 Dick Harter CO .40 1.00
15 Rex Chapman 2.00 5.00
16 Muggsy Bogues 1.50 4.00
17 Kelly Tripucka .40 1.00
18 Robert Reid .40 1.00
19 Kurt Rambis .75 2.00
20 Dave Hoppen .40 1.00
21 Muggsy Bogues IA .75 2.00
22 Hornets Jersey .40 1.00
23 New Jersey Nets Logo .40 1.00
24 Willis Reed CO .75 2.00
25 John Bagley .40 1.00
26 Dennis Hopson .40 1.00
27 Mike McGee .40 1.00
28 Roy Hinson .40 1.00
29 Buck Williams .75 2.00
30 Joe Barry Carroll .40 1.00
31 Roy Hinson IA .40 1.00
32 Nets Jersey .40 1.00
33 New York Knicks Logo .40 1.00
34 Rick Pitino CO 1.25 3.00
35 Mark Jackson 3.00 8.00
36 Trent Tucker .40 1.00
37 Johnny Newman .40 1.00
38 Gerald Wilkins .40 1.00
39 Charles Oakley .40 1.00
40 Patrick Ewing 5.00 12.00
41 Gerald Wilkins IA .40 1.00
42 Knicks Jersey .40 1.00
43 Philadelphia 76ers .40 1.00
44 Jim Lynam CO .40 1.00
45 Maurice Cheeks 1.25 3.00
46 Hersey Hawkins 1.50 4.00
47 Ron Anderson .40 1.00
48 Charles Barkley 8.00 20.00
49 Cliff Robinson .40 1.00
50 Mike Gminski .75 2.00
51 Hersey Hawkins IA .75 2.00
52 76ers Jersey .40 1.00
53 Washington Bullets .40 1.00
54 Wes Unseld CO .75 2.00
55 Jeff Malone .75 2.00
56 Darrell Walker .40 1.00
57 Bernard King .75 2.00
58 Terry Catledge .40 1.00
59 John Williams .40 1.00
60 Dave Feitl .40 1.00
61 Jeff Malone IA .40 1.00
62 Bullets Jersey .40 1.00
63 Atlanta Hawks Logo .40 1.00
64 Mike Fratello CO .40 1.00
65 Doc Rivers 1.00 2.50
66 Spud Webb 1.00 2.50
67 Reggie Theus .75 2.00
68 Dominique Wilkins 4.00 10.00
69 Kevin Willis .75 2.00
70 Moses Malone 1.50 4.00
71 Reggie Theus IA .40 1.00
72 Hawks Jersey .40 1.00
73 Chicago Bulls Logo .40 1.00
74 Doug Collins CO .75 2.00
75 Craig Hodges .40 1.00
76 Michael Jordan 30.00 80.00
77 Scottie Pippen 12.50 30.00
78 Horace Grant 3.00 8.00
79 Brad Sellers .40 1.00
80 Bill Cartwright .75 2.00
81 Brad Sellers IA .40 1.00
82 Bulls Jersey .40 1.00
83 Cleveland Cavaliers .40 1.00
84 Lenny Wilkens CO .75 2.00
85 Mark Price 1.50 4.00
86 Ron Harper 1.50 4.00
87 Hot Rod Williams .40 1.00
88 Mike Sanders .40 1.00
89 Larry Nance .75 2.00
90 Brad Daugherty .75 2.00
91 Mike Sanders IA .40 1.00
92 Cavaliers Jersey .40 1.00
93 Detroit Pistons Logo .40 1.00
94 Chuck Daly CO 1.25 3.00
95 Isiah Thomas 3.00 8.00
96 Joe Dumars 2.50 6.00
97 Dennis Rodman 8.00 20.00
98 Adrian Dantley 1.25 3.00
99 John Salley .75 2.00
100 Bill Laimbeer 1.25 3.00
101 Dennis Rodman IA 5.00 12.00
102 Pistons Jersey .40 1.00
103 Indiana Pacers Logo .40 1.00
104 Dick Versace CO .60 1.50
105 Vern Fleming .40 1.00
106 Reggie Miller 10.00 25.00
107 Chuck Person .75 2.00
108 Herb Williams .40 1.00
109 Steve Stipanovich .40 1.00
110 Rik Smits 2.00 5.00
111 Chuck Person IA .40 1.00
112 Pacers Jersey .40 1.00
113 Milwaukee Bucks Logo .40 1.00
114 Del Harris CO .40 1.00
115 Sidney Moncrief 1.25 3.00
116 Jay Humphries .40 1.00
117 Paul Pressey .40 1.00
118 Ricky Pierce .75 2.00
119 Terry Cummings .75 2.00
120 Jack Sikma .75 2.00
121 Jay Humphries IA .40 1.00
122 Bucks Jersey .40 1.00
123 Mavericks Logo .40 1.00
124 John MacLeod CO .40 1.00
125 Derek Harper .75 2.00
126 Rolando Blackman 1.00 2.50
127 Detlef Schrempf 1.50 4.00
128 Mark Aguirre .75 2.00
129 Sam Perkins .75 2.00
130 James Donaldson .40 1.00
131 Sam Perkins IA .60 1.50
132 Mavericks Jersey .40 1.00
133 Denver Nuggets Logo .40 1.00
134 Doug Moe CO .40 1.00
135 Walter Davis .75 2.00
136 Michael Adams .40 1.00
137 Fat Lever .75 2.00
138 Alex English 1.25 3.00
139 Wayne Cooper .40 1.00
140 Danny Schayes .40 1.00
141 Fat Lever IA .40 1.00
142 Nuggets Jersey .40 1.00
143 Houston Rockets Logo .40 1.00
144 Don Chaney CO .40 1.00
145 Sleepy Floyd .40 1.00
146 Mike Woodson .40 1.00
147 Purvis Short .40 1.00
148 Buck Johnson .40 1.00
149 Otis Thorpe .75 2.00
150 Hakeem Olajuwon 5.00 12.00
151 Otis Thorpe IA .40 1.00
152 Rockets Jersey .40 1.00
153 Miami Heat Logo .40 1.00
154 Ron Rothstein CO .75 2.00
155 Jon Sundvold .40 1.00
156 Kevin Edwards .40 1.00
157 Grant Long .75 2.00
158 Billy Thompson .75 2.00
159 Dwayne Washington .40 1.00
160 Rony Seikaly 1.25 3.00
161 Rony Seikaly IA .40 1.00
162 Heat Jersey .40 1.00
163 San Antonio Spurs .40 1.00
164 Larry Brown CO 2.00 5.00
165 Johnny Dawkins .75 2.00
166 Alvin Robertson .40 1.00
167 Willie Anderson .40 1.00
168 Albert King .40 1.00
169 Greg Anderson .40 1.00
170 Frank Brickowski .40 1.00
171 Willie Anderson IA .40 1.00
172 Spurs Jersey .40 1.00
173 Utah Jazz Logo .40 1.00
174 Jerry Sloan CO 3.00 8.00
175 John Stockton 8.00 20.00
176 Darrell Griffith .75 2.00
177 Marc Iavaroni .40 1.00
178 Thurl Bailey .40 1.00
179 Karl Malone 8.00 20.00
180 Mark Eaton .75 2.00
181 Thurl Bailey IA .40 1.00
182 Jazz Jersey .40 1.00
183 Golden State Warriors .40 1.00
184 Don Nelson CO .75 2.00
185 Mitch Richmond 6.00 15.00
186 Winston Garland .40 1.00
187 Larry Smith .40 1.00
188 Chris Mullin 2.00 5.00
189 Ralph Sampson .75 2.00
190 Manute Bol .75 2.00
191 Ralph Sampson IA .40 1.00
192 Warriors Jersey .40 1.00
193 Los Angeles Clippers .40 1.00
194 Don Casey CO .40 1.00
195 Gary Grant .40 1.00
196 Quintin Dailey .40 1.00
197 Norm Nixon .75 2.00
198 Ken Norman .40 1.00
199 Danny Manning 1.50 4.00
200 Benoit Benjamin .40 1.00
201 Ken Norman IA .40 1.00
202 Clippers Jersey .40 1.00
203 Los Angeles Lakers .40 1.00
204 Pat Riley CO 1.50 4.00
205 Magic Johnson 8.00 20.00
206 Byron Scott 1.25 3.00
207 James Worthy 2.50 6.00
208 A.C. Green 1.50 4.00
209 Mychal Thompson .75 2.00
210 Kareem Abdul-Jabbar 5.00 12.00
211 Byron Scott IA .75 2.00
212 Lakers Jersey .40 1.00
213 Phoenix Suns Logo .40 1.00
214 Cotton Fitzsimmons CO .75 2.00
215 Kevin Johnson 2.00 5.00
216 Dan Majerle 2.00 5.00
217 Eddie Johnson .40 1.00
218 Armon Gilliam .40 1.00
219 Tom Chambers 1.25 3.00
220 Mark West .40 1.00
221 Kevin Johnson IA .75 2.00
222 Suns Jersey .40 1.00
223 Portland Trail .40 1.00
224 Mike Schuler CO .40 1.00
225 Terry Porter .75 2.00
226 Clyde Drexler 6.00 15.00
227 Jerome Kersey .40 1.00
228 Kiki Vandeweghe 1.25 3.00
229 Steve Johnson .40 1.00
230 Kevin Duckworth .40 1.00
231 Jerome Kersey IA .40 1.00
232 Trail Blazers Jersey .40 1.00
233 Sacramento Kings Logo .40 1.00
234 Jerry Reynolds CO .40 1.00
235 Kenny Smith .75 2.00
236 Rodney McCray .40 1.00
237 Derek Smith .75 2.00
238 Ed Pinckney .40 1.00
239 Jim Petersen .40 1.00
240 LaSalle Thompson .40 1.00
241 Kenny Smith IA .40 1.00
242 Kings Jersey .40 1.00
243 Seattle Supersonics .40 1.00
244 Bernie Bickerstaff CO .40 1.00
245 Nate McMillan .75 2.00
246 Dale Ellis .75 2.00
247 Xavier McDaniel .40 1.00
248 Derrick McKey .40 1.00
249 Michael Cage .40 1.00
250 Alton Lister .40 1.00
251 Xavier McDaniel IA .40 1.00
252 Supersonics Jersey .40 1.00
253 AS Puzzle 1.25 3.00
Patrick Ewing
Hakeem Olajuwon
254 AS Puzzle 1.25 3.00
Karl Malone
255 AS Puzzle .40 1.00
256 AS Puzzle .40 1.00
257 AS Puzzle .40 1.00
Fat Lever
258 AS Puzzle .40 1.00
259 Lenny Wilkens CO AS .75 2.00
260 Isiah Thomas AS 1.50 4.00
261 Michael Jordan AS 10.00 25.00
262 Dominique Wilkins AS 2.50 6.00
263 Charles Barkley AS 3.00 8.00
264 Moses Malone AS .75 2.00
265 Mark Jackson AS 1.25 3.00
266 Mark Price AS .75 2.00
267 Larry Nance AS .75 2.00
268 Terry Cummings AS .75 2.00
269 Kevin McHale AS 1.25 3.00
270 Brad Daugherty AS .40 1.00
271 Patrick Ewing AS 2.00 5.00
272 Pat Riley CO AS 1.00 2.50
273 John Stockton AS 5.00 12.00
274 Dale Ellis AS .40 1.00
275 Alex English AS .75 2.00
276 Karl Malone AS 4.00 10.00
277 Hakeem Olajuwon AS 2.50 6.00
278 Kareem Abdul-Jabbar AS 3.00 8.00
279 Clyde Drexler AS 2.50 6.00
280 Chris Mullin AS 1.25 3.00
281 James Worthy AS 1.50 4.00
282 Tom Chambers AS .75 2.00
283 Kevin Duckworth AS .40 1.00
284 Mark Eaton AS .40 1.00
285 Michael Jordan AW 12.50 30.00
286 Mark Jackson AW 1.25 3.00
287 Charles Barkley AW 3.00 8.00
288 Jack Sikma AW .40 1.00
289 Michael Cage AW .40 1.00
290 Mark Eaton AW .40 1.00
291 John Stockton AW 4.00 10.00
292 Doug Moe CO AW .40 1.00
XX Album 6.00 15.00
Dominique Wilkins
Larry Bird

1989-90 Panini Stickers Spanish

The 1989-90 Panini Spanish Basketball set consists of 272 stickers, each measuring approximately 2 1/8" by 3". The stickers were designed to be placed in an album measuring approximately 9" by 11 7/8". The sticker fronts display color player photos and are arranged according to teams within the Atlantic and Central Divisions of the Eastern Conference, and the Midwest and Pacific Divisions of the Western Conference. The set closes with the topical subset: NBA All Stars (244-267), the NBA logo (268) and four Puzzle Cards (269-272).

COMPLETE SET (272) 125.00 275.00
1 Boston Celtics Logo .40 1.00
2 Dennis Johnson .75 2.00
3 Reggie Lewis .75 2.00
4 Kelvin Upshaw .40 1.00
5 Kevin Gamble .40 1.00
6 Larry Bird 8.00 20.00
7 Ed Pinckney .40 1.00
8 Kevin McHale 1.50 4.00
9 Robert Parish .75 2.00
10 Miami Heat Logo .40 1.00
11 Jon Sundvold .40 1.00
12 Rory Sparrow .40 1.00
13 Dwayne Washington .40 1.00
14 Billy Thompson .40 1.00
15 Grant Long .40 1.00
16 Kevin Edwards .40 1.00
17 Pat Cummings .40 1.00
18 Rony Seikaly .40 1.00
19 New Jersey Nets Logo .40 1.00
20 Dennis Hopson .40 1.00
21 Lester Conner .40 1.00
22 Chris Morris .40 1.00
23 Charles Shackleford .40 1.00
24 Purvis Short .40 1.00
25 Roy Hinson .40 1.00
26 Sam Bowie .60 1.50
27 Joe Barry Carroll .40 1.00
28 New York Knicks Logo .40 1.00
29 Mark Jackson 1.00 2.50
30 Rod Strickland .75 2.00
31 Gerald Wilkins .40 1.00
32 Trent Tucker .40 1.00
33 Johnny Newman .40 1.00
34 Kenny Walker .40 1.00
35 Charles Oakley .60 1.50
36 Patrick Ewing 2.50 6.00
37 Philadelphia 76ers Logo .40 1.00
38 Scott Brooks .40 1.00
39 Johnny Dawkins .40 1.00
40 Hersey Hawkins .75 2.00
41 Derek Smith .75 2.00
42 Ron Anderson .40 1.00
43 Charles Barkley 4.00 10.00
44 Rick Mahorn .40 1.00
45 Mike Gminski .40 1.00
46 Washington Bullets Logo .40 1.00
47 Steve Colter .40 1.00
48 Jeff Malone .40 1.00
49 Ledell Eackles .40 1.00
50 Darrell Walker .40 1.00
51 Bernard King .75 2.00
52 Charles Jones .40 1.00
53 Mark Alarie .40 1.00
54 Harvey Grant .40 1.00
55 Atlanta Hawks Logo .40 1.00
56 Anthony Webb .75 2.00
57 Glenn Rivers .75 2.00
58 John Battle .40 1.00
59 Dominique Wilkins 3.00 8.00
60 Cliff Levingston .40 1.00
61 Jon Koncak .40 1.00
62 Antoine Carr .40 1.00
63 Moses Malone 1.25 3.00
64 Chicago Bulls Logo .75 2.00
65 Craig Hodges .40 1.00
66 John Paxson .75 2.00
67 Michael Jordan 20.00 50.00
68 Scottie Pippen 6.00 15.00
69 Charles Davis .40 1.00
70 Horace Grant 1.00 2.50
71 Will Perdue .40 1.00
72 Bill Cartwright .75 2.00
73 Cleveland Cavaliers Logo .40 1.00
74 Mark Price .75 2.00
75 Craig Ehlo .60 1.50
76 Chris Dudley .40 1.00
77 Randolph Keys .40 1.00
78 Larry Nance .75 2.00
79 John Williams .40 1.00
80 Paul Mokeski .40 1.00
81 Wayne Rollins .40 1.00
82 Pistons .40 1.00
83 Isiah Thomas 2.00 5.00
84 Vinnie Johnson .60 1.50
85 Joe Dumars 1.25 3.00
86 Mark Aguirre .60 1.50
87 Dennis Rodman 4.00 10.00
88 John Salley .75 2.00
89 James Edwards .40 1.00
90 Bill Laimbeer .75 2.00
91 Indiana Pacers Logo .40 1.00
92 Reggie Miller 4.00 10.00
93 Vern Fleming .40 1.00
94 Randy Wittman .40 1.00
95 Chuck Person .40 1.00
96 Mike Sanders .40 1.00
97 Rickey Green .40 1.00
98 Lasalle Thompson .40 1.00
99 Rik Smits .75 2.00
100 Milwaukee Bucks Logo .40 1.00
101 Jay Humphries .40 1.00
102 Ricky Pierce .40 1.00
103 Paul Pressey .40 1.00
104 Alvin Robertson .40 1.00
105 Tony Brown .40 1.00
106 Fred Roberts .40 1.00
107 Randy Breuer .40 1.00
108 Jack Sikma .60 1.50
109 Orlando Magic Logo .40 1.00
110 Sam Vincent .40 1.00
111 Reggie Theus .75 2.00
112 Scott Skiles .75 2.00
113 Otis Smith .40 1.00
114 Sidney Green .40 1.00
115 Nick Anderson 1.25 3.00
116 Terry Catledge .40 1.00
117 Mark Acres .40 1.00
118 Hornets .40 1.00
119 Muggsy Bogues 1.00 2.50
120 Dell Curry .40 1.00
121 Rex Chapman .75 2.00
122 Kelly Tripucka .40 1.00
123 Jerry Sichting .40 1.00
124 Brian Rowsom .40 1.00
125 J.R. Reid .40 1.00
126 Stuart Gray .40 1.00
127 Dallas Mavericks Logo .40 1.00
128 Brad Davis .40 1.00
129 Derek Harper .75 2.00
130 Rolando Blackman .75 2.00
131 Adrian Dantley .75 2.00
132 Herb Williams .40 1.00
133 Bill Wennington .40 1.00
134 Sam Perkins .75 2.00
135 James Donaldson .40 1.00
136 Denver Nuggets Logo .40 1.00
137 Walter Davis .75 2.00
138 Michael Adams .40 1.00
139 Lafayette Lever .40 1.00
140 Alex English .75 2.00
141 Todd Lichti .40 1.00
142 Jerome Lane .40 1.00
143 Tim Kempton .40 1.00
144 Blair Rasmussen .40 1.00
145 Houston Rockets Logo .40 1.00
146 Eric Floyd .40 1.00
147 Mike Woodson .40 1.00
148 Derrick Chievous .40 1.00
149 John Lucas .50 1.25
150 Buck Johnson .40 1.00
151 Otis Thorpe .40 1.00
152 Larry Smith .40 1.00
153 Akeem Olajuwon 4.00 10.00
154 Minnesota T'wolves Logo .40 1.00
155 Pooh Richardson .40 1.00
156 Sidney Lowe .40 1.00
157 Doug West .40 1.00
158 Adrian Branch .75 2.00
159 Tony Campbell .40 1.00
160 David Rivers .40 1.00
161 Steve Johnson .40 1.00
162 Brad Lohaus .40 1.00
163 San Antonio Spurs Logo .40 1.00
164 Maurice Cheeks .75 2.00
165 Vernon Maxwell .40 1.00
166 Zarko Paspalj .40 1.00
167 Sean Elliott 2.00 5.00
168 Terry Cummings .75 2.00
169 Frank Brickowski .40 1.00
170 Willie Anderson .40 1.00
171 David Robinson 10.00 25.00
172 Utah Jazz Logo .40 1.00
173 John Stockton 5.00 12.00
174 Darrell Griffith .60 1.50
175 Bobby Hansen .40 1.00
176 Karl Malone 6.00 15.00
177 Mike Brown .40 1.00
178 Thurl Bailey .40 1.00
179 Eric Leckner .40 1.00
180 Mark Eaton .40 1.00
181 Golden State Warrior Logo .40 1.00
182 Winston Garland .40 1.00
183 Mitch Richmond 1.50 4.00
184 Sarunas Marciulionis .75 2.00
185 Terry Teagle .40 1.00
186 Chris Mullin 1.25 3.00
187 Rod Higgins .40 1.00
188 Uwe Blab .40 1.00
189 Manute Bol .40 1.00
190 Los Angeles Clippers Logo .40 1.00
191 Gary Grant .40 1.00
192 Ron Harper .75 2.00
193 Ken Norman .40 1.00
194 Charles Smith .40 1.00
195 Danny Manning .75 2.00
196 Joe Wolf .40 1.00
197 Benoit Benjamin .40 1.00
198 Ken Bannister .40 1.00
199 Los Angeles Lakers Logo .40 1.00
200 Earvin Johnson 6.00 15.00
201 Byron Scott .75 2.00
202 Michael Cooper .75 2.00
203 Orlando Woolridge .40 1.00
204 James Worthy 1.50 4.00
205 A.C. Green .75 2.00
206 Vlade Divac 2.50 6.00
207 Mychal Thompson .40 1.00
208 Phoenix Suns Logo .40 1.00
209 Kevin Johnson .75 2.00
210 Jeff Hornacek 1.50 4.00
211 Greg Grant .40 1.00
212 Dan Majerle .75 2.00
213 Tim Perry .40 1.00
214 Eddie Johnson .40 1.00
215 Tom Chambers .75 2.00
216 Andrew Lang .40 1.00
217 Portland Trail Blazers Logo .40 1.00
218 Clyde Drexler 4.00 10.00
219 Terry Porter .75 2.00
220 Drazen Petrovic 3.00 8.00
221 Jerome Kersey .40 1.00
222 Mark Bryant .40 1.00
223 Danny Young .40 1.00
224 Wayne Cooper .40 1.00
225 Kevin Duckworth .40 1.00
226 Sacramento Kings Logo .40 1.00
227 Danny Ainge 1.25 3.00
228 Michael Jackson .40 1.00
229 Vinny Del Negro .40 1.00
230 Kenny Smith .75 2.00
231 Harold Pressley .40 1.00
232 Rodney McCray .40 1.00
233 Wayman Tisdale .40 1.00
234 Greg Kite .40 1.00
235 Seattle Supersonics Logo .40 1.00
236 Sedale Threatt .40 1.00
237 Avery Johnson 1.25 3.00
238 Nate McMillan .60 1.50
239 Dale Ellis .40 1.00
240 Xavier McDaniel .40 1.00
241 Derrick McKey .40 1.00
242 Michael Cage .40 1.00
243 Olden Polynice .40 1.00
244 Charles Barkley 3.00 8.00
245 Larry Bird 4.00 10.00
246 Tom Chambers .75 2.00
247 Adrian Dantley .40 1.00
248 Clyde Drexler 2.50 6.00
249 Joe Dumars .75 2.00
250 Dale Ellis .40 1.00
251 Patrick Ewing 1.25 3.00
252 A.C. Green .75 2.00
253 Earvin Johnson 4.00 10.00
254 Michael Jordan 12.50 30.00
255 Bill Laimbeer .75 2.00
256 Jeff Malone .40 1.00
257 Karl Malone 3.00 8.00
258 Moses Malone .75 2.00
259 Xavier McDaniel .40 1.00
260 Akeem Olajuwon 2.50 6.00
261 Robert Parish .75 2.00
262 Mark Price .75 2.00
263 Jack Sikma .40 1.00
264 John Stockton 4.00 10.00
265 Isiah Thomas 1.50 4.00
266 Dominique Wilkins 2.00 5.00
267 James Worthy 1.25 3.00
268 NBA Logo .40 1.00
269 Puzzle Card .40 1.00
270 Puzzle Card .40 1.00
271 Puzzle Card .40 1.00
272 Puzzle Card .40 1.00

1990-91 Panini Stickers Spanish

This 217-card set is comprised of stickers and was distributed throughout Europe.

COMPLETE SET (217) 150.00 300.00
1 NBA Logo .40 1.00
2 Boston Celtics Logo .40 1.00
3 Reggie Lewis .60 1.50
4 Larry Bird 5.00 12.00
5 Michael Smith .40 1.00
6 Kevin McHale 1.50 4.00
7 Joe Kleine .40 1.00
8 Robert Parish 1.25 3.00
9 Miami Heat Logo .40 1.00
10 Sherman Douglas .40 1.00
11 Kevin Edwards .40 1.00
12 Glen Rice 2.00 5.00
13 Billy Thompson 1.25 3.00
14 Tellis Frank .60 1.50
15 Rony Seikaly .40 1.00
16 New Jersey Nets Logo .40 1.00
17 Mookie Blaylock .75 2.00
18 Lester Conner .40 1.00
19 Purvis Short .40 1.00
20 Chris Morris .40 1.00
21 Roy Hinson .40 1.00
22 Sam Bowie .60 1.50
23 New York Knicks Logo .40 1.00
24 Maurice Cheeks .75 2.00
25 Mark Jackson 1.25 3.00
26 Gerald Wilkins .40 1.00
27 Kenny Walker .40 1.00
28 Charles Oakley .40 1.00
29 Patrick Ewing 3.00 8.00
30 Philadelphia 76ers Logo .40 1.00
31 Johnny Dawkins .40 1.00
32 Hersey Hawkins .60 1.50
33 Ron Anderson .40 1.00
34 Charles Barkley 4.00 10.00
35 Rick Mahorn .40 1.00
36 Mike Gminski .40 1.00
37 Washington Bullets Logo .40 1.00
38 Ledell Eackles .40 1.00
39 Darrell Walker .40 1.00
40 Bernard King .75 2.00
41 John Williams .40 1.00
42 Mark Alarie .60 1.50
43 Harvey Grant .40 1.00
44 Atlanta Hawks Logo .40 1.00
45 Anthony Webb .75 2.00
46 Doc Rivers .75 2.00
47 Kenny Smith .75 2.00
48 Dominique Wilkins 3.00 8.00
49 Kevin Willis .75 2.00
50 Moses Malone 1.25 3.00
51 Charlotte Hornets Logo .40 1.00
52 Muggsy Bogues .75 2.00
53 Rex Chapman .75 2.00
54 Dell Curry .75 2.00
55 Kelly Tripucka .40 1.00
56 Armon Gilliam .40 1.00
57 J.R. Reid .40 1.00
58 Chicago Bulls Logo .40 1.00
59 Craig Hodges .40 1.00
60 John Paxson .75 2.00
61 Michael Jordan 20.00 50.00
62 Scottie Pippen 5.00 12.00
63 Horace Grant 1.00 2.50
64 Stacey King .40 1.00
65 Cleveland Cavaliers Logo .40 1.00
66 Mark Price .75 2.00
67 Craig Ehlo .60 1.50
68 Winston Bennett .40 1.00
69 John Williams .40 1.00
70 Larry Nance .75 2.00
71 Brad Daugherty .40 1.00
72 Detroit Pistons Logo .40 1.00
73 Isiah Thomas 3.00 8.00
74 Joe Dumars 2.00 5.00
75 Vinnie Johnson .75 2.00
76 Dennis Rodman 2.50 6.00
77 Bill Laimbeer .75 2.00
78 James Edwards .40 1.00
79 Indiana Pacers Logo .40 1.00
80 Vern Fleming .40 1.00
81 Reggie Miller 4.00 10.00
82 Chuck Person .40 1.00
83 LaSalle Thompson .40 1.00
84 Detlef Schrempf .75 2.00
85 Rik Smits .75 2.00
86 Milwaukee Bucks Logo .40 1.00
87 Alvin Robertson .40 1.00
88 Jay Humphries .40 1.00
89 Ricky Pierce .40 1.00
90 Brad Lohaus .40 1.00
91 Jack Sikma .60 1.50
92 Greg Anderson .40 1.00
93 Dallas Mavericks Logo .40 1.00
94 Derek Harper .75 2.00
95 Rolando Blackman .75 2.00
96 Brad Davis .60 1.50
97 Roy Tarpley .40 1.00
98 Herb Williams .40 1.00
99 James Donaldson .40 1.00
100 Denver Nuggets Logo .40 1.00
101 Michael Adams .40 1.00
102 Walter Davis .75 2.00
103 Todd Lichti .40 1.00
104 Jerome Lane .40 1.00
105 Blair Rasmussen .40 1.00
106 Joe Barry Carroll .40 1.00
107 Houston Rockets Logo .40 1.00
108 Eric Floyd .40 1.00
109 Mitchell Wiggins .40 1.00
110 Vernon Maxwell .40 1.00
111 Otis Thorpe .60 1.50
112 Buck Johnson .40 1.00
113 Hakeem Olajuwon 3.00 8.00
114 Minnesota T-wolves Logo .40 1.00
115 Pooh Richardson .40 1.00
116 Tony Campbell .40 1.00
117 Tyrone Corbin .40 1.00
118 Sam Mitchell .60 1.50
119 Tod Murphy .40 1.00
120 Randy Breuer .40 1.00
121 Orlando Magic Logo .40 1.00
122 Scott Skiles .75 2.00
123 Otis Smith .40 1.00
124 Terry Catledge .40 1.00
125 Jerry Reynolds .40 1.00
126 Nick Anderson .75 2.00
127 Sidney Green .40 1.00
128 San Antonio Spurs Logo .40 1.00
129 Rod Strickland .60 1.50
130 Willie Anderson .40 1.00
131 Sean Elliott 1.00 2.50
132 Terry Cummings .75 2.00
133 Frank Brickowski .40 1.00
134 David Robinson 6.00 15.00
135 Utah Jazz Logo .40 1.00
136 John Stockton 6.00 15.00
137 Darrell Griffith .40 1.00
138 Theodore Edwards .40 1.00
139 Karl Malone 5.00 12.00
140 Thurl Bailey .40 1.00
141 Mark Eaton .40 1.00
142 Golden St. Warriors Logo .40 1.00
143 Tim Hardaway 2.00 5.00
144 Mitch Richmond 1.50 4.00
145 Chris Mullin 1.50 4.00
146 Sarunas Marciulionis .75 2.00
147 Terry Teagle .40 1.00
148 Manute Bol .40 1.00
149 L.A. Clippers Logo .40 1.00
150 Gary Grant .40 1.00
151 Ron Harper .75 2.00
152 Ken Norman .40 1.00
153 Charles Smith .40 1.00
154 Danny Manning .75 2.00
155 Benoit Benjamin .40 1.00
156 L.A. Lakers Logo .40 1.00
157 Magic Johnson 6.00 15.00
158 Byron Scott 1.00 2.50
159 James Worthy 1.50 4.00
160 A.C. Green 1.00 2.50
161 Vlade Divac .75 2.00
162 Mychal Thompson .60 1.50
163 Phoenix Suns Logo .40 1.00
164 Kevin Johnson .75 2.00
165 Jeff Hornacek .75 2.00
166 Dan Majerle .75 2.00
167 Tom Chambers .75 2.00
168 Kurt Rambis .75 2.00
169 Mark West .40 1.00
170 Portland Trailblazers Logo .40 1.00
171 Terry Porter .75 2.00
172 Clyde Drexler 4.00 10.00
173 Jerome Kersey .40 1.00
174 Cliff Robinson 1.25 3.00
175 Buck Williams .75 2.00
176 Kevin Duckworth .40 1.00
177 Sacramento Kings Logo .40 1.00
178 Vinny Del Negro .60 1.50
179 Danny Ainge 1.25 3.00
180 Wayman Tisdale .40 1.00
181 Antoine Carr .40 1.00
182 Greg Kite .40 1.00
183 Ralph Sampson .75 2.00
184 Seattle Sonics Logo .40 1.00
185 Nate McMillan .60 1.50
186 Dale Ellis .60 1.50
187 Xavier McDaniel .60 1.50
188 Shawn Kemp 2.00 5.00
189 Derrick McKey .40 1.00
190 Michael Cage .40 1.00
191 Dennis Rodman AW 1.00 2.50
192 Dennis Rodman AW 1.00 2.50
193 Darrell Walker AW .40 1.00
194 Darrell Walker AW .40 1.00
195 Ricky Pierce AW .40 1.00
196 Ricky Pierce AW .40 1.00
197 Isiah Thomas AW 1.00 2.50
198 Isiah Thomas AW 1.00 2.50
199 David Robinson AW 1.50 4.00
200 David Robinson AW 1.50 4.00
201 Magic Johnson AW 1.50 4.00
202 Magic Johnson AW 1.50 4.00
203 Larry Bird AW 2.00 5.00
204 Larry Bird AW 2.00 5.00
205 Michael Jordan AW 4.00 10.00
206 Michael Jordan AW 4.00 10.00
207 Hakeem Olajuwon AW 1.25 3.00
208 Hakeem Olajuwon AW 1.25 3.00
209 Puzzle Card #1 .40 1.00
210 Puzzle Card #2 .40 1.00
211 Puzzle Card #3 .40 1.00
212 Puzzle Card #4 .40 1.00
213 Puzzle Card #5 .40 1.00
214 Puzzle Card #6 .40 1.00
215 Puzzle Card #7 .40 1.00
216 Puzzle Card #8 .40 1.00
217 Puzzle Card #9 .40 1.00

2011 Panini Team Colors National Convention

TC5 Derrick Rose 2.00 5.00
TC6 Joakim Noah 1.25 3.00

2009-10 Panini Threads

COMP.SET w/o RCs (100) 15.00 30.00
RC STATED PRINT RUN 126 TO 700 SETS
ASTERISK CARDS FROM PANINI UPDATE
1 LeBron James 2.00 5.00
2 Dwyane Wade .75 2.00
3 Chris Paul .60 1.50
4 Kobe Bryant 2.00 5.00
5 Dirk Nowitzki .50 1.25
6 Dwight Howard .60 1.50
7 Al Jefferson .40 1.00

8 Chris Bosh .40 1.00
9 Kevin Durant 1.25 3.00
10 Danny Granger .40 1.00
11 Tim Duncan .60 1.50
12 Antawn Jamison .40 1.00
13 Deron Williams .40 1.00
14 Carmelo Anthony .50 1.25
15 Zach Randolph .30 .75
16 Brandon Roy .40 1.00
17 Stephen Jackson .30 .75
18 Pau Gasol .40 1.00
19 Tony Parker .40 1.00
20 David West .40 1.00
21 Devin Harris .40 1.00
22 Joe Johnson .40 1.00
23 Amare Stoudemire .40 1.00
24 Yao Ming .50 1.25
25 Caron Butler .40 1.00
26 Kevin Martin .40 1.00
27 Vince Carter .50 1.25
28 David Lee .30 .75
29 Andre Iguodala .40 1.00
30 Paul Pierce .50 1.25
31 Carlos Boozer .40 1.00
32 Troy Murphy .25 .60
33 Steve Nash .40 1.00
34 Shaquille O'Neal .75 2.00
35 Al Harrington .30 .75
36 Ben Gordon .40 1.00
37 LaMarcus Aldridge .40 1.00
38 Gilbert Arenas .40 1.00
39 Andre Miller .30 .75
40 Chauncey Billups .40 1.00
41 Gerald Wallace .40 1.00
42 Jamal Crawford .30 .75
43 Michael Redd .40 1.00
44 Derrick Rose 1.25 3.00
45 Monta Ellis .40 1.00
46 Hedo Turkoglu .40 1.00
47 Kevin Garnett .75 2.00
48 Richard Jefferson .40 1.00
49 Mehmet Okur .25 .60
50 Baron Davis .40 1.00
51 Rudy Gay .40 1.00
52 Rashard Lewis .30 .75
53 Corey Maggette .30 .75
54 Richard Hamilton .30 .75
55 John Salmons .40 1.00
56 Ron Artest .40 1.00
57 Jameer Nelson .30 .75
58 Russell Westbrook .60 1.50
59 Allen Iverson .50 1.25
60 O.J. Mayo .40 1.00
61 Rajon Rondo .50 1.25
62 Jason Terry .30 .75
63 Mo Williams .30 .75
64 Josh Smith .40 1.00
65 Jeff Green .30 .75
66 Nate Robinson .40 1.00
67 Andris Biedrins .25 .60
68 Tracy McGrady .40 1.00
69 Raymond Felton .30 .75
70 Josh Howard .30 .75
71 Charlie Villanueva .30 .75
72 Jose Calderon .30 .75
73 Ray Allen .40 1.00
74 Andrew Bogut .40 1.00
75 Emeka Okafor .40 1.00
76 Paul Millsap .30 .75
77 Jason Kidd .40 1.00
78 Elton Brand .40 1.00
79 Nene .30 .75
80 T.J. Ford .25 .60
81 Andrew Bynum .50 1.25
82 Randy Foye .25 .60
83 Manu Ginobili .40 1.00
84 Marcus Camby .25 .60
85 Shawn Marion .40 1.00
86 Al Thornton .30 .75
87 Mike Bibby .30 .75
88 Jason Richardson .40 1.00
89 Al Horford .40 1.00
90 Tayshaun Prince .40 1.00
91 Luis Scola .30 .75
92 Brad Miller .30 .75
93 Boris Diaw .30 .75
94 Brook Lopez .40 1.00
95 Lamar Odom .40 1.00
96 Luol Deng .40 1.00
97 Andrea Bargnani .30 .75
98 Jermaine O'Neal .40 1.00
99 Rasheed Wallace .40 1.00
100 Michael Beasley .40 1.00
101 Blake Griffin/640 AU RC 100.00 200.00
102 Hasheem Thabeet/315 AU RC 6.00 15.00
103 James Harden/660 AU RC 20.00 50.00
104 Tyreke Evans/150 AU RC 40.00 100.00
105 Rodrigue Beaubois/640 AU RC 8.00 20.00
106 Jonny Flynn/625 AU RC 6.00 15.00
107 Stephen Curry/625 AU RC 20.00 50.00
108 Jordan Hill/700 AU RC 6.00 15.00
109 Derrick Brown/150 AU RC 12.50 30.00
110 Brandon Jennings/640 AU RC 20.00 50.00
111 Terrence Williams/160 AU RC 6.00 15.00
112 Gerald Henderson/630 AU RC 6.00 15.00
113 Tyler Hansbrough/650 AU RC 10.00 25.00
114 Earl Clark/625 AU RC 6.00 15.00
115 Austin Daye/700 AU RC 6.00 15.00
116 James Johnson/630 AU RC 6.00 15.00
117 Jrue Holiday/630 AU RC 15.00 40.00
118 Ty Lawson/330 AU RC 10.00 25.00
119 Jeff Teague/660 AU RC 8.00 20.00
120 Eric Maynor/126 AU RC 25.00 60.00
121 Darren Collison/160 AU RC 20.00 50.00
122 Dante Cunningham/650 AU RC 6.00 15.00
123 Omri Casspi/660 AU RC 6.00 15.00
124 B.J. Mullens/630 AU RC 6.00 15.00
125 Taj Gibson/330 AU RC 10.00 25.00
126 DeMarre Carroll/630 AU RC 6.00 15.00
127 Wayne Ellington/630 AU RC 6.00 15.00
128 Toney Douglas/630 AU RC 6.00 15.00
129 Jeff Pendergraph/660 AU RC 6.00 15.00
130 DaJuan Summers/630 AU RC 6.00 15.00
131 Sam Young/365 AU RC 6.00 15.00
132 DeJuan Blair/625 AU RC 8.00 20.00
133 Jodie Meeks/625 AU RC 8.00 20.00
134 Chase Budinger/640 AU RC 6.00 15.00
135 Taylor Griffin/640 AU RC 6.00 15.00
136 DeMar DeRozan/700 RC* 10.00 25.00
137 Jonas Jerebko/700 RC* 6.00 15.00
138 Wesley Matthews/683 RC* 10.00 25.00
139 Marcus Thornton/696 RC* 10.00 25.00
140 Jermaine Taylor/696 RC* 6.00 15.00

2009-10 Panini Threads Century Proof Gold

*GOLD: 1.5X TO 4X BASE HI
STATED PRINT RUN 99 SER.#'d SETS

2009-10 Panini Threads Century Proof Orange

*ORANGE: .5X TO 1.25X BASE HI
RANDOM INSERTS IN RETAIL PACKS

2009-10 Panini Threads Century Proof Platinum

*PLATINUM: 3X TO 8X BASE HI
STATED PRINT RUN 25 SER.#'d SETS

2009-10 Panini Threads Century Proof Silver

*SILVER: .75X TO 2X BASE HI
STATED PRINT RUN 249 SER.#'d SETS

2009-10 Panini Threads ABA Legends

COMPLETE SET (10) 6.00 15.00
RANDOM INSERTS IN PACKS
*PROOF: .75X TO 2X BASE HI
PRINT RUN 100 SER.#'d SETS
1 Dan Issel 1.50 4.00
2 Rick Barry 1.50 4.00
3 Artis Gilmore 1.50 4.00
4 George Gervin 1.50 4.00
5 David Thompson 2.00 5.00
6 Louie Dampier 1.50 4.00
7 Moses Malone 1.50 4.00
8 Connie Hawkins 1.50 4.00
9 George McGinnis 1.50 4.00
10 Billy Cunningham 1.50 4.00

2009-10 Panini Threads ABA Legends Autographs

STATED PRINT RUN 25 SER.#'d SETS
1 Dan Issel 10.00 25.00
2 Rick Barry 15.00 30.00
3 Artis Gilmore 20.00 40.00
4 George Gervin 20.00 40.00
5 David Thompson 15.00 30.00
8 Connie Hawkins 25.00 50.00
9 George McGinnis 8.00 20.00

2009-10 Panini Threads Century Collection Materials

STATED PRINT RUN 100 TO 250 SER.#'d SETS
1 Dwight Howard/250 5.00 12.00
2 Tim Duncan/100 5.00 12.00
3 Kobe Bryant/250 8.00 20.00
4 Tracy McGrady/250 3.00 8.00
6 Mike Bibby/250 2.50 6.00
9 Jason Kidd/250 3.00 8.00
10 LaMarcus Aldridge/250 3.00 8.00
11 Michael Beasley/250 3.00 8.00
12 Andre Iguodala/250 3.00 8.00
13 Elton Brand/250 3.00 8.00
14 LeBron James/100 10.00 25.00
17 Chris Paul/250 5.00 12.00
19 Dwyane Wade/250 6.00 15.00

2009-10 Panini Threads Century Collection Materials Prime

*PRIME: .75X TO 2X BASE HI
STATED PRINT RUN 5 TO 25 SER.#'d SETS
SOME UNPRICED DUE TO SCARCITY
8 Dirk Nowitzki/20 8.00 20.00
15 Amare Stoudemire/25 6.00 15.00
18 Gilbert Arenas/25 6.00 15.00
20 Tony Parker/20 6.00 15.00

2009-10 Panini Threads Century Stars

COMPLETE SET (25) 15.00 30.00
RANDOM INSERTS IN PACKS
*PROOF: .6X TO 1.5X BASE HI
PROOF PRINT RUN 100 SER.#'d SETS
1 Joe Johnson .75 2.00
2 Kevin Garnett 1.50 4.00
3 LeBron James 4.00 10.00
4 Jason Kidd .75 2.00
5 Carmelo Anthony 1.00 2.50
6 Yao Ming 1.00 2.50
7 Baron Davis .75 2.00
8 Kobe Bryant 4.00 10.00
9 Chris Paul 1.25 3.00
10 Kevin Durant 2.50 6.00
11 Vince Carter 1.00 2.50
12 Grant Hill 1.00 2.50
13 Tony Parker .75 2.00
14 Carlos Boozer .75 2.00
15 Antawn Jamison .75 2.00
16 Derrick Rose 2.50 6.00
17 Richard Hamilton .60 1.50
18 Danny Granger .75 2.00
19 Dwyane Wade 1.50 4.00
20 Andrew Bogut .75 2.00
21 Devin Harris .75 2.00
22 Nate Robinson .75 2.00
23 Elton Brand .75 2.00
24 Brandon Roy .75 2.00
25 Chris Bosh .75 2.00

2009-10 Panini Threads Century Stars Autographs

STATED PRINT RUN 10 TO 50 SER.#'d SETS
SOME UNPRICED DUE TO SCARCITY
4 Jason Kidd/25 15.00 40.00
8 Kobe Bryant/50 75.00 150.00
13 Tony Parker/25 15.00 40.00
18 Danny Granger/25 8.00 20.00

2009-10 Panini Threads Century Stars Materials

STATED PRINT RUN 100 TO 250 SER.#'d SETS
2 Kevin Garnett/250 6.00 15.00
3 LeBron James/100 10.00 25.00
4 Jason Kidd/250 3.00 8.00
6 Yao Ming/250 4.00 10.00
8 Kobe Bryant/250 8.00 20.00
9 Chris Paul/250 5.00 12.00
10 Kevin Durant/250 6.00 15.00
14 Carlos Boozer/250 3.00 8.00
19 Dwyane Wade/250 6.00 15.00
20 Andrew Bogut/250 3.00 8.00
22 Nate Robinson/250 3.00 8.00
23 Elton Brand/250 3.00 8.00
25 Chris Bosh/250 3.00 8.00

2009-10 Panini Threads Century Stars Materials Prime

*PRIME: .75X TO 2X BASE HI
STATED PRINT RUN 3 TO 25 SER.#'d SETS
SOME UNPRICED DUE TO SCARCITY
21 Devin Harris/25 6.00 15.00

2009-10 Panini Threads Generations

COMPLETE SET (15) 10.00 25.00
RANDOM INSERTS IN PACKS
*PROOF: 1X TO 2.5X BASE HI
PROOF PRINT RUN 100 SER.#'d SETS
1 Jerry West 4.00 10.00
Kobe Bryant
2 Michael Redd .75 2.00
Oscar Robertson
3 Chris Mullin .75 2.00
Stephen Jackson
4 Carmelo Anthony 1.00 2.50
David Thompson
5 Ben Gordon .75 2.00
Isiah Thomas
6 Kevin Johnson .75 2.00
Steve Nash
7 Jordan Hill .75 2.00
Willis Reed
8 Stephen Curry 2.00 5.00
Tim Hardaway
9 Adrian Dantley .75 2.00
Deron Williams
10 Danny Granger .75 2.00
Jalen Rose
11 Pau Gasol .75 2.00
Vlade Divac
12 Kevin Durant 2.50 6.00
Xavier McDaniel
13 John Havlicek 2.50 6.00
Larry Bird
14 Alex English .75 2.00
Chauncey Billups
15 Connie Hawkins .75 2.00
Ron Artest

2009-10 Panini Threads Generations Autographs

STATED PRINT RUN 25 TO 50 SER.#'d SETS
1 Jerry West/25 150.00 300.00
Kobe Bryant
7 Jordan Hill/50 10.00 25.00
Willis Reed
8 Stephen Curry/50 30.00 80.00
Tim Hardaway

2009-10 Panini Threads Generations Materials

STATED PRINT RUN 100 SER.#'d SETS
UNPRICED PRIME PRINT RUN 10 SER.#'d SETS
1 Jerry West 15.00 30.00
Kobe Bryant
3 Chris Mullin 4.00 10.00
Stephen Jackson

2009-10 Panini Threads Jerseys

STATED PRINT RUN 25 TO 100 SER.#'d SETS
1 LeBron James/100 8.00 20.00
2 Dwyane Wade/100 6.00 15.00
3 Chris Paul/100 5.00 12.00
4 Kobe Bryant/100 8.00 20.00
5 Dirk Nowitzki/100 4.00 10.00
6 Dwight Howard/100 5.00 12.00
8 Chris Bosh/100 3.00 8.00
9 Kevin Durant/100 8.00 20.00
11 Tim Duncan/100 5.00 12.00
13 Deron Williams/100 3.00 8.00
16 Brandon Roy/100 3.00 8.00
17 Stephen Jackson/100 2.50 6.00
18 Pau Gasol/100 3.00 8.00
19 Tony Parker/100 3.00 8.00
20 David West/100 3.00 8.00
24 Yao Ming/100 4.00 10.00
28 David Lee/100 2.50 6.00
29 Andre Iguodala/100 3.00 8.00
30 Paul Pierce/100 4.00 10.00
31 Carlos Boozer/100 3.00 8.00
37 LaMarcus Aldridge/100 3.00 8.00
38 Gilbert Arenas/100 3.00 8.00
41 Gerald Wallace/100 3.00 8.00
44 Derrick Rose/100 8.00 20.00
47 Kevin Garnett/100 6.00 15.00
60 O.J. Mayo/100 3.00 8.00
61 Rajon Rondo/100 4.00 10.00
62 Jason Terry/100 2.50 6.00
66 Nate Robinson/100 3.00 8.00
68 Tracy McGrady/100 3.00 8.00
70 Josh Howard/100 2.50 6.00
72 Jose Calderon/100 2.50 6.00
73 Ray Allen/100 3.00 8.00
74 Andrew Bogut/100 3.00 8.00
76 Paul Millsap/100 2.50 6.00
77 Jason Kidd/100 3.00 8.00
78 Elton Brand/100 3.00 8.00
79 Nene/100 2.50 6.00
81 Andrew Bynum/100 4.00 10.00
83 Manu Ginobili/25 3.00 8.00
87 Mike Bibby/100 2.50 6.00
90 Tayshaun Prince/100 3.00 8.00
97 Andrea Bargnani/100 2.50 6.00
98 Jermaine O'Neal/100 3.00 8.00
100 Michael Beasley/100 3.00 8.00

2009-10 Panini Threads Jerseys Prime

*PRIME: .75X TO 2X BASE HI
STATED PRINT RUNS 5 TO 25 SER.#'d SETS
SOME UNPRICED DUE TO SCARCITY
1 LeBron James/25 20.00 50.00
2 Dwyane Wade/25 15.00 40.00
12 Antawn Jamison/25 6.00 15.00
22 Joe Johnson/25 6.00 15.00
23 Amare Stoudemire/25 6.00 15.00
26 Kevin Martin/20 6.00 15.00
35 Al Harrington/25 5.00 12.00
43 Michael Redd/25 6.00 15.00
49 Mehmet Okur/25 4.00 10.00
52 Rashard Lewis/25 5.00 12.00
64 Josh Smith/25 6.00 15.00

2009-10 Panini Threads Kobe Bryant Letters

STATED PRINT RUN 240 SER.#'d SETS
1 Kobe Bryant 125.00 250.00

2009-10 Panini Threads Legends

COMPLETE SET (15) 8.00 20.00
RANDOM INSERTS IN PACKS
*PROOF: .6X TO 1.5X BASE HI
PROOF PRINT RUN 100 SER.#'d SETS
1 Magic Johnson 3.00 8.00
2 Willis Reed 1.25 3.00
3 Kareem Abdul-Jabbar 2.00 5.00
4 John Havlicek 1.25 3.00
5 Isiah Thomas 1.25 3.00
6 Slick Watts 1.25 3.00
7 David Thompson 1.50 4.00
8 Jerry West 1.50 4.00
9 Danny Ainge 1.25 3.00
10 Alex English 1.25 3.00
11 Hal Greer 1.25 3.00
12 Artis Gilmore 1.25 3.00
13 Walt Frazier 1.25 3.00
14 Chris Mullin 1.25 3.00
15 Tom Heinsohn 1.25 3.00

2009-10 Panini Threads Legends Autographs

STATED PRINT RUN 25 SER.#'d SETS
2 Willis Reed 10.00 25.00
4 John Havlicek 20.00 40.00
7 David Thompson 20.00 40.00
8 Jerry West 25.00 50.00
10 Alex English 10.00 25.00
12 Artis Gilmore 10.00 25.00
13 Walt Frazier 10.00 25.00
14 Chris Mullin 15.00 30.00

2009-10 Panini Threads Legends Materials

STATED PRINT RUN 50 TO 100 SER.#'d SETS
*PRIME: .6X TO 1.5X BASE HI
PRIME PRINT RUN 10 TO 25 SETS
SOME PRIME UNPRICED DUE TO SCARCITY
1 Magic Johnson/100 6.00 15.00
3 Kareem Abdul-Jabbar/100 6.00 15.00
5 Isiah Thomas/100 5.00 12.00
8 Jerry West/50 8.00 20.00
9 Danny Ainge/100 5.00 12.00
10 Alex English/100 5.00 12.00
12 Artis Gilmore/100 5.00 12.00
13 Walt Frazier/50 6.00 15.00
14 Chris Mullin/100 5.00 12.00
15 Tom Heinsohn/100 5.00 12.00

2009-10 Panini Threads Rookie Collection Materials

STATED PRINT RUN 250 SER.#'d SETS
*PRIME: .75X TO 2X BASE HI
PRIME PRINT RUN 25 SER.#'d SETS
1 Blake Griffin 15.00 40.00
2 Hasheem Thabeet 2.50 6.00
3 James Harden 8.00 20.00
4 Tyreke Evans 6.00 15.00
5 Jonny Flynn 2.50 6.00
6 Stephen Curry 6.00 15.00
7 Jordan Hill 2.50 6.00
8 DeMar DeRozan 4.00 10.00
9 Brandon Jennings 5.00 12.00
10 Terrence Williams 2.50 6.00
11 Gerald Henderson 2.50 6.00
12 Tyler Hansbrough 4.00 10.00
13 Earl Clark 2.50 6.00
14 Austin Daye 2.50 6.00
15 James Johnson 2.50 6.00
16 Jrue Holiday 5.00 12.00
17 Ty Lawson 4.00 10.00
18 Jeff Teague 3.00 8.00
19 Eric Maynor 2.50 6.00
20 Darren Collison 4.00 10.00
21 Omri Casspi 2.50 6.00
22 B.J. Mullens 2.50 6.00
23 Rodrigue Beaubois 3.00 8.00
24 Taj Gibson 3.00 8.00
25 DeMarre Carroll 2.50 6.00
26 Wayne Ellington 2.50 6.00
27 Toney Douglas 2.50 6.00
28 Jeff Pendergraph 2.50 6.00
29 DaJuan Summers 2.50 6.00
30 Sam Young 2.50 6.00
31 DeJuan Blair 3.00 8.00
32 Jodie Meeks 3.00 8.00
33 Chase Budinger 2.50 6.00
34 Taylor Griffin 2.50 6.00
35 Jermaine Taylor 2.50 6.00

2009-10 Panini Threads Rookie Collection Materials Signatures

STATED PRINT RUN 50 SER.#'d SETS
1 Blake Griffin 100.00 200.00
2 Hasheem Thabeet 8.00 20.00
4 Tyreke Evans 20.00 50.00
5 Jonny Flynn 8.00 20.00
6 Stephen Curry 20.00 50.00
7 Jordan Hill 8.00 20.00
9 Brandon Jennings 15.00 40.00
10 Terrence Williams 8.00 20.00
11 Gerald Henderson 8.00 20.00
12 Tyler Hansbrough 12.00 30.00
13 Earl Clark 8.00 20.00
14 Austin Daye 8.00 20.00
15 James Johnson 8.00 20.00
16 Jrue Holiday 15.00 40.00
17 Ty Lawson 12.00 30.00
18 Jeff Teague 10.00 25.00
21 Omri Casspi 8.00 20.00
22 B.J. Mullens 8.00 20.00
23 Rodrigue Beaubois 10.00 25.00
25 DeMarre Carroll 8.00 20.00
27 Toney Douglas 8.00 20.00
28 Jeff Pendergraph 8.00 20.00
29 DaJuan Summers 8.00 20.00
30 Sam Young 8.00 20.00
31 DeJuan Blair 10.00 25.00
32 Jodie Meeks 10.00 25.00
33 Chase Budinger 8.00 20.00
34 Taylor Griffin 8.00 20.00
35 Jermaine Taylor 8.00 20.00

2009-10 Panini Threads Rookie Collection Materials Prime Signatures

*PRIME: .5X TO 1.25X HI COLUMN
STATED PRINT RUN 25 SER.#'d SETS
1 Blake Griffin 250.00 500.00
17 Ty Lawson 20.00 50.00

2009-10 Panini Threads Rookie Preview Jerseys

STATED PRINT RUN 100 SER.#'d SETS
INSERTED INTO RETAIL PACKS
1 Blake Griffin 20.00 50.00
2 Hasheem Thabeet 3.00 8.00
3 James Harden 10.00 25.00
4 Tyreke Evans 8.00 20.00
5 Jonny Flynn 3.00 8.00
6 Stephen Curry 8.00 20.00
7 Jordan Hill 3.00 8.00
8 DeMar DeRozan 5.00 12.00
9 Brandon Jennings 6.00 15.00
10 Terrence Williams 3.00 8.00
11 Gerald Henderson 3.00 8.00
12 Tyler Hansbrough 5.00 12.00
13 Earl Clark 3.00 8.00
14 Austin Daye 3.00 8.00
15 James Johnson 3.00 8.00
16 Jrue Holiday 6.00 15.00
17 Ty Lawson 5.00 12.00
18 Jeff Teague 4.00 10.00
19 Eric Maynor 3.00 8.00
20 Darren Collison 5.00 12.00
21 Omri Casspi 3.00 8.00
22 B.J. Mullens 3.00 8.00
23 Rodrigue Beaubois 4.00 10.00
24 Taj Gibson 4.00 10.00
25 DeMarre Carroll 3.00 8.00
26 Wayne Ellington 3.00 8.00
27 Toney Douglas 3.00 8.00
28 Jeff Pendergraph 3.00 8.00
29 DaJuan Summers 3.00 8.00
30 Sam Young 3.00 8.00
31 DeJuan Blair 4.00 10.00
32 Chase Budinger 3.00 8.00
33 Jermaine Taylor 3.00 8.00

2009-10 Panini Threads Rookie Preview Jerseys Autographs

STATED PRINT RUN 50 SER.#'d SETS
INSERTED INTO RETAIL PACKS
1 Blake Griffin 125.00 250.00
2 Hasheem Thabeet 6.00 15.00
4 Tyreke Evans 20.00 50.00
5 Jonny Flynn 6.00 15.00
6 Stephen Curry 20.00 50.00
7 Jordan Hill 6.00 15.00
9 Brandon Jennings 12.00 30.00
10 Terrence Williams 6.00 15.00
11 Gerald Henderson 6.00 15.00
12 Tyler Hansbrough 10.00 25.00
13 Earl Clark 6.00 15.00
14 Austin Daye 6.00 15.00
15 James Johnson 6.00 15.00
16 Jrue Holiday 12.00 30.00
17 Ty Lawson 10.00 25.00
18 Jeff Teague 8.00 20.00
21 Omri Casspi 6.00 15.00
22 B.J. Mullens 6.00 15.00
23 Rodrigue Beaubois 8.00 20.00
25 DeMarre Carroll 6.00 15.00
27 Toney Douglas 6.00 15.00
28 Jeff Pendergraph 6.00 15.00
29 DaJuan Summers 6.00 15.00
30 Sam Young 6.00 15.00
31 DeJuan Blair 8.00 20.00
32 Chase Budinger 6.00 15.00
33 Jermaine Taylor 6.00 15.00

2009-10 Panini Threads Silver Signatures

STATED PRINT RUN 10 TO 99 SER.#'d SETS
SOME UNPRICED DUE TO SCARCITY
4 Kobe Bryant/99 100.00 200.00
5 Dirk Nowitzki/25 40.00 100.00
10 Danny Granger/99 6.00 15.00
19 Tony Parker/50 8.00 20.00
21 Devin Harris/50 6.00 15.00
28 David Lee/50 5.00 12.00
29 Andre Iguodala/50 5.00 12.00
71 Charlie Villanueva/50 5.00 12.00
77 Jason Kidd/25 8.00 20.00
87 Mike Bibby/50 5.00 12.00

2009-10 Panini Threads Team Threads Away

COMPLETE SET (50) 25.00 50.00
HOME VERSION: .4X TO 1X AWAY
1 Joe Johnson 1.00 2.50
2 Mike Bibby .75 2.00
3 Paul Pierce 1.25 3.00
4 Rajon Rondo 1.25 3.00
5 Gerald Wallace 1.00 2.50
6 Joakim Noah 1.00 2.50
7 LeBron James 5.00 12.00
8 Shaquille O'Neal 2.00 5.00
9 Dirk Nowitzki 1.25 3.00
10 Shawn Marion 1.00 2.50
11 Carmelo Anthony 1.25 3.00
12 Ben Gordon 1.00 2.50
13 Richard Hamilton .75 2.00
14 Stephen Jackson .75 2.00
15 Tracy McGrady 1.00 2.50
16 Danny Granger 1.00 2.50
17 Baron Davis 1.00 2.50
18 Marcus Camby .60 1.50
19 Kobe Bryant 5.00 12.00
20 Ron Artest 1.00 2.50
21 O.J. Mayo 1.00 2.50
22 Dwyane Wade 2.00 5.00
23 Jermaine O'Neal 1.00 2.50
24 Andrew Bogut 1.00 2.50
25 Michael Redd 1.00 2.50
26 Kevin Love 1.50 4.00
27 Devin Harris 1.00 2.50
28 Rafer Alston .60 1.50
29 Chris Paul 1.50 4.00
30 Peja Stojakovic 1.00 2.50
31 David Lee .75 2.00
32 Nate Robinson 1.00 2.50
33 Kevin Durant 3.00 8.00
34 Dwight Howard 1.50 4.00
35 Vince Carter 1.25 3.00
36 Andre Iguodala 1.00 2.50
37 Elton Brand 1.00 2.50
38 Amare Stoudemire 1.00 2.50
39 Steve Nash 1.00 2.50
40 Brandon Roy 1.00 2.50
41 LaMarcus Aldridge 1.00 2.50
42 Kevin Martin 1.00 2.50
43 Tim Duncan 1.50 4.00
44 Tony Parker 1.00 2.50
45 Chris Bosh 1.00 2.50
46 Hedo Turkoglu 1.00 2.50
47 Deron Williams 1.00 2.50
48 Carlos Boozer 1.00 2.50
49 Antawn Jamison 1.00 2.50
50 Gilbert Arenas 1.00 2.50

2009-10 Panini Threads Team Threads Away Autographs

STATED PRINT RUN 5 TO 25 SER.#'d SETS
*HOME VERSION: .4X TO 1X AWAY
ASTERISK CARDS FROM PANINI UPDATE
2 Mike Bibby/25 30.00 60.00
4 Rajon Rondo/25 30.00 80.00
16 Danny Granger/25* 20.00 40.00
19 Kobe Bryant/25 125.00 250.00
23 Jermaine O'Neal/25 12.00 30.00
26 Kevin Love/25 25.00 50.00
27 Devin Harris/25 12.00 30.00
36 Andre Iguodala/25 12.00 30.00
37 Elton Brand/25 12.00 30.00
44 Tony Parker/25 30.00 80.00
45 Chris Bosh/25* 20.00 50.00
47 Deron Williams/25* 25.00 60.00
48 Carlos Boozer/25 15.00 40.00

2009-10 Panini Threads Triple Threat

COMPLETE SET 6.00 15.00
RANDOM INSERTS IN PACKS
*PROOF: .6X TO 1.5X BASE HI
PROOF PRINT RUN 100 SER.#'d SETS
1 LeBron James 4.00 10.00
2 Chris Paul 1.25 3.00
3 Jason Kidd .75 2.00
4 Kobe Bryant 4.00 10.00
5 Andre Miller .60 1.50
6 Rajon Rondo 1.00 2.50
7 Pau Gasol .75 2.00
8 Tracy McGrady .75 2.00
9 Dwight Howard 1.25 3.00
10 Russell Westbrook 1.25 3.00

2009-10 Panini Threads Triple Threat Autographs

STATED PRINT RUN 50 SER.#'d SETS
3 Jason Kidd 12.00 30.00
4 Kobe Bryant 100.00 200.00

2009-10 Panini Threads Triple Threat Materials

STATED PRINT RUN 90 TO 100 SER.#'d SETS
1 LeBron James/90 10.00 25.00
2 Chris Paul/100 5.00 12.00
3 Jason Kidd/100 3.00 8.00
4 Kobe Bryant/100 8.00 20.00
6 Rajon Rondo/100 4.00 10.00
7 Pau Gasol/95 3.00 8.00
8 Tracy McGrady/100 3.00 8.00
9 Dwight Howard/100 5.00 12.00

2009-10 Panini Threads Triple Threat Materials Prime

*PRIME: .75X TO 2X BASE HI
STATED PRINT RUN 5 TO 25 SER.#'d SETS
SOME UNPRICED DUE TO SCARCITY
4 Kobe Bryant/25 20.00 50.00

2010-11 Panini Threads

COMP.SET w/o RCs (100) 15.00 30.00
ROOKIE PRINT RUN 399 SER.#'d SETS
EXCH.EXPIRATION 5/24/2012
1 Al-Farouq Aminu AU RC 5.00 12.00
2 Andy Rautins AU RC 5.00 12.00
3 Willie Warren AU RC 5.00 12.00
4 Cole Aldrich AU RC 5.00 12.00
5 Craig Brackins AU RC 5.00 12.00
6 Da'Sean Butler AU RC 5.00 12.00
7 Damion James AU RC 5.00 12.00
8 Daniel Orton AU RC 5.00 12.00
9 DeMarcus Cousins AU RC 15.00 40.00
10 Derrick Favors AU RC 10.00 25.00
11 Devin Ebanks AU RC 6.00 15.00
12 Dexter Pittman AU RC 5.00 12.00
13 Dominique Jones AU RC 5.00 12.00
14 Ed Davis AU RC 6.00 15.00
15 Ekpe Udoh AU RC 5.00 12.00
16 Elliot Williams AU RC 5.00 12.00
17 Eric Bledsoe AU RC 8.00 20.00
18 Evan Turner AU RC 10.00 25.00
19 Gani Lawal AU RC 5.00 12.00
20 Gordon Hayward AU RC 10.00 25.00
21 Greg Monroe AU RC 10.00 25.00
22 Greivis Vasquez AU RC 6.00 15.00
23 Hassan Whiteside AU RC 5.00 12.00
24 James Anderson AU RC 5.00 12.00
25 John Wall AU RC 40.00 100.00
26 Xavier Henry AU RC 6.00 15.00
27 Lance Stephenson AU RC 5.00 12.00
28 Larry Sanders AU RC 5.00 12.00
29 Lazar Hayward AU RC 5.00 12.00
30 Luke Babbitt AU RC 5.00 12.00
31 Luke Harangody AU RC 5.00 12.00
32 Patrick Patterson AU RC 8.00 20.00
33 Paul George AU RC 12.00 30.00
34 Quincy Pondexter AU RC 5.00 12.00
35 Stanley Robinson AU RC 5.00 12.00
36 Keith Gallon AU RC 5.00 12.00
37 Trevor Booker AU RC 5.00 12.00
38 Wesley Johnson AU RC 8.00 20.00
39 Andrew Bogut .40 1.00
40 John Salmons .40 1.00
41 Brandon Jennings .40 1.00
42 Michael Beasley .40 1.00
43 Martell Webster .30 .75
44 Kevin Love .50 1.25
45 Brook Lopez .40 1.00
46 Troy Murphy .25 .60
47 Devin Harris .40 1.00
48 Chris Paul .60 1.50
49 David West .40 1.00
50 Marcus Thornton .40 1.00
51 Amare Stoudemire .40 1.00
52 Anthony Randolph .30 .75
53 Danilo Gallinari .40 1.00
54 Raymond Felton .30 .75
55 Kevin Durant 1.25 3.00
56 Russell Westbrook .50 1.25
57 Jeff Green .30 .75
58 Dwight Howard .60 1.50
59 Vince Carter .50 1.25
60 Rashard Lewis .30 .75
61 J.J. Redick .40 1.00
62 Andre Iguodala .40 1.00
63 Allen Iverson .50 1.25
64 Elton Brand .40 1.00
65 Steve Nash .40 1.00
66 Robin Lopez .25 .60
67 Channing Frye .30 .75
68 LaMarcus Aldridge .40 1.00
69 Brandon Roy .40 1.00
70 Andre Miller .30 .75
71 Greg Oden .30 .75
72 Tyreke Evans .50 1.25
73 Samuel Dalembert .25 .60
74 Carl Landry .25 .60
75 Tim Duncan .60 1.50
76 Tony Parker .40 1.00
77 Manu Ginobili .40 1.00
78 Richard Jefferson .40 1.00
79 Andrea Bargnani .30 .75
80 Jose Calderon .30 .75
81 Leandro Barbosa .30 .75
82 Deron Williams .40 1.00
83 Al Jefferson .40 1.00
84 Paul Millsap .30 .75
85 Al Thornton .30 .75
86 Kirk Hinrich .40 1.00
87 Josh Howard .30 .75
88 Joe Johnson .40 1.00
89 Josh Smith .40 1.00
90 Al Horford .30 .75
91 Jamal Crawford .30 .75
92 Paul Pierce .50 1.25
93 Rajon Rondo .50 1.25
94 Kevin Garnett .75 2.00
95 Shaquille O'Neal .75 2.00
96 Stephen Jackson .30 .75
97 Gerald Wallace .40 1.00
98 Gerald Henderson .25 .60
99 Carlos Boozer .40 1.00
100 Derrick Rose 1.25 3.00
101 Luol Deng .40 1.00
102 Joakim Noah .40 1.00
103 Antawn Jamison .40 1.00
104 Daniel Gibson .30 .75
105 Mo Williams
106 Dirk Nowitzki
107 Jason Kidd
108 Jason Terry
109 Carmelo Anthony
110 Chauncey Billups
111 Al Harrington .30 [illegible]
112 Nene .30 [illegible]
113 Ben Gordon .40 1.00
114 Richard Hamilton .30 .75
115 Tracy McGrady .40 1.00
116 Monta Ellis .40 1.00
117 Stephen Curry .50 1.25
118 David Lee .30 .75
119 Shane Battier .30 .75
120 Kevin Martin .40 1.00
121 Luis Scola .30 .75
122 Yao Ming .50 1.25
123 Danny Granger .40 1.00
124 Mike Dunleavy .25 .60
125 Tyler Hansbrough .40 1.00
126 Baron Davis .40 1.00
127 Eric Gordon .40 1.00
128 Chris Kaman .30 .75
129 Kobe Bryant 2.00 5.00
130 Derek Fisher .30 .75
131 Pau Gasol .40 1.00
132 Lamar Odom .40 1.00
133 Rudy Gay .40 1.00
134 Marc Gasol .40 1.00
135 Zach Randolph .30 .75
136 Chris Bosh .40 1.00
137 Dwyane Wade .75 2.00
138 LeBron James 2.00 5.00

2010-11 Panini Threads Century Proof Gold

*GOLD: 1.5X TO 4X BASE HI
STATED PRINT RUN 99 SER.#'d SETS

2010-11 Panini Threads Century Proof Orange

*ORANGE: 1X TO 2.5X BASE HI
STATED PRINT RUN 199 SER.#'d SETS
INSERTED IN RETAIL PACKS ONLY

2010-11 Panini Threads Century Proof Platinum

*PLATINUM: 3X TO 8X BASE HI
STATED PRINT RUN 25 SER.#'d SETS

2010-11 Panini Threads Century Proof Silver

*SILVER: 1X TO 2.5X BASE HI
STATED PRINT RUN 199 SER.#'d SETS

2010-11 Panini Threads All-Time Big Men

COMPLETE SET (25) 12.50 25.00
RANDOM INSERTS IN PACKS
*PROOF: .75X TO 2X BASE HI
PROOF: STATED PRINT RUN 99 SER.#'d SETS
1 Bill Russell 1.50 4.00
2 Kareem Abdul-Jabbar 1.50 4.00
3 Bill Walton 1.00 2.50
4 Artis Gilmore 1.00 2.50
5 Hakeem Olajuwon 1.25 3.00
6 Patrick Ewing 1.25 3.00
7 Walt Bellamy 1.00 2.50
8 Wes Unseld 1.00 2.50
9 Dolph Schayes 1.00 2.50
10 Elvin Hayes 1.00 2.50
11 Karl Malone 1.25 3.00
12 Wayne Embry 1.00 2.50
13 Alonzo Mourning 1.25 3.00
14 Arnie Risen 1.00 2.50
15 Bill Cartwright 1.00 2.50
16 Bob Lanier 1.00 2.50
17 Clyde Lovellette 1.00 2.50
18 Wilt Chamberlain 2.00 5.00
19 Dave Cowens 1.00 2.50
20 David Robinson 1.50 4.00
21 Moses Malone 1.00 2.50
22 Nate Thurmond 1.00 2.50
23 Mark Eaton 1.00 2.50
24 George Mikan 2.00 5.00
25 Robert Parish 1.00 2.50

2010-11 Panini Threads All-Time Big Men Autographs

STATED PRINT RUN 10 TO 49 SER.#'d SETS
SOME UNPRICED DUE TO SCARCITY
1 Bill Russell/25 50.00 120.00
2 Kareem Abdul-Jabbar/25 35.00 70.00
3 Bill Walton/25 10.00 25.00
4 Artis Gilmore/49 6.00 15.00
5 Hakeem Olajuwon/25 20.00 50.00
7 Walt Bellamy/49 6.00 15.00
8 Wes Unseld/49 6.00 15.00
9 Dolph Schayes/49 6.00 15.00
13 Alonzo Mourning/25 25.00 60.00
14 Arnie Risen/49 6.00 15.00
15 Bill Cartwright/49 6.00 15.00
16 Bob Lanier/25 6.00 15.00
17 Clyde Lovellette/25 6.00 15.00
22 Nate Thurmond/25 10.00 25.00
25 Robert Parish/49 6.00 15.00

2010-11 Panini Threads All-Time Big Men Materials

STATED PRINT RUN 399 SER.#'d SETS
5 Hakeem Olajuwon 4.00 10.00
6 Patrick Ewing 4.00 10.00
11 Karl Malone 4.00 10.00
13 Alonzo Mourning 4.00 10.00
23 Mark Eaton 3.00 8.00

2010-11 Panini Threads All-Time Big Men Materials Prime

*PRIME: .75X TO 2X BASE HI
STATED PRINT RUN 50 SER.#'d SETS
2 Kareem Abdul-Jabbar 12.50 30.00
6 Patrick Ewing 12.50 30.00
11 Karl Malone 10.00 25.00
13 Alonzo Mourning 10.00 25.00
16 Bob Lanier 6.00 15.00
19 Dave Cowens 6.00 15.00
25 Robert Parish 6.00 15.00

2010-11 Panini Threads Century Collection Materials

STATED PRINT RUN 399 SER.#'d SETS
*PRIME: .75X TO 2X BASE HI
PRIME STATED PRINT RUN 50 SER.#'d SETS
1 Ben Gordon 3.00 8.00
2 Yi Jianlian 2.50 6.00
3 Wayne Ellington 2.50 6.00
4 Tyler Hansbrough 3.00 8.00
5 Trevor Ariza 2.00 5.00
6 Thaddeus Young 2.00 5.00
7 Terrence Williams 2.00 5.00
8 Samuel Dalembert 2.00 5.00

Ron Artest 3.00 8.00
10 Rodrigue Beaubois 2.50 6.00
11 Luis Scola 2.50 6.00
12 Josh Howard 2.50 6.00
13 Jonny Flynn 2.00 5.00
14 Joakim Noah 3.00 8.00
15 James Harden 4.00 10.00
16 J.J. Barea 3.00 8.00
17 Elton Brand 3.00 8.00
18 Earl Clark 2.00 5.00
19 DeMarre Carroll 2.50 6.00
20 David West 3.00 8.00
21 Brandon Jennings 3.00 8.00
22 Andre Iguodala 3.00 8.00
23 Stephen Curry 4.00 10.00
24 Michael Redd 3.00 8.00
25 James Johnson 3.00 8.00

2010-11 Panini Threads Century Legends

COMPLETE SET (15) 7.50 15.00
RANDOM INSERTS IN PACKS
*PROOF: .6X TO 1.5X BASE HI
PROOF: STATED PRINT RUN 99 SER.#'d SETS
1 Adrian Dantley 1.25 3.00
2 Bob Dandridge 1.25 3.00
3 Calvin Murphy 1.25 3.00
4 Frank Ramsey 1.25 3.00
5 Gary Payton 1.25 3.00
6 Jerry Lucas 1.25 3.00
7 Jerry Sloan 1.25 3.00
8 Jo Jo White 1.25 3.00
9 Kelly Tripucka 1.25 3.00
10 Robert Horry 1.50 4.00
11 Sam Perkins 1.25 3.00
12 Scottie Pippen 2.50 6.00
13 Spencer Haywood 1.25 3.00
14 Toni Kukoc 1.25 3.00
15 World B. Free 1.25 3.00

2010-11 Panini Threads Century Legends Autographs

STATED PRINT RUN 10 TO 50 SER.#'d SETS
SOME UNPRICED DUE TO SCARCITY
1 Adrian Dantley/25 5.00 12.00
2 Bob Dandridge/50 8.00 20.00
4 Frank Ramsey/50 8.00 20.00
9 Kelly Tripucka/25 8.00 20.00
10 Robert Horry/50 20.00 50.00
14 Toni Kukoc/50 20.00 50.00

2010-11 Panini Threads Century Legends Materials

STATED PRINT RUN 399 SER.#'d SETS
5 Gary Payton 3.00 8.00
11 Sam Perkins 3.00 8.00
12 Scottie Pippen 6.00 15.00
14 Toni Kukoc 3.00 8.00

2010-11 Panini Threads Century Legends Materials Prime

*PRIME: .75X TO 2X BASE HI
STATED PRINT RUN 50 SER.#'d SETS
12 Scottie Pippen 25.00 60.00

2010-11 Panini Threads Century Stars

COMPLETE SET (25) 10.00 20.00
RANDOM INSERTS IN PACKS
*PROOF: .6X TO 1.5X BASE HI
PROOF STATED PRINT RUN 99 SER.#'d SETS
1 Al Jefferson .75 2.00
2 Allen Iverson 1.00 2.50
3 Amare Stoudemire .75 2.00
4 Andrea Bargnani .60 1.50
5 Anthony Randolph .60 1.50
6 Carlos Boozer .75 2.00
7 Caron Butler .75 2.00
8 Chauncey Billups .75 2.00
9 Chris Bosh .75 2.00
10 Chris Kaman .60 1.50
11 Chris Paul 1.25 3.00
12 Derrick Rose 2.50 6.00
13 Dirk Nowitzki 1.00 2.50
14 Dwight Howard 1.25 3.00
15 Dwyane Wade 1.50 4.00
16 Joe Johnson .75 2.00
17 Kevin Durant 2.50 6.00
18 Kevin Garnett 1.50 4.00
19 LeBron James 4.00 10.00
20 Paul Pierce 1.00 2.50
21 Rudy Gay .75 2.00
22 Russell Westbrook 1.00 2.50
23 Shaquille O'Neal 1.50 4.00
24 Steve Nash .75 2.00
25 Tim Duncan 1.25 3.00

2010-11 Panini Threads Century Stars Autographs

STATED PRINT RUN 5 TO 25 SER.#'d SETS
SOME UNPRICED DUE TO SCARCITY
4 Andrea Bargnani/25 5.00 12.00
5 Anthony Randolph/25 5.00 12.00
8 Chauncey Billups/25 5.00 12.00
9 Chris Bosh/25 15.00 40.00
22 Russell Westbrook/25 15.00 40.00

2010-11 Panini Threads Century Stars Materials

STATED PRINT RUN 99 TO 399 SER.#'d SETS
1 Al Jefferson/399 3.00 8.00
2 Allen Iverson/99 4.00 10.00
4 Andrea Bargnani/399 2.50 6.00
6 Carlos Boozer/399 3.00 8.00
7 Caron Butler/399 3.00 8.00
8 Chauncey Billups/399 3.00 8.00
13 Dirk Nowitzki/399 4.00 10.00
14 Dwight Howard/399 5.00 12.00
15 Dwyane Wade/399 6.00 15.00
20 Paul Pierce/399 4.00 10.00
23 Shaquille O'Neal/399 6.00 15.00
25 Tim Duncan/399 5.00 12.00

2010-11 Panini Threads Century Stars Materials Prime

*PRIME: .75X TO 2X BASE HI
STATED PRINT RUN 50 SER.#'d SETS
2 Allen Iverson 10.00 25.00
12 Derrick Rose 20.00 50.00
24 Steve Nash 6.00 15.00

2010-11 Panini Threads Jerseys

STATED PRINT RUN 99 TO 399 SER.#'d SETS
39 Andrew Bogut/299 3.00 8.00
41 Brandon Jennings/399 3.00 8.00
42 Michael Beasley/399 3.00 8.00
44 Kevin Love/399 4.00 10.00
47 Devin Harris/299 3.00 8.00
48 Chris Paul/399 5.00 12.00
49 David West/399 3.00 8.00
52 Anthony Randolph/399 2.50 6.00
54 Raymond Felton/399 2.50 6.00
58 Dwight Howard/399 5.00 12.00
59 Vince Carter/399 4.00 10.00
60 Rashard Lewis/399 2.50 6.00
61 J.J. Redick/399 3.00 8.00
62 Andre Iguodala/399 3.00 8.00
63 Allen Iverson/99 4.00 10.00
64 Elton Brand/399 3.00 8.00
65 Steve Nash/399 3.00 8.00
66 Robin Lopez/399 2.00 5.00
67 Channing Frye/399 2.50 6.00
68 LaMarcus Aldridge/399 3.00 8.00
69 Brandon Roy/399 3.00 8.00
70 Andre Miller/399 2.50 6.00
71 Greg Oden/399 2.50 6.00
73 Samuel Dalembert/399 2.00 5.00
75 Tim Duncan/399 5.00 12.00
76 Tony Parker/399 3.00 8.00
77 Manu Ginobili/399 3.00 8.00
78 Richard Jefferson/399 3.00 8.00
79 Andrea Bargnani/399 2.50 6.00
80 Jose Calderon/399 2.50 6.00
81 Leandro Barbosa/399 2.50 6.00
82 Deron Williams/399 3.00 8.00
83 Al Jefferson/399 3.00 8.00
86 Kirk Hinrich/299 3.00 8.00
90 Al Horford/399 2.50 6.00
92 Paul Pierce/399 4.00 10.00
95 Shaquille O'Neal/399 6.00 15.00
96 Stephen Jackson/399 2.50 6.00
98 Gerald Henderson/349 2.00 5.00
99 Carlos Boozer/399 3.00 8.00
102 Joakim Noah/399 3.00 8.00
103 Antawn Jamison/399 3.00 8.00
106 Dirk Nowitzki/399 4.00 10.00
108 Jason Terry/399 2.50 6.00
110 Chauncey Billups/399 3.00 8.00
112 Nene/399 2.50 6.00
113 Ben Gordon/399 3.00 8.00
115 Tracy McGrady/399 3.00 8.00
117 Stephen Curry/199 4.00 10.00
119 Shane Battier/399 2.50 6.00
120 Kevin Martin/399 3.00 8.00
121 Luis Scola/399 2.50 6.00
124 Mike Dunleavy/99 2.00 5.00
125 Tyler Hansbrough/399 3.00 8.00
129 Kobe Bryant/399 8.00 20.00
130 Derek Fisher/399 2.50 6.00
131 Pau Gasol/399 3.00 8.00
132 Lamar Odom/399 3.00 8.00
137 Dwyane Wade/399 6.00 15.00

2010-11 Panini Threads Jerseys Prime

*PRIME: .75X TO 2X BASE HI
STATED PRINT RUN 25 TO 50 SER.#'d SETS
63 Allen Iverson/50 10.00 25.00
65 Steve Nash/50 8.00 20.00
100 Derrick Rose/50 20.00 50.00

2010-11 Panini Threads Rookie Collection Materials

STATED PRINT RUN 399 SER.#'d SETS
*PRIME: .75X TO 2X BASE HI
PRIME STATED PRINT RUN 50 SER.#'d SETS
1 John Wall 8.00 20.00
2 Evan Turner 4.00 10.00
3 Derrick Favors 4.00 10.00
4 Wesley Johnson 3.00 8.00
5 DeMarcus Cousins 6.00 15.00
6 Ekpe Udoh 2.00 5.00
7 Greg Monroe 4.00 10.00
8 Al-Farouq Aminu 2.00 5.00
9 Gordon Hayward 4.00 10.00
10 Paul George 5.00 12.00
11 Cole Aldrich 2.00 5.00
12 Xavier Henry 2.50 6.00
13 Patrick Patterson 3.00 8.00
14 Larry Sanders 2.00 5.00
15 Luke Babbitt 2.00 5.00
16 Eric Bledsoe 3.00 8.00
17 Avery Bradley 4.00 10.00
18 James Anderson 2.00 5.00
19 Craig Brackins 2.00 5.00
20 Elliot Williams 2.00 5.00
21 Trevor Booker 2.00 5.00
22 Damion James 2.00 5.00
23 Dominique Jones 2.00 5.00
24 Quincy Pondexter 2.00 5.00
25 Jordan Crawford 3.00 8.00
26 Greivis Vasquez 2.50 6.00
27 Daniel Orton 2.00 5.00
28 Lazar Hayward 2.00 5.00
29 Dexter Pittman 2.00 5.00
30 Hassan Whiteside 2.00 5.00
31 Andy Rautins 2.00 5.00
32 Lance Stephenson 2.00 5.00
33 Da'Sean Butler 2.00 5.00
34 Devin Ebanks 2.50 6.00
35 Gani Lawal 2.00 5.00

2010-11 Panini Threads Rookie Collection Materials Signatures

STATED PRINT RUN 50 SER.#'d SETS
*SIG.PRIME: .75X TO 2X HI
SIG.PRIME PRINT RUN 25 SER.#'d SETS
1 John Wall 75.00 150.00
2 Evan Turner 12.00 30.00
3 Derrick Favors 12.00 30.00
4 Wesley Johnson 10.00 25.00
5 DeMarcus Cousins 20.00 50.00
6 Ekpe Udoh 6.00 15.00
7 Greg Monroe 12.00 30.00
8 Al-Farouq Aminu 8.00 20.00
9 Gordon Hayward 12.00 30.00
10 Paul George 15.00 40.00
11 Cole Aldrich 6.00 15.00
12 Xavier Henry 8.00 20.00
13 Patrick Patterson 10.00 25.00
14 Larry Sanders 6.00 15.00
15 Luke Babbitt 6.00 15.00
16 Eric Bledsoe 10.00 25.00
17 Avery Bradley 12.00 30.00
18 James Anderson 6.00 15.00
19 Craig Brackins 6.00 15.00
20 Elliot Williams 6.00 15.00
21 Trevor Booker 6.00 15.00
22 Damion James 6.00 15.00
23 Dominique Jones 6.00 15.00
24 Quincy Pondexter 6.00 15.00
25 Jordan Crawford 10.00 25.00
26 Greivis Vasquez 8.00 20.00
27 Daniel Orton 6.00 15.00
28 Lazar Hayward 6.00 15.00
29 Dexter Pittman 6.00 15.00
30 Hassan Whiteside 6.00 15.00
31 Andy Rautins 6.00 15.00
32 Lance Stephenson 6.00 15.00
33 Da'Sean Butler 6.00 15.00
34 Devin Ebanks 8.00 20.00
35 Gani Lawal 6.00 15.00

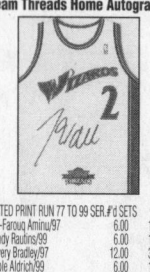

2010-11 Panini Threads Rookie Team Threads Away

COMPLETE SET (40) 20.00 40.00
RANDOM INSERTS IN PACKS
*HOME VERSION: .4X TO 1X BASE HI
HOME VERSION RANDOM INSERTS IN PACKS
1 Al-Farouq Aminu .75 2.00
2 Andy Rautins .75 2.00
3 Avery Bradley 1.50 4.00
4 Cole Aldrich .75 2.00
5 Craig Brackins .75 2.00
6 Darington Hobson .75 2.00
7 Damion James .75 2.00
8 Daniel Orton .75 2.00
9 DeMarcus Cousins 2.50 6.00
10 Derrick Favors 1.50 4.00
11 Brian Zoubek .75 2.00
12 Jeremy Lin 6.00 15.00
13 Dominique Jones .75 2.00
14 Ed Davis 1.00 2.50
15 Ekpe Udoh .75 2.00
16 Elliot Williams .75 2.00
17 Eric Bledsoe 1.25 3.00
18 Evan Turner 1.50 4.00
19 Gani Lawal .75 2.00
20 Gordon Hayward 1.50 4.00
21 Greg Monroe 1.50 4.00
22 Greivis Vasquez 1.00 2.50
23 Hassan Whiteside .75 2.00
24 James Anderson .75 2.00
25 John Wall 3.00 8.00
26 Jordan Crawford 1.25 3.00
27 Lance Stephenson .75 2.00
28 Larry Sanders .75 2.00
29 Lazar Hayward .75 2.00
30 Luke Babbitt .75 2.00
31 Luke Harangody .75 2.00
32 Patrick Patterson 1.25 3.00
33 Paul George 2.00 5.00
34 Quincy Pondexter .75 2.00
35 Stanley Robinson .75 2.00
36 Keith Gallon .75 2.00
37 Trevor Booker .75 2.00
38 Wesley Johnson 1.25 3.00
39 Willie Warren .75 2.00
40 Xavier Henry 1.00 2.50

2010-11 Panini Threads Rookie Team Threads Home Autographs

STATED PRINT RUN 77 TO 99 SER.#'d SETS
1 Al-Farouq Aminu/97 6.00 15.00
2 Andy Rautins/99 6.00 15.00
3 Avery Bradley/97 12.00 30.00
4 Cole Aldrich/99 6.00 15.00
5 Craig Brackins/99 6.00 15.00
6 Darington Hobson/99 6.00 15.00
7 Damion James/99 6.00 15.00
8 Daniel Orton/99 6.00 15.00
9 DeMarcus Cousins/99 20.00 50.00
10 Derrick Favors/99 12.00 30.00
11 Brian Zoubek/99 EXCH 6.00 15.00
12 Jeremy Lin/99 75.00 200.00
13 Dominique Jones/99 6.00 15.00
14 Ed Davis/99 8.00 20.00
15 Ekpe Udoh/99 6.00 15.00
16 Elliot Williams/99 6.00 15.00
17 Eric Bledsoe/99 10.00 25.00
18 Evan Turner/99 12.00 30.00
19 Gani Lawal/99 6.00 15.00
20 Gordon Hayward/99 12.00 30.00
21 Greg Monroe/99 12.00 30.00
22 Greivis Vasquez/99 8.00 20.00
23 Hassan Whiteside/99 6.00 15.00
24 James Anderson/99 6.00 15.00
25 John Wall/99 50.00 125.00
26 Jordan Crawford/99 10.00 25.00
27 Lance Stephenson/99 6.00 15.00
28 Larry Sanders/99 6.00 15.00
29 Lazar Hayward/99 6.00 15.00
30 Luke Babbitt/99 6.00 15.00
31 Luke Harangody/77 6.00 15.00
32 Patrick Patterson/99 10.00 25.00
33 Paul George/99 15.00 40.00
34 Quincy Pondexter/99 6.00 15.00
35 Stanley Robinson/99 EXCH 6.00 15.00
36 Keith Gallon/99 6.00 15.00
37 Trevor Booker/99 6.00 15.00
38 Wesley Johnson/99 10.00 25.00
39 Willie Warren/99 6.00 15.00
40 Xavier Henry/99 8.00 20.00

2010-11 Panini Threads Silver Signatures

STATED PRINT RUN 9 TO 49 SER.#'d SETS
SOME UNPRICED DUE TO SCARCITY
39 Andrew Bogut/24 5.00 12.00
41 Brandon Jennings/24 12.50 30.00
42 Michael Beasley/24 12.50 30.00
44 Kevin Love/24 15.00 40.00
45 Brook Lopez/24 8.00 20.00
47 Devin Harris/24 5.00 12.00
50 Marcus Thornton/49 5.00 12.00
51 Amare Stoudemire/24 12.00 30.00
52 Anthony Randolph/24 8.00 20.00
56 Russell Westbrook/49 12.00 30.00
59 Vince Carter/24 20.00 50.00
61 J.J. Redick/24 10.00 25.00
65 Steve Nash/24 30.00 80.00
66 Robin Lopez/49 4.00 10.00
67 Channing Frye/49 4.00 10.00
68 LaMarcus Aldridge/24 10.00 25.00
69 Brandon Roy/24 10.00 25.00
72 Tyreke Evans/49 10.00 25.00
73 Samuel Dalembert/49 4.00 10.00
74 Carl Landry/49 4.00 10.00
76 Tony Parker/24 6.00 15.00
79 Andrea Bargnani/24 5.00 12.00
82 Deron Williams/24 12.50 30.00
87 Josh Howard/24 4.00 10.00
93 Rajon Rondo/24 12.50 30.00
95 Shaquille O'Neal/24 60.00 120.00
98 Gerald Henderson/49 4.00 10.00
100 Derrick Rose/24 50.00 120.00
101 Luol Deng/24 6.00 15.00
105 Mo Williams/24 5.00 12.00
107 Jason Kidd/24 12.50 30.00
110 Chauncey Billups/24 5.00 12.00
114 Richard Hamilton/24 6.00 15.00
117 Stephen Curry/24 15.00 40.00
125 Tyler Hansbrough/49 5.00 12.00
128 Chris Kaman/24 4.00 10.00
129 Kobe Bryant/24 100.00 200.00
130 Derek Fisher/24 10.00 25.00
131 Pau Gasol/24 20.00 50.00
132 Lamar Odom/24 10.00 25.00
134 Marc Gasol/24 10.00 25.00
135 Zach Randolph/24 5.00 12.00
136 Chris Bosh/24 15.00 40.00

2010-11 Panini Threads Team Threads Away

COMPLETE SET (50) 30.00 60.00
RANDOM INSERTS IN PACKS
*HOME VERSION: .4X TO 1X BASE HI
HOME VERSION RANDOM INSERTS IN PACKS
1 Josh Smith 1.00 2.50
2 Al Horford .75 2.00
3 Shaquille O'Neal 2.00 5.00
4 Kevin Garnett 2.00 5.00
5 Stephen Jackson .75 2.00
6 Derrick Rose 3.00 8.00
7 Carlos Boozer 1.00 2.50
8 Antawn Jamison 1.00 2.50
9 Dirk Nowitzki 1.25 3.00
10 Jason Kidd 1.00 2.50
11 Chauncey Billups 1.00 2.50
12 Chris Andersen 1.00 2.50
13 Tracy McGrady 1.00 2.50
14 Tayshaun Prince 1.00 2.50
15 Monta Ellis 1.00 2.50
16 David Lee .75 2.00
17 Yao Ming 1.25 3.00
18 Kevin Martin 1.00 2.50
19 Darren Collison 1.00 2.50
20 Randy Foye .60 1.50
21 Eric Gordon 1.00 2.50
22 Kobe Bryant 5.00 12.00
23 Pau Gasol 1.00 2.50
24 Marc Gasol 1.00 2.50
25 Zach Randolph .75 2.00
26 LeBron James 5.00 12.00
27 Chris Bosh 1.00 2.50
28 Brandon Jennings 1.00 2.50
29 John Salmons 1.00 2.50
30 Michael Beasley 1.00 2.50
31 Brook Lopez 1.00 2.50
32 Troy Murphy .60 1.50
33 Chris Paul 1.50 4.00
34 David West 1.00 2.50
35 Amare Stoudemire 1.00 2.50
36 Anthony Randolph .75 2.00
37 Kevin Durant 3.00 8.00
38 Russell Westbrook 1.25 3.00
39 Dwight Howard 1.50 4.00
40 Andre Iguodala 1.00 2.50
41 Steve Nash 1.00 2.50
42 Andre Miller .75 2.00
43 Tyreke Evans 1.25 3.00
44 Richard Jefferson 1.00 2.50
45 Andrea Bargnani .75 2.00
46 Leandro Barbosa .75 2.00
47 Deron Williams 1.00 2.50
48 Al Jefferson 1.00 2.50
49 Al Thornton .75 2.00
50 Kirk Hinrich 1.00 2.50

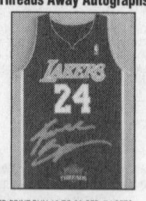

2010-11 Panini Threads Team Threads Away Autographs

STATED PRINT RUN 10 TO 99 SER.#'d SETS
*HOME VERSION: .4X TO 1X BASE HI
HOME PRINT RUN 10 TO 99 SER.#'d SETS
SOME UNPRICED DUE TO SCARCITY
2 Al Horford/49 5.00 12.00
3 Shaquille O'Neal/15 75.00 150.00
10 Jason Kidd/25 12.50 30.00
12 Chris Andersen/25 20.00 50.00
19 Darren Collison/49 5.00 12.00
20 Randy Foye/49 5.00 12.00
22 Kobe Bryant/99 100.00 200.00
24 Marc Gasol/25 12.50 30.00
25 Zach Randolph/49 12.50 30.00
28 Brandon Jennings/49 12.50 30.00
38 Russell Westbrook/49 12.50 30.00
40 Andre Iguodala/25 8.00 20.00
43 Tyreke Evans/49 12.50 30.00
47 Deron Williams/25 15.00 40.00
49 Al Thornton/49 5.00 12.00

2010-11 Panini Threads Triple Threat

COMPLETE SET (10) 7.50 15.00
RANDOM INSERTS IN PACKS
*PROOF: .6X TO 1.5X BASE HI
PROOF STATED PRINT RUN 99 SER.#'d SETS
1 Jason Kidd .75 2.00
2 Deron Williams .75 2.00
3 Andre Iguodala .75 2.00
4 Russell Westbrook 1.00 2.50
5 LeBron James 4.00 10.00
6 Carlos Boozer .75 2.00
7 Rajon Rondo 1.00 2.50
8 Kobe Bryant 4.00 10.00
9 Brandon Roy .75 2.00
10 Steve Nash .75 2.00

2010-11 Panini Threads Triple Threat Autographs

STATED PRINT RUN 5 TO 50 SER.#'d SETS
SOME UNPRICED DUE TO SCARCITY
1 Jason Kidd/15 25.00 60.00
4 Russell Westbrook/50 15.00 40.00
7 Rajon Rondo/15 25.00 60.00
8 Kobe Bryant/50 100.00 200.00
9 Brandon Roy/50 8.00 20.00

2010-11 Panini Threads Triple Threat Materials

STATED PRINT RUN 399 SER.#'d SETS
2 Deron Williams 3.00 8.00
3 Andre Iguodala 3.00 8.00
6 Carlos Boozer 3.00 8.00
8 Kobe Bryant 6.00 15.00
9 Brandon Roy 3.00 8.00

2010-11 Panini Threads Triple Threat Materials Prime

*PRIME: .75X TO 2X BASE HI
STATED PRINT RUN 50 SER.#'d SETS
10 Steve Nash 8.00 20.00

1968-70 Partridge Meats

This black and white (with a little bit of red trim) photo-like card set features players from all three Cincinnati major league sports teams of that time, Cincinnati Reds baseball (BB1-BB18), Cincinnati Bengals football (FB1-FB5), and Cincinnati Royals basketball (BK1-BK2). The cards measure approximately 4" by 5", although there are other sizes sometimes found which are attributable to other years of issue. The cards are blank backed. In addition to the cards listed below, a "Mr. Whopper" card was also issued in honor of an extremely large spokesperson. The Tom Rhoads football card was only recently verified, in 2012, adding to the prevailing thought that these cards were issued over a period of years since its format is slightly different than the other four more well-known football cards in the set.

COMPLETE SET (14) 400.00 800.00
BK1 Adrian Smith 30.00 60.00
BK2 Tom Van Arsdale 30.00 60.00

1977-78 Pepsi All-Stars

This set of eight photos was sponsored by Pepsi. The borderless color player photos measure approximately 8" by 10" and are printed on thick cardboard stock. All the photos depict players either shooting or dunking the ball. The Pepsi logo and the player's name appear in the upper right corner. In blue print the back presents various statistics. The photos are unnumbered and are checklisted below in alphabetical order.

COMPLETE SET (8) 350.00 550.00
1 Rick Barry 15.00 40.00
2 Dave Cowens 15.00 40.00
3 Julius Erving 40.00 75.00
4 Kareem Abdul-Jabbar 40.00 75.00
5 Pete Maravich 150.00 300.00
6 Bob McAdoo 15.00 40.00
7 David Thompson 15.00 40.00
8 Bill Walton 40.00 75.00

1992 Philadelphia Daily News

This nine-card set, which is aptly subtitled "Great Moments in Philadelphia Sports," was sponsored by the Philadelphia Daily News. The fronts of the standard-size cards have red borders and feature miniature reproductions of newspaper front pages with famous headlines and memorable photos. Each card captures a great moment in the history of Philadelphia sports. Sports represented are baseball, (cards 1 and 7-8) hockey, (2) basketball, (3-4) football, (5-6) and boxing (9). The backs are printed in gray, black and white and provide text relating to the event commemorated on the card.

COMPLETE SET (9) 1.40 3.50
3 V .10 .25
Villanova wins NCAA Championship
4 Hoopla .10 .25
Sixers win NBA Championship

1981-82 Philip Morris

This 18-card standard-size set was included in the Champions of American Sport program and features major stars from a variety of sports. The program was issued in conjunction with a traveling exhibition organized by the National Portrait Gallery and the Smithsonian Institution and sponsored by Philip Morris and Miller Brewing Company. The cards are either reproductions of works of art (paintings) or famous photographs of the time. The cards are frequently found with a perforated edge on at least one side. The cards were actually obtained from two perforated pages in the program. There is no notation anywhere on the cards indicating the manufacturer or sponsor.

COMPLETE SET (18) 40.00 100.00
14 Bill Russell 6.00 15.00

1974-75 Picture Buttons

These 11 buttons were issued in 1974, and feature many of the superstar calliber players of the time. Please note that each button was done in full color.

COMPLETE SET (11) 300.00 600.00
1 Kareem Abdul-Jabbar 50.00 100.00
2 Bill Bradley 40.00 80.00
3 Dave DeBusschere 25.00 50.00
4 Walt Frazier 40.00 80.00
5 John Havlicek 50.00 100.00
6 Bob Lanier 25.00 50.00
7 Jerry Lucas 12.50 25.00
8 Pete Maravich 75.00 125.00
9 Willis Reed 40.00 80.00
10 Jerry West 50.00 100.00
11 JoJo White 12.50 25.00

1997 Pinnacle Inside WNBA

The 1997 Pinnacle Inside set was issued in one series totalling 82 cards and honors the first women playing in the WNBA. The set was distributed in cans containing ten cards each with a suggested retail price of $2.99. The fronts feature color action player photos with player information on the backs. The set contains the topical subsets: Hoops Scoops (57-72), and Style & Grace (73-80). Scheduled release date is October, 1997.

COMPLETE SET (81) 12.00 30.00
1 Lisa Leslie RC 2.50 6.00
2 Cynthia Cooper RC 4.00 10.00
3 Rebecca Lobo RC 1.25 3.00
4 Michele Timms RC 1.25 3.00
5 Ruthie Bolton-Holifield RC 1.00 2.50
6 Michelle Edwards RC .40 1.00
7 Vicky Bullett RC .30 .75
8 Tammi Reiss RC .30 .75
9 Penny Toler RC .30 .75
10 Tia Jackson RC .20 .50
11 Rhonda Mapp RC .25 .60
12 Elena Baranova RC .60 1.50
13 Tina Thompson RC 2.50 6.00
14 Merlakia Jones RC .30 .75
15 Tora Suber RC .30 .75
16 Sophia Witherspoon RC .30 .75
17 Tajama Abraham RC .20 .50
18 Jessie Hicks RC .20 .50
19 Tina Nicholson RC .20 .50
20 Tiffany Woosley RC .25 .60
21 Chantel Tremitiere RC .20 .50
22 Daedra Charles RC .20 .50
23 Nancy Lieberman-Cline RC .75 2.00
24 Denique Graves RC .20 .50
25 Toni Foster RC .30 .75
26 Sheryl Swoopes RC 2.50 6.00
27 Kym Hampton RC .30 .75
28 Sharon Manning RC .20 .50
29 Janice Lawrence Braxton RC .20 .50
30 Sue Wicks RC .30 .75
31 Lady Hardmon RC .20 .50
32 Jamila Wideman RC .30 .75
33 Bridgette Gordon RC .20 .50
34 Lynette Woodard RC .50 1.25
35 Kim Perrot RC .75 2.00
36 Teresa Weatherspoon RC 1.50 4.00
37 Andrea Stinson RC .50 1.25
38 Janeth Arcain RC .20 .50
39 Pamela McGee RC .30 .75
40 Tamecka Dixon RC .30 .75
41 Wendy Palmer RC .60 1.50
42 Umeki Webb RC .20 .50
43 Isabelle Fijalkowski RC .20 .50
44 Jennifer Gillom RC .60 1.50
45 Latasha Byears RC .30 .75
46 Haixia Zheng RC .20 .50
47 Kisha Ford RC .20 .50
48 Eva Nemcova RC .40 1.00
49 Penny Moore RC .30 .75
50 Mwadi Mabika RC .20 .50
51 Kim Williams RC .20 .50
52 Wanda Guyton RC .20 .50
53 Vickie Johnson RC .30 .75
54 Deborah Carter RC .20 .50
55 Bridget Pettis RC .20 .50
56 Andrea Congreaves RC .20 .50
57 Haixia Zheng HS .10 .25
58 Tammi Reiss HS .15 .40
59 Jennifer Gillom HS .30 .75
60 Bridgette Gordon HS .10 .25
61 Janice Lawrence Braxton HS .10 .25
62 Cynthia Cooper HS 2.00 5.00
63 Teresa Weatherspoon HS .75 2.00
64 Elena Baranova HS .30 .75
65 Nancy Lieberman-Cline HS .40 1.00
66 Andrea Congreaves HS .10 .25
67 Sophia Witherspoon HS .15 .40
68 Vicky Bullett HS .15 .40
69 Ruthie Bolton-Holifield HS .50 1.25
70 Tina Thompson HS 1.25 3.00
71 Lynette Woodard HS .25 .60
72 Jamila Wideman HS .15 .40
73 Lisa Leslie SG 1.25 3.00
74 Wendy Palmer SG .30 .75
75 Michele Timms SG .60 1.50
76 Ruthie Bolton-Holifield SG .50 1.25
77 Andrea Stinson SG .25 .60
78 Lynette Woodard SG .25 .60
79 Cynthia Cooper SG 2.00 5.00
80 Rebecca Lobo SG .60 1.50
81 Checklist .20 .50

1997 Pinnacle Inside WNBA Court Collection

Randomly inserted in cans at the rate of one in seven, this 82-card set is parallel to the base set and is printed on full silver-foil card stock with bronze foil stamping. To ascertain individual card values, please refer to the multiplier in the header below coupled with the value of the basic card.

COMPLETE SET (81) 40.00 100.00
*COURT: 1.25X TO 3X HI COLUMN

1997 Pinnacle Inside WNBA Executive Collection

Randomly inserted in cans at the rate of one in 47, this 82-card limited production set is parallel to the base set and is printed on prismatic foil with gold foil stamped accents.

*EXEC: 4X TO 10X BASE CARD HI

1997 Pinnacle Inside WNBA Cans

This set of 17 cans feature color action photos of the stars of the league's inaugural season along with their team's logo. Two player cans per team were issued. Each can contained ten cards. A special WNBA can was also distributed. Prices below refer to opened cans.

COMPLETE SET (17) 10.00 25.00
1 Andrea Stinson .50 1.25
2 Vicky Bullett .30 .75
3 Lynette Woodard .50 1.25
4 Michelle Edwards .40 1.00
5 Cynthia Cooper 4.00 10.00
6 Tina Thompson 2.50 6.00
7 Lisa Leslie 2.50 6.00
8 Jamila Wideman .30 .75
9 Teresa Weatherspoon 1.50 4.00
10 Rebecca Lobo 1.25 3.00
11 Michele Timms 1.25 3.00
12 Bridget Pettis .20 .50
13 Bridgette Gordon .20 .50
14 Ruthie Bolton-Holifield 1.00 2.50
15 Wendy Palmer .60 1.50
16 Elena Baranova .60 1.50
17 WNBA League .40 1.00

1997 Pinnacle Inside WNBA My Town

Randomly inserted in cans at the rate of one in 19, this eight-card set features color photos of franchise players printed on a holographic foil card stock with a micro-etched backdrop of the player's team city.

COMPLETE SET (8) 12.00 30.00
1 Lisa Leslie 5.00 12.00
2 Lady Hardmon .40 1.00
3 Michele Timms 2.50 6.00
4 Ruthie Bolton-Holifield 2.00 5.00
5 Andrea Stinson 1.00 2.50
6 Michelle Edwards .75 2.00
7 Cynthia Cooper 8.00 20.00
8 Rebecca Lobo 2.50 6.00

1997 Pinnacle Inside WNBA Team Development

Randomly inserted in cans at the rate of one in 19, this eight-card set features color photos of the WNBA first round draft picks printed on an all-foil card stock with foil stamped treatments.

COMPLETE SET (8) 10.00 25.00
1 Tina Thompson 8.00 20.00
2 Pamela McGee 1.00 2.50
3 Jamila Wideman 1.00 2.50
4 Eva Nemcova 1.25 3.00
5 Tammi Reiss 1.00 2.50
6 Sue Wicks 1.00 2.50
7 Tora Suber 1.00 2.50
8 Toni Foster 1.00 2.50

1998 Pinnacle WNBA

The 1998 Pinnacle WNBA set was issued in one series totalling 85 cards. Each pack came with 10 cards with suggested retail price of $2.49. This was the second year that Pinnacle distributed the only cards for the WNBA. The card fronts carried either an action or posed player shot, and their statistics from the first year of the WNBA.

COMPLETE SET (85) 10.00 25.00
1 Rhonda Blades RC .30 .75
2 Lisa Leslie 1.25 3.00
3 Jennifer Gillom .50 1.25
4 Ruthie Bolton-Holifield .75 2.00
5 Wendy Palmer .50 1.25
6 Sophia Witherspoon .30 .75
7 Eva Nemcova .30 .75
8 Andrea Stinson .50 1.25
9 Heidi Burge RC .30 .75
10 Cynthia Cooper 1.50 4.00
11 Christy Smith RC .30 .75
12 Penny Moore .30 .75
13 Penny Toler .30 .75
14 Bridget Pettis .20 .50

Tora Suber .30 .75
Elena Baranova .50 1.25
Rebecca Lobo .75 2.00
Isabelle Fijalkowski .20 .50
Vicky Bullett .30 .75
Tina Thompson .75 2.00
Andrea Kuklova RC .30 .75
Rita Williams RC .40 1.00
Tamecka Dixon .30 .75
Michele Timms .75 2.00
Bridgette Gordon .20 .50
Tammi Reiss .30 .75
Kym Hampton .30 .75
Janice Braxton .20 .50
Rhonda Mapp .25 .60
Janeth Arcain .20 .50
Lynette Woodard .50 1.25
Tammy Jackson RC .30 .75
Haixia Zheng .20 .50
Toni Foster .30 .75
Chantel Tremitiere .20 .50
Vickie Johnson .30 .75
Michelle Edwards .40 1.00
Wanda Guyton .20 .50
Kim Perrot .60 1.50
Sheryl Swoopes 1.25 3.00
Merlakia Jones .30 .75
Teresa Weatherspoon .75 2.00
Kim Williams .20 .50
Lady Hardmon .20 .50
Latasha Byears .30 .75
Umeki Webb .20 .50
Pamela McGee .30 .75
Nikki McCray RC 1.25 3.00
Cindy Brown RC .75 2.00
Tiffany Woosley .25 .60
Andrea Congreaves .20 .50
Jamila Wideman .30 .75
Mwadi Mabika .20 .50
Murriel Page RC .50 1.25
Mikiko Hagiwara RC .30 .75
Linda Burgess RC .30 .75
Olympia Scott RC .30 .75
Dena Head RC .30 .75
Quacy Barnes RC .30 .75
Suzie McConnell-Serio RC 1.00 2.50
Trena Trice RC .30 .75
Rushia Brown RC .30 .75
Kisha Ford .20 .50
Sharon Manning .20 .50
Tangela Smith RC .30 .75
Jim Lewis CO .20 .50
Nancy Lieberman-Cline CO .75 2.00
Van Chancellor CO .30 .75
Denise Taylor CO .30 .75
Heidi VanDerveer CO .30 .75
Marynell Meadors CO .20 .50
Linda Hill-MacDonald CO .20 .50
Nancy Darsch CO .30 .75
Cheryl Miller CO 1.25 3.00
Julie Rousseau CO .30 .75
Rebecca Lobo P .40 1.00
Jennifer Gillom P .25 .60
Janeth Arcain P .10 .25
Rhonda Mapp P .12 .30
Cynthia Cooper P .75 2.00
Tina Thompson P .40 1.00
Kym Hampton P .15 .40
Cynthia Cooper P .75 2.00
Checklist .20 .50
Checklist .20 .50
6 Sheryl Swoopes PROMO .75 2.00

1998 Pinnacle WNBA Court Collection

ndomly inserted in packs at a rate of one in three, s 85-card set parallels the basic set. The cards ature gold foil, rather than the common silver and atures the title "Court Collection" above the player's ame. The cards are also produced on silver foil. To certain values on individual cards, please refer to the ultiplier in the header, coupled with the value of the ase card.

COURT: 1.25X TO 3X BASE CARD HI

1998 Pinnacle WNBA Arena Collection

andomly inserted in packs at a rate of one in 19, this 5-card set parallels the basic set. The cards feature old foil, rather than the common silver and features e title "Arena Collection" above the player's name. e cards are also produced on a silver sparkle foil. To certain values on individual cards, please refer to the ultiplier in the header, coupled with the value of the ase card.

ARENA: 4X TO 10X BASE CARD HI

1998 Pinnacle WNBA Coast to Coast

andomly inserted in packs at a rate of one in 9, this 0-card set features players who can take it from one nd of the court to another. The card fronts feature a layer photo against silver foil with "Coast 2 Coast" unning along the bottom of the card. The card backs eature commentary.

OMPLETE SET (10) 10.00 25.00
Lynette Woodard 1.00 2.50
Nikki McCray 2.50 6.00
Lisa Leslie 2.50 6.00
Andrea Stinson 1.00 2.50
Eva Nemcova .60 1.50
Cynthia Cooper 3.00 8.00
Teresa Weatherspoon 1.50 4.00
Wendy Palmer 1.00 2.50
Ruthie Bolton-Holifield 1.50 4.00
0 Michele Timms 1.50 4.00

1998 Pinnacle WNBA Number Ones

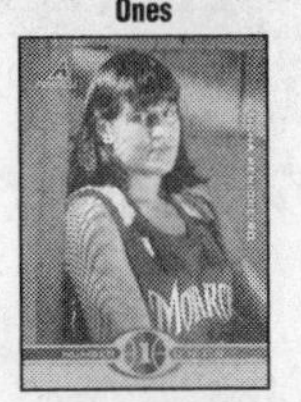

Randomly inserted into packs at a rate of one in 19, this 9-card set features number one draft picks. The card fronts are on silver foil with "Number 1 Ones" across the bottom. Card backs feature a black and white background of the card front with a brief commentary on the player.

COMPLETE SET (9) 8.00 20.00
1 Malgorzata Dydek 2.50 6.00
2 Ticha Penicheiro 3.00 8.00
3 Murriel Page 1.50 4.00
4 Korie Hlede 2.00 5.00
5 Allison Feaster 1.50 4.00
6 Cindy Blodgett 2.00 5.00
7 Tracy Reid 1.25 3.00
8 Alicia Thompson 1.00 2.50
9 Nyree Roberts 1.00 2.50

1998 Pinnacle WNBA Planet Pinnacle

Randomly inserted into packs at a rate of one in 9, this 10-card set features international players. The card fronts feature a posed player shot in a black and red "swirl" against silver foil. Card backs contain a facial shot with commentary.

COMPLETE SET (10) 12.00 30.00
1 Korie Hlede 2.50 6.00
2 Eva Nemcova 1.25 3.00
3 Haixia Zheng .75 2.00
4 Michele Timms 3.00 8.00
5 Ticha Penicheiro 4.00 10.00
6 Elena Baranova 2.00 5.00
7 Rebecca Lobo 3.00 8.00
8 Isabelle Fijalkowski .75 2.00
9 Andrea Congreaves .75 2.00
10 Sheryl Swoopes 5.00 12.00

1968-69 Pipers Minnesota Team Issue

Each of these team-issued photos measure approximately 4 1/4" by 5 1/2" and feature black and white player portraits. The player's name is listed below the photo. The backs are blank. The photos are unnumbered and listed below alphabetically.

COMPLETE SET (10) 35.00 75.00
1 Frank Card 2.00 5.00
2 Connie Hawkins 15.00 40.00
3 Art Heyman 3.00 8.00
4 Arvesta Kelly 2.50 6.00
5 Mike Lewis 2.50 6.00
6 George Sutor 2.00 5.00
7 Steve Vacendak 2.00 5.00
8 Chico Vaughn 2.00 5.00
9 Tom Washington 3.00 8.00
10 Charlie Williams 3.00 8.00

1990-91 Pistons Star

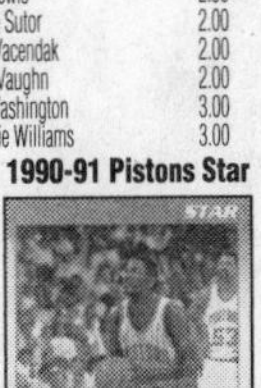

This 14-card standard-size set was produced by Star Company and sponsored by Home Respiratory Health Care, Inc., and the HRHC logo adorns the top of each card back. The front features a color action photo of the player, on a royal blue background that washes out in the middle of the card. In white lettering the player's name, team, and position appear below the picture. In blue lettering the back presents biographical and statistical information in a horizontal format.

COMPLETE SET (14) 1.50 4.00
1 Mark Aguirre .20 .50
2 William Bedford .08 .25
3 Joe Dumars .40 1.00
4 James Edwards .08 .25
5 David Greenwood .08 .25
6 Scott Hastings .08 .25
7 Gerald Henderson .08 .25
8 Vinnie Johnson .20 .50
9 Bill Laimbeer .40 1.00
10 Dennis Rodman .60 1.50
11 John Salley .08 .25
12 Isiah Thomas .40 1.00
13 Chuck Daly CO .20 .50
14 Maia A. Porche PRES .08 .25

1977-78 Pistons Team Issue

These blank-backed black and white photos, which measure 8" by 10" feature members of the 1977-78 Detroit Pistons. Since these photos are unnumbered, we have sequenced them in alphabetical order.

COMPLETE SET (11) 20.00 35.00
1 Roger Brown 1.25 3.00
2 M.L. Carr 3.00 8.00
3 Leon Douglas 1.25 3.00
4 Al Eberhard 1.25 3.00
5 Chris Ford 2.50 6.00
6 Larry Jones 1.25 3.00
7 Al Menendez 1.25 3.00
8 Eric Money 1.25 3.00
9 Willie Norwood 1.25 3.00
10 Howard Porter 1.50 4.00
11 Ralph Simpson 1.50 4.00

1978-79 Pistons Team Issue

These 8" by 10" blank-backed black and white photos feature members of the 1978-79 Detroit Pistons. Since these photos are unnumbered, we have sequenced them in alphabetical order.

COMPLETE SET (13) 20.00 35.00
1 M.L. Carr 1.00 2.50
2 Leon Douglas .75 2.00
3 Chris Ford 1.50 4.00
4 Gus Gerard .75 2.00
5 Bubbles Hawkins .75 2.00
6 Bob Lanier 3.00 8.00
7 John Long .75 2.00
8 Ben Poquette .75 2.00
9 Kevin Porter 1.00 2.50
10 Terry Tyler .75 2.00
11 Dick Vitale CO 5.00 10.00
12 Al Menendez ACO .75 2.00
Mike Abdenor TR
13 Mike Brunker ACO .75 2.00
Richie Adubato ACO

1990-91 Pistons Unocal

This 16-card standard-size set was produced by Hoops for UNOCAL 76 to commemorate the Piston's back to back championship seasons. A photo album to hold the cards was available for 2.76 at all participating UNOCAL 76 filling stations. Beginning on December 1, 1990 and continuing through the end of March, one card was given away each week with a fuel purchase at participating stations. The cards feature color action player photos on white card stock. A blue banner is draped along the top of the picture, and it reads "89-90 Back to Back World Champions." A Lawrence O'Brien trophy is superimposed at the middle of the banner. Player information and the team name are given in a reddish-orange stripe below the picture. On a blue background, the backs have a head shot of the player in the upper left corner, biographical information, and statistics for the player's NBA career. The cards are unnumbered.

COMPLETE SET (16) 3.00 8.00
1 Mark Aguirre .30 .75
2 Chuck Daly CO .60 1.50
3 Joe Dumars .60 1.50
4 James Edwards .20 .50
5 Vinnie Johnson .30 .75
6 Vinnie Johnson .30 .75
(The Shot)
7 Bill Laimbeer .30 .75
8 Lawrence O'Brien .20 .50
Trophy
9 Dennis Rodman .75 2.00
10 John Salley .20 .50
11 Isiah Thomas .75 2.00
12 Isiah Thomas MVP .75 2.00
13 Celebration Card .20 .50
14 Team Photo .50 1.25
15 Two Championship Rings .20 .50
16 1990 World Champions .20 .50

1991-92 Pistons Unocal

This 16-card standard size set marks the second straight year that Hoops has produced a set for UNOCAL 76. The production run was reported to be 2.5 million cards or roughly 157,000 sets. The cards were distributed two per week with a fill up as part of a promotion that began November 28 and ran through March 1992. In addition, 125,000 vinyl photo albums were produced, and collectors who purchased one for 2.76 at participating UNOCAL filling stations received a redemption card that could be exchanged for a complete set. The fronts feature color action player photos framed in yellow on a blue card face. The upper left and lower right corners of the pictures are cut out. On various color panels, the backs carry a color head shot, biography, career summary, and complete statistics. The cards are unnumbered and checklisted below in alphabetical order, with the multi-player cards listed at the end.

COMPLETE SET (16) 3.00 8.00
1 Mark Aguirre .30 .75
2 Dave Bing .40 1.00
3 Chuck Daly CO .30 .75
4 Joe Dumars .60 1.50
5 Joe Dumars .60 1.50
1991 Pistons MVP
6 Bill Laimbeer .30 .75
7 Bill Laimbeer .30 .75
All-Time Leading Rebounder
8 Dennis Rodman .60 1.50
9 John Salley .20 .50
10 Isiah Thomas .75 2.00
11 Isiah Thomas .75 2.00
All-Time Leading Scorer
12 Darrell Walker .20 .50
13 Orlando Woolridge .20 .50
14 Team Photo .50 1.25
1989 World Champs
15 Mark Aguirre .30 .75
Joe Dumars
Bill Laimbeer
Dennis Rodman
Isiah Thomas
Chuck Daly CO
16 Brad Sellers .20 .50
Bob McCann
Charles Thomas
William Bedford
Lance Blanks

2007-08 Pistons Upper Deck

COMPLETE SET (5) 1.25 3.00
1 Richard Hamilton .30 .75
2 Chauncey Billups .40 1.00
3 Tayshaun Prince .40 1.00
4 Rasheed Wallace .40 1.00
5 Chris Webber .40 1.00

2008 Playoff Contenders

This set was released on February 4, 2009. The base set consists of 130 cards.

COMP.SET w/o AU's (50) 8.00 20.00
COMMON CARD (1-50) .25 .60
COMMON AU (51-130) 3.00 8.00
OVERALL AUTO ODDS 5 PER BOX
EXCHANGE DEADLINE 8/4/2010
78 Derrick Rose AU/88 * 150.00 300.00
103 Michael Beasley AU/88 * 30.00 60.00
112 O.J. Mayo AU/88 * 40.00 80.00

2008 Playoff Contenders Playoff Ticket

COMMON CARD (51-130) 1.00 2.50
OVERALL INSERT ODDS 1:3

2009-10 Playoff Contenders

COMP.SET w/o SPs (100) 25.00 50.00
AU RC APPROX.ODDS FOUR PER BOX
UNPRICED CHAMP.TIX PRINT RUN ONE SET
1 Kevin Garnett 1.00 2.50
2 Paul Pierce .60 1.50
3 Rajon Rondo .60 1.50
4 Dirk Nowitzki .60 1.50
5 Jason Terry .40 1.00
6 Josh Howard .40 1.00
7 Shawn Marion .50 1.25
8 Brook Lopez .50 1.25
9 Devin Harris .50 1.25
10 Yi Jianlian .40 1.00
11 Luis Scola .40 1.00
12 Tracy McGrady .50 1.25
13 Trevor Ariza .30 .75
14 Danilo Gallinari .50 1.25
15 Darko Milicic .30 .75
16 David Lee .40 1.00
17 Nate Robinson .50 1.25
18 Allen Iverson .60 1.50
19 Marc Gasol .50 1.25
20 O.J. Mayo .50 1.25
21 Zach Randolph .40 1.00
22 Andre Iguodala .50 1.25
23 Elton Brand .50 1.25
24 Thaddeus Young .30 .75
25 Chris Paul .75 2.00
26 David West .50 1.25
27 Peja Stojakovic .50 1.25
28 Andrea Bargnani .40 1.00
29 Chris Bosh .50 1.25
30 Jarrett Jack .40 1.00
31 Jose Calderon .40 1.00
32 Michael Finley .50 1.25
33 Richard Jefferson .50 1.25
34 Tim Duncan .75 2.00
35 Tony Parker .50 1.25
36 Derrick Rose 1.50 4.00
37 Joakim Noah .50 1.25
38 Tyrus Thomas .40 1.00
39 Carmelo Anthony .60 1.50
40 Chauncey Billups .50 1.25
41 J.R. Smith .50 1.25
42 Nene .40 1.00
43 LeBron James 2.50 6.00
44 Shaquille O'Neal 1.00 2.50
45 Zydrunas Ilgauskas .30 .75
46 Al Jefferson .50 1.25
47 Kevin Love .75 2.00
48 Ryan Gomes .30 .75
49 Ben Gordon .50 1.25
50 Richard Hamilton .40 1.00
51 Tayshaun Prince .50 1.25
52 Andre Miller .40 1.00
53 Brandon Roy .50 1.25
54 LaMarcus Aldridge .50 1.25
55 Rudy Fernandez .40 1.00
56 Danny Granger .50 1.25
57 T.J. Ford .30 .75
58 Troy Murphy .30 .75
59 Jeff Green .40 1.00
60 Kevin Durant 1.50 4.00
61 Russell Westbrook .75 2.00
62 Andrew Bogut .50 1.25
63 Kurt Thomas .30 .75
64 Michael Redd .50 1.25
65 Andrei Kirilenko .40 1.00
66 Deron Williams .50 1.25
67 Mehmet Okur .30 .75
68 Joe Johnson .50 1.25
69 Josh Smith .50 1.25
70 Mike Bibby .40 1.00
71 Anthony Randolph .40 1.00
72 Corey Maggette .40 1.00
73 Stephen Jackson .40 1.00
74 Boris Diaw .40 1.00
75 D.J. Augustin .40 1.00
76 Gerald Wallace .50 1.25
77 Raja Bell .40 1.00
78 Al Thornton .40 1.00
79 Baron Davis .50 1.25
80 Chris Kaman .40 1.00
81 Eric Gordon .50 1.25
82 Daequan Cook .30 .75
83 Dwyane Wade 1.00 2.50
84 Jermaine O'Neal .50 1.25
85 Andrew Bynum .60 1.50
86 Kobe Bryant 2.50 6.00
87 Pau Gasol .50 1.25
88 Ron Artest .50 1.25
89 Dwight Howard .75 2.00
90 Jameer Nelson .40 1.00
91 Vince Carter .60 1.50
92 Amare Stoudemire .50 1.25
93 Grant Hill .60 1.50
94 Steve Nash .50 1.25
95 Antawn Jamison .50 1.25
96 Caron Butler .50 1.25
97 Gilbert Arenas .50 1.25
98 Andres Nocioni .30 .75
99 Kevin Martin .50 1.25
100 Sean May .30 .75
101 Blake Griffin SP AU RC 100.00 200.00
102 Hasheem Thabeet SP AU RC 6.00 15.00
103 James Harden SP AU RC 20.00 50.00
104 Tyreke Evans SP AU RC 20.00 50.00
105 Jonny Flynn SP AU RC 6.00 15.00
106 Stephen Curry SP AU RC 20.00 50.00
107 Jordan Hill SP AU RC 6.00 15.00
108 Brandon Jennings SP AU RC 12.00 30.00
109 Terrence Williams SP AU RC 8.00 20.00
110 Gerald Henderson AU RC 6.00 15.00
111 Tyler Hansbrough SP AU RC 10.00 25.00
112 Earl Clark SP AU RC 6.00 15.00
113 Austin Daye AU RC 6.00 15.00
114 James Johnson AU RC 6.00 15.00
115 Jrue Holiday AU RC 12.00 30.00
116 Ty Lawson AU RC 10.00 25.00
117 Jeff Teague AU RC 8.00 20.00
118 Eric Maynor AU RC 6.00 15.00
119 Darren Collison AU RC 10.00 25.00
120 Omri Casspi AU RC 6.00 15.00
121 B.J. Mullens AU RC 6.00 15.00
122 Rodrigue Beaubois AU RC 8.00 20.00
123 Taj Gibson AU RC 10.00 25.00
124 DeMarre Carroll AU RC 6.00 15.00
125 Wayne Ellington AU RC 6.00 15.00
126 Toney Douglas AU RC 6.00 15.00
127 Jeff Pendergraph AU RC 6.00 15.00
128 Jermaine Taylor AU RC 6.00 15.00
129 Dante Cunningham SP AU RC 6.00 15.00
130 DaJuan Summers AU RC 6.00 15.00
131 Sam Young AU RC 6.00 15.00
132 DeJuan Blair AU RC 8.00 20.00
133 Jodie Meeks AU RC 8.00 20.00
134 Chase Budinger AU RC 6.00 15.00
135 Taylor Griffin AU RC 6.00 15.00
136 Kareem Abdul-Jabbar 2.00 5.00
137 Isiah Thomas 1.25 3.00
138 Bernard King 1.25 3.00
139 Danny Manning 1.25 3.00
140 Larry Bird 4.00 10.00
141 Artis Gilmore 1.25 3.00
142 Jalen Rose 1.25 3.00
143 John Havlicek 1.25 3.00
144 A.C. Green 1.25 3.00
145 Spencer Haywood 1.25 3.00
146 Hal Greer 1.25 3.00
147 Oscar Robertson 1.25 3.00
148 World B. Free 1.25 3.00
149 Sidney Moncrief 1.25 3.00
150 Maurice Cheeks 1.25 3.00

2009-10 Playoff Contenders Classic Tickets Signatures

STATED PRINT RUN 25 SER.#'d SETS
136 Kareem Abdul-Jabbar 40.00 80.00
137 Isiah Thomas 15.00 40.00
138 Bernard King 10.00 25.00
139 Danny Manning 15.00 40.00
140 Larry Bird 75.00 200.00
141 Artis Gilmore 10.00 25.00
142 Jalen Rose 25.00 60.00
143 John Havlicek 25.00 50.00
144 A.C. Green 20.00 50.00
145 Spencer Haywood 10.00 25.00
146 Hal Greer 15.00 30.00
147 Oscar Robertson 100.00 250.00
149 Sidney Moncrief 10.00 25.00
150 Maurice Cheeks 10.00 25.00

2009-10 Playoff Contenders Playoff Tickets

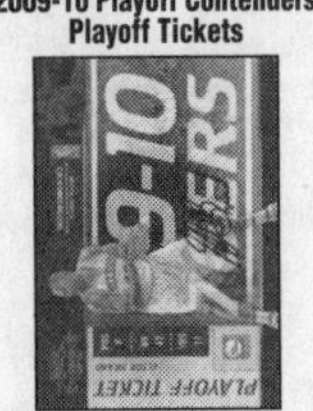

STATED PRINT RUN 5 TO 50 SER.#'d SETS
MOST UNPRICED DUE TO SCARCITY
86 Kobe Bryant/50 100.00 200.00

2009-10 Playoff Contenders Award Contenders

COMPLETE SET (20) 8.00 20.00
RANDOM INSERTS IN PACKS
*BLACK: 1X TO 2.5X BASE HI
BLACK PRINT RUN 50 SER.#'d SETS
*GOLD: .75X TO 2X BASE HI
GOLD PRINT RUN 100 SER.#'d SETS
1 Kobe Bryant 4.00 10.00
2 Danny Granger .75 2.00
3 Al Harrington .60 1.50
4 Ben Gordon .75 2.00
5 Carmelo Anthony 1.00 2.50
6 Chris Bosh .75 2.00
7 Dirk Nowitzki 1.00 2.50
8 Dwyane Wade 1.50 4.00
9 Kevin Love 1.25 3.00
10 LeBron James 4.00 10.00
11 Tony Parker .75 2.00
12 Michael Redd .75 2.00
13 Ray Allen .75 2.00
14 Tim Duncan 1.25 3.00
15 Tracy McGrady .75 2.00
16 Deron Williams .75 2.00
17 Dwight Howard 1.25 3.00
18 Paul Pierce 1.00 2.50
19 Chris Paul 1.25 3.00
20 Chauncey Billups .75 2.00

2009-10 Playoff Contenders Award Contenders Autographs

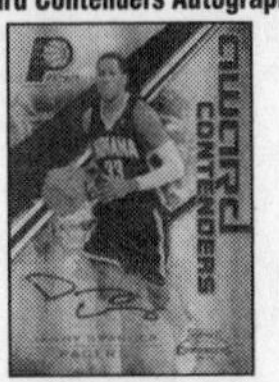

STATED PRINT RUN 5 TO 50 SER.#'d SETS
MOST UNPRICED DUE TO SCARCITY
1 Kobe Bryant/50 100.00 200.00

2009-10 Playoff Contenders Draft Class

COMPLETE SET (25) 10.00 25.00
RANDOM INSERTS IN PACKS
*BLACK: .75X TO 2X BASE HI
BLACK PRINT RUN 50 SER.#'d SETS
*GOLD: .6X TO 1.5X BASE HI
GOLD PRINT RUN 100 SER.#'d SETS
UNPRICED AUTO PRINT RUN 10 SETS
1 Andrea Bargnani 1.00 2.50
2 Adam Morrison 1.00 2.50
3 J.J. Redick 1.25 3.00
4 Jordan Farmar .75 2.00
5 Daniel Gibson 1.00 2.50
6 Greg Oden 1.00 2.50
7 Kevin Durant 4.00 10.00
8 Al Horford 1.25 3.00
9 Mike Conley Jr. 1.00 2.50
10 Yi Jianlian 1.00 2.50
11 Joakim Noah 1.25 3.00
12 Acie Law .75 2.00
13 Thaddeus Young .75 2.00
14 Al Thornton 1.00 2.50
15 Aaron Brooks .75 2.00
16 Ramon Sessions 1.00 2.50
17 Derrick Rose 4.00 10.00
18 Michael Beasley 1.25 3.00
19 Russell Westbrook 2.00 5.00
20 Danilo Gallinari 1.25 3.00
21 Eric Gordon 1.25 3.00
22 D.J. Augustin 1.00 2.50
23 Brook Lopez 1.25 3.00
24 Anthony Randolph 1.00 2.50
25 Paul Millsap 1.00 2.50

2009-10 Playoff Contenders Draft Tandems

COMPLETE SET (20) 15.00 30.00
RANDOM INSERTS IN PACKS
*BLACK: .6X TO 1.5X BASE HI
BLACK PRINT RUN 50 SER.#'d SETS
*GOLD: .5X TO 1.25X BASE HI
GOLD PRINT RUN 100 SER.#'d SETS
UNPRICED AUTO PRINT RUN 10 SETS
1 Hasheem Thabeet 1.25 3.00
Michael Beasley
2 Andrea Bargnani 2.00 5.00
Tim Duncan
3 Chris Bosh 2.00 5.00
Chris Paul
4 Kevin Love 2.00 5.00
Raymond Felton
5 Eric Gordon 1.25 3.00
Randy Foye
6 Chris Kaman 1.00 2.50
Yi Jianlian
7 Amare Stoudemire 1.25 3.00
Joakim Noah
8 James Worthy 1.50 4.00
Larry Johnson
9 Alonzo Mourning 1.50 4.00
Shawn Bradley
10 Dikembe Mutombo 1.25 3.00
Glen Rice
11 Mitch Richmond 1.25 3.00
Sidney Moncrief
12 Corey Brewer 1.25 3.00
Kirk Hinrich
13 Andrew Bynum 1.50 4.00
Paul Pierce
14 Derek Harper 1.50 4.00
Robert Horry
15 Jalen Rose 1.50 4.00
Karl Malone
16 Dan Majerle 1.25 3.00
Tim Hardaway
17 Blake Griffin 8.00 20.00
Magic Johnson
18 Deron Williams 4.00 10.00
James Harden
19 Chris Mullin 3.00 8.00
Stephen Curry
20 Detlef Schrempf 1.25 3.00
Jordan Hill

2009-10 Playoff Contenders Legendary Contenders

COMPLETE SET (20) 10.00 25.00
RANDOM INSERTS IN PACKS
*BLACK: .75X TO 2X BASE HI
BLACK PRINT RUN 50 SER.#'d SETS
*GOLD: .6X TO 1.5X BASE HI
GOLD PRINT RUN 100 SER.#'d SETS
UNPRICED AUTO PRINT RUN 10 SETS
1 Willis Reed 1.50 4.00
2 Shawn Bradley 1.50 4.00
3 Jeff Hornacek 1.50 4.00
5 Dolph Schayes 1.50 4.00
6 Bill Laimbeer 1.50 4.00
7 Kenny Walker 1.50 4.00
8 Connie Hawkins 1.50 4.00
9 Clyde Drexler 2.00 5.00
10 Rony Seikaly 1.50 4.00
11 Larry Johnson 1.50 4.00
12 Cedric Ceballos 1.50 4.00
14 Kurt Rambis 1.50 4.00
15 Joe Dumars 1.50 4.00
16 Bobby Wanzer 1.50 4.00
17 Dan Majerle 1.50 4.00
18 George McGinnis 1.50 4.00
19 Gheorghe Muresan 1.50 4.00

2009-10 Playoff Contenders Lottery Winners

COMPLETE SET (30) 15.00 30.00
RANDOM INSERTS IN PACKS
*BLACK: 1X TO 2.5X BASE HI
BLACK PRINT RUN 50 SER.#'d SETS
*GOLD: .75X TO 2X BASE HI
GOLD PRINT RUN 100 SER.#'d SETS
UNPRICED AUTO PRINT RUN 5 TO 10 SETS
1 LeBron James 4.00 10.00
2 Allen Iverson 1.00 2.50
3 Tim Duncan 1.25 3.00
4 Yao Ming 1.00 2.50
5 Derrick Rose 2.50 6.00
6 Kevin Garnett 1.50 4.00
7 Blake Griffin 5.00 12.00
8 Jason Kidd .75 2.00
9 Carmelo Anthony 1.00 2.50
10 Deron Williams .75 2.00
11 Chris Paul 1.25 3.00
12 Rudy Gay .75 2.00
13 Brandon Roy .75 2.00
14 LaMarcus Aldridge .75 2.00
15 Andrea Bargnani .60 1.50
16 Andre Iguodala .75 2.00
17 Chris Bosh .75 2.00
18 Jeff Green .60 1.50
19 Dwyane Wade 1.50 4.00
20 Chris Kaman .60 1.50
21 Paul Pierce 1.00 2.50
22 Andrew Bynum 1.00 2.50
23 Kevin Durant 2.50 6.00
24 Joakim Noah .75 2.00
25 Al Thornton .60 1.50
26 Charlie Villanueva .60 1.50
27 Emeka Okafor .75 2.00
28 Michael Beasley .75 2.00
29 Mike Bibby .60 1.50
30 Shane Battier .75 2.00

2009-10 Playoff Contenders One-Two Punch

COMPLETE SET (25) 15.00 30.00
RANDOM INSERTS IN PACKS
*BLACK: .6X TO 1.5X BASE HI
BLACK PRINT RUN 50 SER.#'d SETS
*GOLD: .5X TO 1.25X BASE HI
GOLD PRINT RUN 100 SER.#'d SETS
UNPRICED AUTO PRINT RUN 5 TO 10 SETS
1 Brandon Roy 1.50 4.00
Greg Oden
2 Jeff Green 5.00 12.00
Kevin Durant
3 Chris Bosh 1.50 4.00
Hedo Turkoglu
4 Elton Brand 1.50 4.00
Thaddeus Young
5 Anthony Randolph 1.25 3.00
Raja Bell
6 Stephen Jackson 1.25 3.00
Raymond Felton
7 Dirk Nowitzki 2.00 5.00
Josh Howard
8 Ben Gordon 1.50 4.00
Charlie Villanueva
9 Shane Battier 1.50 4.00
Trevor Ariza
10 Chris Kaman 1.25 3.00
Marcus Camby
11 Lamar Odom 1.50 4.00
Pau Gasol
12 Devin Harris 1.50 4.00
Rafer Alston
13 David West 1.50 4.00
Peja Stojakovic
14 Chauncey Billups 1.50 4.00
J.R. Smith
15 Al Jefferson 2.50 6.00
Kevin Love
16 Carlos Boozer 1.50 4.00
Deron Williams
17 O.J. Mayo 1.50 4.00
Rudy Gay
18 Rajon Rondo 2.00 5.00
Ray Allen
19 Leandro Barbosa 1.50 4.00
Steve Nash
20 Al Horford 1.50 4.00
Mike Bibby
21 Derrick Rose 5.00 12.00
Joakim Noah
22 Anderson Varejao 3.00 8.00
Shaquille O'Neal
23 Richard Hamilton 1.50 4.00
Tayshaun Prince
24 Danny Granger 1.50 4.00
Troy Murphy
25 Michael Beasley 1.50 4.00
Udonis Haslem

2009-10 Playoff Contenders Perennial Contenders

COMPLETE SET (20) 10.00 25.00
RANDOM INSERTS IN PACKS
*BLACK: .75X TO 2X BASE HI
BLACK PRINT RUN 50 SER.#'d SETS
*GOLD: .6X TO 1.5X BASE HI
GOLD PRINT RUN 100 SER.#'d SETS
1 Rasheed Wallace 1.00 2.50
2 Joakim Noah 1.00 2.50
3 Shaquille O'Neal 2.00 5.00
4 Jason Terry .75 2.00
5 Chauncey Billups 1.00 2.50
6 Tayshaun Prince 1.00 2.50
7 Tracy McGrady 1.00 2.50
8 Kobe Bryant 5.00 12.00
9 Nate Robinson 1.00 2.50
10 Vince Carter 1.25 3.00
11 Grant Hill 1.25 3.00
12 Greg Oden .75 2.00
13 Tony Parker 1.00 2.50
14 Carlos Boozer 1.00 2.50

15 Ron Artest	1.00	2.50
16 Paul Pierce	1.25	3.00
17 Deron Williams	1.00	2.50
18 Ben Wallace	1.00	2.50
19 LeBron James	5.00	12.00
20 Andre Iguodala	1.00	2.50

2009-10 Playoff Contenders Perennial Contenders Autographs

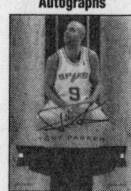

STATED PRINT RUN 5 TO 50 SER.#'d SETS
SOME UNPRICED DUE TO SCARCITY

8 Kobe Bryant/50	100.00	200.00

2009-10 Playoff Contenders Rookie of the Year Contenders

COMPLETE SET (15)	10.00	25.00

RANDOM INSERTS IN PACKS
*BLACK: 1.25X TO 3X BASE HI
BLACK PRINT RUN 50 SER.#'d SETS
*GOLD: .75X TO 2X BASE HI
GOLD PRINT RUN 100 SER.#'d SETS

1 Blake Griffin	6.00	15.00
2 DeJuan Blair	1.25	3.00
3 Omri Casspi	1.00	2.50
4 Chase Budinger	1.00	2.50
5 Hasheem Thabeet	1.00	2.50
6 James Harden	3.00	8.00
7 Brandon Jennings	2.00	5.00
8 Jonny Flynn	1.00	2.50
9 Jordan Hill	1.00	2.50
10 Stephen Curry	2.50	6.00
11 Terrence Williams	1.00	2.50
12 Ty Lawson	1.50	4.00
13 Tyler Hansbrough	1.50	4.00
14 Tyreke Evans	2.50	6.00
15 Taj Gibson	1.25	3.00

2009-10 Playoff Contenders Rookie of the Year Contenders Autographs

STATED PRINT RUN 25 SER.#'d SETS

1 Blake Griffin	175.00	350.00
2 DeJuan Blair	10.00	25.00
3 Omri Casspi	8.00	20.00
4 Chase Budinger	8.00	20.00
5 Hasheem Thabeet	8.00	20.00
6 James Harden	25.00	60.00
7 Brandon Jennings	15.00	40.00
8 Jonny Flynn	8.00	20.00
9 Jordan Hill	8.00	20.00
10 Stephen Curry	20.00	50.00
11 Terrence Williams	8.00	20.00
12 Ty Lawson	12.00	30.00
13 Tyler Hansbrough	12.00	30.00
14 Tyreke Evans	20.00	50.00
15 Taj Gibson	10.00	25.00

2009-10 Playoff Contenders Round Numbers

COMPLETE SET (25)	20.00	40.00

RANDOM INSERTS IN PACKS
*BLACK: .6X TO 1.5X BASE HI
BLACK PRINT RUN 50 SER.#'d SETS
*GOLD: .5X TO 1.25X BASE HI
GOLD PRINT RUN 100 SER.#'d SETS

1 Michael Redd	1.25	3.00
Ramon Sessions		
2 LaMarcus Aldridge	2.00	5.00
Tim Duncan		
3 Chris Bosh	1.25	3.00
Pau Gasol		
4 Ben Gordon	1.50	4.00
Vince Carter		
5 Rashard Lewis	1.00	2.50
Trevor Ariza		
6 Carmelo Anthony	1.50	4.00
Paul Pierce		
7 Dwight Howard	2.00	5.00
Greg Oden		
8 Kevin Garnett	2.50	6.00
Tyler Hansbrough		
9 Blake Griffin	8.00	20.00
Kobe Bryant		
10 Carlos Boozer	1.25	3.00
Paul Millsap		
11 O.J. Mayo	1.25	3.00
Terrence Williams		
12 Brandon Jennings	2.50	6.00
Chris Paul		
13 Steve Nash	2.00	5.00
Ty Lawson		
14 Dwyane Wade	3.00	8.00
Stephen Curry		
15 Monta Ellis	1.25	3.00
Stephen Jackson		
16 Brandon Roy	1.25	3.00
Jonny Flynn		
17 Jason Kidd	3.00	8.00
Tyreke Evans		
18 Derrick Rose	4.00	10.00
James Harden		
19 Andrew Bogut	1.25	3.00
Hasheem Thabeet		
20 Manu Ginobili	1.25	3.00
Mo Williams		
21 Deron Williams	1.25	3.00
Gerald Henderson		
22 Jordan Hill	4.00	10.00
Kevin Durant		
23 Andrea Bargnani	1.50	4.00
Dirk Nowitzki		
24 Amare Stoudemire	1.25	3.00
Elton Brand		
25 Gilbert Arenas	1.25	3.00
Mario Chalmers		

2009-10 Playoff Contenders Round Numbers Autographs

STATED PRINT RUN 10 TO 25 SER.#'d SETS
SOME UNPRICED DUE TO SCARCITY

9 Blake Griffin/25	400.00	800.00
Kobe Bryant		

2010-11 Playoff Contenders Patches

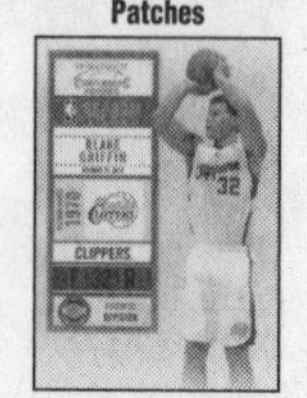

COMP.SET w/o RCs (100)	15.00	40.00

EXCH.EXPIRATION 8/16/2010
UNPRICED CHAMP.TICK.PRINT RUN ONE SET

1 Kobe Bryant	2.50	6.00
2 Pau Gasol	.50	1.25
3 Sasha Vujacic	.30	.75
4 Lamar Odom	.50	1.25
5 Blake Griffin	1.25	3.00
6 Baron Davis	.50	1.25
7 Eric Gordon	.50	1.25
8 Stephen Curry	.60	1.50
9 Monta Ellis	.50	1.25
10 David Lee	.40	1.00
11 Channing Frye	.40	1.00
12 Steve Nash	.50	1.25
13 Robin Lopez	.30	.75
14 Samuel Dalembert	.30	.75
15 Tyreke Evans	.60	1.50
16 Carl Landry	.30	.75
17 Carmelo Anthony	.60	1.50
18 Chauncey Billups	.50	1.25
19 Al Harrington	.40	1.00
20 Chris Andersen	.50	1.25
21 LaMarcus Aldridge	.50	1.25
22 Marcus Camby	.30	.75
23 Brandon Roy	.50	1.25
24 Al Jefferson	.50	1.25
25 Deron Williams	.50	1.25
26 Andrei Kirilenko	.40	1.00
27 Kevin Durant	1.50	4.00
28 Jeff Green	.40	1.00
29 Russell Westbrook	.60	1.50
30 James Harden	.60	1.50
31 Jonny Flynn	.30	.75
32 Anthony Tolliver	.30	.75
33 Kevin Love	.60	1.50
34 Caron Butler	.50	1.25
35 Brendan Haywood	.30	.75
36 Dirk Nowitzki	.60	1.50
37 Jason Kidd	.50	1.25
38 Aaron Brooks	.30	.75
39 Kevin Martin	.50	1.25
40 Yao Ming	.60	1.50
41 DeJuan Blair	.40	1.00
42 Richard Jefferson	.50	1.25
43 Tony Parker	.50	1.25
44 Tim Duncan	.75	2.00
45 Trevor Ariza	.30	.75
46 Chris Paul	.75	2.00
47 David West	.50	1.25
48 Mike Conley Jr.	.40	1.00
49 Marc Gasol	.50	1.25
50 Zach Randolph	.40	1.00
51 O.J. Mayo	.50	1.25
52 Rajon Rondo	.60	1.50
53 Shaquille O'Neal	1.00	2.50
54 Paul Pierce	.60	1.50
55 Kevin Garnett	1.00	2.50
56 Brook Lopez	.50	1.25
57 Terrence Williams	.30	.75
58 Devin Harris	.50	1.25
59 Toney Douglas	.30	.75
60 Amare Stoudemire	.50	1.25
61 Danilo Gallinari	.50	1.25
62 Jrue Holiday	.50	1.25
63 Elton Brand	.50	1.25
64 Andre Iguodala	.50	1.25
65 DeMar DeRozan	.50	1.25
66 Andrea Bargnani	.40	1.00
67 Leandro Barbosa	.40	1.00
68 Joakim Noah	.50	1.25
69 Derrick Rose	1.50	4.00
70 Carlos Boozer	.50	1.25
71 Taj Gibson	.40	1.00
72 Tayshaun Prince	.50	1.25
73 Ben Gordon	.50	1.25
74 Tracy McGrady	.50	1.25
75 Daniel Gibson	.40	1.00
76 Antawn Jamison	.50	1.25
77 Ramon Sessions	.40	1.00
78 Darren Collison	.50	1.25
79 Tyler Hansbrough	.50	1.25
80 Danny Granger	.50	1.25
81 Andrew Bogut	.50	1.25
82 Brandon Jennings	.50	1.25
83 John Salmons	.50	1.25
84 Jamal Crawford	.40	1.00
85 Joe Johnson	.50	1.25
86 Josh Smith	.50	1.25
87 Al Horford	.40	1.00
88 Stephen Jackson	.40	1.00
89 Gerald Henderson	.30	.75
90 Gerald Wallace	.50	1.25
91 Dwyane Wade	1.00	2.50
92 Chris Bosh	.50	1.25
93 LeBron James	2.50	6.00
94 Mike Miller	.50	1.25
95 Dwight Howard	.75	2.00
96 Vince Carter	.60	1.50
97 Jameer Nelson	.40	1.00
98 Al Thornton	.40	1.00
99 JaVale McGee	.40	1.00
100 Andray Blatche	.30	.75
101 John Wall AU RC	40.00	100.00
102 Evan Turner AU RC	12.50	30.00
103 Derrick Favors AU RC	8.00	20.00
104 Wesley Johnson AU RC	6.00	15.00
105 DeMarcus Cousins AU RC	20.00	50.00
106 Ekpe Udoh AU RC	4.00	10.00
107 Greg Monroe AU RC	8.00	20.00
108 Al-Farouq Aminu AU RC	4.00	10.00
109 Gordon Hayward AU RC	10.00	25.00
110 Paul George AU RC	15.00	40.00
111 Cole Aldrich AU RC	4.00	10.00
112 Xavier Henry AU RC	5.00	12.00
113 Ed Davis AU RC	5.00	12.00
114 Patrick Patterson AU RC	6.00	15.00
115 Larry Sanders AU RC	4.00	10.00
116 Luke Babbitt AU RC	4.00	10.00
117 Eric Bledsoe AU RC	8.00	20.00
118 Avery Bradley AU RC	10.00	25.00
119 James Anderson AU RC	4.00	10.00
120 Gary Neal AU RC	8.00	20.00
121 Elliot Williams AU RC	4.00	10.00
122 Trevor Booker AU RC	4.00	10.00
123 Damion James AU RC	4.00	10.00
124 Dominique Jones AU RC	4.00	10.00
125 Quincy Pondexter AU RC	4.00	10.00
126 Jordan Crawford AU RC	6.00	15.00
127 Greivis Vasquez AU RC	6.00	15.00
128 Daniel Orton AU RC	5.00	12.00
129 Lazar Hayward AU RC	4.00	10.00
130 Dexter Pittman AU RC	4.00	10.00
131 Hassan Whiteside AU RC	4.00	10.00
132 Lance Stephenson AU RC	4.00	10.00
133 Gary Forbes AU RC	4.00	10.00
134 Devin Ebanks AU RC	6.00	15.00
135 Gani Lawal AU RC	4.00	10.00
136 Luke Harangody AU RC	4.00	10.00
137 Willie Warren AU RC	4.00	10.00
138 Terrico White AU RC	4.00	10.00
139 Jeremy Evans AU RC	5.00	12.00
140 Timofey Mozgov AU RC	4.00	10.00
141 Jeremy Lin AU RC	75.00	150.00
142 Sherron Collins AU RC	4.00	10.00
143 Armon Johnson AU RC	4.00	10.00
144 Tiago Splitter AU RC	10.00	25.00
145 Landry Fields AU RC	6.00	15.00
146 Andy Rautins AU RC	4.00	10.00
147 Kevin Seraphin AU RC	5.00	12.00
148 Solomon Alabi AU RC	4.00	10.00
149 Derrick Caracter AU RC	6.00	15.00
150 Omer Asik AU RC	8.00	20.00
151 John Wall AU SP	50.00	125.00
152 Evan Turner AU SP	20.00	50.00
153 Derrick Favors AU SP	10.00	25.00
154 Wesley Johnson AU SP	8.00	20.00
155 DeMarcus Cousins AU SP	25.00	60.00
156 Ekpe Udoh AU SP	5.00	12.00
157 Greg Monroe AU SP	10.00	25.00
158 Al-Farouq Aminu AU SP	5.00	12.00
159 Gordon Hayward AU SP	12.00	30.00
160 Paul George AU SP	20.00	50.00
161 Cole Aldrich AU SP	5.00	12.00
162 Xavier Henry AU SP	6.00	15.00
163 Ed Davis AU SP	6.00	15.00
164 Patrick Patterson AU SP	8.00	20.00
165 Larry Sanders AU SP	5.00	12.00
166 Luke Babbitt AU SP	5.00	12.00
167 Eric Bledsoe AU SP	10.00	25.00
168 Avery Bradley AU SP	12.00	30.00
169 James Anderson AU SP	5.00	12.00
170 Gary Neal AU SP	10.00	25.00
171 Elliot Williams AU SP	5.00	12.00
172 Trevor Booker AU SP	5.00	12.00
173 Damion James AU SP	5.00	12.00
174 Dominique Jones AU SP	5.00	12.00
175 Quincy Pondexter AU SP	5.00	12.00
176 Jordan Crawford AU SP	8.00	20.00
177 Greivis Vasquez AU SP	8.00	20.00
178 Daniel Orton AU SP	6.00	15.00
179 Lazar Hayward AU SP	5.00	12.00
180 Dexter Pittman AU SP	5.00	12.00
181 Hassan Whiteside AU SP	5.00	12.00
182 Lance Stephenson AU SP	5.00	12.00
183 Gary Forbes AU SP	6.00	15.00
184 Devin Ebanks AU SP	10.00	25.00
185 Gani Lawal AU SP	5.00	12.00
186 Luke Harangody AU SP	5.00	12.00
187 Willie Warren AU SP	5.00	12.00
188 Terrico White AU SP	5.00	12.00
189 Jeremy Evans AU SP	6.00	15.00
190 Timofey Mozgov AU SP	5.00	12.00
191 Jeremy Lin AU SP	100.00	200.00
192 Sherron Collins AU SP	5.00	12.00
193 Armon Johnson AU SP	5.00	12.00
194 Tiago Splitter AU SP	15.00	40.00
195 Landry Fields AU SP	8.00	20.00
196 Andy Rautins AU SP	5.00	12.00
197 Kevin Seraphin AU SP	6.00	15.00
198 Solomon Alabi AU SP	5.00	12.00
199 Derrick Caracter AU SP	12.00	30.00
200 Omer Asik AU SP	8.00	20.00

2010-11 Playoff Contenders Patches Die Cuts Black

*DC BLACK: 2X TO 5X BASE HI
STATED PRINT RUN 49 SER.#'d SETS

2010-11 Playoff Contenders Patches Die Cuts Gold

*DC GOLD: 1.5X TO 4X BASE HI
STATED PRINT RUN 99 SER.#'d SETS

2010-11 Playoff Contenders Patches Die Cuts Silver

*DC SILVER: 1X TO 2.5X BASE HI
STATED PRINT RUN 299 SER.#'d SETS

2010-11 Playoff Contenders Patches One-Two Punch

COMPLETE SET (25)	20.00	40.00

RANDOM INSERTS IN PACKS
*DC BLACK: 1.25X TO 3X BASE HI
DC BLACK PRINT RUN 49 SER.#'d SETS
*DC GOLD: 1X TO 2.5X BASE HI
DC GOLD PRINT RUN 99 SER.#'d SETS
*DC SILVER: .6X TO 1.5X BASE HI
DC SILVER PRINT RUN 299 SER.#'d SETS

1 Rajon Rondo	1.50	4.00
Shaquille O'Neal		
2 Ray Allen	1.00	2.50
Paul Pierce		
3 Rajon Rondo	1.50	4.00
Kevin Garnett		
4 Derrick Rose	2.50	6.00
Joakim Noah		
5 Brandon Jennings	.75	2.00
Andrew Bogut		
6 Stephen Curry	1.00	2.50
Monta Ellis		
7 Kevin Durant	2.50	6.00
Russell Westbrook		
8 Jason Kidd	1.00	2.50
Dirk Nowitzki		
9 Toney Douglas	.75	2.00
Amare Stoudemire		
10 LeBron James	4.00	10.00
Dwyane Wade		
11 Chris Bosh	4.00	10.00
LeBron James		
12 Blake Griffin	2.00	5.00
Baron Davis		
13 Ben Gordon	.75	2.00
Ben Wallace		
14 Carmelo Anthony	1.00	2.50
Nene		
15 Devin Harris	.75	2.00
Brook Lopez		
16 Joe Johnson	.75	2.00
Al Horford		
17 Jameer Nelson	1.25	3.00
Dwight Howard		
18 Tyreke Evans	1.00	2.50
Carl Landry		
19 Jonny Flynn	.75	2.00
Michael Beasley		
20 Jrue Holiday	.75	2.00
Elton Brand		
21 Chris Paul	1.25	3.00
Emeka Okafor		
22 O.J. Mayo	.75	2.00
Marc Gasol		
23 Kobe Bryant	4.00	10.00
Pau Gasol		
24 Kobe Bryant	4.00	10.00
Derek Fisher		
25 Steve Nash	.75	2.00
Channing Frye		

2010-11 Playoff Contenders Patches Place in History

COMPLETE SET (25)	12.50	30.00

RANDOM INSERTS IN PACKS
*DC BLACK: 1.25X TO 3X BASE HI
DC BLACK PRINT RUN 49 SER.#'d SETS
*DC GOLD: 1X TO 2.5X BASE HI
DC GOLD PRINT RUN 99 SER.#'d SETS
*DC SILVER: .6X TO 1.5X BASE HI
DC SILVER PRINT RUN 299 SER.#'d SETS

1 James Harden	1.00	2.50
2 Brook Lopez	.75	2.00
3 Joakim Noah	.75	2.00
4 J.J. Redick	.75	2.00
5 Andrew Bogut	.75	2.00
6 Andre Iguodala	.75	2.00
7 Carmelo Anthony	1.00	2.50
8 Amare Stoudemire	.75	2.00
9 Pau Gasol	.75	2.00
10 Hedo Turkoglu	.75	2.00
11 Shawn Marion	.75	2.00
12 Dirk Nowitzki	1.00	2.50
13 Chauncey Billups	.75	2.00
14 Kobe Bryant	4.00	10.00
15 Kevin Garnett	1.50	4.00
16 Jason Kidd	.75	2.00
17 Shawn Bradley	.75	2.00
18 Shaquille O'Neal	1.50	4.00
19 Larry Johnson	1.00	2.50
20 Gary Payton	.75	2.00
21 Sean Elliott	.75	2.00
22 Hersey Hawkins	.75	2.00
23 Scottie Pippen	1.50	4.00
24 Walter Berry	.75	2.00
25 Chris Mullin	.75	2.00

2010-11 Playoff Contenders Patches Place in History Autographs Gold

STATED PRINT RUN 10 TO 49 SER.#'d SETS
SOME UNPRICED DUE TO SCARCITY
UNPRICED BLACK PRINT RUN 5 TO 10 SETS

1 James Harden/49	12.00	30.00
2 Brook Lopez/49	6.00	15.00
3 Joakim Noah/49	8.00	20.00
4 J.J. Redick/49	6.00	15.00
5 Andrew Bogut/49	8.00	20.00
6 Andre Iguodala/49	6.00	15.00
8 Amare Stoudemire/49	20.00	50.00
9 Pau Gasol/49	20.00	50.00
12 Dirk Nowitzki/49	40.00	100.00
13 Chauncey Billups/49	8.00	20.00
14 Kobe Bryant/49	125.00	225.00
16 Jason Kidd/49	10.00	25.00
19 Larry Johnson/15	50.00	120.00
20 Gary Payton/49	10.00	25.00
21 Sean Elliott/15	20.00	50.00
22 Hersey Hawkins/49	6.00	15.00
23 Scottie Pippen/49	75.00	150.00
24 Walter Berry/49	6.00	15.00
25 Chris Mullin/49	12.50	30.00

2010-11 Playoff Contenders Patches Rookie of the Year Contenders

COMPLETE SET (15)	10.00	25.00

RANDOM INSERTS IN PACKS
*DC BLACK: 1.25X TO 3X BASE HI
DC BLACK PRINT RUN 49 SER.#'d SETS
*DC GOLD: 1X TO 2.5X BASE HI
DC GOLD PRINT RUN 99 SER.#'d SETS
*DC SILVER: .6X TO 1.5X BASE HI
DC SILVER PRINT RUN 299 SER.#'d SETS

1 John Wall	3.00	8.00
2 Blake Griffin	2.00	5.00
3 Evan Turner	1.50	4.00
4 Wesley Johnson	1.25	3.00
5 Derrick Favors	1.50	4.00
6 DeMarcus Cousins	2.50	6.00
7 Gordon Hayward	1.50	4.00
8 Cole Aldrich	.75	2.00
9 Ekpe Udoh	.75	2.00
10 Ed Davis	1.00	2.50
11 Xavier Henry	1.00	2.50
12 Greg Monroe	1.50	4.00
13 James Anderson	.75	2.00
14 Patrick Patterson	1.25	3.00
15 Al-Farouq Aminu	.75	2.00

2010-11 Playoff Contenders Patches Rookie of the Year Contenders Autographs Gold

STATED PRINT RUN 49 SER.#'d SETS
UNPRICED BLACK PRINT RUN 10 SER.#'d SETS

1 John Wall	100.00	200.00
2 Blake Griffin	80.00	200.00
3 Evan Turner	15.00	40.00
4 Wesley Johnson	12.00	30.00
5 Derrick Favors	15.00	40.00
6 DeMarcus Cousins	25.00	60.00
7 Gordon Hayward	15.00	40.00
8 Cole Aldrich	8.00	20.00
9 Ekpe Udoh	8.00	20.00
10 Ed Davis	10.00	25.00
11 Xavier Henry	10.00	25.00
12 Greg Monroe	15.00	40.00
13 James Anderson	8.00	20.00
14 Patrick Patterson	12.00	30.00
15 Al-Farouq Aminu	8.00	20.00

2010-11 Playoff Contenders Patches Starting Blocks

COMPLETE SET (30)	20.00	40.00

RANDOM INSERTS IN PACKS
*DC BLACK: 1.25X TO 3X BASE HI
DC BLACK PRINT RUN 49 SER.#'d SETS
*DC GOLD: 1X TO 2.5X BASE HI
DC GOLD PRINT RUN 99 SER.#'d SETS
*DC SILVER: .6X TO 1.5X BASE HI
DC SILVER PRINT RUN 299 SER.#'d SETS

1 Tyreke Evans	2.50	6.00
DeMarcus Cousins		
2 Stephen Curry	1.00	2.50
Ekpe Udoh		
3 Marreese Speights	1.50	4.00
Evan Turner		
4 Brook Lopez	1.50	4.00
Derrick Favors		
5 Austin Daye	1.50	4.00
Greg Monroe		
6 Brandon Jennings	.75	2.00
Larry Sanders		
7 DeMarre Carroll	1.00	2.50
Xavier Henry		
8 Derrick Rose	2.50	6.00
Taj Gibson		
9 JaVale McGee	3.00	8.00
John Wall		
10 Jonny Flynn	1.25	3.00
Wesley Johnson		
11 DeMar DeRozan	1.00	2.50
Ed Davis		
12 Danilo Gallinari	.75	2.00
Toney Douglas		
13 Jeremy Evans	1.50	4.00
Gordon Hayward		
14 Brook Lopez	.75	2.00
Damion James		
15 Eric Gordon	2.00	5.00
Blake Griffin		
16 D.J. Augustin	.60	1.50
Gerald Henderson		
17 Thaddeus Young	.75	2.00
Jrue Holiday		
18 Joakim Noah	.75	2.00
James Johnson		
19 Tyler Hansbrough	2.00	5.00
Paul George		
20 Tyreke Evans	1.00	2.50
Omri Casspi		
21 Taj Gibson	.75	2.00
James Johnson		
22 Blake Griffin	2.00	5.00
Al-Farouq Aminu		
23 Aaron Brooks	1.25	3.00
Patrick Patterson		
24 Rodney Stuckey	1.50	4.00
Greg Monroe		
25 Joakim Noah	2.50	6.00
Derrick Rose		
26 Hassan Whiteside	1.00	2.50
Tyreke Evans		
27 Al Horford	1.25	3.00
Jordan Crawford		
28 Andrea Bargnani	.75	2.00
DeMar DeRozan		
29 Rajon Rondo	1.50	4.00
Avery Bradley		
30 Rudy Gay	1.00	2.50
Greivis Vasquez		

2010-11 Playoff Contenders Patches Starting Blocks Autographs Gold

STATED PRINT RUN 25 TO 49 SER.#'d SETS
UNPRICED BLACK PRINT RUN 10 SER.#'d SETS

1 Tyreke Evans/49	25.00	60.00
DeMarcus Cousins		
2 Stephen Curry/49	20.00	50.00
Ekpe Udoh		
4 Brook Lopez/49	12.50	30.00
Derrick Favors		
5 Austin Daye/49	8.00	20.00
Greg Monroe		
6 Brandon Jennings/49	15.00	40.00
Larry Sanders		
7 DeMarre Carroll/49	6.00	15.00
Xavier Henry		
8 Derrick Rose/49	60.00	120.00
Taj Gibson		
9 JaVale McGee/49	50.00	125.00
John Wall		
10 Jonny Flynn/49	10.00	25.00
Wesley Johnson		
11 DeMar DeRozan/49	15.00	40.00
Ed Davis		
12 Danilo Gallinari/25	6.00	15.00
Toney Douglas		
13 Jeremy Evans/49	12.50	30.00
Gordon Hayward		
14 Brook Lopez/49	6.00	15.00
Damion James		
15 Eric Gordon/49	75.00	200.00
Blake Griffin		
16 D.J. Augustin/49	6.00	15.00
Gerald Henderson		
18 Joakim Noah/49	8.00	20.00
James Johnson		
19 Tyler Hansbrough/49	15.00	40.00
Paul George		
20 Tyreke Evans/49	12.50	30.00
Omri Casspi		
21 Taj Gibson/49	8.00	20.00
James Johnson		
22 Blake Griffin/49	60.00	150.00
Al-Farouq Aminu		
23 Aaron Brooks/49	12.50	30.00
Patrick Patterson		
25 Joakim Noah/49	60.00	150.00
Derrick Rose		
26 Hassan Whiteside/49	10.00	25.00
Tyreke Evans		
27 Al Horford/49	6.00	15.00
Jordan Crawford		
28 Andrea Bargnani/49	10.00	25.00
DeMar DeRozan		
29 Rajon Rondo/49	20.00	50.00
Avery Bradley		

2009-10 Playoff National Treasures

COMP.SET w/o RCs (185)	500.00	700.00

1-185 PRINT RUN 99 SER.#'d SETS
186-200 RC PRINT RUN 99 SER.#'d SETS
UNPRICED PLATINUM PRINT RUN 1 TO 5 SETS
UNPRICED SILVER PRINT RUN 10 SETS

1 Kobe Bryant	15.00	40.00
2 LeBron James	15.00	40.00
3 Dwight Howard	5.00	12.00
4 Derrick Rose	10.00	25.00
5 Dwyane Wade	6.00	15.00
6 Kevin Garnett	6.00	15.00
7 Chris Paul	5.00	12.00
8 Paul Pierce	4.00	10.00
9 Shaquille O'Neal	6.00	15.00
10 Pau Gasol	3.00	8.00
11 Carmelo Anthony	4.00	10.00
12 Steve Nash	3.00	8.00
13 David Lee	2.50	6.00
14 Allen Iverson	4.00	10.00
15 Kevin Durant	10.00	25.00
16 Monta Ellis	3.00	8.00
17 Dirk Nowitzki	4.00	10.00
18 Chris Bosh	3.00	8.00
19 Brandon Roy	3.00	8.00
20 Amare Stoudemire	3.00	8.00
21 Joe Johnson	3.00	8.00
22 Zach Randolph	2.50	6.00
23 Carlos Boozer	3.00	8.00
24 Rudy Gay	3.00	8.00
25 Stephen Jackson	2.50	6.00
26 Corey Maggette	2.50	6.00
27 Brook Lopez	3.00	8.00
28 Aaron Brooks	2.00	5.00
29 Rodney Stuckey	3.00	8.00
30 Chris Kaman	2.50	6.00
31 O.J. Mayo	3.00	8.00
32 Tim Duncan	5.00	12.00
33 Al Jefferson	3.00	8.00
34 Andre Iguodala	3.00	8.00
35 Deron Williams	3.00	8.00
36 David West	3.00	8.00
37 Mo Williams	2.50	6.00
38 Gerald Wallace	3.00	8.00
39 Andrea Bargnani	2.50	6.00
40 Antawn Jamison	3.00	8.00
41 Luol Deng	3.00	8.00
42 Al Harrington	2.50	6.00
43 Jamal Crawford	2.50	6.00
44 Jason Terry	2.50	6.00
45 Baron Davis	3.00	8.00
46 Russell Westbrook	5.00	12.00
47 Michael Beasley	3.00	8.00
48 Caron Butler	3.00	8.00
49 Carl Landry	2.00	5.00
50 LaMarcus Aldridge	3.00	8.00
51 Ray Allen	3.00	8.00
52 Trevor Ariza	2.00	5.00
53 Tony Parker	3.00	8.0
54 Chauncey Billups	3.00	8.0
55 Luis Scola	2.50	6.0
56 Josh Smith	3.00	8.0
57 Andrew Bynum	4.00	10.0
58 Marc Gasol	3.00	8.0
59 Jason Richardson	3.00	8.0
60 Jeff Green	2.50	6.0
61 Danny Granger	3.00	8.0
62 Nene	2.50	6.0
63 Vince Carter	4.00	10.0
64 Charlie Villanueva	2.50	6.0
65 Rajon Rondo	4.00	10.0
66 Eric Gordon	3.00	8.0
67 Elton Brand	3.00	8.0
68 D.J. Augustin	2.50	6.0
69 Derek Fisher	2.50	6.0
70 Devin Harris	3.00	8.0
71 Emeka Okafor	3.00	8.0
72 Jason Kidd	3.00	8.0
73 Jermaine O'Neal	3.00	8.0
74 Josh Howard	2.50	6.0
75 Kevin Love	5.00	12.0
76 Lamar Odom	3.00	8.0
77 Mike Bibby	2.50	6.0
78 Randy Foye	2.00	5.0
79 Richard Hamilton	2.50	6.0
80 Ron Artest	3.00	8.0
81 Ronnie Brewer	2.50	6.0
82 Rudy Fernandez	2.50	6.0
83 Ryan Gomes	2.00	5.0
84 Shane Battier	3.00	8.0
85 T.J. Ford	2.00	5.0
86 Ben Gordon	3.00	8.0
87 Rashard Lewis	2.50	6.0
88 Shawn Marion	3.00	8.0
89 Troy Murphy	2.00	5.0
90 Chris Duhon	2.00	5.0
91 Raymond Felton	2.50	6.0
92 Andre Miller	2.50	6.0
93 Jarrett Jack	2.50	6.0
94 Mike Conley Jr.	2.50	6.0
95 Kendrick Perkins	2.50	6.0
96 Chris Andersen	5.00	12.0
97 Greg Oden	2.50	6.0
98 Danilo Gallinari	3.00	8.0
99 Yi Jianlian	2.50	6.0
100 Wilson Chandler	2.50	6.0
101 Ed Macauley LEG	3.00	8.0
102 Bob Cousy LEG	5.00	12.0
103 Bob Pettit LEG	3.00	8.0
104 Dolph Schayes LEG	3.00	8.0
105 Bill Russell LEG	5.00	12.0
106 Bill Sharman LEG	3.00	8.0
107 Elgin Baylor LEG	3.00	8.0
108 Cliff Hagan LEG	3.00	8.0
109 Jerry Lucas LEG	3.00	8.0
110 Oscar Robertson LEG	3.00	8.0
111 Jerry West LEG	4.00	10.0
112 Hal Greer LEG	3.00	8.0
113 Slater Martin LEG	3.00	8.0
114 Frank Ramsey LEG	3.00	8.0
115 Willis Reed LEG	3.00	8.0
116 Jack Twyman LEG	3.00	8.0
117 John Havlicek LEG	3.00	8.0
118 Sam Jones LEG	4.00	10.0
119 Nate Thurmond LEG	3.00	8.0
120 Billy Cunningham LEG	3.00	8.0
121 Tom Heinsohn LEG	3.00	8.0
122 Rick Barry LEG	3.00	8.0
123 Walt Frazier LEG	3.00	8.0
124 Bobby Wanzer LEG	3.00	8.0
125 Clyde Lovellette LEG	3.00	8.0
126 Wes Unseld LEG	3.00	8.0
127 K.C. Jones LEG	3.00	8.00
128 Lenny Wilkens LEG	3.00	8.00
129 Elvin Hayes LEG	3.00	8.00
130 Earl Monroe LEG	3.00	8.00
131 Nate Archibald LEG	3.00	8.00
132 Dave Cowens LEG	3.00	8.00
133 Harry Gallatin LEG	3.00	8.00
134 Connie Hawkins LEG	3.00	8.00
135 Bob Lanier LEG	3.00	8.00
136 Walt Bellamy LEG	3.00	8.00
137 Dan Issel LEG	3.00	8.00
138 Bill Walton LEG	3.00	8.00
139 Kareem Abdul-Jabbar LEG	5.00	12.00
140 Vern Mikkelsen LEG	3.00	8.00
141 George Gervin LEG	3.00	8.00
142 Gail Goodrich LEG	3.00	8.00
143 David Thompson LEG	4.00	10.00
144 Alex English LEG	3.00	8.00
145 Bailey Howell LEG	3.00	8.00
146 Larry Bird LEG	10.00	25.00
147 Marques Haynes LEG	3.00	8.00
148 Arnie Risen LEG	3.00	8.00
149 Kevin McHale LEG	3.00	8.00
150 Bob McAdoo LEG	3.00	8.00
151 Isiah Thomas LEG	3.00	8.00
152 Magic Johnson LEG	8.00	20.00
153 Robert Parish LEG	3.00	8.00
154 James Worthy LEG	4.00	10.00
155 Clyde Drexler LEG	4.00	10.00
156 Lynette Woodard LEG	3.00	8.00
157 Jalen Rose LEG	3.00	8.00
158 Joe Dumars LEG	3.00	8.00
159 Dominique Wilkins LEG	4.00	10.00
160 Adrian Dantley LEG	3.00	8.00
161 Patrick Ewing LEG	4.00	10.00
162 Hakeem Olajuwon LEG	4.00	10.00
163 David Robinson LEG	5.00	12.00
164 John Stockton LEG	5.00	12.00
165 John Kundla LEG	3.00	8.00
166 Earl Lloyd LEG	3.00	8.00
167 Alonzo Mourning LEG	4.00	10.00
168 Bernard King LEG	3.00	8.00
169 Bill Laimbeer LEG	3.00	8.00
170 Scottie Pippen LEG	6.00	15.00
171 Chris Mullin LEG	3.00	8.00
172 Danny Manning LEG	3.00	8.00
173 Dennis Rodman LEG	5.00	12.00
174 Detlef Schrempf LEG	3.00	8.00
175 Dikembe Mutombo LEG	3.00	8.00
176 George McGinnis LEG	3.00	8.00
177 Jeff Hornacek LEG	3.00	8.00
178 Sidney Moncrief LEG	3.00	8.00
179 Pat Riley LEG	3.00	8.00
180 Tom Gola LEG	3.00	8.00
181 Calvin Murphy LEG	3.00	8.00
182 Nancy Lieberman LEG	4.00	10.00
183 Meadowlark Lemon LEG	3.00	8.00
184 Geese Ausbie LEG	3.00	8.00
185 Curly Neal LEG	3.00	8.00
186 Jonas Jerebko RC	8.00	20.00
187 Marcus Thornton RC	12.00	30.00
188 Wesley Matthews RC	15.00	40.00
189 Serge Ibaka RC	25.00	60.00
190 A.J. Price RC	8.00	20.00

on Brockman RC 8.00 20.00
ante Cunningham RC 8.00 20.00
errick Brown RC 8.00 20.00
undiata Gaines RC 8.00 20.00
larcus Landry RC 8.00 20.00
ester Hudson RC 8.00 20.00
anny Green RC 12.00 30.00
avid Andersen RC 8.00 20.00
eMar DeRozan 15.00 40.00
icky Rubio RC 40.00 100.00
lake Griffin JSY AU RC 2000.00 3200.00
asheem Thabeet JSY AU RC 20.00 50.00
ames Harden JSY AU RC 400.00 700.00
yreke Evans JSY AU RC 300.00 600.00
onny Flynn JSY AU RC 30.00 80.00
tephen Curry JSY AU RC 400.00 700.00
ordan Hill JSY AU RC 20.00 50.00
eMar DeRozan JSY AU RC 150.00 325.00
randon Jennings JSY AU RC 250.00 500.00
errence Williams JSY AU RC 40.00 100.00
erald Henderson JSY AU RC 40.00 80.00
yler Hansbrough JSY AU RC 50.00 125.00
arl Clark JSY AU RC 20.00 50.00
ustin Daye JSY AU RC 40.00 80.00
ames Johnson JSY AU RC 25.00 60.00
rue Holiday JSY AU RC 300.00 500.00
y Lawson JSY AU RC 100.00 200.00
eff Teague JSY AU RC 75.00 150.00
ric Maynor JSY AU RC 30.00 80.00
arren Collison JSY AU RC 30.00 80.00
mri Casspi JSY AU RC 50.00 120.00
.J. Mullens JSY AU RC 25.00 60.00
odrigue Beaubois JSY AU RC 40.00 100.00
aj Gibson JSY AU RC 50.00 120.00
eMarre Carroll JSY AU RC 20.00 50.00
Vayne Ellington JSY AU RC 20.00 50.00
oney Douglas JSY AU RC 25.00 60.00
eff Pendergraph JSY AU RC 20.00 50.00
ermaine Taylor JSY AU RC 20.00 50.00
aJuan Summers JSY AU RC 20.00 50.00
am Young JSY AU RC 35.00 70.00
eJuan Blair JSY AU RC 50.00 120.00
odie Meeks JSY AU RC 40.00 80.00
hase Budinger JSY AU RC 40.00 100.00
aylor Griffin JSY AU RC 20.00 50.00
yreke Evans JSY AU/97 75.00 200.00
arren Collison JSY AU 30.00 80.00
asheem Thabeet JSY AU 20.00 50.00

2009-10 Playoff National Treasures Century Gold

UNPRICED PRINT RUN 5 SETS
238 PRINT RUN 25 SER.#'d SETS
lake Griffin JSY AU 3000.00 4000.00
asheem Thabeet JSY AU 25.00 60.00
ames Harden JSY AU 400.00 800.00
yreke Evans JSY AU 400.00 800.00
onny Flynn JSY AU 100.00 200.00
tephen Curry JSY AU 400.00 800.00
ordan Hill JSY AU 25.00 60.00
eMar DeRozan JSY AU 200.00 400.00
randon Jennings JSY AU 300.00 600.00
errence Williams JSY AU 100.00 200.00
erald Henderson JSY AU 40.00 100.00
yler Hansbrough JSY AU 75.00 200.00
arl Clark JSY AU 25.00 60.00
ustin Daye JSY AU 40.00 100.00
ames Johnson JSY AU 25.00 60.00
rue Holiday JSY AU 300.00 600.00
y Lawson JSY AU 125.00 250.00
eff Teague JSY AU 60.00 150.00
ric Maynor JSY AU 25.00 60.00
arren Collison JSY AU 75.00 200.00
mri Casspi JSY AU 25.00 60.00
.J. Mullens JSY AU 25.00 60.00
odrigue Beaubois JSY AU 75.00 150.00
aj Gibson JSY AU 40.00 100.00
eMarre Carroll JSY AU 25.00 60.00
Vayne Ellington JSY AU 25.00 60.00
oney Douglas JSY AU 75.00 150.00
eff Pendergraph JSY AU 25.00 60.00
ermaine Taylor JSY AU 25.00 60.00
aJuan Summers JSY AU 25.00 60.00
am Young JSY AU 30.00 80.00
eJuan Blair JSY AU 125.00 250.00
odie Meeks JSY AU 30.00 80.00
hase Budinger JSY AU 25.00 60.00
aylor Griffin JSY AU 25.00 60.00
yreke Evans JSY AU 200.00 400.00
arren Collison JSY AU 75.00 200.00
asheem Thabeet JSY AU 25.00 60.00

2009-10 Playoff National Treasures 25th Anniversary Team

PLETE SET (10) 25.00 50.00
ED PRINT RUN 25 SER.#'d SETS
lph Schayes 3.00 8.00
b Pettit 3.00 8.00
l Russell 5.00 12.00
orge Mikan 6.00 15.00
b Cousy 5.00 12.00
l Sharman 3.00 8.00
m Jones 4.00 10.00
ul Arizin 3.00 8.00
b Davies 3.00 8.00
ed Auerbach 4.00 10.00

2009-10 Playoff National Treasures 25th Anniversary Team Signatures

ED PRINT RUN 5 TO 25 SER.#'d SETS
E UNPRICED DUE TO SCARCITY
lph Schayes/25 8.00 20.00
l Sharman/25 10.00 25.00

2009-10 Playoff National Treasures 35th Anniversary Team

PLETE SET (10) 30.00 80.00
ED PRINT RUN 35 SER.#'d SETS
reem Abdul-Jabbar 6.00 15.00
in Baylor 4.00 10.00
b Cousy 6.00 15.00
hn Havlicek 4.00 10.00
orge Mikan 8.00 20.00
b Pettit 4.00 10.00
car Robertson 4.00 10.00
l Russell 6.00 15.00
ry West 5.00 12.00
Vilt Chamberlain 8.00 20.00

2009-10 Playoff National Treasures 35th Anniversary Team Signatures

ED PRINT RUN 5 TO 25 SER.#'d SETS
E UNPRICED DUE TO SCARCITY
reem Abdul-Jabbar/25 50.00 100.00
ry West/25 30.00 80.00

2009-10 Playoff National Treasures All Decade Materials

STATED PRINT RUN 10 TO 99 SER.#'d SETS
SOME UNPRICED DUE TO SCARCITY
1 George Mikan/99 12.50 30.00
8 Kareem Abdul-Jabbar/25 8.00 20.00
12 Scottie Pippen/49 10.00 25.00
13 Shaquille O'Neal/49 8.00 20.00
14 Kobe Bryant/99 12.00 30.00
16 Dirk Nowitzki/99 5.00 12.00
17 Tim Duncan/99 6.00 15.00
18 Kevin Garnett/99 8.00 20.00
19 Tracy McGrady/99 4.00 10.00
20 Steve Nash/49 8.00 20.00

2009-10 Playoff National Treasures All Decade Materials Prime

*PRIME: .6X TO 1.5X HI COLUMN
STATED PRINT RUN 5 TO 25 SER.#'d SETS
SOME UNPRICED DUE TO SCARCITY
10 Magic Johnson/25 15.00 40.00
11 Dominique Wilkins/25 8.00 20.00
14 Kobe Bryant/25 25.00 60.00

2009-10 Playoff National Treasures All Decade Materials Signatures

STATED PRINT RUN ONE TO 25 SER.#'d SETS
SOME UNPRICED DUE TO SCARCITY
UNPRICED PRIME PRINT RUN ONE TO 10 SETS
14 Kobe Bryant/25 125.00 250.00

2009-10 Playoff National Treasures All Decade Signatures

STATED PRINT RUN 3 TO 25 SER.#'d SETS
SOME UNPRICED DUE TO SCARCITY
UNPRICED COMBO PRINT RUN FIVE SETS
UNPRICED QUAD PRINT RUN FIVE SETS
UNPRICED TRIO PRINT RUN 3 TO 5 SETS
14 Kobe Bryant/25 125.00 225.00

2009-10 Playoff National Treasures All NBA

STATED PRINT RUN 25 SER.#'d SETS
1 Karl Malone 6.00 15.00
2 Elgin Baylor 5.00 12.00
3 Jerry West 8.00 20.00
4 Kareem Abdul-Jabbar 8.00 20.00
5 Bob Cousy 8.00 20.00
6 Bob Pettit 5.00 12.00
7 Magic Johnson 12.00 30.00
8 Larry Bird 15.00 40.00
9 Oscar Robertson 5.00 12.00
10 Dolph Schayes 5.00 12.00
11 Hakeem Olajuwon 6.00 15.00
12 Kobe Bryant 15.00 40.00
13 George Gervin 5.00 12.00
14 Rick Barry 5.00 12.00
15 Bill Sharman 5.00 12.00
16 David Robinson 8.00 20.00
17 John Havlicek 5.00 12.00
18 Walt Frazier 5.00 12.00
19 Ed Macauley 5.00 12.00
20 Elvin Hayes 5.00 12.00
21 Isiah Thomas 5.00 12.00
22 Jerry Lucas 5.00 12.00
23 Nate Archibald 5.00 12.00
24 Scottie Pippen 10.00 25.00
25 Bill Russell 8.00 20.00

2009-10 Playoff National Treasures All NBA Materials

STATED PRINT RUN 10 TO 99 SER.#'d SETS
SOME UNPRICED DUE TO SCARCITY
1 Karl Malone/99 5.00 12.00
4 Kareem Abdul-Jabbar/25 10.00 25.00
11 Hakeem Olajuwon/99 5.00 12.00
12 Kobe Bryant/99 10.00 25.00
24 Scottie Pippen/49 10.00 25.00

2009-10 Playoff National Treasures All NBA Materials Prime

STATED PRINT RUN 5 TO 25 SER.#'d SETS
SOME UNPRICED DUE TO SCARCITY
1 Karl Malone/25 15.00 30.00
7 Magic Johnson/25 15.00 40.00
11 Hakeem Olajuwon/25 10.00 25.00
12 Kobe Bryant/25 25.00 60.00

2009-10 Playoff National Treasures All NBA Materials Signatures

STATED PRINT RUN ONE TO 25 SER.#'d SETS
SOME UNPRICED DUE TO SCARCITY
UNPRICED PRIME PRINT RUN ONE TO 10 SETS
12 Kobe Bryant/25 125.00 250.00

2009-10 Playoff National Treasures All NBA Signatures

STATED PRINT RUN 4 TO 49 SER.#'d SETS
SOME UNPRICED DUE TO SCARCITY
10 Dolph Schayes/25 8.00 20.00
11 Hakeem Olajuwon/25 20.00 40.00
12 Kobe Bryant/25 125.00 225.00
14 Rick Barry/25
15 Bill Sharman/25 10.00 25.00
18 Walt Frazier/25 20.00 40.00
23 Nate Archibald/49 8.00 20.00

2009-10 Playoff National Treasures Biography Materials

STATED PRINT RUN 49 TO 99 SER.#'d SETS
1 Kobe Bryant/99 10.00 25.00
2 LeBron James/49 10.00 25.00
3 Kevin Durant/49 10.00 25.00
4 Dirk Nowitzki/99 5.00 12.00
5 Dwyane Wade/99 6.00 15.00
6 Carmelo Anthony/99 5.00 12.00
7 Chris Bosh/49 4.00 10.00
8 Dwight Howard/99 6.00 15.00
9 Tim Duncan/99 6.00 15.00
10 Shaquille O'Neal/49 8.00 20.00

2009-10 Playoff National Treasures Biography Materials Prime

*PRIME: .6X TO 1.5X HI COLUMN
STATED PRINT RUN ONE TO 25 SER.#'d SETS
SOME UNPRICED DUE TO SCARCITY
1 Kobe Bryant/25 30.00 80.00
3 Kevin Durant/25 20.00 50.00

2009-10 Playoff National Treasures Biography Materials Autographs

STATED PRINT RUN 3 TO 25 SER.#'d SETS
SOME UNPRICED DUE TO SCARCITY
UNPRICED PRIME PRINT RUN ONE TO 10 SETS
1 Kobe Bryant/25 125.00 250.00

2009-10 Playoff National Treasures Century Materials

STATED PRINT RUN ONE TO 99 SER.#'d SETS
SOME UNPRICED DUE TO SCARCITY
UNPRICED NBA LOGO PRINT RUN 1 TO 2 SETS
UNPRICED NBA TAGS PRINT RUN 1 TO 4 SETS
UNPRICED TEAM LOGO PRINT RUN 1 TO 5 SETS
1 Kobe Bryant/99 12.00 30.00
2 LeBron James/49 12.50 30.00
3 Dwight Howard/99 6.00 15.00
4 Derrick Rose/99 12.00 30.00
5 Dwyane Wade/99 8.00 20.00
6 Kevin Garnett/99 8.00 20.00
7 Chris Paul/99 6.00 15.00
8 Paul Pierce/99 5.00 12.00
9 Shaquille O'Neal/49 8.00 20.00
10 Pau Gasol/99 4.00 10.00
11 Carmelo Anthony/99 5.00 12.00
12 Steve Nash/49 4.00 10.00
13 David Lee/49 3.00 8.00
14 Allen Iverson/99 5.00 12.00
15 Kevin Durant/49 10.00 25.00
16 Monta Ellis/49 4.00 10.00
17 Dirk Nowitzki/99 5.00 12.00
18 Chris Bosh/49 4.00 10.00
19 Brandon Roy/49 4.00 10.00
20 Amare Stoudemire/99 4.00 10.00
21 Joe Johnson/99 4.00 10.00
23 Carlos Boozer/99 4.00 10.00
24 Rudy Gay/99 4.00 10.00
26 Corey Maggette/99 3.00 8.00
27 Brook Lopez/99 4.00 10.00
29 Rodney Stuckey/99 4.00 10.00
30 Chris Kaman/49 3.00 8.00
31 O.J. Mayo/99 4.00 10.00
32 Tim Duncan/99 6.00 15.00
33 Al Jefferson/99 4.00 10.00
34 Andre Iguodala/99 4.00 10.00
35 Deron Williams/25 5.00 12.00
36 David West/99 4.00 10.00
38 Gerald Wallace/99 4.00 10.00
39 Andrea Bargnani/99 3.00 8.00
40 Antawn Jamison/49 4.00 10.00
41 Luol Deng/99 4.00 10.00
44 Jason Terry/99 3.00 8.00
45 Baron Davis/99 4.00 10.00
46 Russell Westbrook/99 6.00 15.00
47 Michael Beasley/99 4.00 10.00
48 Caron Butler/49 4.00 10.00
49 Carl Landry/99 2.50 6.00
50 LaMarcus Aldridge/99 4.00 10.00
51 Ray Allen/99 4.00 10.00
52 Trevor Ariza/99 2.50 6.00
53 Tony Parker/99 4.00 10.00
54 Chauncey Billups/25 4.00 10.00
55 Luis Scola/99 3.00 8.00
56 Josh Smith/99 4.00 10.00
58 Marc Gasol/99 4.00 10.00
59 Jason Richardson/99 4.00 10.00
60 Jeff Green/99 3.00 8.00
61 Danny Granger/99 4.00 10.00
62 Nene/99 3.00 8.00
63 Vince Carter/99 5.00 12.00
65 Rajon Rondo/99 5.00 12.00
66 Eric Gordon/99 4.00 10.00
67 Elton Brand/99 4.00 10.00
68 D.J. Augustin/99 3.00 8.00
69 Derek Fisher/49 6.00 15.00
70 Devin Harris/99 4.00 10.00
71 Emeka Okafor/49 4.00 10.00
73 Jermaine O'Neal/99 4.00 10.00
75 Kevin Love/99 6.00 15.00
76 Lamar Odom/99 4.00 10.00
77 Mike Bibby/99 3.00 8.00
78 Randy Foye/99 2.50 6.00
79 Richard Hamilton/99 3.00 8.00
80 Ron Artest/99 4.00 10.00
82 Rudy Fernandez/99 3.00 8.00
84 Shane Battier/99 4.00 10.00
85 T.J. Ford/99 2.50 6.00
86 Ben Gordon/99 4.00 10.00
87 Rashard Lewis/99 3.00 8.00
88 Shawn Marion/99 4.00 10.00
89 Troy Murphy/99 2.50 6.00
90 Chris Duhon/99 2.50 6.00
91 Raymond Felton/99 3.00 8.00
92 Andre Miller/99 3.00 8.00
94 Mike Conley Jr./99 3.00 8.00
96 Chris Andersen/99 6.00 15.00
97 Greg Oden/99 3.00 8.00
99 Yi Jianlian/99 3.00 8.00
100 Wilson Chandler/99 3.00 8.00
121 Tom Heinsohn/25 4.00 10.00
130 Earl Monroe/25 4.00 10.00
132 Dave Cowens/49 4.00 10.00
135 Bob Lanier/99 5.00 12.00
139 Kareem Abdul-Jabbar/25 8.00 20.00
144 Alex English/25 6.00 15.00
149 Kevin McHale/99 4.00 10.00
153 Robert Parish/49 4.00 10.00
155 Clyde Drexler/25 8.00 20.00
158 Joe Dumars/25 6.00 15.00
161 Patrick Ewing/99 6.00 15.00
162 Hakeem Olajuwon/99 5.00 12.00
167 Alonzo Mourning/99 6.00 15.00
168 Bernard King/99 6.00 15.00
170 Scottie Pippen/49 8.00 20.00
171 Chris Mullin/99 4.00 10.00
172 Danny Manning/99 4.00 10.00
174 Detlef Schrempf/99 6.00 15.00
175 Dikembe Mutombo/99 5.00 12.00
177 Jeff Hornacek/99 4.00 10.00
193 Derrick Brown/25 4.00 10.00

2009-10 Playoff National Treasures Century Materials Prime

*PRIME: .75X TO 2X BASE HI
STATED PRINT RUN ONE TO 25 SER.#'d SETS
SOME UNPRICED DUE TO SCARCITY
4 Derrick Rose/25 25.00 60.00
14 Allen Iverson/25 20.00 40.00
121 Tom Heinsohn/15 10.00 25.00
137 Dan Issel/25 8.00 20.00
144 Alex English/25 8.00 20.00
152 Magic Johnson/25 25.00 60.00
158 Joe Dumars/25 8.00 20.00
159 Dominique Wilkins/25 10.00 25.00
160 Adrian Dantley/25 8.00 20.00
164 John Stockton/25 10.00 25.00
168 Bernard King/25 8.00 20.00
171 Chris Mullin/25 12.50 30.00

2009-10 Playoff National Treasures Century Materials Signatures

STATED PRINT RUN ONE TO 99 SER.#'d SETS
SOME UNPRICED DUE TO SCARCITY
UNPRICED LOGO SIG.PRINT RUN ONE SET
UNPRICED TAG SIG.PRINT RUN ONE SET
UNPRICED TEAM SIG.PRINT RUN 1 TO 5 SETS
1 Kobe Bryant/25 125.00 225.00
14 Allen Iverson/25 60.00 150.00
19 Brandon Roy/25 12.50 30.00
20 Amare Stoudemire/25 15.00 40.00
30 Chris Kaman/49 8.00 20.00
34 Andre Iguodala/49 8.00 20.00
35 Deron Williams/25 12.50 30.00
39 Andrea Bargnani/49 8.00 20.00
45 Baron Davis/99 8.00 20.00
49 Carl Landry/99 8.00 20.00
53 Tony Parker/25 15.00 30.00
54 Chauncey Billups/25 8.00 20.00
57 Andrew Bynum/25 15.00 40.00
68 D.J. Augustin/99 8.00 20.00
71 Emeka Okafor/49 8.00 20.00
85 T.J. Ford/25 8.00 20.00
96 Chris Andersen/99 12.00 30.00
132 Dave Cowens/49 10.00 25.00
144 Alex English/28 8.00 20.00
168 Bernard King/99 8.00 20.00
171 Chris Mullin/49 20.00 40.00
172 Danny Manning/49 12.50 30.00
174 Detlef Schrempf/99 8.00 20.00

2009-10 Playoff National Treasures Century Materials Prime Signatures

STATED PRINT RUN ONE TO 25 SER.#'d SETS
SOME UNPRICED DUE TO SCARCITY
30 Chris Kaman/25 10.00 25.00
34 Andre Iguodala/25 10.00 25.00
49 Carl Landry/25 10.00 25.00
96 Chris Andersen/25 30.00 60.00
132 Dave Cowens/25 15.00 30.00
168 Bernard King/25 10.00 25.00
171 Chris Mullin/25 30.00 80.00
172 Danny Manning/25 15.00 40.00
193 Derrick Brown/25 10.00 25.00

2009-10 Playoff National Treasures Century Signatures

STATED PRINT RUN 5 TO 99 SER.#'d SETS
SOME UNPRICED DUE TO SCARCITY
ASTERISK CARDS FROM PANINI UPDATE
UNPRICED PLAT.SIG PRINT RUN ONE SET
1 Kobe Bryant/25* 125.00 250.00
28 Aaron Brooks/25 6.00 15.00
30 Chris Kaman/25 6.00 15.00
34 Andre Iguodala/25 6.00 15.00
39 Andrea Bargnani/25 6.00 15.00
45 Baron Davis/25 6.00 15.00
46 Russell Westbrook/25 20.00 50.00
47 Michael Beasley/25 8.00 20.00
52 Trevor Ariza/25 6.00 15.00
54 Chauncey Billups/25 8.00 20.00
64 Charlie Villanueva/25 6.00 15.00
68 D.J. Augustin/25 6.00 15.00
70 Devin Harris/25 6.00 15.00
71 Emeka Okafor/25 6.00 15.00
73 Jermaine O'Neal/25 6.00 15.00
74 Josh Howard/25 6.00 15.00
75 Kevin Love/25 20.00 50.00
77 Mike Bibby/25 6.00 15.00
78 Randy Foye/25 6.00 15.00
79 Richard Hamilton/25 6.00 15.00
80 Ron Artest/25 20.00 50.00
81 Ronnie Brewer/25 6.00 15.00
84 Shane Battier/25 8.00 20.00
85 T.J. Ford/25 6.00 15.00
96 Chris Andersen/25 15.00 40.00
104 Dolph Schayes/25 12.50 30.00
108 Cliff Hagan/25 10.00 25.00
112 Hal Greer/25 10.00 25.00
114 Frank Ramsey/25 12.00 30.00
115 Willis Reed/25 10.00 25.00
119 Nate Thurmond/25 10.00 25.00
123 Walt Frazier/25 12.50 30.00
124 Bobby Wanzer/25 10.00 25.00
126 Wes Unseld/25 15.00 40.00
128 Lenny Wilkens/25 10.00 25.00
129 Elvin Hayes/25 15.00 30.00
131 Nate Archibald/25 10.00 25.00
132 Dave Cowens/25 10.00 25.00
133 Harry Gallatin/25 10.00 25.00
137 Dan Issel/17 8.00 20.00
141 George Gervin/25 10.00 25.00
142 Gail Goodrich/25 10.00 25.00
143 David Thompson/25 10.00 25.00
145 Bailey Howell/25 10.00 25.00
147 Marques Haynes/25 15.00 40.00
148 Arnie Risen/25 10.00 25.00
150 Bob McAdoo/25 15.00 30.00
153 Robert Parish/25 15.00 30.00
154 James Worthy/25 30.00 60.00
155 Clyde Drexler/25 20.00 50.00
162 Hakeem Olajuwon/25 25.00 60.00
168 Bernard King/25 10.00 25.00
169 Bill Laimbeer/15 12.50 30.00
171 Chris Mullin/25 15.00 40.00
172 Danny Manning/25 10.00 25.00
174 Detlef Schrempf/25 20.00 50.00
175 Dikembe Mutombo/25 25.00 60.00
176 George McGinnis/25 10.00 25.00
177 Jeff Hornacek/25 10.00 25.00
178 Sidney Moncrief/25 8.00 20.00
179 Pat Riley/25 15.00 40.00
181 Calvin Murphy/25 8.00 20.00
182 Nancy Lieberman/25 8.00 20.00
183 Meadowlark Lemon/25 30.00 60.00
186 Jonas Jerebko/99 8.00 20.00
187 Marcus Thornton/99 25.00 60.00
188 Wesley Matthews/99 25.00 60.00
189 Serge Ibaka/99 100.00 200.00
190 A.J. Price/99 8.00 20.00
191 Jon Brockman/99 6.00 15.00
192 Dante Cunningham/99 6.00 15.00
193 Derrick Brown/99 6.00 15.00
194 Sundiata Gaines/99 6.00 15.00
195 Marcus Landry/99 6.00 15.00
196 Lester Hudson/99 6.00 15.00
197 Danny Green/99 10.00 25.00
198 David Andersen/99 10.00 25.00
199 DeMar DeRozan/99 20.00 50.00
200 Ricky Rubio/99 125.00 250.00

2009-10 Playoff National Treasures Champions

COMPLETE SET (10) 40.00 80.00
STATED PRINT RUN 25 SER.#'d SETS
1 John Kundla 5.00 12.00
2 Vern Mikkelsen 5.00 12.00
3 Earl Lloyd 5.00 12.00
4 Dolph Schayes 5.00 12.00
5 Arnie Risen 5.00 12.00
6 Bobby Wanzer 5.00 12.00
7 Clyde Drexler 6.00 15.00
8 Chauncey Billups 5.00 12.00
9 Shaquille O'Neal 10.00 25.00
10 Tony Parker 5.00 12.00

2009-10 Playoff National Treasures Champions Signature Combos

STATED PRINT RUN 5 TO 25 SER.#'d SETS
SOME UNPRICED DUE TO SCARCITY
UNPRICED QUAD PRINT RUN 5 SER.#'d SETS
3 Dave Cowens/25 30.00 80.00
John Havlicek
4 Elvin Hayes/25 25.00 50.00
Wes Unseld

2009-10 Playoff National Treasures Champions Signatures

STATED PRINT RUN 5 TO 99 SER.#'d SETS
SOME UNPRICED DUE TO SCARCITY
4 Dolph Schayes/25 10.00 25.00
6 Bobby Wanzer/99 8.00 20.00
7 Clyde Drexler/25 20.00 40.00
10 Tony Parker/15 12.00 30.00

2009-10 Playoff National Treasures Colossal Materials

STATED PRINT RUN 5 TO 99 SER.#'d SETS
SOME UNPRICED DUE TO SCARCITY
UNPRICED LOGO PRINT RUNS ONE TO 5 SETS
1 Kobe Bryant/99 12.00 30.00
2 Blake Griffin/25 20.00 50.00
3 Kevin Durant/49 12.00 30.00
4 James Harden/25 10.00 25.00
5 Dirk Nowitzki/99 5.00 12.00
6 Tyreke Evans/25 8.00 20.00
7 Carmelo Anthony/49 5.00 12.00
8 Jonny Flynn/25 3.00 8.00
9 Chris Bosh/25 5.00 12.00
10 Stephen Curry/25 8.00 20.00
11 David Lee/25 3.00 8.00
12 DeMar DeRozan/25 5.00 12.00
14 Brandon Jennings/25 6.00 15.00
15 Steve Nash/49 10.00 25.00
16 Terrence Williams/25 3.00 8.00
18 Omri Casspi/25 3.00 8.00
19 Andre Iguodala/99 4.00 10.00
20 Darren Collison/25 5.00 12.00
22 Taj Gibson/25 4.00 10.00
23 Russell Westbrook/99 6.00 15.00
24 Ty Lawson/25 5.00 12.00
25 Danny Granger/99 4.00 10.00
26 DeJuan Blair/25 4.00 10.00
27 Ray Allen/99 4.00 10.00
28 Chase Budinger/25 3.00 8.00
29 Rajon Rondo/99 5.00 12.00
30 Sam Young/25 3.00 8.00
32 Jrue Holiday/25 6.00 15.00
33 LeBron James/49 15.00 40.00
34 Tyler Hansbrough/25 5.00 12.00
35 Dwyane Wade/99 8.00 20.00
36 Amare Stoudemire/99 4.00 10.00
37 Derrick Rose/99 12.00 30.00
38 Dwight Howard/99 6.00 15.00
40 Tim Duncan/99 6.00 15.00
41 Brandon Roy/49 4.00 10.00
42 Chris Paul/49 6.00 15.00
43 Pau Gasol/99 4.00 10.00
44 Shaquille O'Neal/49 8.00 20.00
45 Josh Smith/99 4.00 10.00
47 Paul Pierce/99 5.00 12.00
48 Eric Gordon/99 4.00 10.00
49 Tony Parker/99 4.00 10.00
50 Kevin Garnett/25 8.00 20.00

2009-10 Playoff National Treasures Colossal Materials Prime

STATED PRINT RUN ONE TO 25 SER.#'d SETS
MOST UNPRICED DUE TO SCARCITY
UNPRICED JSY NO.PRIME PRINT RUN 1 TO 10 SETS
1 Kobe Bryant/25 40.00 100.00

2009-10 Playoff National Treasures Colossal Materials Jersey Numbers

*JSY NUMB: SAME VALUE AS BASE
STATED PRINT RUN 10 TO 99 SER.#'d SETS
SOME UNPRICED DUE TO SCARCITY
23 Russell Westbrook/25 8.00 20.00
27 Ray Allen/25 8.00 20.00
43 Pau Gasol/25 10.00 25.00
47 Paul Pierce/99 5.00 12.00

2009-10 Playoff National Treasures Colossal Materials Signatures

STATED PRINT RUN 3 TO 49 SER.#'d SETS
SOME UNPRICED DUE TO SCARCITY
*JSY NUMBER: .4X TO 1X HI COLUMN
JSY NUMBER PRINT RUN 4 TO 49 SETS
1 Kobe Bryant/25 125.00 250.00
4 James Harden/49 20.00 50.00
6 Tyreke Evans/49 20.00 50.00
8 Jonny Flynn/49 6.00 15.00
9 Chris Bosh/25 15.00 40.00
10 Stephen Curry/49 20.00 50.00
12 DeMar DeRozan/49 10.00 25.00
14 Brandon Jennings/49 12.00 30.00
16 Terrence Williams/49 6.00 15.00
18 Omri Casspi/49 6.00 15.00
19 Andre Iguodala/49 6.00 15.00
20 Darren Collison/49 10.00 25.00
24 Ty Lawson/49 12.00 30.00
26 DeJuan Blair/49 8.00 20.00
28 Chase Budinger/49 6.00 15.00
30 Sam Young/49 6.00 15.00
32 Jrue Holiday/49 12.00 30.00
34 Tyler Hansbrough/49 10.00 25.00
41 Brandon Roy/25 12.50 30.00
49 Tony Parker/15 15.00 40.00

2009-10 Playoff National Treasures Colossal Materials Prime Signatures

STATED PRINT RUN ONE TO 25 SER.#'d SETS
SOME UNPRICED DUE TO SCARCITY
*JSY NUMBER: .4X TO 1X HI COLUMN
JSY NUMBER PRINT RUN ONE TO 25 SETS
12 DeMar DeRozan/25 25.00 60.00
14 Brandon Jennings/25 30.00 80.00
26 DeJuan Blair/25 20.00 50.00
32 Jrue Holiday/25 30.00 80.00

2009-10 Playoff National Treasures NBA Gear Dual

STATED PRINT RUN 10 TO 99 SER.#'d SETS
SOME UNPRICED DUE TO SCARCITY
TAGS NOT PRICED DUE TO SCARCITY
1 Kobe Bryant/99 15.00 30.00
2 LeBron James/49 15.00 30.00
3 Blake Griffin/25 20.00 50.00
5 James Harden/25 10.00 25.00
6 Dwyane Wade/99 6.00 15.00
7 Tyreke Evans/25 8.00 20.00
8 Carmelo Anthony/49 4.00 10.00
9 Jonny Flynn/25 3.00 8.00
10 Chris Paul/99 5.00 12.00
11 Stephen Curry/25 8.00 20.00
12 Dwight Howard/99 5.00 12.00
13 DeMar DeRozan/25 5.00 12.00
14 Earl Clark/25 3.00 8.00
15 Brandon Jennings/25 6.00 15.00
16 Gerald Henderson/25 3.00 8.00
17 Terrence Williams/25 3.00 8.00
18 Toney Douglas/25 3.00 8.00
19 Omri Casspi/25 3.00 8.00
20 Wayne Ellington/25 3.00 8.00
21 Darren Collison/25 5.00 12.00
22 Austin Daye/25 3.00 8.00
23 Taj Gibson/25 4.00 10.00
24 Jeff Teague/25 4.00 10.00
25 Ty Lawson/25 5.00 12.00
26 Eric Maynor/25 3.00 8.00
27 DeJuan Blair/25 4.00 10.00
28 James Johnson/25 3.00 8.00
29 Chase Budinger/25 3.00 8.00
30 Jordan Hill/25 3.00 8.00
31 Sam Young/25 3.00 8.00
32 Hasheem Thabeet/25 3.00 8.00
33 Jrue Holiday/25 6.00 15.00
34 Rodrigue Beaubois/25 4.00 10.00
35 Tyler Hansbrough/25 5.00 12.00

2009-10 Playoff National Treasures NBA Gear Dual Prime

*PRIME: .5X TO 1.25X BASE HI
STATED PRINT RUN 5 TO 49 SER.#'d SETS
SOME UNPRICED DUE TO SCARCITY
1 Kobe Bryant/49 30.00 60.00
3 Blake Griffin/49 30.00 80.00
8 Carmelo Anthony/25 10.00 25.00
10 Chris Paul/20 8.00 20.00
29 Chase Budinger/25 8.00 20.00

2009-10 Playoff National Treasures NBA Gear Dual Signatures

STATED PRINT RUN 3 TO 30 SER.#'d SETS
SOME UNPRICED DUE TO SCARCITY
*PRIME: .5X TO 1.25X HI COLUMN
PRIME PRINT RUN 3 TO 49 SETS
1 Kobe Bryant/25 125.00 250.00
3 Blake Griffin/25 200.00 400.00
5 James Harden/30 25.00 60.00
7 Tyreke Evans/30 25.00 60.00
9 Jonny Flynn/30 6.00 15.00
11 Stephen Curry/30 25.00 60.00
13 DeMar DeRozan/30 10.00 25.00
14 Earl Clark/30 6.00 15.00
15 Brandon Jennings/30 15.00 40.00
16 Gerald Henderson/30 6.00 15.00
17 Terrence Williams/30 6.00 15.00
18 Toney Douglas/30 6.00 15.00
19 Omri Casspi/30 6.00 15.00
20 Wayne Ellington/30 6.00 15.00
21 Darren Collison/30 10.00 25.00
22 Austin Daye/30 6.00 15.00
23 Taj Gibson/30 8.00 20.00
24 Jeff Teague/30 8.00 20.00
25 Ty Lawson/30 10.00 25.00
26 Eric Maynor/25 6.00 15.00
27 DeJuan Blair/30 8.00 20.00
28 James Johnson/30 6.00 15.00
29 Chase Budinger/30 6.00 15.00
30 Jordan Hill/30 6.00 15.00
31 Sam Young/30 6.00 15.00
32 Hasheem Thabeet/30 6.00 15.00
33 Jrue Holiday/30 15.00 40.00
34 Rodrigue Beaubois/30 8.00 20.00
35 Tyler Hansbrough/30 10.00 25.00

2009-10 Playoff National Treasures NBA Gear Trios

STATED PRINT RUN 10 TO 99 SER.#'d SETS
SOME UNPRICED DUE TO SCARCITY
1 Kobe Bryant/99 15.00 30.00
2 LeBron James/49 12.00 30.00
3 Blake Griffin/25 25.00 60.00
5 James Harden/25 12.00 30.00
6 Dwyane Wade/99 8.00 20.00
7 Tyreke Evans/25 10.00 25.00
8 Carmelo Anthony/49 6.00 15.00
9 Jonny Flynn/25 4.00 10.00
10 Chris Paul/99 6.00 15.00
11 Stephen Curry/25 10.00 25.00
12 Dwight Howard/99 6.00 15.00
13 DeMar DeRozan/25 6.00 15.00
14 Earl Clark/25 4.00 10.00
15 Brandon Jennings/25 8.00 20.00
16 Gerald Henderson/25 4.00 10.00
17 Terrence Williams/25 4.00 10.00
18 Toney Douglas/25 4.00 10.00
19 Omri Casspi/25 4.00 10.00
20 Wayne Ellington/25 4.00 10.00
21 Darren Collison/25 6.00 15.00
22 Austin Daye/25 4.00 10.00
23 Taj Gibson/25 5.00 12.00
24 Jeff Teague/25 5.00 12.00
25 Ty Lawson/25 6.00 15.00
26 Eric Maynor/25 4.00 10.00
27 DeJuan Blair/25 5.00 12.00
28 James Johnson/25 4.00 10.00
29 Chase Budinger/25 4.00 10.00
30 Jordan Hill/25 4.00 10.00
31 Sam Young/25 4.00 10.00
32 Hasheem Thabeet/25 4.00 10.00
33 Jrue Holiday/25 8.00 20.00
34 Rodrigue Beaubois/25 5.00 12.00
35 Tyler Hansbrough/25 6.00 15.00

2009-10 Playoff National Treasures NBA Gear Trios Prime

*PRIME: .5X TO 1.25X BASE HI
STATED PRINT RUN 5 TO 49 SER.#'d SETS
SOME UNPRICED DUE TO SCARCITY
1 Kobe Bryant/49 40.00 75.00
8 Carmelo Anthony/49 12.00 30.00
10 Chris Paul/49 12.00 30.00

2009-10 Playoff National Treasures NBA Gear Trios Signatures

STATED PRINT RUN 3 TO 30 SER.#'d SETS
SOME UNPRICED DUE TO SCARCITY
*PRIME: .6X TO 1.5X HI COLUMN
PRIME PRINT RUN 3 TO 49 SETS
1 Kobe Bryant/25 150.00 300.00
5 James Harden/30 25.00 60.00
7 Tyreke Evans/30 25.00 60.00
9 Jonny Flynn/30 6.00 15.00
11 Stephen Curry/30 25.00 60.00
13 DeMar DeRozan/30 10.00 25.00
14 Earl Clark/30 6.00 15.00
15 Brandon Jennings/30 15.00 40.00
16 Gerald Henderson/30 6.00 15.00
17 Terrence Williams/30 6.00 15.00
18 Toney Douglas/30 6.00 15.00
19 Omri Casspi/30 6.00 15.00
20 Wayne Ellington/30 6.00 15.00
21 Darren Collison/30 10.00 25.00
22 Austin Daye/30 6.00 15.00
23 Taj Gibson/30 10.00 25.00
24 Jeff Teague/30 8.00 20.00
25 Ty Lawson/30 10.00 25.00
26 Eric Maynor/25 6.00 15.00
27 DeJuan Blair/30 8.00 20.00
28 James Johnson/30 6.00 15.00
29 Chase Budinger/30 6.00 15.00
30 Jordan Hill/30 6.00 15.00
31 Sam Young/30 6.00 15.00
32 Hasheem Thabeet/30 6.00 15.00
33 Jrue Holiday/30 15.00 40.00
34 Rodrigue Beaubois/30 8.00 20.00
35 Tyler Hansbrough/30 10.00 25.00

2009-10 Playoff National Treasures NBA Greatest

COMPLETE SET (30) 125.00 250.00
PRINT RUN 25 SER.#'d SETS
1 Kareem Abdul-Jabbar 8.00 20.00
2 Nate Archibald 5.00 12.00
3 Rick Barry 5.00 12.00
4 Larry Bird 15.00 40.00
5 Bob Cousy 8.00 20.00
6 Dave Cowens 5.00 12.00
7 Clyde Drexler 6.00 15.00
8 Walt Frazier 5.00 12.00
9 George Gervin 5.00 12.00
10 Hal Greer 5.00 12.00
11 John Havlicek 5.00 12.00
12 Elvin Hayes 5.00 12.00
13 Magic Johnson 12.00 30.00
14 Kevin McHale 5.00 12.00
15 George Mikan 10.00 25.00
16 Earl Monroe 5.00 12.00
17 Shaquille O'Neal 10.00 25.00
18 Robert Parish 5.00 12.00
19 Scottie Pippen 10.00 25.00
20 Willis Reed 5.00 12.00
21 Oscar Robertson 5.00 12.00
22 Bill Russell 8.00 20.00
23 Dolph Schayes 5.00 12.00
24 Isiah Thomas 5.00 12.00
25 Nate Thurmond 5.00 12.00
26 Wes Unseld 5.00 12.00
27 Bill Walton 5.00 12.00
28 Jerry West 6.00 15.00
29 Lenny Wilkens 5.00 12.00
30 James Worthy 6.00 15.00

2009-10 Playoff National Treasures NBA Greatest Materials

STATED PRINT RUN 10 TO 99 SER.#'d SETS
SOME UNPRICED DUE TO SCARCITY
1 Kareem Abdul-Jabbar/25 10.00 25.00
6 Dave Cowens/99 6.00 15.00
7 Clyde Drexler/25 12.00 30.00
14 Kevin McHale/99 6.00 15.00
15 George Mikan/99 12.00 30.00
16 Earl Monroe/25 10.00 25.00
17 Shaquille O'Neal/49 10.00 25.00
18 Robert Parish/49 6.00 15.00
19 Scottie Pippen/49 10.00 25.00

2009-10 Playoff National Treasures NBA Greatest Materials Prime

*PRIME: .6X TO 1.5X HI COLUMN
STATED PRINT RUN 5 TO 25 SER.#'d SETS
SOME UNPRICED DUE TO SCARCITY
13 Magic Johnson/25 15.00 40.00

2009-10 Playoff National Treasures NBA Greatest Materials Signatures

STATED PRINT RUN ONE TO 49 SER.#'d SETS
SOME UNPRICED DUE TO SCARCITY
6 Dave Cowens/49 10.00 25.00
7 Clyde Drexler/49 25.00 50.00

2009-10 Playoff National Treasures NBA Greatest Materials Prime Signatures

STATED PRINT RUN ONE TO 25 SER.#'d SETS
SOME UNPRICED DUE TO SCARCITY
6 Dave Cowens/25 20.00 40.00

2009-10 Playoff National Treasures NBA Greatest Signature Combos

STATED PRINT RUN 5 TO 99 SER.#'d SETS
SOME UNPRICED DUE TO SCARCITY
1 Bob Pettit/25 25.00 50.00
Lenny Wilkens
4 Elvin Hayes/25 25.00 60.00
Wes Unseld
5 Bill Walton/99
Clyde Drexler

2009-10 Playoff National Treasures NBA Greatest Signature Quads

STATED PRINT RUN 3 TO 15 SER.#'d SETS
SOME UNPRICED DUE TO SCARCITY
2 Kevin McHale/15 150.00 300.00
Robert Parish
Bill Walton
Larry Bird

2009-10 Playoff National Treasures NBA Greatest Signatures

STATED PRINT RUN 3 TO 25 SER.#'d SETS
SOME UNPRICED DUE TO SCARCITY
UNPRICED TRIO SIG PRINT RUN 5 SER.#'d SETS
2 Nate Archibald/25 12.00 30.00
6 Dave Cowens/25 12.00 30.00
7 Clyde Drexler/25 25.00 50.00
8 Walt Frazier/25 12.00 30.00
10 Hal Greer/25 12.00 30.00
18 Robert Parish/25 12.00 30.00
20 Willis Reed/25 12.00 30.00
23 Dolph Schayes/25 12.00 30.00
25 Nate Thurmond/25 15.00 40.00
26 Wes Unseld/25 20.00 40.00
27 Bill Walton/25 12.00 30.00
30 James Worthy/25 30.00 60.00

2009-10 Playoff National Treasures Notable Nicknames

STATED PRINT RUN 10 TO 99 SER.#'d SETS
SOME UNPRICED DUE TO SCARCITY
BC Billy Cunningham/55 100.00 200.00
BW Bill Walton/99 40.00 80.00
CD Clyde Drexler/25 100.00 200.00
DC Dave Cowens/99 25.00 60.00
DW Dominique Wilkins/25 200.00 300.00
EH Elvin Hayes/25 100.00 200.00
EM Earl Monroe/99 200.00 500.00
FR Frank Ramsey/49 30.00 80.00
GG George Gervin/99 40.00 70.00
HG Harry Gallatin/49 25.00 60.00
JH John Havlicek/49 75.00 150.00
LB Larry Bird/25 300.00 550.00
NT Nate Thurmond/25 75.00 150.00
OR Oscar Robertson/25 150.00 350.00
WR Willis Reed/99 40.00 80.00
JWE Jerry West/25 150.00 300.00
KB1 Kobe Bryant Mamba/99 700.00 1100.00
KB2 Kobe Bryant MVP/35 600.00 1000.00

2009-10 Playoff National Treasures Pen Pals

STATED PRINT RUN 50 SER.#'d SETS
1 Blake Griffin 100.00 225.00
2 Hasheem Thabeet 6.00 15.00
3 James Harden 20.00 50.00
4 Jordan Hill 6.00 15.00
5 Stephen Curry 25.00 60.00
6 Tyler Hansbrough 10.00 25.00
7 Tyreke Evans 25.00 60.00
8 Blake Griffin 60.00 150.00
Hasheem Thabeet
9 Blake Griffin 75.00 200.00
Tyler Hansbrough
10 Darren Collison 15.00 40.00
Jrue Holiday
11 DeJuan Blair 10.00 25.00
Sam Young
12 Earl Clark 10.00 25.00
Terrence Williams
13 James Harden 12.50 30.00
Jordan Hill
14 James Johnson 10.00 25.00
Jeff Teague
15 Chase Budinger 12.50 30.00
Jordan Hill
16 Ty Lawson 25.00 60.00
Tyler Hansbrough
17 DeJuan Blair 15.00 40.00
Hasheem Thabeet
Jonny Flynn

2009-10 Playoff National Treasures Signature Patches College

STATED PRINT RUN 25 TO 77 SER.#'d SETS
UNPRICED NBA LOGO PRINT RUN 5 TO 10 SETS
UNPRICED NBA LOGOMAN PRINT RUN ONE SET
2 Carmelo Anthony/27 30.00 80.00
3 Bill Walton/77 15.00 40.00
4 Dominique Wilkins/25 15.00 40.00
7 Dave Cowens/27 15.00 40.00
8 Oscar Robertson/27 40.00 100.00
9 David Thompson/27 12.50 30.00
10 Rick Barry/26 12.50 30.00
13 Isiah Thomas/27 15.00 40.00
15 Jerry West/26 40.00 80.00
17 John Havlicek/28 30.00 60.00
19 Kareem Abdul-Jabbar/27 40.00 80.00
25 Magic Johnson/27 40.00 100.00

2009-10 Playoff National Treasures Signature Patches NBA Team

STATED PRINT RUN 49 TO 100 SER.#'d SETS
1 Bill Russell/49 60.00 120.00
2 Carmelo Anthony/53 25.00 60.00
3 Bill Walton/50 10.00 25.00
5 Bob Cousy/54 35.00 70.00
6 Nate Thurmond/53 10.00 25.00
7 Dave Cowens/52 12.00 30.00
8 Oscar Robertson/53 40.00 100.00
9 David Thompson/51 10.00 25.00
10 Rick Barry/51 10.00 25.00
11 Dennis Rodman/53 25.00 60.00
12 Robert Parish/49 12.00 30.00
13 Isiah Thomas/53 12.50 30.00
14 Scottie Pippen/53 100.00 200.00
15 Jerry West/54 30.00 80.00
17 John Havlicek/52 25.00 60.00
18 Steve Nash/25 50.00 100.00
19 Kareem Abdul-Jabbar/54 30.00 60.00
23 Larry Bird/49 60.00 150.00
24 Kobe Bryant/100 100.00 200.00
25 Magic Johnson/51 50.00 120.00

2009-10 Playoff National Treasures Souvenir Cuts

STATED PRINT RUN ONE TO 25 SER.#'d SETS
SOME UNPRICED DUE TO SCARCITY
1 George Mikan/15 125.00 250.00
6 Andy Phillip/25 75.00 200.00
7 Paul Arizin/25 40.00 100.00

2009-10 Playoff National Treasures Timeline Materials Custom Names

STATED PRINT RUN 10 TO 99 SER.#'d SETS
SOME UNPRICED DUE TO SCARCITY
*NICKNAMES: .4X TO 1X BASE HI
1 Kobe Bryant/99 12.00 30.00
2 LeBron James/49 12.00 30.00
3 Tyreke Evans/49 8.00 20.00
4 Brandon Jennings/49 6.00 15.00
5 Stephen Curry/49 8.00 20.00
6 Jonny Flynn/49 3.00 8.00
7 Taj Gibson/49 4.00 10.00
9 Ty Lawson/49 5.00 12.00
10 Shaquille O'Neal/49 8.00 20.00
11 DeJuan Blair/49 4.00 10.00
12 Dirk Nowitzki/99 5.00 12.00
14 Dwyane Wade/99 8.00 20.00
15 Derrick Rose/99 12.00 30.00
16 Carmelo Anthony/49 5.00 12.00
17 David Lee/25 3.00 8.00
18 Chris Bosh/25 4.00 10.00
19 Brook Lopez/99 4.00 10.00
20 Dwight Howard/99 6.00 15.00
21 Joe Johnson/99 4.00 10.00
22 Tim Duncan/99 6.00 15.00
23 James Harden/49 10.00 25.00
24 Steve Nash/25 8.00 20.00
25 Darren Collison/49 5.00 12.00
27 Omri Casspi/49 3.00 8.00
28 Chris Paul/99 6.00 15.00
29 Blake Griffin/49 20.00 50.00
30 Pau Gasol/99 4.00 10.00

2009-10 Playoff National Treasures Timeline Materials Custom Names Prime

*PRIME: .6X TO 1.5X HI COLUMN
STATED PRINT RUN 3 TO 25 SER.#'d SETS
SOME UNPRICED DUE TO SCARCITY
*NICKNAMES: .4X TO 1X BASE HI
1 Kobe Bryant/25 25.00 60.00
29 Blake Griffin/25 40.00 100.00

2009-10 Playoff National Treasures Timeline Materials Custom Names Signatures

STATED PRINT RUN 3 TO 30 SER.#'d SETS
SOME UNPRICED DUE TO SCARCITY
*NICKNAMES: .4X TO 1X BASE HI
1 Kobe Bryant/25 125.00 250.00
3 Tyreke Evans/30 25.00 60.00
4 Brandon Jennings/30 20.00 50.00
5 Stephen Curry/30 25.00 60.00
6 Jonny Flynn/30 8.00 20.00
7 Taj Gibson/30 10.00 25.00
9 Ty Lawson/30 12.00 30.00
11 DeJuan Blair/30 10.00 25.00
17 David Lee/25 15.00 30.00
18 Chris Bosh/25 20.00 50.00
23 James Harden/30 25.00 60.00
25 Darren Collison/30 12.00 30.00
27 Omri Casspi/30 8.00 20.00
29 Blake Griffin/30 200.00 400.00

2009-10 Playoff National Treasures Timeline Materials Custom Names Prime Signatures

STATED PRINT RUN ONE TO 25 SER.#'d SETS
SOME UNPRICED DUE TO SCARCITY
*NICKNAMES: .4X TO 1X BASE HI
4 Brandon Jennings/25 25.00 60.00
5 Stephen Curry/25 30.00 80.00
6 Jonny Flynn/25 10.00 25.00
7 Taj Gibson/25 12.00 30.00
11 DeJuan Blair/25 12.00 30.00
23 James Harden/25 30.00 80.00

2010-11 Playoff National Treasures

1-185 PRINT RUN 99 SER.#'d SETS
JSY AU RC PRINT RUN 71 TO 99 SETS
UNPRICED RC BLACK PRINT RUN ONE SET
UNPRICED SILVER PRINT RUN 10 SETS
UNPRICED PLAT.PRINT RUN ONE TO 5 SETS
1 Josh Smith 4.00 10.00
2 Al Horford 3.00 8.00
3 Jamal Crawford 3.00 8.00
4 Joe Johnson 4.00 10.00
5 Kevin Garnett 8.00 20.00
6 Shaquille O'Neal 8.00 20.00
7 Rajon Rondo 5.00 12.00
8 Ray Allen 4.00 10.00
9 Paul Pierce 5.00 12.00
10 D.J. Augustin 3.00 8.00
11 Stephen Jackson 3.00 8.00
12 Joakim Noah 4.00 10.00
13 Derrick Rose 12.00 30.00
14 Luol Deng 4.00 10.00
15 Carlos Boozer 4.00 10.00
16 Antawn Jamison 4.00 10.00
17 Baron Davis 4.00 10.00
18 Dirk Nowitzki 5.00 12.00
19 Tyson Chandler 3.00 8.00
20 Jason Kidd 4.00 10.00
21 Shawn Marion 4.00 10.00
22 Raymond Felton 3.00 8.00
23 Nene 3.00 8.00
24 Danilo Gallinari 4.00 10.00
25 Ty Lawson 4.00 10.00
26 Tayshaun Prince 4.00 10.00
27 Rodney Stuckey 4.00 10.00
28 Ben Gordon 4.00 10.00
29 Richard Hamilton 3.00 8.00
30 Monta Ellis 4.00 10.00
31 David Lee 3.00 8.00
32 Stephen Curry 5.00 12.00
33 Kevin Martin 4.00 10.00
34 Luis Scola 3.00 8.00
35 Kyle Lowry 3.00 8.00
36 Danny Granger 4.00 10.00
37 Roy Hibbert 3.00 8.00
38 Darren Collison 4.00 10.00
39 Eric Gordon 4.00 10.00
40 Blake Griffin 10.00 25.00
41 Mo Williams 3.00 8.00
42 Kobe Bryant 12.00 30.00
43 Derek Fisher 3.00 8.00
44 Andrew Bynum 5.00 12.00
45 Lamar Odom 4.00 10.00
46 Pau Gasol 4.00 10.00
47 O.J. Mayo 4.00 10.00
48 Rudy Gay 4.00 10.00
49 Mike Conley Jr. 3.00 8.00
50 Zach Randolph 3.00 8.00
51 Dwyane Wade 8.00 20.00
52 Chris Bosh 4.00 10.00
53 Mike Bibby 3.00 8.00
54 LeBron James 12.00 30.00
55 Andrew Bogut 4.00 10.00
56 Brandon Jennings 4.00 10.00
57 John Salmons 4.00 10.00
58 Kevin Love 5.00 12.00
59 Michael Beasley 4.00 10.00
60 Anthony Morrow 2.50 6.00
61 Brook Lopez 4.00 10.00
62 Deron Williams 4.00 10.00
63 Chris Paul 6.00 15.00
64 David West 4.00 10.00
65 Emeka Okafor 4.00 10.00
66 Trevor Ariza 2.50 6.00
67 Amare Stoudemire 4.00 10.00
68 Carmelo Anthony 5.00 12.00
69 Chauncey Billups 4.00 10.00
70 James Harden 5.00 12.00
71 Kevin Durant 12.00 30.00
72 Russell Westbrook 5.00 12.00
73 Dwight Howard 6.00 15.00
74 Jameer Nelson 3.00 8.00
75 Jason Richardson 4.00 10.00
76 Andre Iguodala 4.00 10.00
77 Elton Brand 4.00 10.00
78 Jrue Holiday 4.00 10.00
79 Grant Hill 6.00 15.00
80 Steve Nash 4.00 10.00
81 Vince Carter 5.00 12.00
82 Brandon Roy 4.00 10.00
83 Gerald Wallace 4.00 10.00
84 LaMarcus Aldridge 4.00 10.00
85 Wesley Matthews 4.00 10.00
86 Marcus Thornton 4.00 10.00
87 Tyreke Evans 5.00 12.00
88 Manu Ginobili 4.00 10.00
89 Richard Jefferson 4.00 10.00
90 Tim Duncan 6.00 15.00
91 Tony Parker 4.00 10.00
92 Andrea Bargnani 3.00 8.00
93 DeMar DeRozan 4.00 10.00
94 Leandro Barbosa 3.00 8.00
95 Al Jefferson 4.00 10.00
96 Devin Harris 4.00 10.00
97 Paul Millsap 3.00 8.00
98 Andray Blatche 2.50 6.00
99 Nick Young 3.00 8.00
100 Rashard Lewis 3.00 8.00
101 Julius Erving 8.00 20.00
102 Bill Russell 6.00 15.00
103 Oscar Robertson 5.00 12.00
104 Dave Bing 4.00 10.00
105 Elvin Hayes 4.00 10.00
106 Wilt Chamberlain 8.00 20.00
107 Larry Bird 12.00 30.00
108 Karl Malone 5.00 12.00
109 Jerry Sloan 4.00 10.00
110 Pete Maravich 12.00 30.00
111 Bill Walton 4.00 10.00
112 Scottie Pippen 8.00 20.00
113 Henry Bibby 4.00 10.00
114 Dominique Wilkins 5.00 12.00
115 Kareem Abdul-Jabbar 6.00 15.00
116 Kiki Vandeweghe 4.00 10.00
117 Norm Nixon 4.00 10.00
118 Anfernee Hardaway 10.00 25.00
119 David Robinson 6.00 15.00
120 Kevin McHale 4.00 10.00
121 Dolph Schayes 4.00 10.00
122 Danny Schayes 4.00 10.00
123 Walt Frazier 4.00 10.00
124 Tim Hardaway 4.00 10.00
125 Magic Johnson 10.00 25.00
126 Clyde Drexler 5.00 12.00
127 Dale Ellis 4.00 10.00
128 Bailey Howell 4.00 10.00
129 Mark Price 4.00 10.00
130 Alonzo Mourning 5.00 12.00
131 Byron Scott 4.00 10.00
132 Chris Mullin 4.00 10.00
133 John Salley 4.00 10.00
134 Jerry West 5.00 12.00
135 Dennis Scott 4.00 10.00
136 Walter Berry 4.00 10.00
137 Wes Unseld 4.00 10.00
138 John Stockton 6.00 15.00
139 K.C. Jones 4.00 10.00
140 Rex Chapman 4.00 10.00
141 Patrick Ewing 5.00 12.00
142 Tom Chambers 4.00 10.00
143 Dell Curry 4.00 10.00
144 Hakeem Olajuwon 5.00 12.00
145 Danny Ainge 4.00 10.00
146 Rickey Green 4.00 10.00
147 Dave DeBusschere 4.00 10.00
148 Vlade Divac 4.00 10.00
149 Mark Eaton 4.00 10.00
150 Shawn Kemp 8.00 20.00
151 Jamal Mashburn 4.00 10.00
152 Sam Jones 4.00 10.00
153 Xavier McDaniel 4.00 10.00
154 Elgin Baylor 4.00 10.00
155 David Thompson 5.00 12.00
156 George Gervin 4.00 10.00
157 Albert King 4.00 10.00
158 Isiah Thomas 4.00 10.00
159 Willis Reed 4.00 10.00
160 Walt Bellamy 4.00 10.00
161 Bob Cousy 6.00 15.00
162 Gary Payton 4.00 10.00
163 Jalen Rose 4.00 10.00
164 Chris Webber 4.00 10.00
165 Sean Elliott 4.00 10.00
166 Steve Kerr 4.00 10.00
167 Christian Laettner 5.00 12.00
168 Dan Issel 4.00 10.00
169 Sidney Wicks 4.00 10.00
170 Dan Majerle 4.00 10.00
171 Rick Barry 4.00 10.00
172 George Mikan 8.00 20.00
173 Dikembe Mutombo 4.00 10.00
174 Gail Goodrich 4.00 10.00
175 Darryl Dawkins 4.00 10.00
176 Doc Rivers 4.00 10.00
177 Mitch Richmond 4.00 10.00
178 John Paxson 4.00 10.00
179 John Havlicek 5.00 12.00
180 Moses Malone 4.00 10.00
181 Glen Rice 4.00 10.00
182 Buck Williams 4.00 10.00
183 Ron Harper 4.00 10.00
184 Bob Love 4.00 10.00
185 Dave Cowens 4.00 10.00
186 Devin Ebanks RC 6.00 15.00
187 Craig Brackins RC 5.00 12.00
188 Kevin Seraphin RC 6.00 15.00
189 Omer Asik RC 6.00 15.00
190 Gary Forbes RC 5.00 12.00
191 Semih Erden RC 5.00 12.00
192 Nikola Pekovic RC 8.00 20.00
193 Manny Harris RC 5.00 12.00
194 Jeremy Lin RC 100.00 200.00
195 Jeremy Evans RC 5.00 12.00
196 Eugene Jeter RC 5.00 12.00
197 Samardo Samuels RC 5.00 12.00
198 Ishmael Smith RC 5.00 12.00
199 Armon Johnson RC 5.00 12.00
200 Derrick Caracter RC 5.00 12.00
201 John Wall JSY AU/99 RC 1200.00 2000.00
202 Evan Turner JSY AU/99 RC 175.00 350.00
203 Derrick Favors JSY AU/99 RC 200.00 400.00
204 Wesley Johnson JSY AU/99 RC 75.00 150.00
205 DeMarcus Cousins JSY AU/99 RC350.00 700.00
206 Ekpe Udoh JSY AU/99 RC 40.00 100.00
207 Greg Monroe JSY AU/99 RC 200.00 400.00
208 Al-Farouq Aminu JSY AU/99 RC75.00 150.00
209 Gordon Hayward JSY AU/99 RC150.00 300.00
210 Paul George JSY AU/99 RC 200.00 400.00
211 Cole Aldrich JSY AU/99 RC 30.00 80.00
212 Xavier Henry JSY AU/99 RC 40.00 100.00
213 Ed Davis JSY AU/75 RC 100.00 200.00
214 Patrick Patterson JSY AU/99 RC50.00 125.00
215 Larry Sanders JSY AU/71 RC 30.00 80.00
216 Luke Babbitt JSY AU/99 RC 30.00 80.00
217 Eric Bledsoe JSY AU/86 RC 125.00 250.00
218 Avery Bradley JSY AU/99 RC 100.00 200.00
219 James Anderson JSY AU/99 RC 40.00 100.00
220 Elliot Williams JSY AU/99 RC 30.00 80.00
221 Trevor Booker JSY AU/99 RC 30.00 80.00
222 Damion James JSY AU/99 RC 30.00 80.00
223 Dominique Jones JSY AU/99 RC30.00 80.00
224 Quincy Pondexter JSY AU/99 RC30.00 80.00
225 Jordan Crawford JSY AU/99 RC125.00 250.00
226 Greivis Vasquez JSY AU/99 RC 40.00 100.00
227 Daniel Orton JSY AU/99 RC 30.00 80.00
228 Lazar Hayward JSY AU/99 RC 30.00 80.00
229 Hassan Whiteside JSY AU/99 RC30.00 80.00
230 Terrico White JSY AU/99 RC 30.00 80.00
231 Andy Rautins JSY AU/99 RC 30.00 80.00
232 Lance Stephenson JSY AU/99 RC30.00 80.00
233 Luke Harangody JSY AU/99 RC 30.00 80.00
234 Willie Warren JSY AU/99 RC 30.00 80.00
235 Gani Lawal JSY AU/99 RC 30.00 80.00
236 Dexter Pittman JSY AU/99 RC 30.00 80.00
237 Timofey Mozgov JSY AU/99 RC 30.00 80.00
238 Landry Fields JSY AU/99 RC 50.00 125.00
239 Gary Neal JSY AU/99 RC 50.00 125.00

2010-11 Playoff National Treasures Century Gold

UNPRICED 1-200 PRINT RUN 5 SETS
JSY AU STATED PRINT RUN 25 SETS
201 John Wall JSY AU 1500.00 2500.00
202 Evan Turner JSY AU 200.00 400.00
203 Derrick Favors JSY AU 250.00 500.00
204 Wesley Johnson JSY AU 150.00 300.00
205 DeMarcus Cousins JSY AU 400.00 800.00
206 Ekpe Udoh JSY AU 50.00 125.00
207 Greg Monroe JSY AU 200.00 400.00
208 Al-Farouq Aminu JSY AU 100.00 225.00
209 Gordon Hayward JSY AU 200.00 400.00
210 Paul George JSY AU 300.00 600.00
211 Cole Aldrich JSY AU 50.00 125.00
212 Xavier Henry JSY AU 60.00 150.00
213 Ed Davis JSY AU 150.00 300.00
214 Patrick Patterson JSY AU 80.00 200.00
215 Larry Sanders JSY AU 50.00 125.00
216 Luke Babbitt JSY AU 50.00 125.00
217 Eric Bledsoe JSY AU 175.00 350.00
218 Avery Bradley JSY AU 100.00 250.00
219 James Anderson JSY AU 60.00 150.00
220 Elliot Williams JSY AU 50.00 125.00
221 Trevor Booker JSY AU 50.00 125.00
222 Damion James JSY AU 50.00 125.00
223 Dominique Jones JSY AU 50.00 125.00
224 Quincy Pondexter JSY AU 50.00 125.00
225 Jordan Crawford JSY AU 200.00 400.00
226 Greivis Vasquez JSY AU 60.00 150.00
227 Daniel Orton JSY AU 50.00 125.00
228 Lazar Hayward JSY AU 50.00 125.00
229 Hassan Whiteside JSY AU 50.00 125.00
230 Terrico White JSY AU 50.00 125.00
231 Andy Rautins JSY AU 50.00 125.00
232 Lance Stephenson JSY AU 50.00 125.00
233 Luke Harangody JSY AU 50.00 125.00
234 Willie Warren JSY AU 50.00 125.00
235 Gani Lawal JSY AU 50.00 125.00
236 Dexter Pittman JSY AU 50.00 125.00
237 Timofey Mozgov JSY AU 50.00 125.00
238 Landry Fields JSY AU 150.00 300.00
239 Gary Neal JSY AU 80.00 200.00

2010-11 Playoff National Treasures ABA Legends

STATED PRINT RUN 25 SER.#'d SETS
1 Julius Erving 10.00 25.00
2 Rick Barry 6.00 15.00
3 Moses Malone 6.00 15.00
4 Billy Cunningham 6.00 15.00
5 George Gervin 6.00 15.00
6 Dan Issel 6.00 15.00
7 Connie Hawkins 6.00 15.00
8 Artis Gilmore 6.00 15.00
9 George McGinnis 6.00 15.00
10 Wilt Chamberlain 10.00 25.00

2010-11 Playoff National Treasures ABA Legends Signatures

STATED PRINT RUN 10 TO 99 SER.#'d SETS
SOME UNPRICED DUE TO SCARCITY
2 Rick Barry/99 10.00 25.00
4 Billy Cunningham/99 25.00 60.00
5 George Gervin/25 15.00 40.00
6 Dan Issel/25 12.50 30.00
7 Connie Hawkins/99 15.00 40.00
8 Artis Gilmore/99 10.00 25.00
9 George McGinnis/99 10.00 25.00

2010-11 Playoff National Treasures All Decade

STATED PRINT RUN 25 SER.#'d SETS
1 George Mikan 8.00 20.00
2 Bill Russell 6.00 15.00
3 Elgin Baylor 4.00 10.00
4 Jerry West 6.00 15.00
5 Sam Jones 4.00 10.00
6 Kareem Abdul-Jabbar 6.00 15.00
7 George Gervin 4.00 10.00
8 John Havlicek 5.00 12.00
9 Magic Johnson 10.00 25.00
10 Larry Bird 12.00 30.00
11 Julius Erving 8.00 20.00
12 Kevin McHale 4.00 10.00
13 Dominique Wilkins 5.00 12.00
14 David Robinson 6.00 15.00
15 Clyde Drexler 8.00 20.00
16 Gary Payton 4.00 10.00
17 LeBron James 15.00 40.00
18 Kobe Bryant 15.00 40.00
19 Paul Pierce 4.00 10.00
20 Dirk Nowitzki 4.00 10.00

2010-11 Playoff National Treasures All Decade Materials

STATED PRINT RUN ONE TO 99 SER.#'d SETS
SOME UNPRICED DUE TO SCARCITY
1 George Mikan/25 12.50 30.00
3 Elgin Baylor/49 4.00 10.00
5 Sam Jones/49 4.00 10.00
6 Kareem Abdul-Jabbar/99 8.00 20.00
7 George Gervin/49 4.00 10.00
10 Larry Bird/49 12.00 30.00
11 Julius Erving/49 6.00 15.00
12 Kevin McHale/99 4.00 10.00
13 Dominique Wilkins/25 8.00 20.00
14 David Robinson/99 6.00 15.00
15 Clyde Drexler/99 5.00 12.00
16 Gary Payton/99 4.00 10.00
17 LeBron James/99 12.00 30.00
18 Kobe Bryant/99 12.00 30.00
19 Paul Pierce/99 5.00 12.00
20 Dirk Nowitzki/99 5.00 12.00

2010-11 Playoff National Treasures All Decade Materials Prime

*PRIME: .75X TO 2X BASE HI
STATED PRINT RUN ONE TO 25 SER.#'d SETS
SOME UNPRICED DUE TO SCARCITY
11 Julius Erving/25 15.00 40.00

2010-11 Playoff National Treasures All Decade Materials Signatures

STATED PRINT RUN 5 TO 25 SER.#'d SETS
SOME UNPRICED DUE TO SCARCITY
UNPRICED PRIME PRINT RUN ONE TO 10 SETS
3 Elgin Baylor/25 25.00 60.00
5 Sam Jones/25 15.00 40.00
7 George Gervin/25 20.00 50.00
13 Dominique Wilkins/25 15.00 40.00
14 David Robinson/25 30.00 80.00
15 Clyde Drexler/25 20.00 50.00
16 Gary Payton/25 15.00 40.00
18 Kobe Bryant/25 125.00 250.00
19 Paul Pierce/25 20.00 50.00

2010-11 Playoff National Treasures All Decade Signatures

STATED PRINT RUN 10 TO 25 SER.#'d SETS
SOME UNPRICED DUE TO SCARCITY
UNPRICED COMBO PRINT RUN 5 SETS
UNPRICED QUAD PRINT RUN 5 SETS
UNPRICED TRIO PRINT RUN 5 SETS
3 Elgin Baylor/25 15.00 40.00
5 Sam Jones/25 12.50 30.00
7 George Gervin/25 15.00 40.00
8 John Havlicek/25 15.00 40.00
12 Kevin McHale/25 25.00 60.00
13 Dominique Wilkins/25 15.00 40.00
14 David Robinson/25 30.00 80.00
15 Clyde Drexler/25 25.00 60.00
16 Gary Payton/25 12.50 30.00
18 Kobe Bryant/25 100.00 200.00
19 Paul Pierce/25 15.00 40.00

2010-11 Playoff National Treasures All NBA

STATED PRINT RUN 25 SER.#'d SETS
1 George Mikan 6.00 15.00
2 Bill Walton 3.00 8.00
3 Chris Mullin 3.00 8.00
4 Clyde Drexler 8.00 20.00
5 Connie Hawkins 3.00 8.00
6 Dominique Wilkins 4.00 10.00
7 Earl Monroe 5.00 12.00
8 Gail Goodrich 3.00 8.00
9 Harry Gallatin 3.00 8.00
10 John Stockton 6.00 15.00
11 Moses Malone 3.00 8.00
12 Patrick Ewing 8.00 20.00
13 Sidney Moncrief 3.00 8.00
14 Spencer Haywood 3.00 8.00
15 Tim Hardaway 3.00 8.00
16 Wes Unseld 3.00 8.00
17 Willis Reed 3.00 8.00
18 Alonzo Mourning 10.00 25.00
19 Bernard King 3.00 8.00
20 Julius Erving 6.00 15.00
21 Kevin McHale 3.00 8.00
22 Kevin Durant 10.00 25.00
23 Kobe Bryant 15.00 40.00
24 Kevin Garnett 6.00 15.00
25 Steve Nash 3.00 8.00

2010-11 Playoff National Treasures All NBA Materials

STATED PRINT RUN 25 TO 99 SER.#'d SETS
1 George Mikan/25 12.50 30.00
3 Chris Mullin/49 4.00 10.00
4 Clyde Drexler/99 5.00 12.00
6 Dominique Wilkins/25 8.00 20.00
7 Earl Monroe/99 4.00 10.00
10 John Stockton/99 6.00 15.00
12 Patrick Ewing/99 8.00 20.00
15 Tim Hardaway/49 4.00 10.00
18 Alonzo Mourning/49 6.00 15.00
19 Bernard King/49 4.00 10.00
20 Julius Erving/49 8.00 20.00
21 Kevin McHale/99 4.00 10.00
22 Kevin Durant/49 10.00 25.00
23 Kobe Bryant/99 10.00 25.00
24 Kevin Garnett/99 6.00 15.00
25 Steve Nash/99 4.00 10.00

2010-11 Playoff National Treasures All NBA Materials Prime

*PRIME: .75X TO 2X BASE HI
STATED PRINT RUN ONE TO 25 SER.#'d SETS
SOME UNPRICED DUE TO SCARCITY
7 Earl Monroe/25 12.00 30.00
12 Patrick Ewing/25 25.00 60.00
18 Alonzo Mourning/25 25.00 60.00
20 Julius Erving/25 20.00 50.00
22 Kevin Durant/25 25.00 60.00
23 Kobe Bryant/25 25.00 60.00
24 Kevin Garnett/25 12.00 30.00
25 Steve Nash/25 10.00 25.00

2010-11 Playoff National Treasures All NBA Materials Signatures

STATED PRINT RUN 5 TO 25 SER.#'d SETS
SOME UNPRICED DUE TO SCARCITY
UNPRICED PRIME PRINT RUN 5 TO 10 SETS
3 Chris Mullin/25 15.00 40.00
4 Clyde Drexler/25 25.00 60.00
6 Dominique Wilkins/25 20.00 50.00
7 Earl Monroe/25 12.50 30.00
15 Tim Hardaway/25 12.50 30.00
19 Bernard King/25 10.00 25.00
23 Kobe Bryant/25 125.00 225.00

2010-11 Playoff National Treasures All NBA Signatures

STATED PRINT RUN 10 TO 99 SER.#'d SETS
SOME UNPRICED DUE TO SCARCITY
3 Chris Mullin/49 10.00 25.00
5 Connie Hawkins/99 10.00 25.00
6 Dominique Wilkins/49 12.50 30.00
7 Earl Monroe/25 12.50 30.00
8 Gail Goodrich/99 6.00 15.00
9 Harry Gallatin/99 6.00 15.00
13 Sidney Moncrief/99 6.00 15.00
14 Spencer Haywood/99 6.00 15.00
15 Tim Hardaway/99 10.00 25.00
16 Wes Unseld/99 6.00 15.00
17 Willis Reed/49 8.00 20.00
19 Bernard King/99 8.00 20.00
21 Kevin McHale/25 25.00 60.00
23 Kobe Bryant/99 100.00 200.00
25 Steve Nash/25 30.00 80.00

2010-11 Playoff National Treasures Biography Materials

STATED PRINT RUN 25 TO 99 SER.#'d SETS
1 Kevin Durant/49 10.00 25.00
2 Kobe Bryant/99 12.00 30.00
3 Blake Griffin/25 10.00 25.00
4 LeBron James/99 12.00 30.00
5 Dirk Nowitzki/99 5.00 12.00
6 Derrick Rose/99 12.00 30.00
7 Chris Paul/99 6.00 15.00
8 Zach Randolph/99 3.00 8.00
9 Steve Nash/99 4.00 10.00
10 Tyreke Evans/99 5.00 12.00
11 Al Jefferson/99 4.00 10.00
12 Tony Parker/49 4.00 10.00
13 Stephen Curry/25 5.00 12.00
14 Joakim Noah/99 4.00 10.00
15 Dwight Howard/49 6.00 15.00
16 Kevin Martin/99 4.00 10.00
17 Monta Ellis/99 4.00 10.00
18 Kevin Garnett/99 6.00 15.00
19 Kevin Love/99 5.00 12.00
20 Russell Westbrook/99 5.00 12.00

2010-11 Playoff National Treasures Biography Materials Prime

*PRIME: .75X TO 2X BASE HI
STATED PRINT RUN 5 TO 25 SER.#'d SETS
SOME UNPRICED DUE TO SCARCITY
9 Steve Nash/25 10.00 25.00

2010-11 Playoff National Treasures Biography Materials Autographs

STATED PRINT RUN 10 TO 25 SER.#'d SETS
SOME UNPRICED DUE TO SCARCITY
UNPRICED PRIME PRINT RUN 5 TO 10 SETS
2 Kobe Bryant/25 125.00 225.00
8 Zach Randolph/25 12.50 30.00
10 Tyreke Evans/20 15.00 40.00
11 Al Jefferson/25 8.00 20.00
12 Tony Parker/25 15.00 40.00
13 Stephen Curry/25 15.00 40.00
14 Joakim Noah/25 12.50 30.00
16 Kevin Martin/25 8.00 20.00
17 Monta Ellis/25 10.00 25.00
19 Kevin Love/25 20.00 50.00
20 Russell Westbrook/25 20.00 50.00

2010-11 Playoff National Treasures Century Materials

STATED PRINT RUN ONE TO 99 SER.#'d SETS
SOME UNPRICED DUE TO SCARCITY
UNPRICED LOGO PRINT RUN ONE SET
UNPRICED LOGO SIG PRINT RUN ONE SET
UNPRICED TAG PRINT RUN ONE SET
UNPRICED TAG SIG PRINT RUN ONE SET
1 Josh Smith/25 5.00 12.00
2 Al Horford/25 4.00 10.00
4 Joe Johnson/25 5.00 12.00
5 Kevin Garnett/25 10.00 25.00
6 Shaquille O'Neal/25 10.00 25.00
7 Rajon Rondo/25 6.00 15.00
8 Ray Allen/49 5.00 12.00
9 Paul Pierce/25 6.00 15.00
10 D.J. Augustin/25 4.00 10.00
11 Stephen Jackson/25 4.00 10.00
12 Joakim Noah/25 5.00 12.00
13 Derrick Rose/25 12.00 30.00
14 Luol Deng/25 5.00 12.00
15 Carlos Boozer/25 5.00 12.00
16 Antawn Jamison/25 5.00 12.00
18 Dirk Nowitzki/25 6.00 15.00
19 Tyson Chandler/25 4.00 10.00
20 Jason Kidd/25 5.00 12.00
21 Shawn Marion/25 5.00 12.00
23 Nene/25 4.00 10.00
24 Danilo Gallinari/49 5.00 12.00
25 Ty Lawson/49 5.00 12.00
26 Tayshaun Prince/25 5.00 12.00
27 Rodney Stuckey/15 5.00 12.00
28 Ben Gordon/25 5.00 12.00
29 Richard Hamilton/49 4.00 10.00
30 Monta Ellis/49 5.00 12.00
31 David Lee/25 4.00 10.00
32 Stephen Curry/25 6.00 15.00
33 Kevin Martin/49 5.00 12.00
34 Luis Scola/49 4.00 10.00
35 Kyle Lowry/49 4.00 10
36 Danny Granger/49 5.00 12
37 Roy Hibbert/49 4.00 10
38 Darren Collison/49 5.00 12
39 Eric Gordon/25 5.00 12
40 Blake Griffin/49 12.00 30
41 Mo Williams/25 4.00 10
42 Kobe Bryant/25 15.00 40
43 Derek Fisher/25 4.00 10
44 Andrew Bynum/99 6.00 15
45 Lamar Odom/99 5.00 12
46 Pau Gasol/99 5.00 12
47 O.J. Mayo/25 5.00 12
48 Rudy Gay/25 5.00 12
49 Mike Conley Jr./25 4.00 10
50 Zach Randolph/25 4.00 10
51 Dwyane Wade/25 10.00 25
52 Chris Bosh/49 5.00 12
54 LeBron James/99 12.00 30
55 Andrew Bogut/49 5.00 12
56 Brandon Jennings/49 5.00 12
57 John Salmons/25 5.00 12
58 Kevin Love/25 6.00 15
59 Michael Beasley/25 5.00 12
60 Anthony Morrow/25 3.00 8
61 Brook Lopez/25 5.00 12
63 Chris Paul/25 8.00 20
64 David West/25 5.00 12
65 Emeka Okafor/25 5.00 12
66 Trevor Ariza/49 3.00 8
67 Amare Stoudemire/25 5.00 12
68 Carmelo Anthony/25 6.00 15
69 Chauncey Billups/49 5.00 12
70 James Harden/25 6.00 15
71 Kevin Durant/49 10.00 25
72 Russell Westbrook/49 6.00 15
73 Dwight Howard/25 8.00 20
74 Jameer Nelson/25 4.00 10
75 Jason Richardson/25 5.00 12
76 Andre Iguodala/49 5.00 12
77 Elton Brand/99 5.00 12
78 Jrue Holiday/49 5.00 12
79 Grant Hill/99 8.00 20
80 Steve Nash/99 5.00 12
81 Vince Carter/99 6.00 15
82 Brandon Roy/99 5.00 12
84 LaMarcus Aldridge/99 5.00 12
85 Wesley Matthews/99 5.00 12
87 Tyreke Evans/99 6.00 15
88 Manu Ginobili/99 5.00 12
89 Richard Jefferson/99 5.00 12
90 Tim Duncan/99 8.00 20
91 Tony Parker/49 5.00 12
92 Andrea Bargnani/99 4.00 10
93 DeMar DeRozan/99 5.00 12
94 Leandro Barbosa/99 4.00 10
95 Al Jefferson/99 5.00 12
96 Devin Harris/99 5.00 12
97 Paul Millsap/99 4.00 10
99 Nick Young/99 4.00 10
101 Julius Erving/49 6.00 15
106 Wilt Chamberlain/25 30.00 80
107 Larry Bird/49 12.00 30
108 Karl Malone/99 5.00 12
112 Scottie Pippen/99 8.00 20
114 Dominique Wilkins/25 8.00 20
115 Kareem Abdul-Jabbar/25 6.00 15.
116 Kiki Vandeweghe/99 4.00 10
118 Anfernee Hardaway/99 8.00 20
119 David Robinson/49 6.00 15
120 Kevin McHale/49 4.00 10
126 Clyde Drexler/49 5.00 12
128 Bailey Howell/99 4.00 10
129 Mark Price/99 4.00 10
130 Alonzo Mourning/49 6.00 15
132 Chris Mullin/49 4.00 10
135 Dennis Scott/99 4.00 10
138 John Stockton/99 6.00 15.
141 Patrick Ewing/99 8.00 20.
142 Tom Chambers/25 4.00 10.
144 Hakeem Olajuwon/99 5.00 12.
149 Mark Eaton/49 4.00 10.
152 Sam Jones/49 4.00 10.
154 Elgin Baylor/99 5.00 12
156 George Gervin/49 4.00 10
163 Jalen Rose/99 4.00 10
164 Chris Webber/99 4.00 10
170 Dan Majerle/99 4.00 10
172 George Mikan/25 12.50 30
173 Dikembe Mutombo/99 5.00 12
181 Glen Rice/99 4.00 10.
183 Ron Harper/99 4.00 10.
186 Devin Ebanks/99 6.00 15.
187 Craig Brackins/99 5.00 12.
188 Kevin Seraphin/99 6.00 15.
194 Jeremy Lin/99 100.00 200.

2010-11 Playoff National Treasures Century Materials Prime

*PRIME: 1.25X TO 3X BASE HI
STATED PRINT RUN ONE TO 25 SER.#'d SETS
SOME UNPRICED DUE TO SCARCITY
13 Derrick Rose/25 50.00 125.
42 Kobe Bryant/25 75.00 150.
108 Karl Malone/25 20.00 50.
112 Scottie Pippen/25 40.00 100.
130 Alonzo Mourning/25 20.00 50.
164 Chris Webber/25 12.00 30.
186 Devin Ebanks/25 30.00 80.
194 Jeremy Lin/25 400.00 800.

2010-11 Playoff National Treasures Century Materials Prime Signatures

STATED PRINT RUN ONE TO 25 SER.#'d SETS
SOME UNPRICED DUE TO SCARCITY
2 Al Horford/25 12.00 30.
4 Joe Johnson/25 15.00 40.
10 D.J. Augustin/25 12.00 30.
11 Stephen Jackson/25 12.00 30.
12 Joakim Noah/25 25.00 60.
16 Antawn Jamison/25 12.00 30.
20 Jason Kidd/25 40.00 100.
25 Ty Lawson/25 40.00 100.
30 Monta Ellis/25 25.00 60.
31 David Lee/25 12.00 30.
33 Kevin Martin/25 12.00 30.
36 Danny Granger/25 12.00 30.
37 Roy Hibbert/25 15.00 40.
38 Darren Collison/25 15.00 40.
42 Kobe Bryant/25 175.00 325.
44 Andrew Bynum/25 30.00 80.
48 Rudy Gay/25 12.00 30.
49 Mike Conley Jr./25 12.00 30.
50 Zach Randolph/25 15.00 40.
61 Brook Lopez/25 15.00 40.

ames Harden/25 25.00 60.00
ussell Westbrook/20 75.00 150.00
ameer Nelson/25 15.00 40.00
rue Holiday/25 15.00 40.00
rant Hill/25 150.00 300.00
ince Carter/25 50.00 125.00
randon Roy/25 20.00 50.00
aMarcus Aldridge/25 20.00 50.00
yreke Evans/15 20.00 50.00
ony Parker/25 25.00 60.00
ndrea Bargnani/25 12.00 30.00
eMar DeRozan/25 15.00 40.00
evin Harris/25 12.00 30.00
Kiki Vandeweghe/25 12.00 30.00
Bailey Howell/25 15.00 40.00
Mark Price/25 100.00 175.00
Tom Chambers/15 15.00 40.00
Hakeem Olajuwon/25 30.00 80.00
Dan Issel/25 12.00 30.00
Dan Majerle/25 15.00 40.00
Dikembe Mutombo/25 25.00 60.00
Glen Rice/25 15.00 40.00
Ron Harper/25 25.00 60.00
Devin Ebanks/25 20.00 50.00
Jeremy Lin/25 2000.00 3500.00

2010-11 Playoff National Treasures Century Materials Signatures

TED PRINT RUN ONE TO 99 SER.#'d SETS
E UNPRICED DUE TO SCARCITY
sh Smith/25 8.00 20.00
Horford/25 8.00 20.00
e Johnson/25 8.00 20.00
jon Rondo/49 25.00 60.00
y Allen/25 25.00 60.00
aul Pierce/25 20.00 50.00
D.J. Augustin/99 8.00 20.00
Stephen Jackson/99 8.00 20.00
Joakim Noah/25 15.00 40.00
Antawn Jamison/99 8.00 20.00
Tyson Chandler/35 8.00 20.00
Jason Kidd/25 25.00 60.00
Danilo Gallinari/25 10.00 25.00
Ty Lawson/99 10.00 25.00
Ben Gordon/25 8.00 20.00
Monta Ellis/99 10.00 25.00
David Lee/49 8.00 20.00
Stephen Curry/25 15.00 40.00
Kevin Martin/99 8.00 20.00
Danny Granger/25 8.00 20.00
Roy Hibbert/99 8.00 20.00
Darren Collison/49 8.00 20.00
Mo Williams/99 8.00 20.00
Kobe Bryant/99 100.00 200.00
Derek Fisher/49 10.00 25.00
Andrew Bynum/49 12.50 30.00
Rudy Gay/99 8.00 20.00
Mike Conley Jr./99 8.00 20.00
Zach Randolph/99 8.00 20.00
Andrew Bogut/25 8.00 20.00
Brandon Jennings/25 10.00 25.00
Kevin Love/25 20.00 50.00
Brook Lopez/25 8.00 20.00
Emeka Okafor/25 8.00 20.00
Trevor Ariza/49 8.00 20.00
Chauncey Billups/25 12.50 30.00
James Harden/49 12.00 30.00
Russell Westbrook/49 20.00 50.00
Jameer Nelson/99 8.00 20.00
Andre Iguodala/49 8.00 20.00
Jrue Holiday/49 10.00 25.00
Grant Hill/25 100.00 250.00
Vince Carter/25 25.00 60.00
Brandon Roy/25 12.50 30.00
LaMarcus Aldridge/49 8.00 20.00
Wesley Matthews/99 8.00 20.00
Tyreke Evans/49 12.50 30.00
Tony Parker/25 12.00 30.00
Andrea Bargnani/49 8.00 20.00
DeMar DeRozan/25 8.00 20.00
Al Jefferson/25 8.00 20.00
Devin Harris/25 8.00 20.00
4 Dominique Wilkins/25 15.00 40.00
6 Kiki Vandeweghe/99 8.00 20.00
9 David Robinson/25 40.00 100.00
6 Clyde Drexler/25 25.00 60.00
8 Bailey Howell/99 8.00 20.00
9 Mark Price/49 10.00 25.00
2 Chris Mullin/49 12.50 30.00
2 Tom Chambers/49 8.00 20.00
4 Hakeem Olajuwon/25 25.00 60.00
2 Sam Jones/49 12.50 30.00
4 Elgin Baylor/25 15.00 40.00
3 Jalen Rose/99 8.00 20.00
0 Dan Majerle/99 10.00 25.00
3 Dikembe Mutombo/25 20.00 50.00
1 Glen Rice/49 10.00 25.00
3 Ron Harper/99 10.00 25.00
6 Devin Ebanks/99 12.00 30.00
7 Craig Brackins/99 8.00 20.00
4 Jeremy Lin/99 600.00 1200.00

2010-11 Playoff National Treasures Century Signatures

ATED PRINT RUN ONE TO 99 SER.#'d SETS
ME UNPRICED DUE TO SCARCITY
PRICED PLATINUM PRINT RUN ONE SET
Josh Smith/25 6.00 15.00
Al Horford/25 6.00 15.00
Joe Johnson/25 6.00 15.00
Rajon Rondo/49 20.00 50.00
Ray Allen/25 25.00 60.00
Paul Pierce/25 15.00 40.00
D.J. Augustin/99 6.00 15.00
Stephen Jackson/99 6.00 15.00
Joakim Noah/25 12.00 30.00
Antawn Jamison/99 6.00 15.00
Baron Davis/25 8.00 20.00
Tyson Chandler/20 6.00 15.00
Jason Kidd/25 20.00 50.00
Raymond Felton/99 6.00 15.00
Danilo Gallinari/25 10.00 25.00
Ty Lawson/99 8.00 20.00
Ben Gordon/25 6.00 15.00
Monta Ellis/49 10.00 25.00
David Lee/25 6.00 15.00
Stephen Curry/49 10.00 25.00
Kevin Martin/99 6.00 15.00
Danny Granger/25 6.00 15.00
Roy Hibbert/99 6.00 15.00
Darren Collison/25 6.00 15.00
Mo Williams/99 6.00 15.00
Kobe Bryant/99 100.00 200.00
Derek Fisher/49 8.00 20.00

44 Andrew Bynum/25 12.00 30.00
48 Rudy Gay/99 6.00 15.00
49 Mike Conley Jr./99 6.00 15.00
50 Zach Randolph/49 8.00 20.00
52 Chris Bosh/25 15.00 40.00
53 Mike Bibby/99 6.00 15.00
55 Andrew Bogut/25 8.00 20.00
56 Brandon Jennings/25 8.00 20.00
58 Kevin Love/25 15.00 40.00
61 Brook Lopez/49 6.00 15.00
62 Deron Williams/25 12.50 30.00
65 Emeka Okafor/25 6.00 15.00
66 Trevor Ariza/49 6.00 15.00
69 Chauncey Billups/25 12.50 30.00
70 James Harden/49 12.00 30.00
72 Russell Westbrook/49 20.00 50.00
74 Jameer Nelson/49 6.00 15.00
76 Andre Iguodala/49 8.00 20.00
78 Jrue Holiday/49 6.00 15.00
79 Grant Hill/25 100.00 200.00
80 Steve Nash/25 30.00 70.00
81 Vince Carter/25 15.00 40.00
82 Brandon Roy/25 10.00 25.00
84 LaMarcus Aldridge/25 8.00 20.00
85 Wesley Matthews/99 6.00 15.00
87 Tyreke Evans/49 10.00 25.00
91 Tony Parker/49 10.00 25.00
92 Andrea Bargnani/49 6.00 15.00
93 DeMar DeRozan/25 8.00 20.00
95 Al Jefferson/25 6.00 15.00
96 Devin Harris/99 6.00 15.00
103 Oscar Robertson/25 50.00 120.00
105 Elvin Hayes/49 8.00 20.00
111 Bill Walton/25 10.00 25.00
114 Dominique Wilkins/25 12.50 30.00
116 Kiki Vandeweghe/99 6.00 15.00
120 Kevin McHale/25 15.00 40.00
121 Dolph Schayes/49 6.00 15.00
123 Walt Frazier/49 10.00 25.00
124 Tim Hardaway/75 10.00 25.00
127 Dale Ellis/99 6.00 15.00
128 Bailey Howell/99 6.00 15.00
129 Mark Price/99 12.00 30.00
131 Byron Scott/99 8.00 20.00
132 Chris Mullin/49 12.50 30.00
136 Walter Berry/99 6.00 15.00
137 Wes Unseld/99 6.00 15.00
139 K.C. Jones/20 8.00 20.00
142 Tom Chambers/99 6.00 15.00
143 Dell Curry/99 6.00 15.00
144 Hakeem Olajuwon/25 20.00 50.00
148 Vlade Divac/99 10.00 25.00
149 Mark Eaton/99 6.00 15.00
151 Jamal Mashburn/99 10.00 25.00
152 Sam Jones/49 8.00 20.00
153 Xavier McDaniel/99 6.00 15.00
154 Elgin Baylor/25 15.00 40.00
155 David Thompson/99 6.00 15.00
156 George Gervin/25 10.00 25.00
158 Isiah Thomas/49 8.00 20.00
159 Willis Reed/49 10.00 25.00
160 Walt Bellamy/50 6.00 15.00
162 Gary Payton/25 15.00 40.00
163 Jalen Rose/49 10.00 25.00
165 Sean Elliott/25 15.00 40.00
167 Christian Laettner/49 10.00 25.00
168 Dan Issel/25 6.00 15.00
170 Dan Majerle/99 6.00 15.00
171 Rick Barry/99 8.00 20.00
173 Dikembe Mutombo/49 15.00 40.00
174 Gail Goodrich/99 6.00 15.00
175 Darryl Dawkins/99 6.00 15.00
176 Doc Rivers/49 10.00 25.00
179 John Havlicek/15 15.00 40.00
181 Glen Rice/49 12.50 30.00
183 Ron Harper/99 8.00 20.00
184 Bob Love/99 6.00 15.00
185 Dave Cowens/25 6.00 15.00
186 Devin Ebanks/15 10.00 25.00
187 Craig Brackins/99 8.00 20.00
189 Omer Asik/99 10.00 25.00
190 Gary Forbes/99 8.00 20.00
191 Semih Erden/99 8.00 20.00
192 Nikola Pekovic/99 50.00 125.00
194 Jeremy Lin/99 250.00 500.00
195 Jeremy Evans/99 8.00 20.00
196 Eugene Jeter/99 8.00 20.00
198 Ishmael Smith/49 8.00 20.00
200 Derrick Caracter/99 8.00 20.00

2010-11 Playoff National Treasures Champions

STATED PRINT RUN 25 SER.#'d SETS
1 Bill Russell 6.00 15.00
2 Kareem Abdul-Jabbar 6.00 15.00
3 Oscar Robertson 6.00 15.00
4 David Robinson 6.00 15.00
5 John Havlicek 5.00 12.00
6 Rick Barry 4.00 10.00
7 Hakeem Olajuwon 5.00 12.00
8 Dennis Rodman 8.00 20.00
9 Isiah Thomas 4.00 10.00
10 Robert Horry 5.00 12.00

2010-11 Playoff National Treasures Champions Signatures

STATED PRINT RUN 10 TO 25 SER.#'d SETS
SOME UNPRICED DUE TO SCARCITY
3 Oscar Robertson/25 50.00 125.00
5 John Havlicek/25 20.00 50.00
6 Rick Barry/25 12.50 30.00
7 Hakeem Olajuwon/25 30.00 80.00
8 Dennis Rodman/25 50.00 120.00
9 Isiah Thomas/25 12.50 30.00
10 Robert Horry/25 40.00 100.00

2010-11 Playoff National Treasures Champions Signatures Combos

STATED PRINT RUN 2 TO 20 SER.#'d SETS
UNPRICED QUAD PRINT RUN 2 TO 5 SETS
2 Dennis Rodman/20 30.00 80.00
Bill Laimbeer
7 Paul Pierce/15 50.00 125.00
Rajon Rondo
9 Elvin Hayes/20 20.00 50.00
Wes Unseld
10 Tony Parker/20 20.00 50.00
Robert Horry

2010-11 Playoff National Treasures Colossal Materials

STATED PRINT RUN 5 TO 99 SER.#'d SETS
SOME UNPRICED DUE TO SCARCITY
UNPRICED PRIME PRINT RUN ONE TO 10 SETS
UNPRICED LOGO PRINT RUN ONE TO 5 SETS
UNPRICED LOGO SIG PRINT RUN ONE TO 5 SETS
1 Kevin Durant/49 12.00 30.00
2 Al Horford/99 3.00 8.00
3 Al Jefferson/99 4.00 10.00
4 Alex English/99 4.00 10.00
5 Pau Gasol/99 4.00 10.00
6 Larry Bird/25 12.00 30.00
7 Brook Lopez/49 4.00 10.00
8 John Wall/99 8.00 20.00
9 James Harden/99 5.00 12.00
10 Gary Payton/49 4.00 10.00
11 Patrick Ewing/99 8.00 20.00
12 Ray Allen/49 4.00 10.00
13 DeMarcus Cousins/99 6.00 15.00
14 Derrick Rose/99 12.00 30.00
15 Landry Fields/99 3.00 8.00
16 Kevin Love/99 5.00 12.00
17 Dikembe Mutombo/99 4.00 10.00
18 Kobe Bryant/99 12.50 30.00
19 Evan Turner/99 4.00 10.00
20 Stephen Curry/25 5.00 12.00
21 Tyreke Evans/99 5.00 12.00
22 Wesley Johnson/99 3.00 8.00
23 Rajon Rondo/99 5.00 12.00
24 Blake Griffin/25 10.00 25.00
25 Hakeem Olajuwon/49 6.00 15.00
26 Dwight Howard/49 6.00 15.00
28 Gordon Hayward/99 4.00 10.00
29 Jalen Rose/49 4.00 10.00
30 Jonny Flynn/99 2.50 6.00
31 Bill Laimbeer/99 4.00 10.00
32 Andrew Bogut/49 4.00 10.00
33 Brandon Jennings/49 4.00 10.00
34 Caron Butler/49 4.00 10.00
35 Clyde Drexler/49 8.00 20.00
36 Cole Aldrich/99 2.00 5.00
37 Detlef Schrempf/99 8.00 20.00
38 Eric Bledsoe/99 3.00 8.00
39 Robert Horry/25 6.00 15.00
40 Tim Duncan/99 6.00 15.00
41 Toni Kukoc/45 6.00 15.00
42 Xavier McDaniel/49 4.00 10.00
43 Kelly Tripucka/49 4.00 10.00
44 Luke Babbitt/99 2.00 5.00
46 Robert Parish/20 5.00 12.00
48 Chris Bosh/25 5.00 12.00
49 Xavier Henry/99 2.50 6.00
50 Paul George/99 5.00 12.00

2010-11 Playoff National Treasures Colossal Materials Prime Signatures

STATED PRINT RUN ONE TO 25 SER.#'d SETS
SOME UNPRICED DUE TO SCARCITY
2 Al Horford/25 10.00 25.00
4 Alex English/25 15.00 40.00
8 John Wall/25 125.00 300.00
15 Landry Fields/25 15.00 40.00
18 Kobe Bryant/25 250.00 450.00
19 Evan Turner/25 30.00 80.00
25 Hakeem Olajuwon/25 40.00 100.00
28 Gordon Hayward/25 25.00 60.00
31 Bill Laimbeer/25 15.00 40.00
36 Cole Aldrich/25 10.00 25.00
44 Luke Babbitt/25 10.00 25.00
45 Mark Price/25 50.00 120.00
46 Robert Parish/25 12.50 30.00
49 Xavier Henry/25 15.00 40.00
50 Paul George/25 30.00 80.00

2010-11 Playoff National Treasures Colossal Materials Signatures

STATED PRINT RUN ONE TO 49 SER.#'d SETS
SOME UNPRICED DUE TO SCARCITY
2 Al Horford/25 6.00 15.00
3 Al Jefferson/25 6.00 15.00
4 Alex English/49 6.00 15.00
9 James Harden/20 20.00 50.00
13 DeMarcus Cousins/25 20.00 50.00
15 Landry Fields/49 10.00 25.00
16 Kevin Love/15 15.00 40.00
17 Dikembe Mutombo/25 20.00 50.00
18 Kobe Bryant/20 125.00 225.00
19 Evan Turner/49 12.00 30.00
21 Tyreke Evans/25 12.00 30.00
22 Wesley Johnson/49 10.00 25.00
28 Gordon Hayward/49 12.00 30.00
30 Jonny Flynn/25 6.00 15.00
31 Bill Laimbeer/49 8.00 20.00
32 Andrew Bogut/25 12.50 30.00
33 Brandon Jennings/25 12.50 30.00
34 Caron Butler/23 6.00 15.00
36 Cole Aldrich/49 6.00 15.00
37 Detlef Schrempf/49 10.00 25.00
38 Eric Bledsoe/49 10.00 25.00
41 Toni Kukoc/20 25.00 60.00
42 Xavier McDaniel/20 10.00 25.00
44 Luke Babbitt/49 6.00 15.00
46 Robert Parish/25 8.00 20.00
49 Xavier Henry/49 8.00 20.00
50 Paul George/49 15.00 40.00

2010-11 Playoff National Treasures Colossal Materials Jersey Numbers

STATED PRINT RUN 5 TO 99 SER.#'d SETS
SOME UNPRICED DUE TO SCARCITY
UNPRICED PRIME PRINT RUN ONE TO 10 SETS
1 Kevin Durant/99 12.00 30.00
2 Al Horford/99 3.00 8.00
3 Al Jefferson/99 4.00 10.00
4 Alex English/99 4.00 10.00
5 Pau Gasol/99 4.00 10.00
6 Larry Bird/25 12.00 30.00
7 Brook Lopez/49 4.00 10.00
8 John Wall/99 8.00 20.00
9 James Harden/40 6.00 15.00
10 Gary Payton/49 4.00 10.00
11 Patrick Ewing/99 8.00 20.00
12 Ray Allen/49 4.00 10.00
13 DeMarcus Cousins/99 6.00 15.00
14 Derrick Rose/99 12.00 30.00
15 Landry Fields/99 3.00 8.00
16 Kevin Love/20 6.00 15.00
17 Dikembe Mutombo/99 4.00 10.00
18 Kobe Bryant/49 12.50 30.00
19 Evan Turner/99 4.00 10.00
20 Stephen Curry/25 5.00 12.00
21 Tyreke Evans/99 5.00 12.00
22 Wesley Johnson/99 3.00 8.00
23 Rajon Rondo/99 5.00 12.00
24 Blake Griffin/25 10.00 25.00
25 Hakeem Olajuwon/49 6.00 15.00
26 Dwight Howard/49 6.00 15.00
28 Gordon Hayward/99 4.00 10.00
29 Jalen Rose/49 4.00 10.00
30 Jonny Flynn/99 2.50 6.00
31 Bill Laimbeer/99 4.00 10.00
32 Andrew Bogut/99 4.00 10.00
33 Brandon Jennings/49 4.00 10.00
34 Caron Butler/49 4.00 10.00
35 Clyde Drexler/49 8.00 20.00
36 Cole Aldrich/99 2.00 5.00
37 Detlef Schrempf/99 8.00 20.00
38 Eric Bledsoe/99 3.00 8.00
39 Robert Horry/25 6.00 15.00
40 Tim Duncan/99 6.00 15.00
41 Toni Kukoc/49 6.00 15.00
42 Xavier McDaniel/49 4.00 10.00
43 Kelly Tripucka/99 4.00 10.00
44 Luke Babbitt/99 2.00 5.00
46 Robert Parish/35 4.00 10.00
48 Chris Bosh/25 5.00 12.00
49 Xavier Henry/99 2.50 6.00
50 Paul George/99 5.00 12.00

2010-11 Playoff National Treasures Colossal Materials Jersey Numbers Prime Signatures

STATED PRINT RUN ONE TO 25 SER.#'d SETS
SOME UNPRICED DUE TO SCARCITY
2 Al Horford/25 10.00 25.00
4 Alex English/25 12.00 30.00
9 James Harden/25 20.00 50.00
15 Landry Fields/25 15.00 40.00
19 Evan Turner/25 30.00 80.00
21 Tyreke Evans/15 20.00 50.00
25 Hakeem Olajuwon/15 40.00 100.00
28 Gordon Hayward/25 25.00 60.00
31 Bill Laimbeer/25 15.00 40.00
36 Cole Aldrich/25 10.00 25.00
42 Xavier McDaniel/25 10.00 25.00
43 Kelly Tripucka/20 10.00 25.00
44 Luke Babbitt/25 10.00 25.00
45 Mark Price/15 40.00 100.00
49 Xavier Henry/25 15.00 40.00
50 Paul George/25 30.00 80.00

2010-11 Playoff National Treasures Colossal Materials Jersey Numbers Signatures

STATED PRINT RUN 2 TO 49 SER.#'d SETS
SOME UNPRICED DUE TO SCARCITY
2 Al Horford/25 6.00 15.00
3 Al Jefferson/25 6.00 15.00
4 Alex English/49 6.00 15.00
7 Brook Lopez/25 6.00 15.00
8 John Wall/15 125.00 300.00
9 James Harden/15 20.00 50.00
12 Ray Allen/20 30.00 80.00
13 DeMarcus Cousins/25 20.00 50.00
15 Landry Fields/49 10.00 25.00
17 Dikembe Mutombo/25 25.00 60.00
19 Evan Turner/49 12.00 30.00
22 Wesley Johnson/49 10.00 25.00
28 Gordon Hayward/49 12.00 30.00
29 Jalen Rose/15 30.00 80.00
31 Bill Laimbeer/15 12.50 30.00
32 Andrew Bogut/25 12.50 30.00
33 Brandon Jennings/25 12.50 30.00
34 Caron Butler/25 6.00 15.00
36 Cole Aldrich/49 6.00 15.00
37 Detlef Schrempf/49 10.00 25.00
38 Eric Bledsoe/49 10.00 25.00
41 Toni Kukoc/15 25.00 60.00
42 Xavier McDaniel/49 6.00 15.00
43 Kelly Tripucka/18 6.00 15.00
44 Luke Babbitt/49 6.00 15.00
45 Mark Price/20 40.00 100.00
46 Robert Parish/15 10.00 25.00
49 Xavier Henry/49 8.00 20.00
50 Paul George/49 15.00 40.00

2010-11 Playoff National Treasures Hall of Fame

STATED PRINT RUN 25 SER.#'d SETS
1 Clyde Drexler 8.00 20.00
2 Jerry West 6.00 15.00
3 Larry Bird 15.00 40.00
4 Wes Unseld 5.00 12.00
5 Chris Mullin 5.00 12.00
6 Julius Erving 10.00 25.00
7 Rick Barry 5.00 12.00
8 Oscar Robertson 6.00 15.00
9 Artis Gilmore 5.00 12.00
10 Isiah Thomas 5.00 12.00
11 James Worthy 6.00 15.00
12 Moses Malone 5.00 12.00
13 Dominique Wilkins 6.00 15.00
14 Kareem Abdul-Jabbar 8.00 20.00
15 Dan Issel 5.00 12.00
16 Elgin Baylor 5.00 12.00
17 Robert Parish 5.00 12.00
18 John Stockton 8.00 20.00
19 David Robinson 8.00 20.00
20 Kevin McHale 5.00 12.00
21 Earl Monroe 5.00 12.00
22 Scottie Pippen 15.00 40.00
23 Joe Dumars 5.00 12.00
24 George Mikan 10.00 25.00
25 Bill Russell 8.00 20.00
26 George Gervin 5.00 12.00
27 Dennis Rodman 12.00 30.00
28 Karl Malone 6.00 15.00
29 John Havlicek 6.00 15.00
30 Magic Johnson 12.00 30.00

2010-11 Playoff National Treasures Hall of Fame Materials

STATED PRINT RUN ONE TO 99 SER.#'d SETS
SOME UNPRICED DUE TO SCARCITY
1 Clyde Drexler/25 8.00 20.00
3 Larry Bird/49 12.00 30.00
5 Chris Mullin/49 5.00 12.00
6 Julius Erving/49 8.00 20.00
11 James Worthy/99 5.00 12.00
12 Moses Malone/99 4.00 10.00
13 Dominique Wilkins/25 8.00 20.00
14 Kareem Abdul-Jabbar/99 6.00 15.00
16 Elgin Baylor/49 6.00 15.00
17 Robert Parish/99 4.00 10.00
18 John Stockton/99 6.00 15.00
19 David Robinson/49 6.00 15.00
20 Kevin McHale/99 4.00 10.00
21 Earl Monroe/99 4.00 10.00
22 Scottie Pippen/99 8.00 20.00
23 Joe Dumars/99 4.00 10.00
24 George Mikan/25 12.50 30.00
26 George Gervin/49 4.00 10.00
28 Karl Malone/99 5.00 12.00

2010-11 Playoff National Treasures Hall of Fame Materials Prime

*PRIME: 1X TO 2.5X BASE HI
STATED PRINT RUN ONE TO 25 SER.#'d SETS
SOME UNPRICED DUE TO SCARCITY
15 Dan Issel/25 10.00 25.00
22 Scottie Pippen/25 40.00 100.00
23 Joe Dumars/25 10.00 25.00
28 Karl Malone/25 15.00 40.00

2010-11 Playoff National Treasures Hall of Fame Materials Prime Signatures

STATED PRINT RUN ONE TO 25 SER.#'d SETS
SOME UNPRICED DUE TO SCARCITY
5 Chris Mullin/25 30.00 80.00
9 Artis Gilmore/25 20.00 50.00
10 Isiah Thomas/25 20.00 50.00
11 James Worthy/25 40.00 100.00
15 Dan Issel/25 50.00 120.00
17 Robert Parish/25 15.00 40.00
21 Earl Monroe/25 75.00 200.00
23 Joe Dumars/25 25.00 60.00

2010-11 Playoff National Treasures Hall of Fame Materials Signatures

STATED PRINT RUN ONE TO 49 SER.#'d SETS
SOME UNPRICED DUE TO SCARCITY
1 Clyde Drexler/25 25.00 60.00
5 Chris Mullin/49 20.00 50.00
11 James Worthy/25 25.00 60.00
13 Dominique Wilkins/25 20.00 50.00
16 Elgin Baylor/25 60.00 150.00
17 Robert Parish/25 12.50 30.00
19 David Robinson/25 50.00 120.00
21 Earl Monroe/25 40.00 100.00
23 Joe Dumars/49 12.50 30.00

2010-11 Playoff National Treasures Hall of Fame Signatures

STATED PRINT RUN 10 TO 25 SER.#'d SETS
SOME UNPRICED DUE TO SCARCITY
3 Larry Bird/25 75.00 150.00
4 Wes Unseld/25 25.00 60.00
5 Chris Mullin/25 25.00 60.00
7 Rick Barry/25 20.00 50.00
8 Oscar Robertson/25 100.00 200.00
9 Artis Gilmore/25 15.00 40.00
10 Isiah Thomas/25 12.50 30.00
11 James Worthy/25 25.00 60.00
13 Dominique Wilkins/25 30.00 80.00
15 Dan Issel/25 12.50 30.00
16 Elgin Baylor/25 30.00 80.00
17 Robert Parish/25 12.50 30.00
20 Kevin McHale/25 30.00 80.00
21 Earl Monroe/25 25.00 60.00
23 Joe Dumars/25 12.50 30.00
26 George Gervin/25 20.00 50.00
27 Dennis Rodman/25 50.00 125.00
29 John Havlicek/25 40.00 100.00

2010-11 Playoff National Treasures Hall of Fame Signatures Combos

STATED PRINT RUN 10 TO 50 SER.#'d SETS
SOME UNPRICED DUE TO SCARCITY
UNPRICED QUAD PRINT RUN 5 SETS
UNPRICED TRIO PRINT RUN 5 SETS
3 John Havlicek/25 40.00 100.00
Jerry West
4 Clyde Lovellette/50 10.00 25.00
Dolph Schayes
5 Robert Parish/25 35.00 70.00
Hakeem Olajuwon

2010-11 Playoff National Treasures NBA Gear Dual

STATED PRINT RUN 25 TO 99 SER.#'d SETS
UNPRICED TAG PRINT RUN ONE TO 5 SETS
UNPRICED TAG SIG PRINT RUN ONE TO 5 SETS
1 John Wall/99 10.00 25.00
2 Joakim Noah/99 5.00 12.00
3 Blake Griffin/25 10.00 25.00
4 Tyreke Evans/50 6.00 15.00
5 LeBron James/99 12.00 30.00
6 Evan Turner/99 5.00 12.00
7 Kobe Bryant/99 12.00 30.00
8 DeMarcus Cousins/99 8.00 20.00
9 Kevin Durant/49 10.00 25.00
10 Landry Fields/99 4.00 10.00
11 Stephen Curry/25 6.00 15.00
12 Greg Monroe/99 5.00 12.00
13 Andrew Bogut/49 5.00 12.00
14 Gordon Hayward/99 5.00 12.00
15 Brandon Jennings/99 5.00 12.00
16 Wesley Johnson/99 4.00 10.00
17 LaMarcus Aldridge/99 5.00 12.00
18 Al-Farouq Aminu/99 2.50 6.00
19 Dirk Nowitzki/99 6.00 15.00
20 Paul George/99 6.00 15.00
21 Josh Smith/99 5.00 12.00
22 Xavier Henry/99 3.00 8.00
23 Avery Bradley/99 5.00 12.00
24 Larry Sanders/99 2.50 6.00
25 Cole Aldrich/99 2.50 6.00
26 Luke Babbitt/99 2.50 6.00
27 Greivis Vasquez/99 3.00 8.00
28 Eric Bledsoe/99 4.00 10.00
29 James Anderson/99 2.50 6.00
30 Patrick Patterson/99 4.00 10.00
31 Elliot Williams/99 2.50 6.00
32 Ed Davis/99 3.00 8.00
33 Damion James/99 2.50 6.00
34 Daniel Orton/99 2.50 6.00
35 Lazar Hayward/99 2.50 6.00

2010-11 Playoff National Treasures NBA Gear Dual Prime

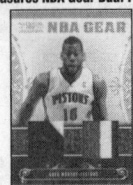

*PRIME STARS: .6X TO 1.5X BASE HI
*PRIME ROOKIES: .75X TO 2X BASE HI
STATED PRINT RUN ONE TO 49 SER.#'d SETS
SOME UNPRICED DUE TO SCARCITY
7 Kobe Bryant/49 40.00 70.00

2010-11 Playoff National Treasures NBA Gear Dual Prime Signatures

STATED PRINT RUN ONE TO 49 SER.#'d SETS
SOME UNPRICED DUE TO SCARCITY
6 Evan Turner/49 15.00 40.00
7 Kobe Bryant/49 150.00 250.00
10 Landry Fields/49 12.00 30.00
12 Greg Monroe/49 15.00 40.00
14 Gordon Hayward/49 15.00 40.00
20 Paul George/25 25.00 60.00
23 Avery Bradley/25 15.00 40.00
24 Larry Sanders/25 10.00 25.00
25 Cole Aldrich/49 8.00 20.00
29 James Anderson/49 8.00 20.00
30 Patrick Patterson/49 12.00 30.00
31 Elliot Williams/25 8.00 20.00
33 Damion James/49 8.00 20.00
34 Daniel Orton/49 8.00 20.00
35 Lazar Hayward/49 8.00 20.00

2010-11 Playoff National Treasures NBA Gear Dual Signatures

STATED PRINT RUN 5 TO 30 SER.#'d SETS
SOME UNPRICED DUE TO SCARCITY
4 Tyreke Evans/30 12.50 30.00
6 Evan Turner/30 12.00 30.00
7 Kobe Bryant/30 100.00 200.00
8 DeMarcus Cousins/30 20.00 50.00
10 Landry Fields/30 10.00 25.00
11 Stephen Curry/25 12.50 30.00
12 Greg Monroe/30 12.00 30.00
14 Gordon Hayward/30 12.00 30.00
15 Brandon Jennings/30 8.00 20.00
16 Wesley Johnson/30 10.00 25.00
18 Al-Farouq Aminu/30 6.00 15.00
20 Paul George/30 15.00 40.00
22 Xavier Henry/30 8.00 20.00
23 Avery Bradley/30 12.00 30.00
24 Larry Sanders/30 6.00 15.00
25 Cole Aldrich/30 6.00 15.00
26 Luke Babbitt/30 6.00 15.00
27 Greivis Vasquez/30 8.00 20.00
28 Eric Bledsoe/30 10.00 25.00
29 James Anderson/30 6.00 15.00
30 Patrick Patterson/30 10.00 25.00
31 Elliot Williams/30 6.00 15.00
32 Ed Davis/30 8.00 20.00
33 Damion James/30 6.00 15.00
34 Daniel Orton/30 6.00 15.00
35 Lazar Hayward/30 6.00 15.00

2010-11 Playoff National Treasures NBA Gear Trios

STATED PRINT RUN 25 TO 99 SER.#'d SETS
1 John Wall/99 12.00 30.00
2 Joakim Noah/99 6.00 15.00
3 Blake Griffin/25 15.00 40.00
4 Tyreke Evans/99 8.00 20.00
5 LeBron James/99 15.00 40.00
6 Evan Turner/99 6.00 15.00
7 Kobe Bryant/99 15.00 40.00
8 DeMarcus Cousins/99 10.00 25.00
9 Kevin Durant/49 10.00 25.00
10 Landry Fields/99 5.00 12.00
11 Stephen Curry/25 8.00 20.00
12 Greg Monroe/99 6.00 15.00
13 Andrew Bogut/49 6.00 15.00
14 Gordon Hayward/99 6.00 15.00
15 Brandon Jennings/49 6.00 15.00
16 Wesley Johnson/99 5.00 12.00
17 LaMarcus Aldridge/99 6.00 15.00
18 Al-Farouq Aminu/99 3.00 8.00
19 Dirk Nowitzki/99 8.00 20.00
20 Paul George/99 8.00 20.00
21 Josh Smith/99 6.00 15.00
22 Xavier Henry/99 4.00 10.00
23 Avery Bradley/99 6.00 15.00
24 Larry Sanders/99 3.00 8.00
25 Cole Aldrich/99 3.00 8.00
26 Luke Babbitt/99 3.00 8.00
27 Greivis Vasquez/99 4.00 10.00
28 Eric Bledsoe/99 5.00 12.00
29 James Anderson/99 3.00 8.00
30 Patrick Patterson/99 5.00 12.00
31 Elliot Williams/99 3.00 8.00
32 Ed Davis/99 4.00 10.00
33 Damion James/99 3.00 8.00
34 Daniel Orton/99 3.00 8.00
35 Lazar Hayward/99 3.00 8.00

2010-11 Playoff National Treasures NBA Gear Trios Prime

*PRIME: .6X TO 1.5X BASE HI
STATED PRINT RUN ONE TO 49 SER.#'d SETS
SOME UNPRICED DUE TO SCARCITY
1 John Wall/49 25.00 60.00
7 Kobe Bryant/49 40.00 100.00

2010-11 Playoff National Treasures NBA Gear Trios Prime Signatures

STATED PRINT RUN ONE TO 49 SER.#'d SETS
SOME UNPRICED DUE TO SCARCITY
4 Tyreke Evans/25 25.00 60.00
6 Evan Turner/49 15.00 40.00
7 Kobe Bryant/49 175.00 350.00
10 Landry Fields/49 12.00 30.00
12 Greg Monroe/49 15.00 40.00
14 Gordon Hayward/49 15.00 40.00
20 Paul George/25 30.00 80.00
24 Larry Sanders/25 12.00 30.00
25 Cole Aldrich/49 10.00 25.00
27 Greivis Vasquez/25 20.00 50.00
29 James Anderson/49 8.00 20.00
30 Patrick Patterson/49 12.00 30.00
33 Damion James/49 8.00 20.00
34 Daniel Orton/49 8.00 20.00
35 Lazar Hayward/49 8.00 20.00

2010-11 Playoff National Treasures NBA Gear Trios Signatures

STATED PRINT RUN 5 TO 30 SER.#'d SETS
SOME UNPRICED DUE TO SCARCITY
4 Tyreke Evans/30 12.50 30.00
6 Evan Turner/30 12.00 30.00
7 Kobe Bryant/30 100.00 225.00
8 DeMarcus Cousins/30 20.00 50.00
10 Landry Fields/30 10.00 25.00
11 Stephen Curry/25 12.50 30.00
12 Greg Monroe/30 12.00 30.00
14 Gordon Hayward/30 12.00 30.00
15 Brandon Jennings/30 10.00 25.00
16 Wesley Johnson/30 10.00 25.00
18 Al-Farouq Aminu/30 6.00 15.00
20 Paul George/30 15.00 40.00
22 Xavier Henry/30 8.00 20.00
23 Avery Bradley/30 15.00 40.00
24 Larry Sanders/30 6.00 15.00
25 Cole Aldrich/30 6.00 15.00
26 Luke Babbitt/30 6.00 15.00
27 Greivis Vasquez/30 10.00 25.00
28 Eric Bledsoe/30 10.00 25.00
29 James Anderson/30 6.00 15.00
30 Patrick Patterson/30 10.00 25.00
31 Elliot Williams/30 6.00 15.00
32 Ed Davis/30 8.00 20.00
33 Damion James/30 6.00 15.00
34 Daniel Orton/30 6.00 15.00
35 Lazar Hayward/30 6.00 15.00

2010-11 Playoff National Treasures Notable Nicknames

STATED PRINT RUN 10 TO 99 SER.#'d SETS
SOME UNPRICED DUE TO SCARCITY
1 David Robinson/25 125.00 250.00
2 Isiah Thomas/49 40.00 100.00
3 Gary Payton/49 40.00 100.00
4 Dennis Rodman/25 100.00 200.00
6 Jason Terry/49 EXCH 30.00 80.00
7 Hakeem Olajuwon/25 75.00 150.00
8 Magic Johnson/10
9 Earl Monroe/25 50.00 120.00
10 Robert Parish/99 15.00 40.00
12 Darryl Dawkins/99 15.00 40.00
13 Larry Johnson/99 30.00 80.00
14 Dan Majerle/99 25.00 60.00
15 James Worthy/25 75.00 150.00
16 David Thompson/99 15.00 40.00
17 Vince Carter/35 75.00 200.00
18 Chris Andersen/99 40.00 100.00
19 Kevin Johnson/49 40.00 100.00
20 LaMarcus Aldridge/25 40.00 100.00
21 Dan Issel/49 25.00 60.00

2010-11 Playoff National Treasures Pen Pals

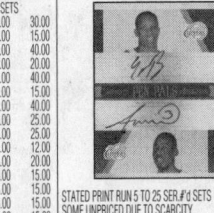

STATED PRINT RUN 5 TO 25 SER.#'d SETS
SOME UNPRICED DUE TO SCARCITY
1 Craig Brackins/25 8.00 20.00
Quincy Pondexter
2 John Wall/25 75.00 200.00
Evan Turner
3 Wesley Johnson/25 20.00 50.00
Gordon Hayward
4 Cole Aldrich/25 8.00 20.00
Xavier Henry
5 Eric Bledsoe/25 12.00 30.00
Al-Farouq Aminu
6 Paul George/25 10.00 25.00
Luke Babbitt
7 Evan Turner/25 15.00 40.00
Xavier Henry
8 Derrick Favors/25 12.00 30.00
Damion James
9 John Wall/15 125.00 250.00
Evan Turner
Derrick Favors
10 Wesley Johnson/15 30.00 80.00
DeMarcus Cousins
Ekpe Udoh
11 Greg Monroe/15 30.00 80.00
Al-Farouq Aminu
Gordon Hayward
12 Wesley Johnson/15 15.00 40.00
Greg Monroe
Dominique Jones
13 DeMarcus Cousins/15 20.00 50.00
Cole Aldrich
Daniel Orton
14 Craig Brackins/15 15.00 40.00
Damion James
Ekpe Udoh

2010-11 Playoff National Treasures Private Signings

STATED PRINT RUN 25 TO 99 SER.#'d SETS
1 Dennis Rodman/25 50.00 120.00
2 Elvin Hayes/99 8.00 20.00
3 Dominique Wilkins/49 15.00 40.00
4 Nate Archibald/99 10.00 25.00
5 Rick Barry/99 10.00 25.00

2010-11 Playoff National Treasures Signature Patches NBA Team

STATED PRINT RUN 10 TO 99 SER.#'d SETS
SOME UNPRICED DUE TO SCARCITY
UNPRICED LOGO PRINT RUN 5 TO 10 SETS
1 Stephen Curry/99 12.50 30.00
2 John Wall/25 125.00 250.00
3 Chris Bosh/25 25.00 60.00
5 Kobe Bryant/49 100.00 200.00
7 Blake Griffin/25 75.00 200.00
9 Jason Terry/49 EXCH 12.50 30.00
10 Jalen Rose/99 6.00 15.00
12 Russell Westbrook/25 25.00 60.00
15 Bill Walton/49 10.00 25.00
16 Elvin Hayes/49 8.00 20.00
17 Kevin Durant/25 125.00 225.00
18 Kevin Love/25 20.00 50.00
21 Adrian Dantley/99 6.00 15.00
22 Earl Monroe/99 12.50 30.00
23 John Havlicek/49 15.00 40.00
25 Joe Dumars/49 12.50 30.00

2010-11 Playoff National Treasures Souvenir Cuts

STATED PRINT RUN ONE TO 30 SER.#'d SETS
SOME UNPRICED DUE TO SCARCITY
7 Paul Arizin/15 30.00 80.00
8 Paul Endacott/30 30.00 80.00
9 Al Cervi/25 25.00 60.00

2010-11 Playoff National Treasures Springfield Bound

STATED PRINT RUN 25 SER.#'d SETS
1 Kobe Bryant 30.00 80.00
2 Shaquille O'Neal 15.00 40.00
3 Jason Kidd 8.00 20.00
4 Steve Nash 8.00 20.00
5 Paul Pierce 10.00 25.00
6 Tim Duncan 12.00 30.00
7 LeBron James 30.00 80.00
8 Ray Allen 8.00 20.00
9 Dirk Nowitzki 10.00 25.00
10 Kevin Garnett 15.00 40.00

2010-11 Playoff National Treasures Springfield Bound Signatures

STATED PRINT RUN 25 SER.#'d SETS
1 Kobe Bryant 125.00 250.00
3 Jason Kidd 20.00 50.00
4 Steve Nash 30.00 80.00
5 Paul Pierce 25.00 60.00
8 Ray Allen 30.00 80.00

2010-11 Playoff National Treasures Timeline Materials Custom Names

STATED PRINT RUN 25 TO 99 SER.#'d SETS
1 Kobe Bryant/99 10.00 25.00
2 Kevin Garnett/49 10.00 25.00
3 Stephen Jackson/99 4.00 10.00
4 Alonzo Mourning/49 10.00 25.00
5 Amare Stoudemire/99 5.00 12.00
6 Andrew Bogut/49 5.00 12.00
7 DeMar DeRozan/99 5.00 12.00
8 Jodie Meeks/99 5.00 12.00
9 Kevin Durant/49 10.00 25.00
10 Paul Pierce/99 6.00 15.00
11 Toney Douglas/99 3.00 8.00
12 Jonny Flynn/99 3.00 8.00
13 Mark Price/99 5.00 12.00
14 Brandon Jennings/49 5.00 12.00
15 Carlos Boozer/99 5.00 12.00
16 DeJuan Blair/99 4.00 10.00
17 Derek Fisher/99 4.00 10.00
18 James Harden/99 6.00 15.00
19 James Jones/99 3.00 8.00
20 Jrue Holiday/99 5.00 12.00
21 LeBron James/99 10.00 25.00
22 Chris Paul/99 8.00 20.00
23 Kevin Love/99 6.00 15.00
24 Lamar Odom/99 5.00 12.00
25 LaMarcus Aldridge/99 5.00 12.00
26 Rajon Rondo/99 6.00 15.00
27 Russell Westbrook/99 6.00 15.00
28 Stephen Curry/25 6.00 15.00
29 Wesley Matthews/99 5.00 12.00
30 Dwight Howard/99 8.00 20.00

2010-11 Playoff National Treasures Timeline Materials Custom Names Prime

*PRIME: .6X TO 1.5X BASE HI
STATED PRINT RUN 5 TO 25 SER.#'d SETS
SOME UNPRICED DUE TO SCARCITY
1 Kobe Bryant/25 25.00 60.00
4 Alonzo Mourning/25 25.00 60.00
9 Kevin Durant/25 30.00 80.00
13 Mark Price/24 10.00 25.00

2010-11 Playoff National Treasures Timeline Materials Custom Names Prime Signatures

STATED PRINT RUN 5 TO 25 SER.#'d SETS
SOME UNPRICED DUE TO SCARCITY
1 Kobe Bryant/25 150.00 325.00
3 Stephen Jackson/20 15.00 40.00
7 DeMar DeRozan/25 15.00 40.00
9 Kevin Durant/25 200.00 400.00
10 Paul Pierce/25 30.00 80.00
11 Toney Douglas/25 10.00 25.00
12 Jonny Flynn/25 10.00 25.00
13 Mark Price/17 30.00 80.00
18 James Harden/23 25.00 60.00
20 Jrue Holiday/23 12.50 30.00
25 LaMarcus Aldridge/16 15.00 40.00

2010-11 Playoff National Treasures Timeline Materials Custom Names Signatures

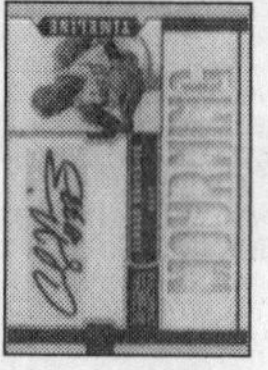

STATED PRINT RUN 10 TO 30 SER.#'d SETS
SOME UNPRICED DUE TO SCARCITY
1 Kobe Bryant/30 100.00 200.00
3 Stephen Jackson/30 6.00 15.00
7 DeMar DeRozan/30 10.00 25.00
8 Jodie Meeks/30 6.00 15.00
10 Paul Pierce/30 15.00 40.00
11 Toney Douglas/30 6.00 15.00
12 Jonny Flynn/30 6.00 15.00
13 Mark Price/30 20.00 50.00
14 Brandon Jennings/30 10.00 25.00
16 DeJuan Blair/30 8.00 20.00
17 Derek Fisher/30 10.00 25.00
18 James Harden/30 15.00 40.00
20 Jrue Holiday/30 8.00 20.00
23 Kevin Love/30 15.00 40.00
25 LaMarcus Aldridge/30 8.00 20.00
26 Rajon Rondo/30 20.00 50.00
27 Russell Westbrook/30 25.00 60.00
28 Stephen Curry/25 12.50 30.00
29 Wesley Matthews/30 6.00 15.00

2010-11 Playoff National Treasures Timeline Materials Custom Team Nicknames

STATED PRINT RUN 10 TO 99 SER.#'d SETS
SOME UNPRICED DUE TO SCARCITY
1 Kobe Bryant/99 10.00 25.00
2 Kevin Garnett/49 10.00 25.00
3 Stephen Jackson/99 4.00 10.00
4 Alonzo Mourning/49 10.00 25.00
5 Amare Stoudemire/99 5.00 12.00
6 Andrew Bogut/49 5.00 12.00
7 DeMar DeRozan/99 5.00 12.00
9 Kevin Durant/49 10.00 25.00
10 Paul Pierce/49 6.00 15.00
11 Toney Douglas/49 3.00 8.00
12 Jonny Flynn/99 3.00 8.00
14 Brandon Jennings/49 5.00 12.00
15 Carlos Boozer/99 5.00 12.00
16 DeJuan Blair/99 4.00 10.00
17 Derek Fisher/25 5.00 12.00
18 James Harden/99 6.00 15.00
19 James Jones/99 3.00 8.00
20 Jrue Holiday/99 5.00 12.00
21 LeBron James/99 10.00 25.00
22 Chris Paul/99 8.00 20.00
23 Kevin Love/99 6.00 15.00
24 Lamar Odom/99 5.00 12.00
25 LaMarcus Aldridge/99 5.00 12.00
26 Rajon Rondo/99 6.00 15.00
27 Russell Westbrook/99 6.00 15.00
28 Stephen Curry/25 6.00 15.00
29 Wesley Matthews/99 5.00 12.00
30 Dwight Howard/99 8.00 20.00
31 Jodie Meeks/99 5.00 12.00

2010-11 Playoff National Treasures Timeline Materials Custom Team Nicknames Prime

*PRIME: .6X TO 1.5X BASE HI
STATED PRINT RUN 2 TO 25 SER.#'d SETS
SOME UNPRICED DUE TO SCARCITY
1 Kobe Bryant/25 25.00 60.00
4 Alonzo Mourning/25 25.00 60.00

2010-11 Playoff National Treasures Timeline Materials Custom Team Nicknames Prime Signatures

STATED PRINT RUN 5 TO 25 SER.#'d SETS
SOME UNPRICED DUE TO SCARCITY
1 Kobe Bryant/23 150.00 325.00
7 DeMar DeRozan/25 15.00 40.00
11 Toney Douglas/17 10.00 25.00
13 Mark Price/20 30.00 80.00
18 James Harden/15 25.00 60.00
25 LaMarcus Aldridge/15 20.00 50.00

2010-11 Playoff National Treasures Timeline Materials Custom Team Nicknames Signatures

STATED PRINT RUN 5 TO 30 SER.#'d SETS
SOME UNPRICED DUE TO SCARCITY
1 Kobe Bryant/30 100.00 200.00
3 Stephen Jackson/30 6.00 15.00
7 DeMar DeRozan/25 10.00 25.00
8 Jodie Meeks/30 6.00 15.00
11 Toney Douglas/30 6.00 15.00
12 Jonny Flynn/30 6.00 15.00
14 Brandon Jennings/30 10.00 25.00
16 DeJuan Blair/30 8.00 20.00
17 Derek Fisher/30 10.00 25.00
18 James Harden/30 15.00 40.00
20 Jrue Holiday/30 8.00 20.00
23 Kevin Love/30 15.00 40.00
25 LaMarcus Aldridge/30 8.00 20.00
27 Russell Westbrook/30 25.00 60.00
28 Stephen Curry/25 12.50 30.00
29 Wesley Matthews/30 6.00 15.00

1977-78 Post Auerbach Tips

These 12 cereal-box cards measure approximately 7 3/16" by 1 3/16" and were available (they formed the back panel of the cereal box) on 15-ounce (cards 1-6) and 20-ounce (cards 7-12) boxes of Post Raisin Bran and Post Grape Nuts. The blank-backed cards feature "NBA" Tips from legendary Boston Celtics coach Red Auerbach. A drawing of him accompanies his description of each line-illustrated play. The cards are numbered on the front.

COMPLETE SET (12) 60.00 120.00
COMMON TIP (1-12) 6.00 12.00

1960 Post Cereal

These large cards measure approximately 7" by 8 3/4". The 1960 Post Cereal Sports Stars set contains nine cards depicting current baseball, football and basketball players. Each card comprised the entire back of a Grape Nuts Flakes Box and is blank backed. The color player photos are set on a colored background surrounded by a wooden frame design, and they are unnumbered (assigned numbers below for reference according to sport). The catalog designation is F278-26.

COMPLETE SET (9) 3000.00 5000.00
BK1 Bob Cousy/(basketball) 200.00 400.00
BK2 Bob Pettit/(basketball) 150.00 300.00

1995 Post Honeycomb Posters

Inserted in specially marked Post Honeycomb Cereal boxes, this set of three posters measures 11" by 17" when unfolded. It carries a color action player photo against a computerized color player portrait. The player's first name in block lettering appears across the top, while his facsimile signature is printed towards the bottom. Instant winners could receive a personally autographed basketball poster of the player depicted on the poster. The back has the official rules and a note about whether the poster is an instant winner. The posters are unnumbered and checklisted below in alphabetical order.

COMPLETE SET (3) 2.00 5.00
1 Patrick Ewing .75 2.00
2 Shawn Kemp .75 2.00
3 Alonzo Mourning .75 2.00

2006-07 Press Pass Legends

Issued in early February 2007, Press Pass Legends features some of the NBA's greatest legends, current players and rookies on a thick card stock with silver foil highlights. An interesting note about the Press Pass Legends product is that it includes the first-ever cut signature of Pete Maravich (serially numbered to five). Card numbers 1-18 showcase the year's rookies and cards 19-70 showcase retired legends and coaches, all in their college uniforms. Also found randomly in the product are exchanges for full-sized basketball autographed by Elton Brand, Richard Hamilton and Lamar Odom. Press Pass hit the market in 18-pack boxes of five cards each and carried an original suggested retail price of $9.00 per pack.

COMPLETE SET (70) 20.00 50.00
UNPRICED PLATINUM PRINT RUN ONE SET
UNPRICED PRESS PLATE PRINT RUN ONE SET
1 Ronnie Brewer .75 2.00
2 J.J. Redick .75 2.00
3 Shelden Williams .60 1.50
4 Adam Morrison .75 2.00
5 Rajon Rondo 2.50 6.00
6 Tyrus Thomas .75 2.00
7 Rodney Carney .60 1.50
8 Shawne Williams .60 1.50
9 Maurice Ager .60 1.50
10 Shannon Brown 1.00 2.50
11 Cedric Simmons .60 1.50
12 Mardy Collins .60 1.50
13 LaMarcus Aldridge 1.50 4.00
14 Hilton Armstrong .60 1.50
15 Rudy Gay 1.00 2.50
16 Marcus Williams .60 1.50
17 Randy Foye .75 2.00
18 Brandon Roy 1.50 4.00
19 Sidney Moncrief .60 1.50
20 Nate Thurmond .60 1.50
21 Larry Nance .60 1.50
22 Sue Bird 2.00 5.00
23 Diana Taurasi 2.00 5.00
24 Jay Bilas .60 1.50
25 Sleepy Floyd .60 1.50
26 Dominique Wilkins .75 2.00
27 Clyde Drexler .75 2.00
27B Clyde Drexler Color 1.00 2.50
28 Elvin Hayes .60 1.50
28B Elvin Hayes Color .75 2.00
29 Hakeem Olajuwon .75 2.00
30 Steve Alford .60 1.50
31 Calbert Cheaney .60 1.50
32 Scott May .60 1.50
33 Isiah Thomas .60 1.50
34 Larry Bird 2.00 5.00
34B Larry Bird 2.50 6.00
35 Connie Hawkins .60 1.50
36 Danny Manning .60 1.50
36B Danny Manning Color .75 2.00
37 Jo Jo White .60 1.50
38 Rex Chapman .60 1.50
39 Dan Issel .60 1.50
40 Pat Riley .75 2.00
41 Pete Maravich 4.00 10.00
42 Wes Unseld .60 1.50
43 Rick Barry .60 1.50
44 Lou Hudson .60 1.50
45 David Robinson 1.00 2.50
46 Spud Webb .60 1.50
47 David Thompson .60 1.50
48 Brad Daugherty .60 1.50
49 Bob McAdoo .60 1.50
50 Sam Perkins .60 1.50
51 Kenny Smith .60 1.50
52 Bill Laimbeer .60 1.50
53 Adrian Dantley .60 1.50
54 John Havlicek .60 1.50
55 A.C. Green .60 1.50
56 Bill Russell 1.25 3.00
57 Walt Frazier .60 1.50
58 Mark Jackson .60 1.50
59 Bernard King .60 1.50
60 Henry Bibby .60 1.50
61 Bill Walton .60 1.50
61B Bill Walton Color .75 2.00
62 Stacey Augmon .60 1.50
63 Reggie Theus .60 1.50
64 Ralph Sampson .60 1.50
65 Jerry West .75 2.00
66 Dean Smith .60 1.50
67 Digger Phelps .60 1.50
68 John Wooden .60 1.50
69 Jerry Tarkanian .60 1.50
70 Larry Bird CL 1.25 3.00
NNO Rip Hamilton Ball 12.50 30.00
NNO Lamar Odom Ball 15.00 40.00
NNO Elton Brand Ball 15.00 40.00

2006-07 Press Pass Legends Bronze

*BRONZE: .5X TO 1.25X BASE HI
PRINT RUN 899 SER.#'d SETS

2006-07 Press Pass Legends Emerald

*EMERALD: 2X TO 5X BASE HI
PRINT RUN 25 SER.#'d SETS

2006-07 Press Pass Legends Gold

*GOLD: 1X TO 2.5X BASE HI
PRINT RUN 99 SER.#'d SETS

2006-07 Press Pass Legends Silver

*SILVER: .6X TO 1.5X BASE HI
PRINT RUN 499 SER.#'d SETS

2006-07 Press Pass Legends Alumni Association

COMPLETE SET (10) 10.00 25.00
STATED ODDS 1:9
1 Sidney Moncrief / Ronnie Brewer 1.50 4.00
2 Jay Bilas / J.J. Redick 2.50 6.00
3 Clyde Drexler / Elvin Hayes 2.00 5.00
4 Isiah Thomas / Steve Alford 2.50 6.00
5 JoJo White / Danny Manning 1.50 4.00
6 Pat Riley / Dan Issel 1.50 4.00
7 Pete Maravich / Tyrus Thomas 6.00 15.00
8 Bob McAdoo / Sam Perkins 1.50 4.00
9 Adrian Dantley / Bill Laimbeer 1.50 4.00
10 Diana Taurasi / Sue Bird 3.00 8.00

2006-07 Press Pass Legends Alumni Association Autographs

PRINT RUN 50 SER.#'d SETS
1 Sidney Moncrief / Ronnie Brewer 15.00 40.00
2 Jay Bilas / J.J. Redick 20.00 40.00
3 Clyde Drexler / Elvin Hayes 20.00 50.00
4 Isiah Thomas / Steve Alford 25.00 60.00
5 JoJo White / Danny Manning 25.00 60.00
6 Pat Riley / Dan Issel 25.00 60.00
9 Adrian Dantley / Bill Laimbeer 25.00 60.00

2006-07 Press Pass Legends Center Court Cuts

RANDOM INSERTS IN PACKS
2 Bill Russell/75 100.00 160.00
2B Bill Russell Red 100.00 200.00

2006-07 Press Pass Legends Legendary Legacy

COMPLETE SET (10) 8.00 20.00
STATED ODDS 1:9
1 Clyde Drexler 1.00 2.50
2 Steve Alford .75 2.00
3 Isiah Thomas .75 2.00
4 Larry Bird 2.50 6.00
5 Danny Manning .75 2.00
6 Pat Riley 1.00 2.50
7 Sam Perkins .75 2.00
8 Bill Walton .75 2.00
9 Jerry West 1.00 2.50
10 Pete Maravich 5.00 12.00

2006-07 Press Pass Legends Legendary Legacy Autographs

PRINT RUN LISTED IN CL BELOW
2 Steve Alford/155 6.00 15.00
3 Isiah Thomas/75 15.00 40.00
4 Larry Bird/50 90.00 180.00
5 Danny Manning/50 15.00 40.00
6 Pat Riley/125 20.00 50.00
7 Sam Perkins/400 6.00 15.00
8 Bill Walton/50 10.00 25.00
9 Jerry West/175 25.00 60.00

2006-07 Press Pass Legends Legendary Legacy Autographs Platinum

PRINT RUNS LISTED IN CL BELOW
SOME UNPRICED DUE TO SCARCITY
2 Steve Alford/25 20.00 50.00
3 Isiah Thomas/25 30.00 60.00
4 Larry Bird/18 100.00 200.00
5 Danny Manning/25 30.00 60.00
6 Pat Riley/25 30.00 80.00
7 Sam Perkins/25 15.00 40.00
9 Jerry West/25 50.00 120.00

2006-07 Press Pass Legends Naismith Award Winners

COMPLETE SET (10) 8.00 20.00
STATED ODDS 1:9
1 Pete Maravich 5.00 12.00
2 Bill Walton .75 2.00
3 David Thompson .75 2.00
4 Scott May .75 2.00
5 Larry Bird 2.50 6.00
6 Ralph Sampson .75 2.00
7 David Robinson 1.25 3.00
8 Danny Manning .75 2.00
9 Calbert Cheaney .75 2.00
10 J.J. Redick 1.00 2.50

2006-07 Press Pass Legends Naismith Award Winners Autographs

PRINT RUNS LISTED IN CL BELOW
2 Bill Walton/75 10.00 25.00
3 David Thompson/275 10.00 25.00
3F David Thompson Red/20 12.00 30.00
4 Scott May/400 5.00 12.00
4A Scott May Red/25 6.00 15.00
6 Ralph Sampson/400 6.00 15.00
6B Ralph Sampson Red 8.00 20.00
7 David Robinson/50 30.00 80.00
8 Danny Manning/100 12.50 30.00
8B Danny Manning Red/49 15.00 40.00
9 Calbert Cheaney/400 5.00 12.00
10 J.J. Redick/275 10.00 25.00
10A J.J. Redick Go Duke/24 25.00 60.00

2006-07 Press Pass Legends Naismith Award Winners Autographs Platinum

PRINT RUNS LISTED IN CL BELOW
SOME UNPRICED DUE TO SCARCITY
2 Bill Walton 15.00 40.00
3 David Thompson 15.00 40.00
5 Larry Bird 100.00 200.00
7 David Robinson 60.00 150.00
8 Danny Manning 20.00 50.00
9 Calbert Cheaney 8.00 20.00

2006-07 Press Pass Legends Saturday Swatches

APPROXIMATE ODDS ONE PER BOX
*PRIME: .6X TO 1.25X BASE HI
PRIME PRINT RUN 50 SER.#'d SETS
1 Ronnie Brewer 4.00 10.00
2 David Lee 2.50 6.00
3 Rodney Carney 3.00 8.00
4 Shannon Brown 5.00 12.00
5 Danny Granger 3.00 8.00
6 Sean May 2.00 5.00
7 LaMarcus Aldridge 6.00 15.00
8 Rudy Gay 5.00 12.00
9 Kyle Lowry 4.00 10.00
10 Chris Paul 6.00 15.00
11 Brandon Roy 6.00 15.00

2006-07 Press Pass Legends Signatures

APPROXIMATELY TWO TO THREE PER BOX
1 LaMarcus Aldridge 10.00 25.00
2 LaMarcus Aldridge Red/25 10.00 25.00
3 Steve Alford 6.00 15.00
5 Steve Alford Red 1987 Champs/25 15.00 40.00
6 Hilton Armstrong 4.00 10.00
9 Stacey Augmon 4.00 10.00
11 Rick Barry 10.00 25.00
12 Rick Barry Go Canes/24 20.00 50.00
13 Rick Barry Red/30 12.50 30.00
14 Henry Bibby 4.00 10.00
19 Henry Bibby Red/22 6.00 15.00
20 Jay Bilas 4.00 10.00
21 Jay Bilas 21 1986 37-3/51 10.00 25.00
51 Larry Bird 40.00 100.00
53 Ronnie Brewer 5.00 12.00
55 Calbert Cheaney 4.00 10.00
59 Adrian Dantley 6.00 15.00
60 Brad Daugherty 4.00 10.00
61 Brad Daugherty Go Heels/35 8.00 20.00
62 Brad Daugherty Red Go Heels/24 10.00 25.00
63 Clyde Drexler 12.50 30.00
64 Eric Sleepy Floyd 4.00 10.00
66 Eric Sleepy Floyd/16 10.00 25.00
67 Eric Sleepy Floyd Red/54 8.00 20.00
68 Randy Foye 5.00 12.00
69 Randy Foye Foyeboy/25 10.00 25.00
70 Randy Foye Red/24 10.00 25.00
71 Walt Frazier 8.00 20.00
75 Rudy Gay 6.00 15.00
78 A.C. Green 4.00 10.00
79 A.C. Green 45/80 6.00 15.00
80 A.C. Green Red/25 8.00 20.00
83 John Havlicek 12.50 30.00
86 Connie Hawkins 12.50 30.00
87 Connie Hawkins Go Hawkeyes/24 20.00 50.00
89 Elvin Hayes 4.00 10.00
90 Elvin Hayes Red/25 8.00 20.00
91 Elvin Hayes Red The Big E/25 15.00 40.00
92 Lou Hudson 4.00 10.00
93 Lou Hudson Red/28 10.00 25.00
94 Dan Issel 8.00 20.00
97 Bernard King 6.00 15.00
98 Bill Laimbeer 10.00 25.00
99 Bill Laimbeer 1978 Final 4/25 20.00 50.00
100 Bill Laimbeer Red/25 20.00 50.00
101 Danny Manning 8.00 20.00
104 Scott May Red 8.00 20.00
105 Sidney Moncrief 6.00 15.00
107 Sidney Moncrief Go Hogs/22 12.50 30.00
108 Sidney Moncrief Red/30 8.00 20.00
109 Adam Morrison 8.00 20.00
110 Adam Morrison Go Zags/37 15.00 30.00
112 Larry Nance 4.00 10.00
114 Larry Nance Red/32 6.00 15.00
116 Hakeem Olajuwon 15.00 40.00
117 Sam Perkins 6.00 15.00
118 Digger Phelps 8.00 20.00
119 Digger Phelps Go Irish/25 10.00 25.00
121 J.J. Redick 12.50 30.00
122 Pat Riley 12.50 30.00
123 David Robinson 30.00 75.00
124 David Robinson Red/24 75.00 150.00
125 Rajon Rondo 15.00 40.00
126 Brandon Roy 10.00 25.00
128 Brandon Roy Red/25 15.00 40.00
129 Ralph Sampson 6.00 15.00
130 Ralph Sampson Red/86 8.00 20.00
131 Kenny Smith 8.00 20.00
132 Kenny Smith Jet/20 12.50 30.00
134 Kenny Smith Red/69 12.50 30.00
135 Kenny Smith Red Jet/26 12.50 30.00
136 Dean Smith 40.00 100.00
138 Jerry Tarkanian 10.00 25.00
142 Jerry Tarkanian Red/23 15.00 40.00
143 Diana Taurasi 8.00 20.00
145 Reggie Theus 4.00 10.
148 Isiah Thomas 10.00 25.
150 Tyrus Thomas 5.00 12.
151 Tyrus Thomas T-Time Geaux Tigers/25 10.00 25.
153 David Thompson 10.00 25.
161 Nate Thurmond 4.00 10.
162 Nate Thurmond Red/25 10.00 25.
165 Wes Unseld 4.00 10.
168 Bill Walton 8.00 20.
169 Bill Walton Red/17 15.00 40.
170 Spud Webb 5.00 12.
171 Jerry West 20.00 50.
175 Jo Jo White 6.00 15.
176 Jo Jo White Red/24 12.50 30.
178 Dominique Wilkins 15.00 40.
179 Dominique Wilkins Red/24 25.00 60.
181 Shelden Williams 4.00 10.
185 John Wooden 75.00 150.
186 John Wooden UCLA/25 75.00 150.

2007-08 Press Pass Legends

Released in October 2007, Press Pass legends boas a 70 card base set that features retired NBA legends, current NBA players and current NBA rookie players. The base cards feature a white backdrop along with a mix of color and black and white photos for certain players. Legends was packed out in boxes that conta three mini-boxes each and each mini-box contains s packs of five cards per. The original suggested retail price per pack was $8.99.

COMPLETE SET (70) 20.00 40.
UNPRICED PLATINUM PRINT RUN ONE SET
UNPRICED PRESS PLATES PRINT RUN ONE SET
1 Jared Dudley .75 2.0
2 Jason Smith .75 2.0
3 Josh McRoberts .75 2.0
4 Taurean Green .75 2.0
5 Javaris Crittenton .75 2.0
6 Glen Davis 1.25 3.
7 Nick Fazekas .75 2.0
8 Aaron Gray .75 2.0
9 Morris Almond .75 2.0
10 Acie Law .75 2.0
11 Aaron Afflalo 1.00 2.5
12 Brandan Wright .75 2.0
13 Nick Young 1.25 3.0
14 Gabe Pruitt .75 2.0
15 Spencer Hawes .75 2.0
16 Sean Elliott .75 2.0
17 Lafette Lever .75 2.0
18 Byron Scott .75 2.0
19 Robert Parish .75 2.0
20 Scottie Pippen 1.25 3.0
21 Dan Majerle 1.00 2.5
22 Tree Rollins .75 2.0
23 Sue Bird 2.00 5.0
24 Jay Bilas .75 2.0
25 Bobby Hurley .75 2.0
26 George Gervin .75 2.0
27 Dominique Wilkins 1.00 2.5
28 Kenny Anderson .75 2.0
29 Willis Reed .75 2.0
30 Larry Bird 2.50 6.0
31 Artis Gilmore .75 2.0
32 JoJo White .75 2.0
33 Rolando Blackman .75 2.0
34 Dan Issel .75 2.0
35 Pete Maravich 2.50 6.0
36 Joe Dumars .75 2.0
37 Hal Greer .75 2.0
38 Rick Barry .75 2.0
39 Glen Rice .75 2.0
40 David Robinson 1.25 3.0
41 Michael Cooper .75 2.0
42 Calvin Murphy .75 2.0
43 John Paxson .75 2.0
44 John Havlicek .75 2.0
45 Jerry Lucas .75 2.0
46 A.C. Green .75 2.0
47 Lenny Wilkens .75 2.0
48 Bill Russell 1.25 3.0
49 Elgin Baylor .75 2.0
50 Alex English .75 2.0
51 Dick McGuire .75 2.0
52 Sherman Douglas .75 2.0
53 Henry Bibby .75 2.0
54 Bill Walton .75 2.0
55 Kiki Vandeweghe .75 2.0
56 Phil Ford .75 2.0
57 George Karl .75 2.0
58 Sam Perkins .75 2.0
59 Kenny Smith .75 2.0
60 James Worthy 1.00 2.5
61 Stacey Augmon .75 2.0
62 Larry Johnson .75 2.0
63 Jerry Tarkanian .75 2.0
64 Gus Williams .75 2.0
65 Nate Archibald .75 2.0
66 Muggsy Bogues .75 2.0
67 Detlef Schrempf .75 2.0
68 Earl Monroe .75 2.0
69 Jerry West 1.00 2.5
70 Jerry Tarkanian / Larry Johnson / Stacy Augmon .75 2.0

2007-08 Press Pass Legends Bronze

*BRONZE: .5X TO 1.25X BASE HI
BRONZE PRINT RUN 899 SER.#'d SETS

2007-08 Press Pass Legends Emerald

*EMERALD: 2.5X TO 6X BASE HI
PRINT RUN 25 SER.#'d SETS

2007-08 Press Pass Legends Gold

*GOLD: 1.25X TO 3X BASE HI
GOLD PRINT RUN 99 SER.#'d SETS

2007-08 Press Pass Legends Silver

*SILVER: .6X TO 1.5X BASE HI
PRINT RUN 499 SER.#'d SETS

007-08 Press Pass Legends All-American

MPLETE SET (11) 8.00 20.00
TED ODDS 1:9
an Elliott .75 2.00
rry Bird 2.50 6.00
en Davis 1.25 3.00
te Maravich 2.50 6.00
vid Robinson 1.25 3.00
hn Paxson .75 2.00
ie Law .75 2.00
ron Afflalo 1.00 2.50
mes Worthy 1.00 2.50
arry Johnson .75 2.00
ick Fazekas .75 2.00

2007-08 Press Pass Legends All-American Autographs

NT RUNS LISTED IN CHECKLIST
PRICED PLATINUM PRINT RUN 25 SETS
H EXPIRATION DATE 10/1/08
ean Elliott/258 6.00 15.00
rry Bird/50 40.00 80.00
en Davis/255 5.00 12.00
hn Paxson/236 8.00 20.00
ohn Paxson Red/23 20.00 40.00
ie Law/245 6.00 15.00
aron Afflalo/232 5.00 12.00
mes Worthy/25 30.00 60.00
arry Johnson/25 25.00 50.00
Nick Fazekas 4.00 10.00
Nick Fazekas Red/31 5.00 12.00

2007-08 Press Pass Legends Alumni Association

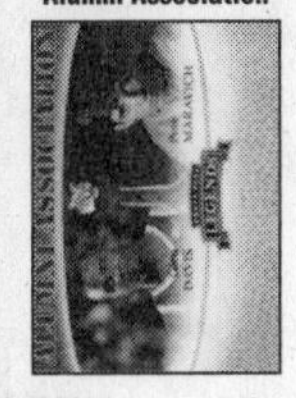

MPLETE SET (10) 10.00 25.00
afayette Lever 2.50 6.00
yron Scott
obby Hurley 4.00 10.00
sh McRoberts
enny Anderson 2.00 5.00
varis Crittenton
te Maravich 4.00 10.00
len Davis
rry Lucas 2.00 5.00
hn Havlicek
enry Bibby 2.00 5.00
iki Vandeweghe
mes Worthy 2.50 6.00
andan Wright
rry Johnson 2.00 5.00
acey Augmon
ick Young 2.00 5.00
us Williams
Detlef Schrempf 2.00 5.00
pencer Hawes

2007-08 Press Pass Legends Alumni Association Autographs

NT RUNS LISTED IN CHECKLIST
afayette Lever/50 15.00 30.00
yron Scott
obby Hurley/48 15.00 30.00
osh McRoberts
enny Anderson/45 10.00 25.00
avaris Crittenton
enry Bibby 10.00 25.00
iki Vandeweghe
ames Worthy 35.00 75.00
randan Wright
arry Johnson 25.00 50.00
acey Augmon
ick Young/46 10.00 25.00
us Williams
NT Sue Bird/25 35.00 75.00
iana Taurasi

2007-08 Press Pass Legends Center Court Cuts

PRINT RUNS LISTED IN CHECKLIST
2 Bill Russell/53 60.00 120.00
2A Bill Russell Red/13 100.00 200.00
2B Bill Russell Red #6/19 100.00 200.00

2007-08 Press Pass Legends Legendary Legacy

COMPLETE SET (10) 8.00 20.00
STATED ODDS 1:9
1 Robert Parish 1.00 2.50
2 Scottie Pippen 1.50 4.00
3 Willis Reed 1.00 2.50
4 Larry Bird 3.00 8.00
5 Joe Dumars 1.00 2.50
6 David Robinson 1.50 4.00
7 Elgin Baylor 1.00 2.50
8 James Worthy 1.25 3.00
9 Nate Archibald 1.00 2.50
10 Earl Monroe 1.00 2.50

2007-08 Press Pass Legends Legendary Legacy Marks

PRINT RUNS LISTED IN CHECKLIST
UNPRICED PLATINUM PRINT RUN ONE TO 25 SETS
1 Robert Parish Red/265 8.00 20.00
2 Scottie Pippen/35 75.00 150.00
2A Scottie Pippen Red/50 75.00 150.00
3 Willis Reed/100 8.00 20.00
4 Larry Bird/50 40.00 80.00
5 Joe Dumars/25 8.00 20.00
7 Elgin Baylor/129 15.00 30.00
8 James Worthy/50 20.00 40.00
9 Nate Archibald/24 8.00 20.00
10 Earl Monroe/42 10.00 25.00
10B Earl Monroe Red/50 10.00 25.00

2007-08 Press Pass Legends Select Swatches

APPROXIMATELY 1:18 PACKS
*PREMIUM: .5X TO 1.25X BASE HI
PREMIUM PRINT RUN 50 SER.#'d SETS
PATCH PRINT RUN 10 SER.#'d SETS
1 Rudy Gay 3.00 8.00
2 Nick Fazekas 3.00 8.00
3 LaMarcus Aldridge 4.00 10.00
4 Acie Law 3.00 8.00
5 Brandan Wright 3.00 8.00
6 Nick Young 5.00 12.00
7 Brandon Roy 4.00 10.00

2007-08 Press Pass Legends Signatures

Sue Bird Birdy/24
Arron Afflalo AAA/4
Arron Afflalo AAA/4
APPROXIMATELY FOUR PER BOX
EXCHANGE EXPIRATION 10/1/08
4 Morris Almond 4.00 10.00
5 Morris Almond Go Rice/25 6.00 15.00
6 Kenny Anderson 5.00 12.00
7 Kenny Anderson Red/48 6.00 15.00
9 Nate Archibald 5.00 12.00
10 Nate Archibald Red/25 15.00 30.00
11 Stacey Augmon 4.00 10.00
13 Stacey Augmon Red/68 6.00 15.00
14 Rick Barry 6.00 15.00
15 Rick Barry Go Canes/35 15.00 30.00
16 Rick Barry Red/40 15.00 30.00
17 Elgin Baylor 15.00 30.00
18 Henry Bibby 4.00 10.00
22 Jay Bilas 5.00 12.00
23 Jay Bilas ESPN Duke 21/39 6.00 15.00
34 Jay Bilas Red/62 10.00 25.00
35 Larry Bird 40.00 80.00
36 Sue Bird 10.00 25.00
38 Sue Bird Red 15.00 30.00
39 Rolando Blackman 6.00 15.00
40 Rolando Blackman Ro Silk/38 20.00 40.00
41 Rolando Blackman Red/25 25.00 50.00
42 Muggsy Bogues 8.00 20.00
43 Muggsy Bogues Go Deacs/26 25.00 50.00
44 Muggsy Bogues Red/52 10.00 25.00
46 Michael Cooper 4.00 10.00
49 Michael Cooper Red 6.00 15.00
51 Javaris Crittenton 4.00 10.00
52 Javaris Crittenton Red/158 5.00 12.00
53 Glen Davis 6.00 15.00
54 Sherman Douglas 4.00 10.00
56 Sherman Douglas Red/82 5.00 12.00
57 Jared Dudley 4.00 10.00
58 Joe Dumars 6.00 15.00
59 Sean Elliott 5.00 12.00
62 Alex English 4.00 10.00
64 Alex English Red 6.00 15.00
69 Phil Ford 5.00 12.00
72 George Gervin 6.00 15.00
74 George Gervin Red/45 10.00 25.00
75 Artis Gilmore 5.00 12.00
76 Artis Gilmore A-Train/199 10.00 25.00
78 Artis Gilmore Red/186 6.00 15.00
79 Artis Gilmore Red A-Train/74 10.00 25.00
81 Aaron Gray 4.00 10.00
84 Hal Greer 6.00 15.00
85 Hal Greer Go Herd/25 15.00 30.00
86 Hal Greer Red/50 10.00 25.00
87 Spencer Hawes 4.00 10.00
91 Spencer Hawes Red/50 5.00 12.00
92 Bobby Hurley 6.00 15.00
94 Bobby Hurley Red/46 15.00 30.00
95 Dan Issel 6.00 15.00
96 Dan Issel The Horse/25 30.00 60.00
98 Larry Johnson 8.00 20.00
99 George Karl 6.00 15.00
103 George Karl Red/57 8.00 20.00
104 Lafayette Lever 4.00 10.00
105 Lafayette Lever Fat/25 25.00 50.00
106 Lafayette Lever Red Fat/50 15.00 30.00
107 Jerry Lucas 10.00 25.00
108 Jerry Lucas Go Bucks/25 30.00 60.00
109 Jerry Lucas Red/50 15.00 30.00
110 Dan Majerle 15.00 30.00
111 Dan Majerle Thunder/25 40.00 80.00
112 Dan Majerle Red/50 25.00 40.00
113 Dick McGuire 6.00 15.00
114 Dick McGuire Red/50 8.00 20.00
115 Dick McGuire Red Tricky/25 15.00 30.00
116 Earl Monroe 8.00 20.00
117 Calvin Murphy 4.00 10.00
118 Calvin Murphy Red/50 6.00 15.00
120 Robert Parish 8.00 20.00
121 John Paxson 6.00 15.00
123 John Paxson Go Irish/14 20.00 40.00
125 Sam Perkins Smooth 6.00 15.00
127 Scottie Pippen 75.00 150.00
129 Willis Reed Go Tigers/25 30.00 75.00
130 Willis Reed Red/25 25.00 50.00
131 Glen Rice 41 5.00 12.00
133 David Robinson 25.00 50.00
137 Tree Rollins 4.00 10.00
140 Tree Rollins Red/46 5.00 12.00
141 Detlef Schrempf 6.00 15.00
142 Detlef Schrempf Go Huskies/25 25.00 50.00
144 Byron Scott 4.00 10.00
146 Byron Scott Red/100 15.00 30.00
147 Jason Smith 4.00 10.00
150 Jerry Tarkanian 5.00 12.00
154 Jerry Tarkanian Red/50 20.00 40.00
155 Lenny Wilkens 4.00 10.00
156 Lenny Wilkens Lefty/25 15.00 30.00
157 Lenny Wilkens Red/50 15.00 30.00
158 Dominique Wilkins 15.00 30.00
160 Dominique Wilkins Red/77 30.00 60.00
162 Dominique Wilkins Red 60.00 120.00
Hum.Hi.Film/23
163 Gus Williams 4.00 10.00
165 Gus Williams Red/50 5.00 12.00
166 James Worthy 25.00 50.00
167 Brandan Wright 10.00 25.00
168 Nick Young 6.00 15.00
169 Josh McRoberts 6.00 15.00

2007-08 Press Pass Legends Student and Teacher Signatures

RANDOM INSERTS IN PACKS
SAJT Stacey Augmon 25.00 60.00
Jerry Tarkanian
SAJT Larry Johnson 30.00 80.00
Jerry Tarkanian

2008-09 Press Pass Legends

COMPLETE SET (70) 15.00 40.00
UNPRICED PLATE PRINT RUN ONE SET
UNPRICED PLATINUM PRINT RUN ONE SET
1 Jerryd Bayless .75 2.00
2 Sonny Weems .75 2.00
3 Trent Plaisted .75 2.00
4 DeVon Hardin .75 2.00
5 Marreese Speights .75 2.00
6 Patrick Ewing Jr. .75 2.00
7 Roy Hibbert 1.25 3.00
8 Eric Gordon 2.00 5.00
9 D.J. White .75 2.00
10 Danilo Gallinari 1.25 3.00
11 Mario Chalmers 1.25 3.00
12 Darrell Jackson .75 2.00
13 Brandon Rush .75 2.00
14 Michael Beasley 1.25 3.00
15 Anthony Randolph 1.00 2.50
16 Joey Dorsey .75 2.00
17 Chris Douglas-Roberts .75 2.00
18 Derrick Rose 6.00 15.00
19 J.J. Hickson 1.00 2.50
20 J.R. Giddens .75 2.00
21 Kosta Koufos .75 2.00
22 Malik Hairston .75 2.00
23 Bryce Taylor .75 2.00
24 Brook Lopez 1.25 3.00
25 Robin Lopez .75 2.00
26 Chris Lofton .75 2.00
27 Candace Parker 6.00 15.00
28 D.J. Augustin .75 2.00
29 DeAndre Jordan 1.50 4.00
30 Kevin Love 3.00 8.00
31 Russell Westbrook 4.00 10.00
32 O.J. Mayo 1.25 3.00
33 Shan Foster .75 2.00
34 Courtney Lee 1.25 3.00
35 Sean Elliott .75 2.00
36 Sidney Moncrief .75 2.00
37 Corliss Williamson .75 2.00
38 Larry Nance .75 2.00
39 Bobby Hurley .75 2.00
40 Sleepy Floyd .75 2.00
41 Clyde Drexler 1.00 2.50
42 Calbert Cheaney .75 2.00
43 Larry Bird 2.50 6.00
44 Danny Manning .75 2.00
45 Rolando Blackman .75 2.00
46 Cliff Hagan .75 2.00
47 Darrell Griffith .75 2.00
48 Bailey Howell .75 2.00
49 David Robinson 1.25 3.00
50 Sidney Lowe .75 2.00
51 Michael Cooper .75 2.00
52 Calvin Murphy .75 2.00
53 Willis Reed .75 2.00
54 Brad Daugherty .75 2.00
55 Nate Archibald .75 2.00
56 James Worthy .75 2.00
57 Jerry Lucas .75 2.00
58 Elgin Baylor .75 2.00
59 Mark Jackson .75 2.00
60 Ernie Grunfeld .75 2.00
61 Bernard King .75 2.00
62 Henry Bibby .75 2.00
63 Gail Goodrich .75 2.00
64 Bill Walton .75 2.00
65 John Wooden 1.00 2.50
66 Stacey Augmon .75 2.00
67 Jerry Tarkanian .75 2.00
68 Gus Williams .75 2.00
69 Jerry West 1.00 2.50
70 UCLA CL .75 2.00

2008-09 Press Pass Legends Bronze

*BRONZE: .5X TO 1.25X BASE HI
BRONZE PRINT RUN 750 SER.#'d SETS

2008-09 Press Pass Legends Emerald

*EMERALD: 1.5X TO 4X BASE HI
EMERALD PRINT RUN 25 SETS

2008-09 Press Pass Legends Gold

*GOLD: .75X TO 2X BASE HI
GOLD PRINT RUN 99 SETS

2008-09 Press Pass Legends Silver

*SILVER: .6X TO 1.5X BASE HI
SILVER PRINT RUN 199 SETS

2008-09 Press Pass Legends All-American

COMPLETE SET (10) 10.00 25.00
STATED ODDS 1:9
1 Sidney Moncrief 1.00 2.50
2 Bobby Hurley 1.00 2.50
3 Larry Bird 3.00 8.00
4 Brandon Rush 1.00 2.50
5 Michael Beasley 1.50 4.00
6 Brad Daugherty 1.00 2.50
7 Derrick Rose 8.00 20.00
8 Candace Parker 8.00 20.00
9 D.J. Augustin 1.00 2.50
10 Kevin Love 4.00 10.00

2008-09 Press Pass Legends All-American Autographs

STATED PRINT RUN 30 TO 271 SER.#'d SETS
1 Sidney Moncrief/271 4.00 10.00
2 Bobby Hurley/195 10.00 25.00
3 Larry Bird/50 40.00 80.00
4 Brandon Rush/159 4.00 10.00
5 Michael Beasley/160 12.50 30.00
6 Brad Daugherty/210 4.00 10.00
7 Derrick Rose/165 50.00 120.00
8 Candace Parker/46 40.00 80.00
9 D.J. Augustin/105 6.00 15.00
10 Kevin Love/78 20.00 50.00
AACC Calbert Cheaney/266 4.00 10.00
AACW Corliss Williamson/165 4.00 10.00
AADG Darrell Griffith/270 4.00 10.00
AADM Danny Manning/169 8.00 20.00
AADR David Robinson/30 50.00 120.00

2008-09 Press Pass Legends All-American Autographs Platinum

STATED PRINT RUN ONE TO 25 SETS
SOME UNPRICED DUE TO SCARCITY
7 Derrick Rose/25 100.00 175.00
8 Candace Parker/25 40.00 100.00
9 D.J. Augustin/25 10.00 25.00
10 Kevin Love/25 25.00 60.00
AADM Danny Manning/25 10.00 25.00
AADR David Robinson/25 50.00 120.00

2008-09 Press Pass Legends Alumni Association

COMPLETE SET (10) 6.00 15.00
STATED ODDS 1:9
1 Sean Elliott 1.50 4.00
Jerryd Bayless
2 Sidney Moncrief 1.25 3.00
Corliss Williamson
3 Calbert Cheaney 1.50 4.00
Eric Gordon
4 Danny Manning 1.50 4.00
Brandon Rush
5 Jerry Lucas 1.25 3.00
Kosta Koufos
7 Gail Goodrich 2.00 5.00
Russell Westbrook
6 Bill Walton 2.00 5.00
Kevin Love
8 Ernie Grunfeld 1.50 4.00
Bernard King
9 Rolando Blackman 2.00 5.00
Michael Beasley
10 Gus Williams 1.50 4.00
O.J. Mayo

2008-09 Press Pass Legends Alumni Association Autographs

STATED PRINT RUN 38 TO 50 SER.#'d SETS
1 Sean Elliott/50 20.00 40.00
Jerryd Bayless
2 Sidney Moncrief/49 10.00 25.00
Corliss Williamson
3 Calbert Cheaney/50 10.00 25.00
Eric Gordon
4 Danny Manning/50 15.00 40.00
Brandon Rush
5 Jerry Lucas/50 10.00 25.00
Kosta Koufos
7 Gail Goodrich/50 35.00 70.00
Russell Westbrook
6 Bill Walton/50 25.00 50.00
Kevin Love
9 Rolando Blackman/49 20.00 50.00
Michael Beasley
10 Gus Williams/50 15.00 40.00
O.J. Mayo
AABLRL Brook Lopez/38 20.00 40.00
Robin Lopez
AAJWBD James Worthy/50 20.00 50.00
Brad Daugherty
AAMCJG Michael Cooper/50 10.00 25.00
J.R. Giddens
AASFRH Sleepy Floyd/50 20.00 40.00
Roy Hibbert

2008-09 Press Pass Legends Legendary Legacy

COMPLETE SET (10) 5.00 12.00
STATED ODDS 1:9
1 Clyde Drexler 1.25 3.00
2 Bobby Hurley 1.00 2.50
3 Larry Bird 3.00 8.00
4 Danny Manning 1.00 2.50
5 Bailey Howell 1.00 2.50
6 David Robinson 1.50 4.00
7 Calvin Murphy 1.00 2.50
8 Jerry Lucas 1.00 2.50
9 Gail Goodrich 1.00 2.50
10 Bill Walton 1.00 2.50

2008-09 Press Pass Legends Legendary Legacy Autographs

STATED PRINT RUN ONE TO 259 SETS
SOME UNPRICED DUE TO SCARCITY
1 Clyde Drexler/98 20.00 50.00
2 Bobby Hurley/200 10.00 25.00
3 Larry Bird/50 40.00 100.00
4 Danny Manning/146 8.00 20.00
5 Bailey Howell/213 5.00 12.00
6 David Robinson/30 40.00 100.00
7 Calvin Murphy/255 5.00 12.00
8 Jerry Lucas/100 6.00 15.00
9 Gail Goodrich/160 5.00 12.00
10 Bill Walton/50 6.00 15.00
10B Bill Walton Red/25* 15.00 40.00
LLBD Brad Daugherty/210 5.00 12.00
LLCW Corliss Williamson/165 5.00 12.00
LLDG Darrell Griffith/259 5.00 12.00
LLJW Jerry West/102 25.00 60.00
LLJW2 Jerry West Red/26* 50.00 100.00
LLJWO James Worthy/50 20.00 50.00

2008-09 Press Pass Legends Legendary Legacy Autographs Platinum

STATED PRINT RUN 4 TO 25 SETS
SOME UNPRICED DUE TO SCARCITY
1 Clyde Drexler 30.00 80.00
2 Bobby Hurley 12.50 30.00
3 Larry Bird 50.00 120.00
4 Danny Manning 10.00 25.00
5 Bailey Howell 10.00 25.00
6 David Robinson 50.00 100.00
7 Calvin Murphy 10.00 25.00
8 Jerry Lucas 10.00 25.00
9 Gail Goodrich/24 10.00 25.00
10 Bill Walton 15.00 40.00
LLBD Brad Daugherty 10.00 25.00
LLJW Jerry West 30.00 60.00
LLJWO James Worthy 25.00 60.00
LLJWO1 James Worthy Big Game/25* 40.00 80.00

2008-09 Press Pass Legends Select Signatures

APPROX.THREE AU's PER MINI BOX
AR Anthony Randolph 4.00 10.00
AR1 Anthony Randolph Red/46* 5.00 12.00
BD Brad Daugherty 4.00 10.00
BH Bailey Howell 6.00 15.00
BH1 Bailey Howell Go Dawgs/25* 10.00 25.00
BH2 Bailey Howell Red/46* 8.00 20.00
BHU Bobby Hurley 8.00 20.00
BHU1 Bobby Hurley Go Duke/25* 60.00 120.00
BHU2 Bobby Hurley Red/46* 10.00 25.00
BK Bernard King 6.00 15.00
BK1 Bernard King Go Vols/18* 25.00 60.00
BK2 Bernard King Red/50* 8.00 20.00
BL Brook Lopez 8.00 20.00
BL2 Brook Lopez Red/25* 10.00 25.00
BR Brandon Rush 4.00 10.00
BW Bill Walton 8.00 20.00
CC Calbert Cheaney 4.00 10.00
CC1 Calbert Cheaney Go Big Red/25* 6.00 15.00
CC2 Calbert Cheaney Red/50* 5.00 12.00
CD Clyde Drexler 15.00 40.00
CD1 Clyde Drexler The Glide/25* 60.00 120.00
CD2 Clyde Drexler Red/50* 25.00 60.00
CDR Chris Douglas-Roberts 4.00 10.00
CDR2 Chris Douglas-Roberts Red/50* 5.00 12.00
CH Cliff Hagan 4.00 10.00
CH2 Cliff Hagen Red/51* 5.00 12.00
CL Courtney Lee 6.00 15.00
CM Calvin Murphy 4.00 10.00
CM1 Calvin Murphy Murph/25* 5.00 12.00
CM2 Calvin Murphy Red/49* 5.00 12.00
CP Candace Parker Red 30.00 80.00
CP1 Candace Parker Blue Go Vols/2* 30.00 80.00
CW Corliss Williamson 4.00 10.00
CW1 Corliss Williamson Big Nasty/15* 8.00 20.00
DA D.J. Augustin 6.00 15.00
DG Darrell Griffith 4.00 10.00
DG2 Darrell Griffith Red/48* 6.00 15.00
DGA Danilo Gallinari 6.00 15.00
DGA2 Danilo Gallinari Red/13* 10.00 25.00
DJ DeAndre Jordan 8.00 20.00
DM Danny Manning 8.00 20.00
DM1 Danny Manning Red/58* 10.00 25.00
DR David Robinson 20.00 40.00
DRO Derrick Rose 50.00 120.00
DRO1 Derrick Rose D.Pooh Rose/25* 125.00 250.00
DRO2 Derrick Rose Red/50* 60.00 150.00
DW D.J. White 4.00 10.00
DW1 D.J. White Red Go IU/25* 10.00 25.00
EB Elgin Baylor 10.00 25.00
EB1 Elgin Baylor Go Chieftains/25* 25.00 60.00
EB2 Elgin Baylor Red/50* 15.00 40.00
EG Eric Gordon 8.00 20.00
EG2 Eric Gordon Red/46* 10.00 25.00
EGR Ernie Grunfeld 5.00 12.00
EGR1 Ernie Grunfeld Red/50* 10.00 25.00
GG Gail Goodrich 5.00 12.00
GW Gus Williams 4.00 10.00
GW2 Gus Williams Red/125* 6.00 15.00
HB Henry Bibby 4.00 10.00
JB Jerryd Bayless 5.00 12.00
JB2 Jerryd Bayless Red/50* 8.00 20.00
JD Joey Dorsey 4.00 10.00
JD1 Joey Dorsey Red The Hulk/47* 6.00 15.00
JG J.R. Giddens 4.00 10.00
JG1 J.R. Giddens Red/54* 5.00 12.00
JL Jerry Lucas 6.00 15.00
JT Jerry Tarkanian 8.00 20.00
JT1 Jerry Tarkanian Red/50* 10.00 25.00
JW Jerry West 25.00 50.00
JWD John Wooden 40.00 80.00
JWO James Worthy 15.00 30.00
JWO1 James Worthy Red/59* 15.00 40.00
KK Kosta Koufos 4.00 10.00
KK2 Kosta Koufos Red/54* 6.00 15.00
KL Kevin Love Red 20.00 50.00
LB Larry Bird 30.00 60.00
LN Larry Nance 4.00 10.00
MB Michael Beasley 8.00 20.00
MB2 Michael Beasley 27/30* 25.00 50.00
MB3 Michael Beasley Red/25* 15.00 40.00
MC Michael Cooper 6.00 15.00
MJ Mark Jackson 5.00 12.00
MS Marreese Speights 4.00 10.00
OM O.J. Mayo 8.00 20.00
OM1 O.J. Mayo Red/39* 10.00 25.00
OM2 O.J. Mayo Red Juice Mayo/50* 20.00 40.00
RB Rolando Blackman 4.00 10.00
RB1 Rolando Blackman Go K-State/25* 10.00 25.00
RB2 Rolando Blackman Red/49* 6.00 15.00
RH Roy Hibbert 8.00 20.00
RL Robin Lopez 5.00 12.00
RL2 Robin Lopez Red/48* 6.00 15.00
RW Russell Westbrook 20.00 50.00
RW2 Russell Westbrook Red/25 20.00 50.00
SA Stacey Augmon 4.00 10.00
SA1 Stacy Augmon Plasticman/25* 15.00 30.00
SA2 Stacy Augmon Red/50* 6.00 15.00
SE Sean Elliott 4.00 10.00
SE1 Sean Elliott Red/50* 10.00 25.00
SF Sleepy Floyd 4.00 10.00
SL Sidney Lowe 4.00 10.00
SM Sidney Moncrief 4.00 10.00
SM1 Sidney Moncrief Super Sid/35* 30.00 60.00

2008-09 Press Pass Legends Select Swatches

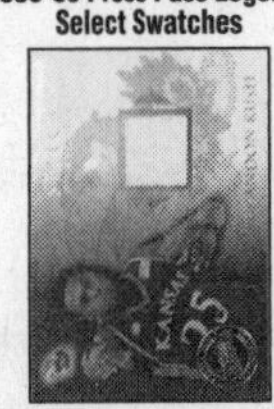

RANDOM INSERTS IN PACKS
UNPRICED PATCH PRINT RUN 10 SETS
*PLATINUM: .6X TO 1.5X BASE
PLATINUM PRINT RUN 50 SER. #'d SETS
SSWAR Anthony Randolph 2.50 6.00
SSWBL Brook Lopez 3.00 8.00
SSWBR Brandon Rush 2.50 6.00
SSWDA D.J. Augustin 2.50 6.00
SSWDR Derrick Rose 10.00 25.00
SSWJD Joey Dorsey 2.50 6.00
SSWRH Roy Hibbert 3.00 8.00
SSWRL Robin Lopez 2.50 6.00
SSWRW Russell Westbrook 6.00 15.00

2008-09 Press Pass Legends Student and Teacher Signatures

PRINT RUN 25 SER.#'d SETS
STBWJW Bill Walton 100.00 200.00
John Wooden
STGGJW Gail Goodrich 60.00 150.00
John Wooden
STHBJW Henry Bibby 75.00 150.00
John Wooden

2009-10 Prestige

COMP.SET w/o RCs (150) 10.00 25.00
1 Joe Johnson .40 1.00
2 Josh Smith .40 1.00
3 Mike Bibby .30 .75
4 Jamal Crawford .30 .75
5 Kevin Garnett .75 2.00
6 Paul Pierce .50 1.25
7 Ray Allen .40 1.00
8 Rajon Rondo .50 1.25
9 Gerald Wallace .40 1.00
10 Boris Diaw .30 .75
11 Emeka Okafor .40 1.00
12 Ben Gordon .40 1.00
13 John Salmons .40 1.00
14 Derrick Rose 1.25 3.00
15 Luol Deng .40 1.00
16 LeBron James 2.00 5.00
17 Mo Williams .30 .75
18 Zydrunas Ilgauskas .25 .60
19 Delonte West .25 .60
20 Shaquille O'Neal .75 2.00
21 Dirk Nowitzki .50 1.25
22 Jason Terry .30 .75
23 Josh Howard .30 .75
24 Jason Kidd .40 1.00
25 Carmelo Anthony .50 1.25
26 Chauncey Billups .40 1.00
27 Nene .30 .75
28 Richard Hamilton .30 .75
29 Allen Iverson .50 1.25
30 Tayshaun Prince .40 1.00
31 Rasheed Wallace .40 1.00
32 Stephen Jackson .30 .75
33 Corey Maggette .30 .75
34 Yao Ming .50 1.25
35 Tracy McGrady .40 1.00
36 Ron Artest .40 1.00
37 Luis Scola .30 .75
38 Danny Granger .40 1.00
39 T.J. Ford .25 .60
40 Mike Dunleavy .25 .60
41 Marquis Daniels .25 .60
42 Zach Randolph .30 .75
43 Al Thornton .30 .75
44 Eric Gordon .40 1.00
45 Baron Davis .40 1.00
46 Kobe Bryant 2.00 5.00
47 Pau Gasol .40 1.00
48 Lamar Odom .40 1.00
49 Derek Fisher .30 .75
50 O.J. Mayo .40 1.00
51 Rudy Gay .40 1.00
52 Marc Gasol .40 1.00
53 Dwyane Wade .75 2.00
54 Jermaine O'Neal .40 1.00
55 Michael Beasley .40 1.00
56 Udonis Haslem .30 .75
57 Michael Redd .40 1.00
58 Charlie Villanueva .30 .75
59 Al Jefferson .40 1.00
60 Ryan Gomes .25 .60
61 Kevin Love .60 1.50
62 Devin Harris .40 1.00
63 Brook Lopez .40 1.00
64 Yi Jianlian .30 .75
65 Chris Paul .60 1.50
66 David West .40 1.00
67 Peja Stojakovic .40 1.00
68 Rasual Butler .25 .60
69 Al Harrington .30 .75
70 Nate Robinson .40 1.00
71 David Lee .30 .75
72 Larry Hughes .30 .75
73 Kevin Durant 1.25 3.00
74 Jeff Green .30 .75
75 Russell Westbrook .60 1.50
76 Dwight Howard .60 1.50
77 Rashard Lewis .40 1.00
78 Hedo Turkoglu .40 1.00
79 Jameer Nelson .40 1.00
80 Vince Carter .50 1.25
81 Andre Iguodala .40 1.00
82 Andre Miller .40 1.00
83 Thaddeus Young .25 .60
84 Elton Brand .40 1.00
85 Amare Stoudemire .40 1.00
86 Steve Nash .40 1.00
87 Jason Richardson .40 1.00
88 Brandon Roy .40 1.00
89 LaMarcus Aldridge .40 1.00
90 Greg Oden .30 .75
91 Kevin Martin .40 1.00
92 Andres Nocioni .25 .60
93 Jason Thompson .25 .60
94 Tony Parker .40 1.00
95 Tim Duncan .60 1.50
96 Manu Ginobili .40 1.00
97 Michael Finley .40 1.00
98 Richard Jefferson .40 1.00
99 Chris Bosh .40 1.00
100 Andrea Bargnani .30 .75
101 Shawn Marion .40 1.00
102 Deron Williams .40 1.00
103 Mehmet Okur .25 .60
104 Carlos Boozer .40 1.00
105 Ronnie Brewer .30 .75
106 Antawn Jamison .40 1.00
107 Caron Butler .40 1.00
108 Nick Young .30 .75
109 Andray Blatche .25 .60
110 Randy Foye .25 .60
111 Kareem Abdul-Jabbar 1.00 2.50
112 Bob Dandridge .60 1.50
113 Alvan Adams .60 1.50
114 A.C. Green .60 1.50
115 Dave Bing .60 1.50
116 Larry Bird 2.00 5.00
117 Nate Thurmond .60 1.50
118 Michael Cooper .60 1.50
119 Bob Cousy 1.00 2.50
120 Adrian Dantley .60 1.50
121 Darryl Dawkins .60 1.50
122 Clyde Drexler .75 2.00

123 Elvin Hayes .60 1.50
124 Walt Frazier .60 1.50
125 World B. Free .60 1.50
126 George Gervin .60 1.50
127 Gail Goodrich .60 1.50
128 Tim Hardaway .60 1.50
129 Connie Hawkins .60 1.50
130 K.C. Jones .60 1.50
131 Bernard King .60 1.50
132 Bob Lanier .60 1.50
133 Dan Majerle .60 1.50
134 Karl Malone .75 2.00
135 Sam Perkins .60 1.50
136 Slick Watts .60 1.50
137 Bob McAdoo .60 1.50
138 Xavier McDaniel .60 1.50
139 Sidney Moncrief .60 1.50
140 Robert Parish .60 1.50
141 Oscar Robertson .60 1.50
142 Paul Silas .60 1.50
143 Moses Malone .60 1.50
144 Dennis Rodman 1.00 2.50
145 Bill Russell 1.00 2.50
146 Bill Bradley .60 1.50
147 Bill Walton .60 1.50
148 Spud Webb .60 1.50
149 Cedric Ceballos .60 1.50
150 Jerry West .75 2.00
151 Blake Griffin RC 6.00 15.00
152 Hasheem Thabeet RC 1.00 2.50
153 James Harden RC 3.00 8.00
154 Tyreke Evans RC 2.50 6.00
155 Blake Griffin College RC 6.00 15.00
156 Jonny Flynn RC 1.00 2.50
157 Stephen Curry RC 2.50 6.00
158 Jordan Hill RC 1.00 2.50
159 DeMar DeRozan RC 1.50 4.00
160 Brandon Jennings SP 15.00 30.00
161 Terrence Williams RC 1.00 2.50
162 Gerald Henderson RC 1.00 2.50
163 Tyler Hansbrough SP 10.00 25.00
164 Earl Clark RC 1.00 2.50
165 Austin Daye RC 1.00 2.50
166 James Johnson RC 1.00 2.50
167 Jrue Holiday RC 2.00 5.00
168 Ty Lawson RC 1.50 4.00
169 Jeff Teague RC 1.25 3.00
170 Eric Maynor RC 1.00 2.50
171 Darren Collison RC 1.50 4.00
172 Hasheem Thabeet UConn RC 1.00 2.50
173 Omri Casspi RC 1.00 2.50
174 B.J. Mullens RC 1.00 2.50
175 Rodrigue Beaubois RC 1.25 3.00
176 Taj Gibson SP 8.00 20.00
177 DeMarre Carroll SP 6.00 15.00
178 Wayne Ellington RC 1.00 2.50
179 Toney Douglas RC 1.00 2.50
180 Tyreke Evans Memphis RC 2.50 6.00
181 Jeff Pendergraph RC 1.00 2.50
182 Jermaine Taylor RC 1.00 2.50
183 Dante Cunningham RC 1.00 2.50
184 DaJuan Summers RC 1.00 2.50
185 Sam Young RC 1.00 2.50
186 DeJuan Blair RC 1.25 3.00
187 Jon Brockman RC 1.00 2.50
188 Derrick Brown RC 1.00 2.50
189 Jodie Meeks RC 1.25 3.00
190 Jonas Jerebko SP 5.00 12.00
191 Marcus Thornton RC 1.50 4.00
192 Chase Budinger RC 1.00 2.50
193 Goran Suton RC 1.00 2.50
194 Danny Green RC 1.50 4.00
195 Taylor Griffin RC 1.00 2.50
196 A.J. Price RC 1.00 2.50
197 Jrue Holiday UCLA RC 2.00 5.00
198 Lester Hudson RC 1.00 2.50
199 Jack McClinton RC 1.00 2.50
200 Patrick Beverley RC 1.00 2.50
201 Blake Griffin RC 6.00 15.00
202 Hasheem Thabeet RC 1.00 2.50
203 James Harden RC 3.00 8.00
204 Tyreke Evans RC 2.50 6.00
205 Jordan Hill Arizona SP 8.00 20.00
206 Jonny Flynn RC 1.00 2.50
207 Stephen Curry RC 2.50 6.00
208 Jordan Hill RC 1.00 2.50
209 DeMar DeRozan RC 1.50 4.00
210 Brandon Jennings RC 2.00 5.00
211 Terrence Williams RC 1.00 2.50
212 Gerald Henderson RC 1.00 2.50
213 Tyler Hansbrough RC 1.50 4.00
214 Earl Clark RC 1.00 2.50
215 Austin Daye RC 1.00 2.50
216 James Johnson RC 1.00 2.50
217 Jrue Holiday RC 2.00 5.00
218 Ty Lawson SP 8.00 20.00
219 Jeff Teague RC 1.25 3.00
220 Eric Maynor SP 6.00 15.00
221 Darren Collison RC 1.50 4.00
222 Tyler Hansbrough RC 1.50 4.00
223 Omri Casspi RC 1.00 2.50
224 B.J. Mullens RC 1.00 2.50
225 Rodrigue Beaubois RC 1.25 3.00
226 Taj Gibson RC 1.25 3.00
227 DeMarre Carroll RC 1.00 2.50
228 Wayne Ellington RC 1.00 2.50
229 Toney Douglas RC 1.00 2.50
230 Stephen Curry Davidson RC 2.50 6.00
231 Jeff Pendergraph RC 1.00 2.50
232 Jermaine Taylor RC 1.00 2.50
233 Dante Cunningham SP 5.00 12.00
234 DaJuan Summers RC 1.00 2.50
235 Sam Young RC 1.00 2.50
236 DeJuan Blair RC 1.25 3.00
237 Jon Brockman RC 1.00 2.50
238 Derrick Brown RC 1.00 2.50
239 Jodie Meeks RC 1.25 3.00
240 Jonas Jerebko RC 1.00 2.50
241 Marcus Thornton RC 1.50 4.00
242 Chase Budinger RC 1.00 2.50
243 Goran Suton RC 1.00 2.50
244 Danny Green RC 1.50 4.00
245 Taylor Griffin RC 1.00 2.50
246 A.J. Price RC 1.00 2.50
247 James Johnson Wake SP 6.00 15.00
248 Lester Hudson RC 1.00 2.50
249 Jack McClinton RC 1.00 2.50
250 Patrick Beverley RC 1.00 2.50
251 Wesley Matthews RC* 1.50 4.00
252 Patrick Mills RC* 1.25 3.00
253 Serge Ibaka RC* 2.50 6.00
254 Marcus Landry RC* 1.00 2.50
255 Sundiata Gaines RC* 1.00 2.50
251A Wesley Matthews AU* 8.00 20.00
252A Patrick Mills AU* 8.00 20.00
253A Serge Ibaka AU* 12.00 30.00
254A Marcus Landry AU* 5.00 12.00
255A Sundiata Gaines AU* 5.00 12.00

2009-10 Prestige Bonus Shots Black Signatures

STATED PRINT RUN 25 TO 250 SER.#'d SETS
ASTERISK CARDS FROM PANINI UPDATE
46 Kobe Bryant/25 100.00 200.00
120 Adrian Dantley/100 6.00 15.00
124 Walt Frazier/100 6.00 15.00
129 Connie Hawkins/100 6.00 15.00
137 Bob McAdoo/50 15.00 30.00
139 Sidney Moncrief/100 6.00 15.00
141 Oscar Robertson/50 20.00 50.00
145 Bill Russell/50 40.00 100.00
147 Bill Walton/50 6.00 15.00
151 Blake Griffin/25 150.00 300.00
153 James Harden/25 25.00 60.00
154 Tyreke Evans/25 20.00 50.00
155 Blake Griffin/25 150.00 300.00
157 Stephen Curry/25 20.00 50.00
158 Jordan Hill/25 6.00 15.00
160 Brandon Jennings/25 12.00 30.00
161 Terrence Williams/25 6.00 15.00
162 Gerald Henderson/25 6.00 15.00
163 Tyler Hansbrough/25 12.00 30.00
164 Earl Clark/25 6.00 15.00
166 James Johnson/25 6.00 15.00
167 Jrue Holiday/25 12.00 30.00
169 Jeff Teague/25 8.00 20.00
171 Darren Collison/50 10.00 25.00
173 Omri Casspi/50 6.00 15.00
174 B.J. Mullens/50 6.00 15.00
175 Rodrigue Beaubois/50 8.00 20.00
176 Taj Gibson/50 8.00 20.00
177 DeMarre Carroll/50 6.00 15.00
179 Toney Douglas/50 6.00 15.00
180 Tyreke Evans/50 15.00 40.00
182 Jermaine Taylor/100 6.00 15.00
183 Dante Cunningham/100 6.00 15.00
186 DeJuan Blair/100 8.00 20.00
188 Derrick Brown/100 6.00 15.00
189 Jodie Meeks/100 8.00 20.00
191 Marcus Thornton/100 10.00 25.00
192 Chase Budinger/100 6.00 15.00
193 Goran Suton/100 6.00 15.00
194 Danny Green/100 10.00 25.00
197 Jrue Holiday/25 12.00 30.00
199 Jack McClinton/100 6.00 15.00
201 Blake Griffin/25 150.00 300.00
202 Hasheem Thabeet/25 6.00 15.00
203 James Harden/25 25.00 60.00
204 Tyreke Evans/25 20.00 50.00
205 Jordan Hill/25 6.00 15.00
207 Stephen Curry/25 20.00 50.00
208 Jordan Hill/25 6.00 15.00
210 Brandon Jennings/25 12.00 30.00
211 Terrence Williams/25 6.00 15.00
212 Gerald Henderson/25 6.00 15.00
213 Tyler Hansbrough/25 12.00 40.00
214 Earl Clark/25 6.00 15.00
216 James Johnson/25 6.00 15.00
217 Jrue Holiday/25 12.00 30.00
219 Jeff Teague/25 8.00 20.00
221 Darren Collison/50 10.00 25.00
222 Tyler Hansbrough/25 12.00 30.00
223 Omri Casspi/50 6.00 15.00
224 B.J. Mullens/50 6.00 15.00
225 Rodrigue Beaubois/50 8.00 20.00
226 Taj Gibson/50 8.00 20.00
227 DeMarre Carroll/50 6.00 15.00
229 Toney Douglas/50 6.00 15.00
230 Stephen Curry/50 15.00 40.00
232 Jermaine Taylor/100 6.00 15.00
233 Dante Cunningham/100 6.00 15.00
236 DeJuan Blair/100 8.00 20.00
238 Derrick Brown/100 6.00 15.00
239 Jodie Meeks/100 8.00 20.00
241 Marcus Thornton/100 10.00 25.00
242 Chase Budinger/100 6.00 15.00
243 Goran Suton/100 6.00 15.00
244 Danny Green/100 10.00 25.00
246 A.J. Price/100 6.00 15.00
247 James Johnson/50 6.00 15.00
249 Jack McClinton/100 6.00 15.00
251 Wesley Matthews/250* 10.00 25.00
252 Patrick Mills/250* 10.00 25.00
253 Serge Ibaka/250* 15.00 40.00
254 Marcus Landry/250* 6.00 15.00
255 Sundiata Gaines/250* 6.00 15.00

2009-10 Prestige Bonus Shots Green

*GREEN 1-150: 3X TO 8X BASE HI
*GREEN 151-250: 1.5X TO 4X BASE HI
STATED PRINT RUN 25 SER.#'d SETS
SP CARDS SAME VALUE AS NON SP
29 Allen Iverson 6.00 15.00

2009-10 Prestige Bonus Shots Orange

*ORANGE 1-150: .75X TO 2X BASE HI
*ORANGE 151-250: .6X TO 1.5X BASE HI
STATED PRINT RUN 300 SER.#'d SETS
SP CARDS SAME VALUE AS NON SP

2009-10 Prestige Draft Picks Light Blue

*BLUE: .4X TO 1X BASE HI
PRINT RUN 999 SER.#'d SETS
SP CARDS SAME VALUE AS NON SP

2009-10 Prestige Draft Picks Light Blue Autographs

STATED PRINT RUN 50 TO 699 SER.#'d SETS
151 Blake Griffin/50 125.00 250.00
153 James Harden/100 12.00 30.00
154 Tyreke Evans/50 15.00 40.00
155 Blake Griffin/50 125.00 250.00
157 Stephen Curry/100 12.00 30.00
158 Jordan Hill/50 4.00 10.00
160 Brandon Jennings/100 8.00 20.00
161 Terrence Williams/100 4.00 10.00
162 Gerald Henderson/50 6.00 15.00
163 Tyler Hansbrough/100 6.00 15.00
164 Earl Clark/100 4.00 10.00
165 Austin Daye/100 4.00 10.00
166 James Johnson/50 4.00 10.00
167 Jrue Holiday/100 8.00 20.00
169 Jeff Teague/100 5.00 12.00
171 Darren Collison/399 6.00 15.00
173 Omri Casspi/499 4.00 10.00
174 B.J. Mullens/499 4.00 10.00
175 Rodrigue Beaubois/499 5.00 12.00
176 Taj Gibson/499 5.00 12.00
177 DeMarre Carroll/499 4.00 10.00
179 Toney Douglas/399 4.00 10.00
180 Tyreke Evans/50 15.00 40.00
181 Jeff Pendergraph/399 4.00 10.00
182 Jermaine Taylor/699 4.00 10.00
183 Dante Cunningham/699 4.00 10.00
186 DeJuan Blair/699 5.00 12.00
188 Derrick Brown/699 4.00 10.00
189 Jodie Meeks/699 5.00 12.00
191 Marcus Thornton/699 6.00 15.00
192 Chase Budinger/699 4.00 10.00
193 Goran Suton/499 4.00 10.00
194 Danny Green/499 6.00 15.00
196 A.J. Price/699 4.00 10.00
197 Jrue Holiday/100 8.00 20.00
199 Jack McClinton/699 4.00 10.00
201 Blake Griffin/50 125.00 250.00
203 James Harden/100 12.00 30.00
204 Tyreke Evans/50 15.00 40.00
205 Jordan Hill/50 4.00 10.00
207 Stephen Curry/100 12.00 30.00
208 Jordan Hill/50 4.00 10.00
210 Brandon Jennings/100 8.00 20.00
211 Terrence Williams/100 4.00 10.00
212 Gerald Henderson/50 6.00 15.00
213 Tyler Hansbrough/100 6.00 15.00
214 Earl Clark/100 4.00 10.00
215 Austin Daye/100 4.00 10.00
216 James Johnson/50 4.00 10.00
217 Jrue Holiday/100 8.00 20.00
219 Jeff Teague/100 5.00 12.00
221 Darren Collison/399 6.00 15.00
222 Tyler Hansbrough/100 6.00 15.00
223 Omri Casspi/499 4.00 10.00
224 B.J. Mullens/499 4.00 10.00
225 Rodrigue Beaubois/499 5.00 12.00
226 Taj Gibson/499 5.00 12.00
227 DeMarre Carroll/499 4.00 10.00
229 Toney Douglas/399 4.00 10.00
230 Stephen Curry/100 12.00 30.00
231 Jeff Pendergraph/100 4.00 10.00
232 Jermaine Taylor/699 4.00 10.00
233 Dante Cunningham/699 4.00 10.00
236 DeJuan Blair/699 5.00 12.00
238 Derrick Brown/699 4.00 10.00
239 Jodie Meeks/699 5.00 12.00
241 Marcus Thornton/699 6.00 15.00
242 Chase Budinger/699 4.00 10.00
243 Goran Suton/499 4.00 10.00
244 Danny Green/499 6.00 15.00
246 A.J. Price/699 4.00 10.00
247 James Johnson/50 4.00 10.00
249 Jack McClinton/699 4.00 10.00

2009-10 Prestige Connections

COMPLETE SET (10) 10.00 25.00
RANDOM INSERTS IN PACKS
1 Luke Walton / Jordan Hill 1.00 2.50
2 Yao Ming / Sun Yue 1.25 3.00
3 Yao Ming / Yi Jianlian 1.25 3.00
4 Marc Gasol / Pau Gasol 1.00 2.50
5 James Posey / David West 1.00 2.50
6 James Johnson / Jeff Teague 1.25 3.00
7 Jrue Holiday / Darren Collison 2.00 5.00
8 Blake Griffin / Tyler Hansbrough 5.00 12.00
9 Dell Curry / Stephen Curry 2.50 6.00
10 Stephen Jackson / Josh Smith 1.00 2.50

2009-10 Prestige Connections Materials

PRINT RUN 250 SER.#'d SETS
UNPRICED PRIME PRINT RUN 10 SETS
6 James Johnson / Jeff Teague 4.00 10.00
7 Jrue Holiday / Darren Collison 5.00 12.00
8 Blake Griffin / Tyler Hansbrough 15.00 40.00

2009-10 Prestige Franchise Favorites

COMPLETE SET (19) 8.00 20.00
RANDOM INSERT IN PACKS
1 Amare Stoudemire .75 2.00
2 Carmelo Anthony 1.00 2.50
3 Chris Bosh .75 2.00
4 Chris Paul 1.25 3.00
5 Deron Williams .75 2.00
6 Dirk Nowitzki 1.00 2.50
7 Dwight Howard 1.25 3.00
8 Dwyane Wade 1.50 4.00
9 Kobe Bryant 4.00 10.00
10 LeBron James 4.00 10.00
11 Paul Pierce 1.00 2.50
12 Tim Duncan 1.25 3.00
13 Yao Ming 1.00 2.50
14 Danny Granger .75 2.00
15 Michael Redd .75 2.00
16 Ben Gordon .75 2.00
17 Gilbert Arenas .75 2.00
18 Kevin Durant 2.50 6.00
19 Brandon Roy .75 2.00

2009-10 Prestige Hardcourt Heroes

COMPLETE SET (20) 6.00 15.00
RANDOM INSERT IN PACKS
1 Joe Johnson .60 1.50
2 Rajon Rondo .75 2.00
3 Ben Gordon .60 1.50
4 LeBron James 3.00 8.00
5 Josh Howard .50 1.25
6 Carmelo Anthony .75 2.00
7 Yao Ming .75 2.00
8 Danny Granger .60 1.50
9 Baron Davis .60 1.50
10 Pau Gasol .60 1.50
11 Jermaine O'Neal .60 1.50
12 Michael Redd .60 1.50
13 Devin Harris .60 1.50
14 David Lee .50 1.25
15 Kevin Durant 2.00 5.00
16 Amare Stoudemire .60 1.50
17 Brandon Roy .60 1.50
18 Tony Parker .60 1.50
19 Chris Bosh .60 1.50
20 Carlos Boozer .60 1.50
BG Blake Griffin PROMO 6.00 15.00

2009-10 Prestige Hardcourt Heroes Materials

STATED PRINT RUN 250 SER.#'d SETS
UNPRICED PRIME PRINT RUN 10 SER.#'d SETS
1 Joe Johnson 3.00 8.00
5 Josh Howard 2.50 6.00
7 Yao Ming 4.00 10.00
11 Jermaine O'Neal 3.00 8.00
14 David Lee 2.50 6.00
17 Brandon Roy 3.00 8.00
19 Chris Bosh 3.00 8.00
20 Carlos Boozer 3.00 8.00

2009-10 Prestige Inside the Numbers

COMPLETE SET (10) 4.00 10.00
RANDOM INSERT IN PACKS
1 Derrick Rose 2.50 6.00
2 Tim Duncan 1.25 3.00
3 Kobe Bryant 4.00 10.00
4 Richard Hamilton .60 1.50
5 T.J. Ford .50 1.25
6 Gilbert Arenas .75 2.00
7 Deron Williams .75 2.00
8 Marcus Camby .50 1.25
9 Chauncey Billups .75 2.00
10 O.J. Mayo .75 2.00

2009-10 Prestige Inside the Numbers Materials

STATED PRINT RUN 100 TO 250 SER.#'d SETS
UNPRICED PRIME PRINT RUN 10 SER.#'d SETS
2 Tim Duncan/150 5.00 12.00
3 Kobe Bryant/100 10.00 25.00
7 Deron Williams/250 3.00 8.00
10 O.J. Mayo/100 3.00 8.00

2009-10 Prestige Inside the Numbers Signatures

STATED PRINT RUN 25 SER.#'d SETS
3 Kobe Bryant 100.00 225.00

2009-10 Prestige NBA Draft Class

COMPLETE SET (34) 25.00 50.00
RANDOM INSERT IN PACKS
1 Blake Griffin 8.00 20.00
2 Hasheem Thabeet 1.25 3.00
3 James Harden 4.00 10.00
4 Tyreke Evans 3.00 8.00
5 Rodrigue Beaubois 1.50 4.00
6 Jonny Flynn 1.25 3.00
7 Stephen Curry 3.00 8.00
8 Jordan Hill 1.25 3.00
9 DeMar DeRozan 2.00 5.00
10 Brandon Jennings 2.50 6.00
11 Terrence Williams 1.25 3.00
12 Gerald Henderson 1.25 3.00
13 Tyler Hansbrough 2.00 5.00
14 Earl Clark 1.25 3.00
15 Austin Daye 1.25 3.00
16 James Johnson 1.25 3.00
17 Jrue Holiday 2.50 6.00
18 Ty Lawson 2.00 5.00
19 Jeff Teague 1.50 4.00
20 Eric Maynor 1.25 3.00
21 Darren Collison 2.00 5.00
23 Omri Casspi 1.25 3.00
24 B.J. Mullens 1.25 3.00
25 Taj Gibson 1.50 4.00
26 DeMarre Carroll 1.25 3.00
27 Wayne Ellington 1.25 3.00
28 Toney Douglas 1.25 3.00
29 Jeff Pendergraph 1.25 3.00
30 DaJuan Summers 1.25 3.00
31 Sam Young 1.25 3.00
32 DeJuan Blair 1.50 4.00
33 Jodie Meeks 1.50 4.00
34 Chase Budinger 1.25 3.00
35 Taylor Griffin 1.25 3.00
36 Patrick Mills 1.50 4.00

2009-10 Prestige NBA Draft Class Autographs

RANDOM INSERTS IN PACKS
1 Blake Griffin 75.00 150.00
2 Hasheem Thabeet 5.00 12.00
3 James Harden 15.00 40.00
4 Tyreke Evans 12.00 30.00
5 Rodrigue Beaubois 6.00 15.00
6 Jonny Flynn 5.00 12.00
7 Stephen Curry 12.00 30.00
8 Jordan Hill 5.00 12.00
10 Brandon Jennings 10.00 25.00
11 Terrence Williams 5.00 12.00
12 Gerald Henderson 5.00 12.00
13 Tyler Hansbrough 8.00 20.00
14 Earl Clark 5.00 12.00
15 Austin Daye 5.00 12.00
16 James Johnson 5.00 12.00
17 Jrue Holiday 10.00 25.00
18 Ty Lawson 8.00 20.00
19 Jeff Teague 6.00 15.00
20 Eric Maynor 5.00 12.00
21 Darren Collison 8.00 20.00
23 Omri Casspi 5.00 12.00
24 B.J. Mullens 5.00 12.00
25 Taj Gibson 6.00 15.00
26 DeMarre Carroll 5.00 12.00
27 Wayne Ellington 5.00 12.00
28 Toney Douglas 5.00 12.00
29 Jeff Pendergraph 5.00 12.00
30 DaJuan Summers/249 5.00 12.00
31 Sam Young 5.00 12.00
32 DeJuan Blair 6.00 15.00
33 Jodie Meeks 6.00 15.00
34 Chase Budinger 5.00 12.00
35 Taylor Griffin 5.00 12.00

2009-10 Prestige NBA Draft Class Autographs Logos

STATED PRINT RUN 124 TO 125 SER.#'d SETS
1 Blake Griffin 100.00 200.00
2 Hasheem Thabeet/124 6.00 15.00
3 James Harden 20.00 50.00
4 Tyreke Evans 20.00 50.00
5 Rodrigue Beaubois 8.00 20.00
6 Jonny Flynn 6.00 15.00
7 Stephen Curry 15.00 40.00
8 Jordan Hill 6.00 15.00
10 Brandon Jennings 12.00 30.00
11 Terrence Williams/124 6.00 15.00
12 Gerald Henderson 6.00 15.00
13 Tyler Hansbrough 10.00 25.00
14 Earl Clark/124 6.00 15.00
15 Austin Daye 6.00 15.00
16 James Johnson 6.00 15.00
17 Jrue Holiday/124 12.00 30.00
18 Ty Lawson 12.00 30.00
19 Jeff Teague 8.00 20.00
20 Eric Maynor 6.00 15.00
21 Darren Collison 10.00 25.00
23 Omri Casspi 6.00 15.00
24 B.J. Mullens 6.00 15.00
25 Taj Gibson 8.00 20.00
26 DeMarre Carroll 6.00 15.00
27 Wayne Ellington 6.00 15.00
28 Toney Douglas 6.00 15.00
29 Jeff Pendergraph 6.00 15.00
30 DaJuan Summers 6.00 15.00
31 Sam Young 6.00 15.00
32 DeJuan Blair 8.00 20.00
33 Jodie Meeks 8.00 20.00
34 Chase Budinger 6.00 15.00
35 Taylor Griffin 6.00 15.00

2009-10 Prestige NBA Draft Class Autographs Logos College

STATED PRINT RUN 93 TO 100 SER.#'d SETS
UNPRICED DRAFT LOGO PRINT RUN 10 SETS
1 Blake Griffin/99 100.00 200.00
2 Hasheem Thabeet/100 8.00 20.00
3 James Harden/100 25.00 60.00
4 Tyreke Evans/100 20.00 50.00
5 Rodrigue Beaubois/100 10.00 25.00
6 Jonny Flynn/100 8.00 20.00
7 Stephen Curry/100 20.00 50.00
8 Jordan Hill/100 8.00 20.00
10 Brandon Jennings/100 25.00 60.00
11 Terrence Williams/100 8.00 20.00
12 Gerald Henderson/100 8.00 20.00
13 Tyler Hansbrough/100 40.00 70.00
14 Earl Clark/100 8.00 20.00
15 Austin Daye/100 8.00 20.00
16 James Johnson/100 8.00 20.00
17 Jrue Holiday/100 15.00 40.00
18 Ty Lawson/98 25.00 60.00
19 Jeff Teague/100 10.00 25.00
21 Darren Collison/100 12.00 30.00
23 Omri Casspi/100 8.00 20.00
24 B.J. Mullens/100 8.00 20.00
25 Taj Gibson/100 10.00 25.00
26 DeMarre Carroll/100 8.00 20.00
27 Wayne Ellington/100 8.00 20.00
28 Toney Douglas/93 8.00 20.00
29 Jeff Pendergraph/100 8.00 20.00
30 DaJuan Summers/100 8.00 20.00
31 Sam Young/98 8.00 20.00
32 DeJuan Blair/100 10.00 25.00
33 Jodie Meeks/99 15.00 40.00
34 Chase Budinger/99 8.00 20.00
35 Taylor Griffin/100 8.00 20.00

2009-10 Prestige Old School

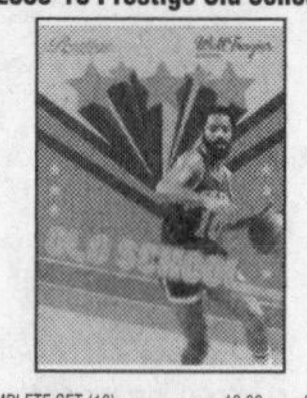

COMPLETE SET (18) 10.00 25.00
RANDOM INSERTS IN PACKS
1 Connie Hawkins 1.50 4.00
2 Bob McAdoo 1.50 4.00
3 Dan Issel 1.50 4.00
4 Kevin McHale 1.50 4.00
5 David Thompson 2.00 5.00
6 Bill Bradley 1.50 4.00
7 Ralph Sampson 1.50 4.00
8 Kenny Walker 1.50 4.00
9 Bryant Reeves 1.50 4.00
10 Dave Cowens 1.50 4.00
11 Joe Dumars 1.50 4.00
12 Oscar Robertson 1.50 4.00
13 Mark Aguirre 1.50 4.00
14 Chris Mullin 1.50 4.00
15 Al Attles 1.50 4.00
16 Walt Frazier 1.50 4.00
17 Dell Curry 1.50 4.00
18 Bill Walton 1.50 4.00

2009-10 Prestige Old School Materials

COMPLETE SET (2) 6.00 15.00
STATED PRINT RUN 250 SER.#'d SETS
4 Kevin McHale 4.00 10.00
14 Chris Mullin 4.00 10.00

2009-10 Prestige Old School Signatures

STATED PRINT RUN 50 TO 100 SER.#'d SETS
ASTERISK CARDS FROM PANINI UPDATE
1 Connie Hawkins*/100 12.50 30.00
2 Bob McAdoo/100 20.00 40.00
3 Dan Issel/100 10.00 25.00
4 Kevin McHale*/100 25.00 60.00
5 David Thompson/100 8.00 20.00
8 Kenny Walker*/100 15.00 40.00
10 Dave Cowens/99 8.00 20.00
12 Oscar Robertson/50 60.00 120.00
14 Chris Mullin*/100 15.00 40.00
15 Al Attles/100 10.00 25.00
16 Walt Frazier*/100 12.50 30.00
17 Dell Curry/96 8.00 20.00
18 Bill Walton/82 15.00 40.00

2009-10 Prestige Playmakers

COMPLETE SET (18) 6.00 15.
RANDOM INSERT IN PACKS
1 Rajon Rondo 1.00 2.
2 Mike Bibby .60 1.
3 D.J. Augustin .60 1.
4 Chauncey Billups .75 2.
5 Danny Granger .75 2.
6 Shane Battier .75 2.
7 Derek Fisher .60 1.
8 Kevin Love 1.25 3.
9 David West .75 2.
10 Nate Robinson .75 2.
11 Russell Westbrook 1.25 3.
12 Jameer Nelson .60 1.
13 Brandon Roy .75 2.
14 Deron Williams .75 2.
15 Jason Terry .60 1.
16 Tayshaun Prince .75 2.
17 Michael Redd .75 2.
18 Devin Harris .75 2.

2009-10 Prestige Playmakers Materials

STATED PRINT RUN 250 SER.#'d SETS
2 Mike Bibby 2.50 6.
6 Shane Battier 3.00 8.
10 Nate Robinson 3.00 8.
13 Brandon Roy 3.00 8.
14 Deron Williams 3.00 8.
15 Jason Terry 2.50 6.

2009-10 Prestige Playmakers Signatures

STATED PRINT RUN 50 TO 100 SER.#'d SETS
ASTERISK CARDS FROM PANINI UPDATE
2 Mike Bibby/100 5.00 12.
8 Kevin Love/50 15.00 40.
11 Russell Westbrook/100 12.50 30.
13 Brandon Roy*/57 10.00 25.
14 Deron Williams*/100 8.00 20.
18 Devin Harris*/100 5.00 12.

2009-10 Prestige Preferred Materials

STATED PRINT RUN 150 TO 250 SETS
UNPRICED PATCH PRINT RUN 10 SER.#'d SETS
1 Brandon Roy/250 3.00 8.
2 Jermaine O'Neal/250 3.00 8.
4 LaMarcus Aldridge/250 3.00 8.
5 David Lee/250 2.50 6.
6 Joe Johnson/250 3.00 8.
7 Elton Brand/250 3.00 8.
8 Dirk Nowitzki/250 4.00 10.
9 Tracy McGrady/250 3.00 8.
10 Tim Duncan/150 5.00 12.

2009-10 Prestige Prestigious Picks Green

STATED PRINT RUN 500 SER.#'d SETS
*BLACK: 1X TO 2.5X BASE HI
BLACK PRINT RUN 25 SER.#'d SETS
*GOLD: .6X TO 1.5X BASE HI
GOLD PRINT RUN 100 SER.#'d SETS
UNPRICED PLATINUM PRINT RUN 10 SETS
1 Blake Griffin 10.00 25.
2 Hasheem Thabeet 1.50 4.
3 James Harden 5.00 12.
4 Tyreke Evans 4.00 10.
5 Jonny Flynn 1.50 4.
6 Stephen Curry 4.00 10.
7 Jordan Hill 1.50 4.
8 DeMar DeRozan 2.50 6.
9 Brandon Jennings 3.00 8.
10 Terrence Williams 1.50 4.
11 Gerald Henderson 1.50 4.
12 Tyler Hansbrough 2.50 6.
13 Earl Clark 1.50 4.
14 Austin Daye 1.50 4.
15 James Johnson 1.50 4.
16 Jrue Holiday 3.00 8.
17 Ty Lawson 2.50 6.
18 Jeff Teague 2.00 5.
19 Eric Maynor 1.50 4.
20 Darren Collison 2.50 6.
21 Omri Casspi 1.50 4.
22 B.J. Mullens 1.50 4.
23 Rodrigue Beaubois 2.00 5.
24 Taj Gibson 2.00 5.
25 DeMarre Carroll 1.50 4.
26 Wayne Ellington 1.50 4
27 Toney Douglas 1.50 4
28 Jeff Pendergraph 1.50 4
29 Jeff Pendergraph 1.50 4
30 DaJuan Summers 1.50 4
31 Sam Young 1.50 4

)eJuan Blair 2.00 5.00
Jodie Meeks 2.00 5.00
Chase Budinger 1.50 4.00
Taylor Griffin 1.50 4.00
Blake Griffin 10.00 25.00
Hasheem Thabeet 1.50 4.00
Jordan Hill 1.50 4.00
Tyler Hansbrough 2.50 6.00
Jonny Flynn 1.50 4.00
James Harden 5.00 12.00
DeMar DeRozan 2.50 6.00
Gerald Henderson 1.50 4.00
Jrue Holiday 3.00 8.00
B.J. Mullens 1.50 4.00
Darren Collison 2.50 6.00
Chase Budinger 1.50 4.00
Wayne Ellington 1.50 4.00
Jodie Meeks 2.00 5.00
Tyreke Evans 4.00 10.00

2009-10 Prestige Prestigious Picks Signatures Black

TED PRINT RUN 50 TO 100 SER.#'d SETS
lake Griffin/100 60.00 150.00
mes Harden/50 20.00 50.00
reke Evans/50 15.00 40.00
ephen Curry/50 15.00 40.00
rdan Hill/50 6.00 15.00
andon Jennings/50 12.00 30.00
Terrence Williams/50 6.00 15.00
Gerald Henderson/50 6.00 15.00
Tyler Hansbrough/50 10.00 25.00
Earl Clark/50 6.00 15.00
Austin Daye/50 6.00 15.00
James Johnson/50 6.00 15.00
Jrue Holiday/50 12.00 30.00
Jeff Teague/50 8.00 20.00
Darren Collison/50 10.00 25.00
Omri Casspi/50 6.00 15.00
B.J. Mullens/50 6.00 15.00
Rodrigue Beaubois/50 8.00 20.00
Taj Gibson/50 8.00 20.00
DeMarre Carroll/50 6.00 15.00
Toney Douglas/50 6.00 15.00
Jeff Pendergraph/50 6.00 15.00
Jeff Pendergraph/50 6.00 15.00
DeJuan Blair/50 8.00 20.00
Jodie Meeks/50 8.00 20.00
Chase Budinger/50 6.00 15.00
Blake Griffin/100 60.00 150.00
Jordan Hill/50 6.00 15.00
Tyler Hansbrough/50 10.00 25.00
James Harden/50 20.00 50.00
Gerald Henderson/50 6.00 15.00
Jrue Holiday/50 12.00 30.00
B.J. Mullens/50 6.00 15.00
Darren Collison/50 10.00 25.00
Chase Budinger/50 6.00 15.00
Jodie Meeks/50 8.00 20.00
Tyreke Evans/50 15.00 40.00

2009-10 Prestige Prestigious Picks Materials Blue

NDOM INSERTS IN PACKS
ACK: 1.25X TO 3X BASE HI
ACK PRINT RUN 25 SER.#'d SETS
OLD: .6X TO 1.5X BASE HI
LD PRINT RUN 50 SER.#'d SETS
EEN: .5X TO 1.25X BASE HI
EEN PRINT RUN 100 SER.#'d SETS
ATINUM PATCH: 1.5X TO 4X BASE HI
ATINUM PRINT RUN 25 SER.#'d SETS
ake Griffin 12.50 30.00
asheem Thabeet 2.00 5.00
ames Harden 6.00 15.00
yreke Evans 5.00 12.00
onny Flynn 2.00 5.00
tephen Curry 5.00 12.00
ordan Hill 2.00 5.00
eMar DeRozan 3.00 8.00
randon Jennings 4.00 10.00
Terrence Williams 2.00 5.00
Gerald Henderson 2.00 5.00
Tyler Hansbrough 3.00 8.00
Earl Clark 2.00 5.00
Austin Daye 2.00 5.00
James Johnson 2.00 5.00
Jrue Holiday 4.00 10.00
Ty Lawson 3.00 8.00
Jeff Teague 2.50 6.00
Eric Maynor 2.00 5.00
Darren Collison 3.00 8.00
Omri Casspi 2.00 5.00
B.J. Mullens 2.00 5.00
Rodrigue Beaubois 2.50 6.00
Taj Gibson 2.50 6.00
DeMarre Carroll 2.00 5.00
Wayne Ellington 2.00 5.00
Toney Douglas 2.00 5.00
Jeff Pendergraph 2.00 5.00
DaJuan Summers 2.00 5.00
Sam Young 2.00 5.00
DeJuan Blair 2.50 6.00
Jodie Meeks 2.50 6.00
Chase Budinger 2.00 5.00
Taylor Griffin 2.00 5.00
Jordan Hill 2.00 5.00
Darren Collison 3.00 8.00
Chase Budinger 2.00 5.00
Jodie Meeks 2.50 6.00
Tyreke Evans 5.00 12.00

2009-10 Prestige Prestigious Pros Black Signatures

STATED PRINT RUN 25 SER.#'d SETS
1 Kobe Bryant 100.00 200.00

2009-10 Prestige Prestigious Pros Green

STATED PRINT RUN 500 SER.#'d SETS
*BLACK: 1.5X TO 4X BASE HI
BLACK PRINT RUN 25 SER.#'d SETS
*GOLD: 1X TO 2.5X BASE HI
GOLD PRINT RUN 100 SER.#'d SETS
UNPRICED PLATINUM PRINT RUN 10 SETS
1 Kobe Bryant 4.00 10.00
2 LeBron James 4.00 10.00
3 Dwyane Wade 1.50 4.00
4 Chris Paul 1.25 3.00
5 Kevin Garnett 1.50 4.00
6 Josh Howard .60 1.50
7 Gilbert Arenas .75 2.00
8 Steve Nash .75 2.00
9 Dirk Nowitzki 1.00 2.50
10 Danny Granger .75 2.00
11 Yao Ming 1.00 2.50
12 Joe Johnson .75 2.00
13 Carmelo Anthony 1.00 2.50
14 Richard Hamilton .60 1.50
15 Stephen Jackson .60 1.50
16 Zach Randolph .60 1.50
17 Rudy Gay .75 2.00
18 Michael Redd .75 2.00
19 Al Jefferson .75 2.00
20 Emeka Okafor .75 2.00
21 Devin Harris .75 2.00
22 Tracy McGrady .75 2.00
23 Ben Gordon .75 2.00
24 Al Harrington .60 1.50
25 Kevin Durant 2.50 6.00
26 Dwight Howard 1.25 3.00
27 Andre Iguodala .75 2.00
28 Brandon Roy .75 2.00
29 Paul Pierce 1.00 2.50
30 Jamal Crawford .60 1.50
31 Kevin Martin .75 2.00
32 Tim Duncan 1.25 3.00
33 Allen Iverson 1.00 2.50
34 Chris Bosh .75 2.00
35 Deron Williams .75 2.00
36 Mo Williams .60 1.50
37 Antawn Jamison .75 2.00
38 Vince Carter 1.00 2.50
39 Ron Artest .75 2.00
40 Amare Stoudemire .75 2.00
41 O.J. Mayo .75 2.00
42 Shawn Marion .75 2.00
43 Chauncey Billups .75 2.00
44 Tony Parker .75 2.00
45 LaMarcus Aldridge .75 2.00
46 Ray Allen .75 2.00
47 Pau Gasol .75 2.00
48 Derrick Rose 2.50 6.00
49 Russell Westbrook 1.25 3.00
50 Richard Jefferson .75 2.00

2009-10 Prestige Prestigious Pros Materials Black

*BLACK: 1.25X TO 3X BASE HI
BLACK PRINT RUN 25 SER.#'d SETS
1A Kobe Bryant AU/25 125.00 225.00

2009-10 Prestige Prestigious Pros Materials Blue

STATED PRINT RUN 150 TO 250 SER.#'d SETS
UNPRICED PLAT.PRINT RUN 10 TO 25 SETS
1 Kobe Bryant/200 10.00 25.00
4 Chris Paul/250 5.00 12.00
5 Kevin Garnett/250 6.00 15.00
6 Josh Howard/250 2.50 6.00
9 Dirk Nowitzki/250 4.00 10.00
11 Yao Ming/250 4.00 10.00
12 Joe Johnson/250 3.00 8.00
19 Al Jefferson/250 3.00 8.00
22 Tracy McGrady/250 3.00 8.00
24 Al Harrington/250 2.50 6.00
26 Dwight Howard/250 5.00 12.00
27 Andre Iguodala/250 3.00 8.00
28 Brandon Roy/250 3.00 8.00
31 Kevin Martin/250 3.00 8.00
32 Tim Duncan/150 5.00 12.00
34 Chris Bosh/250 3.00 8.00
35 Deron Williams/250 3.00 8.00
41 O.J. Mayo/150 3.00 8.00
45 LaMarcus Aldridge/250 3.00 8.00

2009-10 Prestige Prestigious Pros Materials Gold

*GOLD: .6X TO 1.5X BASE HI
GOLD PRINT RUN 50 SER.#'d SETS
1A Kobe Bryant AU/50 100.00 200.00

2009-10 Prestige Prestigious Pros Materials Green

*GREEN: .5X TO 1.25X BASE HI
GREEN PRINT RUN 100 SER.#'d SETS
1A Kobe Bryant AU/100 100.00 200.00

2009-10 Prestige Stars of the NBA

COMPLETE SET (20) 15.00 30.00
RANDOM INSERT IN PACKS
1 LeBron James 4.00 10.00
2 Kobe Bryant 4.00 10.00
3 Dwyane Wade 1.50 4.00
4 Dirk Nowitzki 1.00 2.50
5 Dwight Howard 1.25 3.00
6 Chris Paul 1.25 3.00
7 Shaquille O'Neal 1.50 4.00
8 Kevin Durant 2.50 6.00
9 Danny Granger .75 2.00
10 Kevin Garnett 1.50 4.00
11 Allen Iverson 1.00 2.50
12 Carmelo Anthony 1.00 2.50
13 Yao Ming 1.00 2.50
14 O.J. Mayo .75 2.00
15 Vince Carter 1.00 2.50
16 Tim Duncan 1.25 3.00
17 Chris Bosh .75 2.00
18 Deron Williams .75 2.00
19 Gilbert Arenas .75 2.00
20 Ben Gordon .75 2.00

2009-10 Prestige Stars of the NBA Materials

STATED PRINT RUN 100 TO 250 SER.#'d SETS
UNPRICED PATCH PRINT RUN 10 SER.#'d SETS
2 Kobe Bryant/100 12.50 30.00
4 Dirk Nowitzki/250 4.00 10.00
5 Dwight Howard/250 5.00 12.00
6 Chris Paul/250 5.00 12.00
10 Kevin Garnett/250 6.00 15.00
13 Yao Ming/250 4.00 10.00
14 O.J. Mayo/250 3.00 8.00
16 Tim Duncan/150 5.00 12.00
17 Chris Bosh/250 3.00 8.00
18 Deron Williams/250 3.00 8.00

2009-10 Prestige Stat Stars

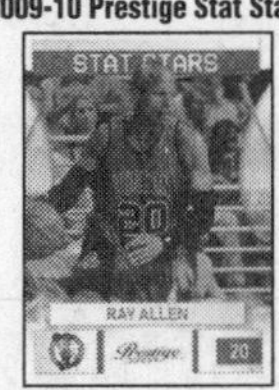

COMPLETE SET (20) 10.00 25.00
RANDOM INSERT IN PACKS
1 O.J. Mayo .75 2.00
2 Kevin Love 1.25 3.00
3 Derrick Rose 2.50 6.00
4 Kevin Durant 2.50 6.00
5 Luis Scola .60 1.50
6 Ramon Sessions .60 1.50
7 Dwyane Wade 1.50 4.00
8 LeBron James 4.00 10.00
9 Kobe Bryant 4.00 10.00
10 Dirk Nowitzki 1.00 2.50
11 Dwight Howard 1.25 3.00
12 Troy Murphy .50 1.25
13 Tim Duncan 1.25 3.00
14 Yao Ming 1.00 2.50
15 Chris Paul 1.25 3.00
16 Deron Williams .75 2.00
17 Jose Calderon .60 1.50
18 Ray Allen .75 2.00
19 Shaquille O'Neal 1.50 4.00
20 Rashard Lewis .60 1.50

2009-10 Prestige Stat Stars Materials

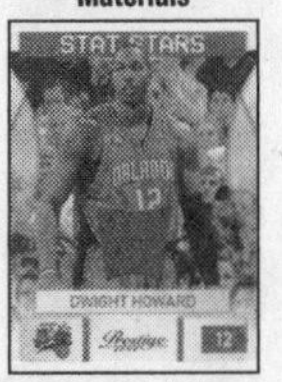

STATED PRINT RUN 150 TO 250 SER.#'d SETS
UNPRICED PRIME PRINT RUN 10 SER.#'d SETS
1 O.J. Mayo/200 3.00 8.00
5 Luis Scola/250 2.50 6.00
9 Kobe Bryant/150 12.50 30.00
10 Dirk Nowitzki/250 4.00 10.00
11 Dwight Howard/250 5.00 12.00
13 Tim Duncan/150 5.00 12.00
14 Yao Ming/250 4.00 10.00
15 Chris Paul/250 5.00 12.00
16 Deron Williams/250 3.00 8.00
17 Jose Calderon/250 2.50 6.00

2009-10 Prestige Super Sophs

COMPLETE SET (9) 6.00 15.00
RANDOM INSERTS IN PACKS
1 Derrick Rose 4.00 10.00
2 Marc Gasol 1.25 3.00
3 Russell Westbrook 2.00 5.00
4 Rudy Fernandez 1.00 2.50
5 O.J. Mayo 1.25 3.00
6 Danilo Gallinari 1.25 3.00
7 Michael Beasley 1.25 3.00
8 Eric Gordon 1.25 3.00
9 Brook Lopez 1.25 3.00

2009-10 Prestige Super Sophs Signatures

STATED PRINT RUN 57 TO 100 SETS
3 Russell Westbrook/57* 12.50 30.00
8 Eric Gordon/100* 8.00 20.00

2009-10 Prestige True Colors

COMPLETE SET (10) 4.00 10.00
RANDOM INSERT IN PACKS
1 Kobe Bryant 4.00 10.00
2 Tim Duncan 1.25 3.00
3 Paul Pierce 1.00 2.50
4 Zydrunas Ilgauskas .50 1.25
5 Dirk Nowitzki 1.00 2.50
6 Jeff Foster .50 1.25
7 Michael Redd .75 2.00
8 Samuel Dalembert .50 1.25
9 Andrei Kirilenko .60 1.50
10 Brendan Haywood .50 1.25

2009-10 Prestige True Colors Materials

STATED PRINT RUN 50 TO 250 SER.#'d SETS
UNPRICED PRIMARY PRINT RUN 10 SETS
1 Kobe Bryant/50 15.00 40.00
2 Tim Duncan/150 5.00 12.00
4 Zydrunas Ilgauskas/250 2.00 5.00
5 Dirk Nowitzki/250 4.00 10.00
6 Jeff Foster/250 2.00 5.00
8 Samuel Dalembert/250 2.00 5.00
9 Andrei Kirilenko/250 2.50 6.00

2009-10 Prestige True Colors Signatures

STATED PRINT RUN 25 SER.#'d SETS
1 Kobe Bryant 100.00 200.00

2010-11 Prestige

COMPLETE SET (250) 60.00 150.00
ASTERISK CARDS INSERTED IN SEASON UPDATE
UNPRICED BONUS BLACK PRINT RUN 10 SETS
1 Al Horford .30 .75
2 Jamal Crawford .30 .75
3 Josh Smith .40 1.00
4 Mike Bibby .30 .75
5 Glen Davis .30 .75
6 Kendrick Perkins .30 .75
7 Kevin Garnett .75 2.00
8 Rajon Rondo .50 1.25
9 Boris Diaw .30 .75
10 D.J. Augustin .30 .75
11 Gerald Wallace .40 1.00
12 Stephen Jackson .30 .75
13 Derrick Rose 1.25 3.00
14 Joakim Noah .40 1.00
15 Luol Deng .40 1.00
16 Taj Gibson .30 .75
17 Anderson Varejao .30 .75
18 Antawn Jamison .40 1.00
19 Anthony Parker .25 .60
20 LeBron James 2.00 5.00
21 Caron Butler .40 1.00
22 Dirk Nowitzki .50 1.25
23 Jason Kidd .40 1.00
24 Shawn Marion .40 1.00
25 Carmelo Anthony .50 1.25
26 Chauncey Billups .40 1.00
27 J.R. Smith .40 1.00
28 Nene .30 .75
29 Ben Gordon .40 1.00
30 Richard Hamilton .30 .75
31 Rodney Stuckey .40 1.00
32 Tayshaun Prince .40 1.00
33 Andris Biedrins .25 .60
34 Anthony Randolph .30 .75
35 Monta Ellis .40 1.00
36 Stephen Curry .50 1.25
37 Aaron Brooks .25 .60
38 Kevin Martin .40 1.00
39 Shane Battier .30 .75
40 Trevor Ariza .25 .60
41 Dahntay Jones .25 .60
42 Danny Granger .40 1.00
43 T.J. Ford .25 .60
44 Troy Murphy .25 .60
45 Baron Davis .40 1.00
46 Blake Griffin 1.00 2.50
47 Chris Kaman .30 .75
48 Eric Gordon .40 1.00
49 Kobe Bryant 2.00 5.00
50 Lamar Odom .40 1.00
51 Pau Gasol .40 1.00
52 Ron Artest .40 1.00
53 Marc Gasol .40 1.00
54 Mike Conley Jr. .30 .75
55 O.J. Mayo .40 1.00
56 Zach Randolph .30 .75
57 Dwyane Wade .75 2.00
58 James Jones .25 .60
59 Jermaine O'Neal .40 1.00
60 Michael Beasley .40 1.00
61 Andrew Bogut .40 1.00
62 Brandon Jennings .40 1.00
63 Ersan Ilyasova .30 .75
64 Luc Mbah a Moute .25 .60
65 Al Jefferson .40 1.00
66 Corey Brewer .25 .60
67 Kevin Love .50 1.25
68 Ramon Sessions .30 .75
69 Brook Lopez .40 1.00
70 Courtney Lee .30 .75
71 Devin Harris .40 1.00
72 Yi Jianlian .30 .75
73 Chris Paul .60 1.50
74 David West .40 1.00
75 Emeka Okafor .40 1.00
76 Marcus Thornton .40 1.00
77 Danilo Gallinari .40 1.00
78 David Lee .30 .75
79 Toney Douglas .25 .60
80 Wilson Chandler .30 .75
81 James Harden .50 1.25
82 Jeff Green .30 .75
83 Kevin Durant 1.25 3.00
84 Russell Westbrook .50 1.25
85 Dwight Howard .60 1.50
86 Jameer Nelson .30 .75
87 Rashard Lewis .30 .75
88 Vince Carter .50 1.25
89 Andre Iguodala .40 1.00
90 Elton Brand .40 1.00
91 Louis Williams .30 .75
92 Thaddeus Young .25 .60
93 Amare Stoudemire .40 1.00
94 Jason Richardson .40 1.00
95 Leandro Barbosa .30 .75
96 Steve Nash .40 1.00
97 Andre Miller .30 .75
98 Brandon Roy .40 1.00
99 Greg Oden .30 .75
100 LaMarcus Aldridge .40 1.00
101 Beno Udrih .25 .60
102 Carl Landry .25 .60
103 Jason Thompson .25 .60
104 Tyreke Evans .50 1.25
105 George Hill .30 .75
106 Manu Ginobili .40 1.00
107 Tim Duncan .60 1.50
108 Tony Parker .40 1.00
109 Andrea Bargnani .30 .75
110 Chris Bosh .40 1.00
111 Hedo Turkoglu .40 1.00
112 Jarrett Jack .30 .75
113 Andrei Kirilenko .30 .75
114 Deron Williams .40 1.00
115 Mehmet Okur .25 .60
116 Paul Millsap .30 .75
117 Al Thornton .30 .75
118 Andray Blatche .25 .60
119 JaVale McGee .30 .75
120 Nick Young .30 .75
121 Alvan Adams .60 1.50
122 Charles Oakley .60 1.50
123 Chris Webber .60 1.50
124 Connie Hawkins .60 1.50
125 Dell Curry .60 1.50
126 Gary Payton .60 1.50
127 Gheorghe Muresan .60 1.50
128 Hal Greer .60 1.50
129 Jalen Rose .60 1.50
130 Jamal Mashburn .60 1.50
131 James Worthy .75 2.00
132 Joe Dumars .60 1.50
133 John Stockton 1.00 2.50
134 K.C. Jones .60 1.50
135 Kelly Tripucka .60 1.50
136 Kurt Rambis .60 1.50
137 Larry Bird 2.00 5.00
138 Larry Johnson .75 2.00
139 Magic Johnson 1.50 4.00
140 Maurice Cheeks .60 1.50
141 Michael Cooper .60 1.50
142 Mike Dunleavy, Sr. .60 1.50
143 Moses Malone .60 1.50
144 Muggsy Bogues .60 1.50
145 Nate Thurmond .60 1.50
146 Pete Maravich 2.00 5.00
147 Quinn Buckner .60 1.50
148 Rolando Blackman .60 1.50
149 Sidney Moncrief .60 1.50
150 Toni Kukoc .60 1.50
151 John Wall RC 5.00 12.00
152 Evan Turner RC 2.50 6.00
153 Derrick Favors RC 2.50 6.00
154 Wesley Johnson RC 2.00 5.00
155 DeMarcus Cousins RC 4.00 10.00
156 Ekpe Udoh RC 1.25 3.00
157 Greg Monroe RC 2.50 6.00
158 Al-Farouq Aminu RC 1.25 3.00
159 Gordon Hayward RC 2.50 6.00
160 Paul George RC 3.00 8.00
161 Cole Aldrich RC 1.25 3.00
162 Xavier Henry RC 1.50 4.00
163 Ed Davis RC 1.50 4.00
164 Patrick Patterson RC 2.00 5.00
165 Larry Sanders RC 1.25 3.00
166 Luke Babbitt RC 1.25 3.00
167 Kevin Seraphin RC 1.50 4.00
168 Eric Bledsoe RC 2.00 5.00
169 Avery Bradley RC 2.50 6.00
170 James Anderson RC 1.25 3.00
171 Craig Brackins RC 1.25 3.00
172 Elliot Williams RC 1.25 3.00
173 Trevor Booker RC 1.25 3.00
174 Damion James RC 1.25 3.00
175 Dominique Jones RC 1.25 3.00
176 Quincy Pondexter RC 1.25 3.00
177 Jordan Crawford RC 2.00 5.00
178 Greivis Vasquez RC 1.50 4.00
179 Daniel Orton RC 1.25 3.00
180 Lazar Hayward RC 1.25 3.00
181 Tibor Pleiss RC 1.25 3.00
182 Dexter Pittman RC 1.25 3.00
183 Hassan Whiteside RC 1.25 3.00
184 Armon Johnson RC 1.25 3.00
185 Brian Zoubek RC 1.25 3.00
186 Terrico White RC 1.25 3.00
187 Jeremy Lin RC 10.00 25.00
188 Andy Rautins RC 1.25 3.00
189 Landry Fields RC 2.00 5.00
190 Lance Stephenson RC 1.25 3.00
191 Jarvis Varnado RC 1.25 3.00
192 Da'Sean Butler RC 1.25 3.00
193 Devin Ebanks RC 1.50 4.00
194 Wesley Johnson RC 2.00 5.00
195 Terrico White RC 1.25 3.00
196 Gani Lawal RC 1.25 3.00
197 Keith Gallon RC 1.25 3.00
198 Lance Stephenson RC 1.25 3.00
199 John Wall RC 5.00 12.00
200 Solomon Alabi RC 1.25 3.00
201 Devin Ebanks RC 1.50 4.00
202 Luke Harangody RC 1.25 3.00
203 Hassan Whiteside RC 1.25 3.00
204 Willie Warren RC 1.25 3.00
205 Andy Rautins RC 1.25 3.00
206 Evan Turner RC 2.50 6.00
207 Keith Gallon RC 1.25 3.00
208 Derrick Caracter RC 1.25 3.00
209 Stanley Robinson RC 1.25 3.00
210 Jeremy Lin RC 10.00 25.00
211 John Wall RC 5.00 12.00
212 Evan Turner RC 2.50 6.00
213 Derrick Favors RC 2.50 6.00
214 Wesley Johnson RC 2.00 5.00
215 DeMarcus Cousins RC 4.00 10.00
216 Ekpe Udoh RC 1.25 3.00
217 Greg Monroe RC 2.50 6.00
218 Al-Farouq Aminu RC 1.25 3.00
219 Gordon Hayward RC 2.50 6.00
220 Paul George RC 3.00 8.00
221 Cole Aldrich RC 1.25 3.00
222 Xavier Henry RC 1.50 4.00
223 Ed Davis RC 1.50 4.00
224 Patrick Patterson RC 2.00 5.00
225 Larry Sanders RC 1.25 3.00
226 Luke Babbitt RC 1.25 3.00
227 Eric Bledsoe RC 2.00 5.00
228 Avery Bradley RC 2.50 6.00
229 James Anderson RC 1.25 3.00
230 Craig Brackins RC 1.25 3.00
231 Elliot Williams RC 1.25 3.00
232 Trevor Booker RC 1.25 3.00
233 Damion James RC 1.25 3.00
234 Dominique Jones RC 1.25 3.00
235 Quincy Pondexter RC 1.25 3.00
236 Jordan Crawford RC 2.00 5.00
237 Greivis Vasquez RC 1.50 4.00
238 Daniel Orton RC 1.25 3.00
239 Lazar Hayward RC 1.25 3.00
240 Dexter Pittman RC 1.25 3.00
241 Da'Sean Butler RC 1.25 3.00
242 Luke Harangody RC 1.25 3.00
243 Willie Warren RC 1.25 3.00
244 Gani Lawal RC 1.25 3.00
245 Stanley Robinson RC 1.25 3.00
246 Gary Neal RC* 2.00 5.00
247 Gary Forbes RC* 1.25 3.00
248 Omer Asik RC* 1.50 4.00
249 Semih Erden RC* 1.25 3.00
250 Timofey Mozgov RC* 1.25 3.00

2010-11 Prestige Bonus Shots Gold

*GOLD 1-120: .75X TO 2X BASE HI
*GOLD 121-245: .5X TO 1.25X BASE HI
GOLD PRINT RUN 249 SER.#'d SETS

2010-11 Prestige Bonus Shots Green

*GREEN 1-120: 4X TO 10X BASE HI
*GREEN 121-150: 2.5X TO 6X BASE HI
*GREEN 151-245: 1.5X TO 4X BASE HI
GREEN PRINT RUN 25 SER.#'d SETS
187 Jeremy Lin 60.00 150.00
210 Jeremy Lin 60.00 150.00

2010-11 Prestige Bonus Shots Orange

*ORANGE 1-150: .6X TO 1.5X BASE HI
*ORANGE 151-245: .4X TO 1X BASE HI
STATED PRINT RUN 499 SER.#'d SETS
RANDOM INSERTS IN RETAIL PACKS

2010-11 Prestige Bonus Shots Purple

*PURPLE 1-120: 2X TO 5X BASE HI
*PURPLE 121-150: 1.25X TO 3X BASE HI
*PURPLE 151-245: 1X TO 2.5X BASE HI
PURPLE PRINT RUN 49 SER.#'d SETS

2010-11 Prestige Bonus Shots Black Signatures

STATED PRINT RUN 25 TO 99 SER.#'d SETS
ASTERISK CARDS INSERTED IN SEASON UPDATE
16 Taj Gibson/25 5.00 12.00
30 Richard Hamilton/50 6.00 15.00
37 Aaron Brooks/99 5.00 12.00
43 T.J. Ford/25 5.00 12.00
46 Blake Griffin/99 50.00 120.00
49 Kobe Bryant/49 75.00 200.00
52 Ron Artest/50 15.00 40.00
59 Jermaine O'Neal/50 5.00 12.00
60 Michael Beasley/25 10.00 25.00
67 Kevin Love/25 10.00 25.00
71 Devin Harris/25 5.00 12.00
75 Emeka Okafor/50 5.00 12.00
76 Marcus Thornton/99 5.00 12.00
79 Toney Douglas/99 5.00 12.00
81 James Harden/99 8.00 20.00
89 Andre Iguodala/50 5.00 12.00
93 Amare Stoudemire/25 20.00 50.00
98 Brandon Roy/50 8.00 20.00
102 Carl Landry/50 5.00 12.00
104 Tyreke Evans/99 10.00 25.00
121 Alvan Adams/50 5.00 12.00
126 Gary Payton/25 20.00 40.00
128 Hal Greer/50 5.00 12.00
145 Nate Thurmond/25 8.00 20.00
149 Sidney Moncrief/50 5.00 12.00
151 John Wall/99 40.00 100.00
152 Evan Turner/25 20.00 50.00
153 Derrick Favors/99 12.00 30.00
154 Wesley Johnson/99 10.00 25.00
155 DeMarcus Cousins/99 20.00 50.00
156 Ekpe Udoh/99 6.00 15.00
158 Al-Farouq Aminu/99 6.00 15.00
161 Cole Aldrich/99 6.00 15.00
162 Xavier Henry/99 8.00 20.00
163 Ed Davis/99 8.00 20.00
164 Patrick Patterson/99 10.00 25.00
166 Luke Babbitt/99 6.00 15.00
167 Kevin Seraphin/25 8.00 20.00
168 Eric Bledsoe/99 12.00 30.00
169 Avery Bradley/99 12.00 30.00
170 James Anderson/99 6.00 15.00
171 Craig Brackins/25 6.00 15.00
175 Dominique Jones/25 6.00 15.00
176 Quincy Pondexter/99 6.00 15.00
177 Jordan Crawford/99 10.00 25.00
179 Daniel Orton/99 6.00 15.00
180 Lazar Hayward/99 6.00 15.00
184 Armon Johnson/99 6.00 15.00
186 Terrico White/99 6.00 15.00
187 Jeremy Lin/99 100.00 200.00
188 Andy Rautins/99 6.00 15.00
189 Landry Fields/99 10.00 25.00
190 Lance Stephenson/99 6.00 15.00
192 Da'Sean Butler/99 6.00 15.00
194 Wesley Johnson/99 10.00 25.00
195 Terrico White/99 6.00 15.00
196 Gani Lawal/99 6.00 15.00
197 Keith Gallon/99 6.00 15.00
198 Lance Stephenson/99 6.00 15.00
199 John Wall/99 40.00 100.00
200 Solomon Alabi/99 6.00 15.00
202 Luke Harangody/99 6.00 15.00
205 Andy Rautins/99 6.00 15.00
206 Evan Turner/25 20.00 50.00
207 Keith Gallon/99 6.00 15.00
210 Jeremy Lin/99 100.00 200.00
211 John Wall/99 40.00 100.00
212 Evan Turner/25 20.00 50.00
213 Derrick Favors/99 12.00 30.00
214 Wesley Johnson/99 10.00 25.00
215 DeMarcus Cousins/99 20.00 50.00
216 Ekpe Udoh/99 6.00 15.00
218 Al-Farouq Aminu/99 6.00 15.00
221 Cole Aldrich/99 6.00 15.00
222 Xavier Henry/99 8.00 20.00
223 Ed Davis/99 8.00 20.00
224 Patrick Patterson/99 10.00 25.00
226 Luke Babbitt/99 6.00 15.00
227 Eric Bledsoe/99 12.00 30.00
228 Avery Bradley/99 12.00 30.00
229 James Anderson/99 6.00 15.00
230 Craig Brackins/25 6.00 15.00
234 Dominique Jones/25 6.00 15.00
235 Quincy Pondexter/99 6.00 15.00
236 Jordan Crawford/99 10.00 25.00
238 Daniel Orton/99 6.00 15.00
239 Lazar Hayward/99 6.00 15.00
241 Da'Sean Butler/99 6.00 15.00
242 Luke Harangody/99 6.00 15.00
244 Gani Lawal/99 6.00 15.00
246 Gary Neal/99* 10.00 25.00
247 Gary Forbes/99* 6.00 15.00
248 Omer Asik/99* 8.00 20.00
249 Semih Erden/99* 6.00 15.00
250 Timofey Mozgov/99* 6.00 15.00

2010-11 Prestige Draft Picks Light Blue

*LIGHT BLUE: .3X TO .8X BASE HI
STATED PRINT RUN 999 SER.#'d SETS

2010-11 Prestige Draft Picks Rights Autographs

STATED PRINT RUN 25 TO 199 SER.#'d SETS
ASTERISK CARDS INSERTED IN SEASON UPDATE
151 John Wall/99 40.00 100.00
152 Evan Turner/25 15.00 40.00
153 Derrick Favors/199 10.00 25.00
154 Wesley Johnson/99 8.00 20.00
155 DeMarcus Cousins/199 15.00 40.00
156 Ekpe Udoh/199 5.00 12.00
158 Al-Farouq Aminu/199 5.00 12.00
161 Cole Aldrich/199 5.00 12.00
162 Xavier Henry/199 6.00 15.00
163 Ed Davis/199 6.00 15.00
164 Patrick Patterson/99 8.00 20.00
166 Luke Babbitt/199 5.00 12.00
167 Kevin Seraphin/25 6.00 15.00
168 Eric Bledsoe/199 8.00 20.00
169 Avery Bradley/199 10.00 25.00
170 James Anderson/199 5.00 12.00
171 Craig Brackins/25 5.00 12.00
175 Dominique Jones/25 10.00 25.00
176 Quincy Pondexter/199 5.00 12.00
177 Jordan Crawford/199 8.00 20.00
179 Daniel Orton/199 5.00 12.00
180 Lazar Hayward/199 5.00 12.00
182 Dexter Pittman/49 5.00 12.00
184 Armon Johnson/199 5.00 12.00
186 Terrico White/199 5.00 12.00
187 Jeremy Lin/199 75.00 200.00
188 Andy Rautins/199 5.00 12.00
189 Landry Fields/199 8.00 20.00
190 Lance Stephenson/199 5.00 12.00
192 Da'Sean Butler/199 5.00 12.00
194 Wesley Johnson/99 8.00 20.00
195 Terrico White/199 5.00 12.00
196 Gani Lawal/199 5.00 12.00
197 Keith Gallon/99 5.00 12.00
198 Lance Stephenson/199 5.00 12.00
199 John Wall/99 40.00 100.00
200 Solomon Alabi/199 5.00 12.00
202 Luke Harangody/99 5.00 12.00
205 Andy Rautins/199 5.00 12.00
206 Evan Turner/25 15.00 50.00
207 Keith Gallon/99 5.00 12.00
210 Jeremy Lin/199 75.00 200.00
211 John Wall/99 40.00 100.00
212 Evan Turner/25 15.00 40.00
213 Derrick Favors/199 10.00 25.00
214 Wesley Johnson/99 8.00 20.00
215 DeMarcus Cousins/199 15.00 40.00
216 Ekpe Udoh/199 5.00 12.00
218 Al-Farouq Aminu/199 5.00 12.00
221 Cole Aldrich/199 5.00 12.00
222 Xavier Henry/199 6.00 15.00
223 Ed Davis/199 6.00 15.00
224 Patrick Patterson/99 8.00 20.00
226 Luke Babbitt/199 5.00 12.00
227 Eric Bledsoe/199 8.00 20.00
228 Avery Bradley/199 10.00 25.00
229 James Anderson/199 5.00 12.00
230 Craig Brackins/25 5.00 12.00
234 Dominique Jones/25 10.00 25.00
235 Quincy Pondexter/199 5.00 12.00
236 Jordan Crawford/199 8.00 20.00
238 Daniel Orton/199 5.00 12.00
239 Lazar Hayward/199 5.00 12.00
240 Dexter Pittman/49 5.00 12.00
244 Gani Lawal/199 5.00 12.00
246 Gary Neal/199* 8.00 20.00
247 Gary Forbes/199* 5.00 12.00
248 Omer Asik/199* 6.00 15.00
249 Semih Erden/199* 5.00 12.00
250 Timofey Mozgov/199* 5.00 12.00

2010-11 Prestige Franchise Favorites

COMPLETE SET (30) 15.00 30.00
RANDOM INSERTS IN PACKS
1 Ray Allen .60 1.50
2 Brook Lopez .60 1.50
3 Al Harrington .50 1.25
4 Allen Iverson .75 2.00
5 Andrea Bargnani .50 1.25
6 Luol Deng .60 1.50
7 Antawn Jamison .60 1.50
8 Tayshaun Prince .60 1.50
9 Danny Granger .60 1.50
10 Brandon Jennings .60 1.50
11 Joe Johnson .60 1.50
12 Stephen Jackson .50 1.25
13 Dwyane Wade 1.25 3.00
14 Dwight Howard 1.00 2.50
15 Al Thornton .50 1.25
16 Dirk Nowitzki .75 2.00
17 Kevin Martin .60 1.50
18 Zach Randolph .50 1.25
19 Chris Paul 1.00 2.50
20 Tim Duncan 1.00 2.50
21 Carmelo Anthony .75 2.00
22 Kevin Love .75 2.00
23 LaMarcus Aldridge .60 1.50
24 Kevin Durant 2.00 5.00

25 Deron Williams .60 1.50
26 Monta Ellis .60 1.50
27 Baron Davis .60 1.50
28 Kobe Bryant 3.00 8.00
29 Steve Nash .60 1.50
30 Tyreke Evans .75 2.00

2010-11 Prestige Franchise Favorites Materials

STATED PRINT RUN 50 TO 249 SER.#'d SETS
*PRIME: .75X TO 2X BASE HI
PRIME PRINT RUN 5 TO 49 SER.#'d SETS
1 Ray Allen/149 3.00 8.00
2 Brook Lopez/249 3.00 8.00
4 Allen Iverson/199 4.00 10.00
5 Andrea Bargnani/249 2.50 6.00
6 Luol Deng/249 3.00 8.00
8 Tayshaun Prince/249 3.00 8.00
9 Danny Granger/249 3.00 8.00
10 Brandon Jennings/249 3.00 8.00
11 Joe Johnson/249 3.00 8.00
13 Dwyane Wade/249 6.00 15.00
14 Dwight Howard/249 5.00 12.00
16 Dirk Nowitzki/249 4.00 10.00
17 Kevin Martin/249 3.00 8.00
19 Chris Paul/249 5.00 12.00
20 Tim Duncan/249 5.00 12.00
21 Carmelo Anthony/249 4.00 10.00
22 Kevin Love/249 4.00 10.00
23 LaMarcus Aldridge/249 3.00 8.00
24 Kevin Durant/50 8.00 20.00
25 Deron Williams/249 3.00 8.00
27 Baron Davis/249 3.00 8.00
28 Kobe Bryant/249 8.00 20.00
29 Steve Nash/249 3.00 8.00
30 Tyreke Evans/249 4.00 10.00

2010-11 Prestige Franchise Favorites Signatures

STATED PRINT RUN 10 TO 49 SER.#'d SETS
SOME UNPRICED DUE TO SCARCITY
10 Brandon Jennings/25 15.00 40.00
22 Kevin Love/25 12.00 30.00
25 Deron Williams/25 10.00 25.00
27 Baron Davis/49 6.00 15.00
28 Kobe Bryant/49 100.00 200.00
30 Tyreke Evans/49 12.00 30.00

2010-11 Prestige Hardcourt Heroes

COMPLETE SET (20) 10.00 25.00
RANDOM INSERTS IN PACKS
1 LeBron James 3.00 8.00
2 Kevin Durant 2.00 5.00
3 David Lee .50 1.25
4 Chris Bosh .60 1.50
5 Pau Gasol .60 1.50
6 Dwight Howard 1.00 2.50
7 Chris Paul 1.00 2.50
8 Carlos Boozer .60 1.50
9 Dirk Nowitzki .75 2.00
10 Dwyane Wade 1.25 3.00
11 Marc Gasol .60 1.50
12 Amare Stoudemire .60 1.50
13 Tim Duncan 1.00 2.50
14 Carmelo Anthony .75 2.00
15 Kobe Bryant 3.00 8.00
16 Deron Williams .60 1.50
17 Gerald Wallace .60 1.50
18 Josh Smith .60 1.50
19 Steve Nash .60 1.50
20 Brook Lopez .60 1.50

2010-11 Prestige Hardcourt Heroes Materials

STATED PRINT RUN 50 TO 249 SER.#'d SETS
*PRIME: .75X TO 2X BASE HI
PRIME PRINT RUN 10 TO 49 SER.#'d SETS
1 LeBron James/50 10.00 25.00
2 Kevin Durant/50 8.00 20.00
4 Chris Bosh/249 3.00 8.00
5 Pau Gasol/249 3.00 8.00
6 Dwight Howard/249 5.00 12.00
7 Chris Paul/249 5.00 12.00
8 Carlos Boozer/249 3.00 8.00
9 Dirk Nowitzki/249 4.00 10.00
10 Dwyane Wade/249 6.00 15.00
11 Marc Gasol/249 3.00 8.00
12 Amare Stoudemire/249 3.00 8.00
13 Tim Duncan/249 5.00 12.00
14 Carmelo Anthony/249 4.00 10.00
15 Kobe Bryant/249 8.00 20.00
16 Deron Williams/249 3.00 8.00
17 Gerald Wallace/249 3.00 8.00
18 Josh Smith/249 3.00 8.00
19 Steve Nash/249 3.00 8.00
20 Brook Lopez/249 3.00 8.00

2010-11 Prestige Hardcourt Heroes Signatures

STATED PRINT RUN 10 TO 25 SER.#'d SETS
12 Amare Stoudemire/25 15.00 40.00
15 Kobe Bryant/25 100.00 200.00
16 Deron Williams/25 12.50 30.00

2010-11 Prestige Inside the Numbers

COMPLETE SET (10) 4.00 10.00
RANDOM INSERTS IN PACKS
1 Danny Granger .60 1.50
2 Dwyane Wade 1.25 3.00
3 Dwight Howard 1.00 2.50
4 Chris Bosh .60 1.50
5 Carmelo Anthony .75 2.00
6 Aaron Brooks .40 1.00
7 Dirk Nowitzki .75 2.00
8 Stephen Jackson .50 1.25
9 David West .60 1.50
10 Zach Randolph .50 1.25

2010-11 Prestige Inside the Numbers Materials

STATED PRINT RUN 149 TO 249 SER.#'d SETS
*PRIME: .75X TO 2X BASE HI
PRIME PRINT RUN 25 TO 49 SER.#'d SETS
1 Danny Granger/149 3.00 8.00
2 Dwyane Wade/249 6.00 15.00
3 Dwight Howard/249 5.00 12.00
4 Chris Bosh/249 3.00 8.00
5 Carmelo Anthony/249 4.00 10.00
7 Dirk Nowitzki/249 4.00 10.00
9 David West/249 3.00 8.00

2010-11 Prestige Inside the Numbers Signatures

STATED PRINT RUN 25 SER.#'d SETS
INSERTED IN PACKS OF SEASON UPDATE
1 Danny Granger* 6.00 15.00

2010-11 Prestige NBA Draft Class

COMPLETE SET (40) 40.00 80.00
STATED PRINT RUN 499 SER.#'d SETS
1 John Wall 5.00 12.00
2 Evan Turner 2.50 6.00
3 Derrick Favors 2.50 6.00
4 Wesley Johnson 2.00 5.00
5 DeMarcus Cousins 4.00 10.00
6 Ekpe Udoh 1.25 3.00
7 Greg Monroe 2.50 6.00
8 Al-Farouq Aminu 1.25 3.00
9 Gordon Hayward 2.50 6.00
10 Paul George 3.00 8.00
11 Cole Aldrich 1.25 3.00
12 Xavier Henry 1.50 4.00
13 Ed Davis 1.50 4.00
14 Patrick Patterson 2.00 5.00
15 Larry Sanders 1.25 3.00
16 Luke Babbitt 1.25 3.00
17 Kevin Seraphin 1.50 4.00
18 Eric Bledsoe 2.00 5.00
19 Avery Bradley 2.50 6.00
20 James Anderson 1.25 3.00
21 Craig Brackins 1.25 3.00
22 Elliot Williams 1.25 3.00
23 Trevor Booker 1.25 3.00
24 Damion James 1.25 3.00
25 Dominique Jones 1.25 3.00
26 Quincy Pondexter 1.25 3.00
27 Jordan Crawford 2.00 5.00
28 Greivis Vasquez 1.50 4.00
29 Daniel Orton 1.25 3.00
30 Lazar Hayward 1.25 3.00
31 Dexter Pittman 1.25 3.00
32 Da'Sean Butler 1.25 3.00
33 Luke Harangody 1.25 3.00
34 Willie Warren 1.25 3.00
35 Gani Lawal 1.25 3.00
36 Hassan Whiteside 1.25 3.00
37 Andy Rautins 1.25 3.00
38 Lance Stephenson 1.25 3.00
39 Devin Ebanks 1.50 4.00
40 Keith Gallon 1.25 3.00

2010-11 Prestige NBA Draft Class Draft Logo Signatures

STATED PRINT RUN 199 TO 499 SER.#'d SETS
LOGOMAN PRINT RUN 10 SER.#'d SETS
LOGOMAN UNPRICED DUE TO SCARCITY
1 John Wall/199 40.00 100.00
2 Evan Turner/199 8.00 20.00
3 Derrick Favors/199 8.00 20.00
4 Wesley Johnson/299 6.00 15.00
5 DeMarcus Cousins/299 15.00 40.00
6 Ekpe Udoh/299 4.00 10.00
7 Greg Monroe/299 8.00 20.00
8 Al-Farouq Aminu/299 4.00 10.00
9 Gordon Hayward/299 8.00 20.00
10 Paul George/299 10.00 25.00
11 Cole Aldrich/299 4.00 10.00
12 Xavier Henry/299 5.00 12.00
13 Ed Davis/299 5.00 12.00
14 Patrick Patterson/299 6.00 15.00
15 Larry Sanders/399 4.00 10.00
16 Luke Babbitt/399 4.00 10.00
17 Kevin Seraphin/399 5.00 12.00
18 Eric Bledsoe/399 6.00 15.00
19 Avery Bradley/396 8.00 20.00
20 James Anderson/399 4.00 10.00
21 Craig Brackins/399 4.00 10.00
22 Elliot Williams/399 4.00 10.00
23 Trevor Booker/399 4.00 10.00
24 Damion James/499 4.00 10.00
25 Dominique Jones/499 4.00 10.00
26 Quincy Pondexter/399 4.00 10.00
27 Jordan Crawford/499 6.00 15.00
28 Greivis Vasquez/499 5.00 12.00
29 Daniel Orton/499 4.00 10.00
30 Lazar Hayward/499 4.00 10.00
31 Dexter Pittman/499 4.00 10.00
32 Da'Sean Butler/499 4.00 10.00
33 Luke Harangody/499 4.00 10.00
34 Willie Warren/399 4.00 10.00
35 Gani Lawal/399 4.00 10.00
36 Hassan Whiteside/399 4.00 10.00
37 Andy Rautins/499 4.00 10.00
38 Lance Stephenson/499 4.00 10.00
39 Devin Ebanks/499 5.00 12.00
40 Keith Gallon/499 4.00 10.00

2010-11 Prestige NBA Draft Class Signatures

STATED PRINT RUN 263 TO 299 SER.#'d SETS
1 John Wall/283 40.00 100.00
2 Evan Turner/299 10.00 25.00
3 Derrick Favors/295 10.00 25.00
4 Wesley Johnson/299 8.00 20.00
5 DeMarcus Cousins/299 15.00 40.00
6 Ekpe Udoh/299 5.00 12.00
7 Greg Monroe/299 10.00 25.00
8 Al-Farouq Aminu/296 5.00 12.00
9 Gordon Hayward/299 10.00 25.00
10 Paul George/299 12.00 30.00
11 Cole Aldrich/299 5.00 12.00
12 Xavier Henry/292 6.00 15.00
13 Ed Davis/299 6.00 15.00
14 Patrick Patterson/299 8.00 20.00
15 Larry Sanders/299 5.00 12.00
16 Luke Babbitt/299 5.00 12.00
17 Kevin Seraphin/299 6.00 15.00
18 Eric Bledsoe/297 8.00 20.00
19 Avery Bradley/298 10.00 25.00
20 James Anderson/299 5.00 12.00
21 Craig Brackins/299 5.00 12.00
22 Elliot Williams/299 5.00 12.00
23 Trevor Booker/294 5.00 12.00
24 Damion James/299 5.00 12.00
25 Dominique Jones/299 5.00 12.00
26 Quincy Pondexter/299 5.00 12.00
27 Jordan Crawford/299 8.00 20.00
28 Greivis Vasquez/299 6.00 15.00
29 Daniel Orton/299 5.00 12.00
30 Lazar Hayward/299 5.00 12.00
31 Dexter Pittman/299 5.00 12.00
32 Da'Sean Butler/299 5.00 12.00
33 Luke Harangody/284 5.00 12.00
34 Willie Warren/292 5.00 12.00
35 Gani Lawal/299 5.00 12.00
36 Hassan Whiteside/263 5.00 12.00
37 Andy Rautins/299 5.00 12.00
38 Lance Stephenson/299 5.00 12.00
39 Devin Ebanks/299 6.00 15.00
40 Keith Gallon/299 5.00 12.00

2010-11 Prestige Old School

COMPLETE SET (20) 15.00 30.00
RANDOM INSERTS IN PACKS
1 Earl Monroe 1.25 3.00
2 George Gervin 1.25 3.00
3 Paul Westphal 1.25 3.00
4 Elgin Baylor 1.25 3.00
5 Doc Rivers 1.25 3.00
6 Gail Goodrich 1.25 3.00
7 Gary Payton 1.25 3.00
8 Isiah Thomas 1.25 3.00
9 Jeff Hornacek 1.25 3.00
10 Kelly Tripucka 1.25 3.00
11 Maurice Cheeks 1.25 3.00
12 Nate Archibald 1.25 3.00
13 Rick Barry 1.25 3.00
14 Sidney Moncrief 1.25 3.00
15 Campy Russell 1.25 3.00
16 Vlade Divac 1.25 3.00
17 Alonzo Mourning 1.50 4.00
18 Sean Elliott 1.25 3.00
19 Cedric Maxwell 1.25 3.00
20 Rolando Blackman 1.25 3.00

2010-11 Prestige Old School Materials

STATED PRINT RUN 25 TO 249 SER.#'d SETS
*PRIME: .75X TO 2X BASE HI
PRIME PRINT RUN 25 TO 49 SER.#'d SETS
1 Earl Monroe/25 6.00 15.00
7 Gary Payton/249 4.00 10.00
9 Jeff Hornacek/149 4.00 10.00
10 Kelly Tripucka/249 4.00 10.00
11 Maurice Cheeks/249 4.00 10.00
17 Alonzo Mourning/249 5.00 12.00
20 Rolando Blackman/249 4.00 10.00

2010-11 Prestige Old School Signatures

STATED PRINT RUN 49 SER.#'d SETS
ASTERISK CARDS INSERTED IN SEASON UPDATE
1 Earl Monroe* 8.00 20.00
2 George Gervin 8.00 20.00
3 Paul Westphal* 8.00 20.00
4 Elgin Baylor* 10.00 25.00
5 Doc Rivers* 10.00 25.00
6 Gail Goodrich 8.00 20.00
7 Gary Payton* 10.00 25.00
8 Isiah Thomas* 12.50 30.00
9 Jeff Hornacek 8.00 20.00
12 Nate Archibald 8.00 20.00
13 Rick Barry 8.00 20.00
14 Sidney Moncrief* 8.00 20.00
15 Campy Russell* 8.00 20.00
16 Vlade Divac* 15.00 40.00
18 Sean Elliott* 15.00 40.00
19 Cedric Maxwell* 8.00 20.00

2010-11 Prestige Playmakers

COMPLETE SET (20) 15.00 30.00
RANDOM INSERTS IN PACKS
1 Steve Nash .75 2.00
2 Chris Paul 1.25 3.00
3 Devin Harris .75 2.00
4 Jose Calderon .60 1.50
5 Stephen Curry 1.00 2.50
6 Tony Parker .75 2.00
7 Baron Davis .75 2.00
8 Andre Iguodala .75 2.00
9 Chris Duhon .50 1.25
10 Mike Conley Jr. .60 1.50
11 Raymond Felton .60 1.50
12 Jason Kidd .75 2.00
13 Brandon Jennings .75 2.00
14 Derrick Rose 2.50 6.00
15 Jameer Nelson .60 1.50
16 LeBron James 4.00 10.00
17 Andre Miller .60 1.50
18 Tyreke Evans 1.00 2.50
19 Darren Collison .75 2.00
20 Jonny Flynn .50 1.25

2010-11 Prestige Playmakers Materials

STATED PRINT RUN 50 TO 249 SER.#'d SETS
*PRIME: .75X TO 2X HI
PRIME PRINT RUN 5 TO 49 SER.#'d SETS
1 Steve Nash/249 3.00 8.00
2 Chris Paul/249 5.00 12.00
3 Devin Harris/249 3.00 8.00
4 Jose Calderon/249 2.50 6.00
5 Stephen Curry/249 4.00 10.00
6 Tony Parker/249 3.00 8.00
7 Baron Davis/249 3.00 8.00
8 Andre Iguodala/249 3.00 8.00
9 Chris Duhon/249 2.00 5.00
10 Mike Conley Jr./100 2.50 6.00
11 Raymond Felton/249 2.50 6.00
12 Jason Kidd/249 3.00 8.00
13 Brandon Jennings/249 3.00 8.00
14 Derrick Rose/149 8.00 20.00
15 Jameer Nelson/249 2.50 6.00
16 LeBron James/50 10.00 25.00
17 Andre Miller/249 2.50 6.00
18 Tyreke Evans/249 4.00 10.00
19 Darren Collison/249 3.00 8.00
20 Jonny Flynn/249 2.00 5.00

2010-11 Prestige Playmakers Signatures

STATED PRINT RUN 10 TO 49 SETS
INSERTED IN PACKS OF SEASON UPDATE
1 Steve Nash/25 30.00 80.00
3 Devin Harris/25 6.00 15.00
5 Stephen Curry/49 10.00 25.00
6 Tony Parker/42 15.00 40.00
13 Brandon Jennings/25 10.00 25.00

2010-11 Prestige Preferred Materials

COMPLETE SET (9) 20.00 40.00
MAT.SIG.PRINT RUN 10 TO 15 SETS
MAT.SIG.UNPRICED DUE TO SCARCITY
2 Allen Iverson/199 5.00 12.00
3 Jason Kidd/249 3.00 8.00
4 Devin Harris/249 3.00 8.00
5 Chris Bosh/249 3.00 8.00
6 Richard Hamilton/249 2.50 6.00
7 Amare Stoudemire/249 3.00 8.00
8 Russell Westbrook/99 4.00 10.00
9 Al Jefferson/249 3.00 8.00
10 Andrea Bargnani/249 2.50 6.00

2010-11 Prestige Preferred Materials Patches

*PATCH: .75X TO 2X BASE HI
STATED PRINT RUN 25 SER.#'d SETS
PATCH SIG.PRINT RUN 5 TO 10 SER.#'d SETS
PATCH SIG.UNPRICED DUE TO SCARCITY
1 Rajon Rondo/25 10.00 25.00

2010-11 Prestige Preferred Materials Signatures

STATED PRINT RUN 10 TO 15 SER.#'d SETS
SOME UNPRICED DUE TO SCARCITY
4 Devin Harris/15 8.00 20.00
5 Chris Bosh/15 12.00 30.00
6 Richard Hamilton/15 8.00 20.00
7 Amare Stoudemire/15 15.00 40.00
10 Andrea Bargnani/15 8.00 20.00

2010-11 Prestige Preferred Signatures

STATED PRINT RUN 10 TO 40 SER.#'d SETS
SOME UNPRICED DUE TO SCARCITY
4 Devin Harris/25 6.00 15.00
7 Amare Stoudemire/40 8.00 20.00
10 Andrea Bargnani/35 6.00 15.00

2010-11 Prestige Prestigious Picks Green

COMPLETE SET (35) 40.00 80.00
STATED PRINT RUN 499 SER.#'d SETS
*BLACK: 1.25X TO 3X BASE HI
BLACK PRINT RUN 25 SER.#'d SETS
*GOLD: .6X TO 1.5X BASE HI
GOLD PRINT RUN 99 SER.#'d SETS
*ORANGE: .6X TO 1.5X BASE HI
ORANGE PRINT RUN 299 SER.#'d SETS
UNPRICED PLATINUM PRINT RUN 10 SETS
1 John Wall 5.00 12.00
2 Evan Turner 2.50 6.00
3 Derrick Favors 2.50 6.00
4 Wesley Johnson 2.00 5.00
5 DeMarcus Cousins 4.00 10.00
6 Ekpe Udoh 1.25 3.00
7 Greg Monroe 2.50 6.00
8 Al-Farouq Aminu 1.25 3.00
9 Gordon Hayward 2.50 6.00
10 Paul George 3.00 8.00
11 Cole Aldrich 1.25 3.00
12 Xavier Henry 1.50 4.00
13 Ed Davis 1.50 4.00
14 Patrick Patterson 2.00 5.00
15 Larry Sanders 1.25 3.00
16 Luke Babbitt 1.25 3.00
17 Eric Bledsoe 2.00 5.00
18 Avery Bradley 2.50 6.00
19 James Anderson 1.25 3.00
20 Craig Brackins 1.25 3.00
21 Elliot Williams 1.25 3.00
22 Trevor Booker 1.25 3.00
23 Damion James 1.25 3.00
24 Dominique Jones 1.25 3.00
25 Quincy Pondexter 1.25 3.00
26 Jordan Crawford 2.00 5.00
27 Greivis Vasquez 1.50 4.00
28 Daniel Orton 1.25 3.00
29 Lazar Hayward 1.25 3.00
30 Dexter Pittman 1.25 3.00
31 Da'Sean Butler 1.25 3.00
32 Luke Harangody 1.25 3.00
33 Willie Warren 1.25 3.00
34 Gani Lawal 1.25 3.00
35 Stanley Robinson 1.25 3.00

2010-11 Prestige Prestigious Picks Materials Green

STATED PRINT RUN 499 SER.#'d SETS
*BLACK: .6X TO 1.5X BASE HI
BLACK PRINT RUN 25 SER.#'d SETS
*GOLD: .5X TO 1.25X BASE HI
GOLD PRINT RUN 99 SER.#'d SETS
UNPRICED PLATINUM PRINT RUN 10 SETS
1 John Wall 8.00 20.00
2 Evan Turner 4.00 10.00
3 Derrick Favors 4.00 10.00
4 Wesley Johnson 3.00 8.00
5 DeMarcus Cousins 6.00 15.00
6 Ekpe Udoh 2.00 5.00
7 Greg Monroe 4.00 10.00
8 Al-Farouq Aminu 2.00 5.00
9 Gordon Hayward 4.00 10.00
10 Paul George 5.00 12.00
11 Cole Aldrich 2.00 5.00
12 Xavier Henry 2.50 6.00
13 Ed Davis 2.50 6.00
14 Patrick Patterson 3.00 8.00
15 Larry Sanders 2.00 5.00
16 Luke Babbitt 2.00 5.00
17 Eric Bledsoe 3.00 8.00
18 Avery Bradley 4.00 10.00
19 James Anderson 2.00 5.00
20 Craig Brackins 2.00 5.00
21 Elliot Williams 2.00 5.00
22 Trevor Booker 2.00 5.00
23 Damion James 2.00 5.00
24 Dominique Jones 2.00 5.00
25 Quincy Pondexter 2.00 5.00
26 Jordan Crawford 3.00 8.00
27 Greivis Vasquez 2.50 6.00
28 Daniel Orton 2.00 5.00
29 Lazar Hayward 2.00 5.00
30 Dexter Pittman 2.00 5.00
31 Da'Sean Butler 2.00 5.00
32 Luke Harangody 2.00 5.00
33 Willie Warren 2.00 5.00
34 Gani Lawal 2.00 5.00

2010-11 Prestige Prestigious Picks Signatures Black

STATED PRINT RUN 25 TO 249 SER.#'d SETS
1 John Wall/49 60.00 150.00
2 Evan Turner/25 12.00 30.00
3 Derrick Favors/249 8.00 20.00
4 Wesley Johnson/249 6.00 15.00
5 DeMarcus Cousins/249 12.00 30.00
6 Ekpe Udoh/249 4.00 10.00
8 Al-Farouq Aminu/249 4.00 10.00
11 Cole Aldrich/249 4.00 10.00
12 Xavier Henry/249 5.00 12.00
13 Ed Davis/249 5.00 12.00
14 Patrick Patterson/149 6.00 15.00
16 Luke Babbitt/249 4.00 10.00
17 Eric Bledsoe/249 6.00 15.00
18 Avery Bradley/249 8.00 20.00
19 James Anderson/249 4.00 10.00
24 Dominique Jones/25 8.00 20.00
25 Quincy Pondexter/249 4.00 10.00
26 Jordan Crawford/249 6.00 15.00
28 Daniel Orton/249 4.00 10.00
29 Lazar Hayward/249 4.00 10.00
30 Dexter Pittman/49 4.00 10.00
31 Da'Sean Butler/49 5.00 12.00
32 Luke Harangody/99 4.00 10.00
34 Gani Lawal/249 4.00 10.00

2010-11 Prestige Prestigious Pros Green

COMPLETE SET (65) 40.00 80.00
STATED PRINT RUN 499 SER.#'d SETS
*BLACK: 1.25X TO 3X BASE HI
BLACK PRINT RUN 25 SER.#'d SETS
*GOLD: .5X TO 1.25X BASE HI
GOLD PRINT RUN 99 SER.#'d SETS
*ORANGE: .6X TO 1.5X BASE HI
ORANGE PRINT RUN 299 SER.#'d SETS
UNPRICED PLATINUM PRINT RUN 10 SETS
1 Ray Allen 1.00 2.50
2 Glen Davis .75 2.00
3 Kevin Garnett 2.00 5.00
4 Yi Jianlian .75 2.00
5 Terrence Williams .60 1.50
6 Bill Walker .60 1.50
7 Chris Duhon .60 1.50
8 Elton Brand 1.00 2.50
9 Thaddeus Young .60 1.50
10 Hedo Turkoglu 1.00 2.50
11 Jose Calderon .75 2.00
12 Joakim Noah 1.00 2.50
13 Kirk Hinrich 1.00 2.50
14 Shaquille O'Neal 2.00 5.00
15 Zydrunas Ilgauskas .60 1.50
16 LeBron James 5.00 12.00
17 Richard Hamilton .75 2.00
18 Rodney Stuckey 1.00 2.50
19 Mike Dunleavy .60 1.50
20 Troy Murphy .60 1.50
21 Andrew Bogut 1.00 2.50
22 Michael Redd 1.00 2.50
23 Al Horford .75 2.00
24 Mike Bibby .75 2.00
25 D.J. Augustin .75 2.00
26 Tyson Chandler .75 2.00
27 Carlos Arroyo .75 2.00
28 Mario Chalmers 1.00 2.50
29 Dwyane Wade 2.00 5.00
30 Marcin Gortat 1.00 2.50
31 Mickael Pietrus .60 1.50
32 Randy Foye .60 1.50
33 Nick Young .75 2.00
34 Shawn Marion 1.00 2.50
35 Caron Butler 1.00 2.50
36 Shane Battier .75 2.00
37 Luis Scola .75 2.00
38 Marc Gasol 1.00 2.50
39 O.J. Mayo 1.00 2.50
40 David West 1.00 2.50
41 Peja Stojakovic 1.00 2.50
42 Richard Jefferson 1.00 2.50
43 Tim Duncan 1.50 4.00
44 Arron Afflalo .60 1.50
45 J.R. Smith 1.00 2.50
46 Kevin Love 1.25 3.00
47 Al Jefferson 1.00 2.50
48 Greg Oden .75 2.00
49 Rudy Fernandez .75 2.00
50 Russell Westbrook 1.25 3.00
51 Jeff Green .75 2.00
52 Andrei Kirilenko .75 2.00
53 Carlos Boozer 1.00 2.50
54 Andris Biedrins .60 1.50
55 Anthony Randolph .75 2.00
56 Baron Davis 1.00 2.50
57 Chris Kaman .75 2.00
58 Derek Fisher .75 2.00
59 Ron Artest 1.00 2.50
60 Kobe Bryant 5.00 12.00
61 Leandro Barbosa .75 2.00
62 Grant Hill 1.25 3.00
63 Channing Frye .75 2.00
64 Omri Casspi .60 1.50
65 Tyreke Evans 1.25 3.00

2010-11 Prestige Prestigious Pros Materials Black

*BLACK: .6X TO 1.5X BASE HI
STATED PRINT RUN 10 TO 25 SER.#'d SETS

2010-11 Prestige Prestigious Pros Materials Gold

*GOLD: .5X TO 1.25X BASE HI
STATED PRINT RUN 25 TO 99 SER.#'d SETS

2010-11 Prestige Prestigious Pros Materials Green

STATED PRINT RUN 50 TO 499 SER.#'d SETS
1 Ray Allen/199 3.00 8.00
2 Glen Davis 2.50 6.00
3 Kevin Garnett 6.00 15.00
5 Terrence Williams 2.00 5.00
6 Bill Walker 2.00 5.00
7 Chris Duhon 2.00 5.00
8 Elton Brand 3.00 8.00
9 Thaddeus Young 2.00 5.00
10 Hedo Turkoglu 3.00 8.00
11 Jose Calderon 2.50 6.00
12 Joakim Noah 3.00 8.00
13 Kirk Hinrich 3.00 8.00
14 Shaquille O'Neal 6.00 15.00
15 Zydrunas Ilgauskas 2.00 5.00
16 LeBron James/50 10.00 25.00
17 Richard Hamilton 2.50 6.00
18 Rodney Stuckey 3.00 8.00
19 Mike Dunleavy 2.00 5.00
20 Troy Murphy 2.00 5.00
21 Andrew Bogut 3.00 8.00
22 Michael Redd 3.00 8.00
23 Al Horford 2.50 6.00
24 Mike Bibby 2.50 6.00
25 D.J. Augustin 2.50 6.00
27 Carlos Arroyo 2.50 6.00
28 Mario Chalmers 3.00 8.00
29 Dwyane Wade 6.00 15.00
30 Marcin Gortat 3.00 8.00
31 Mickael Pietrus 2.00 5.00
32 Randy Foye 2.00 5.00
33 Nick Young 2.50 6.00
34 Shawn Marion 3.00 8.00
35 Caron Butler 3.00 8.00
36 Shane Battier 2.50 6.00
37 Luis Scola 2.50 6.00
38 Marc Gasol 3.00 8.00
39 O.J. Mayo 3.00 8.00
40 David West 3.00 8.00
41 Peja Stojakovic 3.00 8.00
42 Richard Jefferson 3.00 8.00
43 Tim Duncan 5.00 12.00
44 Arron Afflalo 2.00 5.00
45 J.R. Smith 3.00 8.00
46 Kevin Love 4.00 10.00
47 Al Jefferson 3.00 8.00
48 Greg Oden 2.50 6.00
49 Rudy Fernandez 2.50 6.00
50 Russell Westbrook/99 4.00 10.00
51 Jeff Green 2.50 6.00
52 Andrei Kirilenko 2.50 6.00
53 Carlos Boozer 3.00 8.00
54 Andris Biedrins 2.00 5.00
55 Anthony Randolph 2.50 6.00
56 Baron Davis 3.00 8.00
57 Chris Kaman 2.50 6.00
58 Derek Fisher 2.50 6.00
59 Ron Artest 3.00 8.00
60 Kobe Bryant 8.00 20.00
61 Leandro Barbosa 2.50 6.00
62 Grant Hill 6.00 15.00
63 Channing Frye 2.50 6.00
64 Omri Casspi 2.00 5.00
65 Tyreke Evans 4.00 10.00

2010-11 Prestige Prestigious Pros Materials Patches Platinum

*PATCH: .75X TO 2X BASE HI
STATED PRINT RUN 5 TO 25 SER.#'d SETS

2010-11 Prestige Prestigious Pros Signatures Black

STATED PRINT RUN 24 TO 49 SER.#'d SETS
5 Terrence Williams/49 5.00 12.00
25 D.J. Augustin/49 5.00 12.00
32 Randy Foye/49 5.00 12.00
36 Shane Battier/49 5.00 12.00
46 Kevin Love/25 8.00 20.00
56 Baron Davis/49 6.00 15.00
57 Chris Kaman/24 5.00 12.00
59 Ron Artest/25 12.50 30.00
60 Kobe Bryant/49 100.00 200.00
64 Omri Casspi/49 5.00 12.00
65 Tyreke Evans/49 10.00 25.00

2010-11 Prestige Stars of the NBA

COMPLETE SET (14) 15.00 30.00
RANDOM INSERTS IN PACKS
1 Rajon Rondo 1.25 3.00
2 Joe Johnson 1.00 2.50
3 Amare Stoudemire 1.00 2.50
4 Tyreke Evans 1.25 3.00
5 Paul Pierce 1.25 3.00
6 Russell Westbrook 1.25 3.00
7 Kobe Bryant 5.00 12.00
8 Derrick Rose 3.00 8.00
9 Monta Ellis 1.00 2.50
10 David Lee .75 2.00
11 Caron Butler 1.00 2.50
12 LeBron James 5.00 12.00
13 Pau Gasol 1.00 2.50
14 Chauncey Billups 1.00 2.50
15 Kevin Martin 1.00 2.50

2010-11 Prestige Stars of the NBA Materials

STATED PRINT RUN 50 TO 249 SER.#'d SETS
2 Joe Johnson/249 3.00 8.00
3 Amare Stoudemire/249 3.00 8.00
4 Tyreke Evans/249 4.00 10.00
5 Paul Pierce/249 4.00 10.00
6 Russell Westbrook/99 5.00 12.00
7 Kobe Bryant/249 8.00 20.00
8 Derrick Rose/149 10.00 25.00
11 Caron Butler/249 3.00 8.00
12 LeBron James/50 8.00 20.00
13 Pau Gasol/249 3.00 8.00
14 Chauncey Billups/249 3.00 8.00
15 Kevin Martin/249 3.00 8.00

2010-11 Prestige Stars of the NBA Materials Prime

*PRIME: .75X TO 2X HI
STATED PRINT RUN 5 TO 49 SER.#'d SETS
SOME UNPRICED DUE TO SCARCITY

2010-11 Prestige Stars of the NBA Signatures

STATED PRINT RUN 10 TO 25 SER.#'d SETS
SOME UNPRICED DUE TO SCARCITY
3 Amare Stoudemire/25 15.00 40.00
4 Tyreke Evans/25 15.00 40.00
7 Kobe Bryant/25 100.00 200.00

2010-11 Prestige Stat Stars

COMPLETE SET (25) 20.00 40.00
RANDOM INSERTS IN PACKS
1 Kevin Durant 2.50 6.00
2 LeBron James 4.00 10.00
3 Carmelo Anthony 1.00 2.50
4 Kobe Bryant 4.00 10.00
5 Dwyane Wade 1.50 4.00
6 Monta Ellis .75 2.00
7 Dirk Nowitzki 1.00 2.50
8 Dwight Howard 1.25 3.00
9 Marcus Camby .50 1.25
10 Zach Randolph .60 1.50
11 David Lee .60 1.50
12 Pau Gasol .75 2.00
13 Carlos Boozer .75 2.00
14 Steve Nash .75 2.00
15 Chris Paul 1.25 3.00
16 Deron Williams .75 2.00
17 Rajon Rondo 1.00 2.50
18 Jason Kidd .75 2.00
19 Baron Davis .75 2.00
20 Andrew Bogut .75 2.00
21 Josh Smith .75 2.00
22 Brendan Haywood .50 1.25
23 Chris Andersen .75 2.00
24 Samuel Dalembert .50 1.25
25 Brook Lopez .75 2.00

2010-11 Prestige Stat Stars Materials

STATED PRINT RUN 50 TO 249 SER.#'d SETS
*PRIME: .75X TO 2X HI
PRIME PRINT RUN 10 TO 49 SER.#'d SETS
1 Kevin Durant/50 8.00 20.00
2 LeBron James/50 10.00 25.00
3 Carmelo Anthony/249 4.00 10.00
4 Kobe Bryant/249 8.00 20.00
5 Dwyane Wade/249 6.00 15.00
7 Dirk Nowitzki/249 4.00 10.00
8 Dwight Howard/249 5.00 12.00
9 Marcus Camby/249 2.00 5.00
12 Pau Gasol/249 3.00 8.00
13 Carlos Boozer/249 3.00 8.00
14 Steve Nash/249 3.00 8.00
15 Chris Paul/249 5.00 12.00
16 Deron Williams/249 3.00 8.00
18 Jason Kidd/249 3.00 8.00
19 Baron Davis/249 3.00 8.00
20 Andrew Bogut/249 3.00 8.00
21 Josh Smith/249 3.00 8.00
22 Brendan Haywood/249 2.00 5.00
23 Chris Andersen/249 3.00 8.00
24 Samuel Dalembert/249 2.00 5.00
25 Brook Lopez/249 3.00 8.00

2010-11 Prestige Stat Stars Signatures

STATED PRINT RUN 10 TO 25 SER.#'d SETS
SOME UNPRICED DUE TO SCARCITY
4 Kobe Bryant/25 100.00 200.00
16 Deron Williams/25 12.50 30.00
19 Baron Davis/25 10.00 25.00

2010-11 Prestige Super Sophs

COMPLETE SET (5) 4.00 10.00
RANDOM INSERTS IN PACKS
1 Tyreke Evans 1.25 3
2 Brandon Jennings 1.00 2
3 Stephen Curry 1.25 3
4 Darren Collison 1.00 2
5 DeJuan Blair .75 2

2010-11 Prestige Super Sophs Materials

STATED PRINT RUN 249 SER.#'d SETS
*PRIME: .75X TO 2X HI
PRIME PRINT RUN 5 TO 49 SER.#'d SETS
1 Tyreke Evans/249 4.00 10
2 Brandon Jennings/249 3.00 8
3 Stephen Curry/249 4.00 10
4 Darren Collison/249 3.00 8
5 DeJuan Blair/249 2.50 6

2010-11 Prestige Super Sophs Signatures

STATED PRINT RUN 25 SER.#'d SETS
INSERTED IN PACKS OF SEASON UPDATE
2 Brandon Jennings* 10.00 25

2010-11 Prestige True Colors

RANDOM INSERTS IN PACKS
1 Kobe Bryant 4.00 10
2 Tim Duncan 1.25 3
3 Paul Pierce 1.00 2
4 Dirk Nowitzki 1.00 2
5 Tony Parker .75 2

2010-11 Prestige True Colors Materials

STATED PRINT RUN 249 SER.#'d SETS
*PRIME: .75X TO 2X HI
PRIME PRINT RUN 10 TO 49 SER.#'d SETS
1 Kobe Bryant/249 8.00 20
2 Tim Duncan/249 5.00 12
3 Paul Pierce/249 4.00 10
4 Dirk Nowitzki/249 4.00 10
5 Tony Parker/249 3.00 8

2010-11 Prestige True Colors Signatures

STATED PRINT RUN 25 SER.#'d SETS
ASTERISK CARDS INSERTED IN SEASON UPDATE
1 Kobe Bryant/25 100.00 200
5 Tony Parker/25* 15.00 40

2012-13 Prestige

ROOKIES INSERTED ONE PER PACK
UNPRICED BLACK PRINT RUN 10 SETS
1 LaMarcus Aldridge .40
2 Ray Allen .40
3 Al-Farouq Aminu .25
4 JaVale McGee .30
5 Ryan Anderson .30
6 Carmelo Anthony .50
7 Trevor Ariza .25
8 D.J. Augustin .25
9 J.J. Barea .40
10 Andrea Bargnani .30
11 Nicolas Batum .40
12 Michael Beasley .40
13 Rodrigue Beaubois .30
14 DeJuan Blair .30
15 Andrew Bogut .40
16 Trevor Booker .25
17 Carlos Boozer .40
18 Chris Bosh .40
19 Avery Bradley .40
20 Elton Brand .40
21 Kobe Bryant 1.50
22 Andrew Bynum .50
23 Jose Calderon .30
24 Vince Carter .50
25 Mario Chalmers .40
26 Tyson Chandler .30
27 Darren Collison .40
28 Mike Conley .30
29 DeMarcus Cousins .50
30 Jamal Crawford .30
31 Jordan Crawford .40
32 Stephen Curry .40
33 Ed Davis .30
34 Glen Davis .30
35 Boris Diaw .30
36 Luol Deng .40
37 DeMar DeRozan .40
38 Goran Dragic .30
39 Jared Dudley .25
40 Tim Duncan .60
41 Kevin Durant 1.25
42 Devin Ebanks .30
43 Monta Ellis .40
44 Tyreke Evans .40
45 Raymond Felton .30
46 Landry Fields .40
47 Channing Frye .30
48 Danilo Gallinari .30
49 Kevin Garnett .75
50 Marc Gasol .40
51 Pau Gasol .40
52 Rudy Gay .40
53 Paul George .40
54 Taj Gibson .30
55 Manu Ginobili .40
56 Drew Gooden .30
57 Ben Gordon .40
58 Eric Gordon .40
59 Marcin Gortat .40
60 Danny Granger .40
61 Blake Griffin .75
62 Tyler Hansbrough .40
63 James Harden .50
64 Al Harrington .30
65 Gordon Hayward .30
66 Gerald Henderson .25
67 Roy Hibbert .30
68 George Hill .30
69 Grant Hill .50
70 Jrue Holiday .40
71 Al Horford .30
72 Dwight Howard .60
73 Kris Humphries .25
74 Serge Ibaka .40
75 Andre Iguodala .40
76 Ersan Ilyasova .30
77 Jarrett Jack .30
78 Stephen Jackson .30
79 LeBron James 1.50
80 Antawn Jamison .40
81 Al Jefferson .40
82 Brandon Jennings .40
83 Joe Johnson .40
84 DeAndre Jordan .40
85 Chris Kaman .30
86 Jason Kidd .40
87 Carl Landry .25
88 Ty Lawson .40
89 Courtney Lee .30

David Lee .30 .75
Jeremy Lin 1.00 2.50
Brook Lopez .40 1.00
Kevin Love .50 1.25
Kyle Lowry .30 .75
Corey Maggette .30 .75
Shawn Marion .40 1.00
Kevin Martin .40 1.00
Wesley Matthews .40 1.00
O.J. Mayo .40 1.00
Andre Miller .30 .75
Paul Millsap .30 .75
Greg Monroe .40 1.00
Steve Nash .40 1.00
Jameer Nelson .30 .75
Nene .30 .75
Steve Novak .25 .60
Joakim Noah .40 1.00
Dirk Nowitzki .50 1.25
Emeka Okafor .40 1.00
Tony Parker .40 1.00
Chris Paul .60 1.50
Tayshaun Prince .40 1.00
Zach Randolph .30 .75
Jason Richardson .40 1.00
Luke Ridnour .30 .75
Nate Robinson .40 1.00
Rajon Rondo .50 1.25
Derrick Rose 1.25 3.00
Ricky Rubio 1.00 2.50
Luis Scola .30 .75
Ramon Sessions .30 .75
J.R. Smith .40 1.00
Josh Smith .40 1.00
Marreese Speights .25 .60
Amare Stoudemire .40 1.00
Rodney Stuckey .40 1.00
Jeff Teague .30 .75
Jason Terry .30 .75
Jason Thompson .25 .60
Marcus Thornton .40 1.00
Hedo Turkoglu .40 1.00
Evan Turner .40 1.00
Ekpe Udoh .25 .60
Anderson Varejao .30 .75
Dwyane Wade .75 2.00
John Wall .60 1.50
Gerald Wallace .40 1.00
David West .40 1.00
Delonte West .25 .60
Russell Westbrook .50 1.25
Deron Williams .40 1.00
Louis Williams .30 .75
Mo Williams .30 .75
Metta World Peace .40 1.00
Dorell Wright .25 .60
Nick Young .30 .75
Richard Hamilton .30 .75
Thaddeus Young .25 .60
Kirk Hinrich .40 1.00
Paul Pierce .50 1.25
Kyrie Irving RC 5.00 12.00
Derrick Williams RC 2.50 6.00
Brandon Knight RC 2.50 6.00
MarShon Brooks RC 2.00 5.00
Klay Thompson RC 2.50 6.00
Kemba Walker RC 1.50 4.00
Isaiah Thomas RC 1.50 4.00
Kenneth Faried RC 2.00 5.00
Iman Shumpert RC 2.00 5.00
Chandler Parsons RC 1.00 2.50
Tristan Thompson RC 1.50 4.00
Kawhi Leonard RC 2.00 5.00
Jimmer Fredette RC 2.00 5.00
Vernon Macklin RC .60 1.50
Markieff Morris RC 1.25 3.00
Alec Burks RC 1.00 2.50
Norris Cole RC 1.50 4.00
Ivan Johnson RC .75 2.00
Jeremy Pargo RC .60 1.50
Gustavo Ayon RC .75 2.00
Charles Jenkins RC .60 1.50
Nikola Vucevic RC .60 1.50
Donald Sloan RC .60 1.50
Bismack Biyombo RC 1.00 2.50
Tobias Harris RC .75 2.00
Jeremy Tyler RC .60 1.50
Jon Leuer RC .60 1.50
Jan Vesely RC 1.00 2.50
Chris Singleton RC .60 1.50
Enes Kanter RC 1.50 4.00
Jordan Williams RC .75 2.00
Jordan Hamilton RC .60 1.50
Josh Harrellson RC 1.25 3.00
Andrew Goudelock RC .75 2.00
Lavoy Allen RC .75 2.00
Lance Thomas RC .60 1.50
Cory Higgins RC .75 2.00
Nolan Smith RC 1.00 2.50
Marcus Morris RC 1.00 2.50
Trey Thompkins RC .60 1.50
Elliot Williams .25 .60
Terrel Harris RC .60 1.50
Shelvin Mack RC .75 2.00
JaJuan Johnson RC .75 2.00
Reggie Jackson RC .75 2.00
Greg Stiemsma RC 1.00 2.50
E'Twaun Moore RC 1.00 2.50
Josh Selby RC 1.00 2.50
Jimmy Butler RC 1.25 3.00
Cory Joseph RC .60 1.50
Anthony Davis RC 5.00 12.00
Austin Rivers RC 2.00 5.00
Jeremy Lamb RC 1.25 3.00
Michael Kidd-Gilchrist RC 2.50 6.00
Terrence Ross RC 1.25 3.00
Andre Drummond RC 1.25 3.00
Thomas Robinson RC 2.00 5.00
Kendall Marshall RC 1.25 3.00
Terrence Jones RC 1.50 4.00
Meyers Leonard RC 1.00 2.50
Harrison Barnes RC 2.00 5.00
Bradley Beal RC 2.00 5.00
Dion Waiters RC 2.00 5.00
Damian Lillard RC 2.50 6.00
John Henson RC 1.00 2.50
Moe Harkless RC .75 2.00
Royce White RC 1.25 3.00
Tyler Zeller RC 1.25 3.00
Andrew Nicholson RC 1.00 2.50
Evan Fournier RC .75 2.00
Jared Sullinger RC 2.00 5.00
Fab Melo RC 1.25 3.00
Tony Wroten RC .75 2.00
Perry Jones III RC 1.50 4.00
Miles Plumlee RC .75 2.00
Jared Cunningham RC .75 2.00
John Jenkins RC 1.00 2.50
228 Marquis Teague RC 1.25 3.00
229 Festus Ezeli RC .75 2.00
230 Arnett Moultrie RC .60 1.50
231 Bernard James RC .60 1.50
232 Orlando Johnson RC .60 1.50
233 Jeff Taylor RC .60 1.50
234 Quincy Acy RC .75 2.00
235 Justin Harper RC .75 2.00
236 Jae Crowder RC .75 2.00
237 Draymond Green RC .60 1.50
238 Quincy Miller RC .75 2.00
239 Khris Middleton RC .60 1.50
240 Will Barton RC .75 2.00
241 Kim English RC .75 2.00
242 Darius Miller RC 1.25 3.00
243 Doron Lamb RC 1.50 4.00
244 Mike Scott RC .60 1.50
245 Justin Hamilton RC 1.00 2.50
246 Tornike Shengelia RC .60 1.50
247 Kyle O'Quinn RC .60 1.50
248 Robert Sacre RC 1.00 2.50
249 Tyshawn Taylor RC .75 2.00
250 Kris Joseph RC .75 2.00

2012-13 Prestige Bonus Shots Gold

*VETS: 1X TO 2.5X BASE HI
*ROOKIES: .75X TO 2X BASE HI
STATED PRINT RUN 249 SER.#'d SETS
151 Kyrie Irving 12.00 30.00
201 Anthony Davis 12.00 30.00
204 Michael Kidd-Gilchrist 6.00 15.00

2012-13 Prestige All-Stars East

COMPLETE SET (14) 8.00 20.00
RANDOM INSERTS IN RETAIL PACKS
1 Dwyane Wade 1.25 3.00
2 Derrick Rose 2.00 5.00
3 Dwight Howard 1.00 2.50
4 LeBron James 2.50 6.00
5 Carmelo Anthony .75 2.00
6 Chris Bosh .60 1.50
7 Luol Deng .60 1.50
8 Roy Hibbert .50 1.25
9 Andre Iguodala .60 1.50
10 Rajon Rondo .75 2.00
11 Paul Pierce .75 2.00
12 Deron Williams .60 1.50
13 Tom Thibodeau .60 1.50
14 Team Photo 4.00 10.00

2012-13 Prestige All-Stars West

COMPLETE SET (14) 8.00 20.00
RANDOM INSERTS IN RETAIL PACKS
1 Kobe Bryant 2.50 6.00
2 Chris Paul 1.00 2.50
3 Andrew Bynum .75 2.00
4 Blake Griffin 1.25 3.00
5 Kevin Durant 2.00 5.00
6 LaMarcus Aldridge .60 1.50
7 Marc Gasol .60 1.50
8 Kevin Love .75 2.00
9 Steve Nash .60 1.50
10 Dirk Nowitzki .75 2.00
11 Tony Parker .60 1.50
12 Russell Westbrook .75 2.00
13 Scott Brooks .60 1.50
14 Team Photo 4.00 10.00

2012-13 Prestige Connections

COMPLETE SET (25) 12.00 30.00
RANDOM INSERTS IN PACKS
1 Anthony Davis 4.00 10.00
Michael Kidd-Gilchrist
2 Marcus Morris 1.00 2.50
Markieff Morris
3 Russell Westbrook .75 2.00
Kevin Love
4 Jrue Holiday .60 1.50
Darren Collison
5 Vince Carter .75 2.00
Antawn Jamison
6 Jason Terry .60 1.50
Manu Ginobili
7 LaMarcus Aldridge 2.00 5.00
Kevin Durant
8 John Wall 1.00 2.50
Rajon Rondo
9 Chris Paul 1.25 3.00
Blake Griffin
10 DeMar DeRozan .60 1.50
Taj Gibson
11 O.J. Mayo .60 1.50
Nick Young
12 Tony Parker .60 1.50
Nicolas Batum
13 Marc Gasol .60 1.50
Pau Gasol
14 Evan Turner .60 1.50
Mike Conley
15 Derrick Rose 2.00 5.00
Tyreke Evans
16 Tyson Chandler 1.00 2.50
Dwight Howard
17 Steve Nash .75 2.00
Dirk Nowitzki
18 Derek Fisher 2.50 6.00
Kobe Bryant
19 Joakim Noah .60 1.50
Al Horford
20 Dwyane Wade 2.50 6.00
LeBron James
21 Rudy Gay .60 1.50
Ray Allen
22 Richard Hamilton .60 1.50
Ben Gordon
23 Shawn Marion .60 1.50
Amare Stoudemire
24 Karl Malone 1.00 2.50
John Stockton
25 Magic Johnson 2.50 6.00
Larry Bird

2012-13 Prestige Distinctive Ink

RANDOM INSERTS IN PACKS
1 Kevin Durant EXCH 125.00 225.00
2 Kobe Bryant EXCH 100.00 200.00
3 Gordon Hayward 6.00 15.00
4 O.J. Mayo EXCH 10.00 25.00
5 Danilo Gallinari EXCH 6.00 15.00
6 Marcin Gortat EXCH 12.00 30.00
7 Monta Ellis EXCH 10.00 25.00
8 Stephen Jackson EXCH 8.00 20.00
9 Andrew Bogut EXCH 8.00 20.00
10 Danny Granger EXCH 8.00 20.00

2012-13 Prestige Franchise Favorites

COMPLETE SET (25) 10.00 25.00
RANDOM INSERTS IN PACKS
1 Kevin Durant 2.00 5.00
2 Kevin Martin .60 1.50
3 Al Horford .50 1.25
4 Stephen Curry .60 1.50
5 Dirk Nowitzki .75 2.00
6 LeBron James 2.50 6.00
7 Paul Pierce .75 2.00
8 Deron Williams .60 1.50
9 Dwight Howard 1.00 2.50
10 Kobe Bryant 2.50 6.00
11 Blake Griffin 1.25 3.00
12 Ricky Rubio 1.50 4.00
13 Joakim Noah .60 1.50
14 Danny Granger .60 1.50
15 Manu Ginobili .60 1.50
16 Tayshaun Prince .60 1.50
17 Marc Gasol .60 1.50
18 Carmelo Anthony .75 2.00
19 Kyrie Irving 3.00 8.00
20 John Wall 1.00 2.50
21 DeMar DeRozan .60 1.50
22 Andre Iguodala .60 1.50
23 Tony Parker .60 1.50
24 Kevin Love .75 2.00
25 Ty Lawson .60 1.50

2012-13 Prestige Hardcourt Heroes

COMPLETE SET (25) 10.00 25.00
RANDOM INSERTS IN PACKS
1 Rajon Rondo .75 2.00
2 Carmelo Anthony .75 2.00
3 Kevin Durant 2.00 5.00
4 Kobe Bryant 2.50 6.00
5 LeBron James 2.50 6.00
6 Dirk Nowitzki .75 2.00
7 Kevin Love .75 2.00
8 Dwyane Wade 1.25 3.00
9 Derrick Rose 2.00 5.00
10 Dwight Howard 1.00 2.50
11 Tim Duncan 1.00 2.50
12 LaMarcus Aldridge .60 1.50
13 Blake Griffin 1.25 3.00
14 Steve Nash .60 1.50
15 Josh Smith .60 1.50
16 Andrew Bynum .75 2.00
17 Tyreke Evans .60 1.50
18 Russell Westbrook .75 2.00
19 Chris Paul 1.00 2.50
20 Brandon Jennings .60 1.50
21 John Wall 1.00 2.50
22 Kevin Garnett 1.25 3.00
23 Al Jefferson .60 1.50
24 Rudy Gay .60 1.50
25 Monta Ellis .60 1.50

2012-13 Prestige Inside the Numbers Materials

RANDOM INSERTS IN PACKS
1 Kevin Durant 8.00 20.00
2 Kobe Bryant 10.00 25.00
3 Tyson Chandler 2.00 5.00
4 Rajon Rondo 4.00 10.00
5 Ricky Rubio 8.00 20.00
6 Joe Johnson 2.50 6.00
7 Chris Paul 4.00 10.00
8 Steve Nash 2.50 6.00
9 Serge Ibaka 2.50 6.00
10 Dwight Howard 4.00 10.00
11 Mike Conley 2.00 5.00
12 Kevin Love 3.00 8.00
13 Andrew Bynum 3.00 8.00
14 DeAndre Jordan 2.50 6.00
15 Josh Smith 2.50 6.00
16 DeMarcus Cousins 3.00 8.00
17 Blake Griffin 5.00 12.00
18 LeBron James 10.00 25.00
19 Russell Westbrook 3.00 8.00
20 Carmelo Anthony 3.00 8.00
21 Derrick Rose 10.00 25.00
22 Dwyane Wade 5.00 12.00
23 Jose Calderon 2.00 5.00
24 Deron Williams 2.50 6.00
25 John Wall 4.00 10.00
26 Jason Kidd 2.50 6.00
27 Paul Pierce 3.00 8.00
28 LaMarcus Aldridge 2.50 6.00
29 Marcus Camby 2.00 5.00
30 Metta World Peace 2.50 6.00
31 David Lee 2.00 5.00
32 Kyrie Irving 15.00 40.00
33 Stephen Curry 2.50 6.00
34 Tony Parker 2.50 6.00
35 Luol Deng 2.50 6.00
36 Marc Gasol 2.50 6.00
37 Manu Ginobili 2.50 6.00
38 Ryan Anderson 2.00 5.00
39 Kevin Garnett 5.00 12.00
40 Andre Miller 2.00 5.00
41 James Harden 3.00 8.00
42 Antawn Jamison 2.50 6.00
43 Tim Duncan 4.00 10.00
44 Dirk Nowitzki 3.00 8.00
45 Jordan Crawford 2.50 6.00
46 Greg Monroe 2.50 6.00
47 Kenneth Faried 6.00 15.00
48 Baron Davis 2.50 6.00
49 Ty Lawson 2.50 6.00
50 Amare Stoudemire 2.50 6.00

2012-13 Prestige Inside the Numbers Materials Prime

*PRIME: 1.25X TO 3X BASE HI
STATED PRINT RUN 25 SER.#'d SETS
5 Ricky Rubio 30.00 80.00
23 Jose Calderon 10.00 25.00
26 Jason Kidd 10.00 25.00
27 Paul Pierce 12.00 30.00
37 Manu Ginobili 12.00 30.00
47 Kenneth Faried 30.00 80.00

2012-13 Prestige Old School Signatures

STATED PRINT RUN 25 TO 99 SETS
1 Rick Barry/49 15.00 40.00
2 Walt Bellamy/99 6.00 15.00
3 Tom Chambers/99 6.00 15.00
4 Bob Lanier/49 8.00 20.00
5 Spud Webb/99 EXCH 8.00 20.00
6 Kenny Anderson/99 6.00 15.00
7 Rod Strickland/99 6.00 15.00
8 Steve Smith/99 8.00 20.00
9 Vlade Divac/99 EXCH 10.00 25.00
10 Adrian Dantley/99 6.00 15.00
11 Buck Williams/99 EXCH 6.00 15.00
12 Sidney Moncrief/99 6.00 15.00
13 Reggie Theus/99 6.00 15.00
14 Eddie Johnson/99 8.00 20.00
15 Kevin Willis/99 8.00 20.00
16 Larry Johnson/99 EXCH 15.00 40.00
17 Detlef Schrempf/99 10.00 25.00
18 Fat Lever/99 6.00 15.00
19 Kenny Walker/99 12.00 30.00
21 Dikembe Mutombo/49 20.00 50.00
22 Sam Perkins/99 EXCH 6.00 15.00
23 Cedric Ceballos/99 EXCH 8.00 20.00
24 Dan Majerle/99 6.00 15.00
25 Terry Porter/99 8.00 20.00
26 Jamal Mashburn/99 10.00 25.00
27 Danny Manning/49 8.00 20.00
28 Mitch Richmond/99 EXCH 12.00 30.00
29 Glen Rice/49 EXCH 10.00 25.00
30 Chris Mullin/99 12.00 30.00
31 Steve Kerr/49 10.00 25.00
32 Joe Dumars/49 8.00 20.00
33 John Stockton/25
34 Rex Chapman/99 8.00 20.00
35 Kurt Rambis/99 8.00 20.00
36 Robert Parish/49 8.00 20.00
37 Maurice Cheeks/99

2012-13 Prestige Playmakers

RANDOM INSERTS IN PACKS
1 Kobe Bryant 40.00 100.00
2 LeBron James 40.00 100.00
3 Kevin Durant 30.00 80.00
4 Blake Griffin 20.00 50.00
5 Derrick Rose 30.00 80.00
6 Kevin Love 12.00 30.00
7 Dwight Howard 15.00 40.00
8 Deron Williams 10.00 25.00
9 Dirk Nowitzki 12.00 30.00
10 Dwyane Wade 20.00 50.00
11 LaMarcus Aldridge 10.00 25.00
12 Tony Parker 10.00 25.00
13 David Lee 8.00 20.00
14 Russell Westbrook 15.00 40.00
15 Josh Smith 10.00 25.00
16 Rudy Gay 10.00 25.00
17 Brandon Jennings 10.00 25.00
18 Carmelo Anthony 12.00 30.00
19 Al Jefferson 10.00 25.00
20 Chris Paul 15.00 40.00
21 Rajon Rondo 12.00 30.00
22 John Wall 15.00 40.00
23 Joe Johnson 10.00 25.00
24 Paul Pierce 12.00 30.00
25 Danny Granger 10.00 25.00

2012-13 Prestige Prestigious Picks Signatures

RANDOM INSERTS IN PACKS
1 Kyrie Irving 125.00 250.00
2 Derrick Williams 15.00 40.00
3 Enes Kanter 8.00 20.00
4 Tristan Thompson 8.00 20.00
5 Jan Vesely 5.00 12.00
6 Bismack Biyombo 5.00 12.00
7 Brandon Knight 12.00 30.00
8 Kemba Walker 12.00 30.00
9 Jimmer Fredette 10.00 25.00
10 Klay Thompson 20.00 50.00
11 Alec Burks 5.00 12.00
12 Markieff Morris 6.00 15.00
13 Marcus Morris 5.00 12.00
14 Kawhi Leonard 12.00 30.00
15 Nikola Vucevic 3.00 8.00
16 Iman Shumpert 12.00 30.00
17 Chris Singleton 3.00 8.00
18 Tobias Harris 4.00 10.00
19 Nolan Smith 5.00 12.00
20 Kenneth Faried 10.00 25.00
21 Reggie Jackson 4.00 10.00
22 MarShon Brooks 8.00 20.00
23 Jordan Hamilton 3.00 8.00
24 JaJuan Johnson 4.00 10.00
25 Norris Cole 8.00 20.00
26 Cory Joseph 3.00 8.00
27 Jimmy Butler 6.00 15.00
28 Shelvin Mack 4.00 10.00
29 Tyler Honeycutt 3.00 8.00
30 Jordan Williams 4.00 10.00
31 Trey Thompkins 3.00 8.00
32 Chandler Parsons 5.00 12.00
33 Jeremy Tyler 3.00 8.00
34 Jon Leuer 3.00 8.00
35 Darius Morris 4.00 10.00
36 Malcolm Lee 3.00 8.00
37 Charles Jenkins 3.00 8.00
38 Josh Harrellson 6.00 15.00
39 Andrew Goudelock 4.00 10.00
40 Josh Selby 5.00 12.00
41 Isaiah Thomas 8.00 20.00
42 Lavoy Allen 4.00 10.00
43 E'Twaun Moore 5.00 12.00
44 Courtney Fortson 3.00 8.00
45 Anthony Davis 125.00 250.00
46 Michael Kidd-Gilchrist 40.00 100.00
47 Bradley Beal 20.00 50.00
48 Dion Waiters 15.00 40.00
49 Thomas Robinson 25.00 60.00
51 Harrison Barnes 25.00 60.00
52 Terrence Ross 6.00 15.00
53 Andre Drummond 12.00 30.00
54 Austin Rivers 25.00 60.00
55 Meyers Leonard 5.00 12.00
56 Jeremy Lamb EXCH 6.00 15.00
57 Kendall Marshall 8.00 20.00
58 John Henson 8.00 20.00
59 Moe Harkless 4.00 10.00
60 Royce White 8.00 20.00
61 Tyler Zeller 6.00 15.00
62 Terrence Jones 8.00 20.00
63 Andrew Nicholson 5.00 12.00
64 Evan Fournier 4.00 10.00
65 Jared Sullinger 20.00 50.00
66 Fab Melo 8.00 20.00
67 John Jenkins 5.00 12.00
68 Jared Cunningham 4.00 10.00
69 Tony Wroten EXCH 4.00 10.00
70 Miles Plumlee 4.00 10.00
71 Arnett Moultrie 3.00 8.00
72 Perry Jones III 8.00 20.00
73 Marquis Teague 8.00 20.00
74 Festus Ezeli 4.00 10.00
75 Bernard James 3.00 8.00

2012-13 Prestige Prestigious Pros Signatures

RANDOM INSERTS IN PACKS
1 Derrick Rose
2 Kevin Durant EXCH
3 Kobe Bryant EXCH 75.00 150.00
4 Blake Griffin
5 Andrea Bargnani
6 Stephen Curry 8.00 20.00
7 Tyreke Evans EXCH 10.00 25.00
8 Raymond Felton EXCH 5.00 12.00
9 Jeff Teague 4.00 10.00
10 Devin Ebanks 4.00 10.00
11 George Hill 4.00 10.00
12 Mike Conley 4.00 10.00
13 Al Horford
14 Paul Millsap EXCH 6.00 15.00
15 Stephen Jackson 6.00 15.00
16 Ty Lawson
17 Marcus Thornton 5.00 12.00
18 Marcin Gortat EXCH 10.00 25.00
19 Brook Lopez 4.00 10.00
20 Jordan Crawford 4.00 10.00
21 Zach Randolph 4.00 10.00
23 Luol Deng 6.00 15.00
24 Kevin Love 15.00 40.00
25 Derek Fisher 5.00 12.00

2012-13 Prestige Stars of the NBA

COMPLETE SET (25) 8.00 20.00
RANDOM INSERTS IN PACKS
1 Russell Westbrook .75 2.00
2 Pau Gasol .60 1.50
3 Greg Monroe .60 1.50
4 DeMarcus Cousins .75 2.00
5 Chris Bosh .60 1.50
6 Joe Johnson .60 1.50
7 Elton Brand .60 1.50
8 Shawn Marion .60 1.50
9 LeBron James 2.50 6.00
10 Louis Williams .50 1.25
11 Tyson Chandler .50 1.25
12 David Lee .50 1.25
13 Rudy Gay .60 1.50
14 Dirk Nowitzki .75 2.00
15 James Harden .75 2.00
16 Kevin Martin .60 1.50
17 Marcus Thornton .60 1.50
18 Chris Paul 1.00 2.50
19 Brook Lopez .60 1.50
20 Andrew Bogut .60 1.50
21 Ty Lawson .60 1.50
22 Raymond Felton .50 1.25
23 Carlos Boozer .60 1.50
24 Ray Allen .60 1.50
25 Amare Stoudemire .60 1.50

2012-13 Prestige True Colors Materials

RANDOM INSERTS IN PACKS
1 Deron Williams 2.50 6.00
2 Jason Kidd 2.50 6.00
3 Andre Iguodala 2.50 6.00
4 Ricky Rubio 8.00 20.00
5 Danny Granger 2.50 6.00
6 Ryan Anderson 2.00 5.00
7 Paul Millsap 2.00 5.00
8 LeBron James 10.00 25.00
9 Kevin Garnett 5.00 12.00
10 Dwight Howard 4.00 10.00
11 Ty Lawson 2.50 6.00
12 Al Horford 2.00 5.00
13 Steve Nash 2.50 6.00
14 DeMarcus Cousins 3.00 8.00
15 Carmelo Anthony 3.00 8.00
16 Ray Allen 2.50 6.00
17 Tim Duncan 4.00 10.00
18 Eric Gordon 2.50 6.00
19 Kyrie Irving 12.00 30.00
20 Andrea Bargnani 2.00 5.00
21 Russell Westbrook 3.00 8.00
22 Brandon Jennings 2.50 6.00
23 Baron Davis 2.50 6.00
24 Luol Deng 2.50 6.00
25 Stephen Curry 2.50 6.00
26 Kevin Durant 8.00 20.00
27 Jrue Holiday 2.50 6.00
28 Andrew Bynum 3.00 8.00
29 Luis Scola 2.00 5.00
30 Brandon Knight 6.00 15.00
31 Klay Thompson 6.00 15.00
32 Tristan Thompson 4.00 10.00
33 Jordan Crawford 2.50 6.00
34 Drew Gooden 2.00 5.00
35 Danilo Gallinari 2.50 6.00
36 Michael Beasley 2.50 6.00
37 David West 2.50 6.00
38 Raymond Felton 2.00 5.00
39 Kemba Walker 4.00 10.00
40 Kawhi Leonard 5.00 12.00
41 Josh Smith 2.50 6.00
42 Anderson Varejao 2.00 5.00
43 O.J. Mayo 2.50 6.00
44 Mario Chalmers 2.50 6.00
45 Glen Davis 2.00 5.00
46 Mo Williams 2.00 5.00
47 Joakim Noah 2.50 6.00
48 Jared Dudley 2.00 5.00
49 Brook Lopez 2.50 6.00
50 Chris Kaman 2.00 5.00

2012-13 Prestige True Colors Materials Prime

*PRIME: 1.25X TO 3X BASE HI
STATED PRINT RUN 25 SER.#'d SETS
8 LeBron James 40.00 100.00
13 Steve Nash 15.00 40.00
15 Carmelo Anthony 12.00 30.00
16 Ray Allen 12.00 30.00
31 Klay Thompson 40.00 70.00

1980-81 Pride New Orleans WBL

This 11-card set features the 1980-81 New Orleans Pride of the Women's Basketball League. It's believed that 13 cards actually exist, but we only have 11 cards that have been verified at this point in time. According to the backs, these cards were available at Dome Souvenir Stands or at the Pride office. Inside white borders, the fronts display blue-tinted posed action shots. The player's uniform number and autograph are printed on the picture. In blue print on a white background, the backs carry biography, player profile, and a "Trade 'em and win!" contest.

COMPLETE SET (11) 50.00 100.00
1 Kathy Andrykowski 4.00 10.00
2 Sybil Blalock 4.00 10.00
3 Cindy Brogden 7.50 15.00
4 Vicky Chapman 4.00 10.00
5 Beverly Crusoe 4.00 10.00
6 Sharon Farrah 4.00 10.00
7 Eileen Feeney 4.00 10.00
8 Augusta Forest 4.00 10.00
9 Bertha Hardy 4.00 10.00
10 Sue Peters 4.00 10.00
11 Heidi Wayment 4.00 10.00

2008 Prime Cuts Playoff Contenders Autographs

OVERALL AU/MEM ODDS 4 PER BOX
EXCHANGE DEADLINE 6/26/2010
23 O.J. Mayo 30.00 60.00
24 Michael Beasley 15.00 40.00
25 Derrick Rose 150.00 300.00

1985 Prism/Jewel Stickers

These gaudy metallic stickers measure different sizes but most are approximately 2 11/16" by 4". The front features a colorful drawn picture of the player, with the player's name in block lettering, and a facsimile autograph. The picture has rounded corners and a silver border. The backs are blank. The stickers are unnumbered and are checklisted below in alphabetical order by subject.

COMPLETE SET (14) 500.00 1000.00
1 Kareem Abdul-Jabbar 20.00 40.00
2 Larry Bird 40.00 100.00
3 Larry Bird vs 30.00 60.00
James Worthy
4 Julius Erving 30.00 60.00
5 Patrick Ewing 30.00 60.00
6 Magic Johnson 30.00 65.00
7 Michael Jordan 400.00 800.00
8 Moses Malone 6.00 15.00
9 Moses Malone vs 8.00 20.00
Kareem Abdul-Jabbar
10 Sidney Moncrief 4.00 10.00
11 Ralph Sampson 4.00 10.00
12 Isiah Thomas 8.00 20.00
13 Kelly Tripucka 4.00 10.00
14 Buck Williams 4.00 10.00

1989-90 ProCards CBA

The 1989-90 ProCards CBA basketball set contains 207 standard-size cards. The cards were distributed in individual sealed team bags. Reportedly 2,000 sets were produced and distributed. The individual team sets reportedly originally retailed for approximately 3.00 each. The fronts feature posed or action color player photos on a light tan background. Overlaying the upper left corner of the picture is a white circle (representing a basketball), with the CBA logo on it. Just below the circle a basketball rim and net are drawn. The player's name, position, and team are given in black lettering in the lower right corner of the card face. On a gray background with black borders and lettering the horizontally oriented backs present biographical and statistical information. The team logo appears in the cut-out section at the upper right corner. The cards are numbered on the back and arranged according to teams as follows: Sioux Falls SkyForce (1-13), Wichita Falls Texans (14-25), Rapid City Thrillers (26-37), Quad City Thunder (38-50), Pensacola Tornados (51-60), Omaha Racers (61-74, 206-7), Columbus Horizon (75-86), Rockford Lightning (87-100), Albany Patroons (101-114), Santa Barbara Islanders (115-127), Grand Rapids Hoops (128-140), Tulsa Fast Breakers (141-153), LaCrosse Catbirds (154-165), Topeka Sizzlers (166-178), Cedar Rapids Silver Bullets (179-192), and San Jose Jammers (193-205). The set features the first professional cards of Chris Childs, Mario Elie and John Starks.

COMPLETE SET (207) 50.00 120.00
1 Sioux Falls Checklist .30 .75
2 Ben Wilson .30 .75
3 Leonard Harris .40 1.00
4 Laurent Crawford .30 .75
5 Steve Grayer .50 1.25
6 Jim Lampley .30 .75
7 Eric Brown .30 .75
8 Dennis Nutt .50 1.25
9 Ralph Lewis .30 .75
10 Lashun McDaniel .30 .75
11 Leo Parent .30 .75
12 Ron Ekker .30 .75
13 Terry Gould .30 .75
14 Wichita Falls CL .30 .75
15 Mark Peterson .30 .75
16 Greg Van Soelen .30 .75
17 Maurice Selvin .30 .75
18 Michael Tait .40 1.00
19 Deon Hunter .40 1.00
20 Randy Henry .30 .75
21 Kenny McClary .40 1.00
22 Earl Walker .30 .75
23 Jeff Hodge .30 .75
24 Martin Nessley .50 1.25
25 On Court Staff .30 .75
26 Rapid City Checklist .30 .75
27 Daren Queenan .40 1.00
28 Carey Scurry .30 .75
29 Keith Smart 1.25 3.00
30 Jim Thomas .50 1.25
31 Pearl Washington .75 2.00
32 Chris Childs 2.00 5.00
33 Jarvis Basnight .50 1.25
34 Dwight Boyd .30 .75
35 Raymond Brown .40 1.00
36 Sylvester Gray .40 1.00
37 Eric Musselman CO 1.25 3.00
38 Quad City Checklist .30 .75
39 Kenny Gattison 1.25 3.00
40 Lafester Rhodes .30 .75
41 Perry Young .40 1.00
42 Wiley Brown .40 1.00
43 Jose Slaughter .75 2.00
44 Gerald Greene .40 1.00
45 Lloyd Daniels 1.50 4.00
46 Bill Jones .30 .75
47 Sean Couch .30 .75
48 Marty Eggleston .40 1.00
49 Mauro Panaggio CO .40 1.00
50 Dan Panaggio CO .30 .75
51 Pensacola Checklist .30 .75
52 Joe Mullaney CO 1.00 2.50
53 Mark Wade .30 .75
54 Larry Houzer .30 .75
55 Clifford Lett .30 .75
56 Tony Dawson .40 1.00
57 Johnathan Edwards .30 .75
58 Jim Farmer .60 1.50
59 Dwayne Taylor .30 .75
60 Bob McCann .40 1.00
61 Omaha Checklist .30 .75
62 Silks Rodie .30 .75
63 Racers Front Office .30 .75
64 Rodie-Team Mascot .30 .75
65 Tim Price .30 .75
66 Barry Glanzer .30 .75
67 Greg Wiltjer .40 1.00
68 Ron Kellogg .30 .75
69 Tat Hunter .30 .75
70 Reginald Turner .30 .75
71 Jerry Adams .30 .75
72 Roland Gray .30 .75
73 Tim Legler 1.25 3.00
74 Corey Gaines .60 1.50
75 Columbus Checklist .30 .75
76 Gary Youmans .30 .75
77 Kelvin Ransey .75 2.00
78 Chip Engelland 1.50 4.00
79 Brian Martin .30 .75
80 Ray Hall .30 .75
81 Jay Burson .40 1.00
82 Bill Martin .60 1.50
83 Eric Mudd .30 .75
84 Tom Schafer .30 .75
85 Steve Harris .40 1.00
86 Eric Newsome .30 .75
87 Rockford Checklist .30 .75
88 Charley Rosen 1.50 4.00
89 Tom Hart .30 .75
90 Team Picture .30 .75
91 Brent Carmichael .30 .75
92 Fred Cofield .40 1.00
93 Darren Guest .30 .75
94 Bobby Parks .30 .75
95 Elston Turner .60 1.50
96 Adrian McKinnon .30 .75
97 Gary Massey .30 .75
98 Tim Dillon .40 1.00
99 Herb Blunt .30 .75
100 Greg Grissom .30 .75
101 Albany Checklist .30 .75
102 Leroy Witherspoon .30 .75
103 Vincent Askew 2.00 5.00
104 Clinton Smith .30 .75
105 Andre Patterson .40 1.00
106 Jim Ferrer .30 .75
107 Willie Glass .60 1.50
108 Darryl Joe .30 .75
109 Mario Elie 2.50 6.00
110 Dave Popson .75 2.00
111 Danny Pearson .30 .75
112 Doc Nunnally .30 .75
113 Gene Espeland .30 .75
114 Gerald Oliver CO .30 .75
115 Santa Barbara CL .30 .75
116 Luther Burks .50 1.25
117 Brian Christensen .30 .75
118 Kevin Francewar .30 .75
119 Leon Wood 1.00 2.50
120 Derrick Gervin .75 2.00
121 Larry Spriggs .75 2.00
122 Michael Phelps .40 1.00
123 Mike Ratliff .30 .75
124 Steffond Johnson .40 1.00
125 Mitch McMullen .30 .75
126 Sonny Allen .30 .75
127 Don Ford .60 1.50
128 Grand Rapids CL .30 .75
129 Lorenzo Sutton .30 .75
130 Willie Simmons .40 1.00
131 Kenny Fields .40 1.00
132 Winston Crite .30 .75
133 Eric McLaughlin .30 .75
134 Tony Brown .40 1.00
135 Ricky Wilson .40 1.00
136 Milt Newton .40 1.00
137 Albert Springs .30 .75
138 Herbert Crook .40 1.00
139 Mike Mashak ACO .30 .75
140 Jim Sleeper .30 .75
141 Tulsa Checklist .30 .75
142 Terry Faggins .30 .75
143 Ozell Jones .40 1.00
144 Brian Rahilly .30 .75
145 Duane Washington .60 1.50
146 Ron Spivey .30 .75
147 Henry Bibby CO .60 1.50
148 Al Gipson .40 1.00
149 Greg Jones .30 .75
150 Andre Moore .60 1.50
151 Tracy Moore .60 1.50
152 Steve Bontranger .30 .75
153 Bubby Breaker Mascot .30 .75
154 LaCrosse Checklist .30 .75
155 Mike Williams .30 .75
156 Vince Hamilton .40 1.00
157 John Harris .30 .75
158 Tony White .30 .75
159 Todd Alexander .30 .75
160 Richard Johnson .30 .75
161 Leo Rautins 1.00 2.50
162 Dwayne McClain 1.00 2.50
163 Carlos Clark 1.00 2.50
164 Vada Martin .30 .75
165 Flip Saunders 1.50 4.00
166 Topeka Checklist .30 .75
167 Cedric Hunter .30 .75
168 Elfrem Jackson .30 .75
169 Glen Clem .30 .75
170 Mike Richmond .30 .75
171 Jim Rowinski .30 .75
172 Craig Jackson .30 .75
173 Tony Mack .30 .75
174 Hubert Henderson .30 .75
175 Kevin Nixon .30 .75

176 Haywoode Workman 1.25 3.00
177 Porter Cutrell .30 .75
178 Mike Riley .30 .75
179 Cedar Rapids CL .30 .75
180 Bullet Bear .30 .75
181 George Whittaker .30 .75
182 Tom Domako .30 .75
183 Al Lorenzen .30 .75
184 Darryl Johnson .40 1.00
185 Mel Braxton .30 .75
186 Orlando Graham .30 .75
187 Reggie Owens .30 .75
188 John Starks 6.00 15.00
189 Kenny Drummond .30 .75
190 Mark Plansky .30 .75
191 Anthony Blakley .40 1.00
192 Everette Stephens .75 2.00
193 San Jose Checklist .30 .75
194 Cory Russell .30 .75
195 Jim Ellis .30 .75
196 Butch Hays .60 1.50
197 Mike Doktorczyk .30 .75
198 Scooter Barry 1.50 4.00
199 Monroe Douglass .30 .75
200 Scott Fisher .40 1.00
201 David Boone .30 .75
202 Jervis Cole .30 .75
203 Freddie Banks .30 .75
204 Richard Morton .30 .75
205 Dan Williams .30 .75
206 Mike Thibault CO .30 .75
207 Omaha Coaches .30 .75
Omaha Racers

1990-91 ProCards CBA

The 1990-91 ProCards CBA basketball set contains 203 standard-size cards. The individual team sets reportedly originally retailed for approximately 3.00 each. The color player photos on the fronts are framed by a filmstrip design in red on a white card face. The horizontally oriented backs are printed in black on light purple and feature biographical as well as statistical information. The cards are checklisted below according to teams as follows: Omaha Racers (1-16), Cedar Rapids Silver Bullets (17-29), Pensacola Tornados (30-44), Rockford Lightning (45-59), Lacrosse Catbirds (60-71), Rapid City Thrillers (72-81), Sioux Falls Skyforce (82-96), Oklahoma City Cavalry (97-107), Tulsa Fast Breakers (108-118), Wichita Falls Texans (119-134), Quad City Thunder (135-148), Albany Patroons (149-162), Grand Rapids Hoops (163-171), Columbus Horizon (172-183), Yakima Sun Kings (184-192), and San Jose Jammers (193-203). The set contains the first professional card of Anthony Mason.

COMPLETE SET (203) 40.00 100.00
1 Jim Les .75 2.00
2 Ron Moore .25 .60
3 Rod Mason .25 .60
4 Paul Weakly .25 .60
5 Brian Howard .40 1.00
6 Pat Bolden .25 .60
7 Mike Thibault CO .30 .75
8 Tim Legler 1.00 2.50
9 Cedric Hunter .30 .75
10 Mark Peterson .25 .60
11 Greg Wiltjer .40 1.00
12 The Idelman's .25 .60
13 The Silks and Rodie .25 .60
14 Basketball Staff .25 .60
15 Front Office Staff .25 .60
16 Omaha Checklist .25 .60
17 Calvin Duncan .25 .60
18 Pat Durham .40 1.00
19 Steve Grayer .40 1.00
20 Roy Marble .60 1.50
21 Tony Martin .30 .75
22 Shawn McDaniel .25 .60
23 Peter Thibeaux .25 .60
24 Clarence Thompson .25 .60
25 Demone Webster .25 .60
26 A.J. Wynder .40 1.00
27 Steve Kahl .25 .60
28 Steve Bontranger .25 .60
29 Cedar Rapids CL .25 .60
30 Skeeter Henry .40 1.00
31 Eugene McDowell .25 .60
32 Bruce Wheatley .25 .60
33 Mark Wade .30 .75
34 Cheyenne Gibson .25 .60
35 Clifford Lett .30 .75
36 Larry Houzer .25 .60
37 Tony Dawson .25 .60
38 Richard Hollis .30 .75
39 Ed Leonard and Joe Corona .25 .60
40 Front Office Staff .25 .60
41 Torry the Tornado .25 .60
42 Fred Bryan .25 .60
43 Jim Goodman .25 .60
44 Pensacola Checklist .25 .60
45 Joe Fredrick .25 .60
46 Everette Stephens .60 1.50
47 Mario Donaldson .25 .60
48 Dan Godfread .25 .60
49 Haakon Austefjord .25 .60
50 Gary Massey .25 .60
51 Chris Childs 1.25 3.00
52 Gerry Wright .25 .60
53 Marty Conlon 1.00 2.50
54 Tony Costner .25 .60
55 Steve Hayes CO .50 1.25
56 Tom Hart .25 .60
57 Paul Kulick .25 .60
58 Rockford Team Photo .25 .60
59 Rockford Checklist .25 .60
60 Mike Williams .25 .60
61 Brian Rahilly .25 .60
62 Bill Martin .40 1.00
63 Vince Hamilton .30 .75
64 Dwayne McClain .75 2.00
65 Bart Kofoed .40 1.00
66 Dominic Pressley .30 .75
67 Herb Dixon .25 .60
68 Todd Mitchell .30 .75
69 Ben Mitchell .25 .60
70 Flip Saunders 1.25 3.00
71 LaCrosse Checklist .25 .60
72 Keith Smart .75 2.00
73 Stevie Thompson .75 2.00
74 Brian Rowsom .40 1.00
75 Tony Martin .30 .75
76 Joe Ward .25 .60
77 Fennis Dembo .40 1.00
78 Glenn Puddy .25 .60
79 Lanard Copeland .60 1.50
80 Carl Brown .25 .60
81 Rapid City Checklist .25 .60
82 Dennis Nutt .40 1.00
83 Leonard Harris .30 .75
84 Tharon Mayes .30 .75
85 Melvin McCants .40 1.00
86 Tracy Mitchell .30 .75
87 Ken Redfield .30 .75
88 Frank Ross .25 .60
89 Michael Phelps .30 .75
90 Brian Christensen .25 .60
91 Kevin McKenna .60 1.50
92 Steve Raab .25 .60
93 Clay Moser .25 .60
94 Tony Khing .25 .60
95 Little Dude .25 .60
96 Sioux Falls Checklist .25 .60
97 Perry Young .40 1.00
98 Ozell Jones .40 1.00
99 Willie Simmons .25 .60
100 Alvin Heggs .25 .60
101 Kelsey Weems .30 .75
102 Anthony Frederick .30 .75
103 Royce Jeffries .25 .60
104 Darryl McDonald .60 1.50
105 Sgt. Slammer .25 .60
106 Charley Rosen 1.25 3.00
107 Oklahoma City CL .25 .60
108 Keith Wilson .25 .60
109 James Carter .25 .60
110 Tracy Moore .40 1.00
111 Mark Plansky .30 .75
112 Charles Bradley .25 .60
113 Leroy Combs .25 .60
114 Anthony Mason 5.00 12.00
115 Gary Voce .40 1.00
116 Jim Lampley .30 .75
117 Henry Bibby CO .60 1.50
118 Tulsa Checklist .25 .60
119 Texans Logo .25 .60
120 Ennis Whatley .75 2.00
121 Mike Mitchell .40 1.00
122 Derrick Taylor .30 .75
123 Kenny Atkinson .25 .60
124 Jaren Jackson .50 1.25
125 Cedric Ball .25 .60
126 Chris Munk .25 .60
127 Mark Becker .25 .60
128 Rodney Blake .25 .60
129 Kurt Portmann .25 .60
130 Henry James .40 1.00
131 John Treloar ACO .25 .60
132 Dave Whitney ACO .25 .60
133 Mike Davis ACO .50 1.25
134 Wichita Falls CL .25 .60
135 Milt Wagner 1.00 2.50
136 Phil Henderson .60 1.50
137 Tony Harris .25 .60
138 Steve Bardo .40 1.00
139 A.J. Wynder .40 1.00
140 Joel DeBortoli .40 1.00
141 Tim Anderson .25 .60
142 Ron Draper .25 .60
143 Barry Sumpter .30 .75
144 Demone Webster .25 .60
145 Thunderbird Dance Team .25 .60
146 Mauro Panaggio CO .40 1.00
147 Dan Panaggio CO .25 .60
148 Quad City Checklist .25 .60
149 Albert King .40 1.00
150 Keith Smith .25 .60
151 Mario Elie 2.00 5.00
152 Albert Springs .25 .60
153 Jeff Fryer .25 .60
154 Clinton Smith .25 .60
155 Vincent Askew 1.50 4.00
156 Paul Graham .75 2.00
157 Ben McDonald .60 1.50
158 Willie McDuffie .25 .60
159 George Karl CO 3.00 8.00
160 Terry Stotts 1.00 2.50
161 Doc Nunnally .25 .60
162 Albany Checklist .25 .60
163 Reggie Fox .25 .60
164 Sedric Toney .30 .75
165 Ron Draper .25 .60
166 Alex Austin .25 .60
167 Robert Brickey .40 1.00
168 Ricky Blanton .40 1.00
169 Stan Kimbrough .25 .60
170 Ron Cavenall .25 .60
171 Grand Rapids CL .25 .60
172 Darren Henrie .25 .60
173 Duane Washington .50 1.25
174 Barry Stevens .25 .60
175 Craig Neal .25 .60
176 Ron Spivey .25 .60
177 Kerry Hammonds .25 .60
178 Brian Martin .25 .60
179 Jerome Henderson .25 .60
180 John McIntyre .25 .60
181 Chris Childs 1.25 3.00
182 The Jacobson's .25 .60
183 Columbus Checklist .25 .60
184 Luther Burks .25 .60
185 Lee Campbell .25 .60
186 Corey Gaines .40 1.00
187 Mike Higgins .25 .60
188 Ron Kellogg .25 .60
189 Bart Kofoed .40 1.00
190 Jim Rowinski .25 .60
191 Riley Smith .25 .60
192 Yakima Checklist .25 .60
193 Mike Yoest .25 .60
194 Freddie Banks .30 .75
195 Scooter Barry 1.25 3.00
196 Richard Morton .25 .60
197 Kelby Stuckey .25 .60
198 Jervis Cole .25 .60
199 Kenny McClary .30 .75
200 Joe Wallace .25 .60
201 Mark Tillmon .30 .75
202 Greg Butler .30 .75
203 San Jose Checklist .25 .60

1991-92 ProCards CBA

The 1991-92 ProCards CBA basketball set contains 206 standard-size cards. The individual team sets reportedly originally retailed for approximately 3.00 each. The fronts feature a mix of posed and action color player photos, bordered in silver. Two stripes that shade from pink to white accent the pictures on the left and bottom; the CBA logo appears in a circle at their intersection. On a gray background with black borders and lettering, the backs present biographical and statistical information. Seven teams found sponsors that listed their business on the card back, of which four were sports card shops. The cards are numbered on the back and checklisted below according to teams as follows: Bakersfield Jammers (1-11, 72), Wichita Texans (12-24), Rockford Lightning (25-35), Quad City Thunder (36-48), Oklahoma City Cavalry (49-60), Rapid City Thrillers (61-71), Fort Wayne Fury (73-85), Yakima Sun Kings (86-97), Grand Rapids Hoops (98-109), Sioux Falls Skyforce (110-121, 206), Tri-City Chinook (122-135), Columbus Horizon (136-147), LaCrosse Catbirds (148-159), Albany Patroons (160-171), Tulsa Zone (172-183), Omaha Racers (184-195), and Birmingham Bandits (196-205).

COMPLETE SET (206) 30.00 80.00
1 Chris Childs 1.25 3.00
2 Mark Tillmon .30 .75
3 Greg Butler .30 .75
4 Keith Hill .20 .50
5 Jean Derouillere .20 .50
6 Levy Middlebrooks .20 .50
7 Tank Collins .20 .50
8 Sam Williams .20 .50
9 Herman Kull CO .20 .50
10 Don Ford ACO .40 1.00
11 Charles Charlesworth TR .20 .50
12 Calvin Oldham .20 .50
13 Larry Smith .20 .50
14 Trent Jackson .20 .50
15 Rob Rose .40 1.00
16 Walter Bond .40 1.00
17 Jeff Majerle .40 1.00
18 Brad Baldridge .20 .50
19 Kurt Portman .20 .50
20 Cedric Jenkins .30 .75
21 John Treloar CO .20 .50
22 Mike Davis ACO .60 1.50
23 Dave Whitney ACO .20 .50
24 Wichita Falls CL .20 .50
25 Tim Dillon .20 .50
26 Kenny Miller .20 .50
27 Stevie Wise .20 .50
28 Dan Godfread .20 .50
29 Mario Donaldson .20 .50
30 Steve Berger .20 .50
31 Corey Beasley .20 .50
32 Danny Jones .20 .50
33 Lanny Van Eman CO .20 .50
34 Tony Morocco ACO .20 .50
35 Rockford CL .20 .50
36 Bobby Martin .40 1.00
37 Dwight Moody .30 .75
38 Tim Anderson .20 .50
39 A.J. Wynder .40 1.00
40 Keith Robinson .30 .75
41 Steve Scheffler .60 1.50
42 Anthony Bowie 1.00 2.50
43 Tony Harris .40 1.00
44 Barry Mitchell .30 .75
45 Tom Sheehey .20 .50
46 Dan Panaggio CO .20 .50
47 Mike Mashak ACO .20 .50
48 Quad City CL .20 .50
49 Bernard Thompson .40 1.00
50 Daryll Walker .20 .50
51 Darryl Kennedy .30 .75
52 Stevie Thompson .40 1.00
53 Kelsey Weems .30 .75
54 Steve Burtt .40 1.00
55 Junie Lewis .20 .50
56 Chris Harris .20 .50
57 Jeff Hodge .20 .50
58 Demone Webster .20 .50
59 Henry Bibby CO .50 1.25
60 Oklahoma City CL .20 .50
61 Jarvis Basnight .30 .75
62 Ed Horton .30 .75
63 Stanley Brundy .20 .50
64 Irving Thomas .30 .75
65 Nate Johnston .20 .50
66 Keith Smart .75 2.00
67 Larry Robinson .20 .50
68 Michael Anderson .20 .50
69 Eric Musselman CO .60 1.50
70 Duane Ticknor ACO .20 .50
71 Rapid City CL .20 .50
72 Bakersfield CL .20 .50
73 Lyndon Jones .30 .75
74 Warren Bradley .20 .50
75 Anthony Corbitt .20 .50
76 Tony Karasek .20 .50
77 Mark Peterson .20 .50
78 Dan Palombizio .40 1.00
79 Ricky Hall .20 .50
80 John Cooper .40 1.00
81 Carl Thomas .30 .75
82 Travis Williams .20 .50
83 Gerald Oliver CO .20 .50
84 Kevin Kacer TR .50 1.25
Terry Stotts ACO
Dave Carrington ACO
Walter Jordan ACO
85 Fort Wayne CL .20 .50
86 Ronn McMahon .20 .50
87 Sean Tyson .20 .50
88 McKinley Singleton .20 .50
89 Teo Alibegovic .20 .50
90 Joey Johnson .20 .50
91 Riley Smith .20 .50
92 Alex Austin .20 .50
93 Dennis Williams .20 .50
94 Luther Burks .20 .50
95 Bill Klucas CO .20 .50
96 Jack Miller ACO .20 .50
97 Yakima CL .20 .50
98 Roy Fisher .40 1.00
99 Reggie Isaac .20 .50
100 Reggie Jordan .40 1.00
101 Cedric Lewis .40 1.00
102 Jeff Martin .40 1.00
103 Dyron Nix .50 1.25
104 Walter Watts .20 .50
105 Gary Waites .20 .50
106 Gerald Paddio .40 1.00
107 Bruce Stewart CO .20 .50
108 Jeff Burkhamer ACO .20 .50
109 Grand Rapids CL .20 .50
110 Petur Gudmundsson .75 2.00
111 Ralph Lewis .20 .50
112 John Smith .20 .50
113 Tony Farmer .30 .75
114 Matt Roe .40 1.00
115 Darryl McDonald .60 1.50
116 Corey Gaines .40 1.00
117 Richard Rellford .30 .75
118 Ken Redfield .30 .75
119 Chuckie White .20 .50
120 Kevin McKenna CO .50 1.25
121 Clay Moser ACO .20 .50
122 Donald Royal 2.00 5.00
123 Wayne Tinkle .20 .50
124 Jim Usevitch .20 .50
125 Eric Dunn .20 .50
126 Jeffty Connelly .20 .50
127 Alan Pollard .20 .50
128 Clifford Scales .30 .75
129 Harold Wright .20 .50
130 Willie Simms .20 .50
131 Michael Holton .40 1.00
132 Terrill Hall .20 .50
133 Calvin Duncan .20 .50
Guard
Assistant CO
134 Steve Hayes CO .50 1.25
135 Yakima CL .20 .50
136 Duane Washington .50 1.25
137 Kermit Holmes .20 .50
138 Mike Goodson .20 .50
139 Byron Dinkins .40 1.00
140 Leonard Harris .30 .75
141 Louis Banks .20 .50
142 James Bradley .20 .50
143 Jeff King .20 .50
144 Ron Spivey .20 .50
145 Orlando Graham .20 .50
146 Vincent Chickerella CO .20 .50
147 Columbus CL .20 .50
148 Daron Hoges .20 .50
149 Von McDade .20 .50
150 Byron Irvin .40 1.00
151 Patrick Tompkins .20 .50
152 Brian Rahilly .20 .50
153 Kenny Battle .40 1.00
154 Jaren Jackson .40 1.00
155 Troy Truvillion .20 .50
156 Mark Davis .40 1.00
157 Vince Hamilton .25 .60
158 Don Zierden ACO and Mike McCollow ACO .20 .50
159 LaCrosse CL .20 .50
160 Derrick Chievous .40 1.00
161 Jeff Sanders .40 1.00
162 Marc Brown .20 .50
163 Johnnie Hilliad .20 .50
164 Jerry Johnson .20 .50
165 Dave Popson .40 1.00
166 Derrick Rowland .20 .50
167 Jose Slaughter .50 1.25
168 Steve Wright .20 .50
169 Charley Rosen CO 1.00 2.50
170 Lowes Moore ACO .30 .75
171 Albany CL .20 .50
172 Jasper Hooks .20 .50
173 Tracy Moore .30 .75
174 Keith Wilson .20 .50
175 Shawn McDaniel .20 .50
176 Sam Johnson .20 .50
177 Jeff Fryer .20 .50
178 A.C. Carver .20 .50
179 Jawann Oldham .60 1.50
180 Lefty Moore .20 .50
181 Anthony Blakley .40 1.00
182 Steve Bontranger CO .20 .50
183 Tulsa CL .20 .50
184 Cedric Hunter .30 .75
185 Ronnie Grandison .30 .75
186 Ricky Jones .40 1.00
187 Tim Legler .75 2.00
188 Chip Engelland 1.25 3.00
189 Brian Howard .40 1.00
190 Greg Wiltjer .20 .50
191 Rod Mason .20 .50
192 Roland Gray .20 .50
193 Tat Hunter .20 .50
194 Mike Thibault CO .30 .75
195 Omaha CL .20 .50
196 Chris Collier .20 .50
197 Skeeter Henry .30 .75
198 Emmitt Smith .20 .50
199 Anthony Houston .20 .50
200 Michael Cutright .30 .75
201 Michael Ansley .60 1.50
202 Eugene McDowell .20 .50
203 Eric Johnson .20 .50
204 Mo McHone CO .30 .75
205 Birmingham CL .20 .50
206 Sioux Falls CL .20 .50

1987 Pro Basketball Reading Kit

This NBA reading kit was released in 1987. The set features 40-pages (measuring 8 1/2"x14 1/4") of reading material and pictures of star NBA players. Please note that this reading kit was produced using full-color pages.

COMPLETE SET (40) 75.00 135.00
1 Ralph Sampson 1.50 4.00
Hakeem Olajuwon
2 Cheryl Miller 1.50 4.00
3 Paul Arizin 1.00 2.50
4 Walt Frazier 1.25 3.00
5 Joe Fulks 1.00 2.50
6 Manute Bol .75 2.00
7 Referees .75 2.00
8 Bob Pettit 1.25 3.00
9 Patrick Ewing 2.00 5.00
10 Bob Pettit 1.25 3.00
11 Charles Barkley 2.50 6.00
12 Maurice Stokes 1.00 2.50
13 Madison Square Garden .75 2.00
14 Artis Gilmore 1.00 2.50
15 Dr. James Naismith .75 2.00
16 George Mikan 1.25 3.00
17 ABA .75 2.00
18 Spud Webb .75 2.00
19 John Havlicek 1.25 3.00
20 Bob Cousy 2.00 5.00
21 Moses Malone 1.50 4.00
22 Eddie Gottlieb .75 2.00
23 Jerry West 2.50 6.00
24 Dave DeBusschere 1.25 3.00
25 Magic Johnson 3.00 8.00
26 Hall of Fame .75 2.00
27 Minneapolis Lakers .75 2.00
28 Kareem Abdul-Jabbar 3.00 8.00
29 Dolph Schayes 1.00 2.50
30 Elgin Baylor 1.25 3.00
31 Julius Erving 4.00 10.00
32 Jerry Krause .75 2.00
33 Wilt Chamberlain 4.00 10.00
34 Michael Jordan 6.00 15.00
35 Bill Sharman 1.00 2.50
36 Larry Bird 4.00 10.00
37 Bill Russell 3.00 8.00
38 Philadelphia 76ers .75 2.00
39 Oscar Robertson 2.50 6.00
40 Bill Walton 2.00 5.00

1993 Pro Line Live LPs

These 20 limited-print, foil-stamped standard-size cards spotlight top young NFL talent along with three top NBA draft picks. The cards were randomly inserted throughout 1993 Classic Pro Line packs on an average of four per point of purchase box. Each card front features a color player action shot that is borderless on three sides. The right side is edged by a team-colored stripe that carries the player's name in gold foil. The gold-foil limited print seal, which carries the words "One of 40,000," appears at the lower right. In its top half, the back carries another player action shot, followed below by career highlights in a team-colored area at the bottom. The cards are numbered on the back with an "LP" prefix.

COMPLETE SET (20) 6.00 15.00
LP1 Chris Webber .75 2.00
(Dunking football)
LP2 Shaquille O'Neal 1.50 4.00
(Wearing street clothes)
LP3 Jamal Mashburn .10 .30
(Wearing ProLine apparel)

1994 Pro Mags Promos

Produced by Chris Martin Enterprises, Inc., this set 3-card promotional set consists of collectible magnets, each measuring 2 1/8" by 3 3/8". The fronts feature a color player cutout superposed on a gray-streaked background. The player's first name is printed at one of the lower corners. The team logo rounds out the front.

COMPLETE SET (3) 4.00 10.00
1 Shaquille O'Neal UER 2.00 5.00
name spelled O'Neil
2 Grant Hill 1.50 4.00
3 Jason Kidd 2.00 5.00

1994 Pro Mags

Produced by Chris Martin Enterprises, Inc., this set consists of 135 collectible magnets, each measuring 2 1/8" by 3 3/8". The magnets were sold five to a blister pack. A checklist card (printed on glossy paper) and a free team magnet were included in each blister pack. The fronts feature a color player cutout superposed on a gray-streaked background. The player's first name is printed at one of the lower corners, with his last name printed vertically in team color-coded shadow lettering. The team logo rounds out the front. The cards are grouped alphabetically within teams and checklisted below alphabetically according to teams.

COMPLETE SET (135) 40.00 100.00
1 Stacey Augmon .30 .75
2 Mookie Blaylock .30 .75
3 Doug Edwards .25 .60
4 Adam Keefe .25 .60
5 Danny Manning .40 1.00
6 Dee Brown .30 .75
7 Sherman Douglas .25 .60
8 Rick Fox .40 1.00
9 Xavier McDaniel .40 1.00
10 Robert Parish .75 2.00
11 Muggsy Bogues .60 1.50
12 Dell Curry .25 .60
13 Hersey Hawkins .40 1.00
14 Larry Johnson .50 1.25
15 Alonzo Mourning 1.25 3.00
16 B.J. Armstrong .40 1.00
17 Horace Grant .60 1.50
18 Toni Kukoc 1.25 3.00
19 John Paxson .60 1.50
20 Scottie Pippen 2.00 5.00
21 Brad Daugherty .30 .75
22 John Williams .25 .60
23 Chris Mills .40 1.00
24 Larry Nance .50 1.25
25 Gerald Wilkins .40 1.00
26 Doug Smith .25 .60
27 Jim Jackson .75 2.00
28 Popeye Jones .25 .60
29 Jamal Mashburn 1.00 2.50
30 Randy White .25 .60
31 Mahmoud Abdul-Rauf .25 .60
32 LaPhonso Ellis .40 1.00
33 Dikembe Mutombo 1.00 2.50
34 Reggie Williams .25 .60
35 Rodney Rogers .40 1.00
36 Joe Dumars .75 2.00
37 Sean Elliott .75 2.00
38 Allan Houston 1.25 3.00
39 Lindsey Hunter .40 1.00
40 Terry Mills .25 .60
41 Tim Hardaway .60 1.50
42 Chris Mullin .75 2.00
43 Billy Owens .30 .75
44 Latrell Sprewell 1.25 3.00
45 Chris Webber 2.50 6.00
46 Robert Horry .60 1.50
47 Vernon Maxwell .25 .60
48 Hakeem Olajuwon 1.25 3.00
49 Kenny Smith .40 1.00
50 Otis Thorpe .30 .75
51 Dale Davis .30 .75
52 Reggie Miller 1.25 3.00
53 Pooh Richardson .25 .60
54 Rik Smits .30 .75
55 LaSalle Thompson .25 .60
56 Dominique Wilkins 1.25 3.00
57 Ron Harper .60 1.50
58 Mark Jackson .60 1.50
59 Stanley Roberts .25 .60
60 Loy Vaught .30 .75
61 Sam Bowie .40 1.00
62 Vlade Divac .40 1.00
63 George Lynch .30 .75
64 Anthony Peeler .25 .60
65 James Worthy .75 2.00
66 Harold Miner .30 .75
67 Glen Rice .50 1.25
68 Rony Seikaly .30 .75
69 Brian Shaw .40 1.00
70 Steve Smith .50 1.25
71 Vin Baker .40 1.00
72 Theodore Edwards .25 .60
73 Todd Day .25 .60
74 Eric Murdock .25 .60
75 Jon Barry .30 .75
76 Thurl Bailey .30 .75
77 Christian Laettner .60 1.50
78 Chuck Person .30 .75
79 Doug West .25 .60
80 Micheal Williams .25 .60
81 Derrick Coleman .30 .75
82 Rick Mahorn .25 .60
83 Johnny Newman .25 .60
84 Kenny Anderson .30 .75
85 Rex Walters .30 .75
86 Greg Anthony .30 .75
87 Rolando Blackman .60 1.50
88 Patrick Ewing 1.00 2.50
89 Charles Oakley .25 .60
90 John Starks .40 1.00
91 Nick Anderson .30 .75
92 Anfernee Hardaway 2.00 5.00
93 Donald Royal .25 .60
94 Dennis Scott .25 .60
95 Scott Skiles .40 1.00
96 Dana Barros .25 .60
97 Shawn Bradley .30 .75
98 Johnny Dawkins .25 .60
99 Tim Perry .25 .60
100 Clarence Weatherspoon .25 .60
101 Charles Barkley 1.50 4.00
102 Cedric Ceballos .25 .60
103 Malcolm Mackey .25 .60
104 Dan Majerle .60 1.50
105 Danny Ainge .60 1.50
106 Clyde Drexler 1.25 3.00
107 Jerome Kersey .30 .75
108 Rod Strickland .30 .75
109 Buck Williams .40 1.00
110 Clifford Robinson .40 1.00
111 Mitch Richmond 1.00 2.50
112 Lionel Simmons .25 .60
113 Wayman Tisdale .30 .75
114 Walt Williams .25 .60
115 Spud Webb .50 1.25
116 Dale Ellis .30 .75
117 J.R. Reid .25 .60
118 David Robinson 1.25 3.00
119 Dennis Rodman 1.50 4.00
120 Vinny Del Negro .30 .75
121 Kendall Gill .40 1.00
122 Ervin Johnson .25 .60
123 Shawn Kemp .75 2.00
124 Gary Payton 1.25 3.00
125 Sam Perkins .50 1.25
126 Karl Malone 2.00 5.00
127 Tyrone Corbin .25 .60
128 Jeff Hornacek .50 1.25
129 Felton Spencer .25 .60
130 John Stockton 2.00 5.00
131 Michael Adams .25 .60
132 Calbert Cheaney .30 .75
133 Tom Gugliotta .30 .75
134 Don MacLean .25 .60
135 Pervis Ellison .25 .60

1994-95 Pro Mags Rookie Showcase

Produced by Chris Martin Enterprises, Inc., this set of 12 magnets was sold in a cello-wrapped and individually-numbered cardboard sleeve. The sleeve carries a checklist on its back panel and unfolds to reveal the magnets. The magnets measure 2 1/8" by 3 3/8" and have rounded corners. Inside black borders, the fronts display two color player photos, one superposed on the other. The words "Rookie Showcase" are printed above, while the player's name is stamped in gold foil below. The magnets are numbered in the upper left corner.

COMPLETE SET (12) 10.00 25.00
1 Tony Dumas .60 1.50
2 Brian Grant 1.00 2.50
3 Juwan Howard 1.00 2.50
4 Donyell Marshall .60 1.50
5 Eric Mobley .60 1.50
6 Eric Montross .60 1.50
7 Carlos Rogers .60 1.50
8 Jalen Rose 1.50 4.00
9 Charlie Ward .60 1.50
10 Grant Hill 3.00 8.00
11 Glenn Robinson 1.25 3.00
12 Jason Kidd 3.00 8.00

1995 Pro Mags

Produced by Chris Martin Enterprises, this 145-magnet set measures approximately 2 1/4" by 3 1/2 These magnets have rounded corners and were sold packs of five. Each pack included a checklist, printed as a card rather than a magnet. The fronts feature co action player photos with the player's name printed vertically in gold foil along one side. The NBA and team logos are at the bottom. The magnets are checklisted alphabetically according to teams.

COMPLETE SET (145) 60.00 150.
1 Stacey Augmon .75 2.
2 Mookie Blaylock .60 1.
3 Ken Norman .60 1.
4 Steve Smith .75 2.
5 Grant Long .60 1.
6 Eric Williams .60 1.
7 Eric Montross .60 1.
8 Sherman Douglas .60 1.
9 Dee Brown .60 1.
10 Dino Radja .75 2.
11 Larry Johnson 1.00 2.
12 Alonzo Mourning 1.25 3.
13 Muggsy Bogues .75 2.
14 Scott Burrell .60 1.
15 Kendall Gill .60 1.
16 Dennis Rodman 2.00 5.
17 Scottie Pippen 1.50 4.
18 Ron Harper .75 2.
19 Toni Kukoc 1.00 2.
20 Dickey Simpkins .60 1.
21 Danny Ferry .60 1.
22 Tyrone Hill .60 1.
23 Michael Cage .60 1.
24 Chris Mills .60 1.
25 Terrell Brandon .60 1.
26 Jason Kidd 1.50 4.
27 Jamal Mashburn 1.00 2.
28 Tony Dumas .60 1.
29 Roy Tarpley .60 1.
30 Jim Jackson .60 1.
31 Dikembe Mutombo 1.00 2.
32 Jalen Rose 1.25 3.
33 Robert Pack .60 1.
34 Antonio McDyess 1.50 4.
35 Reggie Williams .60 1.
36 Grant Hill 1.50 4.
37 Joe Dumars 1.00 2.
38 Lindsey Hunter .60 1.
39 Allan Houston .75 2.
40 Terry Mills .60 1.
41 Tim Hardaway 1.00 2.
42 Chris Mullin 1.00 2.
43 Joe Smith 1.25 3.
44 Latrell Sprewell 1.00 2.
45 Donyell Marshall .60 1.
46 Hakeem Olajuwon 1.25 3.
47 Robert Horry .75 2.
48 Sam Cassell 1.00 2.
49 Kenny Smith .75 2.
50 Clyde Drexler 1.25 3.
51 Reggie Miller 1.25 3.
52 Mark Jackson 1.00 2.
53 Rik Smits .75 2.
54 Dale Davis .60 1.
55 Derrick McKey .60 1.
56 Loy Vaught .60 1.
57 Terry Dehere .60 1.
58 Lamond Murray .60 1.
59 Eric Piatkowski .75 2.
60 Pooh Richardson .60 1.
61 Vlade Divac 1.00 2.
62 Anthony Peeler .60 1.
63 Nick Van Exel 1.00 2.
64 Cedric Ceballos .60 1.
65 Eddie Jones 1.25 3.
66 Sasha Danilovic .60 1.
67 Glen Rice 1.00 2.
68 Khalid Reeves .60 1.
69 Billy Owens .60 1.
70 Kevin Willis .60 1.
71 Glenn Robinson 1.00 2.
72 Vin Baker .75 2.
73 Todd Day .60 1.
74 Eric Mobley .60 1.
75 Jon Barry .60 1.
76 Isaiah Rider 1.00 2.
77 Christian Laettner .75 2.
78 Kevin Garnett 5.00 12.
79 Doug West .60 1.
80 Sean Rooks .60 1.
81 Derrick Coleman .75 2.
82 Rick Mahorn .60 1.
83 Rex Walters .60 1.
84 Kenny Anderson .75 2.
85 Ed O'Bannon .60 1.
86 Patrick Ewing 1.25 3
87 John Starks .75 2.
88 Charles Oakley .75 2
89 Anthony Mason .60 1.
90 Derek Harper .75 2.
91 Anfernee Hardaway 1.50 4
92 Brian Shaw .60 1.
93 Shaquille O'Neal 2.50 6.
94 Brooks Thompson .60 1.
95 Horace Grant .75 2.
96 Tim Perry .60 1.
97 Sharone Wright .60 1
98 Jerry Stackhouse 2.00 5.
99 Clarence Weatherspoon .60 1
100 Vernon Maxwell .60 1
101 Charles Barkley 1.50 4
102 Danny Manning .75 2
103 Michael Finley 2.00 5
104 Kevin Johnson 1.00 2
105 Wayman Tisdale .60 1.
106 Randolph Childress .60 1.
107 Gary Trent .60 1.
108 James Robinson .60 1.
109 Buck Williams .60 1
110 Clifford Robinson .60 1
111 Corliss Williamson .60 1
112 Bobby Hurley 1.00 2
113 Brian Grant .75 2
114 Mitch Richmond 1.00 2
115 Walt Williams .60 1
116 David Robinson 1.50 4
117 Will Perdue .60 1
118 Chuck Person .60 1.
119 Sean Elliott 1.00 2.
120 Vinny Del Negro .60 1.
121 Ervin Johnson .60 1
122 Shawn Kemp 1.00 2
123 Sam Perkins .60 1
124 Detlef Schrempf 1.00 2
125 Gary Payton 1.00 2
126 Karl Malone 1.25 3
127 John Stockton 1.25 3

elton Spencer	.60	1.50
eff Hornacek	.75	2.00
dam Keefe	.60	1.50
hris Webber	1.25	3.00
wan Howard	1.00	2.50
albert Cheaney	.60	1.50
asheed Wallace	2.00	5.00
heorghe Muresan	.60	1.50
d Pinckney	.60	1.50
ony Massenburg	.60	1.50
amon Stoudamire	1.50	4.00
cie Earl	.60	1.50
vin Robertson	.60	1.50
reg Anthony	.60	1.50
enoit Benjamin	.60	1.50
ntonio Harvey	.60	1.50
yron Scott	1.00	2.50
ryant Reeves	.60	1.50

995-96 Pro Mags Die Cuts

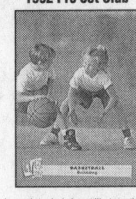

27 magnets were produced by Chris Martin rises. Each magnet measures approximately 3 y 3 1/2". The front features a color action player it with the team name, team logo and player's last on a white background cut in the shape of the ogo and player's name. The player's first name is d in small gold foil letters over his last name with the words "Die-Cut Magnets" above. ly, there are two known variations. One has "Die-agnets" written above the name and the player's ame printed larger, the other has "Die-Cut ets" in the bottom left corner in gold foil and er type on the player's first name. The magnets nnumbered and checklisted below in alphabetical

PLETE SET (27)	12.00	30.00
rles Barkley	2.00	5.00
ick Ewing	1.50	4.00
ernee Hardaway	1.50	4.00
Hardaway	1.25	3.00
nt Hill	1.50	4.00
y Johnson	1.25	3.00
gic Johnson	3.00	8.00
wn Kemp	1.25	3.00
on Kidd	1.50	4.00
rl Malone	1.50	4.00
mal Mashburn	1.25	3.00
eggie Miller	1.50	4.00
aquille O'Neal	2.00	5.00
keem Olajuwon	1.25	3.00
ottie Pippen	1.50	4.00
itch Richmond	1.25	3.00
iah Rider	.75	2.00
vid Robinson	1.50	4.00
enn Robinson	1.25	3.00
nnis Rodman	2.50	6.00
rry Stackhouse	1.50	4.00
hn Stockton	2.00	5.00
amon Stoudamire	1.25	3.00
ck Van Exel	1.25	3.00
hris Webber	1.50	4.00

995 Pro Mags Lost In Space

uced by Chris Martin Enterprises, this 6-magnet easures approximately 2 1/4" by 3 1/2". These ets have rounded corners and were randomly ded with the regular packs. The fronts feature action player photos against a gold foil round with the player's name printed vertically in oil along one side. The NBA and team logos are bottom

PLETE SET (6)	8.00	20.00
Anfernee Hardaway	3.00	8.00
Antonio McDyess	2.50	6.00
saiah Rider	2.00	5.00
Ed O'Bannon	1.00	2.50
Latrell Sprewell	2.00	5.00
Robert Pack	1.25	3.00

95 Pro Mags USA Basketball

uced by Chris Martin Enterprises, this 10-magnet atures the first ten players chosen for the Dream . The magnets measure approximately 2 1/4" by 3 have rounded corners and were sold in packs of The fronts feature a color action player cut-out a red, white, and blue screened background with ords "USA Basketball". Both the player's name ng vertically along the side and a facsimile raph across the bottom are printed in gold foil. ut magnets of each player were also produced, the same action photos as in the regular ets. These die cuts are valued at 2X the values below.

PLETE SET (10)	8.00	20.00
keem Olajuwon	1.25	3.00
nn Robinson	1.00	2.50
l Malone	1.25	3.00
aquille O'Neal	2.50	6.00
ggie Miller	1.25	3.00
vid Robinson	1.50	4.00
n Stockton	1.25	3.00
ernee Hardaway	1.50	4.00
ttie Pippen	1.50	4.00
ant Hill	1.50	4.00

97-98 Pro Mags Heroes of the Locker Room

20-card set was released by Crown Pro to various s across the U.S.. These magnets are not bered and listed below in alphabetical order. Since was designed to be a 20 card set, obviously this incomplete so all additions are appreciated.

PLETE SET	15.00	30.00
be Bryant	6.00	15.00
2 Tim Duncan	4.00	10.00
3 Grant Hill	2.00	5.00
4 Kevin Garnett	2.50	6.00
5 Karl Malone	1.50	4.00
6 Keith Van Horn	1.25	3.00

1992 Pro Set Club

This nine-card standard-size set illustrates the fundamentals of playing basketball. On the fronts, the color action shots of youngsters illustrate the fundamental aspect of the game featured on the card. A special Pro Set Club logo and a lavender bar cut across the bottom of the picture. Within aqua borders, the horizontal backs have an extended caption as well as a question-and-answer trivia feature. The cards are numbered on the back.

COMPLETE SET (9)	2.00	5.00
COMMON CARD (1-9)	.15	.40
9 Basketball Pro Player (David Robinson)	1.00	2.50

1991-92 Pro Set Platinum

The 1991-92 Pro Set Platinum hockey set was released in two series of 150 standard-size cards. The front design features full-bleed glossy color action player photos, with the Pro Set Platinum icon superimposed at the lower right corner. Player names do not appear on the front.

COMPLETE SET (300)	3.00	8.00
COMP.SERIES 1 (150)	1.50	4.00
COMP.SERIES 2 (150)	1.50	4.00
291 Marv Albert CAP	.01	.05

1991 Pro Set Pro Files

These cards measure the standard size. The fronts have full-bleed color photos, with facsimile autographs inscribed across the bottom of the pictures. Reportedly only 150 of each were produced and approximately 100 of each were handed out as part of a contest on the Pro Files TV show. Each week viewers were invited to send in their names and addresses to a Pro Set post office box. All subjects in the set made appearances on the TV show. The show was hosted by Craig James and Tim Brant and was aired on Saturday nights in Dallas and sponsored by Pro Set. The cards were subtitled "Signature Series". The cards are unnumbered and are listed in alphabetical order by subject in the checklist below. All of the cards were facsimile autographed except for Anne Smith who signed all of her cards personally.

COMPLETE SET (13)	120.00	300.00
3 James Donaldson BK holding saxophone)	4.00	10.00
6 Larry Johnson BK	8.00	20.00
13 Herb Williams BK	4.00	10.00

1991-92 Pro Set Prototypes

These standard-size cards were samples produced by Pro Set with the hopes of obtaining an NBA license. The fronts feature full-bleed color action photos, with the player's name and team name printed in two team color-coded bars that overlay the bottom of the picture. These bars intersect a circle displaying the team logo at the lower right corner. The horizontal backs carry biography, statistical (college and pro) information, and career highlights on the left portion, with a blank slot for a player photo on the right portion. The information is "dummy"; for example, Jordan's card back carries some player information on Glen Rice. The words "Prototype For Review Only" are printed on a turquoise triangle at the upper right corner. The cards are numbered "000" on the back and checklisted below in alphabetical order.

1 Tom Chambers	40.00	80.00
2 Patrick Ewing	75.00	200.00
3 Magic Johnson	100.00	250.00
4 Michael Jordan	300.00	600.00
5 Karl Malone	80.00	200.00

1996 Pro Stamps

Produced by Chris Martin Enterprises, this 12-sheet set of stamps features NBA Players against a stamp background. Each sheet contains 12 stamps. The backs of the sheets contain a checklist by team and an offer to "Practice With The Pros". The sheets are numbered in the upper left of the front. The stamps are priced in sheet form. A Pro Stamp Collector Album was also available in special retail boxes. It is priced at the bottom and is not considered part of the set.

COMPLETE SET (12)	12.50	30.00
1 Brooks Thompson	2.00	5.00
Larry Johnson		
Robert Pack		
Mitch Richmond		
Stacey Augmon		
Terry Dehere		
Charles Barkley		
Bryant Reeves		
Derek Harper		
Corliss Williamson		
Rex Walters		
Tyrone Hill		
2 Horace Grant	1.50	4.00
Derrick McKey		
Antonio McDyess		
Brian Grant		
Mookie Blaylock		
Loy Vaught		
Gary Payton		
Benoit Benjamin		
Anthony Mason		
Joe Smith		
Rick Mahorn		
Randolph Childress		
3 Ervin Johnson	1.50	4.00
Dale Davis		
Reggie Williams		
Bobby Hurley		
Ken Norman		
Clifford Robinson		
Detlef Schrempf		
Antonio Harvey		
Charles Oakley		
Latrell Sprewell		
Derrick Coleman		
Gary Trent		
4 Shawn Kemp	1.50	4.00
Rik Smits		
Patrick Ewing		
Corliss Williamson		
Steve Smith		
Buck Williams		
Sam Perkins		
Greg Anthony		
John Starks		
Rony Seiklay		
Grant Long		
James Robinson		
5 Hakeem Olajuwon	2.50	6.00
Cedric Ceballos		
Jason Kidd		
Glen Rice		
Glenn Robinson		
Alvin Robertson		
Toni Kukoc		
David Robinson		
Calbert Cheaney		
Grant Hill		
Isaiah Rider		
Danny Ferry		
6 Robert Horry	1.50	4.00
Nick Van Exel		
Jamal Mashburn		
Sasha Danilovic		
Vin Baker		
Ed Pinckney		
Ron Harper		
Will Perdue		
Juwan Howard		
Joe Dumars		
Dino Radja		
Sean Rooks		
7 Sam Cassell	2.00	5.00
Anthony Peeler		
Tony Dumas		
Charles Barkley		
Khalid Reeves		
Damon Stoudamire		
Scottie Pippen		
Chuck Person		
Chris Webber		
Lindsey Hunter		
Dee Brown		
Doug West		
8 Kenny Smith	2.00	5.00
Vlade Divac		
Roy Tarpley		
Anfernee Hardaway		
Billy Owens		
Tony Massenburg		
Dennis Rodman		
Sean Elliott		
Adam Keefe		
Rasheed Wallace		
Sherman Douglas		
Kevin Garnett		
9 Clyde Drexler	2.00	5.00
Kendall Gill		
Eddie Jones		
Jerry Stackhouse		
Kevin Willis		
Acie Earl		
Wayman Tisdale		
Dickey Simpkins		
Jeff Hornacek		
Gheorghe Muresan		
Eric Montross		
Christian Laettner		
10 Anfernee Hardaway	2.00	5.00
Scott Burrell		
Jim Jackson		
Sharone Wright		
Todd Day		
Pooh Richardson		
Kevin Johnson		
Vinny Del Negro		
Felton Spencer		
Allan Houston		
Eric Williams		
Tyrone Hill		
11 Brian Shaw	2.00	5.00
Muggsy Bogues		
Dikembe Mutombo		
Tim Perry		
Hakeem Olajuwon		
Eric Piatkowski		
Michael Finley		
Reggie Miller		
John Stockton		
Terry Mills		
Ed O'Bannon		
Michael Cage		
12 Dennis Scott	2.00	5.00
Alonzo Mourning		
Jalen Rose		
Walt Williams		
Eric Murdock		
Lamond Murray		
Danny Manning		
Mark Jackson		
Karl Malone		
Tim Hardaway		
Kenny Anderson		
Chris Mills		
NNO Collector's Album	1.25	3.00

1991 Pro Stars Posters

These three posters were folded, cello wrapped, and inserted in Pro Stars cereal boxes. Through an offer on the side panel of the box, the collector could receive another poster by sending in three Pro Stars UPC symbols and 1.00 for postage and handling. In the cello packs, the posters measure approximately 4 1/2" by 4"; they unfold to a narrow poster that measures approximately 4 1/2" by 24". On a background of blue, purple, and bright yellow stars, a cartoon drawing portrays the athlete in an action pose. At the bottom of each poster appears a player profile in English and French. The backsides of all three posters combine to form a composite poster featuring all three players. The posters are unnumbered and listed below alphabetically.

COMPLETE SET (3)	4.00	10.00
2 Michael Jordan	2.00	5.00

1993-94 Quad City Thunder CBA

Released by the Quad City Thunder, this 13-card set features the 1993-94 CBA Champions on a card stock that has blue and red borders.

COMPLETE SET (13)	1.25	3.00
1 Mike Bell	.15	.40
2 Gary Collier	.15	.40
3 Tate George	.20	.50
4 Bill Jones	.15	.40
5 Randolph Keys	.20	.50
6 Richard Manning	.15	.40
7 Kevin Pritchard	.20	.50
8 LaBradford Smith	.15	.40
9 Maurice Stokes	.30	.75
10 Barry Sumpter	.15	.40
11 Shon Tarver	.15	.40
12 Thunder Coaches	.15	.40
13 Team Picture	.15	.40

1979-80 Quaker Iron-Ons

This 10-card set was sponsored by the Quaker Company and was offically licensed by the NBA. Each iron-on measures 4 3/8" by 6 1/8". Card fronts contain a head shot of the player with directions for the iron-on. The backs are blank.

COMPLETE SET (9)	125.00	250.00
1 Kareem Abdul-Jabbar	20.00	40.00
2 Rick Barry	10.00	25.00
3 Julius Erving	25.00	50.00
4 George Gervin	15.00	40.00
5 Elvin Hayes	10.00	20.00
6 Maurice Lucas	5.00	12.00
7 Pete Maravich	45.00	90.00
8 David Thompson	10.00	20.00
9 Paul Westphal	6.00	12.00

1987 Quaker Sports Illustrated Mini Posters

These 7" x 11" mini posters were inserted in boxes of Quaker Chewy Granola Bars. The front contains a full-color player action shot, and says "A Sports Illustrated Poster" in the bottom right corner. The back has an offer to send in four UPC seals in exchange for one of 192 2' x 3' posters listed on the back. The player list is made of mostly baseball, basketball and football but includes ten other categories including surfing, U.S. ski team, Golf and racquetball to name a few. A complete checklist of mini posters is still somewhat questionable. This list includes only the basketball posters known to exist. Any further information that expands on this checklist would be appreciated. The posters are unnumbered and listed below in alphabetical order.

COMPLETE SET (7)	60.00	150.00
1 Larry Bird	12.50	30.00
2 Julius Erving	6.00	15.00
3 Magic Johnson	10.00	25.00
4 Michael Jordan	25.00	60.00
5 Hakeem Olajuwon	8.00	20.00
6 Spud Webb	4.00	10.00
7 Dominique Wilkins	5.00	12.00

1954 Quaker Sports Oddities

This 27-card set features strange moments in sports and was issued as an insert inside Quaker Puffed Rice cereal boxes. Fronts of the cards are drawings depicting the person or the event. In a stripe at the top of the card face appear the words "Sports Oddities." Two colorful drawings fill the remaining space: the left half is a portrait, while the right half is action-oriented. A variety of sports are included. The cards measure approximately 2 1/4" by 3 1/2" and have rounded corners. The last line on the back of each card declares, "It's Odd but True." A person could also buy the complete set for fifteen cents and two box tops from Quaker Puffed Wheat or Quaker Rice. If a collector did send in their material to Quaker Oats the set came back in a specially marked box with the cards in cellophane wrapping. Sets in original wrapping are valued at 1.25x to 1.5X the high column listings in our checklist.

COMPLETE SET (27)	125.00	250.00
5 Harold(Bunny) Levitt/(Free Throws)	15.00	30.00
12 Dartmouth College/ University of Utah/(1944 NCAA Basketball)	7.50	15.00
23 Harlem Globetrotters	20.00	40.00
24 Everett Dean/(Indiana basketball)	12.50	25.00

1961-64 Rawlings

These photos were released during the 1960's by Rawlings to promote their products. Please note that these photos were done in black and white, and have blank backs.

COMPLETE SET (7)	125.00	250.00
1 Richie Guerin	10.00	25.00
2 Cliff Hagan	17.50	35.00
3 John Havlicek	40.00	70.00
4 Gus Johnson	10.00	25.00
5 Bob Pettit	40.00	70.00
6 Frank Ramsey	10.00	25.00
7 Len Wilkens	25.00	60.00

1995 Real Action Pop-Ups

COMPLETE SET (7)	2.50	6.00
4 Pooh Richardson	.40	1.00

1992-93 Reebok Shawn Kemp

Sponsored by Reebok and Olympic Sports, this 7-card set spotlights Shawn Kemp. The first three cards of the set were distributed individually at shoe stores in the Seattle area. The last four cards were available only on a perforated strip; after separation, the cards measure the standard size. The first three cards are much more difficult to obtain than the four-card strip. The fronts feature color action player photos framed by green borders. The player's name is printed vertically in yellow block lettering in the left border. In green and blue print on white, the backs present biography, statistics and sponsor logos. The cards are numbered "X of 7."

COMPLETE SET (7)	15.00	30.00
COMMON CARD (1-3)	3.00	8.00
COMMON CARD (4-7)	1.25	3.00

1998 Reebok Rebecca Lobo Postcard

This postcard features WNBA superstar Rebecca Lobo. The card was distributed by "Go Card" to participating Tower Records stores. The photo is of Rebecca Lobo holding up a Reebok shoe.

1 Rebecca Lobo	1.25	3.00

2005-06 Reflections

Released in late October, this 150-card set features veterans on cards 1-100 and rookies sequentially numbered to 1499 on cards 101-150. All cards are printed on holofoil board and players are set against a background that showcases the featured player's team name. Reflections was packaged in 12-pack boxes where packs contained four cards and carried a suggested retail price of $9.99.

COMP.SET w/o RC's (100)	20.00	50.00
UNPRICED BLACK PRINT RUN ONE SET		
UNPRICED GOLD PRINT RUN 5 SETS		
1 Al Harrington	.50	1.25
2 Josh Smith	.60	1.50
3 Josh Childress	.50	1.25
4 Joe Johnson	.60	1.50
5 Paul Pierce	.75	2.00
6 Antoine Walker	.50	1.25
7 Gary Payton	.60	1.50
8 Al Jefferson	.60	1.50
9 Emeka Okafor	.60	1.50
10 Primoz Brezec	.40	1.00
11 Gerald Wallace	.60	1.50
12 Michael Jordan	5.00	12.00
13 Ben Gordon	.60	1.50
14 Luol Deng	.60	1.50
15 Kirk Hinrich	.60	1.50
16 LeBron James	3.00	8.00
17 Dajuan Wagner	.40	1.00
18 Drew Gooden	.50	1.25
19 Larry Hughes	.50	1.25
20 Dirk Nowitzki	1.00	2.50
21 Jason Terry	.50	1.25
22 Michael Finley	.60	1.50
23 Jerry Stackhouse	.50	1.25
24 Andre Miller	.50	1.25
25 Carmelo Anthony	1.25	3.00
26 Kenyon Martin	.60	1.50
27 Earl Boykins	.40	1.00
28 Rasheed Wallace	.60	1.50
29 Ben Wallace	.60	1.50
30 Richard Hamilton	.50	1.25
31 Chauncey Billups	.60	1.50
32 Baron Davis	.60	1.50
33 Derek Fisher	.50	1.25
34 Jason Richardson	.60	1.50
35 Tracy McGrady	.75	2.00
36 Yao Ming	.75	2.00
37 Juwan Howard	.50	1.25
38 Jermaine O'Neal	.60	1.50
39 Ron Artest	.60	1.50
40 Jamaal Tinsley	.40	1.00
41 Corey Maggette	.50	1.25
42 Elton Brand	.60	1.50
43 Shaun Livingston	.40	1.00
44 Kobe Bryant	3.00	8.00
45 Brian Cook	.40	1.00
46 Lamar Odom	.60	1.50
47 Mike Miller	.60	1.50
48 Pau Gasol	.60	1.50
49 Shane Battier	.50	1.25
50 Shaquille O'Neal	1.25	3.00
51 Dwyane Wade	1.50	4.00
52 Udonis Haslem	.50	1.25
53 Joe Smith	.50	1.25
54 Michael Redd	.60	1.50
55 Desmond Mason	.40	1.00
56 Kevin Garnett	1.25	3.00
57 Wally Szczerbiak	.50	1.25
58 Sam Cassell	.60	1.50
59 Vince Carter	1.00	2.50
60 Jason Kidd	1.00	2.50
61 Richard Jefferson	.60	1.50
62 Jamaal Magloire	.40	1.00
63 J.R. Smith	.60	1.50
64 Bostjan Nachbar	.40	1.00
65 Allan Houston	.40	1.00
66 Stephon Marbury	.50	1.25
67 Jamal Crawford	.50	1.25
68 Dwight Howard	1.25	3.00
69 Grant Hill	.75	2.00
70 Jameer Nelson	.50	1.25
71 Steve Francis	.60	1.50
72 Allen Iverson	1.00	2.50
73 Andre Iguodala	.60	1.50
74 Chris Webber	.60	1.50
75 Samuel Dalembert	.40	1.00
76 Amare Stoudemire	.60	1.50
77 Steve Nash	.75	2.00
78 Quentin Richardson	.50	1.25
79 Shawn Marion	.60	1.50
80 Damon Stoudamire	.50	1.25
81 Zach Randolph	.50	1.25
82 Sebastian Telfair	.50	1.25
83 Peja Stojakovic	.60	1.50
84 Mike Bibby	.60	1.50
85 Cuttino Mobley	.50	1.25
86 Manu Ginobili	.60	1.50
87 Tim Duncan	1.00	2.50
88 Tony Parker	.60	1.50
89 Ray Allen	.60	1.50
90 Rashard Lewis	.60	1.50
91 Luke Ridnour	.50	1.25
92 Ronald Murray	.40	1.00
93 Chris Bosh	.60	1.50
94 Morris Peterson	.40	1.00
95 Rafael Araujo	.40	1.00
96 Andrei Kirilenko	.50	1.25
97 Raul Lopez	.40	1.00
98 Carlos Boozer	.60	1.50
99 Antawn Jamison	.60	1.50
100 Gilbert Arenas	.60	1.50
101 Travis Diener RC	1.50	4.00
102 Julius Hodge RC	1.50	4.00
103 David Lee RC	2.50	6.00
104 Sarunas Jasikevicius RC	1.50	4.00
105 Jason Maxiell RC	1.50	4.00
106 Luther Head RC	1.50	4.00
107 Amir Johnson RC	1.50	4.00
108 Linas Kleiza RC	1.50	4.00
109 Uros Slokar RC	1.50	4.00
110 Andray Blatche RC	2.00	5.00
111 Sean May RC	1.50	4.00
112 Alex Acker RC	1.50	4.00
113 Nate Robinson RC	2.00	5.00
114 Brandon Bass RC	2.00	5.00
115 Ike Diogu RC	1.50	4.00
116 Daniel Ewing RC	1.50	4.00
117 Salim Stoudamire RC	1.50	4.00
118 Dijon Thompson RC	1.50	4.00
119 Danny Granger RC	3.00	8.00
120 Chris Taft RC	1.50	4.00
121 Louis Williams RC	2.50	6.00
122 Channing Frye RC	2.00	5.00
123 Francisco Garcia RC	2.00	5.00
124 Ryan Gomes RC	1.50	4.00
125 Von Wafer RC	1.50	4.00
126 Jarrett Jack RC	1.50	4.00
127 Lawrence Roberts RC	1.50	4.00
128 Ricky Sanchez RC	1.50	4.00
129 C.J. Miles RC	2.00	5.00
130 Ersan Ilyasova RC	2.00	5.00
131 Robert Whaley RC	1.50	4.00
132 Monta Ellis RC	3.00	8.00
133 Bracey Wright RC	1.50	4.00
134 Johan Petro RC	1.50	4.00
135 Will Bynum RC	1.50	4.00
136 Andrew Bynum RC	5.00	12.00
137 Martynas Andriuskevicius RC	1.50	4.00
138 Charlie Villanueva RC	2.00	5.00
139 Antoine Wright RC	1.50	4.00
140 Joey Graham RC	1.50	4.00
141 Wayne Simien RC	1.50	4.00
142 Hakim Warrick RC	2.00	5.00
143 Gerald Green RC	2.00	5.00
144 Marvin Williams RC	2.00	5.00
145 Deron Williams RC	4.00	10.00
146 Rashad McCants RC	1.50	4.00
147 Martell Webster RC	1.50	4.00
148 Raymond Felton RC	2.50	6.00
149 Chris Paul RC	6.00	15.00
150 Andrew Bogut RC	2.50	6.00

2005-06 Reflections Blue

Serially numbered to 50 copies, this set is printed on blue foil and cards 101-150 showcase authentic player autographs.

*BLUE VETS: 1.5X TO 4X BASE HI
*BLUE RCs: 1.5X TO 4X BASE HI
NOT ALL RCs WERE PRODUCED

12 Michael Jordan	25.00	60.00
145 Deron Williams AU	25.00	60.00
149 Chris Paul AU	40.00	100.00

2005-06 Reflections Green

Limited to 25 serially numbered copies, this 140-card set parallels the base set, is printed on green foil, and cards 100-150 contain jersey swatches.

*GREEN VETS: 2.5X TO 6X BASE HI
*GREEN RCs: 1.25X TO 3X BASE HI
NOT ALL RCs WERE PRODUCED

12 Michael Jordan	50.00	120.00

2005-06 Reflections Purple

Randomly seeded in packs, this 150-card set parallels the base Reflections set on a purple foil card with cards 101-150 serially numbered to 250.

*PURPLE VETS: .6X TO 1.5X BASE HI
*PURPLE RCs: .6X TO 1.5X BASE HI

2005-06 Reflections Red

Seeded in packs randomly, this 140-card set parallels cards 1-100 with red backgrounds and sequential numbering to 100. Most of cards 100-150 are also part of the set and are also serially numbered to 100 but also contain jersey swatches.

*RED VETS: 1X TO 2.5X BASE HI

12 Michael Jordan	20.00	50.00

2005-06 Reflections Compare and Contrast Autographs

Randomly seeded in packs, this 40-card set is horizontally designed and showcases two players and their autographs, one on the front and one on the back. Each card is sequentially numbered to 30 copies.

AB Martynas Andriuskevicius Andrew Bogut	20.00	50.00
AK Andre Miller Kirk Hinrich	30.00	60.00
AT Trevor Ariza Dijon Thompson	12.50	30.00
BH Chauncey Billups Richard Hamilton	25.00	50.00
BT Andrew Bogut Chris Taft	20.00	50.00
CO Josh Childress Lamar Odom	12.50	30.00
DF Baron Davis Derek Fisher	12.50	30.00
EF Daniel Ewing Raymond Felton	12.50	30.00
FL Channing Frye David Lee	25.00	60.00
FP Raymond Felton Chris Paul	50.00	120.00
GG Danny Granger Joey Graham	20.00	40.00
GS Ben Gordon J.R. Smith	25.00	50.00
GW Gerald Green Martell Webster	12.50	30.00
IC Ike Diogu Channing Frye	25.00	60.00
IJ Andre Iguodala Richard Jefferson	25.00	50.00
JA Antawn Jamison Gilbert Arenas	12.50	30.00
JJ Richard Jefferson Antawn Jamison	12.50	30.00
JM LeBron James Tracy McGrady	150.00	300.00
LJ Michael Jordan LeBron James	600.00	1000.00
LT Shaun Livingston Sebastian Telfair	12.50	30.00
MF Rashad McCants Raymond Felton	30.00	60.00
MH Yao Ming Dwight Howard	30.00	60.00
MK Stephon Marbury Jason Kidd	30.00	60.00
MM Brad Miller Jamaal Magloire	12.50	30.00
NB Steve Nash Mike Bibby	50.00	100.00
NT Jameer Nelson Sebastian Telfair	12.50	30.00
PW Chris Paul Deron Williams	100.00	200.00
RC Michael Redd Jamal Crawford	12.50	30.00
SF Salim Stoudamire Channing Frye	25.00	60.00
SS Damon Stoudamire Salim Stoudamire	12.50	30.00
VW Charlie Villanueva Hakim Warrick	30.00	60.00
WH Deron Williams Luther Head	75.00	150.00
WM Marvin Williams Sean May	20.00	40.00
WV Marvin Williams Charlie Villanueva	30.00	60.00
WW Antoine Wright Martell Webster	12.50	30.00

2005-06 Reflections Compare and Contrast Jerseys

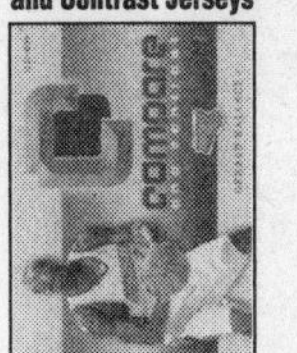

Randomly seeded in packs, this 40-card set is a horizontally designed and places a player and a jersey swatch on each side of the card and is serially numbered to 100 copies.

AJ Allan Houston Jamal Crawford	4.00	10.00
AL Ray Allen Rashard Lewis	5.00	12.00
AR Shareef Abdur-Rahim Zach Randolph	4.00	10.00
BC Caron Butler Brian Cook	4.00	10.00
BJ Kobe Bryant Michael Jordan	40.00	80.00
BM Chris Bosh Donyell Marshall	4.00	10.00
BN Earl Boykins Nene	4.00	10.00
BT Andrew Bogut Chris Taft	5.00	12.00
BW Primoz Brezec Gerald Wallace	4.00	10.00
FM Raymond Felton Rashad McCants	8.00	20.00
FR Derek Fisher Jason Richardson	4.00	10.00
GP Manu Ginobili Tony Parker	10.00	25.00
GS Francisco Garcia Salim Stoudamire	4.00	10.00
GW Gerald Green Martell Webster	4.00	10.00

HC Al Harrington 4.00 10.00
Josh Childress
HT Devin Harris 4.00 10.00
Sebastian Telfair
JJ Michael Jordan 50.00 100.00
LeBron James
LB Raul Lopez 4.00 10.00
Carlos Boozer
MC Brad Miller 4.00 10.00
Eddy Curry
MR Darius Miles 4.00 10.00
Zach Randolph
MS Mike Miller 4.00 10.00
Stromile Swift
OA Jermaine O'Neal 4.00 10.00
Ron Artest
OH Shaquille O'Neal 10.00 25.00
Udonis Haslem
PF Chris Paul 12.50 30.00
Raymond Felton
PR Morris Peterson 4.00 10.00
Jalen Rose
RA Jalen Rose 4.00 10.00
Rafael Araujo
SC Wally Szczerbiak 4.00 10.00
Sam Cassell
SF Salim Stoudamire 4.00 10.00
Channing Frye
SH Jerry Stackhouse 4.00 10.00
Devin Harris
SK Joe Smith 5.00 12.00
Toni Kukoc
SM Wayne Simien 4.00 10.00
Sean May
TJ Jamaal Tinsley 4.00 10.00
Stephen Jackson
WG Deron Williams 6.00 15.00
Francisco Garcia
WI Dajuan Wagner 4.00 10.00
Zydrunas Ilgauskas
WK Chris Webber 8.00 20.00
Kyle Korver
WM Marvin Williams 4.00 10.00
Sean May
WV Hakim Warrick 4.00 10.00
Charlie Villanueva
WW Marvin Williams 4.00 10.00
Hakim Warrick

2005-06 Reflections Compare and Contrast Quad Jerseys

Randomly seeded in packs and limited to 10 serially numbered copies, this 28-card set places two players and their jerseys on each side of the card.
UNPRICED AUTO PRINT RUN 10 SETS
ADHC Gilbert Arenas 8.00 20.00
Juan Dixon
Allan Houston
Jamal Crawford
ALRM Ray Allen 8.00 20.00
Rashard Lewis
Michael Redd
Desmond Mason
BBPW Kobe Bryant 15.00 40.00
Caron Butler
Gary Payton
Antoine Walker
BMIG Elton Brand 6.00 15.00
Corey Maggette
Zydrunas Ilgauskas
Drew Gooden
BNLB Earl Boykins 6.00 15.00
Nene
Raul Lopez
Carlos Boozer
FHMH Steve Francis 8.00 20.00
Grant Hill
Stephon Marbury
Allan Houston
FSFH Marcus Fizer 12.50 30.00
Joe Smith
Steve Francis
Grant Hill
GPBH Manu Ginobili 12.50 30.00
Tony Parker
Chauncey Billups
Richard Hamilton
GSWH Kevin Garnett 12.50 30.00
Wally Szczerbiak
Rasheed Wallace
Richard Hamilton
HCVA Kirk Hinrich 6.00 15.00
Eddy Curry
Nick Van Exel
Shareef Abdur-Rahim
HCWJ Al Harrington 6.00 15.00
Josh Childress
Antoine Walker
Al Jefferson
JASF Stephen Jackson 6.00 15.00
Ron Artest
Jerry Stackhouse
Michael Finley
JGKJ LeBron James 30.00 80.00
Drew Gooden
Jason Kidd
Richard Jefferson
JJBA Michael Jordan 100.00 200.00
LeBron James
Kobe Bryant
Carmelo Anthony
JMSM Joe Johnson 6.00 15.00
Shawn Marion
Sebastian Telfair
Darius Miles
KDPA Kyle Korver 8.00 20.00
Samuel Dalembert
Morris Peterson
Rafael Araujo
LBBC Shaun Livingston 6.00 15.00
Elton Brand
Caron Butler
Brian Cook
MFMW Sean May 10.00 25.00
Raymond Felton
Rashad McCants
Marvin Williams
MJMM Shawn Marion 8.00 20.00
Joe Johnson
Brad Miller
Cuttino Mobley
MNBW Kenyon Martin 6.00 15.00
Nene
Primoz Brezec
Gerald Wallace
PFHW Mickael Pietrus 8.00 20.00
Derek Fisher
Juwan Howard
David Wesley
RPWC Jason Richardson 12.00 30.00
Morris Peterson
Chris Webber
Jamal Crawford
TFMM Jason Terry 10.00 25.00
Michael Finley
Andre Miller
Kenyon Martin

2005-06 Reflections Compare and Contrast Octa Jerseys

Limited to 25 serially numbered copy per, this eleven-card set places eight players along with their jerseys, four per side, on each card.
UNPRICED AUTO PRINT RUN ONE SET
2 Andre Iguodala 15.00 40.00
Al Jefferson
Donta Smith
Beno Udrih
Devin Harris
Shaun Livingston
Jameer Nelson
Delonte West
3 Dwight Howard 30.00 60.00
Ben Gordon
Luol Deng
J.R. Smith
Andrew Bogut
Marvin Williams
Chris Paul
Deron Williams
4 Kobe Bryant 60.00 120.00
Lamar Odom
Caron Butler
Vlade Divac
Mike Bibby
Peja Stojakovic
Brad Miller
Cuttino Mobley
5 LeBron James 60.00 120.00
Drew Gooden
Zydrunas Ilgauskas
Dajuan Wagner
Kirk Hinrich
Luol Deng
Tyson Chandler
Eddy Curry
6 Tim Duncan 30.00 80.00
Tony Parker
Manu Ginobili
Beno Udrih
Dirk Nowitzki
Michael Finley
Jason Terry
Jerry Stackhouse
7 Ray Allen 25.00 60.00
Rashard Lewis
Luke Ridnour
Ronald Murray
Andre Miller
Kenyon Martin
Nene
Earl Boykins
9 Gilbert Arenas 10.00 25.00
Jarvis Hayes
Antawn Jamison
Juan Dixon
Jermaine O'Neal
Ron Artest
Jamaal Tinsley
Stephen Jackson
11 Chris Bosh 25.00 60.00
Jalen Rose
Rafael Araujo
Donyell Marshall
Michael Redd
Desmond Mason
Toni Kukoc
Marcus Fizer
12 Tracy McGrady 40.00 80.00
Yao Ming
David Wesley
Juwan Howard
Pau Gasol
Shane Battier
Stromile Swift
Mike Miller

2005-06 Reflections Fabrics

Inserted in packs at the rate of one in six, this 42-card set is horizontally designed with a player photo on the left and a square swatch of jersey on the right.
*FABRIC BLUE: .6X TO 1.5X BASE HI
*FABRIC GREEN: .75X TO 2X BASE HI
*FABRIC RED: .5X TO 1.25X BASE HI
UNPRICED AUTO PRINT RUN ONE SET
UNPRICED GOLD PRINT RUN 5 SETS
AH Al Harrington 2.00 5.00
AJ Antawn Jamison 2.50 6.00
AK Andrei Kirilenko 2.00 5.00
AM Andre Miller 2.00 5.00
AR Carlos Arroyo 2.00 5.00
AS Amare Stoudemire 2.50 6.00
BD Baron Davis 2.50 6.00
BG Ben Gordon 2.50 6.00
BW Ben Wallace 2.50 6.00
CA Carmelo Anthony 5.00 12.00
CB Chauncey Billups SP 2.50 6.00
CM Corey Maggette 2.00 5.00
DH Dwight Howard 5.00 12.00
DM Desmond Mason SP 2.00 5.00
DN Dirk Nowitzki 4.00 10.00
GA Gilbert Arenas 2.50 6.00
GP Gary Payton 2.50 6.00
JC Jamal Crawford 2.00 5.00
JK Jason Kidd 4.00 10.00
JN Jameer Nelson SP 2.00 5.00
JR J.R. Smith 2.50 6.00
JS Josh Smith 2.50 6.00
KB Kobe Bryant 8.00 20.00
KG Kevin Garnett 5.00 12.00
KK Kyle Korver 2.00 5.00
LD Luol Deng 2.50 6.00
LJ LeBron James 10.00 25.00
LO Lamar Odom 2.50 6.00
MB Mike Bibby 2.50 6.00
MJ Michael Jordan SP 25.00 60.00
MR Michael Redd SP 2.50 6.00
PG Pau Gasol 2.50 6.00
PP Paul Pierce 3.00 8.00
PS Peja Stojakovic 2.50 6.00
RJ Richard Jefferson 2.50 6.00
SB Shane Battier 2.00 5.00
SM Stephon Marbury 2.00 5.00
SN Steve Nash 3.00 8.00
SO Shaquille O'Neal 5.00 12.00
TD Tim Duncan 4.00 10.00
TM Tracy McGrady 3.00 8.00
YM Yao Ming 3.00 8.00

2005-06 Reflections Fabrics Dual Swatch

Inserted in packs, this 42-card set parallels the design of the Fabrics set with two swatches of memorabilia and sequential numbering to 50.
*DUAL SWATCH: .6X TO 1.5X BASE FAB HI
*BLUE: .75X TO 2X BASE FAB HI
BLUE PRINT RUN 25 SER.#'d SETS
UNPRICED AUTO PRINT RUN ONE SET
UNPRICED GOLD PRINT RUN 5 SETS
UNPRICED GREEN PRINT RUN 10 SETS

2005-06 Reflections Fabrics Triple Swatch

Inserted in packs, this 42-card set parallels the design of the Fabrics set enhanced with three swatches of memorabilia and sequential numbering to 25.
*TRIPLE SWATCH: 1.25X TO 3X BASE FAB HI
*BLUE: 1.5X TO 4X BASE FAB HI
BLUE PRINT RUN 20 SER.#'d SETS
UNPRICED AUTO PRINT RUN ONE SET
UNPRICED GOLD PRINT RUN 5 SETS
UNPRICED GREEN PRINT RUN 10 SETS

2005-06 Reflections Signatures

Inserted in packs at the rate of one in 34, this 71-card set features a player photo along the top, a centered autograph sticker and on some cards, sequential numbering to 35. See checklist for details.
STATED ODDS 1:34
SP's/PRINT RUNS LISTED IN CHECKLIST
UNPRICED BLACK PRINT RUN ONE SET
UNPRICED GOLD PRINT RUN 5 SETS
AA Alex Acker 3.00 8.00
AH Al Harrington 3.00 8.00
AI Andre Iguodala/35 10.00 25.00
AJ Antawn Jamison SP 4.00 10.00
AM Andre Miller SP 4.00 10.00
AN Martynas Andriuskevicius 3.00 8.00
AR Carlos Arroyo 8.00 20.00
BG Ben Gordon/35 8.00 20.00
BU Beno Udrih 3.00 8.00
BW Ben Wallace/35 10.00 25.00
CA Carmelo Anthony/35 15.00 40.00
CD Chris Duhon 3.00 8.00
CK Chris Kaman SP 3.00 8.00
CM Corey Maggette SP 3.00 8.00
CW Chris Wilcox SP 3.00 8.00
DA David Harrison 3.00 8.00
DF Derek Fisher 4.00 10.00
DH Dwight Howard/35 15.00 40.00
DM Desmond Mason 3.00 8.00
DS Damon Stoudamire SP 4.00 10.00
DW Dorell Wright 3.00 8.00
FG Francisco Garcia 4.00 10.00
GP Gary Payton/35 10.00 25.00
GR Danny Granger 6.00 15.00
HW Hakim Warrick 4.00 10.00
JA Jalen Rose 4.00 10.00
JG Joey Graham 3.00 8.00
JH Josh Howard SP 3.00 8.00
JJ Jarrett Jack 3.00 8.00
JK Jason Kidd/35 12.50 30.00
JM Jamaal Magloire 3.00 8.00
JN Jameer Nelson SP 3.00 8.00
JO Amir Johnson 3.00 8.00
JP Johan Petro 3.00 8.00
JS Jerry Stackhouse SP 4.00 10.00
JU Julius Hodge 3.00 8.00
JV Jackson Vroman 3.00 8.00
KA Kareem Rush 3.00 8.00
KH Kirk Hinrich/35 10.00 25.00
KM Kevin Martin 3.00 8.00
LH Luther Head 3.00 8.00
LJ LeBron James/35 100.00 200.00
LK Linas Kleiza 3.00 8.00
LU Luke Jackson 3.00 8.00
MD Marquis Daniels SP 3.00 8.00
MJ Michael Jordan/35 300.00 500.00
MP Morris Peterson 3.00 8.00
MW Maurice Williams 3.00 8.00
NR Nate Robinson SP 8.00 20.00
PA Pavel Podkolzin 3.00 8.00
PB Primoz Brezec 3.00 8.00
PP Paul Pierce/35 10.00 25.00
PS Pape Sow 3.00 8.00
RA Rafael Araujo 3.00 8.00
RM Ronald Murray 3.00 8.00
SB Shane Battier 3.00 8.00
SM Stephon Marbury/35 10.00 25.00
SN Steve Nash/35 40.00 100.00
SS Salim Stoudamire 3.00 8.00
SV Sasha Vujacic 3.00 8.00
TA Tony Allen 3.00 8.00
TK Toni Kukoc 8.00 20.00
TM Tracy McGrady/35 15.00 40.00
TR Trevor Ariza 3.00 8.00
UH Udonis Haslem 4.00 10.00
VK Viktor Khryapa 3.00 8.00
WS Wayne Simien SP 3.00 8.00
YM Yao Ming/35 25.00 60.00

2005-06 Reflections Signatures Blue

Inserted in packs, this 95-card set parallels the Signatures set on blue foil and is enhanced with sequential numbering to either 50 or 15. See checklist for details.
*BLUE: .6X TO 1.5X BASE HI
SP/15 NOT PRICED DUE TO SCARCITY
AB Andrew Bogut/50 20.00 50.00
BY Andrew Bynum/50 25.00 60.00
CF Channing Frye/50 10.00 25.00
CP Chris Paul/50 40.00 100.00
CV Charlie Villanueva/50 8.00 20.00
GA Gilbert Arenas/50 8.00 20.00
GG Gerald Green/50 8.00 20.00
JC Josh Childress/50 5.00 12.00
JR J.R. Smith/50 6.00 15.00
JW Jason Williams/50 20.00 50.00
LO Lamar Odom/50 8.00 20.00
MA Marvin Williams/50 8.00 20.00
MB Mike Bibby/50 6.00 15.00
MC Rashad McCants/50 5.00 12.00
PG Pau Gasol/50 10.00 25.00
QR Quentin Richardson/50 5.00 12.00
RF Raymond Felton/50 15.00 40.00
RH Richard Hamilton/50 10.00 25.00
RJ Richard Jefferson/50 5.00 12.00
SL Shaun Livingston/50 5.00 12.00
WE Martell Webster/50 5.00 12.00
WI Deron Williams/50 25.00 60.00

2005-06 Reflections Signatures Green

Inserted in packs, this 95-card set parallels the Signatures set on green foil and is enhanced with sequential numbering to either 25 or 10. See checklist for details.
*GREEN: .75X TO 2X BASE HI
SP/10 NOT PRICED DUE TO SCARCITY
AB Andrew Bogut/25 25.00 60.00
BY Andrew Bynum/25 30.00 80.00
CF Channing Frye/25 12.50 30.00
CP Chris Paul/25 50.00 120.00
CV Charlie Villanueva/25 10.00 25.00
GA Gilbert Arenas/25 10.00 25.00
GG Gerald Green/25 10.00 25.00
JC Josh Childress/25 6.00 15.00
JR J.R. Smith/25 8.00 20.00
JW Jason Williams/25 25.00 60.00
LO Lamar Odom/25 10.00 25.00
MA Marvin Williams/25 10.00 25.00
MB Mike Bibby/25 8.00 20.00
MC Rashad McCants/25 6.00 15.00
PG Pau Gasol/25 12.50 30.00
QR Quentin Richardson/25 6.00 15.00
RF Raymond Felton/25 20.00 50.00
RH Richard Hamilton/25 12.50 30.00
RJ Richard Jefferson/25 6.00 15.00
SE Sean May/25 6.00 15.00
SL Shaun Livingston/25 6.00 15.00
WE Martell Webster/25 6.00 15.00
WI Deron Williams/25 30.00 80.00

2005-06 Reflections Signatures Red

Inserted in packs, this 95-card set parallels the Signatures set on red foil and is enhanced with sequential numbering to either 100 or 25. See checklist for details.
*RED: .5X TO 1.25X BASE HI
BY Andrew Bynum/100 15.00 40.00
CV Charlie Villanueva/100 6.00 15.00
GG Gerald Green/100 6.00 15.00
JC Josh Childress/100 4.00 10.00
JR J.R. Smith/100 5.00 12.00
JW Jason Williams/100 15.00 40.00
MB Mike Bibby/100 5.00 12.00
MC Rashad McCants/100 4.00 10.00
QR Quentin Richardson/100 4.00 10.00
RH Richard Hamilton/100 8.00 20.00
RJ Richard Jefferson/100 4.00 10.00
SE Sean May/100 4.00 10.00

2006-07 Reflections

Released in early September 2006, Reflections features a 149-card base set where cards 1-100 picture NBA veterans and cards 101-149 picture NBA rookies where cards 101-110 are serially numbered to 150 and cards 111-125 are serially numbered to 799 and cards 126-149 are serially numbered to 399. All cards are printed on a thick foil-board card stock.
COMP.SET w/o SP's 25.00 60.00
UNPRICED BLACK PRINT RUN ONE SET
1 Josh Childress .50 1.25
2 Joe Johnson .60 1.50
3 Marvin Williams .60 1.50
4 Dan Dickau .40 1.00
5 Paul Pierce .75 2.00
6 Wally Szczerbiak .50 1.25
7 Raymond Felton .75 2.00
8 Emeka Okafor .60 1.50
9 Kareem Rush .40 1.00
10 Gerald Wallace .60 1.50
11 Tyson Chandler .50 1.25
12 Luol Deng .60 1.50
13 Ben Gordon .60 1.50
14 Michael Jordan 5.00 12.00
15 Larry Hughes .50 1.25
16 Zydrunas Ilgauskas .50 1.25
17 LeBron James 3.00 8.00
18 Donyell Marshall .40 1.00
19 Marquis Daniels .40 1.00
20 Josh Howard .50 1.25
21 Dirk Nowitzki 1.00 2.50
22 Jason Terry .50 1.25
23 Carmelo Anthony .75 2.00
24 Earl Boykins .40 1.00
25 Marcus Camby .50 1.25
26 Kenyon Martin .60 1.50
27 Chauncey Billups .60 1.50
28 Richard Hamilton .50 1.25
29 Rasheed Wallace .60 1.50
30 Baron Davis .60 1.50
31 Ike Diogu .40 1.00
32 Mike Dunleavy .50 1.25
33 Troy Murphy .40 1.00
34 Luther Head .50 1.25
35 Tracy McGrady .75 2.00
36 Yao Ming .75 2.00
37 Jermaine O'Neal .60 1.50
38 Peja Stojakovic .60 1.50
39 Jamaal Tinsley .40 1.00
40 Chris Kaman .50 1.25
41 Sam Cassell .60 1.50
42 Shaun Livingston .40 1.00
43 Cuttino Mobley .50 1.25
44 Kobe Bryant 3.00 8.00
45 Devean George .40 1.00
46 Lamar Odom .60 1.50
47 Pau Gasol .60 1.50
48 Bobby Jackson .40 1.00
49 Mike Miller .60 1.50
50 Shaquille O'Neal 1.25 3.00
51 Dwyane Wade 1.50 4.00
52 Jason Williams .50 1.25
53 Andrew Bogut .60 1.50
54 T.J. Ford .50 1.25
55 Michael Redd .60 1.50
56 Ricky Davis .50 1.25
57 Kevin Garnett 1.25 3.00
58 Troy Hudson .40 1.00
59 Vince Carter .75 2.00
60 Jason Collins .40 1.00
61 Richard Jefferson .60 1.50
62 Jason Kidd 1.00 2.50
63 Desmond Mason .40 1.00
64 Chris Paul 1.25 3.00
65 J.R. Smith .60 1.50
66 Steve Francis .60 1.50
67 Channing Frye .50 1.25
68 Stephon Marbury .50 1.25
69 Dwight Howard 1.00 2.50
70 Darko Milicic .40 1.00
71 Jameer Nelson .50 1.25
72 Andre Iguodala .60 1.50
73 Allen Iverson .75 2.00
74 Chris Webber .60 1.50
75 Boris Diaw .50 1.25
76 Shawn Marion .60 1.50
77 Steve Nash .75 2.00
78 Amare Stoudemire .60 1.50
79 Juan Dixon .40 1.00
80 Darius Miles .40 1.00
81 Sebastian Telfair .40 1.00
82 Ron Artest .60 1.50
83 Mike Bibby .60 1.50
84 Brad Miller .60 1.50
85 Tim Duncan 1.00 2.50
86 Manu Ginobili .60 1.50
87 Robert Horry .50 1.25
88 Tony Parker .60 1.50
89 Ray Allen .60 1.50
90 Rashard Lewis .60 1.50
91 Luke Ridnour .50 1.25
92 Chris Bosh .60 1.50
93 Joey Graham .40 1.00
94 Charlie Villanueva .60 1.50
95 Carlos Boozer .60 1.50
96 Andrei Kirilenko .50 1.25
97 Deron Williams 1.00 2.50
98 Gilbert Arenas .60 1.50
99 Caron Butler .60 1.50
100 Antawn Jamison .60 1.50
101 Adam Morrison RC 3.00 8.00
102 Tyrus Thomas RC 3.00 8.00
103 Rudy Gay RC 4.00 10.00
104 Andrea Bargnani RC 4.00 10.00
105 LaMarcus Aldridge RC 6.00 15.00
106 Brandon Roy RC 6.00 15.00
107 Randy Foye RC 3.00 8.00
108 Marcus Williams RC 2.50 6.00
109 Rodney Carney RC 2.50 6.00
110 Shelden Williams RC 2.50 6.00
111 Patrick O'Bryant RC 1.50 4.00
112 Cedric Simmons RC 1.50 4.00
113 Jordan Farmar RC 1.50 4.00
114 J.J. Redick RC 2.00 5.00
115 Tarence Kinsey RC 1.50 4.00
116 Kevin Pittsnogle RC 1.50 4.00
117 Ronnie Brewer RC 2.00 5.00
118 Shawne Williams RC 1.50 4.00
119 Allan Ray RC 1.50 4.00
120 Shannon Brown RC 2.50 6.00
121 Kyle Lowry RC 2.00 5.00
122 Mardy Collins RC 1.50 4.00
123 Hilton Armstrong RC 1.50 4.00
124 Maurice Ager RC 1.50 4.00
125 Quincy Douby RC 1.50 4.00
126 Rajon Rondo RC 8.00 20.00
127 Mike Gansey RC 2.00 5.00
128 Joel Freeland RC 2.00 5.00
129 Josh Boone RC 2.00 5.00
130 Saer Sene RC 2.00 5.00
131 Denham Brown RC 2.00 5.00
132 Renaldo Balkman RC 2.00 5.00
133 Will Blalock RC 2.00 5.00
134 David Noel RC 2.00 5.00
135 Steve Novak RC 2.00 5.00
136 Solomon Jones RC 2.00 5.00
137 Dee Brown RC 2.00 5.00
138 Hassan Adams RC 2.00 5.00
139 Bobby Jones RC 2.00 5.00
140 Thabo Sefolosha RC 2.50 6.00
141 James White RC 2.00 5.00
142 Paul Davis RC 2.00 5.00
143 P.J. Tucker RC 2.00 5.00
144 Ryan Hollins RC 2.00 5.00
145 Damir Markota RC 2.00 5.00
146 Leon Powe RC 2.00 5.00
147 James Augustine RC 2.00 5.00
148 Alexander Johnson RC 2.00 5.00
149 Daniel Gibson RC 2.50 6.00

2006-07 Reflections Blue

*1-100 BLUE: 2X TO 5X BASE HI
*101-110 BLUE RC: .75X TO 2X BASE HI
*111-125 BLUE RC: 1.25X TO 3X BASE HI
*126-149 BLUE RC: 1X TO 2.5X BASE HI
BLUE PRINT RUN 49 SER.#'d SETS

2006-07 Reflections Copper

*1-100 COPPER: 1.5X TO 4X BASE HI
*101-110 COPPER RC: .5X TO 1.25X BASE HI
*111-125 COPPER RC: .75X TO 2X BASE HI
*126-149 COPPER RC: .6X TO 1.5X BASE HI
COPPER PRINT RUN 99 SER.#'d SETS

2006-07 Reflections Dual Fabric

APPROXIMATE ODDS 1:12
*GOLD FABRIC: .4X TO 1X BASE HI
GOLD PRINT RUN 100 SER.#'d SETS
*COPPER FABRIC: .5X TO 1.25X BASE HI
COPPER PRINT RUN 50 SER.#'d SETS
*PATCH BLUE: 1.25X TO 3X BASE HI
PAT.BLUE PRINT RUN 15 SER.#'d SETS
UNPRICED AUTO PATCH PRINT RUN ONE SET
AH Ray Allen 4.00 10.00
Richard Hamilton
AI Gilbert Arenas 4.00 10.00
Andre Iguodala
AN Rafael Araujo 4.00 10.00
Nene Hilario
AW Carmelo Anthony 5.00 12.00
Hakim Warrick
BC Caron Butler 4.00 10.00
Ben Gordon
BD Carlos Boozer 4.00 10.00
Luol Deng
BG Bruce Bowen 4.00 10.00
Manu Ginobili
BH Elton Brand 5.00 12.00
Dwight Howard
BM Kobe Bryant 10.00 25.00
Tracy McGrady
CB Tyson Chandler 4.00 10.00
Kwame Brown
CR Eddy Curry 4.00 10.00
Zach Randolph
DM Ricky Davis 4.00 10.00
Rashad McCants
DP Tim Duncan 6.00 15.00
Tony Parker
DR Baron Davis 4.00 10.00
Jason Richardson
DS Mike Dunleavy 4.00 10.00
Peja Stojakovic
FR Steve Francis 4.00 10.00
Nate Robinson
FV Channing Frye 4.00 10.00
Charlie Villanueva
FW Raymond Felton 5.00 12.00
Deron Williams
GC Devean George 4.00 10.00
Brian Cook
GJ Kevin Garnett 5.00 12.00
Richard Jefferson
HB Mike Bibby 4.00 10.00
Kirk Hinrich
HH Josh Howard 4.00 10.00
Devin Harris
HR Juwan Howard 4.00 10.00
Jalen Rose
JH Eddie Jones 4.00 10.00
Larry Hughes
JJ Michael Jordan 40.00 100.00
LeBron James
JW Joe Johnson 4.00 10.00
Marvin Williams
KH Jason Kidd 10.00 25.00
Grant Hill
KW Chris Webber 4.00 10.00
Kyle Korver
LF Fred Jones 4.00 10.00
Luke Jackson
LO Rashard Lewis 4.00 10.00
Emeka Okafor
MG Desmond Mason 4.00 10.00
Joey Graham
MI Dikembe Mutombo 4.00 10.00
Zydrunas Ilgauskas
MK Jeff McInnis 4.00 10.00
Nenad Krstic
MM Corey Maggette 4.00 10.00
Cuttino Mobley
MN Steve Nash 5.00
Shawn Marion
NS Steve Nash 5.00
Amare Stoudemire
NT Jameer Nelson 4.00
Sebastian Telfair
NU Bostjan Nachbar 4.00
Beno Udrih
OW Jason Williams 8.00
Shaquille O'Neal
PJ Paul Pierce 4.00
Antawn Jamison
RB Michael Redd 4.00
Andrew Bogut
SJ Wally Szczerbiak 4.00
Al Jefferson
SM Stromile Swift 4.00
Darko Milicic
TO Jamaal Tinsley 4.00
Jermaine O'Neal
WB Ben Wallace 4.00
Chris Bosh
WC Jason Williams 4.00
Sam Cassell
WK Chris Webber 4.00
Andrei Kirilenko
WN Rasheed Wallace 5.00
Dirk Nowitzki
WP Antoine Walker 4.00
Tayshaun Prince

2006-07 Reflections Mirro Image Dual Auto Jersey

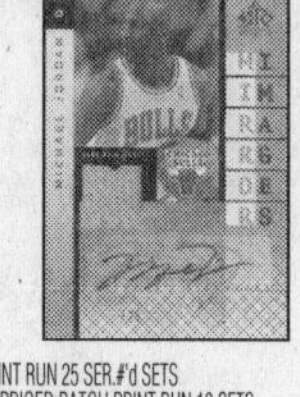

PRINT RUN 25 SER.#'d SETS
UNPRICED PATCH PRINT RUN 10 SETS
AB Ron Artest 12.50
Bruce Bowen
BD Baron Davis 12.50
Chauncey Billups
BH Dwight Howard 25.00
Andrew Bogut
BO Elton Brand 12.50
Emeka Okafor
BP Mike Bibby 50.00
Chris Paul
GB Kevin Garnett 25.00
Chris Bosh
JJ Michael Jordan 450.00
LeBron James
NK Steve Nash 60.00
Jason Kidd
TR Sebastian Telfair 12.50
Nate Robinson

2006-07 Reflections Mirro Image Dual Jersey

PRINT RUN 100 SER.#'d SETS
*PATCHES: .75X TO 2X BASE HI
PATCH PRINT RUN 50 SER.#'d SETS
AB Ron Artest 4.00
Bruce Bowen
BD Baron Davis 4.00
Chauncey Billups
BH Dwight Howard 6.00
Andrew Bogut
BO Elton Brand 4.00
Emeka Okafor
BP Mike Bibby 5.00
Chris Paul
BS Kwame Brown 4.00
Stromile Swift
CI Vince Carter 5.00
Andre Iguodala
CS Josh Childress 4.00
J.R. Smith
DB Tim Duncan 5.00
Elton Brand
DH Larry Hughes 4.00
Marquis Daniels
FM Steve Francis 4.00
Stephon Marbury
FV Channing Frye 4.00
Charlie Villanueva
GB Kevin Garnett 5.00
Chris Bosh
HB Kobe Bryant 8.00
Richard Hamilton
HD Richard Hamilton 4.00
Ricky Davis
HM Grant Hill 10.00
Tracy McGrady
JA LeBron James 20.00
Carmelo Anthony
JH Kirk Hinrich 4.00
Sarunas Jasikevicius
JJ Michael Jordan 50.00
LeBron James
JR Antawn Jamison 4.00
Jason Richardson
KM Andrei Kirilenko 4.00
Darko Milicic
MH Shawn Marion 5.00
Dwight Howard
MO Jamaal Magloire 4.00
Jermaine O'Neal
MP Andre Miller 4.00
Tony Parker
NG Dirk Nowitzki 6.00
Pau Gasol
NK Steve Nash 10.00
Jason Kidd
OM Yao Ming 10.00
Shaquille O'Neal
PR Paul Pierce 4.00
Jason Richardson
RG Michael Redd 4.00
Ben Gordon
RJ Quentin Richardson 4.00
Joe Johnson
SG Wally Szczerbiak 4.00
Manu Ginobili

mare Stoudemire 4.00 10.00
naine O'Neal
amaal Tinsley 4.00 10.00
McInnis
bastian Telfair 4.00 10.00
e Robinson
hris Webber 5.00 12.00
ar Odom

06-07 Reflections Signature Copper

PER: .75X TO 2X SILVER HI
ED PRINT RUN 10-20 SER.#'d SETS
E UNPRICED DUE TO SCARCITY

06-07 Reflections Signature Gold

D: .5X TO 1.25X SILVER HI
ED PRINT RUN 25 TO 50 SER.#'d SETS
ichael Jordan/25 500.00 800.00

06-07 Reflections Signature Silver

OXIMATE ODDS 1:12
RICED BLACK PRINT RUN ONE SET
RICED BLUE PRINT RUN 5 SETS
ndrea Bargnani 8.00 20.00
assan Adams 4.00 10.00
dre Iguodala 5.00 12.00
Jefferson 4.00 10.00
ent Barry 4.00 10.00
uce Bowen 4.00 10.00
aron Davis 5.00 12.00
bby Jackson 4.00 10.00
rad Miller 4.00 10.00
enham Brown 4.00 10.00
andon Roy 12.00 30.00
bby Simmons 4.00 10.00
armelo Anthony 15.00 40.00
hauncey Billups 6.00 15.00
hris Duhon 4.00 10.00
hris Bosh 8.00 20.00
uttino Mobley 4.00 10.00
hris Paul 20.00 50.00
edric Simmons 4.00 10.00
arquis Daniels 4.00 10.00
ee Brown 4.00 10.00
aniel Ewing 4.00 10.00
aniel Gibson 5.00 12.00
wight Howard 10.00 25.00
avid Noel 4.00 10.00
ton Brand 5.00 12.00
meka Okafor 4.00 10.00
aymond Felton 6.00 15.00
ilton Armstrong 4.00 10.00
akeem Olajuwon 10.00 25.00
e Diogu 4.00 10.00
sh Boone 4.00 10.00
e Johnson 5.00 12.00
bby Jones 4.00 10.00
rrett Jack 4.00 10.00
ames White 4.00 10.00
evin Garnett 20.00 50.00
yle Lowry 5.00 12.00
Marcus Aldridge 12.00 30.00
Bron James 100.00 200.00
amar Odom 4.00 10.00
uke Ridnour 4.00 10.00
Maurice Ager 4.00 10.00
Mike Bibby 6.00 15.00
Mardy Collins 4.00 10.00
Michael Redd 5.00 12.00
Marcus Williams 4.00 10.00
teve Novak 4.00 10.00
ate Robinson 5.00 12.00
aul Davis 4.00 10.00
atrick O'Bryant 4.00 10.00
aul Pierce 8.00 20.00
eja Stojakovic 6.00 15.00
J. Tucker 4.00 10.00
uincy Douby 4.00 10.00
on Artest 4.00 10.00
onnie Brewer 5.00 12.00
odney Carney 4.00 10.00
andy Foye 8.00 20.00
udy Gay 8.00 20.00
ichard Jefferson 4.00 10.00
Rashad McCants 4.00 10.00
ajon Rondo 20.00 50.00
onny Turiaf 8.00 20.00
yan Hollins 4.00 10.00
olomon Jones 4.00 10.00
teve Nash 25.00 60.00
helden Williams 4.00 10.00
yrus Thomas 8.00 20.00
ince Carter 15.00 40.00
hawne Williams 4.00 10.00
Marvin Williams 4.00 10.00
Wayne Simien 4.00 10.00

2006-07 Reflections Triple Fabric Gold

T RUN 100 SER.#'d SETS
PPER: .5X TO 1.25X BASE HI
PER PRINT RUN 50 SER.#'d SETS
CHES: 1X TO 2.5X BASE HI
CH PRINT RUN 15 SER.#'d SETS
RICED AUTO PRINT RUN ONE SET
ndray Blatche 2.50 6.00
dre Iguodala 4.00 10.00

AJ Al Jefferson 4.00 10.00
AK Andrei Kirilenko 3.00 8.00
AS Amare Stoudemire 4.00 10.00
AW Antoine Walker 3.00 8.00
BH Brendan Haywood 2.50 6.00
BR Kwame Brown 2.50 6.00
BW Ben Wallace 4.00 10.00
CA Carmelo Anthony 5.00 12.00
CM Corey Maggette 3.00 8.00
DG Danny Granger 4.00 10.00
DH Devin Harris 4.00 10.00
DN Dirk Nowitzki 8.00 20.00
EB Elton Brand 4.00 10.00
GA Gilbert Arenas 4.00 10.00
GE Devean George 2.50 6.00
GO Drew Gooden 3.00 8.00
JH Josh Howard 3.00 8.00
JK Jason Kidd 6.00 15.00
JM Jamaal Magloire 2.50 6.00
JR Jason Richardson 4.00 10.00
JS J.R. Smith 4.00 10.00
KB Kobe Bryant 15.00 40.00
KG Kevin Garnett 8.00 20.00
KH Kirk Hinrich 4.00 10.00
LD Luol Deng 4.00 10.00
LH Larry Hughes 3.00 8.00
LJ LeBron James 20.00 50.00
MB Mike Bibby 4.00 10.00
MC Jeff McInnis 2.50 6.00
MD Mike Dunleavy 3.00 8.00
MG Manu Ginobili 4.00 10.00
MJ Michael Jordan 50.00 120.00
MW Martell Webster 3.00 8.00
PG Pau Gasol 4.00 10.00
PS Peja Stojakovic 4.00 10.00
RD Ricky Davis 3.00 8.00
RF Raymond Felton 5.00 12.00
RJ Richard Jefferson 4.00 10.00
RL Rashard Lewis 4.00 10.00
RM Rashad McCants 2.50 6.00
RS Robert Swift 2.50 6.00
SC Sam Cassell 4.00 10.00
SO Shaquille O'Neal 8.00 20.00
TD Tim Duncan 6.00 15.00
TM Tracy McGrady 5.00 12.00
VC Vince Carter 5.00 12.00
WS Wally Szczerbiak 3.00 8.00
YM Yao Ming 5.00 12.00

1987-88 Rockford Lightning CBA

Produced for the Lightning by the Rockford Litho Centre, this 10-card set features black and white photos on a blue and red card design with player biographies and an advertisement for Gary's Dugout Sports Cards store on the back.

COMPLETE SET (10) 1.50 4.00
COMMON CARD (1-10) .15 .40
1 Fred Cofield .30 .75
2 Bruce Douglas .15 .40
3 John Fox .15 .40
4 Carl Henry .30 .75
5 Jim Lampley .15 .40
6 Pete Myers .30 .75
7 Richard Rellford .15 .40
8 Charley Rosen CO .40 1.00
9 John Schweitz .30 .75
10 David Wood .50 1.25

2001 Rockers Fleer WNBA

Produced by Fleer, this sheet was given away to the first 5000 fans at the last game of the 2001 season at Gund Arena. Cards feature perforated edges, as they were released in the form of a sheet, white borders, and a colored frame around the card to match the team's colors.

COMPLETE SET (9) 4.00 10.00
1 Eva Nemcova 1.25 3.00
2 Ann Wauters 1.25 3.00
3 Merlakia Jones .40 1.00
4 Mery Andrade .40 1.00
5 Cleveland Rockers .40 1.00
6 Rushia Brown .40 1.00
7 Helen Darling .40 1.00
8 Vicky Hall .40 1.00
9 Chasity Melvin .40 1.00

1971-72 Rockets Carnation Milk

Issued on the side of Carnation Milk cartons, the side panels were used to picture members of the 1971-72 Houston Rockets. Since these were unnumbered, the cards are sequenced in alphabetical order.

COMPLETE SET 300.00 600.00
1 Dick Cunningham 30.00 60.00
2 Dick Gibbs 30.00 60.00
3 Elvin Hayes 75.00 150.00
4 Stu Lantz 50.00 100.00
5 Cliff Meely 30.00 60.00
6 Calvin Murphy 50.00 100.00
7 Mike Newlin 40.00 75.00
8 Rudy Tomjanovich 60.00 120.00

1969-70 Rockets Coca-Cola

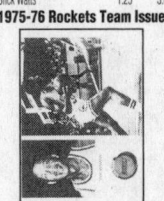

Measuring 8 1/2" by 11", this 9-card set features members from the 1969-70 San Diego Rockets. The fronts feature color close-up shots, with the player's name, weight, age and college. The team logo is located in the lower left corner, with a Coca-Cola logo in the lower right. The backs feature text, the Coca-Cola logo and "Rockets Cage Club", and are not numbered. The photos are listed below in alphabetical order.

COMPLETE SET (9) 60.00 120.00
1 Rick Adelman 8.00 20.00
2 Jim Barnett 5.00 10.00
3 John Block 5.00 10.00
4 Elvin Hayes 12.50 25.00
5 Toby Kimball 5.00 10.00
6 Stu Lantz 8.00 20.00
7 Pat Riley 15.00 30.00
8 John Trapp 5.00 10.00
9 Art Williams 5.00 10.00

1971-72 Rockets Denver Team Issue

Each of these team-issued photos measure approximately 8" by 10" and feature black and white player portraits. The player's name is listed below the photo. Each sheet contains eight photos. The backs are blank. The photos are unnumbered and listed below alphabetically.

COMPLETE SET (2) 15.00 30.00
1 Byron Beck 7.50 15.00
Art Becker
Julian Hammond
Marv Roberts
Ralph Simpson
Dwight Waller
Chuck Williams
Steve Wilson
2 Stan Albeck ACO 10.00 20.00
Larry Brown
Alex Hannum CO
Julius Keye
Del Klone GM
Dave Robisch
Al Smith
Lloyd Williams TR

1968-69 Rockets Jack in the Box

This 14-card set of San Diego Rockets was sponsored by Jack-in-the-Box and available at their restaurants in the greater San Diego area. There is evidence that this set was substantially reissued the following year with cards of Bobby Smith and Bernie Williams replacing the cards of Harry Barnes and Henry Finkel. Bobby Smith's only season with the San Diego Rockets was 1969-70 and Harry Barnes' only season with the San Diego Rockets was 1968-69. The cards only measure approximately 2" by 3" and have the appearance of wallet-size photos. The fronts have posed color head and shoulders shots, with the player's name, team name, team logo, and sponsor's logo below the picture. The backs are blank. The cards are unnumbered and are checklisted below in alphabetical order. The two cards in the set that are more difficult to find are marked by SP in the checklist below. The set features the first professional cards of Rick Adelman, Elvin Hayes, and Pat Riley among others.

COMPLETE SET (14) 50.00 90.00
1 Rick Adelman 2.50 6.00
2 Harry Barnes SP 15.00 40.00
3 Jim Barnett .75 2.00
4 John Block .60 1.50
5 Henry Finkel SP 15.00 40.00
6 Elvin Hayes 4.00 10.00
7 Toby Kimball .60 1.50
8 Don Kojis .60 1.50
9 Stu Lantz 1.25 3.00
10 Pat Riley 5.00 12.00
11 Bobby Smith 1.50 4.00
12 John Trapp .60 1.50
13 Art Williams .60 1.50
14 Bernie Williams 1.00 2.50

1978-79 Rockets Photos

This six card oversized glossy set was released during the 1978-79 season, and features such Rockets stars as Rudy Tomjanovich and Moses Malone. Please note that these black and white cards measure 8"x10", and have blank backs.

COMPLETE SET 15.00 30.00
1 Rick Barry 3.00 8.00
2 Alonzo Bradley 1.00 2.50
3 Jacky Dorsey 1.00 2.50
4 Mike Dunleavy 1.50 4.00
5 Moses Malone 2.50 6.00
6 Calvin Murphy 2.00 5.00
7 Mike Newlin 1.25 3.00
8 Jackie Robinson 1.00 2.50
9 Rudy Tomjanovich 2.00 5.00
10 Slick Watts 1.25 3.00

1975-76 Rockets Team Issue

This 8"x10" set was produced for the Houston Rockets during the 1975-76 season. The set features eight cards of the team's players and coaches Please note that the card of Tom Nissalke was done as a 5"x7" card.

COMPLETE SET (8) 12.50 25.00
1 John Johnson 1.50 4.00
2 Kevin Kunnert 1.25 3.00
3 Mike Newlin 1.50 4.00
4 Ed Ratleff 1.25 3.00
5 Ron Riley 1.25 3.00
6 Rudy White 1.25 3.00
7 Dave Wohl 1.25 3.00
8 Tom Nissalke CO 1.25 3.00

1977-78 Rockets Team Issue

These eight photos featured members of the 1976-77 Houston Rockets. Since they are unnumbered we have sequenced them in alphabetical order.

COMPLETE SET 10.00 20.00
1 John Johnson 1.50 4.00
2 Kevin Kunnert 1.25 3.00
3 Mike Newlin 1.50 4.00
4 Tom Nissalke CO 1.25 3.00
5 Ed Ratleff 1.25 3.00
6 Ron Riley 1.25 3.00
7 Rudy White 1.25 3.00
8 Dave Wohl 1.50 4.00

1990-91 Rockets Team Issue

Each of these Houston Rockets team-issued photos measure approximately 6" by 9" and feature a close-up color player portrait bordered in white. A facsimile autograph and the uniform number accent the front. The backs are blank. The photos are unnumbered and listed below alphabetically.

COMPLETE SET (5) 4.00 10.00
1 Dave Jamerson .30 .75
2 Buck Johnson .30 .75
3 Hakeem Olajuwon 3.00 8.00
4 Otis Thorpe .60 1.50
5 David Wood .30 .75

1971-72 Rockets Team Photo

This black and white press photo, measuring 7 3/4" x 10", was issued for the Houston Rockets' first NBA season. The photo is made up of twelve pictures divided up into three rows. Each individual shot is a close-up of each player. The Houston Rockets' debut logo appears at the bottom middle.

1 Team Photo 6.00 12.00
Curtis Perry
Elvin Hayes
Dick Cunningham
John Egan
Dick Gibbs
Rudy Tomjanovich
Mike Newlin
Jim Davis
Cliff Meely
Calvin Murphy
Stu Lantz
John Vallely

2008-09 Rockets Upper Deck

COMPLETE SET (14) 2.50 6.00
1 Yao Ming .40 1.00
2 Tracy McGrady .30 .75
3 Shane Battier .25 .60
4 Rafer Alston .20 .50
5 Luis Scola .25 .60
6 Chuck Hayes .20 .50
7 Steve Francis .30 .75
8 Luther Head .20 .50
9 Carl Landry .20 .50
10 Dikembe Mutombo .30 .75
11 Ron Artest .30 .75
12 Joey Dorsey .30 .75
13 Rick Adelman CO .20 .50
14 Hakeem Olajuwon .40 1.00

2009-10 Rookies and Stars

COMP.SET w/o SPs (115) 12.50 30.00
AU RC PRINT RUNS LISTED IN CHECKLIST
ASTERISK CARDS FROM PANINI UPDATE
1 Josh Smith .40 1.00
2 Joe Johnson .40 1.00
3 Mike Bibby .30 .75
4 Paul Pierce .50 1.25
5 Ray Allen .40 1.00
6 Rajon Rondo .50 1.25
7 Kevin Garnett .75 2.00
8 Gerald Wallace .40 1.00
9 Boris Diaw .30 .75
10 Raja Bell .30 .75
11 Derrick Rose 1.25 3.00
12 John Salmons .40 1.00
13 Kirk Hinrich .40 1.00
14 LeBron James 2.00 5.00
15 Shaquille O'Neal .75 2.00
16 Mo Williams .30 .75
17 Dirk Nowitzki .50 1.25
18 Josh Howard .30 .75
19 Jason Kidd .40 1.00
20 Jason Terry .30 .75
21 Shawn Marion .40 1.00
22 Carmelo Anthony .50 1.25
23 Chauncey Billups .40 1.00
24 J.R. Smith .40 1.00
25 Richard Hamilton .30 .75
26 Tayshaun Prince .40 1.00
27 Allen Iverson .50 1.25
28 Stephen Jackson .30 .75
29 Corey Maggette .30 .75
30 Monta Ellis .40 1.00
31 Yao Ming .50 1.25
32 Tracy McGrady .40 1.00
33 Trevor Ariza .25 .60
34 Danny Granger .40 1.00
35 Mike Dunleavy .25 .60
36 T.J. Ford .25 .60
37 Al Thornton .30 .75
38 Eric Gordon .40 1.00
39 Kobe Bryant 2.00 5.00
40 Pau Gasol .40 1.00
41 Ron Artest .40 1.00
42 Andrew Bynum .50 1.25
43 Rudy Gay .40 1.00
44 O.J. Mayo .40 1.00
45 Mike Conley Jr. .30 .75
46 Zach Randolph .30 .75
47 Dwyane Wade .75 2.00
48 Michael Beasley .40 1.00
49 Jermaine O'Neal .40 1.00
50 Udonis Haslem .30 .75
51 Michael Redd .40 1.00
52 Ramon Sessions .30 .75
53 Andrew Bogut .40 1.00
54 Al Jefferson .40 1.00
55 Ryan Gomes .25 .60
56 Kevin Love .60 1.50
57 Devin Harris .40 1.00
58 Brook Lopez .40 1.00
59 Rafer Alston .25 .60
60 Chris Paul .60 1.50
61 David West .40 1.00
62 Peja Stojakovic .40 1.00
63 Al Harrington .30 .75
64 Nate Robinson .40 1.00
65 Wilson Chandler .30 .75
66 Kevin Durant 1.25 3.00
67 Jeff Green .30 .75
68 Russell Westbrook .60 1.50
69 Dwight Howard .60 1.50
70 Rashard Lewis .30 .75
71 Jameer Nelson .30 .75
72 Vince Carter .50 1.25
73 Andre Iguodala .40 1.00
74 Elton Brand .40 1.00
75 Thaddeus Young .25 .60
76 Amare Stoudemire .40 1.00
77 Steve Nash .40 1.00
78 Leandro Barbosa .30 .75
79 Channing Frye .30 .75
80 Brandon Roy .40 1.00
81 LaMarcus Aldridge .40 1.00
82 Greg Oden .30 .75
83 Kevin Martin .40 1.00
84 Andres Nocioni .25 .60
85 Spencer Hawes .30 .75
86 Tony Parker .40 1.00
87 Tim Duncan .60 1.50
88 Manu Ginobili .40 1.00
89 Richard Jefferson .40 1.00
90 Chris Bosh .40 1.00
91 Hedo Turkoglu .40 1.00
92 Andrea Bargnani .30 .75
93 Deron Williams .40 1.00
94 Carlos Boozer .40 1.00
95 Andrei Kirilenko .30 .75
96 Ronnie Brewer .30 .75
97 Antawn Jamison .40 1.00
98 Gilbert Arenas .40 1.00
99 Caron Butler .40 1.00
100 Randy Foye .25 .60
101 Kareem Abdul-Jabbar .60 1.50
102 Elvin Hayes .40 1.00
103 Karl Malone .50 1.25
104 Arnie Risen .40 1.00
105 Jalen Rose .40 1.00
106 Dave DeBusschere .40 1.00
107 Artis Gilmore .40 1.00
108 Nate Archibald .40 1.00
109 Mark Eaton .40 1.00
110 Darryl Dawkins .40 1.00
111 Spencer Haywood .40 1.00
112 Bill Cartwright .40 1.00
113 Moses Malone .40 1.00
114 Magic Johnson 1.00 2.50
115 Sleepy Floyd .40 1.00
116 Dante Cunningham RC .75 2.00
117 Jon Brockman RC .75 2.00
118 Jonas Jerebko RC .75 2.00
119 Derrick Brown RC .75 2.00
120 Dionte Christmas RC .75 2.00
121 Marcus Thornton RC 1.25 3.00
122 Danny Green RC 1.25 3.00
123 Goran Suton RC .75 2.00
124 Jack McClinton RC .75 2.00
125 A.J. Price RC .75 2.00
126 Serge Ibaka RC 2.00 5.00
127 DeMar DeRozan RC 1.25 3.00
128 Chris Hunter RC .75 2.00
129 Lester Hudson RC .75 2.00
130 David Andersen RC .75 2.00
131 Blake Griffin AU/449 RC 100.00 200.00
132 Hasheem Thabeet AU/449 RC 6.00 15.00
133 James Harden AU/449 RC 20.00 50.00
134 Tyreke Evans AU/379 RC 20.00 50.00
135 Jonny Flynn AU/449 RC 6.00 15.00
136 Stephen Curry AU/449 RC 15.00 40.00
137 Jordan Hill AU/449 RC 6.00 15.00
138 Dante Cunningham AU/437 RC 6.00 15.00
139 Brandon Jennings AU/379 RC 12.00 30.00
140 Terrence Williams AU/356 RC 6.00 15.00
141 Gerald Henderson AU/449 RC 6.00 15.00
142 Tyler Hansbrough AU/449 RC 10.00 25.00
143 Earl Clark AU/449 RC 6.00 15.00
144 Austin Daye AU/369 RC 6.00 15.00
145 James Johnson AU/449 RC 6.00 15.00
146 Jrue Holiday AU/449 RC 12.00 30.00
147 Ty Lawson AU/369 RC 10.00 25.00
148 Jeff Teague AU/449 RC 8.00 20.00
149 Eric Maynor AU/369 RC 6.00 15.00
150 Darren Collison AU/347 RC 10.00 25.00
151 Omri Casspi AU/449 RC 6.00 15.00
152 B.J. Mullens AU/379 RC 6.00 15.00
153 Rodrigue Beaubois AU/390 RC 8.00 20.00
154 Taj Gibson AU/369 RC 8.00 20.00
155 DeMarre Carroll AU/449 RC 6.00 15.00
156 Wayne Ellington AU/416 RC 6.00 15.00
157 Toney Douglas AU/379 RC 6.00 15.00
158 Jermaine Taylor AU/449 RC 6.00 15.00
159 Jeff Pendergraph AU/449 RC 6.00 15.00
160 DaJuan Summers AU/378 RC 6.00 15.00
161 Sam Young AU/369 RC 6.00 15.00
162 DeJuan Blair AU/449 RC 8.00 20.00
163 Chase Budinger AU/369 RC 6.00 15.00
164 Jodie Meeks AU/449 RC 8.00 20.00
165 Taylor Griffin AU/380 RC 6.00 15.00
166 DeMar Derozan AU/499 RC* 10.00 25.00
167 Wesley Matthews AU/499 RC* 10.00 25.00
168 Serge Ibaka AU/499 RC* 15.00 40.00
169 Marcus Thornton AU/499 RC* 10.00 25.00
170 Jonas Jerebko AU/499 RC* 6.00 15.00

2009-10 Rookies and Stars Gold

*GOLD 1-115: 1X TO 2.5X BASE HI
*GOLD 116-130: .75X TO 2X BASE HI
*GOLD 131-165: .75X TO 2X BASE HI
GOLD 1-130 PRINT RUN 500 SER.#'d SETS
GOLD 131-165 PRINT RUN 25 SER.#'d SETS

2009-10 Rookies and Stars Gold Holofoil

*GOLD STARS: 2X TO 5X BASE HI
*GOLD RCs: 1.25X TO 3X BASE HI
STATED PRINT RUN 250 SER.#'d SETS

2009-10 Rookies and Stars Current NBA Team Patches Signatures

STATED PRINT RUN 199 SER.#'d SETS
1 Kobe Bryant 100.00 200.00

2009-10 Rookies and Stars Dress for Success Materials

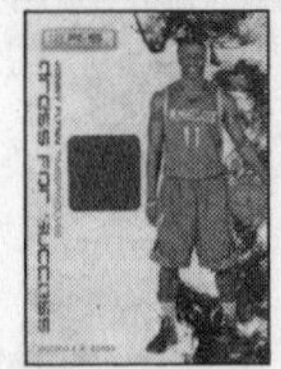

STATED PRINT RUN 299 SER.#'d SETS
*PRIME: 1X TO 2.5X BASE HI
PRIME PRINT RUN 50 SER.#'d SETS
1 Blake Griffin 12.00 30.00
2 Hasheem Thabeet 2.00 5.00
3 James Harden 6.00 15.00
4 Tyreke Evans 5.00 12.00
5 Jonny Flynn 2.00 5.00
6 Stephen Curry 5.00 12.00
7 Jordan Hill 2.00 5.00
8 DeMar DeRozan 3.00 8.00
9 Brandon Jennings 4.00 10.00
10 Terrence Williams 2.00 5.00
11 Gerald Henderson 2.00 5.00
12 Tyler Hansbrough 3.00 8.00
13 Earl Clark 2.00 5.00
14 Austin Daye 2.00 5.00
15 James Johnson 2.00 5.00
16 Jrue Holiday 4.00 10.00
17 Ty Lawson 3.00 8.00
18 Jeff Teague 2.50 6.00
19 Eric Maynor 2.00 5.00
20 Darren Collison 3.00 8.00
21 Omri Casspi 2.00 5.00
22 B.J. Mullens 2.00 5.00
23 Rodrigue Beaubois 2.50 6.00
24 Taj Gibson 2.50 6.00
25 DeMarre Carroll 2.00 5.00
26 Wayne Ellington 2.00 5.00
27 Toney Douglas 2.00 5.00
28 Jermaine Taylor 2.00 5.00
29 Jeff Pendergraph 2.00 5.00
30 DaJuan Summers 2.00 5.00
31 Sam Young 2.00 5.00
32 DeJuan Blair 2.50 6.00
33 Chase Budinger 2.00 5.00
34 Jodie Meeks 2.50 6.00
35 Taylor Griffin 2.00 5.00

2009-10 Rookies and Stars Dress for Success Materials Signatures

STATED PRINT RUN 25 SER.#'d SETS
UNPRICED PRIME SIG PRINT RUN 10 SETS
1 Blake Griffin 150.00 300.00
2 Hasheem Thabeet 6.00 15.00
3 James Harden 25.00 60.00
4 Tyreke Evans 20.00 50.00
5 Jonny Flynn 6.00 15.00
6 Stephen Curry 20.00 50.00
7 Jordan Hill 6.00 15.00
9 Brandon Jennings 12.00 30.00
10 Terrence Williams 6.00 15.00
11 Gerald Henderson 6.00 15.00
12 Tyler Hansbrough 10.00 25.00
13 Earl Clark 6.00 15.00
14 Austin Daye 6.00 15.00
15 James Johnson 6.00 15.00
16 Jrue Holiday 12.00 30.00
18 Jeff Teague 8.00 20.00
21 Omri Casspi 6.00 15.00
22 B.J. Mullens 6.00 15.00
23 Rodrigue Beaubois 8.00 20.00
25 DeMarre Carroll 6.00 15.00
26 Wayne Ellington 6.00 15.00
27 Toney Douglas 6.00 15.00
28 Jermaine Taylor 6.00 15.00
29 Jeff Pendergraph 6.00 15.00
30 DaJuan Summers 6.00 15.00
32 DeJuan Blair 8.00 20.00
33 Chase Budinger 6.00 15.00
34 Jodie Meeks 8.00 20.00
35 Taylor Griffin 6.00 15.00

2009-10 Rookies and Stars Freshman Orientation Materials

STATED PRINT RUN 299 SER.#'d SETS
*PRIME: 1X TO 2.5X BASE HI
PRIME PRINT RUN 50 SER.#'d SETS
1 Blake Griffin 12.00 30.00
2 Hasheem Thabeet 2.00 5.00
3 James Harden 6.00 15.00
4 Tyreke Evans 5.00 12.00
5 Jonny Flynn 2.00 5.00
6 Stephen Curry 5.00 12.00
7 Jordan Hill 2.00 5.00
8 DeMar DeRozan 3.00 8.00
9 Brandon Jennings 4.00 10.00
10 Terrence Williams 2.00 5.00
11 Gerald Henderson 2.00 5.00
12 Tyler Hansbrough 3.00 8.00
13 Earl Clark 2.00 5.00
14 Austin Daye 2.00 5.00
15 James Johnson 2.00 5.00
16 Jrue Holiday 4.00 10.00
17 Ty Lawson 3.00 8.00
18 Jeff Teague 2.50 6.00
19 Eric Maynor 2.00 5.00
20 Darren Collison 3.00 8.00
21 Omri Casspi 2.00 5.00
22 B.J. Mullens 2.00 5.00
23 Rodrigue Beaubois 2.50 6.00
24 Taj Gibson 2.50 6.00
25 DeMarre Carroll 2.00 5.00
26 Wayne Ellington 2.00 5.00
27 Toney Douglas 2.00 5.00
28 Jermaine Taylor 2.00 5.00
29 Jeff Pendergraph 2.00 5.00
30 DaJuan Summers 2.00 5.00
31 Sam Young 2.00 5.00
32 DeJuan Blair 2.50 6.00
33 Chase Budinger 2.00 5.00
34 Jodie Meeks 2.50 6.00
35 Taylor Griffin 2.00 5.00

2009-10 Rookies and Stars Freshman Orientation Materials Signatures

STATED PRINT RUN 25 SER.#'d SETS
UNPRICED PRIME SIG PRINT RUN 10 SETS
1 Blake Griffin 150.00 300.00
2 Hasheem Thabeet 6.00 15.00
3 James Harden 25.00 60.00
4 Tyreke Evans 20.00 50.00
5 Jonny Flynn 6.00 15.00
6 Stephen Curry 20.00 50.00
7 Jordan Hill 6.00 15.00
9 Brandon Jennings 20.00 50.00
10 Terrence Williams 6.00 15.00
11 Gerald Henderson 6.00 15.00
12 Tyler Hansbrough 10.00 25.00
13 Earl Clark 6.00 15.00
14 Austin Daye 6.00 15.00
15 James Johnson 6.00 15.00
16 Jrue Holiday 12.00 30.00
18 Jeff Teague 8.00 20.00
21 Omri Casspi 6.00 15.00
22 B.J. Mullens 6.00 15.00
23 Rodrigue Beaubois 8.00 20.00
24 Taj Gibson 8.00 20.00
25 DeMarre Carroll 6.00 15.00
26 Wayne Ellington 6.00 15.00
27 Toney Douglas 6.00 15.00
28 Jermaine Taylor 6.00 15.00
29 Jeff Pendergraph 6.00 15.00
30 DaJuan Summers 6.00 15.00
32 DeJuan Blair 8.00 20.00
33 Chase Budinger 6.00 15.00
34 Jodie Meeks 8.00 20.00
35 Taylor Griffin 6.00 15.00

2009-10 Rookies and Stars Gold Materials

STATED PRINT RUN 99 TO 250 SER.#'d SETS
1 Josh Smith/250 3.00 8.00
3 Mike Bibby/250 2.50 6.00
13 Kirk Hinrich/250 3.00 8.00
14 LeBron James/250 8.00 20.00
17 Dirk Nowitzki/99 4.00 10.00
18 Josh Howard/250 2.50 6.00
19 Jason Kidd/250 3.00 8.00
20 Jason Terry/250 2.50 6.00
22 Carmelo Anthony/250 4.00 10.00
26 Tayshaun Prince/250 3.00 8.00
28 Stephen Jackson/250 2.50 6.00
31 Yao Ming/250 4.00 10.00
32 Tracy McGrady/250 3.00 8.00
39 Kobe Bryant/99 8.00 20.00
42 Andrew Bynum/250 4.00 10.00
45 Mike Conley Jr./250 2.50 6.00
47 Dwyane Wade/250 6.00 15.00
48 Michael Beasley/250 3.00 8.00
49 Jermaine O'Neal/100 3.00 8.00
50 Udonis Haslem/250 2.50 6.00
51 Michael Redd/250 3.00 8.00
53 Andrew Bogut/250 3.00 8.00
54 Al Jefferson/250 3.00 8.00
56 Kevin Love/250 5.00 12.00
57 Devin Harris/199 3.00 8.00
62 Peja Stojakovic/250 3.00 8.00
63 Al Harrington/250 2.50 6.00
66 Kevin Durant/250 6.00 15.00
69 Dwight Howard/250 5.00 12.00
70 Rashard Lewis/250 2.50 6.00
73 Andre Iguodala/250 3.00 8.00
74 Elton Brand/250 3.00 8.00

75 Thaddeus Young/250 2.00 5.00
76 Amare Stoudemire/250 3.00 8.00
77 Steve Nash/250 3.00 8.00
80 Brandon Roy/250 3.00 8.00
81 LaMarcus Aldridge/250 3.00 8.00
82 Greg Oden/250 2.50 6.00
84 Andres Nocioni/250 2.00 5.00
86 Tony Parker/250 3.00 8.00
87 Tim Duncan/250 5.00 12.00
88 Manu Ginobili/250 3.00 8.00
92 Andrea Bargnani/250 2.50 6.00
93 Deron Williams/250 3.00 8.00
94 Carlos Boozer/250 3.00 8.00
95 Andrei Kirilenko/250 2.50 6.00
127 DeMar DeRozan/250 5.00 12.00

2009-10 Rookies and Stars Gold Stars

COMPLETE SET (15) 8.00 20.00
RANDOM INSERTS IN PACKS
*BLACK: .75X TO 2X BASE HI
BLACK PRINT RUN 100 SER.#'d SETS
*GOLD: .5X TO 1.25X BASE HI
GOLD PRINT RUN 500 SER.#'d SETS
*HOLOFOIL: .6X TO 1.5X BASE HI
HOLO PRINT RUN 250 SER.#'d SETS
1 Dwyane Wade 1.50 4.00
2 Kobe Bryant 4.00 10.00
3 LeBron James 4.00 10.00
4 Dirk Nowitzki 1.00 2.50
5 Danny Granger .75 2.00
6 Kevin Durant 2.50 6.00
7 Chris Paul 1.25 3.00
8 Carmelo Anthony 1.00 2.50
9 Chris Bosh .75 2.00
10 Brandon Roy .75 2.00
11 Joe Johnson .75 2.00
12 Devin Harris .75 2.00
13 Deron Williams .75 2.00
14 Dwight Howard 1.25 3.00
15 Paul Pierce 1.00 2.50

2009-10 Rookies and Stars Gold Stars Materials

RANDOM INSERTS IN PACKS
*PRIME: 1X TO 2.5X BASE HI
PRIME PRINT RUN 10 TO 50 SER.#'d SETS
1 Dwyane Wade 5.00 12.00
2 Kobe Bryant 8.00 20.00
3 LeBron James 8.00 20.00
4 Dirk Nowitzki 3.00 8.00
6 Kevin Durant 6.00 15.00
7 Chris Paul 4.00 10.00
8 Carmelo Anthony 3.00 8.00
9 Chris Bosh 2.50 6.00
10 Brandon Roy 2.50 6.00
11 Joe Johnson 2.50 6.00
12 Devin Harris 2.50 6.00
13 Deron Williams 2.50 6.00
14 Dwight Howard 4.00 10.00

2009-10 Rookies and Stars Gold Stars Signatures

STATED PRINT RUN 10 TO 25 SER.#'d SETS
SOME UNPRICED DUE TO SCARCITY
2 Kobe Bryant/25 100.00 200.00

2009-10 Rookies and Stars Moments in Time

COMPLETE SET (15) 15.00 30.00
RANDOM INSERTS IN PACKS
*BLACK: .75X TO 2X BASE HI
BLACK PRINT RUN 100 SER.#'d SETS
*GOLD: .5X TO 1.25X BASE HI
GOLD PRINT RUN 500 SER.#'d SETS
*HOLOFOIL: .6X TO 1.5X BASE HI
HOLO PRINT RUN 250 SER.#'d SETS
1 Bob Pettit 1.00 2.50
2 Wilt Chamberlain 2.00 5.00
3 John Havlicek 1.00 2.50
4 Bill Russell 1.50 4.00
5 Willis Reed 1.00 2.50
6 Jerry West 1.25 3.00
7 Bill Walton 1.00 2.50
8 Darryl Dawkins 1.00 2.50
9 Magic Johnson 2.50 6.00
10 Spud Webb 1.00 2.50
11 Larry Bird 3.00 8.00
12 Kareem Abdul-Jabbar 1.50 4.00
13 Shaquille O'Neal 2.00 5.00
14 LeBron James 5.00 12.00
15 Kobe Bryant 5.00 12.00

2009-10 Rookies and Stars Prime Cuts

STATED PRINT RUN 25 TO 50 SER.#'d SETS
1 Mike Bibby/50 5.00 12.00
2 Dirk Nowitzki/50 8.00 20.00
3 Tracy McGrady/25 6.00 15.00
4 Elton Brand/50 6.00 15.00
5 Brandon Roy/50 6.00 15.00
6 Michael Beasley/50 6.00 15.00
7 Andre Iguodala/50 6.00 15.00
8 Amare Stoudemire/50 6.00 15.00
9 Andrea Bargnani/50 5.00 12.00
10 Manu Ginobili/50 6.00 15.00
11 Nate Robinson/50 6.00 15.00
12 Al Jefferson/50 6.00 15.00
13 O.J. Mayo/50 6.00 15.00
14 Tony Parker/50 6.00 15.00
15 Carlos Boozer/50 6.00 15.00

2009-10 Rookies and Stars Prime Cuts Signatures

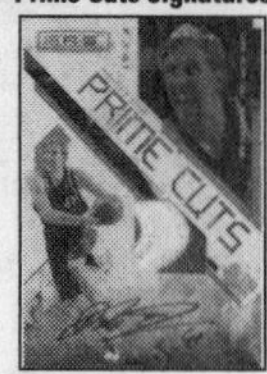

STATED PRINT RUN 25 SER.#'d SETS
1 Mike Bibby 15.00 40.00
2 Dirk Nowitzki 75.00 150.00
6 Michael Beasley 15.00 40.00
15 Carlos Boozer 10.00 25.00

2009-10 Rookies and Stars Retired NBA Team Patches Signatures

STATED PRINT RUN 99 TO 394 SER.#'d SETS
1 Willis Reed/99 10.00 25.00
2 Elvin Hayes/99 8.00 20.00
3 Sidney Moncrief/199 6.00 15.00
4 Danny Manning/199 6.00 15.00
5 Bill Laimbeer/199 10.00 25.00
6 Dan Majerle/99 12.50 30.00
7 Bob Cousy/199 20.00 40.00
8 Earl Monroe/99 12.50 30.00
9 Darryl Dawkins/99 6.00 15.00
10 Adrian Dantley/99 6.00 15.00
11 Byron Scott/199 10.00 25.00
12 Nate Thurmond/199 8.00 20.00
13 Cazzie Russell/199 6.00 15.00
14 Tim Hardaway/199 12.50 30.00
15 Kurt Rambis/99 12.50 30.00
16 Rick Barry/199 12.50 30.00
17 Manute Bol/199 15.00 40.00
18 Artis Gilmore/199 8.00 20.00
19 Spencer Haywood/394 6.00 15.00

2009-10 Rookies and Stars Sharp Shooters

COMPLETE SET (15) 6.00 15.00
RANDOM INSERTS IN PACKS
*BLACK: .75X TO 2X BASE HI
BLACK PRINT RUN 100 SER.#'d SETS
*GOLD: .5X TO 1.25X BASE HI
GOLD PRINT RUN 500 SER.#'d SETS
*HOLOFOIL: .6X TO 1.5X BASE HI
HOLO PRINT RUN 250 SER.#'d SETS
UNPRICED SIG.PRINT RUN 10 SETS
1 Anthony Morrow .75 2.00
2 D.J. Augustin 1.00 2.50
3 Jameer Nelson 1.00 2.50
4 Jason Kapono .75 2.00
5 Kelenna Azubuike .75 2.00
6 Kevin Durant 4.00 10.00
7 Mehmet Okur .75 2.00
8 Mo Williams 1.00 2.50
9 Steve Nash 1.25 3.00
10 Troy Murphy .75 2.00
11 Chauncey Billups 1.25 3.00
12 David West 1.25 3.00
13 Dirk Nowitzki 2.00 5.00
14 Manu Ginobili 1.25 3.00
15 Ray Allen 1.25 3.00

2009-10 Rookies and Stars Sharp Shooters Materials

RANDOM INSERTS IN PACKS
*PRIME: .75X TO 2X BASE HI
PRIME PRINT RUN 50 SER.#'d SETS
6 Kevin Durant 8.00 20.00
9 Steve Nash 3.00 8.00
13 Dirk Nowitzki 4.00 10.00
14 Manu Ginobili 3.00 8.00

2009-10 Rookies and Stars Signatures

STATED PRINT RUN 25 TO 250 SER.#'d SETS
3 Mike Bibby/50 6.00 15.00
17 Dirk Nowitzki/25 40.00 100.00
19 Jason Kidd/25 10.00 25.00
39 Kobe Bryant/25 100.00 225.00
42 Andrew Bynum/25 10.00 25.00
48 Michael Beasley/25 12.00 30.00
56 Kevin Love/25 15.00 40.00
73 Andre Iguodala/25 6.00 15.00
94 Carlos Boozer/50 6.00 15.00
102 Elvin Hayes/25 10.00 25.00
104 Arnie Risen/25 6.00 15.00
107 Artis Gilmore/50 6.00 15.00
108 Nate Archibald/25 12.50 30.00
111 Spencer Haywood/25 8.00 20.00
115 Sleepy Floyd/25 8.00 20.00
117 Jon Brockman/250 5.00 12.00
121 Marcus Thornton/250 8.00 20.00
122 Danny Green/250 8.00 20.00
123 Goran Suton/250 5.00 12.00
124 Jack McClinton/250 5.00 12.00
125 A.J. Price/250 5.00 12.00
129 Lester Hudson/250 5.00 12.00

2009-10 Rookies and Stars Stardom

COMPLETE SET (15) 8.00 20.00
RANDOM INSERTS IN PACKS
*BLACK: .75X TO 2X BASE HI
BLACK PRINT RUN 100 SER.#'d SETS
*GOLD: .5X TO 1.25X BASE HI
GOLD PRINT RUN 500 SER.#'d SETS
*HOLOFOIL: .6X TO 1.5X BASE HI
HOLO PRINT RUN 250 SER.#'d SETS
1 Mike Bibby .75 2.00
2 Rajon Rondo 1.25 3.00
3 Raja Bell .75 2.00
4 Kirk Hinrich 1.00 2.50
5 Shaquille O'Neal 2.00 5.00
6 Jason Terry .75 2.00
7 Chauncey Billups 1.00 2.50
8 Baron Davis 1.00 2.50
9 Kobe Bryant 5.00 12.00
10 O.J. Mayo 1.00 2.50
11 Jermaine O'Neal 1.00 2.50
12 Elton Brand 1.00 2.50
13 Greg Oden .75 2.00
14 Tim Duncan 1.50 4.00
15 Hedo Turkoglu 1.00 2.50

2009-10 Rookies and Stars Stardom Materials

RANDOM INSERTS IN PACKS
1 Mike Bibby 2.00 5.00
4 Kirk Hinrich 2.50 6.00
6 Jason Terry 2.00 5.00
9 Kobe Bryant 8.00 20.00
11 Jermaine O'Neal 2.50 6.00
12 Elton Brand 2.50 6.00
13 Greg Oden 2.00 5.00
14 Tim Duncan 4.00 10.00

2009-10 Rookies and Stars Stardom Signatures

STATED PRINT RUN 50 SER.#'d SETS
1 Mike Bibby 8.00 20.00
9 Kobe Bryant 100.00 200.00

2009-10 Rookies and Stars Statistical Standouts Materials

STATED PRINT RUN 99 TO 299 SER.#'d SETS
*PRIME: .75X TO 2X BASE HI
PRIME PRINT RUN 10 TO 50 SER.#'d SETS
1 Chris Paul/299 5.00 12.00
2 Dirk Nowitzki/299 4.00 10.00
3 Dwyane Wade/299 6.00 15.00
4 Kobe Bryant/99 10.00 25.00
5 LeBron James/299 8.00 20.00
6 Al Jefferson/299 3.00 8.00
8 Dwight Howard/299 5.00 12.00
9 Stephen Jackson/299 2.50 6.00
11 Devin Harris/299 3.00 8.00
12 Joe Johnson/299 3.00 8.00
13 Pau Gasol/299 3.00 8.00
14 Tony Parker/299 3.00 8.00
15 Kevin Martin/299 3.00 8.00

2009-10 Rookies and Stars Statistical Standouts Materials Signatures

STATED PRINT RUN 25 SER.#'d SETS
UNPRICED PRIME SIG PRINT RUN 10 SETS
2 Dirk Nowitzki 50.00 120.00
4 Kobe Bryant 125.00 225.00

2009-10 Rookies and Stars Studio Combo Rookies

COMPLETE SET (10) 10.00 25.00
RANDOM INSERTS IN PACKS
*BLACK: .75X TO 2X BASE HI
BLACK PRINT RUN 100 SER.#'d SETS
*GOLD: .5X TO 1.25X BASE HI
GOLD PRINT RUN 500 SER.#'d SETS
*HOLOFOIL: .6X TO 1.5X BASE HI
HOLO PRINT RUN 250 SER.#'d SETS
1 Blake Griffin / Taylor Griffin 5.00 12.00
2 Chase Budinger / Jordan Hill .75 2.00
3 DeMar DeRozan / Taj Gibson 1.25 3.00
4 Ty Lawson / Tyler Hansbrough 1.25 3.00
5 James Johnson / Jeff Teague 1.00 2.50
6 Darren Collison / Jrue Holiday 1.50 4.00
7 James Harden / Jeff Pendergraph 2.50 6.00
8 DeJuan Blair / Hasheem Thabeet 1.00 2.50
9 Stephen Curry / Tyreke Evans 2.00 5.00
10 Blake Griffin / Tyler Hansbrough 5.00 12.00

2009-10 Rookies and Stars Studio Combo Rookies Materials

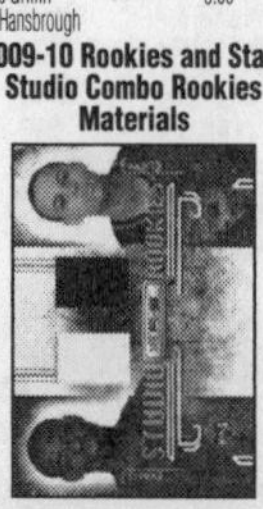

STATED PRINT RUN 299 SER.#'d SETS
*PRIME: 1X TO 2.5X BASE HI
PRIME PRINT RUN 50 SER.#'d SETS
1 Blake Griffin / Taylor Griffin 10.00 25.00
2 Chase Budinger / Jordan Hill 2.00 5.00
3 DeMar DeRozan / Taj Gibson 2.50 6.00
4 Ty Lawson / Tyler Hansbrough 2.50 6.00
5 James Johnson / Jeff Teague 2.00 5.00
6 Darren Collison / Jrue Holiday 3.00 8.00
7 James Harden / Jeff Pendergraph 5.00 12.00
8 DeJuan Blair / Hasheem Thabeet 2.00 5.00
9 Stephen Curry / Tyreke Evans 4.00 10.00
10 Blake Griffin / Tyler Hansbrough 10.00 25.00

2009-10 Rookies and Stars Studio Combo Rookies Signatures

STATED PRINT RUN 50 SER.#'d SETS
1 Blake Griffin / Taylor Griffin 75.00 150.00
2 Chase Budinger / Jordan Hill 10.00 25.00
4 Ty Lawson / Tyler Hansbrough 20.00 50.00
5 James Johnson / Jeff Teague 10.00 25.00
6 Darren Collison / Jrue Holiday 15.00 40.00
7 James Harden / Jeff Pendergraph 10.00 25.00
8 DeJuan Blair / Hasheem Thabeet 12.50 30.00
9 Stephen Curry / Tyreke Evans 40.00 100.00
10 Blake Griffin / Tyler Hansbrough 75.00 200.00

2009-10 Rookies and Stars Team Leaders

COMPLETE SET (30) 20.00 40.00
RANDOM INSERTS IN PACKS
*BLACK: .75X TO 2X BASE HI
BLACK PRINT RUN 100 SER.#'d SETS
*GOLD: .5X TO 1.25X BASE HI
GOLD PRINT RUN 500 SER.#'d SETS
*HOLOFOIL: .6X TO 1.5X BASE HI
HOLO PRINT RUN 250 SER.#'d SETS
1 Joe Johnson / Al Horford / Joe Johnson .75 2.00
2 Paul Pierce / Kevin Garnett / Rajon Rondo 1.50 4.00
3 Gerald Wallace / Emeka Okafor / Raymond Felton .75 2.00
4 Ben Gordon / Joakim Noah / Derrick Rose 2.50 6.00
5 LeBron James / LeBron James / LeBron James 4.00 10.00
6 Dirk Nowitzki / Dirk Nowitzki / Jason Kidd 1.00 2.50
7 Carmelo Anthony / Nene / Chauncey Billups 1.00 2.50
8 Richard Hamilton / Antonio McDyess / Rodney Stuckey .75 2.00
9 Stephen Jackson / Andris Biedrins / Stephen Jackson .75 2.00
10 Yao Ming / Yao Ming / Rafer Alston 1.00 2.50
11 Danny Granger / Troy Murphy / T.J. Ford .75 2.00
12 Al Thornton / Marcus Camby / Baron Davis .75 2.00
13 Kobe Bryant / Pau Gasol / Kobe Bryant 4.00 10.00
14 Rudy Gay / Marc Gasol / Mike Conley Jr. .75 2.00
15 Dwyane Wade / Udonis Haslem / Dwyane Wade 1.50 4.00
16 Michael Redd / Charlie Villanueva / Ramon Sessions .75 2.00
17 Al Jefferson / Al Jefferson / Sebastian Telfair .75 2.00
18 Devin Harris / Brook Lopez / Devin Harris .75 2.00
19 Chris Paul / David West / Chris Paul 1.25 3.00
20 Al Harrington / David Lee / Chris Duhon .75 2.00
21 Kevin Durant / Nick Collison / Earl Watson 2.50 6.00
22 Dwight Howard / Dwight Howard / Hedo Turkoglu 1.25 3.00
23 Andre Iguodala / Samuel Dalembert / Andre Miller .75 2.00
24 Amare Stoudemire / Shaquille O'Neal / Steve Nash 1.50 4.00
25 Brandon Roy / Joel Przybilla / Brandon Roy .75 2.00
26 Kevin Martin / Jason Thompson / Beno Udrih .75 2.00
27 Tony Parker / Tim Duncan / Tony Parker 1.25 3.00
28 Chris Bosh / Chris Bosh / Jose Calderon .75 2.00
29 Deron Williams / Paul Millsap / Deron Williams .75 2.00
30 Antawn Jamison / Antawn Jamison / Caron Butler .75 2.00

2010-11 Rookies and Stars

COMP.SET w/o RCs (115) 12.50 30.00
AU RC PRINT RUNS LISTED IN CHECKLIST
ASTERISK CARDS INSERTED IN SEASON UPDATE
EXCH EXPIRATION 5/10/12
1 Ray Allen .40 1.00
2 Paul Pierce .50 1.25
3 Rajon Rondo .50 1.25
4 Kevin Garnett .75 2.00
5 Brook Lopez .40 1.00
6 Devin Harris .40 1.00
7 Troy Murphy .25 .60
8 Amare Stoudemire .40 1.00
9 Anthony Randolph .30 .75
10 Danilo Gallinari .40 1.00
11 Andre Iguodala .40 1.00
12 Elton Brand .40 1.00
13 Thaddeus Young .25 .60
14 Andrea Bargnani .30 .75
15 Leandro Barbosa .30 .75
16 Jose Calderon .30 .75
17 Carlos Boozer .40 1.00
18 Derrick Rose 1.25 3.00
19 Joakim Noah .40 1.00
20 Luol Deng .40 1.00
21 Antawn Jamison .40 1.00
22 Mo Williams .30 .75
23 Daniel Gibson .30 .75
24 Ben Gordon .40 1.00
25 Richard Hamilton .30 .75
26 Tayshaun Prince .40 1.00
27 Danny Granger .40 1.00
28 Tyler Hansbrough .40 1.00
29 Mike Dunleavy .25 .60
30 Andrew Bogut .40 1.00
31 Brandon Jennings .40 1.00
32 John Salmons .40 1.00
33 Joe Johnson .40 1.00
34 Josh Smith .40 1.00
35 Al Horford .30 .75
36 Jamal Crawford .30 .75
37 Gerald Henderson .25 .60
38 Stephen Jackson .30 .75
39 Gerald Wallace .40 1.00
40 LeBron James 2.00 5.00
41 Dwyane Wade .75 2.00
42 Chris Bosh .40 1.00
43 Dwight Howard .60 1.50
44 Vince Carter .50 1.25
45 J.J. Redick .40 1.00
46 Josh Howard .30 .75
47 Al Thornton .30 .75
48 Gilbert Arenas .40 1.00
49 Kirk Hinrich .40 1.00
50 Dirk Nowitzki .50 1.25
51 Jason Kidd .40 1.00
52 Shawn Marion .40 1.00
53 Caron Butler .40 1.00
54 Kevin Martin .40 1.00
55 Shane Battier .30 .75
56 Luis Scola .30 .75
57 Yao Ming .50 1.25
58 Marc Gasol .40 1.00
59 Rudy Gay .40 1.00
60 Zach Randolph .30 .75
61 Chris Paul .60 1.50
62 Emeka Okafor .40 1.00
63 David West .40 1.00
64 Tim Duncan .60 1.50
65 Tony Parker .40 1.00
66 Richard Jefferson .40 1.00
67 Carmelo Anthony .50 1.25
68 Chauncey Billups .40 1.00
69 Chris Andersen .40 1.00
70 Nene .30 .75
71 Kevin Love .50 1.25
72 Michael Beasley .40 1.00
73 Jonny Flynn .25 .60
74 Brandon Roy .40 1.00
75 Rudy Fernandez .30 .75
76 Greg Oden .30 .75
77 Kevin Durant 1.25 3.00
78 Russell Westbrook .50 1.25
79 Jeff Green .30 .75
80 Deron Williams .40 1.00
81 Al Jefferson .40 1.00
82 Andrei Kirilenko .30 .75
83 Paul Millsap .30 .75
84 David Lee .30 .75
85 Monta Ellis .40 1.00
86 Stephen Curry .50 1.25
87 Eric Gordon .40 1.00
88 Chris Kaman .30 .75
89 Baron Davis .40 1.00
90 Kobe Bryant 2.00 5.00
91 Pau Gasol .40 1.00
92 Lamar Odom .40 1.00
93 Ron Artest .40 1.00
94 Steve Nash .40 1.00
95 Hedo Turkoglu .40 1.00
96 Channing Frye .30 .75
97 Grant Hill .50 1.25
98 Tyreke Evans .50 1.25
99 Samuel Dalembert .25 .60
100 Carl Landry .25 .60
101 Rolando Blackman .40 1.00
102 Joe Dumars .40 1.00
103 Wayne Embry .40 1.00
104 Walt Frazier .40 1.00
105 Gail Goodrich .40 1.00
106 John Havlicek .50 1.25
107 Rod Hundley .40 1.00
108 Phil Jackson .50 1.25
109 K.C. Jones .40 1.00
110 Clyde Lovellette .40 1.00
111 Jerry Lucas .40 1.00
112 Nate McMillan .40 1.00
113 Willis Reed .40 1.00
114 Paul Silas .40 1.00
115 Jerry West .50 1.25
116 Armon Johnson RC .75 2.00
117 Sherron Collins RC .75 2.00
118 Terrico White RC .75 2.00
119 Darington Hobson RC .75 2.00
120 Landry Fields RC 1.25 3.00
121 Tony Gaffney RC .75 2.00
122 Ben Uzoh RC 1.25 3.00
123 Ishmael Smith RC .75 2.00
124 Tweety Carter RC .75 2.00
125 Tiago Splitter RC 1.00 2.50
126 Solomon Alabi RC .75 2.00
127 Magnum Rolle RC .75 2.00
128 Pape Sy RC .75 2.00
129 Jeremy Lin RC 6.00 15.00
130 Derrick Caracter RC .75 2.00
131 Jordan Crawford AU/443 RC 6.00 15.00
132 Luke Harangody AU/460 RC 4.00 10.00
133 Avery Bradley AU/449 RC 8.00 20.00
134 Kevin Seraphin AU/499 RC 5.00 12.00
135 Dominique Jones AU/453 RC 4.00 10.00
136 Greg Monroe AU/454 RC 8.00 20.00
137 Ekpe Udoh AU/457 RC 4.00 10.00
138 Patrick Patterson AU/455 RC 6.00 15.00
139 Lance Stephenson AU/457 RC 4.00 10.00
140 Paul George AU/455 RC 10.00 25.00
141 Eric Bledsoe AU/499 RC 8.00 20.00
142 Willie Warren AU/456 RC 4.00 10.00
143 Al-Farouq Aminu AU/499 RC 4.00 10.00
144 Devin Ebanks AU/455 RC 5.00 12.00
145 Xavier Henry AU/455 RC 5.00 12.00
146 Greivis Vasquez AU/455 RC 5.00 12.00
147 Dexter Pittman AU/455 RC 4.00 10.00
148 Da'Sean Butler AU/455 RC 4.00 10.00
149 Keith Gallon AU/455 RC 4.00 10.00
150 Larry Sanders AU/455 RC 4.00 10.00
151 Lazar Hayward AU/455 RC 4.00 10.00
152 Wesley Johnson AU/452 RC 6.00 15.00
153 Derrick Favors AU/458 RC 8.00 20.00
154 Damion James AU/454 RC 4.00 10.00
155 Craig Brackins AU/455 RC 4.00 10.00
156 Quincy Pondexter AU/461 RC 4.00 10.00
157 Andy Rautins AU/499 RC 4.00 10.00
158 Cole Aldrich AU/450 RC 4.00 10.00
159 Daniel Orton AU/449 RC 4.00 10.00
160 Evan Turner AU/455 RC 8.00 20.00
161 Gani Lawal AU/457 RC 4.00 10.00
162 Elliot Williams AU/461 RC 4.00 10.00
163 Luke Babbitt AU/454 RC 4.00 10.00
164 DeMarcus Cousins AU/454 RC 15.00 40.00
165 Hassan Whiteside AU/458 RC 4.00 10.00
166 James Anderson AU/459 RC 4.00 10.00
167 Ed Davis AU/455 RC 5.00 12.00
168 Gordon Hayward AU/455 RC 8.00 20.00
169 Trevor Booker AU/456 RC 4.00 10.00
170 John Wall AU/454 RC 50.00 125.00
171 Landry Fields AU/499* 6.00 15.00
172 Gary Neal AU/499 RC* 6.00 15.00
173 Omer Asik AU/499 RC* 6.00 15.00
174 Semih Erden AU/411 RC* 4.00 10.00
175 Gary Forbes AU/499 RC* 4.00 10.00

2010-11 Rookies and Stars Gold

*GOLD STARS: 1X TO 2.5X BASE HI
*GOLD 116-130: .6X TO 1.5X BASE HI
*GOLD 131-175: .75X TO 2X BASE HI
GOLD 1-130 PRINT RUN 499 SER.#'d SETS
GOLD 131-175 PRINT RUN 25 SER.#'d SETS
ASTERISK CARDS INSERTED IN SEASON UPDATE
137 Ekpe Udoh AU 12.50 30.00
164 DeMarcus Cousins AU 40.00 100.00

2010-11 Rookies and Stars Gold Holofoil

*HOLO STARS: 2X TO 5X BASE HI
*HOLO RCs: 1.25X TO 3X BASE HI
STATED PRINT RUN 199 SER.#'d SETS

2010-11 Rookies and Stars Gold Materials

STATED PRINT RUN 25 TO 299 SER.#'d SETS
1 Ray Allen/50 3.00 8.00
2 Paul Pierce/299 4.00 10.00
3 Rajon Rondo/299 4.00 10.00
4 Kevin Garnett/50 6.00 15.00
6 Devin Harris/299 3.00 8.00
11 Andre Iguodala/299 3.00 8.00
12 Elton Brand/299 3.00 8.00
13 Thaddeus Young/299 2.00 5.00
14 Andrea Bargnani/299 2.50 6.00
15 Leandro Barbosa/299 2.50 6.00
18 Derrick Rose/50 10.00 25.00
19 Joakim Noah/299 3.00 8.00
20 Luol Deng/50 3.00 8.00
21 Antawn Jamison/299 3.00 8.00
24 Ben Gordon/299 3.00 8.00
26 Tayshaun Prince/299 3.00 8.00
28 Tyler Hansbrough/299 3.00 8.00
29 Mike Dunleavy/99 2.00 5.00
30 Andrew Bogut/100 3.00 8.00
31 Brandon Jennings/299 3.00 8.00
33 Joe Johnson/54 3.00 8.00
37 Gerald Henderson/299 2.00 5.00
38 Stephen Jackson/299 2.50 6.00
39 Gerald Wallace/99 3.00 8.00
41 Dwyane Wade/199 6.00 15.00
43 Dwight Howard/299 5.00 12.00
44 Vince Carter/299 4.00 10.00
45 J.J. Redick/299 3.00 8.00
46 Josh Howard/299 2.50
48 Gilbert Arenas/299 3.00
49 Kirk Hinrich/299 3.00
51 Jason Kidd/50 3.00
52 Shawn Marion/299 3.00
53 Caron Butler/299 3.00
54 Kevin Martin/299 3.00
55 Shane Battier/299 2.50
56 Luis Scola/199 2.50
58 Marc Gasol/99 3.00
59 Rudy Gay/99 3.00
61 Chris Paul/299 5.00
62 Emeka Okafor/299 3.00
63 David West/299 3.00
64 Tim Duncan/299 5.00
65 Tony Parker/299 3.00
66 Richard Jefferson/299 3.00
67 Carmelo Anthony/25 4.00
68 Chauncey Billups/299 3.00
70 Nene/299 2.50
71 Kevin Love/299 4.00
72 Michael Beasley/299 3.00
73 Jonny Flynn/299 2.00
74 Brandon Roy/299 3.00
75 Rudy Fernandez/299 2.50
76 Greg Oden/299 2.50
78 Russell Westbrook/299 4.00
80 Deron Williams/299 3.00
81 Al Jefferson/299 3.00
82 Andrei Kirilenko/299 2.50
86 Stephen Curry/299 4.00
87 Eric Gordon/99 3.00
88 Chris Kaman/150 2.50
89 Baron Davis/100 3.00
91 Pau Gasol/299 3.00
92 Lamar Odom/299 3.00
93 Ron Artest/299 3.00
94 Steve Nash/299 3.00
95 Hedo Turkoglu/299 3.00
96 Channing Frye/299 2.50
99 Samuel Dalembert/299 2.00
101 Rolando Blackman/50 3.00
102 Joe Dumars/99 3.00
118 Terrico White/299 3.00
129 Jeremy Lin/299 30.00

2010-11 Rookies and Star[s] Dress for Success Materia[ls]

STATED PRINT RUN 15 TO 299 SER.#'d SETS
*PRIME: .75X TO 2X BASE HI
PRIME PRINT RUN 10 TO 49 SER.#'d SETS
1 John Wall/299 6.00
2 Andre Miller/299 2.50
3 Evan Turner/299 4.00
4 Wesley Johnson/299 3.00
5 Andris Biedrins/299 2.00
6 Derrick Favors/299 4.00
7 Ekpe Udoh/299 2.00
8 Emeka Okafor/299 3.00
9 Eric Gordon/99 3.00
10 Caron Butler/299 3.00
11 Gani Lawal/299 2.00
12 Gerald Henderson/299 2.00
13 Goran Dragic/199 3.00
14 Gordon Hayward/299 4.00
15 Greg Monroe/299 4.00
16 Greg Oden/299 2.50
17 Greivis Vasquez/299 2.50
18 Hassan Whiteside/299 2.00
19 J.J. Barea/299 4.00
20 J.J. Redick/299 3.00
21 J.R. Smith/299 3.00
22 James Anderson/299 2.00
23 Jeff Green/15 2.50
24 Dwight Howard/299 5.00
25 Jose Calderon/299 2.50
26 Lance Stephenson/299 2.00
27 Marcus Camby/299 2.00
28 Mike Dunleavy/99 2.00
29 DeMarcus Cousins/299 6.00
30 Joakim Noah/299 3.00
31 Xavier Henry/299 2.50
32 Nene/299 2.50
33 Al-Farouq Aminu/299 2.00
34 Larry Sanders/299 2.00
35 Paul George/299 5.00

2010-11 Rookies and Star[s] Dress for Success Materia[ls] Signatures

STATED PRINT RUN 5 TO 25 SER.#'d SETS
PRIME SIG.PRINT RUN 10 SER.#'d SETS
PRIME SIG.UNPRICED DUE TO SCARCITY
1 John Wall/25 100.00
2 Andre Miller/25 6.00
3 Evan Turner/25 15.00
4 Wesley Johnson/25 10.00
6 Derrick Favors/25 20.00
7 Ekpe Udoh/25 6.00
9 Eric Gordon/25 8.00
11 Gani Lawal/25 6.00
12 Gerald Henderson/25 6.00
13 Goran Dragic/25 15.00
14 Gordon Hayward/25 12.00
15 Greg Monroe/25 15.00
17 Greivis Vasquez/25 8.00
18 Hassan Whiteside/25 6.00
19 J.J. Barea/25 20.00
21 J.R. Smith/25 6.00
22 James Anderson/25 6.00
26 Lance Stephenson/25 6.00
27 Marcus Camby/25 6.00
28 Mike Dunleavy/25 6.00
29 DeMarcus Cousins/25 25.00
31 Xavier Henry/25 8.00
33 Al-Farouq Aminu/25 6.00
34 Larry Sanders/25 6.00
35 Paul George/25 15.00

2010-11 Rookies and Star[s] Freshman Orientation Doub[le] Materials

STATED PRINT RUN 399 SER.#'d SETS
*PRIME: 1X TO 2.5X BASE HI
PRIME: PRINT RUN 25 TO 49 SER.#'d SETS
1 John Wall 8.00
2 Evan Turner 4.00
3 Derrick Favors 4.00
4 Wesley Johnson 3.00
5 DeMarcus Cousins 6.00
6 Ekpe Udoh 2.00
7 Greg Monroe 4.00
8 Al-Farouq Aminu 2.00
9 Gordon Hayward 4.00
10 Paul George 5.00
11 Cole Aldrich 2.00
12 Xavier Henry 2.50
13 Patrick Patterson 3.00
14 Larry Sanders 2.00

uke Babbitt 2.00 5.00
ric Bledsoe 3.00 8.00
very Bradley 4.00 10.00
ames Anderson 2.00 5.00
raig Brackins 2.00 5.00
lliot Williams 2.00 5.00
revor Booker 2.00 5.00
amion James 2.00 5.00
Dominique Jones 2.00 5.00
Quincy Pondexter 2.00 5.00
ordan Crawford 3.00 8.00
Greivis Vasquez 2.50 6.00
Daniel Orton 2.00 5.00
azar Hayward 2.00 5.00
Dexter Pittman 2.00 5.00
Hassan Whiteside 2.00 5.00
ance Stephenson 2.00 5.00
a'Sean Butler 2.00 5.00
evin Ebanks 2.50 6.00
Sani Lawal 2.00 5.00
uke Harangody 2.00 5.00

2010-11 Rookies and Stars Freshman Orientation Double Materials Signatures

TED PRINT RUN 49 SER.#'d SETS
ME SIG.PRINT RUN 10 SER.#'d SETS
ME SIG.UNPRICED DUE TO SCARCITY
hn Wall 60.00 150.00
an Turner 12.00 30.00
errick Favors 12.50 30.00
esley Johnson 8.00 20.00
Marcus Cousins 15.00 40.00
pe Udoh 5.00 12.00
eg Monroe 10.00 25.00
-Farouq Aminu 5.00 12.00
ordon Hayward 10.00 25.00
Paul George 12.00 30.00
Cole Aldrich 5.00 12.00
Xavier Henry 6.00 15.00
Patrick Patterson 10.00 25.00
arry Sanders 5.00 12.00
uke Babbitt 6.00 15.00
Eric Bledsoe 10.00 25.00
very Bradley 10.00 25.00
ames Anderson 5.00 12.00
Craig Brackins 5.00 12.00
Elliot Williams 5.00 12.00
Trevor Booker 5.00 12.00
Damion James 5.00 12.00
Dominique Jones 5.00 12.00
Quincy Pondexter 5.00 12.00
ordan Crawford 8.00 20.00
Greivis Vasquez 6.00 15.00
Daniel Orton 5.00 12.00
azar Hayward EXCH 5.00 12.00
Dexter Pittman 5.00 12.00
Hassan Whiteside 5.00 12.00
ance Stephenson 5.00 12.00
Da'Sean Butler 5.00 12.00
Devin Ebanks 10.00 25.00
Sani Lawal 5.00 12.00
uke Harangody 5.00 12.00

2010-11 Rookies and Stars Game Garb Materials

TED PRINT RUN 10 TO 49 SER.#'d SETS
Horford/49 5.00 12.00
n Gordon/49 6.00 15.00
ook Lopez/49 6.00 15.00
aron Butler/25 6.00 15.00
hris Kaman/25 5.00 12.00
anny Granger/15 6.00 15.00
ic Gordon/25 6.00 15.00
rant Hill/49 20.00 50.00
uol Deng/15 6.00 15.00
Nene/49 5.00 12.00
Paul Pierce/49 8.00 20.00
Steve Nash/25 8.00 20.00
Tim Duncan/49 10.00 25.00
Vince Carter/49 8.00 20.00

2010-11 Rookies and Stars me Garb Materials Signatures

TED PRINT RUN 5 TO 49 SER.#'d SETS
ME UNPRICED DUE TO SCARCITY
Horford/25 8.00 20.00
en Gordon/25 8.00 20.00
hris Kaman/49 8.00 20.00
ic Gordon/25 10.00 25.00

2010-11 Rookies and Stars Moments in Time

MPLETE SET (15) 7.50 15.00
DOM INSERTS IN PACKS
ACK: .75X TO 2X BASE HI
CK PRINT RUN 99 SER.#'d SETS
LD: .5X TO 1.25X BASE HI
D PRINT RUN 499 SER.#'d SETS
LO: .6X TO 1.5X BASE HI
O PRINT RUN 199 SER.#'d SETS
ob Cousy 1.25 3.00
gin Baylor .75 2.00
erry West 1.00 2.50
hn Havlicek 1.00 2.50
eorge Gervin .75 2.00
areem Abdul-Jabbar 1.25 3.00
arry Bird 2.50 6.00
lagic Johnson 2.00 5.00
992 USA Men's Olympic Team 2.50 6.00
A.C. Green .75 2.00
John Stockton 1.25 3.00
Karl Malone 1.00 2.50
LeBron James 4.00 10.00
Kobe Bryant 4.00 10.00
Tyreke Evans 1.00 2.50

2010-11 Rookies and Stars Prime Cuts

TED PRINT RUN 25 TO 50 SER.#'d SETS
llen Iverson/50 12.00 30.00
onzo Mourning/50 12.00 30.00
ndre Iguodala/50 10.00 25.00
armelo Anthony/50 12.00 30.00
hris Paul/50 15.00 40.00
yde Drexler/50 12.00 30.00

7 Dirk Nowitzki/50 12.00 30.00
8 Dwight Howard/50 15.00 40.00
9 Dwyane Wade/25 20.00 50.00
10 Gary Payton/50 10.00 25.00
11 John Stockton/50 15.00 40.00
12 Kareem Abdul-Jabbar/50 15.00 40.00
13 Karl Malone/50 12.00 30.00
14 Magic Johnson/50 20.00 50.00
15 Vince Carter/50 12.00 30.00

2010-11 Rookies and Stars Retired NBA Team Patches Signatures

STATED PRINT RUN 54 TO 99 SER.#'d SETS
1 Bill Cartwright/99 15.00 40.00
2 Bob Dandridge/99 8.00 20.00
3 Chris Ford/99 10.00 25.00
4 Dennis Rodman/99 35.00 70.00
5 Gheorghe Muresan/99 EXCH 8.00 20.00
6 Kelly Tripucka/99 6.00 15.00
7 Kevin Johnson/99 EXCH 20.00 50.00
8 Maurice Cheeks/99 6.00 15.00
9 Dominique Wilkins/54 12.50 30.00
10 Xavier McDaniel/99 6.00 15.00

2010-11 Rookies and Stars Sharp Shooters

COMPLETE SET (15) 5.00 12.00
RANDOM INSERTS IN PACKS
*BLACK: .75X TO 2X BASE HI
BLACK: STATED PRINT RUN 99 SER.#'d SETS
*GOLD: .5X TO 1.25X BASE HI
GOLD: STATED PRINT RUN 499 SER.#'d SETS
*HOLO: .6X TO 1.5X BASE HI
HOLO STATED PRINT RUN 199 SER.#'d SETS
1 Dwight Howard 1.50 4.00
2 Kendrick Perkins .75 2.00
3 Nene .75 2.00
4 Marc Gasol 1.00 2.50
5 Andrew Bynum 1.25 3.00
6 Carlos Boozer 1.00 2.50
7 Amare Stoudemire 1.00 2.50
8 Al Horford .75 2.00
9 David Lee .75 2.00
10 Paul Millsap .75 2.00
11 Pau Gasol 1.00 2.50
12 Kevin Garnett 2.00 5.00
13 Chris Bosh 1.00 2.50
14 Tim Duncan 1.50 4.00
15 Rajon Rondo 1.25 3.00

2010-11 Rookies and Stars Sharp Shooters Materials

STATED PRINT RUN 99 SER.#'d SETS
*PRIME: .75X TO 2X BASE HI
PRIME PRINT RUN ONE TO 49 SER.#'d SETS
SOME PRIME UNPRICED DUE TO SCARCITY
1 Dwight Howard 5.00 12.00
3 Nene 2.50 6.00
4 Marc Gasol 3.00 8.00
5 Andrew Bynum 4.00 10.00
8 Al Horford 2.50 6.00
11 Pau Gasol 3.00 8.00
12 Kevin Garnett 6.00 15.00
14 Tim Duncan 5.00 12.00
15 Rajon Rondo 4.00 10.00

2010-11 Rookies and Stars Sharp Shooters Signatures

STATED PRINT RUN 10 TO 49 SER.#'d SETS
SOME UNPRICED DUE TO SCARCITY
4 Marc Gasol/25 12.50 30.00
5 Andrew Bynum/49 8.00 20.00
6 Carlos Boozer/49 6.00 15.00
7 Amare Stoudemire/15 25.00 60.00
8 Al Horford/49 6.00 15.00
9 David Lee/49 6.00 15.00
11 Pau Gasol/15 15.00 40.00
15 Rajon Rondo/15 25.00 60.00

2010-11 Rookies and Stars Signatures

STATED PRINT RUN 5 TO 49 SER.#'d SETS
SOME UNPRICED DUE TO SCARCITY
8 Amare Stoudemire/15 30.00 80.00
11 Andre Iguodala/25 4.00 10.00
14 Andrea Bargnani/49 6.00 15.00
28 Tyler Hansbrough/99 4.00 10.00
37 Gerald Henderson/149 4.00 10.00
46 Josh Howard/99 4.00 10.00
51 Jason Kidd/25 12.50 30.00
55 Shane Battier/49 4.00 10.00
62 Emeka Okafor/25 4.00 10.00
73 Jonny Flynn/199 4.00 10.00
86 Stephen Curry/49 12.50 30.00
89 Baron Davis/25 6.00 15.00
90 Kobe Bryant/99 100.00 200.00
93 Ron Artest/25 10.00 25.00
98 Tyreke Evans/99 10.00 25.00
100 Carl Landry/99 4.00 10.00
105 Gail Goodrich/49 6.00 15.00
106 John Havlicek/25 15.00 40.00
116 Armon Johnson/99 4.00 10.00
118 Terrico White/299 4.00 10.00
120 Landry Fields/349 6.00 15.00
126 Solomon Alabi/350 4.00 10.00
129 Jeremy Lin/499 75.00 150.00

2010-11 Rookies and Stars Stardom

COMPLETE SET (15) 10.00 20.00
RANDOM INSERTS IN PACKS
*BLACK: .75X TO 2X BASE HI
BLACK STATED PRINT RUN 99 SER.#'d SETS
*GOLD: .5X TO 1.25X BASE HI
GOLD STATED PRINT RUN 499 SER.#'d SETS
*HOLO: .6X TO 1.5X BASE HI
HOLO STATED PRINT RUN 199 SER.#'d SETS
1 Kobe Bryant 4.00 10.00
2 LeBron James 4.00 10.00
3 Dirk Nowitzki 1.00 2.50
4 Dwight Howard 1.25 3.00
5 Paul Pierce 1.00 2.50
6 Chris Paul 1.25 3.00
7 Chris Bosh .75 2.00
8 Kevin Durant 2.50 6.00
9 Tyreke Evans 1.00 2.50
10 Steve Nash .75 2.00
11 Deron Williams .75 2.00
12 Derrick Rose 2.50 6.00
13 Dwyane Wade 1.50 4.00
14 Brandon Jennings .75 2.00
15 Carlos Boozer .75 2.00

2010-11 Rookies and Stars Stardom Materials

STATED PRINT RUN 50 TO 99 SER.#'d SETS
1 Kobe Bryant/99 8.00 20.00
3 Dirk Nowitzki/99 4.00 10.00
4 Dwight Howard/99 5.00 12.00
5 Paul Pierce/99 4.00 10.00
6 Chris Paul/99 5.00 12.00
10 Steve Nash/99 3.00 8.00
11 Deron Williams/99 3.00 8.00
12 Derrick Rose/50 10.00 25.00
13 Dwyane Wade/99 6.00 15.00
14 Brandon Jennings/99 3.00 8.00

2010-11 Rookies and Stars Stardom Signatures

STATED PRINT RUN 49 SER.#'d SETS
1 Kobe Bryant 100.00 200.00
9 Tyreke Evans 12.50 30.00
14 Brandon Jennings 10.00 25.00

2010-11 Rookies and Stars Statistical Standouts Materials

STATED PRINT RUN 25 TO 199 SER.#'d SETS
*PRIME: .75X TO 2X BASE HI
PRIME PRINT RUN 5 TO 49 SER.#'d SETS
SOME PRIME UNPRICED DUE TO SCARCITY
2 Carmelo Anthony/25 4.00 10.00
3 Kobe Bryant/199 8.00 20.00
4 Dirk Nowitzki/199 4.00 10.00
6 Joe Johnson/199 3.00 8.00
7 Steve Nash/199 3.00 8.00
8 Deron Williams/199 3.00 8.00
9 Rajon Rondo/199 4.00 10.00
10 Jason Kidd/149 3.00 8.00
11 Dwight Howard/199 5.00 12.00
12 Marcus Camby/199 2.00 5.00
13 Andrew Bogut/100 3.00 8.00
14 Josh Smith/25 3.00 8.00
15 Chris Andersen/199 3.00 8.00

2010-11 Rookies and Stars Statistical Standouts Materials Signatures

STATED PRINT RUN 10 TO 25 SER.#'d SETS
UNPRICED PRIME PRINT RUN 5 TO 10 SETS
3 Kobe Bryant/25 100.00 200.00
6 Joe Johnson/25 10.00 25.00
8 Deron Williams/25 12.50 30.00
9 Rajon Rondo/25 20.00 50.00
10 Jason Kidd/25 20.00 50.00
12 Marcus Camby/25 10.00 25.00
15 Chris Andersen/25 20.00 50.00

2010-11 Rookies and Stars Studio Combo Rookies

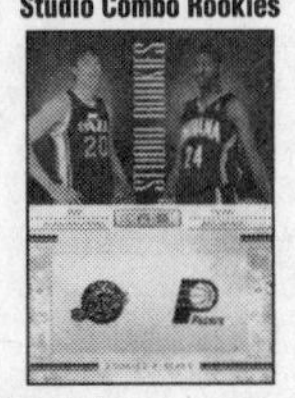

COMPLETE SET (10) 7.50 15.00
RANDOM INSERTS IN PACKS
*BLACK: .75X TO 2X BASE HI
BLACK PRINT RUN 99 SER.#'d SETS
*GOLD: .5X TO 1.25X BASE HI
GOLD PRINT RUN 499 SER.#'d SETS
*HOLO: .6X TO 1.5X BASE HI
HOLO PRINT RUN 199 SER.#'d SETS
1 Evan Turner 3.00 8.00
John Wall
2 Wesley Johnson 1.50 4.00
Derrick Favors
3 Ekpe Udoh 1.50 4.00
DeMarcus Cousins
4 Greg Monroe 1.00 2.50
Al-Farouq Aminu
5 Gordon Hayward 1.50 4.00
Paul George
6 John Wall 4.00 10.00
DeMarcus Cousins
7 Cole Aldrich 1.00 2.50
Xavier Henry
8 Eric Bledsoe 1.50 4.00
Patrick Patterson
9 Devin Ebanks 1.00 2.50
Da'Sean Butler
10 John Wall 2.50 6.00
Daniel Orton

2010-11 Rookies and Stars Studio Combo Rookies Materials

STATED PRINT RUN 399 SER.#'d SETS
*PRIME: .75X TO 2X BASE HI
PRIME PRINT RUN 49 SER.#'d SETS
1 Evan Turner 8.00 20.00
John Wall
2 Wesley Johnson 6.00 15.00
Derrick Favors
3 Ekpe Udoh 4.00 10.00
DeMarcus Cousins
4 Greg Monroe 3.00 8.00
Al-Farouq Aminu
5 Gordon Hayward 4.00 10.00
Paul George
6 John Wall 10.00 25.00
DeMarcus Cousins
7 Cole Aldrich 3.00 8.00
Xavier Henry
8 Eric Bledsoe 5.00 12.00
Patrick Patterson
9 Devin Ebanks 3.00 8.00
Da'Sean Butler
10 John Wall 8.00 20.00
Daniel Orton

2010-11 Rookies and Stars Studio Combo Rookies Signatures

STATED PRINT RUN 49 SER.#'d SETS
1 Evan Turner 60.00 150.00
John Wall
2 Wesley Johnson 15.00 40.00
Derrick Favors
3 Ekpe Udoh 15.00 40.00
DeMarcus Cousins
4 Greg Monroe 10.00 25.00
Al-Farouq Aminu
5 Gordon Hayward 20.00 50.00
Paul George
6 John Wall 60.00 150.00
DeMarcus Cousins
7 Cole Aldrich 10.00 25.00
Xavier Henry
8 Eric Bledsoe 15.00 40.00
Patrick Patterson
9 Devin Ebanks 10.00 25.00
Da'Sean Butler
10 John Wall 40.00 100.00
Daniel Orton

2010-11 Rookies and Stars Superstars

COMPLETE SET (15) 7.50 15.00
RANDOM INSERTS IN PACKS
*BLACK: .75X TO 2X BASE HI
BLACK STATED PRINT RUN 99 SER.#'d SETS
*GOLD: .5X TO 1.25X BASE HI
GOLD STATED PRINT RUN 499 SER.#'d SETS
*HOLO: .6X TO 1.5X BASE HI
HOLO STATED PRINT RUN 199 SER.#'d SETS
1 Kobe Bryant 4.00 10.00
2 LeBron James 4.00 10.00
3 Dwight Howard 1.25 3.00
4 Dwyane Wade 1.50 4.00
5 Kevin Durant 2.50 6.00
6 Steve Nash .75 2.00
7 Dirk Nowitzki 1.00 2.50
8 Andrew Bogut .75 2.00
9 Deron Williams .75 2.00
10 Carmelo Anthony 1.00 2.50
11 Rajon Rondo 1.00 2.50
12 Brandon Roy .75 2.00
13 Tim Duncan 1.25 3.00
14 Josh Smith .75 2.00
15 Chris Bosh .75 2.00

2010-11 Rookies and Stars Superstars Materials

STATED PRINT RUN 25 TO 299 SER.#'d SETS
*PRIME: .75X TO 2X BASE HI
PRIME STATED PRINT RUN 5 TO 49 SETS
SOME PRIME UNPRICED DUE TO SCARCITY
1 Kobe Bryant/299 8.00 20.00
3 Dwight Howard/299 5.00 12.00
4 Dwyane Wade/299 6.00 15.00
6 Steve Nash/299 3.00 8.00
7 Dirk Nowitzki/299 4.00 10.00
8 Andrew Bogut/100 3.00 8.00
9 Deron Williams/299 3.00 8.00
10 Carmelo Anthony/25 4.00 10.00
11 Rajon Rondo/299 4.00 10.00
12 Brandon Roy/299 3.00 8.00
13 Tim Duncan/299 5.00 12.00
14 Josh Smith/25 3.00 8.00

2010-11 Rookies and Stars Superstars Signatures

STATED PRINT RUN 5 TO 49 SER.#'d SETS
SOME UNPRICED DUE TO SCARCITY
1 Kobe Bryant/49 100.00 200.00
9 Deron Williams/25 12.50 30.00
11 Rajon Rondo/15 25.00 60.00
12 Brandon Roy/49 8.00 20.00

2010-11 Rookies and Stars Team Leaders

COMPLETE SET (30) 12.50 25.00
RANDOM INSERTS IN PACKS
*BLACK: .75X TO 2X BASE HI
BLACK STATED PRINT RUN 99 SER.#'d SETS
*GOLD: .5X TO 1.25X BASE HI
GOLD STATED PRINT RUN 499 SER.#'d SETS
*HOLO: .6X TO 1.5X BASE HI
HOLO STATED PRINT RUN 199 SER.#'d SETS
1 Al Horford .75 2.00
Joe Johnson
Josh Smith
2 Kevin Garnett 1.50 4.00
Paul Pierce
Rajon Rondo
3 Gerald Wallace .75 2.00
Stephen Jackson
Boris Diaw
4 Carlos Boozer 2.50 6.00
Luol Deng
Derrick Rose
5 Anderson Varejao .75 2.00
Mo Williams
Antawn Jamison
6 Caron Butler 1.00 2.50
Jason Kidd
Dirk Nowitzki
7 Carmelo Anthony 1.00 2.50
Chauncey Billups
Nene
8 Richard Hamilton .75 2.00
Tayshaun Prince
Ben Gordon
9 Monta Ellis 1.00 2.50
David Lee
Stephen Curry
10 Kevin Martin .75 2.00
Aaron Brooks
Luis Scola
11 Mike Dunleavy .75 2.00
T.J. Ford
Danny Granger
12 Baron Davis .75 2.00
Eric Gordon
Chris Kaman
13 Pau Gasol 4.00 10.00
Lamar Odom
Kobe Bryant
14 Marc Gasol .75 2.00
O.J. Mayo
Zach Randolph
15 Dwyane Wade 4.00 10.00
LeBron James
Chris Bosh
16 Brandon Jennings .75 2.00
John Salmons
Andrew Bogut
17 Kevin Love 1.00 2.50
Michael Beasley
Martell Webster
18 Troy Murphy .75 2.00
Devin Harris
Brook Lopez
19 Chris Paul 1.25 3.00
David West
Trevor Ariza
20 Danilo Gallinari .75 2.00
Amare Stoudemire
Anthony Randolph
21 Kevin Durant 2.50 6.00
Jeff Green
Russell Westbrook
22 Dwight Howard 1.25 3.00
Rashard Lewis
Vince Carter
23 Andre Iguodala .75 2.00
Thaddeus Young
Elton Brand
24 Steve Nash .75 2.00
Jason Richardson
Channing Frye
25 Brandon Roy .75 2.00
LaMarcus Aldridge
Andre Miller
26 Samuel Dalembert 1.00 2.50
Carl Landry
Tyreke Evans
27 Tim Duncan 1.25 3.00
Manu Ginobili
Tony Parker
28 Andrea Bargnani .60 1.50
Jose Calderon
Leandro Barbosa
29 Al Jefferson .75 2.00
Andrei Kirilenko
Deron Williams
30 Josh Howard .75 2.00
Al Thornton
Gilbert Arenas

2010-11 Rookies and Stars Kids Foot Locker

This promotion was offered in late 2010 through early 2011 at participating Kids Foot Locker stores. With every $20 purchase, you received one six-card pack.
COMPLETE SET (6) 6.00 15.00
1 Kobe Bryant 3.00 8.00
2 Wesley Johnson 1.00 2.50
3 Rajon Rondo .75 2.00
4 Derrick Rose 2.00 5.00
5 Evan Turner 1.25 3.00
6 John Wall 2.50 6.00

2009-10 Rookies and Stars Longevity

COMP.SET w/o SPs (115) 15.00 30.00
1 Josh Smith .40 1.00
2 Joe Johnson .40 1.00
3 Mike Bibby .30 .75
4 Paul Pierce .50 1.25
5 Ray Allen .40 1.00
6 Rajon Rondo .50 1.25
7 Kevin Garnett .75 2.00
8 Gerald Wallace .40 1.00
9 Boris Diaw .30 .75
10 Raja Bell .30 .75
11 Derrick Rose 1.25 3.00
12 John Salmons .40 1.00
13 Kirk Hinrich .40 1.00
14 LeBron James 2.00 5.00
15 Shaquille O'Neal .75 2.00
16 Mo Williams .30 .75
17 Dirk Nowitzki .50 1.25
18 Josh Howard .30 .75
19 Jason Kidd .40 1.00
20 Jason Terry .30 .75
21 Shawn Marion .40 1.00
22 Carmelo Anthony .50 1.25
23 Chauncey Billups .40 1.00
24 J.R. Smith .40 1.00
25 Richard Hamilton .30 .75
26 Tayshaun Prince .40 1.00
27 Allen Iverson .50 1.25
28 Stephen Jackson .30 .75
29 Corey Maggette .30 .75
30 Monta Ellis .40 1.00
31 Yao Ming .50 1.25
32 Tracy McGrady .40 1.00
33 Trevor Ariza .25 .60
34 Danny Granger .40 1.00
35 Mike Dunleavy .25 .60
36 T.J. Ford .25 .60
37 Al Thornton .30 .75
38 Eric Gordon .40 1.00
39 Kobe Bryant 2.00 5.00
40 Pau Gasol .40 1.00
41 Ron Artest .40 1.00
42 Andrew Bynum .50 1.25
43 Rudy Gay .40 1.00
44 O.J. Mayo .40 1.00
45 Mike Conley Jr. .30 .75
46 Zach Randolph .30 .75
47 Dwyane Wade .75 2.00
48 Michael Beasley .40 1.00
49 Jermaine O'Neal .40 1.00
50 Udonis Haslem .30 .75
51 Michael Redd .40 1.00
52 Ramon Sessions .30 .75
53 Andrew Bogut .40 1.00
54 Al Jefferson .40 1.00
55 Ryan Gomes .25 .60
56 Kevin Love .60 1.50
57 Devin Harris .40 1.00
58 Brook Lopez .40 1.00
59 Rafer Alston .25 .60
60 Chris Paul .60 1.50
61 David West .40 1.00
62 Peja Stojakovic .40 1.00
63 Al Harrington .30 .75
64 Nate Robinson .40 1.00
65 Wilson Chandler .30 .75
66 Kevin Durant 1.25 3.00
67 Jeff Green .30 .75
68 Russell Westbrook .60 1.50
69 Dwight Howard .60 1.50
70 Rashard Lewis .30 .75
71 Jameer Nelson .30 .75
72 Vince Carter .50 1.25
73 Andre Iguodala .40 1.00
74 Elton Brand .40 1.00
75 Thaddeus Young .25 .60
76 Amare Stoudemire .40 1.00
77 Steve Nash .40 1.00
78 Leandro Barbosa .30 .75
79 Channing Frye .30 .75
80 Brandon Roy .40 1.00
81 LaMarcus Aldridge .40 1.00
82 Greg Oden .30 .75
83 Kevin Martin .40 1.00
84 Andres Nocioni .25 .60
85 Spencer Hawes .30 .75
86 Tony Parker .40 1.00
87 Tim Duncan .60 1.50
88 Manu Ginobili .40 1.00
89 Richard Jefferson .40 1.00
90 Chris Bosh .40 1.00
91 Hedo Turkoglu .40 1.00
92 Andrea Bargnani .30 .75
93 Deron Williams .40 1.00
94 Carlos Boozer .40 1.00
95 Andrei Kirilenko .30 .75
96 Ronnie Brewer .30 .75
97 Antawn Jamison .40 1.00
98 Gilbert Arenas .40 1.00
99 Caron Butler .40 1.00
100 Randy Foye .25 .60
101 Kareem Abdul-Jabbar .60 1.50
102 Elvin Hayes .40 1.00
103 Karl Malone .50 1.25
104 Arnie Risen .40 1.00
105 Jalen Rose .40 1.00
106 Dave DeBusschere .40 1.00
107 Artis Gilmore .40 1.00
108 Nate Archibald .40 1.00
109 Mark Eaton .40 1.00
110 Darryl Dawkins .40 1.00
111 Spencer Haywood .40 1.00
112 Bill Cartwright .40 1.00
113 Moses Malone .40 1.00
114 Magic Johnson 1.00 2.50
115 Sleepy Floyd .40 1.00
116 Dante Cunningham RC .60 1.50
117 Jon Brockman RC .60 1.50
118 Jonas Jerebko RC .60 1.50
119 Derrick Brown RC .60 1.50
120 Dionte Christmas RC .60 1.50
121 Marcus Thornton RC 1.00 2.50
122 Danny Green RC 1.00 2.50
123 Goran Suton RC .60 1.50
124 Jack McClinton RC .60 1.50
125 A.J. Price RC .60 1.50
126 Serge Ibaka RC 1.50 4.00
127 DeMar DeRozan RC 1.00 2.50
128 Chris Hunter RC .60 1.50
129 Lester Hudson RC .60 1.50
130 David Andersen RC .60 1.50

2009-10 Rookies and Stars Longevity Ruby

*1-130 RUBY: 2X TO 5X BASE HI
1-130 RUBY PRINT RUN 250 SER.#'d SETS
131-164 PRINT RUN 43 TO 49 SER.#'d SETS
131 Blake Griffin AU 150.00 300.00
132 Hasheem Thabeet AU 8.00 20.00
133 James Harden AU 25.00 60.00
134 Tyreke Evans AU 20.00 50.00
135 Jonny Flynn AU 8.00 20.00
136 Stephen Curry AU 20.00 50.00
137 Jordan Hill AU 8.00 20.00
139 Brandon Jennings AU 15.00 40.00
140 Terrence Williams AU 8.00 20.00
141 Gerald Henderson AU 8.00 20.00
142 Tyler Hansbrough AU 12.00 30.00
143 Earl Clark AU 8.00 20.00
144 Austin Daye AU 8.00 20.00
145 James Johnson AU/43 8.00 20.00
146 Jrue Holiday AU 15.00 40.00
147 Ty Lawson AU 12.00 30.00
148 Jeff Teague AU 10.00 25.00
149 Eric Maynor AU 8.00 20.00
150 Darren Collison AU 12.00 30.00
151 Omri Casspi AU 8.00 20.00
152 B.J. Mullens AU 8.00 20.00
153 Rodrigue Beaubois AU 10.00 25.00
154 Taj Gibson AU 10.00 25.00
155 DeMarre Carroll AU 8.00 20.00
156 Wayne Ellington AU 8.00 20.00
157 Toney Douglas AU 8.00 20.00
158 Jermaine Taylor AU 8.00 20.00
159 Jeff Pendergraph AU 8.00 20.00
160 DaJuan Summers AU 8.00 20.00
161 Sam Young AU 8.00 20.00
162 DeJuan Blair AU/48 10.00 25.00
163 Chase Budinger AU 8.00 20.00
164 Jodie Meeks AU 10.00 25.00
165 Taylor Griffin AU 8.00 20.00

2009-10 Rookies and Stars Longevity Dress for Success Materials Jerseys

STATED PRINT RUN 299 SER.#'d SETS
1 Blake Griffin 12.00 30.00
2 Hasheem Thabeet 2.00 5.00
3 James Harden 6.00 15.00
4 Tyreke Evans 5.00 12.00
5 Jonny Flynn 2.00 5.00
6 Stephen Curry 5.00 12.00
7 Jordan Hill 2.00 5.00
8 DeMar DeRozan 3.00 8.00
9 Brandon Jennings 4.00 10.00
10 Terrence Williams 2.00 5.00
11 Gerald Henderson 2.00 5.00
12 Tyler Hansbrough 3.00 8.00
13 Earl Clark 2.00 5.00
14 Austin Daye 2.00 5.00
15 James Johnson 2.00 5.00
16 Jrue Holiday 4.00 10.00
17 Ty Lawson 3.00 8.00
18 Jeff Teague 2.50 6.00
19 Eric Maynor 2.00 5.00
20 Darren Collison 3.00 8.00
21 Omri Casspi 2.00 5.00
22 B.J. Mullens 2.00 5.00
23 Rodrigue Beaubois 2.50 6.00
24 Taj Gibson 2.50 6.00
25 DeMarre Carroll 2.00 5.00
26 Wayne Ellington 2.00 5.00
27 Toney Douglas 2.00 5.00
28 Jermaine Taylor 2.00 5.00
29 Jeff Pendergraph 2.00 5.00
30 DaJuan Summers 2.00 5.00
31 Sam Young 2.00 5.00
32 DeJuan Blair 2.50 6.00
33 Chase Budinger 2.00 5.00
34 Jodie Meeks 2.50 6.00
35 Taylor Griffin 2.00 5.00

2009-10 Rookies and Stars Longevity Freshman Orientation Materials Jerseys

STATED PRINT RUN 299 SER.#'d SETS
1 Blake Griffin 12.00 30.00
2 Hasheem Thabeet 2.00 5.00
3 James Harden 6.00 15.00
4 Tyreke Evans 5.00 12.00
5 Jonny Flynn 2.00 5.00
6 Stephen Curry 5.00 12.00
7 Jordan Hill 2.00 5.00
8 DeMar DeRozan 3.00 8.00
9 Brandon Jennings 4.00 10.00
10 Terrence Williams 2.00 5.00
11 Gerald Henderson 2.00 5.00
12 Tyler Hansbrough 3.00 8.00
13 Earl Clark 2.00 5.00
14 Austin Daye 2.00 5.00
15 James Johnson 2.00 5.00
16 Jrue Holiday 4.00 10.00
17 Ty Lawson 3.00 8.00
18 Jeff Teague 2.50 6.00
19 Eric Maynor 2.00 5.00
20 Darren Collison 3.00 8.00
21 Omri Casspi 2.00 5.00
22 B.J. Mullens 2.00 5.00
23 Rodrigue Beaubois 2.50 6.00
24 Taj Gibson 2.50 6.00
25 DeMarre Carroll 2.00 5.00
26 Wayne Ellington 2.00 5.00
27 Toney Douglas 2.00 5.00
28 Jermaine Taylor 2.00 5.00
29 Jeff Pendergraph 2.00 5.00
30 DaJuan Summers 2.00 5.00
31 Sam Young 2.00 5.00
32 DeJuan Blair 2.50 6.00
33 Chase Budinger 2.00 5.00
34 Jodie Meeks 2.50 6.00
35 Taylor Griffin 2.00 5.00

2009-10 Rookies and Stars Longevity Materials Ruby

STATED PRINT RUN 99 TO 250 SER.#'d SETS
*SAPPHIRE: .6X TO 1.5X BASE HI
SAPPHIRE PRINT RUN 25 SER.#'d SETS
1 Josh Smith/250 3.00 8.00
3 Mike Bibby/250 2.50 6.00
13 Kirk Hinrich/250 3.00 8.00
14 LeBron James/250 8.00 20.00
17 Dirk Nowitzki/250 4.00 10.00
18 Josh Howard/250 2.50 6.00
19 Jason Kidd/250 3.00 8.00
20 Jason Terry/250 2.50 6.00
22 Carmelo Anthony/250 4.00 10.00
26 Tayshaun Prince/250 3.00 8.00
31 Yao Ming/250 4.00 10.00
32 Tracy McGrady/250 3.00 8.00
39 Kobe Bryant/99 10.00 25.00
40 Pau Gasol/250 3.00 8.00
42 Andrew Bynum/250 4.00 10.00
44 O.J. Mayo/250 3.00 8.00
45 Mike Conley Jr./250 2.50 6.00
47 Dwyane Wade/250 6.00 15.00
49 Jermaine O'Neal/150 3.00 8.00
50 Udonis Haslem/250 2.50 6.00
51 Michael Redd/250 3.00 8.00
53 Andrew Bogut/250 3.00 8.00
54 Al Jefferson/250 3.00 8.00
56 Kevin Love/250 5.00 12.00
57 Devin Harris/150 3.00 8.00
60 Chris Paul/250 5.00 12.00
62 Peja Stojakovic/250 3.00 8.00
63 Al Harrington/250 2.50 6.00
64 Nate Robinson/250 3.00 8.00
66 Kevin Durant/150 8.00 20.00
69 Dwight Howard/250 5.00 12.00
70 Rashard Lewis/250 2.50 6.00
73 Andre Iguodala/250 3.00 8.00
74 Elton Brand/250 3.00 8.00
75 Thaddeus Young/250 2.00 5.00
76 Amare Stoudemire/250 3.00 8.00
77 Steve Nash/150 3.00 8.00
80 Brandon Roy/250 3.00 8.00
81 LaMarcus Aldridge/250 3.00 8.00
82 Greg Oden/250 2.50 6.00
83 Kevin Martin/250 3.00 8.00
84 Andres Nocioni/250 2.00 5.00
86 Tony Parker/250 3.00 8.00
87 Tim Duncan/250 5.00 12.00
88 Manu Ginobili/250 3.00 8.00
90 Chris Bosh/250 3.00 8.00
92 Andrea Bargnani/250 2.50 6.00
93 Deron Williams/250 3.00 8.00
94 Carlos Boozer/250 3.00 8.00
95 Andrei Kirilenko/250 2.50 6.00
101 Kareem Abdul-Jabbar/250 5.00 12.00
102 Elvin Hayes/250 3.00 8.00
103 Karl Malone/250 4.00 10.00
113 Moses Malone/150 3.00 8.00
115 Sleepy Floyd/250 3.00 8.00
127 DeMar DeRozan/250 5.00 12.00

2009-10 Rookies and Stars Longevity Signatures

STATED PRINT RUN 10 TO 999 SER.#'d SETS
SOME UNPRICED DUE TO SCARCITY
3 Mike Bibby/25 6.00 15.00
19 Jason Kidd/25 10.00 25.00
39 Kobe Bryant/25 100.00 225.00
42 Andrew Bynum/100 8.00 20.00
56 Kevin Love/25 15.00 40.00
102 Elvin Hayes/25 10.00 25.00
104 Arnie Risen/25 6.00 15.00
107 Artis Gilmore/50 6.00 15.00
108 Nate Archibald/25 15.00 30.00
111 Spencer Haywood/25 8.00 20.00
117 Jon Brockman/874 3.00 8.00
121 Marcus Thornton/374 5.00 12.00
122 Danny Green/874 5.00 12.00
123 Goran Suton/773 3.00 8.00
124 Jack McClinton/474 3.00 8.00
125 A.J. Price/474 3.00 8.00
129 Lester Hudson/999 3.00 8.00

2010-11 Rookies and Stars Longevity

COMP.SET w/o RCs (115) 12.50 30.00
EXCH EXPIRATION 5/10/12
1 Ray Allen .40 1.00
2 Paul Pierce .50 1.25
3 Rajon Rondo .50 1.25
4 Kevin Garnett .75 2.00
5 Brook Lopez .40 1.00
6 Devin Harris .40 1.00
7 Troy Murphy .25 .60
8 Amare Stoudemire .40 1.00
9 Anthony Randolph .30 .75
10 Danilo Gallinari .40 1.00
11 Andre Iguodala .40 1.00
12 Elton Brand .40 1.00
13 Thaddeus Young .25 .60
14 Andrea Bargnani .30 .75
15 Leandro Barbosa .30 .75
16 Jose Calderon .30 .75
17 Carlos Boozer .40 1.00
18 Derrick Rose 1.25 3.00
19 Joakim Noah .40 1.00
20 Luol Deng .40 1.00
21 Antawn Jamison .40 1.00
22 Mo Williams .30 .75
23 Daniel Gibson .30 .75
24 Ben Gordon .40 1.00
25 Richard Hamilton .30 .75
26 Tayshaun Prince .40 1.00
27 Danny Granger .40 1.00
28 Tyler Hansbrough .40 1.00
29 Mike Dunleavy .25 .60
30 Andrew Bogut .40 1.00
31 Brandon Jennings .40 1.00
32 John Salmons .40 1.00
33 Joe Johnson .40 1.00
34 Josh Smith .40 1.00
35 Al Horford .30 .75
36 Jamal Crawford .30 .75
37 Gerald Henderson .25 .60
38 Stephen Jackson .30 .75
39 Gerald Wallace .40 1.00
40 LeBron James 2.00 5.00
41 Dwyane Wade .75 2.00
42 Chris Bosh .40 1.00
43 Dwight Howard .60 1.50
44 Vince Carter .50 1.25
45 J.J. Redick .40 1.00
46 Josh Howard .30 .75
47 Al Thornton .30 .75
48 Gilbert Arenas .40 1.00
49 Kirk Hinrich .40 1.00
50 Dirk Nowitzki .50 1.25
51 Jason Kidd .40 1.00
52 Shawn Marion .40 1.00
53 Caron Butler .40 1.00
54 Kevin Martin .40 1.00
55 Shane Battier .30 .75
56 Luis Scola .30 .75
57 Yao Ming .50 1.25
58 Marc Gasol .40 1.00
59 Rudy Gay .40 1.00
60 Zach Randolph .30 .75
61 Chris Paul .60 1.50
62 Emeka Okafor .40 1.00
63 David West .40 1.00
64 Tim Duncan .60 1.50
65 Tony Parker .40 1.00
66 Richard Jefferson .40 1.00
67 Carmelo Anthony .50 1.25
68 Chauncey Billups .40 1.00
69 Chris Andersen .40 1.00
70 Nene .30 .75
71 Kevin Love .50 1.25
72 Michael Beasley .40 1.00
73 Jonny Flynn .25 .60
74 Brandon Roy .40 1.00
75 Rudy Fernandez .30 .75
76 Greg Oden .30 .75
77 Kevin Durant 1.25 3.00
78 Russell Westbrook .50 1.25
79 Jeff Green .30 .75
80 Deron Williams .40 1.00
81 Al Jefferson .40 1.00
82 Andrei Kirilenko .30 .75
83 Paul Millsap .30 .75
84 David Lee .30 .75
85 Monta Ellis .40 1.00
86 Stephen Curry .50 1.25
87 Eric Gordon .40 1.00
88 Chris Kaman .30 .75
89 Baron Davis .40 1.00
90 Kobe Bryant 2.00 5.00
91 Pau Gasol .40 1.00
92 Lamar Odom .40 1.00
93 Ron Artest .40 1.00
94 Steve Nash .40 1.00
95 Hedo Turkoglu .40 1.00
96 Channing Frye .30 .75
97 Grant Hill .50 1.25
98 Tyreke Evans .50 1.25
99 Samuel Dalembert .25 .60
100 Carl Landry .25 .60
101 Rolando Blackman .40 1.00
102 Joe Dumars .40 1.00
103 Wayne Embry .40 1.00
104 Walt Frazier .40 1.00
105 Gail Goodrich .40 1.00
106 John Havlicek .50 1.25
107 Rod Hundley .40 1.00
108 Phil Jackson .50 1.25
109 K.C. Jones .40 1.00
110 Clyde Lovellette .40 1.00
111 Jerry Lucas .40 1.00
112 Nate McMillan .40 1.00
113 Willis Reed .40 1.00
114 Paul Silas .40 1.00
115 Jerry West .50 1.25
116 Armon Johnson RC .60 1.50
117 Sherron Collins RC .60 1.50
118 Terrico White RC .60 1.50
119 Darington Hobson RC .60 1.50
120 Landry Fields RC 1.00 2.50
121 Tony Gaffney RC .60 1.50
122 Ben Uzoh RC 1.00 2.50
123 Ishmael Smith RC .60 1.50
124 Tweety Carter RC .60 1.50
125 Tiago Splitter RC .75 2.00
126 Solomon Alabi RC .60 1.50
127 Magnum Rolle RC .60 1.50
128 Pape Sy RC .60 1.50
129 Jeremy Lin RC 6.00 15.00
130 Derrick Caracter RC .60 1.50

2010-11 Rookies and Stars Longevity Ruby

*RUBY 1-130: 2X TO 5X BASE HI
1-130 RUBY PRINT RUN 250 SER.#'d SETS
131-170 PRINT RUN 5 TO 49 SER.#'d SETS
131 Jordan Crawford AU/49 10.00 25.00
132 Luke Harangody AU/49 6.00 15.00
133 Avery Bradley AU/49 12.00 30.00
134 Kevin Seraphin AU/49 8.00 20.00
135 Dominique Jones AU/49 6.00 15.00
136 Greg Monroe AU/49 12.00 30.00
137 Ekpe Udoh AU/49 6.00 15.00
138 Patrick Patterson AU/49 10.00 25.00
139 Lance Stephenson AU/49 6.00 15.00
140 Paul George AU/49 15.00 40.00
141 Eric Bledsoe AU/49 10.00 25.00
142 Willie Warren AU/49 6.00 15.00
144 Devin Ebanks AU/49 8.00 20.00
145 Xavier Henry AU/49 8.00 20.00
146 Greivis Vasquez AU/49 8.00 20.00
147 Dexter Pittman AU/49 6.00 15.00
148 Da'Sean Butler AU/49 6.00 15.00
149 Keith Gallon AU/49 6.00 15.00
150 Larry Sanders AU/49 6.00 15.00
151 Lazar Hayward AU/49 6.00 15.00
152 Wesley Johnson AU/49 10.00 25.00
153 Derrick Favors AU/49 12.00 30.00
154 Damion James AU/49 6.00 15.00
155 Craig Brackins AU/49 6.00 15.00
156 Quincy Pondexter AU/49 6.00 15.00
157 Andy Rautins AU/49 6.00 15.00
158 Cole Aldrich AU/49 6.00 15.00
159 Daniel Orton AU/49 6.00 15.00
160 Evan Turner AU/49 12.00 30.00
161 Gani Lawal AU/49 6.00 15.00
162 Elliot Williams AU/49 6.00 15.00
163 Luke Babbitt AU/49 6.00 15.00
164 DeMarcus Cousins AU/49 30.00 80.00
165 Hassan Whiteside AU/49 6.00 15.00
166 James Anderson AU/49 6.00 15.00
167 Ed Davis AU/49 8.00 20.00
168 Gordon Hayward AU/49 12.00 30.00
169 Trevor Booker AU/49 6.00 15.00
170 John Wall AU/49 100.00 200.00

2010-11 Rookies and Stars Longevity Sapphire

*SAPPHIRE 1-130: 3X TO 8X BASE HI
1-130 PRINT RUN 25 SER.#'d SETS
UNPRICED 131-170 AU PRINT RUN ONE SET
129 Jeremy Lin 60.00 150.00

2010-11 Rookies and Stars Longevity Dress for Success Materials

STATED PRINT RUN 99 TO 299 SER.#'d SETS
1 John Wall/299 8.00 20.00
2 Andre Miller/299 2.50 6.00
3 Evan Turner/299 4.00 10.00
4 Wesley Johnson/299 3.00 8.00
5 Andris Biedrins/299 2.00 5.00
6 Derrick Favors/299 4.00 10.00
7 Ekpe Udoh/299 2.00 5.00
8 Emeka Okafor/299 3.00 8.00
9 Eric Gordon/99 3.00 8.00
10 Evan Turner/299 4.00 10.00
11 Gani Lawal/299 2.00 5.00
12 Gerald Henderson/299 2.00 5.00
13 Goran Dragic/199 3.00 8.00
14 Gordon Hayward/299 4.00 10.00
15 Greg Monroe/299 4.00 10.00
16 Greg Oden/299 2.50 6.00
17 Greivis Vasquez/299 2.50 6.00
18 Hassan Whiteside/299 2.00 5.00
19 J.J. Barea/299 3.00 8.00
20 J.J. Redick/299 3.00 8.00
21 J.R. Smith/299 3.00 8.00
22 James Anderson/299 2.00 5.00
24 Dwight Howard/299 5.00 12.00
25 Jose Calderon/299 2.50 6.00
26 Lance Stephenson/299 2.00 5.00
27 Marcus Camby/299 2.00 5.00
28 Mike Dunleavy/199 2.00 5.00
29 DeMarcus Cousins/299 6.00 15.00
30 Wesley Johnson/299 3.00 8.00
31 Xavier Henry/299 2.50 6.00
32 Derrick Favors/299 4.00 10.00
33 Al-Farouq Aminu/299 2.00 5.00
34 Larry Sanders/299 2.00 5.00
35 Paul George/299 5.00 12.00

2010-11 Rookies and Stars Longevity Freshman Orientation Materials

STATED PRINT RUN 299 SER.#'d SETS
1 John Wall 8.00 20.00
2 Evan Turner 4.00 10.00
3 Derrick Favors 4.00 10.00
4 Wesley Johnson 3.00 8.00
5 DeMarcus Cousins 6.00 15.00
6 Ekpe Udoh 2.00 5.00
7 Greg Monroe 4.00 10.00
8 Al-Farouq Aminu 2.00 5.00
9 Gordon Hayward 4.00 10.00
10 Paul George 5.00 12.00
11 Cole Aldrich 2.00 5.00
12 Xavier Henry 2.50 6.00
13 Patrick Patterson 3.00 8.00
14 Larry Sanders 2.00 5.00
15 Luke Babbitt 2.00 5.00
16 Eric Bledsoe 3.00 8.00
17 Avery Bradley 4.00 10.00
18 James Anderson 2.00 5.00
19 Craig Brackins 2.00 5.00
20 Elliot Williams 2.00 5.00
21 Trevor Booker 2.00 5.00
22 Damion James 2.00 5.00
23 Dominique Jones 2.00 5.00
24 Quincy Pondexter 2.00 5.00
25 Jordan Crawford 3.00 8.00
26 Greivis Vasquez 2.50 6.00
27 Daniel Orton 2.00 5.00
28 Lazar Hayward 2.00 5.00
29 Dexter Pittman 2.00 5.00
30 Hassan Whiteside 2.00 5.00
31 Lance Stephenson 2.00 5.00
32 Da'Sean Butler 2.00 5.00
33 Devin Ebanks 2.50 6.00
34 Gani Lawal 2.00 5.00
35 Luke Harangody 2.00 5.00

2010-11 Rookies and Stars Longevity Materials Sapphire

STATED PRINT RUN 25 SER.#'d SETS
1 Ray Allen 5.00 12.00
2 Paul Pierce 6.00 15.00
3 Rajon Rondo 6.00 15.00
4 Kevin Garnett 10.00 25.00
6 Devin Harris 5.00 12.00
11 Andre Iguodala 5.00 12.00
12 Elton Brand 5.00 12.00
13 Thaddeus Young 3.00 8.00
15 Leandro Barbosa 4.00 10.00
16 Jose Calderon 4.00 10.00
18 Derrick Rose 15.00 40.00
19 Joakim Noah 5.00 12.00
20 Luol Deng 5.00 12.00
21 Antawn Jamison 5.00 12.00
24 Ben Gordon 5.00 12.00
26 Tayshaun Prince 5.00 12.00
28 Tyler Hansbrough 5.00 12.00
29 Mike Dunleavy 3.00 8.00
30 Andrew Bogut 5.00 12.00
31 Brandon Jennings 5.00 12.00
33 Joe Johnson 5.00 12.00
34 Josh Smith 5.00 12.00
35 Al Horford 4.00 10.00
37 Gerald Henderson 3.00 8.00
38 Stephen Jackson 4.00 10.00
39 Gerald Wallace 5.00 12.00
41 Dwyane Wade 10.00 25.00
43 Dwight Howard 8.00 20.00
44 Vince Carter 6.00 15.00
45 J.J. Redick 5.00 12.00
46 Josh Howard 4.00 10.00
48 Gilbert Arenas 5.00 12.00
49 Kirk Hinrich 5.00 12.00
50 Dirk Nowitzki 6.00 15.00
51 Jason Kidd 5.00 12.00
52 Shawn Marion 5.00 12.00
53 Caron Butler 5.00 12.00
54 Kevin Martin 5.00 12.00
55 Shane Battier 4.00 10.00
56 Luis Scola 4.00 10.00
58 Marc Gasol 5.00 12.00
59 Rudy Gay 5.00 12.00
61 Chris Paul 8.00 20.00
62 Emeka Okafor 5.00 12.00
63 David West 5.00 12.00
64 Tim Duncan 8.00 20.00
65 Tony Parker 5.00 12.00
66 Richard Jefferson 5.00 12.00
67 Carmelo Anthony 6.00 15.00
68 Chauncey Billups 5.00 12.00
69 Chris Andersen 5.00 12.00
70 Nene 4.00 10.00
71 Kevin Love 6.00 15.00
72 Michael Beasley 5.00 12.00
73 Jonny Flynn 3.00 8.00
74 Brandon Roy 5.00 12.00
75 Rudy Fernandez 4.00 10.00
76 Greg Oden 4.00 10.00
78 Russell Westbrook 6.00 15.00
80 Deron Williams 5.00 12.00
82 Andrei Kirilenko 4.00 10.00
86 Stephen Curry 6.00 15.00
88 Chris Kaman 4.00 10.00
89 Baron Davis 5.00 12.00
90 Kobe Bryant 15.00 40.00
91 Pau Gasol 5.00 12.00
92 Lamar Odom 5.00 12.00
93 Ron Artest 5.00 12.00
94 Steve Nash 5.00 12.00
95 Hedo Turkoglu 5.00 12.00
96 Channing Frye 4.00 10.00
97 Grant Hill 10.00 25.00
99 Samuel Dalembert 3.00 8.00
101 Rolando Blackman 5.00 12.00
102 Joe Dumars 5.00 12.00
118 Terrico White 5.00 12.00
129 Jeremy Lin 100.00 200.00

2010-11 Rookies and Stars Longevity Signatures

STATED PRINT RUN 5 TO 799 SER.#'d SETS
SOME UNPRICED DUE TO SCARCITY
8 Amare Stoudemire/15 25.00 60.00
11 Andre Iguodala/25 4.00 10.00
14 Andrea Bargnani/49 5.00 12.00
28 Tyler Hansbrough/99 4.00 10.00
37 Gerald Henderson/149 4.00 10.00
46 Josh Howard/99 4.00 10.00
51 Jason Kidd/25 12.50 30.00
62 Emeka Okafor/25 4.00 10.00
73 Jonny Flynn/199 4.00 10.00
86 Stephen Curry/49 10.00 25.00
89 Baron Davis/20 6.00 15.00
90 Kobe Bryant/49 100.00 200.00
93 Ron Artest/25 12.50 30.00
98 Tyreke Evans/99 10.00 25.00
100 Carl Landry/99 4.00 10.00
105 Gail Goodrich/49 5.00 12.00
106 John Havlicek/25 15.00 40.00
116 Armon Johnson/149 4.00 10.00
117 Sherron Collins/799 4.00 10.00
118 Terrico White/299 4.00 10.00
119 Darington Hobson/799 4.00 10.00
120 Landry Fields/349 6.00 15.00
121 Tony Gaffney/799 4.00 10.00
123 Ishmael Smith/799 4.00 10.00
124 Tweety Carter/499 4.00 10.00
125 Tiago Splitter/799 8.00 20.00
126 Solomon Alabi/350 4.00 10.00
127 Magnum Rolle/799 4.00 10.00
128 Pape Sy/799 4.00 10.00
129 Jeremy Lin/599 75.00 150.00
130 Derrick Caracter/799 4.00 10.00

1978-79 Royal Crown Cola

This set was sponsored by RC Cola, and its logo appears at the top of the card face. The cards were supposedly primarily issued in the southern New England area. The cards were intended to be placed in six-packs of Royal Crown Cola, one per six-pack. The cards measure 3" by 6". The front features a black-and-white head shot framed by a basketball hoop net on red and blue panels. The backs carry a mail-in offer to purchase a Spalding basketball for $6.99. The cards are unnumbered and are checklisted below in alphabetical order. The cards were apparently only licensed by the NBA Players Association since there are no team logos or team markings anywhere on the cards. The set features early professional cards of Walter Davis and Bernard King. Variations of Nate Archibald, Julius Erving, and Walt Frazier cards are reported. They measure 2 1/4" by 9 1/2", have the mail-in offer beneath the picture, and are blank-backed. They are also distinguished by a NBA Players logo, a 1978 MSA (Michael Schlecter Associates) copyright. and a 1978 RC Cola Co. copyright at the bottom.

COMPLETE SET 1500.00 3000.00
1 Kareem Abdul-Jabbar 150.00 300.00
2 Nate Archibald 50.00 100.00
3 Rick Barry 50.00 100.00
4 Jim Chones 25.00 50.00
5 Doug Collins 40.00 80.00
6 Dave Cowens 50.00 100.00
7 Adrian Dantley 45.00 90.00
8 Walter Davis 45.00 85.00
9 John Drew 20.00 45.00
10 Julius Erving 175.00 350.00
11 Walt Frazier 50.00 100.00
12 George Gervin 60.00 120.00
13 Artis Gilmore 45.00 90.00
14 Elvin Hayes 45.00 90.00
15 Dan Issel 45.00 90.00
16 Marques Johnson 35.00 70.00
17 Mickey Johnson 20.00 45.00
18 Bernard King 40.00 80.00
19 Bob Lanier 50.00 100.00
20 Maurice Lucas 35.00 65.00
21 Pete Maravich 300.00 475.00
22 Bob McAdoo 45.00 90.00
23 George McGinnis 30.00 60.00
24 Eric Money 25.00 45.00
25 Earl Monroe 45.00 90.00
26 Calvin Murphy 35.00 75.00
27 Robert Parish 60.00 120.00
28 Billy Paultz 25.00 45.00
29 Jack Sikma 35.00 65.00
30 Ricky Sobers 25.00 45.00
31 David Thompson 60.00 120.00
32 Rudy Tomjanovich 45.00 90.00
33 Wes Unseld 45.00 90.00
34 Norm Van Lier 30.00 60.00
35 Bill Walton 75.00 150.00
36 Marvin Webster 25.00 45.00
37 Scott Wedman 25.00 45.00
38 Paul Westphal 40.00 75.00
39 Jo Jo White 35.00 70.00
40 John Williamson 25.00 45.00
41 Brian Winters 30.00 60.00

1979-80 Royal Crown Cola Cans

The 1979 Royal Crown Cola Cans contain 35 standard-sized cans. The cans were made from steel, and thus are susceptible to rust if they have been in a moisture filled environment. The players head is in an oval picture shaped like a basketball and contains a short biographies below the picture. Each can is numbered "X" of 35. Cans opened from the bottom command up to a 25% premium over the prices listed below.

COMPLETE SET (35) 225.00 450.00
1 Dave Cowens 7.50 15.00
2 Nate Archibald 5.00 10.00
3 Artis Gilmore 7.50 15.00
4 David Thompson 7.50 15.00
5 Bob Lanier 5.00 10.00
6 Rick Barry 10.00 20.00
7 Rudy Tomjanovich 5.00 10.00
8 Kareem Abdul-Jabbar 20.00 40.00
9 Brian Winters 2.00 5.00
10 Bernard King 3.00 8.00
11 Pete Maravich 25.00 50.00
12 Bob McAdoo 5.00 10.00
13 Doug Collins 5.00 10.00
14 George McGinnis 5.00 10.00
15 Walter Davis 2.00 5.00
16 Paul Westphal 5.00 10.00
17 Robert Parish 7.50 15.00
18 Bill Walton 12.50 25.00
19 George Gervin 12.50 25.00
20 Elvin Hayes 7.50 15.00
21 Norm Van Lier 2.00 5.00
22 Dan Issel 7.50 15.00
23 Julius Erving 20.00 40.00
24 Jim Chones 2.00 5.00
25 Jo Jo White 3.00 8.00
26 Calvin Murphy 6.00 12.00
27 Earl Monroe 7.50 15.00
28 Billy Paultz 2.00 5.00
29 John Drew 2.00 5.00
30 John Williamson 2.00 5.00
31 Jack Sikma 3.00 8.00
32 Scott Wedman 2.00 5.00
33 Ricky Sobers 2.00 5.00
34 Maurice Lucas 3.00 8.00
35 Marvin Webster 2.00 5.00

1952 Royal Desserts

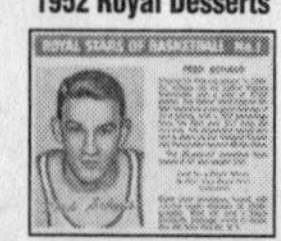

The 1952 Royal Desserts Stars of Basketball set contains eight horizontally oriented cards. The cards formed the backs of Royal Desserts packages of the period; consequently many cards are found with uneven edges stemming from the method of cutting the cards off the box. Each card has its number and the statement "Royal Stars of Basketball" in a red rectangle at the top. The cards measure approximately 2 5/8" by 3 1/4". The cards fronts have a stripe at the top and are divided into halves. The left half has a light-blue tinted head shot of the player and a facsimile autograph, while the right half has career summary. The blue tinted picture contains a facsimile autograph of the player. An album was presumably available as it is advertised on the card. The catalog designation for this scarce set is F219-2. The key card in the set is George Mikan.

COMPLETE SET (8) 7000.00 9500.00
1 Fred Schaus 350.00 700.00
2 Dick McGuire 400.00 850.00
3 Jack Nichols 250.00 500.00
4 Frank Brian 250.00 500.00
5 Joe Fulks 700.00 1200.00
6 George Mikan 3000.00 4000.00
7 Jim Pollard 700.00 1200.00
8 Harry Jeanette 400.00 800.00

1970-71 Royals Cincinnati Team Issue

Measuring 8 1/2" by 11", this 12-photo set features members of the 1970-71 Cincinnati Royals. The fronts feature three photos - one drawing, one head shot and one in-action shot, with the player's name in the lower left and the team name in the lower right. The player's facsimile autograph is located on the in-action shot. The photos are black and white. The backs are black and listed below in alphabetical order.

COMPLETE SET (12) 50.00 100.00
1 Nate Archibald 8.00 20.00
2 Bob Arnzen 2.00 5.00
3 Moe Barr 2.00 5.00
4 Bob Cousy P/CO 12.50 25.00
5 Johnny Green 3.00 8.00
6 Greg Hyder 2.00 5.00
7 Darrall Imhoff 3.00 8.00
8 Sam Lacey 3.00 8.00
9 Charlie Paulk 2.00 5.00
10 Flynn Robinson 3.00 8.00
11 Tom Van Arsdale 3.00 8.00
12 Norm Van Lier 5.00 10.00

1997 Scholastic Ultimate NBA Postcards

These 30 postcards were issued in a Scholastic book entitled "The Ultimate NBA Postcard Book" with an SRP of $7.99. Each postcard is perforated at the top and measures approximately 5 3/4" x 6 1/3". Fronts include a color action shot inside a color border. The player's name is written in block letters on the photo, the player's team is printed at the bottom next to a team logo, and player position is written vertically on the right side. Backs include some "vital statistics" and a small biography. The rest follows the format of a basic postcard. The cards are unnumbered and listed below in alphabetical order.

COMPLETE SET (30) 6.00 15.00
1 Greg Anthony .20 .50
2 Vin Baker .20 .50
3 Shawn Bradley .20 .50
4 Terrell Brandon .20 .50
5 Elden Campbell .20 .50
6 Sam Cassell .30 .75
7 Joe Dumars .40 1.00
8 Patrick Ewing .40 1.00
9 Kevin Garnett 1.50 4.00
10 Kevin Johnson .30 .75
11 Shawn Kemp .25 .60
12 Toni Kukoc .30 .75
13 Karl Malone .60 1.50
14 Jamal Mashburn .30 .75
15 Antonio McDyess .30 .75
16 Alonzo Mourning .40 1.00
17 Dino Radja .20 .50
18 Glen Rice .20 .50
19 Mitch Richmond .30 .75
20 David Robinson .40 1.00
21 Arvydas Sabonis .30 .75
22 Dennis Scott .20 .50
23 Joe Smith .25 .60
24 Steve Smith .30 .75
25 Rik Smits .20 .50
26 John Starks .20 .50
27 Damon Stoudamire .30 .75
28 Loy Vaught .20 .50
29 Clarence Weatherspoon .20 .50
30 Chris Webber .75 2.00

1972 7-11 Cups

Distributed through 7-11 in 1972, these cups feature color portraits of NBA players. They also feature a facsimile autograph and the player's name and team underneath the photo. The "back" side of the cup features statistics and a brief summary on the player. It also contains the 7-11 and NBA Players Association logos. The cups are not numbered and listed below in alphabetical order.

COMPLETE SET 300.00 600.00
1 Kareem Abdul-Jabbar 20.00 40.00
2 Mahdi Abdul-Rahman 5.00 10.00
3 Nate Archibald 8.00 20.00
4 Rick Barry 8.00 20.00
5 Dave Bing 6.00 15.00
6 Austin Carr 5.00 10.00
7 Wilt Chamberlain 25.00 50.00
8 Dave DeBusschere 8.00 20.00
9 Walt Frazier 10.00 20.00
10 Gail Goodrich 6.00 15.00
11 Hal Greer 6.00 15.00
12 Happy Hairston 5.00 10.00
13 John Havlicek 10.00 25.00
14 Connie Hawkins 8.00 20.00
15 Elvin Hayes 10.00 20.00
16 Spencer Haywood 5.00 10.00
17 Lou Hudson 5.00 10.00
18 John Johnson 5.00 10.00
19 Don Kojis 5.00 10.00
20 Bob Lanier 7.50 15.00
21 Kevin Loughery 5.00 10.00
22 Jerry Lucas 6.00 15.00
23 Pete Maravich 50.00 100.00
24 Jack Marin 5.00 10.00
25 Jim McMillian 5.00 10.00
26 Jeff Mullins 5.00 10.00
27 Geoff Petrie 5.00 10.00
28 Willis Reed 8.00 20.00
29 Oscar Robertson 15.00 30.00
30 Paul Silas 6.00 15.00
31 Jerry Sloan 8.00 20.00
32 Elmore Smith 5.00 10.00
33 Nate Thurmond 6.00 15.00
34 Wes Unseld 6.00 15.00
35 Dick Van Arsdale 6.00 12.00
36 Tom Van Arsdale 6.00 12.00
37 Chet Walker 6.00 12.00
38 John Warren 5.00 10.00
39 Jerry West 25.00 50.00
40 Jo Jo White 6.00 15.00

1981 7-Up Jumbos

These thin-stock cards, measuring approximately 5 1/4" x 8 1/2", were given away at 7-Up point-of-purchase displays. With the slogan "Feelin' 7-Up", the cards were produced highlighting the cola's different sports spokesmen of that time. The fronts contain a full-bleed color posed player photograph and a facsimile autograph. The backs have a green border, and some highlights of the player inside a white box. The cards were first available during the 1980-81 basketball season, and therefore Magic Johnson's card is one of his earliest professional pieces. Ann Meyers, another basketball great in her own right, is also represented in the set. Any other additions to this checklist would be greatly appreciated. The cards are unnumbered and checklisted below in alphabetical order.

COMPLETE SET (7) 30.00 75.00
3 Magic Johnson BK 10.00 25.00
5 Ann Meyers BK 6.00 15.00

1976-77 76ers Canada Dry Cans

The 1976-77 Canada Dry Philadelphia 76ers Cans team issue contains at least 14 standard-sized cans which paid tribute to the "Team of the Year 1976-77". Under this caption, the cans contain a 76ers logo and a black and white headshot of the player with the name, uniform number and position below the picture.There is no number given other than the jersey number, thus the set is listed below alphabetically. Cans opened from the bottom command up to a 25% premium over the prices below.The checklist below is thought to be incomplete--any additional input on this series would be appreciated.

COMPLETE SET (14) 37.50 75.00
1 Henry Bibby 2.50 6.00
2 Joe Bryant 2.50 6.00
3 Harvey Catchings 1.50 4.00
4 Darryl Dawkins 5.00 10.00
5 Al Domenico TR 1.50 4.00
6 Mike Dunleavy 3.00 8.00
7 Julius Erving 15.00 30.00
8 Lloyd Free 2.50 6.00
9 Terry Furlow 1.50 4.00
10 Caldwell Jones 2.50 6.00
11 George McGinnis 5.00 10.00
12 Jack McMahon ACO 1.50 4.00
13 Steve Mix 1.50 4.00
14 Gene Shue CO 3.00 8.00

2001-02 76ers Fleer

Released in conjunction with Fleer, this 6-cards set was issued as a team sheet and given away at a Sixers game during the 2001-02 season.

COMPLETE SET (6) 2.00 5.00
NNO Allen Iverson 1.00 2.50
NNO Aaron McKie .30 .75
NNO Eric Snow .30 .75
NNO Team Photo .40 1.00
NNO Larry Brown CO .40 1.00
NNO Dikembe Mutombo .50 1.25

2001-02 76ers Fleer NBA All-Star Jam Session

Issued to fans via a wrapper redemption program at the 2001-02 All-Star Weekend show, Feb 8th-10th, this set was limited to just 7,600 total and was available only at the Fleer booth. The card numbers were not known at press time, so they've been listed in alphabetical order for convenience.

COMPLETE SET (6) 3.00 8.00
1 Speedy Claxton .50 1.25
2 Derrick Coleman .60 1.50
3 Allen Iverson 1.50 4.00
4 Aaron McKie .50 1.25
5 Dikembe Mutombo .75 2.00
6 Eric Snow .50 1.25

1989-90 76ers Kodak

This team photo album was jointly sponsored by Jack's Cameras and Kodak. The photo album consists of three sheets, each measuring approximately 8" by 11" and joined together to form one continuous s The first sheet features a team photo of the Philadelphia 76ers. While the second sheet prese two rows of five cards each, the third sheet prese additional player cards, with the remaining four s filled in by coupons redeemable at Jack's Camera After perforation, the cards measure 2 3/16" by 3 The card front features a color action player photo a red border on white card stock. The player's nar and position are given below the picture, and the logo is sandwiched between the sponsors' logos. backs have the Philadelphia 76ers logo in blue an print. The cards are presented in the album in alphabetical order, with coaches at the end, and w have checklisted them below accordingly. The se features an early professional card of Hersey Haw

COMPLETE SET (16) 6.00
1 Ron Anderson .20
2 Charles Barkley 3.00
3 Scott Brooks .30
4 Lanard Copeland .20
5 Johnny Dawkins .40
6 Mike Gminski .40
7 Hersey Hawkins .75
8 Rick Mahorn .30
9 Kurt Nimphius .20
10 Kenny Payne .20
11 Derek Smith .40
12 Bob Thornton .20
13 Big Shot (Team Mascot) .20
14 Jim Lynam CO .20
15 Fred Carter ACO .20
16 Buzz Braman ACO .75

1975-76 76ers McDonald's Standups

The 1975-76 McDonalds Philadelphia 76ers set contains six blank-backed cards measuring approximately 3 3/4" by 7". The cards were produ by Johnny Pro Enterprises. The cards are die cut, allowing the player pictures to be punched out an displayed. Johnny Pro Enterprises originally sold sets directly to consumers for $1.25 postpaid. The cards are unnumbered and checklisted below in alphabetical order.

COMPLETE SET (6) 6.00
1 Fred Carter 1.25
2 Harvey Catchings 1.25
3 Doug Collins 3.00
4 Billy Cunningham 3.00
5 George McGinnis 2.00
6 Steve Mix 1.25

1979-80 76ers Stand-ups

This set was released during the 1979-80 season, features twelve of the 76er's top players. These ful color player figures were produced on very thick s and stand about ten inches tall. Please note that th stand-ups are not numbered and are listed below alphabetical order.

COMPLETE SET (12) 60.00 12
1 Henry Bibby 3.00
2 Joe Bryant 3.00
3 Harvey Catchings 2.50
4 Doug Collins 7.50 1
5 Darryl Dawkins 6.00 1
6 Mike Dunleavy 5.00 1
7 Julius Erving 30.00 5
8 Lloyd Free 5.00 1
9 Terry Furlow 2.50
10 Caldwell Jones 2.50
11 George McGinnis 5.00 1
12 Steve Mix 2.50

1969-70 76ers Team Issue

Each of these team-issued photos measure approximately 5 3/4" by 7 1/4" and feature black a white player portraits. The player's name is listed below the photo. The backs are blank. The photos unnumbered and listed below alphabetically.

COMPLETE SET (11) 25.00 5
1 Archie Clark 2.00
2 Bill Cunningham 5.00 1
3 Hal Greer 3.00
4 Matt Guokas 2.50
5 Fred Hetzel 1.25
6 Darrall Imhoff 1.25
7 Luke Jackson 2.00
8 Wally Jones 2.00
9 Bud Ogden 1.25
10 Jack Ramsay CO 2.50
11 George Wilson 1.25

1970-71 76ers Team Issue

Measuring 5 1/2" by 7", this 13-photo set was iss for the 1970-71 season. The front photos feature a black and white posed shot with the player's name team directly underneath. The backs are blank, unnumbered, and listed below in alphabetical orde

PLETE SET (13) 20.00 40.00
nis Awtrey 1.00 2.50
hie Clark 1.50 4.00
y Cunningham 3.00 8.00
nnie Dierking 1.25 3.00
d Foster 1.00 2.50
Greer 2.00 5.00
Henry 1.00 2.50
ley Howell 1.25 3.00
e Jackson 1.25 3.00
ally Jones 1.50 4.00
d Ogden 1.00 2.50
ck Ramsay CO 2.00 5.00
m Washington 1.25 3.00

1976-77 76ers Team Issue Black and White

8"x10" set was produced for the Philadelphia
s during the 1976-77 season. The set features 12
k and white cards of the team's players and
hes.

PLETE SET (12) 15.00 30.00
nry Bibby 1.50 4.00
e Bryant 1.50 4.00
d Carter 1.25 3.00
rvey Catchings 1.25 3.00
yd Free 2.00 5.00
eve Mix 1.25 3.00
niel Norman 1.25 3.00
Eugene Dixon Jr. PRES 1.25 3.00
Domenico TR 1.25 3.00
ack McMahon CO 1.25 3.00
ene Shue CO 1.50 4.00
at Williams VP 1.25 3.00

76-77 76ers Team Issue Color

se 12 color blank-backed photos, which measure 4
by 6 1/2" feature members of the Eastern
ference Champions Philadelphia 76ers. These
os were sold in a 12-pack.

PLETE SET (12) 20.00 40.00
nry Bibby 1.25 3.00
e Bryant 1.50 4.00
rvey Catchings .75 2.00
ug Collins 3.00 8.00
rryl Dawkins 2.50 6.00
ke Dunleavy 2.00 5.00
lius Erving 10.00 25.00
oyd Free 2.00 5.00
rry Furlow .75 2.00
aldwell Jones 1.25 3.00
George McGinnis 1.50 4.00
Steve Mix .75 2.00

1948-1950 Safe-T-Card

s from this set were issued in the Washington
area in the late 1940s and early 1950s. Each card
printed in either black or red and features an
t's rendering of a famous area athlete or
sonality from a variety of sports. The card backs
re an ad for Jim Gibbons Cartoon-A-Quiz
vision show along with an ad from a local business.
player's facsimile autograph and team or sport
ation is included on the fronts.

d Auerbach BK 50.00 100.00
Bob Feerick BK 15.00 30.00
Reggie Hermsen BK 15.00 30.00

995 Score Board Phone Card Promo

) Shaquille O'Neal 4.00 10.00
keem Olajuwon

1990-91 SkyBox Prototypes

s ten-card set of prototypes was issued singly as
l as in a complete sheet. The cards were mailed out
rospective dealers and members of the media to
w the unique new design of the inaugural SkyBox
e. The cards are distinguishable by the presence of
d diagonal "prototype" line cutting across the upper
corner of the front. The cards are standard size, 2
by 3 1/2" and are numbered on the back.

MPLETE SET (10) 30.00 80.00
Michael Jordan 15.00 40.00
Dennis Rodman 4.00 10.00
Magic Johnson 6.00 15.00
Rony Seikaly 1.00 2.50
Ricky Pierce 1.00 2.50
Pooh Richardson 1.00 2.50
Kevin Johnson 1.50 4.00
Clyde Drexler 4.00 10.00
David Robinson 5.00 12.00
Karl Malone 6.00 15.00
) SkyBox Logo 2.00 5.00
stributed at 1990 National Convention

1990-91 SkyBox

This 1990-91 set marks SkyBox's entry into the basketball card market. The complete set contains 423 standard-size cards featuring NBA players. The set was released in two series of 300 and 123 cards, respectively. Foil packs for each series contained 15 cards. However, the second series packs contained a mix of players from both series. The second series cards replaced 123 cards from the first series, which then became short-prints compared to other cards in the first series. The front features an action shot of the player on a computer-generated background of various color schemes. The player's name appears in a black stripe at the bottom with the team logo superimposed at the left lower corner. The photo is bordered in gold. The back presents head shots of the player with gold borders on white background. Player statistics are given in a box below the photo. The cards are checklisted below alphabetically according to team. Subsets are Coaches (301-327), Team Checklists (328-354), Lottery Picks (355-365), Updates (366-420), and Checklists (421-423). Rookie Cards of note included in the set are Nick Anderson, Mookie Blaylock, Derrick Coleman, Vlade Divac, Sean Elliott, Danny Ferry, Kendall Gill, Tim Hardaway, Chris Jackson, Avery Johnson, Shawn Kemp, Gary Payton, Drazen Petrovic, Glen Rice, Clifford Robinson and Dennis Scott. First series single prints (SP) are noted below.

COMPLETE SET (423) 10.00 20.00
COMPLETE SERIES 1 (300) 6.00 12.00
COMPLETE SERIES 2 (123) 4.00 8.00
1 John Battle .02 .10
2 Duane Ferrell SP RC .08 .25
3 Jon Koncak .02 .10
4 Cliff Levingston SP .08 .25
5 John Long SP .08 .25
6 Moses Malone .08 .25
7 Doc Rivers .02 .10
8 Kenny Smith SP .08 .25
9 Alexander Volkov .02 .10
10 Spud Webb .02 .10
11 Dominique Wilkins .08 .25
12 Kevin Willis .02 .10
13 John Bagley .02 .10
14 Larry Bird .40 1.00
15 Kevin Gamble .02 .10
16 Dennis Johnson SP .08 .25
17 Joe Kleine .02 .10
18 Reggie Lewis .02 .10
19 Kevin McHale .02 .10
20 Robert Parish .02 .10
21 Jim Paxson SP .08 .25
22 Ed Pinckney .02 .10
23 Brian Shaw .08 .25
24 Michael Smith .02 .10
25 Richard Anderson SP .08 .25
26 Muggsy Bogues .02 .10
27 Rex Chapman .08 .25
28 Dell Curry .02 .10
29 Armon Gilliam .02 .10
30 Michael Holton SP .08 .25
31 Dave Hoppen .02 .10
32 J.R. Reid RC .02 .10
33 Robert Reid SP .08 .25
34 Brian Rowsom SP .08 .25
35 Kelly Tripucka .02 .10
36 Micheal Williams SP UER .08 .25
(Misspelled Michael on card)
37 B.J. Armstrong RC .02 .10
38 Bill Cartwright .02 .10
39 Horace Grant .02 .10
40 Craig Hodges .02 .10
41 Michael Jordan 1.25 3.00
42 Stacey King RC .02 .10
43 Ed Nealy SP .02 .10
44 John Paxson .02 .10
45 Will Perdue .02 .10
46 Scottie Pippen .40 1.00
47 Jeff Sanders SP RC .08 .25
48 Winston Bennett .02 .10
49 Chucky Brown RC .02 .10
50 Brad Daugherty .02 .10
51 Craig Ehlo .02 .10
52 Steve Kerr .08 .25
53 Paul Mokeski SP .08 .25
54 John Morton .02 .10
55 Larry Nance .02 .10
56 Mark Price .02 .10
57 Tree Rollins SP .08 .25
58 Hot Rod Williams .02 .10
59 Steve Alford .02 .10
60 Rolando Blackman .02 .10
61 Adrian Dantley SP .08 .25
62 Brad Davis .02 .10
63 James Donaldson .02 .10
64 Derek Harper .02 .10
65 Anthony Jones SP .08 .25
66 Sam Perkins SP .08 .25
67 Roy Tarpley .02 .10
68 Bill Wennington SP .08 .25
69 Randy White RC .02 .10
70 Herb Williams .02 .10
71 Michael Adams .02 .10
72 Joe Barry Carroll SP .08 .25
73 Walter Davis .02 .10
74 Alex English SP .08 .25
75 Bill Hanzlik .02 .10
76 Tim Kempton SP .08 .25
77 Jerome Lane .02 .10
78 Lafayette Lever SP .08 .25
79 Todd Lichti RC .02 .10
80 Blair Rasmussen .02 .10
81 Danny Schayes SP .08 .25
82 Mark Aguirre .02 .10
83 William Bedford RC .02 .10
84 Joe Dumars .08 .25
85 James Edwards .02 .10
86 David Greenwood SP .08 .25
87 Scott Hastings .02 .10
88 Gerald Henderson SP .08 .25
89 Vinnie Johnson .02 .10
90 Bill Laimbeer .02 .10
91 Dennis Rodman .25 .60
(SkyBox logo in upper right or left)
91B Dennis Rodman .40 1.00
(SkyBox logo in upper left corner)
92 John Salley .02 .10
93 Isiah Thomas .08 .25
94 Manute Bol SP .08 .25
95 Tim Hardaway RC .60 1.50
96 Rod Higgins .02 .10
97 Sarunas Marciulionis RC .02 .10
98 Chris Mullin .08 .25
99 Jim Petersen .02 .10
100 Mitch Richmond .10 .30
101 Mike Smrek .02 .10
102 Terry Teagle SP .08 .25
103 Tom Tolbert RC .02 .10
104 Kelvin Upshaw SP .08 .25
105 Anthony Bowie SP RC .08 .25
106 Adrian Caldwell .02 .10
107 Eric(Sleepy) Floyd .02 .10
108 Buck Johnson .02 .10
109 Vernon Maxwell .02 .10
110 Hakeem Olajuwon .15 .40
111 Larry Smith .02 .10
112A Otis Thorpe ERR .60 1.50
(Front photo actually Mitchell Wiggins)
112B Otis Thorpe COR .02 .10
113A Mitchell Wiggins SP ERR .60 1.50
(Front photo actually Otis Thorpe)
113B Mitchell Wiggins SP COR .08 .25
114 Vern Fleming .02 .10
115 Rickey Green SP .08 .25
116 George McCloud RC .08 .25
117 Reggie Miller .10 .30
118A Dyron Nix SP ERR .60 1.50
(Back photo actually Wayman Tisdale)
118B Dyron Nix SP COR .08 .25
119 Chuck Person .02 .10
120 Mike Sanders .02 .10
121 Detlef Schrempf .02 .10
122 Rik Smits .08 .25
123 LaSalle Thompson .02 .10
124 Benoit Benjamin .02 .10
125 Winston Garland .02 .10
126 Tom Garrick .02 .10
127 Gary Grant .02 .10
128 Ron Harper .02 .10
129 Danny Manning .02 .10
130 Jeff Martin .02 .10
131 Ken Norman .02 .10
132 Charles Smith .02 .10
133 Joe Wolf SP .08 .25
134 Michael Cooper SP .08 .25
135 Vlade Divac RC .25 .60
136 Larry Drew .02 .10
137 A.C. Green .02 .10
138 Magic Johnson .30 .75
139 Mark McNamara SP .08 .25
140 Byron Scott .02 .10
141 Mychal Thompson .02 .10
142 Orlando Woolridge SP .08 .25
143 James Worthy .08 .25
144 Terry Davis RC .02 .10
145 Sherman Douglas RC .02 .10
146 Kevin Edwards .02 .10
147 Tellis Frank SP .08 .25
148 Scott Haffner SP .08 .25
149 Grant Long .02 .10
150 Glen Rice RC .40 1.00
151 Rony Seikaly .02 .10
152 Rory Sparrow SP .08 .25
153 Jon Sundvold .02 .10
154 Billy Thompson .02 .10
155 Greg Anderson .02 .10
156 Ben Coleman SP .08 .25
157 Jeff Grayer RC .02 .10
158 Jay Humphries .02 .10
159 Frank Kornet .02 .10
160 Larry Krystkowiak .02 .10
161 Brad Lohaus .02 .10
162 Ricky Pierce .02 .10
163 Paul Pressey SP .08 .25
164 Fred Roberts .02 .10
165 Alvin Robertson .02 .10
166 Jack Sikma .02 .10
167 Randy Breuer .02 .10
168 Tony Campbell .02 .10
169 Tyrone Corbin .02 .10
170 Sidney Lowe SP .08 .25
171 Sam Mitchell RC .02 .10
172 Tod Murphy .02 .10
173 Pooh Richardson RC .02 .10
174 Donald Royal SP RC .08 .25
175 Brad Sellers SP .08 .25
176 Mookie Blaylock RC .15 .40
177 Sam Bowie .02 .10
178 Lester Conner .02 .10
179 Derrick Gervin .02 .10
180 Jack Haley RC .02 .10
181 Roy Hinson .02 .10
182 Dennis Hopson SP .08 .25
183 Chris Morris .02 .10
184 Pete Myers SP RC .08 .25
185 Purvis Short SP .08 .25
186 Maurice Cheeks .02 .10
187 Patrick Ewing .08 .25
188 Stuart Gray .02 .10
189 Mark Jackson .02 .10
190 Johnny Newman SP .08 .25
191 Charles Oakley .02 .10
192 Brian Quinnett .02 .10
193 Trent Tucker .02 .10
194 Kiki Vandeweghe .02 .10
195 Kenny Walker .02 .10
196 Eddie Lee Wilkins .02 .10
197 Gerald Wilkins .02 .10
198 Mark Acres .02 .10
199 Nick Anderson RC .15 .40
200 Michael Ansley .02 .10
201 Terry Catledge .02 .10
202 Dave Corzine SP .08 .25
203 Sidney Green SP .08 .25
204 Jerry Reynolds .02 .10
205 Scott Skiles .02 .10
206 Otis Smith .02 .10
207 Reggie Theus SP .08 .25
208 Jeff Turner .02 .10
209 Sam Vincent .02 .10
210 Ron Anderson .02 .10
211 Charles Barkley .15 .40
212 Scott Brooks SP .08 .25
213 Lanard Copeland SP .08 .25
214 Johnny Dawkins .02 .10
215 Mike Gminski .02 .10
216 Hersey Hawkins .02 .10
217 Rick Mahorn .02 .10
218 Derek Smith SP .08 .25
219 Bob Thornton .02 .10
220 Tom Chambers .02 .10
221 Greg Grant SP RC .08 .25
222 Jeff Hornacek .02 .10
223 Eddie Johnson .02 .10
224A Kevin Johnson .08 .25
(SkyBox logo in lower right corner)
224B Kevin Johnson .08 .25
(SkyBox logo in upper right corner)
225 Andrew Lang RC .08 .25
226 Dan Majerle .08 .25
227 Mike McGee SP .08 .25
228 Tim Perry .02 .10
229 Kurt Rambis .02 .10
230 Mark West .02 .10
231 Mark Bryant .02 .10
232 Wayne Cooper .02 .10
233 Clyde Drexler .08 .25
234 Kevin Duckworth .02 .10
235 Byron Irvin SP .08 .25
236 Jerome Kersey .02 .10
237 Drazen Petrovic RC .10 .30
238 Terry Porter .02 .10
239 Clifford Robinson RC .15 .40
240 Buck Williams .02 .10
241 Danny Young .02 .10
242 Danny Ainge SP .08 .25
243 Randy Allen SP .08 .25
244A Antoine Carr SP .08 .25
244B Antoine Carr .02 .10
(Wearing Sacramento jersey on back)
245 Vinny Del Negro SP .08 .25
246 Pervis Ellison SP RC .08 .25
247 Greg Kite SP .08 .25
248 Rodney McCray SP .08 .25
249 Harold Pressley SP .08 .25
250 Ralph Sampson .02 .10
251 Wayman Tisdale .02 .10
252 Willie Anderson .02 .10
253 Uwe Blab SP .08 .25
254 Frank Brickowski SP .08 .25
255 Terry Cummings .02 .10
256 Sean Elliott RC .20 .50
257 Caldwell Jones SP .08 .25
258 Johnny Moore SP .08 .25
259 Zarko Paspalj SP .08 .25
260 David Robinson .30 .75
261 Rod Strickland .08 .25
262 David Wingate SP .08 .25
263 Dana Barros RC .08 .25
264 Michael Cage .02 .10
265 Quintin Dailey .02 .10
266 Dale Ellis .02 .10
267 Steve Johnson SP .08 .25
268 Shawn Kemp RC 1.00 2.50
269 Xavier McDaniel .02 .10
270 Derrick McKey .02 .10
271A Nate McMillan SP ERR .08 .25
(Back photo actually
Olden Polynice; first series)
271B Nate McMillan COR .02 .10
(second series)
272 Olden Polynice .02 .10
273 Sedale Threatt .02 .10
274 Thurl Bailey .02 .10
275 Mike Brown .02 .10
276 Mark Eaton .02 .10
277 Blue Edwards RC .02 .10
278 Darrell Griffith .02 .10
279 Bobby Hansen SP .08 .25
280 Eric Johnson .02 .10
281 Eric Leckner SP .08 .25
282 Karl Malone .15 .40
283 Delaney Rudd .02 .10
284 John Stockton .10 .30
285 Mark Alarie .02 .10
286 Steve Colter SP .08 .25
287 Ledell Eackles SP .08 .25
288 Harvey Grant .02 .10
289 Tom Hammonds RC .02 .10
290 Charles Jones .02 .10
291 Bernard King .02 .10
292 Jeff Malone SP .08 .25
293 Darrell Walker .02 .10
294 John Williams .02 .10
295 Checklist 1 SP .08 .25
296 Checklist 2 SP .08 .25
297 Checklist 3 SP .08 .25
298 Checklist 4 SP .08 .25
299 Checklist 5 SP .08 .25
300 Danny Ferry SP RC .20 .50
301 Bob Weiss CO .02 .10
302 Chris Ford CO .02 .10
303 Gene Littles CO .02 .10
304 Phil Jackson CO .10 .30
305 Lenny Wilkens CO .10 .30
306 Richie Adubato CO .02 .10
307 Paul Westhead CO .02 .10
308 Chuck Daly CO .10 .30
309 Don Nelson CO .10 .30
310 Don Chaney CO .02 .10
311 Dick Versace CO .02 .10
312 Mike Schuler CO .02 .10
313 Mike Dunleavy CO .02 .10
314 Ron Rothstein CO .02 .10
315 Del Harris CO .02 .10
316 Bill Musselman CO .02 .10
317 Bill Fitch CO .02 .10
318 Stu Jackson CO .02 .10
319 Matt Guokas CO .02 .10
320 Jim Lynam CO .02 .10
321 Cotton Fitzsimmons CO .02 .10
322 Rick Adelman CO .02 .10
323 Dick Motta CO .02 .10
324 Larry Brown CO .02 .10
325 K.C. Jones CO .10 .30
326 Jerry Sloan CO .10 .30
327 Wes Unseld CO .02 .10
328 Atlanta Hawks TC .02 .10
329 Boston Celtics TC .02 .10
330 Charlotte Hornets TC .02 .10
331 Chicago Bulls TC .10 .30
332 Cleveland Cavaliers TC .02 .10
333 Dallas Mavericks TC .02 .10
334 Denver Nuggets TC .02 .10
335 Detroit Pistons TC .02 .10
336 Golden State Warriors TC .02 .10
337 Houston Rockets TC .02 .10
338 Indiana Pacers TC .02 .10
339 Los Angeles Clippers TC .02 .10
340 Los Angeles Lakers TC .02 .10
341 Miami Heat TC .02 .10
342 Milwaukee Bucks TC .02 .10
343 Minnesota Timberwolves TC .02 .10
344 New Jersey Nets TC .02 .10
345 New York Knicks TC .02 .10
346 Orlando Magic TC .02 .10
347 Philadelphia 76ers TC .02 .10
348 Phoenix Suns TC .02 .10
349 Portland Trail Blazers TC .02 .10
350 Sacramento Kings TC .02 .10
351 San Antonio Spurs TC .02 .10
352 Seattle SuperSonics TC .02 .10
353 Utah Jazz TC .02 .10
354 Washington Bullets TC .02 .10
355 Rumeal Robinson RC .02 .10
356 Kendall Gill RC .50 1.25
357 Chris Jackson RC .25 .60
358 Tyrone Hill RC .20 .50
359 Bo Kimble RC .02 .10
360 Willie Burton RC .02 .10
361 Felton Spencer RC .10 .30
362 Derrick Coleman RC .50 1.25
363 Dennis Scott RC .30 .75
364 Lionel Simmons RC .10 .30
365 Gary Payton RC 2.00 5.00
366 Tim McCormick .02 .10
367 Sidney Moncrief .02 .10
368 Kenny Gattison RC .02 .10
369 Randolph Keys .02 .10
370 Johnny Newman .02 .10
371 Dennis Hopson .02 .10
372 Cliff Levingston .02 .10
373 Derrick Chievous .02 .10
374 Danny Ferry .10 .30
375 Alex English .02 .10
376 Lafayette Lever .02 .10
377 Rodney McCray .02 .10
378 T.R. Dunn .02 .10
379 Corey Gaines .02 .10
380 Avery Johnson RC .30 .75
381 Joe Wolf .02 .10
382 Orlando Woolridge .02 .10
383 Tree Rollins .02 .10
384 Steve Johnson .02 .10
385 Kenny Smith .02 .10
386 Mike Woodson .02 .10
387 Greg Dreiling RC .02 .10
388 Micheal Williams .10 .30
389 Randy Wittman .02 .10
390 Ken Bannister .02 .10
391 Sam Perkins .10 .30
392 Terry Teagle .02 .10
393 Milt Wagner .02 .10
394 Frank Brickowski .02 .10
395 Danny Schayes .02 .10
396 Scott Brooks .02 .10
397 Doug West RC .10 .30
398 Chris Dudley RC .02 .10
399 Reggie Theus .10 .30
400 Greg Grant .02 .10
401 Greg Kite .02 .10
402 Mark McNamara .02 .10
403 Manute Bol .02 .10
404 Rickey Green .02 .10
405 Kenny Battle RC .02 .10
406 Ed Nealy .02 .10
407 Danny Ainge .10 .30
408 Steve Colter .02 .10
409 Bobby Hansen .02 .10
410 Eric Leckner .02 .10
411 Rory Sparrow .02 .10
412 Bill Wennington .02 .10
413 Sidney Green .02 .10
414 David Greenwood .02 .10
415 Paul Pressey .02 .10
416 Reggie Williams .02 .10
417 Dave Corzine .02 .10
418 Jeff Malone .02 .10
419 Pervis Ellison .02 .10
420 Byron Irvin .02 .10
421 Checklist 1 .02 .10
422 Checklist 2 .02 .10
423 Checklist 3 .02 .10
NNO SkyBox Salutes the NBA 2.50 6.00

1991-92 SkyBox Prototypes

Cards from this 20-card standard-size set of prototypes were mailed out to prospective dealers and members of the media to show the new design of the 1991-92 SkyBox issue. The cards are distinguishable by the presence of a black diagonal "prototype" line cutting across the upper left corner of the back. Dennis Rodman and Chris Mullin are supposed to be the two toughest as they were reportedly withdrawn early.

COMPLETE SET (20) 25.00 60.00
24 Rex Chapman 1.00 2.50
86 Dennis Rodman SP 6.00 15.00
95 Chris Mullin SP 3.00 8.00
97 Mitch Richmond 2.50 6.00
114 Reggie Miller 3.00 8.00
130 Charles Smith 1.00 2.50
137 Magic Johnson 5.00 12.00
143 James Worthy 1.50 4.00
173 Pooh Richardson 1.00 2.50
189 Patrick Ewing 2.50 6.00
205 Dennis Scott 1.00 2.50
211 Charles Barkley 4.00 10.00
216 Hersey Hawkins 1.00 2.50
223 Tom Chambers 1.00 2.50
237 Clyde Drexler 2.50 6.00
238 Kevin Duckworth 1.00 2.50
240 Terry Porter 1.00 2.50
242 Buck Williams 1.00 2.50
268 Ricky Pierce 1.00 2.50
294 Bernard King 1.00 2.50

1991-92 SkyBox

The complete 1991-92 SkyBox basketball set contains 659 standard-size cards. The set was released in two series of 350 and 309 cards, respectively. This year SkyBox did not package both first and second series cards in second series packs. The cards were available in 15-card fin-sealed foil packs that feature four different mail-in offers on the back, or 62-card blister packs that contain two (of four) SkyBox logo cards not available in the 15-card foil packs. The fronts feature color action player photos overlaying multi-colored computer-generated geometric shapes and stripes. The pictures are borderless and the card face is white. The player's name appears in different color lettering at the bottom of each card, with the team logo in the lower right corner. In a trapezoid shape, the backs have non-action color player photos. At the bottom biographical and statistical information appear inside a color-striped diagonal. The cards are numbered and checklisted below alphabetically within team order. Subsets are Stats (298-307), Best Single Game Performance (308-312), NBA All-Star Weekend Highlights (313-317), NBA All-Rookie Team (318-322), GQ's "NBA All-Star Style Team" (323-327), Centennial Highlights (328-332), Great Moments from the NBA Finals (333-337), Stay in School (338-344), Checklists (345-350), Team Logos (351-377), Coaches (378-404), Game Frames (405-431), Sixth Man (432-458), Teamwork (459-485), Rising Stars (486-512), Lottery Picks (513-523), Centennial (524-529), 1992 USA Basketball Team (530-546), 1988 USA Basketball Team (547-556), 1984 USA Basketball Team (557-563), The Magic of SkyBox (564-571), SkyBox Salutes (572-576), Skymasters (577-588), Shooting Stars (589-602), Small School Sensations (603-609), NBA Stay in School (610-614), Player Updates (615-653), and Checklists (654-659). As part of a promotion with Cheerios, four SkyBox cards from the basic set were inserted into specially marked 10-ounce and 15-ounce cereal boxes. These cereal boxes appeared on store shelves in December 1991 and January 1992, and they depicted images of SkyBox cards on the front, back, and side panels. An unnumbered gold foil-stamped 1992 USA Basketball Team photo card was randomly inserted into second series foil packs, while the blister packs featured two-card sets of NBA MVPs from the same team for consecutive years. As a mail-in offer a limited Clyde Drexler Olympic card was sent to the first 10,000 respondents in return for teh SkyBox wrappers and 1.00 for postage and handling. Rookie Cards of note include Kenny Anderson, Stacey Augmon, Terrell Brandon, Larry Johnson, Dikembe Mutombo, Steve Smith and John Starks.

COMPLETE SET (659) 30.00 60.00
COMPLETE SERIES 1 (350) 10.00 20.00
COMPLETE SERIES 2 (309) 20.00 40.00
1 John Battle .02 .10
2 Duane Ferrell .02 .10
3 Jon Koncak .02 .10
4 Moses Malone .15 .40
5 Tim McCormick .02 .10
6 Sidney Moncrief .02 .10
7 Doc Rivers .07 .20
8 Rumeal Robinson UER .02 .10
(Drafted 11th; should say 10th)
9 Spud Webb .07 .20
10 Dominique Wilkins .15 .40
11 Kevin Willis .02 .10
12 Larry Bird .60 1.50
13 Dee Brown .02 .10
14 Kevin Gamble .02 .10
15 Joe Kleine .02 .10
16 Reggie Lewis .07 .20
17 Kevin McHale .07 .20
18 Robert Parish .07 .20
19 Ed Pinckney .02 .10
20 Brian Shaw .02 .10
21 Michael Smith .02 .10
22 Stojko Vrankovic .02 .10
23 Muggsy Bogues .07 .20
24 Rex Chapman .07 .20
25 Dell Curry .02 .10
26 Kenny Gattison .02 .10
27 Kendall Gill .07 .20
28 Mike Gminski .02 .10
29 Randolph Keys .02 .10
30 Eric Leckner .02 .10
31 Johnny Newman .02 .10
32 J.R. Reid .02 .10
33 Kelly Tripucka .02 .10
34 B.J. Armstrong .02 .10
35 Bill Cartwright .02 .10
36 Horace Grant .07 .20
37 Craig Hodges .02 .10
38 Dennis Hopson .02 .10
39 Michael Jordan 2.00 5.00
40 Stacey King .02 .10
41 Cliff Levingston .02 .10
42 John Paxson .02 .10
43 Will Perdue .02 .10
44 Scottie Pippen .50 1.25
45 Winston Bennett .02 .10
46 Chucky Brown .02 .10
47 Brad Daugherty .02 .10
48 Craig Ehlo .02 .10
49 Danny Ferry .02 .10
50 Steve Kerr .07 .20
51 John Morton .02 .10
52 Larry Nance .07 .20
53 Mark Price .02 .10
54 Darnell Valentine .02 .10
55 John Williams .02 .10
56 Steve Alford .02 .10
57 Rolando Blackman .02 .10
58 Brad Davis .02 .10
59 James Donaldson .02 .10
60 Derek Harper .07 .20
61 Fat Lever .02 .10
62 Rodney McCray .02 .10
63 Roy Tarpley .02 .10
64 Kelvin Upshaw .02 .10
65 Randy White .02 .10
66 Herb Williams .02 .10
67 Michael Adams .02 .10
68 Greg Anderson .02 .10
69 Anthony Cook .02 .10
70 Chris Jackson .02 .10
71 Jerome Lane .02 .10
72 Marcus Liberty .02 .10
73 Todd Lichti .02 .10
74 Blair Rasmussen .02 .10
75 Reggie Williams .02 .10
76 Joe Wolf .02 .10
77 Orlando Woolridge .02 .10
78 Mark Aguirre .02 .10
79 William Bedford .02 .10
80 Lance Blanks .02 .10
81 Joe Dumars .15 .40
82 James Edwards .02 .10
83 Scott Hastings .02 .10
84 Vinnie Johnson .02 .10
85 Bill Laimbeer .07 .20
86 Dennis Rodman .30 .75
87 John Salley .02 .10
88 Isiah Thomas .15 .40
89 Mario Elie RC .15 .40
90 Tim Hardaway .25 .60
91 Rod Higgins .02 .10
92 Tyrone Hill .07 .20
93 Les Jepsen .02 .10
94 Alton Lister .02 .10
95 Sarunas Marciulionis .02 .10
96 Chris Mullin .15 .40
97 Jim Petersen .02 .10
98 Mitch Richmond .15 .40
99 Tom Tolbert .02 .10
100 Adrian Caldwell .02 .10
101 Eric(Sleepy) Floyd .02 .10
102 Dave Jamerson .02 .10
103 Buck Johnson .02 .10
104 Vernon Maxwell .02 .10
105 Hakeem Olajuwon .25 .60
106 Kenny Smith .02 .10
107 Larry Smith .02 .10
108 Otis Thorpe .07 .20
109 Kennard Winchester RC .02 .10
110 David Wood RC .02 .10
111 Greg Dreiling .02 .10
112 Vern Fleming .02 .10
113 George McCloud .02 .10
114 Reggie Miller .15 .40
115 Chuck Person .02 .10
116 Mike Sanders .02 .10
117 Detlef Schrempf .07 .20
118 Rik Smits .07 .20
119 LaSalle Thompson .02 .10
120 Kenny Williams .02 .10
121 Micheal Williams .02 .10
122 Ken Bannister .02 .10
123 Winston Garland .02 .10
124 Gary Grant .02 .10
125 Ron Harper .07 .20
126 Bo Kimble .02 .10
127 Danny Manning .07 .20
128 Jeff Martin .02 .10
129 Ken Norman .02 .10
130 Olden Polynice .02 .10
131 Charles Smith .02 .10
132 Loy Vaught .02 .10
133 Elden Campbell .07 .20
134 Vlade Divac .07 .20
135 Larry Drew .02 .10
136 A.C. Green .07 .20
137 Magic Johnson .50 1.25
138 Sam Perkins .07 .20
139 Byron Scott .07 .20
140 Tony Smith .02 .10
141 Terry Teagle .02 .10
142 Mychal Thompson .02 .10
143 James Worthy .15 .40
144 Willie Burton .02 .10
145 Bimbo Coles .02 .10
146 Terry Davis .02 .10
147 Sherman Douglas .02 .10
148 Kevin Edwards .02 .10
149 Alec Kessler .02 .10
150 Grant Long .02 .10
151 Glen Rice .15 .40
152 Rony Seikaly .02 .10
153 Jon Sundvold .02 .10
154 Billy Thompson .02 .10
155 Frank Brickowski .02 .10
156 Lester Conner .02 .10
157 Jeff Grayer .02 .10
158 Jay Humphries .02 .10
159 Larry Krystkowiak .02 .10
160 Brad Lohaus .02 .10
161 Dale Ellis .07 .20
162 Fred Roberts .02 .10
163 Alvin Robertson .02 .10
164 Danny Schayes .02 .10
165 Jack Sikma .02 .10
166 Randy Breuer .02 .10
167 Scott Brooks .02 .10
168 Tony Campbell .02 .10
169 Tyrone Corbin .02 .10
170 Gerald Glass .02 .10
171 Sam Mitchell .02 .10
172 Tod Murphy .02 .10
173 Pooh Richardson .02 .10
174 Felton Spencer .02 .10
175 Bob Thornton .02 .10
176 Doug West .02 .10
177 Mookie Blaylock .07 .20
178 Sam Bowie .02 .10
179 Jud Buechler .02 .10
180 Derrick Coleman .07 .20
181 Chris Dudley .02 .10
182 Tate George .02 .10
183 Jack Haley .02 .10
184 Terry Mills RC .15 .40
185 Chris Morris .02 .10
186 Drazen Petrovic .07 .20
187 Reggie Theus .07 .20
188 Maurice Cheeks .02 .10
189 Patrick Ewing .15 .40
190 Mark Jackson .07 .20
191 Jerrod Mustaf .02 .10
192 Charles Oakley .07 .20
193 Brian Quinnett .02 .10
194 John Starks RC .15 .40
195 Trent Tucker .02 .10
196 Kiki Vandeweghe .02 .10
197 Kenny Walker .02 .10
198 Gerald Wilkins .02 .10
199 Mark Acres .02 .10
200 Nick Anderson .07 .20
201 Michael Ansley .02 .10
202 Terry Catledge .02 .10
203 Greg Kite .02 .10
204 Jerry Reynolds .02 .10
205 Dennis Scott .07 .20
206 Scott Skiles .02 .10
207 Otis Smith .02 .10
208 Jeff Turner .02 .10
209 Sam Vincent .02 .10
210 Ron Anderson .02 .10
211 Charles Barkley .25 .60
212 Manute Bol .02 .10
213 Johnny Dawkins .02 .10
214 Armon Gilliam .02 .10
215 Rickey Green .02 .10
216 Hersey Hawkins .07 .20
217 Rick Mahorn .02 .10
218 Brian Oliver .02 .10
219 Andre Turner .02 .10
220 Jayson Williams .15 .40
221 Joe Barry Carroll .02 .10
222 Cedric Ceballos .07 .20
223 Tom Chambers .02 .10
224 Jeff Hornacek .07 .20

225 Kevin Johnson .15 .40
226 Negele Knight .02 .10
227 Andrew Lang .02 .10
228 Dan Majerle .07 .20
229 Xavier McDaniel .02 .10
230 Kurt Rambis .02 .10
231 Mark West .02 .10
232 Alaa Abdelnaby .02 .10
233 Danny Ainge .07 .20
234 Mark Bryant .02 .10
235 Wayne Cooper .02 .10
236 Walter Davis .02 .10
237 Clyde Drexler .15 .40
238 Kevin Duckworth .02 .10
239 Jerome Kersey .02 .10
240 Terry Porter .02 .10
241 Clifford Robinson .07 .20
242 Buck Williams .02 .10
243 Anthony Bonner .02 .10
244 Antoine Carr .02 .10
245 Duane Causwell .02 .10
246 Bobby Hansen .02 .10
247 Jim Les RC .02 .10
248 Travis Mays .02 .10
249 Ralph Sampson .02 .10
250 Lionel Simmons .02 .10
251 Rory Sparrow .02 .10
252 Wayman Tisdale .02 .10
253 Bill Wennington .02 .10
254 Willie Anderson .02 .10
255 Terry Cummings .02 .10
256 Sean Elliott .07 .20
257 Sidney Green .02 .10
258 David Greenwood .02 .10
259 Avery Johnson .07 .20
260 Paul Pressey .02 .10
261 David Robinson .30 .75
262 Dwayne Schintzius .02 .10
263 Rod Strickland .15 .40
264 David Wingate .02 .10
265 Dana Barros .02 .10
266 Benoit Benjamin .02 .10
267 Michael Cage .02 .10
268 Quintin Dailey .02 .10
269 Ricky Pierce .02 .10
270 Eddie Johnson .07 .20
271 Shawn Kemp .40 1.00
272 Derrick McKey .02 .10
273 Nate McMillan .02 .10
274 Gary Payton .40 1.00
275 Sedale Threatt .02 .10
276 Thurl Bailey .02 .10
277 Mike Brown .02 .10
278 Tony Brown .02 .10
279 Mark Eaton .02 .10
280 Blue Edwards .02 .10
281 Darrell Griffith .02 .10
282 Jeff Malone .02 .10
283 Karl Malone .25 .60
284 Delaney Rudd .02 .10
285 John Stockton .15 .40
286 Andy Toolson .02 .10
287 Mark Alarie .02 .10
288 Ledell Eackles .02 .10
289 Pervis Ellison .02 .10
290 A.J. English .02 .10
291 Harvey Grant .02 .10
292 Tom Hammonds .02 .10
293 Charles Jones .02 .10
294 Bernard King .02 .10
295 Darrell Walker .02 .10
296 John Williams .02 .10
297 Haywoode Workman RC .07 .20
298 Muggsy Bogues .02 .10
299 Lester Conner .02 .10
300 Michael Adams .02 .10
301 Chris Mullin Minutes .07 .20
302 Otis Thorpe .02 .10
303 Mitch Richmond .15 .40
Chris Mullin
Tim Hardaway
Highest Scoring Trio
304 Darrell Walker .02 .10
305 Jerome Lane .02 .10
306 John Stockton Assists .07 .20
307 Michael Jordan Points 1.00 2.50
308 Michael Adams .02 .10
309 Larry Smith .02 .10
Jerome Lane
310 Scott Skiles .02 .10
311 Hakeem Olajuwon .15 .40
David Robinson
312 Alvin Robertson .02 .10
313 Stay In School Jam .02 .10
314 Craig Hodges 3P .02 .10
315 Dee Brown SD .02 .10
316 Charles Barkley AS-MVP .15 .40
317 Behind the Scenes .15 .40
Charles Barkley
Joe Dumars
Kevin McHale
318 Derrick Coleman ART .02 .10
319 Lionel Simmons ART .02 .10
320 Dennis Scott ART .02 .10
321 Kendall Gill ART .02 .10
322 Dee Brown ART .02 .10
323 Magic Johnson GQ .25 .60
324 Hakeem Olajuwon GQ .15 .40
325 Kevin Willis .07 .20
Dominique Wilkins
GQ All-Star Style Team
326 Kevin Willis .07 .20
Dominique Wilkins
GQ All-Star Style Team
327 Gerald Wilkins GQ .02 .10
328 Centennial Logo Card .02 .10
329 Old-Fashioned Ball .02 .10
330 Women Take the Court .02 .10
331 The Peach Basket .02 .10
332 James A. Naismith .07 .20
Founder of Basketball
333 Magic Johnson FIN .75 2.00
Michael Jordan
334 Michael Jordan FIN 1.00 2.50
335 Vlade Divac FIN .02 .10
336 John Paxson FIN .02 .10
337 Bulls Starting Five .50 1.25
Great Moments from
the NBA Finals
338 Language Arts .02 .10
339 Mathematics .02 .10
340 Vocational Education .02 .10
341 Social Studies .02 .10
342 Physical Education .02 .10
343 Art .02 .10
344 Science .02 .10
345 Checklist 1 (1-60) .02 .10
346 Checklist 2 (61-120) .02 .10
347 Checklist 3 (121-180) .02 .10
348 Checklist 4 (181-244) .02 .10
349 Checklist 5 (245-305) .02 .10
350 Checklist 6 (306-350) .02 .10
351 Atlanta Hawks TL .02 .10
352 Boston Celtics TL .02 .10
353 Charlotte Hornets TL .02 .10
354 Chicago Bulls TL .02 .10
355 Cleveland Cavaliers TL .02 .10
356 Dallas Mavericks TL .02 .10
357 Denver Nuggets TL .02 .10
358 Detroit Pistons TL .02 .10
359 Golden State Warriors TL .02 .10
360 Houston Rockets TL .02 .10
361 Indiana Pacers TL .02 .10
362 Los Angeles Clippers TL .02 .10
363 Los Angeles Lakers TL .02 .10
364 Miami Heat TL .02 .10
365 Milwaukee Bucks TL .02 .10
366 Minnesota Timberwolves TL .02 .10
367 New Jersey Nets TL .02 .10
368 New York Knicks TL .02 .10
369 Orlando Magic TL .02 .10
370 Philadelphia 76ers TL .02 .10
371 Phoenix Suns TL .02 .10
372 Portland Trail Blazers TL .02 .10
373 Sacramento Kings TL .02 .10
374 San Antonio Spurs TL .02 .10
375 Seattle Supersonics TL .02 .10
376 Utah Jazz TL .02 .10
377 Washington Bullets TL .02 .10
378 Bob Weiss CO .02 .10
379 Chris Ford CO .02 .10
380 Allan Bristow CO .02 .10
381 Phil Jackson CO .07 .20
382 Lenny Wilkens CO .07 .20
383 Richie Adubato CO .02 .10
384 Paul Westhead CO .02 .10
385 Chuck Daly CO .07 .20
386 Don Nelson CO .07 .20
387 Don Chaney CO .02 .10
388 Bob Hill CO RC .02 .10
389 Mike Schuler CO .02 .10
390 Mike Dunleavy CO .02 .10
391 Kevin Loughery CO .02 .10
392 Del Harris CO .02 .10
393 Jimmy Rodgers CO .02 .10
394 Bill Fitch CO .02 .10
395 Pat Riley CO .07 .20
396 Matt Guokas CO .02 .10
397 Jim Lynam CO .02 .10
398 Cotton Fitzsimmons CO .02 .10
399 Rick Adelman CO .02 .10
400 Dick Motta CO .02 .10
401 Larry Brown CO .02 .10
402 K.C. Jones CO .07 .20
403 Jerry Sloan CO .07 .20
404 Wes Unseld CO .07 .20
405 Mo Cheeks GF .02 .10
406 Dee Brown GF .02 .10
407 Rex Chapman GF .02 .10
408 Michael Jordan GF 1.00 2.50
409 John Williams GF .02 .10
410 James Donaldson GF .02 .10
411 Dikembe Mutombo GF .15 .40
412 Isiah Thomas GF .07 .20
413 Tim Hardaway GF .15 .40
414 Hakeem Olajuwon GF .15 .40
415 Detlef Schrempf GF .02 .10
416 Danny Manning GF .02 .10
417 Magic Johnson GF .25 .60
418 Bimbo Coles GF .02 .10
419 Alvin Robertson GF .02 .10
420 Sam Mitchell GF .02 .10
421 Sam Bowie GF .02 .10
422 Mark Jackson GF .02 .10
423 Orlando Magic GF .02 .10
424 Charles Barkley GF .15 .40
425 Dan Majerle GF .02 .10
426 Robert Pack GF .02 .10
427 Wayman Tisdale GF .02 .10
428 David Robinson GF .15 .40
429 Nate McMillan GF .02 .10
430 Karl Malone GF .15 .40
431 Michael Adams GF .02 .10
432 Duane Ferrell SM .02 .10
433 Kevin McHale SM .02 .10
434 Dell Curry SM .02 .10
435 B.J. Armstrong SM .02 .10
436 John Williams SM .02 .10
437 Brad Davis SM .02 .10
438 Marcus Liberty SM .02 .10
439 Mark Aguirre SM .02 .10
440 Rod Higgins SM .02 .10
441 Eric (Sleepy) Floyd SM .02 .10
442 Detlef Schrempf SM .02 .10
443 Loy Vaught SM .02 .10
444 Terry Teagle SM .02 .10
445 Kevin Edwards SM .02 .10
446 Dale Ellis SM .02 .10
447 Tod Murphy SM .02 .10
448 Chris Dudley SM .02 .10
449 Mark Jackson SM .02 .10
450 Jerry Reynolds SM .02 .10
451 Ron Anderson SM .02 .10
452 Dan Majerle SM .02 .10
453 Danny Ainge SM .02 .10
454 Jim Les SM .02 .10
455 Paul Pressey SM .02 .10
456 Ricky Pierce SM .02 .10
457 Mike Brown SM .02 .10
458 Ledell Eackles SM .02 .10
459 Dominique Wilkins .07 .20
Kevin Willis TW
460 Larry Bird .15 .40
Robert Parish TW
461 Rex Chapman .02 .10
Kendall Gill TW
462 Michael Jordan .60 1.50
Scottie Pippen TW
463 Craig Ehlo .02 .10
Mark Price TW
464 Derek Harper .02 .10
Rolando Blackman TW
465 Reggie Williams .02 .10
Chris Jackson TW
466 Isiah Thomas .07 .20
Bill Laimbeer TW
467 Tim Hardaway .07 .20
Chris Mullin TW
468 Vernon Maxwell .02 .10
Kenny Smith TW
469 Reggie Miller .07 .20
Detlef Schrempf TW
470 Charles Smith .02 .10
Danny Manning TW
471 Magic Johnson .15 .40
James Worthy TW
472 Glen Rice .15 .40
Rony Seikaly TW
473 Jay Humphries .02 .10
Alvin Robertson TW
474 Tony Campbell .02 .10
Pooh Richardson TW
475 Derrick Coleman .02 .10
Sam Bowie TW
476 Patrick Ewing .07 .20
Charles Oakley TW
477 Dennis Scott .02 .10
Scott Skiles
478 Charles Barkley .15 .40
Hersey Hawkins TW
479 Kevin Johnson .07 .20
Tom Chambers TW
480 Clyde Drexler .15 .40
Terry Porter TW
481 Lionel Simmons .02 .10
Wayman Tisdale TW
482 Terry Cummings .02 .10
Sean Elliott TW
483 Eddie Johnson .02 .10
Ricky Pierce TW
484 Karl Malone .15 .40
John Stockton TW
485 Harvey Grant .02 .10
Bernard King TW
486 Rumeal Robinson RS .02 .10
487 Dee Brown RS .02 .10
488 Kendall Gill RS .02 .10
489 B.J. Armstrong RS .02 .10
490 Danny Ferry RS .02 .10
491 Randy White RS .02 .10
492 Chris Jackson RS .02 .10
493 Lance Blanks RS .02 .10
494 Tim Hardaway RS .15 .40
495 Vernon Maxwell RS .02 .10
496 Micheal Williams RS .02 .10
497 Charles Smith RS .02 .10
498 Vlade Divac RS .02 .10
499 Willie Burton RS .02 .10
500 Jeff Grayer RS .02 .10
501 Pooh Richardson RS .02 .10
502 Derrick Coleman RS .02 .10
503 John Starks RS .07 .20
504 Dennis Scott RS .02 .10
505 Hersey Hawkins RS .02 .10
506 Negele Knight RS .02 .10
507 Clifford Robinson RS .02 .10
508 Lionel Simmons RS .02 .10
509 David Robinson RS .15 .40
510 Gary Payton RS .20 .50
511 Blue Edwards RS .02 .10
512 Harvey Grant RS .02 .10
513 Larry Johnson RC .60 1.50
514 Kenny Anderson RC .30 .75
515 Billy Owens RC .15 .40
516 Dikembe Mutombo RC .60 1.50
517 Steve Smith RC .60 1.50
518 Doug Smith RC .02 .10
519 Luc Longley RC .15 .40
520 Mark Macon RC .02 .10
521 Stacey Augmon RC .15 .40
522 Brian Williams RC .15 .40
523 Terrell Brandon RC .50 1.25
524 The Ball .02 .10
525 The Basket .02 .10
526 The 24-second Shot .02 .10
527 The Game Program .02 .10
528 The Championship Gift .02 .10
529 Championship Trophy .02 .10
530 Charles Barkley USA .50 1.25
531 Larry Bird USA 1.25 3.00
532 Patrick Ewing USA .30 .75
533 Magic Johnson USA 1.00 2.50
534 Michael Jordan USA 3.00 8.00
535 Karl Malone USA .50 1.25
536 Chris Mullin USA .15 .40
537 Scottie Pippen USA 1.00 2.50
538 David Robinson USA .60 1.50
539 John Stockton USA .30 .75
540 Chuck Daly CO USA .07 .20
541 P.J.Carlesimo CO USA RC .02 .10
542 Mike Krzyzewski CO USA RC .25 .60
543 Lenny Wilkens CO USA .07 .20
544 Team USA 1 1.00 2.50
545 Team USA 2 1.00 2.50
546 Team USA 3 1.00 2.50
547 Willie Anderson USA .02 .10
548 Stacey Augmon USA .15 .40
549 Bimbo Coles USA .02 .10
550 Jeff Grayer USA .02 .10
551 Hersey Hawkins USA .02 .10
552 Dan Majerle USA .02 .10
553 Danny Manning USA .02 .10
554 J.R. Reid USA .02 .10
555 Mitch Richmond USA .30 .75
556 Charles Smith USA .02 .10
557 Vern Fleming USA .02 .10
558 Joe Kleine USA .02 .10
559 Jon Koncak USA .02 .10
560 Sam Perkins USA .02 .10
561 Alvin Robertson USA .02 .10
562 Wayman Tisdale USA .02 .10
563 Jeff Turner USA .02 .10
564 Tony Campbell MAG .02 .10
565 Joe Dumars MAG .07 .20
566 Horace Grant MAG .02 .10
567 Reggie Lewis MAG .02 .10
568 Hakeem Olajuwon MAG .15 .40
569 Sam Perkins MAG .02 .10
570 Chuck Person MAG .02 .10
571 Buck Williams MAG .02 .10
572 Michael Jordan SAL 1.00 2.50
573 Bernard King SAL .02 .10
574 Moses Malone SAL .07 .20
575 Robert Parish SAL .02 .10
576 Pat Riley CO SAL .07 .20
577 Dee Brown SM .02 .10
578 Rex Chapman SM .02 .10
579 Clyde Drexler SM .07 .20
580 Blue Edwards SM .02 .10
581 Ron Harper SM .02 .10
582 Kevin Johnson SM .07 .20
583 Michael Jordan SM 1.00 2.50
584 Shawn Kemp SM .30 .75
585 Xavier McDaniel SM .02 .10
586 Scottie Pippen SM .25 .60
587 Kenny Smith SM .02 .10
588 Dominique Wilkins SM .07 .20
589 Michael Adams SS .02 .10
590 Danny Ainge SS .02 .10
591 Larry Bird SS .30 .75
592 Dale Ellis SS .02 .10
593 Hersey Hawkins SS .02 .10
594 Jeff Hornacek SS .02 .10
595 Jeff Malone SS .02 .10
596 Reggie Miller SS .07 .20
597 Chris Mullin SS .07 .20
598 John Paxson SS .02 .10
599 Drazen Petrovic SS .02 .10
600 Ricky Pierce SS .02 .10
601 Mark Price SS .02 .10
602 Dennis Scott SS .02 .10
603 Manute Bol SMALL .02 .10
604 Jerome Kersey SMALL .02 .10
605 Charles Oakley SMALL .02 .10
606 Scottie Pippen SMALL .25 .60
607 Terry Porter SMALL .02 .10
608 Dennis Rodman SMALL .15 .40
609 Sedale Threatt SMALL .02 .10
610 Business .02 .10
611 Engineering .02 .10
612 Law .02 .10
613 Liberal Arts .02 .10
614 Medicine .02 .10
615 Maurice Cheeks .02 .10
616 Travis Mays .02 .10
617 Blair Rasmussen .02 .10
618 Alexander Volkov .02 .10
619 Rickey Green .02 .10
620 Bobby Hansen .02 .10
621 John Battle .02 .10
622 Terry Davis .02 .10
623 Walter Davis .02 .10
624 Winston Garland .02 .10
625 Scott Hastings .02 .10
626 Brad Sellers .02 .10
627 Darrell Walker .02 .10
628 Orlando Woolridge .02 .10
629 Tony Brown .02 .10
630 James Edwards .02 .10
631 Doc Rivers .07 .20
632 Jack Haley .02 .10
633 Sedale Threatt .02 .10
634 Moses Malone .15 .40
635 Thurl Bailey .02 .10
636 Rafael Addison RC .02 .10
637 Tim McCormick .02 .10
638 Xavier McDaniel .02 .10
639 Charles Shackleford .02 .10
640 Mitchell Wiggins .02 .10
641 Jerrod Mustaf .02 .10
642 Dennis Hopson .02 .10
643 Les Jepsen .02 .10
644 Mitch Richmond .15 .40
645 Dwayne Schintzius .02 .10
646 Spud Webb .07 .20
647 Jud Buechler .02 .10
648 Antoine Carr .02 .10
649 Tyrone Corbin .02 .10
650 Michael Adams .02 .10
651 Ralph Sampson .02 .10
652 Andre Turner .02 .10
653 David Wingate .02 .10
654 Checklist S .02 .10
(351-404)
655 Checklist K .02 .10
(405-458)
656 Checklist Y .02 .10
(459-512)
657 Checklist B .02 .10
(513-563)
658 Checklist O .02 .10
(564-614)
659 Checklist X .02 .10
(615-659)
NNO Clyde Drexler USA 25.00 60.00
(Send-away)
NNO Team USA Card 6.00 12.00

1991-92 SkyBox Blister Inserts

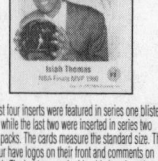

The first four inserts were featured in series one blister packs, while the last two were inserted in series two blister packs. The cards measure the standard size. The first four have logos on their front and comments on the back. The last two are double-sided cards and display most valuable players from the same team for two consecutive years. The cards are numbered on the back with Roman numerals.

COMPLETE SET (6) 1.00 2.50
1 USA Basketball .08 .25
2 Stay in School .08 .25
3 Orlando All-Star .08 .25
4 Inside Stuff .08 .25
5 Magic Johnson .40 1.00
James Worthy
6 Joe Dumars .20 .50
Isiah Thomas

1992-93 SkyBox

The complete 1992-93 SkyBox basketball set contains 413 standard-size cards. The set was released in two series of 327 and 86 cards, respectively. Both series foil packs contained 12 cards each with 36 packs to a box. Suggested retail price was 1.15 per pack. Reported production quantities were approximately 15,000 20-box cases for the first series and 15,000 20-box cases for the second series. The new front design features computer-generated screens of color blended with full-bleed color action photos. The backs carry full-bleed non-action close-up photos overlaid by a column displaying complete statistics and a color stripe with a personal "bio-bit." Cards of second series rookies have a gold seal in the other lower corner. In addition, the second series Draft Pick rookie cards were printed in shorter supply than the other cards in the second series set. First series cards are checklisted below alphabetically according team order. Subsets are Coaches (255-281), Team Tix (282-308), 1992 NBA All-Star Weekend Highlights (309-313), 1992 NBA Finals (314-318), 1992 NBA All-Rookie Team (319), and Public Service (230-321). The set concludes with checklist cards (322-327). The cards are numbered on the back. Special gold-foil stamped cards of Magic Johnson and David Robinson, some personally autographed, were randomly inserted in first series foil packs. Versions of these Johnson and Robinson cards with sparkling silver foil were also produced and one of each accompanied the first 7,500 cases ordered exclusively by hobby accounts. According to SkyBox approximately one of every 36 packs contained either a Magic Johnson or David Robinson SP card. The "Head of the Class" mail-away card features the first six 1992 NBA draft picks. The card was made available to the first 20,000 fans through a mail-in offer for three wrappers from each series of 1992-93 SkyBox cards plus 3.25 for postage and handling. The horizontal front features three color, cut-out player photos against a black background. Three wide vertical stripes in shades of red and violet run behind the players. A gold bar near the bottom carries the phrase "Head of the Class 1992 Top NBA Draft Picks." The back features three player photos similar to the ones on the front. The background design is the same except the wide stripes are green, orange, and blue. A white bar at the lower right corner carries the serial number and production run (20,000). Rookie Cards of note include Tom Gugliotta, Robert Horry, Christian Laettner, Alonzo Mourning, Shaquille O'Neal, Latrell Sprewell and Clarence Weatherspoon.

COMPLETE SET (413) 25.00 50.00
COMPLETE SERIES 1 (327) 15.00 30.00
COMPLETE SERIES 2 (86) 10.00 20.00
1 Stacey Augmon .08 .25
2 Maurice Cheeks .02 .10
3 Duane Ferrell .02 .10
4 Paul Graham .02 .10
5 Jon Koncak .02 .10
6 Blair Rasmussen .02 .10
7 Rumeal Robinson .02 .10
8 Dominique Wilkins .20 .50
9 Kevin Willis .02 .10
10 Larry Bird .75 2.00
11 Dee Brown .02 .10
12 Sherman Douglas .02 .10
13 Rick Fox .08 .25
14 Kevin Gamble .02 .10
15 Reggie Lewis .08 .25
16 Kevin McHale .20 .50
17 Robert Parish .08 .25
18 Ed Pinckney .02 .10
19 Muggsy Bogues .08 .25
20 Dell Curry .02 .10
21 Kenny Gattison .02 .10
22 Kendall Gill .08 .25
23 Mike Gminski .02 .10
24 Tom Hammonds .02 .10
25 Larry Johnson .25 .60
26 Johnny Newman .02 .10
27 J.R. Reid .02 .10
28 B.J. Armstrong .02 .10
29 Bill Cartwright .02 .10
30 Horace Grant .08 .25
31 Michael Jordan 2.50 6.00
32 Stacey King .02 .10
33 John Paxson .02 .10
34 Will Perdue .02 .10
35 Scottie Pippen .60 1.50
36 Scott Williams .02 .10
37 John Battle .02 .10
38 Terrell Brandon .20 .50
39 Brad Daugherty .02 .10
40 Craig Ehlo .02 .10
41 Danny Ferry .02 .10
42 Henry James .02 .10
43 Larry Nance .02 .10
44 Mark Price .02 .10
45 Mike Sanders .02 .10
46 Hot Rod Williams .02 .10
47 Rolando Blackman .02 .10
48 Terry Davis .02 .10
49 Derek Harper .08 .25
50 Donald Hodge .02 .10
51 Mike Iuzzolino .02 .10
52 Fat Lever .02 .10
53 Rodney McCray .02 .10
54 Doug Smith .02 .10
55 Randy White .02 .10
56 Herb Williams .02 .10
57 Greg Anderson .02 .10
58 Walter Davis .02 .10
59 Winston Garland .02 .10
60 Chris Jackson .02 .10
61 Marcus Liberty .02 .10
62 Todd Lichti .02 .10
63 Mark Macon .02 .10
64 Dikembe Mutombo .25 .60
65 Reggie Williams .02 .10
66 Mark Aguirre .02 .10
67 William Bedford .02 .10
68 Lance Blanks .02 .10
69 Joe Dumars .20 .50
70 Bill Laimbeer .08 .25
71 Dennis Rodman .40 1.00
72 John Salley .02 .10
73 Isiah Thomas .20 .50
74 Darrell Walker .02 .10
75 Orlando Woolridge .02 .10
76 Victor Alexander .02 .10
77 Mario Elie .08 .25
78 Chris Gatling .02 .10
79 Tim Hardaway .25 .60
80 Tyrone Hill .02 .10
81 Alton Lister .02 .10
82 Sarunas Marciulionis .02 .10
83 Chris Mullin .20 .50
84 Billy Owens .08 .25
85 Matt Bullard .02 .10
86 Sleepy Floyd .02 .10
87 Avery Johnson .02 .10
88 Buck Johnson .02 .10
89 Vernon Maxwell .02 .10
90 Hakeem Olajuwon .30 .75
91 Kenny Smith .02 .10
92 Larry Smith .02 .10
93 Otis Thorpe .08 .25
94 Dale Davis .02 .10
95 Vern Fleming .02 .10
96 George McCloud .02 .10
97 Reggie Miller .20 .50
98 Chuck Person .02 .10
99 Detlef Schrempf .08 .25
100 Rik Smits .08 .25
101 LaSalle Thompson .02 .10
102 Micheal Williams .02 .10
103 James Edwards .02 .10
104 Gary Grant .02 .10
105 Ron Harper .08 .25
106 Bo Kimble .02 .10
107 Danny Manning .08 .25
108 Ken Norman .02 .10
109 Olden Polynice .02 .10
110 Doc Rivers .08 .25
111 Charles Smith .02 .10
112 Loy Vaught .02 .10
113 Elden Campbell .08 .25
114 Vlade Divac .08 .25
115 A.C. Green .08 .25
116 Jack Haley .02 .10
117 Sam Perkins .08 .25
118 Byron Scott .08 .25
119 Tony Smith .02 .10
120 Sedale Threatt .02 .10
121 James Worthy .20 .50
122 Keith Askins .02 .10
123 Willie Burton .02 .10
124 Bimbo Coles .02 .10
125 Kevin Edwards .02 .10
126 Alec Kessler .02 .10
127 Grant Long .02 .10
128 Glen Rice .20 .50
129 Rony Seikaly .02 .10
130 Brian Shaw .02 .10
131 Steve Smith .25 .60
132 Frank Brickowski .02 .10
133 Dale Ellis .02 .10
134 Jeff Grayer .02 .10
135 Jay Humphries .02 .10
136 Larry Krystkowiak .02 .10
137 Moses Malone .20 .50
138 Fred Roberts .02 .10
139 Alvin Robertson .02 .10
140 Danny Schayes .02 .10
141 Thurl Bailey .02 .10
142 Scott Brooks .02 .10
143 Tony Campbell .02 .10
144 Gerald Glass .02 .10
145 Luc Longley .08 .25
146 Sam Mitchell .02 .10
147 Pooh Richardson .02 .10
148 Felton Spencer .02 .10
149 Doug West .02 .10
150 Rafael Addison .02 .10
151 Kenny Anderson .20 .50
152 Mookie Blaylock .08 .25
153 Sam Bowie .02 .10
154 Derrick Coleman .08 .25
155 Chris Dudley .02 .10
156 Tate George .02 .10
157 Terry Mills .02 .10
158 Chris Morris .02 .10
159 Drazen Petrovic .02 .10
160 Greg Anthony .02 .10
161 Patrick Ewing .20 .50
162 Mark Jackson .08 .25
163 Anthony Mason .20 .50
164 Tim McCormick .02 .10
165 Xavier McDaniel .02 .10
166 Charles Oakley .08 .25
167 John Starks .08 .25
168 Gerald Wilkins .02 .10
169 Nick Anderson .08 .25
170 Terry Catledge .02 .10
171 Jerry Reynolds .02 .10
172 Stanley Roberts .02 .10
173 Dennis Scott .08 .25
174 Scott Skiles .02 .10
175 Jeff Turner .02 .10
176 Sam Vincent .02 .10
177 Brian Williams .02 .10
178 Ron Anderson .02 .10
179 Charles Barkley .30 .75
180 Manute Bol .02 .10
181 Johnny Dawkins .02 .10
182 Armon Gilliam .02 .10
183 Greg Grant .02 .10
184 Hersey Hawkins .08 .25
185 Brian Oliver .02 .10
186 Charles Shackleford .02 .10
187 Jayson Williams .08 .25
188 Cedric Ceballos .08 .25
189 Tom Chambers .02 .10
190 Jeff Hornacek .08 .25
191 Kevin Johnson .20 .50
192 Negele Knight .02 .10
193 Andrew Lang .02 .10
194 Dan Majerle .08 .25
195 Jerrod Mustaf .02 .10
196 Tim Perry .02 .10
197 Mark West .02 .10
198 Alaa Abdelnaby .02 .10
199 Danny Ainge .08 .25
200 Mark Bryant .02 .10
201 Clyde Drexler .20 .50
202 Kevin Duckworth .02 .10
203 Jerome Kersey .02 .10
204 Robert Pack .02 .10
205 Terry Porter .02 .10
206 Clifford Robinson .08 .25
207 Buck Williams .08 .25
208 Anthony Bonner .02 .10
209 Randy Brown .02 .10
210 Duane Causwell .02 .10
211 Pete Chilcutt .02 .10
212 Dennis Hopson .02 .10
213 Jim Les .02 .10
214 Mitch Richmond .20 .50
215 Lionel Simmons .02 .10
216 Wayman Tisdale .02 .10
217 Spud Webb .08 .25
218 Willie Anderson .02 .10
219 Antoine Carr .02 .10
220 Terry Cummings .08 .25
221 Sean Elliott .08 .25
222 Sidney Green .02 .10
223 Vinnie Johnson .02 .10
224 David Robinson .30 .75
225 Rod Strickland .20 .50
226 Greg Sutton .02 .10
227 Dana Barros .02 .10
228 Benoit Benjamin .02 .10
229 Michael Cage .02 .10
230 Eddie Johnson .02 .10
231 Shawn Kemp .40 1.00
232 Derrick McKey .02 .10
233 Nate McMillan .02 .10
234 Gary Payton .40 1.00
235 Ricky Pierce .02 .10
236 David Benoit .02 .10
237 Mike Brown .02 .10
238 Tyrone Corbin .02 .10
239 Mark Eaton .02 .10
240 Blue Edwards .02 .10
241 Jeff Malone .02 .10
242 Karl Malone .30
243 Eric Murdock .02
244 John Stockton .20
245 Michael Adams .02
246 Rex Chapman .02
247 Ledell Eackles .02
248 Pervis Ellison .02
249 A.J. English .02
250 Harvey Grant .02
251 Charles Jones .02
252 Bernard King .02
253 LaBradford Smith .02
254 Larry Stewart .02
255 Bob Weiss CO .02
256 Chris Ford CO .02
257 Allan Bristow CO .02
258 Phil Jackson CO .08
259 Lenny Wilkens CO .08
260 Richie Adubato CO .02
261 Dan Issel CO .02
262 Ron Rothstein CO .02
263 Don Nelson CO .08
264 Rudy Tomjanovich CO .08
265 Bob Hill CO .02
266 Larry Brown CO .08
267 Randy Pfund CO RC .02
268 Kevin Loughery CO .02
269 Mike Dunleavy CO .02
270 Jimmy Rodgers CO .02
271 Chuck Daly CO .08
272 Pat Riley CO .08
273 Matt Guokas CO .02
274 Doug Moe CO .02
275 Paul Westphal CO .02
276 Rick Adelman CO .02
277 Garry St. Jean CO RC .02
278 Jerry Tarkanian CO RC .02
279 George Karl CO .08
280 Jerry Sloan CO .08
281 Wes Unseld CO .08
282 Dominique Wilkins TT .08
283 Reggie Lewis TT .02
284 Kendall Gill TT .02
285 Horace Grant TT .02
286 Brad Daugherty TT .02
287 Derek Harper TT .02
288 Chris Jackson TT .02
289 Isiah Thomas TT .08
290 Chris Mullin TT .08
291 Kenny Smith TT .02
292 Reggie Miller TT .08
293 Ron Harper TT .02
294 Vlade Divac TT .02
295 Glen Rice TT .08
296 Moses Malone TT .08
297 Doug West TT .02
298 Derrick Coleman TT .02
299 Patrick Ewing TT .08
(See also card 305)
300 Scott Skiles TT .02
301 Hersey Hawkins TT .02
302 Kevin Johnson TT .08
303 Clifford Robinson TT .02
304 Spud Webb TT .02
305 David Robinson TT COR .20
305A David Robinson TT ERR .20
(Card misnumbered as 299)
306 Shawn Kemp TT .20
307 John Stockton TT .08
308 Pervis Ellison TT .02
309 Craig Hodges AS .02
310 Magic Johnson AS MVP .30
311 Cedric Ceballos AS SD .02
312 Dennis Rodman .20
Group AS
313 Karl Malone .20
Group AS
314 Michael Jordan MVP 1.25
315 Clyde Drexler FIN .08
316 Danny Ainge PO .08
317 Scottie Pippen FIN .30
318 NBA Champs .20
Michael Jordan
319 Larry Johnson ART .20
Dikembe Mutombo
320 NBA Stay in School .02
321 Boys and Girls .02
322 Checklist 1 .02
323 Checklist 2 .02
324 Checklist 3 .02
325 Checklist 4 .02
326 Checklist 5 .02
327 Checklist 6 .02
328 Adam Keefe SP RC .02
329 Sean Rooks SP RC .02
330 Xavier McDaniel .02
331 Kiki Vandeweghe .02
332 Alonzo Mourning SP RC 1.25
333 Rodney McCray .02
334 Gerald Wilkins .02
335 Tony Bennett SP RC .02
336 LaPhonso Ellis SP RC .20
337 Bryant Stith SP RC .20
338 Isaiah Morris SP RC .02
339 Olden Polynice .02
340 Jeff Grayer .02
341 Byron Houston SP RC .02
342 Latrell Sprewell SP RC 1.50
343 Scott Brooks .02
344 Frank Johnson .02
345 Robert Horry SP RC .20
346 David Wood .02
347 Sam Mitchell .02
348 Pooh Richardson .02
349 Malik Sealy SP RC .20
350 Morlon Wiley .02
351 Mark Jackson .08
352 Stanley Roberts .02
353 Elmore Spencer SP RC .02
354 John Williams .02
355 Randy Woods SP RC .02
356 James Edwards .02
357 Jeff Sanders .02
358 Magic Johnson .60
359 Anthony Peeler SP RC .20
360 Harold Miner SP RC .20
361 John Salley .02
362 Alaa Abdelnaby .02
363 Todd Day SP RC .20
364 Blue Edwards .02
365 Lee Mayberry SP RC .02
366 Eric Murdock .02
367 Mookie Blaylock .08
368 Anthony Avent RC .02
369 Christian Laettner SP RC .40

370 Chuck Person .02 .10
371 Chris Smith SP RC .20 .50
372 Micheal Williams .02 .10
373 Rolando Blackman .02 .10
374 Tony Campbell UER .02 .10
(Back photo actually
Alvin Robertson)
375 Hubert Davis SP RC .20 .50
376 Travis Mays .02 .10
377 Doc Rivers .08 .25
378 Charles Smith .02 .10
379 Rumeal Robinson .02 .10
380 Vinny Del Negro .02 .10
381 Steve Kerr .08 .25
382 Shaquille O'Neal SP RC 5.00 12.00
383 Donald Royal .02 .10
384 Jeff Hornacek .08 .25
385 Andrew Lang .02 .10
386 Tim Perry UER .02 .10
(Alvin Robertson pictured on back)
387 Clarence Weatherspoon SP RC .20 .50
388 Danny Ainge .08 .25
389 Charles Barkley .30 .75
390 Tim Kempton .02 .10
391 Oliver Miller SP RC .20 .50
392 Dave Johnson SP RC .20 .50
393 Tracy Murray SP RC .20 .50
394 Rod Strickland .20 .50
395 Marty Conlon .02 .10
396 Walt Williams SP RC .20 .50
397 Lloyd Daniels RC .02 .10
398 Dale Ellis .02 .10
399 Dave Hoppen .02 .10
400 Larry Smith .02 .10
401 Doug Overton .02 .10
402 Isaac Austin RC .08 .25
403 Jay Humphries .02 .10
404 Larry Krystkowiak .02 .10
405 Tom Gugliotta SP RC .60 1.50
406 Buck Johnson .02 .10
407 Don MacLean SP RC .20 .50
408 Marlon Maxey SP RC .20 .50
409 Corey Williams SP RC .20 .50
410 Special Olympics .08 .25
Dan Majerle
411 Checklist 1 .02 .10
412 Checklist 2 .02 .10
413 Checklist 3 .02 .10
NNO Magic Johnson 2.50 6.00
The Magic Never Ends Silver
NNO David Robinson 1.50 4.00
The Admiral Comes Prepared Silver
NNO David Robinson AU 60.00 150.00
NNO David Robinson 1.50 4.00
The Admiral Comes Prepared Gold
NNO Magic Johnson AU 75.00 200.00
NNO Head of the Class 12.00 30.00
LaPhonso Ellis
Tom Gugliotta
Christian Laettner
Alonzo Mourning
Shaquille O'Neal
Walt Williams
NNO Magic Johnson 2.50 6.00
The Magic Never Ends Gold

1992-93 SkyBox Draft Picks

...is 25-card standard-size insert set showcases the ...st round picks from the 1992 NBA Draft. The cards ...re randomly inserted into 12-card (both series) foil ...cks. According to SkyBox, approximately one out of ...ery eight packs contained a Draft Pick card. The card ...mbering (1-27) reflects the actual order in which ...ch player was selected. Six players (2, 10-11, 15-16, ...) available by the first series cut-off date were issued ...first series foil packs, while the rest of the first round ...cks who signed NBA contracts were issued in second ...ies packs. DP4 and DP17, intended for Jim Jackson ...d Doug Christie respectively, were not issued with ...s set because neither player signed a professional ...ntract in time to be included in the second series. ...ey were issued in 1993-94 first series packs. The ...nts display an opaque metallic gold rectangle set off ...m the player. On a gradated gold background, the ...cks present player profiles. A white rectangle that ...s vertically the length of the card contains statistics. ...e team logo is superimposed on this rectangle. The ...ds are numbered on the back with a "DP" prefix.

...MPLETE SET (25) 12.00 30.00
...MPLETE SERIES 1 (6) 3.00 8.00
...MPLETE SERIES 2 (19) 10.00 25.00
1 Shaquille O'Neal 6.00 15.00
2 Alonzo Mourning 2.00 5.00
3 Christian Laettner .75 2.00
5 LaPhonso Ellis .60 1.50
6 Tom Gugliotta 1.25 3.00
7 Walt Williams .40 1.00
8 Todd Day .40 1.00
9 Clarence Weatherspoon .40 1.00
10 Adam Keefe .15 .40
11 Robert Horry .60 1.50
12 Harold Miner .40 1.00
13 Bryant Stith .40 1.00
14 Malik Sealy .40 1.00
15 Anthony Peeler .40 1.00
16 Randy Woods .15 .40
18 Tracy Murray .40 1.00
19 Don MacLean .15 .40
20 Hubert Davis .40 1.00
21 Jon Barry .40 1.00
22 Oliver Miller .40 1.00
23 Lee Mayberry .15 .40
24 Latrell Sprewell 3.00 8.00
25 Elmore Spencer .15 .40
26 Dave Johnson .15 .40
27 Byron Houston .15 .40

1992-93 SkyBox Olympic Team

Each card in this 12-card standard-size set features an action photo of a team member and his complete statistics from the Olympic Games. According to SkyBox, the cards were randomly inserted into 12-card first series foil packs at a rate of approximately one per six. The backs tell the story of U.S. Men's Olympic Team, from scrimmage in Monte Carlo to the medal ceremony in Barcelona. The cards are numbered on the back with a "USA" prefix.

COMPLETE SET (12) 12.00 30.00
USA1 Clyde Drexler .60 1.50
USA2 Chris Mullin .60 1.50
USA3 John Stockton .60 1.50
USA4 Karl Malone 1.00 2.50
USA5 Scottie Pippen 2.00 5.00
USA6 Larry Bird 2.50 6.00
USA7 Charles Barkley 1.00 2.50
USA8 Patrick Ewing .60 1.50
USA9 Christian Laettner 1.25 3.00
USA10 David Robinson 1.00 2.50
USA11 Michael Jordan 6.00 15.00
USA12 Magic Johnson 2.00 5.00

1992-93 SkyBox David Robinson

This ten-card standard-size insert set provides a look at Robinson at various stages of his life. Included are photos from his childhood, indulging in hobbies, with his family at the Naval Academy and his present day super stardom. The first five cards were randomly inserted in first series 12-card foil packs, while the second five were found in second series packs. According to SkyBox, approximately one of every eight packs contains a David Robinson insert card. The cards feature a different design than the regular issue cards. The fronts display color photos tilted slightly to the left with a special seal overlaying the upper left corner. The surrounding card face shows two colors.

COMPLETE SET (10) 2.00 4.00
COMPLETE SERIES 1 (5) 1.00 2.00
COMPLETE SERIES 2 (5) 1.00 2.00
COMMON CARD (R1-R10) .20 .50

1992-93 SkyBox School Ties

Randomly inserted in 1992-93 SkyBox second series 12-card foil packs at a reported rate of one per four, this 18-card standard-size set consists of six different three-card "School Ties" interlocking cards. When the three cards in each puzzle are placed together, they create a montage of active NBA players from one particular college. The fronts feature several color player photos that have team color-coded picture frames. The team logo appears in a team color-coded banner that is superimposed across the bottom of the picture. The backs have brightly colored backgrounds and display information about the college, the players, and a checklist of the players on the three-card puzzle. The cards are numbered on the back with an "ST" prefix.

COMPLETE SET (18) 7.50 15.00
ST1 Patrick Ewing 1.00 2.50
Alonzo Mourning
ST2 Dikembe Mutombo .20 .50
Eric Floyd
ST3 Reggie Williams .08 .25
David Wingate
ST4 Kenny Anderson .20 .50
Duane Ferrell
ST5 Tom Hammonds .08 .25
Jon Barry
Mark Price
ST6 John Salley .20 .50
Dennis Scott
ST7 Rafael Addison .08 .25
Dave Johnson
ST8 Billy Owens .20 .50
Derrick Coleman
Rony Seikaly
ST9 Sherman Douglas .08 .25
Danny Schayes
ST10 Nick Anderson .20 .50
Kendall Gill
ST11 Derek Harper .08 .25
Eddie Johnson
ST12 Marcus Liberty .08 .25
Ken Norman
ST13 Greg Anthony .20 .50
Stacey Augmon
ST14 Armon Gilliam .20 .50
Larry Johnson
Sidney Green
ST15 Elmore Spencer .08 .25
Gerald Paddio
ST16 James Worthy 4.00 10.00
Michael Jordan
Sam Perkins
ST17 J.R. Reid .08 .25
Pete Chilcutt
Brad Daugherty
Rick Fox
ST18 Hubert Davis .20 .50
Kenny Smith
Scott Williams

1992-93 SkyBox Thunder and Lightning

Randomly inserted into second series 12-card foil packs at a reported rate of one per 40 packs, each card in this nine-card standard-size set features a pair of teammates. There is a photo on each side. The catchword on the front is "Thunder", referring to a dominant power player, while "Lightning" on the back captures the speed of a guard. The cards are highlighted by a litho-foil printing which gives a foil-look to the graphics around the basketball. The cards have color action player photos against a dark background, with computer enhancement around the ball and player. On the front, the power player's name appears at the bottom and is underlined by a thin yellow stripe. The word "Thunder" appears below the stripe. On the horizontal backs, the speed player's name is displayed in the upper right with the same yellow underline, but the word Lightning" appears below it. The cards are numbered on the back with a "TL" prefix.

COMPLETE SET (9) 15.00 40.00
TL1 Dikembe Mutombo 1.50 4.00
Mark Macon
TL2 Buck Williams 1.50 4.00
Clyde Drexler
TL3 Charles Barkley 3.00 8.00
Kevin Johnson
TL4 Pervis Ellison .60 1.50
Michael Adams
TL5 Larry Johnson 1.50 4.00
Muggsy Bogues
TL6 Brad Daugherty .60 1.50
Mark Price
TL7 Shawn Kemp 6.00 15.00
Gary Payton
TL8 Karl Malone 5.00 12.00
John Stockton
TL9 Billy Owens 2.00 5.00
Tim Hardaway

2008-09 SkyBox

This set was released on February 17, 2009. The base set consists of 230 cards. Cards 1-200 feature veterans, and cards 201-230 are rookies. Rookies were inserted at a rate of one in three and the Close Ups subset was inserted at one in 1.25.

COMPLETE SET (230) 40.00 80.00
1 Mike Bibby .25 .60
2 Acie Law .25 .60
3 Al Horford .30 .75
4 Joe Johnson .30 .75
5 Josh Smith .30 .75
6 Marvin Williams .30 .75
7 Ray Allen .30 .75
8 Glen Davis .25 .60
9 Kevin Garnett .60 1.50
10 Paul Pierce .40 1.00
11 Leon Powe .20 .50
12 Rajon Rondo .40 1.00
13 Raymond Felton .25 .60
14 Adam Morrison .30 .75
15 Emeka Okafor .30 .75
16 Boris Diaw .20 .50
17 Gerald Wallace .30 .75
18 Luol Deng .30 .75
19 Ben Gordon .30 .75
20 Kirk Hinrich .30 .75
21 Joakim Noah .30 .75
22 Andres Nocioni .20 .50
23 Tyrus Thomas .25 .60
24 Daniel Gibson .30 .75
25 Zydrunas Ilgauskas .25 .60
26 LeBron James 1.50 4.00
27 Anderson Varejao .25 .60
28 Ben Wallace .30 .75
29 Jose Barea .40 1.00
30 Josh Howard .25 .60
31 Jason Kidd .30 .75
32 Dirk Nowitzki .40 1.00
33 Jason Terry .25 .60
34 Carmelo Anthony .40 1.00
35 Shaun Livingston .20 .50
36 Chauncey Billups .30 .75
37 Kenyon Martin .30 .75
38 J.R. Smith .30 .75
39 Allen Iverson .40 1.00
40 Richard Hamilton .25 .60
41 Jason Maxiell .20 .50
42 Tayshaun Prince .30 .75
43 Rodney Stuckey .40 1.00
44 Rasheed Wallace .30 .75
45 Kelenna Azubuike .20 .50
46 Matt Barnes .20 .50
47 Corey Maggette .25 .60
48 Monta Ellis .30 .75
49 Jamal Crawford .25 .60
50 Stephen Jackson .25 .60
51 Shane Battier .25 .60
52 Luther Head .20 .50
53 Carl Landry .20 .50
54 Tracy McGrady .30 .75
55 Yao Ming .40 1.00
56 Luis Scola .25 .60
57 Mike Dunleavy .25 .60
58 Danny Granger .30 .75
59 Troy Murphy .20 .50
60 T.J. Ford .20 .50
61 Jamaal Tinsley .20 .50
62 Elton Brand .30 .75
63 Chris Kaman .25 .60
64 Ricky Davis .25 .60
65 Baron Davis .30 .75
66 Zach Randolph .25 .60
67 Al Thornton .25 .60
68 Kobe Bryant 1.50 4.00
69 Andrew Bynum .40 1.00
70 Jordan Farmar .20 .50
71 Pau Gasol .30 .75
72 Lamar Odom .30 .75
73 Sasha Vujacic .20 .50
74 Mike Conley Jr. .25 .60
75 Rudy Gay .30 .75
76 Kyle Lowry .30 .75
77 Mike Miller .30 .75
78 Hakim Warrick .25 .60
79 Daequan Cook .20 .50
80 Marcus Camby .20 .50
81 Udonis Haslem .25 .60
82 Shawn Marion .30 .75
83 Alonzo Mourning .40 1.00
84 Dwyane Wade .60 1.50
85 Andrew Bogut .30 .75
86 Richard Jefferson .30 .75
87 Desmond Mason .20 .50
88 Michael Redd .30 .75
89 Ramon Sessions .25 .60
90 Mo Williams .25 .60
91 Corey Brewer .25 .60
92 Randy Foye .30 .75
93 Al Jefferson .30 .75
94 Rashad McCants .20 .50
95 Sebastian Telfair .20 .50
96 Josh Boone .20 .50
97 Vince Carter .40 1.00
98 Devin Harris .30 .75
99 Yi Jianlian .30 .75
100 Keyon Dooling .20 .50
101 Sean Williams .25 .60
102 Tyson Chandler .25 .60
103 Chris Paul .50 1.25
104 Morris Peterson .20 .50
105 Peja Stojakovic .30 .75
106 David West .30 .75
107 Julian Wright .25 .60
108 Al Harrington .25 .60
109 Eddy Curry .20 .50
110 David Lee .25 .60
111 Stephon Marbury .25 .60
112 Cuttino Mobley .25 .60
113 Quentin Richardson .25 .60
114 Keith Bogans .20 .50
115 Maurice Evans .20 .50
116 Dwight Howard .60 1.50
117 Rashard Lewis .25 .60
118 Jameer Nelson .25 .60
119 Hedo Turkoglu .30 .75
120 Samuel Dalembert .20 .50
121 Reggie Evans .20 .50
122 Willie Green .20 .50
123 Andre Iguodala .30 .75
124 Andre Miller .25 .60
125 Thaddeus Young .25 .60
126 Leandro Barbosa .25 .60
127 Jason Richardson .30 .75
128 Grant Hill .40 1.00
129 Steve Nash .30 .75
130 Shaquille O'Neal .60 1.50
131 Amare Stoudemire .30 .75
132 LaMarcus Aldridge .30 .75
133 Steve Blake .20 .50
134 Greg Oden .30 .75
135 Brandon Roy .30 .75
136 Martell Webster .25 .60
137 Beno Udrih .20 .50
138 Ron Artest .30 .75
139 Francisco Garcia .25 .60
140 Kevin Martin .30 .75
141 Brad Miller .25 .60
142 Brent Barry .20 .50
143 Bruce Bowen .20 .50
144 Tim Duncan .50 1.25
145 Michael Finley .30 .75
146 Manu Ginobili .30 .75
147 Tony Parker .30 .75
148 Nick Collison .20 .50
149 Kevin Durant 1.25 3.00
150 Jeff Green .25 .60
151 Earl Watson .20 .50
152 Chris Wilcox .20 .50
153 Damien Wilkins .20 .50
154 Andrea Bargnani .25 .60
155 Chris Bosh .30 .75
156 Jose Calderon .25 .60
157 Jermaine O'Neal .30 .75
158 Jamario Moon .20 .50
159 Anthony Parker .20 .50
160 Carlos Boozer .30 .75
161 Ronnie Brewer .25 .60
162 Andrei Kirilenko .25 .60
163 Kyle Korver .25 .60
164 Mehmet Okur .20 .50
165 Deron Williams .30 .75
166 Gilbert Arenas .30 .75
167 Caron Butler .30 .75
168 Antawn Jamison .30 .75
169 DeShawn Stevenson .20 .50
170 Nick Young .25 .60
171 Al Horford CU .40 1.00
172 Joe Johnson CU .40 1.00
173 Kevin Garnett CU .75 2.00
174 Paul Pierce CU .50 1.25
175 Larry Johnson CU .40 1.00
176 Michael Jordan CU 3.00 8.00
177 LeBron James CU 2.00 5.00
178 Ben Wallace CU .40 1.00
179 Dirk Nowitzki CU .50 1.25
180 Carmelo Anthony CU .50 1.25
181 Allen Iverson CU .50 1.25
182 Isiah Thomas CU .40 1.00
183 Monta Ellis CU .40 1.00
184 Magic Johnson CU 1.00 2.50
185 Kobe Bryant CU 2.00 5.00
186 Dwyane Wade CU .75 2.00
187 Oscar Robertson CU .40 1.00
188 Vince Carter CU .50 1.25
189 Chris Paul CU .60 1.50
190 Patrick Ewing CU .50 1.25
191 Dwight Howard CU .75 2.00
192 Julius Erving CU .75 2.00
193 Steve Nash CU .40 1.00
194 Shaquille O'Neal CU .75 2.00
195 Brandon Roy CU .40 1.00
196 Tim Duncan CU .60 1.50
197 Kevin Durant CU 1.50 4.00
198 Chris Bosh CU .40 1.00
199 Deron Williams CU .40 1.00
200 Gilbert Arenas CU .40 1.00
201 Derrick Rose RC 20.00 50.00
202 Michael Beasley RC 1.50 4.00
203 O.J. Mayo RC 1.50 4.00
204 Russell Westbrook RC 5.00 12.00
205 Kevin Love RC 4.00 10.00
206 Danilo Gallinari RC 1.50 4.00
207 Eric Gordon RC 2.50 6.00
208 Joe Alexander RC 1.00 2.50
209 D.J. Augustin RC 1.00 2.50
210 Brook Lopez RC 1.50 4.00
211 Jerryd Bayless RC 1.00 2.50
212 Jason Thompson RC 1.00 2.50
213 Brandon Rush RC 1.00 2.50
214 Robin Lopez RC 1.00 2.50
215 Roy Hibbert RC 1.50 4.00
216 Alexis Ajinca RC 1.00 2.50
217 George Hill RC 1.50 4.00
218 Donte Greene RC 1.00 2.50
219 J.J. Hickson RC 1.25 3.00
220 D.J. White RC 1.00 2.50
221 Mario Chalmers RC 1.50 4.00
222 Mike Taylor RC 1.00 2.50
223 Kosta Koufos RC 1.00 2.50
224 Kyle Weaver RC 1.00 2.50
225 Rudy Fernandez RC 1.25 3.00
226 Nicolas Batum RC 1.50 4.00
227 Luc Richard Mbah A Moute RC 1.00 2.50
228 Marc Gasol RC 1.50 4.00
229 Darnell Jackson RC 1.00 2.50
230 Richard Hendrix RC 1.00 2.50

2008-09 SkyBox Ruby

*VETS 1-170: 12X TO 30X BASE HI
*SUBSET 171-200: 10X TO 25X BASE HI
*ROOKIES 201-230: 4X TO 10X BASE HI
STATED PRINT RUN 50 SER.#'d SETS
26 LeBron James 60.00 150.00
29 Jose Barea 15.00 40.00
39 Allen Iverson 20.00 50.00
68 Kobe Bryant 60.00 150.00
128 Grant Hill 25.00 60.00
149 Kevin Durant 50.00 125.00
176 Michael Jordan CU 200.00 400.00
181 Allen Iverson CU 20.00 50.00
185 Kobe Bryant CU 60.00 150.00
197 Kevin Durant CU 50.00 125.00
204 Russell Westbrook 60.00 150.00

2008-09 SkyBox Emerald Rookie Autographs

COMBINED AUTO ODDS 1:12
202 Michael Beasley 40.00 100.00
203 O.J. Mayo 40.00 100.00
204 Russell Westbrook 175.00 350.00
205 Kevin Love 150.00 300.00
207 Eric Gordon 40.00 100.00
208 Joe Alexander 8.00 20.00
210 Brook Lopez 12.00 30.00
212 Jason Thompson 8.00 20.00
213 Brandon Rush 8.00 20.00
214 Robin Lopez 8.00 20.00
215 Roy Hibbert 12.00 30.00
216 Alexis Ajinca 8.00 20.00
217 George Hill 12.00 30.00
218 Donte Greene 8.00 20.00
219 J.J. Hickson 10.00 25.00
220 D.J. White 8.00 20.00
221 Mario Chalmers 12.00 30.00
222 Mike Taylor 8.00 20.00
224 Kyle Weaver 8.00 20.00
226 Nicolas Batum 25.00 60.00
227 Luc Richard Mbah A Moute 8.00 20.00
229 Darnell Jackson 8.00 20.00

2008-09 SkyBox Fresh Ink

COMBINED AUTO ODDS 1:12
FICD Chris Duhon 4.00 10.00
FICM Chris Mihm 4.00 10.00
FICW C.J. Watson 4.00 10.00
FIGP Gabe Pruitt 4.00 10.00
FIJF Jordan Farmar 4.00 10.00
FIKD Kevin Durant 50.00 100.00
FIKG Kevin Garnett 40.00 80.00
FIMA Morris Almond 4.00 10.00
FIMW Mario West 4.00 10.00
FIRR Rajon Rondo 10.00 25.00
FISV Sasha Vujacic 4.00 10.00
FIWM Mo Williams 5.00 12.00

2008-09 SkyBox Larger Than Life

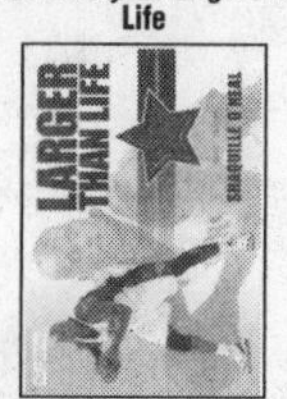

COMBINED MEM.ODDS 1:4
*RETAIL GREEN: .4X TO 1X HI COLUMN
*PATCHES: 1.25X TO 3X HI COLUMN
PATCH PRINT RUN 25 SER.#'d SETS
LLAS Amare Stoudemire 2.00 5.00
LLCA Carmelo Anthony 2.50 6.00
LLDN Dirk Nowitzki 2.50 6.00
LLDW Deron Williams 2.00 5.00
LLEB Elton Brand 2.00 5.00
LLGA Gilbert Arenas 2.00 5.00
LLJJ Joe Johnson 2.00 5.00
LLKB Kobe Bryant 10.00 25.00
LLKG Kevin Garnett 4.00 10.00
LLLJ LeBron James 10.00 25.00
LLME Monta Ellis 2.00 5.00
LLMG Manu Ginobili 2.00 5.00
LLPP Paul Pierce 2.50 6.00
LLRA Ray Allen 2.00 5.00
LLRH Richard Hamilton 2.00 5.00
LLSM Shawn Marion 2.00 5.00
LLSN Steve Nash 2.00 5.00
LLSO Shaquille O'Neal 4.00 10.00
LLTD Tim Duncan 3.00 8.00
LLVC Vince Carter 2.50 6.00

2008-09 SkyBox Metal Universe

COMPLETE SET (100) 75.00 150.00
APPROXIMATE ODDS 1:2
1 Kevin Garnett 2.50 6.00
2 LeBron James 6.00 15.00
3 Dwight Howard 2.50 6.00
4 Kobe Bryant 6.00 15.00
5 Carmelo Anthony 1.50 4.00
6 Tim Duncan 2.00 5.00
7 Yao Ming 1.50 4.00
8 Dwyane Wade 2.50 6.00
9 Dirk Nowitzki 1.50 4.00
10 Jason Kidd 1.25 3.00
11 Allen Iverson 1.50 4.00
12 Tracy McGrady 1.25 3.00
13 Steve Nash 1.25 3.00
14 Ray Allen 1.25 3.00
15 Amare Stoudemire 1.25 3.00
16 Vince Carter 1.50 4.00
17 Shaquille O'Neal 2.50 6.00
18 Chris Bosh 1.25 3.00
19 Gilbert Arenas 1.25 3.00
20 Chauncey Billups 1.25 3.00
21 Paul Pierce 1.50 4.00
22 Chris Paul 2.00 5.00
23 Michael Jordan 15.00 40.00
24 Carlos Boozer 1.25 3.00
25 Manu Ginobili 1.25 3.00
26 Shawn Marion 1.25 3.00
27 Tony Parker 1.25 3.00
28 Baron Davis 1.25 3.00
29 Shane Battier 1.00 2.50
30 Kevin Durant 5.00 12.00
31 Yi Jianlian 1.25 3.00
32 Luis Scola 1.00 2.50
33 Josh Howard 1.00 2.50
34 Marcus Camby .75 2.00
35 Grant Hill 1.50 4.00
36 Michael Redd 1.25 3.00
37 Caron Butler 1.25 3.00
38 Richard Hamilton 1.00 2.50
39 Rasheed Wallace 1.25 3.00
40 Hedo Turkoglu 1.25 3.00
41 Jason Terry 1.00 2.50
42 Tyson Chandler 1.00 2.50
43 Andrew Bogut 1.25 3.00
44 Tayshaun Prince 1.25 3.00
45 Ben Wallace 1.25 3.00
46 Joe Johnson 1.25 3.00
47 T.J. Ford .75 2.00
48 Rashard Lewis 1.00 2.50
49 Jermaine O'Neal 1.25 3.00
50 LaMarcus Aldridge 1.25 3.00
51 Pau Gasol 1.25 3.00
52 Chris Kaman 1.00 2.50
53 Emeka Okafor 1.25 3.00
54 Eddy Curry .75 2.00
55 Al Horford 1.25 3.00
56 Josh Smith 1.25 3.00
57 Gerald Wallace 1.25 3.00
58 Ben Gordon 1.25 3.00
59 Monta Ellis 1.25 3.00
60 Elton Brand 1.25 3.00
61 Rudy Gay 1.25 3.00
62 Al Jefferson 1.25 3.00
63 David West 1.25 3.00
64 Jamal Crawford 1.00 2.50
65 Andre Iguodala 1.25 3.00
66 Brandon Roy 1.25 3.00
67 Greg Oden 1.25 3.00
68 Kevin Martin 1.25 3.00
69 Jamario Moon .75 2.00
70 Deron Williams 1.25 3.00
71 Derrick Rose 25.00 60.00
72 Michael Beasley 2.00 5.00
73 O.J. Mayo 2.00 5.00
74 Russell Westbrook 6.00 15.00
75 Kevin Love 6.00 15.00
76 Danilo Gallinari 2.00 5.00
77 Eric Gordon 3.00 8.00
78 Joe Alexander 1.25 3.00
79 D.J. Augustin 1.25 3.00
80 Brook Lopez 2.00 5.00
81 Jerryd Bayless 1.25 3.00
82 Jason Thompson 1.25 3.00
83 Brandon Rush 1.25 3.00
84 Anthony Randolph 1.50 4.00
85 Robin Lopez 1.25 3.00
86 Marreese Speights 1.25 3.00
87 Roy Hibbert 2.00 5.00
88 Javale McGee 2.00 5.00
89 J.J. Hickson 1.50 4.00
90 Alexis Ajinca 1.25 3.00
91 Ryan Anderson 2.00 5.00
92 Courtney Lee 2.00 5.00
93 Kosta Koufos 1.25 3.00
94 Nicolas Batum 2.00 5.00
95 George Hill 2.00 5.00
96 D.J. White 1.25 3.00
97 J.R. Giddens 1.25 3.00
98 Luc Richard Mbah A Moute 1.25 3.00
99 Marc Gasol 2.00 5.00
100 Rudy Fernandez 1.50 4.00

2008-09 SkyBox Metal Universe Precious Metal Gems Red

*STARS: 8X TO 20X BASE HI
*ROOKIES: 4X TO 10X BASE HI
STATED PRINT RUN 40 SER.#'d SETS
CARDS SERIALLY #'d TO 50
FIRST TEN #'s ARE GREEN
GREEN UNPRICED DUE TO SCARCITY
4 Kobe Bryant 150.00 400.00
8 Dwyane Wade 75.00 150.00
10 Jason Kidd 40.00 100.00
11 Allen Iverson 40.00 100.00
13 Steve Nash 30.00 80.00
23 Michael Jordan 900.00 1500.00
71 Derrick Rose 300.00 600.00
74 Russell Westbrook 250.00 450.00
75 Kevin Love 100.00 250.00
99 Marc Gasol 30.00 80.00

2008-09 SkyBox One on One Dual Memorabilia

COMBINED MEM ODDS 1:4
OOAH Richard Hamilton 3.00 8.00
Ray Allen
OOAJ Gilbert Arenas 6.00 15.00
LeBron James
OOBA Carmelo Anthony 8.00 20.00
Kobe Bryant
OOBB Andrew Bynum 3.00 8.00
Carlos Boozer
OOBG Kevin Garnett 6.00 15.00
Kobe Bryant
OOBH Mike Bibby 3.00 8.00
Kirk Hinrich
OOBM Kenyon Martin 3.00 8.00
Elton Brand
OOBO Shaquille O'Neal 8.00 20.00
Kobe Bryant
OOBP Tony Parker 3.00 8.00
Chauncey Billups
OOCI Andre Iguodala 3.00 8.00
Vince Carter
OODG Pau Gasol 4.00 10.00
Tim Duncan
OODM Tim Duncan 3.00 8.00
Yao Ming
OOGW Kevin Garnett 4.00 10.00
Rasheed Wallace
OOHB Chris Bosh 3.00 8.00
Dwight Howard
OOHG Manu Ginobili 3.00 8.00
Richard Hamilton
OOJA Carmelo Anthony 8.00 20.00
LeBron James
OOKC Jason Kidd 4.00 10.00
Vince Carter
OOMH Shawn Marion 3.00 8.00
Josh Howard
OOMM Corey Maggette 3.00 8.00
Stephon Marbury
OOMO Yao Ming 4.00 10.00
Shaquille O'Neal
OOMW Deron Williams 3.00 8.00
Tracy McGrady
OONG Pau Gasol 4.00 10.00
Dirk Nowitzki
OONP Steve Nash 4.00 10.00
Tony Parker
OOPF Jordan Farmar 3.00 8.00
Tony Parker
OOPJ Paul Pierce 6.00 15.00
LeBron James
OOPP Paul Pierce 3.00 8.00
Tayshaun Prince
OOPW Chris Paul 4.00 10.00
Deron Williams
OORR Jason Richardson 3.00 8.00
Zach Randolph
OOSH Dwight Howard 4.00 10.00
Amare Stoudemire
OOWR Brandon Roy 3.00 8.00
Deron Williams

2008-09 SkyBox Paraph Signatures

COMBINED AUTOGRAPH ODDS 1:12
PSAM Alonzo Mourning 30.00 60.00
PSAT Alando Tucker 4.00 10.00
PSDH Dwight Howard 15.00 40.00
PSJK Jason Kidd 20.00 40.00
PSJN Joakim Noah 4.00 10.00
PSKD Michael Jordan 300.00 550.00
PSLA LaMarcus Aldridge 4.00 10.00
PSPP Paul Pierce 15.00 40.00
PSRJ Richard Jefferson 4.00 10.00
PSTP Tayshaun Prince 4.00 10.00

2008-09 SkyBox Rookie Prevue

COMBINED MEM ODDS 1:4
*RETAIL GREEN: .4X TO 1X HI COLUMN
UNPRICED PATCH PRINT RUN 10 SETS
RPAR Anthony Randolph 2.00 5.00
RPBL Brook Lopez 2.50 6.00
RPDA D.J. Augustin 2.00 5.00
RPDJ DeAndre Jordan 3.00 8.00
RPDR Derrick Rose 12.00 30.00
RPEG Eric Gordon 4.00 10.00
RPGH George Hill 2.50 6.00
RPJA Joe Alexander 2.00 5.00
RPJB Jerryd Bayless 2.00 5.00
RPJH J.J. Hickson 2.00 5.00
RPJT Jason Thompson 2.00 5.00
RPKK Kosta Koufos 2.00 5.00
RPKL Kevin Love 6.00 15.00
RPKW Kyle Weaver 2.00 5.00
RPMB Michael Beasley 2.50 6.00
RPMC Mario Chalmers 2.50 6.00

RPOM O.J. Mayo 2.50 6.00
RPRL Robin Lopez 2.00 5.00
RPSW Sonny Weems 2.00 5.00
RPWS Walter Sharpe 2.00 5.00

2008-09 SkyBox Signature Set Dual

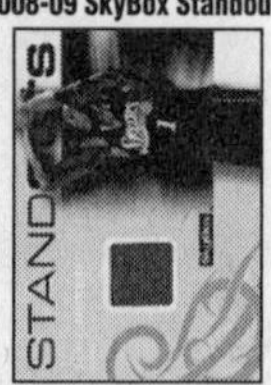

STATED PRINT RUN 23 TO 25 SER.#'d SETS
SSAW Ryan Anderson/25 10.00 25.00
Sean Williams
SSBW C.J. Watson/25 6.00 15.00
Marco Belinelli
SSDG Kevin Durant/25 50.00 125.00
Jeff Green
SSFD Raymond Felton/25 8.00 20.00
Jared Dudley
SSFR Brandon Roy/25 25.00 50.00
Rudy Fernandez
SSGA Rudy Gay/25 8.00 20.00
Darrell Arthur
SSGN Ben Gordon/25 8.00 20.00
Joakim Noah
SSJB Al Jefferson/25 8.00 20.00
Corey Brewer
SSJJ LeBron James/23 350.00 650.00
Michael Jordan
SSJS Ramon Sessions/25 6.00 15.00
Richard Jefferson
SSKJ DeAndre Jordan/25 8.00 20.00
Chris Kaman
SSPG Kevin Garnett/25 100.00 200.00
Paul Pierce
SSPS Tayshaun Prince/25 10.00 25.00
Rodney Stuckey
SSSB J.R. Smith/25 6.00 15.00
Renaldo Balkman
SSSW Jason Smith/25 8.00 20.00
Marreese Speights
SSTS Alando Tucker/25 6.00 15.00
Sean Singletary
SSWC Tyson Chandler/25 8.00 20.00
David West
SSWH Marvin Williams/25 8.00 20.00
Al Horford
SSWV Sasha Vujacic/25 10.00 25.00
Luke Walton

2008-09 SkyBox Standouts

COMBINED MEM ODDS 1:4
*RETAIL GREEN: .4X TO 1X HI COLUMN
*PATCHES: .75X TO 2X HI COLUMN
PATCH PRINT RUN 25 SER.#'d SETS
SOAB Andrew Bynum 4.00 10.00
SOAK Andrei Kirilenko 2.50 6.00
SOBU Beno Udrih 2.00 5.00
SOCK Chris Kaman 2.50 6.00
SODW Deron Williams 3.00 8.00
SOFO Randy Foye 3.00 8.00
SOJC Jarron Collins 2.00 5.00
SOJH Josh Howard 2.50 6.00
SOJR Jason Richardson 3.00 8.00
SOLD Luol Deng 3.00 8.00
SOLH Luther Head 2.00 5.00
SOLR Luke Ridnour 2.50 6.00
SOME Monta Ellis 3.00 8.00
SOPD Paul Davis 2.00 5.00
SORF Raymond Felton 2.50 6.00
SORG Rudy Gay 3.00 8.00
SOSD Samuel Dalembert 2.00 5.00
SOSS Stromile Swift 2.00 5.00
SOUH Udonis Haslem 2.50 6.00
SOZR Zach Randolph 2.50 6.00

1999-00 SkyBox APEX

Replacing the Thunder brand, this was the premiere year for the APEX brand. The set contained 163 cards, featuring 150 veterans and 13 rookies. The cards came eight to a pack with a suggested retail price of $2.69. The rookie cards were inserted at one in 13 packs. Two checklists were also included and inserted at one in six. 50 serial numbered cards were also included that could be redeemed for a Keith Van Horn autographed jersey.
COMPLETE SET (163) 60.00 120.00
COMPLETE SET w/o RC (150) 10.00 25.00
UNPRICED XTREME PRINT RUN ONE SET
1 Paul Pierce .50 1.25
2 Stephon Marbury .25 .60
3 Chris Webber .30 .75
4 Kobe Bryant 1.50 4.00
5 David Robinson .50 1.25
6 Gary Payton .30 .75
7 Kornel David RC .30 .75
8 Glenn Robinson .25 .60
9 Nick Van Exel .25 .60
10 Jelani McCoy .20 .50
11 Charles Oakley .25 .60
12 Michael Finley .30 .75
13 Steve Smith .20 .50
14 Arvydas Sabonis .25 .60
15 Cuttino Mobley .25 .60
16 Eric Piatkowski .25 .60
17 Bobby Jackson .25 .60
18 Keith Van Horn .25 .60
19 Shaquille O'Neal .75 2.00
20 Karl Malone .40 1.00
21 Allan Houston .25 .60
22 Ron Mercer .25 .60
23 Vince Carter .60 1.50
24 Lindsey Hunter .20 .50
25 Scottie Pippen .50 1.25
26 Wesley Person .20 .50
27 Vitaly Potapenko .20 .50
28 Glen Rice .30 .75
29 Tyrone Nesby RC .30 .75
30 Detlef Schrempf .25 .60
31 Clifford Robinson .20 .50
32 Joe Smith .25 .60
33 P.J. Brown .20 .50
34 Christian Laettner .25 .60
35 Avery Johnson .25 .60
36 Kevin Garnett .60 1.50
37 Jason Kidd .50 1.25
38 Kenny Anderson .25 .60
39 Shawn Kemp .30 .75
40 Bison Dele .20 .50
41 Rodney Rogers .20 .50
42 Jamal Mashburn .25 .60
43 Grant Hill .40 1.00
44 Larry Johnson .30 .75
45 Darrell Armstrong .20 .50
46 Shandon Anderson .20 .50
47 Kendall Gill .20 .50
48 Jason Williams .40 1.00
49 Tom Gugliotta .20 .50
50 Ray Allen .30 .75
51 Sam Mitchell .20 .50
52 Brent Barry .25 .60
53 Antawn Jamison .30 .75
54 Chris Mullin .30 .75
55 Alan Henderson .20 .50
56 Derek Anderson .20 .50
57 Tim Thomas .25 .60
58 Anfernee Hardaway .50 1.25
59 Pat Garrity .20 .50
60 Corliss Williamson .20 .50
61 Gary Trent .20 .50
62 Greg Ostertag .20 .50
63 Vin Baker .30 .75
64 LaPhonso Ellis .20 .50
65 Brevin Knight .20 .50
66 Rick Fox .20 .50
67 Bryant Reeves .20 .50
68 Mark Jackson .30 .75
69 John Starks .30 .75
70 Robert Traylor .20 .50
71 Maurice Taylor .20 .50
72 Hersey Hawkins .20 .50
73 Zydrunas Ilgauskas .25 .60
74 Charles Barkley .50 1.25
75 Isaac Austin .20 .50
76 Mike Bibby .30 .75
77 Michael Olowokandi .20 .50
78 Brian Grant .20 .50
79 Felipe Lopez .20 .50
80 Chris Crawford .20 .50
81 Dee Brown .20 .50
82 Antoine Walker .30 .75
83 Vlade Divac .30 .75
84 Rod Strickland .20 .50
85 Dickey Simpkins .20 .50
86 Donyell Marshall .20 .50
87 Larry Hughes .25 .60
88 Rasheed Wallace .30 .75
89 Erick Dampier .20 .50
90 Kerry Kittles .20 .50
91 Mitch Richmond .30 .75
92 Isaiah Rider .20 .50
93 Bobby Phills .20 .50
94 Dirk Nowitzki .60 1.50
95 Cedric Henderson .20 .50
96 Howard Eisley .20 .50
97 Toni Kukoc .30 .75
98 Jalen Rose .25 .60
99 Michael Doleac .20 .50
100 Matt Geiger .20 .50
101 Bryon Russell .20 .50
102 Alvin Williams .20 .50
103 Shawn Bradley .20 .50
104 Latrell Sprewell .30 .75
105 Vernon Maxwell .25 .60
106 Tim Hardaway .30 .75
107 Peja Stojakovic .30 .75
108 Tracy Murray .20 .50
109 Theo Ratliff .25 .60
110 Dikembe Mutombo .30 .75
111 Alonzo Mourning .40 1.00
112 Raef LaFrentz .25 .60
113 Marcus Camby .25 .60
114 Eddie Jones .30 .75
115 Chauncey Billups .30 .75
116 Jayson Williams .20 .50
117 Anthony Mason .20 .50
118 Tracy McGrady .50 1.25
119 John Stockton .40 1.00
120 Matt Harpring .25 .60
121 Mario Elie .20 .50
122 Juwan Howard .25 .60
123 Antonio McDyess .25 .60
124 Ricky Davis .30 .75
125 Reggie Miller .30 .75
126 Allen Iverson .60 1.50
127 Terrell Brandon .20 .50
128 Hakeem Olajuwon .40 1.00
129 Damon Stoudamire .30 .75
130 Randy Brown .20 .50
131 Cedric Ceballos .20 .50
132 Jerry Stackhouse .30 .75
133 Michael Dickerson .20 .50
134 Rik Smits .30 .75
135 Cherokee Parks .20 .50
136 Tim Duncan .60 1.50
137 Shareef Abdur-Rahim .25 .60
138 Derek Fisher .30 .75
139 Bo Outlaw .20 .50
140 Eric Snow .25 .60
141 Jaren Jackson .20 .50
142 Tony Battie .25 .60
143 Derrick Coleman .25 .60
144 Corey Benjamin .20 .50
145 Steve Nash .50 1.25
146 Mookie Blaylock .20 .50
147 Voshon Lenard .20 .50
148 Vinny Del Negro .20 .50
149 Jeff Hornacek .25 .60
150 Patrick Ewing .40 1.00
151 Elton Brand RC 1.50 4.00
152 Steve Francis RC 1.50 4.00
153 Baron Davis RC 2.00 5.00
154 Lamar Odom RC 2.00 5.00
155 Jonathan Bender RC .60 1.50
156 Wally Szczerbiak RC 1.25 3.00
157 Richard Hamilton RC 1.50 4.00
158 Andre Miller RC 1.50 4.00
159 Shawn Marion RC 1.50 4.00
160 Jason Terry RC 1.50 4.00
161 Trajan Langdon RC .60 1.50
162 Aleksandar Radojevic RC .60 1.50
163 Corey Maggette RC 1.25 3.00
P2 Stephon Marbury PROMO 1.00 2.50
NNO Keith Van Horn/50 30.00 80.00
Autographed Jersey

1999-00 SkyBox APEX Xtra

Randomly inserted in hobby packs, this 163-card set parallels the base set. The cards were serially numbered to 50.
*STARS: 25X TO 60X BASE CARD HI
*RCs: 3X TO 8X BASE HI
4 Kobe Bryant 200.00 400.00

1999-00 SkyBox APEX Xtreme

Randomly inserted in hobby packs, this 163-card set parallels the base set. The cards are serially numbered to one.

1999-00 SkyBox APEX Allies

Randomly inserted in packs at one in six, this 15-card set features two superstar teammates on the same card.

COMPLETE SET (15) 5.00 12.00
1 Kobe Bryant 2.50 6.00
Shaquille O'Neal
2 Keith Van Horn .40 1.00
Stephon Marbury
3 John Stockton .60 1.50
Karl Malone
4 Mike Bibby .50 1.25
Shareef Abdur-Rahim
5 Allen Iverson 1.00 2.50
Larry Hughes
6 Michael Olowokandi .30 .75
Maurice Taylor
7 Vince Carter 1.00 2.50
Tracy McGrady
8 Grant Hill .60 1.50
Jerry Stackhouse
9 Jason Williams .60 1.50
Chris Webber
10 Tim Duncan 1.00 2.50
David Robinson
11 Jason Kidd .75 2.00
Tom Gugliotta
12 Vin Baker .50 1.25
Gary Payton
13 Alonzo Mourning .60 1.50
Tim Hardaway
14 Shawn Kemp .50 1.25
Brevin Knight
15 Antonio McDyess .40 1.00
Raef LaFrentz

1999-00 SkyBox APEX Cutting Edge

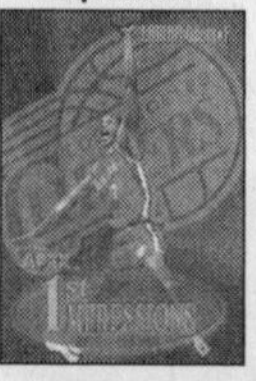

Randomly inserted in packs at one in 24, this 15-card set features players on the cutting edge of superstardom. The cards are die cut.
COMPLETE SET (15) 15.00 30.00
*PLUS: 1.25X TO 3X HI COLUMN
PLUS: STATED ODDS 1:240 HOB/RET
*WARP TEK: 15X TO 40X VALUE
WARP TEK: PRINT RUN 25 SERIAL #'d SETS
1 Allen Iverson 2.00 5.00
2 Paul Pierce 1.50 4.00
3 Vince Carter 2.00 5.00
4 Jason Williams 1.25 3.00
5 Kobe Bryant 8.00 20.00
6 Kevin Garnett 2.00 5.00
7 Stephon Marbury .75 2.00
8 Jason Kidd 1.50 4.00
9 Tim Duncan 2.00 5.00
10 Mike Bibby 1.00 2.50
11 Marcus Camby .75 2.00
12 Michael Olowokandi .60 1.50
13 Antawn Jamison 1.00 2.50
14 Keith Van Horn .75 2.00
15 Raef LaFrentz .75 2.00

1999-00 SkyBox APEX First Impressions

Randomly inserted in packs at one in 12, this 20-card set features the top rookies from the 1999-2000 season. The cards feature embossing and holofoil.
COMPLETE SET (20) 10.00 25.00
1 Jonathan Bender .50 1.25
2 Steve Francis 1.25 3.00
3 Ron Artest 1.25 3.00
4 Baron Davis 1.50 4.00
5 Shawn Marion 1.25 3.00
6 Jason Terry 1.25 3.00
7 Elton Brand 1.25 3.00
8 Kenny Thomas .50 1.25
9 Trajan Langdon .50 1.25
10 Aleksandar Radojevic .50 1.25
11 Corey Maggette 1.00 2.50
12 Jeff Foster .50 1.25
13 Scott Padgett .50 1.25
14 Lamar Odom 1.50 4.00
15 William Avery .50 1.25
16 Andre Miller 1.25 3.00
17 Wally Szczerbiak 1.00 2.50
18 Richard Hamilton 1.25 3.00
19 James Posey .50 1.25
20 Jumaine Jones .50 1.25

1999-00 SkyBox APEX Jam Session

Randomly inserted in packs at one in 96, this 15-card set features the NBA's top stars and aerial artists. The cards feature a die cut design with holofoil stamping on plastic stock.
COMPLETE SET (15) 40.00 80.00
1 Stephon Marbury 2.00 5.00
2 Paul Pierce 4.00 10.00
3 Kobe Bryant 15.00 40.00
4 Keith Van Horn 2.00 5.00
5 Shaquille O'Neal 6.00 15.00
6 Anfernee Hardaway 4.00 10.00
7 Grant Hill 3.00 8.00
8 Antonio McDyess 2.00 5.00
9 Kevin Garnett 5.00 12.00
10 Tracy McGrady 4.00 10.00
11 Shareef Abdur-Rahim 2.00 5.00
12 Shawn Kemp 2.50 6.00
13 Antoine Walker 2.50 6.00
14 Eddie Jones 2.50 6.00
15 Vin Baker 2.50 6.00

1999-00 SkyBox APEX Net Shredders

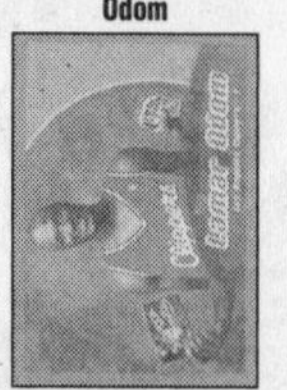

Randomly inserted in packs, this 10-card set features a piece of a game-used net in a card. The nets were obtained from Toronto, Philadelphia, Milwaukee, Sacramento and San Antonio.
1 Vince Carter 30.00 80.00
2 Tracy McGrady 25.00 60.00
3 Allen Iverson 30.00 80.00
4 Larry Hughes 12.00 30.00
5 Glenn Robinson 12.00 30.00
6 Ray Allen 15.00 40.00
7 Jason Williams 20.00 50.00
8 Chris Webber 15.00 40.00
9 Tim Duncan 30.00 80.00
10 David Robinson 25.00 60.00

1999-00 SkyBox APEX Lamar Odom

This one standard-sized card was sent to dealers to announce Fleer/SkyBox's signing of Lamar Odom as a spokesman. The cards are done in the style of 1999-00 SkyBox APEX. The cards are serially numbered out of 2000. Card backs are not numbered.
NNO Lamar Odom 4.00 10.00

2003-04 SkyBox Autographics

Released in late February 2004, this 90-card set places full-color player photos on a tan background with the words "Skybox Autographics" across the middle of the card. Card numbers 1-45 showcase veteran players and cards 46-90 feature rookies and are sequentially numbered to 1500. Autographics was packaged in four pack boxes where packs contained five cards and no suggested retail price was published.
COMP.SET w/o SP's (45) 12.50 30.00
1 Vince Carter .60 1.50
2 Kobe Bryant 2.00 5.00
3 Tony Parker .40 1.00
4 Richard Hamilton .30 .75
5 Jamal Mashburn .30 .75
6 Paul Pierce .50 1.25
7 Allan Houston .30 .75
8 Carlos Boozer .40 1.00
9 Michael Redd .40 1.00
10 Chris Webber .40 1.00
11 Yao Ming .75 2.00
12 Tracy McGrady .50 1.25
13 Zach Randolph .40 1.00
14 Ben Wallace .40 1.00
15 Kenyon Martin .40 1.00
16 Ray Allen .40 1.00
17 Jermaine O'Neal .40 1.00
18 Bonzi Wells .25 .60
19 Ron Artest .40 1.00
20 Peja Stojakovic .40 1.00
21 Dirk Nowitzki .60 1.50
22 Desmond Mason .30 .75
23 Morris Peterson .25 .60
24 Eddy Curry .30 .75
25 Kevin Garnett .75 2.00
26 Rashard Lewis .40 1.00
27 Jason Richardson .40 1.00
28 Amare Stoudemire .60 1.50
29 Steve Francis .40 1.00
30 Allen Iverson .60 1.50
31 Jason Terry .30 .75
32 Pau Gasol .40 1.00
33 Manu Ginobili .50 1.25
34 Reggie Miller .40 1.00
35 Cuttino Mobley .30 .75
36 Mike Bibby .40 1.00
37 Mike Dunleavy .30 .75
38 Jason Kidd .60 1.50
39 Shareef Abdur-Rahim .30 .75
40 Elton Brand .40 1.00
41 Kwame Brown .25 .60
42 Shaquille O'Neal 1.00 2.50
43 Tim Duncan .60 1.50
44 Nene .30 .75
45 Baron Davis .40 1.00
46 Boris Diaw RC 2.00 5.00
47 Luke Walton RC 1.50 4.00
48 Willie Green RC 1.50 4.00
49 Marcus Banks RC 1.50 4.00
50 Dahntay Jones RC 1.50 4.00
51 Leandro Barbosa RC 2.00 5.00
52 Josh Howard RC 1.50 4.00
53 Ndudi Ebi RC 1.50 4.00
54 Chris Bosh RC 3.00 8.00
55 Carmelo Anthony RC 4.00 10.00
56 Zoran Planinic RC 1.50 4.00
57 Aleksandar Pavlovic RC 1.50 4.00
58 Marquis Daniels RC 1.50 4.00
59 Keith McLeod RC 1.50 4.00
60 Ben Handlogten RC 1.50 4.00
61 Francisco Elson RC 1.50 4.00
62 David West RC 2.00 5.00
63 Maurice Williams RC 2.50 6.00
64 Brian Cook RC 1.50 4.00
65 Keith Bogans RC 1.50 4.00
66 Kendrick Perkins RC 2.50 6.00
67 Troy Bell RC 1.50 4.00
68 Kyle Korver RC 2.00 5.00
69 Mickael Pietrus RC 1.50 4.00
70 Maciej Lampe RC 1.50 4.00
71 Steve Blake RC 2.00 5.00
72 Chris Kaman RC 2.00 5.00
73 Curtis Borchardt 1.50 4.00
74 Kirk Hinrich RC 2.00 5.00
75 Dwyane Wade RC 6.00 15.00
76 Zarko Cabarkapa RC 1.50 4.00
77 LeBron James RC 15.00 40.00
78 Jerome Beasley RC 1.50 4.00
79 Nick Collison RC 1.50 4.00
80 Linton Johnson RC 1.50 4.00
81 Udonis Haslem RC 2.00 5.00
82 Travis Outlaw RC 2.00 5.00
83 Jason Kapono RC 1.50 4.00
84 T.J. Ford RC 2.00 5.00
85 Luke Ridnour RC 2.00 5.00
86 Darko Milicic RC 1.50 4.00
87 Mike Sweetney RC 1.50 4.00
88 Jarvis Hayes RC 1.50 4.00
89 Josh Moore RC 1.50 4.00
90 Reece Gaines RC 1.50 4.00

2003-04 SkyBox Autographics Insignia Purple

Randomly inserted in packs, this 90-card set parallels the base set enahnced with purple foil highlights, a purple signature and purple borders. Each card is sequentially numbered to 25.
*PURPLE STARS: 6X TO 15X BASE HI
*PURPLE RCs: 2X TO 5X BASE HI

2003-04 SkyBox Autographics Insignia Silver

Randomly inserted in packs, this 150-card set parallels the base set enhanced with silver background and borders, and each card is sequentially numbered to 150. A Purple version was also inserted and those cards are sequentially numbered to 25.
*SILVER SINGLES: 2.5X TO 6X BASE HI
*SILVER RCs: 1X TO 2X BASE HI

2003-04 SkyBox Autographics Autoclassics

Randomly inserted in packs at the rate of one in 12, this 15-card set features a horizontal design and black and white player photos set against a red white and blue background.
COMPLETE SET (15) 10.00 25.00
1 Vince Carter 1.25 3.00
2 Shawn Marion .75 2.00
3 Tracy McGrady 1.00 2.50
4 David Robinson 1.25 3.00
5 Paul Pierce 1.00 2.50
6 Carmelo Anthony 2.00 5.00
7 Stephon Marbury .60 1.50
8 Jason Richardson .75 2.00
9 Steve Francis .75 2.00
10 Chris Bosh 1.50 4.00
11 Dirk Nowitzki 1.25 3.00
12 Allen Iverson 1.25 3.00
13 Yao Ming 1.50 4.00
14 Shaquille O'Neal 2.00 5.00
15 Tim Duncan 1.25 3.00

2003-04 SkyBox Autographics Autoclassics Memorabilia

Randomly seeded in packs, this 15-card set parallels the base Autoclassics set enhanced with a swatch of game worn memorabilia and sequential numbering to 45. Several other versions of this set were produced: Gold versions are sequentially numbered to five, Signature versions are sequentially numbered to 25 and a one of one signature version.
AI Allen Iverson 20.00 50.00
CA Carmelo Anthony 20.00 50.00
CB Chris Bosh 15.00 40.00
DN Dirk Nowitzki 12.00 30.00
DR David Robinson 12.00 30.00
JR Jason Richardson 8.00 20.00
PP Paul Pierce 10.00 25.00
SF Steve Francis 8.00 20.00
SM Stephon Marbury 6.00 15.00
SM Shawn Marion 8.00 20.00
SO Shaquille O'Neal 20.00 50.00
TD Tim Duncan 12.00 30.00
TM Tracy McGrady 10.00 25.00
VC Vince Carter 12.00 30.00
YM Yao Ming 15.00 40.00

2003-04 SkyBox Autographics Autoclassics Signatures

Randomly inserted, this six-card set parallels the design of the base Autoclassics set enhanced with a cut signature and is sequentially numbered to 25.
UNPRICED GOLD PRINT RUN ONE SET
CA Carmelo Anthony 100.00 200.00
SM Shawn Marion 12.50 30.00
VC Vince Carter 20.00 50.00

2003-04 SkyBox Autographics Autographs

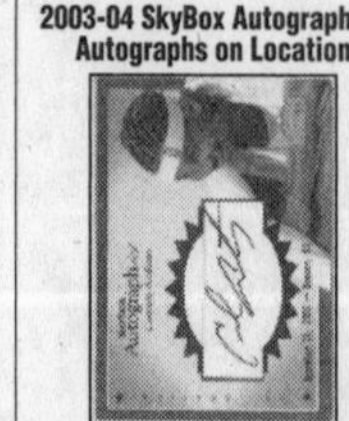

Randomly inserted, this 41-card set places full color player photos along with an embedded cut signature on a blue background with blue borders. Each card is sequentially numbered.
AM Aaron McKie/300 4.00 10.00
AP Aleksandar Pavlovic/300 4.00 10.00
AW Antoine Walker/200 5.00 12.00
BD Boris Diaw/300 5.00 12.00
BM Brad Miller/250 4.00 10.00
CA Carmelo Anthony 20.00 50.00
DJ Dahntay Jones/450 4.00 10.00
DW1 Dwyane Wade/200 30.00 80.00
DW2 David West/350 5.00 12.00
DW3 Dajuan Wagner/200 4.00 10.00
JD Juan Dixon/300 4.00 10.00
JH Josh Howard/200 4.00 10.00
JK Jason Kapono/400 4.00 10.00
KK Kyle Korver/400 5.00 12.00
KR Kareem Rush/300 4.00 10.00
LR Luke Ridnour/500 5.00 12.00
LW Luke Walton/400 4.00 10.00
MB Marcus Banks/400 4.00 10.00
MG Manu Ginobili/200 10.00 25.00
MP Mickael Pietrus/300 4.00 10.00
NH Nene/250 4.00 10.00
PP Paul Pierce/200 8.00 20.00
PS Peja Stojakovic/200 6.00 15.00
RM Ronald Murray/250 4.00 10.00
SA Shareef Abdur-Rahim/250 4.00 10.00
SC Speedy Claxton/300 4.00 10.00
SM Shawn Marion/150 5.00 12.00
TC Tyson Chandler/400 5.00 12.00
TH Travis Hansen/400 4.00 10.00
TM Tracy McGrady/200 10.00 25.00
TP1 Tayshaun Prince/200 5.00 12.00
TP2 Tony Parker/200 8.00 20.00
UH Udonis Haslem/300 5.00 12.00
VC Vince Carter/600 15.00 40.00
WZ Wang Zhizhi/300 8.00 20.00
ZC Zarko Cabarkapa/300 4.00 10.00
ZP Zoran Planinic/300 4.00 10.00

2003-04 SkyBox Autographics Autographs Gold

This 41-card set is a gold parallel to the base Autographs set. Each card is sequentially numbered to 50.
*GOLD: .75X TO 2X BASE AU HI

2003-04 SkyBox Autographics Autographs Silver

Randomly seeded, this 41-card set parallels the base Autographs set enhanced with a silver background and silver borders. Each card is sequentially numbered to 150.
*SILVER: .5X TO 1.25X BASE HI
SM Shawn Marion 5.00 12.00

2003-04 SkyBox Autographics Autographs on Location

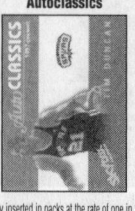

Randomly seeded, this six card set parallels the base Autographs set enhanced with the words, "Autographs on Location" and is sequentially numbered to 99.
AW Antoine Walker 8.00 20.00
CA Carmelo Anthony 30.00 80.00
DW Dwyane Wade 40.00 100.00
PP Paul Pierce 12.50 30.00
TM Tracy McGrady 15.00 40.00
VC Vince Carter 15.00 40.00

2003-04 SkyBox Autographics Autographs Jerseys

Randomly inserted in packs, this seven card set parallels the design of the base Autographs set enhanced with a swatch of a game worn jersey and each card is sequentially numbered to 125.
CA Carmelo Anthony 40.00 80
MP Mickael Pietrus 6.00 15.
TM Tracy McGrady 20.00 50.
TP Tayshaun Prince 6.00 15.
TP Tony Parker 10.00 25.

2003-04 SkyBox Autographics Autographs Patches

This set is a parallel insert and is sequentially numbered to 25.
CA Carmelo Anthony 100.00 200.
TM Tracy McGrady 30.00 80.
TP Tayshaun Prince 12.50 30.

2003-04 SkyBox Autographics Jerseygraphics

Randomly inserted in packs, this 60-card set features a horizontal design with a close-up photo of the player's face along with a square-shaped swatch of game worn jersey. The borders on the card are blue, and each card is sequentially numbered to 350. Silver and Gold versions were also inserted. Silver is sequentially numbered to 150 and Gold to 50.
*GOLD: .6X TO 1.5X BASE HI
AI Allen Iverson/350 4.00 10.
AK Andrei Kirilenko/350 2.50 6.
AS Amare Stoudemire/350 4.00 10.
BD Baron Davis/350 2.50 6.
BW1 Bonzi Wells/350 2.00 5.
BW2 Ben Wallace/350 2.50 6.
CA Carmelo Anthony/350 6.00 15
CB Chris Bosh/350 5.00 12
CK Chris Kaman/350 3.00 8
CW Chris Webber/220 2.50 6
DN Dirk Nowitzki/260 4.00 10
DW1 Dwyane Wade/350 10.00 25
DW2 David West/350 3.00 8
DW3 Dajuan Wagner/350 2.00 5.
EB Elton Brand/350 2.50 6.
EC Eddy Curry/350 2.00 5.
GA Gilbert Arenas/350 2.50 6.
GP Gary Payton/350 2.50 6.
GR Glenn Robinson/350 2.00 5.
JH Jarvis Hayes/350 2.50 6
JK Jason Kidd/350 4.00 10
JO Jermaine O'Neal/350 2.50 6
JR Jason Richardson/350 2.50 6
JS Jerry Stackhouse/350 2.00 5.
KB Kwame Brown/350 2.00 5.
KG Kevin Garnett/350 5.00 12.
KM1 Karl Malone/350 3.00 8.
KM2 Kenyon Martin/350 2.50 6.
LS Latrell Sprewell/350 2.00 5.
MB Mike Bibby/350 2.50 6.
MB Marcus Banks/200 2.50 6.
MD Mike Dunleavy/350 2.00 5.
MF Michael Finley/160 2.50 6.
MG Manu Ginobili/350 3.00 8.
MP1 Mickael Pietrus/200 2.50 6.
MP2 Morris Peterson/350 1.50 4.
MR Michael Redd/350 2.50 6.
MS Mike Sweetney/350 2.50 6.
NH Nene/350 2.00 5.
PG Pau Gasol/350 2.50 6.
PP Paul Pierce/350 3.00 8.
PS Peja Stojakovic/300 2.50 6.
RA Ray Allen/350 2.50 6.
RG Reece Gaines/350 2.50 6.
RH Richard Hamilton/350 2.00 5.
RM Reggie Miller/350 2.50 6.
SA Shareef Abdur-Rahim/350 2.00 5.
SF Steve Francis/350 2.50 6.
SM1 Stephon Marbury/350 2.00 5.
SM2 Shawn Marion/350 2.50 6.
SO Shaquille O'Neal/350 6.00 15.
SP Scottie Pippen/100 8.00 20.
TC Tyson Chandler/350 2.00 5.
TD Tim Duncan/350 4.00 10.
TM Tracy McGrady/350 3.00 8.
TO Travis Outlaw/350 3.00 8.
TP1 Tayshaun Prince/350 2.50 6.
TP2 Tony Parker/350 2.50 6.
VC Vince Carter/350 4.00 10.
YM Yao Ming/350 5.00 12.

2003-04 SkyBox Autographics Jerseygraphics Silver

This is a parallel insert to the Jerseygraphics set where the borders are silver and the cards are sequentially numbered to 150.
*SILVER: .5X TO 1.25X BASE JSY HI
SP Scottie Pippen 8.00 20.

2003-04 SkyBox Autographics Rookies Affirmed

Inserted at the rate of one in four, this 15-card set features a horizontal design and pairs a rookie player with a veteran player. The background is gray and the player photos appear in black and white.
COMPLETE SET (15) 10.00 25.
1 Carmelo Anthony 1.25 3.
Tracy McGrady
2 Chris Bosh 1.00 2.
Vince Carter
3 David West .60 1.
Jamal Mashburn
4 Troy Bell .50 1.
Pau Gasol
5 Mickael Pietrus .50 1.
Jason Richardson
6 Dwyane Wade 2.00 5.
Jerry Stackhouse

nis Haslem .60 1.50
hon Marbury
is Hayes .50 1.25
ald Murray
ce Gaines .50 1.25
y Parker
rcus Banks .60 1.50
Pierce
k Hinrich .60 1.50
e Nash
Bron James 6.00 15.00
e Bryant
ris Kaman 1.00 2.50
Ming
. Ford .75 2.00
n Iverson
rko Milicic .75 2.00
Nowitzki

003-04 SkyBox Autographics ookies Affirmed Game-Used

omly seeded, this 10-card set parallels the base es Affirmed set enhanced with a swatch of game-memorabilia from each of the two players and ential numbering to 500.
CH: 1X TO 2.5X BASE HI
H PRINT RUN 50 SER.#'d SETS
M Carmelo Anthony 8.00 20.00
cy McGrady
C Chris Bosh 6.00 15.00
ce Carter
S David West 4.00 10.00
al Mashburn
L Dwyane Wade 8.00 20.00
y Stackhouse
M Jarvis Hayes 4.00 10.00
ald Murray
P Marcus Banks 4.00 10.00
l Pierce
R Mickael Pietrus 4.00 10.00
on Richardson
P Reece Gaines 4.00 10.00
y Parker
Troy Bell 4.00 10.00
Gasol
W Udonis Haslem 4.00 10.00
phon Marbury

003-04 SkyBox Autographics ookies Affirmed Game-Used Autographs

omly inserted and sequentially numbered to 50, ersion of the Rookies Affirmed set boasts both orabilia swatches and player autographs.
M Carmelo Anthony 75.00 150.00
cy McGrady
L Dwyane Wade 75.00 150.00
y Stackhouse
P Marcus Banks 15.00 40.00
l Pierce

004-05 SkyBox Autographics

sased in June 2005, Autographics boasts a 105-checklist featuring 60 veteran players and 105 es serially numbered to 750. The base cards have ackgrounds with accent team color along the top a facsimile signature in silver foil towards the m. The rookies are similar but do not feature a mile autograph. Skybox Autographics was offered th Hobby and Retail formats where both were aged in five card packs, but Hobby boxes ained 12 packs and retail, 24.
P.SET w/o SP's (60) 15.00 40.00
yane Wade 1.25 3.00
ek Fisher .30 .75
rell Sprewell .30 .75
a Stojakovic .40 1.00
Bron James 2.50 6.00
n Brand .40 1.00
an Houston .30 .75
ris Bosh .40 1.00
rmelo Anthony .75 2.00
haquille O'Neal 1.00 2.50
eve Nash .50 1.25
ntawn Jamison .40 1.00
arko Milicic .25 .60
ichael Redd .40 1.00
hawn Marion .40 1.00
irk Nowitzki .60 1.50
obe Bryant 2.00 5.00
teve Francis .40 1.00
arlos Boozer .40 1.00
arl Malone .50 1.25
.J. Ford .30 .75
arius Miles .25 .60
aul Pierce .50 1.25
ermaine O'Neal .40 1.00
aron Davis .40 1.00
ony Parker .40 1.00
irk Hinrich .40 1.00
hris Kaman .40 1.00
tephon Marbury .30 .75
ashard Lewis .40 1.00
en Wallace .40 1.00
ntoine Walker .40 1.00
mare Stoudemire .50 1.25
ary Payton .40 1.00
ao Ming .75 2.00
ichard Jefferson .40 1.00

37 Tim Duncan .60 1.50
38 Drew Gooden .30 .75
39 Lamar Odom .40 1.00
40 Grant Hill .50 1.25
41 Vince Carter .60 1.50
42 Michael Finley .40 1.00
43 Jason Williams .30 .75
44 Samuel Dalembert .25 .60
45 Andrei Kirilenko .30 .75
46 Jason Kapono .25 .60
47 Reggie Miller .40 1.00
48 Jamaal Magloire .25 .60
49 Ray Allen .40 1.00
50 Kenyon Martin .40 1.00
51 Pau Gasol .40 1.00
52 Allen Iverson .60 1.50
53 Gilbert Arenas .40 1.00
54 Jason Richardson .40 1.00
55 Kevin Garnett .75 2.00
56 Zach Randolph .30 .75
57 Al Harrington .30 .75
58 Tracy McGrady .50 1.25
59 Jason Kidd .60 1.50
60 Chris Webber .40 1.00
61 Andris Biedrins RC 2.00 5.00
62 Robert Swift RC 1.50 4.00
63 Pavel Podkolzine RC 1.50 4.00
64 Kevin Martin RC 2.00 5.00
65 Beno Udrih RC 1.50 4.00
66 David Harrison RC 1.50 4.00
67 Andre Emmett RC 1.50 4.00
68 Emeka Okafor RC 2.50 6.00
69 Dwight Howard RC 5.00 12.00
70 Ben Gordon RC 2.00 5.00
71 Shaun Livingston RC 1.50 4.00
72 Devin Harris RC 2.50 6.00
73 Josh Childress RC 1.50 4.00
74 Luol Deng RC 2.50 6.00
75 Rafael Araujo RC 1.50 4.00
76 Andre Iguodala RC 2.50 6.00
77 Luke Jackson RC 1.50 4.00
78 Sebastian Telfair RC 1.50 4.00
79 Kris Humphries RC 1.50 4.00
80 Al Jefferson RC 2.50 6.00
81 Kirk Snyder RC 1.50 4.00
82 Josh Smith RC 2.50 6.00
83 J.R. Smith RC 2.00 5.00
84 Dorell Wright RC 2.50 6.00
85 Jameer Nelson RC 2.00 5.00
86 Delonte West RC 2.00 5.00
87 Tony Allen RC 2.00 5.00
88 Sasha Vujacic RC 1.50 4.00
89 Andres Nocioni RC 1.50 4.00
90 Royal Ivey RC 1.50 4.00
91 Trevor Ariza RC 1.50 4.00
92 Chris Duhon RC 1.50 4.00
93 John Edwards RC 1.50 4.00
94 Jackson Vroman RC 1.50 4.00
95 Quinton Ross 1.00 2.50
96 Erik Daniels RC 1.50 4.00
97 Anderson Varejao RC 2.00 5.00
98 Lionel Chalmers RC 1.50 4.00
99 Carlos Delfino 1.50 4.00
100 Jared Reiner RC 1.50 4.00
101 Bernard Robinson RC 1.50 4.00
102 Peter John Ramos RC 1.50 4.00
103 D.J. Mbenga RC 1.50 4.00
104 Mario Kasun RC 1.50 4.00
105 Nenad Krstic RC 1.50 4.00

2004-05 SkyBox Autographics Insignia

Inserted randomly in packs, this 105-card set parallels the base Skybox Autographics set enhanced with gold foil highlights and sequential numbering to 150. An Insignia 25 parallel was also released where cards feature purple foil and are sequentially numbered to 25.

*1-60 INSIGNIA: 2.5X TO 6X BASE HI
*61-105 INSIGNIA: .5X TO 1.25X BASE HI

2004-05 SkyBox Autographics Insignia 25

Inserted randomly in packs, this 105-card set parallels the base Skybox Autographics set enhanced with purple foil highlights and sequential numbering to 25.
*1-60 INSIGNIA: 6X TO 15X BASE HI
*61-105 INSIGNIA: 1.5X TO 4X BASE HI

2004-05 SkyBox Autographics Autographs Jerseys

Randomly inserted in packs at the rate of one in 20, this 31-card set features a horizontal design with player photos on the left, a square swatch of jersey on the right and a cut signature below it. Some players were issued and individually numbered, so they are listed in the checklist with print runs. Several different parallels were issued and break down as follows: the 100 set is serially numbered to 100, the 30 set is serially numbered to 30, Embossed is serially numbered to 65 and Embossed 8 is serially numbered to eight.
*AU JSY 100: .5X TO 1.25X BASE AU JSY HI
BASE SER #'d VER. DO NOT HAVE 100 AU
*AU JSY 30: .6X TO 1.5X BASE AU JSY HI
*EMBOSS: .5X TO 1.25X BASE AU JSY HI
*#'d VER.EMBOSS SAME VALUE AS BASE
AJ Antawn Jamison/76 12.50 30.00
AK Andrei Kirilenko 6.00 15.00
BD Baron Davis/24 10.00 25.00
BD Boris Diaw 6.00 15.00
BW Ben Wallace 12.50 30.00
CA Carlos Arroyo 10.00 25.00
CB Carlos Boozer/29 8.00 20.00
CD Carlos Delfino 6.00 15.00
CD Chris Duhon/47 6.00 15.00
DH David Harrison 6.00 15.00
DW David West 6.00 15.00
JD Juan Dixon 6.00 15.00
JH Josh Howard 6.00 15.00
LW Luke Walton 6.00 15.00
MD Mike Dunleavy/20 10.00 25.00
MP Mickael Pietrus 6.00 15.00
NC Nick Collison/53 6.00 15.00
PS Peja Stojakovic/53 15.00 30.00
QR Quinton Ross 6.00 15.00
RH Richard Hamilton/90 15.00 40.00
TO Travis Outlaw 6.00 15.00
VC Vince Carter 12.50 30.00

2004-05 SkyBox Autographics Autographs Patches

Randomly inserted, this 31-card set parallels the base Autographs Jerseys set enhanced with patch swatches and sequential numbering to 75.
PATCHES 10 UNPRICED DUE TO SCARCITY
*AU EMBOSSED: .4X TO 1X BASE HI
AU EMBOSS PRINT RUN 50 SER.#'d SETS
AU EMBOSS 5 UNPRICED DUE TO SCARCITY
AK Andrei Kirilenko 15.00 40.00
AV Anderson Varejao 10.00 25.00
AW Antoine Walker 15.00 40.00
BD Boris Diaw 12.50 30.00
BW Ben Wallace 15.00 40.00
CA Carlos Arroyo 20.00 50.00
CB Carlos Boozer 10.00 25.00
GA Gilbert Arenas 10.00 25.00
JD Juan Dixon 10.00 25.00
LW Luke Walton 10.00 25.00
MD Mike Dunleavy 10.00 25.00
MP Mickael Pietrus 10.00 25.00
NC Nick Collison 10.00 25.00
QR Quinton Ross 10.00 25.00
RH Richard Hamilton 20.00 50.00

2004-05 SkyBox Autographics Future Signs

Inserted in Hobby packs at the rate of one in six and Retail at the rate of one in 12, this 20-card set places player portrait photos on the top in colors that match their team color's highlights wih tan and white borders.

COMPLETE SET (20) 10.00 25.00
1 Andris Biedrins .75 2.00
2 Robert Swift .60 1.50
3 Pavel Podkolzine .60 1.50
4 Ben Gordon .75 2.00
5 Shaun Livingston .60 1.50
6 Devin Harris 1.00 2.50
7 Josh Childress .60 1.50
8 Luol Deng 1.00 2.50
9 Rafael Araujo .60 1.50
10 Luke Jackson .60 1.50
11 Sebastian Telfair .60 1.50
12 Kris Humphries .60 1.50
13 Al Jefferson 1.00 2.50
14 Kirk Snyder .60 1.50
15 Josh Smith 1.00 2.50
16 J.R. Smith .75 2.00
17 Dorell Wright 1.00 2.50
18 Jameer Nelson .75 2.00
19 Delonte West .75 2.00
20 Tony Allen .75 2.00

2004-05 SkyBox Autographics Future Signs Autographs

Randomly seeded in packs at the rate of one in 19, this 16-card set parallels the desing of the Future Signs set enhanced with a player autograph along the bottom of the card.
*AUTO 100: .5X TO 1.25X BASE AU HI
*AUTO 50: .75X TO 2X BASE AU HI
*AUTO EMBOSS: .6X TO 1.5X BASE AU HI
AU EMBOSS PRINT RUN 85 SER.#'d SETS
*AUTO EMBOSS 20: 1X TO 2.5X BASE HI
AB Andris Biedrins 5.00 12.00
AJ Al Jefferson 6.00 15.00
BG Ben Gordon 5.00 12.00
DW Dorell Wright 6.00 15.00
DW2 Delonte West 5.00 12.00
JC Josh Childress 4.00 10.00
JS2 J.R. Smith 5.00 12.00
KH Kris Humphries 4.00 10.00
KS Kirk Snyder 4.00 10.00
LD Luol Deng 6.00 15.00
PP Pavel Podkolzine 4.00 10.00
RA Rafael Araujo 4.00 10.00

2004-05 SkyBox Autographics Future Signs Autographs Patches

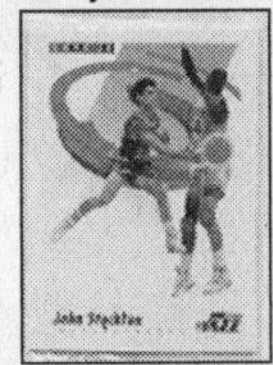

Randomly seeded in packs, this 16-card set parallels the base Future Signs Autographs set but is enhanced with embossed highlights, a patch below the player photo and is sequentially numbered to 70. A parallel version numbered to 20 was also inserted.
JS2 J.R. Smith 12.00 30.00
KH Kris Humphries 10.00 25.00
RA Rafael Araujo 10.00 25.00

2004-05 SkyBox Autographics Jerseygraphics

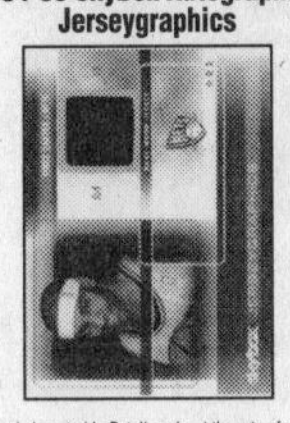

Randomly inserted in Retail packs at the rate of one in 40, this 17-card set features a horizontal design that places player photos on the left and jersey swatches on the right towards the top.
AI Allen Iverson 4.00 10.00
AS Amare Stoudemire 3.00 8.00
BD Boris Diaw 2.00 5.00
CA Carmelo Anthony 5.00 12.00
CB Chris Bosh 2.50 6.00
DN Dirk Nowitzki 4.00 10.00
DW Dajuan Wagner 2.00 5.00
JD Juan Dixon 2.00 5.00
JO Jermaine O'Neal 2.50 6.00
KB Kevin Garnett 5.00 12.00
MD Mike Dunleavy 2.00 5.00
MG Manu Ginobili 3.00 8.00
MJ Marko Jaric 2.00 5.00
MS Mike Sweetney 2.00 5.00
SF Steve Francis 2.50 6.00
SM Stephon Marbury 2.00 5.00
VC Vince Carter 4.00 10.00

2004-05 SkyBox Autographics Master Collection

PRINT RUN 25 SER.#'d SETS
CB Charles Barkley 300.00 600.00
CB2 Carlos Boozer 15.00 40.00
DW Dwyane Wade 100.00 200.00
EB Elton Brand 15.00 40.00
GP Gary Payton 25.00 60.00
LD Luol Deng 30.00 80.00
PS Peja Stojakovic 20.00 50.00
SM Shawn Marion 15.00 40.00
TP Tony Parker 15.00 40.00
VC Vince Carter 30.00 80.00

2004-05 SkyBox Autographics Signature Moves

Inserted in Hobby packs at the rate of one in 12 and Retail at the rate of one in 24, this 10-card set has white borders along the top, full-color player action photos in the middle and is highlighted with irridescent foil.
COMPLETE SET (10) 8.00 20.00
1 Allen Iverson 1.00 2.50
2 LeBron James 4.00 10.00
3 Carmelo Anthony 1.25 3.00
4 Shaquille O'Neal 1.50 4.00
5 Kobe Bryant 3.00 8.00
6 Vince Carter 1.00 2.50
7 Tracy McGrady .75 2.00
8 Jason Kidd 1.00 2.50
9 Kevin Garnett 1.25 3.00
10 Tim Duncan 1.00 2.50

1990-91 SkyBox Broadcasters

These four standard-size cards were issued to the respective NBC announcers to hand out as business cards. Production quantities remain unknown. The cards have the same design as the 1990-91 SkyBox regular issue, with computer-generated backgrounds, gold borders, and photos on both sides. The backs also have biographical information on the announcers. The cards are unnumbered and checklisted below in alphabetical order.
COMPLETE SET (4) 100.00 250.00
1 Bob Costas 40.00 100.00
2 Julie Moran 20.00 40.00
(Michael Jordan on back)
3 Ahmad Rashad 15.00 30.00
4 Pat Riley 40.00 100.00

1991-92 SkyBox Canadian Minis

This set of 50 mini-trading cards was a sports promotion in Canada involving SkyBox and Hostess/Frito Lay. The miniature cards measure 1 1/4" by 1 3/4,". One card was inserted into each specially marked bag of Hostess/Frito Lay products, including Doritos, Ruffles, Cheetos, O'Ryans, and Hostess. It was claimed that nine out of every ten bags contained a card, and in the event that the consumer purchased a bag without a card, a card could be obtained without charge through a mail-in offer. The promotion ran January 20 through March, and was supported by colorful displays at more than 75,000 locations in Canada as well as televisions ads. The card design was identical to the regular issue, with the exception that the backs feature bilingual information.
COMPLETE SET (50) 8.00 20.00
1 Kevin Willis .08 .25
2 Larry Bird 1.00 2.50
3 Kevin McHale .30 .75
4 Robert Parish .20 .50
5 Kendall Gill .20 .50
6 J.R. Reid .08 .25
7 Michael Jordan 2.50 6.00
8 Scottie Pippen .75 2.00
9 Brad Daugherty .08 .25
10 Larry Nance .20 .50
11 Rolando Blackman .20 .50
12 Derek Harper .20 .50
13 Chris Jackson .08 .25
14 Jerome Lane .08 .25
15 Joe Dumars .40 1.00
16 Dennis Rodman .60 1.50
17 Tim Hardaway .40 1.00
18 Chris Mullin .40 1.00
19 Hakeem Olajuwon .60 1.50
20 Otis Thorpe .20 .50
21 Reggie Miller .60 1.50
22 Detlef Schrempf .20 .50
23 Danny Manning .20 .50
24 Charles Smith .08 .25
25 Magic Johnson .75 2.00
26 James Worthy .40 1.00
27 Sherman Douglas .08 .25
28 Rony Seikaly .08 .25
29 Alvin Robertson .08 .25
30 Tony Campbell .08 .25
31 Derrick Coleman .20 .50
32 Charles Oakley .20 .50
33 Dennis Scott .08 .25
34 Scott Skiles .20 .50
35 Charles Barkley .60 1.50
36 Hersey Hawkins .20 .50
37 Jeff Hornacek .20 .50
38 Kevin Johnson .30 .75
39 Clyde Drexler .60 1.50
40 Terry Porter .08 .25
41 Wayman Tisdale .08 .25
42 Terry Cummings .08 .25
43 David Robinson .75 2.00
44 Shawn Kemp .30 .75
45 Ricky Pierce .08 .25
46 Karl Malone .75 2.00
47 John Stockton .75 2.00
48 Harvey Grant .08 .25
49 Bernard King .20 .50
50 Checklist Card .08 .25

1999-00 SkyBox Dominion

The premier release of Dominion replaces the SkyBox Thunder brand. The set was released in one series as a 220-card set with 175 base cards, 20 rookies and two subsets: 3 for All and World Tour. The cards feature a color action shot of the player against a black and white background.
COMPLETE SET (220) 15.00 40.00
1 Jason Williams .25 .60
2 Isaiah Rider .12 .30
3 Tim Hardaway .20 .50
4 Isaac Austin .12 .30
5 Joe Smith .15 .40
6 Mitch Richmond .20 .50
7 Sam Mitchell .12 .30
8 Terrell Brandon .12 .30
9 Grant Long .12 .30
10 Shaquille O'Neal .50 1.25
11 Derrick Coleman .15 .40
12 Rod Strickland .12 .30
13 J.R. Reid .12 .30
14 Tyrone Corbin .12 .30
15 Jeff Hornacek .15 .40
16 Malik Rose .12 .30
17 Terry Davis .12 .30
18 Theo Ratliff .15 .40
19 Kevin Willis .12 .30
20 Raef LaFrentz .15 .40
21 Othella Harrington .12 .30
22 Marcus Camby .15 .40
23 Keon Clark .12 .30
24 Robert Pack .12 .30
25 Sam Mack .12 .30
26 Shawn Kemp .20 .50
27 Nick Anderson .12 .30
28 Bill Wennington .12 .30
29 Steve Smith .12 .30
30 Kobe Bryant 1.00 2.50
31 Bobby Phills .12 .30
32 Cedric Ceballos .12 .30
33 Derek Fisher .20 .50
34 Doug Christie .15 .40
35 Danny Manning .12 .30
36 Eric Murdock .12 .30
37 Glen Rice .20 .50
38 Dikembe Mutombo .20 .50
39 Jason Kidd .30 .75
40 Cedric Henderson .12 .30
41 Rasheed Wallace .20 .50
42 Tim Duncan .40 1.00
43 John Stockton .25 .60
44 Dell Curry .12 .30
45 Muggsy Bogues .15 .40
46 Danny Fortson .12 .30
47 Charles Oakley .15 .40
48 Elden Campbell .12 .30
49 Tony Massenburg .12 .30
50 Kevin Garnett .40 1.00
51 Cherokee Parks .12 .30
52 LaPhonso Ellis .12 .30
53 Sam Cassell .15 .40
54 Shawn Bradley .12 .30
55 David Robinson .30 .75
56 Juwan Howard .15 .40
57 Lindsey Hunter .12 .30
58 Mark Jackson .20 .50
59 Olden Polynice .12 .30
60 Tracy McGrady .30 .75
61 Michael Finley .20 .50
62 Matt Geiger .12 .30
63 Maurice Taylor .12 .30
64 Rex Chapman .12 .30
65 Chris Mullin .20 .50
66 Ray Allen .20 .50
67 Bison Dele .12 .30
68 Dickey Simpkins .12 .30
69 Alvin Williams .12 .30
70 Grant Hill .25 .60
71 Mark Bryant .12 .30
72 Adam Keefe .12 .30
73 Alan Henderson .12 .30
74 Eric Snow .15 .40
75 Matt Harpring .15 .40
76 Jalen Rose .15 .40
77 Derek Harper .15 .40
78 Kerry Kittles .12 .30
79 Tony Battie .15 .40
80 Larry Hughes .15 .40
81 Arvydas Sabonis .15 .40
82 Allan Houston .15 .40
83 Tom Gugliotta .12 .30
84 Reggie Miller .20 .50
85 Dejuan Wheat .12 .30
86 Pat Garrity .12 .30
87 Karl Malone .25 .60
88 Sam Perkins .12 .30
89 Michael Olowokandi .12 .30
90 Anfernee Hardaway .30 .75
91 Bryant Reeves .12 .30
92 Gary Trent .12 .30
93 George Lynch .12 .30
94 Scottie Pippen .30 .75
95 Jerry Stackhouse .20 .50
96 Kendall Gill .12 .30
97 Vin Baker .20 .50
98 Dale Davis .12 .30
99 Charles Barkley .30 .75
100 Allen Iverson .40 1.00
101 Keith Van Horn .15 .40
102 Andrew DeClercq .12 .30
103 Michael Doleac .12 .30
104 Chauncey Billups .20 .50
105 Chris Mills .12 .30
106 Lamond Murray .12 .30
107 Glenn Robinson .15 .40
108 Brian Grant .12 .30
109 Christian Laettner .15 .40
110 Antawn Jamison .20 .50
111 Erick Dampier .12 .30
112 Vernon Maxwell .15 .40
113 Kenny Anderson .15 .40
114 Clarence Weatherspoon .12 .30
115 Corliss Williamson .12 .30
116 Paul Pierce .30 .75
117 Clifford Robinson .12 .30
118 Damon Stoudamire .20 .50
119 Dana Barros .12 .30
120 Stephon Marbury .15 .40
120B Stephon Marbury PROMO .60 1.50
121 Latrell Sprewell .20 .50
122 Tyronn Lue .12 .30
123 Walt Williams .12 .30
124 P.J. Brown .12 .30
125 Gary Payton .20 .50
126 Nick Van Exel .15 .40
127 Bryant Stith .12 .30
128 Eric Piatkowski .15 .40
129 Tyrone Nesby RC .20 .50
130 Ron Mercer .15 .40
131 Hersey Hawkins .12 .30
132 Vlade Divac .20 .50
133 Darrick Martin .12 .30
134 Avery Johnson .15 .40
135 Jaren Jackson .12 .30
136 Brevin Knight .12 .30
137 Wesley Person .12 .30
138 Derek Anderson .12 .30
139 Tim Thomas .15 .40
140 Antonio McDyess .15 .40
141 A.C. Green .20 .50
142 Chris Webber .20 .50
143 Scott Burrell .12 .30
144 John Starks .20 .50
145 Howard Eisley .12 .30
146 Mike Bibby .20 .50
147 Toni Kukoc .20 .50
148 Eddie Jones .20 .50
149 Otis Thorpe .12 .30
150 Shareef Abdur-Rahim .15 .40
151 Calbert Cheaney .12 .30
152 Cuttino Mobley .15 .40
153 Michael Dickerson .12 .30
154 Sean Elliott .20 .50
155 Terry Porter .12 .30
156 Dean Garrett .12 .30
157 Charlie Ward .12 .30
158 Larry Johnson .20 .50
159 Dan Majerle .20 .50
160 Jayson Williams .12 .30
161 Anthony Peeler .12 .30
162 Ron Harper .12 .30
163 Darrell Armstrong .12 .30
164 Kurt Thomas .12 .30
165 Brent Barry .15 .40
166 Lawrence Funderburke .12 .30
167 Terry Cummings .12 .30
168 Jamal Mashburn .15 .40
169 Robert Traylor .12 .30
170 Greg Ostertag .12 .30
171 Brad Miller .20 .50
172 Mario Elie .12 .30
173 Antoine Walker .20 .50
174 Ricky Davis .20 .50
175 Vince Carter .40 1.00
176 Hakeem Olajuwon WT .25 .60
177 Luc Longley WT .12 .30
178 Tim Duncan WT .40 1.00
179 Rick Fox WT .12 .30
180 Zydrunas Ilgauskas WT .15 .40
181 Toni Kukoc WT .20 .50
182 Felipe Lopez WT .12 .30
183 Dikembe Mutombo WT .20 .50
184 Steve Nash WT .30 .75
185 Dirk Nowitzki WT .40 1.00
186 Vitaly Potapenko WT .12 .30
187 Detlef Schrempf WT .15 .40
188 Rik Smits WT .20 .50
189 Vladimir Stepania WT .12 .30
190 Peja Stojakovic WT .20 .50
191 Donyell Marshall 3FA .12 .30
192 Shareef Abdur-Rahim 3FA .15 .40
193 Michael Dickerson 3FA .12 .30
194 Damon Stoudamire 3FA .20 .50
195 Allen Iverson 3FA .40 1.00
196 Grant Hill 3FA .25 .60
197 Scottie Pippen 3FA .30 .75
198 Bryon Russell 3FA .12 .30
199 Alonzo Mourning 3FA .25 .60
200 Patrick Ewing 3FA .25 .60
201 Ron Artest RC .50 1.25
202 William Avery RC .20 .50
203 Lamar Odom RC .60 1.50
204 Baron Davis RC .60 1.50
205 John Celestand RC .20 .50
206 Jumaine Jones RC .20 .50
207 Andre Miller RC .50 1.25
208 Elton Brand RC .50 1.25
209 James Posey RC .20 .50
210 Jason Terry RC .50 1.25
211 Kenny Thomas RC .20 .50
212 Steve Francis RC .50 1.25
213 Wally Szczerbiak RC .40 1.00
214 Richard Hamilton RC .50 1.25
215 Jonathan Bender RC .20 .50
216 Shawn Marion RC .50 1.25
217 Aleksandar Radojevic RC .20 .50
218 Tim James RC .20 .50
219 Trajan Langdon RC .20 .50
220 Corey Maggette RC .40 1.00

1999-00 SkyBox Dominion 2 Point Play

Randomly inserted in packs at one in nine, this 10-card set features two players who are similar in their games.

COMPLETE SET (10) 5.00 12.00
*PLUS: .75X TO 2X HI COLUMN
PLUS: STATED ODDS 1:90
*WARP TEK: 12X TO 30X HI COLUMN
WARP TEK: STATED ODDS 1:900
1 Keith Van Horn .60 1.50
Grant Hill
2 Paul Pierce .75 2.00
Scottie Pippen
3 Tim Duncan 1.00 2.50
Kevin Garnett
4 Kobe Bryant 2.50 6.00
Vince Carter
5 Shaquille O'Neal 1.25 3.00
Michael Olowokandi
6 Chris Webber .50 1.25
Shawn Kemp
7 Jason Williams 1.00 2.50
Allen Iverson
8 Stephon Marbury .75 2.00
Anfernee Hardaway
9 Jason Kidd .75 2.00
Mike Bibby
10 Shareef Abdur-Rahim .40 1.00
Antonio McDyess

1999-00 SkyBox Dominion Game Day 2K

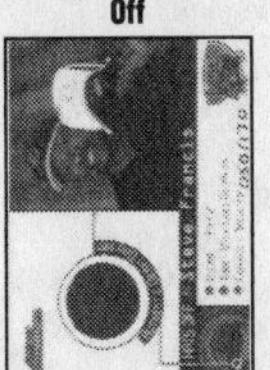

Randomly inserted in packs at one in three, this 20-card set focuses on young players destined to lead the NBA into the next century. The cards are featured on silver foil.
COMPLETE SET (20) 4.00 10.00
*PLUS: 1.5X TO 4X HI COLUMN
PLUS: STATED ODDS 1:30
1 Vince Carter .60 1.50
2 Kobe Bryant 1.50 4.00
3 Dirk Nowitzki .60 1.50
4 Cuttino Mobley .25 .60
5 Kevin Garnett .60 1.50
6 Stephon Marbury .25 .60
7 Shaquille O'Neal .75 2.00
8 Keith Van Horn .25 .60
9 Paul Pierce .50 1.25
10 Jason Williams .40 1.00
11 Mike Bibby .30 .75
12 Michael Dickerson .20 .50
13 Antawn Jamison .30 .75
14 Raef LaFrentz .25 .60
15 Tyrone Nesby .30 .75
16 Ron Mercer .25 .60
17 Tracy McGrady .50 1.25
18 Larry Hughes .25 .60
19 Robert Traylor .20 .50
20 Michael Doleac .20 .50

1999-00 SkyBox Dominion Game Day 2K Warp Tek

Randomly inserted in packs at one in 300, this 20-card set parallels the Game Day 2K insert. To ascertain values on individual cards, please refer to the multiplier in the header, coupled with the value of the base insert.
*WARP TEK: 8X TO 20X VALUE
STATED ODDS 1:300
2 Kobe Bryant 50.00 120.00

1999-00 SkyBox Dominion Hats Off

Randomly inserted in packs, this 14-card set features top players from the 1999 NBA Draft and the hats they wore on Draft Day. Each hat was cut up and a piece from it is mounted on each card. Each card is serially numbered and listed below.
1 Elton Brand/135 25.00 60.00
2 Steve Francis/170 25.00 60.00
3 Baron Davis/170 30.00 80.00
4 Wally Szczerbiak/140 20.00 50.00
5 Richard Hamilton/150 25.00 60.00
6 Andre Miller/140 25.00 60.00
7 Shawn Marion/150 25.00 60.00
8 Jason Terry/170 25.00 60.00
9 Aleksandar Radojevic/135 10.00 25.00

10 William Avery/185 10.00 25.00
11 Ron Artest/140 25.00 50.00
12 James Posey/170 10.00 25.00
13 Tim James/140 10.00 25.00
14 Jumaine Jones/135 10.00 25.00

1999-00 SkyBox Dominion Sky's the Limit

Randomly inserted in packs at one in 24, this 15-card set features talented NBA players who are head and shoulders above the rest of the league. The cards feature silver foil on the front.

COMPLETE SET (15) 12.50 30.00
*PLUS: 1.5X TO 4X HI COLUMN
PLUS: STATED ODDS 1:240
*WARP TEK: 15X TO 40X VALUE
WARP TEK: PRINT RUN 25 SERIAL #'d SETS
1 Kevin Garnett 2.00 5.00
2 Jason Williams 1.25 3.00
3 Grant Hill 1.25 3.00
4 Keith Van Horn .75 2.00
5 Allen Iverson 2.00 5.00
6 Ron Mercer .75 2.00
7 Anfernee Hardaway 1.50 4.00
8 Kobe Bryant 5.00 12.00
9 Shareef Abdur-Rahim .75 2.00
10 Jason Kidd 1.50 4.00
11 Shaquille O'Neal 2.50 6.00
12 Stephon Marbury .75 2.00
13 Paul Pierce 1.50 4.00
14 Tim Duncan 2.00 5.00
15 Vince Carter 2.00 5.00

2000 SkyBox Dominion WNBA

Released for the first time in 2000, this 156-card set features players from the WNBA. Each pack carried 10 cards. Cards featured an action shot of each player against a white background. The player's name and team were in silver foil. The base set contained 104 regular player cards, 22 Expansion Draft cards and 30 Smooth Moves cards.

COMPLETE SET (156) 10.00 25.00
1 Cynthia Cooper 1.25 3.00
2 Sue Wicks .30 .75
3 Clarisse Machanguana RC .20 .50
4 Adrienne Goodson .20 .50
5 Astou Ndiaye RC .60 1.50
6 Crystal Robinson .20 .50
7 Tora Suber .30 .75
8 Lady Hardmon .20 .50
9 Maria Stepanova .20 .50
10 Mwadi Mabika .20 .50
11 Rebecca Lobo .60 1.50
12 Ticha Penicheiro .50 1.25
13 Vicky Bullett .30 .75
14 Adia Barnes .20 .50
15 Andrea Stinson .40 1.00
16 Sheryl Swoopes 1.25 3.00
17 Heather Owen RC .20 .50
18 Andrea Congreaves .20 .50
19 Brandy Reed .30 .75
20 Dawn Staley .50 1.25
21 Jennifer Rizzotti RC 1.00 2.50
22 Latasha Byears .30 .75
23 Merlakia Jones .30 .75
24 Niesa Johnson RC .20 .50
25 Rushia Brown .20 .50
26 Taj McWilliams RC .30 .75
27 Wendy Palmer .50 1.25
28 Krystyna Lara RC .30 .75
29 Andrea Lloyd Curry RC .30 .75
30 Carla McGhee .20 .50
31 DeLisha Milton .20 .50
32 Katie Smith .60 1.50
33 Mery Andrade .20 .50
34 Nikki McCray .50 1.25
35 Ruthie Bolton-Holifield .60 1.50
36 Tamecka Dixon .30 .75
37 Tracy Henderson RC .20 .50
38 Yolanda Griffith .60 1.50
39 LaTonya Johnson .20 .50
40 Coquese Washington .20 .50
41 Chamique Holdsclaw 1.25 3.00
42 Dominique Canty RC .60 1.50
43 Kedra Holland-Corn RC .30 .75
44 Michele Timms .60 1.50
45 Nykesha Sales .30 .75
46 Shalonda Enis RC .20 .50
47 Tamika Whitmore RC .30 .75
48 Tracy Reid .30 .75
49 Kate Starbird .30 .75
50 Amanda Wilson RC .60 1.50
51 Sonia Chase RC .30 .75
52 Elaine Powell .20 .50
53 Michelle Edwards .40 1.00
54 Olympia Scott-Richardson .20 .50
55 Shannon Johnson .20 .50
56 Tammy Jackson .20 .50
57 Ukari Figgs .20 .50
58 Linda Burgess .20 .50
59 Angie Braziel RC .40 1.00
60 Tricia Bader RC .20 .50
61 Adrienne Johnson .30 .75
62 Chasity Melvin RC .20 .50
63 Korie Hlede .30 .75
64 Michelle Griffiths .20 .50
65 Penny Moore .30 .75
66 Sheri Sam .20 .50
67 Tangela Smith .20 .50
68 Val Whiting .20 .50
69 Angie Potthoff .20 .50
70 Cindy Brown .30 .75
71 Kristin Folkl .30 .75
72 Lisa Leslie 1.00 2.50
73 Monica Lamb .20 .50
74 Teresa Weatherspoon .75 2.00
75 Valerie Still RC .60 1.50
76 Tonya Edwards .20 .50
77 Heather Quella RC .30 .75
78 Cass Bauer RC .50 1.25
79 Bridget Pettis .20 .50
80 Cindy Blodgett .30 .75
81 Janeth Arcain .20 .50
82 Kym Hampton .30 .75
83 Margo Dydek .40 1.00
84 Murriel Page .25 .60
85 Sonja Tate .20 .50
86 Vickie Johnson .30 .75
87 Eva Nemcova .30 .75
88 Charlotte Smith .20 .50
89 Venus Lacy RC .20 .50
90 Polina Tzekova RC .20 .50
91 Dalma Ivanyi RC .20 .50
92 Allison Feaster .25 .60
93 Becky Hammon RC 2.50 6.00
94 Amaya Valdemoro RC .30 .75
95 Jennifer Gillom .50 1.25
96 La'Keshia Frett RC .20 .50
97 Markita Aldridge RC .20 .50
98 Natalie Williams .40 1.00
99 Rhonda Mapp .25 .60
100 Suzie McConnell-Serio .40 1.00
101 Tina Thompson .60 1.50
102 Wanda Guyton .20 .50
103 Lisa Harrison RC .50 1.25
104 Andrea Nagy RC .50 1.25
105 Edna Campbell ED .25 .60
106 Nina Bjedov ED RC .20 .50
107 Sonja Henning ED RC .30 .75
108 Toni Foster ED .30 .75
109 Angela Aycock ED RC .30 .75
110 Charmin Smith ED RC .50 1.25
111 Chantel Tremitiere ED .20 .50
112 Gordana Grubin ED RC .20 .50
113 Kara Wolters ED .25 .60
114 Rita Williams ED .25 .60
115 Stephanie McCarty ED .40 1.00
116 Monica Maxwell ED RC .20 .50
117 Debbie Black ED .30 .75
118 Elena Baranova ED .50 1.25
119 Sharon Manning ED .20 .50
120 Molly Goodenbour ED RC .20 .50
121 Alisa Burras ED RC .30 .75
122 Mila Nikolich ED RC .20 .50
123 Jamila Wideman ED .30 .75
124 Michele VanGorp ED .25 .60
125 Sophia Witherspoon ED .30 .75
126 Tari Phillips ED .20 .50
127 Sheri Sam SM .10 .25
128 Mwadi Mabika SM .10 .25
129 Murriel Page SM .12 .30
130 Latasha Byears SM .15 .40
131 Dominique Canty SM .30 .75
132 Crystal Robinson SM .10 .25
133 Cynthia Cooper SM .60 1.50
134 Ruthie Bolton-Holifield SM .30 .75
135 Cindy Brown SM .15 .40
136 Kristin Folkl SM .15 .40
137 Jennifer Gillom SM .25 .60
138 Adrienne Goodson SM .10 .25
139 Vickie Johnson SM .15 .40
140 Merlakia Jones SM .15 .40
141 Rebecca Lobo SM .30 .75
142 Nikki McCray SM .25 .60
143 Suzie McConnell-Serio SM .20 .50
144 DeLisha Milton SM .10 .25
145 Eva Nemcova SM .15 .40
146 Wendy Palmer SM .25 .60
147 Brandy Reed SM .15 .40
148 Nykesha Sales SM .15 .40
149 Andrea Stinson SM .20 .50
150 Michele Timms SM .30 .75
151 Valerie Still SM .30 .75
152 Andrea Nagy SM .25 .60
153 Tonya Edwards SM .10 .25
154 Taj McWilliams SM .15 .40
155 Kedra Holland-Corn SM .15 .40
156 Maria Stepanova SM .10 .25

2000 SkyBox Dominion WNBA Extra

Randomly inserted in packs at one in three, this 156-card set parallels the base set. The cards feature silver foilboard, instead of the regular white stock. To ascertain values on individual cards, please refer to the multiplier in the header below, coupled with the value of the base card.

COMPLETE SET (156) 75.00 150.00
*EXTRA: 1.5X TO 4X BASE CARD HI

2000 SkyBox Dominion WNBA All-WNBA

Randomly inserted in packs at one in 18, this 10-card set features players from the All-WNBA First and Second Teams from 1999. Card backs carry an "AW" prefix.

COMPLETE SET (10) 12.50 30.00
AW1 Sheryl Swoopes 4.00 10.00
AW2 Natalie Williams 1.25 3.00
AW3 Yolanda Griffith 2.00 5.00
AW4 Cynthia Cooper 4.00 10.00
AW5 Ticha Penicheiro 1.50 4.00
AW6 Chamique Holdsclaw 4.00 10.00
AW7 Tina Thompson 2.00 5.00
AW8 Lisa Leslie 3.00 8.00
AW9 Teresa Weatherspoon 2.50 6.00
AW10 Shannon Johnson .60 1.50

2000 SkyBox Dominion WNBA Autographics

Randomly inserted in packs at one in 144, this 12-card set features autographs of top WNBA players. Card backs are not numbered and listed below in alphabetical order.

COMPLETE SET (12) 150.00 300.00
1 Ruthie Bolton-Holifield 15.00 40.00
2 Cynthia Cooper 30.00 80.00
3 Jennifer Gillom 12.00 30.00
4 Yolanda Griffith 15.00 40.00
5 Kedra Holland-Corn 8.00 20.00
6 Lisa Leslie 25.00 60.00
7 Taj McWilliams 8.00 20.00
8 Ticha Penicheiro 12.00 30.00
9 Crystal Robinson 5.00 12.00
10 Andrea Stinson 10.00 25.00
11 Sue Wicks 8.00 20.00
12 Kate Starbird 8.00 20.00

2000 SkyBox Dominion WNBA Girls Rock

Randomly inserted in packs at one in 35, this 10-card set features key players in the WNBA on a die cut foilboard background. Card backs carry a "GR" prefix.

COMPLETE SET (10) 15.00 40.00
GR1 Sheryl Swoopes 5.00 12.00
GR2 Chamique Holdsclaw 5.00 12.00
GR3 Dawn Staley 2.00 5.00
GR4 Katie Smith 2.50 6.00
GR5 Yolanda Griffith 2.50 6.00
GR6 Ticha Penicheiro 2.00 5.00
GR7 Teresa Weatherspoon 3.00 8.00
GR8 Natalie Williams 1.50 4.00
GR9 Lisa Leslie 4.00 10.00
GR10 Cynthia Cooper 5.00 12.00

2000 SkyBox Dominion WNBA Supreme Court

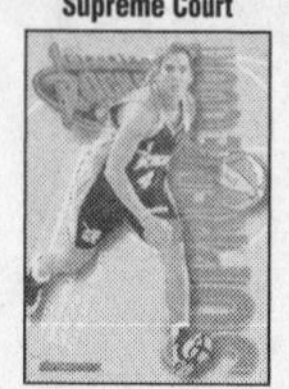

Randomly inserted in packs at one in 12, this 20-card set features the best all-around players in the WNBA. Card backs carry a "SC" prefix.

COMPLETE SET (20) 12.50 30.00
SC1 Dawn Staley 1.50 4.00
SC2 Merlakia Jones 1.00 2.50
SC3 Eva Nemcova 1.00 2.50
SC4 Suzie McConnell-Serio 1.25 3.00
SC5 Cynthia Cooper 4.00 10.00
SC6 Brandy Reed 1.00 2.50
SC7 Katie Smith 2.00 5.00
SC8 Vickie Johnson 1.00 2.50
SC9 Rebecca Lobo 2.00 5.00
SC10 Shannon Johnson .60 1.50
SC11 Nykesha Sales 1.00 2.50
SC12 Jennifer Gillom 1.50 4.00
SC13 Nikki McCray 1.50 4.00
SC14 Michele Timms 2.00 5.00
SC15 Tina Thompson 2.00 5.00
SC16 Ruthie Bolton-Holifield 2.00 5.00
SC17 Wendy Palmer 1.50 4.00
SC18 DeLisha Milton .60 1.50
SC19 Andrea Stinson 1.25 3.00
SC20 Adrienne Goodson .60 1.50

2000 SkyBox Dominion WNBA The Cooper Collection

Randomly inserted in packs at one in six, this eight-card set features different shots of league MVP Cynthia Cooper. Card backs carry a "CC" prefix.

COMPLETE SET (8) 4.00 10.00
COMMON CARD (CC1-CC8) .75 2.00

1995-96 SkyBox Expansion Debut

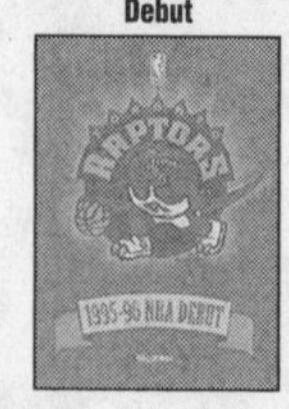

Produced by SkyBox, this two-card set commemorates the debut of the Toronto Raptors and Vancover Grizzlies. Both card fronts carry a red background with the expansion team's logo. Card backs contain a photo of Grant Hill with his commentary on the new teams. The cards are not numbered and listed below in alphabetical order.

COMPLETE SET (2) 2.00 5.00
1 Toronto Raptors 1.25 3.00
Grant Hill
2 Vancover Grizzlies 1.25 3.00
Grant Hill

2004-05 SkyBox Fresh Ink

Issued in February 2005, the Fresh Ink set consists of 120 cards divided up into 90 veteran players and 30 rookies serially numbered to 499. All base cards have wood court borders along the top and bottom where the veteran players have accent colors set to match team colors. Fresh Ink was offered in both Hobby and Retail formats where both were packaged in five card packs while boxes for Hobby contained 18 packs and boxes for Retail contained 24.

COMP.SET w/o SP's (90) 15.00 40.00
UNPRICED PARALLEL ONE EXISTS
1 T.J. Ford .25 .60
2 Pau Gasol .30 .75
3 Kirk Hinrich .30 .75
4 Shawn Marion .30 .75
5 Darius Miles .20 .50
6 Dirk Nowitzki .50 1.25
7 Paul Pierce .40 1.00
8 Theron Smith .20 .50
9 Rasheed Wallace .30 .75
10 Kobe Bryant 1.50 4.00
11 Kevin Garnett .60 1.50
12 Steve Nash .40 1.00
13 Gilbert Arenas .30 .75
14 Udonis Haslem .25 .60
15 Ben Wallace .30 .75
16 Ray Allen .30 .75
17 Elton Brand .30 .75
18 Caron Butler .30 .75
19 Drew Gooden .25 .60
20 Richard Hamilton .25 .60
21 Grant Hill .40 1.00
22 Jason Kapono .20 .50
23 Tony Parker .30 .75
24 Jalen Rose .25 .60
25 Amare Stoudemire .40 1.00
26 Gerald Wallace .30 .75
27 Jason Williams .25 .60
28 LeBron James 2.00 5.00
29 Jamal Crawford .25 .60
30 Earl Boykins .20 .50
31 Michael Finley .30 .75
32 Chris Kaman .30 .75
33 Stephon Marbury .25 .60
34 Shaquille O'Neal .75 2.00
35 Antoine Walker .30 .75
36 Ron Artest .30 .75
37 Samuel Dalembert .20 .50
38 Reece Gaines .20 .50
39 Rashard Lewis .30 .75
40 Desmond Mason .25 .60
41 Jason Richardson .30 .75
42 Wally Szczerbiak .25 .60
43 Bonzi Wells .20 .50
44 Tim Duncan .50 1.25
45 Lamar Odom .30 .75
46 Jermaine O'Neal .30 .75
47 Mickael Pietrus .25 .60
48 Zach Randolph .25 .60
49 Joe Smith .25 .60
50 Allan Houston .25 .60
51 Carmelo Anthony .60 1.50
52 Manu Ginobili .40 1.00
53 Tyronn Lue .20 .50
54 Tayshaun Prince .30 .75
55 Luke Ridnour .25 .60
56 Peja Stojakovic .30 .75
57 Dwyane Wade 1.00 2.50
58 David West .30 .75
59 Allen Iverson .50 1.25
60 Richard Jefferson .30 .75
61 Andrei Kirilenko .25 .60
62 Latrell Sprewell .25 .60
63 Jason Kidd .50 1.25
64 Baron Davis .30 .75
65 Al Harrington .25 .60
66 Jarvis Hayes .20 .50
67 Gary Payton .30 .75
68 Chris Webber .30 .75
69 Vince Carter .50 1.25
70 Eric Williams .20 .50
71 Nene .25 .60
72 Chris Bosh .30 .75
73 Sam Cassell .25 .60
74 Mike Dunleavy .25 .60
75 Steve Francis .30 .75
76 Antawn Jamison .30 .75
77 Joe Johnson .30 .75
78 Corey Maggette .25 .60
79 Jamaal Magloire .20 .50
80 Kenyon Martin .30 .75
81 Reggie Miller .30 .75
82 Yao Ming .60 1.50
83 Dajuan Wagner .20 .50
84 Willie Green .20 .50
85 Shareef Abdur-Rahim .25 .60
86 Tracy McGrady .40 1.00
87 Carlos Arroyo .25 .60
88 Michael Redd .30 .75
89 Alonzo Mourning .40 1.00
90 Mike Bibby .30 .75
91 Luke Jackson RC 1.50 4.00
92 Matt Freije RC 1.50 4.00
93 Kevin Martin RC 2.00 5.00
94 Josh Smith RC 2.50 6.00
95 Kris Humphries RC 1.50 4.00
96 Trevor Ariza RC 1.50 4.00
97 Shaun Livingston RC 1.50 4.00
98 Pavel Podkolzin RC 1.50 4.00
99 Kirk Snyder RC 1.50 4.00
100 Beno Udrih RC 1.50 4.00
101 Tony Allen RC 2.00 5.00
102 Chris Duhon RC 1.50 4.00
103 Josh Childress RC 1.50 4.00
104 David Harrison RC 1.50 4.00
105 Al Jefferson RC 2.50 6.00
106 Rafael Araujo RC 1.50 4.00
107 Andre Emmett RC 1.50 4.00
108 Devin Harris RC 2.50 6.00
109 Andre Iguodala RC 2.50 6.00
110 Emeka Okafor RC 2.50 6.00
111 Dorell Wright RC 2.50 6.00
112 Luol Deng RC 2.50 6.00
113 Dwight Howard RC 5.00 12.00
114 J.R. Smith RC 2.00 5.00
115 Sasha Vujacic RC 1.50 4.00
116 Jameer Nelson RC 2.00 5.00
117 Robert Swift RC 1.50 4.00
118 Sebastian Telfair RC 1.50 4.00
119 Andris Biedrins RC 2.00 5.00
120 Ben Gordon RC 2.00 5.00

2004-05 SkyBox Fresh Ink 50

Randomly inserted in packs, this 120-card set parallels the base set enhanced with sequential numbering to 50 on the back. A Fresh Ink 1 one of one parallel was also randomly seeded in packs.

*50 SINGLES: 3X TO 8X BASE HI
*50 RC's: 1.25X TO 3X BASE HI

2004-05 SkyBox Fresh Ink Autographs

Limited to 199 serially numbered copies of each of the 40 cards, this set is horizontally designed with a small head shot photo in the upper right and the team logo in the upper left. Cut signatures are centered along the bottom of the card. Several different parallel sets were also inserted for the Autographs: Autographs 99 are serially numbered to 99 and have silver foil highlights, Autographs 25 are serially numbered to 25 and have gold highlights, Autographs 1 are done in a one of one numbered format, and a Red foil version was randomly seeded in Retail packs. No odds were given for the red cards.

*AUTO 99: .5X TO 1.25X BASE AU HI
*AUTO 25: .75X TO 2X BASE AU HI
*RED AUTO: .4X TO 1X BASE AU HI
N Nene 5.00 12.00
AJ Al Jefferson 8.00 20.00
AK Andrei Kirilenko 8.00 20.00
AV Anderson Varejao 6.00 15.00
BG Ben Gordon 6.00 15.00
CA Carmelo Anthony 15.00 30.00
CB Carlos Boozer 5.00 12.00
CB Chris Bosh 10.00 25.00
CD Carlos Delfino 5.00 12.00
CD2 Chris Duhon 5.00 12.00
DH David Harrison 5.00 12.00
DH Devin Harris 8.00 20.00
DW Dwyane Wade 30.00 80.00
DW David West 5.00 12.00
GA Gilbert Arenas 8.00 20.00
JC Josh Childress 5.00 12.00
JR Jason Richardson 5.00 12.00
JS Jerry Stackhouse 6.00 15.00
JS2 Josh Smith 8.00 20.00
KH2 K.Humphries Gophers 6.00 15.00
KM Kenyon Martin 8.00 20.00
KS Kirk Snyder 5.00 12.00
LC Lionel Chalmers 5.00 12.00
LD Luol Deng 8.00 20.00
LJ Luke Jackson 5.00 12.00
MB2 Matt Bonner 5.00 12.00
MP Mickael Pietrus 5.00 12.00
MS Mike Sweetney 5.00 12.00
NC Nick Collison 5.00 12.00
QR Quinton Ross 5.00 12.00
RH Richard Hamilton 8.00 20.00
RS Robert Swift 5.00 12.00
TA2 Tony Allen OK State 10.00 25.00
TO Travis Outlaw 5.00 12.00
VC Vince Carter 12.50 30.00

2004-05 SkyBox Fresh Ink Five on Five

Inserted in Hobby packs at the rate of one in 432, this 10-card set features a horizontal design with five small black and white headshots from a single team on one side and five from another rival team on the other.

6 Mike Bibby 6.00 15.00
Kevin Martin
Peja Stojakovic
Chris Webber
Brad Miller
Sebastian Telfair
Darius Miles
Zach Randolph
Shareef Abdur-Rahim
Vladimir Stepania
8 Joe Johnson 8.00 20.00
Steve Nash
Amare Stoudemire
Shawn Marion
Jackson Vroman
Carlos Arroyo
Kirk Snyder
Matt Harpring
Andrei Kirilenko
Carlos Boozer

2004-05 SkyBox Fresh Ink Five on Five Jerseys

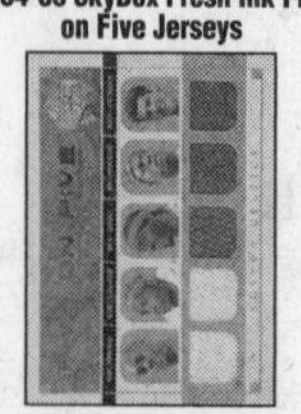

Randomly inserted in Hobby packs, this 10-card set parallels the design of the base Five on Five insert set enhanced with five swatches of game jersey on each side and sequential numbering to 199. A Patch version was also inserted and includes patch swatches and sequential numbering to 10.

1 Manu Ginobili 20.00 50.00
Tony Parker
Tim Duncan
Robert Horry
Radoslav Nestervic
Michael Finley
Marquis Daniels
Josh Howard
Jerry Stackhouse
Dirk Nowitzki
2 Chauncey Billups 30.00 80.00
Tayshaun Prince
Rasheed Wallace
Richard Hamilon
Ben Wallace
Reggie Miller
Jamaal Tinsley
Austin Croshere
Jonathan Bender
David Harrison
3 Sam Cassell 30.00 80.00
Latrell Sprewell
Kevin Garnett
Wally Szczerbiak
Michael Olowokandi
Andre Miller
Earl Boykins
Carmelo Anthony
Nene
Kenyon Martin
4 Vince Carter 20.00 50.00
Jason Kidd
Richard Jefferson
Jason Collins
Zoran Planinic
Dwyane Wade/Eddie Jones
Dorrell Wright
Udonis Haslem
Shaquille O'Neal
5 Gary Payton 30.00 80.00
Marcus Banks
Ricky Davis
Paul Pierce
Raef LeFrentz
Allan Houston
Stephon Marbury
Anfernee Hardaway
Mike Sweetney
Tim Thomas
6 Mike Bibby 20.00 50.00
Kevin Martin
Peja Stojakovic
Chris Webber
Brad Miller
Sebastian Telfair
Darius Miles
Zach Randolph
Shareef Abdur-Rahim
Vladimir Stepania
7 Allen Iverson 25.00 60.00
Willie Green
Andre Iguodala
Kyle Korver
Sam Dalembert
Gilbert Arenas
Larry Hughes
Jarvis Hayes
Antawn Jamison
Kwame Brown
9 Maurice Williams 20.00 50.00
Michael Redd
Desmond Mason
Joe Smith
Keith Van Horn
Baron Davis
J.R. Smith
P.J. Brown
David West
Jamaal Magloire

2004-05 SkyBox Fresh Ink Game Breakers

Randomly inserted in Hobby packs at the rate of one in 18 and Retail at the rate of one in 24, this 15-card set features two players on each card side by side.

COMPLETE SET (15) 30.00 80.00
1 Kevin Garnett 3.00 8.00
Tim Duncan
2 Shaquille O'Neal 2.50 6.00
Alonzo Mourning
3 Stephon Marbury 2.50 6.00
Jason Kidd
4 Larry Bird 8.00 20.00
Magic Johnson
5 Paul Pierce 2.50 6.00
Antoine Walker
6 LeBron James 5.00 12.00
Kobe Bryant
7 Dirk Nowitzki 3.00 8.00
Steve Nash
8 Isiah Thomas 4.00 10.00
Michael Cooper
9 Carmelo Anthony 3.00 8.00
Dwyane Wade
10 Pau Gasol 2.50 6.00
Andrei Kirilenko
11 Reggie Miller 2.50 6.00
Baron Davis
12 Charles Barkley 8.00 20.00
Scottie Pippen
13 Vince Carter 2.50 6.00
Antawn Jamison
14 Tracy McGrady 2.50 6.00
Steve Francis
15 Delonte West 2.00 5.00
Jameer Nelson

2004-05 SkyBox Fresh Ink Game Breakers Jerseys

Randomly inserted in packs, this 15-card set parallels the design of the base Game Breakers insert set enhanced with a swatch of jersey and sequential numbering to 199. A Patch version was released also and contains a game-worn patch and sequential numbering to 49. Patch one of ones also exist.

*PATCHES: .75X TO 2X BASE HI
1 Kevin Garnett 10.00 25.00
Tim Duncan
5 Paul Pierce 6.00 15.00
Antoine Walker
7 Dirk Nowitzki 6.00 15.00
Steve Nash
9 Carmelo Anthony 8.00 20.00
Dwyane Wade
10 Pau Gasol 6.00 15.00
Andrei Kirilenko
11 Reggie Miller 6.00
Baron Davis
13 Vince Carter 6.00
Antawn Jamison
14 Tracy McGrady 6.00
Steve Francis
15 Delonte West 6.00
Jameer Nelson

2004-05 SkyBox Fresh Ink Property Of

Inserted in Hobby packs at the rate of one in three Retail packs at the rate of one in six, this 30-card places players on a gray background set to look li the "Property of" sweat shirts teams use during tra camp.

COMPLETE SET (30) 12.50
1 Josh Childress .60
2 Kevin McHale .75
3 Emeka Okafor 1.00
4 Ben Gordon .75
5 LeBron James 4.00
6 Michael Finley .60
7 Carmelo Anthony 1.25
8 Ben Wallace .60
9 Rick Barry .60
10 Yao Ming 1.25
11 Jermaine O'Neal .60
12 Elton Brand .60
13 Kobe Bryant 3.00
14 Jason Williams .50
15 Dwyane Wade 2.00
16 Michael Redd .60
17 Latrell Sprewell .50
18 Richard Jefferson .60
19 Baron Davis .60
20 Walt Frazier .60
21 Dwight Howard 2.00
22 Allen Iverson 1.00
23 Kevin Johnson .60
24 Clyde Drexler .75
25 Peja Stojakovic .60
26 Manu Ginobili .75
27 Ray Allen .60
28 Chris Bosh .60
29 Andrei Kirilenko .50
30 Elvin Hayes .60

2004-05 SkyBox Fresh Ink Property Of Jerseys

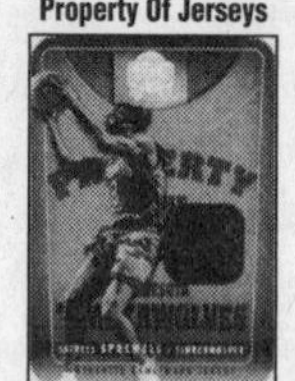

Randomly seeded in packs, this 30-card set paralle the design of the base Property of Insert set enhan with a swatch of jersey and sequential numbering t 199. Three different patch parallel sets were also inserted where one is serially numbered to 99, one 10 and a one of one format.

*PATCHES: .75X TO 2X BASE HI
1 Josh Childress 3.00
6 Michael Finley 3.00
7 Carmelo Anthony 6.00
8 Ben Wallace 3.00
10 Yao Ming 6.00
11 Jermaine O'Neal 3.00
12 Elton Brand 3.00
14 Jason Williams 2.50
15 Dwyane Wade 8.00
16 Michael Redd 3.00
17 Latrell Sprewell 2.50
18 Richard Jefferson 3.00
19 Baron Davis 3.00
21 Dwight Howard 8.00
22 Allen Iverson 5.00
25 Peja Stojakovic 3.00
26 Manu Ginobili 4.00
27 Ray Allen 3.00
29 Andrei Kirilenko 2.50

2004-05 SkyBox Fresh Ink Teammate Tandems

Inserted in Hobby packs at the rate of one in 108 ar Retail packs at the rate of one in 360, this 10-card s features two players from the same team and their h shots side by side.

COMPLETE SET (10) 20.00
1 Yao Ming 4.00
Tracy McGrady
2 Shaquille O'Neal 5.00
Dwyane Wade
3 Michael Finley 4.00
Dirk Nowitzki
4 Richard Hamilton 3.00
Ben Wallace
5 T.J. Ford 3.00
Michael Redd
6 Kevin Garnett 4.00
Latrell Sprewell
7 Richard Jefferson 4.00

n Kidd		
s Bosh	3.00	8.00
Rose		
ael Pietrus	3.00	8.00
n Richardson		
Duncan	4.00	10.00
Parker		

2004-05 SkyBox Fresh Ink eammate Tandems Jerseys

mly inseted in packs, this 10-card set parallels se Teammate Tandems set enhanced with s from each player and sequential numbering to hree patch parallel sets were issued, one serially ered to 49, one numbered to 10 and another in one format.

IL: .4X TO 1X HI COLUMN
L STATED ODDS 1:24 PACKS
CHES: 1X TO 2.5X BASE HI

Ming	6.00	15.00
y McGrady		
hael Finley	8.00	20.00
Nowitzki		
hard Hamilton	5.00	12.00
Wallace		
Ford	5.00	12.00
hael Redd		
in Garnett	6.00	15.00
ell Sprewell		
hard Jefferson	5.00	12.00
on Kidd		
kael Pietrus	5.00	12.00
on Richardson		
m Duncan	6.00	15.00
y Parker		

1999-00 SkyBox Impact

999-00 SkyBox Impact set was released in 2000 as a 200-card set. Each pack contained 10- s and carried a suggested retail price of .99. In ion, a Vince Carter Slam Dunk card was added to et near the end of production, the card is serial bered to 2000. There were also 15 hand- bered autographed versions of this card which inserted into packs.

PLETE SET (200)	12.50	30.00
n Duncan	.30	.75
ug Christie	.12	.30
rk Jackson	.15	.40
ul Pierce	.25	.60
nes Posey RC	.15	.40
eve Smith	.10	.25
arlie Ward	.10	.25
on Brand RC	.40	1.00
ward Eisley	.10	.25
rant Hill	.20	.50
hristian Laettner	.12	.30
orey Maggette RC	.30	.75
cot Pollard	.10	.25
obert Traylor	.10	.25
ick Anderson	.10	.25
at Garrity	.10	.25
ersey Hawkins	.10	.25
roy Hudson	.15	.40
harles Oakley	.12	.30
ary Payton	.15	.40
ik Smits	.15	.40
uggsy Bogues	.12	.30
ale Davis	.10	.25
arry Johnson	.15	.40
ntonio McDyess	.12	.30
lonzo Mourning	.20	.50
cottie Pippen	.25	.60
od Strickland	.10	.25
ntoine Walker	.15	.40
llen Iverson	.30	.75
am Cassell	.12	.30
Mookie Blaylock	.10	.25
im Jackson	.12	.30
Brevin Knight	.10	.25
Anthony Peeler	.10	.25
Bryon Russell	.10	.25
Maurice Taylor	.10	.25
Elden Campbell	.10	.25
Austin Croshere	.10	.25
Keith Van Horn	.12	.30
Raef LaFrentz	.12	.30
Jamal Mashburn	.12	.30
Jermaine O'Neal	.15	.40
Glenn Robinson	.12	.30
Mitch Richmond	.15	.40
Keon Clark	.10	.25
Derrick Coleman	.12	.30
Patrick Ewing	.20	.50
Brian Grant	.10	.25
Kobe Bryant	.75	2.00
Dan Majerle	.15	.40
Ruben Patterson	.10	.25
Walt Williams	.10	.25
Chris Childs	.10	.25
Baron Davis RC	.50	1.25
Richard Hamilton RC	.40	1.00
Voshon Lenard	.10	.25
Vernon Maxwell	.12	.30
Hakeem Olajuwon	.20	.50
Jason Williams	.20	.50
Gary Trent	.10	.25
Kenny Anderson	.12	.30
Shawn Bradley	.10	.25
Obinna Ekezie RC	.15	.40
65 Tom Gugliotta	.10	.25
66 Ron Harper	.10	.25
67 Corey Benjamin	.10	.25
68 Donyell Marshall	.10	.25
69 David Robinson	.25	.60
70 Stephon Marbury	.12	.30
71 Marcus Camby	.12	.30
72 Horace Grant	.12	.30
73 Tim Hardaway	.15	.40
74 Greg Foster	.10	.25
75 Cuttino Mobley	.12	.30
76 Rodney Buford RC	.15	.40
77 Clifford Robinson	.10	.25
78 Isaac Austin	.10	.25
79 Robert Pack	.10	.25
80 Eddie Jones	.15	.40
81 Shawn Marion RC	.40	1.00
82 Anthony Mason	.10	.25
83 Oliver Miller	.10	.25
84 Dirk Nowitzki	.30	.75
85 Jayson Williams	.10	.25
86 Brent Barry	.12	.30
87 P.J. Brown	.10	.25
88 Kelvin Cato	.10	.25
89 Jim McIlvaine	.10	.25
90 Steve Francis RC	.40	1.00
91 Bryant Reeves	.10	.25
92 Jerry Stackhouse	.15	.40
93 Allan Houston	.12	.30
94 Kevin Garnett	.30	.75
95 Karl Malone	.20	.50
96 David Wesley	.10	.25
97 Eddie Robinson RC	.15	.40
98 Ben Wallace	.15	.40
99 Chris Webber	.15	.40
100 Lamar Odom RC	.50	1.25
101 Shandon Anderson	.10	.25
102 Terrell Brandon	.10	.25
103 Jeff Hornacek	.12	.30
104 Terry Mills	.10	.25
105 Tyrone Nesby RC	.15	.40
106 Bo Outlaw	.10	.25
107 Peja Stojakovic	.15	.40
108 Ron Artest RC	.40	1.00
109 Tony Battie	.12	.30
110 Cedric Ceballos	.10	.25
111 Anfernee Hardaway	.25	.60
112 Othella Harrington	.10	.25
113 Dennis Rodman	.30	.75
114 Loy Vaught	.10	.25
115 Malik Rose	.10	.25
116 Vin Baker	.15	.40
117 Charles Barkley	.25	.60
118 Michael Finley	.15	.40
119 Adrian Griffin RC	.15	.40
120 Jason Kidd	.25	.60
121 Gheorghe Muresan	.10	.25
122 Cherokee Parks	.10	.25
123 Glen Rice	.15	.40
124 Bimbo Coles	.10	.25
125 Andrew DeClercq	.10	.25
126 Matt Geiger	.10	.25
127 Bobby Jackson	.12	.30
128 Michael Olowokandi	.10	.25
129 Greg Ostertag	.10	.25
130 Tracy McGrady	.25	.60
131 Rodney Rogers	.10	.25
132 Juwan Howard	.12	.30
133 Terry Cummings	.10	.25
134 Mario Elie	.10	.25
135 Trajan Langdon RC	.15	.40
136 George Lynch	.10	.25
137 Roshown McLeod	.10	.25
138 Joe Smith	.12	.30
139 John Stockton	.20	.50
140 Ray Allen	.15	.40
141 Vince Carter	.30	.75
142 Al Harrington	.15	.40
143 Ron Mercer	.12	.30
144 Vitaly Potapenko	.10	.25
145 Arvydas Sabonis	.12	.30
146 Latrell Sprewell	.15	.40
147 Aaron Williams	.10	.25
148 Shareef Abdur-Rahim	.12	.30
149 Vonteego Cummings RC	.15	.40
150 Shaquille O'Neal	.40	1.00
151 Derek Fisher	.15	.40
152 Todd MacCulloch RC	.15	.40
153 Andre Miller RC	.40	1.00
154 Dikembe Mutombo	.15	.40
155 Ervin Johnson	.10	.25
156 Michael Dickerson	.10	.25
157 A.C. Green	.15	.40
158 Kevin Willis	.10	.25
159 Kerry Kittles	.10	.25
160 Damon Stoudamire	.15	.40
161 Eric Snow	.12	.30
162 Bob Sura	.10	.25
163 Jason Terry RC	.40	1.00
164 Derek Anderson	.10	.25
165 Randy Brown	.10	.25
166 Vlade Divac	.15	.40
167 Chris Gatling	.10	.25
168 Lindsey Hunter	.10	.25
169 Tim Thomas	.12	.30
170 Antawn Jamison	.15	.40
171 Alan Henderson	.10	.25
172 Larry Hughes	.12	.30
173 Shawn Kemp	.15	.40
174 Radoslav Nesterovic RC	.15	.40
175 Scott Padgett	.15	.40
176 Brian Skinner	.10	.25
177 Jerome Williams	.10	.25
178 Corliss Williamson	.10	.25
179 Sean Elliott	.15	.40
180 Wally Szczerbiak RC	.30	.75
181 Toni Kukoc	.15	.40
182 Chucky Atkins RC	.15	.40
183 Jalen Rose	.12	.30
184 Nick Van Exel	.12	.30
185 Rasheed Wallace	.15	.40
186 Avery Johnson	.12	.30
187 Jamie Feick RC	.15	.40
188 Adonal Foyle	.10	.25
189 Devean George RC	.15	.40
190 Mike Bibby	.15	.40
191 Lamond Murray	.10	.25
192 Billy Owens	.10	.25
193 Isaiah Rider	.10	.25
194 Darrell Armstrong	.10	.25
195 Antonio Davis	.10	.25
196 Dale Ellis	.10	.25
197 Tim Young RC	.15	.40
198 Roy Rogers	.10	.25
199 Terry Porter	.10	.25
200 Reggie Miller	.15	.40
P141 Vince Carter PROMO	.60	1.50
NNO Vince Carter COMM/2000	5.00	12.00

1999-00 SkyBox Impact Rewind '99

Inserted one per pack, this 40-card set highlights moments from the 1998-99 NBA season. Card backs carry a "RN" prefix.

COMPLETE SET (40)	6.00	15.00
RN1 Tim Duncan	.50	1.25
RN2 David Robinson	.40	1.00
RN3 Sean Elliott	.25	.60
RN4 Mario Elie	.15	.40
RN5 Avery Johnson	.20	.50
RN6 Malik Rose	.15	.40
RN7 Jaren Jackson	.15	.40
RN8 Tim Duncan	.50	1.25
RN9 Gerald King	.15	.40
RN10 Jerome Kersey	.15	.40
RN11 Steve Kerr	.20	.50
RN12 Antonio Daniels	.15	.40
RN13 Karl Malone	.30	.75
RN14 Vince Carter	.50	1.25
RN15 Karl Malone	.30	.75
RN16 Tim Duncan	.50	1.25
RN17 Alonzo Mourning	.30	.75
RN18 Allen Iverson	.50	1.25
RN19 Jason Kidd	.40	1.00
RN20 Chris Webber	.25	.60
RN21 Grant Hill	.30	.75
RN22 Shaquille O'Neal	.60	1.50
RN23 Gary Payton	.25	.60
RN24 Tim Hardaway	.25	.60
RN25 Kevin Garnett	.50	1.25
RN26 Antonio McDyess	.20	.50
RN27 Hakeem Olajuwon	.30	.75
RN28 Kobe Bryant	1.25	3.00
RN29 John Stockton	.30	.75
RN30 Vince Carter	.50	1.25
RN31 Paul Pierce	.40	1.00
RN32 Jason Williams	.30	.75
RN33 Mike Bibby	.25	.60
RN34 Matt Harpring	.20	.50
RN35 Michael Dickerson	.15	.40
RN36 Cuttino Mobley	.20	.50
RN37 Michael Doleac	.15	.40
RN38 Michael Olowokandi	.15	.40
RN39 Antawn Jamison	.25	.60
RN40 Vince Carter	.50	1.25

1999-00 SkyBox Impact Tattoos

Randomly inserted into packs at 1:4, this 29-card set features temporary tattoos of all the current NBA teams.

COMMON CARD (1-29)	.40	1.00
2 Boston Celtics	.75	2.00
4 Chicago Bulls	.75	2.00
8 Detroit Pistons	.50	1.25
13 Los Angeles Lakers	.75	2.00
18 New York Knicks	.75	2.00
24 San Antonio Spurs	.50	1.25

1991 SkyBox Magic Johnson Video

This standard-size card was enclosed in cellophane and included as an insert with the "Magic Johnson - Always Showtime" VHS video tape. The front features a cut-out action shot of Johnson superimposed on the familiar SkyBox bright colored computer-generated geometric background. In a horizontal format

NNO Magic Johnson	6.00	15.00

2003-04 SkyBox LE

Released in early March 2004, Skybox LE consists of 160 cards divided up as follows: cards 1-110 are veterans and 111-160 are rookies sequentially numbered to 399. Some of the cards are randomly numbered to 99. Base cards have full-color player action photography with white borders and die cut edges (retail versions are not die cut). Skybox LE was packaged in 18-pack boxes where packs contained three cards and carried a suggested retail price of $3.99.

COMP.SET w/o SP's (110)	12.50	30.00
1 Jason Terry	.25	.60
2 Antoine Walker	.30	.75
3 Paul Pierce	.40	1.00
4 Eddy Curry	.25	.60
5 Ricky Davis	.25	.60
6 Jamal Crawford	.25	.60
7 Raef LaFrentz	.20	.50
8 Darius Miles	.20	.50
9 Ray Allen	.30	.75
10 Sam Cassell	.25	.60
11 Andre Miller	.25	.60
12 Dirk Nowitzki	.50	1.25
13 Zach Randolph	.30	.75
14 Tim Duncan	.50	1.25
15 Gary Payton	.30	.75
16 Ben Wallace	.30	.75
17 Michael Finley	.30	.75
18 David Wesley	.20	.50
19 Nick Van Exel	.25	.60
20 Marcus Camby	.25	.60
21 Gilbert Arenas	.30	.75
22 Marcus Haislip	.20	.50
23 Cuttino Mobley	.25	.60
24 Tayshaun Prince	.30	.75
25 Chris Webber	.30	.75
26 Reggie Miller	.30	.75
27 Chauncey Billups	.30	.75
28 Quentin Richardson	.25	.60
29 Mike Dunleavy	.25	.60
30 Karl Malone	.40	1.00
31 Yao Ming	.60	1.50
32 Tyson Chandler	.25	.60
33 Jason Williams	.25	.60
34 Eddie Griffin	.20	.50
35 Eddie Jones	.25	.60
36 Jamaal Tinsley	.20	.50
37 Michael Redd	.30	.75
38 Elton Brand	.30	.75
39 Rashard Lewis	.30	.75
40 Vince Carter	.50	1.25
41 Wally Szczerbiak	.25	.60
42 Chris Wilcox	.20	.50
43 Kenyon Martin	.30	.75
44 Shaquille O'Neal	.75	2.00
45 Baron Davis	.30	.75
46 Pau Gasol	.30	.75
47 Dikembe Mutombo	.30	.75
48 Shane Battier	.25	.60
49 Drew Gooden	.25	.60
50 Lamar Odom	.30	.75
51 Glenn Robinson	.25	.60
52 Tim Thomas	.20	.50
53 Shawn Marion	.30	.75
54 Kevin Garnett	.60	1.50
55 Stephon Marbury	.25	.60
56 Rasheed Wallace	.30	.75
57 Troy Hudson	.20	.50
58 Mike Bibby	.30	.75
59 Jason Kidd	.50	1.25
60 Tony Parker	.30	.75
61 Andrei Kirilenko	.30	.75
62 Manu Ginobili	.40	1.00
63 Kerry Kittles	.20	.50
64 Brent Barry	.20	.50
65 Allan Houston	.25	.60
66 Morris Peterson	.20	.50
67 Tracy McGrady	.40	1.00
68 Matt Harpring	.25	.60
69 Erick Dampier	.20	.50
70 Jerry Stackhouse	.25	.60
71 John Salmons	.30	.75
72 Stephen Jackson	.25	.60
73 Scottie Pippen	.50	1.25
74 Dajuan Wagner	.20	.50
75 Keon Clark	.20	.50
76 Carlos Boozer	.30	.75
77 Steve Nash	.40	1.00
78 Nene	.25	.60
79 Keith Van Horn	.25	.60
80 Earl Boykins	.20	.50
81 Richard Hamilton	.25	.60
82 Jason Richardson	.30	.75
83 Steve Francis	.30	.75
84 Jermaine O'Neal	.30	.75
85 Ron Artest	.30	.75
86 Corey Maggette	.25	.60
87 Kwame Brown	.20	.50
88 Kobe Bryant	1.50	4.00
89 Mike Miller	.30	.75
90 Caron Butler	.30	.75
91 Desmond Mason	.25	.60
92 Latrell Sprewell	.25	.60
93 Richard Jefferson	.30	.75
94 Jamal Mashburn	.25	.60
95 Troy Murphy	.30	.75
96 Peja Stojakovic	.30	.75
97 Allen Iverson	.50	1.25
98 Amare Stoudemire	.50	1.25
99 Rasho Nesterovic	.20	.50
100 Bonzi Wells	.20	.50
101 Bobby Jackson	.20	.50
102 Anfernee Hardaway	.50	1.25
103 Larry Hughes	.25	.60
104 Shareef Abdur-Rahim	.25	.60
105 Hedo Turkoglu	.30	.75
106 Alvin Williams	.20	.50
107 Qyntel Woods	.20	.50
108 Brad Miller	.30	.75
109 Jalen Rose	.25	.60
110 Antonio Davis	.20	.50
111 David West RC	3.00	8.00
112 Boris Diaw RC	3.00	8.00
113 Travis Hansen RC	2.50	6.00
114 Marcus Banks RC	2.50	6.00
115 Kendrick Perkins RC	4.00	10.00
116 Darius Songaila	1.50	4.00
117 Kirk Hinrich/99 RC	10.00	25.00
118 LeBron James/99 RC	300.00	600.00
119 Jason Kapono RC	2.50	6.00
120 Josh Howard RC	2.50	6.00
121 Marquis Daniels RC	2.50	6.00
122 Carmelo Anthony/99 RC	50.00	100.00
123 Darko Milicic/99 RC	8.00	20.00
124 Zaur Pachulia RC	2.50	6.00
125 Mickael Pietrus RC	2.50	6.00
126 Ben Handlogten RC	2.50	6.00
127 James Jones RC	2.50	6.00
128 Chris Kaman RC	3.00	8.00
129 Josh Moore RC	2.50	6.00
130 Brian Cook RC	2.50	6.00
131 Luke Walton RC	2.50	6.00
132 Troy Bell RC	2.50	6.00
133 Dahntay Jones RC	2.50	6.00
134 Dwyane Wade/99 RC	75.00	150.00
135 Udonis Haslem RC	3.00	8.00
136 T.J. Ford/99 RC	10.00	25.00
137 Ndudi Ebi RC	2.50	6.00
138 Zoran Planinic RC	2.50	6.00
139 Raul Lopez	2.50	6.00
140 Francisco Elson RC	2.50	6.00
141 Mike Sweetney RC	2.50	6.00
142 Maciej Lampe RC	2.50	6.00
143 Slavko Vranes RC	2.50	6.00
144 Keith Bogans/99 RC	8.00	20.00
145 Reece Gaines RC	2.50	6.00
146 Willie Green RC	2.50	6.00
147 Kyle Korver RC	3.00	8.00
148 Zarko Cabarkapa RC	2.50	6.00
149 Leandro Barbosa RC	3.00	8.00
150 Travis Outlaw RC	3.00	8.00
151 Curtis Borchardt	2.50	6.00
152 Alex Garcia RC	2.50	6.00
153 Richie Frahm RC	2.50	6.00
154 Nick Collison RC	2.50	6.00
155 Luke Ridnour/99 RC	10.00	25.00
156 Chris Bosh/99 RC	15.00	40.00
157 Aleksandar Pavlovic RC	2.50	6.00
158 Maurice Williams RC	4.00	10.00
159 Jarvis Hayes/99 RC	8.00	20.00
160 Steve Blake RC	3.00	8.00

2003-04 SkyBox LE Retail

COMPLETE SET (160)	30.00	60.00
*VETS: SAME PRICE AS HOBBY		
111 David West RC	1.00	2.50
112 Boris Diaw RC	1.00	2.50
113 Travis Hansen RC	.75	2.00
114 Marcus Banks RC	.75	2.00
115 Kendrick Perkins RC	1.25	3.00
116 Darius Songaila	.50	1.25
117 Kirk Hinrich RC	1.00	2.50
118 LeBron James RC	8.00	20.00
119 Jason Kapono RC	.75	2.00
120 Josh Howard RC	.75	2.00
121 Marquis Daniels RC	.75	2.00
122 Carmelo Anthony RC	2.00	5.00
123 Darko Milicic RC	.75	2.00
124 Zaur Pachulia RC	.75	2.00
125 Mickael Pietrus RC	.75	2.00
126 Ben Handlogten RC	.75	2.00
127 James Jones RC	.75	2.00
128 Chris Kaman RC	1.00	2.50
129 Josh Moore RC	.75	2.00
130 Brian Cook RC	.75	2.00
131 Luke Walton RC	.75	2.00
132 Troy Bell RC	.75	2.00
133 Dahntay Jones RC	.75	2.00
134 Dwyane Wade RC	3.00	8.00
135 Udonis Haslem RC	1.00	2.50
136 T.J. Ford RC	1.00	2.50
137 Ndudi Ebi RC	.75	2.00
138 Zoran Planinic RC	.75	2.00
139 Raul Lopez	.75	2.00
140 Francisco Elson RC	.75	2.00
141 Mike Sweetney RC	.75	2.00
142 Maciej Lampe RC	.75	2.00
143 Slavko Vranes RC	.75	2.00
144 Keith Bogans RC	.75	2.00
145 Reece Gaines RC	.75	2.00
146 Willie Green RC	.75	2.00
147 Kyle Korver RC	1.00	2.50
148 Zarko Cabarkapa RC	.75	2.00
149 Leandro Barbosa RC	1.00	2.50
150 Travis Outlaw RC	1.00	2.50
151 Curtis Borchardt	.75	2.00
152 Alex Garcia RC	.75	2.00
153 Richie Frahm RC	.75	2.00
154 Nick Collison RC	.75	2.00
155 Luke Ridnour RC	1.00	2.50
156 Chris Bosh RC	1.50	4.00
157 Aleksandar Pavlovic RC	.75	2.00
158 Maurice Williams RC	1.25	3.00
159 Jarvis Hayes RC	.75	2.00
160 Steve Blake RC	1.00	2.50

2003-04 SkyBox LE Artist Proofs

Randomly inserted in packs, this 160-card set parallels the base set enhanced with sequential numbering to 50. Two other parallel sets were inserted: Executive one of ones and Photo Proofs which are sequentially numbered to 25.

*AP SINGLES: 5X TO 12X BASE HI
*AP RCs: .75X TO 2X BASE HI
*AP RCs/99: .25X TO .6X BASE HI

2003-04 SkyBox LE Gold Proofs

Randomly seeded in packs, this 160-card set parallels the base Skybox LE set enhanced with sequential numbering to 150.

*GOLD SINGLES: 4X TO 10X BASE HI
*GOLD RC's: .6X TO 1.5X BASE HI
*GOLD RC's/99: .2X TO .5X BASE HI

2003-04 SkyBox LE Photographer Proofs

Randomly seeded in packs, this 160-card set parallels the base set enhanced with the photographer's signature and sequential numbering to 25.

*PP SINGLES: 8X TO 20X BASE HI
*PP RCs: 1.25X TO 3X BASE HI
*PP RCs/99: .4X TO 1X BASE HI

2003-04 SkyBox LE Championship MettLE

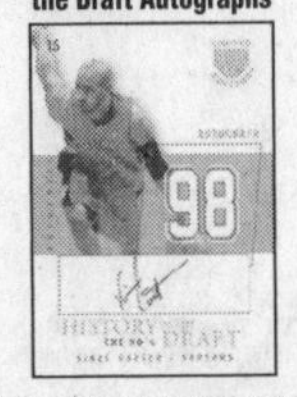

Randomly seeded in packs, this eight-card set features players from America's Team USA Olympic squad. Each card, except for Larry Brown, has a full-color photo and a swatch of game-worn memorabilia. A parallel version of this set was also produced and is sequentially numbered to 10.

RGAI Allen Iverson	12.00	30.00
RGJK Jason Kidd	10.00	25.00
RGJO Jermaine O'Neal	6.00	15.00
RGLB Larry Brown	3.00	8.00
RGMB Mike Bibby	6.00	15.00
RGRA Ray Allen	6.00	15.00
RGTD Tim Duncan	10.00	25.00
RGTM Tracy McGrady	8.00	20.00

2003-04 SkyBox LE History of the Draft Autographs

Randomly inserted in packs, this three-card set features a full-color player action photo with an embedded cut signature. No odds or print run was given for this set.

UNPRICED PARALLEL/10 EXISTS

1 Vince Carter	15.00	40.00
2 Manu Ginobili	12.50	30.00

2003-04 SkyBox LE History of the Draft Autographs 99

Randomly seeded, this six-card set parallels the base HOD Autographs set enhanced with sequential numbering to 99.

*AUTO 50: .5X TO 1.25X AUTO 99

1 Vince Carter	20.00	50.00
2 Manu Ginobili	15.00	40.00
3 Shawn Marion	8.00	20.00
4 Paul Pierce	15.00	30.00
6 Tracy McGrady	10.00	25.00

2003-04 SkyBox LE History of the Draft The 90s

Randomly inserted in packs, this 40-card set utilizes a similar design to the HOD Autographs cards enhanced with a swatch of game used memorabilia and sequential numbering to the last two digits of the year each player was drafted. A version numbered to 50 and one numbered to 10 were also produced.

*PAR.50 SINGLES: .6X TO 1.5X BASE JSY HI

HDAI Allen Iverson/96	5.00	12.00
HDAJ Antawn Jamison/98	3.00	8.00
HDAW Antoine Walker/96	3.00	8.00
HDBD Baron Davis/99	3.00	8.00
HDBW Bonzi Wells/98	2.00	5.00
HDCM Corey Maggette/99	2.50	6.00
HDCW Chris Webber/93	3.00	8.00
HDDN Dirk Nowitzki/98	5.00	12.00
HDEB Elton Brand/99	3.00	8.00
HDGP Gary Payton/90	3.00	8.00
HDGR Glenn Robinson/94	2.50	6.00
HDJK Jason Kidd/94	5.00	12.00
HDJM Jamal Mashburn/93	2.50	6.00
HDJO Jermaine O'Neal/96	3.00	8.00
HDJR Jalen Rose/94	2.50	6.00
HDJS Jerry Stackhouse/95	2.50	6.00
HDJT Jason Terry/99	2.50	6.00
HDKG Kevin Garnett/95	6.00	15.00
HDKV Keith Van Horn/97	2.50	6.00
HDLO Lamar Odom/99	3.00	8.00
HDLS Latrell Sprewell/92	2.50	6.00
HDMB Mike Bibby/98	3.00	8.00
HDMF Michael Finley/95	3.00	8.00
HDMG Manu Ginobili/99	4.00	10.00
HDPP Paul Pierce/98	4.00	10.00
HDPS Peja Stojakovic/96	3.00	8.00
HDRA Ray Allen/96	3.00	8.00
HDRD Ricky Davis/98	2.50	6.00
HDRH Richard Hamilton/99	2.50	6.00
HDRL Rashard Lewis/98	3.00	8.00
HDRW Rasheed Wallace/95	3.00	8.00
HDSA Shareef Abdur-Rahim/96	2.50	6.00
HDSF Steve Francis/99	3.00	8.00
HDSM Shawn Marion/99	3.00	8.00
HDSM Stephon Marbury/96	2.50	6.00
HDSN Steve Nash/96	4.00	10.00
HDSO Shaquille O'Neal/92	8.00	20.00
HDTD Tim Duncan/97	5.00	12.00
HDTM Tracy McGrady/97	4.00	10.00
HDVC Vince Carter/98	5.00	12.00

2003-04 SkyBox LE Jersey Proofs

Randomly inserted in packs, this 50-card set uses the design from the base Skybox LE set enhanced with a square swatch of game used memorabilia. Each card is sequentially numbered to 399. Two parallel versions of this set were also issued: one sequentially numbered to 50 and one numbered to 10.

*PAR.50 SINGLES: .6X TO 1.5X BASE JSY HI

1 Shareef Abdur-Rahim	2.00	5.00
2 Tyson Chandler	2.00	5.00
3 Jalen Rose	2.00	5.00
4 Dirk Nowitzki	4.00	10.00
5 Nene	2.00	5.00
6 Tayshaun Prince	2.50	6.00
7 Richard Hamilton	2.00	5.00
8 Mike Dunleavy	2.00	5.00
9 Steve Francis	2.50	6.00
10 Reggie Miller	2.50	6.00
11 Shane Battier	2.00	5.00
12 Latrell Sprewell	2.00	5.00
13 Richard Jefferson	2.50	6.00
14 Tim Duncan	4.00	10.00
15 Stephon Marbury	2.00	5.00
16 Ray Allen	2.50	6.00
17 Andrei Kirilenko	2.50	6.00
18 Kwame Brown	2.00	5.00
19 Jerry Stackhouse	2.00	5.00
20 Peja Stojakovic	2.50	6.00
21 Chris Webber	2.50	6.00
22 Tony Parker	2.50	6.00
24 Allen Iverson	4.00	10.00
25 Shaquille O'Neal	6.00	15.00
26 Tracy McGrady	3.00	8.00
27 Jason Kidd	4.00	10.00
28 Mike Bibby	2.50	6.00
29 Kevin Garnett	5.00	12.00
30 Amare Stoudemire	4.00	10.00
31 Yao Ming	5.00	12.00
32 Caron Butler	2.50	6.00
33 Jason Richardson	2.50	6.00
34 Paul Pierce	3.00	8.00
35 Steve Nash	3.00	8.00
36 Scottie Pippen	6.00	15.00
37 Ben Wallace	2.50	6.00
38 Jermaine O'Neal	2.50	6.00
39 Karl Malone	3.00	8.00
40 Drew Gooden	2.00	5.00
41 Eddy Curry	2.00	5.00
42 Elton Brand	2.50	6.00
43 Pau Gasol	2.50	6.00
44 Shawn Marion	2.50	6.00
45 Bonzi Wells	2.00	5.00
46 Rasheed Wallace	2.50	6.00
47 Baron Davis	2.50	6.00
48 Kenyon Martin	2.50	6.00
49 Lamar Odom	2.50	6.00
50 Michael Redd	2.50	6.00

2003-04 SkyBox LE League Leaders

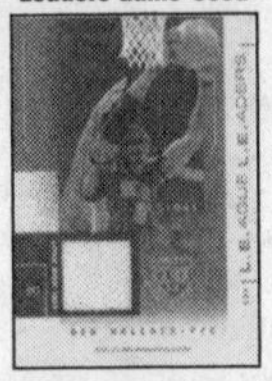

Inserted in packs at the rate of one in 18, this nine-card set focuses on NBA stat leaders. Each card has a full-color player action photo with white borders along the right and bottom of the card. A one of one parallel version was also inserted into packs.

COMPLETE SET (9)	5.00	12.00
1 Tracy McGrady	.75	2.00
2 Ben Wallace	.60	1.50
3 Jason Kidd	1.00	2.50
4 Allen Iverson	1.00	2.50
5 Eddy Curry	.50	1.25
6 Kevin Garnett	1.25	3.00
7 Caron Butler	.60	1.50
8 Amare Stoudemire	1.00	2.50
9 Yao Ming	1.25	3.00

2003-04 SkyBox LE League Leaders Game-Used

Randomly inserted in packs, this nine-card set parallels the design of the base League Leaders set enhanced with a square swatch of game-used memorabilia in the lower left-hand corner of the card. Each card is sequentially numbered to 75. Two parallel versions of this set were also inserted, one is sequentially numbered to 50 and the other is numbered to 10.

*PAR.50 SINGLES: .5X TO 1.25X BASE JSY HI

LLAI Allen Iverson	5.00	12.00
LLAS Amare Stoudemire	5.00	12.00
LLBW Ben Wallace	3.00	8.00
LLCB Caron Butler	3.00	8.00
LLEC Eddy Curry	2.50	6.00
LLJK Jason Kidd	5.00	12.00
LLKG Kevin Garnett	6.00	15.00
LLTM Tracy McGrady	4.00	10.00
LLYM Yao Ming	6.00	15.00

2003-04 SkyBox LE Rare Form

Inserted in packs at the rate of one in 288, this 10-card set features rounded die-cut tops and bottoms, gray borders, an irridescent finish and full-color player action photography. An Executive Proof version of this set was printed as well and these cards are numbered one of one.

1 Vince Carter	5.00	12.00
2 Carmelo Anthony	8.00	20.00
3 Dwyane Wade	12.00	30.00
4 Dajuan Wagner	2.00	5.00
5 Tony Parker	3.00	8.00
6 Caron Butler	3.00	8.00
7 Tyson Chandler	2.50	6.00
8 Chris Bosh	6.00	15.00
9 Jason Richardson	3.00	8.00
10 Jerry Stackhouse	2.50	6.00

2003-04 SkyBox LE Rare Form Autographs

Randomly inserted in packs at the overall odds of one in 18 for all autograph cards, this 19-card set parallels the design for the base Rare Form insert set enhanced with an embedded cut signature. The following cards were not released: 10, 12, 14, 16 and 18. Print runs are listed next to the player.

1 Vince Carter/259	12.50	30.00
2 Carmelo Anthony/190	25.00	60.00
3 Tony Parker/260	10.00	25.00
5 Tyson Chandler	4.00	10.00
6 Troy Bell/350	4.00	10.00
7 Boris Diaw/275	5.00	12.00
8 Mickael Pietrus/290	4.00	10.00
9 Josh Howard/880	4.00	10.00
13 Travis Outlaw	5.00	12.00
15 Brian Cook/490	4.00	10.00
17 Dahntay Jones/350	4.00	10.00
19 Zaur Pachulia/790	4.00	10.00
20 Kendrick Perkins/395	6.00	15.00
21 Tayshaun Prince/100	5.00	12.00
22 Mike Sweetney/130	4.00	10.00
23 Maurice Williams/425	6.00	15.00
24 Travis Hansen/330	4.00	10.00

2003-04 SkyBox LE Rare Form Autographs 150

Randomly seeded, this 24-card set parallels the base Rare Form Autographs set enhanced with sequential numbering to 150.

*AU 50 SINGLES: .5X TO 1.25X AU 150 HI
UNPRICED AUTO SERIAL #'d TO 10 EXIST

1 Vince Carter	15.00	40.00
2 Carmelo Anthony	30.00	80.00
3 Tony Parker	12.50	30.00
4 Caron Butler	5.00	12.00
5 Tyson Chandler	5.00	12.00
6 Troy Bell	5.00	12.00
7 Boris Diaw	6.00	15.00
8 Mickael Pietrus	5.00	12.00
9 Josh Howard	5.00	12.00
10 David West	6.00	15.00
11 Luke Walton	5.00	12.00
13 Travis Outlaw	6.00	15.00
15 Brian Cook	5.00	12.00

17 Dahntay Jones 5.00 12.00
19 Zaur Pachulia 5.00 12.00
20 Kendrick Perkins 8.00 20.00
21 Tayshaun Prince 5.00 12.00
22 Mike Sweetney 5.00 12.00
23 Maurice Williams 8.00 20.00
24 Travis Hansen 5.00 12.00

2003-04 SkyBox LE Rare Form Game-Used

Randomly inserted in packs, this 10-card set parallels the Rare Form insert set design enhanced with a swatch of Game-Used memorabilia and sequential numbering to 99. Two parallel sets were also inserted into packs, a version numbered to 50 and one numbered to 10.

*PAR.50 SINGLES: .5X TO 1.25X BASE JSY HI
RFCA Carmelo Anthony 8.00 20.00
RFCB Chris Bosh 6.00 15.00
RFCB Caron Butler 3.00 8.00
RFDW Dajuan Wagner 2.00 5.00
RFDW Dwyane Wade 12.00 30.00
RFJR Jason Richardson 3.00 8.00
RFJS Jerry Stackhouse 2.50 6.00
RFTC Tyson Chandler 2.50 6.00
RFTP Tony Parker 3.00 8.00
RFVC Vince Carter 5.00 12.00

2003-04 SkyBox LE Sky's the Limit

Randomly seeded in packs at the rate of one in six, this 20-card set places full-color player action photos against a white and blue background. An Executive Proof version of this set was issued also. Each card is numbered one of one.

COMPLETE SET (20) 10.00 25.00
1 Baron Davis .50 1.25
2 Dirk Nowitzki .75 2.00
3 Tayshaun Prince .50 1.25
4 Caron Butler .50 1.25
5 Steve Nash .60 1.50
6 Shawn Marion .50 1.25
7 Scottie Pippen .75 2.00
8 Kobe Bryant 2.50 6.00
9 Tony Parker .50 1.25
10 Amare Stoudemire .75 2.00
11 Jason Richardson .50 1.25
12 Manu Ginobili .60 1.50
13 Drew Gooden .40 1.00
14 Paul Pierce .60 1.50
15 Yao Ming 1.00 2.50
16 LeBron James 5.00 12.00
17 Darko Milicic .50 1.25
18 Carmelo Anthony 1.25 3.00
19 Chris Bosh 1.00 2.50
20 Dwyane Wade 2.00 5.00

2003-04 SkyBox LE Sky's the Limit Game-Used

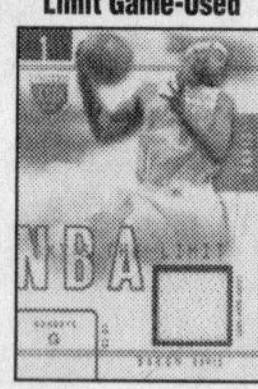

Randomly inserted, this 17-card set parallels the Sky's the Limit insert set enhanced with a swatch of Game-Used memorabilia. Each card is sequentially numbered to 99. Two parallel sets were also produced, one sequentially numbered to 50 and the other numbered to 10.

*PAR.50 SINGLES: .5X TO 1.25X BASE JSY HI
SLBD Baron Davis 3.00 8.00
SLCA Carmelo Anthony 10.00 25.00
SLCB Chris Bosh 6.00 15.00
SLCB Caron Butler 3.00 8.00
SLDG Drew Gooden 2.50 6.00
SLDN Dirk Nowitzki 5.00 12.00
SLDW Dwyane Wade 12.00 30.00
SLJR Jason Richardson 3.00 8.00
SLMG Manu Ginobili 4.00 10.00
SLPP Paul Pierce 4.00 10.00
SLSM Shawn Marion 3.00 8.00
SLSN Steve Nash 4.00 10.00
SLSP Scottie Pippen 8.00 20.00
SLTD Amare Stoudemire 5.00 12.00
SLTP Tayshaun Prince 3.00 8.00
SLTP Tony Parker 3.00 8.00
SLYM Yao Ming 6.00 15.00

2004-05 SkyBox LE

Released in January of 2005, this 125-card set features 75 veterans and 50 rookies. The rookie cards are numbered randomly to either 499 or 99, the ones numbered to 99 are denoted as such in the checklist. Both Hobby and Retail versions of this set were offered where Hobby cards are die cut and retail are not. Hobby and Retail were both packaged in 16-pack boxes, but Hobby packs contained three cards and retail contained five.

COMP.SET w/o SP's (75) 20.00 40.00
1 Tony Parker .30 .75
2 Vince Carter .50 1.25
3 Al Harrington .25 .60
4 Dwyane Wade 1.00 2.50
5 Latrell Sprewell .25 .60
6 Michael Finley .30 .75
7 Caron Butler .30 .75
8 Zach Randolph .25 .60
9 Peja Stojakovic .30 .75
10 Eddy Curry .25 .60
11 Allen Iverson .50 1.25
12 Kirk Hinrich .30 .75
13 Jason Williams .25 .60
14 Hedo Turkoglu .30 .75
15 Manu Ginobili .40 1.00
16 Eddie House .20 .50
17 Reggie Miller .30 .75
18 Steve Francis .30 .75
19 LeBron James 2.00 5.00
20 Dirk Nowitzki .50 1.25
21 Stephon Marbury .25 .60
22 Ray Allen .30 .75
23 Carmelo Anthony .60 1.50
24 Lamar Odom .30 .75
25 Jamaal Magloire .20 .50
26 Shareef Abdur-Rahim .25 .60
27 Chris Webber .30 .75
28 Jason Richardson .25 .60
29 Richard Jefferson .30 .75
30 Richard Hamilton .25 .60
31 Alonzo Mourning .40 1.00
32 Chris Bosh .30 .75
33 Mike Dunleavy .25 .60
34 Andrei Kirilenko .25 .60
35 Tracy McGrady .40 1.00
36 T.J. Ford .25 .60
37 Jason Kidd .50 1.25
38 Carlos Arroyo .25 .60
39 Rasheed Wallace .30 .75
40 Gilbert Arenas .30 .75
41 Kenyon Martin .30 .75
42 Tim Duncan .50 1.25
43 Yao Ming .60 1.50
44 Carlos Boozer .30 .75
45 Michael Redd .30 .75
46 Larry Hughes .25 .60
47 Antoine Walker .25 .60
48 Kevin Garnett .60 1.50
49 Willie Green .20 .50
50 Tyson Chandler .25 .60
51 Elton Brand .30 .75
52 Allan Houston .25 .60
53 Shawn Marion .30 .75
54 Ricky Davis .25 .60
55 Shaquille O'Neal .75 2.00
56 Steve Nash .40 1.00
57 Jarvis Hayes .20 .50
58 Zydrunas Ilgauskas .25 .60
59 Corey Maggette .25 .60
60 Ben Wallace .30 .75
61 Darius Miles .20 .50
62 Drew Gooden .30 .75
63 Pau Gasol .30 .75
64 Jamal Crawford .25 .60
65 Gary Payton .30 .75
66 Jermaine O'Neal .30 .75
67 Jason Kapono .20 .50
68 Marquis Daniels .20 .50
69 Kobe Bryant 1.50 4.00
70 Baron Davis .30 .75
71 Mike Bibby .30 .75
72 Rashard Lewis .30 .75
73 Paul Pierce .40 1.00
74 Sam Cassell .25 .60
75 Amare Stoudemire .40 1.00
76 Dwight Howard/99 RC 12.00 30.00
77 Emeka Okafor/99 RC 6.00 15.00
78 Ben Gordon/99 RC 5.00 12.00
79 Shaun Livingston/99 RC 4.00 10.00
80 Devin Harris/99 RC 6.00 15.00
81 Josh Childress/99 RC 5.00 12.00
82 Luol Deng/99 RC 6.00 15.00
83 Rafael Araujo/99 RC 4.00 10.00
84 Andre Iguodala/99 RC 6.00 15.00
85 Luke Jackson/99 RC 4.00 10.00
86 Andris Biedrins/99 RC 5.00 12.00
87 Robert Swift RC 2.00 5.00
88 Sebastian Telfair/99 RC 4.00 10.00
89 Kris Humphries RC 2.00 5.00
90 Al Jefferson RC 3.00 8.00
91 Kirk Snyder RC 2.00 5.00
92 Josh Smith/99 RC 6.00 15.00
93 J.R. Smith/99 RC 5.00 12.00
94 Dorell Wright RC 2.00 5.00
95 Jameer Nelson/99 RC 5.00 12.00
96 Pavel Podkolzine RC 2.00 5.00
97 Nenad Krstic RC 2.00 5.00
98 Andres Nocioni/99 RC 4.00 10.00
99 Delonte West RC 2.50 6.00
100 Tony Allen RC 2.50 6.00
101 Kevin Martin RC 2.50 6.00
102 Sasha Vujacic/99 RC 4.00 10.00
103 Beno Udrih RC 2.00 5.00
104 David Harrison RC 2.00 5.00
105 Anderson Varejao/99 RC 5.00 12.00
106 Jackson Vroman RC 2.00 5.00
107 Peter John Ramos RC 2.00 5.00
108 Lionel Chalmers RC 2.00 5.00
109 Donta Smith RC 2.00 5.00
110 Andre Emmett RC 2.00 5.00
111 Antonio Burks RC 2.00 5.00
112 Royal Ivey RC 2.00 5.00
113 Chris Duhon/99 RC 4.00 10.00
114 Erik Daniels RC 2.00 5.00
115 Justin Reed RC 2.00 5.00
116 Horace Jenkins RC 2.00 5.00
117 D.J. Mbenga RC 2.00 5.00
118 Trevor Ariza RC 2.00 5.00
119 Tim Pickett RC 2.00 5.00
120 Bernard Robinson RC 2.00 5.00
121 Ibrahim Kutluay RC 2.00 5.00
122 Romain Sato RC 2.00 5.00
123 Luis Flores RC 2.00 5.00
124 Damien Wilkins RC 2.00 5.00
125 Yuta Tabuse/99 RC 8.00 20.00

2004-05 SkyBox LE Retail

Inserted in Retail packs, this 125-card set parallels the base Skybox LE set but is not die cut and the rookie players are not serially numbered.

COMPLETE SET (125) 20.00 50.00
*VETS: SAME PRICE AS HOBBY
76 Dwight Howard RC 2.50 6.00
77 Emeka Okafor RC 1.25 3.00
78 Ben Gordon RC 1.25 3.00
79 Shaun Livingston RC .75 2.00
80 Devin Harris RC 1.25 3.00
81 Josh Childress RC .75 2.00
82 Luol Deng RC 1.25 3.00
83 Rafael Araujo RC .75 2.00
84 Andre Iguodala RC 1.25 3.00
85 Luke Jackson RC .75 2.00
86 Andris Biedrins RC 1.00 2.50
87 Robert Swift RC .75 2.00
88 Sebastian Telfair RC .75 2.00
89 Kris Humphries RC .75 2.00
90 Al Jefferson RC 1.25 3.00
91 Kirk Snyder RC .75 2.00
92 Josh Smith RC 1.25 3.00
93 J.R. Smith RC 1.00 2.50
94 Dorell Wright RC 1.00 2.50
95 Jameer Nelson RC 1.00 2.50
96 Pavel Podkolzine RC .75 2.00
97 Nenad Krstic RC 1.00 2.50
98 Andres Nocioni RC .75 2.00
99 Delonte West RC 1.00 2.50
100 Tony Allen RC 1.00 2.50
101 Kevin Martin RC 1.00 2.50
102 Sasha Vujacic RC .75 2.00
103 Beno Udrih RC .75 2.00
104 David Harrison RC .75 2.00
105 Anderson Varejao RC 1.00 2.50
106 Jackson Vroman RC .75 2.00
107 Peter John Ramos RC .75 2.00
108 Lionel Chalmers RC .75 2.00
109 Donta Smith RC .75 2.00
110 Andre Emmett RC .75 2.00
111 Antonio Burks RC .75 2.00
112 Royal Ivey RC .75 2.00
113 Chris Duhon RC .75 2.00
114 Erik Daniels RC .75 2.00
115 Justin Reed RC .75 2.00
116 Horace Jenkins RC .75 2.00
117 D.J. Mbenga RC .75 2.00
118 Trevor Ariza RC .75 2.00
119 Tim Pickett RC .75 2.00
120 Bernard Robinson RC .75 2.00
121 Ibrahim Kutluay RC .75 2.00
122 Romain Sato RC .75 2.00
123 Luis Flores RC .75 2.00
124 Damien Wilkins RC .75 2.00
125 Yuta Tabuse RC 1.50 4.00

2004-05 SkyBox LE 150

Randomly seeded in packs, this 125-card set parallels the base Skybox LE set enhanced with sequential numbering to 150. Other parallel versions were also issued and these are sequentially numbered to 50, 35 and 15.

*LE 150 1-75 SINGLES: 2X TO 5X BASE HI
*LE 150 RC/499 SINGLES: .6X TO 1.5X BASE HI

2004-05 SkyBox LE 50

Randomly seeded in packs, this 125-card set parallels the base Skybox LE set enhanced with sequential numbering to 50.

*LE 50 1-75 STARS: 3X TO 8X BASE HI
*LE 50 RCs/99: .5X TO 1.25X BASE HI
*LE 50 RCs/499: 1X TO 2.5X BASE HI

2004-05 SkyBox LE 35

Randomly seeded in packs, this 125-card set parallels the base Skybox LE set enhanced with sequential numbering to 35.

*1-75 SINGLES: 4X TO 10X BASE HI
*RCs/99: .6X TO 1.5X BASE HI
*RCs/499: 1.25X TO 3X BASE HI

2004-05 SkyBox LE Jersey Proofs

Randomly inserted in Hobby packs at the rate of one in 60, this 75-card set parallels the design of the base Skybox LE set enhanced with a square jersey swatch. Several different versions of this set were issued and break down as follows: a jersey version sequentially numbered to 99, a patch version that includes a game worn patch swatch sequentially numbered to 50, a patch version sequentially numbered to 15 and a patch version numbered one of one.

*JSY 99 SINGLES: .5X TO 1.25X BASE JSY HI
*PATCH SINGLES: 1X TO 2.5X BASE JSY HI
1 Tony Parker 2.50 6.00
2 Vince Carter 4.00 10.00
3 Al Harrington 2.00 5.00
4 Dwyane Wade 8.00 20.00
5 Latrell Sprewell 2.00 5.00
7 Caron Butler 2.50 6.00
8 Zach Randolph 2.00 5.00
9 Peja Stojakovic 2.50 6.00
10 Eddy Curry 2.00 5.00
11 Allen Iverson 4.00 10.00
12 Kirk Hinrich 2.50 6.00
13 Jason Williams 2.00 5.00
15 Manu Ginobili 3.00 8.00
17 Reggie Miller 2.50 6.00
18 Steve Francis 2.50 6.00
21 Stephon Marbury 2.50 6.00
22 Ray Allen 2.50 6.00
23 Carmelo Anthony 5.00 12.00
24 Lamar Odom 2.50 6.00
26 Shareef Abdur-Rahim 2.00 5.00
28 Jason Richardson 2.50 6.00
32 Chris Bosh 2.50 6.00
33 Mike Dunleavy 2.00 5.00
34 Andrei Kirilenko 2.50 6.00
35 Tracy McGrady 3.00 8.00
36 T.J. Ford 2.00 5.00
39 Rasheed Wallace 2.50 6.00
40 Gilbert Arenas 2.50 6.00
42 Tim Duncan 4.00 10.00
43 Yao Ming 5.00 12.00
44 Carlos Boozer 2.50 6.00
46 Larry Hughes 2.50 6.00
48 Kevin Garnett 5.00 12.00
50 Tyson Chandler 2.00 5.00
51 Elton Brand 2.50 6.00
52 Allan Houston 2.00 5.00
53 Shawn Marion 2.50 6.00
55 Shaquille O'Neal 6.00 15.00
56 Steve Nash 3.00 8.00
59 Corey Maggette 2.50 6.00
60 Ben Wallace 2.50 6.00
61 Darius Miles 2.00 5.00
63 Pau Gasol 2.50 6.00
65 Gary Payton 2.50 6.00
71 Mike Bibby 2.50 6.00
72 Rashard Lewis 2.50 6.00
73 Paul Pierce 3.00 8.00
75 Amare Stoudemire 4.00 10.00

2004-05 SkyBox LE Future Legends

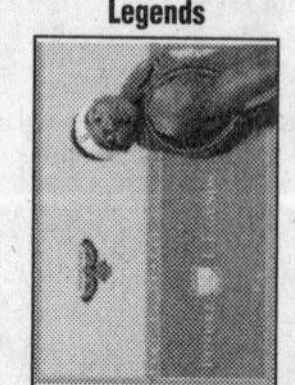

Inserted in packs at the rate of one in 12, this 24-card set is horizontally designed with a player photo on the right and a top/bottom cut design with team colors featured on each. A one of one numbered version of this set was inserted also.

COMPLETE SET (24) 20.00 50.00
1 Dwight Howard 3.00 8.00
2 Jameer Nelson 1.25 3.00
3 Shaun Livingston 1.00 2.50
4 Sebastian Telfair 1.00 2.50
5 Ben Gordon 1.25 3.00
6 Luol Deng 1.50 4.00
7 Josh Childress 1.00 2.50
8 Josh Smith 1.50 4.00
9 Andre Iguodala 1.50 4.00
10 J.R. Smith 1.25 3.00
11 Kris Humphries 1.00 2.50
12 Kirk Snyder 1.00 2.50
13 Devin Harris 1.50 4.00
14 Pavel Podkolzine 1.00 2.50
15 Rafael Araujo 1.00 2.50
16 Robert Swift 1.00 2.50
17 Andris Biedrins 1.25 3.00
18 Luke Jackson 1.00 2.50
19 Chris Duhon 1.00 2.50
20 Dorell Wright 1.50 4.00
21 Tony Allen 1.25 3.00
22 Delonte West 1.25 3.00
23 Yuta Tabuse 2.00 5.00
24 Emeka Okafor 1.50 4.00

2004-05 SkyBox LE Future Legends Jerseys

Randomly inserted in packs, this 21-card set parallels the design of the base Future Legends insert set enhanced with a swatch of jersey and sequential numbering to 75. Several other versions of this set were also issued and break down as follows: Patches serial numbered to 25, Patches Dual serial numbered to 10, Patches Dual one of ones, Patches Autographs serial numbered to 25 and Patches Dual Autographs numbered as one of ones.

*JERSEY 50 SINGLES: .5X TO 1.25X BASE HI
*PATCH: 1X TO 2.5X BASE HI
AB Andris Biedrins 3.00 8.00
AI Andre Iguodala 4.00 10.00
AJ Al Jefferson 4.00 10.00
BG Ben Gordon 3.00 8.00
DH Dwight Howard 8.00 20.00
DH2 Devin Harris 4.00 10.00
DW Dorell Wright 4.00 10.00
DW2 Delonte West 2.50 6.00
FL Sasha Vujacic 2.50 6.00
JC Josh Childress 2.50 6.00
JN Jameer Nelson 3.00 8.00
JS J.R. Smith 3.00 8.00
JS Josh Smith 4.00 10.00
KH Kris Humphries 2.50 6.00
KS Kirk Snyder 2.50 6.00
LD Luol Deng 4.00 10.00
LJ Luke Jackson 2.50 6.00
RA Rafael Araujo 2.50 6.00
SL Shaun Livingston 2.50 6.00
ST Sebastian Telfair 2.50 6.00
TA Tony Allen 3.00 8.00
YT Yuta Tabuse 5.00 12.00

2004-05 SkyBox LE Future Legends of the Draft Patches Autographs

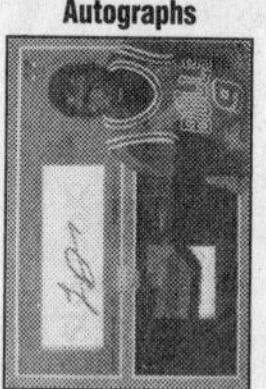

Randomly inserted in packs, this 17-card set parallels the design of the base Draft Jerseys set enhanced with patch swatches and autographs. Each card is serially numbered to 25.

UNPRICED PATCH DUAL PRINT RUN ONE SET
AB Andris Biedrins 10.00 25.00
AJ Al Jefferson 12.00 30.00
BG Ben Gordon 10.00 25.00
DH2 Devin Harris 12.00 30.00
JS Josh Smith 12.00 30.00
JS J.R. Smith 10.00 25.00
KH Kris Humphries 8.00 20.00
KS Kirk Snyder 8.00 20.00
LJ Luke Jackson 8.00 20.00
RA Rafael Araujo 8.00 20.00
ST Sebastian Telfair 8.00 20.00
YT Yuta Tabuse 30.00 80.00

2004-05 SkyBox LE Legends of the Draft

Inserted in Hobby packs at the rate of one in four and Retail packs at the rate of one in eight, this 20-card set features retired greats on a horizontally designed card with a small head shot in the upper right corner, white backgrounds for the top and brown backgrounds for the bottom. A one of one serial numbered version of this set was also produced.

COMPLETE SET (20) 15.00 40.00
1 Oscar Robertson 1.25 3.00
2 Walt Bellamy 1.25 3.00
3 Elgin Baylor 1.25 3.00
4 Cazzie Russell 1.25 3.00
5 Bob Lanier 1.25 3.00
6 Kevin McHale 1.50 4.00
7 Bill Walton 1.25 3.00
8 John Havlicek 1.25 3.00
9 Robert Parish 1.25 3.00
10 Isiah Thomas 1.25 3.00
11 Walt Frazier 1.25 3.00
12 George Gervin 1.25 3.00
13 Nate Archibald 1.25 3.00
14 Bob Cousy 2.00 5.00
15 Rick Barry 1.25 3.00
16 Earl Monroe 1.25 3.00
17 Willis Reed 1.25 3.00
18 Darryl Dawkins 1.25 3.00
19 Wes Unseld 1.25 3.00
20 Pat Riley 1.50 4.00

2004-05 SkyBox LE Legends of the Draft Jerseys

Seeded randomly in packs, this 40-card set parallels the look of the Legends of the draft but replaces retired players with action players, adds a jersey from a game and sequential numbering to 50. Several other versions of this set were issued, one serial numbered to 25, a Dual set serial numbered to 10 and a one of one version. Patch Autograph versions for single players were inserted an serial numbered to 25 and a one of one Patch Autograph Dual set was produced as well.

*PATCH: .6X TO 1.5X BASE HI
PATCH PRINT RUN 25 SER.#'d SETS
AH Anfernee Hardaway 10.00 25.00
AI Allen Iverson 6.00 15.00
AK Andrei Kirilenko 3.00 8.00
AS Amare Stoudemire 5.00 12.00
AW Antoine Walker 4.00 10.00
BD Baron Davis 4.00 10.00
CA Carmelo Anthony 8.00 20.00
CM Corey Maggette 3.00 8.00
CW Chris Webber 4.00 10.00
DN Dirk Nowitzki 6.00 15.00
DW Dwyane Wade 12.00 30.00
EB Elton Brand 4.00 10.00
JK Jason Kidd 6.00 15.00
JO Jermaine O'Neal 4.00 10.00
JR Jason Richardson 4.00 10.00
KM Kenyon Martin 4.00 10.00
LO Lamar Odom 4.00 10.00
MB Mike Bibby 4.00 10.00
PG Pau Gasol 4.00 10.00
PP Paul Pierce 5.00 12.00
RA Ray Allen 4.00 10.00
RH Richard Hamilton 3.00 8.00
RM Reggie Miller 4.00 10.00
RW Rasheed Wallace 4.00 10.00
SF Steve Francis 4.00 10.00
SM Stephon Marbury 3.00 8.00
SM2 Shawn Marion 4.00 10.00
SO Shaquille O'Neal 10.00 25.00
SP Scottie Pippen 20.00 50.00
TD Tim Duncan 6.00 15.00
TP Tony Parker 4.00 10.00
TW Tracy McGrady 5.00 12.00
VC Vince Carter 6.00 15.00
YM Yao Ming 8.00 20.00

2004-05 SkyBox LE Legends of the Draft Jerseys Year

Randomly inserted in packs, this 40-card set parallels the base Legends of the Draft Jerseys insert enhanced with serial numbering to the year each player was drafted.

AI Allen Iverson/96 5.00 12.00
AK Andrei Kirilenko/99 2.50 6.00
AS Amare Stoudemire/102 4.00 10.00
AW Antoine Walker/96 3.00 8.00
BD Baron Davis/99 3.00 8.00
CA Carmelo Anthony/103 6.00 15.00
CM Corey Maggette/99 2.50 6.00
CW Chris Webber/93 3.00 8.00
DN Dirk Nowitzki/98 5.00 12.00
DW Dwyane Wade/103 10.00 25.00
EB Elton Brand/99 3.00 8.00
JK Jason Kidd/94 5.00 12.00
JO Jermaine O'Neal/96 3.00 8.00
JR Jason Richardson/101 3.00 8.00
JS Jerry Stackhouse/95 2.50 6.00
KG Kevin Garnett/95 6.00 15.00
KM Kenyon Martin/100 3.00 8.00
LO Lamar Odom/99 3.00 8.00
MB Mike Bibby/98 3.00 8.00
PG Pau Gasol/101 3.00 8.00
PJ Peja Stojakovic/96 3.00 8.00
PP Paul Pierce/98 4.00 10.00
RA Ray Allen/96 3.00 8.00
RH Richard Hamilton/99 2.50 6.00
RM Reggie Miller/87 3.00 8.00
RW Rasheed Wallace/95 3.00 8.00
SF Steve Francis/99 3.00 8.00
SM2 Shawn Marion/99 3.00 8.00
SN Steve Nash/96 4.00 10.00
SP Scottie Pippen/87 15.00 40.00
TD Tim Duncan/97 5.00 12.00
TP Tony Parker/101 3.00 8.00
TW Tracy McGrady/97 4.00 10.00
VC Vince Carter/98 5.00 12.00
YM Yao Ming/102

2004-05 SkyBox LE Legends of the Draft Patches Autographs

Randomly inserted in packs, this 40-card set parallels the base Legends of the Draft Jerseys insert enhanced with patches and player autographs. Each card is sequentially numbered to 25.

BD Baron Davis 15.00 40.00
CM Corey Maggette 15.00 40.00
DW Dwyane Wade 100.00 200.00
EB Elton Brand 10.00 25.00
JK Jason Kidd 30.00 80.00
JS Jerry Stackhouse 20.00 50.00
KM Kenyon Martin 20.00 50.00
RJ Richard Jefferson 15.00 40.00
SM Stephon Marbury 20.00 50.00
TM Tracy McGrady 30.00 80.00
VC Vince Carter 30.00 80.00

2004-05 SkyBox LE Rare Form

Inserted in Retail packs at the rate of one in 576, this 10-card set is die cut in the middle and places a player on the top half of a card accented by his team's colors. A one of one version of this set was also inserted.

COMPLETE SET (10) 50.00 120.00
1 Shaquille O'Neal 8.00 20.00
2 Dwyane Wade 10.00 25.00
3 Carmelo Anthony 6.00 15.00
4 Kenyon Martin 3.00 8.00
5 Allen Iverson 5.00 12.00
6 Vince Carter 5.00 12.00
7 Kevin Garnett 6.00 15.00
8 Tim Duncan 5.00 12.00
9 LeBron James 20.00 50.00
10 Kobe Bryant 15.00 40.00

2004-05 SkyBox LE Rare Form Jerseys

Randomly inserted in packs, this 10-card set parallels the design of the base Rare Form insert set enhanced with a swatch of game worn jersey and sequential numbering to 50. Several other versions of this set were inserted and break down as follows: Jersey Numbers are serially numbered to featured player's jersey number, Patches contain a patch swatch and are sequentially numbered to 25, Patches Dual feature two players and patches and are sequentially numbered to 10, and Patch Dual one of one's exist.

AI Allen Iverson 6.00 15.00
AS Amare Stoudemire 5.00 12.00
CA Carmelo Anthony 8.00 20.00
DW Dwyane Wade 12.00 30.00
KG Kevin Garnett 8.00 20.00
KM Kenyon Martin 4.00 10.00
SN Steve Nash 5.00 12.00
SO Shaquille O'Neal 10.00 25.00
TD Tim Duncan 6.00 15.00
VC Vince Carter 6.00 15.00

2004-05 SkyBox LE Rare Form Jerseys Numbers

Randomly inserted in packs, this 10-card set parallels the design of the base Rare Form insert set enhanced with a swatch of game worn jersey and sequential numbering to the featured player's jersey number.

STATED PRINT RUN 3 TO 32 SETS
SOME UNPRICED DUE TO SCARCITY
AS Amare Stoudemire/32 6.00 15.00
KG Kevin Garnett/21 10.00 25.00
SO Shaquille O'Neal/32 12.00 30.00
VC Vince Carter/15 12.00 30.00

2004-05 SkyBox LE Sky's the Limit Jerseys

Randomly inserted in packs, this 20-card set places a player photo on the bottom two-thirds of the card and a jersey along the top. Each card is sequentially numbered to 99. Several different versions of the set were issued and break down as follows: Jerseys 50 are sequentially numbered to 50, Patches, which contain a jersey patch are sequentially numbered to 25 and Patches Dual, which contain two jersey patches and are numbered to 10. Patches Dual one of ones were inserted also.

*JSY 50 SINGLES: .5X TO 1.25X BASE JSY
AI Allen Iverson 5.00 12.00
AI2 Andre Iguodala 5.00 12.00
BD Baron Davis 3.00 8.00
BG Ben Gordon 4.00 10.00
DH Devin Harris 5.00 12.00
DH Dwight Howard 10.00 25.00
DN Dirk Nowitzki 5.00 12.00
DW Dwyane Wade 10.00 25.00
DW2 Dorell Wright 5.00 12.00
EB Elton Brand 3.00 8.00
JK Jason Kidd 5.00 12.00
JN Jameer Nelson 4.00 10.00
JS J.R. Smith 4.00 10.00
KH Kirk Hinrich 3.00 8.00
RJ Richard Jefferson 3.00 8.00
SF Steve Francis 3.00 8.00
SL Shaun Livingston 3.00 8.00
ST Sebastian Telfair 3.00 8.00
TM Tracy McGrady 4.00 10.00
YM Yao Ming 6.00 15.00

1991-92 SkyBox Mark and See Minis

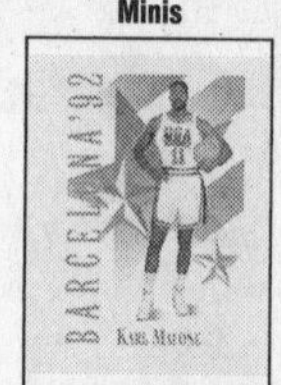

Published by Golden Book (Western Publishing Company Inc.) and SkyBox, this 14-card set was featured on perforated sheets inserted in two 5 1/2" by 8" USA Basketball "Mark and See" booklets (numbered 22381 and 22382). Each booklet came with a special marker, and answers to the multiple-choice questions was revealed by coloring in the blank spaces provided for answers. The first ten cards are perforated, measure approximately 2 1/4" by 2 3/4", and are printed on thin card stock. The fronts are identical to the regular 1991-92 SkyBox II cards, displaying a posed color shot of the player against a computer-generated background consisting of stars and stripes. The words "Barcelona '92" are printed along the left edge. The player's name is at the bottom. In contrast to the regular issue cards, the backs are black-and-white and show a player photo in a flag-shaped icon. A player quote about the Olympic games is featured. Included in the first booklet is a 7 1/4" by 3 1/2" panel that could be cut into three cards, each numbered and measuring approximately 2 3/8" by 3 3/8". It displays the entire team in front of a background showing the words "Barcelona '92" in large red letters above a row of gold stars against a sky scene. The second booklet also featured a 7 1/4" by 3 1/2" panel with a team photo, but it was not numbered and not designed to be cut into smaller player cards. Each card has the complete team listed with the featured players marked by an asterisk.

COMPLETE SET (14) 20.00 50.00
530 Charles Barkley 2.50 6.00
531 Larry Bird 4.00 10.00
532 Patrick Ewing 1.50 4.00
533 Magic Johnson 3.00 8.00
534 Michael Jordan 10.00 25.00
535 Karl Malone 3.00 8.00
536 Chris Mullin 1.25 3.00
537 Scottie Pippen 2.50 6.00
538 David Robinson 2.50 6.00
539 John Stockton 3.00 8.00
544 Team USA Card 1 .75 2.00
Chris Mullin
Charles Barkley
David Robinson
545 Team USA Card 2 2.50 6.00
Michael Jordan
John Stockton
Karl Malone
Magic Johnson
546 Team USA Card 3 1.25 3.00
Patrick Ewing
Larry Bird
Scottie Pippen
NNO Team Photo 1.50 4.00

1993 SkyBox Milestone Pro

These two standard-size promo cards were issu promote the forthcoming 100-card SkyBox Mile (The Dakota Universe) set, which features chara from Milestone Media, the multicultural-themed imprint distributed by DC Comics. Inside a turq frame and a black-and-brown outer border, the f feature cartoon-like caricatures of NBA players, portrayed wearing futuristic body armor. On a b panel, the horizontal backs contain an advertiser for the forthcoming card issue. The cards are unnumbered and checklisted below in alphabeti order.

COMPLETE SET (2) 2.50
1 Magic 1.50
(Magic Johnson)
2 The Admiral 1.50
(David Robinson)

1998-99 SkyBox Molten Me

This was the first year for the Molten Metal set. was issued in 6-card packs with a suggested reta price of $4.99. The set was one series only, conta 150 cards. The set was broken up into 3 different subsets - cards 1-100 was the Metal Smiths sub cards 101-130 was the Heavy Metal subset and c 131-150 was the Supernatural subset. The Metal Smiths subset cards were inserted at four per pac Heavy Metal subset cards were inserted one per p and the Supernatural subset cards were inserted two packs.

COMPLETE SET (150) 25.00
1 Maurice Taylor .10
2 Bison Dele .10
3 Anthony Mason .10
4 John Starks .12
5 Anthony Johnson .10
6 Calbert Cheaney .10
7 Roshown McLeod RC .50
8 Jalen Rose .12
9 Kelvin Cato .10
10 Walter McCarty .10
11 Isaac Austin .10
12 Arvydas Sabonis .12
13 David Wesley .10
14 Jim Jackson .10
15 Elden Campbell .10
16 Michael Doleac RC .50
17 Chris Webber .15
18 Mitch Richmond .15
19 Johnny Newman .10
20 Jayson Williams .10
21 George Lynch .10
22 Ron Harper .12
23 Donyell Marshall .10
24 Derek Fisher .15
25 Matt Harpring RC .60
26 Jason Williams RC 1.25
27 Toni Kukoc .15
28 Clarence Weatherspoon .10
29 Eddie Jones .15
30 Bo Outlaw .10
31 Zydrunas Ilgauskas .12
32 Michael Dickerson RC .50
33 Tyronn Lue RC .50
34 Theo Ratliff .12
35 Dirk Nowitzki RC 3.00
36 Robert Traylor RC .50
37 Gary Trent .10
38 Wesley Person .10
39 Bryce Drew RC .50
40 P.J. Brown .10
41 Joe Smith .12
42 Avery Johnson .10
43 Chris Anstey .10
44 Mario Elie .10
45 Voshon Lenard .10
46 Rex Chapman .10
47 Hersey Hawkins .10
48 Shawn Bradley .10
49 Matt Maloney .10
50 Dan Majerle .15
51 Pat Garrity RC .50
52 Sam Perkins .10
53 Mookie Blaylock .10
54 Al Harrington RC .75
55 Clifford Robinson .10
56 Alan Henderson .10
57 Chris Mullin .15
58 Dennis Scott .10
59 A.C. Green .15
60 Tyrone Hill .10
61 Chauncey Billups .20
62 Michael Finley .15
63 Terrell Brandon .10
64 Detlef Schrempf .15
65 Bonzi Wells RC .50
66 Larry Johnson .10
67 Bryant Reeves .10
68 Raef LaFrentz RC .60
69 Kendall Gill .10
70 Bryon Russell .10
71 Bobby Phills .10
72 Tony Delk .10
73 Lorenzen Wright .10
74 Keon Clark RC .50
75 Billy Owens .10
76 Tracy Murray .10
77 Bobby Jackson .12
78 Sam Cassell .12
79 Corliss Williamson .10

eff Hornacek .12 .30
sPhonso Ellis .10 .25
am Mitchell .10 .25
ean Elliott .15 .40
ohn Wallace .10 .25
ikembe Mutombo .15 .40
ik Smits .12 .30
aiah Rider .10 .25
oe Dumars .15 .40
llan Houston .12 .30
am Mack .10 .25
aul Pierce RC 2.50 6.00
amond Murray .10 .25
lasheed Wallace .15 .40
anny Fortson .10 .25
herokee Parks .10 .25
ntonio Daniels .10 .25
handon Anderson .10 .25
icky Davis RC .75 2.00
odney Rogers .10 .25
Tariq Abdul-Wahad .10 .25
Glenn Robinson .20 .50
Ron Mercer .20 .50
Alonzo Mourning .30 .75
Marcus Camby .20 .50
Steve Smith .20 .50
Tim Hardaway .25 .60
Rod Strickland .15 .40
Reggie Miller .30 .75
Juwan Howard .20 .50
Hakeem Olajuwon .30 .75
John Stockton .30 .75
Antonio McDyess .20 .50
Charles Barkley .40 1.00
Karl Malone .30 .75
Jerry Stackhouse .20 .50
Tracy McGrady .40 1.00
Brevin Knight .15 .40
Gary Payton .25 .60
Derek Anderson .15 .40
Glen Rice .25 .60
David Robinson .40 1.00
Vin Baker .20 .50
Tom Gugliotta .15 .40
Patrick Ewing .30 .75
Ray Allen .30 .75
Anfernee Hardaway .40 1.00
Jason Kidd .40 1.00
Kenny Anderson .20 .50
Kerry Kittles .15 .40
Tim Thomas .25 .60
Shareef Abdur-Rahim .40 1.00
Mike Bibby RC 2.00 5.00
Kobe Bryant 2.00 5.00
Vince Carter RC 4.00 10.00
Tim Duncan .75 2.00
Kevin Garnett .75 2.00
Grant Hill .60 1.50
Larry Hughes RC 1.50 4.00
Allen Iverson .75 2.00
Antawn Jamison RC 2.00 5.00
Michael Jordan 3.00 8.00
Shawn Kemp .40 1.00
Stephon Marbury .50 1.25
Michael Olowokandi RC 1.00 2.50
Shaquille O'Neal 1.00 2.50
Scottie Pippen .60 1.50
Dennis Rodman .75 2.00
Damon Stoudamire .40 1.00
Keith Van Horn .40 1.00
Antoine Walker .40 1.00

998-99 SkyBox Molten Metal Xplosion

s 150-card set parallels the basic set, with the cards ually being metal. The cards were inserted at erent ratios, depending on their subset theme. ds 1-100 (Metal Smiths) were inserted at one in , cards 101-130 (Heavy Metal) were inserted at one 8 and cards 131-150 (Supernatural) were inserted one in 60. To ascertain values on individual cards, ase refer to the multipliers in the header below, pled with the value of the base card.

MPLETE SET (150) 175.00 350.00
100 STARS/RCs: 1X TO 2.5X BASE HI
01-130 STARS: 2X TO 5X BASE HI
31-150 STARS: 4X TO 10X BASE HI
31-150 RCs: 1.5X TO 4X BASE HI
4 Vince Carter 20.00 50.00
7 Dennis Rodman 12.00 30.00

1998-99 SkyBox Molten Metal Fusion

s 50-card set is a semi-parallel of the base set. The only parallels cards 101-150, the Heavy Metal and pernatural subsets. The cards feature die cut chnology. Card 1-30 were inserted at one in 16 cks, while cards 31-50 were randomly inserted and ially numbered to 250. Due to a production blem, 15 of the 20 Supernatural cards were oduced with an incorrect front logo. Thus, these rds were serially numbered to 40, rather than the 0. Five players remain correct, they are Jordan, phon Marbury, Shawn Kemp, Allen Iverson and ant Hill.

Glenn Robinson 1.50 4.00
Ron Mercer 1.50 4.00
Alonzo Mourning 2.50 6.00
Marcus Camby 1.50 4.00
Steve Smith 1.50 4.00
Tim Hardaway 2.00 5.00
Rod Strickland 1.25 3.00
8 Reggie Miller 2.50 6.00
9 Juwan Howard 1.50 4.00
10 Hakeem Olajuwon 2.50 6.00
11 John Stockton 2.50 6.00
12 Antonio McDyess 1.50 4.00
13 Charles Barkley 3.00 8.00
14 Karl Malone 2.50 6.00
15 Jerry Stackhouse 2.00 5.00
16 Tracy McGrady 3.00 8.00
17 Brevin Knight 1.25 3.00
18 Gary Payton 2.00 5.00
19 Derek Anderson 1.25 3.00
20 Glen Rice 2.00 5.00
21 David Robinson 3.00 8.00
22 Vin Baker 1.50 4.00
23 Tom Gugliotta 1.25 3.00
24 Patrick Ewing 2.50 6.00
25 Ray Allen 2.50 6.00
26 Anfernee Hardaway 3.00 8.00
27 Jason Kidd 3.00 8.00
28 Kenny Anderson 1.50 4.00
29 Kerry Kittles 1.25 3.00
30 Tim Thomas 2.00 5.00
31 Shareef Abdur-Rahim 50.00 125.00
32 Mike Bibby 60.00 150.00
33 Kobe Bryant 250.00 600.00
34 Vince Carter 125.00 300.00
35 Tim Duncan 100.00 250.00
36 Kevin Garnett 30.00 80.00
37 Grant Hill 25.00 60.00
38 Larry Hughes 50.00 125.00
39 Allen Iverson 30.00 80.00
40 Antawn Jamison 60.00 150.00
41 Michael Jordan 600.00 1200.00
42 Shawn Kemp 15.00 40.00
43 Stephon Marbury 20.00 50.00
44 Michael Olowokandi 30.00 80.00
45 Shaquille O'Neal 125.00 300.00
46 Scottie Pippen 80.00 200.00
47 Dennis Rodman 125.00 300.00
48 Damon Stoudamire 50.00 125.00
49 Keith Van Horn 50.00 125.00
50 Antoine Walker 50.00 125.00

1998-99 SkyBox Molten Metal Fusion Titanium

This 50-card set parallels the fusion insert using an enhanced design on gold card stock. Cards 1-30, the Heavy Metal subset, are inserted at one in 96 packs, while cards 31-50, the Supernatural subset, are randomly inserted in packs and serially numbered to 40. Due to a production error, 15 of the 20 Supernatural cards were incorrectly serially numbered to 250, rather than to 40.

1 Glenn Robinson 5.00 12.00
2 Ron Mercer 5.00 12.00
3 Alonzo Mourning 8.00 20.00
4 Marcus Camby 5.00 12.00
5 Steve Smith 5.00 12.00
6 Tim Hardaway 6.00 15.00
7 Rod Strickland 4.00 10.00
8 Reggie Miller 8.00 20.00
9 Juwan Howard 5.00 12.00
10 Hakeem Olajuwon 8.00 20.00
11 John Stockton 8.00 20.00
12 Antonio McDyess 5.00 12.00
13 Charles Barkley 10.00 25.00
14 Karl Malone 8.00 20.00
15 Jerry Stackhouse 6.00 15.00
16 Tracy McGrady 10.00 25.00
17 Brevin Knight 4.00 10.00
18 Gary Payton 6.00 15.00
19 Derek Anderson 4.00 10.00
20 Glen Rice 6.00 15.00
21 David Robinson 12.00 30.00
22 Vin Baker 5.00 12.00
23 Tom Gugliotta 4.00 10.00
24 Patrick Ewing 8.00 20.00
25 Ray Allen 8.00 20.00
26 Anfernee Hardaway 10.00 25.00
27 Jason Kidd 10.00 25.00
28 Kenny Anderson 5.00 12.00
29 Kerry Kittles 4.00 10.00
30 Tim Thomas 6.00 15.00
31 Shareef Abdur-Rahim 15.00 40.00
32 Mike Bibby 20.00 50.00
33 Kobe Bryant 80.00 200.00
34 Vince Carter 40.00 100.00
35 Tim Duncan 30.00 80.00
36 Kevin Garnett 100.00 250.00
37 Grant Hill 80.00 200.00
38 Larry Hughes 15.00 40.00
39 Allen Iverson 125.00 300.00
40 Antawn Jamison 20.00 50.00
41 Michael Jordan 1500.00 2500.00
42 Shawn Kemp 50.00 125.00
43 Stephon Marbury 60.00 150.00
44 Michael Olowokandi 10.00 25.00
45 Shaquille O'Neal 40.00 100.00
46 Scottie Pippen 25.00 60.00
47 Dennis Rodman 50.00 125.00
48 Damon Stoudamire 15.00 40.00
49 Keith Van Horn 15.00 40.00
50 Antoine Walker 15.00 40.00

1992-93 SkyBox Nestle

Collectors could obtain two standard-size cards in multi-packs of Nestle Crunch Minis, Nestle Crunch bars, Raisinets, Baby Ruth, and Butterfinger. A special binder to hold the cards was also available through a mail-in offer. These cards are identical to 1992-93 SkyBox series I cards, with the exception that they have no card numbers on them. They are checklisted below in alphabetical order.

COMPLETE SET (50) 60.00 150.00
1 Michael Adams .75 2.00
2 Rolando Blackman 1.00 2.50
3 Manute Bol 1.25 3.00
4 Dee Brown .75 2.00
5 Tony Campbell .75 2.00
6 Derrick Coleman 1.25 3.00
7 Brad Daugherty .75 2.00
8 Clyde Drexler 3.00 8.00
9 Joe Dumars 2.00 5.00
10 Sean Elliott 2.00 5.00
11 Pervis Ellison .75 2.00
12 Kendall Gill 1.25 3.00
13 Tim Hardaway 2.00 5.00
14 Derek Harper 1.25 3.00
15 Hersey Hawkins 1.25 3.00
16 Chris Jackson 1.00 2.50
17 Mark Jackson 1.50 4.00
18 Kevin Johnson 1.50 4.00
19 Shawn Kemp 3.00 8.00
20 Reggie Lewis 1.25 3.00
21 Dan Majerle 1.50 4.00
22 Karl Malone 4.00 10.00
23 Danny Manning 1.25 3.00
24 Reggie Miller 4.00 10.00
25 Chris Mullin 1.50 4.00
26 Dikembe Mutombo 1.50 4.00
27 Charles Oakley 1.25 3.00
28 John Paxson 1.25 3.00
29 Sam Perkins 1.25 3.00
30 Drazen Petrovic 3.00 8.00
31 Ricky Pierce .75 2.00
32 Scottie Pippen 5.00 12.00
33 Terry Porter .75 2.00
34 Mark Price 1.25 3.00
35 J.R. Reid .75 2.00
36 Glen Rice 2.50 6.00
37 Alvin Robertson .75 2.00
38 David Robinson 4.00 10.00
39 Dennis Rodman 4.00 10.00
40 Detlef Schrempf 1.25 3.00
41 Dennis Scott 1.25 3.00
42 Rony Seikaly .75 2.00
43 Scott Skiles 1.25 3.00
44 Charles Smith .75 2.00
45 Kenny Smith .75 2.00
46 John Stockton 5.00 12.00
47 Otis Thorpe 1.25 3.00
48 Wayman Tisdale .75 2.00
49 Dominique Wilkins 3.00 8.00
50 James Worthy 2.50 6.00

1993-94 SkyBox Premium Promos

This six-card standard-size promo set was issued to promote the scheduled November 1993 release of SkyBox I and its inserts. The fronts feature full-bleed color action photos. Cards 1, 3 and 6 below represent the regular issue, and each has a white stripe down one side the card front containing the player's name, position, and team. The SkyBox Premium foil stamp logo appears on the front. The back features a close-up player photo on the top half, and the player's stats and biography on the back. Card 2 below represents the All-Rookie Team inserts and has a black band down the right side of the front containing the player's name and position with the All-Rookie Team logo. The back has a brief biography on a white card face. Card 4 below represents the Showdown Series and has a black foil band stamped along the bottom of the two-player photo on the front, which has the players' names in gold along with the Showdown Series logo. The horizontal back has narrow-cropped close-up photos of each player along the left and right edges with comparative stats between. Card 5 below represents the Center Stage inserts and has the player's name in prismatic silver lettering at the top of front photo and a brief biography on the back. The cards are unnumbered and checklisted below in alphabetical order.

COMPLETE SET (6) 5.00 12.00
1 Michael Jordan 4.00 10.00
2 Christian Laettner .40 1.00
3 Dan Majerle .20 .50
4 Alonzo Mourning .50 1.25
Patrick Ewing
5 Shaquille O'Neal 1.25 3.00
6 David Robinson .75 2.00

1993-94 SkyBox Premium

The 1993-94 SkyBox basketball set contains 341 standard-size cards that were issued in series of 191 and 150 respectively. Cards were issued in 12-card packs with 36 packs per box. The cards feature full-bleed color action photos with a wide white stripe down one side of the front containing the player's name, position, and team. The SkyBox Premium foil stamp logo appears superimposed on the front. The backs display a second player close-up shot on the top half, and the player's statistics and scouting report on the bottom half. The cards are numbered on the back and grouped alphabetically within team order. Subsets are Playoff Performances (4-21), Changing Faces (292-318), and Costacos Brothers Poster Cards (319-338). Rookie Cards of note include Vin Baker, Anfernee Hardaway, Allan Houston, Jamal Mashburn, Nick Van Exel and Chris Webber.The odds of finding a Head of the Class Exchange card are one in 360 first series packs. It was redeemable for a Head of the Class card featuring the top six 1993 draft picks. The redemption date was April 15, 1994.

COMPLETE SET (341) 15.00 30.00
COMPLETE SERIES 1 (191) 7.50 15.00
COMPLETE SERIES 2 (150) 7.50 15.00
1 Checklist .01 .05
2 Checklist .01 .05
3 Checklist .01 .05
4 Larry Johnson PO .05 .15
5 Alonzo Mourning PO .10 .30
6 Hakeem Olajuwon PO .10 .30
7 Brad Daugherty PO .01 .05
8 Oliver Miller PO .01 .05
9 David Robinson PO .10 .30
10 Patrick Ewing PO .05 .15
11 Ricky Pierce PO .01 .05
12 Sam Perkins PO .01 .05
13 John Starks PO .01 .05
14 Michael Jordan PO .75 2.00
15 Dan Majerle PO .01 .05
16 Scottie Pippen PO .20 .50
17 Shawn Kemp PO .10 .30
18 Charles Barkley PO .10 .30
19 Horace Grant PO .01 .05
20 Kevin Johnson PO .01 .05
Michael Jordan
21 John Paxson PO .01 .05
22 David Robinson IS .10 .30
23 NBA On NBC .01 .05
24 Stacey Augmon .01 .05
25 Mookie Blaylock .05 .15
26 Craig Ehlo .01 .05
27 Adam Keefe .01 .05
28 Dominique Wilkins .10 .30
29 Kevin Willis .01 .05
30 Dee Brown .01 .05
31 Sherman Douglas .01 .05
32 Rick Fox .01 .05
33 Kevin Gamble .01 .05
34 Xavier McDaniel .01 .05
35 Robert Parish .05 .15
36 Muggsy Bogues .05 .15
37 Dell Curry .01 .05
38 Kendall Gill .05 .15
39 Larry Johnson .10 .30
40 Alonzo Mourning .20 .50
41 Johnny Newman .01 .05
42 B.J. Armstrong .01 .05
43 Bill Cartwright .01 .05
44 Horace Grant .05 .15
45 Michael Jordan 1.50 4.00
46 John Paxson .01 .05
47 Scottie Pippen .40 1.00
48 Scott Williams .01 .05
49 Terrell Brandon .05 .15
50 Brad Daugherty .01 .05
51 Larry Nance .01 .05
52 Mark Price .01 .05
53 Gerald Wilkins .01 .05
54 John Williams .01 .05
55 Terry Davis .01 .05
56 Derek Harper .05 .15
57 Jim Jackson .05 .15
58 Sean Rooks .01 .05
59 Doug Smith .01 .05
60 Mahmoud Abdul-Rauf .01 .05
61 LaPhonso Ellis .01 .05
62 Mark Macon .01 .05
63 Dikembe Mutombo .10 .30
64 Bryant Stith .01 .05
65 Reggie Williams .01 .05
66 Joe Dumars .10 .30
67 Bill Laimbeer .01 .05
68 Terry Mills .01 .05
69 Alvin Robertson .01 .05
70 Dennis Rodman .25 .60
71 Isiah Thomas .10 .30
72 Victor Alexander .01 .05
73 Tim Hardaway .10 .30
74 Tyrone Hill .01 .05
75 Sarunas Marciulionis .01 .05
76 Chris Mullin .10 .30
77 Billy Owens .01 .05
78 Latrell Sprewell .30 .75
79 Robert Horry .05 .15
80 Vernon Maxwell .01 .05
81 Hakeem Olajuwon .20 .50
82 Kenny Smith .01 .05
83 Otis Thorpe .05 .15
84 Dale Davis .01 .05
85 Reggie Miller .10 .30
86 Pooh Richardson .01 .05
87 Detlef Schrempf .05 .15
88 Malik Sealy .05 .15
89 Rik Smits .05 .15
90 Ron Harper .05 .15
91 Mark Jackson .05 .15
92 Danny Manning .05 .15
93 Stanley Roberts .01 .05
94 Loy Vaught .01 .05
95 Randy Woods .01 .05
96 Sam Bowie .01 .05
97 Doug Christie .05 .15
98 Vlade Divac .05 .15
99 Anthony Peeler .01 .05
100 Sedale Threatt .01 .05
101 James Worthy .10 .30
102 Grant Long .01 .05
103 Harold Miner .01 .05
104 Glen Rice .05 .15
105 John Salley .01 .05
106 Rony Seikaly .01 .05
107 Steve Smith .10 .30
108 Anthony Avent .01 .05
109 Jon Barry .01 .05
110 Frank Brickowski .01 .05
111 Blue Edwards .01 .05
112 Todd Day .01 .05
113 Lee Mayberry .01 .05
114 Eric Murdock .01 .05
115 Thurl Bailey .01 .05
116 Christian Laettner .05 .15
117 Chuck Person .01 .05
118 Doug West .01 .05
119 Micheal Williams .01 .05
120 Kenny Anderson .05 .15
121 Benoit Benjamin .01 .05
122 Derrick Coleman .05 .15
123 Chris Morris .01 .05
124 Rumeal Robinson .01 .05
125 Rolando Blackman .01 .05
126 Patrick Ewing .10 .30
127 Anthony Mason .05 .15
128 Charles Oakley .05 .15
129 Doc Rivers .05 .15
130 Charles Smith .01 .05
131 John Starks .05 .15
132 Nick Anderson .05 .15
133 Shaquille O'Neal .60 1.50
134 Donald Royal .01 .05
135 Dennis Scott .01 .05
136 Scott Skiles .01 .05
137 Brian Williams .01 .05
138 Johnny Dawkins .01 .05
139 Hersey Hawkins .05 .15
140 Jeff Hornacek .05 .15
141 Andrew Lang .01 .05
142 Tim Perry .01 .05
143 Clarence Weatherspoon .01 .05
144 Danny Ainge .05 .15
145 Charles Barkley .20 .50
146 Cedric Ceballos .05 .15
147 Kevin Johnson .05 .15
148 Oliver Miller .01 .05
149 Dan Majerle .05 .15
150 Clyde Drexler .10 .30
151 Harvey Grant .01 .05
152 Jerome Kersey .01 .05
153 Terry Porter .01 .05
154 Clifford Robinson .05 .15
155 Rod Strickland .05 .15
156 Buck Williams .01 .05
157 Mitch Richmond .10 .30
158 Lionel Simmons .01 .05
159 Wayman Tisdale .01 .05
160 Spud Webb .05 .15
161 Walt Williams .01 .05
162 Antoine Carr .01 .05
163 Lloyd Daniels .01 .05
164 Sean Elliott .05 .15
165 Dale Ellis .01 .05
166 Avery Johnson .01 .05
167 J.R. Reid .01 .05
168 David Robinson .20 .50
169 Shawn Kemp .20 .50
170 Derrick McKey .01 .05
171 Nate McMillan .01 .05
172 Gary Payton .20 .50
173 Sam Perkins .05 .15
174 Ricky Pierce .01 .05
175 Tyrone Corbin .01 .05
176 Jay Humphries .01 .05
177 Jeff Malone .01 .05
178 Karl Malone .20 .50
179 John Stockton .10 .30
180 Michael Adams .01 .05
181 Kevin Duckworth .01 .05
182 Pervis Ellison .01 .05
183 Tom Gugliotta .10 .30
184 Don MacLean .01 .05
185 Brent Price .01 .05
186 George Lynch RC .01 .05
187 Rex Walters RC .01 .05
188 Shawn Bradley RC .10 .30
189 Ervin Johnson RC .05 .15
190 Luther Wright RC .01 .05
191 Calbert Cheaney RC .05 .15
192 Craig Ehlo .01 .05
193 Duane Ferrell .01 .05
194 Paul Graham .01 .05
195 Andrew Lang .01 .05
196 Chris Corchiani .01 .05
197 Acie Earl RC .01 .05
198 Dino Radja RC .01 .05
199 Ed Pinckney .01 .05
200 Tony Bennett .01 .05
201 Scott Burrell RC .10 .30
202 Kenny Gattison .01 .05
203 Hersey Hawkins .05 .15
204 Eddie Johnson .01 .05
205 Corie Blount RC .01 .05
206 Steve Kerr .05 .15
207 Toni Kukoc RC .50 1.25
208 Pete Myers .01 .05
209 Danny Ferry .01 .05
210 Tyrone Hill .01 .05
211 Gerald Madkins RC .01 .05
212 Chris Mills RC .10 .30
213 Lucious Harris RC .01 .05
214 Popeye Jones RC .01 .05
215 Jamal Mashburn RC .30 .75
216 Darnell Mee RC .01 .05
217 Rodney Rogers RC .10 .30
218 Brian Williams .01 .05
219 Greg Anderson .01 .05
220 Sean Elliott .05 .15
221 Allan Houston RC .50 1.25
222 Lindsey Hunter RC .10 .30
223 Chris Gatling .01 .05
224 Josh Grant RC .01 .05
225 Keith Jennings .01 .05
226 Avery Johnson .01 .05
227 Chris Webber RC 1.25 3.00
228 Sam Cassell RC .50 1.25
229 Mario Elie .01 .05
230 Richard Petruska RC .01 .05
231 Eric Riley RC .01 .05
232 Antonio Davis RC .15 .40
233 Scott Haskin RC .01 .05
234 Derrick McKey .01 .05
235 Mark Aguirre .01 .05
236 Terry Dehere RC .01 .05
237 Gary Grant .01 .05
238 Randy Woods .01 .05
239 Sam Bowie .01 .05
240 Elden Campbell .01 .05
241 Nick Van Exel RC .40 1.00
242 Manute Bol .01 .05
243 Brian Shaw .01 .05
244 Vin Baker RC .30 .75
245 Brad Lohaus .01 .05
246 Ken Norman .01 .05
247 Derek Strong RC .01 .05
248 Danny Schayes .01 .05
249 Mike Brown .01 .05
250 Luc Longley .05 .15
251 Isaiah Rider RC .25 .60
252 Kevin Edwards .01 .05
253 Armon Gilliam .01 .05
254 Greg Anthony .01 .05
255 Anthony Bonner .01 .05
256 Tony Campbell .01 .05
257 Hubert Davis .01 .05
258 Litterial Green .01 .05
259 Anfernee Hardaway RC 1.00 2.50
260 Larry Krystkowiak .01 .05
261 Todd Lichti .01 .05
262 Dana Barros .01 .05
263 Greg Graham RC .01 .05
264 Warren Kidd RC .01 .05
265 Moses Malone .10 .30
266 A.C. Green .05 .15
267 Joe Kleine .01 .05
268 Malcolm Mackey RC .01 .05
269 Mark Bryant .01 .05
270 Chris Dudley .01 .05
271 Harvey Grant .01 .05
272 James Robinson RC .01 .05
273 Duane Causwell .01 .05
274 Bobby Hurley RC .05 .15
275 Jim Les .01 .05
276 Willie Anderson .01 .05
277 Terry Cummings .01 .05
278 Vinny Del Negro .01 .05
279 Sleepy Floyd .01 .05
280 Dennis Rodman .25 .60
281 Vincent Askew .01 .05
282 Kendall Gill .05 .15
283 Steve Scheffler .01 .05
284 Detlef Schrempf .05 .15
285 David Benoit .01 .05
286 Tom Chambers .01 .05
287 Felton Spencer .01 .05
288 Rex Chapman .01 .05
289 Kevin Duckworth .01 .05
290 Gheorghe Muresan RC .10 .30
291 Kenny Walker .01 .05
292 Andrew Lang CF .01 .05
Craig Ehlo
293 Dino Radja CF .01 .05
Acie Earl
294 Eddie Johnson CF .01 .05
Hersey Hawkins
295 Toni Kukoc CF .10 .30
Corie Blount
296 Tyrone Hill CF .01 .05
Chris Mills
297 Jamal Mashburn CF .10 .30
Popeye Jones
298 Darnell Mee CF .01 .05
Rodney Rogers
299 Lindsey Hunter CF .05 .15
Allan Houston
300 Chris Webber CF .25 .60
Avery Johnson
301 Sam Cassell CF .10 .30
Mario Elie
302 Derrick McKey CF .01 .05
Antonio Davis
303 Terry Dehere CF .01 .05
Mark Aguirre
304 Nick Van Exel CF .10 .30
George Lynch
305 Harold Miner CF .01 .05
Steve Smith
306 Ken Norman CF .05 .15
Vin Baker
307 Mike Brown CF .05 .15
Isaiah Rider
308 Kevin Edwards CF .01 .05
Rex Walters
309 Hubert Davis CF .01 .05
Anthony Bonner
310 Anfernee Hardaway CF .40 1.00
Larry Krystkowiak
311 Moses Malone CF .10 .30
Shawn Bradley
312 Joe Kleine CF .01 .05
A.C. Green
313 Harvey Grant CF .01 .05
Chris Dudley
314 Bobby Hurley CF .10 .30
Mitch Richmond
315 Sleepy Floyd CF .10 .30
Dennis Rodman
316 Kendall Gill CF .01 .05
Detlef Schrempf
317 Felton Spencer CF .01 .05
Luther Wright
318 Calbert Cheaney CF .01 .05
Kevin Duckworth
319 Karl Malone PC .10 .30
320 Alonzo Mourning PC .10 .30
321 Scottie Pippen PC .20 .50
322 Mark Price PC .01 .05
323 LaPhonso Ellis PC .01 .05
324 Joe Dumars PC .05 .15
325 Chris Mullin PC .05 .15
326 Ron Harper PC .01 .05
327 Glen Rice PC .05 .15
328 Christian Laettner PC .01 .05
329 Kenny Anderson PC .01 .05
330 John Starks PC .01 .05
331 Shaquille O'Neal PC .25 .60
332 Charles Barkley PC .10 .30
333 Clifford Robinson PC .01 .05
334 Clyde Drexler PC .05 .15
335 Mitch Richmond PC .05 .15
336 David Robinson PC .10 .30
337 Shawn Kemp PC .10 .30
338 John Stockton PC .05 .15
339 Checklist 4 .01 .05
340 Checklist 5 .01 .05
341 Checklist 6 .01 .05
DP4 Jim Jackson 1992 .60 1.50
DP17 Doug Christie 1992 .15 .40
NNO Head of the Class .60 1.50
Expired Exchange
NNO HOC Card 15.00 30.00
Shawn Bradley
Calbert Cheaney
Anfernee Hardaway
Jamal Mashburn
Isaiah Rider
Chris Webber

1993-94 SkyBox Premium All-Rookies

Randomly inserted in first series 12-card packs at a rate of one in 36, this standard-size five-card set features top rookies from the 1992-93 season. The design features borderless fronts with color action player cutouts set against metallic game-crowd backgrounds. The player's name appears in gold-foil lettering at the upper left. The white back carries a color player head shot along with career highlights.

COMPLETE SET (5) 7.50 15.00
AR1 Shaquille O'Neal 4.00 10.00
AR2 Alonzo Mourning 1.25 3.00
AR3 Christian Laettner .40 1.00
AR4 Tom Gugliotta .75 2.00
AR5 LaPhonso Ellis .10 .30

1993-94 SkyBox Premium Center Stage

Randomly inserted in first series packs at a rate of one in 12, this 9-card standard-size set showcases some of the best players in the NBA. Card fronts feature are borderless fronts with color action player cutouts placed against black backgrounds. The player's name is centered at the top in prismatic silver-foil lettering. The white back features a color action player cutout and player biography.

COMPLETE SET (9) 15.00 30.00
CS1 Michael Jordan 8.00 20.00
CS2 Shaquille O'Neal 4.00 10.00
CS3 Charles Barkley 1.25 3.00
CS4 John Starks .40 1.00
CS5 Larry Johnson .75 2.00
CS6 Hakeem Olajuwon 1.25 3.00
CS7 Kenny Anderson .40 1.00
CS8 Mahmoud Abdul-Rauf .10 .30
CS9 Clifford Robinson .40 1.00

1993-94 SkyBox Premium Draft Picks

These 26 standard-size cards were random inserts in both first series (Nos. 2, 6-8, 12, 15) and second series (the other 20) 12-card packs. The odds of finding one of these cards are one in every 12 packs. Card No. 26 was scheduled to be LSU center Geert Hammink. Hammink decided to play in Europe and his card was pulled. The fronts feature a color player action cutout set off to one side and superposed upon a ghosted posed color player photo. The player's name, the team that drafted him, and his draft pick number appear at the top. The white back carries the player's name, career highlights, and pre-NBA statistics. The cards are numbered on the back with a "DP" prefix. The set is sequenced in draft order.

COMPLETE SET (26) 15.00 40.00
COMPLETE SERIES 1 (9) 4.00 10.00
COMPLETE SERIES 2 (17) 12.00 30.00
DP1 Chris Webber 6.00 15.00
DP2 Shawn Bradley .60 1.50
DP3 Anfernee Hardaway 5.00 12.00
DP4 Jamal Mashburn 1.50 4.00
DP5 Isaiah Rider 1.25 3.00
DP6 Calbert Cheaney .30 .75
DP7 Bobby Hurley .30 .75
DP8 Vin Baker 1.50 4.00
DP9 Rodney Rogers .60 1.50
DP10 Lindsey Hunter .60 1.50
DP11 Allan Houston 2.50 6.00
DP12 George Lynch .20 .50
DP13 Terry Dehere .20 .50
DP14 Scott Haskin .20 .50
DP15 Doug Edwards .20 .50
DP16 Rex Walters .20 .50
DP17 Greg Graham .20 .50
DP18 Luther Wright .20 .50
DP19 Acie Earl .20 .50
DP20 Scott Burrell .60 1.50
DP21 James Robinson .20 .50
DP22 Chris Mills .60 1.50
DP23 Ervin Johnson .30 .75
DP24 Sam Cassell 2.50 6.00
DP25 Corie Blount .20 .50
DP27 Malcolm Mackey .20 .50

1993-94 SkyBox Premium Dynamic Dunks

These nine standard-size cards were random inserts in second series 12-card packs. The odds of finding one of these cards are one in every 36 packs. The horizontal fronts feature color dunking-action player cutouts superposed upon borderless black and gold metallic backgrounds. The player's name appears in gold lettering at the bottom right. The horizontal back carries another color dunking-action player photo. The player's name and a comment on his dunking style appear in white lettering beneath the photo. The set is sequenced in alphabetical order.

COMPLETE SET (9) 12.50 25.00
D1 Nick Anderson .30 .75
D2 Charles Barkley 1.00 2.50
D3 Robert Horry .30 .75
D4 Michael Jordan 10.00 25.00
D5 Shawn Kemp 1.00 2.50
D6 Anthony Mason .30 .75
D7 Alonzo Mourning 1.00 2.50
D8 Hakeem Olajuwon 1.00 2.50
D9 Dominique Wilkins .60 1.50

1993-94 SkyBox Premium Shaq Talk

The 1993-94 SkyBox Shaq Talk set consists of 10 cards that were randomly inserted in first (cards 1-5) and second series (6-10) 12-card packs. The odds of finding one of these cards are reportedly one in every 36 packs. The standard size cards spotlight Shaquille O'Neal. The fronts feature cut-out action shots of Shaq over a ghosted background. The set title is superimposed across the top of the card in red lettering. The white backs have a ghosted SkyBox Premium logo. At the top is a quote from Shaquille regarding game strategy and below is player critique by a basketball analyst. The cards are numbered on the back with a "Shaq Talk" prefix.

COMPLETE SET (10) 15.00 40.00
COMPLETE SERIES 1 (5) 8.00 20.00
COMPLETE SERIES 2 (5) 8.00 20.00
COMMON SHAQ (1-10) 2.00 5.00

1993-94 SkyBox Premium Showdown Series

These 12 standard-size cards were random inserts in first (cards 1-6) and second series (7-12) 12-card packs. The odds of finding one of these cards are one in every six packs. Each front features a borderless color action photo of the two players involved in the "Showdown." Both players' names appear, one vs. the other, in gold lettering within a metallic black stripe near the bottom. The horizontal white back carries a color player close-up for each player on each side. The players' names appear beneath each photo. Comparative statistics fill in the area between the two player photos.

Card	Low	High
COMPLETE SET (12)	3.00	6.00
COMPLETE SERIES 1 (6)	1.50	3.00
COMPLETE SERIES 2 (6)	1.50	3.00
SS1 Alonzo Mourning Patrick Ewing	.15	.40
SS2 Shaquille O'Neal Patrick Ewing	.50	1.25
SS3 Alonzo Mourning Shaquille O'Neal	.60	1.50
SS4 Hakeem Olajuwon Dikembe Mutombo	.20	.50
SS5 David Robinson Hakeem Olajuwon	.25	.60
SS6 David Robinson Dikembe Mutombo	.20	.50
SS7 Shawn Kemp Karl Malone	.25	.60
SS8 Larry Johnson Charles Barkley	.20	.50
SS9 Dominique Wilkins Scottie Pippen	.20	.50
SS10 Joe Dumars Reggie Miller	.08	.25
SS11 Clyde Drexler Michael Jordan	.75	2.00
SS12 Magic Johnson Larry Bird	.60	1.50

1993-94 SkyBox Premium Thunder and Lightning

Randomly inserted in second series packs at a rate of one in 12 packs, this standard-size nine-card set features players pictured on both sides. On one side a guard would be featured and a forward or center on the other side. Borderless on either side, the color action player cutouts set against metallic backgrounds.

Card	Low	High
COMPLETE SET (9)	7.50	15.00
TL1 Jamal Mashburn Jim Jackson	.60	1.50
TL2 Harold Miner Steve Smith	.20	.50
TL3 Isaiah Rider Micheal Williams	.50	1.25
TL4 Derrick Coleman Kenny Anderson	.25	.60
TL5 Patrick Ewing John Starks	.40	1.00
TL6 Shaquille O'Neal Anfernee Hardaway	4.00	10.00
TL7 Shawn Bradley Jeff Hornacek	.20	.50
TL8 Walt Williams Bobby Hurley	.25	.60
TL9 Dennis Rodman David Robinson	1.25	3.00

1993-94 SkyBox Premium USA Tip-Off

The 13-card 1993-94 SkyBox USA Tip-Off set could be only acquired by sending in the USA Exchange card. The USA Exchange cards were randomly inserted in SkyBox series two packs. The Tip-Off redemption expiration was 6/15/94. It should be noted that Michael Jordan is not part of the set. Card fronts and backs feature studio photos of players in their USA Basketball uniforms.

Card	Low	High
COMPLETE SET (14)	10.00	25.00
1 Steve Smith Magic Johnson	1.50	4.00
2 Larry Johnson Charles Barkley	1.00	2.50
3 Patrick Ewing Alonzo Mourning	1.00	2.50
4 Shawn Kemp Karl Malone	1.25	3.00
5 Chris Mullin Dan Majerle	.30	.75
6 John Stockton Mark Price	.50	1.25
7 Christian Laettner Derrick Coleman	.40	1.00
8 Dominique Wilkins Clyde Drexler	.60	1.50
9 Joe Dumars Scottie Pippen	1.25	3.00
10 David Robinson Shaquille O'Neal	2.50	6.00
11 Reggie Miller Larry Bird	2.00	5.00
12 Tim Hardaway	.50	1.25
13 Isiah Thomas	.30	.75
NNO Expired USA Exchange	.60	1.50

1994-95 SkyBox Premium Promo Sheet

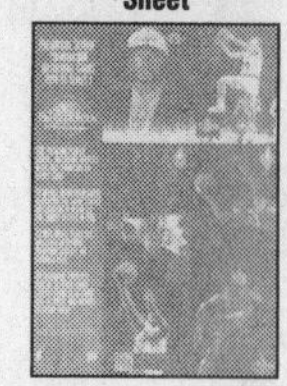

Measuring 7" by 10 1/2", this promo sheet was inserted in Sports Cards magazine to promote the 1994-95 SkyBox second series cards. The perforated sheet features six cards. The cards are priced individually due to numerous sheets torn apart.

Card	Low	High
COMPLETE SET (6)	.75	2.00
255 Glenn Robinson	.40	1.00
295 Scott Skiles	.08	.25
R3 Jamal Mashburn	.15	.40
DP12 Khalid Reeves	.08	.25
SF14 Danny Manning	.15	.40
SU21 Isaiah Rider	.15	.40

1994-95 SkyBox Premium

The 350 standard-size cards that comprise the 1994-95 SkyBox set were issued in two separate series of 200 and 150 cards respectively. Cards were distributed in 12-card hobby and retail packs with a suggested retail price of $1.99 each. Unlike first series packs, each second series pack contained an insert card. Card fronts feature full-bleed action photos with the player's name running down the upper-left corner. The cards are grouped alphabetically within teams and checklisted below alphabetically according to teams. Subsets are NBA on NBC (176-185), Dynamic Duals (186-197), USA Basketball (198), Checklists (298-300), SkySlams (301-313), SkyShots (314-325), SkySwats (326-338), and SkyPilots (339-350). Every first series pack contained an Action and Drama Instant Win game card, offering the chance to play one-on-one with Magic Johnson, or receive a number of other prizes including autographed Hakeem Olajuwon or David Robinson jerseys, a dual autographed Olajuwon/Robinson card or an exclusive Magic Johnson exchange card available only through this promotion. A special three-card panel featuring Johnson, Olajuwon and Robinson was available by mailing in forty first series wrappers before the June 30th, 1995 deadline. Also, three Master Series Preview Press Sheet Exchange cards were randomly seeded into one in every 360 first series packs. The cards were redeemable for 50-card uncut press sheets of SkyBox's new super-premium Emotion cards. The expiration date for the Emotion Press Sheets was March 1, 1995. As a final note, approximately one in every 360 first series retail packs contained an unannounced Hakeem Olajuwon Gold "stealth" card. Approximately one in every 360 second series retail packs contained an unannounced Grant Hill Gold "stealth" card. A standard-size promo card featuring Hakeem Olajuwon was issued to preview the set; a 3 1/2" by 5" jumbo version, distinguished by a gold foil autograph, was issued as a chiptopper in retail boxes. Three 5" by 7" jumbo featuring Grant Hill were also issued as a chiptoppers. Series 1 Sam's retail boxes contained a jumbo Grant Hill Hoops rookie card, Series 2 retail boxes contained a jumbo Grant Hill SkyBox rookie card and Series 2 vintage retail boxes contained a jumbo replica of his Slammin' Universe card. Rookie Cards in this set include Grant Hill, Jason Kidd and Glenn Robinson.

Card	Low	High
COMPLETE SET (350)	15.00	30.00
COMPLETE SERIES 1 (200)	7.50	15.00
COMPLETE SERIES 2 (150)	7.50	15.00
1 Stacey Augmon	.12	.30
2 Mookie Blaylock	.10	.25
3 Doug Edwards	.10	.25
4 Craig Ehlo	.10	.25
5 Adam Keefe	.10	.25
6 Danny Manning	.12	.30
7 Kevin Willis	.10	.25
8 Dee Brown	.10	.25
9 Sherman Douglas	.10	.25
10 Acie Earl	.10	.25
11 Kevin Gamble	.10	.25
12 Xavier McDaniel	.10	.25
13 Dino Radja	.12	.30
14 Muggsy Bogues	.12	.30
15 Scott Burrell	.10	.25
16 Dell Curry	.10	.25
17 LeRon Ellis	.10	.25
18 Hersey Hawkins	.10	.25
19 Larry Johnson	.15	.40
20 Alonzo Mourning	.20	.50
21 B.J. Armstrong	.10	.25
22 Corie Blount	.10	.25
23 Horace Grant	.12	.30
24 Toni Kukoc	.20	.50
25 Luc Longley	.10	.25
26 Scottie Pippen	.30	.75
27 Scott Williams	.10	.25
28 Terrell Brandon	.10	.25
29 Brad Daugherty	.12	.30
30 Tyrone Hill	.10	.25
31 Chris Mills	.10	.25
32 Bobby Phills	.10	.25
33 Mark Price	.15	.40
34 Gerald Wilkins	.10	.25
35 Lucious Harris	.10	.25
36 Jim Jackson	.10	.25
37 Popeye Jones	.10	.25
38 Jamal Mashburn	.15	.40
39 Sean Rooks	.10	.25
40 Mahmoud Abdul-Rauf	.10	.25
41 LaPhonso Ellis	.10	.25
42 Dikembe Mutombo	.15	.40
43 Robert Pack	.10	.25
44 Rodney Rogers	.10	.25
45 Bryant Stith	.10	.25
46 Reggie Williams	.10	.25
47 Joe Dumars	.15	.40
48 Sean Elliott	.15	.40
49 Allan Houston	.15	.40
50 Lindsey Hunter	.10	.25
51 Terry Mills	.10	.25
52 Victor Alexander	.10	.25
53 Tim Hardaway	.15	.40
54 Chris Mullin	.15	.40
55 Billy Owens	.10	.25
56 Latrell Sprewell	.20	.50
57 Chris Webber	.25	.60
58 Sam Cassell	.15	.40
59 Carl Herrera	.10	.25
60 Robert Horry	.15	.40
61 Vernon Maxwell	.10	.25
62 Hakeem Olajuwon	.20	.50
63 Kenny Smith	.12	.30
64 Otis Thorpe	.10	.25
65 Antonio Davis	.10	.25
66 Dale Davis	.10	.25
67 Derrick McKey	.10	.25
68 Reggie Miller	.20	.50
69 Pooh Richardson	.10	.25
70 Rik Smits	.12	.30
71 Haywoode Workman	.10	.25
72 Terry Dehere	.10	.25
73 Harold Ellis	.10	.25
74 Ron Harper	.12	.30
75 Mark Jackson	.15	.40
76 Loy Vaught	.10	.25
77 Dominique Wilkins	.20	.50
78 Elden Campbell	.10	.25
79 Doug Christie	.10	.25
80 Vlade Divac	.15	.40
81 George Lynch	.10	.25
82 Anthony Peeler	.10	.25
83 Sedale Threatt	.10	.25
84 Nick Van Exel	.15	.40
85 Harold Miner	.10	.25
86 Glen Rice	.15	.40
87 John Salley	.10	.25
88 Rony Seikaly	.12	.30
89 Brian Shaw	.10	.25
90 Steve Smith	.12	.30
91 Vin Baker	.15	.40
92 Jon Barry	.10	.25
93 Todd Day	.10	.25
94 Blue Edwards	.10	.25
95 Lee Mayberry	.10	.25
96 Eric Murdock	.10	.25
97 Mike Brown	.10	.25
98 Stacey King	.10	.25
99 Christian Laettner	.12	.30
100 Isaiah Rider	.15	.40
101 Doug West	.10	.25
102 Micheal Williams	.10	.25
103 Kenny Anderson	.12	.30
104 P.J. Brown	.10	.25
105 Derrick Coleman	.12	.30
106 Kevin Edwards	.10	.25
107 Chris Morris	.10	.25
108 Rex Walters	.10	.25
109 Hubert Davis	.10	.25
110 Patrick Ewing	.20	.50
111 Derek Harper	.12	.30
112 Anthony Mason	.10	.25
113 Charles Oakley	.12	.30
114 Charles Smith	.10	.25
115 John Starks	.12	.30
116 Nick Anderson	.10	.25
117 Anfernee Hardaway	.25	.60
118 Shaquille O'Neal	.40	1.00
119 Donald Royal	.10	.25
120 Dennis Scott	.10	.25
121 Scott Skiles	.10	.25
122 Dana Barros	.10	.25
123 Shawn Bradley	.10	.25
124 Johnny Dawkins	.10	.25
125 Greg Graham	.10	.25
126 Clarence Weatherspoon	.10	.25
127 Danny Ainge	.15	.40
128 Charles Barkley	.25	.60
129 Cedric Ceballos	.10	.25
130 A.C. Green	.15	.40
131 Kevin Johnson	.15	.40
132 Dan Majerle	.15	.40
133 Oliver Miller	.10	.25
134 Clyde Drexler	.20	.50
135 Harvey Grant	.10	.25
136 Tracy Murray	.10	.25
137 Terry Porter	.10	.25
138 Clifford Robinson	.10	.25
139 James Robinson	.10	.25
140 Rod Strickland	.10	.25
141 Bobby Hurley	.15	.40
142 Olden Polynice	.10	.25
143 Mitch Richmond	.15	.40
144 Lionel Simmons	.10	.25
145 Wayman Tisdale	.10	.25
146 Spud Webb	.15	.40
147 Walt Williams	.10	.25
148 Willie Anderson	.10	.25
149 Vinny Del Negro	.10	.25
150 Dale Ellis	.10	.25
151 J.R. Reid	.10	.25
152 David Robinson	.25	.60
153 Dennis Rodman	.30	.75
154 Kendall Gill	.10	.25
155 Shawn Kemp	.15	.40
156 Nate McMillan	.10	.25
157 Gary Payton	.15	.40
158 Sam Perkins	.10	.25
159 Ricky Pierce	.10	.25
160 Detlef Schrempf	.15	.40
161 David Benoit	.10	.25
162 Tyrone Corbin	.10	.25
163 Jeff Hornacek	.12	.30
164 Jay Humphries	.10	.25
165 Karl Malone	.20	.50
166 Bryon Russell	.10	.25
167 Felton Spencer	.10	.25
168 John Stockton	.20	.50
169 Michael Adams	.10	.25
170 Rex Chapman	.10	.25
171 Calbert Cheaney	.10	.25
172 Pervis Ellison	.10	.25
173 Tom Gugliotta	.10	.25
174 Don MacLean	.10	.25
175 Gheorghe Muresan	.10	.25
176 Charles Barkley NBC	.25	.60
177 Charles Oakley NBC	.12	.30
178 Hakeem Olajuwon NBC	.20	.50
179 Dikembe Mutombo NBC	.15	.40
180 Scottie Pippen NBC	.30	.75
181 Sam Cassell NBC	.15	.40
182 Karl Malone NBC	.20	.50
183 Reggie Miller PO	.20	.50
184 Patrick Ewing NBC	.20	.50
185 Vernon Maxwell NBC	.10	.25
186 Anfernee Hardaway DD Steve Smith	.25	.60
187 Chris Webber DD Shaquille O'Neal	.40	1.00
188 Jamal Mashburn DD Rodney Rogers	.15	.40
189 Toni Kukoc DD Dino Radja	.20	.50
190 Lindsey Hunter DD Kenny Anderson	.12	.30
191 Latrell Sprewell DD Jim Jackson	.20	.50
192 Clarence Weatherspoon Vin Baker DD	.15	.40
193 Calbert Cheaney DD Chris Mills	.10	.25
194 Isaiah Rider DD Robert Horry	.15	.40
195 Sam Cassell DD Nick Van Exel	.15	.40
196 Gheorghe Muresan DD Shawn Bradley	.10	.25
197 LaPhonso Ellis DD Tom Gugliotta	.10	.25
198 USA Basketball Card	.10	.25
199 Checklist	.10	.25
200 Checklist	.10	.25
201 Sergei Bazarevich RC	.15	.40
202 Tyrone Corbin	.10	.25
203 Grant Long	.10	.25
204 Ken Norman	.10	.25
205 Steve Smith	.12	.30
206 Blue Edwards	.10	.25
207 Greg Minor RC	.15	.40
208 Eric Montross RC	.15	.40
209 Dominique Wilkins	.20	.50
210 Michael Adams	.10	.25
211 Kenny Gattison	.10	.25
212 Darrin Hancock	.15	.40
213 Robert Parish	.15	.40
214 Ron Harper	.12	.30
215 Steve Kerr	.12	.30
216 Will Perdue	.10	.25
217 Dickey Simpkins RC	.15	.40
218 John Battle	.10	.25
219 Michael Cage	.10	.25
220 Tony Dumas RC	.15	.40
221 Jason Kidd RC	.75	2.00
222 Roy Tarpley	.10	.25
223 Dale Ellis	.10	.25
224 Jalen Rose RC	.40	1.00
225 Bill Curley RC	.15	.40
226 Grant Hill RC	.75	2.00
227 Oliver Miller	.10	.25
228 Mark West	.10	.25
229 Tom Gugliotta	.10	.25
230 Ricky Pierce	.10	.25
231 Carlos Rogers RC	.15	.40
232 Clifford Rozier RC	.15	.40
233 Rony Seikaly	.12	.30
234 Tim Breaux	.10	.25
235 Duane Ferrell	.10	.25
236 Mark Jackson	.15	.40
237 Byron Scott	.12	.30
238 John Williams	.10	.25
239 Lamond Murray RC	.15	.40
240 Eric Piatkowski RC	.20	.50
241 Pooh Richardson	.10	.25
242 Malik Sealy	.10	.25
243 Cedric Ceballos	.10	.25
244 Eddie Jones RC	.50	1.25
245 Anthony Miller RC	.15	.40
246 Tony Smith	.10	.25
247 Kevin Gamble	.10	.25
248 Brad Lohaus	.10	.25
249 Billy Owens	.10	.25
250 Khalid Reeves RC	.15	.40
251 Kevin Willis	.10	.25
252 Eric Mobley RC	.15	.40
253 Johnny Newman	.10	.25
254 Ed Pinckney	.10	.25
255 Glenn Robinson RC	.30	.75
256 Howard Eisley	.15	.40
257 Donyell Marshall RC	.15	.40
258 Yinka Dare RC	.15	.40
259 Sean Higgins	.10	.25
260 Jayson Williams	.10	.25
261 Charlie Ward RC	.15	.40
262 Monty Williams RC	.15	.40
263 Horace Grant	.12	.30
264 Brian Shaw	.10	.25
265 Brooks Thompson RC	.15	.40
266 Derrick Alston RC	.15	.40
267 B.J. Tyler RC	.15	.40
268 Scott Williams	.10	.25
269 Sharone Wright RC	.15	.40
270 Antonio Lang RC	.15	.40
271 Danny Manning	.12	.30
272 Wesley Person RC	.15	.40
273 Trevor Ruffin RC	.15	.40
274 Wayman Tisdale	.10	.25
275 Jerome Kersey	.10	.25
276 Aaron McKie RC	.15	.40
277 Frank Brickowski	.10	.25
278 Brian Grant RC	.25	.60
279 Michael Smith RC	.15	.40
280 Terry Cummings	.15	.40
281 Sean Elliott	.15	.40
282 Avery Johnson	.12	.30
283 Moses Malone	.15	.40
284 Chuck Person	.12	.30
285 Vincent Askew	.10	.25
286 Bill Cartwright	.12	.30
287 Sarunas Marciulionis	.10	.25
288 Dontonio Wingfield RC	.15	.40
289 Jay Humphries	.10	.25
290 Adam Keefe	.10	.25
291 Jamie Watson RC	.15	.40
292 Kevin Duckworth	.10	.25
293 Juwan Howard RC	.25	.60
294 Jim McIlvaine RC	.15	.40
295 Scott Skiles	.10	.25
296 Anthony Tucker RC	.15	.40
297 Chris Webber	.25	.60
298 Checklist 201-265	.10	.25
299 Checklist 266-345	.10	.25
300 Checklist 346-350/Inserts	.10	.25
301 Vin Baker SSL	.15	.40
302 Charles Barkley SSL	.25	.60
303 Derrick Coleman SSL	.12	.30
304 Clyde Drexler SSL	.20	.50
305 LaPhonso Ellis SSL	.10	.25
306 Larry Johnson SSL	.15	.40
307 Shawn Kemp SSL	.15	.40
308 Karl Malone SSL	.20	.50
309 Jamal Mashburn SSL	.15	.40
310 Scottie Pippen SSL	.30	.75
311 Dominique Wilkins SSL	.20	.50
312 Walt Williams SSL	.10	.25
313 Sharone Wright SSL	.10	.25
314 B.J. Armstrong SSH	.10	.25
315 Joe Dumars SSH	.15	.40
316 Tony Dumas SSH	.10	.25
317 Tim Hardaway SSH	.15	.40
318 Toni Kukoc SSH	.20	.50
319 Danny Manning SSH	.12	.30
320 Reggie Miller SSH	.20	.50
321 Chris Mullin SSH	.15	.40
322 Wesley Person SSH	.10	.25
323 John Starks SSH	.12	.30
324 John Stockton SSH	.20	.50
325 Clarence Weatherspoon SSH	.10	.25
326 Shawn Bradley SSW	.10	.25
327 Vlade Divac SSW	.15	.40
328 Patrick Ewing SSW	.20	.50
329 Christian Laettner SSW	.12	.30
330 Eric Montross SSW	.10	.25
331 Gheorghe Muresan SSW	.10	.25
332 Dikembe Mutombo SSW	.15	.40
333 Hakeem Olajuwon SSW	.20	.50
334 Robert Parish SSW	.15	.40
335 David Robinson SSW	.25	.60
336 Dennis Rodman SSW	.30	.75
337 Rony Seikaly SSW	.12	.30
338 Rik Smits SSW	.12	.30
339 Kenny Anderson SPI	.12	.30
340 Dee Brown SPI	.10	.25
341 Bobby Hurley SPI	.15	.40
342 Kevin Johnson SPI	.15	.40
343 Jason Kidd SPI	.50	1.25
344 Gary Payton SPI	.15	.40
345 Mark Price SPI	.15	.40
346 Khalid Reeves SPI	.10	.25
347 Jalen Rose SPI	.25	.60
348 Latrell Sprewell SPI	.20	.50
349 B.J. Tyler SPI	.10	.25
350 Charlie Ward SPI	.10	.25
PR Hakeem Olajuwon PROMO	.40	1.00
PR Hakeem Olajuwon JUMBO PROMO	.40	1.00
GHO Grant Hill Gold	5.00	12.00
NNO Grant Hill Hoops JUMBO	2.50	6.00
NNO Hakeem Olajuwon Gold	4.00	10.00
NNO Grant Hill SkyBox JUMBO	2.50	6.00
NNO Grant Hill Slammin' Univ. JUMBO	2.50	6.00
NNO Emotion Sheet A	15.00	30.00
NNO Emotion Sheet B	15.00	30.00
NNO Emotion Exchange A Expired	.40	1.00
NNO Emotion Exchange B Expired	.40	1.00
NNO Emotion Exchange C Expired	.40	1.00
NNO 3rd Prize Game Card Expired	.08	.25
NNO Hakeem Olajuwon David Robinson AU	150.00	300.00
NNO Magic Johnson Exchange Card	2.00	5.00
NNO 3 Card Panel Exchange Magic Johnson Hakeem Olajuwon David Robinson	1.50	4.00

1994-95 SkyBox Premium Center Stage

Randomly inserted in all first series packs at a rate of one in 72, cards from this nine-card standard-size set feature a selection of the game's top stars. Card fronts feature full-color player photos over etched-foil backgrounds.

Card	Low	High
COMPLETE SET (9)	20.00	50.00
CS1 Hakeem Olajuwon	2.50	6.00
CS2 Shaquille O'Neal	6.00	15.00
CS3 Anfernee Hardaway	3.00	8.00
CS4 Chris Webber	3.00	8.00
CS5 Scottie Pippen	4.00	10.00
CS6 David Robinson	3.00	8.00
CS7 Latrell Sprewell	2.50	6.00
CS8 Charles Barkley	3.00	8.00
CS9 Alonzo Mourning	2.50	6.00

1994-95 SkyBox Premium Draft Picks

These 27 standard-size cards were random inserts in both first series (Nos. 2, 9, 10, 14 and 23) and second series (the other 22) packs. The first series cards were randomly seeded into one in every 45 packs. The second series cards were randomly seeded into one in every 18 packs. The set features all twenty-seven first round draft selections from the 1994 NBA draft. The foil card fronts feature a head shot of each player. The cards are numbered with a "DP" prefix. The set is sequenced in draft order.

Card	Low	High
COMPLETE SET (27)	20.00	50.00
COMPLETE SERIES 1 (5)	10.00	20.00
COMPLETE SERIES 2 (22)	12.00	30.00
DP1 Glenn Robinson	2.50	6.00
DP2 Jason Kidd	6.00	15.00
DP3 Grant Hill	4.00	10.00
DP4 Donyell Marshall	.60	1.50
DP5 Juwan Howard	1.00	2.50
DP6 Sharone Wright	.60	1.50
DP7 Lamond Murray	.60	1.50
DP8 Brian Grant	1.00	2.50
DP9 Eric Montross	.60	1.50
DP10 Eddie Jones	3.00	8.00
DP11 Carlos Rogers	.60	1.50
DP12 Khalid Reeves	.60	1.50
DP13 Jalen Rose	1.50	4.00
DP14 Yinka Dare	.60	1.50
DP15 Eric Piatkowski	.75	2.00
DP16 Clifford Rozier	.60	1.50
DP17 Aaron McKie	.60	1.50
DP18 Eric Mobley	.60	1.50
DP19 Tony Dumas	.60	1.50
DP20 B.J. Tyler	.60	1.50
DP21 Dickey Simpkins	.60	1.50
DP22 Bill Curley	.60	1.50
DP23 Wesley Person	.60	1.50
DP24 Monty Williams	.60	1.50
DP25 Greg Minor	.60	1.50
DP26 Charlie Ward	.60	1.50
DP27 Brooks Thompson	.60	1.50

1994-95 SkyBox Premium Grant Hill

Randomly inserted exclusively into one in every 36 second series hobby packs, cards from this 5-card standard-size set highlight the Detroit rookie, and SkyBox spokesperson, in various action shots. Full-color photos are set against a psychedelic background.

Card	Low	High
COMPLETE SET (5)	10.00	25.00
COMMON HILL (GH1-GH5)	3.00	8.00

1994-95 SkyBox Premium Head of the Class

This 6-card standard-size set was available exclusively by mailing in the SkyBox Head of the Class exchange card before the June 15th, 1995 deadline. The Head of the Class exchange card was randomly inserted into one in every 480 first series packs. SkyBox selected six top rookies from the 1994-95 NBA season to be featured in the set. Card fronts feature a full-color player photo against a computer generated textured background. The set is sequenced in alphabetical order.

Card	Low	High
COMPLETE SET (6)	8.00	20.00
1 Grant Hill	4.00	10.00
2 Juwan Howard	1.25	3.00
3 Jason Kidd	4.00	10.00
4 Donyell Marshall	.75	2.00
5 Glenn Robinson	1.50	4.00
6 Sharone Wright	.75	2.00
NNO Checklist Card	.40	1.00
NNO HOC Exchange Card Expired	.75	2.00

1994-95 SkyBox Premium Ragin' Rookies Promos

These standard-size promo cards were issued to preview the 1994-95 SkyBox Premium series. All the cards belong to the Ragin' Rookies insert set. The fronts display full-bleed color action photos with frayed white edges. Across the top of the photo, the player's last name appears in red foil beneath "Ragin' Rookies" in white. The horizontal backs have a player profile on the left portion and a second color player photo on the right. The top left corner is cut off to mark the promotional nature of these cards. The cards are numbered on the back.

Card	Low	High
COMPLETE SET (7)	1.50	4.00
RR8 Lindsey Hunter	.30	.75
RR10 Sam Cassell	.50	1.25
RR13 Nick Van Exel	.50	1.25
RR15 Vin Baker	.50	1.25
RR16 Isaiah Rider	.50	1.25
RR19 Shawn Bradley	.30	.75
RR23 Bryon Russell	.30	.75

1994-95 SkyBox Premium Ragin' Rookies

Randomly inserted into all first series packs at a rate of one in five, cards from this 24-card set feature a selection of the top rookies from the 1993 NBA draft. Full-color action photos feature a scratched border design.

Card	Low	High
COMPLETE SET (24)	10.00	25.00
RR1 Dino Radja	.75	2.00
RR2 Corie Blount	.60	1.50
RR3 Toni Kukoc	1.25	3.00
RR4 Chris Mills	.60	1.50
RR5 Jamal Mashburn	1.00	2.50
RR6 Rodney Rogers	.60	1.50
RR7 Allan Houston	1.00	2.50
RR8 Lindsey Hunter	.60	1.50
RR9 Chris Webber	1.50	4.00
RR10 Sam Cassell	1.00	2.50
RR11 Antonio Davis	.60	1.50
RR12 Terry Dehere	.60	1.50
RR13 Nick Van Exel	1.00	2.50
RR14 George Lynch	.60	1.50
RR15 Vin Baker	1.00	2.50
RR16 Isaiah Rider	1.00	2.50
RR17 P.J. Brown	.60	1.50
RR18 Anfernee Hardaway	1.50	4.00
RR19 Shawn Bradley	.60	1.50
RR20 James Robinson	.60	1.50
RR21 Bobby Hurley	1.00	2.50
RR22 Ervin Johnson	.60	1.50
RR23 Bryon Russell	.60	1.50
RR24 Calbert Cheaney	.60	1.50

1994-95 SkyBox Premium Revolution

Randomly inserted into second series packs at a rate of one in 72, cards from this 10-card standard-size set feature a selection of NBA stars. The horizontal fronts feature full-color player photos against etched-foil backgrounds featuring team colors. The set is sequenced in alphabetical order.

Card	Low	High
COMPLETE SET (10)	20.00	50.
R1 Patrick Ewing	2.50	6.
R2 Grant Hill	5.00	12.
R3 Jamal Mashburn	2.00	5.
R4 Alonzo Mourning	2.50	6.
R5 Dikembe Mutombo	2.00	5.
R6 Shaquille O'Neal	5.00	12.
R7 Scottie Pippen	4.00	10.
R8 Glenn Robinson	2.00	5.
R9 Latrell Sprewell	2.50	6.
R10 Chris Webber	3.00	8.

1994-95 SkyBox Premium SkyTech Force

Randomly inserted into second series packs at a rate one in two, cards from this 30-card standard-size se feature a selection of the NBA's top stars. Card fronts feature foil backgrounds. The player's name is in gol foil on the bottom while the words "SkyTech Force" i printed vertically on the right. The backs contain som career information as well as a color action photo. Th cards are numbered in the upper right with an "SF" prefix and are sequenced in alphabetical order.

Card	Low	High
COMPLETE SET (30)	4.00	10.0
SF1 Kenny Anderson	.20	.5
SF2 B.J. Armstrong	.15	.4
SF3 Charles Barkley	.40	1.0
SF4 Shawn Bradley	.15	.4
SF5 LaPhonso Ellis	.15	.4
SF6 Anfernee Hardaway	.40	1.0
SF7 Bobby Hurley	.25	.6
SF8 Kevin Johnson	.25	.6
SF9 Larry Johnson	.25	.6
SF10 Shawn Kemp	.25	.6
SF11 Jason Kidd	1.25	3.0
SF12 Christian Laettner	.20	.5
SF13 Karl Malone	.30	.7
SF14 Danny Manning	.20	.5
SF15 Chris Mills	.15	.4
SF16 Chris Mullin	.25	.6
SF17 Lamond Murray	.25	.6
SF18 Charles Oakley	.20	.5
SF19 Hakeem Olajuwon	.30	.7
SF20 Gary Payton	.25	.6
SF21 Mark Price	.25	.6
SF22 Dino Radja	.20	.5
SF23 Mitch Richmond	.25	.6
SF24 Clifford Robinson	.15	.4
SF25 David Robinson	.40	1.0
SF26 Dennis Rodman	.50	1.2
SF27 Dickey Simpkins	.25	.6
SF28 John Starks	.20	.5
SF29 John Stockton	.30	.7
SF30 Charlie Ward	.25	.6

1994-95 SkyBox Premium Slammin' Universe

Randomly inserted into second series packs at a rate one in two, cards from this 30-card standard-size set feature a selection of the NBA's top dunkers. The horizontal card fronts feature full-color player action shots against a foil "galaxy" background. The cards a numbered with a "SU" prefix and are sequenced in alphabetical order.

Card	Low	High
COMPLETE SET (30)	4.00	10.0
SU1 Vin Baker	.25	.6
SU2 Dee Brown	.15	.4
SU3 Derrick Coleman	.20	.5
SU4 Clyde Drexler	.30	.7
SU5 Joe Dumars	.25	.6
SU6 Tony Dumas	.25	.6
SU7 Patrick Ewing	.30	.7
SU8 Horace Grant	.20	.5
SU9 Tom Gugliotta	.15	.4
SU10 Grant Hill	1.25	3.0
SU11 Jim Jackson	.15	.4
SU12 Toni Kukoc	.30	.7
SU13 Donyell Marshall	.25	.6
SU14 Jamal Mashburn	.25	.6
SU15 Reggie Miller	.30	.7
SU16 Eric Montross	.25	.6
SU17 Alonzo Mourning	.30	.7
SU18 Dikembe Mutombo	.25	.6
SU19 Shaquille O'Neal	.60	1.5
SU20 Glen Rice	.25	.6
SU21 Isaiah Rider	.25	.6
SU22 Glenn Robinson	.50	1.2
SU23 Jalen Rose	.60	1.5
SU24 Detlef Schrempf	.25	.6
SU25 Steve Smith	.20	.5
SU26 Latrell Sprewell	.30	.7
SU27 Rod Strickland	.15	.4
SU28 B.J. Tyler	.25	.6
SU29 Nick Van Exel	.25	.6
SU30 Dominique Wilkins	.30	.7

1995-96 SkyBox Premium Prom Sheet

Measuring 8" by 10 1/2", this promo sheet was issue to preview the second series of the 1995-96 SkyBox set. The perforated sheet consists of eight cards, with an advertisement in the center of the sheet. The cards are identical their regular issue counterparts includin the card numbers. The cards are priced individually due to numerous sheets torn apart.

Card	Low	High
COMPLETE SET (8)	3.00	8.0
153 Dana Barros	.30	.7
182 Alonzo Mourning	.60	1.5
229 Brent Barry	.40	1.0

erry Stackhouse .75 2.00
im Hardaway .50 1.25
irant Hill .75 2.00
lyde Drexler .60 1.50
Michael Finley .75 2.00

1995-96 SkyBox Premium

1995-96 SkyBox set was issued in two series of and 151 standard-size cards, for a total of 301. cards were issued in 12-card regular packs at a ested retail price of $1.99, and jumbo packs of 20 sold at $3.99. Full-bleed fronts feature a full-color n player cutout against a one-color background of r blue, cyan, yellow or magenta. A computer- rated flame streaks out from the basketball the er is holding. Backs feature a one-color player n shot in a vertical strip on the right side of the s and a full color close-up shot at the bottom left. top right features a player biography and career . The set is arranged and checklisted below abetically according to teams by city. Subsets are t and Center (125-133), Turning Point (134-142), nsion Teams (143-148), Rookies (219-248), or Roll (249-298) and Checklists (299-300). Key kie Cards include Michael Finley, Kevin Garnett, nio McDyess, Joe Smith, Jerry Stackhouse and on Stoudamire. A 5" by 7" jumbo featuring Grant card #226) was issued as a chiptopper in retail s. In addition, parallel lenticular versions of the t Hill and Jerry Stackhouse Meltdown inserts were able through a second series wrapper offer. Both s are unnumbered and feature nifty moving grounds in which a steel wall turns to goo as vorks explode. Collectors had to send in two ppers along with a check or money order for $9.99 card before the December 31st, 1996 deadline.

MPLETE SET (301) 17.50 35.00
MPLETE SERIES 1 (150) 7.50 15.00
MPLETE SERIES 2 (151) 10.00 20.00
acey Augmon .15 .40
ookie Blaylock .12 .30
ant Long .12 .30
eve Smith .15 .40
e Brown .12 .30
erman Douglas .12 .30
ic Montross .12 .30
no Radja .15 .40
ominique Wilkins .25 .60
Muggsy Bogues .15 .40
Scott Burrell .12 .30
Dell Curry .12 .30
Larry Johnson .20 .50
Alonzo Mourning .25 .60
Michael Jordan UER 1.50 4.00
areer block total is wrong
Steve Kerr .15 .40
Toni Kukoc .20 .50
Scottie Pippen .30 .75
Terrell Brandon .12 .30
Tyrone Hill .12 .30
Chris Mills .12 .30
Mark Price .20 .50
John Williams .12 .30
Tony Dumas .12 .30
Jim Jackson .12 .30
Popeye Jones .12 .30
Jason Kidd .30 .75
Jamal Mashburn .20 .50
LaPhonso Ellis .12 .30
Dikembe Mutombo .20 .50
Robert Pack .12 .30
Jalen Rose .25 .60
Bryant Stith .12 .30
Joe Dumars .20 .50
Grant Hill .30 .75
Allan Houston .15 .40
Lindsey Hunter .12 .30
Chris Gatling .12 .30
Tim Hardaway .20 .50
Donyell Marshall .12 .30
Chris Mullin .20 .50
Carlos Rogers .12 .30
Latrell Sprewell .20 .50
Sam Cassell .20 .50
Clyde Drexler .25 .60
Robert Horry .15 .40
Hakeem Olajuwon .25 .60
Kenny Smith .15 .40
Dale Davis .12 .30
Mark Jackson .20 .50
Reggie Miller .25 .60
Rik Smits .15 .40
Lamond Murray .12 .30
Eric Piatkowski .15 .40
Pooh Richardson .12 .30
Rodney Rogers .12 .30
Loy Vaught .12 .30
Elden Campbell .12 .30
Cedric Ceballos .12 .30
Vlade Divac .20 .50
Eddie Jones .25 .60
Anthony Peeler .12 .30
Nick Van Exel .20 .50
Bimbo Coles .12 .30
Billy Owens .12 .30
Khalid Reeves .12 .30
Glen Rice .20 .50
Kevin Willis .12 .30
Vin Baker .15 .40
Todd Day .12 .30
Eric Murdock .12 .30
Glenn Robinson .20 .50
Tom Gugliotta .12 .30
Christian Laettner .15 .40
Isaiah Rider .20 .50
Doug West .12 .30
Kenny Anderson .15 .40
P.J. Brown .12 .30
Derrick Coleman .15 .40
Armon Gilliam .12 .30
Patrick Ewing .25 .60
Derek Harper .15 .40
Anthony Mason .12 .30
84 Charles Oakley .15 .40
85 John Starks .15 .40
86 Nick Anderson .12 .30
87 Horace Grant .15 .40
88 Anfernee Hardaway .30 .75
89 Shaquille O'Neal .50 1.25
90 Dana Barros .12 .30
91 Shawn Bradley .12 .30
92 Clarence Weatherspoon .12 .30
93 Sharone Wright .12 .30
94 Charles Barkley .30 .75
95 Kevin Johnson .20 .50
96 Dan Majerle .20 .50
97 Danny Manning .15 .40
98 Wesley Person .12 .30
99 Clifford Robinson .12 .30
100 Rod Strickland .12 .30
101 Otis Thorpe .12 .30
102 Buck Williams .12 .30
103 Brian Grant .15 .40
104 Olden Polynice .12 .30
105 Mitch Richmond .20 .50
106 Walt Williams .12 .30
107 Vinny Del Negro .12 .30
108 Sean Elliott .20 .50
109 Avery Johnson .15 .40
110 David Robinson .30 .75
111 Dennis Rodman .40 1.00
112 Shawn Kemp .20 .50
113 Gary Payton .20 .50
114 Sam Perkins .12 .30
115 Detlef Schrempf .20 .50
116 David Benoit .12 .30
117 Jeff Hornacek .15 .40
118 Karl Malone .25 .60
119 John Stockton .25 .60
120 Calbert Cheaney .12 .30
121 Juwan Howard .20 .50
122 Don MacLean .12 .30
123 Gheorghe Muresan .12 .30
124 Chris Webber .25 .60
125 Robert Horry FC .15 .40
126 Mark Jackson FC .20 .50
127 Steve Smith FC .15 .40
128 Lamond Murray FC .12 .30
129 Christian Laettner FC .15 .40
130 Kenny Anderson FC .15 .40
131 Anthony Mason FC .12 .30
132 Kevin Johnson FC .20 .50
133 Jeff Hornacek FC .15 .40
134 Larry Johnson TP .20 .50
135 Popeye Jones TP .12 .30
136 Allan Houston TP .15 .40
137 Chris Gatling TP .12 .30
138 Sam Cassell TP .20 .50
139 Anthony Peeler TP .12 .30
140 Vin Baker TP .15 .40
141 Dana Barros TP .12 .30
142 Gheorghe Muresan TP .12 .30
143 Toronto Raptors .12 .30
144 Vancouver Grizzlies .12 .30
145 Glen Rice EXP .20 .50
Muggsy Bogues EXP
146 Nick Anderson EXP .15 .40
Christian Laettner EXP
147 John Salley TF .12 .30
148 Greg Anthony TF .12 .30
149 Checklist #1 .12 .30
150 Checklist #2 .12 .30
151 Craig Ehlo .12 .30
152 Spud Webb .20 .50
153 Dana Barros .12 .30
154 Rick Fox .12 .30
155 Kendall Gill .12 .30
156 Khalid Reeves .12 .30
157 Glen Rice .20 .50
158 Luc Longley .12 .30
159 Dennis Rodman .40 1.00
160 Dickey Simpkins .12 .30
161 Danny Ferry .12 .30
162 Dan Majerle .20 .50
163 Bobby Phills .12 .30
164 Lucious Harris .12 .30
165 George McCloud .12 .30
166 Mahmoud Abdul-Rauf .12 .30
167 Don MacLean .12 .30
168 Reggie Williams .12 .30
169 Terry Mills .12 .30
170 Otis Thorpe .12 .30
171 B.J. Armstrong .12 .30
172 Rony Seikaly .15 .40
173 Chucky Brown .12 .30
174 Mario Elie .12 .30
175 Antonio Davis .12 .30
176 Ricky Pierce .12 .30
177 Terry Dehere .12 .30
178 Rodney Rogers .12 .30
179 Malik Sealy .12 .30
180 Brian Williams .12 .30
181 Sedale Threatt .12 .30
182 Alonzo Mourning .25 .60
183 Lee Mayberry .12 .30
184 Sean Rooks .12 .30
185 Shawn Bradley .12 .30
186 Kevin Edwards .12 .30
187 Hubert Davis .12 .30
188 Charles Smith .12 .30
189 Charlie Ward .12 .30
190 Dennis Scott .12 .30
191 Brian Shaw .12 .30
192 Derrick Coleman .15 .40
193 Richard Dumas .12 .30
194 Vernon Maxwell .12 .30
195 A.C. Green .20 .50
196 Elliot Perry .12 .30
197 John Williams .12 .30
198 Aaron McKie .12 .30
199 Bobby Hurley .20 .50
200 Michael Smith UER .12 .30
front Mike Smith
201 J.R. Reid .12 .30
202 Hersey Hawkins .12 .30
203 Willie Anderson .12 .30
204 Oliver Miller .12 .30
205 Tracy Murray .12 .30
206 Alvin Robertson .12 .30
207 Carlos Rogers UER .12 .30
Card says Rodney Rogers on front with picture
208 John Salley .12 .30
209 Zan Tabak .12 .30
210 Adam Keefe .12 .30
211 Chris Morris .12 .30
212 Greg Anthony .12 .30
213 Blue Edwards .12 .30
214 Kenny Gattison .12 .30
215 Antonio Harvey .12 .30
216 Chris King .12 .30
217 Byron Scott .15 .40
218 Robert Pack .12 .30
219 Alan Henderson RC .20 .50
220 Eric Williams RC .20 .50
221 George Zidek RC .20 .50
222 Jason Caffey RC .20 .50
223 Bob Sura RC .20 .50
224 Cherokee Parks RC .20 .50
225 Antonio McDyess RC .50 1.25
226 Theo Ratliff RC .30 .75
227 Joe Smith RC .40 1.00
228 Travis Best RC .20 .50
229 Brent Barry RC .30 .75
230 Sasha Danilovic RC .20 .50
231 Kurt Thomas RC .20 .50
232 Shawn Respert RC .20 .50
233 Kevin Garnett RC 1.50 4.00
234 Ed O'Bannon RC .20 .50
235 Jerry Stackhouse RC .60 1.50
236 Michael Finley RC .60 1.50
237 Mario Bennett RC .20 .50
238 Randolph Childress RC .20 .50
239 Arvydas Sabonis RC .40 1.00
240 Gary Trent RC .20 .50
241 Tyus Edney RC .20 .50
242 Corliss Williamson RC .20 .50
243 Cory Alexander RC .20 .50
244 Damon Stoudamire RC .50 1.25
245 Greg Ostertag RC .20 .50
246 Lawrence Moten RC .20 .50
247 Bryant Reeves RC .20 .50
248 Rasheed Wallace RC .60 1.50
249 Muggsy Bogues HR .15 .40
250 Dell Curry HR .12 .30
251 Scottie Pippen HR .30 .75
252 Danny Ferry HR .12 .30
253 Mahmoud Abdul-Rauf HR .12 .30
254 Joe Dumars HR .20 .50
255 Tim Hardaway HR .20 .50
256 Chris Mullin HR .20 .50
257 Hakeem Olajuwon HR .25 .60
258 Kenny Smith HR .15 .40
259 Reggie Miller HR .25 .60
260 Rik Smits HR .15 .40
261 Vlade Divac HR .20 .50
262 Doug West HR .12 .30
263 Patrick Ewing HR .25 .60
264 Charles Oakley HR .15 .40
265 Nick Anderson HR .12 .30
266 Dennis Scott HR .12 .30
267 Jeff Turner HR .12 .30
268 Charles Barkley HR .30 .75
269 Kevin Johnson HR .20 .50
270 Clifford Robinson HR .12 .30
271 Buck Williams HR .12 .30
272 Lionel Simmons HR .12 .30
273 David Robinson HR .30 .75
274 Gary Payton HR .20 .50
275 Karl Malone HR .25 .60
276 John Stockton HR .25 .60
277 Steve Smith ELE .15 .40
278 Michael Jordan ELE 1.50 4.00
279 Jim Jackson ELE .12 .30
280 Jason Kidd ELE .30 .75
281 Jamal Mashburn ELE .20 .50
282 Dikembe Mutombo ELE .20 .50
283 Grant Hill ELE .30 .75
284 Tim Hardaway ELE .20 .50
285 Clyde Drexler ELE .25 .60
286 Cedric Ceballos ELE .12 .30
287 Gary Payton ELE .20 .50
288 Billy Owens ELE .12 .30
289 Vin Baker ELE .15 .40
290 Glenn Robinson ELE .20 .50
291 Kenny Anderson ELE .15 .40
292 Anfernee Hardaway ELE .30 .75
293 Shaquille O'Neal ELE .50 1.25
294 Charles Barkley ELE .30 .75
295 Rod Strickland ELE .12 .30
296 Mitch Richmond ELE .20 .50
297 Juwan Howard ELE .20 .50
298 Chris Webber ELE .25 .60
299 Checklist #1 .12 .30
300 Checklist #2 .12 .30
301 Magic Johnson .50 1.25
PR Grant Hill JUMBO 2.50 6.00
NNO Grant Hill 10.00 25.00
Meltdown
NNO Jerry Stackhouse 12.50 30.00
Meltdown

1995-96 SkyBox Premium Atomic

Randomly inserted in all series one packs at a rate of one in four regular packs and one in three jumbo packs, this 15-card standard-size set highlights the play of the NBA's power men. Borderless fronts have etched foil backgrounds with a full-color action player cutout. An atomic symbol surrounds the ball the player is holding and the player's name, team and position are stamped in gold foil at the middle left of the card. Skybox's "Atomic" logo is printed at the bottom left. Backs are numbered with the prefix "A" and have a faded, one color action shot of the player and continues with the basketball as the center of an atomic symbol. Player biography and an inset color photo are set against red bars on the bottom half of the card.

COMPLETE SET (15) 2.50 6.00
A1 Eric Montross .25 .60
A2 Charles Oakley .30 .75
A3 Rik Smits .30 .75
A4 Vlade Divac .40 1.00
A5 Buck Williams .25 .60
A6 Vin Baker .30 .75
A7 Glenn Robinson .40 1.00
A8 Isaiah Rider .40 1.00
A9 Derrick Coleman .30 .75
A10 Clarence Weatherspoon .25 .60
A11 Sharone Wright .25 .60
A12 Brian Grant .30 .75
A13 Jim Jackson .25 .60
A14 Clyde Drexler .50 1.25
A15 Anfernee Hardaway .60 1.50

1995-96 SkyBox Premium Close-Ups

A short player history is the focus of this nine-card standard-size set that features both established players and up-and-coming rookies. The cards were randomly inserted in all series one packs at a rate of one in nine regular packs and one in six jumbo packs. They were also inserted one per special series one Wal-Mart retail pack. Borderless fronts feature an extreme color close-up of the player's face set against an etched foil background. The player's first name is stamped in gold foil script against his last name which is printed larger and in full block letters. The SkyBox logo and "Close-Up" are stamped in gold foil at the bottom left of the card. The backs feature a stretched one-color player photo on the right side of the card. The left side has the player's name, team logo and a short player history printed in black type. The set is sequenced in alphabetical order by team.

COMPLETE SET (9) 10.00 20.00
C1 Scottie Pippen 2.00 5.00
C2 Grant Hill 2.00 5.00
C3 Clyde Drexler 1.50 4.00
C4 Nick Van Exel 1.25 3.00
C5 Tom Gugliotta .75 2.00
C6 Patrick Ewing 1.50 4.00
C7 Charles Barkley 2.00 5.00
C8 Karl Malone 1.50 4.00
C9 Juwan Howard 1.25 3.00

1995-96 SkyBox Premium Dynamic

Randomly inserted at a rate of one in four series one regular packs and one in three series one jumbo packs, this 12-card standard-size set features the most intense NBA players. Fronts feature a full-color action player photo handling a ball that is exploding. The player is set against a bright red etched foil background with the "Dynamic" logo scrawled at an angle across the bottom. The player's name is printed on the bottom right of the card. Full-bleed, one-color backs are numbered with the prefix "D" and picture the player in an action shot and a full color close-up inset. The player's name is printed in white caps and a player profile is printed in black type on tilted red bars. The set is sequenced in alphabetical team order.

COMPLETE SET (12) 2.50 6.00
D1 Larry Johnson .40 1.00
D2 Alonzo Mourning .50 1.25
D3 Dikembe Mutombo .40 1.00
D4 Jalen Rose .50 1.25
D5 Grant Hill .60 1.50
D6 Latrell Sprewell .40 1.00
D7 Reggie Miller .50 1.25
D8 John Starks .30 .75
D9 Calbert Cheaney .25 .60
D10 Dennis Rodman .75 2.00
D11 Detlef Schrempf .40 1.00
D12 Chris Webber .50 1.25

1995-96 SkyBox Premium High Hopes

Randomly inserted in all second series packs at a rate of one in 18, this 20-card set focuses on the hot young stars of the NBA. Borderless fronts feature the player in a full-color action cutout, with "High Hopes" spelled out in red and yellow spark and flame block letters on a black background. The player's name is printed in gold foil at the bottom. Backs have another full-color action cutout set against a back blackground with a player profile printed in white type. "High Hopes" is printed vertically on the right side.

COMPLETE SET (20) 15.00 40.00
HH1 Alan Henderson .75 2.00
HH2 Eric Williams .75 2.00
HH3 George Zidek .75 2.00
HH4 Bob Sura .75 2.00
HH5 Cherokee Parks .75 2.00
HH6 Antonio McDyess 2.00 5.00
HH7 Joe Smith 1.50 4.00
HH8 Brent Barry 1.25 3.00
HH9 Shawn Respert .75 2.00
HH10 Kevin Garnett 6.00 15.00
HH11 Ed O'Bannon .75 2.00
HH12 Jerry Stackhouse 2.50 6.00
HH13 Michael Finley 2.50 6.00
HH14 Arvydas Sabonis 1.50 4.00
HH15 Gary Trent .75 2.00
HH16 Tyus Edney .75 2.00
HH17 Damon Stoudamire 2.00 5.00
HH18 Greg Ostertag .75 2.00
HH19 Bryant Reeves .75 2.00
HH20 Rasheed Wallace 2.50 6.00

1995-96 SkyBox Premium Hot Sparks

Randomly inserted in second series hobby packs only at a rate of one in 12, this 10-card set notes the players who make things happen in the NBA. Fronts have a full-color action cutout with the player's name printed vertically in gold foil on the right side. A mauve computerized image serves as a background. A similar but darker background appears on the back with another full-color action cutout and a player profile printed in white type.

COMPLETE SET (11) 8.00 20.00
HS1 Mookie Blaylock .60 1.50
HS2 Jason Kidd 1.50 4.00
HS3 Tim Hardaway 1.00 2.50
HS4 Nick Van Exel 1.00 2.50
HS5 Kenny Anderson .75 2.00
HS6 Anfernee Hardaway 1.50 4.00
HS7 Rod Strickland .60 1.50
HS8 Gary Payton 1.00 2.50
HS9 Damon Stoudamire 1.50 4.00
HS10 John Stockton 1.25 3.00
HS11 Magic Johnson 2.50 6.00

1995-96 SkyBox Premium Kinetic

Randomly inserted in all first series at a rate of one in four (and one in three jumbo), cards from this 9-card standard-size set highlight the NBA's speed demons. Full-bleed fronts have swirling color swoops and surround a full-color player cutout set against an etched foil background. Player's name and team name are printed in silver foil at the bottom. Borderless backs feature a one-color player cutout and continues with the swoosh patterns. A full-color head shot is inset with a white border and a player profile is printed in black type on gold bars.

COMPLETE SET (9) 1.25 3.00
K1 Mookie Blaylock .25 .60
K2 Tim Hardaway .40 1.00
K3 Lamond Murray UER .25 .60
Mach is spelled Mock
K4 Stacey Augmon .30 .75
K5 Nick Van Exel .40 1.00
K6 Khalid Reeves .25 .60
K7 Kenny Anderson .30 .75
K8 Rod Strickland .25 .60
K9 Gary Payton .40 1.00

1995-96 SkyBox Premium Larger Than Life

Randomly inserted in first series regular and jumbo packs at a rate of one in 48 and one in 36 respectively, this 10-card standard-size set showcases those players who have established themselves in the NBA. A sunburst design is etched into gold foil and serves as a background for the fronts which include a full-color action player cutout. The "Larger Than Life" logo is printed diagonally and upwards from the bottom right and tapers up to the SkyBox logo. The player's first name is printed in lower case black type just above his last name which appears in all caps red type. Backs continue with the sunburst pattern on the gold type. A player profile is printed in black type on the right side and a full-color action cutout appears on the left side. The set is sequenced in alphabetical team order.

COMPLETE SET (10) 30.00 60.00
L1 Michael Jordan 15.00 40.00
L2 Jason Kidd 3.00 8.00
L3 Grant Hill 3.00 8.00
L4 Hakeem Olajuwon 2.50 6.00
L5 Glenn Robinson 2.00 5.00
L6 Patrick Ewing 2.50 6.00
L7 Shaquille O'Neal 5.00 12.00
L8 Charles Barkley 3.00 8.00
L9 David Robinson 3.00 8.00
L10 John Stockton 2.50 6.00

1995-96 SkyBox Premium Lottery Exchange

Hobbyists received this 13-card set after collecting the three separate Lottery Exchange cards randomly inserted into first series packs (each card was seeded at a rate of 1:40 packs). The expiration date for exchanging the cards was June 15th, 1996. The set consists of the first thirteen players selected in the 1995 NBA draft. Card fronts feature a full-color player action cutout set against a murky colored background.

COMPLETE SET (13) 15.00 40.00
1 Joe Smith 1.50 4.00
2 Antonio McDyess 2.00 5.00
3 Jerry Stackhouse 2.50 6.00
4 Rasheed Wallace 2.50 6.00
5 Kevin Garnett 6.00 15.00
6 Bryant Reeves .75 2.00
7 Damon Stoudamire 2.00 5.00
8 Shawn Respert .75 2.00
9 Ed O'Bannon .75 2.00
10 Kurt Thomas .75 2.00
11 Gary Trent .75 2.00
12 Cherokee Parks .75 2.00
13 Corliss Williamson .75 2.00
NNO Exchange Card 2 .40 1.00
NNO Exchange Card 1 .40 1.00
NNO Exchange Card 3 .40 1.00

1995-96 SkyBox Premium Meltdown

Randomly inserted in second series regular packs at a rate of one in 54 and jumbo packs at a rate of one in 42, this 10-card set is a tribute to the league's hottest scorers. Borderless fronts have a foil finish with an image of green and blue melting metal. A full-color player cutout appears on the front with his name and team printed on the bottom. Blue metal showers down in a cascade on the back with a full-color action cutout and a player profile printed in white type.

COMPLETE SET (10) 30.00 80.00
M1 Michael Jordan 15.00 40.00
M2 Dan Majerle 2.00 5.00
M3 Jason Kidd 3.00 8.00
M4 Antonio McDyess 2.50 6.00
M5 Grant Hill 3.00 8.00
M6 Joe Smith 2.00 5.00
M7 Hakeem Olajuwon 2.50 6.00
M8 Shaquille O'Neal 5.00 12.00
M9 Jerry Stackhouse 3.00 8.00
M10 David Robinson 3.00 8.00

1995-96 SkyBox Premium Rookie Prevue

Randomly inserted in first series packs at a rate of one in nine, this 20-card standard-size set focuses on the hot rookies of 1994-95. The borderless fronts include a full-color action player cutout on the right. The player's last name is printed in gold foil across the top with his first name in smaller type underneath the last name. The background is a red and gold sunburst pattern with "Rookie Prevue" in bold block letters on the bottom left. Backs also carry the "Rookie Prevue" logo at the bottom left and a player action cutout on the right. The background continues the red and gold sunburst design and the player's name and a short profile is printed in black type on the upper left side of the back. The set is sequenced in dratt order.

COMPLETE SET (20) 20.00 50.00
RP1 Joe Smith 2.00 5.00
RP2 Antonio McDyess 2.50 6.00
RP3 Jerry Stackhouse 3.00 8.00
RP4 Rasheed Wallace 3.00 8.00
RP5 Bryant Reeves 1.00 2.50
RP6 Damon Stoudamire 2.50 6.00
RP7 Shawn Respert 1.00 2.50
RP8 Ed O'Bannon 1.00 2.50
RP9 Kurt Thomas 1.00 2.50
RP10 Gary Trent 1.00 2.50
RP11 Cherokee Parks 1.00 2.50
RP12 Corliss Williamson 1.00 2.50
RP13 Eric Williams 1.00 2.50
RP14 Brent Barry 1.50 4.00
RP15 Alan Henderson 1.00 2.50
RP16 Bob Sura 1.00 2.50
RP17 Theo Ratliff 1.50 4.00
RP18 Randolph Childress 1.00 2.50
RP19 Michael Finley 3.00 8.00
RP20 George Zidek 1.00 2.50

1995-96 SkyBox Premium Standouts

Randomly inserted in first series packs at a rate of one in 18 regular packs and one in 36 jumbo packs, this 12-card standard-size set spotlights the play of the NBA's hot rookies. The fronts feature the player in a full-color action cutout set against a metallic copper foil. The player stands on top of a circular "Skybox Standouts" logo and his name is stamped in gold foil at the upper right corner. A full-color action player cutout appears on the back and is set against the "Standouts" logo. A player profile appears on the top left of the card and the player's name and team are printed in a reverse type process on a strip of light blue across the bottom.

COMPLETE SET (12) 15.00 30.00
S1 Alonzo Mourning 2.50 6.00
S2 Scottie Pippen 3.00 8.00
S3 Danny Manning 1.50 4.00
S4 Jamal Mashburn 2.00 5.00
S5 Latrell Sprewell 2.00 5.00
S6 Reggie Miller 2.50 6.00
S7 Anfernee Hardaway 3.00 8.00
S8 Brian Grant 1.50 4.00
S9 Shawn Kemp 2.00 5.00
S10 Clifford Robinson 1.25 3.00
S11 Joe Dumars 2.00 5.00
S12 Chris Webber 2.50 6.00

1995-96 SkyBox Premium Standouts Hobby

Randomly inserted exclusivelt into first series hobby packs at a rate of one in 18, this six-card set is a tribute to the league's best. Borderless fronts have gold foil paper and the player's name is stamped in the upper right in a lighter gold foil. A full-color action player cutout appears and stand directly on a circular pattern that reads "Skybox Standouts." Backs have another full-color action cutout with a player profile, the Skybox medallion and a granite-like strip with the player's name and team etched inside.

COMPLETE SET (6) 20.00 50.00
SH1 Michael Jordan 12.00 30.00
SH2 Jason Kidd 4.00 10.00
SH3 Hakeem Olajuwon 3.00 8.00
SH4 Eddie Jones 3.00 8.00
SH5 Shaquille O'Neal 6.00 15.00
SH6 Grant Hill 4.00 10.00

1995-96 SkyBox Premium USA Basketball

Randomly inserted in second series retail packs at a rate of one in 12 and one in every second series jumbo pack and one per series two special retail pack, this set features the first ten players selected to the 1996 USA men's basketball team. Card fronts feature full-color action cutouts of Team USA members pictured in their Olympic togs set against a gray background of a globe.

COMPLETE SET (10) 8.00 20.00
U1 Anfernee Hardaway 1.25 3.00
U2 Grant Hill 1.25 3.00
U3 Karl Malone 1.00 2.50
U4 Reggie Miller 1.00 2.50
U5 Scottie Pippen 1.25 3.00
U6 Hakeem Olajuwon 1.00 2.50
U7 Shaquille O'Neal 2.00 5.00
U8 David Robinson 1.25 3.00
U9 Glenn Robinson .75 2.00
U10 John Stockton 1.00 2.50

1996-97 SkyBox Premium

The 1996-97 Skybox set was issued with a total of 281 cards. The set was issued in two series with series one totaling 131 cards and series two totaling 150. The 12-card packs retail for $2.99 each. The cards are grouped alphabetically within teams. Rookie cards that were available in the first series included Shareef Abdur-Rahim, Kobe Bryant, Marcus Camby, Allen Iverson, Stephon Marbury and Antoine Walker. A Jerry Stackhouse promo was released before the set that is identical to the regular issue card except it does not have a card number on the back. It is listed below at the end of the set.

COMPLETE SET (281) 20.00 35.00
COMPLETE SERIES 1 (131) 12.50 25.00
COMPLETE SERIES 2 (150) 7.50 15.00
1 Mookie Blaylock .12 .30
2 Alan Henderson .12 .30
3 Christian Laettner .15 .40
4 Dikembe Mutombo .20 .50
5 Steve Smith .15 .40
6 Dana Barros .12 .30
7 Rick Fox .12 .30
8 Dino Radja .15 .40
9 Antoine Walker RC .50 1.25
10 Eric Williams .12 .30
11 Dell Curry .12 .30
12 Tony Delk RC .25 .60
13 Matt Geiger .12 .30
14 Glen Rice .20 .50
15 Ron Harper .15 .40
16 Michael Jordan 1.50 4.00
17 Toni Kukoc .20 .50
18 Scottie Pippen .30 .75
19 Dennis Rodman .40 1.00
20 Terrell Brandon .12 .30
21 Danny Ferry .12 .30
22 Chris Mills .12 .30
23 Bobby Phills .12 .30
24 Vitaly Potapenko RC .25 .60
25 Jim Jackson .12 .30
26 Jason Kidd .30 .75
27 Jamal Mashburn .15 .40
28 George McCloud .12 .30
29 Samaki Walker RC .25 .60
30 LaPhonso Ellis .12 .30
31 Antonio McDyess .20 .50
32 Bryant Stith .12 .30
33 Joe Dumars .20 .50
34 Grant Hill .30 .75
35 Lindsey Hunter .12 .30
36 Theo Ratliff .12 .30
37 Otis Thorpe .12 .30
38 Todd Fuller RC .25 .60
39 Chris Mullin .20 .50
40 Joe Smith .15 .40
41 Latrell Sprewell .20 .50
42 Charles Barkley .30 .75
43 Clyde Drexler .25 .60
44 Mario Elie .12 .30
45 Hakeem Olajuwon .25 .60
46 Erick Dampier RC .25 .60
47 Dale Davis .12 .30
48 Derrick McKey .12 .30
49 Reggie Miller .25 .60
50 Rik Smits .15 .40
51 Brent Barry .15 .40
52 Rodney Rogers .12 .30
53 Loy Vaught .12 .30
54 Lorenzen Wright RC .25 .60
55 Kobe Bryant RC 8.00 20.00
56 Cedric Ceballos .12 .30
57 Eddie Jones .20 .50
58 Shaquille O'Neal .50 1.25
59 Nick Van Exel .20 .50
60 Tim Hardaway .20 .50
61 Alonzo Mourning .25 .60
62 Kurt Thomas .12 .30
63 Ray Allen RC 1.00 2.50
64 Vin Baker .15 .40
65 Shawn Respert .12 .30
66 Glenn Robinson .20 .50
67 Kevin Garnett .50 1.25
68 Tom Gugliotta .12 .30
69 Stephon Marbury RC .60 1.50
70 Sam Mitchell .12 .30
71 Shawn Bradley .12 .30
72 Kendall Gill .12 .30
73 Kerry Kittles RC .25 .60

74 Ed O'Bannon .12 .30
75 Patrick Ewing .25 .60
76 Larry Johnson .20 .50
77 Charles Oakley .15 .40
78 John Starks .15 .40
79 John Wallace RC .25 .60
80 Nick Anderson .12 .30
81 Horace Grant .15 .40
82 Anfernee Hardaway .30 .75
83 Dennis Scott .12 .30
84 Derrick Coleman .15 .40
85 Allen Iverson RC 1.25 3.00
86 Jerry Stackhouse .25 .60
87 Clarence Weatherspoon .12 .30
88 Michael Finley .25 .60
89 Robert Horry .15 .40
90 Kevin Johnson .20 .50
91 Steve Nash RC 1.25 3.00
92 Wesley Person .12 .30
93 Aaron McKie .12 .30
94 Jermaine O'Neal RC .60 1.50
95 Clifford Robinson .12 .30
96 Arvydas Sabonis .15 .40
97 Gary Trent .12 .30
98 Tyus Edney .12 .30
99 Brian Grant .15 .40
100 Mitch Richmond .20 .50
101 Billy Owens .12 .30
102 Corliss Williamson .12 .30
103 Vinny Del Negro .12 .30
104 Sean Elliott .20 .50
105 Avery Johnson .15 .40
106 Chuck Person .15 .40
107 David Robinson .30 .75
108 Hersey Hawkins .12 .30
109 Shawn Kemp .20 .50
110 Gary Payton .20 .50
111 Sam Perkins .12 .30
112 Detlef Schrempf .20 .50
113 Marcus Camby RC .40 1.00
114 Carlos Rogers .12 .30
115 Damon Stoudamire .20 .50
116 Zan Tabak .12 .30
117 Antoine Carr .12 .30
118 Jeff Hornacek .15 .40
119 Karl Malone .25 .60
120 Chris Morris .12 .30
121 John Stockton .25 .60
122 Shareef Abdur-Rahim RC .50 1.25
123 Greg Anthony .12 .30
124 Bryant Reeves .12 .30
125 Roy Rogers RC .25 .60
126 Calbert Cheaney .12 .30
127 Juwan Howard .15 .40
128 Gheorghe Muresan .12 .30
129 Chris Webber .25 .60
130 Checklist .12 .30
131 Checklist .12 .30
132 Jon Barry .12 .30
133 Christian Laettner .15 .40
134 Dikembe Mutombo .20 .50
135 Dee Brown .12 .30
136 Todd Day .12 .30
137 David Wesley .12 .30
138 Vlade Divac .20 .50
139 Anthony Goldwire .12 .30
140 Anthony Mason .12 .30
141 Jason Caffey .12 .30
142 Luc Longley .12 .30
143 Tyrone Hill .12 .30
144 Antonio Lang .12 .30
145 Sam Cassell .15 .40
146 Chris Gatling .12 .30
147 Eric Montross .12 .30
148 Ervin Johnson .12 .30
149 Sarunas Marciulionis .12 .30
150 Stacey Augmon .15 .40
151 Grant Long .12 .30
152 Terry Mills .12 .30
153 Kenny Smith .15 .40
154 B.J. Armstrong .12 .30
155 Bimbo Coles .12 .30
156 Charles Barkley .30 .75
157 Brent Price .12 .30
158 Duane Ferrell .12 .30
159 Jalen Rose .15 .40
160 Terry Dehere .12 .30
161 Bo Outlaw .12 .30
162 Corie Blount .12 .30
163 Shaquille O'Neal .50 1.25
164 Rumeal Robinson .12 .30
165 P.J. Brown .12 .30
166 Ronnie Grandison .12 .30
167 Sherman Douglas .12 .30
168 Johnny Newman .12 .30
169 James Robinson .12 .30
170 Doug West .12 .30
171 Robert Pack .12 .30
172 Khalid Reeves .12 .30
173 Chris Childs .12 .30
174 Allan Houston .15 .40
175 Charlie Ward .12 .30
176 Darrell Armstrong RC .40 1.00
177 Gerald Wilkins .12 .30
178 Lucious Harris .12 .30
179 Robert Horry .15 .40
180 Danny Manning .15 .40
181 Kenny Anderson .15 .40
182 Isaiah Rider .15 .40
183 Rasheed Wallace .25 .60
184 Mahmoud Abdul-Rauf .12 .30
185 Cory Alexander .12 .30
186 Vernon Maxwell .12 .30
187 Dominique Wilkins .25 .60
188 Nate McMillan .12 .30
189 Larry Stewart .12 .30
190 Doug Christie .12 .30
191 Hubert Davis .12 .30
192 Walt Williams .12 .30
193 Adam Keefe .12 .30
194 Greg Ostertag .12 .30
195 John Stockton .25 .60
196 George Lynch .12 .30
197 Lee Mayberry .12 .30
198 Tracy Murray .12 .30
199 Rod Strickland .12 .30
200 Shareef Abdur-Rahim ROO .25 .60
201 Ray Allen ROO .50 1.25
202 Shandon Anderson ROO RC .25 .60
203 Kobe Bryant ROO 2.50 6.00
204 Marcus Camby ROO .20 .50
205 Erick Dampier ROO .12 .30
206 Emanual Davis ROO RC .25 .60
207 Tony Delk ROO .25 .60
208 Brian Evans ROO RC .25 .60
209 Derek Fisher ROO RC .50 1.25
210 Todd Fuller ROO .12 .30
211 Dean Garrett ROO RC .25 .60
212 Reggie Geary ROO RC .25 .60
213 Darvin Ham ROO RC .25 .60
214 Othella Harrington ROO RC .25 .60
215 Shane Heal ROO RC .25 .60
216 Allen Iverson ROO .60 1.50
217 Dontae' Jones ROO RC .25 .60
218 Kerry Kittles ROO .12 .30
219 Priest Lauderdale ROO RC .25 .60
220 Randy Livingston ROO RC .25 .60
221 Matt Maloney ROO RC .25 .60
222 Stephon Marbury ROO .30 .75
223 Walter McCarty ROO RC .25 .60
224 Amal McCaskill ROO RC .25 .60
225 Jeff McInnis ROO RC .25 .60
226 Martin Muursepp ROO RC .25 .60
227 Steve Nash ROO .60 1.50
228 Ruben Nembhard ROO RC .25 .60
229 Jermaine O'Neal ROO .30 .75
230 Vitaly Potapenko ROO .12 .30
231 Virginius Praskevicius ROO RC .25 .60
232 Roy Rogers ROO .12 .30
233 Malik Rose ROO RC .30 .75
234 Antoine Walker ROO .25 .60
235 Samaki Walker ROO .12 .30
236 Ben Wallace ROO RC 1.25 3.00
237 John Wallace ROO .12 .30
238 Jerome Williams ROO RC .25 .60
239 Lorenzen Wright ROO .12 .30
240 Sam Cassell PM .15 .40
241 Anfernee Hardaway PM .30 .75
242 Tim Hardaway PM .20 .50
243 Grant Hill PM .30 .75
244 Allan Houston PM .15 .40
245 Juwan Howard PM .15 .40
246 Kevin Johnson PM .20 .50
247 Michael Jordan PM 1.50 4.00
248 Jason Kidd PM .30 .75
249 Karl Malone PM .25 .60
250 Reggie Miller PM .25 .60
251 Gary Payton PM .20 .50
252 Wesley Person PM .12 .30
253 Glen Rice PM .20 .50
254 David Robinson PM .30 .75
255 Steve Smith PM .15 .40
256 Latrell Sprewell PM .20 .50
257 Jerry Stackhouse PM .25 .60
258 Rod Strickland PM .12 .30
259 Nick Van Exel PM .20 .50
260 Charles Barkley DT .30 .75
261 Dale Davis DT .12 .30
262 Patrick Ewing DT .25 .60
263 Michael Finley DT .25 .60
264 Chris Gatling DT .12 .30
265 Armon Gilliam DT .12 .30
266 Tyrone Hill DT .12 .30
267 Robert Horry DT .15 .40
268 Mark Jackson DT .20 .50
269 Shawn Kemp DT .20 .50
270 Jamal Mashburn DT .15 .40
271 Anthony Mason DT .12 .30
272 Alonzo Mourning DT .25 .60
273 Dikembe Mutombo DT .20 .50
274 Shaquille O'Neal DT .50 1.25
275 Isaiah Rider DT .15 .40
276 Dennis Rodman DT .40 1.00
277 Damon Stoudamire DT .20 .50
278 Chris Webber DT .25 .60
279 Jayson Williams DT .12 .30
280 Checklist (132-239) .12 .30
281 Checklist (240-281/inserts) .12 .30
NNO Jerry Stackhouse PROMO .75 2.00

1996-97 SkyBox Premium Rubies

Inserted one card per both series hobby boxes, this 279-card set parallels the basic set. Each "Ruby" card is printed on 24-point stock and features red-foil in the place of the standard gold foil. To ascertain values on individual cards, please refer to the multiplier in the header below, coupled with the value of the base card.
*STARS: 12.5X TO 30X BASE CARD HI
*RCs: 8X TO 20X BASE HI
*PM/DT SUBSET: 8X TO 20X BASE HI
16 Michael Jordan 250.00 450.00
18 Scottie Pippen 12.00 30.00
55 Kobe Bryant 250.00 450.00
85 Allen Iverson 50.00 100.00
203 Kobe Bryant ROO 100.00 200.00
247 Michael Jordan PM 75.00 200.00

1996-97 SkyBox Premium Autographics

Randomly inserted in the following 1996-97 products: Hoops series one and two, SkyBox series one and two, SkyBox Z-Force series one and two and SkyBox EX2000 all at a rate of one in 72, this set features autographs of some of the top stars in the NBA. Card design is identical for each issue and several players had their cards seeded into more than one of the aforementioned products. Card fronts feature a background in the particular player's team colors and an action shot of the player. Most of the cards were autographed vertically along the left side. Card backs are black with a spotlight photo, the player's name and career statistics. The first 100 cards of each player were autographed in blue ink and the remaining number were in black. A couple exceptions include Hakeem Olajuwon and Scottie Pippen, who autographed all of their cards in blue ink only. Also, Kevin Garnett autographed two-thirds of his cards in blue and the rest in black. The cards below are not numbered and are listed alphabetically. As far as set value, the set is considered complete with the Kevin Garnett Black, Hakeem Olajuwon Blue and the Scottie Pippen Blue. Both Olajuwon and Pippen are also listed under the Blue set. Recently, some news of counterfeits have surfaced. The focal cards being reproduced include the Grant Hill, Kevin Garnett and Scottie Pippen. These cards feature no chipping on the edges, a lighter color of black on the back, a fuzzy copyright line and, in general, a poor autograph. These do, however, have the SkyBox logo stamped on the card.
CARDS LISTED BELOW ALPHABETICALLY
BEWARE COUNTERFEITS
1 Ray Allen 40.00 100.00
2 Kenny Anderson 6.00 15.00
3 Nick Anderson 10.00 25.00
4 B.J. Armstrong 8.00 20.00
5 Vincent Askew 5.00 12.00
6 Dana Barros 5.00 12.00
7 Brent Barry 6.00 15.00
8 Travis Best 5.00 12.00
9 Muggsy Bogues 12.50 30.00
10 P.J. Brown 5.00 12.00
11 Randy Brown 6.00 15.00
12 Marcus Camby 12.50 30.00
13 Chris Childs 5.00 12.00
14 Dell Curry 5.00 12.00
15 Andrew DeClercq 5.00 12.00
16 Tony Delk 6.00 15.00
17 Sherman Douglas 5.00 12.00
18 Clyde Drexler 80.00 160.00
19 Tyus Edney 5.00 12.00
20 Michael Finley 12.00 30.00
21 Rick Fox 6.00 15.00
22 Kevin Garnett 125.00 250.00
23 Matt Geiger 5.00 12.00
24 Kendall Gill 6.00 15.00
25 Brian Grant 5.00 12.00
26 Tim Hardaway 12.50 30.00
27 Grant Hill 75.00 150.00
28 Tyrone Hill 5.00 12.00
29 Allan Houston 12.50 30.00
30 Juwan Howard 25.00 60.00
31 Zydrunas Ilgauskas 15.00 40.00
32 Jim Jackson 10.00 25.00
33 Mark Jackson 10.00 25.00
34 Eddie Jones 15.00 40.00
35 Adam Keefe 5.00 12.00
36 Steve Kerr 10.00 25.00
37 Kerry Kittles 15.00 40.00
38 Toni Kukoc 20.00 50.00
39 Andrew Lang 5.00 12.00
40 Voshon Lenard 5.00 12.00
41 Grant Long 5.00 12.00
42 Luc Longley 20.00 50.00
43 George Lynch 5.00 12.00
44 Don MacLean 5.00 12.00
45 Stephon Marbury 25.00 60.00
46 Lee Mayberry 5.00 12.00
47 Walter McCarty 8.00 20.00
48 George McCloud 40.00 80.00
49 Antonio McDyess 35.00 70.00
50 Nate McMillan 6.00 15.00
51 Chris Mills 5.00 12.00
52 Sam Mitchell 5.00 12.00
53 Eric Montross 5.00 12.00
54 Chris Morris 5.00 12.00
55 Lawrence Moten 5.00 12.00
56 Alonzo Mourning 75.00 150.00
57 Gheorghe Muresan 6.00 15.00
58 Steve Nash 250.00 450.00
59 Ed O'Bannon 5.00 12.00
60 Charles Oakley 25.00 60.00
62 Greg Ostertag 5.00 12.00
63 Billy Owens 5.00 12.00
64 Sam Perkins 6.00 15.00
65 Chuck Person 5.00 12.00
66 Wesley Person 5.00 12.00
67 Bobby Phills 6.00 15.00
69 Theo Ratliff 6.00 15.00
70 Glen Rice 6.00 15.00
71 Rodney Rogers 5.00 12.00
72 Byron Scott 6.00 15.00
73 Dennis Scott 5.00 12.00
74 Joe Smith 10.00 25.00
75 Kenny Smith 8.00 20.00
76 Rik Smits 8.00 20.00
77 Eric Snow 5.00 12.00
78 Latrell Sprewell 40.00 70.00
79 Jerry Stackhouse 12.50 30.00
80 John Starks 15.00 40.00
81 Bryant Stith 5.00 12.00
82 Damon Stoudamire 60.00 150.00
83 Rod Strickland 40.00 100.00
84 Bob Sura 5.00 12.00
85 Zan Tabak 5.00 12.00
86 Loy Vaught 5.00 12.00
87 Antoine Walker 15.00 40.00
88 Samaki Walker 6.00 15.00
89 John Wallace 10.00 25.00
90 Bill Wennington 10.00 25.00
91 David Wesley 5.00 12.00
92 Doug West 5.00 12.00
93 Monty Williams 5.00 12.00
94 Joe Wolf 5.00 12.00
95 Sharone Wright 5.00 12.00

1996-97 SkyBox Premium Autographics Blue

Randomly inserted in the following 1996-97 products: Hoops series one and two, SkyBox series one and two, SkyBox Z-Force series one and two and SkyBox E-X2000, this set features the first 100 autographs of some of the top stars in the NBA. Hakeem Olajuwon and Scottie Pippen autographed all of their cards in blue ink only. The cards below are not numbered and are listed alphabetically. Note: John Wallace did not sign any blue cards, so this set is actually complete at 94 cards.
*BLUE: .75X TO 2X VALUE
18 Clyde Drexler 100.00 250.00
22 Kevin Garnett 125.00 250.00
32 Jim Jackson 15.00 40.00
34 Eddie Jones 40.00 100.00
36 Steve Kerr 30.00 80.00
38 Toni Kukoc 75.00 150.00
58 Steve Nash 400.00 800.00
61 Hakeem Olajuwon 100.00 200.00
68 Scottie Pippen 300.00 500.00
78 Latrell Sprewell 40.00 100.00
82 Damon Stoudamire 80.00 200.00

1996-97 SkyBox Premium Close-Ups

Randomly inserted in all series one packs at a rate of one in 24, this 9-card set features a die cut design and gives collectors a close-up view of players in action with a crystal ball in the background.
COMPLETE SET (9) 8.00 20.00
CU1 Anfernee Hardaway 2.00 5.00
CU2 Grant Hill 2.00 5.00
CU3 Juwan Howard 1.00 2.50
CU4 Jason Kidd 2.00 5.00
CU5 Shawn Kemp 1.25 3.00
CU6 Alonzo Mourning 1.50 4.00
CU7 Hakeem Olajuwon 1.50 4.00
CU8 Jerry Stackhouse 1.50 4.00
CU9 Damon Stoudamire 1.25 3.00

1996-97 SkyBox Premium Emerald Autographs

Loosely inserted one in 20 hobby boxes as exchange cards, this 5-card set features autographed base cards. Each card contains green "emerald" foil rather than the standard gold foil. Most of the redemption autographs were returned signed in black ink, however, Marcus Camby redemptions were available in both blue and black ink. The expiration date was February 1, 1998.
E1 Ray Allen 30.00 80.00
E2 Marcus Camby 10.00 25.00
E3 Grant Hill 100.00 175.00
E4 Kerry Kittles 6.00 15.00
E5 Jerry Stackhouse 10.00 25.00
NNO Expired Trade Cards .40 1.00

1996-97 SkyBox Premium Golden Touch

Randomly inserted in all series two packs at a rate of one in 240, this set focuses on veterans and rookies who can make just about any shot on the court. Cards carry a heavily die cut design.
COMPLETE SET (10) 200.00 350.00
1 Vin Baker 6.00 15.00
2 Terrell Brandon 5.00 12.00
3 Allan Houston 6.00 15.00
4 Allen Iverson 15.00 40.00
5 Michael Jordan 175.00 325.00
6 Shawn Kemp 10.00 25.00
7 Karl Malone 10.00 25.00
8 Stephon Marbury 8.00 20.00
9 Latrell Sprewell 8.00 20.00
10 Damon Stoudamire 8.00 20.00

1996-97 SkyBox Premium Intimidators

Randomly inserted in all series two packs at a rate of one in 8, this 20-card set focuses on players who can intimidate on the court. Card fronts feature the player's name and team written vertically around the shot of the player.
COMPLETE SET (20) 15.00 30.00
1 Shareef Abdur-Rahim 1.25 3.00
2 Charles Barkley 1.50 4.00
3 Marcus Camby 1.00 2.50
4 Elden Campbell .60 1.50
5 Derrick Coleman .75 2.00
6 Patrick Ewing 1.25 3.00
7 Michael Finley 1.25 3.00
8 Kevin Garnett 2.50 6.00
9 Jim Jackson .60 1.50
10 Anthony Mason .60 1.50
11 Antonio McDyess 1.00 2.50
12 Alonzo Mourning 1.25 3.00
13 Gheorghe Muresan .60 1.50
14 Dikembe Mutombo 1.00 2.50
15 Shaquille O'Neal 2.50 6.00
16 Isaiah Rider .75 2.00
17 Clifford Robinson .60 1.50
18 David Robinson 1.50 4.00
19 Dennis Rodman 2.00 5.00
20 Clarence Weatherspoon .60 1.50

1996-97 SkyBox Premium Larger Than Life

Randomly inserted in series one hobby packs only at a rate of one in 180, this 18-card set features cards that are presented in 4-color image action photos horizontally. The images are set against a background featuring the player's portrait in the shadow. The player's names are gold foil stamped. Card backs feature a "B" prefix.
COMPLETE SET (18) 150.00 300.00
B1 Shareef Abdur-Rahim 6.00 15.00
B2 Marcus Camby 5.00 12.00
B3 Kevin Garnett 15.00 40.00
B4 Anfernee Hardaway 10.00 25.00
B5 Grant Hill 10.00 25.00
B6 Allen Iverson 15.00 40.00
B7 Michael Jordan 100.00 200.00
B8 Shawn Kemp 6.00 15.00
B9 Stephon Marbury 8.00 20.00
B10 Jamal Mashburn 5.00 12.00
B11 Antonio McDyess 6.00 15.00
B12 Alonzo Mourning 8.00 20.00
B13 Dikembe Mutombo 6.00 15.00
B14 Hakeem Olajuwon 8.00 20.00
B15 Shaquille O'Neal 15.00 40.00
B16 Dennis Rodman 12.00 30.00
B17 Jerry Stackhouse 8.00 20.00
B18 Damon Stoudamire 6.00 15.00

1996-97 SkyBox Premium Net Set

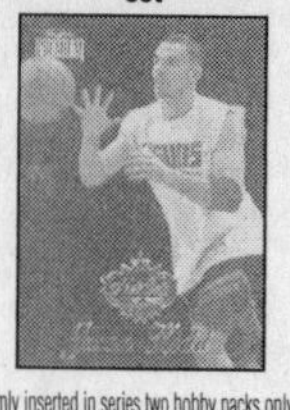

Randomly inserted in series two hobby packs only at a rate of one in 48, this 20-card set focuses on the league's superstars.
COMPLETE SET (20) 100.00 200.00
1 Vin Baker 2.50 6.00
2 Clyde Drexler 4.00 10.00
3 Patrick Ewing 4.00 10.00
4 Anfernee Hardaway 5.00 12.00
5 Grant Hill 5.00 12.00
6 Juwan Howard 2.50 6.00
7 Allen Iverson 8.00 20.00
8 Michael Jordan 25.00 60.00
9 Shawn Kemp 3.00 8.00
10 Jason Kidd 5.00 12.00
11 Karl Malone 4.00 10.00
12 Stephon Marbury 4.00 10.00
13 Alonzo Mourning 4.00 10.00
14 Hakeem Olajuwon 4.00 10.00
15 Shaquille O'Neal 8.00 20.00
16 Scottie Pippen 5.00 12.00
17 David Robinson 5.00 12.00
18 Joe Smith 2.50 6.00
19 Damon Stoudamire 3.00 8.00
20 Chris Webber 4.00 10.00

1996-97 SkyBox Premium New Edition

Randomly inserted in series two retail packs only at a rate of one in 36, this 10-card set focuses on rookies featuring a die cut design that looks similar to the front of a video game machine.
COMPLETE SET (10) 30.00 60.00
1 Shareef Abdur-Rahim 2.00 5.00
2 Ray Allen 4.00 10.00
3 Kobe Bryant 15.00 40.00
4 Marcus Camby 1.50 4.00
5 Allen Iverson 5.00 12.00
6 Kerry Kittles 1.00 2.50
7 Matt Maloney 1.00 2.50
8 Stephon Marbury 2.50 6.00
9 Steve Nash 5.00 12.00
10 Samaki Walker 1.00 2.50

1996-97 SkyBox Premium Rookie Prevue

Randomly inserted in series one packs at a rate of one in 54, this 18-card set focuses on the top 18 players from the 1996 NBA Draft. Card fronts feature a foil background. Card backs are numbered with a "R" prefix.
COMPLETE SET (18) 30.00 80.00
R1 Shareef Abdur-Rahim 2.50 6.00
R2 Ray Allen 5.00 12.00
R3 Kobe Bryant 15.00 40.00
R4 Marcus Camby 2.00 5.00
R5 Erick Dampier 1.25 3.00
R6 Tony Delk 1.25 3.00
R7 Brian Evans 1.25 3.00
R8 Todd Fuller 1.25 3.00
R9 Allen Iverson 6.00 15.00
R10 Kerry Kittles 1.25 3.00
R11 Stephon Marbury 3.00 8.00
R12 Steve Nash 6.00 15.00
R13 Vitaly Potapenko 1.25 3.00
R14 Roy Rogers 1.25 3.00
R15 Antoine Walker 2.50 6.00
R16 Samaki Walker 1.25 3.00
R17 John Wallace 1.25 3.00
R18 Lorenzen Wright 1.25 3.00

1996-97 SkyBox Premium Standouts

Randomly inserted in series one retail packs only at a rate of one in 180, this 9-card set features laser cut photos of standout NBA players which are silhouetted over a foil background which contains a giant basketball net graphic. Card backs are numbered with a "SO" prefix.
COMPLETE SET (9) 50.00 120.00
S01 Grant Hill 10.00 25.00
S02 Juwan Howard 5.00 12.00
S03 Jason Kidd 10.00 25.00
S04 Reggie Miller 8.00 20.00
S05 Shaquille O'Neal 15.00 40.00
S06 Gary Payton 6.00 15.00
S07 Scottie Pippen 10.00 25.00
S08 Mitch Richmond 6.00 15.00
S09 Joe Smith 5.00 12.00

1996-97 SkyBox Premium Thunder and Lightning

Randomly inserted in all series two packs at a rate of one in 144, this 10-card multi-player set focuses on some of the NBA's most deadly combinations. The "outside" card contains the first player while the second player is contained inside the first one.
COMPLETE SET (10) 40.00 100.00
1 Michael Jordan / Scottie Pippen 25.00 60.00
2 Kevin Johnson / Danny Manning 3.00 8.00
3 Grant Hill / Joe Dumars 5.00 12.00
4 Latrell Sprewell / Joe Smith 3.00 8.00
5 Charles Barkley / Hakeem Olajuwon 5.00 12.00
6 Vin Baker / Glenn Robinson 3.00 8.00
7 Patrick Ewing / Larry Johnson 4.00 10.00
8 Shawn Kemp / Gary Payton 3.00 8.00
9 Karl Malone / John Stockton 4.00 10.00
10 Juwan Howard / Chris Webber 4.00 10.00

1996-97 SkyBox Premium Triple Threats

The first nine cards were randomly inserted into first series packs at roughly one per pack. The bonus Triple Threat cards were randomly inserted in first series packs at a rate of one in 240, and feature three members from the NBA Champion Chicago Bulls. These cards differed from the first nine by the use of a metallic background. All card backs were numbered with a "TT" prefix.
COMPLETE SET (9) 1.50 4.00
*RUBY: 10X TO 25X BASE HI
SPs DO NOT HAVE RUBY PARALLEL
TT1 Chris Mullin .40 1.00
TT2 Joe Smith .30 .75
TT3 Latrell Sprewell .40 1.00
TT4 Avery Johnson .30 .75
TT5 Sean Elliott .40 1.00
TT6 David Robinson .60 1.50
TT7 John Stockton .50 1.25
TT8 Karl Malone .50 1.25
TT9 Jeff Hornacek .30 .75
TT10 Dennis Rodman SP 6.00 15.00
TT11 Michael Jordan SP 25.00 60.00
TT12 Scottie Pippen SP 5.00 12.00

1997-98 SkyBox Premium

This 250-card set features borderless color action player images printed on 20 pt. stock with holographic foil stamping and was distributed in eight-card packs with a suggested retail price of $2.59. The backs carry information about the player and career statistics. The second series contained the subset "Team SkyBox" that was inserted into packs at a rate of one in four.
COMPLETE SET (250) 50.00 90.00
COMPLETE SERIES 1 (125) 12.50 25.00
COMPLETE SERIES 2 (125) 40.00 70.00
1 Grant Hill .40 1.00
2 Matt Maloney .15 .40
3 Vinny Del Negro .15 .40
4 Kevin Willis .15 .40
5 Mark Jackson .25 .60
6 Ray Allen .30 .75
7 Derrick Coleman .20 .50
8 Isaiah Rider .15 .40
9 Rod Strickland .15 .40
10 Danny Ferry .15 .40
11 Antonio Davis .15 .40
12 Glenn Robinson .20 .50
13 Cedric Ceballos .15 .40
14 Sean Elliott .25 .60
15 Walt Williams .15 .40
16 Glen Rice .25 .60
17 Clyde Drexler .30 .75
18 Sherman Douglas .15 .40
19 Othella Harrington .15 .40
20 John Stockton .30 .75
21 Priest Lauderdale .15 .40
22 Khalid Reeves .15 .40
23 Kobe Bryant 1.25 3.00
24 Vin Baker UER .20 .50
G.Robinson photo on back
25 Steve Nash .50 1.25
26 Jeff Hornacek .20 .50
27 Tyrone Corbin .15 .40
28 Charles Barkley .40 1.00
29 Michael Jordan 2.00 5.00
30 Latrell Sprewell .25 .60
31 Anfernee Hardaway .40 1.00
32 Steve Kerr .20 .50
33 Joe Smith .20 .50
34 Jermaine O'Neal .30 .75
35 Ron Mercer RC .30 .75
36 Antonio McDyess .20 .50
37 Patrick Ewing .30 .75
38 Avery Johnson .20 .50
39 Toni Kukoc .25 .60
40 Sam Perkins .15 .40
41 Voshon Lenard .15 .40
42 Detlef Schrempf .25 .60
43 Horace Grant .20 .50
44 Luc Longley .15 .40
45 Todd Fuller .15 .40
46 Tim Hardaway .25 .60
47 Nick Anderson .15 .40
48 Scottie Pippen .40 1.00
49 Lindsey Hunter .15 .40
50 Shawn Kemp .25 .60
51 Larry Johnson .25 .60
52 Shawn Bradley .15 .40
53 Martin Muursepp .15 .40
54 Jamal Mashburn .20 .50
55 John Starks .20 .50
56 Rony Seikaly .20 .50
57 Gary Payton .25 .60
58 Juwan Howard .20 .50
59 Vitaly Potapenko .15 .40
60 Reggie Miller .30 .75
61 Alonzo Mourning .30 .75
62 Roy Rogers .15 .40
63 Antoine Walker .25 .60
64 Joe Dumars .25 .60
65 Allan Houston .20 .50
66 Hersey Hawkins .15 .40
67 Dell Curry .15 .40
68 Tony Delk .15 .40
69 Mookie Blaylock .15 .40
70 Derek Harper .15 .40
71 Loy Vaught .15 .40
72 Tom Gugliotta .15 .40
73 Mitch Richmond .25 .60
74 Dikembe Mutombo .25 .60
75 Tony Battie RC .30 .75
76 Derek Fisher .25 .60
77 Jason Kidd .40 1.00
78 Shareef Abdur-Rahim .25
79 Tracy McGrady RC 1.25
80 Anthony Mason .15
81 Mario Elie .15
82 Karl Malone .30
83 Mark Price .25
84 Steve Smith .20
85 LaPhonso Ellis .15
86 Robert Horry .20
87 Wesley Person .15
88 Marcus Camby .25
89 Antonio Daniels RC .25
90 Eddie Jones .25
91 Gary Trent .15
92 Danny Fortson RC .25
93 Chris Childs .15
94 David Robinson .40
95 Bryant Reeves .15
96 Chris Webber .25
97 P.J. Brown .15
98 Tyrone Hill .15
99 Dale Davis .15
100 Allen Iverson .50
101 Jerry Stackhouse .25
102 Arvydas Sabonis .20
103 Damon Stoudamire .25
104 Tim Thomas RC .50
105 Christian Laettner .20
106 Robert Pack .15
107 Lorenzen Wright .15
108 Olden Polynice .15
109 Terrell Brandon .15
110 Theo Ratliff .20
111 Kevin Garnett .50
112 Tim Duncan RC 1.50
113 Bryon Russell .15
114 Chauncey Billups RC 1.00
115 Dale Ellis .15
116 Shaquille O'Neal .60
117 Keith Van Horn RC .50
118 Kenny Anderson .20
119 Dennis Rodman .50
120 Hakeem Olajuwon .30
121 Stephon Marbury .30
122 Kendall Gill .15
123 Kerry Kittles .15
124 Checklist .15
125 Checklist .15
126 Anthony Johnson RC .25
127 Chris Anstey RC .25
128 Dean Garrett .15
129 Rik Smits .20
130 Tracy Murray .15
131 Charles O'Bannon RC .25
132 Eldridge Recasner .15
133 Johnny Taylor RC .25
134 Priest Lauderdale .15
135 Rod Strickland .15
136 Alan Henderson .15
137 Austin Croshere RC .25
138 Buck Williams .15
139 Clifford Robinson .15
140 Darrell Armstrong .15
141 Dennis Scott .15
142 Carl Herrera .15
143 Maurice Taylor RC .25
144 Chris Gatling .15
145 Alvin Williams RC .25
146 Antonio McDyess .20
147 Chauncey Billups .50
148 George McCloud .15
149 George Lynch .15
150 John Thomas RC .25
151 Jayson Williams .15
152 Otis Thorpe .15
153 Serge Zwikker RC .25
154 Chris Crawford RC .25
155 Muggsy Bogues .20
156 Mark Jackson .25
157 Dontonio Wingfield .15
158 Rodrick Rhodes RC .25
159 Sam Cassell .20
160 Hubert Davis .15
161 Clarence Weatherspoon .15
162 Eddie Johnson .15
163 Jacque Vaughn RC .25
164 Mark Price .25
165 Terry Dehere .15
166 Travis Knight .15
167 Charles Smith RC .25
168 David Wesley .15
169 David Wingate .15
170 Todd Day .15
171 Adonal Foyle RC .25
172 Chris Mills .15
173 Paul Grant RC .25
174 Adam Keefe .15
175 Erick Dampier UER .15
back Eric
176 Ervin Johnson .15
177 Lamond Murray .15
178 Vlade Divac .25
179 Bobby Phills .15
180 Brian Williams .15
181 Chris Dudley .15
182 Tyrone Hill .15
183 Donyell Marshall .15
184 Kevin Gamble .15
185 Scot Pollard RC .25
186 Cherokee Parks .15
187 Terry Mills .15
188 Glen Rice .25
189 Shawn Respert .15
190 Terrell Brandon .15
191 Keith Closs RC .25
192 Tariq Abdul-Wahad RC .25
193 Wesley Person .15
194 Chuck Person .20
195 Derek Anderson RC .25
196 Jon Barry .15
197 Chris Mullin .25
198 Ed Gray RC .25
199 Charlie Ward .15
200 Kelvin Cato RC .25
201 Michael Finley .25
202 Rick Fox .15
203 Scott Burrell .15
204 Vin Baker .20
205 Eric Snow .15
206 Isaac Austin .15
207 Keith Booth RC .25
208 Brian Grant .15
209 Chris Webber .25
210 Eric Williams .15
211 Jim Jackson .15
212 Anthony Parker RC .25
213 Brevin Knight RC .25

214 Cory Alexander .15 .40
215 James Robinson .15 .40
216 Bobby Jackson RC .30 .75
217 Bo Outlaw .15 .40
218 God Shammgod RC .25 .60
219 James Cotton RC .25 .60
220 Jud Buechler .15 .40
221 Shandon Anderson .15 .40
222 Kevin Johnson .25 .60
223 Chris Morris .15 .40
224 Shareef Abdur-Rahim TS .50 1.25
225 Ray Allen TS .60 1.50
226 Kobe Bryant TS 2.50 6.00
227 Marcus Camby TS .50 1.25
228 Antonio Daniels TS .50 1.25
229 Tim Duncan TS 3.00 8.00
230 Kevin Garnett TS 1.00 2.50
231 Anfernee Hardaway TS .75 2.00
232 Grant Hill TS .75 2.00
233 Allen Iverson TS 1.00 2.50
234 Bobby Jackson TS .60 1.50
235 Michael Jordan TS 4.00 10.00
236 Shawn Kemp TS .50 1.25
237 Karl Malone TS .60 1.50
238 Stephon Marbury TS .60 1.50
239 Hakeem Olajuwon TS .60 1.50
240 Shaquille O'Neal TS 1.25 3.00
241 Gary Payton TS .50 1.25
242 Scottie Pippen TS .75 2.00
243 David Robinson TS .75 2.00
244 Dennis Rodman TS 1.00 2.50
245 Jerry Stackhouse TS .50 1.25
246 Damon Stoudamire TS .50 1.25
247 Keith Van Horn TS 1.00 2.50
248 Antoine Walker TS .50 1.25
249 Grant Hill CL .40 1.00
250 Hakeem Olajuwon CL .30 .75
NNO Allen Iverson Ruby Shoe 5.00 12.00
NNO Allen Iverson Gold Shoe 1.50 4.00
NNO Allen Iverson Silver Shoe .75 2.00
NNO Allen Iverson Emerald Shoe 12.50 30.00
NNO Allen Iverson Bronze Shoe .50 1.25

1997-98 SkyBox Premium Star Rubies

This 248-card set is a hobby only parallel version of the regular set. The fronts contained a "splattered" red background and red-foil on the "SkyBox" logo. Fewer than 50 sets were produced and serially numbered. To ascertain values on individual cards, please refer to the multipliers in the header, coupled with the value of the base card.
*STARS: 100X TO 200X BASE CARD HI
*RCs: 50X TO 100X BASE HI
*TS: SAME VALUE AS BASE RUBY
1 Grant Hill 150.00 300.00
17 Clyde Drexler 125.00 225.00
20 John Stockton 125.00 250.00
23 Kobe Bryant 2000.00 3200.00
25 Steve Nash 150.00 300.00
28 Charles Barkley 150.00 300.00
29 Michael Jordan 2500.00 4000.00
30 Latrell Sprewell 75.00 150.00
31 Anfernee Hardaway 150.00 300.00
37 Patrick Ewing 80.00 200.00
48 Scottie Pippen 200.00 400.00
50 Shawn Kemp 75.00 150.00
51 Larry Johnson 60.00 150.00
60 Reggie Miller 125.00 250.00
77 Jason Kidd 125.00 250.00
79 Tracy McGrady 200.00 400.00
82 Karl Malone 125.00 250.00
90 Eddie Jones 100.00 200.00
94 David Robinson 150.00 300.00
96 Chris Webber 100.00 200.00
100 Allen Iverson 200.00 400.00
111 Kevin Garnett 175.00 350.00
112 Tim Duncan 400.00 800.00
116 Shaquille O'Neal 250.00 500.00
119 Dennis Rodman 300.00 600.00
120 Hakeem Olajuwon 125.00 250.00
209 Chris Webber 100.00 200.00

1997-98 SkyBox Premium And One

This 10-card set was randomly inserted in series one packs at a rate of one in 96. When the seal was removed from these die cut cards, it could be opened in four directions to reveal a larger player photo in a diamond-shaped "poster" with silver and gold foils. An extra bonus card of the same player is hiding inside.
COMPLETE SET (10) 50.00 100.00
1 Shawn Kemp 3.00 8.00
2 Hakeem Olajuwon 4.00 10.00
3 Charles Barkley 5.00 12.00
4 Antoine Walker 3.00 8.00
5 Dennis Rodman 6.00 15.00
6 Tim Duncan 10.00 25.00
7 Marcus Camby 3.00 8.00
8 Keith Van Horn 3.00 8.00
9 Shareef Abdur-Rahim 3.00 8.00
10 Michael Jordan 25.00 60.00

1997-98 SkyBox Premium Autographics

Randomly inserted in packs of all Fleer/SkyBox products, this set features autographs of some of the NBA's best players. For Hoops 1, these were inserted at a rate of one in 240 hobby and retail packs. For Hoops 2, these were inserted at a rate of one in 144 hobby and retail. For Metal and Metal Championship, these cards were inserted one in 120 hobby and retail. For SkyBox Premium 1 and 2, these cards were inserted one in 72 packs. For SkyBox E-X2001, these cards were inserted one in 60 packs. For SkyBox Z-Force 1 and 2, these cards were inserted one in 120 packs. Both Tracy McGrady and Rasheed Wallace only have Century Marks cards - no regular ones. Those cards are included in the set price, but are priced in the Century Mark set. The cards are not numbered and listed below alphabetically.
1 Shareef Abdur-Rahim 10.00 25.00
2 Cory Alexander 4.00 10.00
3 Kenny Anderson 5.00 12.00
4 Nick Anderson 6.00 15.00
5 Stacey Augmon 5.00 12.00
6 Isaac Austin 4.00 10.00
7 Vin Baker 8.00 20.00
8 Charles Barkley 700.00 1200.00
9 Dana Barros 4.00 10.00
10 Brent Barry 4.00 10.00
11 Tony Battie 5.00 12.00
12 Travis Best 5.00 12.00
13 Corie Blount 4.00 10.00
14 P.J. Brown 4.00 10.00
15 Randy Brown 5.00 12.00
16 Jud Buechler 8.00 20.00
17 Marcus Camby 10.00 25.00
18 Elden Campbell 5.00 12.00
19 Chris Carr 5.00 12.00
20 Kelvin Cato 6.00 15.00
21 Duane Causwell 4.00 10.00
22 Rex Chapman 12.00 30.00
23 Calbert Cheaney 4.00 10.00
24 Randolph Childress 4.00 10.00
25 Derrick Coleman 8.00 20.00
26 Austin Croshere 5.00 12.00
27 Dell Curry 4.00 10.00
28 Ben Davis 4.00 10.00
29 Mark Davis 4.00 10.00
30 Andrew DeClercq 4.00 10.00
31 Tony Delk 4.00 10.00
32 Vlade Divac 15.00 40.00
33 Clyde Drexler 30.00 80.00
34 Joe Dumars 15.00 40.00
35 Howard Eisley 4.00 10.00
36 Danny Ferry 4.00 10.00
37 Michael Finley 10.00 25.00
38 Derek Fisher 10.00 25.00
39 Danny Fortson 8.00 20.00
40 Todd Fuller 4.00 10.00
41 Chris Gatling 4.00 10.00
42 Matt Geiger 4.00 10.00
43 Brian Grant 5.00 12.00
44 Tom Gugliotta 6.00 15.00
45 Tim Hardaway 12.50 30.00
46 Ron Harper 30.00 80.00
47 Othella Harrington 4.00 10.00
48 Grant Hill 75.00 200.00
49 Tyrone Hill 4.00 10.00
50 Allan Houston 12.50 30.00
51 Juwan Howard 10.00 25.00
52 Lindsey Hunter 8.00 20.00
53 Bobby Hurley 4.00 10.00
54 Jim Jackson 8.00 20.00
55 Avery Johnson 6.00 15.00
56 Eddie Johnson 4.00 10.00
57 Ervin Johnson 4.00 10.00
58 Larry Johnson 20.00 50.00
59 Popeye Jones 4.00 10.00
60 Adam Keefe 4.00 10.00
61 Steve Kerr 10.00 25.00
62 Kerry Kittles 10.00 25.00
63 Brevin Knight 5.00 12.00
64 Travis Knight 4.00 10.00
65 George Lynch 4.00 10.00
66 Don MacLean 4.00 10.00
67 Stephon Marbury 20.00 50.00
68 Donny Marshall 5.00 12.00
69 Walter McCarty 5.00 12.00
70 Antonio McDyess 10.00 25.00
72 Ron Mercer 6.00 15.00
73 Reggie Miller 75.00 200.00
74 Chris Mills 4.00 10.00
75 Sam Mitchell 5.00 12.00
76 Chris Morris 4.00 10.00
77 Alonzo Mourning 40.00 100.00
78 Chris Mullin 30.00 60.00
79 Dikembe Mutombo 20.00 50.00
80 Anthony Parker 8.00 20.00
81 Sam Perkins 5.00 12.00
82 Elliot Perry 4.00 10.00
83 Bobby Phills 5.00 12.00
84 Eric Piatkowski 5.00 12.00
85 Scottie Pippen 150.00 325.00
86 Vitaly Potapenko 4.00 10.00
87 Brent Price 4.00 10.00
88 Theo Ratliff 4.00 10.00
89 Glen Rice 10.00 25.00
90 Glenn Robinson 6.00 15.00
91 Dennis Rodman 200.00 400.00
92 Roy Rogers 4.00 10.00
93 Malik Rose 4.00 10.00
94 Joe Smith 8.00 20.00
95 Tony Smith 4.00 10.00
96 Eric Snow 6.00 15.00
97 Jerry Stackhouse Pistons 30.00 80.00
98 Jerry Stackhouse Sixers 10.00 25.00
99 John Starks 12.50 30.00
100 Bryant Stith 4.00 10.00
101 Erick Strickland 4.00 10.00
102 Rod Strickland 10.00 25.00
103 Nick Van Exel 15.00 40.00
104 Keith Van Horn 10.00 25.00
105 David Vaughn 4.00 10.00
106 Jacque Vaughn 4.00 10.00
107 Antoine Walker 10.00 25.00
109 Clarence Weatherspoon 4.00 10.00
110 David Wesley 4.00 10.00
111 Dominique Wilkins 20.00 50.00
112 Gerald Wilkins 4.00 10.00
113 Eric Williams 4.00 10.00
114 John Williams 4.00 10.00
115 Lorenzo Williams 4.00 10.00
116 Monty Williams 4.00 10.00
117 Scott Williams 4.00 10.00
118 Walt Williams 4.00 10.00
119 Lorenzen Wright 4.00 10.00

1997-98 SkyBox Premium Autographics Century Marks

Hand numbered to 100, these embossed cards make up the first hundred cards signed by each athlete. To determine where each card was issued, please refer to the regular SkyBox Autographics set. The cards are not numbered and are listed below alphabetically. To ascertain values on individual cards, please refer to the multiplier in the header below, coupled with the value of the base card.
*CENTURY MARKS: 1.25X TO 3X VALUE
8 Charles Barkley 1000.00 1600.00
33 Clyde Drexler 60.00 150.00
48 Grant Hill 500.00 850.00
62 Kerry Kittles 25.00 60.00
67 Stephon Marbury 50.00 120.00
71 Tracy McGrady 600.00 1000.00
73 Reggie Miller 200.00 400.00
77 Alonzo Mourning 100.00 250.00
85 Scottie Pippen 500.00 900.00
89 Glen Rice 30.00 80.00
91 Dennis Rodman 300.00 600.00
97 Jerry Stackhouse Pistons 60.00 150.00
108 Rasheed Wallace 450.00 750.00
111 Dominique Wilkins 50.00 120.00

1997-98 SkyBox Premium Competitive Advantage

Randomly inserted into series two packs at a rate of one in 96, this 15-card set features some of the best players on die cut, matte finished cards. The cards feature a background of Mount Olympus. Card backs are numbered with a "CA" prefix.
COMPLETE SET (15) 150.00 300.00
CA1 Allen Iverson 10.00 25.00
CA2 Kobe Bryant 30.00 80.00
CA3 Michael Jordan 75.00 150.00
CA4 Shaquille O'Neal 15.00 40.00
CA5 Stephon Marbury 6.00 15.00
CA6 Shareef Abdur-Rahim 5.00 12.00
CA7 Marcus Camby 5.00 12.00
CA8 Kevin Garnett 10.00 25.00
CA9 Dennis Rodman 10.00 25.00
CA10 Anfernee Hardaway 8.00 20.00
CA11 Ray Allen 6.00 15.00
CA12 Scottie Pippen 8.00 20.00
CA13 Shawn Kemp 5.00 12.00
CA14 Hakeem Olajuwon 6.00 15.00
CA15 John Stockton 6.00 15.00

1997-98 SkyBox Premium Golden Touch

Randomly inserted into series two packs at a rate of one in 360, this 15-card die cut set features some of the NBA's biggest superstars on embossed satin gold-foil. Card backs are numbered with a "GT" prefix.
COMPLETE SET (15) 800.00 1300.00
GT1 Michael Jordan 400.00 650.00
GT2 Allen Iverson 30.00 80.00
GT3 Kobe Bryant 175.00 350.00
GT4 Shaquille O'Neal 40.00 100.00
GT5 Stephon Marbury 20.00 50.00
GT6 Marcus Camby 15.00 40.00
GT7 Anfernee Hardaway 40.00 100.00
GT8 Kevin Garnett 30.00 80.00
GT9 Shareef Abdur-Rahim 15.00 40.00
GT10 Dennis Rodman 40.00 100.00
GT11 Grant Hill 30.00 80.00
GT12 Kerry Kittles 10.00 25.00
GT13 Antoine Walker 15.00 40.00
GT14 Scottie Pippen 25.00 60.00
GT15 Damon Stoudamire 15.00 40.00

1997-98 SkyBox Premium Jam Pack

Randomly inserted into series two packs at a rate of one in 18, this 15-card set features stars on the rise on 100% holofoil cardboard. The fronts feature a scenic background that has the players "walking on water". Card backs carry a "JP" prefix.
COMPLETE SET (15) 20.00 40.00
JP1 Ray Allen 2.50 6.00
JP2 Damon Stoudamire 2.00 5.00
JP3 Shawn Kemp 2.00 5.00
JP4 Hakeem Olajuwon 2.50 6.00
JP5 Jerry Stackhouse 2.00 5.00
JP6 John Wallace 1.25 3.00
JP7 Juwan Howard 1.50 4.00
JP8 David Robinson 3.00 8.00
JP9 Gary Payton 2.00 5.00
JP10 Joe Smith 1.50 4.00
JP11 Charles Barkley 3.00 8.00
JP12 Terrell Brandon 1.25 3.00
JP13 Vin Baker 1.50 4.00
JP14 Antonio McDyess 1.50 4.00
JP15 Tim Duncan 5.00 12.00

1997-98 SkyBox Premium Next Game

Randomly inserted in series one packs at the rate of one in six, this 15-card set features color photos of the 1997-98 season's top NBA rookies. The backs carry player information.
COMPLETE SET (15) 5.00 12.00
1 Derek Anderson .30 .75
2 Tony Battie .40 1.00
3 Chauncey Billups 1.25 3.00
4 Kelvin Cato .30 .75
5 Austin Croshere .30 .75
6 Antonio Daniels .30 .75
7 Tim Duncan 2.00 5.00
8 Danny Fortson .30 .75
9 Adonal Foyle .30 .75
10 Tracy McGrady 1.50 4.00
11 Ron Mercer .40 1.00
12 Olivier Saint-Jean .30 .75
13 Maurice Taylor .30 .75
14 Tim Thomas .60 1.50
15 Keith Van Horn .60 1.50

1997-98 SkyBox Premium Premium Players

Randomly inserted in series one packs at the rate of one in 192, this 15-card set features letter box photography in the backsground and a player highlighted in the foreground with silver rainbow foil and team colors.
COMPLETE SET (15) 300.00 550.00
1 Michael Jordan 175.00 350.00
2 Allen Iverson 15.00 40.00
3 Kobe Bryant 50.00 125.00
4 Shaquille O'Neal 20.00 50.00
5 Stephon Marbury 10.00 25.00
6 Marcus Camby 8.00 20.00
7 Anfernee Hardaway 12.00 30.00
8 Kevin Garnett 15.00 40.00
9 Shareef Abdur-Rahim 8.00 20.00
10 Dennis Rodman 15.00 40.00
11 Ray Allen 10.00 25.00
12 Grant Hill 12.00 30.00
13 Kerry Kittles 5.00 12.00
14 Karl Malone 10.00 25.00
15 Scottie Pippen 12.00 30.00

1997-98 SkyBox Premium Reebok Chase Bronze

Inserted one per series one pack, this 15-card set is a partial parallel version of the regular set in three tiers of scarcity (bronze, silver and gold). Allen Iverson also has a special embossed foil card. Please refer to the basic SkyBox set for those values. Card backs carry one of three colors: bronze, gold or silver. The bronze is the base set and is priced below. Please refer to the multipliers in the header to ascertain values for the cards.
COMPLETE SET (15) 2.00 5.00
*GOLD: 12.5X TO 3X BRONZE
*SILVER: .5X TO 1.25X BRONZE
3 Vinny Del Negro .15 .40
5 Mark Jackson .25 .60
12 Glenn Robinson .20 .50
13 Cedric Ceballos .15 .40
17 Clyde Drexler .30 .75
38 Avery Johnson .20 .50
41 Voshon Lenard .15 .40
50 Shawn Kemp .25 .60
81 Mario Elie .15 .40
84 Steve Smith .20 .50
98 Tyrone Hill .15 .40
100 Allen Iverson .50 1.25
106 Robert Pack .15 .40
116 Shaquille O'Neal .60 1.50
118 Kenny Anderson .20 .50

1997-98 SkyBox Premium Rock 'n Fire

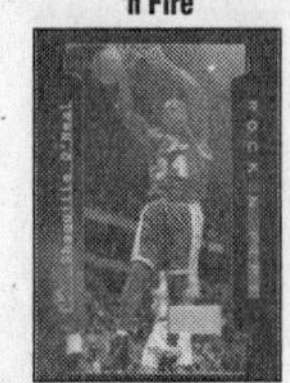

Randomly inserted in series one packs at the rate of one in 18, this 10-card set is reversible and featues a color action photo of a rising basketball star on one side and his portrait on the other with silver foil highlights. The card slides into a frame which carries more player information.
COMPLETE SET (10) 20.00 50.00
1 Allen Iverson 3.00 8.00
2 Kobe Bryant 8.00 20.00
3 Shaquille O'Neal 4.00 10.00
4 Stephon Marbury 2.00 5.00
5 Marcus Camby 1.50 4.00
6 Anfernee Hardaway 2.50 6.00
7 Kevin Garnett 3.00 8.00
8 Shareef Abdur-Rahim 1.50 4.00
9 Damon Stoudamire 1.50 4.00
10 Grant Hill 2.50 6.00

1997-98 SkyBox Premium Silky Smooth

Randomly inserted in series one packs at the rate of one in 360, this 10-card set features a glossy color action player photo with silver and gold holofoil and viewed through a matte coated, laser-cut net which can be opened to expose the card.
COMPLETE SET (10) 175.00 350.00
1 Michael Jordan 100.00 200.00
2 Allen Iverson 12.00 30.00
3 Kobe Bryant 40.00 100.00
4 Shaquille O'Neal 15.00 40.00
5 Stephon Marbury 8.00 20.00
6 Gary Payton 6.00 15.00
7 Anfernee Hardaway 10.00 25.00
8 Kevin Garnett 12.00 30.00
9 Scottie Pippen 10.00 25.00
10 Grant Hill 10.00 25.00

1997-98 SkyBox Premium Star Search

Randomly inserted into series two packs at a rate of one in six, this 15-card set features the top prospects from the 1997 Draft Class. The card fronts, when closed, feature a small photo of the player in front of a curtain. The fronts can be opened to "raise the curtain" on these players to reveal an action shot. Card backs are numbered with a "SS" prefix.
COMPLETE SET (15) 5.00 12.00
SS1 Tim Duncan 2.00 5.00
SS2 Tony Battie .40 1.00
SS3 Keith Van Horn .60 1.50
SS4 Antonio Daniels .30 .75
SS5 Chauncey Billups 1.25 3.00
SS6 Ron Mercer .40 1.00
SS7 Tracy McGrady 1.50 4.00
SS8 Danny Fortson .30 .75
SS9 Brevin Knight .30 .75
SS10 Derek Anderson .30 .75
SS11 Bobby Jackson .40 1.00
SS12 Jacque Vaughn .30 .75
SS13 Tim Thomas .60 1.50
SS14 Austin Croshere .30 .75
SS15 Kelvin Cato .30 .75

1997-98 SkyBox Premium Thunder and Lightning

Randomly inserted into series two packs at a rate of one in 192, this 15-card set features a combination of rainbow holofoil and phosphorescent pigmentation to highlight a collection of stars who use their physical prowess to the team's advantage. Unlike past years, which featured two players, this only features one. One side features the player as "thunder" in his home uniform while the flip side shows him as "lightning" in his away uniform. Card backs are numbered with a "TL" prefix.
COMPLETE SET (15) 200.00 400.00
TL1 Stephon Marbury 8.00 20.00
TL2 Shareef Abdur-Rahim 6.00 15.00
TL3 Shaquille O'Neal 15.00 40.00
TL4 Scottie Pippen 10.00 25.00
TL5 Michael Jordan 125.00 250.00
TL6 Marcus Camby 6.00 15.00
TL7 Kobe Bryant 40.00 100.00
TL8 Kevin Garnett 12.00 30.00
TL9 Kerry Kittles 4.00 10.00
TL10 Grant Hill 10.00 25.00
TL11 Dennis Rodman 15.00 40.00
TL12 Damon Stoudamire 6.00 15.00
TL13 Antoine Walker 6.00 15.00
TL14 Anfernee Hardaway 10.00 25.00
TL15 Allen Iverson 12.00 30.00

1998-99 SkyBox Premium

The 1998-99 SkyBox Premium set was issued with a total of 266 standard size cards. The 8-card packs were released in two series and retailedl for $2.69 each. The fronts feature color game-action photography on ultra thick 20-pt. stock. The cards also carry holographic foil stamping. The rookie subset cards were inserted at a rate of one in four series two packs.
COMPLETE SET (265) 60.00 120.00
COMPLETE SET w/o SP (225) 20.00 40.00
COMPLETE SERIES 1 (125) 12.50 25.00
COMPLETE SERIES 2 (140) 50.00 100.00
1 Tim Duncan .50 1.25
2 Voshon Lenard .15 .40
3 John Starks .20 .50
4 Juwan Howard .20 .50
5 Michael Finley .25 .60
6 Bobby Jackson .20 .50
7 Glenn Robinson .20 .50
8 Antonio McDyess .20 .50
9 Eric Williams .15 .40
10 Zydrunas Ilgauskas .25 .60
11 Terrell Brandon .15 .40
12 Shandon Anderson .15 .40
13 Rod Strickland .15 .40
14 Dennis Rodman .50 1.25
15 Clarence Weatherspoon .15 .40
16 P.J. Brown .15 .40
17 Anfernee Hardaway .40 1.00
18 Dikembe Mutombo .25 .60
19 Patrick Ewing .30 .75
20 Scottie Pippen .40 1.00
21 Shaquille O'Neal .60 1.50
22 Donyell Marshall .15 .40
23 Michael Jordan 2.00 5.00
24 Mark Price .25 .60
25 Jim Jackson .15 .40
26 Isaiah Rider .15 .40
27 Eddie Jones .25 .60
28 Detlef Schrempf .25 .60
29 Corliss Williamson .15 .40
30 Bo Outlaw .15 .40
31 Allen Iverson .50 1.25
32 Luc Longley .15 .40
33 Theo Ratliff .20 .50
34 Antoine Walker .25 .60
35 Lamond Murray .15 .40
36 Avery Johnson .20 .50
37 John Stockton .30 .75
38 David Wesley .15 .40
39 Elden Campbell .15 .40
40 Grant Hill .40 1.00
41 Sam Cassell .20 .50
42 Tracy McGrady .40 1.00
43 Glen Rice .25 .60
44 Kobe Bryant 1.25 3.00
45 John Wallace .15 .40
46 Bobby Phills .15 .40
47 Jerry Stackhouse .25 .60
48 Stephon Marbury .30 .75
49 Jeff Hornacek .20 .50
50 Tom Gugliotta .15 .40
51 Joe Dumars .25 .60
52 Johnny Newman .15 .40
53 Kevin Garnett .50 1.25
54 Dennis Scott .15 .40
55 Anthony Mason .15 .40
56 Rodney Rogers .15 .40
57 Bryon Russell .15 .40
58 Maurice Taylor .15 .40
59 Mookie Blaylock .15 .40
60 Shawn Bradley .15 .40
61 Matt Maloney .15 .40
62 Karl Malone .30 .75
63 Larry Johnson .25 .60
64 Calbert Cheaney .15 .40
65 Steve Smith .20 .50
66 Toni Kukoc .25 .60
67 Reggie Miller .30 .75
68 Jayson Williams .15 .40
69 Gary Payton .25 .60
70 Sean Elliott .25 .60
71 Charles Barkley .40 1.00
72 Tim Hardaway .25 .60
73 Rasheed Wallace .25 .60
74 Tariq Abdul-Wahad .15 .40
75 Kenny Anderson .20 .50
76 Chris Mullin .25 .60
77 Keith Van Horn .25 .60
78 Hersey Hawkins .15 .40
79 Ron Mercer .20 .50
80 Rik Smits .20 .50
81 David Robinson .40 1.00
82 Derek Anderson .15 .40
83 Danny Fortson .15 .40
84 Jason Kidd .40 1.00
85 Chauncey Billups .30 .75
86 Chris Anstey .15 .40
87 Hakeem Olajuwon .30 .75
88 Bryant Reeves .15 .40
89 Anthony Johnson .15 .40
90 Shawn Kemp .25 .60
91 Brevin Knight .15 .40
92 Ray Allen .30 .75
93 Tim Thomas .25 .60
94 Jalen Rose .20 .50
95 Kerry Kittles .15 .40
96 Vin Baker .20 .50
97 Shareef Abdur-Rahim .25 .60
98 Alonzo Mourning .30 .75
99 Joe Smith .20 .50
100 Damon Stoudamire .25 .60
101 Alan Henderson .15 .40
102 Walter McCarty .15 .40
103 Vlade Divac .25 .60
104 Wesley Person .15 .40
105 A.C. Green .25 .60
106 Malik Sealy .15 .40
107 Carl Thomas .15 .40
108 Brent Price .15 .40
109 Mark Jackson .25 .60
110 Lorenzen Wright .15 .40
111 Derek Fisher .25 .60
112 Michael Smith .15 .40
113 Tyrone Hill .15 .40
114 Cherokee Parks .15 .40
115 Kendall Gill .15 .40
116 Darrell Armstrong .15 .40
117 Derrick Coleman .20 .50
118 Rex Chapman .15 .40
119 Arvydas Sabonis .20 .50
120 Billy Owens .15 .40
121 Sam Perkins .15 .40
122 Gary Trent .15 .40
123 Sam Mack .15 .40
124 Tracy Murray .15 .40
125 Allan Houston .20 .50
126 Mitch Richmond .25 .60
127 Carl Herrera .15 .40
128 Ron Harper .20 .50
129 Gary Trent .15 .40
130 Chris Webber .25 .60
131 Antonio Daniels .15 .40
132 Charles Oakley .20 .50
133 Marcus Camby .20 .50
134 Tony Battie .20 .50
135 Otis Thorpe .15 .40
136 Dale Davis .15 .40
137 Chuck Person .20 .50
138 Ervin Johnson .15 .40
139 Jamal Mashburn .20 .50
140 Brian Grant .15 .40
141 Chris Mills .15 .40
142 Doug Christie .15 .40
143 George McCloud .15 .40
144 Todd Fuller .15 .40
145 Jerome Williams .15 .40
146 Chauncey Billups .30 .75
147 Dean Garrett .15 .40
148 Robert Pack .15 .40
149 Clarence Weatherspoon .15 .40
150 Tim Legler .15 .40
151 Bob Sura .15 .40
152 B.J. Armstrong .15 .40
153 Charlie Ward .15 .40
154 Rony Seikaly .25 .60
155 Chris Carr .15 .40
156 Eldridge Recasner .15 .40
157 Michael Stewart .15 .40
158 Jim McIlvaine .15 .40
159 Adam Keefe .15 .40
160 Antonio Davis .15 .40
161 Lawrence Funderburke .15 .40
162 Greg Ostertag .15 .40
163 Dan Majerle .25 .60
164 Dale Ellis .15 .40
165 Greg Anthony .15 .40
166 Chris Whitney .15 .40
167 Eric Piatkowski .20 .50
168 Tom Gugliotta .15 .40
169 Luc Longley .15 .40
170 Antonio McDyess .20 .50
171 George Lynch .15 .40
172 Dell Curry .15 .40
173 Johnny Newman .15 .40
174 Christian Laettner .20 .50
175 Steve Kerr .20 .50
176 Popeye Jones .15 .40
177 Brent Barry .20 .50
178 Billy Owens .15 .40
179 Cherokee Parks .15 .40
180 Derek Harper .20 .50
181 Howard Eisley .15 .40
182 Matt Geiger .15 .40
183 Darrick Martin .15 .40
184 Isaac Austin .15 .40
185 Dennis Scott .15 .40
186 Derrick Coleman .20 .50
187 Sam Perkins .15 .40
188 Latrell Sprewell .25 .60
189 Jud Buechler .15 .40
190 Jason Caffey .15 .40
191 Vlade Divac .25 .60
192 Travis Best .15 .40
193 Loy Vaught .15 .40
194 Mario Elie .15 .40
195 Ed Gray .15 .40
196 Joe Smith .20 .50
197 John Starks .20 .50
198 Anthony Johnson .15 .40
199 Kurt Thomas .15 .40
200 Chris Dudley .15 .40
201 Shareef Abdur-Rahim NF .25 .60
202 Ray Allen NF .30 .75
203 Vin Baker NF .20 .50
204 Charles Barkley NF .40 1.00
205 Kobe Bryant NF 1.25 3.00
206 Tim Duncan NF .50 1.25
207 Anfernee Hardaway NF .40 1.00
208 Grant Hill NF .40 1.00
209 Allen Iverson NF .50 1.25
210 Jason Kidd NF .40 1.00
211 Shawn Kemp NF .25 .60
212 Shaquille O'Neal NF .60 1.50
213 Kerry Kittles NF .15 .40
214 Karl Malone NF .30 .75
215 Stephon Marbury NF .30 .75
216 Ron Mercer NF .20 .50
217 Reggie Miller NF .30 .75
218 Kevin Garnett NF .50 1.25
219 Gary Payton NF .25 .60
220 Scottie Pippen NF .40 1.00
221 David Robinson NF .40 1.00
222 Hakeem Olajuwon NF .30 .75
223 Damon Stoudamire NF .25 .60
224 Keith Van Horn NF .25 .60
225 Antoine Walker NF .25 .60
226 Cory Carr RC .75 2.00
227 Cuttino Mobley RC 1.50 4.00
228 Miles Simon RC .75 2.00
229 J.R. Henderson RC .75 2.00
230 Jason Williams RC 2.00 5.00
231 Felipe Lopez RC .75 2.00
232 Shammond Williams RC .75 2.00
233 Ricky Davis RC 1.25 3.00
234 Vince Carter RC 4.00 10.00
235 Antawn Jamison RC 2.00 5.00
236 Ryan Stack RC .75 2.00
237 Nazr Mohammed RC .75 2.00
238 Sam Jacobson RC .75 2.00
239 Larry Hughes RC 1.50 4.00
240 Ruben Patterson RC .75 2.00
241 Al Harrington RC 1.25 3.00
242 Ansu Sesay RC .75 2.00
243 Vladimir Stepania RC .75 2.00
244 Matt Harpring RC 1.00 2.50
245 Andrae Patterson RC .75 2.00
246 Pat Garrity RC .75 2.00
247 Bonzi Wells RC .75 2.00
248 Bryce Drew RC .75 2.00
249 Toby Bailey RC .75 2.00
250 Michael Doleac RC .75 2.00
251 Michael Dickerson RC .75 2.00
252 Peja Stojakovic RC 2.00 5.00
253 Robert Traylor RC .75 2.00
254 Tyronn Lue RC .75 2.00
255 Dirk Nowitzki RC 5.00 12.00
256 Raef LaFrentz RC 1.00 2.50
257 Jelani McCoy RC .75 2.00
258 Michael Olowokandi RC 1.00 2.50
259 Brian Skinner RC .75 2.00
260 Keon Clark RC .75 2.00
261 Roshown McLeod RC .75 2.00
262 Mike Bibby RC 2.00 5.00
263 Paul Pierce RC 4.00 10.00
264 Tyson Wheeler RC .75 2.00
265 Corey Benjamin RC .75 2.00

1998-99 SkyBox Premium Star Rubies

Serially numbered to 50, this 265-card hobby only parallel offers the same players as the SkyBox base set. SkyBox Premium Star Rubies sparkles with an extra etched ruby holographic foil. In the series two set, rookies are serially numbered to 25. There is no

parallel of the series two Michael Jordan card #266.
*STARS: 50X TO 120X BASE CARD HI
*RCs: 8X TO 20X BASE HI
1 Tim Duncan 80.00 200.00
14 Dennis Rodman 150.00 400.00
17 Anfernee Hardaway 100.00 200.00
20 Scottie Pippen 200.00 400.00
21 Shaquille O'Neal 150.00 300.00
23 Michael Jordan 4000.00 6000.00
27 Eddie Jones 75.00 150.00
31 Allen Iverson 80.00 200.00
40 Grant Hill 100.00 250.00
42 Tracy McGrady 80.00 200.00
44 Kobe Bryant 750.00 1500.00
53 Kevin Garnett 125.00 250.00
67 Reggie Miller 50.00 120.00
71 Charles Barkley 75.00 150.00
84 Jason Kidd 150.00 300.00
87 Hakeem Olajuwon 50.00 120.00
90 Shawn Kemp 100.00 200.00
92 Ray Allen 50.00 120.00
98 Alonzo Mourning 125.00 250.00
188 Latrell Sprewell 50.00 120.00
202 Ray Allen NF 50.00 120.00
204 Charles Barkley NF 75.00 150.00
205 Kobe Bryant NF 750.00 1500.00
206 Tim Duncan NF 80.00 200.00
207 Anfernee Hardaway NF 100.00 200.00
208 Grant Hill NF 100.00 250.00
209 Allen Iverson NF 80.00 200.00
210 Jason Kidd NF 150.00 300.00
211 Shawn Kemp NF 100.00 200.00
212 Shaquille O'Neal NF 150.00 300.00
217 Reggie Miller NF 50.00 120.00
218 Kevin Garnett NF 125.00 250.00
220 Scottie Pippen NF 200.00 400.00
222 Hakeem Olajuwon NF 50.00 120.00
230 Jason Williams 50.00 120.00
234 Vince Carter 600.00 1000.00
252 Peja Stojakovic 50.00 120.00
255 Dirk Nowitzki 600.00 1000.00
262 Mike Bibby 50.00 120.00
263 Paul Pierce 300.00 600.00

1998-99 SkyBox Premium 3D's

Randomly inserted in series one packs at a rate of one in 96, this 15-card insert features color action photography on a special patterned holographic laminant.

COMPLETE SET (15) 300.00 600.00
1 Kobe Bryant 50.00 125.00
2 Anfernee Hardaway 15.00 40.00
3 Allen Iverson 20.00 50.00
4 Michael Jordan 150.00 300.00
5 Stephon Marbury 12.00 30.00
6 Ron Mercer 8.00 20.00
7 Shareef Abdur-Rahim 10.00 25.00
8 Tim Duncan 20.00 50.00
9 Damon Stoudamire 10.00 25.00
10 Kevin Garnett 20.00 50.00
11 Grant Hill 15.00 40.00
12 Scottie Pippen 15.00 40.00
13 Keith Van Horn 10.00 25.00
14 Dennis Rodman 20.00 50.00
15 Shaquille O'Neal 25.00 60.00

1998-99 SkyBox Premium Autographics

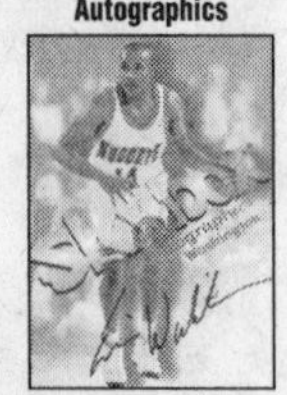

The 1998-99 SkyBox Autographics set consists of many cards and is an insert in all of the SkyBox products (Hoops, Metal, SkyBox, SkyBox Thunder and SkyBox E-X2002). The cards are randomly inserted in packs at a rate of 1:18 for E-X Century, 1:144 for Hoops, 1:68 for Metal, 1:24 for SkyBox Molten Metal, 1:68 for SkyBox Premium series one, 1:24 for SkyBox Premium series two and 1:112 for SkyBox Thunder 1. Allen Iverson signed equal amounts of both black and blue ink cards. The rookies Autographics were originally available via redemption, but were also inserted into packs "live" in later releases. The redemption date for those cards was June 1, 1999. The set is unnumbered and checklisted below in alphabetical order.

1 Tariq Abdul-Wahad 5.00 12.00
2 Shareef Abdur-Rahim 8.00 20.00
3 Cory Alexander 4.00 10.00
4 Ray Allen 20.00 50.00
5 Kenny Anderson 6.00 15.00
6 Nick Anderson 5.00 12.00
7 Chris Anstey 4.00 10.00
8 Isaac Austin 4.00 10.00
9 Vin Baker 10.00 25.00
10 Dana Barros 4.00 10.00
11 Tony Battie 4.00 10.00
12 Corey Benjamin 4.00 10.00
13 Travis Best 4.00 10.00
14 Mike Bibby 10.00 25.00
15 Chauncey Billups 10.00 25.00
16 Corie Blount 4.00 10.00
17 Terrell Brandon 6.00 15.00
18 P.J. Brown 4.00 10.00
19 Scott Burrell 5.00 12.00
20 Jason Caffey 4.00 10.00
21 Marcus Camby 8.00 20.00
22 Elden Campbell 6.00 15.00
23 Chris Carr 4.00 10.00
24 Cory Carr 4.00 10.00
25 Vince Carter 40.00 100.00
26 Kelvin Cato 4.00 10.00
27 Calbert Cheaney 4.00 10.00
28 Keith Closs 4.00 10.00
29 Antonio Daniels 4.00 10.00
30 Dale Davis 8.00 20.00
31 Ricky Davis 10.00 25.00
32 Andrew DeClercq 4.00 10.00
33 Tony Delk 5.00 12.00
34 Michael Dickerson 6.00 15.00
35 Michael Doleac 5.00 12.00
36 Bryce Drew 4.00 10.00
37 Tim Duncan 175.00 350.00
38 Howard Eisley 4.00 10.00
39 Danny Ferry 5.00 12.00
40 Derek Fisher 10.00 25.00
41 Danny Fortson 4.00 10.00
42 Adonal Foyle 4.00 10.00
43 Todd Fuller 4.00 10.00
44 Kevin Garnett 100.00 250.00
45 Pat Garrity 5.00 12.00
46 Brian Grant 5.00 12.00
47 Tom Gugliotta 6.00 15.00
48 Tom Hammonds 4.00 10.00
49 Tim Hardaway 12.50 30.00
50 Matt Harpring 6.00 15.00
51 Othella Harrington 4.00 10.00
52 Hersey Hawkins 8.00 20.00
53 Cedric Henderson 4.00 10.00
54 Grant Hill 150.00 300.00
55 Tyrone Hill 4.00 10.00
56 Allan Houston 12.50 30.00
57 Juwan Howard 10.00 25.00
58 Larry Hughes 10.00 25.00
59 Zydrunas Ilgauskas 15.00 30.00
60 Allen Iverson 175.00 350.00
61 Bobby Jackson 4.00 10.00
62 Antawn Jamison 12.00 30.00
63 Anthony Johnson 4.00 10.00
64 Ervin Johnson 4.00 10.00
65 Larry Johnson 20.00 50.00
66 Eddie Jones 15.00 40.00
67 Adam Keefe 4.00 10.00
68 Shawn Kemp 50.00 120.00
69 Steve Kerr 8.00 20.00
70 Jason Kidd 50.00 120.00
71 Kerry Kittles 6.00 15.00
72 Brevin Knight 5.00 12.00
73 Raef LaFrentz 6.00 15.00
74 Felipe Lopez 4.00 10.00
75 George Lynch 4.00 10.00
76 Karl Malone 250.00 450.00
77 Danny Manning 6.00 15.00
78 Stephon Marbury 10.00 25.00
79 Donyell Marshall 5.00 12.00
80 Tony Massenburg 4.00 10.00
81 Walter McCarty 4.00 10.00
82 Jelani McCoy 4.00 10.00
83 Antonio McDyess 8.00 20.00
84 Tracy McGrady 20.00 50.00
85 Ron Mercer 6.00 15.00
86 Sam Mitchell 4.00 10.00
87 Nazr Mohammed 5.00 12.00
88 Alonzo Mourning 40.00 100.00
89 Chris Mullin 25.00 60.00
90 Dikembe Mutombo 25.00 60.00
91 Hakeem Olajuwon 40.00 100.00
92 Michael Olowokandi 8.00 20.00
93 Elliot Perry 4.00 10.00
94 Bobby Phills 4.00 10.00
95 Eric Piatkowski 4.00 10.00
96 Scottie Pippen 150.00 300.00
97 Scot Pollard 5.00 12.00
98 Vitaly Potapenko 4.00 10.00
99 Brent Price 4.00 10.00
100 Theo Ratliff 5.00 12.00
101 Eldridge Recasner 4.00 10.00
102 Bryant Reeves 5.00 12.00
103 Glen Rice 8.00 20.00
104 Chris Robinson 4.00 10.00
105 David Robinson 100.00 175.00
106 Glenn Robinson 8.00 20.00
107 Dennis Rodman 250.00 500.00
108 Bryon Russell 5.00 12.00
109 Danny Schayes 4.00 10.00
110 Detlef Schrempf 10.00 25.00
111 Rony Seikaly 5.00 12.00
112 Brian Skinner 4.00 10.00
113 Reggie Slater 4.00 10.00
114 Joe Smith 6.00 15.00
115 Steve Smith 8.00 20.00
116 Rik Smits 6.00 15.00
117 Jerry Stackhouse 10.00 25.00
118 John Starks 10.00 25.00
119 Bryant Stith 4.00 10.00
120 Damon Stoudamire 8.00 20.00
121 Mark Strickland 4.00 10.00
122 Rod Strickland 10.00 25.00
123 Bob Sura 4.00 10.00
124 Tim Thomas 5.00 12.00
125 Robert Traylor 5.00 12.00
126 Gary Trent 4.00 10.00
127 Keith Van Horn 6.00 15.00
128 Jacque Vaughn 4.00 10.00
129 Antoine Walker 6.00 15.00
130 Eric Washington 4.00 10.00
131 Clarence Weatherspoon 4.00 10.00
132 Bonzi Wells 8.00 20.00
133 David Wesley 4.00 10.00
134 Eric Williams 4.00 10.00
135 Jason Williams 25.00 50.00
136 Jayson Williams 4.00 10.00
137 Monty Williams 4.00 10.00
138 Walt Williams 4.00 10.00
139 Lorenzen Wright 4.00 10.00

1998-99 SkyBox Premium Autographics Blue

Randomly inserted into the various SkyBox products, this set parallels the basic Autographics insert, but features blue autographs and a serial numbering to 50. Allen Iverson signed equal amounts of blue and black cards, thus, his card is not included in the complete set price. That particular card is also not serial numbered. To ascertain values on individual cards, please refer to the multiplier in the header below, coupled with the value of the autograph.

*BLUE: 1X TO 2.5X VALUE
25 Vince Carter 125.00 300.00
37 Tim Duncan 250.00 600.00
44 Kevin Garnett 200.00 400.00
60 Allen Iverson 200.00 400.00
68 Shawn Kemp 100.00 250.00
70 Jason Kidd 125.00 300.00
76 Karl Malone 500.00 1000.00
84 Tracy McGrady 80.00 200.00
91 Hakeem Olajuwon 80.00 200.00
107 Dennis Rodman 500.00 1000.00
124 Tim Thomas 30.00 80.00

1998-99 SkyBox Premium B.P.O.

Randomly inserted in series two packs at one in six, this 15-card set features the game's brightest young stars. Card fronts feature gold-foil stamping against a black background.

COMPLETE SET (15) 5.00 12.00
1 Ron Mercer .30 .75
2 Shareef Abdur-Rahim .40 1.00
3 Stephon Marbury .50 1.25
4 Tim Thomas .40 1.00
5 Tim Duncan .75 2.00
6 Mike Bibby 1.00 2.50
7 Ray Allen .50 1.25
8 Shawn Kemp .40 1.00
9 Vince Carter 2.00 5.00
10 Antoine Walker .40 1.00
11 Raef LaFrentz .50 1.25
12 Damon Stoudamire .40 1.00
13 Keith Van Horn .40 1.00
14 Kerry Kittles .25 .60
15 Allen Iverson .75 2.00

1998-99 SkyBox Premium Fresh Faces

Randomly inserted in series two packs at a rate of one in 36, this 10-card set focuses on the rookie class from the 1998-99 season.

COMPLETE SET (10) 10.00 25.00
1 Mike Bibby 1.50 4.00
2 Vince Carter 3.00 8.00
3 Al Harrington 1.00 2.50
4 Larry Hughes 1.25 3.00
5 Antawn Jamison 1.50 4.00
6 Raef LaFrentz .75 2.00
7 Michael Olowokandi .75 2.00
8 Paul Pierce 3.00 8.00
9 Robert Traylor .60 1.50
10 Bonzi Wells .60 1.50

1998-99 SkyBox Premium Intimidation Nation

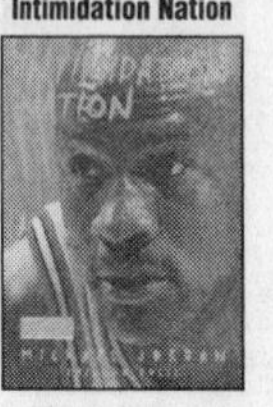

Randomly inserted in series one packs at a rate of one in 360, this 10-card insert set offers gold rainbow holo-foil stamping and features close-up color player photos.

COMPLETE SET (10) 500.00 800.00
1 Shaquille O'Neal 30.00 80.00
2 Kobe Bryant 125.00 250.00
3 Kevin Garnett 25.00 60.00
4 Grant Hill 20.00 50.00
5 Shawn Kemp 15.00 40.00
6 Keith Van Horn 12.00 30.00
7 Antoine Walker 12.00 30.00
8 Michael Jordan 300.00 600.00
9 Gary Payton 12.00 30.00
10 Tim Duncan 25.00 60.00

1998-99 SkyBox Premium Just Cookin'

Randomly inserted in series one packs at a rate of one in 12, this 10-card set features some of the game's top rookies from 1998 on silver holographic foil.

COMPLETE SET (10) 2.50 6.00
1 Maurice Taylor .40 1.00
2 Brevin Knight .40 1.00
3 Tim Thomas .60 1.50
4 Chauncey Billups .75 2.00
5 Chris Anstey .40 1.00
6 Tracy McGrady 1.00 2.50
7 Zydrunas Ilgauskas .60 1.50
8 Antonio Daniels .40 1.00
9 Bobby Jackson .50 1.25
10 Derek Anderson .40 1.00

1998-99 SkyBox Premium Mod Squad

Randomly inserted in series two packs at one in 18, this 16-card set features player's in off the court settings. The cards feature a silver and black foil background.

COMPLETE SET (16) 15.00 40.00
1 Tim Thomas .75 2.00
2 Shaquille O'Neal 2.00 5.00
3 Scottie Pippen 1.25 3.00
4 Kobe Bryant 4.00 10.00
5 Kevin Garnett 1.50 4.00
6 Grant Hill 1.25 3.00
7 Anfernee Hardaway 1.25 3.00
8 Antoine Walker .75 2.00
9 Stephon Marbury 1.00 2.50
10 Kerry Kittles .50 1.25
11 Allen Iverson 1.50 4.00
12 Gary Payton .75 2.00
13 Damon Stoudamire .75 2.00
14 Marcus Camby .60 1.50
15 Shareef Abdur-Rahim .75 2.00
16 Michael Jordan 6.00 15.00

1998-99 SkyBox Premium Net Set

Randomly inserted into series one packs at one in 36, this 15-card set features some of the biggest names in the game on etched silver rainbow foilboard.

COMPLETE SET (15) 25.00 50.00
1 Ron Mercer 1.50 4.00
2 Shawn Kemp 2.00 5.00
3 Brevin Knight 1.25 3.00
4 Maurice Taylor 1.25 3.00
5 Ray Allen 2.50 6.00
6 Dennis Rodman 4.00 10.00
7 Kerry Kittles 1.25 3.00
8 Tim Thomas 2.00 5.00
9 Gary Payton 2.00 5.00
10 Marcus Camby 1.50 4.00
11 Karl Malone 2.50 6.00
12 Juwan Howard 1.50 4.00
13 Zydrunas Ilgauskas 2.00 5.00
14 Scottie Pippen 3.00 8.00
15 Anfernee Hardaway 3.00 8.00

1998-99 SkyBox Premium Slam Funk

Randomly inserted in series two packs at one in 360, this 10-card set highlights players who play above the rim. These plastic cards feature rainbow holo-lamination.

COMPLETE SET (10) 100.00 200.00
1 Kobe Bryant 75.00 200.00
2 Kevin Garnett 15.00 40.00
3 Grant Hill 15.00 40.00
4 Shaquille O'Neal 20.00 50.00
5 Michael Olowokandi 4.00 10.00
6 Tim Duncan 15.00 40.00
7 Antawn Jamison 8.00 20.00
8 Keith Van Horn 8.00 20.00
9 Ron Mercer 6.00 15.00
10 Scottie Pippen 12.00 30.00

1998-99 SkyBox Premium Smooth

Randomly inserted in series one packs at a rate of one 6, this 15-card insert set features color action photos surrounded by a solid black background with silver rainbow holofoil stamping.

COMPLETE SET (15) 3.00 8.00
1 Stephon Marbury .50 1.25
2 Shareef Abdur-Rahim .40 1.00
3 Keith Van Horn .40 1.00
4 Marcus Camby .30 .75
5 Ray Allen .50 1.25
6 Allen Iverson .75 2.00
7 Kerry Kittles .25 .60
8 Tim Thomas .40 1.00
9 Damon Stoudamire .40 1.00
10 Antoine Walker .40 1.00
11 Brevin Knight .25 .60
12 Zydrunas Ilgauskas .40 1.00
13 Ron Mercer .30 .75
14 Maurice Taylor .25 .60
15 Tim Duncan .75 2.00

1998-99 SkyBox Premium Soul of the Game

Randomly inserted in series one packs at a rate of one in 18, this 15-card insert set offers a color action photo on a rainbow foil background that appears to change colors.

COMPLETE SET (15) 30.00 80.00
1 Michael Jordan 30.00 80.00
2 Antoine Walker 1.00 2.50
3 Scottie Pippen 1.50 4.00
4 Grant Hill 1.50 4.00
5 Dennis Rodman 2.00 5.00
6 Kobe Bryant 12.00 30.00
7 Kevin Garnett 2.00 5.00
8 Shaquille O'Neal 2.50 6.00
9 Stephon Marbury 1.25 3.00
10 Kerry Kittles .60 1.50
11 Anfernee Hardaway 1.50 4.00
12 Allen Iverson 2.00 5.00
13 Damon Stoudamire 1.00 2.50
14 Marcus Camby .75 2.00
15 Shareef Abdur-Rahim 1.00 2.50

1998-99 SkyBox Premium That's Jam

Randomly inserted in series two packs at one in 96, this 15-card set features offensive superstars on a clear plastic background.

COMPLETE SET (15) 50.00 120.00
1 Tim Duncan 6.00 15.00
2 Stephon Marbury 4.00 10.00
3 Shareef Abdur-Rahim 3.00 8.00
4 Shaquille O'Neal 8.00 20.00
5 Ron Mercer 2.50 6.00
6 Scottie Pippen 5.00 12.00
7 Antawn Jamison 4.00 10.00
8 Anfernee Hardaway 5.00 12.00
9 Damon Stoudamire 3.00 8.00
10 Allen Iverson 6.00 15.00
11 Keith Van Horn 3.00 8.00
12 Grant Hill 5.00 12.00
13 Kevin Garnett 6.00 15.00
14 Kobe Bryant 20.00 50.00
15 Antoine Walker 3.00 8.00

1999-00 SkyBox Premium

Released in one series, this 150-card set was released in eight-card packs that carried a suggested retail price of $2.69. There were two versions of the 25-card rookie subset: the regular rookie cards, which were portrait cards and not inserted and special action shots, which were inserted at one in eight.

COMPLETE SET (150) 40.00 100.00
COMPLETE SET w/o SP (125) 12.50 30.00
1 Vince Carter .60 1.50
2 Nick Anderson .20 .50
3 Isaiah Rider .20 .50
4 Mitch Richmond .30 .75
5 Danny Fortson .20 .50
6 Kenny Anderson .25 .60
7 Reggie Miller .30 .75
8 Tracy McGrady .50 1.25
9 Steve Nash .50 1.25
10 Robert Traylor .20 .50
11 Tom Gugliotta .20 .50
12 Steve Smith .20 .50
13 Jalen Rose .25 .60
14 Kerry Kittles .20 .50
15 Nick Van Exel .25 .60
16 Raef LaFrentz .25 .60
17 Damon Stoudamire .30 .75
18 Gary Trent .20 .50
19 Jayson Williams .20 .50
20 Brian Grant .20 .50
21 Rod Strickland .20 .50
22 Larry Hughes .25 .60
23 Derek Anderson .20 .50
24 Hakeem Olajuwon .40 1.00
25 Ray Allen .30 .75
26 Gary Payton .30 .75
27 Michael Finley .30 .75
28 Keith Van Horn .25 .60
29 Clifford Robinson .20 .50
30 Shawn Kemp .30 .75
31 Glenn Robinson .25 .60
32 Theo Ratliff .25 .60
33 Lindsey Hunter .20 .50
34 Chris Webber .30 .75
35 Grant Hill .40 1.00
36 Vlade Divac .30 .75
37 Paul Pierce .50 1.25
38 Tyrone Nesby RC .30 .75
39 Larry Johnson .30 .75
40 Bryon Russell .20 .50
41 Antoine Walker .30 .75
42 Michael Olowokandi .20 .50
43 John Stockton .40 1.00
44 Elden Campbell .20 .50
45 Christian Laettner .25 .60
46 Maurice Taylor .20 .50
47 Shareef Abdur-Rahim .25 .60
48 Ricky Davis .30 .75
49 Jerry Stackhouse .30 .75
50 Kobe Bryant 1.50 4.00
51 Jason Williams .40 1.00
52 Mike Bibby .30 .75
53 Eddie Jones .30 .75
54 Antawn Jamison .30 .75
55 Shaquille O'Neal .75 2.00
56 Tim Duncan .60 1.50
57 Cherokee Parks .20 .50
58 Antonio McDyess .25 .60
59 Rasheed Wallace .30 .75
60 Anthony Mason .20 .50
61 Chris Mills .20 .50
62 Glen Rice .30 .75
63 Latrell Sprewell .30 .75
64 Darrell Armstrong .20 .50
65 Sean Elliott .30 .75
66 Juwan Howard .25 .60
67 Brent Barry .25 .60
68 John Starks .30 .75
69 Tim Hardaway .30 .75
70 Marcus Camby .25 .60
71 Anfernee Hardaway .50 1.25
72 Avery Johnson .25 .60
73 Tariq Abdul-Wahad .20 .50
74 Charles Barkley .50 1.25
75 Stephon Marbury .25 .60
76 Jamal Mashburn .25 .60
77 Matt Harpring .25 .60
78 David Robinson .50 1.25
79 Cedric Ceballos .20 .50
80 Terrell Brandon .20 .50
81 Jason Kidd .50 1.25
82 Toni Kukoc .30 .75
83 Michael Dickerson .20 .50
84 Alonzo Mourning .40 1.00
85 Kevin Garnett .60 1.50
86 Matt Geiger .20 .50
87 Vin Baker .30 .75
88 Dikembe Mutombo .30 .75
89 Hersey Hawkins .20 .50
90 Joe Smith .25 .60
91 Charles Oakley .25 .60
92 Ron Mercer .25 .60
93 Rik Smits .30 .75
94 Patrick Ewing .40 1.00
95 Karl Malone .40 1.00
96 Scottie Pippen .50 1.25
97 Zydrunas Ilgauskas .25 .60
98 Sam Cassell .25 .60
99 Detlef Schrempf .25 .60
100 Allen Iverson .60 1.50
101 Elton Brand RC .75 2.00
101A Elton Brand SP 2.00 5.00
102 Steve Francis RC .75 2.00
102A Steve Francis SP 2.00 5.00
103 Baron Davis RC 1.00 2.50
103A Baron Davis SP 2.50 6.00
104 Lamar Odom RC 1.00 2.50
104A Lamar Odom SP 2.50 6.00
105 Jonathan Bender RC .30 .75
105A Jonathan Bender SP .75 2.00
106 Wally Szczerbiak RC .60 1.50
106A Wally Szczerbiak SP 1.50 4.00
107 Richard Hamilton RC .75 2.00
107A Richard Hamilton SP 2.00 5.00
108 Andre Miller RC .75 2.00
108A Andre Miller SP 2.00 5.00
109 Shawn Marion RC .75 2.00
109A Shawn Marion SP 2.00 5.00
110 Jason Terry RC .75 2.00
110A Jason Terry SP 2.00 5.00
111 Trajan Langdon RC .30 .75
111A Trajan Langdon SP .75 2.00
112 Aleksandar Radojevic RC .30 .75
112A Aleksandar Radojevic SP .75 2.00
113 Corey Maggette RC .60 1.50
113A Corey Maggette SP 1.50 4.00
114 William Avery RC .30 .75
114A William Avery SP .75 2.00
115 Vonteego Cummings RC .30 .75
115A Vonteego Cummings SP .75 2.00
116 Ron Artest RC .75 2.00
116A Ron Artest SP 2.00 5.00
117 Cal Bowdler RC .30 .75
117A Cal Bowdler SP .75 2.00
118 James Posey RC .30 .75
118A James Posey SP .75 2.00
119 Quincy Lewis RC .30 .75
119A Quincy Lewis SP .75 2.00
120 Dion Glover RC .30 .75
120A Dion Glover SP .75 2.00
121 Jeff Foster RC .30 .75
121A Jeff Foster SP .75 2.00
122 Kenny Thomas RC .30 .75
122A Kenny Thomas SP .75 2.00
123 Devean George RC .30 .75
123A Devean George SP .75 2.00
124 Scott Padgett RC .30 .75
124A Scott Padgett SP .75 2.00
125 Tim James RC .30 .75
125A Tim James SP .75 2.00

1999-00 SkyBox Premium Star Rubies

Randomly inserted in hobby packs only, this 150-card set parallels the base set using red foil. The regular issue cards 1-125, were serially numbered to 45. The SP versions of cards 101-125 were serially numbered to 25.

*STARS: 30X TO 80X HI COLUMN
*RCs: 12X TO 30X HI
*SPs: 8X TO 20X HI
24 Hakeem Olajuwon 40.00 100.00
35 Grant Hill 75.00 200.00
50 Kobe Bryant 250.00 500.00
55 Shaquille O'Neal 100.00 225.00
56 Tim Duncan 100.00 200.00
71 Anfernee Hardaway 50.00 125.00
78 David Robinson 50.00 125.00
96 Scottie Pippen 100.00 200.00

1999-00 SkyBox Premium Autographics

Randomly inserted in all of the SkyBox products, this 113-card set features autographs of the top NBA stars and rookies. The cards are not numbered and listed below in alphabetical order. The cards were inserted in all products at one in 68, except Hoops Decade, which was inserted at one in 144, Metal, which was inserted at one in 96 and SkyBox Impact, which was inserted at one in 288.

1 Cory Alexander 3.00 8.00
2 Ray Allen 15.00 40.00
3 Darrell Armstrong 3.00 8.00
4 Ron Artest 10.00 25.00
5 William Avery 4.00 10.00
6 Charles Barkley 500.00 900.00
7 Dana Barros 4.00 10.00
8 Corey Benjamin 3.00 8.00
9 Travis Best 3.00 8.00
10 Mike Bibby 10.00 25.00
11 Calvin Booth 3.00 8.00
12 Cal Bowdler 3.00 8.00
13 Bruce Bowen 6.00 15.00
14 P.J. Brown 3.00 8.00
15 Jud Buechler 3.00 8.00
16 Marcus Camby 8.00 20.00
17 Elden Campbell 4.00 10.00
18 Cory Carr 3.00 8.00
19 Vince Carter 15.00 40.00
20 John Celestand 3.00 8.00
21 Dell Curry 3.00 8.00
22 Baron Davis 12.00 30.00
23 Andrew DeClercq 3.00 8.00
24 Tony Delk 4.00 10.00
25 Michael Dickerson 3.00 8.00
26 Michael Doleac 3.00 8.00
27 Bryce Drew 3.00 8.00
28 Obinna Ekezie 3.00 8.00
29 Evan Eschmeyer 4.00 10.00
30 Michael Finley 6.00 15.00
31 Greg Foster 3.00 8.00
32 Jeff Foster 3.00 8.00
33 Steve Francis 10.00 25.00
34 Todd Fuller 3.00 8.00
35 Lawrence Funderburke 3.00 8.00
36 Dean Garrett 3.00 8.00
37 Pat Garrity 3.00 8.00
38 Devean George 4.00 10.00
39 Kendall Gill 5.00 12.00
40 Dion Glover 3.00 8.00
41 Brian Grant 3.00 8.00
42 Paul Grant 3.00 8.00
43 Tom Gugliotta 8.00 20.00
44 Richard Hamilton 12.00 30.00
45 Tim Hardaway 10.00 25.00
46 Matt Harpring 4.00 10.00
47 Al Harrington 4.00 10.00
48 Othella Harrington 3.00 8.00
49 Troy Hudson 3.00 8.00
50 Larry Hughes 8.00 20.00
51 Tim James 3.00 8.00
52 Antawn Jamison 6.00 15.00
53 Anthony Johnson 3.00 8.00
54 Avery Johnson 6.00 15.00
55 Ervin Johnson 3.00 8.00
56 Eddie Jones 15.00 30.00
57 Jumaine Jones 3.00 8.00
58 Adam Keefe 3.00 8.00
59 Shawn Kemp 40.00 100.00
60 Kerry Kittles 6.00 15.00
61 Raef LaFrentz 5.00 12.00
62 Trajan Langdon 5.00 12.00
63 Quincy Lewis 3.00 8.00
64 Felipe Lopez 3.00 8.00
65 Tyronn Lue 3.00 8.00
66 George Lynch 3.00 8.00
67 Sam Mack 3.00 8.00
68 Stephon Marbury 8.00 20.00
69 Shawn Marion 8.00 20.00
70 Tony Massenburg 3.00 8.00
71 Jelani McCoy 3.00 8.00
72 Antonio McDyess 8.00 20.00
73 Tracy McGrady 20.00 40.00
74 Roshown McLeod 3.00 8.00
75 Brad Miller 5.00 12.00
76 Sam Mitchell 3.00 8.00
77 Nazr Mohammed 4.00 10.00
78 Alonzo Mourning 50.00 120.00
79 Tyrone Nesby 3.00 8.00
80 Shaquille O'Neal 75.00 200.00
81 Lamar Odom 8.00 20.00
82 Hakeem Olajuwon 30.00 80.00
83 Michael Olowokandi 8.00 20.00
84 Andrae Patterson 3.00 8.00
85 Eric Piatkowski 4.00 10.00
86 Scottie Pippen 75.00 150.00
87 Scot Pollard 3.00 8.00
88 James Posey 6.00 15.00
89 Brent Price 3.00 8.00
90 Aleksandar Radojevic 3.00 8.00
91 Theo Ratliff 3.00 8.00
92 J.R. Reid 4.00 10.00
93 David Robinson 60.00 150.00
94 Glenn Robinson 8.00 20.00
95 Jalen Rose 12.50 25.00
96 Michael Ruffin 3.00 8.00
97 Wally Szczerbiak 6.00 15.00
98 Joe Smith 6.00 15.00
99 Jerry Stackhouse 8.00 20.00
100 John Starks 10.00 25.00
101 Vladimir Stepania 3.00 8.00
102 Damon Stoudamire 6.00 15.00
103 Maurice Taylor 4.00 10.00
104 Jason Terry 8.00 20.00
105 Kenny Thomas 3.00 8.00
106 Robert Traylor 4.00 10.00
107 Gary Trent 3.00 8.00
108 Antoine Walker 10.00 25.00
109 Chris Webber 100.00 200.00
110 David Wesley 3.00 8.00
111 Aaron Williams 3.00 8.00

Jerome Williams 3.00 8.00
Haywoode Workman 3.00 8.00

1999-00 SkyBox Premium Autographics Blue

ndomly inserted in all SkyBox products, this set is a allel of the regular Autographics insert. The cards ure blue ink and are serially numbered to 50. The ts are not numbered and listed below in habetical order. To ascertain values on individual ts, please refer to the multiplier in the header ow, coupled with the value of the base insert.

UE: .75X TO 2X VALUE
Elden Campbell 10.00 25.00
Vince Carter 50.00 120.00
Baron Davis 40.00 100.00
Steve Francis 25.00 60.00
Richard Hamilton 20.00 50.00
Tracy McGrady 60.00 120.00
Alonzo Mourning 80.00 200.00
Lamar Odom 30.00 80.00
Wally Szczerbiak 20.00 50.00

999-00 SkyBox Premium Back for More

ndomly inserted in packs at one in six, this 15-card focuses on the sensational sophomores for the 99-00 class.

MPLETE SET (15) 5.00 12.00
Mike Bibby .75 2.00
Tyrone Nesby .75 2.00
Ricky Davis .75 2.00
Michael Dickerson .50 1.25
Michael Doleac .50 1.25
Antawn Jamison .75 2.00
Larry Hughes .60 1.50
Matt Harpring .60 1.50
Peja Stojakovic .75 2.00
Raef LaFrentz .60 1.50
Michael Olowokandi .50 1.25
Robert Traylor .50 1.25
Paul Pierce 1.25 3.00
Kornel David .75 2.00
Jason Williams 1.00 2.50

999-00 SkyBox Premium Club Vertical

ndomly inserted in packs, this 10-card set focuses aerial artists on die cut and embossed red-foil rds. The cards are serially numbered to 100.

Vince Carter 40.00 100.00
Tim Duncan 40.00 100.00
Shaquille O'Neal 50.00 125.00
Paul Pierce 30.00 80.00
Kobe Bryant 200.00 500.00
Kevin Garnett 40.00 100.00
Keith Van Horn 15.00 40.00
Jason Williams 25.00 60.00
Grant Hill 60.00 150.00
Allen Iverson 40.00 100.00

1999-00 SkyBox Premium Genuine Coverage

ndomly inserted in packs, this six-card set features watches of game-used jerseys from top NBA stars. e cards are serially numbered and each is listed after e player's name.

Kobe Bryant/340 60.00 150.00
Vince Carter/355 20.00 50.00
Patrick Ewing/450 15.00 40.00
Grant Hill/370 25.00 60.00
Allen Iverson/275 25.00 60.00
Alonzo Mourning/360 15.00 40.00

999-00 SkyBox Premium Good Stuff

ndomly inserted in packs at one in 36, this 10-card et features superstar veterans on fuscia-foil stamped ilver foil.

OMPLETE SET (10) 10.00 25.00
PARALLEL: 8X TO 20X HI COLUMN
PARALLEL: PRINT RUN 99 SERIAL #'d SETS
Kobe Bryant 6.00 15.00
Vince Carter 2.00 5.00
Jason Williams 1.25 3.00
Paul Pierce 1.50 4.00
Tim Duncan 2.00 5.00
Kevin Garnett 2.00 5.00
Grant Hill 1.25 3.00
Keith Van Horn .75 2.00
Allen Iverson 2.00 5.00
Shaquille O'Neal 2.50 6.00

1999-00 SkyBox Premium Majestic

Randomly inserted in packs at one in 12, this 15-card set features some of the games most stylish stars. The cards feature matte-varnished finish.

COMPLETE SET (15) 6.00 15.00
1 Antawn Jamison .60 1.50
2 Jason Kidd 1.00 2.50
3 Ron Mercer .50 1.25
4 Shawn Kemp .60 1.50
5 Stephon Marbury .50 1.25
6 Shaquille O'Neal 1.50 4.00
7 Larry Hughes .50 1.25
8 Kevin Garnett 1.25 3.00
9 Antoine Walker .60 1.50
10 Keith Van Horn .50 1.25
11 Anfernee Hardaway 1.00 2.50
12 Tim Duncan . 1.25 3.00
13 Scottie Pippen 1.00 2.50
14 Shareef Abdur-Rahim .50 1.25
15 Chris Webber .60 1.50

1999-00 SkyBox Premium Prime Time Rookies

Randomly inserted in packs at one in 96, this 15-card set features some of the leagues top rookies on plastic cards with silver and clear patterned holo-foil stamping. Card backs carry a "PT" prefix.

COMPLETE SET (15) 25.00 60.00
PT1 Elton Brand 4.00 10.00
PT2 Steve Francis 4.00 10.00
PT3 Baron Davis 5.00 12.00
PT4 Lamar Odom 5.00 12.00
PT5 Jonathan Bender 1.50 4.00
PT6 Wally Szczerbiak 3.00 8.00
PT7 Richard Hamilton 4.00 10.00
PT8 Andre Miller 4.00 10.00
PT9 Shawn Marion 4.00 10.00
PT10 Jason Terry 4.00 10.00
PT11 Trajan Langdon 1.50 4.00
PT12 Dion Glover 1.50 4.00
PT13 Corey Maggette 3.00 8.00
PT14 William Avery 1.50 4.00
PT15 Tim James 1.50 4.00

1999-00 SkyBox Premium Prime Time Rookies Autographs

Randomly inserted in hobby packs only, this 15-card set features autographed versions of the Prime Time Rookie insert. The cards are serially numbered to 25. Card backs carry a "PT" prefix.

PT1 Elton Brand 40.00 100.00
PT2 Steve Francis 40.00 100.00
PT3 Baron Davis 50.00 125.00
PT4 Lamar Odom 50.00 125.00
PT5 Jonathan Bender 15.00 40.00
PT6 Wally Szczerbiak 30.00 80.00
PT7 Richard Hamilton 40.00 100.00
PT8 Andre Miller 40.00 100.00
PT9 Shawn Marion 40.00 100.00
PT10 Jason Terry 40.00 100.00
PT11 Trajan Langdon 15.00 40.00
PT12 Dion Glover 15.00 40.00
PT13 Corey Maggette 30.00 80.00
PT14 William Avery 15.00 40.00
PT15 Tim James 15.00 40.00

2004-05 SkyBox Premium

Released in May 2005, Skybox Premium consists of a 100-card set divided up into 75 veteran players and 25 rookies serially numbered to 999. Base cards have mostly white in the background with a centered black and white photo offset by a full-color player action photo. Skybox Premium was offered in both Hobby and Retail formats where both were released in five card packs but Hobby boxes contained 12 packs and Retail contained 24.

COMP.SET w/o SP's (75) 15.00 40.00
1 Dwyane Wade 1.25 3.00
2 Rashard Lewis .40 1.00
3 Jermaine O'Neal .40 1.00
4 Ben Wallace .40 1.00
5 Steve Francis .40 1.00
6 Lamar Odom .40 1.00
7 Jason Richardson .40 1.00
8 Jarvis Hayes .25 .60
9 Carmelo Anthony .75 2.00
10 Tony Parker .40 1.00
11 Eddy Curry .30 .75
12 Nene .30 .75
13 Kevin Garnett .75 2.00
14 Darius Miles .25 .60
15 Elton Brand .40 1.00
16 Zach Randolph .30 .75
17 Mike Dunleavy .30 .75
18 Dajuan Wagner .25 .60
19 Steve Nash .50 1.25
20 Ron Artest .40 1.00
21 Ricky Davis .30 .75
22 Antawn Jamison .40 1.00
23 Jamal Mashburn .40 1.00
24 T.J. Ford .30 .75
25 Amare Stoudemire .50 1.25
26 Jason Kapono .25 .60
27 Shawn Marion .40 1.00
28 Corliss Williamson .25 .60
29 Reggie Miller .40 1.00
30 Desmond Mason .30 .75
31 Pau Gasol .40 1.00
32 Baron Davis .40 1.00
33 Allen Iverson .60 1.50
34 Darko Milicic .25 .60
35 Ray Allen .40 1.00
36 Jason Williams .30 .75
37 Michael Redd .40 1.00
38 Yao Ming .75 2.00
39 Antoine Walker .40 1.00
40 Jason Terry .30 .75
41 Sam Cassell .30 .75
42 Richard Jefferson .40 1.00
43 Manu Ginobili .50 1.25
44 Dirk Nowitzki .60 1.50
45 Peja Stojakovic .40 1.00
46 Samuel Dalembert .25 .60
47 Latrell Sprewell .30 .75
48 Gerald Wallace .40 1.00
49 Andrei Kirilenko .30 .75
50 Nick Van Exel .30 .75
51 Jalen Rose .30 .75
52 Shaquille O'Neal 1.00 2.50
53 Shareef Abdur-Rahim .30 .75
54 Tracy McGrady .50 1.25
55 Rasheed Wallace .40 1.00
56 Cuttino Mobley .30 .75
57 Jason Kidd .60 1.50
58 Chris Webber .40 1.00
59 Paul Pierce .50 1.25
60 Mike Bibby .40 1.00
61 Allan Houston .30 .75
62 Kobe Bryant 2.00 5.00
63 Kenyon Martin .40 1.00
64 LeBron James 2.50 6.00
65 Tim Duncan .60 1.50
66 Stephon Marbury .30 .75
67 Kirk Hinrich .40 1.00
68 Chris Bosh .40 1.00
69 Corey Maggette .30 .75
70 Vince Carter .60 1.50
71 Caron Butler .40 1.00
72 Stephen Jackson .30 .75
73 Carlos Boozer .40 1.00
74 Michael Finley .40 1.00
75 Jamal Crawford .30 .75
76 Dwight Howard RC 5.00 12.00
77 Emeka Okafor RC 2.50 6.00
78 Ben Gordon RC 2.00 5.00
79 Shaun Livingston RC 1.50 4.00
80 Devin Harris RC 2.50 6.00
81 Josh Childress RC 1.50 4.00
82 Luol Deng RC 2.50 6.00
83 Rafael Araujo RC 1.50 4.00
84 Andre Iguodala RC 2.50 6.00
85 Luke Jackson RC 1.50 4.00
86 Andris Biedrins RC 2.00 5.00
87 Robert Swift RC 1.50 4.00
88 Sebastian Telfair RC 1.50 4.00
89 Kris Humphries RC 1.50 4.00
90 Al Jefferson RC 2.50 6.00
91 Kirk Snyder RC 1.50 4.00
92 Josh Smith RC 2.50 6.00
93 J.R. Smith RC 2.00 5.00
94 Dorell Wright RC 2.50 6.00
95 Jameer Nelson RC 2.00 5.00
96 Bernard Robinson RC 1.50 4.00
97 Andre Emmett RC 1.50 4.00
98 Delonte West RC 2.00 5.00
99 Tony Allen RC 2.00 5.00
100 Kevin Martin RC 2.00 5.00

2004-05 SkyBox Premium Ruby

Inserted in packs, this 100-card set parallels the base set enhanced with red highlights on the card front and sequential numbering to 75.

*1-75 RUBY: 2.5X TO 6X BASE HI
*76-100 RUBY RC's: 1X TO 2.5X BASE HI

2004-05 SkyBox Premium Autographs

Limited to 100 copies, this 30-card set parallels the look of the base Skybox Premium set but is enhanced with authentic player autographs. A die cut version was also inserted in sets, and no odds were given for these.

*DIE CUTS: .4X TO 1X BASE AU HI
6 Lamar Odom 6.00 15.00
12 Nene 6.00 15.00
22 Antawn Jamison 6.00 15.00
49 Andrei Kirilenko 6.00 15.00
70 Vince Carter 15.00 40.00
78 Ben Gordon 8.00 20.00
82 Luol Deng 10.00 25.00
83 Rafael Araujo 6.00 15.00
85 Luke Jackson 6.00 15.00
86 Andris Biedrins 8.00 20.00
87 Robert Swift 6.00 15.00
89 Kris Humphries 6.00 15.00
91 Kirk Snyder 6.00 15.00
93 J.R. Smith 8.00 20.00
94 Dorell Wright 10.00 25.00
97 Andre Emmett 6.00 15.00
98 Delonte West 8.00 20.00

2004-05 SkyBox Premium Hometown Shout Outs

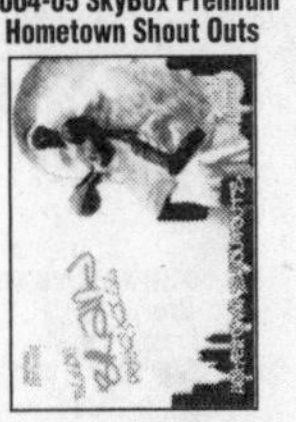

Inserted in packs, this 12-card set features a horizontal design with full-color player photos set against black and white backgrounds. Each card is sequentially numbered, and print runs appear in the checklist.

COMPLETE SET (12) 10.00 25.00
1 Carmelo Anthony/410 1.50 4.00
2 Dwyane Wade/708 2.50 6.00
3 Rasheed Wallace/215 .75 2.00
4 Allen Iverson/757 1.25 3.00
5 Paul Pierce/510 1.00 2.50
6 Richard Jefferson/602 .75 2.00
7 Tim Duncan/340 1.25 3.00
8 Michael Redd/614 .75 2.00
9 Elton Brand/914 .75 2.00
10 LeBron James/330 5.00 12.00
11 Vince Carter/386 1.25 3.00
12 Kobe Bryant/610 4.00 10.00

2004-05 SkyBox Premium Hometown Shout Outs Autographs

Randomly seeded in packs, this 15-card set parallels the design of the base Hometown Shout Outs set enhanced with player autographs. Each card is sequentially numbered and print runs appear in the checklist.

CA Carlos Arroyo/250 15.00 40.00
CA Carmelo Anthony/25 30.00 80.00
CD Carlos Delfino/250 4.00 10.00
DH David Harrison/250 4.00 10.00
DW Dwyane Wade/50 40.00 100.00
HS Ha Seung-Jin/240 4.00 10.00
JJ Joe Johnson/250 5.00 12.00
NC Nick Collison/150 4.00 10.00
PP Paul Pierce 6.00 15.00
RJ Richard Jefferson/75 6.00 15.00
VC Vince Carter 15.00 40.00

2004-05 SkyBox Premium Hometown Shout Outs Jerseys

Randomly seeded in Hobby packs overall at one in six and Retail packs overall at one in 48, this 10-card set parallels the design of the base Hometown Shout Outs set enhanced with player jersey swatches. A Patch version serially numbered to 15 was also issued and contains premium jersey patch swatches.

*JERSEY 75 SINGLES: .6X TO 1.5X BASE HI
AI Allen Iverson 4.00 10.00
CA Carmelo Anthony 5.00 12.00
DW Dwyane Wade 8.00 20.00
EB Elton Brand 2.50 6.00
MR Michael Redd 2.50 6.00
PP Paul Pierce 3.00 8.00
RJ Richard Jefferson 2.50 6.00
RW Rasheed Wallace 2.50 6.00
TD Tim Duncan 4.00 10.00
VC Vince Carter 4.00 10.00

2004-05 SkyBox Premium Parquet Performers

Inserted in Hobby packs at the rate of one in 12, this 15-card set is horizontally designed and showcases great players from the past. Each card features a piece of Floor from the original Boston Garden.

1 Danny Ainge 6.00 15.00
2 Nate Archibald 6.00 15.00
3 Larry Bird 12.50 30.00
4 Kevin McHale 6.00 15.00
5 K.C. Jones 6.00 15.00
7 Pete Maravich 15.00 40.00
8 Jo Jo White 6.00 15.00
9 Robert Parish 8.00 20.00
10 John Havlicek 6.00 15.00
11 Bob Cousy 10.00 25.00
12 Tom Heinsohn 6.00 15.00
13 Dave Cowens 6.00 15.00
14 Bill Sharman 6.00 15.00
15 Sam Jones 6.00 15.00

2004-05 SkyBox Premium Parquet Performers Autographs

Inserted in Hobby packs at the rate of one in 144, this 13-card set parallels the base Parquet Performers set but is autographed. Many of these cards were never issued due to the shut-down of Fleer/Skybox International in the summer of 2005.

BC Bob Cousy 15.00 40.00
BS Bill Sharman 12.50 30.00
DA Danny Ainge 20.00 50.00
DC Dave Cowens 20.00 50.00
KM Kevin McHale 75.00 150.00
NA Nate Archibald 15.00 40.00
RP Robert Parish 15.00 40.00
SJ Sam Jones 12.50 30.00
TH Tom Heinsohn 15.00 40.00

2004-05 SkyBox Premium Performers

Seeded in both Hobby and Retail packs at the rate of one in six, this 20-card set is horizontally designed with a tan background to represent the wood floor of a basketball court and player photos in the top right.

COMPLETE SET (20) 10.00 25.00
1 Tracy McGrady .60 1.50
2 Kenyon Martin .50 1.25
3 Chris Webber .50 1.25
4 Kevin Garnett 1.00 2.50
5 Shaquille O'Neal 1.25 3.00
6 Allen Iverson .75 2.00
7 Steve Francis .50 1.25
8 Manu Ginobili .60 1.50
9 Paul Pierce .60 1.50
10 Ben Wallace .50 1.25
11 Carmelo Anthony 1.00 2.50
12 Peja Stojakovic .50 1.25
13 Richard Hamilton .40 1.00
14 Stephon Marbury .40 1.00
15 Vince Carter .75 2.00
16 Kobe Bryant 2.50 6.00
17 LeBron James 3.00 8.00
18 Dirk Nowitzki .75 2.00
19 Jermaine O'Neal .50 1.25
20 Dwyane Wade 1.50 4.00

2004-05 SkyBox Premium Performers Autographs

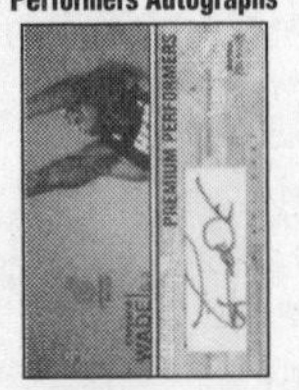

Randomly inserted in packs, this 11-card set parallels the design of the base Premium Performers set enhanced with player autographs and sequential numbering. Print runs are listed in the checklist.

BW Ben Wallace/25 15.00 40.00
CA Carmelo Anthony/25 30.00 80.00
DW Dwyane Wade/50 40.00 100.00
JO Jermaine O'Neal/50 12.50 30.00
KM Kenyon Martin/50 10.00 25.00
MG Manu Ginobili/41 20.00 50.00
PS Peja Stojakovic/100 10.00 25.00
RH Richard Hamilton/78 10.00 25.00
SM Stephon Marbury/50 10.00 25.00
TM Tracy McGrady/43 20.00 50.00
VC Vince Carter 15.00 40.00

2004-05 SkyBox Premium Performers Jerseys

Inserted in Hobby packs at one in six overall and Retail packs at one in 48 overall, this 18-card set parallels the design of the base Premium Performers set enhanced with a swatch of jersey. A Patch version serially numbered to 15 was also inserted.

*JERSEY 75 SINGLES: .6X TO 1.5X BASE HI
AI Allen Iverson 4.00 10.00
BW Ben Wallace 2.50 6.00
CA Carmelo Anthony 5.00 12.00
CW Chris Webber 2.50 6.00
DN Dirk Nowitzki 4.00 10.00
DW Dwyane Wade 8.00 20.00
JO Jermaine O'Neal 2.50 6.00
KG Kevin Garnett 5.00 12.00
KM Kenyon Martin 2.50 6.00
MG Manu Ginobili 3.00 8.00
PP Paul Pierce 3.00 8.00
PS Peja Stojakovic 2.50 6.00
RH Richard Hamilton 2.00 5.00
SF Steve Francis 2.50 6.00
SM Stephon Marbury 2.00 5.00
SO Shaquille O'Neal 6.00 15.00
TM Tracy McGrady 3.00 8.00
VC Vince Carter 4.00 10.00

2004-05 SkyBox Premium Proven Performers

Inserted in both Hobby and Retail packs at the rate of one in 24, this 15-card set is horizontally designed with black backgrounds on the top, gray on the bottom and black and white photos of retired legends.

COMPLETE SET (15) 15.00 40.00
1 Nate Archibald 2.00 5.00
2 Darryl Dawkins 2.00 5.00
3 Walt Frazier 2.00 5.00
4 George Gervin 2.00 5.00
5 John Havlicek 2.00 5.00
6 Robert Parish 2.00 5.00
7 Isiah Thomas 2.00 5.00
8 Earl Monroe 2.00 5.00
9 Oscar Robertson 2.00 5.00
10 Charles Barkley 3.00 8.00
11 Dave Bing 2.00 5.00
12 Magic Johnson 5.00 12.00
13 Bob Cousy 3.00 8.00
14 Bernard King 2.00 5.00
15 Kevin McHale 2.50 6.00

2004-05 SkyBox Premium Proven Performers Autographs

Randomly inserted in packs, this set parallels the base Proven Performers set enhanced with authentic player autographs. Most of these cards were never released due to Fleer/Skybox International closing down in the summer of 2005.

EM Earl Monroe 10.00 25.00
EM2 Earl Monroe JSY 12.50 30.00
GG George Gervin/100 12.50 30.00
MJ Magic Johnson/25 50.00 120.00
NA Nate Archibald 10.00 25.00
RP Robert Parish 12.50 30.00
WF Walt Frazier 10.00 25.00
WF2 Walt Frazier JSY 15.00 40.00

2004-05 SkyBox Premium Proven Performers Jerseys

Inserted in Hobby packs at one in six overall and Retail packs at one in 48 overall, this set parallels the base Proven Performers set enhanced with swatches of jersey. A Patch version numbered to 15 was also inserted.

CB Charles Barkley 12.50 30.00
IT Isiah Thomas 6.00 15.00
KM Kevin McHale 6.00 15.00
RP Robert Parish 6.00 15.00

2004-05 SkyBox Premium Proven Performers Jerseys 75

Randomly seeded, this 12-card set parallels the Performers Jerseys set enhanced with sequential numbering to 75.

*75 SINGLES: .5X TO 1.25X BASE JSY HI
CB Charles Barkley 25.00 60.00

1994 SkyBox Premium Blue Chips Prototypes

Issued in a cello pack, this three-card standard-size (2 1/2" by 3 1/2") set previewed the forthcoming 90-card set that captured scenes from the motion picture "Blue Chips." During the film's opening weekend, February 18-20, 1994, moviegoers at 500 select theaters across the country received these prototype packs. The first card presented an offer to receive a Blue Chips SP card for 6.99. The other two cards displayed full-bleed color shots on their fronts in addition to the movie title and card subtitle. On a background consisting of a ghosted and differently cropped front photo, the backs provide a caption to the photo. The cards are stamped "Prototype" in red and are unnumbered.

COMPLETE SET (3) 1.50 4.00
1 Title card (Mail-in offer) .20 .50
2 Pete Pep Talk 1 (Nick Nolte and team) .40 1.00
3 A Few Tips (Nick Nolte and Shaquille O'Neal) 1.50 4.00

1994 SkyBox Premium Blue Chips

This 90-card standard-size set is based on Paramount Pictures' film, Blue Chips, starring Nick Nolte, NBA stars Shaquille O'Neal and Anfernee Hardaway, former Indiana University star Matt Nover, as well as several other (former and current) players and coaches from college and pro basketball. During the film's opening weekend, Feb. 18-20, the first 1,000 moviegoers received three-card sample packs at each of 500 select theaters across the country. Each sample contained two randomly chosen cards from the 90-card series and an advertisement card. It is reported that a 90-card factory set also exists. The fronts display full-bleed color shots in addition to the movie title and card subtitle. On a background consisting of a ghosted and differently cropped front photo, the backs provide a caption to the photo. The set is subdivided as follows: Story Cards (1-49), Character Cards (50-65), Action Cards (66-72), Behind-the-Scenes (73-88), and Checklists (89-90).

COMPLETE SET (90) 3.00 8.00
1 Pete Pep Talk 1 .01 .05
2 Thousands Cheer .01 .05
3 Stacking Hands .01 .05
4 Two More Points .01 .05
5 You're Outta Here .01 .05
6 Pete Punts .01 .05
7 Q and A .01 .05
8 Pete's Nemesis .01 .05
9 Sympathetic Ear (Bob Cousy listening to Nick Nolte) .08 .25
10 Pete's Dolphin Tank .01 .05
11 Film at 11 .01 .05
12 Gotta Have Heart .01 .05
13 Pete Pep Talk 2 .01 .05
14 Another Game, Another Loss .01 .05
15 Scouting at St. Joe's .01 .05
16 At Home With Butch (Hardaway at home with mother) .08 .25
17 Let's Make A Deal .01 .05
18 Uncle Phil's Big Score .01 .05
19 The First Sighting .01 .05
20 The First Dunk (O'Neal slam dunking) .08 .25
21 Hiring the Tutor (O'Neal introduced to Mary McDonnell) .08 .25
22 A Tutor with Class .01 .05
23 Hometown Parade (Matt Nover) .05 .15
24 Back Home in Indiana .01 .05
25 The Hard Sell (Nolte recruiting Matt Nover) .01 .05
26 Varsity vs. Blue Chips .01 .05
27 Ed Smells Something .01 .05
28 Unfinished Business .01 .05
29 On Campus (Shaquille O'Neal Penny Hardaway Matt Nover girl watching) .08 .25
30 News Crew (O'Neal with microphone in hand) .08 .25
31 Rick's on the Air .05 .15
32 Secret is Revealed .01 .05
33 Unhappy Seeing Happy .01 .05
34 Butch at Practice (Hardaway kneeling, basketball in hand) .08 .25
35 A Few Tips (Nolte coaching O'Neal in practice) .08 .25
36 More Preparation .01 .05
37 Two Old Friends (Nick Nolte Bob Cousy) .08 .25
38 Pete Challenges Tony .01 .05
39 We want Indiana (O'Neal in huddle) .08 .25
40 Taking the Lead (O'Neal shooting) .08 .25
41 Job Well Done (O'Neal on bench) .08 .25
42 On the Move (O'Neal establishing position) .08 .25
43 Fans Go Wild .01 .05
44 The Celebration (O'Neal and Hardaway celebrating) .08 .25
45 Victory Returns .01 .05
46 Ed's Full-Court Press .01 .05
47 Happy's Last Hurrah .01 .05
48 No Longer the Coach .01 .05
49 Always the Teacher .01 .05
50 Coach Bell .01 .05
51 Pete's Assistants .01 .05
52 Vic Roker (Bob Cousy) .08 .25
53 Happy Kuykendall .01 .05
54 Uncle Phil .01 .05
55 Jenny Bell .01 .05
56 Butch McRae (Anfernee Hardaway) .08 .25
57 Neon Bodeaux (Shaquille O'Neal) .08 .25
58 Billy Friedkin (Movie Director) .01 .05
59 Tony .01 .05
60 The Dolphin Girl .01 .05
61 Team 1 .01 .05
62 Team 2 .01 .05
63 Lavada McRae .01 .05
64 Ed Axelby .01 .05
65 Ricky Roe (Matt Nover) .05 .15
66 Under the Hoop (O'Neal playing defense) .08 .25
67 Precision Pass (Hardaway passing) .08 .25
68 Up and In .01 .05
69 Foul .01 .05
70 Out of My Way (O'Neal establishing position) .08 .25
71 Taking a Breather (O'Neal taking breather during timeout) .08 .25
72 Neon at the Line (O'Neal shooting free throw) .08 .25
73 Give Neon the Ball .08 .25
74 Mary McDonnell .01 .05
75 Standing Tall (O'Neal holding net) .08 .25
76 Nick and Rob (Nolte and Cousy conversing on campus) .08 .25
77 Roll Camera (O'Neal joking during filming) .08 .25
78 Nick Nolte and the Crew .01 .05
79 Pre-school with Shaq (O'Neal with pre-school kids) .08 .25
80 Piling On .01 .05
81 Mary Up in Arms (Mary McDonnell in O'Neal's arms) .08 .25
82 Five Blue-Chippers (Penny Hardaway Shaquille O'Neal Matt Nover Nick Nolte William Friedkin) .08 .25
83 The Exorcist (O'Neal making face) .08 .25
84 Checking the Stats (O'Neal reading sports magazine) .08 .25
85 Anfernee's Tricks (Hardaway holding two basketballs) .08 .25
86 The Legendary .01 .05
87 Shaq at Practice (O'Neal holding ball over head) .08 .25
88 Shaq Rehearses (O'Neal posed with basketball in hand) .08 .25
89 Checklist A .01 .05
90 Checklist B .01 .05

1994 SkyBox Premium Blue Chips Foil

Each of the blue chippers, O'Neal, Hardaway, and Nover, is featured on two different foil cards in a bonus insert set randomly inserted in eight-card packs. Reportedly 12,500 of each of the six cards were printed, with each individually numbered ("X of 12,500"). Finally, an SP foil card of O'Neal making the game-winning dunk was available only by mail for 6.99

until 6/1/94 or while supplies lasted. These foil cards utilize the same technology as the "Shaq Talk" insert in the 1993-94 SkyBox Premium series. The cards are numbered on the back with an "F" prefix.

COMPLETE SET (7)	20.00	50.00
F1 Getting to Know Butch McRae Anfernee Hardaway	5.00	12.00
F2 Butch Up Close Anfernee Hardaway	5.00	12.00
F3 Getting to Know Neon Shaquille O'Neal	5.00	12.00
F4 Neon Takes Charge Shaquille O'Neal	5.00	12.00
F5 Getting to Know Ricky Roe, Matt Nover	1.50	4.00
F6 Ricky on the Line Matt Nover	1.50	4.00
SP Neon's game-winner (O'Neal Mail-away)	5.00	12.00

1993-94 SkyBox Premium Pepsi Shaq Attaq

A cover card and four cards featuring horizontal fronts with full-bleed glossy color stills from Shaquille O'Neal's Pepsi commercial were distributed in 5-card cello packs. At the bottom of each photo, the Pepsi logo and "Shaq Attaq" in gold lettering appear. The horizontal back displays a white-bordered still on the left with the Pepsi logo in its upper left. On the right, "SHAQ" appears in gold lettering, with a brief statement about him beneath. The SkyBox logo at the bottom rounds out the card. The cards are numbered on the back.

COMPLETE SET (5)	6.00	15.00
COMMON CARD (1-4)	2.50	6.00
5 Cover Card	.40	1.00

1993-94 SkyBox Schick

Issued in three-card packs inserted in Schick products, the 1993-94 Schick/SkyBox Premium set contains 52 cards that measure the standard size (2 1/2" by 3 1/2"). The fronts feature full-bleed color action photos with a wide white stripe down one side of the card front containing the player's name, position, and team. The SkyBox Premium foil stamp logo appears superimposed on the front. The backs display a second player close-up shot on the top half, and the player's statistics and scouting report on the bottom half. The cards are unnumbered and checklisted below in alphabetical order. The Shawn Bradley card is believed to be a short-print.

COMPLETE SET (52)	50.00	125.00
1 Kenny Anderson	.60	1.50
2 Greg Anthony	.50	1.25
3 Vin Baker	2.00	5.00
4 Stacey Augmon	.50	1.25
5 Corie Blount	.50	1.25
6 Shawn Bradley	1.50	4.00
7 Terrell Brandon	.75	2.00
8 P.J. Brown	1.00	2.50
9 Scott Burrell	.75	2.00
10 Sam Cassell	2.50	6.00
11 Calbert Cheaney	1.00	2.50
12 Doug Christie	.75	2.00
13 Lloyd Daniels	.50	1.25
14 Hubert Davis	.50	1.25
15 Todd Day	.50	1.25
16 Terry Dehere	.50	1.25
17 Acie Earl	.50	1.25
18 LaPhonso Ellis	1.00	2.50
19 Tom Gugliotta	1.50	4.00
20 Anfernee Hardaway	5.00	12.00
21 Scott Haskin	.50	1.25
22 Robert Horry	1.50	4.00
23 Allan Houston	3.00	8.00
24 Lindsey Hunter	1.00	2.50
25 Bobby Hurley	1.00	2.50
26 Jim Jackson	1.50	4.00
27 Ervin Johnson	.60	1.50
28 Adam Keefe	.50	1.25
29 Toni Kukoc	3.00	8.00
30 Christian Laettner	2.00	5.00
31 Malcolm Mackey	.50	1.25
32 Jamal Mashburn	4.00	10.00
33 Oliver Miller	.60	1.50
34 Chris Mills	.75	2.00
35 Harold Miner	1.00	2.50
36 Alonzo Mourning	4.00	10.00
37 Tracy Murray	.50	1.25
38 Shaquille O'Neal	10.00	25.00
39 Anthony Peeler	.60	1.50
40 Dino Radja	1.00	2.50
41 Isaiah Rider	1.00	2.50
42 James Robinson	.50	1.25
43 Rodney Rogers	1.00	2.50
44 Malik Sealy	1.25	3.00
45 Steve Smith	1.50	4.00
46 Elmore Spencer	.50	1.25
47 Latrell Sprewell	2.50	6.00
48 Rex Walters	1.00	2.50
49 Clarence Weatherspoon	.50	1.25
50 Chris Webber	6.00	15.00
51 Walt Williams	.50	1.25
52 Luther Wright	.50	1.25

1993-94 SkyBox Sportslook Promo

This standard-size promo card was offered in the Sportslook magazine. The front displays a full-bleed color player photo with a vertical white bar on the left carrying the player's name in silver lettering. The back has a color player close-up shot on the top portion and a player profile with stats below. The card is unnumbered.

RR8 Magic Johnson	1.00	2.50

1993 SkyBox Story-of-a-Game

This three-card standard-size set was inserted into dual video cassette packs of California-based Strand Home Video's "The Story of a Game." A 32-page basketball booklet was also included in the video pack. Each UV-coated card features off-court full-bleed color photos of David Robinson on the front. The video's logo appears in the upper right, and the SkyBox logo is displayed in the lower left. The backs of the cards have a gray stripe at the top that contains the title and distributor of the video, and a narrow blank pinkish stripe at the bottom. Between these, covering the major portion of the back, are positive statements made by Robinson about the video printed in black over a purplish field that has the video's title in large white upper case lettering.

COMPLETE SET (3)	4.00	10.00
COMMON CARD (1-3)	1.50	4.00

1998-99 SkyBox Thunder

The 1998-99 SkyBox Thunder set consists of 125 standard size cards. The 8-card packs retail for a suggested price of $1.59. The fronts feature a new design with a color image of the player against a contemporary background. The base set is tiered with cards 1-50 coming 4 per pack, cards 51-100 coming 3 per pack and cards 101-125 coming one per pack.

COMPLETE SET (127)	10.00	25.00
1 Kerry Kittles	.12	.30
2 Larry Johnson	.20	.50
3 Hakeem Olajuwon	.25	.60
4 Glenn Robinson	.15	.40
5 Alonzo Mourning	.25	.60
6 Reggie Miller	.25	.60
7 Toni Kukoc	.20	.50
8 Corliss Williamson	.12	.30
9 Nick Van Exel	.15	.40
10 Mookie Blaylock	.12	.30
11 Michael Smith	.12	.30
12 Avery Johnson	.15	.40
13 Brian Williams	.12	.30
14 Doug Christie	.12	.30
15 Danny Fortson	.12	.30
16 Michael Stewart	.12	.30
17 Anthony Peeler	.12	.30
18 Cedric Henderson	.12	.30
19 Lamond Murray	.12	.30
20 Walt Williams	.12	.30
21 Samaki Walker	.12	.30
22 David Wesley	.12	.30
23 Maurice Taylor	.12	.30
24 Todd Fuller	.12	.30
25 Jeff Hornacek	.15	.40
26 Danny Manning	.15	.40
27 Detlef Schrempf	.20	.50
28 Nick Anderson	.12	.30
29 Ron Harper	.15	.40
30 Brian Shaw	.12	.30
31 Bryant Stith	.12	.30
32 Chris Whitney	.12	.30
33 Patrick Ewing	.25	.60
34 Travis Knight	.12	.30
35 Tracy McGrady	.30	.75
36 Dan Majerle	.20	.50
37 Dale Davis	.12	.30
38 Kelvin Cato	.12	.30
39 Zydrunas Ilgauskas	.20	.50
40 Sean Elliott	.20	.50
41 Tony Delk	.12	.30
42 Bobby Phills	.12	.30
43 Clifford Robinson	.12	.30
44 Shawn Bradley	.12	.30
45 Aaron McKie	.12	.30
46 Mark Jackson	.20	.50
47 P.J. Brown	.12	.30
48 Armon Gilliam	.12	.30
49 Ed Gray	.12	.30
50 Olden Polynice	.12	.30
51 Kendall Gill	.12	.30
52 Bryon Russell	.12	.30
53 Dale Ellis	.12	.30
54 Mark Price	.20	.50
55 Donyell Marshall	.12	.30
56 John Starks	.15	.40
57 Jerome Williams	.12	.30
58 Rodney Rogers	.12	.30
59 Michael Finley	.20	.50
60 Marcus Camby	.15	.40
61 Chris Anstey	.12	.30
62 Rodrick Rhodes	.12	.30
63 Derek Anderson	.12	.30
64 Jermaine O'Neal	.20	.50
65 Glen Rice	.20	.50
66 Bryant Reeves	.12	.30
67 Jalen Rose	.15	.40
68 Calbert Cheaney	.12	.30
69 Steve Smith	.15	.40
70 Shandon Anderson	.12	.30
71 Tony Battie	.15	.40
72 Kenny Anderson	.15	.40
73 Tim Hardaway	.20	.50
74 Antonio Daniels	.12	.30
75 Charles Barkley	.30	.75
76 Chauncey Billups	.25	.60
77 Lindsey Hunter	.12	.30
78 Terrell Brandon	.12	.30
79 Anthony Mason	.12	.30
80 Elden Campbell	.12	.30
81 Rasheed Wallace	.20	.50
82 Erick Dampier	.12	.30
83 Tracy Murray	.12	.30
84 Sam Cassell	.15	.40
85 Bobby Jackson	.15	.40
86 Horace Grant	.15	.40
87 Brent Price	.12	.30
88 Allan Houston	.15	.40
89 Brevin Knight	.12	.30
90 Steve Nash	.30	.75
91 Lorenzen Wright	.12	.30
92 Hubert Davis	.12	.30
93 Walter McCarty	.12	.30
94 Jamal Mashburn	.15	.40
95 Dikembe Mutombo	.20	.50
96 Chris Carr	.12	.30
97 Tariq Abdul-Wahad	.12	.30
98 Chris Mullin	.20	.50
99 Charlie Ward	.12	.30
100 Tim Thomas	.20	.50
101 Tim Duncan	.40	1.00
102 Antoine Walker	.20	.50
103 Stephon Marbury	.25	.60
104 Ray Allen	.25	.60
105 Shawn Kemp	.20	.50
106 Michael Jordan	1.50	4.00
107 Gary Payton	.20	.50
108 Kobe Bryant	1.00	2.50
109 Karl Malone	.25	.60
110 Kevin Garnett	.40	1.00
111 Jason Kidd	.30	.75
112 Dennis Rodman	.40	1.00
113 Grant Hill	.30	.75
114 Keith Van Horn	.20	.50
115 Shareef Abdur-Rahim	.20	.50
116 Ron Mercer	.15	.40
117 Allen Iverson	.40	1.00
118 Shaquille O'Neal	.50	1.25
119 Anfernee Hardaway	.30	.75
120 Scottie Pippen	.30	.75
121 David Robinson	.30	.75
122 Vin Baker	.15	.40
123 John Stockton	.25	.60
124 Eddie Jones	.20	.50
125 Juwan Howard	.15	.40
126 Checklist	.12	.30
127 Checklist	.12	.30
NNO Grant Hill SAMPLE	.75	2.00

1998-99 SkyBox Thunder Rave

The 1998-99 SkyBox Thunder Rave set consists of 125 cards and is a parallel to the 1998-99 SkyBox Thunder base set. The cards are randomly inserted in hobby packs only and are serially numbered to 150. To ascertain values on individual cards, please refer to the multiplier in the header, coupled with the value of the base card.

*STARS: 30X TO 80X BASE CARD HI

106 Michael Jordan	300.00	600.00
108 Kobe Bryant	100.00	250.00
112 Dennis Rodman	40.00	100.00
118 Shaquille O'Neal	60.00	150.00

1998-99 SkyBox Thunder Super Rave

The 1998-99 SkyBox Thunder Super Rave set consists of 125 cards and is a parallel to the 1998-99 SkyBox Thunder base set. The cards are randomly inserted in hobby packs only and are serially numbered to 25. To ascertain values on individual cards, please refer to the multiplier in the header, coupled with the value of the base card.

*STARS: 120X TO 300X BASE CARD HI

3 Hakeem Olajuwon	100.00	250.00
6 Reggie Miller	125.00	300.00
35 Tracy McGrady	125.00	300.00
75 Charles Barkley	125.00	300.00
101 Tim Duncan	200.00	500.00
105 Shawn Kemp	125.00	300.00
106 Michael Jordan	4000.00	7000.00
108 Kobe Bryant	2000.00	3500.00
110 Kevin Garnett	200.00	500.00
111 Jason Kidd	125.00	300.00
112 Dennis Rodman	200.00	500.00
113 Grant Hill	125.00	300.00
117 Allen Iverson	150.00	400.00
118 Shaquille O'Neal	300.00	800.00
119 Anfernee Hardaway	125.00	300.00
120 Scottie Pippen	200.00	500.00

1998-99 SkyBox Thunder Boss

The 1998-99 SkyBox Thunder Boss set consists of 20 cards and is an insert to the 1998-99 SkyBox Thunder base set. The cards are randomly inserted in packs at a rate of one in 16. The fronts feature full color action photos of the twenty of the NBA's best players on sculpted embossed cards.

COMPLETE SET (20)	15.00	30.00
1 Shareef Abdur-Rahim	.75	2.00
2 Vin Baker	.60	1.50
3 Tim Duncan	1.50	4.00
4 Kevin Garnett	1.50	4.00
5 Tim Hardaway	.75	2.00
6 Grant Hill	1.25	3.00
7 Michael Jordan	6.00	15.00
8 Shawn Kemp	.75	2.00
9 Jason Kidd	1.25	3.00
10 Karl Malone	1.00	2.50
11 Stephon Marbury	1.00	2.50
12 Ron Mercer	.60	1.50
13 Shaquille O'Neal	2.00	5.00
14 Gary Payton	.75	2.00
15 Scottie Pippen	1.25	3.00
16 Glenn Robinson	.60	1.50
17 John Stockton	1.00	2.50
18 Damon Stoudamire	.75	2.00
19 Keith Van Horn	.75	2.00
20 Antoine Walker	.75	2.00

1998-99 SkyBox Thunder Bringin' It

The 1998-99 SkyBox Thunder Bringin' It set consists of 10 cards and is an insert to the 1998-99 SkyBox Thunder base set. The cards are randomly inserted in packs at a rate of one in 8. The fold-out fronts are silver foil-stamped and provide statistics from ten of the league's most outstanding players.

COMPLETE SET (10)	3.00	8.00
1 Charles Barkley	.60	1.50
2 Anfernee Hardaway	.60	1.50
3 Eddie Jones	.40	1.00
4 Karl Malone	.50	1.25
5 Hakeem Olajuwon	.50	1.25
6 Shaquille O'Neal	1.00	2.50
7 Scottie Pippen	.60	1.50
8 Glen Rice	.40	1.00
9 David Robinson	.60	1.50
10 Dennis Rodman	.75	2.00

1998-99 SkyBox Thunder Flight School

The 1998-99 SkyBox Thunder Flight School set consists of 12 cards and is an insert to the 1998-99 SkyBox Thunder base set. The cards are randomly inserted in hobby packs only at a rate of one in 96. The fronts feature full color action photos complete with "binocular" design.

COMPLETE SET (12)	50.00	120.00
1 Ray Allen	4.00	10.00
2 Kobe Bryant	15.00	40.00
3 Michael Finley	3.00	8.00
4 Kevin Garnett	6.00	15.00
5 Anfernee Hardaway	5.00	12.00
6 Grant Hill	5.00	12.00
7 Allen Iverson	6.00	15.00
8 Eddie Jones	3.00	8.00
9 Michael Jordan	30.00	60.00
10 Shawn Kemp	3.00	8.00
11 Antonio McDyess	2.50	6.00
12 Ron Mercer	2.50	6.00

1998-99 SkyBox Thunder Lift Off

The 1998-99 SkyBox Thunder Lift Off set consists of 10 cards and is an insert to the 1998-99 SkyBox Thunder base set. The cards are randomly inserted in packs at a rate of one in 56. The fronts feature black and white full bleed photos of first and second year standouts "shooting" their teams into the future. Each star is featured on hyperplaid diffraction film-laminated stock.

COMPLETE SET (10)	20.00	50.00
1 Shareef Abdur-Rahim	2.00	5.00
2 Ray Allen	2.50	6.00
3 Kobe Bryant	10.00	25.00
4 Tim Duncan	4.00	10.00
5 Allen Iverson	4.00	10.00
6 Kerry Kittles	1.25	3.00
7 Stephon Marbury	2.50	6.00
8 Ron Mercer	1.50	4.00
9 Keith Van Horn	2.00	5.00
10 Antoine Walker	2.00	5.00

1998-99 SkyBox Thunder Noyz Boyz

The 1998-99 SkyBox Thunder Noyz Boyz set consists of 15 cards and is an insert to the 1998-99 SkyBox Thunder base set. The cards are randomly inserted in packs at a rate of one in 300. The fronts feature color photos of 15 of the NBA's most electric players. The cards are die-cut, foil-stamped and printed on "illusion" stock with material finish.

COMPLETE SET (15)	900.00	1500.00
1 Shareef Abdur-Rahim	20.00	50.00
2 Ray Allen	25.00	60.00
3 Kobe Bryant	200.00	400.00
4 Tim Duncan	40.00	100.00
5 Kevin Garnett	40.00	100.00
6 Anfernee Hardaway	40.00	100.00
7 Grant Hill	30.00	80.00
8 Allen Iverson	40.00	100.00
9 Michael Jordan	450.00	750.00
10 Stephon Marbury	25.00	60.00
11 Shaquille O'Neal	50.00	125.00
12 Scottie Pippen	40.00	100.00
13 Dennis Rodman	50.00	120.00
14 Keith Van Horn	20.00	50.00
15 Antoine Walker	20.00	50.00

1992 SkyBox USA

The 1992 SkyBox USA basketball set contains 110 cards which were distributed in foil-wrap packs. The set includes nine cards of each of the first ten NBA players named to the team, two cards of each coach, and two checklist cards. The set concludes with a "Magic On" subset, representing Johnson's thoughts on his teammates. The wax packs included randomly inserted cards autographed by Magic Johnson and David Robinson as well as a plastic trading card featuring a team photo. However, the autographed cards were not certified. The standard-size cards feature on the fronts full-bleed glossy color action shots, with the player's name and the card's subtitle printed across the top of the picture. On the upper portion, the backs feature a color close-up photo, while the lower portion presents statistics or summarizes the player's professional career.

COMPLETE SET (110)	12.50	25.00
1 Charles Barkley	.10	.30
2 Charles Barkley	.10	.30
3 Charles Barkley	.10	.30
4 Charles Barkley	.10	.30
5 Charles Barkley	.10	.30
6 Charles Barkley	.10	.30
7 Charles Barkley	.10	.30
8 Charles Barkley	.10	.30
9 Charles Barkley	.10	.30
10 Larry Bird	.20	.50
11 Larry Bird	.20	.50
12 Larry Bird	.20	.50
13 Larry Bird	.20	.50
14 Larry Bird	.20	.50
15 Larry Bird	.20	.50
16 Larry Bird	.20	.50
17 Larry Bird	.20	.50
18 Larry Bird	.20	.50
19 Patrick Ewing	.08	.25
20 Patrick Ewing	.08	.25
21 Patrick Ewing	.08	.25
22 Patrick Ewing	.08	.25
23 Patrick Ewing	.08	.25
24 Patrick Ewing	.08	.25
25 Patrick Ewing	.08	.25
26 Patrick Ewing	.08	.25
27 Patrick Ewing	.08	.25
28 Magic Johnson	.20	.50
29 Magic Johnson	.20	.50
30 Magic Johnson	.20	.50
31 Magic Johnson	.20	.50
32 Magic Johnson	.20	.50
33 Magic Johnson	.20	.50
34 Magic Johnson	.20	.50
35 Magic Johnson	.20	.50
36 Magic Johnson	.20	.50
37 Michael Jordan	.60	1.50
38 Michael Jordan	.60	1.50
39 Michael Jordan	.60	1.50
40 Michael Jordan	.60	1.50
41 Michael Jordan	.60	1.50
42 Michael Jordan	.60	1.50
43 Michael Jordan	.60	1.50
44 Michael Jordan	.60	1.50
45 Michael Jordan	.60	1.50
46 Karl Malone	.08	.25
47 Karl Malone	.08	.25
48 Karl Malone	.08	.25
49 Karl Malone	.08	.25
50 Karl Malone	.08	.25
51 Karl Malone	.08	.25
52 Karl Malone	.08	.25
53 Karl Malone	.08	.25
54 Karl Malone	.08	.25
55 Chris Mullin	.08	.25
56 Chris Mullin	.08	.25
57 Chris Mullin	.08	.25
58 Chris Mullin	.08	.25
59 Chris Mullin	.08	.25
60 Chris Mullin	.08	.25
61 Chris Mullin	.08	.25
62 Chris Mullin	.08	.25
63 Chris Mullin	.08	.25
64 Scottie Pippen	.15	.40
65 Scottie Pippen	.15	.40
66 Scottie Pippen	.15	.40
67 Scottie Pippen	.15	.40
68 Scottie Pippen	.15	.40
69 Scottie Pippen	.15	.40
70 Scottie Pippen	.15	.40
71 Scottie Pippen	.15	.40
72 Scottie Pippen	.15	.40
73 David Robinson	.10	.30
74 David Robinson	.10	.30
75 David Robinson	.10	.30
76 David Robinson	.10	.30
77 David Robinson	.10	.30
78 David Robinson	.10	.30
79 David Robinson	.10	.30
80 David Robinson	.10	.30
81 David Robinson	.10	.30
82 John Stockton	.08	.25
83 John Stockton	.08	.25
84 John Stockton	.08	.25
85 John Stockton	.08	.25
86 John Stockton	.08	.25
87 John Stockton	.08	.25
88 John Stockton	.08	.25
89 John Stockton	.08	.25
90 John Stockton	.08	.25
91 P.J. Carlesimo	.08	.25
92 P.J. Carlesimo	.08	.25
93 Chuck Daly	.08	.25
94 Chuck Daly	.08	.25
95 Mike Krzyzewski	.10	.30
96 Mike Krzyzewski	.10	.30
97 Lenny Wilkens	.08	.25
98 Lenny Wilkens	.08	.25
99 Checklist 1-54	.08	.25
100 Checklist 55-110	.08	.25
101 Magic on Barkley	.10	.30
102 Magic on Bird	.20	.50
103 Magic on Ewing	.08	.25
104 Magic on Magic	.20	.50
105 Magic on Jordan	.60	1.50
106 Magic on Malone	.08	.25
107 Magic on Mullin	.08	.25
108 Magic on Pippen	.15	.40
109 Magic on Robinson	.10	.30
110 Magic on Stockton	.08	.25
NNO Plastic Team Card	7.50	15.00

1994 SkyBox USA Prototypes

These eight prototypes were issued to showcase the design of the 1994 SkyBox USA set, which was issued in June 1994. Except for the Dumars and Kemp cards, the front features a borderless color shot of the player in his Team USA uniform posed in front of a portion of the American flag. The fronts of the Dumars and Kemp cards are borderless action shots. The player's name appears in silver foil within a red stripe near the bottom, along with the USA logo. The backs are of several different designs, since the cards represent different subsets, but generally they have a red, white, and blue design. The prototypes are not marked as such and are unnumbered and checklisted below in alphabetical order.

COMPLETE SET (8)	1.50	4.00
1 Derrick Coleman	.08	.25
2 Joe Dumars	.15	.40
3 Magic Johnson	.75	2.00
4 Larry Johnson	.08	.25
5 Shawn Kemp	.25	.60
6 Alonzo Mourning	.30	.75
7 Isiah Thomas	.15	.40
8 Dominique Wilkins	.15	.40

1994 SkyBox USA

These 89 standard-size cards honor the '94 Team USA players. Cards were issued in 10-card packs with 24 packs per box. The borderless fronts feature color posed and action player shots. The player's name appears in silver-foil lettering within a red stripe near the bottom. Each player has a subset of six cards, the backs of which carry information about each player's international experience, NBA rookie year, best game, NBA update, trademark move, and comments on the player by Magic Johnson. In addition, a T-shirt exchange card (one in 300 packs) was available with this product. The offer was valid through October 31, 1994. The On the Court exchange card was redeemable for a a set featuring action from the 1994 Olympic games.

COMPLETE SET (89)	6.00	15.00
1 Alonzo Mourning	.10	.30
2 Alonzo Mourning	.10	.30
3 Alonzo Mourning	.10	.30
4 Alonzo Mourning	.10	.30
5 Alonzo Mourning	.10	.30
6 Alonzo Mourning	.10	.30
7 Larry Johnson	.08	.25
8 Larry Johnson	.08	.25
9 Larry Johnson	.08	.25
10 Larry Johnson	.08	.25
11 Larry Johnson	.08	.25
12 Larry Johnson	.08	.25
13 Shawn Kemp	.10	.30
14 Shawn Kemp	.10	.30
15 Shawn Kemp	.10	.30
16 Shawn Kemp	.10	.30
17 Shawn Kemp	.10	.30
18 Shawn Kemp	.10	.30
19 Mark Price	.08	.25
20 Mark Price	.08	.25
21 Mark Price	.08	.25
22 Mark Price	.08	.25
23 Mark Price	.08	.25
24 Mark Price	.08	.25
25 Steve Smith	.08	.25
26 Steve Smith	.08	.25
27 Steve Smith	.08	.25
28 Steve Smith	.08	.25
29 Steve Smith	.08	.25
30 Steve Smith	.08	.25
31 Dominique Wilkins	.10	.30
32 Dominique Wilkins	.10	.30
33 Dominique Wilkins	.10	.30
34 Dominique Wilkins	.10	.30
35 Dominique Wilkins	.10	.30
36 Dominique Wilkins	.10	.30
37 Derrick Coleman	.08	.25
38 Derrick Coleman	.08	.25
39 Derrick Coleman	.08	.25
40 Derrick Coleman	.08	.25
41 Derrick Coleman	.08	.25
42 Derrick Coleman	.08	.25
43 Isiah Thomas	.10	.30
44 Isiah Thomas	.10	.30
45 Isiah Thomas	.10	.30
46 Isiah Thomas	.10	.30
47 Isiah Thomas	.10	.30
48 Isiah Thomas	.10	.30
49 Joe Dumars	.08	.25
50 Joe Dumars	.08	.25
51 Joe Dumars	.08	.25
52 Joe Dumars	.08	.25
53 Joe Dumars	.08	.25
54 Joe Dumars	.08	.25
55 Dan Majerle	.08	.25
56 Dan Majerle	.08	.25
57 Dan Majerle	.08	.25
58 Dan Majerle	.08	.25
59 Dan Majerle	.08	.25
60 Dan Majerle	.08	.25
61 Tim Hardaway	.10	.30
62 Tim Hardaway	.10	[illegible]
63 Tim Hardaway	.10	[illegible]
64 Tim Hardaway	.10	[illegible]
65 Tim Hardaway	.10	[illegible]
66 Tim Hardaway	.10	[illegible]
67 Shaquille O'Neal	.40	1.0
68 Shaquille O'Neal	.40	1.0
69 Shaquille O'Neal	.40	1.0
70 Shaquille O'Neal	.40	1.0
71 Shaquille O'Neal	.40	1.0
72 Shaquille O'Neal	.40	1.0
73 Reggie Miller	.10	[illegible]
74 Reggie Miller	.10	[illegible]
75 Reggie Miller	.10	[illegible]
76 Reggie Miller	.10	[illegible]
77 Reggie Miller	.10	[illegible]
78 Reggie Miller	.10	[illegible]
79 Don Chaney CO	.10	.3
80 Pete Gillen CO	.10	.3
81 Rick Majerus CO	.10	.3
82 Don Nelson CO	.10	.3
83 '94 USA Team	.08	.2
84 International Rules Time	.08	.2
85 International Rules Court Dimensions	.08	.2
86 International Rules Rules	.08	.2
87 Earvin (Magic) Johnson Passing the Torch	.30	.7
88 David Robinson Passing the Torch	.10	.3
89 Checklist	.08	.2
NNO Expired T-Shirt Exch.	.08	.2

1994 SkyBox USA Gold

Randomly inserted at a rate of 1 in 4 packs, this parallel set features standard-size cards that differ fro[m] their '94 SkyBox USA counterparts only by the embossed gold-foil highlights. The cards are numbered on the back. Please refer to the multiplier provided below (coupled with the prices of the corresponding regular issue cards) to ascertain value

COMPLETE SET (89)	25.00	60.0

*STARS: 1.5X TO 4X HI COLUMN

1994 SkyBox USA Autographs

These scarce chase cards were inserted in SkyBox US[A] packs at a rate of about two per case. Each player signed his "Trademark Move" card from the regular issue set. These are the only seven players known to have signed cards for this product. The signatures are in gold paint, and the cards are embossed with the SkyBox seal to distinguish them from any cards signe[d] after the product's release.

COMPLETE SET (7)	400.00	800.0
11A Larry Johnson	40.00	100.0
17A Shawn Kemp	150.00	300.0
35A Dominique Wilkins	50.00	125.0
47A Isiah Thomas	50.00	125.0
53A Joe Dumars	50.00	125.0
59A Dan Majerle	40.00	100.0
65A Tim Hardaway	60.00	150.0

1994 SkyBox USA Dream Play

Randomly inserted in packs at a rate of one in 35, thes[e] 13 standard-size cards feature on their borderless fronts posed action color cutouts of the players in thei[r] Team USA uniforms set on a dark play diagram background. The player's name appears in prismatic silver-foil lettering at the top. The white back carries play diagrams and descriptions.

COMPLETE SET (13)	6.00	15.00
DP1 Alonzo Mourning	1.00	2.50
DP2 Larry Johnson	.40	1.00
DP3 Shawn Kemp	1.00	2.50
DP4 Mark Price	.20	.50
DP5 Steve Smith	.20	.50
DP6 Dominique Wilkins	.60	1.50
DP7 Derrick Coleman	.20	.50
DP8 Isiah Thomas	.60	1.50
DP9 Joe Dumars	.60	1.50
DP10 Dan Majerle	.40	1.00
DP11 Tim Hardaway	.60	1.50
DP12 Shaquille O'Neal	4.00	10.00
DP13 Reggie Miller	.60	1.50

1994 SkyBox USA Kevin Johnson

This 14-card standard-size set was issued through a wrapper redemption program. The collector received a complete set in exchange for nine wrappers. The offer expired October 31, 1994. The first six cards have the player's name in silver foil lettering, while the next six have the player's name and SkyBox logo in gold foil. The final two cards represent the Dream Play and Portrait insert sets. The silver and gold cards are distinguished in the listing below by "S" and "G" prefixes respectively.

COMPLETE SET (14)	10.00	25.00

Kevin Johnson .75 2.00
Kevin Johnson .20 .50
Kevin Johnson .75 2.00
Kevin Johnson .20 .50
Kevin Johnson .75 2.00
Kevin Johnson .20 .50
Kevin Johnson .75 2.00
Kevin Johnson .20 .50
Kevin Johnson .75 2.00
Kevin Johnson .20 .50
Kevin Johnson .75 2.00
Kevin Johnson .20 .50
4 Kevin Johnson 1.25 3.00
4 Kevin Johnson 5.00 12.00

994 SkyBox USA On The Court

14 card standard-size set was available usively by exchanging the SkyBox USA On the rt trade card before the November 15th, 1994 dline. The trade card was randomly inserted into in every 300 SkyBox USA packs. Each member of am Team II is represented in this set. The set is ed as "On the Court" as all photos were all taken in onto during the World Championships in 1994.
MPLETE SET (14) 6.00 15.00
iah Thomas .60 1.50
m Hardaway .60 1.50
eggie Miller .60 1.50
eve Smith .20 .50
e Dumars .60 1.50
hawn Kemp .60 1.50
Mark Price .20 .50
an Majerle .40 1.00
evin Johnson .40 1.00
Derrick Coleman .20 .50
Alonzo Mourning 1.00 2.50
Dominique Wilkins .60 1.50
Larry Johnson .40 1.00
Shaquille O'Neal 4.00 10.00
D Expired On The ourt Exchange .20 .50

1994 SkyBox USA Portraits

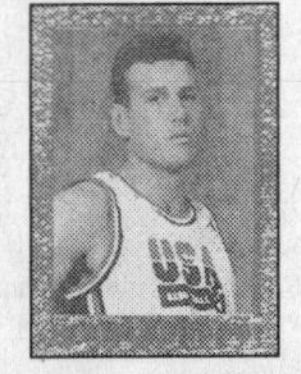

ndomly inserted at a rate of one in 100 packs, these standard-size cards feature embossed gold foil-dered fronts with posed color portraits of the yers in their Team USA uniforms. The player's name pears in embossed lettering within the gold-foil ver margin. The red, white, and blue back carries a te from the player.
MPLETE SET (13) 40.00 80.00
Alonzo Mourning 5.00 12.00
2 Larry Johnson 2.50 6.00
3 Shawn Kemp 4.00 10.00
4 Mark Price 2.00 5.00
5 Steve Smith 2.00 5.00
5 Dominique Wilkins 3.00 8.00
7 Derrick Coleman 2.50 6.00
8 Isiah Thomas 3.00 8.00
9 Joe Dumars 3.00 8.00
10 Dan Majerle 2.50 6.00
11 Tim Hardaway 3.00 8.00
12 Shaquille O'Neal 15.00 40.00
13 Reggie Miller 4.00 10.00

1996 SkyBox USA

e 1996 SkyBox USA set, featuring members of eam Team 3, was issued in one series totalling 60 ds. The 6-card packs retailed for $1.99 each. The features the topical subsets: Grant's Slant (1-10), ag Book (11-20), Playing for Pride (21-30), ntribution (31-50), Coaches (51-54) and Awesome ros (55-59). Card fronts feature an Olympic ring ckground with an action shot of the player.
OMPLETE SET (60) 5.00 12.00
Anfernee Hardaway GS .25 .60
Grant Hill GS .25 .60
Karl Malone GS .20 .50
Reggie Miller GS .20 .50
Scottie Pippen GS .25 .60
Hakeem Olajuwon GS .25 .60
Shaquille O'Neal GS .40 1.00
David Robinson GS .25 .60
Glenn Robinson GS .15 .40
John Stockton GS .20 .50
Anfernee Hardaway .25 .60
Grant Hill .25 .60
Karl Malone .20 .50
Reggie Miller .20 .50
Scottie Pippen .25 .60
Hakeem Olajuwon .25 .60
Shaquille O'Neal .40 1.00
David Robinson .25 .60
Glenn Robinson .15 .40
John Stockton .20 .50
Anfernee Hardaway .25 .60
Grant Hill .25 .60
Karl Malone .20 .50
Reggie Miller .20 .50

25 Scottie Pippen .25 .60
26 Hakeem Olajuwon .20 .50
27 Shaquille O'Neal .40 1.00
28 David Robinson .25 .60
29 Glenn Robinson .15 .40
30 John Stockton .20 .50
31 Anfernee Hardaway .25 .60
32 Grant Hill .25 .60
33 Karl Malone .20 .50
34 Reggie Miller .20 .50
35 Scottie Pippen .25 .60
36 Hakeem Olajuwon .20 .50
37 Shaquille O'Neal .40 1.00
38 David Robinson .25 .60
39 Glenn Robinson .15 .40
40 Glenn Robinson .15 .40
41 Anfernee Hardaway .25 .60
42 Grant Hill .25 .60
43 Karl Malone .20 .50
44 Reggie Miller .20 .50
45 Scottie Pippen .25 .60
46 Hakeem Olajuwon .20 .50
47 Shaquille O'Neal .40 1.00
48 David Robinson .25 .60
49 Glenn Robinson .15 .40
50 John Stockton .20 .50
51 Lenny Wilkens CO .15 .40
52 Bobby Cremins .15 .40
53 Clem Haskins .15 .40
54 Jerry Sloan .15 .40
55 Shaquille O'Neal .30 .75
Anfernee Hardaway AD
56 Karl Malone .15 .40
John Stockton AD
57 David Robinson .15 .40
Hakeem Olajuwon AD
58 Scottie Pippen .15 .40
Grant Hill AD
59 Reggie Miller .15 .40
Glenn Robinson AD
60 Checklist .08 .25
NNO Grant Hill 1.25 3.00
Promo Sheet

1996 SkyBox USA Bronze

Randomly inserted in hobby and retail packs at a rate of one in 12, this set features the first ten players selected to the 1996 USA men's basketball team. Card fronts feature foil printing and UV coating.
COMPLETE SET (10) 8.00 20.00
*SPARKLE: .5X TO 1.25X VALUE
SPARKLE: STATED ODDS 1:18 HOBBY
B1 Anfernee Hardaway 1.50 4.00
B2 Grant Hill 1.50 4.00
B3 Karl Malone 1.25 3.00
B4 Reggie Miller 1.25 3.00
B5 Scottie Pippen 1.50 4.00
B6 Hakeem Olajuwon 1.25 3.00
B7 Shaquille O'Neal 2.50 6.00
B8 David Robinson 1.50 4.00
B9 Glenn Robinson 1.00 2.50
B10 John Stockton 1.25 3.00

1996 SkyBox USA Gold

Randomly inserted in hobby and retail packs at a rate of one in 120, this set features the first ten players selected to the 1996 men's USA basketball team. Card fronts feature foil printing and UV coating.
COMPLETE SET (10) 40.00 100.00
*SPARKLE: .5X TO 1.25X VALUE
SPARKLE: STATED ODDS 1:180 HOBBY
G1 Anfernee Hardaway 8.00 20.00
G2 Grant Hill 8.00 20.00
G3 Karl Malone 6.00 15.00
G4 Reggie Miller 6.00 15.00
G5 Scottie Pippen 8.00 20.00
G6 Hakeem Olajuwon 6.00 15.00
G7 Shaquille O'Neal 12.00 30.00
G8 David Robinson 8.00 20.00
G9 Glenn Robinson 5.00 12.00
G10 John Stockton 6.00 15.00

1996 SkyBox USA Quads

Randomly inserted in packs at a rate of one in 3, this 15-card set features the first ten players selected to the 1996 USA men's basketball team. The standard-sized cards actually feature four preforated mini quadrant cards. These mini cards are replicas of the basic issue cards. Each of the original ten members of the team have their own quads. In addition, the final five quads are based on the following themes: Power, Versatility, Passing, Defense and Scoring.
COMPLETE SET (15) 5.00 12.00
Q1 Anfernee Hardaway .75 2.00
Q2 Grant Hill .75 2.00
Q3 Karl Malone .60 1.50
Q4 Reggie Miller .60 1.50
Q5 Scottie Pippen .75 2.00
Q6 Hakeem Olajuwon .60 1.50
Q7 Shaquille O'Neal 1.25 3.00
Q8 David Robinson .75 2.00
Q9 Glenn Robinson .50 1.25
Q10 John Stockton .60 1.50
Q11 Karl Malone Power .40 1.00
Shaquille O'Neal
Hakeem Olajuwon
David Robinson
Q12 Grant Hill Versatility .40 1.00
Scottie Pippen
Anfernee Hardaway
Glenn Robinson
Q13 A.Hardaway Passing .40 1.00
John Stockton
Grant Hill
Reggie Miller
Q14 Scottie Pippen Defense .40 1.00
John Stockton
Hakeem Olajuwon
David Robinson
Q15 Karl Malone Scoring .40 1.00
(Reggie Miller
Shaquille O'Neal
Glenn Robinson

1996 SkyBox USA Silver

Randomly inserted in hobby and retail packs at a rate of one in 48, this set features the first ten players selected to the 1996 men's USA basketball team. Card fronts feature foil printing and UV coating.
COMPLETE SET (10) 20.00 50.00
*SPARKLE: .5X TO 1.25X VALUE
SPARKLE: STATED ODDS 1:72 HOBBY
S1 Anfernee Hardaway 4.00 10.00
S2 Grant Hill 4.00 10.00
S3 Karl Malone 3.00 8.00
S4 Reggie Miller 3.00 8.00
S5 Scottie Pippen 4.00 10.00
S6 Hakeem Olajuwon 3.00 8.00
S7 Shaquille O'Neal 6.00 15.00
S8 David Robinson 4.00 10.00
S9 Glenn Robinson 2.50 6.00
S10 John Stockton 3.00 8.00

1996 SkyBox USA Wrapper Exchange

This 25-card set was available via a wrapper exchange program. Sets could be obtained by sending in 10 wrappers along with $3 for postage and handling before the December 31, 1996 deadline. The set contains cards for Charles Barkley and Mitch Richmond, two late additions to the team, and has all of the subset and insert cards that they would have had if they were in the basic set.
COMPLETE SET (25) 5.00 12.00
61 Charles Barkley GS .25 .60
62 Mitch Richmond GS .15 .40
63 Charles Barkley BB .25 .60
64 Mitch Richmond BB .15 .40
65 Charles Barkley PP .25 .60
66 Mitch Richmond PP .15 .40
67 Charles Barkley CON .25 .60
68 Mitch Richmond CON .15 .40
69 Charles Barkley CON .25 .60
70 Mitch Richmond CON .15 .40
71 Charles Barkley .15 .40
Mitch Richmond AD
B11 Charles Barkley Bronze .60 1.50
B12 Mitch Richmond Bronze .40 1.00
G11 Charles Barkley Gold 1.50 4.00
G12 Mitch Richmond Gold 1.00 2.50
Q16 Charles Barkley Quad 1.00 2.50
Q17 Mitch Richmond Quad .60 1.50
S11 Charles Barkley Silver 1.00 2.50
S12 Mitch Richmond Silver .60 1.50
BS11 Charles Barkley Bronze Sparkle .60 1.50
BS12 Mitch Richmond Bronze Sparkle .40 1.00
GS11 Charles Barkley Gold Sparkle 1.50 4.00
GS12 Mitch Richmond Gold Sparkle 1.00 2.50
SS11 Charles Barkley Silver Sparkle 1.00 2.50
SS12 Mitch Richmond Silver Sparkle .60 1.50

1996 SkyBox USA Texaco

This 14-card set was available in 3-card packs through a joint promotion between Texaco and Fleer/SkyBox. Packs could be obtained with a 8-gallon fill-up (one) or for $.89 per pack. The card fronts have a gray background with a full player shot. The player's name is in red foil on the card front.
COMPLETE SET (14) 2.00 5.00
1 Charles Barkley .40 1.00
2 Anfernee Hardaway .40 1.00
3 Grant Hill .40 1.00
4 Karl Malone .30 .75
5 Reggie Miller .30 .75
6 Hakeem Olajuwon .30 .75
7 Shaquille O'Neal .60 1.50
8 Scottie Pippen .40 1.00
9 Mitch Richmond .25 .60
10 David Robinson .40 1.00
11 Glenn Robinson .25 .60
12 John Stockton .30 .75
13 Lenny Wilkens CO .25 .60
14 Team Card .25 .60

1991 Smokey's Larry Johnson

This seven-card set was sponsored by Smokey's Sportscards, Inc. (Las Vegas, Nevada) in honor of Larry Johnson, the 1990-91 NCAA Player of the Year. Set production was limited to 49,500, and the unique set number appears on a cardboard picture frame that accompanies the seven cards. The standard-size cards have high gloss color action photos on the front, with gold borders on a black card face. Johnson's name is written in aqua and white lettering at the bottom of the card. Inside a gold border, the glossy backs have a black marble design. A color mugshot of Johnson appears at the top of each back, and an extended caption to the card appears in a pale green rectangle. The promo card was distributed at the 1991 National Convention and at the FanFest in Toronto as a Smokey's advertisement. A total of 72,000 cards were printed, with each bearing a unique serial number on the back.
COMPLETE SET (7) 2.00 5.00
COMMON CARD (1-7) .40 1.00
PR Larry Johnson PROMO .50 1.25

2001 Sol Fleer WNBA

This set was produced by Fleer and handed out at the August 10th Sol's game to the first 5000 ticket-holders. Cards feature perforated edges, as they were released in the form of a sheet, white borders, and a colored frame around the card to match the team's colors.
COMPLETE SET (9) 4.00 10.00
1 Debbie Black .40 1.00
2 Katrina Colleton .40 1.00
3 Tracy Reid .40 1.00
4 Kisha Ford .40 1.00
5 Kristen Rasmussen .40 1.00
6 Sandy Brondello 1.50 4.00
7 Marlies Askamp .40 1.00
8 Ron Rothstein .40 1.00
9 Sheri Sam .40 1.00

1994-95 SP

The complete 1994-95 SP set (issued by Upper Deck) consists of 165-card standard size cards issued in eight-card packs (suggested retail price $3.99). Boxes were distributed exclusively to hobby dealers. The set features full-bleed fronts with color action photos. There is a gold strip down the left side with the player name while the team name is at the bottom. The backs feature another color action photo with the statistics at the bottom and a gold hologram at the bottom left. The only subset is Premier Prospects (1-30) which highlights rookies. Unlike the regular player cards, these rookie-focused cards have a full-bleed gold foil background with a silver foil pyramid at the bottom with the player's name in it. The backs have a vertical color player photo on the right and statistics on the left. After the Premier Prospects subset, the cards are grouped alphabetically within teams. Two parallel Michael Jordan cards (red and silver), both numbered MJ1, were randomly inserted into packs. The cards feature feature photos from Jordan's return with the words "He's Back March 19, 1995" in red foil. The red version was inserted at a ratio of one in every 30 packs. The silver version was inserted at a ratio of one in every 192 packs. Rookie Cards of note in this set include Grant Hill, Juwan Howard, Eddie Jones, Jason Kidd and Glenn Robinson.
COMPLETE SET (165) 15.00 30.00
1 Glenn Robinson FOIL RC .60 1.50
2 Jason Kidd FOIL RC 2.00 5.00
3 Grant Hill FOIL RC 2.00 5.00
4 Donyell Marshall FOIL RC .30 .75
5 Juwan Howard FOIL RC .50 1.25
6 Sharone Wright FOIL RC .30 .75
7 Lamond Murray FOIL RC .30 .75
8 Brian Grant FOIL RC .50 1.25
9 Eric Montross FOIL RC .30 .75
10 Eddie Jones FOIL RC 1.00 2.50
11 Carlos Rogers FOIL RC .30 .75
12 Khalid Reeves FOIL RC .30 .75
13 Jalen Rose FOIL RC .75 2.00
14 Eric Piatkowski FOIL RC .40 1.00
15 Clifford Rozier FOIL RC .30 .75
16 Aaron McKie FOIL RC .30 .75
17 Eric Mobley FOIL RC .30 .75
18 Tony Dumas FOIL RC .30 .75
19 B.J. Tyler FOIL RC .30 .75
20 Dickey Simpkins FOIL RC .30 .75
21 Bill Curley FOIL RC .30 .75
22 Wesley Person FOIL RC .30 .75
23 Monty Williams FOIL RC .30 .75
24 Greg Minor FOIL RC .30 .75
25 Charlie Ward FOIL RC .30 .75
26 Brooks Thompson FOIL RC .30 .75
27 Trevor Ruffin FOIL RC .30 .75
28 Derrick Alston FOIL RC .30 .75
29 Michael Smith FOIL RC .30 .75
30 Dontonio Wingfield FOIL RC .30 .75
31 Stacey Augmon .15 .40
32 Steve Smith .15 .40
33 Mookie Blaylock .12 .30
34 Grant Long .12 .30
35 Ken Norman .12 .30
36 Dominique Wilkins .25 .60
37 Dino Radja .15 .40
38 Dee Brown .12 .30
39 David Wesley .12 .30
40 Rick Fox .12 .30
41 Alonzo Mourning .25 .60
42 Larry Johnson .20 .50
43 Hersey Hawkins .12 .30
44 Scott Burrell .12 .30
45 Muggsy Bogues .15 .40
46 Scottie Pippen .40 1.00
47 Toni Kukoc .25 .60
48 B.J. Armstrong .12 .30
49 Will Perdue .12 .30
50 Ron Harper .15 .40
51 Mark Price .20 .50
52 Tyrone Hill .12 .30
53 Chris Mills .12 .30
54 John Williams .12 .30
55 Bobby Phills .12 .30
56 Jim Jackson .12 .30
57 Jamal Mashburn .20 .50
58 Popeye Jones .12 .30
59 Roy Tarpley .12 .30
60 Lorenzo Williams .12 .30
61 Mahmoud Abdul-Rauf .12 .30
62 Rodney Rogers .12 .30
63 Bryant Stith .12 .30
64 Dikembe Mutombo .20 .50
65 Robert Pack .12 .30
66 Joe Dumars .20 .50
67 Terry Mills .12 .30
68 Oliver Miller .12 .30
69 Lindsey Hunter .12 .30
70 Mark West .12 .30
71 Latrell Sprewell .25 .60
72 Tim Hardaway .20 .50
73 Ricky Pierce .12 .30
74 Rony Seikaly .15 .40
75 Tom Gugliotta .15 .40
76 Hakeem Olajuwon .25 .60
77 Clyde Drexler .25 .60
78 Vernon Maxwell .12 .30
79 Robert Horry .20 .50
80 Sam Cassell .25 .60
81 Reggie Miller .25 .60
82 Rik Smits .15 .40
83 Derrick McKey .12 .30
84 Mark Jackson .12 .30
85 Dale Davis .12 .30
86 Loy Vaught .12 .30
87 Terry Dehere .12 .30
88 Malik Sealy .12 .30
89 Pooh Richardson .12 .30
90 Tony Massenburg .12 .30
91 Cedric Ceballos .12 .30
92 Nick Van Exel .20 .50
93 George Lynch .12 .30
94 Vlade Divac .20 .50
95 Elden Campbell .12 .30
96 Glen Rice .20 .50
97 Kevin Willis .12 .30
98 Billy Owens .12 .30
99 Bimbo Coles .12 .30
100 Harold Miner .12 .30
101 Vin Baker .20 .50
102 Todd Day .12 .30
103 Marty Conlon .12 .30
104 Lee Mayberry .12 .30
105 Eric Murdock .12 .30
106 Isaiah Rider .20 .50
107 Doug West .12 .30
108 Christian Laettner .15 .40
109 Sean Rooks .12 .30
110 Stacey King .12 .30
111 Derrick Coleman .15 .40
112 Kenny Anderson .15 .40
113 Chris Morris .12 .30
114 Armon Gilliam .12 .30
115 Benoit Benjamin .12 .30
116 Patrick Ewing .25 .60
117 Charles Oakley .15 .40
118 John Starks .15 .40
119 Derek Harper .15 .40
120 Charles Smith .12 .30
121 Shaquille O'Neal .50 1.25
122 Anfernee Hardaway .30 .75
123 Nick Anderson .12 .30
124 Horace Grant .15 .40
125 Donald Royal .12 .30
126 Clarence Weatherspoon .12 .30
127 Dana Barros .12 .30
128 Jeff Malone .12 .30
129 Willie Burton .12 .30
130 Shawn Bradley .12 .30
131 Charles Barkley .30 .75
132 Kevin Johnson .20 .50
133 Danny Manning .15 .40
134 Dan Majerle .20 .50
135 A.C. Green .20 .50
136 Otis Thorpe .12 .30
137 Clifford Robinson .12 .30
138 Rod Strickland .12 .30
139 Buck Williams .12 .30
140 James Robinson .12 .30
141 Mitch Richmond .20 .50
142 Walt Williams .12 .30
143 Olden Polynice .12 .30
144 Spud Webb .20 .50
145 Duane Causwell .12 .30
146 David Robinson .30 .75
147 Dennis Rodman .40 1.00
148 Sean Elliott .20 .50
149 Avery Johnson .15 .40
150 J.R. Reid .12 .30
151 Shawn Kemp .20 .50
152 Gary Payton .30 .75
153 Detlef Schrempf .20 .50
154 Nate McMillan .12 .30
155 Kendall Gill .12 .30
156 Karl Malone .25 .60
157 John Stockton .25 .60
158 Jeff Hornacek .15 .40
159 Felton Spencer .12 .30
160 David Benoit .12 .30
161 Chris Webber .30 .75
162 Rex Chapman .12 .30
163 Don MacLean .12 .30
164 Calbert Cheaney .12 .30
165 Scott Skiles .12 .30
P23 Michael Jordan PROMO 4.00 10.00
MJ1R Michael Jordan Red 2.00 5.00
MJ1S Michael Jordan Silver 8.00 20.00

1994-95 SP Die Cuts

This is a parallel set to the regular SP issue. These die cuts appear one per pack. The only difference other than the die cut design is the silver hologram in the bottom left of the back instead of the gold hologram in the regular set and all cards are numbered with a "D" prefix. Please refer to the multipliers provided below (coupled with prices of the regular issue SP cards) to ascertain value.
COMPLETE SET (165) 20.00 50.00
*STARS: 1X TO 2.5X BASE CARD HI
*RCs: .75X TO 2X BASE HI

1994-95 SP Holoviews

Cards from this 36-card standard size set were randomly inserted in packs at a rate of one in five. The set features a mixture of NBA stars coupled with a wide selection of 1994-95 rookies. The fronts feature color action photos with a hologram of company spokesperson Shawn Kemp on the left with the player's name in silver just to the right. In addition, a holographic head shot of each player is placed in the lower left corner. The backs have a black and white photo on the right and player information on the left.
COMPLETE SET (36) 20.00 50.00
*DIE CUTS: 1X TO 2.5X HI COLUMN
DIE CUTS: STATED ODDS 1:75
PC1 Eric Montross .50 1.25
PC2 Dominique Wilkins 1.00 2.50
PC3 Larry Johnson .75 2.00
PC4 Dickey Simpkins .50 1.25
PC5 Jalen Rose 1.25 3.00
PC6 Latrell Sprewell 1.00 2.50
PC7 Carlos Rogers .50 1.25
PC8 Lamond Murray .50 1.25
PC9 Eddie Jones 1.50 4.00
PC10 Cedric Ceballos .50 1.25
PC11 Khalid Reeves .50 1.25
PC12 Glenn Robinson 1.00 2.50
PC13 Christian Laettner .60 1.50
PC14 Derrick Coleman .60 1.50
PC15 Vin Baker .50 1.25
PC16 Donyell Marshall .50 1.25
PC17 Kenny Anderson .60 1.50
PC18 Sharone Wright .50 1.25
PC19 Wesley Person .50 1.25
PC20 Brian Grant .75 2.00
PC21 Mitch Richmond .75 2.00
PC22 Shawn Kemp .75 2.00
PC23 Gary Payton .75 2.00
PC24 Juwan Howard .75 2.00
PC25 Stacey Augmon .60 1.50
PC26 Aaron McKie .50 1.25
PC27 Clifford Rozier .50 1.25
PC28 Eric Piatkowski .60 1.50
PC29 Shaquille O'Neal 3.00 8.00
PC30 Charlie Ward .50 1.25
PC31 Monty Williams .50 1.25
PC32 Jason Kidd 2.50 6.00
PC33 Bill Curley .50 1.25
PC34 Grant Hill 2.50 6.00
PC35 Jamal Mashburn .75 2.00
PC36 Nick Van Exel .75 2.00

1995-96 SP

The 1995-96 Upper Deck SP set was issued in one series totalling 167 cards. The 8-card packs, distributed exclusively to hobby outlets, retailed for $4.19 each. The first 147 cards are grouped by team alphabetically by city. The set ends with the rookie-based subset Premier Prospects (148-167) which feature a totally different design to the basic cards. Card stock thickness was upgraded from the previous year. A special Hakeem Olajuwon Commemorative card (celebrating his achievement of becoming only the ninth player in NBA history to score 20,000 points and grab 10,000 rebounds) was randomly seeded into 1 in every 359 packs. Rookie Cards of note in this set include Michael Finley, Kevin Garnett, Antonio McDyess, Jerry Stackhouse and Damon Stoudamire.
COMPLETE SET (167) 12.00 30.00
1 Stacey Augmon .20 .50
2 Mookie Blaylock .15 .40
3 Andrew Lang .15 .40
4 Steve Smith .20 .50
5 Spud Webb .25 .60
6 Dana Barros .15 .40
7 Dee Brown .15 .40
8 Todd Day .15 .40
9 Rick Fox .15 .40
10 Eric Montross .15 .40
11 Dino Radja .20 .50
12 Kenny Anderson .15 .40
13 Scott Burrell .15 .40
14 Dell Curry .15 .40
15 Matt Geiger .15 .40
16 Larry Johnson .25 .60
17 Glen Rice .25 .60
18 Steve Kerr .25 .60
19 Toni Kukoc .25 .60
20 Luc Longley .15 .40
21 Scottie Pippen .40 1.00
22 Dennis Rodman .50 1.25
23 Michael Jordan 2.00 5.00
24 Terrell Brandon .15 .40
25 Michael Cage .15 .40
26 Danny Ferry .15 .40
27 Chris Mills .15 .40
28 Bobby Phills .15 .40
29 Tony Dumas .15 .40
30 Jim Jackson .15 .40
31 Popeye Jones .15 .40
32 Jason Kidd .40 1.00
33 Jamal Mashburn .25 .60
34 Mahmoud Abdul-Rauf .15 .40
35 LaPhonso Ellis .15 .40
36 Dikembe Mutombo .25 .60
37 Jalen Rose .30 .75
38 Bryant Stith .15 .40
39 Joe Dumars .25 .60
40 Grant Hill .40 1.00
41 Lindsey Hunter .20 .50
42 Allan Houston .20 .50
43 Otis Thorpe .15 .40
44 B.J. Armstrong .15 .40
45 Tim Hardaway .25 .60
46 Chris Mullin .25 .60
47 Latrell Sprewell .25 .60
48 Rony Seikaly .20 .50
49 Sam Cassell .25 .60
50 Clyde Drexler .30 .75
51 Robert Horry .20 .50
52 Hakeem Olajuwon .30 .75
53 Kenny Smith .20 .50
54 Dale Davis .15 .40
55 Derrick McKey .15 .40
56 Reggie Miller .30 .75
57 Ricky Pierce .15 .40
58 Rik Smits .20 .50
59 Lamond Murray .15 .40
60 Rodney Rogers .15 .40
61 Malik Sealy .15 .40
62 Loy Vaught .15 .40
63 Brian Williams .15 .40
64 Elden Campbell .15 .40
65 Cedric Ceballos .15 .40
66 Magic Johnson .60 1.50
67 Eddie Jones .30 .75
68 Nick Van Exel .25 .60
69 Bimbo Coles .15 .40
70 Alonzo Mourning .30 .75
71 Billy Owens .15 .40
72 Kevin Willis .15 .40
73 Vin Baker .20 .50
74 Benoit Benjamin .15 .40
75 Sherman Douglas .15 .40
76 Lee Mayberry .15 .40
77 Glenn Robinson .25 .60
78 Tom Gugliotta .15 .40
79 Christian Laettner .20 .50
80 Sam Mitchell .15 .40
81 Terry Porter .15 .40
82 Isaiah Rider .25 .60
83 Shawn Bradley .15 .40
84 P.J. Brown .15 .40
85 Kendall Gill .15 .40
86 Armon Gilliam .15 .40
87 Jayson Williams .15 .40
88 Patrick Ewing .30 .75
89 Derek Harper .20 .50
90 Anthony Mason .20 .50
91 Charles Oakley .20 .50
92 John Starks .20 .50
93 Nick Anderson .15 .40
94 Horace Grant .20 .50
95 Anfernee Hardaway .40 1.00
96 Shaquille O'Neal .60 1.50
97 Dennis Scott .15 .40
98 Derrick Coleman .20 .50
99 Vernon Maxwell .15 .40
100 Trevor Ruffin .15 .40
101 Clarence Weatherspoon .15 .40
102 Sharone Wright .15 .40
103 Charles Barkley .40 1.00
104 A.C. Green .25 .60
105 Kevin Johnson .25 .60
106 Wesley Person .15 .40
107 John Williams .15 .40
108 Chris Dudley .15 .40
109 Harvey Grant .15 .40
110 Aaron McKie .15 .40
111 Clifford Robinson .15 .40
112 Rod Strickland .15 .40
113 Brian Grant .20 .50
114 Sarunas Marciulionis .15 .40
115 Olden Polynice .15 .40
116 Mitch Richmond .25 .60
117 Walt Williams .15 .40
118 Vinny Del Negro .15 .40
119 Sean Elliott .25 .60
120 Avery Johnson .20 .50
121 Chuck Person .20 .50
122 David Robinson .40 1.00
123 Hersey Hawkins .15 .40
124 Shawn Kemp .25 .60
125 Gary Payton .25 .60
126 Sam Perkins .15 .40
127 Detlef Schrempf .25 .60
128 Oliver Miller .15 .40
129 Tracy Murray .15 .40
130 Ed Pinckney .15 .40
131 Alvin Robertson .15 .40
132 Zan Tabak .15 .40
133 Jeff Hornacek .20 .50
134 Adam Keefe .15 .40
135 Karl Malone .30 .75
136 Chris Morris .15 .40
137 John Stockton .30 .75
138 Greg Anthony .15 .40
139 Blue Edwards .15 .40
140 Kenny Gattison .15 .40
141 Chris King .15 .40
142 Bryon Russell .20 .50
143 Calbert Cheaney .15 .40
144 Juwan Howard .25 .60
145 Gheorghe Muresan .15 .40
146 Robert Pack .15 .40
147 Chris Webber .30 .75
148 Alan Henderson RC .25 .60
149 Eric Williams RC .25 .60
150 George Zidek RC .25 .60
151 Bob Sura RC .25 .60
152 Antonio McDyess RC .60 1.50
153 Theo Ratliff RC .40 1.00
154 Joe Smith RC .50 1.25
155 Brent Barry RC .40 1.00
156 Sasha Danilovic RC .25 .60
157 Kurt Thomas RC .25 .60
158 Shawn Respert RC .25 .60
159 Kevin Garnett RC 5.00 12.00
160 Ed O'Bannon RC .25 .60
161 Jerry Stackhouse RC 1.50 4.00
162 Michael Finley RC .75 2.00
163 Arvydas Sabonis RC .50 1.25
164 Cory Alexander RC .25 .60
165 Damon Stoudamire RC .60 1.50
166 Bryant Reeves RC .25 .60
167 Rasheed Wallace RC .75 2.00
C1 Hakeem Olajuwon COMM 5.00 12.00
P23 Michael Jordan PROMO 4.00 10.00

1995-96 SP All-Stars

Randomly inserted in packs at a rate of one in five, this 30-card set features the 24 players from the 1996 NBA All-Star game in addition to six potential future All-Star athletes. Each card features a double die-cut design and silver foil stamping.
COMPLETE SET (30) 25.00 60.00
*GOLD: 2X TO 5X HI COLUMN
GOLD: STATED ODDS 1:61
AS1 Anfernee Hardaway 1.25 3.00
AS2 Michael Jordan 8.00 20.00
AS3 Grant Hill 1.25 3.00
AS4 Scottie Pippen 1.25 3.00
AS5 Shaquille O'Neal 2.00 5.00
AS6 Vin Baker .60 1.50
AS7 Terrell Brandon .50 1.25
AS8 Patrick Ewing 1.00 2.50
AS9 Juwan Howard .75 2.00
AS10 Reggie Miller 1.00 2.50
AS11 Alonzo Mourning 1.00 2.50
AS12 Glen Rice .75 2.00
AS13 Clyde Drexler 1.00 2.50
AS14 Jason Kidd 1.25 3.00
AS15 Charles Barkley 1.25 3.00
AS16 Shawn Kemp .75 2.00
AS17 Hakeem Olajuwon 1.00 2.50
AS18 Sean Elliott .75 2.00
AS19 Karl Malone 1.00 2.50
AS20 Dikembe Mutombo .75 2.00
AS21 Gary Payton .75 2.00
AS22 Mitch Richmond .75 2.00
AS23 David Robinson 1.25 3.00
AS24 John Stockton 1.00 2.50
AS25 Jerry Stackhouse 1.25 3.00
AS26 Damon Stoudamire 1.00 2.50
AS27 Rasheed Wallace 1.25 3.00
AS28 Kevin Garnett 3.00 8.00
AS29 Antonio McDyess 1.00 2.50
AS30 Joe Smith .75 2.00

1995-96 SP Holoviews

Randomly inserted in packs at a rate of one in seven, this 40-card set features a selection of youngsters and veteran stars from all 29 teams. Each card utilizes the special Holoview technology and features four holographic head shot images in the background.
COMPLETE SET (40) 40.00 100.00
PC1 Mookie Blaylock 1.00 2.50
PC2 Eric Williams .75 2.00

1995-96 SP Holoviews

PC3 Larry Johnson	1.50	4.00
PC4 George Zidek	.75	2.00
PC5 Michael Jordan	12.00	30.00
PC6 Bob Sura	.75	2.00
PC7 Jason Kidd	2.50	6.00
PC8 Cherokee Parks	.75	2.00
PC9 Antonio McDyess	2.00	5.00
PC10 Grant Hill	2.50	6.00
PC11 Theo Ratliff	1.25	3.00
PC12 Joe Smith	1.50	4.00
PC13 Latrell Sprewell	1.50	4.00
PC14 Hakeem Olajuwon	2.00	5.00
PC15 Travis Best	.75	2.00
PC16 Brent Barry	1.25	3.00
PC17 Nick Van Exel	1.50	4.00
PC18 Kurt Thomas	.75	2.00
PC19 Shawn Respert	.75	2.00
PC20 Glenn Robinson	1.50	4.00
PC21 Christian Laettner	1.25	3.00
PC22 Ed O'Bannon	.75	2.00
PC23 Patrick Ewing	2.00	5.00
PC24 Anfernee Hardaway	2.50	6.00
PC25 Shaquille O'Neal	4.00	10.00
PC26 Jerry Stackhouse	2.50	6.00
PC27 Mario Bennett	.75	2.00
PC28 Michael Finley	2.50	6.00
PC29 Randolph Childress	.75	2.00
PC30 Brian Grant	1.25	3.00
PC31 Mitch Richmond	1.50	4.00
PC32 Cory Alexander	.75	2.00
PC33 David Robinson	2.50	6.00
PC34 Sherrell Ford	.75	2.00
PC35 Shawn Kemp	1.50	4.00
PC36 Damon Stoudamire	2.00	5.00
PC37 Greg Ostertag	.75	2.00
PC38 Bryant Reeves	.75	2.00
PC39 Juwan Howard	1.50	4.00
PC40 Rasheed Wallace	2.50	6.00

1995-96 SP Holoviews Die Cuts

Randomly inserted in packs at a rate of one in 76, this 40-card set parallels the more common Holoview inserts. Unlike the basic Holoview inserts, each Holoview Die Cut insert features a tiled, die cut top border.

*DIE CUTS: 1.5X TO 4X HI COLUMN

PC5 Michael Jordan	60.00	150.00
PC13 Latrell Sprewell	8.00	20.00

1995-96 SP Jordan Collection

Randomly inserted at a rate of one in every 29 packs, these four cards cards continue the collection of Michael Jordan commemorative cards issued across all of Upper Deck's various 1995-96 brands.

COMPLETE SET (4)	12.00	30.00
COMMON CARD (JC17-JC20)	4.00	10.00

1996-97 SP

The 1996-97 SP set was issued in one series totalling 146 cards. The set contains the topical subset Premier Prospects (127-146). Cards were issued in 8-card packs with a suggested retail price of $3.99. Card fronts feature a player shot with his name running horizontally across the bottom and the player's team running vertically across the side.

COMPLETE SET (146)	17.50	35.00
1 Mookie Blaylock	.15	.40
2 Christian Laettner	.20	.50
3 Dikembe Mutombo	.25	.60
4 Steve Smith	.20	.50
5 Dana Barros	.15	.40
6 Rick Fox	.15	.40
7 Dino Radja	.20	.50
8 Eric Williams	.15	.40
9 Dell Curry	.15	.40
10 Vlade Divac	.25	.60
11 Anthony Mason	.15	.40
12 Glen Rice	.25	.60
13 Scottie Pippen	.40	1.00
14 Toni Kukoc	.25	.60
15 Luc Longley	.15	.40
16 Michael Jordan	2.00	5.00
17 Dennis Rodman	.50	1.25
18 Terrell Brandon	.15	.40
19 Tyrone Hill	.15	.40
20 Bobby Phills	.15	.40
21 Bob Sura	.15	.40
22 Chris Gatling	.15	.40
23 Jim Jackson	.15	.40
24 Sam Cassell	.20	.50
25 Jamal Mashburn	.20	.50
26 Dale Ellis	.15	.40
27 LaPhonso Ellis	.15	.40
28 Mark Jackson	.25	.60
29 Antonio McDyess	.25	.60
30 Bryant Stith	.15	.40
31 Joe Dumars	.25	.60
32 Grant Hill	.40	1.00
33 Lindsey Hunter	.15	.40
34 Otis Thorpe	.15	.40
35 Chris Mullin	.25	.60
36 Mark Price	.25	.60
37 Joe Smith	.20	.50
38 Latrell Sprewell	.25	.60
39 Charles Barkley	.40	1.00
40 Clyde Drexler	.30	.75
41 Mario Elie	.15	.40
42 Hakeem Olajuwon	.30	.75
43 Travis Best	.15	.40
44 Dale Davis	.15	.40
45 Reggie Miller	.30	.75
46 Rik Smits	.20	.50
47 Pooh Richardson	.15	.40
48 Rodney Rogers	.15	.40
49 Malik Sealy	.15	.40
50 Loy Vaught	.15	.40
51 Elden Campbell	.15	.40
52 Robert Horry	.20	.50
53 Eddie Jones	.25	.60
54 Shaquille O'Neal	.60	1.50
55 Nick Van Exel	.25	.60
56 Sasha Danilovic	.15	.40
57 Tim Hardaway	.25	.60
58 Dan Majerle	.25	.60
59 Alonzo Mourning	.30	.75
60 Vin Baker	.20	.50
61 Sherman Douglas	.15	.40
62 Armon Gilliam	.15	.40
63 Glenn Robinson	.25	.60
64 Kevin Garnett	.60	1.50
65 Tom Gugliotta	.15	.40
66 Terry Porter	.15	.40
67 Doug West	.15	.40
68 Shawn Bradley	.15	.40
69 Kendall Gill	.15	.40
70 Robert Pack	.15	.40
71 Jayson Williams	.15	.40
72 Chris Childs	.15	.40
73 Patrick Ewing	.30	.75
74 Allan Houston	.20	.50
75 Larry Johnson	.25	.60
76 John Starks	.20	.50
77 Nick Anderson	.15	.40
78 Horace Grant	.20	.50
79 Anfernee Hardaway	.40	1.00
80 Dennis Scott	.15	.40
81 Derrick Coleman	.20	.50
82 Mark Davis	.15	.40
83 Jerry Stackhouse	.30	.75
84 Clarence Weatherspoon	.15	.40
85 Cedric Ceballos	.15	.40
86 Kevin Johnson	.25	.60
87 Jason Kidd	.40	1.00
88 Danny Manning	.20	.50
89 Wesley Person	.15	.40
90 Kenny Anderson	.20	.50
91 Isaiah Rider	.20	.50
92 Clifford Robinson	.15	.40
93 Arvydas Sabonis	.20	.50
94 Rasheed Wallace	.30	.75
95 Mahmoud Abdul-Rauf	.15	.40
96 Brian Grant	.20	.50
97 Olden Polynice	.15	.40
98 Mitch Richmond	.25	.60
99 Corliss Williamson	.15	.40
100 Sean Elliott	.25	.60
101 Avery Johnson	.20	.50
102 David Robinson	.40	1.00
103 Dominique Wilkins	.30	.75
104 Hersey Hawkins	.15	.40
105 Jim McIlvaine	.15	.40
106 Shawn Kemp	.25	.60
107 Gary Payton	.25	.60
108 Detlef Schrempf	.25	.60
109 Doug Christie	.15	.40
110 Popeye Jones	.15	.40
111 Damon Stoudamire	.25	.60
112 Walt Williams	.15	.40
113 Jeff Hornacek	.20	.50
114 Karl Malone	.30	.75
115 Greg Ostertag	.15	.40
116 Bryon Russell	.15	.40
117 John Stockton	.30	.75
118 Greg Anthony	.15	.40
119 Blue Edwards	.15	.40
120 Anthony Peeler	.15	.40
121 Bryant Reeves	.15	.40
122 Calbert Cheaney	.15	.40
123 Juwan Howard	.20	.50
124 Gheorghe Muresan	.15	.40
125 Rod Strickland	.15	.40
126 Chris Webber	.30	.75
127 Antoine Walker RC	.75	2.00
128 Tony Delk RC	.40	1.00
129 Vitaly Potapenko RC	.40	1.00
130 Samaki Walker RC	.40	1.00
131 Todd Fuller RC	.40	1.00
132 Erick Dampier RC	.40	1.00
133 Lorenzen Wright RC	.40	1.00
134 Kobe Bryant RC	8.00	20.00
135 Derek Fisher RC	.75	2.00
136 Ray Allen RC	2.00	5.00
137 Stephon Marbury RC	1.00	2.50
138 Kerry Kittles RC	.40	1.00
139 Walter McCarty RC	.40	1.00
140 John Wallace RC	.40	1.00
141 Allen Iverson RC	2.50	6.00
142 Steve Nash RC	4.00	10.00
143 Jermaine O'Neal RC	1.00	2.50
144 Marcus Camby RC	.60	1.50
145 Shareef Abdur-Rahim RC	.75	2.00
146 Roy Rogers RC	.40	1.00
S16 Michael Jordan Sample	2.50	6.00

1996-97 SP Game Film

Randomly inserted in packs at a rate of one in 120, this 10-card set uses slide photography and video film to capture the moves of each particular player. Card backs contain a "GF" prefix.

COMPLETE SET (10)	75.00	150.00
GF1 Michael Jordan	30.00	80.00
GF2 Kevin Garnett	10.00	25.00
GF3 Charles Barkley	6.00	15.00
GF4 Anfernee Hardaway	6.00	15.00
GF5 Shaquille O'Neal	12.00	30.00
GF6 Jim Jackson	2.50	6.00
GF7 Dennis Rodman	8.00	20.00
GF8 Alonzo Mourning	5.00	12.00
GF9 Grant Hill	6.00	15.00
GF10 Shawn Kemp	4.00	10.00

1996-97 SP Holoviews

Randomly inserted in packs at a rate of one in 10, this 40-card set features the top NBA players with Holoview technology. Unlike past years, there is no die-cut parallel. Card backs are numbered with a "PC" prefix.

COMPLETE SET (40)	75.00	150.00
PC1 Mookie Blaylock	1.00	2.50
PC2 Antoine Walker	2.00	5.00
PC3 Eric Williams	1.00	2.50
PC4 Tony Delk	1.00	2.50
PC5 Michael Jordan	15.00	40.00
PC6 Dennis Rodman	3.00	8.00
PC7 Vitaly Potapenko	1.00	2.50
PC8 Bob Sura	1.00	2.50
PC9 Jamal Mashburn	1.25	3.00
PC10 Antonio McDyess	1.50	4.00
PC11 Grant Hill	2.50	6.00
PC12 Joe Smith	1.25	3.00
PC13 Latrell Sprewell	1.50	4.00
PC14 Charles Barkley	2.50	6.00
PC15 Hakeem Olajuwon	2.00	5.00
PC16 Erick Dampier	1.00	2.50
PC17 Lorenzen Wright	1.00	2.50
PC18 Kobe Bryant	30.00	60.00
PC19 Shaquille O'Neal	4.00	10.00
PC20 Alonzo Mourning	2.00	5.00
PC21 Ray Allen	4.00	10.00
PC22 Kevin Garnett	4.00	10.00
PC23 Stephon Marbury	2.50	6.00
PC24 Kerry Kittles	1.00	2.50
PC25 Walter McCarty	1.00	2.50
PC26 John Wallace	1.00	2.50
PC27 Anfernee Hardaway	2.50	6.00
PC28 Allen Iverson	5.00	12.00
PC29 Jerry Stackhouse	2.00	5.00
PC30 Steve Nash	5.00	12.00
PC31 Jermaine O'Neal	2.50	6.00
PC32 Brian Grant	1.25	3.00
PC33 Mitch Richmond	1.50	4.00
PC34 David Robinson	2.50	6.00
PC35 Shawn Kemp	1.50	4.00
PC36 Marcus Camby	1.50	4.00
PC37 Damon Stoudamire	1.50	4.00
PC38 John Stockton	2.00	5.00
PC39 Shareef Abdur-Rahim	2.00	5.00
PC40 Juwan Howard	1.25	3.00

1996-97 SP Inside Info

Inserted as a chiptopper at one per box, this 17-card set features several action and portrait photos of the players. In addition, each card has a special slide-out portion containing more information. The basic set contains 16 cards and the 17th is for Michael Jordan commemorating his 25,000 point.

COMPLETE SET (17)	50.00	120.00
*GOLD: 1.25X TO 3X HI COLUMN		
GOLD: RANDOM INSERTS IN BOXES		
IN1 Charles Barkley	4.00	10.00
IN2 Kevin Garnett	6.00	15.00
IN3 Anfernee Hardaway	4.00	10.00
IN4 Grant Hill	4.00	10.00
IN5 Allen Iverson	6.00	15.00
IN6 Jason Kidd	4.00	10.00
IN7 Shawn Kemp	2.50	6.00
IN8 Antonio McDyess	2.50	6.00
IN9 Dikembe Mutombo	2.50	6.00
IN10 Shaquille O'Neal	6.00	15.00
IN11 Hakeem Olajuwon	3.00	8.00
IN12 Dennis Rodman	5.00	12.00
IN13 Jerry Stackhouse	3.00	8.00
IN14 John Stockton	3.00	8.00
IN15 Damon Stoudamire	2.50	6.00
IN16 Chris Webber	3.00	8.00
IN17 Michael Jordan 25K	15.00	40.00

1996-97 SP Rookie Jumbos

Released in special retail outlets, this 20-card set featured 5" by 7" cards of the rookie subset from 96-97 SP. The set originally carried a retail price of $19.99.

COMPLETE SET (20)	12.00	30.00
1 Antoine Walker	1.25	3.00
2 Tony Delk	.60	1.50
3 Vitaly Potapenko	.60	1.50
4 Samaki Walker	.60	1.50
5 Todd Fuller	.60	1.50
6 Erick Dampier	.60	1.50
7 Lorenzen Wright	.60	1.50
8 Kobe Bryant	12.50	30.00
9 Derek Fisher	1.25	3.00
10 Ray Allen	2.50	6.00
11 Stephon Marbury	1.50	4.00
12 Kerry Kittles	.60	1.50
13 Walter McCarty	.60	1.50
14 John Wallace	.60	1.50
15 Allen Iverson	3.00	8.00
16 Steve Nash	3.00	8.00
17 Jermaine O'Neal	1.50	4.00
18 Marcus Camby	1.00	2.50
19 Shareef Abdur-Rahim	1.25	3.00
20 Roy Rogers	.60	1.50

1996-97 SP SPx Force

Randomly inserted in packs at a rate of one in 360, this 5-card set features the holoview technology of four players per card divided into particular themes: Scoring, Rebounding, Playmakers, Defenders and All-Around Talents. In addition, the All-Around Talents card also came in four different autographed versions, with each player individually signing 100 cards. Each of the autographed cards are sequentially numbered.

F1 Michael Jordan	30.00	80.00
Jerry Stackhouse		
Mitch Richmond		
Latrell Sprewell		
F2 Shawn Kemp	15.00	40.00
Dennis Rodman		
Charles Barkley		
Juwan Howard		
F3 Mookie Blaylock	10.00	25.00
Nick Van Exel		
Stephon Marbury		
Damon Stoudamire		
F4 Marcus Camby	10.00	25.00
Erick Dampier		
Anfernee Hardaway		
Antonio McDyess		
F5 Michael Jordan	30.00	80.00
Anfernee Hardaway		
Shawn Kemp		
Damon Stoudamire		
F5A Michael Jordan AU	1000.00	2000.00
F5B Anfernee Hardaway AU	125.00	250.00
F5C Shawn Kemp AU	175.00	350.00
F5D Damon Stoudamire AU	75.00	150.00

1997-98 SP Authentic

This is the first year that the brand name SP has changed over to SP Authentic, due to the heavy inclusion of autographs and memorabilia. The set size is 176 cards that were issued in five-card packs which carried a suggested retail price of $4.99.

COMPLETE SET (176)	60.00	120.00
1 Steve Smith	.30	.75
2 Dikembe Mutombo	.40	1.00
3 Christian Laettner	.30	.75
4 Mookie Blaylock	.25	.60
5 Alan Henderson	.25	.60
6 Antoine Walker	.40	1.00
7 Ron Mercer RC	1.00	2.50
8 Walter McCarty	.25	.60
9 Kenny Anderson	.30	.75
10 Travis Knight	.25	.60
11 Dana Barros	.25	.60
12 Glen Rice	.40	1.00
13 Vlade Divac	.40	1.00
14 Dell Curry	.25	.60
15 David Wesley	.25	.60
16 Bobby Phills	.25	.60
17 Anthony Mason	.25	.60
18 Toni Kukoc	.40	1.00
19 Dennis Rodman	.75	2.00
20 Ron Harper	.30	.75
21 Steve Kerr	.30	.75
22 Scottie Pippen	.60	1.50
23 Michael Jordan	3.00	8.00
24 Shawn Kemp	.40	1.00
25 Wesley Person	.25	.60
26 Derek Anderson RC	.75	2.00
27 Zydrunas Ilgauskas	.40	1.00
28 Brevin Knight RC	.75	2.00
29 Michael Finley	.40	1.00
30 Shawn Bradley	.25	.60
31 A.C. Green	.40	1.00
32 Hubert Davis	.25	.60
33 Dennis Scott	.25	.60
34 Tony Battie RC	1.00	2.50
35 Bobby Jackson RC	1.00	2.50
36 LaPhonso Ellis	.25	.60
37 Bryant Stith	.25	.60
38 Dean Garrett	.25	.60
39 Danny Fortson RC	.75	2.00
40 Grant Hill	.60	1.50
41 Brian Williams	.25	.60
42 Lindsey Hunter	.25	.60
43 Malik Sealy	.25	.60
44 Jerry Stackhouse	.40	1.00
45 Muggsy Bogues	.30	.75
46 Joe Smith	.30	.75
47 Donyell Marshall	.25	.60
48 Erick Dampier	.25	.60
49 Bimbo Coles	.25	.60
50 Charles Barkley	.60	1.50
51 Hakeem Olajuwon	.50	1.25
52 Clyde Drexler	.50	1.25
53 Kevin Willis	.25	.60
54 Mario Elie	.25	.60
55 Reggie Miller	.50	1.25
56 Rik Smits	.30	.75
57 Chris Mullin	.40	1.00
58 Antonio Davis	.25	.60
59 Dale Davis	.25	.60
60 Mark Jackson	.40	1.00
61 Brent Barry	.30	.75
62 Loy Vaught	.25	.60
63 Rodney Rogers	.25	.60
64 Lamond Murray	.25	.60
65 Maurice Taylor RC	.75	2.00
66 Shaquille O'Neal	1.00	2.50
67 Eddie Jones	.40	1.00
68 Kobe Bryant	2.00	5.00
69 Nick Van Exel	.30	.75
70 Robert Horry	.30	.75
71 Tim Hardaway	.40	1.00
72 Jamal Mashburn	.30	.75
73 Alonzo Mourning	.50	1.25
74 Isaac Austin	.25	.60
75 P.J. Brown	.25	.60
76 Ray Allen	.50	1.25
77 Glenn Robinson	.30	.75
78 Ervin Johnson	.25	.60
79 Terrell Brandon	.25	.60
80 Tyrone Hill	.25	.60
81 Stephon Marbury	.50	1.25
82 Kevin Garnett	.75	2.00
83 Tom Gugliotta	.25	.60
84 Chris Carr	.25	.60
85 Cherokee Parks	.25	.60
86 Sam Cassell	.30	.75
87 Chris Gatling	.25	.60
88 Kendall Gill	.25	.60
89 Keith Van Horn RC	1.50	4.00
90 Jayson Williams	.25	.60
91 Kerry Kittles	.25	.60
92 Patrick Ewing	.50	1.25
93 Larry Johnson	.40	1.00
94 Chris Childs	.25	.60
95 John Starks	.30	.75
96 Charles Oakley	.30	.75
97 Allan Houston	.30	.75
98 Mark Price	.40	1.00
99 Anfernee Hardaway	.60	1.50
100 Rony Seikaly	.30	.75
101 Horace Grant	.30	.75
102 Bo Outlaw	.25	.60
103 Clarence Weatherspoon	.25	.60
104 Allen Iverson	.75	2.00
105 Jim Jackson	.25	.60
106 Theo Ratliff	.30	.75
107 Tim Thomas RC	1.50	4.00
108 Danny Manning	.30	.75
109 Jason Kidd	.60	1.50
110 Kevin Johnson	.40	1.00
111 Rex Chapman	.25	.60
112 Clifford Robinson	.25	.60
113 Antonio McDyess	.30	.75
114 Damon Stoudamire	.40	1.00
115 Isaiah Rider	.25	.60
116 Arvydas Sabonis	.30	.75
117 Rasheed Wallace	.40	1.00
118 Brian Grant	.25	.60
119 Gary Trent	.25	.60
120 Mitch Richmond	.40	1.00
121 Corliss Williamson	.25	.60
122 Lawrence Funderburke RC	.75	2.00
123 Olden Polynice	.25	.60
124 Billy Owens	.25	.60
125 Avery Johnson	.30	.75
126 Sean Elliott	.40	1.00
127 David Robinson	.60	1.50
128 Tim Duncan RC !	7.50	15.00
129 Jaren Jackson	.25	.60
130 Detlef Schrempf	.40	1.00
131 Gary Payton	.40	1.00
132 Vin Baker	.30	.75
133 Hersey Hawkins	.25	.60
134 Dale Ellis	.25	.60
135 Sam Perkins	.25	.60
136 Marcus Camby	.40	1.00
137 John Wallace	.25	.60
138 Doug Christie	.25	.60
139 Chauncey Billups RC	5.00	12.00
140 Walt Williams	.25	.60
141 Karl Malone	.50	1.25
142 Bryon Russell	.25	.60
143 Jeff Hornacek	.30	.75
144 Greg Ostertag	.25	.60
145 John Stockton	.50	1.25
146 Shandon Anderson	.25	.60
147 Shareef Abdur-Rahim	.40	1.00
148 Bryant Reeves	.25	.60
149 Antonio Daniels RC	.75	2.00
150 Otis Thorpe	.25	.60
151 Blue Edwards	.25	.60
152 Chris Webber	.40	1.00
153 Juwan Howard	.30	.75
154 Rod Strickland	.25	.60
155 Calbert Cheaney	.25	.60
156 Tracy Murray	.25	.60
157 Chauncey Billups FW	1.50	4.00
158 Ed Gray FW RC	.75	2.00
159 Tony Battie FW	.50	1.25
160 Keith Van Horn FW	.75	2.00
161 Cedric Henderson FW RC	.75	2.00
162 Kelvin Cato FW RC	.75	2.00
163 Tariq Abdul-Wahad FW RC	.75	2.00
164 Derek Anderson FW	.40	1.00
165 Tim Duncan FW	2.50	6.00
166 Tracy McGrady FW RC	6.00	15.00
167 Ron Mercer FW	.50	1.25
168 Bobby Jackson FW	.50	1.25
169 Antonio Daniels FW	.40	1.00
170 Zydrunas Ilgauskas FW	.40	1.00
171 Maurice Taylor FW	.40	1.00
172 Tim Thomas FW	.75	2.00
173 Brevin Knight FW	.40	1.00
174 Lawrence Funderburke FW	.40	1.00
175 Jacque Vaughn FW RC	.75	2.00
176 Danny Fortson FW	.40	1.00
SPA23 Michael Jordan PROMO	3.00	8.00

1997-98 SP Authentic Authentics

Randomly inserted into packs at an overall rate of one in 288, this 20-card set features redemption cards for various pieces of memorabilia (both signed and unsigned) from Michael Jordan, Anfernee Hardaway and Shawn Kemp. The cards are not numbered and are listed below in alphabetical order by player. Some cards are not priced below due to insufficient market information.

AH1 Anfernee Hardaway	200.00	350.00
Signed Black Jersey/100		
AH2 Anfernee Hardaway	125.00	250.00
Signed Blue Jersey/190		
AH3 Anfernee Hardaway	25.00	50.00
Signed Sports Illustrated/300		
AH4 Anfernee Hardaway	15.00	30.00
Unsigned 8x10 photo/300		
MJ1 Michael Jordan	1000.00	2000.00
Signed Jersey/50		
MJ2 Michael Jordan	450.00	700.00
Signed 16x20 Photo/100		
MJ3 Michael Jordan	35.00	60.00
Unsigned 2-card set/500		
MJ4 Michael Jordan	35.00	60.00
Unsigned 8x10 Photo/400		
MJ5 Michael Jordan	15.00	40.00
Unsigned Gold Card/250		
MJ6 Michael Jordan	200.00	400.00
Unsigned Game Night Card/100		
MJ6B Michael Jordan	200.00	400.00
Unsigned Game Night Card/100		
MJ6C Michael Jordan	200.00	400.00
Unsigned Game Night Card/100		
MJ6D Michael Jordan	200.00	400.00
Unsigned Game Night Card/100		
MJ6E Michael Jordan	200.00	400.00
Unsigned Game Night Card/100		
MJ7 Michael Jordan	30.00	80.00
Unsigned Blow-up Poster/200		
MJ8 Michael Jordan	1200.00	2000.00
Signed Game Night Card/23		
SK1 Shawn Kemp	300.00	500.00
Signed Sonics Jersey/35		
SK2 Shawn Kemp	40.00	80.00
Signed All-Star Photo/104		
SK3 Shawn Kemp	40.00	80.00
Signed Mini-ball/100		
NNO SP Uncut Sheet/200	90.00	150.00

1997-98 SP Authentic BuyBack

Randomly inserted into packs at a rate of one in 309 packs, this 36-card set features 15 different player autographs on past SP issued cards and/or inserts. Each card is different in regards to how many each player signed and those numbers have been provided by Upper Deck.

1 Shareef Abdur-Rahim 96-7/192	20.00	50.00
2 Vin Baker 94-5/17	12.50	30.00
3 Vin Baker 95-6/71	12.50	30.00
4 Vin Baker 95-6AS/83	12.50	30.00
5 Clyde Drexler 94-5/141	30.00	80.00
6 Clyde Drexler 95-6/200	30.00	80.00
7 Clyde Drexler 96-7/63	30.00	80.00
8 Anfernee Hardaway 94-5/77	75.00	150.00
9 Anfernee Hardaway 95-6/100	75.00	150.00
10 Anfernee Hardaway 96-7/31	100.00	200.00
11 Tim Hardaway 94-5/126	30.00	80.00
12 Tim Hardaway 95-6/84	30.00	80.00
13 Tim Hardaway 96-7/43	30.00	80.00
14 Juwan Howard 94-5/50	15.00	40.00
15 Juwan Howard 95-6/300	12.50	30.00
16 Juwan Howard 95-6AS/50	12.50	30.00
17 Juwan Howard 96-7/33	12.50	30.00
18 Eddie Jones 94-5/50	25.00	60.00
19 Eddie Jones 95-6/87	20.00	50.00
20 Eddie Jones 96-7/18	20.00	50.00
21 Michael Jordan 94-5MJ1R/55	1000.00	2000.00
22 Jason Kidd 94-5/50	75.00	150.00
23 Jason Kidd 95-6/300	50.00	100.00
24 Jason Kidd 95-6AS/43	50.00	100.00
25 Jason Kidd 96-7/43	50.00	100.00
26 Kerry Kittles 96-7/201	12.50	30.00
27 Karl Malone 94-5/187	60.00	120.00
28 Karl Malone 95-6/36	60.00	120.00
29 Glen Rice 95-6AS78	12.50	30.00
30 Glen Rice 96-7/47	12.50	30.00
31 Mitch Richmond 94-5/95	12.50	30.00
32 Mitch Richmond 95-6/83	12.50	30.00
33 Mitch Richmond 96-7/39	12.50	30.00
34 Damon Stoudamire 95-6/35	30.00	80.00
35 Damon Stoudamire 96-7/36	25.00	60.00
36 Antoine Walker 96-7/132	15.00	40.00

1997-98 SP Authentic Premium Portraits

Randomly inserted into packs at a rate of one in 1,528, this seven-card set features an autograph from some of the top stars in the NBA. Card backs are numbered with the player's initials.

DP Damon Stoudamire	30.00	80.00
EP Eddie Jones	50.00	120.00
JP Jason Kidd	100.00	200.00
KP Kerry Kittles	25.00	60.00
MP Dikembe Mutombo	30.00	80.00
RP Glen Rice	25.00	60.00
TP Tim Hardaway	40.00	80.00

1997-98 SP Authentic Profiles 1

Randomly inserted into packs at a rate of one in three, this 40-card set profiles some of the leagues best players. Card backs are numbered with a "P" prefix.

COMPLETE SET (40)	30.00	60.00
*PRO.2: 1.25X TO 3X HI COLUMN		
PRO.2: STATED ODDS 1:12		
P1 Michael Jordan	4.00	10.00
P2 Glen Rice	.50	1.25
P3 Brent Barry	.40	1.00
P4 LaPhonso Ellis	.30	.75
P5 Allen Iverson	1.00	2.50
P6 Dikembe Mutombo	.50	1.25
P7 Charles Barkley	.75	2.00
P8 Antoine Walker	.50	1.25
P9 Karl Malone	.60	1.50
P10 Jason Kidd	.75	2.00
P11 Gary Payton	.50	1.25
P12 Kevin Garnett	1.00	2.50
P13 Keith Van Horn	.50	1.25
P14 Glenn Robinson	.40	1.00
P15 Michael Finley	.50	1.25
P16 Hakeem Olajuwon	.60	1.50
P17 Chris Webber	.50	1.25
P18 Mitch Richmond	.50	1.25
P19 Marcus Camby	.50	1.25
P20 Tim Hardaway	.50	1.25
P21 Shawn Kemp	.50	1.25
P22 Reggie Miller	.60	1.50
P23 Shaquille O'Neal	1.25	3.00
P24 Chauncey Billups	1.00	2.50
P25 Grant Hill	.75	2.00
P26 Shareef Abdur-Rahim	.50	1.25
P27 David Robinson	.75	2.00
P28 Scottie Pippen	.75	2.00
P29 Juwan Howard	.40	1.00
P30 Anfernee Hardaway	.75	2.00
P31 Jerry Stackhouse	.50	1.25
P32 Kobe Bryant	2.50	6.00
P33 Patrick Ewing	.60	1.50
P34 Alonzo Mourning	.60	1.50
P35 John Stockton	.60	1.50
P36 Kenny Anderson	.40	1.00
P37 Tim Duncan	1.50	4.00
P38 Stephon Marbury	.60	1.50
P39 Dennis Rodman	1.00	2.5
P40 Joe Smith	.40	1.0

1997-98 SP Authentic Profiles

Randomly inserted into packs, this 40-card set parallels both the regular Profiles 1 and 2, but is die cut and is serially numbered on the back to 100. Card backs carry a "P" prefix. To ascertain values on individual cards, please refer to the multiplier in the header below, coupled with the value of the base card.

*STARS: 20X TO 50X VALUE

*RCs: 15X TO 40X VALUE

P1 Michael Jordan	600.00	800.0
P11 Gary Payton	30.00	80.0
P12 Kevin Garnett	75.00	150.0
P16 Hakeem Olajuwon	40.00	100.0
P27 David Robinson	50.00	125.0
P28 Scottie Pippen	50.00	125.0
P30 Anfernee Hardaway	75.00	150.0
P32 Kobe Bryant	300.00	550.0
P39 Dennis Rodman	100.00	200.0

1997-98 SP Authentic Sign of the Times

Randomly inserted into packs at a rate of one in 42, this 22-card set features autographs of several different NBA players. Card backs are numbered with the player's initials.

AH Allan Houston	20.00	50.0
AJ Avery Johnson	8.00	20.0
BB Brent Barry	6.00	15.0
BW Brian Williams	10.00	25.0
CM Chris Mullin	15.00	40.0
DM Dikembe Mutombo	15.00	40.0
DS Damon Stoudamire	6.00	15.0
EJ Eddie Jones	15.00	40.0
GM Gheorghe Muresan	6.00	15.0
GP Gary Payton	25.00	50.0
GR Glen Rice	8.00	20.0
HW Juwan Howard	8.00	20.0
KJ Kevin Johnson	25.00	60.0
KK Kerry Kittles	5.00	12.0
LH Lindsey Hunter	5.00	12.0
MB Mookie Blaylock	5.00	12.0
MR Mitch Richmond	10.00	25.0
SC Sam Cassell	6.00	15.0
SE Sean Elliott	10.00	25.0
TE Terrell Brandon	6.00	15.0
TG Tom Gugliotta	5.00	12.0
TH Tim Hardaway	15.00	40.0
VB Vin Baker	8.00	20.0

1997-98 SP Authentic Sign of the Times Stars and Rookies

Randomly inserted into packs at a rate of one in 113, this 12-card set features autographs of some of the top stars and rookies from 1997-98. Card backs are numbered with the player's initials.

AW Antoine Walker	8.00	20.0
CD Clyde Drexler	40.00	100.0
CH Chauncey Billups	12.50	30.0
JK Jason Kidd	100.00	200.0
JS John Stockton TRADE	25.00	50.0
Did not sign		
KM Karl Malone	75.00	150.0
KV Keith Van Horn	6.00	15.0
MJ Michael Jordan	4000.00	6500.0
RO Ron Mercer	5.00	12.0
SA Shareef Abdur-Rahim	10.00	25.0
TB Tony Battie	5.00	12.0

1998-99 SP Authentic

The 1998-99 SP Authentic set contained 120 cards and was released in five-card packs with a suggested retail price of $4.99. The set also featured short-printed rookie F/X cards featuring the top 30 rookies. Each of the rookie cards were serially numbered to 3500.

COMPLETE SET w/o RC (90)	20.00	40.00
1 Michael Jordan	1.25	3.00
2 Michael Jordan	1.25	3.00
3 Michael Jordan	1.25	3.00
4 Michael Jordan	1.25	3.00
5 Michael Jordan	1.25	3.00
6 Michael Jordan	1.25	3.00
7 Michael Jordan	1.25	3.00
8 Michael Jordan	1.25	3.00
9 Michael Jordan	1.25	3.00
10 Michael Jordan	1.25	3.00
11 Steve Smith	.25	.60
12 Dikembe Mutombo	.30	.75
13 Alan Henderson	.20	.50
14 Antoine Walker	.30	.75
15 Ron Mercer	.25	.60
16 Kenny Anderson	.25	.60
17 Derrick Coleman	.25	.60
18 David Wesley	.20	.50
19 Glen Rice	.30	.75
20 Toni Kukoc	.30	.75
21 Ron Harper	.25	.60
22 Brent Barry	.25	.60
23 Shawn Kemp	.30	.75
24 Zydrunas Ilgauskas	.30	.75
25 Brevin Knight	.20	.50
26 Michael Finley	.30	.75
27 Steve Nash	.50	1.25
28 Cedric Ceballos	.20	.50
29 Antonio McDyess	.25	.60
30 Nick Van Exel	.25	.60
31 Grant Hill	.50	1.25
32 Jerry Stackhouse	.30	.75

Bison Dele	.20	.50
John Starks	.25	.60
Chris Mills	.20	.50
Hakeem Olajuwon	.40	1.00
Charles Barkley	.50	1.25
Scottie Pippen	.50	1.25
Reggie Miller	.40	1.00
Chris Mullin	.30	.75
Rik Smits	.25	.60
Lamond Murray	.20	.50
Maurice Taylor	.20	.50
Kobe Bryant	1.50	4.00
Dennis Rodman	.60	1.50
Shaquille O'Neal	.75	2.00
Alonzo Mourning	.40	1.00
Tim Hardaway	.30	.75
Jamal Mashburn	.25	.60
Ray Allen	.40	1.00
Glenn Robinson	.25	.60
Terrell Brandon	.20	.50
Kevin Garnett	.60	1.50
Stephon Marbury	.40	1.00
Joe Smith	.25	.60
Keith Van Horn	.30	.75
Kendall Gill	.20	.50
Jayson Williams	.20	.50
Patrick Ewing	.40	1.00
Allan Houston	.25	.60
Larry Johnson	.30	.75
Anfernee Hardaway	.50	1.25
Horace Grant	.25	.60
Allen Iverson	.60	1.50
Tim Thomas	.30	.75
Jason Kidd	.50	1.25
Tom Gugliotta	.20	.50
Rex Chapman	.20	.50
Damon Stoudamire	.30	.75
Isaiah Rider	.20	.50
Rasheed Wallace	.30	.75
Chris Webber	.30	.75
Vlade Divac	.30	.75
Corliss Williamson	.20	.50
Tim Duncan	.60	1.50
David Robinson	.50	1.25
Sean Elliott	.30	.75
Detlef Schrempf	.30	.75
Vin Baker	.25	.60
Gary Payton	.30	.75
Doug Christie	.20	.50
Tracy McGrady	.50	1.25
Karl Malone	.40	1.00
John Stockton	.40	1.00
Jeff Hornacek	.25	.60
Shareef Abdur-Rahim	.30	.75
Bryant Reeves	.20	.50
Juwan Howard	.25	.60
Mitch Richmond	.30	.75
Rod Strickland	.20	.50
Michael Olowokandi RC	3.00	8.00
Mike Bibby RC	8.00	20.00
Raef LaFrentz RC	3.00	8.00
Antawn Jamison RC	6.00	15.00
Vince Carter RC	25.00	60.00
Robert Traylor RC	2.50	6.00
Jason Williams RC	10.00	25.00
Larry Hughes RC	8.00	20.00
Dirk Nowitzki RC	40.00	100.00
Paul Pierce RC	20.00	50.00
Bonzi Wells RC	2.50	6.00
Michael Doleac RC	2.50	6.00
Keon Clark RC	2.50	6.00
Michael Dickerson RC	2.50	6.00
Matt Harpring RC	3.00	8.00
Bryce Drew RC	2.50	6.00
Pat Garrity RC	2.50	6.00
Roshown McLeod RC	2.50	6.00
Ricky Davis RC	6.00	15.00
Brian Skinner RC	2.50	6.00
Tyronn Lue RC	2.50	6.00
Felipe Lopez RC	2.50	6.00
Al Harrington RC	8.00	20.00
Sam Jacobson RC	2.50	6.00
Cory Carr RC	2.50	6.00
Corey Benjamin RC	2.50	6.00
Nazr Mohammed RC	2.50	6.00
Rashard Lewis RC	10.00	25.00
Peja Stojakovic RC	10.00	25.00
Andrae Patterson RC	2.50	6.00
P Michael Jordan PROMO	2.00	5.00

1998-99 SP Authentic Authentics

andomly inserted in packs at one in 864, this 27-card et features memorabilia redemption cards. Each card ppears in different quantities and could be redeemed r special pieces of memorabilia. Card backs carry a " prefix. Only one of each card was available for the ame-worn authentics (T18-T27). These cards are, erefore, not priced.

Larry Bird/10 Autographed NBA Ball	400.00	600.00
Julius Erving/25 Signed SI Cover	125.00	250.00
Anfernee Hardaway/200 Signed SI Cover	25.00	50.00
Anfernee Hardaway/200 Signed 8x10 photo	25.00	50.00
Tim Hardaway/125 Signed Mini-ball	20.00	40.00
Tim Hardaway/150 Signed 8x10 First version	12.50	25.00
Tim Hardaway/75 Signed 8x10 Second version	20.00	40.00
Juwan Howard/150 Signed Mini-ball	12.50	25.00
Eddie Jones/50 Signed Mini-ball	20.00	40.00
0 Eddie Jones/100 Signed 8x10	15.00	30.00
1 Michael Jordan/23 Signed black jersey	1500.00	2500.00
2 Michael Jordan/23 Signed white jersey	1500.00	2500.00
3 Shawn Kemp/150 Signed 8x10	20.00	40.00
4 Shawn Kemp/30 Signed jersey	200.00	400.00
5 Gary Payton/75 Signed SI Cover	50.00	100.00
6 Scottie Pippen/25 Signed Ball	150.00	300.00
7 Forum Floor Pieces/23	125.00	250.00

1998-99 SP Authentic First Class

Randomly inserted in packs at one in seven, this 30-card set features the NBA's hottest stars featured on a unique die cut design. Card backs carry a "FC" prefix.

COMPLETE SET (30)	15.00	40.00
FC1 Michael Jordan	4.00	10.00
FC2 Dikembe Mutombo	.50	1.25
FC3 Antoine Walker	.50	1.25
FC4 Glen Rice	.50	1.25
FC5 Toni Kukoc	.50	1.25
FC6 Shawn Kemp	.50	1.25
FC7 Michael Finley	.50	1.25
FC8 Raef LaFrentz	.60	1.50
FC9 Grant Hill	.75	2.00
FC10 Antawn Jamison	1.25	3.00
FC11 Scottie Pippen	.75	2.00
FC12 Reggie Miller	.60	1.50
FC13 Michael Olowokandi	.60	1.50
FC14 Kobe Bryant	2.50	6.00
FC15 Tim Hardaway	.50	1.25
FC16 Ray Allen	.60	1.50
FC17 Kevin Garnett	1.00	2.50
FC18 Keith Van Horn	.50	1.25
FC19 Allan Houston	.40	1.00
FC20 Anfernee Hardaway	.75	2.00
FC21 Allen Iverson	1.00	2.50
FC22 Jason Kidd	.75	2.00
FC23 Damon Stoudamire	.50	1.25
FC24 Jason Williams	1.25	3.00
FC25 Tim Duncan	1.00	2.50
FC26 Gary Payton	.50	1.25
FC27 Vince Carter	2.50	6.00
FC28 Karl Malone	.60	1.50
FC29 Mike Bibby	1.25	3.00
FC30 Mitch Richmond	.50	1.25

1998-99 SP Authentic MICHAEL

Randomly inserted in packs at one in 144, this 15-card set features Michael Jordan on Ionix technology. Card backs carry a "M" prefix.

COMPLETE SET (15)	150.00	300.00
COMMON CARD (M1-15)	12.00	30.00

1998-99 SP Authentic NBA 2K

Randomly inserted in packs at one in 23, this 20-card set looks at the future of the NBA, highlighting the stars of tomorrow. Card backs carry a "2K" prefix.

COMPLETE SET (20)	25.00	60.00
2K1 Michael Olowokandi	1.25	3.00
2K2 Mike Bibby	2.50	6.00
2K3 Raef LaFrentz	1.25	3.00
2K4 Antawn Jamison	2.50	6.00
2K5 Vince Carter	5.00	12.00
2K6 Robert Traylor	1.00	2.50
2K7 Jason Williams	2.50	6.00
2K8 Larry Hughes	2.00	5.00
2K9 Dirk Nowitzki	6.00	15.00
2K10 Paul Pierce	5.00	12.00
2K11 Cuttino Mobley	2.00	5.00
2K12 Michael Doleac	1.00	2.50
2K13 Corey Benjamin	1.00	2.50
2K14 Michael Dickerson	1.00	2.50
2K15 Allen Iverson	2.00	5.00
2K16 Kobe Bryant	5.00	12.00
2K17 Tim Duncan	2.00	5.00
2K18 Keith Van Horn	1.00	2.50
2K19 Kevin Garnett	2.00	5.00
2K20 Grant Hill	1.50	4.00

1998-99 SP Authentic Sign of the Times Bronze

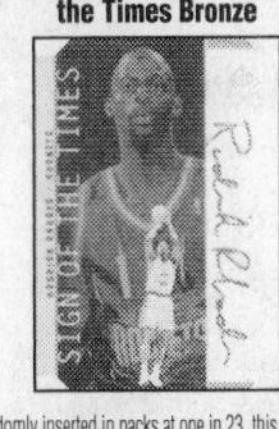

Randomly inserted in packs at one in 23, this 45-card set features autographs of NBA players. The cards are numbered by initials.

AM Antonio McDyess	6.00	15.00
AV Avery Johnson	8.00	20.00
BE Blue Edwards	5.00	12.00
BG Brian Grant	5.00	12.00
BK Brevin Knight	5.00	12.00
BL Mookie Blaylock	6.00	15.00
BP Bobby Phills	5.00	12.00
BR Bryon Russell	6.00	15.00
CB Chauncey Billups	8.00	20.00
CC Chris Carr	5.00	12.00
CH Calbert Cheaney	5.00	12.00
DA Derek Anderson	6.00	15.00
DC Doug Christie	6.00	15.00
DK Derek Fisher	8.00	20.00
DM Donyell Marshall	5.00	12.00
DN Danny Manning	6.00	15.00
DT Detlef Schrempf	10.00	25.00
DV David Wesley	5.00	12.00
ED Erick Dampier	5.00	12.00
EG Ed Gray	5.00	12.00
GR Glen Rice	6.00	15.00
HG Horace Grant	12.50	30.00
HW Juwan Howard	6.00	15.00
JH Jeff Hornacek	15.00	40.00
JR Jalen Rose	10.00	25.00
JW Jerome Williams	5.00	12.00
JY Jayson Williams	5.00	12.00
KA Kenny Anderson	6.00	15.00
LH Lindsey Hunter	5.00	12.00
LJ Larry Johnson	15.00	30.00
MG Tracy McGrady	20.00	50.00
MI Michael Finley	6.00	15.00
MK Mark Jackson	8.00	20.00
NA Nick Anderson	10.00	25.00
OH Othella Harrington	5.00	12.00
PJ P.J. Brown	5.00	12.00
RH Ron Harper	20.00	50.00
RR Rodrick Rhodes	5.00	12.00
SE Sean Elliott	10.00	25.00
TB Terrell Brandon	6.00	15.00
TK Toni Kukoc	15.00	40.00
TQ Tariq Abdul-Wahad	5.00	12.00
TR Theo Ratliff	5.00	12.00
TY Maurice Taylor	5.00	12.00
WM Walter McCarty	5.00	12.00

1998-99 SP Authentic Sign of the Times Gold

Randomly inserted in packs at one in 864, this 4-card set features a super-rare die cut autograph of NBA players. Card backs are numbered by the player's initials.

AI Allen Iverson	150.00	300.00
AW Antoine Walker	15.00	40.00
MJ Michael Jordan	1500.00	2500.00
TH Tim Hardaway	25.00	60.00

1998-99 SP Authentic Sign of the Times Silver

Randomly inserted in packs at one in 115, this 13-card set features autographs of NBA players. Card backs carry the player's initials.

AJ Antawn Jamison	10.00	25.00
DR Dennis Rodman	75.00	200.00
HO Hakeem Olajuwon	25.00	60.00
LR Larry Hughes	12.00	30.00
MB Mike Bibby	10.00	25.00
MO Michael Olowokandi	5.00	12.00
MT Dikembe Mutombo	15.00	40.00
PN Anfernee Hardaway	50.00	125.00
RL Raef LaFrentz	5.00	12.00
RM Ron Mercer	8.00	20.00
RT Robert Traylor	5.00	12.00
SH Shawn Kemp	40.00	100.00
VC Vince Carter	50.00	120.00

1999-00 SP Authentic

Released in May 2000, the 1999-00 SP Authentic product contained 135 cards, offered in five-card packs with a suggested retail price of $4.99. The base set contained 90 veterans and 45 rookies. The rookie subset was serially numbered to 1500.

COMPLETE SET (135)	200.00	400.00
COMPLETE SET w/o RC (90)	15.00	40.00
1 Dikembe Mutombo	.40	1.00
2 Jim Jackson	.30	.75
3 Alan Henderson	.25	.60
4 Antoine Walker	.40	1.00
5 Paul Pierce	.60	1.50
6 Kenny Anderson	.30	.75
7 Eddie Jones	.40	1.00
8 Derrick Coleman	.30	.75
9 Anthony Mason	.25	.60
10 Chris Carr	.25	.60
11 Hersey Hawkins	.25	.60
12 B.J. Armstrong	.25	.60
13 Shawn Kemp	.40	1.00
14 Bob Sura	.25	.60
15 Lamond Murray	.25	.60
16 Michael Finley	.40	1.00
17 Cedric Ceballos	.25	.60
18 Dirk Nowitzki	.75	2.00
19 Erick Strickland	.25	.60
20 Antonio McDyess	.30	.75
21 Nick Van Exel	.30	.75
22 Grant Hill	.50	1.25
23 Jerry Stackhouse	.40	1.00
24 Lindsey Hunter	.25	.60
25 Christian Laettner	.30	.75
26 Antawn Jamison	.40	1.00
27 Chris Mills	.25	.60
28 Larry Hughes	.30	.75
29 Charles Barkley	.60	1.50
30 Hakeem Olajuwon	.50	1.25
31 Cuttino Mobley	.30	.75
32 Reggie Miller	.40	1.00
33 Jalen Rose	.30	.75
34 Rik Smits	.40	1.00
35 Maurice Taylor	.25	.60
36 Derek Anderson	.25	.60
37 Tyrone Nesby RC	.40	1.00
38 Kobe Bryant	2.00	5.00
39 Shaquille O'Neal	1.00	2.50
40 Glen Rice	.40	1.00
41 Tim Hardaway	.40	1.00
42 Alonzo Mourning	.50	1.25
43 Jamal Mashburn	.30	.75
44 Ray Allen	.40	1.00
45 Sam Cassell	.30	.75
46 Glenn Robinson	.30	.75
47 Kevin Garnett	.75	2.00
48 Terrell Brandon	.25	.60
49 Joe Smith	.30	.75
50 Stephon Marbury	.30	.75
51 Keith Van Horn	.30	.75
52 Jamie Feick RC	.40	1.00
53 Kerry Kittles	.25	.60
54 Allan Houston	.30	.75
55 Latrell Sprewell	.40	1.00
56 Patrick Ewing	.50	1.25
57 Darrell Armstrong	.25	.60
58 Ron Mercer	.30	.75
59 Michael Doleac	.25	.60
60 Allen Iverson	.75	2.00
61 Toni Kukoc	.40	1.00
62 Eric Snow	.30	.75
63 Anfernee Hardaway	.60	1.50
64 Jason Kidd	.60	1.50
65 Tom Gugliotta	.25	.60
66 Scottie Pippen	.60	1.50
67 Steve Smith	.25	.60
68 Damon Stoudamire	.40	1.00
69 Jason Williams	.50	1.25
70 Peja Stojakovic	.40	1.00
71 Chris Webber	.40	1.00
72 Vlade Divac	.40	1.00
73 Tim Duncan	.75	2.00
74 David Robinson	.60	1.50
75 Avery Johnson	.30	.75
76 Gary Payton	.40	1.00
77 Vin Baker	.40	1.00
78 Vernon Maxwell	.30	.75
79 Vince Carter	.75	2.00
80 Tracy McGrady	.60	1.50
81 Doug Christie	.30	.75
82 Karl Malone	.50	1.25
83 John Stockton	.50	1.25
84 Jeff Hornacek	.30	.75
85 Mike Bibby	.40	1.00
86 Shareef Abdur-Rahim	.30	.75
87 Othella Harrington	.25	.60
88 Mitch Richmond	.40	1.00
89 Juwan Howard	.30	.75
90 Rod Strickland	.25	.60
91 Elton Brand RC	8.00	20.00
92 Steve Francis RC	8.00	20.00
93 Baron Davis RC	12.00	30.00
94 Lamar Odom RC	10.00	25.00
95 Jonathan Bender RC	3.00	8.00
96 Wally Szczerbiak RC	6.00	15.00
97 Richard Hamilton RC	8.00	20.00
98 Andre Miller RC	8.00	20.00
99 Shawn Marion RC	8.00	20.00
100 Jason Terry RC	8.00	20.00
101 Trajan Langdon RC	3.00	8.00
102 Aleksandar Radojevic RC	3.00	8.00
103 Corey Maggette RC	6.00	15.00
104 William Avery RC	3.00	8.00
105 Ron Artest RC	8.00	20.00
106 James Posey RC	3.00	8.00
107 Quincy Lewis RC	3.00	8.00
108 Dion Glover RC	3.00	8.00
109 Kenny Thomas RC	3.00	8.00
110 Devean George RC	3.00	8.00
111 Tim James RC	3.00	8.00
112 Vonteego Cummings RC	3.00	8.00
113 Jumaine Jones RC	3.00	8.00
114 Scott Padgett RC	3.00	8.00
115 Adrian Griffin RC	3.00	8.00
116 Anthony Carter RC	3.00	8.00
117 Todd MacCulloch RC	3.00	8.00
118 Chucky Atkins RC	3.00	8.00
119 Obinna Ekezie RC	3.00	8.00
120 Eddie Robinson RC	3.00	8.00
121 Michael Ruffin RC	3.00	8.00
122 Laron Profit RC	3.00	8.00
123 Cal Bowdler RC	3.00	8.00
124 Chris Herren RC	3.00	8.00
125 Milt Palacio RC	3.00	8.00
126 Jeff Foster RC	3.00	8.00
127 Ryan Bowen RC	3.00	8.00
128 Tim Young RC	3.00	8.00
129 Derrick Dial RC	3.00	8.00
130 Greg Buckner RC	3.00	8.00
131 Rodney Buford RC	3.00	8.00
132 Evan Eschmeyer RC	3.00	8.00
133 Jermaine Jackson RC	3.00	8.00
134 John Celestand RC	3.00	8.00
135 Ryan Robertson RC	3.00	8.00
KG Kevin Garnett PROMO	.75	2.00

1999-00 SP Authentic Athletic

Randomly inserted in packs at one in 12, this 12-card set featured players best known for their head-turning athletic moves. Card backs carry an "A" prefix.

COMPLETE SET (12)	8.00	20.00
A1 Grant Hill	.75	2.00
A2 Shareef Abdur-Rahim	.50	1.25
A3 Jason Kidd	1.00	2.50
A4 Vince Carter	1.25	3.00
A5 Steve Francis	1.50	4.00
A6 Scottie Pippen	1.00	2.50
A7 Paul Pierce	1.00	2.50
A8 Kobe Bryant	3.00	8.00
A9 Stephon Marbury	.50	1.25
A10 Michael Finley	.60	1.50
A11 Eddie Jones	.60	1.50
A12 Kevin Garnett	1.25	3.00

1999-00 SP Authentic Authentics

Randomly inserted in packs at one in 15000, this 10-card set features memorabilia redemption cards good for an autographed authentic jersey of the featured athlete. Only 100 total cards were available - ten cards per player.

1999-00 SP Authentic BuyBack

Randomly inserted in packs at one in 288, this 120-card set features previous SP/SP Authentic cards bought back by Upper Deck, autographed by the players. Print runs for each card are listed below. The cards are listed in alphabetical order. Some of the tougher cards are unpriced, but are listed below for checklisting purposes.

LOWER PRINT RUNS UNPRICED

2 Mike Bibby 98-9SPA2K/42	20.00	50.00
3A Kobe Bryant Redemption	40.00	100.00
8 Kobe Bryant 98-9SPA/132	150.00	300.00
9 Kevin Garnett 95-6SP/21	100.00	200.00
11 Kevin Garnett 96-7SP/21	100.00	200.00
15 Kevin Garnett 98-9SPA/NNO	50.00	100.00
18 Brian Grant 94-5SP/NNO	6.00	15.00
22 Brian Grant 95-6SP/NNO	6.00	15.00
25 Brian Grant 96-7SP/16	15.00	40.00
26 Brian Grant 97-8SPA/16	15.00	40.00
27 Tom Gugliotta 94-5SP/24	10.00	25.00
29 Tom Gugliotta 95-6SP/24	10.00	25.00
30 Tom Gugliotta 96-7SP/24	10.00	25.00
32 Tom Gugliotta 98-9SPA/110	6.00	15.00
33 Anfernee Hardaway 94-5SP/30	100.00	200.00
35 Anfernee Hardaway 95-6SP/30	100.00	200.00
40 Anfernee Hardaway 98-9SPA/32	100.00	200.00
43 Larry Hughes 98-9SPA2K/90	25.00	60.00
44 Mark Jackson 94-5SP NNO	6.00	15.00
48 Antawn Jamison 98-9SPAFC/NNO	15.00	40.00
50 Eddie Jones 94-5SP/NNO	30.00	80.00
52 Eddie Jones 95-6SP/NNO	10.00	25.00
54 Eddie Jones 96-7SP/NNO	10.00	25.00
60 Brevin Knight 97-8SPA/24	10.00	25.00
61 Brevin Knight 98-9SPA/NNO	6.00	15.00
63 Raef LaFrentz 98-9SPAFC/NNO	6.00	15.00
64 Raef LaFrentz 98-9SPA2K/NNO	6.00	15.00
65 Karl Malone 94-5SP/NNO	30.00	75.00
74 Jermaine O'Neal 96-7SP/170	40.00	100.00
77 Glen Rice 94-5SP/41	15.00	40.00
79 Glen Rice 95-6SP/NNO	8.00	20.00
82 Glen Rice 96-7SP/41	15.00	40.00
85 Glen Rice 98-9SPA/NNO	8.00	20.00
87 Jalen Rose 94-5SP/100	25.00	60.00
88 Jalen Rose 95-6SP/120	12.50	30.00
89 Jerry Stackhouse 95-6SP/NNO	25.00	60.00
94 Jerry Stackhouse 96-7SP/16	40.00	100.00
96 Jerry Stackhouse 97-8SPA/25	40.00	100.00
97 Jerry Stackhouse 98-9SPA/NNO	12.50	30.00
98 Damon Stoudamire 95-6SP/NNO	10.00	25.00
100 Damon Stoudamire 95-6SPHo/35	25.00	60.00
102 Damon Stoudamire 96-7SP/31	25.00	60.00
105 Damon Stoudamire 98-9SPA/NNO	10.00	25.00
108 Maurice Taylor 97-8SPA/20	12.50	30.00
109 Maurice Taylor 98-9SPA/NNO	6.00	15.00
111 Robert Traylor 98-9SPA2K/NNO	6.00	15.00
112 Antoine Walker 96-7SP/NNO	15.00	40.00
114 Antoine Walker 97-8SPA/19	25.00	60.00
115 Antoine Walker 98-9SPA/NNO	12.50	30.00
117 Jayson Williams 95-6SP/NNO	6.00	15.00
118 Jayson Williams 96-7SP/33	8.00	20.00
120 Jayson Williams 98-9SPA/NNO	6.00	15.00

1999-00 SP Authentic First Class

Randomly inserted in packs at one in 12, this 12-card set featured the more talented players in the NBA. The cards carry a "FC" prefix.

COMPLETE SET (12)	6.00	15.00
FC1 Kevin Garnett	1.25	3.00
FC2 Kobe Bryant	3.00	8.00
FC3 Gary Payton	.60	1.50
FC4 Tim Hardaway	.60	1.50
FC5 Antonio McDyess	.50	1.25
FC6 Allan Houston	.50	1.25
FC7 Jason Kidd	1.00	2.50
FC8 Reggie Miller	.60	1.50
FC9 Jason Williams	.75	2.00
FC10 Allen Iverson	1.25	3.00
FC11 David Robinson	1.00	2.50
FC12 Shaquille O'Neal	1.50	4.00

1999-00 SP Authentic Maximum Force

Randomly inserted in packs at one in four, this 15-card set highlighted the stars who make a strong impact on the game. Card backs carry a "M" prefix.

COMPLETE SET (15)	4.00	10.00
M1 Karl Malone	.50	1.25
M2 Antawn Jamison	.40	1.00
M3 Shareef Abdur-Rahim	.30	.75
M4 Tim Duncan	.75	2.00
M5 Allen Iverson	.75	2.00
M6 Michael Finley	.40	1.00
M7 Kevin Garnett	.75	2.00
M8 Kobe Bryant	2.00	5.00
M9 Gary Payton	.40	1.00
M10 Keith Van Horn	.30	.75
M11 Chris Webber	.40	1.00
M12 Glenn Robinson	.30	.75
M13 Alonzo Mourning	.50	1.25
M14 Antoine Walker	.40	1.00
M15 Antonio McDyess	.30	.75

1999-00 SP Authentic Premier Powers

Randomly inserted in packs at one in 72, this nine-card set captured the sheer domination of some of the NBA's most irresistible forces. Card backs carry a "P" prefix.

COMPLETE SET (9)	20.00	50.00
P1 Kobe Bryant	8.00	20.00
P2 Kevin Garnett	3.00	8.00
P3 Tim Duncan	3.00	8.00
P4 Elton Brand	4.00	10.00
P5 Vince Carter	3.00	8.00
P6 Lamar Odom	5.00	12.00
P7 Grant Hill	2.00	5.00
P8 Shaquille O'Neal	4.00	10.00
P9 Allen Iverson	3.00	8.00

1999-00 SP Authentic Sign of the Times

Randomly inserted in packs at one in 23, this 58-card set features autographs from NBA stars and rookies. Card backs are numbered by the players initials.

AC Anthony Carter	4.00	10.00
AD Antonio Davis	4.00	10.00
AG Adrian Griffin	4.00	10.00
AH Al Harrington	4.00	10.00
AJ Antawn Jamison	6.00	15.00
AL Alan Henderson	4.00	10.00
AM Andre Miller	4.00	10.00
AN Anfernee Hardaway	60.00	150.00
AW Antoine Walker	10.00	25.00
BD Baron Davis	10.00	25.00
BG Brian Grant	4.00	10.00
BR Brevin Knight	4.00	10.00
BW Bonzi Wells	4.00	10.00
CA Chucky Atkins	4.00	10.00
CM Corey Maggette	6.00	15.00
CR Austin Croshere	4.00	10.00
CT Cuttino Mobley	4.00	10.00
DA Darrell Armstrong	4.00	10.00
DG Dion Glover	4.00	10.00
DN Dirk Nowitzki	50.00	120.00
DS Damon Stoudamire	8.00	20.00
EJ Eddie Jones	10.00	25.00
GR Glen Rice	8.00	20.00
JB Jonathan Bender	4.00	10.00
JO Jermaine O'Neal	6.00	15.00
JP James Posey	4.00	10.00
JR Jalen Rose	8.00	20.00
JS Jerry Stackhouse	6.00	15.00
JT Jason Terry	6.00	15.00
JY Jayson Williams	4.00	10.00
KB Kobe Bryant	100.00	200.00
KG Kevin Garnett	50.00	100.00
KM Karl Malone	40.00	100.00
LH Larry Hughes	8.00	20.00
LM Lamond Murray	4.00	10.00
MB Mike Bibby	4.00	10.00
MD Antonio McDyess	8.00	20.00
ME Mario Elie	6.00	15.00
MI Michael Dickerson	4.00	10.00
MJ Michael Jordan	900.00	1400.00
MK Mark Jackson	4.00	10.00
MT Maurice Taylor	4.00	10.00
QL Quincy Lewis	4.00	10.00
RA Ron Artest	8.00	20.00
RH Richard Hamilton	6.00	15.00
RL Raef LaFrentz	4.00	10.00
RP Ruben Patterson	4.00	10.00
RT Robert Traylor	4.00	10.00
SF Steve Francis	6.00	15.00
SH Shawn Marion	6.00	15.00
SM Sam Mack	4.00	10.00
SU Bob Sura	4.00	10.00
TG Tom Gugliotta	4.00	10.00
TL Trajan Langdon	4.00	10.00
TN Tyrone Nesby	4.00	10.00
TR Tracy McGrady	15.00	40.00
WA William Avery	4.00	10.00
WS Wally Szczerbiak	4.00	10.00

1999-00 SP Authentic Sign of the Times Gold

Randomly inserted in packs, this 57-card set parallels the regular Sign of the Times autographed insert. Each card features gold foil and is serially numbered to 25. Michael Jordan was the only player that did not have a Gold parallel.

*GOLD: 1.5X TO 4X BASE AUTO

KB Kobe Bryant	300.00	600.00

1999-00 SP Authentic Supremacy

Randomly inserted in packs at one in 24, this nine-card set features the "go-to guys" when the game is on the line. Card backs carry a "S" prefix.

COMPLETE SET (9)	8.00	20.00
S1 Vince Carter	1.50	4.00
S2 Shaquille O'Neal	2.00	5.00
S3 Tim Duncan	1.50	4.00
S4 Kevin Garnett	1.50	4.00
S5 Jason Williams	1.00	2.50
S6 Stephon Marbury	.60	1.50
S7 Gary Payton	.75	2.00
S8 Kobe Bryant	4.00	10.00
S9 Grant Hill	1.00	2.50

2000-01 SP Authentic

The 2000-01 SP Authentic product released in June, 2001 and featured a 136-card base set that was broken into tiers as follows: Base Veterans (1-90), and Rookies (91-136) that were serial numbered to either 500, 1250, or 2000 (please see print runs below). Each pack contained five cards and carried a suggested retail price of $4.99.

COMP.SET w/o SP's (90)	10.00	25.00
1 Jason Terry	.40	1.00
2 Alan Henderson	.25	.60
3 Lorenzen Wright	.25	.60
4 Paul Pierce	.50	1.25
5 Antoine Walker	.30	.75
6 Bryant Stith	.25	.60
7 Jamal Mashburn	.30	.75
8 Baron Davis	.40	1.00
9 David Wesley	.25	.60
10 Elton Brand	.40	1.00
11 Ron Artest	.40	1.00
12 Ron Mercer	.25	.60
13 Andre Miller	.30	.75
14 Lamond Murray	.25	.60
15 Jim Jackson	.25	.60
16 Michael Finley	.40	1.00
17 Dirk Nowitzki	.60	1.50
18 Steve Nash	.60	1.50
19 Antonio McDyess	.30	.75
20 Nick Van Exel	.30	.75
21 Raef LaFrentz	.25	.60
22 Jerry Stackhouse	.30	.75
23 Chucky Atkins	.25	.60
24 Joe Smith	.30	.75
25 Antawn Jamison	.40	1.00
26 Larry Hughes	.30	.75
27 Mookie Blaylock	.30	.75
28 Steve Francis	.40	1.00
29 Hakeem Olajuwon	.50	1.25
30 Cuttino Mobley	.30	.75
31 Reggie Miller	.40	1.00
32 Jermaine O'Neal	.40	1.00
33 Jalen Rose	.30	.75
34 Travis Best	.25	.60
35 Lamar Odom	.40	1.00
36 Corey Maggette	.30	.75
37 Eric Piatkowski	.25	.60
38 Shaquille O'Neal	1.00	2.50
39 Kobe Bryant	2.00	5.00
40 Isaiah Rider	.30	.75
41 Horace Grant	.30	.75
42 Eddie Jones	.40	1.00
43 Brian Grant	.25	.60
44 Tim Hardaway	.40	1.00
45 Ray Allen	.40	1.00
46 Glenn Robinson	.30	.75
47 Sam Cassell	.30	.75
48 Kevin Garnett	.75	2.00
49 Terrell Brandon	.25	.60
50 Chauncey Billups	.40	1.00
51 Wally Szczerbiak	.30	.75
52 Stephon Marbury	.30	.75
53 Keith Van Horn	.30	.75
54 Aaron Williams	.25	.60
55 Latrell Sprewell	.30	.75
56 Allan Houston	.30	.75
57 Glen Rice	.30	.75
58 Tracy McGrady	.60	1.50
59 Grant Hill	.50	1.25
60 Darrell Armstrong	.25	.60
61 Allen Iverson	.75	2.00
62 Dikembe Mutombo	.40	1.00
63 Aaron McKie	.25	.60
64 Jason Kidd	.60	1.50
65 Clifford Robinson	.25	.60
66 Shawn Marion	.40	1.00
67 Damon Stoudamire	.30	.75

68 Steve Smith .30 .75
69 Rasheed Wallace .40 1.00
70 Chris Webber .40 1.00
71 Jason Williams .40 1.00
72 Peja Stojakovic .40 1.00
73 Tim Duncan .75 2.00
74 David Robinson .60 1.50
75 Derek Anderson .25 .60
76 Gary Payton .40 1.00
77 Rashard Lewis .40 1.00
78 Patrick Ewing .50 1.25
79 Vince Carter .75 2.00
80 Charles Oakley .30 .75
81 Antonio Davis .25 .60
82 Karl Malone .50 1.25
83 John Stockton .50 1.25
84 John Starks .25 .60
85 Shareef Abdur-Rahim .30 .75
86 Mike Bibby .40 1.00
87 Michael Dickerson .25 .60
88 Richard Hamilton .30 .75
89 Mitch Richmond .30 .75
90 Christian Laettner .25 .60
91 Kenyon Martin AU/500 RC 12.00 30.00
92 Stromile Swift AU/500 RC 5.00 12.00
93 Darius Miles AU/500 RC 5.00 12.00
94 Marcus Fizer/1250 RC 2.50 6.00
95 Mike Miller AU/500 RC 10.00 25.00
96 DerMarr Johnson AU/500 RC 5.00 12.00
97 Chris Mihm/1250 RC 2.50 6.00
98 Jamal Crawford/1250 RC 4.00 10.00
99 Joel Przybilla/2000 RC 2.00 5.00
100 Keyon Dooling/1250 RC 2.50 6.00
101 Jerome Moiso/1250 RC 2.50 6.00
102 Etan Thomas/2000 RC 2.00 5.00
103 Courtney Alexander/1250 RC 2.50 6.00
104 Mateen Cleaves/1250 RC 2.50 6.00
105 Jason Collier/2000 RC 2.00 5.00
106 Hedo Turkoglu/1250 RC 5.00 12.00
107 Desmond Mason/1250 RC 3.00 8.00
108 Quentin Richardson/1250 RC 4.00 10.00
109 Jamaal Magloire/1250 RC 2.50 6.00
110 Speedy Claxton/2000 RC 2.00 5.00
111 Morris Peterson AU/500 RC 5.00 12.00
112 Donnell Harvey/2000 RC 2.00 5.00
113 DeShawn Stevenson/1250 RC 3.00 8.00
114 Jake Tsakalidis/2000 RC 2.00 5.00
115 Soumaila Samake/2000 RC 2.00 5.00
116 Erick Barkley/2000 RC 2.00 5.00
117 Mark Madsen/2000 RC 2.00 5.00
118 A.J. Guyton/1250 RC 2.50 6.00
119 Olumide Oyedeji/2000 RC 2.00 5.00
120 Eddie House/1250 RC 2.50 6.00
121 Eduardo Najera/2000 RC 2.00 5.00
122 Lavor Postell/2000 RC 2.00 5.00
123 Hanno Mottola/1250 RC 2.50 6.00
124 Ira Newble/2000 RC 2.00 5.00
125 Chris Porter/1250 RC 2.50 6.00
126 Ruben Wolkowyski/2000 RC 2.00 5.00
127 Pepe Sanchez/2000 RC 2.00 5.00
128 Stephen Jackson/1250 RC 4.00 10.00
129 Marc Jackson/1250 RC 2.50 6.00
130 Dragan Tarlac/2000 RC 2.00 5.00
131 Lee Nailon/2000 2.00 5.00
132 Mike Penberthy/1250 RC 2.50 6.00
133 Mark Blount/2000 RC 2.00 5.00
134 Dan Langhi/2000 RC 2.00 5.00
135 Daniel Santiago/2000 RC 3.00 8.00
136 Wang Zhizhi AU/500 RC 20.00 50.00
S1 Kobe Bryant PROMO 1.00 2.50

2000-01 SP Authentic Athletic

Randomly inserted into packs at one in 24, this 7-card insert features some of the most athletic players in the NBA. Card backs carry an "A" prefix.

COMPLETE SET (7) 5.00 12.00
A1 Allen Iverson 1.25 3.00
A2 Elton Brand .60 1.50
A3 Antonio McDyess .50 1.25
A4 Vince Carter 1.25 3.00
A5 Kobe Bryant 3.00 8.00
A6 Grant Hill .75 2.00
A7 Kevin Garnett 1.25 3.00

2000-01 SP Authentic BuyBack

Randomly inserted in packs at one in 2500, this insert set features previous SP/SP Authentic cards bought back by Upper Deck, and autographed by the players. Print runs for each card are listed below. The cards are listed in alphabetical order. Some of the tougher cards are unpriced, but are listed below for checklisting purposes. Each card was accompanied by a certificate of authenticity from Upper Deck, and all of the UDA holograms carry an "AAA" prefix to the numbering.

MOST AU'S NOT PRICED DUE TO SCARCITY
20 Kevin Garnett 95-6SP/21 150.00 300.00
45 Tim Hardaway 98-9SPA/40 15.00 40.00
61 Michael Jordan 94-5SP/23 750.00 1500.00
84 Tracy McGrady 98-9SPA/20 75.00 150.00
85 Tracy McGrady 99-0SPA/27 50.00 100.00
105 Jerry Stackhouse 95-6SP/22 40.00 100.00
110 Antoine Walker 96-7SP/24 30.00 80.00

2000-01 SP Authentic First Class

Randomly inserted into packs at one in 24, this 7-card insert features players that are first class citizens on and off the court. Card backs carry a "FC" prefix.

COMPLETE SET (7) 6.00 15.00
FC1 Shareef Abdur-Rahim .50 1.25
FC2 Kevin Garnett 1.25 3.00
FC3 Baron Davis .60 1.50
FC4 Shaquille O'Neal 1.50 4.00
FC5 Rashard Lewis .60 1.50
FC6 Paul Pierce .75 2.00
FC7 Kobe Bryant 3.00 8.00

2000-01 SP Authentic Premier Powers

Randomly inserted into packs at one in 24, this 7-card insert features some of the most overpowering players in the NBA. Card backs carry an "P" prefix.

COMPLETE SET (7) 6.00 15.00
P1 Chris Webber .60 1.50
P2 Allen Iverson 1.25 3.00
P3 Kobe Bryant 3.00 8.00
P4 Rasheed Wallace .60 1.50
P5 Tracy McGrady 1.00 2.50
P6 Kevin Garnett 1.25 3.00
P7 Tim Duncan 1.25 3.00

2000-01 SP Authentic Sign of the Times

Randomly inserted in packs at one in 23, this 48-card set features autographs from NBA stars and rookies. Card backs are numbered by the players initials. Please note that a few of the players packed out as exchange cards, and must be redeemed no later that 01/18/02.

AC Austin Croshere 4.00 10.00
AJ Antawn Jamison 4.00 10.00
AM Antonio McDyess 4.00 10.00
AR Darrell Armstrong 4.00 10.00
AW Antoine Walker 6.00 15.00
CA Courtney Alexander 4.00 10.00
CM Chris Mihm 4.00 10.00
DA Darius Miles 4.00 10.00
DE Desmond Mason 5.00 12.00
DH Donnell Harvey 4.00 10.00
DJ DerMarr Johnson 4.00 10.00
DN Dirk Nowitzki 40.00 100.00
DS DeShawn Stevenson 5.00 12.00
EB Erick Barkley 4.00 10.00
EJ Eddie Jones 5.00 12.00
ET Etan Thomas 4.00 10.00
FI Marcus Fizer 4.00 10.00
GP Gary Payton 12.50 30.00
JA Jamaal Magloire 4.00 10.00
JB Jonathan Bender 4.00 10.00
JC Jamal Crawford 6.00 15.00
JM Jerome Moiso 4.00 10.00
JO Jermaine O'Neal 6.00 15.00
JP Joel Przybilla 4.00 10.00
JR Jalen Rose 4.00 10.00
JS Jerry Stackhouse 6.00 15.00
KB Kobe Bryant SP 75.00 150.00
KG Kevin Garnett SP 40.00 80.00
KM Kenyon Martin 6.00 15.00
MA Corey Maggette 4.00 10.00
MB Mike Bibby 6.00 15.00
MC Mateen Cleaves 4.00 10.00
MF Michael Finley 8.00 20.00
MK Mike Miller 6.00 15.00
MM Mark Madsen 4.00 10.00
MN Mamadou N'Diaye 4.00 10.00
MP Mike Penberthy 4.00 10.00
MP Morris Peterson 4.00 10.00
QR Quentin Richardson 6.00 15.00
RH Richard Hamilton 6.00 15.00
RM Reggie Miller 50.00 120.00
SC Speedy Claxton 4.00 10.00
SF Steve Francis 5.00 12.00
SJ Stephen Jackson 10.00 25.00
SM Shawn Marion 5.00 12.00
SS Stromile Swift 4.00 10.00
TM Tracy McGrady 12.50 30.00
TT Tim Thomas 4.00 10.00

2000-01 SP Authentic Sign of the Times Platinum

Randomly inserted in packs at one in 287, this 28-card set features autographs from NBA stars and rookies. Card backs are numbered by the players initials. Please note that a few of the players packed out as exchange cards, and must be redeemed no later that 01/18/02. Also be aware that there were only 200 serial-numbered sets produced unless noted below.

*PLATINUM: .6X TO 1.5X BASIC SIGN
KG Kevin Garnett/21 150.00 300.00
MJ Michael Jordan/23 1000.00 2000.00

2000-01 SP Authentic Sign of the Times Double

Randomly inserted into packs at one in 287, this 18-card insert set features dual-player autographs from both NBA veterans and rookies. Please note that a few of the cards packed out as exchange cards, and must be redeemed no later that 01/18/02.

CADH Courtney Alexander / Donnell Harvey 5.00 12.00
DADS Darius Miles / DeShawn Stevenson 6.00 15.00
DAQR Darius Miles / Quentin Richardson 6.00 15.00
FIJC Marcus Fizer / Jamal Crawford 5.00 12.00
JCDS Jamal Crawford / DeShawn Stevenson 5.00 12.00
KBKG Kobe Bryant / Kevin Garnett 125.00 250.00
KBKM Kobe Bryant / Kenyon Martin 80.00 160.00
KBSF Kobe Bryant / Steve Francis 80.00 200.00
KBTM Kobe Bryant / Tracy McGrady 100.00 200.00
KGKM Kevin Garnett / Kenyon Martin 60.00 120.00
KMDA Kenyon Martin / Darius Miles 10.00 25.00
KMDJ Kenyon Martin / DerMarr Johnson 6.00 15.00
KMFI Kenyon Martin / Marcus Fizer 5.00 12.00
KMSJ Kenyon Martin / Stephen Jackson 8.00 20.00
KMSS Kenyon Martin / Stromile Swift 20.00 50.00
MCMP Mateen Cleaves / Morris Peterson 6.00 15.00
MJDR Michael Jordan / Julius Erving 600.00 1000.00
MJKB Michael Jordan / Kobe Bryant 600.00 1000.00

2000-01 SP Authentic Sign of the Times Triple

Randomly inserted into packs, this 6-card insert set features three player autographs from both NBA veterans and rookies. Please note that a few of the cards packed out as exchange cards, and must be redeemed no later that 01/18/02. Also be aware that there were only 25 serial numbered sets produced.

DRMGLB Julius Erving / Magic Johnson / Larry Bird 300.00 600.00
KBKGKM Kobe Bryant / Kevin Garnett / Kenyon Martin 200.00 400.00
KBMJKG Kobe Bryant / Michael Jordan / Kevin Garnett 1000.00 2000.00
KBMJMG Kobe Bryant / Michael Jordan / Magic Johnson 1000.00 2000.00
KMSJMJ Kenyon Martin / Stephen Jackson / Marc Jackson 40.00 100.00
KMSSDA Kenyon Martin / Stromile Swift / Darius Miles 40.00 100.00

2000-01 SP Authentic Special Forces

Randomly inserted into packs at one in 24, this 7-card insert features some of the best shooters in the NBA. Card backs carry an "SF" prefix.

COMPLETE SET (7) 5.00 12.00
SF1 Kobe Bryant 3.00 8.00
SF2 Steve Francis .60 1.50
SF3 Eddie Jones .60 1.50
SF4 Shaquille O'Neal 1.50 4.00
SF5 Stephon Marbury .50 1.25
SF6 Lamar Odom .60 1.50
SF7 Kevin Garnett 1.25 3.00

2000-01 SP Authentic Spectacular

Randomly inserted into packs at one in 24, this 7-card insert features players that have a knack for getting on the nightly highlight reels. Card backs carry an "SP" prefix.

COMPLETE SET (7) 5.00 12.00
SP1 Kobe Bryant 3.00 8.00
SP2 Chris Webber .60 1.50
SP3 Latrell Sprewell .50 1.25
SP4 Vince Carter 1.25 3.00
SP5 Rashard Lewis .60 1.50
SP6 Tim Duncan 1.25 3.00
SP7 Karl Malone .75 2.00

2000-01 SP Authentic Supremacy

Randomly inserted in packs at one in 24, this 7-card set features the "go-to guys" when the game is on the line. Card backs carry a "S" prefix.

COMPLETE SET (7) 6.00 15.00
S1 Shaquille O'Neal 1.50 4.00
S2 Tim Duncan 1.25 3.00
S3 Kevin Garnett 1.25 3.00
S4 Allen Iverson 1.25 3.00
S5 Kobe Bryant 3.00 8.00
S6 Vince Carter 1.25 3.00
S7 Jason Kidd 1.00 2.50

2001-02 SP Authentic

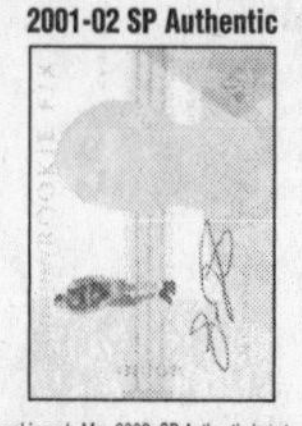

Released in early May 2002, SP Authentic boasts a 165-card set divided up into 90 base cards, 50 rookie cards, numbers 91-140, and 15 Spectaculars, numbers 141-165, which are sequentially numbered to 1000. Veteran cards feature full color player action photos are set against a colored background centered on an all-white embossed card stock. The rookie cards are divided up as follows: card numbers 91-106 are sequentially numbered to 1600 and have gray scale portraits of the player, orange highlights, and a piece of film with a picture from a game. Card numbers 107-115 are sequentially numbered to 550 and share the same design. Card numbers 116-131 are sequentially numbered to 1525 and also feature the same design with green highlights instead of yellow, and have authentic player autographs instead of a film cell. Card numbers 132-140 are sequentially numbered to 700 and are also autographed. SP Authentic was packaged in 24-pack boxes with packs containing five cards and carried a suggested retail price of $4.99.

COMP.SET w/o SP's (90) 20.00 40.00
1 Shareef Abdur-Rahim .30 .75
2 Jason Terry .40 1.00
3 Dion Glover .25 .60
4 Paul Pierce .50 1.25
5 Antoine Walker .30 .75
6 Kenny Anderson .30 .75
7 Baron Davis .40 1.00
8 David Wesley .25 .60
9 Jamal Mashburn .30 .75
10 Jalen Rose .30 .75
11 Fred Hoiberg .25 .60
12 Marcus Fizer .25 .60
13 Andre Miller .30 .75
14 Lamond Murray .25 .60
15 Chris Mihm .25 .60
16 Dirk Nowitzki .60 1.50
17 Steve Nash .60 1.50
18 Michael Finley .40 1.00
19 Nick Van Exel .30 .75
20 Antonio McDyess .30 .75
21 Juwan Howard .30 .75
22 James Posey .25 .60
23 Jerry Stackhouse .30 .75
24 Clifford Robinson .25 .60
25 Ben Wallace .40 1.00
26 Antawn Jamison .40 1.00
27 Larry Hughes .30 .75
28 Danny Fortson .25 .60
29 Steve Francis .40 1.00
30 Cuttino Mobley .30 .75
31 Reggie Miller .40 1.00
32 Al Harrington .30 .75
33 Jermaine O'Neal .40 1.00
34 Darius Miles .25 .60
35 Elton Brand .40 1.00
36 Lamar Odom .40 1.00
37 Corey Maggette .30 .75
38 Kobe Bryant 2.00 5.00
39 Shaquille O'Neal 1.00 2.50
40 Rick Fox .30 .75
41 Lindsey Hunter .25 .60
42 Stromile Swift .25 .60
43 Michael Dickerson .25 .60
44 Jason Williams .30 .75
45 Alonzo Mourning .50 1.25
46 Eddie Jones .30 .75
47 Anthony Carter .25 .60
48 Ray Allen .40 1.00
49 Glenn Robinson .30 .75
50 Sam Cassell .30 .75
51 Kevin Garnett .75 2.00
52 Terrell Brandon .25 .60
53 Wally Szczerbiak .30 .75
54 Joe Smith .30 .75
55 Jason Kidd .60 1.50
56 Kenyon Martin .40 1.00
57 Mark Jackson .30 .75
58 Allan Houston .30 .75
59 Latrell Sprewell .30 .75
60 Marcus Camby .30 .75
61 Tracy McGrady .60 1.50
62 Grant Hill .50 1.25
63 Mike Miller .40 1.00
64 Allen Iverson .75 2.00
65 Dikembe Mutombo .40 1.00
66 Aaron McKie .25 .60
67 Stephon Marbury .30 .75
68 Shawn Marion .40 1.00
69 Anfernee Hardaway .60 1.50
70 Rasheed Wallace .40 1.00
71 Bonzi Wells .25 .60
72 Derek Anderson .25 .60
73 Chris Webber .40 1.00
74 Mike Bibby .40 1.00
75 Peja Stojakovic .40 1.00
76 Tim Duncan .75 2.00
77 David Robinson .60 1.50
78 Antonio Daniels .25 .60
79 Gary Payton .40 1.00
80 Rashard Lewis .40 1.00
81 Desmond Mason .30 .75
82 Vince Carter .60 1.50
83 Morris Peterson .25 .60
84 Antonio Davis .25 .60
85 Karl Malone .50 1.25
86 John Stockton .50 1.25
87 Donyell Marshall .25 .60
88 Richard Hamilton .30 .75
89 Courtney Alexander .25 .60
90 Michael Jordan 6.00 15.00
91 Tierre Brown RC 2.00 5.00
92 Damone Brown RC 2.00 5.00
93 Michael Bradley RC 2.00 5.00
94 Kedrick Brown RC 2.00 5.00
95 Alton Ford RC 2.00 5.00
96 Jason Collins RC 2.00 5.00
97 Antonis Fotsis RC 2.00 5.00
98 Mengke Bateer RC 2.00 5.00
99 Trenton Hassell RC 2.00 5.00
100 Jamison Brewer RC 2.00 5.00
101 Bobby Simmons RC 2.00 5.00
102 Mike James RC 2.00 5.00
103 Oscar Torres RC 2.00 5.00
104 Brandon Armstrong RC 2.00 5.00
105 Will Solomon RC 2.00 5.00
106 Vladimir Radmanovic RC 2.00 5.00
107 Kirk Haston RC 3.00 8.00
108 Gerald Wallace RC 5.00 12.00
109 Andrei Kirilenko RC 8.00 20.00
110 Joseph Forte RC 3.00 8.00
111 Brendan Haywood RC 4.00 10.00
112 Zach Randolph RC 8.00 20.00
113 DeSagana Diop RC 3.00 8.00
114 Shane Battier RC 6.00 15.00
115 Pau Gasol RC 10.00 25.00
116 Alvin Jones AU RC 3.00 8.00
117 Zeljko Rebraca AU RC 3.00 8.00
118 Kenny Satterfield AU RC 3.00 8.00
119 Jarron Collins AU RC 3.00 8.00
120 Ruben Boumtje-Boumtje AU RC 3.00 8.00
121 Loren Woods AU RC 3.00 8.00
122 Earl Watson AU RC 3.00 8.00
123 Jeff Trepagnier AU RC 3.00 8.00
124 Brian Scalabrine AU RC 3.00 8.00
125 Terence Morris AU RC 3.00 8.00
126 Gilbert Arenas AU RC 10.00 25.00
127 Samuel Dalembert AU RC 4.00 10.00
128 Jeryl Sasser AU RC 3.00 8.00
129 Rodney White AU RC 3.00 8.00
130 Eddie Griffin AU RC 3.00 8.00
131 Tyson Chandler AU RC 5.00 12.00
132 Steven Hunter AU RC 4.00 10.00
133 Troy Murphy AU RC 6.00 15.00
134 Richard Jefferson AU RC 8.00 20.00
135 Joe Johnson AU RC 12.50 30.00
136 Eddy Curry AU RC 6.00 15.00
137 Jason Richardson AU RC 8.00 20.00
138 Tony Parker AU RC 20.00 50.00
139 Jamaal Tinsley AU RC 5.00 12.00
140 Kwame Brown AU RC 4.00 10.00
141 Paul Pierce SPEC 2.00 5.00
142 Tim Duncan SPEC 3.00 8.00
143 Stephon Marbury SPEC 1.25 3.00
144 Shareef Abdur-Rahim SPEC 1.25 3.00
145 Ray Allen SPEC 1.50 4.00
146 Bonzi Wells SPEC 1.00 2.50
147 Kenyon Martin SPEC 1.50 4.00
148 Darius Miles SPEC 1.00 2.50
149 Baron Davis SPEC 1.50 4.00
150 Dirk Nowitzki SPEC 2.50 6.00
151 Antoine Walker SPEC 1.25 3.00
152 Mike Miller SPEC 1.50 4.00
153 Shawn Marion SPEC 1.50 4.00
154 Jason Kidd SPEC 2.50 6.00
155 Elton Brand SPEC 1.50 4.00
156 Antawn Jamison SPEC 1.50 4.00
157 Rashard Lewis SPEC 1.50 4.00
158 Steve Francis SPEC 1.50 4.00
159 Tracy McGrady SPEC 2.50 6.00
160 Kobe Bryant SPEC 10.00 25.00
161 Allen Iverson SPEC 4.00 10.00
162 Vince Carter SPEC 3.00 8.00
163 Shaquille O'Neal SPEC 5.00 12.00
164 Kevin Garnett SPEC 4.00 10.00
165 Michael Jordan SPEC 15.00 40.00
PROMO Michael Jordan PROMO 4.00 10.00

2001-02 SP Authentic Dual Signatures

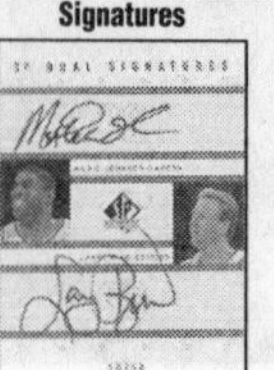

Randomly inserted in packs, this six card set features two autographs from NBA superstars on each card. Small square portrait photos appear of each of the featured players where a signing box is left next to them for authentic player autographs. Each card is squentially numbered to 50.

DR/LB Julius Erving / Larry Bird 150.00 300.00
KB/MG Kobe Bryant / Magic Johnson 200.00 400.00
MG/LB Magic Johnson / Larry Bird 150.00 300.00
MJ/DR Michael Jordan / Julius Erving 500.00 1000.00
MJ/KB Michael Jordan / Kobe Bryant 600.00 1200.00
TC/EC Tyson Chandler / Eddy Curry 40.00 100.00

2001-02 SP Authentic Rookie Authentics

Randomly seeded in packs, this 23-card set is designed horizontally with full color player photos on the left and a large square jersey swatch on the right. Each card is sequentially numbered to 1275.

RAAK Andrei Kirilenko 6.00 15.00
RABA Brandon Armstrong 2.50 6.00
RAEC Eddy Curry 4.00 10.00
RAEG Eddie Griffin 2.50 6.00
RAGW Gerald Wallace 4.00 10.00
RAJA Jarron Collins 2.50 6.00
RAJC Jason Collins 2.50 6.00
RAJF Joseph Forte 2.50 6.00
RAJJ Joe Johnson 6.00 15.00
RAJR Jason Richardson 5.00 12.00
RAJS Jeryl Sasser 2.50 6.00
RAKB Kedrick Brown 2.50 6.00
RAKW Kwame Brown 2.50 6.00
RAMB Michael Bradley 2.50 6.00
RARJ Richard Jefferson 5.00 12.00
RARW Rodney White 2.50 6.00
RASD Samuel Dalembert 3.00 8.00
RASH Steven Hunter 2.50 6.00
RATC Tyson Chandler 4.00 10.00
RATH Trenton Hassell 2.50 6.00
RATM Terence Morris 2.50 6.00
RATP Tony Parker 10.00 25.00
RAVR Vladimir Radmanovic 2.50 6.00

2001-02 SP Authentic Signatures

Randomly seeded in packs, this 24-card set is horizontally designed with full color player action photos on the right side and a white strip on the bottom third of the card where player autographs appear. Each card is sequentially numbered to 390.

UNPRICED TRIPLE AUTO PRINT RUN 10 SETS
AJ Alvin Jones 4.00 10.00
DJ DerMarr Johnson 4.00 10.00
EG Eddie Griffin 4.00 10.00
GA Gilbert Arenas 15.00 40.00
GW Gerald Wallace 6.00 15.00
JC Jason Collins 4.00 10.00
JJ Joe Johnson 10.00 25.00
JR Jason Richardson 8.00 20.00
JS Jeryl Sasser 4.00 10.00
JT Jamaal Tinsley 5.00 12.00
KM Kenyon Martin 8.00 20.00
KS Kenny Satterfield 4.00 10.00
KW Kwame Brown 4.00 10.00
LW Loren Woods 4.00 10.00
MM Mike Miller 5.00 12.00
MP Morris Peterson 4.00 10.00
QR Quentin Richardson 5.00 12.00
RJ Richard Jefferson 8.00 20.00
RW Rodney White 4.00 10.00
SH Steven Hunter 4.00 10.00
TC Tyson Chandler 10.00 25.00
TM Troy Murphy 6.00 15.00
TP Tony Parker 20.00 50.00
VR Vladimir Radmanovic 4.00 10.00

2001-02 SP Authentic Star Signatures

Randomly inserted in packs, this six card set utilizes the same design as the Star Signatures with cards sequentially numbered to 75.

DMS Darius Miles 15.00 30.00
JKS Jason Kidd 25.00 60.00
KBS Kobe Bryant 125.00 250.00
KGS Kevin Garnett 40.00 100.00
MJS Michael Jordan 400.00 800.00
SAS Shareef Abdur-Rahim 15.00 30.00

2001-02 SP Authentic Superstar Authentics

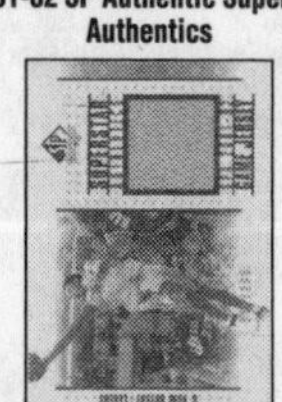

Randomly seeded in packs, this seven card set is designed horizontally with full color player photos on the left and a large square jersey swatch on the right. Each card is sequentially numbered to 200.

SAAI Allen Iverson 10.00 25.00
SACW Chris Webber 8.00 20.00
SAJK Jason Kidd 8.00 20.00
SAKB Kobe Bryant 20.00 50.00
SAKG Kevin Garnett 10.00 25.00
SAMJ Michael Jordan 80.00 160.00
SATM Tracy McGrady 8.00 20.00

2002-03 SP Authentic

Released in April 2003, SP Authentic was issued as a 203-card set divided up as follows: Veteran cards 1-100, SP Specials veterans card numbers 101-142 (sequentially numbered to 2000), Autographed Rook card numbers 143-174 (sequentially numbered to 1500), and Rookie cards numbers 175-203 (sequentially numbered to 1500). Several veteran players also had autographed versions of their base cards inserted into the product. These cards are denoted as "A" versions and are not included in the base set price or card count. Base cards have white borders and a white background with gray hatch mark along the left and right side of the card. SP Authentic was packaged in 24-pack boxes where packs contain five cards and carried a suggested retail price of $4.9

COMP.SET w/o SP's (100) 15.00 40.0
1 Glenn Robinson .30 .7
2 Shareef Abdur-Rahim .30 .7
3 Jason Terry .30 .7
4 Theo Ratliff .25 .6
5 Paul Pierce .50 1.2
5A Paul Pierce AU 12.50 30.0
6 Antoine Walker .30 .7
6A Antoine Walker AU 8.00 20.0
7 Tony Delk .25 .6
8 Vin Baker .30 .7
9 Jalen Rose .30 .7
10 Eddy Curry .30 .7
11 Tyson Chandler .30 .7
11A Tyson Chandler AU 8.00 20.0
12 Marcus Fizer .25 .6
12A Marcus Fizer AU 5.00 12.0
13 Darius Miles .25 .6
14 Zydrunas Ilgauskas .30 .7
15 Dirk Nowitzki .60 1.5
16 Michael Finley .40 1.0
17 Steve Nash .50 1.2
18 Raef LaFrentz .25 .6
19 Juwan Howard .30 .7
20 Rodney White .25 .6
21 Ben Wallace .40 1.0
22 Richard Hamilton .30 .7
23 Chauncey Billups .40 1.0
24 Chucky Atkins .25 .6
25 Jason Richardson .40 1.0
26 Antawn Jamison .40 1.0
27 Gilbert Arenas .40 1.0
28 Steve Francis .40 1.0
29 Cuttino Mobley .30 .7
30 Jermaine O'Neal .40 1.0
30A Jermaine O'Neal AU 8.00 20.0
31 Jamaal Tinsley .25 .6
32 Reggie Miller .40 1.0
33 Ron Artest .40 1.0
34 Elton Brand .40 1.0
35 Andre Miller .30 .7
36 Michael Olowokandi .25 .6
37 Kobe Bryant 2.00 5.0
38 Shaquille O'Neal 1.00 2.5
39 Robert Horry .30 .7
40 Derek Fisher .30 .7
41 Pau Gasol .50 1.2
42 Shane Battier .40 1.0
43 Eddie Jones .30 .7
44 Brian Grant .25 .6
45 Malik Allen .25 .6
46 Gary Payton .40 1.0
47 Sam Cassell .30 .7
48 Kevin Garnett .75 2.0
49 Wally Szczerbiak .25 .6
50 Troy Hudson .25 .6
51 Radoslav Nesterovic .25 .6
52 Jason Kidd .60 1.5
53 Richard Jefferson .40 1.0
54 Kenyon Martin .40 1.0
54A Kenyon Martin AU 8.00 20.0
55 Kerry Kittles .25 .6
56 Baron Davis .40 1.0
57 Jamal Mashburn .30 .7
58 David Wesley .25 .6
59 P.J. Brown .25 .6
60 Jamaal Magloire .25 .6
60A Jamaal Magloire AU 5.00 12.0
61 Allan Houston .30 .7
62 Kurt Thomas .25 .6
63 Latrell Sprewell .30 .7
64 Clarence Weatherspoon .25 .6
65 Tracy McGrady .60 1.5
66 Grant Hill .50 1.2
67 Mike Miller .40 1.0
67A Mike Miller AU 8.00 20.0
68 Allen Iverson .60 1.5
69 Keith Van Horn .30 .7
70 Stephon Marbury .30 .7
71 Shawn Marion .40 1.0
72 Anfernee Hardaway .60 1.5
73 Rasheed Wallace .40 1.0
74 Derek Anderson .25 .6
75 Scottie Pippen .60 1.5
76 Bonzi Wells .25 .6
77 Chris Webber .40 1.0
78 Mike Bibby .40 1.0
78A Mike Bibby AU 6.00 15.0
79 Peja Stojakovic .40 1.0
80 Hedo Turkoglu .40 1.0
81 Vlade Divac .30 .7
82 Tim Duncan .75 2.0
83 David Robinson .60 1.5
84 Tony Parker .50 1.2
85 Steve Smith .30 .7
86 Ray Allen .40 1.0
87 Rashard Lewis .40 1.0
88 Brent Barry .25 .6
89 Elden Campbell .25 .6
90 Vince Carter .60 1.5
91 Morris Peterson .25 .6
92 Antonio Davis .25 .6
93 Alvin Williams .25 .6
94 Karl Malone .50 1.2
95 John Stockton .50 1.2
96 Andrei Kirilenko .50 1.2
97 DeShawn Stevenson .25 .6

A DeShawn Stevenson AU 5.00 12.00
Jerry Stackhouse .30 .75
Michael Jordan 3.00 8.00
0 Kwame Brown .25 .60
1 Kobe Bryant SPEC 5.00 12.00
2 Allen Iverson SPEC 1.50 4.00
3 Pau Gasol SPEC 1.25 3.00
4 Antoine Walker SPEC .75 2.00
5 Jermaine O'Neal SPEC 1.00 2.50
6 Ray Allen SPEC 1.00 2.50
7 Baron Davis SPEC 1.00 2.50
8 Tim Duncan SPEC 2.00 5.00
9 Rashard Lewis SPEC 1.00 2.50
0 Michael Jordan SPEC 8.00 20.00
1 Stephon Marbury SPEC .75 2.00
2 Shareef Abdur-Rahim SPEC .75 2.00
3 Vince Carter SPEC 1.50 4.00
4 Allan Houston SPEC .75 2.00
5 Dirk Nowitzki SPEC 1.50 4.00
6 Grant Hill SPEC 1.25 3.00
7 Mike Bibby SPEC 1.00 2.50
8 Derek Anderson SPEC .60 1.50
9 Shaquille O'Neal SPEC 2.50 6.00
0 Steve Francis SPEC 1.00 2.50
1 Richard Jefferson SPEC 1.00 2.50
2 Ben Wallace SPEC 1.00 2.50
3 Jason Kidd SPEC 1.50 4.00
4 Jalen Rose SPEC .75 2.00
5 Paul Pierce SPEC 1.25 3.00
26 Michael Finley SPEC 1.00 2.50
27 Jamal Mashburn SPEC .75 2.00
28 Elton Brand SPEC 1.00 2.50
9 Rasheed Wallace SPEC 1.00 2.50
0 Gary Payton SPEC 1.00 2.50
1 Tracy McGrady SPEC 1.50 4.00
2 Richard Hamilton SPEC .75 2.00
3 Chris Webber SPEC 1.00 2.50
4 Karl Malone SPEC 1.25 3.00
5 Darius Miles SPEC .60 1.50
6 Shawn Marion SPEC 1.00 2.50
7 Kevin Garnett SPEC 2.00 5.00
8 Eddie Jones SPEC .75 2.00
9 Jason Richardson SPEC 1.00 2.50
0 Glenn Robinson SPEC .75 2.00
1 Jerry Stackhouse SPEC .75 2.00
2 Shane Battier SPEC 1.00 2.50
3 Yao Ming AU RC 20.00 50.00
4 Jay Williams AU RC 4.00 10.00
5 Drew Gooden AU RC 5.00 12.00
6 Nikoloz Tskitishvili AU RC 3.00 8.00
7 DaJuan Wagner AU RC 3.00 8.00
8 Nene Hilario AU RC 4.00 10.00
9 Chris Wilcox AU RC 3.00 8.00
0 Amare Stoudemire AU RC 15.00 40.00
1 Caron Butler AU RC 6.00 15.00
2 Jared Jeffries AU RC 3.00 8.00
3 Melvin Ely AU RC 3.00 8.00
4 Marcus Haislip AU RC 3.00 8.00
5 Fred Jones AU RC 3.00 8.00
6 Bostjan Nachbar AU RC 3.00 8.00
7 Jiri Welsch AU RC 3.00 8.00
8 Juan Dixon AU RC 4.00 10.00
9 Curtis Borchardt AU RC 3.00 8.00
0 Ryan Humphrey AU RC 3.00 8.00
1 Kareem Rush AU RC 3.00 8.00
2 Qyntel Woods AU RC 3.00 8.00
3 Casey Jacobsen AU RC 3.00 8.00
4 Tayshaun Prince AU RC 5.00 12.00
5 Frank Williams AU RC 3.00 8.00
6 John Salmons AU RC 4.00 10.00
7 Chris Jefferies AU RC 3.00 8.00
8 Dan Dickau AU RC 3.00 8.00
9 Carlos Boozer AU RC 6.00 15.00
0 Marko Jaric AU 3.00 8.00
1 Sam Clancy AU RC 3.00 8.00
2 Manu Ginobili AU RC 15.00 40.00
3 Vincent Yarbrough AU RC 3.00 8.00
4 Gordan Giricek AU RC 3.00 8.00
5 Predrag Savovic RC 1.50 4.00
6 Mike Dunleavy RC 2.00 5.00
7 Tamar Slay RC 1.50 4.00
8 Rasual Butler RC 1.50 4.00
9 Reggie Evans RC 1.50 4.00
0 Igor Rakocevic RC 1.50 4.00
1 Juaquin Hawkins RC 1.50 4.00
2 J.R. Bremer RC 1.50 4.00
3 Cezary Trybanski RC 1.50 4.00
4 Junior Harrington RC 1.50 4.00
5 Efthimios Rentzias RC 1.50 4.00
6 Smush Parker RC 1.50 4.00
7 Jamal Sampson RC 1.50 4.00
8 Roger Mason RC 1.50 4.00
9 Robert Archibald RC 1.50 4.00
0 Mehmet Okur RC 1.50 4.00
1 Dan Gadzuric RC 1.50 4.00
2 Pat Burke RC 1.50 4.00
3 Lonny Baxter RC 1.50 4.00
4 Tito Maddox RC 1.50 4.00
5 Jannero Pargo RC 1.50 4.00
6 Ronald Murray RC 1.50 4.00
7 Mike Wilks RC 1.50 4.00
8 Mike Batiste RC 1.50 4.00
9 Chris Owens RC 1.50 4.00
0 Raul Lopez RC 1.50 4.00
1 Antoine Rigaudeau RC 1.50 4.00
2 Ken Johnson RC 1.50 4.00
3 Maceo Baston RC 1.50 4.00
NO Michael Jordan PROMO 2.00 5.00

2002-03 SP Authentic Limited

andomly seeded in packs, this 203-card set parallels e base set enhanced with gold highlights in the ackground and sequential numbering-Limited ersions were also issued for the autograph cards. The arallel breaks down as follows: Cards 1-142 are equentially numbered to 100, Cards 143-203 are equentially numbered to 50.

-100 STARS: 3X TO 8X BASE CARD HI
1-100 AU's: .75X TO 2X BASE CARD HI
101-142 SPEC: 1.25X TO 3X BASE CARD HI
RCs: 1.5X TO 4X BASE CARD HI
50 Amare Stoudemire AU 100.00 200.00
51 Caron Butler AU 40.00 100.00

2002-03 SP Authentic Dual Excellence Signatures

Randomly inserted in packs, this six-card set features two players and two player autographs on each card. Small square portrait photos of the players appear on the top and the bottom of the card, next to which is an authentic player autograph. Each card is sequentially numbered to 25.

JEKA Julius Erving 150.00 300.00
Kareem Abdul-Jabbar
KBJK Kobe Bryant 175.00 350.00
Jason Kidd
KBMB Kobe Bryant 125.00 250.00
Mike Bibby
MJLB Michael Jordan 500.00 1000.00
Larry Bird

2002-03 SP Authentic Marks of Distinction

Randomly inserted in packs, this 10-card set features both current and retired NBA players. Full color player portraits are bordered with gold and set on a card with gray and white borders. Each card is autographed and sequentially numbered to 50.

BRM Bill Russell 150.00 300.00
DRM Julius Erving 75.00 200.00
JKM Jason Kidd 75.00 150.00
JRM Jason Richardson 30.00 80.00
JWM Jay Williams 20.00 50.00
KAM Kareem Abdul-Jabbar 75.00 150.00
KBM Kobe Bryant 200.00 400.00
KGM Kevin Garnett 60.00 150.00
LBM Larry Bird 200.00 350.00
MJM Michael Jordan 500.00 1000.00

2002-03 SP Authentic SP Dual Signatures

Randomly inserted at the rate of one Dual or Single Signature per box, this 12-card set places one player photo on the top next to his signature and the same on the bottom. All cards have gold foil highlights.

ASCJ Amare Stoudemire 15.00 40.00
Casey Jacobsen
CWME Chris Wilcox 6.00 15.00
Melvin Ely
DRKA Julius Erving SP 100.00 250.00
Kareem Abdul-Jabbar
DWCB DaJuan Wagner 10.00 25.00
Carlos Boozer
EGMJ Manu Ginobili 15.00 40.00
Marko Jaric
JJJD Juan Dixon 6.00 15.00
Jared Jeffries
JKKM Jason Kidd 20.00 50.00
Kenyon Martin
JWTC Jay Williams SP 15.00 40.00
Tyson Chandler
KBKA Kobe Bryant SP 200.00 400.00
Kareem Abdul-Jabbar
MJKB Michael Jordan SP 700.00 1200.00
Kobe Bryant
PPAW Paul Pierce 25.00 60.00
Antoine Walker
YMJW Yao Ming 25.00 60.00
Jay Williams

2002-03 SP Authentic SP Signatures

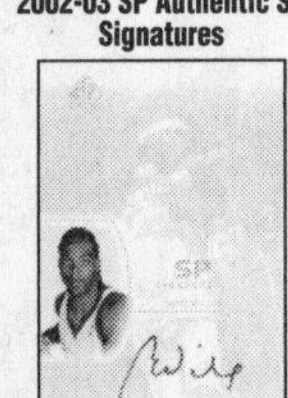

Randomly inserted in packs at the rate of one single or one dual signature per box, this 40-card set places full-color player portraits in the lower left hand corner set against a gray-scale action photo in the background. All cards contain authentic player autographs.

AW Antoine Walker 5.00 12.00
BN Bostjan Nachbar 3.00 8.00
CA Carlos Boozer 6.00 15.00
CB Chauncey Billups 6.00 15.00
CU Curtis Borchardt 3.00 8.00
CW Chris Wilcox 3.00 8.00
DD Dan Dickau 3.00 8.00
DG Dan Gadzuric 3.00 8.00
DR Julius Erving SP 50.00 120.00
DS DeShawn Stevenson 3.00 8.00
DW DaJuan Wagner 3.00 8.00
EG Manu Ginobili 20.00 50.00
ET Etan Thomas 3.00 8.00
FW Frank Williams 3.00 8.00
GW Gerald Wallace 6.00 15.00
JD Juan Dixon 4.00 10.00
JK Jason Kidd 15.00 40.00
JM Jamaal Magloire 3.00 8.00
JO Jermaine O'Neal 4.00 10.00
JR Jason Richardson 4.00 10.00
JS John Salmons 4.00 10.00
JW Jay Williams 6.00 15.00
KA Kareem Abdul-Jabbar 50.00 100.00
KB Kobe Bryant SP 125.00 250.00
KG Kevin Garnett SP 50.00 120.00
KM Kenyon Martin 6.00 15.00
KR Kareem Rush 3.00 8.00
LB Larry Bird 100.00 200.00
MB Mike Bibby 5.00 12.00
MF Marcus Fizer 3.00 8.00
MJ Michael Jordan SP 600.00 1000.00
MM Mike Miller 5.00 12.00
MO Jerome Moiso 4.00 10.00
PP Paul Pierce 12.50 30.00
PS Peja Stojakovic 6.00 15.00
SC Sam Clancy 3.00 8.00
SM Shawn Marion SP 8.00 20.00
TC Tyson Chandler 5.00 12.00
WE Jiri Welsch 3.00 8.00
YM Yao Ming 25.00 50.00

2002-03 SP Authentic Beckett.com Samples

Randomly inserted in Beckett Basketball Collector issue #155, this 100-card set parallels the base SP Authentic set enhanced with a silver foil stamp along the bottom of the card that reads, "UD PROMO."

SAMPLES: .75X TO 2X BASE HI

2003-04 SP Authentic

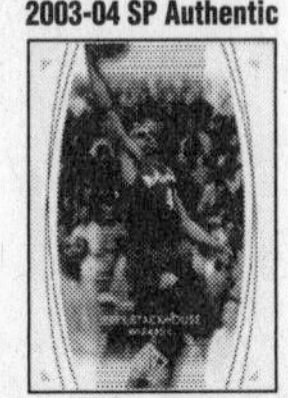

Released in March 2004, this 189-card set is divided up as follows: cards 1-90 are base veteran cards with framed oval full-color player photos; 91-132 and 144 are spectaculars cards sequentially numbered to 3999 with full-color player photos set on an "S" shaped wave background; 133-147 are rookie players sequentially numbered to 999; 148-153 are rookie players sequentially numbered to 500; and 154-189 are autographed rookie cards sequentially numbered to 1250. SP Authentic was packed in 24-pack boxes of five cards each and carried a suggested retail price of $4.99.

COMP.SET w/o SP's (90) 15.00 40.00
1 Shareef Abdur-Rahim .30 .75
2 Theo Ratliff .25 .60
3 Jason Terry .30 .75
4 Raef LaFrentz .25 .60
5 Vin Baker .25 .60
6 Paul Pierce .50 1.25
7 Antonio Davis .25 .60
8 Scottie Pippen .60 1.50
9 Tyson Chandler .30 .75
10 Dajuan Wagner .25 .60
11 Carlos Boozer .40 1.00
12 Zydrunas Ilgauskas .30 .75
13 Dirk Nowitzki .60 1.50
14 Antoine Walker .40 1.00
15 Steve Nash .50 1.25
16 Michael Finley .40 1.00
17 Earl Boykins .25 .60
18 Andre Miller .30 .75
19 Nene .30 .75
20 Chauncey Billups .40 1.00
21 Richard Hamilton .30 .75
22 Ben Wallace .40 1.00
23 Clifford Robinson .25 .60
24 Jason Richardson .40 1.00
25 Nick Van Exel .30 .75
26 Yao Ming .75 2.00
27 Cuttino Mobley .30 .75
28 Steve Francis .40 1.00
29 Jermaine O'Neal .40 1.00
30 Reggie Miller .40 1.00
31 Ron Artest .40 1.00
32 Elton Brand .40 1.00
33 Corey Maggette .30 .75
34 Quentin Richardson .30 .75
35 Kobe Bryant 2.00 5.00
36 Karl Malone .50 1.25
37 Gary Payton .40 1.00
38 Shaquille O'Neal 1.00 2.50
39 Pau Gasol .40 1.00
40 Bonzi Wells .25 .60
41 Mike Miller .40 1.00
42 Lamar Odom .40 1.00
43 Eddie Jones .30 .75
44 Caron Butler .40 1.00
45 Toni Kukoc .40 1.00
46 Desmond Mason .30 .75
47 Michael Redd .40 1.00
48 Latrell Sprewell .30 .75
49 Kevin Garnett .75 2.00
50 Sam Cassell .30 .75
51 Richard Jefferson .40 1.00
52 Kenyon Martin .40 1.00
53 Jason Kidd .60 1.50
54 Jamal Mashburn .30 .75
55 Baron Davis .40 1.00
56 David Wesley .25 .60
57 Allan Houston .30 .75
58 Stephon Marbury .30 .75
59 Keith Van Horn .30 .75
60 Gordan Giricek .25 .60
61 Drew Gooden .30 .75
62 Tracy McGrady .50 1.25
63 Glenn Robinson .30 .75
64 Allen Iverson .60 1.50
65 Eric Snow .25 .60
66 Amare Stoudemire .60 1.50
67 Antonio McDyess .30 .75
68 Shawn Marion .40 1.00
69 Zach Randolph .40 1.00
70 Damon Stoudamire .30 .75
71 Rasheed Wallace .40 1.00
72 Peja Stojakovic .40 1.00
73 Chris Webber .40 1.00
74 Mike Bibby .40 1.00
75 Brad Miller .40 1.00
76 Tony Parker .40 1.00
77 Tim Duncan .60 1.50
78 Manu Ginobili .50 1.25
79 Vladimir Radmanovic .25 .60
80 Ray Allen .40 1.00
81 Rashard Lewis .40 1.00
82 Morris Peterson .25 .60
83 Vince Carter .60 1.50
84 Jalen Rose .30 .75
85 Andrei Kirilenko .40 1.00
86 Matt Harpring .30 .75
87 Carlos Arroyo .30 .75
88 Gilbert Arenas .40 1.00
89 Larry Hughes .30 .75
90 Jerry Stackhouse .30 .75
91 Kobe Bryant SPEC 5.00 12.00
92 Jason Kidd SPEC 1.50 4.00
93 Rasheed Wallace SPEC 1.00 2.50
94 Jalen Rose SPEC .75 2.00
95 Tim Duncan SPEC 1.50 4.00
96 Shareef Abdur-Rahim SPEC .75 2.00
97 Baron Davis SPEC 1.00 2.50
98 Pau Gasol SPEC 1.00 2.50
99 Allen Iverson SPEC 1.50 4.00
100 Yao Ming SPEC 2.00 5.00
101 Gary Payton SPEC 1.00 2.50
102 Ray Allen SPEC 1.00 2.50
103 Tracy McGrady SPEC 1.25 3.00
104 Amare Stoudemire SPEC 1.50 4.00
105 Tony Parker SPEC 1.00 2.50
106 Stephon Marbury SPEC .75 2.00
107 Richard Hamilton SPEC .75 2.00
108 Chris Webber SPEC 1.00 2.50
109 Elton Brand SPEC 1.00 2.50
110 Jerry Stackhouse SPEC .75 2.00
111 Andre Miller SPEC .75 2.00
112 Kevin Garnett SPEC 2.00 5.00
113 Jason Richardson SPEC 1.00 2.50
114 Allan Houston SPEC .75 2.00
115 Dajuan Wagner SPEC .60 1.50
116 Richard Jefferson SPEC 1.00 2.50
117 Shaquille O'Neal SPEC 2.50 6.00
118 Latrell Sprewell SPEC .75 2.00
119 Rashard Lewis SPEC 1.00 2.50
120 Steve Nash SPEC 1.25 3.00
121 Desmond Mason SPEC .75 2.00
122 Mike Bibby SPEC 1.00 2.50
123 Shawn Marion SPEC 1.00 2.50
124 Vince Carter SPEC 1.50 4.00
125 Caron Butler SPEC 1.00 2.50
126 Gilbert Arenas SPEC 1.00 2.50
127 Dirk Nowitzki SPEC 1.50 4.00
128 Paul Pierce SPEC 1.25 3.00
129 Jermaine O'Neal SPEC 1.00 2.50
130 Andrei Kirilenko SPEC 1.00 2.50
131 Michael Jordan SPEC 8.00 20.00
132 Steve Francis SPEC 1.00 2.50
133 T.J. Ford RC 3.00 8.00
134 Kirk Hinrich RC 3.00 8.00
135 Nick Collison RC 2.50 6.00
136 Maurice Carter RC 2.50 6.00
137 Francisco Elson RC 2.50 6.00
138 Udonis Haslem 3.00 8.00
139 Jon Stefansson RC 2.50 6.00
140 Richie Frahm RC 2.50 6.00
141 Ronald Dupree RC 2.50 6.00
142 Josh Moore RC 2.50 6.00
143 Alex Garcia RC 2.50 6.00
144 Zach Randolph SPEC 1.00 2.50
145 Ben Handlogten RC 2.50 6.00
146 Devin Brown RC 2.50 6.00
147 Marquis Daniels RC 2.50 6.00
148 LeBron James AU RC 500.00 850.00
149 Darko Milicic AU RC 6.00 15.00
150 Carmelo Anthony AU RC 75.00 150.00
151 Chris Bosh AU RC 30.00 80.00
152 Dwyane Wade AU RC 125.00 300.00
153 Jarvis Hayes AU RC 6.00 15.00
154 Mickael Pietrus AU RC 4.00 10.00
155 Chris Kaman AU RC 5.00 12.00
156 Dahntay Jones AU RC 4.00 10.00
157 Marcus Banks AU RC 4.00 10.00
158 Luke Ridnour AU RC 5.00 12.00
159 Reece Gaines AU RC 4.00 10.00
160 Troy Bell AU RC 4.00 10.00
161 Mike Sweetney AU RC 4.00 10.00
162 David West AU RC 8.00 20.00
163 Aleksandar Pavlovic AU RC 4.00 10.00
164 Steve Blake AU RC 5.00 12.00
165 Boris Diaw AU RC 5.00 12.00
166 Zoran Planinic AU RC 4.00 10.00
167 Travis Outlaw AU RC 5.00 12.00
168 Brian Cook AU RC 4.00 10.00
169 Jerome Beasley AU RC 4.00 10.00
170 Ndudi Ebi AU RC 4.00 10.00
171 Kendrick Perkins AU RC 6.00 15.00
172 Leandro Barbosa AU RC 5.00 12.00
173 Josh Howard AU RC 4.00 10.00
174 Maciej Lampe AU RC 4.00 10.00
175 Jason Kapono AU RC 4.00 10.00
176 Luke Walton AU RC 4.00 10.00
177 Slavko Vranes AU RC 4.00 10.00
178 Zarko Cabarkapa AU RC 4.00 10.00
179 Zaur Pachulia AU RC 4.00 10.00
180 Maurice Williams AU RC 6.00 15.00
181 Brandon Hunter AU RC 4.00 10.00
182 Keith Bogans AU RC 4.00 10.00
183 Travis Hansen AU RC 4.00 10.00
184 Theron Smith AU RC 4.00 10.00
185 Willie Green AU RC 4.00 10.00
186 James Jones AU RC 4.00 10.00
187 Kyle Korver AU RC 5.00 12.00
188 Udonis Haslem AU RC 5.00 12.00
189 James Lang AU RC 4.00 10.00

2003-04 SP Authentic Limited

Randomly inserted, this 189-card set parallels the base SP Authentic set where cards 1-147 are enhanced with sequential numbering to 100, cards 148-153 are sequentially numbered to 50 and cards 154-189 are sequentially numbered to 100.

*1-90 SINGLES: 2X TO 5X BASE HI
*91-132 SPEC: .75X TO 2X BASE HI
*133-147 RCs: .75X TO 2X BASE HI
*154-189 AU RCs: .6X TO 1.5X BASE HI
35 Kobe Bryant 12.00 30.00
91 Kobe Bryant SPEC 12.00 30.00
148 LeBron James AU 800.00 1300.00
151 Chris Bosh AU 60.00 150.00

2003-04 SP Authentic Limited Extra

Randomly seeded, this 189-card set parallels the base set enhanced with sequential numbering to 25.

*1-90 SINGLES: 6X TO 15X BASE HI
*91-132 SPEC: 2.5X TO 6X BASE HI
*133-147 RCs: 1.25X TO 3X BASE HI
*154-189 AU RCs: 1X TO 2.5X BASE HI
131 Michael Jordan SPEC 75.00 150.00
180 Maurice Williams AU 30.00 80.00

2003-04 SP Authentic Signatures

Inserted in packs with all other autographs at the overall odds of one in 24, this 59-card set utilizes a horizontal design with full-color player action photos on the right and authentic player autographs on the left.

ADA Antonio McDyess 5.00 12.00
AJA Antawn Jamison 5.00 12.00
AMJ Andre Miller 4.00 10.00
CAA Corey Maggette 4.00 10.00
CBA Chauncey Billups 8.00 20.00
CHA Chris Bosh 20.00 50.00
CKA Chris Kaman 5.00 12.00
COA Carlos Boozer 4.00 10.00
CYA Carmelo Anthony SP 30.00 80.00
DAA Darius Miles 4.00 10.00
DEA Desmond Mason 4.00 10.00
DJA Dahntay Jones 4.00 10.00
DMA Darko Milicic 4.00 10.00
DRA David Robinson 30.00 60.00
DWA Dajuan Wagner 4.00 10.00
DYA Dwyane Wade 50.00 120.00
ECA Eddy Curry 4.00 10.00
EGA Manu Ginobili 15.00 40.00
GAA Gilbert Arenas 8.00 20.00
GGA Gordan Giricek 4.00 10.00
GPA Gary Payton 10.00 25.00
GWA Gerald Wallace 4.00 10.00
JAA Jarvis Hayes 4.00 10.00
JEA Julius Erving 30.00 80.00
JHA Josh Howard 4.00 10.00
JKA Jason Kidd 12.00 30.00
JOA Jason Kapono 4.00 10.00
JRA Jason Richardson SP 6.00 15.00
JSA Jerry Stackhouse 5.00 12.00
KBA Kobe Bryant SP 100.00 200.00
KGA Kevin Garnett SP 30.00 80.00
KKA Kyle Korver 5.00 12.00
KOA Keith Bogans 4.00 10.00
LBA Larry Bird 75.00 150.00
LJA LeBron James SP 300.00 550.00
LOA Lamar Odom 6.00 15.00
LWA Luke Walton 4.00 10.00
MAA Marcus Banks 4.00 10.00
MBA Mike Bibby 4.00 10.00
MJA Michael Jordan SP 300.00 650.00
MOA Morris Peterson 4.00 10.00
MPA Mickael Pietrus 4.00 10.00
MSA Mike Sweetney 4.00 10.00
MWA Maurice Williams 6.00 15.00
NEA Ndudi Ebi 4.00 10.00
PEA Patrick Ewing 125.00 250.00
PPA Paul Pierce 10.00 25.00
PSA Peja Stojakovic 6.00 15.00
RHA Richard Hamilton 6.00 15.00
SAA Shareef Abdur-Rahim 4.00 10.00
SBA Shane Battier 4.00 10.00
SMA Shawn Marion 6.00 15.00
SVA Slavko Vranes 4.00 10.00
TBA Troy Bell 4.00 10.00
TMA Tracy McGrady 15.00 40.00
TPA Tony Parker 8.00 20.00
YMA Yao Ming 15.00 40.00
ZOA Alonzo Mourning 20.00 50.00
ZPA Zoran Planinic 4.00 10.00

2003-04 SP Authentic Signatures Dual

Inserted in packs at the rate of one in 288, this 29-card set pairs players where one is on the top and one is on the bottom and their signatures. Small portrait photos appear on the right while the autographs appear on the left.

AKA Shareef Abdur-Rahim 12.00 30.00
Jason Kidd
ASA Gilbert Arenas 8.00 20.00
Jerry Stackhouse
BBA Troy Bell 8.00 20.00
Shane Battier
BMA Larry Bird SP 175.00 325.00
Alonzo Mourning
BRA Brent Barry 8.00 20.00
Luke Ridnour
BSA Mike Bibby 15.00 30.00
Peja Stojakovic
CRA Eddy Curry 8.00 20.00
Jalen Rose
CWA Brian Cook 10.00 25.00
Luke Walton
ESA Julius Erving SP 50.00 100.00
Amare Stoudemire
GBA Kevin Garnett SP 150.00 300.00
Kobe Bryant
HAD Richard Hamilton 25.00 60.00
Chauncey Billups
HPA Brandon Hunter 8.00 20.00
Paul Pierce
JAA LeBron James SP 600.00 1000.00
Carmelo Anthony
JJA Michael Jordan SP 1200.00 1800.00
LeBron James
KJA Jason Kidd SP 20.00 50.00
Richard Jefferson
MDA Shawn Marion 8.00 20.00
Leandro Barbosa
MGA Tracy McGrady SP 15.00 40.00
Reece Gaines
MIA Darko Milicic SP 20.00 40.00
Chauncey Billups
MLA Antonio McDyess 8.00 20.00
Maciej Lampe
MSA Andre Miller 8.00 20.00
Reece Gaines
NAA Nene SP 30.00 60.00
Carmelo Anthony
OPA Travis Outlaw 8.00 20.00
Kendrick Perkins
OWA Lamar Odom 30.00 60.00
Dwyane Wade
PBA Morris Peterson 12.50 30.00
Chris Bosh
PGA Tony Parker 20.00 50.00
Manu Ginobili
PKA Gary Payton SP 125.00 250.00
Kobe Bryant
RPA Jason Richardson 8.00 20.00
Mickael Pietrus
SRA John Stockton 60.00 150.00
David Robinson
WMA DaJuan Wagner 8.00 20.00
Darius Miles

2003-04 SP Authentic Signatures Triple

Randomly inserted, the design of this set is very similar to the Dual Signatures insert with one more player added. There are nine cards in the set and each card is sequentially numbered to 15.

AMN Carmelo Anthony 150.00 300.00
Andre Miller
Nene
HPW Jarvis Hayes 40.00 100.00
Mickael Pietrus
David West
JJB LeBron James 2000.00 3500.00
Michael Jordan
Kobe Bryant
KPB Jason Kidd 100.00 200.00
Tony Parker
Marcus Banks
MBK Darko Milicic 75.00 150.00
Chris Bosh
Chris Kaman
MRP Tracy McGrady 100.00 200.00
Jason Richardson
Paul Pierce
PBJ Gary Payton 250.00 500.00
Kobe Bryant
Magic Johnson
SMB Amare Stoudemire 100.00 200.00
Shawn Marion
Leandro Barbosa

2003-04 SP Authentic SPGU Authentic Fabrics Dual

Randomly inserted in packs, this 12-card set features a horizontal design with two players, one on each of the left and right side of the card with two swatches of jersey in the center. Each card is sequentially numbered to 50.

UNPRICED QUAD PRINT RUN 10 SETS
AMJ Carmelo Anthony 20.00 40.00
Andre Miller
BGJ Troy Bell 6.00 15.00
Pau Gasol
BOJ Kobe Bryant 30.00 80.00
Luke Walton
GMJ Reece Gaines 8.00 20.00
Tracy McGrady
HSJ Jarvis Hayes 6.00 15.00
Jerry Stackhouse
HTJ Travis Hansen 6.00 15.00
Jason Terry
KBJ Chris Kaman 6.00 15.00
Elton Brand
MSJ Darko Milicic 8.00 20.00
Amare Stoudemire
PRJ Mickael Pietrus 6.00 15.00
Jason Richardson
SHJ Mike Sweetney 6.00 15.00
Allan Houston
WBJ Dwyane Wade 25.00 60.00
Caron Butler

2003-04 SP Authentic SPGU Authentic Fabrics Triple

Randomly inserted, this 12-card set places three players and three swatches of game used fabric on a card where each is sequentially numbered to 25.

CCP Tyson Chandler 50.00 120.00
Eddy Curry
Scottie Pippen
DMW Baron Davis 12.50 30.00
Jamal Mashburn
David West
GSE Kevin Garnett 20.00 50.00
Latrell Sprewell
Ndudi Ebi
JJM LeBron James 200.00 400.00
Michael Jordan
Tracy McGrady
JMW LeBron James 150.00 300.00
Darko Milicic
Dwyane Wade
MBJ Mike Miller 12.50 30.00
Shane Battier
Dahntay Jones
MML Antonio McDyess 12.50 30.00
Shawn Marion
Maciej Lampe
MRK Desmond Mason 30.00 80.00
Michael Redd
Toni Kukoc
POB Gary Payton 75.00 150.00
Shaquille O'Neal
Kobe Bryant
VRP Nick Van Exel 12.50 30.00
Jason Richardson
Mickael Pietrus

2003-04 SP Authentic SPGU Rookie Authentic Fabrics

Randomly inserted, this 30-card set uses the same design as SP Game Used Authentic Fabrics with the SP Authentic logo appearing on the card instead. Full-color player photos appear on the right while a square swatch of memorabilia appears on the left. A Patch version was also issued, and these cards are sequentially numbered to 50.

APJ Aleksandar Pavlovic 4.00 10.00
BDJ Boris Diaw 5.00 12.00
CHJ Chris Bosh 8.00 20.00
CKJ Chris Kaman 5.00 12.00
CYJ Carmelo Anthony 12.00 30.00
DEJ David West 5.00 12.00
DJJ Dahntay Jones 4.00 10.00
DMJ Darko Milicic 4.00 10.00
DYJ Dwyane Wade 20.00 50.00
JHJ Jarvis Hayes 4.00 10.00
JKJ Jason Kapono 4.00 10.00
JOJ Josh Howard 4.00 10.00
KOJ Keith Bogans 4.00 10.00
KPJ Zoran Planinic 4.00 10.00
KPJ Kendrick Perkins 6.00 15.00
LBJ Leandro Barbosa 5.00 12.00
LJJ LeBron James 100.00 200.00
LRJ Luke Ridnour 5.00 12.00
LWJ Luke Walton 4.00 10.00
MAJ Marcus Banks 4.00 10.00
MIJ Mike Sweetney 4.00 10.00
MLJ Maciej Lampe 4.00 10.00
MPJ Mickael Pietrus 4.00 10.00
NEJ Ndudi Ebi 4.00 10.00
RGJ Reece Gaines 4.00 10.00
SBJ Steve Blake 5.00 12.00
TBJ Troy Bell 4.00 10.00
THJ Travis Hansen 4.00 10.00
TOJ Travis Outlaw 5.00 12.00
ZCJ Zarko Cabarkapa 4.00 10.00

2003-04 SP Authentic SPGU Rookie Authentic Patches

This 30-card set is a parallel insert to the SPGU Rookie Authentic Fabrics set enhanced with premium patch memorabilia swatches and sequential numbering to 50.

*PATCHES: 1X TO 2.5X BASE FAB HI
LJP LeBron James 150.00 400.00

2003-04 SP Authentic SPGU Rookie Exclusive Autographs Update

Randomly seeded in packs, this seven card set utilizes the design from the SP Game Used Rookie Exclusive Autographs set with the SP Authentic logo prominently displayed. Each card is sequentially numbered to 100. Please note that upon release, card number R49 was not issued.

R43 Mike Sweetney 8.00 20.00
R44 Francisco Elson 8.00 20.00
R45 Marquis Daniels 8.00 20.00
R46 Theron Smith 8.00 20.00
R47 Willie Green 8.00 20.00
R48 Udonis Haslem 10.00 25.00
R50 James Jones 8.00 20.00

2004-05 SP Authentic

Issued in March, SP Authentic consists of a 186-card set with 90 veteran cards, 40 Essentials subset cards (91-130) sequentially numbered to 2999, 10 rookie cards (131-140) sequentially numbered to 999, 39 autographed rookie cards (141-145, 147-180) sequentially numbered to 1499, six different autographed versions of card 146 (all sequentially numbered to 10) and six autographed rookie cards sequentially numbered to 999 (181-186) SP Authentic was packaged in 24-pack boxes where packs contained five cards and carried a SRP of $4.99.

COMP.SET w/o SP's (90)
1 Al Harrington .30 .75
2 Antoine Walker .40 1.00
3 Tony Delk .25 .60
4 Gary Payton .40 1.00
5 Mark Blount .25 .60
6 Paul Pierce .50 1.25
7 Kareem Rush .25 .60
8 Gerald Wallace .40 1.00
9 Jason Kapono .25 .60
10 Eddy Curry .30 .75
11 Kirk Hinrich .40 1.00
12 Tyson Chandler .30 .75
13 Drew Gooden .30 .75
14 LeBron James 2.50 6.00
15 Zydrunas Ilgauskas .30 .75
16 Dirk Nowitzki .60 1.50
17 Jason Terry .30 .75
18 Michael Finley .40 1.00
19 Carmelo Anthony .75 2.00
20 Kenyon Martin .40 1.00
21 Andre Miller .30 .75
22 Ben Wallace .40 1.00
23 Chauncey Billups .40 1.00
24 Rasheed Wallace .40 1.00
25 Derek Fisher .30 .75
26 Jason Richardson .40 1.00
27 Speedy Claxton .25 .60
28 Juwan Howard .30 .75
29 Tracy McGrady .50 1.25
30 Yao Ming .75 2.00
31 Jermaine O'Neal .40 1.00
32 Reggie Miller .40 1.00
33 Fred Jones .25 .60
34 Corey Maggette .30 .75
35 Elton Brand .40 1.00
36 Kerry Kittles .25 .60
37 Caron Butler .40 1.00
38 Kobe Bryant 2.00 5.00
39 Lamar Odom .40 1.00
40 Bonzi Wells .25 .60
41 Jason Williams .30 .75
42 Pau Gasol .40 1.00
43 Dwyane Wade 1.25 3.00
44 Eddie Jones .30 .75
45 Shaquille O'Neal 1.00 2.50
46 Desmond Mason .30 .75
47 Keith Van Horn .30 .75
48 Michael Redd .40 1.00
49 Kevin Garnett .75 2.00
50 Latrell Sprewell .30 .75
51 Sam Cassell .30 .75
52 Vince Carter .60 1.50
53 Jason Kidd .60 1.50

54 Richard Jefferson .40 1.00
55 Baron Davis .40 1.00
56 Jamaal Magloire .25 .60
57 P.J. Brown .25 .60
58 Allan Houston .30 .75
59 Jamal Crawford .30 .75
60 Stephon Marbury .30 .75
61 Hedo Turkoglu .40 1.00
62 Grant Hill .50 1.25
63 Steve Francis .40 1.00
64 Allen Iverson .60 1.50
65 Glenn Robinson .30 .75
66 Kyle Korver .30 .75
67 Amare Stoudemire .50 1.25
68 Shawn Marion .40 1.00
69 Steve Nash .50 1.25
70 Darius Miles .25 .60
71 Shareef Abdur-Rahim .30 .75
72 Zach Randolph .30 .75
73 Chris Webber .40 1.00
74 Mike Bibby .40 1.00
75 Peja Stojakovic .40 1.00
76 Manu Ginobili .50 1.25
77 Tim Duncan .60 1.50
78 Tony Parker .40 1.00
79 Rashard Lewis .40 1.00
80 Ray Allen .40 1.00
81 Ronald Murray .25 .60
82 Donyell Marshall .25 .60
83 Jalen Rose .30 .75
84 Chris Bosh .40 1.00
85 Andrei Kirilenko .30 .75
86 Carlos Boozer .40 1.00
87 Matt Harpring .30 .75
88 Antawn Jamison .40 1.00
89 Gilbert Arenas .40 1.00
90 Larry Hughes .30 .75
91 Bill Russell ESS 2.00 5.00
92 Larry Bird ESS 4.00 10.00
93 Paul Pierce ESS 1.50 4.00
94 Michael Jordan ESS 10.00 25.00
95 LeBron James ESS 8.00 20.00
96 Dirk Nowitzki ESS 2.00 5.00
97 Carmelo Anthony ESS 2.50 6.00
98 Ben Wallace ESS 1.25 3.00
99 Isiah Thomas ESS 1.25 3.00
100 Tracy McGrady ESS 1.50 4.00
101 Yao Ming ESS 2.50 6.00
102 Jermaine O'Neal ESS 1.25 3.00
103 Reggie Miller ESS 1.25 3.00
104 Elton Brand ESS 1.25 3.00
105 Kareem Abdul-Jabbar ESS 2.00 5.00
106 Kobe Bryant ESS 6.00 15.00
107 Magic Johnson ESS 3.00 8.00
108 Wilt Chamberlain ESS 2.50 6.00
109 Pau Gasol ESS 1.25 3.00
110 Dwyane Wade ESS 4.00 10.00
111 Shaquille O'Neal ESS 3.00 8.00
112 Michael Redd ESS 1.25 3.00
113 Oscar Robertson ESS 1.25 3.00
114 Kevin Garnett ESS 2.50 6.00
115 Sam Cassell ESS 1.00 2.50
116 Jason Kidd ESS 2.00 5.00
117 Baron Davis ESS 1.25 3.00
118 Stephon Marbury ESS 1.00 2.50
119 Steve Francis ESS 1.25 3.00
120 Allen Iverson ESS 2.00 5.00
121 Julius Erving ESS 2.50 6.00
122 Amare Stoudemire ESS 1.50 4.00
123 Shawn Marion ESS 1.25 3.00
124 Chris Webber ESS 1.25 3.00
125 Peja Stojakovic ESS 1.25 3.00
126 Tim Duncan ESS 2.00 5.00
127 Ray Allen ESS 1.25 3.00
128 Vince Carter ESS 2.00 5.00
129 Andrei Kirilenko ESS 1.00 2.50
130 John Stockton ESS 2.00 5.00
131 Emeka Okafor RC 3.00 8.00
132 Mario Kasun RC 2.00 5.00
133 Andre Barrett RC 2.00 5.00
134 Ha Seung-Jin RC 2.00 5.00
135 Horace Jenkins RC 2.00 5.00
136 Tony Bobbitt RC 2.00 5.00
137 Luis Flores RC 2.00 5.00
138 John Edwards RC 2.00 5.00
139 Beno Udrih RC 2.00 5.00
140 Erik Daniels RC 2.00 5.00
141 Nenad Krstic AU RC 4.00 10.00
142 Yuta Tabuse AU RC 15.00 30.00
143 Pape Sow AU RC 4.00 10.00
144 Andres Nocioni AU RC 4.00 10.00
145 Bernard Robinson AU RC 4.00 10.00
147 Trevor Ariza AU RC 4.00 10.00
148 Damien Wilkins AU RC 4.00 10.00
149 Justin Reed AU RC 4.00 10.00
150 Chris Duhon AU RC 4.00 10.00
151 Royal Ivey AU RC 4.00 10.00
152 Antonio Burks AU RC 4.00 10.00
153 Andre Emmett AU RC 4.00 10.00
154 Donta Smith AU RC 4.00 10.00
155 Lionel Chalmers AU RC 4.00 10.00
156 P.J. Ramos AU RC 4.00 10.00
157 Jackson Vroman AU RC 4.00 10.00
158 Anderson Varejao AU RC 5.00 12.00
159 David Harrison AU RC 4.00 10.00
160 D.J. Mbenga AU RC 4.00 10.00
161 Sasha Vujacic AU RC 4.00 10.00
162 Kevin Martin AU RC 10.00 25.00
163 Tony Allen AU RC 5.00 12.00
164 Delonte West AU RC 5.00 12.00
165 Romain Sato AU RC 4.00 10.00
166 Viktor Khryapa AU RC 4.00 10.00
167 Pavel Podkolzine AU RC 4.00 10.00
168 Jameer Nelson AU RC 5.00 12.00
169 Dorell Wright AU RC 6.00 15.00
170 J.R. Smith AU RC 6.00 15.00
171 Josh Smith AU RC 8.00 20.00
172 Kirk Snyder AU RC 4.00 10.00
173 Al Jefferson AU RC 10.00 25.00
174 Kris Humphries AU RC 4.00 10.00
175 Sebastian Telfair AU RC 4.00 10.00
176 Robert Swift AU RC 4.00 10.00
177 Andris Biedrins AU RC 5.00 12.00
178 Luke Jackson AU RC 4.00 10.00
179 Andre Iguodala AU RC 10.00 25.00
180 Rafael Araujo AU RC 4.00 10.00
181 Luol Deng AU RC 10.00 25.00
182 Josh Childress AU RC 6.00 15.00
183 Devin Harris AU RC 10.00 25.00
184 Shaun Livingston AU RC 6.00 15.00
185 Ben Gordon AU RC 10.00 25.00
186 Dwight Howard AU RC 80.00 160.00

2004-05 SP Authentic Limited

Randomly inserted in packs, this 185-card set parallels the base set enhanced with sequential numbering to 100. Note that card number 146 was not issued. Also printed was a Limited Extra parallel and those cards are sequentially numbered to 25.

*1-90: 2.5X TO 6X BASE HI
*91-130 ESS: .75X TO 2X BASE HI
*131-140 RC: 1X TO 2.5X BASE HI
*141-180 AU RC: .6X TO 1.5X BASE HI
*181-186 AU RC: .5X TO 1.25X BASE HI
186 Dwight Howard AU 150.00 300.00

2004-05 SP Authentic Limited Extra

Randomly inserted in packs, this 185-card set parallels the base set enhanced with sequential numbering to 25.

*1-90: 6X TO 15X BASE HI
*91-130 ESS: 2X TO 5X BASE HI
*131-140 RC: 1.25X TO 3X BASE HI
*141-180 AU RC: 1X TO 2.5X BASE HI
*181-186 AU RC: .6X TO 1.5X BASE HI
CARD 146 NOT ISSUED
142 Yuta Tabuse AU 75.00 150.00
171 Josh Smith AU 30.00 80.00
173 Al Jefferson AU 40.00 100.00
179 Andre Iguodala AU 40.00 100.00
181 Luol Deng AU 40.00 100.00
185 Ben Gordon AU 40.00 100.00
186 Dwight Howard AU 250.00 450.00

2004-05 SP Authentic Fabrics Dual

Randomly inserted, this 25-card set places two players, top and bottom, along with a swatch of jersey and sequential numbering to 100. Triple player versions sequentially numbered to 25 and Quadruple player versions numbered to ten were also randomly seeded in packs.

UNPRICED QUAD PRINT RUN 10 SER.#'d SETS
AH Trevor Ariza 5.00 12.00
Allan Houston
AM Rafael Araujo 5.00 12.00
Donyell Marshall
BJ Kobe Bryant 50.00 120.00
LeBron James
BO Caron Butler 5.00 12.00
Lamar Odom
BS Andris Biedrins 5.00 12.00
Kirk Snyder
CW Josh Childress 5.00 12.00
Antoine Walker
DB Luol Deng 8.00 20.00
Elton Brand
DP Chris Duhon 12.50 30.00
Scottie Pippen
HB Kris Humphries 5.00 12.00
Carlos Boozer
HF Dwight Howard 10.00 25.00
Steve Francis
HO David Harrison 5.00 12.00
Jermaine O'Neal
HS Devin Harris 8.00 20.00
Jerry Stackhouse
HW Richard Hamilton 10.00 25.00
Rasheed Wallace
IR Andre Iguodala 8.00 20.00
Glenn Robinson
JA Antawn Jamison 5.00 12.00
Gilbert Arenas
JJ LeBron James 100.00 200.00
Michael Jordan
JP Al Jefferson 8.00 20.00
Gary Payton
KB Andrei Kirilenko 5.00 12.00
Carlos Boozer
KJ Nenad Krstic 5.00 12.00
Richard Jefferson
LM Shaun Livingston 5.00 12.00
Corey Maggette
MM Kenyon Martin 5.00 12.00
Andre Miller
MW Kevin Martin 8.00 20.00
Chris Webber
SM J.R. Smith 5.00 12.00
Jamal Mashburn
TM Sebastian Telfair 5.00 12.00
Darius Miles

2004-05 SP Authentic Fabrics Triple

Inserted randomly, this seven card set features three player head shots and three player jerseys along with sequential numbering to 25.

BSA Larry Bird 30.00 80.00
Peja Stojakovic
Ray Allen
GBR Ben Gordon 30.00 80.00
Kobe Bryant
Oscar Robertson
JAJ Michael Jordan 80.00 200.00
Carmelo Anthony
LeBron James
JSC Magic Johnson 40.00 100.00
John Stockton
Bob Cousy
JSG LeBron James 40.00 100.00
Amare Stoudemire
Pau Gasol
NFT Dirk Nowitzki 15.00 40.00
Michael Finley
Jason Terry
OMT Jermaine O'Neal 15.00 40.00
Reggie Miller
Jamaal Tinsley
ROO David Robinson 40.00 100.00
Hakeem Olajuwon
Shaquille O'Neal

2004-05 SP Authentic Fabrics Patches

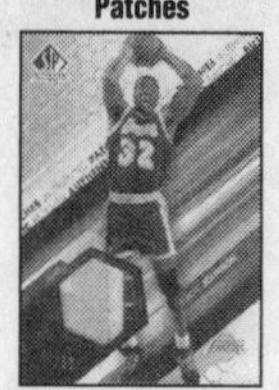

Inserted in packs, this 42-card set parallels the design of the Authentic Fabrics insert set enhanced with a swatch of game-worn patch. Each card is sequentially numbered to 50.

AI Andre Iguodala 10.00 25.00
AJ Al Jefferson 10.00 25.00
AK Andrei Kirilenko 5.00 12.00
AR Rafael Araujo 6.00 15.00
AS Amare Stoudemire 8.00 20.00
BD Baron Davis 6.00 15.00
BG Ben Gordon 8.00 20.00
BI Andris Biedrins 8.00 20.00
CA Carmelo Anthony 12.00 30.00
DE Devin Harris 10.00 25.00
DH Dwight Howard 20.00 50.00
DN Dirk Nowitzki 10.00 25.00
DW Dorell Wright 10.00 25.00
JC Josh Childress 6.00 15.00
JE Julius Erving 15.00 40.00
JK Jason Kidd 10.00 25.00
JN Jameer Nelson 8.00 20.00
JR J.R. Smith 8.00 20.00
JS Josh Smith 10.00 25.00
KB Kobe Bryant 30.00 80.00
KG Kevin Garnett 12.00 30.00
KH Kris Humphries 6.00 15.00
KS Kirk Snyder 6.00 15.00
LB Larry Bird 30.00 80.00
LD Luol Deng 10.00 25.00
LJ LeBron James 40.00 100.00
LU Luke Jackson 6.00 15.00
MA Magic Johnson 30.00 80.00
MJ Michael Jordan 125.00 250.00
PP Paul Pierce 10.00 25.00
PS Peja Stojakovic 6.00 15.00
RA Ray Allen 12.50 30.00
SH Shawn Marion 6.00 15.00
SL Shaun Livingston 6.00 15.00
SM Stephon Marbury 5.00 12.00
SO Shaquille O'Neal 40.00 80.00
ST Sebastian Telfair 6.00 15.00
TD Tim Duncan 10.00 25.00
TM Tracy McGrady 8.00 20.00
TP Tony Parker 6.00 15.00
YM Yao Ming 12.00 30.00
YT Anderson Varejao

2004-05 SP Authentic Fabrics Autographs

Limited to 50 copies, this set places players on a background set to match team colors, a swatch of jersey in the lower right corner and an authentic player autograph.

AI Andre Iguodala 25.00 60.00
AJ Al Jefferson 25.00 60.00
AK Andrei Kirilenko 8.00 20.00
AR Rafael Araujo 8.00 20.00
AS Amare Stoudemire 30.00 80.00
BD Baron Davis 8.00 20.00
BG Ben Gordon 25.00 60.00
BI Andris Biedrins 10.00 25.00
BW Ben Wallace 12.50 30.00
CA Carmelo Anthony 30.00 80.00
DE Devin Harris 12.00 30.00
DH Dwight Howard 60.00 150.00
DW Dorell Wright 12.00 30.00
JC Josh Childress 8.00 20.00
JE Julius Erving 60.00 150.00
JK Jason Kidd 20.00 50.00
JN Jameer Nelson 12.50 30.00
JR J.R. Smith 25.00 60.00
JS Josh Smith 25.00 60.00
JW Jason Williams 40.00 100.00
KB Kobe Bryant 150.00 300.00
KG Kevin Garnett 40.00 100.00
KH Kris Humphries 8.00 20.00
KS Kirk Snyder 8.00 20.00
LB Larry Bird 100.00 200.00
LD Luol Deng 25.00 60.00
LJ LeBron James 150.00 300.00
LU Luke Jackson 8.00 20.00
MA Magic Johnson 75.00 150.00
MJ Michael Jordan 400.00 650.00
PG Pau Gasol 12.50 30.00
PP Paul Pierce 25.00 60.00
PS Peja Stojakovic 12.50 30.00
RA Ray Allen 40.00 100.00
SH Shawn Marion 12.50 30.00
SL Shaun Livingston 8.00 20.00
SM Stephon Marbury 15.00 40.00
ST Sebastian Telfair 8.00 20.00
TM Tracy McGrady 30.00 80.00
YM Yao Ming 30.00 80.00

2004-05 SP Authentic Fabrics Rookies

Inserted in packs at the combined rate of all memorabilia cards at one in 24, this 42-card set parallels the design of the Authentic Fabrics insert set but focuses on rookie players.

AB Antonio Burks SP 3.00 8.00
AE Andre Emmett 2.50 6.00
AI Andre Iguodala 4.00 10.00
AJ Al Jefferson 4.00 10.00
AV Anderson Varejao 3.00 8.00
BG Ben Gordon 3.00 8.00
BI Andris Biedrins 3.00 8.00
BR Bernard Robinson 2.50 6.00
CD Chris Duhon 2.50 6.00
DA David Harrison 2.50 6.00
DE Devin Harris 4.00 10.00
DH Dwight Howard 8.00 20.00
DS Donta Smith 2.50 6.00
DW Dorell Wright 4.00 10.00
HS Ha Seung-Jin 2.50 6.00
JC Josh Childress 2.50 6.00
JN Jameer Nelson 3.00 8.00
JR J.R. Smith 3.00 8.00
JS Josh Smith SP 5.00 12.00
JV Jackson Vroman 2.50 6.00
KH Kris Humphries 2.50 6.00
KM Kevin Martin 3.00 8.00
KS Kirk Snyder 2.50 6.00
LC Lionel Chalmers 2.50 6.00
LD Luol Deng 4.00 10.00
LU Luke Jackson 2.50 6.00
MF Matt Freije 2.50 6.00
NK Nenad Krstic 2.50 6.00
PR Peter John Ramos 2.50 6.00
RA Rafael Araujo 2.50 6.00
RS Robert Swift SP 2.50 6.00
SL Shaun Livingston 2.50 6.00
ST Sebastian Telfair 2.50 6.00
SV Sasha Vujacic 2.50 6.00
TA Tony Allen 3.00 8.00
TR Trevor Ariza 2.50 6.00
WE Delonte West 3.00 8.00

2004-05 SP Authentic Signatures

Inserted at a combined rate for all autographed cards at one in 24, this 97-card set employs a horizontal design where player photos appear on the left and an autograph appears on the right.

AB Antonio Burks 4.00 10.00
AE Andre Emmett 4.00 10.00
AH Al Harrington 4.00 10.00
AI Andre Iguodala 8.00 20.00
AJ Antawn Jamison 5.00 12.00
AK Andrei Kirilenko 4.00 10.00
AL Al Jefferson 10.00 25.00
AM Andre Miller 4.00 10.00
AN Antonio McDyess 5.00 12.00
AR Rafael Araujo 4.00 10.00
AS Amare Stoudemire 12.50 30.00
AV Anderson Varejao 5.00 12.00
AY Carlos Arroyo 15.00 40.00
BD Baron Davis 5.00 12.00
BE Ben Wallace 15.00 40.00
BG Ben Gordon 10.00 25.00
BI Andris Biedrins 5.00 12.00
BK Bernard King 8.00 20.00
BO Carlos Boozer 4.00 10.00
BR Bill Russell 60.00 150.00
BU Beno Udrih 4.00 10.00
BW Bill Walton 10.00 25.00
CA Carmelo Anthony 20.00 50.00
CD Chris Duhon 4.00 10.00
CH Chauncey Billups 6.00 15.00
CL Clyde Drexler 15.00 40.00
CM Corey Maggette 4.00 10.00
CR Jamal Crawford 4.00 10.00
DE Devin Harris 6.00 15.00
DF Derek Fisher 5.00 12.00
DH Dwight Howard 30.00 80.00
DM Desmond Mason 4.00 10.00
DR David Robinson 40.00 80.00
DS Donta Smith 4.00 10.00
DW Dorell Wright 6.00 15.00
GA Gilbert Arenas 6.00 15.00
GP Gary Payton 8.00 20.00
HA David Harrison 4.00 10.00
HO Hakeem Olajuwon 20.00 50.00
JA Jason Richardson 4.00 10.00
JC Josh Childress 4.00 10.00
JE Julius Erving 40.00 100.00
JH Josh Howard 4.00 10.00
JK Jason Kidd 15.00 40.00
JN Jameer Nelson 5.00 12.00
JO John Stockton 50.00 120.00
JR J.R. Smith 8.00 20.00
JS Josh Smith 8.00 20.00
JV Jackson Vroman 4.00 10.00
JW Jason Williams 15.00 40.00
KB Kobe Bryant 100.00 200.00
KE Kevin Martin 5.00 12.00
KG Kevin Garnett 25.00 60.00
KH Kris Humphries 4.00 10.00
KI Kirk Hinrich 10.00 25.00
KS Kirk Snyder 4.00 10.00
LB Larry Bird 75.00 150.00
LC Lionel Chalmers 4.00 10.00
LD Luol Deng 8.00 20.00
LJ LeBron James 150.00 300.00
LO Lamar Odom 5.00 12.00
LU Luke Jackson 4.00 10.00
MA Magic Johnson 75.00 150.00
MB Mike Bibby 4.00 10.00
MD Marquis Daniels 4.00 10.00
MJ Michael Jordan 300.00 600.00
MR Michael Redd 4.00 10.00
NK Nenad Krstic 4.00 10.00
NO Andres Nocioni 4.00 10.00
PA Pavel Podkolzine 4.00 10.00
PE Peter John Ramos 4.00 10.00
PG Pau Gasol 12.50 30.00
PP Paul Pierce 10.00 25.00
PR Pat Riley 12.50 30.00
PS Peja Stojakovic 5.00 12.00
RH Richard Hamilton 6.00 15.00
RI Royal Ivey 4.00 10.00
RJ Richard Jefferson 4.00 10.00
RN Dennis Rodman 50.00 120.00
RO Jalen Rose 6.00 15.00
RS Robert Swift 4.00 10.00
RY Ray Allen 15.00 40.00
SA Shareef Abdur-Rahim 4.00 10.00
SC Sam Cassell EXCH 4.00 10.00
SH Shawn Marion 6.00 15.00
SM Stephon Marbury 8.00 20.00
ST Sebastian Telfair 4.00 10.00
SV Sasha Vujacic 4.00 10.00
TA Tony Allen 5.00 12.00
TM Tracy McGrady 15.00 40.00
TP Tony Parker 8.00 20.00
WE Delonte West 5.00 12.00
WF Walt Frazier 10.00 25.00
WR Willis Reed 10.00 25.00
YM Yao Ming 15.00 40.00
ZR Zach Randolph 4.00 10.00

2004-05 SP Authentic Signatures Dual

Inserted at the rate of one in 288, this 74-card set utilizes some of the design aspects of the Signatures insert but places two players and two autographs on each card front. Triple player versions sequentially numbered to 15 and Quadruple player versions sequentially numbered to ten were also inserted.

UNPRICED TRIPLE PRINT RUN 15 SETS
UNPRICED QUAD PRINT RUN 10 SETS
AB Carlos Arroyo 30.00 80.00
Carlos Boozer
AJ Tony Allen 40.00 80.00
Al Jefferson
AM Carmelo Anthony SP 30.00 60.00
Andre Miller
AR S.Abdur-Rahim 10.00 25.00
Zach Randolph
BB Ben Wallace 25.00 60.00
Chauncey Billups
BJ Larry Bird/25 150.00 300.00
Magic Johnson
BO Kobe Bryant SP 125.00 300.00
Lamar Odom
CA Jamal Crawford 10.00 25.00
Trevor Ariza
CB Sam Cassell 15.00 40.00
Mike Bibby
CL Lionel Chalmers 10.00 25.00
Shaun Livingston
CS Josh Childress 10.00 25.00
Donta Smith
CT Carmelo Anthony/25 50.00 100.00
Tracy McGrady
DH Luol Deng 15.00 40.00
Kirk Hinrich
DJ Dwight Howard 40.00 100.00
J.R. Smith
DM Baron Davis 10.00 25.00
Jamaal Magloire
DS Baron Davis 12.50 30.00
J.R. Smith
EB Andre Emmett 10.00 25.00
Antonio Burks
GC Kevin Garnett SP 40.00 80.00
Sam Cassell
GD Ben Gordon/25 12.50 30.00
Luol Deng
GH Ben Gordon 30.00 80.00
Richard Hamilton
GM Kevin Garnett/25 50.00 100.00
Tracy McGrady
HD Devin Harris 12.50 30.00
Marquis Daniels
HG Dwight Howard/25 75.00 200.00
Ben Gordon
HJ Devin Harris 10.00 25.00
Jerry Stackhouse
HN Dwight Howard/25 40.00 100.00
Jameer Nelson
HR Hakeem Olajuwon/25 100.00 200.00
David Robinson
HS Al Harrington 10.00 25.00
Josh Smith
JA Antawn Jamison 12.50 30.00
Gilbert Arenas
JJ Michael Jordan/25 400.00 800.00
LeBron James
JK Richard Jefferson 10.00 25.00
Nenad Krstic
JW Al Jefferson 25.00 60.00
Delonte West
KD Kevin Garnett/25 100.00 200.00
Dwight Howard
KH Andrei Kirilenko 10.00 25.00
Kris Humphries
KJ Jason Kidd 20.00 50.00
Richard Jefferson
KK Jason Kidd 15.00 40.00
Nenad Krstic
KR Bernard King/25 40.00 80.00
Willis Reed
LC LeBron James/25 200.00 400.00
Carmelo Anthony
LK Lebron James/25 300.00 600.00
Kobe Bryant
LL LeBron James 100.00 250.00
Luke Jackson
MB Kevin Martin 10.00 25.00
Mike Bibby
MC Stephon Marbury 10.00 25.00
Jamal Crawford
MJ Marquis Daniels 10.00 25.00
Josh Howard
ML Corey Maggette 10.00 25.00
Shaun Livingston
MM Tracy McGrady/25 75.00 150.00
Yao Ming
MP Andre Miller 15.00 40.00
Tony Parker
NW Jameer Nelson 12.50 30.00
Delonte West
OR Lamar Odom 10.00 25.00
Kareem Rush
PH Pavel Podkolzine 10.00 25.00
Devin Harris
PM Gary Payton/25 30.00 80.00
Stephon Marbury
PU Tony Parker 20.00 50.00
Beno Udrih
RB Jason Richardson 20.00 40.00
Andris Biedrins
RD Robert Swift 10.00 25.00
Damien Wilkins
RF Jason Richardson 12.50 30.00
Derek Fisher
RL Ray Allen 20.00 50.00
Luke Ridnour
RM Michael Redd SP 10.00 25.00
Desmond Mason
RO Bill Russell/25 100.00 200.00
Hakeem Olajuwon
SA John Stockton/25 100.00 200.00
Andrei Kirilenko
SB Peja Stojakovic SP 15.00 40.00
Mike Bibby
SD Amare Stoudemire/25 25.00 60.00
Luol Deng
SH Kirk Snyder 10.00 25.00
Kris Humphries
SK John Stockton/25 100.00 200.00
Jason Kidd
SM Amare Stoudemire SP 50.00 100.00
Shawn Marion
SW J.R. Smith 12.50 30.00
Dorell Wright
TN Sebastian Telfair/25 12.50 30.00
Jameer Nelson
WB Jason Williams 20.00 50.00
Shane Battier

2005-06 SP Authentic

Released in January 2006, SP Authentic consists of 157 cards where cards 1-90 feature veteran players, cards 91-132 feature rookie autograph cards serially numbered to 1299 and cards 133-157 feature rookies serially numbered to 999. Base cards have white backgrounds with color accents set to match team colors. SP Authentic was packaged in 24-pack boxes of five cards each and upon release, carried a $4.99 SRP.

COMP.SET w/o SP's (90) 15.00 40.00
1 Boris Diaw .30 .75
2 Josh Childress .30 .75
3 Josh Smith .40 1.00
4 Antoine Walker .30 .75
5 Al Jefferson .40 1.00
6 Paul Pierce .50 1.25
7 Kareem Rush .25 .60
8 Emeka Okafor .40 1.00
9 Gerald Wallace .40 1.00
10 Ben Gordon .40 1.00
11 Kirk Hinrich .40 1.00
12 Michael Jordan 3.00 8.00
13 Drew Gooden .30 .75
14 LeBron James 2.00 5.00
15 Luke Jackson .25 .60
16 Dirk Nowitzki .60 1.50
17 Jason Terry .30 .75
18 Josh Howard .40 1.00
19 Nene Hilario .30 .75
20 Carmelo Anthony .75 2.00
21 Kenyon Martin .40 1.00
22 Ben Wallace .40 1.00
23 Chauncey Billups .40 1.00
24 Rasheed Wallace .40 1.00
25 Baron Davis .40 1.00
26 Jason Richardson .40 1.00
27 Mike Dunleavy .30 .75
28 David Wesley .25 .60
29 Tracy McGrady .50 1.25
30 Yao Ming .50 1.25
31 Jamaal Tinsley .25 .60
32 Jermaine O'Neal .40 1.00
33 Fred Jones .25 .60
34 Corey Maggette .30 .75
35 Elton Brand .40 1.00
36 Shaun Livingston .25 .60
37 Caron Butler .40 1.00
38 Kobe Bryant 2.00 5.00
39 Wilt Chamberlain .75 2.00
40 Jason Williams .30 .75
41 Pau Gasol .40 1.00
42 Shane Battier .30 .75
43 Udonis Haslem .30 .75
44 Dwyane Wade 1.00 2.50
45 Shaquille O'Neal .75 2.00
46 Desmond Mason .25 .60
47 T.J. Ford .30 .75
48 Michael Redd .40 1.00
49 Kevin Garnett .75 2.00
50 Wally Szczerbiak .30 .75
51 Ndudi Ebi .25 .60
52 Jason Kidd .60 1.50
53 Richard Jefferson .40 1.00
54 Vince Carter .60 1.50
55 Lee Nailon .25 .60
56 J.R. Smith .40 1.00
57 Jamaal Magloire .25 .60
58 Jamal Crawford .30 .75
59 Stephon Marbury .30 .75
60 Quentin Richardson .30 .75
61 Dwight Howard .75 2.00
62 Grant Hill .50 1.25
63 Steve Francis .40 1.00
64 Allen Iverson .60 1.50
65 Andre Iguodala .40 1.00
66 Chris Webber .40 1.00
67 Amare Stoudemire .40 1.00
68 Shawn Marion .40 1.00
69 Steve Nash .50 1.25
70 Sebastian Telfair .30 .75
71 Darius Miles .25 .60
72 Zach Randolph .30 .75
73 Brad Miller .40 1.00
74 Mike Bibby .40 1.00
75 Peja Stojakovic .40 1.00
76 Manu Ginobili .40 1.00
77 Tim Duncan .60 1.50
78 Tony Parker .40 1.00
79 Luke Ridnour .30
80 Rashard Lewis .40 1.
81 Ray Allen .40 1.
82 Chris Bosh .40 1.
83 Morris Peterson .25
84 Jalen Rose .40 1.
85 Andrei Kirilenko .30
86 Carlos Boozer .40 1.
87 John Stockton .75 2.
88 Antawn Jamison .40 1.
89 Gilbert Arenas .40 1.
90 Brendan Haywood .25
91 Andrew Bogut AU RC 8.00 20.
92 Marvin Williams AU RC 6.00 15.
93 Deron Williams AU RC 25.00 60.
94 Chris Paul AU RC 60.00 150.
95 Raymond Felton AU RC 8.00 20.
96 Martell Webster AU RC 5.00 12.
97 Charlie Villanueva AU RC 6.00 15.
98 Channing Frye AU RC 6.00 15.
99 Brandon Bass AU RC 8.00 20.
100 Travis Diener AU RC 5.00 12.
101 Andray Blatche AU RC 6.00 15.
102 Monta Ellis AU RC 15.00 40.
103 Sean May AU RC 5.00 12.
104 Rashad McCants AU RC 5.00 12.
105 Antoine Wright AU RC 5.00 12.
106 Joey Graham AU RC 5.00 12.
107 Danny Granger AU RC 10.00 25.
108 Gerald Green AU RC 8.00 20.
109 Hakim Warrick AU RC 6.00 15.
110 Julius Hodge AU RC 5.00 12.
111 Sarunas Jasikevicius AU RC 5.00 12.
112 Martynas Andriuskevicius AU RC 5.00 12.
113 Francisco Garcia AU RC 6.00 15.
114 Luther Head AU RC 5.00 12.
115 Nate Robinson AU RC 10.00 25.
116 Jason Maxiell AU RC 5.00 12.
117 Wayne Simien AU RC 5.00 12.
118 David Lee AU RC 8.00 20.
119 Daniel Ewing AU RC 5.00 12.
120 Louis Williams AU RC 10.00 25.
121 Salim Stoudamire AU RC 5.00 12.
122 Jarrett Jack AU RC 5.00 12.
123 Andrew Bynum AU RC 15.00 40.
124 C.J. Miles AU RC 6.00 15.
125 Ersan Ilyasova AU RC 6.00 15.
126 Will Bynum AU RC 5.00 12.
127 Lawrence Roberts AU RC 5.00 12.
128 Dijon Thompson AU RC 5.00 12.
129 Johan Petro AU RC 5.00 12.
130 Bracey Wright AU RC 5.00 12.
131 Ike Diogu AU RC 5.00 12.
132 Ryan Gomes AU RC 5.00 12.
133 Ronnie Price RC 2.00 5.
134 Alan Anderson RC 2.00 5.
135 Esteban Batista RC 2.00 5.
136 Linas Kleiza RC 2.00 5.
137 Eddie Basden RC 2.00 5.
138 Josh Powell RC 2.00 5.
139 Kevin Burleson RC 2.00 5.
140 Von Wafer RC 2.00 5.
141 Rawle Marshall RC 2.00 5.
142 Gerald Fitch RC 2.00 5.
143 Robert Whaley RC 2.00 5.
144 Orien Greene RC 2.00 5.
145 Fabricio Oberto RC 2.00 5.
146 Amir Johnson RC 2.00 5.
147 Shavlik Randolph RC 2.00 5.
148 Arvydas Macijauskas RC 2.00 5.
149 Alex Acker RC 2.00 5.
150 James Singleton RC 2.00 5.
151 Anthony Roberson RC 2.00 5.
152 Earl Barron RC 2.00 5.
153 Dwayne Jones RC 2.00 5.
154 Sean Banks RC 2.00 5.
155 Sharrod Ford RC 2.00 5.
156 Andre Owens RC 2.00 5.
157 Donell Taylor RC 2.00 5.

2005-06 SP Authentic Limited Extra Autographs

Limited from 9 to 25 serially numbered copies, this 2 card set parallels part of the base veteran set enhance with authentic player autographs.

SOME UNPRICED DUE TO SCARCITY
5 Al Jefferson/25 8.00 20.0
9 Gerald Wallace/25 8.00 20.0
14 LeBron James/25 250.00 500.0
30 Yao Ming/25 40.00 100.0
70 Sebastian Telfair/25 8.00 20.0
82 Chris Bosh/25 25.00 60.0
84 Jalen Rose/25 8.00 20.0
88 Antawn Jamison/25 8.00 20.0

2005-06 SP Authentic Limited Extra Patches

Limited to 25 serially numbered copies, this 52-card set parallels part of the base veteran set enhanced wi premium patch swatches in the front lower left hand corner.

*PATCH: 8X TO 20X BASE HI
38 Kobe Bryant 40.00 100.0
39 Wilt Chamberlain 100.00 200.0
47 Oscar Robertson 60.00 120.0
62 Grant Hill 12.50 30.0
66 Chris Webber 12.50 30.0
76 Manu Ginobili 12.50 30.0
87 John Stockton 50.00 100.0

2005-06 SP Authentic Limited Extra Rookie Autographs

Limited to 25 serially numbered copies, this 42-card set parallels most of the base rookie set enhanced wi gold foil highlights and jersey swatches.

91 Andrew Bogut JSY 40.00 100.0
92 Marvin Williams JSY 15.00 40.0
93 Deron Williams JSY 100.00 200.0
94 Chris Paul JSY 250.00 500.0
95 Raymond Felton JSY 40.00 100.0
96 Martell Webster JSY 12.00 30.0
97 Charlie Villanueva JSY 15.00 40.0
98 Channing Frye JSY 15.00 40.0
99 Brandon Bass JSY 15.00 40.0
100 Travis Diener JSY 12.00 30.0
101 Andray Blatche JSY 15.00 40.0
102 Monta Ellis JSY 60.00 120.0
103 Sean May JSY 12.00 30.0
104 Rashad McCants JSY 12.00 30.0
105 Antoine Wright JSY 12.00 30.0
106 Joey Graham JSY 12.00 30.0
107 Danny Granger JSY 25.00 60.0
108 Gerald Green JSY 30.00 80.0
109 Hakim Warrick JSY 15.00 40.0
110 Julius Hodge JSY 15.00 40.0
111 Sarunas Jasikevicius JSY 12.00 30.0
112 Martynas Andriuskevicius JSY 12.00 30.0
113 Francisco Garcia JSY 15.00 40.0
114 Luther Head JSY 12.00 30.0
115 Nate Robinson JSY 15.00 40.0
116 Jason Maxiell JSY 12.00 30.0

7 Wayne Simien JSY 12.00 30.00
8 David Lee JSY 20.00 50.00
9 Daniel Ewing JSY 12.00 30.00
0 Louis Williams JSY 20.00 50.00
1 Salim Stoudamire JSY 12.00 30.00
2 Jarrett Jack JSY 12.00 30.00
3 Andrew Bynum JSY 100.00 200.00
4 C.J. Miles JSY 15.00 40.00
5 Ersan Ilyasova JSY 15.00 40.00
6 Will Bynum 10.00 25.00
7 Lawrence Roberts 10.00 25.00
8 Dijon Thompson 10.00 25.00
9 Johan Petro 10.00 25.00
0 Bracey Wright 10.00 25.00
1 Ike Diogu 10.00 25.00
2 Ryan Gomes 10.00 25.00

2005-06 SP Authentic Limited Rookie Autographs

nited to 100 serially numbered copies, this 42-card t parallels most of the base rookie set enhanced with ld foil highlights and jersey swatches.

Andrew Bogut 15.00 40.00
Marvin Williams 10.00 25.00
Deron Williams 30.00 80.00
Chris Paul 40.00 100.00
Raymond Felton 12.00 30.00
Martell Webster 8.00 20.00
Charlie Villanueva 10.00 25.00
Channing Frye 10.00 25.00
Brandon Bass 10.00 25.00
0 Travis Diener 8.00 20.00
1 Andray Blatche 10.00 25.00
2 Monta Ellis 15.00 40.00
3 Sean May 8.00 20.00
4 Rashad McCants 8.00 20.00
5 Antoine Wright 8.00 20.00
6 Joey Graham 8.00 20.00
7 Danny Granger 15.00 40.00
8 Gerald Green 10.00 25.00
9 Hakim Warrick 10.00 25.00
0 Julius Hodge 8.00 20.00
1 Sarunas Jasikevicius 8.00 20.00
2 Martynas Andriuskevicius 8.00 20.00
3 Francisco Garcia 10.00 25.00
4 Luther Head 8.00 20.00
5 Nate Robinson 10.00 25.00
6 Jason Maxiell 8.00 20.00
7 Wayne Simien 8.00 20.00
8 David Lee 12.00 30.00
9 Daniel Ewing 8.00 20.00
0 Louis Williams 12.00 30.00
1 Salim Stoudamire 8.00 20.00
2 Jarrett Jack 8.00 20.00
3 Andrew Bynum 30.00 80.00
4 C.J. Miles 10.00 25.00
5 Ersan Ilyasova 10.00 25.00
6 Will Bynum 8.00 20.00
7 Lawrence Roberts 8.00 20.00
8 Dijon Thompson 8.00 20.00
9 Johan Petro 8.00 20.00
0 Bracey Wright 8.00 20.00
1 Ike Diogu 8.00 20.00
2 Ryan Gomes 8.00 20.00

2005-06 SP Authentic Limited Rookie Patches

ndomly seeded in packs, this 34-card set parallels st of the base rookie set enhanced with with a atch of patch. Only 100 copies of each card were nted, however, they're contained in the regular kie card print run, so these will be numbered from 299 through 100/1299.

Andrew Bogut 40.00 100.00
Marvin Williams 15.00 40.00
Deron Williams 100.00 200.00
Chris Paul 150.00 400.00
Raymond Felton 40.00 100.00
Martell Webster 12.00 30.00
Charlie Villanueva 15.00 40.00
Channing Frye 15.00 40.00
Brandon Bass 15.00 40.00
Travis Diener 12.00 30.00
Andray Blatche 15.00 40.00
2 Monta Ellis 50.00 120.00
3 Sean May 12.00 30.00
4 Rashad McCants 12.00 30.00
5 Antoine Wright 12.00 30.00
6 Joey Graham 12.00 30.00
7 Danny Granger 25.00 60.00
Gerald Green 15.00 40.00
Hakim Warrick 15.00 40.00
Julius Hodge 12.00 30.00
Sarunas Jasikevicius 12.00 30.00
2 Martynas Andriuskevicius 12.00 30.00
Francisco Garcia 15.00 40.00
Luther Head 12.00 30.00
Nate Robinson 15.00 40.00
Jason Maxiell 12.00 30.00
7 Wayne Simien 12.00 30.00
David Lee 20.00 50.00
Daniel Ewing 12.00 30.00
Louis Williams 20.00 50.00
Salim Stoudamire 12.00 30.00
2 Jarrett Jack 12.00 30.00
3 Andrew Bynum 100.00 200.00
4 C.J. Miles 15.00 40.00

2005-06 SP Authentic Limited Rookies

nited to 100 serially numbered copies, this 25-card parallels part of the base rookie set enhanced with pper highlights and backgrounds.

*LIMITED: 1X TO 2.5X BASE HI
*EXTRA: 1.5X TO 4X BASE HI
EXTRA PRINT RUN 25 SER.#'d SETS

2005-06 SP Authentic Limited Warm Ups

Limited to 100 serially numbered copies, this 53-card set parallels part of the base veteran set enhanced with warm-up swatches in the lower left hand corner.

3 Josh Smith 3.00 8.00
4 Antoine Walker 2.50 6.00
7 Kareem Rush 2.00 5.00
13 Drew Gooden 2.50 6.00
15 Luke Jackson 2.00 5.00
16 Dirk Nowitzki 5.00 12.00
17 Jason Terry 2.50 6.00
18 Josh Howard 3.00 8.00
19 Nene Hilario 2.50 6.00
21 Kenyon Martin 3.00 8.00
24 Rasheed Wallace 3.00 8.00
26 Jason Richardson 3.00 8.00
27 Mike Dunleavy 2.50 6.00
28 David Wesley 2.00 5.00
31 Jamaal Tinsley 2.00 5.00
32 Jermaine O'Neal 3.00 8.00
33 Fred Jones 2.00 5.00
34 Corey Maggette 2.50 6.00
35 Elton Brand 3.00 8.00
36 Shaun Livingston 2.00 5.00
37 Caron Butler 3.00 8.00
38 Kobe Bryant 12.50 30.00
39 Wilt Chamberlain 20.00 50.00
40 Jason Williams 2.50 6.00
43 Udonis Haslem 2.50 6.00
45 Shaquille O'Neal 6.00 15.00
46 Desmond Mason 2.00 5.00
50 Wally Szczerbiak 2.50 6.00
51 Ndudi Ebi 2.00 5.00
53 Richard Jefferson 3.00 8.00
55 Lee Nailon 2.00 5.00
58 Jamal Crawford 2.50 6.00
60 Quentin Richardson 2.50 6.00
62 Grant Hill 4.00 10.00
63 Steve Francis 3.00 8.00
66 Chris Webber 3.00 8.00
67 Amare Stoudemire 3.00 8.00
71 Darius Miles 2.00 5.00
72 Zach Randolph 2.50 6.00
73 Brad Miller 3.00 8.00
74 Mike Bibby 3.00 8.00
75 Peja Stojakovic 3.00 8.00
76 Manu Ginobili 3.00 8.00
77 Tim Duncan 5.00 12.00
78 Tony Parker 3.00 8.00
79 Luke Ridnour 2.50 6.00
80 Rashard Lewis 3.00 8.00
81 Ray Allen 3.00 8.00
83 Morris Peterson 2.00 5.00
86 Carlos Boozer 3.00 8.00
87 John Stockton 6.00 15.00
89 Gilbert Arenas 3.00 8.00
90 Brendan Haywood 2.00 5.00

2005-06 SP Authentic Limited Warm Ups Autographs

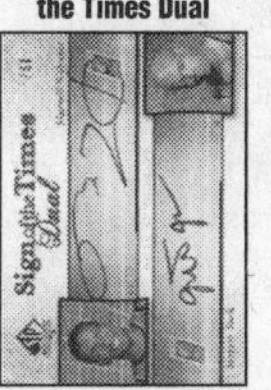

Limited to 100 serially numbered copies, this 53-card set parallels part of the base veteran set enhanced with warm-up swatches in the lower left hand corner and authentic player autographs.

2 Josh Childress 6.00 15.00
5 Al Jefferson 6.00 15.00
6 Paul Pierce 15.00 40.00
9 Gerald Wallace 6.00 15.00
10 Ben Gordon 10.00 25.00
12 Michael Jordan 250.00 450.00
14 LeBron James 175.00 350.00
20 Carmelo Anthony 20.00 50.00
22 Ben Wallace 10.00 25.00
23 Chauncey Billups 6.00 15.00
25 Baron Davis 6.00 15.00
29 Tracy McGrady 20.00 50.00
30 Yao Ming 20.00 50.00
41 Pau Gasol 10.00 25.00
49 Kevin Garnett 25.00 60.00
52 Jason Kidd 15.00 40.00
56 J.R. Smith 6.00 15.00
57 Jamaal Magloire 6.00 15.00
59 Stephon Marbury 12.50 30.00
61 Dwight Howard 25.00 60.00
65 Andre Iguodala 6.00 15.00
69 Steve Nash 40.00 80.00
70 Sebastian Telfair 6.00 15.00
82 Chris Bosh 12.50 30.00
84 Jalen Rose 6.00 15.00
85 Andrei Kirilenko 6.00 15.00
88 Antawn Jamison 6.00 15.00

2005-06 SP Authentic Sensational Sigs

Inserted in packs randomly, this 42-card set features both veterans and rookies where player photos appear on the right, a team-uniform colored border appears on the left and an autograph appears centered along the bottom.

AB Andray Blatche 5.00 12.00
AL Al Jefferson 4.00 10.00
AN Martynas Andriuskevicius 4.00 10.00
AW Antoine Wright 4.00 10.00
BB Brandon Bass 5.00 12.00
BK Bernard King 6.00 15.00
CJ C.J. Miles 5.00 12.00
CM Cuttino Mobley 4.00 10.00
CT Chris Taft 4.00 10.00
CV Charlie Villanueva 5.00 12.00
CW Chris Wilcox 4.00 10.00
DE Daniel Ewing 4.00 10.00
DT Dijon Thompson 4.00 10.00
EI Ersan Ilyasova 5.00 12.00
GG Gerald Green 5.00 12.00
GW Gerald Wallace 5.00 12.00
HW Hakim Warrick 5.00 12.00
ID Ike Diogu 4.00 10.00
JA Jason Maxiell 4.00 10.00
JH Julius Hodge 4.00 10.00
KK Kyle Korver 5.00 12.00
LJ LeBron James SP 125.00 250.00
LR Lawrence Roberts 4.00 10.00
LW Louis Williams 6.00 15.00
MA Martell Webster 4.00 10.00
MD Marquis Daniels 4.00 10.00
ME Monta Ellis 12.00 30.00
MJ Michael Jordan SP 300.00 500.00
MW Maurice Williams 4.00 10.00
RF Raymond Felton 6.00 15.00
RG Ryan Gomes 4.00 10.00
RM Rashad McCants 4.00 10.00
SB Shane Battier 4.00 10.00
SJ Sarunas Jasikevicius 4.00 10.00
SM Sean May 4.00 10.00
TA Tony Allen 4.00 10.00
UH Udonis Haslem 5.00 12.00
WB Will Bynum 4.00 10.00

2005-06 SP Authentic Sign of the Times All-Stars

Found randomly seeded in packs, this 24-card set is horizontally designed with player images on the left, the set name in gold foil on right side at the top and an autograph at the bottom. Each card is serially numbered to 50.

AJ Antawn Jamison 6.00 15.00
AK Andrei Kirilenko 6.00 15.00
AM Antonio McDyess 6.00 15.00
BL Bill Laimbeer 15.00 40.00
BM Brad Miller 6.00 15.00
GA Gilbert Arenas 6.00 15.00
GP Gary Payton 10.00 25.00
GR Glenn Robinson 10.00 25.00
JK Jason Kidd 12.50 30.00
JM Jamaal Magloire 6.00 15.00
KG Kevin Garnett 20.00 50.00
LJ LeBron James 200.00 400.00
PP Paul Pierce 12.50 30.00
SA Shareef Abdur-Rahim 6.00 15.00
SC Sam Cassell 6.00 15.00
SM Stephon Marbury 8.00 20.00
SN Steve Nash 40.00 100.00
ST Jerry Stackhouse 8.00 20.00
TM Tracy McGrady 12.50 30.00
WA Ben Wallace 12.50 30.00
YM Yao Ming 20.00 50.00

2005-06 SP Authentic Sign of the Times Dual

Randomly inserted, this 24-card set places two players, their photos and their autographs on horizontally designed cards that utilize team jersey colors and gold foil highlights. Each card is serially numbered to 50.
UNPRICED TRIPLE PRINT RUN 15 SETS

BF Andrew Bogut / Channing Frye 15.00 40.00
BH Chris Bosh / Dwight Howard 25.00 60.00
BW Andrew Bogut / Marvin Williams 15.00 40.00
CB Chauncey Billups / Ben Wallace 20.00 50.00
FL Channing Frye / David Lee 12.50 30.00
FM Raymond Felton / Sean May 12.50 30.00
GB Francisco Garcia / Mike Bibby 12.50 30.00
GJ Danny Granger / Sarunas Jasikevivius 12.50 30.00
GM Gerald Green / Tracy McGrady 20.00 50.00
GW Pau Gasol / Hakim Warrick 12.50 30.00
HK Julius Hodge / Linas Kleiza 12.50 30.00
HR Luther Head / Nate Robinson 12.50 30.00
JG Al Jefferson / Gerald Green 12.50 30.00
JH LeBron James / Dwight Howard 150.00 300.00
JJ LeBron James / Michael Jordan 600.00 900.00
MO Yao Ming / Hakeem Olajuwon 25.00 60.00
NL Curly Neal / Meadowlark Lemon 40.00 80.00
PW Chris Paul / Deron Williams 100.00 200.00
VG Charlie Villanueva / Joey Graham 12.50 30.00
WB Martell Webster / Andrew Bynum 20.00 50.00
WJ Martell Webster / Jarrett Jack 12.50 30.00
WP Marvin Williams / Chris Paul 40.00 100.00
WS Marvin Williams / Salim Stoudamire 12.50 30.00

2005-06 SP Authentic Sign of the Times Legends

Found randomly seeded in packs, this 23-card set is horizontally designed with player images on the left, the set name in gold foil on right side at the top and an autograph at the bottom. Each card is serially numbered to 25.

BK Bob Knight 30.00 80.00
BR Bill Russell 100.00 200.00
BW Bill Walton 20.00 50.00
DR Dennis Rodman 75.00 150.00
EH Elvin Hayes 20.00 50.00
GG George Gervin 20.00 50.00
HO Hakeem Olajuwon 20.00 50.00
IT Isiah Thomas 20.00 50.00
JE Julius Erving 50.00 100.00
JH John Stockton 100.00 200.00
JW John Wooden 75.00 150.00
KA Kareem Abdul-Jabbar 50.00 120.00
LB Larry Bird 100.00 200.00
LW Lenny Wilkens 20.00 50.00
LY Larry Brown 20.00 50.00
MA Magic Johnson 75.00 150.00
MJ Michael Jordan 500.00 900.00
PR Pat Riley 20.00 50.00
RP Robert Parish 20.00 50.00
SP Scottie Pippen 150.00 300.00
WF Walt Frazier 20.00 50.00
WR Willis Reed 20.00 50.00

2005-06 SP Authentic Sign of the Times Rookies

Found randomly seeded in packs, this 25-card set is horizontally designed with player images on the left, the set name in gold foil on right side at the top and an autograph at the bottom. Each card is serially numbered to 100.

AB Andrew Bogut 10.00 25.00
AN Andrew Bynum 25.00 60.00
CF Channing Frye 8.00 20.00
CP Chris Paul 50.00 120.00
CV Charlie Villanueva 8.00 20.00
DG Danny Granger 12.00 30.00
DT Dijon Thompson 6.00 15.00
DW Deron Williams 15.00 40.00
FG Francisco Garcia 8.00 20.00
GE Gerald Green 8.00 20.00
HW Hakim Warrick 8.00 20.00
ID Ike Diogu 6.00 15.00
JA Jason Maxiell 6.00 15.00
JG Joey Graham 6.00 15.00
JJ Jarrett Jack 6.00 15.00
JP Johan Petro 6.00 15.00
JU Julius Hodge 6.00 15.00
LH Luther Head 6.00 15.00
MW Marvin Williams 8.00 20.00
NR Nate Robinson 8.00 20.00
RF Raymond Felton 10.00 25.00
RM Rashad McCants 6.00 15.00
SE Sean May 6.00 15.00
SS Salim Stoudamire 6.00 15.00
WE Martell Webster 6.00 15.00

2005-06 SP Authentic Sign of the Times Veterans

Found randomly seeded in packs, this 25-card set is horizontally designed with player images on the left, the set name in gold foil on right side at the top and an autograph at the bottom. Each card is serially numbered to 75.

AH Al Harrington 6.00 15.00
AL Al Jefferson 6.00 15.00
CA Carlos Boozer 6.00 15.00
CB Chauncey Billups 10.00 25.00
CH Chris Bosh 10.00 25.00
CM Cuttino Mobley 6.00 15.00
DH Dwight Howard 15.00 40.00
DS Damon Stoudamire 6.00 15.00
GW Gerald Wallace 6.00 15.00
JC Josh Childress 6.00 15.00
JN Jameer Nelson 6.00 15.00
JR Jalen Rose 8.00 20.00
KH Kirk Hinrich 6.00 15.00
KK Kyle Korver 6.00 15.00
LO Lamar Odom 8.00 20.00
MD Marquis Daniels 6.00 15.00
MP Morris Peterson 6.00 15.00
PG Pau Gasol 10.00 25.00
RH Richard Hamilton 10.00 25.00
RJ Richard Jefferson 6.00 15.00
SB Shane Battier 6.00 15.00
SI J.R. Smith 6.00 15.00
TA Trevor Ariza 6.00 15.00
UH Udonis Haslem 6.00 15.00

2006-07 SP Authentic

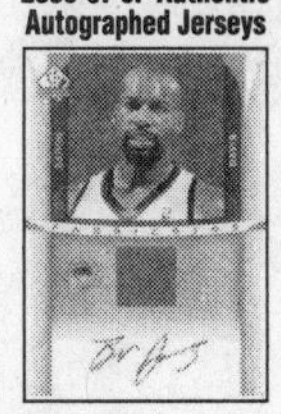

Issued in late April 2007, SP Authentic boasts a clean design with a white background and pictures veteran players on card numbers 1-90, rookies serially numbered to 199 on cards 91-100, autograph rookies serially numbered to 999 on cards 101-122 and autograph rookies serially numbered to 299 on cards 124-132. All rookie autographs are signed directly on-card. SP Authentic is packaged in 24-pack boxes of five cards each and carried an initial suggested retail price of $4.99 per pack.

COMP.SET w/o SP's (100) 15.00 35.00
1 Joe Johnson .40 1.00
2 Marvin Williams .40 1.00
3 Josh Childress .30 .75
4 Paul Pierce .50 1.25
5 Sebastian Telfair .25 .60
6 Gerald Green .30 .75
7 Emeka Okafor .40 1.00
8 Raymond Felton .50 1.25
9 Gerald Wallace .40 1.00
10 Ben Wallace .40 1.00
11 Ben Gordon .40 1.00
12 Kirk Hinrich .40 1.00
13 LeBron James 2.00 5.00
14 Zydrunas Ilgauskas .30 .75
15 Drew Gooden .30 .75
16 Jason Terry .30 .75
17 Dirk Nowitzki .60 1.50
18 Devin Harris .40 1.00
19 Carmelo Anthony .50 1.25
20 Kenyon Martin .40 1.00
21 Andre Miller .30 .75
22 Chauncey Billups .40 1.00
23 Richard Hamilton .30 .75
24 Rasheed Wallace .40 1.00
25 Jason Richardson .40 1.00
26 Baron Davis .40 1.00
27 Troy Murphy .25 .60
28 Tracy McGrady .50 1.25
29 Yao Ming .50 1.25
30 Shane Battier .30 .75
31 Jermaine O'Neal .40 1.00
32 Sarunas Jasikevicius .30 .75
33 Al Harrington .30 .75
34 Elton Brand .40 1.00
35 Sam Cassell .40 1.00
36 Chris Kaman .30 .75
37 Kobe Bryant 2.00 5.00
38 Lamar Odom .40 1.00
39 Vladimir Radmanovic .25 .60
40 Pau Gasol .40 1.00
41 Hakim Warrick .30 .75
42 Damon Stoudamire .30 .75
43 Shaquille O'Neal .75 2.00
44 Dwyane Wade 1.00 2.50
45 Alonzo Mourning .50 1.25
46 Andrew Bogut .40 1.00
47 Charlie Villanueva .40 1.00
48 Michael Redd .40 1.00
49 Kevin Garnett .75 2.00
50 Ricky Davis .30 .75
51 Rashad McCants .25 .60
52 Vince Carter .50 1.25
53 Jason Kidd .60 1.50
54 Richard Jefferson .40 1.00
55 Chris Paul .75 2.00
56 Peja Stojakovic .40 1.00
57 Tyson Chandler .30 .75
58 Stephon Marbury .30 .75
59 Channing Frye .30 .75
60 Nate Robinson .40 1.00
61 Grant Hill .50 1.25
62 Dwight Howard .60 1.50
63 Jameer Nelson .30 .75
64 Allen Iverson .50 1.25
65 Andre Iguodala .40 1.00
66 Kyle Korver .30 .75
67 Steve Nash .50 1.25
68 Amare Stoudemire .40 1.00
69 Shawn Marion .40 1.00
70 Jamaal Magloire .25 .60
71 Martell Webster .30 .75
72 Jarrett Jack .30 .75
73 Mike Bibby .40 1.00
74 Ron Artest .40 1.00
75 Brad Miller .40 1.00
76 Tony Parker .40 1.00
77 Tim Duncan .60 1.50
78 Manu Ginobili .40 1.00
79 Ray Allen .40 1.00
80 Rashard Lewis .40 1.00
81 Luke Ridnour .30 .75
82 Chris Bosh .40 1.00
83 T.J. Ford .30 .75
84 Joey Graham .25 .60
85 Carlos Boozer .40 1.00
86 Andrei Kirilenko .30 .75
87 Deron Williams .60 1.50
88 Gilbert Arenas .40 1.00
89 Antawn Jamison .40 1.00
90 Andray Blatche .25 .60
91 Adam Morrison RC 2.50 6.00
92 Alexander Johnson RC 2.00 5.00
93 J.J. Redick RC 2.50 6.00
94 Vassilis Spanoulis RC 2.00 5.00
95 Jorge Garbajosa RC 2.00 5.00
96 Leon Powe RC 2.00 5.00
97 Chris Quinn RC 2.00 5.00
98 Tarence Kinsey RC 2.00 5.00
99 Yakhouba Diawara RC 2.00 5.00
100 Robert Hite RC 2.00 5.00
101 Thabo Sefolosha AU RC 8.00 20.00
102 Ronnie Brewer AU RC 8.00 20.00
103 Cedric Simmons AU RC 6.00 15.00
104 Dee Brown AU RC 6.00 15.00
105 Craig Smith AU RC 6.00 15.00
106 Rodney Carney AU RC 6.00 15.00
107 Pops Mensah-Bonsu AU RC 6.00 15.00
108 Shawne Williams AU RC 6.00 15.00
109 Quincy Douby AU RC 6.00 15.00
110 Renaldo Balkman AU RC 6.00 15.00
111 Rajon Rondo AU RC 30.00 80.00
112 Marcus Williams AU RC 6.00 15.00
113 Josh Boone AU RC 6.00 15.00
114 Kyle Lowry AU RC 8.00 20.00
115 Shannon Brown AU RC 10.00 25.00
116 Jordan Farmar AU RC 6.00 15.00
117 Sergio Rodriguez AU RC 6.00 15.00
118 Maurice Ager AU RC 6.00 15.00
119 Mardy Collins AU RC 6.00 15.00
120 James White AU RC 6.00 15.00
121 Steve Novak AU RC 6.00 15.00
122 Solomon Jones AU RC 6.00 15.00
123 Andrea Bargnani AU RC 12.00 30.00
124 LaMarcus Aldridge AU RC 25.00 60.00
125 Tyrus Thomas AU RC 10.00 25.00
126 Shelden Williams AU RC 8.00 20.00
127 Brandon Roy AU RC 20.00 50.00
128 Randy Foye AU RC 10.00 25.00
129 Rudy Gay AU RC 15.00 40.00
130 Patrick O'Bryant AU RC 8.00 20.00
131 Saer Sene AU RC 8.00 20.00
132 Hilton Armstrong AU RC 8.00 20.00

2006-07 SP Authentic Gold

*1-90 GOLD: 4X TO 10X BASE HI
*91-100 GOLD RCs: 1X TO 2.5X BASE HI
*101-122 GOLD AU RCs: 1X TO 2.5X BASE HI
*123-132 GOLD AU RCs: .75X TO 2X BASE HI
GOLD PRINT RUN 25 SER.#'d SETS
127 Brandon Roy AU 50.00 120.00

2006-07 SP Authentic Autographed Jerseys

PRINT RUN 50 SER.#'d SETS

AI Andre Iguodala 6.00 15.00
AJ Al Jefferson 8.00 20.00
AM Alonzo Mourning 40.00 80.00
AR Allan Ray 5.00 12.00
BD Baron Davis 10.00 25.00
BG Ben Gordon 10.00 25.00
BI Chauncey Billups 6.00 15.00
CB Chris Bosh 12.50 30.00
CM Corey Maggette 5.00 12.00
CP Chris Paul 25.00 60.00
CS Craig Smith 5.00 12.00
DI Boris Diaw 5.00 12.00
DN David Noel 5.00 12.00
DW Deron Williams 12.50 30.00
JK Jason Kidd 15.00 40.00
JS J.R. Smith 5.00 12.00
KD Keyon Dooling 5.00 12.00
KH Kirk Hinrich 10.00 25.00
KK Kyle Korver 5.00 12.00
LB Leandro Barbosa 6.00 15.00
LH Larry Hughes 6.00 15.00
LR Luke Ridnour 5.00 12.00
MA Maurice Ager 5.00 12.00
MB Mike Bibby 6.00 15.00
MD Marquis Daniels 5.00 12.00
MJ Mike James 5.00 12.00
QD Quincy Douby 5.00 12.00
RB Raja Bell 12.50 30.00
RF Raymond Felton 6.00 15.00
RJ Richard Jefferson 5.00 12.00
RM Rashad McCants 5.00 12.00
SM Sean May 5.00 12.00
TC Tyson Chandler 5.00 12.00
TF T.J. Ford 5.00 12.00
TP Tayshaun Prince 6.00 15.00

2006-07 SP Authentic Autographed Jerseys Dual

PRINT RUN 25 SER.#'d SETS

DBD Mike Bibby / Quincy Douby 12.50 30.00
DBH Chauncey Billups / Richard Hamilton 12.50 30.00
DCP Chris Paul / Tyson Chandler 20.00 40.00
DCR Mardy Collins / Quentin Richardson 8.00 20.00
DDH Chris Duhon / Kirk Hinrich 12.50 30.00
DDO Baron Davis / Patrick O'Bryant 8.00 20.00
DFB Channing Frye / Renaldo Balkman 8.00 20.00
DHB Larry Hughes / Shannon Brown 8.00 20.00
DKI Kyle Korver / Andre Iguodala 12.50 30.00
DKJ Jason Kidd / Richard Jefferson 25.00 60.00
DNM David Noel / Rashad McCants 8.00 20.00

2006-07 SP Authentic Autographed Jerseys Triple

PRINT RUN 15 SER.#'d SETS
UNPRICED QUAD PRINT RUN 5 SETS

CFR Mardy Collins / Channing Frye / Quentin Richardson 20.00 50.00
JEJ Michael Jordan / LeBron James / Julius Erving 750.00 1000.00
MMD Tracy McGrady / Yao Ming / Clyde Drexler 100.00 200.00
NDP Chris Paul / Steve Nash / Baron Davis 100.00 200.00

2006-07 SP Authentic Chirography

APPROXIMATE ODDS 1:30
*GOLD: .6X TO 1.5X BASE HI
PRINT RUN 25 SER.#'d SETS

AI Andre Iguodala 6.00 15.00
BE Charlie Bell 4.00 10.00
BG Ben Gordon 6.00 15.00
BM Brad Miller 4.00 10.00
BO Chris Bosh 12.50 30.00
BR Brandon Roy 12.50 30.00
CB Chauncey Billups 5.00 12.00
CM Corey Maggette 4.00 10.00
DG Danny Granger 4.00 10.00
DM Damir Markota 4.00 10.00
DW Deron Williams 10.00 25.00
FG Francisco Garcia 4.00 10.00
GG Gerald Green 4.00 10.00
HW Hakim Warrick 4.00 10.00
IU Ime Udoka 4.00 10.00
JA Antawn Jamison 5.00 12.00
JG Joey Graham 4.00 10.00
JJ Jarrett Jack 4.00 10.00
JK Jason Kapono 4.00 10.00
JS J.R. Smith 5.00 12.00
KI Jason Kidd 8.00 20.00
KK Kyle Korver 6.00 15.00
LA LaMarcus Aldridge 12.50 30.00
LB Leandro Barbosa 4.00 10.00
LR Luke Ridnour 4.00 10.00
MI Mile Ilic 4.00 10.00
MW Martell Webster 4.00 10.00
NO Steve Novak 5.00 12.00
NR Nate Robinson 6.00 15.00
PA Paul Millsap 8.00 20.00
PM Pops Mensah-Bonsu 4.00 10.00
QR Quentin Richardson 4.00 10.00
RB Raja Bell 8.00 20.00
RH Ryan Hollins 4.00 10.00
RJ Richard Jefferson 4.00 10.00
RM Rashad McCants 4.00 10.00
RR Rajon Rondo 25.00 60.00
RT Ronny Turiaf 5.00 12.00
SA Shareef Abdur-Rahim 4.00 10.00
SB Shannon Brown 5.00 12.00
SJ Solomon Jones 4.00 10.00
SK Steve Kerr 6.00 15.00
SM Sean May 4.00 10.00
SN Steve Nash 25.00 60.00
SR Sergio Rodriguez 4.00 10.00
SW Shawne Williams 4.00 10.00
TC Tyson Chandler 5.00 12.00
TF T.J. Ford 4.00 10.00
TM Tracy McGrady 10.00 25.00
TP Tayshaun Prince 5.00 12.00
TS Thabo Sefolosha 6.00 15.00
TT Tyrus Thomas 8.00 20.00
VC Vince Carter 12.50 30.00
WI Shelden Williams 4.00 10.00

2006-07 SP Authentic Fabrics

APPROXIMATE ODDS 1:24

AB Andrew Bogut 2.50 6.00
AI Andre Iguodala 2.50 6.00
AJ Antawn Jamison 2.50 6.00
AM Alonzo Mourning 3.00 8.00
AW Antoine Walker 2.00 5.00
BL Bill Laimbeer 2.50 6.00
BW Ben Wallace 2.50 6.00
CA Carmelo Anthony 3.00 8.00
CB Chauncey Billups 2.50 6.00
CM Corey Maggette 2.00 5.00
CP Chris Paul 5.00 12.00
DM Darko Milicic 2.00 5.00
DN Dirk Nowitzki 4.00 10.00
DR David Robinson 4.00 10.00
GG George Gervin 2.50 6.00
GP Gary Payton 2.50 6.00
HO Hakeem Olajuwon 3.00 8.00
JC Josh Childress 2.00 5.00
JK Jason Kidd 4.00 10.00
KA Kareem Abdul-Jabbar 8.00 20.00
KB Kobe Bryant 8.00 20.00
KH Kirk Hinrich 2.50 6.00
LH Larry Hughes 2.00 5.00
LJ LeBron James 10.00 25.00
LO Lamar Odom 2.50 6.00
MA Donyell Marshall 2.00 5.00
MJ Michael Jordan 20.00 50.00
MW Marvin Williams 2.50 6.00
NR Nate Robinson 2.50 6.00
PP Paul Pierce 3.00 8.00
RW Rasheed Wallace 2.50 6.00
SE Sean Elliott 2.50 6.00
SO Shaquille O'Neal 5.00 12.00
TC Tyson Chandler 2.00 5.00
TM Tracy McGrady 3.00 8.00
TP Tayshaun Prince 2.50 6.00
VC Vince Carter 3.00 8.00
WF Walt Frazier 2.50 6.00
YM Yao Ming 3.00 8.00
ZI Zydrunas Ilgauskas 2.00 5.00

2006-07 SP Authentic Fabrics Dual

PRINT RUN 100 SER.#'d SETS
BI Kobe Bryant 15.00 40.00
Allen Iverson
DR David Robinson 12.50 30.00
Tim Duncan
GM Kevin Garnett 5.00 12.00
Rashad McCants
GW Pau Gasol 5.00 12.00
Hakim Warrick
JJ Michael Jordan 40.00 80.00
LeBron James
JP Chris Paul 15.00 40.00
LeBron James
KC Vince Carter 10.00 25.00
Jason Kidd
MA Carmelo Anthony 5.00 12.00
Kenyon Martin
MF Stephon Marbury 5.00 12.00
Walt Frazier
MJ Tracy McGrady 20.00 40.00
LeBron James
MM Michael Jordan 40.00 100.00
Magic Johnson
NH Dirk Nowitzki 5.00 12.00
Devin Harris
NS Steve Nash 8.00 20.00
Amare Stoudemire
PB Larry Bird 20.00 40.00
Paul Pierce

2006-07 SP Authentic Fabrics Triple

PRINT RUN 50 SER.#'d SETS
BOF Kobe Bryant 15.00 40.00
Lamar Odom
Jordan Farmar
DMO Shaquille O'Neal 15.00 40.00
Yao Ming
Tim Duncan
GFR Randy Foye 10.00 25.00
Rudy Gay
J.J. Redick
JEB Michael Jordan 50.00 125.00
Larry Bird
Julius Erving
MMN Tracy McGrady 12.50 30.00
Yao Ming
Steve Novak
NMS Steve Nash 15.00 40.00
Amare Stoudemire
Shawn Marion

2006-07 SP Authentic Fabrics Quad

PRINT RUN 25 SER.#'d SETS
ARSA LaMarcus Aldridge 25.00 60.00
Brandon Roy
Hilton Armstrong
Cedric Simmons
IGJB LeBron James 30.00 80.00
Zydrunas Ilgauskas
Drew Gooden
Shannon Brown
KCJW Richard Jefferson 20.00 50.00
Vince Carter
Jason Kidd
Marcus Williams
WHGT Ben Gordon 20.00 50.00
Kirk Hinrich
Ben Wallace
Tyrus Thomas
WWMO Shaquille O'Neal 25.00 60.00
Antoine Walker
Jason Williams
Alonzo Mourning

2006-07 SP Authentic Rookie Autographed Patches

PRINT RUN 30 SER.#'d SETS
UNPRICED LOGO PRINT RUN ONE SET
AB Andrea Bargnani 50.00 100.00
BJ Bobby Jones 12.00 30.00
BR Brandon Roy 125.00 250.00
HA Hilton Armstrong 12.00 30.00
JB Josh Boone 12.00 30.00
JF Jordan Farmar 12.00 30.00
JG Jorge Garbajosa 12.00 30.00
JW James White 12.00 30.00
LA LaMarcus Aldridge 60.00 150.00
MA Maurice Ager 12.00 30.00
MW Marcus Williams 12.00 30.00
PD Paul Davis 12.00 30.00
PO Patrick O'Bryant 12.00 30.00
PT P.J. Tucker 12.00 30.00
RB Ronnie Brewer 15.00 40.00
RC Rodney Carney 12.00 30.00
RF Randy Foye 15.00 40.00
RG Rudy Gay 40.00 80.00
RR Rajon Rondo 150.00 300.00
SB Shannon Brown 20.00 50.00
SN Steve Novak 12.00 30.00
SS Saer Sene 12.00 30.00
SW Shelden Williams 12.00 30.00
WI Shawne Williams 12.00 30.00

2006-07 SP Authentic Rookie Exclusives Jerseys

APPROXIMATE ODDS 1:30
*PATCH: 1.5X TO 4X BASE HI
PATCH PRINT RUN 25 SER.#'d SETS
AB Andrea Bargnani 4.00 10.00
AR Allan Ray 2.50 6.00
BR Brandon Roy 6.00 15.00
CS Cedric Simmons 2.50 6.00
DE Dee Brown 2.50 6.00
DN David Noel 2.50 6.00
JB Josh Boone 2.50 6.00
JF Jordan Farmar 2.50 6.00
JG Jorge Garbajosa 2.50 6.00
JW James White 2.50 6.00
MA Maurice Ager 2.50 6.00
MC Mardy Collins 2.50 6.00
MW Marcus Williams 2.50 6.00
PD Paul Davis 2.50 6.00
PO Patrick O'Bryant 2.50 6.00
QD Quincy Douby 2.50 6.00
RB Renaldo Balkman 2.50 6.00
RC Rodney Carney 2.50 6.00
RF Randy Foye 3.00 8.00
RG Rudy Gay 4.00 10.00
RO Ronnie Brewer 3.00 8.00
RR Rajon Rondo 6.00 15.00
SB Shannon Brown 4.00 10.00
SJ Solomon Jones 2.50 6.00
SM Craig Smith 2.50 6.00
SN Steve Novak 2.50 6.00
SS Saer Sene 2.50 6.00
TS Thabo Sefolosha 3.00 8.00
TT Tyrus Thomas 3.00 8.00
WI Shawne Williams 2.50 6.00

2006-07 SP Authentic Rookie Exclusives Jerseys Autographs

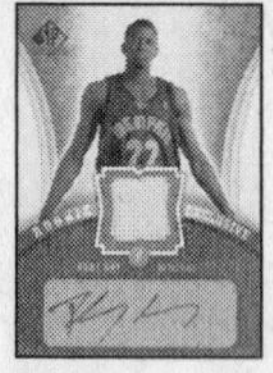

PRINT RUN 60 SER.#'d SETS
AB Andrea Bargnani 20.00 50.00
BR Brandon Roy 30.00 80.00
DE Dee Brown 8.00 20.00
DN David Noel 8.00 20.00
JB Josh Boone 8.00 20.00
JF Jordan Farmar 8.00 20.00
JG Jorge Garbajosa 8.00 20.00
JW James White 8.00 20.00
MA Maurice Ager 8.00 20.00
MC Mardy Collins 8.00 20.00
MW Marcus Williams 8.00 20.00
PD Paul Davis 8.00 20.00
PO Patrick O'Bryant 8.00 20.00
QD Quincy Douby 8.00 20.00
RB Renaldo Balkman 8.00 20.00
RC Rodney Carney 8.00 20.00
RF Randy Foye 10.00 25.00
RG Rudy Gay 15.00 40.00
RO Ronnie Brewer 10.00 25.00
RR Rajon Rondo 50.00 120.00
SB Shannon Brown 12.00 30.00
SJ Solomon Jones 8.00 20.00
SM Craig Smith 8.00 20.00
SN Steve Novak 8.00 20.00
SS Saer Sene 8.00 20.00
TS Thabo Sefolosha 10.00 25.00
TT Tyrus Thomas 10.00 25.00
WI Shawne Williams 8.00 20.00

2006-07 SP Authentic Sign of the Times All-Stars

PRINT RUN 50 SER.#'d SETS
AD Adrian Dantley 6.00 15.00
AJ Antawn Jamison 6.00 15.00
BD Baron Davis 6.00 15.00
BL Bill Laimbeer 15.00 40.00
BM Brad Miller 6.00 15.00
CB Chris Bosh 10.00 25.00
CD Clyde Drexler 15.00 40.00
CH Connie Hawkins 6.00 15.00
DA Brad Daugherty 6.00 15.00
DR David Robinson 40.00 80.00
JK Jason Kidd 20.00 40.00
JM Jamaal Magloire 6.00 15.00
MR Michael Ray Richardson 6.00 15.00
PP Paul Pierce 10.00 25.00
PS Peja Stojakovic 6.00 15.00
RH Richard Hamilton 8.00 20.00
RO Dennis Rodman 30.00 80.00
SE Sean Elliott 12.50 30.00
SN Steve Nash 50.00 100.00
TM Tracy McGrady 15.00 40.00
VC Vince Carter 25.00 60.00
YM Yao Ming 15.00 40.00

2006-07 SP Authentic Sign of the Times Legends

PRINT RUN 25 SER.#'d SETS
BK Bernard King 8.00 20.00
BW Bill Walton 20.00 50.00
CM Cedric Maxwell 8.00 20.00
FR World B. Free 10.00 25.00
HO Hakeem Olajuwon 20.00 40.00
JE Julius Erving 50.00 100.00
LB Larry Bird 60.00 120.00
MA Magic Johnson 60.00 120.00
ME Mark Eaton 8.00 20.00
MJ Michael Jordan 300.00 600.00
NA Nate Archibald 8.00 20.00
PW Paul Westphal 8.00 20.00
SP Sam Perkins 8.00 20.00
TC Tom Chambers 8.00 20.00
WF Walt Frazier 15.00 40.00

2006-07 SP Authentic Sign of the Times Rookies

PRINT RUN 100 SER.#'d SETS
AB Andrea Bargnani 12.00 30.00
AR Allan Ray 4.00 10.00
BR Brandon Roy 15.00 40.00
CS Cedric Simmons 4.00 10.00
HA Hassan Adams 4.00 10.00
HI Hilton Armstrong 4.00 10.00
JB Josh Boone 4.00 10.00
KL Kyle Lowry 5.00 12.00
LA LaMarcus Aldridge 10.00 25.00
MC Mardy Collins 4.00 10.00
PM Pops Mensah-Bonsu 4.00 10.00
PO Patrick O'Bryant 4.00 10.00
QD Quincy Douby 4.00 10.00
RB Renaldo Balkman 4.00 10.00
RC Rodney Carney 4.00 10.00
RF Randy Foye 5.00 12.00
RG Rudy Gay 8.00 20.00
RH Ryan Hollins 4.00 10.00
RR Rajon Rondo 25.00 60.00
SB Shannon Brown 6.00 15.00
SS Saer Sene 4.00 10.00
SW Shelden Williams 4.00 10.00
TS Thabo Sefolosha 5.00 12.00
TT Tyrus Thomas 5.00 12.00
WB Will Blalock 4.00 10.00

2006-07 SP Authentic Sign of the Times Veterans

PRINT RUN 75 SER.#'d SETS
BG Ben Gordon 12.50 30.00
BM Brad Miller 4.00 10.00
BO Chris Bosh 12.50 30.00
CB Chauncey Billups 6.00 15.00
CM Corey Maggette 4.00 10.00
DG Danny Granger 4.00 10.00
DS DeShawn Stevenson 4.00 10.00
DW Deron Williams 10.00 25.00
GG Gerald Green 4.00 10.00
HW Hakim Warrick 4.00 10.00
JJ Jarrett Jack 4.00 10.00
KH Kirk Hinrich 12.50 30.00
LB Leandro Barbosa 4.00 10.00
MJ Mike James 4.00 10.00
MW Marvin Williams 4.00 10.00
RB Raja Bell 8.00 20.00
RJ Richard Jefferson 4.00 10.00
TF T.J. Ford 4.00 10.00

2006-07 SP Authentic Sign of the Times Dual

PRINT RUN 100 SER.#'d SETS
UNLESS LISTED IN CHECKLIST
UNPRICED QUAD PRINT RUN 5 SETS
UNPRICED TRIPLE PRINT RUN 10 SETS
SDAB Andrea Bargnani/15 25.00 60.00
LaMarcus Aldridge
SDAM Maurice Ager/15 12.50 30.00
Pops Mensah-Bonsu
SDAR Allan Ray/15 30.00 80.00
Rajon Rondo
SDBA Hassan Adams 10.00 25.00
Josh Boone
SDBB Dee Brown 10.00 25.00
Ronnie Brewer
SDBF Chris Bosh 20.00 40.00
T.J. Ford
SDCN Rodney Carney 10.00 25.00
Steve Novak
SDFB Channing Frye 10.00 25.00
Renaldo Balkman
SDGB Daniel Gibson 10.00 25.00
Shannon Brown
SDHA James Augustine/15 12.50 30.00
Ryan Hollins
SDHB Richard Hamilton/15 12.50 30.00
Chauncey Billups
SDHG Ben Gordon 20.00 50.00
Kirk Hinrich
SDIJ Andre Iguodala 20.00 40.00
Bobby Jones
SDJJ Michael Jordan 500.00 850.00
LeBron James
SDKD Baron Davis 20.00 40.00
Jason Kidd
SDKN Jason Kidd/15 50.00 120.00
Steve Nash
SDMA Carmelo Anthony/15 60.00 150.00
Tracy McGrady
SDMD Brad Miller/15 10.00 25.00
Paul Davis
SDOH Raymond Felton 15.00 30.00
Emeka Okafor
SDPB Will Blalock/15 10.00 25.00
Tayshaun Prince
SDPJ Paul Pierce 25.00 50.00
Richard Jefferson
SDRJ Rajon Rondo/15 30.00 80.00
Al Jefferson
SDRK Kyle Korver/15 15.00 40.00
Quentin Richardson
SDRR Brandon Roy/15 30.00 80.00
Sergio Rodriguez
SDSA Cedric Simmons 10.00 25.00
Hilton Armstrong
SDSJ DeShawn Stevenson/15 10.00 25.00
Antawn Jamison
SDTS Thabo Sefolosha/15 10.00 25.00
Tyrus Thomas
SDWA Delonte West/15 10.00 25.00
Tony Allen
SDWG Hakim Warrick/15 15.00 40.00
Rudy Gay
SDWJ Shelden Williams/15 10.00 25.00
Solomon Jones
SDWR Ben Wallace/15 60.00 120.00
Dennis Rodman
SDWW Shawne Williams 10.00 25.00
James White

2007-08 SP Authentic

Released in February 2008, SP Authentic features a 153-card set where cards 1-100 picture veteran players, cards 101-106 picture rookie players and are sequentially numbered to 299, cards 107-113 picture rookie players along with authentic autographs and sequential numbering to 999, cards 114-117 picture rookie players along with authentic autographs and sequential numbering to 299, cards 118 and 119 picture rookie players with authentic autographs and sequential numbering to 999 and cards 122-153 picture rookie players with both premium patch swatches and authentic autographs along with sequential numbering to either 599, 399 or 299. SP Authentic is packaged in 24-pack boxes of five cards each and carried an intial suggested retail price of $4.99.

COMP.SET w/o SP's (100) 25.00 50.00
UNPRICED DIE CUT PRINT RUN 10 SETS
1 Brandon Roy .60 1.50
2 Channing Frye .40 1.00
3 Jarrett Jack .40 1.00
4 LaMarcus Aldridge .60 1.50
5 Delonte West .40 1.00
6 Johan Petro .30 .75
7 Nick Collison .30 .75
8 Joe Johnson .50 1.25
9 Josh Smith .50 1.25
10 Marvin Williams .50 1.25
11 Hakim Warrick .40 1.00
12 Pau Gasol .50 1.25
13 Rudy Gay .50 1.25
14 Al Jefferson .50 1.25
15 Paul Pierce .60 1.50
16 Ray Allen .60 1.50
17 Andrew Bogut .50 1.25
18 Charlie Villanueva .50 1.25
19 Maurice Williams .40 1.00
20 Michael Redd .40 1.00
21 Kevin Garnett 1.00 2.50
22 Randy Foye .50 1.25
23 Ricky Davis .40 1.00
24 Emeka Okafor .50 1.25
25 Gerald Wallace .50 1.25
26 Jason Richardson .50 1.25
27 David Lee .40 1.00
28 Eddy Curry .30 .75
29 Stephon Marbury .40 1.00
30 Zach Randolph .40 1.00
31 Brad Miller .40 1.00
32 Kevin Martin .50 1.25
33 Mike Bibby .50 1.25
34 Ron Artest .50 1.25
35 Jamaal Tinsley .30 .75
36 Jermaine O'Neal .50 1.25
37 Mike Dunleavy .40 1.00
38 Andre Iguodala .50 1.25
39 Andre Miller .40 1.00
40 Rodney Carney .30 .75
41 Chris Paul 1.00 2.50
42 David West .50 1.25
43 Tyson Chandler .40 1.00
44 Corey Maggette .40 1.00
45 Cuttino Mobley .40 1.00
46 Elton Brand .50 1.25
47 Darko Milicic .30 .75
48 Dwight Howard .75 2.00
49 Hedo Turkoglu .50 1.25
50 Rashard Lewis .40 1.00
51 Antawn Jamison .50 1.25
52 Caron Butler .50 1.25
53 Gilbert Arenas .50 1.25
54 Jason Kidd .50 1.25
55 Richard Jefferson .50 1.25
56 Vince Carter .60 1.50
57 Baron Davis .50 1.25
58 Monta Ellis .50 1.25
59 Stephen Jackson .40 1.00
60 Jordan Farmar .30 .75
61 Kobe Bryant 2.50 6.00
62 Lamar Odom .50 1.25
63 Alonzo Mourning .60 1.50
64 Dwyane Wade 1.25 3.00
65 Shaquille O'Neal 1.00 2.50
66 Allen Iverson .60 1.50
67 Carmelo Anthony .60 1.50
68 Marcus Camby .30 .75
69 Andrea Bargnani .60 1.50
70 Chris Bosh .50 1.25
71 Jose Calderon .40 1.00
72 T.J. Ford .40 1.00
73 Ben Gordon .50 1.25
74 Ben Wallace .50 1.25
75 Kirk Hinrich .50 1.25
76 Luol Deng .50 1.25
77 Larry Hughes .40 1.00
78 LeBron James 2.50 6.00
79 Zydrunas Ilgauskas .40 1.00
80 Andrei Kirilenko .40 1.00
81 Carlos Boozer .50 1.25
82 Deron Williams .75 2.00
83 Mehmet Okur .30 .75
84 Luther Head .40 1.00
85 Tracy McGrady .50 1.25
86 Yao Ming .60 1.50
87 Chauncey Billups .50 1.25
88 Rasheed Wallace .50 1.25
89 Richard Hamilton .40 1.00
90 Tayshaun Prince .50 1.25
91 Manu Ginobili .50 1.25
92 Tim Duncan .75 2.00
93 Tony Parker .50 1.25
94 Amare Stoudemire .60 1.50
95 Grant Hill .60 1.50
96 Shawn Marion .50 1.25
97 Steve Nash .60 1.50
98 Dirk Nowitzki .60 1.50
99 Jason Terry .40 1.00
100 Josh Howard .40 1.00
101 Greg Oden/299 RC 5.00 12.00
102 Yi Jianlian/299 RC 6.00 15.00
103 Brandan Wright/299 RC 4.00 10.00
104 Thaddeus Young/299 RC 5.00 12.00
105 Nick Young/299 RC 6.00 15.00
106 Jamario Moon/299 RC 4.00 10.00
106B Guillermo Diaz/299 4.00 10.00
107 Marco Belinelli AU/999 RC 5.00 12.00
108 Darryl Watkins AU/999 RC 5.00 12.00
109 Oleksiy Pecherov AU/999 RC 5.00 12.00
110 Juan Carlos Navarro AU/999 RC 5.00 12.00
111 JamesOn Curry AU/999 RC 5.00 12.00
112 Demetris Nichols AU/999 RC 5.00 12.00
113 Herbert Hill AU/999 RC 5.00 12.00
114 Coby Karl/299 RC 4.00 10.00
115 Darius Washington/299 4.00 10.00
116 Glen Davis AU/999 RC 8.00 20.00
117 Cheikh Samb/299 RC 4.00 10.00
118 Ramon Sessions AU/999 RC 8.00 20.00
119 Luis Scola AU/999 RC 8.00 20.00
122 Spencer Hawes JSY AU/599 RC 6.00 15.00
123 Acie Law JSY AU/599 RC 6.00 15.00
124 Julian Wright JSY AU/599 RC 6.00 15.00
125 Al Thornton JSY AU/599 RC 6.00 15.00
126 Rodney Stuckey JSY AU/599 RC10.00 25.00
127 Sean Williams JSY AU/599 RC 6.00 15.00
128 Javaris Crittenton JSY AU/599 RC6.00 15.00
129 Jason Smith JSY AU/599 RC 6.00 15.00
130 Daequan Cook JSY AU/599 RC 6.00 15.00
131 Jared Dudley JSY AU/599 RC 6.00 15.00
132 Wilson Chandler JSY AU/599 RC10.00 25.00
133 Morris Almond JSY AU/599 RC 6.00 15.00
134 Arron Afflalo JSY AU/599 RC 8.00 20.00
135 Alando Tucker JSY AU/599 RC 6.00 15.00
136 Carl Landry JSY AU/599 RC 6.00 15.00
137 Gabe Pruitt JSY AU/599 RC 6.00 15.00
138 Aaron Brooks/299 RC 4.00 10.00
139 Nick Fazekas JSY AU/599 RC 6.00 15.00
140 Jermareo Davidson JSY AU/599 RC6.00 15.00
141 Josh McRoberts JSY AU/599 RC 6.00 15.00
142 Glen Davis/299 RC 6.00 15.00
143 Adam Haluska JSY AU/599 RC 6.00 15.00
147 Dominic McGuire JSY AU/599 RC6.00 15.00
148 Aaron Gray JSY AU/599 RC 6.00 15.00
149 Taurean Green JSY AU/599 RC 6.00 15.00
150 D.J. Strawberry JSY AU/599 RC 6.00 15.00
151 Chris Richard JSY AU/399 RC 6.00 15.00
152 Kevin Durant JSY AU/299 RC 600.00 1100.00
153 Al Horford JSY AU/299 RC 15.00 40.00
154 Mike Conley Jr. JSY AU/299 RC20.00 50.00
155 Jeff Green JSY AU/299 RC 15.00 40.00
156 Corey Brewer JSY AU/299 RC 15.00 40.00
157 Joakim Noah JSY AU/299 RC 30.00 80.00

2007-08 SP Authentic Retail

The Retail version of SP Authentic differs from the Hobby version in that the cards display the "SP" logo rather than the full "SP Authentic" logo, and the rookie cards are not autographed or serially numbered.

COMPLETE SET (153) 30.00 80.00
*VETS: .25X TO .6X HOBBY SP
101 Greg Oden RC 1.50 4.00
102 Yi Jianlian RC 2.00 5.00
103 Brandan Wright RC 1.25 3.00
104 Thaddeus Young RC 1.50 4.00
105 Nick Young RC 2.00 5.00
106 Jamario Moon RC 1.25 3.00
106B Guillermo Diaz 1.25 3.00
107 Marco Belinelli RC 1.25 3.00
108 Darryl Watkins RC 1.25 3.00
109 Oleksiy Pecherov RC 1.25 3.00
110 Juan Carlos Navarro RC 1.25 3.00
111 JamesOn Curry RC 1.25 3.00
112 Demetris Nichols RC 1.25 3.00
113 Herbert Hill RC 1.25 3.00
114 Coby Karl RC 1.25 3.00
115 Darius Washington 1.25 3.00
116 Louis Amundson RC 1.25 3.00
117 Cheikh Samb RC 1.25 3.00
118 Ramon Sessions RC 2.00 5.00
119 Luis Scola RC 2.00 5.00
122 Spencer Hawes RC 1.25 3.00
123 Acie Law RC 1.25 3.00
124 Julian Wright RC 1.25 3.00
125 Al Thornton RC 1.25 3.00
126 Rodney Stuckey RC 2.00 5.00
127 Sean Williams RC 1.25 3.00
128 Javaris Crittenton RC 1.25 3.00
129 Jason Smith RC 1.25 3.00
130 Daequan Cook RC 1.25 3.00
131 Jared Dudley RC 1.25 3.00
132 Wilson Chandler RC 2.00 5.00
133 Morris Almond RC 1.25 3.00
134 Arron Afflalo RC 1.50 4.00
135 Alando Tucker RC 1.25 3.00
136 Carl Landry RC 1.25 3.00
137 Gabe Pruitt RC 1.25 3.00
138 Aaron Brooks RC 1.25 3.00
139 Nick Fazekas RC 1.25 3.00
140 Jermareo Davidson RC 1.25 3.00
141 Josh McRoberts RC 1.25 3.00
142 Glen Davis RC 2.00 5.00
143 Adam Haluska RC 1.25 3.00
147 Dominic McGuire RC 1.25 3.00
148 Aaron Gray RC 1.25 3.00
149 Taurean Green RC 1.25 3.00
150 D.J. Strawberry RC 1.25 3.00
151 Chris Richard RC 1.25 3.00
152 Kevin Durant RC 10.00 25.00
153 Al Horford RC 1.50 4.00
154 Mike Conley Jr. RC 2.00 5.00
155 Jeff Green RC 1.50 4.00
156 Corey Brewer RC 1.50 4.00
157 Joakim Noah RC 3.00 8.00

2007-08 SP Authentic By The Number Career Points

PRINT RUN 75 SER.#'d SETS
*JERSEY NUMB: .5X TO 1.25X BASE HI
JSY NUM PRINT RUN 25 SER.#'d SETS
*RC YEAR SAME VALUE AS POINTS
RC YEAR PRINT RUN 50 SER.#'d SETS
EXCH EXPIRE DATE 1/28/10
BNAD Adrian Dantley 8.00 20.00
BNAH Al Harrington 8.00 20.00
BNAJ Al Jefferson 8.00 20.00
BNAU James Augustine 8.00 20.00
BNBA Leandro Barbosa 8.00 20.00
BNBD Baron Davis 15.00 30.00
BNBJ Bobby Jackson 8.00 20.00
BNBM Brad Miller 8.00 20.00
BNBR Brandon Roy 20.00 40.00
BNBW Bill Walton 15.00 30.00
BNCA Carmelo Anthony 25.00 60.00
BNCH Tom Chambers 8.00 20.00
BNDA Brad Daugherty 8.00 20.00
BNDG Daniel Gibson 15.00 30.00
BNDH Dwight Howard 30.00 80.00
BNDM Donyell Marshall 8.00 20.00
BNDW Deron Williams 15.00 40.00
BNHA Hilton Armstrong 8.00 20.00
BNHO Hakeem Olajuwon 20.00 40.00
BNJA Antawn Jamison 15.00 30.00
BNJJ Jarrett Jack 8.00 20.00
BNJO Michael Jordan/23 400.00 600.00
BNJW Jamaal Wilkes 8.00 20.00
BNKB Kobe Bryant/24 200.00 400.00
BNKH Kirk Hinrich 20.00 40.00
BNLA LaMarcus Aldridge 15.00 40.00
BNLB Larry Bird 75.00 150.00
BNLJ LeBron James 150.00 325.00
BNMJ Magic Johnson 75.00 150.00
BNPE Morris Peterson 8.00 20.00
BNPM Paul Millsap 8.00 20.00
BNPP Paul Pierce 15.00 30.00
BNQR Quentin Richardson 8.00 20.00
BNRB Rick Barry 15.00 30.00
BNRG Rudy Gay 15.00 30.00
BNRR Rajon Rondo 25.00 60.00
BNSA Shareef Abdur-Rahim 8.00 20.00
BNSH Spencer Haywood 8.00 20.00
BNSK Steve Kerr 10.00 25.00
BNSM Sidney Moncrief 8.00 20.00
BNSP Sam Perkins 8.00 20.00
BNTC Terry Cummings 8.00 20.00
BNTP Tayshaun Prince 10.00 25.00
BNTT Tyrus Thomas 10.00 25.00
BNTY Tyson Chandler 8.00 20.00
BNVC Vince Carter 20.00 40.00
BNWF Walt Frazier 15.00 40.00
BNYM Yao Ming 25.00 50.00

2007-08 SP Authentic Chirography

RANDOM INSERTS IN PACKS
EXCH EXPIRE DATE 1/28/10
CRAD Adrian Dantley 6.00 15.00
CRAJ Antawn Jamison 4.00 10.00
CRAM Alonzo Mourning 20.00 40.00
CRBD Baron Davis 6.00 15.00
CRCM Chris Mihm 4.00 10.00
CRDR Dennis Rodman 20.00 50.00
CRDW Deron Williams 10.00 25.00
CRFG Francisco Garcia 4.00 10.00
CRJO Magic Johnson 40.00 100.00
CRLJ LeBron James 125.00 250.00
CRRO Brandon Roy 10.00 25.00
CRRP Robert Parish 6.00 15.00
CRSA Shareef Abdur-Rahim 4.00 10.00
CRSP Sam Perkins 6.00 15.00
CRTP Tayshaun Prince 6.00 15.00
CRWE Jerry West 40.00 100.00
CRWF Walt Frazier 15.00 40.00

2007-08 SP Authentic Chirography Gold

STATED PRINT RUN 5 TO 25 SER.#'d SETS
EXCHANGE EXPIRATION 1/28/10
CRAB Andrea Bargnani 8.00 20.00
CRAD Adrian Dantley 15.00 30.00
CRAM Alonzo Mourning 60.00 120.00
CRBD Baron Davis 15.00 40.00
CRBJ Bobby Jackson 8.00 20.00
CRBW Bill Walton 15.00 40.00
CRCD Chuck Daly 40.00 80.00
CRCH Connie Hawkins 20.00 40.00
CRDA Brad Daugherty 15.00 30.00
CRDG Daniel Gibson 15.00 30.00
CRDN Don Nelson 20.00 40.00
CRDR Dennis Rodman 25.00 60.00
CRDT David Thompson 15.00 30.0
CRDW Deron Williams 20.00 50.0
CRFG Francisco Garcia 8.00 20.0
CRHO Hakeem Olajuwon 25.00 50.
CRJK Jason Kidd 20.00 40.
CRJO Magic Johnson 60.00 120.
CRJW Jamaal Wilkes 10.00 25.
CRLB Leandro Barbosa 15.00 30.
CRMB Mike Bibby 8.00 20.
CRMI Andre Miller 8.00 20.
CRMP Mark Price 20.00 50.
CRPA Tony Parker 20.00 40.
CRPP Paul Pierce 25.00 50.
CRRB Rick Barry 20.00 40.
CRRO Brandon Roy 25.00 60.
CRRP Robert Parish 20.00 50.
CRSB Shannon Brown 12.50 30.
CRSN Steve Nash 50.00 100.
CRSP Sam Perkins 15.00 30.
CRST John Stockton 40.00 80.
CRTC Tom Chambers 8.00 20.
CRTY Tyson Chandler 15.00 30.
CRWA Don Slick Watts 8.00 20.
CRWE Jerry West 60.00 150.
CRWF Walt Frazier 8.00 20.

2007-08 SP Authentic Destination Stardom

COMPLETE SET (30) 20.00 40.
RANDOM INSERTS IN PACKS
DS1 Kevin Durant 6.00 15.
DS2 Al Horford 1.00 2.
DS3 Mike Conley Jr. 1.00 2.
DS4 Jeff Green 1.00 2.
DS5 Corey Brewer 1.00 2.
DS6 Joakim Noah 2.00 5.
DS7 Spencer Hawes .75 2.
DS8 Acie Law .75 2.
DS9 Julian Wright .75 2.
DS10 Al Thornton .75 2.
DS11 Rodney Stuckey 1.25 3.
DS12 Sean Williams .75 2.
DS13 Marco Belinelli .75 2.
DS14 Javaris Crittenton .75 2.
DS15 Jason Smith .75 2.
DS16 Daequan Cook .75 2.
DS17 Jared Dudley .75 2.
DS18 Wilson Chandler 1.25 3.
DS19 Morris Almond .75 2.
DS20 Arron Afflalo 1.00 2.
DS21 Alando Tucker .75 2.
DS22 Glen Davis 1.25 3.
DS23 Carl Landry .75 2.
DS24 Gabe Pruitt .75 2.
DS25 Luis Scola 1.25 3.
DS26 Nick Fazekas .75 2.
DS27 Jermareo Davidson .75 2.
DS28 Josh McRoberts .75 2.
DS29 Kyrylo Fesenko .75 2.
DS30 Aaron Gray .75 2.

2007-08 SP Authentic Profiles

COMPLETE SET (60) 25.00 50.
RANDOM INSERTS IN PACKS
AP1 Acie Law 1.00 2.
AP2 Al Horford 1.25 3.
AP3 Al Thornton 1.00 2.
AP4 Arron Afflalo 1.25 3.
AP5 Corey Brewer 1.25 3.
AP6 Daequan Cook 1.00 2.
AP7 Jared Dudley 1.00 2.
AP8 Jason Smith 1.00 2.
AP9 Javaris Crittenton 1.00 2.
AP10 Jeff Green 1.25 3.
AP11 Joakim Noah 2.50 6.
AP12 Julian Wright 1.00 2.
AP13 Kevin Durant 8.00 20.
AP14 Marco Belinelli 1.00 2.
AP15 Mike Conley Jr. 1.50 4.
AP16 Morris Almond 1.00 2.
AP17 Rodney Stuckey 1.50 4.
AP18 Sean Williams 1.00 2.
AP19 Spencer Hawes 1.00 2.
AP20 Wilson Chandler 1.50 4.
AP21 Allen Iverson 1.25 3.
AP22 Carlos Boozer 1.00 2.
AP23 Carmelo Anthony 1.25 3.
AP24 Chauncey Billups 1.00 2.
AP25 Chris Bosh 1.00 2.
AP26 Dirk Nowitzki 1.25 3.
AP27 Dwyane Wade 2.50 6.
AP28 Gilbert Arenas 1.00 2.
AP29 Jason Kidd 1.25 3.
AP30 Kevin Garnett 2.00 5.
AP31 Kobe Bryant 5.00 12.
AP32 LeBron James 5.00 12.
AP33 Ray Allen 1.00 2.
AP34 Shaquille O'Neal 2.00 5.
AP35 Steve Nash 1.25 3.
AP36 Tim Duncan 1.50 4.
AP37 Tony Parker 1.00 2.
AP38 Tracy McGrady 1.00 2.
AP39 Vince Carter 1.25 3.
AP40 Yao Ming 1.25 3.
AP41 Adrian Dantley 1.00 2.
AP42 Bill Walton 1.00 2.
AP43 Chris Mullin 1.25 3.
AP44 David Robinson 1.50 4.
AP45 Elvin Hayes 1.00 2.
AP46 George Gervin 1.00 2.
AP47 Hakeem Olajuwon 1.25 3.
AP48 Jerry West 1.25 3.

49 John Stockton 1.50 4.00
50 Julius Erving 2.00 5.00
51 Kareem Abdul-Jabbar 1.50 4.00
52 Karl Malone 1.25 3.00
53 Larry Bird 3.00 8.00
54 Magic Johnson 2.50 6.00
55 Michael Jordan 8.00 20.00
56 Moses Malone 1.00 2.50
57 Oscar Robertson 1.00 2.50
58 Rick Barry 1.00 2.50
59 Robert Parish 1.00 2.50
60 Wilt Chamberlain 2.00 5.00

2007-08 SP Authentic Recruiting Class 2007

ATED PRINT RUN 60 TO 75 SER.#'d SETS
ITY NAME: SAME VALUE AS BASE
Y NAME STATED PRINT RUN 50 SETS
PRICED DRAFT POS.PRINT RUN 15 SETS
EAM NAME: .5X TO 1.25X BASE HI
AM NAME STATED PRINT RUN 25 SETS
CH EXPIRE DATE 1/28/10
AA Arron Afflalo/75 8.00 20.00
AB Aaron Brooks/75 6.00 15.00
AH Al Horford/75 12.50 30.00
AL Acie Law/75 6.00 15.00
AT Al Thornton/75 6.00 15.00
CB Corey Brewer/75 8.00 20.00
CL Carl Landry/75 6.00 15.00
DC Daequan Cook/75 6.00 15.00
DM Dominic McGuire/75 6.00 15.00
DU Jared Dudley/75 6.00 15.00
GD Glen Davis/75 10.00 25.00
GP Gabe Pruitt/75 6.00 15.00
JC Javaris Crittenton/75 6.00 15.00
JD Jermareo Davidson/75 6.00 15.00
JG Jeff Green/75 8.00 20.00
JM Josh McRoberts/75 6.00 15.00
JN Joakim Noah/75 30.00 80.00
JS Jason Smith/75 6.00 15.00
JW Julian Wright/75 6.00 15.00
KD Kevin Durant/60 175.00 350.00
MA Morris Almond/75 6.00 15.00
MB Marco Belinelli/75 6.00 15.00
MC Mike Conley Jr./75 10.00 25.00
NF Nick Fazekas/75 6.00 15.00
RS Rodney Stuckey/75 10.00 25.00
SH Spencer Hawes/75 6.00 15.00
SW Sean Williams/75 6.00 15.00
TG Taurean Green/75 6.00 15.00
TU Alando Tucker/75 6.00 15.00
WC Wilson Chandler/75 10.00 25.00

2007-08 SP Authentic Rookie Autographs

INT RUNS LISTED IN CHECKLIST
PRICED LOGO PRINT RUN ONE SET
SERTED INTO RETAIL SP PACKS
2 Spencer Hawes/599 6.00 15.00
3 Acie Law/100 6.00 15.00
4 Julian Wright/100 6.00 15.00
5 Al Thornton/599 6.00 15.00
6 Rodney Stuckey/599 10.00 25.00
7 Sean Williams/100 6.00 15.00
8 Javaris Crittenton/100 6.00 15.00
9 Jason Smith/100 6.00 15.00
0 Daequan Cook/100 6.00 15.00
1 Jared Dudley/100 6.00 15.00
2 Wilson Chandler/599 10.00 25.00
3 Morris Almond/100 6.00 15.00
4 Aaron Afflalo/599 8.00 20.00
5 Alando Tucker/100 6.00 15.00
6 Carl Landry/100 6.00 15.00
7 Gabe Pruitt/100 6.00 15.00
8 Aaron Brooks/599 6.00 15.00
9 Nick Fazekas/599 6.00 15.00
0 Jermareo Davidson/100 6.00 15.00
1 Josh McRoberts/599 6.00 15.00
2 Glen Davis/599 10.00 25.00
3 Adam Haluska/599 6.00 15.00
7 Dominic McGuire/100 6.00 15.00
8 Aaron Gray/100 6.00 15.00
9 Taurean Green/599 6.00 15.00
0 D.J. Strawberry/599 6.00 15.00
1 Chris Richard/100 6.00 15.00
2 Kevin Durant/399 250.00 450.00
3 Al Horford/399 8.00 20.00
4 Mike Conley Jr./100 10.00 25.00
5 Jeff Green/399 8.00 20.00
6 Corey Brewer/100 8.00 20.00
7 Joakim Noah/100 15.00 40.00

2007-08 SP Authentic Sign of the Times Dual

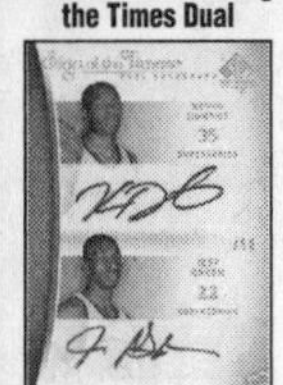

NT RUN 16 TO 50 SER.#'d SETS
PRICED TRIPLE PRINT RUN 10 SETS
PRICED QUAD PRINT RUN 5 SETS
PRICED SIXES PRINT RUN 5 SETS
CH EXPIRE DATE 1/28/10
AR LaMarcus Aldridge 25.00 50.00
randon Roy
AW Deron Williams 10.00 25.00
mes Augustine
D Paul Davis 8.00 20.00
nannon Brown
G Mike Bibby 10.00 25.00
ancisco Garcia
B Boris Diaw 10.00 25.00
eandro Barbosa
G Kevin Durant 100.00 250.00
ff Green
M Michael Jordan 300.00 500.00
Dennis Rodman
STFB T.J. Ford 10.00 25.00
Josh Boone
STGC Rudy Gay 15.00 40.00
Mike Conley Jr.
STGM Donyell Marshall 8.00 20.00
Daniel Gibson
STGN Aaron Gray 15.00 30.00
Joakim Noah
STGR Rajon Rondo 20.00 40.00
Daniel Gibson
STHM Al Harrington 8.00 20.00
Paul Millsap
STJA Solomon Jones 8.00 20.00
James Augustine
STJC Al Jefferson 15.00 40.00
Rodney Carney
STJR Magic Johnson 50.00 100.00
Pat Riley
STJS Antawn Jamison 8.00 20.00
DeShawn Stevenson
STLA Maurice Ager 8.00 20.00
Kyle Lowry
STMD Chris Mihm 8.00 20.00
Paul Davis
STMG Hal Greer 8.00 20.00
Andre Miller
STMN Sean May/31 8.00 20.00
David Noel
STMP Paul Millsap 8.00 20.00
Leon Powe
STMS Maurice Ager 8.00 20.00
Shannon Brown
STMT Alonzo Mourning 20.00 50.00
Tyrus Thomas
STOS Hakeem Olajuwon 25.00 50.00
Ralph Sampson
STPD Tayshaun Prince 15.00 30.00
Adrian Dantley
STPJ Tayshaun Prince 100.00 200.00
LeBron James
STPW Tony Parker 15.00 40.00
Deron Williams
STRP Rajon Rondo 20.00 40.00
Gabe Pruitt
STSA Cedric Simmons 8.00 20.00
Hilton Armstrong
STSJ Sean May 8.00 20.00
Jared Dudley
STWA Bill Walton 15.00 30.00
LaMarcus Aldridge
STWD Damien Wilkins 8.00 20.00
Yakhouba Diawara
STWJ Shelden Williams 8.00 20.00
Solomon Jones
STWP Bill Walton 20.00 40.00
Robert Parish

2008-09 SP Authentic

This set was released on February 3, 2009. The base set consists of 141 cards.
COMP.SET w/o SP's (100) 25.00 50.00
UNPRICED DIE CUT PRINT RUN 10 SETS
UNPRICED RC LOGOMAN PRINT RUN ONE SET
1 Dwyane Wade 1.00 2.50
2 Alonzo Mourning .60 1.50
3 Daequan Cook .30 .75
4 Kevin Durant 2.00 5.00
5 Jeff Green .40 1.00
6 Chris Wilcox .30 .75
7 Al Jefferson .50 1.25
8 Corey Brewer .40 1.00
9 Randy Foye .50 1.25
10 Rudy Gay .50 1.25
11 Mike Conley Jr. .40 1.00
12 Mike Miller .50 1.25
13 Jamal Crawford .40 1.00
14 Eddy Curry .30 .75
15 Quentin Richardson .40 1.00
16 Stephon Marbury .40 1.00
17 Chris Kaman .40 1.00
18 Marcus Camby .30 .75
19 Baron Davis .50 1.25
20 Michael Redd .50 1.25
21 Richard Jefferson .50 1.25
22 Mo Williams .40 1.00
23 Emeka Okafor .50 1.25
24 Gerald Wallace .50 1.25
25 Jason Richardson .50 1.25
26 Joakim Noah .50 1.25
27 Luol Deng .50 1.25
28 Ben Gordon .50 1.25
29 Michael Jordan 4.00 10.00
30 Vince Carter .60 1.50
31 Yi Jianlian .50 1.25
32 Devin Harris .50 1.25
33 T.J. Ford .30 .75
34 Danny Granger .50 1.25
35 Mike Dunleavy .40 1.00
36 Ron Artest .50 1.25
37 Kevin Martin .50 1.25
38 Brad Miller .40 1.00
39 Brandon Roy .50 1.25
40 LaMarcus Aldridge .50 1.25
41 Greg Oden .50 1.25
42 Corey Maggette .40 1.00
43 Al Harrington .40 1.00
44 Monta Ellis .50 1.25
45 Al Horford .50 1.25
46 Joe Johnson .50 1.25
47 Josh Smith .50 1.25
48 Mike Bibby .40 1.00
49 Andre Iguodala .50 1.25
50 Andre Miller .40 1.00
51 Thaddeus Young .40 1.00
52 Chris Bosh .50 1.25
53 Jermaine O'Neal .50 1.25
54 Jose Calderon .40 1.00
55 Antawn Jamison .50 1.25
56 Caron Butler .50 1.25
57 Gilbert Arenas .50 1.25
58 LeBron James 2.50 6.00
59 Daniel Gibson .50 1.25
60 Anderson Varejao .40 1.00
61 Allen Iverson .60 1.50
62 Carmelo Anthony .60 1.50
63 Elton Brand .50 1.25
64 Jason Kidd .50 1.25
65 Dirk Nowitzki .60 1.50
66 Josh Howard .40 1.00
67 Dwight Howard 1.00 2.50
68 Hedo Turkoglu .50 1.25
69 Rashard Lewis .40 1.00
70 Deron Williams .50 1.25
71 Carlos Boozer .50 1.25
72 Andrei Kirilenko .40 1.00
73 Ronnie Brewer .40 1.00
74 Shaquille O'Neal 1.00 2.50
75 Steve Nash .50 1.25
76 Amare Stoudemire .50 1.25
77 Leandro Barbosa .40 1.00
78 Yao Ming .60 1.50
79 Tracy McGrady .50 1.25
80 Shane Battier .40 1.00
81 Luis Scola .40 1.00
82 Tim Duncan .75 2.00
83 Tony Parker .50 1.25
84 Manu Ginobili .50 1.25
85 Chris Paul .75 2.00
86 David West .50 1.25
87 Tyson Chandler .40 1.00
88 Peja Stojakovic .50 1.25
89 Kobe Bryant 2.50 6.00
90 Pau Gasol .50 1.25
91 Lamar Odom .50 1.25
92 Andrew Bynum .60 1.50
93 Chauncey Billups .50 1.25
94 Richard Hamilton .40 1.00
95 Rasheed Wallace .50 1.25
96 Tayshaun Prince .50 1.25
97 Kevin Garnett 1.00 2.50
98 Paul Pierce .60 1.50
99 Ray Allen .50 1.25
100 Rajon Rondo .60 1.50
101 Alexis Ajinca AU/199 RC 8.00 20.00
102 Joe Alexander JSY AU/499 RC 8.00 20.00
103 Ryan Anderson JSY AU/499 RC 12.00 30.00
104 Darrell Arthur JSY AU/499 RC 8.00 20.00
105 D.J. Augustin JSY AU/299 RC 15.00 40.00
106 Jerryd Bayless JSY AU/299 RC 20.00 50.00
107 Michael Beasley JSY AU/299 RC25.00 60.00
108 Mario Chalmers JSY AU/499 RC15.00 40.00
109 Joe Crawford AU/199 RC 8.00 20.00
110 Joey Dorsey JSY AU/499 RC 8.00 20.00
111 C.D-Roberts JSY AU/499 RC 8.00 20.00
112 Patrick Ewing Jr. JSY AU/499 RC8.00 20.00
113 Danilo Gallinari AU/199 RC 25.00 60.00
114 J.R. Giddens JSY AU/499 RC 8.00 20.00
115 Eric Gordon JSY AU/299 RC 75.00 150.00
116 Donte Greene JSY AU/499 RC 10.00 25.00
117 Malik Hairston AU/199 RC 8.00 20.00
118 Roy Hibbert JSY AU/499 RC 12.00 30.00
119 J.J. Hickson JSY AU/499 RC 10.00 25.00
120 George Hill JSY AU/499 RC 15.00 40.00
121 DeAndre Jordan JSY AU/499 RC15.00 40.00
122 Kosta Koufos JSY AU/499 RC 8.00 20.00
123 Courtney Lee JSY AU/499 RC 12.00 30.00
124 Brook Lopez JSY AU/299 RC 25.00 60.00
125 Robin Lopez JSY AU/499 RC 8.00 20.00
126 Kevin Love JSY AU/299 RC 150.00 300.00
127 O.J. Mayo JSY AU/299 RC 30.00 80.00
128 JaVale McGee JSY AU/499 RC 15.00 40.00
129 Anthony Randolph JSY AU/499 RC15.00 40.00
130 Derrick Rose JSY AU/299 RC 600.00 1000.00
131 Brandon Rush JSY AU/299 RC 15.00 40.00
132 Walter Sharpe JSY AU/499 RC 8.00 20.00
133 Sean Singletary AU/199 RC 8.00 20.00
134 Marreese Speights JSY AU/499 RC8.00 20.00
135 Mike Taylor AU/199 RC 8.00 20.00
136 Jason Thompson JSY AU/499 RC8.00 20.00
137 Kyle Weaver JSY AU/499 RC 8.00 20.00
138 Sonny Weems JSY AU/499 RC 8.00 20.00
139 Russell Westbrook JSY AU/299 RC150.00 300.00
140 D.J. White JSY AU/499 RC 8.00 20.00
147 Rudy Fernandez JSY AU/499 RC10.00 25.00

2008-09 SP Authentic Retail

COMP.SET w/o RCs (100) 10.00 25.00
*VETS: .25X TO .6X BASE HOBBY
SOME AU RC UNPRICED DUE TO SCARCITY
104 Darrell Arthur AU RC 15.00 40.00
107 Michael Beasley AU RC 50.00 120.00
108 Mario Chalmers AU RC 40.00 100.00
109 Joe Crawford AU RC 15.00 40.00
112 Patrick Ewing Jr. AU RC 15.00 40.00
113 Danilo Gallinari AU RC 25.00 60.00
121 DeAndre Jordan AU RC 30.00 80.00
127 O.J. Mayo AU RC 50.00 120.00
128 Javale McGee AU RC 30.00 80.00
130 Derrick Rose AU RC 900.00 1500.00
132 Walter Sharpe AU RC 15.00 40.00
137 Kyle Weaver AU RC 15.00 40.00
138 Sonny Weems AU RC 15.00 40.00
139 Russell Westbrook AU RC 250.00 500.00

2008-09 SP Authentic Chirography

COMBINED AUTO ODDS 1:12
CAD Adrian Dantley 5.00 12.00
CAE Alex English 5.00 12.00
CAG Artis Gilmore 5.00 12.00
CBD Brad Daugherty 5.00 12.00
CBL Bob Lanier 5.00 12.00
CBS Bill Sharman 8.00 20.00
CBW Buck Williams 5.00 12.00
CDD Darryl Dawkins 6.00 15.00
CDR Dennis Rodman 20.00 50.00
CDT David Thompson 6.00 15.00
CDW Don Watts 5.00 12.00
CGG George Gervin 8.00 20.00
CGM George McGinnis 5.00 12.00
CGO Gail Goodrich 10.00 25.00
CGR Glen Rice 15.00 30.00
CJE Julius Erving 30.00 60.00
CJH John Havlicek 20.00 40.00
CJS John Salley 6.00 15.00
CLB Larry Bird 40.00 80.00
CMC Maurice Cheeks 5.00 12.00
CMJ Michael Jordan 350.00 550.00
CNT Nate Thurmond 6.00 15.00
CRB Rick Barry 8.00 20.00
CRO David Robinson 40.00 80.00
CRP Robert Parish 10.00 25.00
CSJ Sam Jones 12.50 30.00
CSK Steve Kerr 8.00 20.00
CTH Tom Heinsohn 8.00 20.00
CTS Tom Sanders 8.00 20.00
CVD Vlade Divac 15.00 40.00
CWF Walt Frazier 12.50 30.00
CWI Dominique Wilkins 15.00 30.00
CXM Xavier McDaniel 6.00 15.00

2008-09 SP Authentic Destination Stardom

COMPLETE SET (30) 15.00 40.00
STATED ODDS 1:3
DS1 Derrick Rose 6.00 15.00
DS2 Michael Beasley 1.25 3.00
DS3 O.J. Mayo 1.25 3.00
DS4 Russell Westbrook 4.00 10.00
DS5 Kevin Love 3.00 8.00
DS6 Danilo Gallinari 1.25 3.00
DS7 Eric Gordon 2.00 5.00
DS8 Joe Alexander .75 2.00
DS9 D.J. Augustin .75 2.00
DS10 Brook Lopez 1.25 3.00
DS11 Jerryd Bayless .75 2.00
DS12 Jason Thompson .75 2.00
DS13 Brandon Rush .75 2.00
DS14 Anthony Randolph 1.00 2.50
DS15 Robin Lopez .75 2.00
DS16 Marreese Speights .75 2.00
DS17 Roy Hibbert 1.25 3.00
DS18 Javale McGee 1.25 3.00
DS19 J.J. Hickson 1.00 2.50
DS20 Alexis Ajinca .75 2.00
DS21 Courtney Lee 1.25 3.00
DS22 D.J. White .75 2.00
DS23 J.R. Giddens .75 2.00
DS24 Joey Dorsey .75 2.00
DS25 Sonny Weems .75 2.00
DS26 Mario Chalmers 1.25 3.00
DS27 Sun Yue 1.00 2.50
DS28 Rudy Fernandez 1.00 2.50
DS29 Marc Gasol 1.25 3.00
DS30 Hamed Haddadi .75 2.00

2008-09 SP Authentic Limited Memorabilia

RANDOM INSERTS IN PACKS
SPLAD Darrell Arthur 2.50 6.00
SPLAR Anthony Randolph 3.00 8.00
SPLBL Brook Lopez 4.00 10.00
SPLBR Brandon Rush 2.50 6.00
SPLCD Chris Douglas-Roberts 2.50 6.00
SPLDA D.J. Augustin 2.50 6.00
SPLDG Donte Greene 2.50 6.00
SPLDJ DeAndre Jordan 5.00 12.00
SPLDR Derrick Rose 25.00 60.00
SPLEG Eric Gordon 6.00 15.00
SPLGH George Hill 4.00 10.00
SPLJA Joe Alexander 2.50 6.00
SPLJB Jerryd Bayless 2.50 6.00
SPLJD Joey Dorsey 2.50 6.00
SPLJG J.R. Giddens 2.50 6.00
SPLJH J.J. Hickson 3.00 8.00
SPLJM Javale McGee 4.00 10.00
SPLJT Jason Thompson 2.50 6.00
SPLKK Kosta Koufos 2.50 6.00
SPLKL Kevin Love 10.00 25.00
SPLKW Kyle Weaver 2.50 6.00
SPLMB Michael Beasley 4.00 10.00
SPLMC Mario Chalmers 4.00 10.00
SPLMS Marreese Speights 2.50 6.00
SPLOM O.J. Mayo 4.00 10.00
SPLRA Ryan Anderson 4.00 10.00
SPLRF Rudy Fernandez 3.00 8.00
SPLRL Robin Lopez 2.50 6.00
SPLSW Sonny Weems 2.50 6.00
SPLWS Walter Sharpe 2.50 6.00

2008-09 SP Authentic Profiles

COMPLETE SET (60) 30.00 60.00
STATED ODDS 1:3
AP1 Charles Oakley .75 2.00
AP2 Dominique Wilkins 1.00 2.50
AP3 James Worthy .75 2.00
AP4 Joe Dumars .75 2.00
AP5 Julius Erving 1.50 4.00
AP6 Kareem Abdul-Jabbar 1.25 3.00
AP7 Larry Bird 2.50 6.00
AP8 Larry Johnson .75 2.00
AP9 Magic Johnson 2.00 5.00
AP10 Michael Jordan 6.00 15.00
AP11 Muggsy Bogues .75 2.00
AP12 Oscar Robertson .75 2.00
AP13 Rick Mahorn .75 2.00
AP14 Spud Webb .75 2.00
AP15 Vlade Divac .75 2.00
AP16 Al Horford .75 2.00
AP17 Amare Stoudemire .75 2.00
AP18 Carlos Boozer .75 2.00
AP19 Chris Bosh .75 2.00
AP20 David West .75 2.00
AP21 Dirk Nowitzki 1.00 2.50
AP22 Dwight Howard 1.50 4.00
AP23 Kevin Garnett 1.50 4.00
AP24 LeBron James 4.00 10.00
AP25 Pau Gasol .75 2.00
AP26 Rasheed Wallace .75 2.00
AP27 Shaquille O'Neal 1.50 4.00
AP28 Shawn Marion .75 2.00
AP29 Tim Duncan 1.25 3.00
AP30 Yao Ming 1.00 2.50
AP31 Allen Iverson 1.00 2.50
AP32 Baron Davis .75 2.00
AP33 Carmelo Anthony 1.00 2.50
AP34 Chauncey Billups .75 2.00
AP35 Chris Paul 1.25 3.00
AP36 Deron Williams .75 2.00
AP37 Dwyane Wade 1.50 4.00
AP38 Joe Johnson .75 2.00
AP39 Kevin Durant 3.00 8.00
AP40 Kobe Bryant 4.00 10.00
AP41 Paul Pierce 1.00 2.50
AP42 Steve Nash .75 2.00
AP43 Tony Parker .75 2.00
AP44 Tracy McGrady .75 2.00
AP45 Vince Carter 1.00 2.50
AP46 Derrick Rose 6.00 15.00
AP47 Michael Beasley 1.25 3.00
AP48 O.J. Mayo 1.25 3.00
AP49 Russell Westbrook 4.00 10.00
AP50 Kevin Love 3.00 8.00
AP51 Danilo Gallinari 1.25 3.00
AP52 Sun Yue 1.00 2.50
AP53 Jason Thompson .75 2.00
AP54 Eric Gordon 2.00 5.00
AP55 Rudy Fernandez 1.00 2.50
AP56 Marc Gasol 1.25 3.00
AP57 D.J. Augustin .75 2.00
AP58 Jerryd Bayless .75 2.00
AP59 Luc Richard Mbah A Moute .75 2.00
AP60 Hamed Haddadi .75 2.00

2008-09 SP Authentic Recruiting Class City Name

TOTAL PRINT RUNS LISTED
RCCBL Brook Lopez/13 30.00 80.00
RCCBW Bill Walker/26 25.00 50.00
RCCDA Darrell Arthur/34 20.00 40.00
RCCDG Danilo Gallinari/13 30.00 80.00
RCCDJ D.J. Augustin/16 30.00 60.00
RCCDR Derrick Rose/23 300.00 600.00
RCCDW D.J. White/38 15.00 30.00
RCCEG Eric Gordon/17 50.00 120.00
RCCGH George Hill/40 25.00 50.00
RCCJA Joe Alexander/24 15.00 30.00
RCCJB Jerryd Bayless/20 40.00 80.00
RCCJC Joe Crawford/34 15.00 30.00
RCCJG J.R. Giddens/26 20.00 50.00
RCCJH J.J. Hickson/36 30.00 60.00
RCCJM Javale McGee/31 25.00 60.00
RCCJT Jason Thompson/25 25.00 50.00
RCCKL Kevin Love/48 75.00 150.00
RCCMB Michael Beasley/17 50.00 120.00
RCCMS Marreese Speights/30 20.00 50.00
RCCOM O.J. Mayo/35 50.00 120.00
RCCPE Patrick Ewing Jr./37 15.00 30.00
RCCRA Ryan Anderson/29 20.00 40.00
RCCRH Roy Hibbert/37 25.00 50.00
RCCRL Robin Lopez/27 15.00 30.00
RCCRW Russell Westbrook/19 175.00 350.00
RCCSS Sean Singletary/27 15.00 30.00
RCCWS Walter Sharpe/14 15.00 30.00

2008-09 SP Authentic Recruiting Class Full Name

TOTAL PRINT RUNS LISTED
RCNAR Anthony Randolph/75 15.00 30.00
RCNBR Brandon Rush/66 15.00 30.00
RCNBW Bill Walker/80 15.00 30.00
RCNDA Darrell Arthur/78 15.00 30.00
RCNDJ D.J. Augustin/80 20.00 50.00
RCNDR Derrick Rose/66 300.00 550.00
RCNDW D.J. White/77 15.00 30.00
RCNGH George Hill/80 15.00 40.00
RCNJA Joe Alexander/72 15.00 30.00
RCNJB Jerryd Bayless/65 15.00 40.00
RCNJC Joe Crawford/77 15.00 30.00
RCNJG J.R. Giddens/81 15.00 30.00
RCNJM Javale McGee/77 15.00 40.00
RCNJT Jason Thompson/65 15.00 40.00
RCNKL Kevin Love/18 100.00 250.00
RCNMB Michael Beasley/70 30.00 80.00
RCNMS Marreese Speights/80 15.00 30.00
RCNOM O.J. Mayo/30 50.00 120.00
RCNPE Patrick Ewing Jr./84 15.00 30.00
RCNRA Ryan Anderson/84 15.00 30.00
RCNRH Roy Hibbert/70 20.00 40.00
RCNRL Robin Lopez/80 15.00 30.00
RCNRW Russell Westbrook/64 75.00 150.00
RCNSS Sean Singletary/84 15.00 30.00
RCNWS Walter Sharpe/84 15.00 30.00

2008-09 SP Authentic Sign of the Times Dual

PRINT RUN 50 SER.#'d SETS
UNPRICED QUAD PRINT RUN 5 SETS
UNPRICED TRIPLE PRINT RUN 10 SETS
SDAR LaMarcus Aldridge 25.00 50.00
Brandon Roy
SDBB Shane Battier 8.00 20.00
Ronnie Brewer
SDBW Marco Belinelli 6.00 15.00
C.J. Watson
SDCC Mike Conley Jr. 8.00 20.00
Mike Conley Sr.
SDCO Emeka Okafor 6.00 15.00
Tyson Chandler
SDDG Kevin Durant 40.00 100.00
Jeff Green
SDFF Raymond Felton 6.00 15.00
Randy Foye
SDGC Rudy Gay 6.00 15.00
Mike Conley Jr.
SDGH Al Horford 25.00 50.00
Kevin Garnett
SDHA Walter Herrmann 6.00 15.00
Arron Afflalo
SDHM Al Horford 8.00 20.00
Jamario Moon
SDIS Rodney Stuckey 10.00 25.00
Andre Iguodala
SDJS Josh Boone 6.00 15.00
Sean Williams
SDJW Richard Jefferson 6.00 15.00
Mo Williams
SDKB Chauncey Billups 15.00 30.00
Jason Kidd
SDKJ Chris Kaman 6.00 15.00
Al Jefferson
SDKK Coby Karl 6.00 15.00
George Karl
SDMI Andre Iguodala 6.00 15.00
Andre Miller
SDOB Lamar Odom 8.00 20.00
Carlos Boozer
SDPA Ray Allen 40.00 80.00
Paul Pierce
SDPH Tayshaun Prince 20.00 40.00
Dwight Howard
SDPP Tony Parker 35.00 75.00
Chris Paul
SDSB Andrew Bynum 12.50 30.00
Amare Stoudemire
SDSV J.R. Smith 6.00 15.00
Sasha Vujacic
SDTS Al Thornton 8.00 20.00
Luis Scola
SDVR Sasha Vujacic 15.00 40.00
Rajon Rondo
SDWG David West 10.00 25.00
Rudy Gay
SDWL Luke Walton 8.00 20.00
Carl Landry

2008-09 SP Authentic Varsity Letters Legends City Name

TOTAL PRINT RUNS LISTED
SOME UNPRICED DUE TO SCARCITY
VLBD Brad Daugherty/18* 15.00 40.00
VLBL Bob Lanier/14* 30.00 60.00
VLBR Bill Russell/13* 125.00 250.00
VLDR Dennis Rodman/12* 125.00 225.00
VLDW Don Watts/13* 15.00 40.00
VLMP Mark Price/18* 150.00 300.00
VLRB Rick Barry/19* 40.00 80.00
VLRM Rick Mahorn/14* 25.00 60.00
VLRO David Robinson/15* 100.00 200.00
VLSJ Sam Jones/13* 50.00 120.00
VLTC Tom Chambers/11* 25.00 50.00

2008-09 SP Authentic Varsity Letters Legends Full Name

TOTAL PRINT RUNS LISTED
VLBD Brad Daugherty/39* 10.00 25.00
VLBL Bob Lanier/18* 20.00 40.00
VLBR Bill Russell/22* 125.00 250.00
VLDR Dennis Rodman/24* 25.00 60.00
VLDW Don Watts/39* 12.50 30.00
VLGR Glen Rice/24* 75.00 150.00
VLMB Muggsy Bogues/36* 60.00 150.00
VLMJ Michael Jordan/26* 900.00 1500.00
VLMP Mark Price/36* 125.00 250.00
VLRB Rick Barry/27* 30.00 60.00
VLRO David Robinson/26* 75.00 150.00
VLSJ Sam Jones/24* 60.00 120.00
VLTC Tom Chambers/33* 15.00 40.00

2008-09 SP Authentic Varsity Letters Veterans City Name

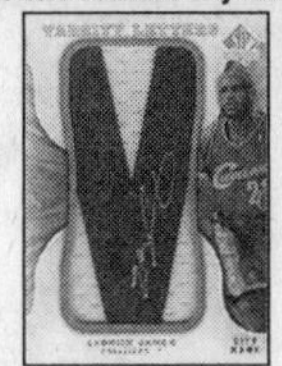

TOTAL PRINT RUNS LISTED
SOME UNPRICED DUE TO SCARCITY
VVAB Andrew Bogut/14* 15.00 30.00
VVAH Al Horford/39* 15.00 30.00
VVAM Alonzo Mourning/27* 100.00 200.00
VVAT Alando Tucker/48* 15.00 30.00
VVBG Ben Gordon/23* 25.00 50.00
VVCK Chris Kaman/17* 15.00 30.00
VVCL Carl Landry/14* 25.00 60.00
VVCP Chris Paul/10* 150.00 300.00
VVDC Daequan Cook/42* 15.00 30.00
VVDH Dwight Howard/22* 50.00 120.00
VVJA Antawn Jamison/17* 30.00 60.00
VVJF Jordan Farmar/28* 15.00 30.00
VVKB Kobe Bryant/16* 300.00 500.00
VVKD Kevin Durant/19* 150.00 300.00
VVKG Kevin Garnett/13* 75.00 150.00
VVLJ LeBron James/18* 350.00 600.00
VVLW Luke Walton/28* 15.00 30.00
VVMC Mike Conley Jr./16* 20.00 50.00
VVMW Mario West/32* 15.00 30.00
VVQR Quentin Richardson/42* 15.00 30.00
VVRJ Richard Jefferson/29* 15.00 30.00
VVRS Ramon Sessions/39* 15.00 30.00
VVST Rodney Stuckey/21* 20.00 50.00
VVSV Sasha Vujacic/44* 20.00 40.00

2008-09 SP Authentic Varsity Letters Veterans Full Name

TOTAL PRINT RUN LISTED
VVAH Al Horford/81* 10.00 25.00
VVAM Alonzo Mourning/56* 75.00 150.00
VVAT Alando Tucker/84* 10.00 25.00
VVBD Baron Davis/60* 10.00 25.00
VVBG Ben Gordon/63* 20.00 40.00
VVBY Andrew Bynum/55* 25.00 60.00
VVCK Chris Kaman/60* 10.00 25.00
VVCL Carl Landry/90* 15.00 30.00
VVCP Chris Paul/54* 50.00 100.00
VVDC Daequan Cook/88* 10.00 25.00
VVDH Dwight Howard/60* 30.00 80.00
VVDW David West/72* 10.00 25.00
VVJA Antawn Jamison/65* 15.00 30.00
VVJF Jordan Farmar/84* 20.00 40.00
VVKB Kobe Bryant/20* 300.00 500.00
VVKD Kevin Durant/22* 150.00 300.00
VVKG Kevin Garnett/24* 75.00 150.00
VVLJ LeBron James/22* 300.00 500.00
VVLW Luke Walton/80* 10.00 25.00
VVMC Mike Conley Jr./60* 15.00 40.00
VVMW Mario West/72* 10.00 25.00
VVQR Quentin Richardson/85* 10.00 25.00
VVRJ Richard Jefferson/80* 10.00 25.00
VVRS Ramon Sessions/91* 10.00 25.00
VVST Rodney Stuckey/78* 15.00 40.00
VVSV Sasha Vujacic/84* 10.00 25.00

2008-09 SP Authentic Vital Signs

COMBINED AUTO ODDS 1:12
VSAH Al Horford 4.00 10.00
VSBG Ben Gordon 6.00 15.00
VSDF Derek Fisher 8.00 20.00
VSDH Dwight Howard 15.00 30.00
VSDL David Lee 4.00 10.00
VSDW David West 6.00 15.00
VSJB Josh Boone 4.00 10.00
VSJG Jeff Green 5.00 12.00
VSKB Kobe Bryant 125.00 250.00
VSKD Kevin Durant 50.00 125.00
VSKG Kevin Garnett 35.00 75.00
VSLJ LeBron James 200.00 350.00
VSLW Luke Walton 4.00 10.00
VSRF Rudy Fernandez 8.00 20.00
VSRG Rudy Gay 4.00 10.00
VSRS Rodney Stuckey 4.00 10.00
VSSE Ramon Sessions 5.00 12.00
VSTC Tyson Chandler 4.00 10.00

2010-11 SP Authentic

Released in May, 2011, the 2010-11 SP Authentic set was issued in six-card packs with 24 packs per box.

The base issue cards are complete at a 100-card set and the autographs are complete at a 42-card set. For the autographs, most players had their last names used, although #203, #209, #221 and #240 used the word "Rookie" to spell out their Lettermen individual sets. To obtain the full print runs on the autographs take the number of letters in their last name (or "Rookie" for the numbers listed above) and multiply that by the serial-numbering on the actual card.

COMP.SET w/o RCs (100) 8.00 20.00
AU PRINT RUN 149 TO 299 SER.#'d SETS
1 Michael Jordan 2.50 6.00
2 Jerry West .40 1.00
3 Bill Walton .30 .75
4 Bill Russell .50 1.25
5 David Robinson .50 1.25
6 Hakeem Olajuwon .40 1.00
7 Alonzo Mourning .40 1.00
8 Christian Laettner .40 1.00
9 Magic Johnson .75 2.00
10 George Gervin .30 .75
11 Clyde Drexler .40 1.00
12 Dominique Wilkins .40 1.00
13 John Stockton .50 1.25
14 Larry Bird 1.00 2.50
15 James Worthy .40 1.00
16 Julius Erving .60 1.50
17 Bruce Bowen .20 .50
18 Phil Ford .30 .75
19 Bobby Jones .30 .75
20 B.J. Armstrong .30 .75
21 Rick Barry .30 .75
22 Elgin Baylor .30 .75
23 LeBron James 1.50 4.00
24 Jim Jackson .20 .50
25 Larry Brown .30 .75
26 Bill Cartwright .30 .75
27 Cynthia Cooper .40 1.00
28 Walter Davis .30 .75
29 Adrian Dantley .30 .75
30 Brad Daugherty .30 .75
31 Hubert Davis .30 .75
32 Vlade Divac .30 .75
33 Rick Fox .30 .75
34 Walt Frazier .30 .75
35 Gail Goodrich .30 .75
36 Darrell Griffith .30 .75
37 Anfernee Hardaway .75 2.00
38 James Harden .40 1.00
39 Robert Horry .40 1.00
40 John Havlicek .40 1.00
41 Steve Alford .30 .75
42 Rod Hundley .30 .75
43 Lauren Jackson .40 1.00
44 Mark Jackson .30 .75
45 Avery Johnson .30 .75
46 Larry Johnson .40 1.00
47 Rex Walters .20 .50
48 Shawn Kemp .50 1.25
49 Toni Kukoc .30 .75
50 Bill Laimbeer .30 .75
51 Lonnie Shelton .30 .75
52 Freddie Lewis .30 .75
53 George Lynch .30 .75
54 Danny Manning .30 .75
55 Sam Perkins .30 .75
56 Greg Anthony .20 .50
57 Bill Sharman .30 .75
58 Candace Parker .50 1.25
59 Terry Porter .25 .60
60 Glen Rice .30 .75
61 Micheal Ray Richardson .30 .75
62 Mateen Cleaves .30 .75
63 Dennis Rodman .50 1.25
64 Derrick Rose 1.00 2.50
65 Pat Riley .30 .75
66 Calbert Cheaney .30 .75
67 Cazzie Russell .30 .75
68 Bobby Hurley .30 .75
69 Jack Sikma .30 .75
70 Sam Cassell .30 .75
71 Jerry Sloan .30 .75
72 Kenny Smith .30 .75
73 J.R. Reid .20 .50
74 Tim Hardaway .30 .75
75 David Thompson .40 1.00
76 Reggie Theus .30 .75
77 Rudy Tomjanovich .30 .75
78 Chet Walker .30 .75
79 Russell Westbrook .40 1.00
80 Marion Jones .40 1.00
81 Steve Fisher .40 1.00
82 Tom Izzo .30 .75
83 Roy Williams .60 1.50
84 Bill Self .40 1.00
85 Jim Boeheim .40 1.00
86 Gary Williams .40 1.00
87 Mike Montgomery .30 .75
88 Jim Calhoun .40 1.00
89 Billy Donovan .30 .75
90 Mark Few .30 .75
91 Ben Howland .30 .75
92 Thad Matta .30 .75
93 Bruce Pearl .30 .75
94 Bob Huggins .30 .75
95 Bo Ryan .30 .75
96 Tubby Smith .30 .75
97 Sean Miller .30 .75
98 Rick Majerus .30 .75
99 Jay Wright .30 .75
100 Jamie Dixon .30 .75
201 Hassan Whiteside AU 5.00 12.00
Serial 299, Print Run 2691
202 Terrico White AU 6.00 15.00
Serial 299, Print Run 1495
203 Andy Rautins AU 10.00 25.00
Serial 299, Print Run 1794
204 Derrick Favors AU 15.00 40.00
Serial 149, Print Run 894
205 Al-Farouq Aminu AU 6.00 15.00
Serial 149, Print Run 745
206 Cole Aldrich AU 10.00 25.00
Serial 149, Print Run 1043
207 DeMarcus Cousins AU 25.00 60.00
Serial 149, Print Run 1043
208 Ed Davis AU 8.00 20.00
Serial 149, Print Run 745
209 Hamady N'Diaye AU 5.00 12.00
Serial 299, Print Run 1794
210 Greg Monroe AU 15.00 40.00
Serial 149, Print Run 894
211 Brian Zoubek AU 8.00 20.00
Serial 149, Print Run 894
212 Manny Harris AU 5.00 12.00
Serial 299, Print Run 1794
213 Damion James AU 5.00 12.00
Serial 149, Print Run 745
214 Stanley Robinson AU 5.00 12.00
Serial 149, Print Run 1192
215 Armon Johnson AU 5.00 12.00
Serial 299, Print Run 2093
216 Craig Brackins AU 5.00 12.00
Serial 299, Print Run 2093
217 Gani Lawal AU 5.00 12.00
Serial 299, Print Run 1495
218 Luke Babbitt AU 5.00 12.00
Serial 299, Print Run 2093
219 Dominique Jones AU 5.00 12.00
Serial 299, Print Run 1495
220 Xavier Henry AU 8.00 20.00
Serial 149, Print Run 745
221 Solomon Alabi AU 5.00 12.00
Serial 299, Print Run 1794
222 Jordan Crawford AU 8.00 20.00
Serial 299, Print Run 2392
223 Eric Bledsoe AU 15.00 40.00
Serial 149, Print Run 1043
224 Jerome Jordan AU 5.00 12.00
Serial 149, Print Run 894
225 James Anderson AU 5.00 12.00
Serial 299, Print Run 2392
226 Dexter Pittman AU 5.00 12.00
Serial 299, Print Run 2093
227 Da'Sean Butler AU 8.00 20.00
Serial 149, Print Run 894
228 Trevor Booker AU 6.00 15.00
Serial 299, Print Run 1794
229 Ekpe Udoh AU 8.00 20.00
Serial 149, Print Run 596
230 Sherron Collins AU 8.00 20.00
Serial 299, Print Run 2093
231 Deon Thompson AU 10.00 25.00
Serial 149, Print Run 1192
232 Gordon Hayward AU 15.00 40.00
Serial 149, Print Run 1043
233 Scottie Reynolds AU 5.00 12.00
Serial 149, Print Run 1192
234 Jarvis Varnado AU EXCH 5.00 12.00
Serial 149, Print Run 1043
235 Quincy Pondexter AU 8.00 20.00
Serial 299, Print Run 2691
236 Luke Harangody AU 5.00 12.00
Serial 299, Print Run 2691
237 Paul George AU 20.00 50.00
Serial 149, Print Run 894
238 Greivis Vasquez AU 12.50 30.00
Serial 299, Print Run 2093
239 Aubrey Coleman AU 5.00 12.00
Serial 149, Print Run.1043
240 Lazar Hayward AU 5.00 12.00
Serial 299, Print Run 1794
241 Elliot Williams AU 5.00 12.00
Serial 299, Print Run 2392
242 Devin Ebanks AU 10.00 25.00
Serial 299, Print Run 1794

2010-11 SP Authentic By The Letter Legend Last Name

This autograph set was randomly inserted into packs and features the Lettermen style. To obtain the complete print run, take the actual serial-numbering on the card and multiply that by the player's last name. The only exceptions appear to be for Jim Jackson and Robert Horry, which should spell out "Legend".

STATED PRINT RUN 30 TO 149 SER.#'d SETS
LAJ Avery Johnson 10.00 25.00
Serial 75, Print Run 525
LAM Alonzo Mourning 60.00 150.00
Serial 30, Print Run 240
LBC Bill Cartwright 10.00 25.00
Serial 30, Print Run 300
LBJ B.J. Armstrong 10.00 25.00
Serial 149, Print Run 1341
LBL Bill Laimbeer 10.00 25.00
Serial 149, Print Run 1192
LBS Bill Sharman 15.00 40.00
Serial 30, Print Run 210
LBW Bill Walton 15.00 40.00
Serial 30, Print Run 180
LCA Sam Cassell 10.00 25.00
Serial 149, Print Run 1043
LCC Cynthia Cooper 10.00 25.00
Serial 30, Print Run 180
LCL Christian Laettner 15.00 40.00
Serial 75, Print Run 600
LCP Candace Parker EXCH 20.00 50.00
Serial 149, Print Run 894
LCW Chet Walker 10.00 25.00
Serial 75, Print Run 450
LDA Danny Manning 30.00 80.00
Serial 30, Print Run 210
LDR Derrick Rose EXCH 90.00 175.00
Serial 149, Print Run 596
LDT David Thompson 10.00 25.00
Serial 30, Print Run 240
LEB Elgin Baylor 15.00 40.00
Serial 30, Print Run 180
LGG Gail Goodrich 15.00 40.00
Serial 30, Print Run 240
LHO Hakeem Olajuwon 30.00 80.00
Serial 30, Print Run 240
LJE Julius Erving EXCH 50.00 120.00
Serial 30, Print Run 180
LJH James Harden 15.00 40.00
Serial 30, Print Run 180
LJJ Jim Jackson 10.00 25.00
Serial 149, Print Run 694
LJR J.R. Reid 10.00 25.00
Serial 149, Print Run 596
LJS Jerry Sloan 10.00 25.00
Serial 75, Print Run 375
LKS Kenny Smith 12.50 30.00
Serial 30, Print Run 150
LLB Larry Bird 75.00 150.00
Serial 30, Print Run 120
LLJ LeBron James 175.00 350.00
Serial 30, Print Run 150
LMJ Michael Jordan 400.00 800.00
Serial 30, Print Run 180
LRF Rick Fox 20.00 50.00
Serial 30, Print Run 90
LRI Glen Rice 30.00 80.00
Serial 30, Print Run 120
LRO David Robinson 60.00 150.00
Serial 30, Print Run 240
LRU Bill Russell 75.00 150.00
Serial 30, Print Run 210
LRW Russell Westbrook EXCH 20.00 50.00
Serial 149, Print Run 1341
LRY Robert Horry 15.00 40.00
Serial 149, Print Run 894
LSA Steve Alford 10.00 25.00
Serial 149, Print Run 894
LSC Sidney Crosby 150.00 300.00
Serial 30, Print Run 180
LTP Terry Porter 12.50 30.00
Serial 75, Print Run 450

2010-11 SP Authentic Chirography

STATED ODDS 1:128 PACKS
CAH Anfernee Hardaway 50.00 120.00
CCP Candace Parker 10.00 25.00
CDE DeMarcus Cousins 30.00 80.00
CDF Derrick Favors 15.00 40.00
CHR Robert Horry 20.00 50.00
CJJ Jim Jackson 8.00 20.00
CRF Rick Fox 8.00 20.00

2010-11 SP Authentic Holo F/X

COMPLETE SET (42) 30.00 80.00
STATED ODDS 1:6 PACKS
1 Derrick Rose 3.00 8.00
2 Walt Frazier 1.00 2.50
3 Christian Laettner 1.25 3.00
4 Robert Horry 1.25 3.00
5 Anfernee Hardaway 2.50 6.00
6 Julius Erving 2.00 5.00
7 Larry Bird 3.00 8.00
8 Jim Jackson .60 1.50
9 Elgin Baylor 1.00 2.50
10 Tim Hardaway 1.00 2.50
11 Dennis Rodman 1.50 4.00
12 Kenny Smith 1.00 2.50
13 Jerry West 1.25 3.00
14 Bill Russell 1.50 4.00
15 Xavier Henry 1.25 3.00
16 Greg Anthony .60 1.50
17 Magic Johnson 2.50 6.00
18 George Gervin 1.00 2.50
19 Hakeem Olajuwon 1.25 3.00
20 David Robinson 1.50 4.00
21 LeBron James 5.00 12.00
22 Ed Davis 1.25 3.00
23 Michael Jordan 8.00 20.00
24 Greg Monroe 2.00 5.00
25 Bill Walton 1.00 2.50
26 Cazzie Russell 1.00 2.50
27 Alonzo Mourning 1.25 3.00
28 Rick Fox 1.00 2.50
29 Candace Parker 1.50 4.00
30 Danny Manning 1.00 2.50
31 Clyde Drexler 1.25 3.00
32 Derrick Favors 2.00 5.00
33 Al-Farouq Aminu 1.00 2.50
34 DeMarcus Cousins 3.00 8.00
35 Larry Johnson 1.25 3.00
36 James Worthy 1.25 3.00
37 David Thompson 1.25 3.00
38 Jim Boeheim 1.25 3.00
39 Bill Self 1.00 2.50
40 Roy Williams 2.00 5.00
41 Ben Howland 1.00 2.50
42 Tom Izzo 1.00 2.50

2010-11 SP Authentic Holo F/X Die Cuts

*HOLO DC: 2X TO 5X BASE HI
STATED ODDS 1:144 PACKS
11 Dennis Rodman 12.50 30.00
21 LeBron James 50.00 120.00
23 Michael Jordan 100.00 200.00
27 Alonzo Mourning 15.00 40.00

2010-11 SP Authentic Jordan Brand Classic

RANDOM INSERTS IN PACKS
JCDA Ed Davis 2.50 6.00
JCDE Devin Ebanks 2.50 6.00
JCEB Devin Ebanks 2.50 6.00
JCED Ed Davis 2.50 6.00
JCGM Greg Monroe 4.00 10.00
JCMG Greg Monroe 4.00 10.00
JCMO Greg Monroe 4.00 10.00

2010-11 SP Authentic Michael Jordan Supreme Court Floor

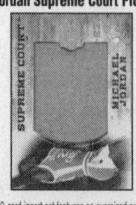

This 40-card insert set features an oversized swatch of North Carolina floor. The set was broken up into four tiers (which are also written on the back of each card) which feature "Common" for cards 1-10, "Uncommon" for 11-20, "Rare" for 21-30 and "Ultra Rare" for 31-40. The common versions feature a light blue color, the uncommon feature a red color, the rare feature a black color and the ultra rare feature a brown color. The cards were inserted at an overall rate of 1:48 packs.

COMMON FLOOR (1-10) 12.00 30.00
UNCOMMON FLOOR (11-20) 15.00 40.00
RARE FLOOR (21-30) 20.00 50.00
ULTRA RARE FLOOR (31-40) 40.00 100.00
UNPRICED AUTO PRINT RUN 5 SETS

2010-11 SP Authentic Sign of the Times

STATED ODDS 1:128 PACKS
UNPRICED DUAL PRINT RUN 10 SETS
UNPRICED QUAD PRINT RUN 2 TO 5 SETS
UNPRICED TRIPLE PRINT RUN 8 SETS
SAD Adrian Dantley 3.00 8.00
SBC Bobby Cremins 3.00 8.00
SBD Billy Donovan 10.00 25.00
SBH Bob Huggins 15.00 40.00
SBW Bill Walton 15.00 40.00
SCB Craig Brackins 3.00 8.00
SDM Danny Manning 8.00 20.00
SDR Derrick Rose 60.00 150.00
SDW Donald Williams 3.00 8.00
SEB Elgin Baylor 8.00 20.00
SFL Freddie Lewis 3.00 8.00
SGE George Gervin 10.00 25.00
SGL Gani Lawal 3.00 8.00
SHA John Havlicek 40.00 100.00
SJA James Anderson 3.00 8.00
SJD Jamie Dixon 10.00 25.00
SJO Magic Johnson 50.00 120.00
SJS Jack Sikma 3.00 8.00
SLB Larry Bird 60.00 150.00
SLE LeBron James 100.00 200.00
SLJ LeBron James 100.00 200.00
SMC Michael Cooper 3.00 8.00
SMF Mark Few 3.00 8.00
SMI Michael Jordan 300.00 550.00
SMJ Michael Jordan 300.00 550.00
SMM Mike Montgomery 3.00 8.00
SMR Micheal Ray Richardson 3.00 8.00
SRM Rick Majerus 3.00 8.00
SRW Russell Westbrook 25.00 60.00
SRX Rex Walters 3.00 8.00
SSC Sam Cassell 3.00 8.00
SSK Shawn Kemp 50.00 120.00
SSP Sam Perkins 6.00 15.00
STB Trevor Booker 3.00 8.00
STK Toni Kukoc 20.00 50.00
STS Tubby Smith 3.00 8.00
SWE Bruce Weber 4.00 10.00
SWF Walt Frazier 10.00 25.00

2011-12 SP Authentic

COMPLETE SET (100) 40.00 100.00
1 Michael Jordan 2.00 5.00
2 LeBron James 1.25 3.00
3 Grant Hill .40 1.00
4 Walt Frazier .30 .75
5 Anfernee Hardaway .75 2.00
6 Alonzo Mourning .40 1.00
7 Julius Erving .60 1.50
8 David Robinson .50 1.25
9 Russell Westbrook .40 1.00
10 Magic Johnson .75 2.00
11 Derrick Rose 1.00 2.50
12 Hakeem Olajuwon .40 1.00
13 Clyde Drexler .40 1.00
14 James Worthy .40 1.00
15 Larry Bird 1.00 2.50
16 Tristan Thompson .60 1.50
17 Jimmer Fredette .75 2.00
18 Alec Burks .40 1.00
19 Bismack Biyombo .40 1.00
20 Justin Harper .30 .75
21 Demetri McCamey .25 .60
22 Nolan Smith .40 1.00
23 Klay Thompson 1.00 2.50
24 Nikola Vucevic .25 .60
25 JaJuan Johnson .30 .75
26 Reggie Jackson .30 .75
27 Kawhi Leonard .75 2.00
28 Tobias Harris .30 .75
29 MarShon Brooks .75 2.00
30 Tyler Honeycutt .25 .60
31 Marcus Morris .40 1.00
32 Markieff Morris .50 1.25
33 Norris Cole .60 1.50
34 Cory Joseph .25 .60
35 Shelvin Mack .30 .75
36 Jordan Williams .30 .75
37 Chandler Parsons .40 1.00
38 Chris Singleton .25 .60
39 Jonas Valanciunas .50 1.25
40 Donatas Motiejunas .30 .75
41 Jon Leuer .25 .60
42 Malcolm Lee .25 .60
43 Charles Jenkins .25 .60
44 Travis Leslie .25 .60
45 Josh Selby .40 1.00
46 Keith Benson .25 .60
47 E'Twaun Moore .40 1.00
48 Matt Howard .30 .75
49 Scotty Hopson .25 .60
50 Durrell Summers .30 .75
51 LeBron James FX 2.50 6.00
52 Michael Jordan FX 5.00 12.00
53 Alonzo Mourning FX .75 2.00
54 Larry Johnson FX .75 2.00
55 Magic Johnson FX 1.50 4.00
56 Clyde Drexler FX .75 2.00
57 Hakeem Olajuwon FX .75 2.00
58 John Havlicek FX .75 2.00
59 David Robinson FX 1.00 2.50
60 Julius Erving FX 1.25 3.00
61 Mark Jackson FX .60 1.50
62 Adrian Dantley FX .60 1.50
63 Dennis Rodman FX 1.25 3.00
64 Danny Manning FX 1.00 2.50
65 Gail Goodrich FX .60 1.50
66 Anfernee Hardaway FX 1.50 4.00
67 Glen Rice FX .60 1.50
68 Hal Greer FX .60 1.50
69 Derrick Rose FX 2.00 5.00
70 Grant Hill FX 1.00 2.50
71 Russell Westbrook FX .75 2.00
72 Bill Laimbeer FX .60 1.50
73 Walt Frazier FX .60 1.50
74 Bill Russell FX 1.00 2.50
75 James Worthy FX .75 2.00
76 Rick Barry FX .60 1.50
77 Jerry West FX .75 2.00
78 Larry Bird FX 2.00 5.00
79 Bill Walton FX .60 1.50
80 Elgin Baylor FX .60 1.50
81 David Thompson FX .60 1.50
82 Tim Hardaway FX .60 1.50
83 Jack Sikma FX .60 1.50
84 Chet Walker FX .60 1.50
85 Tristan Thompson FX 1.50 4.00
86 Jonas Valanciunas FX 1.25 3.00
87 Jimmer Fredette FX 2.00 5.00
88 Kawhi Leonard FX 2.00 5.00
89 Bismack Biyombo FX 1.00 2.50
90 Klay Thompson FX 2.50 6.00
91 Alec Burks FX 1.00 2.50
92 Markieff Morris FX 1.25 3.00
93 Marcus Morris FX 1.00 2.50
94 Nikola Vucevic FX .60 1.50
95 Chris Singleton FX .60 1.50
96 Tobias Harris FX .75 2.00
97 Nolan Smith FX 1.00 2.50
98 Reggie Jackson FX .75 2.00
99 JaJuan Johnson FX .75 2.00
100 Cory Joseph FX .60 1.50

2011-12 SP Authentic Autographs

RANDOM INSERTS IN PACKS
FB FX PRINT RUN 3 TO 50 SER.#'d SETS
SOME FB FX UNPRICED DUE TO SCARCITY
1 Michael Jordan 300.00 500.00
2 LeBron James 100.00 200.00
3 Grant Hill 100.00 200.00
4 Walt Frazier 12.00 30.00
5 Anfernee Hardaway 40.00 100.00
6 Alonzo Mourning 30.00 80.00
7 Julius Erving 40.00 100.00
8 David Robinson 30.00 80.00
9 Russell Westbrook 10.00 25.00
10 Magic Johnson 50.00 120.00
11 Derrick Rose 75.00 150.00
12 Hakeem Olajuwon 30.00 80.00
13 Clyde Drexler 40.00 100.00
14 James Worthy 15.00 40.00
15 Larry Bird 50.00 125.00
16 Tristan Thompson 12.00 30.00
17 Jimmer Fredette 15.00 40.00
18 Alec Burks 8.00 20.00
19 Bismack Biyombo 8.00 20.00
20 Justin Harper 6.00 15.00
21 Demetri McCamey 5.00 12.00
22 Nolan Smith 8.00 20.00
23 Klay Thompson 25.00 60.00
24 Nikola Vucevic EXCH 5.00 12.00
25 JaJuan Johnson 8.00 20.00
26 Reggie Jackson 6.00 15.00
27 Kawhi Leonard 15.00 40.00
28 Tobias Harris 6.00 15.00
29 MarShon Brooks 15.00 40.00
30 Tyler Honeycutt 5.00 12.00
31 Marcus Morris 8.00 20.00
32 Markieff Morris 10.00 25.00
33 Norris Cole 15.00 40.00
34 Cory Joseph 5.00 12.00
35 Shelvin Mack 6.00 15.00
36 Jordan Williams 6.00 15.00
37 Chandler Parsons 8.00 20.00
38 Chris Singleton 5.00 12.00
41 Jon Leuer 5.00 12.00
42 Malcolm Lee 5.00 12.00
43 Charles Jenkins 5.00 12.00
44 Travis Leslie 5.00 12.00
45 Josh Selby 8.00 20.00
46 Keith Benson 5.00 12.00
47 E'Twaun Moore 12.00 30.00
48 Matt Howard 6.00 15.00
49 Scotty Hopson 5.00 12.00
50 Durrell Summers 6.00 15.00
62 Adrian Dantley FX/50 6.00 15.00
72 Bill Laimbeer FX/50 6.00 15.00
82 Tim Hardaway FX/50 8.00 20.00
83 Jack Sikma FX/50 6.00 15.00
84 Chet Walker FX/50 6.00 15.00
85 Tristan Thompson FX/50 20.00 50.00
87 Jimmer Fredette FX/50 75.00 200.00
88 Kawhi Leonard FX/50 25.00 60.00
89 Bismack Biyombo FX/50 12.00 30.00
90 Klay Thompson FX/50 75.00 150.00
91 Alec Burks FX/50 15.00 40.00
92 Markieff Morris FX/50 15.00 40.00
93 Marcus Morris FX/50 12.00 30.00
95 Chris Singleton FX/50 8.00 20.00
96 Tobias Harris FX/50 20.00 50.00
97 Nolan Smith FX/50 12.00 30.00
98 Reggie Jackson FX/50 10.00 25.00
99 JaJuan Johnson FX/50 10.00 25.00
100 Cory Joseph FX/50 8.00 20.00

2011-12 SP Authentic Autographs Gold

STATED PRINT RUN 3 TO 25 SER.#'d SETS
SOME UNPRICED DUE TO SCARCITY
17 Jimmer Fredette/25 175.00 350.00
22 Nolan Smith/25 20.00 50.00
23 Klay Thompson/25 75.00 200.00
28 Tobias Harris/25 25.00 60.00
29 MarShon Brooks/25 60.00 150.00
47 E'Twaun Moore/25 40.00 100.00

2011-12 SP Authentic By The Letter

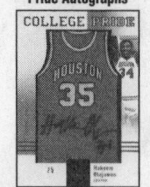

STATED PRINT RUN 5 TO 100 SER.#'d SETS
TOTAL PRINT RUN LISTED WITH ASTERISK
BLAM Alonzo Mourning 50.00 120.00
Serial 5; Print Run 50
BLBD Billy Donovan 15.00 40.00
Serial 30; Print Run 210
BLBL Bill Laimbeer 6.00 15.00
Serial 75; Print Run 675
BLBR Bill Russell 100.00 200.00
Serial 5; Print Run 15
BLCD Clyde Drexler 40.00 100.00
Serial 5; Print Run 35
BLCL Christian Laettner 15.00 40.00
Serial 100; Print Run 400
BLDM Danny Manning 20.00 50.00
Serial 25; Print Run 150
BLDR Derrick Rose 100.00 200.00
Serial 5; Print Run 35
BLDT David Thompson 10.00 25.00
Serial 25; Print Run 175
BLGA Greg Anthony 6.00 15.00
Serial 100; Print Run 400
BLGG Gail Goodrich 12.00 30.00
Serial 10; Print Run 40
BLGH Grant Hill 100.00 200.00
Serial 15; Print Run 60
BLHO Hakeem Olajuwon 40.00 100.00
Serial 5; Print Run 35
BLJE Julius Erving 50.00 120.00
Serial 5; Print Run 25
BLJW Jay Wright 8.00 20.00
Serial 15; Print Run 135
BLLB Larry Bird 75.00 150.00
Serial 5; Print Run 60
BLLJ LeBron James 100.00 200.00
Serial 23; Print Run 345
BLMB Mike Brey 6.00 15.00
Serial 25; Print Run 225
BLMJ Michael Jordan 300.00 550.00
Serial 23; Print Run 299
BLRB Rick Barry 12.50 30.00
Serial 10; Print Run 50
BLRO David Robinson 60.00 150.00
Serial 5; Print Run 20
BLRW Russell Westbrook 25.00 60.00
Serial 75; Print Run 300
BLRY Bo Ryan 15.00 40.00
Serial 25; Print Run 225
BLSF Steve Fisher 8.00 20.00
Serial 50; Print Run 200
BLTH Tim Hardaway 10.00 25.00
Serial 100; Print Run 400
BLWA Bill Walton 20.00 50.00
Serial 10; Print Run 40
BLWE Jerry West 50.00 125.00
Serial 5; Print Run 60
BLAD1 Adrian Dantley 6.00 15.00
Serial D,N/25; Print Run 50
BLAD2 Adrian Dantley 6.00 15.00
Serial A,E,M,O,R,T/50; Print Run 350
BLBC1 Bill Cartwright 6.00 15.00
Serial A,C,N,R,S/25; Print Run 225
BLBC2 Bill Cartwright 6.00 15.00
Serial F,O,I/50; Print Run 150
BLBH1 Ben Howland 8.00 20.00
Serial U/15; Print Run 15
BLBH2 Ben Howland 6.00 15.00
Serial A,C,L/30; Print Run 90
BLCR1 Cazzie Russell 8.00 20.00
Serial M/25; Print Run 25
BLCR2 Cazzie Russell 8.00 20.00
Serial A,C,G,H,I,N/50; Print Run 350
BLCW1 Chet Walker 6.00 15.00
Serial B,Y/10; Print Run 20
BLCW2 Chet Walker 6.00 15.00
Serial A,D,E,L,R/25; Print Run 125
BLDG1 Darrell Griffith 8.00 20.00
Serial V/25; Print Run 25
BLDG2 Darrell Griffith 6.00 15.00
Serial E,I,L,O,S,U/75; Print Run 675
BLEB1 Elgin Baylor 10.00 25.00
Serial E,T/25; Print Run 100
BLEB2 Elgin Baylor 10.00 25.00
Serial A,L,S/75; Print Run 225
BLFL1 Freddie Lewis 6.00 15.00
Serial Z/100; Print Run 100
BLFL2 Freddie Lewis 6.00 15.00
Serial A,E,I,N,O,R,S,T/50; Print Run 550
BLGR1 Glen Rice 10.00 25.00
Serial M/25; Print Run 25
BLGR2 Glen Rice 10.00 25.00
Serial A,C,G,H,I,N/75; Print Run 525
BLGW1 Gary Williams 25.00 60.00
Serial M,Y/15; Print Run 30
BLGW2 Gary Williams 25.00 60.00
Serial A,D,L,N,R/25; Print Run 150
BLJC1 Jim Calhoun 12.50 30.00
Serial N/25; Print Run 50
BLJC2 Jim Calhoun 12.50 30.00
Serial C,O,U/50; Print Run 150
BLJD1 Jamie Dixon 6.00 15.00
Serial P,T/10; Print Run 30
BLJD2 Jamie Dixon 6.00 15.00
Serial B,G,H,I,R,S,U/35; Print Run 245
BLJJ1 Jim Jackson 8.00 20.00
Serial H,I,O/100; Print Run 400
BLJJ2 Jim Jackson 8.00 20.00
Serial A,E,S,T/50; Print Run 250
BLJR1 J.R. Reid 10.00 25.00
Serial C,N/10; Print Run 30
BLJR2 J.R. Reid 10.00 25.00
Serial A,H,I,L,O,R,T/15; Print Run 150
BLLS1 Lonnie Shelton 6.00 15.00
Serial A,E,T/50; Print Run 250
BLLS2 Lonnie Shelton 6.00 15.00
Serial G,N,O,R,S/75; Print Run 450
BLRH1 Robert Horry 8.00 20.00
Serial B/50; Print Run 50
BLRH2 Robert Horry 6.00 15.00
Serial A,L,M/100; Print Run 600
BLSC1 Sam Cassell 6.00 15.
Serial A,E,T/25; Print Run 125
BLSC2 Sam Cassell 6.00 15.
Serial D,I,L,O,R,S/75; Print Run 450
BLSC3 Sam Cassell 6.00 15.
Serial F/100; Print Run 100
BLTM1 Thad Matta 10.00 25.
Serial O/20; Print Run 40
BLTM2 Thad Matta 10.00 25.
Serial A,E,H,I,S,T/35; Print Run 245
BLTS1 Tubby Smith 8.00 20.
Serial M/10; Print Run 10
BLTS2 Tubby Smith 8.00 20.
Serial N/15; Print Run 30
BLTS3 Tubby Smith 6.00 15.
Serial A,E,I,O,S,T/25; Print Run 150

2011-12 SP Authentic College Pride Autographs

STATED PRINT RUN 5 TO 40 SER.#'d SETS
SOME UNPRICED DUE TO SCARCITY
UNPRICED PARALLEL PRINT RUN 3 TO 10 SETS
CJAL Solomon Alabi/40 6.00 15.
CJBA B.J. Armstrong/40 15.00 40.
CJBD Billy Donovan/40 15.00 40.
CJBH Ben Howland/40 8.00 20.
CJBL Bill Laimbeer/40 8.00 20.
CJBS Bill Self/40 20.00 50.
CJBW Bill Walton/40 15.00 40.
CJCL Christian Laettner/40 25.00 60.
CJCR Cazzie Russell/40 15.00 40.
CJDC DeMarcus Cousins/40 30.00 80.
CJDM Danny Manning/40 20.00 50.
CJDT David Thompson/40 12.50 30.
CJEB Elgin Baylor/40 12.50 30.
CJFL Freddie Lewis/40 6.00 15.
CJGR Glen Rice/40 25.00 60.
CJHU Bobby Hurley/40 30.00 80.
CJJB Jim Boeheim/40 30.00 80.
CJJO Michael Jordan/40 300.00 600.
CJKS Kenny Smith/40 15.00 40.
CJLJ LeBron James/40 100.00 200.
CJLU Luke Babbitt/40 6.00 15.
CJRT Reggie Theus/40 10.00 25.
CJRU Russell Westbrook/40 35.00 70.
CJSA Steve Alford/40 15.00 40.
CJSC Sam Cassell/40 6.00 15.
CJSH Bill Sharman/40 8.00 20.
CJTH Tim Hardaway/40 15.00 40.
CJTS Tubby Smith/40 6.00 15.
CJWR Jay Wright/40 12.50 30.

2011-12 SP Authentic Home Court Signatures

RANDOM INSERTS IN PACKS
HCAD Adrian Dantley 8.00 20.
HCAH Anfernee Hardaway 50.00 120.
HCAM Alonzo Mourning 30.00 80.
HCBC Bill Cartwright 8.00 20.
HCBD Brad Daugherty 8.00 20.
HCBH Bobby Hurley 8.00 20.
HCBL Bill Laimbeer 8.00 20.
HCBM Bob McAdoo 8.00 20.
HCBR Bill Russell 75.00 150.
HCBW Bill Walton 10.00 25.
HCCL Christian Laettner 10.00 25.
HCCR Cazzie Russell 10.00 25.
HCDG Darrell Griffith 8.00 20.
HCDM Danny Manning 15.00 40.
HCDR David Robinson 50.00 125.
HCDT David Thompson 12.00 30.
HCEB Elgin Baylor 8.00 20.
HCGH Grant Hill 75.00 200.
HCGO Gail Goodrich 10.00 25.
HCGR Glen Rice 12.00 30.
HCHO Hakeem Olajuwon 50.00 125.
HCJA Jim Jackson 8.00 20.
HCJE Julius Erving 50.00 120.
HCJH John Havlicek 50.00 125.
HCJJ JaJuan Johnson 8.00 20.
HCJW James Worthy 20.00 50.
HCLB Larry Bird 125.00 225.
HCLJ LeBron James 100.00 200.
HCLO Brook Lopez 8.00 20.
HCMA Magic Johnson 50.00 125.
HCMJ Michael Jordan 500.00 800.
HCNS Nolan Smith 10.00 25.
HCRB Rick Barry 10.00 25.
HCRF Rick Fox 8.00 20.
HCRH Robert Horry 8.00 20.
HCRT Reggie Theus 8.00 20.
HCSC Sam Cassell 8.00 20.
HCSM Kenny Smith 8.00 20.
HCSP Sam Perkins 8.00 20.
HCTO Rudy Tomjanovich 8.00 20.
HCWE Jerry West 50.00 125.

2011-12 SP Authentic Jordan Brand Classic

NDOM INSERTS IN PACKS

HO Scotty Hopson	1.25	3.00
LE Malcolm Lee	1.25	3.00
ML Malcolm Lee	1.25	3.00
SH Scotty Hopson	1.25	3.00
BCCJ Cory Joseph	1.25	3.00
BCSE Josh Selby	2.00	5.00
BCTH Tobias Harris	1.50	4.00
BCTT Tristan Thompson	3.00	8.00

2011-12 SP Authentic Jordan Brand Classic Autographs

NDOM INSERTS IN PACKS

CCJ Cory Joseph	6.00	15.00
CSE Josh Selby	10.00	25.00
CTH Tobias Harris	10.00	25.00
CTT Tristan Thompson	15.00	40.00

2011-12 SP Authentic North Carolina Floor

NDOM INSERTS IN PACKS

NCBD Brad Daugherty	4.00	10.00
NCBP Buzz Peterson	4.00	10.00
NCJO Michael Jordan	10.00	25.00
NCJR J.R. Reid	4.00	10.00
NCJW James Worthy	5.00	12.00
NCKS Kenny Smith	4.00	10.00
NCMI Michael Jordan	10.00	25.00
NCMJ Michael Jordan	10.00	25.00
NCPE Sam Perkins	4.00	10.00
NCRE J.R. Reid	4.00	10.00
NCSM Kenny Smith	4.00	10.00
NCSP Sam Perkins	4.00	10.00
NCWF Joe Wolf	4.00	10.00
NCWO James Worthy	5.00	12.00

2011-12 SP Authentic North Carolina Floor Autographs

ATED PRINT RUN 10 TO 75 SER.#'d SETS
ME UNPRICED DUE TO SCARCITY

NCBD Brad Daugherty/75	10.00	25.00
NCBP Buzz Peterson/75	10.00	25.00
NCJO Michael Jordan/23	400.00	600.00
NCJR J.R. Reid/75	10.00	25.00
NCMI Michael Jordan/23	400.00	600.00
NCMJ Michael Jordan/23	400.00	600.00
NCPE Sam Perkins/75	12.00	30.00
NCRE J.R. Reid/75	10.00	25.00
NCSP Sam Perkins/75	12.00	30.00
NCWF Joe Wolf/75	10.00	25.00

2011-12 SP Authentic Sign of the Times Dual

MMON CARD	8.00	20.00
ATED PRINT RUN ONE TO 30 SETS		
ME UNPRICED DUE TO SCARCITY		
PRICED QUAD PRINT RUN 4 SETS		
LD Adrian Dantley/30	8.00	20.00
Bill Laimbeer		
PD Sam Perkins/30	12.00	30.00
Brad Daugherty		
SP Sam Perkins/30	12.00	30.00
Kenny Smith		

2011-12 SP Authentic Sign of the Times Triple

ATED PRINT RUN ONE TO 25 SETS		
ME UNPRICED DUE TO SCARCITY		
BCH Jim Calhoun/25	12.00	30.00
Billy Donovan		
Ben Howland		
SPD Kenny Smith/25	15.00	40.00
Brad Daugherty		
Sam Perkins		

1994-95 SP Championship

e premier edition of the 1994-95 SP Championship ies (made by Upper Deck) consists of 135 standard e cards issued in six-card foil packs, each with a, ggested retail price of $2.99. SP Championship ds were shipped exclusively to retail outlets. Card ts feature full-bleed, color action photos with a foil Championship logo. The player's name runs up the e of the card in small gold foil print. Team name is tained in a foil oval. After a Road to the Finals (1- subset, the cards are grouped alphabetically within n order. Rookie Cards of note in this set include nt Hill, Juwan Howard, Eddie Jones, Jason Kidd d Glenn Robinson.

MPLETE SET (135)	15.00	30.00
Mookie Blaylock RF	.10	.25
ominique Wilkins RF	.20	.50
lonzo Mourning RF	.20	.50
Michael Jordan RF	1.50	4.00
Mark Price RF	.15	.40
amal Mashburn RF	.15	.40
ikembe Mutombo RF	.15	.40
rant Hill RF	.40	1.00
9 Latrell Sprewell RF	.20	.50
10 Hakeem Olajuwon RF	.20	.50
11 Reggie Miller RF	.20	.50
12 Loy Vaught RF	.10	.25
13 Nick Van Exel RF	.15	.40
14 Glen Rice RF	.15	.40
15 Glenn Robinson RF	.15	.40
16 Isaiah Rider RF	.15	.40
17 Kenny Anderson RF	.12	.30
18 Patrick Ewing RF	.20	.50
19 Shaquille O'Neal RF	.40	1.00
20 Dana Barros RF	.10	.25
21 Charles Barkley RF	.25	.60
22 Clifford Robinson RF	.10	.25
23 Mitch Richmond RF	.15	.40
24 David Robinson RF	.25	.60
25 Shawn Kemp RF	.15	.40
26 Karl Malone RF	.20	.50
27 Chris Webber RF	.25	.60
28 Stacey Augmon	.12	.30
29 Mookie Blaylock	.10	.25
30 Grant Long	.10	.25
31 Steve Smith	.12	.30
32 Dee Brown	.10	.25
33 Eric Montross RC	.15	.40
34 Dino Radja	.12	.30
35 Dominique Wilkins	.20	.50
36 Muggsy Bogues	.12	.30
37 Scott Burrell	.10	.25
38 Larry Johnson	.15	.40
39 Alonzo Mourning	.20	.50
40 B.J. Armstrong	.10	.25
41 Michael Jordan	3.00	8.00
42 Toni Kukoc	.20	.50
43 Scottie Pippen	.30	.75
44 Tyrone Hill	.10	.25
45 Chris Mills	.10	.25
46 Mark Price	.15	.40
47 John Williams	.10	.25
48 Jim Jackson	.10	.25
49 Jason Kidd RC	.75	2.00
50 Jamal Mashburn	.15	.40
51 Roy Tarpley	.10	.25
52 Mahmoud Abdul-Rauf	.10	.25
53 Dikembe Mutombo	.15	.40
54 Rodney Rogers	.10	.25
55 Bryant Stith	.10	.25
56 Joe Dumars	.15	.40
57 Grant Hill RC	.75	2.00
58 Lindsey Hunter	.10	.25
59 Terry Mills	.10	.25
60 Tim Hardaway	.15	.40
61 Donyell Marshall RC	.15	.40
62 Chris Mullin	.15	.40
63 Latrell Sprewell	.20	.50
64 Sam Cassell	.15	.40
65 Clyde Drexler	.20	.50
66 Vernon Maxwell	.10	.25
67 Hakeem Olajuwon	.20	.50
68 Dale Davis	.10	.25
69 Mark Jackson	.15	.40
70 Reggie Miller	.20	.50
71 Rik Smits	.12	.30
72 Terry Dehere	.10	.25
73 Lamond Murray RC	.15	.40
74 Pooh Richardson	.10	.25
75 Loy Vaught	.10	.25
76 Cedric Ceballos	.10	.25
77 Vlade Divac	.15	.40
78 Eddie Jones RC	.50	1.25
79 Nick Van Exel	.15	.40
80 Bimbo Coles	.10	.25
81 Billy Owens	.10	.25
82 Glen Rice	.15	.40
83 Kevin Willis	.10	.25
84 Vin Baker	.15	.40
85 Marty Conlon	.10	.25
86 Eric Murdock	.10	.25
87 Glenn Robinson RC	.30	.75
88 Tom Gugliotta	.10	.25
89 Christian Laettner	.12	.30
90 Isaiah Rider	.15	.40
91 Doug West	.10	.25
92 Kenny Anderson	.12	.30
93 Benoit Benjamin	.10	.25
94 Derrick Coleman	.12	.30
95 Armon Gilliam	.10	.25
96 Patrick Ewing	.20	.50
97 Derek Harper	.12	.30
98 Charles Oakley	.12	.30
99 John Starks	.12	.30
100 Nick Anderson	.10	.25
101 Horace Grant	.12	.30
102 Anfernee Hardaway	.25	.60
103 Shaquille O'Neal	.40	1.00
104 Dana Barros	.10	.25
105 Shawn Bradley	.10	.25
106 Clarence Weatherspoon	.10	.25
107 Sharone Wright RC	.15	.40
108 Charles Barkley	.25	.60
109 Kevin Johnson	.15	.40
110 Dan Majerle	.15	.40
111 Wesley Person RC	.15	.40
112 Terry Porter	.10	.25
113 Clifford Robinson	.10	.25
114 Rod Strickland	.10	.25
115 Buck Williams	.10	.25
116 Brian Grant RC	.25	.60
117 Mitch Richmond	.15	.40
118 Spud Webb	.15	.40
119 Walt Williams	.10	.25
120 Vinny Del Negro	.10	.25
121 Sean Elliott	.15	.40
122 David Robinson	.25	.60
123 Dennis Rodman	.30	.75
124 Kendall Gill	.10	.25
125 Shawn Kemp	.15	.40
126 Gary Payton	.15	.40
127 Detlef Schrempf	.15	.40
128 David Benoit	.10	.25
129 Jeff Hornacek	.12	.30
130 Karl Malone	.20	.50
131 John Stockton	.20	.50
132 Rex Chapman	.10	.25
133 Calbert Cheaney	.10	.25
134 Juwan Howard RC	.25	.60
135 Chris Webber	.25	.60

1994-95 SP Championship Die Cuts

This 135-card parallel set is identical to the regular SP Championship series except for the die cut design on the cards as well as the silver hologram on their backs. One die cut card was inserted in each pack. Please refer to the multipliers provide in the header to ascertain prices.

COMPLETE SET (135)	30.00	60.00
*DIE CUT: 1X TO 2.5X BASE CARD HI		

1994-95 SP Championship Future Playoff Heroes

Randomly inserted at a rate of 1 in every 40 packs, this 10-card standard-size set spotlights up-and-coming NBA stars who figure to be Playoff Heroes in the coming years. Unlike, the glossy regular issue cards, these inserts feature a throwback design element incorporating basic cardboard-style backgrounds against glossy color player action photos. The set is sequenced in alphabetical order.

COMPLETE SET (10)	15.00	40.00
*DIE CUTS: 2.5X TO 6X HI COLUMN		
DIE CUTS: STATED ODDS 1:300		
F1 Brian Grant	1.25	3.00
F2 Anfernee Hardaway	2.50	6.00
F3 Grant Hill	4.00	10.00
F4 Eddie Jones	2.50	6.00
F5 Jamal Mashburn	1.50	4.00
F6 Shaquille O'Neal	4.00	10.00
F7 Isaiah Rider	1.50	4.00
F8 Glenn Robinson	1.50	4.00
F9 Latrell Sprewell	2.00	5.00
F10 Chris Webber	2.50	6.00

1994-95 SP Championship Playoff Heroes

Randomly inserted at a rate of one in every 15 packs, this 10-card standard size set features active NBA Playoff performers. Unlike, the glossy regular issue cards, these inserts feature a throwback design element incorporating basic cardboard-style backgrounds against glossy color player action photos. A number of cards slipped through production with scuffed logos on front. In addition, some others also had "Future Playoff Heroes" logos rather than the regular "Playoff Heroes" logos. None of these variations trade for a premium. The set is sequenced in alphabetical order.

COMPLETE SET (10)	15.00	40.00
*DIE CUTS: 2X TO 5X HI COLUMN		
DIE CUTS: STATED ODDS 1:225		
P1 Charles Barkley	1.50	4.00
P2 Michael Jordan	12.00	30.00
P3 Shawn Kemp	1.00	2.50
P4 Moses Malone	1.00	2.50
P5 Reggie Miller	1.25	3.00
P6 Alonzo Mourning	1.25	3.00
P7 Dikembe Mutombo	1.00	2.50
P8 Hakeem Olajuwon	1.25	3.00
P9 Robert Parish	1.00	2.50
P10 John Stockton	1.25	3.00

1995-96 SP Championship

The 1995-96 SP Championship set was issued in one series totaling 146 cards. The 6-card packs retailed for $2.99 each. The set, issued in early-May, 1996 to retail outlets only, features full color action shots against an all-foil background with player name, team and a head shot along the front borders. The set is sequenced in alphabetical order by team and includes many of the top stars in the 1996 playoffs along with a special subset: Race for the Playoffs (118-146). Rookie Cards of note include Michael Finley, Kevin Garnett, Antonio McDyess, Jerry Stackhouse and Damon Stoudamire.

COMPLETE SET (146)	15.00	40.00
1 Stacey Augmon	.20	.50
2 Mookie Blaylock	.15	.40
3 Alan Henderson RC	.25	.60
4 Steve Smith	.20	.50
5 Dana Barros	.15	.40
6 Dee Brown	.15	.40
7 Eric Montross	.15	.40
8 Dino Radja	.20	.50
9 Eric Williams RC	.25	.60
10 Kenny Anderson	.20	.50
11 Larry Johnson	.25	.60
12 Glen Rice	.25	.60
13 George Zidek RC	.25	.60
14 Toni Kukoc	.25	.60
15 Scottie Pippen	.40	1.00
16 Dennis Rodman	.50	1.25
17 Michael Jordan	2.00	5.00
18 Terrell Brandon	.15	.40
19 Danny Ferry	.15	.40
20 Chris Mills	.15	.40
21 Bobby Phills	.15	.40
22 Jim Jackson	.15	.40
23 Popeye Jones	.15	.40
24 Jason Kidd	.40	1.00
25 Jamal Mashburn	.25	.60
26 Mahmoud Abdul-Rauf	.15	.40
27 Dale Ellis	.15	.40
28 Antonio McDyess RC	.60	1.50
29 Dikembe Mutombo	.25	.60
30 Joe Dumars	.25	.60
31 Grant Hill	.40	1.00
32 Allan Houston	.20	.50
33 Otis Thorpe	.15	.40
34 Tim Hardaway	.25	.60
35 Chris Mullin	.25	.60
36 Latrell Sprewell	.25	.60
37 Joe Smith RC	.50	1.25
38 Sam Cassell	.25	.60
39 Clyde Drexler	.30	.75
40 Robert Horry	.20	.50
41 Hakeem Olajuwon	.30	.75
42 Dale Davis	.15	.40
43 Derrick McKey	.15	.40
44 Reggie Miller	.30	.75
45 Rik Smits	.20	.50
46 Brent Barry RC	.40	1.00
47 Lamond Murray	.15	.40
48 Loy Vaught	.15	.40
49 Brian Williams	.15	.40
50 Cedric Ceballos	.15	.40
51 Magic Johnson	.60	1.50
52 Eddie Jones	.30	.75
53 Nick Van Exel	.25	.60
54 Sasha Danilovic RC	.25	.60
55 Alonzo Mourning	.30	.75
56 Billy Owens	.15	.40
57 Kevin Willis	.15	.40
58 Vin Baker	.20	.50
59 Sherman Douglas	.15	.40
60 Lee Mayberry	.15	.40
61 Glenn Robinson	.25	.60
62 Kevin Garnett RC	2.50	6.00
63 Tom Gugliotta	.15	.40
64 Christian Laettner	.20	.50
65 Isaiah Rider	.25	.60
66 Chris Childs	.15	.40
67 Kendall Gill	.15	.40
68 Armon Gilliam	.15	.40
69 Ed O'Bannon RC	.25	.60
70 Patrick Ewing	.30	.75
71 Derek Harper	.20	.50
72 Charles Oakley	.20	.50
73 John Starks	.20	.50
74 Horace Grant	.20	.50
75 Anfernee Hardaway	.40	1.00
76 Shaquille O'Neal	.60	1.50
77 Dennis Scott	.15	.40
78 Derrick Coleman	.20	.50
79 Trevor Ruffin	.15	.40
80 Jerry Stackhouse RC	.75	2.00
81 Clarence Weatherspoon	.15	.40
82 Charles Barkley	.40	1.00
83 Michael Finley RC	.75	2.00
84 Kevin Johnson	.25	.60
85 Danny Manning	.20	.50
86 Randolph Childress RC	.25	.60
87 Clifford Robinson	.15	.40
88 Arvydas Sabonis RC	.50	1.25
89 Rod Strickland	.15	.40
90 Tyus Edney RC	.25	.60
91 Brian Grant	.20	.50
92 Mitch Richmond	.25	.60
93 Walt Williams	.15	.40
94 Sean Elliott	.25	.60
95 Avery Johnson	.20	.50
96 Chuck Person	.20	.50
97 David Robinson	.40	1.00
98 Shawn Kemp	.25	.60
99 Gary Payton	.25	.60
100 Sam Perkins	.15	.40
101 Detlef Schrempf	.25	.60
102 Ed Pinckney	.15	.40
103 Tracy Murray	.15	.40
104 Alvin Robertson	.15	.40
105 Damon Stoudamire RC	.60	1.50
106 Jeff Hornacek	.20	.50
107 Karl Malone	.30	.75
108 Chris Morris	.15	.40
109 John Stockton	.30	.75
110 Greg Anthony	.15	.40
111 Blue Edwards	.15	.40
112 Bryant Reeves RC	.25	.60
113 Byron Scott	.20	.50
114 Juwan Howard	.25	.60
115 Gheorghe Muresan	.15	.40
116 Rasheed Wallace RC	.75	2.00
117 Chris Webber	.30	.75
118 Mookie Blaylock RP	.15	.40
119 Dana Barros RP	.15	.40
120 Larry Johnson RP	.25	.60
121 Michael Jordan RP	2.00	5.00
122 Terrell Brandon RP	.15	.40
123 Jason Kidd RP	.40	1.00
124 Mahmoud Abdul-Rauf RP	.15	.40
125 Grant Hill RP	.40	1.00
126 Latrell Sprewell RP	.25	.60
127 Hakeem Olajuwon RP	.30	.75
128 Reggie Miller RP	.30	.75
129 Loy Vaught RP	.15	.40
130 Magic Johnson RP	.60	1.50
131 Alonzo Mourning RP	.30	.75
132 Vin Baker RP	.20	.50
133 Tom Gugliotta RP	.15	.40
134 Ed O'Bannon RP	.25	.60
135 Patrick Ewing RP	.30	.75
136 Anfernee Hardaway RP	.40	1.00
137 Jerry Stackhouse RP	.50	1.25
138 Charles Barkley RP	.40	1.00
139 Clifford Robinson RP	.15	.40
140 Mitch Richmond RP	.25	.60
141 David Robinson RP	.40	1.00
142 Shawn Kemp RP	.25	.60
143 Damon Stoudamire RP	.40	1.00
144 John Stockton RP	.30	.75
145 Bryant Reeves RP	.15	.40
146 Juwan Howard RP	.25	.60

1995-96 SP Championship Champions of the Court

Randomly inserted in packs at a rate of one in 6, cards from this 30-card set feature one top star from each NBA team and an additional card of Michael Jordan. In this special horizontal design, there is one action color photo on the left side and the same action photo in black and white on the right side. The main feature of the card is a cel photo featuring a headshot with a protective film covering the cell photo on the front of the card. When you turn the card over you see the same photo of the player. Each card is printed on special transparent chromium material. Unpeeled cards are priced below. Peeled cards are valued at about ten to twenty-five percent less.

COMPLETE SET (30)	50.00	100.00
*DIE CUTS: 2X TO 5X HI COLUMN		
DIE CUTS: STATED ODDS 1:75		
C1 Steve Smith	1.00	2.50
C2 Dino Radja	1.00	2.50
C3 Glen Rice	1.25	3.00
C4 Scottie Pippen	2.00	5.00
C5 Terrell Brandon	.75	2.00
C6 Jason Kidd	2.00	5.00
C7 Dikembe Mutombo	1.25	3.00
C8 Grant Hill	2.00	5.00
C9 Joe Smith	1.25	3.00
C10 Hakeem Olajuwon	1.50	4.00
C11 Reggie Miller	1.50	4.00
C12 Loy Vaught	.75	2.00
C13 Magic Johnson	3.00	8.00
C14 Alonzo Mourning	1.50	4.00
C15 Vin Baker	1.00	2.50
C16 Kevin Garnett	5.00	12.00
C17 Ed O'Bannon	.60	1.50
C18 Patrick Ewing	1.50	4.00
C19 Shaquille O'Neal	3.00	8.00
C20 Jerry Stackhouse	2.00	5.00
C21 Charles Barkley	2.00	5.00
C22 Clifford Robinson	.75	2.00
C23 Mitch Richmond	1.25	3.00
C24 David Robinson	2.00	5.00
C25 Shawn Kemp	1.25	3.00
C26 Damon Stoudamire	1.50	4.00
C27 John Stockton	1.50	4.00
C28 Bryant Reeves	.60	1.50
C29 Juwan Howard	1.25	3.00
C30 Michael Jordan	10.00	25.00

1995-96 SP Championship Championship Shots

Inserted at a rate of one per magazine and Wal-Mart pack, as well as randomly in one in every three regular retail packs, this 20-card set features intense, closeup shots of many of the top NBA stars. Despite their status as inserts, these cards are actually easier to pull from packs than regular-issue cards. The design is highlighted by a horizontal, silver-foil, saw-tooth die cut element on the side border.

COMPLETE SET (20)	10.00	20.00
*GOLD: 3X TO 8X HI COLUMN		
GOLD: STATED ODDS 1:62		
S1 Antonio McDyess	.60	1.50
S2 Nick Van Exel	.50	1.25
S3 Michael Finley	.75	2.00
S4 Anfernee Hardaway	.75	2.00
S5 Latrell Sprewell	.50	1.25
S6 Brian Grant	.40	1.00
S7 Juwan Howard	.50	1.25
S8 Ed O'Bannon	.25	.60
S9 Kevin Garnett	2.00	5.00
S10 Charles Barkley	.75	2.00
S11 Joe Smith	.50	1.25
S12 Patrick Ewing	.60	1.50
S13 Brent Barry	.40	1.00
S14 Dennis Rodman	1.00	2.50
S15 Jerry Stackhouse	.75	2.00
S16 Michael Jordan	4.00	10.00
S17 Jalen Rose	.60	1.50
S18 Jamal Mashburn	.50	1.25
S19 Theo Ratliff	.40	1.00
S20 Shaquille O'Neal	1.25	3.00

1995-96 SP Championship Jordan Collection

Randomly inserted in packs at a rate of one in 29, this 4-card set completes the run of Jordan cards across Upper Deck's 1995-96 brands.

COMPLETE SET (4)	12.00	30.00
COMMON CARD (JC21-JC24)	4.00	10.00

2000-01 SP Game Floor

The 2000-01 SP Game Floor product was released in May, 2001 and featured a 100-card base set that was broken into tiers as follows: Base Veterans (1-60), and Rookies (61-100) that were serial numbered to 300. Each pack contained three cards, and carried a suggested retail price of $19.99 per pack.

1 Jason Terry	1.00	2.50
2 Toni Kukoc	.75	2.00
3 Antoine Walker	.75	2.00
4 Paul Pierce	1.25	3.00
5 Jamal Mashburn	.75	2.00
6 Baron Davis	1.00	2.50
7 Elton Brand	1.00	2.50
8 Ron Mercer	.60	1.50
9 Andre Miller	.75	2.00
10 Lamond Murray	.60	1.50
11 Michael Finley	1.00	2.50
12 Dirk Nowitzki	1.50	4.00
13 Antonio McDyess	.75	2.00
14 Nick Van Exel	.75	2.00
15 Jerry Stackhouse	.75	2.00
16 Joe Smith	.75	2.00
17 Antawn Jamison	1.00	2.50
18 Larry Hughes	.75	2.00
19 Steve Francis	1.00	2.50
20 Maurice Taylor	.60	1.50
21 Jalen Rose	.75	2.00
22 Reggie Miller	1.00	2.50
23 Lamar Odom	1.00	2.50
24 Corey Maggette	.75	2.00
25 Kobe Bryant	5.00	12.00
26 Shaquille O'Neal	2.50	6.00
27 Horace Grant	.75	2.00
28 Eddie Jones	1.00	2.50
29 Tim Hardaway	1.00	2.50
30 Glenn Robinson	.75	2.00
31 Ray Allen	1.00	2.50
32 Kevin Garnett	2.00	5.00
33 Terrell Brandon	.60	1.50
34 Wally Szczerbiak	.75	2.00
35 Stephon Marbury	.75	2.00
36 Keith Van Horn	.75	2.00
37 Latrell Sprewell	.75	2.00
38 Allan Houston	.75	2.00
39 Tracy McGrady	1.50	4.00
40 Darrell Armstrong	.60	1.50
41 Allen Iverson	2.00	5.00
42 Dikembe Mutombo	1.00	2.50
43 Jason Kidd	1.50	4.00
44 Shawn Marion	1.00	2.50
45 Rasheed Wallace	1.00	2.50
46 Damon Stoudamire	.75	2.00
47 Chris Webber	1.00	2.50
48 Jason Williams	1.00	2.50
49 Tim Duncan	2.00	5.00
50 David Robinson	1.50	4.00
51 Gary Payton	1.00	2.50
52 Rashard Lewis	1.00	2.50
53 Vince Carter	2.00	5.00
54 Charles Oakley	.75	2.00
55 Karl Malone	1.25	3.00
56 John Stockton	1.25	3.00
57 Shareef Abdur-Rahim	.75	2.00
58 Mike Bibby	1.00	2.50
59 Richard Hamilton	.75	2.00
60 Mitch Richmond	.75	2.00
61 Kenyon Martin RC	6.00	15.00
62 Marc Jackson RC	2.50	6.00
63 Darius Miles RC	2.50	6.00
64 Morris Peterson RC	2.50	6.00
65 Mike Miller RC	5.00	12.00
66 Quentin Richardson RC	4.00	10.00
67 DerMarr Johnson RC	2.50	6.00
68 Chris Mihm RC	2.50	6.00
69 Jamal Crawford RC	4.00	10.00
70 Joel Przybilla RC	2.50	6.00
71 Keyon Dooling RC	2.50	6.00
72 Jerome Moiso RC	2.50	6.00
73 Mike Penberthy RC	2.50	6.00
74 Courtney Alexander RC	2.50	6.00
75 Mateen Cleaves RC	2.50	6.00
76 Wang Zhizhi RC	6.00	15.00
77 Hedo Turkoglu RC	5.00	12.00
78 Desmond Mason RC	3.00	8.00
79 Marcus Fizer RC	2.50	6.00
80 Jamaal Magloire RC	2.50	6.00
81 Stromile Swift RC	2.50	6.00
82 DeShawn Stevenson RC	3.00	8.00
83 Stephen Jackson RC	4.00	10.00
84 Erick Barkley RC	2.50	6.00
85 Mark Madsen RC	2.50	6.00
86 Dan Langhi RC	2.50	6.00
87 Hanno Mottola RC	2.50	6.00
88 Paul McPherson RC	2.50	6.00
89 Eddie House RC	2.50	6.00
90 Chris Porter RC	2.50	6.00
91 Jason Collier RC	2.50	6.00
92 Speedy Claxton RC	2.50	6.00
93 Ruben Wolkowyski RC	2.50	6.00
94 A.J. Guyton RC	2.50	6.00
95 Donnell Harvey RC	2.50	6.00
96 Ira Newble RC	2.50	6.00
97 Lee Nailon	2.50	6.00
98 Pepe Sanchez RC	2.50	6.00
99 Eduardo Najera RC	2.50	6.00
100 David Vanterpool RC	2.50	6.00

2000-01 SP Game Floor Authentic Fabric/Floor Combos

Randomly inserted into packs at one in 10, this 14-card insert features a swatch of both game-used jersey and floor. Card backs carry the player's initials followed by the letter "C". A gold version sequentially numbered to 25 was also issued.

*GOLD: 2.5X TO 6X HI		
AIC Allen Iverson	6.00	15.00
DMC Darius Miles	3.00	8.00
JKC Jason Kidd	5.00	12.00
JMC Jamal Mashburn	2.50	6.00
KAC Karl Malone	4.00	10.00
KBC Kobe Bryant	15.00	40.00
KGC Kevin Garnett	6.00	15.00
MAC Marc Jackson	3.00	8.00
MDC Antonio McDyess	2.50	6.00
PPC Paul Pierce	4.00	10.00
RLC Rashard Lewis	3.00	8.00
SMC Stephon Marbury	2.50	6.00
SOC Shaquille O'Neal	8.00	20.00
TMC Tracy McGrady	5.00	12.00

2000-01 SP Game Floor Authentic Floor

Randomly inserted into packs at one per pack, this 60-card insert features a swatch of actual game-used floor. Card backs carry the player's initials as numbering.

AH Allan Houston AS	2.00	5.00
AH2 Allan Houston	2.00	5.00
AI Allen Iverson	5.00	12.00
AM Andre Miller	2.00	5.00
BD Baron Davis	2.50	6.00
CA Courtney Alexander	2.50	6.00
CP Chris Porter	2.50	6.00
CW Chris Webber	2.50	6.00
DE Desmond Mason	3.00	8.00
DJ DerMarr Johnson	2.50	6.00
DM Darius Miles	2.50	6.00
DS DeShawn Stevenson	3.00	8.00
DV David Robinson	4.00	10.00
EJ Eddie Jones	2.50	6.00
FI Marcus Fizer	2.50	6.00
GP Gary Payton	2.50	6.00
GR Glenn Robinson	2.00	5.00
JK Jason Kidd	4.00	10.00
JM Jamaal Magloire	2.50	6.00
JP Joel Przybilla	2.50	6.00
JS Jerry Stackhouse	2.00	5.00
JT Jason Terry	2.50	6.00
JW Jason Williams	2.50	6.00
KA Karl Malone	3.00	8.00
KB Kobe Bryant AS	8.00	20.00
KB2 Kobe Bryant	8.00	20.00
KE Khalid El-Amin	2.50	6.00
KG Kevin Garnett AS	5.00	12.00
KG2 Kevin Garnett	5.00	12.00
KM Kenyon Martin	6.00	15.00
LS Latrell Sprewell AS	2.00	5.00
LS2 Latrell Sprewell	2.00	5.00
MA Marc Jackson	2.50	6.00
MC Mateen Cleaves	2.50	6.00
MD Antonio McDyess AS	2.00	5.00
MD2 Antonio McDyess	2.00	5.00
MF Michael Finley	2.50	6.00
MJ Michael Jordan	20.00	50.00
MM Mike Miller	5.00	12.00
MP Morris Peterson	2.50	6.00
MT Dikembe Mutombo	2.50	6.00
PP Paul Pierce	3.00	8.00
PS Peja Stojakovic	2.50	6.00
QR Quentin Richardson	4.00	10.00
RA Ray Allen	2.50	6.00
RA2 Ray Allen AS	2.50	6.00
RL Rashard Lewis	2.50	6.00
RW Rasheed Wallace AS	2.50	6.00
RW2 Rasheed Wallace	2.50	6.00
SA Shareef Abdur-Rahim	2.00	5.00
SF Steve Francis	2.50	6.00
SH Shawn Marion	2.50	6.00
SJ Stephen Jackson	4.00	10.00
SM Stephon Marbury AS	2.00	5.00
SM2 Stephon Marbury	2.00	5.00
SO Shaquille O'Neal	6.00	15.00
SP Scottie Pippen	4.00	10.00
SS Stromile Swift	2.50	6.00
TM Tracy McGrady	4.00	10.00
WS Wally Szczerbiak	2.00	5.00

2000-01 SP Game Floor Authentic Floor Autographs

Randomly inserted into packs, this 17-card insert features a swatch of actual game-used floor plus an authentic autograph from the depicted player. Card backs carry the player's initials followed by the letter "A" as numbering. Please note that there were only 200 of each of these cards produced (with exception to Bryant, Jordan, and Garnett).

CAA Courtney Alexander/200	5.00	12.00
DJA DerMarr Johnson/200	5.00	12.00
DMA Darius Miles/200	5.00	12.00
DSA DeShawn Stevenson/200	6.00	15.00
FIA Marcus Fizer/200	5.00	12.00
JPA Joel Przybilla/200	5.00	12.00
JSA Jerry Stackhouse/200	8.00	20.00
KGA Kevin Garnett/21	150.00	300.00
KMA Kenyon Martin/200	12.00	30.00
MAA Marc Jackson/200	5.00	12.00
MJA Michael Jordan/23	400.00	800.00
MMA Mike Miller/200	10.00	25.00
MPA Morris Peterson/200	5.00	12.00
SFA Steve Francis/200	8.00	20.00
SJA Stephen Jackson/200	8.00	20.00
SSA Stromile Swift/200	5.00	12.00

2000-01 SP Game Floor Authentic Floor Combos

Randomly inserted into packs at one in ten, this 30-card insert features two swatches of game-used floor. Card backs carry a "C" prefix. A gold version sequentially numbered to 100 was also issued.

*GOLD: .75X TO 2X BASE COMBO HI		
C1 Allen Iverson	10.00	25.00
Shaquille O'Neal		
C2 Marc Jackson	4.00	10.00
Stephen Jackson		
C3 Stephon Marbury	5.00	12.00
Steve Francis		
C4 Chris Webber	5.00	12.00
Jason Williams		
C5 Darius Miles	4.00	10.00
Marc Jackson		
C6 Michael Jordan	60.00	120.00
Larry Bird		
C7 Kenyon Martin	5.00	12.00
Chris Webber		
C8 Kenyon Martin	4.00	10.00
DerMarr Johnson		
C9 Kenyon Martin	4.00	10.00
Marc Jackson		
C10 Kenyon Martin	4.00	10.00
Stephen Jackson		
C11 Kevin Garnett	6.00	15.00
Chris Webber		
C12 Kevin Garnett	6.00	15.00
Tracy McGrady		
C13 Kobe Bryant	10.00	25.00
Allen Iverson		

C14 Kobe Bryant 10.00 25.00
Chris Webber
C15 Kobe Bryant 6.00 15.00
Darius Miles
C16 Kobe Bryant 10.00 25.00
Jason Kidd
C17 Michael Jordan 30.00 80.00
Karl Malone
C18 Karl Malone 25.00 60.00
John Stockton
C19 Kobe Bryant 8.00 20.00
Kenyon Martin
C20 Kobe Bryant 10.00 25.00
Kevin Garnett
C21 Kobe Bryant 10.00 25.00
Kevin Garnett
C22 Kobe Bryant 50.00 100.00
Larry Bird
C23 Jason Williams 5.00 12.00
Peja Stojakovic
C24 Kobe Bryant 50.00 120.00
Michael Jordan
C25 Kobe Bryant 15.00 40.00
Shaquille O'Neal
C26 Kobe Bryant 8.00 20.00
Steve Francis
C27 Kobe Bryant 8.00 20.00
Tracy McGrady
C28 Jason Kidd 5.00 12.00
Shawn Marion
C29 Mateen Cleaves 4.00 10.00
Morris Peterson
C30 Kevin Garnett 5.00 12.00
Rasheed Wallace

2002-03 SP Game Used

Released in September 2002, SP Game Used boasts a 144-card set with several different components. Card numbers 1-102 feature veteran players and place full color action photos agains a white and blue or gray background on the side of the card where the player picture is. Several jersey cards are mixed in with these 102 cards. Jersey cards are denoted by "JSY" in the price guide. Overall odds point to at least one Jersey and or Autographed card per pack. Rookie cards share most design aspects except the blue or gray background is centered with two blocks of color on either side set to match the featured player's team colors. All rookie cards are sequentially numbered to 900. SP Game Used was packaged in six pack boxes where packs contained three cards and carried a suggested retail price of $29.99.

1 Shareef Abdur-Rahim JSY 2.50 6.00
2 DerMarr Johnson JSY 2.00 5.00
3 Jason Terry JSY 2.50 6.00
4 Antoine Walker JSY 2.50 6.00
5 Paul Pierce SP JSY 12.50 30.00
6 Kedrick Brown JSY 2.00 5.00
7 Tony Battie 1.25 3.00
8 Jamal Mashburn JSY 2.50 6.00
9 Baron Davis 2.00 5.00
10 David Wesley 1.25 3.00
11 Jalen Rose 1.50 4.00
12 Eddy Curry JSY 2.50 6.00
13 Tyson Chandler JSY 2.50 6.00
14 Marcus Fizer JSY 2.00 5.00
15 Lamond Murray 1.25 3.00
16 Andre Miller JSY 2.50 6.00
17 Chris Mihm JSY 2.00 5.00
18 Ricky Davis 1.50 4.00
19 Dirk Nowitzki 3.00 8.00
20 Michael Finley 2.00 5.00
21 Steve Nash 2.50 6.00
22 Nick Van Exel 1.50 4.00
23 Antonio McDyess JSY 2.50 6.00
24 Juwan Howard 1.50 4.00
25 James Posey 1.25 3.00
26 Jerry Stackhouse 1.50 4.00
27 Clifford Robinson 1.25 3.00
28 Ben Wallace 2.00 5.00
29 Antawn Jamison 2.00 5.00
30 Jason Richardson SP JSY 6.00 15.00
31 Gilbert Arenas 2.00 5.00
32 Steve Francis 2.00 5.00
33 Cuttino Mobley 1.50 4.00
34 Eddie Griffin JSY 2.00 5.00
35 Reggie Miller JSY 3.00 8.00
36 Jermaine O'Neal 2.00 5.00
37 Jamaal Tinsley JSY 2.00 5.00
38 Elton Brand 2.00 5.00
39 Darius Miles JSY 2.00 5.00
40 Lamar Odom JSY 3.00 8.00
41 Corey Maggette JSY 2.50 6.00
42 Kobe Bryant SP JSY 20.00 50.00
43 Shaquille O'Neal 5.00 12.00
44 Derek Fisher 1.50 4.00
45 Devean George 1.25 3.00
46 Pau Gasol 2.50 6.00
47 Jason Williams 1.50 4.00
48 Shane Battier 2.00 5.00
49 Stromile Swift 1.25 3.00
50 Alonzo Mourning 2.50 6.00
51 Eddie Jones 1.50 4.00
52 Brian Grant 1.25 3.00
53 Ray Allen 2.00 5.00
54 Glenn Robinson 1.50 4.00
55 Sam Cassell 1.50 4.00
56 Kevin Garnett SP JSY 12.50 30.00
57 Wally Szczerbiak JSY 2.50 6.00
58 Terrell Brandon JSY 2.00 5.00
59 Chauncey Billups JSY 3.00 8.00
60 Jason Kidd SP JSY 12.50 30.00
61 Richard Jefferson 2.00 5.00
62 Kenyon Martin JSY 3.00 8.00
63 Brandon Armstrong JSY 2.00 5.00
64 Keith Van Horn 1.50 4.00
65 Allan Houston 1.50 4.00
66 Latrell Sprewell 1.50 4.00
67 Kurt Thomas 1.25 3.00
68 Tracy McGrady 3.00 8.00
69 Mike Miller JSY 3.00 8.00
70 Darrell Armstrong JSY 2.00 5.00
71 Allen Iverson JSY 5.00 12.00
72 Dikembe Mutombo JSY 3.00 8.00
73 Aaron McKie 1.25 3.00
74 Stephon Marbury 1.50 4.00
75 Shawn Marion 2.00 5.00
76 Joe Johnson JSY 3.00 8.00
77 Anfernee Hardaway 3.00 8.00
78 Rasheed Wallace 2.00 5.00
79 Damon Stoudamire 1.50 4.00
80 Scottie Pippen 3.00 8.00
81 Chris Webber 2.00 5.00
82 Peja Stojakovic 2.00 5.00
83 Mike Bibby JSY 3.00 8.00
84 Gerald Wallace JSY 3.00 8.00
85 Tim Duncan 4.00 10.00
86 David Robinson 3.00 8.00
87 Tony Parker JSY 4.00 10.00
88 Gary Payton 2.00 5.00
89 Rashard Lewis 2.00 5.00
90 Desmond Mason 1.50 4.00
91 Vladimir Radmanovic JSY 2.00 5.00
92 Morris Peterson 1.25 3.00
93 Antonio Davis 1.25 3.00
94 Vince Carter 3.00 8.00
95 Karl Malone 2.50 6.00
96 John Stockton JSY 4.00 10.00
97 Donyell Marshall 1.25 3.00
98 Andrei Kirilenko 2.00 5.00
99 Richard Hamilton 1.50 4.00
100 Michael Jordan SP JSY 60.00 150.00
101 Courtney Alexander JSY 2.00 5.00
102 Kwame Brown JSY 2.00 5.00
103 Jay Williams RC 5.00 12.00
104 Yao Ming RC 12.00 30.00
105 Drew Gooden RC 6.00 15.00
106 DaJuan Wagner RC 4.00 10.00
107 Curtis Borchardt RC 4.00 10.00
108 Amare Stoudemire RC 10.00 25.00
109 Caron Butler RC 6.00 15.00
110 Jared Jeffries RC 4.00 10.00
111 Chris Wilcox RC 4.00 10.00
112 Qyntel Woods RC 4.00 10.00
113 Casey Jacobsen RC 4.00 10.00
114 Melvin Ely RC 4.00 10.00
115 Kareem Rush RC 4.00 10.00
116 Mike Dunleavy RC 5.00 12.00
117 Dan Dickau RC 4.00 10.00
118 Juan Dixon RC 5.00 12.00
119 Sam Clancy RC 4.00 10.00
120 Tayshaun Prince RC 5.00 12.00
121 Dan Gadzuric RC 4.00 10.00
122 Chris Jefferies RC 4.00 10.00
123 Steve Logan RC 4.00 10.00
124 Vincent Yarbrough RC 4.00 10.00
125 Fred Jones RC 4.00 10.00
126 Efthimios Rentzias RC 4.00 10.00
127 Nene Hilario RC 5.00 12.00
128 Rod Grizzard RC 4.00 10.00
129 Matt Barnes RC 5.00 12.00
130 Nikoloz Tskitishvili RC 4.00 10.00
131 Bostjan Nachbar RC 4.00 10.00
132 Marcus Haislip RC 4.00 10.00
133 Jamal Sampson RC 4.00 10.00
134 Frank Williams RC 4.00 10.00
135 Tito Maddox RC 4.00 10.00
136 Carlos Boozer RC 8.00 20.00
137 Jiri Welsch RC 4.00 10.00
138 John Salmons RC 5.00 12.00
139 Predrag Savovic RC 4.00 10.00
140 Marko Jaric 4.00 10.00
141 Robert Archibald RC 4.00 10.00
142 Manu Ginobili RC 10.00 25.00
143 Chris Owens RC 4.00 10.00
144 Ryan Humphrey RC 4.00 10.00

2002-03 SP Game Used Autographed Jerseys

Randomly inserted in packs, this 24-card set parallels the base SP Game Used set design enhanced with a square swatch of game jersey somewhere on the bottom quarter of the card and authentic player autographs. Each card is sequentially numbered to 100.

1 Shareef Abdur-Rahim 8.00 20.00
2 DerMarr Johnson 8.00 20.00
4 Antoine Walker 10.00 25.00
6 Kedrick Brown 8.00 20.00
12 Eddy Curry 8.00 20.00
13 Tyson Chandler 10.00 25.00
14 Marcus Fizer 8.00 20.00
16 Andre Miller 10.00 25.00
34 Eddie Griffin 8.00 20.00
39 Darius Miles 10.00 25.00
40 Lamar Odom 12.50 30.00
41 Corey Maggette 8.00 20.00
57 Wally Szczerbiak 10.00 25.00
58 Terrell Brandon 10.00 25.00
61 Richard Jefferson 10.00 25.00
62 Kenyon Martin 15.00 40.00
63 Brandon Armstrong 8.00 20.00
69 Mike Miller 12.50 30.00
84 Gerald Wallace 12.50 30.00
87 Tony Parker 15.00 40.00
91 Vladimir Radmanovic 8.00 20.00
101 Courtney Alexander 8.00 20.00
102 Kwame Brown 10.00 25.00

2002-03 SP Game Used Autographed SP Jerseys

Randomly inserted in packs, this six card set features full-color player photography set against a peach and white background. The letters "SP" appear on the bottom third of the card with a half diamond shaped jersey starting on the edge of the S from SP. Every card is autographed and sequentially numbered to 25.

42 Kobe Bryant 200.00 400.00
56 Kevin Garnett 75.00 200.00
60 Jason Kidd 40.00 100.00
100 Michael Jordan 500.00 800.00

2002-03 SP Game Used Rookies Gold

Randomly inserted in packs, this 42-card set parallels the base SP Game Used set enhanced with gold backgrounds and gold SP Game Used logos. Each card is sequentially numbered to 50.

*GOLD: 1.25X TO 3X BASE CARD HI

2002-03 SP Game Used All-Star Apparel

Randomly inserted in packs at the combined odds of one in one for all jersey and autograph sets, this 24-card set places a small portrait style photograph in the upper right hand corner tinted in a color to match the player's team below which is a square swatch of game worn jersey on a silver/blue background.

*GOLD: .75X TO 2X HI
GOLD: STATED PRINT RUN 100 SETS

AKAS Andrei Kirilenko 3.00 8.00
AMAS Alonzo Mourning 4.00 10.00
BHAS Brendan Haywood 2.00 5.00
CMAS Chris Mihm 2.00 5.00
DMAS Desmond Mason 2.50 6.00
DNAS Dirk Nowitzki 5.00 12.00
GIAS Gilbert Arenas 3.00 8.00
GPAS Gary Payton 3.00 8.00
GWAS Gerald Wallace 3.00 8.00
KBAS Kobe Bryant 15.00 40.00
KDAS Jason Kidd 5.00 12.00
KMAS Kenyon Martin 3.00 8.00
LNAS Lee Nailon 2.00 5.00
MFAS Marcus Fizer 2.00 5.00
MGAS Magic Johnson 10.00 25.00
MJAS Michael Jordan 40.00 100.00
MMAS Mike Miller 3.00 8.00
PGAS Pau Gasol 4.00 10.00
QRAS Quentin Richardson 2.50 6.00
SFAS Steve Francis 3.00 8.00
SNAS Steve Nash 4.00 10.00
SSAS Steve Smith 2.50 6.00
WSAS Wally Szczerbiak 2.50 6.00
ZRAS Zelijko Rebraca 2.00 5.00

2002-03 SP Game Used Authentic Fabrics Dual

Randomly inserted in packs, this 28-card set showcases two players with small full color photos centered at the top and two small swatchs of game used memorabilia along the bottom. Each card is sequentially numbered to 100.

UNPRICED QUAD PRINT RUN 10 SETS
UNPRICED DUAL AU PRINT RUN 10 SETS

AMCMJ Andre Miller 6.00 15.00
Chris Mihm
BDJMJ Baron Davis 6.00 15.00
Jamal Mashburn
CMLOJ Corey Maggette 6.00 15.00
Lamar Odom
CWPSJ Chris Webber 10.00 25.00
Peja Stojakovic
DNMFJ Dirk Nowitzki 15.00 40.00
Michael Finley
DNSNJ Dirk Nowitzki 15.00 40.00
Steve Nash
DRTPJ David Robinson 20.00 50.00
Tony Parker
EBKMJ Elton Brand 12.50 30.00
Karl Malone
ECTCJ Eddy Curry 6.00 15.00
Tyson Chandler
JPJHJ James Posey 6.00 15.00
Juwan Howard
JTTPJ Jamaal Tinsley 10.00 25.00
Tony Parker
KBAIJ Kobe Bryant 30.00 80.00
Allen Iverson
KBKGJ Kobe Bryant 25.00 60.00
Kevin Garnett
KGTBJ Kevin Garnett 8.00 20.00
Terrell Brandon
KGWSJ Kevin Garnett 8.00 20.00
Wally Szczerbiak
KMJSJ Karl Malone 20.00 50.00
John Stockton
KMKVJ Kenyon Martin 6.00 15.00
Keith Van Horn
KWCAJ Kwame Brown 6.00 15.00
Courtney Alexander
MFTHJ Marcus Fizer 6.00 15.00
Trenton Hassell
MJKBJ Michael Jordan 60.00 150.00
Kobe Bryant
MJMGJ Michael Jordan 60.00 150.00
Magic Johnson
PPAWJ Paul Pierce 15.00 40.00
Antoine Walker
RAGRJ Ray Allen 12.50 30.00
Glenn Robinson
RMJOJ Reggie Miller 15.00 40.00
Jemaine O'Neal
RWDSJ Rasheed Wallace 12.50 30.00
Damon Stoudamire
SADJJ Shareef Abdur-Rahim 6.00 15.00
DerMarr Johnson
SMSMJ Stephon Marbury 10.00 25.00
Shawn Marion
TMMMJ Tracy McGrady 12.50 30.00
Mike Miller

2002-03 SP Game Used Authentic Fabrics Triple

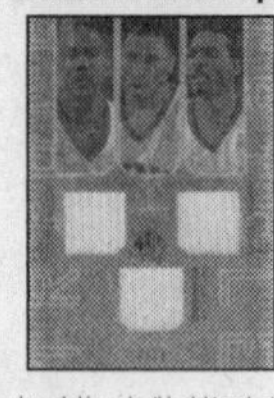

Randomly seeded in packs, this eight card set features three players with three pictures centered along the top of the card and three swatches of game used memorabilia along the bottom. Note: The cards are not numbered numerically on the card backs. They're listed this way to fit in our publications-ie: #1 is actually AW/PP/KA-J and so on. Each card is sequentially numbered to 25.

1 Antoine Walker 30.00 80.00
Paul Pierce
Kenny Anderson
2 Chris Webber 30.00 80.00
Peja Stojakovic
Mike Bibby
3 Jason Terry 20.00 50.00
Shareef Abdur-Rahim
DerMarr Johnson
4 Kobe Bryant 100.00 200.00
Rick Fox
Robert Horry
5 Karl Malone 40.00 100.00
John Stockton
Andrei Kirilenko
6 Antonio McDyess 20.00 50.00
Juwan Howard
James Posey
7 Michael Jordan 100.00 250.00
Kobe Bryant
Kevin Garnett
8 Stephon Marbury 50.00 120.00
Shawn Marion
Anfernee Hardaway

2002-03 SP Game Used Authentic Patches

Inserted in packs, this 18-card set places a blue-tone portrait photo of the featured player on the left side of the card and a multi-color patch swatch in the upper right hand corner. A stripe of color runs from the patch down to the bottom of the card in the showcased team's colors. Each card is sequentially numbered to 100.

UNPRICED TRIPLE PRINT RUN 10 SETS

AWP Antoine Walker 10.00 25.00
BDP Baron Davis 12.00 30.00
CMP Corey Maggette 10.00 25.00
DJP DerMarr Johnson 8.00 20.00
DMP Darius Miles 8.00 20.00
GWP Gerald Wallace 12.00 30.00
JRP Jason Richardson 12.00 30.00
KBP Kobe Bryant 75.00 200.00
KGP Kevin Garnett 40.00 100.00
KWP Kwame Brown 8.00 20.00
LSP Latrell Sprewell 15.00 40.00
MJP Michael Jordan 125.00 300.00
PPP Paul Pierce 15.00 40.00
QRP Quentin Richardson 10.00 25.00
SAP Shareef Abdur-Rahim 10.00 25.00
TBP Terrell Brandon 8.00 20.00
TPP Tony Parker 15.00 40.00
WSP Wally Szczerbiak 10.00 25.00

2002-03 SP Game Used Autographed Authentic Patches

Randomly inserted in packs, this 15-card set parallels the design of the base Authentic Patches insert enhanced with authentic player autographs and sequential numbering to 50.

UNPRICED DUAL PRINT RUN 5 SETS

AWAP Antoine Walker 30.00 80.00
CMAP Corey Maggette 15.00 40.00
DJAP DerMarr Johnson 15.00 40.00
DMAP Darius Miles 15.00 40.00
GWAP Gerald Wallace 30.00 80.00
KBAP Kobe Bryant 400.00 800.00
KGAP Kevin Garnett 125.00 250.00
KWAP Kwame Brown 15.00 40.00
MJAP Michael Jordan 600.00 1200.00
PPAP Paul Pierce 40.00 100.00
QRAP Quentin Richardson 15.00 40.00
TBAP Terrell Brandon 15.00 40.00
TPAP Tony Parker 30.00 80.00
WSAP Wally Szczerbiak 15.00 40.00

2002-03 SP Game Used Dual Authentic Patches

Randomly seeded in packs, this six card set features a horizontal card design with a patch swatch in the upper left hand corner and lower right hand corner next to which is a streached black and gray-scale portrait of each player. Cards are sequentially numbered to 25.

KBJKP Kobe Bryant 100.00 250.00
Jason Kidd
KBJRP Kobe Bryant 100.00 250.00
Jason Richardson
KBKGP Kobe Bryant 125.00 300.00
Kevin Garnett
KBMGP Kobe Bryant 125.00 300.00
Magic Johnson
MJKBP Michael Jordan 250.00 500.00
Kobe Bryant
MJMGP Michael Jordan 300.00 500.00
Magic Johnson

2002-03 SP Game Used Extra SIGnificance

Randomly inserted in packs, this 10-card set is divided in half with a color photo and autograph of each of the featured players, one on the top and one on the bottom. Each card is sequentially numbered to 25. A Gold version sequentially numbered to 5 was also released.

DMLO Darius Miles 25.00 60.00
Lamar Odom
JKKM Jason Kidd 40.00 100.00
Kenyon Martin
JRJT Jason Richardson 25.00 60.00
Jamaal Tinsley
KBJK Kobe Bryant 200.00 400.00
Jason Kidd
KBJR Kobe Bryant 100.00 250.00
Jason Richardson
KBKG Kobe Bryant 200.00 400.00
Kevin Garnett
KBMA Kobe Bryant 300.00 600.00
Magic Johnson
KGTC Kevin Garnett 40.00 100.00
Tyson Chandler
MJKB Michael Jordan 400.00 800.00
Kobe Bryant
MJMA Michael Jordan 400.00 800.00
Magic Johnson

2002-03 SP Game Used SIGnificance

Randomly seeded in packs, this 29-card set looks very similar to the base SP Game Used cards with the word, SIGnificance in the upper right hand corner and an authentic player autograph in the lower right hand corner. A Gold version sequentially numbered to 50 was also issued.

*GOLD: .75X TO 2X SIGNIFICANCE HI

AW Antoine Walker 6.00 15.00
CM Corey Maggette 4.00 10.00
DJ DerMarr Johnson 4.00 10.00
DS DeShawn Stevenson 4.00 10.00
EG Eddie Griffin 4.00 10.00
HM Hanno Mottola 4.00 10.00
JA Jamaal Magloire 4.00 10.00
JS Jerry Stackhouse 6.00 15.00
JT Jamaal Tinsley 4.00 10.00
KE Kedrick Brown 4.00 10.00
KM Kenyon Martin 6.00 15.00
KW Kwame Brown 4.00 10.00
LH Larry Hughes 4.00 10.00
LM Lamond Murray 4.00 10.00
LW Loren Woods 4.00 10.00
MB Michael Bradley 4.00 10.00
MF Marcus Fizer 4.00 10.00
MK Mark Madsen 4.00 10.00
MM Mike Miller 6.00 15.00
MO Terence Morris 4.00 10.00
MP Morris Peterson 4.00 10.00
QR Quentin Richardson 4.00 10.00
RJ Richard Jefferson 5.00 12.00
RM Ron Mercer 4.00 10.00
RW Rodney White 4.00 10.00
SD Samuel Dalembert 4.00 10.00
TC Tyson Chandler 8.00 20.00
TM Troy Murphy 4.00 10.00
WS Wally Szczerbiak 4.00 10.00

2002-03 SP Game Used Special SIGnificance

Seeded in packs, this 10-card set looks similar to the SIGnificance set with the words, "Special SIGnificance" in a black box in the upper right hand corner with an authentic player autograph in the lower right hand corner. Each card is sequentially numbered to 50. A Gold version sequentially numbered to 10 was also inserted in packs.

AM Andre Miller 10.00 25.00
DM Darius Miles 10.00 25.00
JK Jason Kidd 30.00 80.00
JR Jason Richardson 15.00 40.00
KB Kobe Bryant 150.00 300.00
KG Kevin Garnett 30.00 80.00
LO Lamar Odom 15.00 40.00
MJ Michael Jordan 400.00 800.00
PP Paul Pierce 25.00 60.00
SA Shareef Abdur-Rahim 10.00 25.00
TM Troy Murphy 10.00 25.00

2002-03 SP Game Used UD Rookie Exclusive Autographs

Randomly inserted in packs, this 23-card set places full color player action photography on the left side of the card and a cut authentic player autograph on the right side of the card. Each card is sequentially numbered to 100.

RKAS Amare Stoudemire 75.00 150.00
RKCA Caron Butler 12.00 30.00
RKCH Chris Jefferies 8.00 20.00
RKCJ Casey Jacobsen 8.00 20.00
RKCW Chris Wilcox 8.00 20.00
RKDD Dan Dickau 8.00 20.00
RKDG Drew Gooden 12.00 30.00
RKDW DaJuan Wagner 8.00 20.00
RKEL Melvin Ely 8.00 20.00
RKFJ Fred Jones 8.00 20.00
RKFW Frank Williams 8.00 20.00
RKJD Juan Dixon 10.00 25.00
RKJJ Jared Jeffries 8.00 20.00
RKJS John Salmons 10.00 25.00
RKJW Jay Williams 10.00 25.00
RKKR Kareem Rush 8.00 20.00
RKMH Marcus Haislip 8.00 20.00
RKNH Nene Hilario 10.00 25.00
RKNT Nikoloz Tskitishvili 8.00 20.00
RKQW Qyntel Woods 8.00 20.00
RKRH Ryan Humphrey 8.00 20.00
RKTP Tayshaun Prince 10.00 25.00
RKYM Yao Ming 75.00 150.00

2003-04 SP Game Used

Issued in August 2003, this 148-card set is divided up into 94 veteran player cards which are a mix of base and jersey cards (inserted overall at 1:1 along with the Legendary Fabrics, All-Star Apparel and Authentic Fabrics), 12 Michael Jordan Tribute cards sequentially numbered to 999 (card numbers 95-106) and 41 rookie cards (card numbers 107-148) sequentially numbered to 999. Base cards have white borders with accent colors to match team jerseys, the MJ Tribute cards have red and blue borders around the photos and white borders on the outside of the card and rookie cards have colored backgrounds to match jersey color and black and white designs towards the bottom of the card. SP Game Used was packaged in six-pack boxes where packs contained three cards and carried a suggested retail price of $29.99.

1 Shareef Abdur-Rahim 1.25 3.00
2 Glenn Robinson 1.25 3.00
3 Jason Terry JSY 2.50 6.00
4 Paul Pierce 2.00 5.00
5 Antoine Walker 1.50 4.00
6 Eddy Curry 1.25 3.00
7 Tyson Chandler JSY 2.50 6.00
8 Jalen Rose JSY 2.50 6.00
9 Jay Williams JSY 2.00 5.00
10 DaJuan Wagner JSY 2.00 5.00
11 Darius Miles JSY 2.00 5.00
12 Carlos Boozer JSY 3.00 8.00
13 Steve Nash 2.00 5.00
14 Michael Finley 1.50 4.00
15 Nick Van Exel 1.25 3.00
16 Dirk Nowitzki JSY 5.00 12.00
17 Rodney White 1.00 2.50
18 Marcus Camby 1.25 3.00
19 Nikoloz Tskitishvili 1.00 2.50
20 Nene Hilario JSY 2.50 6.00
21 Richard Hamilton 1.25 3.00
22 Chauncey Billups 1.50 4.00
23 Ben Wallace 1.50 4.00
24 Gilbert Arenas 1.50 4.00
25 Troy Murphy 1.50 4.00
26 Jason Richardson JSY 3.00 8.00
27 Antawn Jamison JSY 3.00 8.00
28 Cuttino Mobley 1.25 3.00
29 Steve Francis 1.50 4.00
30 Eddie Griffin 1.00 2.50
31 Jermaine O'Neal 1.50 4.00
32 Reggie Miller 1.50 4.00
33 Jamaal Tinsley JSY 2.00 5.00
34 Lamar Odom 1.50 4.00
35 Chris Wilcox 1.00 2.50
36 Marko Jaric 1.00 2.50
37 Elton Brand JSY 3.00 8.00
38 Andre Miller JSY 2.50 6.00
39 Kobe Bryant 8.00 20.00
40 Shaquille O'Neal 4.00 10.00
41 Gary Payton 1.50 4.00
42 Kareem Rush JSY 2.00 5.00
43 Mike Miller 1.50 4.00
44 Shane Battier JSY 2.50 6.00
45 Pau Gasol JSY 3.00 8.00
46 Eddie Jones 1.25 3.00
47 Brian Grant 1.00 2.50
48 Caron Butler JSY 3.00 8.00
49 Joe Smith 1.25 3.00
50 Desmond Mason 1.25 3.00
51 Toni Kukoc 1.50 4.00
52 Wally Szczerbiak 1.25 3.00
53 Kevin Garnett JSY 6.00 15.00
54 Alonzo Mourning 2.00 5.00
55 Kenyon Martin 1.50 4.0
56 Jason Kidd JSY 5.00 12.0
57 Richard Jefferson JSY 3.00 8.0
58 Baron Davis 1.50 4.0
59 Jamal Mashburn JSY 2.50 6.0
60 Latrell Sprewell 1.25 3.0
61 Allan Houston 1.25 3.0
62 Antonio McDyess 1.25 3.0
63 Juwan Howard 1.25 3.0
64 Drew Gooden JSY 2.50 6.0
65 Tracy McGrady JSY 4.00 10.0
66 Keith Van Horn 1.25 3.0
67 Aaron McKie 1.00 2.5
68 Allen Iverson JSY 5.00 12.0
69 Stephon Marbury 1.25 3.0
70 Shawn Marion 1.50 4.0
71 Anfernee Hardaway 2.50 6.0
72 Joe Johnson 1.50 4.0
73 Amare Stoudemire JSY 5.00 12.0
74 Rasheed Wallace 1.50 4.0
75 Scottie Pippen 2.50 6.0
76 Mike Bibby 1.50 4.0
77 Peja Stojakovic 1.50 4.0
78 Gerald Wallace 1.50 4.0
79 Chris Webber JSY 3.00 8.0
80 Tim Duncan 2.50 6.0
81 Manu Ginobili 2.00 5.0
82 Tony Parker JSY 3.00 8.0
83 Ray Allen 1.50 4.0
84 Rashard Lewis JSY 3.00 8.0
85 Morris Peterson 1.00 2.5
86 Antonio Davis 1.00 2.5
87 Vince Carter 2.50 6.0
88 John Stockton JSY 4.00 10.0
89 Karl Malone JSY 4.00 10.0
90 Jerry Stackhouse 1.25 3.0
91 Michael Jordan 10.00 25.0
92 Michael Jordan JSY 50.00 100.0
93 Kobe Bryant JSY 15.00 40.0
94 Yao Ming JSY 6.00 15.0
95 Michael Jordan Tribute 10.00 25.0
96 Michael Jordan Tribute 10.00 25.0
97 Michael Jordan Tribute 10.00 25.0
98 Michael Jordan Tribute 10.00 25.0
99 Michael Jordan Tribute 10.00 25.0
100 Michael Jordan Tribute 10.00 25.0
101 Michael Jordan Tribute 10.00 25.0
102 Michael Jordan Tribute 10.00 25.0
103 Michael Jordan Tribute 10.00 25.0
104 Michael Jordan Tribute 10.00 25.0
105 Michael Jordan Tribute 10.00 25.0
106 Michael Jordan Tribute 10.00 25.0
107 LeBron James RC 40.00 100.0
108 Darko Milicic RC 3.00 8.0
109 Carmelo Anthony RC 8.00 20.0
110 Chris Bosh RC 6.00 15.0
111 Dwyane Wade RC 12.00 30.0
112 Chris Kaman RC 4.00 10.0
113 Kirk Hinrich RC 4.00 10.0
114 T.J. Ford RC 4.00 10.0
115 Mike Sweetney RC 3.00 8.0
116 Jarvis Hayes RC 3.00 8.0
117 Mickael Pietrus RC 3.00 8.0
118 Nick Collison RC 3.00 8.0
119 Marcus Banks RC 3.00 8.0
120 Luke Ridnour RC 4.00 10.0
121 Reece Gaines RC 3.00 8.0
122 Troy Bell RC 3.00 8.0
123 Zarko Cabarkapa RC 3.00 8.0
124 David West RC 4.00 10.0
125 Aleksandar Pavlovic RC 3.00 8.0
126 Dahntay Jones RC 3.00 8.0
127 Boris Diaw RC 4.00 10.0
128 Zoran Planinic RC 3.00 8.0
129 Travis Outlaw RC 4.00 10.0
130 Brian Cook RC 3.00 8.0
131 Carlos Delfino RC 4.00 10.0
132 Ndudi Ebi RC 3.00 8.0
133 Kendrick Perkins RC 5.00 12.0
134 Leandro Barbosa RC 4.00 10.0
135 Josh Howard RC 3.00 8.0
136 Maciej Lampe RC 3.00 8.0
137 Jason Kapono RC 3.00 8.0
138 Luke Walton RC 3.00 8.0
139 Jerome Beasley RC 3.00 8.0
140 Sofoklis Schortsanitis RC 3.00 8.0
141 Mario Austin RC 3.00 8.0
142 Travis Hansen RC 3.00 8.0
143 Steve Blake RC 4.00 10.0
144 Slavko Vranes RC 3.00 8.0
145 Zaur Pachulia RC 3.00 8.0
146 Keith Bogans RC 3.00 8.0
147 Matt Bonner RC 4.00 10.0
148 Maurice Williams RC 5.00 12.

2003-04 SP Game Used Gold

Randomly inserted in packs, this 148-card set parall the base set enhanced with gold highlights. Cards 1- are sequentially numbered to 100, with the jersey ca from 1-94 sequentially numbered to 50. Both the Michael Jordan Tribute and rookie cards are sequentially numbered to 50.

*1-94 SINGLES: .5X TO 1.25X BASE HI
*1-94 JSY SINGLES: .6X TO 1.5X BASE HI
COMMON MJ TRIB (95-106) 20.00 50.
*107-148 RC SINGLES: 1X TO 2.5X BASE HI
107 Lebron James 200.00 400.
111 Dwyane Wade 50.00 120.

2003-04 SP Game Used All Sta Apparel

Randomly inserted at one in one along with the othe memorabilia cards mentioned in the main set blurb, this 18-card set features a black background with fu color player action photography along with a swatch All-Star worn memorabilia. A gold version was also issued and is sequentially numbered to 100.

*GOLD SINGLES: .75X TO 2X BASE CARD HI

AKAS Andrei Kirilenko 2.50 6.
BWAS Ben Wallace 2.50 6.
DGAS Drew Gooden 2.00 5.
DMAS Desmond Mason 2.00 5.
GAAS Gilbert Arenas 2.50 6.
GGAS Gordan Giricek 1.50 4.
JAAS Marko Jaric 1.50 4.

S Jason Richardson 2.50 6.00
S Jamaal Tinsley 1.50 4.00
S Kobe Bryant 10.00 25.00
S Nene Hilario 2.00 5.00
S Richard Jefferson 2.50 6.00
S Shawn Marion 2.50 6.00
S Tim Duncan 4.00 10.00
S Troy Murphy 2.50 6.00
S Tony Parker 2.50 6.00
S Yao Ming 5.00 12.00
S Zydrunas Ilgauskas 2.00 5.00

2003-04 SP Game Used Authentic Fabrics

domly inserted at one in one along with the other mentioned in the main set blurb, this 77-card set es full-color player action photos on the right of card and a square swatch of memorabilia in the er left. The far upper left-hand corner prominently lays the SP Game Used Logo. A Gold version of set was also inserted and cards are sequentially bered to 100.

Antonio Davis 2.00 5.00
Allan Houston 2.00 5.00
Anfernee Hardaway 4.00 10.00
Aaron McKie 2.00 5.00
Alonzo Mourning 3.00 8.00
Antoine Walker 2.50 6.00
Baron Davis 2.50 6.00
Bostjan Nachbar 2.00 5.00
Ben Wallace 2.50 6.00
Chauncey Billups 2.50 6.00
Chris Jefferies 2.00 5.00
Chris Wilcox 2.00 5.00
Dan Dickau 2.00 5.00
Devean George 2.00 5.00
Desmond Mason 2.00 5.00
Dikembe Mutombo 2.50 6.00
David Robinson 4.00 10.00
David Wesley 2.00 5.00
dy Curry 2.00 5.00
Manu Ginobili 3.00 8.00
Eddie Griffin 2.00 5.00
ddie Jones 2.00 5.00
Eric Snow 2.00 5.00
arcus Fizer 2.00 5.00
Fred Jones 2.00 5.00
Frank Williams 2.00 5.00
Gordan Giricek 2.00 5.00
Grant Hill 3.00 8.00
Gary Payton 2.50 6.00
Glenn Robinson 2.00 5.00
Gerald Wallace 2.50 6.00
Marko Jaric 2.00 5.00
Juan Dixon 2.00 5.00
ared Jeffries 2.00 5.00
Joe Johnson 2.50 6.00
ermaine O'Neal 2.50 6.00
ohn Salmons 2.50 6.00
Jiri Welsch 2.00 5.00
wame Brown 2.00 5.00
obe Bryant 15.00 40.00
edrick Brown 2.00 5.00
Kenyon Martin 2.50 6.00
urt Thomas 2.00 5.00
eith Van Horn 2.00 5.00
eBron James 40.00 100.00
amar Odom 2.50 6.00
atrell Sprewell 2.00 5.00
Shawn Marion 2.50 6.00
Mike Bibby 2.50 6.00
Marcus Camby 2.00 5.00
Melvin Ely 2.00 5.00
Michael Finley 2.50 6.00
Marcus Haislip 2.00 5.00
Michael Jordan 40.00 100.00
Mike Miller 2.50 6.00
Morris Peterson 1.50 4.00
Nikoloz Tskitishvilli 2.00 5.00
Paul Pierce 3.00 8.00
Peja Stojakovic 2.50 6.00
Quentin Richardson 2.00 5.00
Qyntel Woods 2.00 5.00
Ray Allen 2.50 6.00
Rasual Butler 2.00 5.00
Richard Hamilton 2.00 5.00
Reggie Miller 2.50 6.00
Rasheed Wallace 2.50 6.00
Shareef Abdur Rahim 2.00 5.00
Steve Francis 2.50 6.00
Stephon Marbury 2.00 5.00
Steve Nash 3.00 8.00
Scottie Pippen 5.00 12.00
erry Stackhouse 2.00 5.00
Tim Duncan 4.00 10.00
Toni Kukoc 2.50 6.00
Vin Baker 2.00 5.00
Charlie Ward 2.00 5.00
Wally Szczerbiak 2.00 5.00

2003-04 SP Game Used Authentic Fabrics Autographs

omly seeded in packs, this 29-card set parallels ok of the Authentic Fabrics insert set enhanced fade to white bottom and authentic player raphs. Each card is sequentially numbered to

Antawn Jamison 8.00 20.00
Amare Stoudemire 15.00 40.00
Corey Maggette 8.00 20.00
David Robinson 30.00 80.00
DaJuan Wagner 8.00 20.00
Manu Ginobili 15.00 40.00
Etan Thomas 5.00 12.00
Fred Jones 5.00 12.00
Gilbert Arenas 8.00 20.00
Gerald Wallace 8.00 20.00
Jason Kidd 25.00 60.00
Jerome Moiso 5.00 12.00
Jermaine O'Neal 12.50 30.00
Jason Richardson 10.00 25.00
Jerry Stackhouse 8.00 20.00
Jamaal Tinsley 8.00 20.00
Jay Williams 8.00 20.00
Kobe Bryant 125.00 250.00

LOAJ Lamar Odom 10.00 25.00
MBAJ Mike Bibby 12.50 30.00
PPAJ Paul Pierce 15.00 40.00
PSAJ Peja Stojakovic 10.00 25.00
RJAJ Richard Jefferson 8.00 20.00
ROAJ Jalen Rose 8.00 20.00
SFAJ Steve Francis 8.00 20.00
SMAJ Shawn Marion 10.00 25.00
TMAJ Tracy McGrady 20.00 50.00
TPAJ Tony Parker 12.50 30.00
YMAJ Yao Ming 30.00 80.00

2003-04 SP Game Used Authentic Fabrics Gold

This set is a parallel insert to the base Authentic Fabrics insert set and cards are sequentially numbered to 100.

*GOLD SINGLES: .6X TO 1.5X BASE HI
AHJ Anfernee Hardaway 10.00 25.00
SPJ Scottie Pippen 10.00 25.00

2003-04 SP Game Used Authentic Fabrics Dual

Randomly inserted in packs, this 38-card set features a horizontal design with player photos on both the left and right of the card and two swatches of game used memorabilia. Each card is sequentially numbered to 100.

UNPRICED QUAD PRINT RUN 10 SETS
AIKVJ Allen Iverson 10.00 25.00
Keith Van Horn
AMQRJ Andre Miller 5.00 12.00
Quentin Richardson
ASCJJ Amare Stoudemire 6.00 15.00
Casey Jacobsen
AWVBJ Antoine Walker 5.00 12.00
Vin Baker
BDJMJ Baron Davis 5.00 12.00
Jamal Mashburn
BWCBJ Ben Wallace 8.00 20.00
Chauncey Billups
CBDMJ Carlos Boozer 5.00 12.00
Darius Miles
CBRBJ Caron Butler 5.00 12.00
Rasual Butler
DMKMJ Kenyon Martin 6.00 15.00
Dikembe Mutombo
DNSNJ Dirk Nowitzki 10.00 25.00
Steve Nash
EBMEJ Elton Brand 5.00 12.00
Melvin Ely
EJAMJ Eddie Jones 6.00 15.00
Alonzo Mourning
GAAJJ Gilbert Arenas 5.00 12.00
Antawn Jamison
GHDGJ Grant Hill 6.00 15.00
Drew Gooden
GPTKJ Gary Payton 12.50 30.00
Toni Kukoc
JHMCJ Juwan Howard 5.00 12.00
Marcus Camby
JRECJ Jalen Rose 5.00 12.00
Eddy Curry
JSWZJ Joe Smith 5.00 12.00
Wally Szczerbiak
JTDDJ Jason Terry 5.00 12.00
Dan Dickau
JTJOJ Jamaal Tinsley 5.00 12.00
Jermaine O'Neal
KBDFJ Kobe Bryant 20.00 50.00
Derek Fisher
KGTHJ Kevin Garnett 10.00 25.00
Troy Hudson
KMJSJ John Stockton 15.00 30.00
Karl Malone
LSAHJ Latrell Sprewell 5.00 12.00
Allan Houston
MFRLJ Michael Finley 5.00 12.00
Raef LaFrentz
MJKBJ Michael Jordan 60.00 150.00
Kobe Bryant
MJMAJ Michael Jordan 75.00 150.00
Magic Johnson
NHNTJ Nene 5.00 12.00
Nikoloz Tskitishvili
PGMMJ Pau Gasol 6.00 15.00
Mike Miller
PPKBJ Paul Pierce 5.00 12.00
Kedrick Brown
RJJKJ Richard Jefferson 6.00 15.00
Jason Kidd
RMFJJ Reggie Miller 5.00 12.00
Fred Jones
RWSPJ Rasheed Wallace 15.00 30.00
Scottie Pippen
SAGRJ Shareef Abdur-Rahim 5.00 12.00
Glenn Robinson
SMAHJ Stephon Marbury 12.00 30.00
Anfernee Hardaway
TMGGJ Tracy McGrady 8.00 20.00
Gordan Giricek
TPRHJ Tayshaun Prince 6.00 15.00
Richard Hamilton
WZCWJ Wang ZhiZhi 5.00 12.00
Chris Wilcox

2003-04 SP Game Used Authentic Fabrics Dual Autographs

Randomly seeded, this 48-card set parallels the design of the Authentic Fabrics Dual set enhanced with a fade to white bottom and two authentic player autographs.

Each card is sequentially numbered to 50. Also included were several cards numbered to 15. Those cards are denoted in our checklist.

SOME NOT PRICED DUE TO SCARCITY
1 Andre Miller 30.00 60.00
Jason Kidd
2 Andre Miller 20.00 40.00
Lamar Odom
3 Andre Miller 10.00 25.00
Marko Jaric
4 Chauncey Billups 20.00 40.00
Tayshaun Prince
5 Corey Maggette 10.00 25.00
Andre Miller
6 Gordan Giricek 10.00 25.00
Drew Gooden
7 Drew Gooden 30.00 60.00
Paul Pierce
8 DaJuan Wagner 15.00 30.00
Carlos Boozer
9 Manu Ginobili 30.00 60.00
Marko Jaric
10 Eddie Griffin 10.00 25.00
Steve Francis
11 Gilbert Arenas 10.00 25.00
Jason Richardson
12 Gordan Giricek 20.00 40.00
Tony Parker
13 Peja Stojakovic 10.00 25.00
Gerald Wallace
14 Jason Kidd 20.00 50.00
Jamaal Tinsley
16 Jason Kidd 20.00 50.00
Richard Jefferson
17 Jermaine O'Neal 40.00 100.00
Kevin Garnett
18 Jalen Rose 10.00 25.00
Marcus Fizer
19 Jason Richardson 10.00 25.00
Richard Jefferson
20 Jason Richardson 20.00 40.00
Tony Parker
22 Jerry Stackhouse 10.00 25.00
Juan Dixon
23 Jamaal Tinsley 15.00 30.00
Tony Parker
24 Jay Williams 20.00 40.00
Carlos Boozer
25 Jay Williams 15.00 30.00
Marcus Fizer
26 Kobe Bryant 100.00 200.00
Mike Bibby
28 Lamar Odom 10.00 25.00
Chris Wilcox
29 Mike Bibby 10.00 25.00
Peja Stojakovic
31 Melvin Ely 10.00 25.00
Lamar Odom
32 Morris Peterson 10.00 25.00
Jason Richardson
33 Richard Hamilton 20.00 40.00
Chauncey Billups
34 Richard Jefferson 15.00 30.00
Mike Bibby
35 Steve Francis/15 150.00 300.00
Kobe Bryant
36 Steve Francis 40.00 80.00
Yao Ming
37 Shawn Marion 25.00 50.00
Amare Stoudemire
39 Tracy McGrady/15 100.00 200.00
Kevin Garnett
41 Tony Parker 40.00 80.00
Manu Ginobili
42 Tony Parker 10.00 25.00
Marko Jaric

2003-04 SP Game Used Authentic Fabrics Triple

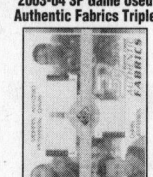

Randomly inserted, this six-card set places three players and three swatches of authentic memorabilia on the card. Each card is sequentially numbered to 25, and note the prominent display of the SP Game Used logo.

2 DaJuan Wagner 12.50 30.00
Darius Miles
Carlos Boozer
3 Jalen Rose 12.50 30.00
Tyson Chandler
Jay Williams
4 John Stockton 30.00 80.00
Karl Malone
Andrei Kirilenko
6 Chris Jefferies 12.50 30.00
Morris Peterson
Antonio Davis
8 Pau Gasol 20.00 50.00
Shane Battier
Mike Miller
9 Ray Allen 20.00 50.00
Rashard Lewis
Joe Forte

2003-04 SP Game Used Authentic Patches

Randomly seeded, this 59-card set places full-color player photos at the top of the card and a centered square swatch of game-used patch on the bottom. Each card is sequentially numbered to 100.

AHP Allan Houston 8.00 20.00
AIP Allen Iverson 20.00 50.00
AJP Antawn Jamison 10.00 25.00
AMP Alonzo Mourning 20.00 50.00
ASP Amare Stoudemire 15.00 40.00
AWP Antoine Walker 10.00 25.00
BDP Baron Davis 10.00 25.00
CBP Caron Butler 10.00 25.00
CWP Chris Webber 12.50 30.00
DNP Dirk Nowitzki 15.00 40.00
DRR David Robinson 12.00 30.00
DWP DaJuan Wagner 6.00 15.00
EBP Elton Brand 10.00 25.00
EJP Eddie Jones 15.00 40.00
GAP Gilbert Arenas 10.00 25.00
GHP Grant Hill 12.00 30.00
GPP Gary Payton 10.00 25.00
HAP Anfernee Hardaway 20.00 50.00
HTP Hedo Turkoglu 10.00 25.00
JJP Jared Jeffries 6.00 15.00
JKP Jason Kidd 15.00 40.00
JMP Jamal Mashburn 8.00 20.00
JOP Jermaine O'Neal 10.00 25.00
JRP Jason Richardson 10.00 25.00
JSP John Stockton 12.00 30.00
JTP Jamaal Tinsley 6.00 15.00
JWP Jay Williams 6.00 15.00
KAP Karl Malone 12.00 30.00
KBP Kobe Bryant 40.00 100.00
KGP Kevin Garnett 20.00 50.00
KJP Kareem Abdul-Jabbar 30.00 80.00
KMP Kenyon Martin 10.00 25.00
KRP Kareem Rush 6.00 15.00
KVP Keith Van Horn 8.00 20.00
LOP Lamar Odom 10.00 25.00
LSP Latrell Sprewell 10.00 25.00
MAP Magic Johnson 30.00 60.00
MBP Mike Bibby 10.00 25.00
MCP Antonio McDyess 8.00 20.00
MIP Andre Miller 8.00 20.00
MJP Michael Jordan 100.00 250.00
NHP Nene Hilario 10.00 25.00
PGP Pau Gasol 10.00 25.00
PPP Paul Pierce 12.00 30.00
RAP Ray Allen 10.00 25.00
RHP Richard Hamilton 8.00 20.00
RJP Richard Jefferson 10.00 25.00
RLP Rashard Lewis 10.00 25.00
RMP Reggie Miller 10.00 25.00
RWP Rasheed Wallace 10.00 25.00
SBP Shane Battier 8.00 20.00
SFP Steve Francis 10.00 25.00
SHP Shawn Marion 10.00 25.00
SMP Stephon Marbury 8.00 20.00
SPP Scottie Pippen 30.00 80.00
TMP Tracy McGrady 12.00 30.00
WSP Wally Szczerbiak 8.00 20.00
WZP Wang Zhi Zhi 10.00 25.00
YMP Yao Ming 20.00 50.00

2003-04 SP Game Used Authentic Patches Autographs

Randomly inserted in packs, this 35-card set parallels the design of the Authentic Patches insert set enhanced with authentic player autographs. Each card is sequentially numbered to 50.

AJAP Antawn Jamison 15.00 40.00
ASAP Amare Stoudemire 40.00 100.00
BIAP Chauncey Billups 15.00 40.00
BOAP Carlos Boozer 15.00 40.00
CBAP Caron Butler 30.00 60.00
DDAP Dan Dickau 15.00 40.00
DGAP Drew Gooden 15.00 40.00
DJAP DerMarr Johnson 15.00 40.00
DWAP DaJuan Wagner 15.00 40.00
EGAP Manu Ginobili 30.00 80.00
ETAP Etan Thomas 15.00 40.00
GAAP Gilbert Arenas 25.00 50.00
GWAP Gerald Wallace 15.00 40.00
JDAP Juan Dixon 15.00 40.00
JKAP Jason Kidd 50.00 120.00
JMAP Jerome Moiso 15.00 40.00
JOAP Jermaine O'Neal 15.00 40.00
JRAP Jason Richardson 20.00 50.00
JSAP Jerry Stackhouse 25.00 60.00
JWAP Jay Williams 25.00 50.00
KBAP Kobe Bryant 200.00 450.00
LOAP Lamar Odom 15.00 40.00
MBAP Mike Bibby 15.00 40.00
MJAP Michael Jordan 600.00 1000.00
NHAP Nene Hilario 15.00 40.00
PPAP Paul Pierce 40.00 80.00
PSAP Peja Stojakovic 20.00 50.00
RHAP Richard Hamilton 20.00 50.00
RJAP Richard Jefferson 15.00 40.00
ROAP Jalen Rose 15.00 40.00
SFAP Steve Francis 30.00 60.00
SMAP Shawn Marion 20.00 50.00
TMAP Tracy McGrady 30.00 80.00
TPAP Tony Parker 30.00 60.00
YMAP Yao Ming 40.00 100.00

2003-04 SP Game Used Authentic Patches Dual

Randomly inserted, this eight-card set utilizes the design of the Authentic Patches set but places two players and two patch swatches on each card. Cards are sequentially numbered to 25. An autographed version was also issued and these cards are sequentially numbered to five.

UNPRICED AUTO PRINT RUN 5 SETS
UNPRICED TRIPLE PRINT RUN 10 SETS
2 Jason Richardson 25.00 60.00
Antawn Jamison
3 Kobe Bryan 50.00 120.00
Kareem Rush
4 Michael Jordan 100.00 250.00
Kobe Bryant
5 Michael Jordan 125.00 300.00
Larry Bird
6 Peja Stojakovic 25.00 60.00
Gordan Giricek
7 Steve Nash 40.00 100.00
Rick Fox
8 Tracy McGrady 25.00 60.00
Darius Miles

2003-04 SP Game Used Extra SIGnificance

Randomly inserted in packs, this 10-card set features a horizontal design with one player photo appearing on the right and the other on the left with both autographs in the middle. Each card is sequentially numbered to 25. A Gold parallel version of this set was also produced and those cards are sequentially numbered to five.

ASTM Amare Stoudemire 50.00 120.00
Tracy McGrady
KAMJ Kareem Abdul-Jabbar 150.00 300.00
Magic Johnson
MJLB Michael Jordan 350.00 650.00
Larry Bird
PSMB Peja Stojakovic 25.00 60.00
Mike Bibby
YMKA Yao Ming 75.00 200.00
Kareem Abdul-Jabbar

2003-04 SP Game Used Legendary Fabrics

Randomly inserted at the rate of one in one along with the rest of the sets mentioned in the main set blurb, this 11-card set focuses on retired NBA Greats. Each card places a black and white image of the player on the left side of the card and a swatch of memorabilia on the right. An autographed version including most of the players from this set was issued.

BRLO Bill Russell 20.00 50.00
DWL Dominique Wilkins 8.00 20.00
EJL Magic Johnson 12.50 30.00
JEL Julius Erving 12.50 30.00
KML Kevin McHale 8.00 20.00
LBL Larry Bird 15.00 40.00
MJL Michael Jordan 50.00 120.00
ORL Oscar Robertson 10.00 25.00
WCL Wilt Chamberlain 35.00 70.00

2003-04 SP Game Used Legendary Fabrics Autographs

This set is an autographed parallel to the Legendary Fabrics set, limited to just 100 serial numbered sets.

2 Bill Russell 100.00 250.00
3 Larry Bird 80.00 200.00
4 Julius Erving 60.00 150.00
5 Magic Johnson 60.00 150.00
6 Kareem Abdul-Jabbar 40.00 100.00
7 Dominique Wilkins 40.00 100.00

2003-04 SP Game Used Rookie Exclusive Autographs

This 42-card set is sequentially numbered to 100 and was randomly inserted in packs. Player photos appear on the right side of the card while an embedded cut signature appears centered below the photo.

RE1 Lebron James 900.00 1400.00
RE2 Darko Milicic 8.00 20.00
RE3 Carmelo Anthony 75.00 200.00
RE4 Chris Bosh 40.00 100.00
RE5 Chris Kaman 10.00 25.00
RE6 Reece Gaines 8.00 20.00
RE7 Mickael Pietrus 8.00 20.00
RE8 Marcus Banks 8.00 20.00
RE9 Troy Bell 8.00 20.00
RE10 Zarko Cabarkapa 8.00 20.00
RE11 David West 10.00 25.00
RE12 Aleksandar Pavlovic 8.00 20.00
RE13 Dahntay Jones 8.00 20.00
RE14 Boris Diaw 10.00 25.00
RE15 Zoran Planinic 8.00 20.00
RE16 Travis Outlaw 10.00 25.00
RE17 Brian Cook 8.00 20.00
RE18 Leandro Barbosa 10.00 25.00
RE19 Josh Howard 8.00 20.00
RE20 Maciej Lampe 8.00 20.00
RE21 Jason Kapono 8.00 20.00
RE22 Luke Walton 8.00 20.00
RE23 Jerome Beasley 8.00 20.00
RE24 Sofoklis Schortsanitis 8.00 20.00
RE25 Mario Austin 8.00 20.00
RE26 Travis Hansen 8.00 20.00
RE27 Steve Blake 10.00 25.00
RE28 Slavko Vranes 8.00 20.00
RE29 Zaur Pachulia 8.00 20.00
RE30 Keith Bogans 8.00 20.00
RE31 Matt Bonner 10.00 25.00
RE32 Maurice Williams 12.00 30.00
RE33 Kyle Korver 10.00 25.00
RE34 Rick Rickert 8.00 20.00
RE35 Brandon Hunter 8.00 20.00
RE36 Jarvis Hayes 8.00 20.00
RE37 Ndudi Ebi 8.00 20.00
RE38 Kendrick Perkins 12.00 30.00
RE39 Dwyane Wade 250.00 500.00
RE40 Luke Ridnour 10.00 25.00
RE41 James Lang 8.00 20.00
RE42 Carlos Delfino 10.00 25.00

2003-04 SP Game Used SIGnificance

Inserted in packs, this 58-card set places full-color player photos along the top and leaves a low-detailed area on the bottom for player autographs. Each card is sequentially numbered to 100. Two other versions of this set were inserted: a Gold version sequentially numbered to 10, and a Marks version sequentially numbered to 25.

AJ Antawn Jamison 6.00 15.00
AM Antonio McDyess 5.00 12.00
AM Andre Miller 4.00 10.00
AS Amare Stoudemire 12.00 30.00
BI Chauncey Billups 8.00 20.00
BO Carlos Boozer 6.00 15.00
BW Bill Walton 10.00 25.00
CB Caron Butler 8.00 20.00
CJ Chris Jefferies 4.00 10.00
CM Corey Maggette 4.00 10.00
DA Dan Gadzuric 4.00 10.00
DD Dan Dickau 4.00 10.00
DG Drew Gooden 4.00 10.00
DJ DerMarr Johnson 4.00 10.00
DR David Robinson 30.00 80.00
DWO DaJuan Wagner 6.00 15.00
EGO Manu Ginobili 12.00 30.00
ET Etan Thomas 4.00 10.00
FJ Fred Jones 4.00 10.00
GA Gilbert Arenas 8.00 20.00
GG Gordon Giricek 4.00 10.00
GR Eddie Griffin 4.00 10.00
GW Gerald Wallace 6.00 15.00
HU Ryan Humphrey 4.00 10.00
IM George Gervin 10.00 25.00
JD Juan Dixon 4.00 10.00
JK Jason Kidd 20.00 50.00
JM Jerome Moiso 6.00 15.00
JO Jermaine O'Neal 8.00 20.00
JR Jason Richardson 8.00 20.00
JS Jerry Stackhouse 6.00 15.00
JT Jamaal Tinsley 6.00 15.00
JW Jay Williams 8.00 20.00
KA Kareem Abdul-Jabbar 30.00 80.00
KB Kobe Bryant 100.00 200.00
KG Kevin Garnett 30.00 80.00
LO Lamar Odom 8.00 20.00
MB Mike Bibby 8.00 20.00
MJ Michael Jordan/23 300.00 550.00
MP Morris Peterson 4.00 10.00
NH Nene Hilario 5.00 12.00
NW Dominique Wilkins 15.00 40.00
PP Paul Pierce 15.00 40.00
PS Peja Stojakovic 6.00 15.00
QW Qyntel Woods 4.00 10.00
RE Reggie Evans 4.00 10.00
RH Richard Hamilton 8.00 20.00
RJ Richard Jefferson 6.00 15.00
RO Jalen Rose 6.00 15.00
SF Steve Francis 8.00 20.00
SM Shawn Marion 8.00 20.00
TM Tracy McGrady 15.00 40.00
TP Tony Parker 15.00 40.00
WI Chris Wilcox 4.00 10.00
WZ Wang Zhi Zhi 8.00 20.00
YM Yao Ming 20.00 50.00

2003-04 SP Game Used SIGnificant Marks

This set is a parallel insert to the SIGnificance set enhanced with sequential numbering to 75.

AJSM Antawn Jamison 10.00 25.00
AMSM Andre Miller 8.00 20.00
ANSM Antonio McDyess 10.00 25.00
ASSM Amare Stoudemire 25.00 60.00
BOSM Carlos Boozer 10.00 25.00
BWSM Bill Walton 15.00 40.00
CBSM Caron Butler 15.00 40.00
CMSM Corey Maggette 8.00 20.00
CWSM Chris Wilcox 8.00 20.00
DGSM Drew Gooden 8.00 20.00
DJSM DerMarr Johnson 8.00 20.00
DRSM David Robinson 40.00 100.00
DWSM DaJuan Wagner 8.00 20.00
EGSM Manu Ginobili 20.00 50.00
ETSM Etan Thomas 8.00 20.00
GASM Gilbert Arenas 10.00 25.00
GESM George Gervin 15.00 40.00
GGSM Gordon Giricek 8.00 20.00
GRSM Eddie Griffin 8.00 20.00
GWSM Gerald Wallace 10.00 25.00
JDSM Juan Dixon 8.00 20.00
JKSM Jason Kidd 25.00 60.00
JMSM Jerome Moiso 8.00 20.00
JOSM Jermaine O'Neal 10.00 25.00
JRSM Jason Richardson 10.00 25.00
JSSM Jerry Stackhouse 10.00 25.00
JWSM Jay Williams 10.00 25.00
LOSM Lamar Odom 15.00 30.00
MBSM Mike Bibby 15.00 30.00
MPSM Morris Peterson 8.00 20.00
PPSM Paul Pierce 20.00 50.00
PSSM Peja Stojakovic 12.50 30.00
RHSM Richard Hamilton 10.00 25.00
RJSM Richard Jefferson 10.00 25.00
ROSM Jalen Rose 10.00 25.00
SFSM Steve Francis 10.00 25.00
SMSM Shawn Marion 12.50 30.00
TMSM Tracy McGrady 20.00 50.00
TPSM Tony Parker 20.00 50.00
YMSM Yao Ming 30.00 80.00

2003-04 SP Game Used SIGnificant Numbers

This set is a parallel insert to the SIGnificance set and each player signed copies totaling his jersey number.

MOST NOT PRICED DUE TO SCARCITY
AS32 Amare Stoudemire/32 60.00 150.00
JR23 Jason Richardson/23 25.00 60.00
KG21 Kevin Garnett/21 100.00 200.00
MJ23 Michael Jordan/23 500.00 800.00
PP34 Paul Pierce/34 40.00 100.00

2004-05 SP Game Used

Issued in September 2004, SP Game Used consists of 162 card where cards 1-60 are base veterans, cards 61-90 are veteran jersey cards inserted at the combined rate for all memorabilia at one per pack, cards 91-132 feature rookies and are sequentially numbered to 999 and cards 133-162 are part of a LeBron James season in review subset and are sequentially numbered to 999. SP Game used was packaged in six pack boxes where packs contained three cards each and carried a SRP of $29.99..

UNPRICED LIMITED PARALLEL PRINT RUN ONE SET
1 Tony Delk .60 1.50
2 Boris Diaw .75 2.00
3 Ricky Davis .75 2.00
4 Gary Payton 1.00 2.50
5 Gerald Wallace 1.00 2.50
6 Jason Kapono .60 1.50
7 Tyson Chandler .75 2.00
8 Kirk Hinrich 1.00 2.50
9 Dajuan Wagner .60 1.50
10 Zydrunas Ilgauskas .75 2.00
11 Jerry Stackhouse .75 2.00
12 Michael Finley 1.00 2.50
13 Andre Miller .75 2.00
14 Nene .75 2.00
15 Richard Hamilton .75 2.00
16 Rasheed Wallace 1.00 2.50
17 Derek Fisher .75 2.00
18 Mike Dunleavy .75 2.00
19 Tracy McGrady 1.25 3.00
20 Jim Jackson .60 1.50
21 Reggie Miller 1.00 2.50
22 Jermaine O'Neal 1.00 2.50
23 Elton Brand 1.00 2.50
24 Corey Maggette .75 2.00
25 Lamar Odom 1.00 2.50
26 Caron Butler 1.00 2.50
27 Pau Gasol 1.00 2.50
28 Bonzi Wells .60 1.50
29 Dwyane Wade 3.00 8.00
30 Shaquille O'Neal 2.50 6.00
31 Michael Redd 1.00 2.50
32 T.J. Ford .75 2.00
33 Latrell Sprewell .75 2.00
34 Sam Cassell .75 2.00
35 Jason Kidd 1.50 4.00
36 Richard Jefferson 1.00 2.50
37 Baron Davis 1.00 2.50
38 Jamaal Magloire .60 1.50
39 Allan Houston .75 2.00
40 Stephon Marbury .75 2.00
41 Steve Francis 1.00 2.50
42 Cuttino Mobley .75 2.00
43 Glenn Robinson .75 2.00
44 Kenny Thomas .60 1.50
45 Shawn Marion 1.00 2.50
46 Amare Stoudemire 1.25 3.00
47 Zach Randolph .75 2.00
48 Damon Stoudamire .75 2.00
49 Chris Webber 1.00 2.50
50 Peja Stojakovic 1.00 2.50
51 Manu Ginobili 1.25 3.00
52 Tim Duncan 1.50 4.00
53 Rashard Lewis 1.00 2.50
54 Ray Allen 1.00 2.50
55 Jalen Rose .75 2.00
56 Vince Carter 1.50 4.00
57 Carlos Boozer 1.00 2.50
58 Andrei Kirilenko .75 2.00

59 Larry Hughes	.75	2.00
60 Gilbert Arenas	1.00	2.50
61 Paul Pierce JSY	3.00	8.00
62 Eddy Curry JSY	2.00	5.00
63 LeBron James JSY	12.50	30.00
64 Antawn Jamison JSY	2.50	6.00
65 Dirk Nowitzki JSY	4.00	10.00
66 Antoine Walker JSY	2.50	6.00
67 Carmelo Anthony JSY	5.00	12.00
68 Ben Wallace JSY	2.50	6.00
69 Jason Richardson JSY	2.50	6.00
70 Yao Ming JSY	5.00	12.00
71 Michael Jordan JSY	40.00	100.00
72 Kobe Bryant JSY	10.00	25.00
73 Quentin Richardson JSY	2.00	5.00
74 Jason Williams JSY	2.00	5.00
75 Eddie Jones JSY	2.00	5.00
76 Keith Van Horn JSY	2.00	5.00
77 Kevin Garnett JSY	5.00	12.00
78 Kenyon Martin JSY	2.50	6.00
79 Jamal Mashburn JSY	2.50	6.00
80 Kurt Thomas JSY	2.00	5.00
81 Juwan Howard JSY	2.00	5.00
82 Allen Iverson JSY	4.00	10.00
83 Joe Johnson JSY	2.50	6.00
84 Shareef Abdur-Rahim JSY	2.00	5.00
85 Mike Bibby JSY	2.50	6.00
86 Tony Parker JSY	2.50	6.00
87 Luke Ridnour JSY	2.00	5.00
88 Jalen Rose JSY	2.00	5.00
89 Gordan Giricek JSY	2.00	5.00
90 Juan Dixon JSY	2.00	5.00
91 Emeka Okafor RC	5.00	12.00
92 Dwight Howard RC	10.00	25.00
93 Shaun Livingston RC	3.00	8.00
94 Luol Deng RC	5.00	12.00
95 Ben Gordon RC	4.00	10.00
96 Devin Harris RC	5.00	12.00
97 Andre Iguodala RC	5.00	12.00
98 Andris Biedrins RC	4.00	10.00
99 Josh Childress RC	3.00	8.00
100 Josh Smith RC	5.00	12.00
101 Jameer Nelson RC	4.00	10.00
102 J.R. Smith RC	4.00	10.00
103 Sergei Monia RC	3.00	8.00
104 Sebastian Telfair RC	3.00	8.00
105 Pavel Podkolzine RC	3.00	8.00
106 Luke Jackson RC	3.00	8.00
107 Dorell Wright RC	5.00	12.00
108 Robert Swift RC	3.00	8.00
109 Anderson Varejao RC	4.00	10.00
110 Sasha Vujacic RC	3.00	8.00
111 Rafael Araujo RC	3.00	8.00
112 Al Jefferson RC	5.00	12.00
113 Kris Humphries RC	3.00	8.00
114 Kirk Snyder RC	3.00	8.00
115 Peter John Ramos RC	3.00	8.00
116 Beno Udrih RC	3.00	8.00
117 Viktor Khryapa RC	3.00	8.00
118 David Harrison RC	3.00	8.00
119 Trevor Ariza RC	3.00	8.00
120 Ha Seung-Jin RC	3.00	8.00
121 Kevin Martin RC	4.00	10.00
122 Delonte West RC	4.00	10.00
123 Blake Stepp RC	3.00	8.00
124 Chris Duhon RC	3.00	8.00
125 Tony Allen RC	4.00	10.00
126 Donta Smith RC	3.00	8.00
127 Andre Emmett RC	3.00	8.00
128 Royal Ivey RC	3.00	8.00
129 Nenad Krstic RC	3.00	8.00
130 Romain Sato RC	3.00	8.00
131 Antonio Burks RC	3.00	8.00
132 Lionel Chalmers RC	3.00	8.00
133 LeBron James SIR	4.00	10.00
134 LeBron James SIR	4.00	10.00
135 LeBron James SIR	4.00	10.00
136 LeBron James SIR	4.00	10.00
137 LeBron James SIR	4.00	10.00
138 LeBron James SIR	4.00	10.00
139 LeBron James SIR	4.00	10.00
140 LeBron James SIR	4.00	10.00
141 LeBron James SIR	4.00	10.00
142 LeBron James SIR	4.00	10.00
143 LeBron James SIR	4.00	10.00
144 LeBron James SIR	4.00	10.00
145 LeBron James SIR	4.00	10.00
146 LeBron James SIR	4.00	10.00
147 LeBron James SIR	4.00	10.00
148 LeBron James SIR	4.00	10.00
149 LeBron James SIR	4.00	10.00
150 LeBron James SIR	4.00	10.00
151 LeBron James SIR	4.00	10.00
152 LeBron James SIR	4.00	10.00
153 LeBron James SIR	4.00	10.00
154 LeBron James SIR	4.00	10.00
155 LeBron James SIR	4.00	10.00
156 LeBron James SIR	4.00	10.00
157 LeBron James SIR	4.00	10.00
158 LeBron James SIR	4.00	10.00
159 LeBron James SIR	4.00	10.00
160 LeBron James SIR	4.00	10.00
161 LeBron James SIR	4.00	10.00
162 LeBron James SIR	4.00	10.00

2004-05 SP Game Used Parallel

Randomly inserted in packs, this 162-card set parallels the base set enhanced with sequential numbering to 100 for cards 1-90 and sequential numbering to 50 for cards 91-162. An LTD parallel was also inserted and these cards are numbered in a one of one format.
*1-60: .75X TO 2X BASE HI
*61-90: .6X TO 1.5X BASE HI
*91-132: 1X TO 2.5X BASE HI
*133-162: 1.5X TO 4X BASE HI

2004-05 SP Game Used All-Star Apparel

Randomly seeded with all memorabilia cards at the rate of one in one, this six-card set features jerseys of players from the Got Milk Rookie Challenge game and the logo from the 2004 NBA All-Star Game in Los Angeles. A Gold Parallel version was also inserted and these cards are numbered to 100.
*GOLD SINGLES: .6X TO 1.5X BASE JSY HI

BO Carlos Boozer	2.50	6.00
CM Cuttino Mobley	2.00	5.00
MD Mike Dunleavy	2.00	5.00
NH Nene	2.00	5.00
RM Ronald Murray	2.00	5.00
UH Udonis Haslem	2.00	5.00

2004-05 SP Game Used All-Star Sigs

Limited to 25 copies, this 30-card set features a small head shot of some of the games greatest all-stars along with a sticker autograph. A Gold parallel version of this set was also produced and these cards are numbered to the featured player's total number of All-Star appearances.
UNPRICED GOLD PRINT RUN ONE TO 14 SETS

AK Andrei Kirilenko	12.50	30.00
BD Baron Davis	12.50	30.00
BM Brad Miller	10.00	25.00
BR Bill Russell	100.00	200.00
CD Clyde Drexler	30.00	80.00
DE Dennis Rodman	75.00	150.00
DR David Robinson	90.00	175.00
GP Gary Payton	20.00	50.00
JE Julius Erving	40.00	100.00
JK Jason Kidd	25.00	60.00
JS John Stockton	60.00	150.00
KB Kobe Bryant	125.00	250.00
KG Kevin Garnett	50.00	120.00
LB Larry Bird	75.00	150.00
MJ Michael Jordan	400.00	700.00
MR Michael Redd	10.00	25.00
PP Paul Pierce	25.00	60.00
RM Reggie Miller	40.00	100.00
RP Robert Parish	15.00	40.00
SA Shareef Abdur-Rahim	10.00	25.00
SM Stephon Marbury	10.00	25.00
WF Walt Frazier	15.00	40.00
YM Yao Ming	30.00	80.00
ZO Alonzo Mourning	60.00	150.00

2004-05 SP Game Used Authentic Fabrics

Inserted at the combined odds of one per pack for all memorabilia cards, this 83-card set features colored backgrounds and a square swatch of memorabilia centered towards the bottom of the card. A Gold version sequentially numbered to 100 and a Patch version in a one of one format were also inserted.
SP INFO.PROVIDED BY UPPER DECK
*GOLD SINGLES: .6X TO 1.5X BASE JSY HI

AH Anfernee Hardaway	6.00	15.00
AJ Antawn Jamison	2.50	6.00
AK Andrei Kirilenko	2.00	5.00
AM Aaron McKie	2.00	5.00
AN Andre Miller	2.00	5.00
AS Amare Stoudemire	3.00	8.00
BD Baron Davis	2.50	6.00
BO Boris Diaw	2.00	5.00
CA Carlos Boozer	2.50	6.00
CB Caron Butler	2.50	6.00
CH Chauncey Billups	2.50	6.00
CJ Casey Jacobsen SP	2.00	5.00
CM Corey Maggette	2.00	5.00
CW Chris Wilcox	2.00	5.00
DA Derek Anderson	1.50	4.00
DB Shane Battier	2.00	5.00
DF Derek Fisher	2.00	5.00
DG Drew Gooden	2.00	5.00
DI Dikembe Mutombo	2.50	6.00
DM Darius Miles	2.00	5.00
DW David Wesley	2.00	5.00
EB Elton Brand	2.50	6.00
EC Eddy Curry	2.00	5.00
EG Manu Ginobili	3.00	8.00
EJ Eddie Jones SP	2.00	5.00
FJ Fred Jones	2.00	5.00
GA Gilbert Arenas	2.50	6.00
GG Gordan Giricek SP	2.00	5.00
GR Glenn Robinson	2.00	5.00
JA Marko Jaric SP	2.00	5.00
JD Juan Dixon SP	2.00	5.00
JH Jarvis Hayes	2.00	5.00
JI Jiri Welsch	2.00	5.00
JJ Joe Johnson	2.50	6.00
JK Jason Kidd SP	4.00	10.00
JM Jamaal Magloire	2.00	5.00
JO Jermaine O'Neal	2.50	6.00
JR Jalen Rose	2.00	5.00
JS Jerry Stackhouse	2.00	5.00
JT Jason Terry	2.00	5.00
JW Jason Williams	2.00	5.00
KB Kobe Bryant SP	12.00	30.00
KK Kerry Kittles	1.50	4.00
KR Kareem Rush SP	2.00	5.00
KT Kurt Thomas SP	2.00	5.00
KV Keith Van Horn SP	2.00	5.00
LE Rashard Lewis	2.50	6.00
LH Larry Hughes SP	2.00	5.00
LJ LeBron James	15.00	40.00
LO Lamar Odom	2.50	6.00
LR Luke Ridnour	2.00	5.00
LS Latrell Sprewell	2.00	5.00
MA Jamal Mashburn	2.50	6.00
MB Mike Bibby	2.50	6.00
MD Antonio McDyess	2.00	5.00
MI Mike Dunleavy	2.00	5.00
MJ Michael Jordan SP	50.00	100.00
MM Mike Miller	2.50	6.00
MO Morris Peterson	1.50	4.00
MP Mickael Pietrus	2.00	5.00
MR Michael Redd	2.50	6.00
NH Nene	2.00	5.00
NV Nick Van Exel	2.00	5.00
OL Michael Olowokandi	2.00	5.00
PG Pau Gasol	2.50	6.00
PR Tayshaun Prince	2.50	6.00
PS Peja Stojakovic	2.50	6.00
QR Quentin Richardson	2.00	5.00
RA Ray Allen	2.50	6.00
RH Richard Hamilton	2.00	5.00
RL Raef LaFrentz	2.00	5.00
RM Reggie Miller	3.00	8.00
SB Shane Battier	2.00	5.00
SJ Stephen Jackson	2.00	5.00
SM Shawn Marion SP	2.50	6.00
SS Stromile Swift SP	2.00	5.00
ST Stephon Marbury	2.00	5.00
TC Tyson Chandler	2.00	5.00
TD Tim Duncan	4.00	10.00
TK Toni Kukoc	2.00	5.00
TP Tony Parker	2.50	6.00
TR Theo Ratliff	2.00	5.00
WS Wally Szczerbiak	2.00	5.00
ZI Zydrunas Ilgauskas SP	2.00	5.00

2004-05 SP Game Used Authentic Fabrics Autographs

Randomly inserted in packs, this 31-card set parallels the design aspects of the base Authentic Fabrics set enhanced with a player autograph and sequential numbering to 100.

AJ Antawn Jamison	8.00	20.00
AK Andrei Kirilenko	8.00	20.00
AM Andre Miller	8.00	20.00
AN Antonio McDyess	8.00	20.00
AS Amare Stoudemire	20.00	50.00
BD Baron Davis	10.00	25.00
CA Carmelo Anthony	25.00	60.00
CM Corey Maggette	8.00	20.00
DW Dwyane Wade	60.00	150.00
GA Gilbert Arenas	10.00	25.00
GP Gary Payton	15.00	40.00
JC Jamal Crawford	8.00	20.00
JK Jason Kidd	25.00	60.00
JR Jason Richardson	10.00	25.00
KB Kobe Bryant	100.00	200.00
KG Kevin Garnett	50.00	100.00
LJ LeBron James	150.00	300.00
LO Lamar Odom	10.00	25.00
MB Mike Bibby	8.00	20.00
MJ Michael Jordan	300.00	600.00
PG Pau Gasol	20.00	50.00
PP Paul Pierce	15.00	40.00
RJ Richard Jefferson	8.00	20.00
RM Reggie Miller	40.00	100.00
SA Shareef Abdur-Rahim	8.00	20.00
SC Sam Cassell	8.00	20.00
SH Shawn Marion	8.00	20.00
SM Stephon Marbury	20.00	50.00
TM Tracy McGrady	20.00	50.00
YM Yao Ming	25.00	60.00
ZR Zach Randolph	10.00	25.00

2004-05 SP Game Used Authentic Fabrics Dual

Randomly inserted, this 38-card set utilizes some design aspects of the single player Authentic Fabrics cards but is horizontally designed with two players and two swatches of memorabilia. Each card is sequentially numbered to 100.
UNPRICED DUAL PATCH PRINT RUN 10 SETS
UNPRICED LOGO PRINT RUN ONE SET
UNPRICED QUAD PRINT RUN 10 SETS

AL Ray Allen	4.00	10.00
Rashard Lewis		
BJ Kobe Bryant	50.00	120.00
LeBron James		
BM Elton Brand	4.00	10.00
Corey Maggette		
BR Chris Bosh	4.00	10.00
Jalen Rose		
CB Wilt Chamberlain	50.00	120.00
Kobe Bryant		
CC Jamal Crawford	4.00	10.00
Tyson Chandler		
DM Baron Davis	4.00	10.00
Jamal Mashburn		
FM Steve Francis	8.00	20.00
Yao Ming		
GF Devean George	4.00	10.00
Derek Fisher		
GP Manu Ginobili	10.00	25.00
Tony Parker		
GW Pau Gasol	6.00	15.00
Jason Williams		
HG Juwan Howard	4.00	10.00
Reece Gaines		
HH Larry Hughes	4.00	10.00
Jarvis Hayes		
IS Allen Iverson	8.00	20.00
Eric Snow		
JB Michael Jordan	60.00	150.00
Kobe Bryant		
JJ LeBron James	100.00	200.00
Michael Jordan		
JT Michael Jordan	50.00	120.00
Isiah Thomas		
KM Jason Kidd	6.00	15.00
Kenyon Martin		
MA Darous Miles	4.00	10.00
Shareef Abdur-Rahim		
MB Mike Miller	4.00	10.00
Shane Battier		
MI Tracy McGrady	10.00	25.00
Allen Iverson		
NN Dirk Nowitzki	6.00	15.00
Steve Nash		
OM Shaquille O'Neal	12.50	30.00
Karl Malone		
PB Paul Pierce	25.00	60.00
Larry Bird		
PS James Posey	4.00	10.00
Stromile Swift		
RA Zach Randolph	4.00	10.00
Shareef Abdur-Rahim		
RD David Robinson	15.00	40.00
Tim Duncan		
RJ Jason Richardson	4.00	10.00
Richard Jefferson		
RK Glenn Robinson	4.00	10.00
Kyle Korver		
RV Michael Redd	4.00	10.00
Keith Van Horn		
RW Kareem Rush	4.00	10.00
Luke Walton		
SC Latrell Sprewell	8.00	20.00
Sam Cassell		
SK John Stockton	12.50	30.00
Andrei Kirilenko		
SM Amare Stoudemire	8.00	20.00
Shawn Marion		
SW Peja Stojakovic	8.00	20.00
Chris Webber		
TS Kurt Thomas	4.00	10.00
Mike Sweetney		
WH Ben Wallace	8.00	20.00
Richard Hamilton		
WO Dwyane Wade	10.00	25.00
Lamar Odom		

2004-05 SP Game Used Authentic Fabrics Dual Autographs

Randomly inserted, this 42-card set utilizes some design aspects of the single player Authentic Fabrics cards but is horizontally designed with two players, two swatches of memorabilia and two autographs. Each card is sequentially numbered to 50.

AJ Carmelo Anthony/15	250.00	500.00
LeBron James		
AM Carmelo Anthony	40.00	80.00
Andre Miller		
AR Shareef Abdur-Rahim	20.00	50.00
Zach Randolph		
AS Gilbert Arenas	15.00	40.00
Jerry Stackhouse		
BA Mike Bibby	15.00	40.00
Gilbert Arenas		
BG Chauncey Billups	60.00	120.00
Kevin Garnett		
BH Chauncey Billups	25.00	60.00
Richard Hamilton		
BJ Mike Bibby	15.00	40.00
Richard Jefferson		
BM Shane Battier	15.00	40.00
Corey Maggette		
BP Kobe Bryant	100.00	200.00
Gary Payton		
BS Chris Bosh	30.00	80.00
Stephon Marbury		
DM Baron Davis	40.00	80.00
Reggie Miller		
GB Pau Gasol	30.00	80.00
Shane Battier		
GC Kevin Garnett	50.00	100.00
Sam Cassell		
GM Kevin Garnett/15	100.00	200.00
Tracy McGrady		
JB LeBron James	150.00	300.00
Carlos Boozer		
JJ Michael Jordan/15	500.00	1000.00
LeBron James		
JM LeBron James	200.00	400.00
Yao Ming		
KG Andrei Kirilenko	20.00	50.00
- Pau Gasol		
KJ Jason Kidd	40.00	80.00
Richard Jefferson		
MA Darius Miles	15.00	40.00
Shareef Abdur-Rahim		
MG Tracy McGrady	30.00	60.00
Drew Gooden		
MH Andre Miller	15.00	40.00
Nene		
MJ Reggie Miller	40.00	100.00
Fred Jones		
MK Stephon Marbury	50.00	120.00
Jason Kidd		
MM Shawn Marion	15.00	40.00
Antonio McDyess		
MP Tracy McGrady	40.00	80.00
Paul Pierce		
MR Alonzo Mourning	60.00	120.00
Richard Jefferson		
MW Corey Maggette	15.00	40.00
Chris Wilcox		
PB Paul Pierce/15	125.00	250.00
Larry Bird		
PF Gary Payton	25.00	60.00
Derek Fisher		
PM Paul Pierce	15.00	40.00
Marcus Banks		
RJ Jason Richardson	15.00	40.00
Fred Jones		
RP Jason Richardson	15.00	40.00
Mickael Pietrus		
RR Zach Randolph	15.00	40.00
Jason Richardson		
SA Shawn Marion	40.00	80.00
Amare Stoudemire		
SM Amare Stoudemire	30.00	60.00
Antonio McDyess		
WD Chris Wilcox	15.00	40.00
Juan Dixon		
WH Dwyane Wade	60.00	120.00
Udonis Haslem		
WO Dwyane Wade	60.00	120.00
Lamar Odom		

2004-05 SP Game Used Authentic Fabrics Triple

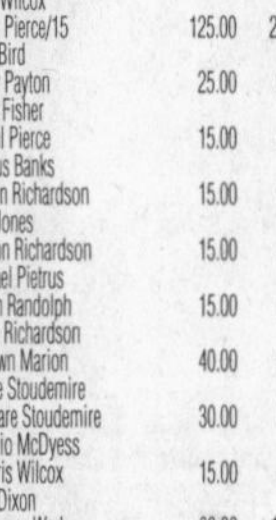

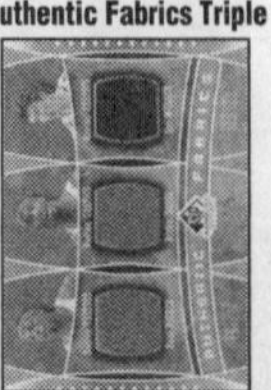

Limted to 25 and randomly seeded, this nine card set features three players and three swatches of game worn memorabilia.

JBJ Michael Jordan	125.00	250.00
Kobe Bryant		
LeBron James		
JBW LeBron James	20.00	50.00
Carlos Boozer		
DaJuan Wagner		
MKJ Kenyon Martin	10.00	25.00
Kerry Kittles		
Richard Jefferson		
PDW Paul Pierce	12.50	30.00
Ricky Davis		
Jiri Welsch		
RSA Zach Randolph	10.00	25.00
Damon Stoudamire		
Derek Anderson		
RVD Jason Richardson	10.00	25.00
Nick Van Exel		
Mike Dunleavy		

2004-05 SP Game Used Authentic Patches

Randomly seeded and limited to 100 serial numbered copies, this 57-card set has a gray border along the bottom and a premium patch swatch in the lower left hand corner. Dual player versions serially numbered to 25 and Triple player versions serially numbered to 10 were also produced and inserted.
UNPRICED TRIPLE PRINT RUN 10 SETS

AK Andrei Kirilenko	5.00	12.00
AL Ray Allen	8.00	20.00
AM Andre Miller	5.00	12.00
AS Amare Stoudemire	8.00	20.00
AW Antoine Walker	6.00	15.00
BW Ben Wallace	6.00	15.00
CA Carmelo Anthony	12.00	30.00
CB Chris Bosh	6.00	15.00
CH Chauncey Billups	6.00	15.00
CM Cuttino Mobley	5.00	12.00
CO Corey Maggette	5.00	12.00
CW Chris Webber	8.00	20.00
DG Drew Gooden	5.00	12.00
DM Darius Miles	4.00	10.00
DN Dirk Nowitzki	10.00	25.00
DW Dwyane Wade	20.00	50.00
EC Eddy Curry	5.00	12.00
EG Manu Ginobili	8.00	20.00
GA Gilbert Arenas	6.00	15.00
GP Gary Payton	6.00	15.00
JC Jamal Crawford	5.00	12.00
JH Jarvis Hayes	4.00	10.00
JR Jalen Rose	5.00	12.00
JS Jerry Stackhouse	5.00	12.00
JT Jason Terry	5.00	12.00
JW Jason Williams	8.00	20.00
KB Kobe Bryant	50.00	125.00
KE Kenyon Martin	6.00	15.00
KG Kevin Garnett	12.00	30.00
KM Karl Malone	8.00	20.00
LH Larry Hughes	5.00	12.00
LJ LeBron James	30.00	80.00
LO Lamar Odom	6.00	15.00
LS Latrell Sprewell	6.00	15.00
MB Mike Bibby	6.00	15.00
MF Michael Finley	6.00	15.00
MJ Michael Jordan	100.00	200.00
MP Morris Peterson	4.00	10.00
MR Michael Redd	6.00	15.00
NH Nene	5.00	12.00
NV Nick Van Exel	5.00	12.00
PG Pau Gasol	6.00	15.00
PP Paul Pierce	8.00	20.00
PS Peja Stojakovic	6.00	15.00
QR Quentin Richardson	5.00	12.00
RH Richard Hamilton	5.00	12.00
RJ Richard Jefferson	6.00	15.00
RL Rashard Lewis	6.00	15.00
RM Reggie Miller	12.50	30.00
SA Shareef Abdur-Rahim	5.00	12.00
SF Steve Francis	6.00	15.00
SH Shawn Marion	6.00	15.00
SM Stephon Marbury	5.00	12.00
SN Steve Nash	8.00	20.00
TM Tracy McGrady	8.00	20.00
TP Tony Parker	6.00	15.00
ZR Zach Randolph	5.00	12.00

2004-05 SP Game Used Authentic Patches Autographs

Randomly seeded in packs, this 30-card set parallels the design of the Authentic Patches set enhanced with a player autograph and sequential numbering to 50. Dual Autographed versions serially numbered to five were also inserted.

AJ Antawn Jamison	15.00	40.00
AK Andrei Kirilenko	15.00	40.00
AM Andre Miller	15.00	40.00
AN Antonio McDyess	15.00	40.00
AS Amare Stoudemire	25.00	60.00
BD Baron Davis	15.00	40.00
CA Carmelo Anthony	60.00	150.00
CM Corey Maggette	15.00	40.00
DW Dwyane Wade	125.00	250.00
GA Gilbert Arenas	15.00	40.00
GP Gary Payton	20.00	50.00
JC Jamal Crawford	15.00	40.00
JK Jason Kidd	60.00	120.00
JR Jason Richardson	15.00	40.00
KB Kobe Bryant	150.00	300.00
KG Kevin Garnett	75.00	150.00
LJ LeBron James	200.00	450.00
LO Lamar Odom	20.00	50.00
MB Mike Bibby	15.00	40.00
PG Pau Gasol	30.00	80.00
PP Paul Pierce	40.00	80.00
RJ Richard Jefferson	15.00	40.00
RM Reggie Miller	75.00	200.00
SA Shareef Abdur-Rahim	15.00	40.00
SC Sam Cassell	15.00	40.00
SH Shawn Marion	20.00	50.00
SM Stephon Marbury	20.00	50.00
TM Tracy McGrady	40.00	100.00
YM Yao Ming	40.00	100.00
ZR Zach Randolph	15.00	40.00

2004-05 SP Game Used Authentic Patches Dual

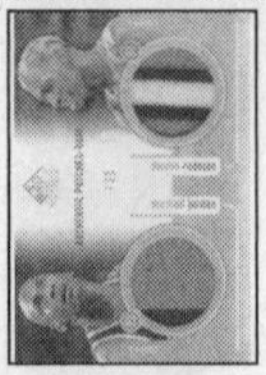

Inserted randomly in packs, this eight card set utilizes some of the design aspects of the Authentic Patches set but is horizontally designed with two players and two memorabilia patches. Each card is limited to 25 serially numbered copies.

AG Antawn Jamison	20.00	50.00
Gilbert Arenas		
CR Wilt Chamberlain	175.00	300.00
Bill Russell		
JA LeBron James	50.00	120.00
Carmelo Anthony		
JB Michael Jordan	175.00	300.00
Kobe Bryant		
JR Michael Jordan	100.00	200.00
Dennis Rodman		

2004-05 SP Game Used Endorsed Numbers

Inserted randomly, this 88-card set is limited to each specific player's jersey number and has a sticker signature across the middle.
SOME NOT PRICED DUE TO SCARCITY

AJ Antawn Jamison/33	12.50	30.00
AK Andrei Kirilenko/47	20.00	50.00
AN Antonio McDyess/24	20.00	50.00
BB Brent Barry/31	15.00	40.00
BH Brandon Hunter/56	5.00	12.00
BM Brad Miller/52	12.50	30.00
CD Clyde Drexler/22	100.00	200.00
CK Chris Kaman/35	5.00	12.00
CM Cedric Maxwell/31	10.00	25.00
CW Chris Wilcox/54	5.00	12.00
DA David Robinson/50	75.00	150.00
DJ Dahntay Jones/30	5.00	12.00
DM Darko Milicic/31	15.00	40.00
DR Dennis Rodman/91	50.00	120.00
FE Francisco Elson/56	6.00	15.00
GP Gary Payton/20	20.00	50.00
GR Glenn Robinson/31	12.00	30.00
JA Jason Kapono/24	5.00	12.00
JJ James Jones/33	6.00	15.00
KG Kevin Garnett/21	30.00	80.00
KK Kyle Korver/26	15.00	40.00
LB Larry Bird/33	100.00	200.00
LJ LeBron James/23	200.00	400.00
MA Magic Johnson/32	75.00	150.00
MJ Michael Jordan/23	300.00	600.00
ML Maciej Lampe/30	8.00	20.00
MR Michael Redd/22	12.50	30.00
MS Mike Sweetney/50	5.00	12.00
MW Maurice Williams/25	5.00	12.00
NH Nene/31	8.00	20.00
PG Pau Gasol/16	30.00	80.00
PP Paul Pierce/34	20.00	50.00
RH Richard Hamilton/32	12.50	30.00
RJ Richard Jefferson/24	10.00	25.00
RM Reggie Miller/31	40.00	100.00
SA Shareef Abdur-Rahim/33	10.00	25.00
SC Sam Cassell/19	15.00	40.00
SH Shawn Marion/31	15.00	40.00
TO Travis Outlaw/25	6.00	15.00
WG Willie Green/33	5.00	12.00
WZ Wang Zhizhi/15	15.00	40.00
ZO Alonzo Mourning/33	75.00	150.00
ZP Zaza Pachulia/27	5.00	12.00
ZR Zach Randolph/50	10.00	25.00

2004-05 SP Game Used Legendary Fabrics

Inserted at the combined rate for memorabilia cards at one per pack, this 11-card set places a player photo above an "L" shaped swatch of game used memorabilia.

BR Bill Russell	8.00	20.00
CD Clyde Drexler	6.00	15.00
DR Dennis Rodman	8.00	20.00
GG George Gervin	5.00	12.00
IT Isiah Thomas	5.00	12.00
JE Julius Erving	10.00	25.00
JS John Stockton	8.00	20.00
LB Larry Bird	15.00	40.00
MA Magic Johnson	12.00	30.00
MJ Michael Jordan	40.00	100.00
WF Walt Frazier	5.00	12.00

2004-05 SP Game Used Legendary Fabrics Autograp

Seeded in packs randomly, this 11-card set paralle the Legendary Fabrics set enhanced with player autographs and sequential numbering to 100.

BR Bill Russell	100.00	20
CD Clyde Drexler	25.00	6
DR Dennis Rodman	100.00	25
GG George Gervin	15.00	4
IT Isiah Thomas	25.00	6
JE Julius Erving	50.00	10
JS John Stockton	75.00	15
LB Larry Bird	100.00	20
MA Magic Johnson	75.00	15
MJ Michael Jordan	300.00	55
WF Walt Frazier	15.00	4

2004-05 SP Game Used Rook Exclusive Autographs

Randomly inserted in packs, this 51-card set is horizontally designed with a player photo and eith cut signature or a sticker signature centered along bottom. Each card is limited to 100 serially numbe copies.

RE1 Andre Emmett	6.00	1
RE2 Andre Iguodala	20.00	5
RE3 Al Jefferson	40.00	10
RE4 Anderson Varejao	12.50	3
RE5 Ben Gordon	15.00	4
RE6 Andris Biedrins	8.00	2
RE7 Blake Stepp	6.00	1
RE8 Antonio Burks	6.00	1
RE9 Beno Udrih	6.00	1
RE10 Chris Duhon	6.00	1
RE11 David Harrison	6.00	1
RE12 Delonte West	12.50	3
RE13 Dwight Howard	80.00	20
RE14 Dorell Wright	10.00	2
RE15 Donta Smith	6.00	1
RE16 Devin Harris	15.00	4
RE17 Ha Seung-Jin	10.00	2
RE18 Josh Childress	6.00	1
RE19 Jameer Nelson	10.00	2
RE20 J.R. Smith	12.50	3
RE21 Pape Sow	6.00	
RE22 Jackson Vroman	6.00	
RE23 Kris Humphries	6.00	
RE24 Kevin Martin	25.00	
RE25 Kirk Snyder	6.00	
RE26 Lionel Chalmers	6.00	
RE27 Luol Deng	15.00	4
RE28 Luke Jackson	6.00	
RE29 Matt Freije	6.00	
RE30 Pavel Podkolzine	6.00	
RE31 Peter John Ramos	6.00	
RE32 Rafael Araujo	6.00	
RE33 Robert Swift	6.00	
RE34 Romain Sato	6.00	
RE35 Shaun Livingston	10.00	
RE36 Sergei Monia	6.00	
RE37 Sebastian Telfair	6.00	
RE38 Sasha Vujacic	6.00	
RE39 Tony Allen	8.00	
RE40 Tim Pickett	6.00	
RE41 Trevor Ariza	6.00	
RE42 Viktor Khryapa	6.00	
RE43 David Young	6.00	
RE44 Royal Ivey	6.00	
RE45 Christian Drejer	6.00	
RE46 Bernard Robinson	6.00	
RE48 Justin Reed	6.00	
RE49 Darius Rice	6.00	
RE50 Ricky Minard	6.00	
RE51 Nenad Krstic	6.00	
NNO Josh Smith	20.00	5

2004-05 SP Game Used SIGnificance

Limited to 100 copies, this 111-card set features photos and an unshaded basketball along the bot in which autographs appear. Gold versions limite 10 were produced along with dual signatures, numbered to 25, and dual gold signatures, numb to five.

AJ Antawn Jamison	5.00	
AK Andrei Kirilenko	6.00	
AL Al Harrington	5.00	
AM Andre Miller	5.00	
AS Amare Stoudemire	12.50	
BB Brent Barry	5.00	
BC Bob Cousy	25.00	
BD Baron Davis	5.00	
BE Jerome Beasley	5.00	
BH Brandon Hunter	5.00	
BL Steve Blake	5.00	
BM Brad Miller	6.00	
BO Carlos Boozer	5.00	
BR Bill Russell	60.00	1

Bill Walton 10.00 25.00
Carmelo Anthony 25.00 60.00
Clyde Drexler 20.00 50.00
Cedric Maxwell 5.00 12.00
Chauncey Billups 8.00 20.00
Chris Kaman 5.00 12.00
Corey Maggette 5.00 12.00
Chuck Daly 20.00 40.00
Darryl Dawkins 8.00 20.00
Derek Fisher 6.00 15.00
Drew Gooden 5.00 12.00
Dan Dickau 5.00 12.00
Darko Milicic 5.00 12.00
David Robinson 40.00 80.00
David Thompson 5.00 12.00
Dwyane Wade 40.00 100.00
Dahntay Jones 5.00 12.00
Eddy Curry 5.00 12.00
Francisco Elson 5.00 12.00
Fred Jones 5.00 12.00
Gilbert Arenas 6.00 15.00
George Gervin 8.00 20.00
Gordan Giricek 5.00 12.00
Gary Payton 10.00 25.00
Glenn Robinson 5.00 12.00
Gerald Wallace 5.00 12.00
siah Thomas 20.00 50.00
Jamaal Wilkes 8.00 20.00
Jon Barry 5.00 12.00
Juan Dixon 5.00 12.00
Julius Erving 30.00 80.00
Josh Howard 5.00 12.00
James Jones 5.00 12.00
Jason Kidd 12.50 30.00
Jerome Moiso 5.00 12.00
John Salley 8.00 20.00
Jalen Rose 6.00 15.00
John Stockton 40.00 100.00
Jamaal Tinsley 5.00 12.00
James Worthy 30.00 60.00
Jason Kapono 5.00 12.00
Kobe Bryant 100.00 200.00
K.C. Jones 8.00 20.00
Keith Bogans 5.00 12.00
Kevin Garnett 30.00 80.00
Kyle Korver 8.00 20.00
Kareem Rush 5.00 12.00
Kurt Rambis 12.50 30.00
Larry Bird 50.00 120.00
Leandro Barbosa 5.00 12.00
LeBron James 125.00 250.00
Lamar Odom 6.00 15.00
Luke Ridnour 5.00 12.00
Magic Johnson 50.00 120.00
Mike Bibby 6.00 15.00
Mickael Pietrus 5.00 12.00
Michael Jordan 300.00 500.00
Morris Peterson 5.00 12.00
Michael Redd 5.00 12.00
Mike Sweetney 5.00 12.00
Maurice Williams 5.00 12.00
Nene 5.00 12.00
Primoz Brezec 5.00 12.00
Pau Gasol 15.00 40.00
Zoran Planinic 5.00 12.00
Paul Pierce 10.00 25.00
Pat Riley 15.00 40.00
Reece Gaines 5.00 12.00
Richard Hamilton 6.00 15.00
Jason Richardson 6.00 15.00
Richard Jefferson 5.00 12.00
Reggie Miller 40.00 100.00
Dennis Rodman 50.00 120.00
Robert Parish 8.00 20.00
Shareef Abdur-Rahim 5.00 12.00
Shane Battier 6.00 15.00
Sam Cassell 5.00 12.00
Shawn Marion 8.00 20.00
Stephon Marbury 12.50 30.00
Jerry Stackhouse 6.00 15.00
Spud Webb 8.00 20.00
Troy Bell 5.00 12.00
Tracy McGrady 20.00 50.00
Travis Outlaw 5.00 12.00
Tony Parker 6.00 15.00
Theron Smith 5.00 12.00
Walt Frazier 8.00 20.00
Willie Green 5.00 12.00
Willis Reed 10.00 25.00
Wes Unseld 8.00 20.00
Wang Zhizhi 8.00 20.00
Yao Ming 20.00 50.00
Zarko Cabarkapa 5.00 12.00
Alonzo Mourning 20.00 50.00
Zaza Pachulia 5.00 12.00
Zach Randolph 6.00 15.00

2004-05 SP Game Used SIGnificance Duals

ndomly inserted and limited to 25 copies, this 30-
d set places two players and two autographs on
h card.
PRICED GOLD PRINT RUN 5 SETS
Carmelo Anthony 300.00 600.00
ichael Jordan
Brent Barry 15.00 40.00
on Barry
Kobe Bryant 150.00 300.00
agic Johnson
Carlos Boozer 20.00 50.00
ndrei Kirilenko
Eddy Curry 20.00 50.00
amal Crawford
Darryl Dawkins 50.00 120.00
ulius Erving
Baron Davis 40.00 100.00
iah Thomas
Kevin Garnett 75.00 150.00
am Cassell
Kevin Garnett 150.00 300.00
ll Russell
K.C. Jones 30.00 80.00
ob Cousy
LeBron James 700.00 1200.00
ichael Jordan

KS Jason Kidd 100.00 200.00
John Stockton
LK Larry Bird 100.00 200.00
K.C. Jones
MD Tracy McGrady 75.00 150.00
Clyde Drexler
MJ Cedric Maxwell 15.00 40.00
K.C. Jones
MP Cedric Maxwell 40.00 100.00
Robert Parish
MS Stephon Marbury 20.00 50.00
Mike Sweetney
PB Paul Pierce 75.00 150.00
Larry Bird
RJ Kurt Rambis 75.00 150.00
Magic Johnson
RP Michael Redd 15.00 40.00
Zaur Pachulia
RW Kareem Rush 15.00 40.00
Luke Walton
SE Amare Stoudemire 75.00 150.00
Julius Erving
WE Dwyane Wade 125.00 250.00
Julius Erving

2004-05 SP Game Used SIGnificant Numbers

Randomly seeded in packs, this 12-card set is horizontally designed with both an autograph and a swatch of memorabilia. Each card is limited to the featured player's jersey number.
STATED PRINT RUN ONE TO 50 SETS
SOME NOT PRICED DUE TO SCARCITY
AK Andrei Kirilenko/47 25.00 60.00
AS Amare Stoudemire/32 30.00 80.00
CA Carmelo Anthony/15 100.00 200.00
DR David Robinson/50 40.00 100.00
LJ LeBron James/23 250.00 400.00
MA Magic Johnson/32 90.00 180.00
MJ Michael Jordan/23 300.00 600.00

2004-05 SP Game Used Wood Impressions

Limited to 75 copies and randomly seeded in packs, this 42-card set places a player photo above a swatch of wood that is autographed.
AK Andrei Kirilenko 15.00 40.00
AM Andre Miller 10.00 25.00
AS Amare Stoudemire 15.00 40.00
BC Bob Cousy 25.00 60.00
BD Baron Davis 12.00 30.00
CA Carmelo Anthony 30.00 80.00
CD Clyde Drexler 30.00 80.00
CH Chauncey Billups 15.00 40.00
CM Corey Maggette 10.00 25.00
DR Dennis Rodman 100.00 200.00
DT David Thompson 15.00 40.00
DW Dwyane Wade 75.00 150.00
FE Francisco Elson 10.00 25.00
GG George Gervin 12.50 30.00
GP Gary Payton 12.50 30.00
IT Isiah Thomas 15.00 40.00
JC Jamal Crawford 10.00 25.00
JE Julius Erving 40.00 80.00
JH Josh Howard 10.00 25.00
JK Jason Kidd 25.00 60.00
JR Jason Richardson 10.00 25.00
JS John Stockton 75.00 150.00
JW James Worthy 25.00 60.00
KB Kobe Bryant 100.00 200.00
KG Kevin Garnett 50.00 120.00
KK Kyle Korver 10.00 25.00
LJ LeBron James 175.00 350.00
LO Lamar Odom 10.00 25.00
MA Magic Johnson 75.00 150.00
MD Marquis Daniels 10.00 25.00
MJ Michael Jordan 350.00 600.00
PG Pau Gasol 20.00 50.00
PP Paul Pierce 15.00 40.00
RJ Richard Jefferson 10.00 25.00
RM Reggie Miller 40.00 100.00
SA Shareef Abdur-Rahim 10.00 25.00
SM Shawn Marion 12.50 30.00
SW Spud Webb 12.50 30.00
TM Tracy McGrady 30.00 80.00
WR Willis Reed 15.00 40.00
YM Yao Ming 40.00 80.00
ZR Zach Randolph 10.00 25.00

2005-06 SP Game Used

Released in November 2004, SP Game Used boasts a 150-card set where cards 1-100 feature veterans and cards 101-150 feature rookie players serially numbered to 999. Base cards have white and gray backgrounds with highlights set to match team colors. SP Game Used was packaged in six pack boxes of three cards each and carried a suggested retail price of $29.99.

Each pack contains either an autograph or memorabilia cards.
UNPRICED PARALLEL PRINT RUN ONE SET
UNPRICED PARALLEL PRINT RUN 10 SETS
1 Al Harrington .75 2.00
2 Josh Smith 1.00 2.50
3 Josh Childress .75 2.00
4 Joe Johnson 1.00 2.50
5 Paul Pierce 1.25 3.00
6 Antoine Walker .75 2.00
7 Gary Payton 1.00 2.50
8 Al Jefferson 1.00 2.50
9 Emeka Okafor 1.00 2.50
10 Primoz Brezec .60 1.50
11 Gerald Wallace 1.00 2.50
12 Michael Jordan 8.00 20.00
13 Ben Gordon 1.00 2.50
14 Luol Deng 1.00 2.50
15 Eddy Curry .75 2.00
16 LeBron James 5.00 12.00
17 Dajuan Wagner .60 1.50
18 Drew Gooden .75 2.00
19 Larry Hughes .75 2.00
20 Dirk Nowitzki 1.50 4.00
21 Marquis Daniels .60 1.50
22 Michael Finley 1.00 2.50
23 Jerry Stackhouse .75 2.00
24 Andre Miller .75 2.00
25 Carmelo Anthony 2.00 5.00
26 Kenyon Martin 1.00 2.50
27 Nene .75 2.00
28 Rasheed Wallace 1.00 2.50
29 Ben Wallace 1.00 2.50
30 Richard Hamilton .75 2.00
31 Chauncey Billups 1.00 2.50
32 Baron Davis 1.00 2.50
33 Derek Fisher .75 2.00
34 Jason Richardson 1.00 2.50
35 Tracy McGrady 1.25 3.00
36 Yao Ming 1.25 3.00
37 Juwan Howard .75 2.00
38 Jermaine O'Neal 1.00 2.50
39 Ron Artest 1.00 2.50
40 Jamaal Tinsley .60 1.50
41 Corey Maggette .75 2.00
42 Elton Brand 1.00 2.50
43 Shaun Livingston .60 1.50
44 Kobe Bryant 5.00 12.00
45 Brian Cook .60 1.50
46 Lamar Odom 1.00 2.50
47 Bonzi Wells .60 1.50
48 Pau Gasol 1.00 2.50
49 Shane Battier .75 2.00
50 Shaquille O'Neal 2.00 5.00
51 Dwyane Wade 2.50 6.00
52 Dorell Wright .60 1.50
53 Eddie Jones .75 2.00
54 Joe Smith .75 2.00
55 Michael Redd 1.00 2.50
56 Desmond Mason .60 1.50
57 Kevin Garnett 2.00 5.00
58 Wally Szczerbiak .75 2.00
59 Sam Cassell 1.00 2.50
60 Vince Carter 1.50 4.00
61 Jason Kidd 1.50 4.00
62 Richard Jefferson 1.00 2.50
63 Jamaal Magloire .60 1.50
64 J.R. Smith 1.00 2.50
65 Bostjan Nachbar .60 1.50
66 Allan Houston .60 1.50
67 Stephon Marbury .75 2.00
68 Jamal Crawford .75 2.00
69 Dwight Howard 2.00 5.00
70 Grant Hill 1.25 3.00
71 Jameer Nelson .75 2.00
72 Steve Francis 1.00 2.50
73 Allen Iverson 1.50 4.00
74 Andre Iguodala 1.00 2.50
75 Chris Webber 1.00 2.50
76 Samuel Dalembert .60 1.50
77 Amare Stoudemire 1.00 2.50
78 Steve Nash 1.25 3.00
79 Quentin Richardson .75 2.00
80 Shawn Marion 1.00 2.50
81 Darius Miles .60 1.50
82 Zach Randolph .75 2.00
83 Shareef Abdur-Rahim .75 2.00
84 Peja Stojakovic 1.00 2.50
85 Mike Bibby 1.00 2.50
86 Manu Ginobili 1.00 2.50
87 Tim Duncan 1.50 4.00
88 Tony Parker 1.00 2.50
89 Ray Allen 1.00 2.50
90 Rashard Lewis 1.00 2.50
91 Robert Swift .60 1.50
92 Ronald Murray .60 1.50
93 Chris Bosh 1.00 2.50
94 Morris Peterson .60 1.50
95 Rafael Araujo .60 1.50
96 Andrei Kirilenko .75 2.00
97 Raul Lopez .60 1.50
98 Carlos Boozer 1.00 2.50
99 Antawn Jamison 1.00 2.50
100 Gilbert Arenas 1.00 2.50
101 Andrew Bynum RC 10.00 25.00
102 Julius Hodge RC 3.00 8.00
103 David Lee RC 5.00 12.00
104 Sarunas Jasikevicius RC 3.00 8.00
105 Ike Diogu RC 3.00 8.00
106 Luther Head RC 3.00 8.00
107 Jason Maxiell RC 3.00 8.00
108 Linas Kleiza RC 3.00 8.00
109 Amir Johnson RC 3.00 8.00
110 Andray Blatche RC 4.00 10.00
111 Sean May RC 3.00 8.00
112 Alex Acker RC 3.00 8.00
113 Nate Robinson RC 4.00 10.00
114 Brandon Bass RC 4.00 10.00
115 Ricky Sanchez RC 3.00 8.00
116 Daniel Ewing RC 3.00 8.00
117 Salim Stoudamire RC 3.00 8.00
118 Dijon Thompson RC 3.00 8.00
119 Danny Granger RC 6.00 15.00
120 Raymond Felton RC 5.00 12.00
121 Louis Williams RC 5.00 12.00
122 Channing Frye RC 4.00 10.00
123 Francisco Garcia RC 4.00 10.00
124 Ryan Gomes RC 3.00 8.00
125 Ersan Ilyasova RC 4.00 10.00
126 Jarrett Jack RC 3.00 8.00
127 Lawrence Roberts RC 3.00 8.00
128 Bracey Wright RC 3.00 8.00
129 C.J. Miles RC 4.00 10.00
130 Will Bynum RC 3.00 8.00
131 Travis Diener RC 3.00 8.00
132 Monta Ellis RC 6.00 15.00
133 Martell Webster RC 3.00 8.00
134 Johan Petro RC 3.00 8.00
135 Uros Slokar RC 3.00 8.00
136 Von Wafer RC 3.00 8.00
137 Martynas Andriuskevicius RC 3.00 8.00
138 Charlie Villanueva RC 4.00 10.00
139 Antoine Wright RC 3.00 8.00
140 Joey Graham RC 3.00 8.00
141 Wayne Simien RC 3.00 8.00
142 Hakim Warrick RC 4.00 10.00
143 Gerald Green RC 4.00 10.00
144 Marvin Williams RC 4.00 10.00
145 Deron Williams RC 8.00 20.00
146 Rashad McCants RC 3.00 8.00
147 Robert Whaley RC 3.00 8.00
148 Chris Taft RC 3.00 8.00
149 Chris Paul RC 12.00 30.00
150 Andrew Bogut RC 5.00 12.00

2005-06 SP Game Used 100

Randomly seeded in packs, this 150-card set parallels the base set enhanced with serial numbering to 100.
*1-100 VETERANS: .75X TO 2X BASE HI
*101-150 RC's: .5X TO 1.25X BASE HI

2005-06 SP Game Used 50

Randomly seeded in packs, this 150-card set parallels the base set enhanced with serial numbering to 50.
*1-100 VETERANS: 1.25X TO 3X BASE HI
*101-150 RCs: .6X TO 1.5X BASE HI
12 Michael Jordan 30.00 80.00

2005-06 SP Game Used 25

Randomly seeded in packs, this 150-card set parallels the base set enhanced with serial numbering to 25.
*1-100 VETERANS: 2X TO 5X BASE HI
*101-150 RCs: .75X TO 2X BASE HI
12 Michael Jordan 50.00 125.00

2005-06 SP Game Used Jerseys

Randomly inserted in packs, this 97-card set parallels the design of the base set enhanced with a jersey swatch, gold foil highlights and sequential numbering to 100.
1J Al Harrington 2.50 6.00
2J Josh Smith 3.00 8.00
3J Josh Childress 2.50 6.00
4J Joe Johnson 3.00 8.00
5J Paul Pierce 4.00 10.00
6J Antoine Walker 2.50 6.00
7J Gary Payton 3.00 8.00
8J Al Jefferson 3.00 8.00
10J Primoz Brezec 2.00 5.00
11J Gerald Wallace 3.00 8.00
12J Michael Jordan 40.00 100.00
13J Ben Gordon 3.00 8.00
14J Luol Deng 3.00 8.00
15J Eddy Curry 2.50 6.00
16J LeBron James 15.00 40.00
17J Dajuan Wagner 2.00 5.00
18J Drew Gooden 2.50 6.00
19J Larry Hughes 2.50 6.00
20J Dirk Nowitzki 5.00 12.00
21J Marquis Daniels 2.00 5.00
22J Michael Finley 3.00 8.00
23J Jerry Stackhouse 2.50 6.00
24J Andre Miller 2.50 6.00
25J Carmelo Anthony 6.00 15.00
26J Kenyon Martin 3.00 8.00
27J Nene 2.50 6.00
28J Rasheed Wallace 3.00 8.00
29J Ben Wallace 3.00 8.00
30J Richard Hamilton 2.50 6.00
31J Chauncey Billups 3.00 8.00
32J Baron Davis 3.00 8.00
33J Derek Fisher 2.50 6.00
34J Jason Richardson 3.00 8.00
35J Tracy McGrady 4.00 10.00
36J Yao Ming 4.00 10.00
37J Juwan Howard 2.50 6.00
38J Jermaine O'Neal 3.00 8.00
39J Ron Artest 3.00 8.00
40J Jamaal Tinsley 2.00 5.00
41J Corey Maggette 2.50 6.00
42J Elton Brand 3.00 8.00
43J Shaun Livingston 2.00 5.00
44J Kobe Bryant 15.00 40.00
45J Brian Cook 2.00 5.00
46J Lamar Odom 3.00 8.00
47J Bonzi Wells 2.00 5.00
48J Pau Gasol 3.00 8.00
49J Shane Battier 2.50 6.00
50J Shaquille O'Neal 6.00 15.00
51J Dwyane Wade 8.00 20.00
52J Dorell Wright 2.00 5.00
53J Eddie Jones 2.50 6.00
54J Joe Smith 2.50 6.00
55J Michael Redd 3.00 8.00
56J Desmond Mason 2.00 5.00
57J Kevin Garnett 6.00 15.00
58J Wally Szczerbiak 2.50 6.00
59J Sam Cassell 3.00 8.00
61J Jason Kidd 5.00 12.00
62J Richard Jefferson 3.00 8.00
63J Jamaal Magloire 2.00 5.00
64J J.R. Smith 3.00 8.00
65J Bostjan Nachbar 2.00 5.00
66J Allan Houston 2.00 5.00
67J Stephon Marbury 2.50 6.00
68J Jamal Crawford 2.50 6.00
69J Dwight Howard 6.00 15.00
70J Grant Hill 4.00 10.00
71J Jameer Nelson 2.50 6.00
72J Steve Francis 3.00 8.00
74J Andre Iguodala 3.00 8.00
75J Chris Webber 3.00 8.00
76J Samuel Dalembert 2.00 5.00
77J Amare Stoudemire 3.00 8.00
78J Steve Nash 4.00 10.00
79J Quentin Richardson 2.50 6.00
80J Shawn Marion 3.00 8.00
81J Darius Miles 2.00 5.00
82J Zach Randolph 2.50 6.00
83J Shareef Abdur-Rahim 2.50 6.00
84J Peja Stojakovic 3.00 8.00
85J Mike Bibby 3.00 8.00
86J Manu Ginobili 3.00 8.00
87J Tim Duncan 5.00 12.00
88J Tony Parker 3.00 8.00
89J Ray Allen 3.00 8.00
90J Rashard Lewis 3.00 8.00
91J Robert Swift 2.00 5.00
92J Ronald Murray 2.00 5.00
93J Chris Bosh 3.00 8.00
94J Morris Peterson 2.00 5.00
95J Rafael Araujo 2.00 5.00
96J Andrei Kirilenko 2.50 6.00
97J Raul Lopez 2.00 5.00
98J Carlos Boozer 3.00 8.00
99J Antawn Jamison 3.00 8.00
100J Gilbert Arenas 3.00 8.00

2005-06 SP Game Used Authentic Fabrics

Inserted at the rate of one per pack, this 100-card set features both veteran and rookie players with a centered image at the top of the card and a centered swatch of jersey at the bottom.
*GOLD: .5X TO 1.25X BASE FAB HI
GOLD PRINT RUN 100 SER.#'d SETS
*PATCHES: 2X TO 5X BASE HI
PATCH PRINT RUN 75 SER.#'d SETS
UNPRICED LOGO PRINT RUN ONE SET
AB Andris Biedrins 2.00 5.00
AE Andre Emmett 2.00 5.00
AH Anfernee Hardaway 6.00 15.00
AI Andre Iguodala 2.50 6.00
AJ Al Jefferson 2.50 6.00
AK Andrei Kirilenko 2.00 5.00
AM Antonio McDyess 2.00 5.00
AN Antawn Jamison 2.50 6.00
AR Ron Artest 2.50 6.00
AS Amare Stoudemire 2.50 6.00
BC Brian Cook 2.00 5.00
BD Baron Davis 2.50 6.00
BE Ben Wallace 2.50 6.00
BG Ben Gordon 2.50 6.00
BJ Bobby Jackson 2.00 5.00
BR Bernard Robinson 2.00 5.00
BW Bonzi Wells 2.00 5.00
CA Carmelo Anthony 5.00 12.00
CB Carlos Boozer 2.50 6.00
CD Carlos Delfino 2.00 5.00
CM Corey Maggette 2.00 5.00
CU Cuttino Mobley 2.00 5.00
CW Corliss Williamson 2.00 5.00
DE Devean George 2.00 5.00
DG Drew Gooden 2.00 5.00
DH Dwight Howard 5.00 12.00
DJ Damon Jones 2.00 5.00
DM Darius Miles 2.00 5.00
DN Dirk Nowitzki 4.00 10.00
DS Darius Songaila 2.00 5.00
EB Elton Brand 2.50 6.00
EC Eddy Curry 2.00 5.00
EJ Eddie Jones 2.00 5.00
GP Gary Payton 2.50 6.00
GR Glenn Robinson 2.00 5.00
GW Gerald Wallace 2.50 6.00
JA Jason Kapono 2.00 5.00
JD Juan Dixon 2.00 5.00
JH Jarvis Hayes 2.00 5.00
JJ Jim Jackson 2.00 5.00
JK Jason Kidd 4.00 10.00
JM Jamaal Magloire 2.00 5.00
JN Jameer Nelson 2.00 5.00
JO Jermaine O'Neal 2.50 6.00
JR Jason Richardson 2.50 6.00
JS Joe Smith 2.00 5.00
KB Kobe Bryant 12.50 30.00
KE Kevin Martin 2.50 6.00
KG Kevin Garnett 5.00 12.00
KH Kris Humphries 2.00 5.00
KM Kenyon Martin 2.50 6.00
KS Kirk Snyder 2.00 5.00
KW Kwame Brown 2.00 5.00
LA Larry Hughes 2.00 5.00
LD Luol Deng 2.50 6.00
LH Lucious Harris 2.00 5.00
LJ LeBron James 15.00 40.00
LO Raul Lopez 2.00 5.00
LU Luke Jackson 2.00 5.00
MA Malik Rose 2.00 5.00
MB Mike Bibby 2.50 6.00
MD Marquis Daniels 2.00 5.00
MG Manu Ginobili 2.50 6.00
MI Mike Dunleavy 2.00 5.00
MJ Michael Jordan 30.00 80.00
MP Morris Peterson SP 1.50 4.00
MR Michael Redd SP 2.50 6.00
MT Maurice Taylor 2.00 5.00
NK Nenad Krstic 2.00 5.00
NT Nikoloz Tskitishvili 2.00 5.00
PP Paul Pierce 3.00 8.00
PS Peja Stojakovic 2.50 6.00
QR Quentin Richardson 2.00 5.00
RA Ray Allen 2.50 6.00
RF Rafael Araujo 2.00 5.00
RG Reece Gaines 2.00 5.00
RH Richard Hamilton 2.00 5.00
RJ Richard Jefferson 2.50 6.00
RL Rashard Lewis 2.50 6.00
RM Ronald Murray 2.00 5.00
RR Rodney Rogers 2.00 5.00
SD Samuel Dalembert 2.00 5.00
SF Steve Francis 2.50 6.00
SM Stephon Marbury 2.00 5.00
SN Steve Nash 3.00 8.00
SO Shaquille O'Neal 5.00 12.00
ST Sebastian Telfair 2.00 5.00
SV Sasha Vujacic 2.00 5.00
TA Tony Allen SP 2.00 5.00
TC Tyson Chandler 2.00 5.00
TD Tim Duncan 4.00 10.00
TH Troy Hudson 2.00 5.00
TM Tracy McGrady 3.00 8.00
TP Tony Parker 2.50 6.00
UH Udonis Haslem 2.00 5.00
VR Vladimir Radmanovic 2.00 5.00
WG Willie Green 2.00 5.00
WI Kevin Willis 2.00 5.00
WS Wally Szczerbiak 2.00 5.00
YM Yao Ming 3.00 8.00

2005-06 SP Game Used Authentic Fabrics Autographs

Randomly seeded in packs, this 29-card set places player photos at the top of the card, a swatch of memorabilia in the center and a player autograph along the bottom. Each card is serially numbered to 100.
AB Andris Biedrins/100 5.00 12.00
AH Al Harrington/100 5.00 12.00
AJ Antawn Jamison/100 5.00 12.00
AK Andrei Kirilenko/100 8.00 20.00
AR Carlos Arroyo/100 15.00 40.00
BD Baron Davis/100 10.00 25.00
BG Ben Gordon/100 12.50 30.00
BM Brad Miller/100 5.00 12.00
CM Corey Maggette/100 5.00 12.00
DG Drew Gooden/100 5.00 12.00
DH Dwight Howard/100 20.00 50.00
DM Desmond Mason/100 5.00 12.00
DS Damon Stoudamire/100 5.00 12.00
DW Dorell Wright/100 5.00 12.00
GA Gilbert Arenas/100 8.00 20.00
JM Jamaal Magloire/100 5.00 12.00
JW Jason Williams/100 15.00 40.00
KH Kirk Hinrich/100 12.50 30.00
LJ LeBron James/100 200.00 400.00
MB Mike Bibby/100 5.00 12.00
MJ Michael Jordan/23 500.00 900.00
MR Michael Redd/100 5.00 12.00
PP Paul Pierce/100 20.00 50.00
QR Quentin Richardson/100 5.00 12.00
RJ Richard Jefferson/100 5.00 12.00
SM Shawn Marion/100 12.50 30.00
SN Steve Nash/100 50.00 120.00
TM Tracy McGrady/100 30.00 60.00

2005-06 SP Game Used Authentic Fabrics Autographs Patches

Randomly seeded in packs, this 30-card set parallels the design of the Authentic Fabrics Autographs set enhanced with a patch swatch gold highlights and sequential numbering to 25.
AB Andris Biedrins/25 15.00 40.00
AH Al Harrington/25 15.00 40.00
AJ Antawn Jamison/25 15.00 40.00
AK Andrei Kirilenko/25 25.00 60.00
AR Carlos Arroyo/25 40.00 80.00
BD Baron Davis/25 15.00 40.00
BM Brad Miller/25 15.00 40.00
CM Corey Maggette/25 15.00 40.00
DG Drew Gooden/25 15.00 40.00
DH Dwight Howard/25 40.00 100.00
DM Desmond Mason/25 15.00 40.00
DW Dorell Wright/25 15.00 40.00
GA Gilbert Arenas/25 15.00 40.00
JM Jamaal Magloire/25 15.00 40.00
JW Jason Williams/25 60.00 150.00
KH Kirk Hinrich/25 25.00 60.00
LJ LeBron James/25 250.00 500.00
MB Mike Bibby/25 15.00 40.00
MR Michael Redd/25 15.00 40.00
PP Paul Pierce/25 25.00 60.00
QR Quentin Richardson/25 15.00 40.00
RJ Richard Jefferson/25 15.00 40.00
SM Shawn Marion/25 20.00 50.00
SN Steve Nash/25 80.00 160.00
TM Tracy McGrady/25 60.00 120.00

2005-06 SP Game Used Authentic Fabrics Dual

Randomly seeded in packs, this 41-card set features two players side by side, two swatches of memorabilia and sequential numbering to 100. A Gold version sequentially numbered to 50, a Patches version sequentially numbered to 15 and a Patches Gold version sequentially numbered to 10 were also produced.
*GOLD: .5X TO 1.25X BASE FAB HI
UNPRICED PATCH PRINT RUN 15 SETS
UNPRICED PATCH GOLD PRINT RUN 10 SETS
AL Ray Allen 8.00 20.00
Rashard Lewis
AT Al Jefferson 5.00 12.00
Tony Allen
BC Brad Miller 5.00 12.00
Cuttino Mobley
BJ Kobe Bryant 40.00 80.00
LeBron James
BL Carlos Boozer 5.00 12.00
Raul Lopez
BO Kobe Bryant 15.00 40.00
Lamar Odom
BP Chris Bosh 5.00 12.00
Morris Peterson
CS Sam Cassell 5.00 12.00
Wally Szczerbiak
DH Juan Dixon 5.00 12.00
Jarvis Hayes
DS Marquis Daniels 5.00 12.00
Jerry Stackhouse
GJ Drew Gooden 5.00 12.00
Luke Jackson
GP Manu Ginobili 8.00 20.00
Tony Parker
GW Pau Gasol 5.00 12.00
Bonzi Wells
HB Richard Hamilton 6.00 15.00
Chauncey Billups
HC Kirk Hinrich 5.00 12.00
Eddy Curry
HN Dwight Howard 6.00 15.00
Jameer Nelson
HS Kris Humphries 5.00 12.00
Kirk Snyder
JA Antawn Jamison 5.00 12.00
Gilbert Arenas
JH Damon Jones 5.00 12.00
Udonis Haslem
JJ LeBron James 60.00 120.00
Michael Jordan
JS Joe Johnson 5.00 12.00
Shawn Marion
KJ Jason Kidd 8.00 20.00
Richard Jefferson
MB Corey Maggette 5.00 12.00
Elton Brand
MC Stephon Marbury 5.00 12.00
Jamal Crawford
MM Andre Miller 5.00 12.00
Kenyon Martin
MR Ronald Murray 5.00 12.00
Vladimir Radmanovic
MS Jamaal Magloire 5.00 12.00
J.R. Smith
MT Darius Miles 5.00 12.00
Sebastian Telfair
NF Dirk Nowitzki 8.00 20.00
Michael Finley
OA Jermaine O'Neal 5.00 12.00
Ron Artest
OJ Shaquille O'Neal 10.00 25.00
Eddie Jones
RA Zach Randolph 5.00 12.00
Shareef Abdur-Rahim
RF Jason Richardson 5.00 12.00
Derek Fisher
RK Bernard Robinson 5.00 12.00
Jason Kapono
RM Michael Redd 5.00 12.00
Desmond Mason
RP Dennis Rodman 25.00 60.00
Scottie Pippen
SC Josh Smith 5.00 12.00
Josh Childress
TS Isiah Thomas 8.00 20.00
John Stockton
WI Chris Webber 5.00 12.00
Andre Iguodala
WP Antoine Walker 5.00 12.00
Gary Payton
WW Rasheed Wallace 5.00 12.00
Ben Wallace

2005-06 SP Game Used Authentic Fabrics Dual Autographs

Randomly seeded in packs, this 30-card set parallels the design of the Authentic Fabrics Dual set enhanced with player autographs and sequential numbering to 50.
UNPRICED PATCH PRINT RUN 5 SETS
AJ Kareem Abdul-Jabbar 150.00 300.00
Magic Johnson
AM Carmelo Anthony 20.00 50.00
Andre Miller
AT Al Jefferson 12.50 30.00
Tony Allen
BH Chauncey Billups 15.00 40.00
Richard Hamilton
BS Mike Bibby 20.00 40.00
Peja Stojakovic
CH Josh Childress 12.50 30.00
Al Harrington
DD Baron Davis 20.00 40.00
Mike Dunleavy
GH Ben Gordon 20.00 50.00
Kirk Hinrich
GW Pau Gasol 25.00 60.00
Jason Williams
HN Dwight Howard 20.00 50.00
Jameer Nelson
IK Andre Iguodala 25.00 50.00
Kyle Korver
JA Antawn Jamison 15.00 40.00
Gilbert Arenas
JJ LeBron James 600.00 1100.00
Michael Jordan
KB Andrei Kirilenko 12.50 30.00
Carlos Boozer
KJ Jason Kidd 20.00 50.00
Richard Jefferson
ML Corey Maggette 12.50 30.00
Shaun Livingston
MW Corey Maggette 12.50 30.00
Chris Wilcox
MY Tracy McGrady 40.00 80.00
Yao Ming
PP Paul Pierce 30.00 80.00
Gary Payton
PR Scottie Pippen 225.00 400.00
Dennis Rodman
RM Michael Redd 12.50 30.00
Desmond Mason
RP Jalen Rose 12.50 30.00
Morris Peterson
SD Jerry Stackhouse 12.50 30.00
Marquis Daniels
SM J.R. Smith 12.50 30.00
Jamaal Magloire
ST Damon Stoudamire 12.50 30.00
Sebastian Telfair
VO Sasha Vujacic 12.50 30.00
Lamar Odom
WB Gerald Wallace 12.50 30.00
Primoz Brezec

2005-06 SP Game Used Authentic Fabrics Triple

Randomly seeded in packs, this 10-card set features three player photos along the top of the card and three swatches of memorabilia along the bottom. Each card is serially numbered to 25.
UNPRICED TRIPLE GOLD PRINT RUN 15 SETS
UNPRICED TRIPLE PATCH PRINT RUN 10 SETS
UNPRICED TRIPLE PATCH GOLD PRINT RUN 3 SETS
BML Elton Brand 12.50 30.00
Corey Maggette
Shaun Livingston
DJW Samuel Dalembert 15.00 40.00
Andre Iguodala
Chris Webber
DPG Tim Duncan 20.00 50.00
Tony Parker
Manu Ginobili
DRD Baron Davis 12.50 30.00
Jason Richardson
Mike Dunleavy
JAH Antawn Jamison 12.50 30.00
Gilbert Arenas
Jarvis Hayes
JJB LeBron James 150.00 300.00
Michael Jordan
Kobe Bryant
NFD Dirk Nowitzki 20.00 50.00
Michael Finley
Marquis Daniels
OAT Jermaine O'Neal 12.50 30.00
Ron Artest
Jamaal Tinsley
PJA Paul Pierce 15.00 40.00
Al Jefferson
Tony Allen

2005-06 SP Game Used Authentic Tags

Randomly inserted in packs, this 21-card set features a player image along the top and three swatches of memorabilia from jersey logos and tags along the bottom. Cards are serially numbered to just three copies.
NOT PRICED DUE TO SCARCITY
UNPRICED AUTO PRINT RUN ONE SET

2005-06 SP Game Used By the Letter

Seeded in packs randomly, this 10-card set features a player image on the left of the card and a full letter from the player's nameplate on the back of his uniform. The total number of cards for each player is limited to the number of letters in the player's last name.
NOT PRICED DUE TO SCARCITY

2005-06 SP Game Used Legendary Fabrics

Randomly seeded in packs, this 12-card set features NBA legends along with a swatch of memorabilia.
BK Bernard King 6.00 15.00
BR Bill Russell 12.50 30.00
CD Clyde Drexler 6.00 15.00
DR Dennis Rodman 12.50 30.00
GG George Gervin 6.00 15.00
HO Hakeem Olajuwon 6.00 15.00
JS John Stockton 10.00 25.00
KA Kareem Abdul-Jabbar 8.00 20.00
LB Larry Bird 15.00 40.00
MJ Michael Jordan 50.00 100.00
MJ2 Magic Johnson 12.50 30.00
SP Scottie Pippen 15.00 40.00

2005-06 SP Game Used Legendary Fabrics Autographs

Found in packs randomly, this set features NBA legends, a swatch of memorabilia and an authentic autograph. Each card is serially numbered to 23 or 50 copies.
BK Bernard King/50 12.50 30.00
BR Bill Russell/50 100.00 225.00
DR Dennis Rodman/50 75.00 150.00
GG George Gervin/50 12.50 30.00
HO Hakeem Olajuwon/50 30.00 80.00
JS John Stockton/50 60.00 150.00
LB Larry Bird/50 75.00 150.00
MA Magic Johnson/50 50.00 125.00
MJ Michael Jordan/23 700.00 1000.00
SP Scottie Pippen/50 125.00 250.00

2005-06 SP Game Used Materials

Limited to 10 serially numbered copies, this seven card set features both current players and NBA legends along with a swatch of memorabilia.
NOT PRICED DUE TO SCARCITY
UNPRICED LIMITED PRINT RUN 5 SETS
UNPRICED EXTRA PRINT RUN ONE SET

2005-06 SP Game Used Rookie Exclusive Autographs

Found in packs randomly, this 52-card set is horizontally designed with a player photo along the top and a cut signature embedded in the middle. Cards are serially numbered to 100.
AA Alex Acker 8.00 20.00
AB Andray Blatche 10.00 25.00
AJ Amir Johnson 8.00 20.00
AN Andrew Bogut 12.00 30.00
AW Antoine Wright 8.00 20.00
BB Brandon Bass 10.00 25.00
BW Bracey Wright 8.00 20.00
BY Andrew Bynum 25.00 60.00
CF Channing Frye 10.00 25.00
CJ C.J. Miles 10.00 25.00
CP Chris Paul 100.00 200.00
CT Chris Taft 8.00 20.00
CV Charlie Villanueva 10.00 25.00
DE Daniel Ewing 8.00 20.00
DG Danny Granger 15.00 40.00
DL David Lee 12.00 30.00
DT Dijon Thompson 8.00 20.00
DW Deron Williams 40.00 100.00
EI Ersan Ilyasova 10.00 25.00
FG Francisco Garcia 10.00 25.00
GG Gerald Green 10.00 25.00
HW Hakim Warrick 10.00 25.00
ID Ike Diogu 8.00 20.00
JG Joey Graham 8.00 20.00
JH Julius Hodge 8.00 20.00
JJ Jarrett Jack 8.00 20.00
JM Jason Maxiell 8.00 20.00
JP Johan Petro 8.00 20.00
LH Luther Head 8.00 20.00
LK Linas Kleiza 8.00 20.00
LR Lawrence Roberts 8.00 20.00
LW Louis Williams 12.00 30.00
MA Martell Webster 8.00 20.00
ME Monta Ellis 20.00 50.00
MG Mickael Gelabale 8.00 20.00
MW Marvin Williams 10.00 25.00
MY Martynas Andriuskevicius 8.00 20.00
NR Nate Robinson 15.00 40.00
RA Rashad McCants 8.00 20.00
RF Raymond Felton 15.00 40.00
RG Ryan Gomes 8.00 20.00
RS Ricky Sanchez 8.00 20.00
RT Ronny Turiaf 8.00 20.00
RW Robert Whaley 8.00 20.00
SJ Sarunas Jasikevicius 8.00 20.00
SM Sean May 8.00 20.00
SS Salim Stoudamire 8.00 20.00
TD Travis Diener 8.00 20.00
US Uros Slokar 8.00 20.00
VW Von Wafer 8.00 20.00
WB Will Bynum 8.00 20.00
WS Wayne Simien 8.00 20.00

2005-06 SP Game Used Signature Numbers

Found randomly inserted in packs, this 40-card set features a player photo set against a background that displays his jersey number along with a player autograph. Cards are serially numbered to each specific player's jersey number.
SOME NOT PRICED DUE TO SCARCITY
AKO Andrei Kirilenko/47 ERR 12.50 30.00
Yao Ming Autograph
CA Carmelo Anthony/15 25.00 60.00
DR Dennis Rodman/91 50.00 100.00
JN Jameer Nelson/14 12.50 30.00
KK Kyle Korver/26 12.50 30.00
LB Larry Bird/33 100.00 200.00
MA Magic Johnson/32 60.00 120.00
MJ Michael Jordan/23 600.00 1200.00
MR Michael Redd/22 12.50 30.00
PG Pau Gasol/16 20.00 50.00
PP Paul Pierce/34 15.00 40.00
ST Sebastian Telfair/31 12.50 30.00
UH Udonis Haslem/40 12.50 30.00

2005-06 SP Game Used SIGnificance

Seeded in packs randomly, this 120-card set is horizontally designed and utilizes some of the design elements of the base set along with player autographs and sequential numbering to 100.
*SIG 25: .75X TO 2X BASE HI
SIG 25 PRINT RUN 25 SER.#'d SETS
UNPRICED SIG 10 PRINT RUN 10 SETS
AB Andray Blatche 5.00 12.00
AH Al Harrington 4.00 10.00
AI Andre Iguodala 5.00 12.00
AJ Antawn Jamison 4.00 10.00
AKO Andrei Kirilenko ERR 8.00 20.00
Yao Ming Autograph
AL Al Jefferson 4.00 10.00
AM Antonio McDyess 5.00 12.00
AN Martynas Andriuskevicius 4.00 10.00
AR Carlos Arroyo 10.00 25.00
AW Antoine Wright 4.00 10.00
BB Brandon Bass 5.00 12.00
BD Baron Davis 5.00 12.00
BE Bernard King 6.00 15.00
BG Ben Gordon 8.00 20.00
BK Bob Knight 25.00 50.00
BL Bill Laimbeer 6.00 15.00
BM Brad Miller 4.00 10.00
BO Andrew Bogut 8.00 20.00
BU Beno Udrih 4.00 10.00
BW Bracey Wright 4.00 10.00
BY Andrew Bynum 15.00 40.00
CB Carlos Boozer 4.00 10.00
CD Clyde Drexler 15.00 40.00
CF Channing Frye 6.00 15.00
CH Chauncey Billups 6.00 15.00
CJ C.J. Miles 5.00 12.00
CM Corey Maggette 4.00 10.00
CN Curly Neal 20.00 40.00
CO Michael Cooper 6.00 15.00
CP Chris Paul 30.00 80.00
CS Chris Bosh 8.00 20.00
CT Chris Taft 4.00 10.00
CV Charlie Villanueva 5.00 12.00
DA Daniel Ewing 4.00 10.00
DD Dan Dickau 4.00 10.00
DE Desmond Mason 4.00 10.00
DF Derek Fisher 6.00 15.00
DG Danny Granger 15.00 30.00
DH Dwight Howard 15.00 30.00
DL David Lee 6.00 15.00
DM Darko Milicic 4.00 10.00
DP Dan Patrick 10.00 25.00
DR Dennis Rodman 25.00 60.00
DS Damon Stoudamire 4.00 10.00
DT Dijon Thompson 4.00 10.00
DW Deron Williams 20.00 50.00
ED Erik Daniels 4.00 10.00
EH Elvin Hayes 6.00 15.00
EI Ersan Ilyasova 5.00 12.00
FG Francisco Garcia 5.00 12.00
GA Gilbert Arenas 6.00 15.00
GG George Gervin 10.00 25.00
GW Gerald Wallace 5.00 12.00
HO Hakeem Olajuwon 15.00 40.00
HW Hakim Warrick 10.00 25.00
ID Ike Diogu 4.00 10.00
IT Isiah Thomas 12.50 30.00
JA Jamal Crawford 4.00 10.00
JC Josh Childress 4.00 10.00
JD Juan Dixon 4.00 10.00
JG Joey Graham 4.00 10.00
JH Julius Hodge 4.00 10.00
JJ Jarrett Jack 4.00 10.00
JK Jason Kidd 10.00 25.00
JM Jamaal Magloire 4.00 10.00
JO John Edwards 4.00 10.00
JP Johan Petro 4.00 10.00
JR J.R. Smith 5.00 12.00
JV Jackson Vroman 4.00 10.00
JW John Wooden 50.00 120.00
KA Jason Kapono 4.00 10.00
KE Kevin Martin 5.00 12.00
KH Kris Humphries 4.00 10.00
KI Kirk Hinrich 6.00 15.00
KK Kyle Korver 5.00 12.00
KM Kenny Mayne 6.00 15.00
LA Larry Brown 15.00 40.00
LC Linda Cohn 10.00 25.00
LD Luol Deng 6.00 15.00
LF Luis Flores 4.00 10.00
LH Luther Head 4.00 10.00
LJ LeBron James 100.00 200.00
LO Lamar Odom 5.00 12.00
LR Lawrence Roberts 4.00 10.00
LU Louis Williams 6.00 15.00
LW Lenny Wilkens 10.00 25.00
MA Marvin Williams 5.00 12.00
MB Mike Bibby 5.00 12.00
MC Mark Cuban 10.00 25.00
MD Marquis Daniels 4.00 10.00
ME Monta Ellis 12.50 30.00
MI Andre Miller 4.00 10.00
MJ Michael Jordan 250.00 500.00
ML Meadowlark Lemon 12.50 30.00
MP Morris Peterson 4.00 10.00
MR Michael Redd 5.00 12.00
MW Maurice Williams 4.00 10.00
NR Nate Robinson 6.00 15.00
PG Pau Gasol 8.00 20.00
PS Pape Sow 4.00 10.00
QR Quentin Richardson 4.00 10.00
RF Raymond Felton 8.00 20.00
RJ Richard Jefferson 4.00 10.00
RM Ronald Murray 4.00 10.00
RT Ronny Turiaf 6.00 15.00
SB Steve Blake 4.00 10.00
SH Shane Battier 4.00 10.00
SV Sasha Vujacic 4.00 10.00
TA Tony Allen 4.00 10.00
TD Travis Diener 4.00 10.00
TR Trevor Ariza 4.00 10.00
UH Udonis Haslem 4.00 10.00
VK Viktor Khryapa 4.00 10.00
VW Von Wafer 4.00 10.00
WE Martell Webster 4.00 10.00
WF Walt Frazier 10.00 25.00
WI Jason Williams 15.00 30.00
WR Willis Reed 8.00 20.00
WS Wayne Simien 4.00 10.00

2005-06 SP Game Used SIGnificance Dual

Randomly inserted in packs, this 30 cards set utilizes some of the design elements of the SIGnificance set but places two players and two autographs on each card along with sequential numbering to 25.
UNPRICED DUAL GOLD PRINT RUN 5 SETS
BW Larry Brown 35.00 75.00
Lenny Wilkens
DO Clyde Drexler 75.00 150.00
Hakeem Olajuwon
EI Julius Erving 50.00 120.00
Andre Iguodala
FR Walt Frazier 35.00 75.00
Willis Reed
FS Channing Frye 15.00 40.00
Salim Stoudamire
GH Gerald Green 15.00 40.00
Hakim Warrick
GW Pau Gasol 35.00 75.00
Jason Williams
HG Kirk Hinrich 40.00 100.00
Ben Gordon
HH Devin Harris 20.00 50.00
Josh Howard
HN Dwight Howard 25.00 60.00
Jameer Nelson
IS Andre Iguodala 50.00 100.00
J.R. Smith
JJ Michael Jordan 500.00 1000.00
LeBron James
KB Andrei Kirilenko 15.00 40.00
Carlos Boozer
KJ Jason Kidd 30.00 80.00
Richard Jefferson
KW Bob Knight 125.00 250.00
John Wooden
MA Stephon Marbury 15.00 40.00
Trevor Ariza
MM Magic Johnson 450.00 750.00
Michael Jordan
MP Mike Bibby 30.00 60.00
Peja Stojakovic
NL Curly Neal 75.00 150.00
Meadowlark Lemon
NR Steve Nash 80.00 160.00
Quentin Richardson
PF Chris Paul 75.00 150.00
Raymond Felton
PR Scottie Pippen 200.00 350.00
Dennis Rodman
RB Bill Russell 200.00 350.00
Larry Bird
TJ Isiah Thomas 80.00 160.00
Magic Johnson
TL Sebastian Telfair 15.00 40.00
Shaun Livingston
WH Deron Williams 60.00 120.00
Luther Head
WM Marvin Williams 25.00 50.00
Sean May
YM Yao Ming 60.00 120.00
Tracy McGrady

2005-06 SP Game Used SIGnificant Numbers Autographs

Found randomly in packs, this 12-card set features the same design as the SIGnificance set enhanced with a swatch of memorabilia and sequential numbering to the featured players jersey number.
SOME NOT PRICED DUE TO SCARCITY
UNPRICED PATCH PRINT RUN FIVE SETS
DR Dennis Rodman/91 50.00 100.00
KA Kareem Abdul-Jabbar/33 50.00 125.00
LB Larry Bird/33 80.00 200.00
LJ LeBron James/23 300.00 500.00
MA Magic Johnson/32 60.00 150.00
MJ Michael Jordan/23 350.00 600.00

2005-06 SP Game Used Superstar Exclusive Autographs

Randomly seeded in packs, this 35-card set parallels the design of the Rookie Exclusive Autographs with player photos, cut signatures and sequential numbering to either 25 or 100.
AJ Antawn Jamison/25 10.00 25.00
BD Baron Davis/25 10.00 25.00
BG Ben Gordon/25 15.00 40.00
BK Bernard King/100 10.00 25.00
CB Chris Bosh/25 12.50 30.00
DE Devin Harris/25 10.00 25.00
DH Dwight Howard/25 35.00 70.00
JC Josh Childress/25 10.00 25.00
JK Jason Kidd/25 20.00 50.00
JN Jameer Nelson/25 10.00 25.00
JS John Salley/100 10.00 25.00
KH Kirk Hinrich/25 10.00 25.00
LD Luol Deng/25 12.50 30.00
LJ LeBron James/25 150.00 300.00
MB Mike Bibby/25 10.00 25.00
MJ Michael Jordan/25 300.00 600.00
MR Michael Redd/25 10.00 25.00
PG Pau Gasol/25 10.00 25.00
PS Peja Stojakovic/25 15.00 40.00
RH Richard Hamilton/25 15.00 40.00
RJ Richard Jefferson/25 10.00 25.00
SL Shaun Livingston/25 10.00 25.00
SM Stephon Marbury/25 15.00 40.00
SN Steve Nash/25 60.00 120.00
TM Tracy McGrady/25 30.00 80.00
WR Willis Reed/100 12.50 30.00
YM Yao Ming/25 25.00 60.00

2006-07 SP Game Used

Issued in late October 2006, SP Game Used boasts a 249-card base set where card numbers 1-100 picture veteran players, cards 101-200 picture veteran players along with a swatch jersey and card numbers 201-249 picture rookies sequentially numbered to 999. SP Game Used is packaged in single packs of five cards each and carried an initial suggested retail price of $29.99.
COMP.SET w/o SP's (100) 25.00 60.00
UNPRICED RAINBOW PRINT RUN 10 SETS
1 Al Harrington .60 1.50
2 Joe Johnson .75 2.00
3 Salim Stoudamire .50 1.25
4 Tony Allen .50 1.25
5 Dan Dickau .50 1.25
6 Gerald Green .60 1.50
7 Michael Olowokandi .50 1.25
8 Brevin Knight .50 1.25
9 Peja Stojakovic .75 2.00
10 Gerald Wallace .75 2.00
11 Luol Deng .75 2.00
12 Chris Duhon .50 1.25
13 Mike Sweetney .50 1.25
14 Drew Gooden .60 1.50
15 Luke Jackson .50 1.25
16 Damon Jones .50 1.25
17 Eric Snow .50 1.25
18 Erick Dampier .50 1.25
19 Marquis Daniels .50 1.25
20 Jerry Stackhouse .60 1.50
21 Jason Terry .60 1.50
22 Earl Boykins .50 1.25
23 Marcus Camby .60 1.50
24 Kenyon Martin .75 2.00
25 Andre Miller .60 1.50
26 Kelvin Cato .50 1.25
27 Lindsey Hunter .50 1.25
28 Antonio McDyess .60 1.50
29 Mike Dunleavy .60 1.50
30 Derek Fisher .60 1.50
31 Troy Murphy .50 1.25
32 Rafer Alston .50 1.25
33 Juwan Howard .60 1.50
34 Stromile Swift .50 1.25
35 Austin Croshere .50 1.25
36 Stephen Jackson .60 1.50
37 Jamaal Tinsley .50 1.25
38 Sam Cassell .75 2.00
39 Chris Kaman .60 1.50
40 Yaroslav Korolev .50 1.25
41 Cuttino Mobley .60 1.50
42 Devean George .50 1.25
43 Smush Parker .50 1.25
44 Ronny Turiaf .60 1.50
45 Shane Battier .60 1.50
46 Bobby Jackson .50 1.25
47 Mike Miller .75 2.00
48 Damon Stoudamire .60 1.50
49 Alonzo Mourning 1.00 2.50
50 Gary Payton .75 2.00
51 Dwyane Wade 2.00 5.00
52 Jason Williams .60 1.50
53 T.J. Ford .60 1.50
54 Jamaal Magloire .50 1.25
55 Maurice Williams .60 1.50
56 Marcus Banks .50 1.25
57 Eddie Griffin .50 1.25
58 Troy Hudson .50 1.25
59 Jason Collins .50 1.25
60 Nenad Krstic .50 1.25
61 Antoine Wright .50 1.25
62 P.J. Brown .50 1.25
63 Speedy Claxton .50 1.25
64 Marc Jackson .50 1.25
65 Jamal Crawford .60 1.50
66 Eddy Curry .60 1.50
67 Quentin Richardson .60 1.50
68 Carlos Arroyo .60 1.50
69 Keyon Dooling .50 1.25
70 Darko Milicic .50 1.25
71 Steven Hunter .50 1.25
72 Allen Iverson 1.00 2.50
73 Kyle Korver .60 1.50
74 Raja Bell .60 1.50
75 Boris Diaw .60 1.50
76 Kurt Thomas .50 1.25
77 Steve Blake .50 1.25
78 Darius Miles .50 1.25
79 Joel Przybilla .50 1.25
80 Ha Seung-Jin .50 1.25
81 Shareef Abdur-Rahim .60 1.50
82 Brad Miller .75 2.00
83 Kenny Thomas .50 1.25
84 Bonzi Wells .50 1.25
85 Brent Barry .50 1.25
86 Bruce Bowen .50 1.25
87 Michael Finley .75 2.00
88 Robert Horry .60 1.50
89 Luke Ridnour .60 1.50
90 Robert Swift .50 1.25
91 Chris Wilcox .50 1.25
92 Rafael Araujo .50 1.25
93 Jose Calderon .60 1.50
94 Mike James .50 1.25
95 Matt Harpring .60 1.50
96 Kris Humphries .50 1.25
97 Jason Richardson .75 2.00
98 Gilbert Arenas .75 2.00
99 Antonio Daniels .50 1.25
100 Brendan Haywood .50 1.25
101 Josh Childress JSY 2.00 5.00
102 Josh Smith JSY 2.50 6.00
103 Marvin Williams JSY 2.50 6.00
104 Al Jefferson JSY 2.50 6.00
105 Paul Pierce JSY 3.00 8.00
106 Wally Szczerbiak JSY 2.00 5.00
107 Raymond Felton JSY 3.00 8.00
108 Sean May JSY 1.50 4.00
109 Emeka Okafor JSY 2.50 6.00
110 Tyson Chandler JSY 2.00 5.00
111 Ben Gordon JSY 2.50 6.00
112 Kirk Hinrich JSY 2.50 6.00
113 Michael Jordan SP JSY 30.00 75.00
114 Larry Hughes JSY 2.00 5.00
115 Zydrunas Ilgauskas JSY 2.00 5.00
116 LeBron James JSY 10.00 25.00
117 Devin Harris JSY 2.50 6.00
118 Josh Howard JSY 2.00 5.00
119 Dirk Nowitzki JSY 4.00 10.00
120 Carmelo Anthony JSY 3.00 8.00
121 Julius Hodge JSY 2.00 5.00
122 Linas Kleiza JSY 2.00 5.00
123 Chauncey Billups JSY 2.50 6.00
124 Tayshaun Prince JSY 2.50 6.00
125 Ben Wallace JSY 2.50 6.00
126 Rasheed Wallace JSY 2.50 6.00
127 Baron Davis JSY 2.50 6.00
128 Ike Diogu JSY 2.00 5.00
129 Jason Richardson JSY 2.50 6.00
130 Chris Taft JSY 2.00 5.00
131 Luther Head JSY 2.00 5.00
132 Tracy McGrady JSY 3.00 8.00
133 Yao Ming JSY 3.00 8.00
134 Danny Granger JSY 2.50 6.00
135 Sarunas Jasikevicius JSY 2.00 5.00
136 Jermaine O'Neal JSY 2.50 6.00
137 Peja Stojakovic SP JSY 2.50 6.00
138 Elton Brand JSY 2.50 6.00
139 Shaun Livingston JSY 2.00 5.00
140 Corey Maggette JSY 2.00 5.00
141 Kwame Brown JSY 2.00 5.00
142 Kobe Bryant JSY 10.00 25.00
143 Andrew Bynum JSY 4.00 10.00
144 Lamar Odom JSY 2.50 6.00
145 Pau Gasol JSY 2.50 6.00
146 Eddie Jones JSY 2.00 5.00
147 Hakim Warrick JSY 2.00 5.00
148 Shaquille O'Neal JSY 5.00 12.00
149 Wayne Simien JSY 2.00 5.00
150 Antoine Walker JSY 2.00 5.00
151 Andrew Bogut JSY 2.50 6.00
152 Ersan Ilyasova JSY 2.00 5.00
153 Michael Redd JSY 2.50 6.00
154 Ricky Davis JSY 2.00 5.00
155 Kevin Garnett JSY 5.00 12.00
156 Rashad McCants JSY 2.00 5.00
157 Bracey Wright JSY 2.00 5.00
158 Vince Carter JSY 3.00 8.00
159 Richard Jefferson JSY 2.50 6.00
160 Jason Kidd JSY 4.00 10.00
161 Jeff McInnis JSY 2.00 5.00
163 Chris Paul JSY 5.00 12.00
164 J.R. Smith JSY 2.50 6.00
165 David West JSY 2.50 6.00
166 Steve Francis JSY 2.50 6.00
167 Channing Frye JSY 2.00 5.00
168 Stephon Marbury JSY 2.00 5.00
169 Nate Robinson JSY 2.50 6.00
170 Grant Hill JSY 3.00 8.00
171 Dwight Howard JSY 4.00 10.00
172 Jameer Nelson JSY 2.00 5.00
173 Samuel Dalembert JSY 2.00 5.00
174 Andre Iguodala JSY 2.50 6.00
175 Chris Webber JSY 2.50 6.00
176 Shawn Marion JSY 2.50 6.00
177 Steve Nash JSY 3.00 8.00
178 Amare Stoudemire JSY 2.50 6.00
179 Zach Randolph JSY 2.00 5.00
180 Sebastian Telfair JSY 1.50 4.00
181 Martell Webster JSY 2.00 5.00
182 Ron Artest JSY 2.50 6.00
183 Mike Bibby JSY 2.50 6.00
184 Francisco Garcia JSY 2.00 5.00
185 Tim Duncan JSY 4.00 10.00
186 Manu Ginobili JSY 2.50 6.00
187 Tony Parker JSY 2.50 6.00
188 Ray Allen JSY 2.50 6.00
189 Rashard Lewis JSY 2.50 6.00
190 Johan Petro JSY 2.00 5.00
191 Chris Bosh JSY 2.50 6.00
192 Joey Graham JSY 2.00 5.00
193 Charlie Villanueva JSY 2.50 6.00
194 Carlos Boozer JSY 2.50 6.00
195 Andrei Kirilenko JSY 2.00 5.00
196 C.J. Miles JSY 2.00 5.00
197 Deron Williams JSY 4.00 10.00
198 Andray Blatche JSY 2.00 5.00
199 Caron Butler JSY 2.50 6.00
200 Antawn Jamison JSY 2.50 6.00
201 Andrea Bargnani RC 4.00 10.00
202 LaMarcus Aldridge RC 6.00 15.00
203 Adam Morrison RC 3.00 8.00
204 Tyrus Thomas RC 3.00 8.00
205 Shelden Williams RC 2.50 6.00
206 Brandon Roy RC 6.00 15.00
207 Randy Foye RC 3.00 8.00
208 Rudy Gay RC 4.00 10.00
209 Patrick O'Bryant RC 2.50 6.00
210 Saer Sene RC 2.50 6.00
211 J.J. Redick RC 3.00 8.00
212 Hilton Armstrong RC 2.50 6.00
213 Thabo Sefolosha RC 3.00 8.00
214 Ronnie Brewer RC 3.00 8.00
215 Cedric Simmons RC 2.50 6.00
216 Rodney Carney RC 2.50 6.00
217 Shawne Williams RC 2.50 6.00
218 Hassan Adams RC 2.50 6.00
219 Quincy Douby RC 2.50 6.00
220 Renaldo Balkman RC 2.50 6.00
221 Rajon Rondo RC 10.00 25.00
222 Marcus Williams RC 2.50 6.00
223 Josh Boone RC 2.50 6.00
224 Kyle Lowry RC 3.00 8.00
225 Shannon Brown RC 4.00 10.00
226 Jordan Farmar RC 2.50 6.00
227 Maurice Ager RC 2.50 6.00
228 Mardy Collins RC 2.50 6.00
229 Will Blalock RC 2.50 6.00
230 James White RC 2.50 6.00
231 Steve Novak RC 2.50 6.00
232 Solomon Jones RC 2.50 6.00
233 Paul Davis RC 2.50 6.00
234 P.J. Tucker RC 2.50 6.00
235 Craig Smith RC 2.50 6.00
236 Bobby Jones RC 2.50 6.00
237 David Noel RC 2.50 6.00
238 Denham Brown RC 2.50 6.00
239 James Augustine RC 2.50 6.00
240 Daniel Gibson RC 3.00 8.00
241 Ryan Hollins RC 2.50 6.00
242 Alexander Johnson RC 2.50 6.00
243 Dee Brown RC 2.50 6.00
244 Paul Millsap RC 4.00 10.00
245 Leon Powe RC 2.50 6.00
246 Mike Gansey RC 2.50 6.00
247 Tarence Kinsey RC 2.50 6.00
248 Damir Markota RC 2.50 6.00
249 J.R. Pinnock RC 2.50 6.00
250 Kevin Pittsnogle RC 2.50 6.00

2006-07 SP Game Used Gold

*1-100 GOLD: .75X TO 2X BASE HI
*101-200 JSY GOLD: .5X TO 1.25X BASE HI
*201-249 RCs GOLD: .6X TO 1.5X BASE HI
PRINT RUN 100 SER.#'d SETS

2006-07 SP Game Used Patche

*PATCH: 1.25X TO 3X BASE HI
STATED PRINT RUN 25 SER.#'d SETS
170 Grant Hill 15.00 40.
175 Chris Webber 15.00 40.

2006-07 SP Game Used All-Sta Memorabilia

PRINT RUN 100 SER.#'d SETS
*PATCHES: .75X TO 2X BASE HI
PATCH PRINT RUN 25 SER.#'d SETS
AB Andrew Bogut 4.00 10.
AI Andre Iguodala 4.00 10.
AN Andres Nocioni 2.50 6.
BG Ben Gordon 4.00 10.
BO Chris Bosh 4.00 10.
BW Ben Wallace 4.00 10.
CB Chauncey Billups 4.00 10.
CF Channing Frye 3.00 8.
CP Chris Paul 8.00 20.
CV Charlie Villanueva 4.00 10.
DG Danny Granger 4.00 10.
DH Devin Harris 4.00 10.
DJ Dahntay Jones 2.50 6.
DN Dirk Nowitzki 6.00 15.
DW Delonte West 3.00 8.
EB Elton Brand 4.00 10.
EO Emeka Okafor 4.00 10.
GA Gilbert Arenas 4.00 10.
HW Hakim Warrick 3.00 8.
JS Josh Smith 4.00 10.
JT Jason Terry 3.00 8.
KB Kobe Bryant 15.00 40.
LD Luol Deng 4.00 10.
LH Luther Head 3.00 8.
LJ LeBron James 15.00 40.
NK Nenad Krstic 2.50 6.
NR Nate Robinson 4.00 10.
PG Pau Gasol 4.00 10.
PP Paul Pierce 5.00 12.
QR Quentin Richardson 3.00 8.
RA Ray Allen 5.00 12.
RH Richard Hamilton 3.00 8.
RI Royal Ivey 2.50 6.
RW Rasheed Wallace 4.00 10.
SJ Sarunas Jasikevicius 3.00 8.
SM Shawn Marion 4.00 10.
SO Shaquille O'Neal 8.00 20.
TD Tim Duncan 6.00 15.
TF T.J. Ford 3.00 8.
TP Tony Parker 4.00 10.
VC Vince Carter 5.00 12.
WI Deron Williams 6.00 15.

2006-07 SP Game Used Authentic Fabrics Dual

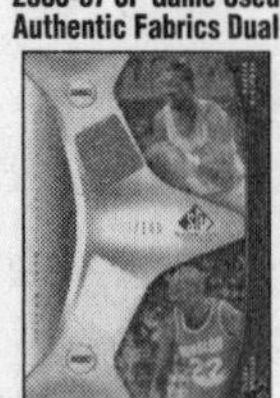

PRINT RUN 100 SER.#'d SETS
AD Ron Artest 3.00 8
Quincy Douby
AI Allen Iverson 6.00 15
Andre Iguodala
AJ Al Jefferson 3.00 8.
Tony Allen
AR Richard Jefferson 3.00 8.
Antoine Wright
AW Ray Allen 3.00 8.
Chris Wilcox
BF Chris Bosh 3.00 8
T.J. Ford
BG Caron Butler 3.00 8
Ben Gordon
BM C.J. Miles 3.00 8
Ronnie Brewer
CA Tyson Chandler 3.00 8.
Hilton Armstrong
CJ Josh Childress 3.00 8.
Solomon Jones
CL LeBron James 12.00 30
Carmelo Anthony
CM Corey Maggette 3.00 8
Sam Cassell
DI Samuel Dalembert 3.00 8
Andre Iguodala
DM Ricky Davis 3.00 8
Rashad McCants
DR Baron Davis 3.00 8
Jason Richardson
DS Drew Gooden 3.00 8
Shannon Brown
DT Mike Dunleavy 3.00 8
Chris Taft
FC Eddy Curry 3.00 8

anning Frye
Steve Francis 3.00 8.00
ephon Marbury
teve Francis 3.00 8.00
te Robinson
Raymond Felton 4.00 10.00
rvin Williams
Mike Bibby 3.00 8.00
ncisco Garcia
oey Graham 3.00 8.00
se Calderon
Hakim Warrick 3.00 8.00
dy Gay
Richard Hamilton 4.00 10.00
auncey Billups
osh Howard 3.00 8.00
vin Harris
eBron James 8.00 20.00
rry Hughes
Andre Miller 3.00 8.00
ius Hodge
Kirk Hinrich 3.00 8.00
ke Sweetney
Kirk Hinrich 4.00 10.00
rus Thomas
llen Iverson 4.00 10.00
dney Carney
drunas Ilgauskas 10.00 25.00
Bron James
ntawn Jamison 3.00 8.00
bert Arenas
Magic Johnson 25.00 60.00
rry Bird
ichael Jordan 40.00 80.00
Bron James
Jarrett Jack 3.00 8.00
artell Webster
oe Johnson 3.00 8.00
sh Smith
oe Johnson 3.00 8.00
arvin Williams
Bernard King 6.00 15.00
alt Frazier
Andrei Kirilenko 3.00 8.00
eron Williams
Shaun Livingston 3.00 8.00
sh Childress
Rashard Lewis 3.00 8.00
han Petro
Jamaal Magloire 3.00 8.00
Marcus Aldridge
Raymond Felton 3.00 8.00
an May
Juwan Howard 4.00 10.00
acy McGrady
Cuttino Mobley 3.00 8.00
aun Livingston
Corey Maggette 3.00 8.00
uttino Mobley
Dirk Nowitzki 5.00 12.00
au Gasol
Grant Hill 3.00 8.00
meer Nelson
Hakeem Olajuwon 8.00 20.00
yde Drexler
Lamar Odom 4.00 10.00
rdan Farmar
Emeka Okafor 3.00 8.00
ean May
Zach Randolph 3.00 8.00
aurice Ager
Luke Ridnour 4.00 10.00
ke Jackson
Paul Pierce 3.00 8.00
ajon Rondo
Rashad McCants 4.00 10.00
andy Foye
Michael Redd 3.00 8.00
harlie Villanueva
Wally Szczerbiak 3.00 8.00
ny Allen
Wally Szczerbiak 3.00 8.00
ebastian Telfair
Jason Williams 3.00 8.00
ayne Simien
Maurice Taylor 3.00 8.00
dy Curry
Chris Taft 3.00 8.00
e Diogu
Jason Terry 3.00 8.00
osh Howard
Kurt Thomas 4.00 10.00
mare Stoudemire
Jamaal Tinsley 3.00 8.00
hawne Williams
Deron Williams 6.00 15.00
ee Brown
Juan Dixon 3.00 8.00
artell Webster
Chris Webber 5.00 12.00
yle Korver
David West 3.00 8.00
edric Simmons
Marvin Williams 3.00 8.00
helden Williams

2006-07 SP Game Used Authentic Fabrics Dual Autographs

TED PRINT RUN 15 TO 50 SER.#'d SETS
Ron Artest 12.50 30.00
ill Laimbeer
Chris Paul 30.00 80.00
ilton Armstrong
Ron Artest 10.00 25.00
eja Stojakovic
Mike Bibby 12.50 30.00
on Artest
Tyson Chandler 12.50 30.00
ndrew Bogut
Elton Brand 25.00 60.00
evin Garnett
Andrew Bogut 15.00 40.00
rsan Ilyasova
Mike Bibby 15.00 40.00

Brad Miller
BP Chauncey Billups 15.00 40.00
Tayshaun Prince
BR Nate Robinson 12.50 30.00
Renaldo Balkman
BW Carlos Boozer 20.00 50.00
Deron Williams
CB Tyson Chandler 8.00 20.00
Kwame Brown
CJ Vince Carter 15.00 40.00
Richard Jefferson
DL Marquis Daniels 8.00 20.00
Shaun Livingston
DT Baron Davis 8.00 20.00
Chris Taft
FT T.J. Ford 8.00 20.00
P.J. Tucker
GB Mike Bibby 8.00 20.00
Francisco Garcia
GH Kevin Garnett 50.00 120.00
Dwight Howard
GM Kevin Garnett 20.00 50.00
Rashad McCants
HG Hakim Warrick 12.50 30.00
Rudy Gay
HM Larry Hughes 8.00 20.00
Donyell Marshall
IK Kyle Korver 12.50 30.00
Andre Iguodala
IR Andre Iguodala 8.00 20.00
Nate Robinson
JA LeBron James/15 125.00 250.00
Carmelo Anthony
JJ Michael Jordan/15 600.00 1000.00
LeBron James
JW Joe Johnson 12.50 30.00
Marvin Williams
KC Jason Kidd 25.00 60.00
Vince Carter
KD Jason Kidd 12.50 30.00
Baron Davis
KF Bernard King 20.00 50.00
Walt Frazier
KJ Jason Kidd 12.50 30.00
Richard Jefferson
KS Kyle Korver 8.00 20.00
Peja Stojakovic
LS Shaun Livingston 8.00 20.00
J.R. Smith
MA Yao Ming/15 50.00 120.00
Kareem Abdul-Jabbar
MB Donyell Marshall 8.00 20.00
Carlos Boozer
MF Rashad McCants 10.00 25.00
Raymond Felton
MJ Tracy McGrady/15 125.00 250.00
LeBron James
ML Cuttino Mobley 8.00 20.00
Shaun Livingston
MM Corey Maggette 8.00 20.00
Cuttino Mobley
NB Steve Nash/15 50.00 120.00
Chauncey Billups
OB Lamar Odom 8.00 20.00
Kwame Brown
OD Hakeem Olajuwon/15 100.00 200.00
Clyde Drexler
OG Lamar Odom 8.00 20.00
Joey Graham
OJ Lamar Odom 8.00 20.00
Al Jefferson
PJ Paul Pierce 20.00 50.00
Al Jefferson
PT Sebastian Telfair 8.00 20.00
Kevin Pittsnogle
RC Quentin Richardson 8.00 20.00
Eddy Curry
RH Luke Ridnour 8.00 20.00
Kirk Hinrich
RJ Quentin Richardson 8.00 20.00
Joe Johnson
SC Tyson Chandler 8.00 20.00
Cedric Simmons
TG Chris Taft 8.00 20.00
Francisco Garcia
TR Sebastian Telfair 8.00 20.00
Nate Robinson
WB Andrew Bogut 12.50 30.00
Marvin Williams
WJ Antawn Jamison 8.00 20.00
Marvin Williams
WP Chris Paul 40.00 100.00
Deron Williams

2006-07 SP Game Used Authentic Fabrics Dual Patches

*PATCHES: 1X TO 2.5X BASE HI
PRINT RUN 25 SER.#'d SETS
CL LeBron James 30.00 80.00
Carmelo Anthony

2006-07 SP Game Used Authentic Fabrics Dual Patches Autographs

STATED PRINT RUN 5 TO 25 SER.#'d SETS
SOME UNPRICED DUE TO SCARCITY
AL Ron Artest/25 15.00 40.00
Bill Laimbeer
AP Chris Paul/25 40.00 100.00
Hilton Armstrong
BC Tyson Chandler/25 15.00 40.00
Andrew Bogut
BM Mike Bibby/25 20.00 50.00
Brad Miller
BW Carlos Boozer/25 25.00 60.00
Deron Williams
CB Tyson Chandler/25 10.00 25.00
Kwame Brown
CJ Vince Carter/25 20.00 50.00
Richard Jefferson
DL Marquis Daniels/25 10.00 25.00
Shaun Livingston
DT Baron Davis/25 10.00 25.00
Chris Taft
GM Kevin Garnett/25 25.00 60.00
Rashad McCants
HG Hakim Warrick/25 15.00 40.00
Rudy Gay
IK Kyle Korver/25 15.00 40.00
Andre Iguodala
IR Andre Iguodala/25 10.00 25.00
Nate Robinson
KC Jason Kidd/25 30.00 80.00
Vince Carter
KD Jason Kidd/25 15.00 40.00
Baron Davis
KF Bernard King/25 30.00 80.00
Walt Frazier
KJ Jason Kidd/25 25.00 60.00
Richard Jefferson
KS Kyle Korver/25 10.00 25.00
Peja Stojakovic
MB Donyell Marshall/25 10.00 25.00
Carlos Boozer
MF Rashad McCants/25 12.50 30.00
Raymond Felton
MM Corey Maggette/25 10.00 25.00
Cuttino Mobley
OJ Lamar Odom/25 10.00 25.00
Al Jefferson
PT Sebastian Telfair/25 10.00 25.00
Kevin Pittsnogle
RH Luke Ridnour/25 10.00 25.00
Kirk Hinrich
TG Chris Taft/25 10.00 25.00
Francisco Garcia
TR Sebastian Telfair/25 10.00 25.00
Nate Robinson

2006-07 SP Game Used Authentic Fabrics Triple

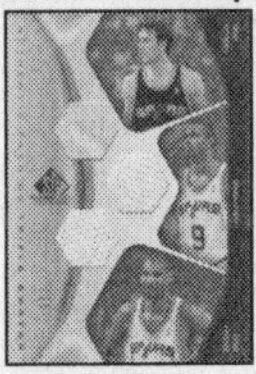

PRINT RUN 25 SER.#'d SETS
UNPRICED PATCH PRINT RUN 10 SETS
ASJ Wally Szczerbiak 12.50 30.00
Al Jefferson
Tony Allen
BAJ Kobe Bryant 30.00 80.00
LeBron James
Carmelo Anthony
BBB Elton Brand 12.50 30.00
Shane Battier
Carlos Boozer
BGF Chris Bosh 12.50 30.00
T.J. Ford
Joey Graham
BOV Lamar Odom 12.50 30.00
Kwame Brown
Sasha Vujacic
DMO Tim Duncan 30.00 80.00
Hakeem Olajuwon
Yao Ming
DPG Tim Duncan 25.00 60.00
Tony Parker
Manu Ginobili
DRD Jason Richardson 12.50 30.00
Mike Dunleavy
Ike Diogu
GHO Kevin Garnett 20.00 50.00
Dwight Howard
Jermaine O'Neal
HBP Richard Hamilton 15.00 40.00
Chauncey Billups
Tayshaun Prince
HDG Kirk Hinrich 15.00 40.00
Luol Deng
Ben Gordon
IKB Zydrunas Ilgauskas 12.50 30.00
Nenad Krstic
Andrew Bogut
JMM Antawn Jamison 12.50 30.00
Jeff McInnis
Sean May
KCJ Jason Kidd 15.00 40.00
Vince Carter
Richard Jefferson
MRR Stephon Marbury 12.50 30.00
Quentin Richardson
Nate Robinson
MWP Desmond Mason 15.00 40.00
David West
Chris Paul
NKS Dirk Nowitzki 15.00 40.00
Andrei Kirilenko
Peja Stojakovic
NMS Steve Nash 20.00 50.00
Shawn Marion
Amare Stoudemire
WIK Chris Webber 15.00 40.00
Allen Iverson
Kyle Korver

2006-07 SP Game Used Legendary Fabrics

PRINT RUN 100 SER.#'d SETS
BK Bernard King 5.00 12.00
BL Bill Laimbeer 6.00 15.00
BR Bill Russell 15.00 40.00
CD Clyde Drexler 8.00 20.00
DR Dennis Rodman 8.00 20.00
GG George Gervin 5.00 12.00
HO Hakeem Olajuwon 8.00 20.00
JE Julius Erving 10.00 25.00
JH Jeff Hornacek 6.00 15.00
JS John Starks 6.00 15.00
KA Kareem Abdul-Jabbar 8.00 20.00
LB Larry Bird 12.50 30.00
MA Magic Johnson 10.00 25.00
MJ Michael Jordan 30.00 75.00
NA Nate Archibald 5.00 12.00
RP Robert Parish 5.00 12.00
SE Sean Elliott 5.00 12.00
SK Steve Kerr 5.00 12.00
ST John Stockton 8.00 20.00
WF Walt Frazier 5.00 12.00

2006-07 SP Game Used Legendary Fabrics Autographs

PRINT RUN 10 TO 50 SER.#'d SETS
BK Bernard King/50 10.00 25.00
BL Bill Laimbeer/50 10.00 25.00
CD Clyde Drexler/50 30.00 80.00
GG George Gervin/50 10.00 25.00
HO Hakeem Olajuwon/50 25.00 60.00
JE Julius Erving/10 75.00 150.00
JH Jeff Hornacek/50 20.00 50.00
JS John Starks/50 30.00 60.00
KA Kareem Abdul-Jabbar/10 60.00 120.00
LB Larry Bird/10 125.00 225.00
MA Magic Johnson/50 75.00 150.00
MJ Michael Jordan/50 500.00 800.00
NA Nate Archibald/50 12.50 30.00
RP Robert Parish/50 12.50 30.00
SK Steve Kerr/50 12.50 30.00
WF Walt Frazier/50 12.50 30.00

2006-07 SP Game Used Rookie Exclusive Autographs

PRINT RUN 100 SER.#'d SETS
AB Andrea Bargnani 10.00 25.00
AD Hassan Adams 6.00 15.00
AR Allan Ray 6.00 15.00
BA Renaldo Balkman 6.00 15.00
BJ Bobby Jones 6.00 15.00
BR Brandon Roy 15.00 40.00
CS Cedric Simmons 6.00 15.00
DB Denham Brown 6.00 15.00
DE Dee Brown 6.00 15.00
DG Daniel Gibson 8.00 20.00
DN David Noel 6.00 15.00
HA Hilton Armstrong 6.00 15.00
JA James Augustine 6.00 15.00
JB Josh Boone 6.00 15.00
JF Jordan Farmar 6.00 15.00
JW James White 6.00 15.00
KL Kyle Lowry 8.00 20.00
KP Kevin Pittsnogle 6.00 15.00
LA LaMarcus Aldridge 15.00 40.00
MA Maurice Ager 6.00 15.00
MC Mardy Collins 6.00 15.00
MG Mike Gansey 6.00 15.00
MW Marcus Williams 6.00 15.00
PD Paul Davis 6.00 15.00
PO Patrick O'Bryant 6.00 15.00
PT P.J. Tucker 6.00 15.00
QD Quincy Douby 6.00 15.00
RB Ronnie Brewer 8.00 20.00
RC Rodney Carney 6.00 15.00
RF Randy Foye 8.00 20.00
RG Rudy Gay 12.50 30.00
RH Ryan Hollins 6.00 15.00
RR Rajon Rondo 30.00 80.00
SB Shannon Brown 10.00 25.00
SJ Solomon Jones 6.00 15.00
SM Craig Smith 6.00 15.00
SN Steve Novak 6.00 15.00
SS Saer Sene 6.00 15.00
SW Shelden Williams 6.00 15.00
TT Tyrus Thomas 10.00 25.00
WI Shawne Williams 6.00 15.00

2006-07 SP Game Used SIGnificance

PRINT RUN 23 TO 100 SER.#'d SETS
AB Andrew Bogut/100 5.00 12.00
AH Hilton Armstrong/100 4.00 10.00
AI Andre Iguodala/100 4.00 10.00
AJ Al Jefferson/100 4.00 10.00
AU James Augustine/25 4.00 10.00
BA Andrea Bargnani/100 8.00 20.00
BB Brent Barry/100 4.00 10.00
BI Chauncey Billups/100 6.00 15.00
BJ Bobby Jackson/100 4.00 10.00
BK Bernard King/100 6.00 15.00
BM Brad Miller/100 4.00 10.00
BN Denham Brown/100 4.00 10.00
BR Brandon Roy/100 15.00 40.00
BW Bill Walton/100 8.00 20.00
CA Carmelo Anthony/50 20.00 50.00
CD Clyde Drexler/100 12.50 30.00
CE Cedric Simmons/25 4.00 10.00
CM Cuttino Mobley/100 4.00 10.00
CS Craig Smith/100 4.00 10.00
CT Chris Taft/100 4.00 10.00
DB Dee Brown/100 4.00 10.00
DE Daniel Ewing/100 4.00 10.00
DG Daniel Gibson/100 5.00 12.00
DH Dwight Howard/100 12.50 30.00
DJ Dwayne Jones/100 4.00 10.00
DM Donyell Marshall/100 4.00 10.00
DN David Noel/100 4.00 10.00
DS DeShawn Stevenson/100 4.00 10.00
DW Deron Williams/100 8.00 20.00
EC Eddy Curry/100 4.00 10.00
EI Ersan Ilyasova/100 4.00 10.00
FG Francisco Garcia/100 4.00 10.00
FR Randy Foye/100 6.00 15.00
HA Hassan Adams/100 4.00 10.00
HW Hakim Warrick/100 4.00 10.00
JB Bobby Jones/100 4.00 10.00
JG Joey Graham/100 4.00 10.00
JK Jason Kapono/100 4.00 10.00
JO Amir Johnson/100 4.00 10.00
JW James White/100 4.00 10.00
KB Kwame Brown/100 4.00 10.00
KG Kevin Garnett/100 20.00 50.00
KH Kirk Hinrich/100 6.00 15.00
KK Kyle Korver/100 4.00 10.00
KL Kyle Lowry/100 5.00 12.00
LA LaMarcus Aldridge/100 10.00 25.00
LB Larry Bird/25 75.00 150.00
LH Larry Hughes/100 4.00 10.00
LJ LeBron James/23 150.00 300.00
LO Lamar Odom/100 5.00 12.00
LR Luke Ridnour/100 4.00 10.00
MA Maurice Ager/100 4.00 10.00
MB Mike Bibby/100 4.00 10.00
MD Marquis Daniels/100 4.00 10.00
MI Michael Jordan/23 300.00 550.00
NR Nate Robinson/100 4.00 10.00
NS Steve Novak/100 4.00 10.00
PO Patrick O'Bryant/100 4.00 10.00
PP Paul Pierce/100 10.00 25.00
PS Peja Stojakovic/100 5.00 12.00
QD Quincy Douby/100 4.00 10.00
RB Renaldo Balkman/100 4.00 10.00
RC Rodney Carney/100 4.00 10.00
RG Rudy Gay/100 6.00 15.00
RH Ryan Hollins/100 4.00 10.00
RJ Richard Jefferson/100 4.00 10.00
RM Rashad McCants/100 4.00 10.00
RT Ronny Turiaf/100 8.00 20.00
SB Shannon Brown/100 6.00 15.00
SC Speedy Claxton/100 4.00 10.00
SW Shelden Williams/100 4.00 10.00
TP Tayshaun Prince/100 6.00 15.00
TT Tyrus Thomas/100 10.00 25.00
VC Vince Carter/100 12.50 30.00
VW Von Wafer/100 4.00 10.00
WI Marvin Williams/100 4.00 10.00
WM Marcus Williams/100 4.00 10.00
YK Yaroslav Korolev/100 4.00 10.00
YM Yao Ming/100 15.00 40.00

2006-07 SP Game Used SIGnificance Dual

PRINT RUN 10 TO 50 SER.#'d SETS
SOME UNPRICED DUE TO SCARCITY
AL Ron Artest 20.00 50.00
Bill Laimbeer
AP Chris Paul 15.00 40.00
Hilton Armstrong
AR LaMarcus Aldridge 40.00 100.00
Brandon Roy
AS Ron Artest 12.50 30.00
Peja Stojakovic
BJ Amir Johnson 8.00 20.00
Will Blalock
BP Chauncey Billups 15.00 40.00
Tayshaun Prince
BR Brent Barry 10.00 25.00
Nate Robinson
BT Kwame Brown 15.00 40.00
Ronny Turiaf
BW Andrew Bogut 12.50 30.00
Marvin Williams
CB Tyson Chandler 8.00 20.00
Andrew Bogut
CJ Vince Carter 20.00 40.00
Richard Jefferson
DL Marquis Daniels 10.00 25.00
Shaun Livingston
EK Daniel Ewing 8.00 20.00
Yaroslav Korolev
FO Francisco Garcia 8.00 20.00
Orien Greene
FS Randy Foye 20.00 50.00
Craig Smith
FT T.J. Ford 12.50 30.00
P.J. Tucker
GG Joey Graham 8.00 20.00
Stephen Graham
GH Kevin Garnett 40.00 100.00
Dwight Howard
GM Kevin Garnett 20.00 50.00
Rashad McCants
HR Richard Jefferson 8.00 20.00
Hassan Adams
IR Andre Iguodala 10.00 25.00
Nate Robinson
JR Al Jefferson 15.00 40.00
Rajon Rondo
JS Joe Johnson 8.00 20.00
Salim Stoudamire
JW Antawn Jamison 12.50 30.00
Marvin Williams
KF Bernard King 25.00 60.00
Walt Frazier
KS Kyle Korver 10.00 25.00
Peja Stojakovic
LD Shaun Livingston 8.00 20.00
Paul Davis
ME Cuttino Mobley 8.00 20.00
Daniel Ewing
MF Rashad McCants 12.50 30.00
Raymond Felton
MK Cuttino Mobley 8.00 20.00
Chris Kaman
OJ Lamar Odom 10.00 25.00
Al Jefferson
OW Lamar Odom 8.00 20.00
Von Wafer
PJ Paul Pierce 12.50 30.00
Al Jefferson
PR Rajon Rondo 15.00 40.00
Kevin Pittsnogle
RC Quentin Richardson 8.00 20.00
Eddy Curry
RJ Quentin Richardson 8.00 20.00
Joe Johnson
RK Quentin Richardson 10.00 25.00
Bernard King
SI Bobby Simmons 8.00 20.00
Ersan Ilyasova
TE Chris Taft 10.00 25.00
Monta Ellis
TH Kirk Hinrich 10.00 25.00
Tyrus Thomas
TR Sebastian Telfair 8.00 20.00
Nate Robinson
WB Marcus Williams 8.00 20.00
Josh Boone
WE Deron Williams 10.00 25.00
Daniel Ewing
WJ Bobby Jackson 8.00 20.00
Hakim Warrick
WS Shelden Williams 8.00 20.00
Solomon Jones

2006-07 SP Game Used Significant Numbers

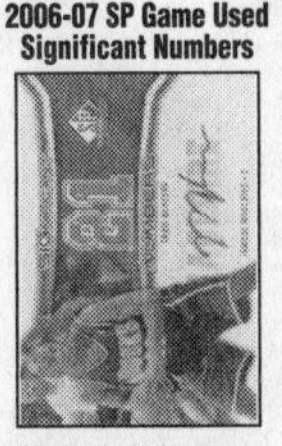

CARDS #'d TO PLAYER'S JSY NUMBER
SOME UNPRICED DUE TO SCARCITY
BK Bernard King/30 15.00 40.00
BL Bill Laimbeer/40 30.00 80.00
BM Brad Miller/52 6.00 15.00
BO Bobby Jones/11 15.00 40.00
CA Carmelo Anthony/15 60.00 120.00
CD Clyde Drexler/22 50.00 100.00
CO Corey Maggette/50 8.00 20.00
CT Chris Taft/21 10.00 25.00
DM Donyell Marshall/24 6.00 15.00
DR Dennis Rodman/91 40.00 100.00
EC Eddy Curry/34 6.00 15.00
EI Ersan Ilyasova/23 6.00 15.00
FG Francisco Garcia/32 8.00 20.00
GG George Gervin/44 20.00 50.00
HA Hilton Armstrong/12 15.00 40.00
HO Hakeem Olajuwon/34 40.00 80.00
HW Hakim Warrick/21 10.00 25.00
JM Jamaal Magloire/20 8.00 20.00
JO Michael Jordan/23 400.00 650.00
JW James White/100 6.00 15.00
KA Kareem Abdul-Jabbar/33 75.00 150.00
KG Kevin Garnett/21 40.00 80.00
KK Kyle Korver/26 12.50 30.00
KW Kwame Brown/54 10.00 25.00
LA LaMarcus Aldridge/12 60.00 150.00
LB Larry Bird/33 125.00 250.00
LH Larry Hughes/32 15.00 40.00
LJ LeBron James/23 150.00 400.00
NS Steve Novak/20 10.00 25.00
PO Patrick O'Bryant/26 10.00 25.00
PP Paul Pierce/34 20.00 50.00
PS Peja Stojakovic/16 15.00 40.00
RC Rodney Carney/25 12.50 30.00
RE Renaldo Balkman/32 10.00 25.00
RF Raymond Felton/20 20.00 50.00
RG Rudy Gay/22 25.00 60.00
RJ Richard Jefferson/24 10.00 25.00
RP Robert Parish/00 12.00 30.00
SE Sean Elliott/32 15.00 40.00
SJ Solomon Jones/44 6.00 15.00
SK Steve Kerr/25 40.00 75.00
SL Shaun Livingston/14 20.00 50.00
SM J.R. Smith/23 15.00 40.00
SN Steve Nash/13 60.00 120.00
TE Sebastian Telfair/31 12.50 30.00
TP Tayshaun Prince/22 20.00 50.00
TT Tyrus Thomas/24 25.00 60.00
VC Vince Carter/15 30.00 80.00
WF Walt Frazier/10 25.00 60.00
WI Marvin Williams/24 12.50 30.00
YM Yao Ming/11 60.00 120.00

2007-08 SP Game Used

This 190-card set was released in September, 2007. The set was issued in five-card packs which came six packs to a box and 10 boxes to a case where packs carried an initial SRP of $50. Cards numbered 1-100 feature veterans in team alphabetical order while cards 101-140 feature veterans with game-used jersey swatches attached and the set concludes with cards 141-190 featuring 2007-08 rookies. The jersey cards were issued at a stated rate of approximately one per pack and the rookies were issued to a stated print run of 999 serial numbered sets.

COMP.SET w/o SP's (100) 35.00 70.00
1 Joe Johnson 1.00 2.50
2 Marvin Williams 1.00 2.50
3 Josh Smith 1.00 2.50
4 Al Jefferson 1.00 2.50
5 Paul Pierce 1.25 3.00
6 Delonte West .75 2.00
7 Raymond Felton 1.25 3.00
8 Gerald Wallace 1.00 2.50
9 Emeka Okafor 1.00 2.50
10 Michael Jordan 8.00 20.00
11 Ben Gordon 1.00 2.50
12 Luol Deng 1.00 2.50
13 Kirk Hinrich 1.00 2.50
14 LeBron James 5.00 12.00
15 Larry Hughes .75 2.00
16 Zydrunas Ilgauskas .75 2.00
17 Dirk Nowitzki 1.25 3.00
18 Josh Howard .75 2.00
19 Jason Terry .75 2.00
20 Allen Iverson 1.25 3.00
21 Carmelo Anthony 1.25 3.00
22 Marcus Camby .60 1.50
23 J.R. Smith 1.00 2.50
24 Chauncey Billups 1.00 2.50
25 Rasheed Wallace 1.00 2.50
26 Richard Hamilton .75 2.00
27 Tayshaun Prince 1.00 2.50
28 Jason Richardson 1.00 2.50
29 Baron Davis 1.00 2.50
30 Monta Ellis 1.00 2.50
31 Tracy McGrady 1.00 2.50
32 Yao Ming 1.25 3.00
33 Rafer Alston .60 1.50
34 Jermaine O'Neal 1.00 2.50
35 Danny Granger 1.00 2.50
36 Jamaal Tinsley .60 1.50
37 Elton Brand 1.00 2.50
38 Corey Maggette .75 2.00
39 Cuttino Mobley .75 2.00
40 Kobe Bryant 5.00 12.00
41 Lamar Odom 1.00 2.50
42 Luke Walton .60 1.50
43 Kwame Brown .60 1.50
44 Pau Gasol 1.00 2.50
45 Mike Miller 1.00 2.50
46 Hakim Warrick .75 2.00
47 Dwyane Wade 2.50 6.00
48 Shaquille O'Neal 2.00 5.00
49 Jason Williams .75 2.00
50 Michael Redd 1.00 2.50
51 Mo Williams .75 2.00
52 Andrew Bogut 1.00 2.50
53 Kevin Garnett 2.00 5.00
54 Ricky Davis .75 2.00
55 Mike James .60 1.50
56 Vince Carter 1.25 3.00
57 Jason Kidd 1.25 3.00
58 Nenad Krstic .60 1.50
59 Richard Jefferson 1.00 2.50
60 Stephon Marbury .75 2.00
61 Eddy Curry .60 1.50
62 Jamal Crawford .75 2.00
63 David Lee .75 2.00
64 Chris Paul 2.00 5.00
65 Tyson Chandler .75 2.00
66 David West 1.00 2.50
67 Peja Stojakovic 1.00 2.50
68 Dwight Howard 1.50 4.00
69 Grant Hill 1.25 3.00
70 Jameer Nelson .75 2.00
71 Andre Miller .75 2.00
72 Andre Iguodala 1.00 2.50
73 Kyle Korver .75 2.00
74 Steve Nash 1.25 3.00
75 Amare Stoudemire 1.25 3.00
76 Shawn Marion 1.00 2.50
77 Leandro Barbosa .75 2.00
78 Brandon Roy 1.25 3.00
79 Zach Randolph .75 2.00
80 LaMarcus Aldridge 1.25 3.00
81 Mike Bibby 1.00 2.50
82 Kevin Martin 1.00 2.50
83 Ron Artest 1.00 2.50
84 Tony Parker 1.00 2.50
85 Manu Ginobili 1.00 2.50
86 Tim Duncan 1.50 4.00
87 Rashard Lewis .75 2.00
88 Ray Allen 1.00 2.50
89 Chris Wilcox .60 1.50
90 T.J. Ford .75 2.00
91 Chris Bosh 1.00 2.50
92 Juan Dixon .60 1.50
93 Andrea Bargnani 1.25 3.00
94 Carlos Boozer 1.00 2.50
95 Mehmet Okur .60 1.50
96 Deron Williams 1.50 4.00
97 Gilbert Arenas 1.00 2.50
98 Antawn Jamison 1.00 2.50
99 Caron Butler 1.00 2.50
100 DeShawn Stevenson .60 1.50
101 Al Jefferson JSY 3.00 8.00
102 Allen Iverson JSY 4.00 10.00
103 Amare Stoudemire JSY 3.00 8.00
104 Andre Iguodala JSY 3.00 8.00
105 Andre Miller JSY 2.50 6.00
106 Ben Gordon JSY 3.00 8.00
107 Bruce Bowen JSY 2.00 5.00
108 Carmelo Anthony JSY 4.00 10.00
109 Charlie Villanueva JSY 3.00 8.00
110 Corey Maggette JSY 2.50 6.00
111 Danny Granger JSY 3.00 8.00
112 Darko Milicic JSY 2.00 5.00
113 Devin Harris JSY 3.00 8.00
114 Dirk Nowitzki JSY 4.00 10.00
115 Donyell Marshall JSY 2.00 5.00
116 Drew Gooden JSY 2.50 6.00
117 Dwight Howard JSY 5.00 12.00
118 Elton Brand JSY 3.00 8.00
119 Gilbert Arenas JSY 3.00 8.00
120 Grant Hill JSY 4.00 10.00
121 Jason Kidd JSY 3.00 8.00
122 Jason Richardson JSY 3.00 8.00
123 Jermaine O'Neal JSY 3.00 8.00
124 Kevin Garnett JSY 6.00 15.00
125 Kobe Bryant JSY 8.00 20.00
126 LeBron James JSY 10.00 25.00
127 Luol Deng JSY 3.00 8.00
128 Manu Ginobili JSY 3.00 8.00
129 Mike Bibby JSY 3.00 8.00
130 Nenad Krstic JSY 2.00 5.00
131 Pau Gasol JSY 3.00 8.00
132 Paul Pierce JSY 4.00 10.00
133 Rashard Lewis JSY 2.50 6.00
134 Ray Allen JSY 3.00 8.00
135 Richard Jefferson JSY 3.00 8.00
136 Shaquille O'Neal JSY 6.00 15.00
137 Shaun Livingston JSY 2.00 5.00
138 Shawn Marion JSY 3.00 8.00
139 Tayshaun Prince JSY 3.00 8.00

140 Tim Duncan JSY 5.00 12.00
141 Greg Oden RC 2.50 6.00
142 Kevin Durant RC 15.00 40.00
143 Al Horford RC 2.50 6.00
144 Mike Conley Jr. RC 3.00 8.00
145 Jeff Green RC 2.50 6.00
146 Dominic McGuire RC 2.00 5.00
147 Corey Brewer RC 2.50 6.00
148 Brandan Wright RC 3.00 8.00
149 Joakim Noah RC 5.00 12.00
150 Spencer Hawes RC 2.00 5.00
151 Acie Law RC 2.00 5.00
152 Thaddeus Young RC 2.50 6.00
153 Julian Wright RC 2.00 5.00
154 Al Thornton RC 2.00 5.00
155 Rodney Stuckey RC 3.00 8.00
156 Nick Young RC 3.00 8.00
157 Sean Williams RC 2.00 5.00
158 Marco Belinelli RC 2.00 5.00
159 Javaris Crittenton RC 2.00 5.00
160 Jason Smith RC 2.00 5.00
161 Daequan Cook RC 2.00 5.00
162 Jared Dudley RC 2.00 5.00
163 Wilson Chandler RC 3.00 8.00
164 Morris Almond RC 2.00 5.00
165 Aaron Brooks RC 2.00 5.00
166 Arron Afflalo RC 2.50 6.00
167 Alando Tucker RC 2.00 5.00
168 Petteri Koponen RC 2.00 5.00
169 Carl Landry RC 2.00 5.00
170 Gabe Pruitt RC 2.00 5.00
171 Marcus Williams RC 2.00 5.00
172 Nick Fazekas RC 2.00 5.00
173 Glen Davis RC 3.00 8.00
174 Jermareo Davidson RC 2.00 5.00
175 Josh McRoberts RC 2.00 5.00
176 Chris Richard RC 2.00 5.00
177 Derrick Byars RC 2.00 5.00
178 Adam Haluska RC 2.00 5.00
179 Reyshawn Terry RC 2.00 5.00
180 Jared Jordan RC 2.00 5.00
181 Aaron Gray RC 2.00 5.00
182 JamesOn Curry RC 2.00 5.00
183 Taurean Green RC 2.00 5.00
184 Demetris Nichols RC 2.00 5.00
185 Herbert Hill RC 2.00 5.00
186 Brad Newley RC 2.00 5.00
187 Ramon Sessions RC 3.00 8.00
188 Sammy Mejia RC 2.00 5.00
189 D.J. Strawberry RC 2.00 5.00
190 Stephane Lasme RC 2.00 5.00

2007-08 SP Game Used Gold

*1-100 GOLD: 1.5X TO 4X BASE HI
*101-140 GOLD JSY: 1X TO 2.5X BASE HI
*141-190 GOLD RC: 1.5X TO 4X BASE HI
PRINT RUN 25 SER.#'d SETS
142 Kevin Durant 150.00 300.00

2007-08 SP Game Used All-Star Jersey

PRINT RUN 199 SER.#'d SETS
*PATCHES: 1.25X TO 3X BASE HI
PATCH PRINT RUN 50 SER.#'d SETS
ASAB Andrew Bogut 3.00 8.00
ASBG Ben Gordon 3.00 8.00
ASBO Carlos Boozer 3.00 8.00
ASBR Brandon Roy 4.00 10.00
ASBY Andrew Bynum 4.00 10.00
ASCB Chauncey Billups 3.00 8.00
ASCP Chris Paul 6.00 15.00
ASDH Dwight Howard 5.00 12.00
ASDJ Damon Jones 2.00 5.00
ASDL David Lee 2.50 6.00
ASDN Dirk Nowitzki 4.00 10.00
ASFE Raymond Felton 4.00 10.00
ASGA Gilbert Arenas 3.00 8.00
ASGG Gerald Green 2.50 6.00
ASJF Jordan Farmar 2.00 5.00
ASJG Jorge Garbajosa 2.50 6.00
ASJH Josh Howard 2.50 6.00
ASJJ Joe Johnson 3.00 8.00
ASJK Jason Kidd 3.00 8.00
ASJO Jermaine O'Neal 3.00 8.00
ASKB Kobe Bryant 10.00 25.00
ASLH Luther Head 2.50 6.00
ASLJ LeBron James 15.00 30.00
ASMM Mike Miller 3.00 8.00
ASMO Mehmet Okur 2.00 5.00
ASMW Marcus Williams 2.00 5.00
ASPM Paul Millsap 2.50 6.00
ASPP Paul Pierce 4.00 10.00
ASRA Ray Allen 3.00 8.00
ASRF Randy Foye 3.00 8.00
ASSN Steve Nash 4.00 10.00
ASSP Smush Parker 2.00 5.00
ASTP Tony Parker 4.00 10.00
ASTT Tyrus Thomas 3.00 8.00
ASYM Yao Ming 4.00 10.00

2007-08 SP Game Used Authentic Fabrics

APPROXIMATE ODDS ONE PER BOX
*PATCHES: 1X TO 2.5X BASE HI
PATCH PRINT RUN 75 SER.#'d SETS
AFAB Andrew Bynum 4.00 10.00
AFAI Allen Iverson 4.00 10.00
AFAJ Antawn Jamison 3.00 8.00
AFAM Alonzo Mourning 4.00 10.00
AFBR Brandon Roy 4.00 10.00
AFCB Chauncey Billups 3.00 8.00
AFCP Chris Paul 6.00 15.00
AFCW Chris Webber 3.00 8.00
AFDW Deron Williams 5.00 12.00
AFEB Elton Brand 3.00 8.00
AFGW Gerald Wallace 3.00 8.00
AFJO Jermaine O'Neal 3.00 8.00
AFJR Jason Richardson 3.00 8.00
AFLJ LeBron James 10.00 25.00
AFMG Manu Ginobili 3.00 8.00
AFMJ Michael Jordan 25.00 60.00
AFPG Pau Gasol 3.00 8.00
AFQD Quincy Douby 2.00 5.00
AFRW Rasheed Wallace 3.00 8.00
AFYM Yao Ming 4.00 10.00

2007-08 SP Game Used Authentic Fabrics Dual

PRINT RUN 99 SER.#'d SETS
*PATCH: .75X TO 2X BASE HI
PATCH PRINT RUN 50 SER.#'d SETS
AB Gilbert Arenas 4.00 10.00
Caron Butler
AI Allen Iverson 8.00 20.00
Carmelo Anthony
AW Ron Artest 4.00 10.00
Antoine Walker
BJ Mike Bibby 4.00 10.00
Mike James
BS Bruce Bowen 4.00 10.00
Josh Smith
BV Andrew Bogut 4.00 10.00
Charlie Villanueva
CJ Vince Carter 5.00 12.00
Richard Jefferson
CO Marcus Camby 4.00 10.00
Mehmet Okur
DB Antonio Daniels 4.00 10.00
Andray Blatche
DM Ricky Davis 4.00 10.00
Kenyon Martin
DW Luol Deng 4.00 10.00
Marvin Williams
FL Raymond Felton 4.00 10.00
Shaun Livingston
GD Manu Ginobili 6.00 15.00
Tim Duncan
GJ Kevin Garnett 5.00 12.00
Mike James
HB Brendan Haywood 4.00 10.00
Kwame Brown
HD Larry Hughes 4.00 10.00
Marquis Daniels
HJ Al Harrington 4.00 10.00
Antawn Jamison
HP Richard Hamilton 4.00 10.00
Tayshaun Prince
HT Devin Harris 4.00 10.00
Jamaal Tinsley
HW Rasheed Wallace 4.00 10.00
Richard Hamilton
JJ LeBron James 40.00 100.00
Michael Jordan
JK Jason Williams 4.00 10.00
Kirk Hinrich
JP Richard Jefferson 4.00 10.00
Tayshaun Prince
JS Josh Smith 4.00 10.00
Josh Childress
KN Nenad Krstic 4.00 10.00
Nene
KR Kyle Korver 4.00 10.00
Michael Redd
LB David Lee 4.00 10.00
Carlos Boozer
LP Rashard Lewis 4.00 10.00
Morris Peterson
MD Andre Miller 4.00 10.00
Baron Davis
MG Corey Maggette 4.00 10.00
Danny Granger
MH Sean May 4.00 10.00
Udonis Haslem
MI Yao Ming 5.00 12.00
Zydrunas Ilgauskas
MK Alonzo Mourning 5.00 12.00
Andrei Kirilenko
MN Darko Milicic 4.00 10.00
Jameer Nelson
MT Stephon Marbury 4.00 10.00
Jason Terry
OW Lamar Odom 4.00 10.00
Luke Walton
PD Mickael Pietrus 4.00 10.00
Mike Dunleavy
PS Paul Pierce 4.00 10.00
Peja Stojakovic
RB Zach Randolph 4.00 10.00
Andrew Bynum
RH Jalen Rose 6.00 15.00
Grant Hill
RR Nate Robinson 4.00 10.00
Quentin Richardson
RW Luke Ridnour 4.00 10.00
Chris Wilcox
SK Stromile Swift 4.00 10.00
Tarence Kinsey
SR Wally Szczerbiak 4.00 10.00
Allan Ray
WA Chris Webber 5.00 12.00
LaMarcus Aldridge
WB Delonte West 4.00 10.00
Earl Boykins
WC Drew Gooden 4.00 10.00
Tyson Chandler
WH Gerald Wallace 4.00 10.00
Josh Howard
WM Ben Wallace 4.00 10.00
Brad Miller
WS David West 4.00 10.00
J.R. Smith

2007-08 SP Game Used Authentic Fabrics Triple

PRINT RUN 50 SER.#'d SETS
*PATCHES: .75X TO 2X BASE HI
PATCH PRINT RUN 25 SER.#'d SETS
AMB Ron Artest 5.00 12.00
Quincy Douby
Mike Bibby
ASO Hilton Armstrong 5.00 12.00
Saer Sene
Patrick O'Bryant
BBA Andray Blatche 5.00 12.00
Andrew Bynum
LaMarcus Aldridge
BGM Kobe Bryant 30.00 75.00
Kevin Garnett
Tracy McGrady
BMK Beno Udrih 5.00 12.00
Manu Ginobili
Steve Kerr
CBW Brian Cook 5.00 12.00
Kwame Brown
Luke Walton
FMW Raymond Felton 5.00 12.00
Sean May
Gerald Wallace
HJB Al Harrington 5.00 12.00
Antawn Jamison
Carlos Boozer
HLN Devin Harris 5.00 12.00
Shaun Livingston
David Noel
ICA Allen Iverson 8.00 20.00
Marcus Camby
Carmelo Anthony
IKD Andre Iguodala 5.00 12.00
Kyle Korver
Samuel Dalembert
JGC Fred Jones 6.00 15.00
Gerald Green
Vince Carter
JJJ LeBron James 75.00 200.00
Michael Jordan
Magic Johnson
KNM Nenad Krstic 5.00 12.00
Nene
Darko Milicic
LAR Rashard Lewis 5.00 12.00
Ray Allen
Luke Ridnour
LRR David Lee 5.00 12.00
Nate Robinson
Quentin Richardson
MCI Alonzo Mourning 10.00 25.00
Tyson Chandler
Zydrunas Ilgauskas
MHG Donyell Marshall 5.00 12.00
Larry Hughes
Drew Gooden
MHR Brad Miller 5.00 12.00
Udonis Haslem
Zach Randolph
MNS Shawn Marion 10.00 25.00
Steve Nash
Amare Stoudemire
MTW Andre Miller 5.00 12.00
Jamaal Tinsley
Jason Williams
NBW Jameer Nelson 5.00 12.00
Earl Boykins
Delonte West
PGD Tony Parker 20.00 40.00
Manu Ginobili
Tim Duncan
PWH Tayshaun Prince 8.00 20.00
Chris Webber
Richard Hamilton
RSD J.J. Redick 8.00 20.00
J.R. Smith
Mike Dunleavy
SKW John Stockton 6.00 15.00
Andrei Kirilenko
Deron Williams
SRC Josh Smith 5.00 12.00
Jason Richardson
Josh Childress
WBB Ben Wallace 5.00 12.00
Bruce Bowen
Shane Battier
WGP Martell Webster 5.00 12.00
Danny Granger
Johan Petro
WRR Martell Webster 6.00 15.00
Brandon Roy
Zach Randolph

2007-08 SP Game Used Authentic Fabrics Quad

PRINT RUN 25 SER.#'d SETS
UNPRICED PATCH PRINT RUN 10 SETS
ABPB Ron Artest 20.00 40.00
Bruce Bowen
Mickael Pietrus
Caron Butler
BHWR Elton Brand 15.00 30.00
Grant Hill
Rasheed Wallace
Zach Randolph
ESDO Mark Eaton 30.00 60.00
John Stockton
Clyde Drexler
Hakeem Olajuwon
GCMM Kevin Garnett 30.00 60.00
Vince Carter
Tracy McGrady
Shawn Marion
JDSH Richard Jefferson 15.00 30.00
Ricky Davis
J.R. Smith
Larry Hughes
JOHK LeBron James 40.00 80.00
Shaquille O'Neal
Dwight Howard
Jason Kidd
KDNF Andrei Kirilenko 15.00 30.00
Paul Davis
Nene
Channing Frye
MOVG Sean May 15.00 30.00
Lamar Odom
Charlie Villanueva
Drew Gooden
NDAS Dirk Nowitzki 20.00 40.00
Tim Duncan
Carmelo Anthony
Amare Stoudemire
RFSH Michael Redd 30.00 60.00
Michael Finley
Peja Stojakovic
Richard Hamilton
RMLC Allan Ray 15.00 30.00
Stephon Marbury
Shaun Livingston
Sam Cassell
WMMB Ben Wallace 15.00 30.00
Brad Miller
Darko Milicic
Kwame Brown

2007-08 SP Game Used Cut from the Cloth

APPROXIMATELY ONE PER BOX
*PATCHES: 1.25X TO 3X BASE HI
PATCH PRINT RUN 25 SER.#'d SETS
CCAB Andrew Bogut 2.50 6.00
CCAH Al Harrington 2.00 5.00
CCAK Andrei Kirilenko 2.00 5.00
CCAM Alonzo Mourning 5.00 12.00
CCBC Brian Cook 2.00 5.00
CCBH Brendan Haywood 2.00 5.00
CCBR Brandon Roy 3.00 8.00
CCCB Caron Butler 2.50 6.00
CCCH Chauncey Billups 2.50 6.00
CCCP Chris Paul 5.00 12.00
CCCR Charlie Villanueva 2.50 6.00
CCDW Deron Williams 4.00 10.00
CCEB Elton Brand 2.50 6.00
CCJH Josh Howard 2.50 6.00
CCJJ J.J. Redick 2.50 6.00
CCJR Jason Richardson 2.50 6.00
CCJS Josh Smith 2.50 6.00
CCKH Kirk Hinrich 2.50 6.00
CCLH Larry Hughes 2.00 5.00
CCLO Lamar Odom 2.50 6.00
CCMR Michael Redd 2.50 6.00
CCMW Martell Webster 2.00 5.00
CCNR Nate Robinson 2.50 6.00
CCPS Peja Stojakovic 2.50 6.00
CCRW Rasheed Wallace 2.50 6.00
CCSM Stephon Marbury 2.50 6.00
CCSN Steve Nash 3.00 8.00
CCTM Tracy McGrady 2.50 6.00
CCTP Tony Parker 2.50 6.00
CCVC Vince Carter 3.00 8.00

2007-08 SP Game Used Hardcourt Classics

PRINT RUN 199 SER.#'d SETS
*PATCH: 1X TO 2.5X BASE HI
PATCH PRINT RUN 25 SER.#'d SETS
HCAD Antonio Daniels 2.00 5.00
HCAS Amare Stoudemire 3.00 8.00
HCBC Brian Cardinal 2.00 5.00
HCBH Brendan Haywood 2.00 5.00
HCBL Andray Blatche 2.00 5.00
HCBW Ben Wallace 3.00 8.00
HCCD Chris Duhon 2.00 5.00
HCCF Channing Frye 2.50 6.00
HCCM Corey Maggette 2.50 6.00
HCDH Dwight Howard 5.00 12.00
HCDS Damon Stoudamire 2.50 6.00
HCDT Donell Taylor 2.00 5.00
HCDW Dorell Wright 2.00 5.00
HCEH Eddie House 2.00 5.00
HCEP Eric Piatkowski 2.00 5.00
HCGO Ben Gordon 3.00 8.00
HCHW Hakim Warrick 2.50 6.00
HCJC Jason Collins 2.00 5.00
HCJH Juwan Howard 2.50 6.00
HCJJ Jerome James 2.00 5.00
HCJK Jason Kapono 2.00 5.00
HCJM Jeff McInnis 2.00 5.00
HCJN Jameer Nelson 2.50 6.00
HCJP James Posey 2.00 5.00
HCJR Jalen Rose 2.50 6.00
HCJS James Singleton 2.00 5.00
HCJT Jake Tsakalidis 2.00 5.00
HCJW Jason Williams 2.50 6.00
HCKB Keith Bogans 2.00 5.00
HCKG Kevin Garnett 6.00 15.00
HCKH Kirk Hinrich 2.50 6.00
HCLA LeBron James 8.00 20.00
HCLD Luol Deng 3.00 8.00
HCLH Luther Head 2.50 6.00
HCLJ Linton Johnson 2.00 5.00
HCLW Lorenzen Wright 2.00 5.00
HCMJ Marc Jackson 2.00 5.00
HCMM Mikki Moore 2.00 5.00
HCMR Michael Redd 3.00 8.00
HCMS Mike Sweetney 2.00 5.00
HCMW Mike Wilks 2.00 5.00
HCNR Nate Robinson 3.00 8.00
HCOH Othella Harrington 2.00 5.00
HCPA Jannero Pargo 2.00 5.00
HCPB Pat Burke 2.00 5.00
HCPG Pau Gasol 3.00 8.00
HCQD Quincy Douby 2.00 5.00
HCQR Quentin Richardson 2.50 6.00
HCSB Shannon Brown 3.00 8.00
HCSM Shawn Marion 3.00 8.00
HCSO Shaquille O'Neal 6.00 15.00
HCST DeShawn Stevenson 2.00 5.00
HCTA Trevor Ariza 2.00 5.00
HCUH Udonis Haslem 2.50 6.00
HCWS Wally Szczerbiak 2.50 6.00

2007-08 SP Game Used Rookie Exclusives Autographs

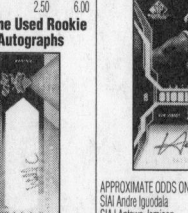

PRINT RUN 100 SER.#'d SETS
REAA Arron Afflalo 10.00 25.00
REAB Aaron Brooks 8.00 20.00
REAG Aaron Gray 8.00 20.00
REAH Adam Haluska 8.00 20.00
REAL Acie Law 8.00 20.00
REAT Al Thornton 8.00 20.00
RECB Corey Brewer 10.00 25.00
RECL Carl Landry 8.00 20.00
RECU JamesOn Curry 8.00 20.00
REDA Jermareo Davidson 8.00 20.00
REDB Derrick Byars 8.00 20.00
REDC Daequan Cook 8.00 20.00
REDS D.J. Strawberry 8.00 20.00
REGD Glen Davis 12.00 30.00
REGP Gabe Pruitt 8.00 20.00
REHH Herbert Hill 8.00 20.00
REHO Al Horford 20.00 50.00
REJC Javaris Crittenton 8.00 20.00
REJD Jared Dudley 8.00 20.00
REJG Jeff Green 12.00 30.00
REJJ Jared Jordan 8.00 20.00
REJM Josh McRoberts 8.00 20.00
REJN Joakim Noah 30.00 80.00
REJS Jason Smith 8.00 20.00
REJW Julian Wright 8.00 20.00
REKD Kevin Durant 125.00 250.00
REMC Mike Conley Jr. 12.00 30.00
REMW Marcus Williams 5.00 12.00
RENF Nick Fazekas 8.00 20.00
REPK Petteri Koponen 8.00 20.00
RERS Rodney Stuckey 12.00 30.00
RERT Reyshawn Terry 8.00 20.00
RESH Spencer Hawes 8.00 20.00
RESL Stephane Lasme 8.00 20.00
RETG Taurean Green 8.00 20.00
RETU Alando Tucker 8.00 20.00
REWC Wilson Chandler 12.00 30.00

2007-08 SP Game Used Signature Swatch

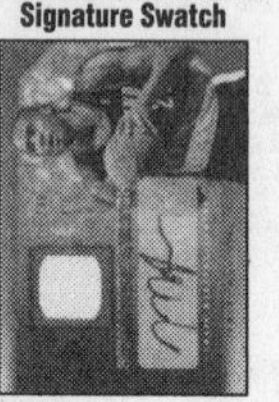

PRINT RUN 30 SER.#'d SETS
SSAI Andre Iguodala 6.00 15.00
SSAJ Antawn Jamison 10.00 25.00
SSAM Alonzo Mourning 25.00 60.00
SSAR Allan Ray 6.00 15.00
SSBB Bruce Bowen 8.00 20.00
SSBD Baron Davis 12.50 30.00
SSBG Ben Gordon 12.50 30.00
SSBJ Bobby Jones 6.00 15.00
SSBM Brad Miller 6.00 15.00
SSBR Brandon Roy 15.00 30.00
SSCA Carmelo Anthony 20.00 50.00
SSCB Chris Bosh 15.00 40.00
SSCF Channing Frye 6.00 15.00
SSCM Corey Maggette 6.00 15.00
SSCP Chris Paul 20.00 50.00
SSCS Cedric Simmons 6.00 15.00
SSDN David Noel 6.00 15.00
SSDS DeShawn Stevenson 6.00 15.00
SSDW Deron Williams 20.00 40.00
SSEO Emeka Okafor 6.00 15.00
SSFO Randy Foye 8.00 20.00
SSGW Gerald Wallace 8.00 20.00
SSHA Hilton Armstrong 6.00 15.00
SSJK Jason Kidd 20.00 40.00
SSJM Jamaal Magloire 6.00 15.00
SSJO Jermaine O'Neal 10.00 25.00
SSJS J.R. Smith 6.00 15.00
SSKB Kobe Bryant 100.00 200.00
SSLA LaMarcus Aldridge 20.00 40.00
SSLH Larry Hughes 6.00 15.00
SSLJ LeBron James 100.00 200.00
SSMA Maurice Ager 6.00 15.00
SSMB Mike Bibby 8.00 20.00
SSMC Mardy Collins 6.00 15.00
SSMI Andre Miller 6.00 15.00
SSMJ Michael Jordan 300.00 550.00
SSNO Steve Novak 6.00 15.00
SSPA Tony Parker 10.00 25.00
SSPD Paul Davis 6.00 15.00
SSPP Paul Pierce 20.00 50.00
SSPS Peja Stojakovic 8.00 20.00
SSQD Quincy Douby 6.00 15.00
SSQR Quentin Richardson 6.00 15.00
SSRF Raymond Felton 6.00 15.00
SSRH Richard Hamilton 8.00 20.00
SSRJ Richard Jefferson 6.00 15.00
SSSA Sean May 6.00 15.00
SSSB Shannon Brown 6.00 15.00
SSSM Craig Smith 6.00 15.00
SSSN Steve Nash 25.00 60.00
SSSS Saer Sene 6.00 15.00
SSTM Tracy McGrady 20.00 50.00
SSTP Tayshaun Prince 6.00 15.00
SSVC Vince Carter 20.00 50.00
SSWB Will Blalock 6.00 15.00
SSYM Yao Ming 25.00 60.00

2007-08 SP Game Used Signature Swatch Patch

*PATCH: .75X TO 2X HI COLUMN
PATCH PRINT RUN 15 SER.#'d SETS
SSAM Alonzo Mourning 75.00 150.00
SSCP Chris Paul 75.00 150.00

2007-08 SP Game Used SIGnificance

APPROXIMATE ODDS ONE PER BOX
SIAI Andre Iguodala 4.00 10.00
SIAJ Antawn Jamison 4.00 10.00
SIAM Andre Miller 4.00 10.00
SIBA Leandro Barbosa 4.00 10.00
SIBD Baron Davis 5.00 12.00
SIBG Ben Gordon 8.00 20.00
SIBM Brad Miller 4.00 10.00
SIBR Brandon Roy 10.00 25.00
SICA Carmelo Anthony 20.00 50.00
SICB Chris Bosh 10.00 25.00
SICD Chris Duhon 4.00 10.00
SICM Corey Maggette 4.00 10.00
SICP Chris Paul 15.00 40.00
SICS Craig Smith 4.00 10.00
SIDB Dee Brown 4.00 10.00
SIDR Clyde Drexler 20.00 40.00
SIDW Deron Williams 8.00 20.00
SIHA Hassan Adams 4.00 10.00
SIHO Hakeem Olajuwon 20.00 50.00
SIHW Hakim Warrick 4.00 10.00
SIIU Ime Udoka 4.00 10.00
SIJA James Augustine 4.00 10.00
SIJE Julius Erving 40.00 80.00
SIJG Joey Graham 4.00 10.00
SIJJ Jarrett Jack 4.00 10.00
SIJK Jason Kidd 12.50 30.00
SIJS J.R. Smith 4.00 10.00
SIKB Kobe Bryant 75.00 150.00
SILA LaMarcus Aldridge 8.00 20.00
SILB Larry Bird 40.00 100.00
SILJ LeBron James 80.00 160.00
SIMC Mardy Collins 4.00 10.00
SINO Steve Novak 4.00 10.00
SIPM Paul Millsap 4.00 10.00
SIPP Paul Pierce 10.00 25.00
SIRB Raja Bell 4.00 10.00
SIRG Rudy Gay 6.00 15.00
SISN Steve Nash 40.00 80.00
SIST John Stockton 50.00 100.00
SISW Shelden Williams 4.00 10.00
SITM Tracy McGrady 15.00 30.00
SITS Thabo Sefolosha 4.00 10.00
SIVC Vince Carter 15.00 40.00
SIVS Vassilis Spanoulis 4.00 10.00
SIWB Will Blalock 4.00 10.00

2007-08 SP Game Used SIGnificance Dual

PRINT RUN 50 SER.#'d SETS
SP PRINT RUN 25 SER.#'d SETS
UNLESS LISTED IN CHECKLIST
SDAR LaMarcus Aldridge 15.00 40.00
Brandon Roy
SDBA Nate Archibald 12.00 30.00
Muggsy Bogues
SDBB Raja Bell 15.00 30.00
Leandro Barbosa
SDBJ Kobe Bryant SP 200.00 325.00
LeBron James
SDBM Mike Bibby 10.00 25.00
Brad Miller
SDBO Jermaine O'Neal SP 75.00 150.00
Kobe Bryant
SDCL Tyson Chandler 10.00 25.00
David Lee
SDCM Vince Carter SP 40.00 80.00
Tracy McGrady
SDCO Eddy Curry 10.00 25.00
Emeka Okafor
SDCS Tyson Chandler 10.00 25.00
Peja Stojakovic
SDDH Al Harrington 10.00 25.00
Baron Davis
SDDS Chris Duhon 10.00 25.00
Thabo Sefolosha
SDER Julius Erving SP 125.00 225.00
Bill Russell
SDFC Walt Frazier 10.00 25.00
Mardy Collins
SDFG Jorge Garbajosa 10.00 25.00
T.J. Ford
SDFR Cazzie Russell SP 35.00 75.00
Walt Frazier
SDFS Craig Smith 10.00 25.00
Randy Foye
SDGR Rudy Gay SP 30.00 60.00
Brandon Roy
SDHD Chris Duhon/15 30.00 60.00
Kirk Hinrich
SDJI Richard Jefferson 10.00 25.00
Mile Ilic
SDJS Antawn Jamison 10.00
DeShawn Stevenson
SDKC Jason Kidd SP 30.00
Vince Carter
SDKK Steve Kerr 10.00
Jason Kapono
SDKR Dennis Rodman SP 60.00
Steve Kerr
SDLF Channing Frye 10.00
David Lee
SDLM Rick Mahorn SP 40.00
Bill Laimbeer
SDMI Andre Miller 10.00
Andre Iguodala
SDMM Tracy McGrady SP 60.00
Yao Ming
SDMW Sean May 10.00
Marvin Williams
SDNB Steve Novak 10.00
Will Blalock
SDOF Raymond Felton 10.00
Emeka Okafor
SDOM Calvin Murphy/20 40.00
Hakeem Olajuwon
SDPB Muggsy Bogues 20.00
Robert Parish
SDPC Vince Carter SP 30.00
Paul Pierce
SDSP Peja Stojakovic 20.00
Chris Paul
SDSS John Stockton SP 125.00
Steve Nash
SDST Tyrus Thomas 10.00
J.R. Smith
SDTB Tayshaun Prince 10.00
Will Blalock

2007-08 SP Game Used Significant Numbers Autogra

PRINT RUNS LISTED IN CHECKLIST
SOME UNPRICED DUE TO SCARCITY
AM Alonzo Mourning/33 75.00
AR Allan Ray/20 8.00
BL Bill Laimbeer/40 15.00
BM Brad Miller/52 8.00
CA Carmelo Anthony/15 40.00
CD Clyde Drexler/22 60.00
CF Channing Frye/44 15.00
CM Corey Maggette/50 8.00
CS Cedric Simmons/15 8.00
DD Darryl Dawkins/53 10.00
DL David Lee/42 20.00
DM Donyell Marshall/24 8.00
DN David Noel/34 8.00
HW Hakim Warrick/21 8.00
KB Kobe Bryant/24 150.00
KK Kyle Korver/26 8.00
LA LaMarcus Aldridge/12 40.00
LB Larry Bird/33 100.00
LJ1 LeBron James/23 175.00
LJ2 LeBron James/23 175.00
MC Mardy Collins/25 8.00
ME Mark Eaton/53 8.00
MJ Michael Jordan/23 450.00
MP Morris Peterson/24 8.00
MS Saer Sene/18 8.00
NO Steve Novak/20 8.00
PD Paul Davis/40 8.00
PP Paul Pierce/34 40.00
QR Quentin Richardson/23 8.00
RC Rodney Carney/25 8.00
RG Rudy Gay/22 20.00
RH Richard Hamilton/32 15.00
SK Steve Kerr/25 20.00
SM Sean May/42 8.00
SN Steve Nash/13 50.00
ST John Stockton/12 100.00
TP Tayshaun Prince/22 20.00
TT Tyrus Thomas/24 20.00
YM Yao Ming/11 75.00

2007-08 SP Game Used Significant Numbers Non-Au Patch

PRINT RUNS LISTED IN CHECKLIST
SOME UNPRICED DUE TO SCARCITY
AG Maurice Ager/13 6.00
AM Alonzo Mourning/33 40.00
AR Allan Ray/20 6.00
BJ Bobby Jackson/35 6.00
BL Bill Laimbeer/40 10.00
BM Brad Miller/52 6.00
CA Carmelo Anthony/15 25.00
CF Channing Frye/44 6.00
CM Corey Maggette/50 6.00
CS Cedric Simmons/15 6.00
DD Darryl Dawkins/53 6.00
DH Dwight Howard/12 25.00
DM Donyell Marshall/24 6.00
DN David Noel/34 6.00
DR David Robinson/55 30.00
EB Elton Brand/42 6.00
HW Hakim Warrick/21 6.00
JN Jameer Nelson/14 6.00
JR Jason Richardson/23 20.00
KB Kobe Bryant/24 50.00
KH Kirk Hinrich/12 20.00
KK Kyle Korver/26 15.00
LA LaMarcus Aldridge/12 15.00
LB Larry Bird/33 25.00
LH Larry Hughes/32 6.00

Card	Low	High
LeBron James/23	60.00	120.00
LeBron James/23	60.00	120.00
Magic Johnson/32	30.00	60.00
Mike Bibby/10	15.00	30.00
Mardy Collins/25	6.00	15.00
Mark Eaton/53	15.00	30.00
Manu Ginobili/20	10.00	25.00
Michael Jordan/23	125.00	225.00
Saer Sene/18	6.00	15.00
Marvin Williams/24	8.00	20.00
Steve Novak/20	8.00	20.00
Paul Davis/40	6.00	15.00
Paul Pierce/34	15.00	30.00
Peja Stojakovic/16	10.00	25.00
Quentin Richardson/23	6.00	15.00
Rodney Carney/25	8.00	20.00
Rudy Gay/22	10.00	25.00
Richard Hamilton/32	10.00	25.00
Richard Jefferson/24	6.00	15.00
Dennis Rodman/91	20.00	50.00
Sean Elliott/32	20.00	40.00
Steve Kerr/25	20.00	40.00
Sean May/42	6.00	15.00
Steve Nash/13	25.00	50.00
John Stockton/12	30.00	60.00
Tyrus Thomas/24	10.00	25.00
Vince Carter/15	20.00	50.00
Walt Frazier/10	20.00	40.00
Yao Ming/11	20.00	40.00

2007-08 SP Game Used Swatch of Class

PROXIMATE ODDS ONE PER BOX
ATCHES: 1.5X TO 4X BASE HI
TCH PRINT RUN 25 SER.#'d SETS

Card	Low	High
CD Clyde Drexler	5.00	12.00
DD Darryl Dawkins	4.00	10.00
DE Dennis Rodman	6.00	15.00
DR David Robinson	5.00	12.00
JE Julius Erving	6.00	15.00
JS John Stockton	4.00	10.00
LB Larry Bird	6.00	15.00
MA Magic Johnson	6.00	15.00
MJ Michael Jordan	20.00	50.00
RP Robert Parish	4.00	10.00

2009-10 SP Game Used

Card	Low	High
MP. SET w/o SPs (100)	30.00	60.00
OKIE PRINT RUN 399 SER.#'d SETS		
Al Harrington	.75	2.00
Al Horford	1.00	2.50
Al Jefferson	1.00	2.50
Al Thornton	.75	2.00
Allen Iverson	1.25	3.00
Andre Iguodala	1.00	2.50
Andre Miller	.75	2.00
Andrea Bargnani	.75	2.00
Antawn Jamison	1.00	2.50
Baron Davis	1.00	2.50
Ben Gordon	1.00	2.50
Ben Wallace	1.00	2.50
Beno Udrih	.60	1.50
Brad Miller	.75	2.00
Brandon Roy	1.00	2.50
Carlos Boozer	1.00	2.50
Carmelo Anthony	1.25	3.00
Chauncey Billups	1.00	2.50
Chris Bosh	1.00	2.50
Chris Duhon	.60	1.50
Chris Paul	1.50	4.00
Courtney Lee	.75	2.00
D.J. Augustin	.75	2.00
Danny Granger	1.00	2.50
David Lee	.75	2.00
David West	1.00	2.50
Derek Fisher	.75	2.00
Deron Williams	1.00	2.50
Derrick Rose	3.00	8.00
DeShawn Stevenson	.60	1.50
Devin Harris	1.00	2.50
Dirk Nowitzki	1.25	3.00
Dwight Howard	1.50	4.00
Dwyane Wade	2.00	5.00
Elton Brand	1.00	2.50
Eric Gordon	1.00	2.50
Gilbert Arenas	1.00	2.50
Hedo Turkoglu	1.00	2.50
Jamal Crawford	.75	2.00
Jason Kidd	1.00	2.50
Jason Richardson	1.00	2.50
Jeff Green	.75	2.00
Jermaine O'Neal	1.00	2.50
Jerryd Bayless	.75	2.00
Joe Johnson	1.00	2.50
Jose Calderon	.75	2.00
Josh Howard	.75	2.00
Josh Smith	1.00	2.50
Kenyon Martin	1.00	2.50
Kevin Durant	3.00	8.00
Kevin Garnett	2.00	5.00
Kevin Love	1.50	4.00
Kevin Martin	1.00	2.50
Kobe Bryant	5.00	12.00
Lamar Odom	1.00	2.50
LaMarcus Aldridge	1.00	2.50
LeBron James	5.00	12.00
Luis Scola	.75	2.00
Luke Ridnour	.75	2.00
Luol Deng	1.00	2.50
Manu Ginobili	1.00	2.50
Marc Gasol	1.00	2.50
Mario Chalmers	1.00	2.50
64 Michael Beasley	1.00	2.50
65 Michael Redd	1.00	2.50
66 Mike Bibby	.75	2.00
67 Mike Dunleavy	.60	1.50
68 Mo Williams	.75	2.00
69 Monta Ellis	1.00	2.50
70 O.J. Mayo	1.00	2.50
71 Pau Gasol	1.00	2.50
72 Paul Pierce	1.25	3.00
73 Peja Stojakovic	1.00	2.50
74 Quentin Richardson	.75	2.00
75 Raja Bell	.75	2.00
76 Ray Allen	1.00	2.50
77 Raymond Felton	.75	2.00
78 Richard Hamilton	.75	2.00
79 Richard Jefferson	1.00	2.50
80 Rodney Stuckey	1.00	2.50
81 Ron Artest	1.00	2.50
82 Ronnie Brewer	.75	2.00
83 Rudy Fernandez	.75	2.00
84 Rudy Gay	1.00	2.50
85 Russell Westbrook	1.50	4.00
86 Sebastian Telfair	.60	1.50
87 Shaquille O'Neal	2.00	5.00
88 Shawn Marion	1.00	2.50
89 Stephen Jackson	.75	2.00
90 Steve Nash	1.00	2.50
91 T.J. Ford	.60	1.50
92 Tayshaun Prince	1.00	2.50
93 Thaddeus Young	.60	1.50
94 Tim Duncan	1.50	4.00
95 Tony Parker	1.00	2.50
96 Tracy McGrady	1.00	2.50
97 Tyson Chandler	.75	2.00
98 Vince Carter	1.25	3.00
99 Yao Ming	1.25	3.00
100 Yi Jianlian	.75	2.00
101 A.J. Price RC	4.00	10.00
102 B.J. Mullens RC	4.00	10.00
103 Blake Griffin RC	25.00	60.00
104 Brandon Jennings RC	8.00	20.00
105 Chase Budinger RC	4.00	10.00
106 DaJuan Summers RC	4.00	10.00
107 Rodrigue Beaubois RC	5.00	12.00
108 Danny Green RC	6.00	15.00
109 Dante Cunningham RC	4.00	10.00
110 Darren Collison RC	6.00	15.00
111 DeJuan Blair RC	5.00	12.00
112 DeMar DeRozan RC	6.00	15.00
113 Derrick Brown RC	4.00	10.00
114 Earl Clark RC	4.00	10.00
115 Eric Maynor RC	4.00	10.00
116 Gerald Henderson RC	4.00	10.00
117 Hasheem Thabeet RC	4.00	10.00
118 James Harden RC	12.00	30.00
119 James Johnson RC	4.00	10.00
120 Jeff Pendergraph RC	4.00	10.00
121 Jeff Teague RC	5.00	12.00
122 Jonny Flynn RC	4.00	10.00
123 Jordan Hill RC	4.00	10.00
124 Austin Daye RC	4.00	10.00
125 Jrue Holiday RC	8.00	20.00
126 Marcus Thornton RC	6.00	15.00
127 Nick Calathes RC	4.00	10.00
128 Omri Casspi RC	4.00	10.00
129 Patrick Mills RC	5.00	12.00
130 Ricky Rubio RC	20.00	50.00
131 Sam Young RC	4.00	10.00
132 Sergio Llull RC	4.00	10.00
133 Stephen Curry RC	10.00	25.00
134 Taj Gibson RC	5.00	12.00
135 Terrence Williams RC	4.00	10.00
136 Toney Douglas RC	4.00	10.00
137 Ty Lawson RC	6.00	15.00
138 Tyler Hansbrough RC	6.00	15.00
139 Jermaine Taylor RC	4.00	10.00
140 Tyreke Evans RC	10.00	25.00
141 DeMarre Carroll RC	4.00	10.00
142 Wayne Ellington RC	4.00	10.00

2009-10 SP Game Used 3 Star Swatches

PRINT RUN 299 SER.#'d SETS
*SWATCH 125: .5X TO 1.25X BASE HI
*SWATCH 50: .6X TO 1.5X BASE HI
*SWATCH 35: .75X TO 2X BASE HI

Card	Low	High
3SAGA Gilbert Arenas	5.00	12.00
Ray Allen		
Kevin Garnett		
3SAHW Ray Allen	4.00	10.00
Ben Gordon		
Richard Hamilton		
3SARB Brandon Roy	4.00	10.00
LaMarcus Aldridge		
Jerryd Bayless		
3SASY Shaquille O'Neal	5.00	12.00
Andrew Bynum		
Yao Ming		
3SAWI Luke Walton	4.00	10.00
Andre Iguodala		
Gilbert Arenas		
3SBAH Kobe Bryant	10.00	25.00
Ron Artest		
Dwight Howard		
3SBFR Randy Foye	4.00	10.00
Keith Bogans		
Brandon Rush		
3SBGJ LeBron James	12.50	30.00
Kobe Bryant		
Kevin Garnett		
3SBHM Josh Howard	4.00	10.00
Caron Butler		
Paul Millsap		
3SBIM Moses Malone	4.00	10.00
Andre Iguodala		
Elton Brand		
3SBJD Kobe Bryant	25.00	60.00
LeBron James		
Kevin Durant		
3SBMH Kobe Bryant	12.50	30.00
Dwight Howard		
Tracy McGrady		
3SBMJ Kobe Bryant	15.00	40.00
LeBron James		
Oscar Robertson		
3SBOB Andrea Bargnani	4.00	10.00
Chris Bosh		
Jermaine O'Neal		
3SBOF Kobe Bryant	10.00	25.00
Horace Grant		
Shaquille O'Neal		
3SBWC Brandan Wright	4.00	10.00
Shannon Brown		
Wilson Chandler		
3SBWM Paul Millsap	4.00	10.00
Deron Williams		
Carlos Boozer		
3SCFM Vince Carter	5.00	12.00
Raymond Felton		
Sean May		
3SCGM Vince Carter	5.00	12.00
Tracy McGrady		
George Gervin		
3SCMA Carmelo Anthony	5.00	12.00
Shawn Marion		
Vince Carter		
3SCMP Vince Carter	6.00	15.00
Tracy McGrady		
Scottie Pippen		
3SDFA Jordan Farmar	4.00	10.00
Baron Davis		
Arron Afflalo		
3SDGP George Gervin	5.00	12.00
Tim Duncan		
Tony Parker		
3SDGR Tim Duncan	5.00	12.00
George Gervin		
David Robinson		
3SDHP Tim Duncan	5.00	12.00
Josh Howard		
Chris Paul		
3SDMF Baron Davis	4.00	10.00
Jordan Farmar		
Spud Webb		
3SDMO Tim Duncan	6.00	15.00
Yao Ming		
Shaquille O'Neal		
3SDPR Tim Duncan	6.00	15.00
Tony Parker		
David Robinson		
3SDWC Mario Chalmers	4.00	10.00
Chris Douglas-Roberts		
D.J. White		
3SEFC Monta Ellis	4.00	10.00
Javaris Crittenton		
Jordan Farmar		
3SEGH Patrick Ewing	4.00	10.00
Roy Hibbert		
Jeff Green		
3SEHO Shaquille O'Neal	6.00	15.00
Patrick Ewing		
Dwight Howard		
3SELR Patrick Ewing	4.00	10.00
Nate Robinson		
David Lee		
3SGAS Donte Greene	4.00	10.00
Walter Sharpe		
Joe Alexander		
3SGCH Vince Carter	5.00	12.00
Grant Hill		
Kevin Garnett		
3SGCO Kevin Garnett	5.00	12.00
Jermaine O'Neal		
Vince Carter		
3SGMN Kevin Garnett	5.00	12.00
Dirk Nowitzki		
Shawn Marion		
3SGMO Yao Ming	5.00	12.00
Pau Gasol		
Shaquille O'Neal		
3SGNA Kevin Garnett	6.00	15.00
Dirk Nowitzki		
Carmelo Anthony		
3SGNB Dirk Nowitzki	5.00	12.00
Kevin Garnett		
Chris Bosh		
3SGPA Kevin Garnett	5.00	12.00
Carmelo Anthony		
Tayshaun Prince		
3SGYL Robin Lopez	4.00	10.00
Aaron Gray		
Thaddeus Young		
3SHAR Ray Allen	4.00	10.00
J.J. Redick		
Jeff Hornacek		
3SHBA Richard Hamilton	4.00	10.00
Gilbert Arenas		
Chauncey Billups		
3SHDP Scottie Pippen	12.00	30.00
Derrick Rose		
Luol Deng		
3SHFT Rudy Fernandez	4.00	10.00
Richard Hamilton		
Alando Tucker		
3SHHL Luther Head	4.00	10.00
Carl Landry		
Josh Howard		
3SHIP Richard Hamilton	4.00	10.00
Allen Iverson		
Tayshaun Prince		
3SHIW Allen Iverson	4.00	10.00
Richard Hamilton		
Rasheed Wallace		
3SHJK DeAndre Jordan	4.00	10.00
Roy Hibbert		
Kosta Koufos		
3SHMS Jeff Hornacek	5.00	12.00
John Stockton		
Karl Malone		
3SHWD Luke Walton	4.00	10.00
Quincy Douby		
Al Harrington		
3SIBJ Magic Johnson	6.00	15.00
Chauncey Billups		
Allen Iverson		
3SJBJ LeBron James	50.00	125.00
Michael Jordan		
Kobe Bryant		
3SJGP Horace Grant	25.00	60.00
Michael Jordan		
Scottie Pippen		
3SJMJ Michael Jordan	25.00	60.00
Magic Johnson		
Karl Malone		
3SJWS John Stockton	6.00	15.00
Deron Williams		
Magic Johnson		
3SKPS Jason Kidd	5.00	12.00
John Stockton		
Chris Paul		
3SLGH Horace Grant	5.00	12.00
Rashard Lewis		
Dwight Howard		
3SLHD David Lee	4.00	10.00
Udonis Haslem		
Paul Davis		
3SMBD Corey Maggette	4.00	10.00
Carlos Boozer		
Luol Deng		
3SMBO Yao Ming	5.00	12.00
Andrew Bynum		
Shaquille O'Neal		
3SMBR O.J. Mayo	10.00	25.00
Derrick Rose		
Michael Beasley		
3SMCD Michael Cooper	5.00	12.00
Clyde Drexler		
Karl Malone		
3SMCK Karl Malone	4.00	10.00
Carlos Boozer		
Mehmet Okur		
3SMDO Corey Maggette	4.00	10.00
Baron Davis		
Lamar Odom		
3SMER Corey Maggette	4.00	10.00
Monta Ellis		
Anthony Randolph		
3SMGP Karl Malone	6.00	15.00
Scottie Pippen		
George Gervin		
3SMHH Josh Howard	4.00	10.00
Larry Hughes		
Corey Maggette		
3SMHL Carl Landry	4.00	10.00
Luis Scola		
Tracy McGrady		
3SMME Corey Maggette	4.00	10.00
Monta Ellis		
Chris Mullin		
3SMMO Shawn Marion	4.00	10.00
Jermaine O'Neal		
Kenyon Martin		
3SMPT Scottie Pippen	5.00	12.00
Tyrus Thomas		
Corey Maggette		
3SMSM Amare Stoudemire	6.00	15.00
Moses Malone		
Yao Ming		
3SMTO Al Harrington	4.00	10.00
Jermaine O'Neal		
Jamaal Tinsley		
3SMUW Shelden Williams	4.00	10.00
Beno Udrih		
Brad Miller		
3SMWH Jermaine O'Neal	5.00	12.00
Udonis Haslem		
Dwyane Wade		
3SNAK Ryan Anderson	4.00	10.00
Kosta Koufos		
Steve Novak		
3SNAR Brandon Roy	5.00	12.00
Gilbert Arenas		
Steve Nash		
3SNGM Steve Nash	6.00	15.00
Yao Ming		
Kevin Garnett		
3SNHB Joakim Noah	4.00	10.00
Al Horford		
Corey Brewer		
3SNIM Steve Nash	6.00	15.00
Allen Iverson		
Stephon Marbury		
3SNKP Tony Parker	6.00	15.00
Jason Kidd		
Steve Nash		
3SOJC Lamar Odom	6.00	15.00
Michael Cooper		
Magic Johnson		
3SPAG Kevin Garnett	8.00	20.00
Ray Allen		
Paul Pierce		
3SPMG David Robinson	5.00	12.00
Horace Grant		
Karl Malone		
3SRBG Brandon Rush	5.00	12.00
J.R. Giddens		
Michael Beasley		
3SSJC Jason Kidd	6.00	15.00
Steve Nash		
Chris Paul		
3SSMR Wally Szczerbiak	4.00	10.00
Luke Ridnour		
Mike Miller		
3SSOT Stromile Swift	5.00	12.00
Shaquille O'Neal		
Tyrus Thomas		
3STBS Tyrus Thomas	4.00	10.00
Ronnie Brewer		
Cedric Simmons		
3STFP Jamaal Tinsley	5.00	12.00
T.J. Ford		
Chris Paul		
3STGW Eric Gordon	4.00	10.00
Isiah Thomas		
D.J. White		
3STRC Javaris Crittenton	4.00	10.00
Jamaal Tinsley		
Nate Robinson		
3STSN Tyrus Thomas	4.00	10.00
Joakim Noah		
Luol Deng		
3STUW Jamaal Tinsley	4.00	10.00
Beno Udrih		
Deron Williams		
3STWB Jamaal Tinsley	4.00	10.00
Delonte West		
Raymond Felton		
3SWDG Kevin Durant	10.00	25.00
Jeff Green		
Russell Westbrook		
3SWTR Al Thornton	4.00	10.00
Anthony Randolph		
Jason Thompson		
3SWWH Rasheed Wallace	5.00	12.00
Ben Wallace		
Dwight Howard		

2009-10 SP Game Used 4 on 4 Fabrics

STATED PRINT RUN 99 SER.#'d SETS
*SWATCH 65: .4X TO 1X BASE HI

Card	Low	High
FFGUARD Clyde Drexler	40.00	100.00
Walt Frazier		
Spud Webb		
Michael Jordan		
Steve Kerr		
John Stockton		
Jeff Hornacek		
Dan Majerle		
FFSTARS Dan Majerle	20.00	50.00
Chris Mullin		
George Gervin		
Moses Malone		
Walt Frazier		
Clyde Drexler		
Hakeem Olajuwon.		
Willis Reed		
FF01CFINL Allen Iverson	15.00	40.00
Shaquille O'Neal		
David Robinson		
Kobe Bryant		
Ray Allen		
Horace Grant		
Dikembe Mutombo		
Raja Bell		
FF02CFINL Jason Kidd	15.00	40.00
Devean George		
Kobe Bryant		
Kenyon Martin		
Shaquille O'Neal		
Jason Collins		
Richard Jefferson		
Peja Stojakovic		
FF03FINL Jason Kidd	12.00	30.00
David Robinson		
Tim Duncan		
Tony Parker		
Kenyon Martin		
Steve Kerr		
Jason Collins		
Richard Jefferson		
FF04FINL Shaquille O'Neal	12.50	30.00
Karl Malone		
Tayshaun Prince		
Richard Hamilton		
Rasheed Wallace		
Chauncey Billups		
Luke Walton		
Kobe Bryant		
FF05FINL Chauncey Billups	10.00	25.00
Tony Parker		
Manu Ginobili		
Bruce Bowen		
Tim Duncan		
Rasheed Wallace		
Richard Hamilton		
Tayshaun Prince		
FF06FINL Shaquille O'Neal	12.00	30.00
Alonzo Mourning		
Dwyane Wade		
Udonis Haslem		
Dirk Nowitzki		
Josh Howard		
Jason Terry		
Devin Harris		
FF07FINL Tim Duncan	15.00	40.00
Bruce Bowen		
Manu Ginobili		
Tony Parker		
LeBron James		
Wally Szczerbiak		
Zydrunas Ilgauskas		
Daniel Gibson		
FF2009AS LeBron James	25.00	60.00
Chris Paul		
Amare Stoudemire		
Dwyane Wade		
Yao Ming		
Dwight Howard		
Kobe Bryant		
Kevin Garnett		
FF80STAR James Worthy	20.00	50.00
Magic Johnson		
Michael Cooper		
Larry Bird		
Robert Parish		
Spud Webb		
Dennis Rodman		
Bill Laimbeer		
FF90EAST Bill Laimbeer	40.00	100.00
Isiah Thomas		
Dennis Rodman		
Joe Dumars		
Steve Kerr		
Michael Jordan		
Horace Grant		
Scottie Pippen		
FF90STAR Scottie Pippen	40.00	100.00
Michael Jordan		
David Robinson		
Patrick Ewing		
Hakeem Olajuwon		
Clyde Drexler		
Dan Majerle		
Karl Malone		
FF90WEST John Stockton	15.00	40.00
Karl Malone		
Jeff Hornacek		
Tom Chambers		
Michael Cooper		
Magic Johnson		
Vlade Divac		
James Worthy		
FF91FINL James Worthy	40.00	100.00
Vlade Divac		
Magic Johnson		
Michael Cooper		
Michael Jordan		
Steve Kerr		
Horace Grant		
Scottie Pippen		
FFATLCHA Marvin Williams	8.00	20.00
Joe Johnson		
Josh Smith		
Al Horford		
Emeka Okafor		
Raja Bell		
Raymond Felton		
Gerald Wallace		
FFATLDAL Al Horford	8.00	20.00
Joe Johnson		
Mike Bibby		
Marvin Williams		
Jason Terry		
Josh Howard		
Dirk Nowitzki		
Jason Kidd		
FFATLMIA Marvin Williams	8.00	20.00
Mike Bibby		
Al Horford		
Acie Law		
Dwyane Wade		
Udonis Haslem		
Jermaine O'Neal		
Mario Chalmers		
FFATLORL Acie Law	8.00	20.00
Al Horford		
Mike Bibby		
Joe Johnson		
Rashard Lewis		
Jameer Nelson		
Dwight Howard		
Courtney Lee		
FFATLWAS Joe Johnson	8.00	20.00
Marvin Williams		
Acie Law		
Josh Smith		
Gilbert Arenas		
Caron Butler		
Dominic McGuire		
DeShawn Stevenson		
FFBOSLAL Rajon Rondo	20.00	50.00
Paul Pierce		
Andrew Bynum		
Jordan Farmar		
Pau Gasol		
Kobe Bryant		
Kevin Garnett		
Ray Allen		
FFBOSNET Ray Allen	10.00	25.00
Kevin Garnett		
Vince Carter		
Devin Harris		
Paul Pierce		
Rajon Rondo		
Chris Douglas-Roberts		
Brook Lopez		
FFBOSNYK Rajon Rondo	10.00	25.00
Paul Pierce		
Wilson Chandler		
Quentin Richardson		
Al Harrington		
Nate Robinson		
Kevin Garnett		
Ray Allen		
FFBOSPHI Ray Allen	10.00	25.00
Kevin Garnett		
Paul Pierce		
J.R. Giddens		
Marreese Speights		
Andre Miller		
Andre Iguodala		
Elton Brand		
FFBOSTOR Glen Davis	10.00	25.00
Paul Pierce		
Kevin Garnett		
Ray Allen		
Shawn Marion		
Jose Calderon		
Andrea Bargnani		
Chris Bosh		
FFCENTER Patrick Ewing	20.00	50.00
Willis Reed		
Hakeem Olajuwon		
Wilt Chamberlain		
Robert Parish		
Moses Malone		
David Robinson		
Bill Laimbeer		
FFCHAMIA Emeka Okafor	8.00	20.00
D.J. Augustin		
Michael Beasley		
Daequan Cook		
Jermaine O'Neal		
Jamaal Magloire		
Juwan Howard		
Raymond Felton		
FFCHAORL Sean May	8.00	20.00
Raja Bell		
Jameer Nelson		
Courtney Lee		
Dwight Howard		
J.J. Redick		
D.J. Augustin		
Emeka Okafor		
FFCHAWAS Nick Young	8.00	20.00
Javaris Crittenton		
Javale McGee		
Mike James		
Sean May		
Juwan Howard		
Gerald Wallace		
Boris Diaw		
FFCHICLE LeBron James	12.00	30.00
Ben Wallace		
Zydrunas Ilgauskas		
Delonte West		
Ben Gordon		
Luol Deng		
Joakim Noah		
Derrick Rose		
FFCHIDET Derrick Rose	12.00	30.00
Luol Deng		
Kirk Hinrich		
Ben Gordon		
Tayshaun Prince		
Allen Iverson		
Rasheed Wallace		
Rodney Stuckey		
FFCHIIND Roy Hibbert	10.00	25.00
Mike Dunleavy		
T.J. Ford		
Danny Granger		
Kirk Hinrich		
Luol Deng		
Derrick Rose		
Tyrus Thomas		
FFCHIMIL Derrick Rose	10.00	25.00
Joakim Noah		
Luol Deng		
Aaron Gray		
Charlie Villanueva		
Luke Ridnour		
Michael Redd		
Richard Jefferson		
FFCLEDET Rodney Stuckey	12.00	30.00
Arron Afflalo		
Kwame Brown		
Richard Hamilton		
LeBron James		
Wally Szczerbiak		
Zydrunas Ilgauskas		
Daniel Gibson		
FFCLEIND Lorenzen Wright	12.00	30.00
J.J. Hickson		
Wally Szczerbiak		
LeBron James		
Jarrett Jack		
Jamaal Tinsley		
Marquis Daniels		
Josh McRoberts		
FFCLEMIL Richard Jefferson	12.00	30.00
Andrew Bogut		
Luke Ridnour		
LeBron James		
Zydrunas Ilgauskas		
Ben Wallace		
Joe Alexander		
Daniel Gibson		
FFCLEPHO Daniel Gibson	12.00	30.00
Zydrunas Ilgauskas		
Ben Wallace		
LeBron James		
Amare Stoudemire		
Shaquille O'Neal		
Steve Nash		
Grant Hill		
FFDALHOU Brian Cook	8.00	20.00
Tracy McGrady		
Yao Ming		
Brent Barry		
Jason Kidd		
Josh Howard		
Shawne Williams		
Antoine Wright		
FFDALMEM Devean George	8.00	20.00
Gerald Green		
Dirk Nowitzki		
Jason Terry		
Rudy Gay		
Darius Miles		
Mike Conley Jr.		
O.J. Mayo		
FFDALNEW Tyson Chandler	8.00	20.00
Chris Paul		
Morris Peterson		
Antonio Daniels		
Dirk Nowitzki		
Josh Howard		
Jason Kidd		
Gerald Green		
FFDALSAN Antoine Wright	8.00	20.00
James Singleton		
Dirk Nowitzki		
Jason Terry		
George Hill		
Tony Parker		
Bruce Bowen		
Michael Finley		
FFDENMIN Chauncey Billups	8.00	20.00
Carmelo Anthony		
Linas Kleiza		
Renaldo Balkman		
Jason Collins		
Mike Miller		
Sebastian Telfair		
Craig Smith		
FFDENOKL Nene	8.00	20.00
{Sonny Weems		
J.R. Smith		
Kenyon Martin		
Nenad Krstic		
Kyle Weaver		
Jeff Green		
Russell Westbrook		
FFDENPOR Chauncey Billups	8.00	20.00
Johan Petro		
Sonny Weems		
Renaldo Balkman		
Jerryd Bayless		
Martell Webster		
Sergio Rodriguez		
Channing Frye		
FFDENUTA Kyle Korver	10.00	25.00
Deron Williams		
Kosta Koufos		
Morris Almond		
Sonny Weems		
Linas Kleiza		
Kenyon Martin		
Carmelo Anthony		
FFDETIND Jamaal Tinsley	8.00	20.00
Danny Granger		
Brandon Rush		
Roy Hibbert		
Kwame Brown		
Arron Afflalo		
Rodney Stuckey		
Walter Sharpe		
FFDETMIL Allen Iverson	8.00	20.00
Rasheed Wallace		
Tayshaun Prince		
Richard Hamilton		
Joe Alexander		
Michael Redd		
Andrew Bogut		
Richard Jefferson		
FFDETNEW Chris Paul	8.00	20.00
Morris Peterson		
Peja Stojakovic		
Tyson Chandler		
Tayshaun Prince		
Rasheed Wallace		
Allen Iverson		
Rodney Stuckey		
FFEAST6M Wally Szczerbiak	8.00	20.00
Richard Hamilton		
Nick Young		
D.J. Augustin		
Jermaine O'Neal		
Michael Beasley		
Tyrus Thomas		
Al Harrington		
FFEASTAS Chris Bosh	20.00	50.00
Dwight Howard		
Ray Allen		
Kevin Garnett		

Dwyane Wade
Joe Johnson
Paul Pierce
LeBron James
FFEASTCE Zydrunas Ilgauskas 8.00 20.00
Rasheed Wallace
Emeka Okafor
Andrew Bogut
Al Horford
Dwight Howard
Andrea Bargnani
David Lee
FFEASTPF Chris Bosh 10.00 25.00
Kevin Garnett
Rashard Lewis
Josh Smith
Udonis Haslem
Elton Brand
Antawn Jamison
Ben Wallace
FFEASTPG Rodney Stuckey 10.00 25.00
Gilbert Arenas
T.J. Ford
Derrick Rose
Mike Bibby
Andre Miller
Jameer Nelson
Devin Harris
FFEASTSF Shawn Marion 15.00 40.00
Andre Iguodala
Paul Pierce
Luol Deng
Danny Granger
Richard Jefferson
LeBron James
Tayshaun Prince
FFEASTSG Allen Iverson 10.00 25.00
Michael Redd
Ben Gordon
Dwyane Wade
Joe Johnson
Quentin Richardson
Vince Carter
Ray Allen
FFEASVWES Gilbert Arenas 30.00 80.00
LeBron James
Shaquille O'Neal
Paul Pierce
Kobe Bryant
Kevin Garnett
Jason Kidd
Tracy McGrady
FFFORWRD James Worthy 15.00 40.00
Kevin McHale
Horace Grant
Larry Bird
Scottie Pippen
Chris Mullin
Karl Malone
Tom Chambers
FFGOLLAC Monta Ellis 8.00 20.00
Corey Maggette
Marco Belinelli
Brandan Wright
Chris Kaman
Baron Davis
Steve Novak
Mardy Collins
FFGOLLAL Brandan Wright 12.00 30.00
Anthony Randolph
Monta Ellis
Corey Maggette
Jordan Farmar
Luke Walton
Shannon Brown
Kobe Bryant
FFGOLPHO Monta Ellis 8.00 20.00
Corey Maggette
Anthony Randolph
Brandan Wright
Robin Lopez
Alando Tucker
Steve Nash
Grant Hill
FFGOLSAC Brandan Wright 8.00 20.00
Anthony Randolph
Corey Maggette
Monta Ellis
Andres Nocioni
Beno Udrih
Spencer Hawes
Donte Greene
FFHOUMEM Darrell Arthur 10.00 25.00
Hakim Warrick
Rudy Gay
O.J. Mayo
Yao Ming
Tracy McGrady
Kyle Lowry
Aaron Brooks
FFHOUNEW Aaron Brooks 8.00 20.00
Ron Artest
Tracy McGrady
Shane Battier
James Posey
Hilton Armstrong
Antonio Daniels
Peja Stojakovic
FFHOUSAN Shane Battier 8.00 20.00
Ron Artest
Brent Barry
Luis Scola
Michael Finley
George Hill
Manu Ginobili
Tim Duncan
FFINDMIL Joe Alexander 8.00 20.00
Roy Hibbert
Josh McRoberts
Luke Ridnour
Charlie Villanueva
Keith Bogans
T.J. Ford
Marquis Daniels
FFLACLAL Al Thornton 12.00 30.00
Baron Davis
Marcus Camby
DeAndre Jordan
Kobe Bryant
Adam Morrison
Andrew Bynum
Trevor Ariza
FFLACPHO DeAndre Jordan 8.00 20.00
Baron Davis
Zach Randolph
Mardy Collins
Robin Lopez
Alando Tucker
Louis Amundson
Jason Richardson
FFLACSAC Jason Thompson 8.00 20.00
Kevin Martin
Kenny Thomas
Andres Nocioni
Al Thornton
Eric Gordon
Zach Randolph
Chris Kaman
FFLALPHO Steve Nash 15.00 40.00
Shaquille O'Neal
Amare Stoudemire
Jared Dudley
Luke Walton
Jordan Farmar
Kobe Bryant
Lamar Odom
FFLALSAC Lamar Odom 12.00 30.00
Kobe Bryant
Pau Gasol
Trevor Ariza
Andres Nocioni
Kevin Martin
Beno Udrih
Jason Thompson
FFMEMNEW Chris Paul 8.00 20.00
Hilton Armstrong
Julian Wright
Tyson Chandler
Darko Milicic
O.J. Mayo
Mike Conley Jr.
Darrell Arthur
FFMEMSAN Mike Conley Jr. 8.00 20.00
Darko Milicic
Hakim Warrick
Rudy Gay
Tim Duncan
Bruce Bowen
Manu Ginobili
Tony Parker
FFMIAORL Dwyane Wade 10.00 25.00
Jermaine O'Neal
Michael Beasley
Mario Chalmers
Jameer Nelson
Rafer Alston
Courtney Lee
Dwight Howard
FFMIAUTA Mario Chalmers 8.00 20.00
Udonis Haslem
Jermaine O'Neal
Dwyane Wade
Andrei Kirilenko
Mehmet Okur
Carlos Boozer
Deron Williams
FFMIAWAS Antawn Jamison 8.00 20.00
Oleksiy Pecherov
Juan Dixon
DeShawn Stevenson
Dorell Wright
Udonis Haslem
Daequan Cook
Mario Chalmers
FFMINOKL Brian Cardinal 8.00 20.00
Randy Foye
Rodney Carney
Sebastian Telfair
Kyle Weaver
Robert Swift
Desmond Mason
Kevin Durant
FFMINPOR Al Jefferson 8.00 20.00
Randy Foye
Craig Smith
Kevin Love
Jerryd Bayless
Brandon Roy
LaMarcus Aldridge
Rudy Fernandez
FFMINUTA Kevin Love 8.00 20.00
Craig Smith
Randy Foye
Al Jefferson
Ronnie Brewer
Carlos Boozer
Mehmet Okur
Andrei Kirilenko
FFNETNYK Brook Lopez 8.00 20.00
Chris Douglas-Roberts
Quentin Richardson
Al Harrington
David Lee
Wilson Chandler
Vince Carter
Devin Harris
FFNETPHI Vince Carter 10.00 25.00
Elton Brand
Jason Smith
Andre Iguodala
Andre Miller
Chris Douglas-Roberts
Brook Lopez
Maurice Ager
FFNETTOR Josh Boone 10.00 25.00
Brook Lopez
Chris Douglas-Roberts
Vince Carter
Shawn Marion
Andrea Bargnani
Chris Bosh
Jason Kapono
FFNEWMEM Rudy Gay 8.00 20.00
Hakim Warrick
Darius Miles
Tyson Chandler
O.J. Mayo
Peja Stojakovic
Antonio Daniels
Morris Peterson
FFNEWSAN Morris Peterson 8.00 20.00
Chris Paul
Peja Stojakovic
James Posey
George Hill
Tony Parker
Bruce Bowen
Michael Finley
FFNYKPHI Marreese Speights 8.00 20.00
Andre Miller
Andre Iguodala
Thaddeus Young
Nate Robinson
Al Harrington
Quentin Richardson
Wilson Chandler
FFNYKTOR Wilson Chandler 8.00 20.00
Al Harrington
Nate Robinson
David Lee
Shawn Marion
Chris Bosh
Andrea Bargnani
Jose Calderon
FFOKLPOR LaMarcus Aldridge 10.00 25.00
Brandon Roy
Channing Frye
Sergio Rodriguez
Kevin Durant
Desmond Mason
Thabo Sefolosha
Russell Westbrook
FFOKLUTA D.J. White 8.00 20.00
Kyle Weaver
Jeff Green
Robert Swift
Kyle Korver
Jarron Collins
Morris Almond
Paul Millsap
FFORLPOR Martell Webster 10.00 25.00
Brandon Roy
LaMarcus Aldridge
Rudy Fernandez
Courtney Lee
Dwight Howard
Jameer Nelson
Rashard Lewis
FFORLWAS Rashard Lewis 8.00 20.00
Jameer Nelson
Dwight Howard
J.J. Redick
Mike James
Andray Blatche
Nick Young
Dominic McGuire
FFPHITOR Andrea Bargnani 8.00 20.00
Chris Bosh
Jason Kapono
Joey Graham
Andre Iguodala
Andre Miller
Jason Smith
Elton Brand
FFPHOSAC Andres Nocioni 10.00 25.00
Jason Thompson
Spencer Hawes
Kenny Thomas
Shaquille O'Neal
Steve Nash
Jason Richardson
Louis Amundson
FFPORUTA Mehmet Okur 8.00 20.00
Paul Millsap
Kosta Koufos
Deron Williams
Rudy Fernandez
LaMarcus Aldridge
Brandon Roy
Jerryd Bayless
FFSACLAC Chris Kaman 8.00 20.00
Eric Gordon
Ricky Davis
Al Thornton
Andres Nocioni
Cedric Simmons
Spencer Hawes
Donte Greene
FFWEST6M Andrei Kirilenko 8.00 20.00
Mike Miller
Rudy Fernandez
James Posey
J.R. Smith
Manu Ginobili
Ron Artest
Lamar Odom
FFWESTAS Kobe Bryant 20.00 50.00
Dirk Nowitzki
Yao Ming
Tony Parker
Chauncey Billups
Chris Paul
Shaquille O'Neal
Amare Stoudemire
FFWESTCE Shaquille O'Neal 10.00 25.00
Al Jefferson
Mehmet Okur
Tyson Chandler
Marc Gasol
Nene
Yao Ming
Andrew Bynum
FFWESTPF Dirk Nowitzki 10.00 25.00
Pau Gasol
Luis Scola
Kenyon Martin
Tim Duncan
LaMarcus Aldridge
Carlos Boozer
Amare Stoudemire
FFWESTPG Steve Nash 10.00 25.00
Deron Williams
Chris Paul
Baron Davis
Tony Parker
Chauncey Billups
Jason Kidd
Russell Westbrook
FFWESTSF Kevin Durant 10.00 25.00
Josh Howard
Shane Battier
Carmelo Anthony
Michael Finley
Peja Stojakovic
Rudy Gay
Grant Hill
FFWESTSG Jason Richardson 12.50 30.00
Randy Foye
Ronnie Brewer
O.J. Mayo
Brandon Roy
Eric Gordon
Tracy McGrady
Kobe Bryant

2009-10 SP Game Used Combo Materials

STATED PRINT RUN 499 SER.#'d SETS
*MATERIAL 155: .5X TO 1.25X BASE HI
*MATERIAL 50: .6X TO 1.5X BASE HI
*MATERIAL 35: .6X TO 1.5X BASE HI
CM23 LeBron James 30.00 80.00
Michael Jordan
CMAA Carmelo Anthony 4.00 10.00
Gilbert Arenas
CMAB Gilbert Arenas 3.00 8.00
Caron Butler
CMAG Kevin Garnett 5.00 12.00
Ray Allen
CMAN Ray Allen 4.00 10.00
Dirk Nowitzki
CMAP Tony Parker 4.00 10.00
Gilbert Arenas
CMAT Carmelo Anthony 4.00 10.00
Tyrus Thomas
CMBA Chauncey Billups 3.00 8.00
Gilbert Arenas
CMBH Udonis Haslem 3.00 8.00
Elton Brand
CMBJ Kobe Bryant 15.00 40.00
LeBron James
CMBL Carlos Boozer 3.00 8.00
David Lee
CMBM Andrea Bargnani 4.00 10.00
Yao Ming
CMBO Kobe Bryant 8.00 20.00
Lamar Odom
CMBP Chauncey Billups 3.00 8.00
Tony Parker
CMBS Kobe Bryant 10.00 25.00
Shaquille O'Neal
CMCA Vince Carter 6.00 15.00
Carmelo Anthony
CMCB Chris Bosh 4.00 10.00
Vince Carter
CMCG Rudy Gay 3.00 8.00
Michael Cooper
CMCH Vince Carter 4.00 10.00
Grant Hill
CMCJ Corey Maggette 3.00 8.00
Josh Howard
CMCN Dirk Nowitzki 5.00 12.00
Vince Carter
CMCR Corey Maggette 3.00 8.00
Rudy Gay
CMCS Chris Bosh 3.00 8.00
Shawn Marion
CMCT Tyrus Thomas 4.00 10.00
Vince Carter
CMDB Baron Davis 3.00 8.00
Chauncey Billups
CMDD Baron Davis 3.00 8.00
Chris Kaman
CMDG Horace Grant 3.00 8.00
Vlade Divac
CMDH Dwight Howard 5.00 12.00
Tim Duncan
CMDJ Magic Johnson 5.00 12.00
Baron Davis
CMDO Jermaine O'Neal 3.00 8.00
Luol Deng
CMDR Dwight Howard 4.00 10.00
Rasheed Wallace
CMDT Tracy McGrady 5.00 12.00
Dwyane Wade
CMDW Baron Davis 4.00 10.00
Deron Williams
CMFB Jordan Farmar 8.00 20.00
Kobe Bryant
CMFF T.J. Ford 3.00 8.00
Raymond Felton
CMGA Gilbert Arenas 5.00 12.00
Kevin Garnett
CMGB Kevin Garnett 5.00 12.00
Chris Bosh
CMGN Kevin Garnett 6.00 15.00
Dirk Nowitzki
CMGO Kevin Garnett 5.00 12.00
Shaquille O'Neal
CMGP Horace Grant 8.00 20.00
Scottie Pippen
CMGS Scottie Pippen 8.00 20.00
George Gervin
CMHB Chauncey Billups 3.00 8.00
Richard Hamilton
CMHD Luol Deng 3.00 8.00
Larry Hughes
CMHG Richard Hamilton 3.00 8.00
Rudy Gay
CMHI Larry Hughes 3.00 8.00
Andre Iguodala
CMHJ Joe Johnson 3.00 8.00
Grant Hill
CMHM Jeff Hornacek 4.00 10.00
Karl Malone
CMHO Grant Hill 5.00 12.00
Shaquille O'Neal
CMHS Jeff Hornacek 6.00 15.00
John Stockton
CMHT Jamaal Tinsley 3.00 8.00
Larry Hughes
CMIB Chauncey Billups 4.00 10.00
Allen Iverson
CMIM Zydrunas Ilgauskas 4.00 10.00
Yao Ming
CMIP Allen Iverson 4.00 10.00
Chris Paul
CMIT Al Thornton 3.00 8.00
Andre Iguodala
CMIW Allen Iverson 4.00 10.00
Deron Williams
CMJA Michael Jordan 20.00 50.00
Ray Allen
CMJB Kobe Bryant 30.00 80.00
Michael Jordan
CMJD Magic Johnson 5.00 12.00
Clyde Drexler
CMJJ Magic Johnson 25.00 60.00
Michael Jordan
CMJK Joe Johnson 8.00 20.00
Kobe Bryant
CMJL Lamar Odom 3.00 8.00
Jermaine O'Neal
CMJM Josh Howard 3.00 8.00
Shawn Marion
CMJP Michael Jordan 25.00 60.00
Scottie Pippen
CMKK Kevin Garnett 5.00 12.00
Karl Malone
CMKM Jason Kidd 5.00 12.00
Tracy McGrady
CMKP Kevin Garnett 5.00 12.00
Paul Pierce
CMKT Jason Kidd 4.00 10.00
Jamaal Tinsley
CMLG Rashard Lewis 3.00 8.00
Jeff Green
CMLM Magic Johnson 12.50 30.00
LeBron James
CMLO Mehmet Okur 3.00 8.00
Rashard Lewis
CMLS Scottie Pippen 12.00 30.00
LeBron James
CMMB Yao Ming 4.00 10.00
Andrea Bargnani
CMMC Michael Cooper 4.00 10.00
Karl Malone
CMMD Mike Miller 3.00 8.00
Drew Gooden
CMMG Mike Miller 3.00 8.00
Rudy Gay
CMMH Josh Howard 3.00 8.00
Shawn Marion
CMMJ LeBron James 10.00 25.00
Karl Malone
CMMN Dan Majerle 4.00 10.00
Steve Nash
CMMO Shaquille O'Neal 5.00 12.00
Yao Ming
CMMP Scottie Pippen 6.00 15.00
Karl Malone
CMMS Karl Malone 6.00 15.00
John Stockton
CMMT Al Thornton 3.00 8.00
Desmond Mason
CMMW Kenyon Martin 3.00 8.00
Luke Walton
CMNS John Stockton 5.00 12.00
Steve Nash
CMOC Vince Carter 4.00 10.00
Lamar Odom
CMOG Lamar Odom 3.00 8.00
Pau Gasol
CMOO Mehmet Okur 4.00 10.00
Shaquille O'Neal
CMPG Carmelo Anthony 4.00 10.00
Paul Pierce
CMPI Paul Pierce 3.00 8.00
Andre Iguodala
CMPR Chris Paul 4.00 10.00
Brandon Roy
CMRE Luke Ridnour 3.00 8.00
Monta Ellis
CMRJ Jordan Farmar 3.00 8.00
Raymond Felton
CMSA Stephon Marbury 4.00 10.00
Allen Iverson
CMSM Wally Szczerbiak 3.00 8.00
Chris Mullin
CMSO Shaquille O'Neal 5.00 12.00
Amare Stoudemire
CMSS Stromile Swift 3.00 8.00
Wally Szczerbiak
CMUS John Stockton 4.00 10.00
Beno Udrih
CMWG Ben Wallace 3.00 8.00
Pau Gasol
CMWH Luther Head 4.00 10.00
Deron Williams
CMWM Shelden Williams 3.00 8.00
Javale McGee

2009-10 SP Game Used Combo Patches

STATED PRINT RUN 99 SER.#'d SETS
CPR Nene 5.00 12.00
Zach Randolph
CPAA Joe Alexander 5.00 12.00
Ryan Anderson
CPAB Ben Wallace 8.00 20.00
Antonio McDyess
CPAG Trevor Ariza 5.00 12.00
Jeff Green
CPAM Marcus Camby 6.00 15.00
Antonio McDyess
CPAT Arron Afflalo 5.00 12.00
Alando Tucker
CPAW Ryan Anderson 5.00 12.00
Sean Williams
CPBB Brian Cardinal 5.00 12.00
Ben Wallace
CPBC Rodney Carney 5.00 12.00
Shane Battier
CPBF Mike Bibby 6.00 15.00
Raymond Felton
CPBJ Jason Collins 5.00 12.00
Brandan Wright
CPBY Thaddeus Young 6.00 15.00
Shannon Brown
CPCC Mike Conley Jr. 6.00 15.00
Javaris Crittenton
CPCE Tyson Chandler 6.00 15.00
Marcus Camby
CPCH Brendan Haywood 5.00 12.00
Brian Cardinal
CPCI Jamal Crawford 10.00 25.00
Allen Iverson
CPCM Javaris Crittenton 5.00 12.00
Dominic McGuire
CPCS Rodney Stuckey 6.00 15.00
Speedy Claxton
CPCW Wilson Chandler 5.00 12.00
Sean Williams
CPDA Ryan Anderson 5.00 12.00
Samuel Dalembert
CPDG Kevin Durant 8.00 20.00
Jeff Green
CPDH Vlade Divac 6.00 15.00
Spencer Hawes
CPDW Julian Wright 8.00 20.00
Kevin Durant
CPEM Karl Malone 12.00 30.00
Patrick Ewing
CPER Rashard Lewis 5.00 12.00
Eric Gordon
CPFD Michael Finley 12.00 30.00
Kevin Durant
CPFG Michael Finley 6.00 15.00
Manu Ginobili
CPGA Carmelo Anthony 12.00 30.00
Kevin Garnett
CPGB Manu Ginobili 5.00 12.00
Jerryd Bayless
CPGC Aaron Gray 5.00 12.00
Wilson Chandler
CPGF Manu Ginobili 6.00 15.00
Rudy Fernandez
CPGG Kevin Garnett 10.00 25.00
Pau Gasol
CPGH Manu Ginobili 6.00 15.00
George Hill
CPGK Manu Ginobili 5.00 12.00
Jason Kapono
CPGL David Lee 6.00 15.00
Drew Gooden
CPGM Manu Ginobili 8.00 20.00
Adam Morrison
CPGO Pau Gasol 5.00 12.00
Jermaine O'Neal
CPGS Gerald Green 5.00 12.00
Wally Szczerbiak
CPHG Kirk Hinrich 6.00 15.00
Manu Ginobili
CPHW Brendan Haywood 5.00 12.00
Brandan Wright
CPID Allen Iverson 12.00 30.00
Kevin Durant
CPIS Allen Iverson 8.00 20.00
Rodney Stuckey
CPIW Allen Iverson 8.00 20.00
Rasheed Wallace
CPJB Keith Bogans 5.00 12.00
Richard Jefferson
CPJC Jason Collins 5.00 12.00
Jason Smith
CPJG Manu Ginobili 5.00 12.00
Richard Jefferson
CPJL Robin Lopez 5.00 12.00
DeAndre Jordan
CPJR Jamaal Tinsley 5.00 12.00
Beno Udrih
CPJT Richard Jefferson 5.00 12.00
Alando Tucker
CPKG Manu Ginobili 6.00 15.00
Steve Kerr
CPKK Karl Malone 12.00 30.00
Kevin McHale
CPMC Darko Milicic 5.00 12.00
Mike Conley Jr.
CPMD Morris Almond 5.00 12.00
Mike Dunleavy
CPMG Josh McRoberts 5.00 12.00
Jeff Green
CPMI Zydrunas Ilgauskas 8.00 20.00
Mikki Moore
CPMK Kosta Koufos 8.00 20.00
Karl Malone
CPMN Josh McRoberts 5.00 12.00
Joakim Noah
CPMP Scottie Pippen 20.00 50.00
Karl Malone
CPMT Jason Thompson 6.00 15.00
Javale McGee
CPMW Julian Wright 5.00 12.00
Josh McRoberts
CPNB Mike Bibby 5.00 12.00
Nick Young
CPND Joakim Noah 15.00 40.00
Kevin Durant
CPNG Jeff Green 8.00 20.00
Joakim Noah
CPNH Grant Hill 10.00 25.00
Steve Nash
CPNI Steve Nash 8.00 20.00
Allen Iverson
CPNL Robin Lopez 5.00 12.00
Joakim Noah
CPNW Joakim Noah 6.00 15.00
Julian Wright
CPOB Jerryd Bayless 5.00 12.00
Travis Outlaw
CPOD Chris Kaman 5.00 12.00
Patrick O'Bryant
CPPC Javaris Crittenton 6.00 15.00
Oleksiy Pecherov
CPPK Karl Malone 8.00 20.00
Pau Gasol
CPPM Gabe Pruitt 5.00 12.00
Dominic McGuire
CPRH George Hill 6.00 15.00
David Robinson
CPRP David Robinson 8.00 20.00
Robert Parish
CPRR Zach Randolph 6.00 15.00
Jason Richardson
CPRS Anthony Randolph 5.00 12.00
Walter Sharpe
CPSB Jerryd Bayless 5.00 12.00
J.R. Smith
CPSR Jason Richardson 6.00 15.00
Wally Szczerbiak
CPST Tyson Chandler 5.00 12.00
Sean Williams
CPSW Brandan Wright 5.00 12.00
Jason Smith
CPTC Jamaal Tinsley 5.00 12.00
Mike Conley Jr.
CPTL Robin Lopez 5.00 12.00
Jason Thompson
CPTS Jason Thompson 5.00 12.00
Marreese Speights
CPTY Nick Young 5.00 12.00
Reggie Theus
CPWA Sean Williams 5.00 12.00
Ryan Anderson
CPWB Lorenzen Wright 5.00 12.00
Kwame Brown
CPWH Spencer Hawes 5.00 12.00
Brandan Wright
CPWM Marreese Speights 5.00 12.00
Wilson Chandler
CPWW Brandan Wright 6.00 15.00
Hakim Warrick

2009-10 SP Game Used Fabric Foursomes

PRINT RUN 199 SER.#'d SETS
*MATERIAL 125: SAME VALUE
*MATERIAL 50: .75X TO 2X HI
*MATERIAL 35: .75X TO 2X HI
F4AATB Aaron Brooks 4.00 10.00
Arron Afflalo
Morris Almond
Alando Tucker
F4AHLB Aaron Brooks 4.00 10.00
Carl Landry
Ron Artest
Yao Ming
F4ALAH Courtney Lee 4.00 10.00
George Hill
Ryan Anderson
Darrell Arthur
F4AWDA Chris Douglas-Roberts 4.00 10.00
Ryan Anderson
Sean Williams
Maurice Ager
F4BDGP Tim Duncan 12.50 30.00
Scottie Pippen
Kevin Garnett
Kobe Bryant
F4BGBR Kobe Bryant 15.00 30.0
George Gervin
David Robinson
Larry Bird
F4BIJO Kobe Bryant 20.00 40.0
Shaquille O'Neal
Allen Iverson
LeBron James
F4BJWL Acie Law 4.00 10.0
Marvin Williams
Joe Johnson
Mike Bibby
F4BMCS Josh Smith 10.00 25.0
Kobe Bryant
Vince Carter
Desmond Mason
F4BMDI Andre Iguodala 5.00 12.0
Andre Miller
Samuel Dalembert
Elton Brand
F4BMMJ LeBron James 10.00 25.0
Yao Ming
Elton Brand
Kenyon Martin
F4BNGN Kobe Bryant 10.00 25.0
Kevin Garnett
Dirk Nowitzki
Steve Nash
F4BOGB Andrew Bynum 15.00 30.0
Lamar Odom
Kobe Bryant
Pau Gasol
F4BOWB Carlos Boozer 4.00 10.0
Mehmet Okur
Deron Williams
Ronnie Brewer
F4CGAW Ron Artest 6.00 15.0
Kevin Garnett
Ben Wallace
Marcus Camby
F4CHBL Vince Carter 4.00 10.0
Josh Boone
Brook Lopez
Devin Harris
F4DBCM Juan Dixon 4.00 10.0
Javale McGee
Javaris Crittenton
Caron Butler
F4DBPH George Hill 8.00 20.0
Tim Duncan
Bruce Bowen
Tony Parker
F4DDFG Danny Granger 5.00 12.0
T.J. Ford
Marquis Daniels
Mike Dunleavy
F4DFPG Tony Parker 6.00 15.0
Manu Ginobili
Tim Duncan
Michael Finley
F4DGNR Ben Gordon 12.50 30.0
Luol Deng
Joakim Noah
Derrick Rose
F4DHGC Al Horford 8.00 20.0
Mike Conley Jr.
Kevin Durant
Jeff Green
F4DIOR Allen Iverson 10.00 25.0
Shaquille O'Neal
Tim Duncan
David Robinson
F4DKIC Tim Duncan 6.00 15.0
Jason Kidd
Vince Carter
Allen Iverson
F4DMBA D.J. Augustin 5.00 12.0
Sean May
Boris Diaw
Gerald Wallace
F4DMIO Allen Iverson 10.00 25.0
Karl Malone
Shaquille O'Neal
Tim Duncan
F4DTGJ Baron Davis 6.00 15.0
DeAndre Jordan
Eric Gordon
Al Thornton
F4EMHO Shaquille O'Neal 8.00 20.0
Yao Ming
Dwight Howard
Patrick Ewing
F4FCDC Wilson Chandler 4.00 10.0
Daequan Cook
Jared Dudley
Rudy Fernandez
F4GCGM Marc Gasol 6.00 15.0
O.J. Mayo
Mike Conley Jr.
Rudy Gay
F4GCKS Tom Chambers 8.00 20.0
John Stockton
Bernard King
Kevin Garnett
F4GFRW Shelden Williams 4.00 10.0
Randy Foye
Brandon Roy
Rudy Gay
F4GGLA Eric Gordon 6.00 15.0
Joe Alexander
Kevin Love
Brook Lopez
F4GHTG Aaron Gray 4.00 10.0
Tyrus Thomas
Luol Deng
Kirk Hinrich
F4HAPD Gabe Pruitt 4.00 10.0
Glen Davis
Tony Allen
Eddie House
F4HBAS Richard Hamilton 4.00 10.0
Arron Afflalo
Walter Sharpe
Kwame Brown
F4HBYM Brendan Haywood 4.00 10.0
Andray Blatche
Nick Young
Dominic McGuire
F4HCRG Eddy Curry 4.00 10.0
Nate Robinson
Al Harrington
Quentin Richardson
F4HEOR Patrick Ewing 10.00 25.
David Robinson
Shaquille O'Neal

rant Hill
HMHA Roy Hibbert 4.00 10.00
aVale McGee
.J. Hickson
lexis Ajinca
HNSS Cedric Simmons 4.00 10.00
ndres Nocioni
arry Hughes
habo Sefolosha
HOBA Juwan Howard 4.00 10.00
erald Wallace
meka Okafor
).J. Augustin
HSGR Nate Robinson 4.00 10.00
)wight Howard
erald Green
osh Smith
DPD Robert Parish 10.00 25.00
lyde Drexler
llen Iverson
drian Dantley
WJW LeBron James 8.00 20.00
Ben Wallace
ydrunas Ilgauskas
)elonte West
IWPS Tayshaun Prince 6.00 15.00
Allen Iverson
Rasheed Wallace
Rodney Stuckey
JASB Caron Butler 4.00 10.00
Gilbert Arenas
Antawn Jamison
DeShawn Stevenson
JBVA Joe Alexander 4.00 10.00
Andrew Bogut
Charlie Villanueva
Richard Jefferson
JDWC DeAndre Jordan 4.00 10.00
Joey Dorsey
Mario Chalmers
Kyle Weaver
JMCA Michael Jordan 40.00 100.00
Wilt Chamberlain
Kareem Abdul-Jabbar
Karl Malone
JOMR Karl Malone 30.00 80.00
Hakeem Olajuwon
Michael Jordan
David Robinson
JORD LeBron James 12.50 30.00
Brandon Roy
Emeka Okafor
Kevin Durant
JPST Chris Paul 10.00 25.00
Isiah Thomas
John Stockton
Magic Johnson
JRRB Richard Jefferson 5.00 12.00
Andrew Bogut
Luke Ridnour
Michael Redd
JSWH Josh Smith 4.00 10.00
Marvin Williams
Al Horford
Joe Johnson
KBCB Andrea Bargnani 8.00 20.00
Jose Calderon
Jason Kapono
Chris Bosh
KKMM C.J. Miles 4.00 10.00
Paul Millsap
Andrei Kirilenko
Kyle Korver
KNHW Antoine Wright 6.00 15.00
Jason Kidd
Josh Howard
Dirk Nowitzki
LHBR Rashard Lewis 5.00 12.00
Jameer Nelson
J.J. Redick
Dwight Howard
LHNL Dwight Howard 6.00 15.00
Courtney Lee
Jameer Nelson
Rashard Lewis
MBAN Kenyon Martin 5.00 12.00
Carmelo Anthony
Chauncey Billups
Nene
MBMS Tracy McGrady 6.00 15.00
Shane Battier
Yao Ming
Luis Scola
MBRW Michael Beasley 12.00 30.00
Derrick Rose
O.J. Mayo
Russell Westbrook
MDGW Russell Westbrook 8.00 20.00
Desmond Mason
Jeff Green
Kevin Durant
MEWR Anthony Randolph 4.00 10.00
Brandan Wright
Corey Maggette
Monta Ellis
MMBL Kevin Love 4.00 10.00
Corey Brewer
Mike Miller
Al Jefferson
MMMD Joey Dorsey 5.00 12.00
Yao Ming
Tracy McGrady
Dikembe Mutombo
MNDG Paul Millsap 4.00 10.00
Rudy Gay
Steve Novak
Daniel Gibson
MUDT Andres Nocioni 4.00 10.00
Spencer Hawes
Beno Udrih
Jason Thompson
MWCB Michael Beasley 5.00 12.00
Daequan Cook
Dorell Wright
Jamaal Magloire
MWHC Dwyane Wade 5.00 12.00
Udonis Haslem
Jermaine O'Neal
Mario Chalmers
MYSS Jason Smith 4.00 10.00
Marreese Speights
Donyell Marshall
Thaddeus Young
NHSO Grant Hill 6.00 15.00
Shaquille O'Neal
Amare Stoudemire
Steve Nash
NKMW Steve Nash 5.00 12.00

Deron Williams
Andre Miller
Jason Kidd
F4NWBL Acie Law 4.00 10.00
Joakim Noah
Brandan Wright
Corey Brewer
F4ODRB Travis Outlaw 4.00 10.00
Sergio Rodriguez
Brandon Roy
Jerryd Bayless
F4ORMW Moses Malone 6.00 15.00
Oscar Robertson
Dominique Wilkins
Hakeem Olajuwon
F4PAGR Kevin Garnett 12.50 30.00
Ray Allen
Rajon Rondo
Paul Pierce
F4PCSP Tyson Chandler 5.00 12.00
Chris Paul
Morris Peterson
Peja Stojakovic
F4POMR Shaquille O'Neal 8.00 20.00
David Robinson
Alonzo Mourning
Hakeem Olajuwon
F4SJMG Mike Miller 4.00 10.00
Antawn Jamison
Ben Gordon
John Starks
F4SKBW Renaldo Balkman 4.00 10.00
Sonny Weems
Linas Kleiza
J.R. Smith
F4SWGH Daniel Gibson 4.00 10.00
Lorenzen Wright
J.J. Hickson
Wally Szczerbiak
F4TGSW Devean George 4.00 10.00
James Singleton
Shawne Williams
Jason Terry
F4TJFS Al Jefferson 4.00 10.00
Sebastian Telfair
Randy Foye
Craig Smith
F4TMRH Brandon Rush 4.00 10.00
Roy Hibbert
Josh McRoberts
Jamaal Tinsley
F4TYSW Julian Wright 4.00 10.00
Al Thornton
Rodney Stuckey
Thaddeus Young
F4WARF Martell Webster 5.00 12.00
Rudy Fernandez
LaMarcus Aldridge
Brandon Roy
F4WBOF Emeka Okafor 4.00 10.00
Gerald Wallace
Raja Bell
Raymond Felton
F4WGGS D.J. White 4.00 10.00
Walter Sharpe
Donte Greene
J.R. Giddens
F4WKWW D.J. White 4.00 10.00
Kyle Weaver
Russell Westbrook
Nenad Krstic
F4WMEO Jerry West 10.00 25.00
Patrick Ewing
Karl Malone
Shaquille O'Neal
F4YCSW Sean Williams 4.00 10.00
Nick Young
Javaris Crittenton
Jason Smith

2009-10 SP Game Used Logo Men

STATED PRINT RUN ONE TO 18 SER.#'d SETS
MOST UNPRICED DUE TO SCARCITY
LOGOBI Chauncey Billups/16 50.00 120.00
LOGODN Dirk Nowitzki/14 250.00 400.00
LOGOJO Jermaine O'Neal/15 50.00 120.00
LOGOKG Kevin Garnett/18 250.00 400.00
LOGOPP Paul Pierce/14 150.00 300.00

2009-10 SP Game Used Multi Marks Dual

RANDOM INSERTS IN PACKS
MDAA Andris Biedrins 8.00 20.00
Andray Blatche
MDAB Corey Brewer 10.00 25.00
Ron Artest
MDAD Al Horford 8.00 20.00
Darrell Arthur
MDAG D.J. Augustin 8.00 20.00
Eric Gordon
MDAH LaMarcus Aldridge 10.00 25.00
Al Horford
MDAN Joakim Noah 10.00 25.00
LaMarcus Aldridge
MDAT Tyson Chandler 15.00 30.00
Andrew Bynum
MDAW Spud Webb 10.00 25.00
Kenny Anderson
MDBA Josh Boone 8.00 20.00
Ryan Anderson
MDBB Corey Brewer 8.00 20.00
Bobby Brown
MDBC Mike Conley Jr. 10.00 25.00
Andrew Bynum
MDBJ Bobby Brown 10.00 25.00
Jose Barea
MDBL Brandon Bass 8.00 20.00
Robin Lopez
MDBM Tracy McGrady 20.00 40.00
Michael Beasley
MDBN Joakim Noah 10.00 25.00
Andray Blatche
MDBR Brandon Rush 8.00 20.00
Chris Bosh
MDBS Marreese Speights 8.00 20.00
Andray Blatche
MDBT Al Thornton 10.00 25.00
Andrew Bynum
MDBW Bobby Brown 8.00 20.00
Kyle Weaver
MDCA Tyson Chandler 8.00 20.00
Hilton Armstrong
MDCB Vince Carter 15.00 40.00
Michael Beasley
MDCG Artis Gilmore 8.00 20.00
Tom Chambers
MDCH Tyson Chandler 15.00 30.00
Dwight Howard
MDCM O.J. Mayo 12.00 30.00
Mike Conley Jr.
MDCT Mike Conley Jr. 8.00 20.00
Mike Taylor
MDDA Arron Afflalo 8.00 20.00
Keyon Dooling
MDDG Eric Gordon 10.00 25.00
Boris Diaw
MDDW Marvin Williams 35.00 70.00
Kevin Durant
MDDX Will Bynum 8.00 20.00
Morris Almond
MDEB Larry Bird 60.00 120.00
Julius Erving
MDEW Julius Erving 50.00 100.00
Dominique Wilkins
MDFB Rudy Fernandez 8.00 20.00
Nicolas Batum
MDGB Andrew Bogut 30.00 60.00
Kevin Garnett
MDGD Gail Goodrich 40.00 80.00
Kevin Durant
MDGL Carl Landry 8.00 20.00
Aaron Gray
MDGN Jameer Nelson 15.00 30.00
Pau Gasol
MDGP Kevin Garnett 30.00 80.00
Tony Parker
MDGR Danny Granger 15.00 40.00
Brandon Rush
MDGT Jason Thompson 8.00 20.00
Eric Gordon
MDGW Eric Gordon 20.00 50.00
Russell Westbrook
MDHG Spencer Haywood 8.00 20.00
Jeff Green
MDHM Yao Ming 20.00 50.00
Dwight Howard
MDHR Michael Redd 12.50 30.00
Jeff Hornacek
MDJB Antawn Jamison 10.00 25.00
Chris Bosh
MDJD Chris Duhon 8.00 20.00
Bobby Jackson
MDJK Kevin Love 12.50 30.00
Julian Wright
MDJM Julian Wright 8.00 20.00
Michael Beasley
MDJS DeAndre Jordan 8.00 20.00
Walter Sharpe
MDJW Mo Williams 100.00 200.00
LeBron James
MDKD Adrian Dantley 8.00 20.00
Bernard King
MDKT Jason Kidd 25.00 60.00
Isiah Thomas
MDLB Kevin Love 12.50 30.00
Corey Brewer
MDLM LeBron James 100.00 200.00
Mo Williams
MDLP Tayshaun Prince 12.50 30.00
Bob Lanier
MDLS Ramon Sessions 8.00 20.00
Acie Law
MDLW Brook Lopez 8.00 20.00
Sean Williams
MDMB O.J. Mayo 15.00 40.00
Michael Beasley
MDMD Clyde Drexler 40.00 80.00
Yao Ming
MDMH Josh McRoberts 8.00 20.00
Spencer Hawes
MDML Kevin Love 20.00 50.00
O.J. Mayo
MDMR Yao Ming 50.00 100.00
David Robinson
MDNM Yao Ming 40.00 80.00
Steve Nash
MDNS Dominique Wilkins 250.00 500.00
Michael Jordan
MDNT David West 8.00 20.00
Antawn Jamison
MDPB Corey Brewer 15.00 30.00
Tony Parker
MDPH Al Horford 12.50 30.00
Bob Pettit
MDPS Tayshaun Prince 10.00 25.00
Rodney Stuckey
MDRA D.J. Augustin 8.00 20.00
Micheal Ray Richardson
MDRB Jerryd Bayless 10.00 25.00
Brandon Roy
MDRM Derrick Rose 60.00 120.00
O.J. Mayo
MDRN Joakim Noah 25.00 50.00
Dennis Rodman
MDRS Brandon Roy 15.00 30.00
Rodney Stuckey
MDSC Damon Stoudamire 8.00 20.00
Sam Cassell
MDSN Bruce Bowen 8.00 20.00
Jerryd Bayless
MDSR Rodney Stuckey 30.00 80.00
Derrick Rose
MDSW Chet Walker 30.00 60.00
John Stockton
MDTG Al Thornton 8.00 20.00
Danilo Gallinari
MDTR Derrick Rose 30.00 80.00
Tyrus Thomas
MDVB Michael Beasley 15.00 30.00
Kiki Vandeweghe
MDVF Jordan Farmar 8.00 20.00
Sasha Vujacic
MDVP Kiki Vandeweghe 15.00 30.00
Robert Parish
MDWA Alexis Ajinca 8.00 20.00
Sean Williams
MDWB Julian Wright 8.00 20.00
Jerryd Bayless
MDWC Mike Conley Jr. 8.00 20.00
Mo Williams
MDWD Joey Dorsey 8.00 20.00
Chris Wilcox
MDWJ Darnell Jackson 8.00 20.00
Julian Wright
MDWL Brook Lopez 8.00 20.00
Shelden Williams
MDWR Mo Williams 10.00 25.00
Rajon Rondo

2009-10 SP Game Used Multi Marks Triple

STATED PRINT RUN 4 TO 100 SER.#'d SETS
SOME UNPRICED DUE TO SCARCITY
MTARB Corey Brewer/50 10.00 25.00
Brandon Roy
B.J. Armstrong
MTARC B.J. Armstrong/75 10.00 25.00
Brandon Roy
Mike Conley Jr.
MTBAT LaMarcus Aldridge/60 20.00 50.00
Al Thornton
Chris Bosh
MTBBC Mike Conley Jr./100 10.00 25.00
Corey Brewer
Bobby Brown
MTBBS Josh Boone/75 10.00 25.00
Nicolas Batum
Marreese Speights
MTBCT Mike Conley Jr./100 10.00 25.00
Mike Taylor
Corey Brewer
MTBMG Josh McRoberts/50 12.50 30.00
Chris Bosh
Danilo Gallinari
MTBNT Al Thornton/100 10.00 25.00
Josh Boone
Joakim Noah
MTBWJ DeAndre Jordan/75 10.00 25.00
Julian Wright
Renaldo Balkman
MTDLW Luol Deng/75 20.00 50.00
Courtney Lee
Russell Westbrook
MTFBA Jose Barea/75 15.00 40.00
Arron Afflalo
Randy Foye
MTFBG Bobby Brown/100 10.00 25.00
Eric Gordon
Rudy Fernandez
MTFHS Rudy Fernandez/75 10.00 25.00
Sean Singletary
J.J. Hickson
MTFNC Mike Conley Jr./100 15.00 40.00
Rudy Fernandez
Joakim Noah
MTGNW Joakim Noah/50 15.00 40.00
Rudy Gay
Julian Wright
MTGWA Julian Wright/75 10.00 25.00
Joe Alexander
Francisco Garcia
MTHAB Jeff Hornacek/14 30.00 60.00
Jerryd Bayless
Ray Allen
MTJGJ LeBron James/25 500.00 800.00
Kevin Garnett
Michael Jordan
MTJWJ LeBron James/75 100.00 200.00
Darnell Jackson
Mo Williams
MTMBH Donyell Marshall/50 10.00 25.00
Alfredo Tito Horford
Andris Biedrins
MTMHT Isiah Thomas/18 50.00 100.00
Dwight Howard
Yao Ming
MTMLW O.J. Mayo/100 50.00 120.00
Kevin Love
Russell Westbrook
MTMNW Josh McRoberts/25 15.00 30.00
Julian Wright
Joakim Noah
MTMRG Derrick Rose/75 40.00 100.00
Danilo Gallinari
Brandon Rush
MTMWH Yao Ming/40 25.00 50.00
Bill Walton
Al Horford
MTMWS Mario West/50 10.00 25.00
Josh McRoberts
Walter Sharpe
MTNBC Mike Conley Jr./100 10.00 25.00
Corey Brewer
Joakim Noah
MTNSB Jason Smith/75 10.00 25.00
Joakim Noah
Bobby Brown
MTNTB Nicolas Batum/75 10.00 25.00
Al Thornton
Joakim Noah
MTOBG Lamar Odom/75 10.00 25.00
Eric Gordon
Bobby Brown
MTOMM Yao Ming/25 75.00 150.00
Tracy McGrady
Hakeem Olajuwon
MTPBG Will Bynum/75 10.00 25.00
Morris Peterson
Jeff Green
MTRWK Pat Riley/14 30.00 80.00
George Karl
Paul Westphal
MTSCC Mario Chalmers/75 10.00 25.00
Rodney Stuckey
Mike Conley Jr.
MTWGB Jerryd Bayless/75 15.00 40.00
Eric Gordon
Spud Webb
MTWGK Marvin Williams/100 10.00 25.00
Rudy Gay
Kosta Koufos
MTWMG Josh McRoberts/50 10.00 25.00
David West
Jeff Green
MTWTC Mike Conley Jr./75 10.00 25.00
Mo Williams
Alando Tucker

2009-10 SP Game Used Multi Marks Quad

STATED PRINT RUN 5 TO 99 SER.#'d SETS
SOME UNPRICED DUE TO SCARCITY
MQBBMG Bobby Brown/25 12.00 30.00
Corey Brewer
O.J. Mayo
Danilo Gallinari
MQBBRW Bobby Brown/25 75.00 200.00
Michael Beasley
Derrick Rose
Russell Westbrook
MQBCMG Bobby Brown/25 15.00 40.00
O.J. Mayo
Mike Conley Jr.
Eric Gordon
MQBHHS Walter Sharpe/99 12.00 30.00
Darnell Jackson
Roy Hibbert
Shannon Brown
MQBLGA Danilo Gallinari/99 12.00 30.00
Bobby Brown
Brook Lopez
Alexis Ajinca
MQBRBG Bruce Bowen/50 12.00 30.00
Brandon Roy
Eric Gordon
Bobby Brown
MQBRRB Andris Biedrins/50 12.00 30.00
Anthony Randolph
Brandon Roy
Jerryd Bayless
MQCBWL Vince Carter/50 25.00 60.00
Sean Williams
Corey Brewer
Kevin Love
MQCMRB Jerryd Bayless/50 50.00 125.00
Mike Conley Jr.
O.J. Mayo
Derrick Rose
MQGBNG Joakim Noah/50 40.00 100.00
Danilo Gallinari
Chris Bosh
Kevin Garnett
MQGJNB Pau Gasol/25 125.00 250.00
Jameer Nelson
Michael Beasley
LeBron James
MQGMHB Michael Beasley/50 50.00 100.00
Al Horford
Kevin Garnett
Yao Ming
MQGTGW Daniel Gibson/50 25.00 60.00
Eric Gordon
Al Thornton
Russell Westbrook
MQHGWD Julian Wright/50 12.00 30.00
Chris Douglas-Roberts
Al Harrington
Ben Gordon
MQHJWH Kirk Hinrich/99 12.00 30.00
George Hill
Jarrett Jack
Kyle Weaver
MQHNHL Dwight Howard/50 40.00 100.00
Joakim Noah
Al Horford
Kevin Love
MQJBRW LeBron James/25 200.00 400.00
Derrick Rose
Michael Beasley
Russell Westbrook
MQJMBR Joakim Noah/50 15.00 40.00
Andray Blatche
Antawn Jamison
Anthony Randolph
MQJWWW Sean Williams/32 12.00 30.00
Shelden Williams
Antawn Jamison
Julian Wright
MQKBPW Jason Kidd/50 40.00 80.00
Chauncey Billups
Tony Parker
Deron Williams
MQMBRW Michael Beasley/50 75.00 200.00
Derrick Rose
O.J. Mayo
Russell Westbrook
MQMDMH Vlade Divac/50 30.00 60.00
Spencer Hawes
Yao Ming
Tracy McGrady
MQMDSF Walt Frazier/15 75.00 150.00
Alonzo Mourning
John Stockton
Brad Daugherty
MQMMBO Alonzo Mourning/25 75.00 200.00
Jermaine O'Neal
Yao Ming
Andrew Bynum
MQMPBR Renaldo Balkman/99 12.00 30.00
Donyell Marshall
Tayshaun Prince
Anthony Randolph
MQMSCM Rashad McCants/50 12.00 30.00
Luc Mbah a Moute
Rodney Stuckey
Mike Conley Jr.
MQNBRL Corey Brewer/50 50.00 120.00
Kevin Love
Derrick Rose
Joakim Noah
MQOCHL Dwight Howard/50 40.00 100.00
Lamar Odom
Kevin Love
Vince Carter
MQPBMG Danilo Gallinari/50 12.00 30.00
Gabe Pruitt
O.J. Mayo
Corey Brewer
MQRCMR O.J. Mayo/50 50.00 120.00
Mike Conley Jr.
Brandon Roy
Derrick Rose
MQTCMG Mike Conley Jr./50 20.00 50.00
O.J. Mayo
Al Thornton
Eric Gordon
MQTHLA Alexis Ajinca/50 12.00 30.00
Brook Lopez
Spencer Hawes
Tyrus Thomas
MQWPBB Tayshaun Prince/50 15.00 40.00
David West
Corey Brewer
Chris Bosh

2009-10 SP Game Used Retro Rookie Exclusives

STATED PRINT RUN 5 TO 300 SER.#'d SETS
SOME UNPRICED DUE TO SCARCITY
RRAE Alex English/180 8.00 20.00
RRAM Alonzo Mourning/25 60.00 120.00
RRAR B.J. Armstrong/278 10.00 25.00
RRAS Amare Stoudemire/15 25.00 50.00
RRBC Bill Cartwright/150 8.00 20.00
RRBD Brad Daugherty/300 8.00 20.00
RRBK Bernard King/250 10.00 25.00
RRBM Bob McAdoo/300 8.00 20.00
RRBP Bob Pettit/70 15.00 40.00
RRBR Brandon Roy/50 10.00 25.00
RRBS Bill Sharman/100 8.00 20.00
RRBW Bill Walton/100 10.00 25.00
RRCB Chauncey Billups/100 8.00 20.00
RRCD Clyde Drexler/25 25.00 60.00
RRCR Cazzie Russell/75 8.00 20.00
RRDH Dwight Howard/25 20.00 40.00
RRDN Don Nelson/100 12.00 30.00
RRDR Dennis Rodman/35 25.00 60.00
RRDW Dominique Wilkins/50 20.00 40.00
RREB Elgin Baylor/50 15.00 30.00
RRGG George Gervin/75 8.00 20.00
RRGO Gail Goodrich/100 8.00 20.00
RRGR Glen Rice/55 12.50 30.00
RRHG Horace Grant/50 8.00 20.00
RRHL Hal Greer/50 15.00 30.00
RRJA LeBron James/23 150.00 300.00
RRJK Jason Kidd/25 20.00 40.00
RRJO Jermaine O'Neal/60 10.00 25.00
RRJW James Worthy/25 20.00 50.00
RRKA Kareem Abdul-Jabbar/25 40.00 100.00
RRKD Kevin Durant/25 75.00 150.00
RRKG Kevin Garnett/25 25.00 60.00
RRKV Kiki Vandeweghe/170 8.00 20.00
RRLA LaMarcus Aldridge/50 10.00 25.00
RRLD Luol Deng/100 8.00 20.00
RRLJ Larry Johnson/25 30.00 60.00
RRLO Lamar Odom/100 8.00 20.00
RRMJ Michael Jordan/23 300.00 500.00
RRMP Mark Price/300 10.00 25.00
RROR Oscar Robertson/25 30.00 80.00
RRPA Tony Parker/25 15.00 30.00
RRPR Pat Riley/25 15.00 30.00
RRQR Quentin Richardson/250 8.00 20.00
RRRB Rick Barry/75 15.00 30.00
RRRG Rudy Gay/100 8.00 20.00
RRRM Rick Mahorn/80 8.00 20.00
RRRO Rolondo Blackman/165 8.00 20.00
RRSC Bill Laimbeer/260 8.00 20.00
RRTC Tom Chambers/100 8.00 20.00
RRTM Tracy McGrady/25 20.00 40.00
RRYM Yao Ming/25 20.00 40.00

2009-10 SP Game Used Rookie Exclusive Signatures

STATED PRINT RUN 100 SER.#'d SETS
READ Austin Daye 6.00 15.00
REAP A.J. Price 6.00 15.00
REBM B.J. Mullens 6.00 15.00
REBR Derrick Brown 6.00 15.00
REBU Chase Budinger 6.00 15.00
RECA DeMarre Carroll 6.00 15.00
RECU Dante Cunningham 6.00 15.00
REDC Darren Collison 10.00 25.00
REDG Danny Green 10.00 25.00
REDS DaJuan Summers 6.00 15.00
REEC Earl Clark 6.00 15.00
REEM Eric Maynor 6.00 15.00
REGH Gerald Henderson 6.00 15.00
REGR Taylor Griffin 6.00 15.00
REGS Goran Suton 6.00 15.00
REHA James Harden 20.00 50.00
REJB Jon Brockman 6.00 15.00
REJE Jonas Jerebko 8.00 20.00
REJF Jonny Flynn 6.00 15.00
REJH Jrue Holiday 12.00 30.00
REJJ James Johnson 6.00 15.00
REJM Jack McClinton 6.00 15.00
REJP Jeff Pendergraph 6.00 15.00
REJT Jeff Teague 8.00 20.00
RELH Lester Hudson 6.00 15.00
REMT Marcus Thornton 10.00 25.00
RENC Nick Calathes 6.00 15.00
REOC Omri Casspi 6.00 15.00
REPB Patrick Beverley 6.00 15.00
RERB Rodrigue Beaubois 8.00 20.00
RERR Ricky Rubio 100.00 200.00
RERV Robert Vaden 6.00 15.00
RESC Stephen Curry 15.00 40.00
RESL Sergio Llull 6.00 15.00
RESY Sam Young 6.00 15.00
RETA Jermaine Taylor 6.00 15.00
RETD Toney Douglas 6.00 15.00
RETG Taj Gibson 8.00 20.00
RETL Ty Lawson 12.00 30.00
REWE Wayne Ellington 6.00 15.00

2009-10 SP Game Used Signature Fabrics

RANDOM INSERTS IN PACKS
SFAA Arron Afflalo 4.00 10.00
SFAB Andrew Bogut 5.00 12.00
SFAJ Al Jefferson 4.00 10.00
SFAL Morris Almond 4.00 10.00
SFAM Alonzo Mourning 25.00 60.00
SFAR Anthony Randolph 5.00 12.00
SFAT Al Thornton 4.00 10.00
SFBD Boris Diaw 4.00 10.00
SFBL Brook Lopez 5.00 12.00
SFBO Bruce Bowen 5.00 12.00
SFBR Brandon Roy 15.00 30.00
SFBY Andrew Bynum 10.00 25.00
SFCB Chauncey Billups 6.00 15.00
SFCD Clyde Drexler 30.00 80.00
SFCH Chris Bosh 10.00 25.00
SFCJ C.J. Miles 4.00 10.00
SFCL Carl Landry 4.00 10.00
SFCO Corey Brewer 5.00 12.00
SFCR Javaris Crittenton 4.00 10.00
SFDC Daequan Cook 4.00 10.00
SFDE Derrick Rose 75.00 150.00
SFDG Chris Douglas-Roberts 4.00 10.00
SFDH Dwight Howard 20.00 40.00
SFDM Desmond Mason 4.00 10.00
SFDO Donyell Marshall 4.00 10.00
SFDR David Robinson 40.00 80.00
SFDS DeShawn Stevenson 5.00 12.00
SFDW Dominique Wilkins 15.00 30.00
SFEG Eric Gordon 5.00 12.00
SFGR Jeff Green 6.00 15.00
SFHA Spencer Hawes 4.00 10.00
SFJA Antawn Jamison 5.00 12.00
SFJC Javaris Crittenton 4.00 10.00
SFJD Joey Dorsey 4.00 10.00
SFJF Jordan Farmar 5.00 12.00
SFJG Jeff Green 5.00 12.00
SFJH J.J. Hickson 4.00 10.00
SFJK Jason Kidd 12.50 30.00
SFJM Javale McGee 5.00 12.00
SFJN Joakim Noah 6.00 15.00
SFJO DeAndre Jordan 6.00 15.00
SFJR J.R. Giddens 4.00 10.00
SFJS Jason Smith 4.00 10.00
SFJW Julian Wright 4.00 10.00
SFJY Jared Dudley 4.00 10.00
SFKD Kevin Durant 50.00 125.00
SFKG Kevin Garnett 40.00 100.00
SFKK Kosta Koufos 4.00 10.00
SFKL Kevin Love 20.00 50.00
SFKW Kyle Weaver 4.00 10.00
SFLB Larry Bird 50.00 125.00
SFLD Luol Deng 8.00 20.00
SFLE Courtney Lee 8.00 20.00
SFLJ LeBron James 175.00 350.00
SFLK Linas Kleiza 4.00 10.00
SFLO Lamar Odom 6.00 15.00
SFLS Luis Scola 5.00 12.00
SFMA Mario Chalmers 4.00 10.00
SFMB Michael Beasley 12.50 30.00
SFMC Mike Conley Jr. 5.00 12.00
SFMI Mike Conley Jr. 5.00 12.00
SFMJ Michael Jordan 350.00 650.00
SFMO Jamario Moon 5.00 12.00
SFMP Morris Peterson 4.00 10.00
SFMS Josh McRoberts 5.00 12.00
SFMW Marvin Williams 5.00 12.00
SFNE Donte Greene 4.00 10.00
SFNO Joakim Noah 10.00 25.00
SFPA Tony Parker 8.00 20.00
SFPG Pau Gasol 20.00 50.00
SFQR Quentin Richardson 4.00 10.00
SFRA Ron Artest 10.00 25.00
SFRB Renaldo Balkman 4.00 10.00
SFRF Rudy Fernandez 6.00 15.00
SFRG Rudy Gay 5.00 12.00
SFRJ Richard Jefferson 6.00 15.00
SFRO Dennis Rodman 25.00 60.00
SFRS Ramon Sessions 6.00 15.00
SFRU Brandon Rush 4.00 10.00
SFRW Russell Westbrook 20.00 50.00
SFSM Josh Smith 5.00 12.00
SFSW Sean Williams 4.00 10.00
SFTA Trevor Ariza 8.00 20.00
SFTM Tracy McGrady 12.50 30.00
SFTP Tayshaun Prince 5.00 12.00
SFTT Tyrus Thomas 6.00 15.00
SFTU Alando Tucker 4.00 10.00
SFVC Vince Carter 40.00 80.00
SFWI Mo Williams 12.00 30.00
SFWR Julian Wright 5.00 12.00
SFWS Walter Sharpe 4.00 10.00

2009-10 SP Game Used SIGnificance

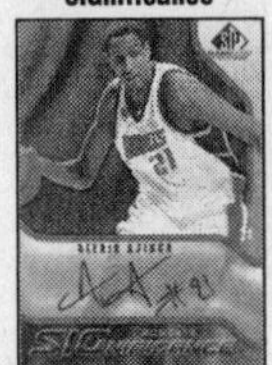

RANDOM INSERTS IN PACKS
UNPRICED GOLD PRINT RUN 10 SETS
SAA Alexis Ajinca 4.00 10.00
SAB Andrew Bogut 5.00 12.00
SAG Aaron Gray 4.00 10.00
SAJ Al Jefferson 5.00 12.00
SAL Acie Law 4.00 10.00
SAN Ryan Anderson 4.00 10.00
SAR Darrell Arthur 4.00 10.00
SAT Al Thornton 4.00 10.00
SAV Anderson Varejao 4.00 10.00
SBB Bobby Brown 4.00 10.00
SBC Corey Brewer 4.00 10.00
SBD Boris Diaw 5.00 12.00

SBJ Josh Boone 4.00 10.00
SBL Brook Lopez 5.00 12.00
SBP Bob Pettit 6.00 15.00
SBR Bobby Brown 4.00 10.00
SBU Beno Udrih 4.00 10.00
SBW Bill Walker 4.00 10.00
SBY Andrew Bynum 8.00 20.00
SCA M.L. Carr 6.00 15.00
SCB Chauncey Billups 6.00 15.00
SCD Chris Duhon 4.00 10.00
SCH Chris Bosh 6.00 15.00
SCL Carl Landry 4.00 10.00
SCM Chris Mihm 4.00 10.00
SCO Corey Brewer 4.00 10.00
SCR Caron Butler 4.00 10.00
SDA D.J. Augustin 4.00 10.00
SDC Daequan Cook 4.00 10.00
SDE DeAndre Jordan 6.00 15.00
SDG Danilo Gallinari 5.00 12.00
SDJ Darnell Jackson 4.00 10.00
SDO Joey Dorsey 4.00 10.00
SDR Derrick Rose 50.00 120.00
SDW Dominique Wilkins 12.00 30.00
SEG Eric Gordon 6.00 15.00
SGA Danilo Gallinari 4.00 10.00
SGI Artis Gilmore 6.00 15.00
SGP Gabe Pruitt 4.00 10.00
SJA Antawn Jamison 5.00 12.00
SJB Jerryd Bayless 5.00 12.00
SJC Javaris Crittenton 4.00 10.00
SJD Jared Dudley 4.00 10.00
SJF Jordan Farmar 5.00 12.00
SJG Jeff Green 5.00 12.00
SJH J.J. Hickson 4.00 10.00
SJJ Jarrett Jack 4.00 10.00
SJM Javale McGee 4.00 10.00
SJN Joakim Noah 8.00 20.00
SJO Joe Alexander 5.00 12.00
SJS Jason Smith 4.00 10.00
SJT Jason Thompson 4.00 10.00
SKD Kevin Durant 100.00 200.00
SKG Kevin Garnett 30.00 60.00
SKK Kosta Koufos 4.00 10.00
SKL Kevin Love 15.00 40.00
SKW Kyle Weaver 4.00 10.00
SLA Louis Amundson 4.00 10.00
SLD Luol Deng 6.00 15.00
SLE Courtney Lee 5.00 12.00
SLM Luc Mbah A Moute 4.00 10.00
SLO Kyle Lowry 4.00 10.00
SMA Morris Almond 4.00 10.00
SMJ Josh McRoberts 4.00 10.00
SMK Maurice Cheeks 5.00 12.00
SMS Marreese Speights 5.00 12.00
SMT Mike Taylor 4.00 10.00
SMW Mo Williams 5.00 12.00
SNO Joakim Noah 6.00 15.00
SOD Lamar Odom 5.00 12.00
SOM O.J. Mayo 8.00 20.00
SOR Oscar Robertson 75.00 150.00
SPA Tony Parker 6.00 15.00
SPM Paul Millsap 4.00 10.00
SQR Quentin Richardson 4.00 10.00
SRA Ron Artest 6.00 15.00
SRJ Richard Jefferson 5.00 12.00
SRL Robin Lopez 5.00 12.00
SRM Rashad McCants 4.00 10.00
SRS Ramon Sessions 6.00 15.00
SRU Brandon Rush 4.00 10.00
SRW Russell Westbrook 15.00 40.00
SSH Spencer Hawes 4.00 10.00
SSJ Josh Smith 5.00 12.00
SSM Jason Smith 4.00 10.00
SSS Sean Singletary 4.00 10.00
SST Rodney Stuckey 4.00 10.00
SSV Sasha Vujacic 5.00 12.00
SSW Spud Webb 5.00 12.00
STC Tom Chambers 5.00 12.00
STY Tyson Chandler 5.00 12.00
SWA Walter Sharpe 4.00 10.00
SWI Deron Williams 10.00 25.00
SWS Shelden Williams 4.00 10.00
SYM Yao Ming 10.00 25.00

2009-10 SP Game Used Six Star Swatches 65

STATED PRINT RUN 65 SER.#'d SETS
*BASE SIX STAR: .4X TO 1X BASE HI
BASE SIX STAR PRINT RUN 99 SETS

6SAGWMHM O.J. Mayo 15.00 30.00
Deron Williams
Al Horford
Carmelo Anthony
Ben Gordon
Adam Morrison
6SAIDENO Kobe Bryant 40.00 100.00
Magic Johnson
Kevin Garnett
Dwight Howard
Michael Jordan
Shaquille O'Neal
6SAJBWHO Gilbert Arenas 20.00 50.00
LeBron James
Dwyane Wade
Jermaine O'Neal
Dwight Howard
Chris Bosh
6SALLBWS Courtney Lee 8.00 20.00
Marreese Speights
Jerryd Bayless
D.J. Augustin
Brook Lopez
Kyle Weaver
6SAMNDSG Maurice Ager 8.00 20.00
Paul Millsap
Craig Smith
Daniel Gibson
Steve Novak
Shannon Brown
6SAWGGDS Joey Dorsey 8.00 20.00
J.R. Giddens
Walter Sharpe
Darrell Arthur
Donte Greene
D.J. White
6SBAGCPR Vince Carter 20.00 50.00
Tayshaun Prince
Ray Allen
Dennis Rodman
Kevin Garnett
Kobe Bryant
6SBAMMDL Courtney Lee 10.00 25.00
Shawn Marion
Ray Allen
Mike Bibby
Corey Maggette
Mike Dunleavy
6SBAMPSA Amare Stoudemire 15.00 30.00
Ray Allen
Tony Parker
Carmelo Anthony
Shawn Marion
Kobe Bryant
6SBDGIJO Kobe Bryant 25.00 50.00
Kevin Garnett
Tim Duncan
Shaquille O'Neal
LeBron James
Allen Iverson
6SBDKGWW LeBron James 20.00 50.00
Rasheed Wallace
Tim Duncan
Kevin Garnett
Kobe Bryant
Jason Kidd
6SBDNGIN Dirk Nowitzki 20.00 50.00
Kobe Bryant
Kevin Garnett
Tim Duncan
Allen Iverson
Steve Nash
6SBISHOP Shaquille O'Neal 40.00 100.00
George Gervin
Larry Bird
Michael Jordan
Magic Johnson
Dwight Howard
6SBJKAHD Bernard King 15.00 30.00
Clyde Drexler
Devin Harris
Kobe Bryant
Carmelo Anthony
Richard Jefferson
6SBLHAKH Kosta Koufos 8.00 20.00
Ryan Anderson
J.J. Hickson
Mario Chalmers
George Hill
Courtney Lee
6SBMDMFV Andrew Bynum 8.00 20.00
Channing Frye
Ike Diogu
Rashad McCants
Charlie Villanueva
Sean May
6SBNAIMI Steve Nash 15.00 40.00
Zydrunas Ilgauskas
Allen Iverson
Kobe Bryant
Stephon Marbury
Ray Allen
6SBNAMIJ Ray Allen 25.00 50.00
Kobe Bryant
Magic Johnson
Allen Iverson
Chris Paul
Steve Nash
6SBPCJHN Vince Carter 15.00 30.00
Antawn Jamison
Dirk Nowitzki
Larry Hughes
Paul Pierce
Mike Bibby
6SBPFWWW Marvin Williams 8.00 20.00
Chris Paul
Martell Webster
Deron Williams
Andrew Bogut
Raymond Felton
6SBROCKR Michael Jordan 30.00 80.00
Steve Kerr
Scottie Pippen
Magic Johnson
Vlade Divac
James Worthy
6SBSWDSB Quincy Douby 8.00 20.00
Renaldo Balkman
Shawne Williams
Cedric Simmons
Ronnie Brewer
Thabo Sefolosha
6SCBCRBG Jason Richardson 8.00 20.00
Kwame Brown
Tyson Chandler
Shane Battier
Eddy Curry
Pau Gasol
6SCBKFCS Jason Kidd 10.00 25.00
Tracy McGrady
Mike Bibby
Tyson Chandler
Marcus Camby
Stromile Swift
6SCBRKSO Andrei Kirilenko 8.00 20.00
Zach Randolph
Tyson Chandler
Peja Stojakovic
Jermaine O'Neal
Shane Battier
6SCJMGGP Ben Gordon 10.00 25.00
Manu Ginobili
Antawn Jamison
Kevin Martin
Vince Carter
Mike Miller
6SCMGMAW Marcus Camby 8.00 20.00
Ben Wallace
Alonzo Mourning
Dikembe Mutombo
Ron Artest
Kevin Garnett
6SCMSOSB Andrew Bynum 8.00 20.00
Donyell Marshall
Josh Smith
Peja Stojakovic
Emeka Okafor
Tyson Chandler
6SDACKSC D.J. Augustin 8.00 20.00
Shelden Williams
Corey Brewer
Al Horford
Chris Duhon
Kevin Durant
6SDBICMG Pau Gasol 20.00 40.00
Tim Duncan
Elton Brand
Mike Miller
Vince Carter
Allen Iverson
6SDBJBPS Tayshaun Prince 8.00 20.00
Caron Butler
Juan Dixon
Carlos Boozer
Chris Bosh
Luis Scola
6SDGMKGS Pau Gasol 12.50 30.00
Kevin Garnett
Kenyon Martin
Tim Duncan
Andrei Kirilenko
Amare Stoudemire
6SDGMNOH Mehmet Okur 10.00 25.00
Tim Duncan
Kevin Garnett
Josh Howard
Dirk Nowitzki
Tracy McGrady
6SDHCBRW Al Horford 15.00 30.00
Michael Beasley
Derrick Rose
Mike Conley Jr.
Kevin Durant
Russell Westbrook
6SDICBMC Mike Conley Jr. 10.00 25.00
Allen Iverson
Baron Davis
Steve Nash
Andre Miller
Chauncey Billups
6SDIHSHJ Tim Duncan 10.00 25.00
Dwight Howard
Amare Stoudemire
Al Jefferson
Zydrunas Ilgauskas
Brendan Haywood
6SDIMJHR Allen Iverson 15.00 40.00
LeBron James
Dwight Howard
Yao Ming
Tim Duncan
Derrick Rose
6SDKMNPM Tim Duncan 15.00 30.00
Tony Parker
Yao Ming
Tracy McGrady
Dirk Nowitzki
Jason Kidd
6SDNSAPR Dirk Nowitzki 15.00 30.00
Tim Duncan
Carmelo Anthony
Brandon Roy
Chris Paul
Amare Stoudemire
6SDSHBOM Richard Hamilton 8.00 20.00
Wally Szczerbiak
Baron Davis
Andre Miller
Elton Brand
Lamar Odom
6SDWHBGC Al Horford 8.00 20.00
Mike Conley Jr.
Corey Brewer
Brandan Wright
Kevin Durant
Jeff Green
6SEGMBJB Carlos Boozer 20.00 40.00
LeBron James
Larry Bird
George Gervin
Julius Erving
Shawn Marion
6SFACDCB Wilson Chandler 8.00 20.00
Aaron Brooks
Daequan Cook
Rudy Fernandez
Morris Almond
Jared Dudley
6SFRLBRB Josh Boone 8.00 20.00
Sergio Rodriguez
Rajon Rondo
Kyle Lowry
Jordan Farmar
Shannon Brown
6SGAALBT Eric Gordon 8.00 20.00
Joe Alexander
Jerryd Bayless
D.J. Augustin
Brook Lopez
Jason Thompson
6SGFOARS Randy Foye 8.00 20.00
Hilton Armstrong
Rudy Gay
Mouhamed Sene
J.J. Redick
Patrick O'Bryant
6SGGMBPO Chris Bosh 10.00 25.00
Yao Ming
Kevin Garnett
Pau Gasol
Jermaine O'Neal
Chris Paul
6SGWGWGR Hakim Warrick 8.00 20.00
Danny Granger
Gerald Green
Antoine Wright
Joey Graham
Nate Robinson
6SHCBJBO Joe Johnson 10.00 25.00
Chauncey Billups
Shaquille O'Neal
Vince Carter
Caron Butler
Richard Hamilton
6SHCNAGH Richard Hamilton 10.00 25.00
Gilbert Arenas
Vince Carter
Ben Gordon
Devin Harris
Dirk Nowitzki
6SHKSAPT Larry Hughes 8.00 20.00
Gabe Pruitt
Jason Thompson
Kyle Korver
Morris Almond
Robert Swift
6SJAHPGG Danny Granger 10.00 25.00
Rudy Gay
Chris Paul
LeBron James
Carmelo Anthony
Devin Harris
6SJMAKBW Chris Bosh 15.00 30.00
Carmelo Anthony
Dwyane Wade
LeBron James
Chris Kaman
Darko Milicic
6SKAJBWH LeBron James 20.00 40.00
Dwyane Wade
Ray Allen
Chris Bosh
Dwight Howard
Jason Kidd
6SKASCDY Kobe Bryant 15.00 30.00
Yao Ming
Allen Iverson
David West
Steve Nash
Carlos Boozer
6SKJEMCA Mehmet Okur 10.00 25.00
Emeka Okafor
Javale McGee
Channing Frye
Kevin Garnett
Al Horford
6SLADKAY Yao Ming 15.00 30.00
Dwight Howard
Andrea Bargnani
Kwame Brown
LeBron James
Andrew Bogut
6SLILYRO John Stockton 30.00 80.00
Karl Malone
Isiah Thomas
Magic Johnson
Michael Jordan
Scottie Pippen
6SLKJGHM Luther Head 8.00 20.00
Linas Kleiza
David Lee
Monta Ellis
Francisco Garcia
Jarrett Jack
6SLOGANO Magic Johnson 25.00 60.00
Kobe Bryant
Kevin Garnett
Derrick Rose
Michael Jordan
Russell Westbrook
6SMASONC Michael Jordan 30.00 80.00
David Robinson
Magic Johnson
Hakeem Olajuwon
Shaquille O'Neal
Karl Malone
6SMBRGLW Kevin Love 15.00 40.00
Eric Gordon
O.J. Mayo
Derrick Rose
Michael Beasley
Russell Westbrook
6SMGSADR Carmelo Anthony 12.50 30.00
David Robinson
Clyde Drexler
Kevin Garnett
Amare Stoudemire
Karl Malone
6SMGSWDN Amare Stoudemire 10.00 25.00
Mike Dunleavy
Yao Ming
Chris Wilcox
Drew Gooden
Nene
6SMJSSRN Nene 8.00 20.00
J.R. Smith
Kenyon Martin
Josh Smith
Richard Jefferson
Brandon Rush
6SMMMGEK Karl Malone 15.00 40.00
George Gervin
Alonzo Mourning
Bernard King
Patrick Ewing
Hakeem Olajuwon
6SMMMMCS Kenyon Martin 8.00 20.00
Jamal Crawford
Stromile Swift
Mike Miller
Darius Miles
Desmond Mason
6SMOWADB Kevin Durant 10.00 25.00
Darko Milicic
Emeka Okafor
LaMarcus Aldridge
Michael Beasley
Marvin Williams
6SMTMAGK Ron Artest 8.00 20.00
Shawn Marion
Jason Terry
Devean George
Corey Maggette
Andrei Kirilenko
6SNBKDBP Steve Nash 15.00 30.00
Chris Paul
Baron Davis
Jason Kidd
Mike Bibby
Chauncey Billups
6SNOAHLU Michael Jordan 50.00 125.00
Julius Erving
Kevin Garnett
Kobe Bryant
LeBron James
Kevin Durant
6SNTHMWG Richard Hamilton 10.00 25.00
Daniel Gibson
Steve Nash
Deron Williams
Jason Terry
Andre Miller
6SNTYHWL Joakim Noah 8.00 20.00
Acie Law
Thaddeus Young
Spencer Hawes
Al Thornton
Julian Wright
6SNWVUMD Kevin Martin 8.00 20.00
Beno Udrih
Dorell Wright
Jameer Nelson
Sasha Vujacic
Chris Duhon
6SOBPTCW Chris Bosh 8.00 20.00
Lamar Odom
Tyrus Thomas
Chris Paul
Mike Conley Jr.
Russell Westbrook
6SOHDGHI Emeka Okafor 10.00 25.00
Ben Gordon
Luol Deng
Andre Iguodala
Dwight Howard
Devin Harris
6SOMNJHP Hakeem Olajuwon 15.00 40.00
Tracy McGrady
Dwight Howard
Dirk Nowitzki
Robert Parish
LeBron James
6SPBMFGO Vlade Divac 20.00 40.00
Karl Malone
Shaquille O'Neal
Horace Grant
Dennis Rodman
Kobe Bryant
6SPEJBMB Paul Pierce 25.00 60.00
Larry Bird
Julius Erving
Michael Beasley
LeBron James
O.J. Mayo
6SPHJWBJ Antawn Jamison 10.00 25.00
Richard Hamilton
Rasheed Wallace
Chauncey Billups
Paul Pierce
Joe Johnson
6SPNCJRM Paul Pierce 20.00 50.00
Dirk Nowitzki
LeBron James
O.J. Mayo
Richard Jefferson
Michael Redd
6SPWSDFA Amare Stoudemire 8.00 20.00
Morris Peterson
Joe Alexander
Ben Wallace
Luol Deng
Raymond Felton
6SRAGDRL Acie Law 8.00 20.00
George Hill
DeShawn Stevenson
Richard Jefferson
Luke Ridnour
Rashad McCants
6SRHMRLS Anthony Randolph 8.00 20.00
Robin Lopez
Brandon Rush
Roy Hibbert
Javale McGee
Marreese Speights
6SRHOWHF Kirk Hinrich 8.00 20.00
Luke Walton
Josh Howard
Travis Outlaw
Luke Ridnour
T.J. Ford
6SRHSPWD Michael Redd 10.00 25.00
Deron Williams
Chris Paul
Dwight Howard
Josh Smith
Kevin Durant
6SRWJJCH Gerald Wallace 8.00 20.00
Joe Johnson
Brendan Haywood
Zach Randolph
Richard Jefferson
Jason Collins
6SSJOPRD Amare Stoudemire 20.00 40.00
LeBron James
Brandon Roy
Chris Paul
Emeka Okafor
Kevin Durant
6SSKWRGC Wally Szczerbiak 8.00 20.00
Daniel Gibson
Andrei Kirilenko
Marvin Williams
Rajon Rondo
Wilson Chandler
6SSLRADS Ron Artest 8.00 20.00
Rashard Lewis
Josh Smith
Jason Richardson
Mike Dunleavy
Wally Szczerbiak
6SSOHSBO Emeka Okafor 8.00 20.00
Stromile Swift
Josh Smith
Jermaine O'Neal
Andrew Bynum
Dwight Howard
6SSSTSJH J.R. Smith 8.00 20.00
Josh Smith
Rajon Rondo
Al Jefferson
Sebastian Telfair
Robert Swift
6STADCPO Jamaal Tinsley 8.00 20.00
Mehmet Okur
Jarron Collins
Gilbert Arenas
Samuel Dalembert
Tony Parker
6STAMBRW Tyrus Thomas 8.00 20.00
Andrea Bargnani
Adam Morrison
Brandon Roy
LaMarcus Aldridge
Shelden Williams
6STEAKKS Shaquille O'Neal 10.00 25.00
Allen Iverson
Kwame Brown
Elton Brand
Kenyon Martin
Tim Duncan
6STORGER Michael Jordan 30.00 80.00
Kareem Abdul-Jabbar
Wilt Chamberlain
Hakeem Olajuwon
Moses Malone
Karl Malone
6SWAPDTL Alando Tucker 8.00 20.00
Arron Afflalo
Carl Landry
Wilson Chandler
Gabe Pruitt
Glen Davis
6SWDJWWC Sonny Weems 8.00 20.00
Mario Chalmers
DeAndre Jordan
Brook Lopez
Chris Douglas-Roberts
Kyle Weaver
6SWHFWGL Jeff Green 10.00 25.00
Raymond Felton
Shelden Williams
Kevin Love
Dwyane Wade
Devin Harris
6SYCSSBW Jason Smith 8.00 20.00
Sean Williams
Marco Belinelli
Rodney Stuckey
Javaris Crittenton
Nick Young

2009-10 SP Game Used Triple Patch

STATED PRINT RUN 60 SER.#'d SETS

TPADD Quincy Douby 10.00 25.00
Ray Allen
Mike Dunleavy
TPAMS Peja Stojakovic 12.00 30.00
Ray Allen
Manu Ginobili
TPASG Ray Allen 12.00 30.00
Kevin Garnett
Wally Szczerbiak
TPASR Peja Stojakovic 8.00 20.00
Anthony Randolph
Ron Artest
TPAWA Ryan Anderson 8.00 20.00
Darrell Arthur
Kyle Weaver
TPAYS Nick Young 8.00 20.00
Rodney Stuckey
Nate Archibald
TPBDL Kobe Bryant 35.00 70.00
Kevin Love
Kevin Durant
TPBFC Mike Conley Jr. 8.00 20.00
Mike Bibby
Kirk Hinrich
TPBGW Aaron Gray 8.00 20.00
Andray Blatche
Brandan Wright
TPBHG Brendan Haywood 8.00 20.00
Elton Brand
Drew Gooden
TPBLM Dominic McGuire 8.00 20.00
Corey Brewer
Carl Landry
TPBMN Joakim Noah 10.00 25.00
Josh McRoberts
Kwame Brown
TPBRJ Kwame Brown 8.00 20.00
Jerome James
Malik Rose
TPBSW Shane Battier 8.00 20.00
Stromile Swift
Sean Williams
TPCCD Jarron Collins 8.00 20.00
Jason Collins
Glen Davis
TPCMB Glen Davis 8.00 20.00
Shawn Marion
Jerryd Bayless
TPCOY Tom Chambers 8.00 20.00
Travis Outlaw
Thaddeus Young
TPDAD Glen Davis 8.00 20.00
Hilton Armstrong
Ike Diogu
TPDBM Tim Duncan 15.00 40.00
Elton Brand
Alonzo Mourning
TPDCS Ricky Davis 8.00 20.00
Tyson Chandler
Thabo Sefolosha
TPDMD Chris Douglas-Roberts 8.00 20.00
Luol Deng
Adam Morrison
TPDSB Shannon Brown 8.00 20.00
Peja Stojakovic
Ricky Davis
TPDSG Peja Stojakovic 8.00 20.00
Mike Dunleavy
Manu Ginobili
TPDWA Antoine Wright 8.00 20.00
Antonio Daniels
Arron Afflalo
TPDYC Juan Dixon 8.00 20.00
Javaris Crittenton
Nick Young
TPFRT Sergio Rodriguez 8.00 20.00
Alando Tucker
Randy Foye
TPFRY Zach Randolph 8.00 20.00
Al Thornton
Thaddeus Young
TPGCN Nene 15.00 30.00
Kevin Garnett
Wilson Chandler
TPGHT Aaron Gray 8.00 20.00
Al Horford
Jason Thompson
TPGKS Mouhamed Sene 12.50 30.00
Nenad Krstic
Pau Gasol
TPGPD Glen Davis 10.00 25.00
Gabe Pruitt
Kevin Garnett
TPGRA Kevin Garnett 15.00 40.00
David Robinson
Darrell Arthur
TPGRB Zach Randolph 10.00 25.00
Andris Biedrins
Kevin Garnett
TPHAW Brandan Wright 8.00 20.00
Arron Afflalo
Brendan Haywood
TPHCY Tyson Chandler 10.00 25.00
Al Harrington
Thaddeus Young
TPHGF Rudy Fernandez 8.00 20.00
Francisco Garcia
Josh Howard
TPIAG Allen Iverson 10.00 25.00
Eric Gordon
D.J. Augustin
TPICG Allen Iverson 20.00 50.00
Daniel Gibson
Rajon Rondo
TPIMR Derrick Rose 25.00 60.00
Allen Iverson
O.J. Mayo
TPITF Allen Iverson 10.00 25.00
Sebastian Telfair
Raymond Felton
TPJLB Aaron Brooks 8.00 20.00
Acie Law
Bobby Jackson
TPJRB Brent Barry 8.00 20.00
Dirk Nowitzki
Mike Dunleavy
TPJSC Mike Dunleavy 8.00 20.00
Cedric Simmons
Daequan Cook
TPKKM Michael Beasley 25.00 50.00
Kevin Garnett
Karl Malone
TPKSN Mouhamed Sene 8.00 20.00
Nenad Krstic
Nene
TPLAR Rajon Rondo 8.00 20.0
Ron Artest
Rashard Lewis
TPLGB Kyle Lowry 8.00 20.0
J.R. Giddens
Jerryd Bayless
TPLGR Rudy Gay 10.00 25.0
Rajon Rondo
Rashard Lewis
TPLJA Rashard Lewis 8.00 20.0
Morris Almond
Richard Jefferson
TPMCT Sebastian Telfair 8.00 20.0
Tyson Chandler
Shawn Marion
TPMCY Shawn Marion 8.00 20.0
Thaddeus Young
Tyson Chandler
TPMGB Corey Brewer 8.00 20.0
Devean George
Desmond Mason
TPMGF Kevin Garnett 20.00 50.0
Willis Reed
Karl Malone
TPMGK Karl Malone 20.00 40.0
Bernard King
Kevin Garnett
TPMJG LeBron James 25.00 60.0
Rudy Gay
Kevin Garnett
TPMMM Karl Malone 20.00 50.0
Patrick Ewing
Dikembe Mutombo
TPMMS J.R. Smith 8.00 20.0
Richard Jefferson
Desmond Mason
TPMNG Jeff Green 8.00 20.0
Josh McRoberts
Joakim Noah
TPMRH Derrick Rose 25.00 50.0
George Hill
O.J. Mayo
TPMRW Corey Maggette 10.00 25.0
Dwyane Wade
Quentin Richardson
TPMWW Brad Miller 8.00 20.0
Brandan Wright
Sean Williams
TPNFT Kirk Hinrich 8.00 20.0
Sebastian Telfair
Steve Nash
TPNGD Steve Nash 15.00 40.0
Kevin Garnett
Kevin Durant
TPOWD Glen Davis 8.00 20.0
Shelden Williams
Mehmet Okur
TPPFF Jordan Farmar 8.00 20.0
Shannon Brown
Trevor Ariza
TPPSW Julian Wright 8.00 20.0
Jason Smith
Johan Petro
TPRAW Jason Richardson 8.00 20.0
Julian Wright
LaMarcus Aldridge
TPRDS Juan Dixon 8.00 20.0
Jason Richardson
J.R. Smith
TPRGB J.R. Giddens 8.00 20.0
Anthony Randolph
Jerryd Bayless
TPSAY Nick Young 8.00 20.0
Peja Stojakovic
Morris Almond
TPSDG Glen Davis 8.00 20.0
Jason Smith
Jeff Green
TPSIA LaMarcus Aldridge 8.00 20.0
Wally Szczerbiak
Zydrunas Ilgauskas
TPSRD Michael Redd 8.00 20.0
Mike Dunleavy
Wally Szczerbiak
TPSSW Wally Szczerbiak 8.00 20.0
Peja Stojakovic
Shawne Williams
TPSWB Corey Brewer 8.00 20.0
DeShawn Stevenson
Delonte West
TPSYC Wally Szczerbiak 8.00 20.0
Thaddeus Young
Wilson Chandler
TPSYW Thaddeus Young 8.00 20.0
Stromile Swift
Sean Williams
TPTFD Jared Dudley 8.00 20.0
Jamaal Tinsley
Jordan Farmar
TPTNS Jameer Nelson 8.00 20.0
Jamaal Tinsley
James Singleton
TPVSG Charlie Villanueva 8.00 20.0
Cedric Simmons
J.R. Giddens
TPWAJ Joey Dorsey 8.00 20.0
Anthony Randolph
Wally Szczerbiak
TPWAT Arron Afflalo 8.00 20.0
Mike Conley Jr.
Alando Tucker
TPWMD Rasheed Wallace 8.00 20.0
Al Thornton
Sean May
TPWRW Bill Walton 20.00 50.0
Karl Malone
Dennis Rodman
TPYHS Al Horford 8.00 20.0
Thaddeus Young
Walter Sharpe

2007-08 SP Rookie Edition

Released in March 2008, SP Rookie Edition boasts a 210-card set where cards 1-60 feature veteran players on a horizontal design with black borders and gold fo

lights, cards 61-104 feature rookie players on a
ilar design, cards 105-120 feature rookie players
cards which employ the design of the 1996-97 SP
cards 121-150 feature rookie players on cards
ch employ the design of the 1997-98 SP Authentic
cards 151-180 feature rookie players on cards
ch employ the design of the 1994-95 SP rookie foil
and cards 181-210 feature a mix of retired legends,
eran players and rookies on cards which frame a
or portrait style photo against a white background.
Rookie Edition is packaged in 14-pack boxes of
it cards each and carried an intial SRP of $4.99 per
k.

Card	Low	High
ndre Iguodala	.50	1.25
ndre Miller	.40	1.00
erald Wallace	.50	1.25
ason Richardson	.50	1.25
ndrew Bogut	.50	1.25
lichael Redd	.50	1.25
en Gordon	.50	1.25
en Wallace	.50	1.25
eBron James	2.50	6.00
Larry Hughes	.40	1.00
Paul Pierce	.60	1.50
Ray Allen	.50	1.25
Elton Brand	.50	1.25
Pau Gasol	.50	1.25
Kyle Lowry	.50	1.25
Joe Johnson	.50	1.25
Josh Smith	.50	1.25
Dwyane Wade	1.25	3.00
Shaquille O'Neal	1.00	2.50
Chris Paul	1.00	2.50
Morris Peterson	.30	.75
Carlos Boozer	.50	1.25
Michael Jordan	4.00	10.00
Deron Williams	.75	2.00
Mehmet Okur	.30	.75
Ron Artest	.50	1.25
Mike Bibby	.50	1.25
Eddy Curry	.30	.75
Zach Randolph	.40	1.00
Kobe Bryant	2.50	6.00
Lamar Odom	.50	1.25
Dwight Howard	.75	2.00
Rashard Lewis	.40	1.00
Dirk Nowitzki	.60	1.50
Josh Howard	.40	1.00
Jason Kidd	.50	1.25
Vince Carter	.60	1.50
Allen Iverson	.60	1.50
Carmelo Anthony	.60	1.50
Jermaine O'Neal	.50	1.25
Tayshaun Prince	.50	1.25
Chauncey Billups	.50	1.25
Richard Hamilton	.40	1.00
T.J. Ford	.40	1.00
Chris Bosh	.50	1.25
Tracy McGrady	.50	1.25
Yao Ming	.60	1.50
Tim Duncan	.75	2.00
Tony Parker	.50	1.25
Amare Stoudemire	.50	1.25
Shawn Marion	.50	1.25
Steve Nash	.60	1.50
Chris Wilcox	.30	.75
Kevin Garnett	1.00	2.50
Brandon Roy	.60	1.50
LaMarcus Aldridge	.60	1.50
Baron Davis	.50	1.25
Caron Butler	.50	1.25
Gilbert Arenas	.50	1.25
Antawn Jamison	.50	1.25
Kevin Durant RC	5.00	12.00
2 Al Horford RC	.75	2.00
3 Mike Conley Jr. RC	1.00	2.50
Jeff Green RC	.75	2.00
Corey Brewer RC	.75	2.00
Joakim Noah RC	1.50	4.00
Spencer Hawes RC	.60	1.50
Acie Law RC	.60	1.50
Julian Wright RC	.60	1.50
Al Thornton RC	.60	1.50
Rodney Stuckey RC	1.00	2.50
2 Sean Williams RC	.60	1.50
3 Marco Belinelli RC	.60	1.50
Javaris Crittenton RC	.60	1.50
Jason Smith RC	.60	1.50
Daequan Cook RC	.60	1.50
Jared Dudley RC	.60	1.50
Wilson Chandler RC	1.00	2.50
Morris Almond RC	.60	1.50
Aaron Brooks RC	.60	1.50
Arron Afflalo RC	.75	2.00
2 Alando Tucker RC	.60	1.50
3 Carl Landry RC	.60	1.50
4 Gabe Pruitt RC	.60	1.50
5 Juan Carlos Navarro RC	.60	1.50
6 Yi Jianlian RC	1.00	2.50
7 Glen Davis RC	1.00	2.50
8 Jermareo Davidson RC	.60	1.50
9 Thaddeus Young RC	.75	2.00
0 Brandan Wright RC	.60	1.50
1 Luis Scola RC	1.00	2.50
2 Chris Richard RC	.60	1.50
3 Adam Haluska RC	.60	1.50
4 D.J. Strawberry RC	.60	1.50
5 Darryl Watkins RC	.60	1.50
6 Cheikh Samb RC	.60	1.50
7 Greg Oden RC	.75	2.00
8 Aaron Gray RC	.60	1.50
9 JamesOn Curry RC	.60	1.50
00 Taurean Green RC	.60	1.50
01 Demetris Nichols RC	.60	1.50
02 Nick Young RC	1.00	2.50
03 Ramon Sessions RC	1.00	2.50
04 Coby Karl RC	.60	1.50
05 Jason Smith 96-97	1.00	2.50
06 Kevin Durant 96-97	8.00	20.00
07 Al Horford 96-97	1.25	3.00
08 Mike Conley Jr. 96-97	1.50	4.00
09 Jeff Green 96-97	1.25	3.00
10 Corey Brewer 96-97	1.25	3.00
11 Joakim Noah 96-97	2.50	6.00
12 Spencer Hawes 96-97	1.00	2.50
13 Acie Law 96-97	1.00	2.50
14 Julian Wright 96-97	1.00	2.50
15 Al Thornton 96-97	1.00	2.50
16 Rodney Stuckey 96-97	1.50	4.00
17 Sean Williams 96-97	1.00	2.50
18 Marco Belinelli 96-97	1.00	2.50
19 Javaris Crittenton 96-97	1.00	2.50
20 Jason Smith 96-97	1.00	2.50
121 Kevin Durant 97-98	12.00	30.00
122 Al Horford 97-98	2.00	5.00
123 Mike Conley Jr. 97-98	2.50	6.00
124 Jeff Green 97-98	2.00	5.00
125 Corey Brewer 97-98	2.00	5.00
126 Joakim Noah 97-98	4.00	10.00
127 Spencer Hawes 97-98	1.50	4.00
128 Acie Law 97-98	1.50	4.00
129 Julian Wright 97-98	1.50	4.00
130 Al Thornton 97-98	1.50	4.00
131 Rodney Stuckey 97-98	2.50	6.00
132 Sean Williams 97-98	1.50	4.00
133 Marco Belinelli 97-98	1.50	4.00
134 Javaris Crittenton 97-98	1.50	4.00
135 Jason Smith 97-98	1.50	4.00
136 Daequan Cook 97-98	1.50	4.00
137 Jared Dudley 97-98	1.50	4.00
138 Wilson Chandler 97-98	2.50	6.00
139 Brandan Wright 97-98	1.50	4.00
140 Aaron Brooks 97-98	1.50	4.00
141 Alando Tucker 97-98	1.50	4.00
142 Carl Landry 97-98	1.50	4.00
143 Gabe Pruitt 97-98	1.50	4.00
144 D.J. Strawberry 97-98	1.50	4.00
145 Yi Jianlian 97-98	2.50	6.00
146 Glen Davis 97-98	2.50	6.00
147 Greg Oden 97-98	2.00	5.00
148 Aaron Gray 97-98	1.50	4.00
149 Taurean Green 97-98	1.50	4.00
150 D.J. Strawberry 97-98	1.50	4.00
151 Kevin Durant 94-95	12.00	30.00
152 Al Horford 94-95	2.00	5.00
153 Mike Conley Jr. 94-95	2.50	6.00
154 Jeff Green 94-95	2.00	5.00
155 Corey Brewer 94-95	2.00	5.00
156 Joakim Noah 94-95	4.00	10.00
157 Spencer Hawes 94-95	1.50	4.00
158 Acie Law 94-95	1.50	4.00
159 Julian Wright 94-95	1.50	4.00
160 Al Thornton 94-95	1.50	4.00
161 Rodney Stuckey 94-95	2.50	6.00
162 Sean Williams 94-95	1.50	4.00
163 Marco Belinelli 94-95	1.50	4.00
164 Javaris Crittenton 94-95	1.50	4.00
165 Jason Smith 94-95	1.50	4.00
166 Daequan Cook 94-95	1.50	4.00
167 Jared Dudley 94-95	1.50	4.00
168 Wilson Chandler 94-95	2.50	6.00
169 Morris Almond 94-95	1.50	4.00
170 Aaron Brooks 94-95	1.50	4.00
171 Arron Afflalo 94-95	2.00	5.00
172 Alando Tucker 94-95	1.50	4.00
173 Carl Landry 94-95	1.50	4.00
174 Gabe Pruitt 94-95	1.50	4.00
175 Darius Washington 94-95	1.50	4.00
176 Oleksiy Pecherov 94-95	1.50	4.00
177 Luis Scola 94-95	2.50	6.00
178 Greg Oden 94-95	2.00	5.00
179 Dominique Wilkins 94-95	2.00	5.00
180 Yi Jianlian 94-95	2.50	6.00
181 Carmelo Anthony 98-99	2.00	5.00
182 B.J. Armstrong 98-99	1.50	4.00
183 Larry Bird 98-99	5.00	12.00
184 Steve Novak 98-99	1.00	2.50
185 Kobe Bryant 98-99	8.00	20.00
186 Vince Carter 98-99	2.00	5.00
187 Tom Chambers 98-99	1.50	4.00
188 Baron Davis 98-99	1.50	4.00
189 Boris Diaw 98-99	1.25	3.00
190 Hilton Armstrong 98-99	1.00	2.50
191 Hal Greer 98-99	1.50	4.00
192 Keyon Dooling 98-99	1.00	2.50
193 LeBron James 98-99	8.00	20.00
194 Antawn Jamison 98-99	1.50	4.00
195 Magic Johnson 98-99	4.00	10.00
196 Michael Jordan 98-99	12.00	30.00
197 Danny Manning 98-99	1.50	4.00
198 Tracy McGrady 98-99	1.50	4.00
199 Chris Mihm 98-99	.60	1.50
200 Yao Ming 98-99	2.00	5.00
201 Steve Nash 98-99	2.00	5.00
202 Hakeem Olajuwon 98-99	2.00	5.00
203 Tony Parker 98-99	1.50	4.00
204 Paul Pierce 98-99	2.00	5.00
205 Quentin Richardson 98-99	1.25	3.00
206 Dennis Rodman 98-99	2.50	6.00
207 DeShawn Stevenson 98-99	1.00	2.50
208 John Stockton 98-99	2.50	6.00
209 Shelden Williams 98-99	1.00	2.50
210 Dominique Wilkins 98-99	2.00	5.00

2007-08 SP Rookie Edition 1994-95 SP Rookie Autographs

OVERALL AUTO ODDS 1:7

Card	Low	High
151 Kevin Durant	100.00	200.00
152 Al Horford	6.00	15.00
153 Mike Conley Jr.	8.00	20.00
154 Jeff Green	6.00	15.00
155 Corey Brewer	6.00	15.00
156 Joakim Noah	12.00	30.00
157 Spencer Hawes	5.00	12.00
158 Acie Law	5.00	12.00
159 Julian Wright	5.00	12.00
160 Al Thornton	5.00	12.00
161 Rodney Stuckey	8.00	20.00
162 Sean Williams	5.00	12.00
163 Marco Belinelli	5.00	12.00
164 Javaris Crittenton	5.00	12.00
165 Jason Smith	5.00	12.00
166 Daequan Cook	5.00	12.00
167 Jared Dudley	5.00	12.00
168 Wilson Chandler	8.00	20.00
169 Morris Almond	5.00	12.00
170 Aaron Brooks	5.00	12.00
171 Arron Afflalo	6.00	15.00
172 Alando Tucker	5.00	12.00
173 Carl Landry	5.00	12.00
174 Gabe Pruitt	5.00	12.00
175 Ramon Sessions	8.00	20.00
176 Oleksiy Pecherov	5.00	12.00
179 Ramon Sessions	8.00	20.00

2007-08 SP Rookie Edition 1996-97 SP Rookie Autographs

OVERALL AUTO ODDS 1:7

Card	Low	High
106 Kevin Durant	100.00	200.00
107 Al Horford	6.00	15.00
108 Mike Conley Jr.	8.00	20.00
109 Jeff Green	6.00	15.00
110 Corey Brewer	6.00	15.00
111 Joakim Noah	12.00	30.00
112 Spencer Hawes	5.00	12.00
113 Acie Law	5.00	12.00
114 Julian Wright	5.00	12.00
115 Al Thornton	5.00	12.00
116 Rodney Stuckey	8.00	20.00
117 Sean Williams	5.00	12.00
118 Marco Belinelli	5.00	12.00
119 Javaris Crittenton	5.00	12.00
120 Jason Smith	5.00	12.00

2007-08 SP Rookie Edition 1997-98 SP Rookie Autographs

OVERALL AUTO ODDS 1:7

Card	Low	High
121 Kevin Durant	100.00	200.00
122 Al Horford	6.00	15.00
123 Mike Conley Jr.	8.00	20.00
124 Jeff Green	6.00	15.00
125 Corey Brewer	6.00	15.00
126 Joakim Noah	12.00	30.00
127 Spencer Hawes	5.00	12.00
128 Acie Law	5.00	12.00
129 Julian Wright	5.00	12.00
130 Al Thornton	5.00	12.00
131 Rodney Stuckey	8.00	20.00
132 Sean Williams	5.00	12.00
133 Marco Belinelli	5.00	12.00
134 Javaris Crittenton	5.00	12.00
135 Jason Smith	5.00	12.00
136 Daequan Cook	5.00	12.00
137 Jared Dudley	5.00	12.00
138 Wilson Chandler	8.00	20.00
140 Aaron Brooks	5.00	12.00
141 Alando Tucker	5.00	12.00
142 Carl Landry	5.00	12.00
143 Gabe Pruitt	5.00	12.00
146 Glen Davis	8.00	20.00
148 Aaron Gray	5.00	12.00
149 Taurean Green	5.00	12.00
144 D.J. Strawberry	5.00	12.00

2007-08 SP Rookie Edition 1998-99 SP Autographs

OVERALL AUTO ODDS 1:7

Card	Low	High
181 Carmelo Anthony	20.00	50.00
182 B.J. Armstrong	6.00	15.00
183 Larry Bird	40.00	80.00
184 Steve Novak	5.00	12.00
185 Kobe Bryant	80.00	160.00
186 Vince Carter	20.00	40.00
187 Tom Chambers	5.00	12.00
188 Baron Davis	6.00	15.00
189 Boris Diaw	5.00	12.00
190 Hilton Armstrong	5.00	12.00
191 Hal Greer	6.00	15.00
193 LeBron James	150.00	300.00
194 Antawn Jamison	6.00	15.00
195 Magic Johnson	40.00	80.00
196 Michael Jordan	500.00	700.00
197 Danny Manning	8.00	20.00
198 Tracy McGrady	15.00	30.00
199 Chris Mihm	5.00	12.00
200 Yao Ming	15.00	40.00
201 Steve Nash	40.00	80.00
202 Hakeem Olajuwon	20.00	50.00
203 Tony Parker	12.50	25.00
204 Paul Pierce	12.50	25.00
205 Quentin Richardson	5.00	12.00
206 Dennis Rodman	25.00	60.00
207 DeShawn Stevenson	5.00	12.00
208 John Stockton	50.00	100.00
209 Shelden Williams	5.00	12.00

2007-08 SP Rookie Edition Rookie Autographs

OVERALL AUTO ODDS 1:7

Card	Low	High
61 Kevin Durant	100.00	200.00
62 Al Horford	6.00	15.00
63 Mike Conley Jr.	8.00	20.00
64 Jeff Green	6.00	15.00
65 Corey Brewer	6.00	15.00
66 Joakim Noah	12.00	30.00
67 Spencer Hawes	5.00	12.00
68 Acie Law	5.00	12.00
69 Julian Wright	5.00	12.00
70 Al Thornton	5.00	12.00
71 Rodney Stuckey	8.00	20.00
72 Sean Williams	5.00	12.00
73 Marco Belinelli	5.00	12.00
74 Javaris Crittenton	5.00	12.00
75 Jason Smith	5.00	12.00
76 Daequan Cook	5.00	12.00
77 Jared Dudley	5.00	12.00
78 Wilson Chandler	8.00	20.00
79 Morris Almond	5.00	12.00
80 Aaron Brooks	5.00	12.00
81 Arron Afflalo	6.00	15.00
82 Alando Tucker	5.00	12.00
83 Carl Landry	5.00	12.00
84 Gabe Pruitt	5.00	12.00
85 Juan Navarro	5.00	12.00
87 Glen Davis	8.00	20.00
88 Jermareo Davidson	5.00	12.00
92 Chris Richard	5.00	12.00
93 Adam Haluska	5.00	12.00
94 D.J. Strawberry	5.00	12.00
96 Cheikh Samb	5.00	12.00
98 Aaron Gray	5.00	12.00
99 JamesOn Curry	5.00	12.00
100 Taurean Green	5.00	12.00
101 Demetris Nichols	5.00	12.00
103 Ramon Sessions	8.00	20.00
104 Coby Karl	5.00	12.00
105 D.J. Strawberry	5.00	12.00

2007-08 SP Rookie Edition SP Limited Jerseys

RANDOM INSERTS IN PACKS

Card	Low	High
SPAB Andrea Bargnani	3.00	8.00
SPAH Al Horford	3.00	8.00
SPAJ Antawn Jamison	2.50	6.00
SPAL Acie Law	2.50	6.00
SPAS Amare Stoudemire	2.50	6.00
SPAT Al Thornton	2.50	6.00
SPBI Chauncey Billups	2.50	6.00
SPBO Chris Bosh	2.50	6.00
SPBW Brandan Wright	2.50	6.00
SPCA Carmelo Anthony	3.00	8.00
SPCB Corey Brewer	3.00	8.00
SPCP Chris Paul	5.00	12.00
SPDC Daequan Cook	2.50	6.00
SPDH Dwight Howard	4.00	10.00
SPDW Deron Williams	4.00	10.00
SPEO Emeka Okafor	2.50	6.00
SPGD Glen Davis	4.00	10.00
SPJC Javaris Crittenton	2.50	6.00
SPJD Jared Dudley	2.50	6.00
SPJG Jeff Green	3.00	8.00
SPJN Joakim Noah	6.00	15.00
SPJS Jason Smith	2.50	6.00
SPJW Julian Wright	2.50	6.00
SPKB Kobe Bryant	8.00	20.00
SPKD Kevin Durant	15.00	40.00
SPKG Kevin Garnett	5.00	12.00
SPLA LaMarcus Aldridge	3.00	8.00
SPLJ LeBron James	8.00	20.00
SPMC Mike Conley Jr.	4.00	10.00
SPNY Nick Young	4.00	10.00
SPRG Rudy Gay	2.50	6.00
SPRS Rodney Stuckey	4.00	10.00
SPSH Spencer Hawes	2.50	6.00
SPSO Shaquille O'Neal	5.00	12.00
SPSW Sean Williams	2.50	6.00
SPTD Tim Duncan	4.00	10.00
SPTM Tracy McGrady	2.50	6.00
SPTP Tayshaun Prince	2.50	6.00
SPTT Tyrus Thomas	2.50	6.00
SPTY Thaddeus Young	3.00	8.00
SPVC Vince Carter	3.00	8.00
SPYM Yao Ming	3.00	8.00

2007-08 SP Rookie Threads

Released in April 2008, SP Rookie Threads boasts an 83-card base set where cards 1-42 feature veterans, cards 43-48 feature rookies serially numbered to 199, cards 49-60 feature rookies with autographs sequentially numbered to 199 and cards 61-83 feature rookies with autographs sequentially numbered to 799. SP Rookie Threads is packaged in six-pack boxes where packs contain five cards and carried an initial SRP of $50 per pack.

Card	Low	High
COMP.SET w/o SP's (42)	20.00	40.00
1 Allen Iverson	.60	1.50
2 Amare Stoudemire	.50	1.25
3 Andre Iguodala	.50	1.25
4 Andrea Bargnani	.60	1.50
5 Baron Davis	.50	1.25
6 Ben Gordon	.50	1.25
7 Brandon Roy	.60	1.50
8 Carmelo Anthony	.60	1.50
9 Chauncey Billups	.50	1.25
10 Chris Bosh	.50	1.25
11 Chris Paul	1.00	2.50
12 David Lee	.40	1.00
13 Deron Williams	.75	2.00
14 Dirk Nowitzki	.60	1.50
15 Dwight Howard	.75	2.00
16 Dwyane Wade	1.25	3.00
17 Elton Brand	.50	1.25
18 Emeka Okafor	.50	1.25
19 Gilbert Arenas	.50	1.25
20 Jason Kidd	.50	1.25
21 Jermaine O'Neal	.50	1.25
22 Kevin Garnett	1.00	2.50
23 Kirk Hinrich	.50	1.25
24 Kobe Bryant	2.50	6.00
25 LaMarcus Aldridge	.60	1.50
26 LeBron James	2.50	6.00
27 Luke Ridnour	.40	1.00
28 Marvin Williams	.50	1.25
29 Michael Jordan	4.00	10.00
30 Michael Redd	.50	1.25
31 Mike Bibby	.50	1.25
32 Paul Pierce	.60	1.50
33 Randy Foye	.50	1.25
34 Rudy Gay	.50	1.25
35 Shaquille O'Neal	1.00	2.50
36 Stephon Marbury	.40	1.00
37 Steve Nash	.60	1.50
38 Tim Duncan	.75	2.00
39 Tony Parker	.50	1.25
40 Tracy McGrady	.50	1.25
41 Vince Carter	.60	1.50
42 Yao Ming	.60	1.50
43 Greg Oden RC	3.00	8.00
44 Yi Jianlian RC	4.00	10.00
45 Brandan Wright RC	2.50	6.00
46 Thaddeus Young RC	3.00	8.00
47 Nick Young RC	4.00	10.00
48 Juan Carlos Navarro RC	2.50	6.00
49 Kevin Durant JSY AU RC	250.00	450.00
50 Al Horford JSY AU RC	10.00	25.00
51 Mike Conley Jr. JSY AU RC	12.00	30.00
52 Jeff Green JSY AU RC	10.00	25.00
53 Corey Brewer JSY AU RC	10.00	25.00
54 Joakim Noah JSY AU RC	20.00	50.00
55 Spencer Hawes JSY AU RC	8.00	20.00
56 Acie Law JSY AU RC	8.00	20.00
57 Julian Wright JSY AU RC	8.00	20.00
58 Al Thornton JSY AU RC	8.00	20.00
59 Rodney Stuckey JSY AU RC	12.00	30.00
60 Jason Smith JSY AU RC	8.00	20.00
61 Taurean Green JSY AU RC	4.00	10.00
62 Javaris Crittenton JSY AU RC	4.00	10.00
63 Sean Williams JSY AU RC	4.00	10.00
64 Daequan Cook JSY AU RC	4.00	10.00
65 Jared Dudley JSY AU RC	4.00	10.00
66 Wilson Chandler JSY AU RC	6.00	15.00
67 Morris Almond JSY AU RC	4.00	10.00
68 Aaron Brooks JSY AU RC	4.00	10.00
69 Arron Afflalo JSY AU RC	5.00	12.00
70 Alando Tucker JSY AU RC	4.00	10.00
71 Aaron Gray JSY AU RC	4.00	10.00
72 Carl Landry JSY AU RC	4.00	10.00
73 Gabe Pruitt JSY AU RC	4.00	10.00
74 Nick Fazekas JSY AU RC	4.00	10.00
75 Adam Haluska JSY AU RC	4.00	10.00
76 Glen Davis JSY AU RC	6.00	15.00
77 Josh McRoberts JSY AU RC	4.00	10.00
78 Herbert Hill JSY AU RC	4.00	10.00
79 Jermareo Davidson JSY AU RC	4.00	10.00
80 Chris Richard JSY AU RC	4.00	10.00
81 Dominic McGuire JSY AU RC	4.00	10.00
83 Demetris Nichols JSY AU RC	4.00	10.00
84 D.J. Strawberry JSY AU RC	4.00	10.00

2007-08 SP Rookie Threads Maximum Threads

PRINT RUN 25 SER.#'d SETS

Card	Low	High
MTBG Ben Gordon	6.00	15.00
MTCA Carmelo Anthony	8.00	20.00
MTCB Chris Bosh	6.00	15.00
MTDH Dwight Howard	10.00	25.00
MTDN Dirk Nowitzki	10.00	25.00
MTDR David Robinson	15.00	30.00
MTDW Deron Williams	10.00	25.00
MTHO Hakeem Olajuwon	8.00	20.00
MTJS John Stockton	10.00	25.00
MTKA Kareem Abdul-Jabbar	10.00	25.00
MTKB Kobe Bryant	20.00	50.00
MTKG Kevin Garnett	12.00	30.00
MTLA LaMarcus Aldridge	8.00	20.00
MTLB Larry Bird	20.00	50.00
MTSO Shaquille O'Neal	12.00	30.00
MTTM Tracy McGrady	6.00	15.00
MTTT Tyrus Thomas	6.00	15.00
MTVC Vince Carter	8.00	20.00
MTYM Yao Ming	8.00	20.00

2007-08 SP Rookie Threads Portraits Autographs

STATED COMBINED AUTO ODDS 1:1.2

Card	Low	High
POAJ Al Jefferson	5.00	12.00
POBG Ben Gordon	5.00	12.00
POCA Carmelo Anthony	15.00	30.00
PODR David Robinson	25.00	60.00
POHO Hakeem Olajuwon	15.00	30.00
POJE Julius Erving	25.00	60.00
POJO Michael Jordan	200.00	350.00
POKB Kobe Bryant	75.00	150.00
POLB Larry Bird	40.00	80.00
POLJ LeBron James	100.00	200.00
POMB Mike Bibby	5.00	12.00
POMJ Magic Johnson	40.00	80.00
POSN Steve Nash	25.00	60.00
POTP Tayshaun Prince	6.00	15.00
POVC Vince Carter	12.00	30.00

2007-08 SP Rookie Threads Rookie Threads

ONE MEMORABILIA CARD PER PACK
*PARALLEL: .5X TO 1.25X BASE HI
PRINT RUN 199 SER.#'d SETS

Card	Low	High
RTAA Arron Afflalo	3.00	8.00
RTAB Aaron Brooks	2.50	6.00
RTAG Aaron Gray	2.50	6.00
RTAH Al Horford	3.00	8.00
RTAL Acie Law	2.50	6.00
RTAT Al Thornton	2.50	6.00
RTBW Brandan Wright	2.50	6.00
RTCB Corey Brewer	3.00	8.00
RTCL Carl Landry	2.50	6.00
RTCR Chris Richard	2.50	6.00
RTDA Jermareo Davidson	2.50	6.00
RTDC Daequan Cook	2.50	6.00
RTDM Dominic McGuire	2.50	6.00
RTDN Demetris Nichols	2.50	6.00
RTDS D.J. Strawberry	2.50	6.00
RTGD Glen Davis	4.00	10.00
RTGP Gabe Pruitt	2.50	6.00
RTHA Adam Haluska	2.50	6.00
RTHH Herbert Hill	2.50	6.00
RTJC Javaris Crittenton	2.50	6.00
RTJD Jared Dudley	2.50	6.00
RTJG Jeff Green	3.00	8.00
RTJM Josh McRoberts	2.50	6.00
RTJN Joakim Noah	6.00	15.00
RTJS Jason Smith	2.50	6.00
RTJW Julian Wright	2.50	6.00
RTKD Kevin Durant	12.00	30.00
RTMA Morris Almond	2.50	6.00
RTMC Mike Conley Jr.	4.00	10.00
RTNF Nick Fazekas	2.50	6.00
RTNY Nick Young	4.00	10.00
RTRS Rodney Stuckey	4.00	10.00
RTSH Spencer Hawes	2.50	6.00
RTSW Sean Williams	2.50	6.00
RTTG Taurean Green	2.50	6.00
RTTU Alando Tucker	2.50	6.00
RTTY Thaddeus Young	3.00	8.00
RTWC Wilson Chandler	4.00	10.00

2007-08 SP Rookie Threads Rookie Threads Patch

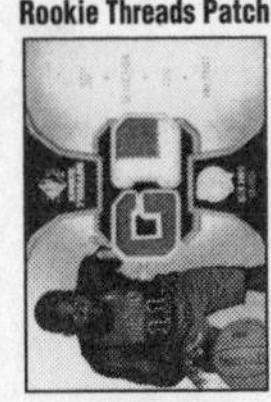

*PATCH: .6X TO 1.5X BASE HI
PATCH PRINT RUN 50 SER.#'d SETS

Card	Low	High
RTKD Kevin Durant	40.00	80.00

2007-08 SP Rookie Threads Rookie Threads Dual

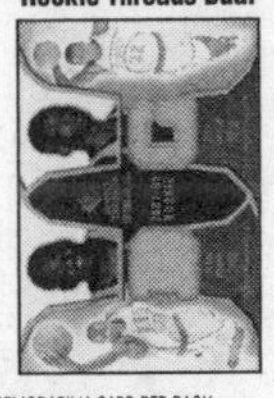

ONE MEMORABILIA CARD PER PACK
*PARALLEL: .5X TO 1.25X BASE HI
PARALLEL PRINT RUN 99 SER.#'d SETS

Card	Low	High
AS Morris Almond	3.00	8.00
Rodney Stuckey		
BR Corey Brewer	3.00	8.00
Chris Richard		
CC Mike Conley Jr.	3.00	8.00
Daequan Cook		
DG Kevin Durant	6.00	15.00
Jeff Green		
DH Kevin Durant	6.00	15.00
Al Horford		
HB Al Horford	3.00	8.00
Corey Brewer		
HL Al Horford	3.00	8.00
Acie Law		
LB Aaron Brooks	3.00	8.00
Carl Landry		
MD Glen Davis	4.00	10.00
Josh McRoberts		
NB Corey Brewer	4.00	10.00
Joakim Noah		
NC Wilson Chandler	3.00	8.00
Demetris Nichols		
SA Arron Afflalo	4.00	10.00
Rodney Stuckey		
SH Spencer Hawes	4.00	10.00
Rodney Stuckey		
TS Alando Tucker	4.00	10.00
D.J. Strawberry		
TW Julian Wright	4.00	10.00
Al Thornton		
WW Brandan Wright	3.00	8.00
Julian Wright		
WY Brandan Wright	3.00	8.00
Thaddeus Young		
YC Thaddeus Young	3.00	8.00
Javaris Crittenton		
YP Nick Young	3.00	8.00
Gabe Pruitt		
YY Nick Young	3.00	8.00
Thaddeus Young		

2007-08 SP Rookie Threads Rookie Threads Patch Dual

PRINT RUN 25 SER.#'d SETS

Card	Low	High
DG Kevin Durant	30.00	60.00
Jeff Green		
DH Kevin Durant	30.00	60.00
Al Horford		
MD Josh McRoberts	8.00	20.00
Glen Davis		
NB Joakim Noah	8.00	20.00
Corey Brewer		
YC Thaddeus Young	6.00	15.00
Javaris Crittenton		
YY Thaddeus Young	6.00	15.00
Nick Young		

2007-08 SP Rookie Threads Rookie Threads Triple

MEMORABILIA ODDS ON PER PACK
*PARALLEL: .5X TO 1.25X BASE HI
PARALLEL PRINT RUN 50 SER.#'d SETS

Card	Low	High
ACB Arron Afflalo	5.00	12.00
Aaron Brooks		
Daequan Cook		
DCW Sean Williams	4.00	10.00
Wilson Chandler		
Glen Davis		
DGW Kevin Durant	10.00	25.00
Jeff Green		
Julian Wright		
DHC Al Horford	10.00	25.00
Mike Conley Jr.		
Kevin Durant		
DYW Kevin Durant	10.00	25.00
Thaddeus Young		
Brandan Wright		
GSP Gabe Pruitt	4.00	10.00
Taurean Green		
D.J. Strawberry		
GYC Aaron Gray	4.00	10.00
Thaddeus Young		
Javaris Crittenton		
NDS D.J. Strawberry	5.00	12.00
Glen Davis		
Joakim Noah		
NGR Chris Richard	5.00	12.00
Taurean Green		
Joakim Noah		
NHB Joakim Noah	5.00	12.00
Corey Brewer		
Al Horford		
PLC Gabe Pruitt	4.00	10.00
Mike Conley Jr.		
Acie Law		
SHW Jason Smith	4.00	10.00
Sean Williams		
Spencer Hawes		
TCB Al Thornton	4.00	10.00
Daequan Cook		
Corey Brewer		
TLC Alando Tucker	4.00	10.00
Carl Landry		
Mike Conley Jr.		
TYW Thaddeus Young	4.00	10.00
Julian Wright		
Al Thornton		
YCS Nick Young	4.00	10.00
Javaris Crittenton		
Rodney Stuckey		
YYW Thaddeus Young	4.00	10.00
Brandan Wright		
Nick Young		

2007-08 SP Rookie Threads Rookie Threads Patch Triple

PRINT RUN 15 SER.#'d SETS

Card	Low	High
ACB Arron Afflalo	10.00	25.00
Daequan Cook		
Aaron Brooks		
DCW Glen Davis	10.00	25.00
Wilson Chandler		
Sean Williams		
DGW Kevin Durant	50.00	100.00
Jeff Green		
Julian Wright		
DHC Kevin Durant	50.00	100.00
Al Horford		
Mike Conley Jr.		
GSP Gabe Pruitt	8.00	20.00
Taurean Green		
D.J. Strawberry		
NDS Joakim Noah	15.00	30.00
Glen Davis		
D.J. Strawberry		
NHB Joakim Noah	15.00	30.00
Al Horford		
Corey Brewer		
SHW Jason Smith	8.00	20.00
Spencer Hawes		
Sean Williams		
TYW Al Thornton	15.00	30.00
Thaddeus Young		
Julian Wright		
YYW Thaddeus Young	10.00	25.00
Nick Young		
Brandan Wright		

2007-08 SP Rookie Threads Rookie Threads Patch Autographs

PRINT RUN 25 SER.#'d SETS

Card	Low	High
RTAA Arron Afflalo	12.00	30.00
RTAB Aaron Brooks	10.00	25.00
RTAH Al Horford	12.00	30.00
RTAL Acie Law	10.00	25.00
RTAT Al Thornton	10.00	25.00
RTCL Carl Landry	10.00	25.00
RTDS D.J. Strawberry	10.00	25.00
RTGD Glen Davis	15.00	40.00
RTJD Jared Dudley	10.00	25.00
RTJG Jeff Green	12.00	30.00
RTJN Joakim Noah	30.00	80.00
RTJS Jason Smith	10.00	25.00
RTKD Kevin Durant	300.00	600.00
RTMC Mike Conley Jr.	15.00	40.00
RTRS Rodney Stuckey	15.00	40.00
RTSH Spencer Hawes	10.00	25.00

RTSW Sean Williams 10.00 25.00
RTTG Taurean Green 10.00 25.00
RTTU Alando Tucker 10.00 25.00
RTWC Wilson Chandler 15.00 40.00

2007-08 SP Rookie Threads Rookie Threads Patch Dual Autographs

PRINT RUN 15 SER.#'d SETS
UNPRICED TRIPLE PRINT RUN 10 SETS
BR Corey Brewer 12.50 30.00
Chris Richard
CC Daequan Cook 20.00 40.00
Mike Conley Jr.
DH Kevin Durant 250.00 450.00
Al Horford
HB Al Horford 40.00 75.00
Corey Brewer
HL Al Horford 15.00 40.00
Acie Law
NB Joakim Noah 25.00 60.00
Corey Brewer
SA Arron Afflalo 25.00 50.00
Rodney Stuckey
SH Rodney Stuckey 25.00 50.00
Spencer Hawes
TW Al Thornton 15.00 40.00
Julian Wright

2007-08 SP Rookie Threads Rookies Gold

*43-48 GOLD: .75X TO 2X BASE HI
*49-60 GOLD: SAME VALUE AS BASE
*61-84 GOLD: .75X TO 2X BASE HI
GOLD PRINT RUN 50 SER.#'d SETS
UNPRICED SILVER PRINT RUN ONE SET
49 Kevin Durant JSY AU 300.00 550.00

2007-08 SP Rookie Threads Scripted in Time

COMBINED AUTO ODDS 1:1.2
AJ Al Jefferson 4.00 10.00
BB Bruce Bowen 4.00 10.00
BD Baron Davis 6.00 15.00
CP Chris Paul 25.00 60.00
DG Daniel Gibson 5.00 12.00
DH Dwight Howard 20.00 40.00
DL David Lee 4.00 10.00
EO Emeka Okafor 4.00 10.00
GR Danny Granger 5.00 12.00
JO Jermaine O'Neal 4.00 10.00
KH Kirk Hinrich 4.00 10.00
KK Kyle Korver 4.00 10.00
KL Kyle Lowry 4.00 10.00
LA LaMarcus Aldridge 10.00 25.00
LB Leandro Barbosa 4.00 10.00
LH Larry Hughes 4.00 10.00
LP Leon Powe 5.00 12.00
PO Patrick O'Bryant 4.00 10.00
PP Paul Pierce 8.00 20.00
RC Rodney Carney 4.00 10.00
RR Rajon Rondo 12.50 30.00
SB Shannon Brown 4.00 10.00
TF T.J. Ford 4.00 10.00
TM Tracy McGrady 10.00 25.00
TT Tyrus Thomas 4.00 10.00
YM Yao Ming 15.00 30.00

2007-08 SP Rookie Threads Signing Day

COMBINED AUTO ODDS 1:1.2
SDAA Arron Afflalo 4.00 10.00
SDAB Aaron Brooks 3.00 8.00
SDAG Aaron Gray 3.00 8.00
SDAH Al Horford 6.00 15.00
SDAL Acie Law 3.00 8.00
SDAT Al Thornton 3.00 8.00
SDCB Corey Brewer 4.00 10.00
SDCK Coby Karl 3.00 8.00
SDCL Carl Landry 3.00 8.00
SDCR Chris Richard 3.00 8.00
SDDA Jermareo Davidson 3.00 8.00
SDDC Daequan Cook 3.00 8.00
SDDN Demetris Nichols 3.00 8.00
SDDS D.J. Strawberry 3.00 8.00
SDGD Glen Davis 5.00 12.00
SDGP Gabe Pruitt 3.00 8.00
SDHA Adam Haluska 3.00 8.00
SDHH Herbert Hill 3.00 8.00
SDJC Javaris Crittenton 3.00 8.00
SDJD Jared Dudley 3.00 8.00
SDJG Jeff Green 4.00 10.00
SDJM Josh McRoberts 3.00 8.00
SDJN Joakim Noah 8.00 20.00
SDJS Jason Smith 3.00 8.00
SDJW Julian Wright 3.00 8.00
SDKD Kevin Durant 125.00 225.00
SDLS Luis Scola 5.00 12.00
SDMA Morris Almond 3.00 8.00
SDMB Marco Belinelli 3.00 8.00
SDMC Mike Conley Jr. 5.00 12.00
SDNF Nick Fazekas 3.00 8.00
SDRS Ramon Sessions 5.00 12.00
SDRS Rodney Stuckey 5.00 12.00
SDSH Spencer Hawes 3.00 8.00
SDSW Sean Williams 3.00 8.00
SDTG Taurean Green 3.00 8.00
SDTU Alando Tucker 3.00 8.00
SDWC Wilson Chandler 5.00 12.00

2007-08 SP Rookie Threads SP Marks Dual

PRINT RUN 50 SER.#'d SETS
UNPRICED QUAD PRINT RUN 10 SER.#'d SETS
UNPRICED SIX PRINT RUN 5 SER.#'d SETS
MDAR LaMarcus Aldridge 20.00 40.00
Brandon Roy
MDAS Arron Afflalo 10.00 25.00
Rodney Stuckey
MDCJ Vince Carter 20.00 40.00
Antawn Jamison
MDCM Vince Carter 25.00 60.00
Tracy McGrady
MDDA Alonzo Mourning 20.00 40.00
Daequan Cook
MDDB Baron Davis 15.00 40.00
Marco Belinelli
MDDG Kevin Durant 125.00 250.00
Jeff Green
MDDH Baron Davis 10.00 25.00
Al Harrington
MDGC Rudy Gay 8.00 20.00
Mike Conley Jr.
MDHB Spencer Hawes 8.00 20.00
Mike Bibby
MDHD Horace Grant 20.00 50.00
Dwight Howard
MDHG Kirk Hinrich 12.50 30.00
Ben Gordon
MDJP Tayshaun Prince 8.00 20.00
Richard Jefferson
MDKA Steve Kerr 20.00 40.00
B.J. Armstrong
MDKP Jason Kidd 20.00 50.00
Tony Parker
MDLG David Lee 8.00 20.00
Rudy Gay
MDMW Yao Ming 20.00 40.00
Bill Walton
MDOM Yao Ming 30.00 60.00
Hakeem Olajuwon
MDPD Paul Pierce/26 20.00 40.00
Adrian Dantley
MDPS Rodney Stuckey 15.00 30.00
Tayshaun Prince
MDPW Chris Paul 50.00 100.00
Deron Williams
MDRG Taurean Green 10.00 25.00
Brandon Roy
MDRR David Robinson 40.00 80.00
Dennis Rodman
MDTM Al Thornton 20.00 40.00
Danny Manning
MDTN Tyrus Thomas 15.00 30.00
Joakim Noah
MDWH Al Horford 25.00 50.00
Dominique Wilkins

2007-08 SP Rookie Threads SP Marks Triple

PRINT RUN 25 SER.#'d SETS
ARM LaMarcus Aldridge 15.00 40.00
Brandon Roy
Josh McRoberts
CAW Tyson Chandler 10.00 25.00
Hilton Armstrong
Julian Wright
CBP Rodney Carney 10.00 25.00
Josh Boone
Leon Powe
CRA Mardy Collins 10.00 25.00
Rajon Rondo
Arron Afflalo
FFR Randy Foye 20.00 40.00
Rajon Rondo
Raymond Felton
GGP Francisco Garcia 10.00 25.00
Daniel Gibson
Gabe Pruitt
GIS Ben Gordon 10.00 25.00
Andre Iguodala
Rodney Stuckey
JBJ Kobe Bryant 800.00 1200.00
LeBron James
Michael Jordan
JFB Randy Foye 15.00 30.00
Corey Brewer
Al Jefferson
JGH Ben Gordon 20.00 40.00
Adam Haluska
Antawn Jamison
JMN Antawn Jamison 10.00 25.00
Sean May
David Noel
MRC Alonzo Mourning 50.00 100.00
Pat Riley
Daequan Cook
OMM Alonzo Mourning 50.00 100.00
Yao Ming
Hakeem Olajuwon
PAJ Carmelo Anthony 20.00 50.00
Richard Jefferson
Tayshaun Prince
PDB Morris Peterson 10.00 25.00
Shannon Brown
Paul Davis
PJH Antawn Jamison 20.00 40.00
Al Harrington
Paul Pierce
PRM Rajon Rondo 20.00 50.00
Randolph Morris
Tayshaun Prince

2007-08 SP Rookie Threads SP Threads

ONE MEMORABILIA CARD PER PACK
SPAI Andre Iguodala 4.00 10.00
SPAK Andrei Kirilenko 3.00 8.00
SPAS Amare Stoudemire 4.00 10.00
SPBL Bill Laimbeer 4.00 10.00
SPCA Carmelo Anthony 5.00 12.00
SPCD Clyde Drexler 5.00 12.00
SPCF Channing Frye 3.00 8.00
SPCP Chris Paul 8.00 20.00
SPDG Drew Gooden 3.00 8.00
SPDH Dwight Howard 6.00 15.00
SPDN Dirk Nowitzki 5.00 12.00
SPDR David Robinson 6.00 15.00
SPDW Deron Williams 6.00 15.00
SPIV Allen Iverson 5.00 12.00
SPJA LeBron James 12.50 30.00
SPJK Jason Kidd 4.00 10.00
SPKB Kobe Bryant 12.50 30.00
SPKG Kevin Garnett 8.00 20.00
SPLA LaMarcus Aldridge 5.00 12.00
SPLJ LeBron James 12.50 30.00
SPMJ Michael Jordan 25.00 60.00
SPPR Tayshaun Prince 4.00 10.00
SPRH Richard Hamilton 3.00 8.00
SPRO Dennis Rodman 6.00 15.00
SPSL Shaun Livingston 3.00 8.00
SPSM Shawn Marion 4.00 10.00
SPSN Steve Nash 5.00 12.00
SPSO Shaquille O'Neal 8.00 20.00
SPST Stephon Marbury 3.00 8.00
SPTD Tim Duncan 6.00 15.00
SPTP Tony Parker 4.00 10.00
SPVC Vince Carter 5.00 12.00
SPYM Yao Ming 5.00 12.00

2007-08 SP Rookie Threads SP Threads Patch

*PATCH: .75X TO 2X BASE HI
ONE MEMORABILIA CARD PER PACK
SPKB Kobe Bryant 40.00 80.00

2008-09 SP Rookie Threads

This set was released on December 10, 2008. The base set consists of 100 cards. Cards 1-60 feature veterans, while cards 61-66 are rookies serial numbered of 99. Cards 67-94 feature autographed jersey rookies serial numbered of 599, and cards 95-100 are autographed jersey rookies serial numbered of 399.

COMP.SET w/o SPs (60) 20.00 50.00
1 Antawn Jamison .60 1.50
2 Gilbert Arenas .60 1.50
3 Carlos Boozer .60 1.50
4 Deron Williams .60 1.50
5 Jermaine O'Neal .60 1.50
6 Chris Bosh .60 1.50
7 Jeff Green .50 1.25
8 Kevin Durant 2.50 6.00
9 Tim Duncan 1.00 2.50
10 Tony Parker .60 1.50
11 Beno Udrih .40 1.00
12 Kevin Martin .60 1.50
13 Brandon Roy .60 1.50
14 Greg Oden .60 1.50
15 Amare Stoudemire .60 1.50
16 Steve Nash .60 1.50
17 Thaddeus Young .50 1.25
18 Andre Iguodala .60 1.50
19 Hedo Turkoglu .60 1.50
20 Dwight Howard 1.25 3.00
21 Jamal Crawford .50 1.25
22 Stephon Marbury .50 1.25
23 David West .60 1.50
24 Chris Paul 1.00 2.50
25 Yi Jianlian .60 1.50
26 Vince Carter .75 2.00
27 Al Jefferson .60 1.50
28 Corey Brewer .50 1.25
29 Richard Jefferson .60 1.50
30 Michael Redd .60 1.50
31 Dwyane Wade 1.25 3.00
32 Shawn Marion .60 1.50
33 Mike Conley Jr. .50 1.25
34 Rudy Gay .60 1.50
35 Pau Gasol .60 1.50
36 Kobe Bryant 3.00 8.00
37 Al Thornton .50 1.25
38 Baron Davis .60 1.50
39 Danny Granger .60 1.50
40 T.J. Ford .40 1.00
41 Tracy McGrady .60 1.50
42 Yao Ming .75 2.00
43 Stephen Jackson .50 1.25
44 Monta Ellis .60 1.50
45 Richard Hamilton .50 1.25
46 Chauncey Billups .60 1.50
47 Allen Iverson .75 2.00
48 Carmelo Anthony .75 2.00
49 Jason Kidd .60 1.50
50 Dirk Nowitzki .75 2.00
51 LeBron James 3.00 8.00
52 Ben Wallace .60 1.50
53 Ben Gordon .60 1.50
54 Joakim Noah .60 1.50
55 Gerald Wallace .60 1.50
56 Jason Richardson .60 1.50
57 Kevin Garnett 1.25 3.00
58 Paul Pierce .75 2.00
59 Al Horford .60 1.50
60 Joe Johnson .60 1.50
61 James Gist RC 2.00 5.00
62 Danilo Gallinari RC 3.00 8.00
63 Malik Hairston RC 2.00 5.00
64 Mike Taylor RC 2.00 5.00
65 Joe Crawford RC 2.00 5.00
66 Trent Plaisted RC 2.00 5.00
67 Russell Westbrook JSY AU RC 50.00 125.00
68 Sonny Weems JSY AU RC 5.00 12.00
69 Joe Alexander JSY AU RC 5.00 12.00
70 D.J. Augustin JSY AU RC 5.00 12.00
71 Brook Lopez JSY AU RC 8.00 20.00
72 Jason Thompson JSY AU RC 5.00 12.00
73 Brandon Rush JSY AU RC 5.00 12.00
74 Anthony Randolph JSY AU RC 6.00 15.00
75 Robin Lopez JSY AU RC 5.00 12.00
76 Marreese Speights JSY AU RC 5.00 12.00
77 Roy Hibbert JSY AU RC 10.00 25.00
78 JaVale McGee JSY AU RC 8.00 20.00
79 J.J. Hickson JSY AU RC 6.00 15.00
80 Kyle Weaver JSY AU RC 5.00 12.00
81 Ryan Anderson JSY AU RC 8.00 20.00
82 Courtney Lee JSY AU RC 8.00 20.00
83 Kosta Koufos JSY AU RC 5.00 12.00
84 George Hill JSY AU RC 8.00 20.00
85 Darrell Arthur JSY AU RC 5.00 12.00
86 Donte Greene JSY AU RC 5.00 12.00
87 D.J. White JSY AU RC 5.00 12.00
88 J.R. Giddens JSY AU RC 5.00 12.00
89 Walter Sharpe JSY AU RC 5.00 12.00
90 Joey Dorsey JSY AU RC 5.00 12.00
91 Mario Chalmers JSY AU RC 8.00 20.00
92 DeAndre Jordan JSY AU RC 12.00 30.00
93 Chris Douglas-Roberts JSY AU RC5.00 12.00
94 Patrick Ewing Jr. JSY AU RC 4.00 10.00
95 Derrick Rose JSY AU RC 175.00 350.00
96 Michael Beasley JSY AU RC 15.00 40.00
97 O.J. Mayo JSY AU RC 15.00 40.00
98 Kevin Love JSY AU RC 50.00 125.00
99 Eric Gordon JSY AU RC 25.00 60.00
100 Jerryd Bayless JSY AU RC 10.00 25.00

2008-09 SP Rookie Threads Authorization

APPROXIMATE ODDS 1:12
AUAB Andrew Bynum 10.00 25.00
AUAH Al Horford 5.00 12.00
AUBR Bill Russell 60.00 120.00
AUBW Bill Walton 8.00 20.00
AUCB Chauncey Billups 6.00 15.00
AUCP Chris Paul 20.00 50.00
AUCW Chris Wilcox 5.00 12.00
AUDH Dwight Howard 15.00 40.00
AUJA LeBron James 100.00 200.00
AUJM Jamario Moon 5.00 12.00
AUJP John Paxson 8.00 20.00
AUKA Kareem Abdul-Jabbar 50.00 100.00
AUKB Kobe Bryant 100.00 200.00
AUKD Kevin Durant 100.00 175.00
AULJ Larry Johnson 25.00 60.00
AULS Luis Scola 5.00 12.00
AUMJ Michael Jordan 300.00 500.00
AUMW Maurice Williams 5.00 12.00
AURG Rudy Gay 6.00 15.00
AUTC Tom Chambers 5.00 12.00
AUWF Walt Frazier 6.00 15.00

2008-09 SP Rookie Threads Letters of Introduction

CARDS #'d TO LETTERS IN FULL NAME
SOME NOT PRICED DUE TO SCARCITY
LICD Chris Douglas-Roberts/19* 12.00 30.00
LIJB Jerryd Bayless/13* 12.00 30.00
LIMB Michael Beasley/14* 25.00 60.00
LIMS Marreese Speights/16* 12.00 30.00

2008-09 SP Rookie Threads Rookie Threads

APPROXIMATE ODDS 1:3
*PARALLEL 125: .4X TO 1X BASE HI
PARALLEL PRINT RUN 125 SER.#'d SETS
*PATCH: 1X TO 2.5X HI COLUMN
PATCH PRINT RUN 35 SER.#'d SETS
RTAR Anthony Randolph 2.50 6.00
RTBR Brandon Rush 2.00 5.00
RTCL Courtney Lee 3.00 8.00
RTDA D.J. Augustin 2.00 5.00
RTDR Derrick Rose 15.00 40.00
RTEG Eric Gordon 5.00 12.00
RTGH George Hill 3.00 8.00
RTGR Donte Greene 2.00 5.00
RTJA Joe Alexander 2.00 5.00
RTJB Jerryd Bayless 2.00 5.00
RTJD Joey Dorsey 2.00 5.00
RTJG J.R. Giddens 2.00 5.00
RTJH J.J. Hickson 2.50 6.00
RTJT Jason Thompson 2.00 5.00
RTKL Kevin Love 8.00 20.00
RTMB Michael Beasley 3.00 8.00
RTMC Mario Chalmers 3.00 8.00
RTMS Marreese Speights 2.00 5.00
RTOM O.J. Mayo 3.00 8.00
RTSW Sonny Weems 2.00 5.00

2008-09 SP Rookie Threads Rookie Threads Dual

APPROXIMATE ODDS 1:6
RTDAB D.J. Augustin 3.00 8.00
Jerryd Bayless
RTDAL Kevin Love 4.00 10.00
Joe Alexander
RTDBC Michael Beasley 5.00 12.00
Mario Chalmers
RTDBH Jerryd Bayless 3.00 8.00
George Hill
RTDBR Derrick Rose 10.00 25.00
Michael Beasley
RTDDD Joey Dorsey 3.00 8.00
Chris Douglas-Roberts
RTDGA Eric Gordon 4.00 10.00
Joe Alexander
RTDGD Donte Greene 3.00 8.00
Joey Dorsey
RTDGW Eric Gordon 3.00 8.00
D.J. White
RTDLL Brook Lopez 4.00 10.00
Robin Lopez
RTDLW Russell Westbrook 8.00 20.00
Kevin Love
RTDMR O.J. Mayo 10.00 25.00
Derrick Rose
RTDRC Brandon Rush 4.00 10.00
Mario Chalmers
RTDWH Sonny Weems 4.00 10.00
George Hill

2008-09 SP Rookie Threads Rookie Threads Dual Parallel

*PARALLEL: .5X TO 1.25X BASE HI
PRINT RUN 50 SER.#'d SETS
RTDAM O.J. Mayo 5.00 12.00
Darrell Arthur
RTDAW D.J. Augustin 4.00 10.00
Kyle Weaver
RTDDA Ryan Anderson 4.00 10.00
Chris Douglas-Roberts
RTDGJ Eric Gordon 5.00 12.00
DeAndre Jordan
RTDHM Roy Hibbert 5.00 12.00
Javale McGee
RTDRL Brandon Rush 5.00 12.00
Courtney Lee
RTDTE Jason Thompson 4.00 10.00
Patrick Ewing Jr.
RTDTS Jason Thompson 4.00 10.00
Marreese Speights
RTDWW Russell Westbrook 5.00 12.00
D.J. White

2008-09 SP Rookie Threads Rookie Threads Dual Patch

*PATCH: 1X TO 2.5X BASE HI
PRINT RUN 25 SER.#'d SETS
RTDAM O.J. Mayo 10.00 25.00
Darrell Arthur
RTDAW D.J. Augustin 8.00 20.00
Kyle Weaver
RTDDA Ryan Anderson 8.00 20.00
Chris Douglas-Roberts
RTDGJ Eric Gordon 10.00 25.00
DeAndre Jordan
RTDHM Roy Hibbert 10.00 25.00
Javale McGee
RTDRL Brandon Rush 10.00 25.00
Courtney Lee
RTDTE Jason Thompson 8.00 20.00
Patrick Ewing Jr.
RTDTS Jason Thompson 8.00 20.00
Marreese Speights
RTDWW Russell Westbrook 10.00 25.00
D.J. White

2008-09 SP Rookie Threads Rookie Threads Triple

APPROXIMATE ODDS 1:6
*PARALLEL: .75X TO 2X BASE HI
PARALLEL PRINT RUN 15 SER.#'d SETS
*PATCH: 1.25X TO 3X BASE HI
PATCH PRINT RUN 15 SER.#'d SETS
RTTAGH George Hill 3.00 8.00
Darrell Arthur
Donte Greene
RTTAGW Russell Westbrook 4.00 10.00
Eric Gordon
D.J. Augustin
RTTALA Brook Lopez 3.00 8.00
Joe Alexander
D.J. Augustin
RTTARW Derrick Rose 10.00 25.00
Russell Westbrook
D.J. Augustin
RTTBLA Michael Beasley 5.00 12.00
Kevin Love
Joe Alexander
RTTDWE Sonny Weems 3.00 8.00
Chris Douglas-Roberts
Patrick Ewing Jr.
RTTGWH Sonny Weems 3.00 8.00
George Hill
Donte Greene
RTTHGS J.R. Giddens 3.00 8.00
Walter Sharpe
J.J. Hickson
RTTHMH J.J. Hickson 4.00 10.00
Roy Hibbert
Javale McGee
RTTJLK DeAndre Jordan 3.00 8.00
Kosta Koufos
Robin Lopez
RTTJWC Mario Chalmers 4.00 10.00
DeAndre Jordan
Kyle Weaver
RTTLAK Ryan Anderson 3.00 8.00
Courtney Lee
Kosta Koufos
RTTLDA Brook Lopez 3.00 8.00
Ryan Anderson
Chris Douglas-Roberts
RTTMBR Derrick Rose 10.00 25.00
Michael Beasley
O.J. Mayo
RTTMGB O.J. Mayo 4.00 10.00
Eric Gordon
Jerryd Bayless
RTTMRG Derrick Rose 10.00 25.00
O.J. Mayo
Eric Gordon
RTTRAC Brandon Rush 3.00 8.00
Darrell Arthur
Mario Chalmers
RTTRDD Derrick Rose 10.00 25.00
Joey Dorsey
Chris Douglas-Roberts
RTTRLS Marreese Speights 3.00 8.00
Anthony Randolph
Robin Lopez
RTTRSC Mario Chalmers 3.00 8.00
Marreese Speights
Brandon Rush
RTTRTB Brandon Rush 3.00 8.00
Jerryd Bayless
Jason Thompson
RTTWES Patrick Ewing Jr. 3.00 8.00
Walter Sharpe
D.J. White
RTTWGD D.J. White 3.00 8.00
J.R. Giddens
Joey Dorsey

2008-09 SP Rookie Threads Rookies Parallel

PRINT RUNS LISTED IN CHECKLIST
SOME NOT PRICED DUE TO SCARCITY
61 James Gist/59 3.00 8.00
63 Malik Hairston/47 3.00 8.00
64 Mike Taylor/55 3.00 8.00
65 Joe Crawford/58 3.00 8.00
66 Trent Plaisted/37 3.00 8.00
68 Sonny Weems JSY AU/39 10.00 25.00
71 Brook Lopez JSY AU/10 50.00 120.00
73 Brandon Rush JSY AU/13 12.00 30.00
74 Anthony Randolph JSY AU/14 60.00 120.00
75 Robin Lopez JSY AU/15 15.00 40.00
76 Marreese Speights JSY AU/16 20.00 50.00
77 Roy Hibbert JSY AU/17 20.00 50.00
78 Javale McGee JSY AU/18 20.00 50.00
79 J.J. Hickson JSY AU/19 15.00 40.00
80 Kyle Weaver JSY AU/38 10.00 25.00
81 Ryan Anderson JSY AU/21 15.00 40.00
82 Courtney Lee JSY AU/22 15.00 40.00
83 Kosta Koufos JSY AU/23 10.00 25.00
84 George Hill JSY AU/26 15.00 40.00
85 Darrell Arthur JSY AU/27 10.00 25.00
86 Donte Greene JSY AU/28 10.00 25.00
87 D.J. White JSY AU/29 10.00 25.00
88 J.R. Giddens JSY AU/30 10.00 25.00
89 Walter Sharpe JSY AU/32 10.00 25.00
90 Joey Dorsey JSY AU/33 10.00 25.00
91 Mario Chalmers JSY AU/34 15.00 40.00
92 DeAndre Jordan JSY AU/35 20.00 50.00
93 Chris Douglas-Roberts JSY AU/4010.00 25.00
94 Patrick Ewing Jr. JSY AU/43 10.00 25.00

2008-09 SP Rookie Threads Scripted in Time

RANDOM INSERTS IN PACKS
SITAB Andrew Bynum 10.00 25.00
SITAJ Al Jefferson 4.00 10.00
SITBB Bruce Bowen 4.00 10.00
SITBD Baron Davis 4.00 10.00
SITBG Ben Gordon 4.00 10.00
SITDH Dwight Howard 15.00 40.00
SITEO Emeka Okafor 4.00 10.00
SITGR Danny Granger 5.00 12.00
SITHA Hilton Armstrong 4.00 10.00
SITHE Luther Head 4.00 10.00
SITJG Jeff Green 5.00 12.00
SITJS Jason Smith 4.00 10.00
SITKA Kelenna Azubuike 6.00 15.00
SITKL Kyle Lowry 4.00 10.00
SITLA LaMarcus Aldridge 6.00 15.00
SITLH Larry Hughes 4.00 10.00
SITLP Leon Powe 6.00 15.00
SITPM Paul Millsap 8.00 20.00
SITPP Paul Pierce 12.50 30.00
SITRA Ray Allen 12.50 30.00
SITRC Rodney Carney 4.00 10.00
SITRJ Richard Jefferson 5.00 12.00
SITRS Rodney Stuckey 8.00 20.00
SITSB Shane Battier 4.00 10.00
SITSJ Solomon Jones 4.00 10.00
SITTF T.J. Ford 4.00 10.00
SITTM Tracy McGrady 12.50 30.00
SITTP Tayshaun Prince 5.00 12.00
SITTT Tyrus Thomas 4.00 10.00
SITYM Yao Ming 20.00 50.00

2008-09 SP Rookie Threads Signing Day

APPROXIMATE ODDS 1:6
SDAR Anthony Randolph 5.00 12.00
SDBL Brook Lopez 6.00 15.00
SDBR Brandon Rush 4.00 10.00
SDCD Chris Douglas-Roberts 4.00 10.00
SDDA D.J. Augustin 4.00 10.00
SDDG Danilo Gallinari 6.00 15.00
SDDR Derrick Rose 150.00 300.00
SDDW D.J. White 4.00 10.00
SDEG Eric Gordon 15.00 40.00
SDGH George Hill 6.00 15.00
SDGR Donte Greene 4.00 10.00
SDJA Joe Alexander 4.00 10.00
SDJC Joe Crawford 4.00 10.00
SDJD Joey Dorsey 4.00 10.00
SDJG J.R. Giddens 4.00 10.00
SDJH J.J. Hickson 5.00 12.00
SDJT Jason Thompson 4.00 10.00
SDKK Kosta Koufos 4.00 10.00
SDKL Kevin Love 25.00 60.00
SDMB Michael Beasley 15.00 40.00
SDMC Mario Chalmers 8.00 20.00
SDMH Malik Hairston 4.00 10.00
SDMS Marreese Speights 4.00 10.00
SDOM O.J. Mayo 15.00 40.00
SDPE Patrick Ewing Jr. 4.00 10.00
SDRH Roy Hibbert 6.00 15.00
SDRL Robin Lopez 4.00 10.00
SDRW Russell Westbrook 30.00 80.00
SDSW Sonny Weems 4.00 10.00

2008-09 SP Rookie Threads SP Threads

APPROXIMATE ODDS 1:4
TAB Andrea Bargnani 2.00 5.00
TAI Allen Iverson 5.00 12.00
TAK Andrei Kirilenko 2.00 5.00
TAS Amare Stoudemire 2.50 6.00
TBO Andrew Bogut 2.50 6.00
TCB Caron Butler 2.50 6.00
TCH Chris Bosh 2.50 6.00
TDG Daniel Gibson 2.50 6.00
TDH Devin Harris 2.50 6.00
TDN Dirk Nowitzki 3.00 8.00
TEB Elton Brand 2.50 6.00
TGH Grant Hill 4.00 10.00
THO Dwight Howard 5.00 12.00
TJG Jeff Green 2.00 5.00
TJH Josh Howard 2.00 5.00
TJJ Joe Johnson 2.50 6.00
TJK Jason Kidd 2.50 6.00
TJR Jason Richardson 2.50 6.00
TJS Josh Smith 2.50 6.00
TKD Kevin Durant 10.00 25.00
TKG Kevin Garnett 5.00 12.00
TKH Kirk Hinrich 2.50 6.00
TLD Luol Deng 2.50 6.00
TLJ LeBron James 8.00 20.00
TMG Manu Ginobili 2.50 6.00
TPG Pau Gasol 2.50 6.00
TRA Ray Allen 2.50 6.00
TRH Richard Hamilton 2.00 5.00
TSL Shaun Livingston 2.00 5.00
TSM Shawn Marion 2.50 6.00
TTD Tim Duncan 4.00 10.00

2008-09 SP Rookie Threads SP Threads Patch

*PATCH: 1X TO 2.5X BASE HI
RANDOM INSERTS IN PACKS
TGH Grant Hill 30.00 60.00
TLJ LeBron James 25.00 60.00

2008-09 SP Rookie Threads SP Threads Dual

APPROXIMATE ODDS 1:5
TDAP Scottie Pippen 10.00 25.00
Carmelo Anthony
TDBJ Kobe Bryant 35.00 70.00
Michael Jordan
TDDD Clyde Drexler 10.00 25.00
Kevin Durant
TDEA Julius Erving 5.00 12.00
Gilbert Arenas
TDEJ Patrick Ewing 6.00 15.00
Al Jefferson
TDGM Kevin McHale 6.00 15.00
Kevin Garnett
TDHK Jeff Hornacek 6.00 15.00
Kyle Korver
TDHO Shaquille O'Neal 8.00 20.00
Dwight Howard
TDIR Allen Iverson 6.00 15.00
Brandon Roy

JB Larry Bird 12.50 30.00
eBron James
KJ Magic Johnson 8.00 20.00
ason Kidd
MB Carlos Boozer 5.00 12.00
arl Malone
MW Alonzo Mourning 5.00 12.00
ean Williams
PT Isiah Thomas 5.00 12.00
hris Paul
RM Dan Majerle 5.00 12.00
Michael Redd
SP John Starks 5.00 12.00
ony Parker
SR David Robinson 6.00 15.00
mare Stoudemire
WL Bill Laimbeer 5.00 12.00
Rasheed Wallace
WS Deron Williams 5.00 12.00
John Stockton

2008-09 SP Rookie Threads SP Threads Dual Patch

NDOM INSERTS IN PACKS
AP Carmelo Anthony 30.00 80.00
Scottie Pippen
BJ Michael Jordan 40.00 100.00
Kobe Bryant
DD Clyde Drexler 20.00 50.00
Kevin Durant
EA Julius Erving 15.00 40.00
Gilbert Arenas
EJ Patrick Ewing 15.00 40.00
Al Jefferson
GM Kevin Garnett 15.00 40.00
Kevin McHale
HK Jeff Hornacek 10.00 25.00
Kyle Korver
HO Dwight Howard 20.00 50.00
Shaquille O'Neal
IR Allen Iverson 12.00 30.00
Brandon Roy
JB LeBron James 20.00 50.00
Larry Bird
KJ Jason Kidd 15.00 40.00
Magic Johnson
MW Sean Williams 20.00 40.00
Alonzo Mourning
PT Isiah Thomas 12.50 30.00
Chris Paul
RM Michael Redd 10.00 25.00
Dan Majerle
SP John Starks 15.00 30.00
Tony Parker
WL Rasheed Wallace 10.00 25.00
Bill Laimbeer

2003-04 SP Signature Edition

eleased in March 2004, SP Signature Edition boasts a 25-card set divided up as follows: Cards 1-100 are eteran base cards with player photos on the left and olored borders on the right to match the player's eam; cards 101-142 are rookies sequentially umbered to 499 which are horizontally designed with layer photos on the right and the player's team logo n the left; cards 143-222 are sequentially numbered o the player's jersey number and have a colored order along the bottom and gray background on the op; and cards 223-225 feature celebrities Spike Lee, ummer Sanders and Cheryl Miller. A Legendary Cut hick Hearn one of one autograph was also inserted. P Signature Edition was packaged in one-pack boxes f three cards each and carried a suggested retail price f $60. Each "Pack" came with a collectible metal tin-oth black and white versions were available for each layer.

COMP.SET w/o SP's (100) 30.00 80.00
1 Shareef Abdur-Rahim .50 1.25
2 Jason Terry .50 1.25
3 Theo Ratliff .40 1.00
4 Raef LaFrentz .40 1.00
5 Paul Pierce .75 2.00
6 Larry Bird 2.00 5.00
7 Jalen Rose .50 1.25
8 Scottie Pippen 1.00 2.50
9 Michael Jordan 5.00 12.00
10 Dennis Rodman .75 2.00
11 Dajuan Wagner .40 1.00
12 Darius Miles .40 1.00
13 Carlos Boozer .60 1.50
14 Zydrunas Ilgauskas .50 1.25
15 Dirk Nowitzki 1.00 2.50
16 Steve Nash .75 2.00
17 Antoine Walker .60 1.50
18 Antawn Jamison .60 1.50
19 Andre Miller .50 1.25
20 Nene .50 1.25
21 Nikoloz Tskitishvili .40 1.00
22 Ben Wallace .60 1.50
23 Richard Hamilton .50 1.25
24 Chauncey Billups .60 1.50
25 Nick Van Exel .50 1.25
26 Jason Richardson .60 1.50
27 Mike Dunleavy .50 1.25
28 Yao Ming 1.25 3.00
29 Steve Francis .60 1.50
30 Cuttino Mobley .50 1.25
31 Reggie Miller .60 1.50
32 Jermaine O'Neal .60 1.50
33 Jamaal Tinsley .40 1.00
34 Chris Wilcox .40 1.00
35 Elton Brand .60 1.50
36 Wang Zhizhi .50 1.25
37 Corey Maggette .50 1.25
38 Kobe Bryant 3.00 8.00
39 Shaquille O'Neal 1.50 4.00
40 Gary Payton .60 1.50
41 Karl Malone .75 2.00
42 Pau Gasol .60 1.50
43 Shane Battier .50 1.25
44 Mike Miller .60 1.50
45 Caron Butler .60 1.50
46 Eddie Jones .50 1.25
47 Lamar Odom .60 1.50
48 Brian Grant .40 1.00
49 Desmond Mason .50 1.25
50 Michael Redd .60 1.50
51 Tim Thomas .40 1.00
52 Wally Szczerbiak .50 1.25
53 Kevin Garnett 1.25 3.00
54 Latrell Sprewell .50 1.25
55 Sam Cassell .50 1.25
56 Richard Jefferson .60 1.50
57 Kenyon Martin .60 1.50
58 Jason Kidd 1.00 2.50
59 Alonzo Mourning .75 2.00
60 Jamal Mashburn .50 1.25
61 Baron Davis .60 1.50
62 David Wesley .40 1.00
63 Allan Houston .50 1.25
64 Keith Van Horn .50 1.25
65 Antonio McDyess .50 1.25
66 Gordan Giricek .40 1.00
67 Tracy McGrady .75 2.00
68 Drew Gooden .50 1.25
69 Grant Hill .75 2.00
70 Glenn Robinson .50 1.25
71 Allen Iverson 1.00 2.50
72 Julius Erving 1.25 3.00
73 Eric Snow .40 1.00
74 Shawn Marion .60 1.50
75 Amare Stoudemire 1.00 2.50
76 Stephon Marbury .50 1.25
77 Bonzi Wells .40 1.00
78 Rasheed Wallace .60 1.50
79 Derek Anderson .40 1.00
80 Zach Randolph .60 1.50
81 Mike Bibby .60 1.50
82 Chris Webber .60 1.50
83 Peja Stojakovic .60 1.50
84 Brad Miller .60 1.50
85 Tony Parker .60 1.50
86 Tim Duncan 1.00 2.50
87 Manu Ginobili .75 2.00
88 David Robinson 1.00 2.50
89 Rashard Lewis .60 1.50
90 Ray Allen .60 1.50
91 Vladimir Radmanovic .40 1.00
92 Morris Peterson .40 1.00
93 Vince Carter 1.00 2.50
94 Antonio Davis .40 1.00
95 Andrei Kirilenko .60 1.50
96 Matt Harpring .50 1.25
97 Jarron Collins .40 1.00
98 Gilbert Arenas .60 1.50
99 Jerry Stackhouse .50 1.25
100 Kwame Brown .40 1.00
101 LeBron James RC 50.00 120.00
102 Darko Milicic RC 4.00 10.00
103 Carmelo Anthony RC 12.00 30.00
104 Chris Bosh RC 8.00 20.00
105 Dwyane Wade RC 15.00 40.00
106 Chris Kaman RC 5.00 12.00
107 Kirk Hinrich RC 5.00 12.00
108 T.J. Ford RC 5.00 12.00
109 Mike Sweetney RC 4.00 10.00
110 Jarvis Hayes RC 4.00 10.00
111 Mickael Pietrus RC 4.00 10.00
112 Nick Collison RC 4.00 10.00
113 Marcus Banks RC 4.00 10.00
114 Luke Ridnour RC 5.00 12.00
115 Reece Gaines RC 4.00 10.00
116 Troy Bell RC 4.00 10.00
117 Zarko Cabarkapa RC 4.00 10.00
118 David West RC 5.00 12.00
119 Aleksandar Pavlovic RC 4.00 10.00
120 Dahntay Jones RC 4.00 10.00
121 Boris Diaw RC 5.00 12.00
122 Zoran Planinic RC 4.00 10.00
123 Travis Outlaw RC 5.00 12.00
124 Brian Cook RC 4.00 10.00
125 James Lang RC 4.00 10.00
126 Ndudi Ebi RC 4.00 10.00
127 Kendrick Perkins RC 6.00 15.00
128 Leandro Barbosa RC 5.00 12.00
129 Josh Howard RC 4.00 10.00
130 Maciej Lampe RC 4.00 10.00
131 Jason Kapono RC 4.00 10.00
132 Luke Walton RC 4.00 10.00
133 Jerome Beasley RC 4.00 10.00
134 Willie Green RC 4.00 10.00
135 James Jones RC 4.00 10.00
136 Travis Hansen RC 4.00 10.00
137 Steve Blake RC 5.00 12.00
138 Slavko Vranes RC 4.00 10.00
139 Zaur Pachulia RC 4.00 10.00
140 Keith Bogans RC 4.00 10.00
141 Kyle Korver RC 5.00 12.00
142 Brandon Hunter RC 4.00 10.00
144 LeBron James/23 80.00 200.00
145 Michael Jordan/23 75.00 150.00
146 Darius Miles/21 6.00 15.00
148 Gary Payton/20 12.50 30.00
152 Ray Allen/34 10.00 25.00
153 Paul Pierce/34 12.50 30.00
154 Carmelo Anthony/15 25.00 60.00
160 Andrei Kirilenko/47 6.00 15.00
162 Nene/31 6.00 15.00
163 Elton Brand/42 6.00 15.00
168 Jerry Stackhouse/42 8.00 20.00
171 Darko Milicic/31 15.00 40.00
174 Glenn Robinson/31 6.00 15.00
175 Tim Duncan/21 25.00 60.00
177 Scottie Pippen/33 50.00 120.00
178 Richard Hamilton/32 8.00 20.00
179 Corey Maggette/50 6.00 15.00
182 Amare Stoudemire/32 12.50 30.00
185 Dirk Nowitzki/41 12.50 30.00
187 Magic Johnson/32 25.00 60.00
188 Michael Redd/22 6.00 15.00
190 Rasheed Wallace/30 12.50 30.00
192 Jason Terry/31 6.00 15.00
196 Kevin Garnett/21 25.00 60.00
203 Mike Miller/33 6.00 15.00
207 Morris Peterson/24 6.00 15.00
209 Jason Richardson/23 6.00 15.00
210 Shaquille O'Neal/34 25.00 60.00
211 Desmond Mason/24 6.00 15.00
212 Jamal Mashburn/24 6.00 15.00
213 Shawn Marion/31 8.00 20.00
214 Manu Ginobili/20 10.00 25.00
215 Larry Bird/33 50.00 120.00
216 Antawn Jamison/33 6.00 15.00
217 Reggie Miller/31 15.00 40.00
218 Pau Gasol/16 10.00 25.00
222 Vince Carter/15 20.00 50.00
223 Spike Lee 1.50 4.00
224 Summer Sanders 1.25 3.00
225 Cheryl Miller .75 2.00

2003-04 SP Signature Edition Gold

Randomly seeded in packs, this 100-card set parallels card numbers 1-100 from the base set and the cards are enhanced with gold foil highlights and sequential numbering to 100.
*GOLD SINGLES: 1.5X TO 4X BASE HI

2003-04 SP Signature Edition Autographed Parallel

Randomly inserted, this 84-card set is a skip-numbered parallel where veteran players, 1-100, signed cards numbered to their jersey number and rookie players signed cards sequentially numbered to 25.
SOME NOT PRICED DUE TO SCARCITY
SKIP-NUMBERED PARALLEL SET
A5 Paul Pierce/34 30.00 80.00
A6 Larry Bird/33 125.00 250.00
A9 Michael Jordan/23 500.00 800.00
A10 Dennis Rodman/91 60.00 150.00
A12 Darius Miles/21 10.00 25.00
A18 Antawn Jamison/33 15.00 40.00
A20 Nene/31 15.00 40.00
A23 Richard Hamilton/32 15.00 40.00
A26 Jason Richardson/23 15.00 40.00
A31 Reggie Miller/31 80.00 160.00
A34 Chris Wilcox/54 10.00 25.00
A36 Wang Zhizhi/16 15.00 40.00
A37 Corey Maggette/50 10.00 25.00
A40 Gary Payton/20 30.00 80.00
A43 Shane Battier/31 15.00 40.00
A53 Kevin Garnett/21 100.00 200.00
A56 Richard Jefferson/24 15.00 40.00
A65 Antonio McDyess/34 20.00 40.00
A74 Shawn Marion/31 25.00 60.00
A83 Peja Stojakovic/16 50.00 120.00
A87 Manu Ginobili/20 40.00 100.00
A92 Morris Peterson/24 10.00 25.00
A99 Jerry Stackhouse/42 15.00 40.00
A101 LeBron James 1000.00 1500.00
A102 Darko Milicic 12.00 30.00
A103 Carmelo Anthony 150.00 300.00
A104 Chris Bosh 100.00 200.00
A105 Dwyane Wade 400.00 750.00
A106 Chris Kaman 15.00 40.00
A107 Kirk Hinrich 15.00 40.00
A108 T.J. Ford 15.00 40.00
A109 Mike Sweetney 12.00 30.00
A110 Jarvis Hayes 12.00 30.00
A111 Mickael Pietrus 12.00 30.00
A112 Nick Collison 12.00 30.00
A113 Marcus Banks 12.00 30.00
A114 Luke Ridnour 15.00 40.00
A115 Reece Gaines 12.00 30.00
A116 Troy Bell 12.00 30.00
A117 Zarko Cabarkapa 12.00 30.00
A118 David West 20.00 50.00
A119 Aleksandar Pavlovic 12.00 30.00
A120 Dahntay Jones 12.00 30.00
A121 Boris Diaw 15.00 40.00
A122 Zoran Planinic 12.00 30.00
A123 Travis Outlaw 15.00 40.00
A124 Brian Cook 12.00 30.00
A125 James Lang 12.00 30.00
A126 Ndudi Ebi 12.00 30.00
A127 Kendrick Perkins 20.00 50.00
A128 Leandro Barbosa 15.00 40.00
A129 Josh Howard 12.00 30.00
A130 Maciej Lampe 12.00 30.00
A131 Jason Kapono 12.00 30.00
A132 Luke Walton 12.00 30.00
A133 Jerome Beasley 12.00 30.00
A134 Willie Green 12.00 30.00
A135 James Jones 12.00 30.00
A136 Travis Hansen 12.00 30.00
A137 Steve Blake 15.00 40.00
A138 Slavko Vranes 12.00 30.00
A139 Zaur Pachulia 12.00 30.00
A140 Keith Bogans 12.00 30.00
A141 Kyle Korver 15.00 40.00
A142 Brandon Hunter 12.00 30.00

2003-04 SP Signature Edition Alumni Associates Signatures

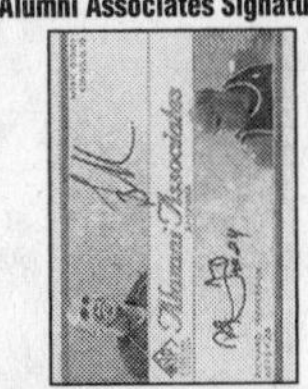

Randomly inserted, this 11-card set pairs players from the same college, with one on the top and one on the bottom, where each player signed the card. Each card is sequentially numbered to 100.
AK Shareef Abdur-Rahim 15.00 40.00
Jason Kidd
AW Gilbert Arenas 15.00 40.00
Luke Walton
BJ Mike Bibby 15.00 40.00
Richard Jefferson
DB Mike Dunleavy 15.00 40.00
Shane Battier
FD Steve Francis 15.00 40.00
Juan Dixon
MJ Corey Maggette 15.00 40.00
Dahntay Jones
MW Antonio McDyess 15.00 40.00
Gerald Wallace
PG Paul Pierce 20.00 50.00
Drew Gooden
PR Morris Peterson 15.00 40.00
Jason Richardson
SJ Jerry Stackhouse 15.00 40.00
Antawn Jamison
WM Reggie Miller 40.00 100.00
Bill Walton

2003-04 SP Signature Edition Celebrity Signings

Randomly inserted in packs, this three-card set features celebrities and their autographs. No odds were given for Cheryl Miller and Summer Sanders, but Spike Lee's card is sequentially numbered to 32. A gold version where Cheryl and Summer are sequentially numbered to 50 and Spike is sequentially numbered to 15 was also inserted in packs.
*GOLD: .6X TO 1.5X BASE AU HI
CM Cheryl Miller 12.50 30.00
SL Spike Lee/32 100.00 200.00
SS Summer Sanders 20.00 50.00

2003-04 SP Signature Edition Famous Nicknames

Randomly seeded in packs, this 30-card set places player photos on the left side of the card and autographs on the right along with a caption stating the player's nickname. Several players have more than one version and others signed to specific amounts listed in our checklist whereas everone else signed to 25.
AS Amare Stoudemire/25 75.00 150.00
The Future
BB Brent Barry/25 25.00 60.00
Bones
CA Carmelo Anthony/25 200.00 400.00
Melo
CB Chauncey Billups/25 25.00 60.00
Smooth
CM Cuttino Mobley/25 25.00 60.00
DM Desmond Mason/25 25.00 60.00
Dmase
DR Dennis Rodman/100 150.00 300.00
The Worm
EG Manu Ginobili/25 125.00 225.00
Manu
GA Gilbert Arenas/25 50.00 120.00
GA
GG George Gervin/25 40.00 100.00
Iceman
GP Gary Payton/25 50.00 120.00
The Glove
GR Glenn Robinson/25 25.00 60.00
Big Dog
JE Julius Erving/25 100.00 225.00
Dr. J
JR Jason Richardson/25 25.00 60.00
KG1 Kevin Garnett/25 125.00 250.00
The Kid
KG2 Kevin Garnett/25 125.00 250.00
LJ1 LeBron James/25 750.00 1500.00
King
LJ2 LeBron James/25 750.00 1500.00
Bron
LJ3 LeBron James/25 750.00 1500.00
The Chosen One
LO Lamar Odom/25 25.00 60.00
LO
MB Mike Bibby/25 40.00 100.00
Dime
NH Nene/25 25.00 60.00
Baby Boy
PP Paul Pierce/25 60.00 150.00
The Truth
RH Richard Hamilton/25 25.00 60.00
Rip
RO David Robinson/100 100.00 200.00
The Admiral
SF Steve Francis/25 40.00 100.00
SL Spike Lee/25 150.00 300.00
Mars
SM Shawn Marion/25 40.00 100.00
Matrix
TM Tracy McGrady/25 100.00 200.00
T-Mac
YM Yao Ming/25 100.00 200.00

2003-04 SP Signature Edition INKcredible INKscriptions

Randomly inserted, this 13-card set features a full-color player photo on the left and an authentic autograph with a special caption on the right. Several players have more than one version, and each card is sequentially numbered to 25.
BW Bill Walton/HOF 20.00 50.00
CA Carmelo Anthony/#3 Draft Pick 150.00 300.00
DM Darko Milicic/#2 Draft Pick 25.00 60.00
GG George Gervin/Hall of Fame 96 40.00 100.00
GP Gary Payton 30.00 80.00
JE Julius Erving/HOF 1993 75.00 200.00
JK Jason Kidd/All NBA 50.00 120.00
JR1 Jason Richardson 20.00 50.00
JR2 Jason Richardson 20.00 50.00
KG Kevin Garnett/All NBA 75.00 200.00
LJ LeBron James 700.00 1200.00
PS Peja Stojakovic/03 3Pt Champ 40.00 100.00

2003-04 SP Signature Edition Marquee Marks

Inserted in packs, this nine card set pairs two players from a team, one in the upper left corner and the other in the lower right where they signed next to their picture. Each card is sequentially numbered to 100 unless specified in our checklist.
AN Carmelo Anthony/75 30.00 80.00
Nene
BP Kobe Bryant/100 125.00 250.00
Gary Payton
DD Mike Dunleavy Sr./100 15.00 40.00
Mike Dunleavy Jr.
JM0 LeBron James/100 150.00 300.00
Darius Miles
JS Magic Johnson/75 150.00 300.00
John Stockton
LM Spike Lee/25 250.00 500.00
Reggie Miller
MM Cheryl Miller/100 75.00 150.00
Reggie Miller
MS Cheryl Miller/100 25.00 60.00
Summer Sanders
WW Bill Walton/100 20.00 50.00
Luke Walton

2003-04 SP Signature Edition National Treasures

This six-card set pairs players who hail from the same country. Small head-shots appear of each player, one on the top and the other on the bottom and both autographs appear in the middle of the card. Each card is sequentially numbered to 100.
NT1 Nene 12.50 30.00
Leandro Barbosa
NT2 Peja Stojakovic 12.50 30.00
Zarko Cabarkapa
NT3 Boris Diaw 12.50 30.00
Mickael Pietrus
NT4 Yao Ming 100.00 200.00
Wang Zhizhi
NT5 Tony Parker 20.00 50.00
Mickael Pietrus
NT6 Darko Milicic 12.50 30.00
Zoran Planinic

2003-04 SP Signature Edition Rookie INKorporated

Randomly inserted in packs, this 28-card set showcases this year's rookies with a small photo in the lower left hand corner and an autograph on the right. Each card is sequentially numbered to 100.
AP Aleksandar Pavlovic 5.00 12.00
BC Brian Cook 5.00 12.00
BD Boris Diaw 6.00 15.00
CA Carmelo Anthony 50.00 120.00
CB Chris Bosh 25.00 60.00
CK Chris Kaman 6.00 15.00
DJ Dahntay Jones 5.00 12.00
DM Darko Milicic 5.00 12.00
DY Dwyane Wade 125.00 250.00
HO Josh Howard 5.00 12.00
JH Jarvis Hayes 5.00 12.00
JK Jason Kapono 5.00 12.00
KP Kendrick Perkins 8.00 20.00
LB Leandro Barbosa 6.00 15.00
LJ LeBron James 350.00 700.00
LR Luke Ridnour 6.00 15.00
LW Luke Walton 5.00 12.00
MB Marcus Banks 5.00 12.00
ML Maciej Lampe 5.00 12.00
MP Mickael Pietrus 5.00 12.00
MS Mike Sweetney 5.00 12.00
NE Ndudi Ebi 5.00 12.00
RG Reece Gaines 5.00 12.00
TB Troy Bell 5.00 12.00
TO Travis Outlaw 6.00 15.00
WE David West 6.00 15.00
ZC Zarko Cabarkapa 5.00 12.00
ZP Zoran Planinic 5.00 12.00

2003-04 SP Signature Edition Scripts for Success

Randomly inserted in packs, this 28-card set features a horizontal design where full-color player action photos appear on the right and an authentic player autograph appears on the left. Each card is sequentially numbered to 250.
AP Aleksandar Pavlovic 4.00 10.00
BC Brian Cook 4.00 10.00
BD Boris Diaw 5.00 12.00
CB Chris Bosh 15.00 40.00
CK Chris Kaman 5.00 12.00
DJ Dahntay Jones 4.00 10.00
DM Darko Milicic 4.00 10.00
DY Dwyane Wade 60.00 150.00
HO Josh Howard 4.00 10.00
JH Jarvis Hayes 4.00 10.00
JK Jason Kapono 4.00 10.00
KP Kendrick Perkins 6.00 15.00
LB Leandro Barbosa 5.00 12.00
LR Luke Ridnour 5.00 12.00
LW Luke Walton 4.00 10.00
MB Marcus Banks 4.00 10.00
ML Maciej Lampe 4.00 10.00
MP Mickael Pietrus 4.00 10.00
MS Mike Sweetney 4.00 10.00
MW Maurice Williams 6.00 15.00
NE Ndudi Ebi 4.00 10.00
RG Reece Gaines 4.00 10.00
TB Troy Bell 4.00 10.00
TO Travis Outlaw 5.00 12.00
WE David West 5.00 12.00
ZA Zaur Pachulia 4.00 10.00
ZC Zarko Cabarkapa 4.00 10.00
ZP Zoran Planinic 4.00 10.00

2003-04 SP Signature Edition Signatures

Randomly seeded in packs at the rate of one in one along with the sets mentioned in the main set blurb, this 77-card set places player busts (from the waist up) on the left side of the card and authentic autographs on the right. Each card is highlighted with silver foil.
AJ Antawn Jamison 4.00 10.00
AM Antonio McDyess SP 5.00 12.00
AP Aleksandar Pavlovic 3.00 8.00
BA Marcus Banks 3.00 8.00
BD Boris Diaw 4.00 10.00
BO Carlos Boozer 5.00 12.00
CA Carmelo Anthony SP 40.00 80.00
CB Chauncey Billups 8.00 20.00
CH Chris Bosh 20.00 40.00
CK Chris Kaman 4.00 10.00
CM Corey Maggette 3.00 8.00
CW Chris Wilcox 3.00 8.00
DA Darius Miles SP 5.00 12.00
DG Drew Gooden 3.00 8.00
DJ Dahntay Jones 3.00 8.00
DM Darko Milicic 3.00 8.00
DR Dennis Rodman SP 75.00 150.00
DU Mike Dunleavy Sr. 5.00 12.00
DY Dwyane Wade 50.00 120.00
EG Manu Ginobili 12.50 30.00
GA Gilbert Arenas 8.00 20.00
GG George Gervin 10.00 25.00
GP Gary Payton SP 15.00 40.00
HW Josh Howard 3.00 8.00
JD Juan Dixon 3.00 8.00
JE Julius Erving SP 30.00 80.00
JH Jarvis Hayes 3.00 8.00
JK Jason Kidd 10.00 25.00
JL James Lang 3.00 8.00
JR Jason Richardson 6.00 15.00
JS Jerry Stackhouse 6.00 15.00
KB Kobe Bryant 100.00 200.00
KG Kevin Garnett 25.00 60.00
KO Jason Kapono 3.00 8.00
KP Kendrick Perkins 10.00 25.00
LB Larry Bird SP 75.00 150.00
LE Leandro Barbosa 4.00 10.00
LJ LeBron James 250.00 500.00
LO Lamar Odom SP 6.00 15.00
LR Luke Ridnour 4.00 10.00
LW Luke Walton 3.00 8.00
MA Magic Johnson SP 60.00 150.00
MB Mike Bibby 6.00 15.00
MD Mike Dunleavy 5.00 12.00
MI Andre Miller 3.00 8.00
MJ Michael Jordan 400.00 700.00
MK Mickael Pietrus 3.00 8.00
ML Maciej Lampe 3.00 8.00
MP Morris Peterson 3.00 8.00
MS Mike Sweetney SP 3.00 8.00
MW Maurice Williams 5.00 12.00
NE Ndudi Ebi 3.00 8.00
NH Nene 3.00 8.00
PE Patrick Ewing 75.00 150.00
PP Paul Pierce 15.00 30.00
PS Peja Stojakovic 6.00 15.00
RG Reece Gaines 3.00 8.00
RH Richard Hamilton 6.00 15.00
RJ Richard Jefferson 3.00 8.00
RL Rashard Lewis SP 6.00 15.00
RM Reggie Miller 50.00 125.00
RO Jalen Rose 6.00 15.00
SA Shareef Abdur-Rahim SP 6.00 15.00
SF Steve Francis 6.00 15.00
SM Shawn Marion SP 6.00 15.00
ST John Stockton SP 50.00 120.00
TB Troy Bell 3.00 8.00
TM Tracy McGrady 12.50 30.00
TO Travis Outlaw 4.00 10.00
TP Tony Parker 10.00 25.00
WA Bill Walton SP 12.50 30.00
WE David West 4.00 10.00
WG Dajuan Wagner SP 3.00 8.00
WZ Wang Zhizhi SP 6.00 15.00
YM Yao Ming 20.00 50.00
ZC Zarko Cabarkapa 3.00 8.00
ZP Zoran Planinic 3.00 8.00

2003-04 SP Signature Edition Signatures Gold

Randomly inserted, this 77-card set parallels the base Signatures set enhanced with gold foil highlights and sequential numbering to 50.
*GOLD SINGLES: .75X TO 2X BASE AU HI
CA Carmelo Anthony 100.00 200.00
CH Chris Bosh 40.00 100.00
DM Darko Milicic 6.00 15.00
DR Dennis Rodman 100.00 200.00
DY Dwyane Wade 150.00 300.00
GP Gary Payton 25.00 60.00
LB Larry Bird 80.00 200.00
LJ LeBron James 600.00 1200.00
MA Magic Johnson 100.00 200.00
MJ Michael Jordan 600.00 1000.00
PE Patrick Ewing 100.00 200.00
WA Bill Walton 15.00 40.00

2003-04 SP Signature Edition Signatures Triple

Randomly seeded in packs, this 10-card set lines up three player photos and autographs, from top to bottom, and cards are sequentially numbered to 25.
BPG Kobe Bryant 250.00 500.00
Gary Payton
Kevin Garnett
BSW Mike Bibby 100.00 200.00
Peja Stojakovic
Gerald Wallace
JJM LeBron James 1000.00 2000.00
Michael Jordan
Tracy McGrady
JMA LeBron James 600.00 1000.00
Darko Milicic
Carmelo Anthony
KJP Jason Kidd 75.00 150.00
Richard Jefferson
Zoran Planinic
MGG Tracy McGrady 75.00 150.00
Drew Gooden
Reece Gaines
MGJ Kevin Garnett 400.00 800.00
Tracy McGrady
LeBron James
MHB Darko Milicic 75.00 150.00
Richard Hamilton
Chauncey Billups
MJM Reggie Miller 80.00 200.00
Jalen Rose
Andre Miller
RJP Antawn Jamison 30.00 80.00
Jason Richardson
Mickael Pietrus

2003-04 SP Signature Edition Tins

COMPLETE SET 6.00 15.00
*BLACK TINS: .6X TO 1.5X BASE HI
NNO Carmelo Anthony .75 2.00
NNO Michael Jordan 2.50 6.00
NNO Tracy McGrady .40 1.00
NNO Kobe Bryant 1.50 4.00
NNO Darko Milicic .30 .75
NNO LeBron James 3.00 8.00

2004-05 SP Signature Edition

Released in June 2005, SP Signature Edition is made up of a 242-card set where cards 1-100 feature veteran players, 101-142 feature rookie jersey sequentially numbered to 499 and cards 143-242 are serially numbered to the featured player's jersey number. SP Signature was sold in three card tins and the SRP was $60.
1 Antoine Walker .60 1.50
2 Al Harrington .50 1.25
3 Boris Diaw .50 1.25
4 Paul Pierce .75 2.00
5 Ricky Davis .50 1.25
6 Gary Payton .60 1.50
7 Gerald Wallace .60 1.50
8 Emeka Okafor RC 3.00 8.00
9 Jahidi White .40 1.00
10 Eddy Curry .50 1.25
11 Kirk Hinrich .60 1.50
12 Michael Jordan 5.00 12.00
13 LeBron James 4.00 10.00
14 Dajuan Wagner .40 1.00
15 Jeff McInnis .40 1.00
16 Drew Gooden .50 1.25
17 Dirk Nowitzki 1.00 2.50
18 Michael Finley .60 1.50
19 Jerry Stackhouse .50 1.25
20 Jason Terry .50 1.25
21 Kenyon Martin .60 1.50
22 Andre Miller .50 1.25
23 Carmelo Anthony 1.25 3.00
24 Nene .50 1.25
25 Chauncey Billups .60 1.50
26 Rasheed Wallace .60 1.50
27 Ben Wallace .60 1.50
28 Richard Hamilton .50 1.25
29 Derek Fisher .50 1.25
30 Jason Richardson .60 1.50
31 Mike Dunleavy .50 1.25
32 Yao Ming 1.25 3.00
33 Tracy McGrady .75 2.00
34 Juwan Howard .50 1.25
35 Jermaine O'Neal .60 1.50
36 Reggie Miller .60 1.50
37 Ron Artest .60 1.50
38 Jamaal Tinsley .40 1.00
39 Elton Brand .60 1.50
40 Corey Maggette .50 1.25
41 Marko Jaric .40 1.00
42 Kerry Kittles .40 1.00
43 Kobe Bryant 3.00 8.00
44 Chucky Atkins .40 1.00
45 Lamar Odom .60 1.50
46 Caron Butler .60 1.50
47 Pau Gasol .60 1.50
48 Jason Williams .50 1.25
49 Bonzi Wells .40 1.00
50 Shaquille O'Neal 1.50 4.00
51 Dwyane Wade 2.00 5.00
52 Eddie Jones .50 1.25
53 Michael Redd .60 1.50
54 Desmond Mason .50 1.25
55 T.J. Ford .50 1.25
56 Latrell Sprewell .50 1.25
57 Kevin Garnett 1.25 3.00
58 Sam Cassell .50 1.25
59 Troy Hudson .40 1.00
60 Vince Carter 1.00 2.50
61 Richard Jefferson .60 1.50
62 Jason Kidd 1.00 2.50
63 Jamal Mashburn .60 1.50
64 Baron Davis .60 1.50
65 Jamaal Magloire .40 1.00
66 Allan Houston .50 1.25
67 Jamal Crawford .50 1.25
68 Stephon Marbury .50 1.25
69 Grant Hill .75 2.00
70 Cuttino Mobley .50 1.25
71 Steve Francis .60 1.50
72 Glenn Robinson .50 1.25
73 Allen Iverson 1.00 2.50
74 Kyle Korver .50 1.25
75 Amare Stoudemire .75 2.00
76 Steve Nash .75 2.00
77 Quentin Richardson .50 1.25
78 Shawn Marion .60 1.50
79 Shareef Abdur-Rahim .50 1.25
80 Damon Stoudamire .50 1.25
81 Zach Randolph .50 1.25
82 Darius Miles .40 1.00
83 Peja Stojakovic .60 1.50
84 Chris Webber .60 1.50
85 Mike Bibby .60 1.50
86 Tony Parker .60 1.50
87 Tim Duncan 1.00 2.50
88 Manu Ginobili .75 2.00
89 Ronald Murray .40 1.00
90 Ray Allen .60 1.50
91 Rashard Lewis .60 1.50
92 Chris Bosh .60 1.50
93 Jalen Rose .50 1.25
94 Rafer Alston .40 1.00
95 Andrei Kirilenko .50 1.25
96 Matt Harpring .50 1.25
97 Carlos Boozer .60 1.50
98 Gilbert Arenas .60 1.50
99 Jarvis Hayes .40 1.00
100 Antawn Jamison .60 1.50
101 Dwight Howard JSY RC 10.00 25.00
102 Ben Gordon JSY RC 4.00 10.00
103 Shaun Livingston JSY RC 3.00 8.00
104 Devin Harris JSY RC 5.00 12.00
105 Josh Childress JSY RC 3.00 8.00
106 Luol Deng JSY RC 5.00 12.00
107 Rafael Araujo JSY RC 3.00 8.00
108 Andre Iguodala JSY RC 5.00 12.00
109 Luke Jackson JSY RC 3.00 8.00
110 Sebastian Telfair JSY RC 3.00 8.00
111 Kris Humphries JSY RC 3.00 8.00
112 Al Jefferson JSY RC 5.00 12.00
113 Kirk Snyder JSY RC 3.00 8.00
114 Josh Smith JSY RC 5.00 12.00
115 J.R. Smith JSY RC 4.00 10.00
116 Dorell Wright JSY RC 5.00 12.00
117 Jameer Nelson JSY RC 4.00 10.00
118 Delonte West JSY RC 4.00 10.00
119 Tony Allen JSY RC 4.00 10.00
120 Kevin Martin JSY RC 4.00 10.00
121 David Harrison JSY RC 3.00 8.00
122 Anderson Varejao JSY RC 4.00 10.00
123 Jackson Vroman JSY RC 3.00 8.00
124 Lionel Chalmers JSY RC 3.00 8.00
125 Andre Emmett JSY RC 3.00 8.00
126 Chris Duhon JSY RC 3.00 8.00
127 Bernard Robinson JSY RC 3.00 8.00
128 Tim Pickett RC 2.00 5.00
129 Nenad Krstic JSY RC 3.00 8.00
130 Andris Biedrins JSY RC 4.00 10.00
131 Robert Swift RC 2.00 5.00
132 Andres Nocioni RC 2.00 5.00
133 Justin Reed RC 2.00 5.00
134 Romain Sato RC 2.00 5.00
135 Sasha Vujacic JSY RC 3.00 8.00
136 Beno Udrih RC 2.00 5.00
137 Peter John Ramos JSY RC 3.00 8.00
138 Donta Smith JSY RC 3.00 8.00
139 Antonio Burks RC 2.00 5.00
140 Yuta Tabuse JSY RC 6.00 15.00
141 Trevor Ariza JSY RC 3.00 8.00
142 Matt Freije JSY RC 3.00 8.00
143 Drew Gooden/90 4.00 10.00
144 Elton Brand/42 4.00 10.00
145 Shawn Marion/31 6.00 15.00

Card	Low	High
148 Dirk Nowitzki/41	6.00	15.00
149 Pau Gasol/16	6.00	15.00
152 Devin Harris/34	6.00	15.00
165 Shaquille O'Neal/32	12.50	30.00
166 Shareef Abdur-Rahim/33	4.00	10.00
167 Jason Terry/31	4.00	10.00
171 Zach Randolph/50	5.00	12.00
172 Dave DeBusschere/22	10.00	25.00
176 Gary Payton/20	8.00	20.00
180 Michael Redd/22	4.00	10.00
181 Peja Stojakovic/16	8.00	20.00
183 Luke Jackson/33	4.00	10.00
184 Richard Hamilton/32	6.00	15.00
185 Kevin Garnett/21	12.00	30.00
188 Sebastian Telfair/31	4.00	10.00
191 David Robinson/50	10.00	25.00
192 Jerry Stackhouse/42	4.00	10.00
193 Kris Humphries/43	4.00	10.00
194 Dennis Rodman/91	6.00	15.00
199 Michael Jordan/23	75.00	150.00
200 Magic Johnson/32	15.00	40.00
207 George Gervin/44	6.00	15.00
212 Bernard King/30	4.00	10.00
214 Grant Hill/33	8.00	20.00
215 J.R. Smith/23	8.00	20.00
216 LeBron James/23	25.00	60.00
218 Amare Stoudemire/32	8.00	20.00
221 Larry Bird/33	15.00	40.00
222 Reggie Miller/31	12.00	30.00
224 Andrei Kirilenko/47	6.00	15.00
228 Corey Maggette/50	4.00	10.00
233 Hakeem Olajuwon/34	6.00	15.00
234 Richard Jefferson/24	4.00	10.00
235 Tim Duncan/21	12.00	30.00
236 Ray Allen/34	10.00	25.00
238 Paul Pierce/34	8.00	20.00
240 Willis Reed/19	5.00	12.00
242 Manu Ginobili/20	6.00	15.00

2004-05 SP Signature Edition 25

Randomly inserted, this 142-card set parallels the first 142 cards of the SP Signature edition base set and is enhanced with sequential numbering to 25. Some of the rookies autographed their cards.
MOST RC PLAYERS ARE AUTOGRAPHED
SOME NOT PRICED DUE TO SCARCITY

Card	Low	High
12 Michael Jordan	75.00	150.00
69 Grant Hill	12.00	30.00
101 Dwight Howard JSY AU	175.00	350.00
102 Ben Gordon JSY AU	20.00	50.00
104 Devin Harris JSY AU	25.00	60.00
108 Andre Iguodala JSY AU	40.00	100.00
112 Al Jefferson JSY AU	40.00	100.00
114 Josh Smith JSY AU	20.00	50.00
117 Jameer Nelson JSY AU	12.00	30.00
118 Delonte West JSY AU	12.00	30.00
119 Tony Allen JSY AU	12.00	30.00
122 Anderson Varejao JSY AU	12.00	30.00
126 Chris Duhon JSY AU	10.00	25.00
129 Nenad Krstic JSY AU	10.00	25.00
130 Andris Biedrins JSY AU	12.00	30.00
141 Trevor Ariza JSY AU	10.00	25.00

2004-05 SP Signature Edition Autographed Parallel

Randomly seeded in packs, this 42-card set parallels most of the veteran players in the set and are enhanced with autographs and sequential numbering to the featured player's jersey number.
CARDS #'d TO PLAYER JSY NUMBER
CARDS WITH ASTERISK ISSUED AS EXCH

Card	Low	High
A4 Paul Pierce/34*	20.00	50.00
A6 Gary Payton/20	25.00	60.00
A12 Michael Jordan/23*	300.00	600.00
A13 LeBron James/23	200.00	400.00
A19 Jerry Stackhouse/42	15.00	40.00
A22 Andre Miller/24	12.50	30.00
A23 Carmelo Anthony/15	75.00	150.00
A28 Richard Hamilton/32	15.00	40.00
A30 Jason Richardson/23	12.50	30.00
A36 Reggie Miller/31	50.00	120.00
A40 Corey Maggette/50	12.50	30.00
A47 Pau Gasol/16	25.00	60.00
A53 Michael Redd/22	12.50	30.00
A57 Kevin Garnett/21	60.00	150.00
A65 Jamaal Magloire/21	12.50	30.00
A75 Amare Stoudemire/32	40.00	100.00
A78 Shawn Marion/31	15.00	40.00
A79 Shareef Abdur-Rahim/33	15.00	40.00
A81 Zach Randolph/50	12.50	30.00
A95 Andrei Kirilenko/47	15.00	40.00

2004-05 SP Signature Edition AKA Autographs

Limited to either 50 or 100 copies, this 49-card set is horizontally designed and features both an autograph and a nickname inscription.

Card	Low	High
AL Al Jefferson Big Al/100	15.00	40.00
AM Antonio McDyess/100	10.00	25.00
AR Rafael Araujo Hoffa/100	10.00	25.00
AS Amare Stoudemire Future/50	50.00	100.00
BC Bob Cousy Cooz/50	20.00	50.00
BG Ben Gordon M.S.G./50	20.00	50.00
BW Ben Wallace Big Ben/50	40.00	80.00
CA Carlos Arroyo New Maestro/100	25.00	60.00
CD Clyde Drexler The Glide/50	50.00	100.00
CH Chris Duhon C-Doo/100	10.00	25.00
DF Derek Fisher Fish/100	15.00	40.00
DG Drew Gooden Truth/100	10.00	25.00
DH Dwight Howard DeBo/100	25.00	60.00
DR Dennis Rodman The Worm/50	60.00	120.00
DS Damon Stoudamire ROY 96/100	12.00	30.00
DW Delonte West Redz/100	12.00	30.00
EC Eddy Curry ECity/100	10.00	25.00
GP Gary Payton	20.00	50.00
GW Gerald Wallace	10.00	25.00
HO Hakeem Olajuwon The Dream/50	50.00	125.00
JA Jason Williams JW/100	30.00	80.00
JC Josh Childress Real Deal/50	15.00	40.00
JM Jamaal Magloire Big Cat/100	10.00	25.00
JS Josh Smith JSmoove/100	15.00	40.00
JV Jackson Vroman Jax/100	10.00	25.00
JW John Wooden	75.00	150.00
KA Kenny Anderson	10.00	25.00
KE Kevin Martin K-Mart/100	12.00	30.00
KG Kevin Garnett KG/100	40.00	80.00
KH Kirk Hinrich Capt. Kirk/50	25.00	60.00
LJ LeBron James Bron/100	150.00	300.00
LO Lamar Odom/50	15.00	40.00
MB Mike Bibby	25.00	60.00
MR Michael Redd Silky/50	15.00	40.00
PP Paul Pierce Truth/50	25.00	60.00
RH Richard Hamilton RIP/50	25.00	60.00
RM Ronald Murray Flip/100	10.00	25.00
RT Robert Traylor Tractor/100	10.00	25.00
RY Ray Allen	20.00	50.00
SA Shareef Abdur-Rahim Reef/50	15.00	40.00
SE Sebastian Telfair Bassy/50	15.00	40.00
SM Shawn Marion Matrix/50	20.00	50.00
ST Stephon Marbury	20.00	50.00
TK1 Toni Kukoc Croatian Sensation/100	25.00	60.00
TK2 Toni Kukoc Pink Panther/100	20.00	50.00
TM Tracy McGrady T-Mac/50	30.00	60.00
AU Stacey Augmon Plastic Man/100	15.00	40.00

2004-05 SP Signature Edition Alumni Associates

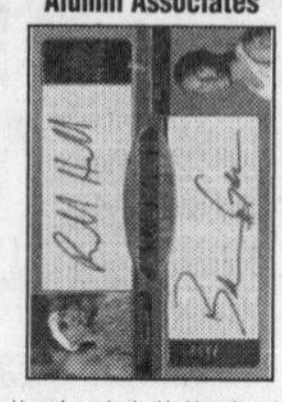

Inserted in packs randomly, this 11-card set places two players who attended the same college along with their autographs. Each card is sequentially numbered to 100.

Card	Low	High
AB Gilbert Arenas / Mike Bibby	15.00	40.00
BD Carlos Boozer / Chris Duhon	15.00	40.00
CS Lionel Chalmers / Romain Sato	10.00	25.00
DA Baron Davis / Trevor Ariza	10.00	25.00
HG Richard Hamilton / Ben Gordon	25.00	50.00
JI Richard Jefferson / Andre Iguodala	15.00	40.00
JJ Fred Jones / Luke Jackson	10.00	25.00
KD Kirk Hinrich / Drew Gooden	20.00	50.00
MD Corey Maggette / Luol Deng	15.00	40.00
NW Jameer Nelson / Delonte West	15.00	30.00

2004-05 SP Signature Edition Celebrity Signings

No odds were given on the packs for this set, but the three cards are of celebrities and place a photo on the top of the card and an autograph on the bottom.

Card	Low	High
CS7 Nelly	25.00	60.00
CS8 Jamie Foxx	25.00	60.00
CS9 Mark Cuban	15.00	40.00

2004-05 SP Signature Edition INKredible INKscriptions

Randomly seeded and sequentially numbered to 25, this 45-card set is horizontally designed with a player photo on the left and an autograph and an inscription on the right.

Card	Low	High
AK Andrei Kirilenko	15.00	40.00
AS Amare Stoudemire	30.00	80.00
BD Baron Davis Bdiddy	30.00	80.00
BG Ben Gordon 04 NCAA Champ	40.00	100.00
BG2 Ben Gordon Draft Pick #3	40.00	100.00
BK Bob Knight	25.00	60.00
CA1 Carmelo Anthony Final 4 MVP	50.00	120.00
CA2 Carmelo Anthony 03 NCAA Champ	50.00	120.00
CA3 Carmelo Anthony Melo	60.00	150.00
CD Clyde Drexler Phi Slamma Jamma	75.00	150.00
CH Chauncey Billups 04 Finals MVP	25.00	60.00
DE Devin Harris Big 10 POY	20.00	50.00
DE2 Devin Harris Draft Pick #5	20.00	50.00
DH Dwight Howard 04 Naismith AW	75.00	150.00
DH2 Dwight Howard Draft Pick #1	75.00	150.00
DH3 Dwight Howard	75.00	150.00
DR David Robinson The Admiral	75.00	150.00
HO Hakeem Olajuwon Phi Slamma Jamma	40.00	100.00
JA Jalen Rose Fab Five	15.00	40.00
JC Josh Childress 04 Pac 10 POY	15.00	40.00
JE Julius Erving Dr. J	75.00	150.00
JH Josh Howard	15.00	40.00
JN Jameer Nelson John Wooden AW	20.00	50.00
JR J.R.Smith McDonald's MVP	30.00	80.00
JR2 J.R. Smith	20.00	50.00
KG Kevin Garnett 2004 MVP	50.00	120.00
KS Kirk Snyder 04 WAC POY	15.00	40.00
LJ1 LeBron James King James	300.00	500.00
LJ2 LeBron James 04 Naismith AW	300.00	600.00
LJ3 LeBron James 04 ROY	300.00	500.00
MA Magic Johnson	150.00	300.00
PS Peja Stojakovic 3 Time All-Star	30.00	80.00
RA1 Rafeal Araujo 04 Mount.West POY	15.00	40.00
RH Richard Hamilton 04 NBA Champs	15.00	40.00
SL1 Shaun Livingston Draft Pick #4	15.00	40.00
SL2 Shaun Livingston Geezy	15.00	40.00
ST1 Sebastian Telfair 3 Time PSAL Champ	15.00	40.00
TA1 Tony Allen 2004 Big 12 POY	15.00	40.00
TA2 Tony Allen	15.00	40.00
TM Tracy McGrady 5 Time All-Star	40.00	100.00
WI Jason Williams White Chocolate	75.00	150.00

2004-05 SP Signature Edition Marks of Distinction

Randomly inserted and sequentially numbered to 25, this 30-card set places player photos towards the top and autographs on the bottom.

Card	Low	High
AK Andrei Kirilenko	10.00	25.00
BD Baron Davis	10.00	25.00
BK Bernard King	12.50	30.00
BR Bill Russell	100.00	200.00
BW Ben Wallace	20.00	50.00
CA Carmelo Anthony	40.00	100.00
CD Clyde Drexler	40.00	100.00
DH Dwight Howard	75.00	150.00
DR David Robinson	75.00	150.00
HO Hakeem Olajuwon	30.00	80.00
IT Isiah Thomas	25.00	60.00
JE Julius Erving	75.00	150.00
JK Jason Kidd	40.00	100.00
JR Jason Richardson	10.00	25.00
JS John Stockton	100.00	200.00
KB Kobe Bryant	125.00	250.00
KG Kevin Garnett	50.00	120.00
KH Kirk Hinrich	20.00	50.00
LB Larry Bird	100.00	200.00
LJ LeBron James	150.00	300.00
MA Magic Johnson	75.00	150.00
MJ Michael Jordan	350.00	600.00
PG Pau Gasol	15.00	40.00
PP Paul Pierce	15.00	40.00
PS Peja Stojakovic	15.00	40.00
RA Ray Allen	20.00	50.00
SM Stephon Marbury	15.00	40.00
TM Tracy McGrady	40.00	100.00
YM Yao Ming	40.00	100.00

2004-05 SP Signature Edition Marquee Marks

This seven card set was randomly seeded in packs and is horizontally designed with two great players from the same franchise along with their autographs. Each card is limited to 100 copies.

Card	Low	High
JB Magic Johnson / Kobe Bryant	125.00	250.00
KR Bernard King / Willis Reed	12.50	30.00
MM Yao Ming / Tracy McGrady	30.00	80.00
MT Stephon Marbury / Sebastian Telfair	12.50	30.00
NL Curly Neal / Meadowlark Lemon	50.00	100.00
SB Peja Stojakovic / Mike Bibby	15.00	40.00
SH J.R. Smith / Dwight Howard	40.00	100.00

2004-05 SP Signature Edition Pride of a Nation

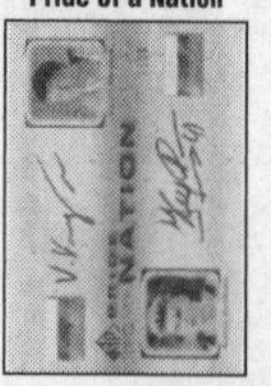

Randomly inserted in packs, this five-card set places two players from the same nation along with their autographs and country flag on the card front. Each card is sequentially numbered to 100.

Card	Low	High
BV Primoz Brezec / Sasha Vujacic	10.00	25.00
KG Toni Kukoc / Gordan Giricek	20.00	50.00
KK Viktor Khryapa / Andrei Kirilenko	10.00	25.00
KP Andrei Kirilenko / Pavel Podkolzin	10.00	25.00
VU Sasha Vujacic / Beno Udrih	10.00	25.00

2004-05 SP Signature Edition Quadruple Authentic Signatures

Randomly inserted, this nine-card set features four players and four signatures on gold foil on the card front. Each card is sequentially numbered to 15.
SOME NOT PRICED DUE TO SCARCITY

Card	Low	High
BJJB Kobe Bryant / Magic Johnson / LeBron James / Larry Bird	500.00	800.00
CBPP Bob Cousy / Larry Bird / Paul Pierce / Gary Payton	125.00	250.00
KSJM Jason Kidd / John Stockton / Magic Johnson / Stephon Marbury	200.00	400.00
SMGK Peja Stojakovic / Yao Ming / Pau Gasol / Andrei Kirilenko	100.00	200.00
WOMR Ben Wallace / Hakeem Olajuwon / Yao Ming / David Robinson	200.00	350.00

2004-05 SP Signature Edition Rookie Auto Drafts

Limited to each specific player's draft position, this 44-card set is horizontally designed with a player photo on the left and the draft board and an authentic autograph on the right.
MOST NOT PRICED DUE TO SCARCITY

Card	Low	High
AE Andre Emmett/35	6.00	15.00
AN Antonio Burks/36	6.00	15.00
AV Anderson Varejao/30	10.00	25.00
BR Bernard Robinson/45	6.00	15.00
BU Beno Udrih/28	15.00	40.00
CD Chris Duhon/38	10.00	25.00
DA David Harrison/29	6.00	15.00
DW Dorell Wright/19	20.00	50.00
JN Jameer Nelson/20	10.00	25.00
JR J.R. Smith/18	25.00	60.00
JS Josh Smith/17	25.00	60.00
JU Justin Reed/40	6.00	15.00
KM Kevin Martin/26	12.50	30.00
KS Kirk Snyder/16	15.00	40.00
LC Lionel Chalmers/33	6.00	15.00
LF Luis Flores/55	6.00	15.00
MF Matt Freije/53	6.00	15.00
NK Nenad Krstic/24	15.00	40.00
PP Pavel Podkolzin/21	12.50	30.00
PR Peter John Ramos/32	6.00	15.00
PS Pape Sow/47	6.00	15.00
RI Royal Ivey/37	6.00	15.00
RO Romain Sato/52	6.00	15.00
SV Sasha Vujacic/27	10.00	25.00
TP Tim Pickett/44	6.00	15.00
TR Trevor Ariza/43	6.00	15.00
WE Delonte West/24	15.00	40.00

2004-05 SP Signature Edition Rookie GRAPHiti

Randomly seeded in packs, this 40-card set is horizontally designed with a player photo and an autograph in the foreground and a graphiti style background. Each card is serially numbered to 200.

Card	Low	High
AB Andris Biedrins	5.00	12.00
AE Andre Emmett	4.00	10.00
AI Andre Iguodala	6.00	15.00
AJ Al Jefferson	6.00	15.00
AN Andres Nocioni	4.00	10.00
AV Anderson Varejao	5.00	12.00
BG Ben Gordon	5.00	12.00
BR Bernard Robinson	4.00	10.00
BU Beno Udrih	4.00	10.00
CD Chris Duhon	4.00	10.00
DA David Harrison	4.00	10.00
DE Devin Harris	6.00	15.00
DH Dwight Howard	20.00	50.00
DW Dorell Wright	6.00	15.00
JC Josh Childress	4.00	10.00
JN Jameer Nelson	5.00	12.00
JR J.R. Smith	5.00	12.00
JS Josh Smith	6.00	15.00
JU Justin Reed	4.00	10.00
JV Jackson Vroman	4.00	10.00
KH Kris Humphries	4.00	10.00
KM Kevin Martin	5.00	12.00
KS Kirk Snyder	4.00	10.00
LC Lionel Chalmers	4.00	10.00
LD Luol Deng	6.00	15.00
LF Luis Flores	4.00	10.00
LJ Luke Jackson	4.00	10.00
MF Matt Freije	4.00	10.00
NK Nenad Krstic	4.00	10.00
PR Peter John Ramos	4.00	10.00
RA Rafael Araujo	4.00	10.00
RS Robert Swift	4.00	10.00
SL Shaun Livingston	4.00	10.00
ST Sebastian Telfair	4.00	10.00
SV Sasha Vujacic	4.00	10.00
TA Tony Allen	5.00	12.00
TP Tim Pickett	4.00	10.00
TR Trevor Ariza	4.00	10.00
WE Delonte West	5.00	12.00
YT Yuta Tabuse	8.00	20.00

2004-05 SP Signature Edition Rookies INKorporated

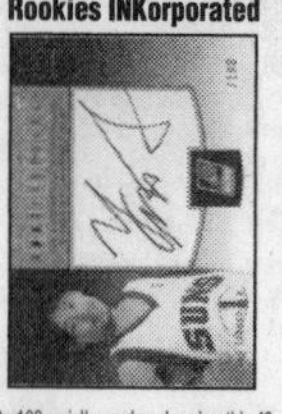

Limited to 100 serially numbered copies, this 40-card set places rookie photos on the left and has a white-out box on the right for autographs.

Card	Low	High
AB Andris Biedrins	6.00	15.00
AE Andre Emmett	5.00	12.00
AI Andre Iguodala	8.00	20.00
AJ Al Jefferson	8.00	20.00
AN Andres Nocioni	5.00	12.00
AV Anderson Varejao	6.00	15.00
BG Ben Gordon	6.00	15.00
BR Bernard Robinson	5.00	12.00
BU Beno Udrih	5.00	12.00
CD Chris Duhon	5.00	12.00
DA David Harrison	5.00	12.00
DE Devin Harris	8.00	20.00
DH Dwight Howard	40.00	80.00
DW Dorell Wright	8.00	20.00
JC Josh Childress	5.00	12.00
JN Jameer Nelson	6.00	15.00
JR J.R. Smith	6.00	15.00
JS Josh Smith	8.00	20.00
JV Jackson Vroman	5.00	12.00
KH Kris Humphries	5.00	12.00
KM Kevin Martin	6.00	15.00
KS Kirk Snyder	5.00	12.00
LC Lionel Chalmers	5.00	12.00
LD Luol Deng	8.00	20.00
LF Luis Flores	5.00	12.00
LJ Luke Jackson	5.00	12.00
MF Matt Freije	5.00	12.00
NK Nenad Krstic	5.00	12.00
PR Peter John Ramos	5.00	12.00
RA Rafael Araujo	5.00	12.00
RS Robert Swift	5.00	12.00
SL Shaun Livingston	5.00	12.00
ST Sebastian Telfair	5.00	12.00
SV Sasha Vujacic	5.00	12.00
TA Tony Allen	6.00	15.00
TP Tim Pickett	5.00	12.00
TR Trevor Ariza	5.00	12.00
WE Delonte West	6.00	15.00
YT Yuta Tabuse	10.00	25.00

2004-05 SP Signature Edition Scripts for Success

Seeded in packs randomly and limited to 25 copies, this 40-card set is horizontally designed, has a colored border along the bottom and a player photo and autograph set to a white background on the top.

Card	Low	High
AB Andris Biedrins	12.00	30.00
AE Andre Emmett	10.00	25.00
AI Andre Iguodala	15.00	40.00
AJ Al Jefferson	15.00	40.00
BG Ben Gordon	12.00	30.00
BR Bernard Robinson	10.00	25.00
BU Beno Udrih	10.00	25.00
CD Chris Duhon	10.00	25.00
DA David Harrison	10.00	25.00
DE Devin Harris	15.00	40.00
DH Dwight Howard	40.00	100.00
DW Dorell Wright	15.00	40.00
JN Jameer Nelson	12.00	30.00
JR J.R. Smith	12.00	30.00
JS Josh Smith	15.00	40.00
JV Jackson Vroman	10.00	25.00
KH Kris Humphries	10.00	25.00
KM Kevin Martin	12.00	30.00
KS Kirk Snyder	10.00	25.00
LD Luol Deng	15.00	40.00
MF Matt Freije	10.00	25.00
NK Nenad Krstic	10.00	25.00
PR Peter John Ramos	10.00	25.00
RA Rafael Araujo	10.00	25.00
RS Robert Swift	10.00	25.00
SL Shaun Livingston	10.00	25.00
ST Sebastian Telfair	10.00	25.00
SV Sasha Vujacic	10.00	25.00
TA Tony Allen	12.00	30.00
TP Tim Pickett	10.00	25.00
TR Trevor Ariza	10.00	25.00
WE Delonte West	12.00	30.00
YT Yuta Tabuse	40.00	100.00

2004-05 SP Signature Edition Signatures

Inserted at the overall odds of one per pack along with all other autographs, this 99-card set is horizontally designed with a player photo on the left and autographed gold foil on the right. A gold parallel was also inserted and those cards are sequentially numbered to ten.

Card	Low	High
AB Andris Biedrins	4.00	10.00
AE Andre Emmett	3.00	8.00
AH Al Harrington	3.00	8.00
AI Andre Iguodala	6.00	15.00
AJ Al Jefferson	6.00	15.00
AK Andrei Kirilenko	6.00	15.00
AL Ray Allen	10.00	25.00
AN Antawn Jamison	6.00	15.00
AR Carlos Arroyo	6.00	15.00
AS Amare Stoudemire	10.00	25.00
AV Anderson Varejao	4.00	10.00
BC Bob Cousy	20.00	50.00
BD Baron Davis	5.00	12.00
BE Beno Udrih	3.00	8.00
BG Ben Gordon	5.00	12.00
BK Bernard King	6.00	15.00
BM Brad Miller	3.00	8.00
BO Carlos Boozer	4.00	10.00
BR Bill Russell SP	75.00	150.00
BU Antonio Burks	3.00	8.00
BW Ben Wallace	10.00	25.00
CD Chris Duhon	3.00	8.00
CL Clyde Drexler	12.50	30.00
CM Corey Maggette	3.00	8.00
CR Jamal Crawford SP	8.00	20.00
DA David Harrison	3.00	8.00
DE Dennis Rodman	50.00	100.00
DF Derek Fisher	6.00	15.00
DH Dwight Howard	30.00	65.00
DM Desmond Mason	3.00	8.00
DR David Robinson SP	30.00	80.00
DS Donta Smith	3.00	8.00
GG George Gervin	10.00	25.00
HA Devin Harris	5.00	12.00
IT Isiah Thomas SP	12.50	30.00
IV Royal Ivey	3.00	8.00
JA Jason Richardson	5.00	12.00
JE Julius Erving SP	40.00	100.00
JH Josh Howard	4.00	10.00
JK Jason Kidd SP	12.00	30.00
JN Jameer Nelson	4.00	10.00
JR J.R. Smith	4.00	10.00
JV Jackson Vroman	3.00	8.00
KB Kobe Bryant SP	80.00	160.00
KG Kevin Garnett SP	25.00	60.00
KH Kris Humphries	3.00	8.00
KI Kirk Hinrich	8.00	20.00
KM Kevin Martin	4.00	10.00
KR Kareem Rush	3.00	8.00
KS Kirk Snyder	3.00	8.00
LB Larry Bird SP	50.00	120.00
LC Lionel Chalmers	3.00	8.00
LD Luol Deng	5.00	12.00
LF Luis Flores	3.00	8.00
LJ LeBron James	150.00	300.00
LU Luke Jackson	3.00	8.00
MB Mike Bibby SP	5.00	12.00
MD Marquis Daniels	3.00	8.00
MJ Michael Jordan SP	350.00	600.00
MR Michael Redd	5.00	12.00
NK Nenad Krstic	3.00	8.00
NO Andres Nocioni	3.00	8.00
PG Pau Gasol	8.00	20.00
PR Peter John Ramos	3.00	8.00
RA Rafael Araujo	3.00	8.00
RE Justin Reed	3.00	8.00
RH Richard Hamilton	5.00	12.00
RJ Richard Jefferson	5.00	12.00
RM Reggie Miller SP	25.00	60.00
RO Bernard Robinson	3.00	8.00
RS Robert Swift	3.00	8.00
SA Romain Sato	3.00	8.00
SC Sam Cassell	4.00	10.00
SF Shareef Abdur-Rahim	5.00	12.00
SH Shawn Marion	6.00	15.00
SL Shaun Livingston	3.00	8.00
SM Josh Smith	5.00	12.00
SV Sasha Vujacic	3.00	8.00
TA Tony Allen	4.00	10.00
TM Tracy McGrady SP	15.00	40.00
TP Tony Parker	6.00	15.00
TP2 T.Parker AU Both Sides	15.00	40.00
TR Trevor Ariza	3.00	8.00
WE Delonte West	4.00	10.00
WR Dorell Wright	5.00	12.00
YM Yao Ming SP	20.00	50.00
ZO Alonzo Mourning SP	10.00	25.00
ZR Zach Randolph	3.00	8.00

2004-05 SP Signature Edition Signatures Dual

Limited to 100 copies for most and 25 copies for the short printed cards, this 38-card set utilizes some of the design elements of the Signatures set but is horizontally designed and places two players on the card front.

Card	Low	High
AA Andre Emmett / Antonio Burks	8.00	20.00
AM Carmelo Anthony SP / Tracy McGrady	50.00	120.00
AT Shareef Abdur-Rahim / Sebastian Telfair	8.00	20.00
BH Chauncey Billups / Richard Hamilton	15.00	40.00
BJ Kobe Bryant SP / Michael Jordan	700.00	1200.00
BM Mike Bibby / Kevin Martin	10.00	25.00
BS Carlos Boozer / Kirk Snyder	8.00	20.00
CS Josh Childress / Josh Smith	10.00	25.00
DH Marquis Daniels / Devin Harris	10.00	25.00
DP Baron Davis / Tony Parker	12.50	30.00
DS Baron Davis / J.R. Smith	10.00	25.00
DT Delonte West / Tony Allen	10.00	25.00
EJ Julius Erving SP / Michael Jordan	400.00	700.00
GC Kevin Garnett / Sam Cassell	25.00	60.00
GD Ben Gordon / Luol Deng	15.00	40.00
GH Kevin Garnett SP / Dwight Howard	75.00	150.00
HN Dwight Howard / Jameer Nelson	20.00	50.00
JB LeBron James SP / Kobe Bryant	300.00	550.00
JH LeBron James SP / Dwight Howard	200.00	400.00
JJ Michael Jordan SP / LeBron James	400.00	800.00
JR Antawn Jamison / Peter John Ramos	8.00	20.00
JV Luke Jackson / Anderson Varejao	8.00	20.00
KH Andrei Kirilenko / Kris Humphries	8.00	20.00
KJ Jason Kidd / Richard Jefferson	15.00	40.00
KM Bernard King SP / Stephon Marbury	12.00	30.00
LC Shaun Livingston / Lionel Chalmers	8.00	20.00
LM Larry Bird SP / Magic Johnson	250.00	400.00
MH Reggie Miller / David Harrison	20.00	50.00
OR Lamar Odom / Kareem Rush	8.00	20.00
PA Morris Peterson / Rafael Araujo	8.00	20.00
PP Paul Pierce / Gary Payton	20.00	50.00
RB Bill Russell SP / Larry Bird	175.00	350.00
RS Zach Randolph / Damon Stoudamire	8.00	20.00
SM Amare Stoudemire / Shawn Marion	15.00	40.00
VM Jackson Vroman / (Shawn Marion	8.00	20.00
WR Ben Wallace SP / Dennis Rodman	25.00	60.00

2004-05 SP Signature Edition SP Signs

Serially numbered to either 100 or 50, this 90-card set places a player photo and an autograph on a design that is highlighted by the featured player's team colors.

Card	Low	High
AE Andre Emmett/100	5.00	12.00
AH Al Harrington/100	5.00	12.00
AI Andre Iguodala/50	12.00	30.00
AJ Al Jefferson/100	8.00	20.00
AK Andrei Kirilenko/50	8.00	20.00
AL Ray Allen/100	10.00	25.00
AM Andre Miller/100	5.00	12.00
AN Antawn Jamison/100	5.00	12.00
AR Carlos Arroyo/100	8.00	20.00
AS Amare Stoudemire/100	15.00	40.00
AV Anderson Varejao/100	6.00	15.00
BC Bob Cousy/50	20.00	50.00
BD Baron Davis/50	8.00	20.00
BE Beno Udrih/100	5.00	12.00
BG Ben Gordon/50	8.00	20.00
BI Bill Walton/100	10.00	25.00
BK Bernard King/50	10.00	25.00
BM Brad Miller/100	5.00	12.00
BO Carlos Boozer/100	5.00	12.00
BR Bill Russell/50	75.00	150.00
BU Antonio Burks/100	5.00	12.00
BW Ben Wallace/50	15.00	40.00
CA Carmelo Anthony/50	25.00	60.00
CB Chauncey Billups/100	8.00	20.00
CD Chris Duhon/100	5.00	12.00
CL Clyde Drexler/50	25.00	60.00
CM Corey Maggette/100	5.00	12.00
DA David Harrison/100	5.00	12.00
DE Dennis Rodman/50	40.00	100.00
DG Drew Gooden/100	5.00	12.00
DH Dwight Howard/100	30.00	80.00
DW Dorell Wright/100	8.00	20.00
ED Erik Daniels/100	5.00	12.00
GG George Gervin/100	10.00	25.00
HA Devin Harris/50	10.00	25.00
HO Hakeem Olajuwon/50	25.00	60.00
HS Ha Seung-Jin/100	5.00	12.00
IT Isiah Thomas/100	15.00	40.00
JC Josh Childress/50	6.00	15.00
JE Julius Erving/50	40.00	100.00
JH Josh Howard/100	5.00	12.00
JK Jason Kidd/50	12.50	30.00
JM Jamaal Magloire/100	5.00	12.00
JN Jameer Nelson/100	6.00	15.00
JR J.R. Smith/100	6.00	15.00
JS John Stockton/50	60.00	150.00
JU Justin Reed/100	5.00	12.00
JV Jackson Vroman/100	5.00	12.00
JW Jason Williams/100	25.00	60.00
KB Kobe Bryant/50	100.00	200.00
KH Kris Humphries/100	5.00	12.00
KI Kirk Hinrich/50	8.00	20.00
KM Kevin Martin/100	6.00	15.00
KS Kirk Snyder/100	5.00	12.00
LB Larry Bird/50	75.00	150.00
LC Lionel Chalmers/100	5.00	12.00
LD Luol Deng/50	10.00	25.00
LF Luis Flores/100	5.00	12.00
LJ LeBron James/50	150.00	300.00
LO Lamar Odom/50	12.00	30.00
LU Luke Jackson/100	5.00	12.00
MA Magic Johnson/100	50.00	120.00
MB Mike Bibby/100	8.00	20.00
MC Michael Cooper/100	10.00	25.00
MJ Michael Jordan/100	300.00	600.00
MR Michael Redd/50	8.00	20.00
NO Andres Nocioni/100	5.00	12.00
PA Pape Sow/100	5.00	12.00
PG Pau Gasol/100	8.00	20.00
PP Paul Pierce/50	12.50	30.00
PR Pat Riley/50	15.00	40.00
PS Peja Stojakovic/50	12.50	30.00
RA Rafael Araujo/100	5.00	12.00
RH Richard Hamilton/50	12.50	30.00
RJ Richard Jefferson/100	5.00	12.00
SA Romain Sato/100	5.00	12.00
SC Sam Cassell/100	5.00	12.00
SF Shareef Abdur-Rahim/100	5.00	12.00
SL Shaun Livingston/50	6.00	15.00
SM Josh Smith/50	10.00	25.00

Scottie Pippen/100 200.00 350.00
Stephon Marbury/100 8.00 20.00
Tony Allen/100 6.00 15.00
Sebastian Telfair/100 5.00 12.00
Tracy McGrady/100 20.00 50.00
Tony Parker/100 6.00 15.00
Trevor Ariza/100 5.00 12.00
Delonte West/100 6.00 15.00
Walt Frazier/100 12.50 30.00
Yao Ming/50 30.00 80.00

2004-05 SP Signature Edition Triple Authentic Signatures

ndomly seeded and serially numbered to 25, this -card set parallels the design of the Sigantures but ces three players and their autographs on the card nt.

D Shareef Abdur-Rahim 30.00 80.00
ach Randolph
Clyde Drexler
A Kobe Bryant 250.00 450.00
Magic Johnson
Kareem Abdul-Jabbar
E Larry Bird 250.00 500.00
Magic Johnson
Julius Erving
J Larry Bird 75.00 150.00
Paul Pierce
Al Jefferson
MS Baron Davis 20.00 50.00
Jamaal Magloire
J.R. Smith
OH Ben Gordon 25.00 60.00
Luol Deng
Kirk Hinrich
MH Kevin Garnett 100.00 200.00
Tracy McGrady
Dwight Howard
BW Richard Hamilton 25.00 60.00
Chauncey Billups
Ben Wallace
J LeBron James 600.00 1000.00
Carmelo Anthony
Michael Jordan
J Michael Jordan 700.00 1200.00
Kobe Bryant
LeBron James
IA LeBron James 250.00 500.00
Dwight Howard
Carmelo Anthony
TH Shaun Livingston 12.50 30.00
Sebastian Telfair
Devin Harris
MM Hakeem Olajuwon 100.00 200.00
Yao Ming
Tracy McGrady
CS Josh Smith 25.00 60.00
Josh Childress
Donta Smith
KH John Stockton 100.00 200.00
Andrei Kirilenko
Kris Humphries

2005-06 SP Signature Edition

ssued in March 2006, SP Signature Edition features a 42-card set where cards 1-100 picture veterans and ards 101-142 picture rookies serially numbered to 99. Base cards have a white border with the player's ame on the right and background colors to match layer jersey colors. Signature Edition was packaged in hree-card tins that carried an initial $60 SRP.

COMP.SET w/o SP's (100) 50.00 100.00
Josh Smith .60 1.50
2 Josh Childress .50 1.25
3 Joe Johnson .60 1.50
4 Paul Pierce .75 2.00
5 Ricky Davis .50 1.25
6 Al Jefferson .60 1.50
7 Emeka Okafor .60 1.50
8 Kareem Rush .40 1.00
9 Gerald Wallace .60 1.50
10 Michael Jordan 5.00 12.00
11 Ben Gordon .60 1.50
12 Luol Deng .60 1.50
13 Kirk Hinrich .60 1.50
14 LeBron James 3.00 8.00
15 Larry Hughes .50 1.25
16 Zydrunas Ilgauskas .50 1.25
17 Donyell Marshall .40 1.00
18 Dirk Nowitzki 1.00 2.50
19 Jason Terry .50 1.25
20 Josh Howard .60 1.50
21 Devin Harris .60 1.50
22 Carmelo Anthony 1.25 3.00
23 Marcus Camby .50 1.25
24 Andre Miller .50 1.25
25 Kenyon Martin .60 1.50
26 Chauncey Billups .60 1.50
27 Ben Wallace .60 1.50
28 Richard Hamilton .50 1.25
29 Jason Richardson .60 1.50
30 Troy Murphy .50 1.25
31 Baron Davis .60 1.50
32 Tracy McGrady .75 2.00
33 Yao Ming .75 2.00
34 Stromile Swift .40 1.00
35 Jermaine O'Neal .60 1.50
36 Ron Artest .60 1.50
37 Stephen Jackson .50 1.25
38 Corey Maggette .50 1.25
39 Shaun Livingston .40 1.00
40 Chris Wilcox .40 1.00
41 Elton Brand .60 1.50
42 Kobe Bryant 3.00 8.00
43 Kwame Brown .40 1.00
44 Lamar Odom .60 1.50
45 Pau Gasol .60 1.50
46 Damon Stoudamire .50 1.25
47 Lorenzen Wright .40 1.00
48 Shaquille O'Neal 1.25 3.00
49 Dwyane Wade 1.50 4.00
50 Antoine Walker .50 1.25
51 Jason Williams .50 1.25
52 Desmond Mason .40 1.00
53 Michael Redd .60 1.50
54 Maurice Williams .50 1.25
55 Kevin Garnett 1.25 3.00
56 Marko Jaric .40 1.00
57 Wally Szczerbiak .50 1.25
58 Jason Kidd 1.00 2.50
59 Richard Jefferson .60 1.50
60 Vince Carter 1.00 2.50
61 Jamaal Magloire .40 1.00
62 J.R. Smith .60 1.50
63 Speedy Claxton .40 1.00
64 Stephon Marbury .50 1.25
65 Quentin Richardson .50 1.25
66 Mike Sweetney .40 1.00
67 Grant Hill .75 2.00
68 Dwight Howard 1.25 3.00
69 Steve Francis .60 1.50
70 Allen Iverson 1.00 2.50
71 Samuel Dalembert .40 1.00
72 Kyle Korver .50 1.25
73 Chris Webber .60 1.50
74 Steve Nash .75 2.00
75 Amare Stoudemire .60 1.50
76 Shawn Marion .60 1.50
77 Sebastian Telfair .50 1.25
78 Zach Randolph .50 1.25
79 Juan Dixon .40 1.00
80 Mike Bibby .60 1.50
81 Peja Stojakovic .60 1.50
82 Brad Miller .60 1.50
83 Tim Duncan 1.00 2.50
84 Manu Ginobili .60 1.50
85 Robert Horry .50 1.25
86 Tony Parker .60 1.50
87 Ray Allen .60 1.50
88 Rashard Lewis .60 1.50
89 Vladimir Radmanovic .40 1.00
90 Chris Bosh .60 1.50
91 Rafer Alston .40 1.00
92 Jalen Rose .60 1.50
93 Andrei Kirilenko .50 1.25
94 Matt Harpring .50 1.25
95 Carlos Boozer .60 1.50
96 Mehmet Okur .40 1.00
97 Gilbert Arenas .60 1.50
98 Antawn Jamison .60 1.50
99 Caron Butler .60 1.50
100 Antonio Daniels .40 1.00
101 Andrew Bogut RC 4.00 10.00
102 Marvin Williams RC 3.00 8.00
103 Deron Williams RC 6.00 15.00
104 Chris Paul RC 10.00 25.00
105 Raymond Felton RC 4.00 10.00
106 Martell Webster RC 2.50 6.00
107 Charlie Villanueva RC 3.00 8.00
108 Channing Frye RC 3.00 8.00
109 Ike Diogu RC 2.50 6.00
110 Andrew Bynum RC 8.00 20.00
111 Sean May RC 2.50 6.00
112 Rashad McCants RC 2.50 6.00
113 Antoine Wright RC 2.50 6.00
114 Joey Graham RC 2.50 6.00
115 Danny Granger RC 5.00 12.00
116 Gerald Green RC 3.00 8.00
117 Hakim Warrick RC 3.00 8.00
118 Julius Hodge RC 2.50 6.00
119 Nate Robinson RC 3.00 8.00
120 Jarrett Jack RC 2.50 6.00
121 Francisco Garcia RC 3.00 8.00
122 Luther Head RC 2.50 6.00
123 Johan Petro RC 2.50 6.00
124 Jason Maxiell RC 2.50 6.00
125 Linas Kleiza RC 2.50 6.00
126 Wayne Simien RC 2.50 6.00
127 David Lee RC 4.00 10.00
128 Salim Stoudamire RC 2.50 6.00
129 Daniel Ewing RC 2.50 6.00
130 Brandon Bass RC 3.00 8.00
131 C.J. Miles RC 3.00 8.00
132 Ersan Ilyasova RC 3.00 8.00
133 Travis Diener RC 2.50 6.00
134 Monta Ellis RC 5.00 12.00
135 Chris Taft RC 2.50 6.00
136 Martynas Andriuskevicius RC 2.50 6.00
137 Louis Williams RC 4.00 10.00
138 Bracey Wright RC 2.50 6.00
139 Robert Whaley RC 2.50 6.00
140 Andray Blatche RC 3.00 8.00
141 Ryan Gomes RC 2.50 6.00
142 Sarunas Jasikevicius RC 2.50 6.00

2005-06 SP Signature Edition Gold

Randomly inserted in packs, this 142-card set parallels the base SP Signature Edition set enhanced with gold background highlights and sequential numbering to 25.

*1-100 GOLD: 3X TO 8X BASE HI
*101-142 GOLD: 1.25X TO 3X BASE HI
10 Michael Jordan 60.00 150.00

2005-06 SP Signature Edition INKredible INKscriptions

Found randomly in packs, these cards are serially numbered to either 50 or 100 and horizontally designed with player photos on the left and authentic autographs on the right. Some players signed inscriptions rather than their names.

AB Andrew Bogut/50 20.00 50.00
AJ Al Jefferson/100 6.00 15.00
AK Andrei Kirilenko/50 12.00 30.00
BB Brent Barry/100 8.00 20.00
BI Bill Walton/100 20.00 50.00
BJ Bobby Jackson/100 6.00 15.00
BK Bob Knight/50 40.00 80.00
BL Bill Laimbeer/100 20.00 50.00
BR Brandon Bass/100 10.00 25.00
CB Chris Bosh/50 15.00 40.00
CH Chauncey Billups/100 20.00 50.00
CP Chris Paul/50 75.00 150.00
DA David Robinson/50 50.00 120.00
DR Dennis Rodman/50 50.00 100.00
EB Elton Brand/50 8.00 20.00
EH Elvin Hayes/100 12.50 30.00
EO Emeka Okafor/100 12.50 30.00
GE George Gervin/100 12.50 30.00
GG Gerald Green/100 8.00 20.00
HO Hakeem Olajuwon/50 25.00 60.00
HW Hakim Warrick/100 8.00 20.00
IT Isiah Thomas/50 20.00 50.00
JE Julius Erving/50 50.00 120.00
JG Joey Graham/100 6.00 15.00
JH Julius Hodge/100 6.00 15.00
KA Kareem Abdul-Jabbar/50 100.00 200.00
KW Kwame Brown/100 6.00 15.00
LB LeBron James/50 300.00 550.00
LH Larry Hughes/100 6.00 15.00
LW Louis Williams/100 10.00 25.00
MJ Magic Johnson/50 100.00 200.00
MW Marvin Williams/50 10.00 25.00
NR Nate Robinson/100 20.00 50.00
PP Paul Pierce/50 25.00 60.00
QR Quentin Richardson/100 6.00 15.00
RA Ron Artest/50 15.00 40.00
RF Raymond Felton/100 25.00 50.00
RM Rashad McCants/100 6.00 15.00
RP Robert Parish/50 25.00 60.00
SE Sean May/100 6.00 15.00
SM Stephon Marbury/50 10.00 25.00
SN Steve Nash/50 75.00 150.00
SP Scottie Pippen/50 100.00 200.00
SS Salim Stoudamire/100 6.00 15.00
TM Tracy McGrady/50 15.00 40.00
WS Wayne Simien/100 6.00 15.00
YM Yao Ming/50 30.00 80.00

2005-06 SP Signature Edition Marks of Distinction

Limited to 40 serially numbered copies, this 41-card set places full color player photos along the top of the card and sticker autograph on the bottom over a white background.

AB Andrew Bogut 15.00 40.00
AJ Antawn Jamison 8.00 20.00
AN Andrew Bynum 20.00 50.00
AW Antoine Wright 8.00 20.00
CB Chris Bosh 12.50 30.00
CF Channing Frye 10.00 25.00
CH Chauncey Billups 10.00 25.00
CM Cuttino Mobley 8.00 20.00
CP Chris Paul 60.00 150.00
CV Charlie Villanueva 10.00 25.00
DG Danny Granger 12.50 30.00
DH Dwight Howard 15.00 40.00
DR Dennis Rodman 20.00 50.00
DW Deron Williams 15.00 40.00
FG Francisco Garcia 10.00 25.00
GG Gerald Green 10.00 25.00
HO Hakeem Olajuwon 20.00 50.00
HW Hakim Warrick 10.00 25.00
IT Isiah Thomas 20.00 50.00
JG Joey Graham 8.00 20.00
JH Julius Hodge 8.00 20.00
JJ Jarrett Jack 8.00 20.00
JK Jason Kidd 15.00 50.00
JS J.R. Smith 8.00 20.00
LB Larry Bird 50.00 120.00
LJ LeBron James 200.00 400.00
LO Lamar Odom 10.00 25.00
MA Magic Johnson 50.00 120.00
MJ Michael Jordan 400.00 700.00
MR Michael Redd 8.00 20.00
MV Marvin Williams 10.00 25.00
MW Martell Webster 8.00 20.00
NR Nate Robinson 12.50 30.00
PP Paul Pierce 12.50 30.00
RF Raymond Felton 15.00 40.00
RM Rashad McCants 8.00 20.00
SM Sean May 8.00 20.00
ST Stephon Marbury 12.50 30.00
TC Tyson Chandler 8.00 20.00
TM Tracy McGrady 20.00 50.00
YM Yao Ming 20.00 50.00

2005-06 SP Signature Edition Rookie GRAPHiti

Randomly inserted in packs, this horizontally designed cards places full color player photos on the left and autograph on the right of a yellow and orange background. Each card is serially numbered to 100.

AB Andray Blatche 6.00 15.00
AW Antoine Wright 5.00 12.00
BB Brandon Bass 6.00 15.00
BW Bracey Wright 5.00 12.00
CT Chris Taft 5.00 12.00
DE Daniel Ewing 5.00 12.00
DL David Lee 8.00 20.00
DT Dijon Thompson 5.00 12.00
EI Ersan Ilyasova 6.00 15.00
GG Gerald Green 6.00 15.00
HW Hakim Warrick 6.00 15.00
JG Joey Graham 5.00 12.00
JH Julius Hodge 5.00 12.00
JM Jason Maxiell 5.00 12.00
LK Linas Kleiza 5.00 12.00
LR Lawrence Roberts 5.00 12.00
LW Louis Williams 8.00 20.00
MA Martynas Andriuskevicius 5.00 12.00
ME Monta Ellis 15.00 40.00
NR Nate Robinson 10.00 25.00
RG Ryan Gomes 5.00 12.00
SJ Sarunas Jasikevicius 5.00 12.00
SM Sean May 5.00 12.00
SS Salim Stoudamire 5.00 12.00
TD Travis Diener 5.00 12.00

2005-06 SP Signature Edition Rookies INKorporated

Randomly seeded an serially numbered out of 50, this 25-card set has bronze highlights and borders to match team colors around a portrait-style photo of the featured player. Autographs are centered along the bottom of the card.

AB Andrew Bogut 12.50 30.00
AN Andrew Bynum 20.00 50.00
AW Antoine Wright 6.00 15.00
CF Channing Frye 8.00 20.00
CP Chris Paul 60.00 150.00
CV Charlie Villanueva 8.00 20.00
DG Danny Granger 12.00 30.00
DW Deron Williams 15.00 40.00
FG Francisco Garcia 8.00 20.00
GG Gerald Green 8.00 20.00
HW Hakim Warrick 8.00 20.00
ID Ike Diogu 6.00 15.00
JG Joey Graham 6.00 15.00
JH Julius Hodge 6.00 15.00
JJ Jarrett Jack 6.00 15.00
JM Jason Maxiell 6.00 15.00
JP Johan Petro 6.00 15.00
MA Marvin Williams 8.00 20.00
MW Martell Webster 6.00 15.00
NR Nate Robinson 12.50 30.00
RF Raymond Felton 12.50 30.00
RM Rashad McCants 6.00 15.00
SM Sean May 6.00 15.00
WS Wayne Simien 6.00 15.00

2005-06 SP Signature Edition Scripts for Success

Randomly inserted in packs, this 54-card set is horizontally designed with a player photo on the left and an autograph on the right. Each card features blue-silver highlights and is sequentially numbered to 200.

*SILVER: .6X TO 1.5X BASE HI
SILVER PRINT RUN 50 SER.#'d SETS
*GOLD: .75X TO 2X BASE HI
GOLD PRINT RUN 25 SER.#'d SETS
AB Andrew Bogut 6.00 15.00
AD Andray Blatche 5.00 12.00
AL Al Jefferson 4.00 10.00
AN Andrew Bynum 12.00 30.00
AW Antoine Wright 4.00 10.00
BB Brandon Bass 5.00 12.00
BR Bruce Bowen 5.00 12.00
BW Bracey Wright 4.00 10.00
CF Channing Frye 5.00 12.00
CP Chris Paul 40.00 100.00
CT Chris Taft 4.00 10.00
CV Charlie Villanueva 5.00 12.00
DD Dan Dickau 4.00 10.00
DE Daniel Ewing 4.00 10.00
DG Danny Granger 8.00 20.00
DH Dwight Howard 12.00 30.00
DL David Lee 6.00 15.00
DS Damon Stoudamire 4.00 10.00
DT Dijon Thompson 4.00 10.00
DW Deron Williams 10.00 25.00
EI Ersan Ilyasova 5.00 12.00
FG Francisco Garcia 5.00 12.00
GG Gerald Green 5.00 12.00
HW Hakim Warrick 5.00 12.00
ID Ike Diogu 4.00 10.00
IT Isiah Thomas 10.00 25.00
JA Jamaal Magloire 4.00 10.00
JG Joey Graham 4.00 10.00
JH Julius Hodge 4.00 10.00
JJ Jarrett Jack 4.00 10.00
JM Jason Maxiell 4.00 10.00
JP Johan Petro 4.00 10.00
JR J.R. Smith 4.00 10.00
KK Kyle Korver 4.00 10.00
LH Luther Head 4.00 10.00
LK Linas Kleiza 4.00 10.00
LO Lamar Odom 5.00 12.00
LR Lawrence Roberts 4.00 10.00
MA Martynas Andriuskevicius 4.00 10.00
MD Marquis Daniels 4.00 10.00
ME Monta Ellis 12.50 30.00
MV Marvin Williams 5.00 12.00
PP Paul Pierce 10.00 25.00
QR Quentin Richardson 4.00 10.00
RF Raymond Felton 6.00 15.00
RG Ryan Gomes 4.00 10.00
RM Rashad McCants 4.00 10.00
RP Robert Parish 8.00 20.00
SA Shareef Abdur-Rahim 4.00 10.00
SJ Sarunas Jasikevicius 4.00 10.00
SM Sean May 4.00 10.00
SS Salim Stoudamire 4.00 10.00
TD Travis Diener 4.00 10.00
WS Wayne Simien 4.00 10.00

2005-06 SP Signature Edition Signatures

Inserted at approximately one per pack, this 127-card set places a player photo at the top of the card, an autograph along the bottom, a strip between the two in team uniform colors and black and gray borders.

*GOLD: .75X TO 2X BASE AU HI
GOLD PRINT RUN 25 SER.#'d SETS
UNPRICED TRIPLE PRINT RUN 10 SETS
AB Andrew Bogut 6.00 15.00
AD Andre Miller 4.00 10.00
AI Andre Iguodala 5.00 12.00
AJ Antawn Jamison 4.00 10.00
AK Andrei Kirilenko 4.00 10.00
AL Al Jefferson 4.00 10.00
AN Andris Biedrins 4.00 10.00
AN Andrew Bynum 12.00 30.00
AR Amir Johnson 4.00 10.00
AW Antoine Wright 4.00 10.00
AY Carlos Arroyo 10.00 25.00
BA Bracey Wright 4.00 10.00
BB Brent Barry 4.00 10.00
BD Baron Davis 4.00 10.00
BJ Bobby Jackson 4.00 10.00
BK Bernard King 5.00 12.00
BL Bill Laimbeer 12.50 30.00
BM Brad Miller 4.00 10.00
BO Bob Knight SP 25.00 60.00
BR Brandon Bass 5.00 12.00
BS Bobby Simmons 4.00 10.00
BT Andray Blatche 5.00 12.00
BW Bruce Bowen 5.00 12.00
CA Carmelo Anthony SP 20.00 40.00
CB Carlos Boozer SP 4.00 10.00
CD Chris Duhon 4.00 10.00
CF Channing Frye 5.00 12.00
CH Chauncey Billups 6.00 15.00
CJ C.J. Miles 5.00 12.00
CM Corey Maggette 4.00 10.00
CP Chris Paul 40.00 100.00
CR Chris Bosh 8.00 20.00
CT Chris Taft 4.00 10.00
CU Cuttino Mobley 4.00 10.00
CV Charlie Villanueva 5.00 12.00
CW Chris Wilcox 4.00 10.00
DA Darko Milicic 4.00 10.00
DD Dan Dickau 4.00 10.00
DE Daniel Ewing 4.00 10.00
DG Danny Granger 8.00 20.00
DH David Harrison 4.00 10.00
DL David Lee 6.00 15.00
DM Desmond Mason 4.00 10.00
DO Donyell Marshall 4.00 10.00
DR Dennis Rodman 20.00 50.00
DS Damon Stoudamire 4.00 10.00
DW Deron Williams 12.00 30.00
EB Elton Brand SP 4.00 10.00
EH Elvin Hayes 6.00 15.00
EO Emeka Okafor 4.00 10.00
ES Ersan Ilyasova 5.00 12.00
FG Francisco Garcia 5.00 12.00
GE George Gervin 8.00 20.00
GG Gerald Green 5.00 12.00
GO Gordan Giricek 4.00 10.00
GP Gary Payton 8.00 20.00
GW Gerald Wallace 5.00 12.00
HA Josh Howard 4.00 10.00
HD Dwight Howard 12.00 30.00
HO Hakeem Olajuwon SP 15.00 40.00
HW Hakim Warrick 5.00 12.00
ID Ike Diogu 4.00 10.00
IT Isiah Thomas 10.00 25.00
JA Jason Kidd 10.00 25.00
JC Josh Childress 4.00 10.00
JG Joey Graham 4.00 10.00
JH Julius Hodge 4.00 10.00
JJ Jarrett Jack 4.00 10.00
JK Jason Kapono 4.00 10.00
JM Jason Maxiell 4.00 10.00
JO Joe Johnson 5.00 12.00
JP Johan Petro 4.00 10.00
JR J.R. Smith 4.00 10.00
JS James Singleton 4.00 10.00
KA Kareem Abdul-Jabbar SP 30.00 80.00
KB Kwame Brown 4.00 10.00
KD Keyon Dooling 4.00 10.00
KH Kirk Hinrich 6.00 15.00
KK Kyle Korver 4.00 10.00
KR Kris Humphries 4.00 10.00
LE Luke Jackson 4.00 10.00
LH Larry Hughes 4.00 10.00
LJ LeBron James 125.00 250.00
LK Linas Kleiza 4.00 10.00
LO Lamar Odom 5.00 12.00
LR Lawrence Roberts 4.00 10.00
LU Luther Head 4.00 10.00
LW Louis Williams 6.00 15.00
MA Martynas Andriuskevicius 4.00 10.00
MC Antonio McDyess 4.00 10.00
MD Marquis Daniels 4.00 10.00
ME Monta Ellis 10.00 25.00
MJ Michael Jordan SP 250.00 500.00
ML Jamaal Magloire 4.00 10.00
MP Morris Peterson 4.00 10.00
MR Michael Redd 4.00 10.00
MW Marvin Williams 5.00 12.00
NR Nate Robinson 5.00 12.00
OG Orien Greene 4.00 10.00
PP Paul Pierce 8.00 20.00
RA Ron Artest 6.00 15.00
RF Raymond Felton 6.00 15.00
RG Ryan Gomes 4.00 10.00
RH Richard Hamilton 5.00 12.00
RI Luke Ridnour 4.00 10.00
RM Rashad McCants 4.00 10.00
RP Robert Parish 10.00 25.00
SA Shareef Abdur-Rahim 4.00 10.00
SE Sean May 4.00 10.00
SI Scottie Pippen 75.00 150.00
SJ Sarunas Jasikevicius 4.00 10.00
SK Steve Kerr 8.00 20.00
SM Stephon Marbury 6.00 15.00
SP Speedy Claxton 4.00 10.00
SS Salim Stoudamire 4.00 10.00
ST Stromile Swift 4.00 10.00
TA Tony Allen 4.00 10.00
TC Tyson Chandler 4.00 10.00
TD Travis Diener 4.00 10.00
TM Tracy McGrady 12.50 30.00
TP Tayshaun Prince 6.00 15.00
VC Vince Carter 15.00 40.00
VR Vladimir Radmanovic 4.00 10.00
VW Von Wafer 4.00 10.00
WA Bill Walton 8.00 20.00
WS Wayne Simien 4.00 10.00
YM Yao Ming 20.00 50.00

2005-06 SP Signature Edition Signatures Dual

Serially numbered to 25, this 29-card set places two player photos and two autographs surrounded by team colors on a horizontally designed card with black and bronze highlights.

AH Carmelo Anthony 40.00 80.00
Julius Hodge
BB Andrew Bogut 25.00 60.00
Andrew Bynum
BJ Larry Bird 200.00 300.00
Magic Johnson
BM Elton Brand 15.00 40.00
Corey Maggette
BP Chauncey Billups 40.00 80.00
Tayshaun Prince
DD Ike Diogu 15.00 40.00
Baron Davis
FM Raymond Felton 15.00 40.00
Sean May
FR Channing Frye 25.00 60.00
Nate Robinson
GS Ben Gordon 15.00 40.00
J.R. Smith
GW Pau Gasol 15.00 40.00
Hakim Warrick
JG Al Jefferson 25.00 60.00
Gerald Green
JH LeBron James 200.00 300.00
Larry Hughes
MK Stephon Marbury 30.00 80.00
Jason Kidd
MM Yao Ming 40.00 100.00
Tracy McGrady
MR Stephon Marbury 15.00 40.00
Nate Robinson
MS Tracy McGrady 20.00 50.00
Stromile Swift
NB Steve Nash 75.00 150.00
Chauncey Billups
PG Paul Pierce 20.00 50.00
Gerald Green
PS Chris Paul 60.00 120.00
J.R. Smith
RP Dennis Rodman 200.00 400.00
Scottie Pippen
TS Isiah Thomas 100.00 200.00
John Stockton
VG Charlie Villanueva 15.00 40.00
Joey Graham
WD Hakim Warrick 15.00 40.00
Ike Diogu
WJ Martell Webster 15.00 40.00
Jarrett Jack
WM Deron Williams 25.00 60.00
C.J. Miles
WP Marvin Williams 50.00 100.00
Chris Paul
WS Marvin Williams 15.00 40.00
Salim Stoudamire

2006-07 SP Signature Edition

Released in late March 2007, SP Signature Edition showcases a 142-card set where veteran players serially numbered to 499 are pictured on card numbers 1-100 and rookie players serially numbered to 299 are pictured on card numbers 101-142. SP Signature Edition is packaged in single-pack tins of five cards each and carried an initial suggested retail price of $60.00.

1 Josh Childress .75 2.00
2 Joe Johnson 1.00 2.50
3 Marvin Williams 1.00 2.50
4 Al Jefferson 1.00 2.50
5 Paul Pierce 1.25 3.00
6 Sebastian Telfair .60 1.50
7 Raymond Felton 1.25 3.00
8 Emeka Okafor 1.00 2.50
9 Gerald Wallace 1.00 2.50
10 Ben Gordon 1.00 2.50
11 Kirk Hinrich 1.00 2.50
12 Ben Wallace 1.00 2.50
13 Drew Gooden .75 2.00
14 LeBron James 5.00 12.00
15 Donyell Marshall .60 1.50
16 Devin Harris 1.00 2.50
17 Josh Howard .75 2.00
18 Dirk Nowitzki 1.50 4.00
19 Jason Terry .75 2.00
20 Carmelo Anthony 1.25 3.00
21 Kenyon Martin 1.00 2.50
22 J.R. Smith 1.00 2.50
23 Chauncey Billups 1.00 2.50
24 Richard Hamilton .75 2.00
25 Rasheed Wallace 1.00 2.50
26 Baron Davis 1.00 2.50
27 Troy Murphy .60 1.50
28 Jason Richardson 1.00 2.50
29 Rafer Alston .60 1.50
30 Shane Battier .75 2.00
31 Tracy McGrady 1.25 3.00
32 Yao Ming 1.25 3.00
33 Marquis Daniels .60 1.50
34 Al Harrington .75 2.00
35 Jermaine O'Neal 1.00 2.50
36 Elton Brand 1.00 2.50
37 Sam Cassell 1.00 2.50
38 Chris Kaman .75 2.00
39 Corey Maggette .75 2.00
40 Kobe Bryant 5.00 12.00
41 Lamar Odom 1.00 2.50
42 Kwame Brown .60 1.50
43 Eddie Jones .75 2.00
44 Mike Miller 1.00 2.50
45 Hakim Warrick .75 2.00
46 Pau Gasol 1.00 2.50
47 Alonzo Mourning 1.25 3.00
48 Shaquille O'Neal 2.00 5.00
49 Dwyane Wade 2.50 6.00
50 Jason Williams .75 2.00
51 Andrew Bogut 1.00 2.50
52 Michael Redd 1.00 2.50
53 Charlie Villanueva 1.00 2.50
54 Kevin Garnett 2.00 5.00
55 Mike James .60 1.50
56 Rashad McCants .60 1.50
57 Vince Carter 1.25 3.00
58 Richard Jefferson 1.00 2.50
59 Jason Kidd 1.50 4.00
60 Tyson Chandler .75 2.00
61 Desmond Mason .60 1.50
62 Chris Paul 2.00 5.00
63 Peja Stojakovic 1.00 2.50
64 Steve Francis 1.00 2.50
65 Stephon Marbury .75 2.00
66 Quentin Richardson .75 2.00
67 Nate Robinson 1.00 2.50
68 Carlos Arroyo .75 2.00
69 Dwight Howard 1.50 4.00
70 Darko Milicic .60 1.50
71 Andre Iguodala 1.00 2.50
72 Allen Iverson 1.25 3.00
73 Kyle Korver .75 2.00
74 Chris Webber 1.00 2.50
75 Boris Diaw .75 2.00
76 Shawn Marion 1.00 2.50
77 Steve Nash 1.25 3.00
78 Amare Stoudemire 1.00 2.50
79 Jamaal Magloire .60 1.50
80 Zach Randolph .75 2.00
81 Martell Webster .75 2.00
82 Ron Artest 1.00 2.50
83 Brad Miller 1.00 2.50
84 Mike Bibby 1.00 2.50
85 Tim Duncan 1.50 4.00
86 Michael Finley 1.00 2.50
87 Manu Ginobili 1.00 2.50
88 Tony Parker 1.00 2.50
89 Ray Allen 1.00 2.50
90 Rashard Lewis 1.00 2.50
91 Luke Ridnour .75 2.00
92 Chris Bosh 1.00 2.50
93 T.J. Ford .75 2.00
94 Joey Graham .60 1.50
95 Carlos Boozer 1.00 2.50
96 Andrei Kirilenko .75 2.00
97 Deron Williams 1.50 4.00
98 Gilbert Arenas 1.00 2.50
99 Caron Butler 1.00 2.50
100 Antawn Jamison 1.00 2.50
101 Andrea Bargnani RC 4.00 10.00
102 LaMarcus Aldridge RC 6.00 15.00
103 Adam Morrison RC 3.00 8.00
104 Tyrus Thomas RC 3.00 8.00
105 Shelden Williams RC 2.50 6.00
106 Brandon Roy RC 6.00 15.00
107 Randy Foye RC 3.00 8.00
108 Rudy Gay RC 4.00 10.00
109 Patrick O'Bryant RC 2.50 6.00
110 Saer Sene RC 2.50 6.00
111 J.J. Redick RC 3.00 8.00
112 Hilton Armstrong RC 2.50 6.00
113 Thabo Sefolosha RC 3.00 8.00
114 Ronnie Brewer RC 3.00 8.00
115 Cedric Simmons RC 2.50 6.00
116 Rodney Carney RC 2.50 6.00
117 Shawne Williams RC 2.50 6.00
118 Quincy Douby RC 2.50 6.00
119 Renaldo Balkman RC 2.50 6.00
120 Rajon Rondo RC 10.00 25.00
121 Marcus Williams RC 2.50 6.00
122 Josh Boone RC 2.50 6.00
123 Kyle Lowry RC 3.00 8.00
124 Shannon Brown RC 4.00 10.00
125 Jordan Farmar RC 2.50 6.00
126 Sergio Rodriguez RC 2.50 6.00
127 Maurice Ager RC 2.50 6.00
128 Mardy Collins RC 2.50 6.00
129 James White RC 2.50 6.00
130 Steve Novak RC 2.50 6.00
131 Solomon Jones RC 2.50 6.00
132 Paul Davis RC 2.50 6.00
133 P.J. Tucker RC 2.50 6.00
134 Craig Smith RC 2.50 6.00
135 Bobby Jones RC 2.50 6.00
136 David Noel RC 2.50 6.00
137 James Augustine RC 2.50 6.00
138 Daniel Gibson RC 3.00 8.00
139 Marcus Vinicius RC 2.50 6.00
140 Dee Brown RC 2.50 6.00
141 Ryan Hollins RC 2.50 6.00
142 Hassan Adams RC 2.50 6.00

2006-07 SP Signature Edition Gold

*1-100 GOLD: 2X TO 5X BASE HI
*101-142 GOLD: 1.25X TO 3X BASE HI
PRINT RUN 25 SER.#'d SETS

2006-07 SP Signature Edition AKA Signings

PRINT RUN 25 TO 50 SER.#'d SETS
AB Andrea Bargnani/25 20.00 50.00
AD Adrian Dantley/50 12.50 30.00
BB Brent Barry/50 15.00 40.00
BG Ben Gordon/25 20.00 50.00
BL Bill Laimbeer/50 25.00 60.00
BR Bill Russell/25 100.00 225.00
BS Byron Scott/50 12.50 30.00
CA Carmelo Anthony/25 50.00 100.00
CB Chauncey Billups/50 20.00 50.00
CD Clyde Drexler/25 50.00 100.00
CS Cedric Simmons/50 5.00 12.00
DD Darryl Dawkins/50 20.00 50.00
DN David Noel/50 5.00 12.00
DR Dennis Rodman/25 60.00 120.00
EH Elvin Hayes/25 15.00 40.00
GG George Gervin/50 20.00 50.00
HA Hilton Armstrong/50 5.00 12.00
HO Hakeem Olajuwon/25 30.00 75.00
JB Josh Boone/50 5.00 12.00
JE Julius Erving/25 60.00 150.00
JF Jordan Farmar/50 5.00 12.00
JK Jason Kidd/25 20.00 50.00
JW James White/50 5.00 12.00
KH Kirk Hinrich/25 40.00 80.00
LA LaMarcus Aldridge/25 25.00 60.00
LJ LeBron James/25 250.00 400.00
MA Maurice Ager/25 5.00 12.00
MJ Magic Johnson/25 60.00 120.00
MP Morris Peterson/50 5.00 12.00
NA Nate Archibald/50 12.50 30.00
PD Paul Davis/50 5.00 12.00
PO Patrick O'Bryant/50 5.00 12.00
PP Paul Pierce/25 30.00 80.00
QD Quincy Douby/50 5.00 12.00
RB Renaldo Balkman/50 5.00 12.00
RF Randy Foye/50 6.00 15.00
RJ Richard Jefferson/25 8.00 20.00
RR Rajon Rondo/50 25.00 60.00
SM Craig Smith/50 5.00 12.00
SW Shelden Williams/50 5.00 12.00
TM Tracy McGrady/25 20.00 50.00
TT Tyrus Thomas/25 12.50 30.00
VC Vince Carter/25 30.00 60.00

2006-07 SP Signature Edition Alumni Associations

PRINT RUN 50 SER.#'d SETS
AB Hilton Armstrong 10.00 25.00
Josh Boone
AF LaMarcus Aldridge 15.00 40.00
T.J. Ford
AJ Hassan Adams 10.00 25.00
Richard Jefferson
BA Maurice Ager 10.00 25.00
Shannon Brown
BJ Chris Bosh 12.50 30.00
Jarrett Jack
BT Brandon Bass 12.50 30.00
Tyrus Thomas
DF Baron Davis 10.00 25.00
Jordan Farmar
DJ Dee Brown 10.00 25.00
James Augustine
GG Ben Gordon 25.00 60.00
Rudy Gay
GT Daniel Gibson 10.00 25.00
P.J. Tucker
JB Joe Johnson 12.50 30.00
Ronnie Brewer
JR Bobby Jones 20.00 50.00
Brandon Roy
MF Rashad McCants 15.00 40.00
Raymond Felton
NM David Noel 10.00 25.00
Sean May
RF Allan Ray 10.00 25.00
Randy Foye
RP Rajon Rondo 20.00 50.00
Tayshaun Prince
WC Marvin Williams 15.00 40.00
Vince Carter
WO Marcus Williams 10.00 25.00
Emeka Okafor

2006-07 SP Signature Edition Five Star Autographs

PRINT RUN 10 SER.#'d SETS
BATFR Andrea Bargnani 150.00 300.00
LaMarcus Aldridge
Tyrus Thomas
Randy Foye
Brandon Roy
DWEHF Baron Davis 30.00 60.00
Bill Walton
Mark Eaton
Ryan Hollins
Jordan Farmar
HGDTS Kirk Hinrich 150.00 300.00
Ben Gordon
Chris Duhon
Tyrus Thomas
Thabo Sefolosha
WDWAR Bill Walton 225.00 350.00
Clyde Drexler
Martell Webster

LaMarcus Aldridge
Brandon Roy

2006-07 SP Signature Edition Four Star Autographs

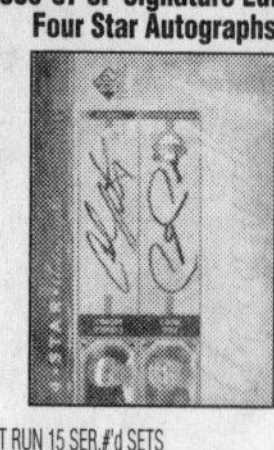

PRINT RUN 15 SER.#'d SETS
APMJ Carmelo Anthony 300.00 450.00
Paul Pierce
Tracy McGrady
LeBron James
BATW Andrea Bargnani 75.00 150.00
LaMarcus Aldridge
Tyrus Thomas
Shelden Williams
DWAR Clyde Drexler 150.00 250.00
Bill Walton
LaMarcus Aldridge
Brandon Roy
GHST Ben Gordon 20.00 50.00
Kirk Hinrich
Thabo Sefolosha
Tyrus Thomas
JEBJ Michael Jordan 900.00 1500.00
Julius Erving
Larry Bird
Magic Johnson
KICJ Kyle Korver 20.00 50.00
Andre Iguodala
Rodney Carney
Bobby Jones
ODMM Hakeem Olajuwon 125.00 250.00
Clyde Drexler
Yao Ming
Tracy McGrady
OGGH Emeka Okafor 40.00 100.00
Ben Gordon
Rudy Gay
Richard Hamilton
PKNB Chris Paul 100.00 225.00
Jason Kidd
Steve Nash
Chauncey Billups

2006-07 SP Signature Edition Hoops Inc. Autographs

PRINT RUN 50 SER.#'d SETS
*GOLD: .5X TO 1.25X BASE HI
GOLD PRINT RUN 25 SER.#'d SETS
AD Adrian Dantley 8.00 20.00
CH Connie Hawkins 8.00 20.00
DJ Dennis Johnson 25.00 60.00
EH Elvin Hayes 6.00 15.00
FW Walt Frazier 8.00 20.00
GG George Gervin 12.50 30.00
HG Hal Greer 6.00 15.00
JS Jack Sikma 6.00 15.00
MB Muggsy Bogues 8.00 20.00
MC Michael Cooper 8.00 20.00
ME Mark Eaton 6.00 15.00
MR Micheal Ray Richardson 6.00 15.00
NA Nate Archibald 8.00 20.00
NT Nate Thurmond 6.00 15.00
PW Paul Westphal 8.00 20.00
RP Robert Parish 10.00 25.00
RS Ralph Sampson 8.00 20.00
RT Reggie Theus 6.00 15.00
SK Steve Kerr 8.00 20.00
SP Sam Perkins 8.00 20.00
SW Spud Webb 10.00 25.00
WT Wayman Tisdale 6.00 15.00

2006-07 SP Signature Edition INKredible INKscriptions

PRINT RUN 50 TO 100 SER.#'d SETS
AB Andrea Bargnani/50 15.00 40.00
AJ Antawn Jamison/100 8.00 20.00
AR Allan Ray/50 5.00 12.00
BG Ben Gordon/50 15.00 40.00
BJ Bobby Jones/100 5.00 12.00
BM Brad Miller/100 5.00 12.00
BR Brandon Roy/50 20.00 50.00
CE Cedric Simmons/50 5.00 12.00
CS Craig Smith/100 5.00 12.00
DG Daniel Gibson/50 8.00 20.00
DM Damir Markota/100 5.00 12.00
DN David Noel/100 5.00 12.00
DW Deron Williams/50 25.00 60.00
GW Gerald Wallace/50 8.00 20.00
HA Hassan Adams/100 5.00 12.00
HI Hilton Armstrong/100 5.00 12.00
JA James Augustine/100 5.00 12.00
JB Josh Boone/50 5.00 12.00
JF Jordan Farmar/100 5.00 12.00
JW James White/100 5.00 12.00
KK Kyle Korver/50 15.00 40.00
LA LaMarcus Aldridge/50 15.00 40.00
LB Leandro Barbosa/100 5.00 12.00
MJ Mike James/100 5.00 12.00
NO Steve Novak/100 5.00 12.00
NR Nate Robinson/100 10.00 25.00
PD Paul Davis/50 5.00 12.00
PM Pops Mensah-Bonsu/100 5.00 12.00
PT P.J. Tucker/100 5.00 12.00
QD Quincy Douby/100 5.00 12.00
RB Raja Bell/50 15.00 40.00
RE Renaldo Balkman/100 5.00 12.00
RF Raymond Felton/100 12.50 30.00
RG Rudy Gay/50 12.50 30.00
RJ Richard Jefferson/50 6.00 15.00
SB Shannon Brown/50 12.50 30.00
SJ Solomon Jones/100 5.00 12.00
SN Steve Nash/50 125.00 250.00
SR Sergio Rodriguez/50 6.00 15.00
SS Saer Sene/100 5.00 12.00
SW Shelden Williams/50 5.00 12.00
TF T.J. Ford/100 5.00 12.00
TP Tayshaun Prince 12.50 30.00
TS Thabo Sefolosha/50 12.50 30.00
TT Tyrus Thomas/50 8.00 20.00
WB Will Blalock/100 5.00 12.00
WI Shawne Williams/50 5.00 12.00

2006-07 SP Signature Edition Marks of Distinction

PRINT RUN 50 SER.#'d SETS
AB Andrea Bargnani 15.00 40.00
AH Al Harrington 5.00 12.00
AI Andre Iguodala 5.00 12.00
BA Renaldo Balkman 5.00 12.00
BD Baron Davis 5.00 12.00
BG Ben Gordon 15.00 40.00
BM Brad Miller 5.00 12.00
BR Brandon Roy 15.00 40.00
CB Chauncey Billups 8.00 20.00
CH Chris Bosh 10.00 25.00
CM Corey Maggette 5.00 12.00
CS Cedric Simmons 5.00 12.00
DB Dee Brown 5.00 12.00
EO Emeka Okafor 10.00 25.00
HA Hassan Adams 5.00 12.00
JA James Augustine 5.00 12.00
JB Josh Boone 5.00 12.00
JF Jordan Farmar 5.00 12.00
JJ Jarrett Jack 5.00 12.00
JO Joe Johnson 8.00 20.00
KL Kyle Lowry 6.00 15.00
LB Leandro Barbosa 5.00 12.00
MA Maurice Ager 5.00 12.00
MB Mike Bibby 5.00 12.00
MC Mardy Collins 5.00 12.00
MJ Michael Jordan 300.00 550.00
MW Marcus Williams 5.00 12.00
ON Jermaine O'Neal 6.00 15.00
PO Patrick O'Bryant 5.00 12.00
PP Paul Pierce 10.00 25.00
PS Peja Stojakovic 5.00 12.00
QD Quincy Douby 5.00 12.00
RC Rodney Carney 5.00 12.00
RF Randy Foye 6.00 15.00
RG Rudy Gay 10.00 25.00
RH Richard Hamilton 8.00 20.00
RJ Richard Jefferson 5.00 12.00
RO Ronnie Brewer 6.00 15.00
RR Rajon Rondo 25.00 60.00
SN Steve Novak 5.00 12.00
SR Sergio Rodriguez 5.00 12.00
SS Saer Sene 5.00 12.00
SW Shawne Williams 5.00 12.00
TP Tayshaun Prince 8.00 20.00
TS Thabo Sefolosha 6.00 15.00
WI Shelden Williams 5.00 12.00

2006-07 SP Signature Edition Rookie GRAPHiti

PRINT RUN 50 SER.#'d SETS
*GOLD: .5X TO 1.25X BASE HI
GOLD PRINT RUN 25 SER.#'d SETS
AB Andrea Bargnani 15.00 40.00
BR Brandon Roy 12.00 30.00
CS Cedric Simmons 5.00 12.00
HA Hilton Armstrong 5.00 12.00
JB Josh Boone 5.00 12.00
JF Jordan Farmar 5.00 12.00
KL Kyle Lowry 6.00 15.00
LA LaMarcus Aldridge 15.00 40.00
MA Maurice Ager 5.00 12.00
MW Marcus Williams 5.00 12.00
PO Patrick O'Bryant 5.00 12.00
QD Quincy Douby 5.00 12.00
RB Renaldo Balkman 5.00 12.00
RC Rodney Carney 5.00 12.00
RF Randy Foye 6.00 15.00
RG Rudy Gay 8.00 20.00
RO Ronnie Brewer 6.00 15.00
RR Rajon Rondo 25.00 60.00
SB Shannon Brown 8.00 20.00
SR Sergio Rodriguez 5.00 12.00
SS Saer Sene 5.00 12.00
SW Shelden Williams 5.00 12.00
TS Thabo Sefolosha 6.00 15.00
TT Tyrus Thomas 10.00 25.00
WI Shawne Williams 5.00 12.00

2006-07 SP Signature Edition Signature Style

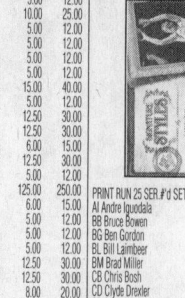

PRINT RUN 25 SER.#'d SETS
AI Andre Iguodala 8.00 20.00
BB Bruce Bowen 8.00 20.00
BG Ben Gordon 15.00 40.00
BL Bill Laimbeer 30.00 75.00
BM Brad Miller 8.00 20.00
CB Chris Bosh 15.00 40.00
CD Clyde Drexler 50.00 120.00
CP Chris Paul 25.00 60.00
DR David Robinson 60.00 150.00
GG George Gervin 20.00 50.00
HO Hakeem Olajuwon 20.00 50.00
JE Julius Erving 50.00 100.00
JK Jason Kidd 20.00 50.00
JS John Stockton 60.00 150.00
KA Kareem Abdul-Jabbar 60.00 120.00
KK Kyle Korver 10.00 25.00
LB Larry Bird 60.00 120.00
LJ LeBron James 125.00 250.00
MA Magic Johnson 60.00 120.00
MB Mike Bibby 8.00 20.00
PS Peja Stojakovic 8.00 20.00
RO Dennis Rodman 30.00 80.00
RP Robert Parish 12.50 30.00
SK Steve Kerr 30.00 60.00
SN Steve Nash 75.00 150.00
TM Tracy McGrady 30.00 80.00
VC Vince Carter 25.00 60.00
YM Yao Ming 25.00 60.00

2006-07 SP Signature Edition Signatures

APPROXIMATE ODDS ONE PER PACK
UNPRICED GOLD PRINT RUN 10 SETS
AB Andrea Bargnani 6.00 15.00
AH Al Harrington 3.00 8.00
AJ Al Jefferson 3.00 8.00
AM Maurice Ager 3.00 8.00
AR Hilton Armstrong 3.00 8.00
BA Leandro Barbosa 3.00 8.00
BB Brent Barry 3.00 8.00
BD Baron Davis 4.00 10.00
BO Chris Bosh 10.00 25.00
BR Ronnie Brewer 4.00 10.00
CA Carmelo Anthony 20.00 40.00
CB Chauncey Billups 5.00 12.00
CD Clyde Drexler 12.50 30.00
CM Corey Maggette 3.00 8.00
CP Chris Paul 20.00 50.00
CS Cedric Simmons 3.00 8.00
DB Dee Brown 3.00 8.00
DG Daniel Gibson 4.00 10.00
DM Damir Markota 3.00 8.00
DN David Noel 3.00 8.00
DR David Robinson 30.00 75.00
DS DeShawn Stevenson 3.00 8.00
EO Emeka Okafor 4.00 10.00
FO Randy Foye 4.00 10.00
GG George Gervin 8.00 20.00
GR Danny Granger 3.00 8.00
HA Hassan Adams 3.00 8.00
HO Hakeem Olajuwon 12.50 30.00
IU Ime Udoka 3.00 8.00
JA James Augustine 3.00 8.00
JB Josh Boone 3.00 8.00
JC Josh Childress 3.00 8.00
JF Jordan Farmar 3.00 8.00
JG Jorge Garbajosa 3.00 8.00
JJ Jarrett Jack 3.00 8.00
JK Jason Kidd 8.00 20.00
JM Mike James 3.00 8.00
JN Antawn Jamison 4.00 10.00
JO Avery Johnson 5.00 12.00
JS J.R. Smith 3.00 8.00
JW James White 3.00 8.00
KA Kareem Abdul-Jabbar 40.00 80.00
KK Kyle Korver 6.00 15.00
KL Kyle Lowry 4.00 10.00
LA LaMarcus Aldridge 8.00 20.00
LB Larry Bird 50.00 100.00
LJ LeBron James 100.00 225.00
LR Luke Ridnour 3.00 8.00
MA Magic Johnson 60.00 120.00
MC Mardy Collins 3.00 8.00
ME Pops Mensah-Bonsu 3.00 8.00
MI Mile Ilic 3.00 8.00
MJ Michael Jordan 350.00 650.00
MO Cuttino Mobley 3.00 8.00
MP Morris Peterson 3.00 8.00
MW Marvin Williams 3.00 8.00
NO Steve Novak 3.00 8.00
NR Nate Robinson 3.00 8.00
OG Orien Greene 3.00 8.00
PD Paul Davis 3.00 8.00
PM Paul Millsap 5.00 12.00
PO Patrick O'Bryant 3.00 8.00
PT P.J. Tucker 3.00 8.00
QD Quincy Douby 3.00 8.00
RA Allan Ray 3.00 8.00
RC Rodney Carney 3.00 8.00
RE Renaldo Balkman 3.00 8.00
RG Rudy Gay 5.00 12.00
RH Ryan Hollins 3.00 8.00
RM Rashad McCants 3.00 8.00
RO Dennis Rodman 25.00 60.00
RR Rajon Rondo 15.00 40.00
RT Reggie Theus 3.00 8.00
RU Bill Russell 75.00 150.00
RY Brandon Roy 10.00 25.00
SB Shannon Brown 5.00 12.00
SJ Solomon Jones 3.00 8.00
SK Steve Kerr 8.00 20.00
SM Craig Smith 3.00 8.00
SR Sergio Rodriguez 3.00 8.00
SS Saer Sene 3.00 8.00
ST John Stockton 60.00 120.00
SW Shawne Williams 3.00 8.00
TF T.J. Ford 3.00 8.00
TS Thabo Sefolosha 4.00 10.00
TT Tyrus Thomas 4.00 10.00
VC Vince Carter 20.00 50.00
WB Will Blalock 3.00 8.00
WE Spud Webb 8.00 20.00
WI Shelden Williams 3.00 8.00
WT Wayman Tisdale 8.00 20.00
YK Yaroslav Korolev 3.00 8.00
YM Yao Ming 10.00 25.00

2006-07 SP Signature Edition Signs of Success

PRINT RUN 25 SER.#'d SETS
UNPRICED GOLD PRINT RUN 10 SETS
AB Andrea Bargnani 25.00 60.00
AI Andre Iguodala 8.00 20.00
AR Allan Ray 5.00 12.00
BJ Bobby Jones 5.00 12.00
BR Brandon Roy 20.00 50.00
CS Cedric Simmons 5.00 12.00
DB Dee Brown 5.00 12.00
DG Danny Granger 6.00 15.00
DM Damir Markota 5.00 12.00
DN David Noel 5.00 12.00
GG Gerald Green 5.00 12.00
HA Hassan Adams 5.00 12.00
HI Hilton Armstrong 5.00 12.00
JB Josh Boone 5.00 12.00
JC Josh Childress 5.00 12.00
JF Jordan Farmar 5.00 12.00
JS J.R. Smith 8.00 20.00
KL Kyle Lowry 6.00 15.00
LB Leandro Barbosa 5.00 12.00
LR Luke Ridnour 5.00 12.00
MA Maurice Ager 5.00 12.00
ME Pops Mensah-Bonsu 5.00 12.00
MJ Mike James 5.00 12.00
MW Marcus Williams 5.00 12.00
OG Orien Greene 5.00 12.00
PM Paul Millsap 8.00 20.00
PO Patrick O'Bryant 5.00 12.00
PT P.J. Tucker 5.00 12.00
QD Quincy Douby 5.00 12.00
RC Rodney Carney 5.00 12.00
RF Randy Foye 6.00 15.00
RG Rudy Gay 10.00 25.00
RH Ryan Hollins 5.00 12.00
RO Ronnie Brewer 6.00 15.00
RR Rajon Rondo 25.00 60.00
SB Shannon Brown 8.00 20.00
SJ Solomon Jones 5.00 12.00
SM Craig Smith 5.00 12.00
SN Steve Novak 5.00 12.00
SR Sergio Rodriguez 5.00 12.00
SS Saer Sene 5.00 12.00
TS Thabo Sefolosha 6.00 15.00
TT Tyrus Thomas 10.00 25.00
WB Will Blalock 5.00 12.00
WE Martell Webster 5.00 12.00
WI Shelden Williams 5.00 12.00

2006-07 SP Signature Edition Three Star Autographs

PRINT RUN 25 SER.#'d SETS
ATG LaMarcus Aldridge 20.00 40.00
P.J. Tucker
Daniel Gibson
BBF Andrea Bargnani 80.00 160.00
Chris Bosh
T.J. Ford
BBM Ronnie Brewer 15.00 40.00
Dee Brown
Paul Millsap
BCF Renaldo Balkman 15.00 40.00
Mardy Collins
Channing Frye
BDM Mike Bibby 15.00 40.00
Quincy Douby
Brad Miller
BPB Chauncey Billups 15.00 40.00
Tayshaun Prince
Will Blalock
CWJ Josh Childress 15.00 40.00
Shelden Williams
Solomon Jones
DFH Baron Davis 15.00 40.00
Jordan Farmar
Ryan Hollins
GGW Danny Granger 15.00 40.00
Orien Greene
Shawne Williams
GLW Rudy Gay 20.00 50.00
Kyle Lowry
Hakim Warrick
JKC Bobby Jones 15.00 40.00
Kyle Korver
Rodney Carney
JMS Mike James 15.00 40.00
Rashad McCants
Craig Smith
MMN Yao Ming 50.00 100.00
Tracy McGrady
Steve Novak
OBM Emeka Okafor 20.00 50.00
Josh Boone
Donyell Marshall
PRR Paul Pierce 75.00 150.00
Rajon Rondo
Allan Ray
PWF Chris Paul 60.00 120.00
Deron Williams
Raymond Felton
RFW Brandon Roy 20.00 50.00
Randy Foye
Marcus Williams
SAC Cedric Simmons 15.00 40.00
Hilton Armstrong
Tyson Chandler
SSR Saer Sene 20.00 50.00
Thabo Sefolosha
Sergio Rodriguez
TSG Tyrus Thomas 40.00 80.00
Thabo Sefolosha
Ben Gordon
WBA Marcus Williams 15.00 40.00
Josh Boone
Hassan Adams

2006-07 SP Signature Edition Two Star Autographs

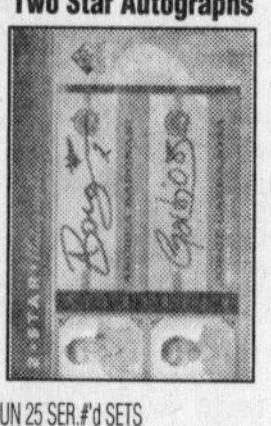

PRINT RUN 25 SER.#'d SETS
AM Maurice Ager 8.00 20.00
Pops Mensah-Bonsu
BC Renaldo Balkman 8.00 20.00
Mardy Collins
BG Andrea Bargnani 60.00 120.00
Jorge Garbajosa
BM Ronnie Brewer 20.00 50.00
Paul Millsap
BW Bruce Bowen 10.00 25.00
James White
CJ Rodney Carney 8.00 20.00
Bobby Jones
DA Chris Duhon 10.00 25.00
B.J. Armstrong
FT T.J. Ford 8.00 20.00
P.J. Tucker
GB Shannon Brown 8.00 20.00
Daniel Gibson
GG Danny Granger 8.00 20.00
Orien Greene
GL Rudy Gay 12.50 30.00
Kyle Lowry
HF Ryan Hollins 10.00 25.00
Jordan Farmar
HW Connie Hawkins 15.00 40.00
Paul Westphal
IR Andre Iguodala 12.50 30.00
Nate Robinson
JC Joe Johnson 8.00 20.00
Josh Childress
JD Antawn Jamison 10.00 25.00
Brad Daugherty
JG Al Jefferson 12.50 30.00
Gerald Green
JS Antawn Jamison 8.00 20.00
DeShawn Stevenson
JW Jarrett Jack 8.00 20.00
Martell Webster
KN Kyle Korver 12.50 30.00
Steve Novak
MA Brad Miller 8.00 20.00
Shareef Abdur-Rahim
MD Corey Maggette 8.00 20.00
Paul Davis
OG Emeka Okafor 8.00 20.00
Ben Gordon
PB Tayshaun Prince 8.00 20.00
Will Blalock
PG Morris Peterson 8.00 20.00
Joey Graham
RR Rajon Rondo 15.00 40.00
Allan Ray
RS Luke Ridnour 8.00 20.00
Saer Sene
SA Cedric Simmons 8.00 20.00
Hilton Armstrong
SF Byron Scott 25.00 50.00
Jordan Farmar
SJ Craig Smith 8.00 20.00
Mike James
TT Tyrus Thomas 15.00 40.00
Thabo Sefolosha
WB Dee Brown 12.50 30.00
Deron Williams
WH Al Harrington 8.00 20.00
Shawne Williams
WJ Hakim Warrick 8.00 20.00
Richard Jefferson

2009-10 SP Signature Edition

COMPLETE SET (100) 30.00 60.00
1 Al Harrington .75 2.00
2 Al Horford 1.00 2.50
3 Al Jefferson 1.00 2.50
4 Al Thornton .75 2.00
5 Allen Iverson 1.25 3.00
6 Andre Iguodala 1.00 2.50
7 Andre Miller .75 2.00
8 Andrea Bargnani .75 2.00
9 Antawn Jamison 1.00 2.50
10 Baron Davis 1.00 2.50
11 Ben Gordon 1.00 2.50
12 Ben Wallace 1.00 2.50
13 Beno Udrih .60 1.50
14 Brad Miller .75 2.00
15 Brandon Roy 1.00 2.50
16 Carlos Boozer 1.00 2.50
17 Carmelo Anthony 1.25 3.00
18 Chauncey Billups 1.00 2.50
19 Chris Bosh 1.00 2.50
20 Chris Duhon .60 1.50
21 Chris Paul 1.50 4.00
22 Courtney Lee .75 2.00
23 D.J. Augustin .75 2.00
24 Danny Granger 1.00 2.50
25 David Lee .75 2.00
26 David West 1.00 2.50
27 Derek Fisher .75 2.00
28 Deron Williams 1.00 2.50
29 Derrick Rose 3.00 8.00
30 DeShawn Stevenson .60 1.50
31 Devin Harris 1.00 2.50
32 Dirk Nowitzki 1.25 3.00
33 Dwight Howard 1.50 4.00
34 Dwyane Wade 2.00 5.00
35 Elton Brand 1.00 2.50
36 Eric Gordon 1.00 2.50
37 Gilbert Arenas 1.00 2.50
38 Hedo Turkoglu 1.00 2.50
39 Jamal Crawford .75 2.00
40 Jason Kidd 1.00 2.50
41 Jason Richardson 1.00 2.50

2009-10 SP Signature Edition

42 Jeff Green .75 2.00
43 Jermaine O'Neal 1.00 2.50
44 Jerryd Bayless .75 2.00
45 Joe Johnson 1.00 2.50
46 Jose Calderon .75 2.00
47 Josh Howard .75 2.00
48 Josh Smith 1.00 2.50
49 Kenyon Martin 1.00 2.50
50 Kevin Durant 3.00 8.00
51 Kevin Garnett 2.00 5.00
52 Kevin Love 1.50 4.00
53 Kevin Martin 1.00 2.50
54 Kobe Bryant 5.00 12.00
55 Lamar Odom 1.00 2.50
56 LaMarcus Aldridge 1.00 2.50
57 LeBron James 5.00 12.00
58 Luis Scola .75 2.00
59 Luke Ridnour .75 2.00
60 Luol Deng 1.00 2.50
61 Manu Ginobili 1.00 2.50
62 Marc Gasol 1.00 2.50
63 Mario Chalmers 1.00 2.50
64 Michael Beasley 1.00 2.50
65 Michael Redd 1.00 2.50
66 Mike Bibby .75 2.00
67 Mike Dunleavy .60 1.50
68 Mo Williams .75 2.00
69 Monta Ellis 1.00 2.50
70 O.J. Mayo 1.00 2.50
71 Pau Gasol 1.00 2.50
72 Paul Pierce 1.25 3.00
73 Peja Stojakovic 1.00 2.50
74 Quentin Richardson .75 2.00
75 Raja Bell .75 2.00
76 Ray Allen 1.00 2.50
77 Raymond Felton .75 2.00
78 Richard Hamilton .75 2.00
79 Richard Jefferson 1.00 2.50
80 Rodney Stuckey 1.00 2.50
81 Ron Artest 1.00 2.50
82 Ronnie Brewer .75 2.00
83 Rudy Fernandez .75 2.00
84 Rudy Gay 1.00 2.50
85 Russell Westbrook 1.50 4.00
86 Sebastian Telfair .60 1.50
87 Shaquille O'Neal 2.00 5.00
88 Shawn Marion 1.00 2.50
89 Stephen Jackson .75 2.00
90 Steve Nash 1.00 2.50
91 T.J. Ford .60 1.50
92 Tayshaun Prince 1.00 2.50
93 Thaddeus Young .60 1.50
94 Tim Duncan 1.50 4.00
95 Tony Parker 1.00 2.50
96 Tracy McGrady 1.00 2.50
97 Tyson Chandler .75 2.00
98 Vince Carter 1.25 3.00
99 Yao Ming 1.25 3.00
100 Yi Jianlian .75 2.00

2009-10 SP Signature Edition 2 Star Signatures

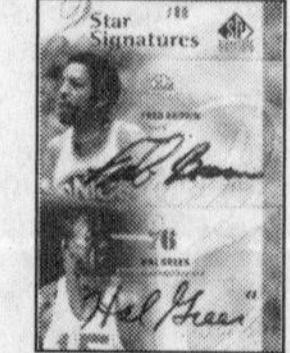

STATED PRINT RUN 23 TO 299 SER.#'d SETS
2SAB Morris Almond 6.00 15.00
Aaron Brooks/99
2SAH George Hill 6.00 15.00
Kelenna Azubuike/199
2SBA Nicolas Batum 6.00 15.00
Alexis Ajinca/199
2SBG Fred Brown 6.00 15.00
Hal Greer/80
2SBO Kwame Brown 6.00 15.00
Patrick O'Bryant/65
2SBS Jose Barea 10.00 25.00
Ramon Sessions/99
2SBW Fred Brown 6.00 15.00
Lenny Wilkens/60

CV Ernie Vandeweghe 6.00 15.00
l Cervi/60
DD Keyon Dooling 6.00 15.00
hris Douglas-Roberts/99
DS Baron Davis 6.00 15.00
odney Stuckey/99
FB Rudy Fernandez 6.00 15.00
icolas Batum/199
FJ Jarrett Jack 6.00 15.00
aymond Felton/60
FR Rudy Fernandez 8.00 20.00
ajon Rondo/199
GB Carlos Boozer 10.00 25.00
orace Grant/49
GD Pau Gasol 12.50 30.00
rad Daugherty/60
GS Pau Gasol 15.00 30.00
Josh Smith/30
HC Eddy Curry 6.00 15.00
Al Harrington/99
JA Arron Afflalo 8.00 20.00
Jose Barea/99
JJ LeBron James 500.00 800.00
Michael Jordan/23
JR John Paxson 40.00 80.00
Ron Harper/35
KD Billy Donovan 30.00 60.00
Bobby Knight/60
LB Bill Sharman 15.00 30.00
Lenny Wilkens/30
LD Brad Daugherty 10.00 25.00
Bill Laimbeer/60
LG Courtney Lee 6.00 15.00
J.R. Giddens/199
LH George Hill 6.00 15.00
Courtney Lee/199
LS Jack Sikma 8.00 20.00
Bill Laimbeer/65
SMB Corey Maggette 6.00 15.00
Shane Battier/30
SMD Mike Bibby 6.00 15.00
D.J. Augustin/99
SMS Tom Sanders 15.00 30.00
Bob McAdoo/89
SMW Brad Miller 6.00 15.00
Chris Wilcox/119
SND Brad Daugherty 6.00 15.00
Larry Nance/60
SNH Larry Nance 6.00 15.00
Spencer Haywood/60
SPH Tom Heinsohn 10.00 25.00
Robert Parish/79
SPS J.R. Smith 6.00 15.00
Morris Peterson/40
SRA Micheal Ray Richardson 6.00 15.00
Kenny Anderson/60
SRB Rajon Rondo 10.00 25.00
Aaron Brooks/199
SSA Jason Smith 6.00 15.00
Ryan Anderson/60
SSB Jack Sikma 6.00 15.00
Fred Brown/69
SSD Chuck Daly 20.00 40.00
Jerry Sloan/40
SSG Jerry Sloan 10.00 25.00
Gail Goodrich/60
SSM Ramon Sessions 8.00 20.00
Luc Mbah A Moute/99
SSR Spencer Haywood 8.00 20.00
Robert Parish/99
SSS Josh Smith 12.50 30.00
Amare Stoudemire/40
SSW Stromile Swift 6.00 15.00
Shelden Williams/60
STS David Thompson 10.00 25.00
Josh Smith/30
STT Jason Thompson 6.00 15.00
Al Thornton/99
SWA Spud Webb 6.00 15.00
Kenny Anderson/60
SWF Spud Webb 10.00 25.00
Derek Fisher/99
SWI Andre Iguodala 8.00 20.00
Gerald Wallace/30
SWS Jerry Sloan 20.00 50.00
Chet Walker/60

2009-10 SP Signature Edition 3 Star Signatures

STATED PRINT RUN 10 TO 199 SER.#'d SETS
SOME UNPRICED DUE TO SCARCITY
3SABA Nicolas Batum 6.00 15.00
Alexis Ajinca
Louis Amundson/199
3SABM Hilton Armstrong 10.00 25.00
Nicolas Batum
Javale McGee/199
3SACG J.R. Giddens 6.00 15.00
Javaris Crittenton
D.J. Augustin/99
3SADW Darrell Arthur 6.00 15.00
Jared Dudley
D.J. White/99
3SALH Courtney Lee 8.00 20.00
Kelenna Azubuike
George Hill/199
3SBBG J.R. Giddens 10.00 25.00
Aaron Brooks
Jose Barea/199
3SBBW Bruce Bowen 6.00 15.00
Sean Williams
Corey Brewer/99
3SBDA Josh Boone 6.00 15.00
Chris Douglas-Roberts
Ryan Anderson/199
3SBDS Mike Bibby 10.00 25.00
Rodney Stuckey
Baron Davis/49
3SBGA Marc Gasol 10.00 25.00
Nicolas Batum
Ryan Anderson/199
3SBSC Aaron Brooks 6.00 15.00
Mario Chalmers
Ramon Sessions/199
3SCHV Eddy Curry 10.00 25.00
Spencer Haywood
Ernie Vandeweghe/35
3SDSG Artis Gilmore 10.00 25.00
Jack Sikma
Brad Daugherty/35
3SDWL Mo Williams 8.00 20.00
Courtney Lee
Keyon Dooling/35
3SDWP Bill Walton 30.00 60.00
Terry Porter
Clyde Drexler/49
3SESL DaJuan Summers 10.00 25.00
Wayne Ellington
Ty Lawson/99
3SFAH Rudy Fernandez 10.00 25.00
Lionel Hollins
Kenny Anderson/35
3SFBS Rudy Fernandez 10.00 25.00
Ramon Sessions
Jose Barea/199
3SFCH Daequan Cook 6.00 15.00
George Hill
Rudy Fernandez/49
3SFRB Aaron Brooks 8.00 20.00
Rajon Rondo
Rudy Fernandez/199
3SFRS Ramon Sessions 12.50 30.00
T.J. Ford
Rajon Rondo/39
3SFWP Spud Webb 8.00 20.00
Derek Fisher
Terry Porter/49
3SFWR Mo Williams 15.00 40.00
Derek Fisher
Rajon Rondo/99
3SGRD Horace Grant 40.00 80.00
David Robinson
Billy Donovan/25
3SGSM Hal Greer 15.00 40.00
Tom Sanders
Slater Martin/40
3SHBG Fred Brown 25.00 60.00
John Havlicek
Gail Goodrich/10
3SHHR Ricky Rubio 50.00 125.00
Gerald Henderson
James Harden/99
3SHKH Spencer Haywood 8.00 20.00
Bernard King
Al Harrington/35
3SHWB Al Harrington 10.00 25.00
Chris Bosh
Gerald Wallace/35
3SJFB Jose Barea 15.00 40.00
Bobby Jackson
Raymond Felton/49
3SJRA Kareem Abdul-Jabbar 900.00 1200.00
Bill Russell
Michael Jordan/10
3SLGM Carl Landry 6.00 15.00
Donte Greene
Luc Mbah A Moute/99
3SMGP Pau Gasol 30.00 80.00
Brad Miller
Robert Parish/25
3SMPA Louis Amundson 6.00 15.00
Oleksiy Pecherov
Donyell Marshall/95
3SMSW Mario West 6.00 15.00
DeShawn Stevenson
Corey Maggette/120
3SOAI Andre Iguodala 25.00 50.00
Carmelo Anthony
Lamar Odom/25
3SOMH Alonzo Mourning 60.00 120.00
Dwight Howard
Hakeem Olajuwon/35
3SOTW Tyrus Thomas 8.00 20.00
Emeka Okafor
Julian Wright/50
3SPPS Robert Parish 15.00 30.00
Tom Sanders
Paul Pierce/49
3SPTR Dennis Rodman 40.00 70.00
John Paxson
Reggie Theus/25
3SRAH George Hill 10.00 25.00
Rajon Rondo
Morris Almond/99
3SRSB Rodney Stuckey 15.00 30.00
Rajon Rondo
Aaron Brooks/49
3SRSC Rajon Rondo 10.00 25.00
Mario Chalmers
Ramon Sessions/99
3SSHG Spencer Haywood 15.00 30.00
Jack Sikma
Jeff Green/49
3SSSB Amare Stoudemire 8.00 20.00
Josh Smith
Brandon Bass/30
3SSWS Tom Sanders 15.00 40.00
Chet Walker
Jerry Sloan/55
3STMB David Thompson 15.00 30.00
Don Buse
Bob McAdoo/55
3SWAP Kenny Anderson 12.00 30.00
Terry Porter
Spud Webb/35
3SWHW Jerry West 30.00 80.00
Lenny Wilkens
Cliff Hagan/30
3SWMS Luc Mbah A Moute 8.00 20.00
Walter Sharpe
Bill Walker/199
3SWRP Pat Riley 20.00 40.00
Jamaal Wilkes
Jim Price/35

2009-10 SP Signature Edition 4 Star Signatures

STATED PRINT RUN 10 TO 99 SER.#'d SETS
SOME UNPRICED DUE TO SCARCITY
4SBCHH Chase Budinger 15.00 40.00
Gerald Henderson
Earl Clark
James Harden/99
4SBPGG Paul Pierce 200.00 400.00
Kobe Bryant
Pau Gasol
Kevin Garnett/25
4SBWKO Patrick O'Bryant 10.00 25.00
Chris Wilcox
Kwame Brown
Chris Kaman/39
4SCMBK Chris Kaman 10.00 25.00
Carlos Boozer
Eddy Curry
Brad Miller/75
4SGBLL Michael Beasley 20.00 50.00
Brook Lopez
Kevin Love
Marc Gasol/75
4SGCRV Hal Greer 25.00 50.00
Ernie Vandeweghe
Arnie Risen
Al Cervi/39
4SGLDG Pau Gasol 25.00 50.00
Horace Grant
Bill Laimbeer
Brad Daugherty/39
4SHHME Gerald Henderson 15.00 40.00
Wayne Ellington
Eric Maynor
Jrue Holiday/99
4SJDFR Bobby Jackson 20.00 40.00
Keyon Dooling
Rajon Rondo
Raymond Felton/99
4SKDAP Jason Kidd 30.00 60.00
Kenny Anderson
Baron Davis
Terry Porter/39
4SKPAH Ron Harper 40.00 80.00
Steve Kerr
B.J. Armstrong
John Paxson/99
4SMESC DaJuan Summers 15.00 30.00
Wayne Ellington
Earl Clark
B.J. Mullens/99
4SMRGW Russell Westbrook 75.00 200.00
Eric Gordon
O.J. Mayo
Derrick Rose/75
4SNDSG Pau Gasol 20.00 40.00
Brad Daugherty
Jack Sikma
Larry Nance/39
4SOWMI Lamar Odom 10.00 25.00
Andre Iguodala
Donyell Marshall
Gerald Wallace/39
4SPKJA Paul Pierce 150.00 300.00
Carmelo Anthony
Bernard King
LeBron James/25
4SPLHR Tom Heinsohn 25.00 50.00
Jim Loscutoff
Robert Parish
Dino Radja/39
4SRBBS Rajon Rondo 30.00 80.00
Aaron Brooks
Jose Barea
Ramon Sessions/99
4SSSNK Jerry Sloan 40.00 100.00
Don Nelson
Bill Sharman
George Karl/39
4SSWSG Jerry Sloan 30.00 80.00
Tom Sanders
Chet Walker
Gail Goodrich/39
4STDJW LeBron James 150.00 300.00
Darryl Dawkins
David Thompson
Dominique Wilkins/39
4SWFMG Rudy Fernandez 15.00 30.00
Paul Millsap
Gerald Wallace
Jeff Green/39
4SWGBS Gerald Wallace 25.00 60.00
Carlos Boozer
Josh Smith
Pau Gasol/39
4SWRAP Spud Webb 25.00 60.00
Rajon Rondo
Kenny Anderson
Terry Porter/39
4SWSCM Slater Martin 40.00 80.00
Dave Cowens
Bill Sharman
Jerry West/39

2009-10 SP Signature Edition INKredible

STATED PRINT RUN 15 TO 499 SER.#'d SETS
SOME UNPRICED DUE TO SCARCITY
IAA Alexis Ajinca/499 3.00 8.00
IAB Aaron Brooks/399 4.00 10.00
IAC Al Cervi/99 8.00 20.00
IAF Arron Afflalo/399 3.00 8.00
IAM Alonzo Mourning/49 20.00 50.00
IAR Anthony Randolph/169 6.00 15.00
IAU D.J. Augustin/199 4.00 10.00
IBA Jose Barea/199 15.00 40.00
IBB Bobby Brown/499 3.00 8.00
IBC Bill Cartwright/99 8.00 20.00
IBD Baron Davis/75 4.00 10.00
IBE Michael Beasley/99 12.50 30.00
IBI Mike Bibby/50 4.00 10.00
IBL Andray Blatche/99 4.00 10.00
IBR Brad Davis/99 4.00 10.00
IBW Bill Walker/499 4.00 10.00
ICA Carmelo Anthony/49 20.00 50.00
ICB Corey Brewer/99 3.00 8.00
ICD Chris Douglas-Roberts/499 3.00 8.00
ICL Clyde Lovellette/99 6.00 15.00
ICM Corey Maggette/75 4.00 10.00
ICW Chet Walker/99 6.00 15.00
IDA Brad Daugherty/139 5.00 12.00
IDF Derek Fisher/149 8.00 20.00
IDG Daniel Gibson/50 4.00 10.00
IDJ Darnell Jackson/499 3.00 8.00
IDM Donyell Marshall/199 3.00 8.00
IDO Billy Donovan/49 20.00 40.00
IDR Derrick Rose/99 75.00 150.00
IDW D.J. White/399 3.00 8.00
IEG Eric Gordon/99 6.00 15.00
IGA Danilo Gallinari/199 4.00 10.00
IGD Glen Davis/499 4.00 10.00
IGG George Gervin/149 6.00 15.00
IGH George Hill/399 4.00 10.00
IGP Gabe Pruitt/499 3.00 8.00
IGR Donte Greene/399 4.00 10.00
IJB Jerryd Bayless/199 4.00 10.00
IJD Joey Dorsey/499 3.00 8.00
IJG Jeff Green/99 4.00 10.00
IJL Jim Loscutoff/99 5.00 12.00
IJN Joakim Noah/149 10.00 25.00
IJO DeAndre Jordan/499 6.00 15.00
IJP Jim Price/99 3.00 8.00
IJS Jack Sikma/399 4.00 10.00
IJW Jerry West/49 25.00 50.00
IKA Kenny Anderson/99 5.00 12.00
IKL Kevin Love/199 15.00 40.00
ILA Louis Amundson/199 4.00 10.00
ILB Larry Bird/25 50.00 100.00
ILE Courtney Lee/99 6.00 15.00
ILJ LeBron James/23 125.00 250.00
ILM Luc Mbah A Moute/499 3.00 8.00
ILN Larry Nance/99 5.00 12.00
ILO Brook Lopez/199 5.00 12.00
IMA Morris Almond/99 3.00 8.00
IMB Marco Belinelli/399 3.00 8.00
IMC Mario Chalmers/499 4.00 10.00
IMJ Michael Jordan/23 350.00 650.00
IML Meadowlark Lemon/65 25.00 50.00
IMR Micheal Ray Richardson/149 4.00 10.00
IMT Mike Taylor/499 3.00 8.00
IMW Marvin Williams/99 4.00 10.00
INB Nicolas Batum/499 6.00 15.00
IOM O.J. Mayo/99 10.00 25.00
IPG Pau Gasol/75 15.00 30.00
IRA Ray Allen/25 20.00 50.00
IRB Renaldo Balkman/50 3.00 8.00
IRH Roy Hibbert/149 5.00 12.00
IRJ Richard Jefferson/115 5.00 12.00
IRP Robert Parish/149 6.00 15.00
IRR Rajon Rondo/299 15.00 40.00
IRS Ramon Sessions/199 4.00 10.00
IRU Brandon Rush/99 4.00 10.00
IRW Russell Westbrook/149 20.00 50.00
ISH Spencer Haywood/299 4.00 10.00
ISI James Silas/99 6.00 15.00
ISJ Sam Jones/35 20.00 40.00
ISL Jerry Sloan/99 6.00 15.00
ISM Josh Smith/119 4.00 10.00
ISO Sonny Weems/499 3.00 8.00
ISS Sean Singletary/499 3.00 8.00
ISW Spud Webb/299 5.00 12.00
ITS Tom Sanders/149 8.00 20.00
IWA Darrell Walker/99 4.00 10.00
IWE David West/149 4.00 10.00
IWI Chris Wilcox/279 3.00 8.00
IYM Yao Ming/49 15.00 30.00

2009-10 SP Signature Edition Signature Rookies

STATED PRINT RUN 199 SER.#'d SETS
RAD Austin Daye 5.00 12.00
RAJ A.J. Price 5.00 12.00
RBM B.J. Mullens 5.00 12.00
RBR Derrick Brown 5.00 12.00
RBU Chase Budinger 5.00 12.00
RCU Dante Cunningham 5.00 12.00
RDC Darren Collison 8.00 20.00
RDG Danny Green 8.00 20.00
RDS DaJuan Summers 5.00 12.00
REC Earl Clark 5.00 12.00
REM Eric Maynor 5.00 12.00
RGH Gerald Henderson 5.00 12.00
RGI Taylor Griffin 5.00 12.00
RHA James Harden 15.00 40.00
RHO Jrue Holiday 10.00 25.00
RJE Jonas Jerebko 5.00 12.00
RJF Jonny Flynn 5.00 12.00
RJJ James Johnson 5.00 12.00
RJP Jeff Pendergraph 5.00 12.00
RJT Jeff Teague 6.00 15.00
RMT Marcus Thornton 8.00 20.00
ROC Omri Casspi 5.00 12.00
RPB Patrick Beverley 5.00 12.00
RRR Ricky Rubio 75.00 150.00
RSC Stephen Curry 12.00 30.00
RSY Sam Young 5.00 12.00
RTA Jermaine Taylor 5.00 12.00
RTD Toney Douglas 5.00 12.00
RTG Taj Gibson 6.00 15.00
RTL Ty Lawson 8.00 20.00
RWE Wayne Ellington 8.00 20.00

2009-10 SP Signature Edition SIGnificance

STATED PRINT RUN 25 TO 499 SER.#'d SETS
SAA Alexis Ajinca/399 3.00 8.00
SAG Aaron Gray/499 3.00 8.00
SAJ Al Jefferson/249 4.00 10.00
SAL Acie Law/99 3.00 8.00
SAN Ryan Anderson/399 3.00 8.00
SAT Al Thornton/299 4.00 10.00
SAV Anderson Varejao/99 4.00 10.00
SBB Bobby Brown/499 3.00 8.00
SBC Corey Brewer/49 5.00 12.00
SBD Boris Diaw/109 5.00 12.00
SBJ Josh Boone/399 3.00 8.00
SBL Brook Lopez/199 4.00 10.00
SBR Bobby Brown/499 3.00 8.00
SBU Beno Udrih/99 3.00 8.00
SBW Bill Walker/499 3.00 8.00
SBY Andrew Bynum/199 8.00 20.00
SCA M.L. Carr/99 5.00 12.00
SCB Chauncey Billups/89 5.00 12.00
SCD Chris Duhon/99 3.00 8.00
SCH Chris Bosh/45 12.00 30.00
SCL Carl Landry/249 4.00 10.00
SCO Corey Brewer/49 4.00 10.00
SCR Caron Butler/99 5.00 12.00
SDA D.J. Augustin/199 4.00 10.00
SDC Daequan Cook/149 3.00 8.00
SDE DeAndre Jordan/499 6.00 15.00
SDG Danilo Gallinari/149 4.00 10.00
SDH Dwight Howard/49 15.00 30.00
SDJ Darnell Jackson/499 4.00 10.00
SDO Joey Dorsey/499 3.00 8.00
SDR Derrick Rose/49 75.00 200.00
SEG Eric Gordon/99 6.00 15.00
SGA Danilo Gallinari/149 5.00 12.00
SGI Artis Gilmore/25 10.00 25.00
SGP Gabe Pruitt/499 3.00 8.00
SJA Antawn Jamison/149 4.00 10.00
SJC Javaris Crittenton/105 3.00 8.00
SJD Jared Dudley/99 3.00 8.00
SJF Jordan Farmar/99 4.00 10.00
SJG Jeff Green/99 5.00 12.00
SJH J.J. Hickson/249 3.00 8.00
SJJ Jarrett Jack/30 4.00 10.00
SJM Javale McGee/399 4.00 10.00
SJN Joakim Noah/125 8.00 20.00
SJO Joe Alexander/249 4.00 10.00
SJS Jason Smith/399 3.00 8.00
SJT Jason Thompson/249 3.00 8.00
SKK Kosta Koufos/399 3.00 8.00
SKL Kevin Love/149 15.00 40.00
SKW Kyle Weaver/499 3.00 8.00
SLA Louis Amundson/349 3.00 8.00
SLD Luol Deng/40 5.00 12.00
SLE Courtney Lee/399 4.00 10.00
SLM Luc Mbah A Moute/499 3.00 8.00
SLO Kyle Lowry/99 3.00 8.00
SMA Morris Almond/199 3.00 8.00
SMB Michael Beasley/49 8.00 20.00
SMC Mario Chalmers 4.00 10.00
SMI Mike Conley Jr./49 6.00 15.00
SMJ Josh McRoberts/99 4.00 10.00
SMK Maurice Cheeks/99 4.00 10.00
SMS Marreese Speights/249 5.00 12.00
SMT Mike Taylor/499 3.00 8.00
SMW Mo Williams/299 5.00 12.00
SJO Joakim Noah/125 8.00 20.00
SOD Lamar Odom/149 8.00 20.00
SOM O.J. Mayo/99 10.00 25.00
SOR Oscar Robertson/25 40.00 80.00
SPA Tony Parker/65 10.00 25.00
SQR Quentin Richardson/379 4.00 10.00
SRA Ron Artest/25 6.00 15.00
SRL Robin Lopez/249 4.00 10.00
SRM Rashad McCants/99 4.00 10.00
SRS Ramon Sessions/199 4.00 10.00
SRU Brandon Rush/299 4.00 10.00
SRW Russell Westbrook/199 15.00 40.00
SSH Spencer Hawes/199 4.00 10.00
SSJ Josh Smith/99 5.00 12.00
SSM Jason Smith/399 3.00 8.00
SSS Sean Singletary/499 3.00 8.00
SST Rodney Stuckey/125 4.00 10.00
SSV Sasha Vujacic/99 5.00 12.00
SSW Spud Webb/199 5.00 12.00
STC Tom Chambers/99 5.00 12.00
STY Tyson Chandler/139 3.00 8.00
SWI Deron Williams/50 10.00 25.00
SWS Shelden Williams/199 4.00 10.00
SYM Yao Ming/49 15.00 40.00

1972-73 Spalding

Each of these seven photos measures 8 1/2" by 11". The fronts feature black-and-white action or posed player photos with a brown outer border that looks like a picture frame and a white inner border. The player's name and the words "Spalding Advisory Staff" appear in a gold bar under the photo. The backs are blank. The cards are unnumbered and checklisted below in alphabetical order.

COMPLETE SET (7) 150.00 300.00
1 Rick Barry 25.00 60.00
2 Rick Barry 25.00 60.00
(Action Shot)
3 Wilt Chamberlain 50.00 120.00
(Philadelphia)
4 Wilt Chamberlain 50.00 120.00
(San Francisco)
5 Julius Erving 40.00 100.00
6 Gail Goodrich 20.00 50.00
7 Luke Jackson 10.00 25.00

2001 Sparks Fleer WNBA

Sponsored by Melissa's and issued in conjunction with Fleer, this 9-card sheet was handed out at the August 8, 2001 game to the first 5000 ticket-holders. Cards feature perforated edges, as they were released in the form of a sheet, white borders, and a colored frame around the card to match the team's colors.

COMPLETE SET (9) 5.00 12.00
1 Temecka Dixon .40 1.00
2 Lisa Leslie 2.50 6.00
3 Ukari Figgs .40 1.00
4 Delisha Milton .40 1.00
5 L.A. Sparks .40 1.00
Melissa's
6 Mwadi Mabika .40 1.00
7 Rhonda Mapp .40 1.00
8 Michael Cooper .40 1.00
9 Latasha Byears .40 1.00

1953 Sport Magazine Premiums

This 10-card set features 5 1/2" by 7" color portraits and was issued as a subscription premium by Sport Magazine. These photos were taken by noted sports photographer Ozzie Sweet. Each features a top player from a number of different sports. The photo backs are blank and unnumbered. We've checklisted the set below in alphabetical order.

COMPLETE SET (10) 30.00 60.00
2 Bob Cousy BK 7.50 15.00

1996 Sported/Match

This 15-card set was produced by the British company Howitt Printing and features cards that "pop-up" when pulled. The basic card front for the first ten cards features a photo of the player against a black background with the title "Sported! World Class Winners" running vertically along the right-side of the card. The final five-cards feature a blue background with the title "Match World Class Winners" running vertically along the right side of the card. When the cards are pulled open, they reveal some statistics and the player's greatest Sported!or Match moment.

COMPLETE SET (15) 10.00 25.00
2 Michael Jordan BK 8.00 20.00
7 Shaquille O'Neal BK 3.00 8.00

1933 Sport Kings

The cards in this 48-card set measure 2 3/8" by 2 7/8". The 1933 Sport Kings set, issued by the Goudey Gum Company, contains cards for the most famous athletic heroes of the times. No less than 18 different sports are represented in the set. The baseball cards of Cobb, Hubbell, and Ruth, and the football cards of Rockne, Grange and Thorpe command premium prices. The cards were issued in one-card penny packs which came 100 packs to a box along with a piece of gum. The catalog designation for this set is R338.

COMPLETE SET 10000.00 16000.00
3 Nat Holman/(basketball) 200.00 350.00
5 Ed Wachter/(basketball) 75.00 125.00
32 Joe Lapchick UER 250.00 400.00
spelled Lopchick on front/(basketball)
33 Eddie Burke/(basketball) 125.00 250.00

2007 Sportkings

4 Larry Bird 6.00 15.00
16 Magic Johnson 6.00 15.00
30 Bill Russell 15.00 30.00
44 Dominique Wilkins 4.00 10.00
46 John Wooden 6.00 15.00

2007 Sportkings Mini

*MINIS: 1X TO 2X BASIC
ONE PER PACK
ANNOUNCED PRINT RUN 93 SETS

2007 Sportkings Autograph Gold

*GOLD: 1.2X TO 2X BASIC
RANDOM INSERTS IN PACKS
ANNOUNCED PRINT RUN 10 SETS
ABR Bill Russell 125.00 200.00
ALB Larry Bird 90.00 150.00

2007 Sportkings Autograph Silver

RANDOM INSERTS IN PACKS
ANNOUNCED PRINT RUN B/WN 95-99 PER
ABR Bill Russell 75.00 125.00
ADW Dominique Wilkins 15.00 30.00
AJW John Wooden 75.00 150.00
ALB Larry Bird 60.00 100.00
AMJ Magic Johnson 50.00 80.00

2007 Sportkings Autograph Memorabilia Gold

*GOLD/10: 1.2X TO 2X SILVER/40
ANNOUNCED PRINT RUN 10 SETS
AMLB Larry Bird Jsy 125.00 200.00

2007 Sportkings Autograph Memorabilia Silver

RANDOM INSERTS IN PACKS
ANNOUNCED PRINT RUN 40 SETS
AMDW Dominique Wilkins Jsy 20.00 40.00
AMJW John Wooden Jkt 75.00 150.00
AMLB Larry Bird Jsy 70.00 120.00
AMMJ Magic Johnson Jsy 60.00 100.00

2007 Sportkings Cityscapes Silver

ANNOUNCED PRINT RUN 20 SETS
*GOLD: .5X TO 1.2X BASIC
GOLD ANNOUNCED PRINT RUN 10 SETS
RANDOM INSERTS IN PACKS
CS04 Carl Yastrzemski Jsy 20.00 40.00
Larry Bird Jsy
Boston
CS06 Ted Williams Jsy 40.00 80.00
Larry Bird Jsy
Boston
CS08 Magic Johnson Jsy 20.00 40.00
Terry Sawchuk Jsy
Los Angeles

2007 Sportkings Decades Silver

ANNOUNCED PRINT RUN 20 SETS
*GOLD: .5X TO 1.2X BASIC
GOLD ANNOUNCED PRINT RUN 10 SETS
RANDOM INSERTS IN PACKS
D05 Hulk Hogan Shirt 50.00 100.00
Don Mattingly Jsy
Magic Johnson Jsy/1980s

2007 Sportkings Double Memorabilia Gold

*GOLD: .6X TO 1.5X BASIC
RANDOM INSERTS IN PACKS
ANNOUNCED PRINT RUN 10 SETS
DM15, DM16 ANNOUNCED PRINT RUN 1 PER
NO DM15, DM16 PRICING DUE TO SCARCITY

2007 Sportkings Double Memorabilia Silver

RANDOM INSERTS IN PACKS
ANNOUNCED PRINT RUN 4-40 SETS
DM15, DM16 ANNOUNCED PRINT RUN 4 PER
NO DM15, DM16 PRICING DUE TO SCARCITY
DM2 Larry Bird Jkt-Jsy 15.00 40.00
DM3 Magic Johnson Jsy-Shorts 12.50 30.00

2007 Sportkings Patch Silver

ANNOUNCED PRINT RUN 20 SETS
P28-P30 ANNOUNCED PRINT RUN 4 PER
NO P28-P30 PRICING DUE TO SCARCITY
*GOLD: .6X TO 1.2X BASIC
GOLD ANNOUNCED PRINT RUN 10 SETS
GOLD P28-P30 ANCD. PRINT RUN 1 PER
GOLD P28-P30 NO PRICING AVAILABLE
RANDOM INSERTS IN PACKS
P2 Dominque Wilkins Jsy 10.00 25.00
P5 John Wooden Jkt 20.00 50.00
P6 Larry Bird Jsy 30.00 60.00
P7 Larry Bird Jkt 30.00 60.00
P9 Magic Johnson Jsy 20.00 50.00

2007 Sportkings Single Memorabilia Silver

RANDOM INSERTS IN PACKS
ANNOUNCED PRINT RUN 90 SETS
SM3, SM13 ANNOUNCED PRINT RUN 4 PER
NO SM3, SM13 PRICING DUE TO SCARCITY
SM34 Dominique Wilkins Jsy 4.00 15.00
SM35 John Wooden Jkt 10.00 25.00
SM36 Larry Bird Shorts 10.00 25.00
SM37 Larry Bird Jsy 10.00 25.00
SM38 Larry Bird Jkt 10.00 25.00
SM39 Magic Johnson Jsy 8.00 20.00
SM40 Magic Johnson Shorts 8.00 20.00

2007 Sportkings Triple Memorabilia Silver

ANNOUNCED PRINT RUN 10 SETS
TM7, TM8 ANNOUNCED PRINT RUN 4 PER
NO TM7, TM8 PRICING DUE TO SCARCITY
GOLD ANNOUNCED PRINT RUN 1 SET
NO GOLD PRICING DUE TO SCARCITY
RANDOM INSERTS IN PACKS
TM01 Larry Bird Jkt-Jsy-Shorts 50.00 100.00
TM09 Larry Bird Jsy 50.00 100.00
Magic Johnson Jsy
Dominique Wilkins Jsy

2008 Sportkings

FIVE CARDS PER BOX
55 Hakeem Olajuwon 4.00 8.00
56 Dolph Schayes 5.00 10.00
57 Robert Parish 4.00 8.00
67 Meadowlark Lemon 5.00 10.00
85 Walt Frazier 4.00 8.00
108 Oscar Robertson 5.00 10.00

2008 Sportkings Mini

*MINI: 1X TO 2X BASIC
ONE PER BOX

2008 Sportkings Autograph Silver

ANNOUNCED PRINT RUN B/WN 20-90 PER
RANDOM INSERTS IN PACKS
DS Dolph Schayes/90 * 20.00 40.00
HO Hakeem Olajuwon/80 * 15.00 30.00
RP Robert Parish/80 * 10.00 25.00
OR1 Oscar Robertson/50 * 50.00 100.00
OR2 Oscar Robertson/50 * 50.00 100.00
WF1 Walt Frazier/40 * 15.00 30.00
WF2 Walt Frazier/40 * 15.00 30.00
MLE1 Meadowlark Lemon/40 * 25.00 50.00
MLE2 Meadowlark Lemon/40 * 25.00 50.00

2008 Sportkings Autograph Memorabilia Silver

ANNOUNCED PRINT RUN B/WN 15-50 PER
NO GOLD PRICING DUE TO SCARCITY
RANDOM INSERTS IN PACKS
HO Hakeem Olajuwon/40 * 20.00 40.00
MLE1 Meadowlark Lemon/40 * 30.00 60.00
MLE2 Meadowlark Lemon/30 * 30.00 60.00
RP Robert Parish/40 * 15.00 30.00
WF1 Walt Frazier/40 * 20.00 40.00
WF2 Walt Frazier/40 * 20.00 40.00

2008 Sportkings Cityscapes Double Silver

RANDOM INSERTS IN PACKS
2 Deion Sanders 15.00 40.00
Dominique Wilkins
Atlanta

2008 Sportkings Cityscapes Triple Silver

RANDOM INSERTS IN PACKS
1 Larry Bird 30.00 60.00
Roger Clemens
Robert Parish
Boston

2008 Sportkings Decades Silver

RANDOM INSERTS IN PACKS
4 Dan Marino 30.00 60.00
Mark Messier
Robert Parish
5 Brett Hull 20.00 50.00
Michael Irvin
Hakeem Olajuwon

2008 Sportkings Double Memorabilia Silver

RANDOM INSERTS IN PACKS
7 Robert Parrish 15.00 40.00
Larry Bird

2008 Sportkings Passing the Torch Silver

RANDOM INSERTS IN PACKS

2008 Sportkings Patch Silver

RANDOM INSERTS IN PACKS
9 Hakeem Olajuwon 10.00 25.00
23 Robert Parish 12.50 30.00
25 Walt Frazier 12.50 30.00

2008 Sportkings Single Memorabilia Silver

RANDOM INSERTS IN PACKS
16 Hakeem Olajuwon 6.00 15.00
29 Meadowlark Lemon 8.00 20.00
35 Robert Parish 6.00 15.00
41 Walt Frazier 6.00 15.00

2008 Sportkings Triple Memorabilia Silver

RANDOM INSERTS IN PACKS
14 Hakeem Olajuwon 20.00 50.00
Magic Johnson
Larry Bird

2009 Sportkings

COMPLETE SET (52) 250.00 450.00
COMMON CARD (109-160) 5.00 12.00
SEMISTARS 6.00 15.00
UNLISTED STARS 8.00 20.00
112 Rick Barry 5.00 12.00
113 Jerry West 6.00 15.00
120 George Mikan 6.00 15.00
124 Pete Maravich 15.00 40.00
157 Lisa Leslie 8.00 20.00

2009 Sportkings Mini

*MINI: .6X TO 1.5X BASIC CARDS
STATED ODDS ONE PER BOX
UNPRICED SILVER PRINT RUN 7 SETS
UNPRICED GOLD PRINT RUN 3 SETS

2009 Sportkings Autograph Silver

ANNOUNCED PRINT RUN B/WN 15-70 PER
UNPRICED GOLD PRINT RUN 10
JWE1 Jerry West/50* 30.00 60.00
JWE2 Jerry West/50* 30.00 60.00

LLE1 Lisa Leslie/40* 25.00 50.00
LLE2 Lisa Leslie/40* 25.00 50.00
RBA1 Rick Barry/70* 20.00 40.00
RBA2 Rick Barry/70* 20.00 40.00

2009 Sportkings Autograph Memorabilia Silver

ANNOUNCED PRINT RUN B/WN 15-40 PER
UNPRICED GOLD PRINT RUN 10
RANDOM INSERTS IN PACKS
LLE1 Lisa Leslie Jsy/40* 25.00 50.00
LLE2 Lisa Leslie Jsy/40* 25.00 50.00

2009 Sportkings Double Memorabilia Silver

ANNOUNCED PRINT RUN B/WN 1-19
UNPRICED GOLD PRINT RUN 1
RANDOM INSERTS IN PACKS
14 Lisa Leslie Jsy/19* 20.00 40.00
Jackie Joyner-Kersee Shirt

2009 Sportkings Patch Silver

ANNOUNCED PRINT RUN B/WN 4-19
UNPRICED GOLD PRINT RUN 1 SET
RANDOM INSERTS IN PACKS
10 Lisa Leslie/19* 15.00 30.00

2009 Sportkings Single Memorabilia Silver

ANNOUNCED PRINT RUN B/WN 4-29
UNPRICED GOLD PRINT RUN B/WN 1-4
RANDOM INSERTS IN PACKS
19 Lisa Leslie Jsy/29* 10.00 25.00

2010 Sportkings

COMPLETE SET (48) 150.00 300.00
COMP.SET w/o ALI SP (47) 100.00 200.00
168 Wilt Chamberlain 6.00 15.00
169 Bobby Knight 5.00 12.00
173 Sheryl Swoopes 4.00 10.00
174 Dennis Rodman 5.00 12.00
202 Curly Neal 5.00 12.00

2010 Sportkings Mini

COMPLETE SET (48) 175.00 350.00
*MINI: .5X TO 1.2X BASIC CARDS
STATED ODDS 1:2

2010 Sportkings Autograph Silver

ANNOUNCED PRINT RUN 10-50
UNPRICED GOLD PRINT RUN 5-10
ACN1 Curly Neal/40* 20.00 40.00
ACN2 Curly Neal/40* 20.00 40.00
ADR1 Dennis Rodman/40* 25.00 50.00
ADR2 Dennis Rodman/40* 25.00 50.00
ABKN1 Bobby Knight/25* 30.00 60.00
ABKN2 Bobby Knight/25* 30.00 60.00
ABKN3 Bobby Knight/25* 30.00 60.00
ASSW1 Sheryl Swoopes/40* 15.00 30.00
ASSW2 Sheryl Swoopes/40* 15.00 30.00

2010 Sportkings Autograph Memorabilia Silver

ANNOUNCED PRINT RUN 10-40
UNPRICED GOLD PRINT RUN 5-10
AMCN1 Curly Neal Shorts/40* 25.00 50.00
AMCN2 Curly Neal Shorts/40* 25.00 50.00
AMDR1 Dennis Rodman/40* 30.00 60.00
AMDR2 Dennis Rodman/40* 30.00 60.00
AMBKN1 Bobby Knight Shirt/20* 40.00 80.00
AMBKN2 Bobby Knight Shirt/20* 40.00 80.00
AMBKN3 Bobby Knight Shirt/20* 40.00 80.00
AMSSW1 Sheryl Swoopes Jsy/40* 20.00 40.00
AMSSW2 Sheryl Swoopes Jsy/40* 20.00 40.00

2010 Sportkings Double Memorabilia Silver

STATED PRINT RUN 20 UNLESS NOTED
DM7 Wilt Chamberlain 40.00 100.00
Curly Neal
DM9 Sheryl Swoopes 10.00 25.00
Lisa Leslie

2010 Sportkings Gold Medal Winners Cut Autographs

STATED PRINT RUN X SER.#'d SETS
UNPRICED DUE TO SCARCITY
GMWAD Anne Donovan

2010 Sportkings Patch Silver

STATED PRINT RUN 20
UNPRICED GOLD PRINT RUN 10
P4 Sheryl Swoopes 10.00 25.00

2010 Sportkings Single Memorabilia Silver

STATED PRINT RUN 26 UNLESS NOTED
SM4 Bobby Knight 10.00 20.00
SM7 Curly Neal 6.00 12.00
SM8 Dennis Rodman 10.00 20.00
SM26 Sheryl Swoopes 6.00 12.00
SM30 Wilt Chamberlain 20.00 40.00

2010 Sportkings Triple Memorabilia Silver

SILVER PRINT RUN 4-20
UNPRICED GOLD PRINT RUN 1-10
TM3 Wilt Chamberlain 20.00 40.00
Curly Neal
Dennis Rodman

2012 Sportkings

218 Jackie Stiles 4.00 10.00
219 David Robinson 4.00 10.00
220 Bill Walton 4.00 10.00
221 Isiah Thomas 4.00 10.00
222 Dick Vitale 4.00 10.00

2012 Sportkings Mini

*MINI: .5X TO 1.2X BASIC CARDS
RANDOM INSERT IN PACKS

2012 Sportkings Autograph Memorabilia Silver

ANNOUNCED PRINT RUN 15-50
AMBW1 Bill Walton/40* 12.00 25.00
AMBW2 Bill Walton/40* 12.00 25.00
AMDRO1 David Robinson/40* 40.00 80.00
AMDRO2 David Robinson/40* 40.00 80.00
AMITH1 Isiah Thomas/40* 12.00 25.00
AMITH2 Isiah Thomas/40* 12.00 25.00
AMJST1 Jackie Stiles/50* 12.00 25.00
AMJST2 Jackie Stiles/50* 12.00 25.00

2012 Sportkings Autographs Silver

ANNOUNCED PRINT RUN 15-130
ABW1 Bill Walton/40* 10.00 20.00
ABW2 Bill Walton/40* 10.00 20.00
ADRO1 David Robinson/40* 30.00 60.00
ADRO2 David Robinson/40* 30.00 60.00
ADV1 Dick Vitale/90* 20.00 40.00
ADV2 Dick Vitale/90* 20.00 40.00
AITH1 Isiah Thomas/40* 12.00 25.00
AITH2 Isiah Thomas/40* 12.00 25.00
AJST1 Jackie Stiles/50* 10.00 20.00
AJST2 Jackie Stiles/50* 10.00 20.00

2012 Sportkings Cityscapes Double Silver

ANNOUNCED PRINT RUN 30
CS8 Isiah Thomas 15.00 30.00
Gordie Howe
CS10 Scottie Pippen 25.00 50.00
Frank Thomas

2012 Sportkings Double Memorabilia Silver

ANNOUNCED PRINT RUN 60
DM5 David Robinson 10.00 20.00
Bill Walton

2012 Sportkings Premium Back

*SINGLES: .5X TO 1.2X BASIC CARDS
STATED ODDS ONE PER PACK

2012 Sportkings Premium Back Redemption Paintings

ANNOUNCED PRINT RUN 1
UNPRICED DUE TO SCARCITY
AVAILABLE VIA PREMIUM BACK EXCHANGE
8 Bob Cousy
12 Charles Barkley
18 Elgin Baylor
31 Julius Erving
32 Kareem Abdul-Jabbar
33 Kobe Bryant
35 LeBron James
38 Michael Jordan
48 Shaquille O'Neal

2012 Sportkings Premium Back Redemption Quad Memorabilia

STATED PRINT RUN 10 SER. #'d SETS
UNPRICED DUE TO SCARCITY
AVAILABLE VIA PREMIUM BACK EXCHANGE
SKEQM02 Roberto Alomar
Bjorn Borg
Clyde Drexler
Maurice Richard
SKEQM03 David Robinson
Rickey Henderson
Rod Carew
Billy Graham
SKEQM04 Ken Griffey Jr.
Patrick Roy
Ben Hogan
Scottie Pippen
SKEQM06 Fernando Valenzuela
Bill Walton
Franco Harris
Julio Cesar Chavez
SKEQM08 Seattle Slew
Isiah Thomas
Payne Stewart
Tito Ortiz
SKEQM09 Tony Gwynn
Bob Hayes
Larry Bird
Steve Yzerman

2012 Sportkings Premium Back Redemption Sketches

ANNOUNCED PRINT RUN 1
UNPRICED DUE TO SCARCITY
AVAILABLE VIA PREMIUM BACK EXCHANGE
1 Adolph Rupp
2 Al McGuire
19 Bill Walton
27 Bobby Knight
43 Dean Smith
44 Denny Crum
52 Don Haskins
56 Everett Dean
57 Forrest Allen
59 Frank McGuire
69 Gary Williams
75 Hank Iba
76 Harold E. Foster
84 Howard Hobson
97 Jerry Tarkanian
98 Jim Boeheim
99 Jim Calhoun
104 Joe B. Hall
109 John Thompson
110 John Wooden
115 Jud Heathcote
117 Ken Loeffler
119 Larry Brown
122 Lute Olson
132 Mike Krzyzewski
135 Nat Holman
141 Pete Newell
151 Rick Pitino
154 Rollie Massimino
157 Roy Williams
165 Steve Fisher
174 Tubby Smith
182 Wilt Chamberlain

2012 Sportkings Quad Memorabilia Silver

ANNOUNCED PRINT RUN 30
QM5 David Robinson 15.00 30.00
Bill Walton
Isiah Thomas
Scottie Pippen

2012 Sportkings Single Memorabilia Silver

ANNOUNCED PRINT RUN 90
SM9 David Robinson 7.50 15.00
SM10 Jackie Stiles 7.50 15.00
SM11 Isiah Thomas 7.50 15.00
SM12 Bill Walton 7.50 15.00

2012 Sportkings Triple Memorabilia Silver

ANNOUNCED PRINT RUN 30
TM5 David Robinson 15.00 30.00
Kyle Petty
Gale Sayers

2008 Sportkings National Convention VIP Promo

7 Larry Bird 4.00 10.00
Nat Holman
13 Bill Russell 3.00 8.00
Joe Lapchick

2009 Sportkings National Convention VIP Promo

COMPLETE SET (7)
1 Ivan Lendl 4.00 10.00
Phil Esposito
Rusty Wallace
Ken Shamrock
Rick Barry
Mike Tyson
4 Jerry West 5.00 12.00
Byron Nelson
Fred Perry
Mark Martin
Minnesota Fats
Jerry Rice

2010 Sportkings National Convention VIP Promo

6 Wilt Chamberlain 1.50 4.00
8 Dennis Rodman 1.25 3.00
21 Curly Neal 1.25 3.00

1994-95 Sports Action Basket

Released during the 1994-95 season, this 172-card set packed out in Sports Action Basket magazine. Each card is numbered on the back, the first two digits refer to the issue number, and the last two digits refer to the individual card. The set features many NBA players, coaches, and cheerleaders. Oddities include Jack Nicholson and Michael Jordan as a baseball player.

COMPLETE SET (172) 200.00 500.00
5301 Dan Majerle 2.00 5.00
5302 Ron Harper 2.00 5.00
5303 Muggsy Bogues 1.50 4.00
5304 Shaquille O'Neal 8.00 20.00
5305 Larry Johnson 1.50 4.00
5306 Jalen Rose 3.00 8.00
5307 Nate McMillan 1.25 3.00
5308 Clippers Cheerleaders .40 1.00
5309 Kenny Smith 1.25 3.00
5310 Gorilla Mascot .60 1.50
5311 Michael Young 1.25 3.00
5312 David Robinson 5.00 12.00
5313 Jason Kidd 8.00 20.00
5314 Richard Dacoury 1.25 3.00
5315 Damon Bailey 1.50 4.00
5316 Dennis Rodman 3.00 8.00
5317 Michael Jordan 20.00 50.00
5318 B.J. Armstrong 1.25 3.00
5501 Billy Owens 1.25 3.00
5502 Alonzo Mourning 3.00 8.00
5503 Yann Bonato 1.25 3.00
5504 Isiah Thomas 2.50 6.00
5505 Glenn Robinson 3.00 8.00
5506 Karl Malone 5.00 12.00
5507 Dikembe Mutombo 2.50 6.00
5508 Hakeem Olajuwon 3.00 8.00
5509 Rony Seikaly 1.25 3.00
5510 Vernon Maxwell 1.25 3.00
5511 Stephane Ostrowski 1.25 3.00
5512 Arvydas Sabonis 3.00 8.00
5513 Yinka Dare 1.25 3.00
5514 Jamal Mashburn 3.00 8.00
5515 Buck Williams 1.50 4.00
5516 Mookie Blaylock 1.25 3.00
5517 Charles Barkley 5.00 12.00
5518 Patrick Ewing 3.00 8.00
5601 Scott Skiles 1.50 4.00
5602 Terry Porter 1.25 3.00
5603 Dominique Wilkins 3.00 8.00
5604 Stuff Mascot .40 1.00
5605 Anthony Peeler 1.25 3.00
5606 Donyell Marshall 1.50 4.00
5607 Chris Webber 3.00 8.00
5608 Alexander Volkov 2.00 5.00
5609 Pooh Richardson 1.25 3.00
5610 Robert Parish 1.50 4.00
5611 Isaiah Rider 1.50 4.00
5612 Steve Smith 1.50 4.00
5613 Michael Adams 1.25 3.00
5614 John Lucas Foundation .75 2.00
5615 Michael Jordan 20.00 50.00
5616 Sarunas Marciulionis 2.00 5.00
5617 Gerald Wilkins 1.50 4.00
5618 Miami Cheerleader .75 2.00
5701 Charlotte Mascot .40 1.00
5702 Brad Daugherty 1.25 3.00
5703 Chris Mullin 2.50 6.00
5704 Don MacLean 1.25 3.00
5705 Vlade Divac 1.50 4.00
5706 Danny Ainge 2.00 5.00
5707 Mark Jackson 2.00 5.00
5708 Lakers Cheerleaders 1.25 3.00
5709 B.J. Armstrong 1.50 4.00
5710 Nikos Gallis 2.00 5.00
5711 Joe Dumars 2.50 6.00
5712 Antoine Rigaudeau 2.00 5.00
5713 Rik Smits 1.25 3.00
5714 Charles Oakley 1.25 3.00
5715 Shawn Kemp 2.00 5.00
5716 Chris Webber 3.00 8.00
5717 Bill Varner 1.25 3.00
5718 Christian Laettner 2.00 5.00
5801 John Stockton 6.00 15.00
5802 Mitch Richmond 2.50 6.00
5803 Charles Barkley 5.00 12.00
5804 Latrell Sprewell 2.50 6.00
5805 Danny Manning 1.50 4.00
5806 Miami Mascot .40 1.00
5807 Bulls Mascot .40 1.00
5808 Kevin Willis 1.25 3.00
5809 Micheal Williams 1.25 3.00
5810 Magic Johnson 6.00 15.00
5811 Kevin Johnson 1.50 4.00
5812 Dennis Rodman 3.00 8.00
5813 John Starks 1.50 4.00
5814 Gheorghe Muresan 1.25 3.00
5815 Orlando Cheerleader 1.25 3.00
5816 Jeff Hornacek 2.00 5.00
5817 Clyde Drexler 4.00 10.00
5818 Dell Curry 1.25 3.00
5901 Jimmy Jackson 1.50 4.00
5902 Byron Scott 2.00 5.00
5903A Sam Cassell 2.00 5.00
5903B Otis Thorpe UER 1.25 3.00
Should have been numbered 5904
5905 San Antonio Mascot .40 1.00
5906 James Worthy 2.50 6.00
5907 A.C. Green 2.00 5.00
5908 Cleveland Cheerleader 1.25 3.00
5909 John Paxson 1.50 4.00
5910 Doug Christie 1.25 3.00
5911 Derrick Coleman 1.25 3.00
5912 Sean Rooks 1.25 3.00
5913 Turbo Mascot .40 1.00
5914 Charles Smith 1.25 3.00
5915 Derrick McKey 1.25 3.00
5916 Cherokee Parks 1.25 3.00
5917 Felton Spencer 1.25 3.00
5918 Derrick Phelps 1.25 3.00
6001 Steve Smith 1.50 4.00
6002 Tim Hardaway 2.00 5.00
6003 Dee Brown 1.25 3.00
6004 Reggie Miller 4.00 10.00
6005 Mark Price 2.00 5.00
6006 Jack Nicholson 2.00 5.00
6007 Kenny Anderson 1.25 3.00
6008 Jimmy Jackson 1.50 4.00
6009 Dikembe Mutombo 2.50 6.00
6010 Charles Oakley 1.25 3.00
6011 Muggsy Bogues 1.50 4.00
6012 Dan Majerle 2.00 5.00
6013 Mahmoud Abdul-Rauf .75 2.00
6014 B.J. Armstrong 1.50 4.00
6015 Nick Van Exel 2.50 6.00
6016 Kevin Johnson 1.50 4.00
6017 John Stockton 6.00 15.00
6018 Detlef Schrempf 1.50 4.00
6101 Scottie Pippen 5.00 12.00
6102 LaPhonso Ellis 1.25 3.00
6103 Sherman Douglas 1.25 3.00
6104 Isaiah Rider 1.50 4.00
6105 Vinny Del Negro 1.25 3.00
6106 Gary Payton 3.00 8.00
6107 Mookie Blaylock 1.25 3.00
6108 Christian Laettner 2.00 5.00
6109 Kevin Willis 1.25 3.00
6110 Harold Miner 1.25 3.00
6111 Chris Webber 3.00 8.00
6112 Rod Strickland 1.25 3.00
6113 Derrick Coleman 1.25 3.00
6114 Larry Johnson 1.50 4.00
6115 Rony Seikaly 1.25 3.00
6116 Derrick Coleman 1.25 3.00
6117 Larry Johnson 1.50 4.00
6118 Karl Malone 5.00 12.00
6201 Dell Curry 1.25 3.00
6202 Joe Dumars 2.50 6.00
6203 Robert Horry 2.00 5.00
6204 Glen Rice 2.00 5.00
6205 Hakeem Olajuwon 3.00 8.00
6206 Danny Ainge 1.50 4.00
6207 Oklahoma Cheerleader .75 2.00
6208 J.R. Reid 1.25 3.00
6209 Derrick McKey 1.25 3.00
6210 Shaquille O'Neal 8.00 20.00
6211 Christian Laettner 2.00 5.00
6212 John Starks 1.50 4.00
6213 Vernon Maxwell 1.25 3.00
6214 Charles Barkley 5.00 12.00
6215 Clyde Drexler 4.00 10.00
6216 Doug Smith 1.25 3.00
6217 Gators Cheerleader 1.25 3.00
6218 David Robinson 4.00 10.00
5406 Detlef Schrempf 1.50 4.00
5407 Anfernee Hardaway 3.00 8.00
5409 Reggie Miller 4.00 10.00
5410 Spud Webb 1.50 4.00
5412 Eric Montross 1.25 3.00
5415 Hakeem Olajuwon 3.00 8.00
5417 Glen Rice 2.00 5.00
5418 Kenny Anderson 1.25 3.00
6302 Craig Ehlo 1.25 3.00
6306 Jamal Mashburn 3.00 8.00

1995 Sports Action Basket

This oversized 41-card set was released in France in 1995. The set features four subsets: Ecris a ta Star (Write to your star) (ES), Legend of the NBA (LN), Star of the NBA (SN), and Back Court (BC). Please note that these cards are not numbered and are listed below in Alphabetical order.

COMPLETE SET (41) 150.00 300.00
1 Charles Barkley SN 3.00 8.00
2 Larry Bird LN 6.00 15.00
3 Dee Brown SN 1.25 3.00
4 Sam Cassell SN 2.00 5.00
5 Vlade Divac ES 2.00 5.00
6 Patrick Ewing SN 2.50 6.00
7 Horace Grant SN 1.50 4.00
8 Anfernee Hardaway ES 3.00 8.00
9 Anfernee Hardaway SN 3.00 8.00
10 Grant Hill ES 3.00 8.00
11 Jeff Hornacek SN 1.50 4.00
12 Bobby Hurley SN 2.00 5.00
13 Jim Jackson SN 1.25 3.00
14 Magic Johnson LN 5.00 12.00
15 Vinnie Johnson SN 1.25 3.00
16 Michael Jordan SN 15.00 40.00
17 Michael Jordan HOME UER ES 15.00 40.00
18 Michael Jordan AWAY ES 15.00 40.00
19 Shawn Kemp SN 2.00 5.00
20 Shawn Kemp BC 2.00 5.00
21 Jason Kidd SN 3.00 8.00
22 Toni Kukoc SN 2.00 5.00
23 Christian Laettner ES 1.50 4.00
24 Karl Malone HOME ES 2.50 6.00
25 Karl Malone AWAY UER ES 2.50 6.00
26 Anthony Mason SN 1.25 3.00
27 Antonio McDyess SN 2.50 6.00
28 Nate McMillan SN 1.25 3.00
29 Reggie Miller SN 2.50 6.00
30 Chris Mullin SN 2.00 5.00
31 Alonzo Mourning ES 2.50 6.00
32 Shaquille O'Neal ES 5.00 12.00
33 Hakeem Olajuwon UER ES 2.50 6.00
34 Hakeem Olajuwon SN 2.50 6.00
35 Gary Payton SN 2.00 5.00
36 Mitch Richmond SN 2.00 5.00
37 Mitch Richmond ES 2.00 5.00
38 Isaiah Rider SN 2.00 5.00
39 Dennis Rodman SN 4.00 10.00
40 Arvydas Sabonis SN 2.00 5.00
41 Nick Van Exel SN 2.00 5.00

1995 Sports Action Basket Sticker Panels

This set was released in France in 1995 by Sports Action Basket. The set features eight 4 5/8" by 6 1/2" sticker panels that features top NBA players and team logos. Please note that these panels are not numbered.

COMPLETE SET (7) 25.00 60.00
1 Hakeem Olajuwon 8.00 20.00
Michael Jordan
Jalen Rose
Charles Barkley
Chris Webber
Magic Cheerleader
Reggie Miller
Georgia Tech
Shawn Kemp
2 Miami Hurricanes 3.00 8.00
The Intimidator
Rebels Logo
Grant Hill
Dennis Rodman
Anfernee Hardaway
Lakers Cheerleader
Muggsy Bogues
Shaquille O'Neal
Scottie Pippen
3 Clyde Drexler 3.00 8.00
Robert Horry
Mitch Richmond
Mortal Kombat
Jimmy Jackson
Derek Harper
Mookie Blaylock
Vinny Del Negro
Dee Brown
4 Gorilla Mascot 3.00 8.00
Space Player
Horace Grant
James Robinson
Danny Ferry
David Robinson
Doug Smith
Kendall Gill
Mahmoud Abdul-Rauf
Mitch Richmond
5 Mitch Richmond 4.00 10.00
Dennis Rodman
Shaquille O'Neal
Jason Kidd
Knicks Cheerleader
Penny Hardaway
Larry Johnson
Charles Barkley
Isaiah Rider
6 Dee Brown 3.00 8.00
Karl Malone
Rik Smits
Chris Mullin
Joe Dumars
Shaquille O'Neal
Sean Elliott
John Starks
Pedrag Danilovic
7 KO 4.00 10.00
Playground Attitude
Dennis Rodman
Pacers Mascot
Charles Barkley
John Stockton
Don MacLean
Billy Owens
Coach Attitude

1996 Sports Action Basket Punch Outs

This 10-card set was released in 1996, and features players from the Chicago Bulls and the Seattle Supersonics. These player action-figures were printed on a very thick stock, and measure roughly 4 3/4" x 6 1/4". All of Bulls' players are featured on a white bordered card, the Sonics' players were issued on a light yellow bordered card.

COMPLETE SET (10) 40.00 100.00
1 Michael Jordan 20.00 50.00
2 Steve Kerr 2.00 5.00
3 Toni Kukoc 3.00 8.00
4 Scottie Pippen 5.00 12.00
5 Dennis Rodman 5.00 12.00
6 Frank Brickowski 2.00 5.00
7 Hersey Hawkins 2.00 5.00
8 Shawn Kemp 4.00 10.00
9 Gary Payton 4.00 10.00
10 Detlef Schrempf 2.00 5.00

1987 Sports Cube Game

3 1/2" by 5 3/8" cards with nine black and white portrait shots on front and questions on the back
COMPLETE SET (3) 8.00 20.00
1 James Naismith 6.00 15.00
Babe Ruth
America's Cup
Knute Rockne
Vince Lombardi
Herb Brooks
Jack Johnson
Bobby Jones
Jim Thorpe

1978 Sports I.D. Patches

This patch set was issued in 1978, and featured many of the NBA's top players or teams. Each patch was done in full color, and measured 3" x 5". Each patch is unnumbered and is listed below in alphabetical order.

COMPLETE SET (6) 60.00 120.00
1 Darryl Dawkins 5.00 10.00
2 Julius Erving 20.00 40.00
3 Dan Issel 12.50 25.00
4 Bobby Jones 7.50 15.00
5 Nuggets Team Photo 7.50 15.00
6 Spurs Team Photo 7.50 15.00
7 David Thompson 7.50 15.00

1989 Sports Illustrated for Kids I

Since its debut issue in January 1989, SI for Kids has included a perforated sheet of nine standard-size cards bound into each magazine. The cards were consecutively numbered 1-324 through December 1991. The athletes featured represent an extremely wide spectrum of sports. Each card features color photos with variously colored borders. The borders are as follows: aqua (1-108), green (109-207), woodgrain (208-216), red (217-315), marble (316-324). The player's name is printed in a white bar at the top, while his or her sport appears at the bottom. The backs carry biographical information, career highlights, and a trivia question with answer. The cards' magazine issue date appears on the back in very small type. Although originally distributed in sheet form, the cards are frequently traded as singles. Thus, they are priced individually. The value of an intact sheet is equal to the sum of the nine cards plus a premium of up to 20%.

4 Larry Bird BK 4.00 10.00
6 Isiah Thomas BK .60 1.50
10 Mark Jackson BK .40 1.00
16 Michael Jordan BK 20.00 35.00
23 Dominique Wilkins BK .40 1.00
27 Magic Johnson BK 4.00 10.00
29 Charles Barkley BK 2.00 5.00
34 Alex English BK .40 1.00
42 Kareem Abdul-Jabbar BK 1.50 4.00
44 Hakeem Olajuwon BK 1.50 4.00
77 Patrick Ewing BK 1.25 3.00
89 Karl Malone BK 2.00 5.00
91 Joe Dumars BK .40 1.00
93 Chris Mullin BK .40 1.00
97 Bridgette Gordon BK .40 1.00
101 Nancy Lieberman-Cline BK .40 1.00
104 John Stockton BK 1.00 2.50
107 Michael Cooper BK .40 1.00

1990 Sports Illustrated for Kids I

113 James Worthy BK .50 1.25
117 Jack Sikma BK .15 .40
119 Sandra Hodge BK .75 2.00
123 Brad Daugherty BK .10 .30
124 Dale Ellis BK .15 .40
129 Bill Laimbeer BK .10 .30
131 David Robinson BK 2.00 5.00
137 Moses Malone BK .50 1.25
139 J.R. Reid BK .10 .30
145 Reggie Miller BK .75 2.00
150 Rex Chapman BK .15 .40
160 Scottie Pippen BK 2.00 5.00
164 Jennifer Azzi BK .50 1.25
192 Dennis Rodman BK 2.00 5.00
199 Lynette Woodard BK .30 .75
200 Terry Cummings BK .15 .40
204 Kevin Johnson BK .50 1.25
208 Wilt Chamberlain BK 1.50 4.00

1991 Sports Illustrated for Kids I

217 Tom Chambers BK .15 .40
221 Clyde Drexler BK 1.25 3.00
223 Teresa Edwards BK .50 1.25
226 Ricky Pierce BK .15 .40
230 Bernard King BK .30 .75
235 Kevin McHale BK .50 1.25
239 Charles Smith HK .10 .30
244 Rolando Blackman BK .10 .30
246 Vlade Divac BK .30 .75
255 Kevin Duckworth BK .10 .30
263 Alvin Robertson BK .10 .30
274 Daedra Charles BK .60 1.50
281 Sonja Henning BK .40 1.00
302 Tim Hardaway BK .40 1.00
307 Chuck Person BK .15 .40
309 Hersey Hawkins BK .15 .40
310 Venus Lacy BK .75 2.00
323 Bill Russell BK 1.25 3.00

1992 Sports Illustrated for Kids II

Since its debut issue in January 1989, SI for Kids has included a perforated sheet of nine standard-size cards bound into each magazine. In January 1992, the card numbers started over again at 1. This listing comprises the cards contained from that magazine through the last 2000 issue. The athletes featured represent an extremely wide spectrum of sports. Each card features color photos with borders of various designs and colors. The borders are as follows: navy (1-9, 19-99), clouds (10-18, 55-63, 226-234), marble (100-108, 208-216, 316-324), pink (109-207), purple (217-225), blue (235-315), gold/silver (325-486), clouds (487-495) and gold/silver (496-621). The athlete's name is printed at the top while his or her sport appears at the bottom. The backs carry biographical information, career highlights, and a trivia question with answer. The cards' magazine issue date appears on the back in very small type. Although originally distributed in sheet form, the cards are frequently traded as singles. Thus, they are priced individually. The value of an intact sheet is equal to the sum of the nine cards plus a premium of up to 20 percent. The cards labeled as "MC" were issued in SI for Kids as part of a milk promotion.

4 Michael Jordan BK 8.00 20.00
8 Dee Brown BK .10 .30
19 Dominique Wilkins BK .40 1.00
25 Derrick Coleman BK .20 .50
31 Mitch Richmond BK .30 .75
35 David Robinson BK 1.25 3.00
37 Robert Parish BK .40 1.00
41 Dikembe Mutombo BK .60 1.50
46 Shawn Kemp BK .75 2.00
67 Dawn Staley BK .30 .75
85 Larry Johnson BK .40 1.00
92 Michael Adams BK .10 .30
97 Detlef Schrempf BK .30 .75
104 Julius Erving BK 1.25 3.00

1993 Sports Illustrated for Kids II

109 Drazen Petrovic BK .10 .30
122 Karl Malone BK 1.25 3.00
124 Horace Grant BK .60 1.50
127 Chris Mullin BK .20 .50
131 Shaquille O'Neal BK 3.00 8.00
140 Charles Barkley BK 1.25 3.00
147 Spud Webb BK .20 .50
155 Cliff Robinson BK .10 .30
164 Val Whiting BK .10 .30
166 Patrick Ewing BK .75 2.00
184 Sheryl Swoopes BK 1.25 3.00
193 Christian Laettner BK .30 .75
213 Oscar Robertson BK .75 2.00

1994 Sports Illustrated for Kids II

238 Hakeem Olajuwon BK .75 2.00
242 Dennis Rodman BK 1.25 3.00
249 Alonzo Mourning BK .75 2.00
250 John Starks BK .30 .75
260 Chris Webber BK .60 1.50
264 Danny Manning BK .20 .50
269 Lisa Leslie BK 1.25 3.00
279 Anfernee Hardaway BK 1.50 4.00
286 Mark Price BK .15 .40
295 Latrell Sprewell BK .40 1.00
299 Dikembe Mutombo BK .40 1.00
308 B.J. Armstrong BK .20 .50
316 Ann Meyers BK .30 .75
322 Bill Bradley BK .60 1.50

1996 Sports Illustrated for Kids II

440 Glen Rice BK .30 .75
444 Katrina McClain BK .30 .75
449 Alonzo Mourning BK .40 1.00
452 Teresa Edwards BK .20 .50
kid photo
458 David Robinson BK .40 1.00
kid photo
461 Mahmoud Abdul-Rauf BK .10 .30
468 Rik Smits BK .40 1.00
469 Juwan Howard BK .40 1.00
473 Magic Johnson BK 1.25 3.00
482 Dennis Rodman BK .75 2.00
484 Clifford Robinson BK .10 .30
487 Oscar Robertson BK .75 2.00
494 Cheryl Miller BK .30 .75
504 Jennifer Rizzotti BK .50 1.25
514 Shawn Kemp BK .75 2.00
522 Gheorghe Muresan BK .15 .40
523 Arvydas Sabonis BK .20 .50
530 Trooper Johnson BK .08 .25
533 Jerry Stackhouse BK .30 .75
534 Lisa Leslie BK .60 1.50
537 Michael Finley BK .40 1.00

1997 Sports Illustrated for Kids II

541 Kevin Garnett BK 1.25 3.00
545 Shaquille O'Neal BK 1.00 2.50
549 Kara Wolters BK .30 .75
550 Damon Stoudamire BK .60 1.50
556 Shawn Bradley BK .15 .40
560 Charles Barkley BK .75 2.00
572 Anfernee Hardaway .40 1.00
Ken Griffey Jr.
April Fool
580 Kevin Johnson BK .30 .75
584 Anfernee Hardaway BK .75 2.00
587 Grant Hill BK .60 1.50
597 Tom Gugliotta BK .20 .50
599 Hakeem Olajuwon BK .60 1.50
603 Chamique Holdsclaw BK .40 1.00
605 Mark Jackson BK .15 .40
612 Michele Timms BK .15 .40
614 Tim Hardaway BK .30 .75
622 Patrick Ewing BK .30 .75
cartoon
626 Lisa Leslie BK .40 1.00
cartoon
631 Scottie Pippen BK .50 1.25
635 Cynthia Cooper BK 1.25 3.00
637 John Stockton BK .60 1.50
642 Ruthie Bolton-Holifield BK 1.50 4.00
643 Gary Payton BK .40 1.00

1998 Sports Illustrated for Kids II

651 Natalie Williams BK .30 .75
653 Glen Rice BK .15 .40
655 Chris Webber BK .30 .75
668 Shawn Kemp BK .50 1.25
670 Tim Duncan BK .75 2.00
689 Reggie Miller BK .40 1.00
691 Keith Van Horn BK .30 .75
696 Rod Strickland BK .15 .40
698 Vin Baker BK .20 .50
700 Yolanda Griffith BK .20 .50
707 Dikembe Mutombo BK .30 .75
716 Jason Kidd BK .40 1.00
726 Antoine Walker BK .60 1.50
730 Dennis Rodman BK .30 .75
731 Karl Malone BK .60 1.50
739 Kobe Bryant BK 2.00 5.00
741 Mookie Blaylock BK .15 .40
745 Tina Thompson BK .30 .75
748 Stephon Marbury BK .30 .75
756 Katie Smith BK .20 .50

1999 Sports Illustrated for Kids II

760 Steve Kerr BK .15 .40
762 Debbie Black BK .08 .25
769 Shareef Abdur-Rahim BK .40 1.00
775 Michael Jordan BK 2.00 5.00
776 Michael Jordan BK 2.00 5.00
777 Michael Jordan BK 2.00 5.00
778 Michael Jordan BK 2.00 5.00
779 Michael Jordan BK 2.00 5.00
780 Michael Jordan BK 2.00 5.00
781 Michael Jordan BK 2.00 5.00
782 Michael Jordan BK 2.00 5.00
783 Michael Jordan BK 2.00 5.00
785 David Robinson BK .75 2.00
787 Sheryl Swoopes BK .75 2.00
793 Alonzo Mourning BK .30 .75
803 Eddie Jones BK .30 .75
810 Mitch Richmond BK .30 .75
811 Allen Iverson BK .75 2.00
819 Jennifer Gillom BK .40 1.00
821 Vince Carter BK 1.25 3.00
823 Teresa Weatherspoon BK .60 1.50
827 Brian Grant BK .15 .40
830 Darrell Armstrong BK .10 .30
835 Suzie McConnell-Serio BK .40 1.00
838 Gary Payton BK .40 1.00
842 Kobe Bryant BK 2.00 5.00
845 Cynthia Cooper BK .75 2.00
847 Avery Johnson BK .15 .40
851 Shaquille O'Neal BK 1.00 2.50
853 Ticha Penicheiro BK .20 .50
857 Kendall Gill BK .15 .40
859 Nykesha Sales BK .40 1.00

000 Sports Illustrated for Kids II

Michael Jordan BK	2.00	5.00
Alonzo Mourning BK	.30	.75
Reggie Miller BK	.40	1.00
Scottie Pippen BK	.30	.75
Allan Houston BK	.15	.40
John Stockton BK	.30	.75
Grant Hill BK	.30	.75
Rasheed Wallace BK	.40	1.00
Jeff Hornacek BK	.15	.40
Tim Duncan BK	.60	1.50
Sean Elliott BK	.15	.40
Elton Brand BK	.15	.40
Natalie Williams BK	.20	.50
Glenn Robinson BK	.15	.40
Vince Carter BK	.75	2.00
Sheryl Swoopes	.75	2.00
ythnia Cooper		
ina Thompson		
asketball		
Jalen Rose BK	.10	.30
Katie Smith BK	.20	.50
Jason Kidd BK	.40	1.00

001 Sports Illustrated for Kids

ce its debut issue in January 1989, SI for Kids has luded a perforated sheet of nine standard-size cards und into each magazine. In December 2000, for the cond time, the card numbers started over again at 1. e athletes featured represent an extremely wide ectrum of sports. The athlete's name is printed at the while his or her sport appears at the bottom. The cks carry biographical information, career highlights, d a trivia question with answer. The cards' magazine ue date appears on the back in very small type. hough originally distributed in sheet form, the cards e frequently traded as singles. Thus, they are priced dividually. The value of an intact sheet is equal to the n of the nine cards plus a premium of up to 20 rcent.

MPLETE SET (108)	25.00	50.00
Kevin Garnett BK	.75	2.00
Jason Williams BK	.07	.20
Steve Francis BK	.20	.50
Ray Allen BK	.40	1.00
Latrell Sprewell BK	.08	.25
Tim Hardaway BK	.08	.25
Allen Iverson BK	1.00	2.50
Stephon Marbury BK	.15	.40
Sheryl Swoopes BK	.40	1.00
Jerry Stackhouse BK	.08	.25
Antonio McDyess BK	.15	.40
Dirk Nowitzki BK	.40	1.00
Dawn Staley BK	.15	.40
Kobe Bryant BK	1.25	3.00
Damon Stoudamire BK	.20	.50
Tracy McGrady BK	.40	1.00
Ruth Riley BK	.40	1.00
Karl Malone BK	.30	.75
Tim Duncan BK	.30	.75
Jackie Stiles BK	.40	1.00
Dikembe Mutombo BK	.08	.25
Shaquille O'Neal BK	1.00	2.50
Mike Miller BK	.15	.40
03 Aaron McKie BK	.10	.30
07 Predrag Stojakoic BK	.30	.75

2002 Sports Illustrated for Kids

3 Vince Carter BK	.60	1.50
7 Lisa Leslie BK	.30	.75
20 Chris Webber BK	.40	1.00
25 Glenn Robinson BK	.10	.30
28 Kevin Garnett BK	.50	1.25
0 Baron Davis BK	.40	1.00
8 Jason Kidd BK	.40	1.00
2 Darius Miles BK	.60	1.50
7 Jermaine O'Neal BK	.20	.50
9 Michael Jordan BK	2.00	5.00
4 Penny Hardaway BK	.10	.30
6 Andre Miller BK	.20	.50
1 Lauren Jackson BK	.75	2.00
7 Antoine Walker BK	.20	.50
1 Chamique Holdsclaw BK	.20	.50
3 Ben Wallace BK	.20	.50
5 Sue Bird BK	.20	.50
4 Gary Payton BK	.10	.30
8 Pau Gasol BK	.07	.20
0 Mike Bibby BK	.07	.20
2 Corliss Williamson BK	.07	.20
0 Robert Horry BK	.07	.20
2 Tamika Catchings BK	.10	.30
10 Jason Richardson BK	.08	.25
12 Alonzo Mourning BK	.20	.50
9 Antoine Walker BK	.20	.50
24 Nikki Teasley BK	.07	.20

2003 Sports Illustrated for Kids

nce its debut issue in January 1989, SI for Kids has cluded a perforated sheet of nine standard-size cards ound into each magazine. In January 2001, for the econd time, the card numbers started over at 1. Listed elow are the cards issued in magazines that carry 003 cover dates. The athletes featured represent an xtremely wide spectrum of sports. Although originally istributed in sheet form, the cards are frequently aded as singles. Thus, they are priced individually. he value of an intact sheet is equal to the sum of the ine cards plus a premium of up to 20 percent.

27 Tracy McGrady BK	.40	1.00
31 Rasheed Wallace BK	.30	.75
36 Luke Walton BK	.20	.50
40 Shareef Abdur-Rahim BK	.20	.50
44 Sheryl Swoopes BK	.30	.75
49 Kenyon Martin BK	.20	.50
54 Steve Nash BK	.40	1.00
56 Jerry Stackhouse BK	.20	.50
64 LeBron James BK	4.00	10.00
66 Tim Duncan BK	.40	1.00
68 Diana Taurasi WNBA	.40	1.00
73 Stephon Marbury BK	.30	.75
75 Jamal Mashburn BK	.20	.50
82 Chris Webber BK	.20	.50
84 Carmelo Anthony BK	.50	1.25
88 Tony Parker BK	.30	.75
91 Paul Pierce BK	.30	.75
93 Kobe Bryant BK	1.25	3.00
97 Tina Thompson WNBA	.20	.50
99 Nick Van Exel BK	.20	.50
03 Richard Jefferson BK	.20	.50
05 Shannon Johnson WNBA	.30	.75
09 Yao Ming BK	.75	1.25
11 Richard Hamilton BK	.20	.50
17 Drew Gooden BK	.20	.50
23 Michael Finley BK	.20	.50
26 Allen Iverson BK	.40	1.00
28 Jermaine O'Neal BK	.20	.50
32 Swin Cash Women's BK	.40	1.00

2004 Sports Illustrated for Kids

ONE NINE-CARD SHEET PER MAGAZINE

334 Shaquille O'Neal BK	.40	1.00
338 Michael Jordan BK	2.00	5.00
344 Steve Francis BK	.20	.50
350 Raymond Felton BK	.20	.50
354 Vince Carter BK	.40	1.00
355 Lauren Jackson BK	.40	1.00
362 Peja Stojakovic BK	.20	.50
368 Nicole Powell Women's BK	.30	.75
372 Jason Kidd BK	.30	.75
378 Michael Redd BK	.20	.50
380 Kevin Garnett BK	.30	.75
382 Sue Bird WNBA	.60	1.50
387 Andrei Kirilienko BK	.20	.50
390 Mike Bibby BK	.20	.50
392 LeBron James BK	1.25	3.00
397 Theo Ratliff BK	.20	.50
401 Corey Maggette BK	.20	.50
407 Dwayne Wade BK	.60	1.50
412 Chamique Holdsclaw WNBA	.40	1.00
419 Carmelo Anthony BK	.40	1.00
425 Dirk Nowitzki BK	.40	1.00
432 Diana Taurasi WNBA	1.00	2.50
433 Ron Artest BK	.20	.50
437 Manu Ginobili BK	.20	.50

2005 Sports Illustrated for Kids

445 Nykesha Sales WNBA	.30	.75
449 Sam Cassell BK	.20	.50
456 Carlos Boozer BK	.20	.50
457 Chris Paul BK	.75	2.00
464 Amare Stoudemire BK	.30	.75
468 Rashad McCants BK	.20	.50
473 Shaquille O'Neal BK	.40	1.00
477 Emeka Okafor BK	.20	.50
482 Allen Iverson BK	.40	1.00
486 Seimone Augustus College BK	.30	.75
489 Lisa Leslia WNBA	.50	1.25
491 Ray Allen BK	.30	.75
500 Shawn Marion BK	.20	.50
502 Gilbert Arenas BK	.30	.75
510 Ban Wallace BK	.20	.50
511 Cuttino Mobley BK	.20	.50
515 Chris Bosh BK	.30	.75
517 Tina Thompson WNBA	.40	1.00
525 Paul Pierce BK	.30	.75
529 Vince Carter BK	.40	1.00
533 Ben Gordon BK	.30	.75
539 Troy Murphy BK	.20	.50

2006 Sports Illustrated for Kids

6 Dee Brown BK	.20	.50
8 Sheryl Swoopes BK	.40	1.00
14 Jason Richardson BK	.20	.50
16 Chris Webber BK	.20	.50
19 Richard Hamilton BK	.20	.50
23 Manu Ginobili BK	.20	.50
29 Marcus Camby BK	.20	.50
31 J.J. Redick BK	.60	1.50
38 Dirk Nowitzki BK	.40	1.00
43 Cheryl Ford WNBA	.40	1.00
46 Adam Morrison BK	.60	1.50
51 Steve Nash BK	.40	1.00
56 Jason Terry BK	.20	.50
58 Ivory Latta Women's BK	.60	1.50
63 Pau Gasol BK	.20	.50
64 Lindsay Whalen WNBA	.30	.75
66 Dwight Howard BK	.40	1.00
71 Courtney Paris BK	.40	1.00
74 Chauncey Billups BK	.20	.50
80 Tamika Catchings WNBA	.40	1.00
84 Tracy McGrady BK	.40	1.00
89 Alana Beard WNBA	.30	.75
97 Boris Diaw BK	.20	.50
99 Swin Cash WNBA	.40	1.00
101 Kirk Hinrich BK	.20	.50
105 Joakim Noah BK	.20	.50
107 Cappie Pondexter WNBA	.40	1.00

2007 Sports Illustrated for Kids

ONE NINE-CARD SHEET PER MAGAZINE

116 Chris Paul BK	1.25	3.00
118 Kevin Love HS BK	1.00	2.50
122 O.J. Mayo HS BK	1.25	3.00
126 Maya Moore HS BK	.20	.50
129 Tim Duncan BK	.40	1.00
130 Joe Johnson BK	.20	.50
134 Lindsey Harding BK	.20	.50
137 Zach Randolph BK	.20	.50
141 Tyler Hansbrough BK	.75	2.00
142 Candace Parker BK	2.00	5.00
147 Kevin Durant BK	4.00	10.00
148 Andre Iguodala BK	.30	.75
152 Crystal Langhorne BK	.20	.50
155 Josh Howard BK	.30	.75
157 DeAnna Nolan WNBA	.20	.50
161 Caron Butler BK	.20	.50
163 Tina Charles BK	.20	.50
167 Carlos Boozer BK	.20	.50
174 Luol Deng BK	.20	.50
175 Katie Douglas WBNA	.30	.75
186 Brandon Roy BK	.75	2.00
188 Michelle Snow WNBA	.20	.50
194 Tony Parker BK	.40	1.00
199 Candice Wiggins BK	.20	.50
204 Kevin Martin BK	.20	.50
208 Penny Taylor WNBA	.30	.75
212 Kobe Bryant BK	.75	2.00
214 D.J. Augustin BK	.30	.75

2008 Sports Illustrated for Kids

226 Armintie Price BK	.20	.50
230 Yao Ming BK	.30	.75
234 Deron Williams BK	.40	1.00
237 Kevin Garnett BK	.75	2.00
238 Michael Beasley BK	.40	1.00
245 Derrick Rose BK	3.00	8.00
249 Chris Kaman BK	.20	.50
250 Rashard Lewis BK	.20	.50
255 Ray Allen BK	.30	.75
256 Epiphanny Prince BK	.20	.50
260 Al Jefferson BK	.20	.50
263 David West BK	.20	.50
270 Lauren Jackson BK	.40	1.00
276 Allen Iverson BK	.40	1.00
281 Rudy Gay BK	.25	.60
283 Sophia Young BK	.20	.50
289 Chris Bosh BK	.25	.60
302 Paul Pierce BK	.30	.75
304 Stephen Curry BK	.75	2.00
312 Kobe Bryant BK	.75	2.00
317 Al Horford BK	.20	.50
321 Luke Harangody BK	.40	1.00

2009 Sports Illustrated for Kids

335 Manu Ginobili BK	.30	.75
342 Alana Beard BK	.20	.50
347 Kevin Garnett ART BK	.40	1.00
351 Dwyane Wade ART BK	.60	1.50
353 Nate Robinson BK	.20	.50
357 Kevin Durant BK	.60	1.50
364 Candace Parker BK	.40	1.00
368 Mo Williams BK	.20	.50
372 Derrick Rose BK	.75	2.00
373 Maya Moore BK	.75	2.00
381 LeBron James BK	.75	2.00
383 Dwight Howard BK	.40	1.00
388 Danny Granger BK	.20	.50
395 Diana Taurasi BK	.40	1.00
397 Pau Gasol BK	.20	.50
401 Carmelo Anthony BK	.30	.75
408 Rajon Rondo BK	.30	.75
409 Swin Cash BK	.40	1.00
417 Dirk Nowitzki BK	.40	1.00
429 Devin Harris BK	.20	.50
431 Jayne Appel BK	.20	.50

2010 Sports Illustrated for Kids

433 Marc Gasol BK	.25	.60
440 Joakim Noah BK	.40	1.00
444 Amare Stoudemire BK	.25	.60
448 Tyreke Evans BK	.30	.75
453 Tim Duncan BK	.40	1.00
458 Monta Ellis BK	.20	.50
462 Deron Williams BK	.30	.75
467 Sherron Collins BK	.20	.50
471 Steve Nash BK	.40	1.00
472 Russell Westbrook BK	.40	1.00
478 Joe Johnson BK	.20	.50
483 Carlos Boozer BK	.20	.50
492 Derek Fisher BK	.20	.50
494 Rebekkah Brunson BK	.20	.50
498 Josh Smith BK	.20	.50
505 Jason Kidd BK	.30	.75
512 Zach Randolph BK	.20	.50
517 Lauren Jackson BK	.40	1.00
522 Andre Iguodala BK	.20	.50
523 Diana Taurasi BK		
528 Kobe Bryant BK	.75	2.00
530 Andrew Bogut BK	.25	.60

2011 Sports Illustrated for Kids

5 Chris Paul BK	.40	1.00
9 John Wall BK	.40	1.00
15 Blake Griffin BK	.40	1.00
17 Kevin Love BK	.40	1.00
23 LeBron James BK	.75	2.00
25 Brittney Griner BK	1.25	3.00
30 Kevin Durant BK	.75	2.00
35 Jimmer Fredette BK	1.50	4.00
37 Kemba Walker BK	1.25	3.00
41 Derrick Rose BK	.75	2.00
48 Dirk Nowitzki BK	.40	1.00
59 Jason Terry BK	.20	.50
65 Tina Charles BK	.20	.50
72 Dwyane Wade BK	.60	1.50
78 Dwight Howard BK	.40	1.00
85 Angel McCoughtry BK	.20	.50
87 Harrison Barnes BK	1.25	3.00
93 Carmelo Anthony BK	.30	.75
94 Skylar Diggins BK	.20	.50

2012 Sports Illustrated for Kids

105 Terrence Jones BK	.40	1.00
114 LaMarcus Aldridge BK	.25	.60
116 Kyle Lowry BK	.20	.50
122 Kevin Durant BK	.75	2.00
124 Deron Williams BK	.25	.60
129 Kobe Bryant BK	.75	2.00
130 Joakim Noah BK	.25	.60
138 Chris Paul BK	.40	1.00
143 Seimone Augustus BK	.20	.50
145 Rajon Rondo BK	.40	1.00
149 LeBron James BK	.75	2.00
154 Sylvia Fowles BK	.20	.50
158 Tim Duncan BK	.40	1.00

1977-79 Sportscaster Series 1

COMPLETE SET (24)	17.50	35.00
124 Pete Maravich BK	3.00	8.00

1977-79 Sportscaster Series 2

COMPLETE SET (24)	30.00	60.00
203 Kareem Abdul-Jabbar BK	2.00	4.00
209 USA-USSR USA vs. Russia Basketball Sergei Belov	1.00	2.00

1977-79 Sportscaster Series 3

COMPLETE SET (24)	15.00	30.00
315 Julius Erving BK	3.00	6.00

1977-79 Sportscaster Series 4

COMPLETE SET (24)	15.00	30.00
412 Bill Russell BK	3.00	6.00
414 Dave Cowens BK	1.00	2.00
415 Rick Barry BK	1.00	2.00

1977-79 Sportscaster Series 5

COMPLETE SET (24)	12.50	25.00
510 Referee's Signals Olympic Action Basketball	.75	1.50
519 The 1969-70 Knickerbockers Knicks vs. Lakers Basketball	1.00	2.00

1977-79 Sportscaster Series 6

COMPLETE SET (24)	12.50	25.00
608 The UCLA Dynasty UCLA In Action Basketball	1.50	3.00
621 George McGinnis BK	.75	1.50

1977-79 Sportscaster Series 7

COMPLETE SET (24)	15.00	30.00
712 A Laboratory Sport USA vs. Russia Basketball	1.00	2.00
713 Walt Frazier BK	1.50	3.00
720 Wilt Chamberlain BK	5.00	10.00

1977-79 Sportscaster Series 8

COMPLETE SET (24)	12.50	25.00
810 Jerry West BK	2.50	5.00

1977-79 Sportscaster Series 9

COMPLETE SET (24)	15.00	30.00
912 Nate Archibald BK	1.00	2.00
916 A Game for Giants USA vs. Russia Basketball	1.25	2.50

1977-79 Sportscaster Series 10

COMPLETE SET (24)	17.50	35.00
1018 John Havlicek BK	1.50	4.00

1977-79 Sportscaster Series 11

COMPLETE SET (25)	20.00	40.00
1124A UCLA vs Houston ERR Bill Walton Basketball	10.00	20.00
1124B UCLA vs. Houston COR Lew Alcindor Basketball	5.00	10.00

1977-79 Sportscaster Series 12

COMPLETE SET (24)	12.50	25.00
1213 Wes Unseld BK	1.00	2.50

1977-79 Sportscaster Series 13

COMPLETE SET (24)	12.50	25.00
1304 The European Championship Cup Ignis Varese Tea Basketball	.50	1.00
1310 Lakers Win 33 In A Row: Wilt Chamberlain Jerry West Basketball	2.00	4.00

1977-79 Sportscaster Series 14

COMPLETE SET (24)	17.50	35.00
1412 Emil Zatopek Track and Field	.50	1.00
1418 Oscar Robertson BK	2.00	4.00

1977-79 Sportscaster Series 16

COMPLETE SET (24)	15.00	30.00
1614 Elgin Baylor BK	1.25	2.50
1624 Dick Button Figure Skating	1.00	2.00

1977-79 Sportscaster Series 18

COMPLETE SET (24)	12.50	25.00
1820 Jackie Chazalon BK	.50	1.00

1977-79 Sportscaster Series 19

COMPLETE SET (24)	25.00	50.00
1914 Bob Pettit BK	1.00	2.00

1977-79 Sportscaster Series 20

COMPLETE SET (24)	7.50	15.00
2021 24-Second Clock Sixers' Player Basketball	.75	1.50

1977-79 Sportscaster Series 21

COMPLETE SET (24)	15.00	30.00
2114 Clarence(Bevo) Francis Basketball	.50	1.00

1977-79 Sportscaster Series 22

COMPLETE SET (24)	15.00	30.00
2208 Milwaukee Bucks/1970-1971 Bucks vs. Knicks Lew Alcindor Basketball	1.50	3.00

1977-79 Sportscaster Series 23

COMPLETE SET (24)	20.00	40.00
2303 Lingo Pete Maravich Basketball	1.50	3.00

1977-79 Sportscaster Series 26

COMPLETE SET (24)	15.00	30.00
2624 Villeurbanne BK	.25	.50

1977-79 Sportscaster Series 30

COMPLETE SET (24)	12.50	25.00
3010 Fouls and Penalties Hawks vs. Bulls Basketball	.50	1.00
3012 Podoloff Cup Kareem Abdul-Jabbar Basketball	1.50	3.00
3013 NBA All-Star Game Randy Smith Basketball	1.00	2.00

1977-79 Sportscaster Series 33

COMPLETE SET (24)	10.00	20.00
3304 Pivot Play Bill Walton Basketball	2.50	5.00

1977-79 Sportscaster Series 34

COMPLETE SET (24)	15.00	30.00
3414 Defenses College Action Basketball	.50	1.00

1977-79 Sportscaster Series 35

COMPLETE SET (24)	15.00	30.00
3506 The Highest Scoring Game Julius Erving Basketball	3.00	6.00

1977-79 Sportscaster Series 36

COMPLETE SET (26)	15.00	30.00
3608A Artis Gilmore ERR Basketball/(Pictures Phil Ford and the Four-corner Offense; see 3612)	1.50	3.00
3608B Artis Gilmore COR Basketball	1.50	3.00
3612A The Four Corner ERR Offense Bulls vs. Bullets Basketball/(Pictures Artis Gilmore; see 3608)	1.50	3.00
3612B The Four Corner COR Offense Phil Ford	1.50	3.00
3622 The NCAA Tournament Kentucky vs. Duke Basketball	2.50	5.00

1977-79 Sportscaster Series 38

COMPLETE SET (24)	20.00	40.00
3811 Paul Westphal Basketball	1.00	2.00
3812 Biddy-Basket Playground Game Basketball	.50	1.00

1977-79 Sportscaster Series 39

COMPLETE SET (24)	7.50	15.00
3910 Maccabi of Tel Aviv Maccabi Team Basketball	.50	1.00
3915 Doug Collins BK	1.50	3.00

1977-79 Sportscaster Series 40

COMPLETE SET (24)	10.00	20.00
4007 Marques Johnson BK	2.00	4.00
4009 Walter Davis BK	2.00	4.00

1977-79 Sportscaster Series 42

COMPLETE SET (24)	15.00	30.00
4202 Bernard King BK	1.00	2.00

1977-79 Sportscaster Series 43

COMPLETE SET (24)	12.50	25.00
4301 The Washington Bullets Bullets vs. Sonics Basketball	1.00	2.00
4318 Power Forward Maurice Lucas Basketball	1.25	2.50

1977-79 Sportscaster Series 44

COMPLETE SET (24)	12.50	25.00
4416 Butch Lee BK	.75	1.50
4421 3-Guard Offense Phil Chenier Basketball	1.00	2.00

1977-79 Sportscaster Series 52

COMPLETE SET (24)	10.00	20.00
5224 Hank Luisetti BK	1.25	2.50

1977-79 Sportscaster Series 53

COMPLETE SET (24)	15.00	30.00
5322 Jack Sikma BK	1.25	2.50
5323 John Walker Track and Field	.75	1.50

1977-79 Sportscaster Series 54

COMPLETE SET (24)	15.00	30.00
5415 George Mikan BK	5.00	10.00
5423 Manuel Raga BK	.75	1.50

1977-79 Sportscaster Series 55

COMPLETE SET (24)	12.50	25.00
5518 Leonard Robinson BK	.75	1.50

1977-79 Sportscaster Series 56

COMPLETE SET (24)	37.50	75.00
5611 Marvin Webster BK	2.00	4.00

1977-79 Sportscaster Series 59

COMPLETE SET (24)	50.00	100.00
5905 David Thompson BK	4.00	8.00

1977-79 Sportscaster Series 60

COMPLETE SET (24)	37.50	75.00
6008 Carol Blazejowski BK	3.00	6.00

1977-79 Sportscaster Series 61

COMPLETE SET (24)	50.00	100.00
6110 Bill Bradley Beyond Sports	7.50	15.00

1977-79 Sportscaster Series 62

COMPLETE SET (24)	40.00	80.00
6209 Calvin Murphy BK	2.50	5.00

1977-79 Sportscaster Series 63

COMPLETE SET (24)	30.00	60.00
6305 First TV Game Burke Crotty Basketball	1.00	2.00
6320 Austin Carr BK	2.00	4.00

1977-79 Sportscaster Series 64

COMPLETE SET (24)	25.00	50.00
6404 Chinese Tour Mu Tieh-Chu Basketball	1.00	2.00
6405 Olympic Games Honors Tables USA vs. Russia Basketball	2.50	5.00
6424 Three Officials Three Referees Basketball	1.00	2.00

1977-79 Sportscaster Series 65

COMPLETE SET (24)	40.00	80.00
6502 Wilt Chamberlain In Volleyball Volleyball	6.00	12.00
6515 20,000 Point Club Hal Greer Basketball	2.50	5.00

1977-79 Sportscaster Series 66

COMPLETE SET (24)	37.50	75.00
6611 Hall of Fame Basketball	2.00	4.00

1977-79 Sportscaster Series 67

COMPLETE SET (24)	40.00	80.00
6702 Nancy Lieberman BK	5.00	10.00
6711 Bob Morse BK	2.00	4.00

1977-79 Sportscaster Series 70

COMPLETE SET (24)	30.00	60.00
7021 Kurt Thomas The Rings Gymnastics	3.00	6.00

1977-79 Sportscaster Series 73

COMPLETE SET (24)	40.00	80.00
7303 Rudy Tomjanovich BK	5.00	10.00

1977-79 Sportscaster Series 74

COMPLETE SET (24)	200.00	400.00
7407 A Pro Oddity Eric Money Basketball	2.00	4.00
7418 Larry Bird BK	150.00	300.00

1977-79 Sportscaster Series 76

COMPLETE SET (24)	30.00	60.00
7608 The Longest Shot Rudy Williams Basketball	1.00	2.00
7614 Inge Nissen BK	2.00	4.00

1977-79 Sportscaster Series 77

COMPLETE SET (24)	150.00	300.00
7705 Kevin Porter BK	2.50	5.00
7721 Nat Holman Joe Lapchick BK	4.00	8.00

1977-79 Sportscaster Series 78

COMPLETE SET (24)	150.00	300.00
7802 Earvin Johnson BK	100.00	200.00
7824 Dave Bing BK	4.00	8.00

1977-79 Sportscaster Series 79

COMPLETE SET (24)	60.00	120.00
7910 Ouliana Semenova BK	4.00	8.00
7915 Phil Ford BK	2.50	5.00
7919 Women's Basketball League Randi Burdick Basketball	2.00	4.00

1977-79 Sportscaster Series 81

COMPLETE SET (24)	62.50	125.00
8102 Lenny Wilkens BK	7.50	15.00

1977-79 Sportscaster Series 82

COMPLETE SET (24)	50.00	100.00
8202 Moses Malone BK	7.50	15.00
8215 Academic Basketball Team Greg Kelser Basketball	3.00	6.00

1977-79 Sportscaster Series 83

COMPLETE SET (24)	62.50	125.00
8307 Three-Point Field Goal: Louis Dampier Basketball	3.00	6.00
8317 Dutch Dehnert BK	3.00	6.00

1977-79 Sportscaster Series 84

COMPLETE SET (24)	60.00	120.00
8409 United Basketball Association Mike Riordan Basketball	3.00	6.00

1977-79 Sportscaster Series 85

COMPLETE SET (24)	62.50	125.00
8515 Women's Draft Pat Colasurdo Basketball	2.00	4.00
8522 F.P. Naismith Award Mike Scheib Alton Byrd Basketball	3.00	6.00

1977-79 Sportscaster Series 86

COMPLETE SET (24)	50.00	100.00
8608 Danny Ainge BB BK	25.00	50.00

1977-79 Sportscaster Series 102

COMPLETE SET (24)	75.00	150.00
10202 Ray Meyer BK	7.50	15.00

1977-79 Sportscaster Series 103

COMPLETE SET (24)	87.50	175.00
10304 Ann Meyers BK	10.00	20.00

1997 Sports Time USBL

Distributed in two 25-card series sets, this 50-card set was produced by Sports Time, Inc. and features some of the best players who have played in the United States Basketball League. Card fronts feature a somewhat fuzzy action photo with the player's name running vertically along the left border. Card backs feature same photo as front, with bio and statistics.

COMPLETE SET (50)	8.00	20.00
1 Norris Coleman	.08	.25
2 Anthony Mason	1.25	3.00
3 Michael Anderson	.08	.25
4 Dallas Comegys	.20	.50
5 Anthony Pullard	.08	.25
6 Darrell Armstrong	.08	.25
7 Kermit Holmes	.08	.25
8 Lloyd Daniels	.30	.75
9 Roy Tarpley	.40	1.00
10 Paul Graham	.20	.50
11 Nantambu Willingham	.08	.25
12 Michael Ray Richardson World B. Free	.40	1.00
13 Richard Dumas	.20	.50
14 International All-Star Tour	.08	.25
15 Keith Jennings	.20	.50
16 Duane Washington	.20	.50
17 Wes Matthews	.20	.50
18 Michael Adams	.40	1.00
19 First USBL Game John Hot Rod Williams	.30	.75
20 Chuck Nevitt	.20	.50
21 The Awards Muggsy Bogues	.40	1.00
22 The First Game Michael Adams	.08	.25
23 The Beginning Daniel T. Meisenheimer	.08	.25
24 Charlie Ward	.75	2.00
25 Oliver Lee	.08	.25
26 Greg Sutton	.08	.25
27 1991 USBL Championship Paul Graham	.08	.25
28 Miami Tropics	.08	.25
29 New Haven Skyhawks	.08	.25
30 Back to Back Champions Miami Tropics	.08	.25
31 Springfield Fame	.08	.25
32 Nate Johnson	.08	.25
33 Muggsy Bogues	1.25	3.00
34 Chris Collier	.08	.25
35 Sandhi Ortiz-Delvalle	.08	.25
36 Henri Abrams	.08	.25
37 Dan Cyrulik	.08	.25
38 Charles Smith	.30	.75
39 Mark Boyd	.08	.25
40 Tim Legler	.40	1.00
41 Jerry Ice Reynolds	.20	.50
42 Road to the NBA Richard Dumas	.08	.25
43 Anthony Mason CL	.40	1.00
44 Richard Dumas CL	.08	.25
45 Atlanta Trojans Atlantic City Seagulls	.08	.25
46 Connecticut Skyhawks Florida Sharks	.08	.25
47 Jacksonville Barracudas Long Island Surf	.08	.25
48 New Hampshire Thunder Loons Philadelphia Power	.08	.25
49 Portland Wave Raleigh Cougars	.08	.25
50 Tampa Bay Windjammers Westchester Kings	.08	.25

1972 Sportscope Arena Great Moments in Basketball

Issued in 1972 by Sportscope, Inc. these items have been described as arena card booklets. We are not sure if the checklist is complete and will continue to add as we find other players.

1 Lew Alcindor Wilt Chamberlain	40.00	75.00
2 Lew Alcindor Bob Lanier	40.00	75.00
3 Lew Alcindor Willis Reed Bill Bradley	40.00	75.00
4 Dave Bing Oscar Robertson	25.00	50.00
5 Austin Carr	15.00	30.00
6 Wilt Chamberlain Lew Alcindor	50.00	100.00
7 Wilt Chamberlain Jerry Lucas	75.00	150.00
8 Dave Cowens	25.00	50.00
9 Billy Cunningham Phil Jackson	25.00	50.00
10 Dave DeBusschere	25.00	50.00
11 Walt Frazier	25.00	50.00
12 Gail Goodrich	20.00	40.00
13 John Havlicek	25.00	50.00
14 Pete Maravich	75.00	150.00
15 Jack Marin	15.00	30.00
16 Jack Newman	15.00	30.00
17 Unidentified Chicago Bulls #18	15.00	30.00
18 Dick VanArsdale Walt Frazier	20.00	40.00
19 Lenny Wilkens	25.00	50.00

1976 Sportstix

This blank-backed irregularly shaped sticker features a borderless color player action photo. The team markings were crudely obliterated from the photo. The one basketball sticker is part of a larger multi-sport release. The stickers came in packs of five.

1 Dave DeBusschere	7.50	15.00

1996 SPx

The premier edition of Upper Deck's super-premium SPx basketball set contains 50 cards featuring only the top stars and youngsters in the NBA. The set marked a number of technological "firsts" in the basketball card market including first stand-alone all-Holoview set and first complete, perimeter die cut set. To create the holoview imagery, each athlete was videotaped while rotating on a turntable. The individual frames of videotape were then synthesized to produce a 50-degree, three-dimensional picture. Each card features super premium 32 point thick stock. Each pack contained only one card and carried a suggested retail price of $2.99. Each box contained 36 packs. In addition, to the 50 regular cards, a special Record Breaker card commemorating Michael Jordan's eighth scoring title (1:75 packs) and Tribute card commemorating Anfernee Hardaway's accomplishments in the NBA (1:24 packs) were issued. Also, two separate trade cards were available for signed Jordan and Hardaway cards. The odds of receiving a Jordan trade card were 1:34,560 packs. The Hardaway trade card was more than 25 times easier to pull at a rate of 1,345 packs. The Jordan AU was issued with a card sized certificate of authenticity, and the Upper Deck Authenticated hologram sticker on these cards carries a "BAC" or "BAD" prefix to the serial number.

COMPLETE SET (50)	25.00	60.00
1 Stacey Augmon	.60	1.50
2 Mookie Blaylock	.50	1.25
3 Eric Montross	.50	1.25
4 Eric Williams	.50	1.25
5 Larry Johnson	.75	2.00
6 George Zidek	.50	1.25
7 Jason Caffey	.50	1.25
8 Michael Jordan	8.00	20.00
9 Chris Mills	.50	1.25
10 Bob Sura	.50	1.25
11 Jason Kidd	1.25	3.00
12 Jamal Mashburn	.60	1.50
13 Antonio McDyess	.75	2.00
14 Jalen Rose	.60	1.50
15 Grant Hill	1.25	3.00
16 Theo Ratliff	.60	1.50
17 Joe Smith	.60	1.50
18 Latrell Sprewell	.75	2.00
19 Hakeem Olajuwon	1.00	2.50
20 Reggie Miller	1.00	2.50
21 Rik Smits	.60	1.50
22 Brent Barry	.60	1.50
23 Lamond Murray	.50	1.25
24 Magic Johnson	2.00	5.00
25 Eddie Jones	.75	2.00
26 Nick Van Exel	.75	2.00
27 Alonzo Mourning	1.00	2.50
28 Kurt Thomas	.50	1.25
29 Vin Baker	.60	1.50
30 Glenn Robinson	.75	2.00
31 Kevin Garnett	2.00	5.00
32 Ed O'Bannon	.50	1.25
33 Patrick Ewing	1.00	2.50
34 Anfernee Hardaway	1.25	3.00
35 Shaquille O'Neal	2.00	5.00
36 Jerry Stackhouse	1.00	2.50
37 Charles Barkley	1.25	3.00
38 Michael Finley	1.00	2.50
39 Randolph Childress	.75	2.00
40 Gary Trent	.50	1.25
41 Brian Grant	.60	1.50
42 Mitch Richmond	.75	2.00
43 David Robinson	1.25	3.00
44 Shawn Kemp	.75	2.00
45 Gary Payton	.75	2.00
46 Damon Stoudamire	.75	2.00
47 Karl Malone	1.00	2.50
48 John Stockton	1.00	2.50
49 Bryant Reeves	.50	1.25
50 Rasheed Wallace	1.00	2.50
R1 Michael Jordan Record Breaker	6.00	15.00
T1 Anfernee Hardaway Tribute	1.50	4.00
NNO Anfernee Hardaway AU	40.00	100.00
NNO Anfernee Hardaway Expired Exchange	15.00	30.00
NNO Michael Jordan AU	600.00	1200.00
NNO Michael Jordan Expired Exchange	300.00	600.00

1996 SPx Gold

Cards in this set of 50 were randomly issued in packs at a rate of one in seven and parallel the regular issue set. The cards are differentiated by gold borders on the front. Please refer to the multiplier below, coupled with the value of the basic card, to determine individual card value.

COMPLETE SET (50)	50.00	120.00

*GOLD: .75X TO 2X BASE CARD HI

1996 SPx Holoview Heroes

Cards in this set of ten were randomly issued at a rate of one in every 24 packs and feature ten NBA players with the potential to be named to the NBA Hall of Fame. These die-cut cards feature a combination of lithograph and holoview technology.

COMPLETE SET (10) 20.00 50.00
H1 Michael Jordan 12.00 30.00
H2 Jason Kidd 2.50 6.00
H3 Grant Hill 2.50 6.00
H4 Joe Smith 1.25 3.00
H5 Magic Johnson 4.00 10.00
H6 Antonio McDyess 1.50 4.00
H7 Anfernee Hardaway 2.50 6.00
H8 Jerry Stackhouse 2.00 5.00
H9 Damon Stoudamire 1.50 4.00
H10 Shaquille O'Neal 4.00 10.00

1997 SPx

The 1997 SPx set was issued in one series totaling 50 cards and was distributed in one-card packs at a suggested retail of $3.49. This perimeter die-cut set features combinations of holographic, lithographic and Holoview images printed on super premium 32 point card stock. The cards were released after the 1997 NBA Playoffs and carry information from the first half of the 1996-97 NBA season. The cards are numbered with an "SPx" prefix. A Michael Jordan "sample" card was released prior to the regular set. It is listed below at the end of the set.

COMPLETE SET (50) 50.00 100.00
1 Mookie Blaylock .60 1.50
2 Antoine Walker 1.00 2.50
3 Eric Williams .60 1.50
4 Tony Delk .60 1.50
5 Michael Jordan 8.00 20.00
6 Dennis Rodman 2.00 5.00
7 Vitaly Potapenko .60 1.50
8 Bob Sura .60 1.50
9 Jamal Mashburn .75 2.00
10 Samaki Walker .60 1.50
11 Antonio McDyess .75 2.00
12 Joe Dumars 1.00 2.50
13 Grant Hill 1.50 4.00
14 Joe Smith .75 2.00
15 Latrell Sprewell 1.00 2.50
16 Charles Barkley 1.50 4.00
17 Hakeem Olajuwon 1.25 3.00
18 Erick Dampier .60 1.50
19 Reggie Miller 1.25 3.00
20 Brent Barry .75 2.00
21 Lorenzen Wright .60 1.50
22 Kobe Bryant 10.00 25.00
23 Eddie Jones 1.00 2.50
24 Shaquille O'Neal 2.50 6.00
25 Alonzo Mourning 1.25 3.00
26 Kurt Thomas .60 1.50
27 Vin Baker .75 2.00
28 Glenn Robinson .75 2.00
29 Kevin Garnett 2.00 5.00
30 Stephon Marbury 1.25 3.00
31 Kerry Kittles .60 1.50
32 Patrick Ewing 1.25 3.00
33 Larry Johnson 1.00 2.50
34 Anfernee Hardaway 1.50 4.00
35 Allen Iverson 2.00 5.00
36 Jerry Stackhouse 1.00 2.50
37 Kevin Johnson 1.00 2.50
38 Steve Nash 2.00 5.00
39 Jermaine O'Neal 1.25 3.00
40 Mitch Richmond 1.00 2.50
41 David Robinson 1.50 4.00
42 Shawn Kemp 1.00 2.50
43 Gary Payton 1.00 2.50
44 Marcus Camby 1.00 2.50
45 Damon Stoudamire 1.00 2.50
46 Karl Malone 1.25 3.00
47 John Stockton 1.25 3.00
48 Shareef Abdur-Rahim 1.00 2.50
49 Bryant Reeves .60 1.50
50 Juwan Howard .75 2.00
SPX5 Michael Jordan PROMO 8.00 20.00

1997 SPx Gold

Randomly inserted in packs at a rate of one in nine, this 50-card parallel set is a gold version of the regular set. To ascertain values of individual cards, please refer to the multiplier in the header, coupled with the value of the basic card.

*STARS: .75X TO 2X BASE CARD HI
5 Michael Jordan 20.00 50.00
22 Kobe Bryant 25.00 60.00

1997 SPx Holoview Heroes

Randomly inserted in packs at a rate of one in 75, this 20-card set features color photos of some of the best performers in the NBA on a vertical die-cut card format. Card backs are numbered with a "H" prefix.

COMPLETE SET (20) 150.00 300.00
H1 Michael Jordan 50.00 125.00
H2 Grant Hill 10.00 25.00
H3 Reggie Miller 8.00 20.00
H4 Joe Smith 5.00 12.00
H5 Kevin Garnett 12.00 30.00
H6 Mitch Richmond 6.00 15.00
H7 Allen Iverson 12.00 30.00
H8 Patrick Ewing 8.00 20.00
H9 Hakeem Olajuwon 8.00 20.00
H10 David Robinson 10.00 25.00
H11 Anfernee Hardaway 12.00 30.00
H12 Juwan Howard 5.00 12.00
H13 Gary Payton 6.00 15.00
H14 Dennis Rodman 12.00 30.00
H15 Shaquille O'Neal 15.00 40.00
H16 Charles Barkley 10.00 25.00
H17 Damon Stoudamire 6.00 15.00
H18 Shawn Kemp 6.00 15.00
H19 Glenn Robinson 5.00 12.00
H20 John Stockton 8.00 20.00

1997 SPx ProMotion

Randomly inserted in packs at a rate of one in 430, this five-card set features back-to-back Holoview images. Card fronts actually picture three shots of the player.

COMPLETE SET (5) 150.00 300.00
1 Michael Jordan 100.00 250.00
2 Damon Stoudamire 12.00 30.00
3 Anfernee Hardaway 20.00 50.00
4 Shawn Kemp 15.00 40.00
5 Antonio McDyess 10.00 25.00

1997 SPx ProMotion Autographs

This five-card set is a parallel set to the regular SPx Pro Motion set and is similar in design. The difference is the autograph of the pictured player on the card. Only 100 of these autographed cards are available for each player and are hand numbered.

1 Michael Jordan 2000.00 3500.00
2 Damon Stoudamire 75.00 125.00
3 Anfernee Hardaway 175.00 350.00
4 Shawn Kemp 125.00 250.00
5 Antonio McDyess 75.00 125.00

1997-98 SPx

The 1998 SPx set was the final that used the "holoview" technology. The 50-card set was packaged in three-card packs with a suggested retail price of $5.99. The set also featured redemption cards for a "Piece of History" which was a framed, uncut, Hardcourt HoloView sheet. That card is priced at the bottom of the set.

COMPLETE SET (50) 25.00 60.00
1 Mookie Blaylock .40 1.00
2 Dikembe Mutombo .60 1.50
3 Chauncey Billups RC 3.00 8.00
4 Antoine Walker .60 1.50
5 Glen Rice .60 1.50
6 Michael Jordan 6.00 15.00
7 Scottie Pippen 1.00 2.50
8 Dennis Rodman 1.25 3.00
9 Shawn Kemp .60 1.50
10 Michael Finley .60 1.50
11 Tony Battie RC 1.00 2.50
12 LaPhonso Ellis .40 1.00
13 Grant Hill 1.00 2.50
14 Joe Dumars .60 1.50
15 Joe Smith .50 1.25
16 Clyde Drexler .75 2.00
17 Charles Barkley 1.00 2.50
18 Hakeem Olajuwon .75 2.00
19 Reggie Miller .75 2.00
20 Brent Barry .50 1.25
21 Kobe Bryant 3.00 8.00
22 Shaquille O'Neal 1.50 4.00
23 Alonzo Mourning .75 2.00
24 Glenn Robinson .50 1.25
25 Kevin Garnett 1.25 3.00
26 Stephon Marbury .75 2.00
27 Keith Van Horn RC 1.50 4.00
28 Patrick Ewing .75 2.00
29 Anfernee Hardaway 1.00 2.50
30 Allen Iverson 1.25 3.00
31 Kevin Johnson .60 1.50
32 Antonio McDyess .50 1.25
33 Jason Kidd 1.00 2.50
34 Kenny Anderson .50 1.25
35 Rasheed Wallace .60 1.50
36 Mitch Richmond .60 1.50
37 Tim Duncan RC 5.00 12.00
38 David Robinson 1.00 2.50
39 Vin Baker .50 1.25
40 Gary Payton .60 1.50
41 Marcus Camby .60 1.50
42 Tracy McGrady RC 4.00 10.00
43 Damon Stoudamire .60 1.50
44 Karl Malone .75 2.00
45 John Stockton .75 2.00
46 Shareef Abdur-Rahim .60 1.50
47 Antonio Daniels RC .75 2.00
48 Bryant Reeves .40 1.00
49 Juwan Howard .50 1.25
50 Chris Webber .60 1.50
T1 Piece of History Trade 4.00 10.00

1997-98 SPx Sky

Inserted one per pack, this 50-card set parallels the basic set using a "sky" background. The cards feature light blue borders and light blue coloring throughout the card front. To ascertain individual card values, please refer to the multiplier in the header below coupled with the value of the basic card.

COMPLETE SET (50) 30.00 80.00
*STARS: .5X TO 1.25X BASE CARD HI
*RCs: .4X TO 1X BASE HI

1997-98 SPx Bronze

Inserted at one in three packs, this 50-card set parallels the basic set. The cards contain bronze borders and bronze coloring throughout the card front. To ascertain individual card values, please refer to the multiplier in the header below coupled with the value of the basic card.

COMPLETE SET (50) 60.00 150.00
*STARS: .75X TO 2X BASE CARD HI
*RCs: .6X TO 1.5X BASE HI

1997-98 SPx Silver

Randomly inserted into packs at a rate of one in six, this 50-card set parallels the basic set. The cards feature silver borders and silver coloring throughout the card front. To ascertain individual card values, please refer to the multiplier in the header below coupled with the value of the basic card.

*STARS: 1.25X TO 3X BASE CARD HI
*RCs: 1X TO 2.5X BASE HI

1997-98 SPx Gold

Randomly inserted into packs at one in 17, this 50-card set parallels the basic set. Cards have gold borders and gold coloring throughout the card front. To ascertain individual card values, please refer to the multiplier in the header below coupled with the value of the basic card.

*STARS: 4X TO 10X BASE CARD HI
*RCs: 2X TO 5X BASE HI

1997-98 SPx Grand Finale

Randomly inserted into packs, this 50-card parallel set features serial numbering to 50 on the card backs. To ascertain values on individual cards, please refer to the multiplier in the header below, coupled with the value of the base card.

*STARS: 30X TO 80X BASE CARD HI
*RCs: 12.5X TO 30X BASE HI
3 Chauncey Billups 150.00 300.00
6 Michael Jordan 1500.00 3000.00
7 Scottie Pippen 150.00 300.00
8 Dennis Rodman 250.00 500.00
9 Shawn Kemp 100.00 200.00
13 Grant Hill 125.00 250.00
16 Clyde Drexler 125.00 225.00
17 Charles Barkley 150.00 300.00
18 Hakeem Olajuwon 125.00 250.00
19 Reggie Miller 125.00 250.00
21 Kobe Bryant 500.00 800.00
22 Shaquille O'Neal 250.00 500.00
25 Kevin Garnett 175.00 350.00
29 Anfernee Hardaway 125.00 250.00
30 Allen Iverson 125.00 300.00
37 Tim Duncan 300.00 500.00
38 David Robinson 150.00 300.00
42 Tracy McGrady 175.00 350.00
44 Karl Malone 125.00 250.00
45 John Stockton 125.00 250.00
50 Chris Webber 100.00 200.00

1997-98 SPx Hardcourt Holoview

Randomly inserted into packs at a rate of one in 54, this 20-card set features key NBA players using several "holoview" poses.

COMPLETE SET (20) 200.00 400.00
HH1 Michael Jordan 75.00 200.00
HH2 Allen Iverson 15.00 40.00
HH3 Antoine Walker 6.00 15.00
HH4 Chris Webber 6.00 15.00
HH5 Glenn Robinson 5.00 12.00
HH6 Kevin Garnett 12.00 30.00
HH7 Shareef Abdur-Rahim 6.00 15.00
HH8 Keith Van Horn 5.00 12.00
HH9 Kobe Bryant 40.00 100.00
HH10 Glen Rice 6.00 15.00
HH11 Damon Stoudamire 6.00 15.00
HH12 Hakeem Olajuwon 8.00 20.00
HH13 Mookie Blaylock 4.00 10.00
HH14 Shaquille O'Neal 20.00 50.00
HH15 Stephon Marbury 8.00 20.00
HH16 Chauncey Billups 10.00 25.00
HH17 Anfernee Hardaway 10.00 25.00
HH18 Tim Duncan 20.00 50.00
HH19 Mitch Richmond 6.00 15.00
HH20 Grant Hill 10.00 25.00

1997-98 SPx ProMotion

Randomly inserted into packs at a rate of one in 252, this 10-card set features the player against several "holoview" poses.

COMPLETE SET (10) 250.00 500.00
PM1 Michael Jordan 175.00 350.00
PM2 Shaquille O'Neal 30.00 80.00
PM3 Tim Duncan 75.00 150.00
PM4 Shareef Abdur-Rahim 12.00 30.00
PM5 Grant Hill 20.00 50.00
PM6 Karl Malone 15.00 40.00
PM7 Anfernee Hardaway 20.00 50.00
PM8 Keith Van Horn 12.00 30.00
PM9 Kevin Garnett 25.00 60.00
PM10 Damon Stoudamire 12.00 30.00

1999-00 SPx

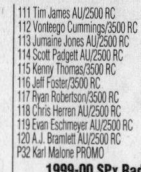

The 1999-00 version of SPx was released by Upper Deck as a 120-card set. The set was divided into 90 veterans and 30 rookies, which had either signed or unsigned cards. The unsigned rookies were serially numbered to 3500. The signed rookies were serially numbered to either 2500 or 500, depending on the player. The cards are designed below. Each pack contained four cards and carried a suggested retail price of $5.99. Please note that card "P32" was given out to dealers and members of the hobby press as a promotional card.

COMPLETE SET w/o RC (90) 18.00 30.00
UNPRICED SPECTRUM SERIAL #'d TO 1
1 Dikembe Mutombo .50 1.25
2 Alan Henderson .30 .75
3 Antoine Walker .50 1.25
4 Paul Pierce .75 2.00
5 Kenny Anderson .40 1.00
6 Eddie Jones .50 1.25
7 David Wesley .30 .75
8 Elden Campbell .30 .75
9 Toni Kukoc .50 1.25
10 Dickey Simpkins .30 .75
11 Shawn Kemp .50 1.25
12 Brevin Knight .30 .75
13 Michael Finley .50 1.25
14 Cedric Ceballos .30 .75
15 Dirk Nowitzki 1.00 2.50
16 Antonio McDyess .40 1.00
17 Nick Van Exel .40 1.00
18 Chauncey Billups .50 1.25
19 Grant Hill .60 1.50
20 Jerry Stackhouse .50 1.25
21 Bison Dele .30 .75
22 Lindsey Hunter .30 .75
23 Antawn Jamison .50 1.25
24 Donyell Marshall .30 .75
25 John Starks .50 1.25
26 Chris Mills .30 .75
27 Hakeem Olajuwon .60 1.50
28 Scottie Pippen .75 2.00
29 Charles Barkley .75 2.00
30 Reggie Miller .50 1.25
31 Rik Smits .50 1.25
32 Jalen Rose .40 1.00
33 Chris Mullin .50 1.25
34 Maurice Taylor .30 .75
35 Michael Olowokandi .30 .75
36 Shaquille O'Neal 1.25 3.00
37 Kobe Bryant 2.50 6.00
38 Glen Rice .50 1.25
39 Tim Hardaway .50 1.25
40 Alonzo Mourning .60 1.50
41 Dan Majerle .50 1.25
42 P.J. Brown .30 .75
43 Glenn Robinson .40 1.00
44 Ray Allen .50 1.25
45 Sam Cassell .40 1.00
46 Tim Thomas .40 1.00
47 Kevin Garnett 1.00 2.50
48 Bobby Jackson .40 1.00
49 Joe Smith .40 1.00
50 Stephon Marbury .40 1.00
51 Keith Van Horn .40 1.00
52 Jayson Williams .30 .75
53 Patrick Ewing .60 1.50
54 Latrell Sprewell .50 1.25
55 Allan Houston .40 1.00
56 Marcus Camby .40 1.00
57 Bo Outlaw .30 .75
58 Darrell Armstrong .30 .75
59 Allen Iverson 1.00 2.50
60 Theo Ratliff .40 1.00
61 Larry Hughes .40 1.00
62 Jason Kidd .75 2.00
63 Tom Gugliotta .30 .75
64 Clifford Robinson .30 .75
65 Brian Grant .30 .75
66 Jermaine O'Neal .50 1.25
67 Rasheed Wallace .50 1.25
68 Damon Stoudamire .50 1.25
69 Jason Williams .60 1.50
70 Chris Webber .50 1.25
71 Vlade Divac .50 1.25
72 Avery Johnson .40 1.00
73 Tim Duncan 1.00 2.50
74 David Robinson .75 2.00
75 Sean Elliott .50 1.25
76 Gary Payton .50 1.25
77 Vin Baker .50 1.25
78 Jelani McCoy .30 .75
79 Charles Oakley .40 1.00
80 Vince Carter 1.00 2.50
81 Tracy McGrady .75 2.00
82 Doug Christie .40 1.00
83 Karl Malone .60 1.50
84 John Stockton .60 1.50
85 Shareef Abdur-Rahim .40 1.00
86 Bryant Reeves .30 .75
87 Mike Bibby .50 1.25
88 Juwan Howard .40 1.00
89 Mitch Richmond .50 1.25
90 Rod Strickland .30 .75
91 Elton Brand RC 6.00 15.00
92 Steve Francis AU/500 RC 12.00 30.00
93 Baron Davis AU/500 RC 30.00 60.00
94 Lamar Odom/3500 RC 8.00 20.00
95 Jonathan Bender/3500 RC 2.50 6.00
96 Wally Szczerbiak AU/500 RC 10.00 25.00
97 Richard Hamilton AU/2500 RC 8.00 20.00
98 Andre Miller AU/500 RC 12.00 30.00
99 Shawn Marion AU/2500 RC 8.00 20.00
100 Jason Terry AU/2500 RC 8.00 20.00
101 Trajan Langdon AU/2500 RC 3.00 8.00
102 Venson Hamilton/3500 RC 2.50 6.00
103 Corey Maggette AU/500 RC 10.00 25.00
104 William Avery AU/2500 RC 3.00 8.00
105 Dion Glover/3500 RC 2.50 6.00
106 Ron Artest AU RC 8.00 20.00
107 Cal Bowdler/3500 RC 2.50 6.00
108 James Posey AU/2500 RC 3.00 8.00
109 Quincy Lewis AU/2500 RC 3.00 8.00
110 Devean George AU/2500 RC 3.00 8.00
111 Tim James AU/2500 RC 3.00 8.00
112 Vonteego Cummings/3500 RC 2.50 6.00
113 Jumaine Jones AU/2500 RC 3.00 8.00
114 Scott Padgett AU/2500 RC 3.00 8.00
115 Kenny Thomas/3500 RC 2.50 6.00
116 Jeff Foster/3500 RC 2.50 6.00
117 Ryan Robertson/3500 RC 2.50 6.00
118 Chris Herren AU/2500 RC 5.00 12.00
119 Evan Eschmeyer AU/2500 RC 3.00 8.00
120 A.J. Bramlett AU/2500 RC 3.00 8.00
P32 Karl Malone PROMO .50 1.25

1999-00 SPx Radiance

Randomly inserted in packs, this 120-card set parallels the base set. The cards are serially numbered to 100. To ascertain values on individual cards, please refer to the multiplier in the header, coupled with the value of the base card.

*STARS: 8X TO 20X BASE CARD HI
11 Shawn Kemp 20.00 50.00
19 Grant Hill 20.00 50.00
37 Kobe Bryant 60.00 150.00
91 Elton Brand 20.00 50.00
92 Steve Francis 20.00 50.00
93 Baron Davis 25.00 60.00
94 Lamar Odom 25.00 60.00
95 Jonathan Bender 8.00 20.00
96 Wally Szczerbiak 15.00 40.00
97 Richard Hamilton 20.00 50.00
98 Andre Miller 20.00 50.00
99 Shawn Marion 20.00 50.00
100 Jason Terry 20.00 50.00
101 Trajan Langdon 8.00 20.00
102 Venson Hamilton 8.00 20.00
103 Corey Maggette 15.00 40.00
104 William Avery 8.00 20.00
105 Dion Glover 8.00 20.00
106 Ron Artest 20.00 50.00
107 Cal Bowdler 8.00 20.00
108 James Posey 8.00 20.00
109 Quincy Lewis 8.00 20.00
110 Devean George 8.00 20.00
111 Tim James 8.00 20.00
112 Vonteego Cummings 8.00 20.00
113 Jumaine Jones 8.00 20.00
114 Scott Padgett 8.00 20.00
115 Kenny Thomas 8.00 20.00
116 Jeff Foster 8.00 20.00
117 Ryan Robertson 8.00 20.00
118 Chris Herren 8.00 20.00
119 Evan Eschmeyer 8.00 20.00
120 A.J. Bramlett 8.00 20.00

1999-00 SPx Decade of Jordan

Randomly inserted in packs at one in nine, this 10-card set features each card dedicated to each year of the decade of the 90's. Card backs carry a "J" prefix.

COMPLETE SET (10) 15.00 30.00
COMMON CARD (J1-J10) 2.00 5.00

1999-00 SPx Masters

Randomly inserted in packs at one in 17, this 15-card set features the most masterful offensive performers in the NBA. Card backs carry a "M" prefix.

COMPLETE SET (15) 20.00 40.00
M1 Michael Jordan 10.00 25.00
M2 Vince Carter 2.50 6.00
M3 Tim Duncan 2.50 6.00
M4 Allen Iverson 2.50 6.00
M5 Gary Payton 1.25 3.00
M6 Shareef Abdur-Rahim 1.00 2.50
M7 Keith Van Horn 1.00 2.50
M8 Grant Hill 1.50 4.00
M9 Kobe Bryant 6.00 15.00
M10 Kevin Garnett 2.50 6.00
M11 Karl Malone 1.50 4.00
M12 Allan Houston 1.00 2.50
M13 Jason Kidd 2.00 5.00
M14 Antoine Walker 1.25 3.00
M15 Jason Williams 1.50 4.00

1999-00 SPx Prolifics

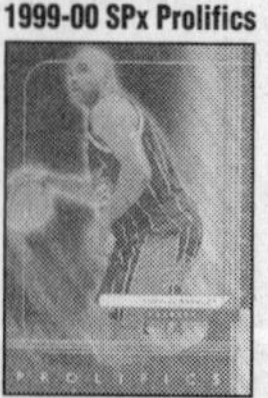

Randomly inserted in packs at one in 17, this 15-card set highlights stars who command the attention of the finest defenders in the league. Card backs carry a "P" prefix.

COMPLETE SET (15) 12.50 25.00
P1 Michael Jordan 8.00 20.00
P2 Karl Malone 1.00 2.50
P3 Jason Kidd 1.25 3.00
P4 Reggie Miller .75 2.00
P5 Glen Rice .75 2.00
P6 Hakeem Olajuwon 1.00 2.50
P7 Mitch Richmond .75 2.00
P8 Shawn Kemp .75 2.00
P9 Patrick Ewing 1.00 2.50
P10 Dikembe Mutombo .75 2.00
P11 Scottie Pippen 1.25 3.00
P12 John Stockton 1.00 2.50
P13 David Robinson 1.25 3.00
P14 Tim Hardaway .75 2.00
P15 Charles Barkley 1.25 3.00

1999-00 SPx Spxcitement

Randomly inserted in packs at one in three, this 20-card set features the top players in the league who provide fans with the most electrifying moves. Card backs carry a "S" prefix.

COMPLETE SET (20) 5.00 12.00
S1 Antoine Walker .40 1.00
S2 Antonio McDyess .30 .75
S3 Antawn Jamison .40 1.00
S4 Vin Baker .40 1.00
S5 Juwan Howard .30 .75
S6 Brian Grant .25 .60
S7 Brevin Knight .25 .60
S8 Glenn Robinson .30 .75
S9 Stephon Marbury .30 .75
S10 Reggie Miller .40 1.00
S11 Nick Van Exel .30 .75
S12 Alonzo Mourning .50 1.25
S13 David Robinson .60 1.50
S14 Hakeem Olajuwon .50 1.25
S15 Toni Kukoc .40 1.00
S16 Maurice Taylor .25 .60
S17 Darrell Armstrong .25 .60
S18 Latrell Sprewell .40 1.00
S19 Tom Gugliotta .25 .60
S20 Michael Jordan 4.00 10.00

1999-00 SPx Spxtreme

Randomly inserted in packs at one in six, this 20-card set focuses on the most collectible players that makes them the fan favorites that they are. Card backs carry a "X" prefix.

COMPLETE SET (20) 8.00 20.00
X1 Michael Jordan 5.00 12.00
X2 Tim Hardaway .60 1.50
X3 Marcus Camby .50 1.25
X4 Jason Williams .75 2.00
X5 Shareef Abdur-Rahim .50 1.25
X6 Keith Van Horn .50 1.25
X7 Glen Rice .60 1.50
X8 Gary Payton .60 1.50
X9 Grant Hill .75 2.00
X10 Allan Houston .50 1.25
X11 Ray Allen .60 1.50
X12 Michael Finley .60 1.50
X13 Shawn Kemp .60 1.50
X14 Shaquille O'Neal 1.50 4.00
X15 Paul Pierce 1.00 2.50
X16 Mike Bibby .60 1.50
X17 Michael Olowokandi .40 1.00
X18 Damon Stoudamire .60 1.50
X19 Mitch Richmond .60 1.50
X20 Eddie Jones .60 1.50

1999-00 SPx Starscape

Randomly inserted in packs at one in nine, this 10-card set features the players that are worth the price of admission, every time they take the court. Card backs carry a "ST" prefix.

COMPLETE SET (10) 5.00 12.00
ST1 Michael Jordan 4.00 10.00
ST2 John Stockton .60 1.50
ST3 Antonio McDyess .40 1.00
ST4 Alonzo Mourning .60 1.50
ST5 Shaquille O'Neal 1.25 3.00
ST6 Stephon Marbury .40 1.00
ST7 Chris Webber .50 1.25
ST8 Charles Barkley .75 2.00
ST9 Antawn Jamison .50 1.25
ST10 Scottie Pippen .75 2.00

1999-00 SPx Winning Materials

Randomly inserted in packs at one in 252, this eight-card set features an authentic jersey swatch and a piece of a game-worn shoe or uniform from some of the top players in the NBA. WM3 and WM7 do not exist. Two signed versions of Winning Material also exist, each numbered to the player's jersey number. The two were Michael Jordan to 23 and Karl Malone to 32. Card backs carry a "WM" prefix.

WM1 Michael Jordan 125.00 300.00
WM1A Michael Jordan AU/23 1000.00 2000.00
WM2 Karl Malone 12.50 30.00
WM2A Karl Malone AU/32 100.00 200.00
WM4 Kobe Bryant 30.00 80.00
WM5 Paul Pierce 12.50 30.00
WM6 Kevin Garnett 15.00 40.00
WM8 Shaquille O'Neal 20.00 50.00
WM9 David Robinson 12.50 30.00
WM10 Charles Barkley 15.00 40.00

2000-01 SPx

The 2000-01 SPx product was released in early December, 2001, and features a 138-card base set. The base set is broken into tiers as follows: 90 Veterans (1-90), and 48 Rookies. Rookies 91/93-98/138 are serial numbered to 4500, Rookies 99-104 are serial numbered to 2500, Rookies 105-110 are serial numbered to 500, Rookies 92/111-130/136-137 are serial numbered to 2500, and Rookies 131-15 are serial numbered to 900. Each pack contains four cards are carried a suggested retail price of $4.99.

COMPLETE SET w/o RC (90) 20.00 40.00
1 Dikembe Mutombo .50 1.25
2 Jim Jackson .30 .75
3 Jason Terry .50 1.25
4 Paul Pierce .60 1.50
5 Kenny Anderson .40 1.00
6 Antoine Walker .40 1.00
7 Derrick Coleman .40 1.00
8 Baron Davis .50 1.25
9 David Wesley .30 .75
10 Elton Brand .50 1.25
11 Ron Artest .50 1.25
12 Corey Benjamin .30 .75
13 Trajan Langdon .30 .75
14 Lamond Murray .30 .75
15 Andre Miller .40 1.00
16 Michael Finley .50 1.25
17 Gary Trent .30 .75
18 Dirk Nowitzki .75 2.00
19 Antonio McDyess .40 1.00
20 Nick Van Exel .40 1.00
21 Raef LaFrentz .30 .75
22 Jerry Stackhouse .40 1.00
23 Michael Curry .30 .75
24 Jerome Williams .30 .75
25 Larry Hughes .40 1.00
26 Antawn Jamison .50 1.25
27 Mookie Blaylock .40 1.00
28 Hakeem Olajuwon .60 1.50
29 Steve Francis .50 1.25
30 Shandon Anderson .30 .75
31 Reggie Miller .50 1.25
32 Jalen Rose .40 1.00
33 Austin Croshere .30 .75
34 Lamar Odom .50 1.25
35 Michael Olowokandi .30 .75
36 Tyrone Nesby .50 1.25
37 Shaquille O'Neal 1.25 3.00
38 Kobe Bryant 2.50 6.00
39 Robert Horry .40 1.00
40 Ron Harper .40 1.00
41 Alonzo Mourning .60 1.50
42 Eddie Jones .50 1.25
43 Tim Hardaway .50 1.25
44 Glenn Robinson .40 1.00
45 Sam Cassell .40 1.00
46 Ray Allen .50 1.25
47 Tim Thomas .30 .75
48 Kevin Garnett 1.00 2.50
49 Terrell Brandon .30 .75
50 Wally Szczerbiak .40 1.00
51 Keith Van Horn .40 1.00
52 Stephon Marbury .40 1.00
53 Jamie Feick .30 .75
54 Latrell Sprewell .40 1.00
55 Marcus Camby .40 1.00
56 Allan Houston .40 1.00
57 Grant Hill .60 1.50
58 Tracy McGrady .75 2.00
59 Darrell Armstrong .30 .75
60 Allen Iverson 1.00 2.50
61 Toni Kukoc .40 1.00
62 Theo Ratliff .30 .75
63 Anfernee Hardaway .75 2.00
64 Jason Kidd .75 2.00
65 Shawn Marion .50 1.25
66 Steve Smith .40 1.00
67 Rasheed Wallace .50 1.25
68 Scottie Pippen .75 2.00
69 Bonzi Wells .30 .75
70 Jason Williams .50 1.25
71 Vlade Divac .40 1.00
72 Chris Webber .50 1.25
73 David Robinson .75 2.00
74 Sean Elliott .40 1.00
75 Tim Duncan 1.00 2.50
76 Gary Payton .50 1.25
77 Rashard Lewis .50 1.25
78 Vin Baker .40 1.00
79 Vince Carter 1.00 2.50
80 Muggsy Bogues .40 1.00
81 Antonio Davis .30 .75
82 Karl Malone .60 1.50
83 John Stockton .60 1.50
84 Bryon Russell .30 .75
85 Shareef Abdur-Rahim .40 1.00
86 Michael Dickerson .30 .75
87 Mike Bibby .50 1.25
88 Mitch Richmond .40 1.00
89 Richard Hamilton .40 1.00
90 Juwan Howard .40 1.00
91 Lavor Postell RC 1.00 2.50
92 Mark Madsen JSY AU RC 3.00 8.00
93 Soumaila Samake RC 1.00 2.50
94 Michael Redd RC 2.50 6.00
95 Paul McPherson RC 1.00 2.50
96 Ruben Wolkowyski RC 1.00 2.50
97 Daniel Santiago RC 1.50 4.00
98 Pepe Sanchez RC 1.00 2.50
99 Marc Jackson RC 1.50 4.00
100 Khalid El-Amin RC 1.50 4.00
101 Iakovos Tsakalidis RC 1.50 4.00
102 Jabari Smith RC 1.50 4.00

3 Jason Hart RC 1.50 4.00
4 Stephen Jackson RC 2.50 6.00
5 Eduardo Najera RC 2.50 6.00
6 Hanno Mottola RC 2.50 6.00
7 Eddie House RC 2.50 6.00
8 Dan Langhi RC 2.50 6.00
9 A.J. Guyton RC 2.50 6.00
0 Chris Porter RC 2.50 6.00
1 Mike Miller JSY AU RC 6.00 15.00
2 Keyon Dooling JSY AU RC 3.00 8.00
3 Courtney Alexander JSY AU RC 3.00 8.00
4 Desmond Mason JSY AU RC 4.00 10.00
5 Jamaal Magloire JSY AU RC 3.00 8.00
6 DeShawn Stevenson JSY AU RC 4.00 10.00
7 Dermarr Johnson JSY AU RC 3.00 8.00
8 Mateen Cleaves JSY AU RC 3.00 8.00
9 Morris Peterson JSY AU RC 3.00 8.00
0 Jerome Moiso JSY AU RC 3.00 8.00
1 Donnell Harvey JSY AU RC 3.00 8.00
2 Quentin Richardson JSY AU RC 5.00 12.00
3 Jamal Crawford JSY AU RC 10.00 25.00
24 Erick Barkley JSY AU RC 3.00 8.00
25 Hedo Turkoglu JSY AU RC 6.00 15.00
26 Etan Thomas JSY AU RC 3.00 8.00
27 Mamadou N'Diaye JSY AU RC 3.00 8.00
28 Joel Przybilla JSY AU RC 3.00 8.00
29 Jason Collier JSY AU RC 3.00 8.00
30 Speedy Claxton JSY AU RC 3.00 8.00
31 Kenyon Martin JSY AU RC 10.00 25.00
32 Stromile Swift JSY AU RC 4.00 10.00
33 Darius Miles JSY AU RC 4.00 10.00
34 Marcus Fizer JSY AU RC 4.00 10.00
35 Chris Mihm JSY AU RC 4.00 10.00
36 Jake Voskuhl JSY AU RC 3.00 8.00
37 Pete Mickeal JSY AU RC 3.00 8.00
38 Dalibor Bagaric RC 1.00 2.50

2000-01 SPx Spectrum

andomly inserted in packs, this 138-card set parallels e base set. The cards are serially numbered to 25. To scertain values on individual cards, please refer to the ultiplier in the header, coupled with the value of the ase card.

STARS: 15X TO 40X BASE CARD HI
7 Grant Hill 30.00 80.00
1 Lavor Postell 10.00 25.00
2 Mark Madsen JSY AU 20.00 50.00
3 Soumaila Samake 10.00 25.00
4 Michael Redd 25.00 60.00
5 Paul McPherson 10.00 25.00
6 Ruben Wolkowyski 10.00 25.00
7 Daniel Santiago 15.00 40.00
8 Pepe Sanchez 10.00 25.00
9 Marc Jackson 10.00 25.00
00 Khalid El-Amin 10.00 25.00
01 Iakovos Tsakalidis 10.00 25.00
02 Jabari Smith 10.00 25.00
03 Jason Hart 10.00 25.00
04 Stephen Jackson 15.00 40.00
05 Eduardo Najera 10.00 25.00
06 Hanno Mottola 10.00 25.00
07 Eddie House 10.00 25.00
08 Dan Langhi 10.00 25.00
09 A.J. Guyton 10.00 25.00
10 Chris Porter 10.00 25.00
11 Mike Miller JSY AU 40.00 100.00
12 Keyon Dooling JSY AU 20.00 50.00
13 Courtney Alexander JSY AU 20.00 50.00
14 Desmond Mason JSY AU 25.00 60.00
15 Jamaal Magloire JSY AU 20.00 50.00
16 DeShawn Stevenson JSY AU 25.00 60.00
17 Dermarr Johnson JSY AU 20.00 50.00
18 Mateen Cleaves JSY AU 20.00 50.00
19 Morris Peterson JSY AU 20.00 50.00
120 Jerome Moiso JSY AU 20.00 50.00
121 Donnell Harvey JSY AU 20.00 50.00
122 Quentin Richardson JSY AU 30.00 80.00
123 Jamal Crawford JSY AU 30.00 80.00
124 Erick Barkley JSY AU 20.00 50.00
125 Hedo Turkoglu JSY AU 40.00 100.00
126 Etan Thomas JSY AU 20.00 50.00
127 Mamadou N'Diaye JSY AU 20.00 50.00
128 Joel Przybilla JSY AU 20.00 50.00
129 Jason Collier JSY AU 20.00 50.00
130 Speedy Claxton JSY AU 20.00 50.00
131 Kenyon Martin JSY AU 50.00 125.00
132 Stromile Swift JSY AU 20.00 50.00
133 Darius Miles JSY AU 20.00 50.00
134 Marcus Fizer JSY AU 20.00 50.00
135 Chris Mihm JSY AU 20.00 50.00
136 Jake Voskuhl JSY AU 20.00 50.00
137 Pete Mickeal JSY AU 20.00 50.00
138 Dalibor Bagaric 10.00 25.00

2000-01 SPx Masters

Randomly inserted in packs at one in 8, this 11-card insert set features NBA players that have mastered the game of basketball. Card backs carry a "M" prefix.

COMPLETE SET (11) 6.00 15.00
M1 Michael Jordan 3.00 8.00
M2 Kobe Bryant 2.00 5.00
M3 Steve Francis .40 1.00
M4 Elton Brand .40 1.00
M5 Tim Duncan .75 2.00
M6 Jason Kidd .60 1.50
M7 Kevin Garnett .75 2.00
M8 Karl Malone .50 1.25
M9 Shaquille O'Neal 1.00 2.50
M10 Gary Payton .40 1.00
M11 Vince Carter .75 2.00

2000-01 SPx Spxcitement

Randomly inserted into packs at one in 5, this 20-card insert set features players that always bring excitement to the game. Card backs carry a "S" prefix.

COMPLETE SET (20) 7.50 15.00
S1 Kobe Bryant 2.00 5.00
S2 Gary Payton .40 1.00
S3 Rasheed Wallace .40 1.00
S4 Jason Williams .40 1.00
S5 Ray Allen .40 1.00
S6 Tim Duncan .75 2.00
S7 Stephon Marbury .30 .75
S8 Allen Iverson .75 2.00
S9 Jerry Stackhouse .30 .75
S10 Kevin Garnett .75 2.00
S11 Antawn Jamison .40 1.00
S12 Paul Pierce .50 1.25
S13 Lamar Odom .40 1.00
S14 Elton Brand .40 1.00
S15 Vince Carter .75 2.00
S16 Antonio McDyess .30 .75
S17 Michael Finley .40 1.00
S18 Jalen Rose .30 .75
S19 Richard Hamilton .30 .75
S20 Jason Kidd .60 1.50

2000-01 SPx Spxtreme

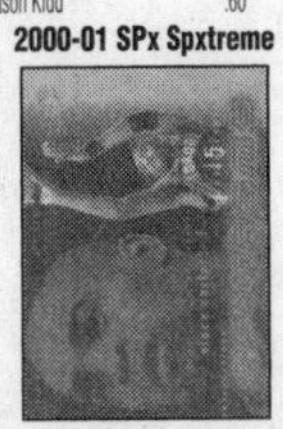

Randomly inserted into packs at one in 8, this 11-card insert set features players that play extremely hard every night . Card backs carry a "X" prefix.

COMPLETE SET (11) 5.00 12.00
X1 Kevin Garnett .75 2.00
X2 Steve Francis .40 1.00
X3 Chris Webber .40 1.00
X4 Elton Brand .40 1.00
X5 Shareef Abdur-Rahim .30 .75
X6 Larry Hughes .30 .75
X7 Vince Carter .75 2.00
X8 Kobe Bryant 2.00 5.00
X9 Scottie Pippen .60 1.50
X10 Anfernee Hardaway .60 1.50
X11 Shaquille O'Neal 1.00 2.50

2000-01 SPx UD Authentics Rookie Exclusives

Randomly inserted into packs, this 5-card insert features authentic autographs of top rookies from the 2000-01 season. Card backs carry the player's initials as numbering. Please note that the Kenyon Martin card packed out as an exchange card and must be redeemed by 8/03/01.

DM Darius Miles 8.00 20.00
KM Kenyon Martin 20.00 50.00
MF Marcus Fizer 8.00 20.00
MI Mike Miller 15.00 40.00
SS Stromile Swift 8.00 20.00

2000-01 SPx Winning Materials

Randomly inserted in packs at one in 72, this 27-card set features an authentic jersey swatch and another swatch of memorabilia including shorts, shoes, and warm-ups. Card backs carry the players initials as numbering. Also note that there are autographed versions of these cards that were seeded into packs at one in 252.

BR1 Bryon Russell 3.00 8.00
CM1 Chris Mihm 5.00 12.00
DM1 DerMarr Johnson 5.00 12.00
JS1 John Stockton 6.00 15.00
KB1 Kobe Bryant JSY/WM 15.00 40.00
KB2 Kobe Bryant JSY/Shoe 40.00 100.00
KB3 Kobe Bryant WM/Shoe 40.00 100.00
KG1 Kevin Garnett JSY/WM 10.00 25.00
KG2 Kevin Garnett JSY/SS 10.00 25.00
KG3 Kevin Garnett JSY/Shorts 10.00 25.00
KM1 Kenyon Martin 12.00 30.00
MF1 Marcus Fizer 5.00 12.00
MM1 Karl Malone JSY/Shorts 6.00 15.00
MM3 Karl Malone JSY/Shoe 10.00 25.00
TB1 Terrell Brandon JSY/WM 3.00 8.00
WS1 Wally Szczerbiak JSY/WM 4.00 10.00
WS2 Wally Szczerbiak JSY/SS 4.00 10.00
DMA1 DerMarr Johnson AU 6.00 15.00
KBA1 Kobe Bryant JSY/WM AU 100.00 250.00
KBA2 Kobe Bryant JSY/Shoe AU 100.00 250.00
KBA3 Kobe Bryant WM/Shoe AU 100.00 250.00
KGA1 Kevin Garnett JSY/WM AU 30.00 80.00
KGA2 Kevin Garnett JSY/SS AU 50.00 125.00
KMA1 Kenyon Martin AU 10.00 25.00
MFA1 Marcus Fizer AU 6.00 15.00
MJA1 Michael Jordan JSY/WM AU 300.00 600.00
MJA2 Michael Jordan WM/Shoe AU 500.00 800.00

2001-02 SPx

Released in February 2002, SPx features a 173-card set consisting of 90 base cards and 50 rookie players with three versions of card numbers 91-111. Rookie versions are differentiated as follows: version "A" has a blue background, version "B" has a green background, and version "C" has a red background. These cards are horizontally designed with a player photo, a swatch of a jersey, and a "cut signature" placed inside the card. Card numbers 91-105 are sequentially numbered to 800, and card numbers 106-111 are sequentially numbered to 250. The set was released without card numbers 112-120, and card numbers 121-140 feature a purple letter "R" on the left side of the card and player photos on the right, and are squentially numbered to 1999. SPx was packaged in 18-pack boxes where packs contained four cards and carried a suggested retail price of $6.99.

COMP.SET w/o SP's (90) 30.00 60.00
1 Jason Terry .50 1.25
2 Shareef Abdur-Rahim .40 1.00
3 DerMarr Johnson .30 .75
4 Paul Pierce .60 1.50
5 Antoine Walker .40 1.00
6 Kenny Anderson .40 1.00
7 Baron Davis .50 1.25
8 Jamal Mashburn .40 1.00
9 David Wesley .30 .75
10 Ron Mercer .30 .75
11 Ron Artest .50 1.25
12 Marcus Fizer .30 .75
13 Andre Miller .40 1.00
14 Lamond Murray .30 .75
15 Chris Mihm .30 .75
16 Michael Finley .50 1.25
17 Dirk Nowitzki .75 2.00
18 Steve Nash .75 2.00
19 Antonio McDyess .40 1.00
20 Nick Van Exel .40 1.00
21 Raef LaFrentz .30 .75
22 Jerry Stackhouse .40 1.00
23 Chucky Atkins .30 .75
24 Corliss Williamson .30 .75
25 Antawn Jamison .50 1.25
26 Larry Hughes .40 1.00
27 Chris Porter .30 .75
28 Steve Francis .50 1.25
29 Cuttino Mobley .40 1.00
30 Maurice Taylor .30 .75
31 Reggie Miller .50 1.25
32 Jalen Rose .40 1.00
33 Jermaine O'Neal .50 1.25
34 Darius Miles .30 .75
35 Elton Brand .50 1.25
36 Lamar Odom .50 1.25
37 Quentin Richardson .40 1.00
38 Kobe Bryant 2.50 6.00
39 Shaquille O'Neal 1.25 3.00
40 Rick Fox .40 1.00
41 Derek Fisher .40 1.00
42 Stromile Swift .30 .75
43 Jason Williams .40 1.00
44 Michael Dickerson .30 .75
45 Alonzo Mourning .60 1.50
46 Eddie Jones .40 1.00
47 Anthony Carter .30 .75
48 Glenn Robinson .40 1.00
49 Ray Allen .50 1.25
50 Sam Cassell .40 1.00
51 Kevin Garnett 1.00 2.50
52 Wally Szczerbiak .40 1.00
53 Terrell Brandon .30 .75
54 Chauncey Billups .50 1.25
55 Kenyon Martin .50 1.25
56 Keith Van Horn .40 1.00
57 Jason Kidd .75 2.00
58 Latrell Sprewell .40 1.00
59 Allan Houston .40 1.00
60 Marcus Camby .40 1.00
61 Tracy McGrady .75 2.00
62 Mike Miller .50 1.25
63 Grant Hill .60 1.50
64 Allen Iverson 1.00 2.50
65 Dikembe Mutombo .50 1.25
66 Aaron McKie .30 .75
67 Stephon Marbury .40 1.00
68 Shawn Marion .50 1.25
69 Tom Gugliotta .30 .75
70 Rasheed Wallace .50 1.25
71 Damon Stoudamire .40 1.00
72 Bonzi Wells .30 .75
73 Chris Webber .50 1.25
74 Peja Stojakovic .50 1.25
75 Mike Bibby .50 1.25
76 Tim Duncan 1.00 2.50
77 David Robinson .75 2.00
78 Antonio Daniels .30 .75
79 Gary Payton .50 1.25
80 Rashard Lewis .50 1.25
81 Desmond Mason .40 1.00
82 Vince Carter .75 2.00
83 Morris Peterson .30 .75
84 Antonio Davis .30 .75
85 Karl Malone .60 1.50
86 John Stockton .60 1.50
87 Donyell Marshall .30 .75
88 Richard Hamilton .40 1.00
89 Courtney Alexander .30 .75
90 Michael Jordan 8.00 20.00
91A Tony Parker JSY AU RC 20.00 50.00
91B Tony Parker JSY AU RC 20.00 50.00
91C Tony Parker JSY AU RC 20.00 50.00
92A Jamaal Tinsley JSY AU RC 4.00 10.00
92B Jamaal Tinsley JSY AU RC 4.00 10.00
92C Jamaal Tinsley JSY AU RC 4.00 10.00
93A Samuel Dalembert JSY AU RC 4.00 10.00
93B Samuel Dalembert JSY AU RC 4.00 10.00
93C Samuel Dalembert JSY AU RC 4.00 10.00
94A Gerald Wallace JSY AU RC 5.00 12.00
94B Gerald Wallace JSY AU RC 5.00 12.00
94C Gerald Wallace JSY AU RC 5.00 12.00
95A Brandon Armstrong JSY AU RC 3.00 8.00
95B Brandon Armstrong JSY AU RC 3.00 8.00
95C Brandon Armstrong JSY AU RC 3.00 8.00
96A Jeryl Sasser JSY AU RC 3.00 8.00
96B Jeryl Sasser JSY AU RC 3.00 8.00
96C Jeryl Sasser JSY AU RC 3.00 8.00
97A Jason Collins JSY AU RC 3.00 8.00
97B Jason Collins JSY AU RC 3.00 8.00
97C Jason Collins JSY AU RC 3.00 8.00
98A Michael Bradley JSY AU RC 3.00 8.00
98B Michael Bradley JSY AU RC 3.00 8.00
98C Michael Bradley JSY AU RC 3.00 8.00
99A Steven Hunter JSY AU RC 3.00 8.00
99B Steven Hunter JSY AU RC 3.00 8.00
99C Steven Hunter JSY AU RC 3.00 8.00
100A Troy Murphy JSY AU RC 5.00 12.00
100B Troy Murphy JSY AU RC 5.00 12.00
100C Troy Murphy JSY AU RC 5.00 12.00
101A Richard Jefferson JSY AU RC 6.00 15.00
101B Richard Jefferson JSY AU RC 6.00 15.00
101C Richard Jefferson JSY AU RC 6.00 15.00
102A Vladimir Radmanov JSY AU RC 3.00 8.00
102B Vladimir Radmanov JSY AU RC 3.00 8.00
102C Vladimir Radmanov JSY AU RC 3.00 8.00
103A Kedrick Brown JSY AU RC 3.00 8.00
103B Kedrick Brown JSY AU RC 3.00 8.00
103C Kedrick Brown JSY AU RC 3.00 8.00
104A J.Johnson JSY AU ERR RC 8.00 20.00
Photo of Joseph Forte
104B J.Johnson JSY AU ERR RC 8.00 20.00
Photo of Joseph Forte
104C J.Johnson JSY AU ERR RC 8.00 20.00
Photo of Joseph Forte
104D Joe Johnson JSY AU COR RC 8.00 20.00
104E Joe Johnson JSY AU COR RC 8.00 20.00
104F Joe Johnson JSY AU COR RC 8.00 20.00
105A Kirk Haston JSY AU RC 3.00 8.00
105B Kirk Haston JSY AU RC 3.00 8.00
105C Kirk Haston JSY AU RC 3.00 8.00
106A Rodney White JSY AU RC 5.00 12.00
106B Rodney White JSY AU RC 5.00 12.00
106C Rodney White JSY AU RC 5.00 12.00
107A Eddie Griffin JSY AU RC 5.00 12.00
107B Eddie Griffin JSY AU RC 5.00 12.00
107C Eddie Griffin JSY AU RC 5.00 12.00
108A Jason Richardson JSY AU RC 10.00 25.00
108B Jason Richardson JSY AU RC 10.00 25.00
108C Jason Richardson JSY AU RC 10.00 25.00
109A Eddy Curry JSY AU RC 8.00 20.00
109B Eddy Curry JSY AU RC 8.00 20.00
109C Eddy Curry JSY AU RC 8.00 20.00
110A Tyson Chandler JSY AU RC 10.00 25.00
110B Tyson Chandler JSY AU RC 10.00 25.00
110C Tyson Chandler JSY AU RC 10.00 25.00
111A Kwame Brown JSY AU RC 5.00 12.00
111B Kwame Brown JSY AU RC 5.00 12.00
111C Kwame Brown JSY AU RC 5.00 12.00
121 Shane Battier RC 4.00 10.00
122 Brendan Haywood RC 2.50 6.00
123 Joseph Forte RC 2.00 5.00
124 Zach Randolph RC 6.00 15.00
125 DeSagana Diop RC 2.00 5.00
126 Damone Brown RC 2.00 5.00
127 Andrei Kirilenko RC 5.00 12.00
128 Trenton Hassell RC 2.00 5.00
129 Gilbert Arenas RC 3.00 8.00
130 Earl Watson RC 2.00 5.00
131 Kenny Satterfield RC 2.00 5.00
132 Will Solomon RC 2.00 5.00
133 Bobby Simmons RC 2.00 5.00
134 Brian Scalabrine RC 2.00 5.00
135 Charlie Bell RC 2.00 5.00
136 Zeljko Rebraca RC 2.00 5.00
137 Loren Woods RC 2.00 5.00
138 Terence Morris RC 2.00 5.00
139 Jamison Brewer RC 2.00 5.00
140 Pau Gasol RC 6.00 15.00
NNO Kobe Bryant PROMO 2.00 5.00

2001-02 SPx Spectrum

Randomly inserted in packs, this 173-card set parallels the base SPx set enhanced with sequential numbering to 25. Three versions of the rookie cards exist. Please see base set blurb for version and color breakdown of these cards.

*1-90 STARS: 15X TO 40X BASE CARD HI
*91-105 RCs: 2X TO 5X HI
*106-111 RCs: 1.25X TO 3X HI
*121-140 RCs: 2.5X TO 6X HI
91-111 HAS THREE VERSIONS ALL EQUAL
91A Tony Parker JSY AU 75.00 200.00
108A Jason Richardson JSY AU 50.00 120.00

2001-02 SPx Winning Materials

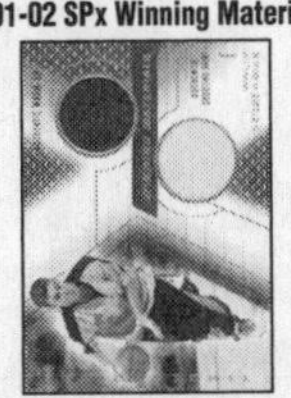

Randomly inserted in packs at the rate of one in 18, this 20-card set features a horizontal design with a player photo on the left and two swatches of game materials on the right. The breakdown of materials on each card appears after the player's name in the descriptions below.

AH Anfernee Hardaway Shorts/WU 6.00 15.00
AI Allen Iverson JSY/Shorts 8.00 20.00
CB Chauncey Billups JSY/WU 4.00 10.00
KB Kobe Bryant JSY/WU 20.00 50.00
KE Kenyon Martin Shorts/Shirt 4.00 10.00
KG Kevin Garnett JSY/WU 8.00 20.00
KG2 Kevin Garnett WU/Shirt 8.00 20.00
KM Karl Malone JSY/JSY 5.00 12.00
KM2 Karl Malone WU/Shorts 5.00 12.00
KV Keith Van Horn WU/JSY 3.00 8.00
LP Lavor Postell Shirt/Pr.JSY 2.50 6.00
MM Mike Miller WU/Shirt 4.00 10.00
MO Michael Olowokandi Shirt/WU 2.50 6.00
RH Richard Hamilton WU/Shirt 3.00 8.00
SM Shawn Marion WU/Shirt 4.00 10.00
SS Stromile Swift WU/Shirt 2.50 6.00
ST John Stockton JSY/Pr.JSY 5.00 12.00
ST2 John Stockton JSY/Shirt 5.00 12.00
TB Terrell Brandon WU/Shirt 2.50 6.00
WS Wally Szczerbiak WU/Shirt 3.00 8.00

2002-03 SPx

Released in December 2002, SPx conatins 162 cards and is broken down as follows: Cards 1-90 are veterans, cards 91-110 are Flashback Fabrics veteran jersey autographs, cards 111-132 are rookie jersey autographs (sequentially numbered to 999), cards 133-138 are rookies sequentially numbered to 1599, cards 139-147 are rookies sequentially numbered to 2599, and cards 148-162 are rookies sequentailly numbered to 2999. Base cards showcase a horizontal design which places a full color player action photo next to a close-up portrait style photo. All Autograph cards have "cut signatures" embedded in them, and the Flashback Fabrics have an F shaped jersey swatch and the rookies have an R shaped jersey swatch. SPx was packaged in 18-pack boxes where packs contained four cards and carried a suggested retail price of $4.99.

COMP.SET w/o SP's (90) 25.00 60.00
1 Shareef Abdur-Rahim .40 1.00
2 Jason Terry .40 1.00
3 Glenn Robinson .40 1.00
4 Paul Pierce .60 1.50
5 Antoine Walker .40 1.00
6 Kedrick Brown .30 .75
7 Vin Baker .40 1.00
8 Jalen Rose .40 1.00
9 Tyson Chandler .40 1.00
10 Eddy Curry .40 1.00
11 Ricky Davis .40 1.00
12 Chris Mihm .30 .75
13 Darius Miles .30 .75
14 Dirk Nowitzki .75 2.00
15 Michael Finley .50 1.25
16 Steve Nash .60 1.50
17 Raef LaFrentz .30 .75
18 James Posey .30 .75
19 Juwan Howard .40 1.00
20 Richard Hamilton .40 1.00
21 Ben Wallace .50 1.25
22 Chauncey Billups .50 1.25
23 Antawn Jamison .50 1.25
24 Jason Richardson .50 1.25
25 Steve Francis .50 1.25
26 Eddie Griffin .30 .75
27 Cuttino Mobley .40 1.00
28 Reggie Miller .50 1.25
29 Jamaal Tinsley .30 .75
30 Jermaine O'Neal .50 1.25
31 Elton Brand .50 1.25
32 Andre Miller .40 1.00
33 Lamar Odom .50 1.25
34 Kobe Bryant 2.50 6.00
35 Shaquille O'Neal 1.25 3.00
36 Robert Horry .40 1.00
37 Devean George .30 .75
38 Pau Gasol .60 1.50
39 Shane Battier .50 1.25
40 Jason Williams .40 1.00
41 Alonzo Mourning .60 1.50
42 Eddie Jones .40 1.00
43 Brian Grant .30 .75
44 Ray Allen .50 1.25
45 Tim Thomas .30 .75
46 Kevin Garnett 1.00 2.50
47 Terrell Brandon .30 .75
48 Wally Szczerbiak .40 1.00
49 Jason Kidd .75 2.00
50 Richard Jefferson .50 1.25
51 Kenyon Martin .50 1.25
52 Baron Davis .50 1.25
53 Jamal Mashburn .40 1.00
54 David Wesley .30 .75
55 P.J. Brown .30 .75
56 Allan Houston .40 1.00
57 Antonio McDyess .40 1.00
58 Latrell Sprewell .40 1.00
59 Tracy McGrady .75 2.00
60 Mike Miller .50 1.25
61 Darrell Armstrong .30 .75
62 Allen Iverson .75 2.00
63 Keith Van Horn .40 1.00
64 Stephon Marbury .40 1.00
65 Shawn Marion .50 1.25
66 Anfernee Hardaway .75 2.00
67 Rasheed Wallace .50 1.25
68 Damon Stoudamire .40 1.00
69 Scottie Pippen .75 2.00
70 Chris Webber .50 1.25
71 Mike Bibby .50 1.25
72 Peja Stojakovic .50 1.25
73 Hedo Turkoglu .50 1.25
74 Tim Duncan 1.00 2.50
75 David Robinson .75 2.00
76 Tony Parker .60 1.50
77 Steve Smith .40 1.00
78 Gary Payton .50 1.25
79 Rashard Lewis .50 1.25
80 Brent Barry .30 .75
81 Desmond Mason .40 1.00
82 Vince Carter .75 2.00
83 Morris Peterson .30 .75
84 Antonio Davis .30 .75
85 Karl Malone .60 1.50
86 John Stockton .60 1.50
87 Andrei Kirilenko .50 1.25
88 Jerry Stackhouse .40 1.00
89 Michael Jordan 4.00 10.00
90 Kwame Brown .30 .75
91 Jason Richardson JSY AU 8.00 20.00
92 Tyson Chandler JSY AU 6.00 15.00
93 Kenyon Martin JSY AU 15.00 30.00
94 Gerald Wallace JSY AU SP 6.00 15.00
95 Kareem Abdul-Jabbar JSY AU SP 60.00 120.00
96 Morris Peterson JSY AU SP 6.00 15.00
97 Andre Miller JSY AU 6.00 15.00
98 Quentin Richardson JSY AU 6.00 15.00
99 Mike Miller JSY AU 6.00 15.00
100 Jermaine O'Neal JSY AU SP 10.00 25.00
101 Marcus Fizer JSY AU 6.00 15.00
102 Mike Bibby JSY AU 10.00 25.00
103 Chauncey Billups JSY AU SP 10.00 25.00
104 Lamar Odom JSY AU SP 12.50 30.00
105 Antoine Walker JSY AU 10.00 25.00
106 Paul Pierce JSY AU 15.00 30.00
107 Jason Kidd JSY AU SP 20.00 40.00
108 Kevin Garnett JSY AU SP 75.00 150.00
109 Kobe Bryant JSY AU SP 150.00 300.00
110 Michael Jordan JSY AU SP 500.00 750.00
111 Chris Jefferies JSY AU RC 4.00 10.00
112 John Salmons JSY AU RC 5.00 12.00
113 Tayshaun Prince JSY AU RC 5.00 12.00
114 Casey Jacobsen JSY AU RC 4.00 10.00
115 Qyntel Woods JSY AU RC 4.00 10.00
116 Kareem Rush JSY AU RC 4.00 10.00
117 Ryan Humphrey JSY AU RC 4.00 10.00
118 Carlos Boozer JSY AU RC 8.00 20.00
119 Sam Clancy JSY AU RC 4.00 10.00
120 Fred Jones JSY AU RC 4.00 10.00
121 Marcus Haislip JSY AU RC 4.00 10.00
122 Melvin Ely JSY AU RC 4.00 10.00
123 Jared Jeffries JSY AU RC 4.00 10.00
124 Dan Gadzuric JSY AU RC 4.00 10.00
125 Amare Stoudemire JSY AU RC 15.00 40.00
126 Caron Butler JSY AU RC 6.00 15.00
127 Nene Hilario JSY AU RC 5.00 12.00
128 DaJuan Wagner JSY AU RC 4.00 10.00
129 Nikoloz Tskitishvili JSY AU RC 4.00 10.00
130 Drew Gooden JSY AU RC 6.00 15.00
131 Jay Williams JSY AU RC 5.00 12.00
132 Yao Ming JSY AU RC 40.00 80.00
133 Mike Dunleavy RC 2.00 5.00
134 Frank Williams RC 1.50 4.00
135 Jiri Welsch RC 1.50 4.00
136 Dan Dickau RC 1.50 4.00
137 Efthimios Rentzias RC 1.50 4.00
138 Chris Wilcox RC 1.50 4.00
139 Curtis Borchardt RC 1.50 4.00
140 Predrag Savovic RC 1.50 4.00
141 Tito Maddox RC 1.50 4.00
142 Roger Mason RC 1.50 4.00
143 Juan Dixon RC 2.00 5.00
144 Pat Burke RC 1.50 4.00
145 Marko Jaric 1.50 4.00
146 Gordan Giricek RC 1.50 4.00
147 Juaquin Hawkins RC 1.50 4.00
148 Vincent Yarbrough RC 1.50 4.00
149 Robert Archibald RC 1.50 4.00
150 Bostjan Nachbar RC 1.50 4.00
151 Jamal Sampson RC 1.50 4.00
152 Lonny Baxter RC 1.50 4.00
153 J.R. Bremer RC 1.50 4.00
154 Cezary Trybanski RC 1.50 4.00
155 Manu Ginobili RC 4.00 10.00
156 Raul Lopez RC 1.50 4.00
157 Rasual Butler RC 1.50 4.00
158 Tamar Slay RC 1.50 4.00
159 Ronald Murray RC 1.50 4.00
160 Igor Rakocevic RC 1.50 4.00
161 Reggie Evans RC 1.50 4.00
162 Jannero Pargo RC 1.50 4.00

2002-03 SPx Spectrum

Randomly inserted in packs, this 162-card set parallels the base SPx set enhanced with gold highlights. Each card is sequentially numbered to 25. Cards 91-110 feature both a swatch of jersey and an autograph and are serially numbered to one.

*1-90 STARS: 10X TO 25X BASE CARD HI
*111-132 RCs: 2X TO 5X HI
*133-162 RCs: 3X TO 8X HI
28 Reggie Miller 15.00 40.00
34 Kobe Bryant 100.00 200.00
89 Michael Jordan 150.00 300.00
125 Amare Stoudemire JSY AU 150.00 300.00

2002-03 SPx Winning Combos

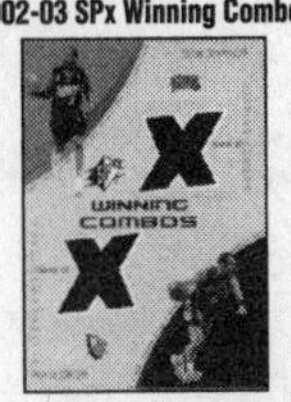

Inserted in packs at the rate of one in 18, this 20-card set places player photos in the upper left hand corner and in the lower right hand corner. Next to the player photos, there is an X shaped swatch of game worn memorabilia. An Autograph parallel for six cards was also inserted and sequentially numbered to 10.

AIJK Allen Iverson SP 6.00 15.00
Jason Kidd
BDJM Baron Davis 4.00 10.00
Jamal Mashburn
BHKW Brendan Haywood 4.00 10.00
Kwame Brown
CWPS Chris Webber 4.00 10.00
Peja Stojakovic
ECTC Eddy Curry 4.00 10.00
Tyson Chandler
JTJO Jamaal Tinsley 4.00 10.00
Jermaine O'Neal
KBAI Kobe Bryant SP 12.50 30.00
Allen Iverson
KBJK Kobe Bryant 10.00 25.00
Jason Kidd
KBTM Kobe Bryant SP 12.50 30.00
Tracy McGrady
KGWS Kevin Garnett 5.00 12.00
Wally Szczerbiak
KMJS Karl Malone 6.00 15.00
John Stockton
KMRJ Kenyon Martin 4.00 10.00
Richard Jefferson
MJKB Michael Jordan SP 50.00 120.00
Kobe Bryant
PPAW Paul Pierce 5.00 12.00
Antoine Walker
QRLO Quentin Richardson 4.00 10.00
Lamar Odom
SADJ Shareef Abdur-Rahim 4.00 10.00
DerMarr Johnson
SMSM Stephon Marbury 4.00 10.00
Shawn Marion
TMMM Tracy McGrady SP 6.00 15.00
Mike Miller
WCKB Wilt Chamberlain SP 50.00 120.00
Kobe Bryant
WCMJ Wilt Chamberlain SP 150.00 300.00
Michael Jordan

2002-03 SPx Winning Materials

Inserted in packs at the rate of one in 18, this 19-card set features a horizontal design with a player photo in the lower right hand corner and two X shaped swatches of game used memorabilia.

AMW Antonio McDyess JSY/WU 3.00 8.00
BDW Baron Davis JSY/WU 4.00 10.00
CWW Chris Webber JSY/WU 4.00 10.00
DNW Dirk Nowitzki Shorts/WU 6.00 15.00
DRW David Robinson JSY/WU 6.00 15.00
EBW Elton Brand Shorts/WU 4.00 10.00
JKW Jason Kidd Shirt/WU 6.00 15.00
KBW Kobe Bryant Shorts/WU 15.00 40.00
KGW Kevin Garnett Shorts/WU 8.00 20.00
KMW Kenyon Martin Shirt/WU 4.00 10.00
MJW Michael Jordan Shirt/JSY SP 60.00 150.00
MMW Mike Miller JSY/Shirt 4.00 10.00
PPW Paul Pierce Shirt/WU 5.00 12.00
PSW Peja Stojakovic JSY/WU 4.00 10.00
RHW Richard Hamilton Shirt/WU 3.00 8.00
RJW Richard Jefferson Shirt/WU 4.00 10.00
SHW Shawn Marion Shirt/WU 4.00 10.00
SMW Stephon Marbury Shirt/WU 3.00 8.00
TMW Tracy McGrady Shirt/WU SP 8.00 20.00

2002-03 SPx Winning Materials Autographs

Randomly seeded in packs, this 12-card set uses the same design as the Winning Materials insert set enhanced with a gold background and an authentic player autograph. Each card is sequentially numbered to 23 or 100.

AMA Andre Miller/100 10.00 25.00
JKA Jason Kidd/100 40.00 100.00
JWA Jay Williams/100 10.00 25.00
KBA Kobe Bryant/100 125.00 250.00
KGA Kevin Garnett/100 40.00 100.00
KMA Kenyon Martin/100 12.00 30.00
MBA Mike Bibby/100 10.00 25.00
MJA Michael Jordan/23 500.00 1000.00
MMA Mike Miller/100 10.00 25.00
PPA Paul Pierce/100 20.00 50.00
QRA Quentin Richardson/100 10.00 25.00
TCA Tyson Chandler/100 10.00 25.00

2003-04 SPx

Released in December 2003, this 206-card set is broken down as follows: Cards 1-90 feature veteran players on a horizontal design with full-color player action photos on the right and a gray-scale portrait photo on the left; cards 91-132 are Spxcellence cards sequentially numbered to 3999; cards 133-150 are rookie cards sequentially numbered to 2999; cards 151-156 feature rookie jersey autograph cards sequentially numbered to 750; cards 157-165 feature rookie jersey autograph cards sequentially numbered to 1250; cards 166-185 feature rookie jersey autograph cards sequentially numbered to 1999; and cards 186-206 feature veteran jersey autograph cards sequentially numbered to random amounts. SPx was packaged in 18-pack boxes where packs contained four cards plus one promo and carried a suggested retail price of $6.99

COMP.SET w/o SP's (90) 25.00 60.00
1 Shafreef Abdur-Rahim .40 1.00
2 Jason Terry .40 1.00
3 Theo Ratliff .30 .75
4 Paul Pierce .60 1.50
5 Raef LaFrentz .30 .75
6 Vin Baker .30 .75
7 Jalen Rose .40 1.00
8 Tyson Chandler .40 1.00
9 Michael Jordan 4.00 10.00
10 Dajuan Wagner .30 .75
11 Darius Miles .30 .75
12 Carlos Boozer .50 1.25
13 Dirk Nowitzki .75 2.00
14 Antoine Walker .50 1.25
15 Steve Nash .60 1.50
16 Nene .40 1.00
17 Marcus Camby .40 1.00
18 Andre Miller .40 1.00
19 Richard Hamilton .40 1.00
20 Ben Wallace .50 1.25
21 Chauncey Billups .50 1.25
22 Nick Van Exel .40 1.00
23 Jason Richardson .50 1.25
24 Speedy Claxton .30 .75
25 Steve Francis .50 1.25
26 Yao Ming 1.00 2.50
27 Cuttino Mobley .40 1.00
28 Reggie Miller .50 1.25
29 Jamaal Tinsley .30 .75
30 Jermaine O'Neal .50 1.25
31 Elton Brand .50 1.25
32 Corey Maggette .40 1.00
33 Quentin Richardson .40 1.00
34 Kobe Bryant 2.50 6.00

35 Karl Malone .60 1.50
36 Shaquille O'Neal 1.25 3.00
37 Gary Payton .50 1.25
38 Pau Gasol .50 1.25
39 Shane Battier .40 1.00
40 Mike Miller .50 1.25
41 Eddie Jones .40 1.00
42 Lamar Odom .50 1.25
43 Caron Butler .50 1.25
44 Michael Redd .50 1.25
45 Joe Smith .40 1.00
46 Desmond Mason .40 1.00
47 Kevin Garnett 1.00 2.50
48 Latrell Sprewell .40 1.00
49 Michael Olowokandi .30 .75
50 Jason Kidd .75 2.00
51 Richard Jefferson .50 1.25
52 Kenyon Martin .50 1.25
53 Baron Davis .50 1.25
54 Jamal Mashburn .40 1.00
55 David Wesley .30 .75
56 Allan Houston .40 1.00
57 Antonio McDyess .40 1.00
58 Keith Van Horn .40 1.00
59 Tracy McGrady .60 1.50
60 Grant Hill .60 1.50
61 Drew Gooden .40 1.00
62 Juwan Howard .40 1.00
63 Allen Iverson .75 2.00
64 Glenn Robinson .40 1.00
65 Eric Snow .30 .75
66 Stephon Marbury .50 1.25
67 Shawn Marion .50 1.25
68 Amare Stoudemire .75 2.00
69 Rasheed Wallace .50 1.25
70 Bonzi Wells .30 .75
71 Damon Stoudamire .40 1.00
72 Chris Webber .50 1.25
73 Mike Bibby .50 1.25
74 Peja Stojakovic .50 1.25
75 Brad Miller .50 1.25
76 Tim Duncan .75 2.00
77 Tony Parker .50 1.25
78 Manu Ginobili .60 1.50
79 Ray Allen .50 1.25
80 Rashard Lewis .50 1.25
81 Vladimir Radmanovic .30 .75
82 Vince Carter .75 2.00
83 Morris Peterson .30 .75
84 Antonio Davis .30 .75
85 Raul Lopez .50 1.25
86 Matt Harpring .40 1.00
87 Andrei Kirilenko .50 1.25
88 Jerry Stackhouse .40 1.00
89 Gilbert Arenas .50 1.25
90 Larry Hughes .40 1.00
91 Allen Iverson 1.50 4.00
92 Dirk Nowitzki 1.50 4.00
93 Kobe Bryant 5.00 12.00
94 Michael Jordan 8.00 20.00
95 Vince Carter 1.50 4.00
96 Shaquille O'Neal 2.50 6.00
97 Yao Ming 2.00 5.00
98 Amare Stoudemire 1.50 4.00
99 Paul Pierce 1.25 3.00
100 Jason Richardson 1.00 2.50
101 Steve Francis 1.00 2.50
102 Jermaine O'Neal 1.00 2.50
103 Karl Malone 1.25 3.00
104 Tracy McGrady 1.25 3.00
105 Stephon Marbury .75 2.00
106 Chris Webber 1.00 2.50
107 Tim Duncan 1.50 4.00
108 Ray Allen 1.00 2.50
109 Antoine Walker 1.00 2.50
110 Steve Nash 1.25 3.00
111 Elton Brand 1.00 2.50
112 Rashard Lewis 1.00 2.50
113 Jerry Stackhouse .75 2.00
114 Shawn Marion 1.00 2.50
115 Mike Bibby 1.00 2.50
116 Tony Parker 1.00 2.50
117 Michael Finley 1.00 2.50
118 Allan Houston .75 2.00
119 Richard Hamilton .75 2.00
120 Ben Wallace 1.00 2.50
121 Reggie Miller 1.00 2.50
122 Richard Jefferson 1.00 2.50
123 Glenn Robinson .75 2.00
124 Rasheed Wallace 1.00 2.50
125 Gilbert Arenas 1.00 2.50
126 Jason Kidd 1.50 4.00
127 Latrell Sprewell .75 2.00
128 Kevin Garnett 2.00 5.00
129 Caron Butler 1.00 2.50
130 Pau Gasol 1.00 2.50
131 Alonzo Mourning 1.25 3.00
132 Gary Payton 1.00 2.50
133 Kirk Hinrich RC 4.00 10.00
134 T.J. Ford RC 4.00 10.00
135 Nick Collison RC 3.00 8.00
136 Keith McLeod RC 3.00 8.00
137 Jon Stefansson RC 3.00 8.00
138 Britton Johnsen RC 3.00 8.00
139 Matt Carroll RC 3.00 8.00
140 Linton Johnson RC 3.00 8.00
141 Francisco Elson RC 3.00 8.00
142 Willie Green RC 3.00 8.00
143 Kyle Korver RC 4.00 10.00
144 Theron Smith RC 3.00 8.00
145 Brandon Hunter RC 3.00 8.00
146 Josh Moore RC 3.00 8.00
147 Marquis Daniels RC 3.00 8.00
148 James Lang RC 3.00 8.00
149 Udonis Haslem RC 4.00 10.00
150 Alex Garcia RC 3.00 8.00
151 LeBron James JSY AU RC 700.00 1200.00
152 Darko Milicic JSY AU RC 6.00 15.00
153 Carmelo Anthony JSY AU RC 75.00 150.00
154 Chris Bosh JSY AU RC 30.00 80.00
155 Dwyane Wade JSY AU RC 150.00 300.00
156 Chris Kaman JSY AU RC 8.00 20.00
157 Jarvis Hayes JSY AU RC 5.00 12.00
158 Mickael Pietrus JSY AU RC 5.00 12.00
159 Dahntay Jones JSY AU RC 5.00 12.00
160 Marcus Banks JSY AU RC 5.00 12.00
161 Luke Ridnour JSY AU RC 6.00 15.00
162 Reece Gaines JSY AU RC 5.00 12.00
163 Troy Bell JSY AU RC 5.00 12.00
164 Mike Sweetney JSY AU RC 5.00 12.00
165 David West JSY AU RC 6.00 15.00
166 Aleksandar Pavlovic JSY AU RC 4.00 10.00
167 Mo Williams JSY AU RC 6.00 15.00
168 Boris Diaw JSY AU RC 5.00 12.00
169 Zoran Planinic JSY AU RC 4.00 10.00
170 Travis Outlaw JSY AU RC 5.00 12.00
171 Brian Cook JSY AU RC 4.00 10.00
172 Jerome Beasley JSY AU RC 4.00 10.00
173 Ndudi Ebi JSY AU RC 4.00 10.00
174 Kendrick Perkins JSY AU RC 6.00 15.00
175 Leandro Barbosa JSY AU RC 5.00 12.00
176 Josh Howard JSY AU RC 4.00 10.00
177 Maciej Lampe JSY AU RC 4.00 10.00
178 Jason Kapono JSY AU RC 4.00 10.00
179 Luke Walton JSY AU RC 4.00 10.00
180 Slavko Vranes JSY AU RC 4.00 10.00
181 Zarko Cabarkapa JSY AU RC 4.00 10.00
182 Travis Hansen JSY AU RC 4.00 10.00
183 Steve Blake JSY AU RC 5.00 12.00
184 Zaur Pachulia JSY AU RC 4.00 10.00
185 Keith Bogans JSY AU RC 4.00 10.00
186 Michael Jordan JSY AU/23 500.00 800.00
187 Kobe Bryant JSY AU/25 150.00 300.00
188 Kevin Garnett JSY AU/150 50.00 100.00
189 Richard Jefferson JSY AU/215 10.00 25.00
190 Gilbert Arenas JSY AU/215 10.00 25.00
191 Antawn Jamison JSY AU/215 10.00 25.00
192 Tracy McGrady JSY AU/50 25.00 60.00
193 Steve Francis JSY AU/100 15.00 40.00
194 Yao Ming JSY AU/100 30.00 60.00
195 Amare Stoudemire JSY AU/215 20.00 50.00
196 Shareef Abdur-Rahim JSY AU/34210.00 25.00
197 Shane Battier JSY AU/280 10.00 25.00
198 Tony Parker JSY AU/200 10.00 25.00
199 Andre Miller JSY AU/215 10.00 25.00
200 Shawn Marion JSY AU/265 10.00 25.00
201 Richard Hamilton JSY AU/215 10.00 25.00
202 Lamar Odom JSY AU/215 10.00 25.00
203 Jerry Stackhouse JSY AU/215 10.00 25.00
204 Antonio McDyess JSY AU/230 10.00 25.00
205 Manu Ginobili JSY AU/215 15.00 40.00
206 Drew Gooden JSY AU/215 10.00 25.00

2003-04 SPx Spectrum

Randomly inserted in packs, this 206-card set parallels the base SPx set where cards 1-185 are sequentially numbered to 25 and cards 186-206 are numbered one of one.

*1-90 SINGLES: 5X TO 12X BASE HI
*91-132 SINGLES: 2.5X TO 6X BASE HI
*133-150 RCs: 1X TO 2.5X BASE HI
*151-156 RCs: .75X TO 2X BASE HI
*157-165 RCs: 1X TO 2.5X BASE HI
*166-185 RCs: 1.25X TO 3X BASE HI
9 Michael Jordan 100.00 200.00
60 Grant Hill 12.50 30.00
94 Michael Jordan 100.00 200.00
151 LeBron James JSY AU 2000.00 3000.00
153 Carmelo Anthony JSY AU 300.00 600.00
154 Chris Bosh JSY AU 150.00 300.00
155 Dwyane Wade JSY AU 400.00 800.00

2003-04 SPx Winning Materials

Randomly seeded at the rate of one in 18, this 42-card set features a horizontal design where player photos appear on the left and swatches of game-worn memorabilia appear in the center.

WM1 Shaquille O'Neal SP 10.00 25.00
WM2 Paul Pierce 5.00 12.00
WM3 Anfernee Hardaway 6.00 15.00
WM4 Nene 3.00 8.00
WM5 Jay Williams 2.50 6.00
WM6 Tony Parker 4.00 10.00
WM7 Stephon Marbury 3.00 8.00
WM8 Gary Payton 4.00 10.00
WM9 Vlade Divac 3.00 8.00
WM10 Reggie Miller SP 8.00 20.00
WM11 Jermaine O'Neal 4.00 10.00
WM12 Baron Davis 4.00 10.00
WM13 Jamal Mashburn 3.00 8.00
WM14 Darius Miles 2.50 6.00
WM15 David Robinson 6.00 15.00
WM16 Kwame Brown 2.50 6.00
WM17 Karl Malone 5.00 12.00
WM18 Joe Smith 3.00 8.00
WM19 Steve Nash 5.00 12.00
WM20 Richard Jefferson 4.00 10.00
WM21 Antonio McDyess 3.00 8.00
WM22 Caron Butler 4.00 10.00
WM23 Andre Miller 3.00 8.00
WM24 Shane Battier 3.00 8.00
WM25 Steve Francis 4.00 10.00
WM26 Elton Brand 4.00 10.00
WM27 Lamar Odom 4.00 10.00
WM28 Jason Richardson 4.00 10.00
WM29 Antawn Jamison 4.00 10.00
WM30 Kurt Thomas 2.50 6.00
WM31 Pau Gasol 4.00 10.00
WM32 Allen Iverson 6.00 15.00
WM33 Jason Kidd 6.00 15.00
WM34 Dirk Nowitzki 6.00 15.00
WM35 Chris Webber 4.00 10.00
WM36 Amare Stoudemire 6.00 15.00
WM37 Tracy McGrady 5.00 12.00
WM38 Tim Duncan 6.00 15.00
WM39 Kevin Garnett 8.00 20.00
WM40 LeBron James SP 50.00 120.00
WM41 Kobe Bryant SP 15.00 40.00
WM42 Michael Jordan SP 40.00 100.00

2003-04 SPx Winning Materials Autographs

Randomly seeded in packs, this 15-card set parallels the design of the base Winning Materials insert set enhanced with a second swatch of memorabilia, authentic player autographs and sequential numbering to 100.

AJ Antawn Jamison 10.00 25.00
AM Andre Miller 8.00 20.00
CB Caron Butler 10.00 25.00
DW Dajuan Wagner 8.00 20.00
JM Jerome Moiso 8.00 20.00
JT Jamaal Tinsley 8.00 20.00
KB Kobe Bryant 125.00 250.00
MA Marko Jaric 8.00 20.00
MB Mike Bibby 15.00 40.00
NH Nene 8.00 20.00
PS Peja Stojakovic 15.00 40.00
RH Richard Hamilton 10.00 25.00
RJ Richard Jefferson 8.00 20.00
SF Steve Francis 15.00 40.00
YM Yao Ming 30.00 80.00

2003-04 SPx Winning Materials Combos

Randomly inserted at the rate of one in 18, this 42-card set places one player on the left and another on the right with a swatch of game worn material from each. An autographed version of the set was also produced where cards are sequentially numbered to 10.

WC1 Pau Gasol 5.00 12.00
Stromile Swift
WC2 Marko Jaric 5.00 12.00
Andre Miller
WC3 Peja Stojakovic 6.00 15.00
Mike Bibby
WC4 Richard Jefferson 6.00 15.00
Jason Kidd
WC5 Gilbert Arenas 4.00 10.00
Jason Richardson
WC6 Tony Parker 5.00 12.00
Rasho Nesterovic
WC7 Marcus Fizer 4.00 10.00
Tyson Chandler
WC8 Tracy McGrady 8.00 20.00
Amare Stoudemire
WC9 Kevin Garnett 8.00 20.00
Wally Szczerbiak
WC10 Brad Miller 5.00 12.00
Reggie Miller
WC11 Cuttino Mobley 4.00 10.00
Steve Francis
WC12 Michael Finley 5.00 12.00
Steve Nash
WC13 Dirk Nowitzki 5.00 12.00
Eduardo Najera
WC14 Desmond Mason 4.00 10.00
Gary Payton
WC15 Julius Erving 12.50 30.00
Magic Johnson
WC16 Andrei Kirilenko 5.00 12.00
Karl Malone
WC17 Jalen Rose 4.00 10.00
Eddy Curry
WC18 Juwan Howard 4.00 10.00
Nene
WC19 Keith Van Horn 4.00 10.00
Aaron McKie
WC20 Carlos Boozer 4.00 10.00
Chris Mihm
WC21 Corey Maggette 4.00 10.00
Michael Olowokandi
WC22 Derek Fisher 10.00 25.00
Kobe Bryant
WC23 Larry Hughes 4.00 10.00
Kwame Brown
WC24 Mike Miller 4.00 10.00
Shane Battier
WC25 Quentin Richardson 4.00 10.00
Lamar Odom
WC26 Theo Ratliff 4.00 10.00
Jason Terry
WC27 Shareef Abdur-Rahim 4.00 10.00
Jason Terry
WC28 Peja Stojakovic 5.00 12.00
Brad Miller
WC29 Dikembe Mutombo 4.00 10.00
Brandon Armstrong
WC30 Darius Miles 4.00 10.00
Carlos Boozer
WC31 Baron Davis 4.00 10.00
David Wesley
WC32 Elton Brand 4.00 10.00
Corey Maggette
WC33 Ray Allen 4.00 10.00
Rashard Lewis
WC34 Kenyon Martin 4.00 10.00
Dikembe Mutombo
WC35 Andrei Kirilenko 4.00 10.00
DeShawn Stevenson
WC36 Anfernee Hardaway 5.00 12.00
Joe Johnson
WC37 Chauncey Billups 4.00 10.00
Richard Hamilton
WC38 Chris Webber 4.00 10.00
Hedo Turkoglu
WC39 Jamaal Magloire 4.00 10.00
Jamal Mashburn
WC40 DerMarr Johnson 4.00 10.00
Jason Terry
WC41 LeBron James SP 30.00 80.00
Darko Milicic
WC42 Kobe Bryant SP 40.00 100.00
Michael Jordan

2003-04 SPx Winning Materials Combos Autographs

This six-card set is a partial parallel of the Winning Materials Combos set enhanced with autographs and sequential numbering to 10.

2004-05 SPx

Released in November 2004, this 168 card set features veteran players on cards 1-90, rookies serially numbered to 1999 on cards 91-111, rookies serially numbered to 99 on cards 112-117, jersey/autographed rookies serially numbered to 1999 on cards 118-139, jersey/autographed rookies serially numbered to 750 on cards 140-147, and veteran flashback autograph on cards 148-168. Every card in the set is horizontally designed. SPx was packaged in 18 pack boxes where packs contained four cards and carried a SRP of $6.99.

COMP.SET w/o SP's (90) 25.00 60.00
1 Antoine Walker .50 1.25
2 Al Harrington .40 1.00
3 Boris Diaw .40 1.00
4 Paul Pierce .60 1.50
5 Ricky Davis .40 1.00
6 Gary Payton .50 1.25
7 Jahidi White .30 .75
8 Jason Kapono .30 .75
9 Gerald Wallace .50 1.25
10 Eddy Curry .40 1.00
11 Kirk Hinrich .50 1.25
12 Tyson Chandler .40 1.00
13 LeBron James 3.00 8.00
14 Drew Gooden .40 1.00
15 Dajuan Wagner .30 .75
16 Dirk Nowitzki .75 2.00
17 Michael Finley .50 1.25
18 Jerry Stackhouse .40 1.00
19 Carmelo Anthony 1.00 2.50
20 Kenyon Martin .50 1.25
21 Nene .40 1.00
22 Chauncey Billups .50 1.25
23 Richard Hamilton .40 1.00
24 Ben Wallace .50 1.25
25 Mike Dunleavy .40 1.00
26 Jason Richardson .50 1.25
27 Derek Fisher .40 1.00
28 Yao Ming 1.00 2.50
29 Jim Jackson .30 .75
30 Tracy McGrady .60 1.50
31 Jermaine O'Neal .50 1.25
32 Reggie Miller .50 1.25
33 Stephen Jackson .40 1.00
34 Elton Brand .50 1.25
35 Corey Maggette .40 1.00
36 Chris Kaman .50 1.25
37 Kobe Bryant 2.50 6.00
38 Chris Mihm .30 .75
39 Lamar Odom .50 1.25
40 Pau Gasol .50 1.25
41 Jason Williams .40 1.00
42 Bonzi Wells .30 .75
43 Shaquille O'Neal 1.25 3.00
44 Dwyane Wade 1.50 4.00
45 Eddie Jones .40 1.00
46 Michael Redd .50 1.25
47 Desmond Mason .40 1.00
48 T.J. Ford .40 1.00
49 Latrell Sprewell .40 1.00
50 Kevin Garnett 1.00 2.50
51 Sam Cassell .40 1.00
52 Richard Jefferson .50 1.25
53 Alonzo Mourning .60 1.50
54 Jason Kidd .75 2.00
55 Jamal Mashburn .40 1.00
56 Baron Davis .50 1.25
57 Jamaal Magloire .30 .75
58 Allan Houston .40 1.00
59 Jamal Crawford .40 1.00
60 Stephon Marbury .40 1.00
61 Cuttino Mobley .40 1.00
62 Hedo Turkoglu .50 1.25
63 Steve Francis .50 1.25
64 Glenn Robinson .40 1.00
65 Allen Iverson .75 2.00
66 Aaron McKie .30 .75
67 Amare Stoudemire .60 1.50
68 Steve Nash .60 1.50
69 Shawn Marion .50 1.25
70 Shareef Abdur-Rahim .50 1.25
71 Damon Stoudamire .40 1.00
72 Zach Randolph .50 1.25
73 Peja Stojakovic .50 1.25
74 Chris Webber .50 1.25
75 Mike Bibby .50 1.25
76 Tony Parker .50 1.25
77 Tim Duncan .75 2.00
78 Manu Ginobili .60 1.50
79 Ronald Murray .30 .75
80 Ray Allen .50 1.25
81 Rashard Lewis .50 1.25
82 Chris Bosh .50 1.25
83 Vince Carter .75 2.00
84 Jalen Rose .40 1.00
85 Andrei Kirilenko .40 1.00
86 Carlos Boozer .50 1.25
87 Carlos Arroyo .40 1.00
88 Gilbert Arenas .50 1.25
89 Jarvis Hayes .30 .75
90 Antawn Jamison .50 1.25
91 Matt Freije RC 2.50 6.00
92 Horace Jenkins RC 2.50 6.00
93 Luis Flores RC 2.50 6.00
94 Jared Reiner RC 2.50 6.00
95 D.J. Mbenga RC 2.50 6.00
96 Pape Sow RC 2.50 6.00
97 Erik Daniels RC 2.50 6.00
98 Arthur Johnson RC 2.50 6.00
99 John Edwards RC 2.50 6.00
100 Andre Barrett RC 2.50 6.00
101 Romain Sato RC 2.50 6.00
102 Tim Pickett RC 2.50 6.00
103 Bernard Robinson RC 2.50 6.00
104 Justin Reed RC 2.50 6.00
105 Andres Nocioni RC 2.50 6.00
106 Awvee Storey RC 2.50 6.00
107 Damien Wilkins RC 2.50 6.00
108 Nenad Krstic JSY AU RC 4.00 10.00
109 Viktor Khryapa RC 2.50 6.00
110 Royal Ivey RC 2.50 6.00
111 Antonio Burks RC 2.50 6.00
112 Robert Swift RC 12.00 30.00
113 Trevor Ariza RC 12.00 30.00
114 Chris Duhon RC 12.00 30.00
115 Beno Udrih RC 12.00 30.00
116 Pavel Podkolzine RC 12.00 30.00
117 Emeka Okafor RC 20.00 50.00
118 Yuta Tabuse JSY AU RC 8.00 20.00
119 Andre Emmett JSY AU RC 4.00 10.00
120 Sasha Vujacic JSY AU RC 4.00 10.00
121 Lionel Chalmers JSY AU RC 4.00 10.00
122 J.R. Smith JSY AU RC 8.00 20.00
123 Dorell Wright JSY AU RC 6.00 15.00
124 Jameer Nelson JSY AU RC 5.00 12.00
125 Andris Biedrins JSY AU RC 5.00 12.00
126 Jackson Vroman JSY AU RC 4.00 10.00
127 Anderson Varejao JSY AU RC 5.00 12.00
128 Delonte West JSY AU RC 5.00 12.00
129 Tony Allen JSY AU RC 5.00 12.00
130 Kevin Martin JSY AU RC 5.00 12.00
131 Rafael Araujo JSY AU RC 4.00 10.00
132 David Harrison JSY AU RC 4.00 10.00
133 Kris Humphries JSY AU RC 4.00 10.00
134 Al Jefferson JSY AU RC 10.00 25.00
135 Kirk Snyder JSY AU RC 4.00 10.00
136 Peter J.Ramos JSY AU RC 4.00 10.00
137 Luke Jackson JSY AU RC 4.00 10.00
138 Donta Smith JSY AU RC 4.00 10.00
139 Josh Smith JSY AU RC 8.00 20.00
140 Sebastian Telfair JSY AU RC 6.00 15.00
141 Andre Iguodala JSY AU RC 10.00 25.00
142 Luol Deng JSY AU RC 12.00 30.00
143 Josh Childress JSY AU RC 6.00 15.00
144 Devin Harris JSY AU RC 10.00 25.00
145 Shaun Livingston JSY AU RC 6.00 15.00
146 Ben Gordon JSY AU RC 8.00 20.00
147 Dwight Howard JSY AU RC 75.00 150.00
149 Pau Gasol AU 12.50 30.00
150 Jason Kidd AU 20.00 50.00
151 Richard Hamilton AU 15.00 40.00
152 Amare Stoudemire AU 15.00 40.00
153 Chauncey Billups AU 12.50 30.00
154 Mike Bibby AU 12.50 30.00
155 Jason Richardson AU 12.50 30.00
156 LeBron James AU SP 150.00 300.00
157 Larry Bird AU SP 75.00 150.00
158 Reggie Miller AU 30.00 80.00
159 Kevin Garnett AU 40.00 100.00
160 Baron Davis AU 12.50 30.00
162 Magic Johnson AU SP 50.00 120.00
163 Tracy McGrady AU 40.00 80.00
164 Yao Ming AU 25.00 60.00
165 Michael Jordan AU SP 300.00 500.00
166 Andrei Kirilenko AU 12.50 30.00
167 Stephon Marbury AU 12.50 30.00
168 Shawn Marion AU 12.50 30.00

2004-05 SPx Spectrum

Randomly inserted in packs, this 168-card set parallels the base SPx set enhanced with sequential numbering to 25 on cards 1-147 and one of one numberings for cards 148-168.

*1-90: 4X TO 10X BASE HI
*91-111: 1.25X TO 3X BASE HI
*112-117: .25X TO .6X BASE HI
*108, 118-139: 1.5X TO 4X BASE HI
*140-147: 1X TO 2.5X BASE HI
118 Yuta Tabuse JSY AU 60.00 150.00
122 J.R. Smith JSY AU 50.00 120.00
128 Delonte West JSY AU 40.00 100.00
130 Kevin Martin JSY AU 40.00 100.00
134 Al Jefferson JSY AU 100.00 200.00
139 Josh Smith JSY AU 75.00 150.00
141 Andre Iguodala JSY AU 100.00 200.00
142 Luol Deng JSY AU 100.00 200.00
144 Devin Harris JSY AU 75.00 150.00
146 Ben Gordon JSY AU 40.00 100.00

2004-05 SPx Throwback

Randomly inserted in packs, this 120-card set parallels the base set with yellow highlights. Cards 1-90 are serially numbered to 120, and the rookie cards were inserted at the rate of one in 252. A Throwback Spectrum parallel was also inserted and these cards are serially numbered one of one.

*1-90 THROW: .75X TO 2X BASE HI
*118-139 JSY RCs: .75X TO 2X BASE HI
*140-147 JSY RCs: .5X TO 1.25X BASE HI
118 Yuta Tabuse JSY AU 30.00 80.00
134 Al Jefferson JSY AU 40.00 100.00
139 Josh Smith JSY AU 25.00 60.00
141 Andre Iguodala JSY AU 30.00 80.00
142 Luol Deng JSY AU 15.00 40.00
144 Devin Harris JSY AU 20.00 50.00
146 Ben Gordon JSY AU 20.00 50.00

2004-05 SPx Winning Materials

Seeded in packs at the rate of one in 15, this 40-card set is horizontally designed with a player photo on the left and an "X" shaped swatch of memorabilia on the right.

AI Allen Iverson 5.00 12.00
AK Andrei Kirilenko 2.50 6.00
AS Amare Stoudemire 4.00 10.00
BD Baron Davis 3.00 8.00
BM Brad Miller 3.00 8.00
BW Ben Wallace 3.00 8.00
CA Carmelo Anthony 6.00 15.00
CB Carlos Boozer 3.00 8.00
DA David Wesley 2.00 5.00
DH Dwight Howard 8.00 20.00
DM Darius Miles 2.00 5.00
DN Dirk Nowitzki 5.00 12.00
DS DeShawn Stevenson 2.00 5.00
DW Dajuan Wagner 2.00 5.00
EB Elton Brand 3.00 8.00
EC Eddy Curry 2.50 6.00
JC Jamal Crawford 2.50 6.00
JK Jason Kidd 5.00 12.00
JM Jamaal Magloire 2.00 5.00
JO Jermaine O'Neal 3.00 8.00
KB Kobe Bryant 10.00 25.00
KG Kevin Garnett 6.00 15.00
LJ LeBron James SP 12.00 30.00
MB Mike Bibby 3.00 8.00
MJ Michael Jordan SP 30.00 80.00
PG Pau Gasol 3.00 8.00
PP Paul Pierce 4.00 10.00
PS Peja Stojakovic 3.00 8.00
RA Ray Allen 3.00 8.00
RJ Richard Jefferson 3.00 8.00
RM Reggie Miller 3.00 8.00
SA Shareef Abdur-Rahim 2.50 6.00
SM Shawn Marion 3.00 8.00
SN Steve Nash 4.00 10.00
SO Shaquille O'Neal 8.00 20.00
ST Stephon Marbury 2.50 6.00
TD Tim Duncan 5.00 12.00
TM Tracy McGrady 4.00 10.00
WS Wally Szczerbiak 2.50 6.00
YM Yao Ming 6.00 15.00

2004-05 SPx Winning Materials Autographs

Serially numbered to 100, this 34-card set parallels the design of the Winning Materials insert enhanced with an autograph.

AI Andre Iguodala 15.00 40.00
AK Andrei Kirilenko 10.00 25.00
AS Amare Stoudemire 25.00 60.00
BD Baron Davis 15.00 40.00
BG Ben Gordon 12.00 30.00
BM Brad Miller 10.00 25.00
CA Carmelo Anthony 25.00 60.00
CB Carlos Boozer 10.00 25.00
DE Devin Harris 15.00 40.00
DF Derek Fisher 12.50 30.00
DH Dwight Howard 60.00 120.00
JA Jason Richardson 10.00 25.00
JC Jamal Crawford 10.00 25.00
JK Jason Kidd 20.00 50.00
JR Jalen Rose 12.50 30.00
JS John Stockton 60.00 150.00
KB Kobe Bryant 100.00 200.00
KG Kevin Garnett 50.00 100.00
LB Larry Bird 75.00 150.00
LD Luol Deng 15.00 40.00
LJ LeBron James 200.00 400.00
LO Lamar Odom 12.50 30.00
MA Magic Johnson 75.00 150.00
MJ Michael Jordan 400.00 650.00
PP Paul Pierce 15.00 40.00
RJ Richard Jefferson 10.00 25.00
RM Reggie Miller 40.00 80.00
SA Shareef Abdur-Rahim 10.00 25.00
SL Shaun Livingston 10.00 25.00
SM Shawn Marion 12.50 30.00
ST Stephon Marbury 15.00 40.00
TE Sebastian Telfair 10.00 25.00
TM Tracy McGrady 30.00 80.00
YM Yao Ming 30.00 80.00

2004-05 SPx Winning Materials Combos

Inserted at the rate of one in 15, this 42-card set uses some of the design elements from the Winning Materials set but places two players with swatches of memorabilia. An Autographed version sequentially numbered to 10 was also inserted.

UNPRICED AUTO PRINT RUN 10 SETS
AJ Antoine Walker 5.00 12.00
Josh Smith
AK Antawn Jamison 5.00 12.00
Kwame Brown
AM Carmelo Anthony 6.00 15.00
Andre Miller
BA Chris Bosh 5.00 12.00
Rafael Araujo
BJ Kobe Bryant 20.00 50.00
LeBron James
BO Kobe Bryant 10.00 25.00
Lamar Odom
BP Marcus Banks 5.00 12.00
Gary Payton
DG Luol Deng 8.00 20.00
Ben Gordon
DM Baron Davis 5.00 12.00
Jamaal Magloire
DP Tim Duncan 8.00 20.00
Tony Parker
ES Andre Emmett 5.00 12.00
Stromile Swift
FM Steve Francis 5.00 12.00
Cuttino Mobley
GC Kevin Garnett 8.00 20.00
Sam Cassell
GD Manu Ginobili 10.00 25.00
Tim Duncan
GM Kevin Garnett 10.00 25.00
Tracy McGrady
II Allen Iverson 8.00 20.00
Andre Iguodala
JB Michael Jordan 40.00 100.00
Kobe Bryant
JC John Stockton 10.00 25.00
Carlos Boozer
JJ LeBron James SP 60.00 150.00
Michael Jordan
JS LeBron James 15.00 40.00
Eric Snow
KA Kenyon Martin 5.00 12.00
Andre Miller
KB Andrei Kirilenko SP 5.00 12.00
Carlos Boozer
KC Karl Malone 5.00 12.00
Caron Butler
KJ Jason Kidd 6.00 15.00
Richard Jefferson
LA LeBron James SP 15.00 40.00
Carmelo Anthony
MB Corey Maggette 5.00 12.00
Elton Brand
MC Stephon Marbury 5.00 12.00
Jamal Crawford
MH Stephon Marbury 5.00 12.00
Allan Houston
MM Yao Ming 8.00 20.00
Tracy McGrady
MS Shawn Marion 6.00 15.00
Amare Stoudemire
MT Darius Miles 5.00 12.00
Sebastian Telfair
NH Dirk Nowitzki 6.00 15.00
Devin Harris
NW Jameer Nelson 5.00 12.00
Delonte West
OH Shaquille O'Neal 8.00 20.00
Dwight Howard
OM Jermaine O'Neal 6.00 15.00
Reggie Miller
PJ Paul Pierce 8.00 20.00
Al Jefferson
PM Pau Gasol 5.00 12.00
Mike Miller
RD Jason Richardson 5.00 12.00
Mike Dunleavy
SB Peja Stojakovic 5.00 12.00
Mike Bibby
SD Shareef Abdur-Rahim 5.00 12.00
Darius Miles
SN Amare Stoudemire 8.00 20.00
Steve Nash
TH Jamal Tinsley 5.00 12.00
David Harrison

2005-06 SPx

Released in December 2005, SPx consists of a 154-card set where cards 1-90 picture veterans on all-foil cards with an "X" design behind full color player photos, cards 91-120 picture rookies on an all foil cards stock and are sequentially numbered to 1499, cards 121-146 are horizontally designed and picture rookie players with a swatch of memorabilia and an embedded cut signature serially numbered to 1499 (with a few exceptions--card 124 is serially numbered to 99, card 133 is serially numbered to 99, card 136 is serially numbered to 1458 and card 141 is serially numbered to 99), and cards 147-154 picture rookies, same design as cards 121-146, but are serially numbered to 750. SPx was packaged in 18-pack boxes where packs contain four cards and carried an initial SRP of $6.99.

COMP.SET w/o SP's (90) 20.00 50.00
1 Josh Childress .40 1.00
2 Josh Smith .50 1.25
3 Al Harrington .40 1.00
4 Antoine Walker .40 1.00
5 Gary Payton .50 1.25
6 Paul Pierce .60 1.50
7 Kareem Rush .30 .75
8 Emeka Okafor .50 1.25
9 Gerald Wallace .50 1.25
10 Michael Jordan 4.00 10.00
11 Kirk Hinrich .50 1.25
12 Ben Gordon .60 1.50
13 Drew Gooden .40 1.00
14 Larry Hughes .40 1.00
15 LeBron James 2.50 6.00
16 Zydrunas Ilgauskas .40 1.00
17 Dirk Nowitzki .75 2.00
18 Jason Terry .40 1.00
19 Michael Finley .50 1.25
20 Carmelo Anthony 1.00 2.50
21 Kenyon Martin .50 1.25
22 Andre Miller .40 1.00
23 Ben Wallace .50 1.25
24 Chauncey Billups .50 1.25
25 Richard Hamilton .40 1.00
26 Troy Murphy .40 1.00
27 Jason Richardson .50 1.25
28 Baron Davis .50 1.25
29 Tracy McGrady .60 1.50
30 Yao Ming .60 1.50
31 David Wesley .30 .75
32 Jermaine O'Neal .50 1.25
33 Jamaal Tinsley .30 .75
34 Ron Artest .50 1.25
35 Corey Maggette .40 1.00
36 Elton Brand .50 1.25
37 Bobby Simmons .30 .75
38 Caron Butler .50 1.25
39 Kobe Bryant 2.50 6.00
40 Lamar Odom .50 1.25
41 Mike Miller .50 1.25
42 Jason Williams .40 1.00
43 Pau Gasol .50 1.25
44 Dwyane Wade 1.25 3.00
45 Eddie Jones .40 1.00
46 Shaquille O'Neal 1.00 2.50
47 Desmond Mason .30 .75
48 Keith Van Horn .40 1.00
49 Michael Redd .50 1.25
50 Kevin Garnett 1.00 2.50
51 Latrell Sprewell .40 1.00
52 Sam Cassell .50 1.25
53 Vince Carter .75 2.00

Jason Kidd .75 2.00
Richard Jefferson .50 1.25
Dan Dickau .30 .75
Jamaal Magloire .30 .75
J.R. Smith .50 1.25
Jamal Crawford .40 1.00
Stephon Marbury .40 1.00
Quentin Richardson .40 1.00
Dwight Howard 1.00 2.50
Grant Hill .60 1.50
Steve Francis .50 1.25
Allen Iverson .75 2.00
Andre Iguodala .50 1.25
Chris Webber .50 1.25
Amare Stoudemire .50 1.25
Shawn Marion .50 1.25
Steve Nash .60 1.50
Damon Stoudamire .40 1.00
Shareef Abdur-Rahim .40 1.00
Zach Randolph .40 1.00
Brad Miller .50 1.25
Mike Bibby .50 1.25
Peja Stojakovic .50 1.25
Manu Ginobili .50 1.25
Tim Duncan .75 2.00
Tony Parker .50 1.25
Rashard Lewis .50 1.25
Ray Allen .50 1.25
Luke Ridnour .40 1.00
Rafer Alston .30 .75
Jalen Rose .50 1.25
Chris Bosh .50 1.25
Andrei Kirilenko .40 1.00
Carlos Boozer .50 1.25
Matt Harpring .40 1.00
Antawn Jamison .50 1.25
Gilbert Arenas .50 1.25
Bracey Wright RC 2.00 5.00
Chris Taft RC 2.00 5.00
Jose Calderon RC 2.00 5.00
Dijon Thompson RC 2.00 5.00
Esteban Batista RC 2.00 5.00
Linas Kleiza RC 2.00 5.00
Earl Barron RC 2.00 5.00
Ike Diogu RC 2.00 5.00
Alan Anderson RC 2.00 5.00
0 Shavlik Randolph RC 2.00 5.00
1 Eddie Basden RC 2.00 5.00
2 Johan Petro RC 2.00 5.00
3 Ersan Ilyasova RC 2.50 6.00
4 Dwayne Jones RC 2.00 5.00
5 Aaron Miles RC 2.00 5.00
6 James Singleton RC 2.00 5.00
7 Von Wafer RC 2.00 5.00
8 Josh Powell RC 2.00 5.00
9 Yaroslav Korolev RC 2.00 5.00
0 Ronnie Price RC 2.00 5.00
1 Andray Blatche RC 2.50 6.00
2 Robert Whaley RC 2.00 5.00
3 Donell Taylor RC 2.00 5.00
4 Orien Greene RC 2.00 5.00
5 Lawrence Roberts RC 2.00 5.00
6 Amir Johnson RC 2.00 5.00
7 Matt Walsh RC 2.00 5.00
8 Fabricio Oberto RC 2.00 5.00
9 Arvydas Macijauskas RC 2.00 5.00
20 Alex Acker RC 2.00 5.00
21 Salim Stoudamire JSY AU RC 4.00 10.00
22 Francisco Garcia JSY AU RC 5.00 12.00
23 Daniel Ewing JSY AU RC 4.00 10.00
24 Nate Robinson JSY AU/199 RC 30.00 75.00
25 Luther Head JSY AU RC 4.00 10.00
26 Louis Williams JSY AU RC 6.00 15.00
27 Jarrett Jack JSY AU RC 4.00 10.00
28 Jason Maxiell JSY AU/1453 RC 4.00 10.00
29 Wayne Simien JSY AU RC 4.00 10.00
30 Julius Hodge JSY AU RC 4.00 10.00
31 C.J. Miles JSY AU RC 5.00 12.00
32 Andrew Bynum JSY AU RC 15.00 40.00
33 Monta Ellis JSY AU/99 RC 100.00 200.00
34 Joey Graham JSY AU RC 4.00 10.00
35 Antoine Wright JSY AU RC 4.00 10.00
36 Sean May JSY AU/1458 RC 4.00 10.00
37 Channing Frye JSY AU RC 5.00 12.00
38 Gerald Green JSY AU RC 5.00 12.00
39 Sarunas Jasikevicius JSY AU RC 4.00 10.00
40 Danny Granger JSY AU RC 8.00 20.00
41 Hakim Warrick JSY AU/99 RC 15.00 40.00
42 David Lee JSY AU RC 6.00 15.00
43 Brandon Bass JSY AU RC 5.00 12.00
44 Ryan Gomes JSY AU RC 4.00 10.00
45 Martynas Andriuskevicius JSY AU RC4.00 10.00
46 Travis Diener JSY AU RC 4.00 10.00
47 Martell Webster JSY AU RC 6.00 15.00
48 Rashad McCants JSY AU RC 6.00 15.00
49 Deron Williams JSY AU RC 25.00 60.00
50 Charlie Villanueva JSY AU RC 8.00 20.00
51 Raymond Felton JSY AU RC 10.00 25.00
52 Andrew Bogut JSY AU RC 10.00 25.00
53 Chris Paul JSY AU RC 75.00 150.00
54 Marvin Williams JSY AU RC 8.00 20.00

2005-06 SPx Spectrum

ound at random in packs, this 154-card set parallels he base SPx set enhanced with holofoil highlights and equential numbering to 25.
1-90 SPECTRUM: 4X TO 10X BASE HI
91-120 RCs: 1.25X TO 3X BASE HI
121-146 RCs: 1.5X TO 4X BASE HI
147-154 RCs: 1X TO 2.5X BASE HI
124, 133, 141 RC SP: .75X TO 2X BASE HI
0 Michael Jordan 50.00 120.00
32 Andrew Bynum JSY AU 60.00 150.00
33 Monta Ellis JSY AU 150.00 300.00
49 Deron Williams JSY AU 100.00 200.00
51 Raymond Felton JSY AU 50.00 120.00
52 Andrew Bogut JSY AU 50.00 120.00
53 Chris Paul JSY AU 250.00 500.00

2005-06 SPx Flashback Fabrics

Randomly seeded in packs, this 40-card set features a horizontal design with player photos on the left, a jersey swatch on the right and an embedded signature towards the bottom of the card. Though print runs or odds were never released, it is believed 25 cards for each player are in circulation.
UNPRICED SPECTRUM PRINT RUN ONE SET
AK Andrei Kirilenko 8.00 20.00
BD Baron Davis 8.00 20.00
BG Ben Gordon 10.00 25.00
BO Carlos Boozer 8.00 20.00
BW Ben Wallace 8.00 20.00
CA Carmelo Anthony 20.00 50.00
CB Chauncey Billups 10.00 25.00
CH Chris Bosh 10.00 25.00
DH Dwight Howard 15.00 40.00
DR David Robinson 25.00 60.00
GA Gilbert Arenas 10.00 25.00
HO Hakeem Olajuwon 20.00 50.00
IT Isiah Thomas 20.00 50.00
JC Josh Childress 8.00 20.00
JK Jason Kidd 12.50 30.00
JR J.R. Smith 8.00 20.00
JS John Stockton 50.00 120.00
KH Kirk Hinrich 10.00 25.00
LB Larry Bird 60.00 120.00
LD Luol Deng 8.00 20.00
LJ LeBron James SP 200.00 400.00
LO Lamar Odom 10.00 25.00
MA Magic Johnson 50.00 100.00
MB Mike Bibby 8.00 20.00
MJ Michael Jordan SP 300.00 600.00
PG Pau Gasol 8.00 20.00
PP Paul Pierce 12.50 30.00
PS Peja Stojakovic 8.00 20.00
QR Quentin Richardson 8.00 20.00
RH Richard Hamilton 8.00 20.00
RJ Richard Jefferson 8.00 20.00
SE Sean May 8.00 20.00
SL Shaun Livingston 8.00 20.00
SN Steve Nash 30.00 80.00
ST Stephon Marbury 8.00 20.00
TM Tracy McGrady 15.00 40.00
UH Udonis Haslem 8.00 20.00
VC Vince Carter 15.00 40.00
WF Walt Frazier 20.00 50.00
YM Yao Ming 15.00 40.00

2005-06 SPx SPxcitement Rookies

Serially numbered to 1999, this 20-card set features full color player action photos, and a border along the left that morphs into a SPxcitement logo along the bottom of the card.
*SPECTRUM: 1.25X TO 3X BASE HI
SPECTRUM PRINT RUN 99 SER.#'d SETS
UNPRICED AUTO PRINT RUN 5 SETS
XCR1 Chris Paul 4.00 10.00
XCR2 Marvin Williams 1.25 3.00
XCR3 Andrew Bogut 1.50 4.00
XCR4 Hakim Warrick 1.25 3.00
XCR5 Rashad McCants 1.00 2.50
XCR6 Raymond Felton 1.50 4.00
XCR7 Sean May 1.00 2.50
XCR8 Charlie Villanueva 1.25 3.00
XCR9 Gerald Green 1.25 3.00
XCR10 Danny Granger 2.00 5.00
XCR11 Deron Williams 2.50 6.00
XCR12 Martell Webster 1.00 2.50
XCR13 Andrew Bynum 3.00 8.00
XCR14 Channing Frye 1.25 3.00
XCR15 Joey Graham 1.00 2.50
XCR16 Ike Diogu 1.00 2.50
XCR17 Antoine Wright 1.00 2.50
XCR18 Julius Hodge 1.00 2.50
XCR19 Nate Robinson 1.25 3.00
XCR20 Jarrett Jack 1.00 2.50

2005-06 SPx SPxcitement Veterans

Limited to 999 serially numbered copies, this 40-card set places full color player photos in the center of a design that features a colored square in the background set to match team colors with white borders along the top and bottom and black borders on the sides.
*SPECTRUM: 1X TO 2.5X BASE HI
SPECTRUM PRINT RUN 99 SER.#'d SETS
UNPRICED AUTO PRINT RUN 5 SETS
XCV1 Gary Payton 1.00 2.50
XCV2 Paul Pierce 1.25 3.00
XCV3 Michael Jordan 8.00 20.00
XCV4 Ben Gordon 1.00 2.50
XCV5 Kirk Hinrich 1.00 2.50
XCV6 LeBron James 5.00 12.00
XCV7 Carmelo Anthony 2.00 5.00
XCV8 Ben Wallace 1.00 2.50
XCV9 Chauncey Billups 1.00 2.50
XCV10 Richard Hamilton .75 2.00
XCV11 Baron Davis 1.00 2.50
XCV12 Tracy McGrady 1.25 3.00
XCV13 Yao Ming 1.25 3.00
XCV14 Kobe Bryant 5.00 12.00
XCV15 Lamar Odom 1.00 2.50
XCV16 Pau Gasol 1.00 2.50
XCV17 Jason Williams .75 2.00
XCV18 Michael Redd 1.00 2.50
XCV19 Jason Kidd 1.50 4.00
XCV20 Richard Jefferson 1.00 2.50
XCV21 J.R. Smith 1.00 2.50
XCV22 Stephon Marbury .75 2.00
XCV23 Dwight Howard 2.00 5.00
XCV24 Jameer Nelson .75 2.00
XCV25 Andre Iguodala 1.00 2.50
XCV26 Kyle Korver .75 2.00
XCV27 Quentin Richardson .75 2.00
XCV28 Steve Nash 1.25 3.00
XCV29 Damon Stoudamire .75 2.00
XCV30 Mike Bibby 1.00 2.50
XCV31 Peja Stojakovic 1.00 2.50
XCV32 Chris Bosh 1.00 2.50
XCV33 Andrei Kirilenko .75 2.00
XCV34 Antawn Jamison 1.00 2.50
XCV35 Carlos Boozer 1.00 2.50
XCV36 Hakeem Olajuwon 1.25 3.00
XCV37 Isiah Thomas 1.00 2.50
XCV38 Dennis Rodman 1.50 4.00
XCV39 Scottie Pippen 1.50 4.00
XCV40 John Stockton 2.00 5.00

2005-06 SPx Winning Materials

Inserted in packs at the rate of one in 18, this 41-card set is horizontally designed with a player photo in the middle and a two swatches of memorabilia, one on each side of the player.
*SPECTRUM: .75X TO 2X BASE HI
SPECTRUM PRINT RUN 25 SER.#'d SETS
AB Andrew Bogut 5.00 12.00
AS Amare Stoudemire 3.00 8.00
BD Baron Davis 3.00 8.00
CA Carmelo Anthony 6.00 15.00
CB Chris Bosh 3.00 8.00
CP Chris Paul 8.00 20.00
CW Chris Webber 3.00 8.00
DE Deron Williams 6.00 15.00
DN Dirk Nowitzki 5.00 12.00
EB Elton Brand 3.00 8.00
GA Gilbert Arenas 3.00 8.00
GG Gerald Green 4.00 10.00
GH Grant Hill 4.00 10.00
JK Jason Kidd 5.00 12.00
JO Jermaine O'Neal 3.00 8.00
JR Jason Richardson 3.00 8.00
KB Kobe Bryant 10.00 25.00
KG Kevin Garnett 6.00 15.00
KM Kenyon Martin 3.00 8.00
LJ LeBron James 10.00 25.00
MF Michael Finley 3.00 8.00
MG Manu Ginobili 3.00 8.00
MJ Michael Jordan 30.00 80.00
MW Marvin Williams 4.00 10.00
PG Pau Gasol 3.00 8.00
PP Paul Pierce 4.00 10.00
PS Peja Stojakovic 3.00 8.00
QR Quentin Richardson 2.50 6.00
RA Ray Allen 3.00 8.00
RL Rashard Lewis 3.00 8.00
SF Steve Francis 3.00 8.00
SM Shawn Marion 3.00 8.00
SN Steve Nash 4.00 10.00
SO Shaquille O'Neal 6.00 15.00
ST Stephon Marbury 2.50 6.00
TD Tim Duncan 5.00 12.00
TM Tracy McGrady 4.00 10.00
TP Tony Parker 3.00 8.00
VC Vince Carter 5.00 12.00
YM Yao Ming 4.00 10.00
ZI Zydrunas Ilgauskas 2.50 6.00

2005-06 SPx Winning Materials Autographs

Serially numbered to either 50 or 25 copies, this 18-card set parallels the design of the Winning Materials set enhanced with player autographs. See checklist for serial number details.
AB Andrew Bogut/50 20.00 50.00
BG Ben Gordon/50 15.00 40.00
CA Carmelo Anthony/25 30.00 80.00
CB Chauncey Billups/50 15.00 40.00
CH Chris Bosh/50 15.00 40.00
CP Chris Paul/50 60.00 150.00
DE Deron Williams/50 25.00 60.00
GG Gerald Green/50 15.00 40.00
KH Kirk Hinrich/50 12.50 30.00
LJ LeBron James/50 200.00 350.00
MB Mike Bibby/50 12.50 30.00
MJ Michael Jordan/25 400.00 700.00
MW Marvin Williams/50 15.00 40.00
PS Peja Stojakovic/50 12.50 30.00
QR Quentin Richardson/50 12.50 30.00
SN Steve Nash/25 60.00 120.00

2005-06 SPx Winning Materials Combos

Inserted at the rate of one in 18, this 42-card set features two players and two swatches of memorabilia.
*SPECTRUM: .75X TO 2X BASE HI
SPECTRUM PRINT RUN 25 SER.#'d SETS
UNPRICED AUTO PRINT RUN 10 SETS
AL Ray Allen / Rashard Lewis 4.00 10.00
AN Carmelo Anthony / Nene 5.00 12.00
BB Kobe Bryant / Caron Butler 8.00 20.00
BH Chauncey Billups / Richard Hamilton 6.00 15.00
BP Brad Miller / Peja Stojakovic 4.00 10.00
BS Ryan Bowen / Stromile Swift 4.00 10.00
CL Sam Cassell / Shaun Livingston 4.00 10.00
DC Luol Deng / Tyson Chandler 4.00 10.00
DG Tim Duncan / Manu Ginobili 6.00 15.00
DW Samuel Dalembert / Chris Webber 4.00 10.00
FN Steve Francis / Jameer Nelson 4.00 10.00
GC Devean George / Brian Cook 4.00 10.00
GH Ben Gordon / Kirk Hinrich 4.00 10.00
GS Kevin Garnett / Wally Szczerbiak 6.00 15.00
HH Dwight Howard / Grant Hill 6.00 15.00
HM Allan Houston / Stephon Marbury 4.00 10.00
HW Udonis Haslem / Dorell Wright 4.00 10.00
JA Antawn Jamison / Gilbert Arenas 4.00 10.00
JI LeBron James / Zydrunas Ilgauskas 10.00 25.00
JJ Michael Jordan SP / LeBron James 40.00 100.00
KB Andrei Kirilenko / Carlos Boozer 4.00 10.00
KJ Jason Kidd / Richard Jefferson 5.00 12.00
KM Linas Kleiza / Kenyon Martin 4.00 10.00
MB Corey Maggette / Elton Brand 4.00 10.00
MS Shawn Marion / Amare Stoudemire 5.00 12.00
MY Tracy McGrady / Yao Ming 6.00 15.00
NR Steve Nash / Shawn Marion 5.00 12.00
NT Dirk Nowitzki / Jason Terry 4.00 10.00
OT Jermaine O'Neal / Jamaal Tinsley 4.00 10.00
PJ Paul Pierce / Al Jefferson 4.00 10.00
PU Tony Parker / Beno Udrih 4.00 10.00
RA Jalen Rose / Rafael Araujo 4.00 10.00
RD Jason Richardson / Baron Davis 4.00 10.00
RM Zach Randolph / Darius Miles 4.00 10.00
RR Luke Ridnour / Vladimir Radmanovic 4.00 10.00
RW Kareem Rush / Gerald Wallace 4.00 10.00
SM J.R. Smith / Jamaal Magloire 4.00 10.00
TH Jason Terry / Devin Harris 4.00 10.00
WP Antoine Walker / Gary Payton 4.00 10.00
WS Dajuan Wagner / Eric Snow 4.00 10.00
WW David Wesley / Charlie Ward 4.00 10.00
YO Yao Ming / Shaquille O'Neal 6.00 15.00

2006-07 SPx

Released in late February 2007, SPx features a 152-card set where cards 1-100 utilize a foil-board design with an "X" in the background and picture veterans, cards 101-121 utilize a similar design and picture rookies serially numbered to 1999, cards 122-127 utilize a horizontal design including both a cut signature and a jersey swatch and picture rookies serially numbered to 299, and cards 127-152 utilize the same horizontal design and picture rookies serially numbered to 1199. SPx is packaged in 18-pack boxes of four cards each and carried a suggested retail price of $6.99 per pack.
COMP.SET w/o RC's (100) 25.00 60.00
1 Joe Johnson .50 1.25
2 Salim Stoudamire .30 .75
3 Marvin Williams .50 1.25
4 Tony Allen .30 .75
5 Al Jefferson .50 1.25
6 Paul Pierce .60 1.50
7 Raymond Felton .60 1.50
8 Emeka Okafor .50 1.25
9 Gerald Wallace .50 1.25
10 Tyson Chandler .40 1.00
11 Ben Gordon .50 1.25
12 Michael Jordan 4.00 10.00
13 Drew Gooden .40 1.00
14 Zydrunas Ilgauskas .40 1.00
15 LeBron James 2.50 6.00
16 Devin Harris .50 1.25
17 Dirk Nowitzki .75 2.00
18 Jason Terry .40 1.00
19 Carmelo Anthony .60 1.50
20 Andre Miller .40 1.00
21 Eduardo Najera .30 .75
22 Chauncey Billups .50 1.25
23 Richard Hamilton .40 1.00
24 Ben Wallace .50 1.25
25 Rasheed Wallace .50 1.25
26 Baron Davis .50 1.25
27 Troy Murphy .30 .75
28 Jason Richardson .50 1.25
9 Rafer Alston .30 .75
30 Tracy McGrady .60 1.50
31 Yao Ming .60 1.50
32 Sarunas Jasikevicius .40 1.00
33 Jermaine O'Neal .50 1.25
34 Peja Stojakovic .50 1.25
35 Elton Brand .50 1.25
36 Sam Cassell .50 1.25
37 Chris Kaman .40 1.00
38 Shaun Livingston .30 .75
39 Kobe Bryant 2.50 6.00
40 Lamar Odom .50 1.25
41 Ronny Turiaf .40 1.00
42 Pau Gasol .50 1.25
43 Mike Miller .50 1.25
44 Damon Stoudamire .40 1.00
45 Shaquille O'Neal 1.00 2.50
46 Wayne Simien .30 .75
47 Dwyane Wade 1.25 3.00
48 Jason Williams .40 1.00
49 Andrew Bogut .50 1.25
50 T.J. Ford .40 1.00
51 Jamaal Magloire .30 .75
52 Michael Redd .50 1.25
53 Ricky Davis .40 1.00
54 Kevin Garnett 1.00 2.50
55 Rashad McCants .30 .75
56 Vince Carter .60 1.50
57 Richard Jefferson .50 1.25
58 Jason Kidd .75 2.00
59 Speedy Claxton .30 .75
60 Desmond Mason .30 .75
61 Chris Paul 1.00 2.50
62 Steve Francis .50 1.25
63 Channing Frye .40 1.00
64 Stephon Marbury .40 1.00
65 Nate Robinson .50 1.25
66 Carlos Arroyo .40 1.00
67 Grant Hill .60 1.50
68 Dwight Howard .75 2.00
69 Jameer Nelson .40 1.00
70 Andre Iguodala .50 1.25
71 Allen Iverson .60 1.50
72 Chris Webber .50 1.25
73 Boris Diaw .40 1.00
74 Shawn Marion .50 1.25
75 Steve Nash .60 1.50
76 Amare Stoudemire .50 1.25
77 Zach Randolph .40 1.00
78 Sebastian Telfair .30 .75
79 Martell Webster .40 1.00
80 Shareef Abdur-Rahim .40 1.00
81 Ron Artest .50 1.25
82 Mike Bibby .50 1.25
83 Brad Miller .50 1.25
84 Tim Duncan .75 2.00
85 Michael Finley .50 1.25
86 Manu Ginobili .50 1.25
87 Tony Parker .50 1.25
88 Ray Allen .50 1.25
89 Rashard Lewis .50 1.25
90 Chris Wilcox .30 .75
91 Chris Bosh .50 1.25
92 Joey Graham .30 .75
93 Charlie Villanueva .50 1.25
94 Carlos Boozer .50 1.25
95 Andrei Kirilenko .40 1.00
96 C.J. Miles .30 .75
97 Deron Williams .75 2.00
98 Gilbert Arenas .50 1.25
99 Caron Butler .50 1.25
100 Antawn Jamison .50 1.25
101 Adam Morrison RC 2.50 6.00
102 Alexander Johnson RC 2.00 5.00
103 Damir Markota RC 2.00 5.00
104 J.J. Redick RC 2.50 6.00
105 Will Blalock RC 2.00 5.00
106 Leon Powe RC 2.00 5.00
107 Thabo Sefolosha RC 2.50 6.00
108 Pops Mensah-Bonsu RC 2.00 5.00
109 Robert Hite RC 2.00 5.00
110 Tarence Kinsey RC 2.00 5.00
111 Vassilis Spanoulis RC 2.00 5.00
112 Yakhouba Diawara RC 2.00 5.00
113 Daniel Gibson RC 2.50 6.00
114 Hassan Adams RC 2.00 5.00
115 James Augustine RC 2.00 5.00
116 Chris Quinn RC 2.00 5.00
117 Mardy Collins RC 2.00 5.00
118 Paul Millsap RC 3.00 8.00
119 P.J. Tucker RC 2.00 5.00
120 Ryan Hollins RC 2.00 5.00
121 Saer Sene RC 2.00 5.00
122 Andrea Bargnani JSY AU RC 15.00 40.00
123 LaMarcus Aldridge JSY AU RC 25.00 60.00
124 Tyrus Thomas JSY AU RC 12.00 30.00
125 Shelden Williams JSY AU RC 10.00 25.00
126 Brandon Roy JSY AU RC 25.00 60.00
127 Randy Foye JSY AU RC 12.00 30.00
128 Paul Davis JSY AU RC 5.00 12.00
129 Solomon Jones JSY AU RC 5.00 12.00
130 David Noel JSY AU RC 5.00 12.00
131 Allan Ray JSY AU RC 5.00 12.00
132 Bobby Jones JSY AU RC 5.00 12.00
133 Cedric Simmons JSY AU RC 5.00 12.00
134 Dee Brown JSY AU RC 5.00 12.00
135 Shawne Williams JSY AU RC 5.00 12.00
136 Hilton Armstrong JSY AU RC 5.00 12.00
137 James White JSY AU RC 5.00 12.00
138 Jordan Farmar JSY AU RC 5.00 12.00
139 Josh Boone JSY AU RC 5.00 12.00
140 Kyle Lowry JSY AU RC 6.00 15.00
141 Marcus Williams JSY AU RC 5.00 12.00
142 Maurice Ager JSY AU RC 5.00 12.00
143 Patrick O'Bryant JSY AU RC 5.00 12.00
144 Quincy Douby JSY AU RC 5.00 12.00
145 Rajon Rondo JSY AU RC 30.00 75.00
146 Renaldo Balkman JSY AU RC 5.00 12.00
147 Rodney Carney JSY AU RC 5.00 12.00
148 Ronnie Brewer JSY AU RC 6.00 15.00
149 Rudy Gay JSY AU RC 10.00 25.00
150 Shannon Brown JSY AU RC 8.00 20.00
151 Steve Novak JSY AU RC 5.00 12.00
152 Craig Smith JSY AU RC 5.00 12.00

2006-07 SPx Spectrum

*1-100 SPECTRUM: 4X TO 10X BASE HI
*101-121 RCs: 1.25X TO 3X BASE HI
*122-127 RCs: 1.25X TO 3X BASE HI
*128-152 RCs: 1.25X TO 3X BASE HI
SPECTRUM PRINT RUN 25 SER.#'d SETS
12 Michael Jordan 60.00 150.00
39 Kobe Bryant 30.00 80.00
126 Brandon Roy JSY AU 100.00 250.00
145 Rajon Rondo JSY AU 125.00 250.00

2006-07 SPx Flashback Fabrics

APPROXIMATE ODDS 1:72
UNPRICED SPECTRUM PRINT RUN ONE SET
FFAB Andrew Bynum 5.00 12.00
FFAI Allen Iverson 4.00 10.00
FFAJ Antawn Jamison 3.00 8.00
FFAK Andrei Kirilenko 2.50 6.00
FFAW Antoine Walker 2.50 6.00
FFBB Bruce Bowen 2.00 5.00
FFBG Ben Gordon 3.00 8.00
FFBM Brad Miller 3.00 8.00
FFCB Carlos Boozer 3.00 8.00
FFCF Channing Frye 2.50 6.00
FFCW Chris Webber 3.00 8.00
FFDG Drew Gooden 2.50 6.00
FFDH Devin Harris 3.00 8.00
FFDM Desmond Mason 2.00 5.00
FFDR Dennis Rodman 10.00 25.00
FFGA Gilbert Arenas 3.00 8.00
FFGE Devean George 2.00 5.00
FFGG George Gervin 5.00 12.00
FFGH Grant Hill 4.00 10.00
FFID Ike Diogu 2.00 5.00
FFJC Jamal Crawford 2.50 6.00
FFJN Jameer Nelson 2.50 6.00
FFJR Jason Richardson 3.00 8.00
FFJS John Stockton 8.00 20.00
FFJT Jason Terry 2.50 6.00
FFLD Luol Deng 3.00 8.00
FFLH Luther Head 2.50 6.00
FFLO Lamar Odom 3.00 8.00
FFMG Manu Ginobili 3.00 8.00
FFMJ Magic Johnson 8.00 20.00
FFQR Quentin Richardson 2.50 6.00
FFRJ Richard Jefferson 3.00 8.00
FFRO David Robinson 6.00 15.00
FFRW Rasheed Wallace 3.00 8.00
FFSD Samuel Dalembert 2.00 5.00
FFSE Sean Elliott 3.00 8.00
FFSJ Sarunas Jasikevicius 2.50 6.00
FFSM Sean May 2.00 5.00
FFWF Walt Frazier 5.00 12.00
FFWR Antoine Wright 2.00 5.00
FFWS Wally Szczerbiak 2.50 6.00

2006-07 SPx Flashback Fabrics Autographs

APPROXIMATE ODDS 1:144
UNPRICED SPECTRUM PRINT RUN ONE SET
FFBD Baron Davis 6.00 15.00
AFFAB Andrew Bogut 8.00 20.00
AFFAI Andre Iguodala 8.00 20.00
AFFAJ Al Jefferson 6.00 15.00
AFFBK Bernard King 10.00 25.00
AFFBL Bill Laimbeer 10.00 25.00
AFFCA Carmelo Anthony 20.00 50.00
AFFCB Chris Bosh 12.50 30.00
AFFCD Clyde Drexler 25.00 60.00
AFFCM Corey Maggette 6.00 15.00
AFFDG Danny Granger 6.00 15.00
AFFDW Deron Williams 12.50 30.00
AFFFG Francisco Garcia 6.00 15.00
AFFHO Hakeem Olajuwon 20.00 50.00
AFFHW Hakim Warrick 6.00 15.00
AFFJG Joey Graham 6.00 15.00
AFFJS J.R. Smith 6.00 15.00
AFFKK Kyle Korver 8.00 20.00
AFFLB Larry Bird 60.00 120.00
AFFLH Larry Hughes 8.00 20.00
AFFLJ LeBron James 150.00 300.00
AFFMD Marquis Daniels 6.00 15.00
AFFMJ Michael Jordan 300.00 600.00
AFFMW Marvin Williams 6.00 15.00
AFFNR Nate Robinson 6.00 15.00
AFFPP Paul Pierce 10.00 25.00
AFFPS Peja Stojakovic 8.00 20.00
AFFRA Ron Artest 8.00 20.00
AFFRF Raymond Felton 6.00 15.00
AFFRP Robert Parish 12.50 30.00
AFFSK Steve Kerr 20.00 50.00
AFFSL Shaun Livingston 6.00 15.00
AFFSN Steve Nash 40.00 80.00
AFFST Sebastian Telfair 6.00 15.00
AFFTC Tyson Chandler 6.00 15.00
AFFTM Tracy McGrady 30.00 60.00
AFFVC Vince Carter 25.00 50.00
AFFWE Martell Webster 6.00 15.00
AFFYK Yaroslav Korolev 6.00 15.00
AFFYM Yao Ming 15.00 40.00

2006-07 SPx SPxcitement

COMPLETE SET 30.00 75.00
APPROXIMATE ODDS ONE PER PACK
UNPRICED AUTO PRINT RUN 10 SETS
SPX1 Andrea Bargnani 1.25 3.00
SPX2 LaMarcus Aldridge 2.00 5.00
SPX3 Adam Morrison 1.00 2.50
SPX4 Tyrus Thomas 1.00 2.50
SPX5 Shelden Williams .75 2.00
SPX6 Brandon Roy 2.00 5.00
SPX7 Rudy Gay 1.25 3.00
SPX8 Saer Sene .75 2.00
SPX9 Hilton Armstrong .75 2.00
SPX10 Thabo Sefolosha 1.00 2.50
SPX11 Ronnie Brewer 1.00 2.50
SPX12 Cedric Simmons .75 2.00
SPX13 Rodney Carney .75 2.00
SPX14 Quincy Douby .75 2.00
SPX15 Rajon Rondo 3.00 8.00
SPX16 Renaldo Balkman .75 2.00
SPX17 Steve Novak .75 2.00
SPX18 Maurice Ager .75 2.00
SPX19 Mardy Collins .75 2.00
SPX20 James White .75 2.00
SPX21 Craig Smith .75 2.00
SPX22 Bobby Jones .75 2.00
SPX23 Dee Brown .75 2.00
SPX24 Will Blalock .75 2.00
SPX25 Daniel Gibson 1.00 2.50
SPX26 Michael Jordan 6.00 15.00
SPX27 Larry Bird 2.50 6.00
SPX28 Bill Russell 1.50 4.00
SPX29 Julius Erving 1.50 4.00
SPX30 Moses Malone .75 2.00
SPX31 Robert Parish .75 2.00
SPX32 Magic Johnson 2.00 5.00
SPX33 Walt Frazier .75 2.00
SPX34 Dennis Rodman 1.25 3.00
SPX35 Kareem Abdul-Jabbar 1.25 3.00
SPX36 Hakeem Olajuwon 1.00 2.50
SPX37 Zach Randolph .60 1.50
SPX38 Clyde Drexler 1.00 2.50
SPX39 David Robinson 1.25 3.00
SPX40 John Stockton 1.25 3.00
SPX41 Marvin Williams .75 2.00
SPX42 Joe Johnson .75 2.00
SPX43 Paul Pierce 1.00 2.50
SPX44 Emeka Okafor .75 2.00
SPX45 Raymond Felton 1.00 2.50
SPX46 Ben Gordon .75 2.00
SPX47 Kirk Hinrich .75 2.00
SPX48 LeBron James 4.00 10.00
SPX49 Zydrunas Ilgauskas .60 1.50
SPX50 Dirk Nowitzki 1.25 3.00
SPX51 Jason Terry .60 1.50
SPX52 Carmelo Anthony 1.00 2.50
SPX53 Kenyon Martin .75 2.00
SPX54 Chauncey Billups .75 2.00
SPX55 Richard Hamilton .60 1.50
SPX56 Ben Wallace .75 2.00
SPX57 Baron Davis .75 2.00
SPX58 Jason Richardson .75 2.00
SPX59 Tracy McGrady 1.00 2.50
SPX60 Yao Ming 1.00 2.50
SPX61 Jermaine O'Neal .75 2.00
SPX62 Peja Stojakovic .75 2.00
SPX63 Elton Brand .75 2.00
SPX64 Sam Cassell .75 2.00
SPX65 Kobe Bryant 4.00 10.00
SPX66 Pau Gasol .75 2.00
SPX67 Shaquille O'Neal 1.50 4.00
SPX68 Dwyane Wade 2.00 5.00
SPX69 Gary Payton .75 2.00
SPX70 Kevin Garnett 1.50 4.00
SPX71 Vince Carter 1.00 2.50
SPX72 Jason Kidd 1.25 3.00
SPX73 Chris Paul 1.50 4.00
SPX74 Stephon Marbury .60 1.50
SPX75 Grant Hill 1.00 2.50
SPX76 Dwight Howard 1.25 3.00
SPX77 Allen Iverson 1.00 2.50
SPX78 Chris Webber .75 2.00
SPX79 Shawn Marion .75 2.00
SPX80 Amare Stoudemire .75 2.00
SPX81 Steve Nash 1.00 2.50
SPX82 Ron Artest .75 2.00
SPX83 Tim Duncan 1.25 3.00
SPX84 Manu Ginobili .75 2.00
SPX85 Tony Parker .75 2.00
SPX86 Ray Allen .75 2.00
SPX87 Chris Bosh .75 2.00
SPX88 Charlie Villanueva .75 2.00
SPX89 Andrei Kirilenko .60 1.50
SPX90 Gilbert Arenas .75 2.00
SPX91 Antawn Jamison .75 2.00
SPX92 Carlos Boozer .75 2.00
SPX93 Deron Williams 1.25 3.00
SPX94 Rashard Lewis .75 2.00
SPX95 Michael Finley .75 2.00
SPX96 Josh Howard .60 1.50
SPX97 Boris Diaw .60 1.50
SPX98 Andre Iguodala .75 2.00
SPX99 Mike Bibby .75 2.00

2006-07 SPx Winning Combos

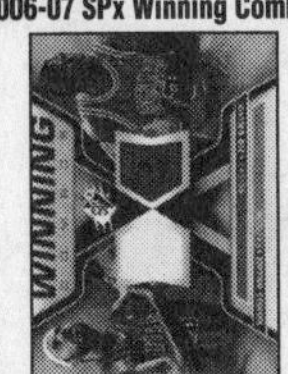

APPROXIMATE ODDS 1:20
WCAP Ray Allen / Johan Petro 5.00 12.00
WCBB Kwame Brown / Andrew Bynum 3.00 8.00
WCBG Mike Bibby / Francisco Garcia 3.00 8.00
WCBM Kobe Bryant / Tracy McGrady 8.00 20.00
WCBV Chris Bosh / Charlie Villanueva 3.00 8.00
WCCD Tyson Chandler / Luol Deng 3.00 8.00
WCCF Eddy Curry / Channing Frye 3.00 8.00
WCCR Jamal Crawford / Nate Robinson 3.00 8.00
WCDG Luol Deng / Ben Gordon 3.00 8.00
WCDH Marquis Daniels / Devin Harris 3.00 8.00
WCDI Samuel Dalembert / Andre Iguodala 3.00 8.00
WCDP Tim Duncan / Tony Parker 5.00 12.00
WCDR Baron Davis / Jason Richardson 3.00 8.00
WCGH Kevin Garnett 8.00 20.00

Dwight Howard		
WCGJ Danny Granger	3.00	8.00
Sarunas Jasikevicius		
WCGW Devean George	3.00	8.00
Luke Walton		
WCHB Richard Hamilton	3.00	8.00
Chauncey Billups		
WCHG Larry Hughes	3.00	8.00
Drew Gooden		
WCHN Grant Hill	3.00	8.00
Jameer Nelson		
WCHS Kirk Hinrich	3.00	8.00
Wayne Simien		
WCIK Zydrunas Ilgauskas	3.00	8.00
Nenad Krstic		
WCJA Al Jefferson	3.00	8.00
Tony Allen		
WCJB Antawn Jamison	3.00	8.00
Caron Butler		
WCJG Eddie Jones	3.00	8.00
Pau Gasol		
WCJJ Michael Jordan	40.00	100.00
LeBron James		
WCJW Richard Jefferson	3.00	8.00
Antoine Wright		
WCKC Jason Kidd	4.00	10.00
Vince Carter		
WCKW Andrei Kirilenko	3.00	8.00
Deron Williams		
WCMB Corey Maggette	3.00	8.00
Elton Brand		
WCMI Jamaal Magloire	3.00	8.00
Ersan Ilyasova		
WCMO Yao Ming	6.00	15.00
Shaquille O'Neal		
WCMR Stephon Marbury	3.00	8.00
Quentin Richardson		
WCNS Steve Nash	5.00	12.00
Amare Stoudemire		
WCOM Emeka Okafor	3.00	8.00
Sean May		
WCPD David West	3.00	8.00
Peja Stojakovic		
WCPM Paul Pierce	3.00	8.00
Shawn Marion		
WCRB Michael Redd	3.00	8.00
Andrew Bogut		
WCRD Zach Randolph	3.00	8.00
Juan Dixon		
WCSA Amare Stoudemire	5.00	12.00
Carmelo Anthony		
WCSH Stromile Swift	3.00	8.00
Luther Head		
WCSP J.R. Smith	4.00	10.00
Chris Paul		
WCSW Wally Szczerbiak	3.00	8.00
Delonte West		
WCTN Jason Terry	3.00	8.00
Dirk Nowitzki		
WCTO Jamaal Tinsley	3.00	8.00
Jermaine O'Neal		
WCTW Sebastian Telfair	3.00	8.00
Martell Webster		
WCWJ Dahntay Jones	3.00	8.00
Hakim Warrick		
WCWK Chris Webber	3.00	8.00
Kyle Korver		
WCWM Rashad McCants	3.00	8.00
Bracey Wright		
WCWS Antoine Walker	3.00	8.00
Wayne Simien		
WCWW Rasheed Wallace	3.00	8.00
Ben Wallace		

2006-07 SPx Winning Materials

RANDOM INSERTS IN PACKS

WMAI Andre Iguodala	3.00	8.00
WMAJ Al Jefferson	3.00	8.00
WMBD Baron Davis	3.00	8.00
WMBO Chris Bosh	3.00	8.00
WMBW Ben Wallace	3.00	8.00
WMCA Carmelo Anthony	4.00	10.00
WMCB Chauncey Billups	3.00	8.00
WMCF Channing Frye	2.50	6.00
WMCM Corey Maggette	2.50	6.00
WMCP Chris Paul	6.00	15.00
WMCV Charlie Villanueva	3.00	8.00
WMDG Drew Gooden	2.50	6.00
WMDH Dwight Howard	5.00	12.00
WMDJ Dahntay Jones	2.00	5.00
WMDN Dirk Nowitzki	5.00	12.00
WMDW Delonte West	2.50	6.00
WMEB Elton Brand	3.00	8.00
WMEO Emeka Okafor	3.00	8.00
WMGA Gilbert Arenas	3.00	8.00
WMGR Danny Granger	3.00	8.00
WMID Ike Diogu	2.00	5.00
WMJH Josh Howard	2.50	6.00
WMJK Jason Kidd	5.00	12.00
WMJO Jermaine O'Neal	3.00	8.00
WMKB Kobe Bryant	10.00	25.00
WMKG Kevin Garnett	6.00	15.00
WMLD Luol Deng	3.00	8.00
WMLH Luther Head	2.50	6.00
WMLJ LeBron James	10.00	25.00
WMMA Shawn Marion	3.00	8.00
WMMJ Michael Jordan	30.00	75.00
WMMR Michael Redd	3.00	8.00
WMNK Nenad Krstic	2.00	5.00
WMPG Pau Gasol	3.00	8.00
WMPP Paul Pierce	4.00	10.00
WMRA Ray Allen	3.00	8.00
WMRH Richard Hamilton	2.50	6.00
WMRW Rasheed Wallace	3.00	8.00
WMSD Samuel Dalembert	2.00	5.00
WMSL Shaun Livingston	2.00	5.00
WMSM Stephon Marbury	2.50	6.00
WMSN Steve Nash	4.00	10.00
WMSO Shaquille O'Neal	6.00	15.00
WMTD Tim Duncan	5.00	12.00
WMTM Tracy McGrady	4.00	10.00
WMTP Tony Parker	3.00	8.00
WMVC Vince Carter	4.00	10.00
WMWS Wally Szczerbiak	2.50	6.00
WMYM Yao Ming	4.00	10.00
WMZI Zydrunas Ilgauskas	2.50	6.00

2007-08 SPx

This 140-card set was released in December, 2007. The set was issued into the hobby in three-card packs which came 10 packs to a box and 10 boxes to a case. Cards numbered 1-90 feature veterans while cards 91-140 feature 2007-08 NBA rookies. In that grouping, cards numbered 101-140 have both a signature and a player-worn jersey swatch. The serial numbering for the rookies was arranged this way: Cards numbered 91-110 were issued to a stated print run of 299 serial numbered sets while cards 111-140 were issued to a stated print run of 825 serial numbered sets. SPx is packaged in 10-pack boxes where packs contain three cards and carried an initial SRP of $20.

COMP.SET w/o SP's (90)	25.00	50.00
UNPRICED SPECTRUM PRINT RUN 10 SETS		
1 Chauncey Billups	.50	1.25
2 Tayshaun Prince	.50	1.25
3 Richard Hamilton	.40	1.00
4 Rasheed Wallace	.50	1.25
5 Zydrunas Ilgauskas	.40	1.00
6 Larry Hughes	.40	1.00
7 LeBron James	2.50	6.00
8 T.J. Ford	.40	1.00
9 Andrea Bargnani	.60	1.50
10 Chris Bosh	.50	1.25
11 Shaquille O'Neal	1.00	2.50
12 Dwyane Wade	1.25	3.00
13 Udonis Haslem	.40	1.00
14 Ben Wallace	.50	1.25
15 Ben Gordon	.50	1.25
16 Luol Deng	.50	1.25
17 Kirk Hinrich	.50	1.25
18 Vince Carter	.60	1.50
19 Richard Jefferson	.50	1.25
20 Jason Kidd	.50	1.25
21 Gilbert Arenas	.50	1.25
22 Caron Butler	.50	1.25
23 Antawn Jamison	.50	1.25
24 Dwight Howard	.75	2.00
25 Jameer Nelson	.40	1.00
26 Jermaine O'Neal	.50	1.25
27 Danny Granger	.50	1.25
28 Mike Dunleavy	.40	1.00
29 Andre Iguodala	.50	1.25
30 Kyle Korver	.40	1.00
31 Gerald Wallace	.50	1.25
32 Emeka Okafor	.50	1.25
33 Jason Richardson	.50	1.25
34 Eddy Curry	.30	.75
35 Stephon Marbury	.40	1.00
36 Quentin Richardson	.40	1.00
37 David Lee	.40	1.00
38 Marvin Williams	.50	1.25
39 Josh Smith	.50	1.25
40 Joe Johnson	.50	1.25
41 Michael Redd	.50	1.25
42 Andrew Bogut	.50	1.25
43 Paul Pierce	.60	1.50
44 Al Jefferson	.50	1.25
45 Ray Allen	.50	1.25
46 Dirk Nowitzki	.60	1.50
47 Jerry Stackhouse	.40	1.00
48 Jason Terry	.40	1.00
49 Josh Howard	.40	1.00
50 Amare Stoudemire	.50	1.25
51 Steve Nash	.60	1.50
52 Leandro Barbosa	.40	1.00
53 Shawn Marion	.50	1.25
54 Tony Parker	.50	1.25
55 Tim Duncan	.75	2.00
56 Manu Ginobili	.50	1.25
57 Michael Finley	.50	1.25
58 Andrei Kirilenko	.40	1.00
59 Carlos Boozer	.50	1.25
60 Deron Williams	.75	2.00
61 Mehmet Okur	.30	.75
62 Tracy McGrady	.50	1.25
63 Yao Ming	.60	1.50
64 Carmelo Anthony	.60	1.50
65 Allen Iverson	.60	1.50
66 Marcus Camby	.30	.75
67 Kobe Bryant	2.50	6.00
68 Lamar Odom	.50	1.25
69 Baron Davis	.50	1.25
70 Al Harrington	.40	1.00
71 Stephen Jackson	.40	1.00
72 Elton Brand	.50	1.25
73 Corey Maggette	.40	1.00
74 Shaun Livingston	.30	.75
75 David West	.50	1.25
76 Chris Paul	1.00	2.50
77 Tyson Chandler	.40	1.00
78 Kevin Garnett	1.00	2.50
79 Ricky Davis	.40	1.00
80 Randy Foye	.50	1.25
81 Kevin Martin	.50	1.25
82 Ron Artest	.50	1.25
83 Mike Bibby	.50	1.25
84 Steve Francis	.50	1.25
85 Brandon Roy	.60	1.50
86 Jarrett Jack	.40	1.00
87 Delonte West	.40	1.00
88 Rashard Lewis	.40	1.00
89 Pau Gasol	.50	1.25
90 Mike Miller	.50	1.25
91 Greg Oden RC	8.00	20.00
92 Thaddeus Young RC	4.00	10.00
93 Brandan Wright RC	3.00	8.00
94 Yi Jianlian RC	5.00	12.00
95 Nick Young RC	5.00	12.00
96 Chris Richard RC	3.00	8.00
97 Marco Belinelli RC	3.00	8.00
98 Juan Carlos Navarro RC	3.00	8.00
99 Sammy Mejia RC	3.00	8.00
100 Kyrylo Fesenko RC	3.00	8.00
101 Kevin Durant JSY AU RC	250.00	400.00
102 Al Horford JSY AU RC	12.00	30.00
103 Mike Conley Jr. JSY AU RC	15.00	40.00
104 Jeff Green JSY AU RC	12.00	30.00
105 Corey Brewer JSY AU RC	12.00	30.00
106 Joakim Noah JSY AU RC	25.00	60.00
107 Spencer Hawes JSY AU RC	10.00	25.00
108 Acie Law JSY AU RC	10.00	25.00
109 Julian Wright JSY AU RC	10.00	25.00
110 Al Thornton JSY AU RC	10.00	25.00
111 Javaris Crittenton JSY AU RC	5.00	12.00
112 Daequan Cook JSY AU RC	5.00	12.00
113 Jared Dudley JSY AU RC	5.00	12.00
114 Wilson Chandler JSY AU RC	8.00	20.00
115 Morris Almond JSY AU RC	5.00	12.00
116 Arron Afflalo JSY AU RC	6.00	15.00
117 Alando Tucker JSY AU RC	5.00	12.00
118 Carl Landry JSY AU RC	5.00	12.00
119 Gabe Pruitt JSY AU RC	5.00	12.00
120 Marcus Williams JSY AU RC	5.00	12.00
121 Nick Fazekas JSY AU RC	5.00	12.00
122 Jermareo Davidson JSY AU RC	5.00	12.00
123 Josh McRoberts JSY AU RC	5.00	12.00
124 Glen Davis JSY AU RC	8.00	20.00
125 Adam Haluska JSY AU RC	5.00	12.00
126 Reyshawn Terry JSY AU RC	5.00	12.00
127 Jared Jordan JSY AU RC	5.00	12.00
128 Stephane Lasme JSY AU RC	5.00	12.00
129 Aaron Gray JSY AU RC	5.00	12.00
130 Taurean Green JSY AU RC	5.00	12.00
131 Demetris Nichols JSY AU RC	5.00	12.00
132 Herbert Hill JSY AU RC	5.00	12.00
133 Aaron Brooks JSY AU RC	5.00	12.00
134 D.J. Strawberry JSY AU RC	5.00	12.00
135 Dominic McGuire JSY AU RC	5.00	12.00
136 Jason Smith JSY AU RC	5.00	12.00
137 Sean Williams JSY AU RC	5.00	12.00
138 Derrick Byars JSY AU RC	5.00	12.00
139 Ramon Sessions JSY AU RC	8.00	20.00
140 Rodney Stuckey JSY AU RC	8.00	20.00

2007-08 SPx Radiance

*1-90 RADIANCE: 3X TO 8X BASE HI
*91-110 RC RAD: 1X TO 2.5X BASE HI
*111-140 RC RAD: 1.5X TO 4X BASE HI
RADIANCE PRINT RUN 25 SER.#'d SETS

101 Kevin Durant JSY AU	600.00	1100.00

2007-08 SPx Duel Scripts

PRINT RUN 10 TO 25 SER.#'d SETS
SOME UNPRICED DUE TO SCARCITY

BB Bruce Bowen/25	10.00	25.00
Leandro Barbosa		
BJ LeBron James/10	350.00	500.00
Kobe Bryant		
CJ Corey Brewer/25	12.50	30.00
Joakim Noah		
EB Larry Bird/25	100.00	200.00
Julius Erving		
GD Clyde Drexler/25	40.00	80.00
George Gervin		
HG Richard Hamilton/25	10.00	25.00
Daniel Gibson		
HH Richard Hamilton/25	20.00	40.00
Larry Hughes		
IJ Al Jefferson/25	20.00	40.00
Andre Iguodala		
JA LeBron James/25	225.00	350.00
Carmelo Anthony		
JE Michael Jordan/25	400.00	650.00
Julius Erving		
LM Larry Bird/25	150.00	300.00
Magic Johnson		
NA Norm Nixon/25	15.00	30.00
Nate Archibald		
NP Steve Nash/25	60.00	120.00
Tony Parker		
SJ Magic Johnson/25	100.00	200.00
John Stockton		
WR Bill Russell/25	125.00	250.00
Jerry West		

2007-08 SPx Endorsements

RANDOM INSERTS IN PACKS

AA Arron Afflalo	5.00	12.00
AH Al Horford	5.00	12.00
AI Andre Iguodala	4.00	10.00
AL Acie Law	4.00	10.00
BR Bill Russell	75.00	150.00
BW Bill Walton	8.00	20.00
CA Carmelo Anthony	15.00	30.00
CB Corey Brewer	5.00	12.00
CD Clyde Drexler	15.00	40.00
DH Dwight Howard	20.00	50.00
GG George Gervin	8.00	20.00
HO Hakeem Olajuwon	15.00	40.00
JG Jeff Green	5.00	12.00
JN Joakim Noah	12.00	30.00
JO Jermaine O'Neal	4.00	10.00
KB Kobe Bryant	80.00	200.00
KD Kevin Durant	100.00	200.00
LJ LeBron James	80.00	200.00
MC Mike Conley Jr.	6.00	15.00
MI Michael Jordan	200.00	400.00
RJ Richard Jefferson	4.00	10.00
SH Spencer Hawes	4.00	10.00
TM Tracy McGrady	10.00	25.00
TP Tony Parker	6.00	15.00
VC Vince Carter	15.00	40.00
WF Walt Frazier	10.00	25.00
YM Yao Ming	20.00	40.00

2007-08 SPx Flashback Fabrics

RANDOM INSERTS IN PACKS
*PARALLEL: 1X TO 2.5X BASE HI
PARALLEL PRINT RUN 25 SER.#'d SETS

AW Antoine Walker	2.00	5.00
BB Bruce Bowen	2.00	5.00
BD Boris Diaw	2.00	5.00
BU Caron Butler	2.50	6.00
CB Carlos Boozer	2.50	6.00
CV Charlie Villanueva	2.50	6.00
CW Chris Webber	2.50	6.00
DG Danny Granger	2.50	6.00
DN Dirk Nowitzki	3.00	8.00
DW Deron Williams	4.00	10.00
EO Emeka Okafor	2.50	6.00
GA Gilbert Arenas	2.50	6.00
JK Jason Kidd	2.50	6.00
JR Jason Richardson	2.50	6.00
JT Jason Terry	2.00	5.00
JW Jason Williams	2.00	5.00
KA Jason Kapono	2.00	5.00
KG Kevin Garnett	5.00	12.00
KM Kenyon Martin	2.50	6.00
LJ LeBron James	15.00	30.00
LO Lamar Odom	2.50	6.00
MA Stephon Marbury	2.00	5.00
MB Mike Bibby	2.50	6.00
MC Marcus Camby	2.00	5.00
MF Michael Finley	2.50	6.00
MO Alonzo Mourning	5.00	12.00
N Nene	2.00	5.00
PG Pau Gasol	2.50	6.00
PP Paul Pierce	3.00	8.00
PS Peja Stojakovic	2.50	6.00
RA Ray Allen	2.50	6.00
RL Rashard Lewis	2.00	5.00
RW Rasheed Wallace	2.50	6.00
SC Sam Cassell	2.50	6.00
SF Steve Francis	2.50	6.00
SM Shawn Marion	2.50	6.00
SO Shaquille O'Neal	5.00	12.00
TC Tyson Chandler	2.00	5.00
TD Tim Duncan	4.00	10.00
UH Udonis Haslem	2.00	5.00
ZR Zach Randolph	2.00	5.00

2007-08 SPx Flashback Fabrics Autographs

STATED PRINT RUN 10 TO 25 SER.#'d SETS
SOME UNPRICED DUE TO SCARCITY
UNPRICED PARALLEL PRINT RUN ONE TO 10 SETS

AD Adrian Dantley/25	8.00	20.00
AH Al Harrington/25	8.00	20.00
AI Andre Iguodala/25	8.00	20.00
AJ Al Jefferson/25	8.00	20.00
BD Baron Davis/25	12.50	30.00
BG Ben Gordon/25	12.50	30.00
BO Chris Bosh/25	15.00	40.00
BR Bill Russell/25	75.00	150.00
CD Clyde Drexler/25	25.00	50.00
CP Chris Paul/25	30.00	60.00
DH Dwight Howard/25	40.00	80.00
HO Hakeem Olajuwon/25	20.00	50.00
JA Antawn Jamison/25	8.00	20.00
JE Julius Erving/25	40.00	100.00
JO Jermaine O'Neal/25	8.00	20.00
JS John Stockton/25	50.00	100.00
LB Larry Bird/25	75.00	150.00
LJ LeBron James/25.	125.00	250.00
MI Michael Jordan/25	350.00	650.00
MJ Magic Johnson/25	50.00	100.00
MR Michael Ray Richardson/25	8.00	20.00
NA Nate Archibald/25	15.00	30.00
PA Tony Parker/25	15.00	30.00
QR Quentin Richardson/25	8.00	20.00
RH Richard Hamilton/25	15.00	30.00
RJ Richard Jefferson/25	8.00	20.00
RO Brandon Roy/25	15.00	30.00
RT Reggie Theus/25	15.00	30.00
SK Steve Kerr/25	15.00	30.00
SN Steve Nash/25	40.00	100.00
TC Tyson Chandler/25	8.00	20.00
TM Tracy McGrady/25	20.00	50.00
TP Tayshaun Prince/25	8.00	20.00
VC Vince Carter/25	15.00	40.00
WF Walt Frazier/25	15.00	30.00
YM Yao Ming/25	25.00	50.00

2007-08 SPx Freshman Orientation

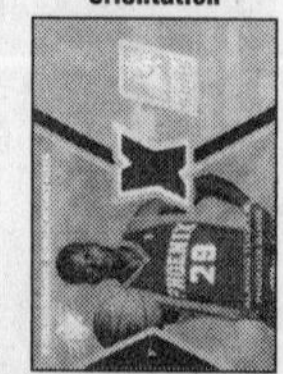

APPROXIMATE ODDS TWO PER BOX
*PATCHES: 1X TO 2.5X BASE HI
PATCH PRINT RUN 25 SER.#'d SETS

AA Arron Afflalo	3.00	8.00
AB Aaron Brooks	2.50	6.00
AH Al Horford	3.00-	8.00
AL Acie Law	2.50	6.00
AT Al Thornton	2.50	6.00
BW Brandan Wright	2.50	6.00
CB Corey Brewer	3.00	8.00
CL Carl Landry	2.50	6.00
DC Daequan Cook	2.50	6.00
GD Glen Davis	4.00	10.00
GP Gabe Pruitt	2.50	6.00
JC Javaris Crittenton	2.50	6.00
JD Jared Dudley	2.50	6.00
JG Jeff Green	3.00	8.00
JM Josh McRoberts	2.50	6.00
JN Joakim Noah	6.00	15.00
JS Jason Smith	2.50	6.00
JW Julian Wright	2.50	6.00
KD Kevin Durant	12.00	30.00
MA Morris Almond	2.50	6.00
MC Mike Conley Jr.	4.00	10.00
MW Marcus Williams	2.50	6.00
NF Nick Fazekas	2.50	6.00
NY Nick Young	4.00	10.00
RS Rodney Stuckey	4.00	10.00
SH Spencer Hawes	2.50	6.00
SW Sean Williams	2.50	6.00
TU Alando Tucker	2.50	6.00
TY Thaddeus Young	3.00	8.00
WC Wilson Chandler	4.00	10.00

2007-08 SPx Freshman Orientation Autographs

PRINT RUN 25 TO 50 SER.#'d SETS
UNPRICED LOGO PRINT RUN ONE SET

AA Arron Afflalo/50	8.00	20.00
AB Aaron Brooks/25	6.00	15.00
AH Al Horford/25	8.00	20.00
AL Acie Law/25	6.00	15.00
AT Al Thornton/25	6.00	15.00
CB Corey Brewer/25	8.00	20.00
CL Carl Landry/50	6.00	15.00
GP Gabe Pruitt/50	6.00	15.00
JC Javaris Crittenton/25	6.00	15.00
JD Jared Dudley/25	6.00	15.00
JG Jeff Green/25	8.00	20.00
JM Josh McRoberts/50	6.00	15.00
JN Joakim Noah/25	25.00	60.00
KD Kevin Durant/25	250.00	500.00
MA Morris Almond/50	6.00	15.00
MC Mike Conley Jr./25	10.00	25.00
NF Nick Fazekas/50	6.00	15.00
NY Nick Young/25	10.00	25.00
RS Rodney Stuckey/25	10.00	25.00
SW Sean Williams/25	6.00	15.00
TU Alando Tucker/25	6.00	15.00
WC Wilson Chandler/50	10.00	25.00

2007-08 SPx Freshman Orientation Tandems

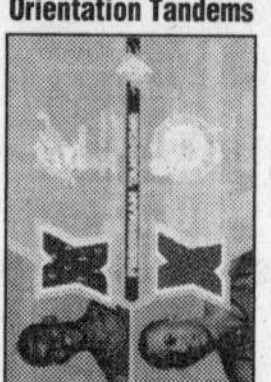

RANDOM INSERTS IN PACKS
*PATCHES: .75X TO 2X BASE HI
PATCH PRINT RUN 15 SER.#'d SETS
UNPRICED AUTO PRINT RUN 10 SER.#'d SETS

AA Aaron Brooks	4.00	10.00
Arron Afflalo		
AB Morris Almond	3.00	8.00
Aaron Brooks		
AS Rodney Stuckey	4.00	10.00
Arron Afflalo		
CW Sean Williams	3.00	8.00
Wilson Chandler		
DD Jared Dudley	3.00	8.00
Jermareo Davidson		
DG Kevin Durant	8.00	20.00
Jeff Green		
DH Kevin Durant	8.00	20.00
Al Horford		
DW Sean Williams	3.00	8.00
Jared Dudley		
HB Al Horford	5.00	12.00
Corey Brewer		
HS Spencer Hawes	3.00	8.00
Jason Smith		
LC Mike Conley Jr.	3.00	8.00
Acie Law		
NB Corey Brewer	5.00	12.00
Joakim Noah		
PD Glen Davis	4.00	10.00
Gabe Pruitt		
TC Al Thornton	3.00	8.00
Javaris Crittenton		
TL Alando Tucker	3.00	8.00
Carl Landry		
WW Julian Wright	3.00	8.00
Brandan Wright		
YC Thaddeus Young	3.00	8.00
Javaris Crittenton		
YP Nick Young	3.00	8.00
Gabe Pruitt		
YS Thaddeus Young	3.00	8.00
Jason Smith		

2007-08 SPx Freshman Orientation Triples

RANDOM INSERTS IN PACKS
UNPRICED PATCH PRINT RUN 5 SETS
UNPRICED AUTO PRINT RUN 5 SER.#'d SETS

ACC Daequan Cook	3.00	8.00
Javaris Crittenton		
Morris Almond		
DGC Kevin Durant	10.00	25.00
Jeff Green		
Mike Conley Jr.		
DLC Carl Landry	3.00	8.00
Wilson Chandler		
Glen Davis		
NHB Al Horford	6.00	15.00
Corey Brewer		
Joakim Noah		
SLC Mike Conley Jr.	4.00	10.00
Acie Law		
Rodney Stuckey		
STW Sean Williams	3.00	8.00
Jason Smith		
Alando Tucker		
TYD Thaddeus Young	3.00	8.00
Al Thornton		
Jared Dudley		
WGW Jeff Green	4.00	10.00
Julian Wright		
Brandan Wright		
YAB Nick Young	4.00	10.00
Aaron Brooks		
Arron Afflalo		

2007-08 SPx Super Scripts

APPROXIMATELY ONE PER BOX

AB Andrea Bargnani	4.00	10.00
AH Al Horford	5.00	12.00
AI Andre Iguodala	4.00	10.00
AJ Antawn Jamison	4.00	10.00
AL Acie Law	4.00	10.00
AT Al Thornton	4.00	10.00
BD Boris Diaw	4.00	10.00
BO Chris Bosh	10.00	25.00
BR Brandon Roy	10.00	25.00
CA Carmelo Anthony	15.00	40.00
CP Chris Paul	20.00	50.00
DA Baron Davis	6.00	15.00
DG Daniel Gibson	4.00	10.00
DH Dwight Howard	15.00	40.00
DJ D.J. Strawberry	4.00	10.00
EO Emeka Okafor	4.00	10.00
JE Al Jefferson	4.00	10.00
JG Jeff Green	5.00	12.00
JJ Jarrett Jack	4.00	10.00
JN Joakim Noah	10.00	25.00
KB Kobe Bryant	125.00	250.00
KD Kevin Durant	100.00	200.00
KK Kyle Korver	4.00	10.00
LB Leandro Barbosa	4.00	10.00
LH Larry Hughes	4.00	10.00
LJ LeBron James	150.00	300.00
MC Mike Conley Jr.	6.00	15.00
PR Tayshaun Prince	4.00	10.00
QR Quentin Richardson	4.00	10.00
RF Randy Foye	4.00	10.00
RH Richard Hamilton	4.00	10.00
RJ Richard Jefferson	4.00	10.00
RM Rashad McCants	4.00	10.00
SH Spencer Hawes	4.00	10.00
SM Sean May	4.00	10.00
TC Tyson Chandler	4.00	10.00
TF T.J. Ford	4.00	10.00
TP Tony Parker	8.00	20.00
VC Vince Carter	15.00	30.00

2007-08 SPx Winning Materials Jersey Numbers

APPROXIMATELY TWO PER BOX
UNPRICED PATCH PRINT RUN 15 SETS
*STAT JSY: SAME VALUE
APPROXIMATELY TWO PER BOX
UNPRICED STAT PATCH PRINT RUN 10 SETS

AB Andrea Bargnani	3.00	8.00
AH Al Harrington	2.00	5.00
AJ Al Jefferson	2.50	6.00
AK Andrei Kirilenko	2.00	5.00
AM Alonzo Mourning	5.00	12.00
AR Ron Artest	2.50	6.00
AS Amare Stoudemire	2.50	6.00
AW Antoine Walker	2.00	5.00
BB Bruce Bowen	2.00	5.00
BD Baron Davis	2.50	6.00
BG Ben Gordon	2.50	6.00
BI Chauncey Billups	2.50	6.00
BM Brad Miller	2.00	5.00
BO Andrew Bogut	2.50	6.00
BR Brandon Roy	3.00	8.00
BU Caron Butler	2.50	6.00
BY Andrew Bynum	3.00	8.00
CA Carmelo Anthony	3.00	8.00
CB Carlos Boozer	2.50	6.00
CH Chris Bosh	2.50	6.00
CM Corey Maggette	2.00	5.00
CP Chris Paul	5.00	12.00
CV Charlie Villanueva	2.50	6.00
CW Chris Webber	2.50	6.00
DE Deron Williams	4.00	10.00
DG Danny Granger	2.50	6.00
DH Dwight Howard	4.00	10.00
DI Boris Diaw	2.00	5.00
DW Delonte West	2.00	5.00
EC Eddy Curry	2.00	5.00
GG Gerald Green	2.00	5.00
GH Grant Hill	3.00	8.00
GO Drew Gooden	2.00	5.0
GP Gary Payton	2.50	6.0
HA Devin Harris	2.50	6.0
IG Andre Iguodala	2.50	6.0
JA Antawn Jamison	2.50	6.0
JH Josh Howard	2.00	5.0
JJ Joe Johnson	2.50	6.0
JK Jarrett Jack	2.00	5.0
JO Jermaine O'Neal	2.50	6.0
JR Jason Richardson	2.50	6.0
JS J.R. Smith	2.50	6.0
JT Jason Terry	2.00	5.0
JW Jason Williams	2.00	5.0
KB Kobe Bryant	8.00	20.0
KG Kevin Garnett	5.00	12.0
KH Kirk Hinrich	2.50	6.0
KM Kenyon Martin	2.50	6.0
LD Luol Deng	2.50	6.0
LH Larry Hughes	2.00	5.0
LJ LeBron James	10.00	25.0
LO Lamar Odom	2.50	6.0
MA Sean May	2.00	5.0
MB Mike Bibby	2.50	6.0
MC Antonio McDyess	2.00	5.0
MF Michael Finley	2.50	6.0
MG Manu Ginobili	2.50	6.0
MI Andre Miller	2.00	5.0
MR Michael Redd	2.50	6.0
MW Marvin Williams	2.50	6.0
NH Nene	2.00	5.0
PG Pau Gasol	2.50	6.0
PS Peja Stojakovic	2.50	6.0
QR Quentin Richardson	2.00	5.0
RA Ray Allen	2.50	6.0
RF Raymond Felton	3.00	8.0
RG Rudy Gay	2.50	6.0
RH Richard Hamilton	2.00	5.0
RJ Richard Jefferson	2.50	6.0
RL Rashard Lewis	2.00	5.0
RW Rasheed Wallace	2.50	6.0
SC Sam Cassell	2.50	6.0
SH Shawn Marion	2.50	6.0
SL Shaun Livingston	2.00	5.0
SM Josh Smith	2.50	6.0
SN Steve Nash	3.00	8.0
SO Shaquille O'Neal	5.00	12.0
ST Stephon Marbury	2.00	5.0
TD Tim Duncan	4.00	10.0
TJ T.J. Ford	2.00	5.0
TM Tracy McGrady	2.50	6.0
TP Tayshaun Prince	2.50	6.0
VC Vince Carter	3.00	8.0
WE David West	2.50	6.0
WI Chris Wilcox	2.00	5.0
WS Wally Szczerbiak	2.00	5.0
YM Yao Ming	3.00	8.0
ZI Zydrunas Ilgauskas	2.00	5.0
ZR Zach Randolph	2.00	5.0

2007-08 SPx Winning Materials Combos

RANDOM INSERTS IN PACKS
*PATCHES: 1X TO 2.5X BASE HI
PATCH PRINT RUN 50 SER.#'d SETS

AA Allen Iverson	6.00	15.0
Alonzo Mourning		
BA Ron Artest	3.00	8.0
Mike Bibby		
BF Chris Bosh	4.00	10.0
T.J. Ford		
BO Chris Bosh	3.00	8.0
Jermaine O'Neal		
BP Chauncey Billups	3.00	8.0
Tayshaun Prince		
CL Eddy Curry	3.00	8.0
David Lee		
DH Baron Davis	3.00	8.0
Al Harrington		
DP Tim Duncan	4.00	10.0
Tony Parker		
FM Raymond Felton	3.00	8.0
Sean May		
GF Kevin Garnett	4.00	10.0
Randy Foye		
GG Pau Gasol	3.00	8.0
Rudy Gay		
GH Drew Gooden	3.00	8.0
Kirk Hinrich		
GO Jermaine O'Neal	3.00	8.0
Danny Granger		
HB Richard Hamilton	4.00	10.0
Chauncey Billups		
HH Dwight Howard	5.00	12.0
Grant Hill		
HJ LeBron James	6.00	15.0
Larry Hughes		
JA Gilbert Arenas	3.00	8.0
Antawn Jamison		
JG Al Jefferson	3.00	8.0
Gerald Green		
KB Carlos Boozer	3.00	8.0
Andrei Kirilenko		
KC Vince Carter	4.00	10.0
Jason Kidd		
KL Kobe Bryant	6.00	15.0
Lamar Odom		
LW Rashard Lewis	3.00	8.0
Chris Wilcox		
MA Carmelo Anthony	4.00	10.0
Kenyon Martin		
MB Elton Brand	3.00	8.0
Corey Maggette		
MI Andre Iguodala	3.00	8.0
Andre Miller		
MM Yao Ming	5.00	12.0
Tracy McGrady		
MR Stephon Marbury	3.00	8.0
Zach Randolph		
NH Dirk Nowitzki	4.00	10.0
Josh Howard		
NJ Nene	3.00	8.0
J.R. Smith		
PA Ray Allen	5.00	12.0
Paul Pierce		
RB Andrew Bogut	3.00	8.0

Michael Redd
Emeka Okafor 3.00 8.00
Jason Richardson
Amare Stoudemire 4.00 10.00
Boris Diaw
W Marvin Williams 3.00 8.00
Josh Smith
G Ben Gordon 3.00 8.00
Ben Wallace
M Deron Williams 4.00 10.00
Paul Millsap
P Jason Williams 3.00 8.00
Gary Payton
W Chris Webber 4.00 10.00
Rasheed Wallace

2007-08 SPx Winning Materials Combos Patches Autographs

PRINT RUN 8 TO 25 SER.#'d SETS
SOME UNPRICED DUE TO SCARCITY
P Chauncey Billups/15 25.00 60.00
Tayshaun Prince
G Pau Gasol/25 30.00 60.00
Rudy Gay
D Amare Stoudemire/25 30.00 80.00
Boris Diaw
W Marvin Williams/25 30.00 60.00
Josh Smith
M Deron Williams/25 30.00 60.00
Paul Millsap

2007-08 SPx Winning Materials Triples

RANDOM INSERTS IN PACKS
PATCHES: .75X TO 2X BASE HI
PATCH PRINT RUN 25 SER.#'d SETS
UNPRICED AUTO PRINT RUN 5 SER.#'d SETS
MN Carmelo Anthony 6.00 15.00
Kenyon Martin
Nene
MJ Kobe Bryant 15.00 40.00
LeBron James
Tracy McGrady
AW Marcus Camby 4.00 10.00
Ben Wallace
Ron Artest
PM Richard Hamilton 5.00 12.00
Tayshaun Prince
Antonio McDyess
AB Gilbert Arenas 4.00 10.00
Caron Butler
Antawn Jamison
SW Joe Johnson 4.00 10.00
Marvin Williams
Josh Smith
CJ Vince Carter 5.00 12.00
Jason Kidd
Richard Jefferson
BL Elton Brand 4.00 10.00
Corey Maggette
Shaun Livingston
IP Steve Nash 6.00 15.00
Tony Parker
Allen Iverson
MS Steve Nash 5.00 12.00
Amare Stoudemire
Shawn Marion
AG Paul Pierce 4.00 10.00
Al Jefferson
Gerald Green
GB Tony Parker 5.00 12.00
Manu Ginobili
Bruce Bowen
MO Shaquille O'Neal 8.00 20.00
Alonzo Mourning
Gary Payton
BV Andrew Bogut 4.00 10.00
Michael Redd
Charlie Villanueva
MF Emeka Okafor 4.00 10.00
Sean May
Raymond Felton
NH Dirk Nowitzki 5.00 12.00
Josh Howard
Jason Terry
DG Ben Wallace 4.00 10.00
Luol Deng
Ben Gordon
HR Chris Webber 4.00 10.00
Juwan Howard
Jalen Rose
GJ Zydrunas Ilgauskas 4.00 10.00
Larry Hughes
Drew Gooden

2008-09 SPx

This set was released on November 19, 2008. The base set consists of 178 cards. Cards 1-90 feature veterans, and cards 91-110 are rookies serial numbered of 99. Cards 111-130 are autographed jersey rookie cards serial numbered of 99, and cards 131-178 are autographed jersey rookie cards serial numbered of 699. Each of these has both home and away versions, which are valued the same.

COMP.SET w/o SP's (90) 30.00 60.00
UNPRICED SPECTRUM PRINT RUN ONE SET
1 Kevin Garnett 1.25 3.00
2 Ray Allen .60 1.50
3 Paul Pierce .75 2.00
4 Chauncey Billups .60 1.50
5 Rasheed Wallace .60 1.50
6 Richard Hamilton .50 1.25
7 Tayshaun Prince .60 1.50
8 Dwight Howard 1.25 3.00
9 Hedo Turkoglu .60 1.50
10 Rashard Lewis .50 1.25
11 Daniel Gibson .60 1.50
12 Ben Wallace .60 1.50
13 LeBron James 3.00 8.00
14 Antawn Jamison .60 1.50
15 Caron Butler .60 1.50
16 Gilbert Arenas .60 1.50
17 Chris Bosh .60 1.50
18 Jamario Moon .40 1.00
19 T.J. Ford .40 1.00
20 Andre Iguodala .60 1.50
21 Andre Miller .50 1.25
22 Thaddeus Young .60 1.50
23 Al Horford .60 1.50
24 Joe Johnson .60 1.50
25 Josh Smith .60 1.50
26 Danny Granger .60 1.50
27 Jermaine O'Neal .60 1.50
28 Devin Harris .60 1.50
29 Yi Jianlian .60 1.50
30 Vince Carter .75 2.00
31 Ben Gordon .60 1.50
32 Joakim Noah .60 1.50
33 Luol Deng .60 1.50
34 Emeka Okafor .60 1.50
35 Gerald Wallace .60 1.50
36 Jason Richardson .60 1.50
37 Andrew Bogut .60 1.50
38 Michael Redd .60 1.50
39 Richard Jefferson .60 1.50
40 Eddy Curry .40 1.00
41 Jamal Crawford .60 1.50
42 Stephon Marbury .50 1.25
43 Zach Randolph .50 1.25
44 Daequan Cook .40 1.00
45 Dwyane Wade 1.25 3.00
46 Shawn Marion .60 1.50
47 Jordan Farmar .40 1.00
48 Kobe Bryant 3.00 8.00
49 Pau Gasol .60 1.50
50 Lamar Odom .60 1.50
51 Chris Paul 1.00 2.50
52 David West .60 1.50
53 Peja Stojakovic .60 1.50
54 Manu Ginobili .60 1.50
55 Tim Duncan 1.00 2.50
56 Tony Parker .60 1.50
57 Carlos Boozer .60 1.50
58 Deron Williams .60 1.50
59 Mehmet Okur .40 1.00
60 Luis Scola .50 1.25
61 Tracy McGrady .60 1.50
62 Yao Ming .75 2.00
63 Amare Stoudemire .60 1.50
64 Shaquille O'Neal 1.25 3.00
65 Steve Nash .60 1.50
66 Jason Kidd .60 1.50
67 Dirk Nowitzki .75 2.00
68 Josh Howard .50 1.25
69 Allen Iverson .75 2.00
70 Carmelo Anthony .75 2.00
71 Kenyon Martin .60 1.50
72 Elton Brand .60 1.50
73 Monta Ellis .60 1.50
74 Stephen Jackson .50 1.25
75 Brandon Roy .60 1.50
76 Greg Oden .60 1.50
77 LaMarcus Aldridge .60 1.50
78 Francisco Garcia .50 1.25
79 Kevin Martin .60 1.50
80 Ron Artest .60 1.50
81 Al Thornton .50 1.25
82 Chris Kaman .50 1.25
83 Baron Davis .60 1.50
84 Al Jefferson .60 1.50
85 Corey Brewer .50 1.25
86 Mike Conley Jr. .50 1.25
87 Rudy Gay .60 1.50
88 Damien Wilkins .40 1.00
89 Jeff Green .50 1.25
90 Kevin Durant 2.50 6.00
91 Danilo Gallinari RC 5.00 12.00
92 Rudy Fernandez RC 6.00 15.00
93 Sean Singletary RC 3.00 8.00
94 Othello Hunter RC 3.00 8.00
95 Shan Foster RC 3.00 8.00
96 Mike Taylor RC 3.00 8.00
97 Joe Crawford RC 3.00 8.00
98 Thomas Gardner RC 3.00 8.00
99 Nicolas Batum RC 8.00 20.00
100 Malik Hairston RC 3.00 8.00
101 Danilo Gallinari RC 5.00 12.00
102 Rudy Fernandez RC 6.00 15.00
103 Sean Singletary RC 3.00 8.00
104 Othello Hunter RC 3.00 8.00
105 Shan Foster RC 3.00 8.00
106 Mike Taylor RC 3.00 8.00
107 Joe Crawford RC 3.00 8.00
108 Thomas Gardner RC 3.00 8.00
109 Nicolas Batum RC 8.00 20.00
110 Malik Hairston RC 3.00 8.00
111 Derrick Rose JSY AU RC 300.00 600.00
112 Michael Beasley JSY AU RC 25.00 60.00
113 O.J. Mayo JSY AU RC 25.00 60.00
114 Russell Westbrook JSY AU RC 100.00 200.00
115 Kevin Love JSY AU RC 75.00 150.00
116 Eric Gordon JSY AU RC 30.00 80.00
117 D.J. Augustin JSY AU RC 8.00 20.00
118 Jerryd Bayless JSY AU RC 8.00 20.00
119 Brook Lopez JSY AU RC 12.00 30.00
120 Brandon Rush JSY AU RC 8.00 20.00
121 Derrick Rose JSY AU RC 300.00 600.00
122 Michael Beasley JSY AU RC 25.00 60.00
123 O.J. Mayo JSY AU RC 25.00 60.00
124 Russell Westbrook JSY AU RC 100.00 200.00
125 Kevin Love JSY AU RC 75.00 150.00
126 Eric Gordon JSY AU RC 30.00 80.00
127 D.J. Augustin JSY AU RC 8.00 20.00
128 Jerryd Bayless JSY AU RC 8.00 20.00
129 Brook Lopez JSY AU RC 12.00 30.00
130 Brandon Rush JSY AU RC 8.00 20.00
131 Joe Alexander JSY AU RC 5.00 12.00
132 Jason Thompson JSY AU RC 5.00 12.00
133 Anthony Randolph JSY AU RC 6.00 15.00
134 Robin Lopez JSY AU RC 5.00 12.00
135 Marreese Speights JSY AU RC 5.00 12.00
136 Roy Hibbert JSY AU RC 8.00 20.00
137 Javale McGee JSY AU RC 8.00 20.00
138 J.J. Hickson JSY AU RC 6.00 15.00
139 Ryan Anderson JSY AU RC 8.00 20.00
140 Courtney Lee JSY AU RC 8.00 20.00
141 Kosta Koufos JSY AU RC 5.00 12.00
142 George Hill JSY AU RC 8.00 20.00
143 Darrell Arthur JSY AU RC 5.00 12.00
144 Donte Greene JSY AU RC 5.00 12.00
145 D.J. White JSY AU RC 5.00 12.00
146 J.R. Giddens JSY AU RC 5.00 12.00
147 Walter Sharpe JSY AU RC 5.00 12.00
148 Joey Dorsey JSY AU RC 5.00 12.00
149 Mario Chalmers JSY AU RC 8.00 20.00
150 DeAndre Jordan JSY AU RC 10.00 25.00
151 Kyle Weaver JSY AU RC 5.00 12.00
152 Sonny Weems JSY AU RC 5.00 12.00
153 Chris Douglas-Roberts JSY AU RC5.00 12.00
154 Patrick Ewing Jr. JSY AU RC 5.00 12.00
155 Joe Alexander JSY AU RC 5.00 12.00
156 Jason Thompson JSY AU RC 5.00 12.00
157 Anthony Randolph JSY AU RC 6.00 15.00
158 Robin Lopez JSY AU RC 5.00 12.00
159 Marreese Speights JSY AU RC 5.00 12.00
160 Roy Hibbert JSY AU RC 8.00 20.00
161 Javale McGee JSY AU RC 8.00 20.00
162 J.J. Hickson JSY AU RC 6.00 15.00
163 Ryan Anderson JSY AU RC 8.00 20.00
164 Courtney Lee JSY AU RC 8.00 20.00
165 Kosta Koufos JSY AU RC 5.00 12.00
166 George Hill JSY AU RC 8.00 20.00
167 Darrell Arthur JSY AU RC 5.00 12.00
168 Donte Greene JSY AU RC 5.00 12.00
169 D.J. White JSY AU RC 5.00 12.00
170 J.R. Giddens JSY AU RC 5.00 12.00
171 Walter Sharpe JSY AU RC 5.00 12.00
172 Joey Dorsey JSY AU RC 5.00 12.00
173 Mario Chalmers JSY AU RC 8.00 20.00
174 DeAndre Jordan JSY AU RC 10.00 25.00
175 Kyle Weaver JSY AU RC 5.00 12.00
176 Sonny Weems JSY AU RC 5.00 12.00
177 Chris Douglas-Roberts JSY AU RC5.00 12.00
178 Patrick Ewing Jr. JSY AU RC 5.00 12.00

2008-09 SPx Radiance

*1-90 RADIANCE: 5X TO 12X BASE HI
*91-110 RAD: .6X TO 1.5X BASE HI
*111-178 RAD: .75X TO 2X BASE HI
PRINT RUN 25 SER.#'d SETS
137 Javale McGee JSY AU 20.00 50.00
139 Ryan Anderson JSY AU 15.00 40.00

2008-09 SPx Dual Scripts

STATED PRINT RUN 25 TO 50 SER.#'d SETS
DSAB Morris Almond/50 5.00 12.00
Aaron Brooks
DSAG Eric Gordon/50 15.00 40.00
D.J. Augustin
DSAT Alando Tucker/50 5.00 12.00
Kelenna Azubuike
DSBA Arron Afflalo/50 5.00 12.00
Mike Bibby
DSBG Corey Brewer/50 5.00 12.00
Jeff Green
DSBM Chauncey Billups/50 5.00 12.00
Andre Miller
DSBR Derrick Rose/50 100.00 250.00
Michael Beasley
DSBT Al Thornton/50 10.00 25.00
Andrew Bynum
DSCB Javaris Crittenton/50 5.00 12.00
Aaron Brooks
DSCP Paul Pierce/50 30.00 80.00
Vince Carter
DSEE Patrick Ewing/25 60.00 120.00
Patrick Ewing Jr.
DSFL Acie Law/50 6.00 15.00
Raymond Felton
DSFS D.J. Strawberry/50 5.00 12.00
Jordan Farmar
DSGL Kevin Love/50 30.00 80.00
Danilo Gallinari
DSGS Ramon Sessions/50 5.00 12.00
Daniel Gibson
DSGW Julian Wright/50 5.00 12.00
Rudy Gay
DSIM Jamario Moon/50 5.00 12.00
Andre Iguodala
DSKH Spencer Hawes/50 6.00 15.00
Chris Kaman
DSLL Brook Lopez/50 10.00 25.00
Robin Lopez
DSMW O.J. Mayo/50 40.00 80.00
Russell Westbrook
DSPC Mike Conley Jr./50 25.00 60.00
Chris Paul
DSPN Joakim Noah/50 15.00 40.00
Tayshaun Prince
DSPS Gabe Pruitt/50 6.00 15.00
Ramon Sessions
DSPW Sean Williams/50 5.00 12.00
Leon Powe
DSRB Jerryd Bayless/50 6.00 15.00
Brandon Rush
DSSS Jason Smith/50 5.00 12.00
Rodney Stuckey
DSTA Joe Alexander/50 5.00 12.00
Jason Thompson
DSWL David West/50 5.00 12.00
Carl Landry

2008-09 SPx Endorsements

STATED PRINT RUN 12 TO 25 SER.#'d SETS
SPXBR Bill Russell/25 75.00 150.00
SPXCP Chris Paul/25 30.00 80.00
SPXDR David Robinson/25 30.00 80.00
SPXJE Julius Erving/25 30.00 80.00
SPXJS John Stockton/12 60.00 120.00
SPXKB Kobe Bryant/24 100.00 225.00
SPXKD Kevin Durant/25 60.00 120.00
SPXKG Kevin Garnett/25 50.00 100.00
SPXLB Larry Bird/25 50.00 100.00
SPXLJ LeBron James/23 125.00 250.00
SPXMJ Magic Johnson/25 30.00 80.00
SPXOR Oscar Robertson/25 50.00 100.00
SPXSN Steve Nash/25 30.00 80.00
SPXYM Yao Ming/25 30.00 80.00

2008-09 SPx Freshman Orientation

STATED ODDS 1:1.5
*PATCH: .75X TO 2X BASE HI
PATCH PRINT RUN 25 SER.#'d SETS
FOAD Darrell Arthur 2.50 6.00
FOAR Anthony Randolph 3.00 8.00
FOBL Brook Lopez 4.00 10.00
FOBR Brandon Rush 2.50 6.00
FOCD Chris Douglas-Roberts 2.50 6.00
FODA D.J. Augustin 2.50 6.00
FODG Donte Greene 2.50 6.00
FODR Derrick Rose 15.00 40.00
FODW D.J. White 2.50 6.00
FOEG Eric Gordon 6.00 15.00
FOGH George Hill 4.00 10.00
FOJA Joe Alexander 2.50 6.00
FOJB Jerryd Bayless 2.50 6.00
FOJG J.R. Giddens 2.50 6.00
FOJH J.J. Hickson 3.00 8.00
FOJM Javale McGee 4.00 10.00
FOJT Jason Thompson 2.50 6.00
FOKK Kosta Koufos 2.50 6.00
FOKL Kevin Love 8.00 20.00
FOMB Michael Beasley 4.00 10.00
FOMC Mario Chalmers 4.00 10.00
FOMS Marreese Speights 2.50 6.00
FOOM O.J. Mayo 4.00 10.00
FOPE Patrick Ewing Jr. 2.50 6.00
FORA Ryan Anderson 4.00 10.00
FORH Roy Hibbert 4.00 10.00
FORL Robin Lopez 2.50 6.00
FORW Russell Westbrook 8.00 20.00
FOSW Sonny Weems 2.50 6.00
FOWS Walter Sharpe 2.50 6.00

2008-09 SPx Signature Block

COMBINED AUTO/MEM ODDS 1:10
SBAJ Antawn Jamison 4.00 10.00
SBAM Alonzo Mourning 40.00 100.00
SBBA B.J. Armstrong 4.00 10.00
SBCM Chris Mullin 20.00 50.00
SBDF Derek Fisher 8.00 20.00
SBDH Dwight Howard 12.50 30.00
SBDM Danny Manning 5.00 12.00
SBDW Dominique Wilkins 15.00 30.00
SBFG Francisco Garcia 4.00 10.00
SBKG Kevin Garnett 30.00 80.00
SBLH Larry Hughes 4.00 10.00
SBLO Lamar Odom 8.00 20.00
SBLS Luis Scola 4.00 10.00
SBMC Maurice Cheeks 5.00 12.00
SBMJ Michael Jordan 250.00 450.00
SBMR Micheal Ray Richardson 4.00 10.00
SBPO Patrick O'Bryant 4.00 10.00
SBQR Quentin Richardson 4.00 10.00
SBSM Sidney Moncrief 4.00 10.00
SBSP Sam Perkins 4.00 10.00
SBTC Tom Chambers 4.00 10.00
SBVC Vince Carter 12.50 30.00

2008-09 SPx Super Scripts

COMBINED AUTO/MEM ODDS 1:10
SSAL Acie Law 3.00 8.00
SSBI Chauncey Billups 4.00 10.00
SSBO Chris Bosh 8.00 20.00
SSCM Chris Mihm 3.00 8.00
SSDH Dwight Howard 10.00 25.00
SSDS D.J. Strawberry 3.00 8.00
SSFG Francisco Garcia 3.00 8.00
SSJC Javaris Crittenton 3.00 8.00
SSJD Jared Dudley 3.00 8.00
SSJF Jordan Farmar 5.00 12.00
SSJN Joakim Noah 8.00 20.00
SSJS Jason Smith 3.00 8.00
SSJW Julian Wright 3.00 8.00
SSKB Kobe Bryant 80.00 160.00
SSKD Kevin Durant 40.00 100.00
SSKG Kevin Garnett 30.00 80.00
SSKK Kyle Korver 3.00 8.00
SSMA Morris Almond 3.00 8.00
SSMW Mario West 3.00 8.00
SSRS Ramon Sessions 4.00 10.00
SSSH Spencer Hawes 3.00 8.00
SSSW Sean Williams 3.00 8.00
SSWI Shelden Williams 3.00 8.00

2008-09 SPx Triple Scripts

PRINT RUN 25 SER.#'d SETS
TSBWA Kobe Bryant 200.00 400.00
Kareem Abdul-Jabbar
Jerry West
TSMMS Tracy McGrady 40.00 100.00
Yao Ming
Luis Scola
TSNKP Tony Parker 75.00 150.00
Jason Kidd
Steve Nash
TSPAG Kevin Garnett 300.00 600.00
Paul Pierce
Ray Allen
TSPWR Chris Paul 50.00 120.00
Deron Williams
Brandon Roy
TSRBM Derrick Rose 150.00 300.00
Michael Beasley
O.J. Mayo
TSSHB Dwight Howard 60.00 150.00
Amare Stoudemire
Andrew Bynum
TSWJA LeBron James 150.00 300.00
Carmelo Anthony
David West

2008-09 SPx Winning Materials Initials

STATED ODDS 1:1.5
*JSY NUM: .4X TO 1X BASE HI
*PATCHES: 1X TO 2.5X BASE HI
PATCH PRINT RUN 25 SER.#'d SETS
UNPRICED JSY AUTO PRINT RUN 10 SETS
UNPRICED PATCH AUTO PRINT RUN 5 SETS
WMIAB Andrew Bynum 3.00 8.00
WMIAI Allen Iverson 3.00 8.00
WMIAJ Antawn Jamison 2.50 6.00
WMIAM Andre Miller 2.00 5.00
WMIAS Amare Stoudemire 2.50 6.00
WMIAT Al Thornton 2.00 5.00
WMIBG Ben Gordon 2.50 6.00
WMIBR Brandon Roy 2.50 6.00
WMICA Carmelo Anthony 3.00 8.00
WMICB Chris Bosh 2.50 6.00
WMICM Corey Maggette 2.00 5.00
WMICP Chris Paul 4.00 10.00
WMIDG Daniel Gibson 2.50 6.00
WMIDH Dwight Howard 5.00 12.00
WMIDN Dirk Nowitzki 3.00 8.00
WMIEB Elton Brand 2.50 6.00
WMIEO Emeka Okafor 2.50 6.00
WMIGD Glen Davis 2.00 5.00
WMIHA Hilton Armstrong 2.00 5.00
WMIIG Andre Iguodala 2.50 6.00
WMIJF Jordan Farmar 1.50 4.00
WMIJG Jeff Green 2.00 5.00
WMIJH Josh Howard 2.00 5.00
WMIJK Jason Kidd 2.50 6.00
WMIJO Jermaine O'Neal 2.50 6.00
WMIJS J.R. Smith 2.50 6.00
WMIKB Kobe Bryant 10.00 25.00
WMIKD Kevin Durant 10.00 25.00
WMIKG Kevin Garnett 5.00 12.00
WMIKH Kirk Hinrich 2.50 6.00
WMILA LaMarcus Aldridge 2.50 6.00
WMILH Larry Hughes 2.00 5.00
WMILJ LeBron James 10.00 25.00
WMILO Lamar Odom 2.50 6.00
WMIPP Paul Pierce 3.00 8.00
WMIRA Ray Allen 2.50 6.00
WMIRF Raymond Felton 2.00 5.00
WMIRG Rudy Gay 2.50 6.00
WMIRL Rashard Lewis 2.00 5.00
WMISO Shaquille O'Neal 5.00 12.00
WMISW Shelden Williams 2.00 5.00
WMITM Tracy McGrady 2.50 6.00
WMITP Tayshaun Prince 2.50 6.00
WMIVC Vince Carter 3.00 8.00
WMIYM Yao Ming 3.00 8.00

2008-09 SPx Winning Materials Combos

STATED ODDS 1:1.5
*PATCHES: 1.25X TO 3X HI COLUMN
PATCH PRINT RUN 25 SER.#'d SETS
UNPRICED AUTO PATCH PRINT RUN 5 SETS
WMCAD Kevin Durant 8.00 20.00
Carmelo Anthony
WMCAG Ray Allen 6.00 15.00
Kevin Garnett
WMCAR Brandon Roy 3.00 8.00
LaMarcus Aldridge
WMCBB Andrea Bargnani 3.00 8.00
Chris Bosh
WMCBF Jordan Farmar 4.00 10.00
Andrew Bynum
WMCBG Kobe Bryant 6.00 15.00
Pau Gasol
WMCBJ LeBron James 12.50 30.00
Kobe Bryant
WMCBL Acie Law 3.00 8.00
Mike Bibby
WMCBM Ronnie Brewer 3.00 8.00
Paul Millsap
WMCBO Andrea Bargnani 3.00 8.00
Jermaine O'Neal
WMCBW Deron Williams 3.00 8.00
Carlos Boozer
WMCCH Devin Harris 3.00 8.00
Vince Carter
WMCCL Shaun Livingston 3.00 8.00
Marcus Camby
WMCCN Kenyon Martin 3.00 8.00
Nene
WMCCT Al Thornton 3.00 8.00
Marcus Camby
WMCDG Jeff Green 6.00 15.00
Kevin Durant
WMCDM Manu Ginobili 4.00 10.00
Tim Duncan
WMCEJ Magic Johnson 6.00 15.00
Julius Erving
WMCEW Brandan Wright 3.00 8.00
Monta Ellis
WMCFD Raymond Felton 3.00 8.00
Jermareo Davidson
WMCFW Martell Webster 3.00 8.00
Channing Frye
WMCGD Ben Gordon 3.00 8.00
Luol Deng
WMCGP Paul Pierce 6.00 15.00
Kevin Garnett
WMCHB Chauncey Billups 3.00 8.00
Richard Hamilton
WMCHG Drew Gooden 3.00 8.00
Larry Hughes
WMCHN Dirk Nowitzki 3.00 8.00
Josh Howard
WMCIA Carmelo Anthony 4.00 10.00
Allen Iverson
WMCIY Andre Iguodala 3.00 8.00
Thaddeus Young
WMCJB Antawn Jamison 3.00 8.00
Caron Butler
WMCJF Randy Foye 3.00 8.00
Al Jefferson
WMCJH Joe Johnson 3.00 8.00
Al Horford
WMCJP Michael Jordan 25.00 60.00
Scottie Pippen
WMCJS Josh Smith 3.00 8.00
Joe Johnson
WMCKN Dirk Nowitzki 4.00 10.00
Jason Kidd
WMCKO Andrei Kirilenko 3.00 8.00
Mehmet Okur
WMCLH Dwight Howard 3.00 8.00
Rashard Lewis
WMCMB Elton Brand 3.00 8.00
Andre Miller
WMCMD Kevin Martin 3.00 8.00
Quincy Douby
WMCMH Shawn Marion 3.00 8.00
Udonis Haslem
WMCMM Tracy McGrady 4.00 10.00
Yao Ming
WMCMR Nate Robinson 3.00 8.00
Stephon Marbury
WMCMS John Stockton 4.00 10.00
Karl Malone
WMCNH Steve Nash 6.00 15.00
Grant Hill
WMCPG Tony Parker 4.00 10.00
Manu Ginobili
WMCPM Dan Majerle 8.00 20.00
Mark Price
WMCPW Chris Paul 5.00 12.00
Deron Williams
WMCPY Nick Young 3.00 8.00
Oleksiy Pecherov
WMCRB Andrew Bogut 3.00 8.00
Michael Redd
WMCRP Gabe Pruitt 3.00 8.00
Rajon Rondo
WMCRR Quentin Richardson 3.00 8.00
Zach Randolph
WMCRT Isiah Thomas 5.00 12.00
Dennis Rodman
WMCRW Jason Richardson 3.00 8.00
Gerald Wallace
WMCSE John Starks 6.00 15.00
Patrick Ewing
WMCSH Dwight Howard 4.00 10.00
Amare Stoudemire
WMCSO Amare Stoudemire 4.00 10.00
Shaquille O'Neal
WMCSP Peja Stojakovic 4.00 10.00
Chris Paul
WMCTN Joakim Noah 3.00 8.00
Tyrus Thomas
WMCWJ Ben Wallace 6.00 15.00
LeBron James
WMCWO Emeka Okafor 3.00 8.00
Gerald Wallace
WMCWP Tayshaun Prince 3.00 8.00
Rasheed Wallace

2008-09 SPx Winning Materials Trios

COMBINED MEM STATED ODDS 1:1.5
*PATCH: 1.5X TO 4X BASE HI
PATCH PRINT RUN 15 SER.#'d SETS
UNPRICED AUTO PRINT RUN 3 SER.#'d SETS
WMTBBG Andrea Bargnani 4.00 10.00
Chris Bosh
Joey Graham
WMTBGB Kobe Bryant 10.00 25.00
Pau Gasol
Andrew Bynum
WMTBJS Josh Smith 4.00 10.00
Joe Johnson
Mike Bibby
WMTBLS Luis Scola 4.00 10.00
Carl Landry
Shane Battier
WMTBWB Deron Williams 5.00 12.00
Carlos Boozer
Ronnie Brewer
WMTCBH Josh Boone 4.00 10.00
Vince Carter
Devin Harris
WMTCKT Al Thornton 4.00 10.00
Marcus Camby
Chris Kaman
WMTCSP Peja Stojakovic 5.00 12.00
Chris Paul
Tyson Chandler
WMTDMG Kevin Martin 4.00 10.00
Quincy Douby
Francisco Garcia
WMTDPG Tony Parker 6.00 15.00
Tim Duncan
Manu Ginobili
WMTGFW Danny Granger 4.00 10.00
T.J. Ford
Shawne Williams
WMTHDG Ben Gordon 4.00 10.00
Luol Deng
Kirk Hinrich
WMTHWS Rodney Stuckey 4.00 10.00
Richard Hamilton
Rasheed Wallace
WMTJBY Antawn Jamison 4.00 10.00
Caron Butler
Nick Young
WMTJMF Randy Foye 4.00 10.00
Al Jefferson
Rashad McCants
WMTKIA Carmelo Anthony 6.00 15.00
Allen Iverson
Kenyon Martin
WMTKNH Dirk Nowitzki 5.00 12.00
Josh Howard
Jason Kidd
WMTLAH Dwight Howard 5.00 12.00
Rashard Lewis
Carlos Arroyo
WMTMEW Brandan Wright 4.00 10.00
Monta Ellis
Corey Maggette
WMTMIY Andre Iguodala 4.00 10.00
Andre Miller
Thaddeus Young
WMTMMH Shawn Marion 4.00 10.00
Udonis Haslem
Alonzo Mourning
WMTMRC Jamal Crawford 4.00 10.00
Stephon Marbury
Zach Randolph
WMTNSO Amare Stoudemire 6.00 15.00
Shaquille O'Neal
Steve Nash
WMTPAG Ray Allen 10.00 25.00
Kevin Garnett
Paul Pierce
WMTPDG Jeff Green 6.00 15.00
Kevin Durant
Johan Petro
WMTRRB Andrew Bogut 4.00 10.00
Michael Redd
Luke Ridnour
WMTRWO Emeka Okafor 4.00 10.00
Gerald Wallace
Jason Richardson
WMTTGF Rudy Gay 4.00 10.00
Tyrus Thomas
Jordan Farmar
WMTWAR Brandon Roy 4.00 10.00
LaMarcus Aldridge
Martell Webster
WMTWJG Ben Wallace 6.00 15.00
LeBron James
Daniel Gibson

1998-99 SPx Finite

This was the first year for SPx to move from a "Holoview" based set to a serially numbered set. The full set consists of 210 cards that carried an SRP of $5.99. The base set was divided up into five smaller sets all with different numbering. The base set contained 90 cards, serially numbered to 10,000. The Star Power subset contained 60 cards, serially numbered to 5,400. The SPx 2000 subset contained 30 cards, serially numbered to 4,050. The Top Flight subset contained 20 cards, serially numbered to 3,390. Finally, the Finite Excellence subset contained 10 cards, serially numbered to 1,770. In addition, rookie cards were inserted into boxes of Upper Deck 2 in two-card packs. The cards were serially numbered to 2,500. Cards 227 and 228 do not exist, since those particular rookies did not sign NBA contracts. The cards are considered rookie cards, but the set is not included in the complete set price.

1 Michael Jordan 6.00 15.00
2 Hakeem Olajuwon 1.00 2.50
3 Keith Van Horn .75 2.00
4 Rasheed Wallace .75 2.00
5 Mookie Blaylock .50 1.25
6 Bobby Jackson .60 1.50
7 Detlef Schrempf .75 2.00
8 Antonio McDyess .60 1.50
9 Lamond Murray .50 1.25
10 Chris Mullin .75 2.00
11 Zydrunas Ilgauskas .75 2.00
12 Tracy Murray .50 1.25
13 Jerry Stackhouse .75 2.00
14 Avery Johnson .60 1.50
15 Larry Johnson .75 2.00
16 Alan Henderson .50 1.25
17 David Wesley .50 1.25
18 Kevin Willis .50 1.25

19 Eddie Jones .75 2.00
20 Horace Grant .60 1.50
21 Ray Allen 1.00 2.50
22 Derrick Coleman .60 1.50
23 Derek Anderson .50 1.25
24 Tim Hardaway .75 2.00
25 Danny Fortson .50 1.25
26 Tariq Abdul-Wahad .50 1.25
27 Charles Barkley 1.25 3.00
28 Sam Cassell .60 1.50
29 Kevin Garnett 1.50 4.00
30 Jeff Hornacek .60 1.50
31 Isaac Austin .50 1.25
32 Allan Houston .60 1.50
33 David Robinson 1.25 3.00
34 Tracy McGrady 1.25 3.00
35 LaPhonso Ellis .50 1.25
36 Shawn Kemp .75 2.00
37 Glenn Robinson .60 1.50
38 Shareef Abdur-Rahim .75 2.00
39 Vin Baker .60 1.50
40 Rik Smits .60 1.50
41 Jason Kidd 1.25 3.00
42 Erick Dampier .50 1.25
43 Shawn Bradley .50 1.25
44 Anfernee Hardaway 1.25 3.00
45 John Stockton 1.00 2.50
46 Calbert Cheaney .50 1.25
47 Terrell Brandon .50 1.25
48 Hubert Davis .50 1.25
49 Patrick Ewing 1.00 2.50
50 Kobe Bryant 4.00 10.00
51 Gary Payton .75 2.00
52 Marcus Camby .60 1.50
53 Bryant Reeves .50 1.25
54 Reggie Miller 1.00 2.50
55 Antoine Walker .75 2.00
56 Scottie Pippen 1.25 3.00
57 Hersey Hawkins .50 1.25
58 John Starks .60 1.50
59 Dikembe Mutombo .75 2.00
60 Damon Stoudamire .75 2.00
61 Rodney Rogers .50 1.25
62 Nick Anderson .50 1.25
63 Brian Williams .50 1.25
64 Ron Mercer .60 1.50
65 Donyell Marshall .50 1.25
66 Glen Rice .75 2.00
67 Michael Finley .75 2.00
68 Tim Duncan 1.50 4.00
69 Stephon Marbury 1.00 2.50
70 Antonio Daniels .50 1.25
71 Chauncey Billups 1.00 2.50
72 Kerry Kittles .50 1.25
73 Brian Grant .50 1.25
74 Anthony Mason .50 1.25
75 Allen Iverson 1.50 4.00
76 Juwan Howard .60 1.50
77 Grant Hill 1.25 3.00
78 Tony Delk .50 1.25
79 Olden Polynice .50 1.25
80 Alonzo Mourning 1.00 2.50
81 Karl Malone 1.00 2.50
82 Isaiah Rider .50 1.25
83 Shaquille O'Neal 2.00 5.00
84 Steve Smith .60 1.50
85 Kenny Anderson .60 1.50
86 Toni Kukoc .75 2.00
87 Anthony Peeler .50 1.25
88 Tim Thomas .75 2.00
89 Nick Van Exel .60 1.50
90 Jamal Mashburn .60 1.50
91 Reggie Miller SP 1.50 4.00
92 Juwan Howard SP 1.00 2.50
93 Glen Rice SP 1.25 3.00
94 Grant Hill SP 2.00 5.00
95 Maurice Taylor SP .75 2.00
96 Vin Baker SP 1.00 2.50
97 Tim Thomas SP 1.25 3.00
98 Bobby Jackson SP 1.00 2.50
99 Damon Stoudamire SP 1.25 3.00
100 Michael Jordan SP 10.00 25.00
101 Eddie Jones SP 1.25 3.00
102 Keith Van Horn SP 1.25 3.00
103 Dikembe Mutombo SP 1.25 3.00
104 Brevin Knight SP .75 2.00
105 Shawn Bradley SP .75 2.00
106 Lamond Murray SP .75 2.00
107 Tim Duncan SP 2.50 6.00
108 Bryant Reeves SP .75 2.00
109 Antoine Walker SP 1.25 3.00
110 John Stockton SP 1.50 4.00
111 Nick Anderson SP .75 2.00
112 Chris Mullin SP 1.25 3.00
113 Glenn Robinson SP 1.00 2.50
114 Kevin Garnett SP 2.50 6.00
115 Michael Stewart SP .75 2.00
116 Antonio McDyess SP 1.00 2.50
117 Jim Jackson SP .75 2.00
118 Chauncey Billups SP 1.50 4.00
119 Sam Cassell SP 1.00 2.50
120 Dennis Rodman SP 2.50 6.00
121 Rasheed Wallace SP 1.25 3.00
122 Brian Williams SP .75 2.00
123 Anfernee Hardaway SP 2.00 5.00
124 Scottie Pippen SP 2.00 5.00
125 Terrell Brandon SP .75 2.00
126 Michael Finley SP 1.25 3.00
127 Kerry Kittles SP .75 2.00
128 Toni Kukoc SP 1.25 3.00
129 Hakeem Olajuwon SP 1.50 4.00
130 Tim Hardaway SP 1.25 3.00
131 Shareef Abdur-Rahim SP 1.25 3.00
132 Donyell Marshall SP .75 2.00
133 David Robinson SP 2.00 5.00
134 LaPhonso Ellis SP .75 2.00
135 Ray Allen SP 1.50 4.00
136 Nick Van Exel SP 1.00 2.50
137 Patrick Ewing SP 1.50 4.00
138 Anthony Mason SP .75 2.00
139 Shaquille O'Neal SP 3.00 8.00
140 Shawn Kemp SP 1.25 3.00
141 Stephon Marbury SP 1.50 4.00
142 Karl Malone SP 1.50 4.00
143 Allen Iverson SP 2.50 6.00
144 Kenny Anderson SP 1.00 2.50
145 Marcus Camby SP 1.00 2.50
146 Steve Smith SP 1.00 2.50
147 Gary Payton SP 1.25 3.00
148 Jason Kidd SP 2.00 5.00
149 Alonzo Mourning SP 1.50 4.00
150 Charles Barkley SP 2.00 5.00
151 Kobe Bryant SPx 10.00 25.00
152 Ron Mercer SPx 1.50 4.00
153 Maurice Taylor SPx 1.25 3.00
154 Tim Duncan SPx 4.00 10.00
155 Shareef Abdur-Rahim SPx 2.00 5.00
156 Eddie Jones SPx 2.00 5.00
157 Chauncey Billups SPx 2.50 6.00
158 Derek Anderson SPx 1.25 3.00
159 Bobby Jackson SPx 1.50 4.00
160 Stephon Marbury SPx 2.50 6.00
161 Anfernee Hardaway SPx 3.00 8.00
162 Zydrunas Ilgauskas SPx 2.00 5.00
163 Allen Iverson SPx 4.00 10.00
164 Antoine Walker SPx 2.00 5.00
165 Tracy McGrady SPx 3.00 8.00
166 Rasheed Wallace SPx 2.00 5.00
167 Jason Kidd SPx 3.00 8.00
168 Kevin Garnett SPx 4.00 10.00
169 Damon Stoudamire SPx 2.00 5.00
170 Brevin Knight SPx 1.25 3.00
171 Tim Thomas SPx 2.00 5.00
172 Danny Fortson SPx 1.25 3.00
173 Jermaine O'Neal SPx 2.00 5.00
174 Keith Van Horn SPx 2.00 5.00
175 Ray Allen SPx 2.50 6.00
176 Kerry Kittles SPx 1.25 3.00
177 Vin Baker SPx 1.50 4.00
178 Allan Houston SPx 1.50 4.00
179 Alan Henderson SPx 1.25 3.00
180 Bryon Russell SPx 1.25 3.00
181 Michael Jordan TF 20.00 50.00
182 Maurice Taylor TF 1.50 4.00
183 Isaiah Rider TF 1.50 4.00
184 Antonio McDyess TF 2.00 5.00
185 Anfernee Hardaway TF 4.00 10.00
186 Glenn Robinson TF 2.00 5.00
187 Dikembe Mutombo TF 2.50 6.00
188 Shawn Kemp TF 2.50 6.00
189 Tracy McGrady TF 4.00 10.00
190 Reggie Miller TF 3.00 8.00
191 Derek Anderson TF 1.50 4.00
192 Allan Houston TF 2.00 5.00
193 Michael Finley TF 2.50 6.00
194 Nick Van Exel TF 2.00 5.00
195 Juwan Howard TF 2.00 5.00
196 LaPhonso Ellis TF 1.50 4.00
197 Ron Mercer TF 2.00 5.00
198 Glen Rice TF 2.50 6.00
199 Joe Smith TF 2.00 5.00
200 Kobe Bryant TF 12.00 30.00
201 Michael Jordan FE 30.00 80.00
202 Karl Malone FE 5.00 12.00
203 Hakeem Olajuwon FE 5.00 12.00
204 David Robinson FE 6.00 15.00
205 Shaquille O'Neal FE 10.00 25.00
206 John Stockton FE 5.00 12.00
207 Grant Hill FE 6.00 15.00
208 Tim Hardaway FE 4.00 10.00
209 Scottie Pippen FE 6.00 15.00
210 Gary Payton FE 4.00 10.00
211 Michael Olowokandi RC 3.00 8.00
212 Mike Bibby RC 6.00 15.00
213 Raef LaFrentz RC 3.00 8.00
214 Antawn Jamison RC 6.00 15.00
215 Vince Carter RC 12.00 30.00
216 Robert Traylor RC 2.50 6.00
217 Jason Williams RC 6.00 15.00
218 Larry Hughes RC 5.00 12.00
219 Dirk Nowitzki RC 15.00 40.00
220 Paul Pierce RC 12.00 30.00
221 Bonzi Wells RC 2.50 6.00
222 Michael Doleac RC 2.50 6.00
223 Keon Clark RC 2.50 6.00
224 Michael Dickerson RC 2.50 6.00
225 Matt Harpring RC 3.00 8.00
226 Bryce Drew RC 2.50 6.00
229 Pat Garrity RC 2.50 6.00
230 Roshown McLeod RC 2.50 6.00
231 Ricky Davis RC 4.00 10.00
232 Brian Skinner RC 2.50 6.00
233 Tyronn Lue RC 2.50 6.00
234 Felipe Lopez RC 2.50 6.00
235 Al Harrington RC 4.00 10.00
236 Ruben Patterson RC 2.50 6.00
237 Jelani McCoy RC 2.50 6.00
238 Corey Benjamin RC 2.50 6.00
239 Nazr Mohammed RC 2.50 6.00
240 Rashard Lewis RC 6.00 15.00
S1 Michael Jordan PROMO 5.00 12.00

1998-99 SPx Finite Extreme

This one of one serial numbered parallel was randomly inserted into packs of series one SPx Finite.

1998-99 SPx Finite Radiance

This set parallels the base set and was divided up into five smaller sets all with different numbering. The base set contained 90 cards, serially numbered to 5,000. The Star Power subset contained 60 cards, serially numbered to 2,700. The SPx 2000 subset contained 30 cards, serially numbered to 2,025. The Top Flight subset contained 20 cards, serially numbered to 1,130. Finally, the Finite Excellence subset contained 10 cards, serially numbered to 590. In addition, cards of rookies were inserted into boxes of Upper Deck 2 in two-card packs. The cards were serially numbered to 1,500. Two of the cards do not exist (227 and 228) due to rookies not signing NBA contracts. The rookie set is not included in the complete set price. To ascertain values on individual cards, please refer to the multiplier in the header, coupled with the base card.

*1-90 STARS: .6X TO 1.5X BASE HI
*91-150 STARS: .75X TO 2X BASE HI
*151-180 STARS: .6X TO 1.5X BASE HI
*181-200 STARS: .75X TO 2X BASE HI
*201-210 STARS: .75X TO 2X BASE HI
211-240 RCs: .4X TO 1X BASE HI
215 Vince Carter 15.00 40.00

1998-99 SPx Finite Spectrum

This set parallels the base set and was divided up into five smaller sets all with different numbering. The base set contained 90 cards, serially numbered to 350. The Star Power subset contained 60 cards, serially numbered to 250. The SPx 2000 subset contained 30 cards, serially numbered to 75. The Top Flight subset contained 20 cards, serially numbered to 50. Finally, the Finite Excellence subset contained 10 cards, serially numbered to 25. In addition, cards of rookies were inserted into boxes of Upper Deck 2 in two-card packs. The cards were serially numbered to 25. Two of the cards do not exist (227 and 228) due to rookies not signing NBA contracts. The rookie set is not included in the complete set price.

*1-90 STARS: 5X TO 12X BASE HI
*91-150 STARS: 4X TO 10X BASE HI
*151-180 STARS: 4X TO 10X BASE HI
*181-200 STARS: 4X TO 10X BASE HI
*201-210 STARS: 5X TO 12X BASE HI
*211-240 RCs: 8X TO 20X BASE HI
1 Michael Jordan 200.00 400.00
100 Michael Jordan SP 250.00 500.00
151 Kobe Bryant SPx 250.00 500.00
181 Michael Jordan TF 750.00 1500.00
185 Anfernee Hardaway TF 50.00 125.00
188 Shawn Kemp TF 40.00 100.00
200 Kobe Bryant TF 300.00 600.00
201 Michael Jordan FE 2200.00 3000.00
209 Scottie Pippen FE 100.00 250.00
215 Vince Carter 500.00 1000.00
219 Dirk Nowitzki 600.00 1200.00
240 Rashard Lewis 125.00 300.00

1979-80 Spurs Police

This set contains 15 cards measuring approximately 2 5/8" by 4 1/8" featuring the San Antonio Spurs. Backs contain safety tips, "Tips from the Spurs." The set was also sponsored by Handy Dan and were put out by Express News and Handy Dan in conjunction with the Police Department.

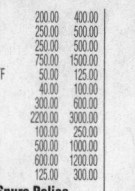

COMPLETE SET (15) 3.00 6.00
1 Mike Evans .25 .60
2 Billy Paultz .30 .75
12 Mike Gale .25 .60
13 James Silas .30 .75
21 Irv Kiffin .25 .60
30 Paul Griffin .25 .60
31 Kevin Restani .25 .60
35 Larry Kenon .30 .75
44 George Gervin 1.50 4.00
53 Mark Olberding .25 .60
54 Wiley Peck .25 .60
NNO Bob Bass .25 .60
NNO George Karl ACO .40 1.00
NNO Bernie LaReau .25 .60
NNO Doug Moe CO .40 1.00

1988-89 Spurs Police/Diamond Shamrock

This eight-card set of San Antonio Spurs is one of two that were sponsored by Diamond Shamrock, a regional oil retailer and convenience store chain headquartered in San Antonio. One set had a tear-off tab, and one card was given out each week at San Antonio Diamond Shamrock CornerStore locations with each 3.00 purchase or purchase of eight gallons of gas. It is reported that 100,000 sets were printed. This promotion included weekly drawings for pairs of tickets and a final drawing to determine the winners of the Grand Prize and other prizes. The expiration of the contest to "Win A Road Trip With The Spurs" was May 21, 1989. The other set was donated to the San Antonio Police Department and distributed to kids in the San Antonio area by patrolmen on the night shift; 50,000 sets were produced. The cards measure approximately 2 1/2" by 3 9/16" and except for the tear-off tab, the two sets are identical. The front features a color action player photo with a white border (only the Robinson card has a posed shot). The card front has a distinctive black background with a white pinstripe pattern. Three color bands (aqua, red, and orange) overlay the top of the picture, with the team logo in the middle. The player's name is given in the aqua band below the picture. The back has biographical information and a player safety tip in a gray box. The San Antonio Police and sponsor logos appear at the bottom. The cards are unnumbered and checklisted below in alphabetical order, with jersey number after the player's name. The set may have received additional multiple printings in order to capitalize on the popularity of the David Robinson card, which was printed a year earlier than his 1989-90 Hoops Rookie Card.

COMPLETE SET (8) 3.50 7.00
1 Greg Anderson 33 .20 .50
2 Willie Anderson 40 .25 .60
3 Frank Brickowski 43 .25 .60
4 Larry Brown CO .40 1.00
5 Dallas Comegys 22 .25 .60
6 Johnny Dawkins 24 .30 .75
7 Alvin Robertson 21 .20 .50
8 David Robinson 50 2.50 6.00

1976-77 Spurs Team Issue

This 8" x 10" set was produced for the San Antonio Spurs during the 1976-77 season. The set features eight black and white cards of the team's players.

COMPLETE SET (8) 12.50 25.00
1 Mike D'Antoni 2.00 5.00
2 Louie Dampier 2.00 5.00
3 Coby Dietrick 1.25 3.00
4 Mike Gale 1.25 3.00
5 Billy Paultz 1.50 4.00
6 James Silas 1.50 4.00
7 Ken Smith 1.25 3.00
8 Henry Ward 1.25 3.00

2007 Spurs Upper Deck

Distributed by Upper Deck, this set originally was available in three 9-card perforated sheets.

COMPLETE SET (27) 10.00 20.00
1 Tony Parker .75 2.00
2 Brent Barry .40 1.00
3 Tony Parker .75 2.00
4 Jackie Butler .40 1.00
5 2007 NBA Champions .40 1.00
6 Matt Bonner .40 1.00
7 Bruce Bowen .40 1.00
8 Gregg Popovich CO .60 1.50
9 Bruce Bowen .60 1.50
Michael Finley
10 Manu Ginobili .75 2.00
11 Francisco Elson .40 1.00
12 Manu Ginobili .75 2.00
13 James White .40 1.00
14 4 Time NBA Champions .40 1.00
15 Melvin Ely .40 1.00
16 Michael Finley .75 2.00
17 The Coyote .40 1.00
18 Fabricio Oberto .40 1.00
Brent Barry
19 Tim Duncan 1.00 2.50
20 Jacque Vaughn .40 1.00
21 Tim Duncan 1.00 2.50
22 Fabricio Oberto .40 1.00
23 2007 Conference Champs .40 1.00
24 Beno Udrih .40 1.00
25 Robert Horry .75 2.00
26 Tim Duncan 1.00 2.50
Tony Parker CL
27 Robert Horry .75 2.00

1971-72 Squires Virginia Team Issue

Each of these team-issued photos measure approximately 8" by 10" and feature black and white player portraits on two sheets. The player's name and vitals are listed below the photo. Each sheet contains either seven or eight player portraits. The backs are blank. The photos are unnumbered and listed below alphabetically. Julius Erving is featured in his rookie season.

COMPLETE SET (2) 25.00 50.00
1 Bill Bunting 20.00 40.00
Jim Eakins
Julius Erving
George Irvine
Neil Johnson
Mike Maloy
Doug Moe
Dana Pagett
2 Al Bianchi CO 7.50 15.00
Earl M. Foreman PRES
Charlie Scott
Ray Scott
Willie Sojourner
Adrian Smith
Roland Taylor

2000 St. Vincent Stamps

NNO1 Michael Jordan 2.00 5.00
NNO2 Michael Jordan Full Sheet 8.00 20.00

1992-93 Stadium Club

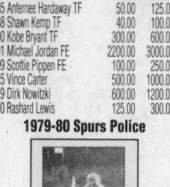

The complete 1992-93 Stadium Club basketball set (created by Topps) consists of 400 standard-size cards, having been issued in two 200-card series. Both first and second series packs contained 15 cards with a suggested retail price of $1.79 per pack. Topps also issued, late in the season, second series 23-card jumbo packs. A Stadium Club membership form was inserted in every 15-card pack. The basic card fronts feature full-bleed color action player photos. The team name and player's name appear in gold foil stripes that cut across the bottom of the card and intersect the Stadium Club logo. On a colorful background of a basketball in a net, the horizontal backs present biography, The Sporting News Skills Rating System, player evaluation, 1991-92 season and career statistics, and a miniature representation of the player's first Topps card, which is confusingly referenced as "Topps Rookie Card" by Topps. The first series closes and the second series begins with a Members Choice (191-210) subset. Rookie Cards of note include Tom Gugliotta, Robert Horry, Christian Laettner, Alonzo Mourning, Shaquille O'Neal, Latrell Sprewell and Clarence Weatherspoon.

COMPLETE SET (400) 25.00 55.00
COMPLETE SERIES 1 (200) 10.00 20.00
COMPLETE SERIES 2 (200) 15.00 35.00
1 Michael Jordan 3.00 8.00
2 Greg Anthony .02 .10
3 Otis Thorpe .10 .30
4 Jim Les .02 .10
5 Kevin Willis .02 .10
6 Derek Harper .10 .30
7 Elden Campbell .10 .30
8 A.J. English .02 .10
9 Kenny Gattison .02 .10
10 Drazen Petrovic .02 .10
11 Chris Mullin .25 .60
12 Mark Price .02 .10
13 Karl Malone .40 1.00
14 Gerald Glass .02 .10
15 Negele Knight .02 .10
16 Mark Macon .02 .10
17 Michael Cage .02 .10
18 Kevin Edwards .02 .10
19 Sherman Douglas .02 .10
20 Ron Harper .10 .30
21 Clifford Robinson .10 .30
22 Byron Scott .10 .30
23 Antoine Carr .02 .10
24 Greg Dreiling .02 .10
25 Bill Laimbeer .10 .30
26 Hersey Hawkins .10 .30
27 Will Perdue .02 .10
28 Todd Lichti .02 .10
29 Gary Grant .02 .10
30 Sam Perkins .10 .30
31 Jayson Williams .10 .30
32 Magic Johnson .75 2.00
33 Larry Bird 1.00 2.50
34 Chris Morris .02 .10
35 Nick Anderson .10 .30
36 Scott Hastings .02 .10
37 Ledell Eackles .02 .10
38 Robert Pack .02 .10
39 Dana Barros .02 .10
40 Anthony Bonner .02 .10
41 J.R. Reid .02 .10
42 Tyrone Hill .02 .10
43 Rik Smits .10 .30
44 Kevin Duckworth .02 .10
45 LaSalle Thompson .02 .10
46 Brian Williams .02 .10
47 Willie Anderson .02 .10
48 Ken Norman .02 .10
49 Mike Iuzzolino .02 .10
50 Isiah Thomas .25 .60
51 Alec Kessler .02 .10
52 Johnny Dawkins .02 .10
53 Avery Johnson .02 .10
54 Stacey Augmon .10 .30
55 Charles Oakley .10 .30
56 Rex Chapman .02 .10
57 Charles Shackleford .02 .10
58 Jeff Ruland .02 .10
59 Craig Ehlo .02 .10
60 Jon Koncak .02 .10
61 Danny Schayes .02 .10
62 David Benoit .02 .10
63 Robert Parish .10 .30
64 Mookie Blaylock .10 .30
65 Sean Elliott .10 .30
66 Mark Aguirre .02 .10
67 Scott Williams .02 .10
68 Doug West .02 .10
69 Kenny Anderson .25 .60
70 Randy Brown .02 .10
71 Muggsy Bogues .10 .30
72 Spud Webb .10 .30
73 Sedale Threatt .02 .10
74 Chris Gatling .02 .10
75 Derrick McKey .02 .10
76 Sleepy Floyd .02 .10
77 Chris Jackson .02 .10
78 Thurl Bailey .02 .10
79 Steve Smith .30 .75
80 Cedric Ceballos .02 .10
81 Anthony Bowie .02 .10
82 John Williams .02 .10
83 Paul Graham .02 .10
84 Willie Burton .02 .10
85 Vernon Maxwell .02 .10
86 Stacey King .02 .10
87 B.J. Armstrong .02 .10
88 Kevin Gamble .02 .10
89 Terry Catledge .02 .10
90 Jeff Malone .02 .10
91 Sam Bowie .02 .10
92 Orlando Woolridge .02 .10
93 Steve Kerr .10 .30
94 Eric Leckner .02 .10
95 Loy Vaught .02 .10
96 Jud Buechler .02 .10
97 Doug Smith .02 .10
98 Sidney Green .02 .10
99 Jerome Kersey .02 .10
100 Patrick Ewing .25 .60
101 Ed Nealy .02 .10
102 Shawn Kemp .50 1.25
103 Luc Longley .10 .30
104 George McCloud .02 .10
105 Ron Anderson .02 .10
106 Moses Malone UER .25 .60
(Rookie Card is 1975-76, not 1976-77)
107 Tony Smith .02 .10
108 Terry Porter .02 .10
109 Blair Rasmussen .02 .10
110 Bimbo Coles .02 .10
111 Grant Long .02 .10
112 John Battle .02 .10
113 Brian Oliver .02 .10
114 Tyrone Corbin .02 .10
115 Benoit Benjamin .02 .10
116 Rick Fox .10 .30
117 Rafael Addison .02 .10
118 Danny Young .02 .10
119 Fat Lever .02 .10
120 Terry Cummings .10 .30
121 Felton Spencer .02 .10
122 Joe Kleine .02 .10
123 Johnny Newman .02 .10
124 Gary Payton .50 1.25
125 Kurt Rambis .02 .10
126 Vlade Divac .10 .30
127 John Paxson .02 .10
128 Lionel Simmons .02 .10
129 Randy Wittman .02 .10
130 Winston Garland .02 .10
131 Jerry Reynolds .02 .10
132 Dell Curry .02 .10
133 Fred Roberts .02 .10
134 Michael Adams .02 .10
135 Charles Jones .02 .10
136 Frank Brickowski .02 .10
137 Alton Lister .02 .10
138 Horace Grant .10 .30
139 Greg Sutton .02 .10
140 John Starks .10 .30
141 Detlef Schrempf .10 .30
142 Rodney Monroe .02 .10
143 Pete Chilcutt .02 .10
144 Mike Brown .02 .10
145 Rony Seikaly .02 .10
146 Donald Hodge .02 .10
147 Kevin McHale .25 .60
148 Ricky Pierce .02 .10
149 Brian Shaw .02 .10
150 Reggie Williams .02 .10
151 Kendall Gill .10 .30
152 Tom Chambers .02 .10
153 Jack Haley .02 .10
154 Terrell Brandon .25 .60
155 Dennis Scott .10 .30
156 Mark Randall .02 .10
157 Kenny Payne .02 .10
158 Bernard King .02 .10
159 Tate George .02 .10
160 Scott Skiles .02 .10
161 Pervis Ellison .02 .10
162 Marcus Liberty .02 .10
163 Rumeal Robinson .02 .10
164 Anthony Mason .25 .60
165 Les Jepsen .02 .10
166 Kenny Smith .02 .10
167 Randy White .02 .10
168 Dee Brown .02 .10
169 Chris Dudley .02 .10
170 Armon Gilliam .02 .10
171 Eddie Johnson .02 .10
172 A.C. Green .10 .30
173 Darrell Walker .02 .10
174 Bill Cartwright .02 .10
175 Mike Gminski .02 .10
176 Tom Tolbert .02 .10
177 Buck Williams .10 .30
178 Mark Eaton .02 .10
179 Danny Manning .10 .30
180 Glen Rice .25 .60
181 Sarunas Marciulionis .02 .10
182 Danny Ferry .02 .10
183 Chris Corchiani .02 .10
184 Dan Majerle .10 .30
185 Alvin Robertson .02 .10
186 Vern Fleming .02 .10
187 Kevin Lynch .02 .10
188 John Williams .02 .10
189 Checklist 1-100 .02 .10
190 Checklist 101-200 .02 .10
191 David Robinson MC .25 .60
192 Larry Johnson MC .25 .60
193 Derrick Coleman MC .02 .10
194 Larry Bird MC .50 1.25
195 Billy Owens MC .02 .10
196 Dikembe Mutombo MC .25 .60
197 Charles Barkley MC .25 .60
198 Scottie Pippen MC .40 1.00
199 Clyde Drexler MC .10 .30
200 John Stockton MC .10 .30
201 Shaquille O'Neal MC 3.00 8.00
202 Chris Mullin MC .10 .30
203 Glen Rice MC .10 .30
204 Isiah Thomas MC .10 .30
205 Karl Malone MC .25 .60
206 Christian Laettner MC .25 .60
207 Patrick Ewing MC .10 .30
208 Dominique Wilkins MC .10 .30
209 Alonzo Mourning MC .50 1.25
210 Michael Jordan MC 1.50 4.00
211 Tim Hardaway .30 .75
212 Rodney McCray .02 .10
213 Larry Johnson .30 .75
214 Charles Smith .02 .10
215 Kevin Brooks .02 .10
216 Kevin Johnson .25 .60
217 Duane Cooper RC .02 .10
218 Christian Laettner UER RC .50 1.25
(Missing '92 Draft Pick logo)
219 Tim Perry .02 .10
220 Hakeem Olajuwon .40 1.00
221 Lee Mayberry RC .02 .10
222 Mark Bryant .02 .10
223 Robert Horry RC .25 .60
224 Tracy Murray UER RC .10 .30
(Missing '92 Draft Pick logo)
225 Greg Grant .02 .10
226 Rolando Blackman .02 .10
227 James Edwards UER .02 .10
(Rookie Card is 1978-79, not 1980-81)
228 Sean Green .02 .10
229 Buck Johnson .02 .10
230 Andrew Lang .02 .10
231 Tracy Moore RC .02 .10
232 Adam Keefe UER RC .02 .10
(Missing '92 Draft Pick logo)
233 Tony Campbell .02 .10
234 Rod Strickland .25 .60
235 Terry Mills .02 .10
236 Billy Owens .10 .30
237 Bryant Stith UER RC .10 .30
(Missing '92 Draft Pick logo)
238 Tony Bennett UER RC .02 .10
(Missing '92 Draft Pick logo)
239 David Wood .02 .10
240 Jay Humphries .02 .10
241 Doc Rivers .10 .30
242 Wayman Tisdale .02 .10
243 Litterial Green RC .02 .10
244 Jon Barry .10 .30
245 Brad Daugherty .02 .10
246 Nate McMillan .02 .10
247 Shaquille O'Neal RC 6.00 15.00
248 Chris Smith RC .02 .10
249 Duane Ferrell .02 .10
250 Anthony Peeler RC .10 .30
251 Gundars Vetra RC .02 .10
252 Danny Ainge .10 .30
253 Mitch Richmond .25 .60
254 Malik Sealy RC .10 .30
255 Brent Price RC .10 .30
256 Xavier McDaniel .02 .10
257 Bobby Phills RC .25 .60
258 Donald Royal .02 .10
259 Olden Polynice .02 .10
260 Dominique Wilkins UER .25 .60
(Scoring 10,000th point& should be 20,000th)
261 Larry Krystkowiak .02 .10
262 Duane Causwell .02 .10
263 Todd Day RC .10 .30
264 Sam Mack RC .10 .30
265 John Stockton .25 .60
266 Eddie Lee Wilkins .02 .10
267 Gerald Glass .02 .10
268 Robert Pack .02 .10
269 Gerald Wilkins .02 .10
270 Reggie Lewis .10 .30
271 Scott Brooks .02 .10
272 Randy Woods UER RC .02 .10
(Missing '92 Draft Pick logo)
273 Dikembe Mutombo .30 .75
274 Kiki Vandeweghe .02 .10
275 Rich King .02 .10
276 Jeff Turner .02 .10
277 Vinny Del Negro .02 .10
278 Marlon Maxey RC .02 .10
279 Elmore Spencer UER RC .02 .10
(Missing '92 Draft Pick logo)
280 Cedric Ceballos .10 .30
281 Alex Blackwell RC .02 .10
282 Terry Davis .02 .10
283 Morlon Wiley .02 .10
284 Trent Tucker .02 .10
285 Carl Herrera .02 .10
286 Eric Anderson RC .02 .10
287 Clyde Drexler .25 .60
288 Tom Gugliotta RC .75 2.00
289 Dale Ellis .02 .10
290 Lance Blanks .02 .10
291 Tom Hammonds .02 .10
292 Eric Murdock .02 .10
293 Walt Williams RC .25 .60
294 Gerald Paddio .02 .10
295 Brian Howard RC .02 .10
296 Ken Williams .02 .10
297 Alonzo Mourning RC 1.50 4.00
298 Larry Nance .02 .10
299 Jeff Grayer .02 .10
300 Dave Johnson RC .02 .10
301 Bob McCann RC .02 .10
302 Bart Kofoed .02 .10
303 Anthony Cook .02 .10
304 Radisav Curcic RC .02 .10
305 John Crotty RC .02 .10
306 Brad Sellers .02 .10
307 Marcus Webb RC .02 .10
308 Winston Garland .02 .10
309 Walter Palmer .02 .10
310 Rod Higgins .02 .10
311 Travis Mays .02 .10
312 Alex Stivrins RC .02 .10
313 Greg Kite .02 .10
314 Dennis Rodman .50 1.25
315 Mike Sanders .02 .10
316 Ed Pinckney .02 .10
317 Harold Miner RC .10 .30
318 Pooh Richardson .02 .10
319 Oliver Miller RC .10 .30
320 Latrell Sprewell RC 2.00 5.00
321 Anthony Pullard RC .02 .10
322 Mark Randall .02 .10
323 Jeff Hornacek .10 .30
324 Rick Mahorn UER .02 .10
(Rookie Card is 1981-82, not 1992-93)
325 Sean Rooks RC .02 .10
326 Paul Pressey .02 .10
327 James Worthy .25 .60
328 Matt Bullard .02 .10
329 Reggie Smith RC .02 .10
330 Don MacLean UER RC .02 .10
(Missing '92 Draft Pick logo)
331 John Williams UER .02 .10
(Rookie Card erroneously shows Hot Rod)
332 Frank Johnson .02 .10
333 Hubert Davis UER RC .10 .30
(Missing '92 Draft Pick logo)
334 Lloyd Daniels RC .02 .10
335 Steve Bardo RC .02 .10
336 Jeff Sanders .02 .10
337 Tree Rollins .02 .10
338 Micheal Williams .02 .10
339 Lorenzo Williams RC .02 .10
340 Harvey Grant .02 .10
341 Avery Johnson .02 .10
342 Bo Kimble .02 .10
343 LaPhonso Ellis UER RC .25 .60
(Missing '92 Draft Pick logo)
344 Mookie Blaylock .10 .30
345 Isaiah Morris UER RC .02 .10
(Missing '92 Draft Pick logo)
346 Clarence Weatherspoon RC .25 .60
347 Manute Bol .02 .10
348 Victor Alexander .02 .10
349 Corey Williams RC .02 .10
350 Byron Houston RC .02 .10
351 Stanley Roberts .02 .10
352 Anthony Avent RC .02 .10
353 Vincent Askew .02 .10
354 Herb Williams .02 .10
355 J.R. Reid .02 .10
356 Brad Lohaus .02 .10
357 Reggie Miller .25 .60
358 Blue Edwards .02 .10
359 Tom Tolbert .02 .10
360 Charles Barkley .40 1.00
361 David Robinson .40 1.00
362 Dale Davis .02 .10
363 Robert Werdann UER RC .02 .10
(Missing '92 Draft Pick logo)
364 Chuck Person .02 .10
365 Alaa Abdelnaby .02 .10
366 Dave Jamerson .02 .10
367 Scottie Pippen .75 2.00
368 Mark Jackson .10 .30
369 Keith Askins .02 .10
370 Marty Conlon .02 .10
371 Chucky Brown .02 .10
372 LaBradford Smith .02 .10
373 Tim Kempton .02 .10
374 Sam Mitchell .02 .10
375 John Salley .02 .10
376 Mario Elie .10 .30
377 Mark West .02 .10
378 David Wingate .02 .10
379 Jaren Jackson RC .10 .30
380 Rumeal Robinson .02 .10
381 Kennard Winchester .02 .10
382 Walter Bond RC .02 .10
383 Isaac Austin RC .10 .30
384 Derrick Coleman .10 .30
385 Larry Smith .02 .10
386 Joe Dumars .25 .60
387 Matt Geiger UER RC .10 .30
(Missing '92 Draft Pick logo)
388 Stephen Howard RC .02 .10
389 William Bedford .02 .10
390 Jayson Williams .10 .30
391 Kurt Rambis .02 .10
392 Keith Jennings RC .02 .10
393 Steve Kerr UER .10 .30
(The words key stat are repeated on back)
394 Larry Stewart .02 .10
395 Danny Young .02 .10
396 Doug Overton .02 .10
397 Mark Acres .02 .10

John Bagley .02 .10
Checklist 201-300 .02 .10
Checklist 301-400 .02 .10

1992-93 Stadium Club Beam Team

mprised of some of the NBA's biggest stars, "Beam am" cards commemorate Topps' 1993 sponsorship a six-minute NBA laser animation show called ams Above the Rim. The show premiered at the 1993 A All-Star Game. Afterwards, the laser show barked on a ten-city tour and was featured in either pre-game or half-time events in ten NBA arenas. ese cards were randomly inserted in second series -card packs at a rate of one in 36. The color action yer photos on the fronts are bordered on two sides an angled silver light beam border design with a ht refracting pattern. The player's name appears on a ite-outlined burnt orange bar superimposed over a sketball icon at the bottom. The backs present a lor head shot and, on a basketball icon, career hlights.

MPLETE SET (21) 75.00 150.00
Michael Jordan 25.00 60.00
Dominique Wilkins 1.50 4.00
Shawn Kemp 2.50 6.00
Clyde Drexler 1.50 4.00
Scottie Pippen 5.00 12.00
Chris Mullin 1.50 4.00
Reggie Miller 1.50 4.00
Glen Rice 1.50 4.00
Jeff Hornacek .75 2.00
Jeff Malone .60 1.50
John Stockton 1.50 4.00
Kevin Johnson 1.50 4.00
Mark Price .60 1.50
Tim Hardaway 2.00 5.00
Charles Barkley 2.50 6.00
Hakeem Olajuwon 2.50 6.00
Karl Malone 2.50 6.00
Patrick Ewing 1.50 4.00
Dennis Rodman 3.00 8.00
David Robinson 2.50 6.00
Shaquille O'Neal 25.00 60.00

1993-94 Stadium Club

e 1993-94 Stadium Club set consists of 360 andard-size cards issued in two series of 180 cards. rds were issued in 12 and 20-card packs. There re 24 twelve-card packs per box. The full-bleed nts feature glossy color action photos. The player's me is superimposed on the lower portion of the ture in white and gold foil lettering. The borderless cks are divided in half vertically with a torn effect. e left side sports a vertical player photo and on the ht side, over a purple background, is biography and yer's name and team. A brief section named "The zz" provides career highlights. A multi-colored box ts the 1992-93 statistics, career statistics and a pps Skills Rating System that provides a score cluding player intimidation, mobility, shooting range d defense. Subsets featured are Triple Double (1-11, 1-111) and High Court (61-69, 170-178) and erspersed NBA Draft Picks. Card number 345 was ver issued. Due to an error in numbering, both Toni koc and Chris Corchiani are numbered 336. rchiani is actually listed on the checklist card as mber 345, thus we've listed him below in that order. okie Cards of note in this set include Vin Baker, fernee Hardaway, Allan Houston, Toni Kukoc, Jamal ashburn, Nick Van Exel and Chris Webber.

MPLETE SET (360) 20.00 40.00
MPLETE SERIES 1 (180) 10.00 20.00
MPLETE SERIES 2 (180) 10.00 20.00
Michael Jordan TD 1.00 2.50
Kenny Anderson TD .02 .10
Steve Smith TD .07 .20
Kevin Gamble TD .02 .10
Detlef Schrempf TD .02 .10
Larry Johnson TD .07 .20
Brad Daugherty TD .02 .10
Rumeal Robinson TD .02 .10
Micheal Williams TD .02 .10
David Robinson TD .15 .40
Sam Perkins TD .02 .10
Thurl Bailey .02 .10
Sherman Douglas .02 .10
Larry Stewart .02 .10
Kevin Johnson .07 .20
Bill Cartwright .02 .10
Larry Nance .02 .10
P.J. Brown RC .15 .40
Tony Bennett .02 .10
Robert Parish .07 .20
David Benoit .02 .10
Detlef Schrempf .07 .20
Hubert Davis .02 .10
Donald Hodge .02 .10
Hersey Hawkins .07 .20
Mark Jackson .07 .20
Reggie Williams .02 .10
Lionel Simmons .02 .10
Ron Harper .07 .20
Chris Mills RC .15 .40
Danny Schayes .02 .10
J.R. Reid .02 .10
Willie Burton .02 .10
Greg Anthony .02 .10
Elden Campbell .02 .10
Ervin Johnson RC .07 .20
Scott Brooks .02 .10
Johnny Newman .02 .10
39 Rex Chapman .02 .10
40 Chuck Person .02 .10
41 John Williams .02 .10
42 Anthony Bowie .02 .10
43 Negele Knight .02 .10
44 Tyrone Corbin .02 .10
45 Jud Buechler .02 .10
46 Adam Keefe .02 .10
47 Glen Rice .07 .20
48 Tracy Murray .02 .10
49 Rick Mahorn .02 .10
50 Vlade Divac .07 .20
51 Eric Murdock .02 .10
52 Isaiah Morris .02 .10
53 Bobby Hurley RC .07 .20
54 Mitch Richmond .15 .40
55 Danny Ainge .07 .20
56 Dikembe Mutombo .15 .40
57 Jeff Hornacek .07 .20
58 Tony Campbell .02 .10
59 Vinny Del Negro .02 .10
60 Xavier McDaniel HC .02 .10
61 Scottie Pippen HC .25 .60
62 Larry Nance HC .02 .10
63 Dikembe Mutombo HC .07 .20
64 Hakeem Olajuwon HC .15 .40
65 Dominique Wilkins HC .07 .20
66 Clarence Weatherspoon HC .02 .10
67 Chris Morris HC .02 .10
68 Patrick Ewing HC .07 .20
69 Kevin Willis HC .02 .10
70 Jon Barry .02 .10
71 Jerry Reynolds .02 .10
72 Sarunas Marciulionis .02 .10
73 Mark West .02 .10
74 B.J. Armstrong .02 .10
75 Greg Kite .02 .10
76 LaSalle Thompson .02 .10
77 Randy White .02 .10
78 Alaa Abdelnaby .02 .10
79 Kevin Brooks .02 .10
80 Vern Fleming .02 .10
81 Doc Rivers .07 .20
82 Shawn Bradley RC .15 .40
83 Wayman Tisdale .02 .10
84 Olden Polynice .02 .10
85 Michael Cage .02 .10
86 Harold Miner .02 .10
87 Doug Smith .02 .10
88 Tom Gugliotta .15 .40
89 Hakeem Olajuwon .25 .60
90 Loy Vaught .02 .10
91 James Worthy .15 .40
92 John Paxson .02 .10
93 Jon Koncak .02 .10
94 Lee Mayberry .02 .10
95 Clarence Weatherspoon .02 .10
96 Mark Eaton .02 .10
97 Rex Walters RC .02 .10
98 Alvin Robertson .02 .10
99 Dan Majerle .07 .20
100 Shaquille O'Neal .75 2.00
101 Derrick Coleman TD .02 .10
102 Hersey Hawkins TD .02 .10
103 Scottie Pippen TD .25 .60
104 Scott Skiles TD .02 .10
105 Rod Strickland TD .02 .10
106 Pooh Richardson TD .02 .10
107 Tom Gugliotta TD .07 .20
108 Mark Jackson TD .02 .10
109 Dikembe Mutombo TD .07 .20
110 Charles Barkley TD .15 .40
111 Otis Thorpe TD .02 .10
112 Malik Sealy .02 .10
113 Mark Macon .02 .10
114 Dee Brown .02 .10
115 Nate McMillan .02 .10
116 John Starks .07 .20
117 Clyde Drexler .15 .40
118 Antoine Carr .02 .10
119 Doug West .02 .10
120 Victor Alexander .02 .10
121 Kenny Gattison .02 .10
122 Spud Webb .07 .20
123 Rumeal Robinson .02 .10
124 Tim Kempton .02 .10
125 Karl Malone .25 .60
126 Randy Woods .02 .10
127 Calbert Cheaney RC .07 .20
128 Johnny Dawkins .02 .10
129 Dominique Wilkins .15 .40
130 Horace Grant .07 .20
131 Bill Laimbeer .02 .10
132 Kenny Smith .02 .10
133 Sedale Threatt .02 .10
134 Brian Shaw .02 .10
135 Dennis Scott .02 .10
136 Mark Bryant .02 .10
137 Xavier McDaniel .02 .10
138 David Wood .02 .10
139 Luther Wright RC .02 .10
140 Lloyd Daniels .02 .10
141 Marlon Maxey UER .02 .10
(Name spelled Maxley on the front)
142 Pooh Richardson .02 .10
143 Jeff Grayer .02 .10
144 LaPhonso Ellis .02 .10
145 Gerald Wilkins .02 .10
146 Dell Curry .02 .10
147 Duane Causwell .02 .10
148 Tim Hardaway .15 .40
149 Isiah Thomas .15 .40
150 Doug Edwards RC .02 .10
151 Anthony Peeler .02 .10
152 Tate George .02 .10
153 Terry Davis .02 .10
154 Sam Perkins .07 .20
155 John Salley .02 .10
156 Vernon Maxwell .02 .10
157 Anthony Avent .02 .10
158 Clifford Robinson .07 .20
159 Corie Blount RC .02 .10
160 Gerald Paddio .02 .10
161 Blair Rasmussen .02 .10
162 Carl Herrera .02 .10
163 Chris Smith .02 .10
164 Pervis Ellison .02 .10
165 Rod Strickland .07 .20
166 Jeff Malone .02 .10
167 Danny Ferry .02 .10
168 Kevin Lynch .02 .10
169 Michael Jordan 2.00 5.00
170 Derrick Coleman HC .02 .10
171 Jerome Kersey HC .02 .10
172 David Robinson HC .15 .40
173 Shawn Kemp HC .15 .40
174 Karl Malone HC .15 .40
175 Shaquille O'Neal HC .30 .75
176 Alonzo Mourning HC .15 .40
177 Charles Barkley HC .15 .40
178 Larry Johnson HC .07 .20
179 Checklist 1-90 .02 .10
180 Checklist 91-180 .02 .10
181 Michael Jordan FF .75 2.00
182 Dominique Wilkins FF .05 .15
183 Dennis Rodman FF .10 .30
184 Scottie Pippen FF .20 .50
185 Larry Johnson FF .07 .20
186 Karl Malone FF .10 .30
187 Clarence Weatherspoon FF .01 .05
188 Charles Barkley FF .10 .30
189 Patrick Ewing FF .07 .20
190 Derrick Coleman FF .01 .05
191 LaBradford Smith .01 .05
192 Derek Harper .05 .15
193 Ken Norman .01 .05
194 Rodney Rogers RC .10 .30
195 Chris Dudley .01 .05
196 Gary Payton .20 .50
197 Andrew Lang .01 .05
198 Billy Owens .01 .05
199 Bryon Russell RC .10 .30
200 Patrick Ewing .10 .30
201 Stacey King .01 .05
202 Grant Long .01 .05
203 Sean Elliott .05 .15
204 Muggsy Bogues .05 .15
205 Kevin Edwards .01 .05
206 Dale Davis .01 .05
207 Dale Ellis .01 .05
208 Terrell Brandon .05 .15
209 Kevin Gamble .01 .05
210 Robert Horry .05 .15
211 Moses Malone UER .15 .40
Birthdate on back is 1993
212 Gary Grant .01 .05
213 Bobby Hurley .05 .15
214 Larry Krystkowiak .01 .05
215 A.C. Green .05 .15
216 Christian Laettner .05 .15
217 Orlando Woolridge .01 .05
218 Craig Ehlo .01 .05
219 Terry Porter .01 .05
220 Jamal Mashburn RC .40 1.00
221 Kevin Duckworth .01 .05
222 Shawn Kemp .20 .50
223 Frank Brickowski .01 .05
224 Chris Webber RC 1.25 3.00
225 Charles Oakley .05 .15
226 Jay Humphries .01 .05
227 Steve Kerr .05 .15
228 Tim Perry .01 .05
229 Sleepy Floyd .01 .05
230 Bimbo Coles .01 .05
231 Eddie Johnson .01 .05
232 Terry Mills .01 .05
233 Danny Manning .05 .15
234 Isaiah Rider RC .30 .75
235 Darnell Mee RC .01 .05
236 Haywoode Workman .01 .05
237 Scott Skiles .01 .05
238 Otis Thorpe .05 .15
239 Mike Peplowski RC .01 .05
240 Eric Leckner .01 .05
241 Johnny Newman .01 .05
242 Benoit Benjamin .01 .05
243 Doug Christie .05 .15
244 Acie Earl RC .01 .05
245 Luc Longley .05 .15
246 Tyrone Hill .01 .05
247 Allan Houston RC .50 1.25
248 Joe Kleine .01 .05
249 Mookie Blaylock .05 .15
250 Anthony Bonner .01 .05
251 Luther Wright .01 .05
252 Todd Day .01 .05
253 Kendall Gill .05 .15
254 Mario Elie .01 .05
255 Pete Myers UER .01 .05
Card has born in 1993
256 Jim Les .01 .05
257 Stanley Roberts .01 .05
258 Michael Adams .01 .05
259 Hersey Hawkins .05 .15
260 Shawn Bradley .07 .20
261 Scott Haskin RC .01 .05
262 Corie Blount .01 .05
263 Charles Smith .01 .05
264 Armon Gilliam .01 .05
265 Jamal Mashburn NW .10 .30
266 Anfernee Hardaway NW .50 1.25
267 Shawn Bradley NW .07 .20
268 Chris Webber NW .60 1.50
269 Bobby Hurley NW .01 .05
270 Isaiah Rider NW .10 .30
271 Dino Radja NW .01 .05
272 Chris Mills NW .05 .15
273 Nick Van Exel NW .10 .30
274 Lindsey Hunter NW .07 .20
275 Toni Kukoc NW .10 .30
276 Popeye Jones NW .01 .05
277 Chris Mills .15 .40
278 Ricky Pierce .01 .05
279 Negele Knight .01 .05
280 Kenny Walker .01 .05
281 Nick Van Exel RC .40 1.00
282 Derrick Coleman UER .05 .15
(Career stats listed under '92-93)
283 Popeye Jones RC .01 .05
284 Derrick McKey .01 .05
285 Rick Fox .01 .05
286 Jerome Kersey .01 .05
287 Steve Smith .10 .30
288 Brian Williams .01 .05
289 Chris Mullin .10 .30
290 Terry Cummings .01 .05
291 Donald Royal .01 .05
292 Alonzo Mourning .20 .50
293 Mike Brown .01 .05
294 Latrell Sprewell .30 .75
295 Oliver Miller .01 .05
296 Terry Dehere RC .01 .05
297 Detlef Schrempf .05 .15
298 Sam Bowie UER .01 .05
(Last name Bowe on front)
299 Chris Morris .01 .05
300 Scottie Pippen .40 1.00
301 Warren Kidd RC .01 .05
302 Don MacLean .01 .05
303 Sean Rooks .01 .05
304 Matt Geiger .01 .05
305 Dennis Rodman .25 .60
306 Reggie Miller .10 .30
307 Vin Baker RC .30 .75
308 Anfernee Hardaway RC 1.00 2.50
309 Lindsey Hunter RC .10 .30
310 Stacey Augmon .01 .05
311 Randy Brown .01 .05
312 Anthony Mason .05 .15
313 John Stockton .10 .30
314 Sam Cassell RC .50 1.25
315 Buck Williams .01 .05
316 Bryant Stith .01 .05
317 Brad Daugherty .01 .05
318 Dino Radja RC .01 .05
319 Rony Seikaly .01 .05
320 Charles Barkley .25 .60
321 Avery Johnson .01 .05
322 Mahmoud Abdul-Rauf .01 .05
323 Larry Johnson .10 .30
324 Micheal Williams .01 .05
325 Mark Aguirre .01 .05
326 Jim Jackson .05 .15
327 Antonio Harvey RC .01 .05
328 David Robinson .20 .50
329 Calbert Cheaney .02 .10
330 Kenny Anderson .07 .20
331 Walt Williams .02 .10
332 Kevin Willis .01 .05
333 Nick Anderson .05 .15
334 Rik Smits .05 .15
335 Joe Dumars .15 .40
336 Toni Kukoc RC .50 1.25
337 Harvey Grant .01 .05
338 Tom Chambers .01 .05
339 Blue Edwards .01 .05
340 Mark Price .01 .05
341 Ervin Johnson .05 .15
342 Rolando Blackman .01 .05
343 Scott Burrell RC .10 .30
344 Gheorghe Muresan RC .10 .30
345 Chris Corchiani UER 336 .01 .05
346 Richard Petruska RC .01 .05
347 Dana Barros .01 .05
348 Hakeem Olajuwon FF .10 .30
349 Dee Brown FF .01 .05
350 John Starks FF .01 .05
351 Ron Harper FF .01 .05
352 Chris Webber FF .60 1.50
353 Dan Majerle FF .01 .05
354 Clyde Drexler FF .05 .15
355 Shawn Kemp FF .10 .30
356 David Robinson FF .10 .30
357 Chris Morris FF .01 .05
358 Shaquille O'Neal FF .25 .60
359 Checklist .01 .05
360 Checklist .01 .05

1993-94 Stadium Club First Day Issue

Randomly inserted in first and second series foil packs at a rate of 1 in 24, the First Day Issue set parallels that of the basic Stadium Club set. Each of the 360 standard-size cards have a prismatic silver First Day logo in one upper corner. Topps announced that there were 1,000 of each card produced. Collectors should exercise caution when trading in these cards as some unscrupulous parties attempted to transfer the First Day logo from common First Day cards on to regular issue star cards. To ascertain values on individual cards, please refer to the multiplier in the header, coupled with the value of the base card.

*SER.1 STARS: 10X TO 20X BASE CARD HI
*SER.2 STARS: 25X TO 50X HI
*SER.1 RCs: 7.5X TO 15X BASE HI
*SER.2 RCs: 20X TO 40X HI

1993-94 Stadium Club Beam Team

Randomly inserted in first and second series 12-card and 20-card foil packs at a rate of one in 24, cards from this standard-size 27-card set features a selection of top NBA stars and rookies. Cards were issued in two series of 13 and 14, respectively. The design consists of borderless fronts with color player action photos set against game-crowd backgrounds. Silver metallic beams appear near the bottom above the player's name. The horizontal back carries a color action photo on one side, with player profile on the other. The cards are numbered on the back as "X of 27."

COMPLETE SET (27) 20.00 50.00
COMPLETE SERIES 1 (13) 12.00 30.00
COMPLETE SERIES 2 (14) 8.00 20.00
1 Shaquille O'Neal 3.00 8.00
2 Mark Price .20 .50
3 Patrick Ewing .50 1.25
4 Michael Jordan 10.00 25.00
5 Charles Barkley .60 1.50
6 Reggie Miller .50 1.25
7 Derrick Coleman .30 .75
8 Dominique Wilkins .50 1.25
9 Karl Malone .60 1.50
10 Alonzo Mourning .60 1.50
11 Tim Hardaway .50 1.25
12 Hakeem Olajuwon .60 1.50
13 David Robinson .60 1.50
14 Dan Majerle .30 .75
15 Larry Johnson .50 1.25
16 LaPhonso Ellis .20 .50
17 Nick Van Exel 1.00 2.50
18 Scottie Pippen 1.50 4.00
19 John Stockton .50 1.25
20 Bobby Hurley .30 .75
21 Chris Webber 3.00 8.00
22 Jamal Mashburn .60 1.50
23 Anfernee Hardaway 2.50 6.00
24 Isaiah Rider .60 1.50
25 Ken Norman .20 .50
26 Danny Manning .30 .75
27 Calbert Cheaney .30 .75

1993-94 Stadium Club Big Tips

Randomly inserted about one in every four packs, these 27 team logo cards measure the standard size. The horizontal black fronts are framed by a thin white line and carry the words "NBA Showdown '94," the NBA logo and the team name and logo within a team-colored stripe across the bottom. The back carries game hints for the Electronic Arts NBA Showdown '94 and a videogame offer. The logo cards are unnumbered and checklisted below in alphabetical team order.

COMPLETE SET (27) 2.50 5.00
COMMON CARD (1-27) .08 .25

1993-94 Stadium Club Frequent Flyer Points

Randomly inserted in second series packs were 100 different Frequent Flyer point cards with 20 of the best NBA jumpshot stars each having five different point cards. The insertion rate was one in every six packs. Upon collecting 50 points or more for one particular player the collector could send the cards to Topps and receive a limited edition Frequent Flyer Upgrade card for the same player. The blue-bordered fronts features a rainbow colored map of the United States with a diagram of when, where and how many points the player scored. The players name appears in yellow in the upper right. The purple-bordered back features the rules on a ghosted sky background.

COMPLETE SET (100) 10.00 25.00
1 Charles Barkley .10 .30
2 Dee Brown .02 .10
3 Derrick Coleman .05 .15
4 Clyde Drexler .07 .20
5 Patrick Ewing .07 .20
6 Ron Harper .05 .15
7 Larry Johnson .05 .15
8 Shawn Kemp .08 .25
9 Dan Majerle .05 .15
10 Karl Malone .20 .50
11 Chris Morris .02 .10
12 Hakeem Olajuwon .10 .30
13 Shaquille O'Neal .40 1.00
14 Scottie Pippen .25 .60
15 David Robinson .10 .30
16 Dennis Rodman .10 .30
17 John Starks .05 .15
18 Clarence Weatherspoon .02 .10
19 Chris Webber .50 1.25
20 Dominique Wilkins .07 .20

1993-94 Stadium Club Frequent Flyer Upgrades

Cards from this 20-card standard size set are based upon the Frequent Flyer subsets in the basic 1993-94 Stadium Club issue. Upgrades are identical to the basic cards with the exception of a chromium like metallic gloss and Upgrade logo on front. Upgrades were available only through a mail offer based on Frequent Flyer Point cards which were randomly inserted at a rate of 1 in every 6 second series packs. Each of the 21 players featured in the Frequent Flyer subsets (except for Michael Jordan) had five different point cards (based upon point totals derived from actual games during the season) making for a total of 100 different point cards. Since none of the point cards feature player photos, none trade for a premium and are priced below as expired point cards. To obtain a Frequent Flyer Upgrade card, collectors had to accumulate 50 points or more of an individual player and redeem them by September 15, 1994.

COMPLETE SET (20) 45.00 75.00
182 Dominique Wilkins 2.00 5.00
183 Dennis Rodman 3.00 8.00
184 Scottie Pippen 5.00 12.00
185 Larry Johnson 2.00 5.00
186 Karl Malone 3.00 8.00
187 Clarence Weatherspoon .50 1.25
188 Charles Barkley 3.00 8.00
189 Patrick Ewing 2.00 5.00
190 Derrick Coleman 1.00 2.50
348 Hakeem Olajuwon 3.00 8.00
349 Dee Brown .50 1.25
350 John Starks 1.00 2.50
351 Ron Harper 1.00 2.50
352 Chris Webber 10.00 25.00
353 Dan Majerle 1.00 2.50
354 Clyde Drexler 2.00 5.00
355 Shawn Kemp 2.50 6.00
356 David Robinson 2.50 6.00
357 Chris Morris .50 1.25
358 Shaquille O'Neal 10.00 25.00
NNO Expired Point Cards .08 .25

1993-94 Stadium Club Rim Rockers

Randomly inserted in second series 12-card packs at a rate of one in 24, these six standard-size cards feature some of the NBA's top dunkers. Fronts contain color player action shots. The player's name appears near the bottom. His first name is printed in white lowercase lettering; his last is gold-foil stamped in uppercase lettering. The back carries another borderless color player action shot, but its right side is ghosted, blue-screened, and overprinted with career highlights in white lettering. The cards are numbered on the back as "X of 6."

COMPLETE SET (6) 3.00 6.00
1 Shaquille O'Neal 1.50 4.00
2 Harold Miner .07 .20
3 Charles Barkley .50 1.25
4 Dominique Wilkins .30 .75
5 Shawn Kemp .40 1.00
6 Robert Horry .10 .30

1993-94 Stadium Club Super Teams

Randomly inserted in first series 12 and 20-card foil packs at a rate of one in 24, cards from this standard-size 27-card set feature borderless fronts with color team action photos. The team name appears in gold-foil lettering at the bottom. The back features the NBA Super Team Card rules. If the team shown on the card won its division, conference or league championship, the collector could have redeemed it for special prizes until Nov. 1, 1994. Atlanta, Houston, New York and Seattle were all winners. Their cards are currently in shorter supply than non-winner Super Team cards. The four winning teams are designated below with a "W". In addition, Conference, Division and Finals winner cards have "C", "D" and "F" designations.

COMPLETE SET (27) 7.50 15.00
1 Atlanta Hawks WD .15 .40
(Kevin Willis
Dominique Wilkins)
2 Boston Celtics .15 .40
(Xavier McDaniel
Robert Parish)
3 Charlotte Hornets .75 2.00
(Larry Johnson
Alonzo Mourning)
4 Chicago Bulls .15 .40
(Horace Grant)
5 Cleveland Cavaliers .15 .40
(Brad Daugherty
John Williams)
6 Dallas Mavericks .15 .40
(Group photo)
7 Denver Nuggets .75 2.00
(Dikembe Mutombo
Kevin Brooks)
8 Detroit Pistons .15 .40
(Group photo)
9 Golden State Warriors .15 .40
(Group photo)
10 Houston Rockets WCDF 2.50 6.00
(Group photo)
11 Indiana Pacers .15 .40
(Group photo)
12 Los Angeles Clippers .15 .40
(Danny Manning
Ron Harper)
13 Los Angeles Lakers .15 .40
(Group photo)
14 Miami Heat .15 .40
(John Salley
Willie Burton)
15 Milwaukee Bucks .15 .40
(Group photo)
16 Minnesota Timberwolves .75 2.00
(Christian Laettner
Felton Spencer)
17 New Jersey Nets .15 .40
(Derrick Coleman)
18 New York Knicks WCD 1.00 2.50
(Patrick Ewing)
19 Orlando Magic 2.50 6.00
(Shaquille O'Neal)
20 Philadelphia 76ers .15 .40
(Clarence Weatherspoon
Jeff Hornacek)
21 Phoenix Suns .50 1.25
(Charles Barkley
Dan Majerle)
22 Portland Trail Blazers .15 .40
(Buck Williams)
23 Sacramento Kings .15 .40
(Lionel Simmons)
24 San Antonio Spurs .50 1.25
(David Robinson)
25 Seattle Supersonics WD .75 2.00
(Shawn Kemp)
26 Utah Jazz .15 .40
(Group photo)
27 Washington Bullets .15 .40
(Group photo)

1993-94 Stadium Club Super Teams Division Winners

Collectors who pulled either a Hawks, Knicks, Rockets or Sonics Super Team insert card (randomly inserted in 1993-94 Stadium Club series 1 packs) could exchange the card for an 11-card Division Winners team set. The offer expired November 1, 1994. The cards are identical to their regular issue counterparts, except for the gold-foil Division Winner logo on their fronts. In the listing below, the suffixes H, K, R, and S have been added to denote Hawks, Knicks, Rockets and Supersonics.

COMPLETE BAG HAWKS (11) 3.00 6.00
COMPLETE BAG KNICKS (11) 3.00 6.00
COMPLETE BAG ROCKETS (11) 5.00 10.00
COMPLETE BAG SONICS (11) 5.00 10.00
H46 Adam Keefe .20 .50
H93 Jon Koncak .20 .50
H129 Dominique Wilkins .50 1.25
H150 Doug Edwards DP .20 .50
H197 Andrew Lang .20 .50
H218 Craig Ehlo .20 .50
H233 Danny Manning .40 1.00
H249 Mookie Blaylock .40 1.00
H310 Stacey Augmon .20 .50
H332 Kevin Willis .20 .50
K23 Hubert Davis .20 .50
K34 Greg Anthony .20 .50
K81 Doc Rivers .40 1.00
K116 John Starks .40 1.00
K192 Derek Harper .40 1.00
K200 Patrick Ewing 1.00 2.50
K225 Charles Oakley .40 1.00
K250 Anthony Bonner .20 .50
K263 Charles Smith .20 .50
K312 Anthony Mason .40 1.00
R37 Scott Brooks .20 .50
R89 Hakeem Olajuwon 2.50 6.00
R132 Kenny Smith .20 .50
R156 Vernon Maxwell .20 .50
R162 Carl Herrera .20 .50
R210 Robert Horry 1.00 2.50

R238 Otis Thorpe .40 1.00
R254 Mario Elie .20 .50
R314 Sam Cassell 1.25 3.00
R346 Richard Petruska .20 .50
S85 Michael Cage .20 .50
S115 Nate McMillan .20 .50
S154 Sam Perkins .40 1.00
S173 Shawn Kemp HC .50 1.25
S196 Gary Payton 2.50 6.00
S222 Shawn Kemp 1.50 4.00
S253 Kendall Gill .40 1.00
S278 Ricky Pierce .20 .50
S297 Detlef Schrempf .40 1.00
S341 Ervin Johnson .40 1.00
HD1 Hawks DW Super Team .20 .50
KD18 Knicks DW Super Team .20 .50
RD10 Rocket DW Super Team .20 .50
SD25 Sonics DW Super Team .20 .50

1993-94 Stadium Club Super Teams Master Photos

Collectors who pulled either a Knicks or Rockets Super Team insert card (randomly inserted in 1993-94 Stadium Club series 1 packs) could exchange the card via mail for a 11-card Master Photo set. The expiration date for the offer was November 1, 1994. Measuring 5" by 7", the cards are numbered on the back "X of 10." In the listing below, the suffixes K and R have been added to denote Knicks and Rockets.

COMPLETE BAG KNICKS (11) 5.00 10.00
COMPLETE BAG ROCKETS (11) 7.50 15.00
K1 Greg Anthony .30 .75
K2 Anthony Bonner .30 .75
K3 Hubert Davis .30 .75
K4 Patrick Ewing 1.50 4.00
K5 Derek Harper .60 1.50
K6 Anthony Mason .60 1.50
K7 Charles Oakley .60 1.50
K8 Doc Rivers .60 1.50
K9 Charles Smith .30 .75
K10 John Starks .60 1.50
KMP Knicks MP Superteam .30 .75
R1 Scott Brooks .30 .75
R2 Sam Cassell 2.00 5.00
R3 Mario Elie .30 .75
R4 Carl Herrera .30 .75
R5 Robert Horry 1.50 4.00
R6 Vernon Maxwell .30 .75
R7 Hakeem Olajuwon 4.00 10.00
R8 Richard Petruska .30 .75
R9 Kenny Smith .30 .75
R10 Otis Thorpe .60 1.50
RMP Rockets MP Superteam .30 .75

1993-94 Stadium Club Super Teams NBA Finals

This parallel issue to the 1993-94 Stadium Club set was redeemable only by mail in exchange for the Houston Rockets Super Team card (randomly inserted into 1993-94 Stadium Club series 1 packs.) The card had to be mailed in before the Nov. 1st, 1994 deadline. A gold-foil NBA Finals logo on the front distinguishes these cards from their regular issue counterparts. Please refer to the multipliers provided below (coupled with the prices of the corresponding regular issue cards) to ascertain value.

COMPLETE SET (361) 35.00 60.00
*SER.1 STARS: 1.25X TO 2.5X VALUE
*SER.2 STARS: 1.5X TO 3X VALUE
*SER.1 RC's: 1X TO 2X VALUE
*SER.2 RC's: 1.25X TO 2.5X VALUE

1994-95 Stadium Club

The 362 standard size cards that comprise the 1994-95 Stadium Club set were issued in two separate series of 182 and 180 cards each. Cards were primarily distributed in 12-card packs, each with a suggested retail price of $2.00. Full-bleed fronts feature full-color action shots with player's name placed along the bottom in foil. Topical subsets featured are College Teammates (100-114), Draft Picks (172, 179-182), All-Import (201-205, 251-255), Back Court Tandem (226-230, 276-280, 326-330), and Faces of the Game (353-362). Other topical subsets, such as Thru the Glass as well as First and Second Round '94 Draft Picks, are scattered throughout the set. Autographed cards of Reggie Miller were randomly inserted one per box into special retail boxes. Rookie Cards of note include Grant Hill, Juwan Howard, Eddie Jones, Jason Kidd and Glenn Robinson.

COMPLETE SET (362) 15.00 40.00
COMPLETE SERIES 1 (182) 8.00 20.00
COMPLETE SERIES 2 (180) 8.00 20.00
1 Patrick Ewing .20 .50
2 Patrick Ewing TG .20 .50
3 Bimbo Coles .10 .25
4 Elden Campbell .10 .25
5 Brent Price .10 .25
6 Hubert Davis .10 .25
7 Donald Royal .10 .25
8 Tim Perry .10 .25
9 Chris Webber .25 .60
10 Chris Webber TG .25 .60
11 Brad Daugherty .12 .30
12 P.J. Brown .10 .25
13 Charles Barkley .25 .60
14 Mario Elie .10 .25
15 Tyrone Hill .10 .25
16 Anfernee Hardaway .25 .60
17 Anfernee Hardaway TG .25 .60
18 Toni Kukoc .20 .50
19 Chris Morris .10 .25

20 Gerald Wilkins .10 .25
21 David Benoit .10 .25
22 Kevin Duckworth .10 .25
23 Derrick Coleman .12 .30
24 Adam Keefe .10 .25
25 Marlon Maxey .10 .25
26 Vern Fleming .10 .25
27 Jeff Malone .10 .25
28 Rodney Rogers .10 .25
29 Terry Mills .10 .25
30 Doug West .10 .25
31 Doug West TTG .10 .25
32 Shaquille O'Neal .40 1.00
33 Scottie Pippen .30 .75
34 Lee Mayberry .10 .25
35 Dale Ellis .10 .25
36 Cedric Ceballos .10 .25
37 Lionel Simmons .10 .25
38 Kenny Gattison .10 .25
39 Popeye Jones .10 .25
40 Jerome Kersey .10 .25
41 Jerome Kersey TTG .10 .25
42 Larry Stewart .10 .25
43 Rod Strickland .10 .25
44 Chris Mills .10 .25
45 Latrell Sprewell .20 .50
46 Haywoode Workman .10 .25
47 Charles Smith .10 .25
48 Detlef Schrempf .15 .40
49 Gary Grant .10 .25
50 Gary Grant TTG .10 .25
51 Tom Chambers .15 .40
52 J.R. Reid .10 .25
53 Mookie Blaylock .10 .25
54 Mookie Blaylock TTG .10 .25
55 Rony Seikaly .12 .30
56 Isaiah Rider .15 .40
57 Isaiah Rider TTG .15 .40
58 Nick Anderson .10 .25
59 Victor Alexander .10 .25
60 Lucious Harris .10 .25
61 Mark Macon .10 .25
62 Otis Thorpe .10 .25
63 Randy Woods .10 .25
64 Clyde Drexler .20 .50
65 Dikembe Mutombo .15 .40
66 Todd Day .10 .25
67 Greg Anthony .10 .25
68 Sherman Douglas .10 .25
69 Chris Mullin .15 .40
70 Kevin Johnson .15 .40
71 Kendall Gill .10 .25
72 Dennis Rodman .30 .75
73 Dennis Rodman TG .30 .75
74 Jeff Turner .10 .25
75 John Stockton .20 .50
76 John Stockton TTG .20 .50
77 Doug Edwards .10 .25
78 Jim Jackson .10 .25
79 Hakeem Olajuwon .20 .50
80 Glen Rice .15 .40
81 Christian Laettner .12 .30
82 Terry Porter .10 .25
83 Joe Dumars .15 .40
84 David Wingate .10 .25
85 B.J. Armstrong .10 .25
86 Derrick McKey .10 .25
87 Elmore Spencer .10 .25
88 Walt Williams .10 .25
89 Shawn Bradley .10 .25
90 Acie Earl .10 .25
91 Acie Earl TTG .10 .25
92 Randy Brown .10 .25
93 Grant Long .10 .25
94 Terry Dehere .10 .25
95 Spud Webb .15 .40
96 Lindsey Hunter .10 .25
97 Blair Rasmussen .10 .25
98 Tim Hardaway .15 .40
99 Kevin Edwards .10 .25
100 Patrick Ewing CT .20 .50
Reggie Williams CT
101 Chuck Person CT .25 .60
Charles Barkley CT
102 Mahmoud Abdul-Rauf CT .40 1.00
Shaquille O'Neal CT
103 Rony Seikaly CT .12 .30
Derrick Coleman CT
104 Hakeem Olajuwon CT .20 .50
Clyde Drexler CT
105 Chris Mullin CT .15 .40
Mark Jackson CT
106 Robert Horry CT .20 .50
Latrell Sprewell CT
107 Pooh Richardson CT .20 .50
Reggie Miller CT
108 Dennis Scott CT .12 .30
Kenny Anderson CT
109 Kendall Gill CT .10 .25
Ken Norman CT
110 Scott Skiles CT .10 .25
Kevin Willis CT
111 Terry Mills CT .15 .40
Glen Rice CT
112 Christian Laettner CT .15 .40
Bobby Hurley CT
113 Stacey Augmon CT .15 .40
Larry Johnson CT
114 Sam Perkins CT .20 .50
James Worthy CT
115 Carl Herrera .10 .25
116 Sam Bowie .10 .25
117 Gary Payton .15 .40
118 Danny Ainge .15 .40
119 Danny Ainge TTG .15 .40
120 Luc Longley .10 .25
121 Antonio Davis .10 .25
122 Terry Cummings .15 .40
123 Terry Cummings TTG .15 .40
124 Mark Price .15 .40
125 Jamal Mashburn .15 .40
126 Mahmoud Abdul-Rauf .10 .25
127 Charles Oakley .12 .30
128 Steve Smith .12 .30
129 Vin Baker .15 .40
130 Robert Horry .15 .40
131 Doug Christie .10 .25
132 Wayman Tisdale .10 .25
133 Wayman Tisdale TTG .10 .25
134 Muggsy Bogues .12 .30
135 Dino Radja .12 .30
136 Jeff Hornacek .12 .30
137 Gheorghe Muresan .10 .25
138 Loy Vaught .10 .25
139 Loy Vaught TTG .10 .25
140 Benoit Benjamin .10 .25
141 Johnny Dawkins .10 .25
142 Allan Houston .15 .40
143 Jon Barry .10 .25
144 Reggie Miller .20 .50
145 Kevin Willis .10 .25
146 James Worthy .20 .50
147 James Worthy TTG .20 .50
148 Scott Burrell .10 .25
149 Tom Gugliotta .10 .25
150 LaPhonso Ellis .10 .25
151 Doug Smith .10 .25
152 A.C. Green .15 .40
153 A.C. Green TTG .15 .40
154 George Lynch .10 .25
155 Sam Perkins .10 .25
156 Corie Blount .10 .25
157 Xavier McDaniel .10 .25
158 Xavier McDaniel TTG .10 .25
159 Eric Murdock .10 .25
160 David Robinson .25 .60
161 Karl Malone .20 .50
162 Karl Malone TTG .20 .50
163 Clarence Weatherspoon .10 .25
164 Calbert Cheaney .10 .25
165 Tom Hammonds .10 .25
166 Tom Hammonds TTG .10 .25
167 Alonzo Mourning .20 .50
168 Clifford Robinson .10 .25
169 Micheal Williams .10 .25
170 Ervin Johnson .10 .25
171 Mike Gminski .10 .25
172 Jason Kidd RC .75 2.00
173 Anthony Bonner .10 .25
174 Stacey King .10 .25
175 Rex Chapman .10 .25
176 Greg Graham .10 .25
177 Stanley Roberts .10 .25
178 Mitch Richmond .15 .40
179 Eric Montross RC .15 .40
180 Eddie Jones RC .50 1.25
181 Grant Hill RC .75 2.00
182 Donyell Marshall RC .15 .40
183 Glenn Robinson RC .30 .75
184 Dominique Wilkins .20 .50
185 Mark Price .15 .40
186 Anthony Mason .10 .25
187 Tyrone Corbin .10 .25
188 Dale Davis .10 .25
189 Nate McMillan .10 .25
190 Jason Kidd .50 1.25
191 John Salley .10 .25
192 Keith Jennings .10 .25
193 Mark Bryant .10 .25
194 Sleepy Floyd .10 .25
195 Grant Hill .50 1.25
196 Joe Kleine .10 .25
197 Anthony Peeler .10 .25
198 Malik Sealy .10 .25
199 Kenny Walker .10 .25
200 Donyell Marshall .15 .40
201 Vlade Divac AI .15 .40
202 Dino Radja AI .12 .30
203 Carl Herrera AI .10 .25
204 Olden Polynice AI .10 .25
205 Patrick Ewing AI .20 .50
206 Willie Anderson .10 .25
207 Mitch Richmond .15 .40
208 John Crotty .10 .25
209 Tracy Murray .10 .25
210 Juwan Howard RC .25 .60
211 Robert Parish .15 .40
212 Steve Kerr .12 .30
213 Anthony Bowie .10 .25
214 Tim Breaux .10 .25
215 Sharone Wright RC .15 .40
216 Brian Williams .10 .25
217 Rick Fox .10 .25
218 Harold Miner .10 .25
219 Duane Ferrell .10 .25
220 Lamond Murray RC .15 .40
221 Blue Edwards .10 .25
222 Bill Cartwright .12 .30
223 Sergei Bazarevich RC .15 .40
224 Herb Williams .10 .25
225 Brian Grant RC .25 .60
226 Derek Harper BCT .12 .30
John Starks
227 Rod Strickland BCT .20 .50
Clyde Drexler
228 Kevin Johnson BCT .15 .40
Dan Majerle
229 Lindsey Hunter BCT .15 .40
Joe Dumars
230 Tim Hardaway BCT .20 .50
Latrell Sprewell
231 Bill Wennington .10 .25
232 Brian Shaw .10 .25
233 Jamie Watson RC .15 .40
234 Chris Whitney .10 .25
235 Eric Montross .10 .25
236 Kenny Smith .12 .30
237 Andrew Lang .10 .25
238 Lorenzo Williams .10 .25
239 Dana Barros .10 .25
240 Eddie Jones .30 .75
241 Harold Ellis .10 .25
242 James Edwards .10 .25
243 Don MacLean .10 .25
244 Ed Pinckney .10 .25
245 Carlos Rogers RC .15 .40
246 Michael Adams .10 .25
247 Rex Walters .10 .25
248 John Starks .12 .30
249 Terrell Brandon .10 .25
250 Khalid Reeves RC .15 .40
251 Dominique Wilkins AI .20 .50
252 Toni Kukoc AI .20 .50
253 Rick Fox AI .10 .25
254 Detlef Schrempf AI .15 .40
255 Rik Smits AI .12 .30
256 Johnny Dawkins .10 .25
257 Dan Majerle .15 .40
258 Mike Brown .10 .25
259 Byron Scott .12 .30
260 Jalen Rose RC .40 1.00
261 Byron Houston .10 .25
262 Frank Brickowski .10 .25
263 Vernon Maxwell .10 .25
264 Craig Ehlo .10 .25
265 Yinka Dare RC .15 .40
266 Dee Brown .10 .25
267 Felton Spencer .10 .25
268 Harvey Grant .10 .25
269 Nick Van Exel .15 .40
270 Bob Martin .10 .25
271 Hersey Hawkins .10 .25
272 Scott Williams .10 .25
273 Sarunas Marciulionis .10 .25
274 Kevin Gamble .10 .25
275 Clifford Rozier RC .15 .40
276 B.J. Armstrong BCT .12 .30
Ron Harper
277 John Stockton BCT .20 .50
Jeff Hornacek
278 Bobby Hurley BCT .15 .40
Mitch Richmond
279 Anfernee Hardaway BCT .25 .60
Dennis Scott
280 Jason Kidd BCT .50 1.25
Jim Jackson
281 Ron Harper .12 .30
282 Chuck Person .12 .30
283 John Williams .10 .25
284 Robert Pack .10 .25
285 Aaron McKie RC .15 .40
286 Chris Smith .10 .25
287 Horace Grant .12 .30
288 Oliver Miller .10 .25
289 Derek Harper .12 .30
290 Eric Mobley RC .15 .40
291 Scott Skiles .10 .25
292 Olden Polynice .10 .25
293 Mark Jackson .15 .40
294 Wayman Tisdale .10 .25
295 Tony Dumas RC .15 .40
296 Bryon Russell .10 .25
297 Vlade Divac .15 .40
298 David Wesley .10 .25
299 Askia Jones RC .15 .40
300 B.J. Tyler RC .15 .40
301 Hakeem Olajuwon AI .20 .50
302 Luc Longley AI .10 .25
303 Rony Seikaly AI .12 .30
304 Sarunas Marciulionis AI .10 .25
305 Dikembe Mutombo AI .15 .40
306 Ken Norman .10 .25
307 Dell Curry .10 .25
308 Danny Ferry .10 .25
309 Shawn Kemp .15 .40
310 Dickey Simpkins RC .15 .40
311 Johnny Newman .10 .25
312 Dwayne Schintzius .10 .25
313 Sean Elliott .15 .40
314 Sean Rooks .10 .25
315 Bill Curley RC .15 .40
316 Bryant Stith .10 .25
317 Pooh Richardson .10 .25
318 Jim McIlvaine RC .15 .40
319 Dennis Scott .10 .25
320 Wesley Person RC .15 .40
321 Bobby Hurley .15 .40
322 Armon Gilliam .10 .25
323 Rik Smits .12 .30
324 Tony Smith .10 .25
325 Monty Williams RC .15 .40
326 Gary Payton BCT .15 .40
Kendall Gill
327 Mookie Blaylock BCT .12 .30
Stacey Augmon
328 Mark Jackson BCT .20 .50
Reggie Miller
329 Sam Cassell BCT .15 .40
Vernon Maxwell
330 Harold Miner BCT .15 .40
Khalid Reeves
331 Vinny Del Negro .10 .25
332 Billy Owens .10 .25
333 Mark West .10 .25
334 Matt Geiger .10 .25
335 Greg Minor RC .15 .40
336 Larry Johnson .15 .40
337 Donald Hodge .10 .25
338 Aaron Williams RC .15 .40
339 Jay Humphries .10 .25
340 Charlie Ward RC .15 .40
341 Scott Brooks .10 .25
342 Stacey Augmon .12 .30
343 Will Perdue .10 .25
344 Dale Ellis .10 .25
345 Brooks Thompson RC .15 .40
346 Manute Bol .10 .25
347 Kenny Anderson .12 .30
348 Willie Burton .10 .25
349 Michael Cage .10 .25
350 Danny Manning .12 .30
351 Ricky Pierce .10 .25
352 Sam Cassell .15 .40
353 Reggie Miller FG .20 .50
354 David Robinson FG .25 .60
355 Shaquille O'Neal FG .40 1.00
356 Scottie Pippen FG .30 .75
357 Alonzo Mourning FG .20 .50
358 Clarence Weatherspoon FG .10 .25
359 Derrick Coleman FG .12 .30
360 Charles Barkley FG .25 .60
361 Karl Malone FG .20 .50
362 Chris Webber FG .25 .60
NNO Reggie Miller AU 20.00 50.00

1994-95 Stadium Club First Day Issue

This set parallels the basic issue 1994-95 Stadium Club set. First Day cards were randomly inserted into both series packs at a rate of one in 24. The cards differ from their regular issue counterparts in that each First Day card has a gold-foil "First Day Issue" logo on front. To ascertain values on individual cards, please refer to the multiplier in the header, coupled with the value of the base card.

*STARS: 6X TO 15X BASE CARD HI
*RCs: 5X TO 12X BASE HI

1994-95 Stadium Club Beam Team

Randomly inserted at a rate of 1 in every 24 second series packs, this 27-card standard-size set features a star player from each NBA team spotlit with lazer light foil. The borderless fronts feature a player photo with his name in the upper left corner and the words "Beam Team" in funky lettering on the bottom. The backs are split between a player photo and some notes. Vital statistics are in the lower left corner and the cards are numbered in the lower corner as "X" of 27. The set is sequenced in alphabetical order by team.

COMPLETE SET (27) 25.00 50.00
1 Mookie Blaylock .50 1.25
2 Dominique Wilkins 1.00 2.50
3 Alonzo Mourning 1.00 2.50
4 Toni Kukoc 1.00 2.50
5 Mark Price .75 2.00
6 Jason Kidd 4.00 10.00
7 Jalen Rose 2.00 5.00
8 Grant Hill 4.00 10.00
9 Latrell Sprewell 1.00 2.50
10 Hakeem Olajuwon 1.00 2.50
11 Reggie Miller 1.00 2.50
12 Lamond Murray .75 2.00
13 George Lynch .50 1.25
14 Khalid Reeves .75 2.00
15 Glenn Robinson 1.50 4.00
16 Donyell Marshall .75 2.00
17 Derrick Coleman .60 1.50
18 Patrick Ewing 1.00 2.50
19 Shaquille O'Neal 4.00 10.00
20 Clarence Weatherspoon .50 1.25
21 Charles Barkley 1.25 3.00
22 Clifford Robinson .50 1.25
23 Bobby Hurley .75 2.00
24 David Robinson 1.25 3.00
25 Shawn Kemp .75 2.00
26 Karl Malone 1.00 2.50
27 Chris Webber 1.25 3.00

1994-95 Stadium Club Clear Cut

Randomly inserted in all first series packs at a rate of one in 12, cards from this 27-card acetate set spotlight one key player from each NBA team. The set has "see through" fronts with some statistical information on the back. The player is identified on the right side of the card and the words "Clear Cut" are located in the bottom right. The set is sequenced in alphabetical order by team.

COMPLETE SET (27) 10.00 25.00
1 Stacey Augmon .50 1.25
2 Dino Radja .50 1.25
3 Alonzo Mourning .75 2.00
4 Scottie Pippen 2.50 6.00
5 Gerald Wilkins .40 1.00
6 Jamal Mashburn .60 1.50
7 Dikembe Mutombo .60 1.50
8 Lindsey Hunter .40 1.00
9 Chris Mullin .60 1.50
10 Hakeem Olajuwon .75 2.00
11 Reggie Miller .75 2.00
12 Gary Grant .40 1.00
13 Doug Christie .40 1.00
14 Steve Smith .50 1.25
15 Vin Baker .60 1.50
16 Christian Laettner .50 1.25
17 Derrick Coleman .50 1.25
18 Charles Oakley .50 1.25
19 Dennis Scott .40 1.00
20 Clarence Weatherspoon .40 1.00
21 Charles Barkley 1.50 4.00
22 Clifford Robinson .40 1.00
23 Mitch Richmond .60 1.50
24 David Robinson 1.00 2.50
25 Shawn Kemp .60 1.50
26 Karl Malone .75 2.00
27 Don MacLean .40 1.00

1994-95 Stadium Club Dynasty and Destiny

This 20-card standard-size set was randomly inserted in first series foil packs at a rate of one in six and were also inserted one per first series rack pack. This set features a mixture of youthful phenoms paired up with a matching veteran star. The borderless fronts feature player photos, the player's name in the upper left corner and either the word "Destiny" or "Dynasty" in the lower right. The back has a player photo in a lower corner with a brief note and stats on the other side.

COMPLETE SET (20) 4.00 10.00
1A Mark Price .40 1.00
1B Kenny Anderson .30 .75
2A Karl Malone .50 1.25
2B Derrick Coleman .30 .75
3A John Stockton .50 1.25
3B Anfernee Hardaway .60 1.50
4A Mitch Richmond .40 1.00
4B Jim Jackson .25 .60
5A James Worthy .50 1.25
5B Jamal Mashburn .40 1.00
6A Patrick Ewing .50 1.25
6B Alonzo Mourning .50 1.25
7A Hakeem Olajuwon .50 1.25
7B Shaquille O'Neal 1.00 2.50
8A Clyde Drexler .50 1.25
8B Isaiah Rider .40 1.00
9A Scottie Pippen .75 2.00
9B Latrell Sprewell .50 1.25
10A Charles Barkley .60 1.50
10B Chris Webber .60 1.50

1994-95 Stadium Club Rising Stars

Randomly inserted in all first series packs at a rate of one in 24, cards from this 10-card standard-size set feature a selection of young NBA stars. Card fronts feature full-color player action shots cut out against etched-foil backgrounds, with a prismatic galaxy design.

COMPLETE SET (12) 12.00 30.00
1 Kenny Anderson 1.00 2.50
2 Latrell Sprewell 1.50 4.00
3 Jamal Mashburn 1.25 3.00
4 Alonzo Mourning 1.50 4.00
5 Shaquille O'Neal 6.00 15.00
6 LaPhonso Ellis .75 2.00
7 Chris Webber 3.00 8.00
8 Isaiah Rider 1.25 3.00
9 Dikembe Mutombo 1.25 3.00
10 Anfernee Hardaway 3.00 8.00
11 Antonio Davis .75 2.00
12 Robert Horry 1.25 3.00

1994-95 Stadium Club Super Skills

Randomly inserted at a rate of 1 in every 24 second series 12-card packs and seeded one per second series retail rack pack, cards from this 25-card standard-size set feature Topps selection of the five top players at each position in the NBA. Card fronts feature a multi-hued rainbow foil background.

COMPLETE SET (25) 10.00 25.00
1 Mark Price .50 1.25
2 Tim Hardaway .50 1.25
3 Kevin Johnson .50 1.25
4 John Stockton .60 1.50
5 Mookie Blaylock .30 .75
6 Reggie Miller .60 1.50
7 Jeff Hornacek .40 1.00
8 Latrell Sprewell .60 1.50
9 John Starks .40 1.00
10 Nate McMillan .30 .75
11 Chris Mullin .50 1.25
12 Toni Kukoc .60 1.50
13 Anthony Mason .30 .75
14 Robert Horry .50 1.25
15 Scottie Pippen 1.00 2.50
16 Charles Barkley .75 2.00
17 Dennis Rodman 1.00 2.50
18 Karl Malone .60 1.50
19 Chris Webber .75 2.00
20 Charles Oakley .40 1.00
21 Patrick Ewing .60 1.50
22 Shaquille O'Neal 1.25 3.00
23 Dikembe Mutombo .50 1.25
24 David Robinson .75 2.00
25 Hakeem Olajuwon .60 1.50

1994-95 Stadium Club Super Teams

Randomly inserted in all first series packs at a rate of one in 24, cards from this 27-card standard-size set feature an action shot or group photo from each team in the league. Teams that won either their Division, their Conference or the NBA Finals were redeemable for special team sets or other prizes. The expiration date for Super Team cards was December 31st, 1995. The five winning cards (Houston, Indiana, Orlando, Phoenix and San Antonio) carry "W" designations. In addition "C", "D" and "F" designations are used to denote conference, division and finals winners.

COMPLETE SET (27) 12.00 30.00
1 Atlanta Hawks .40 1.00
Kevin Willis
2 Boston Celtics .40 1.00
Group
3 Charlotte Hornets .40 1.00
Muggsy Bogues
4 Chicago Bulls .40 1.00
Group
5 Cleveland Cavaliers .40 1.00
Danny Ferry
6 Dallas Mavericks .40 1.00
Jim Jackson
7 Denver Nuggets .40 1.00
Rodney Rogers
8 Detroit Pistons .40 1.00
Joe Dumars
9 Golden State Warriors 2.00 5.00
Chris Webber
10 Houston Rockets WCF 4.00 10.00
Hakeem Olajuwon
11 Indiana Pacers WD .40 1.00
Rik Smits
12 LA Clippers .40 1.00
Group
13 L.A. Lakers .40 1.00
Nick Van Exel
14 Miami Heat .40 1.00
Glen Rice
15 Milwaukee Bucks .40 1.00
Vin Baker
16 Minnesota Timberwolves .40 1.00
Christian Laettner
17 New Jersey Nets .40 1.00
Chris Morris
18 New York Knicks .40 1.00
Group
19 Orlando Magic WCD 6.00 15.00
Shaquille O'Neal
20 Philadelphia 76ers .40 1.00
Dana Barros
21 Phoenix Suns WD 2.00 5.00
Charles Barkley
22 Portland Trail Blazers .40 1.00
Group
23 Sacramento Kings .40 1.00
Olden Polynice
24 San Antonio Spurs WD .40 1.00
Group
25 Seattle Supersonics .40 1.00
Group
26 Utah Jazz 1.00 2.50
John Stockton
27 Washington Bullets .40 1.00
Group

1994-95 Stadium Club Super Teams Division Winners

Each of these four team sets was available exclusively by mailing in the corresponding winning Super Team card before the December 31st, 1995 deadline. Super Team cards were randomly seeded in all first series Stadium Club packs at a rate of one in 24. The card design parallels the regular issue Stadium Club cards except for the gold foil "Division Winner" logo on each card front. The cards are listed below alphabetically according to teams; the prefixes M, P, SP, and SU have been added to denote Magic, Pacers, Spurs and Suns respectively.

COMP.BAG MAGIC (11) 6.00 12.00
COMP.BAG PACERS (11) 1.50 3.00
COMP.BAG SPURS (11) 2.50 5.00
COMP.BAG SUNS (11) 3.00 6.00
M7 Donald Royal .20 .50
M16 Anfernee Hardaway 1.50 4.00
M32 Shaquille O'Neal 2.50 6.00
M58 Nick Anderson .20 .50
M74 Jeff Turner .20 .50
M213 Anthony Bowie .20 .50
M232 Brian Shaw .20 .50
M287 Horace Grant .25 .60
M319 Dennis Scott .20 .50
M345 Brooks Thompson .30 .75
MD19 Magic DW Super Team .40 1.00
P26 Vern Fleming .20 .50
P46 Haywoode Workman .20 .50
P86 Derrick McKey .20 .50
P121 Antonio Davis .20 .50
P144 Reggie Miller .40 1.00
P188 Dale Davis .20 .50
P219 Duane Ferrell .20 .50
P259 Byron Scott .25 .60
P293 Mark Jackson .30 .75
P323 Rik Smits .25 .60
PD11 Pacers DW Super Team .40 1.00
SP52 J.R. Reid .20 .50
SP72 Dennis Rodman 1.00 2.50
SP73 Dennis Rodman TG 1.00 2.50
SP122 Terry Cummings .30 .75
SP160 David Robinson .75 2.00
SP206 Willie Anderson .20 .50
SP282 Chuck Person .25 .60
SP313 Sean Elliott .30 .75
SP331 Vinny Del Negro .20 .50
SP354 David Robinson FG .75 2.00
SPD24 Spurs DW Super Team .40 1.00
SU13 Charles Barkley 1.00 2.50
SU70 Kevin Johnson .30 .75
SU118 Danny Ainge .30 .75
SU152 A.C. Green .30 .75
SU196 Joe Kleine .20 .50
SU257 Dan Majerle .30 .75
SU294 Wayman Tisdale .20 .50
SU320 Wesley Person .30 .75
SU350 Danny Manning .25 .60
SU360 Charles Barkley FG 1.00 2.50
SUD21 Suns DW Super Team .40 1.00

1994-95 Stadium Club Super Teams Master Photos

Each of these two over-sized (5" by 7") team sets were available exclusively by mailing in the corresponding winning Super Team card before the December 31st, 1995 deadline. Super Team cards were randomly seeded in all first series Stadium Club packs at a rate of one in 24. The card design loosely parallels the corresponding regular issue Stadium Club cards but the bold, wildly designed borders and separate numbering sequences create distinctive differences. The cards are listed below alphabetically according to teams; the prefixes M and R have been added to denote Magic and Rockets respectively.

COMP.BAG MAGIC (11) 7.50 15.00
COMP.BAG ROCKETS (11) 4.00 8.00
M1 Nick Anderson .30 .75
M2 Anthony Bowie .30 .75
M3 Jeff Turner .30 .75
M4 Dennis Scott .30 .75
M5 Horace Grant .40 1.00
M6 Shaquille O'Neal 4.00 10.00
M7 Brooks Thompson .50 1.25
M8 Anfernee Hardaway 2.50 6.00
M9 Donald Royal .30 .75
M10 Brian Shaw .30 .75
MM19 Magic MP Super Team .40 1.00
R1 Tim Breaux .30 .75
R2 Scott Brooks .30 .75
R3 Clyde Drexler 1.25 3.00
Hakeem Olajuwon CT
R4 Hakeem Olajuwon 1.50 4.00
R5 Sam Cassell .50 1.25
R6 Vernon Maxwell .30 .75
R7 Mario Elie .30 .75
R8 Carl Herrera .30 .75
R9 Kenny Smith .40 1.00
R10 Robert Horry .50 1.25
MR10 Rockets MP Super Team .40 1.00

1994-95 Stadium Club Super Teams NBA Finals

Available exclusively by redeeming the Stadium Club Super Teams Houston Rockets card before the December 31st, 1995 deadline, this 362-card standard-size set parallels the basic issue 1994-95 Stadium Club set except for the gold foil NBA Finals logo placed on each card front. Please refer to the multipliers provided below (coupled with the value of the corresponding regular issue card) to ascertain value.

COMPLETE SET (363) 35.00 80.00
*STARS: 1.25X TO 2.5X VALUE

1994-95 Stadium Club Team of the Future

Randomly inserted at a rate of 1 in every 24 second series packs, this 10-card standard-size set is comprised of tomorrow's superstars. Card fronts feature color player action shots against brilliant gold, etched-foil backgrounds.

COMPLETE SET (10) 10.00 25.00
1 Anfernee Hardaway 2.00 5.00
2 Latrell Sprewell 1.50 4.00
3 Grant Hill 3.00 8.00
4 Chris Webber 2.00 5.00
5 Shaquille O'Neal 3.00 8.00
6 Jason Kidd 3.00 8.00
7 Jim Jackson .75 2.00
8 Jamal Mashburn 1.25 3.00
9 Glenn Robinson 1.25 3.00
10 Alonzo Mourning 1.50 4.00

1995-96 Stadium Club

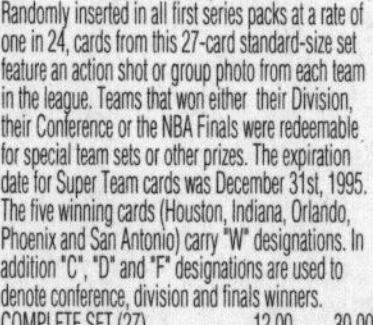

The 1995-96 Stadium Club basketball set was issued in two series of 180 and 181 standard-size cards, for total of 361. Cards were distributed in 13-card regular packs at a suggested retail price of \$2.50, and in 24-card jumbo packs. The packs were distributed in 24-piece boxes. Fronts are full-bleed full-color action player shots. The player's name appears in etched foil against an exploding star background and his team's name is printed in gold foil at the bottom. Backs feature a close-up head shot and a full-color action photo with a blue background. The player's name is printed at the top as is his biography, player profile and '94-95 statistics. A category statistic chart appears on the lower right side of the chart. Second series cards included these variations. The "Rookie Cards" as well as other subset cards were issued in basic hobby and retail packs with a silver prismatic foil. These cards were also issued one per special retail pack with a gold/orange-type foil background. Subsets include 1[illegible] cards of players from the two expansion teams (Vancouver Grizzlies and Toronto Raptors), 29 "Extreme Corps" and six "Trans-Action" cards. A parallel version of every subset card was inserted in rack and jumbo packs. The parallel versions of the subset cards feature silver and blue diffraction foil around the player's name and team name. These foil variations are priced at equal value.

COMPLETE SET (361) 25.00 50.0[illegible]
COMPLETE SERIES 1 (180) 15.00 25.0[illegible]
COMPLETE SERIES 2 (181) 10.00 25.0[illegible]
1 Michael Jordan 2.00 5.0[illegible]
2 Glenn Robinson .25 [illegible]
3 Jason Kidd .40 1.0[illegible]
4 Clyde Drexler .30 [illegible]
5 Horace Grant .20 [illegible]
6 Allan Houston .20 [illegible]
7 Xavier McDaniel .15 [illegible]
8 Jeff Hornacek .20 [illegible]
9 Vlade Divac .25 [illegible]
10 Juwan Howard .25 [illegible]
11 Keith Jennings EXP .15 [illegible]
12 Grant Long .15 [illegible]
13 Jalen Rose .30 [illegible]
14 Malik Sealy .15 [illegible]
15 Gary Payton .25 [illegible]
16 Danny Ferry .15 [illegible]
17 Glen Rice .25 [illegible]
18 Randy Brown .15 [illegible]
19 Greg Graham .15 [illegible]
20 Kenny Anderson UER .20 [illegible]
Name is spelled Kenney
21 Aaron McKie .15 [illegible]
22 John Salley EXP .15 [illegible]
23 Darrin Hancock .15 [illegible]
24 Carlos Rogers .15 [illegible]
25 Vin Baker .20 [illegible]
26 Bill Wennington .15 [illegible]
27 Kenny Smith .20 [illegible]
28 Sherman Douglas .15 [illegible]
29 Terry Davis .15 [illegible]
30 Grant Hill .40 1.0[illegible]
31 Reggie Miller .30 [illegible]
32 Anfernee Hardaway .40 1.0[illegible]
33 Patrick Ewing .30 [illegible]
34 Charles Barkley .40 1.0[illegible]
35 Eddie Jones .30 [illegible]
36 Kevin Duckworth .15 [illegible]
37 Tom Hammonds .15 [illegible]
38 Craig Ehlo .15 [illegible]
39 Micheal Williams .15 [illegible]
40 Alonzo Mourning .30 [illegible]
41 John Williams .15 [illegible]
42 Felton Spencer .15 [illegible]
43 Lamond Murray .15 [illegible]
44 Dontonio Wingfield EXP .15 [illegible]
45 Rik Smits .20 [illegible]
46 Donyell Marshall .15 [illegible]
47 Clarence Weatherspoon .15 [illegible]
48 Kevin Edwards .15 [illegible]
49 Charlie Ward .15 [illegible]
50 David Robinson .40 1.0[illegible]
51 James Robinson .15 [illegible]
52 Bill Cartwright .20 [illegible]
53 Bobby Hurley .25 [illegible]
54 Kevin Gamble .15 [illegible]
55 B.J. Tyler EXP .15 [illegible]
56 Chris Smith .15 [illegible]
57 Wesley Person .15 [illegible]
58 Tim Breaux .15 [illegible]
59 Mitchell Butler .15 [illegible]
60 Toni Kukoc .25 [illegible]
61 Roy Tarpley .15 [illegible]
62 Todd Day .15 [illegible]
63 Anthony Peeler .15 [illegible]
64 Brian Williams .15 [illegible]
65 Muggsy Bogues .20 [illegible]
66 Jerome Kersey EXP .15 [illegible]
67 Eric Piatkowski .20 [illegible]
68 Tim Perry .15 [illegible]
69 Chris Gatling .15 [illegible]
70 Mark Price .25 [illegible]
71 Terry Mills .15 [illegible]
72 Anthony Avent .15 [illegible]
73 Matt Geiger .15 [illegible]
74 Walt Williams .15 [illegible]
75 Sean Elliott .25 [illegible]
76 Ken Norman .15 [illegible]
77 Kendall Gill TA .15 [illegible]
78 Byron Houston .15 [illegible]
79 Rick Fox .15 [illegible]
80 Derek Harper .20 [illegible]
81 Rod Strickland .15 [illegible]
82 Bryon Russell .15 [illegible]
83 Antonio Davis .15 [illegible]
84 Isaiah Rider .25 [illegible]
85 Kevin Johnson .25 [illegible]
86 Derrick Coleman .20 [illegible]
87 Doug Overton .15 [illegible]
88 Hersey Hawkins TA .15 [illegible]
89 Popeye Jones .15 [illegible]
90 Dickey Simpkins .15 [illegible]

Rodney Rogers TA .15 .40
Rex Chapman TA .15 .40
Spud Webb TA .25 .60
Lee Mayberry .15 .40
Cedric Ceballos .15 .40
Tyrone Hill .15 .40
Bill Curley .15 .40
Jeff Turner .15 .40
Tyrone Corbin TA .15 .40
0 John Stockton .30 .75
1 Mookie Blaylock EC .15 .40
2 Dino Radja EC .20 .50
3 Alonzo Mourning EC .30 .75
4 Scottie Pippen EC .40 1.00
5 Terrell Brandon EC .15 .40
6 Jim Jackson EC .15 .40
7 Mahmoud Abdul-Rauf EC .15 .40
8 Grant Hill EC .40 1.00
9 Tim Hardaway EC .25 .60
0 Hakeem Olajuwon EC .30 .75
1 Rik Smits EC .20 .50
2 Loy Vaught EC .15 .40
3 Vlade Divac EC .25 .60
4 Kevin Willis EC .15 .40
5 Glenn Robinson EC .25 .60
6 Christian Laettner EC .20 .50
7 Derrick Coleman EC .20 .50
8 Patrick Ewing EC .30 .75
9 Shaquille O'Neal EC .60 1.50
0 Dana Barros EC .15 .40
21 Charles Barkley EC .40 1.00
22 Rod Strickland EC .15 .40
23 Brian Grant EC .20 .50
24 David Robinson EC .40 1.00
25 Shawn Kemp EC .25 .60
26 Oliver Miller EC .15 .40
27 Karl Malone EC .30 .75
28 Benoit Benjamin EC .15 .40
29 Chris Webber EC .30 .75
30 Dan Majerle .25 .60
31 Calbert Cheaney .15 .40
32 Mark Jackson .25 .60
3 Greg Anthony EXP .15 .40
4 Scott Burrell .15 .40
5 Detlef Schrempf .25 .60
6 Marty Conlon .15 .40
7 Rony Seikaly .20 .50
8 Olden Polynice .15 .40
9 Terry Cummings .25 .60
0 Stacey Augmon .20 .50
1 Bryant Stith .15 .40
2 Sean Higgins .15 .40
3 Antoine Carr .15 .40
4 Blue Edwards EXP .15 .40
5 A.C. Green .25 .60
6 Bobby Phills .15 .40
7 Terry Dehere .15 .40
8 Sharone Wright .15 .40
9 Nick Anderson .15 .40
50 Jim Jackson .15 .40
1 Eric Montross .15 .40
2 Doug West .15 .40
3 Charles Smith .15 .40
4 Will Perdue .15 .40
5 Gerald Wilkins EXP .15 .40
56 Robert Horry .20 .50
57 Robert Parish .25 .60
58 Lindsey Hunter .15 .40
59 Harvey Grant .15 .40
0 Tim Hardaway .25 .60
1 Sarunas Marciulionis .15 .40
2 Khalid Reeves .15 .40
53 Bo Outlaw .15 .40
54 Dale Davis .15 .40
55 Nick Van Exel .25 .60
56 Byron Scott EXP .20 .50
57 Steve Smith .20 .50
58 Brian Grant .20 .50
9 Avery Johnson .20 .50
0 Dikembe Mutombo .25 .60
1 Tom Gugliotta .15 .40
2 Armon Gilliam .15 .40
3 Shawn Bradley .15 .40
4 Herb Williams .15 .40
5 Dino Radja .20 .50
76 Billy Owens .15 .40
7 Kenny Gattison EXP .15 .40
8 J.R. Reid .15 .40
9 Otis Thorpe .15 .40
0 Sam Cassell .25 .60
1 Sam Cassell .25 .60
2 Pooh Richardson .15 .40
3 Johnny Newman .15 .40
4 Dennis Scott .15 .40
35 Will Perdue .15 .40
6 Andrew Lang .15 .40
7 Karl Malone .30 .75
8 Buck Williams .15 .40
9 P.J. Brown .15 .40
0 Khalid Reeves .15 .40
1 Kevin Willis .15 .40
2 Robert Pack .15 .40
3 Joe Dumars .25 .60
4 Sam Perkins .15 .40
5 Dan Majerle .25 .60
6 John Williams .15 .40
7 Reggie Williams .15 .40
8 Greg Anthony .15 .40
9 Steve Kerr .20 .50
0 Richard Dumas .15 .40
01 Dee Brown .15 .40
02 Zan Tabak .15 .40
03 David Wood .15 .40
04 Duane Causwell .15 .40
05 Sedale Threatt .15 .40
06 Hubert Davis .15 .40
07 Donald Hodge .15 .40
08 Duane Ferrell .15 .40
09 Sam Mitchell .15 .40
0 Adam Keefe .15 .40
1 Clifford Robinson .15 .40
2 Rodney Rogers .15 .40
3 Jayson Williams .15 .40
4 Brian Shaw .15 .40
5 Luc Longley .15 .40
6 Don MacLean .15 .40
7 Rex Chapman .15 .40
8 Wayman Tisdale .15 .40
9 Shawn Kemp .25 .60
0 Chris Webber .30 .75
1 Antonio Harvey .15 .40
2 Sarunas Marciulionis .15 .40
3 Jeff Malone .15 .40
4 Chucky Brown .15 .40
5 Greg Minor .15 .40
6 Clifford Rozier .15 .40
227 Derrick McKey .15 .40
228 Tony Dumas .15 .40
229 Oliver Miller .15 .40
230 Charles Oakley .20 .50
231 Fred Roberts .15 .40
232 Glen Rice .25 .60
233 Terry Porter .15 .40
234 Mark Macon .15 .40
235 Michael Cage .15 .40
236 Eric Murdock .15 .40
237 Vinny Del Negro .15 .40
238 Spud Webb .25 .60
239 Mario Elie .15 .40
240 Blue Edwards .15 .40
241 Dontonio Wingfield .15 .40
242 Brooks Thompson .15 .40
243 Alonzo Mourning .30 .75
244 Dennis Rodman .50 1.25
245 Lorenzo Williams .15 .40
246 Haywoode Workman .15 .40
247 Loy Vaught .15 .40
248 Vernon Maxwell .15 .40
249 Lionel Simmons .15 .40
250 Chris Childs .15 .40
251 Mahmoud Abdul-Rauf .15 .40
252 Vincent Askew .15 .40
253 Chris Morris .15 .40
254 Elliot Perry .15 .40
255 Dell Curry .15 .40
256 Dana Barros .15 .40
257 Terrell Brandon .15 .40
258 Monty Williams .15 .40
259 Corie Blount .15 .40
260 B.J. Armstrong .15 .40
261 Jim McIlvaine .15 .40
262 Otis Thorpe .15 .40
263 Sean Rooks .15 .40
264 Tony Massenburg .15 .40
265 Steve Smith .20 .50
266 Ron Harper .20 .50
267 Dale Ellis .15 .40
268 Clyde Drexler .30 .75
269 Jamie Watson .15 .40
270 Doc Rivers .20 .50
271 Derrick Alston .15 .40
272 Eric Mobley .15 .40
273 Ricky Pierce .15 .40
274 David Wesley .15 .40
275 John Starks .20 .50
276 Chris Mullin .25 .60
277 Ervin Johnson .15 .40
278 Jamal Mashburn .25 .60
279 Joe Kleine .15 .40
280 Mitch Richmond .25 .60
281 Chris Mills .15 .40
282 Bimbo Coles .15 .40
283 Larry Johnson .25 .60
284 Stanley Roberts .15 .40
285 Rex Walters .15 .40
286 Donald Royal .15 .40
287 Benoit Benjamin .15 .40
288 Chris Dudley .15 .40
289 Elden Campbell .15 .40
290 Mookie Blaylock .15 .40
291 Hersey Hawkins .15 .40
292 Anthony Mason .15 .40
293 Latrell Sprewell .25 .60
294 Harold Miner .15 .40
295 Scott Williams .15 .40
296 David Benoit .15 .40
297 Christian Laettner .20 .50
298 LaPhonso Ellis .15 .40
299 Gheorghe Muresan .15 .40
300 Kendall Gill .15 .40
301 Eddie Johnson .15 .40
302 Terry Cummings .25 .60
303 Chuck Person .20 .50
304 Michael Smith .15 .40
305 Mark West .15 .40
306 Willie Anderson .15 .40
307 Pervis Ellison .15 .40
308 Brian Williams .15 .40
309 Danny Manning .20 .50
310 Hakeem Olajuwon .30 .75
311 Scottie Pippen .40 1.00
312 Jon Koncak .15 .40
313 Sasha Danilovic RC .25 .60
314 Lucious Harris .15 .40
315 Yinka Dare .15 .40
316 Eric Williams RC .25 .60
317 Gary Trent RC .25 .60
318 Theo Ratliff RC .40 1.00
319 Lawrence Moten RC .25 .60
320 Jerome Allen RC .25 .60
321 Tyus Edney RC .25 .60
322 Loren Meyer RC .25 .60
323 Michael Finley RC .75 2.00
324 Alan Henderson RC .25 .60
325 Bob Sura RC .25 .60
326 Joe Smith RC .50 1.25
327 Damon Stoudamire RC .60 1.50
328 Sherrell Ford RC .25 .60
329 Jerry Stackhouse RC .75 2.00
330 George Zidek RC .25 .60
331 Brent Barry RC .40 1.00
332 Shawn Respert RC .25 .60
333 Rasheed Wallace RC .75 2.00
334 Antonio McDyess RC .60 1.50
335 David Vaughn RC .25 .60
336 Cory Alexander RC .25 .60
337 Jason Caffey RC .25 .60
338 Frankie King RC .25 .60
339 Travis Best RC .25 .60
340 Greg Ostertag RC .25 .60
341 Ed O'Bannon RC .25 .60
342 Kurt Thomas RC .25 .60
343 Kevin Garnett RC 2.00 5.00
344 Bryant Reeves RC .25 .60
345 Corliss Williamson RC .25 .60
346 Cherokee Parks RC .25 .60
347 Junior Burrough RC .25 .60
348 Randolph Childress RC .25 .60
349 Lou Roe RC .25 .60
350 Mario Bennett RC .25 .60
351 Dikembe Mutombo XP .25 .60
352 Larry Johnson XP .25 .60
353 Vlade Divac XP .25 .60
354 Karl Malone XP .30 .75
355 John Stockton XP .30 .75
356 Alonzo Mourning TA .30 .75
357 Glen Rice TA .25 .60
358 Dan Majerle TA .25 .60
359 John Williams TA .15 .40
360 Mark Price TA .25 .60
361 Magic Johnson .60 1.50

1995-96 Stadium Club Beam Team

Randomly inserted in all first and second series packs, this 20-card standard-size set features Topps' annual selection of their Beam Team stars. First series cards were randomly seeded into one in every 18 hobby and retail packs. Second series cards were randomly seeded into one in every 36 hobby packs and one in every 72 retail packs. Card front design from first to second series is radically different. First series cards feature borderless fronts with full-color action player cutouts set against a dark background of laser beams. Second series cards feature very bright neon green, yellow and red die cut backgrounds set against a cut out action shot of the featured player.

COMPLETE SET (20) 40.00 80.00
COMPLETE SERIES 1 (10) 5.00 12.00
COMPLETE SERIES 2 (10) 35.00 70.00
BT1 David Robinson 1.50 4.00
BT2 Juwan Howard 1.00 2.50
BT3 Mitch Richmond 1.00 2.50
BT4 Reggie Miller 1.25 3.00
BT5 Glenn Robinson 1.00 2.50
BT6 Shaquille O'Neal 2.50 6.00
BT7 Shawn Kemp 1.00 2.50
BT8 Karl Malone 1.25 3.00
BT9 Jamal Mashburn 1.00 2.50
BT10 Alonzo Mourning 1.25 3.00
BT11 Charles Barkley 4.00 10.00
BT12 Hakeem Olajuwon 2.50 6.00
BT13 Kenny Anderson 1.50 4.00
BT14 Michael Jordan 20.00 50.00
BT15 Dikembe Mutombo 2.00 5.00
BT16 Rod Strickland 1.25 3.00
BT17 Patrick Ewing 2.50 6.00
BT18 Latrell Sprewell 2.00 5.00
BT19 Grant Hill 4.00 10.00
BT20 Cedric Ceballos 1.25 3.00

1995-96 Stadium Club Draft Picks

Randomly inserted in series one packs, this set of 15 skip-numbered standard-size cards is numbered in the order of the 1995 NBA draft. Some draft picks are missing in the series one collection but those cards were not included in the second series. Full-bleed fronts picture the player in full-color action shots with the TSC logo at the top. "NBA Draft Pick" and the player's name are printed in red type at the bottom of the card. Blue and white backs are numbered according to place in draft with the player's name is printed in lower case white type at the top. The white areas resemble torn, crumpled paper and contain the player's biography, college statistics and a player profile, which is printed vertically in black type on the lower right side of the back.

COMPLETE SET (15) 3.00 8.00
2 Antonio McDyess .60 1.50
3 Jerry Stackhouse .75 2.00
4 Rasheed Wallace .75 2.00
5 Kevin Garnett 2.00 5.00
6 Bryant Reeves .25 .60
8 Shawn Respert .25 .60
9 Ed O'Bannon .25 .60
11 Gary Trent .25 .60
12 Cherokee Parks .25 .60
15 Brent Barry .40 1.00
16 Alan Henderson .25 .60
17 Bob Sura .25 .60
18 Theo Ratliff .40 1.00
19 Randolph Childress .25 .60
22 George Zidek .25 .60

1995-96 Stadium Club Extreme

This 24-card set was randomly inserted in packs at a rate of 1:9; however, special cards like Power Zone and Warp Speed were inserted in packs at a rate of 1:18. The cards are borderless and standard sized. They carry color action shots that are up close and personal! The Topps logo can be found in either upper corner. The player's name is written in gold lettering at either bottom corner and is set in a firework-type display of colors. The player's team name is also written in gold and is also located in either bottom corner of the card. The backs have another action shot of the player along with a head shot. His career stats are listed as well as a short bio.

13 Jalen Rose .30 .75
26 Bill Wennington .15 .40
31 Reggie Miller .30 .75
34 Charles Barkley .40 1.00
41 John Williams .15 .40
49 Charlie Ward .15 .40
56 Chris Smith .15 .40
64 Brian Williams .15 .40
65 Muggsy Bogues .20 .50
72 Anthony Avent .15 .40
96 Tyrone Hill .15 .40
117 Derrick Coleman .20 .50
125 Shawn Kemp .25 .60
143 Antoine Carr .15 .40
147 Terry Dehere .15 .40
148 Sharone Wright .15 .40
149 Nick Anderson .15 .40
153 Charles Smith .15 .40
168 Brian Grant .20 .50
179 Otis Thorpe .15 .40

1995-96 Stadium Club Intercontinental

Featuring NBA stars born outside the U.S., this 10-card set was a special bonus found only in 1995-96 Stadium Club Australian packs. On the horizontal fronts, color action player cutouts are superposed over longitude and latitude markings (in silver foil) and continents (in gold foil). On a computer-generated background, the backs provide biographical information and career highlight.

COMPLETE SET (10) 4.00 10.00
IC1 Hakeem Olajuwon 3.00 8.00
IC2 Dikembe Mutombo 1.00 2.50
IC3 Bill Wennington .60 1.50
IC4 Rick Fox .60 1.50
IC5 Carl Herrera .60 1.50
IC6 Rony Seikaly .75 2.00
IC7 Rik Smits .75 2.00
IC8 Dino Radja .75 2.00
IC9 Sarunas Marciulionis .60 1.50
IC10 Luc Longley .60 1.50

1995-96 Stadium Club Nemeses

Randomly inserted in series one packs at a rate of one in 18, this 10-card standard-size set portrays arch rivals on each side of the card. Both sides are silver and blue etched foil with alternating full-color action cutouts of the players. Both sides carry a smaller full-color shot of each player's nemesis looking on. Each side carries a highlight of a game when one player got the better of the other. The "Nemeses" logo appears at the top of each side in gold etched foil.

COMPLETE SET (10) 20.00 50.00
N1 Hakeem Olajuwon / David Robinson 2.50 6.00
N2 Patrick Ewing / Rik Smits 2.00 5.00
N3 John Stockton / Kevin Johnson 2.00 5.00
N4 Shaquille O'Neal / Alonzo Mourning 4.00 10.00
N5 Charles Barkley / Karl Malone 2.50 6.00
N6 Scottie Pippen / Grant Hill 4.00 10.00
N7 Anfernee Hardaway / Kenny Anderson 2.50 6.00
N8 Reggie Miller / John Starks 2.00 5.00
N9 Toni Kukoc / Dino Radja 2.00 5.00
N10 Michael Jordan / Joe Dumars 10.00 25.00

1995-96 Stadium Club Power Zone

Randomly inserted in first and second series packs, this set of twelve standard-size cards feature the men who drive to the basket with authority. First series cards were randomly seeded into one in every 36 hobby and retail packs. Second series cards were randomly seeded into one in every 48 hobby and retail packs. First and second series card design differ radically. The first series cards feature borderless fronts with full-color action player cutouts set against a silver diffracted foil background. Second series cards contain a foil-etched background.

COMPLETE SET (12) 20.00 40.00
COMPLETE SERIES 1 (6) 10.00 20.00
COMPLETE SERIES 2 (6) 10.00 20.00
PZ1 Shaquille O'Neal 5.00 12.00
PZ2 Charles Barkley 3.00 8.00
PZ3 Patrick Ewing 2.50 6.00
PZ4 Karl Malone 2.50 6.00
PZ5 Larry Johnson 2.00 5.00
PZ6 Derrick Coleman 1.50 4.00
PZ7 Hakeem Olajuwon 2.50 6.00
PZ8 David Robinson 3.00 8.00
PZ9 Shawn Kemp 2.00 5.00
PZ10 Dennis Rodman 4.00 10.00
PZ11 Alonzo Mourning 2.50 6.00
PZ12 Vin Baker 1.50 4.00

1995-96 Stadium Club Reign Men

Randomly inserted in second-series hobby and retail packs at a rate of one in 48, this 10-card set features the NBA's slam dunk kings. Card fronts have a foil-etched background with the card name "Reign Men" running vertically along the right side. Card backs are horizontal with a head shot of the player, biographical information and a brief commentary. The cards are numbered with an "RM" prefix.

COMPLETE SET (10) 20.00 50.00
RM1 Shawn Kemp 2.00 5.00
RM2 Michael Jordan 12.50 30.00
RM3 Larry Johnson 2.00 5.00
RM4 Grant Hill 3.00 8.00
RM5 Isaiah Rider 2.00 5.00
RM6 Sean Elliott 2.00 5.00
RM7 Scottie Pippen 3.00 8.00
RM8 Robert Horry 1.50 4.00
RM9 Kendall Gill 1.25 3.00
RM10 Jerry Stackhouse 3.00 8.00

1995-96 Stadium Club Spike Says

Filmmaker Spike Lee picks his 10 favorite NBA players and tells us all about them in his inimitable style. Cards in this 10-piece set were randomly inserted at a rate of one in every 12 retail packs and one in every 24 hobby packs. Card fronts are full bleed action shots with the player's name and the set name in silver refractive foil. Spike Lee is also pictured on each card front in a small circle in the lower right. Card backs are horizontal with Spike Lee's commentary on the player. The cards are numbered with a "SS" prefix.

COMPLETE SET (10) 10.00 20.00
SS1 Michael Jordan 6.00 15.00
SS2 Alonzo Mourning 1.00 2.50
SS3 Reggie Miller 1.00 2.50
SS4 Patrick Ewing 1.00 2.50
SS5 Charles Barkley 1.25 3.00
SS6 Kenny Anderson .60 1.50
SS7 Scottie Pippen 1.25 3.00
SS8 Jerry Stackhouse 1.25 3.00
SS9 Shaquille O'Neal 2.00 5.00
SS10 John Starks .60 1.50

1995-96 Stadium Club Warp Speed

Randomly inserted in first and second series packs, this 12-card standard-size set features the players with the quickest first steps in the league. First series cards were randomly seeded in hobby and retail packs at a rate of one in 36. Second series cards were randonmly seeded in hobby and retail packs at a rate of one in 48. First and second series card designs differ radically. First series features full-bleed fronts, a full-color action player cutout with a trailing ghost image set against a silver foil "outer space" background with shiny silver flecks. The "Warp Speed" logo appears vertically on the left side and the player's name printed in red at the bottom. Second series cards feature cur out action shots of each player set against a silver foil, vortex background.

COMPLETE SET (12) 20.00 50.00
COMPLETE SERIES 1 (6) 12.00 30.00
COMPLETE SERIES 2 (6) 8.00 20.00
WS1 Michael Jordan 12.00 30.00
WS2 Kevin Johnson 1.50 4.00
WS3 Gary Payton 1.50 4.00
WS4 Anfernee Hardaway 2.50 6.00
WS5 Mookie Blaylock 1.00 2.50
WS6 Tim Hardaway 1.50 4.00
WS7 Scottie Pippen 2.50 6.00
WS8 Jason Kidd 2.50 6.00
WS9 Grant Hill 2.50 6.00
WS10 Nick Van Exel 1.50 4.00
WS11 Kenny Anderson 1.25 3.00
WS12 Latrell Sprewell 1.50 4.00

1995-96 Stadium Club Wizards

Randomly inserted exclusively in series one hobby packs at a rate of one in 24, this 10-card standard-size set features the best ball handlers in the game. Borderless etched foil fronts feature the player in a full-color action cutout with the Blue etched foil "Wizard" logo at the top. The player's name is stamped in gold foil at the bottom.

COMPLETE SET (10) 12.50 30.00
W1 Nick Van Exel 2.00 5.00
W2 Tim Hardaway 2.00 5.00
W3 Mookie Blaylock 1.25 3.00
W4 Gary Payton 2.00 5.00
W5 Jason Kidd 3.00 8.00
W6 Kenny Anderson 1.50 4.00
W7 John Stockton 2.50 6.00
W8 Kevin Johnson 2.00 5.00
W9 Muggsy Bogues 1.50 4.00
W10 Anfernee Hardaway 3.00 8.00

1995-96 Stadium Club X-2

Randomly inserted exclusively in second series hobby packs at a rate of one in 24 and second series retail packs at one in 48, this 10-card set showcases elite players who averaged double-doubles last season. Card fronts have an etched "X" in the background with an action shot. Card backs contain the same background with biographical and statistical information.

COMPLETE SET (10) 10.00 25.00
X1 Hakeem Olajuwon 2.00 5.00
X2 Shaquille O'Neal 4.00 10.00
X3 David Robinson 2.50 6.00
X4 Patrick Ewing 2.00 5.00
X5 Charles Barkley 2.50 6.00
X6 Karl Malone 2.00 5.00
X7 Derrick Coleman 1.25 3.00
X8 Shawn Kemp 1.50 4.00
X9 Vin Baker 1.25 3.00
X10 Vlade Divac 1.50 4.00

1996-97 Stadium Club Promos

These promotional cards, issued before the product's release date, look identical to the 1996-97 Stadium Club cards bearing the same card numbers. The only differentiation can be found in the copyright information on the backs of the cards. The promos have only two lines of white type whereas the cards from the regular set have four lines. The front of the Damon Stoudamire promo has his name correctly written so it reads from the bottom to the top of the card unlike the regular issue that has the name reading from top to bottom.

COMPLETE SET (6) 1.50 4.00
1 Scottie Pippen .60 1.50
33 Arvydas Sabonis .30 .75
46 Damon Stoudamire .40 1.00
47 Elden Campbell .25 .60
77 Nick Anderson .25 .60
78 David Robinson .60 1.50

1996-97 Stadium Club

The 180-card Stadium Club set features embossed, foil color action player photos printed on 20 pt. stock, making them noticeably sturdier than previous Stadium Club releases. The cards were released in two series, each containing 90 cards. Cards were distributed in eight-card packs with a suggested retail price of $2.50. The fronts feature full-color game action photography with the players name running vertically up the right side of the card in an embossed foil strip. No subsets or Rookie Cards were included in the first series set. Two Moments or Rookies insert cards were guaranteed to be in each first series pack.

COMPLETE SET (180) 10.00 25.00
COMPLETE SERIES 1 (90) 4.00 10.00
COMPLETE SERIES 2 (90) 6.00 15.00
1 Scottie Pippen .40 1.00
2 Dale Davis .15 .40
3 Horace Grant .20 .50
4 Gheorghe Muresan .15 .40
5 Elliot Perry .15 .40
6 Carlos Rogers .15 .40
7 Glenn Robinson .25 .60
8 Avery Johnson .20 .50
9 Dee Brown .15 .40
10 Grant Hill .40 1.00
11 Tyus Edney .15 .40
12 Patrick Ewing .30 .75
13 Jason Kidd .40 1.00
14 Clifford Robinson .15 .40
15 Robert Horry .20 .50
16 Dell Curry .15 .40
17 Terry Porter .15 .40
18 Shaquille O'Neal .60 1.50
19 Bryant Stith .15 .40
20 Shawn Kemp .25 .60
21 Kurt Thomas .15 .40
22 Pooh Richardson .15 .40
23 Bob Sura .15 .40
24 Olden Polynice .15 .40
25 Lawrence Moten .15 .40
26 Kendall Gill .15 .40
27 Cedric Ceballos .15 .40
28 Latrell Sprewell .25 .60
29 Christian Laettner .20 .50
30 Jamal Mashburn .20 .50
31 Jerry Stackhouse .30 .75
32 John Stockton .30 .75
33 Arvydas Sabonis .20 .50
34 Detlef Schrempf .25 .60
35 Toni Kukoc .25 .60
36 Sasha Danilovic .15 .40
37 Dana Barros .15 .40
38 Loy Vaught .15 .40
39 John Starks .20 .50
40 Marty Conlon .15 .40
41 Antonio McDyess .25 .60
42 Michael Finley .30 .75
43 Tom Gugliotta .15 .40
44 Terrell Brandon .15 .40
45 Derrick McKey .15 .40
46 Damon Stoudamire .25 .60
47 Elden Campbell .15 .40
48 Luc Longley .15 .40
49 B.J. Armstrong .15 .40
50 Lindsey Hunter .15 .40
51 Glen Rice .25 .60
52 Shawn Respert .15 .40
53 Cory Alexander .15 .40
54 Tim Legler .15 .40
55 Bryant Reeves .15 .40
56 Anfernee Hardaway .40 1.00
57 Charles Barkley .40 1.00
58 Mookie Blaylock .15 .40
59 Kevin Garnett .60 1.50
60 Hersey Hawkins .15 .40
61 Ed O'Bannon .15 .40
62 George Zidek .15 .40
63 Mitch Richmond .25 .60
64 Derrick Coleman .20 .50
65 Chris Webber .30 .75
66 Bobby Phills .15 .40
67 Rik Smits .20 .50
68 Jeff Hornacek .20 .50
69 Sam Cassell .20 .50
70 Gary Trent .15 .40
71 LaPhonso Ellis .15 .40
72 Oliver Miller .15 .40
73 Rex Chapman .15 .40
74 Jim Jackson .15 .40
75 Eric Williams .15 .40
76 Brent Barry .20 .50
77 Nick Anderson .15 .40
78 David Robinson .40 1.00
79 Calbert Cheaney .15 .40
80 Joe Smith .20 .50
81 Steve Kerr .20 .50
82 Wayman Tisdale .15 .40
83 Steve Smith .20 .50
84 Clyde Drexler .30 .75
85 Theo Ratliff .15 .40
86 Charlie Ward .15 .40
87 Karl Malone .30 .75
88 Clarence Weatherspoon .15 .40
89 Greg Anthony .15 .40
90 Shawn Bradley .15 .40
91 Otis Thorpe .15 .40
92 Larry Johnson .25 .60
93 Sharone Wright .15 .40
94 Charles Barkley .40 1.00
95 Wesley Person .15 .40
96 Dikembe Mutombo .25 .60
97 Eddie Jones .25 .60
98 Juwan Howard .20 .50
99 Grant Hill .40 1.00
100 Chris Carr RC .25 .60
101 Michael Jordan 2.00 5.00
102 Vincent Askew .15 .40
103 Gary Payton .25 .60
104 Chris Mills .15 .40
105 Reggie Miller .30 .75
106 Don MacLean .15 .40
107 John Stockton .30 .75
108 Mahmoud Abdul-Rauf .15 .40
109 P.J. Brown .15 .40
110 Kenny Anderson .20 .50
111 Mark Price .25 .60
112 Derek Harper .20 .50
113 Dino Radja .20 .50
114 Terry Dehere .15 .40
115 Mark Jackson .25 .60
116 Vin Baker .20 .50
117 Dennis Scott .15 .40
118 Sean Elliott .25 .60
119 Lee Mayberry .15 .40
120 Vlade Divac .25 .60
121 Joe Dumars .25 .60
122 Isaiah Rider .20 .50
123 Hakeem Olajuwon .30 .75
124 Robert Pack .15 .40
125 Jalen Rose .20 .50
126 Allan Houston .20 .50
127 Nate McMillan .15 .40
128 Rod Strickland .15 .40
129 Sean Rooks .15 .40
130 Dennis Rodman .50 1.25
131 Alonzo Mourning .30 .75
132 Danny Ferry .15 .40
133 Sam Cassell .20 .50
134 Brian Grant .20 .50
135 Karl Malone .30 .75
136 Chris Gatling .15 .40
137 Tom Gugliotta .15 .40
138 Hubert Davis .15 .40
139 Lucious Harris .15 .40
140 Rony Seikaly .20 .50
141 Alan Henderson .15 .40
142 Mario Elie .15 .40
143 Vinny Del Negro .15 .40
144 Harvey Grant .15 .40
145 Muggsy Bogues .20 .50
146 Rodney Rogers .15 .40
147 Kevin Johnson .25 .60
148 Anthony Peeler .15 .40
149 Jon Koncak .15 .40
150 Ricky Pierce .15 .40
151 Todd Day .15 .40
152 Tyrone Hill .15 .40
153 Nick Van Exel .25 .60
154 Rasheed Wallace .30 .75
155 Jayson Williams .15 .40
156 Sherman Douglas .15 .40
157 Bryon Russell .15 .40
158 Ron Harper .20 .50
159 Stacey Augmon .20 .50
160 Antonio Davis .15 .40
161 Tim Hardaway .25 .60
162 Charles Oakley .20 .50
163 Billy Owens .15 .40
164 Sam Perkins .15 .40
165 Chris Whitney .15 .40
166 Matt Geiger .15 .40
167 Andrew Lang .15 .40
168 Danny Manning .20 .50
169 Doug Christie .15 .40
170 George Lynch .15 .40
171 Malik Sealy .15 .40
172 Eric Montross .15 .40
173 Rick Fox .15 .40
174 Chris Mullin .25 .60
175 Ken Norman .15 .40
176 Sarunas Marciulionis .15 .40
177 Kevin Garnett .60 1.50
178 Brian Shaw .15 .40
179 Will Perdue .15 .40
180 Scott Williams .15 .40
NNO Checklist .15 .40

1996-97 Stadium Club Matrix

Randomly inserted into series 1 packs only at the rate of one in 12, this 90-card set is a parallel set to the series 1 base cards of the regular Stadium set. The difference in design lies in the Power Matrix technology used in the printing of this semi-parallel set. To ascertain values of individual cards, please refer to the multiplier in the header, coupled with the value of the basic card.

*STARS: 5X TO 12X BASE CARD HI

1996-97 Stadium Club Class Acts

Randomly inserted in all series two packs at a rate of one in 24, this 20-card dual player set features players who were either college teammates or went to the same school. The cards incorporated the use of the Finest technology. Card backs were numbered with a "CA" prefix.

COMPLETE SET (10) 30.00 60.00
*ATO.REF: 2X TO 5X HI
ATO.REF: SER.2 STATED ODDS 1:192 H/R
*REF: 1X TO 2.5X HI COLUMN
REF: SER.2 STATED ODDS 1:96 H/R

CA1 Michael Jordan 10.00 25.00
Jerry Stackhouse
CA2 Patrick Ewing 1.50 4.00
Alonzo Mourning
CA3 Gary Payton 1.25 3.00
Brent Barry
CA4 Chris Webber 1.50 4.00
Juwan Howard
CA5 Christian Laettner 2.00 5.00
Grant Hill
CA6 Shareef Abdur-Rahim 2.50 6.00
Jason Kidd
CA7 Clyde Drexler 2.50 6.00
Hakeem Olajuwon
CA8 Stephon Marbury 1.50 4.00
Kenny Anderson
CA9 Anfernee Hardaway 2.00 5.00
Lorenzen Wright
CA10 Allen Iverson 3.00 8.00
Dikembe Mutombo

1996-97 Stadium Club Finest Reprints

Randomly inserted in series one packs at the rate of one in 24 hobby and one in 20 retail, this 25-card set features reprints of 25 of the 50 greatest NBA players as they appeared on their first Topps, Star Co., or Bowman cards. Cards utilize the Finest technology. The remaining 25 cards were issued in 1996-97 Topps series two.

2 Nate Archibald 1.25 3.00
4 Charles Barkley 3.00 8.00
5 Rick Barry 1.25 3.00
6 Elgin Baylor 1.25 3.00
7 Dave Bing 1.25 3.00
8 Larry Bird 6.00 15.00
Julius Erving
Magic Johnson
10 Bob Cousy 3.00 8.00
12 Billy Cunningham 1.25 3.00
13 Dave DeBusschere 1.25 3.00
15 Julius Erving 2.50 6.00
17 Walt Frazier 1.25 3.00
18 George Gervin 1.25 3.00
19 Hal Greer 1.25 3.00
24 Michael Jordan 15.00 40.00
26 Karl Malone 3.00 8.00
28 Pete Maravich 4.00 10.00
29 Kevin McHale 1.50 4.00
34 Robert Parish 1.25 3.00
35 Bob Pettit 1.25 3.00
36 Scottie Pippen 3.00 8.00
41 Dolph Schayes 1.25 3.00
44 Isiah Thomas 1.25 3.00
48 Jerry West 3.00 8.00
49 Lenny Wilkens UER 1.25 3.00
50 James Worthy 1.50 4.00

1996-97 Stadium Club Finest Reprints Refractors

Randomly inserted in series one packs at the rate of one in 96 hobby and one in 80 retail, this 25-card set is distinguished in design from the regular Topps Stars Reprint set by the refractor quality of the card. To ascertain values on individual cards, please refer to the multiplier in the header below, coupled with the value of the base card.

*STARS: 1.25X TO 3X VALUE
24 Michael Jordan 100.00 200.00

1996-97 Stadium Club Fusion

Randomly inserted in both series hobby packs at a rate of one in 24, this 32-card set features color player photos on fusion laser cut cards. Each card displays one player and fits together with another card creating a larger image. Only the cards displaying the correct teammates can be "fused" together. Card backs are numbered with a "F" prefix.

COMPLETE SET (32) 70.00 140.00
COMPLETE SERIES 1 (16) 50.00 100.00
COMPLETE SERIES 2 (16) 20.00 40.00
F1 Michael Jordan 20.00 50.00
F2 Chris Webber 2.50 6.00
F3 Glenn Robinson 2.00 5.00
F4 Glen Rice 2.00 5.00
F5 Gary Payton 2.00 5.00
F6 Rik Smits 1.50 4.00
F7 Grant Hill 3.00 8.00
F8 Horace Grant 1.50 4.00
F9 Scottie Pippen 3.00 8.00
F10 Gheorghe Muresan 1.25 3.00
F11 Vin Baker 1.50 4.00
F12 Dell Curry 1.25 3.00
F13 Shawn Kemp 2.00 5.00
F14 Reggie Miller 2.50 6.00
F15 Joe Dumars 2.00 5.00
F16 Anfernee Hardaway 3.00 8.00
F17 Charles Barkley 3.00 8.00
F18 Juwan Howard 1.50 4.00
F19 Patrick Ewing 2.50 6.00
F20 John Stockton 2.50 6.00
F21 David Robinson 3.00 8.00
F22 Cedric Ceballos 1.25 3.00
F23 Alonzo Mourning 2.50 6.00
F24 Mookie Blaylock 1.25 3.00
F25 Clyde Drexler 2.50 6.00
F26 Rod Strickland 1.25 3.00
F27 Larry Johnson 2.00 5.00
F28 Karl Malone 2.50 6.00
F29 Sean Elliott 2.00 5.00
F30 Shaquille O'Neal 5.00 12.00
F31 Tim Hardaway 2.00 5.00
F32 Dikembe Mutombo 2.00 5.00

1996-97 Stadium Club Gallery Player's Private Issue

Randomly inserted at a rate of one in 96 series 2 hobby packs, this 18-card set completes the 1995-96 Topps Gallery Player's Private Issue set. Cards are identical to the 1995-96 release. For pricing, please refer to the 1995-96 Topps Gallery Player's Private Issue set.

COMPLETE SET (18) 200.00 400.00

1996-97 Stadium Club Golden Moments

Five Golden Moment cards (GM1-M5) highlighted memorable events in the NBA from 1995 and 1996. These cards feature record-breaking occasions. The cards feature sturdy 20 pt. stock, actual event photography and were seeded at an approximate rate of one per first series pack.

COMPLETE SET (5) 1.50 4.00
GM1 Robert Parish .25 .60
GM2 John Stockton .30 .75
GM3 Michael Jordan 1.50 4.00
Dennis Rodman
GM4 Dennis Scott .15 .40
GM5 Hakeem Olajuwon .30 .75

1996-97 Stadium Club High Risers

Randomly inserted in second series packs at a rate of one in 36, this 15-card set features a combination of Power Matrix and embossed technologies. The set features some of the NBA's best players above the rim. Card backs carry a "HR" prefix.

COMPLETE SET (15) 30.00 80.00
HR1 Scottie Pippen 3.00 8.00
HR2 Anfernee Hardaway 3.00 8.00
HR3 Vin Baker 1.50 4.00
HR4 Brent Barry 1.50 4.00
HR5 Clyde Drexler 2.50 6.00
HR6 Kevin Garnett 5.00 12.00
HR7 Grant Hill 3.00 8.00
HR8 Michael Finley 2.50 6.00
HR9 Jerry Stackhouse 2.50 6.00
HR10 Isaiah Rider 1.50 4.00
HR11 Shaquille O'Neal 5.00 12.00
HR12 Antonio McDyess 2.00 5.00
HR13 Shawn Kemp 2.00 5.00
HR14 Michael Jordan 15.00 40.00
HR15 Juwan Howard 1.50 4.00

1996-97 Stadium Club Mega Heroes

Randomly inserted in second series retail packs only at a rate of one in 20, this 9-card set features NBA players who have famous nicknames. Card fronts feature different themes depending on the player's particular nickname. Card backs carry a "MH" prefix.

COMPLETE SET (9) 6.00 15.00
MH1 Dennis Rodman 2.00 5.00
MH2 David Robinson 1.50 4.00
MH3 Karl Malone 1.25 3.00
MH4 Clyde Drexler 1.25 3.00
MH5 Anfernee Hardaway 1.50 4.00
MH6 Hakeem Olajuwon 1.25 3.00
MH7 Charles Oakley .75 2.00
MH8 Joe Smith .75 2.00
MH9 Glenn Robinson 1.00 2.50

1996-97 Stadium Club Rookie Showcase

Randomly inserted in all series two packs at a rate of one in 12, this 25-card set features Topps first shot at holography. The cards focus on rookies and feature a "two-shot" hologram. Card backs carry a "RS" prefix.

COMPLETE SET (25) 40.00 80.00
RS1 Marcus Camby 1.50 4.00
RS2 Shareef Abdur-Rahim 2.00 5.00
RS3 Stephon Marbury 2.50 6.00
RS4 Ray Allen 4.00 10.00
RS5 Antoine Walker 2.00 5.00
RS6 Lorenzen Wright 1.00 2.50
RS7 Kerry Kittles 1.00 2.50
RS8 Samaki Walker 1.00 2.50
RS9 Erick Dampier 1.00 2.50
RS10 Todd Fuller 1.00 2.50
RS11 Kobe Bryant 10.00 25.00
RS12 Steve Nash 5.00 12.00
RS13 Tony Delk 1.00 2.50
RS14 Jermaine O'Neal 2.50 6.00
RS15 John Wallace 1.00 2.50
RS16 Walter McCarty 1.00 2.50
RS17 Dontae' Jones 1.00 2.50
RS18 Roy Rogers 1.00 2.50
RS19 Derek Fisher 2.00 5.00
RS20 Martin Muursepp 1.00 2.50
RS21 Jerome Williams 1.00 2.50
RS22 Brian Evans 1.00 2.50
RS23 Priest Lauderdale 1.00 2.50
RS24 Travis Knight 1.00 2.50
RS25 Allen Iverson 5.00 12.00

1996-97 Stadium Club Rookies 1

This set of 25 standard-sized cards feature most of the top rookies selected in the first round of the 1996 NBA Draft. These cards were seeded at an approximate rate of one per first series pack. Cards are printed on sturdy 20 pt. stock and were the first cards released to picture the rookies in their pro uniforms. Card fronts feature full color, borderless photographs with the word "Rookie" running down the side of the card. A number of the top foreign draft picks were excluded from the set.

COMPLETE SET (25) 7.50 15.00
R1 Allen Iverson 1.25 3.00
R2 Marcus Camby .40 1.00
R3 Shareef Abdur-Rahim .50 1.25
R4 Stephon Marbury .60 1.50
R5 Ray Allen 1.00 2.50
R6 Antoine Walker .50 1.25
R7 Lorenzen Wright .25 .60
R8 Kerry Kittles .25 .60
R9 Samaki Walker .25 .60
R10 Erick Dampier .25 .60
R11 Todd Fuller .25 .60
R12 Kobe Bryant 4.00 10.00
R13 Steve Nash 1.25 3.00
R14 Tony Delk .25 .60
R15 Jermaine O'Neal .60 1.50
R16 John Wallace .25 .60
R17 Walter McCarty .25 .60
R18 Dontae Jones .25 .60
R19 Roy Rogers .25 .60
R20 Derek Fisher .50 1.25
R21 Martin Muursepp .25 .60
R22 Jerome Williams .25 .60
R23 Brian Evans .25 .60
R24 Priest Lauderdale .25 .60
R25 Travis Knight .25 .60

1996-97 Stadium Club Rookies 2

This set of 20 standard-sized cards feature most of the top rookies selected in the first round of the 1996 NBA Draft. These cards were seeded at an approximate rate of one per second series pack. Cards are printed on 20 pt. stock.

COMPLETE SET (20) 7.50 15.00
R1 Shareef Abdur-Rahim .50 1.25
R2 Tony Delk .25 .60
R3 Priest Lauderdale .25 .60
R4 Roy Rogers .25 .60
R5 Lorenzen Wright .25 .60
R6 Stephon Marbury .60 1.50
R7 Derek Fisher .50 1.25
R8 John Wallace .25 .60
R9 Kobe Bryant 4.00 10.00
R10 Kerry Kittles .25 .60
R11 Antoine Walker .50 1.25
R12 Steve Nash 1.25 3.00
R13 Erick Dampier .25 .60
R14 Walter McCarty .25 .60
R15 Vitaly Potapenko .25 .60
R16 Allen Iverson 1.25 3.00
R17 Marcus Camby .40 1.00
R18 Todd Fuller .25 .60
R19 Ray Allen 1.00 2.50
R20 Jermaine O'Neal .60 1.50

1996-97 Stadium Club Shining Moments

The fifteen Shining Moments cards showcase the slamming and jamming plays that made the '95-96 season memorable. The cards feature sturdy 20 pt. stock, actual event photography and were seeded at an approximate rate of one per first series pack

COMPLETE SET (15) 3.00 8.00
SM1 Charles Barkley .40 1.00
SM2 Michael Jordan 2.00 5.00
SM3 Karl Malone .30 .75
SM4 Hakeem Olajuwon .30 .75
SM5 John Stockton .30 .75
SM6 Patrick Ewing .30 .75
SM7 Reggie Miller .30 .75
SM8 David Robinson .40 1.00
SM9 Dennis Rodman .50 1.25
SM10 Damon Stoudamire .25 .60
SM11 Brent Barry .20 .50
SM12 Tim Legler .15 .40
SM13 Jason Kidd .40 1.00
SM14 Terrell Brandon .15 .40
SM15 Allen Iverson 1.25 3.00

1996-97 Stadium Club Special Forces

Randomly inserted in series one packs at a rate of one in 20, this 10-card retail only set features color action photos of super-charged stars printed with the Electra-Etch foil technology. There appears to be different levels of etching on the cards, with some etched very deep and heavy and some barely etched, if at all.

COMPLETE SET (10) 15.00 40.00
SF1 Anfernee Hardaway 2.00 5.00
SF2 Grant Hill 2.00 5.00
SF3 Shawn Kemp 1.25 3.00
SF4 Michael Jordan 12.00 30.00
SF5 Shaquille O'Neal 3.00 8.00
SF6 Scottie Pippen 2.00 5.00
SF7 Damon Stoudamire 1.25 3.00
SF8 Jerry Stackhouse 1.50 4.00
SF9 Gary Payton 1.25 3.00
SF10 Dennis Rodman 2.50 6.00

1996-97 Stadium Club Top Crop

Randomly inserted in series one packs at a rate of one in 24, this 12-card set features color action player photos on double-sided Power Matrix cards with NBA All-Stars from both the East and the West Conferences pitted against each other. One side displays an all-star player from the Eastern Conference with the other side carrying the corresponding Western Conference all-star player.

COMPLETE SET (12) 20.00 50.00
TC1 Shaquille O'Neal 4.00 10.00
Hakeem Olajuwon
TC2 Alonzo Mourning 1.50 4.00
Dikembe Mutombo
TC3 Patrick Ewing 2.00 5.00
David Robinson
TC4 Grant Hill 2.00 5.00
Sean Elliott
TC5 Scottie Pippen 2.00 5.00
Shawn Kemp
TC6 Vin Baker 1.50 4.00
Karl Malone
TC7 Juwan Howard 2.00 5.00
Charles Barkley
TC8 Glen Rice 1.50 4.00
Clyde Drexler
TC9 Michael Jordan 10.00 25.00
Gary Payton
TC10 Terrell Brandon 1.50 4.00
John Stockton
TC11 Reggie Miller 1.50 4.00
Mitch Richmond
TC12 Anfernee Hardaway 2.00 5.00
Jason Kidd

1996-97 Stadium Club Welcome Additions

The 25 Welcome Addition cards showcase the new additions that NBA teams made in the off-season. The cards feature sturdy 20 pt. stock and were seeded at an approximate rate of one per second series pack.

COMPLETE SET (25) 2.00 5.00
WA1 Charles Barkley .40 1.00
WA2 Armon Gilliam .15 .40
WA3 Larry Johnson .25 .60
WA4 Felton Spencer .15 .40
WA5 Isaiah Rider .20 .50
WA6 Kevin Willis .15 .40
WA7 Mahmoud Abdul-Rauf .15 .40
WA8 Chris Childs .15 .40
WA9 Robert Horry .20 .50
WA10 Dan Majerle .25 .60
WA11 Robert Pack .15 .40
WA12 Rod Strickland .15 .40
WA13 Tyrone Corbin .15 .40
WA14 Anthony Mason .15 .40
WA15 Derek Harper .20 .50
WA16 Kenny Anderson .20 .50
WA17 Hubert Davis .15 .40
WA18 Allan Houston .20 .50
WA19 Shaquille O'Neal .60 1.50
WA20 Brent Price .15 .40
WA21 Ervin Johnson .15 .40
WA22 Craig Ehlo .15 .40
WA23 Jalen Rose .20 .50
WA24 Oliver Miller .15 .40
WA25 Mark West .15 .40

1997-98 Stadium Club Promos

These six standard-size promo cards issued to preview the 97-98 Stadium Club set. They are numbered the same as the regular cards in the 97-8 Stadium Club set. The cards have slick photo stock on the front with a shiny foil-embossed logo. The player's name is found at the bottom inside an effervescent blue strip. The backs are filled with commentary and player statistics. The last three years of the player's performance are highlighted and given rankings based on others who played the same position. Most likely, the only difference between these promos and the regular set will be the small white lines of trademark information on the back of the card. This is not definite, but if past trends are followed, it may very well be the case.

COMPLETE SET (6) 2.00 5.00
21 Glen Rice .50 1.25
41 Reggie Miller .60 1.50
87 Patrick Ewing .60 1.50
95 Antoine Walker .50 1.25
115 Karl Malone .60 1.50
169 Kenny Anderson .40 1.00

1997-98 Stadium Club

The 1997-98 Stadium Club first series was issued with a total of 120 cards and was distributed in 10-card packs for a suggested retail price of $3.00. The fronts feature full-bleed color action player photos embossed and printed on 20 pt. stock and containing a new holographic foil logo. The backs carry expanded career and previous season statistics, including the player's ranking among other players at the same position. The cards of series one are the odd numbered cards.

COMPLETE SET (240) 22.50 45.00
COMPLETE SERIES 1 (120) 12.50 25.00
COMPLETE SERIES 2 (120) 10.00 20.00
1 Scottie Pippen .40 1.00
2 Bryon Russell .15 .40
3 Muggsy Bogues .20 .50
4 Gary Payton .25 .60
5 Ron Harper 2.00 5.00
Michael Jordan
Scottie Pippen
Dennis Rodman
6 Corliss Williamson .15 .40
7 Samaki Walker .15 .40
8 Allan Houston .20 .50
9 Ray Allen .30 .75
10 Nick Van Exel .20 .50
11 Chris Mullin .25 .60
12 Popeye Jones .15 .40
13 Horace Grant .20 .50
14 Rik Smits .20 .50
15 Wayman Tisdale .15 .40
16 Donny Marshall .15 .40
17 Rod Strickland .15 .40
18 Rod Strickland .15 .40
19 Greg Anthony .15 .40
20 Lindsey Hunter .15 .40
21 Glen Rice .25 .60
22 Anthony Goldwire .15 .40
23 Mahmoud Abdul-Rauf .15 .40
24 Sean Elliott .25 .60
25 Cory Alexander .15 .40
26 Tyrone Corbin .15 .40
27 Sam Perkins .15 .40
28 Brian Shaw .15 .40
29 Doug Christie .15 .40
30 Mark Jackson .25 .60
31 Christian Laettner .20 .50
32 Damon Stoudamire .25 .60
33 Eric Williams .15 .40
34 Glenn Robinson .20 .50
35 Brooks Thompson .15 .40
36 Derrick Coleman .20 .50
37 Theo Ratliff .20 .50
38 Ron Harper .20 .50
39 Hakeem Olajuwon .30 .75
40 Mitch Richmond .25 .60
41 Reggie Miller .30 .75
42 Reggie Miller .30 .75
43 Shaquille O'Neal .60 1.50
44 Zydrunas Ilgauskas .25 .60
45 Jamal Mashburn .20 .50
46 Isaiah Rider .15 .40
47 Tom Gugliotta .15 .40
48 Rex Chapman .15 .40
49 Lorenzen Wright .15 .40
50 Pooh Richardson .15 .40
51 Armon Gilliam .15 .40
52 Kevin Johnson .25 .60
53 Kerry Kittles .15 .40
54 Kerry Kittles .15 .40
55 Charles Oakley .20 .50
56 Dennis Rodman .50 1.25
57 Greg Ostertag .15 .40
58 Todd Fuller .15 .40
59 Mark Davis .15 .40
60 Erick Strickland RC .25 .60
61 Clifford Robinson .15 .40
62 Nate McMillan .15 .40
63 Steve Kerr .20 .50
64 Bob Sura .15 .40
65 Danny Ferry .15 .40
66 Loy Vaught .15 .40
67 A.C. Green .25 .60
68 John Stockton .30 .75
69 Terry Mills .15 .40
70 Voshon Lenard .15 .40
71 Matt Maloney .15 .40
72 Charlie Ward .15 .40
73 Brent Barry .20 .50
74 Chris Webber .25 .60
75 Stephon Marbury .30 .75
76 Bryant Stith .15 .40
77 Shareef Abdur-Rahim .25 .60
78 Sean Rooks .15 .40
79 Rony Seikaly .20 .50
80 Brent Price .15 .40
81 Wesley Person .15 .40
82 Michael Smith .15 .40
83 Gary Trent .15 .40
84 Dan Majerle .25 .60
85 Rex Walters .15 .40
86 Clarence Weatherspoon .15 .40
87 Patrick Ewing .30 .75
88 B.J. Armstrong .15 .40
89 Travis Best .15 .40
90 Steve Smith .20 .50
91 Vitaly Potapenko .15 .40
92 Derek Strong .15 .40
93 Michael Finley .25 .60
94 Will Perdue .15 .40
95 Antoine Walker .25 .60
96 Chuck Person .20 .50
97 Mookie Blaylock .15 .40
98 Eric Snow .15 .40
99 Tony Delk .15 .40
100 Mario Elie .15 .40
101 Terrell Brandon .15 .40
102 Shawn Bradley .15 .40
103 Latrell Sprewell .25 .60
104 Latrell Sprewell .25 .60
105 Tim Hardaway .25 .60
106 Terry Porter .15 .40
107 Darrell Armstrong .15 .40
108 Rasheed Wallace .25 .60
109 Vinny Del Negro .15 .40
110 Tracy Murray .15 .40
111 Lawrence Moten .15 .40
112 Lamond Murray .15 .40
113 Juwan Howard .20 .50
114 Juwan Howard .20 .50
115 Karl Malone .30 .75
116 Aaron McKie .15 .40
117 Shawn Respert .15 .40
118 Michael Jordan 2.00 5.00
119 Shawn Kemp .25 .60
120 Arvydas Sabonis .20 .50
121 Tyus Edney .15 .40
122 Bryant Reeves .15 .40
123 Jason Kidd .40 1.00
124 Dikembe Mutombo .25 .60
125 Allen Iverson .50 1.25
126 Allen Iverson .50 1.25
127 Larry Johnson .25 .60
128 Jerry Stackhouse .25 .60
129 Kendall Gill .15 .40
130 Kendall Gill .15 .40
131 Vin Baker .20 .50
132 Joe Dumars .25 .60
133 Calbert Cheaney .15 .40
134 Alonzo Mourning .30 .75
135 Isaac Austin .15 .40
136 Joe Smith .20 .50
137 Elden Campbell .15 .40
138 Kevin Garnett .50 1.25
139 Malik Sealy .15 .40
140 John Starks .20 .50
141 Clyde Drexler .30 .75
142 Matt Geiger .15 .40
143 Mark Price .25 .60
144 Buck Williams .15 .40
145 Grant Hill .40 1.00
146 Kobe Bryant 1.25 3.00
147 Dale Ellis .15 .40
148 Jason Caffey .15 .40
149 Toni Kukoc .25 .60
150 Avery Johnson .20 .50
151 Alan Henderson .15 .40
152 Walt Williams .15 .40
153 Greg Minor .15 .40
154 Calbert Cheaney .15 .40
155 Vlade Divac .25 .60
156 Greg Foster .15 .40
157 LaPhonso Ellis .15 .40
158 Charles Barkley .40 1.00
159 Antonio Davis .15 .40
160 Roy Rogers .15 .40
161 Robert Horry .20 .50
162 Sam Cassell .20 .50
163 Chris Carr .15 .40
164 Robert Pack .15 .40
165 Sam Cassell .20 .50
166 Rodney Rogers .15 .40
167 Chris Childs .15 .40
168 Shandon Anderson .15 .40
169 Kenny Anderson .20 .50
170 Anthony Mason .15 .40
171 Olden Polynice .15 .40
172 David Wingate .15 .40
173 David Robinson .40 1.00
174 Billy Owens .15 .40
175 Detlef Schrempf .25 .60
176 Carlos Rogers .15 .40
177 Marcus Camby .25 .60
178 Dana Barros .15 .40
179 Shandon Anderson .15 .40
180 Jayson Williams .15 .40
181 Eldridge Recasner .15 .40
182 Doug West .15 .40
183 Kevin Willis .15 .40
184 Eddie Johnson .15 .40
185 Derek Fisher .25 .60
186 Eddie Jones .25 .60
187 Sherman Douglas .15 .40
188 Anthony Peeler .15 .40
189 Danny Manning .20 .50
190 Stacey Augmon .20 .50
191 Hersey Hawkins .15 .40
192 Micheal Williams .15 .40
193 Jeff Hornacek .20 .50
194 Anfernee Hardaway .40 1.00
195 Harvey Grant .15 .40
196 Nick Anderson .15 .40
197 Luc Longley .15 .40
198 Andrew Lang .15 .40
199 P.J. Brown .15 .40
200 Cedric Ceballos .15 .40
201 Tim Duncan RC 1.50 4.00
202 Ervin Johnson TRAN .15 .40
203 Keith Van Horn RC .50 1.25
204 David Wesley TRAN .15 .40
205 Chauncey Billups RC 1.00 2.50
206 Jim Jackson TRAN .15 .40
207 Antonio Daniels RC .25 .60
208 Travis Knight TRAN .15 .40
209 Tony Battie RC .30 .75
210 Bobby Phills TRAN .15 .40
211 Bobby Jackson RC .30 .75
212 Otis Thorpe TRAN .15 .40
213 Tim Thomas RC .50 1.25
214 Chris Mullin TRAN .25 .60
215 Adonal Foyle RC .25 .60
216 Brian Williams TRAN .15 .40
217 Tracy McGrady RC 1.25 3.00
218 Tyus Edney TRAN .15 .40
219 Danny Fortson RC .25 .60
220 Clifford Robinson TRAN .15 .40
221 Olivier Saint-Jean RC .25 .60
222 Vin Baker TRAN .20 .50
223 Austin Croshere RC .25 .60
224 John Wallace TRAN .15 .40
225 Derek Anderson RC .25 .60
226 Kelvin Cato RC .25 .60
227 Maurice Taylor RC .25 .60
228 Scot Pollard RC .25 .60
229 John Thomas RC .25 .60
230 Dean Garrett TRAN .15 .40
231 Brevin Knight RC .25 .60
232 Ron Mercer RC .30 .75
233 Johnny Taylor RC .25 .60
234 Antonio McDyess TRAN .20 .50
235 Ed Gray RC .25 .60
236 Terrell Brandon TRAN .15 .40
237 Anthony Parker RC .25 .60
238 Shawn Kemp TRAN .25 .60
239 Paul Grant RC .25 .60
240 Dennis Scott TRAN .15 .40

1997-98 Stadium Club First Day Issue

Randomly inserted in both series retail packs only at the rate of one in 24, this 240-card set parallels the base set. The cards are reportedly limited to 200 each. Card fronts contain the theme First Day Issue written in gold foil above the player's name. To ascertain values on individual cards, please refer to the multiplier in the header below, coupled with the value of the base card.

*STARS: 12.5X TO 30X BASE CARD HI
*RCs: 6X TO 15X BASE HI
5 Bulls - Team of the 90's 125.00 250.00
Ron Harper
Michael Jordan
Scottie Pippen
Dennis Rodman
118 Michael Jordan 125.00 250.00

1997-98 Stadium Club One Of A Kind

Randomly inserted in both series hobby only packs, with series one inserted at the rate of one in 86 and series two inserted at one in 69, this 240-card set parallels the base set. The cards are serially numbered to 150. Card fronts differ by carrying a metal look. To ascertain values on individual cards, please refer to the multiplier in the header below, coupled with the value of the base card.

*STARS: 25X TO 60X BASE CARD HI
*RCs: 12.5X TO 30X BASE HI
118 Michael Jordan 450.00 750.00
146 Kobe Bryant 100.00 250.00

1997-98 Stadium Club Printing Plates

This 120-card hobby only set is parallel to the base set and features the actual printing plates used to produce the cards. Each player is featured on a plate that provided one of the four colors (cyan, magenta, yellow, and black) used in the printing. There are no premiums for any particular color.

1997-98 Stadium Club Bowman's Best Previews

Randomly inserted in packs at the rate of one in 24, this 10-card set is a sneak preview of the Bowman's Best series and features color action player photos with a section of a large gold basketball in the background. Card backs are numbered with a BBP prefix.

*ATO.REF: 2X TO 5X HI
ATO.REF: SER.1/2 STATED ODDS 1:192 H/R
*REF: 1.25X TO 3X HI COLUMN
REF: SER.1/2 STATED ODDS 1:96 H/R
BBP1 Allen Iverson 2.00 5.0
BBP2 Gary Payton 1.00 2.5
BBP3 Grant Hill 1.50 4.0
BBP4 Anfernee Hardaway 1.50 4.0
BBP5 Karl Malone 1.25 3.0
BBP6 Glen Rice 1.00 2.5
BBP7 Antoine Walker 1.00 2.5
BBP8 Alonzo Mourning 1.25 3.0
BBP9 Shareef Abdur-Rahim 1.00 2.5
BBP10 Shaquille O'Neal 2.50 6.0
BBP11 Maurice Taylor .50 1.2
BBP12 Chauncey Billups 2.00 5.0
BBP13 Paul Grant .50 1.2
BBP14 Tony Battie .60 1.5
BBP15 Austin Croshere .50 1.2
BBP16 Brevin Knight .50 1.2
BBP17 Bobby Jackson .60 1.5
BBP18 Johnny Taylor .50 1.2
BBP19 Scot Pollard .50 1.2
BBP20 Tariq Abdul-Wahad .50 1.2

1997-98 Stadium Club Co-Signers

Randomly inserted in both series, with series one inserted at one in 387 hobby and series two at one in 309 hobby, this 12-card set features a color action photo of a different player on each side of the card along with an authentic autograph of each player. Each of these double-sided cards are stamped with th Topps Certified Autograph issue stamp to ensure authenticity. The cards were inserted within three groups at different levels. Group "A", or cards CO1-CO4 were inserted at one in 15,483. Group "B", or cards CO5-CO8 were inserted at one in 5,161. Group "C", or cards CO9-CO12 were inserted at one in 430 packs. Card backs carry a CO prefix.

CO1 Karl Malone 700.00 1200.0
Kobe Bryant
CO2 Juwan Howard 75.00 150.0
Hakeem Olajuwon
CO3 John Starks 75.00 150.0
Joe Smith
CO4 Clyde Drexler 100.00 200.0
Tim Hardaway
CO5 Kobe Bryant 150.00 300.0
John Starks
CO6 Hakeem Olajuwon 100.00 200.0
Clyde Drexler
CO7 Tim Hardaway 20.00 50.0
Juwan Howard
CO8 Joe Smith 50.00 120.0
Karl Malone
CO9 Juwan Howard 20.00 50.0
Clyde Drexler
CO10 Hakeem Olajuwon 25.00 60.0
Tim Hardaway
CO11 Joe Smith 60.00 150.0
Kobe Bryant
CO12 Karl Malone 60.00 150.0
John Starks
CO13 Dikembe Mutombo 40.00 100.0
Chauncey Billups
CO14 Keith Van Horn 125.00 250.0
Chris Webber
CO15 Karl Malone 75.00 150.0
Kerry Kittles
CO16 Ron Mercer 25.00 60.0
Antoine Walker
CO17 Chris Webber 125.00 250.0
Karl Malone
CO18 Antoine Walker 40.00 80.0
Dikembe Mutombo
CO19 Kerry Kittles 20.00 50.0
Keith Van Horn
CO20 Chauncey Billups 20.00 50.0
Ron Mercer
CO21 Antoine Walker 20.00 50.0
Chauncey Billups
CO22 Dikembe Mutombo 20.00 50.0
Ron Mercer
CO23 Keith Van Horn 40.00 80.0
Karl Malone
CO24 Chris Webber 50.00 120.0
Kerry Kittles

1997-98 Stadium Club Hardcourt Heroics

Randomly inserted in series one packs at the rate of one in 12, this 10-card set features color player imag of some of the greatest NBA stars printed on a bright, colorful background with unilluster technology. Card backs are numbered with a H prefix.

COMPLETE SET (10) 8.00 20.0
H1 Michael Jordan 6.00 15.0
H2 Gary Payton .50 1.2
H3 Charles Barkley .75 2.0
H4 Mitch Richmond .50 1.2
H5 Shawn Kemp .50 1.2
H6 Anfernee Hardaway .75 2.0
H7 Vin Baker .40 1.0
H8 Shaquille O'Neal 1.25 3.0
H9 Scottie Pippen .75 2.0
H10 Grant Hill .75 2.0

1997-98 Stadium Club Hardwood Hopefuls

ndomly inserted in series one packs at the rate of
e in 36, this 10-card set features color action photos
he top 1997 NBA Draft Picks printed on rainbow foil
ds. Card backs are numbered with a HH prefix.
MPLETE SET (10) 6.00 15.00
1 Brevin Knight .50 1.25
2 Adonal Foyle .50 1.25
3 Keith Van Horn 1.00 2.50
4 Tim Duncan 3.00 8.00
5 Danny Fortson .50 1.25
6 Tracy McGrady 2.50 6.00
7 Tony Battie .60 1.50
8 Chauncey Billups 2.00 5.00
9 Austin Croshere .50 1.25
10 Antonio Daniels .50 1.25

1997-98 Stadium Club Hoop Screams

ndomly inserted in series one packs at the rate of
e in 12, this 10-card set features color action photos
players who display intensity around the rim by their
me faces. Card backs are numbered with a HS prefix.

MPLETE SET (10) 6.00 15.00
1 Shaquille O'Neal 1.25 3.00
2 Cedric Ceballos .30 .75
3 Kevin Garnett 1.00 2.50
4 Shawn Kemp .50 1.25
5 Jerry Stackhouse .50 1.25
6 Grant Hill .75 2.00
7 Patrick Ewing .60 1.50
8 Marcus Camby .50 1.25
9 Kobe Bryant 2.50 6.00
10 Michael Jordan 5.00 12.00

1997-98 Stadium Club Never Compromise

ndomly inserted into series two packs at a rate of
e in 36, this 20-card set focuses on players who
er compromise in their game play. Card backs carry
NC" prefix.
MPLETE SET (20) 30.00 80.00
1 Michael Jordan 12.00 30.00
2 Karl Malone 2.00 5.00
3 Hakeem Olajuwon 2.00 5.00
4 Kevin Garnett 3.00 8.00
5 Dikembe Mutombo 1.50 4.00
6 Gary Payton 1.50 4.00
7 Grant Hill 2.50 6.00
8 Charles Barkley 2.50 6.00
9 Shaquille O'Neal 4.00 10.00
10 Anfernee Hardaway 2.50 6.00
11 Tim Duncan 5.00 12.00
12 Keith Van Horn 1.50 4.00
13 Tracy McGrady 4.00 10.00
14 Tim Thomas 1.50 4.00
15 Austin Croshere .75 2.00
16 Maurice Taylor .75 2.00
17 Chauncey Billups 3.00 8.00
18 Adonal Foyle .75 2.00
19 Tony Battie 1.00 2.50
20 Bobby Jackson 1.00 2.50

1997-98 Stadium Club Royal Court

ndomly inserted into series two packs at a rate of
e in 12, this 20-card set features the elite players in
NBA. The card fronts feature a Royal Court logo
ainst a silver foil background. Card backs carry a
C" prefix.
MPLETE SET (20) 20.00 50.00
1 Scottie Pippen 1.50 4.00
2 Karl Malone 1.25 3.00
3 Gary Payton 1.00 2.50
4 Kobe Bryant 5.00 12.00
5 Antoine Walker 1.00 2.50
6 Michael Jordan 8.00 20.00
7 Shaquille O'Neal 2.50 6.00
8 Dikembe Mutombo 1.00 2.50
9 Hakeem Olajuwon 1.25 3.00
10 Grant Hill 1.50 4.00
11 Tim Duncan 3.00 8.00
12 Keith Van Horn 1.00 2.50
13 Chauncey Billups 2.00 5.00
14 Antonio Daniels .50 1.25
15 Tony Battie .60 1.50
16 Bobby Jackson .60 1.50
17 Tim Thomas 1.00 2.50
18 Adonal Foyle .50 1.25
19 Tracy McGrady 2.50 6.00
20 Danny Fortson .50 1.25

1997-98 Stadium Club Triumvirate

Randomly inserted in both series retail packs only at one in 48, these cards feature three NBA teammates that can be fused together. These laser cut cards use Luminous technology. Card backs are numbered with a "T" prefix.
*LUM.CARDS: 1.25X TO 3X BASE TRIUMV.
LUM: SER.1/2 STATED ODDS 1:192 RET
*ILLUM.CARDS: 2X TO 5X BASE TRIUMV.
ILLUM: SER.1/2 STATED ODDS 1:384 RET
T1A Scottie Pippen 5.00 12.00
T1B Michael Jordan 100.00 175.00
T1C Dennis Rodman 10.00 25.00
T2A Ray Allen 4.00 10.00
T2B Vin Baker 2.50 6.00
T2C Glenn Robinson 2.50 6.00
T3A Juwan Howard 2.50 6.00
T3B Chris Webber 3.00 8.00
T3C Rod Strickland 2.00 5.00
T4A Christian Laettner 2.50 6.00
T4B Dikembe Mutombo 3.00 8.00
T4C Steve Smith 2.50 6.00
T5A Tom Gugliotta 2.00 5.00
T5B Kevin Garnett 6.00 15.00
T5C Stephon Marbury 4.00 10.00
T6A Charles Barkley 5.00 12.00
T6B Hakeem Olajuwon 4.00 10.00
T6C Clyde Drexler 4.00 10.00
T7A John Stockton 4.00 10.00
T7B Karl Malone 4.00 10.00
T7C Bryon Russell 2.00 5.00
T8A Larry Johnson 3.00 8.00
T8B Patrick Ewing 4.00 10.00
T8C Allan Houston 2.50 6.00
T9A Tim Hardaway 3.00 8.00
T9B Michael Jordan 100.00 175.00
T9C Anfernee Hardaway 5.00 12.00
T10A Glen Rice 3.00 8.00
T10B Scottie Pippen 5.00 12.00
T10C Grant Hill 5.00 12.00
T11A Dikembe Mutombo 3.00 8.00
T11B Patrick Ewing 4.00 10.00
T11C Alonzo Mourning 4.00 10.00
T12A Ron Mercer 2.00 5.00
T12B Keith Van Horn 3.00 8.00
T12C Tracy McGrady 8.00 20.00
T13A Gary Payton 3.00 8.00
T13B John Stockton 4.00 10.00
T13C Stephon Marbury 4.00 10.00
T14A Karl Malone 4.00 10.00
T14B Charles Barkley 5.00 12.00
T14C Kevin Garnett 6.00 15.00
T15A David Robinson 5.00 12.00
T15B Hakeem Olajuwon 4.00 10.00
T15C Shaquille O'Neal 8.00 20.00
T16A Antonio Daniels 1.50 4.00
T16B Tim Duncan 10.00 25.00
T16C Adonal Foyle 1.50 4.00

1998-99 Stadium Club Promos

This 6-card promotional set was issued to dealers and members of the press to promote the 1998-99 Stadium Club product. Please note that the card backs carry a "PP" prefix.
COMPLETE SET (6) 2.00 5.00
PP1 Shareef Abdur-Rahim .40 1.00
PP2 Shaquille O'Neal 1.00 2.50
PP3 Keith Van Horn .40 1.00
PP4 Kevin Garnett .75 2.00
PP5 Tracy McGrady .60 1.50
PP6 Tim Hardaway .40 1.00

1998-99 Stadium Club

The 1998-99 Stadium Club set was issued with a total of 240 standard size cards, with each series containing 120 cards. The 10-card packs retail for a suggested price of $3.00 each. The fronts feature color action photography on a borderless design and were printed on a 20-point stock card. The rookies were redemption cards, originally numbered DP1-DP20. The redemption cards came back as cards numbered 101-120, thus making them rookie cards.
COMPLETE SET (240) 90.00 180.00
COMPLETE SERIES 1 (120) 75.00 150.00
COMP.SERIES 1 w/o RC (100) 7.50 15.00
COMPLETE SERIES 2 (120) 15.00 30.00
1 Eddie Jones .25 .60
2 Matt Geiger .15 .40
3 Ray Allen .30 .75
4 Billy Owens .15 .40
5 Larry Johnson .25 .60
6 Jerry Stackhouse .25 .60
7 Travis Best .15 .40
8 Sam Cassell .20 .50
9 Isaiah Rider .15 .40
10 Walter McCarty .15 .40
11 Hakeem Olajuwon .30 .75
12 Detlef Schrempf .25 .60
13 Chris Garner .15 .40
14 Voshon Lenard .15 .40
15 Kevin Garnett .50 1.25
16 Doug Christie .15 .40
17 Dikembe Mutombo .25 .60
18 Terrell Brandon .15 .40
19 Brevin Knight .15 .40
20 Dan Majerle .25 .60
21 Keith Van Horn .25 .60
22 Jim Jackson .15 .40
23 Theo Ratliff .20 .50
24 Anthony Peeler .15 .40
25 Tim Hardaway .25 .60
26 Bo Outlaw .15 .40
27 Blue Edwards .15 .40
28 Khalid Reeves .15 .40
29 David Wesley .15 .40
30 Toni Kukoc .25 .60
31 Jaren Jackson .15 .40
32 Mario Elie .15 .40
33 Nick Anderson .15 .40
34 Derek Anderson .15 .40
35 Rodney Rogers .15 .40
36 Jalen Rose .20 .50
37 Corliss Williamson .15 .40
38 Tyrone Corbin .15 .40
39 Antonio Davis .15 .40
40 Chris Mills .15 .40
41 Clarence Weatherspoon .15 .40
42 George Lynch .15 .40
43 Kelvin Cato .15 .40
44 Anthony Mason .15 .40
45 Tracy McGrady .40 1.00
46 Lamond Murray .15 .40
47 Mookie Blaylock .15 .40
48 Tracy Murray .15 .40
49 Ron Harper .20 .50
50 Tom Gugliotta .15 .40
51 Allan Houston .20 .50
52 Arvydas Sabonis .20 .50
53 Brian Williams .15 .40
54 Brian Shaw .15 .40
55 John Stockton .30 .75
56 Rick Fox .15 .40
57 Hersey Hawkins .15 .40
58 Danny Manning .20 .50
59 Chris Carr .15 .40
60 Lindsey Hunter .15 .40
61 Donyell Marshall .15 .40
62 Michael Jordan 2.00 5.00
63 Mark Strickland .15 .40
64 LaPhonso Ellis .15 .40
65 Rod Strickland .15 .40
66 David Robinson .40 1.00
67 Cedric Ceballos .15 .40
68 Christian Laettner .20 .50
69 Anthony Goldwire .15 .40
70 Armon Gilliam .15 .40
71 Shaquille O'Neal .60 1.50
72 Sherman Douglas .15 .40
73 Kendall Gill .15 .40
74 Charlie Ward .15 .40
75 Allen Iverson .50 1.25
76 Shawn Kemp .25 .60
77 Travis Knight .15 .40
78 Gary Payton .25 .60
79 Cedric Henderson .15 .40
80 Matt Bullard .15 .40
81 Steve Kerr .20 .50
82 Shawn Bradley .15 .40
83 Antonio McDyess .20 .50
84 Robert Horry .20 .50
85 Darrick Martin .15 .40
86 Derek Strong .15 .40
87 Shandon Anderson .15 .40
88 Lawrence Funderburke .15 .40
89 Brent Price .15 .40
90 Reggie Miller .30 .75
91 Shareef Abdur-Rahim .25 .60
92 Jeff Hornacek .20 .50
93 Antoine Carr .15 .40
94 Greg Anthony .15 .40
95 Rex Chapman .15 .40
96 Antoine Walker .25 .60
97 Bobby Jackson .20 .50
98 Calbert Cheaney .15 .40
99 Avery Johnson .20 .50
100 Jason Kidd .40 1.00
101 Michael Olowokandi RC 2.50 6.00
102 Mike Bibby RC 5.00 12.00
103 Raef LaFrentz RC 2.50 6.00
104 Antawn Jamison RC 5.00 12.00
105 Vince Carter RC 10.00 25.00
106 Robert Traylor RC 2.00 5.00
107 Jason Williams RC 5.00 12.00
108 Larry Hughes RC 4.00 10.00
109 Dirk Nowitzki RC 12.00 30.00
110 Paul Pierce RC 10.00 25.00
111 Bonzi Wells RC 2.00 5.00
112 Michael Doleac RC 2.00 5.00
113 Keon Clark RC 2.00 5.00
114 Michael Dickerson RC 2.00 5.00
115 Matt Harpring RC 2.50 6.00
116 Bryce Drew RC 2.00 5.00
117 Pat Garrity RC 2.00 5.00
118 Roshown McLeod RC 2.00 5.00
119 Ricky Davis RC 3.00 8.00
120 Brian Skinner RC 2.00 5.00
121 Dee Brown .15 .40
122 Hubert Davis .15 .40
123 Vitaly Potapenko .15 .40
124 Ervin Johnson .15 .40
125 Chris Gatling .15 .40
126 Darrell Armstrong .15 .40
127 Glen Rice .25 .60
128 Ben Wallace .25 .60
129 Sam Mitchell .15 .40
130 Joe Dumars .25 .60
131 Terry Davis .15 .40
132 A.C. Green .25 .60
133 Alan Henderson .15 .40
134 Ron Mercer .20 .50
135 Brian Grant .15 .40
136 Chris Childs .15 .40
137 Rony Seikaly .25 .60
138 Pete Chilcutt .15 .40
139 Anfernee Hardaway .40 1.00
140 Bryon Russell .15 .40
141 Tim Thomas .25 .60
142 Erick Dampier .15 .40
143 Charles Barkley .40 1.00
144 Mark Jackson .25 .60
145 Bryant Reeves .15 .40
146 Tyrone Hill .15 .40
147 Rasheed Wallace .25 .60
148 Tim Duncan .50 1.25
149 Steve Smith .20 .50
150 Alonzo Mourning .30 .75
151 Danny Fortson .15 .40
152 Aaron Williams .15 .40
153 Andrew DeClercq .15 .40
154 Elden Campbell .15 .40
155 Don Reid .15 .40
156 Rik Smits .20 .50
157 Adonal Foyle .15 .40
158 Muggsy Bogues .20 .50
159 Chris Mullin .25 .60
160 Randy Brown .15 .40
161 Kenny Anderson .20 .50
162 Tariq Abdul-Wahad .15 .40
163 P.J. Brown .15 .40
164 Jayson Williams .15 .40
165 Grant Hill .40 1.00
166 Clifford Robinson .15 .40
167 Damon Stoudamire .25 .60
168 Aaron McKie .15 .40
169 Erick Strickland .15 .40
170 Kobe Bryant 1.25 3.00
171 Karl Malone .30 .75
172 Eric Piatkowski .20 .50
173 Rodrick Rhodes .15 .40
174 Sean Elliott .25 .60
175 John Wallace .15 .40
176 Derek Fisher .25 .60
177 Maurice Taylor .15 .40
178 Wesley Person .15 .40
179 Jamal Mashburn .20 .50
180 Patrick Ewing .30 .75
181 Howard Eisley .15 .40
182 Michael Finley .25 .60
183 Juwan Howard .20 .50
184 Matt Maloney .15 .40
185 Glenn Robinson .20 .50
186 Zydrunas Ilgauskas .25 .60
187 Dana Barros .15 .40
188 Stacey Augmon .20 .50
189 Bobby Phills .15 .40
190 Kerry Kittles .15 .40
191 Vin Baker .20 .50
192 Stephon Marbury .30 .75
193 Peja Stojakovic RC .60 1.50
194 Michael Olowokandi .30 .75
195 Mike Bibby .60 1.50
196 Raef LaFrentz .30 .75
197 Antawn Jamison .60 1.50
198 Vince Carter 1.25 3.00
199 Robert Traylor .25 .60
200 Jason Williams .60 1.50
201 Larry Hughes .50 1.25
202 Dirk Nowitzki 1.50 4.00
203 Paul Pierce 1.25 3.00
204 Bonzi Wells .25 .60
205 Michael Doleac .25 .60
206 Keon Clark .25 .60
207 Michael Dickerson .25 .60
208 Matt Harpring .30 .75
209 Bryce Drew .25 .60
210 Pat Garrity .25 .60
211 Roshown McLeod .25 .60
212 Ricky Davis .40 1.00
213 Brian Skinner .25 .60
214 Tyronn Lue RC .25 .60
215 Felipe Lopez RC .25 .60
216 Al Harrington RC .40 1.00
217 Sam Jacobson RC .25 .60
218 Vladimir Stepania RC .25 .60
219 Corey Benjamin RC .25 .60
220 Nazr Mohammed RC .25 .60
221 Tom Gugliotta TRAN .15 .40
222 Derrick Coleman TRAN .20 .50
223 Mitch Richmond TRAN .25 .60
224 John Starks TRAN .20 .50
225 Antonio McDyess TRAN .20 .50
226 Joe Smith TRAN .20 .50
227 Bobby Jackson TRAN .20 .50
228 Luc Longley TRAN .15 .40
229 Isaac Austin TRAN .15 .40
230 Chris Webber TRAN .25 .60
231 Chauncey Billups TRAN .30 .75
232 Sam Perkins TRAN .15 .40
233 Loy Vaught TRAN .20 .50
234 Antonio Daniels TRAN .15 .40
235 Brent Barry TRAN .20 .50
236 Latrell Sprewell TRAN .25 .60
237 Vlade Divac TRAN .25 .60
238 Marcus Camby TRAN .20 .50
239 Charles Oakley TRAN .20 .50
240 Scottie Pippen TRAN .40 1.00

1998-99 Stadium Club First Day Issue

Randomly inserted in both series retail packs at 1:44, this 240-card set is a parallel to the base set. The cards feature the set name "First Day Issue" on the card front - and are serially numbered to 200 on the card back. The draft pick cards from series one, which did not originally have a First Day Issue parallel, were included in series two packs. To ascertain values on individual cards, please refer to the multiplier in the header, coupled with the value of the base card.
*STARS: 12.5X TO 30X BASE CARD HI
*SER.1 RCs: 1X TO 2.5X BASE HI
*SER.2 RCs: 6X TO 15X BASE HI
62 Michael Jordan 250.00 500.00
105 Vince Carter 50.00 120.00
109 Dirk Nowitzki 50.00 120.00
170 Kobe Bryant 50.00 120.00

1998-99 Stadium Club One Of A Kind

Randomly inserted in both series hobby packs only at one in 56 for series one and one in 55 for series two, this 240-card set is a parallel to the base set. The cards feature the One of a Kind logo on the card front - and are serially numbered to 150 on the card back. To ascertain values on individual cards, please refer to the multiplier in the header, coupled with the value of the base card.
*STARS: 15X TO 40X BASE CARD HI
*SER.1 RCs: 1.25X TO 3X BASE HI
*SER.2 RCs: 8X TO 20X BASE HI
62 Michael Jordan 250.00 500.00
105 Vince Carter 60.00 150.00

1998-99 Stadium Club Printing Plates

Randomly inserted in home team advantage packs only, this 960-card set is a parallel of the base set. Each printing plate is a "one of one", but each card has four different color versions: Black, Cyan, Magenta and Yellow.

1998-99 Stadium Club Chrome

Randomly inserted into both series packs at a rate of one in 12, this 20-card set features NBA stars on a chromium background. The card backs are numbered with a SCC prefix.
COMPLETE SET (40) 20.00 50.00
COMPLETE SERIES 1 (20) 10.00 25.00
COMPLETE SERIES 2 (20) 10.00 25.00
*REF: 1X TO 2.5X HI COLUMN
REF: SER.1/2 STATED ODDS 1:48 H/R
SCC1 Alonzo Mourning 1.00 2.50
SCC2 Scottie Pippen 1.25 3.00
SCC3 Patrick Ewing 1.00 2.50
SCC4 Vin Baker .60 1.50
SCC5 Glenn Robinson .60 1.50
SCC6 Kobe Bryant 4.00 10.00
SCC7 Charles Barkley 1.25 3.00
SCC8 Chris Mullin .75 2.00
SCC9 Steve Smith .60 1.50
SCC10 Stephon Marbury 1.00 2.50
SCC11 Zydrunas Ilgauskas .75 2.00
SCC12 Jayson Williams .50 1.25
SCC13 Juwan Howard .60 1.50
SCC14 Grant Hill 1.25 3.00
SCC15 Damon Stoudamire .75 2.00
SCC16 Ron Mercer .60 1.50
SCC17 Tim Duncan 1.50 4.00
SCC18 Michael Finley .75 2.00
SCC19 Glen Rice .75 2.00
SCC20 Karl Malone 1.00 2.50
SCC21 Eddie Jones .75 2.00
SCC22 Dikembe Mutombo .75 2.00
SCC23 Keith Van Horn .75 2.00
SCC24 Jason Kidd 1.25 3.00
SCC25 Shaquille O'Neal 2.00 5.00
SCC26 Kevin Garnett 1.50 4.00
SCC27 Allen Iverson 1.50 4.00
SCC28 Shawn Kemp .75 2.00
SCC29 Gary Payton .75 2.00
SCC30 Shareef Abdur-Rahim .75 2.00
SCC31 Mike Bibby 1.50 4.00
SCC32 Raef LaFrentz .75 2.00
SCC33 Jason Williams 1.50 4.00
SCC34 Paul Pierce 3.00 8.00
SCC35 Michael Doleac .60 1.50
SCC36 Michael Dickerson .60 1.50
SCC37 Bryce Drew .60 1.50
SCC38 Roshown McLeod .60 1.50
SCC39 Felipe Lopez .60 1.50
SCC40 Al Harrington 1.00 2.50

1998-99 Stadium Club Co-Signers

Randomly inserted into both series hobby packs an overall rate of one in 209, this 24-card set features two autographs of NBA players on one side. The cards are stamped with the "Certified Autograph Issue" stamp to ensure authenticity. Specific odds on Group A (CO1-CO4) are one in 8,337, Group B (CO5-CO8) are one in 2,792, Group C (CO9-CO12) are one in 233, Group A (CO13-CO16) are one in 11,618, Group B (CO17-CO20) are one in 3,873 and Group C (CO21-CO24) are 1:323. The card backs are numbered with a CO prefix.
CO1 Tim Duncan / Kobe Bryant 900.00 1500.00
CO2 Larry Johnson / Damon Stoudamire 100.00 200.00
CO3 Antoine Walker / Jason Kidd 125.00 225.00
CO4 Gary Payton / Shareef Abdur-Rahim 100.00 200.00
CO5 Kobe Bryant / Larry Johnson 175.00 350.00
CO6 Tim Duncan / Damon Stoudamire 80.00 200.00
CO7 Shareef Abdur-Rahim / Antoine Walker 30.00 80.00
CO8 Gary Payton / Jason Kidd 80.00 200.00
CO9 Damon Stoudamire / Kobe Bryant 60.00 150.00
CO10 Larry Johnson / Tim Duncan 60.00 120.00
CO11 Jason Kidd / Shareef Abdur-Rahim 20.00 50.00
CO12 Antoine Walker / Gary Payton 20.00 50.00
CO13 Tim Duncan / Eddie Jones 125.00 250.00
CO14 Jayson Williams / Vin Baker 30.00 80.00
CO15 Eddie Jones / Jayson Williams 15.00 40.00
CO16 Vin Baker / Tim Duncan 50.00 100.00
CO17 Eddie Jones / Vin Baker 15.00 40.00
CO18 Tim Duncan / Jayson Williams 40.00 80.00
CO19 Antawn Jamison / Michael Olowokandi 15.00 40.00
CO20 Vince Carter / Mike Bibby 30.00 80.00
CO21 Michael Olowokandi / Vince Carter 40.00 80.00
CO22 Mike Bibby / Antawn Jamison 40.00 100.00
CO23 Antawn Jamison / Vince Carter 60.00 150.00
CO24 Mike Bibby / Michael Olowokandi 25.00 60.00

1998-99 Stadium Club Never Compromise

Randomly inserted in both series packs at a rate of one in 12, this 20-card set features ten of the most dependable players in the NBA. Card backs are numbered with a NC prefix.
COMPLETE SET (20) 12.00 30.00
COMPLETE SERIES 1 (10) 6.00 15.00
COMPLETE SERIES 2 (10) 6.00 15.00
NC1 Michael Jordan 5.00 12.00
NC2 Kobe Bryant 2.50 6.00
NC3 Vin Baker .40 1.00
NC4 Tim Duncan 1.00 2.50
NC5 Eddie Jones .50 1.25
NC6 Shawn Kemp .50 1.25
NC7 Grant Hill .75 2.00
NC8 Antoine Walker .50 1.25
NC9 Karl Malone .60 1.50
NC10 Scottie Pippen .75 2.00
NC11 Michael Olowokandi .50 1.25
NC12 Mike Bibby 1.00 2.50
NC13 Raef LaFrentz .50 1.25
NC14 Antawn Jamison 1.00 2.50
NC15 Vince Carter 2.00 5.00
NC16 Robert Traylor .40 1.00
NC17 Jason Williams 1.00 2.50
NC18 Bryce Drew .40 1.00
NC19 Paul Pierce 2.00 5.00
NC20 Felipe Lopez .40 1.00

1998-99 Stadium Club Never Compromise Oversized

Inserted one per hobby box, this 8-card set are blow-up versions of the Never Compromise insert. The card backs are numbered with a NC prefix. To ascertain values on individual cards, please refer to the multiplier in the header, coupled with the value of the base insert.
1 Kobe Bryant 3.00 8.00
2 Vin Baker .50 1.25
3 Tim Duncan 1.25 3.00
4 Eddie Jones .60 1.50
5 Shawn Kemp .60 1.50
6 Antoine Walker .60 1.50
7 Karl Malone .75 2.00
8 Scottie Pippen 1.00 2.50

1998-99 Stadium Club Prime Rookies

Randomly inserted in packs at a rate of one in 16, this 10-card set features redemption cards for some of the top rookies from the 1998 class. The card backs are numbered with a P prefix.
COMPLETE SET (10) 30.00 60.00
P1 Michael Olowokandi 2.00 5.00
P2 Mike Bibby 4.00 10.00
P3 Raef LaFrentz 2.00 5.00
P4 Antawn Jamison 4.00 10.00
P5 Vince Carter 10.00 25.00
P6 Robert Traylor 1.50 4.00
P7 Jason Williams 4.00 10.00
P8 Larry Hughes 3.00 8.00
P9 Dirk Nowitzki 12.00 30.00
P10 Paul Pierce 8.00 20.00

1998-99 Stadium Club Royal Court

Randomly inserted in series two packs at one in 24, this 15-card set features the best veteran player's - and some top rookies in the NBA against a holographic card front. Card backs are numbered with a RC prefix.
COMPLETE SET (15) 15.00 40.00
RC1 Gary Payton .75 2.00
RC2 Kobe Bryant 4.00 10.00
RC3 Tim Duncan 1.50 4.00
RC4 Scottie Pippen 1.25 3.00
RC5 Allen Iverson 1.50 4.00
RC6 Shaquille O'Neal 2.00 5.00
RC7 Stephon Marbury 1.00 2.50
RC8 Antoine Walker .75 2.00
RC9 Michael Jordan 6.00 15.00
RC10 Keith Van Horn .75 2.00
RC11 Michael Olowokandi .75 2.00
RC12 Mike Bibby 1.50 4.00
RC13 Antawn Jamison 1.50 4.00
RC14 Robert Traylor .60 1.50
RC15 Roshown McLeod .60 1.50

1998-99 Stadium Club Statliners

Randomly inserted into series one packs at a rate of one in 8, this 20-card set features some of the NBA's premier veterans featuring a photo from their finest statistical performance of the previous season. Card backs are numbered with a S prefix.
COMPLETE SET (20) 15.00 40.00
S1 Karl Malone .75 2.00
S2 Michael Jordan 5.00 12.00
S3 Antoine Walker .60 1.50
S4 Tim Duncan 1.25 3.00
S5 Grant Hill 1.00 2.50
S6 Allen Iverson 1.25 3.00
S7 Kevin Garnett 1.25 3.00
S8 Gary Payton .60 1.50
S9 Shareef Abdur-Rahim .60 1.50
S10 Shawn Kemp .60 1.50
S11 Stephon Marbury .75 2.00
S12 Vin Baker .50 1.25
S13 Ray Allen .75 2.00
S14 Glen Rice .60 1.50
S15 Dikembe Mutombo .60 1.50
S16 Shaquille O'Neal 1.50 4.00
S17 Kobe Bryant 3.00 8.00
S18 Scottie Pippen 1.00 2.50
S19 Keith Van Horn .60 1.50
S20 David Robinson 1.00 2.50

1998-99 Stadium Club Triumvirate

Randomly inserted into both series hobby packs at a rate of one in 24, this 48-card set features three players from the same team or same theme that interlock to form one card. The non-clear background of the cards are "solid". Card backs are numbered with a T prefix.
*LUMINESCENT: 1X TO 2.5X HI COLUMN
LUM: SER.1/2 STATED ODDS 1:96 HOB
*ILLUMINATOR: 2X TO 5X HI
ILLUM: SER.1/2 STATED ODDS 1:192 HOB
T1A Kenny Anderson 1.00 2.50
T1B Antoine Walker 1.25 3.00
T1C Ron Mercer 1.00 2.50
T2A Kobe Bryant 8.00 20.00
T2B Shaquille O'Neal 3.00 8.00
T2C Eddie Jones 1.25 3.00
T3A Stephon Marbury 1.50 4.00
T3B Kevin Garnett 2.50 6.00
T3C Tom Gugliotta .75 2.00
T4A Jayson Williams .75 2.00
T4B Keith Van Horn 1.25 3.00
T4C Kerry Kittles .75 2.00
T5A Kevin Johnson 1.25 3.00
T5B Antonio McDyess 1.00 2.50
T5C Jason Kidd 2.00 5.00
T6A Avery Johnson 1.00 2.50
T6B David Robinson 2.00 5.00
T6C Tim Duncan 2.50 6.00
T7A Vin Baker 1.00 2.50
T7B Gary Payton 1.25 3.00
T7C Detlef Schrempf 1.25 3.00
T8A John Stockton 1.50 4.00
T8B Karl Malone 1.50 4.00
T8C Jeff Hornacek 1.00 2.50
T9A Shaquille O'Neal 3.00 8.00
T9B David Robinson 2.00 5.00
T9C Hakeem Olajuwon 1.50 4.00
T10A Dikembe Mutombo 1.25 3.00
T10B Alonzo Mourning 1.50 4.00
T10C Patrick Ewing 1.50 4.00
T11A Tim Duncan 2.50 6.00
T11B Kevin Garnett 2.50 6.00
T11C Shareef Abdur-Rahim 1.25 3.00
T12A Shawn Kemp 1.25 3.00
T12B Grant Hill 2.00 5.00
T12C Antoine Walker 1.25 3.00
T13A Kobe Bryant 8.00 20.00
T13B Gary Payton 1.25 3.00
T13C Stephon Marbury 1.50 4.00
T14A Ray Allen 1.50 4.00
T14B Allen Iverson 2.50 6.00
T14C Anfernee Hardaway 2.00 5.00
T15A Antawn Jamison 3.00 8.00
T15B Michael Olowokandi 1.50 4.00
T15C Raef LaFrentz 1.50 4.00
T16A Robert Traylor 1.25 3.00
T16B Larry Hughes 2.50 6.00
T16C Vince Carter 6.00 15.00

1998-99 Stadium Club Wing Men

Randomly inserted in series two packs at one in 12, this 20-card set features superstar player moves on the hardcourt. Card backs carry a "W" prefix.
COMPLETE SET (20) 15.00 30.00
W1 Kobe Bryant 3.00 8.00
W2 Tim Duncan 1.25 3.00
W3 Michael Finley .60 1.50
W4 Kevin Garnett 1.25 3.00
W5 Shawn Kemp .60 1.50
W6 Grant Hill 1.00 2.50
W7 Eddie Jones .60 1.50
W8 Tim Thomas .60 1.50
W9 Vin Baker .50 1.25
W10 Antoine Walker .60 1.50
W11 Steve Smith .50 1.25
W12 Glen Rice .60 1.50
W13 Ron Mercer .50 1.25
W14 Allen Iverson 1.25 3.00
W15 Ray Allen .75 2.00
W16 Glenn Robinson .50 1.25
W17 Kerry Kittles .40 1.00
W18 Vince Carter 2.50 6.00
W19 Larry Hughes 1.00 2.50
W20 Paul Pierce 2.50 6.00

1999-00 Stadium Club

The 1999-00 version of Stadium Club was released in just one series, containing 201 cards. The cards were issued in six-card packs with a suggested retail price of $2. Within the base set, there were 150 veterans, 16 Transaction subset cards, 9 USA Women's Basketball Team subset cards and 26 Rookie cards, inserted one in three.

COMPLETE SET (201) 25.00 60.00
COMPLETE SET w/o RC (175) 12.50 30.00
1 Allen Iverson .50 1.25
2 Chris Crawford .15 .40
3 Chris Webber .25 .60
4 Antawn Jamison .25 .60
5 Karl Malone .30 .75
6 Sam Cassell .20 .50
7 Kerry Kittles .15 .40
8 Tim Thomas .20 .50
9 Chauncey Billups .25 .60
10 Shawn Bradley .15 .40
11 Alan Henderson .15 .40
12 David Wesley .15 .40
13 Glenn Robinson .20 .50
14 Mitch Richmond .25 .60
15 Luc Longley .15 .40
16 Shareef Abdur-Rahim .20 .50
17 Christian Laettner .20 .50
18 Anthony Mason .15 .40
19 Randy Brown .15 .40
20 Charles Barkley .40 1.00
21 Bob Sura .15 .40
22 Bobby Jackson .20 .50
23 Arvydas Sabonis .20 .50
24 Tracy Murray .15 .40
25 Matt Harpring .20 .50
26 Shawn Kemp .25 .60
27 Travis Best .15 .40
28 Ruben Patterson .15 .40
29 Mike Bibby .25 .60
30 Vlade Divac .25 .60
31 Tyrone Hill .15 .40
32 David Robinson .40 1.00
33 Keith Van Horn .20 .50
34 Alvin Williams .15 .40
35 Juwan Howard .20 .50
36 Shaquille O'Neal .60 1.50
37 Dale Davis .15 .40
38 Alonzo Mourning .30 .75
39 Michael Olowokandi .15 .40
40 Jason Caffey .15 .40
41 Andrew DeClercq .15 .40
42 Jud Buechler .15 .40
43 Toni Kukoc .25 .60
44 Dikembe Mutombo .25 .60
45 Steve Nash .40 1.00
46 Eddie Jones .25 .60
47 Reggie Miller .25 .60
48 Rick Fox .15 .40
49 Larry Hughes .25 .60
50 Tim Duncan .50 1.25
51 Jerome Williams .15 .40
52 Rod Strickland .15 .40
53 Anthony Peeler .15 .40
54 Greg Ostertag .15 .40
55 Patrick Ewing .30 .75
56 Grant Hill .30 .75
57 Derrick Coleman .20 .50
58 Raef LaFrentz .20 .50
59 Mark Bryant .15 .40
60 Rik Smits .20 .50
61 Latrell Sprewell .25 .60
62 John Starks .25 .60
63 Brevin Knight .15 .40
64 Cuttino Mobley .20 .50
65 Clarence Weatherspoon .15 .40
66 Marcus Camby .20 .50
67 Stephon Marbury .20 .50
68 Tom Gugliotta .15 .40
69 Vince Carter .50 1.25
70 Vladimir Stepania .15 .40
71 Chris Mullin .25 .60
72 Tyrone Nesby RC .20 .50
73 Kornel David RC .25 .60
74 Elden Campbell .15 .40
75 Lindsey Hunter .15 .40
76 Chris Childs .15 .40
77 Ervin Johnson .15 .40
78 Rasheed Wallace .25 .60
79 Jeff Hornacek .25 .60
80 Matt Geiger .15 .40
81 Antoine Walker .25 .60
82 Jason Williams .30 .75
83 Robert Horry .25 .60
84 Jaren Jackson .15 .40
85 Kendall Gill .15 .40
86 Dan Majerle .25 .60
87 Bobby Phills .15 .40
88 Eric Piatkowski .20 .50
89 Robert Traylor .15 .40
90 Cory Carr .15 .40
91 P.J. Brown .15 .40
92 Terrell Brandon .15 .40
93 Corliss Williamson .15 .40
94 Bryant Reeves .15 .40
95 Larry Johnson .25 .60
96 Keith Closs .15 .40
97 Gary Trent .15 .40
98 Walter McCarty .15 .40
99 Wesley Person .15 .40
100 Chris Mills .15 .40
101 Glen Rice .25 .60
102 Peja Stojakovic .25 .60
103 Jason Kidd .40 1.00
104 Dirk Nowitzki .50 1.25
105 Bryon Russell .15 .40
106 Vin Baker .25 .60
107 Darrell Armstrong .20 .50
108 Eric Snow .20 .50
109 Hakeem Olajuwon .30 .75
110 Tracy McGrady .40 1.00
111 Kenny Anderson .20 .50
112 Jalen Rose .20 .50
113 Greg Anthony .15 .40
114 Tim Hardaway .25 .60
115 Doug Christie .20 .50
116 Allan Houston .20 .50
117 Kobe Bryant 1.25 3.00
118 Kevin Garnett .50 1.25
119 Vitaly Potapenko .15 .40
120 Steve Kerr .20 .50
121 Nick Van Exel .20 .50
122 Jerry Stackhouse .25 .60
123 Derek Fisher .25 .60
124 Donyell Marshall .15 .40
125 Mark Jackson .25 .60
126 Ray Allen .25 .60
127 Avery Johnson .20 .50
128 Michael Doleac .15 .40
129 Charles Oakley .20 .50
130 Gary Payton .25 .60
131 Theo Ratliff .20 .50
132 Cedric Ceballos .15 .40
133 Paul Pierce .40 1.00
134 Michael Finley .25 .60
135 Malik Sealy .15 .40
136 Brian Grant .15 .40
137 John Stockton .30 .75
138 Chris Whitney .15 .40
139 Maurice Taylor .15 .40
140 Antonio McDyess .20 .50
141 Adrian Griffin RC .25 .60
142 Vernon Maxwell .20 .50
143 Jamal Mashburn .20 .50
144 Jayson Williams .15 .40
145 Joe Smith .20 .50
146 Clifford Robinson .15 .40
147 Mario Elie .15 .40
148 Damon Stoudamire .25 .60
149 Felipe Lopez .15 .40
150 Rex Chapman .15 .40
151 Antonio Davis TRAN .15 .40
152 Mookie Blaylock TRAN .15 .40
153 Ron Mercer TRAN .20 .50
154 Horace Grant TRAN .20 .50
155 Steve Smith TRAN .15 .40
156 Isaiah Rider TRAN .15 .40
157 Tariq Abdul-Wahad TRAN .15 .40
158 Michael Dickerson TRAN .15 .40
159 Nick Anderson TRAN .15 .40
160 Jim Jackson TRAN .20 .50
161 Hersey Hawkins TRAN .15 .40
162 Brent Barry TRAN .20 .50
163 Shandon Anderson TRAN .15 .40
164 Scottie Pippen TRAN .40 1.00
165 Isaac Austin TRAN .15 .40
166 Anfernee Hardaway TRAN .40 1.00
167 Natalie Williams USA .30 .75
168 Teresa Edwards USA .30 .75
169 Yolanda Griffith USA .40 1.00
170 Nikki McCray USA .30 .75
171 Katie Smith USA .50 1.25
172 Chamique Holdsclaw USA 1.50 4.00
173 Dawn Staley USA .40 1.00
174 Ruthie Bolton-Holifield USA .30 .75
175 Lisa Leslie USA .75 2.00
176 Elton Brand RC 1.25 3.00
177 Steve Francis RC 1.25 3.00
178 Baron Davis RC 1.50 4.00
179 Lamar Odom RC 1.50 4.00
180 Jonathan Bender RC .50 1.25
181 Wally Szczerbiak RC 1.00 2.50
182 Richard Hamilton RC 1.25 3.00
183 Andre Miller RC 1.25 3.00
184 Shawn Marion RC 1.25 3.00
185 Jason Terry RC 1.25 3.00
186 Trajan Langdon RC .50 1.25
187 Aleksandar Radojevic RC .50 1.25
188 Corey Maggette RC 1.00 2.50
189 William Avery RC .50 1.25
190 DeMarco Johnson RC .50 1.25
191 Ron Artest RC 1.25 3.00
192 Cal Bowdler RC .50 1.25
193 James Posey RC .50 1.25
194 Quincy Lewis RC .50 1.25
195 Scott Padgett RC .50 1.25
196 Jeff Foster RC .50 1.25
197 Kenny Thomas RC .50 1.25
198 Devean George RC .50 1.25
199 Tim James RC .50 1.25
200 Vonteego Cummings RC .50 1.25
201 Jumaine Jones RC .50 1.25

1999-00 Stadium Club First Day Issue

Randomly inserted in retail packs at a rate of one in 26, this 201-card set parallels the base set. The cards are serially numbered to 150. To ascertain values on individual cards, please refer to the multiplier in the header, coupled with the value of the base card.

*STARS: 10X TO 25X BASE CARD HI
*RCs: 2X TO 5X BASE HI

1999-00 Stadium Club One of a Kind

Randomly inserted in hobby packs at one in 22, this 201-card set parallels the base set. The cards are serially numbered to 150. To ascertain values on individual cards, please refer to the multiplier in the header, coupled with the value of the base card.

*STARS: 10X TO 25X BASE CARD HI
*RCs: 2X TO 5X BASE HI

1999-00 Stadium Club Printing Plates

Randomly inserted in Home Team Advantage packs only at one in 79, this 804-card set parallels the base set. Each one of one printing plate was produced in four colors: Black, Cyan, Magenta and Yellow. A sticker on the card back helps to reveal which player is on the front.

1999-00 Stadium Club 3x3

Randomly inserted in packs at one in 27, this 30-card set features ten groups of three top-notch players arranged by position with laser cut designs.

COMPLETE SET (30) 50.00 120.00
*LUMINESCENT: .75X TO 2X HI COLUMN
LUM: STATED ODDS 1:108 H/R, 1:54 HTA
ILLUMINATOR: 1.5X TO 4X HI COLUMN
ILLUM: STATED ODDS 1:216 H/R, 1:108 HTA
1A Vince Carter 3.00 8.00
1B Shareef Abdur-Rahim 1.25 3.00
1C Grant Hill 2.00 5.00
2A Allen Iverson 3.00 8.00
2B Stephon Marbury 1.25 3.00
2C Jason Williams 2.00 5.00
3A Kevin Garnett 3.00 8.00
3B Antoine Walker 1.50 4.00
3C Scottie Pippen 2.50 6.00
4A Kobe Bryant 8.00 20.00
4B Eddie Jones 1.50 4.00
4C Michael Finley 1.50 4.00
5A Tim Duncan 3.00 8.00
5B Keith Van Horn 1.25 3.00
5C Antonio McDyess 1.25 3.00
6A Shaquille O'Neal 4.00 10.00
6B Alonzo Mourning 2.00 5.00
6C Dikembe Mutombo 1.50 4.00
7A Karl Malone 2.00 5.00
7B Chris Webber 1.50 4.00
7C Shawn Kemp 1.50 4.00
8A John Stockton 2.00 5.00
8B Gary Payton 1.50 4.00
8C Jason Kidd 2.50 6.00
9A Elton Brand 2.50 6.00
9B Lamar Odom 3.00 8.00
9C Wally Szczerbiak 2.00 5.00
10A Steve Francis 2.50 6.00
10B Baron Davis 3.00 8.00
10C Jason Terry 2.50 6.00

1999-00 Stadium Club Chrome Previews

Randomly inserted in packs at one in 24, this 20-card set parallels some of the base cards using chromium technology. Card backs carry a "SCC" prefix.

COMPLETE SET (20) 15.00 40.00
*REF: 1.25X TO 3X HI COLUMN
REF: STATED ODDS 1:120 H/R, 1:60 HTA
*JUMBO: .4X TO 1X HI
JUMBO: ONE PER HOB/HTA BOX
*JUMBO REF: 1.5X TO 4X HI
JUMBO REF: STATED ODDS 1:12 H, 1:8 HTA
SCC1 Kevin Garnett 1.50 4.00
SCC2 Grant Hill 1.00 2.50
SCC3 Vince Carter 1.50 4.00
SCC4 Allen Iverson 1.50 4.00
SCC5 Shareef Abdur-Rahim .60 1.50
SCC6 Stephon Marbury .60 1.50
SCC7 Kobe Bryant 4.00 10.00
SCC8 Keith Van Horn .60 1.50
SCC9 Tim Duncan 1.50 4.00
SCC10 Shaquille O'Neal 2.00 5.00
SCC11 Jason Williams 1.00 2.50
SCC12 Scottie Pippen 1.25 3.00
SCC13 Gary Payton .75 2.00
SCC14 Karl Malone 1.00 2.50
SCC15 Elton Brand 2.00 5.00
SCC16 Steve Francis 2.00 5.00
SCC17 Baron Davis 2.50 6.00
SCC18 Lamar Odom 2.50 6.00
SCC19 Ron Artest 2.50 6.00
SCC20 Corey Maggette 1.50 4.00

1999-00 Stadium Club Co-Signers

Randomly inserted in hobby packs only at an overall rate of one in 254, this 26-card set features double-autographed cards. The insert rate on each individual group is: "A" 1:3294, "B" 1:2202, "C" 1:733 and "D" 1:550. Group A features cards CS1-CS8, Group B cards CS9-CS14, Group C features cards CS15-CS20 and Group D cards CS21-CS26. Card backs carry a "CS" prefix.

CS1 Tim Duncan 150.00 300.00
Tracy McGrady
CS2 Tim Duncan 60.00 120.00
Marcus Camby
CS3 Tim Duncan 100.00 200.00
Elton Brand
CS4 Tim Duncan 125.00 250.00
Steve Francis
CS5 Tim Duncan 75.00 150.00
Shawn Marion
CS6 Tim Duncan 50.00 120.00
Jonathan Bender
CS7 Tim Duncan 50.00 120.00
Wally Szczerbiak
CS8 Tim Duncan 60.00 120.00
Corey Maggette
CS9 Tracy McGrady 50.00 100.00
Steve Francis
CS10 Corey Maggette 20.00 40.00
Shawn Marion
CS11 Marcus Camby 25.00 50.00
Gary Payton
CS12 Elton Brand 20.00 40.00
Shareef Abdur-Rahim
CS13 Paul Pierce 20.00 50.00
Jonathan Bender
CS14 Tom Gugliotta 15.00 40.00
Wally Szczerbiak
CS15 Tracy McGrady 20.00 50.00
Corey Maggette
CS16 Steve Francis 25.00 60.00
Shawn Marion
CS17 Gary Payton 15.00 40.00
Jonathan Bender
CS18 Paul Pierce 25.00 60.00
Marcus Camby
CS19 Elton Brand 12.50 30.00
Tom Gugliotta
CS20 Wally Szczerbiak 15.00 40.00
Shareef Abdur-Rahim
CS21 Tracy McGrady 20.00 50.00
Shawn Marion
CS22 Steve Francis 15.00 40.00
Corey Maggette
CS23 Gary Payton 25.00 60.00
Paul Pierce
CS24 Jonathan Bender 12.50 30.00
Marcus Camby
CS25 Elton Brand 12.50 30.00
Wally Szczerbiak
CS26 Tom Gugliotta 12.50 30.00
Shareef Abdur-Rahim

1999-00 Stadium Club Lone Star Signatures

Randomly inserted in packs, this 13-card set features autographs of top NBA stars and rookies. The cards were inserted at an overall rate of one in 389. The cards are broken up into the following groups: Group 1 (LS1) 1:28620, Group 2 (LS2-LS5) 1:4871, Group 3 (LS6-LS7) 1:7269, Group 4 (LS8-LS10) 1:1024, Group 5 (LS11-LS12) 1:1215 and Group 6 (LS13) 1:2544.

LS1 Tim Duncan 175.00 350.00
LS2 Shawn Marion 8.00 20.00
LS3 Jonathan Bender 6.00 15.00
LS4 Wally Szczerbiak 8.00 20.00
LS5 Corey Maggette 10.00 25.00
LS6 Gary Payton 30.00 60.00
LS7 Tom Gugliotta 20.00 40.00
LS8 Steve Francis 8.00 20.00
LS9 Elton Brand 6.00 15.00
LS10 Tracy McGrady 25.00 60.00
LS11 Paul Pierce 15.00 30.00
LS12 Shareef Abdur-Rahim 6.00 15.00
LS13 Marcus Camby 6.00 15.00

1999-00 Stadium Club Never Compromise

Randomly inserted in packs at one in 12, this 30-card set features players who leave it all on the hardwood divided into three groups of ten - Rookies, Stars and Legends. Card backs carry a "NC" prefix.

COMPLETE SET (30) 15.00 40.00
*GAME-VIEW STARS: 6X TO 15X HI COLUMN
*GAME-VIEW RCs: 5X TO 12X HI COLUMN
GAME-VIEW: STATED ODDS 1:220 H, 1:88 HTA
GAME-VIEW: PRINT RUN 100 SERIAL #'d SETS
NC1 Elton Brand 1.00 2.50
NC2 Steve Francis 1.00 2.50
NC3 Baron Davis 1.25 3.00
NC4 Lamar Odom 1.25 3.00
NC5 Jonathan Bender .40 1.00
NC6 Wally Szczerbiak .75 2.00
NC7 Richard Hamilton 1.00 2.50
NC8 Andre Miller 1.00 2.50
NC9 Corey Maggette .75 2.00
NC10 Jason Terry 1.00 2.50
NC11 Kevin Garnett 1.25 3.00
NC12 Grant Hill .75 2.00
NC13 Vince Carter 1.25 3.00
NC14 Allen Iverson 1.25 3.00
NC15 Shareef Abdur-Rahim .50 1.25
NC16 Stephon Marbury .50 1.25
NC17 Kobe Bryant 3.00 8.00
NC18 Keith Van Horn .50 1.25
NC19 Tim Duncan 1.25 3.00
NC20 Shaquille O'Neal 1.50 4.00
NC21 Karl Malone .75 2.00
NC22 Scottie Pippen 1.00 2.50
NC23 David Robinson 1.00 2.50
NC24 John Stockton .75 2.00
NC25 Charles Barkley 1.00 2.50
NC26 Gary Payton .60 1.50
NC27 Hakeem Olajuwon .60 1.50
NC28 Alonzo Mourning .75 2.00
NC29 Reggie Miller .60 1.50
NC30 Mitch Richmond .60 1.50

1999-00 Stadium Club Onyx Extreme

Randomly inserted in packs at one in eight, this 10-card set features black styrene cards with silver foil stamping that highlights players whose moves defy the norm. Card backs carry an "OE" prefix.

COMPLETE SET (10) 3.00 8.00
*DIE CUTS: 1.25X TO 3X HI COLUMN
DIE CUTS: STATED ODDS 1:40 H/R, 1:30 HTA
OE1 Antonio McDyess .40 1.00
OE2 Antoine Walker .50 1.25
OE3 Jason Williams .60 1.50
OE4 Chris Webber .60 1.50
OE5 David Robinson .75 2.00
OE6 Wally Szczerbiak 1.00 2.50
OE7 Jason Kidd .75 2.00
OE8 Shawn Kemp .50 1.25
OE9 Aleksandar Radojevic .50 1.25
OE10 Tim Duncan 1.00 2.50

1999-00 Stadium Club Picture Ending

Randomly inserted in packs at one in 12, this 10-card set features memorable buzzer-beating plays from the 1999 NBA Playoffs. Card backs carry a "PE" prefix.

COMPLETE SET (10) 2.50 6.00
PE1 Allan Houston .40 1.00
PE2 John Stockton .60 1.50
PE3 Sean Elliott .50 1.25
PE4 Latrell Sprewell .50 1.25
PE5 Darrell Armstrong .30 .75
PE6 Marcus Camby .40 1.00
PE7 Keith Van Horn .40 1.00
PE8 Antoine Walker .50 1.25
PE9 Larry Johnson .50 1.25
PE10 Avery Johnson .40 1.00

1999-00 Stadium Club Pieces of Patriotism

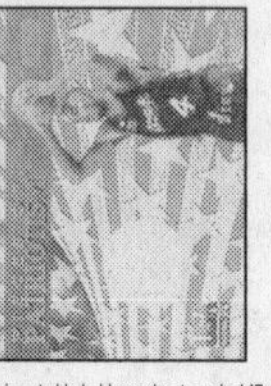

Randomly inserted in hobby packs at one in 147, this nine-card set features game-used jersey cards from player's who particiapted in the qualifiying Tournament of the Americas for the 2000 Summer Olympic Games. Card backs carry a "P" prefix.

P1 Allan Houston 6.00 15.00
P2 Kevin Garnett 10.00 25.00
P3 Gary Payton 8.00 20.00
P4 Steve Smith 6.00 15.00
P5 Tim Hardaway 6.00 15.00
P6 Tim Duncan 12.00 30.00
P7 Jason Kidd 8.00 20.00
P8 Tom Gugliotta 6.00 15.00
P9 Vin Baker 6.00 15.00

2000-01 Stadium Club Promos

This 6-card promotional set was issued to dealers and members of the press to promote the 2000-01 Stadium Club product. Please note that the card backs carry a "PP" prefix.

COMPLETE SET (6) 2.00 5.00
PP1 Shaquille O'Neal 1.25 3.00
PP2 Latrell Sprewell .40 1.00
PP3 Ray Allen .50 1.25
PP4 Clifford Robinson .30 .75
PP5 Corey Maggette .40 1.00
PP6 John Stockton .60 1.50

2000-01 Stadium Club

The 2000-01 Stadium Club product was released in January, 2001 and featured a 175-card base set that was broken into tiers as follows: Base Veterans (1-150), and Rookies (151-175) that were inserted into packs at 1:4 hobby/retail and 1:1 HTA. Each pack contained seven cards, and carried a suggested retail price of $2.50.

COMPLETE SET (175) 30.00 60.00
COMPLETE SET w/o RC (150) 10.00 25.00
1 Baron Davis .25 .60
2 Adrian Griffin .15 .40
3 Dikembe Mutombo .25 .60
4 Andre Miller .20 .50
5 Kenny Anderson .20 .50
6 Keon Clark .15 .40
7 Larry Hughes .20 .50
8 Ruben Patterson .15 .40
9 Shandon Anderson .15 .40
10 Reggie Miller .25 .60
11 Lamar Odom .25 .60
12 John Stockton .30 .75
13 Rod Strickland .15 .40
14 Michael Dickerson .15 .40
15 Quincy Lewis .15 .40
16 Vin Baker .20 .50
17 Vince Carter .50 1.25
18 Avery Johnson .20 .50
19 Michael Finley .25 .60
20 Eric Snow .15 .40
21 Kevin Garnett .50 1.25
22 Rodney Rogers .15 .40
23 Bonzi Wells .15 .40
24 Jason Kidd .40 1.00
25 Toni Kukoc .20 .50
26 Darrell Armstrong .15 .40
27 Larry Johnson .25 .60
28 Kendall Gill .15 .40
29 Wally Szczerbiak .20 .50
30 Tim Thomas .15 .40
31 Dan Majerle .20 .50
32 Karl Malone .30 .75
33 Juwan Howard .20 .50
34 Kobe Bryant 1.25 3.00
35 Bryant Reeves .15 .40
36 Cuttino Mobley .20 .50
37 Mookie Blaylock .20 .50
38 Jerome Williams .15 .40
39 James Posey .15 .40
40 Shawn Bradley .15 .40
41 Tim Hardaway .25 .60
42 Theo Ratliff .15 .40
43 Damon Stoudamire .20 .50
44 Derrick Coleman .20 .50
45 Ron Artest .25 .60
46 Antoine Walker .20 .50
47 Jason Terry .25 .60
48 Antonio McDyess .20 .50
49 Jonathan Bender .15 .40
50 Shaquille O'Neal .60 1.50
51 Anthony Carter .15 .40
52 Ray Allen .25 .60
53 Joe Smith .20 .50
54 Marcus Camby .20 .50
55 Keith Van Horn .20 .50
56 Charlie Ward .15 .40
57 John Amaechi .15 .40
58 Tom Gugliotta .15 .40
59 Allan Houston .20 .50
60 Anfernee Hardaway .40 1.00
61 Scottie Pippen .40 1.00
62 Jason Williams .25 .60
63 Steve Smith .20 .50
64 David Robinson .40 1.00
65 Gary Payton .25 .60
66 Robert Horry .20 .50
67 Greg Ostertag .15 .40
68 Mike Bibby .25 .60
69 Tim Duncan .50 1.25
70 Richard Hamilton .20 .50
71 Bryon Russell .15 .40
72 Charles Oakley .20 .50
73 Rashard Lewis .25 .60
74 Chris Webber .25 .60
75 Arvydas Sabonis .20 .50
76 Allen Iverson .50 1.25
77 Bo Outlaw .15 .40
78 Elden Campbell .15 .40
79 Dirk Nowitzki .40 1.00
80 Elton Brand .25 .60
81 Brevin Knight .15 .40
82 David Wesley .15 .40
83 Raef LaFrentz .15 .40
84 Antawn Jamison .25 .60
85 Hakeem Olajuwon .30 .75
86 Jamie Feick .15 .40
87 Jalen Rose .20 .50
88 Michael Olowokandi .15 .40
89 Rick Fox .15 .40
90 Austin Croshere .15 .40
91 Glenn Robinson .20 .50
92 Stephon Marbury .20 .50
93 Clifford Robinson .15 .40
94 Derek Fisher .25 .60
95 Vlade Divac .15 .40
96 Jim Jackson .15 .40
97 Paul Pierce .30 .75
98 Corey Benjamin .15 .40
99 Lamond Murray .15 .40
100 Steve Francis .25 .60
101 Mitch Richmond .15 .40
102 Othella Harrington .15 .40
103 Nick Anderson .15 .40
104 Antonio Davis .15 .40
105 Ervin Johnson .15 .40
106 Rasheed Wallace .25 .60
107 Shawn Marion .25 .60
108 Latrell Sprewell .20 .50
109 Terrell Brandon .15 .40
110 Sam Cassell .20 .50
111 Shareef Abdur-Rahim .20 .50
112 Travis Best .15 .40
113 Tyrone Nesby .25 .60
114 Alan Henderson .15 .40
115 Vonteego Cummings .15 .40
116 Kelvin Cato .15 .40
117 Jerry Stackhouse .20 .50
118 Nick Van Exel .20 .50
119 Corliss Williamson TRAN .15 .40
120 Doug Christie TRAN .15 .40
121 Horace Grant TRAN .15 .40
122 Glen Rice TRAN .20 .50
123 Patrick Ewing TRAN .30 .75
124 Dale Davis TRAN .15 .40
125 Brian Grant TRAN .15 .40
126 Shawn Kemp TRAN .15 .40
127 Cedric Ceballos TRAN .15 .40
128 Christian Laettner TRAN .15 .40
129 Lindsey Hunter TRAN .15 .40
130 Donyell Marshall TRAN .15 .40
131 Robert Pack TRAN .15 .40
132 Danny Fortson TRAN .15 .40
133 Howard Eisley TRAN .15 .40
134 Andrew DeClercq TRAN .15 .40
135 Mark Jackson TRAN .15 .40
136 Grant Hill TRAN .30 .75
137 Tracy McGrady TRAN .40 1.00
138 Maurice Taylor TRAN .15 .40
139 Derek Anderson TRAN .15 .40
140 Corey Maggette TRAN .20 .50
141 Jermaine O'Neal TRAN .25 .60
142 Ben Wallace TRAN .25 .60
143 Ron Mercer TRAN .15 .40
144 John Starks TRAN .15 .40
145 Erick Strickland TRAN .15 .40
146 Isaiah Rider TRAN .15 .40
147 Eddie Jones TRAN .25 .60
148 Anthony Mason TRAN .15 .40
149 P.J. Brown TRAN .15 .40
150 Jamal Mashburn TRAN .15 .40
151 Kenyon Martin RC 1.00 2.50
152 Stromile Swift RC .40 1.00
153 Darius Miles RC .40 1.00
154 Marcus Fizer RC .40 1.00
155 Mike Miller RC .75 2.00
156 DerMarr Johnson RC .40 1.00
157 Chris Mihm RC .40 1.00
158 Jamal Crawford RC .60 1.50
159 Joel Przybilla RC .40 1.00
160 Keyon Dooling RC .40 1.00
161 Jerome Moiso RC .40 1.00
162 Etan Thomas RC .40 1.00
163 Courtney Alexander RC .40 1.00
164 Mateen Cleaves RC .40 1.00
165 Jason Collier RC .40 1.00
166 Desmond Mason RC .40 1.00
167 Quentin Richardson RC .50 1.25
168 Jamaal Magloire RC .40 1.00
169 Speedy Claxton RC .40 1.00
170 Morris Peterson RC .40 1.00
171 Donnell Harvey RC .40 1.00
172 DeShawn Stevenson RC .50 1.25
173 Mamadou N'Diaye RC .40 1.00
174 Erick Barkley RC .40 1.00
175 Mark Madsen RC .40 1.00

2000-01 Stadium Club 11 x 14 Autographs

Randomly inserted into packs at one in 1675 Hobby/Retail, and 1:656 HTA, this 12-card exchange set features 11x14 autographs of some of the most popular players in the NBA. Please note that each of these 11x14's originally packed out as exchange ca Each player is listed below in alphabetical order.

IVERSON WAS NEVER REDEEMED
1 Ron Artest 8.00 20.
2 Elton Brand 8.00 20.
3 Mateen Cleaves 8.00 20.
4 Jamal Crawford 8.00 20.
5 Tim Duncan 60.00 120.
6 Steve Francis 8.00 20.
7 Larry Hughes 8.00 20.
9 Magic Johnson 60.00 120.
10 Tracy McGrady 20.00 50.
11 Shaquille O'Neal 60.00 120.
12 Latrell Sprewell 30.00 80.

2000-01 Stadium Club Beam Team

Randomly inserted in packs at one in 67 Hobby/Reta and 1:26 HTA, this 30-card set features the NBA's k players. Card backs carry a "BT" prefix.

BT1 Tim Duncan 30.00 80.
BT2 Shaquille O'Neal 40.00 100.
BT3 Kevin Garnett 30.00 80.
BT4 Vince Carter 30.00 80.
BT5 Kobe Bryant 80.00 200.
BT6 Allen Iverson 30.00 80.
BT7 Steve Francis 15.00 40.
BT8 Chris Webber 15.00 40.
BT9 Elton Brand 15.00 40.
BT10 Larry Hughes 12.00 30.
BT11 Lamar Odom 15.00 40.
BT12 Shareef Abdur-Rahim 12.00 30.
BT13 Jason Kidd 25.00 60.
BT14 Gary Payton 15.00 40.
BT15 Antonio McDyess 12.00 30.
BT16 Jason Williams 15.00 40.
BT17 Karl Malone 20.00 50.
BT18 Eddie Jones 15.00 40.
BT19 Scottie Pippen 25.00 60.
BT20 Latrell Sprewell 12.00 30.
BT21 Paul Pierce 20.00 50.
BT22 Michael Finley 15.00 40.
BT23 Jerry Stackhouse 12.00 30.
BT24 Jalen Rose 12.00 30.
BT25 Antoine Walker 12.00 30.
BT26 Anfernee Hardaway 25.00 60.
BT27 Mike Bibby 15.00 40.
BT28 Kenyon Martin 40.00 100.
BT29 Stromile Swift 15.00 40.
BT30 Darius Miles 15.00 40.

2000-01 Stadium Club Captur the Action

Randomly inserted into packs at one in 8 hobby/reta and 1:2 HTA, this 14-card insert features players tha capture the attention of the fans better than anyone e on the court. Card backs carry a "CA" prefix.

COMPLETE SET (14) 8.00 20.
CA1 Shaquille O'Neal 1.25 3.
CA2 Kobe Bryant 3.00 8.
CA3 Vince Carter 1.00 2.
CA4 Kevin Garnett 1.00 2.
CA5 Allen Iverson 1.00 2.
CA6 Steve Francis .50 1.
CA7 Tracy McGrady .75 2.
CA8 Tim Duncan 1.00 2.
CA9 Elton Brand .50 1.
CA10 Lamar Odom .50 1.
CA11 Larry Hughes .40 1.
CA12 Chris Webber .50 1.
CA13 Antonio McDyess .40 1.
CA14 Gary Payton .50 1.

2000-01 Stadium Club Captur the Action Game View

Randomly inserted in hobby packs only at 1:278, th 14-card set parallels the Capture the Action insert. T cards were serially numbered to 100. To ascertain values on individual cards, please refer to the multiplier in the header, coupled with the value of th base insert.

*GAME VIEW: 5X TO 12X BASE HI
CA2 Kobe Bryant 100.00 200

2000-01 Stadium Club Co-Signers

Randomly inserted into packs at one in 649 hobby/retail and 1:252 HTA, this 12-card insert set features authentic dual-autographs from players like Magic Johnson and Shaquille O'Neal. Card backs c a "CS" prefix.

CS1 Magic Johnson 200.00 400.

haquille O'Neal		
2 Magic Johnson	60.00	150.00
lateen Cleaves		
3 Shaquille O'Neal	250.00	450.00
im Duncan		
4 Tim Duncan	60.00	150.00
lton Brand		
5 Elton Brand	20.00	50.00
on Artest		
6 Allen Iverson	100.00	200.00
teve Francis		
7 Steve Francis	12.50	30.00
lateen Cleaves		
9 Tracy McGrady	30.00	80.00
atrell Sprewell		
10 Allen Iverson	75.00	150.00
amal Crawford		
11 Tracy McGrady	40.00	100.00
ddie Jones		
12 Ron Artest	12.50	30.00
amal Crawford		

2000-01 Stadium Club Game Jerseys

ndomly inserted into packs at one in 20 hobby/retail d 1:8 HTA, this 96-card insert set features authentic atches of game-used jerseys from players like Paul rce and Grant Hill. Card backs carry a "SC" prefix owed by the city's initials.

AH1 Dikembe Mutombo	3.00	8.00
AH2 Jason Terry	3.00	8.00
AH3 Jim Jackson	2.00	5.00
AH4 Alan Henderson	2.00	5.00
AH5 Cal Bowdler	2.00	5.00
AH6 DerMarr Johnson	2.00	5.00
AH7 Chris Crawford	2.00	5.00
AH8 Lorenzen Wright	2.00	5.00
AH9 Roshown McLeod	2.00	5.00
AH10 Dion Glover	2.00	5.00
AH11 Anthony Johnson	2.00	5.00
AH12 Hanno Mottola	2.00	5.00
BC1 Antoine Walker	2.50	6.00
BC2 Paul Pierce	4.00	10.00
BC3 Kenny Anderson	2.50	6.00
BC4 Adrian Griffin	2.00	5.00
BC5 Vitaly Potapenko	2.00	5.00
BC6 Walter McCarty	2.00	5.00
BC7 Tony Battie	2.00	5.00
LC1 Jeff McInnis	2.00	5.00
LC2 Michael Olowokandi	2.00	5.00
LC3 Tyrone Nesby	3.00	8.00
LC4 Derek Strong	2.00	5.00
LC5 Corey Maggette	2.50	6.00
LC6 Eric Piatkowski	2.00	5.00
LC7 Brian Skinner	2.00	5.00
LC8 Darius Miles	2.00	5.00
LC9 Keyon Dooling	3.00	8.00
LC10 Quentin Richardson	3.00	8.00
LC11 Sean Rooks	2.00	5.00
LL1 Shaquille O'Neal	8.00	20.00
LL2 Horace Grant	2.50	6.00
LL3 Robert Horry	2.50	6.00
LL4 Rick Fox	2.50	6.00
LL5 Brian Shaw	2.00	5.00
LL6 Ron Harper	2.50	6.00
LL7 Tyronn Lue	2.00	5.00
LL8 Isaiah Rider	2.50	6.00
LL9 Greg Foster	2.00	5.00
LL10 Mark Madsen	2.00	5.00
LL11 Devean George	2.00	5.00
NJ1 Stephon Marbury	2.50	6.00
NJ2 Keith Van Horn	2.50	6.00
NJ3 Kendall Gill	2.00	5.00
NJ4 Evan Eschmeyer	2.00	5.00
NJ5 Soumaila Samake	2.00	5.00
NJ6 Stephen Jackson	3.00	8.00
NJ7 Johnny Newman	2.00	5.00
NJ8 Jim McIlvaine	2.00	5.00
NJ9 Lucious Harris	2.00	5.00
NJ10 Sherman Douglas	2.00	5.00
NJ11 Kenyon Martin	5.00	12.00
NJ12 Aaron Williams	2.00	5.00
OM1 Grant Hill	4.00	10.00
OM2 Tracy McGrady	5.00	12.00
OM3 Darrell Armstrong	2.00	5.00
OM4 Michael Doleac	2.00	5.00
OM5 Pat Garrity	2.00	5.00
OM6 Dee Brown	2.00	5.00
OM7 Bo Outlaw	2.00	5.00
OM8 John Amaechi	2.00	5.00
OM9 Mike Miller	4.00	10.00
OM10 Monty Williams	2.00	5.00
OM11 Andrew DeClercq	2.00	5.00
OM12 Don Reid	2.00	5.00
PS1 Jason Kidd	5.00	12.00
PS2 Anfernee Hardaway	5.00	12.00
PS3 Tom Gugliotta	2.00	5.00
PS4 Shawn Marion	3.00	8.00
PS5 Clifford Robinson	2.00	5.00
PS6 Rodney Rogers	2.00	5.00
PS7 Chris Dudley	2.00	5.00
PS8 Rex Chapman	2.00	5.00
PS9 Iakovos Tsakalidis	2.00	5.00
PS10 Tony Delk	2.00	5.00
PS11 Mario Elie	2.00	5.00
PS12 Corie Blount	2.00	5.00
VG1 Shareef Abdur-Rahim	2.50	6.00
VG2 Mike Bibby	3.00	8.00
VG3 Michael Dickerson	2.00	5.00
VG4 Othella Harrington	2.00	5.00
VG5 Bryant Reeves	2.00	5.00
VG6 Damon Jones	3.00	8.00
VG7 Brent Price	2.00	5.00
VG8 Stromile Swift	2.00	5.00
VG9 Grant Long	2.00	5.00
VG10 Doug West	2.00	5.00
VG11 Tony Massenburg	2.00	5.00
VG12 Isaac Austin	2.00	5.00
WW1 Mitch Richmond	2.50	6.00
WW2 Juwan Howard	2.50	6.00
WW3 Rod Strickland	2.50	6.00
WW4 Richard Hamilton	2.50	6.00
WW5 Jahidi White	2.00	5.00
SCWW6 Michael Smith	2.00	5.00
SCWW7 Chris Whitney	2.00	5.00

2000-01 Stadium Club Head to Head Game Jerseys

Randomly inserted into packs at one in 96 HTA, this 10-card insert set features authentic swatches of game-used jerseys from players like Grant Hill and Jason Kidd. Card backs carry a "HH" prefix.

HH1 Kenyon Martin Antoine Walker	5.00	12.00
HH2 Stromile Swift Darius Miles	5.00	12.00
HH3 Grant Hill Shareef Abdur-Rahim	6.00	15.00
HH4 Juwan Howard Keith Van Horn	5.00	12.00
HH5 Keyon Dooling Jason Kidd	6.00	15.00
HH6 DerMarr Johnson Paul Pierce	5.00	12.00
HH7 Quentin Richardson Shawn Marion	5.00	12.00
HH8 Stephon Marbury Kenny Anderson	5.00	12.00
HH9 Tracy McGrady Anfernee Hardaway	8.00	20.00
HH10 Jason Terry Mike Bibby	5.00	12.00

2000-01 Stadium Club Lone Star Signatures

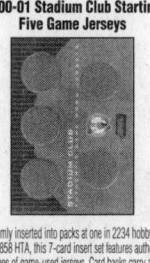

Randomly inserted into packs at one in 237 hobby/retail and 1:92 HTA, this 12-card insert set features authentic autgraphs from players like Magic Johnson and Shaquille O'Neal. Card backs carry a "LS" prefix followed by the player's initials.

LSAI Allen Iverson	75.00	200.00
LSEB Elton Brand	6.00	15.00
LSEJ Eddie Jones	8.00	20.00
LSJC Jamal Crawford	6.00	15.00
LSLS Latrell Sprewell	25.00	60.00
LSMC Mateen Cleaves	6.00	15.00
LSMJ Magic Johnson	40.00	100.00
LSRA Ron Artest	6.00	15.00
LSSF Steve Francis	8.00	20.00
LSSO Shaquille O'Neal	60.00	120.00
LSTD Tim Duncan	100.00	175.00
LSTM Tracy McGrady	20.00	50.00

2000-01 Stadium Club Starting Five Game Jerseys

Randomly inserted into packs at one in 2234 hobby and 1:858 HTA, this 7-card insert set features authentic swatches of game-used jerseys. Card backs carry a "SF" prefix followed by the team's initials.

SFAH Jason Terry Jimmy Jackson LaPhonso Ellis Allen Henderson Dikembe Mutombo	15.00	40.00
SFBC Kenny Anderson Paul Pierce Antoine Walker Jerome Moiso Vitaly Potapenko	50.00	120.00
SFNJN Stephon Marbury Kendall Gill Keith Van Horn Kenyon Martin Jim McIlvaine	40.00	80.00
SFOM Darrell Armstrong Tracy McGrady Grant Hill Bo Outlaw John Amaechi	40.00	80.00
SFPS Jason Kidd Anfernee Hardaway Shawn Marion Tom Gugliotta Clifford Robinson	75.00	150.00
SFVG Mike Bibby Michael Dickerson Shareef Abdur-Rahim Stromile Swift Bryant Reeves	30.00	80.00
SFWW Rod Strickland Mitch Richmond Richard Hamilton Juwan Howard Jahidi White	30.00	80.00

2000-01 Stadium Club Striking Distance

Randomly inserted into packs at one in 8 hobby/retail and 1:3 HTA, this 20-card insert set features players that are capable of taking over the game at any time. Card backs carry a "SD" prefix.

COMPLETE SET (20)	15.00	30.00
SD1 Reggie Miller	.60	1.50
SD2 Tim Duncan	1.25	3.00
SD3 Allen Iverson	1.25	3.00
SD4 Kevin Garnett	1.25	3.00
SD5 Vince Carter	1.25	3.00
SD6 Kobe Bryant	3.00	8.00
SD7 Shaquille O'Neal	1.50	4.00
SD8 Chris Webber	.60	1.50
SD9 Elton Brand	.60	1.50
SD10 Steve Francis	.60	1.50
SD11 Lamar Odom	.60	1.50
SD12 Gary Payton	.60	1.50
SD13 Karl Malone	.75	2.00
SD14 Latrell Sprewell	.50	1.25
SD15 Ray Allen	.60	1.50
SD16 Stephon Marbury	.50	1.25
SD17 Rasheed Wallace	.60	1.50
SD18 Jason Williams	.60	1.50
SD19 Scottie Pippen	1.00	2.50
SD20 Eddie Jones	.60	1.50

2001-02 Stadium Club

Released in late October 2001, this 134-card set features full color action photography on a borderless card stock with a colored bar containing the player's name and the Stadium Club logo along the bottom. The set is divided up into 101 veteran cards and 33 rookies inserted at the rate of one in four and one per pack in Home Team Advantage. In addition to the rookie card, HTA packs also contain two parallel cards. Stadium Club was packed out in six card packs and sixteen card HTA packs. Regular boxes contained 24 packs and retailed for $3.00 per pack, while HTA boxes contained 10 packs and retailed for $6.00 per pack.

COMP.SET w/o SP's (101)	12.50	25.00
1 Dikembe Mutombo	.25	.60
2 Clifford Robinson	.15	.40
3 Bonzi Wells	.15	.40
4 Peja Stojakovic	.25	.60
5 Gary Payton	.25	.60
6 Morris Peterson	.15	.40
7 Patrick Ewing	.30	.75
8 Terrell Brandon	.15	.40
9 Tim Thomas	.15	.40
10 Kobe Bryant	1.25	3.00
11 Hakeem Olajuwon	.30	.75
12 Marc Jackson	.15	.40
13 Wang Zhizhi	.20	.50
14 Andre Miller	.20	.50
15 Elton Brand	.25	.60
16 Eddie Robinson	.15	.40
17 Jason Terry	.25	.60
18 Allan Houston	.20	.50
19 Grant Hill	.30	.75
20 Tim Duncan	.50	1.25
21 Kevin Garnett	.50	1.25
22 Jahidi White	.15	.40
23 Michael Dickerson	.15	.40
24 Karl Malone	.30	.75
25 Chris Webber	.25	.60
26 Scottie Pippen	.40	1.00
27 Latrell Sprewell	.20	.50
28 Keith Van Horn	.20	.50
29 Ray Allen	.25	.60
30 Alonzo Mourning	.30	.75
31 Lamar Odom	.25	.60
32 Jalen Rose	.20	.50
33 Ben Wallace	.25	.60
34 Shaquille O'Neal	.60	1.50
35 Antonio McDyess	.20	.50
36 Dirk Nowitzki	.40	1.00
37 Marcus Fizer	.15	.40
38 Jamal Mashburn	.20	.50
39 Paul Pierce	.30	.75
40 DerMarr Johnson	.15	.40
41 Steve Nash	.40	1.00
42 Jerry Stackhouse	.20	.50
43 Larry Hughes	.20	.50
44 Cuttino Mobley	.20	.50
45 Horace Grant	.20	.50
46 Eddie Jones	.20	.50
47 Wally Szczerbiak	.20	.50
48 Marcus Camby	.20	.50
49 Jamal Crawford	.20	.50
50 Vince Carter	.40	1.00
51 Donyell Marshall	.15	.40
52 Shareef Abdur-Rahim	.20	.50
53 Courtney Alexander	.15	.40
54 Kenny Anderson	.20	.50
55 Ron Mercer	.15	.40
56 Lamond Murray	.15	.40
57 Michael Finley	.25	.60
58 Raef LaFrentz	.15	.40
59 Reggie Miller	.25	.60
60 Steve Francis	.25	.60
61 Rick Fox	.20	.50
62 Tim Hardaway	.25	.60
63 Glenn Robinson	.20	.50
64 LaPhonso Ellis	.20	.50
65 Kenyon Martin	.25	.60
66 Jason Williams	.20	.50
67 Derek Anderson	.15	.40
68 Eric Snow	.15	.40
69 Darius Miles	.15	.40
70 Antawn Jamison	.25	.60
71 Mateen Cleaves	.15	.40
72 Jason Kidd	.40	1.00
73 Rasheed Wallace	.25	.60
74 Chris Porter	.15	.40
75 Tracy McGrady	.40	1.00
76 Aaron McKie	.15	.40
77 Baron Davis	.25	.60
78 Toni Kukoc	.20	.50
79 Antoine Walker	.20	.50
80 Shawn Marion	.25	.60
81 Mike Miller	.25	.60
82 Stephon Marbury	.20	.50
83 Glen Rice	.20	.50
84 David Robinson	.40	1.00
85 Rashard Lewis	.25	.60
86 John Stockton	.30	.75
87 Stromile Swift	.15	.40
88 Richard Hamilton	.20	.50
89 Desmond Mason	.20	.50
90 Brian Grant	.15	.40
91 Keyon Dooling	.15	.40
92 Jermaine O'Neal	.25	.60
93 Nick Van Exel	.20	.50
94 Tom Gugliotta	.15	.40
95 Darrell Armstrong	.15	.40
96 Sam Cassell	.20	.50
97 Mike Bibby	.25	.60
98 DeShawn Stevenson	.15	.40
99 Antonio Davis	.15	.40
100 Allen Iverson	.50	1.25
101 Kwame Brown RC	.75	2.00
102 Tyson Chandler RC	1.25	3.00
103 Pau Gasol RC	2.50	6.00
104 Eddy Curry RC	1.25	3.00
105 Jason Richardson RC	1.50	4.00
106 Shane Battier RC	1.50	4.00
107 Eddie Griffin RC	.75	2.00
108 DeSagana Diop RC	.75	2.00
109 Rodney White RC	.75	2.00
110 Joe Johnson RC	2.00	5.00
111 Kedrick Brown RC	.75	2.00
112 Vladimir Radmanovic RC	.75	2.00
113 Richard Jefferson RC	1.50	4.00
114 Troy Murphy RC	1.25	3.00
115 Steven Hunter RC	.75	2.00
116 Kirk Haston RC	.75	2.00
117 Michael Bradley RC	.75	2.00
118 Jason Collins RC	.75	2.00
119 Zach Randolph RC	2.00	5.00
120 Brendan Haywood RC	1.00	2.50
121 Joseph Forte RC	.75	2.00
122 Jeryl Sasser RC	.75	2.00
123 Brandon Armstrong RC	.75	2.00
124 Gerald Wallace RC	1.25	3.00
125 Samuel Dalembert RC	1.00	2.50
126 Jamaal Tinsley RC	1.00	2.50
127 Tony Parker RC	3.00	8.00
128 Trenton Hassell RC	.75	2.00
129 Gilbert Arenas RC	1.25	3.00
130 Omar Cook RC	.75	2.00
131 Jeff Trepagnier RC	.75	2.00
132 Loren Woods RC	.75	2.00
133 Terence Morris RC	.75	2.00
134 Michael Jordan	6.00	15.00

2001-02 Stadium Club Parallel

Randomly inserted in packs at the rate of one in four for card numbers 1-100 and one in 12 for card number 101-133, this 134-card set parallels the base stadium club set with the original Topps Stadium Club logo at the bottom of the card. This logo looks like an aerial photo of a stadium with pennant flags.

134 Michael Jordan	15.00	40.00

2001-02 Stadium Club Co-Signers

Randomly inserted in packs at a rate of 1:68, this 4-card hobby exclusive insert set features dual players and their autographs. The horizontally designed set is standard size and set on borderless cards. The fronts include color photos of each featured player along with his printed name, autograph, and team name.

CS2 Shaquille O'Neal Kareem Abdul-Jabbar	125.00	250.00
CS3 Baron Davis Jason Terry	25.00	60.00
SCATRI Magic Johnson Kareem Abdul-Jabbar Shaquille O'Neal	300.00	500.00

2001-02 Stadium Club Dunkus Colossus

Randomly inserted in packs at a rate of 1:4, this 15-card insert set showcases NBA leapers flaunting their most powerful and acrobatic dunks.

COMPLETE SET (15)	5.00	12.00
DC1 Baron Davis	.40	1.00
DC2 Vince Carter	.60	1.50
DC3 Tracy McGrady	.60	1.50
DC4 Shawn Marion	.40	1.00
DC5 Kevin Garnett	.75	2.00
DC6 Darius Miles	.25	.60
DC7 Steve Francis	.40	1.00
DC8 Chris Webber	.40	1.00
DC9 Alonzo Mourning	.50	1.25
DC10 Rasheed Wallace	.40	1.00
DC11 Tim Duncan	.75	2.00
DC12 Antonio McDyess	.30	.75
DC13 Jerry Stackhouse	.30	.75
DC14 Jermaine O'Neal	.40	1.00
DC15 Shaquille O'Neal	1.00	2.50

2001-02 Stadium Club Lone Star Signatures

Randomly inserted in packs at the rate of one in 18, this 18-card set features full color player action photography coupled with authentic player autographs. Each card is enhanced with the "Topps Certified Autograph" stamp of authenticity.

LSAH Al Harrington	5.00	12.00
LSAJ Antawn Jamison	5.00	12.00
LSCA Courtney Alexander	5.00	12.00
LSEB Elton Brand	5.00	12.00
LSEMJ Magic Johnson	40.00	100.00
LSGA Gilbert Arenas	15.00	30.00
LSHT Hedo Turkoglu	5.00	12.00
LSIT Iakovos Tsakalidis	5.00	12.00
LSJF Joseph Forte	5.00	12.00
LSJT Jason Terry	5.00	12.00
LSKAJ Kareem Abdul-Jabbar	40.00	80.00
LSKS Kenny Satterfield	5.00	12.00
LSMJ Marc Jackson	5.00	12.00
LSPS Peja Stojakovic	6.00	15.00
LSSB Shane Battier	5.00	12.00
LSSM Shawn Marion	5.00	12.00
LSSO Shaquille O'Neal	40.00	100.00
LSTM Troy Murphy	6.00	15.00

2001-02 Stadium Club Maximus Rejectus

This 10-card insert set is randomly inserted in packs at a rate of 1:8. The standard size set features the 10 top shot-swatters in the league set against a borderless background. Color action shots grace the front of the cards as the featured player "swats" for the ball.

MR1 Chris Webber	.50	1.25
MR2 Shaquille O'Neal	1.25	3.00
MR3 Tim Duncan	1.00	2.50
MR4 Kevin Garnett	1.00	2.50
MR5 Darius Miles	.30	.75
MR6 Theo Ratliff	.30	.75
MR7 Dikembe Mutombo	.50	1.25
MR8 Jermaine O'Neal	.50	1.25
MR9 Alonzo Mourning	.60	1.50
MR10 Marcus Camby	.40	1.00

2001-02 Stadium Club NBA Call Signs

This 10-card insert set is randomly inserted in packs at a rate of 1:24. The set highlights 10 NBA stars and their nicknames. The standard size cards have a full color action shot set against a borderless backdrop. The featured player's nickname is boldly printed below the photo along with his actual name.

COMPLETE SET (10)	10.00	25.00
CS1 Steve Francis	1.00	2.50
CS2 Shaquille O'Neal	2.50	6.00
CS3 Allen Iverson	2.00	5.00
CS4 Tracy McGrady	1.50	4.00
CS5 Vince Carter	1.50	4.00
CS6 Lamar Odom	1.00	2.50
CS7 Gary Payton	1.00	2.50
CS8 Stephon Marbury	.75	2.00
CS9 Karl Malone	1.25	3.00
CS10 Glenn Robinson	.75	2.00

2001-02 Stadium Club Stroke of Genius

Randomly inserted along with Traction and Touch of Class cards at the rate of one per box, this 15-card set features a horizontal card design with full color player action photos on the right side of the card and a circular game worn memorabilia swatch on the left. Cards are enhanced with gold foil stamping.

SGAI Allen Iverson	8.00	20.00
SGBD Baron Davis	4.00	10.00
SGCW Chris Webber	4.00	10.00
SGDM Darius Miles	2.50	6.00
SGGP Gary Payton	4.00	10.00
SGGR Glenn Robinson	3.00	8.00
SGJK Jason Kidd	6.00	15.00
SGJS John Stockton	5.00	12.00
SGKM Karl Malone	5.00	12.00
SGKW Jason Williams	3.00	8.00
SGRM Reggie Miller	4.00	10.00
SGRW Rasheed Wallace	4.00	10.00
SGSM Shawn Marion	4.00	10.00
SGSO Shaquille O'Neal	10.00	25.00
SGSXM Stephon Marbury	3.00	8.00

2001-02 Stadium Club Stroke of Genius Autographs

Randomly inserted in Hobby packs only, this three card set utilizes the card design from the base Stroke of Genius insert set enhanced with authentic player autographs.

SGASM Shawn Marion/31	20.00	50.00
SGASO Shaquille O'Neal/34	100.00	200.00

2001-02 Stadium Club Touch of Class

Randomly inserted along with Traction and Stroke of Genius cards at the rate of one per box, this 15-card set features a horizontal card design with full color player action photos on the right side of the card and a circular game worn sneaker swatch on the left. Cards are enhanced with gold foil stamping.

TCAFM Antonio McDyess	3.00	8.00
TCAM Andre Miller	3.00	8.00
TCDN Dirk Nowitzki	6.00	15.00
TCEB Elton Brand	4.00	10.00
TCJS Jerry Stackhouse	3.00	8.00
TCJT Jason Terry	4.00	10.00
TCKM Kenyon Martin	4.00	10.00
TCMF Michael Finley	4.00	10.00
TCMJ Marc Jackson	2.50	6.00
TCMM Mike Miller	4.00	10.00
TCPP Paul Pierce	5.00	12.00
TCRA Ray Allen	4.00	10.00
TCSF Steve Francis	4.00	10.00
TCTD Tim Duncan	8.00	20.00
TCTM Tracy McGrady	6.00	15.00

2001-02 Stadium Club Touch of Class Autographs

Randomly inserted in Hobby packs only, this three card set utilizes the card stock from the base Touch of Class insert set and cards are enhanced with authentic player autographs.

TCAEB Elton Brand/42	20.00	50.00
TCATD Tim Duncan/21	200.00	400.00

2001-02 Stadium Club Traction

Randomly inserted along with Touch of Class and Stroke of Genius cards at the rate of one per box, this nine card set features full color player action photos set with a circular swatch of a game used shoe. The right edge of the card is white and contains the Stadium Club Logo in the top corner.

TAJ Antawn Jamison	6.00	15.00
TBD Baron Davis	6.00	15.00
TEB Elton Brand	6.00	15.00
TJT Jason Terry	6.00	15.00
TPS Peja Stojakovic	6.00	15.00
TRH Richard Hamilton	5.00	12.00
TSM Shawn Marion	6.00	15.00
TSO Shaquille O'Neal	15.00	40.00
TTD Tim Duncan	12.00	30.00

2001-02 Stadium Club Traction Autographs

Randomly inserted in HTA packs only, this nine card set parallels the base Stadium Club Traction insert set enhanced with certified player autographs and the Topps Certified Autograph foil stamp in the lower right hand corner.

SOME NOT PRICED DUE TO SCARCITY

TAJ Antawn Jamison/33	25.00	60.00
TEB Elton Brand/21	25.00	60.00
TJT Jason Terry/31	25.00	60.00
TPS Peja Stojakovic/16	40.00	100.00
TRH Richard Hamilton/16	30.00	80.00
TSM Shawn Marion/31	30.00	80.00
TSO Shaquille O'Neal/34	150.00	300.00

2002-03 Stadium Club

Released in late October 2002, this 133-card set is divided up into 100 veteran players and 33 rookie players. Base cards are extra glossy and borderless, and in the spirit of the Stadium Club line, the photography is incredible. Along the bottom of each card, note: both horizontal and vertical versions were available, is a gold stripe with the players name off to the left and above and the Stadium Club logo off to the right and below. Rookie card stated odds were one in three. Stadium Club was packaged in 24-pack boxes where packs contained six cards and carried a suggested retail price of $3.00.

COMPLETE SET (133)	50.00	100.00
COMP.SET w/o SP's (100)	10.00	25.00
1 Shaquille O'Neal	.60	1.50
2 Pau Gasol	.30	.75
3 Allen Iverson	.40	1.00
4 Bonzi Wells	.15	.40
5 Mike Bibby	.25	.60
6 Rashard Lewis	.25	.60
7 Aaron McKie	.15	.40
8 Shane Battier	.25	.60
9 Kenyon Martin	.25	.60
10 Tim Duncan	.50	1.25
11 Richard Jefferson	.25	.60
12 Jalen Rose	.20	.50
13 Antoine Walker	.20	.50
14 Michael Finley	.25	.60
15 Clifford Robinson	.15	.40
16 Antawn Jamison	.25	.60
17 Reggie Miller	.25	.60
18 Elton Brand	.25	.60
19 Robert Horry	.20	.50
20 Kevin Garnett	.50	1.25
21 Baron Davis	.25	.60
22 Latrell Sprewell	.20	.50
23 Glenn Robinson	.20	.50
24 Wally Szczerbiak	.20	.50
25 Tracy McGrady	.40	1.00
26 Stephon Marbury	.20	.50
27 Rasheed Wallace	.25	.60
28 Doug Christie	.15	.40
29 Desmond Mason	.20	.50
30 Vince Carter	.40	1.00
31 Andrei Kirilenko	.25	.60
32 Richard Hamilton	.20	.50
33 Jamaal Tinsley	.15	.40
34 Steve Francis	.25	.60
35 Ben Wallace	.25	.60
36 Juwan Howard	.20	.50
37 Dirk Nowitzki	.40	1.00
38 Andre Miller	.20	.50
39 Elden Campbell	.15	.40
40 Paul Pierce	.30	.75
41 Shareef Abdur-Rahim	.20	.50
42 John Stockton	.30	.75
43 Gary Payton	.25	.60
44 David Robinson	.40	1.00
45 Scottie Pippen	.40	1.00
46 Morris Peterson	.15	.40
47 Mike Miller	.25	.60
48 Marcus Camby	.20	.50
49 Joe Smith	.20	.50
50 Kobe Bryant	1.25	3.00
51 Alonzo Mourning	.30	.75
52 Ray Allen	.25	.60
53 Keith Van Horn	.20	.50
54 Grant Hill	.30	.75
55 Dikembe Mutombo	.25	.60
56 Shawn Marion	.25	.60
57 Peja Stojakovic	.25	.60
58 Tony Parker	.30	.75
59 Keon Clark	.15	.40
60 Brendan Haywood	.15	.40
61 Derek Anderson	.15	.40
62 Allan Houston	.20	.50
63 Brian Grant	.15	.40
64 Lamar Odom	.25	.60
65 Jermaine O'Neal	.25	.60
66 Kenny Anderson	.20	.50
67 Dermarr Johnson	.15	.40
68 Lamond Murray	.15	.40
69 Jason Richardson	.25	.60
70 Rodney Rogers	.15	.40
71 Rick Fox	.20	.50
72 Tim Thomas	.15	.40
73 Darrell Armstrong	.15	.40
74 Anfernee Hardaway	.40	1.00
75 Chris Webber	.25	.60
76 Derrick Coleman	.20	.50
77 Karl Malone	.30	.75
78 Antonio Davis	.15	.40
79 Jason Terry	.20	.50
80 Wang Zhizhi	.15	.40
81 Steve Nash	.30	.75
82 Eddy Curry UER Jamal Crawford pic on front	.20	.50
83 Tim Hardaway	.25	.60
84 Corliss Williamson	.15	.40
85 Eddie Griffin	.15	.40
86 Darius Miles	.15	.40
87 Jason Williams	.20	.50
88 Sam Cassell	.20	.50
89 Kwame Brown	.15	.40
90 Jason Kidd	.40	1.00
91 Jamal Mashburn	.20	.50
92 Jamaal Magloire	.15	.40
93 Tyson Chandler	.20	.50
94 Jumaine Jones	.15	.40
95 Antonio McDyess	.20	.50
96 Jerry Stackhouse	.20	.50
97 Gilbert Arenas	.25	.60
98 Cuttino Mobley	.20	.50
99 Eddie Jones	.20	.50
100 Michael Jordan	2.00	5.00
101 Yao Ming RC	2.50	6.00
102 Jay Williams RC	1.00	2.50
103 Mike Dunleavy RC	1.00	2.50
104 Drew Gooden RC	1.25	3.00
105 Nikoloz Tskitishvili RC	.75	2.00
106 DaJuan Wagner RC	.75	2.00
107 Nene Hilario RC	1.00	2.50
108 Chris Wilcox RC	.75	2.00
109 Amare Stoudemire RC	2.00	5.00
110 Caron Butler RC	1.25	3.00
111 Jared Jeffries RC	.75	2.00
112 Melvin Ely RC	.75	2.00
113 Marcus Haislip RC	.75	2.00
114 Fred Jones RC	.75	2.00
115 Bostjan Nachbar RC	.75	2.00
116 Dan Dickau RC	.75	2.00
117 Juan Dixon RC	1.00	2.50
118 Dan Gadzuric RC	.75	2.00
119 Ryan Humphrey RC	.75	2.00
120 Kareem Rush RC	.75	2.00
121 Qyntel Woods RC	.75	2.00
122 Casey Jacobsen RC	.75	2.00
123 Tayshaun Prince RC	1.00	2.50
124 Frank Williams RC	.75	2.00
125 John Salmons RC	1.00	2.50
126 Chris Jefferies RC	.75	2.00
127 Sam Clancy RC	.75	2.00
128 Ronald Murray RC	.75	2.00
129 Roger Mason RC	.75	2.00
130 Robert Archibald RC	.75	2.00
131 Vincent Yarbrough RC	.75	2.00
132 Darius Songaila RC	.75	2.00
133 Carlos Boozer RC	1.50	4.00

2002-03 Stadium Club 10th Anniversary Parallel

Randomly inserted at one per pack for veterans and with rookies sequentially numbered to 1000, this 133-card set parallels the base set enhanced with a gold strip that reads "10th Anniversary Stadium Club Basketball" along the bottom of the card.

*STARS: .5X TO 1.25X BASE CARD HI
*RCs: .75X TO 2X BASE CARD HI

100 Michael Jordan	4.00	10.00

2002-03 Stadium Club Photo Proof Parallel

Randomly seeded in packs, this 133-card set parallels the Stadium Club base set order enhanced with a silver "film" effect along the left side and the words, "Photo Proof." All foil highlights on the cards are silver and veteran players are sequentially numbered to 500, while rookie players are sequentially numbered to 100.

*STARS: 3X TO 8X BASE CARD HI
*RCs: 3X TO 8X BASE CARD HI

100 Michael Jordan	20.00	50.00

2002-03 Stadium Club All-Star Coverage Relics

Inserted in packs, this 15-card set features a horizontal design with a red white and blue motif. A red stripe appears along the left side of the card, full color player photos appear next to this and are set against a gray background featuring the Ben Franklin Philadelphia All-Star Game logo in white. Next to this is a blue stripe in which a circular piece of game used memorabilia is placed and another gray stripe next to that with the player's name in white. Each card is sequentially numbered to 700.

ASAI Allen Iverson	5.00	12.00
ASBH Brendan Haywood	2.00	5.00
ASDLM Darius Miles	2.00	5.00
ASEB Elton Brand	3.00	8.00
ASJK Jason Kidd	5.00	12.00
ASJO Jermaine O'Neal	3.00	8.00
ASJR Jason Richardson	3.00	8.00
ASKM Kenyon Martin	3.00	8.00
ASPG Pau Gasol	4.00	10.00
ASPS Peja Stojakovic	3.00	8.00
ASSB Shane Battier	3.00	8.00
ASSF Steve Francis	3.00	8.00
ASTD Tim Duncan	6.00	15.00
ASTM Tracy McGrady	5.00	12.00
ASTP Tony Parker	4.00	10.00

2002-03 Stadium Club All-Star Coverage Relics Autographs

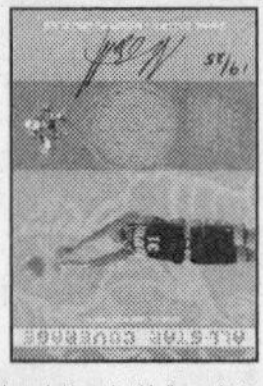

Randomly seeded in packs, this five card set parallels the look of the base All-Star Coverage Relics insert set enhanced with authentic player autographs. Each card is sequentially numbered to 25.

ASAEB Elton Brand	25.00	60.00
ASAJO Jermaine O'Neal	25.00	60.00
ASASB Shane Battier	25.00	60.00
ASATD Tim Duncan	125.00	250.00

2002-03 Stadium Club Beam Team

Inserted in packs, this 20-card set showcases the brightest stars of the NBA on an all foil-board card with full-color player action photos set against a silver background with a gold arch through it. Each card is sequentially numbered to 500.

BT1 Shaquille O'Neal	8.00	20.00
BT2 Michael Jordan	30.00	80.00
BT3 Antoine Walker	2.50	6.00
BT4 Vince Carter	5.00	12.00
BT5 Darius Miles	2.00	5.00
BT6 Jerry Stackhouse	2.50	6.00
BT7 Kevin Garnett	6.00	15.00
BT8 Tim Duncan	6.00	15.00
BT9 Kobe Bryant	15.00	40.00
BT10 Steve Francis	3.00	8.00
BT11 Chris Webber	3.00	8.00
BT12 Richard Jefferson	3.00	8.00
BT13 Dirk Nowitzki	5.00	12.00
BT14 Antawn Jamison	3.00	8.00
BT15 DaJuan Wagner	3.00	8.00
BT16 Caron Butler	5.00	12.00
BT17 Mike Dunleavy	4.00	10.00
BT18 Kareem Rush	3.00	8.00
BT19 Amare Stoudemire	8.00	20.00
BT20 Drew Gooden	5.00	12.00

2002-03 Stadium Club Co-Signers

Seeded in packs at the rate of 1:2224, this two card set pairs players on cards with two authentic player autographs and two full color player photos.

CS1 Shaquille O'Neal / Tim Duncan	175.00	350.00
CS2 Elton Brand / Shawn Marion	30.00	80.00

2002-03 Stadium Club Dual Relics

Randomly seeded, this 10-card set places two players, one on each side of the card in full-color action with a gray strip and two circular swatches of game used memorabilia through the middle. Each card is sequentially numbered to 100.

CC1 Tracy McGrady / Steve Francis	15.00	40.00
CC2 Shaquille O'Neal / Tim Duncan	20.00	50.00
CC3 Allen Iverson / Shaquille O'Neal	20.00	50.00
CC4 Tim Duncan / Jersey/Warmup	15.00	40.00
CC5 Shaquille O'Neal / Jersey/Warmup	25.00	60.00
CC6 Michael Finley / Dirk Nowitzki	15.00	40.00
CC7 John Stockton / Karl Malone	15.00	40.00
CC8 Ray Allen / Glenn Robinson	15.00	40.00
CC9 Chris Webber / Peja Stojakovic	15.00	40.00
CC10 Paul Pierce / Baron Davis	15.00	40.00

2002-03 Stadium Club Frequent Flyers Relics

Inserted in packs, this 14-card set showcases players in mid air with a trapezoidal swatch of game used memorabilia. Backgrounds feature a cloudy sky along the top, a true-life stadium background in the middle and an all-white background along the bottom where the swatch of memorabilia resides. Each card is sequentially numbered-print runs are listed below.

FFAH Anfernee Hardaway/700	5.00	12.00
FFDN Dirk Nowitzki/700	5.00	12.00
FFJT Jason Terry/200	4.00	10.00
FFPP Paul Pierce/700	4.00	10.00
FFQR Quentin Richardson/350	2.50	6.00
FFRA Ray Allen/700	3.00	8.00
FFRL Raef Lafrentz/700	2.00	5.00
FFRW Rasheed Wallace/350	3.00	8.00
FFSM Stephon Marbury/700	2.50	6.00
FFSO Shaquille O'Neal/700	8.00	20.00
FFSDM Shawn Marion/700	3.00	8.00
FFTD Tim Duncan/700	6.00	15.00
FFTM Tracy McGrady/700	5.00	12.00

2002-03 Stadium Club Frequent Flyers Relics Autographs

Randomly seeded in packs, this five card set utilizes the same design as the base Frequent Flyers Relics set enhanced with authentic player autographs. Each card is sequentially numbered to 25.

FFAJT Jason Terry	20.00	50.00
FFARL Raef LaFrentz	20.00	50.00
FFASO Shaquille O'Neal	150.00	300.00
FFATD Tim Duncan	125.00	250.00
FFASDM Shawn Marion	30.00	80.00

2002-03 Stadium Club Lone Star Signatures

Randomly inserted in packs, this 25-card set features a full color player action photo towards the top of the card, a border with a fingerprint pattern along the left side, and a red stripe through the middle (horizontally) to separate the white autograph space from the photo. Each card contains a gold foil Topps authentication stamp and is sequentially numbered. Print runs are listed below.

LSAM Aaron McKie/250	5.00	12.00
LSDB Damone Brown/500	5.00	12.00
LSDG Drew Gooden/100	8.00	20.00
LSDW DaJuan Wagner/100	5.00	12.00
LSEB Elton Brand/100	8.00	20.00
LSFJ Fred Jones/100	5.00	12.00
LSFW Frank Williams/100	5.00	12.00
LSJF Joseph Forte/250	5.00	12.00
LSJT Jake Tsakalidis/500	5.00	12.00
LSKB Kwame Brown/250	5.00	12.00
LSKS Kenny Satterfield/250	5.00	12.00
LSLP Lavor Postell/1000	5.00	12.00
LSMB Mike Bibby/500	6.00	15.00
LSMD Mike Dunleavy/100	6.00	15.00
LSRH Richard Hamilton/500	6.00	15.00
LSSM Shawn Marion/200	8.00	20.00
LSSO Shaquille O'Neal/1000	40.00	80.00
LSTM Troy Murphy/250	5.00	12.00
LSYM Yao Ming/100	25.00	60.00

2002-03 Stadium Club Reprint Relics

Randomly inserted in packs, this 10-card set uses a horizontal design and places a photo of the featured player's Stadium Club rookie card on the left and a parallelogram-shaped swatch of game-used memorabilia on the right. Each card is sequentially numbered to 700.

SCCW Chris Webber	4.00	10.00
SCDM Darius Miles	2.50	6.00
SCDN Dirk Nowitzki	6.00	15.00
SCEB Elton Brand	4.00	10.00
SCJK Jason Kidd	6.00	15.00
SCMF Michael Finley	4.00	10.00
SCPG Pau Gasol	5.00	12.00
SCRA Ray Allen	4.00	10.00
SCSO Shaquille O'Neal	10.00	25.00
SCTD Tim Duncan	8.00	20.00

2002-03 Stadium Club The Hustlers

Randomly inserted in packs at the rate of one in four, this 20-card set is horizontally designed with gold and white borders along the left and right side of the card and full-color player action photos in the middle. The words, "The Hustlers" appear in the left border and the player's name appears in the right.

COMPLETE SET (20)	10.00	25.00
H1 Baron Davis	.50	1.25
H2 Jamaal Tinsley	.30	.75
H3 Karl Malone	.60	1.50
H4 Kevin Garnett	1.00	2.50
H5 Tim Duncan	1.00	2.50
H6 Kenyon Martin	.50	1.25
H7 Michael Jordan	4.00	10.00
H8 Vince Carter	.75	2.00
H9 Kobe Bryant	2.50	6.00
H10 Alonzo Mourning	.60	1.50
H11 Shaquille O'Neal	1.25	3.00
H12 Chris Webber	.50	1.25
H13 Paul Pierce	.60	1.50
H14 Tony Parker	.60	1.50
H15 Jason Kidd	.75	2.00
H16 Antonio McDyess	.40	1.00
H17 Eddie Jones	.40	1.00
H18 Michael Finley	.50	1.25
H19 Tracy McGrady	.75	2.00
H20 Gary Payton	.50	1.25

2002-03 Stadium Club Urban Legends

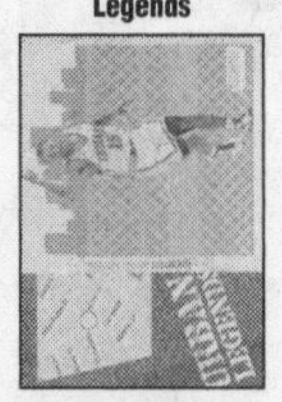

Randomly seeded in packs at the rate of one in eight, this ten card set also uses a horizontal design with a background reminiscent of black top on the left side that contains a map quest map of the player's home town. Full color phots are set against an urban background with buildings and a chain link fence.

COMPLETE SET (10)	3.00	8.00
UL1 Allen Iverson	.60	1.50
UL2 Kobe Bryant	2.00	5.00
UL3 Elton Brand	.40	1.00
UL4 Jamaal Tinsley	.25	.60
UL5 Vince Carter	.60	1.50
UL6 Kevin Garnett	.75	2.00
UL7 Gary Payton	.40	1.00
UL8 Ron Artest	.40	1.00
UL9 Kenny Anderson	.30	.75
UL10 Stephon Marbury	.30	.75

2002-03 Stadium Club Beckett.com Samples

Issued by Topps, this 129-card set was inserted at one per magazine for Beckett Basketball Card Monthly #149. This set parallels the base Stadium Club set but is enhanced with a gold foil Beckett.com stamp in the upper right hand corner. The following cards were not produced: #30 Vince Carter, #50 Kobe Bryant, #100 Michael Jordan, and #102 Jay Williams. Card numbers 101-133 were shortprinted by three times over the base cards.

*SINGLES: .75X TO 2X BASE STADIUM HI

2007-08 Stadium Club Promos

PP1 Dwyane Wade	1.00	2.50
PP2 Carmelo Anthony	.50	1.25
PP3 Larry Bird / Magic Johnson	1.25	3.00

2007-08 Stadium Club

This 150-card set was released in December, 2007. The set was issued into the hobby in six card packs, with an $20 SRP, which came 12 packs to a box, six boxes to a carton and two cartons to a case. Cards numbered 1-80 feature veterans, with cards numbered 81-100 featuring retired greats and cards numbered 1-150 featuring 2007-08 NBA rookies. The Rookie Cards were issued to a stated print run of 1999 serial numbered sets. A card for a signed 8" by 10" Greg Oden photo was randomly inserted into packs as well.

COMP.SET w/o SP's (100)	20.00	50.00
EXCH EXPIRE DATE 1/31/10		
UNPRICED PP PLATINUM PRINT RUN ONE SET		
UNPRICED RC SPRFRCTR PRINT RUN ONE SET		
1 Amare Stoudemire	.40	1.00
2 Baron Davis	.40	1.00
3 Dwyane Wade	1.00	2.50
4 Chris Bosh	.40	1.00
5 Josh Smith	.40	1.00
6 Tyson Chandler	.30	.75
7 Al Jefferson	.40	1.00
8 Deron Williams	.60	1.50
9 Andre Iguodala	.40	1.00
10 Jermaine O'Neal	.40	1.00
11 Yao Ming	.50	1.25
12 Kirk Hinrich	.40	1.00
13 Steve Nash	.50	1.25
14 Jameer Nelson	.30	.75
15 Carmelo Anthony	.50	1.25
16 Pau Gasol	.40	1.00
17 Andrew Bynum	.50	1.25
18 Gerald Wallace	.40	1.00
19 Carlos Boozer	.40	1.00
20 Rasheed Wallace	.40	1.00
21 Tim Duncan	.60	1.50
22 Michael Redd	.40	1.00
23 LeBron James	2.00	5.00
24 Kobe Bryant	2.00	5.00
25 Richard Jefferson	.40	1.00
26 Mike Bibby	.40	1.00
27 Ben Gordon	.40	1.00
28 Caron Butler	.40	1.00
29 Corey Maggette	.30	.75
30 Kevin Garnett	.75	2.00
31 Shawn Marion	.40	1.00
32 Shaquille O'Neal	.75	2.00
33 Allen Iverson	.50	1.25
34 Eddy Curry	.25	.60
35 Chris Wilcox	.25	.60
36 T.J. Ford	.30	.75
37 LaMarcus Aldridge	.50	1.25
38 Drew Gooden	.30	.75
39 Antawn Jamison	.40	1.00
40 Richard Hamilton	.30	.75
41 Dirk Nowitzki	.50	1.25
42 Elton Brand	.40	1.00
43 Jason Richardson	.40	1.00
44 Paul Pierce	.50	1.25
45 Manu Ginobili	.40	1.00
46 Danny Granger	.40	1.00
47 Andrei Kirilenko	.30	.75
48 Jarrett Jack	.30	.75
49 Andre Miller	.30	.75
50 Gilbert Arenas	.40	1.00
51 Mehmet Okur	.25	.60
52 Rudy Gay	.40	1.00
53 Ben Wallace	.40	1.00
54 Tayshaun Prince	.40	1.00
55 Jason Kidd	.40	1.00
56 Josh Howard	.30	.75
57 Daniel Gibson	.40	1.00
58 Rafer Alston	.25	.60
59 Monta Ellis	.40	1.00
60 Dwight Howard	.60	1.50
61 Chauncey Billups	.40	1.00
62 Joe Johnson	.40	1.00
63 Kevin Martin	.40	1.00
64 Ray Allen	.40	1.00
65 Luol Deng	.40	1.00
66 Raymond Felton	.50	1.25
67 Lamar Odom	.40	1.00
68 Mo Williams	.30	.75
69 Tony Parker	.40	1.00
70 Brandon Roy	.50	1.25
71 Tracy McGrady	.40	1.00
72 Marcus Camby	.25	.60
73 Stephon Marbury	.30	.75
74 Jason Terry	.30	.75
75 Randy Foye	.40	1.00
76 Vince Carter	.50	1.25
77 Andrea Bargnani	.50	1.25
78 Chris Paul	.75	2.00
79 Rashard Lewis	.30	.75
80 Leandro Barbosa	.30	.75
81 Larry Johnson	1.00	2.50
82 Patrick Ewing	1.25	3.00
83 Hakeem Olajuwon	1.25	3.00
84 Clyde Drexler	1.25	3.00
85 David Robinson	1.50	4.00
86 Bill Walton	1.00	2.50
87 Wilt Chamberlain	2.00	5.00
88 Bill Russell	1.50	4.00
89 Bob Lanier	1.00	2.50
90 Dennis Rodman	1.50	4.00
91 John Stockton	1.50	4.00
92 Isiah Thomas	1.00	2.50
93 Magic Johnson	2.50	6.00
94 Larry Bird	3.00	8.00
95 Elgin Baylor	1.00	2.50
96 Oscar Robertson	1.00	2.50
97 Joe Barry Carroll	1.00	2.50
98 James Worthy	1.25	3.00
99 Pete Maravich	3.00	8.00
100 Kenny Smith	1.00	2.50
101 Greg Oden RC	2.00	5.00
102 Kevin Durant RC	12.00	30.00
103 Al Horford RC	2.00	5.00
104 Mike Conley Jr. RC	2.50	6.00
105 Jeff Green RC	2.00	5.00
106 Yi Jianlian RC	2.50	6.00
107 Corey Brewer RC	2.00	5.00
108 Brandan Wright RC	1.50	4.00
109 Joakim Noah RC	4.00	10.00
110 Spencer Hawes RC	1.50	4.00
111 Acie Law RC	1.50	4.00
112 Thaddeus Young RC	2.00	5.00
113 Julian Wright RC	1.50	4.00
114 Al Thornton RC	1.50	4.00
115 Rodney Stuckey RC	2.50	6.00
116 Nick Young RC	2.50	6.00
117 Sean Williams RC	1.50	4.00
118 Marco Belinelli RC	1.50	4.00
119 Javaris Crittenton RC	1.50	4.00
120 Jason Smith RC	1.50	4.00
121 Daequan Cook RC	1.50	4.00
122 Jared Dudley RC	1.50	4.00
123 Wilson Chandler RC	2.50	6.00
124 D.J. Strawberry RC	1.50	4.00
125 Morris Almond RC	1.50	4.00
126 Aaron Brooks RC	1.50	4.00
127 Arron Afflalo RC	2.00	5.00
128 Luis Scola RC	2.50	6.00
129 Alando Tucker RC	1.50	4.00
130 Carl Landry RC	1.50	4.00
131 Gabe Pruitt RC	1.50	4.00
132 Marcus Williams RC	1.50	4.00
133 Nick Fazekas RC	1.50	4.00
134 Glen Davis RC	2.50	6.00
135 Jermareo Davidson RC	1.50	4.00
136 Josh McRoberts RC	1.50	4.00
137 Oleksiy Pecherov RC	1.50	4.00
138 Derrick Byars RC	1.50	4.00
139 Adam Haluska RC	1.50	4.00
140 Reyshawn Terry RC	1.50	4.00
141 Jared Jordan RC	1.50	4.00
142 Stephane Lasme RC	1.50	4.00
143 Dominic McGuire RC	1.50	4.00
144 Aaron Gray RC	1.50	4.00
145 JamesOn Curry RC	1.50	4.00
146 Taurean Green RC	1.50	4.00
147 Demetris Nichols RC	1.50	4.00
148 Herbert Hill RC	1.50	4.00
149 Ramon Sessions RC	2.50	6.00
150 Sammy Mejia RC	1.50	4.00
NNO Greg Oden AU 8x10	100.00	200.00

2007-08 Stadium Club Chrome Rookie Refractors

*REFRACTORS: .5X TO 1.25X BASE HI
REF.PRINT RUN 999 SER.#'d SETS

102 Kevin Durant	25.00	50.00

2007-08 Stadium Club Chrome Rookie Refractors Gold

*REF.GOLD: 1.25X TO 3X BASE HI
PRINT RUN 99 SER.#'d SETS

102 Kevin Durant	100.00	200.00

2007-08 Stadium Club Chrome Rookie X-Fractors

*X-FRACTOR: 1.5X TO 4X BASE HI
PRINT RUN 50 SER.#'d SETS

102 Kevin Durant	150.00	300.00

2007-08 Stadium Club Chrome Rookie X-Fractors Autographs

GROUP A ODDS 1:66, GROUP B 1:30
GROUP C ODDS 1:9

101 Greg Oden B	12.00	30.00
106 Yi Jianlian A	8.00	20.00
108 Brandan Wright A	5.00	12.00
110 Spencer Hawes B	5.00	12.00
111 Acie Law B	5.00	12.00
112 Thaddeus Young C	6.00	15.00
115 Rodney Stuckey C	8.00	20.00
116 Nick Young A	8.00	20.00
117 Sean Williams C	5.00	12.00
118 Marco Belinelli C	5.00	12.00
119 Javaris Crittenton C	5.00	12.00
120 Jason Smith B	5.00	12.00
121 Daequan Cook C	5.00	12.00
122 Jared Dudley B	5.00	12.00
123 Wilson Chandler C	8.00	20.00
125 Morris Almond C	5.00	12.00
126 Aaron Brooks C	5.00	12.00
127 Arron Afflalo C	6.00	15.00
132 Marcus Williams C	5.00	12.00
133 Nick Fazekas C	5.00	12.00

2007-08 Stadium Club First Day Issue

*1-80 VETS: .6X TO 1.5X BASE HI
*81-100 RETIRED: .5X TO 1.25X BASE HI
PRINT RUN 1999 SER.#'d SETS

2007-08 Stadium Club Photographer's Proof Silver

*SILVER 1-80: .75X TO 2X BASE HI
*SILVER 81-100: .6X TO 1.5X BASE HI
SILVER PRINT RUN 199 SER.#'d SETS

2007-08 Stadium Club Beam Team Autographs

GROUP A ODDS 1:110, GROUP B 1:141
GROUP C ODDS 1:38, GROUP D 1:26
GROUP E ODDS 1:20, GROUP F 1:44
*AU GOLD: .5X TO 1.25X BASE HI
GOLD PRINT RUN 25 SER.#'d SETS

AB Andrea Bargnani A	8.00	20.00
ABY Andrew Bynum B	15.00	40.00
AI Andre Iguodala A	5.00	12.00
AM Adam Morrison A	6.00	15.00
BD Baron Davis C	10.00	25.00
BG Ben Gordon A	12.50	30.00
CA Carmelo Anthony A	15.00	40.00
CB Carlos Boozer A	6.00	15.00
CBI Chauncey Billups B	6.00	15.00
CBO Chris Bosh A	12.00	30.00
CD Chris Duhon D	5.00	12.00
CF Channing Frye D	5.00	12.00
CM Corey Maggette E	5.00	12.00
DG Danny Granger F	5.00	12.00
DL David Lee E	5.00	12.00
DW Dwyane Wade A	30.00	60.00
DWI Deron Williams C	12.50	30.00
EO Emeka Okafor A	6.00	15.00
GW Gerald Wallace C	5.00	12.00
HT Hedo Turkoglu E	5.00	12.00
JC Josh Childress C	5.00	12.00
JF Jordan Farmar A	10.00	25.00
JH Josh Howard B	5.00	12.00
JO Jermaine O'Neal A	6.00	15.00
KH Kirk Hinrich B	8.00	20.00
MJ Mike James E	5.00	12.00
MW Marcus Williams D	5.00	12.00
MWE Martell Webster D	5.00	12.00
RA Ray Allen A	15.00	30.00
RB Raja Bell E	5.00	12.00
RF Raymond Felton C	5.00	12.00
SC Speedy Claxton F	5.00	12.00
SD Samuel Dalembert E	5.00	12.00
SO Shaquille O'Neal A	80.00	160.00
TJF T.J. Ford C	5.00	12.00
TP Tony Parker A	15.00	40.00
UH Udonis Haslem D	5.00	12.00
VC Vince Carter A	15.00	40.00

2007-08 Stadium Club Beam Team Relics

GROUP A ODDS 1:30, GROUP B 1:40
GROUP C ODDS 1:6, GROUP D 1:6
*GOLD: .5X TO 1.5X BASE HI
GOLD PRINT RUN 99 SER.#'d SETS

AB Andrea Bargnani D	4.00	10.00
AI Allen Iverson A	4.00	10.00
AIG Andre Iguodala C	3.00	8.00
AS Amare Stoudemire A	3.00	8.00
BD Baron Davis B	3.00	8.00
BG Ben Gordon A	3.00	8.00
CA Carmelo Anthony A	4.00	10.00
CB Carlos Boozer A	3.00	8.00
CBI Chauncey Billups C	3.00	8.00
CBO Chris Bosh C	3.00	8.00
DH Dwight Howard C	5.00	12.00
DN Dirk Nowitzki D	4.00	10.00
DW Dwyane Wade D	6.00	15.00
DWI Deron Williams D	5.00	12.00
JK Jason Kidd A	3.00	8.00
JO Jermaine O'Neal D	3.00	8.00
KB Kobe Bryant C	8.00	20.00
LD Luol Deng D	3.00	8.00
SN Steve Nash C	4.00	10.00
SO Shaquille O'Neal D	6.00	15.00
TD Tim Duncan C	5.00	12.00
TM Tracy McGrady C	3.00	8.00
TP Tony Parker C	3.00	8.00
VC Vince Carter B	4.00	10.00
YM Yao Ming C	4.00	10.00

2007-08 Stadium Club Full Court Press Relics

PRINT RUN 499 SER.#'d SETS
*GOLD: .5X TO 1.25X BASE HI
GOLD PRINT RUN 50 SER.#'d SETS
*DUAL: SAME VALUE AS BASE
DUAL PRINT RUN 199 SER.#'d SETS
*DUAL GOLD: .6X TO 1.5X BASE HI
DUAL GOLD PRINT RUN 25 SER.#'d SETS
*TRIPLE: .5X TO 1.25X BASE HI
TRIPLE PRINT RUN 99 SET.#'d SETS
UNPRICED TRIPLE GOLD PRINT RUN 10 SETS

AA Arron Afflalo	3.00	8.00
AB Aaron Brooks	2.50	6.00
AH Al Horford	3.00	8.00
AJ Al Jefferson	2.50	6.00
AL Acie Law	2.50	6.00
AS Amare Stoudemire	2.50	6.00
AT Al Thornton	2.50	6.00
ATU Alando Tucker	2.50	6.00
BD Baron Davis	2.50	6.00
BW Brandan Wright	2.50	6.00
BWA Ben Wallace	2.50	6.00
CA Carmelo Anthony	3.00	8.00
CB Corey Brewer	3.00	8.00
CBO Chris Bosh	2.50	6.00
CP Chris Paul	5.00	12.00
DC Daequan Cook	2.50	6.00
DH Dwight Howard	4.00	10.00
DN Dirk Nowitzki	3.00	8.00
DR David Robinson	4.00	10.00
DW Dwyane Wade	6.00	15.00
DWI Dominique Wilkins	3.00	8.00
EB Elton Brand	2.50	6.00
GD Glen Davis	4.00	10.00
GO Greg Oden	3.00	8.00
IT Isiah Thomas	2.50	6.00
JC Javaris Crittenton	2.50	6.00
JD Jared Dudley	2.50	6.00
JG Jeff Green	3.00	8.00
JK Jason Kidd	2.50	6.00
JM Josh McRoberts	2.50	6.00
JN Joakim Noah	6.00	15.00
JS Jason Smith	2.50	6.00
JW Julian Wright	2.50	6.00
KB Kobe Bryant	8.00	20.00
LB Larry Bird	8.00	20.00
MC Mike Conley Jr.	4.00	10.00
MJ Magic Johnson	6.00	15.0
NY Nick Young	4.00	10.0
RJ Richard Jefferson	2.50	6.0
RS Rodney Stuckey	4.00	10.0
SH Spencer Hawes	2.50	6.0
SN Steve Nash	3.00	8.0
SO Shaquille O'Neal	5.00	12.0
SW Sean Williams	2.50	6.0
TD Tim Duncan	4.00	10.0
TM Tracy McGrady	2.50	6.0
TY Thaddeus Young	3.00	8.0
VC Vince Carter	3.00	8.0
WC Wilson Chandler	4.00	10.0
YM Yao Ming	3.00	8.0

2007-08 Stadium Club Future Foundation Autographs Relics Dual

GROUP A ODDS 1:2050, GROUP B 1:1175
GROUP C ODDS 1:176

AW Carmelo Anthony / Marcus Williams	15.00	40.0
BL Chauncey Billups / Acie Law C	15.00	40.0
BW Chris Bosh / Brandan Wright	20.00	50.0
DC Baron Davis / Javaris Crittenton	12.00	30.0
IY Andre Iguodala / Thaddeus Young	12.00	30.0
OH Jermaine O'Neal / Spencer Hawes	12.00	30.
RO Bill Russell / Greg Oden	300.00	450.
RW Dennis Rodman / Sean Williams	25.00	50.0
WT Dominique Wilkins / Al Thornton	15.00	40.
WY Dwyane Wade / Nick Young	30.00	80.

2007-08 Stadium Club Super Teams

PRINT RUN 50 SER.#'d SETS

ATL Atlanta Hawks	5.00	12.
BOS Boston Celtics	10.00	25.
CHA Charlotte Bobcats	5.00	12.
CHI Chicago Bulls	6.00	15.
CLE Cleveland Cavaliers	10.00	25.
DAL Dallas Mavericks	6.00	15.
DEN Denver Nuggets	6.00	15.
DET Detroit Pistons	5.00	12.
GST Golden State Warriors	5.00	12.
HOU Houston Rockets	5.00	12.
IND Indiana Pacers	5.00	12.
LAC Los Angeles Clippers	5.00	12.
LAL Los Angeles Lakers	10.00	25.
MEM Memphis Grizzlies	5.00	12.
MIA Miami Heat	6.00	15.
MIL Milwaukee Bucks	5.00	12.
MIN Minnesota Timberwolves	5.00	12.
NJE New Jersey Nets	5.00	12.
NOR New Orleans Hornets	5.00	12.
NYC New York Knicks	6.00	15.
ORL Orlando Magic	6.00	15.
PHI Philadelphia 76ers	5.00	12.
PHO Phoenix Suns	6.00	15.
POR Portland Trail Blazers	5.00	12.
SAC Sacramento Kings	5.00	12.
SAN San Antonio Spurs	6.00	15.
SEA Seattle SuperSonics	6.00	15.
TOR Toronto Raptors	5.00	12.
UTA Utah Jazz	5.00	12.
WAS Washington Wizards	5.00	12.

2007-08 Stadium Club Super Teams Rookie Black Refracto

These cards were available via a redemption (for the complete set) from the 2007-08 Stadium Club Super Teams promotion. If you were holding a card from a team that won their division, you received the Refrac set.

COMPLETE SET (50)	100.00	200.
UNPRICED SUPERFR. VIA CHAMP.ST WINNER		
UNPRICED X-FRACTOR VIA CONF.ST WINNER		
101 Greg Oden	2.50	6.
102 Kevin Durant	30.00	80.
103 Al Horford	2.50	6.
104 Mike Conley Jr.	3.00	8.
105 Jeff Green	2.50	6.
106 Yi Jianlian	3.00	8.
107 Corey Brewer	2.50	6.
108 Brandan Wright	2.00	5.
109 Joakim Noah	5.00	12.
110 Spencer Hawes	2.00	5.
111 Acie Law	2.00	5.
112 Thaddeus Young	2.50	6.
113 Julian Wright	2.00	5.
114 Al Thornton	2.00	5.
115 Rodney Stuckey	3.00	8.
116 Nick Young	3.00	8.
117 Sean Williams	2.00	5.
118 Marco Belinelli	2.00	5.
119 Javaris Crittenton	2.00	5.
120 Jason Smith	2.00	5.
121 Daequan Cook	2.00	5.
122 Jared Dudley	2.00	5.
123 Wilson Chandler	3.00	8.
124 D.J. Strawberry	2.00	5.
125 Morris Almond	2.00	5.
126 Aaron Brooks	2.00	5.
127 Arron Afflalo	2.50	6
128 Luis Scola	3.00	8
129 Alando Tucker	2.00	5
130 Carl Landry	2.00	5.
131 Gabe Pruitt	2.00	5.
132 Marcus Williams	2.00	5.
133 Nick Fazekas	2.00	5.
134 Glen Davis	3.00	8.
135 Jermareo Davidson	2.00	5.
136 Josh McRoberts	2.00	5.
137 Oleksiy Pecherov	2.00	5.
138 Derrick Byars	2.00	5.
139 Adam Haluska	2.00	5.
140 Reyshawn Terry	2.00	5.

1 Jared Jordan 2.00 5.00
2 Stephane Lasme 2.00 5.00
3 Dominic McGuire 2.00 5.00
4 Aaron Gray 2.00 5.00
5 JamesOn Curry 2.00 5.00
6 Taurean Green 2.00 5.00
7 Demetris Nichols 2.00 5.00
8 Herbert Hill 2.00 5.00
9 Ramon Sessions 3.00 8.00
0 Sammy Mejia 2.00 5.00

1999-00 Stadium Club Chrome

buting in 1999/00, the base set contained 150 cards nted on 23-point stock. Most of the cards were allels of the Stadium Club set, with some updated otography on rookies and free agents. Each pack ntained five cards with a suggested retail price of .00.

MPLETE SET (150) 25.00 60.00
Allen Iverson .60 1.50
Chris Webber .30 .75
Antawn Jamison .30 .75
Karl Malone .40 1.00
Sam Cassell .25 .60
Kerry Kittles .20 .50
Tim Thomas .25 .60
Shawn Bradley .20 .50
David Wesley .20 .50
Glenn Robinson .25 .60
Mitch Richmond .30 .75
Shareef Abdur-Rahim .25 .60
Christian Laettner .25 .60
Anthony Mason .20 .50
Randy Brown .20 .50
Charles Barkley .50 1.25
Bobby Jackson .25 .60
Matt Harpring .25 .60
Shawn Kemp .30 .75
Ruben Patterson .20 .50
Mike Bibby .30 .75
Vlade Divac .30 .75
David Robinson .50 1.25
Keith Van Horn .25 .60
Juwan Howard .25 .60
Shaquille O'Neal .75 2.00
Alonzo Mourning .40 1.00
Michael Olowokandi .20 .50
Andrew DeClercq .20 .50
Toni Kukoc .30 .75
Dikembe Mutombo .30 .75
Steve Nash .50 1.25
Eddie Jones .30 .75
Reggie Miller .30 .75
Larry Hughes .25 .60
Tim Duncan .60 1.50
Jerome Williams .20 .50
Rod Strickland .20 .50
Patrick Ewing .40 1.00
Grant Hill .40 1.00
Derrick Coleman .25 .60
Raef LaFrentz .25 .60
Rik Smits .30 .75
Latrell Sprewell .30 .75
John Starks .30 .75
Cuttino Mobley .25 .60
Marcus Camby .25 .60
Stephon Marbury .25 .60
Tom Gugliotta .20 .50
Vince Carter .60 1.50
Chris Mullin .30 .75
Tyrone Nesby RC .50 1.25
Elden Campbell .20 .50
Lindsey Hunter .20 .50
Rasheed Wallace .30 .75
Jeff Hornacek .25 .60
Matt Geiger .20 .50
Antoine Walker .30 .75
Jason Williams .40 1.00
Robert Horry .30 .75
Kendall Gill .20 .50
Dan Majerle .30 .75
Robert Traylor .20 .50
P.J. Brown .20 .50
Terrell Brandon .20 .50
Corliss Williamson .20 .50
Bryant Reeves .20 .50
Larry Johnson .30 .75
Keith Closs .20 .50
Walter McCarty .20 .50
Wesley Person .20 .50
Chris Mills .20 .50
Glen Rice .30 .75
Jason Kidd .50 1.25
Dirk Nowitzki .60 1.50
Bryon Russell .20 .50
Vin Baker .30 .75
Darrell Armstrong .20 .50
Eric Snow .25 .60
Hakeem Olajuwon .40 1.00
Tracy McGrady .50 1.25
Kenny Anderson .25 .60
Jalen Rose .25 .60
Tim Hardaway .30 .75
Doug Christie .25 .60
Allan Houston .25 .60
Kobe Bryant 1.50 4.00
Kevin Garnett .60 1.50
Steve Kerr .25 .60
Nick Van Exel .25 .60
Jerry Stackhouse .30 .75
Derek Fisher .30 .75
Donyell Marshall .20 .50
Mark Jackson .30 .75
Ray Allen .30 .75
Avery Johnson .25 .60
Michael Doleac .20 .50
Charles Oakley .25 .60
Gary Payton .30 .75
Theo Ratliff .25 .60
Cedric Ceballos .20 .50
Paul Pierce .50 1.25
Michael Finley .30 .75
Brian Grant .20 .50
John Stockton .40 1.00
Maurice Taylor .20 .50
107 Antonio McDyess .25 .60
108 Adrian Griffin RC .50 1.25
109 Jamal Mashburn .25 .60
110 Jayson Williams .20 .50
111 Joe Smith .25 .60
112 Clifford Robinson .20 .50
113 Mario Elie .20 .50
114 Damon Stoudamire .30 .75
115 Felipe Lopez .20 .50
116 Antonio Davis TRAN .20 .50
117 Mookie Blaylock TRAN .20 .50
118 Ron Mercer TRAN .25 .60
119 Horace Grant TRAN .25 .60
120 Steve Smith TRAN .20 .50
121 Isaiah Rider TRAN .20 .50
122 Tariq Abdul-Wahad TRAN .20 .50
123 Michael Dickerson TRAN .20 .50
124 Nick Anderson TRAN .20 .50
125 Jim Jackson TRAN .25 .60
126 Hersey Hawkins TRAN .20 .50
127 Brent Barry TRAN .25 .60
128 Shandon Anderson TRAN .20 .50
129 Scottie Pippen TRAN .50 1.25
130 Isaac Austin TRAN .20 .50
131 Anfernee Hardaway TRAN .50 1.25
132 Elton Brand RC 1.25 3.00
133 Steve Francis RC 1.25 3.00
134 Baron Davis RC 1.50 4.00
135 Lamar Odom RC 1.50 4.00
136 Jonathan Bender RC .50 1.25
137 Wally Szczerbiak RC 1.00 2.50
138 Richard Hamilton RC 1.25 3.00
139 Andre Miller RC 1.25 3.00
140 Shawn Marion RC 1.25 3.00
141 Jason Terry RC 1.25 3.00
142 Trajan Langdon RC .50 1.25
143 Aleksandar Radojevic RC .50 1.25
144 Corey Maggette RC 1.00 2.50
145 William Avery RC .50 1.25
146 Ron Artest RC 1.25 3.00
147 Cal Bowdler RC .50 1.25
148 James Posey RC .50 1.25
149 Quincy Lewis RC .50 1.25
150 Scott Padgett RC .50 1.25

1999-00 Stadium Club Chrome First Day Issue

Randomly inserted in packs at one in 47, this 150-card set parallels the base set. The cards feature the "First Day Issue" logo on the front and all cards are serially numbered to 100 on the back. To ascertain values on individual cards, please refer to the mutiplier in the header, coupled with the value of the base card.
*STARS: 10X TO 25X BASE CARD HI
*RCs: 3X TO 8X BASE HI

1999-00 Stadium Club Chrome First Day Issue Refractors

Randomly inserted in packs at one in 186, this 150-card set parallels the base set. The cards feature the "First Day Issue" logo on the front and all cards are serially numbered to 25 on the back. The cards also feature the "classic" Refractor technology.
*STARS: 40X TO 100X BASE CARD HI
*RCs: 8X TO 20X BASE HI
87 Kobe Bryant 250.00 500.00

1999-00 Stadium Club Chrome Refractors

Randomly inserted in packs at one in 12, this 150-card set parallels the base set. The cards feature the "classic" Refractor technology. To ascertain values on individual cards, please refer to the mutiplier in the header, coupled with the value of the base card.
*STARS: 2X TO 5X BASE CARD HI
*RCs: 1.25X TO 3X BASE HI

1999-00 Stadium Club Chrome Clear Shots

Randomly inserted in packs at one in 16, this 10-card set features NBA rookies shot from both the front and the back at the same time. The cards are printed on ClearChrome technology. Card backs carry a "CS" prefix.
COMPLETE SET (10) 4.00 10.00
*REF: 1X TO 2.5X HI COLUMN
REF: STATED ODDS 1:80
CS1 Lamar Odom 1.00 2.50
CS2 Elton Brand .75 2.00
CS3 Steve Francis .75 2.00
CS4 Shawn Marion .75 2.00
CS5 Wally Szczerbiak .60 1.50
CS6 Richard Hamilton .75 2.00
CS7 Andre Miller .75 2.00
CS8 Jason Terry .75 2.00
CS9 Baron Davis 1.00 2.50
CS10 Jonathan Bender .30 .75

1999-00 Stadium Club Chrome Eyes of the Game

Randomly inserted in packs at one in 24, this 10-card set features players who possess the "eye" to hit the key shot or make the key pass. The cards are printed on ClearChrome techonology. Card backs carry an "EG" prefix.
COMPLETE SET (10) 10.00 25.00
*REF: 1.25X TO 3X HI COLUMN
REF: STATED ODDS 1:120
EG1 Jason Kidd 1.50 4.00
EG2 Jason Williams 1.25 3.00
EG3 Gary Payton 1.00 2.50
EG4 Kevin Garnett 2.00 5.00
EG5 Vince Carter 2.00 5.00
EG6 Kobe Bryant 5.00 12.00
EG7 Stephon Marbury .75 2.00
EG8 Allen Iverson 2.00 5.00
EG9 Alonzo Mourning 1.25 3.00
EG10 John Stockton 1.25 3.00

1999-00 Stadium Club Chrome True Colors

Randomly inserted in packs at one in eight, this 10-card set features players that show their "true colors" at crunch time. Card backs carry a "TC" prefix.
COMPLETE SET (10) 3.00 8.00
*REF: 1X TO 2.5X HI COLUMN
REF: STATED ODDS 1:40
TC1 Gary Payton .40 1.00
TC2 Stephon Marbury .30 .75
TC3 Karl Malone .50 1.25
TC4 Kevin Garnett .75 2.00
TC5 Allen Iverson .75 2.00
TC6 Vince Carter .75 2.00
TC7 Grant Hill .50 1.25
TC8 Shaquille O'Neal 1.00 2.50
TC9 Reggie Miller .40 1.00
TC10 Tim Duncan .75 2.00

1999-00 Stadium Club Chrome Visionaries

Randomly inserted in packs at one in 32, this 10-card set showcases young stars destined for NBA glory. Card backs carry a "V" prefix.
COMPLETE SET (10) 12.50 30.00
*REF: 1X TO 2.5X HI COLUMN
REF: STATED ODDS 1:160
V1 Vince Carter 2.50 6.00
V2 Tim Duncan 2.50 6.00
V3 Jason Williams 1.50 4.00
V4 Lamar Odom 4.00 10.00
V5 Steve Francis 3.00 8.00
V6 Paul Pierce 2.00 5.00
V7 Tracy McGrady 2.00 5.00
V8 Elton Brand 3.00 8.00
V9 Shawn Marion 3.00 8.00
V10 Antawn Jamison 1.25 3.00

1993 Stadium Club Members Only

This 59-card standard-size set was mailed out to Stadium Club Members in four separate mailings. Each box contained several sports. The fronts have full-bleed color action player photos with the words "Members Only" printed in gold foil at the bottom along with the player's name and the Stadium Club logo. On a multi-colored background, the horizontal backs carry player information and a computer generated drawing of a baseball player. The cards are unnumbered and checklisted below alphabetically according to sport as follows: baseball (1-28), basketball (29-44), football (45-53), and hockey (54-59).
COMPLETE SET (59) 10.00 20.00
29 Danny Ainge .08 .25
30 Mark Eaton .07 .20
31 Patrick Ewing .25 .60
32 Anfernee Hardaway .25 .60
33 Carl Herrera .08 .25
Rockets Tie Mark
for Best Start
34 Michael Jordan 1.25 3.00
35 Hakeem Olajuwon .40 1.00
36 Shaquille O'Neal .75 2.00
37 Cliff Robinson .08 .25
38 David Robinson .40 1.00
39 Brian Shaw .07 .20
40 John Stockton .25 .60
41 Isiah Thomas .15 .40
42 Chris Webber .75 2.00
43 Dominique Wilkins .15 .40
44 Micheal Williams .07 .20

1994-95 Stadium Club Members Only 50

Topps produced a 50-card boxed set for each of the four major sports. With their club membership, members received one set of their choice and had the option of purchasing additional sets for $10.00 each. The 45 Stadium Club Cards in the basketball set represent 11 of the top NBA players in each division from 1994-95 with an extra player from the Central Division. The five Topps Rookie Picks cards (46-50) represent the top five players from the 1994 NBA Draft and are all given a special Finest style refractive foil coating. The color action photos on the fronts have brightly-colored backgrounds and carry the distinctive Topps Stadium Club Members Only gold foil seal. The backs present a second color photo and player profile.
COMP.FACT SET (50) 15.00 40.00
1 Shaquille O'Neal .75 2.00
2 Charles Oakley .25 .60
3 Chris Webber .50 1.25
4 Dominique Wilkins .40 1.00
5 Kenny Anderson .25 .60
6 Kevin Willis .20 .50
7 Anfernee Hardaway .50 1.25
8 Derrick Coleman .25 .60
9 Clarence Weatherspoon .20 .50
10 Glen Rice .30 .75
11 Patrick Ewing .40 1.00
12 Reggie Miller .40 1.00
13 Scottie Pippen .60 1.50
14 Steve Smith .25 .60
15 Alonzo Mourning .40 1.00
16 Vin Baker .30 .75
17 Tyrone Hill .20 .50
18 Joe Dumars .30 .75
19 Mookie Blaylock .20 .50
20 Michael Jordan 2.50 6.00
21 Larry Johnson .30 .75
22 Mark Price .30 .75
23 Rik Smits .25 .60
24 Hakeem Olajuwon .40 1.00
25 Karl Malone .40 1.00
26 Jamal Mashburn .30 .75
27 Sean Elliott .30 .75
28 Christian Laettner .25 .60
29 Dikembe Mutombo .30 .75
30 John Stockton .40 1.00
31 Clyde Drexler .40 1.00
32 Tom Gugliotta .20 .50
33 Mahmoud Abdul-Rauf .20 .50
34 David Robinson .50 1.25
35 Chris Mullin .30 .75
36 Shawn Kemp .30 .75
37 Mitch Richmond .30 .75
38 Clifford Robinson .20 .50
39 Cedric Ceballos .20 .50
40 Charles Barkley .50 1.25
41 Loy Vaught .20 .50
42 Gary Payton .30 .75
43 Walt Williams .20 .50
44 Nick Van Exel .30 .75
45 Kevin Johnson .30 .75
46 Glenn Robinson TRP 2.00 5.00
47 Jason Kidd TRP 5.00 12.00
48 Grant Hill TRP 5.00 12.00
49 Donyell Marshall TRP 1.00 2.50
50 Juwan Howard TRP 1.50 4.00

1995-96 Stadium Club Members Only 50

For the second straight season, Ttopps produced a 50-card boxed set for Basketball fans. Cards number 46 through 50 featured leading rookies and were printed using Finest technology.
COMP.FACT SET (50) 10.00 25.00
1 Magic Johnson .75 2.00
2 Steve Smith .25 .60
3 Scottie Pippen .50 1.25
4 David Robinson .50 1.25
5 Jason Kidd .50 1.25
6 Dikembe Mutombo .30 .75
7 Sean Elliott .30 .75
8 Rik Smits .25 .60
9 Brian Grant .25 .60
10 Hakeem Olajuwon .40 1.00
11 Greg Anthony .20 .50
12 Mitch Richmond .30 .75
13 Clyde Drexler .40 1.00
14 Mahmoud Abdul-Rauf .20 .50
15 Larry Johnson .30 .75
16 Mookie Blaylock .20 .50
17 Clarence Weatherspoon .20 .50
18 Grant Hill .50 1.25
19 Vin Baker .25 .60
20 Patrick Ewing .40 1.00
21 Charles Barkley .50 1.25
22 Glenn Robinson .30 .75
23 Dino Radja .25 .60
24 Charles Oakley .25 .60
25 Anfernee Hardaway .50 1.25
26 Jamal Mashburn .30 .75
27 John Stockton .40 1.00
28 Isaiah Rider .30 .75
29 Cedric Ceballos .20 .50
30 Shaquille O'Neal .75 2.00
31 Shawn Kemp .30 .75
32 Juwan Howard .30 .75
33 Alonzo Mourning .40 1.00
34 Tom Gugliotta .20 .50
35 Karl Malone .40 1.00
36 Clifford Robinson .20 .50
37 Chris Webber .40 1.00
38 Latrell Sprewell .30 .75
39 Loy Vaught .20 .50
40 Michael Jordan 2.50 6.00
41 Reggie Miller .40 1.00
42 Terrell Brandon .20 .50
43 Armon Gilliam .20 .50
44 Gary Payton .30 .75
45 Glen Rice .30 .75
46 Jerry Stackhouse FIN 2.00 5.00
47 Michael Finley FIN 2.00 5.00
48 Joe Smith FIN 1.25 3.00
49 Damon Stoudamire FIN 1.50 4.00
50 Brent Barry FIN 1.00 2.50

1996-97 Stadium Club Members Only 55

Topps produced a 55-card boxed set for each of the four major sports. With their club membership, members received one set of their choice and had the option of purchasing additional sets for $15.00 each. The 50 Stadium Club Cards in the basketball set represent the top NBA players in each division. The five Topps Rookie player cards (51-55) represent the top players from the 1996-97 NBA season and are all given a special Finest style foil coating. The color action photos on the fronts are full bleed with the player in a gold circle and carry the distinctive Topps Stadium Club Members Only gold foil seal. The backs present a second color photo and player profile.
COMP.FACT SET (55) 50.00 120.00
1 Scottie Pippen .50 1.25
2 Dikembe Mutombo .30 .75
3 Antonio McDyess .30 .75
4 Mark Jackson .30 .75
5 Vin Baker .25 .60
6 Kendall Gill .20 .50
7 Kenny Anderson .25 .60
8 Karl Malone .40 1.00
9 Chris Webber .40 1.00
10 David Robinson .50 1.25
11 Cedric Ceballos .20 .50
12 Patrick Ewing .40 1.00
13 Alonzo Mourning .40 1.00
14 Latrell Sprewell .30 .75
15 Terrell Brandon .20 .50
16 Anthony Mason .20 .50
17 Joe Dumars .30 .75
18 Hakeem Olajuwon .40 1.00
19 Brent Barry .25 .60
20 Shaquille O'Neal .75 2.00
21 Kevin Garnett .75 2.00
22 Anfernee Hardaway .50 1.25
23 Jerry Stackhouse .40 1.00
24 Mitch Richmond .30 .75
25 Gary Payton .30 .75
26 Damon Stoudamire .30 .75
27 Christian Laettner .25 .60
28 Dino Radja .25 .60
29 Shawn Bradley .20 .50
30 John Stockton .40 1.00
31 Sean Elliott .30 .75
32 Jason Kidd .50 1.25
33 Allan Houston .25 .60
34 Glenn Robinson .30 .75
35 Tim Hardaway .30 .75
36 Reggie Miller .40 1.00
37 Charles Barkley .50 1.25
38 Joe Smith .25 .60
39 Grant Hill .50 1.25
40 LaPhonso Ellis .20 .50
41 Michael Jordan 2.50 6.00
42 Glen Rice .30 .75
43 Rony Seikaly .25 .60
44 Shawn Kemp .30 .75
45 Juwan Howard .25 .60
46 Tyrone Hill .20 .50
47 Michael Finley .40 1.00
48 Loy Vaught .20 .50
49 Arvydas Sabonis .25 .60
50 Brian Grant .25 .60
51 Kerry Kittles Finest 3.00 8.00
52 Kobe Bryant Finest 30.00 80.00
53 Stephon Marbury Finest 8.00 20.00
54 Allen Iverson Finest 15.00 40.00
55 Shareef Abdur-Rahim Finest 6.00 15.00

1992-93 Stadium Club Members Only Parallel

Available exclusively through Topps members Only Club, this set was sold in complete factory set form for $199. A total of 10,000 factory sets were printed. The set includes parallel cards of the 400-card basic Stadium Club set from that year in addition to the 21-card Beam Team insert set. The numbering for Members Only cards is identical to the regular issue Stadium Club cards from that year. Members Only cards are readily distinguishable by the gold "Members Only" logo stamped onto the front of each card.
COMPLETE SET (421) 100.00 250.00
1 Michael Jordan 10.00 25.00
2 Greg Anthony .10 .30
3 Otis Thorpe .20 .50
4 Jim Les .10 .30
5 Kevin Willis .10 .30
6 Derek Harper .25 .60
7 Elden Campbell .20 .50
8 A.J. English .10 .30
9 Kenny Gattison .10 .30
10 Drazen Petrovic 1.50 4.00
11 Chris Mullin .75 2.00
12 Mark Price .60 1.50
13 Karl Malone 1.50 4.00
14 Gerald Glass .10 .30
15 Negele Knight .10 .30
16 Mark Macon .10 .30
17 Michael Cage .10 .30
18 Kevin Edwards .10 .30
19 Sherman Douglas .10 .30
20 Ron Harper .40 1.00
21 Clifford Robinson .20 .50
22 Byron Scott .40 1.00
23 Antoine Carr .10 .30
24 Greg Dreiling .10 .30
25 Bill Laimbeer .40 1.00
26 Hersey Hawkins .20 .50
27 Will Perdue .10 .30
28 Todd Lichti .10 .30
29 Gary Grant .10 .30
30 Sam Perkins .40 1.00
31 Jayson Williams .20 .50
32 Magic Johnson 2.50 6.00
33 Larry Bird 3.00 8.00
34 Chris Morris .10 .30
35 Nick Anderson .20 .50
36 Scott Hastings .10 .30
37 Ledell Eackles .10 .30
38 Robert Pack .10 .30
39 Dana Barros .10 .30
40 Anthony Bonner .10 .30
41 J.R. Reid .10 .30
42 Tyrone Hill .10 .30
43 Rik Smits .30 .75
44 Kevin Duckworth .10 .30
45 LaSalle Thompson .10 .30
46 Brian Williams .10 .30
47 Willie Anderson .10 .30
48 Ken Norman .10 .30
49 Mike Iuzzolino .10 .30
50 Isiah Thomas .75 2.00
51 Alec Kessler .10 .30
52 Johnny Dawkins .10 .30
53 Avery Johnson .40 1.00
54 Stacey Augmon .20 .50
55 Charles Oakley .20 .50
56 Rex Chapman .40 1.00
57 Charles Shackleford .10 .30
58 Jeff Ruland .10 .30
59 Craig Ehlo .10 .30
60 Jon Koncak .10 .30
61 Danny Schayes .10 .30
62 David Benoit .10 .30
63 Robert Parish .40 1.00
64 Mookie Blaylock .20 .50
65 Sean Elliott .40 1.00
66 Mark Aguirre .30 .75
67 Scott Williams .10 .30
68 Doug West .10 .30
69 Kenny Anderson .30 .75
70 Randy Brown .10 .30
71 Muggsy Bogues .40 1.00
72 Spud Webb .40 1.00
73 Sedale Threatt .10 .30
74 Chris Gatling .10 .30
75 Derrick McKey .10 .30
76 Sleepy Floyd .10 .30
77 Chris Jackson .10 .30
78 Thurl Bailey .10 .30
79 Steve Smith .60 1.50
80 Cedric Ceballos .10 .30
81 Anthony Bowie .10 .30
82 John Williams .10 .30
83 Paul Graham .10 .30
84 Willie Burton .10 .30
85 Vernon Maxwell .10 .30
86 Stacey King .10 .30
87 B.J. Armstrong .20 .50
88 Kevin Gamble .10 .30
89 Terry Catledge .10 .30
90 Jeff Malone .20 .50
91 Sam Bowie .30 .75
92 Orlando Woolridge .10 .30
93 Steve Kerr .40 1.00
94 Eric Leckner .10 .30
95 Loy Vaught .10 .30
96 Jud Buechler .10 .30
97 Doug Smith .10 .30
98 Sidney Green .10 .30
99 Jerome Kersey .10 .30
100 Patrick Ewing 1.00 2.50
101 Ed Nealy .10 .30
102 Shawn Kemp 1.00 2.50
103 Luc Longley .30 .75
104 George McCloud .10 .30
105 Ron Anderson .10 .30
106 Moses Malone UER .40 1.00
(Rookie Card is 1975-76, not 1976-77)
107 Tony Smith .10 .30
108 Terry Porter .20 .50
109 Blair Rasmussen .10 .30
110 Bimbo Coles .10 .30
111 Grant Long .10 .30
112 John Battle .10 .30
113 Brian Oliver .10 .30
114 Tyrone Corbin .10 .30
115 Benoit Benjamin .10 .30
116 Rick Fox .30 .75
117 Rafael Addison .10 .30
118 Danny Young .10 .30
119 Fat Lever .10 .30
120 Terry Cummings .20 .50
121 Felton Spencer .10 .30
122 Joe Kleine .10 .30
123 Johnny Newman .10 .30
124 Gary Payton 1.50 4.00
125 Kurt Rambis .30 .75
126 Vlade Divac .30 .75
127 John Paxson .40 1.00
128 Lionel Simmons .10 .30
129 Randy Wittman .10 .30
130 Winston Garland .10 .30
131 Jerry Reynolds .10 .30
132 Dell Curry .10 .30
133 Fred Roberts .10 .30
134 Michael Adams .10 .30
135 Charles Jones .10 .30
136 Frank Brickowski .10 .30
137 Alton Lister .10 .30
138 Horace Grant .40 1.00
139 Greg Sutton .10 .30
140 John Starks .30 .75
141 Detlef Schrempf .30 .75
142 Rodney Monroe .10 .30
143 Pete Chilcutt .10 .30
144 Mike Brown .10 .30
145 Rony Seikaly .10 .30
146 Donald Hodge .10 .30
147 Kevin McHale .60 1.50
148 Ricky Pierce .10 .30
149 Brian Shaw .10 .30
150 Reggie Williams .10 .30
151 Kendall Gill .30 .75
152 Tom Chambers .30 .75
153 Jack Haley .10 .30
154 Terrell Brandon .30 .75
155 Dennis Scott .20 .50
156 Mark Randall .10 .30
157 Kenny Payne .10 .30
158 Bernard King .30 .75
159 Tate George .10 .30
160 Scott Skiles .40 1.00
161 Pervis Ellison .10 .30
162 Marcus Liberty .10 .30
163 Rumeal Robinson .10 .30
164 Anthony Mason .30 .75
165 Les Jepsen .10 .30
166 Kenny Smith .20 .50
167 Randy White .10 .30
168 Dee Brown .10 .30
169 Chris Dudley .10 .30
170 Armon Gilliam .10 .30
171 Eddie Johnson .10 .30
172 A.C. Green .40 1.00
173 Darrell Walker .10 .30
174 Bill Cartwright .20 .50
175 Mike Gminski .10 .30
176 Tom Tolbert .20 .50
177 Buck Williams .30 .75
178 Mark Eaton .10 .30
179 Danny Manning .30 .75
180 Glen Rice .40 1.00
181 Sarunas Marciulionis .30 .75
182 Danny Ferry .10 .30
183 Chris Corchiani .10 .30
184 Dan Majerle .50 1.25
185 Alvin Robertson .10 .30
186 Vern Fleming .10 .30
187 Kevin Lynch .10 .30
188 John Williams .10 .30
189 Checklist 1-100 .10 .30
190 Checklist 101-200 .10 .30
191 David Robinson MC .75 2.00
192 Larry Johnson MC .30 .75
193 Derrick Coleman MC .10 .30
194 Larry Bird MC 1.50 4.00
195 Billy Owens MC .10 .30
196 Dikembe Mutombo MC .40 1.00
197 Charles Barkley MC .75 2.00
198 Scottie Pippen MC 1.00 2.50
199 Clyde Drexler MC .75 2.00
200 John Stockton MC 1.00 2.50
201 Shaquille O'Neal MC 4.00 10.00
202 Chris Mullin MC .40 1.00
203 Glen Rice MC .30 .75
204 Isiah Thomas MC .50 1.25
205 Karl Malone MC .75 2.00
206 Christian Laettner MC 1.00 2.50
207 Patrick Ewing MC .50 1.25
208 Dominique Wilkins MC .60 1.50
209 Alonzo Mourning MC 2.00 5.00
210 Michael Jordan MC 5.00 12.00
211 Tim Hardaway MC .60 1.50
212 Rodney McCray .10 .30
213 Larry Johnson .30 .75
214 Charles Smith .10 .30
215 Kevin Brooks .10 .30
216 Kevin Johnson .30 .75
217 Duane Cooper .10 .30
218 Christian Laettner UER 2.00 5.00
(Missing '92 Draft Pick logo)
219 Tim Perry .10 .30
220 Hakeem Olajuwon 1.25 3.00
221 Lee Mayberry .10 .30
222 Mark Bryant .10 .30
223 Robert Horry 1.50 4.00
224 Tracy Murray UER .20 .50
(Missing '92 Draft Pick logo)
225 Greg Grant .10 .30
226 Rolando Blackman .30 .75
227 James Edwards UER .10 .30
(Rookie Card is 1978-79, not 1980-81)
228 Sean Green .10 .30
229 Buck Johnson .10 .30
230 Andrew Lang .10 .30
231 Tracy Moore .10 .30
232 Adam Keefe UER .20 .50
(Missing '92 Draft Pick logo)
233 Tony Campbell .10 .30
234 Rod Strickland .20 .50
235 Terry Mills .10 .30
236 Billy Owens .20 .50
237 Bryant Stith UER .20 .50
(Missing '92 Draft Pick logo)
238 Tony Bennett UER .10 .30
(Missing '92 Draft Pick logo)
239 David Wood .10 .30
240 Jay Humphries .10 .30
241 Doc Rivers .30 .75
242 Wayman Tisdale .10 .30
243 Litterial Green .10 .30
244 Jon Barry .30 .75
245 Brad Daugherty .10 .30
246 Nate McMillan .20 .50
247 Shaquille O'Neal 10.00 25.00
248 Chris Smith .10 .30
249 Duane Ferrell .10 .30
250 Anthony Peeler .30 .75
251 Gundars Vetra .10 .30
252 Danny Ainge .40 1.00
253 Mitch Richmond .60 1.50
254 Malik Sealy .40 1.00
255 Brent Price .20 .50
256 Xavier McDaniel .10 .30
257 Bobby Phills .30 .75
258 Donald Royal .10 .30
259 Olden Polynice .10 .30
260 Dominique Wilkins UER 1.00 2.50
(Scoring 10,000th point & should be 20,000th)
261 Larry Krystkowiak .10 .30
262 Duane Causwell .10 .30
263 Todd Day .20 .50
264 Sam Mack .20 .50
265 John Stockton 1.50 4.00
266 Eddie Lee Wilkins .10 .30
267 Gerald Glass .10 .30
268 Robert Pack .10 .30
269 Gerald Wilkins .10 .30
270 Reggie Lewis .20 .50
271 Scott Brooks .10 .30
272 Randy Woods UER .10 .30
(Missing '92 Draft Pick logo)
273 Dikembe Mutombo .60 1.50
274 Kiki Vandeweghe .40 1.00
275 Rich King .10 .30
276 Jeff Turner .20 .50
277 Vinny Del Negro .10 .30
278 Marlon Maxey .10 .30
279 Elmore Spencer UER .10 .30
(Missing '92 Draft Pick logo)
280 Cedric Ceballos .20 .50
281 Alex Blackwell .10 .30
282 Terry Davis .10 .30
283 Morlon Wiley .10 .30
284 Trent Tucker .10 .30
285 Carl Herrera .10 .30
286 Eric Anderson .10 .30
287 Clyde Drexler 1.25 3.00
288 Tom Gugliotta 2.50 6.00
289 Dale Ellis .10 .30
290 Lance Blanks .10 .30
291 Tom Hammonds .10 .30
292 Eric Murdock .10 .30
293 Walt Williams .30 .75
294 Gerald Paddio .10 .30
295 Brian Howard .10 .30
296 Ken Williams .10 .30
297 Alonzo Mourning 4.00 10.00
298 Larry Nance .30 .75
299 Jeff Grayer .10 .30
300 Dave Johnson .10 .30
301 Bob McCann .10 .30
302 Bart Kofoed .10 .30
303 Anthony Cook .10 .30
304 Radisav Curcic .10 .30
305 John Crotty .10 .30
306 Brad Sellers .10 .30
307 Marcus Webb .10 .30
308 Winston Garland .10 .30
309 Walter Palmer .10 .30
310 Rod Higgins .10 .30
311 Travis Mays .10 .30
312 Alex Stivrins .10 .30
313 Greg Kite .10 .30
314 Dennis Rodman 1.25 3.00
315 Mike Sanders .10 .30
316 Ed Pinckney .10 .30
317 Harold Miner .20 .50
318 Pooh Richardson .10 .30
319 Oliver Miller .20 .50
320 Latrell Sprewell 2.00 5.00
321 Anthony Pullard .10 .30
322 Mark Randall .10 .30
323 Jeff Hornacek .40 1.00
324 Rick Mahorn UER .10 .30
(Rookie Card is 1981-82, not 1992-93)
325 Sean Rooks .10 .30
326 Paul Pressey .10 .30
327 James Worthy .60 1.50
328 Matt Bullard .10 .30
329 Reggie Smith .10 .30
330 Don MacLean UER .20 .50
(Missing '92 Draft Pick logo)
331 John Williams UER .10 .30
(Rookie Card erroneously shows Hot Rod)
332 Frank Johnson .10 .30
333 Hubert Davis UER .20 .50
(Missing '92 Draft Pick logo)
334 Lloyd Daniels .10 .30
335 Steve Bardo .10 .30
336 Jeff Sanders .10 .30
337 Tree Rollins .10 .30
338 Micheal Williams .10 .30
339 Lorenzo Williams .10 .30
340 Harvey Grant .10 .30
341 Avery Johnson .40 1.00
342 Bo Kimble .10 .30
343 LaPhonso Ellis UER .30 .75
(Missing '92 Draft Pick logo)
344 Mookie Blaylock .20 .50
345 Isaiah Morris UER .10 .30
(Missing '92 Draft Pick logo)
346 Clarence Weatherspoon .30 .75

347 Manute Bol .10 .30
348 Victor Alexander .10 .30
349 Corey Williams .10 .30
350 Byron Houston .10 .30
351 Stanley Roberts .10 .30
352 Anthony Avent .10 .30
353 Vincent Askew .10 .30
354 Herb Williams .10 .30
355 J.R. Reid .10 .30
356 Brad Lohaus .10 .30
357 Reggie Miller 1.00 2.50
358 Blue Edwards .10 .30
359 Tom Tolbert .20 .50
360 Charles Barkley 1.25 3.00
361 David Robinson 1.25 3.00
362 Dale Davis .20 .50
363 Robert Werdann UER .10 .30
(Missing '92 Draft Pick logo)
364 Chuck Person .10 .30
365 Alaa Abdelnaby .10 .30
366 Dave Jamerson .10 .30
367 Scottie Pippen 2.00 5.00
368 Mark Jackson .50 1.25
369 Keith Askins .10 .30
370 Marty Conlon .10 .30
371 Chucky Brown .10 .30
372 LaBradford Smith .10 .30
373 Tim Kempton .10 .30
374 Sam Mitchell .10 .30
375 John Salley .20 .50
376 Mario Elie .20 .50
377 Mark West .10 .30
378 David Wingate .10 .30
379 Jaren Jackson .20 .50
380 Rumeal Robinson .10 .30
381 Kennard Winchester .10 .30
382 Walter Bond .10 .30
383 Isaac Austin .20 .50
384 Derrick Coleman .20 .50
385 Larry Smith .10 .30
386 Joe Dumars .60 1.50
387 Matt Geiger UER .10 .30
(Missing '92 Draft Pick logo)
388 Stephen Howard .10 .30
389 William Bedford .10 .30
390 Jayson Williams .20 .50
391 Kurt Rambis .30 .75
392 Keith Jennings .10 .30
393 Steve Kerr UER .30 .75
(The words key stat are repeated on back)
394 Larry Stewart .10 .30
395 Danny Young .10 .30
396 Doug Overton .10 .30
397 Mark Acres .10 .30
398 John Bagley .10 .30
399 Checklist 201-300 .10 .30
400 Checklist 301-400 .10 .30
BT1 Michael Jordan 20.00 50.00
BT2 Dominique Wilkins 2.50 6.00
BT3 Shawn Kemp 1.50 4.00
BT4 Clyde Drexler 2.50 6.00
BT5 Scottie Pippen 2.50 6.00
BT6 Chris Mullin 1.50 4.00
BT7 Reggie Miller 2.00 5.00
BT8 Glen Rice 1.25 3.00
BT9 Jeff Hornacek 1.25 3.00
BT10 Jeff Malone .75 2.00
BT11 John Stockton 3.00 8.00
BT12 Kevin Johnson 1.00 2.50
BT13 Mark Price 1.00 2.50
BT14 Tim Hardaway 1.50 4.00
BT15 Charles Barkley 2.50 6.00
BT16 Hakeem Olajuwon 2.00 5.00
BT17 Karl Malone 2.50 6.00
BT18 Patrick Ewing 1.50 4.00
BT19 Dennis Rodman 2.00 5.00
BT20 David Robinson 2.50 6.00
BT21 Shaquille O'Neal 15.00 40.00

1993-94 Stadium Club Members Only Parallel

For the second straight year, Topps offered a special parallel set of their complete Stadium Club product (regular-issue and insert cards included) through their Members Only club. The set was available to members only in factory set form and was offered for $229 plus shipping and handling.

COMPLETE SET (414) 100.00 250.00
1 Michael Jordan TD 5.00 12.00
2 Kenny Anderson TD .10 .30
3 Steve Smith TD .30 .75
4 Kevin Gamble TD .10 .30
5 Detlef Schrempf TD .20 .50
6 Larry Johnson TD .20 .50
7 Brad Daugherty TD .10 .30
8 Rumeal Robinson TD .10 .30
9 Micheal Williams TD .10 .30
10 David Robinson TD .60 1.50
11 Sam Perkins TD .20 .50
12 Thurl Bailey .10 .30
13 Sherman Douglas .10 .30
14 Larry Stewart .10 .30
15 Kevin Johnson .30 .75
16 Bill Cartwright .20 .50
17 Larry Nance .20 .50
18 P.J.Brown RC .40 1.00
19 Tony Bennett .10 .30
20 Robert Parish .40 1.00
21 David Benoit .10 .30
22 Detlef Schrempf .30 .75
23 Hubert Davis .10 .30
24 Donald Hodge .10 .30
25 Hersey Hawkins .20 .50
26 Mark Jackson .40 1.00
27 Reggie Williams .10 .30
28 Lionel Simmons .10 .30
29 Ron Harper .40 1.00
30 Chris Mills RC .30 .75
31 Danny Schayes .10 .30
32 J.R. Reid .10 .30
33 Willie Burton .10 .30
34 Greg Anthony .10 .30
35 Elden Campbell .10 .30
36 Ervin Johnson RC .20 .50
37 Scott Brooks .10 .30
38 Johnny Newman .10 .30
39 Rex Chapman .30 .75
40 Chuck Person .10 .30
41 John Williams .10 .30
42 Anthony Bowie .10 .30
43 Negele Knight .10 .30
44 Tyrone Corbin .10 .30
45 Jud Buechler .10 .30
46 Adam Keefe .10 .30
47 Glen Rice .40 1.00
48 Tracy Murray .10 .30
49 Rick Mahorn .10 .30
50 Vlade Divac .30 .75
51 Eric Murdock .10 .30
52 Isaiah Morris .10 .30
53 Bobby Hurley .20 .50
54 Mitch Richmond .60 1.50
55 Danny Ainge .40 1.00
56 Dikembe Mutombo .40 1.00
57 Jeff Hornacek .40 1.00
58 Tony Campbell .10 .30
59 Vinny Del Negro .10 .30
60 Xavier McDaniel HC .10 .30
61 Scottie Pippen HC 1.25 3.00
62 Larry Nance HC .20 .50
63 Dikembe Mutombo HC .30 .75
64 Hakeem Olajuwon HC .60 1.50
65 Dominique Wilkins HC .60 1.50
66 Clarence Weatherspoon HC .10 .30
67 Chris Morris HC .10 .30
68 Patrick Ewing HC .40 1.00
69 Kevin Willis HC .10 .30
70 Jon Barry .10 .30
71 Jerry Reynolds .10 .30
72 Sarunas Marciulionis .20 .50
73 Mark West .10 .30
74 B.J. Armstrong .20 .50
75 Greg Kite .10 .30
76 LaSalle Thompson .10 .30
77 Randy White .10 .30
78 Alaa Abdelnaby .10 .30
79 Kevin Brooks .10 .30
80 Vern Fleming .10 .30
81 Doc Rivers .30 .75
82 Shawn Bradley .40 1.00
83 Wayman Tisdale .10 .30
84 Olden Polynice .10 .30
85 Michael Cage .10 .30
86 Harold Miner .10 .30
87 Doug Smith .10 .30
88 Tom Gugliotta .30 .75
89 Hakeem Olajuwon 1.00 2.50
90 Loy Vaught .10 .30
91 James Worthy .60 1.50
92 John Paxson .30 .75
93 Jon Koncak .10 .30
94 Lee Mayberry .10 .30
95 Clarence Weatherspoon .10 .30
96 Mark Eaton .10 .30
97 Rex Walters .20 .50
98 Alvin Robertson .10 .30
99 Dan Majerle .40 1.00
100 Shaquille O'Neal 3.00 8.00
101 Derrick Coleman TD .20 .50
102 Hersey Hawkins TD .20 .50
103 Scottie Pippen TD 1.25 3.00
104 Scott Skiles TD .30 .75
105 Rod Strickland TD .10 .30
106 Pooh Richardson TD .10 .30
107 Tom Gugliotta TD .40 1.00
108 Mark Jackson TD .40 1.00
109 Dikembe Mutombo TD .30 .75
110 Charles Barkley TD .60 1.50
111 Otis Thorpe TD .10 .30
112 Malik Sealy .20 .50
113 Mark Macon .10 .30
114 Dee Brown .10 .30
115 Nate McMillan .20 .50
116 John Starks .30 .75
117 Clyde Drexler 1.00 2.50
118 Antoine Carr .10 .30
119 Doug West .10 .30
120 Victor Alexander .10 .30
121 Kenny Gattison .10 .30
122 Spud Webb .30 .75
123 Rumeal Robinson .10 .30
124 Tim Kempton .10 .30
125 Karl Malone 1.50 4.00
126 Randy Woods .10 .30
127 Calbert Cheaney .20 .50
128 Johnny Dawkins .10 .30
129 Dominique Wilkins 1.00 2.50
130 Horace Grant .30 .75
131 Bill Laimbeer .40 1.00
132 Kenny Smith .20 .50
133 Sedale Threatt .10 .30
134 Brian Shaw .10 .30
135 Dennis Scott .10 .30
136 Mark Bryant .10 .30
137 Xavier McDaniel .10 .30
138 David Wood .10 .30
139 Luther Wright .10 .30
140 Lloyd Daniels .10 .30
141 Marlon Maxey UER .10 .30
(Name spelled Maxley on the front)
142 Pooh Richardson .10 .30
143 Jeff Grayer .10 .30
144 LaPhonso Ellis .10 .30
145 Gerald Wilkins .10 .30
146 Dell Curry .10 .30
147 Duane Causwell .10 .30
148 Tim Hardaway .75 2.00
149 Isiah Thomas .75 2.00
150 Doug Edwards .10 .30
151 Anthony Peeler .10 .30
152 Tate George .10 .30
153 Terry Davis .10 .30
154 Sam Perkins .30 .75
155 John Salley .20 .50
156 Vernon Maxwell .10 .30
157 Anthony Avent .10 .30
158 Clifford Robinson .20 .50
159 Corie Blount .10 .30
160 Gerald Paddio .10 .30
161 Blair Rasmussen .10 .30
162 Carl Herrera .10 .30
163 Chris Smith .10 .30
164 Pervis Ellison .10 .30
165 Rod Strickland .20 .50
166 Jeff Malone .10 .30
167 Danny Ferry .10 .30
168 Kevin Lynch .10 .30
169 Michael Jordan 8.00 20.00
170 Derrick Coleman HC .10 .30
171 Jerome Kersey HC .15 .40
172 David Robinson HC .60 1.50
173 Shawn Kemp HC .40 1.00
174 Karl Malone HC 1.00 2.50
175 Shaquille O'Neal HC 2.00 5.00
176 Alonzo Mourning HC .40 1.00
177 Charles Barkley HC .75 2.00
178 Larry Johnson HC .20 .50
179 Checklist 1-90 .10 .30
180 Checklist 91-180 .10 .30
181 Michael Jordan FF 4.00 10.00
182 Dominique Wilkins FF .75 2.00
183 Dennis Rodman FF .75 2.00
184 Scottie Pippen FF 1.25 3.00
185 Larry Johnson FF .20 .50
186 Karl Malone FF 1.00 2.50
187 Clarence Weatherspoon FF .10 .30
188 Charles Barkley FF .75 2.00
189 Patrick Ewing FF .40 1.00
190 Derrick Coleman FF .20 .50
191 LaBradford Smith .10 .30
192 Derek Harper .20 .50
193 Ken Norman .10 .30
194 Rodney Rogers .60 1.50
195 Chris Dudley .10 .30
196 Gary Payton 1.00 2.50
197 Andrew Lang .10 .30
198 Billy Owens .10 .30
199 Bryon Russell .30 .75
200 Patrick Ewing .75 2.00
201 Stacey King .10 .30
202 Grant Long .10 .30
203 Sean Elliott .40 1.00
204 Muggsy Bogues .40 1.00
205 Kevin Edwards .10 .30
206 Dale Davis .10 .30
207 Dale Ellis .10 .30
208 Terrell Brandon .20 .50
209 Kevin Gamble .10 .30
210 Robert Horry .40 1.00
211 Moses Malone UER .40 1.00
(Birthdate on back is 1993)
212 Gary Grant .10 .30
213 Bobby Hurley .10 .30
214 Larry Krystkowiak .10 .30
215 A.C. Green .40 1.00
216 Christian Laettner .40 1.00
217 Orlando Woolridge .10 .30
218 Craig Ehlo .10 .30
219 Terry Porter .20 .50
220 Jamal Mashburn 1.50 4.00
221 Kevin Duckworth .10 .30
222 Shawn Kemp .75 2.00
223 Frank Brickowski .10 .30
224 Chris Webber 6.00 15.00
225 Charles Oakley .20 .50
226 Jay Humphries .10 .30
227 Steve Kerr .40 1.00
228 Tim Perry .10 .30
229 Sleepy Floyd .10 .30
230 Bimbo Coles .10 .30
231 Eddie Johnson .10 .30
232 Terry Mills .10 .30
233 Danny Manning .30 .75
234 Isaiah Rider 1.25 3.00
235 Darnell Mee .10 .30
236 Haywoode Workman .10 .30
237 Scott Skiles .40 1.00
238 Otis Thorpe .20 .50
239 Mike Peplowski .10 .30
240 Eric Leckner .10 .30
241 Johnny Newman .10 .30
242 Benoit Benjamin .10 .30
243 Doug Christie .10 .30
244 Acie Earl RC .10 .30
245 Luc Longley .20 .50
246 Tyrone Hill .10 .30
247 Allan Houston 2.00 5.00
248 Joe Kleine .10 .30
249 Mookie Blaylock .20 .50
250 Anthony Bonner .10 .30
251 Luther Wright .10 .30
252 Todd Day .10 .30
253 Kendall Gill .30 .75
254 Mario Elie .10 .30
255 Pete Myers .10 .30
256 Jim Les .10 .30
257 Stanley Roberts .10 .30
258 Michael Adams .10 .30
259 Hersey Hawkins .30 .75
260 Shawn Bradley .30 .75
261 Scott Haskin .10 .30
262 Corie Blount .10 .30
263 Charles Smith .10 .30
264 Armon Gilliam .10 .30
265 Jamal Mashburn NW 1.00 2.50
266 Anfernee Hardaway NW 2.50 6.00
267 Shawn Bradley NW .30 .75
268 Chris Webber NW 3.00 8.00
269 Bobby Hurley NW .30 .75
270 Isaiah Rider NW .60 1.50
271 Dino Radja NW .20 .50
272 Chris Mills NW .30 .75
273 Nick Van Exel NW .40 1.00
274 Lindsey Hunter NW .30 .75
275 Toni Kukoc NW 1.00 2.50
276 Popeye Jones NW .10 .30
277 Chris Mills .30 .75
278 Ricky Pierce .10 .30
279 Negele Knight .10 .30
280 Kenny Walker .10 .30
281 Nick Van Exel 2.00 5.00
282 Derrick Coleman UER .20 .50
(Career stats listed under '92-93)
283 Popeye Jones RC .20 .50
284 Derrick McKey .10 .30
285 Rick Fox .30 .75
286 Jerome Kersey .10 .30
287 Steve Smith .30 .75
288 Brian Williams .10 .30
289 Chris Mullin .40 1.00
290 Terry Cummings .20 .50
291 Donald Royal .10 .30
292 Alonzo Mourning .75 2.00
293 Mike Brown .10 .30
294 Latrell Sprewell 1.25 3.00
295 Oliver Miller .10 .30
296 Terry Dehere .10 .30
297 Detlef Schrempf .30 .75
298 Sam Bowie UER .20 .50
(Last name Bowe on front)
299 Chris Morris .10 .30
300 Scottie Pippen 2.00 5.00
301 Warren Kidd .10 .30
302 Don MacLean .10 .30
303 Sean Rooks .10 .30
304 Matt Geiger .10 .30
305 Dennis Rodman 1.00 2.50
306 Reggie Miller .75 2.00
307 Vin Baker 1.25 3.00
308 Anfernee Hardaway 3.00 8.00
309 Lindsey Hunter .40 1.00
310 Stacey Augmon .20 .50
311 Randy Brown .10 .30
312 Anthony Mason .20 .50
313 John Stockton 1.25 3.00
314 Sam Cassell 1.50 4.00
315 Buck Williams .30 .75
316 Bryant Stith .10 .30
317 Brad Daugherty .10 .30
318 Dino Radja .10 .30
319 Rony Seikaly .10 .30
320 Charles Barkley 1.00 2.50
321 Avery Johnson .40 1.00
322 Mahmoud Abdul-Rauf .10 .30
323 Larry Johnson .40 1.00
324 Micheal Williams .10 .30
325 Mark Aguirre .30 .75
326 Jim Jackson .50 1.25
327 Antonio Harvey .10 .30
328 David Robinson 1.25 3.00
329 Calbert Cheaney .20 .50
330 Kenny Anderson .20 .50
331 Walt Williams .10 .30
332 Kevin Willis .10 .30
333 Nick Anderson .20 .50
334 Rik Smits .20 .50
335 Joe Dumars .60 1.50
336 Toni Kukoc 2.50 6.00
337 Harvey Grant .10 .30
338 Tom Chambers .30 .75
339 Blue Edwards .10 .30
340 Mark Price .40 1.00
341 Ervin Johnson .20 .50
342 Rolando Blackman .30 .75
343 Scott Burrell .30 .75
344 Gheorghe Muresan .30 .75
345 Chris Corchiani .10 .30
346 Richard Petruska .10 .30
347 Dana Barros .10 .30
348 Hakeem Olajuwon FF .30 .75
349 Dee Brown FF .10 .30
350 John Starks FF .20 .50
351 Ron Harper FF .20 .50
352 Chris Webber FF 3.00 8.00
353 Dan Majerle FF .30 .75
354 Clyde Drexler FF .60 1.50
355 Shawn Kemp FF .40 1.00
356 David Robinson FF .60 1.50
357 Chris Morris FF .10 .30
358 Shaquille O'Neal FF 1.50 4.00
359 Checklist .10 .30
360 Checklist .10 .30
BT1 Shaquille O'Neal 5.00 12.00
BT2 Mark Price .50 1.25
BT3 Patrick Ewing 1.25 3.00
BT4 Michael Jordan 12.50 30.00
BT5 Charles Barkley 1.50 4.00
BT6 Reggie Miller 1.25 3.00
BT7 Derrick Coleman .30 .75
BT8 Dominique Wilkins 1.25 3.00
BT9 Karl Malone 2.50 6.00
BT10 Alonzo Mourning 1.25 3.00
BT11 Tim Hardaway 1.25 3.00
BT12 Hakeem Olajuwon 1.50 4.00
BT13 David Robinson 1.50 4.00
BT14 Dan Majerle .60 1.50
BT15 Larry Johnson .60 1.50
BT16 LaPhonso Ellis .30 .75
BT17 Nick Van Exel 2.00 5.00
BT18 Scottie Pippen 3.00 8.00
BT19 John Stockton 3.00 8.00
BT20 Bobby Hurley .40 1.00
BT21 Chris Webber 8.00 20.00
BT22 Jamal Mashburn 1.50 4.00
BT23 Anfernee Hardaway 6.00 15.00
BT24 Isaiah Rider 1.50 4.00
BT25 Ken Norman .30 .75
BT26 Danny Manning .40 1.00
BT27 Calbert Cheaney .50 1.25
ST1 Atlanta .40 1.00
Dominique Wilkins
ST2 Boston .30 .75
Robert Parish
ST3 Charlotte .50 1.25
Larry Johnson
Alonzo Mourning
ST4 Chicago .30 .75
Horace Grant
ST5 Cleveland .10 .30
Brad Daugherty
ST6 Dallas .10 .30
Group
ST7 Denver .40 1.00
Dikembe Mutombo
ST8 Detroit .10 .30
Group
ST9 Golden State .10 .30
Group
ST10 Houston .10 .30
Group
ST11 Indiana .10 .30
Group
ST12 L.A.Clippers .30 .75
Danny Manning
ST13 L.A.Lakers .10 .30
Group
ST14 Miami .10 .30
John Salley
ST15 Milwaukee .10 .30
Group
ST16 Minnesota .30 .75
Christian Laettner
ST17 New Jersey .10 .30
Derrick Coleman
ST18 New York .40 1.00
Patrick Ewing
ST19 Orlando 1.50 4.00
Shaquille O'Neal
ST20 Philadelphia .15 .40
Clarence Weatherspoon
ST21 Phoenix .50 1.25
Charles Barkley
ST22 Portland .10 .30
Buck Williams
ST23 Sacramento .10 .30
Lionel Simmons
ST24 San Antonio .50 1.25
David Robinson
ST25 Seattle .40 1.00
Shawn Kemp
ST26 Utah .10 .30
Group
ST27 Washington .10 .30
Group

1994-95 Stadium Club Members Only Parallel

This 509 card set parallels the complete mainstream 1994-95 Stadium Club run (including all basic issue and insert cards). Topps printed only as many sets as were ordered through their Members Only collector's club, until the maximum of 7,500 sets was reached. To reserve a set, members had to send in an order form or call a toll free number before February 28, 1995. The factory set cost 199.00 plus 10.00 for shipping and handling, and it included a Members Only Edition portfolio with display sheets. The fronts are identical to the regular issue, except for the Members Only emblem. Also the NBA Super Team cards have different backs than the retail product, making them ineligible for prizes. An embossed, autographed card featuring Reggie Miller was included in the set.

COMPLETE SET (509) 125.00 300.00
1 Patrick Ewing .75 2.00
2 Patrick Ewing TG .75 2.00
3 Bimbo Coles .40 1.00
4 Elden Campbell .40 1.00
5 Brent Price .40 1.00
6 Hubert Davis .40 1.00
7 Donald Royal .40 1.00
8 Tim Perry .40 1.00
9 Chris Webber 1.00 2.50
10 Chris Webber TG 1.00 2.50
11 Brad Daugherty .50 1.25
12 P.J. Brown .40 1.00
13 Charles Barkley 1.25 3.00
14 Mario Elie .40 1.00
15 Tyrone Hill .40 1.00
16 Anfernee Hardaway 1.25 3.00
17 Anfernee Hardaway TG 1.25 3.00
18 Toni Kukoc .75 2.00
19 Chris Morris .40 1.00
20 Gerald Wilkins .40 1.00
21 David Benoit .40 1.00
22 Kevin Duckworth .40 1.00
23 Derrick Coleman .50 1.25
24 Adam Keefe .40 1.00
25 Marlon Maxey .40 1.00
26 Vern Fleming .40 1.00
27 Jeff Malone .40 1.00
28 Rodney Rogers .40 1.00
29 Terry Mills .40 1.00
30 Doug West .40 1.00
31 Doug West TG .40 1.00
32 Shaquille O'Neal 2.50 6.00
33 Scottie Pippen 1.50 4.00
34 Lee Mayberry .40 1.00
35 Dale Ellis .40 1.00
36 Cedric Ceballos .40 1.00
37 Lionel Simmons .40 1.00
38 Kenny Gattison .40 1.00
39 Popeye Jones .40 1.00
40 Jerome Kersey .40 1.00
41 Jerome Kersey TG .40 1.00
42 Larry Stewart .40 1.00
43 Rod Strickland .40 1.00
44 Chris Mills .40 1.00
45 Latrell Sprewell .75 2.00
46 Haywoode Workman .40 1.00
47 Charles Smith .40 1.00
48 Detlef Schrempf .60 1.50
49 Gary Grant .40 1.00
50 Gary Grant TG .40 1.00
51 Tom Chambers .60 1.50
52 J.R. Reid .40 1.00
53 Mookie Blaylock .40 1.00
54 Mookie Blaylock TG .40 1.00
55 Rony Seikaly .50 1.25
56 Isaiah Rider .60 1.50
57 Isaiah Rider TG .60 1.50
58 Nick Anderson .40 1.00
59 Victor Alexander .40 1.00
60 Lucious Harris .40 1.00
61 Mark Macon .40 1.00
62 Otis Thorpe .40 1.00
63 Randy Woods .40 1.00
64 Clyde Drexler .75 2.00
65 Dikembe Mutombo .60 1.50
66 Todd Day .40 1.00
67 Greg Anthony .40 1.00
68 Sherman Douglas .40 1.00
69 Chris Mullin .60 1.50
70 Kevin Johnson .60 1.50
71 Kendall Gill .40 1.00
72 Dennis Rodman 1.25 3.00
73 Dennis Rodman TG 1.25 3.00
74 Jeff Turner .40 1.00
75 John Stockton .75 2.00
76 John Stockton TG .75 2.00
77 Doug Edwards .40 1.00
78 Jim Jackson .40 1.00
79 Hakeem Olajuwon .75 2.00
80 Glen Rice .60 1.50
81 Christian Laettner .50 1.25
82 Terry Porter .40 1.00
83 Joe Dumars .60 1.50
84 David Wingate .40 1.00
85 B.J. Armstrong .40 1.00
86 Derrick McKey .40 1.00
87 Elmore Spencer .40 1.00
88 Walt Williams .40 1.00
89 Shawn Bradley .40 1.00
90 Acie Earl .40 1.00
91 Acie Earl TTG .40 1.00
92 Randy Brown .40 1.00
93 Grant Long .40 1.00
94 Terry Dehere .40 1.00
95 Spud Webb .60 1.50
96 Lindsey Hunter .40 1.00
97 Blair Rasmussen .40 1.00
98 Tim Hardaway .60 1.50
99 Kevin Edwards .40 1.00
100 Patrick Ewing CT .75 2.00
Reggie Williams CT
101 Chuck Person CT 1.00 2.50
Charles Barkley CT
102 Mahmoud Abdul-Rauf CT 1.50 4.00
Shaquille O'Neal CT
103 Rony Seikaly CT .50 1.25
Derrick Coleman CT
104 Hakeem Olajuwon CT .75 2.00
Clyde Drexler CT
105 Chris Mullin CT .60 1.50
Mark Jackson CT
106 Robert Horry CT .75 2.00
Latrell Sprewell CT
107 Pooh Richardson CT .75 2.00
Reggie Miller CT
108 Dennis Scott CT .50 1.25
Kenny Anderson CT
109 Kendall Gill CT .40 1.00
Ken Norman CT
110 Scott Skiles CT .40 1.00
Kevin Willis CT
111 Terry Mills CT .60 1.50
Glen Rice CT
112 Christian Laettner CT .60 1.50
Bobby Hurley CT
113 Stacey Augmon CT .60 1.50
Larry Johnson CT
114 Sam Perkins CT .75 2.00
James Worthy CT
115 Carl Herrera .40 1.00
116 Sam Bowie .40 1.00
117 Gary Payton .60 1.50
118 Danny Ainge .60 1.50
119 Danny Ainge TG .60 1.50
120 Luc Longley .40 1.00
121 Antonio Davis .40 1.00
122 Terry Cummings .60 1.50
123 Terry Cummings TG .60 1.50
124 Mark Price .60 1.50
125 Jamal Mashburn .60 1.50
126 Mahmoud Abdul-Rauf .40 1.00
127 Charles Oakley .50 1.25
128 Steve Smith .50 1.25
129 Vin Baker .60 1.50
130 Robert Horry .60 1.50
131 Doug Christie .40 1.00
132 Wayman Tisdale .40 1.00
133 Wayman Tisdale TG .40 1.00
134 Muggsy Bogues .50 1.25
135 Dino Radja .50 1.25
136 Jeff Hornacek .50 1.25
137 Gheorghe Muresan .40 1.00
138 Loy Vaught .40 1.00
139 Loy Vaught TG .40 1.00
140 Benoit Benjamin .40 1.00
141 Johnny Dawkins .40 1.00
142 Allan Houston .60 1.50
143 Jon Barry .40 1.00
144 Reggie Miller .75 2.00
145 Kevin Willis .40 1.00
146 James Worthy .75 2.00
147 James Worthy TG .75 2.00
148 Scott Burrell .40 1.00
149 Tom Gugliotta .40 1.00
150 LaPhonso Ellis .40 1.00
151 Doug Smith .40 1.00
152 A.C. Green .60 1.50
153 A.C. Green TG .60 1.50
154 George Lynch .40 1.00
155 Sam Perkins .40 1.00
156 Corie Blount .40 1.00
157 Xavier McDaniel .40 1.00
158 Xavier McDaniel TG .40 1.00
159 Eric Murdock .40 1.00
160 David Robinson 1.00 2.50
161 Karl Malone .75 2.00
162 Karl Malone TG .75 2.00
163 Clarence Weatherspoon .40 1.00
164 Calbert Cheaney .40 1.00
165 Tom Hammonds .40 1.00
166 Tom Hammonds TG .40 1.00
167 Alonzo Mourning .75 2.00
168 Clifford Robinson .40 1.00
169 Micheal Williams .40 1.00
170 Ervin Johnson .40 1.00
171 Mike Gminski .40 1.00
172 Jason Kidd 4.00 10.00
173 Anthony Bonner .40 1.00
174 Stacey King .40 1.00
175 Rex Chapman .40 1.00
176 Greg Graham .40 1.00
177 Stanley Roberts .40 1.00
178 Mitch Richmond .60 1.50
179 Eric Montross .60 1.50
180 Eddie Jones 2.00 5.00
181 Grant Hill 4.00 10.00
182 Donyell Marshall .60 1.50
183 Glenn Robinson 1.25 3.00
184 Dominique Wilkins .75 2.00
185 Mark Price .60 1.50
186 Anthony Mason .40 1.00
187 Tyrone Corbin .40 1.00
188 Dale Davis .40 1.00
189 Nate McMillan .40 1.00
190 Jason Kidd 3.00 8.00
191 John Salley .40 1.00
192 Keith Jennings .40 1.00
193 Mark Bryant .40 1.00
194 Sleepy Floyd .40 1.00
195 Grant Hill 3.00 8.00
196 Joe Kleine .40 1.00
197 Anthony Peeler .40 1.00
198 Malik Sealy .40 1.00
199 Kenny Walker .40 1.00
200 Donyell Marshall .60 1.50
201 Vlade Divac AI .60 1.50
202 Dino Radja AI .50 1.25
203 Carl Herrera AI .40 1.00
204 Olden Polynice AI .40 1.00
205 Patrick Ewing AI .75 2.00
206 Willie Anderson .40 1.00
207 Mitch Richmond .60 1.50
208 John Crotty .40 1.00
209 Tracy Murray .40 1.00
210 Juwan Howard 1.00 2.50
211 Robert Parish .60 1.50
212 Steve Kerr .50 1.25
213 Anthony Bowie .40 1.00
214 Tim Breaux .40 1.00
215 Sharone Wright .60 1.50
216 Brian Williams .40 1.00
217 Rick Fox .40 1.00
218 Harold Miner .40 1.00
219 Duane Ferrell .40 1.00
220 Lamond Murray .60 1.50
221 Blue Edwards .40 1.00
222 Bill Cartwright .50 1.25
223 Sergei Bazarevich .60 1.50
224 Herb Williams .40 1.00
225 Brian Grant 1.00 2.50
226 Derek Harper BCT .50 1.25
John Starks
227 Rod Strickland BCT .75 2.00
Clyde Drexler
228 Kevin Johnson BCT .60 1.50
Dan Majerle
229 Lindsey Hunter BCT .60 1.50
Joe Dumars
230 Tim Hardaway BCT .75 2.00
Latrell Sprewell
231 Bill Wennington .40 1.00
232 Brian Shaw .40 1.00
233 Jamie Watson .60 1.50
234 Chris Whitney .40 1.00
235 Eric Montross .60 1.50
236 Kenny Smith .50 1.25
237 Andrew Lang .40 1.00
238 Lorenzo Williams .40 1.00
239 Dana Barros .40 1.00
240 Eddie Jones 2.00 5.00
241 Harold Ellis .40 1.00
242 James Edwards .40 1.00
243 Don MacLean .40 1.00
244 Ed Pinckney .40 1.00
245 Carlos Rogers .60 1.50
246 Michael Adams .40 1.00
247 Rex Walters .40 1.00
248 John Starks .50 1.25
249 Terrell Brandon .40 1.00
250 Khalid Reeves .60 1.50
251 Dominique Wilkins AI .75 2.00
252 Toni Kukoc AI .75 2.00
253 Rick Fox AI .40 1.00
254 Detlef Schrempf AI .60 1.50
255 Rik Smits AI .50 1.25
256 Johnny Dawkins .40 1.0
257 Dan Majerle .60 1.5
258 Mike Brown .40 1.0
259 Byron Scott .50 1.2
260 Jalen Rose 1.50 4.0
261 Byron Houston .40 1.0
262 Frank Brickowski .40 1.0
263 Vernon Maxwell .40 1.0
264 Craig Ehlo .40 1.0
265 Yinka Dare .60 1.5
266 Dee Brown .40 1.0
267 Felton Spencer .40 1.0
268 Harvey Grant .40 1.0
269 Nick Van Exel .60 1.5
270 Bob Martin .40 1.0
271 Hersey Hawkins .40 1.0
272 Scott Williams .40 1.0
273 Sarunas Marciulionis .40 1.0
274 Kevin Gamble .40 1.0
275 Clifford Rozier .60 1.5
276 B.J. Armstrong BCT .50 1.2
Ron Harper
277 John Stockton BCT .75 2.
Jeff Hornacek
278 Bobby Hurley BCT .60 1.5
Mitch Richmond
279 Anfernee Hardaway BCT 1.00 2.5
Dennis Scott
280 Jason Kidd BCT 3.00 8.0
Jim Jackson
281 Ron Harper .50 1.2
282 Chuck Person .50 1.2
283 John Williams .40 1.0
284 Robert Pack .40 1.0
285 Aaron McKie .60 1.5
286 Chris Smith .40 1.0
287 Horace Grant .50 1.2
288 Oliver Miller .40 1.
289 Derek Harper .50 1.2
290 Eric Mobley .60 1.2
291 Scott Skiles .40 1.
292 Olden Polynice .40 1.
293 Mark Jackson .60 1.
294 Wayman Tisdale .40 1.
295 Tony Dumas .60 1.
296 Bryon Russell .40 1.0
297 Vlade Divac .60 1.5
298 David Wesley .40 1.0
299 Askia Jones .60 1.5
300 B.J. Tyler .60 1.
301 Hakeem Olajuwon AI .75 2.
302 Luc Longley AI .40 1.
303 Rony Seikaly AI .50 1.2
304 Sarunas Marciulionis AI .40 1.
305 Dikembe Mutombo AI .60 1.
306 Ken Norman .40 1.
307 Dell Curry .40 1.
308 Danny Ferry .40 1.
309 Shawn Kemp .60 1.5
310 Dickey Simpkins .60 1.5
311 Johnny Newman .40 1.
312 Dwayne Schintzius .40 1.
313 Sean Elliott .60 1.5
314 Sean Rooks .40 1.
315 Bill Curley .60 1.
316 Bryant Stith .40 1.
317 Pooh Richardson .40 1.
318 Jim McIlvaine .60 1.
319 Dennis Scott .40 1.
320 Wesley Person .60 1.
321 Bobby Hurley .60 1.
322 Armon Gilliam .40 1.
323 Rik Smits .50 1.
324 Tony Smith .40 1.
325 Monty Williams .60 1.
326 Gary Payton BCT .60 1.
Kendall Gill
327 Mookie Blaylock BCT .50 1.
Stacey Augmon
328 Mark Jackson BCT .75 2.
Reggie Miller
329 Sam Cassell BCT .60 1.
Vernon Maxwell
330 Harold Miner BCT .60 1.
Khalid Reeves
331 Vinny Del Negro .40 1.
332 Billy Owens .40 1.
333 Mark West .40 1.
334 Matt Geiger .40 1.
335 Greg Minor .60 1.
336 Larry Johnson .60 1.
337 Donald Hodge .40 1.
338 Aaron Williams .60 1.
339 Jay Humphries .40 1.
340 Charlie Ward .60 1
341 Scott Brooks .40 1
342 Stacey Augmon .50 1
343 Will Perdue .50 1
344 Dale Ellis .40 1.
345 Brooks Thompson .60 1.
346 Manute Bol .40 1
347 Kenny Anderson .50 1.
348 Willie Burton .40 1.
349 Michael Cage .40 1.
350 Danny Manning .50 1
351 Ricky Pierce .40 1.
352 Sam Cassell .60 1
353 Reggie Miller FG .75 2
354 David Robinson FG 1.00 2
355 Shaquille O'Neal FG 1.50 4
356 Scottie Pippen FG 1.25 3
357 Alonzo Mourning FG .75 2
358 Clarence Weatherspoon FG .40 1
359 Derrick Coleman FG .50 1
360 Charles Barkley FG 1.00 2
361 Karl Malone FG .75 2.
362 Chris Webber FG 1.00 2
BT1 Mookie Blaylock .40 1.
BT2 Dominique Wilkins .75 2
BT3 Alonzo Mourning .75 2
BT4 Toni Kukoc .75 2
BT5 Mark Price .60 1
BT6 Jason Kidd 3.00 8
BT7 Jalen Rose 1.50 4
BT8 Grant Hill 3.00 8
BT9 Latrell Sprewell .75 2
BT10 Hakeem Olajuwon .75 2
BT11 Reggie Miller .75 2
BT12 Lamond Murray .60 1
BT13 George Lynch .40 1
BT14 Khalid Reeves .60 1
BT15 Glenn Robinson 1.25 3
BT16 Donyell Marshall .60 1
BT17 Derrick Coleman .50 1
BT18 Patrick Ewing .75 2
BT19 Shaquille O'Neal 1.50 4
BT20 Clarence Weatherspoon .40 1
BT21 Charles Barkley 1.00 2

22 Clifford Robinson .40 1.00
23 Bobby Hurley .60 1.50
24 David Robinson 1.00 2.50
25 Shawn Kemp .60 1.50
26 Karl Malone .75 2.00
27 Chris Webber 1.00 2.50
1 Stacey Augmon .50 1.25
2 Dino Radja .50 1.25
3 Alonzo Mourning .75 2.00
4 Scottie Pippen 1.25 3.00
5 Gerald Wilkins .40 1.00
6 Jamal Mashburn .60 1.50
7 Dikembe Mutombo .60 1.50
8 Lindsey Hunter .40 1.00
9 Chris Mullin .60 1.50
10 Hakeem Olajuwon .75 2.00
11 Reggie Miller .75 2.00
12 Gary Grant .40 1.00
13 Doug Christie .40 1.00
14 Steve Smith .50 1.25
15 Vin Baker .60 1.50
16 Christian Laettner .50 1.25
17 Derrick Coleman .50 1.25
18 Charles Oakley .50 1.25
19 Dennis Scott .40 1.00
20 Clarence Weatherspoon .40 1.00
21 Charles Barkley 1.00 2.50
22 Clifford Robinson .40 1.00
23 Mitch Richmond .60 1.50
24 David Robinson 1.00 2.50
25 Shawn Kemp .60 1.50
26 Karl Malone .75 2.00
27 Don MacLean .40 1.00
1A Mark Price .60 1.50
1B Kenny Anderson .50 1.25
2A Karl Malone .75 2.00
2B Derrick Coleman .50 1.25
3A John Stockton .75 2.00
3B Anfernee Hardaway 1.00 2.50
4A Mitch Richmond .60 1.50
4B Jim Jackson .40 1.00
5A James Worthy .75 2.00
5B Jamal Mashburn .60 1.50
6A Patrick Ewing .75 2.00
6B Alonzo Mourning .75 2.00
7A Hakeem Olajuwon .75 2.00
7B Shaquille O'Neal 1.50 4.00
8A Clyde Drexler .75 2.00
8B Isaiah Rider .60 1.50
9A Scottie Pippen 1.25 3.00
9B Latrell Sprewell .75 2.00
10A Charles Barkley 1.00 2.50
10B Chris Webber 1.00 2.50
1 Kenny Anderson .50 1.25
2 Latrell Sprewell .75 2.00
3 Jamal Mashburn .60 1.50
4 Alonzo Mourning .75 2.00
5 Shaquille O'Neal 1.50 4.00
6 LaPhonso Ellis .40 1.00
7 Chris Webber 1.00 2.50
8 Isaiah Rider .60 1.50
9 Dikembe Mutombo .60 1.50
10 Anfernee Hardaway 1.00 2.50
11 Antonio Davis .40 1.00
12 Robert Horry .60 1.50
1 Mark Price .60 1.50
2 Tim Hardaway .60 1.50
3 Kevin Johnson .60 1.50
4 John Stockton .75 2.00
5 Mookie Blaylock .40 1.00
6 Reggie Miller .75 2.00
7 Jeff Hornacek .50 1.25
8 Latrell Sprewell .75 2.00
9 John Starks .50 1.25
10 Nate McMillan .40 1.00
11 Chris Mullin .60 1.50
12 Toni Kukoc .75 2.00
13 Anthony Mason .40 1.00
14 Robert Horry .60 1.50
15 Scottie Pippen 1.25 3.00
16 Charles Barkley 1.00 2.50
17 Dennis Rodman 1.25 3.00
18 Karl Malone .75 2.00
19 Chris Webber 1.00 2.50
20 Charles Oakley .50 1.25
21 Patrick Ewing .75 2.00
22 Shaquille O'Neal 1.50 4.00
23 Dikembe Mutombo .60 1.50
24 David Robinson 1.00 2.50
25 Hakeem Olajuwon .75 2.00
1 Atlanta Hawks .40 1.00
Craig Ehlo
2 Boston Celtics .40 1.00
Group
3 Charlotte Hornets .40 1.00
Group
4 Chicago Bulls .40 1.00
Group
5 Cleveland Cavaliers .40 1.00
Group
6 Dallas Mavericks .40 1.00
Jim Jackson
7 Denver Nuggets .40 1.00
Group
8 Detroit Pistons .40 1.00
Joe Dumars
9 Golden State Warriors 1.00 2.50
Chris Webber
10 Houston Rockets .75 2.00
Hakeem Olajuwon
11 Indiana Pacers .50 1.25
Rik Smits
12 Los Angeles Clippers .40 1.00
Group
13 Los Angeles Lakers .60 1.50
Nick Van Exel
14 Miami Heat .40 1.00
Group
15 Milwaukee Bucks .60 1.50
Vin Baker
16 Minnesota Timberwolves .40 1.00
Group
17 New Jersey Nets .40 1.00
Group
18 New York Knicks .40 1.00
Group
19 Orlando Magic 1.50 4.00
Shaquille O'Neal
20 Philadelphia 76ers .40 1.00
Group
21 Phoenix Suns .40 1.00
Group
22 Portland Trail Blazers .40 1.00
Group
23 Sacramento Kings .40 1.00
Olden Polynice
24 San Antonio Spurs .40 1.00
Group

ST25 Seattle Supersonics .40 1.00
Group
ST26 Utah Jazz .75 2.00
John Stockton
ST27 Washington Bullets .40 1.00
Group
TF1 Anfernee Hardaway 1.00 2.50
TF2 Latrell Sprewell .75 2.00
TF3 Grant Hill 3.00 8.00
TF4 Chris Webber 1.00 2.50
TF5 Shaquille O'Neal 1.50 4.00
TF6 Jason Kidd 3.00 8.00
TF7 Jim Jackson .40 1.00
TF8 Jamal Mashburn .60 1.50
TF9 Glenn Robinson 1.25 3.00
TF10 Alonzo Mourning .75 2.00
NNO Reggie Miller AU 15.00 40.00

1995-96 Stadium Club Members Only Parallel I

Unlike previous years, Topps decided to split up their Members Only parallel sets into separate series. Issued only in factory set form and offered for sale through their Members Only Collectors Club, this 291-card set parallels the cards offered from the mainstream 1995-96 Stadium Club first series product (including both regular issue and insert cards). The set consists of all 180 basic issue first series cards plus the following insert cards: Beam Team 1, Draft Picks (a skip-numbered set), Intercontinental (only offered elsewhere in Australian boxes), Nemeses, Power Zone 1, Warp Speed 1 and Wizards. In addition, Topps included both blue and red foil versions of all the subset cards within the 180-card basic issue (X-Pansion, Trans-Action and Extreme Corps).

COMPLETE SET (291) 120.00 300.00
1 Michael Jordan 8.00 20.00
2 Glenn Robinson .75 2.00
3 Jason Kidd 1.25 3.00
4 Clyde Drexler 1.00 2.50
5 Horace Grant .60 1.50
6 Allan Houston .60 1.50
7 Xavier McDaniel .50 1.25
8 Jeff Hornacek .60 1.50
9 Vlade Divac .75 2.00
10 Juwan Howard .75 2.00
11EB Keith Jennings EXP Blue .50 1.25
11ER Keith Jennings EXP Red .50 1.25
12 Grant Long .50 1.25
13 Jalen Rose 1.00 2.50
14 Malik Sealy .50 1.25
15 Gary Payton .75 2.00
16 Danny Ferry .50 1.25
17 Glen Rice .75 2.00
18 Randy Brown .50 1.25
19 Greg Graham .50 1.25
20 Kenny Anderson .60 1.50
21 Aaron McKie .50 1.25
22EB John Salley EXP Blue .50 1.25
22ER John Salley EXP Red .50 1.25
23 Darrin Hancock .50 1.25
24 Carlos Rogers .50 1.25
25 Vin Baker .60 1.50
26 Bill Wennington .50 1.25
27 Kenny Smith .60 1.50
28 Sherman Douglas .50 1.25
29 Terry Davis .50 1.25
30 Grant Hill 1.25 3.00
31 Reggie Miller 1.00 2.50
32 Anfernee Hardaway 1.25 3.00
33 Patrick Ewing 1.00 2.50
34 Charles Barkley 1.25 3.00
35 Eddie Jones 1.00 2.50
36 Kevin Duckworth .50 1.25
37 Tom Hammonds .50 1.25
38 Craig Ehlo .50 1.25
39 Micheal Williams .50 1.25
40 Alonzo Mourning 1.00 2.50
41 John Williams .50 1.25
42 Felton Spencer .50 1.25
43 Lamond Murray .50 1.25
44EB Dontonio Wingfield EXP Blue .50 1.25
44ER Dontonio Wingfield EXP Red .50 1.25
45 Rik Smits .60 1.50
46 Donyell Marshall .50 1.25
47 Clarence Weatherspoon .50 1.25
48 Kevin Edwards .50 1.25
49 Charlie Ward .50 1.25
50 David Robinson 1.25 3.00
51 James Robinson .50 1.25
52 Bill Cartwright .60 1.50
53 Bobby Hurley .75 2.00
54 Kevin Gamble .50 1.25
55EB B.J. Tyler EXP Blue .50 1.25
55ER B.J. Tyler EXP Red .50 1.25
56 Chris Smith .50 1.25
57 Wesley Person .50 1.25
58 Tim Breaux .50 1.25
59 Mitchell Butler .50 1.25
60 Toni Kukoc .75 2.00
61 Roy Tarpley .50 1.25
62 Todd Day .50 1.25
63 Anthony Peeler .50 1.25
64 Brian Williams .50 1.25
65 Muggsy Bogues .60 1.50
66EB Jerome Kersey EXP Blue .50 1.25
66ER Jerome Kersey EXP Red .50 1.25
67 Eric Piatkowski .60 1.50
68 Tim Perry .50 1.25
69 Chris Gatling .50 1.25
70 Mark Price .75 2.00
71 Terry Mills .50 1.25
72 Anthony Avent .50 1.25
73 Matt Geiger .50 1.25
74 Walt Williams .50 1.25
75 Sean Elliott .75 2.00
76 Ken Norman .50 1.25
77TB Kendall Gill TA Blue .50 1.25
77TR Kendall Gill TA Red .50 1.25
78 Byron Houston .50 1.25
79 Rick Fox .50 1.25
80 Derek Harper .60 1.50
81 Rod Strickland .50 1.25
82 Bryon Russell .50 1.25
83 Antonio Davis .50 1.25
84 Isaiah Rider .75 2.00
85 Kevin Johnson .75 2.00
86 Derrick Coleman .60 1.50
87 Doug Overton .50 1.25
88TB Hersey Hawkins TA Blue .50 1.25
88TR Hersey Hawkins TA Red .50 1.25
89 Popeye Jones .50 1.25
90 Dickey Simpkins .50 1.25
91TB Rodney Rogers TA Blue .50 1.25
91TR Rodney Rogers TA Red .50 1.25
92TB Rex Chapman TA Blue .50 1.25
92TR Rex Chapman TA Red .50 1.25
93TB Spud Webb TA Blue .75 2.00
93TR Spud Webb TA Red .75 2.00
94 Lee Mayberry .50 1.25
95 Cedric Ceballos .50 1.25
96 Tyrone Hill .50 1.25
97 Bill Curley .50 1.25
98 Jeff Turner .50 1.25
99TB Tyrone Corbin TA Blue .50 1.25
99TR Tyrone Corbin TA Red .50 1.25
100 John Stockton 1.00 2.50
101B Mookie Blaylock EC Blue .50 1.25
101R Mookie Blaylock EC Red .50 1.25
102B Dino Radja EC Blue .60 1.50
102R Dino Radja EC Red .60 1.50
103B Alonzo Mourning EC Blue 1.00 2.50
103R Alonzo Mourning EC Red 1.00 2.50
104B Scottie Pippen EC Blue 1.25 3.00
104R Scottie Pippen EC Red 1.25 3.00
105B Terrell Brandon EC Blue .50 1.25
105R Terrell Brandon EC Red .50 1.25
106B Jim Jackson EC Blue .50 1.25
106R Jim Jackson EC Red .50 1.25
107B Mahmoud Abdul-Rauf EC Blue .50 1.25
107R Mahmoud Abdul-Rauf EC Red .50 1.25
108B Grant Hill EC Blue 1.25 3.00
108R Grant Hill EC Red 1.25 3.00
109B Tim Hardaway EC Blue .75 2.00
109R Tim Hardaway EC Red .75 2.00
110B Hakeem Olajuwon EC Blue 1.00 2.50
110R Hakeem Olajuwon EC Red 1.00 2.50
111B Rik Smits EC Blue .60 1.50
111R Rik Smits EC Red .60 1.50
112B Loy Vaught EC Blue .50 1.25
112R Loy Vaught EC Red .50 1.25
113B Vlade Divac EC Blue .75 2.00
113R Vlade Divac EC Red .75 2.00
114B Kevin Willis EC Blue .50 1.25
114R Kevin Willis EC Red .50 1.25
115B Glenn Robinson EC Blue .75 2.00
115R Glenn Robinson EC Red .75 2.00
116B Christian Laettner EC Blue .60 1.50
116R Christian Laettner EC Red .60 1.50
117B Derrick Coleman EC Blue .60 1.50
117R Derrick Coleman EC Red .60 1.50
118B Patrick Ewing EC Blue 1.00 2.50
118R Patrick Ewing EC Red 1.00 2.50
119B Shaquille O'Neal EC Blue 2.00 5.00
119R Shaquille O'Neal EC Red 2.00 5.00
120B Dana Barros EC Blue .50 1.25
120R Dana Barros EC Red .50 1.25
121B Charles Barkley EC Blue 1.25 3.00
121R Charles Barkley EC Red 1.25 3.00
122B Rod Strickland EC Blue .50 1.25
122R Rod Strickland EC Red .50 1.25
123B Brian Grant EC Blue .60 1.50
123R Brian Grant EC Red .60 1.50
124B David Robinson EC Blue 1.25 3.00
124R David Robinson EC Red 1.25 3.00
125B Shawn Kemp EC Blue .75 2.00
125R Shawn Kemp EC Red .75 2.00
126B Oliver Miller EC Blue .50 1.25
126R Oliver Miller EC Red .50 1.25
127B Karl Malone EC Blue 1.00 2.50
127R Karl Malone EC Red 1.00 2.50
128B Benoit Benjamin EC Blue .50 1.25
128R Benoit Benjamin EC Red .50 1.25
129B Chris Webber EC Blue 1.00 2.50
129R Chris Webber EC Red 1.00 2.50
130 Dan Majerle .75 2.00
131 Calbert Cheaney .50 1.25
132 Mark Jackson .75 2.00
133EB Greg Anthony EXP Blue .50 1.25
133ER Greg Anthony EXP Red .50 1.25
134 Scott Burrell .50 1.25
135 Detlef Schrempf .75 2.00
136 Marty Conlon .50 1.25
137 Rony Seikaly .60 1.50
138 Olden Polynice .50 1.25
139 Terry Cummings .75 2.00
140 Stacey Augmon .60 1.50
141 Bryant Stith .50 1.25
142 Sean Higgins .50 1.25
143 Antoine Carr .50 1.25
144EB Blue Edwards EXP Blue .50 1.25
144ER Blue Edwards EXP Red .50 1.25
145 A.C. Green .75 2.00
146 Bobby Phills .50 1.25
147 Terry Dehere .50 1.25
148 Sharone Wright .50 1.25
149 Nick Anderson .50 1.25
150 Jim Jackson .50 1.25
151 Eric Montross .50 1.25
152 Doug West .50 1.25
153 Charles Smith .50 1.25
154 Will Perdue .50 1.25
155EB Gerald Wilkins EXP Blue .50 1.25
155ER Gerald Wilkins EXP Red .50 1.25
156 Robert Horry .60 1.50
157 Robert Parish .75 2.00
158 Lindsey Hunter .50 1.25
159 Harvey Grant .50 1.25
160 Tim Hardaway .75 2.00
161 Sarunas Marciulionis .50 1.25
162 Khalid Reeves .50 1.25
163 Bo Outlaw .50 1.25
164 Dale Davis .50 1.25
165 Nick Van Exel .75 2.00
166EB Byron Scott EXP Blue .60 1.50
166ER Byron Scott EXP Red .60 1.50
167 Steve Smith .60 1.50
168 Brian Grant .60 1.50
169 Avery Johnson .60 1.50
170 Dikembe Mutombo .75 2.00
171 Tom Gugliotta .50 1.25
172 Armon Gilliam .50 1.25
173 Shawn Bradley .50 1.25
174 Herb Williams .50 1.25
175 Dino Radja .60 1.50
176 Billy Owens .50 1.25
177EB Kenny Gattison EXP Blue .50 1.25
177ER Kenny Gattison EXP Red .50 1.25
178 J.R. Reid .50 1.25
179 Otis Thorpe .50 1.25
180 Sam Cassell .75 2.00
N1 Hakeem Olajuwon 2.50 6.00
David Robinson
N2 Patrick Ewing 2.00 5.00
Rik Smits
N3 John Stockton 2.00 5.00
Kevin Johnson
N4 Shaquille O'Neal 4.00 10.00
Alonzo Mourning
N5 Charles Barkley 2.50 6.00
Karl Malone
N6 Scottie Pippen 2.50 6.00
Grant Hill
N7 Anfernee Hardaway 2.50 6.00
Kenny Anderson
N8 Reggie Miller 2.00 5.00
John Starks
N9 Toni Kukoc 1.50 4.00
Dino Radja
N10 Michael Jordan 15.00 40.00
Joe Dumars
BT1 David Robinson 2.50 6.00
BT2 Juwan Howard 1.50 4.00
BT3 Mitch Richmond 1.50 4.00
BT4 Reggie Miller 2.00 5.00
BT5 Vin Baker 1.25 3.00
BT6 Shaquille O'Neal 4.00 10.00
BT7 Shawn Kemp 1.50 4.00
BT8 Karl Malone 2.00 5.00
BT9 Jamal Mashburn 1.50 4.00
BT10 Alonzo Mourning 2.00 5.00
DP2 Antonio McDyess 2.50 6.00
DP3 Jerry Stackhouse 3.00 8.00
DP4 Rasheed Wallace 3.00 8.00
DP5 Kevin Garnett 8.00 20.00
DP6 Bryant Reeves 1.00 2.50
DP8 Shawn Respert 1.00 2.50
DP9 Ed O'Bannon 1.00 2.50
DP11 Gary Trent 1.00 2.50
DP12 Cherokee Parks 1.00 2.50
DP15 Brent Barry 1.50 4.00
DP16 Alan Henderson 1.00 2.50
DP17 Bob Sura 1.00 2.50
DP18 Theo Ratliff 1.50 4.00
DP19 Randolph Childress 1.00 2.50
DP22 George Zidek 1.00 2.50
IC1 Hakeem Olajuwon 2.00 5.00
IC2 Dikembe Mutombo 1.50 4.00
IC3 Bill Wennington 1.00 2.50
IC4 Rick Fox 1.00 2.50
IC5 Carl Herrera 1.00 2.50
IC6 Rony Seikaly 1.25 3.00
IC7 Rik Smits 1.25 3.00
IC8 Dino Radja 1.25 3.00
IC9 Sarunas Marciulionis 1.00 2.50
IC10 Luc Longley 1.00 2.50
PZ1 Shaquille O'Neal 4.00 10.00
PZ2 Charles Barkley 2.50 6.00
PZ3 Patrick Ewing 2.00 5.00
PZ4 Karl Malone 2.00 5.00
PZ5 Larry Johnson 1.50 4.00
PZ6 Derrick Coleman 1.25 3.00
WS1 Michael Jordan 15.00 40.00
WS2 Kevin Johnson 1.50 4.00
WS3 Gary Payton 1.50 4.00
WS4 Anfernee Hardaway 2.50 6.00
WS5 Mookie Blaylock 1.00 2.50
WS6 Tim Hardaway 1.50 4.00
WZ1 Nick Van Exel 1.50 4.00
WZ2 Tim Hardaway 1.50 4.00
WZ3 Mookie Blaylock 1.00 2.50
WZ4 Gary Payton 1.50 4.00
WZ5 Jason Kidd 2.50 6.00
WZ6 Kenny Anderson 1.25 3.00
WZ7 John Stockton 2.00 5.00
WZ8 Kevin Johnson 1.50 4.00
WZ9 Muggsy Bogues 1.25 3.00
WZ10 Anfernee Hardaway 2.50 6.00

1995-96 Stadium Club Members Only Parallel II

This 233-card set parallels the cards offered from the mainstream 1995-96 Stadium Club second series product (including both regular issue and insert cards). The set consists of all 181 basic issue second series cards plus the following insert cards: Beam Team 2, Power Zone 2, Reign Men, Spike Says, Warp Speed 2 and X-2.

COMPLETE SET (233) 120.00 300.00
181 Sam Cassell .75 2.00
182 Pooh Richardson .50 1.25
183 Johnny Newman .50 1.25
184 Dennis Scott .50 1.25
185 Will Perdue .50 1.25
186 Andrew Lang .50 1.25
187 Karl Malone 1.00 2.50
188 Buck Williams .50 1.25
189 P.J. Brown .50 1.25
190 Khalid Reeves .50 1.25
191 Kevin Willis .50 1.25
192 Robert Pack .50 1.25
193 Joe Dumars .75 2.00
194 Sam Perkins .50 1.25
195 Dan Majerle .75 2.00
196 John Williams .50 1.25
197 Reggie Williams .50 1.25
198 Greg Anthony .50 1.25
199 Steve Kerr .60 1.50
200 Richard Dumas .50 1.25
201 Dee Brown .50 1.25
202 Zan Tabak .50 1.25
203 David Wood .50 1.25
204 Duane Causwell .50 1.25
205 Sedale Threatt .50 1.25
206 Hubert Davis .50 1.25
207 Donald Hodge .50 1.25
208 Duane Ferrell .50 1.25
209 Sam Mitchell .50 1.25
210 Adam Keefe .50 1.25
211 Clifford Robinson .50 1.25
212 Rodney Rogers .50 1.25
213 Jayson Williams .50 1.25
214 Brian Shaw .50 1.25
215 Luc Longley .50 1.25
216 Don MacLean .50 1.25
217 Rex Chapman .50 1.25
218 Wayman Tisdale .50 1.25
219 Shawn Kemp .75 2.00
220 Chris Webber 1.00 2.50
221 Antonio Harvey .50 1.25
222 Sarunas Marciulionis .50 1.25
223 Jeff Malone .50 1.25
224 Chucky Brown .50 1.25
225 Greg Minor .50 1.25
226 Clifford Rozier .50 1.25
227 Derrick McKey .50 1.25
228 Tony Dumas .50 1.25
229 Oliver Miller .50 1.25
230 Charles Oakley .60 1.50
231 Fred Roberts .50 1.25
232 Glen Rice .75 2.00
233 Terry Porter .50 1.25
234 Mark Macon .50 1.25
235 Michael Cage .50 1.25
236 Eric Murdock .50 1.25
237 Vinny Del Negro .50 1.25
238 Spud Webb .75 2.00
239 Mario Elie .50 1.25
240 Blue Edwards .50 1.25
241 Dontonio Wingfield .50 1.25
242 Brooks Thompson .50 1.25
243 Alonzo Mourning 1.00 2.50
244 Dennis Rodman 1.50 4.00
245 Lorenzo Williams .50 1.25
246 Haywoode Workman .50 1.25
247 Loy Vaught .50 1.25
248 Vernon Maxwell .50 1.25
249 Lionel Simmons .50 1.25
250 Chris Childs .50 1.25
251 Mahmoud Abdul-Rauf .50 1.25
252 Vincent Askew .50 1.25
253 Chris Morris .50 1.25
254 Elliot Perry .50 1.25
255 Dell Curry .50 1.25
256 Dana Barros .50 1.25
257 Terrell Brandon .50 1.25
258 Monty Williams .50 1.25
259 Corie Blount .50 1.25
260 B.J. Armstrong .50 1.25
261 Jim McIlvaine .50 1.25
262 Otis Thorpe .50 1.25
263 Sean Rooks .50 1.25
264 Tony Massenburg .50 1.25
265 Steve Smith .60 1.50
266 Ron Harper .60 1.50
267 Dale Ellis .50 1.25
268 Clyde Drexler 1.00 2.50
269 Jamie Watson .50 1.25
270 Doc Rivers .60 1.50
271 Derrick Alston .50 1.25
272 Eric Mobley .50 1.25
273 Ricky Pierce .50 1.25
274 David Wesley .50 1.25
275 John Starks .60 1.50
276 Chris Mullin .75 2.00
277 Ervin Johnson .50 1.25
278 Jamal Mashburn .75 2.00
279 Joe Kleine .50 1.25
280 Mitch Richmond .75 2.00
281 Chris Mills .50 1.25
282 Bimbo Coles .50 1.25
283 Larry Johnson .75 2.00
284 Stanley Roberts .50 1.25
285 Rex Walters .50 1.25
286 Donald Royal .50 1.25
287 Benoit Benjamin .50 1.25
288 Chris Dudley .50 1.25
289 Elden Campbell .50 1.25
290 Mookie Blaylock .50 1.25
291 Hersey Hawkins .50 1.25
292 Anthony Mason .50 1.25
293 Latrell Sprewell .75 2.00
294 Harold Miner .50 1.25
295 Scott Williams .50 1.25
296 David Benoit .50 1.25
297 Christian Laettner .60 1.50
298 LaPhonso Ellis .50 1.25
299 Gheorghe Muresan .50 1.25
300 Kendall Gill .50 1.25
301 Eddie Johnson .50 1.25
302 Terry Cummings .75 2.00
303 Chuck Person .60 1.50
304 Michael Smith .50 1.25
305 Mark West .50 1.25
306 Willie Anderson .50 1.25
307 Pervis Ellison .50 1.25
308 Brian Williams .50 1.25
309 Danny Manning .60 1.50
310 Hakeem Olajuwon 1.00 2.50
311 Scottie Pippen 1.25 3.00
312 Jon Koncak .50 1.25
313 Sasha Danilovic .75 2.00
314 Lucious Harris .50 1.25
315 Yinka Dare .50 1.25
316 Eric Williams .75 2.00
317 Gary Trent .75 2.00
318 Theo Ratliff 1.25 3.00
319 Lawrence Moten .75 2.00
320 Jerome Allen .75 2.00
321 Tyus Edney .75 2.00
322 Loren Meyer .75 2.00
323 Michael Finley 2.50 6.00
324 Alan Henderson .75 2.00
325 Bob Sura .75 2.00
326 Joe Smith 1.50 4.00
327 Damon Stoudamire 2.00 5.00
328 Sherrell Ford .75 2.00
329 Jerry Stackhouse 2.50 6.00
330 George Zidek .75 2.00
331 Brent Barry 1.25 3.00
332 Shawn Respert .75 2.00
333 Rasheed Wallace 2.50 6.00
334 Antonio McDyess 2.00 5.00
335 David Vaughn .75 2.00
336 Cory Alexander .75 2.00
337 Jason Caffey .75 2.00
338 Frankie King .75 2.00
339 Travis Best .75 2.00
340 Greg Ostertag .75 2.00
341 Ed O'Bannon .75 2.00
342 Kurt Thomas .75 2.00
343 Kevin Garnett 12.50 30.00
344 Bryant Reeves .75 2.00
345 Corliss Williamson .75 2.00
346 Cherokee Parks .75 2.00
347 Junior Burrough .75 2.00
348 Randolph Childress .75 2.00
349 Lou Roe .75 2.00
350 Mario Bennett .75 2.00
351 Dikembe Mutombo .75 2.00
352 Larry Johnson .75 2.00
353 Vlade Divac .75 2.00
354 Karl Malone 1.00 2.50
355 John Stockton 1.00 2.50
356 Alonzo Mourning 1.00 2.50
357 Glen Rice .75 2.00
358 Dan Majerle .75 2.00
359 John Williams .50 1.25
360 Mark Price .75 2.00
361 Magic Johnson 2.00 5.00
B11 Charles Barkley 2.50 6.00
B12 Hakeem Olajuwon 2.00 5.00
B13 Kenny Anderson 1.25 3.00
B14 Michael Jordan 15.00 40.00
B15 Dikembe Mutombo 1.50 4.00
B16 Rod Strickland 1.00 2.50
B17 Patrick Ewing 2.00 5.00
B18 Latrell Sprewell 1.50 4.00
B19 Grant Hill 2.50 6.00
B20 Cedric Ceballos 1.00 2.50
X1 Hakeem Olajuwon 2.00 5.00
X2 Shaquille O'Neal 4.00 10.00
X3 David Robinson 2.50 6.00
X4 Patrick Ewing 2.00 5.00
X5 Charles Barkley 2.50 6.00
X6 Karl Malone 2.00 5.00
X7 Derrick Coleman 1.25 3.00
X8 Shawn Kemp 1.50 4.00
X9 Vin Baker 1.25 3.00
X10 Vlade Divac 1.50 4.00
PZ7 Hakeem Olajuwon 2.00 5.00
PZ8 David Robinson 2.50 6.00
PZ9 Shawn Kemp 1.50 4.00
PZ10 Dennis Rodman 3.00 8.00
PZ11 Alonzo Mourning 2.00 5.00
PZ12 Vin Baker 1.25 3.00
RM1 Shawn Kemp 1.50 4.00
RM2 Michael Jordan 15.00 40.00
RM3 Larry Johnson 1.50 4.00
RM4 Grant Hill 2.50 6.00
RM5 Isaiah Rider 1.50 4.00
RM6 Sean Elliott 1.50 4.00
RM7 Scottie Pippen 2.50 6.00
RM8 Robert Horry 1.25 3.00
RM9 Kendall Gill 1.00 2.50
RM10 Jerry Stackhouse 5.00 12.00
SS1 Michael Jordan 15.00 40.00
SS2 Alonzo Mourning 2.00 5.00
SS3 Reggie Miller 2.00 5.00
SS4 Patrick Ewing 2.00 5.00
SS5 Charles Barkley 2.50 6.00
SS6 Kenny Anderson 1.25 3.00
SS7 Scottie Pippen 2.50 6.00
SS8 Jerry Stackhouse 5.00 12.00
SS9 Shaquille O'Neal 4.00 10.00
SS10 John Starks 1.25 3.00
WS7 Scottie Pippen 2.50 6.00
WS8 Jason Kidd 2.50 6.00
WS9 Grant Hill 2.50 6.00
WS10 Nick Van Exel 1.50 4.00
WS11 Kenny Anderson 1.25 3.00
WS12 Latrell Sprewell 1.50 4.00

1996-97 Stadium Club Members Only Parallel I

This 173-card set parallels the cards offered from the mainstream 1996-97 Stadium Club first series product (including both regular issue and insert cards). The set consists of all 90 basic issue first series cards plus the following insert cards: Fusion 1, Golden Moments, Rookies 1, Shining Moments, Special Forces and Top Crop. Cards feature the Members Only logo running diagonally in the background.

COMPLETE SET (173) 150.00 400.00
1 Scottie Pippen 1.50 4.00
2 Dale Davis .60 1.50
3 Horace Grant .75 2.00
4 Gheorghe Muresan .60 1.50
5 Elliot Perry .60 1.50
6 Carlos Rogers .60 1.50
7 Glenn Robinson 1.00 2.50
8 Avery Johnson .75 2.00
9 Dee Brown .60 1.50
10 Grant Hill 1.50 4.00
11 Tyus Edney .60 1.50
12 Patrick Ewing 1.25 3.00
13 Jason Kidd 1.50 4.00
14 Clifford Robinson .60 1.50
15 Robert Horry .75 2.00
16 Dell Curry .60 1.50
17 Terry Porter .60 1.50
18 Shaquille O'Neal 2.50 6.00
19 Bryant Stith .60 1.50
20 Shawn Kemp 1.00 2.50
21 Kurt Thomas .60 1.50
22 Pooh Richardson .60 1.50
23 Bob Sura .60 1.50
24 Olden Polynice .60 1.50
25 Lawrence Moten .60 1.50
26 Kendall Gill .60 1.50
27 Cedric Ceballos .60 1.50
28 Latrell Sprewell 1.00 2.50
29 Christian Laettner .75 2.00
30 Jamal Mashburn .75 2.00
31 Jerry Stackhouse 1.25 3.00
32 John Stockton 1.25 3.00
33 Arvydas Sabonis .75 2.00
34 Detlef Schrempf 1.00 2.50
35 Toni Kukoc 1.00 2.50
36 Sasha Danilovic .60 1.50
37 Dana Barros .60 1.50
38 Loy Vaught .60 1.50
39 John Starks .75 2.00
40 Marty Conlon .60 1.50
41 Antonio McDyess 1.00 2.50
42 Michael Finley 1.25 3.00
43 Tom Gugliotta .60 1.50
44 Terrell Brandon .60 1.50
45 Derrick McKey .60 1.50
46 Damon Stoudamire 1.00 2.50
47 Elden Campbell .60 1.50
48 Luc Longley .60 1.50
49 B.J. Armstrong .60 1.50
50 Lindsey Hunter .60 1.50
51 Glen Rice 1.00 2.50
52 Shawn Respert .60 1.50
53 Cory Alexander .60 1.50
54 Tim Legler .60 1.50
55 Bryant Reeves .60 1.50
56 Anfernee Hardaway 1.50 4.00
57 Charles Barkley 1.50 4.00
58 Mookie Blaylock .60 1.50
59 Kevin Garnett 2.50 6.00
60 Hersey Hawkins .60 1.50
61 Ed O'Bannon .60 1.50
62 George Zidek .60 1.50
63 Mitch Richmond 1.00 2.50
64 Derrick Coleman .75 2.00
65 Chris Webber 1.25 3.00
66 Bobby Phills .60 1.50
67 Rik Smits .75 2.00
68 Jeff Hornacek .75 2.00
69 Sam Cassell .75 2.00
70 Gary Trent .60 1.50
71 LaPhonso Ellis .60 1.50
72 Oliver Miller .60 1.50
73 Rex Chapman .60 1.50
74 Jim Jackson .60 1.50
75 Eric Williams .60 1.50
76 Brent Barry .75 2.00
77 Nick Anderson .60 1.50
78 David Robinson 1.50 4.00
79 Calbert Cheaney .60 1.50
80 Joe Smith .75 2.00
81 Steve Kerr .75 2.00
82 Wayman Tisdale .60 1.50
83 Steve Smith .75 2.00
84 Clyde Drexler 1.25 3.00
85 Theo Ratliff .60 1.50
86 Charlie Ward .60 1.50
87 Karl Malone 1.25 3.00
88 Clarence Weatherspoon .60 1.50
89 Greg Anthony .60 1.50
90 Shawn Bradley .60 1.50
F1 Michael Jordan 15.00 40.00
F2 Chris Webber 2.00 5.00
F3 Glenn Robinson 1.50 4.00
F4 Glen Rice 1.50 4.00
F5 Gary Payton 1.50 4.00
F6 Rik Smits 1.25 3.00
F7 Grant Hill 2.50 6.00
F8 Horace Grant 1.25 3.00
F9 Scottie Pippen 2.50 6.00
F10 Gheorghe Muresan 1.00 2.50
F11 Vin Baker 1.25 3.00
F12 Dell Curry 1.00 2.50
F13 Shawn Kemp 1.50 4.00
F14 Reggie Miller 2.00 5.00
F15 Joe Dumars 1.50 4.00
F16 Anfernee Hardaway 2.50 6.00
R1 Allen Iverson 20.00 50.00
R2 Marcus Camby 6.00 15.00
R3 Shareef Abdur-Rahim 8.00 20.00
R4 Stephon Marbury 10.00 25.00
R5 Ray Allen 15.00 40.00
R6 Antoine Walker 8.00 20.00
R7 Lorenzen Wright 4.00 10.00
R8 Kerry Kittles 4.00 10.00
R9 Samaki Walker 4.00 10.00
R10 Erick Dampier 4.00 10.00
R11 Todd Fuller 4.00 10.00
R12 Kobe Bryant 60.00 150.00
R13 Steve Nash 20.00 50.00
R14 Tony Delk 4.00 10.00
R15 Jermaine O'Neal 10.00 25.00
R16 John Wallace 4.00 10.00
R17 Walter McCarty 4.00 10.00
R18 Dontae' Jones 4.00 10.00
R19 Roy Rogers 4.00 10.00
R20 Derek Fisher 8.00 20.00
R21 Martin Muursepp 4.00 10.00
R22 Jerome Williams 4.00 10.00
R23 Brian Evans 4.00 10.00
R24 Priest Lauderdale 4.00 10.00
R25 Travis Knight 4.00 10.00
GM1 Robert Parish 1.00 2.50
GM2 John Stockton 1.25 3.00
GM3 Michael Jordan 8.00 20.00
Toni Kukoc
Dennis Rodman
GM4 Dennis Scott .60 1.50
GM5 Hakeem Olajuwon 1.25 3.00
SF1 Anfernee Hardaway 2.50 6.00
SF2 Grant Hill 2.50 6.00
SF3 Shawn Kemp 1.50 4.00
SF4 Michael Jordan 15.00 40.00
SF5 Shaquille O'Neal 4.00 10.00
SF6 Scottie Pippen 2.50 6.00
SF7 Damon Stoudamire 1.50 4.00
SF8 Jerry Stackhouse 2.00 5.00
SF9 Gary Payton 1.50 4.00
SF10 Dennis Rodman 3.00 8.00
SM1 Charles Barkley 1.50 4.00
SM2 Michael Jordan 8.00 20.00
SM3 Karl Malone 1.25 3.00
SM4 Hakeem Olajuwon 1.25 3.00
SM5 John Stockton 1.25 3.00
SM6 Patrick Ewing 1.25 3.00
SM7 Reggie Miller 1.25 3.00
SM8 David Robinson 1.50 4.00
SM9 Dennis Rodman 2.00 5.00
SM10 Damon Stoudamire 1.00 2.50
SM11 Brent Barry .75 2.00
SM12 Tim Legler .60 1.50
SM13 Jason Kidd 1.50 4.00
SM14 Terrell Brandon .60 1.50
SM15 Allen Iverson 5.00 12.00
TC1 Hakeem Olajuwon 4.00 10.00
Shaquille O'Neal
TC2 Dikembe Mutombo 2.00 5.00
Alonzo Mourning
TC3 David Robinson 2.50 6.00
Patrick Ewing
TC4 Sean Elliott 2.50 6.00
Grant Hill
TC5 Shawn Kemp 2.50 6.00
Scottie Pippen
TC6 Karl Malone 2.00 5.00
Vin Baker
TC7 Charles Barkley 2.50 6.00
Juwan Howard
TC8 Clyde Drexler 2.00 5.00
Glen Rice
TC9 Gary Payton 15.00 40.00
Michael Jordan
TC10 John Stockton 2.00 5.00
Terrell Brandon
TC11 Mitch Richmond 2.00 5.00
Reggie Miller
TC12 Jason Kidd 2.50 6.00
Anfernee Hardaway

1996-97 Stadium Club Members Only Parallel II

This 210-card set parallels the cards offered from the mainstream 1996-97 Stadium Club second series product (including both regular issue and insert cards). The set consists of all 90 basic issue second series cards plus the following insert cards: Class Acts, Fusion 2, High Risers, Mega Heroes, Rookie Showcase, Rookies 2 and Welcome Additions. Cards feature the Members Only logo running diagonally in the background.

COMPLETE SET (210) 200.00 500.00
91 Otis Thorpe .60 1.50
92 Larry Johnson 1.00 2.50
93 Sharone Wright .60 1.50
94 Charles Barkley 1.50 4.00
95 Wesley Person .60 1.50
96 Dikembe Mutombo 1.00 2.50
97 Eddie Jones 1.00 2.50
98 Juwan Howard .75 2.00
99 Grant Hill 1.50 4.00
100 Chris Carr 1.00 2.50
101 Michael Jordan 8.00 20.00
102 Vincent Askew .60 1.50
103 Gary Payton 1.00 2.50
104 Chris Mills .60 1.50
105 Reggie Miller 1.25 3.00
106 Don MacLean .60 1.50
107 John Stockton 1.25 3.00
108 Mahmoud Abdul-Rauf .60 1.50
109 P.J. Brown .60 1.50
110 Kenny Anderson .75 2.00
111 Mark Price 1.00 2.50
112 Derek Harper .75 2.00
113 Dino Radja .75 2.00
114 Terry Dehere .60 1.50
115 Mark Jackson 1.00 2.50
116 Vin Baker .75 2.00
117 Dennis Scott .60 1.50
118 Sean Elliott 1.00 2.50
119 Lee Mayberry .60 1.50
120 Vlade Divac 1.00 2.50
121 Joe Dumars 1.00 2.50
122 Isaiah Rider .75 2.00
123 Hakeem Olajuwon 1.25 3.00
124 Robert Pack .60 1.50

125 Jalen Rose .75 2.00
126 Allan Houston .75 2.00
127 Nate McMillan .60 1.50
128 Rod Strickland .60 1.50
129 Sean Rooks .60 1.50
130 Dennis Rodman 2.00 5.00
131 Alonzo Mourning 1.25 3.00
132 Danny Ferry .60 1.50
133 Sam Cassell .75 2.00
134 Brian Grant .75 2.00
135 Karl Malone 1.25 3.00
136 Chris Gatling .60 1.50
137 Tom Gugliotta .60 1.50
138 Hubert Davis .60 1.50
139 Lucious Harris .60 1.50
140 Rony Seikaly .75 2.00
141 Alan Henderson .60 1.50
142 Mario Elie .60 1.50
143 Vinny Del Negro .60 1.50
144 Harvey Grant .60 1.50
145 Muggsy Bogues .75 2.00
146 Rodney Rogers .60 1.50
147 Kevin Johnson 1.00 2.50
148 Anthony Peeler .60 1.50
149 Jon Koncak .60 1.50
150 Ricky Pierce .60 1.50
151 Todd Day .60 1.50
152 Tyrone Hill .60 1.50
153 Nick Van Exel 1.00 2.50
154 Rasheed Wallace 1.25 3.00
155 Jayson Williams .60 1.50
156 Sherman Douglas .60 1.50
157 Bryon Russell .60 1.50
158 Ron Harper .75 2.00
159 Stacey Augmon .75 2.00
160 Antonio Davis .60 1.50
161 Tim Hardaway 1.00 2.50
162 Charles Oakley .75 2.00
163 Billy Owens .60 1.50
164 Sam Perkins .60 1.50
165 Chris Whitney .60 1.50
166 Matt Geiger .60 1.50
167 Andrew Lang .60 1.50
168 Danny Manning .75 2.00
169 Doug Christie .60 1.50
170 George Lynch .60 1.50
171 Malik Sealy .60 1.50
172 Eric Montross .60 1.50
173 Rick Fox .60 1.50
174 Chris Mullin 1.00 2.50
175 Ken Norman .60 1.50
176 Sarunas Marciulionis .60 1.50
177 Kevin Garnett 2.50 6.00
178 Brian Shaw .60 1.50
179 Will Perdue .60 1.50
180 Scott Williams .60 1.50
F17 Charles Barkley 2.50 6.00
F18 Juwan Howard 1.25 3.00
F19 Patrick Ewing 2.00 5.00
F20 John Stockton 2.00 5.00
F21 David Robinson 2.50 6.00
F22 Cedric Ceballos 1.00 2.50
F23 Alonzo Mourning 2.00 5.00
F24 Mookie Blaylock 1.00 2.50
F25 Clyde Drexler 2.00 5.00
F26 Rod Strickland 1.00 2.50
F27 Larry Johnson 1.50 4.00
F28 Karl Malone 2.00 5.00
F29 Sean Elliott 1.50 4.00
F30 Shaquille O'Neal 4.00 10.00
F31 Tim Hardaway 1.50 4.00
F32 Dikembe Mutombo 1.50 4.00
R1 Shareef Abdur-Rahim 8.00 20.00
R2 Tony Delk 4.00 10.00
R3 Priest Lauderdale 4.00 10.00
R4 Roy Rogers 4.00 10.00
R5 Lorenzen Wright 4.00 10.00
R6 Stephon Marbury 10.00 25.00
R7 Derek Fisher 8.00 20.00
R8 John Wallace 4.00 10.00
R9 Kobe Bryant 60.00 150.00
R10 Kerry Kittles 4.00 10.00
R11 Antoine Walker 8.00 20.00
R12 Steve Nash 20.00 50.00
R13 Erick Dampier 4.00 10.00
R14 Walter McCarty 4.00 10.00
R15 Vitaly Potapenko 4.00 10.00
R16 Allen Iverson 20.00 50.00
R17 Marcus Camby 6.00 15.00
R18 Todd Fuller 4.00 10.00
R19 Ray Allen 15.00 40.00
R20 Jermaine O'Neal 10.00 25.00
CA1 Michael Jordan 15.00 40.00
Jerry Stackhouse
CA2 Patrick Ewing 2.00 5.00
Alonzo Mourning
CA3 Brent Barry 1.50 4.00
Gary Payton
CA4 Chris Webber 2.00 5.00
Juwan Howard
CA5 Christian Laettner 2.50 6.00
Grant Hill
CA6 Jason Kidd 3.00 8.00
Shareef Abdur-Rahim
CA7 Clyde Drexler 2.00 5.00
Hakeem Olajuwon
CA8 Kenny Anderson 4.00 10.00
Stephon Marbury
CA9 Anfernee Hardaway 2.50 6.00
Lorenzen Wright
CA10 Dikembe Mutombo 8.00 20.00
Allen Iverson
HR1 Scottie Pippen 2.50 6.00
HR2 Anfernee Hardaway 2.50 6.00
HR3 Vin Baker 1.25 3.00
HR4 Brent Barry 1.25 3.00
HR5 Clyde Drexler 2.00 5.00
HR6 Kevin Garnett 4.00 10.00
HR7 Grant Hill 2.50 6.00
HR8 Michael Finley 2.00 5.00
HR9 Jerry Stackhouse 2.00 5.00
HR10 Isaiah Rider 1.25 3.00
HR11 Shaquille O'Neal 4.00 10.00
HR12 Antonio McDyess 1.50 4.00
HR13 Shawn Kemp 1.50 4.00
HR14 Michael Jordan 15.00 40.00
HR15 Juwan Howard 1.25 3.00
MH1 Dennis Rodman 3.00 8.00
MH2 David Robinson 2.50 6.00
MH3 Karl Malone 2.00 5.00
MH4 Clyde Drexler 2.00 5.00
MH5 Anfernee Hardaway 2.50 6.00
MH6 Hakeem Olajuwon 2.00 5.00
MH7 Charles Oakley 1.25 3.00
MH8 Joe Smith 1.25 3.00
MH9 Glenn Robinson 1.50 4.00
RS1 Marcus Camby 2.50 6.00
RS2 Shareef Abdur-Rahim 3.00 8.00
RS3 Stephon Marbury 4.00 10.00
RS4 Ray Allen 6.00 15.00
RS5 Antoine Walker 3.00 8.00
RS6 Lorenzen Wright 1.50 4.00
RS7 Kerry Kittles 1.50 4.00
RS8 Samaki Walker 1.50 4.00
RS9 Erick Dampier 1.50 4.00
RS10 Todd Fuller 1.50 4.00
RS11 Kobe Bryant 60.00 150.00
RS12 Steve Nash 8.00 20.00
RS13 Tony Delk 1.50 4.00
RS14 Jermaine O'Neal 4.00 10.00
RS15 John Wallace 1.50 4.00
RS16 Walter McCarty 1.50 4.00
RS17 Dontae' Jones 1.50 4.00
RS18 Roy Rogers 1.50 4.00
RS19 Derek Fisher 3.00 8.00
RS20 Martin Muursepp 1.50 4.00
RS21 Jerome Williams 1.50 4.00
RS22 Brian Evans 1.50 4.00
RS23 Priest Lauderdale 1.50 4.00
RS24 Travis Knight 1.50 4.00
RS25 Allen Iverson 8.00 20.00
WA1 Charles Barkley 1.50 4.00
WA2 Armon Gilliam .60 1.50
WA3 Larry Johnson 1.00 2.50
WA4 Felton Spencer .60 1.50
WA5 Isaiah Rider .75 2.00
WA6 Kevin Willis .60 1.50
WA7 Mahmoud Abdul-Rauf .60 1.50
WA8 Chris Childs .60 1.50
WA9 Robert Horry .75 2.00
WA10 Dan Majerle 1.00 2.50
WA11 Robert Pack .60 1.50
WA12 Rod Strickland .60 1.50
WA13 Tyrone Corbin .60 1.50
WA14 Anthony Mason .60 1.50
WA15 Derek Harper .75 2.00
WA16 Kenny Anderson .75 2.00
WA17 Hubert Davis .60 1.50
WA18 Allan Houston .75 2.00
WA19 Shaquille O'Neal 2.50 6.00
WA20 Brent Price .60 1.50
WA21 Ervin Johnson .60 1.50
WA22 Craig Ehlo .60 1.50
WA23 Jalen Rose .75 2.00
WA24 Oliver Miller .60 1.50
WA25 Mark West .60 1.50

1997-98 Stadium Club Members Only Parallel I

The series one version of the Members Only set contained 201 cards which included a parallel of the basic set and the following inserts: Bowman's Best Previews, Hardcourt Heroics, Hardwood Hopefuls, Hoop Screams and Triumvirate. All cards feature "Members Only" strips running diagonally along the card back except for Bowman's Best Previews, which have no distinguishing logos and Triumvirate which has the "Members Only" strip running diagonally on the card front.

COMPLETE SET (184) 200.00 400.00
1 Scottie Pippen 2.00 5.00
3 Muggsy Bogues 1.00 2.50
5 Bulls - Team of the 90's 12.00 30.00
Ron Harper
Michael Jordan
Scottie Pippen
Dennis Rodman
7 Samaki Walker .75 2.00
9 Ray Allen 1.50 4.00
11 Chris Mullin 1.25 3.00
13 Horace Grant 1.00 2.50
15 Wayman Tisdale .75 2.00
17 Rod Strickland .75 2.00
19 Greg Anthony .75 2.00
21 Glen Rice 1.25 3.00
23 Mahmoud Abdul-Rauf .75 2.00
25 Cory Alexander .75 2.00
27 Sam Perkins .75 2.00
29 Doug Christie .75 2.00
31 Christian Laettner 1.00 2.50
33 Eric Williams .75 2.00
35 Brooks Thompson .75 2.00
37 Theo Ratliff 1.00 2.50
39 Hakeem Olajuwon 1.50 4.00
41 Reggie Miller 1.50 4.00
43 Shaquille O'Neal 3.00 8.00
45 Jamal Mashburn 1.00 2.50
47 Tom Gugliotta .75 2.00
49 Lorenzen Wright .75 2.00
51 Armon Gilliam .75 2.00
53 Kerry Kittles .75 2.00
55 Bo Outlaw .75 2.00
57 Greg Ostertag .75 2.00
59 Mark Davis .75 2.00
61 Clifford Robinson .75 2.00
63 Steve Kerr 1.00 2.50
65 Danny Ferry .75 2.00
67 A.C. Green 1.25 3.00
69 Terry Mills .75 2.00
71 Matt Maloney .75 2.00
73 Brent Barry 1.00 2.50
75 Stephon Marbury 1.50 4.00
77 Shareef Abdur-Rahim 1.25 3.00
79 Rony Seikaly 1.00 2.50
81 Wesley Person .75 2.00
83 Gary Trent .75 2.00
85 Rex Walters .75 2.00
87 Patrick Ewing 1.50 4.00
89 Travis Best .75 2.00
91 Vitaly Potapenko .75 2.00
93 Michael Finley 1.25 3.00
95 Antoine Walker 1.25 3.00
97 Mookie Blaylock .75 2.00
99 Tony Delk .75 2.00
101 Terrell Brandon .75 2.00
103 Latrell Sprewell 1.25 3.00
105 Tim Hardaway 1.25 3.00
107 Darrell Armstrong .75 2.00
109 Vinny Del Negro .75 2.00
111 Lawrence Moten .75 2.00
113 Juwan Howard 1.00 2.50
115 Karl Malone 1.50 4.00
117 Shawn Respert .75 2.00
119 Shawn Kemp 1.25 3.00
121 Tyus Edney .75 2.00
123 Jason Kidd 2.00 5.00
125 Allen Iverson 2.50 6.00
127 Larry Johnson 1.25 3.00
129 Kendall Gill .75 2.00
131 Vin Baker 1.00 2.50
133 Calbert Cheaney .75 2.00
135 Isaac Austin .75 2.00
137 Elden Campbell .75 2.00
139 Malik Sealy .75 2.00
141 Clyde Drexler 1.50 4.00
143 Mark Price 1.25 3.00
145 Grant Hill 2.00 5.00
147 Dale Ellis .75 2.00
149 Toni Kukoc 1.25 3.00
151 Alan Henderson .75 2.00
153 Greg Minor .75 2.00
155 Vlade Divac 1.25 3.00
157 LaPhonso Ellis .75 2.00
159 Antonio Davis .75 2.00
161 Robert Horry 1.00 2.50
163 Chris Carr .75 2.00
165 Sam Cassell 1.00 2.50
167 Chris Childs .75 2.00
169 Kenny Anderson 1.00 2.50
171 Olden Polynice .75 2.00
173 David Robinson 2.00 5.00
175 Detlef Schrempf 1.25 3.00
177 Marcus Camby 1.25 3.00
179 Shandon Anderson .75 2.00
181 Eldridge Recasner .75 2.00
183 Kevin Willis .75 2.00
185 Derek Fisher 1.25 3.00
187 Sherman Douglas .75 2.00
189 Danny Manning 1.00 2.50
191 Hersey Hawkins .75 2.00
193 Jeff Hornacek 1.00 2.50
195 Harvey Grant .75 2.00
197 Luc Longley .75 2.00
199 P.J. Brown .75 2.00
201 Tim Duncan 8.00 20.00
203 Keith Van Horn 2.50 6.00
205 Chauncey Billups 5.00 12.00
207 Antonio Daniels 1.25 3.00
209 Tony Battie 1.50 4.00
211 Bobby Jackson 1.50 4.00
213 Tim Thomas 2.50 6.00
215 Adonal Foyle 1.25 3.00
217 Tracy McGrady 6.00 15.00
219 Danny Fortson 1.25 3.00
221 Olivier Saint-Jean 1.25 3.00
223 Austin Croshere 1.25 3.00
225 Derek Anderson 1.25 3.00
227 Maurice Taylor 1.25 3.00
229 John Thomas 1.25 3.00
231 Brevin Knight 1.25 3.00
233 Johnny Taylor 1.25 3.00
235 Ed Gray 1.25 3.00
237 Anthony Parker 1.25 3.00
239 Paul Grant 1.25 3.00
H1 Michael Jordan 15.00 40.00
H2 Gary Payton 1.50 4.00
H3 Charles Barkley 2.50 6.00
H4 Mitch Richmond 1.50 4.00
H5 Shawn Kemp 1.50 4.00
H6 Anfernee Hardaway 2.50 6.00
H7 Vin Baker 1.25 3.00
H8 Shaquille O'Neal 4.00 10.00
H9 Scottie Pippen 2.50 6.00
H10 Grant Hill 2.50 6.00
T1A Scottie Pippen 2.50 6.00
T1B Michael Jordan 15.00 40.00
T1C Dennis Rodman 3.00 8.00
T2A Ray Allen 2.00 5.00
T2B Vin Baker 1.25 3.00
T2C Glenn Robinson 1.25 3.00
T3A Juwan Howard 1.25 3.00
T3B Chris Webber 1.50 4.00
T3C Rod Strickland 1.00 2.50
T4A Christian Laettner 1.25 3.00
T4B Dikembe Mutombo 1.50 4.00
T4C Steve Smith 1.25 3.00
T5A Tom Gugliotta 1.00 2.50
T5B Kevin Garnett 3.00 8.00
T5C Stephon Marbury 2.00 5.00
T6A Charles Barkley 2.50 6.00
T6B Hakeem Olajuwon 2.00 5.00
T6C Clyde Drexler 2.00 5.00
T7A John Stockton 2.00 5.00
T7B Karl Malone 2.00 5.00
T7C Bryon Russell 1.00 2.50
T8A Larry Johnson 1.50 4.00
T8B Patrick Ewing 2.00 5.00
T8C Allan Houston 1.25 3.00
HH1 Brevin Knight .75 2.00
HH2 Adonal Foyle .75 2.00
HH3 Keith Van Horn 1.50 4.00
HH4 Tim Duncan 5.00 12.00
HH5 Danny Fortson .75 2.00
HH6 Tracy McGrady 4.00 10.00
HH7 Tony Battie 1.00 2.50
HH8 Chauncey Billups 3.00 8.00
HH9 Austin Croshere .75 2.00
HH10 Antonio Daniels .75 2.00
HS1 Shaquille O'Neal 4.00 10.00
HS2 Cedric Ceballos 1.00 2.50
HS3 Kevin Garnett 3.00 8.00
HS4 Shawn Kemp 1.50 4.00
HS5 Jerry Stackhouse 1.50 4.00
HS6 Grant Hill 2.50 6.00
HS7 Patrick Ewing 2.00 5.00
HS8 Marcus Camby 1.50 4.00
HS9 Kobe Bryant 8.00 20.00
HS10 Michael Jordan 15.00 40.00
BBP1 Allen Iverson 3.00 8.00
BBP2 Gary Payton 1.50 4.00
BBP3 Grant Hill 2.50 6.00
BBP4 Anfernee Hardaway 2.50 6.00
BBP5 Karl Malone 2.00 5.00
BBP6 Glen Rice 1.50 4.00
BBP7 Antoine Walker 1.50 4.00
BBP8 Alonzo Mourning 2.00 5.00
BBP9 Shareef Abdur-Rahim 1.50 4.00
BBP10 Shaquille O'Neal 4.00 10.00

1997-98 Stadium Club Members Only Parallel II

The series two version of the Members Only set contained cards which included a parallel of the basic set and the following inserts: Bowman's Best Previews, Never Comprimise, Royal Court and Triumvirate. All cards feature "Members Only" strips running diagonally along the card back.

COMPLETE SET (194) 200.00 400.00
2 Bryon Russell .75 2.00
4 Gary Payton 1.25 3.00
6 Corliss Williamson .75 2.00
8 Allan Houston 1.00 2.50
10 Nick Van Exel 1.00 2.50
12 Popeye Jones .75 2.00
14 Rik Smits 1.00 2.50
16 Donny Marshall .75 2.00
18 Rod Strickland .75 2.00
20 Lindsey Hunter .75 2.00
22 Anthony Goldwire .75 2.00
24 Tyrone Corbin .75 2.00
26 Sean Elliott 1.25 3.00
28 Brian Shaw .75 2.00
30 Mark Jackson 1.25 3.00
32 Damon Stoudamire 1.25 3.00
34 Glenn Robinson 1.00 2.50
36 Derrick Coleman 1.00 2.50
38 Ron Harper 1.00 2.50
40 Mitch Richmond 1.25 3.00
42 Reggie Miller 1.50 4.00
44 Zydrunas Ilgauskas 1.25 3.00
46 Isaiah Rider .75 2.00
48 Rex Chapman .75 2.00
50 Pooh Richardson .75 2.00
52 Kevin Johnson 1.25 3.00
54 Kerry Kittles .75 2.00
56 Dennis Rodman 2.50 6.00
58 Todd Fuller .75 2.00
60 Erick Strickland 1.25 3.00
62 Nate McMillan .75 2.00
64 Bob Sura .75 2.00
66 Loy Vaught .75 2.00
68 John Stockton 1.50 4.00
70 Voshon Lenard .75 2.00
72 Charlie Ward .75 2.00
74 Chris Webber 1.25 3.00
76 Bryant Stith .75 2.00
78 Sean Rooks .75 2.00
80 Brent Price .75 2.00
82 Michael Smith .75 2.00
84 Dan Majerle 1.25 3.00
86 Clarence Weatherspoon .75 2.00
88 B.J. Armstrong .75 2.00
90 Steve Smith 1.00 2.50
92 Derek Strong .75 2.00
94 Will Perdue .75 2.00
96 Chuck Person 1.00 2.50
98 Eric Snow .75 2.00
100 Mario Elie .75 2.00
102 Shawn Bradley .75 2.00
104 Latrell Sprewell 1.25 3.00
106 Terry Porter .75 2.00
108 Rasheed Wallace 1.25 3.00
110 Tracy Murray .75 2.00
112 Lamond Murray .75 2.00
114 Juwan Howard 1.00 2.50
116 Aaron McKie .75 2.00
118 Michael Jordan 10.00 25.00
120 Arvydas Sabonis 1.00 2.50
122 Bryant Reeves .75 2.00
124 Dikembe Mutombo 1.25 3.00
126 Allen Iverson 2.50 6.00
128 Jerry Stackhouse 1.25 3.00
130 Kendall Gill .75 2.00
132 Joe Dumars 1.25 3.00
134 Alonzo Mourning 1.50 4.00
136 Joe Smith 1.00 2.50
138 Kevin Garnett 2.50 6.00
140 John Starks 1.00 2.50
142 Matt Geiger .75 2.00
144 Buck Williams .75 2.00
146 Kobe Bryant 6.00 15.00
148 Jason Caffey .75 2.00
150 Avery Johnson 1.00 2.50
152 Walt Williams .75 2.00
154 Calbert Cheaney .75 2.00
156 Greg Foster .75 2.00
158 Charles Barkley 2.00 5.00
160 Roy Rogers .75 2.00
162 Sam Cassell 1.00 2.50
164 Robert Pack .75 2.00
166 Rodney Rogers .75 2.00
168 Shandon Anderson .75 2.00
170 Anthony Mason .75 2.00
172 David Wingate .75 2.00
174 Billy Owens .75 2.00
176 Carlos Rogers .75 2.00
178 Dana Barros .75 2.00
180 Jayson Williams .75 2.00
182 Doug West .75 2.00
184 Eddie Johnson .75 2.00
186 Eddie Jones 1.25 3.00
188 Anthony Peeler .75 2.00
190 Stacey Augmon 1.00 2.50
192 Micheal Williams .75 2.00
194 Anfernee Hardaway 2.00 5.00
196 Nick Anderson .75 2.00
198 Andrew Lang .75 2.00
200 Cedric Ceballos .75 2.00
202 Ervin Johnson TRAN .75 2.00
204 David Wesley TRAN .75 2.00
206 Jim Jackson TRAN .75 2.00
208 Travis Knight TRAN .75 2.00
210 Bobby Phills TRAN .75 2.00
212 Otis Thorpe TRAN .75 2.00
214 Chris Mullin TRAN 1.25 3.00
216 Brian Williams TRAN .75 2.00
218 Tyus Edney TRAN .75 2.00
220 Clifford Robinson TRAN .75 2.00
222 Vin Baker TRAN 1.00 2.50
224 John Wallace TRAN .75 2.00
226 Kelvin Cato 1.25 3.00
228 Scot Pollard 1.25 3.00
230 Dean Garrett TRAN .75 2.00
232 Ron Mercer 1.50 4.00
234 Antonio McDyess TRAN 1.00 2.50
236 Terrell Brandon TRAN .75 2.00
238 Shawn Kemp TRAN 1.25 3.00
240 Dennis Scott TRAN .75 2.00
T9A Tim Hardaway 1.50 4.00
T9B Michael Jordan 15.00 40.00
T9C Anfernee Hardaway 2.50 6.00
T10A Glen Rice 1.50 4.00
T10B Scottie Pippen 2.50 6.00
T10C Grant Hill 2.50 6.00
T11A Dikembe Mutombo 1.50 4.00
T11B Patrick Ewing 2.00 5.00
T11C Alonzo Mourning 2.00 5.00
T12A Ron Mercer 1.00 2.50
T12B Keith Van Horn 1.50 4.00
T12C Tracy McGrady 4.00 10.00
T13A Gary Payton 1.50 4.00
T13B John Stockton 2.00 5.00
T13C Stephon Marbury 2.00 5.00
T14A Karl Malone 2.00 5.00
T14B Charles Barkley 2.50 6.00
T14C Kevin Garnett 3.00 8.00
T15A David Robinson 2.50 6.00
T15B Hakeem Olajuwon 2.00 5.00
T15C Shaquille O'Neal 4.00 10.00
T16A Antonio Daniels .75 2.00
T16B Tim Duncan 5.00 12.00
T16C Adonal Foyle .75 2.00
NC1 Michael Jordan 15.00 40.00
NC2 Karl Malone 2.00 5.00
NC3 Hakeem Olajuwon 2.00 5.00
NC4 Kevin Garnett 3.00 8.00
NC5 Dikembe Mutombo 1.50 4.00
NC6 Gary Payton 1.50 4.00
NC7 Grant Hill 2.50 6.00
NC8 Charles Barkley 2.50 6.00
NC9 Shaquille O'Neal 4.00 10.00
NC10 Anfernee Hardaway 2.50 6.00
NC11 Tim Duncan 5.00 12.00
NC12 Keith Van Horn 1.50 4.00
NC13 Tracy McGrady 4.00 10.00
NC14 Tim Thomas 1.50 4.00
NC15 Austin Croshere .75 2.00
NC16 Maurice Taylor .75 2.00
NC17 Chauncey Billups 3.00 8.00
NC18 Adonal Foyle .75 2.00
NC19 Tony Battie 1.00 2.50
NC20 Bobby Jackson 1.00 2.50
RC1 Scottie Pippen 2.50 6.00
RC2 Karl Malone 2.00 5.00
RC3 Gary Payton 1.50 4.00
RC4 Kobe Bryant 8.00 20.00
RC5 Antoine Walker 1.50 4.00
RC6 Michael Jordan 15.00 40.00
RC7 Shaquille O'Neal 4.00 10.00
RC8 Dikembe Mutombo 1.50 4.00
RC9 Hakeem Olajuwon 2.00 5.00
RC10 Grant Hill 2.50 6.00
RC11 Tim Duncan 5.00 12.00
RC12 Keith Van Horn 1.50 4.00
RC13 Chauncey Billups 3.00 8.00
RC14 Antonio Daniels .75 2.00
RC15 Tony Battie 1.00 2.50
RC16 Bobby Jackson 1.00 2.50
RC17 Tim Thomas 1.50 4.00
RC18 Adonal Foyle .75 2.00
RC19 Tracy McGrady 4.00 10.00
RC20 Danny Fortson .75 2.00
BBP11 Maurice Taylor .75 2.00
BBP12 Chauncey Billups 3.00 8.00
BBP13 Paul Grant .75 2.00
BBP14 Tony Battie 1.00 2.50
BBP15 Austin Croshere .75 2.00
BBP16 Brevin Knight .75 2.00
BBP17 Bobby Jackson 1.00 2.50
BBP18 Johnny Taylor .75 2.00
BBP19 Scot Pollard .75 2.00
BBP20 Tariq Abdul-Wahad .75 2.00

1983 Star All-Star Game

This was the first NBA set issued by Star Company. The 30-card standard-size set was issued in a clear, sealed plastic bag and distributed through hobby dealers. According to information provided on the order forms, Star Company printed 15,000 sets. The sets originally retailed for $2.50 to $5.00 each. Each card has a blue border on the front and blue print on the back. The set commemorates the 1983 NBA All-Star Game held in Los Angeles. Many of the cards feature players in their All-Star uniforms. There are two unnumbered cards in the set listed at the end of the checklist below. The cards are numbered on the back with the order of the numbering essentially alphabetical according to the player's name. The set features the first professional card of Isiah Thomas.

COMPLETE SET (32) 40.00 100.00
1 Julius Erving CL ! 4.00 10.00
2 Larry Bird 8.00 20.00
3 Maurice Cheeks 1.00 2.50
4 Julius Erving 4.00 10.00
5 Marques Johnson 1.25 3.00
6 Bill Laimbeer 1.25 3.00
7 Moses Malone 2.00 5.00
8 Sidney Moncrief 1.25 3.00
9 Robert Parish 2.00 5.00
10 Reggie Theus 1.25 3.00
11 Isiah Thomas 6.00 15.00
12 Andrew Toney 1.25 3.00
13 Buck Williams 1.25 3.00
14 Kareem Abdul-Jabbar 3.00 8.00
15 Alex English 2.00 5.00
16 George Gervin 2.50 6.00
17 Artis Gilmore 1.25 3.00
18 Magic Johnson 6.00 15.00
19 Maurice Lucas 1.25 3.00
20 Jim Paxson 1.25 3.00
21 Jack Sikma 1.25 3.00
22 David Thompson 2.00 5.00
23 Kiki Vandeweghe 1.25 3.00
24 Jamaal Wilkes 1.25 3.00
25 Gus Williams 1.25 3.00
26 Julius Erving MVP 4.00 10.00
27 Reggie Theus RB 2.00 5.00
Moses Malone
28 All-Star All-Time 1.25 3.00
Leaders (East Coast Line)
29 Larry Bird 5.00 12.00
Robert Parish
30 Sidney Moncrief IA 1.25 3.00
xx Artis Gilmore 1.25 3.00
Alex English
Ad on back
xx Kareem Abdul-Jabbar 3.00 8.00
(Uncut sheet offer on back)
BAG Complete sealed bag (32) 40.00 100.00

1983-84 Star

This set of 276 standard-size cards was issued in four series during the first six months of 1984. Several teams in the first series (1-100) are difficult to obtain due to extensive miscuts (all of which, according to the company, were destroyed) in the initial production process. The team sets were issued in clear sealed bags. Many of the team bags were distributed to hobby dealers through a small group of Star Co. master distributors. According to Star Company's original sales materials and order forms, reportedly 5,000 team bags were printed for each team although quality control problems with the early sets apparently reduced that number considerably. The retail price per bag was $2.50 to $5 for most of the teams. Color borders around the fronts and color printing on the backs correspond to team colors. Cards are numbered according to team order. Extended Rookie Cards include Mark Aguirre, Danny Ainge, Rolando Blackman, Tom Chambers, Clyde Drexler, Dale Ellis, Derek Harper, Larry Nance, Rickey Pierce, Isiah Thomas, Dominique Wilkins, Buck Williams and James Worthy. A promotional card of Sidney Moncrief was produced in limited quantities, but it was numbered 39 rather than 38 as it was in the regular set. There is typically a slight discount on sales of opened team bags.

COMPLETE SET (275) 1200.00 1800.00
1 Julius Erving SP ! 20.00 50.00
2 Maurice Cheeks SP 3.00 8.00
3 Franklin Edwards SP 2.00 5.00
4 Marc Iavaroni SP 2.50 6.00
5 Clemon Johnson SP 2.00 5.00
6 Bobby Jones SP 4.00 10.00
7 Moses Malone SP 8.00 20.00
8 Leo Rautins SP 2.00 5.00
9 Clint Richardson SP 2.00 5.00
10 Sedale Threatt SP XRC 4.00 10.00
11 Andrew Toney SP XRC 6.00 15.00
12 Sam Williams SP 2.00 5.00
13 Magic Johnson SP ! 25.00 60.00
14 Kareem Abdul-Jabbar SP 15.00 40.00
15 Michael Cooper SP 6.00 15.00
16 Calvin Garrett SP 2.00 5.00
17 Mitch Kupchak SP 2.50 6.00
18 Bob McAdoo SP 5.00 12.00
19 Mike McGee SP 2.00 5.00
20 Swen Nater SP 2.00 5.00
21 Kurt Rambis SP XRC 8.00 20.00
22 Byron Scott SP XRC 10.00 25.00
23 Larry Spriggs SP 2.00 5.00
24 Jamaal Wilkes SP 5.00 12.00
25 James Worthy SP XRC 20.00 50.00
26 Larry Bird SP ! 100.00 250.00
27 Danny Ainge SP XRC 30.00 50.00
28 Quinn Buckner SP 4.00 10.00
29 M.L. Carr SP 4.00 10.00
30 Carlos Clark SP 4.00 10.00
31 Gerald Henderson SP 4.00 10.00
32 Dennis Johnson SP 8.00 20.00
33 Cedric Maxwell SP 4.00 10.00
34 Kevin McHale SP ! 12.50 30.00
35 Robert Parish SP ! 10.00 25.00
36 Scott Wedman SP 4.00 10.00
37 Greg Kite SP XRC 4.00 10.00
38 Sidney Moncrief SP 5.00 12.00
39A Sidney Moncrief SP 8.00 20.00
(Promotional card)
39B Nate Archibald SP 6.00 15.00
40 Randy Breuer SP XRC 2.00 5.00
41 Junior Bridgeman SP 2.00 5.00
42 Harvey Catchings SP 2.00 5.00
43 Kevin Grevey SP 2.00 5.00
44 Marques Johnson SP 4.00 10.00
45 Bob Lanier SP 6.00 15.00
46 Alton Lister SP XRC 2.00 5.00
47 Paul Mokeski SP XRC 2.00 5.00
48 Paul Pressey SP XRC 2.00 5.00
49 Mark Aguirre SP XRC 25.00 60.00
50 Rolando Blackman SP XRC 25.00 60.00
51 Pat Cummings SP 6.00 15.00
52 Brad Davis SP XRC 8.00 20.00
53 Dale Ellis SP XRC 25.00 60.00
54 Bill Garnett SP 6.00 15.00
55 Derek Harper SP XRC 30.00 60.00
56 Kurt Nimphius SP 6.00 15.00
57 Jim Spanarkel SP 6.00 15.00
58 Elston Turner SP 6.00 15.00
59 Jay Vincent SP XRC 20.00 40.00
60 Mark West SP XRC 10.00 20.00
61 Bernard King 4.00 10.00
62 Bill Cartwright 3.00 8.00
63 Len Elmore 1.50 4.00
64 Eric Fernsten 1.50 4.00
65 Ernie Grunfeld 1.50 4.00
66 Louis Orr 1.50 4.00
67 Leonard Robinson 1.50 4.00
68 Rory Sparrow XRC 2.00 5.00
69 Trent Tucker XRC 2.00 5.00
70 Darrell Walker XRC 2.00 5.00
71 Marvin Webster 1.50 4.00
72 Ray Williams 1.50 4.00
73 Ralph Sampson XRC 5.00 12.00
74 James Bailey 1.50 4.00
75 Phil Ford 1.50 4.00
76 Elvin Hayes 4.00 10.00
77 Caldwell Jones 1.50 4.00
78 Major Jones 1.50 4.00
79 Allen Leavell 1.50 4.00
80 Lewis Lloyd 1.50 4.00
81 Rodney McCray XRC 2.00 5.00
82 Robert Reid 2.00 5.00
83 Terry Teagle XRC 2.00 5.00
84 Wally Walker 1.50 4.00
85 Kelly Tripucka XRC 2.00 5.00
86 Kent Benson 1.50 4.00
87 Earl Cureton 1.50 4.00
88 Lionel Hollins 1.50 4.00
89 Vinnie Johnson 2.00 5.00
90 Bill Laimbeer 3.00 8.00
91 Cliff Levingston XRC 2.00 5.00
92 John Long 1.50 4.00
93 David Thirdkill 1.50 4.00
94 Isiah Thomas XRC 40.00 100.00
95 Ray Tolbert 1.50 4.00
96 Terry Tyler 1.50 4.00
97 Jim Paxson 3.00 8.00
98 Kenny Carr 1.50 4.00
99 Wayne Cooper 1.50 4.00
100 Clyde Drexler XRC 80.00 160.00
101 Jeff Lamp XRC 3.00 8.00
102 Lafayette Lever XRC 3.00 8.00
103 Calvin Natt 1.50 4.00
104 Audie Norris 1.50 4.00
105 Tom Piotrowski 1.50 4.00
106 Mychal Thompson 1.50 4.00
107 Darnell Valentine XRC 2.00 5.00
108 Pete Verhoeven 1.50 4.00
109 Walter Davis 3.00 8.00
110 Alvan Adams 2.00 5.00
111 James Edwards 2.00 5.00
112 Rod Foster XRC 2.00 5.00
113 Maurice Lucas 2.00 5.00
114 Kyle Macy 1.50 4.00
115 Larry Nance XRC 8.00 20.00
116 Charles Pittman 1.50 4.00
117 Rick Robey 1.50 4.00
118 Mike Sanders XRC 2.00 5.00
119 Alvin Scott 1.50 4.00
120 Paul Westphal 3.00 8.0
121 Bill Walton 6.00 15.0
122 Michael Brooks 1.50 4.0
123 Terry Cummings XRC 5.00 12.0
124 James Donaldson XRC 2.00 5.0
125 Craig Hodges XRC 2.00 5.0
126 Greg Kelser XRC 2.00 5.0
127 Hank McDowell 1.50 4.0
128 Billy McKinney 1.50 4.0
129 Norm Nixon 2.00 5.0
130 Ricky Pierce UER XRC/ 3.00 8.0
Misspelled Rickey
on both sides)
131 Derek Smith XRC 2.00 5.0
132 Jerome Whitehead 1.50 4.0
133 Adrian Dantley 4.00 10.0
134 Mitchell Anderson 1.50 4.0
135 Thurl Bailey XRC 3.00 8.0
136 Tom Boswell 1.50 4.0
137 John Drew 1.50 4.0
138 Mark Eaton XRC 4.00 10.0
139 Jerry Eaves 1.50 4.0
140 Rickey Green XRC 2.00 5.0
141 Darrell Griffith 1.50 4.0
142 Bobby Hansen XRC 2.00 5.0
143 Rich Kelley 1.50 4.0
144 Jeff Wilkins 1.50 4.0
145 Buck Williams XRC 7.50 15.0
146 Otis Birdsong 1.50 4.0
147 Darwin Cook 1.50 4.0
148 Darryl Dawkins 3.00 8.0
149 Mike Gminski 1.50 4.0
150 Reggie Johnson 1.50 4.0
151 Albert King XRC 2.00 5.0
152 Mike O'Koren 1.50 4.0
153 Kelvin Ransey 1.50 4.0
154 Micheal Ray Richardson 1.50 4.0
155 Clarence Walker 1.50 4.0
156 Bill Willoughby 1.50 4.0
157 Steve Stipanovich XRC 2.00 5.0
158 Butch Carter 1.50 4.0
159 Edwin Leroy Combs 1.50 4.0
160 George L. Johnson 1.50 4.0
161 Clark Kellogg XRC 3.00 8.0
162 Sidney Lowe XRC 2.00 5.0
163 Kevin McKenna 1.50 4.0
164 Jerry Sichting XRC 2.00 5.0
165 Brook Steppe 1.50 4.0
166 Jimmy Thomas 1.50 4.0
167 Granville Waiters 1.50 4.0
168 Herb Williams XRC 2.00 5.0
169 Dave Corzine 1.50 4.0
170 Wallace Bryant 1.50 4.0
171 Quintin Dailey XRC 2.00 5.0
172 Sidney Green XRC 2.00 5.0
173 David Greenwood 1.50 4.0
174 Rod Higgins XRC 2.00 5.0
175 Clarence Johnson 1.50 4.0
176 Ronnie Lester 3.00 8.0
177 Jawann Oldham 1.50 4.0
178 Ennis Whatley XRC 2.00 5.0
179 Mitchell Wiggins XRC 2.00 5.0
180 Orlando Woolridge XRC 3.00 8.0
181 Kiki Vandeweghe XRC 5.00 12.0
182 Richard Anderson 1.50 4.0
183 Howard Carter 1.50 4.0
184 T.R. Dunn 1.50 4.0
185 Keith Edmonson 1.50 4.0
186 Alex English 5.00 12.0
187 Mike Evans 1.50 4.0
188 Bill Hanzlik XRC 2.00 5.0
189 Dan Issel 4.00 10.0
190 Anthony Roberts 1.50 4.0
191 Danny Schayes XRC 2.00 5.0
192 Rob Williams 1.50 4.0
193 Jack Sikma 3.00 8.0
194 Fred Brown 1.50 4.0
195 Tom Chambers XRC 10.00 25.0
196 Steve Hawes 1.50 4.0
197 Steve Hayes 1.50 4.0
198 Reggie King 1.50 4.0
199 Scooter McCray 1.50 4.0
200 Jon Sundvold XRC 2.00 5.0
201 Danny Vranes 1.50 4.0
202 Gus Williams 2.00 5.0
203 Al Wood 1.50 4.0
204 Jeff Ruland XRC 2.00 5.0
205 Greg Ballard 1.50 4.0
206 Charles Davis 1.50 4.0
207 Darren Daye 1.50 4.0
208 Michael Gibson 1.50 4.0
209 Frank Johnson XRC 3.00 8.0
210 Joe Kopicki 1.50 4.0
211 Rick Mahorn 2.00 5.0
212 Jeff Malone XRC 3.00 8.0
213 Tom McMillen 1.50 4.0
214 Ricky Sobers 1.50 4.0
215 Bryan Warrick 1.50 4.0
216 Billy Knight 1.50 4.0
217 Don Buse 1.50 4.0
218 Larry Drew XRC 2.00 5.0
219 Eddie Johnson XRC 4.00 10.0
220 Joe Meriweather 1.50 4.0
221 Larry Micheaux 1.50 4.0
222 Ed Nealy XRC 2.00 5.0
223 Mark Olberding 1.50 4.0
224 Dave Robisch 1.50 4.0
225 Reggie Theus 3.00 8.0
226 LaSalle Thompson XRC 2.00 5.0
227 Mike Woodson 1.50 4.0
228 World B. Free 2.00 5.0
229 John Bagley XRC 2.00 5.0
230 Jeff Cook 1.50 4.0
231 Geoff Crompton 1.50 4.0
232 John Garris 1.50 4.0
233 Stewart Granger 1.50 4.0
234 Roy Hinson XRC 2.00 5.0
235 Phil Hubbard 1.50 4.
236 Geoff Huston 1.50 4.
237 Ben Poquette 1.50 4.0
238 Cliff Robinson 1.50 4.0
239 Lonnie Shelton 1.50 4.0
240 Paul Thompson 1.50 4.0
241 George Gervin 5.00 12.0
242 Gene Banks 1.50 4.
243 Ron Brewer 1.50 4.
244 Artis Gilmore 3.00 8.
245 Edgar Jones 1.50 4.
246 John Lucas 2.00 5.
247A Mike Mitchell ERR 1.50 4.
Photo and Name actually Mark McNamara
247B Mike Mithcell ERR 3.00 8.
Photo actually Mark McNamara, correct name
248A M.McNamara ERR XRC 2.00 5.
Photo and Name actually Mike Mitchell
248B M.McNamara ERR XRC 3.00 8.
Photo actually Mike Mitchell, correct name

249 Johnny Moore 1.50 4.00
250 John Paxson XRC 6.00 15.00
251 Fred Roberts XRC 2.00 5.00
252 Joe Barry Carroll 1.50 4.00
253 Mike Bratz 1.50 4.00
254 Don Collins 1.50 4.00
255 Lester Conner 1.50 4.00
256 Chris Engler 1.50 4.00
257 Sleepy Floyd XRC 4.00 10.00
258 Wallace Johnson 1.50 4.00
259 Pace Mannion 1.50 4.00
260 Purvis Short 1.50 4.00
261 Larry Smith 1.50 4.00
262 Darren Tillis 1.50 4.00
263 Dominique Wilkins XRC 90.00 180.00
264 Rickey Brown 1.50 4.00
265 Johnny Davis 1.50 4.00
266 Mike Glenn XRC 2.00 5.00
267 Scott Hastings XRC 2.00 5.00
268 Eddie Johnson 1.50 4.00
269 Mark Landsberger 1.50 4.00
270 Billy Paultz 1.50 4.00
271 Doc Rivers XRC 12.50 30.00
272 Tree Rollins 2.00 5.00
273 Dan Roundfield 1.50 4.00
274 Sly Williams 1.50 4.00
275 Randy Wittman XRC 2.00 5.00
BAG1 76ers sealed bag (12) 50.00 100.00
BAG2 Blazers sealed bag (12) 100.00 200.00
BAG3 Bucks sealed bag (11) 25.00 50.00
BAG4 Bullets sealed bag (12) 12.50 30.00
BAG5 Bulls sealed bag (12) 20.00 50.00
BAG6 Cavs sealed bag (13) 12.50 30.00
BAG7 Celtics sealed bag (12) 150.00 350.00
BAG8 Clippers sealed bag (12) 20.00 50.00
BAG9 Hawks sealed bag (14) 125.00 225.00
BAG10 Jazz sealed bag (12) 12.50 30.00
BAG11 Kings sealed bag (12) 12.50 30.00
BAG12 Knicks sealed bag (12) 17.50 35.00
BAG13 Lakers sealed bag (13) 60.00 150.00
BAG14 Mavs sealed bag (12) 80.00 200.00
BAG15 Nets sealed bag (12) 12.50 30.00
BAG16 Nuggets sealed bag (12) 15.00 40.00
BAG17 Pacers sealed bag (12) 12.50 30.00
BAG18 Pistons sealed bag (12) 60.00 120.00
BAG19 Rockets sealed bag (12) 12.50 30.00
BAG20 Sonics sealed bag (11) 20.00 40.00
BAG21 Spurs sealed bag (11) 12.50 30.00
BAG22 Suns sealed bag (12) 20.00 50.00
BAG23 Warriors sealed bag (11) 12.50 30.00

1983-84 Star All-Rookies

This set features the ten members of the 1982-83 NBA All-Rookie Team. The standard-size cards have a yellow border around the fronts of the cards. The set was issued in a sealed plastic bag and distributed through hobby dealers. It originally retailed for about $2.50 to $5. The set was issued late summer of 1983 and features the Star '84 logo on the front of each card. The cards are numbered on the backs with the order of the numbering alphabetical according to the player's last name.

COMPLETE SET (10) 15.00 35.00
1 Terry Cummings 2.50 6.00
2 Quintin Dailey 1.25 3.00
3 Rod Higgins 1.25 3.00
4 Clark Kellogg 1.25 3.00
5 Lafayette Lever 1.25 3.00
6 Paul Pressey 1.25 3.00
7 Trent Tucker 1.25 3.00
8 Dominique Wilkins ! 8.00 20.00
9 Rob Williams 1.25 3.00
10 James Worthy 5.00 12.00
BAG Complete sealed bag (10) 12.50 30.00

1983-84 Star Sixers Champs

This set of 25 standard-size cards is devoted to Philadelphia's NBA Championship victory over the Los Angeles Lakers in 1983. Reportedly 10,000 sets were printed. Majority of the distribution was done at the Spectrum, the 76ers home arena. The cards have a red border around the fronts of the cards and red printing on the backs. The set was issued in late summer of 1983 and features the Star '84 logo on the front of each card.

COMPLETE SET (25) 20.00 50.00
Moses Malone CL 1.50 4.00
Billy Cunningham CO 1.25 3.00
Moses Malone 3.00 8.00
Kareem Abdul-Jabbar
Julius Erving IA 3.00 8.00
Clint Richardson IA 1.25 3.00
Andrew Toney IA 1.25 3.00
7 Phila. 113, LA 107 1.25 3.00
Game 1 Boxscore
Bobby Jones IA 1.25 3.00
Maurice Cheeks IA 1.25 3.00
10 Julius Erving IA 3.00 8.00
11 Andrew Toney IA 1.25 3.00
12 Phila. 103, LA 93 1.25 3.00
Game 2 Boxscore
13 Serious Sixers 1.25 3.00
(Pre-Game Lineup)
14 Moses Malone IA 1.50 4.00
15 Clemon Johnson IA 1.25 3.00
16 Maurice Cheeks IA 1.25 3.00
17 Phila. 111, LA 94 1.25 3.00
Game 3 Boxscore
18 Julius Erving IA 3.00 8.00
19 Bobby Jones 1.25 3.00
Sixth Man of Year
20 Moses Malone IA 1.50 4.00
21 World Champs 1.25 3.00
Phila. 115, LA 108
Game 4 Boxscore
22 Julius Erving 3.00 8.00
Series Stats
23 Moses Malone 1.50 4.00
Philly in a Sweep
Prior World Champs
24 Julius Erving 3.00 8.00
Basking in Glory

25 Moses Malone MVP 1.50 4.00
BAG Complete sealed bag (25) 20.00 50.00

1984 Star All-Star Game

This set of 25 standard-size cards features participants in the 34th Annual NBA All-Star Game held in Denver. The cards have a white border around the fronts of the cards and blue printing on the backs. Cards feature the Star '84 logo on the front. The cards are ordered with the East All-Stars on cards 2-13 and the West All-Stars on cards 14-25. The cards are on the backs and are in alphabetical order by division.

COMPLETE SET (25) 40.00 100.00
1 Isiah Thomas CL 4.00 10.00
2 Larry Bird 15.00 30.00
3 Otis Birdsong 1.25 3.00
4 Julius Erving 6.00 15.00
5 Bernard King 2.00 5.00
6 Bill Laimbeer 2.50 6.00
7 Kevin McHale 3.00 8.00
8 Sidney Moncrief 2.00 5.00
9 Robert Parish 2.00 5.00
10 Jeff Ruland 1.25 3.00
11 Isiah Thomas 5.00 12.00
(Magic Johnson also shown on card)
12 Andrew Toney 1.25 3.00
13 Kelly Tripucka 1.25 3.00
14 Kareem Abdul-Jabbar 5.00 12.00
15 Mark Aguirre 1.25 3.00
16 Adrian Dantley 2.00 5.00
17 Walter Davis 1.25 3.00
18 Alex English 2.00 5.00
19 George Gervin 2.50 6.00
20 Rickey Green 1.25 3.00
21 Magic Johnson 12.50 25.00
22 Jim Paxson 1.25 3.00
23 Ralph Sampson 2.00 5.00
24 Jack Sikma 2.00 5.00
25 Kiki Vandeweghe 2.00 5.00
BAG Complete sealed bag (25) 40.00 100.00

1984 Star All-Star Game Denver Police

This 34-card standard-size set was distributed as individual cards by the Denver Police in the months following the NBA All-Star Game held in Denver. Reportedly 10,000 sets were produced. The set was composed of participants in the All-Star Game (1-25) and the Slam Dunk contest (26-34). The cards have a white border around the fronts and blue printing on the backs. Cards feature the Star '84 logo on the fronts and safety tips on the backs.

COMPLETE SET (34) 100.00 200.00
1 Isiah Thomas CL 3.00 8.00
2 Larry Bird 20.00 40.00
3 Otis Birdsong 1.25 3.00
4 Julius Erving 6.00 15.00
5 Bernard King 2.00 5.00
6 Bill Laimbeer 2.50 6.00
7 Kevin McHale 4.00 10.00
8 Sidney Moncrief 2.00 5.00
9 Robert Parish 3.00 8.00
10 Jeff Ruland 1.25 3.00
11 Isiah Thomas 6.00 15.00
Magic Johnson
12 Andrew Toney 1.25 3.00
13 Kelly Tripucka 1.25 3.00
14 Kareem Abdul-Jabbar 6.00 15.00
15 Mark Aguirre 2.00 5.00
16 Adrian Dantley 2.00 5.00
17 Walter Davis 2.00 5.00
18 Alex English 2.50 6.00
19 George Gervin 2.50 6.00
20 Rickey Green 1.25 3.00
21 Magic Johnson 15.00 30.00
22 Jim Paxson 1.25 3.00
23 Ralph Sampson 2.00 5.00
24 Jack Sikma 2.00 5.00
25 Kiki Vandeweghe 2.00 5.00
26 Michael Cooper SD 2.00 5.00
27 Clyde Drexler SD 10.00 25.00
28 Julius Erving SD 6.00 15.00
29 Darrell Griffith SD 2.00 5.00
30 Edgar Jones SD 1.25 3.00
31 Larry Nance SD 2.50 6.00
32 Ralph Sampson SD 2.00 5.00
33 Dominique Wilkins SD 10.00 25.00
34 Orlando Woolridge SD 1.25 3.00

1984 Star Award Banquet

This 24-card standard-size set was produced for the NBA to be given away at the Awards Banquet which took place following the conclusion of the 1983-84 season. According to a 1984 Star Company press release, only 3,000 sets were produced. The cards highlighted award winners from the 1983-84 season. Cards have a blue border around the fronts of the cards and pink and blue printing on the backs. The set was issued in June of 1984 and features the Star '84 logo on the front of each card.

COMPLETE SET (24) 40.00 100.00
1 1984 Award Winners 1.25 3.00
Checklist
2 Frank Layden CO 1.25 3.00
3 Ralph Sampson ROY 1.25 3.00
4 Adrian Dantley 1.25 3.00
Comeback Player of the Year
5 Kevin McHale 2.00 5.00
Sixth Man
6 Magic Johnson POY 6.00 15.00
7 Sidney Moncrief 1.25 3.00
Defensive Player
8 Larry Bird MVP 8.00 20.00
9 Larry Nance 2.00 5.00
Slam Dunk Champ
10 Larry Bird LL 4.00 10.00
Darrell Griffith LL
Artis Gilmore LL
Adrian Dantley LL
11 Magic Johnson LL 3.00 8.00
Rickey Green LL
Mark Eaton LL
Moses Malone LL
12 Isiah Thomas AS MVP 2.50 6.00
13 Adrian Dantley LL 1.25 3.00
14 Artis Gilmore LL 1.25 3.00
15 Larry Bird LL 8.00 20.00
16 Darrell Griffith LL 1.25 3.00
17 Magic Johnson LL 6.00 15.00
18 Rickey Green LL 1.25 3.00
19 Mark Eaton LL 1.25 3.00
20 Moses Malone LL 2.00 5.00
21 Kareem Abdul-Jabbar 4.00 10.00
David Stern
22 Bobby Jones 2.00 5.00
Michael Cooper
Tree Rollins#Sidney Moncrief
Maurice Cheeks
All-Defensive Team
23 Ralph Sampson 2.00 5.00
Steve Stipanovich
Byron Scott
Jeff Malone
Thurl Bailey
Darrell Walker
All-Rookie Team
24 Larry Bird 6.00 15.00
Magic Johnson
Isiah Thomas
Kareem Abdul--Jabbar
Bernard King
All-NBA Team
BAG Complete sealed bag (24) 40.00 100.00

1984 Star Larry Bird

This set contains 18 standard-size cards highlighting the career of basketball great Larry Bird. Cards have a green border around the fronts of the cards and green printing on the backs. Cards feature Star '84 logo on the front as they were released in May of 1984.

COMPLETE SET (18) 40.00 75.00
COMMON L.BIRD (1-18) 2.00 5.00
BAG Complete sealed bag (18) 40.00 75.00

1984 Star Celtics Champs

This set of 25 standard-size cards is devoted to Boston's NBA Championship victory over the Los Angeles Lakers in 1984. Cards have a green border around the fronts of the cards and green printing on the backs. The set was issued in summer of 1984 and features the Star '84 logo on the front of each card. The set includes two of the three Red Auerbach cards ever printed.

COMPLETE SET (25) 100.00 200.00
1 Red Auerbach CL 4.00 10.00
Cedric Maxwell
David Stern COMM
2 Kareem Abdul-Jabbar IA 4.00 10.00
Robert Parish
3 Kevin McHale IA 2.50 6.00
4 Larry Bird IA 10.00 25.00
5 Magic Johnson IA 8.00 20.00
6 K.C. Jones CO 2.50 6.00
Danny Ainge
7 Larry Bird IA 10.00 25.00
8 Kareem Abdul-Jabbar IA 3.00 8.00
Kevin McHale
9 James Worthy IA 2.50 6.00
10 Magic Johnson IA 8.00 20.00
11 Magic Johnson IA 25.00 50.00
Larry Bird
12 Danny Ainge IA 3.00 8.00
James Worthy
13 M.L.Carr 1.25 3.00
Cedric Maxwell
14 Larry Bird IA 15.00 35.00
15 Pat Riley CO IA 3.00 8.00
16 Kareem Abdul-Jabbar 4.00 10.00
17 Robert Parish IA 2.00 5.00
18 Kareem Abdul-Jabbar IA 4.00 10.00
19 Dennis Johnson IA 2.00 5.00
20 Kareem Abdul-Jabbar IA 4.00 10.00
21 K.C. Jones CO 2.00 5.00
22 M.L. Carr IA 1.25 3.00
23 Red Auerbach ! 4.00 10.00
24 Larry Bird MVP ! 20.00 40.00
25 Boston Garden ! 4.00 10.00
BAG Complete sealed bag (25) 100.00 200.00

1984 Star Slam Dunk

An 11-card standard-size set highlighting the revival of the Slam Dunk contest (during the 1984 All-Star Weekend in Denver) was produced by the Star Company in 1984. The cards have a white border around the fronts and blue printing on the backs. The Star '84 logo are featured on the front.

COMPLETE SET (11) 30.00 60.00
1 Group Photo 6.00 15.00
(checklist back)
2 Michael Cooper 2.00 5.00
3 Clyde Drexler 8.00 20.00
4 Julius Erving 6.00 15.00
5 Darrell Griffith 2.00 5.00
6 Edgar Jones 1.25 3.00
7 Larry Nance 2.50 6.00
8 Ralph Sampson 2.00 5.00
9 Dominique Wilkins UER 8.00 20.00
10 Orlando Woolridge 2.00 5.00
11 Larry Nance 2.50 6.00
1984 Slam Dunk Champ
BAG Complete sealed bag (11) 30.00 60.00

1984-85 Star

This set of 288 standard-size cards was issued in three series during the first five months of 1985 by Star Company. The set is comprised of team sets that were issued in clear sealed bags. Many of these team bags were distributed to hobby dealers through a small group of Star Company master distributors and retailed for $2.50-$5. According to Star Company's original sales materials and order forms, reportedly 3,000 team bags were printed for each team. The cards have a colored border around the fronts of the cards according to the team with corresponding color printing on the backs. Cards are organized numerically by team. The set also features a special subset (195-200) honoring Gold Medal-winning players from the 1984 Olympic basketball competition as well as a subset of NBA specials (281-288). Michael Jordan's Extended Rookie Card appears in this set. Other Extended Rookie's include Charles Barkley, Craig Ehlo, Hakeem Olajuwon, Alvin Robertson, Sam Perkins, John Stockton and Otis Thorpe. There is typically a slight discount on sales of opened team bags.

COMPLETE SET (288) 3500.00 4500.00
1 Larry Bird 30.00 80.00
2 Danny Ainge 6.00 12.00
3 Quinn Buckner 1.50 4.00
4 Rick Carlisle 4.00 10.00
5 M.L. Carr 1.50 4.00
6 Dennis Johnson 3.00 8.00
7 Greg Kite 1.50 4.00
8 Cedric Maxwell 1.50 4.00
9 Kevin McHale 8.00 20.00
10 Robert Parish 5.00 12.00
11 Scott Wedman 1.50 4.00
12 Larry Bird 15.00 40.00
1983-84 NBA MVP
13 Marques Johnson 1.50 4.00
14 Junior Bridgeman 1.50 4.00
15 Michael Cage XRC 2.00 5.00
16 Harvey Catchings 1.50 4.00
17 James Donaldson 1.50 4.00
18 Lancaster Gordon 1.50 4.00
19 Jay Murphy 1.50 4.00
20 Norm Nixon 1.50 4.00
21 Derek Smith 1.50 4.00
22 Bill Walton 8.00 20.00
23 Bryan Warrick 1.50 4.00
24 Rory White 1.50 4.00
25 Bernard King 3.00 8.00
26 James Bailey 1.50 4.00
27 Ken Bannister 1.50 4.00
28 Butch Carter 1.50 4.00
29 Bill Cartwright 3.00 8.00
30 Pat Cummings 1.50 4.00
31 Ernie Grunfeld 1.50 4.00
32 Louis Orr 1.50 4.00
33 Leonard Robinson 1.50 4.00
34 Rory Sparrow 1.50 4.00
35 Trent Tucker 1.50 4.00
36 Darrell Walker 1.50 4.00
37 Eddie Lee Wilkins XRC 2.00 5.00
38 Alvan Adams 1.50 4.00
39 Walter Davis 2.00 5.00
40 James Edwards 1.50 4.00
41 Rod Foster 1.50 4.00
42 Michael Holton 1.50 4.00
43 Jay Humphries XRC 2.00 5.00
44 Charles Jones 1.50 4.00
45 Maurice Lucas 1.50 4.00
46 Kyle Macy 1.50 4.00
47 Larry Nance 4.00 10.00
48 Charles Pittman 1.50 4.00
49 Rick Robey 1.50 4.00
50 Mike Sanders 1.50 4.00
51 Alvin Scott 1.50 4.00
52 Clark Kellogg 1.50 4.00
53 Tony Brown 1.50 4.00
54 Devin Durrant 1.50 4.00
55 Vern Fleming XRC 2.00 5.00
56 Bill Garnett 1.50 4.00
57 Stuart Gray UER 1.50 4.00
(Photo actually Tony Brown)
58 Jerry Sichting 1.50 4.00
59 Terence Stansbury 1.50 4.00
60 Steve Stipanovich 1.50 4.00
61 Jimmy Thomas 1.50 4.00
62 Granville Waiters 1.50 4.00
63 Herb Williams 1.50 4.00
64 Artis Gilmore 2.00 5.00
65 Gene Banks 1.50 4.00
66 Ron Brewer 1.50 4.00
67 George Gervin 8.00 20.00
68 Edgar Jones 1.50 4.00
69 Ozell Jones 1.50 4.00
70 Mark McNamara 1.50 4.00
71 Mike Mitchell 1.50 2.00
72 Johnny Moore 1.50 4.00
73 John Paxson 2.00 5.00
74 Fred Roberts 1.50 4.00
75 Alvin Robertson XRC 2.00 5.00
76 Dominique Wilkins 20.00 40.00
77 Rickey Brown 1.50 4.00
78 Antoine Carr XRC 2.00 5.00
79 Mike Glenn 1.50 4.00
80 Scott Hastings 1.50 4.00
81 Eddie Johnson 1.50 4.00
82 Cliff Levingston 1.50 4.00
83 Leo Rautins 1.50 4.00
84 Doc Rivers 4.00 10.00
85 Tree Rollins 1.50 4.00
86 Randy Wittman 1.50 4.00
87 Sly Williams 1.50 4.00
88 Darryl Dawkins 2.00 5.00
89 Otis Birdsong 1.50 4.00
90 Darwin Cook 1.50 4.00
91 Mike Gminski 1.50 4.00
92 George L. Johnson 1.50 4.00
93 Albert King 1.50 4.00
94 Mike O'Koren 1.50 4.00
95 Kelvin Ransey 1.50 4.00
96 M.R. Richardson 1.50 4.00
97 Wayne Sappleton 1.50 4.00
98 Jeff Turner XRC 2.00 5.00
99 Buck Williams 2.00 5.00
100 Michael Wilson 1.50 4.00
101 Michael Jordan XRC 1200.00 2200.00
102 Dave Corzine 2.00 5.00
103 Quintin Dailey 2.00 5.00
104 Sidney Green 2.00 5.00
105 David Greenwood 2.00 5.00
106 Rod Higgins 2.00 5.00
107 Steve Johnson 2.00 5.00
108 Caldwell Jones 2.00 5.00
109 Wes Matthews 2.00 5.00
110 Jawann Oldham 2.00 5.00
111 Ennis Whatley 2.00 5.00
112 Orlando Woolridge 2.00 5.00
113 Tom Chambers 3.00 8.00
114 Cory Blackwell 1.50 4.00
115 Frank Brickowski XRC 2.00 5.00
116 Gerald Henderson 1.50 4.00
117 Reggie King 1.50 4.00
118 Tim McCormick XRC 2.00 5.00
119 John Schweitz 1.50 4.00
120 Jack Sikma 2.00 5.00
121 Ricky Sobers 1.50 4.00
122 Jon Sundvold 1.50 4.00
123 Danny Vranes 1.50 4.00
124 Al Wood 1.50 4.00
125 Terry Cummings UER 3.00 8.00
(Robert Cummings on card back)
126 Randy Breuer 1.50 4.00
127 Charles Davis 1.50 4.00
128 Mike Dunleavy 2.00 5.00
129 Kenny Fields 1.50 4.00
130 Kevin Grevey 1.50 4.00
131 Craig Hodges 1.50 4.00
132 Alton Lister 1.50 4.00
133 Larry Micheaux 1.50 4.00
134 Paul Mokeski 1.50 4.00
135 Sidney Moncrief 3.00 8.00
136 Paul Pressey 1.50 4.00
137 Alex English 3.00 8.00
138 Wayne Cooper 1.50 4.00
139 T.R. Dunn 1.50 4.00
140 Mike Evans 1.50 4.00
141 Bill Hanzlik 1.50 4.00
142 Dan Issel 5.00 12.00
143 Joe Kopicki 1.50 4.00
144 Lafayette Lever 2.00 5.00
145 Calvin Natt 1.50 4.00
146 Danny Schayes 1.50 4.00
147 Elston Turner 1.50 4.00
148 Willie White 1.50 4.00
149 Purvis Short 1.50 4.00
150 Chuck Aleksinas 1.50 4.00
151 Mike Bratz 1.50 4.00
152 Steve Burtt 1.50 4.00
153 Lester Conner 1.50 4.00
154 Sleepy Floyd 2.00 5.00
155 Mickey Johnson 1.50 4.00
156 Gary Plummer 1.50 4.00
157 Larry Smith 1.50 4.00
158 Peter Thibeaux 1.50 4.00
159 Jerome Whitehead 1.50 4.00
160 Othell Wilson 1.50 4.00
161 Kiki Vandeweghe 2.00 5.00
162 Sam Bowie XRC 4.00 10.00
163 Kenny Carr 1.50 4.00
164 Steve Colter 1.50 4.00
165 Clyde Drexler ! 20.00 40.00
166 Audie Norris 1.50 4.00
167 Jim Paxson 1.50 4.00
168 Tom Scheffler 1.50 4.00
169 Bernard Thompson 1.50 4.00
170 Mychal Thompson 1.50 4.00
171 Darnell Valentine 1.50 4.00
172 Magic Johnson ! 25.00 60.00
173 Kareem Abdul-Jabbar 15.00 40.00
174 Michael Cooper 4.00 10.00
175 Earl Jones 1.50 4.00
176 Mitch Kupchak 2.00 5.00
177 Ronnie Lester 1.50 4.00
178 Bob McAdoo 4.00 10.00
179 Mike McGee 1.50 4.00
180 Kurt Rambis 3.00 8.00
181 Byron Scott 4.00 10.00
182 Larry Spriggs 1.50 4.00
183 Jamaal Wilkes 3.00 8.00
184 James Worthy 6.00 15.00
185 Gus Williams 1.50 4.00
186 Greg Ballard 1.50 4.00
187 Dudley Bradley 1.50 4.00
188 Darren Daye 1.50 4.00
189 Frank Johnson 1.50 4.00
190 Charles Jones 1.50 4.00
191 Rick Mahorn 1.50 4.00
192 Jeff Malone 1.50 4.00
193 Tom McMillen 1.50 4.00
194 Jeff Ruland 1.50 4.00
195 Michael Jordan OLY ! 150.00 300.00
196 Vern Fleming OLY 2.00 5.00
197 Sam Perkins OLY 4.00 10.00
198 Alvin Robertson OLY 2.00 5.00
199 Jeff Turner OLY 2.00 5.00
200 Leon Wood OLY 2.00 5.00
201 Moses Malone 6.00 12.00
202 Charles Barkley XRC 60.00 150.00
203 Maurice Cheeks 2.00 5.00
204 Julius Erving 20.00 40.00
205 Clemon Johnson 1.50 4.30
206 George L. Johnson 1.50 4.00
207 Bobby Jones 3.00 8.00
208 Clint Richardson 1.50 4.00
209 Sedale Threatt 1.50 4.00
210 Andrew Toney 2.00 5.00
211 Sam Williams 1.50 4.00
212 Leon Wood XRC 2.00 5.00
213 Mel Turpin XRC 2.00 5.00
214 Ron Anderson XRC 2.00 5.00
215 John Bagley 1.50 4.00
216 Johnny Davis 1.50 4.00
217 World B. Free 1.50 4.00
218 Roy Hinson 1.50 4.00
219 Phil Hubbard 1.50 4.00
220 Edgar Jones 1.50 4.00
221 Ben Poquette 1.50 4.00
222 Lonnie Shelton 1.50 4.00
223 Mark West 1.50 4.00
224 Kevin Williams 1.50 4.00
225 Mark Eaton 2.00 5.00
226 Mitchell Anderson 1.50 4.00
227 Thurl Bailey 1.50 4.00
228 Adrian Dantley 3.00 8.00
229 Rickey Green 1.50 4.00
230 Darrell Griffith 1.50 4.00
231 Rich Kelley 1.50 4.00
232 Pace Mannion 1.50 4.00
233 Billy Paultz 1.50 4.00
234 Fred Roberts 1.50 4.00
235 John Stockton XRC 80.00 200.00
236 Jeff Wilkins 1.50 4.00
237 Hakeem Olajuwon XRC ! 100.00 200.00
238 Craig Ehlo XRC 7.50 15.00
239 Lionel Hollins 1.50 4.00
240 Allen Leavell 1.50 4.00
241 Lewis Lloyd 1.50 4.00
242 John Lucas 1.50 4.00
243 Rodney McCray 1.50 4.00
244 Hank McDowell 1.50 4.00
245 Larry Micheaux 1.50 4.00
246 Jim Petersen XRC 2.00 5.00
247 Robert Reid 1.50 4.00
248 Ralph Sampson 2.00 5.00
249 Mitchell Wiggins 1.50 4.00
250 Mark Aguirre 2.00 5.00
251 Rolando Blackman 2.00 5.00
252 Wallace Bryant 1.50 4.00
253 Brad Davis 1.50 4.00
254 Dale Ellis 2.00 5.00
255 Derek Harper 2.00 5.00
256 Kurt Nimphius 1.50 4.00
257 Sam Perkins XRC 6.00 15.00
258 Charlie Sitton 1.50 4.00
259 Tom Sluby 1.50 4.00
260 Jay Vincent 1.50 4.00
261 Isiah Thomas 10.00 25.00
262 Kent Benson 1.50 4.00
263 Earl Cureton 1.50 4.00
264 Vinnie Johnson 1.50 4.00
265 Bill Laimbeer 2.00 5.00
266 John Long 1.50 4.00
267 Dan Roundfield 1.50 4.00
268 Kelly Tripucka 1.50 4.00
269 Terry Tyler 1.50 4.00
270 Reggie Theus 2.00 5.00
271 Don Buse 1.50 4.00
272 Larry Drew 1.50 4.00
273 Eddie Johnson 1.50 4.00
274 Billy Knight 1.50 4.00
275 Joe Meriweather 1.50 4.00
276 Mark Olberding 1.50 4.00
277 LaSalle Thompson 1.50 4.00
278 Otis Thorpe XRC 4.00 10.00
279 Pete Verhoeven 1.50 4.00
280 Mike Woodson 1.50 4.00
281 Julius Erving SPEC ! 8.00 20.00
282 Kareem Abdul-Jabbar SPEC ! 8.00 20.00
283 Dan Issel SPEC ! 3.00 8.00
284 Bernard King SPEC ! 2.00 5.00
285 Moses Malone SPEC ! 4.00 10.00
286 Mark Eaton SPEC ! 2.00 5.00
287 Isiah Thomas SPEC ! 6.00 15.00
288 Michael Jordan SPEC ! 125.00 300.00
BAG1 76ers sealed bag (12) 125.00 225.00
BAG2 Blazers sealed bag (11) 40.00 80.00
BAG3 Bucks sealed bag (12) 12.50 30.00
BAG4 Bullets sealed bag (10) 12.50 30.00
BAG5 Bulls sealed bag (12) 2000.00 2600.00
BAG6 Cavs sealed bag (12) 12.50 30.00
BAG7 Celtics sealed bag (12) 60.00 150.00
BAG8 Clippers sealed bag (12) 12.50 30.00
BAG9 Hawks sealed bag (12) 25.00 60.00
BAG10 Jazz sealed bag (12) 125.00 225.00
BAG11 Kings sealed bag (11) 10.00 25.00
BAG12 Knicks sealed bag (13) 15.00 40.00
BAG13 Lakers sealed bag (13) 60.00 150.00
BAG14 Mavs sealed bag (11) 15.00 40.00
BAG15 Nets sealed bag (13) 12.50 30.00
BAG16 Nuggets sealed bag (12) 12.50 30.00
BAG17 Pacers sealed bag (12) 12.50 30.00
BAG18 Pistons sealed bag (9) 20.00 50.00
BAG19 Rockets sealed bag (13) 125.00 225.00
BAG20 Sonics sealed bag (12) 12.50 30.00
BAG21 Spurs sealed bag (12) 15.00 40.00
BAG22 Suns sealed bag (14) 12.50 30.00
BAG23 Warriors sealed bag (12) 12.50 30.00
BAG24 Olympic sealed bag (14) 350.00 650.00

1984-85 Star Arena

These sets were produced to be sold in the arena of each of the five teams featured in this set. The teams are Boston, Dallas, Milwaukee, Los Angeles Lakers and Philadelphia. Each set is different from the team's regular issue set in that the photography and card backs are different. Shortly after distribution began, Bob Lanier announced his retirement and his cards were withdrawn from the Milwaukee set. Cards measure 2 1/2" by 3 1/2" and have a colored border around the fronts according to team. Corresponding color printing is on the backs. Celtics feature Star '85 logo on the front while the other four teams feature the Star '84 logo on the front. The cards are ordered alphabetically by team using prefixes A-E.

COMPLETE SET (48) 125.00 250.00
COMPLETE SET (49) w/Lanier 250.00 500.00
A1 Larry Bird 20.00 40.00
A2 Danny Ainge 2.50 6.00
A3 Rick Carlisle 2.50 6.00
A4 Dennis Johnson 3.00 8.00
A5 Cedric Maxwell 1.25 3.00
A6 Kevin McHale 3.00 8.00
A7 Robert Parish 2.50 6.00
A8 Scott Wedman 1.25 3.00
A9 Robert Parish 10.00 25.00
Larry Bird
Kevin McHale
Jimmy Rodgers CO
K.C. Jones CO
Chris Ford CO
B1 Mark Aguirre UER 2.50 6.00
Aguirre is incorrectly spelled Aguire
B2 Rolando Blackman 2.50 6.00
B3 Brad Davis 1.25 3.00
B4 Dale Ellis 1.50 4.00
B5 Bill Garnett 1.25 3.00
B6 Derek Harper UER 2.50 6.00
(Mike Harper on both sides with Mike's birthdate ,etc.)
B7 Kurt Nimphius 1.25 3.00
B8 Jim Spanarkel 1.25 3.00
B9 Elston Turner 1.25 3.00
B10 Jay Vincent 1.25 3.00
B11 Mark West 1.25 3.00
C1 Nate Archibald 2.50 6.00
C2 Junior Bridgeman 1.25 3.00
C3 Mike Dunleavy 2.50 6.00
C4 Kevin Grevey 1.25 3.00
C5 Marques Johnson 2.50 6.00
C6 Bob Lanier SP 125.00 250.00
C7 Alton Lister 1.25 3.00
C8 Sidney Moncrief 2.50 6.00
C9 Paul Pressey 1.25 3.00
D1 Kareem Abdul-Jabbar 8.00 20.00
D2 Michael Cooper 2.50 6.00
D3 Magic Johnson 12.50 30.00
D4 Mike McGee 1.25 3.00
D5 Swen Nater 1.25 3.00
D6 Kurt Rambis 3.00 8.00
D7 Byron Scott 3.00 8.00
D8 James Worthy 4.00 10.00
D9 Magic Johnson AS 10.00 25.00
Kareem Abdul-Jabbar
D10 Kareem Abdul-Jabbar LL 6.00 15.00
E1 Julius Erving 6.00 15.00
E2 Maurice Cheeks 1.50 4.00
E3 Franklin Edwards 1.25 3.00
E4 Marc Iavaroni 1.50 4.00
E5 Clemon Johnson 1.25 3.00
E6 Bobby Jones 2.50 6.00
E7 Moses Malone 3.00 8.00
E8 Clint Richardson 1.25 3.00
E9 Andrew Toney 1.50 4.00
E10 Sam Williams 1.25 3.00
BAG1 76ers sealed bag (10) 25.00 40.00
BAG2 Bucks sealed bag (8) 10.00 25.00
BAG3 Celtics sealed bag (9) 40.00 80.00
BAG4 Lakers sealed bag (10) 40.00 100.00
BAG5 Mavs sealed bag (11) 12.50 30.00

1984-85 Star Court Kings 5x7

This over-sized 50-card set was issued as two series of 25. Cards measure approximately 5" by 7" and have a yellow (first series 1-25) or blue (second series 26-50) colored border around the fronts of the cards and blue and yellow printing on the backs. These large cards feature the Star '85 logo on the front. The set features early professional cards of Charles Barkley, Michael Jordan and Hakeem Olajuwon.

COMPLETE SET (50) 200.00 400.00
1 Kareem Abdul-Jabbar 6.00 12.00
2 Jeff Ruland 1.50 4.00
3 Mark Aguirre 2.00 5.00
4 Julius Erving 5.00 12.00
5 Kelly Tripucka 1.50 4.00
6 Buck Williams 2.00 5.00
7 Sidney Moncrief 2.00 5.00
8 World B. Free 1.50 4.00
9 Bill Walton 3.00 8.00
10 Purvis Short 1.50 4.00
11 Rickey Green 1.50 4.00
12 Dominique Wilkins 5.00 12.00
13 Jim Paxson 1.50 4.00
14 Ralph Sampson 2.00 5.00
15 Magic Johnson 10.00 20.00
16 Reggie Theus 2.00 5.00
17 Moses Malone 3.00 8.00
18 Larry Bird 12.50 30.00
19 Larry Nance 2.00 5.00
20 Clark Kellogg 1.50 4.00
21 Jack Sikma 1.50 4.00
22 Alex English 2.00 5.00
23 Bernard King 1.50 4.00
24 Dave Corzine 1.50 4.00
25 George Gervin 3.00 8.00
26 Michael Jordan 100.00 200.00
27 Rolando Blackman 2.00 5.00
28 Dan Issel 3.00 8.00
29 Maurice Cheeks 1.50 4.00
30 Isiah Thomas 6.00 15.00
31 Robert Parish 3.00 8.00
32 Mark Eaton 1.50 4.00
33 Sam Perkins 3.00 8.00
34 Artis Gilmore 2.00 5.00
35 Andrew Toney 1.50 4.00
36 Adrian Dantley 1.50 4.00
37 Terry Cummings 1.50 4.00
38 Orlando Woolridge 1.50 4.00
39 Tom.Chambers 2.00 5.00
40 Gus Williams 1.50 4.00
41 Charles Barkley 20.00 40.00
42 Kevin McHale 5.00 12.00
43 Otis Birdsong 1.50 4.00
44 Sam Bowie 2.00 5.00
45 Darrell Griffith 1.50 4.00
46 Kiki Vandeweghe 2.00 5.00
47 Hakeem Olajuwon 20.00 35.00
48 Marques Johnson 1.50 4.00
49 James Worthy 4.00 10.00
50 Mel Turpin 1.50 4.00
BAG1 Series 1 sealed bag (25) 60.00 120.00
BAG2 Series 2 sealed bag (25) 200.00 325.00

1984-85 Star Julius Erving

This set contains 18 standard-size cards highlighting the career of basketball great Julius Erving. The cards have a red border around the fronts of the cards and red printing on the backs. Cards feature Star '85 logo on the front although they were released in the summer of 1984.

COMPLETE SET (18) 40.00 80.00
COMMON J.ERVING (1-18) 2.00 5.00
1 Julius Erving Checklist 2.50 6.00
18 Julius Erving 2.50 6.00
The Future
BAG1 Complete sealed bag (19) 40.00 80.00

1985 Star Kareem Abdul-Jabbar

The 1985 Star Kareem Abdul-Jabbar set is an 18-card standard-size tribute set. Most of the photos on the fronts are from the early 1980s. Card backs provide various statistics and tidbits of information about Abdul-Jabbar. The set's basic design is identical to those of the Star Company's regular NBA sets. The cards show a Star '85 logo in the upper right corner. The front borders are Lakers' purple.

COMPLETE SET (18) 20.00 50.00
COMMON JABBAR (1-18) 1.50 4.00
1 Kareem Abdul-Jabbar 2.00 5.00
Checklist Card
18 Kareem Abdul-Jabbar 2.00 5.00
The Future
BAG1 Complete sealed bag (18) 20.00 50.00

1985 Star Coaches

The 1984-85 Star NBA Coaches set is a ten-card standard-size set depicting some of the NBA's best known coaches. The set's basic design is identical to those of the Star Company's regular NBA sets. The front borders are royal blue, and the backs show each man's coaching records. Statistics for ex-players are NOT included. The cards show a Star '85 logo in the upper right corner. Coaching statistics on the card backs only go up through the 1983-84 NBA season.

COMPLETE SET (10) 10.00 25.00
1 John Bach 1.25 3.00
2 Hubie Brown 1.25 3.00
3 Cotton Fitzsimmons 1.25 3.00
4 Kevin Loughery 1.25 3.00
5 John MacLeod 1.25 3.00
6 Doug Moe 1.25 3.00
7 Don Nelson 1.25 3.00
8 Jack Ramsay 1.25 3.00
9 Pat Riley 2.50 6.00
10 Lenny Wilkens UER 2.00 5.00
(Name misspelled on card back)
BAG1 Complete sealed bag (10) 10.00 25.00

1985 Star Crunch'n'Munch All-Stars

The 1985 Star Crunch'n'Munch NBA All-Stars set is an 11-card standard-size set featuring the ten starting players in the 1985 NBA All-Star Game plus a checklist card. The set was produced for the Crunch 'n' Munch Food Company and was originally available to the hobby exclusively through Don Guilbert of Woonsocket, Rhode Island. The set's basic design is identical to those of the Star Company's regular NBA sets. The cards show a Star '85 logo in the upper right corner. The front borders are yellowish orange and the backs show each player's All-Star Game record.

COMPLETE SET (11) 250.00 400.00
1 All-Star CL 2.50 6.00
2 Larry Bird 40.00 80.00
3 Julius Erving 12.50 30.00
4 Michael Jordan ! 125.00 300.00
5 Moses Malone 4.00 10.00
6 Isiah Thomas 6.00 15.00
7 Kareem Abdul-Jabbar 8.00 20.00
8 Adrian Dantley 4.00 10.00
9 George Gervin 5.00 12.00
10 Magic Johnson 30.00 60.00
11 Ralph Sampson 4.00 10.00
BAG1 Complete sealed bag (11) 250.00 400.00

1985 Star Gatorade Slam Dunk

This nine-card set was given to the people who attended the 1985 All-Star Weekend Banquet at Indianapolis. Cards measure the standard size and have a green border around the fronts of the cards and green printing on the backs. Cards feature the Star '85 and Gatorade logos on the fronts. Since Terence Stansbury was a late substitute in the Slam Dunk contest for Charles Barkley, both cards were produced, but the Barkley card was not released at that time. However, the Barkley card has since surfaced in the marketplace. The Barkley card is unnumbered and shows him dunking.

COMPLETE SET (9) 150.00 275.00
1 Slam Dunk CL 2.50 6.00
2 Larry Nance 2.50 6.00
3 Terence Stansbury 1.50 4.00
4 Clyde Drexler 10.00 25.00
5 Julius Erving 10.00 25.00
6 Darrell Griffith 1.50 4.00
7 Michael Jordan 100.00 250.00
8 Dominique Wilkins 10.00 25.00
9 Orlando Woolridge 1.50 4.00
BAG1 Complete sealed bag (11) 150.00 275.00
NNO Charles Barkley SP 40.00 80.00
(Withdrawn)

1985 Star Last 11 ROY's

The 1985 Star Rookies of the Year set is an 11-card standard-size set depicting each of the NBA's ROY award winners from the 1974-75 through 1984-85 seasons. Michael Jordan's card only shows his collegiate statistics while all others provide NBA statistics up through the 1983-84 season. Cards of Darrell Griffith and Jamaal Wilkes show the Star '86 logo in the upper right corner while all others in the set show Star '85. The set's basic design is identical to those of the Star Company's regular NBA sets and the front borders are off-white. The set is sequenced in reverse chronological order according to when each player won the ROY.

COMPLETE SET (11) 175.00 275.00
1 Michael Jordan 100.00 250.00
2 Ralph Sampson 2.00 5.00
3 Terry Cummings 2.00 5.00
4 Buck Williams 2.00 5.00
5 Darrell Griffith 2.00 5.00
6 Larry Bird 40.00 80.00
7 Phil Ford 2.00 5.00
8 Walter Davis 2.00 5.00
9 Adrian Dantley 2.50 6.00
10 Alvan Adams 2.00 5.00
11 Jamaal Wilkes 2.00 5.00
BAG1 Complete sealed bag (11) 175.00 275.00

1985 Star Lite All-Stars

This 13-card standard-size set was given to the people who attended the 1985 All-Star Weekend Banquet at Indianapolis. The set was issued in a clear, sealed plastic bag. Cards have a blue border around the fronts of the cards and blue printing on the backs. Cards feature the Star '85 and Lite Beer logos on the fronts. Players featured are the 1985 NBA All-Star starting line-ups and coaches. A cropping variation on card #4, Michael Jordan, has been noted in the checklist. The variation features Jordan's hair right up tight to the top white outline border.

COMPLETE SET (13) 125.00 250.00
1 1985 NBA All-Stars 2.00 5.00
2 Larry Bird 30.00 60.00
3 Julius Erving 6.00 15.00
4 Michael Jordan ! 100.00 175.00
5 Moses Malone 3.00 8.00
6 Isiah Thomas 3.00 8.00
7 K.C. Jones CO 2.00 5.00
8 Kareem Abdul-Jabbar 7.50 15.00
9 Adrian Dantley 2.00 5.00
10 George Gervin 3.00 8.00
11 Magic Johnson 20.00 40.00
12 Ralph Sampson 2.00 5.00
13 Pat Riley CO 2.50 6.00
4A Michael Jordan VAR
Variation in cropping with hair touching border
BAG1 Complete sealed bag (13) 125.00 250.00

1985 Star Schick Legends

This 24-card set was given to the people who attended the 1985 All-Star Weekend Banquet at Indianapolis. Cards measure 2 1/2" by 3 1/2" and have a yellow border around the fronts of the cards and yellow and black printing on the backs. Cards feature the Star '85 and Schick logos on the fronts. Players featured were participants in the Schick NBA Legends Classic. The cards are numbered on the back; the numbering corresponds to alphabetical order by player.

COMPLETE SET (25) 25.00 60.00
1 Schick NBA Legends CL 1.25 3.00
2 Rick Barry 2.50 6.00
3 Zelmo Beaty 1.25 3.00
4 Walt Bellamy 1.50 4.00
5 Dave Bing 1.50 4.00
6 Roger Brown 1.25 3.00
7 Bob Cousy 2.50 6.00
8 Mel Daniels 1.50 4.00
9 Bob Davies 1.50 4.00
10 Dave DeBusschere 2.00 5.00
11 Walt Frazier 2.50 6.00
12 John Havlicek 3.00 8.00
13 Connie Hawkins 2.50 6.00
14 Tom Heinsohn 2.00 5.00
15 Red Holzman CO 1.50 4.00
16 Johnny Kerr 1.25 3.00
17 Bobby Leonard 1.25 3.00
18 Pete Maravich 12.50 30.00
19 Earl Monroe 2.50 6.00
20 Bob Pettit 3.00 8.00
21 Oscar Robertson 4.00 10.00
22 Nate Thurmond 2.00 5.00
23 Dick Van Arsdale 1.25 3.00
24 Tom Van Arsdale 1.25 3.00
25 George Yardley 1.25 3.00
BAG1 Complete sealed bag (25) 30.00 80.00

1985 Star Slam Dunk Supers 5x7

This ten-card set uses actual photography from the 1985 Slam Dunk contest in Indianapolis held during the NBA All-Star Weekend. Cards measure approximately 5" by 7" and have a red border around the fronts of the cards and red printing on the backs. Cards feature Star '85 logo on the fronts. The set ordering for these numbered cards is alphabetical by subject's name.

COMPLETE SET (10) 125.00 250.00
1 Group Photo CL 20.00 40.00
2 Clyde Drexler 12.50 25.00
3 Julius Erving 10.00 25.00
4 Darrell Griffith 2.00 5.00
5 Michael Jordan 100.00 175.00
6 Larry Nance 3.00 8.00
7 Terence Stansbury 2.00 5.00
8 Dominique Wilkins 6.00 15.00
9 Orlando Woolridge 2.00 5.00
10 Dominique Wilkins 6.00 15.00
(1985 Slam Dunk Champ)
BAG1 Complete sealed bag (10) 125.00 250.00

1985 Star Team Supers 5x7

This 40-card set is actually eight team sets of five each except for the Sixers having ten players included. Cards measure approximately 5" by 7" and have a colored border around the fronts of the cards according to the team with corresponding color printing on the backs. Cards feature Star '85 logo on the front. Cards are numbered below by assigning a team prefix based on the initials of the team, for example, BC for Boston Celtics.

COMPLETE SET (40) 250.00 450.00
BC1 Larry Bird 15.00 30.00
BC2 Robert Parish 3.00 8.00
BC3 Kevin McHale 4.00 10.00
BC4 Dennis Johnson 3.00 8.00
BC5 Danny Ainge 3.00 8.00
CB1 Michael Jordan 100.00 200.00
CB2 Orlando Woolridge 1.50 4.00
CB3 Quintin Dailey 1.50 4.00
CB4 Dave Corzine 1.50 4.00
CB5 Steve Johnson 1.50 4.00
DP1 Isiah Thomas 5.00 12.00
DP2 Kelly Tripucka 1.50 4.00
DP3 Vinnie Johnson 1.50 4.00
DP4 Bill Laimbeer 2.00 5.00
DP5 John Long 1.50 4.00
HR1 Ralph Sampson 2.00 5.00
HR2 Hakeem Olajuwon 20.00 40.00
HR3 Lewis Lloyd 1.50 4.00
HR4 Rodney McCray 1.50 4.00
HR5 Lionel Hollins 1.50 4.00
LA1 Kareem Abdul-Jabbar 8.00 20.00
LA2 Magic Johnson 15.00 40.00
LA3 James Worthy 4.00 10.00
LA4 Byron Scott 2.00 5.00
LA5 Bob McAdoo 3.00 8.00
MB1 Terry Cummings 2.00 5.00
MB2 Sidney Moncrief 2.00 5.00
MB3 Paul Pressey 1.50 4.00
MB4 Mike Dunleavy 2.00 5.00
MB5 Alton Lister 1.50 4.00
PS1 Julius Erving 8.00 20.00
PS2 Maurice Cheeks 2.00 5.00
PS3 Bobby Jones 2.00 5.00
PS4 Clemon Johnson 1.50 4.00
PS5 Leon Wood 2.00 5.00
PS6 Moses Malone 4.00 10.00
PS7 Andrew Toney 1.50 4.00
PS8 Charles Barkley 25.00 50.00
PS9 Clint Richardson 1.50 4.00
PS10 Sedale Threatt 1.50 4.00
BAG1a 76ers sealed blue bag (5) 30.00 60.00
BAG1b 76ers sealed white bag (5) 12.50 30.00
BAG2 Bucks sealed bag (5) 6.00 15.00
BAG3 Bulls sealed bag (5) 100.00 200.00
BAG4 Celtics sealed bag (5) 25.00 50.00
BAG5 Lakers sealed bag (5) 30.00 60.00
BAG6 Pistons sealed bag (5) 10.00 20.00
BAG7 Rockets sealed bag (5) 20.00 40.00

1985-86 Star

This 172-card standard-size set was produced by the Star Company and features players in the NBA. Cards were released in two groups, 1-94 and 95-172. The team sets were issued in clear sealed bags. Many of these team bags were distributed to hobby dealers through a small group of Star Company master distributors. The original wholesale price per bag was $2-$3 for most of the teams. According to Star Company's original sales materials and order forms, reportedly 2,000 team bags were printed for each team and an additional 2,200 team sets were printed for the more popular teams of that time. Cards are numbered in team order. Borders are colored according to team. Card backs are very similar to the other Star basketball sets except that the player statistics go up through the 1984-85 season. Extended Rookie Cards in this set include Patrick Ewing and Kevin Willis. There is typically a slight discount on sales of opened team bags. Cards of Celtics players (95-102) have either green or white borders. Many cards in this set (particularly 95-176) have been counterfeited and are prevalent on the market. Among those affected are the Ewing Extended Rookie Card (166) and Jordan (117).

COMPLETE BAG SET (172) 750.00 1250.00
1 Maurice Cheeks ! 2.50 6.00
2 Charles Barkley ! 25.00 50.00
3 Julius Erving ! 8.00 20.00
4 Clemon Johnson 1.00 2.50
5 Bobby Jones ! 1.50 4.00
6 Moses Malone ! 3.00 8.00
7 Sedale Threatt ! 1.00 2.50
8 Andrew Toney 1.50 4.00
9 Leon Wood 1.00 2.50
10 Isiah Thomas UER 6.00 15.00
(No Pistons logo on card front)
11 Kent Benson 1.00 2.50
12 Earl Cureton 1.00 2.50
13 Vinnie Johnson 1.50 4.00
14 Bill Laimbeer 2.50 6.00
15 John Long 1.00 2.50
16 Rick Mahorn 1.00 2.50
17 Kelly Tripucka 1.00 2.50
18 Hakeem Olajuwon ! 15.00 40.00
19 Allen Leavell 1.00 2.50
20 Lewis Lloyd 1.00 2.50
21 John Lucas 1.00 2.50
22 Rodney McCray 1.00 2.50
23 Robert Reid 1.00 2.50
24 Ralph Sampson 1.50 4.00
25 Mitchell Wiggins 1.00 2.50
26 Kareem Abdul-Jabbar 10.00 25.00
27 Michael Cooper 3.00 8.00
28 Magic Johnson 25.00 60.00
29 Mitch Kupchak 2.00 5.00
30 Maurice Lucas 2.00 5.00
31 Kurt Rambis 2.50 6.00
32 Byron Scott 3.00 8.00
33 James Worthy 6.00 15.00
34 Larry Nance 2.50 6.00
35 Alvan Adams 1.50 4.00
36 Walter Davis 1.50 4.00
37 James Edwards 1.00 2.50
38 Jay Humphries 1.00 2.50
39 Charles Pittman 1.00 2.50
40 Rick Robey 1.00 2.50
41 Mike Sanders 1.00 2.50
42 Dominique Wilkins 12.50 30.00
43 Scott Hastings 1.00 2.50
44 Eddie Johnson 1.00 2.50
45 Cliff Levingston 1.00 2.50
46 Tree Rollins 1.00 2.50
47 Doc Rivers UER 2.50 6.00
(Ray Williams is pictured on the front)
48 Kevin Willis XRC 5.00 12.00
49 Randy Wittman 1.00 2.50
50 Alex English 3.00 8.00
51 Wayne Cooper 1.00 2.50
52 T.R. Dunn 1.00 2.50
53 Mike Evans 1.00 2.50
54 Lafayette Lever 1.50 4.00
55 Calvin Natt 1.00 2.50
56 Danny Schayes 1.50 4.00
57 Elston Turner 1.00 2.50
58 Buck Williams 2.50 6.00
59 Otis Birdsong 1.00 2.50
60 Darwin Cook 1.00 2.50
61 Darryl Dawkins 1.50 4.00
62 Mike Gminski 1.00 2.50
63 Mickey Johnson 1.00 2.50
64 Mike O'Koren 1.00 2.50
65 Micheal Ray Richardson 1.00 2.50
66 Tom Chambers 2.50 6.00
67 Gerald Henderson 1.00 2.50
68 Tim McCormick 1.00 2.50
69 Jack Sikma 1.50 4.00
70 Ricky Sobers 1.00 2.50
71 Danny Vranes 1.00 2.50
72 Al Wood 1.00 2.50
73 Danny Young XRC 1.50 4.00
74 Reggie Theus 1.50 4.00
75 Larry Drew 1.00 2.50
76 Eddie Johnson 1.50 4.00
77 Mark Olberding 1.00 2.50
78 LaSalle Thompson 1.00 2.50
79 Otis Thorpe 1.50 4.00
80 Mike Woodson 1.50 4.00
81 Clark Kellogg 1.50 4.00
82 Quinn Buckner 1.00 2.50
83 Vern Fleming 1.00 2.50
84 Bill Garnett 1.00 2.50
85 Terence Stansbury 1.00 2.50
86 Steve Stipanovich 1.00 2.50
87 Herb Williams 1.00 2.50
88 Marques Johnson 1.50 4.00
89 Michael Cage 1.50 4.00
90 Franklin Edwards 1.00 2.50
91 Cedric Maxwell 1.00 2.50
92 Derek Smith 1.00 2.50
93 Rory White 1.00 2.50
94 Jamaal Wilkes 1.50 4.00
95G Larry Bird Green 20.00 40.00
95W Larry Bird White 25.00 60.00
96G Danny Ainge Green 4.00 10.00
96W Danny Ainge White 6.00 15.00
97G Dennis Johnson Green 3.00 8.00
98G Kevin McHale Green 6.00 12.00
98W Kevin McHale White 8.00 20.00
99G Robert Parish Green 3.00 8.00
99W Robert Parish White 5.00 12.00
100G Jerry Sichting Green 1.00 2.50
101G Bill Walton Green 6.00 12.00
102G Scott Wedman Green 1.00 2.50
103 Kiki Vandeweghe 1.50 4.00
104 Sam Bowie 1.50 4.00
105 Kenny Carr 1.00 2.50
106 Clyde Drexler ! 20.00 50.00
107 Jerome Kersey XRC 3.00 8.00
108 Jim Paxson 1.50 4.00
109 Mychal Thompson 1.50 4.00
110 Gus Williams 1.50 4.00
111 Darren Daye 1.00 2.50
112 Jeff Malone 1.50 4.00
113 Tom McMillen 1.50 4.00
114 Cliff Robinson 1.00 2.50
115 Dan Roundfield 1.00 2.50
116 Jeff Ruland 1.50 4.00
117 Michael Jordan ! 200.00 500.00
118 Gene Banks 1.50 4.00
119 Dave Corzine 1.50 4.00
120 Quintin Dailey 1.50 4.00
121 George Gervin 6.00 15.00
122 Jawann Oldham 1.50 4.00
123 Orlando Woolridge 1.50 4.00
124 Terry Cummings 2.50 6.00
125 Craig Hodges 1.00 2.50
126 Alton Lister 1.00 2.50
127 Paul Mokeski 1.00 2.50
128 Sidney Moncrief 2.50 6.00
129 Ricky Pierce 1.50 4.00
130 Paul Pressey 1.00 2.50
131 Purvis Short 1.00 2.50
132 Joe Barry Carroll 1.00 2.50
133 Lester Conner 1.00 2.50
134 Sleepy Floyd 1.50 4.00
135 Geoff Huston 1.00 2.50
136 Larry Smith 1.00 2.50
137 Jerome Whitehead 1.00 2.50
138 Adrian Dantley 2.50 6.00
139 Mitchell Anderson 1.00 2.50
140 Thurl Bailey 1.50 4.00
141 Mark Eaton 1.50 4.00
142 Rickey Green 1.00 2.50
143 Darrell Griffith 1.50 4.00
144 John Stockton 40.00 70.00
145 Artis Gilmore 2.50 6.00
146 Marc Iavaroni 1.50 4.00
147 Steve Johnson 1.00 2.50
148 Mike Mitchell 1.00 2.50
149 Johnny Moore 1.00 2.50
150 Alvin Robertson 1.00 2.50
151 Jon Sundvold 1.00 2.50
152 World B. Free 1.50 4.00
153 John Bagley 1.00 2.50
154 Johnny Davis 1.00 2.50
155 Roy Hinson 1.00 2.50
156 Phil Hubbard 1.00 2.50
157 Ben Poquette 1.00 2.50
158 Mel Turpin 1.00 2.50
159 Rolando Blackman 2.50 6.00
160 Mark Aguirre 2.50 6.00
161 Brad Davis 1.50 4.00
162 Dale Ellis 1.50 4.00
163 Derek Harper 2.50 6.00
164 Sam Perkins 2.50 6.00
165 Jay Vincent 1.00 2.50
166 Patrick Ewing XRC 60.00 150.00
167 Bill Cartwright 1.50 4.00
168 Pat Cummings 1.00 2.50
169 Ernie Grunfeld 1.50 4.00
170 Rory Sparrow 1.00 2.50
171 Trent Tucker 1.00 2.50
172 Darrell Walker 1.50 4.00
97W Dennis Johnson White 5.00 12.00
100W Jerry Sichting White 1.50 4.00
101W Bill Walton White 8.00 20.00
102W Scott Wedman White 1.50 4.00
BAG1 76ers sealed bag (9) 30.00 70.00
BAG2 Blazers sealed bag (7) 30.00 70.00
BAG3 Bucks sealed bag (7) 8.00 20.00
BAG4 Bullets sealed bag (7) 8.00 20.00
BAG5 Bulls sealed bag (7) 400.00 600.00
BAG6 Cavs sealed bag (7) 8.00 20.00
BAG7 Celtics grn sealed bag (8) 30.00 80.00
BAG8 Celtics wht sealed bag (8) 50.00 120.00
BAG9 Clippers sealed bag (7) 8.00 20.00
BAG10 Hawks sealed bag (8) 20.00 40.00
BAG11 Jazz sealed bag (7) 30.00 80.00
BAG12 Kings sealed bag (7) 8.00 20.00
BAG13 Knicks sealed bag (7) 100.00 175.00
BAG14 Lakers SP sealed bag (8) 50.00 120.00
BAG15 Mavs sealed bag (7) 10.00 25.00
BAG16 Nets sealed bag (8) 8.00 20.00
BAG17 Nuggets sealed bag (8) 8.00 20.00
BAG18 Pacers sealed bag (7) 8.00 20.00
BAG19 Pistons sealed bag (8) 15.00 30.00
BAG20 Rockets sealed bag (8) 25.00 60.00
BAG21 Sonics sealed bag (8) 8.00 20.00
BAG22 Spurs sealed bag (7) 8.00 20.00
BAG23 Suns sealed bag (8) 8.00 20.00
BAG24 Warriors sealed bag (7) 8.00 20.00

1985-86 Star All-Rookie Team

The 1985-86 Star NBA All-Rookie Team is an 11-card standard-size set that features 11 top rookies from the previous (1984-85) season. The set's basic design is identical to those of the Star Company's regular NBA sets. The front borders are red and the backs include each player's collegiate statistics. Alvin Robertson's card shows the Star '86 logo in the upper right corner. All others in the set show Star '85.

COMPLETE SET (11) 250.00 350.00
1 Hakeem Olajuwon 25.00 50.00
2 Michael Jordan 100.00 250.00
3 Charles Barkley 25.00 60.00
4 Sam Bowie 2.50 6.00
5 Sam Perkins 2.50 6.00
6 Vern Fleming 2.00 5.00
7 Otis Thorpe 2.00 5.00
8 John Stockton 30.00 60.00
9 Kevin Willis 2.50 6.00
10 Tim McCormick 2.00 5.00
11 Alvin Robertson 2.00 5.00
BAG1 Complete sealed bag (11) 250.00 350.00

1985-86 Star Lakers Champs

The 1985-86 Star Lakers NBA Champs set is an 18-card standard-size set commemorating the Los Angeles Lakers' 1985 NBA Championship. Each card depicts action from the Championship series. The front borders are off-white. The backs feature game and series summaries plus other related information. The set's basic design is identical to those of the Star Company's regular NBA sets. The cards show a Star '86 logo in the upper right corner.

COMPLETE SET (18) 30.00 80.00
1 Kareem Abdul-Jabbar 5.00 12.00
Jerry Buss OWN
2 Larry Bird IA 6.00 15.00
3 Dennis Johnson IA 1.25 3.00
4 Danny Ainge IA 2.00 5.00
5 Byron Scott IA 1.25 3.00
6 Kevin McHale IA 2.50 6.00
7 Magic Johnson IA 6.00 15.00
8 Kareem Abdul-Jabbar MVP 3.00 8.00
Robert Parish
9 Larry Bird IA 6.00 15.00
10 Kareem Abdul-Jabbar IA 3.00 8.00
11 Danny Ainge IA 2.00 5.00
Michael Cooper
12 Pat Riley CO 2.00 5.00
13 K.C. Jones CO 1.25 3.00
14 Magic Johnson IA 6.00 15.00
15 Boston Playoff Stats 2.50 6.00
(action under basket)
16 Road To The Title 1.25 3.00
17 Prior World Champs I 1.25 3.00
(riding on float)
18 Ronald Reagan 15.00 30.00
Lakers Champs II
BAG1 Complete sealed bag (18) 30.00 80.00

1986 Star Best of the Best

The Star Company reportedly produced only 1,400 sets and planned to release them in 1986. However, they were not issued until as late as 1990. This set and the Magic Johnson set were printed on the same uncut sheet. No factory-sealed bags exist for this set due to the fact that the sets were cut from the sheets years after the original printing. It is understood that the uncut sheets were sold to hobbyists who cut the sheets and packaged sets to be sold into the hobby. The cards measure the standard size. The fronts feature color action photos with white inner borders and a blue card face. The player's name, position, and team name appear at the bottom. The set title "Best of the Best" appears in a white circle at the lower left corner. The backs are white with blue borders and contain biography and statistics. The cards are numbered and arranged in alphabetical order.

COMPLETE SET (15) 50.00 120.00
1 Kareem Abdul-Jabbar 2.50 6.00
2 Charles Barkley 6.00 15.00
3 Larry Bird 5.00 12.00
4 Tom Chambers 1.00 2.50
5 Terry Cummings 1.00 2.50
6 Julius Erving 3.00 8.00
7 Patrick Ewing 4.00 10.00
8 Magic Johnson 5.00 12.00
9 Michael Jordan 40.00 100.00
10 Moses Malone 1.50 4.00
11 Hakeem Olajuwon 4.00 10.00
12 John Stockton 4.00 10.00
13 Isiah Thomas 2.50 6.00
14 Dominique Wilkins 3.00 8.00
15 James Worthy 2.50 6.00

1986 Star Best of the New/Old

The Star Company distributed these sets to dealers who purchased 1985-86 complete sets. Dealers received one set for every five regular sets purchased. The cards measure the standard size. The cards are unnumbered and checklisted below in alphabetical order. The Best of the New are numbered 1-4 and the Best of the Old are numbered 5-8. The numbering is alphabetical within each group. Counterfeiting has been a problem with the Best of the New series.

COMPLETE SET (8) 225.00 450.00
COMPLETE NEW SET (4) 75.00 150.00
COMPLETE OLD SET (4) 150.00 300.00
1 Patrick Ewing 10.00 25.00
2 Michael Jordan 60.00 150.00
3 Hakeem Olajuwon 10.00 25.00
4 Ralph Sampson 2.00 5.00
5 Kareem Abdul-Jabbar 50.00 100.00
6 Julius Erving 60.00 120.00
7 George Gervin 30.00 60.00
8 Bill Walton 30.00 60.00
BAG1 Complete old sealed bag (4) 150.00 300.00
BAG2 Complete new sealed bag (4) 75.00 150.00

1986 Star Court Kings

The 1986 Star Court Kings set contains 33 standard-size cards which feature many of the NBA's top players. The set's basic design is identical to those of the Star Company's regular NBA sets. The front borders are yellow, and the backs have career narrative summaries of each player but no statistics. The cards show a Star '86 logo in the upper right corner. The cards are numbered in the upper left corner of the reverse. The numbering is alphabetical by last name.

COMPLETE SET (33) 100.00 200.00
1 Mark Aguirre 1.25 3.00
2 Kareem Abdul-Jabbar 5.00 12.00
3 Charles Barkley ! 8.00 20.00
4 Larry Bird ! 8.00 20.00
5 Rolando Blackman 1.25 3.00
6 Tom Chambers 1.25 3.00
7 Maurice Cheeks 1.25 3.00
8 Terry Cummings 1.25 3.00
9 Adrian Dantley 1.25 3.00
10 Darryl Dawkins 1.25 3.00
11 Mark Eaton 1.25 3.00
12 Alex English 1.50 4.00
13 Julius Erving 5.00 12.00
14 Patrick Ewing ! 5.00 12.00
15 George Gervin 2.50 6.00
16 Darrell Griffith 1.25 3.00
17 Magic Johnson 6.00 15.00
18 Michael Jordan 75.00 150.00
19 Clark Kellogg 1.25 3.00
20 Bernard King 1.25 3.00
21 Moses Malone 1.50 4.00
22 Kevin McHale 2.50 6.00
23 Sidney Moncrief 1.50 4.00
24 Larry Nance 1.50 4.00
25 Hakeem Olajuwon 5.00 12.00
26 Robert Parish 2.00 5.00
27 Ralph Sampson 1.25 3.00
28 Isiah Thomas 2.50 6.00
29 Andrew Toney 1.25 3.00
30 Kelly Tripucka 1.25 3.00
31 Kiki Vandeweghe 1.25 3.00
32 Dominique Wilkins UER 4.00 10.00
33 James Worthy 3.00 8.00
BAG1 Complete sealed bag (33) 100.00 200.00

1986 Star Magic Johnson

This 10-card set highlights the career of Magic Johnson. The Star Company reportedly produced only 1,400 sets of these cards and planned to release them in 1986. However, they were not issued until perhaps as late as 1990. This set and the Best of the Best set were printed on the same uncut sheet. Star directly sold sheets to hobbyists who cut them and sold sets to the hobby. The cards measure the standard size. The cards are unnumbered and checklisted below in alphabetical order.

COMPLETE SET (10) 30.00 60.00
COMMON CARD (1-10) 3.00 8.00

1986 Star Michael Jordan

The 1986 Star Michael Jordan set contains ten cards highlighting his career. There were reportedly only 2,800 sets produced. They were originally available to the hobby exclusively through Dan Stickney of Michigan. Sets were originally issued in sealed plastic bags. The card backs contain various bits of information about Jordan. The set's basic design is identical to those of the Star Company's regular NBA sets. The front borders are red. The cards show a Star '86 logo in the upper right corner. The cards measure approximately 2 1/2" by 3 1/2". The cards are numbered in the upper left corner of the reverse. Collectors should beware of counterfeits.

COMPLETE SET (10) 300.00 500.00
COMMON CARD (1-10) 30.00 60.00
BAG1 Complete sealed bag (10) 300.00 500.00

1990 Star Charles Barkley

This 11-card set measures the standard size. The fronts feature color action shots, with red borders that wash out in the middle of the card face. The horizontally oriented backs are printed in red on white and have various kinds of player information. Reportedly there were 5000 regular sets produced; 250 limited edition glossy sets. Glossy cards are valued at five times the values of the regular cards.

COMPLETE SET (11) 1.25 3.00
COMMON CARD (1-11) .20 .50

1990 Star Dee Brown

This 11-card set measures the standard size. The fror feature color action shots, with green borders that wa out in the middle of the card face. The horizontally oriented backs are printed in green on white and have various kinds of player information. Reportedly there were 5000 regular sets produced; 250 limited edition glossy sets. Glossy cards are valued at five times the values of the regular cards.

COMPLETE SET (11) .75 2.0
COMMON CARD (1-11) .10 .2

1990 Star Tom Chambers

This 11-card set measures the standard size. The fror feature color action shots, with orange borders that wash out in the middle of the card face. The horizontally oriented backs are printed in orange on white and have various kinds of player information. Reportedly there were 5000 regular sets produced; 25 limited edition glossy sets. Glossy cards are valued a five times the values of the regular cards.

COMPLETE SET (11) .75 2.0
COMMON CARD (1-11) .12 .3

1990 Star Derrick Coleman I

This 11-card set measures the standard size. The fron feature color action shots, with blue borders that wash out in the middle of the card face. The horizontally oriented backs are printed in blue on white and have various kinds of player information. Reportedly there were 5000 regular sets produced; 250 limited edition glossy sets. Glossy cards are valued at five times the values of the regular cards.

COMPLETE SET (11) .75 2.0
COMMON CARD (1-11) .12 .3

1990 Star Derrick Coleman II

This 11-card set measures the standard size. The fron feature color action shots, with red borders that wash out in the middle of the card face. The horizontally oriented backs are printed in red on white and have various kinds of player information. Reportedly there were 5000 regular sets produced; 250 limited edition glossy sets. Glossy cards are valued at five times the values of the regular cards.

COMPLETE SET (11) .75 2.0
COMMON CARD (1-11) .12 .3

1990 Star Clyde Drexler

This 11-card set measures the standard size. The fron feature color action shots, with red borders that wash out in the middle of the card face. The horizontally oriented backs are printed in red on white and have various kinds of player information. Reportedly there were 5000 regular sets produced; 250 limited edition glossy sets. Glossy cards are valued at five times the values of the regular cards.

COMPLETE SET (11) 1.25 3.0
COMMON CARD (1-11) .25 .6

1990 Star Patrick Ewing

This 11-card set measures the standard size. The fron feature color action shots, with orange borders that wash out in the middle of the card face. The horizontally oriented backs are printed in blue on whit and have various kinds of player information. Reportedly there were 5000 regular sets produced; 25 limited edition glossy sets. Glossy cards are valued a five times the values of the regular cards.

COMPLETE SET (11) 1.25 3.0
COMMON CARD (1-11) .15 .4

1990 Star Tim Hardaway

This 11-card set measures the standard size. The fron feature color action shots, with yellow borders that wash out in the middle of the card face. The horizontally oriented backs are printed in blue on whit and have various kinds of player information. Reportedly there were 5000 regular sets produced; 25 limited edition glossy sets. Glossy cards are valued at five times the values of the regular cards.

COMPLETE SET (11) .75 2.0
COMMON CARD (1-11) .15 .4

1990 Star Kevin Johnson

This 11-card set measures the standard size. The fron feature color action shots, with orange borders that wash out in the middle of the card face. The horizontally oriented backs are printed in purple on white and have various kinds of player information. Reportedly there were 5000 regular sets produced; 25 limited edition glossy sets. Glossy cards are valued a five times the values of the regular cards.

COMPLETE SET (11) .75 2.0
COMMON CARD (1-11) .10 .3

1990 Star Karl Malone

This 11-card set measures the standard size. The fron feature color action shots, with green borders that wa out in the middle of the card face. The horizontally oriented backs are printed in green on white and have

ous kinds of player information. Reportedly there 5000 regular sets produced; 250 limited edition sy sets. Glossy cards are valued at five times the es of the regular cards.
IPLETE SET (11) 1.25 3.00
IMON CARD (1-11) .20 .50

1990 Star Hakeem Olajuwon

s 11-card set measures the standard size. The fronts ure color action shots, with yellow borders that h out in the middle of the card face. The zontally oriented backs are printed in red on white have various kinds of player information. ortedly there were 5000 regular sets produced; 250 ted edition glossy sets. Glossy cards are valued at times the values of the regular cards.
IPLETE SET (11) 1.25 3.00
IMON CARD (1-11) .20 .50

1990 Star David Robinson I

s 11-card set measures the standard size. The fronts ure color action shots, with blue borders that wash in the middle of the card face. The horizontally nted backs are printed in blue on white and have ous kinds of player information. Reportedly there 5000 regular sets produced; 250 limited edition sy sets. Glossy cards are valued at five times the es of the regular cards.
IPLETE SET (11) 2.00 5.00
IMON CARD (1-11) .30 .75

1990 Star David Robinson II

s 11-card set measures the standard size. The fronts ure color action shots, with black borders that wash in the middle of the card face. The horizontally nted backs are printed in black on white and have ous kinds of player information. Reportedly there 5000 regular sets produced; 250 limited edition sy sets. Glossy cards are valued at five times the es of the regular cards.
IPLETE SET (11) 1.50 4.00
IMON CARD (1-11) .25 .60

1990 Star David Robinson III

s 11-card set measures the standard size. The fronts ure color action shots, with purple borders that h out in the middle of the card face. The zontally oriented backs are printed in purple on te and have various kinds of player information. ortedly there were 5000 regular sets produced; 250 ted edition glossy sets. Glossy cards are valued at times the values of the regular cards.
IPLETE SET (11) 1.50 4.00
IMON CARD (1-11) .30 .75

1990 Star John Stockton

s 11-card set measures the standard size. The fronts ure color action shots, with purple borders that h out in the middle of the card face. The zontally oriented backs are printed in purple on te and have various kinds of player information. ortedly there were 5000 regular sets produced; 250 ted edition glossy sets. Glossy cards are valued at times the values of the regular cards.
IPLETE SET (11) 1.50 4.00
IMON CARD (1-11) .20 .50

1990 Star Isiah Thomas

s 11-card set measures the standard size. The fronts ture color action shots, with purple borders that h out in the middle of the card face. The zontally oriented backs are printed in purple on te and have various kinds of player information. ortedly there were 5000 regular sets produced; 250 ted edition glossy sets. Glossy cards are valued at times the values of the regular cards.
IPLETE SET (11) 1.25 3.00
IMON CARD (1-11) .20 .50

1990 Star Dominique Wilkins

s 11-card set measures the standard size. The fronts ture color action shots, with yellow borders that h out in the middle of the card face. The zontally oriented backs are printed in red on white have various kinds of player information. ortedly there were 5000 regular sets produced; 250 ted edition glossy sets. Glossy cards are valued at five times the values of the regular cards.
COMPLETE SET (11) 1.25 3.00
COMMON CARD (1-11) .20 .50

1990 Star James Worthy

This 11-card set measures the standard size. The fronts feature color action shots, with yellow borders that wash out in the middle of the card face. The horizontally oriented backs are printed in purple on white and have various kinds of player information. Reportedly there were 5000 regular sets produced; 250 limited edition glossy sets. Glossy cards are valued at five times the values of the regular cards.
COMPLETE SET (11) 1.25 3.00
COMMON CARD (1-11) .15 .40

1990-91 Star Promos

These 18 promo cards showcase outstanding NBA players. The standard-size cards feature color action player photos on the obverse. The pictures have different color borders, which wash out as one approaches the middle of the card face. In white lettering the player's name, team, and "Promo" appear below the picture. The reverses are blank. The cards are unnumbered and are checklisted below in alphabetical order. Reportedly there were 1400 promo sets and 50 glossy promo sets produced. The glossy promos are valued at four times the values of the regular cards.
COMPLETE SET (18) 16.00 40.00
1 Charles Barkley 2.50 6.00
2 Dee Brown .40 1.00
3 Tom Chambers .40 1.00
4 Derrick Coleman I .60 1.50
5 Derrick Coleman II .40 1.00
6 Clyde Drexler 1.25 3.00
7 Patrick Ewing 1.25 3.00
8 Tim Hardaway 1.50 4.00
9 Kevin Johnson .75 2.00
10 Karl Malone 3.00 8.00
11 Hakeem Olajuwon 2.00 5.00
12 David Robinson I 2.00 5.00
13 David Robinson II 2.00 5.00
14 David Robinson III 2.00 5.00
15 John Stockton 2.00 5.00
16 Isiah Thomas .75 2.00
17 Dominique Wilkins .75 2.00
18 James Worthy .75 2.00

1993-94 Star

The 1993-94 Star basketball set consists of 100 standard-size cards featuring past and current NBA players. The cards were packaged in nine-card foil packs, and randomly inserted special coupons enabled the collector to win special autograph cards, uncut sheets, and other memorabilia. The fronts feature color player action photos with team color-coded borders. The player's name appears above the photo at the upper right. The card's subtitle appears below the photo at the lower left. The back has a color player action shot on the left side with the player's name, bio and profile alongside to the right. All NBA team names and logos have been airbrushed from the players' uniforms.
COMPLETE SET (100) 6.00 15.00
1 Larry Bird .40 1.00
Career Stats 1979-1987
2 Chris Mullin .08 .25
Pro Season Stats
3 Harold Miner .05 .15
Collegiate Record
4 Tom Gugliotta UER .05 .15
Personal Data/(Misspelled Guggliotta on front and back)
5 Christian Laettner .08 .25
College and NBA Record
6 Tim Hardaway .10 .30
Collegiate Stats
7 Shawn Kemp .15 .40
NBA Regular Season Stats
8 Walt Frazier .08 .25
Collegiate Record
9 John Starks .08 .25
Career Highlights
10 Charles Barkley .15 .40
Collegiate Stats
11 Robert Parish .10 .30
Pro Stats 1
12 Chris Mullin .08 .25
Playoff Stats
13 Kevin McHale .10 .30
Collegiate Stats
14 Scott Burrell .05 .15
Career Stats
15 Harold Miner .05 .15
1992/93 Season 1
16 Richard Dumas .05 .15
Career Stats
17 Larry Bird .40 1.00
Career Stats 1988-1992
18 Xavier McDaniel .05 .15
Collegiate Stats
19 Christian Laettner .08 .25
1992-93 Season 1
20 Shawn Kemp .15 .40
NBA Playoff Stats
21 Tom Gugliotta UER .05 .15
Collegiate Record/(Misspelled Guggliotta on front and back)
22 Walt Frazier .08 .25
Career Stats 1
23 Tim Hardaway .10 .30
Regular Season Stats
24 John Starks .08 .25
Personal Info
25 Charles Barkley .15 .40
Pro Season Stats
26 Robert Parish .10 .30
Pro Stats 2
27 Bill Walton .08 .25
Collegiate Stats
28 Xavier McDaniel .05 .15
Regular Season Stats
29 Chris Mullin .08 .25
All-Star Stats
30 Scott Burrell .05 .15
1992/93 Season
31 Shawn Kemp .15 .40
1992/93 Season
32 Oliver Miller .05 .15
Career Stats
33 Larry Bird .40 1.00
All-Star Stats
34 Richard Dumas .05 .15
1992/93 Season
35 Kevin McHale .10 .30
Pro Stats
36 Oliver Miller .05 .15
Collegiate Info
37 Harold Miner .05 .15
1992/93 Season 2
38 Christian Laettner .08 .25
1992/93 Season 2
39 Charles Barkley .15 .40
Pro Season Stats
40 Tom Gugliotta UER .05 .15
Career Highs/(Misspelled Guggliotta on front and back)
41 John Starks .08 .25
1992/93 Season 1
42 Tim Hardaway .10 .30
Playoff
All-Star Stats
43 Robert Parish .10 .30
All-Star Stats
44 Scott Burrell .05 .15
Collegiate Info 1
45 Bill Walton .08 .25
Regular Season Stats
46 Xavier McDaniel .05 .15
Playoff Stats
47 Richard Dumas .05 .15
Career Highs
48 Walt Frazier .08 .25
Career Stats 2
49 Oliver Miller .05 .15
1992/93 Season 1
50 Charles Barkley .15 .40
All-Star Stats
51 Larry Bird .40 1.00
Playoff Stats
52 Chris Mullin .08 .25
Career Best
53 Shawn Kemp .15 .40
Pro Info
54 Christian Laettner .08 .25
College Info
55 Robert Parish .10 .30
Playoff Stats
56 John Starks .08 .25
1992/93 Season 2
57 Xavier McDaniel .05 .15
Pro Info
58 Bill Walton .08 .25
Playoff
All-Star Stats
59 Harold Miner .05 .15
Personal Info
60 Richard Dumas .05 .15
Collegiate Info
61 Oliver Miller .05 .15
1992/93 Season 2
62 Tom Gugliotta UER .05 .15
Colliegiate Info/(Misspelled Guggliotta on front and back)
63 Scott Burrell .05 .15
Collegiate Info 2
64 Tim Hardaway .10 .30
Pro Info 1
65 Walt Frazier .08 .25
NBA Playoff Record
66 Larry Bird .40 1.00
Career Highlights
67 Shawn Kemp .15 .40
Personal Info
68 Kevin McHale .10 .30
All-Star Stats
69 Xavier McDaniel .05 .15
Personal Data
70 John Starks .08 .25
NBA Regular Season and Playoff Record
71 Bill Walton .08 .25
Career Info 1
72 Christian Laettner .08 .25
Personal Data and Collegiate Record
73 Chris Mullin .08 .25
1992/93 Season
74 Walt Frazier .08 .25
NBA All-Star Game Record
75 Charles Barkley .15 .40
Playoff Stats
76 Oliver Miller .05 .15
Personal Info
77 Kevin McHale .10 .30
Playoff Stats
78 Robert Parish .10 .30
Career Highs
79 Larry Bird .40 1.00
All-Time Standings
80 Harold Miner .05 .15
Collegiate Info
81 Kevin McHale .10 .30
Career Highs
82 Tim Hardaway .10 .30
Pro Info 2
83 Tom Gugliotta UER .05 .15
Personal Data and 1992/93 Stats (Misspelled Guggliotta on front and back)
84 Bill Walton .08 .25
Career Info 2
85 Shawn Kemp .15 .40
Personal Data
86 Scott Burrell .05 .15
Personal Data
87 Richard Dumas .05 .15
Personal Info
88 Charles Barkley .15 .40
Pro Info
89 Bill Walton .08 .25
Personal Info
90 Kevin McHale .10 .30
Personal Data
91 Christian Laettner .08 .25
Personal Info
92 Walt Frazier .08 .25
Personal Data
93 John Starks .08 .25
Collegiate and CBA Regular Season Record
94 Harold Miner .05 .15
Personal Data and NBA Regular Season Record
95 Robert Parish .10 .30
Personal Info
96 Tim Hardaway .10 .30
Personal Data
97 Tom Gugliotta UER .05 .15
1992/93 Season Misspelled Guggliotta on front and back)
98 Larry Bird .40 1.00
Personal Data
99 Chris Mullin .08 .25
Personal Info
100 Charles Barkley .15 .40
Personal Info

2009-10 Studio

COMPLETE SET (150) 30.00 60.00
UNPRICED PLATINUM PRINT RUN ONE SET
UNPRICED PRESS PLATES PRINT RUN ONE SET
1 Andrew Bynum .60 1.50
2 Derek Fisher .40 1.00
3 Kobe Bryant 2.50 6.00
4 Lamar Odom .50 1.25
5 Carmelo Anthony .60 1.50
6 Chauncey Billups .50 1.25
7 Chris Andersen .75 2.00
8 Brandon Roy .50 1.25
9 LaMarcus Aldridge .50 1.25
10 Rudy Fernandez .40 1.00
11 Manu Ginobili .50 1.25
12 Tim Duncan .75 2.00
13 Tony Parker .50 1.25
14 Luis Scola .40 1.00
15 Shane Battier .50 1.25
16 Tracy McGrady .50 1.25
17 Dirk Nowitzki .60 1.50
18 Jason Kidd .50 1.25
19 Jason Terry .40 1.00
20 Josh Howard .40 1.00
21 Chris Paul .75 2.00
22 David West .50 1.25
23 Peja Stojakovic .50 1.25
24 Rasual Butler .30 .75
25 Andrei Kirilenko .40 1.00
26 Carlos Boozer .50 1.25
27 Deron Williams .50 1.25
28 Amare Stoudemire .50 1.25
29 Grant Hill .60 1.50
30 Jason Richardson .50 1.25
31 Steve Nash .50 1.25
32 Anthony Randolph .40 1.00
33 Corey Maggette .40 1.00
34 Monta Ellis .50 1.25
35 Raja Bell .40 1.00
36 Marc Gasol .50 1.25
37 Mike Conley Jr. .40 1.00
38 O.J. Mayo .50 1.25
39 Rudy Gay .50 1.25
40 Al Jefferson .50 1.25
41 Kevin Love .75 2.00
42 Ryan Gomes .30 .75
43 Jeff Green .40 1.00
44 Kevin Durant 1.50 4.00
45 Russell Westbrook .75 2.00
46 Al Thornton .40 1.00
47 Chris Kaman .40 1.00
48 Eric Gordon .50 1.25
49 Andres Nocioni .30 .75
50 Francisco Garcia .40 1.00
51 Kevin Martin .50 1.25
52 LeBron James 2.50 6.00
53 Mo Williams .40 1.00
54 Shaquille O'Neal 1.00 2.50
55 Kevin Garnett 1.00 2.50
56 Paul Pierce .60 1.50
57 Rajon Rondo .60 1.50
58 Ray Allen .50 1.25
59 Dwight Howard .75 2.00
60 Jameer Nelson .40 1.00
61 Rashard Lewis .40 1.00
62 Al Horford .50 1.25
63 Joe Johnson .50 1.25
64 Josh Smith .50 1.25
65 Mike Bibby .40 1.00
66 Dwyane Wade 1.00 2.50
67 Jermaine O'Neal .50 1.25
68 Michael Beasley .50 1.25
69 Derrick Rose 1.50 4.00
70 Joakim Noah .50 1.25
71 John Salmons .50 1.25
72 Andre Iguodala .50 1.25
73 Elton Brand .50 1.25
74 Thaddeus Young .30 .75
75 Ben Gordon .50 1.25
76 Richard Hamilton .40 1.00
77 Tayshaun Prince .50 1.25
78 Danny Granger .50 1.25
79 Mike Dunleavy .30 .75
80 T.J. Ford .30 .75
81 Troy Murphy .30 .75
82 Boris Diaw .40 1.00
83 Gerald Wallace .50 1.25
84 Stephen Jackson .40 1.00
85 Raymond Felton .40 1.00
86 Andrew Bogut .50 1.25
87 Luke Ridnour .40 1.00
88 Michael Redd .50 1.25
89 Brook Lopez .50 1.25
90 Devin Harris .50 1.25
91 Yi Jianlian .40 1.00
92 Andrea Bargnani .40 1.00
93 Chris Bosh .50 1.25
94 Jose Calderon .40 1.00
95 Al Harrington .40 1.00
96 David Lee .40 1.00
97 Wilson Chandler .40 1.00
98 Antawn Jamison .50 1.25
99 Caron Butler .50 1.25
100 Mike Miller .50 1.25
101 Wes Unseld .50 1.25
102 Arnie Risen .50 1.25
103 Bailey Howell .50 1.25
104 Bill Cartwright .50 1.25
105 Byron Scott .50 1.25
106 Darryl Dawkins .50 1.25
107 Jeff Hornacek .50 1.25
108 Jerry Lucas .50 1.25
109 Kelly Tripucka .50 1.25
110 Manute Bol .50 1.25
111 Mark Eaton .50 1.25
112 Michael Cage .50 1.25
113 Mitch Richmond .50 1.25
114 Norm Nixon .50 1.25
115 Paul Westphal .50 1.25
116 Rick Barry .50 1.25
117 Ron Harper .50 1.25
118 Spencer Haywood .50 1.25
119 Dennis Rodman .75 2.00
120 Anfernee Hardaway 1.25 3.00
121 Ty Lawson RC 1.50 4.00
122 Jeff Pendergraph RC 1.00 2.50
123 DeJuan Blair RC 1.25 3.00
124 Jermaine Taylor RC 1.00 2.50
125 Rodrigue Beaubois RC 1.25 3.00
126 Darren Collison RC 1.50 4.00
127 Eric Maynor RC 1.00 2.50
128 Earl Clark RC 1.00 2.50
129 Stephen Curry RC 2.50 6.00
130 DeMarre Carroll RC 1.00 2.50
131 Hasheem Thabeet RC 1.00 2.50
132 Jonny Flynn RC 1.00 2.50
133 Wayne Ellington RC 1.00 2.50
134 B.J. Mullens RC 1.00 2.50
135 James Harden RC 3.00 8.00
136 Blake Griffin RC 6.00 15.00
137 Omri Casspi RC 1.00 2.50
138 Tyreke Evans RC 2.50 6.00
139 Jeff Teague RC 1.25 3.00
140 James Johnson RC 1.00 2.50
141 Taj Gibson RC 1.25 3.00
142 Jrue Holiday RC 2.00 5.00
143 Austin Daye RC 1.00 2.50
144 Tyler Hansbrough RC 1.50 4.00
145 Gerald Henderson RC 1.00 2.50
146 Brandon Jennings RC 2.00 5.00
147 Terrence Williams RC 1.00 2.50
148 DeMar DeRozan RC 1.50 4.00
149 Jordan Hill RC 1.00 2.50
150 Toney Douglas RC 1.00 2.50

2009-10 Studio Proofs Bronze

*BRONZE: .6X TO 1.5X BASE HI
STATED PRINT RUN 199 SER.#'d SETS

2009-10 Studio Proofs Gold

*GOLD: 1.5X TO 4X BASE HI
STATED PRINT RUN 49 SER.#'d SETS
44 Kevin Durant 8.00 20.00

2009-10 Studio Proofs Gold Signatures

STATED PRINT RUN 5 TO 25 SER.#'d SETS
SOME UNPRICED DUE TO SCARCITY
UNPRICED PLAT.SIG PRINT RUN ONE SET
3 Kobe Bryant/25 125.00 250.00
13 Tony Parker/25 10.00 25.00
41 Kevin Love/25 15.00 40.00
48 Eric Gordon/25 8.00 20.00
57 Rajon Rondo/25 20.00 40.00
80 T.J. Ford/25 8.00 15.00
101 Wes Unseld/25 10.00 25.00
105 Byron Scott/25 8.00 20.00
107 Jeff Hornacek/25 10.00 25.00
121 Ty Lawson/25 12.00 30.00
122 Jeff Pendergraph/25 8.00 20.00
123 DeJuan Blair/25 10.00 25.00
124 Jermaine Taylor/25 8.00 20.00
125 Rodrigue Beaubois/25 10.00 25.00
126 Darren Collison/25 12.00 30.00
127 Eric Maynor/25 8.00 20.00
128 Earl Clark/25 8.00 20.00
129 Stephen Curry/25 40.00 100.00
130 DeMarre Carroll/25 8.00 20.00
131 Hasheem Thabeet/25 8.00 20.00
132 Jonny Flynn/25 8.00 20.00
133 Wayne Ellington/25 8.00 20.00
134 B.J. Mullens/25 8.00 20.00
135 James Harden/25 25.00 60.00
136 Blake Griffin/25 125.00 250.00
137 Omri Casspi/25 8.00 20.00
138 Tyreke Evans/25 40.00 100.00
139 Jeff Teague/25 10.00 25.00
140 James Johnson/25 8.00 20.00
141 Taj Gibson/25 10.00 25.00
142 Jrue Holiday/25 15.00 40.00
143 Austin Daye/25 8.00 20.00
144 Tyler Hansbrough/25 12.00 30.00
145 Gerald Henderson/25 8.00 20.00
146 Brandon Jennings/25 15.00 40.00
147 Terrence Williams/25 8.00 20.00
149 Jordan Hill/25 8.00 20.00
150 Toney Douglas/25 8.00 20.00

2009-10 Studio Proofs Silver

*SILVER: .75X TO 2X BASE HI
STATED PRINT RUN 99 SER.#'d SETS

2009-10 Studio Proofs Silver Signatures

STATED PRINT RUN ONE TO 49 SER.#'d SETS
SOME UNPRICED DUE TO SCARCITY
3 Kobe Bryant/49 125.00 225.00
13 Tony Parker/49 8.00 20.00
41 Kevin Love/49 10.00 25.00
42 Ryan Gomes/25 5.00 12.00
45 Russell Westbrook/25 15.00 40.00
47 Chris Kaman/25 6.00 15.00
48 Eric Gordon/49 5.00 12.00
57 Rajon Rondo/49 12.50 30.00
58 Ray Allen/25 20.00 40.00
67 Jermaine O'Neal/25 6.00 15.00
68 Michael Beasley/25 8.00 20.00
78 Danny Granger/25 10.00 25.00
80 T.J. Ford/49 5.00 10.00
90 Devin Harris/25 8.00 20.00
96 David Lee/25 8.00 20.00
101 Wes Unseld/49 8.00 20.00
103 Bailey Howell/25 15.00 30.00
105 Byron Scott/49 6.00 15.00
107 Jeff Hornacek/49 8.00 20.00
110 Manute Bol/25 20.00 50.00
119 Dennis Rodman/25 20.00 40.00
121 Ty Lawson/49 10.00 25.00
122 Jeff Pendergraph/49 6.00 15.00
123 DeJuan Blair/49 8.00 20.00
124 Jermaine Taylor/49 6.00 15.00
125 Rodrigue Beaubois/49 8.00 20.00
126 Darren Collison/49 10.00 25.00
127 Eric Maynor/49 6.00 15.00
128 Earl Clark/49 6.00 15.00
129 Stephen Curry/49 30.00 80.00
130 DeMarre Carroll/49 6.00 15.00
131 Hasheem Thabeet/49 6.00 15.00
132 Jonny Flynn/49 6.00 15.00
133 Wayne Ellington/49 6.00 15.00
134 B.J. Mullens/49 6.00 15.00
135 James Harden/49 20.00 50.00
136 Blake Griffin/49 100.00 200.00
137 Omri Casspi/49 6.00 15.00
138 Tyreke Evans/49 30.00 80.00
139 Jeff Teague/49 8.00 20.00
140 James Johnson/49 6.00 15.00
141 Taj Gibson/49 8.00 20.00
142 Jrue Holiday/49 12.00 30.00
143 Austin Daye/49 6.00 15.00
144 Tyler Hansbrough/49 10.00 25.00
145 Gerald Henderson/49 6.00 15.00
146 Brandon Jennings/49 12.00 30.00
147 Terrence Williams/49 6.00 15.00
149 Jordan Hill/49 6.00 15.00
150 Toney Douglas/49 6.00 15.00

2009-10 Studio Essence

COMPLETE SET (15) 7.50 15.00
RANDOM INSERTS IN PACKS
*PROOF: .75X TO 2X BASE HI
PROOF PRINT RUN 199 SER.#'d SETS
1 Al Jefferson .75 2.00
2 Andre Iguodala .75 2.00
3 Andrew Bynum 1.00 2.50
4 Baron Davis .75 2.00
5 Charlie Villanueva .60 1.50
6 Chris Bosh .75 2.00
7 Chris Kaman .60 1.50
8 Devin Harris .75 2.00
9 Emeka Okafor .75 2.00
10 Josh Howard .60 1.50
11 Rajon Rondo 1.00 2.50
12 Randy Foye .50 1.25
13 Ronnie Brewer .60 1.50
14 Rudy Fernandez .60 1.50
15 Trevor Ariza .50 1.25

2009-10 Studio Essence Materials

STATED PRINT RUN 149 TO 249 SER.#'d SETS
1 Al Jefferson/249 3.00 8.00
2 Andre Iguodala/249 3.00 8.00
3 Andrew Bynum/149 4.00 10.00
4 Baron Davis/249 3.00 8.00
5 Charlie Villanueva/249 2.50 6.00
6 Chris Bosh/249 3.00 8.00
7 Chris Kaman/149 2.50 6.00
10 Josh Howard/249 2.50 6.00

2009-10 Studio Essence Signatures

STATED PRINT RUN 49 TO 99 SER.#'d SETS
ASTERISK CARDS FROM PANINI UPDATE
2 Andre Iguodala/99 5.00 12.00
3 Andrew Bynum/49* 8.00 20.00
4 Baron Davis/49* 5.00 12.00
7 Chris Kaman/99 4.00 10.00
8 Devin Harris/99 4.00 10.00
10 Josh Howard/49 4.00 10.00
11 Rajon Rondo/49* 15.00 40.00
12 Randy Foye/99 4.00 10.00
13 Ronnie Brewer/99 4.00 10.00

2009-10 Studio Heritage

COMPLETE SET (20) 20.00 40.00
RANDOM INSERTS IN PACKS
*PROOFS: .6X TO 1.5X BASE HI
PROOF PRINT RUN 199 SER.#'d SETS
1 Elvin Hayes 1.25 3.00
2 Jerry West 1.50 4.00
3 Spencer Haywood 1.25 3.00
4 Sidney Moncrief 1.25 3.00
5 Sam Perkins 1.25 3.00
6 Robert Parish 1.25 3.00
7 Rick Barry 1.25 3.00
8 Paul Westphal 1.25 3.00
9 Nate Archibald 1.25 3.00
10 Moses Malone 1.25 3.00
11 Magic Johnson 3.00 8.00
12 Lou Hudson 1.25 3.00
13 Lenny Wilkens 1.25 3.00
14 Isiah Thomas 1.25 3.00
15 George Gervin 1.25 3.00
16 Frank Ramsey 1.25 3.00
17 Dolph Schayes 1.25 3.00
18 David Thompson 1.50 4.00
19 Darryl Dawkins 1.25 3.00
20 Connie Hawkins 1.25 3.00

2009-10 Studio Heritage Materials

STATED PRINT RUN 99 TO 249 SER.#'d SETS
2 Jerry West/99 6.00 15.00
6 Robert Parish/249 4.00 10.00
10 Moses Malone/99 4.00 10.00
11 Magic Johnson/249 8.00 20.00
14 Isiah Thomas/249 4.00 10.00
15 George Gervin/99 4.00 10.00

2009-10 Studio Heritage Signatures

STATED PRINT RUN 49 TO 99 SER.#'d SETS
1 Elvin Hayes/99 10.00 25.00
2 Jerry West/49 40.00 80.00
3 Spencer Haywood/99 8.00 20.00
4 Sidney Moncrief/99 8.00 20.00
5 Sam Perkins/99 8.00 20.00
6 Robert Parish/99 8.00 20.00
7 Rick Barry/99 8.00 20.00
8 Paul Westphal/99 8.00 20.00
9 Nate Archibald/99 8.00 20.00
11 Magic Johnson/49 40.00 100.00
13 Lenny Wilkens/99 8.00 20.00
14 Isiah Thomas/93 10.00 25.00
15 George Gervin/99 10.00 25.00
16 Frank Ramsey/99 15.00 40.00
17 Dolph Schayes/99 8.00 20.00
18 David Thompson/99 8.00 20.00

2009-10 Studio Masterstrokes

COMPLETE SET (20) 20.00 40.00
RANDOM INSERTS IN PACKS
*PROOFS: .6X TO 1.5X BASE HI
PROOF PRINT RUN 199 SER.#'d SETS
1 Al Jefferson 1.00 2.50
2 Andre Iguodala 1.00 2.50
3 Carlos Boozer 1.00 2.50
4 Carmelo Anthony 1.25 3.00
5 Danilo Gallinari 1.00 2.50
6 Dwight Howard 1.50 4.00
7 Jason Kidd 1.00 2.50
8 Joe Johnson 1.00 2.50
9 Kevin Martin 1.00 2.50
10 Kobe Bryant 5.00 12.00
11 LeBron James 5.00 12.00
12 Manu Ginobili 1.00 2.50
13 O.J. Mayo 1.00 2.50
14 Paul Pierce 1.25 3.00
15 Kevin Durant 3.00 8.00
16 Tracy McGrady 1.00 2.50
17 Dwyane Wade 2.00 5.00
18 Chris Bosh 1.00 2.50
19 Stephen Jackson .75 2.00
20 Tayshaun Prince 1.00 2.50

2009-10 Studio Masterstrokes Materials

STATED PRINT RUN 50 TO 249 SER.#'d SETS
1 Al Jefferson/249 3.00 8.00
2 Andre Iguodala/249 3.00 8.00
3 Carlos Boozer/249 3.00 8.00
4 Carmelo Anthony/249 4.00 10.00
5 Danilo Gallinari/249 3.00 8.00
6 Dwight Howard/249 5.00 12.00
8 Joe Johnson/50 3.00 8.00
10 Kobe Bryant/249 8.00 20.00
11 LeBron James/249 8.00 20.00
12 Manu Ginobili/249 3.00 8.00
14 Paul Pierce/199 4.00 10.00
16 Tracy McGrady/199 3.00 8.00
17 Dwyane Wade/249 6.00 15.00
18 Chris Bosh/249 3.00 8.00
20 Tayshaun Prince/249 3.00 8.00

2009-10 Studio Masterstrokes Signatures

STATED PRINT RUN 49 TO 99 SER.#'d SETS
2 Andre Iguodala/81 8.00 20.00
3 Carlos Boozer/99 8.00 20.00
7 Jason Kidd/49 15.00 40.00
10 Kobe Bryant/99 100.00 200.00
16 Tracy McGrady/49 10.00 25.00
18 Chris Bosh/99 10.00 25.00

2009-10 Studio Materials

STATED PRINT RUN 10 TO 249 SER.#'d SETS
SOME UNPRICED DUE TO SCARCITY
1 Andrew Bynum/249 4.00 10.00
3 Kobe Bryant/249 8.00 20.00
5 Carmelo Anthony/249 4.00 10.00
6 Chauncey Billups/249 3.00 8.00
7 Chris Andersen/249 5.00 12.00
8 Brandon Roy/249 3.00 8.00
9 LaMarcus Aldridge/249 3.00 8.00
11 Manu Ginobili/249 3.00 8.00
12 Tim Duncan/249 5.00 12.00
13 Tony Parker/249 3.00 8.00
14 Luis Scola/249 2.50 6.00
15 Shane Battier/249 3.00 8.00
16 Tracy McGrady/249 3.00 8.00
17 Dirk Nowitzki/249 4.00 10.00
18 Jason Kidd/249 3.00 8.00
19 Jason Terry/249 2.50 6.00
20 Josh Howard/249 2.50 6.00
21 Chris Paul/249 5.00 12.00
22 David West/249 3.00 8.00
25 Andrei Kirilenko/149 2.50 6.00
26 Carlos Boozer/249 3.00 8.00
27 Deron Williams/249 3.00 8.00
28 Amare Stoudemire/249 3.00 8.00
34 Monta Ellis/249 3.00 8.00
37 Mike Conley Jr./249 2.50 6.00
40 Al Jefferson/249 3.00 8.00
41 Kevin Love/249 5.00 12.00
42 Ryan Gomes/249 2.00 5.00
46 Al Thornton/249 2.50 6.00
47 Chris Kaman/149 2.50 6.00
49 Andres Nocioni/249 2.00 5.00
52 LeBron James/249 8.00 20.00
53 Mo Williams/249 2.50 6.00
54 Shaquille O'Neal/249 6.00 15.00
55 Kevin Garnett/249 6.00 15.00
56 Paul Pierce/199 4.00 10.00
58 Ray Allen/249 3.00 8.00
59 Dwight Howard/249 5.00 12.00
60 Jameer Nelson/249 2.50 6.00
61 Rashard Lewis/249 2.50 6.00
62 Al Horford/249 3.00 8.00
63 Joe Johnson/50 3.00 8.00
64 Josh Smith/249 3.00 8.00
65 Mike Bibby/50 2.50 6.00
66 Dwyane Wade/249 6.00 15.00
67 Jermaine O'Neal/50 3.00 8.00
68 Michael Beasley/249 3.00 8.00
69 Derrick Rose/50 10.00 25.00
70 Joakim Noah/249 3.00 8.00
72 Andre Iguodala/249 3.00 8.00
73 Elton Brand/249 3.00 8.00
74 Thaddeus Young/249 2.00 5.00
75 Ben Gordon/199 3.00 8.00
76 Richard Hamilton/249 2.50 6.00
77 Tayshaun Prince/249 3.00 8.00
82 Boris Diaw/249 2.50 6.00
83 Gerald Wallace/249 3.00 8.00
85 Raymond Felton/249 2.50 6.00
92 Andrea Bargnani/100 2.50 6.00
93 Chris Bosh/249 3.00 8.00
94 Jose Calderon/249 2.50 6.00
95 Al Harrington/25 2.50 6.00
96 David Lee/249 2.50 6.00
98 Antawn Jamison/249 3.00 8.00
113 Mitch Richmond/249 6.00 15.00
116 Rick Barry/199 3.00 8.00
117 Ron Harper/249 8.00 20.00
120 Anfernee Hardaway/249 10.00 25.00
121 Ty Lawson/249 3.00 8.00
122 Jeff Pendergraph/249 2.00 5.00
123 DeJuan Blair/249 2.50 6.00
124 Jermaine Taylor/249 2.00 5.00
125 Rodrigue Beaubois/249 2.50 6.00
126 Darren Collison/249 3.00 8.00
127 Eric Maynor/249 2.00 5.00
128 Earl Clark/249 2.00 5.00
129 Stephen Curry/249 5.00 12.00
130 DeMarre Carroll/249 2.00 5.00
131 Hasheem Thabeet/249 2.00 5.00
132 Jonny Flynn/249 2.00 5.00
133 Wayne Ellington/249 2.00 5.00
134 B.J. Mullens/249 2.00 5.00
135 James Harden/249 6.00 15.00
136 Blake Griffin/249 12.00 30.00
137 Omri Casspi/249 2.00 5.00
138 Tyreke Evans/249 5.00 12.00
139 Jeff Teague/249 2.50 6.00
140 James Johnson/249 2.00 5.00
141 Taj Gibson/249 2.50 6.00
142 Jrue Holiday/249 4.00 10.00
143 Austin Daye/249 2.00 5.00
144 Tyler Hansbrough/249 3.00 8.00
145 Gerald Henderson/249 2.00 5.00
146 Brandon Jennings/249 4.00 10.00
147 Terrence Williams/249 2.00 5.00
148 DeMar DeRozan/249 3.00 8.00
149 Jordan Hill/249 2.00 5.00
150 Toney Douglas/249 2.00 5.00

2009-10 Studio Signatures

STATED PRINT RUN 5 TO 199 SER.#'d SETS
SOME UNPRICED DUE TO SCARCITY

Card	Low	High
3 Kobe Bryant/49	125.00	225.00
13 Tony Parker/25	10.00	25.00
15 Shane Battier/50	5.00	12.00
41 Kevin Love/25	15.00	40.00
45 Russell Westbrook/99	15.00	40.00
47 Chris Kaman/99	5.00	12.00
48 Eric Gordon/99	6.00	15.00
57 Rajon Rondo/50	15.00	40.00
58 Ray Allen/25	25.00	60.00
67 Jermaine O'Neal/25	6.00	15.00
68 Michael Beasley/50	6.00	15.00
78 Danny Granger/25	10.00	25.00
80 T.J. Ford/99	5.00	10.00
90 Devin Harris/49	5.00	12.00
93 Chris Bosh/25	20.00	40.00
96 David Lee/25	8.00	20.00
101 Wes Unseld/50	8.00	20.00
103 Bailey Howell/49	10.00	25.00
110 Manute Bol/50	20.00	40.00
116 Rick Barry/25	10.00	25.00
119 Dennis Rodman/25	20.00	50.00
121 Ty Lawson/199	8.00	20.00
122 Jeff Pendergraph/199	5.00	12.00
123 DeJuan Blair/199	6.00	15.00
124 Jermaine Taylor/199	5.00	12.00
125 Rodrigue Beaubois/199	6.00	15.00
126 Darren Collison/199	8.00	20.00
127 Eric Maynor/199	5.00	12.00
128 Earl Clark/199	5.00	12.00
129 Stephen Curry/199	12.00	30.00
130 DeMarre Carroll/199	5.00	12.00
131 Hasheem Thabeet/199	5.00	12.00
132 Jonny Flynn/199	5.00	12.00
133 Wayne Ellington/199	5.00	12.00
134 B.J. Mullens/199	5.00	12.00
135 James Harden/199	15.00	40.00
136 Blake Griffin/199	75.00	150.00
137 Omri Casspi/199	5.00	12.00
138 Tyreke Evans/199	12.00	30.00
139 Jeff Teague/199	6.00	15.00
140 James Johnson/199	5.00	12.00
141 Taj Gibson/199	6.00	15.00
142 Jrue Holiday/199	10.00	25.00
143 Austin Daye/199	5.00	12.00
144 Tyler Hansbrough/199	8.00	20.00
145 Gerald Henderson/199	5.00	12.00
146 Brandon Jennings/199	10.00	25.00
147 Terrence Williams/199	5.00	12.00
149 Jordan Hill/199	5.00	12.00
150 Toney Douglas/199	5.00	12.00

2009-10 Studio Skylines

Card	Low	High
COMPLETE SET (30)	25.00	50.00
RANDOM INSERTS IN PACKS		
*PROOFS: .6X TO 1.5X BASE HI		
PROOF PRINT RUN 199 SER.#'d SETS		
1 Mike Bibby	.75	2.00
2 Rajon Rondo	1.25	3.00
3 Gerald Henderson	1.00	2.50
4 Derrick Rose	3.00	8.00
5 LeBron James	5.00	12.00
6 Jason Terry	.75	2.00
7 Chauncey Billups	1.00	2.50
8 Ben Gordon	1.00	2.50
9 Stephen Curry	2.50	6.00
10 Tracy McGrady	1.00	2.50
11 Danny Granger	1.00	2.50
12 Blake Griffin	6.00	15.00
13 Kobe Bryant	5.00	12.00
14 O.J. Mayo	1.00	2.50
15 Dwyane Wade	2.00	5.00
16 Andrew Bogut	1.00	2.50
17 Kevin Love	1.50	4.00
18 Devin Harris	1.00	2.50
19 Chris Paul	1.50	4.00
20 Nate Robinson	1.00	2.50
21 Russell Westbrook	1.50	4.00
22 Dwight Howard	1.50	4.00
23 Elton Brand	1.00	2.50
24 Steve Nash	1.00	2.50
25 Brandon Roy	1.00	2.50
26 Kevin Martin	1.00	2.50
27 Tim Duncan	1.50	4.00
28 Chris Bosh	1.00	2.50
29 Deron Williams	1.00	2.50
30 Gilbert Arenas	1.00	2.50

2009-10 Studio Skylines Materials

STATED PRINT RUN 50 TO 249 SER.#'d SETS

Card	Low	High
1 Mike Bibby/50	2.50	6.00
3 Gerald Henderson/249	2.50	6.00
4 Derrick Rose/50	10.00	25.00
5 LeBron James/249	8.00	20.00
6 Jason Terry/249	2.50	6.00
7 Chauncey Billups/249	3.00	8.00
8 Ben Gordon/199	3.00	8.00
9 Stephen Curry/249	6.00	15.00
10 Tracy McGrady/249	3.00	8.00
12 Blake Griffin/249	15.00	40.00
13 Kobe Bryant/249	8.00	20.00
15 Dwyane Wade/249	6.00	15.00
17 Kevin Love/249	5.00	12.00
19 Chris Paul/249	5.00	12.00
20 Nate Robinson/249	3.00	8.00
22 Dwight Howard/249	5.00	12.00
23 Elton Brand/249	3.00	8.00
25 Brandon Roy/249	3.00	8.00
27 Tim Duncan/249	5.00	12.00
28 Chris Bosh/249	3.00	8.00
29 Deron Williams/249	3.00	8.00
30 Gilbert Arenas/249	3.00	8.00

2009-10 Studio Skylines Signatures

STATED PRINT RUN 49 TO 99 SER.#'d SETS
ASTERISK CARDS FROM PANINI UPDATE

Card	Low	High
1 Mike Bibby/99	6.00	15.00
2 Rajon Rondo/99*	15.00	40.00
3 Gerald Henderson/99	6.00	15.00
7 Chauncey Billups/99	8.00	20.00
9 Stephen Curry/99	25.00	60.00
10 Tracy McGrady/49	10.00	25.00
11 Danny Granger/99*	8.00	20.00
12 Blake Griffin/99	100.00	200.00
13 Kobe Bryant/99	100.00	200.00
17 Kevin Love/99	15.00	40.00
18 Devin Harris/99	6.00	15.00
21 Russell Westbrook/99	20.00	50.00
28 Chris Bosh/99	10.00	25.00
29 Deron Williams/92	10.00	25.00

2009-10 Studio Team Studio

Card	Low	High
COMPLETE SET (15)	10.00	25.00
RANDOM INSERTS IN PACKS		
*PROOFS: .75X TO 2X BASE HI		
PROOF PRINT RUN 199 SER.#'d SETS		
1 Kobe Bryant Pau Gasol	4.00	10.00
2 Dwight Howard Rashard Lewis	1.25	3.00
3 Tim Duncan Tony Parker	1.25	3.00
4 Kevin Garnett Ray Allen	1.50	4.00
5 Dirk Nowitzki Josh Howard	1.00	2.50
6 LeBron James Shaquille O'Neal	4.00	10.00
7 Dwyane Wade Daequan Cook	1.50	4.00
8 Carmelo Anthony Chauncey Billups	1.00	2.50
9 Carlos Boozer Andrei Kirilenko	.75	2.00
10 Al Harrington David Lee	.60	1.50
11 Chris Bosh Andrea Bargnani	.75	2.00
12 Bill Laimbeer Joe Dumars	.75	2.00
13 Larry Bird Kevin McHale	2.50	6.00
14 Magic Johnson Kareem Abdul-Jabbar	2.00	5.00
15 George McGinnis Moses Malone	.75	2.00

2009-10 Studio Team Studio Materials

STATED PRINT RUN 25 TO 249 SER.#'d SETS

Card	Low	High
1 Kobe Bryant/249 Pau Gasol	10.00	25.00
2 Dwight Howard/249 Rashard Lewis	4.00	10.00
3 Tim Duncan/249 Tony Parker	6.00	15.00
4 Kevin Garnett/249 Ray Allen	6.00	15.00
5 Dirk Nowitzki/249 Josh Howard	6.00	15.00
6 LeBron James/249 Shaquille O'Neal	12.50	30.00
7 Dwyane Wade/249 Daequan Cook	4.00	10.00
8 Carmelo Anthony/249 Chauncey Billups	5.00	12.00
9 Carlos Boozer/249 Andrei Kirilenko	4.00	10.00
10 Al Harrington/25 David Lee	6.00	15.00
11 Chris Bosh/249 Andrea Bargnani	4.00	10.00
13 Larry Bird/249 Kevin McHale	10.00	25.00
14 Magic Johnson/249 Kareem Abdul-Jabbar	10.00	25.00
15 George McGinnis/249 Moses Malone	4.00	10.00

1992-93 Suns 25th

Celebrating the 25th anniversary of the Suns' franchise, this 26-card standard-size set was sponsored by The Arizona Republic and The Phoenix Gazette. Each card pictures the Suns' team leader for a particular year, beginning in 1968-69 and ending in 1992-93. The cards feature action player photos. The entire card face, including the picture, exhibits a yellowish beige tint. The player's name appears below the photo, the year above. A purple border design frames the photo, name, and year. The outer edge of the card is enhanced by faded purple shading giving the card an older look. The horizontal backs present biographical information and team statistics for that particular year. There are two back versions with and without sponsor's logo; without seems to be slightly more difficult.

Card	Low	High
COMPLETE SET (26)	6.00	15.00
1 Gail Goodrich	.75	2.00
2 Connie Hawkins	.75	2.00
3 Dick Van Arsdale	.40	1.00
4 Paul Silas	.40	1.00
5 Neil Walk	.20	.50
6 Charlie Scott	.25	.60
7 Curtis Perry	.20	.50
8 Curtis Perry	.20	.50
9 Alvan Adams	.25	.60
10 Garfield Heard	.20	.50
11 Walter Davis	.40	1.00
12 Paul Westphal	.40	1.00
13 Don Buse	.20	.50
14 Truck Robinson	.25	.60
15 Kyle Macy	.40	1.00
16 Dennis Johnson	.50	1.25
17 Maurice Lucas	.40	1.00
18 Larry Nance	.40	1.00
19 Walter Davis	.40	1.00
20 Jeff Hornacek	.40	1.00
21 Eddie Johnson	.30	.75
22 Tyrone Corbin	.20	.50
23 Tom Chambers	.30	.75
24 Kevin Johnson	.40	1.00
25 Dan Majerle	.40	1.00
26 Charles Barkley	1.25	3.00

1976-77 Suns 8 x 10

This 8x10 set was produced for the Phoenix Suns during the 1976-77 season. The set features nice black and white cards of the team's players and coaches.

Card	Low	High
COMPLETE SET (9)	25.00	50.00
1 Dennis Awtrey	1.25	3.00
2 Al Bianchi CO	1.50	4.00
3 Jerry Colangelo GM	1.25	3.00
4 Keith Erickson	1.25	3.00
5 Butch Feher	1.25	3.00
6 Garfield Heard	2.00	5.00
7 Ron Lee	1.25	3.00
8 John McLeod CO	1.25	3.00
9 Curtis Perry	1.25	3.00
10 Joe Proski TR	1.25	3.00
11 Ricky Sobers	1.25	3.00
12 Ira Terrell	1.25	3.00
13 Dick Van Arsdale	2.00	5.00
14 Tom Van Arsdale	1.50	4.00
15 Dick Van Arsdale Tom Van Arsdale	2.00	5.00
16 Paul Westphal	2.50	6.00

1970-71 Suns A1 Premium Beer

These scarce cards are black and white and come with unperforated tabs. The cards were actually the advertising-oriented price tabs for six-packs of A1 Premium Beer. The set features members of the Phoenix Suns. There are three variations primarily based on the price marked on the tab; they are 95 cents (most common), 98 cents (tougher to find), and no price listed. Those not specifically identified in the checklist below are the 95 cents varieties. In terms of size, they resemble bookmarks, each measuring approximately 2 1/4" by 8 3/4". The top of each ad has a circular A-1 Premium Beer emblem. Immediately below the price for the six-pack appears; this can be either 95 or 98 cents, or on some ads no price was given. The black-and-white photo itself measures approximately 2 1/4" by 3 3/8" and features a posed action shot of the player. The backs are blank. The cards are unnumbered and are checklisted below in alphabetical order.

Card	Low	High
COMPLETE SET (13)	900.00	1700.00
1A Mel Counts (95 cents)	50.00	100.00
1B Mel Counts (98 cents)	60.00	120.00
2 Lamar Green	40.00	85.00
3 Clem Haskins	75.00	150.00
4 Connie Hawkins (98 cents)	250.00	450.00
5 Greg Howard	40.00	85.00
6 Paul Silas	125.00	225.00
7 Fred Taylor CO	40.00	85.00
8A Dick Van Arsdale ERR (Reversed negative; no price)	100.00	175.00
8B Dick Van Arsdale COR (No price)	75.00	150.00
9A Neal Walk (95 cents)	50.00	100.00
9B Neal Walk (No price)	60.00	120.00
10 John Wetzel (No price)	50.00	100.00

1968-69 Suns Carnation Milk

This 12-card set of Phoenix Suns was sponsored by Carnation Milk and was issued as panels on the sides of milk cartons. The fronts feature a player pose and brief biographical information near the photo. The bottom of the panels indicate "WIN, 440 Home Game tickets to be given away." The cards measure approximately 3 1/2" by 7 1/2" and are blank backed. The cards are unnumbered and are checklisted below in alphabetical order. Bob Warlick was only with the Phoenix Suns during the last half of the 1968-69 season. The set features the first professional card of Gail Goodrich.

Card	Low	High
COMPLETE SET (12)	800.00	1400.00
1 Jim Fox	60.00	125.00
2 Gail Goodrich	200.00	400.00
3 Gary Gregor	50.00	100.00
4 Neil Johnson	60.00	125.00
5 John Kerr CO	90.00	170.00
6 Dave Lattin	60.00	125.00
7 Stan McKenzie	40.00	80.00
8 McCoy McLemore	40.00	80.00
9 Dick Snyder	40.00	80.00
10 Dick Van Arsdale	75.00	150.00
11 Bob Warlick	60.00	125.00
12 George Wilson	40.00	80.00

1969-70 Suns Carnation Milk

This ten-card set features members of the Phoenix Suns and was produced by Carnation Milk. The cards show white backgrounds with blue and white drawings of the players. Playing tips (in red type) are found at the bottom of each card. Player statistics were on the opposite milk carton panel and hence were not saved in most cases. The cards measure approximately 3 1/2" by 7 1/2". The backs are blank. The cards are unnumbered and are checklisted below in alphabetical order. The set features the first professional card of Connie Hawkins.

Card	Low	High
COMPLETE SET (10)	700.00	1100.00
1 Jerry Chambers	35.00	70.00
2 Jim Fox	35.00	70.00
3 Gail Goodrich	100.00	200.00
4 Connie Hawkins	200.00	400.00
5 Stan McKenzie	35.00	70.00
6 Paul Silas	100.00	200.00
7 Dick Snyder	35.00	70.00
8 Dick Van Arsdale	50.00	100.00
9 Neal Walk	60.00	120.00
10 Gene Williams	35.00	70.00

1970-71 Suns Carnation Milk

This ten-card set features members of the Phoenix Suns and was produced by Carnation Milk. The cards have solid red backgrounds or orange backgrounds if the cards were from diet milk cartons. Apparently the entire set was issued in both color backgrounds. The cards measure approximately 3 1/2" by 7 1/2". The backs are blank. The cards are unnumbered and are checklisted below in alphabetical order.

Card	Low	High
COMPLETE SET (10)	400.00	800.00
1 Mel Counts	30.00	60.00
2 Lamar Green	25.00	50.00
3 Art Harris	25.00	50.00
4 Clem Haskins	40.00	80.00
5 Connie Hawkins	125.00	250.00
6 Gus Johnson	60.00	120.00
7 Otto Moore	25.00	50.00
8 Paul Silas	60.00	120.00
9 Dick Van Arsdale	40.00	80.00
10 Neal Walk	30.00	60.00

1971-72 Suns Carnation Milk

This five-card set features members of the Phoenix Suns and was produced by Carnation Milk and issued as panels on the sides of milk cartons. The cards measure approximately 3 1/2" by 7 1/2". The backs are blank. The cards are unnumbered and are checklisted below in alphabetical order.

Card	Low	High
COMPLETE SET (5)	200.00	400.00
1 Connie Hawkins	100.00	200.00
2 Otto Moore	25.00	50.00
3 Fred Taylor CO	25.00	50.00
4 Neal Walk	30.00	60.00
5 John Wetzel	30.00	60.00

1972-73 Suns Carnation Milk

This 12-card set features members of the Phoenix Suns and was produced by Carnation Milk and issued as panels on the sides of milk cartons. The picture and text are in the team's colors, purple and orange. The cards measure approximately 3 1/2" by 7 1/2". The backs are blank. The cards are unnumbered and are checklisted below in alphabetical order.

Card	Low	High
COMPLETE SET (12)	400.00	800.00
1 Mel Counts	30.00	60.00
2 Lamar Green	25.00	50.00
3 Clem Haskins	40.00	80.00
4 Connie Hawkins	100.00	200.00
5 Gus Johnson	50.00	100.00
6 Dennis Layton	30.00	60.00
7 Otto Moore	25.00	50.00
8 Fred Taylor CO	25.00	50.00
9 Dick Van Arsdale	40.00	80.00
10 Bill VanBredaKolff CO	25.00	50.00
11 Neal Walk	30.00	60.00
12 John Wetzel	30.00	60.00

1987-88 Suns Circle K

This 15-card set was sponsored by Circle K stores. The cards were issued in three strips of five player cards each, plus a coupon. After perforation, the cards measure the standard size. The front features a posed color player photo, with white and purple borders on white card stock. Player information is given below the picture, and team and sponsor logos in the lower corners round out the card face. In a horizontal format the back has biographical and statistical information. The cards are unnumbered and are checklist below in alphabetical order. The set features the first professional cards of Jeff Hornacek and Armon Gilliam.

Card	Low	High
COMPLETE SET (15)	12.00	30.00
1 Alvan Adams	1.25	3.00
2 Herb Brown ACO	.75	2.00
3 Jeff Cook	.75	2.00
4 Winston Crite	.60	1.50
5 Walter Davis	1.50	4.00
6 James Edwards	1.00	2.50
7 Armon Gilliam	2.50	6.00
8 Jeff Hornacek	4.00	10.00
9 Jay Humphries	1.00	2.50
10 Eddie Johnson	1.50	4.00
11 Larry Nance	2.00	5.00
12 Joe Proski TR	.60	1.50
13 Mike Sanders	.60	1.50
14 Bernard Thompson	.60	1.50
15 John Wetzel CO	.60	1.50

1975-76 Suns Fan Grabber

The 1975-76 Phoenix Suns set contains 16 cards, including 12 player cards. The fronts feature black and white pictures, and the backs are blank. The dimensions are approximately 3 1/2" by 4 3/8". The set commemorates the Suns' Western Conference Championship. The cards are unnumbered and are checklisted below in alphabetical order. The set features Alvan Adams' first professional card. These cards were available through at the Fan Grabber concession stands at all Suns playoff games.

Card	Low	High
COMPLETE SET (16)	10.00	25.00
1 Alvan Adams	2.00	5.00
2 Dennis Awtrey	.60	1.50
3 Al Bianchi GM	.60	1.50
4 Jerry Colangelo VP	1.00	2.50
5 Keith Erickson	1.25	3.00
6 Nate Hawthorne	.60	1.50
7 Garfield Heard	1.00	2.50
8 Phil Lumpkin	.60	1.50
9 John MacLeod CO	.75	2.00
10 Curtis Perry	.75	2.00
11 Joe Proski TR	.60	1.50
12 Pat Riley	7.50	15.00
13 Ricky Sobers	1.00	2.50
14 Dick Van Arsdale	1.25	3.00
15 Paul Westphal	3.00	8.00
16 John Wetzel	.40	1.00

1982-83 Suns Giant Service

The 1982-83 Giant Self Service Stations Phoenix Suns set contains three cards each measuring approximately 3 1/4" by 4 1/2". The fronts have color photos while the backs show detailed career highlights and statistics. Each card has a safety tip on back. Apparently during the course of the promotion, one card was given out each month until the end of the season, Walter Davis in January, Maurice Lucas in February, and Larry Nance in March. In addition to being available at gas stations, the cards were also distributed at the Phoenix Suns' Arena on "Giant Service Station Night".

Card	Low	High
COMPLETE SET (3)	6.00	15.00
1 Walter Davis January	3.00	7.00
2 Maurice Lucas February	2.00	5.00
3 Larry Nance March	4.00	9.00

1972-73 Suns Holsum

Sponsored by Holsum Bread in Phoenix, Arizona, these inserts were available in loaves of bread. Each one measures approximately 2 1/2" by 4", is printed on glossy paper, and is devoted to a different Sun player and basketball topic. While the front displays a player portrait, the back carries a Holsum bread advertisement. The trifold insert unfolds to reveal player biography, basketball tips, and records and facts. All print is in light blue lettering; the fronts and backs are accented with red-orange as well. The inserts are unnumbered and checklisted below in alphabetical order.

Card	Low	High
COMPLETE SET (9)	100.00	175.00
1 Corky Calhoun	8.00	20.00
2 Lamar Green	8.00	20.00
3 Clem Haskins	15.00	30.00
4 Connie Hawkins	60.00	120.00
5 Dennis Layton	8.00	20.00
6 Charlie Scott	25.00	50.00
7 Dick Van Arsdale	15.00	30.00
8 Neal Walk	10.00	20.00
9 Walt Wesley	8.00	20.00

1977-78 Suns Humpty Dumpty Discs

The 1977-78 Humpty Dumpty Phoenix Suns set contains 12 discs measuring approximately 3 1/4" in diameter. The blankbacked discs are printed on thick stock. The fronts feature small black and white facial photos surrounded by a purple border with orange trim. Players are numbered below in alphabetical order by subject. The set features Walter Davis' first professional card.

Card	Low	High
COMPLETE SET (12)	15.00	30.00
1 Alvan Adams	1.25	3.00
2 Dennis Awtrey	.75	2.00
3 Mike Bratz	1.00	2.50
4 Don Buse	1.00	2.50
5 Walter Davis	7.50	15.00
6 Bayard Forrest	.75	2.00
7 Garfield Heard	1.25	3.00
8 Ron Lee	.75	2.00
9 Curtis Perry	.75	2.00
10 Alvin Scott	.75	2.00
11 Ira Terrell	1.00	2.50
12 Paul Westphal	2.50	6.00

1980-81 Suns Pepsi

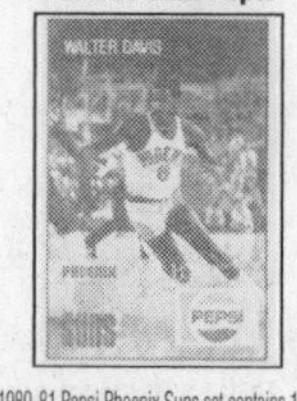

The 1980-81 Pepsi Phoenix Suns set contains 12 numbered cards attached to a bumper sticker-sized promotional flyer/entry blank. The cards were part of a promotion featuring the fans' selection of their Suns' dream team. The entire strip measures approximately 2 7/8" by 11" whereas the cards themselves are standard size, 2 1/2" by 3 1/2". The strips were perforated twice to allow for the card and two ads. The strips were found in six-packs and eight-packs of Pepsi-Cola in the Phoenix area. The fronts feature color photos, and the backs include statistics and biographical information.

Card	Low	High
COMPLETE SET (12)	5.00	10.00
1 Walter Davis	1.25	3.00
2 Alvin Scott	.30	.75
3 Johnny High	.30	.75
4 Dennis Johnson	1.25	3.00
5 Alvan Adams	.75	2.00
6 Rich Kelley	.30	.75
7 Truck Robinson	.60	1.50
8 Joel Kramer	.50	1.25
9 Jeff Cook	.30	.75
10 Mike Niles	.30	.75
11 Kyle Macy	.60	1.50
12 John MacLeod CO	.30	.75

1981-82 Suns Pepsi

The 1981-82 Pepsi Phoenix Suns set contains 12 numbered cards attached to a bumper sticker-sized promotional flyer/entry blank. The cards were part of a promotion featuring the fans' selection of their Suns' dream team. A coupon attached to the card could be redeemed for a ticket to the game. The entire strip measures approximately 2 7/8" by 11" whereas the cards themselves are approximately standard size, 2 1/2" by 3 1/2". The strips were perforated twice to allow for the card and two ads. The strips were found in six-packs and eight-packs of Pepsi-Cola in the Phoenix area. The fronts feature color photos, and the backs include statistics and biographical information. The set features Larry Nance's first professional card.

Card	Low	High
COMPLETE SET (12)	20.00	50.00
1 Alvan Adams	2.00	5.00
2 Dudley Bradley	1.25	3.00
3 Jeff Cooke	1.25	3.00
4 Walter Davis	4.00	10.00
5 The Gorilla	2.00	5.00
6 Dennis Johnson	4.00	10.00
7 Joel Kramer	1.50	4.00
8 John MacLeod CO	1.50	4.00
9 Kyle Macy	2.00	5.00
10 Larry Nance	6.00	15.00
11 Truck Robinson	2.00	5.00
12 Alvin Scott	1.25	3.00

1984-85 Suns Police

This set contains 16 cards measuring 2 5/8" by 4 1/8" featuring the Phoenix Suns. This set was issued in the Summer of 1984. Backs contain safety tips ("Suns Tips") and are written in purple print with an orange accent color. The set was sponsored by Kiwanis, the Suns, the NBA, and the Phoenix Police. The cards are unnumbered except for uniform number.

Card	Low	High
COMPLETE SET (16)	20.00	40.00
4 Kyle Macy	1.50	4.00
6 Walter Davis	3.00	8.00
7 Mike Sanders	.75	2.00
8 Rick Robey	1.50	4.00
10 Rod Foster	.75	2.00
14 Alvin Scott	.75	2.00
20 Maurice Lucas	1.50	4.00
22 Larry Nance	4.00	10.00
32 Charles Pittman	.75	2.00
33 Alvan Adams	1.50	4.00
44 Paul Westphal	2.50	6.00
53 James Edwards	1.50	4.00
NNO Suns Mascot	1.50	4.00
NNO John MacLeod CO	.75	2.00
NNO Al Bianchi ACO	.75	2.00
NNO Joe Proski TR	.75	2.00

1990-91 Suns Smokey

This five-card set of Phoenix Suns was sponsored b the USDA Forest Service in cooperation with several other federal agencies. The cards were given away a specific Phoenix Suns home game. The cards are oversized and measure approximately 3" by 5". The front features a color action player photo, with the Smokey Bear logo superimposed on the top left edg of the picture and the team logo on the bottom right edge. The picture is bordered in purple and has a shadow format. The team name and player's name a given in purple lettering on a peach-colored background. The back presents brief biographical information and features a fire prevention cartoon starring Smokey the Bear. The cards are unnumbere and are checklisted below in alphabetical order. Edd Johnson was apparently pulled from distribution aft he was traded and hence his card is a little tougher find than the other four players.

Card	Low	High
COMPLETE SET (5)	9.00	18.
1 Tom Chambers	1.50	4.
2 Jeff Hornacek	1.50	4.
3 Eddie Johnson SP	2.50	6.
4 Kevin Johnson	2.50	6.
5 Dan Majerle	2.00	5.

1972-73 Suns Team Issue

Each of these team-issued photos measure approximately 8" by 10" and feature two black and white player photos - one a portrait and the other a posed action shot. The player's name is listed below the portrait. The backs are blank. The photos are unnumbered and listed below alphabetically.

Card	Low	High
COMPLETE SET (10)	25.00	50.(
1 Corky Calhoun	1.25	3.(
2 Mel Counts	1.25	3.(
3 Lamar Green	1.25	3.(
4 Clem Haskins	2.50	6.(
5 Connie Hawkins	7.50	15.(
6 Gus Johnson	2.00	5.(
7 Dennis Mo Layton	1.25	3.(
8 Charlie Scott	3.00	8.(
9 Dick Van Arsdale	2.00	5.(
10 Neal Walk	1.50	4.(

1973-74 Suns Team Issue

Measuring approximately 8" by 10", these photos feature members of the 1973-74 Phoenix Suns.

Card	Low	High
COMPLETE SET	15.00	30.(
1 Dick Van Arsdale	1.50	4.(
2 Neal Walk	1.25	3.(
3 Dennis Scott	1.50	4.(
4 Lamar Green	1.25	3.(
5 Clem Haskins	1.25	3.(
6 Mike Bantom	1.25	3.(
7 Jim Owens	1.25	3.(
8 Bob Christian	1.25	3.(
9 Corky Calhoun	1.25	3.(
10 Gary Melchionni	1.25	3.(
11 Keith Erickson	1.25	3.(
12 Bill Chamberlain	1.25	3.(

1974-75 Suns Team Issue

This set of 11 oversized cards picture a face shot of t player to the left, a posed shot to the right and career statistics at the bottom left. The set is black and white The cards are not numbered and checklisted below ir alphabetical order.

Card	Low	High
COMPLETE SET (11)	17.50	35.0
1 Dennis Awtrey	1.25	3.0
2 Mike Bantom	1.25	3.0
3 Keith Erickson	1.50	4.0
4 Nate Hawthorne	1.25	3.0
5 Gary Melchionni	1.25	3.0
6 Jim Owens	1.25	3.0
7 Curtis Perry	1.25	3.0
8 Fred Saunders	1.25	3.0
9 Charlie Scott	2.50	6.0
10 Dick Van Arsdale	1.50	4.0
11 Earl Williams	1.25	3.0

1975-76 Suns Team Issue

Measuring 8" by 10", this 14-card set features members of the Phoenix Suns. The set features black and white photos with the backs being blank. The ca are not numbered and checklisted below in alphabetical order.

Card	Low	High
COMPLETE SET (14)	17.50	35.(
1 Alvan Adams	1.50	4.(
2 Dennis Awtrey	.75	2.(
3 Keith Erickson	1.25	3.(
4 Nate Hawthorne	.75	2.(
5 Phil Lumpkin	.75	2.(
6 John MacLeod CO	1.25	3.(
7 Curtis Perry	.75	2.(
8 Joe Proski TR	.75	2.(
9 Pat Riley	5.00	10.(
10 Fred Saunders	.75	2.(
11 John Shumate	1.25	3.(
12 Ricky Sobers	.75	2.(
13 Paul Westphal	2.00	5.(
14 John Wetzel	.75	2.(

1977-78 Suns Team Issue

s 12-card set was released during the 1977-78 ason, and features all of the Phoenix Suns players n that year. Please note that these cards are slightly ersized at 3x5, and the card backs are blank.

OMPLETE SET (12) 20.00 40.00
lvan Adams 2.00 5.00
ennis Awtrey 1.25 3.00
Mike Bratz 1.25 3.00
Don Buse 1.25 3.00
Walter Davis 3.00 8.00
Bayard Forrest 1.25 3.00
Greg Griffin 1.25 3.00
Garfield Heard 1.50 4.00
Ron Lee 1.25 3.00
Curtis Perry 1.25 3.00
Alvin Scott 1.25 3.00
Paul Westphal 2.00 5.00

1988-89 Suns Team Issue

is seven-card set of Phoenix Suns measures proximately 5" by 8". The front has a black and white tion player photo with white borders. In the white ace below the picture appears the player's name, sey number, position, and the team logo. The backs e blank. The cards are unnumbered and we have ecklisted them below in alphabetical order. Tyrone orbin, Kevin Johnson, and Mark West came to the uns on February 25, 1988. Tyrone Corbin was lected in the expansion draft on June 15, 1989 and nny Gattison was waived by the Suns on September , 1989. The set includes Kevin Johnson's first ofessional card.

OMPLETE SET (7) 10.00 25.00
Tyrone Corbin 1.50 4.00
Kenny Gattison 1.00 2.50
Armon Gilliam 1.50 4.00
Jeff Hornacek 2.00 5.00
Eddie Johnson 1.25 3.00
Kevin Johnson 5.00 12.00
Mark West 1.00 2.50

2001-02 Suns Topps

eleased by Topps in conjunction with Sprite, this set atures a horizontal design with the Suns logo in the ackground. Our information on this set is incomplete. you have information regarding this release, please ontact us at basketballmag@beckett.com.

OMPLETE SET (8) 2.00 5.00
52 Anfernee Hardaway .75 2.00
53 Tom Gugliotta .30 .75
55 Clifford Robinson .30 .75
56 Rodney Rogers .30 .75
57 Chris Dudley .30 .75
58 Scott Skiles CO .30 .75
59 The Gorilla MASCOT .25 .60
NO Phoenix Suns .25 .60

1992-93 Suns Topps/Circle K Stickers

ssued in four three-sticker vertical strips, this 12-icker set features white-bordered color player action hotos, with the peel-away backs doubling as weepstakes entry forms to win one of 50 autographed uns posters. Each sticker measures approximately 2 /8" by 3 3/8". The photos are framed by orange and hite stripes, and each player's name appears at the ottom within a purple bar. The strips are numbered as eries 1-4, and the players are listed below in lphabetical order; S1 signifies sticker strip one. The et was sponsored by Circle K for the benefit of Boys lub charity.

OMPLETE SET (12) 4.00 10.00
Danny Ainge S1 .60 1.50
Charles Barkley S3 1.50 4.00
Cedric Ceballos S3 .30 .75
Tom Chambers S4 .60 1.50
Frank Johnson S1 .20 .50
Kevin Johnson S1 .60 1.50
Tom Kempton S4 .08 .25
Negele Knight S2 .08 .25
Dan Majerle S2 .60 1.50
0 Oliver Miller S3 .20 .50
1 Jerrod Mustaf S4 .08 .25
2 Mark West S2 .08 .25

1976-77 Suns

The 1976-77 Phoenix Suns set contains 12 horizontal player cards measuring 3 1/2" by 4 3/8". The fronts have circular black and white photos framed by the Suns' orange and purple logo. The backs are blank.

COMPLETE SET (12) 6.00 15.00
1 Alvan Adams 1.25 3.00
2 Dennis Awtrey .60 1.50
3 Keith Erickson 1.25 3.00
4 Butch Feher .60 1.50
5 Garfield Heard 1.00 2.50
6 Ron Lee .60 1.50
7 Curtis Perry .60 1.50
8 Ricky Sobers 1.00 2.50
9 Ira Terrell .75 2.00
10 Dick Van Arsdale 1.25 3.00
11 Tom Van Arsdale 1.25 3.00
12 Paul Westphal 2.00 5.00

1987-88 Suns Wendy's

This four-card set of Phoenix Suns was sponsored by Wendy's and measures approximately 5" by 8". Wendy's logo appears only on the Larry Nance card, whereas the others say "Don't Foul Out, Say No To Drugs" in the upper left corner. The front has a black and white action player photo with white borders. In the white action below the picture appears the player's name, jersey number, position, the team logo, and the words, "A commitment to quality." The backs are blank. The cards are unnumbered and we have checklisted them below in alphabetical order. Jay Humphries, Larry Nance, and Mike Sanders were traded away from the Suns on February 25, 1988.

COMPLETE SET (4) 6.00 15.00
1 Jay Humphries 2.00 5.00
2 Larry Nance 4.00 10.00
3 Mike Sanders 1.25 3.00
4 Bernard Thompson 1.25 3.00

1988 Supercampioni

This 56-sticker multisport set was available at Fina gas stations in Italy. Each sticker measures 1 3/4" by 2 7/16". The fronts display a color action photo inside a red inner border and a blue outer border. The bottom wider border carries the team emblem and, in a yellow bar, the player's name. The backs have a Fina advertisement and the sticker number. The players portrayed on stickers 31-38 are from Tracer Milano.

COMPLETE SET (8) 15.00 35.00
31 Robert Brunamonti .75 2.00
32 Michael D'Antoni 4.00 10.00
33 Walter Magnifico 2.50 6.00
34 Pier Luigi Marzorati .75 2.00
35 Bob McAdoo 5.00 12.00
36 Dino Meneghin 2.00 5.00
37 Antonello Riva 2.00 5.00
38 Renato Villalta .75 2.00

1974-75 Supersonics KTW-1250 Milk Cartons

These cards measure approximately 3 1/4" by 2 5/8" and feature drawings of the featured person in navy blue on a yellow background. A brief profile of the person appears in navy below the drawing. The cards are unnumbered and checklisted below in alphabetical order.

COMPLETE SET (2) 60.00 120.00
1 Wayne Cody ANN 10.00 20.00
2 Bill Russell GM 50.00 100.00

1990-91 Supersonics Kayo

This 14-card standard-size set was produced by Kayo Cards as a give-away to fans attending the April 13, 1991 Seattle Supersonics home game. A total of 10,000 sets supposedly were produced. The cards are numbered on the back. The set features early professional cards of Shawn Kemp and Gary Payton.

COMPLETE SET (14) 3.00 8.00
1 Shawn Kemp 1.00 2.50
2 Scott Meents .15 .40
3 Derrick McKey .25 .60
4 Michael Cage .25 .60
5 Benoit Benjamin .08 .25
6 Dave Corzine .08 .25
7 K.C. Jones CO .30 .75
8 Quintin Dailey .08 .25
9 Ricky Pierce .25 .60
10 Eddie Johnson .25 .60
11 Nate McMillan .40 1.00
12 Gary Payton 1.50 4.00
13 Sedale Threatt .08 .25
14 Dana Barros .20 .50

1993-94 Supersonics Playoff Taco Time

This four-card playoff subset was released in May 1994. Measuring 3 1/2" by 5" and featuring cartoon-like caricatures, these four cards combine to form 2 two-card pictures on their fronts (see 1-2 and 3-4 below); on their backs, they combine to form a four-card composite of Squatch wearing a Sonic uniform. The cards are unnumbered.

COMPLETE SET (4) 2.00 5.00
COMMON CARD (1-4) .50 1.25

1978-79 Supersonics Police

This set contains 16 unnumbered cards measuring 2 5/8" by 4 1/8" featuring the Seattle Supersonics. The set was sponsored by the Washington State Crime Prevention Association, Kiwanis Club, and local law enforcement agencies. The year of issue is printed in the lower right corner of the reverse. Backs contain safety tips ("Tips from the Sonics") and are written in black ink with blue accent. The cards are listed below in alphabetical order. The set features early professional cards of Dennis Johnson and Jack Sikma.

COMPLETE SET (16) 10.00 20.00
1 Fred Brown .75 2.00
2 Joe Hassett .30 .75
3 Dennis Johnson 1.50 4.00
4 John Johnson .30 .75
5 Tom LaGarde .40 1.00
6 Lonnie Shelton .50 1.25
7 Jack Sikma 1.00 2.50
8 Paul Silas 1.00 2.50
9 Dick Snyder .30 .75
10 Wally Walker .30 .75
11 Gus Williams .75 2.00
12 Len Wilkens CO 2.00 5.00
13 Les Habegger ACO .30 .75
14 Frank Furtado TR .30 .75
15 T. Wheedle mascot .30 .75
16 Team Photo .75 2.00

1979-80 Supersonics Police

This set contains 16 numbered cards measuring 2 5/8" by 4 1/8" featuring the Seattle Supersonics. Backs contain safety tips ("Tips for the Sonics") and are written in blue ink with red accent. The cards are numbered and dated in the lower right corner of the obverse. The set was sponsored by the Washington State Crime Prevention Association, Kiwanis, Coca Cola, Rainier Bank, and local area law enforcement agencies. The set features the first professional card of Vinnie Johnson.

COMPLETE SET (16) 7.50 15.00
1 Gus Williams .60 1.50
2 James Bailey .30 .75
3 Jack Sikma .60 1.50
4 Tom LaGarde .30 .75
5 Paul Silas .75 2.00
6 Lonnie Shelton .40 1.00
7 T. Wheedle (Mascot) .20 .50
8 Vinnie Johnson 1.25 3.00
9 Dennis Johnson 1.00 2.50
10 Wally Walker .40 1.00
11 Les Habegger ACO .25 .60
12 Frank Furtado TR .25 .60
13 Fred Brown .60 1.50
14 John Johnson .30 .75
15 Team Photo 1.00 2.50
16 Len Wilkens CO 1.00 2.50

1983-84 Supersonics Police

This set contains 16 cards measuring 2 5/8" by 4 1/8" featuring the Seattle Supersonics. Backs contain safety tips ("Tips from the Sonics") and are written in blue ink with a red accent. The set was also sponsored by the Washington State Crime Prevention Association, Kiwanis, Coca Cola, Ernst Home Centers, and area law enforcement agencies. The year of issue is given at the bottom right corner of the obverse. The cards are numbered on the back. The set features an early professional card of Tom Chambers.

COMPLETE SET (16) 3.00 8.00
1 Reggie King .30 .75
2 Frank Furtado TR .25 .60
3 Tom Chambers 1.25 3.00
4 Dave Harshman ACO .25 .60
5 Gus Williams .40 1.00
6 T. Wheedle (Mascot) .25 .60
7 Scooter McCray .30 .75
8 Jack Sikma .40 1.00
9 Al Wood .25 .60
10 Bob Blackburn ANN .25 .60
11 Danny Vranes .30 .75
12 Charles Bradley .25 .60
13 Steve Hawes .30 .75
14 Jon Sundvold .30 .75
15 Fred Brown .40 1.00
16 Lenny Wilkens CO .75 2.00

1979-80 Supersonics Portfolio

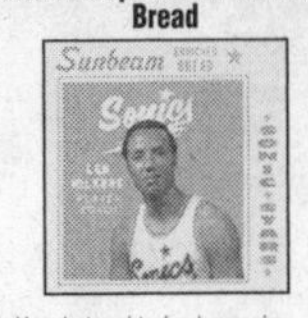

These limited collector prints of Seattle Supersonics were produced by artist Bill Vanderdasson and measure 11" by 14". Each print depicts a player in game action. While ten of the prints are in black and white on a gray background, the Sikma print is in full color. Each print has a hand-drawn border with rounded corners. The backs are blank. Dennis Awtrey was acquired from Boston on January 17, 1979 and left the SuperSonics via free agency on August 14, 1980. Dennis Johnson was traded to the Phoenix Suns on June 4, 1980.

COMPLETE SET (11) 22.50 45.00
1 Dennis Awtrey 1.25 3.00
2 Fred Brown 3.00 8.00
3 Dennis Johnson 5.00 10.00
4 John Johnson 1.25 3.00
5 Tom LaGarde 1.25 3.00
6 Lonnie Shelton 1.50 4.00
7 Jack Sikma 3.00 8.00
8 Paul Silas 3.00 8.00
9 Dick Snyder 1.25 3.00
10 Wally Walker 1.50 4.00
11 Gus Williams 2.50 6.00

1971-72 Supersonics Reed

These 13 pencil drawings of the 1971-72 Supersonics were drawn by Ashby Reed during the 1971-72 season. Each photo measures approximately 8 1/2" x 10". Each photo is black and white with a blank back.

COMPLETE SET (13) 25.00 50.00
1 Fred Brown 2.50 6.00
2 Barry Clemens 1.25 3.00
3 Pete Cross 1.25 3.00
4 Jake Ford 1.25 3.00
5 Spencer Haywood 3.00 8.00
6 Garfield Heard 1.50 4.00
7 Don Kojis 1.25 3.00
8 Bob Rule 1.25 3.00
9 Don Smith 1.25 3.00
10 Dick Snyder 1.25 3.00
11 Rod Thorn ACO 1.50 4.00
12 Lenny Wilkens 5.00 10.00
13 Lee Winfield 1.25 3.00

1973-74 Supersonics Shur-Fresh

The 1973-74 Shur-Fresh Seattle Supersonics set contains 12 cards measuring approximately 2 3/4" square. There are ten player cards and two coach cards. The cards have plastic bread ties attached to them. The fronts have color photos and the backs have biographical information. Cards are unnumbered so they are listed below in alphabetical order. The set features one of the few cards of Hall of Famer Bill Russell. Bill Russell's card may be slightly more difficult as a consumer could earn tickets to a Sonics game for five different cards of which one needed to be Russell's.

COMPLETE SET (12) 50.00 100.00
1 John Brisker 5.00 10.00
2 Fred Brown 10.00 20.00
3 Emmette Bryant ACO 3.00 8.00
4 Jim Fox 5.00 10.00
5 Dick Gibbs 3.00 8.00
6 Spencer Haywood 6.00 15.00
7 Bill Russell CO 30.00 60.00
8 Jim McDaniels 6.00 12.00
9 Kennedy McIntosh 3.00 8.00
10 Dick Snyder 3.00 8.00
11 Bud Stallworth 3.00 8.00
12 Lee Winfield 3.00 8.00

1990-91 Supersonics Smokey

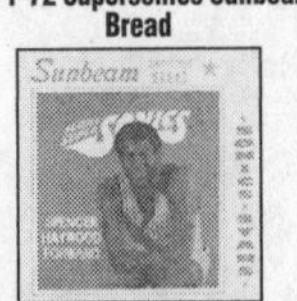

This 16-card set was sponsored by the USDA Forest Service in conjunction with other federal agencies. The cards were issued in a sheet of four rows of four cards each. After perforation, they measure the standard size. The front features a color action player photo, with the Smokey the Bear logo in the lower left corner. The front is done in the team's colors: border and lettering in yellow on a green background. The team name is inscribed above the picture, with the player's name below. The back presents biographical information and a fire prevention cartoon starring Smokey. The set features early professional cards of Shawn Kemp and Gary Payton.

COMPLETE SET (16) 6.00 15.00
1 Dana Barros .60 1.50
2 Michael Cage .60 1.50
3 Dave Corzine .40 1.00
4 Quintin Dailey .40 1.00
5 Dale Ellis .60 1.50
6 K.C. Jones CO .60 1.50
7 Shawn Kemp 1.50 4.00
8 Bob Kloppenburg CO .40 1.00
9 Xavier McDaniel .40 1.00
10 Derrick McKey .60 1.50
11 Nate McMillan .75 2.00
12 Scott Meents .40 1.00
13 Kip Motta CO .40 1.00
14 Gary Payton 3.00 8.00
15 Olden Polynice .40 1.00
16 Sedale Threatt .40 1.00

1969-70 Supersonics Sunbeam Bread

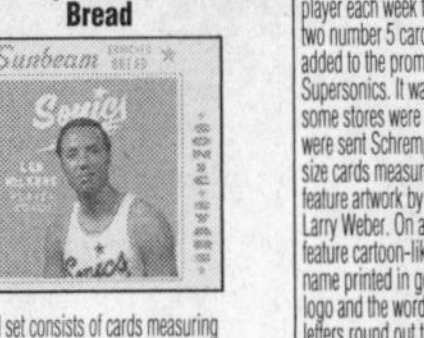

This 11-card set consists of cards measuring approximately 2 3/4" by 2 3/4". The cards were attached to plastic bread ties and issued on loaves of Sunbeam Bread. The cards of either Tom Meschery or Len Wilkens along with any four other player cards could be redeemed by a fan 16 years of age or younger for a free ticket to a 1969-70 Seattle Supersonics game. The card fronts feature a color posed photo of each player shot from the waist up. The team and player name are given in white lettering in the picture. The photo has a thin red border, with the words "Sunbeam Enriched Bread" across the top of the card face. The words "Sonic Stars" are written vertically along the right side of the picture. Cards show the team's schedule for the 1969-70 season. Cards are unnumbered so they are listed below in alphabetical order.

COMPLETE SET (11) 50.00 100.00
1 Lucius Allen 10.00 20.00
2 Bob Boozer 6.00 12.00
3 Barry Clemens 5.00 10.00
4 Art Harris 5.00 10.00
5 Tom Meschery SP 7.50 15.00
6 Erwin Mueller 5.00 10.00
7 Dorie Murrey 5.00 10.00
8 Bob Rule 6.00 12.00
9 John Tresvant 5.00 10.00
10 Len Wilkens P/CO SP 20.00 40.00
11 Seattle Coliseum DP 5.00 10.00

1970-71 Supersonics Sunbeam Bread

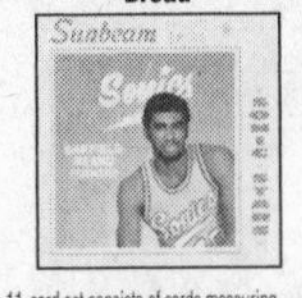

This 11-card set consists of cards measuring approximately 2 3/4" by 2 3/4". The cards were attached to plastic bread ties and issued on loafs of Sunbeam Bread. The front features a color posed photo of each player shot from the waist up. The team and player name are given in white lettering in the picture. The photo has a thin red border, with the words "Sunbeam Enriched Bread" across the top of the card face. The words "Sonic Stars" are written vertically along the right side of the picture. The back has a career summary of the player and an offer for fans 16 years of age or younger to complete and send in a set of five different Sonic players (including Tom Meschery or Len Wilkens) for a complimentary ticket to a 1970-71 Seattle Supersonics home game. Cards are unnumbered so they are listed below in alphabetical order.

COMPLETE SET (11) 50.00 100.00
1 Tom Black 5.00 10.00
2 Barry Clemens 5.00 10.00
3 Pete Cross 5.00 10.00
4 Jake Ford 5.00 10.00
5 Garfield Heard 6.00 15.00
6 Don Kojis 6.00 12.00
7 Tom Meschery SP 6.00 15.00
8 Dick Snyder 5.00 10.00
9 Len Wilkens P/CO SP 20.00 40.00
10 Lee Winfield 5.00 10.00
11 Seattle Coliseum 5.00 10.00

1971-72 Supersonics Sunbeam Bread

This 11-card set consists of cards measuring approximately 2 3/4" by 2 3/4". The cards were attached to plastic bread ties and issued on loafs of Sunbeam Bread. The front features a color posed photo of each player shot from the waist up. The team and player name are given in white lettering in the picture. The photo has a thin red border, with the words "Sunbeam Enriched Bread" across the top of the card face. The words "Sonic Stars" are written vertically along the right side of the picture. Cards are unnumbered so they are listed below in alphabetical order.

COMPLETE SET (11) 50.00 100.00
1 Pete Cross 5.00 10.00
2 Jake Ford 5.00 10.00
3 Spencer Haywood 10.00 20.00
4 Garfield Heard 7.50 15.00
5 Don Kojis 6.00 12.00
6 Bob Rule 6.00 12.00
7 Don Smith 5.00 10.00
8 Dick Snyder 5.00 10.00
9 Len Wilkens P/CO 15.00 30.00
10 Lee Winfield 5.00 10.00
11 Sonics Coliseum 5.00 10.00

1993-94 Supersonics Taco Time

Alrak Enterprises produced this set as a promotion for Taco Time Restaurants of Western Washington. Individual cards were available free with the purchase of a Taco Time "Happy Meal" or could be purchased at participating restaurants for 99 cents with any food purchase. The promotion featured a different Sonic player each week for 12 consecutive weeks. There are two number 5 cards because Detlef Schrempf was added to the promotion after his trade to the Seattle Supersonics. It was reported that during week five, some stores were sent McKey by mistake while others were sent Schrempf in short numbers. The postcard-size cards measure approximately 3 1/2" by 5" and feature artwork by sports and comic book illustrator Larry Weber. On a colored background, the fronts feature cartoon-like caricatures, with the player's first name printed in gold-foil letters at the top. The team's logo and the words "Not in our house" also in gold-foil letters round out the front. With Seattle's night skyline as a background, the horizontal backs show a color player portrait, the player's name, biographical information, and his favorite Taco Time menu item. The cards are numbered on the back.

COMPLETE SET (9) 9.00 18.00
1 Nate McMillan 1.25 3.00
2 Sam Perkins 1.25 3.00
3 Gary Payton 2.50 6.00
4 Ricky Pierce .75 2.00
5A Derrick McKey .75 2.00
5B Detlef Schrempf 1.25 3.00
6 Shawn Kemp 1.50 4.00
7 George Karl CO .75 2.00
8 Kendall Gill 1.00 2.50
9 Michael Cage .75 2.00

1967-68 Supersonics Team Issue

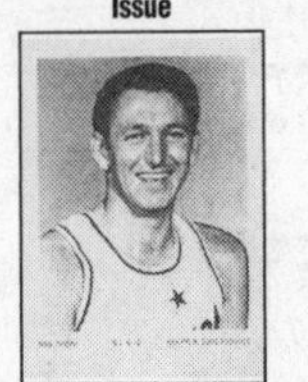

Each of these team issued photos measure approximately 4" by 5" and feature black and white close-up player portraits. The backs are blank. The photos are not numbered and listed below alphabetically.

COMPLETE SET (12) 100.00 200.00
1 Henry Akin 7.50 15.00
2 Walt Hazzard 15.00 30.00
3 Tommy Kron 7.50 15.00
4 Plummer Lott 7.50 15.00
5 Tom Meschery 10.00 20.00
6 Dorie Murrey 7.50 15.00
7 Bud Olsen 7.50 15.00
8 Bob Rule 10.00 20.00
9 Rod Thorn 10.00 20.00
10 Al Tucker 7.50 15.00
11 Bob Weiss 10.00 20.00
12 George Wilson 7.50 15.00

1968-69 Supersonics Team Issue

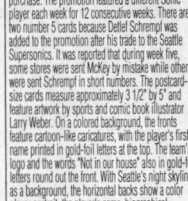

This 5x7 set was produced for the Seattle Supersonics during the 1968-69 season. The set features 12 black and white cards of the team's players.

COMPLETE SET (12) 60.00 120.00
1 Dorie Murrey 5.00 10.00
2 Tom Meschery 6.00 12.00
3 Len Wilkens 12.50 25.00
4 Al Hairston 5.00 10.00
5 Art Harris 5.00 10.00
6 Bob Kauffman 5.00 10.00
7 Rod Thorn 6.00 12.00
8 Al Tucker 5.00 10.00
9 Bob Rule 6.00 12.00
10 Plummer Lott 5.00 10.00
11 Tommy Kron 5.00 10.00
12 Joe Kennedy 5.00 10.00

1975-76 Supersonics Team Issue

This 8" x10" set was produced for the Seattle Supersonics during the 1975-76 season. The set features eight black and white cards of the team's players.

COMPLETE SET (8) 10.00 20.00
1 Mike Bantom 1.25 3.00
2 Rod Derline 1.25 3.00
3 Herm Gilliam 1.25 3.00
4 Leonard Gray 1.25 3.00
5 Willie Norwood 1.25 3.00
6 Frank Oleynick 1.25 3.00
7 Bruce Seals 1.25 3.00
8 Talvin Skinner 1.25 3.00

1976-77 Supersonics Team Issue

This 8" x10" set was produced for the Seattle Supersonics during the 1976-77 season. The set features nine black and white cards of the team's players and coaches.

COMPLETE SET (9) 12.50 25.00
1 Mike Bantom 1.25 3.00
2 Tommy Burleson 1.50 4.00
3 Leonard Gray 1.25 3.00
4 Mike Green 1.25 3.00
5 Willie Norwood 1.25 3.00
6 Frank Oleynick 1.25 3.00
7 Bruce Seals 1.25 3.00
8 Slick Watts 1.25 3.00
9 Bob Wilkerson 1.50 4.00

1978-79 Supersonics Team Issue

Each of these team-issued photos measure approximately 5 7/8" by 9" and feature color close-up player portraits with white borders. A facsimile autograph appears at the bottom. The backs are blank. The photos are unnumbered and listed below alphabetically.

COMPLETE SET (11) 17.50 35.00
1 Fred Brown 2.50 6.00
2 Al Fleming .75 2.00
3 Joe Hassett .75 2.00
4 Dennis Johnson 3.00 8.00
5 John Johnson .75 2.00
6 Jack Sikma 2.50 6.00
7 Paul Silas 2.50 6.00
8 Wally Walker 1.00 2.50
9 Marvin Webster 1.25 3.00
10 Gus Williams 2.00 5.00
11 Cover Photo (Smaller versions of all ten photos) 2.00 5.00

1978-79 Supersonics Team Issue 8 X 10

This seven photo set was released during the 1978-79 season. The set features many of the players on that years team. Please note that these cards measure 8" x 10" and are listed below in alphabetical order.

COMPLETE SET (7) 12.50 25.00
1 Fred Brown 2.00 5.00
2 Dennis Johnson 2.00 5.00
3 John Johnson 1.50 4.00
4 Lonnie Shelton 1.25 3.00
5 Jack Sikma 2.00 5.00
6 Wally Walker 1.50 4.00
7 Gus Williams 1.25 3.00

1983-84 Supersonics Team Issue

This 6" x 8" set was produced for the Seattle Supersonics during the 1983-84 season. The set features 12 black and white cards of the team's players.

COMPLETE SET (12) 12.00 30.00
1 Fred Brown 1.50 4.00
2 Al Wood .75 2.00
3 David Thompson 1.50 4.00
4 Scooter McCray .75 2.00
5 Jack Sikma 1.50 4.00
6 Gus Williams 1.25 3.00
7 Lenny Wilkens CO 1.50 4.00
8 Tom Chambers 1.50 4.00
9 Steve Hawes .75 2.00
10 Steve Hayes .75 2.00
11 Clay Johnson .75 2.00
12 Danny Vranes .75 2.00

1990-91 Supersonics Team Issue

Measuring 3 3/8" by 4 3/4", these cards feature on their fronts black-and-white action photos. On white card stock, the backs carry a headshot, biography, and a facsimile autograph. The cards are unnumbered and checklisted below in alphabetical order.

COMPLETE SET (6) 10.00 25.00
1 Benoit Benjamin 1.25 3.00
2 Eddie Johnson 1.50 4.00
3 K.C. Jones CO 1.50 4.00
4 Shawn Kemp 3.00 8.00

5 Derrick McKey	1.50	4.00
6 Gary Payton	5.00	12.00

1980 Superstar Matchbook

These collector issued matchbooks were issued in the New England area in 1980 and featured superstars from all sports but with an emphasis on players who made their fame in New England. Since these are unnumbered, we have sequenced them in alphabetical order.

COMPLETE SET	30.00	60.00
2 Larry Bird	5.00	10.00

2001-02 Sweet Shot

Released in December 2001, Upper Deck Sweet Shot is a 120-card set divided up into 90 base cards and 30 rookie cards. Veteran cards have a white border and a bronze background with a basketball centered in the desing. Photos are full color action shots, and the the bottom of the card has bronze foil highlights. The rookie breakdown is as follows: card numbers 91-110 utilize the same card design with a shift from bronze to silver on both the background and the foil highlights, and are sequentially numbered to 1200. Card numbers 111-120 have full color backgrounds, gold foil highlights, and are sequentially numbered to 600. Sweet Shot was packaged in 18-pack boxes with four cards per pack and carried a suggested retail price of $9.99.

COMP.SET w/o SP's	20.00	40.00
1 Jason Terry	.30	.75
2 Shareef Abdur-Rahim	.25	.60
3 Toni Kukoc	.25	.60
4 Paul Pierce	.40	1.00
5 Antoine Walker	.25	.60
6 Kenny Anderson	.25	.60
7 Baron Davis	.30	.75
8 Jamal Mashburn	.25	.60
9 David Wesley	.20	.50
10 Ron Mercer	.20	.50
11 Ron Artest	.30	.75
12 A.J. Guyton	.20	.50
13 Andre Miller	.25	.60
14 Lamond Murray	.20	.50
15 Chris Mihm	.20	.50
16 Michael Finley	.30	.75
17 Dirk Nowitzki	.50	1.25
18 Steve Nash	.50	1.25
19 Antonio McDyess	.25	.60
20 Nick Van Exel	.25	.60
21 Raef LaFrentz	.20	.50
22 Jerry Stackhouse	.25	.60
23 Chucky Atkins	.20	.50
24 Corliss Williamson	.20	.50
25 Antawn Jamison	.30	.75
26 Marc Jackson	.20	.50
27 Larry Hughes	.25	.60
28 Steve Francis	.30	.75
29 Cuttino Mobley	.25	.60
30 Maurice Taylor	.20	.50
31 Reggie Miller	.30	.75
32 Jalen Rose	.25	.60
33 Jermaine O'Neal	.30	.75
34 Darius Miles	.20	.50
35 Elton Brand	.30	.75
36 Corey Maggette	.25	.60
37 Quentin Richardson	.25	.60
38 Kobe Bryant	1.50	4.00
39 Shaquille O'Neal	.75	2.00
40 Rick Fox	.25	.60
41 Derek Fisher	.25	.60
42 Stromile Swift	.20	.50
43 Jason Williams	.25	.60
44 Michael Dickerson	.20	.50
45 Alonzo Mourning	.40	1.00
46 Eddie Jones	.25	.60
47 Anthony Carter	.20	.50
48 Glenn Robinson	.25	.60
49 Ray Allen	.30	.75
50 Sam Cassell	.25	.60
51 Kevin Garnett	.60	1.50
52 Chauncey Billups	.30	.75
53 Terrell Brandon	.20	.50
54 Joe Smith	.25	.60
55 Kenyon Martin	.30	.75
56 Keith Van Horn	.25	.60
57 Jason Kidd	.50	1.25
58 Latrell Sprewell	.25	.60
59 Allan Houston	.25	.60
60 Marcus Camby	.25	.60
61 Tracy McGrady	.50	1.25
62 Mike Miller	.30	.75
63 Grant Hill	.40	1.00
64 Allen Iverson	.60	1.50
65 Dikembe Mutombo	.30	.75
66 Aaron McKie	.20	.50
67 Stephon Marbury	.25	.60
68 Shawn Marion	.30	.75
69 Tom Gugliotta	.20	.50
70 Rasheed Wallace	.30	.75
71 Damon Stoudamire	.25	.60
72 Bonzi Wells	.20	.50
73 Chris Webber	.30	.75
74 Peja Stojakovic	.30	.75
75 Mike Bibby	.30	.75
76 Tim Duncan	.60	1.50
77 David Robinson	.50	1.25
78 Antonio Daniels	.20	.50
79 Gary Payton	.30	.75
80 Rashard Lewis	.30	.75
81 Desmond Mason	.25	.60
82 Vince Carter	.50	1.25
83 Morris Peterson	.20	.50
84 Antonio Davis	.20	.50
85 Karl Malone	.40	1.00
86 John Stockton	.40	1.00
87 Donyell Marshall	.20	.50
88 Richard Hamilton	.25	.60
89 Courtney Alexander	.20	.50
90 Michael Jordan	6.00	15.00
91 Zach Randolph RC	5.00	12.00
92 Troy Murphy RC	3.00	8.00
93 Michael Bradley RC	2.00	5.00
94 Vladimir Radmanovic RC	2.00	5.00
95 Kirk Haston RC	2.00	5.00
96 Joseph Forte RC	2.00	5.00
97 Jamaal Tinsley RC	2.50	6.00
98 Jason Collins RC	2.00	5.00
99 Brendan Haywood RC	2.50	6.00
100 Richard Jefferson RC	4.00	10.00
101 Gerald Wallace RC	3.00	8.00
102 Jeryl Sasser RC	2.00	5.00
103 Samuel Dalembert RC	2.50	6.00
104 Tony Parker RC	8.00	20.00
105 Kedrick Brown RC	2.00	5.00
106 Brandon Armstrong RC	2.00	5.00
107 Steven Hunter RC	2.00	5.00
108 Andrei Kirilenko RC	5.00	12.00
109 Primoz Brezec RC	2.00	5.00
110 Terence Morris RC	2.00	5.00
111 Eddie Griffin RC	2.50	6.00
112 DeSagana Diop RC	2.50	6.00
113 Tyson Chandler RC	4.00	10.00
114 Joe Johnson RC	6.00	15.00
115 Rodney White RC	2.50	6.00
116 Eddy Curry RC	4.00	10.00
117 Shane Battier RC	5.00	12.00
118 Jason Richardson RC	5.00	12.00
119 Kwame Brown RC	2.50	6.00
120 Pau Gasol RC	8.00	20.00

2001-02 Sweet Shot Rookie Memorabilia

Randomly inserted in packs, this 28-card set features rookie layers coupled with a swatch of game-worn memorabilia. Player portrait photos appear on the left in color, and a swatch of jersey appears in the lower right hand corner. Card numbers 91-110 are sequentially numbered to 1200, and card numbers 111-120 are sequentially numbered to 600. The card numbers and order parallel that of the base set. Samuel Dalembert #103 and Kedrick Brown #105 do not have jersey cards, therefore, those numbers do not exist.

91 Zach Randolph	6.00	15.00
92 Troy Murphy	4.00	10.00
93 Michael Bradley	2.50	6.00
94 Vladimir Radmanovic	2.50	6.00
95 Kirk Haston	2.50	6.00
96 Joseph Forte	2.50	6.00
97 Jamaal Tinsley	3.00	8.00
98 Jason Collins	2.50	6.00
99 Brendan Haywood	3.00	8.00
100 Richard Jefferson	5.00	12.00
101 Gerald Wallace	4.00	10.00
102 Jeryl Sasser	2.50	6.00
104 Tony Parker	10.00	25.00
106 Brandon Armstrong	2.50	6.00
107 Steven Hunter	2.50	6.00
108 Andrei Kirilenko	6.00	15.00
109 Primoz Brezec	2.50	6.00
110 Terence Morris	2.50	6.00
111 Eddie Griffin	4.00	10.00
112 DeSagana Diop	4.00	10.00
113 Tyson Chandler	6.00	15.00
114 Joe Johnson	10.00	25.00
115 Rodney White	4.00	10.00
116 Eddy Curry	6.00	15.00
117 Shane Battier	8.00	20.00
118 Jason Richardson	8.00	20.00
119 Kwame Brown	4.00	10.00
120 Pau Gasol	12.00	30.00

2001-02 Sweet Shot Game Jerseys

Inserted one in every 18 packs, this 25-card set showcases an oval swatch of a jersey in the upper right hand corner. The card background is green with full color player action photos, a gray-scale portrait photo on the left side and silver foil highlights.

AI Allen Iverson	6.00	15.00
AJ Antawn Jamison	3.00	8.00
AW Antoine Walker	2.50	6.00
BD Baron Davis	3.00	8.00
CM Corey Maggette	2.50	6.00
CW Chris Webber	5.00	12.00
DJ DerMarr Johnson	2.00	5.00
DM Darius Miles	2.00	5.00
JM Jamal Mashburn	2.50	6.00
JT Jason Terry	3.00	8.00
KB Kobe Bryant	15.00	40.00
KE Kenyon Martin	3.00	8.00
KG Kevin Garnett	6.00	15.00
KM Karl Malone	4.00	10.00
KV Keith Van Horn	2.50	6.00
LH Larry Hughes	2.50	6.00
MF Marcus Fizer	2.00	5.00
MM Mike Miller	3.00	8.00
RM Ron Mercer	2.00	5.00
SM Shawn Marion	3.00	8.00
ST John Stockton	4.00	10.00
TB Terrell Brandon	2.00	5.00
TK Toni Kukoc	2.50	6.00
TM Tracy McGrady	5.00	12.00
WS Wally Szczerbiak	2.50	6.00

2001-02 Sweet Shot Hot Spot Floor

Inserted one in every 18 packs, this 28-card set features large swatches of floor set next to a full color player photo. The background fades from orange around the swatch into a "wood floor" background on the bottom and the words "Hot Spot Floor" on the top, and cards contain red foil highlights.

AHF Allan Houston	2.50	6.00
AMF Andre Miller	2.50	6.00
BWF Bonzi Wells	2.00	5.00
DEF Desmond Mason	2.50	6.00
DVF David Robinson	5.00	12.00
EJF Eddie Jones	2.50	6.00
JKF Jason Kidd	5.00	12.00
JMF Jamal Mashburn	2.50	6.00
JOF Jermaine O'Neal	3.00	8.00
JSF Jerry Stackhouse	2.50	6.00
JTF Jason Terry	3.00	8.00
KBF Kobe Bryant	15.00	40.00
KGF Kevin Garnett	6.00	15.00
LSF Latrell Sprewell	2.50	6.00
MAF Marc Jackson	2.00	5.00
MJF Michael Jordan	60.00	150.00
QRF Quentin Richardson	2.50	6.00
RAF Ray Allen	3.00	8.00
RHF Richard Hamilton	2.50	6.00
RLF Rashard Lewis	3.00	8.00
RMF Reggie Miller	5.00	12.00
RWF Rasheed Wallace	3.00	8.00
SFF Steve Francis	3.00	8.00
SHF Shawn Marion	3.00	8.00
SMF Stephon Marbury	2.50	6.00
SPF Scottie Pippen	8.00	20.00
TMF Tracy McGrady	5.00	12.00
WSF Wally Szczerbiak	2.50	6.00

2001-02 Sweet Shot Network Executives

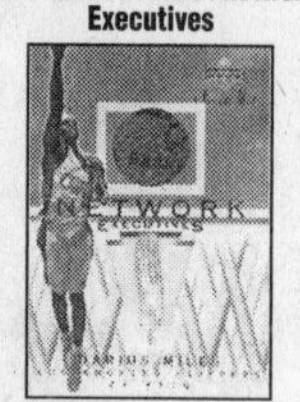

Inserted one in every 108 packs, this 8 card set features combination of pieces of game used basketballs and nets on each card, with the corresponding player. Player action photos appear along the left side of the card, and the bottom background is a rim and basketball net. The swatch of basketball appears on the top half of the card, and the swatch of net is set to mix in with the bottom background.

AGN A.J. Guyton	6.00	15.00
AJN Antawn Jamison	10.00	25.00
DJN DerMarr Johnson	6.00	15.00
DMN Darius Miles	6.00	15.00
JAN Jason Terry	10.00	25.00
QRN Quentin Richardson	8.00	20.00
RHN Richard Hamilton	8.00	20.00
RMN Ron Mercer	6.00	15.00

2001-02 Sweet Shot Signature Shots

Inserted one in 18 packs, this 24 cards set features an authentic autograph signed on a piece of basketball-like material with the corresponding player on front. The back of the card is numbered with the player's initials.

AWS Antoine Walker	5.00	12.00
DAS Darrell Armstrong	5.00	12.00
DES Desmond Mason	5.00	12.00
DJS DerMarr Johnson	5.00	12.00
ECS Eddy Curry	5.00	12.00
EGS Eddie Griffin	5.00	12.00
HUS Steven Hunter	5.00	12.00
JJS Joe Johnson	8.00	20.00
JMS Jamal Mashburn	5.00	12.00
JPS Joel Przybilla	5.00	12.00
JRS Jason Richardson	6.00	15.00
JSS Jerry Stackhouse	6.00	15.00
KBS Kobe Bryant	125.00	250.00
KES Kenyon Martin	6.00	15.00
KGS Kevin Garnett	25.00	60.00
KWS Kwame Brown	5.00	12.00
LHS Larry Hughes	5.00	12.00
MJS Michael Jordan	300.00	600.00
PPS Paul Pierce	12.00	30.00
RJS Richard Jefferson	6.00	15.00
SSS Stromile Swift	5.00	12.00
TCS Tyson Chandler	6.00	15.00
TMS Troy Murphy	6.00	15.00
WSS Wally Szczerbiak	6.00	15.00

2001-02 Sweet Shot Three-point Shots

Numbered to each player's jersey, this 15 card insert features a piece of game used jersey, floor, and autograph of the corresponding player shown on the front of the card. The back of the card is numbered with the player's initials.

DE Desmond Mason/24	30.00	80.00
DM Darius Miles/21	20.00	50.00
JM Jamal Mashburn/24	30.00	80.00
JS Jerry Stackhouse/42	30.00	80.00
KG Kevin Garnett/21	100.00	200.00
MJ Michael Jordan/23	600.00	1000.00
MM Mike Miller/50	20.00	50.00
PP Paul Pierce/34	40.00	100.00

2002-03 Sweet Shot

This 132-card standard-size was issued in four card packs with an $9.99 SRP which came 12 packs to a box. Cards numbered 1-90 featured veterans while cards 91 through 123 featured rookies and were issued to a stated print run of 999 copies and cards 124 through 132 featured rookies and were issued to a stated print run of 499 cards.

COMP.SET w/o SP's (90)	15.00	40.00
1 Shareef Abdur-Rahim	.25	.60
2 Jason Terry	.25	.60
3 Glenn Robinson	.25	.60
4 Paul Pierce	.40	1.00
5 Antoine Walker	.25	.60
6 Kedrick Brown	.20	.50
7 Vin Baker	.25	.60
8 Jalen Rose	.25	.60
9 Eddy Curry	.25	.60
10 Tyson Chandler	.25	.60
11 Zydrunas Ilgauskas	.25	.60
12 Chris Mihm	.20	.50
13 Darius Miles	.20	.50
14 Dirk Nowitzki	.50	1.25
15 Michael Finley	.30	.75
16 Steve Nash	.40	1.00
17 Raef LaFrentz	.20	.50
18 James Posey	.20	.50
19 Juwan Howard	.25	.60
20 Richard Hamilton	.25	.60
21 Ben Wallace	.30	.75
22 Chauncey Billups	.30	.75
23 Jason Richardson	.30	.75
24 Antawn Jamison	.30	.75
25 Steve Francis	.30	.75
26 Eddie Griffin	.20	.50
27 Cuttino Mobley	.25	.60
28 Reggie Miller	.30	.75
29 Jamaal Tinsley	.20	.50
30 Jermaine O'Neal	.30	.75
31 Elton Brand	.30	.75
32 Lamar Odom	.30	.75
33 Andre Miller	.25	.60
34 Kobe Bryant	1.50	4.00
35 Shaquille O'Neal	.75	2.00
36 Devean George	.20	.50
37 Pau Gasol	.40	1.00
38 Shane Battier	.30	.75
39 Jason Williams	.25	.60
40 Eddie House	.20	.50
41 Eddie Jones	.25	.60
42 Brian Grant	.20	.50
43 Ray Allen	.30	.75
44 Tim Thomas	.20	.50
45 Kevin Garnett	.60	1.50
46 Terrell Brandon	.20	.50
47 Wally Szczerbiak	.25	.60
48 Joe Smith	.25	.60
49 Jason Kidd	.50	1.25
50 Richard Jefferson	.30	.75
51 Kenyon Martin	.30	.75
52 Dikembe Mutombo	.30	.75
53 Jamal Mashburn	.25	.60
54 Baron Davis	.30	.75
55 David Wesley	.20	.50
56 Allan Houston	.25	.60
57 Antonio McDyess	.25	.60
58 Latrell Sprewell	.25	.60
59 Tracy McGrady	.50	1.25
60 Mike Miller	.30	.75
61 Darrell Armstrong	.20	.50
62 Allen Iverson	.50	1.25
63 Keith Van Horn	.25	.60
64 Stephon Marbury	.25	.60
65 Shawn Marion	.30	.75
66 Anfernee Hardaway	.50	1.25
67 Rasheed Wallace	.30	.75
68 Bonzi Wells	.20	.50
69 Scottie Pippen	.50	1.25
70 Chris Webber	.30	.75
71 Mike Bibby	.30	.75
72 Peja Stojakovic	.30	.75
73 Hedo Turkoglu	.30	.75
74 Tim Duncan	.60	1.50
75 David Robinson	.50	1.25
76 Tony Parker	.40	1.00
77 Steve Smith	.25	.60
78 Gary Payton	.30	.75
79 Rashard Lewis	.30	.75
80 Desmond Mason	.25	.60
81 Brent Barry	.20	.50
82 Vince Carter	.50	1.25
83 Morris Peterson	.20	.50
84 Antonio Davis	.20	.50
85 Karl Malone	.40	1.00
86 John Stockton	.40	1.00
87 Andrei Kirilenko	.30	.75
88 Jerry Stackhouse	.25	.60
89 Michael Jordan	2.50	6.00
90 Kwame Brown	.20	.50
91 Efthimios Rentzias RC	2.00	5.00
92 Marko Jaric	2.00	5.00
93 Rasual Butler RC	2.00	5.00
94 Predrag Savovic RC	2.00	5.00
95 Sam Clancy RC	2.00	5.00
96 Lonny Baxter RC	2.00	5.00
97 Raul Lopez RC	2.00	5.00
98 Rod Grizzard RC	2.00	5.00
99 Tito Maddox RC	2.00	5.00
100 Carlos Boozer RC	4.00	10.00
101 Dan Gadzuric RC	2.00	5.00
102 Vincent Yarbrough RC	2.00	5.00
103 Robert Archibald RC	2.00	5.00
104 Roger Mason RC	2.00	5.00
105 Ronald Murray RC	2.00	5.00
106 Dan Dickau RC	2.00	5.00
107 Chris Jefferies RC	2.00	5.00
108 John Salmons RC	2.50	6.00
109 Frank Williams RC	2.00	5.00
110 Tayshaun Prince RC	2.50	6.00
111 Casey Jacobsen RC	2.00	5.00
112 Qyntel Woods RC	2.00	5.00
113 Kareem Rush RC	2.00	5.00
114 Ryan Humphrey RC	2.00	5.00
115 Curtis Borchardt RC	2.00	5.00
116 Juan Dixon RC	2.50	6.00
117 Jiri Welsch RC	2.00	5.00
118 Bostjan Nachbar RC	2.00	5.00
119 Fred Jones RC	2.00	5.00
120 Marcus Haislip RC	2.00	5.00
121 Melvin Ely RC	2.00	5.00
122 Jared Jeffries RC	2.00	5.00
123 Caron Butler RC	3.00	8.00
124 Amare Stoudemire RC	8.00	20.00
125 Chris Wilcox RC	3.00	8.00
126 Nene Hilario RC	4.00	10.00
127 DaJuan Wagner RC	3.00	8.00
128 Nikoloz Tskitishvili RC	3.00	8.00
129 Drew Gooden RC	5.00	12.00
130 Mike Dunleavy RC	4.00	10.00
131 Jay Williams RC	4.00	10.00
132 Yao Ming RC	10.00	25.00

2002-03 Sweet Shot Jerseys

Issued at a stated rate of one in 12, these 19 cards feature game-used jersey swatches of NBA players. A Gold version sequentially numbered to 50 was also inserted in packs.

*GOLD: .75X TO 2X JERSEYS HI

AIJ Allen Iverson	5.00	12.00
AJJ Antawn Jamison	3.00	8.00
BDJ Baron Davis	3.00	8.00
DJJ DerMarr Johnson	2.00	5.00
HTJ Hedo Turkoglu	3.00	8.00
JMJ Jamal Mashburn	2.50	6.00
JOJ Jermaine O'Neal	3.00	8.00
JSJ Joe Smith	2.50	6.00
KBJ Kobe Bryant	15.00	40.00
KGJ Kevin Garnett	6.00	15.00
KVJ Keith Van Horn	2.50	6.00
MCJ Antonio McDyess	2.50	6.00
MJJ Michael Jordan	30.00	80.00
PPJ Paul Pierce	4.00	10.00
RHJ Richard Hamilton	2.50	6.00
SFJ Steve Francis	3.00	8.00
SMJ Stephon Marbury	2.50	6.00
SNJ Steve Nash	4.00	10.00
WSJ Wally Szczerbiak	2.50	6.00

2002-03 Sweet Shot Off the Glass

Inserted at a stated rate of one in 84, these cards were made with a plexiglass feel and feature 12 leading NBA players.

G1 Michael Jordan	30.00	80.00
G2 Kobe Bryant	20.00	50.00
G3 Kevin Garnett	8.00	20.00
G4 Allen Iverson	6.00	15.00
G5 Shaquille O'Neal	10.00	25.00
G6 Vince Carter	6.00	15.00
G7 Paul Pierce	5.00	12.00
G8 Jason Kidd	6.00	15.00
G9 Steve Francis	4.00	10.00
G10 Tim Duncan	8.00	20.00
G11 Jay Williams	5.00	12.00
G12 Yao Ming	12.00	30.00

2002-03 Sweet Shot Signature Shots

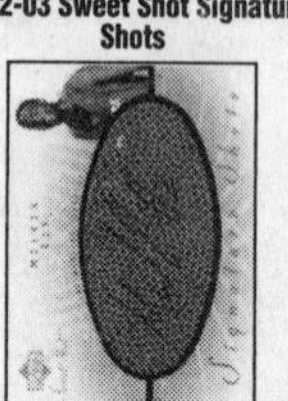

Inserted at a stated rate of one in 24, these 30 cards feature authentic autographs from mainly current NBA players. Retired superstars Larry Bird, Magic Johnson and Julius Erving also signed cards in this set. A few of these cards were issued in shorter supply and we have printed the stated print run when known.

AS Amare Stoudemire	15.00	40.00
AW Antoine Walker	8.00	20.00
CB Caron Butler	8.00	20.00
CW Chris Wilcox	5.00	12.00
DG Drew Gooden	8.00	20.00
DS DeShawn Stevenson	5.00	12.00
DW DaJuan Wagner	5.00	12.00
JE Julius Erving SP	75.00	150.00
JJ Jared Jeffries	5.00	12.00
JK Jason Kidd	15.00	40.00
JR Jason Richardson	8.00	20.00
JW Jay Williams	6.00	15.00
KB Kobe Bryant SP	125.00	250.00
KM Kenyon Martin	6.00	15.00
LB Larry Bird	75.00	150.00
LO Lamar Odom	6.00	15.00
ME Melvin Ely	5.00	12.00
MF Marcus Fizer	5.00	12.00
MG Magic Johnson	60.00	120.00
MJ Michael Jordan SP	400.00	700.00
MP Morris Peterson	5.00	12.00
NH Nene Hilario	6.00	15.00
NT Nikoloz Tskitishvili	5.00	12.00
PP Paul Pierce	12.50	30.00
QR Quentin Richardson	5.00	12.00
RJ Richard Jefferson	6.00	15.00
RM Ron Mercer/34	6.00	15.00
SA Shareef Abdur-Rahim	5.00	12.00
TC Tyson Chandler	6.00	15.00
YM Yao Ming	25.00	60.00

2002-03 Sweet Shot Sweet Swatches

Inserted at a stated rate of one in 12, these 20 cards feature game-worn swatches from NBA players. A Gold version was also inserted in packs where cards are sequentially numbered to 100.

*GOLD: .6X TO 1.5X SWATCH HI

AMS Andre Miller	2.50	6.00
AWS Antoine Walker	2.50	6.00
BDS Baron Davis	3.00	8.00
CWS Chris Webber	3.00	8.00
DMS Darius Miles	2.00	5.00
DNS Dirk Nowitzki	5.00	12.00
ECS Eddy Curry	2.50	6.00
JMS Jamal Mashburn	2.50	6.00
KBS Kobe Bryant	15.00	40.00
KES Kenyon Martin	3.00	8.00
KGS Kevin Garnett	6.00	15.00
KMS Karl Malone	4.00	10.00
KWS Kwame Brown	2.00	5.00
LOS Lamar Odom	3.00	8.00
MMS Mike Miller	3.00	8.00
RHS Robert Horry	2.50	6.00
SMS Shawn Marion	3.00	8.00
TBS Terrell Brandon	2.00	5.00
TMS Tracy McGrady	5.00	12.00
WSS Wally Szczerbiak	2.50	6.00

2002-03 Sweet Shot Three-Point Shots

Randomly inserted into packs, these 17 cards feature not only a "shirt" piece but also an authentic autograph of the featured player. Each of these cards were issued to the player's jersey number.

MFA Marcus Fizer/21	20.00	50.00
MGA Magic Johnson/32	150.00	300.00
MJA Michael Jordan/23	500.00	1000.00
MMA Mike Miller/50	20.00	50.00
MPA Morris Peterson/24	20.00	50.00
PPA Paul Pierce/34	75.00	150.00

2003-04 Sweet Shot

Released in November 2003, Sweet Shot boasts a 144-card set divided up as follows: cards 1-90 are base veterans with a full color player action photo, borders set to look like a basketball and a colored ribbon on the left side of the card that matches the player's team colors. Cards 91-96 feature rookies and have white borders and are sequentially numbered to 799. Cards 97-132 feature rookies and a white border on the left and a basketball texture on the right. The middle of each card, where the player's photo is, is printed on metal. Cards 133-144 feature Michael Jordan and are seuqentially numbered to 799. Sweet Shot was packaged in 12-pack boxes where packs contained four cards and carried a suggested retail price of $9.99.

COMP.SET w/o SP's (90)	15.00	40.00
1 Shareef Abdur-Rahim	.25	.60
2 Jason Terry	.25	.60
3 Theo Ratliff	.20	.50
4 Paul Pierce	.40	1.00
5 Antoine Walker	.30	.75
6 Vin Baker	.20	.50
7 Jalen Rose	.25	.60
8 Tyson Chandler	.25	.60
9 Jay Williams	.20	.50
10 Dajuan Wagner	.20	.50
11 Zydrunas Ilgauskas	.25	.60
12 Darius Miles	.20	.50
13 Dirk Nowitzki	.50	1.25
14 Antawn Jamison	.30	.75
15 Steve Nash	.40	1.00
16 Nene Hilario	.25	.60
17 Marcus Camby	.25	.60
18 Andre Miller	.25	.60
19 Richard Hamilton	.25	.60
20 Ben Wallace	.30	.75
21 Chauncey Billups	.30	.75
22 Nick Van Exel	.25	.60
23 Jason Richardson	.30	.75
24 Erick Dampier	.20	.50
25 Steve Francis	.30	.75
26 Yao Ming	.60	1.50
27 Cuttino Mobley	.25	.60
28 Reggie Miller	.30	.75
29 Jamaal Tinsley	.20	.50
30 Jermaine O'Neal	.30	.75
31 Elton Brand	.30	.75
32 Corey Maggette	.25	.60
33 Marko Jaric	.20	.50
34 Kobe Bryant	1.50	4.00
35 Gary Payton	.30	.75
36 Shaquille O'Neal	.75	2.00
37 Karl Malone	.40	1.00
38 Pau Gasol	.30	.75
39 Shane Battier	.25	.60
40 Mike Miller	.30	.75
41 Eddie Jones	.25	.60
42 Lamar Odom	.30	.75
43 Caron Butler	.30	.75
44 Michael Redd	.30	.75
45 Joe Smith	.25	.60
46 Desmond Mason	.25	.60
47 Kevin Garnett	.60	1.50
48 Wally Szczerbiak	.25	.60
49 Latrell Sprewell	.25	.60
50 Jason Kidd	.50	1.25
51 Richard Jefferson	.30	.75
52 Kenyon Martin	.30	.75
53 Baron Davis	.30	.75
54 Jamal Mashburn	.25	.60
55 David Wesley	.20	.50
56 Allan Houston	.25	
57 Antonio McDyess	.25	
58 Keith Van Horn	.25	
59 Tracy McGrady	.40	1.
60 Grant Hill	.40	1.
61 Drew Gooden	.25	
62 Allen Iverson	.50	1.
64 Eric Snow	.20	
64A Glenn Robinson	.25	
65 Stephon Marbury	.25	
66 Shawn Marion	.30	
67 Amare Stoudemire	.50	1.
68 Rasheed Wallace	.30	
69 Bonzi Wells	.20	
70 Damon Stoudamire	.25	
71 Chris Webber	.30	
72 Mike Bibby	.30	
73 Peja Stojakovic	.30	
74 Vlade Divac	.25	
75 Tim Duncan	.50	1.
76 David Robinson	.50	1.
77 Tony Parker	.30	
78 Manu Ginobili	.40	1.
79 Ray Allen	.30	
80 Rashard Lewis	.30	
81 Vladimir Radmanovic	.20	
82 Vince Carter	.50	1.
83 Morris Peterson	.20	
84 Antonio Davis	.20	
85 Keon Clark	.20	
86 John Stockton	.40	1.0
87 Andrei Kirilenko	.30	
88 Jerry Stackhouse	.25	
89 Kwame Brown	.20	
90 Larry Hughes	.25	
91 LeBron James RC	50.00	125.
92 Darko Milicic RC	5.00	12.0
93 Carmelo Anthony RC	12.00	30.0
94 Chris Bosh RC	10.00	25.0
95 Dwyane Wade RC	20.00	50.0
96 Chris Kaman RC	6.00	15.0
97 Kirk Hinrich RC	5.00	12.0
98 T.J. Ford RC	5.00	12.0
99 Mike Sweetney RC	4.00	10.0
100 Jarvis Hayes RC	4.00	10.0
101 Mickael Pietrus RC	4.00	10.0
102 Nick Collison RC	4.00	10.0
103 Marcus Banks RC	4.00	10.0
104 Luke Ridnour RC	5.00	12.0
105 Reece Gaines RC	4.00	10.0
106 Troy Bell RC	4.00	10.0
107 Zarko Cabarkapa RC	4.00	10.0
108 David West RC	5.00	12.0
109 Aleksandar Pavlovic RC	4.00	10.0
110 Dahntay Jones RC	4.00	10.0
111 Boris Diaw RC	5.00	12.0
112 Zoran Planinic RC	4.00	10.0
113 Travis Outlaw RC	5.00	12.0
114 Brian Cook RC	4.00	10.0
115 Carlos Delfino RC	5.00	12.0
116 Ndudi Ebi RC	4.00	10.0
117 Kendrick Perkins RC	6.00	15.0
118 Leandro Barbosa RC	5.00	12.0
119 Josh Howard RC	4.00	10.0
120 Jason Kapono RC	4.00	10.0
121 Luke Walton RC	4.00	10.0
122 Jerome Beasley RC	4.00	10.0
123 Kyle Korver RC	5.00	12.0
124 Maciej Lampe RC	4.00	10.0
125 Travis Hansen RC	4.00	10.0
126 Steve Blake RC	5.00	12.0
127 Willie Green RC	4.00	10.0
128 Slavko Vranes RC	4.00	10.0
129 Keith Bogans RC	4.00	10.0
130 Maurice Williams RC	6.00	15.0
131 Matt Bonner RC	5.00	12.0
132 Zaur Pachulia RC	4.00	10.0
133 Michael Jordan	10.00	25.0
134 Michael Jordan	10.00	25.0
135 Michael Jordan	10.00	25.0
136 Michael Jordan	10.00	25.0
137 Michael Jordan	10.00	25.0
138 Michael Jordan	10.00	25.0
139 Michael Jordan	10.00	25.0
140 Michael Jordan	10.00	25.0
141 Michael Jordan	10.00	25.0
142 Michael Jordan	10.00	25.0
143 Michael Jordan	10.00	25.0
144 Michael Jordan	10.00	25.0

2003-04 Sweet Shot Jerseys

Inserted at the rate of one in 12, this 30-card set place full-color player photos on the left of the card and a swatch of game-worn jersey on the right.

AHJ Allan Houston	2.00	5.0
AIJ Allen Iverson	4.00	10.0
ASJ Amare Stoudemire	4.00	10.0
AWJ Antoine Walker	2.50	6.0
BDJ Baron Davis	2.50	6.0
CWJ Chris Webber	2.50	6.0
DNJ Dirk Nowitzki	4.00	10.0
DRJ David Robinson	6.00	15.00
DWJ DaJuan Wagner	2.00	5.0
GAJ Gilbert Arenas	2.50	6.0
GHJ Grant Hill	3.00	8.0
JKJ Jason Kidd	4.00	10.0
JOJ Jermaine O'Neal	2.50	6.0
JSJ John Stockton	3.00	8.0
KBJ Kobe Bryant SP	12.00	30.0
KGJ Kevin Garnett	5.00	12.0
KMJ Kenyon Martin	2.50	6.0
LJJ LeBron James	40.00	100.0
LSJ Latrell Sprewell	2.00	5.00
MAJ Shawn Marion	2.50	6.00
MJJ Michael Jordan SP	25.00	60.00
PPJ Paul Pierce	3.00	8.00
RAJ Ray Allen	2.50	6.00
SFJ Steve Francis	2.50	6.00
SMJ Stephon Marbury	2.00	5.00
SNJ Steve Nash	3.00	8.00
SPJ Scottie Pippen	6.00	15.00
TDJ Tim Duncan	4.00	10.00
TMJ Tracy McGrady	3.00	8.00
YMJ Yao Ming	5.00	12.0

2003-04 Sweet Shot Signature Shots

serted at the rate of one in 24, this 42-card set is rizontally desiged with a full-color player photo and autographed swatch of basketball embedded in the rd.

J Antawn Jamison 5.00 12.00
M Antonio McDyess 5.00 12.00
S Amare Stoudemire 10.00 25.00
Marcus Banks 5.00 12.00
Chauncey Billups 8.00 20.00
V Bill Walton 12.50 30.00
A Carmelo Anthony 40.00 100.00
B Caron Butler 5.00 12.00
K Chris Kaman 6.00 15.00
J DerMarr Johnson 5.00 12.00
M Darko Milicic 5.00 12.00
R David Robinson SP 30.00 60.00
W DaJuan Wagner 5.00 12.00
G Manu Ginobili 15.00 40.00
A Gilbert Arenas 6.00 15.00
Julius Erving SP 30.00 80.00
K Jason Kidd SP 12.50 30.00
R Jason Richardson 6.00 15.00
S Jerry Stackhouse 6.00 15.00
Kareem Abdul-Jabbar SP 40.00 80.00
B Kobe Bryant SP 100.00 200.00
B Larry Bird SP 50.00 120.00
LeBron James 250.00 500.00
R Luke Ridnour 6.00 15.00
A Magic Johnson SP 50.00 100.00
B Mike Bibby SP 8.00 20.00
I Andre Miller 5.00 12.00
J Michael Jordan SP 300.00 600.00
P Mickael Pietrus 5.00 12.00
P Paul Pierce 15.00 30.00
S Peja Stojakovic 6.00 15.00
G Reece Gaines 5.00 12.00
H Richard Hamilton 8.00 20.00
Richard Jefferson 6.00 15.00
O Jalen Rose SP 6.00 15.00
B Shane Battier 6.00 15.00
F Steve Francis 6.00 15.00
M Shawn Marion 6.00 15.00
M Tracy McGrady SP 20.00 50.00
O Travis Outlaw 6.00 15.00
P Tony Parker 8.00 20.00
M Yao Ming 20.00 50.00

2003-04 Sweet Shot Sweet Spot Signatures

serted at the rate of one in 168, this 41-card set is orizontally designed with an embedded autographed aseball sweet spot swatch.

JA Antawn Jamison/49 15.00 40.00
MA Antonio McDyess 15.00 40.00
SA Amare Stoudemire 30.00 80.00
AA Marcus Banks/49 15.00 40.00
IA Chauncey Billups 15.00 40.00
WA Bill Walton 25.00 60.00
AA Carmelo Anthony/49 125.00 225.00
BA Caron Butler 15.00 40.00
KA Chris Kaman/49 15.00 40.00
JA DerMarr Johnson 15.00 40.00
MA Darko Milicic/49 15.00 40.00
RA David Robinson/49 75.00 150.00
GA Manu Ginobili 30.00 80.00
AA Gilbert Arenas 15.00 40.00
EA Julius Erving 100.00 200.00
KA Jason Kidd/44 40.00 100.00
RA Jason Richardson 15.00 40.00
SA Jerry Stackhouse/49 15.00 40.00
AA Kareem Abdul-Jabbar/49 75.00 150.00
BA Kobe Bryant/50 175.00 350.00
BA Larry Bird/50 100.00 200.00
JA LeBron James/49 750.00 1200.00
RA Luke Ridnour/49 15.00 40.00
MAA Magic Johnson/49 75.00 200.00
MBA Mike Bibby/39 25.00 60.00
MIA Andre Miller 15.00 40.00
MJA Michael Jordan/23 500.00 1000.00
MPA Mickael Pietrus/49 15.00 40.00
PA Paul Pierce 25.00 60.00
PSA Peja Stojakovic 15.00 40.00
RGA Reece Gaines 15.00 40.00
RHA Richard Hamilton 15.00 40.00
RJA Richard Jefferson/49 15.00 40.00
ROA Jalen Rose/44 15.00 40.00
SBA Shane Battier 15.00 40.00
SFA Steve Francis/40 20.00 50.00
SMA Shawn Marion 15.00 40.00
TMA Tracy McGrady/49 40.00 100.00
TOA Travis Outlaw/49 15.00 40.00
PA Tony Parker 20.00 50.00
MA Yao Ming 60.00 120.00

2003-04 Sweet Shot Sweet Swatches

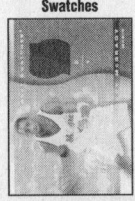

Inserted at the rate of one in 12, this 33-card set is horizontally designed with a player photo to the left and a swatch of game-worn jersey in the upper right hand corner.

AHSS Allan Houston 2.00 5.00
AISS Allen Iverson 4.00 10.00
ASSS Amare Stoudemire 4.00 10.00
BDSS Baron Davis 2.50 6.00
CWSS Chris Webber SP 5.00 12.00
DNSS Dirk Nowitzki 4.00 10.00
DSSS Damon Stoudamire SP 2.00 5.00
ECSS Eddy Curry 2.00 5.00
JKSS Jason Kidd 4.00 10.00
JOSS Jermaine O'Neal 2.50 6.00
JRSS Jalen Rose 2.00 5.00
JSSS Joe Smith 2.00 5.00
JTSS Jamaal Tinsley 2.00 5.00
JWSS Jay Williams 2.00 5.00
KBSS Kobe Bryant SP 15.00 40.00
KGSS Kevin Garnett 5.00 12.00
LOSS Lamar Odom 2.50 6.00
LSSS Latrell Sprewell 2.00 5.00
MCSS Marcus Camby 2.00 5.00
MJSS Michael Jordan SP 40.00 100.00
MMSS Mike Miller 2.50 6.00
PPSS Paul Pierce 3.00 8.00
RISS Jason Richardson 2.50 6.00
RMSS Reggie Miller 2.50 6.00
SBSS Shane Battier 2.00 5.00
SFSS Steve Francis 2.50 6.00
SHSS Shawn Marion 2.50 6.00
SMSS Stephon Marbury 2.00 5.00
TBSS Terrell Brandon 2.00 5.00
TCSS Tyson Chandler 2.00 5.00
TMSS Tracy McGrady 3.00 8.00
WSSS Wally Szczerbiak 2.00 5.00
YMSS Yao Ming SP 6.00 15.00

2003-04 Sweet Shot Three-Point Shots

Randomly inserted, this 41-card set has cards sequentially numbered to featured player's jersey number and places two swatches of game-worn memorabilia along with a cut signature in the center of the card.

MOST UNPRICED DUE TO SCARCITY
AJ3 Antawn Jamison/33 25.00 60.00
AM3 Antonio McDyess/34 25.00 60.00
AS3 Amare Stoudemire/32 100.00 200.00
CA3 Carmelo Anthony/15 150.00 300.00
DR3 David Robinson/50 50.00 120.00
EG3 Manu Ginobili/20 30.00 80.00
JA3 Marko Jaric/20 25.00 60.00
JS3 Jerry Stackhouse/42 40.00 80.00
KA3 K.Abdul-Jabbar/33 75.00 200.00
LB3 Larry Bird/33 75.00 200.00
LJ3 LeBron James/23 900.00 1500.00
MA3 Magic Johnson/32 150.00 300.00
MI3 Andre Milller/24 25.00 60.00
MJ3 Michael Jordan/23 600.00 1000.00
MP3 Morris Peterson/24 25.00 60.00
PP3 Paul Pierce/34 50.00 120.00
PS3 Peja Stojakovic/16 60.00 150.00
RH3 Richard Hamilton/32 25.00 60.00
RJ3 Richard Jefferson/24 25.00 60.00
SB3 Shane Battier/31 25.00 60.00
SM3 Shawn Marion/31 30.00 60.00

2004-05 Sweet Shot

Released in February 2005, Sweet Shot consists of a 136-card set where cards 1-90 feature veteran players, cards 91-130 feature rookies sequentially numbered to 1250 and cards 131-136 feature rookies sequentially numbered to 499. Sweet Shot was packaged in 12-pack boxes with four cards per pack and a pack SRP of $9.99.

COMP.SET w/o SP's (90) 15.00 40.00
1 Antoine Walker .30 .75
2 Al Harrington .25 .60
3 Boris Diaw .25 .60
4 Paul Pierce .40 1.00
5 Ricky Davis .25 .60
6 Gary Payton .30 .75
7 Gerald Wallace .30 .75
8 Jason Kapono .20 .50
9 Jahidi White .20 .50
10 Eddy Curry .25 .60
11 Kirk Hinrich .30 .75
12 Antonio Davis .20 .50
13 LeBron James 2.00 5.00
14 Dajuan Wagner .20 .50
15 Jeff McInnis .20 .50
16 Dirk Nowitzki .50 1.25
17 Michael Finley .30 .75
18 Jerry Stackhouse .25 .60
19 Kenyon Martin .30 .75
20 Andre Miller .25 .60
21 Carmelo Anthony .60 1.50
22 Chauncey Billups .30 .75
23 Rasheed Wallace .30 .75
24 Ben Wallace .30 .75
25 Derek Fisher .25 .60
26 Jason Richardson .30 .75
27 Mike Dunleavy .25 .60
28 Yao Ming .60 1.50
29 Tracy McGrady .40 1.00
30 Juwan Howard .25 .60
31 Jermaine O'Neal .30 .75
32 Reggie Miller .30 .75
33 Ron Artest .30 .75
34 Elton Brand .30 .75
35 Corey Maggette .25 .60
36 Marko Jaric .20 .50
37 Kobe Bryant 1.50 4.00
38 Karl Malone .40 1.00
39 Lamar Odom .30 .75
40 Pau Gasol .30 .75
41 Jason Williams .25 .60
42 Bonzi Wells .20 .50
43 Shaquille O'Neal .75 2.00
44 Dwyane Wade 1.00 2.50
45 Eddie Jones .25 .60
46 Michael Redd .30 .75
47 Desmond Mason .25 .60
48 T.J. Ford .25 .60
49 Latrell Sprewell .25 .60
50 Kevin Garnett .60 1.50
51 Sam Cassell .25 .60
52 Aaron Williams .20 .50
53 Richard Jefferson .30 .75
54 Jason Kidd .50 1.25
55 Jamal Mashburn .30 .75
56 Baron Davis .30 .75
57 Jamaal Magloire .20 .50
58 Allan Houston .25 .60
59 Jamal Crawford .25 .60
60 Stephon Marbury .25 .60
61 Keith Bogans .20 .50
62 Cuttino Mobley .25 .60
63 Steve Francis .30 .75
64 Glenn Robinson .25 .60
65 Allen Iverson .50 1.25
66 Kenny Thomas .20 .50
67 Amare Stoudemire .40 1.00
68 Steve Nash .40 1.00
69 Quentin Richardson .25 .60
70 Shareef Abdur-Rahim .25 .60
71 Damon Stoudamire .25 .60
72 Zach Randolph .25 .60
73 Peja Stojakovic .30 .75
74 Chris Webber .30 .75
75 Mike Bibby .30 .75
76 Tony Parker .30 .75
77 Tim Duncan .50 1.25
78 Manu Ginobili .40 1.00
79 Ronald Murray .20 .50
80 Ray Allen .30 .75
81 Rashard Lewis .30 .75
82 Chris Bosh .30 .75
83 Vince Carter .50 1.25
84 Jalen Rose .25 .60
85 Andrei Kirilenko .25 .60
86 Matt Harpring .25 .60
87 Carlos Boozer .30 .75
88 Gilbert Arenas .30 .75
89 Jarvis Hayes .20 .50
90 Antawn Jamison .30 .75
91 Anderson Varejao RC 2.50 6.00
92 Jackson Vroman RC 2.00 5.00
93 Peter John Ramos RC 2.00 5.00
94 Lionel Chalmers RC 2.00 5.00
95 Donta Smith RC 2.00 5.00
96 Andre Emmett RC 2.00 5.00
97 Antonio Burks RC 2.00 5.00
98 Royal Ivey RC 2.00 5.00
99 Chris Duhon RC 2.00 5.00
100 Albert Miralles RC 2.00 5.00
101 Justin Reed RC 2.00 5.00
102 David Young RC 2.00 5.00
103 Trevor Ariza RC 2.00 5.00
104 Luol Deng RC 3.00 8.00
105 Rafael Araujo RC 2.00 5.00
106 Andre Iguodala RC 3.00 8.00
107 Luke Jackson RC 2.00 5.00
108 Andris Biedrins RC 2.50 6.00
109 Robert Swift RC 2.00 5.00
110 Sebastian Telfair RC 2.00 5.00
111 Kris Humphries RC 2.00 5.00
112 Al Jefferson RC 3.00 8.00
113 Kirk Snyder RC 2.00 5.00
114 Josh Smith RC 3.00 8.00
115 J.R. Smith RC 2.50 6.00
116 Dorell Wright RC 3.00 8.00
117 Jameer Nelson RC 2.50 6.00
118 Pavel Podkolzine RC 2.00 5.00
119 Viktor Khryapa RC 2.00 5.00
120 Sergei Monia RC 2.00 5.00
121 Nenad Krstic RC 2.00 5.00
122 Tim Pickett RC 2.00 5.00
123 Bernard Robinson RC 2.00 5.00
124 Yuta Tabuse RC 4.00 10.00
125 Delonte West RC 2.50 6.00
126 Tony Allen RC 2.50 6.00
127 Kevin Martin RC 2.50 6.00
128 Sasha Vujacic RC 2.00 5.00
129 Beno Udrih RC 2.00 5.00
130 David Harrison RC 2.00 5.00
131 Dwight Howard RC 10.00 25.00
132 Emeka Okafor RC 5.00 12.00
133 Ben Gordon RC 4.00 10.00
134 Shaun Livingston RC 3.00 8.00
135 Devin Harris RC 5.00 12.00
136 Josh Childress RC 3.00 8.00

2004-05 Sweet Shot Jerseys

Inserted randomly in packs at the rate of one in 12, this 42-card set features borders along the top and bottom of the card, full color pictures and square swatch of jersey.

AI Allen Iverson 4.00 10.00
AJ Antawn Jamison SP 2.50 6.00
AK Andrei Kirilenko 2.00 5.00
AN Andre Iguodala 4.00 10.00
BG Ben Gordon 3.00 8.00
CA Carmelo Anthony 5.00 12.00
CB Chris Bosh 2.50 6.00
CW Chris Webber 2.50 6.00
DE Devin Harris 4.00 10.00
DH Dwight Howard 8.00 20.00
EB Elton Brand 2.50 6.00
EG Manu Ginobili SP 3.00 8.00
IT Isiah Thomas 2.50 6.00
JC Josh Childress 2.50 6.00
JK Jason Kidd 4.00 10.00
JN Jameer Nelson 3.00 8.00
JO Jermaine O'Neal 2.50 6.00
JR J.R. Smith 3.00 8.00
JS Josh Smith 4.00 10.00
KB Kobe Bryant 10.00 25.00
KG Kevin Garnett 5.00 12.00
KM Kenyon Martin 2.50 6.00
LB Larry Bird 15.00 40.00
LD Luol Deng 4.00 10.00
LJ LeBron James 12.50 30.00
LS Latrell Sprewell 2.00 5.00
LU Luke Jackson 2.50 6.00
MJ Michael Jordan SP 60.00 120.00
MR Michael Redd 2.50 6.00
PP Paul Pierce 3.00 8.00
PS Peja Stojakovic 2.50 6.00
RA Rafael Araujo 2.50 6.00
RH Richard Hamilton 2.00 5.00
RJ Richard Jefferson 2.50 6.00
SF Steve Francis 2.50 6.00
SL Shaun Livingston 2.50 6.00
SN Steve Nash 3.00 8.00
SN Dirk Nowitzki 4.00 10.00
SO Shaquille O'Neal 6.00 15.00
ST Sebastian Telfair 2.50 6.00
TD Tim Duncan 4.00 10.00
TM Tracy McGrady 3.00 8.00

2004-05 Sweet Shot Signature Shots

Inserted at one in 12, this 42-card set is horizontally designed with a player photo appearing along the top and an autographed swatch of basketball along the bottom.

*COLOR PARALLEL: 1X TO 2.5X BASE HI
*SP COLOR PARALLEL: .6X TO 1.5X BASE HI
WHITE/BLUE/RED STATED ODDS 1:960
UNPRICED STARS/STRIPES PRINT RUN 10 SETS
S & S NOT PRICED DUE TO SCARCITY
AI Andre Iguodala 6.00 15.00
AK Andrei Kirilenko 5.00 12.00
AS Amare Stoudemire 10.00 25.00
BG Ben Gordon 5.00 12.00
BK Bernard King 6.00 15.00
BM Brad Miller 4.00 10.00
CA Carmelo Anthony 15.00 40.00
CB Carlos Boozer 4.00 10.00
CD Clyde Drexler 12.50 30.00
CH Josh Childress 4.00 10.00
DE Devin Harris 6.00 15.00
DH Dwight Howard 25.00 60.00
DR Dennis Rodman 20.00 50.00
DW Dwyane Wade SP 40.00 100.00
HO Hakeem Olajuwon 15.00 40.00
JC Jamal Crawford SP 8.00 20.00
JE Julius Erving SP 40.00 100.00
JH Josh Howard 4.00 10.00
JK Jason Kidd 12.50 30.00
JN Jameer Nelson 5.00 12.00
JO John Stockton SP 50.00 120.00
JR J.R. Smith 5.00 12.00
JS Josh Smith 6.00 15.00
JW Jamaal Wilkes 5.00 12.00
KB Kobe Bryant SP 125.00 250.00
KG Kevin Garnett 40.00 70.00
LB Larry Bird SP 60.00 150.00
LD Luol Deng 6.00 15.00
LJ LeBron James 100.00 200.00
LU Luke Jackson 4.00 10.00
MA Magic Johnson SP 40.00 100.00
MD Marquis Daniels 4.00 10.00
MJ Michael Jordan SP 250.00 500.00
PR Pat Riley 12.00 30.00
RA Rafael Araujo 4.00 10.00
SE Sebastian Telfair 4.00 10.00
SL Shaun Livingston 4.00 10.00
SM Shawn Marion 4.00 10.00
ST Stephon Marbury 6.00 15.00
TM Tracy McGrady 10.00 25.00
WF Walt Frazier SP 12.00 30.00
YM Yao Ming SP 30.00 60.00

2004-05 Sweet Shot Swatches

Seeded randomly in packs at the rate of one in 12, this 42-card set is bordered on the top and the bottom and has an "S" shaped swatch of memorabilia.

AH Allan Houston 2.00 5.00
AI Allen Iverson 4.00 10.00
AK Andrei Kirilenko 2.00 5.00
AM Andre Miller 2.00 5.00
AS Amare Stoudemire 3.00 8.00
AW Antoine Walker 2.50 6.00
BD Baron Davis 2.50 6.00
CA Carmelo Anthony 5.00 12.00
CB Carlos Boozer 2.50 6.00
CM Corey Maggette 2.00 5.00
DN Dirk Nowitzki 4.00 10.00
DR David Robinson 4.00 10.00
EC Eddy Curry 2.00 5.00
EG Manu Ginobili 3.00 8.00
GA Gilbert Arenas 2.50 6.00
GP Gary Payton 2.50 6.00
JA Jalen Rose 2.00 5.00
JO Jermaine O'Neal 2.50 6.00
JR Jason Richardson 2.50 6.00
JT Jason Terry 2.00 5.00
KB Kobe Bryant 10.00 25.00
KG Kevin Garnett 5.00 12.00
KM Kenyon Martin 2.50 6.00
LJ LeBron James 15.00 40.00
LO Lamar Odom 2.50 6.00
MF Michael Finley 2.50 6.00
MJ Michael Jordan SP 60.00 120.00
NH Nene 2.00 5.00
PP Paul Pierce 3.00 8.00
PS Peja Stojakovic 2.50 6.00
QR Quentin Richardson 2.00 5.00
RJ Richard Jefferson 2.50 6.00
RM Reggie Miller 2.50 6.00
RW Rasheed Wallace 2.50 6.00
SC Sam Cassell 2.00 5.00
SH Shawn Marion 2.50 6.00
SM Stephon Marbury 2.00 5.00
SO Shaquille O'Neal 6.00 15.00
TD Tim Duncan 4.00 10.00
TM Tracy McGrady 3.00 8.00
TP Tony Parker 2.50 6.00
YM Yao Ming 5.00 12.00

2004-05 Sweet Shot Sweet Spot Signatures

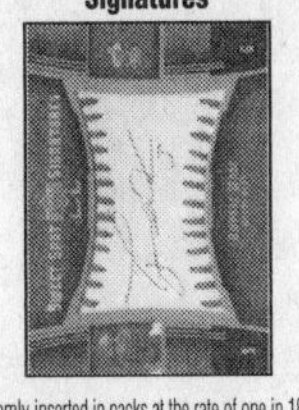

Randomly inserted in packs at the rate of one in 180, this 41-card set features an embedded and autographed sweet spot from a baseball.

AI Andre Iguodala 12.00 30.00
AK Andrei Kirilenko 15.00 40.00
AS Amare Stoudemire 20.00 50.00
BG Ben Gordon 12.00 30.00
BK Bernard King 25.00 60.00
BM Brad Miller 8.00 20.00
CA Carmelo Anthony 40.00 80.00
CB Carlos Boozer 8.00 20.00
CD Clyde Drexler 25.00 60.00
CH Josh Childress 8.00 20.00
CK Chris Kaman 8.00 20.00
DE Devin Harris 12.00 30.00
DH Dwight Howard 50.00 120.00
DR Dennis Rodman 50.00 120.00
DW Dwyane Wade 60.00 150.00
JC Jamal Crawford 8.00 20.00
JE Julius Erving 60.00 120.00
JH Josh Howard 8.00 20.00
JK Jason Kidd 30.00 80.00
JN Jameer Nelson 10.00 25.00
JO John Stockton 100.00 200.00
JR J.R. Smith 12.00 30.00
JS Josh Smith 12.00 30.00
JW Jamaal Wilkes 10.00 25.00
KB Kobe Bryant 125.00 250.00
KG Kevin Garnett 50.00 120.00
LB Larry Bird 125.00 250.00
LD Luol Deng 12.00 30.00
LJ LeBron James 125.00 300.00
LU Luke Jackson 8.00 20.00
MA Magic Johnson 60.00 150.00
MD Marquis Daniels 8.00 20.00
MJ Michael Jordan 350.00 600.00
PR Pat Riley 15.00 40.00
RA Rafael Araujo 8.00 20.00
SE Sebastian Telfair 8.00 20.00
SL Shaun Livingston 8.00 20.00
SM Shawn Marion 8.00 20.00
ST Stephon Marbury 15.00 40.00
TM Tracy McGrady 40.00 80.00
WF Walt Frazier 12.50 30.00

2004-05 Sweet Shot Three Point Shots

Randomly seeded in packs, this 41-card set features a horizontal design with two swatches of jersey and a cut signature. Each card is serially numbered to the player's jersey number.

SOME NOT PRICED DUE TO SCARCITY
AK Andrei Kirilenko/47 15.00 40.00
AS Amare Stoudemire/32 75.00 150.00
BM Brad Miller/52 15.00 40.00
CA Carmelo Anthony/15 100.00 200.00
CD Clyde Drexler/22 75.00 150.00
DE Devin Harris/34 25.00 60.00
DR Dennis Rodman/91 50.00 120.00
JA Jason Richardson/23 15.00 40.00
JR J.R. Smith/23 25.00 60.00
KG Kevin Garnett/21 75.00 150.00
LB Larry Bird/33 150.00 300.00
LJ LeBron James/23 250.00 450.00
LU Luke Jackson/33 15.00 40.00
MA Magic Johnson/32 100.00 200.00
MR Michael Redd/22 15.00 40.00
RA Rafael Araujo/55 15.00 40.00
RH Richard Hamilton/32 40.00 100.00
RJ Richard Jefferson/24 15.00 40.00
SM Shawn Marion/31 40.00 100.00

2005-06 Sweet Shot

Released in December 2005, Sweet Shot boasts a 150-card set where cards 1-100 feature veteran players on cards where the backgraound is oval and framing the player in colors to match team colors, cards 101-142 feature rookies on a basketball style background serially numbered to 1599 and cards 143-150 are serially numbered to 499. Sweet Shot was packaged in 12-pack boxes where each pack contained four cards and carried a $9.99 SRP.

COMP.SET w/o SP's (100) 15.00 40.00
1 Al Harrington .30 .75
2 Josh Smith .40 1.00
3 Josh Childress .30 .75
4 Tyronn Lue .25 .60
5 Paul Pierce .50 1.25
6 Antoine Walker .30 .75
7 Gary Payton .40 1.00
8 Al Jefferson .40 1.00
9 Emeka Okafor .40 1.00
10 Primoz Brezec .25 .60
11 Gerald Wallace .40 1.00
12 Michael Jordan 3.00 8.00
13 Ben Gordon .40 1.00
14 Luol Deng .40 1.00
15 Kirk Hinrich .40 1.00
16 LeBron James 2.00 5.00
17 Luke Jackson .25 .60
18 Drew Gooden .30 .75
19 Larry Hughes .30 .75
20 Dirk Nowitzki .60 1.50
21 Jason Terry .30 .75
22 Michael Finley .40 1.00
23 Jerry Stackhouse .30 .75
24 Andre Miller .30 .75
25 Carmelo Anthony .75 2.00
26 Kenyon Martin .40 1.00
27 Earl Boykins .25 .60
28 Rasheed Wallace .40 1.00
29 Ben Wallace .40 1.00
30 Richard Hamilton .30 .75
31 Chauncey Billups .40 1.00
32 Baron Davis .40 1.00
33 Derek Fisher .30 .75
34 Jason Richardson .40 1.00
35 Tracy McGrady .50 1.25
36 Yao Ming .50 1.25
37 Juwan Howard .30 .75
38 Jermaine O'Neal .40 1.00
39 Ron Artest .40 1.00
40 Jamaal Tinsley .25 .60
41 Corey Maggette .30 .75
42 Elton Brand .40 1.00
43 Shaun Livingston .25 .60
44 Kobe Bryant 2.00 5.00
45 Brian Cook .25 .60
46 Lamar Odom .40 1.00
47 Mike Miller .40 1.00
48 Pau Gasol .40 1.00
49 Shane Battier .30 .75
50 Shaquille O'Neal .75 2.00
51 Dwyane Wade 1.00 2.50
52 Udonis Haslem .30 .75
53 Joe Smith .30 .75
54 Michael Redd .40 1.00
55 Desmond Mason .25 .60
56 Kevin Garnett .75 2.00
57 Wally Szczerbiak .30 .75
58 Sam Cassell .40 1.00
59 Vince Carter .60 1.50
60 Jason Kidd .60 1.50
61 Richard Jefferson .40 1.00
62 Jamaal Magloire .25 .60
63 J.R. Smith .40 1.00
64 Speedy Claxton .25 .60
65 Allan Houston .25 .60
66 Stephon Marbury .30 .75
67 Jamal Crawford .30 .75
68 Dwight Howard .75 2.00
69 Grant Hill .50 1.25
70 Jameer Nelson .30 .75
71 Steve Francis .40 1.00
72 Allen Iverson .60 1.50
73 Andre Iguodala .40 1.00
74 Chris Webber .40 1.00
75 Kyle Korver .30 .75
76 Amare Stoudemire .40 1.00
77 Steve Nash .50 1.25
78 Quentin Richardson .30 .75
79 Shawn Marion .40 1.00
80 Damon Stoudamire .30 .75
81 Zach Randolph .30 .75
82 Sebastian Telfair .30 .75
83 Peja Stojakovic .40 1.00
84 Mike Bibby .40 1.00
85 Cuttino Mobley .30 .75
86 Manu Ginobili .40 1.00
87 Tim Duncan .60 1.50
88 Tony Parker .40 1.00
89 Ray Allen .40 1.00
90 Rashard Lewis .40 1.00
91 Luke Ridnour .30 .75
92 Ronald Murray .25 .60
93 Chris Bosh .40 1.00
94 Morris Peterson .25 .60
95 Jalen Rose .40 1.00
96 Andrei Kirilenko .30 .75
97 Raul Lopez .25 .60
98 Carlos Boozer .40 1.00
99 Antawn Jamison .40 1.00
100 Gilbert Arenas .40 1.00
101 Ike Diogu RC 2.00 5.00
102 Julius Hodge RC 2.00 5.00
103 David Lee RC 3.00 8.00
104 Linas Kleiza RC 2.00 5.00
105 Jason Maxiell RC 2.00 5.00
106 Luther Head RC 2.00 5.00
107 Jose Calderon RC 2.00 5.00
108 Brandon Bass RC 2.50 6.00
109 Ricky Sanchez RC 2.00 5.00
110 Andray Blatche RC 2.50 6.00
111 Sean May RC 2.00 5.00
112 Travis Diener RC 2.00 5.00
113 Nate Robinson RC 2.50 6.00
114 Von Wafer RC 2.00 5.00
115 James Singleton RC 2.00 5.00
116 Daniel Ewing RC 2.00 5.00
117 Salim Stoudamire RC 2.00 5.00
118 Dijon Thompson RC 2.00 5.00
119 Danny Granger RC 4.00 10.00
120 Will Bynum RC 2.00 5.00
121 Louis Williams RC 3.00 8.00
122 Channing Frye RC 2.50 6.00
123 Francisco Garcia RC 2.50 6.00
124 Ryan Gomes RC 2.00 5.00
125 Ronnie Price RC 2.00 5.00
126 Jarrett Jack RC 2.00 5.00
127 Alan Anderson RC 2.00 5.00
128 Ersan Ilyasova RC 2.50 6.00
129 C.J. Miles RC 2.50 6.00
130 Arvydas Macijauskas RC 2.00 5.00
131 Bracey Wright RC 2.00 5.00
132 Monta Ellis RC 4.00 10.00
133 Chris Taft RC 2.00 5.00
134 Johan Petro RC 2.00 5.00
135 Yaroslav Korolev RC 2.00 5.00
136 Andrew Bynum RC 6.00 15.00
137 Martynas Andriuskevicius RC 2.00 5.00
138 Charlie Villanueva RC 2.50 6.00
139 Antoine Wright RC 2.00 5.00
140 Joey Graham RC 2.00 5.00
141 Wayne Simien RC 2.00 5.00
142 Hakim Warrick RC 2.50 6.00
143 Gerald Green RC 4.00 10.00
144 Marvin Williams RC 4.00 10.00
145 Deron Williams RC 8.00 20.00
146 Rashad McCants RC 3.00 8.00
147 Raymond Felton RC 5.00 12.00
148 Martell Webster RC 3.00 8.00
149 Chris Paul RC 12.00 30.00
150 Andrew Bogut RC 5.00 12.00

2005-06 Sweet Shot Gold

Inserted in packs, this 150-card set parallels the base set with gold foil highlights where cards 1-100 are serially numbered to 199 and cards 101-150 are serially numbered to 100.

*GOLD STARS: 1X TO 2.5X BASE HI
*GOLD RC's 101-142: .75X TO 2X BASE HI
*GOLD RC's 143-150: .5X TO 1.25X BASE HI
12 Michael Jordan 10.00 25.00

2005-06 Sweet Shot Spectrum

Inserted in packs, this 150-card set parallels the base set with holofoil highlights where cards 1-100 are serially numbered to 75 and cards 101-150 are serially numbered to 50.

*SPEC STARS: 2X TO 5X BASE HI
*SPEC RCs 101-142: 1X TO 2.5X BASE HI
*SPEC RCs 143-150: .6X TO 1.5X BASE HI
12 Michael Jordan 20.00 50.00

2005-06 Sweet Shot Jerseys

Randomly inserted in packs, this 100-card set is horizontally designed with a full color player photo on the left and an "S" shaped swatch of memorabilia on the right. Cards are serially numbered to either 125 or 250.

*GOLD: .6X TO 1.5X BASE HI
GOLD PRINT RUN 50 TO 99 SER.#'d SETS
AB Andrew Bogut/125 5.00 12.00
AK Andrei Kirilenko/125 2.50 6.00
AN Andris Biedrins/125 2.50 6.00
AR Rafael Araujo/250 2.00 5.00
AS Amare Stoudemire/125 3.00 8.00
AT Antoine Wright/250 3.00 8.00
AW Antoine Walker/250 2.50 6.00
BB Bruce Bowen/125 2.00 5.00
BD Baron Davis/125 3.00 8.00
BG Ben Gordon/125 3.00 8.00
CA Carmelo Anthony/125 6.00 15.00
CB Caron Butler/250 3.00 8.00
CM Corey Maggette/125 2.50 6.00
CP Chris Paul/125 8.00 20.00
CV Charlie Villanueva/125 4.00 10.00
CW Chris Webber/250 3.00 8.00
DA Dajuan Wagner/250 2.00 5.00
DE Devin Harris/100 3.00 8.00
DF Derek Fisher/125 2.50 6.00
DG Devean George/125 2.00 5.00
DH Dwight Howard/125 6.00 15.00
DI Dikembe Mutombo/125 3.00 8.00
DM Darius Miles/250 2.00 5.00
DN Dirk Nowitzki/125 5.00 12.00
DO Dorell Wright/125 2.00 5.00
DR Dennis Rodman/125 5.00 12.00
DS DeShawn Stevenson/125 2.00 5.00
DW Deron Williams/125 6.00 15.00
EB Elton Brand/125 3.00 8.00
EC Eddy Curry/250 2.50 6.00
GA Gilbert Arenas/125 3.00 8.00
GG Gerald Green/250 4.00 10.00
GH Grant Hill/125 4.00 10.00
GR Danny Granger/250 5.00 12.00
HW Hakim Warrick/125 4.00 10.00
JA Jamal Crawford/125 2.50 6.00
JC Jason Collins/125 2.00 5.00
JH Josh Howard/50 3.00 8.00
JJ Jarrett Jack/250 3.00 8.00
JK Jason Kidd/125 5.00 12.00
JO Jermaine O'Neal/250 3.00 8.00
JR Jalen Rose/250 3.00 8.00
JS J.R. Smith/125 3.00 8.00
JT Jason Terry/250 2.50 6.00
JU Julius Hodge/125 3.00 8.00
KB Kobe Bryant/125 8.00 20.00
KD Keyon Dooling/250 2.00 5.00
KG Kevin Garnett/125 6.00 15.00
KM Kenyon Martin/250 3.00 8.00
KR Kareem Rush/250 2.00 5.00
KT Kurt Thomas/125 2.00 5.00
KW Kwame Brown/250 2.00 5.00
LB Larry Bird/125 10.00 25.00
LD Luol Deng/125 3.00 8.00
LH Larry Hughes/125 2.50 6.00
LJ LeBron James/125 10.00 25.00
LU Luke Jackson/125 2.00 5.00
LW Luke Walton/125 2.00 5.00
MA Magic Johnson/125 8.00 20.00
MD Mike Dunleavy/250 2.50 6.00
MG Manu Ginobili/250 3.00 8.00
MI Michael Finley/250 3.00 8.00
MJ Michael Jordan/125 40.00 80.00
MK Marko Jaric/125 2.00 5.00
MS Mike Sweetney/125 2.00 5.00
MW Marvin Williams/125 4.00 10.00
NH Nene/125 2.50 6.00
NR Nate Robinson/125 4.00 10.00
PG Pau Gasol/125 3.00 8.00
PP Paul Pierce/125 4.00 10.00
PS Peja Stojakovic/125 3.00 8.00
QR Quentin Richardson/125 2.50 6.00
RA Ray Allen/125 3.00 8.00
RD Ricky Davis/250 2.50 6.00
RF Raymond Felton/125 5.00 12.00
RI Jason Richardson/125 3.00 8.00
RJ Richard Jefferson/125 3.00 8.00
RL Rashard Lewis/125 3.00 8.00
RM Rashad McCants/125 3.00 8.00
RS Robert Swift/125 2.00 5.00
RW Rasheed Wallace/250 3.00 8.00
SC Sam Cassell/250 3.00 8.00
SD Samuel Dalembert/250 2.00 5.00
SF Steve Francis/250 3.00 8.00

SH Shawn Marion/125 3.00 8.00
SJ Sarunas Jasikevicius/125 3.00 8.00
SM Sean May/125 3.00 8.00
SN Steve Nash/125 4.00 10.00
SO Shaquille O'Neal/125 6.00 15.00
ST Stephon Marbury/125 2.50 6.00
TC Tyson Chandler/250 2.50 6.00
TD Tim Duncan/125 5.00 12.00
TM Tracy McGrady/250 4.00 10.00
WA Charlie Ward/250 2.00 5.00
WE Martell Webster/125 3.00 8.00
WI Chris Wilcox/125 2.00 5.00
WS Wayne Simien/250 3.00 8.00
YM Yao Ming/125 4.00 10.00
ZI Zydrunas Ilgauskas/125 2.50 6.00
ZR Zach Randolph/250 2.50 6.00

2005-06 Sweet Shot Signature Shots

Inserted in packs at the rate of one in 12, this 63-card set is horizontally designed with a player photo on the left and a cut signature embedded in the card on a basketball textured swatch.

AB Andrew Bogut 8.00 20.00
AI Andre Iguodala 5.00 12.00
AK Andrei Kirilenko 5.00 12.00
BG Ben Gordon 6.00 15.00
BK Bob Knight SP 25.00 60.00
BM Brad Miller 5.00 12.00
CD Clyde Drexler 12.50 30.00
CF Channing Frye 6.00 15.00
CP Chris Paul 30.00 80.00
CV Charlie Villanueva 6.00 15.00
DE Devin Harris 5.00 12.00
DH Dwight Howard 15.00 40.00
DW Deron Williams 15.00 40.00
HW Hakim Warrick 6.00 15.00
ID Ike Diogu 5.00 12.00
JA Jamaal Wilkes 6.00 15.00
JG Joey Graham 5.00 12.00
JN Jameer Nelson 5.00 12.00
JR J.R. Smith 5.00 12.00
JW John Wooden SP 60.00 150.00
KA Kareem Abdul-Jabbar SP 50.00 100.00
LA Larry Brown 10.00 25.00
LB Larry Bird SP 50.00 120.00
LD Luol Deng 5.00 12.00
LJ LeBron James 125.00 250.00
MA Magic Johnson SP 50.00 120.00
MJ Michael Jordan SP 300.00 550.00
MW Marvin Williams 6.00 15.00
RM Rashad McCants 5.00 12.00
SH Shawn Marion 5.00 12.00
SL Shaun Livingston 5.00 12.00
SM Sean May 5.00 12.00
SN Steve Nash SP 30.00 80.00
ST Sebastian Telfair 5.00 12.00
WE Martell Webster 5.00 12.00

2005-06 Sweet Shot Signature Shots Acetate

Randomly seeded and limited to 75 or 25 serially numbered copies, this horizontally designed set places full color pictures on the top of the card and an acetate cut signature in the middle.

AB Andrew Bogut/75 15.00 40.00
AN Andrew Bynum/75 30.00 80.00
CA Carmelo Anthony/25 25.00 60.00
CF Channing Frye/75 12.00 30.00
CP Chris Paul/75 75.00 150.00
DH Dwight Howard/75 20.00 50.00
DR Dennis Rodman/75 60.00 150.00
DW Deron Williams/75 25.00 60.00
GE Gerald Green/75 12.00 30.00
HW Hakim Warrick/75 12.00 30.00
ID Ike Diogu/75 10.00 25.00
IT Isiah Thomas/75 15.00 40.00
JG Joey Graham/75 10.00 25.00
JK Jason Kidd/75 15.00 40.00
JW John Wooden/75 60.00 150.00
LB Larry Bird/25 75.00 150.00
LJ LeBron James/25 200.00 400.00
MJ Michael Jordan/25 250.00 500.00
MW Marvin Williams/75 12.00 30.00
RF Raymond Felton/75 15.00 40.00
RJ Richard Jefferson/75 10.00 25.00
RM Rashad McCants/75 10.00 25.00
SM Sean May/75 10.00 25.00
SN Steve Nash/75 40.00 100.00
SP Scottie Pippen/75 100.00 200.00
TM Tracy McGrady/75 25.00 50.00
WE Martell Webster/75 10.00 25.00
YM Yao Ming/75 25.00 60.00

2005-06 Sweet Shot Signature Shots Wood

Limited to either 35 or 15 serially numbered copies, this set parallels the design of the acetate set but employs an autographed wood swatch.
SOME UNPRICED DUE TO SCARCITY

AB Andrew Bogut/35 20.00 50.00
AN Andrew Bynum/35 40.00 100.00
CF Channing Frye/35 15.00 40.00
CP Chris Paul/35 75.00 200.00
DH Dwight Howard/35 25.00 60.00
DR Dennis Rodman/35 60.00 150.00
DW Deron Williams/35 30.00 80.00
GE Gerald Green/35 15.00 40.00
HW Hakim Warrick/35 15.00 40.00
ID Ike Diogu/35 12.00 30.00
IT Isiah Thomas/35 20.00 50.00
JG Joey Graham/35 12.00 30.00
JK Jason Kidd/35 20.00 50.00
JW John Wooden/35 60.00 150.00
MW Marvin Williams/35 15.00 40.00
RF Raymond Felton/35 20.00 50.00
RJ Richard Jefferson/35 12.50 30.00
RM Rashad McCants/35 12.00 30.00
SM Sean May/35 12.00 30.00
SN Steve Nash/35 60.00 150.00
SP Scottie Pippen/35 100.00 250.00
TM Tracy McGrady/35 30.00 60.00
WE Martell Webster/35 12.00 30.00
YM Yao Ming/35 30.00 80.00

2005-06 Sweet Shot Sweet Swatches

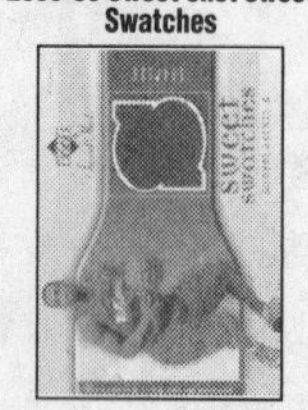

Randomly seeded in packs, this 99-card set is horizontally designed with player photos on the left and an "S" shaped swatch of memorabilia on the right. Cards are serially numbered to either 250 to 125.
*GOLD: .6X TO 1.5X BASE HI
GOLD PRINT RUN 50 TO 99 SETS

AB Andrew Bogut/125 5.00 12.00
AK Andrei Kirilenko/125 2.50 6.00
AN Andris Biedrins/125 2.50 6.00
AR Rafael Araujo/125 2.00 5.00
AS Amare Stoudemire/125 3.00 8.00
AT Antoine Wright/250 3.00 8.00
AW Antoine Walker/250 2.50 6.00
BB Bruce Bowen/125 2.00 5.00
BD Baron Davis/250 3.00 8.00
BG Ben Gordon/125 3.00 8.00
CA Carmelo Anthony/125 6.00 15.00
CB Caron Butler/250 3.00 8.00
CM Corey Maggette/125 2.50 6.00
CP Chris Paul/125 8.00 20.00
CV Charlie Villanueva/125 4.00 10.00
CW Chris Webber/250 3.00 8.00
DA Dajuan Wagner/250 2.00 5.00
DE Devin Harris/125 3.00 8.00
DF Derek Fisher/250 2.50 6.00
DG Devean George/125 2.00 5.00
DH Dwight Howard/125 6.00 15.00
DI Dikembe Mutombo/250 3.00 8.00
DM Darius Miles/250 2.00 5.00
DN Dirk Nowitzki/125 5.00 12.00
DO Dorell Wright/125 2.00 5.00
DS DeShawn Stevenson/250 2.00 5.00
DW Deron Williams/125 6.00 15.00
EB Elton Brand/125 3.00 8.00
EC Eddy Curry/250 2.50 6.00
GA Gilbert Arenas/125 3.00 8.00
GG Gerald Green/125 4.00 10.00
GH Grant Hill/125 4.00 10.00
GR Danny Granger/250 5.00 12.00
HW Hakim Warrick/125 4.00 10.00
JA Jamal Crawford/125 2.50 6.00
JC Jason Collins/125 2.00 5.00
JH Josh Howard/125 3.00 8.00
JK Jason Kidd/125 5.00 12.00
JL Jalen Rose/250 3.00 8.00
JO Jermaine O'Neal/125 3.00 8.00
JR J.R. Smith/125 3.00 8.00
JT Jason Terry/250 2.50 6.00
JU Julius Hodge/125 3.00 8.00
KB Kobe Bryant/125 8.00 20.00
KD Keyon Dooling/250 2.00 5.00
KG Kevin Garnett/125 6.00 15.00
KK Kyle Korver/125 2.50 6.00
KM Kenyon Martin/250 3.00 8.00
KR Kareem Rush/250 2.00 5.00
KT Kurt Thomas/250 2.00 5.00
KW Kwame Brown/250 2.00 5.00
LD Luol Deng/125 3.00 8.00
LH Larry Hughes/125 2.50 6.00
LJ LeBron James/125 12.50 30.00
LR Luke Ridnour/250 2.50 6.00
LU Luke Jackson/125 2.00 5.00
LW Luke Walton/125 2.00 5.00
MB Mike Bibby/125 3.00 8.00
MD Mike Dunleavy/125 2.50 6.00
MG Manu Ginobili/125 3.00 8.00
MI Michael Finley/250 3.00 8.00
MJ Michael Jordan/125 40.00 80.00
MK Marko Jaric/250 2.00 5.00
MS Mike Sweetney/125 2.00 5.00
MW Marvin Williams/125 4.00 10.00
NH Nene/125 2.50 6.00
NR Nate Robinson/125 4.00 10.00
PG Pau Gasol/250 3.00 8.00
PP Paul Pierce/125 4.00 10.00
PS Peja Stojakovic/125 3.00 8.00
QR Quentin Richardson/250 2.50 6.00
RA Ray Allen/125 3.00 8.00
RD Ricky Davis/250 2.50 6.00
RF Raymond Felton/250 5.00 12.00
RI Jason Richardson/125 3.00 8.00
RL Rashard Lewis/125 3.00 8.00
RM Rashad McCants/125 3.00 8.00
RN Ron Artest/125 3.00 8.00
RS Robert Swift/250 2.00 5.00
RW Rasheed Wallace/250 3.00 8.00
SC Sam Cassell/250 3.00 8.00
SD Samuel Dalembert/250 2.00 5.00
SH Shawn Marion/125 3.00 8.00
SJ Sarunas Jasikevicius/250 3.00 8.00
SM Sean May/125 3.00 8.00
SN Steve Nash/125 4.00 10.00
SO Shaquille O'Neal/125 6.00 15.00
ST Stephon Marbury/125 2.50 6.00
TC Tyson Chandler/250 2.50 6.00
TD Tim Duncan/125 5.00 12.00
TM Tracy McGrady/250 4.00 10.00
TP Tony Parker/125 3.00 8.00
WA Charlie Ward/250 2.00 5.00
WE Martell Webster/125 3.00 8.00
WI Chris Wilcox/250 2.00 5.00
WS Wayne Simien/125 3.00 8.00
YM Yao Ming/125 4.00 10.00
ZI Zydrunas Ilgauskas/125 2.50 6.00
ZR Zach Randolph/125 2.50 6.00

2005-06 Sweet Shot Three Point Shots

Seeded in packs randomly, this 32-card set is horizontally designed with a full color player photo in the center, two swatches of memorabilia on the sides and an authentic player autograph centered at the bottom of the card on vellum. Print runs provided by Upper Deck.
SOME UNPRICED DUE TO SCARCITY

CM Corey Maggette/50 10.00 25.00
DR Dennis Rodman/91 50.00 120.00
LB Larry Bird/33 75.00 150.00
LJ LeBron James/23 300.00 600.00
MJ Michael Jordan/23 400.00 700.00
PG Pau Gasol/16 20.00 50.00
PS Peja Stojakovic/16 20.00 50.00
RF Raymond Felton/20 25.00 60.00
RH Richard Hamilton/32 15.00 40.00
RJ Richard Jefferson/24 10.00 25.00
SM Sean May/42 10.00 25.00
SP Scottie Pippen/33 200.00 350.00

2006-07 Sweet Shot

Released in mid December 2006, the 137-card Sweet Shot set pictures veterans on cards 1-90, autograph rookies sequentially numbered to 799 on cards 91-115, autograph rookies sequentially numbered to 250 on cards 121-132 and rookies sequentially numbered to 99 on cards 133-137. All rookie autographs are signed on a swatch shaped like the surface of a basketball. Sweet Shot is packaged in 12-pack boxes of four cards each and carried an initial suggested retail price of $9.99 per pack.

COMP.SET w/o SP's (90) 15.00 40.00
1 Josh Childress .30 .75
2 Joe Johnson .40 1.00
3 Marvin Williams .40 1.00
4 Al Jefferson .40 1.00
5 Paul Pierce .50 1.25
6 Wally Szczerbiak .30 .75
7 Raymond Felton .50 1.25
8 Emeka Okafor .40 1.00
9 Gerald Wallace .40 1.00
10 Ben Gordon .40 1.00
11 Kirk Hinrich .40 1.00
12 Michael Jordan 3.00 8.00
13 Larry Hughes .30 .75
14 Zydrunas Ilgauskas .30 .75
15 LeBron James 2.00 5.00
16 Marquis Daniels .25 .60
17 Dirk Nowitzki .60 1.50
18 Jason Terry .30 .75
19 Carmelo Anthony .50 1.25
20 Marcus Camby .30 .75
21 Kenyon Martin .40 1.00
22 Chauncey Billups .40 1.00
23 Richard Hamilton .30 .75
24 Ben Wallace .40 1.00
25 Baron Davis .40 1.00
26 Mike Dunleavy .30 .75
27 Jason Richardson .40 1.00
28 Rafer Alston .25 .60
29 Tracy McGrady .50 1.25
30 Yao Ming .50 1.25
31 Austin Croshere .25 .60
32 Jermaine O'Neal .40 1.00
33 Peja Stojakovic .40 1.00
34 Elton Brand .40 1.00
35 Sam Cassell .40 1.00
36 Shaun Livingston .25 .60
37 Kwame Brown .25 .60
38 Kobe Bryant 2.00 5.00
39 Lamar Odom .40 1.00
40 Pau Gasol .40 1.00
41 Bobby Jackson .25 .60
42 Hakim Warrick .30 .75
43 Shaquille O'Neal .75 2.00
44 Dwyane Wade 1.00 2.50
45 Jason Williams .30 .75
46 Andrew Bogut .40 1.00
47 T.J. Ford .30 .75
48 Jamaal Magloire .25 .60
49 Ricky Davis .30 .75
50 Kevin Garnett .75 2.00
51 Rashad McCants .25 .60
52 Vince Carter .50 1.25
53 Richard Jefferson .40 1.00
54 Jason Kidd .60 1.50
55 Desmond Mason .25 .60
56 Chris Paul .75 2.00
57 J.R. Smith .40 1.00
58 Channing Frye .30 .75
59 Stephon Marbury .30 .75
60 Quentin Richardson .30 .75
61 Carlos Arroyo .30 .75
62 Dwight Howard .60 1.50
63 Darko Milicic .25 .60
64 Andre Iguodala .40 1.00
65 Allen Iverson .50 1.25
66 Chris Webber .40 1.00
67 Boris Diaw .30 .75
68 Shawn Marion .40 1.00
69 Steve Nash .50 1.25
70 Juan Dixon .25 .60
71 Zach Randolph .30 .75
72 Sebastian Telfair .25 .60
73 Ron Artest .40 1.00
74 Mike Bibby .40 1.00
75 Brad Miller .40 1.00
76 Tim Duncan .60 1.50
77 Manu Ginobili .40 1.00
78 Tony Parker .40 1.00
79 Ray Allen .40 1.00
80 Rashard Lewis .40 1.00
81 Luke Ridnour .30 .75
82 Chris Bosh .40 1.00
83 Joey Graham .25 .60
84 Charlie Villanueva .40 1.00
85 Carlos Boozer .40 1.00
86 Andrei Kirilenko .30 .75
87 Deron Williams .60 1.50
88 Gilbert Arenas .40 1.00
89 Caron Butler .40 1.00
90 Antawn Jamison .40 1.00
91 David Noel AU RC 5.00 12.00
92 James Augustine AU RC 5.00 12.00
93 Kyle Lowry AU RC 6.00 15.00
94 Bobby Jones AU RC 5.00 12.00
95 Solomon Jones AU RC 5.00 12.00
96 Craig Smith AU RC 5.00 12.00
97 Josh Boone AU RC 5.00 12.00
98 Jordan Farmar AU RC 5.00 12.00
99 Marcus Williams AU RC 5.00 12.00
100 Hassan Adams AU RC 5.00 12.00
101 Dee Brown AU RC 5.00 12.00
102 Denham Brown AU RC 5.00 12.00
103 Steve Novak AU RC 5.00 12.00
104 James White AU RC 5.00 12.00
105 Daniel Gibson AU RC 6.00 15.00
106 Renaldo Balkman AU RC 5.00 12.00
107 P.J. Tucker AU RC 5.00 12.00
108 Saer Sene AU RC 5.00 12.00
109 Thabo Sefolosha AU RC 6.00 15.00
110 Maurice Ager AU RC 5.00 12.00
111 Rajon Rondo AU RC 20.00 50.00
112 Shawne Williams AU RC 5.00 12.00
113 Mardy Collins AU RC 5.00 12.00
114 Paul Davis AU RC 5.00 12.00
115 Quincy Douby AU RC 5.00 12.00
121 Rodney Carney AU RC 6.00 15.00
122 Randy Foye AU RC 8.00 20.00
123 Ronnie Brewer AU RC 8.00 20.00
124 Cedric Simmons AU RC 6.00 15.00
125 Andrea Bargnani AU RC 10.00 25.00
126 LaMarcus Aldridge AU RC 15.00 40.00
127 Tyrus Thomas AU RC 8.00 20.00
128 Rudy Gay AU RC 10.00 25.00
129 Shelden Williams AU RC 6.00 15.00
130 Patrick O'Bryant AU RC 6.00 15.00
131 Hilton Armstrong AU RC 6.00 15.00
132 Brandon Roy AU RC 15.00 40.00
133 Adam Morrison RC 6.00 15.00
134 J.J. Redick RC 6.00 15.00
135 Alexander Johnson RC 5.00 12.00
136 Damir Markota RC 5.00 12.00
137 Leon Powe RC 5.00 12.00
138 Ryan Hollins RC 5.00 12.00
139 Tarence Kinsey RC 5.00 12.00
140 Jorge Garbajosa RC 5.00 12.00

2006-07 Sweet Shot Gold

*1-90 GOLD: 1.25X TO 3X BASE HI
1-90 GOLD PRINT RUN 199 SER.#'d SETS
*91-115 AU RC GOLD: 1.5X TO 4X BASE HI
*116-132 AU RC GOLD: 1.25X TO 3X BASE HI
*133-140 ROOKIE GOLD: 1X TO 2.5X BASE HI
91-140 GOLD PRINT RUN 25 SER.#'d SETS

2006-07 Sweet Shot Signature Shots Acetate

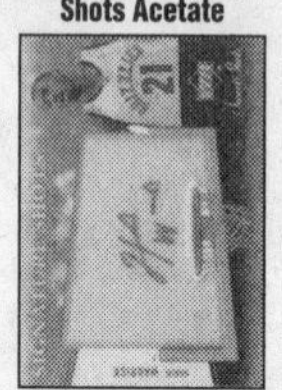

PRINT RUN 25 SER.#'d SETS

BB Brent Barry 25.00 60.00
BD Baron Davis 10.00 25.00
CF Channing Frye 10.00 25.00
DG Danny Granger 10.00 25.00
EI Ersan Ilyasova 10.00 25.00
HW Hakim Warrick 12.50 30.00
JC Josh Childress 10.00 25.00
JJ Joe Johnson 10.00 25.00
JS J.R. Smith 10.00 25.00
KK Kyle Korver 10.00 25.00
KV Kiki Vandeweghe 10.00 25.00
LJ LeBron James 200.00 350.00
LW Louis Williams 10.00 25.00
MJ Michael Jordan 300.00 600.00
MW Marvin Williams 10.00 25.00
PP Paul Pierce 15.00 40.00
PS Peja Stojakovic 25.00 60.00
RF Raymond Felton 12.50 30.00
RM Rashad McCants 10.00 25.00
RT Ronny Turiaf 10.00 25.00
ST John Starks 20.00 50.00
TC Tyson Chandler 10.00 25.00
TP Tayshaun Prince 15.00 40.00
VC Vince Carter 40.00 80.00
WF Walt Frazier 12.50 30.00

2006-07 Sweet Shot Signature Shots Leather

APPROXIMATELY ONE PER BOX

AI Andre Iguodala 5.00 12.00
AU James Augustine 5.00 12.00
BB Brent Barry 6.00 15.00
BC Carlos Boozer 5.00 12.00
BJ Bobby Jones 5.00 12.00
BR Bill Russell SP 100.00 200.00
CA Carmelo Anthony 15.00 40.00
CB Chris Bosh SP 12.50 30.00
CD Chris Duhon 5.00 12.00
CF Channing Frye 5.00 12.00
CK Chris Kaman 5.00 12.00
CM Cuttino Mobley 5.00 12.00
CP Chris Paul SP 30.00 80.00
CT Chris Taft 5.00 12.00
DC Clyde Drexler 12.50 30.00
DG Danny Granger 5.00 12.00
DH Dwight Howard 12.50 30.00
DN David Noel 5.00 12.00
DR David Robinson SP 20.00 50.00
EC Eddy Curry 5.00 12.00
EI Ersan Ilyasova 5.00 12.00
FR Randy Foye 8.00 20.00
GW Gerald Wallace 5.00 12.00
HO Hakeem Olajuwon 15.00 40.00
HW Hakim Warrick 5.00 12.00
ID Ike Diogu 5.00 12.00
JA Al Jefferson 5.00 12.00
JB Josh Boone 5.00 12.00
JC Josh Childress 5.00 12.00
JE Julius Erving SP 25.00 60.00
JF Jordan Farmar 5.00 12.00
JJ Joe Johnson 6.00 15.00
JR Jalen Rose 5.00 12.00
JS J.R. Smith 5.00 12.00
KB Kwame Brown 5.00 12.00
KD Keyon Dooling 5.00 12.00
KK Kyle Korver 5.00 12.00
KL Kyle Lowry 6.00 15.00
KV Kiki Vandeweghe 6.00 15.00
LH Larry Hughes 5.00 12.00
LJ LeBron James SP 100.00 200.00
LR Luke Ridnour 5.00 12.00
LW Louis Williams 5.00 12.00
MC Corey Maggette 5.00 12.00
ME Monta Ellis 5.00 12.00
MW Marvin Williams 5.00 12.00
NR Nate Robinson 6.00 15.00
PS Peja Stojakovic SP 8.00 20.00
QR Quentin Richardson 5.00 12.00
RA Ron Artest SP 10.00 25.00
RB Ronnie Brewer 8.00 20.00
RC Rodney Carney 5.00 12.00
RF Raymond Felton 5.00 12.00
RJ Richard Jefferson 5.00 12.00
RM Rashad McCants 5.00 12.00
RT Ronny Turiaf 12.50 30.00
SC Craig Smith 5.00 12.00
SE Sean Elliott 8.00 20.00
SK Steve Kerr 8.00 20.00
SL Shaun Livingston 5.00 12.00
SO Solomon Jones 5.00 12.00
ST John Starks 20.00 50.00
SV Sasha Vujacic 5.00 12.00
TC Tyson Chandler 5.00 12.00
TM Tracy McGrady 10.00 25.00
TP Tayshaun Prince 6.00 15.00
TS Sebastian Telfair 5.00 12.00
VC Vince Carter SP 25.00 50.00
VW Von Wafer 5.00 12.00
WF Walt Frazier 6.00 15.00
WM Martell Webster 5.00 12.00
YK Yaroslav Korolev 5.00 12.00
YM Yao Ming 12.50 30.00

2006-07 Sweet Shot Stitches

APPROXIMATE ODDS ONE PER BOX
*GOLD: .6X TO 1.5X BASE HI
GOLD PRINT RUN 50 SER.#'d SETS

AK Andrei Kirilenko 2.00 5.00
AM Andre Miller 2.00 5.00
AS Amare Stoudemire 2.50 6.00
BD Baron Davis 2.50 6.00
CA Carmelo Anthony 3.00 8.00
CM Corey Maggette 2.00 5.00
DG Drew Gooden 2.00 5.00
DN Dirk Nowitzki 4.00 10.00
GA Gilbert Arenas 2.50 6.00
GH Grant Hill 3.00 8.00
JH Josh Howard 2.00 5.00
JK Jason Kidd 4.00 10.00
JM Jamaal Magloire 2.00 5.00
JO Jermaine O'Neal 2.50 6.00
JT Jamaal Tinsley 2.00 5.00
KG Kevin Garnett 5.00 12.00
KK Kyle Korver 2.00 5.00
LD Luol Deng 2.50 6.00
LJ LeBron James SP 10.00 25.00
MA Shawn Marion 2.50 6.00
MB Mike Bibby 2.50 6.00
MC Jeff McInnis 2.00 5.00
MJ Michael Jordan SP 40.00 80.00
MP Mickael Pietrus 2.00 5.00
PP Paul Pierce 3.00 8.00
RL Rashard Lewis 2.50 6.00
SD Samuel Dalembert 2.00 5.00
SF Steve Francis 2.50 6.00
SM Stephon Marbury 2.00 5.00
SO Shaquille O'Neal 5.00 12.00
SS Stromile Swift 2.00 5.00
TA Tony Allen 2.00 5.00
TC Tyson Chandler 2.00 5.00
TD Tim Duncan 4.00 10.00
TM Tracy McGrady 3.00 8.00
TP Tony Parker 2.50 6.00
VC Vince Carter 3.00 8.00
WS Wally Szczerbiak 2.00 5.00
YM Yao Ming 3.00 8.00
ZI Zydrunas Ilgauskas 2.00 5.00

2006-07 Sweet Shot Swatches Dual

PRINT RUN 199 SER.#'d SETS
*DUAL GOLD: .6X TO 1.5X BASE HI
GOLD PRINT RUN 25 SER.#'d SETS

AH Rafer Alston 4.00 10.00
Luther Head
AK Ray Allen 4.00 10.00
Kyle Korver
AL Ray Allen 4.00 10.00
Rashard Lewis
AN Carmelo Anthony 5.00 12.00
Nene
AT Al Jefferson 4.00 10.00
Tony Allen
BB Kwame Brown 4.00 10.00
Andrew Bynum
BD Andris Biedrins 4.00 10.00
Ike Diogu
BG Chris Bosh 4.00 10.00
Joey Graham
BL Elton Brand 4.00 10.00
Shaun Livingston
BM Mike Bibby 4.00 10.00
Brad Miller
BV Andrew Bogut 4.00 10.00
Charlie Villanueva
CH Brendan Haywood 4.00 10.00
Caron Butler
CJ Vince Carter 6.00 15.00
Richard Jefferson
CP Tyson Chandler 5.00 12.00
Chris Paul
CW David West 4.00 10.00
Tyson Chandler
DB Baron Davis 4.00 10.00
Chauncey Billups
DG Tim Duncan 6.00 15.00
Manu Ginobili
DI Samuel Dalembert 4.00 10.00
Andre Iguodala
DP Tim Duncan 6.00 15.00
Tony Parker
DW Juan Dixon 4.00 10.00
Martell Webster
FM Steve Francis 4.00 10.00
Stephon Marbury
GJ Drew Gooden 10.00 25.00
LeBron James
GM Kevin Garnett 5.00 12.00
Shawn Marion
GS Peja Stojakovic 4.00 10.00
Manu Ginobili
GW Pau Gasol 4.00 10.00
Hakim Warrick
HB Richard Hamilton 4.00 10.00
Chauncey Billups
HG Kirk Hinrich 4.00 10.00
Ben Gordon
HI Larry Hughes 4.00 10.00
Zydrunas Ilgauskas
JA Antawn Jamison 4.00 10.00
Gilbert Arenas
JG Danny Granger 4.00 10.00
Sarunas Jasikevicius
JJ Michael Jordan 40.00 80.00
LeBron James
JW Joe Johnson 4.00 10.00
Marvin Williams
KJ Jason Kidd 15.00 40.00
LeBron James
KW Andrei Kirilenko 5.00 12.00
Deron Williams
LP Rashard Lewis 4.00 10.00
Johan Petro
MB Kobe Bryant 10.00 25.00
Tracy McGrady
MD Jamaal Magloire 4.00 10.00
Juan Dixon
MH Darko Milicic 5.00 12.00
Dwight Howard
MK Jeff McInnis 4.00 10.00
Nenad Krstic
MM Tracy McGrady 6.00 15.00
Yao Ming
MO Yao Ming 10.00 25.00
Shaquille O'Neal
MR Corey Maggette 4.00 10.00
Michael Redd
MS Alonzo Mourning 4.00 10.00
Wayne Simien
NH Dirk Nowitzki 6.00 15.00
Josh Howard
NM Steve Nash 6.00 15.00
Shawn Marion
OF Emeka Okafor 4.00 10.00
Raymond Felton
PP Tony Parker 5.00 12.00
Chris Paul
PS Paul Pierce 4.00 10.00
Wally Szczerbiak
RD Jason Richardson 4.00 10.00
Mike Dunleavy
RF Nate Robinson 4.00 10.00
Channing Frye
SD Amare Stoudemire 5.00 12.00
Boris Diaw
TC Maurice Taylor 4.00 10.00
Eddy Curry
TO Jamaal Tinsley 4.00 10.00
Jermaine O'Neal
TS Kurt Thomas 5.00 12.00
Amare Stoudemire
UG Beno Udrih 4.00 10.00
Manu Ginobili
WC Josh Childress 4.00 10.00
Marvin Williams
WD Ben Wallace 5.00 12.00
Luol Deng
WH Richard Hamilton 6.00 15.00
Ben Wallace
WK Chris Webber 4.00 10.00
Kyle Korver
WP Rasheed Wallace 6.00 15.00
Tayshaun Prince

2006-07 Sweet Shot Sweet Spot Signatures

RANDOM INSERTS IN PACKS

AJ Antawn Jamison 10.00 25.00
BD Baron Davis 10.00 25.00
CA Carmelo Anthony 30.00 80.00
CD Clyde Drexler 40.00 80.00
CP Chris Paul 35.00 75.00
HO Hakeem Olajuwon 25.00 60.00
JC Josh Childress 10.00 25.00
JO Magic Johnson 50.00 120.00
KA Kareem Abdul-Jabbar 60.00 120.00
KK Kyle Korver 10.00 25.00
LB Larry Bird 50.00 125.00
LJ LeBron James SP 125.00 250.00
PP Paul Pierce 20.00 50.00
PS Peja Stojakovic 12.50 30.00
RA Ron Artest 15.00 40.00
RF Raymond Felton 15.00 40.00
RM Rashad McCants 10.00 25.00
TC Tyson Chandler 10.00 25.00
TP Tayshaun Prince 10.00 25.00
VC Vince Carter 40.00 80.00
YM Yao Ming 25.00 60.00

2007-08 Sweet Shot

This 132-card set was released in December, 2007. The set was issued into the hobby in five-card packs (boxes) which came 20 to a case and packs carried an initial SRP of $75. Cards numbered 1-90 feature NBA veterans in their 2006-07 alphabetical team order while cards 91-132 feature NBA rookies all of which have signatures. Every card in this set is serial numbered with cards 1-90 having a stated print run of 350 serial numbered sets, cards 91-102 having a stated print run of 299 serial numbered sets and cards 103-132 having a stated print run of 699 serial numbered sets.

1 Joe Johnson 1.00 2.50
2 Marvin Williams 1.00 2.50
3 Josh Smith 1.00 2.50
4 Al Jefferson 1.00 2.50
5 Paul Pierce 1.25 3.00
6 Ray Allen 1.00 2.50
7 Adam Morrison 1.00 2.50
8 Raymond Felton 1.25 3.00
9 Gerald Wallace 1.00 2.50
10 Jason Richardson 1.00 2.50
11 Ben Gordon 1.00 2.50
12 Luol Deng 1.00 2.50
13 Ben Wallace 1.00 2.50
14 Michael Jordan 8.00 20.00
15 Larry Hughes .75 2.00
16 LeBron James 5.00 12.00
17 Zydrunas Ilgauskas .75 2.00
18 Dirk Nowitzki 1.25 3.00
19 Josh Howard .75 2.00
20 Jason Terry .75 2.00
21 Allen Iverson 1.25 3.00
22 Nene .75 2.00
23 Carmelo Anthony 1.25 3.00
24 Chauncey Billups 1.00 2.50
25 Richard Hamilton .75 2.00
26 Tayshaun Prince 1.00 2.50
27 Baron Davis 1.00 2.50
28 Stephen Jackson .75 2.00
29 Brandan Wright RC 1.50 4.00
30 Tracy McGrady 1.00 2.50
31 Yao Ming 1.25 3.00
32 Shane Battier .75 2.00
33 Jermaine O'Neal 1.00 2.50
34 Danny Granger 1.00 2.50
35 Elton Brand 1.00 2.50
36 Corey Maggette .75 2.00
37 Kobe Bryant 5.00 12.00
38 Lamar Odom 1.00 2.50
39 Luke Walton .60 1.50
40 Rudy Gay 1.00 2.50
41 Pau Gasol 1.00 2.50
42 Dwyane Wade 2.50 6.00
43 Antoine Walker .75 2.00
44 Shaquille O'Neal 2.00 5.00
45 Michael Redd 1.00 2.50
46 Maurice Williams .75 2.00
47 Andrew Bogut 1.00 2.50
48 Yi Jianlian RC 2.50 6.00
49 Kevin Garnett 2.00 5.00
50 Ricky Davis .75 2.00
51 Randy Foye 1.00 2.50
52 Vince Carter 1.25 3.00
53 Jason Kidd 1.00 2.50
54 Richard Jefferson 1.00 2.50
55 Tyson Chandler .75 2.00
56 David West 1.00 2.50
57 Chris Paul 2.00 5.00
58 Eddy Curry .60 1.50
59 Jamal Crawford .75 2.00
60 Stephon Marbury .75 2.00
61 Zach Randolph .75 2.00
62 Dwight Howard 1.50 4.00
63 Grant Hill 1.25 3.00
64 Andre Miller .75 2.00
65 Thaddeus Young RC 2.00 5.00
66 Andre Iguodala 1.00 2.50
67 Steve Nash 1.25 3.00
68 Amare Stoudemire 1.00 2.50
69 Shawn Marion 1.00 2.50
70 Brandon Roy 1.25 3.00
71 Greg Oden RC 2.00 5.00
72 Ron Artest 1.00 2.50
73 Mike Bibby 1.00 2.50
74 Kevin Martin 1.00 2.50
75 Tim Duncan 1.50 4.00
76 Manu Ginobili 1.00 2.50
77 Tony Parker 1.00 2.50
78 Wally Szczerbiak .75 2.00
79 Delonte West .75 2.00
80 Rashard Lewis .75 2.00
81 T.J. Ford .75 2.00
82 Chris Bosh 1.00 2.50
83 Andrea Bargnani 1.25 3.00
84 Carlos Boozer 1.00 2.50
85 Mehmet Okur .60 1.50
86 Deron Williams 1.50 4.00
87 Gilbert Arenas 1.00 2.50
88 Antawn Jamison 1.00 2.50
89 Caron Butler 1.00 2.50
90 Nick Young RC 2.50 6.00
91 Al Horford AU RC 8.00 20.00
92 Acie Law AU RC 6.00 15.00

Joakim Noah AU RC 15.00 40.00
Marco Belinelli AU RC 6.00 15.00
Al Thornton AU RC 6.00 15.00
Javaris Crittenton AU RC 6.00 15.00
Mike Conley Jr. AU RC 10.00 25.00
Corey Brewer AU RC 8.00 20.00
Julian Wright AU RC 6.00 15.00
Spencer Hawes AU RC 6.00 15.00
Kevin Durant AU RC 125.00 225.00
2 Jeff Green AU RC 8.00 20.00
3 Daequan Cook AU RC 5.00 12.00
4 Jared Dudley AU RC 5.00 12.00
5 Wilson Chandler AU RC 8.00 20.00
6 Rodney Stuckey AU RC 8.00 20.00
7 Morris Almond AU RC 5.00 12.00
3 Arron Afflalo AU RC 6.00 15.00
9 Alando Tucker AU RC 5.00 12.00
0 Sean Williams AU RC 5.00 12.00
Carl Landry AU RC 5.00 12.00
2 Gabe Pruitt AU RC 5.00 12.00
3 Marcus Williams AU RC 5.00 12.00
4 Nick Fazekas AU RC 5.00 12.00
5 Jermareo Davidson AU RC 5.00 12.00
6 Josh McRoberts AU RC 5.00 12.00
7 Aaron Brooks AU RC 5.00 12.00
3 Derrick Byars AU RC 5.00 12.00
9 Adam Haluska AU RC 5.00 12.00
0 Reyshawn Terry AU RC 5.00 12.00
1 Jared Jordan AU RC 5.00 12.00
2 Stephane Lasme AU RC 5.00 12.00
3 Aaron Gray AU RC 5.00 12.00
4 Renaldas Seibutis AU RC 5.00 12.00
5 Taurean Green AU RC 5.00 12.00
6 Demetris Nichols AU RC 5.00 12.00
7 Herbert Hill AU RC 5.00 12.00
8 Sammy Mejia AU RC 5.00 12.00
9 D.J. Strawberry AU RC 5.00 12.00
0 Chris Richard AU RC 5.00 12.00
1 Glen Davis AU RC 8.00 20.00
2 Jason Smith AU RC 5.00 12.00

2007-08 Sweet Shot Rookie Stitches

RINT RUN 99 SER.#'d SETS
PATCHES: 1X TO 2.5X BASE HI
TCH PRINT RUN 10 SER.#'d SETS
H Al Horford 4.00 10.00
Acie Law 3.00 8.00
T Al Thornton 3.00 8.00
V Brandan Wright 3.00 8.00
3 Corey Brewer 4.00 10.00
C Daequan Cook 3.00 8.00
C Javaris Crittenton 3.00 8.00
D Jared Dudley 3.00 8.00
G Jeff Green 4.00 10.00
N Joakim Noah 8.00 20.00
S Jason Smith 3.00 8.00
V Julian Wright 3.00 8.00
D Kevin Durant 25.00 60.00
C Mike Conley Jr. 5.00 12.00
Y Nick Young 5.00 12.00
S Rodney Stuckey 5.00 12.00
H Spencer Hawes 3.00 8.00
V Sean Williams 3.00 8.00
Y Thaddeus Young 4.00 10.00
C Wilson Chandler 5.00 12.00

2007-08 Sweet Shot Signature Kicks White Leather

RINT RUN 24 TO 40 SER.#'d SETS
NPRICED BLACK PRINT RUN 5 TO 10 SETS
A Arron Afflalo/40 10.00 25.00
G Aaron Gray/40 8.00 20.00
H Al Harrington/40 8.00 20.00
J Antawn Jamison/40 20.00 40.00
L Morris Almond/40 8.00 20.00
G Ben Gordon/40 10.00 25.00
R Brandon Roy/40 10.00 25.00
S Craig Smith/40 8.00 20.00
G Daniel Gibson/40 10.00 25.00
L David Lee/40 10.00 25.00
N David Noel/40 8.00 20.00
R Dennis Rodman/40 25.00 50.00
W Deron Williams/40 20.00 40.00
O Al Horford/40 12.50 30.00
A James Augustine/40 8.00 20.00
B Josh Boone/40 8.00 20.00
C Javaris Crittenton/40 8.00 20.00
G Jorge Garbajosa/40 10.00 25.00
W Julian Wright/40 8.00 20.00
B Kobe Bryant/24 175.00 325.00
D Kevin Durant/40 150.00 300.00
L Kyle Lowry/40 8.00 20.00
A LaMarcus Aldridge/40 15.00 30.00
B Leandro Barbosa/40 10.00 25.00
J LeBron James/40 100.00 200.00
P Leon Powe/40 8.00 20.00
MC Mardy Collins/40 8.00 20.00
PM Paul Millsap/40 8.00 20.00
F Randy Foye/40 8.00 20.00
S Rodney Stuckey/40 12.00 30.00
SJ Solomon Jones/40 8.00 20.00
P Tayshaun Prince/40 15.00 30.00

2007-08 Sweet Shot Signature Shots

PRINT RUNS LISTED IN CHECKLIST
SOME NOT PRICED DUE TO SCARCITY
AB Andrea Bargnani/25 10.00 25.00
AD Adrian Dantley/98 5.00 12.00
AH Al Harrington/50 4.00 10.00
AI Andre Iguodala/50 6.00 15.00
AJ Antawn Jamison/50 5.00 12.00
AM Alonzo Mourning/25 60.00 120.00
BA B.J. Armstrong/98 8.00 20.00
BB Bruce Bowen/97 4.00 10.00
BD Baron Davis/50 8.00 20.00
BE Raja Bell/25 15.00 30.00
BG Ben Gordon/369 6.00 15.00
BI Larry Bird/50 40.00 80.00
BL Bill Laimbeer/197 6.00 15.00
BM Brad Miller/99 4.00 10.00
BS Bill Sharman/50 10.00 25.00
BW Bill Walton/25 20.00 40.00
CD Chris Duhon/297 4.00 10.00
CH Tyson Chandler/98 4.00 10.00
CR Cazzie Russell/25 10.00 25.00
CS Cedric Simmons/98 4.00 10.00
CW Shawne Williams/195 4.00 10.00
DB Dee Brown/195 4.00 10.00
DH Dwight Howard/50 20.00 40.00
DL David Lee/197 4.00 10.00
DN David Noel/150 4.00 10.00
DO Keyon Dooling/197 4.00 10.00
DR Dennis Rodman/25 25.00 60.00
DW Deron Williams/409 10.00 25.00
DX Clyde Drexler/25 40.00 80.00
EO Emeka Okafor/25 10.00 25.00
FG Francisco Garcia/97 4.00 10.00
GR Glen Rice/50 4.00 10.00
HA Hilton Armstrong/195 4.00 10.00
HG Horace Grant/50 15.00 40.00
HK Connie Hawkins/50 15.00 30.00
HO Hakeem Olajuwon/25 20.00 40.00
JA James Augustine/195 4.00 10.00
JB Josh Boone/195 4.00 10.00
JG Jorge Garbajosa/97 4.00 10.00
JK Jason Kidd/20 20.00 40.00
JN Magic Johnson/50 50.00 100.00
JO Avery Johnson/50 8.00 20.00
JR J.R. Smith/197 4.00 10.00
JW Jamaal Wilkes/98 6.00 15.00
KA Kareem Abdul-Jabbar/50 30.00 60.00
KD Kevin Durant/99 100.00 200.00
KL Kyle Lowry/189 4.00 10.00
LB Leandro Barbosa/197 4.00 10.00
LH Larry Hughes/50 4.00 10.00
LJ LeBron James/54 100.00 200.00
LP Leon Powe/197 4.00 10.00
MA Maurice Ager/225 4.00 10.00
MC Mardy Collins/195 4.00 10.00
MD Marquis Daniels/195 4.00 10.00
MI Mile Ilic/195 4.00 10.00
PD Paul Davis/195 4.00 10.00
PM Paul Millsap/97 4.00 10.00
PO Patrick O'Bryant/197 4.00 10.00
PP Paul Pierce/50 12.50 30.00
PR Pat Riley/25 25.00 50.00
QR Quentin Richardson/25 4.00 10.00
RB Ronnie Brewer/149 4.00 10.00
RC Rodney Carney/220 4.00 10.00
RF Raymond Felton/197 5.00 12.00
RH Ryan Hollins/219 4.00 10.00
RI Rick Mahorn/97 6.00 15.00
RR Rajon Rondo/97 12.50 30.00
RS Randolph Morris/195 4.00 10.00
RT Ronny Turiaf/195 6.00 15.00
SB Shannon Brown/195 4.00 10.00
SC Craig Smith/195 4.00 10.00
SF Stromile Swift/220 4.00 10.00
SJ Solomon Jones/195 4.00 10.00
SK Steve Kerr/50 8.00 20.00
SN Steve Nash/25 40.00 80.00
SP Sam Perkins/98 5.00 12.00
SR Sergio Rodriguez/195 4.00 10.00
SS Saer Sene/195 4.00 10.00
SW Shelden Williams/197 4.00 10.00
TC Tom Chambers/195 4.00 10.00
TF T.J. Ford/197 4.00 10.00
TM Tracy McGrady/50 10.00 25.00
TT Tyrus Thomas/25 15.00 30.00
VC Vince Carter/25 25.00 60.00
WD Walter Davis/32 5.00 12.00
WF Walt Frazier/25 20.00 50.00
WI Marvin Williams/399 5.00 12.00
WI2 Damien Wilkins/195 4.00 10.00
WO John Wooden/103 60.00 150.00
WT Wayman Tisdale/97 10.00 25.00
WU Wes Unseld/25 10.00 25.00
YD Yakhouba Diawara/195 4.00 10.00

2007-08 Sweet Shot Signature Shots Acetate

PRINT RUN 10 TO 25 SER.#'d SETS
UNPRICED DUAL PRINT RUN 15 SER.#'d SETS
BR Brandon Roy/25 30.00 60.00
DH Dwight Howard/25 25.00 60.00
JB Josh Boone/25 6.00 15.00
KD Kevin Durant/25 150.00 300.00
LA LaMarcus Aldridge/25 10.00 25.00
LJ LeBron James/25 125.00 250.00
LW Lenny Wilkens/25 12.50 30.00
MA Maurice Ager/25 6.00 15.00
PP Paul Pierce/25 30.00 60.00
RF Randy Foye/25 8.00 20.00
RG Rudy Gay/25 15.00 40.00
SI Cedric Simmons/25 6.00 15.00
SN Steve Nash/25 50.00 100.00
YM Yao Ming/25 20.00 40.00

2007-08 Sweet Shot Signature Shots Black Ink

PRINT RUNS LISTED IN CHECKLIST
SOME NOT PRICED DUE TO SCARCITY
AD Adrian Dantley/50 6.00 15.00
AJ Antawn Jamison/50 5.00 12.00
BA B.J. Armstrong/50 10.00 25.00
BB Bruce Bowen/97 4.00 10.00
BG Ben Gordon/92 6.00 15.00
BI Larry Bird/50 40.00 80.00
BL Bill Laimbeer/25 15.00 30.00
BS Bill Sharman/32 10.00 25.00
CH Tyson Chandler/25 6.00 15.00
CM Corey Maggette/50 6.00 15.00
CR Cazzie Russell/50 6.00 15.00
CS Cedric Simmons/98 4.00 10.00
CW Shawne Williams/195 4.00 10.00
DB Dee Brown/195 4.00 10.00
DG Daniel Gibson/97 6.00 15.00
DH Dwight Howard/45 15.00 40.00
DL David Lee/98 4.00 10.00
DN David Noel/69 4.00 10.00
DO Keyon Dooling/98 4.00 10.00
FG Francisco Garcia/97 4.00 10.00
FO Randy Foye/99 4.00 10.00
HA Hilton Armstrong/97 4.00 10.00
JA James Augustine/195 4.00 10.00
JB Josh Boone/195 4.00 10.00
JG Jorge Garbajosa/97 4.00 10.00
JO Avery Johnson/98 6.00 15.00
JR J.R. Smith/25 8.00 20.00
JW Jamaal Wilkes/25 15.00 30.00
KB Kobe Bryant/24 200.00 375.00
KD Kevin Durant/99 100.00 200.00
KL Kyle Lowry/189 4.00 10.00
LB Leandro Barbosa/197 4.00 10.00
LJ LeBron James/23 100.00 225.00
LP Leon Powe/100 4.00 10.00
LR Luke Ridnour/98 4.00 10.00
MA Maurice Ager/97 4.00 10.00
MC Mardy Collins/97 4.00 10.00
MD Marquis Daniels/97 4.00 10.00
MI Mile Ilic/97 4.00 10.00
PD Paul Davis/97 4.00 10.00
PM Paul Millsap/97 4.00 10.00
PO Patrick O'Bryant/98 4.00 10.00
RB Ronnie Brewer/97 4.00 10.00
RC Rodney Carney/98 4.00 10.00
RF Raymond Felton/98 5.00 12.00
RH Ryan Hollins/97 4.00 10.00
RI Rick Mahorn/97 6.00 15.00
RR Rajon Rondo/97 12.50 30.00
RS Randolph Morris/97 4.00 10.00
RT Ronny Turiaf/99 6.00 15.00
SB Shannon Brown/49 8.00 20.00
SC Craig Smith/195 4.00 10.00
SF Stromile Swift/98 4.00 10.00
SJ Solomon Jones/97 4.00 10.00
SP Sam Perkins/98 5.00 12.00
SR Sergio Rodriguez/97 4.00 10.00
SS Saer Sene/97 4.00 10.00
SW Shelden Williams/50 4.00 10.00
TC Tom Chambers/50 5.00 12.00
TF T.J. Ford/25 6.00 15.00
TM Tracy McGrady/41 12.50 30.00
WI Marvin Williams/25 8.00 20.00
WI2 Damien Wilkins/195 4.00 10.00
WT Wayman Tisdale/97 10.00 25.00
YD Yakhouba Diawara/99 4.00 10.00

2007-08 Sweet Shot Signature Shots White Ink

STATED PRINT RUN ONE TO 191 SER.#'d SETS
MOST NOT PRICED DUE TO SCARCITY
KK Kyle Korver/191 4.00 10.00

2007-08 Sweet Shot Sweet Spot Signatures

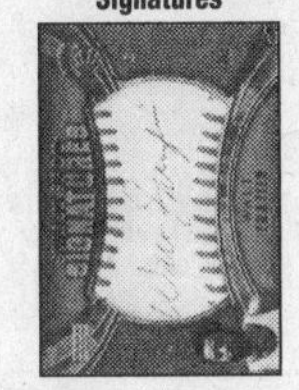

PRINT RUNS LISTED IN CHECKLIST
SOME NOT PRICED DUE TO SCARCITY
UNPRICED GOLD PRINT RUN 1 TO 5 SETS
BR Brandon Roy/50 20.00 40.00
CS Craig Smith/50 6.00 15.00
DG Daniel Gibson/50 10.00 25.00
HG Horace Grant/25 25.00 60.00
HW Hakim Warrick/70 6.00 15.00
JN Joakim Noah/50 25.00 60.00
KD Kevin Durant/35 175.00 350.00
LA LaMarcus Aldridge/50 20.00 40.00
LJ LeBron James/23 150.00 300.00
MJ Michael Jordan/23 450.00 650.00
MO Randolph Morris/50 6.00 15.00
RG Rudy Gay/50 12.50 30.00
RM Rick Mahorn/50 12.50 30.00
SR Sergio Rodriguez/50 6.00 15.00
TG Taurean Green/50 6.00 15.00
TT Tyrus Thomas/25 30.00 60.00
WF Walt Frazier/50 15.00 40.00
YD Yakhouba Diawara/50 6.00 15.00

2007-08 Sweet Shot Sweet Spot Signatures Silver Stitch

PRINT RUNS LISTED IN CHECKLIST
SOME NOT PRICED DUE TO SCARCITY
CS Craig Smith/20 8.00 20.00
DG Daniel Gibson/20 8.00 20.00
JG Jorge Garbajosa/20 8.00 20.00
RM Rick Mahorn/20 20.00 40.00
SR Sergio Rodriguez/20 8.00 20.00

2007-08 Sweet Shot Sweet Stitches

RANDOM INSERTS IN PACKS
*PATCHES: 1X TO 2.5X BASE HI
PATCH PRINT RUN 35 SER.#'d SETS
AI Allen Iverson 3.00 8.00
AR Ron Artest 2.50 6.00
BR Elton Brand 2.50 6.00
CA Carmelo Anthony 3.00 8.00
CM Corey Maggette 2.00 5.00
CW Chris Wilcox 2.00 5.00
DE Desmond Mason 2.00 5.00
DG Devean George 2.00 5.00
DH Devin Harris 2.50 6.00
DM Darko Milicic 2.00 5.00
DU Mike Dunleavy 2.00 5.00
FJ Fred Jones 2.00 5.00
GH Grant Hill 3.00 8.00
JO Jermaine O'Neal 2.50 6.00
JR Jason Richardson 2.50 6.00
JS J.R. Smith 2.50 6.00
KB Kobe Bryant 8.00 20.00
KG Kevin Garnett 5.00 12.00
LH Larry Hughes 2.00 5.00
LJ LeBron James 8.00 20.00
MA Martynas Andriuskevicius 2.00 5.00
MD Marquis Daniels 2.00 5.00
MG Manu Ginobili 2.50 6.00
PA Tony Parker 2.50 6.00
PG Pau Gasol 2.50 6.00
RA Ray Allen 2.50 6.00
RJ Richard Jefferson 2.50 6.00
RL Rashard Lewis 2.00 5.00
RW Rasheed Wallace 2.50 6.00
SD Samuel Dalembert 2.00 5.00
SF Steve Francis 2.50 6.00
SI Wayne Simien 2.00 5.00
SL Shaun Livingston 2.00 5.00
SM Sean May 2.00 5.00
SO Shaquille O'Neal 5.00 12.00
TD Tim Duncan 4.00 10.00
TP Tayshaun Prince 2.50 6.00
WS Wally Szczerbiak 2.00 5.00
ZI Zydrunas Ilgauskas 2.00 5.00
ZR Zach Randolph 2.00 5.00

2007-08 Sweet Shot Sweet Swatches Dual

RANDOM INSERTS IN PACKS
*PATCHES: 1.25X TO 3X BASE HI
PATCH PRINT RUN 25 SER.#'d SETS
AG Ray Allen 6.00 15.00
 Kevin Garnett
AS Martynas Andriuskevicius 3.00 8.00
 Thabo Sefolosha
BB Kwame Brown 3.00 8.00
 Andrew Bynum
BD Elton Brand 3.00 8.00
 Paul Davis
BF Kobe Bryant 8.00 20.00
 Jordan Farmar
BG Manu Ginobili 4.00 10.00
 Bruce Bowen
CJ Richard Jefferson 5.00 12.00
 Vince Carter
CS Tyson Chandler 3.00 8.00
 Cedric Simmons
DD Mike Dunleavy 3.00 8.00
 Marquis Daniels
DG Luol Deng 4.00 10.00
 Ben Gordon
DP Tim Duncan 5.00 12.00
 Tony Parker
DT Ricky Davis 3.00 8.00
 Sebastian Telfair
FB Shane Battier 3.00 8.00
 Steve Francis
GH Devean George 3.00 8.00
 Devin Harris
HB Grant Hill 6.00 15.00
 Raja Bell
HJ LeBron James 6.00 15.00
 Larry Hughes
HW Richard Hamilton 3.00 8.00
 Rasheed Wallace
IA Allen Iverson 6.00 15.00
 Carmelo Anthony
IM Darko Milicic 3.00 8.00
 Zydrunas Ilgauskas
JG Luke Jackson 3.00 8.00
 Joey Graham
JJ Michael Jordan 40.00 70.00
 LeBron James
KB Andrei Kirilenko 3.00 8.00
 Caron Butler
LH Dwight Howard 3.00 8.00
 Rashard Lewis
MC Stephon Marbury 3.00 8.00
 Mardy Collins
MG Donyell Marshall 3.00 8.00
 Drew Gooden
MH Yao Ming 4.00 10.00
 Luther Head
ML Corey Maggette 3.00 8.00
 Shaun Livingston
MR Desmond Mason 3.00 8.00
 Michael Redd
MS Amare Stoudemire 6.00 15.00
 Shawn Marion
NA Trevor Ariza 3.00 8.00
 Jameer Nelson
NH Dirk Nowitzki 4.00 10.00
 Josh Howard
PG Kevin Garnett 5.00 12.00
 Paul Pierce
RD Ronnie Brewer 3.00 8.00
 Dee Brown
RF Jason Richardson 3.00 8.00
 Raymond Felton
SG Pau Gasol 3.00 8.00
 Stromile Swift
SP Peja Stojakovic 4.00 10.00
 Chris Paul
SW Wally Szczerbiak 3.00 8.00
 Delonte West
TD Ike Diogu 3.00 8.00
 Jamaal Tinsley
WR Jalen Rose 5.00 12.00
 Chris Webber
WW Chris Wilcox 3.00 8.00
 Damien Wilkins

2009 Sweet Spot Signatures Red Stitch Blue Ink

OVERALL AUTO ODDS 1:3 HOBBY
PRINT RUNS B/WN 2-199 COPIES PER
NO PRICING ON QTY 25 OR LESS
EXCHANGE DEADLINE 10/7/2011
LJ LeBron James/15 150.00 300.00

2009 Sweet Spot Signatures Red Stitch Green Ink

OVERALL AUTO ODDS 1:3 HOBBY
ANNOUNCED PRINT RUNS LISTED
PRINT RUN INFO PROVIDED BY UD
EXCHANGE DEADLINE 10/7/2011
LJ LeBron James/25 * 125.00 250.00

2006 Sweet Spot Update Spokesmen Signatures

OVERALL AUTO ODDS 1:6
UNPRICED AU PRINT RUN 5-20
4 Michael Jordan/20 400.00 700.00

1951 Syracuse National Glasses

These glasses were given out to a select few fans at a Syracuse National game in 1951. The glasses have a silhouette of the player on them along with their name. Since they are unnumbered we have sequenced them in alphabetical order.

COMPLETE SET (9) 500.00 850.00
1 Al Cervi 50.00 100.00
2 Billy Gabor 25.00 50.00
3 Alex Hannum 60.00 120.00
4 Noble Jorgensen 25.00 50.00
5 George Ratkovicz 25.00 50.00
6 Dolph Schayes 250.00 400.00
7 Paul Seymour 60.00 120.00
8 Front Office Personnel 25.00 50.00
9 Onodoga Cty War Memorial 25.00 50.00

1958-59 Syracuse Nationals

This set consists of 8" by 10" glossy photos of the 1955-56 Syracuse Nationals. Originally the photos sold for 25 cents each, or the entire set for $2.00. The order blank also included an offer for a 32-page record book that could be purchased for 50 cents. The photos are unnumbered and checklisted below in alphabetical order. We have dated this set 1958-59 as it was Hal Greer's and Connie Dierking's rookie NBA season and Togo Palazzi's last full NBA season.

COMPLETE SET (11) 800.00 1600.00
1 Al Bianchi 75.00 150.00
2 Ed Conlin 65.00 125.00
3 Larry Costello 75.00 150.00
4 Connie Dierking 75.00 150.00
5 Hal Greer 100.00 200.00
6 Bob Hopkins 65.00 125.00
7 John Kerr 100.00 200.00
8 Togo Palazzi 65.00 125.00
9 Dolph Schayes 150.00 300.00
10 Paul Seymour 65.00 125.00
11 Team Photo 75.00 150.00

1962-63 Syracuse Nationals

These photos, which measure 8" by 10", feature members of the Syracuse Nationals. Since these photos are unnumbered, we have sequenced them in alphabetical order.

COMPLETE SET 400.00 800.00
1 Al Bianchi 30.00 60.00
2 Len Chappell 25.00 50.00
3 Larry Costello 40.00 80.00
4 Dave Gambee 25.00 50.00
5 Hal Greer 60.00 120.00
6 Alex Hannum 30.00 60.00
7 Swede Halbrook 25.00 50.00
8 John Kerr 50.00 100.00
9 Paul Neuman 25.00 50.00
10 Joe Roberts 25.00 50.00
11 Dolph Schayes 75.00 150.00
12 Lee Shaffer 25.00 50.00

1998 Taco Bell Shaquille O'Neal

Inserted into various Taco Bell Home Original dinners, this card is shorter than a standard sized card and features a 3-D shot of Shaquille O'Neal dunking. The card back is not numbered and features a black and white promotional ad stating "Pile On The Fun with Taco Bell".

1 Shaquille O'Neal 4.00 10.00

1984-85 Tampa Bay Thrillers

This oversized card was released during the 1984-85 season by Eckerd Drug Store, it features ten of the Tampa Bay Thriller's players and coaches. Please note that this 8x11 black and white card is not numbered and has a blank back.

1 Jeff Rosenberg PRES 4.00 10.00
 Bill Musselman CO
 Charles Jones
 James Banks
 Les Craft
 Marc Glass
 Steve Hayes
 Perry Moss
 Freeman Williams
 Ron Valentine

1980-81 TCMA CBA

The 1980-81 Continental Basketball Association set, produced by TCMA, features 45 black and white photos of the players along with the team name in red along the side of the front of the card. The sets were originally available direct from the CBA for 5.50. The backs contain brief biographical data and statistics, the CBA logo, the team logo and the card number. A 1981 TCMA copyright date also appears on the back. The standard-size cards are printed on white cardboard backs.

COMPLETE SET (45) 40.00 80.00
1 Chubby Cox 1.25 3.00
2 Sylvester Cuyler 1.00 2.50
3 Harry Davis .75 2.00
4 Danny Salisbury .75 2.00
5 Cazzie Russell 6.00 12.00
6 Al Green 1.00 2.50
7 Rick Wilson .75 2.00
8 Jim Brogan .75 2.00
9 Andre McCarter 2.50 6.00
10 Jerry Baskerville 1.25 3.00
11 James Woods .75 2.00
12 Geoff Crompton 1.25 3.00
13 Korky Nelson .75 2.00
14 George Karl CO 7.50 15.00
15 Stan Pietkiewicz 1.25 3.00
16 Raymond Townsend 2.00 5.00
17 Lenny Horton .75 2.00
18 Carl Bailey .75 2.00
19 Ken Jones .75 2.00
20 Rory Sparrow 3.00 8.00
21 Mauro Panaggio CO 1.50 4.00
22 Glenn Hagan 1.25 3.00
23 Larry Fogle 1.25 3.00
24 Wayne Abrams .75 2.00
25 Jerry Christian .75 2.00
26 Edgar Jones 1.50 4.00
27 Jerry Radocha .75 2.00
28 Greg Jackson 1.00 2.50
29 Eddie Mast P/CO 1.25 3.00
30 Ron Davis 1.25 3.00
31 Tico Brown 1.00 2.50
32 Freeman Blade 1.00 2.50
33 Bill Klucas CO 1.00 2.50
34 Melvin Davis 1.00 2.50
35 James Hardy .75 2.00
36 Brad Davis 4.00 10.00
37 Andre Wakefield .75 2.00
38 Brett Vroman 1.25 3.00
39 Larry Knight .75 2.00
40 Mel Bennett .75 2.00
41 Stan Eckwood .75 2.00
42 Andrew Parker .75 2.00
43 Billy Ray (Dunk) Bates 1.50 4.00
44 Matt Teahan .75 2.00
45 Carlton Green .75 2.00

1981-82 TCMA CBA

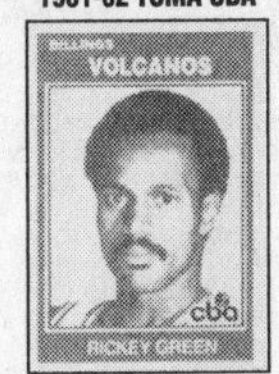

This 90-card standard-size set features black and white photos surrounded by a red frame line in which the player's name and team are printed. The Continental Basketball Association (CBA) logo appears in black on the front of the card. The back of the card contains the card number, career statistics, brief biographical data, and the team and CBA logos. A TCMA copyright date appears on the back.

COMPLETE SET (90) 60.00 150.00
1 1981 CBA Champions 2.00 5.00
 Rochester Zeniths/(Previous champions listed on back)
2 Wayne Abrams .75 2.00
3 Pete Taylor .75 2.00
4 George Torres .75 2.00
5 Henry Bibby 3.00 8.00
6 Rufus Harris .75 2.00
7 Donnie Koonce .75 2.00
8 Jeff Wilkins 1.50 4.00
9 Kurt Nimphius 1.25 3.00
10 Billy Ray(Dunk) Bates 1.50 4.00
11 James Lee 1.25 3.00
12 Marlon Redmond .75 2.00
13 Gary Mazza CO .75 2.00
14 Tony Fuller 1.25 3.00
15 Brad Davis 3.00 8.00
16 Joe Cooper 1.25 3.00
17 Andra Griffin .75 2.00
18 Rudy White 1.25 3.00
19 Ricky Williams .75 2.00
20 Glenn Hagan 1.25 3.00
21 Ernie Graham .75 2.00
22 Kevin Graham .75 2.00
23 Billy Reid .75 2.00
24 Mauro Panaggio CO 1.25 3.00
25 Bo Ellis 1.50 4.00
26 Ollie Matson 1.25 3.00
27 Tony Turner .75 2.00
28 Leo Papile CO .75 2.00
29 Larry Holmes .75 2.00
30 Steve Hayes 2.00 5.00
31 Carl Bailey .75 2.00
32 Tico Brown 1.25 3.00
33 Percy Davis .75 2.00
34 Al Leslie .75 2.00
35 Ken Dennard 1.50 4.00
36 Larry Spriggs 3.00 8.00
37 John Smith .75 2.00
38 Kenny Natt 1.25 3.00
39 Harry Heineken .75 2.00
40 Lowes Moore .75 2.00
41 Curtis Berry .75 2.00
42 Freeman Blade CO 1.25 3.00
43 Larry Lawrence .75 2.00
44 Purvis Miller .75 2.00
45 Ron Valentine .75 2.00
46 Charles Floyd .75 2.00
47 Greg Cornelius .75 2.00
48 Clay Johnson 2.00 5.00
49 Bill Klucas CO 1.25 3.00
50 Cazzie Russell P/CO 4.00 10.00
51 Craig Shelton 1.50 4.00
52 Dave Britton .75 2.00
53 Ken Green .75 2.00
54 Stan Pawlak CO 1.25 3.00
55 Rich Yonakor .75 2.00
56 Darryl Gladden .75 2.00
57 Norman Black .75 2.00
58 Pete Harris .75 2.00
59 Anthony Roberts .75 2.00
60 Jawann Oldham 1.50 4.00
61 Sam Clancy 2.00 5.00
62 Andre McCarter 2.00 5.00
63 Joe Merten .75 2.00
64 Eddie Moss .75 2.00
65 Brad Branson .75 2.00
66 Lenny Horton .75 2.00
67 Jerome Henderson .75 2.00
68 Terry Stotts 2.00 5.00
69 Tony Wells .75 2.00
70 Rickey Green 3.00 8.00
71 Don Newman .75 2.00
72 Randy Owens .75 2.00
73 Erv Giddings .75 2.00
74 Barry Young .75 2.00
75 Jim Brogan .75 2.00
76 Richard Johnson .75 2.00
77 George Karl CO 4.00 10.00
78 U.S. Reed 1.25 3.00
79 Fran Greenberg .75 2.00
 (PR Director)
80 Ron Davis .75 2.00
81 Larry Fogle 1.00 2.50
82 Clarence Kea .75 2.00
83 Steve Craig 1.25 3.00
84 Harry Davis .75 2.00
85 Jacky Dorsey .75 2.00
86 Herb Gray .75 2.00
87 Randy Johnson .75 2.00
88 Jim Drucker COMM .75 2.00
89 Lynbert Johnson .75 2.00
90 Checklist 1-90 .75 2.00

1982-83 TCMA CBA

This third Continental Basketball Association set from TCMA features 90 black and white standard-size cards with red frame lines. The CBA logo, the player's name, physical data, team name, and team logo appear on the front, as does the card number. The back of the cards form a large puzzle. The cards were apparently issued in two series of 45 cards each.

COMPLETE SET (90) 50.00 125.00
1 Cazzie Russell CO 3.00 8.00
2 Boot Bond .75 2.00
3 Ron Charles 1.00 2.50
4 Charles Pittman 1.50 4.00
5 Calvin Garrett 2.00 5.00
6 Willie Jones .60 1.50
7 Riley Clarida .60 1.50
8 Jim Johnstone .60 1.50
9 Bobby Potts .60 1.50
10 Lowes Moore .75 2.00
11 Dwight Anderson 3.00 8.00
12 John Coughran .60 1.50
13 Mike Evans 1.50 4.00
14 Alan Hardy .60 1.50
15 Willie Smith .60 1.50
16 Oliver Mack 2.00 5.00
17 Checklist 1-45 .60 1.50
18 Picture 1 .60 1.50
 (Action under basket)
19 James Lee 1.25 3.00
20 Kenny Natt 1.25 3.00
21 Cyrus Mann .60 1.50
22 Bobby Cattage .75 2.00
23 Garry Witts .60 1.50
24 Bill Klucas CO .75 2.00
25 Al Smith 1.00 2.50
26 B.B. Fontenet .60 1.50
27 Chris Giles .60 1.50
28 Barry Young .75 2.00
29 Horace Wyatt 1.00 2.50
30 Robert Smith .75 2.00
31 Ron Baxter 1.00 2.50
32 Charlie Jones .75 2.00
33 Tico Brown 1.00 2.50
34 John McCullough .60 1.50
35 Dan Callandrillo 1.00 2.50
36 John Leonard 1.00 2.50
37 Sam Worthen 1.00 2.50
38 Dale Wilkinson .75 2.00
39 Gary Johnson .60 1.50
40 Dean Meminger CO 1.25 3.00
41 Lloyd Terry .60 1.50
42 Mike Schultz .75 2.00
43 Darryl Gladden .60 1.50
44 Clarence Kea .75 2.00
45 Charlie Floyd .60 1.50
46 Skip Dillard 1.25 3.00
47 Craig Tucker .60 1.50
48 Gib Hinz .60 1.50
49 Tom Sienkiewicz .75 2.00

50 Larry Spriggs 2.00 5.00
51 Perry Moss .60 1.50
52 Gerald Sims .60 1.50
53 Alan Taylor .60 1.50
54 James Terry .60 1.50
55 John Nillen CO .60 1.50
56 Steve Burks .60 1.50
57 Anthony Martin .60 1.50
58 Purvis Miller .75 2.00
59 Kevin Smith .60 1.50
60 John Neumann CO 1.00 2.50
61 Mike Davis 1.25 3.00
62 Gary Carter 1.25 3.00
63 Checklist 46-90 .60 1.50
64 Picture 2 .60 1.50
(Action under basket)
65 Charles Thompson .60 1.50
66 John Douglas .60 1.50
67 John Schweitz 1.25 3.00
68 Kevin Figaro .60 1.50
69 John Smith .60 1.50
70 Joe Cooper 1.00 2.50
71 Tony Brown 1.25 3.00
72 Mike Wilson .60 1.50
73 Wayne Abrams .60 1.50
74 T.X. Martin .60 1.50
75 Joe Merten .60 1.50
76 Joe Kopicki 1.00 2.50
77 Carl Nicks 1.00 2.50
78 Wayne Kreklow .60 1.50
79 Tony Guy .75 2.00
80 Dave Harshman CO .60 1.50
81 Bob Davis .60 1.50
82 Gary Mazza CO .60 1.50
83 Randy Owens .60 1.50
84 David Burns .60 1.50
85 Erv Giddings .60 1.50
86 JoJo Hunter 1.00 2.50
87 Frankie Sanders .60 1.50
88 Dave Richardson .60 1.50
89 Lionel Garrett .60 1.50
90 Marvin Barnes 3.00 8.00

1982-83 TCMA Lancaster CBA

This set features 30 black and white standard-sized cards with blue border on front. The card backs contain statistics and are numbered on the back. Many of the poses are in action shots. The set is printed on dark cardboard. All cards feature players or personnel of the Lancaster Lightning (Continental Basketball Association) team which won the 1981-82 CBA Championship.

COMPLETE SET (30) 14.00 35.00
1 Lightning Wins 1982 1.25 3.00
CBA Championship
2 1982-83 Lancaster .60 1.50
Lightning Team Picture
3 Dr. Seymour Kilstein PRES .40 1.00
4 Cazzie Russell CO 2.00 5.00
5 Cazzie Russell CO IA 2.00 5.00
6 Ed Koback 1.00 2.50
Operations
7 Bob Danforth .40 1.00
Marketing
8 Henry Bibby IA 1.25 3.00
9 Joe Cooper .75 2.00
10 Joe Cooper IA .60 1.50
11 Curtis Berry .75 2.00
12 Curtis Berry IA .60 1.50
13 James Lee 1.00 2.50
14 James Lee IA .75 2.00
15 Ed Sherod IA .60 1.50
16 Charlie Floyd .40 1.00
17 Charlie Floyd IA .40 1.00
18 Darryl Gladden .40 1.00
19 Darryl Gladden IA .40 1.00
20 Tom Sienkiewicz .75 2.00
21 Tom Sienkiewicz IA .60 1.50
22 Stan Williams .40 1.00
23 Willie Redden .40 1.00
24 Reginald Gaines .40 1.00
25 Gary (Cat) Johnson .75 2.00
26 Gary (Cat) Johnson IA .60 1.50
27 Keith Hilliard .40 1.00
28 Keith Hilliard IA .40 1.00
29 Donald Seals .40 1.00
30 Rufus Harris .75 2.00

1981 TCMA NBA

This 44-card standard-sized set features some of the all-time great basketball players. The fronts feature a color posed photo of the player, while the back has name, career summary, and career highlights.

COMPLETE SET (44) 40.00 100.00
1 Alex Hannum .75 2.00
2 Larry Foust .40 1.00
3 George Mikan 5.00 12.00
4 Mel(Hutch) Hutchins .40 1.00
5 Bob Pettit 1.50 4.00
6 Willis Reed 1.25 3.00
7 Adolph Schayes 1.25 3.00
8 Vern Mikkelsen SP 5.00 12.00
9 Cazzie Russell .60 1.50
10 Dick Van Arsdale .60 1.50
11 Lenny Wilkens 1.25 3.00
12 Ray Felix .60 1.50
13 Ed Macauley 1.00 2.50
14 Clyde Lovellette .75 2.00
15 Slater(Dugie) Martin .75 2.00
16 Bill Russell 6.00 15.00
17 Oscar Robertson SP 6.00 15.00
18 Bill Bradley 2.00 5.00
19 Elgin Baylor 3.00 8.00
20 Bill Sharman 2.00 5.00
21 Tom(Satch) Sanders 1.00 2.50
22 Dave Bing .75 2.00
23 Carl Braun .75 2.00
24 Frank Selvy .75 2.00
25 George Yardley .60 1.50
26 Dick McGuire .60 1.50
27 Leroy Ellis .40 1.00
28 Jack Twyman .75 2.00
29 Nate Thurmond 1.25 3.00
30 Walt Frazier 1.50 4.00
31 John(Red) Kerr 1.25 3.00
32 Jerry West 4.00 10.00
33 John Egan SP 2.50 6.00
34 Jim Loscutoff 1.00 2.50
35 Bob Leonard .60 1.50
36 Rick Barry 1.25 3.00
37 Gene Shue .75 2.00
38 Jerry Lucas 1.00 2.50
39 Dave DeBusschere 1.25 3.00
40 Johnny Green 1.00 2.50
Charles Tyra
Carl Braun
Richie Guerin
John George
41 Bob Cousy 4.00 10.00
42 Walter Bellamy .60 1.50
43 Billy Cunningham .75 2.00
44 Wilt Chamberlain 6.00 15.00

1990 The National Michael Jordan Promo

This standard-sized card was issued to promote the upcoming "The National" sports-only newspaper. The card front features the newspaper name at the top with Jordan shooting over Ewing. The card back features information about the new newspaper. The card is not numbered.

NNO Michael Jordan 12.00 30.00

2008-09 Thunder Upper Deck

COMPLETE SET (14) 2.50 6.00
1 Kevin Durant 1.25 3.00
2 Earl Watson .20 .50
3 Nick Collison .20 .50
4 Jeff Green .25 .60
5 Chris Wilcox .20 .50
6 Damien Wilkins .20 .50
7 Johan Petro .20 .50
8 Robert Swift .20 .50
9 Mouhamed Sene .20 .50
10 Desmond Mason .20 .50
11 Russell Westbrook 1.50 4.00
12 D.J. White .30 .75
13 P.J. Carlesimo CO .20 .50
14 Kyle Weaver .30 .75

1989-90 Timberwolves Burger King

This seven-card set was sponsored by Burger King to commemorate the inaugural season of the Minnesota Timberwolves. The cards were issued with a (9" by 12") Player Cards Collector Set, which included on the inside a 1989-90 game schedule and slots to hold the cards. The standard size cards feature on the fronts color action player photos, with dark blue borders on white card stock. A banner reading "Inaugural Season" overlays the top of the picture. The team name and logo at the top and player identification below the picture round out the card face. The backs have biographical and statistical information, with the team logo and a blue stripe (with player's name in white) appearing at the top of the cards. The cards are unnumbered. Brad Lohaus is considered somewhat tougher to find since he was supposedly pulled from the set and replaced by Randy Breuer during the promotion. The set features the first professional card of Jerome "Pooh" Richardson.

COMPLETE SET (7) 1.50 4.00
19 Tony Campbell .30 .75
23 Tyrone Corbin .40 1.00
24 Pooh Richardson .60 1.50
35 Sidney Lowe .30 .75
42 Sam Mitchell .40 1.00
45 Randy Breuer .30 .75
54 Brad Lohaus .30 .75

2009-10 Timeless Treasures

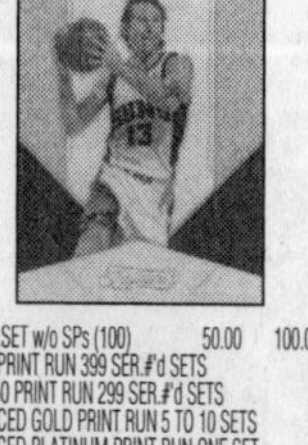

COMP.SET w/o SPs (100) 50.00 100.00
1-100 PRINT RUN 399 SER.#'d SETS
101-150 PRINT RUN 299 SER.#'d SETS
UNPRICED GOLD PRINT RUN 5 TO 10 SETS
UNPRICED PLATINUM PRINT RUN ONE SET
1 Kobe Bryant 5.00 12.00
2 LeBron James 5.00 12.00
3 Chris Paul 1.50 4.00
4 Dwight Howard 1.50 4.00
5 Dwyane Wade 2.00 5.00
6 Dirk Nowitzki 1.25 3.00
7 Danny Granger 1.00 2.50
8 Kevin Durant 3.00 8.00
9 Pau Gasol 1.00 2.50
10 Amare Stoudemire 1.00 2.50
11 Chris Bosh 1.00 2.50
12 Brandon Roy 1.00 2.50
13 Kevin Garnett 2.00 5.00
14 Al Jefferson 1.00 2.50
15 Deron Williams 1.00 2.50
16 Chauncey Billups 1.00 2.50
17 Steve Nash 1.00 2.50
18 Tim Duncan 1.50 4.00
19 Andre Iguodala 1.00 2.50
20 Jason Kidd 1.00 2.50
21 Devin Harris 1.00 2.50
22 Joe Johnson 1.00 2.50
23 Gerald Wallace 1.00 2.50
24 Vince Carter 1.25 3.00
25 Paul Pierce 1.25 3.00
26 Brook Lopez 1.00 2.50
27 Kevin Martin 1.00 2.50
28 Antawn Jamison 1.00 2.50
29 David West 1.00 2.50
30 Carmelo Anthony 1.25 3.00
31 Troy Murphy .60 1.50
32 Rashard Lewis .75 2.00
33 Elton Brand 1.00 2.50
34 Josh Smith 1.00 2.50
35 Baron Davis 1.00 2.50
36 Ray Allen 1.00 2.50
37 Carlos Boozer 1.00 2.50
38 David Lee .75 2.00
39 Derrick Rose 3.00 8.00
40 Rajon Rondo 1.25 3.00
41 O.J. Mayo 1.00 2.50
42 Nene .75 2.00
43 Andrea Bargnani .75 2.00
44 Charlie Villanueva .75 2.00
45 Ben Gordon 1.00 2.50
46 Mike Bibby .75 2.00
47 Tony Parker 1.00 2.50
48 Andrew Bynum 1.25 3.00
49 Russell Westbrook 1.50 4.00
50 Anthony Randolph .75 2.00
51 Eric Gordon 1.00 2.50
52 Jeff Green .75 2.00
53 Shaquille O'Neal 2.00 5.00
54 Aaron Brooks .60 1.50
55 Chris Kaman .75 2.00
56 D.J. Augustin .75 2.00
57 Emeka Okafor 1.00 2.50
58 Derek Fisher .75 2.00
59 Jermaine O'Neal 1.00 2.50
60 Josh Howard .75 2.00
61 Kevin Love 1.50 4.00
62 Lamar Odom 1.00 2.50
63 Michael Beasley 1.00 2.50
64 Richard Hamilton .75 2.00
65 Ron Artest 1.00 2.50
66 Ronnie Brewer .75 2.00
67 Rudy Fernandez .75 2.00
68 Ryan Gomes .60 1.50
69 Shane Battier 1.00 2.50
70 T.J. Ford .60 1.50
71 Tracy McGrady 1.00 2.50
72 Trevor Ariza .60 1.50
73 Greg Oden .75 2.00
74 Nate Archibald 1.00 2.50
75 Al Cervi 1.00 2.50
76 Bob Cousy 1.50 4.00
77 Harry Gallatin 1.00 2.50
78 Gail Goodrich 1.00 2.50
79 Hal Greer 1.00 2.50
80 John Havlicek 1.00 2.50
81 Connie Hawkins 1.00 2.50
82 Elvin Hayes 1.00 2.50
83 Bob McAdoo 1.00 2.50
84 Pete Maravich 3.00 8.00
85 Bill Russell 1.50 4.00
86 Dolph Schayes 1.00 2.50
87 Bill Sharman 1.00 2.50
88 David Thompson 1.25 3.00
89 Nate Thurmond 1.00 2.50
90 Jack Twyman 1.00 2.50
91 Wes Unseld 1.00 2.50
92 Bill Walton 1.00 2.50
93 Bobby Wanzer 1.00 2.50
94 Frank Ramsey 1.00 2.50
95 Willis Reed 1.00 2.50
96 Pat Riley 1.00 2.50
97 Xavier McDaniel 1.00 2.50
98 Oscar Robertson 1.00 2.50
99 Lenny Wilkens 1.00 2.50
100 James Worthy 1.25 3.00
101 Blake Griffin AU RC 75.00 150.00
102 Hasheem Thabeet AU RC 5.00 12.00
103 James Harden AU RC 15.00 40.00
104 Tyreke Evans AU RC 15.00 40.00
105 Jonny Flynn AU RC 5.00 12.00
106 Stephen Curry AU RC 15.00 40.00
107 Jordan Hill AU RC 5.00 12.00
108 Ricky Rubio AU RC 50.00 125.00
109 Brandon Jennings AU RC 10.00 25.00
110 Terrence Williams AU RC 5.00 12.00
111 Gerald Henderson AU RC 5.00 12.00
112 Tyler Hansbrough AU RC 8.00 20.00
113 Earl Clark AU RC 5.00 12.00
114 Austin Daye AU RC 5.00 12.00
115 James Johnson AU RC 5.00 12.00
116 Jrue Holiday AU RC 10.00 25.00
117 Ty Lawson AU RC 8.00 20.00
118 Jeff Teague AU RC 6.00 15.00
119 Eric Maynor AU RC 5.00 12.00
120 Darren Collison AU RC 8.00 20.00
121 Omri Casspi AU RC 5.00 12.00
122 B.J. Mullens AU RC 5.00 12.00
123 Rodrigue Beaubois AU RC 6.00 15.00
124 Taj Gibson AU RC 6.00 15.00
125 DeMarre Carroll AU RC 5.00 12.00
126 Wayne Ellington AU RC 5.00 12.00
127 Toney Douglas AU RC 5.00 12.00
128 Jeff Pendergraph AU RC 5.00 12.00
129 Jermaine Taylor AU RC 5.00 12.00
130 DaJuan Summers AU RC 5.00 12.00
131 Sam Young AU RC 5.00 12.00
132 DeJuan Blair AU RC 6.00 15.00
133 Jodie Meeks AU RC 6.00 15.00
134 Chase Budinger AU RC 5.00 12.00
135 Taylor Griffin AU RC 5.00 12.00
136 Marcus Thornton AU RC 8.00 20.00
137 Danny Green AU RC 8.00 20.00
138 Derrick Brown AU RC 5.00 12.00
139 Jonas Jerebko AU RC 5.00 12.00
140 Serge Ibaka AU RC 12.00 30.00
141 Jon Brockman AU RC 5.00 12.00
142 Dante Cunningham AU RC 5.00 12.00
143 Wesley Matthews AU RC 8.00 20.00
144 A.J. Price AU RC 5.00 12.00
145 Lester Hudson AU RC 5.00 12.00
146 Marcus Landry AU RC 5.00 12.00
147 Sundiata Gaines AU RC 5.00 12.00
148 David Andersen AU RC 5.00 12.00
149 Patrick Mills AU RC 10.00 25.00
150 DeMar DeRozan AU RC 15.00 30.00

2009-10 Timeless Treasures Silver

*SILVER 1-100: 1.5X TO 4X BASE HI
SILVER 1-100 PRINT RUN 25 SER.#'d SETS
*SILVER RC/25: .6X TO 1.5X BASE HI
SILVER/10 UNPRICED DUE TO SCARCITY
103 James Harden AU/25 30.00 80.00

2009-10 Timeless Treasures Championship Season Combos Materials

STATED PRINT RUN 25 SER.#'d SETS
UNPRICED PRIME PRINT RUN 5 SER.#'d SETS
1 Kevin Garnett 10.00 25.00
Ray Allen
2 Kevin Garnett 8.00 20.00
Rajon Rondo
3 Rajon Rondo 10.00 25.00
Ray Allen
4 Kobe Bryant 15.00 40.00
Pau Gasol

2009-10 Timeless Treasures Championship Season Materials

STATED PRINT RUN 50 TO 100 SER.#'d SETS
UNPRICED PRIME PRINT RUN 5 TO 25 SETS
UNPRICED TAG PRINT RUN 3 TO 6 SETS
UNPRICED TAG LOGO PRINT RUN 1 TO 2 SETS
UNPRICED TAG NBA SIGS PRINT RUN 1 TO 2 SETS
UNPRICED TEAM LOGO PRINT RUN 1 TO 2 SETS
UNPRICED TEAM LOGO SIGS PRINT RUN 1-3 SETS
UNPRICED NBA LOGO PRINT RUN 1 TO 3 SETS
UNPRICED NBA LOGO SIGS PRINT RUN 1 TO 3 SETS
1 Kevin Garnett/100 6.00 15.00
2 Rajon Rondo/100 4.00 10.00
3 Ray Allen/100 3.00 8.00
4 Pau Gasol/50 5.00 12.00
5 Kobe Bryant/100 10.00 25.00
6 Dwyane Wade/100 6.00 15.00
7 Tim Duncan/100 5.00 12.00
8 Tony Parker/100 3.00 8.00
10 Tom Heinsohn/100 3.00 8.00
11 Kareem Abdul-Jabbar/100 5.00 12.00
12 Manu Ginobili/100 3.00 8.00

2009-10 Timeless Treasures Championship Season Materials Laundry Tags Signatures

STATED PRINT RUN ONE TO 12 SER.#'d SETS
MOST UNPRICED DUE TO SCARCITY
3 Ray Allen/12 50.00 100.00

2009-10 Timeless Treasures Championship Season Materials Signatures

STATED PRINT RUN 5 TO 25 SER.#'d SETS
SOME UNPRICED DUE TO SCARCITY
UNPRICED PRIME PRINT RUN 5 TO 10 SETS
2 Rajon Rondo/25 30.00 60.00
3 Ray Allen/25 30.00 80.00
11 Kareem Abdul-Jabbar/25 40.00 80.00

2009-10 Timeless Treasures Championship Season Quad Materials

STATED PRINT RUN 25 TO 50 SER.#'d SETS
UNPRICED PRIME PRINT RUN 5 SER.#'d SETS
1 Dwyane Wade/50 10.00 25.00
Kevin Garnett
Kobe Bryant
Tim Duncan
2 Kareem Abdul-Jabbar/25 15.00 30.00
Kobe Bryant
Nate Archibald
Tom Heinsohn

2009-10 Timeless Treasures Championship Season Triple Materials

STATED PRINT RUN 25 SER.#'d SETS
UNPRICED PRIME PRINT RUN 5 SER.#'d SETS
1 Kevin Garnett/25 15.00 40.00
Rajon Rondo
Ray Allen

2009-10 Timeless Treasures HOF Combos Materials

STATED PRINT RUN 10 TO 50 SER.#'d SETS
UNPRICED PRIME PRINT RUN 5 SER.#'d SETS
1 Kareem Abdul-Jabbar/50 15.00 40.00
George Mikan
2 Larry Bird/50 10.00 25.00
Kevin McHcHale
3 Joe Dumars/50 6.00 15.00
Isiah Thomas
4 Alex English/50 5.00 12.00
Dan Issel
5 Tom Heinsohn/50 6.00 15.00
Dave Cowens
6 Dave Cowens/50 6.00 15.00
John Havlicek
7 Hakeem Olajuwon/50 10.00 25.00
Clyde Drexler

2009-10 Timeless Treasures HOF Materials Jerseys

STATED PRINT RUN 5 TO 50 SER.#'d SETS
UNPRICED PRIME PRINT RUN 5 SER.#'d SETS
1 George Mikan/50 15.00 40.00
2 Kareem Abdul-Jabbar/50 6.00 15.00
3 John Stockton/50 6.00 15.00
4 Tom Heinsohn/50 5.00 12.00
5 Adrian Dantley/50 4.00 10.00
6 Alex English/50 4.00 10.00
7 Earl Monroe/50 5.00 12.00
8 George Gervin/50 5.00 12.00
9 Dominique Wilkins/50 5.00 12.00
10 Dave Cowens/50 5.00 12.00
11 Joe Dumars/50 5.00 12.00
12 Jerry West/50 6.00 15.00
13 Isiah Thomas/50 4.00 10.00
14 Walt Frazier/50 4.00 10.00
15 Robert Parish/50 4.00 10.00
16 Rick Barry/50 4.00 10.00
17 Moses Malone/50 4.00 10.00
18 Magic Johnson/50 8.00 20.00
21 Kevin McHale/50 5.00 12.00
22 Dan Issel/50 4.00 10.00
23 Bob Lanier/50 4.00 10.00
24 Clyde Drexler/50 5.00 12.00
25 Clyde Drexler/50 5.00 12.00
29 Hakeem Olajuwon/50 5.00 12.00
30 Patrick Ewing/50 8.00 20.00

2009-10 Timeless Treasures HOF Materials Jerseys Signatures

STATED PRINT RUN 5 TO 25 SER.#'d SETS
UNPRICED PRIME PRINT RUN 10 SER.#'d SETS
2 Kareem Abdul-Jabbar/25 50.00 100.00
8 George Gervin/25 15.00 40.00
9 Dominique Wilkins/25 15.00 40.00
10 Dave Cowens/25 12.50 30.00
13 Isiah Thomas/25 12.50 30.00
14 Walt Frazier/25 12.50 30.00
15 Robert Parish/25 12.50 30.00
18 Magic Johnson/25 50.00 100.00
19 Larry Bird/25 50.00 100.00
22 Dan Issel/25 12.50 30.00
24 Clyde Drexler/25 25.00 50.00
25 Clyde Drexler/25 25.00 50.00
26 John Havlicek/25 20.00 40.00

2009-10 Timeless Treasures HOF Quad Materials

STATED PRINT RUN 10 TO 50 SER.#'d SETS
SOME NOT PRICED DUE TO SCARCITY
UNPRICED PRIME PRINT RUN 5 SER.#'d SETS
1 George Mikan/50 30.00 80.00
Kareem Abdul-Jabbar
Jerry West
Magic Johnson
2 Adrian Dantley/50 15.00 30.00
Joe Dumars
Isiah Thomas
Bob Lanier
3 Tom Heinsohn/50 20.00 40.00
Dave Cowens
John Havlicek
Larry Bird

2009-10 Timeless Treasures HOF Signatures Silver

STATED PRINT RUN 35 SER.#'d SETS
UNPRICED GOLD PRINT RUN 10 SER.#'d SETS
UNPRICED PLATINUM PRINT RUN ONE SET
2 Kareem Abdul-Jabbar 40.00 80.00
8 George Gervin 10.00 25.00
10 Dave Cowens 8.00 20.00
13 Isiah Thomas 8.00 20.00
15 Robert Parish 8.00 20.00
18 Magic Johnson 40.00 80.00
19 Larry Bird 40.00 80.00
24 Clyde Drexler 25.00 50.00
25 Clyde Drexler 20.00 50.00
26 John Havlicek 20.00 40.00
31 Wes Unseld 12.50 30.00
32 Bob Cousy 20.00 40.00
33 Oscar Robertson 40.00 80.00
34 Bill Russell 50.00 120.00

2009-10 Timeless Treasures Home and Road Gamers

STATED PRINT RUN 25 TO 100 SER.#'d SETS
UNPRICED PRIME PRINT RUNS 1 TO 10 SETS
1 Kevin Garnett/50 8.00 20.00
2 Deron Williams/50 4.00 10.00
3 Tracy McGrady/50 4.00 10.00
4 Tim Duncan/50 6.00 15.00
5 Kevin McHale/50 6.00 15.00
6 Kobe Bryant/50 15.00 40.00
7 Kareem Abdul-Jabbar/25 8.00 20.00
8 LeBron James/100 12.00 30.00
9 Dwight Howard/100 6.00 15.00
10 Shaquille O'Neal/100 8.00 20.00
11 Vince Carter/100 5.00 12.00
12 Dirk Nowitzki/100 5.00 12.00
14 Jason Kidd/100 4.00 10.00
15 Dan Issel/50 4.00 10.00
16 Chris Paul/100 6.00 15.00
17 LaMarcus Aldridge/100 4.00 10.00
18 Karl Malone/50 5.00 12.00
19 Dwyane Wade/50 8.00 20.00
20 Dikembe Mutombo/100 4.00 10.00
21 Kevin Durant/100 10.00 25.00
22 Hakeem Olajuwon/100 5.00 12.00
23 Elton Brand/100 4.00 10.00
24 Isiah Thomas/50 4.00 10.00
26 Brandon Roy/100 4.00 10.00
27 David Lee/50 4.00 10.00
28 Al Jefferson/100 4.00 10.00
29 Brook Lopez/100 4.00 10.00

2009-10 Timeless Treasures Home and Road Gamers Signatures

STATED PRINT RUN ONE TO 25 SER.#'d SETS
SOME NOT PRICED DUE TO SCARCITY
UNPRICED PRIME PRINT RUN ONE TO 10 SETS
2 Deron Williams/25 20.00 50.00
3 Tracy McGrady/25 20.00 40.00
6 Kobe Bryant/25 150.00 300.00
15 Dan Issel/25 12.00 30.00
20 Dikembe Mutombo/25 30.00 60.00
24 Isiah Thomas/25 20.00 40.00
27 David Lee/20 12.00 30.00

2009-10 Timeless Treasures Materials Jerseys

STATED PRINT RUN 50 TO 100 SER.#'d SETS
UNPRICED PRIME PRINT RUN 1 TO 10 SETS
TAGS PRINT RUN ONE SER.#'d SET
TAGS INK PRINT RUN ONE SER.#'d SET
TAGS NBA LOGO PRINT RUN ONE SET
TAGS NBA LOGO INK PRINT RUN ONE SET
TAGS TEAM LOGO PRINT RUN ONE SET
TAGS TEAM LOGO INK PRINT RUN ONE SET
TAGS NOT PRICED DUE TO SCARCITY
1 Kobe Bryant/100 8.00 20.00
2 LeBron James/100 8.00 20.00
3 Chris Paul/100 5.00 12.00
4 Dwight Howard/100 5.00 12.00
5 Dwyane Wade/100 6.00 15.00
6 Dirk Nowitzki/100 4.00 10.00
7 Danny Granger/100 3.00 8.00
8 Kevin Durant/100 8.00 20.00
9 Pau Gasol/100 3.00 8.00
10 Amare Stoudemire/100 3.00 8.00
11 Chris Bosh/100 3.00 8.00
12 Brandon Roy/100 3.00 8.00
13 Kevin Garnett/100 6.00 15.00
14 Al Jefferson/100 3.00 8.00
15 Deron Williams/100 3.00 8.00
16 Chauncey Billups/100 3.00 8.00
18 Tim Duncan/100 5.00 12.00
19 Andre Iguodala/100 3.00 8.00
20 Jason Kidd/100 3.00 8.00
21 Devin Harris/100 3.00 8.00
22 Joe Johnson/100 3.00 8.00
23 Gerald Wallace/100 3.00 8.00
24 Vince Carter/100 4.00 10.00
25 Paul Pierce/100 4.00 10.00
26 Brook Lopez/100 3.00 8.00
28 Antawn Jamison/100 3.00 8.00
29 David West/100 3.00 8.00
30 Carmelo Anthony/100 4.00 10.00
31 Troy Murphy/100 2.00 5.00
32 Rashard Lewis/100 2.50 6.00
33 Elton Brand/100 3.00 8.00
34 Josh Smith/100 3.00 8.00
35 Baron Davis/100 3.00 8.00
36 Ray Allen/100 3.00 8.00
37 Carlos Boozer/100 3.00 8.00
38 David Lee/100 2.50 6.00
40 Rajon Rondo/100 4.00 10.00
41 O.J. Mayo/100 3.00 8.00
42 Nene/100 2.50 6.00
43 Andrea Bargnani/100 2.50 6.00
44 Charlie Villanueva/100 2.50 6.00
45 Ben Gordon/100 3.00 8.00
46 Mike Bibby/100 2.50 6.00
48 Andrew Bynum/100 4.00 10.00
49 Russell Westbrook/100 5.00 12.00
50 Anthony Randolph/100 2.50 6.00
51 Eric Gordon/100 3.00 8.00
52 Jeff Green/100 2.50 6.00
53 Shaquille O'Neal/100 6.00 15.00
54 Aaron Brooks/100 2.00 5.00
55 Chris Kaman/100 2.50 6.00
56 D.J. Augustin/100 2.50 6.00
57 Emeka Okafor/100 3.00 8.00
61 Kevin Love/100 5.00 12.00
63 Michael Beasley/100 3.00 8.00
64 Richard Hamilton/100 2.50 6.00
67 Rudy Fernandez/100 2.50 6.00
68 Ryan Gomes/100 2.00 5.00
69 Shane Battier/100 3.00 8.00
70 T.J. Ford/100 2.00 5.00
71 Tracy McGrady/100 3.00 8.00
73 Greg Oden/100 2.50 6.00
80 John Havlicek/50 6.00 15.00
91 Wes Unseld/50 4.00 10.00

2009-10 Timeless Treasures Materials Jerseys Ink

STATED PRINT RUN ONE TO 100 SER.#'d SETS
SOME UNPRICED DUE TO SCARCITY
1 Kobe Bryant/100 100.00 200.00
3 Danny Granger/50 8.00 20.00
5 Chris Bosh/50 15.00 30.00
7 Deron Williams/50 12.50 30.00
10 Jason Kidd/25 25.00 50.00
11 Devin Harris/50 8.00 20.00
15 Ray Allen/50 25.00 50.00
18 Rajon Rondo/50 25.00 50.00
20 Tony Parker/45 10.00 25.00
22 Russell Westbrook/50 20.00 50.00
23 Eric Gordon/50 12.50 30.00
25 Tracy McGrady/50 15.00 30.00
27 Tyreke Evans/50 30.00 80.00
28 Brandon Jennings/100 12.00 30.00
29 Blake Griffin/100 100.00 200.00
30 Omri Casspi/50 8.00 20.00

2009-10 Timeless Treasures Materials Jerseys Prime Ink

STATED PRINT RUN ONE TO 25 SER.#'d SETS
SOME UNPRICED DUE TO SCARCITY
1 Kobe Bryant/25 200.00 350.00
3 Danny Granger/25 10.00 25.00
5 Chris Bosh/25 20.00 50.00
7 Deron Williams/25 15.00 40.00
11 Devin Harris/25 10.00 25.00
15 Ray Allen/25 30.00 60.00
16 Carlos Boozer/25 15.00 30.00
17 David Lee/25 10.00 25.00
18 Rajon Rondo/25 30.00 80.00
20 Tony Parker/25 20.00 40.00
22 Russell Westbrook/25 40.00 100.00
23 Eric Gordon/25 15.00 40.00
27 Tyreke Evans/25 75.00 150.00
28 Brandon Jennings/25 30.00 80.00
29 Blake Griffin/25 200.00 400.00
30 Omri Casspi/25 15.00 30.00

2009-10 Timeless Treasures MVP Materials

STATED PRINT RUN 10 TO 100 SER.#'d SETS
SOME UNPRICED DUE TO SCARCITY
TAGS NBA LOGO PRINT RUN ONE TO TWO SETS
TAGS NBA LOGO SIGS PRINT RUN ONE SET
TAGS TEAM LOGO PRINT RUN 1 TO 2 SETS
TAGS SIGS PRINT RUN 1 TO 4 SETS
TAGS TEAM LOGO SIGS PRINT RUN ONE SET
TAGS NOT PRICED DUE TO SCARCITY
1 Dirk Nowitzki/100 5.00 12.00
2 LeBron James/90 10.00 25.00
3 Kobe Bryant/100 10.00 25.00
6 Larry Bird/100 12.00 30.00
7 Karl Malone/100 5.00 12.00

2009-10 Timeless Treasures MVP Materials Prime

PRINT RUNS 10 TO 25 SER.#'d SETS
SOME UNPRICED DUE TO SCARCITY
2 LeBron James/25 25.00 60.00
5 Tim Duncan/25 12.00 30.00
7 Karl Malone/25 10.00 25.00

2009-10 Timeless Treasures MVP Materials MVP

STATED PRINT RUN 5 TO 25 SER.#'d SETS
SOME UNPRICED DUE TO SCARCITY
1 Dirk Nowitzki/25 8.00 20.00
2 LeBron James/25 15.00 40.00
3 Kobe Bryant/25 15.00 40.00
6 Larry Bird/25 15.00 40.00
7 Karl Malone/25 10.00 25.00

2009-10 Timeless Treasures MVP Materials MVP Prime

STATED PRINT RUN 5 TO 25 SER.#'d SETS
SOME UNPRICED DUE TO SCARCITY
5 Tim Duncan/25 20.00 50.00
7 Karl Malone/25 15.00 40.00

2009-10 Timeless Treasures MVP Materials Quads

UNPRICED PRIME PRINT RUN 10 SETS
1 Dirk Nowitzki/25 30.00 60.00
Kobe Bryant
LeBron James
Steve Nash

2009-10 Timeless Treasures MVP Materials Signatures

STATED PRINT RUN 25 SER.#'d SETS
UNPRICED PRIME PRINT RUN 10 SER.#'d SETS
1 Dirk Nowitzki/25 50.00 120.00
3 Kobe Bryant/25 100.00 200.00
6 Larry Bird/25 50.00 100.00

2009-10 Timeless Treasures NBA Apprentice Materials

STATED PRINT RUN 100 SER.#'d SETS
*PRIME: .75X TO 2X BASE HI
PRIME PRINT RUNS 1 TO 99 SER.#'d SETS
SOME PRIME UNPRICED DUE TO SCARCITY
TAGS PRINT RUN ONE SET
TAGS NBA LOGO PRINT RUN ONE SET
TAGS NBA LOGO SIGS PRINT RUN ONE SET
TAGS SIGS PRINT RUN ONE SET
TAGS TEAM LOGO PRINT RUN ONE SET
TAGS TEAM LOGO SIGS PRINT RUN ONE SET
TAGS NOT PRICED DUE TO SCARCITY
1 Blake Griffin 12.50 30.00
2 Hasheem Thabeet 2.50 6.00
3 James Harden 8.00 20.00
4 Tyreke Evans 6.00 15.00
5 Jonny Flynn 2.50 6.00
6 Stephen Curry 6.00 15.00
7 Jordan Hill 2.50 6.00
8 DeMar DeRozan 4.00 10.00
9 Brandon Jennings 5.00 12.00
10 Terrence Williams 2.50 6.00
11 Gerald Henderson 2.50 6.00
12 Tyler Hansbrough 4.00 10.00
13 Earl Clark 2.50 6.00
14 Austin Daye 2.50 6.00
15 James Johnson 2.50 6.00
16 Jrue Holiday 5.00 12.00
17 Ty Lawson 4.00 10.00
18 Jeff Teague 3.00 8.00
19 Eric Maynor 2.50 6.00
20 Darren Collison 4.00 10.00
21 Omri Casspi 2.50 6.00
22 B.J. Mullens 2.50 6.00
23 Rodrigue Beaubois 3.00 8.00
24 Taj Gibson 3.00 8.00
25 DeMarre Carroll 2.50 6.00
26 Wayne Ellington 2.50 6.00
27 Toney Douglas 2.50 6.00
28 Jeff Pendergraph 2.50 6.00
29 Jermaine Taylor 2.50 6.00
30 DaJuan Summers 2.50 6.00
31 Sam Young 2.50 6.00
32 DeJuan Blair 3.00 8.00
33 Jodie Meeks 3.00 8.00
34 Chase Budinger 2.50 6.00
35 Taylor Griffin 2.50 6.00

2009-10 Timeless Treasures NBA Apprentice Materials Signatures

STATED PRINT RUN 50 SER.#'d SETS
UNPRICED PRIME PRINT RUN 10 SER.#'d SETS
1 Blake Griffin 100.00 200.00
2 Hasheem Thabeet 5.00 12.00
3 James Harden 20.00 50.00
4 Tyreke Evans 12.00 30.00
5 Jonny Flynn 5.00 12.00
6 Stephen Curry 12.00 30.00
7 Jordan Hill 5.00 12.00
9 Brandon Jennings 10.00 25.00
10 Terrence Williams 5.00 12.00
11 Gerald Henderson 5.00 12.00
12 Tyler Hansbrough 8.00 20.00
13 Earl Clark 5.00 12.00
14 Austin Daye 5.00 12.00
16 Jrue Holiday 10.00 25.00
18 Jeff Teague 6.00 15.00
19 Eric Maynor 5.00 12.00
20 Darren Collison 8.00 20.00
21 Omri Casspi 5.00 12.00
22 B.J. Mullens 5.00 12.00
23 Rodrigue Beaubois 6.00 15.00
24 Taj Gibson 6.00 15.00
25 DeMarre Carroll 5.00 12.00
26 Wayne Ellington 5.00 12.00
27 Toney Douglas 5.00 12.00
28 Jeff Pendergraph 5.00 12.00
30 DaJuan Summers 5.00 12.00
31 Sam Young 5.00 12.00
32 DeJuan Blair 6.00 15.00
33 Jodie Meeks 6.00 15.00
34 Chase Budinger 5.00 12.00
35 Taylor Griffin 5.00 12.00

2009-10 Timeless Treasures NBA Apprentice Combo Materials

STATED PRINT RUN 100 SER.#'d SETS
UNPRICED PRIME PRINT RUN 10 SER.#'d SETS
1 Blake Griffin 12.00 30.00
Brandon Jennings
2 Blake Griffin 12.00 30.00
Tyreke Evans
3 Brandon Jennings 5.00 12.00
Tyreke Evans
4 James Johnson 2.50 6.00
Taj Gibson
5 Hasheem Thabeet 2.00 5.00
Sam Young
6 Brandon Jennings 4.00 10.00
Jodie Meeks
7 Jonny Flynn 2.00 5.00
Wayne Ellington
8 Jordan Hill 2.00 5.00
Toney Douglas
9 James Harden 6.00 15.00
B.J. Mullens
10 Tyreke Evans 5.00 12.00
Omri Casspi
11 Ty Lawson 5.00 12.00
Tyreke Evans
12 Ty Lawson 4.00 10.00

Brandon Jennings
Stephen Curry 5.00 12.00
Jonny Flynn
James Harden 6.00 15.00
Stephen Curry
Omri Casspi 2.50 6.00
DeJuan Blair

2009-10 Timeless Treasures NBA Apprentice Combo Signatures

TATED PRINT RUN 25 SER.#'d SETS
Blake Griffin 75.00 150.00
Taylor Griffin
Hasheem Thabeet 8.00 20.00
Sam Young
James Harden 12.00 30.00
B.J. Mullens
Tyreke Evans 30.00 80.00
Omri Casspi
Jonny Flynn 8.00 20.00
Wayne Ellington
Jordan Hill 8.00 20.00
Toney Douglas
Brandon Jennings 15.00 40.00
Jodie Meeks
Tyler Hansbrough 12.50 30.00
A.J. Price
0 Earl Clark 8.00 20.00
Taylor Griffin
2 James Johnson 10.00 25.00
Taj Gibson
3 Darren Collison 15.00 40.00
Marcus Thornton
6 Hasheem Thabeet 8.00 20.00
A.J. Price
9 DeJuan Blair 8.00 20.00
Sam Young
20 Jordan Hill 8.00 20.00
Chase Budinger
21 Earl Clark 10.00 25.00
Terrence Williams
22 Jrue Holiday 15.00 30.00
Darren Collison
23 James Harden 12.00 30.00
Jeff Pendergraph
24 Brandon Jennings 75.00 150.00
Tyreke Evans
25 Blake Griffin 100.00 200.00
Tyler Hansbrough

2009-10 Timeless Treasures NBA Apprentice Quad Materials

STATED PRINT RUN 100 SER.#'d SETS
UNPRICED PRIME PRINT RUN ONE TO 10 SETS
1 Blake Griffin 12.50 30.00
Hasheem Thabeet
James Harden
Tyreke Evans
2 Jonny Flynn 6.00 15.00
Stephen Curry
Jordan Hill
DeMar DeRozan
3 Brandon Jennings 5.00 12.00
Terrence Williams
Gerald Henderson
Tyler Hansbrough
4 Blake Griffin 12.50 30.00
Jordan Hill
DeJuan Blair
Tyler Hansbrough
5 Tyreke Evans 6.00 15.00
Jonny Flynn
Brandon Jennings
Ty Lawson
6 Brandon Jennings 6.00 15.00
Tyreke Evans
James Harden
Ty Lawson
7 Darren Collison 5.00 12.00
DeJuan Blair
Jonny Flynn
Omri Casspi
8 DeJuan Blair 12.50 30.00
Omri Casspi
Tyler Hansbrough
Blake Griffin
9 Eric Maynor 5.00 12.00
Darren Collison
Stephen Curry
Toney Douglas
10 Blake Griffin 12.50 30.00
James Harden
Tyreke Evans
Brandon Jennings
11 DeMar DeRozan 5.00 12.00
Jordan Hill
Jrue Holiday
Terrence Williams
12 Taj Gibson 5.00 12.00
Brandon Jennings
Tyler Hansbrough
James Johnson
13 Ty Lawson 5.00 12.00
Wayne Ellington
James Harden
Jonny Flynn
14 DeJuan Blair 5.00 12.00
Chase Budinger
Hasheem Thabeet
Darren Collison
15 Blake Griffin 12.50 30.00
Omri Casspi
Stephen Curry
Tyreke Evans

2009-10 Timeless Treasures NBA Apprentice Triple Materials

STATED PRINT RUN 100 SER.#'d SETS
UNPRICED PRIME PRINT RUN ONE TO 10 SETS
1 Tyler Hansbrough 5.00 12.00
Ty Lawson
Wayne Ellington
2 Blake Griffin 10.00 25.00
Hasheem Thabeet
James Harden
3 Tyreke Evans 5.00 12.00
Jonny Flynn
Stephen Curry
4 Jordan Hill 5.00 12.00
DeMar DeRozan
Brandon Jennings
5 Terrence Williams 5.00 12.00
Gerald Henderson
Tyler Hansbrough
6 Blake Griffin 10.00 25.00
Tyreke Evans
Brandon Jennings
7 Tyreke Evans 5.00 12.00
Jonny Flynn
Brandon Jennings
8 Tyreke Evans 5.00 12.00
Ty Lawson
Brandon Jennings
9 James Harden 5.00 12.00
Stephen Curry
Chase Budinger
10 Blake Griffin 10.00 25.00
Tyler Hansbrough
DeJuan Blair
11 Omri Casspi 6.00 15.00
Blake Griffin
DeJuan Blair
12 Ty Lawson 5.00 12.00
Jonny Flynn
Stephen Curry
13 Tyreke Evans 5.00 12.00
Brandon Jennings
Omri Casspi
14 Tyreke Evans 5.00 12.00
Ty Lawson
Omri Casspi
15 Blake Griffin 10.00 25.00
Tyler Hansbrough
Omri Casspi

2009-10 Timeless Treasures Private Signings

STATED PRINT RUN 20 TO 100 SER.#'d SETS
1 Kobe Bryant/100 100.00 200.00
2 Steve Nash/20 40.00 100.00
3 Tracy McGrady/25 12.00 30.00
4 Danny Granger/25 10.00 25.00
5 Carmelo Anthony/25 25.00 50.00
6 Bill Russell/25 50.00 120.00
7 Bill Walton/25 15.00 30.00
8 Bob Cousy/25 20.00 50.00
9 Chris Bosh/20 20.00 40.00
10 Dave Cowens/25 15.00 30.00
11 David Thompson/25 10.00 25.00
12 Dennis Rodman/25 25.00 60.00
13 Isiah Thomas/25 10.00 25.00
14 Jerry West/25 30.00 60.00
15 John Havlicek/25 20.00 40.00
16 Kareem Abdul-Jabbar/25 40.00 80.00
17 Kevin Love/25 20.00 50.00
18 Kevin McHale/25 25.00 60.00
19 Larry Bird/25 40.00 100.00
20 Magic Johnson/25 40.00 100.00
21 Dominique Wilkins/20 12.00 30.00
22 Nate Thurmond/25 10.00 25.00
23 Oscar Robertson/25 40.00 80.00
24 Pau Gasol/25 30.00 60.00
25 Rajon Rondo/25 25.00 50.00
26 Ray Allen/25 25.00 60.00
27 Rick Barry/25 10.00 25.00
28 Robert Parish/25 10.00 25.00
29 Scottie Pippen/25 150.00 300.00
30 Tony Parker/20 15.00 30.00

2009-10 Timeless Treasures Rookie Year Materials

STATED PRINT RUN 25 TO 100 SER.#'d SETS
*PRIME: 1X TO 2.5X BASE HI
PRIME PRINT RUN 25 SER.#'d SETS
TAGS PRINT RUN ONE TO 6 SETS
TAGS NBA LOGO PRINT RUN 1 TO 3 SETS
TAGS NBA LOGO SIG.PRINT RUN ONE TO 3 SETS
TAGS SIGS PRINT RUN ONE TO 9 SETS
TAGS TEAM LOGO PRINT RUN 1 TO 3 SETS
TAGS TEAM LOGO SIG.PRINT RUN 1 TO 3 SETS
NBA LOGO PRINT RUN ONE TO 4 SETS
NBA LOGO SIGS PRINT RUN ONE TO 4 SETS
TAGS AND LOGOS UNPRICED DUE TO SCARCITY
1 Dwight Howard/50 5.00 12.00
2 Chris Paul/50 5.00 12.00
3 LeBron James/100 10.00 25.00
4 Kobe Bryant/100 10.00 25.00
5 Brandon Roy/100 3.00 8.00
6 Derrick Rose/50 10.00 25.00
7 Carmelo Anthony/100 4.00 10.00
8 Andre Iguodala/100 3.00 8.00
9 Shaquille O'Neal/100 6.00 15.00
10 Deron Williams/100 3.00 8.00
11 Kevin Garnett/100 6.00 15.00
12 Kevin Durant/100 10.00 25.00
13 Brandon Jennings/25 10.00 25.00
14 Dikembe Mutombo/100 6.00 15.00
15 Tracy McGrady/100 3.00 8.00

2009-10 Timeless Treasures Rookie Year Materials Signatures

STATED PRINT RUN ONE TO 50 SER.#'d SETS
SOME UNPRICED DUE TO SCARCITY
4 Kobe Bryant/50 100.00 225.00
6 Derrick Rose/25 125.00 250.00
10 Deron Williams/25 15.00 30.00
13 Brandon Jennings/25 25.00 60.00
14 Dikembe Mutombo/25 30.00 60.00
15 Tracy McGrady/25 25.00 50.00

2009-10 Timeless Treasures Rookie Year Materials Prime Signatures

STATED PRINT RUN ONE TO 25 SER.#'d SETS
SOME UNPRICED DUE TO SCARCITY
4 Kobe Bryant/25 200.00 350.00
6 Derrick Rose/25 150.00 300.00

2009-10 Timeless Treasures Rookie Year Materials Quads

STATED PRINT RUN 25 SER.#'d SETS
UNPRICED PRIME PRINT RUN 5 SER.#'d SETS
1 LeBron James 25.00 50.00
Kobe Bryant
Chris Paul
Dwight Howard
2 Kevin Garnett 40.00 100.00
Shaquille O'Neal
Kobe Bryant
LeBron James
3 LeBron James 15.00 30.00
Dwight Howard
Andre Iguodala
Carmelo Anthony
4 Kevin Garnett 25.00 60.00
Shaquille O'Neal
Tracy McGrady
Kobe Bryant
5 Kevin Garnett 30.00 80.00
Dwight Howard
Dikembe Mutombo
Shaquille O'Neal

2009-10 Timeless Treasures Rookie Year Materials ROY

STATED PRINT RUN 25 TO 100 SER.#'d SETS
2 Chris Paul/25 12.50 30.00
3 LeBron James/100 15.00 40.00
5 Brandon Roy/25 6.00 15.00
9 Shaquille O'Neal/100 15.00 40.00
12 Kevin Durant/100 12.50 30.00

2009-10 Timeless Treasures Rookie Year Materials ROY Prime

STATED PRINT RUN ONE TO 25 SER.#'d SETS
SOME UNPRICED DUE TO SCARCITY
2 Chris Paul/25 20.00 40.00
3 LeBron James/25 40.00 100.00
12 Kevin Durant/25 25.00 60.00

2009-10 Timeless Treasures Rookie Year Materials ROY Prime Signatures

STATED PRINT RUN 25 SER.#'d SETS
UNPRICED ROY SIG PRINT RUN 10 SETS
6 Derrick Rose/25 250.00 400.00

2009-10 Timeless Treasures Signatures Silver

STATED PRINT RUN 25 TO 100 SER.#'d SETS
UNPRICED GOLD PRINT RUN 10 SER.#'d SETS
UNPRICED PLATINUM PRINT RUN ONE SET
1 Kobe Bryant 100.00 200.00
7 Danny Granger 5.00 12.00
9 Pau Gasol 25.00 50.00
11 Chris Bosh 12.50 30.00
15 Deron Williams 10.00 25.00
21 Devin Harris 5.00 12.00
36 Ray Allen 20.00 50.00
39 Derrick Rose 75.00 150.00
40 Rajon Rondo 20.00 40.00
41 O.J. Mayo 15.00 30.00
44 Charlie Villanueva 5.00 12.00
47 Tony Parker 8.00 20.00
49 Russell Westbrook 15.00 40.00
51 Eric Gordon 6.00 15.00
54 Aaron Brooks 5.00 12.00
56 D.J. Augustin 5.00 12.00
57 Emeka Okafor 6.00 15.00
59 Jermaine O'Neal 6.00 15.00
60 Josh Howard 5.00 12.00
61 Kevin Love 15.00 40.00
63 Michael Beasley 8.00 20.00
66 Ronnie Brewer 5.00 12.00
68 Ryan Gomes 8.00 20.00
69 Shane Battier 5.00 12.00
70 T.J. Ford 5.00 12.00
71 Tracy McGrady 15.00 40.00
72 Trevor Ariza 6.00 15.00
74 Nate Archibald 8.00 20.00
75 Al Cervi 6.00 15.00
76 Bob Cousy 20.00 50.00
77 Harry Gallatin 5.00 12.00
78 Gail Goodrich 8.00 20.00
79 Hal Greer 8.00 20.00
80 John Havlicek 15.00 30.00
82 Elvin Hayes 5.00 12.00
83 Bob McAdoo 10.00 25.00
86 Dolph Schayes 8.00 20.00
87 Bill Sharman 8.00 20.00
88 David Thompson 8.00 20.00
89 Nate Thurmond 8.00 20.00
91 Wes Unseld 6.00 15.00
92 Bill Walton 10.00 25.00
93 Bobby Wanzer 6.00 15.00
94 Frank Ramsey 10.00 25.00
95 Willis Reed 8.00 20.00
96 Pat Riley 15.00 30.00
98 Oscar Robertson 30.00 60.00
99 Lenny Wilkens 6.00 15.00
100 James Worthy 20.00 50.00

2009-10 Timeless Treasures Souvenir Cuts

STATED PRINT RUN ONE TO 25 SER.#'d SETS
SOME UNPRICED DUE TO SCARCITY
1 George Mikan/25 100.00 200.00
8 Hank Luisetti/15 50.00 125.00
9 Andy Phillip/15 100.00 175.00
13 Paul Arizin/25 30.00 60.00

2009-10 Timeless Treasures Souvenir Cuts Materials

STATED PRINT RUN 25 SER.#'d SETS
1 George Mikan/25 125.00 250.00

2009-10 Timeless Treasures Statistical Champions Materials

STATED PRINT RUN 50 TO 100 SER.#'d SETS
UNPRICED PRIME PRINT RUN 10 SER.#'d SETS
1 George Gervin/50 5.00 12.00
2 John Stockton/50 6.00 15.00
3 Dwight Howard/100 5.00 12.00
4 Kobe Bryant/100 10.00 25.00
5 Chris Paul/100 5.00 12.00

2009-10 Timeless Treasures Statistical Champions Materials Signatures

STATED PRINT RUN 50 SER.#'d SETS
UNPRICED PRIME PRINT RUN 10 SER.#'d SETS
1 George Gervin/50 15.00 40.00
4 Kobe Bryant/50 100.00 200.00

2010-11 Timeless Treasures

COMP.SET w/o RCs (100) 50.00 100.00
UNPRICED GOLD PRINT RUN 10 SETS
UNPRICED PLATINUM PRINT RUN ONE SET
1 Kobe Bryant 5.00 12.00
2 Pau Gasol 1.00 2.50
3 Derek Fisher .75 2.00
4 Andrew Bynum 1.25 3.00
5 Caron Butler 1.00 2.50
6 Dirk Nowitzki 1.25 3.00
7 Jason Kidd 1.00 2.50
8 Jason Terry .75 2.00
9 Grant Hill 1.25 3.00
10 Jason Richardson 1.00 2.50
11 Robin Lopez .60 1.50
12 Steve Nash 1.00 2.50
13 Carmelo Anthony 1.25 3.00
14 Chauncey Billups 1.00 2.50
15 Chris Andersen 1.00 2.50
16 Nene .75 2.00
17 Al Jefferson 1.00 2.50
18 Deron Williams 1.00 2.50
19 Mehmet Okur .60 1.50
20 Paul Millsap .75 2.00
21 Brandon Roy 1.00 2.50
22 Greg Oden .75 2.00
23 LaMarcus Aldridge 1.00 2.50
24 Marcus Camby .60 1.50
25 George Hill .75 2.00
26 Manu Ginobili 1.00 2.50
27 Tim Duncan 1.50 4.00
28 Tony Parker 1.00 2.50
29 James Harden 1.25 3.00
30 Jeff Green .75 2.00
31 Kevin Durant 3.00 8.00
32 Russell Westbrook 1.25 3.00
33 Aaron Brooks .60 1.50
34 Kevin Martin 1.00 2.50
35 Luis Scola .75 2.00
36 Yao Ming 1.25 3.00
37 Marc Gasol 1.00 2.50
38 Rudy Gay 1.00 2.50
39 Zach Randolph .75 2.00
40 Chris Paul 1.50 4.00
41 Marcus Thornton 1.00 2.50
42 Trevor Ariza .60 1.50
43 Chris Kaman .75 2.00
44 Eric Gordon 1.00 2.50
45 Baron Davis 1.00 2.50
46 David Lee .75 2.00
47 Monta Ellis 1.00 2.50
48 Stephen Curry 1.25 3.00
49 Carl Landry .60 1.50
50 Samuel Dalembert .60 1.50
51 Tyreke Evans 1.25 3.00
52 Kevin Love 1.25 3.00
53 Michael Beasley 1.00 2.50
54 Sebastian Telfair .60 1.50
55 Anderson Varejao .75 2.00
56 Antawn Jamison 1.00 2.50
57 Mo Williams .75 2.00
58 Dwight Howard 1.50 4.00
59 J.J. Redick 1.00 2.50
60 Vince Carter 1.25 3.00
61 Al Horford .75 2.00
62 Joe Johnson 1.00 2.50
63 Josh Smith 1.00 2.50
64 Kendrick Perkins .75 2.00
65 Paul Pierce 1.25 3.00
66 Rajon Rondo 1.25 3.00
67 Shaquille O'Neal 2.00 5.00
68 Chris Bosh 1.00 2.50
69 Dwyane Wade 2.00 5.00
70 LeBron James 5.00 12.00
71 Andrew Bogut 1.00 2.50
72 Brandon Jennings 1.00 2.50
73 Michael Redd 1.00 2.50
74 D.J. Augustin .75 2.00
75 Gerald Wallace 1.00 2.50
76 Stephen Jackson .75 2.00
77 Carlos Boozer 1.00 2.50
78 Derrick Rose 3.00 8.00
79 Luol Deng 1.00 2.50
80 Andrea Bargnani .75 2.00
81 DeMar DeRozan 1.00 2.50
82 Leandro Barbosa .75 2.00
83 Danny Granger 1.00 2.50
84 Darren Collison 1.00 2.50
85 Troy Murphy .60 1.50
86 Amare Stoudemire 1.00 2.50
87 Anthony Randolph .75 2.00
88 Danilo Gallinari 1.00 2.50
89 Ben Wallace 1.00 2.50
90 Richard Hamilton .75 2.00
91 Tracy McGrady 1.00 2.50
92 Andre Iguodala 1.00 2.50
93 Louis Williams .75 2.00
94 Thaddeus Young .60 1.50
95 Al Thornton .75 2.00
96 JaVale McGee .75 2.00
97 Josh Howard .75 2.00
98 Anthony Morrow .60 1.50
99 Brook Lopez 1.00 2.50
100 Devin Harris 1.00 2.50
101 John Wall AU/299 RC 40.00 100.00
102 Evan Turner AU/299 RC 10.00 25.00
103 Derrick Favors AU/299 RC 8.00 20.00
104 Wesley Johnson AU/299 RC 6.00 15.00
105 DeMarcus Cousins AU/299 RC 12.00 30.00
106 Ekpe Udoh AU/299 RC 4.00 10.00
107 Greg Monroe AU/299 RC 8.00 20.00
108 Al-Farouq Aminu AU/299 RC 4.00 10.00
109 Gordon Hayward AU/299 RC 8.00 20.00
110 Paul George AU/298 RC 10.00 25.00
111 Cole Aldrich AU/299 RC 4.00 10.00
112 Xavier Henry AU/299 RC 5.00 12.00
113 Ed Davis AU/298 RC 5.00 12.00
114 Patrick Patterson AU/299 RC 6.00 15.00
115 Larry Sanders AU/299 RC 4.00 10.00
116 Luke Babbitt AU/299 RC 4.00 10.00
117 Kevin Seraphin AU/299 RC 5.00 12.00
118 Eric Bledsoe AU/299 RC 6.00 15.00
119 Avery Bradley AU/299 RC 8.00 20.00
120 James Anderson AU/299 RC 4.00 10.00
121 Craig Brackins AU/299 RC 4.00 10.00
122 Elliot Williams AU/299 RC 4.00 10.00
123 Trevor Booker AU/299 RC 4.00 10.00
124 Damion James AU/299 RC 4.00 10.00
125 Dominique Jones AU/299 RC 4.00 10.00
126 Quincy Pondexter AU/299 RC 4.00 10.00
127 Jordan Crawford AU/299 RC 6.00 15.00
128 Greivis Vasquez AU/299 RC 5.00 12.00
129 Daniel Orton AU/299 RC 4.00 10.00
130 Lazar Hayward AU/299 RC 4.00 10.00
131 Jeremy Lin AU/299 RC 75.00 200.00
132 Dexter Pittman AU/299 RC 4.00 10.00
133 Hassan Whiteside AU/286 RC 4.00 10.00
134 Armon Johnson AU/299 RC 4.00 10.00
135 Terrico White AU/299 RC 4.00 10.00
136 Darington Hobson AU/298 RC 4.00 10.00
137 Andy Rautins AU/297 RC 4.00 10.00
138 Landry Fields AU/299 RC 6.00 15.00
139 Lance Stephenson AU/299 RC 4.00 10.00
140 Jarvis Varnado AU/299 RC 4.00 10.00
141 Sherron Collins AU/299 RC 4.00 10.00
142 Devin Ebanks AU/299 RC 5.00 12.00
143 Gani Lawal AU/249 RC 4.00 10.00
144 Timofey Mozgov AU/299 RC 4.00 10.00
145 Solomon Alabi AU/299 RC 4.00 10.00
146 Luke Harangody AU/299 RC 4.00 10.00
147 Willie Warren AU/298 RC 4.00 10.00
148 Jeremy Evans AU/299 RC 4.00 10.00
149 Derrick Caracter AU/299 RC 4.00 10.00
150 Stanley Robinson AU/299 RC 4.00 10.00

2010-11 Timeless Treasures Silver

*1-100 SILVER: 1.5X TO 4X BASE HI
*101-150 SILVER: .6X TO 1.5X BASE HI
STATED PRINT RUN 25 SER.#'d SETS
9 Grant Hill 8.00 20.00
131 Jeremy Lin AU 200.00 400.00

2010-11 Timeless Treasures Championship Season Materials

STATED PRINT RUN 10 TO 99 SER.#'d SETS
SOME UNPRICED DUE TO SCARCITY
UNPRICED LOGOMAN PRINT RUN ONE SET
UNPRICED TAG PRINT RUN 1 TO 5 SETS
UNPRICED TAG TEAM LOGO ONE SET
1 Andrew Bynum/99 5.00 12.00
2 Derek Fisher/99 3.00 8.00
3 Derek Fisher/99 3.00 8.00
4 Glen Davis/99 3.00 8.00
5 Hakeem Olajuwon/99 5.00 12.00
6 Joe Dumars/99 4.00 10.00
7 Kevin Garnett/99 8.00 20.00
8 Kobe Bryant/99 10.00 25.00
9 Lamar Odom/99 4.00 10.00
10 Luke Walton/99 2.50 6.00
12 Manu Ginobili/99 4.00 10.00
13 Pau Gasol/99 4.00 10.00
14 Pau Gasol/99 4.00 10.00
16 Ron Artest/99 4.00 10.00
17 Scottie Pippen/99 8.00 20.00
18 Tim Duncan/49 6.00 15.00
19 Tim Duncan/99 6.00 15.00
20 Tony Parker/49 4.00 10.00

2010-11 Timeless Treasures Championship Season Materials Combos

STATED PRINT RUN 10 TO 25 SER.#'d SETS
SOME UNPRICED DUE TO SCARCITY
UNPRICED PRIME PRINT RUN 5 SETS
1 Andrew Bynum/25 8.00 20.00
Pau Gasol
2 Lamar Odom/25 6.00 15.00
Luke Walton
3 Derek Fisher/25 8.00 20.00
Pau Gasol
5 Tim Duncan/25 8.00 20.00
Tony Parker
7 Hakeem Olajuwon/25 15.00 40.00
Scottie Pippen
8 Derek Fisher/25 10.00 25.00
Ron Artest

2010-11 Timeless Treasures Championship Season Materials Prime

*PRIME: .6X TO 1.5X BASE HI
STATED PRINT RUN 5 TO 25 SER.#'d SETS
SOME UNPRICED DUE TO SCARCITY
6 Joe Dumars/25 8.00 20.00
13 Pau Gasol/25 8.00 20.00
14 Pau Gasol/25 8.00 20.00
15 Ray Allen/25 6.00 15.00

2010-11 Timeless Treasures Championship Season Materials Quads

STATED PRINT RUN 10 TO 25 SER.#'d SETS
SOME UNPRICED DUE TO SCARCITY
UNPRICED PRIME PRINT RUN 5 SER.#'d SETS
1 Andrew Bynum/25 15.00 40.00
Derek Fisher
Kobe Bryant
Lamar Odom
2 Luke Walton/25 20.00 50.00
Pau Gasol
Ron Artest
Kobe Bryant

2010-11 Timeless Treasures Championship Season Materials Signatures

STATED PRINT RUN 10 TO 25 SER.#'d SETS
SOME UNPRICED DUE TO SCARCITY
2 Derek Fisher/25 20.00 50.00
3 Derek Fisher/25 20.00 50.00
8 Kobe Bryant/25 100.00 200.00
16 Ron Artest/25 15.00 40.00
17 Scottie Pippen/25 125.00 250.00
20 Tony Parker/25 10.00 25.00

2010-11 Timeless Treasures Championship Season Materials Triple

STATED PRINT RUN 10 TO 25 SER.#'d SETS
SOME UNPRICED DUE TO SCARCITY
UNPRICED PRIME PRINT RUN 5 SER.#'d SETS
1 Manu Ginobili/25 10.00 25.00
Tim Duncan
Tony Parker
2 Glen Davis/25 10.00 25.00
Kevin Garnett
Ray Allen

2010-11 Timeless Treasures HOF Materials Combos

STATED PRINT RUN 25 TO 50 SER.#'d SETS
1 Larry Bird/50 15.00 40.00
Magic Johnson
2 John Stockton/50 10.00 25.00
Karl Malone
3 Isiah Thomas/25 6.00 15.00
Joe Dumars
5 Dave Cowens/50 6.00 15.00
Robert Parish
6 Scottie Pippen/50 8.00 20.00
Clyde Drexler
7 Moses Malone/25 6.00 15.00
Karl Malone
9 Dominique Wilkins/50 10.00 25.00
Scottie Pippen
10 George Mikan/50 15.00 40.00
Kareem Abdul-Jabbar

2010-11 Timeless Treasures HOF Materials Combos Prime

STATED PRINT RUN 10 TO 50 SER.#'d SETS
SOME UNPRICED DUE TO SCARCITY
1 Larry Bird/50 25.00 60.00
Magic Johnson
2 John Stockton/50 20.00 50.00
Karl Malone
3 Isiah Thomas/50 8.00 20.00
Joe Dumars
5 Dave Cowens/25 8.00 20.00
Robert Parish
7 Moses Malone/50 10.00 25.00
Karl Malone
8 Rick Barry/45 8.00 20.00
Dan Issel

2010-11 Timeless Treasures HOF Materials Jerseys

STATED PRINT RUN 5 TO 50 SER.#'d SETS
SOME UNPRICED DUE TO SCARCITY
UNPRICED PRIME PRINT RUN 5 SER.#'d SETS
5 David Robinson/50 6.00 15.00
6 Dave Cowens/50 4.00 10.00
7 Magic Johnson/50 6.00 15.00
15 Dominique Wilkins/50 5.00 12.00
21 Wes Unseld/50 4.00 10.00
28 Bob Lanier/50 4.00 10.00
33 Karl Malone/50 5.00 12.00
34 Kevin McHale/50 4.00 10.00
35 Hakeem Olajuwon/50 5.00 12.00

2010-11 Timeless Treasures HOF Materials Jerseys Signatures

STATED PRINT RUN 5 TO 25 SER.#'d SETS
SOME UNPRICED DUE TO SCARCITY
UNPRICED PRIME SIG PRINT RUN 4 TO 10 SETS
6 Dave Cowens/25 8.00 20.00
15 Dominique Wilkins/25 20.00 50.00
21 Wes Unseld/25 8.00 20.00
28 Bob Lanier/25 10.00 25.00
34 Kevin McHale/25 25.00 60.00

2010-11 Timeless Treasures HOF Materials Quads

STATED PRINT RUN 10 TO 50 SER.#'d SETS
SOME UNPRICED DUE TO SCARCITY
1 Geroge Mikan/50 20.00 50.00
Bob Lanier
Patrick Ewing
Hakeem Olajuwon
2 Larry Bird/50 20.00 50.00
Dennis Johnson
Robert Parish
Dave Cowens
3 Dominique Wilkins/50 10.00 25.00
Alex English
Kevin McHale
Karl Malone
5 Larry Bird/50 25.00 60.00
Magic Johnson
Kareem Abdul-Jabbar
Robert Parish

2010-11 Timeless Treasures HOF Materials Quads Prime

STATED PRINT RUN 5 TO 50 SER.#'d SETS
SOME UNPRICED DUE TO SCARCITY
2 Larry Bird/50 30.00 80.00
Dennis Johnson
Robert Parish
Dave Cowens
5 Larry Bird/50 40.00 100.00
Magic Johnson
Kareem Abdul-Jabbar
Robert Parish

2010-11 Timeless Treasures HOF Signatures Silver

STATED PRINT RUN 10 TO 49 SER.#'d SETS
SOME UNPRICED DUE TO SCARCITY
UNPRICED GOLD PRINT RUN 5 TO 10 SETS
UNPRICED PLATINUM PRINT RUN ONE SET
2 Bill Walton/25 10.00 25.00
3 Elgin Baylor/25 12.50 30.00
4 Calvin Murphy/25 6.00 15.00
6 Dave Cowens/25 8.00 20.00
9 James Worthy/25 25.00 60.00
10 Bobby Wanzer/25 6.00 15.00
11 David Thompson/25 6.00 15.00
12 Adrian Dantley/25 6.00 15.00
13 Clyde Drexler/25 25.00 60.00
17 Joe Dumars/25 12.50 30.00
18 Oscar Robertson/25 40.00 100.00
19 Rick Barry/25 6.00 15.00
20 Gail Goodrich/49 6.00 15.00
21 Wes Unseld/25 8.00 20.00
22 K.C. Jones/25 6.00 15.00
23 Bob McAdoo/25 15.00 40.00
24 Dolph Schayes/25 6.00 15.00
25 Lenny Wilkens/25 6.00 15.00
26 Jerry West/25 30.00 80.00
27 Elvin Hayes/25 10.00 25.00
28 Bob Lanier/25 6.00 15.00
29 Sam Jones/25 12.00 30.00
30 Connie Hawkins/25 12.00 30.00
31 Hal Greer/25 6.00 15.00
32 George Gervin/25 15.00 40.00
34 Kevin McHale/25 20.00 50.00

2010-11 Timeless Treasures Home and Road Gamers

STATED PRINT RUN 10 TO 99 SER.#'d SETS
SOME UNPRICED DUE TO SCARCITY
UNPRICED PRIME PRINT RUN 1 TO 10 SETS
1 Hakeem Olajuwon/99 5.00 12.00
3 Dominique Wilkins/99 5.00 12.00
4 Kevin McHale/99 4.00 10.00
5 Dikembe Mutombo/99 4.00 10.00
6 Sleepy Floyd/49 4.00 10.00
7 Gary Payton/99 4.00 10.00
8 Glen Rice/99 4.00 10.00
9 Patrick Ewing/99 8.00 20.00
11 Karl Malone/99 5.00 12.00
12 Joe Johnson/49 4.00 10.00
13 Mike Bibby/99 3.00 8.00
14 Paul Pierce/99 5.00 12.00
15 Boris Diaw/99 3.00 8.00
16 Joakim Noah/99 4.00 10.00
17 Dirk Nowitzki/99 5.00 12.00
18 Jason Terry/99 3.00 8.00
19 Chris Andersen/99 4.00 10.00
20 J.R. Smith/99 4.00 10.00
21 Jeff Foster/99 2.50 6.00
22 Eric Gordon/49 4.00 10.00
23 Pau Gasol/99 4.00 10.00
25 Michael Redd/99 4.00 10.00
26 David West/99 4.00 10.00
27 James Harden/99 5.00 12.00
28 Dwight Howard/99 6.00 15.00
29 Jameer Nelson/99 3.00 8.00
30 LaMarcus Aldridge/99 4.00 10.00

2010-11 Timeless Treasures Home and Road Gamers Signatures

STATED PRINT RUN 10 TO 25 SER.#'d SETS
SOME UNPRICED DUE TO SCARCITY
UNPRICED PRIME PRINT RUN 5 TO 10 SETS
3 Dominique Wilkins/25 20.00 50.00
4 Kevin McHale/25 25.00 60.00
5 Dikembe Mutombo/25 20.00 50.00
6 Sleepy Floyd/25 10.00 25.00
7 Gary Payton/25 20.00 50.00
12 Joe Johnson/25 12.50 30.00
16 Joakim Noah/25 20.00 50.00
19 Chris Andersen/25 20.00 50.00
20 J.R. Smith/25 8.00 20.00
27 James Harden/25 12.00 30.00
30 LaMarcus Aldridge/25 12.50 30.00

2010-11 Timeless Treasures Materials Jerseys

STATED PRINT RUN ONE TO 99 SER.#'d SETS
SOME UNPRICED DUE TO SCARCITY
UNPRICED PRIME PRINT RUN 2 TO 10 SETS
UNPRICED TAG PRINT RUN ONE TO 5 SETS
UNPRICED TAG TEAM LOGO 1 TO 5 SETS
1 Kobe Bryant/99 10.00 25.00
2 Pau Gasol/49 3.00 8.00
5 Caron Butler/99 3.00 8.00
6 Dirk Nowitzki/99 4.00 10.00
7 Jason Kidd/99 3.00 8.00
8 Jason Terry/99 2.50 6.00
9 Grant Hill/99 4.00 10.00
10 Jason Richardson/99 3.00 8.00
12 Steve Nash/99 3.00 8.00
13 Carmelo Anthony/99 4.00 10.00
14 Chauncey Billups/99 3.00 8.00
16 Nene/99 2.50 6.00
17 Al Jefferson/99 3.00 8.00
18 Deron Williams/49 3.00 8.00
19 Mehmet Okur/99 2.00 5.00
21 Brandon Roy/99 3.00 8.00
22 Greg Oden/99 2.50 6.00
23 LaMarcus Aldridge/99 3.00 8.00
26 Manu Ginobili/99 3.00 8.00
27 Tim Duncan/99 5.00 12.00
28 Tony Parker/99 3.00 8.00
29 James Harden/99 4.00 10.00
32 Russell Westbrook/49 4.00 10.00
35 Luis Scola/99 2.50 6.00
37 Marc Gasol/99 3.00 8.00
38 Rudy Gay/35 3.00 8.00
39 Zach Randolph/99 2.50 6.00
40 Chris Paul/99 5.00 12.00
43 Chris Kaman/99 2.50 6.00
44 Eric Gordon/49 3.00 8.00
45 Baron Davis/99 3.00 8.00
48 Stephen Curry/30 4.00 10.00
50 Samuel Dalembert/99 2.00 5.00
51 Tyreke Evans/99 4.00 10.00
52 Kevin Love/99 4.00 10.00
56 Antawn Jamison/99 3.00 8.00
58 Dwight Howard/99 5.00 12.00
59 J.J. Redick/99 3.00 8.00
60 Vince Carter/99 4.00 10.00
61 Al Horford/99 2.50 6.00
62 Joe Johnson/99 3.00 8.00
63 Josh Smith/49 3.00 8.00
65 Paul Pierce/30 4.00 10.00
68 Chris Bosh/99 3.00 8.00
69 Dwyane Wade/99 6.00 15.00
70 LeBron James/99 10.00 25.00
72 Brandon Jennings/99 3.00 8.00
73 Michael Redd/99 3.00 8.00
74 D.J. Augustin/99 2.50 6.00
75 Gerald Wallace/25 3.00 8.00
78 Derrick Rose/99 10.00 25.00
79 Luol Deng/99 3.00 8.00
80 Andrea Bargnani/99 2.50 6.00
81 DeMar DeRozan/99 3.00 8.00
82 Leandro Barbosa/99 2.50 6.00
84 Darren Collison/49 3.00 8.00
86 Amare Stoudemire/49 3.00 8.00
88 Danilo Gallinari/99 3.00 8.00
92 Andre Iguodala/99 3.00 8.00
94 Thaddeus Young/99 2.00 5.00
97 Josh Howard/99 2.50 6.00
99 Brook Lopez/25 3.00 8.00

2010-11 Timeless Treasures Materials Jerseys Ink

STATED PRINT RUN ONE TO 99 SER.#'d SETS
SOME UNPRICED DUE TO SCARCITY
1 Al Horford/49 6.00 15.00
3 Baron Davis/49 6.00 15.00
4 Brandon Jennings/99 10.00 25.00
5 Brook Lopez/25 6.00 15.00
7 Derrick Rose/25 80.00 200.00
8 J.J. Redick/49 12.50 30.00
9 Joakim Noah/49 12.50 30.00
10 Joe Johnson/25 10.00 25.00
11 J.R. Smith/49 6.00 15.00
12 Kevin Love/49 12.50 30.00
13 LaMarcus Aldridge/49 10.00 25.00
16 Ron Artest/25 15.00 40.00
17 Stephen Curry/35 15.00 40.00
18 Steve Nash/20 30.00 80.00
19 Tony Parker/99 8.00 20.00
20 Alex English/25 8.00 20.00

21 Alvan Adams/99 6.00 15.00
22 Chris Mullin/99 15.00 40.00
24 Danny Manning/99 6.00 15.00
26 Gary Payton/49 12.50 30.00
28 John Stockton/25 40.00 100.00
29 Mark Aguirre/99 10.00 25.00
30 Robert Parish/25 8.00 20.00

2010-11 Timeless Treasures Materials Jerseys Prime Ink

STATED PRINT RUN 2 TO 25 SER.#'d SETS
SOME UNPRICED DUE TO SCARCITY
UNPRICED TAG PRINT RUN ONE TO TWO SETS
UNPRICED TAG TEAM PRINT RUN ONE SET
16 Ron Artest/20 20.00 50.00
17 Stephen Curry/25 20.00 50.00
19 Tony Parker/25 20.00 50.00
20 Alex English/25 10.00 25.00
21 Alvan Adams/25 10.00 25.00
30 Robert Parish/15 12.50 30.00

2010-11 Timeless Treasures MVP Materials

STATED PRINT RUN 10 TO 99 SER.#'d SETS
SOME UNPRICED DUE TO SCARCITY
UNPRICED LOGOMAN PRINT RUN ONE SET
UNPRICED TAG PRINT RUN ONE TO 5 SETS
UNPRICED TAG TEAM PRINT RUN ONE TO 4 SETS
1 Allen Iverson/99 5.00 12.00
2 Karl Malone/99 5.00 12.00
3 Kobe Bryant/25 15.00 40.00
4 LeBron James/99 10.00 25.00
7 Tim Duncan/49 6.00 15.00

2010-11 Timeless Treasures MVP Materials MVP

STATED PRINT RUN 5 TO 25 SER.#'d SETS
SOME UNPRICED DUE TO SCARCITY
UNPRICED SIG PRINT RUN 5 TO 10 SETS
UNPRICED SIG PRIME PRINT RUN 5 TO 10 SETS
1 Allen Iverson/25 6.00 15.00
2 Karl Malone/25 6.00 15.00
4 LeBron James/25 15.00 40.00

2010-11 Timeless Treasures MVP Materials MVP Prime

STATED PRINT RUN 5 TO 25 SER.#'d SETS
SOME UNPRICED DUE TO SCARCITY
1 Allen Iverson/25 12.50 30.00
2 Karl Malone/25 15.00 40.00
4 LeBron James/25 25.00 60.00
5 LeBron James/25 25.00 60.00

2010-11 Timeless Treasures MVP Materials Prime

STATED PRINT RUN 5 TO 25 SER.#'d SETS
SOME UNPRICED DUE TO SCARCITY
1 Allen Iverson/25 12.50 30.00
2 Karl Malone/25 15.00 40.00
4 LeBron James/25 25.00 60.00
5 LeBron James/25 25.00 60.00
7 Tim Duncan/25 12.50 30.00

2010-11 Timeless Treasures MVP Materials Quads

STATED PRINT RUN 25 SER.#'d SETS
UNPRICED PRIME PRINT RUN 10 SER.#'d SETS
1 Allen Iverson 20.00 50.00
Karl Malone
Magic Johnson
LeBron James
2 Allen Iverson 12.50 30.00
Karl Malone
Magic Johnson
Tim Duncan

2010-11 Timeless Treasures MVP Materials Signatures

STATED PRINT RUN 10 TO 25 SER.#'d SETS
SOME UNPRICED DUE TO SCARCITY
UNPRICED LOGOMAN SIG PRINT RUN ONE SET
UNPRICED PRIME SIG PRINT RUN 5 TO 10 SETS
UNPRICED TAG SIG PRINT RUN ONE SET
UNPRICED TAG TEAM SIG PRINT RUN ONE SET
1 Allen Iverson/25 75.00 150.00
3 Kobe Bryant/25 100.00 200.00

2010-11 Timeless Treasures NBA Apprentice Materials

STATED PRINT RUN 99 SER.#'d SETS
*PRIME: .75X TO 2X BASE HI
PRIME PRINT RUN ONE TO 25 SETS
SOME UNPRICED DUE TO SCARCITY
UNPRICED LOGOMAN PRINT RUN ONE TO 5 SETS
UNPRICED TAG PRINT RUN ONE TO 5 SETS
1 John Wall 8.00 20.00
2 Evan Turner 4.00 10.00
3 Derrick Favors 4.00 10.00
4 Wesley Johnson 3.00 8.00
5 DeMarcus Cousins 6.00 15.00
6 Ekpe Udoh 2.00 5.00
7 Greg Monroe 4.00 10.00
8 Al-Farouq Aminu 2.00 5.00
9 Gordon Hayward 4.00 10.00
10 Paul George 5.00 12.00
11 Cole Aldrich 2.00 5.00
12 Xavier Henry 2.50 6.00
13 Ed Davis 2.50 6.00
14 Patrick Patterson 3.00 8.00
15 Larry Sanders 2.00 5.00
16 Luke Babbitt 2.00 5.00
17 Eric Bledsoe 3.00 8.00
18 Avery Bradley 4.00 10.00
19 James Anderson 2.00 5.00
20 Craig Brackins 2.00 5.00
21 Elliot Williams 2.00 5.00
22 Trevor Booker 2.00 5.00
23 Damion James 2.00 5.00
24 Dominique Jones 2.00 5.00
25 Quincy Pondexter 2.00 5.00
26 Jordan Crawford 3.00 8.00
27 Greivis Vasquez 2.50 6.00
28 Daniel Orton 2.00 5.00
29 Lazar Hayward 2.00 5.00
30 Dexter Pittman 2.00 5.00
31 Hassan Whiteside 2.00 5.00
32 Terrico White 2.00 5.00
33 Andy Rautins 2.00 5.00
34 Lance Stephenson 2.00 5.00
35 Timofey Mozgov 2.00 5.00
36 Devin Ebanks 2.50 6.00
37 Gani Lawal 2.00 5.00
38 Kevin Seraphin 2.50 6.00
39 Luke Harangody 2.00 5.00
40 Willie Warren 2.00 5.00

2010-11 Timeless Treasures NBA Apprentice Materials Combos

STATED PRINT RUN 99 SER.#'d SETS
UNPRICED PRIME PRINT RUN 10 SETS
1 John Wall 8.00 20.00
Evan Turner
2 John Wall 10.00 25.00
DeMarcus Cousins
3 Evan Turner 5.00 12.00
Derrick Favors
4 Derrick Favors 4.00 10.00
Wes Johnson
5 Wes Johnson 5.00 12.00
DeMarcus Cousins
6 Greg Monroe 3.00 8.00
Terrico White
7 Al-Farouq Aminu 4.00 10.00
Eric Bledsoe
8 Luke Harangody 3.00 8.00
Avery Bradley
9 Greivis Vasquez 3.00 8.00
Xavier Henry
10 Cole Aldrich 3.00 8.00
Xavier Henry
11 Ekpe Udoh 4.00 10.00
Gordon Hayward
12 Paul George 4.00 10.00
Lance Stephenson
13 Damion James 3.00 8.00
Dexter Pittman
14 Ed Davis 4.00 10.00
Patrick Patterson
15 Eric Bledsoe 4.00 10.00
Daniel Orton

2010-11 Timeless Treasures NBA Apprentice Materials Quads

STATED PRINT RUN 99 SER.#'d SETS
UNPRICED PRIME PRINT RUN 4 TO 10 SETS
1 John Wall 10.00 25.00
Evan Turner
Derrick Favors
Wes Johnson
2 John Wall 20.00 50.00
DeMarcus Cousins
Patrick Patterson
Eric Bledsoe
3 DeMarcus Cousins 6.00 15.00
Ekpe Udoh
Greg Monroe
Al-Farouq Aminu
4 Gordon Hayward 4.00 10.00
Paul George
Cole Aldrich
Xavier Henry
5 Dexter Pittman 4.00 10.00
Hassan Whiteside
Cole Aldrich
Daniel Orton
6 Ekpe Udoh 5.00 12.00
Greg Monroe
Patrick Patterson
Larry Sanders
7 Ed Davis 5.00 12.00
Greivis Vasquez
Al-Farouq Aminu
Derrick Favors
8 Evan Turner 6.00 15.00
Luke Harangody
Ed Davis
Damion James
9 Larry Sanders 4.00 10.00
Paul George
Kevin Seraphin
Greg Monroe
10 Timofey Mozgov 4.00 10.00
Trevor Booker
Jordan Crawford
Dexter Pittman
11 Elliot Williams 5.00 12.00
Wes Johnson
Gordon Hayward
Luke Babbitt
12 Willie Warren 4.00 10.00
Gani Lawal
Hassan Whiteside
Devin Ebanks
13 Dominique Jones 5.00 12.00
Patrick Patterson
Quincy Pondexter
James Anderson
14 Willie Warren 4.00 10.00
Avery Bradley
Damion James
Kevin Seraphin
15 Devin Ebanks 4.00 10.00
Timofey Mozgov
Andy Rautins
Wes Johnson

2010-11 Timeless Treasures NBA Apprentice Materials Signatures

STATED PRINT RUN 50 SER.#'d SETS
UNPRICED LOGO.SIG PRINT RUN ONE TO 5 SETS
UNPRICED PRIME SIG PRINT RUN ONE TO 10 SETS
UNPRICED TAG SIG PRINT RUN ONE TO 5 SETS
UNPRICED TAG TEAM SIG PRINT RUN ONE SET
1 John Wall 75.00 150.00
2 Evan Turner 15.00 40.00
3 Derrick Favors 10.00 25.00
4 Wesley Johnson 8.00 20.00
5 DeMarcus Cousins 20.00 50.00
6 Ekpe Udoh 5.00 12.00
7 Greg Monroe 10.00 25.00
8 Al-Farouq Aminu 5.00 12.00
9 Gordon Hayward 10.00 25.00
10 Paul George 12.00 30.00
11 Cole Aldrich 5.00 12.00
12 Xavier Henry 6.00 15.00
13 Ed Davis 6.00 15.00
14 Patrick Patterson 8.00 20.00
15 Larry Sanders 5.00 12.00
16 Luke Babbitt 5.00 12.00
17 Eric Bledsoe 8.00 20.00
18 Avery Bradley 10.00 25.00
19 James Anderson 5.00 12.00
20 Craig Brackins 5.00 12.00
21 Elliot Williams 5.00 12.00
22 Trevor Booker 5.00 12.00
23 Damion James 5.00 12.00
24 Dominique Jones 5.00 12.00
25 Quincy Pondexter 5.00 12.00
26 Jordan Crawford 8.00 20.00
27 Greivis Vasquez 6.00 15.00
28 Daniel Orton 5.00 12.00
29 Lazar Hayward 5.00 12.00
30 Dexter Pittman 5.00 12.00
31 Hassan Whiteside 5.00 12.00
32 Terrico White 5.00 12.00
33 Andy Rautins 5.00 12.00
34 Lance Stephenson 5.00 12.00
35 Timofey Mozgov 5.00 12.00
36 Devin Ebanks 6.00 15.00
37 Gani Lawal 5.00 12.00
38 Kevin Seraphin 8.00 20.00
39 Luke Harangody 5.00 12.00
40 Willie Warren 5.00 12.00

2010-11 Timeless Treasures NBA Apprentice Materials Triple

STATED PRINT RUN 99 SER.#'d SETS
UNPRICED PRIME PRINT RUN 3 TO 10 SETS
1 John Wall 8.00 20.00
Evan Turner
Derrick Favors
2 Wes Johnson 5.00 12.00
DeMarcus Cousins
Ekpe Udoh
3 Greg Monroe 4.00 10.00
Al-Farouq Aminu
Gordon Hayward
4 Paul George 3.00 8.00
Cole Aldrich
Xavier Henry
5 Ed Davis 4.00 10.00
Patrick Patterson
Larry Sanders
6 Luke Babbitt 4.00 10.00
Eric Bledsoe
Avery Bradley
7 James Anderson 3.00 8.00
Craig Brackins
Elliot Williams
8 Trevor Booker 3.00 8.00
Damion James
Dominique Jones
9 Quincy Pondexter 3.00 8.00
Jordan Crawford
Greivis Vasquez
10 Daniel Orton 3.00 8.00
Lazar Hayward
Dexter Pittman
11 Hassan Whiteside 3.00 8.00
Terrico White
Andy Rautins
12 Lance Stephenson 3.00 8.00
Timofey Mozgov
Devin Ebanks
13 Gani Lawal 3.00 8.00
Kevin Seraphin
Luke Harangody
14 John Wall 12.50 30.00
DeMarcus Cousins
Patrick Patterson
15 Patrick Patterson 5.00 12.00
Eric Bledsoe
Daniel Orton

2010-11 Timeless Treasures NBA Apprentice Signatures Combos

STATED PRINT RUN 25 SER.#'d SETS
1 John Wall 50.00 125.00
Evan Turner
2 John Wall 50.00 125.00
DeMarcus Cousins
3 Evan Turner 15.00 40.00
Derrick Favors
4 Derrick Favors 12.50 30.00
Wesley Johnson
5 Wesley Johnson 15.00 40.00
DeMarcus Cousins
6 Greg Monroe 12.50 30.00
Terrico White
7 Al-Farouq Aminu 12.50 30.00
Eric Bledsoe
8 Luke Harangody 8.00 20.00
Avery Bradley
9 Greivis Vasquez 10.00 25.00
Xavier Henry
10 Cole Aldrich 8.00 20.00
Xavier Henry
11 Ekpe Udoh 10.00 25.00
Gordon Hayward
12 Paul George 10.00 25.00
Lance Stephenson
13 Damion James 8.00 20.00
Dexter Pittman
14 Ed Davis 12.50 30.00
Patrick Patterson
15 Eric Bledsoe 12.50 30.00
Daniel Orton

2010-11 Timeless Treasures NBA Draft Lottery Patches

STATED PRINT RUN 10 TO 140 SER.#'d SETS
SOME UNPRICED DUE TO SCARCITY
1 John Wall/10
2 Evan Turner/20 25.00 60.00
3 Derrick Favors/30 15.00 40.00
4 Wesley Johnson/40 10.00 25.00
5 DeMarcus Cousins/50 20.00 50.00
6 Ekpe Udoh/60 6.00 15.00
7 Greg Monroe/70 10.00 25.00
8 Al-Farouq Aminu/80 6.00 15.00
9 Gordon Hayward/90 10.00 25.00
10 Paul George/100 10.00 25.00
11 Cole Aldrich/110 6.00 15.00
12 Xavier Henry/120 6.00 15.00
13 Ed Davis/130 6.00 15.00
14 Patrick Patterson/140 8.00 20.00

2010-11 Timeless Treasures Rookie Year Materials

STATED PRINT RUN ONE TO 99 SER.#'d SETS
SOME UNPRICED DUE TO SCARCITY
UNPRICED LOGO.PRINT RUN ONE TO 4 SETS
UNPRICED TAG PRINT RUN ONE TO 5 SETS
UNPRICED TAG TEAM PRINT RUN 1 TO 2 SETS
1 Al Horford/99 2.50 6.00
2 Al Thornton/99 2.50 6.00
3 Andre Iguodala/99 3.00 8.00
4 Andrea Bargnani/49 2.50 6.00
5 Chris Paul/99 5.00 12.00
6 Daequan Cook/99 2.00 5.00
7 Deron Williams/99 3.00 8.00
8 Dikembe Mutombo/99 3.00 8.00
9 Dwight Howard/99 5.00 12.00
10 Jameer Nelson/99 2.50 6.00
11 Jeff Green/99 2.50 6.00
12 Joakim Noah/49 3.00 8.00
13 Kevin Durant/99 8.00 20.00
14 Kevin Garnett/99 6.00 15.00
15 LeBron James/99 10.00 25.00
16 Luis Scola/99 2.50 6.00
17 Mike Conley Jr./20 2.50 6.00
18 Nate Robinson/49 3.00 8.00
19 O.J. Mayo/99 3.00 8.00
20 Patrick Ewing/99 5.00 12.00
22 Paul Pierce/99 4.00 10.00
23 Rodney Stuckey/49 3.00 8.00
24 Shaquille O'Neal/99 10.00 25.00
25 Thaddeus Young/49 2.00 5.00
26 Zydrunas Ilgauskas/99 2.00 5.00
27 Andrew Bogut/99 3.00 8.00

2010-11 Timeless Treasures Rookie Year Materials Prime

PRIME: .75X TO 2X BASE HI
STATED PRINT RUN ONE TO 25 SER.#'d SETS
SOME UNPRICED DUE TO SCARCITY
8 Dikembe Mutombo/25 10.00 25.00
12 Joakim Noah/25 8.00 20.00
17 Mike Conley Jr./25 5.00 12.00
26 Zydrunas Ilgauskas/25 5.00 12.00

2010-11 Timeless Treasures Rookie Year Materials Prime Signatures

STATED PRINT RUN 5 TO 25 SER.#'d SETS
SOME UNPRICED DUE TO SCARCITY
2 Al Thornton/25 10.00 25.00
3 Andre Iguodala/15 12.00 30.00
7 Deron Williams/25 20.00 50.00
8 Dikembe Mutombo/25 20.00 50.00
12 Joakim Noah/25 20.00 50.00
27 Andrew Bogut/25 10.00 25.00

2010-11 Timeless Treasures Rookie Year Materials Quads

STATED PRINT RUN 25 SER.#'d SETS
UNPRICED PRIME PRINT RUN 5 SETS
1 Chris Paul 12.50 30.00
Nate Robinson
Deron Williams
Andrew Bogut
2 Dikembe Mutombo 25.00 60.00
Patrick Ewing
Shaquille O'Neal
Kevin Garnett
3 Paul Pierce 25.00 60.00
LeBron James
Kevin Durant
Dwight Howard
4 Andre Iguodala 6.00 15.00
Andrea Bargnani
Luis Scola
Joakim Noah
5 Al Horford 6.00 15.00
Al Thornton
Mike Conley Jr.
Rodney Stuckey

2010-11 Timeless Treasures Rookie Year Materials ROY

STATED PRINT RUN 99 SER.#'d SETS
*PRIME: 1X TO 2.5X BASE HI
PRIME PRINT RUN ONE TO 25 SETS
SOME PRIME UNPRICED DUE TO SCARCITY
5 Chris Paul 5.00 12.00
13 Kevin Durant 8.00 20.00
15 LeBron James 10.00 25.00
20 Patrick Ewing 5.00 12.00
24 Shaquille O'Neal 10.00 25.00

2010-11 Timeless Treasures Rookie Year Materials ROY Signatures

STATED PRINT RUN 10 TO 25 SER.#'d SETS
SOME UNPRICED DUE TO SCARCITY
13 Kevin Durant/25 100.00 200.00

2010-11 Timeless Treasures Rookie Year Materials Signatures

STATED PRINT RUN 10 TO 50 SER.#'d SETS
SOME UNPRICED DUE TO SCARCITY
UNPRICED LOGOMAN SIG PRINT RUN ONE SET
UNPRICED TAG SIG PRINT RUN ONE TO 2 SETS
UNPRICED TAG TEAM SIG PRINT RUN ONE SET
1 Al Horford/50 5.00 12.00
2 Al Thornton/50 5.00 12.00
3 Andre Iguodala/50 6.00 15.00
4 Andrea Bargnani/25 5.00 12.00
7 Deron Williams/50 12.50 30,00
8 Dikembe Mutombo/50 15.00 40.00
13 Kevin Durant/25 100.00 200.00
27 Andrew Bogut/50 8.00 20.00

2010-11 Timeless Treasures Signatures Silver

STATED PRINT RUN 10 TO 99 SER.#'d SETS
SOME UNPRICED DUE TO SCARCITY
UNPRICED GOLD PRINT RUN 5 TO 10 SETS
UNPRICED PLATINUM PRINT RUN ONE SET
1 Kobe Bryant/99 100.00 200.00
7 Jason Kidd/25 12.50 30.00
11 Robin Lopez/25 5.00 12.00
17 Al Jefferson/49 5.00 12.00
23 LaMarcus Aldridge/25 8.00 20.00
28 Tony Parker/99 8.00 20.00
29 James Harden/25 10.00 25.00
32 Russell Westbrook/99 20.00 50.00
33 Aaron Brooks/99 5.00 12.00
37 Marc Gasol/49 8.00 20.00
41 Marcus Thornton/15 5.00 12.00
46 David Lee/49 6.00 15.00
48 Stephen Curry/20 15.00 40.00
49 Carl Landry/99 6.00 15.00
51 Tyreke Evans/99 10.00 25.00
52 Kevin Love/19 15.00 40.00
53 Michael Beasley/49 12.50 30.00
57 Mo Williams/49 5.00 12.00
64 Kendrick Perkins/25 6.00 15.00
66 Rajon Rondo/25 15.00 40.00
68 Chris Bosh/49 15.00 40.00
71 Andrew Bogut/49 5.00 12.00
74 D.J. Augustin/99 5.00 12.00
78 Derrick Rose/25 75.00 150.00
80 Andrea Bargnani/49 5.00 12.00
81 DeMar DeRozan/49 6.00 15.00
83 Danny Granger/99 5.00 12.00
84 Darren Collison/99 5.00 12.00
87 Anthony Randolph/99 5.00 12.00
88 Danilo Gallinari/49 5.00 12.00
90 Richard Hamilton/25 6.00 15.00
91 Tracy McGrady/40 12.50 30.00
92 Andre Iguodala/49 5.00 12.00
97 Josh Howard/25 5.00 12.00
99 Brook Lopez/25 6.00 15.00
100 Devin Harris/49 5.00 12.00

2010-11 Timeless Treasures Timeless Signatures Silver

STATED PRINT RUN 10 TO 25 SER.#'d SETS
SOME UNPRICED DUE TO SCARCITY
UNPRICED GOLD PRINT RUN 5 TO 10 SETS
UNPRICED PLATINUM PRINT RUN ONE SET
10 John Stockton/25 40.00 100.00

1957-58 Topps

The 1957-58 Topps basketball set of 80 cards was Topps first basketball issue. Topps did not produce another basketball set until it released a test issue in 1968. A major set followed in 1969. Cards were issued in 5-cent packs (six cards per pack, 24 per box) and measure the standard size. A number of cards in the set were double printed (indicated by DP in checklist below). The set contains 49 double prints, 30 single prints and one quadruple print (No. 24 Bob Pettit). Card backs give statistical information from the 1956-57 NBA season. Bill Russell's Rookie Card is part of the set. Other Rookie Cards include Paul Arizin, Nat "Sweetwater" Clifton, Bob Cousy, Cliff Hagan, Tom Heinsohn, Rod Hundley, Red Kerr, Clyde Lovellette, Pettit, Dolph Schayes, Bill Sharman and Jack Twyman. The set contains the only card of Maurice Stokes. Topps also produced a three-card advertising panel featuring the fronts of Walt Davis, Joe Graboski and Cousy with an advertisement for the upcoming Topps basketball set on the combined reverse.

COMPLETE SET (80) 3000.00 5500.00
1 Nat Clifton RC DP 75.00 150.00
2 George Yardley DP RC 40.00 70.00
3 Neil Johnston DP RC 25.00 55.00
4 Carl Braun DP 30.00 50.00
5 Bill Sharman DP RC 65.00 125.00
6 George King DP RC 15.00 40.00
7 Kenny Sears DP RC 15.00 40.00
8 Dick Ricketts DP RC 15.00 40.00
9 Jack Nichols DP 15.00 25.00
10 Paul Arizin DP RC 30.00 80.00
11 Chuck Noble DP 15.00 25.00
12 Slater Martin DP RC 30.00 60.00
13 Dolph Schayes DP RC 25.00 60.00
14 Dick Atha DP 15.00 25.00
15 Frank Ramsey DP RC 40.00 80.00
16 Dick McGuire DP RC 25.00 50.00
17 Bob Cousy DP RC 175.00 350.00
18 Larry Foust DP RC 15.00 40.00
19 Tom Heinsohn RC 125.00 225.00
20 Bill Thieben DP 15.00 25.00
21 Don Meineke DP RC 15.00 40.00
22 Tom Marshall 25.00 40.00
23 Dick Garmaker 25.00 40.00
24 Bob Pettit QP RC 60.00 120.00
25 Jim Krebs DP RC 15.00 40.00
26 Gene Shue DP RC 40.00 60.00
27 Ed Macauley DP RC 30.00 60.00
28 Vern Mikkelsen RC 40.00 100.00
29 Willie Naulls RC 30.00 60.00
30 Walter Dukes DP RC 30.00 45.00
31 Dave Piontek DP 15.00 25.00
32 Johnny Red Kerr RC 60.00 100.00
33 Larry Costello DP RC 30.00 50.00
34 Woody Sauldsberry DP RC 15.00 40.00
35 Ray Felix RC 30.00 45.00
36 Ernie Beck 25.00 40.00
37 Cliff Hagan RC 60.00 100.00
38 Guy Sparrow DP 15.00 25.00
39 Jim Loscutoff RC 40.00 60.00
40 Arnie Risen DP 30.00 45.00
41 Joe Graboski 25.00 40.00
42 Maurice Stokes DP RC UER 60.00 100.00
Text refers to
N.F.L. Record
43 Rod Hundley DP RC 50.00 100.00
44 Tom Gola DP RC 50.00 80.00
45 Med Park RC 30.00 45.00
46 Mel Hutchins DP 15.00 25.00
47 Larry Friend DP 15.00 25.00
48 Lennie Rosenbluth DP RC 30.00 50.00
49 Walt Davis 25.00 40.00
50 Richie Regan RC 30.00 45.00
51 Frank Selvy DP RC 30.00 50.00
52 Art Spoelstra DP 15.00 25.00
53 Bob Hopkins RC 25.00 40.00
54 Earl Lloyd RC 30.00 50.00
55 Phil Jordan DP 15.00 25.00
56 Bob Houbregs DP RC 25.00 40.00
57 Lou Tsioropoulos DP 15.00 25.00
58 Ed Conlin RC 30.00 45.00
59 Al Bianchi RC 50.00 80.00
60 George Dempsey RC 30.00 45.00
61 Chuck Share 25.00 40.00
62 Harry Gallatin DP RC 30.00 50.00
63 Bob Harrison 25.00 40.00
64 Bob Burrow DP 15.00 25.00
65 Win Wilfong DP 15.00 25.00
66 Jack McMahon DP RC 15.00 40.00
67 Jack George 25.00 40.00
68 Charlie Tyra DP 15.00 25.00
69 Ron Sobie 25.00 40.00
70 Jack Coleman 25.00 40.00
71 Jack Twyman DP RC 65.00 110.00
72 Paul Seymour RC 30.00 45.00
73 Jim Paxson DP RC 35.00 55.00
74 Bob Leonard RC 30.00 50.00
75 Andy Phillip 40.00 60.00
76 Joe Holup 25.00 40.00
77 Bill Russell RC 700.00 1100.00
78 Clyde Lovellette DP RC 50.00 100.00
79 Ed Fleming DP 15.00 25.00
80 Dick Schnittker RC 60.00 120.00

1968-69 Topps Test

This set was apparently a limited test issue produced by Topps. The cards measure the standard size. The fronts feature a black and white "action" pose of the player, on white card stock. The player's name, team, and height are given below the picture. The horizontally oriented card backs form a composite of Wilt Chamberlain. The set is dated as 1968-69 since Earl Monroe's first season was 1967-68. The set features the first professional cards of Dave Bing, Bill Bradley, Dave DeBusschere, John Havlicek, Earl Monroe, and Willis Reed, among others.

COMPLETE SET (22) 18000.00 24000.00
1 Wilt Chamberlain 3000.00 4000.00
2 Hal Greer 400.00 800.00
3 Chet Walker 250.00 500.00
4 Bill Russell 3000.00 4000.00
5 John Havlicek UER 1600.00 2200.00
(Misspelled Havilcek)
6 Cazzie Russell 300.00 600.00
7 Willis Reed 500.00 850.00
8 Bill Bradley 500.00 850.00
9 Odie Smith 200.00 450.00
10 Dave Bing 500.00 850.00
11 Dave DeBusschere 500.00 850.00
12 Earl Monroe 500.00 850.00
13 Nate Thurmond 400.00 800.00
14 Jim King 200.00 450.00
15 Len Wilkens 500.00 900.00
16 Bill Bridges 200.00 450.00
17 Zelmo Beaty 300.00 600.00
18 Elgin Baylor 1400.00 2000.00
19 Jerry West 2400.00 3000.00
20 Jerry Sloan 600.00 900.00
21 Jerry Lucas 500.00 850.00
22 Oscar Robertson 1500.00 2000.00

1969-70 Topps

The 1969-70 Topps set of 99 cards was Topps' first major basketball issue since 1957. Cards were issued in 10-cent packs (10 cards per pack, 24 packs per box) and measure 2 1/2" by 4 11/16". The set features the first card of Lew Alcindor (later Kareem Abdul-Jabbar). Other notable Rookie Cards in the set are Dave Bing, Bill Bradley, Billy Cunningham, Dave DeBusschere, Walt Frazier, John Havlicek, Connie Hawkins, Elvin Hayes, Jerry Lucas, Earl Monroe, Don Nelson, Willis Reed, Nate Thurmond and Wes Unseld. The set was printed on a sheet of 99 cards (nine rows of eleven across) with the checklist card occupying the lower right corner of the sheet. As a result, the checklist is prone to wear and very difficult to obtain in Near Mint or better condition.

COMPLETE SET (99) 1000.00 1800.00
1 Wilt Chamberlain 40.00 100.00
2 Gail Goodrich RC 15.00 30.00
3 Cazzie Russell RC 8.00 15.00
4 Darrall Imhoff RC 2.50 6.00
5 Bailey Howell 3.00 8.00
6 Lucius Allen RC 5.00 10.00
7 Tom Boerwinkle RC 2.50 6.00
8 Jimmy Walker RC 3.00 8.00
9 John Block RC 2.50 6.00
10 Nate Thurmond RC 15.00 30.00
11 Gary Gregor 1.50 4.00
12 Gus Johnson RC 6.00 15.00
13 Luther Rackley 1.50 4.00
14 Jon McGlocklin RC 15.00 30.00
15 Connie Hawkins RC 15.00 40.00
16 Johnny Egan 1.50 4.00
17 Jim Washington 1.50 4.00
18 Dick Barnett RC 3.00 8.00
19 Tom Meschery 3.00 8.00
20 John Havlicek RC 25.00 60.00
21 Eddie Miles 1.50 4.00
22 Walt Wesley 2.50 6.00
23 Rick Adelman RC 4.00 10.00
24 Al Attles 3.00 8.00
25 Lew Alcindor RC 125.00 250.00
26 Jack Marin RC 3.00 8.00
27 Walt Hazzard RC 4.00 10.00
28 Connie Dierking 1.50 4.00
29 Keith Erickson RC 4.00 10.00
30 Bob Rule RC 5.00 10.00
31 Dick Van Arsdale RC 4.00 10.00
32 Archie Clark RC 4.00 10.00
33 Terry Dischinger RC 1.50 4.00
34 Henry Finkel RC 1.50 4.00
35 Elgin Baylor 10.00 25.00
36 Ron Williams 1.50 4.00
37 Loy Petersen 1.50 4.00
38 Guy Rodgers 3.00 8.00
39 Toby Kimball 1.50 4.00
40 Billy Cunningham RC 10.00 25.00
41 Joe Caldwell RC 3.00 8.00
42 Leroy Ellis RC 2.50 6.00
43 Bill Bradley RC 25.00 60.00
44 Len Wilkens UER 10.00 25.00
(Misspelled Wilkins
on card back)
45 Jerry Lucas RC 12.50 30.00
46 Neal Walk RC 2.50 6.00
47 Emmette Bryant RC 2.50 6.00
48 Bob Kauffman RC 1.50 4.00
49 Mel Counts RC 2.50 6.00
50 Oscar Robertson 15.00 40.00
51 Jim Barnett RC 3.00 8.00
52 Don Smith 1.50 4.00
53 Jim Davis 1.50 4.00
54 Wally Jones RC 2.50 6.00
55 Dave Bing RC 12.50 30.00
56 Wes Unseld RC 15.00 30.00
57 Joe Ellis 1.50 4.00
58 John Tresvant 1.50 4.00
59 Larry Siegfried RC 2.50 6.00
60 Willis Reed RC 15.00 30.00
61 Paul Silas RC 6.00 15.00
62 Bob Weiss RC 3.00 8.00
63 Willie McCarter 1.50 4.00
64 Don Kojis RC 1.50 4.00
65 Lou Hudson RC 8.00 20.00
66 Jim King 1.50 4.00
67 Luke Jackson RC 2.50 6.00
68 Len Chappell RC 1.50 4.00
69 Ray Scott 1.50 4.00
70 Jeff Mullins RC 4.00 10.00
71 Howie Komives 1.50 4.00
72 Tom Sanders RC 5.00 10.00
73 Dick Snyder 1.50 4.00
74 Dave Stallworth RC 2.50 6.00
75 Elvin Hayes RC 15.00 40.00
76 Art Harris 1.50 4.00
77 Don Ohl 2.50 6.00
78 Bob Love RC 15.00 30.00
79 Tom Van Arsdale RC 5.00 12.00
80 Earl Monroe RC 12.50 30.00
81 Greg Smith 1.50 4.00
82 Don Nelson RC 15.00 30.00
83 Happy Hairston RC 3.00 8.00
84 Hal Greer 6.00 12.00
85 Dave DeBusschere RC 15.00 30.00
86 Bill Bridges RC 3.00 8.00
87 Herm Gilliam RC 2.50 6.00
88 Jim Fox 1.50 4.00
89 Bob Boozer 2.50 6.00
90 Jerry West 25.00 60.00
91 Chet Walker RC 6.00 15.00
92 Flynn Robinson RC 2.50 6.00
93 Clyde Lee 1.50 4.00
94 Kevin Loughery RC 5.00 12.00
95 Walt Bellamy 5.00 10.00
96 Art Williams 1.50 4.00
97 Adrian Smith RC 2.50 6.00
98 Walt Frazier RC 20.00 50.00
99 Checklist 1-99 100.00 200.00

1969-70 Topps Rulers

The 1969-70 Topps basketball cartoon poster inserts are clever color cartoon drawings of NBA players, with "ruler" markings on the left edge of the insert. These paper-thin posters measure approximately 2 1/2" by 9 7/8". The player's height is indicated in an arrow pointing towards the ruler, and the top of the player's head corresponds to this line on the ruler. The inserts are numbered and contain the player's name and team in an oval near the bottom of the insert. As might be expected, these inserts make the players look both taller and thinner than they actually are. Insert number 5 was never issued; it was intended to be Bill Russell. The inserts came with gum packs (one per pack) of Topps regular issue basketball cards of that year.

COMPLETE SET (23) 200.00 400.00
1 Walt Bellamy 3.00 8.00
2 Jerry West 20.00 40.00
3 Bailey Howell 3.00 8.00
4 Elvin Hayes 7.50 15.00
6 Bob Rule 3.00 8.00

Gail Goodrich	5.00	10.00
Jeff Mullins	3.00	8.00
John Havlicek	15.00	30.00
0 Lew Alcindor	40.00	100.00
1 Wilt Chamberlain	30.00	80.00
2 Nate Thurmond	5.00	12.00
3 Hal Greer	4.00	10.00
4 Lou Hudson	3.00	8.00
5 Jerry Lucas	6.00	12.00
6 Dave Bing	6.00	12.00
7 Walt Frazier	7.50	15.00
8 Gus Johnson	3.00	8.00
9 Willis Reed	7.50	15.00
0 Earl Monroe	7.50	15.00
1 Billy Cunningham	6.00	15.00
2 Wes Unseld	5.00	12.00
3 Bob Boozer	3.00	8.00
4 Oscar Robertson	17.50	35.00

1970-71 Topps

The 1970-71 Topps basketball card set of 175 color cards continued the larger-size (2 1/2" by 4 11/16") format established the previous year. Cards were issued in 10-cent wax packs with 10 cards per pack and 24 packs per box. Cards numbered 106 to 115 contain the previous season's NBA first and second team All-Star selections. The first six cards in the set (1-6) feature the statistical league leaders from the previous season. The last eight cards in the set (168-175) summarize the results of the previous season's NBA championship playoff series won by the Knicks over the Lakers. The key Rookie Cards in this set are Pete Maravich, Calvin Murphy and Pat Riley. There are 22 short-printed cards in the first series which are marked SP in the checklist below.

COMPLETE SET (175)	700.00	1200.00
1 Lew Alcindor	15.00	40.00
Jerry West		
Elvin Hayes LL		
2 Jerry West	15.00	40.00
Lew Alcindor		
Elvin Hayes LL SP		
3 Johnny Green	2.00	5.00
Darrall Imhoff		
Lou Hudson LL		
4 Flynn Robinson	5.00	10.00
Chet Walker		
Jeff Mullins LL SP		
5 Elvin Hayes	12.50	30.00
Wes Unseld		
Lew Alcindor LL		
6 Len Wilkens	6.00	12.00
Walt Frazier		
Clem Haskins LL SP		
7 Bill Bradley	15.00	40.00
8 Ron Williams	1.00	2.50
9 Otto Moore	1.00	2.50
10 John Havlicek SP !	30.00	70.00
11 George Wilson RC	1.00	2.50
12 John Trapp	1.00	2.50
13 Pat Riley RC	15.00	40.00
14 Jim Washington	1.00	2.50
15 Bob Rule	1.50	4.00
16 Bob Weiss	1.50	4.00
17 Neil Johnson	1.00	2.50
18 Walt Bellamy	2.50	6.00
19 McCoy McLemore	1.00	2.50
20 Earl Monroe	7.50	15.00
21 Wally Anderzunas	1.00	2.50
22 Guy Rodgers	1.50	4.00
23 Rick Roberson	1.00	2.50
24 Checklist 1-110	20.00	40.00
25 Jimmy Walker	1.50	4.00
26 Mike Riordan RC	2.50	6.00
27 Henry Finkel	1.00	2.50
28 Joe Ellis	1.00	2.50
29 Mike Davis	1.00	2.50
30 Lou Hudson	2.50	6.00
31 Lucius Allen SP	4.00	10.00
32 Toby Kimball SP	3.00	8.00
33 Luke Jackson SP	3.00	8.00
34 Johnny Egan	3.00	8.00
35 Leroy Ellis SP	4.00	10.00
36 Jack Marin SP	4.00	10.00
37 Joe Caldwell SP	4.00	10.00
38 Keith Erickson	2.50	6.00
39 Don Smith	1.00	2.50
40 Flynn Robinson	1.50	4.00
41 Bob Boozer	1.00	2.50
42 Howie Komives	1.00	2.50
43 Dick Barnett	1.50	4.00
44 Stu Lantz RC	1.50	4.00
45 Dick Van Arsdale	2.50	6.00
46 Jerry Lucas	5.00	10.00
47 Don Chaney RC	5.00	12.00
48 Ray Scott	1.00	2.50
49 Dick Cunningham SP	4.00	10.00
50 Wilt Chamberlain	20.00	50.00
51 Kevin Loughery	1.50	4.00
52 Stan McKenzie	1.00	2.50
53 Fred Foster	1.00	2.50
54 Jim Davis	1.00	2.50
55 Walt Wesley	1.00	2.50
56 Bill Hewitt	1.00	2.50
57 Darrall Imhoff	1.00	2.50
58 John Block	1.00	2.50
59 Al Attles SP	4.00	10.00
60 Chet Walker	2.50	6.00
61 Luther Rackley	1.00	2.50
62 Jerry Chambers SP RC	4.00	10.00
63 Bob Dandridge RC	3.00	8.00
64 Dick Snyder	1.00	2.50
65 Elgin Baylor	18.00	30.00
66 Connie Dierking	1.00	2.50
67 Steve Kuberski RC	1.00	2.50
68 Tom Boerwinkle	1.00	2.50
69 Paul Silas	2.50	6.00
70 Elvin Hayes	18.00	30.00
71 Bill Bridges	1.50	4.00
72 Wes Unseld	7.50	15.00
73 Herm Gilliam	1.00	2.50
74 Bobby Smith SP RC	4.00	10.00
75 Lew Alcindor	20.00	50.00
76 Jeff Mullins	1.50	4.00
77 Happy Hairston	1.50	4.00
78 Dave Stallworth SP	3.00	8.00
79 Fred Hetzel	1.00	2.50
80 Len Wilkens SP	12.00	25.00
81 Johnny Green RC	2.50	6.00
82 Erwin Mueller	1.00	2.50
83 Wally Jones	1.50	4.00
84 Bob Love	3.00	8.00
85 Dick Garrett RC	1.00	2.50
86 Don Nelson SP	12.00	25.00
87 Neal Walk SP	3.00	8.00
88 Larry Siegfried	1.00	2.50
89 Gary Gregor	1.00	2.50
90 Nate Thurmond	3.00	8.00
91 John Warren	1.00	2.50
92 Gus Johnson	2.50	6.00
93 Gail Goodrich	7.50	15.00
94 Dorie Murrey	1.00	2.50
95 Cazzie Russell SP	5.00	12.00
96 Terry Dischinger	1.00	2.50
97 Norm Van Lier SP RC	7.50	15.00
98 Jim Fox	1.00	2.50
99 Tom Meschery	1.00	2.50
100 Oscar Robertson	15.00	40.00
101A Checklist 111-175	15.00	30.00
(1970-71 in black)		
101B Checklist 111-175	15.00	30.00
(1970-71 in white)		
102 Rich Johnson	1.00	2.50
103 Mel Counts	1.50	4.00
104 Bill Hosket SP RC	3.00	8.00
105 Archie Clark	1.50	4.00
106 Walt Frazier AS	5.00	10.00
107 Jerry West AS	12.50	25.00
108 Billy Cunningham AS SP	5.00	12.00
109 Connie Hawkins AS	3.00	8.00
110 Willis Reed AS	3.00	8.00
111 Nate Thurmond AS	2.00	5.00
112 John Havlicek AS	15.00	30.00
113 Elgin Baylor AS	8.00	20.00
114 Oscar Robertson AS	12.00	20.00
115 Lou Hudson AS	1.50	4.00
116 Emmette Bryant	1.25	3.00
117 Greg Howard	1.25	3.00
118 Rick Adelman	2.00	5.00
119 Barry Clemens	1.25	3.00
120 Walt Frazier	18.00	30.00
121 Jim Barnes RC	1.25	3.00
122 Bernie Williams	1.25	3.00
123 Pete Maravich RC	150.00	300.00
124 Matt Guokas RC	3.00	8.00
125 Dave Bing	6.00	12.00
126 John Tresvant	1.25	3.00
127 Shaler Halimon	1.25	3.00
128 Don Ohl	1.25	3.00
129 Fred Carter RC	2.50	6.00
130 Connie Hawkins	8.00	20.00
131 Jim King	1.25	3.00
132 Ed Manning RC	2.50	6.00
133 Adrian Smith	1.25	3.00
134 Walt Hazzard	2.50	6.00
135 Dave DeBusschere	7.50	15.00
136 Don Kojis	1.25	3.00
137 Calvin Murphy RC	15.00	40.00
138 Nate Bowman	1.25	3.00
139 Jon McGlocklin	2.00	5.00
140 Billy Cunningham	8.00	20.00
141 Willie McCarter	1.25	3.00
142 Jim Barnett	1.25	3.00
143 Jo Jo White RC	10.00	20.00
144 Clyde Lee	1.25	3.00
145 Tom Van Arsdale	2.50	6.00
146 Len Chappell	1.25	3.00
147 Lee Winfield	1.25	3.00
148 Jerry Sloan RC	10.00	25.00
149 Art Harris	1.25	3.00
150 Willis Reed	10.00	20.00
151 Art Williams	1.25	3.00
152 Don May	1.25	3.00
153 Loy Petersen	1.25	3.00
154 Dave Gambee	1.25	3.00
155 Hal Greer	2.50	6.00
156 Dave Newmark	1.25	3.00
157 Jimmy Collins	1.25	3.00
158 Bill Turner	1.25	3.00
159 Eddie Miles	1.25	3.00
160 Jerry West	20.00	50.00
161 Bob Quick	1.25	3.00
162 Fred Crawford	1.25	3.00
163 Tom Sanders	2.50	6.00
164 Dale Schlueter	1.25	3.00
165 Clem Haskins RC	4.00	10.00
166 Greg Smith	1.25	3.00
167 Rod Thorn RC	3.00	8.00
168 Playoff G1	5.00	10.00
Willis Reed		
169 Playoff G2	2.00	5.00
Dick Garnett		
170 Playoff G3	5.00	10.00
Dave DeBusschere		
171 Playoff G4	8.00	20.00
Jerry West		
172 Playoff G5	8.00	20.00
Bill Bradley		
173 Playoff G6	8.00	20.00
Wilt Chamberlain		
174 Playoff G7	6.00	12.00
Walt Frazier		
175 Knicks Celebrate	10.00	20.00
(New York Knicks, World Champs)		

1970-71 Topps Poster

This set of 24 large (8" by 10") thin paper posters was issued as an insert in second series wax packs along with the 1970-71 Topps regular basketball cards. The posters are in full color and contain the player's name and his team near the upper left of the poster. The number appears in the border at the lower right, and a Topps copyright date and a 1968 National Basketball Player's Association copyright date appears in the border at the left.

COMPLETE SET (24)	100.00	200.00
1 Walt Frazier	5.00	12.00
2 Joe Caldwell	2.00	5.00
3 Willis Reed	5.00	10.00
4 Elvin Hayes	10.00	20.00
5 Jeff Mullins	2.50	6.00
6 Oscar Robertson	12.50	25.00
7 Dave Bing	4.00	10.00
8 Jerry Sloan	4.00	10.00
9 Leroy Ellis	2.00	5.00
10 Hal Greer	3.00	8.00
11 Emmette Bryant	2.00	5.00
12 Bob Rule	6.00	12.00
(Bill Russell in background)		
13 Lew Alcindor	20.00	45.00
14 Chet Walker	3.00	8.00
15 Jerry West	15.00	30.00
16 Billy Cunningham	3.00	8.00
17 Wilt Chamberlain	15.00	40.00
18 John Havlicek	12.50	25.00
19 Lou Hudson	2.00	5.00
20 Earl Monroe	3.00	8.00
21 Wes Unseld	3.00	8.00
22 Connie Hawkins	5.00	10.00
23 Tom Van Arsdale	2.00	5.00
24 Len Chappell	2.00	5.00

1971-72 Topps

The 1971-72 Topps basketball set of 233 witnessed a return to the standard-sized card, i.e., 2 1/2" by 3 1/2". Cards were issued in 10-card, 10 cent packs with 24 packs per box. National Basketball Association players are depicted on cards 1 to 144 and American Basketball Association players are depicted on cards 145 to 233. The set was produced on two sheets. The second production sheet contained the ABA players (145-233) as well as 31 double-printed cards (NBA players) from the first sheet. These DP's are indicated in the checklist below. Subsets include NBA Playoffs (133-137), NBA Statistical Leaders (138-143) and ABA Statistical Leaders (146-151). The key Rookie Cards in this set are Nate Archibald, Rick Barry, Larry Brown, Dave Cowens, Spencer Haywood, Dan Issel, Bob Lanier, Rudy Tomjanovich and Doug Moe.

COMPLETE SET (233)	500.00	750.00
1 Oscar Robertson !	8.00	20.00
2 Bill Bradley	6.00	15.00
3 Jim Fox	.60	1.50
4 John Johnson RC	.75	2.00
5 Luke Jackson	.75	2.00
6 Don May DP	.60	1.50
7 Kevin Loughery	.75	2.00
8 Terry Dischinger	.60	1.50
9 Neal Walk	.75	2.00
10 Elgin Baylor	7.50	15.00
11 Rick Adelman	1.00	2.50
12 Clyde Lee	.60	1.50
13 Jerry Chambers	.60	1.50
14 Fred Carter	.75	2.00
15 Tom Boerwinkle DP	.60	1.50
16 John Block	.60	1.50
17 Dick Barnett	.75	2.00
18 Henry Finkel	.60	1.50
19 Norm Van Lier	1.50	4.00
20 Spencer Haywood RC	4.00	10.00
21 George Johnson	.60	1.50
22 Bobby Lewis	.60	1.50
23 Bill Hewitt	.60	1.50
24 Walt Hazzard DP	1.50	4.00
25 Happy Hairston	.75	2.00
26 George Wilson	.60	1.50
27 Lucius Allen	.75	2.00
28 Jim Washington	.60	1.50
29 Nate Archibald RC	6.00	15.00
30 Willis Reed	3.00	8.00
31 Erwin Mueller	.60	1.50
32 Art Harris	.60	1.50
33 Pete Cross	.75	2.00
34 Geoff Petrie RC	2.00	5.00
35 John Havlicek	6.00	15.00
36 Larry Siegfried	.60	1.50
37 John Tresvant DP	.60	1.50
38 Ron Williams	.60	1.50
39 Lamar Green DP	.60	1.50
40 Bob Rule DP	.75	2.00
41 Jim McMillian RC	.75	2.00
42 Wally Jones	.75	2.00
43 Bob Boozer	.60	1.50
44 Eddie Miles	.60	1.50
45 Bob Love DP	2.00	5.00
46 Claude English	.60	1.50
47 Dave Cowens RC	10.00	25.00
48 Emmette Bryant	.60	1.50
49 Dave Stallworth	.75	2.00
50 Jerry West	8.00	20.00
51 Joe Ellis	.60	1.50
52 Walt Wesley DP	.60	1.50
53 Howie Komives	.60	1.50
54 Paul Silas	1.50	4.00
55 Pete Maravich DP	10.00	25.00
56 Gary Gregor	.60	1.50
57 Sam Lacey RC	1.50	4.00
58 Calvin Murphy DP	2.50	6.00
59 Bob Dandridge	.75	2.00
60 Hal Greer	1.50	4.00
61 Keith Erickson	1.50	4.00
62 Joe Cooke	.60	1.50
63 Bob Lanier RC	12.50	30.00
64 Don Kojis	.60	1.50
65 Walt Frazier	4.00	10.00
66 Chet Walker DP	1.50	4.00
67 Dick Garrett	.60	1.50
68 John Trapp	.75	2.00
69 Jo Jo White	2.50	6.00
70 Wilt Chamberlain	20.00	35.00
71 Dave Sorenson	.60	1.50
72 Jim King	.60	1.50
73 Cazzie Russell	1.50	4.00
74 Jon McGlocklin	.75	2.00
75 Tom Van Arsdale	.75	2.00
76 Dale Schlueter	.60	1.50
77 Gus Johnson DP	1.50	4.00
78 Dave Bing	2.50	6.00
79 Billy Cunningham	3.00	8.00
80 Len Wilkens	3.00	8.00
81 Jerry Lucas DP	2.00	5.00
82 Don Chaney	1.50	4.00
83 McCoy McLemore	.60	1.50
84 Bob Kauffman DP	.60	1.50
85 Dick Van Arsdale	1.50	4.00
86 Johnny Green	.75	2.00
87 Jerry Sloan	2.00	5.00
88 Luther Rackley DP	.60	1.50
89 Shaler Halimon	.60	1.50
90 Jimmy Walker	.75	2.00
91 Rudy Tomjanovich RC	6.00	15.00
92 Levi Fontaine	.60	1.50
93 Bobby Smith	.75	2.00
94 Bob Arnzen	.60	1.50
95 Wes Unseld DP	2.50	6.00
96 Clem Haskins DP	1.50	4.00
97 Jim Davis	.60	1.50
98 Steve Kuberski	.60	1.50
99 Mike Davis DP	.60	1.50
100 Lew Alcindor	12.50	30.00
101 Willie McCarter	.60	1.50
102 Charlie Paulk	.60	1.50
103 Lee Winfield	.60	1.50
104 Jim Barnett	.60	1.50
105 Connie Hawkins DP	2.50	6.00
106 Archie Clark DP	.75	2.00
107 Dave DeBusschere	2.50	6.00
108 Stu Lantz DP	.75	2.00
109 Don Smith	.60	1.50
110 Lou Hudson	1.50	4.00
111 Leroy Ellis	.60	1.50
112 Jack Marin	.75	2.00
113 Matt Guokas	.75	2.00
114 Don Nelson	3.00	8.00
115 Jeff Mullins DP	.75	2.00
116 Walt Bellamy	2.50	6.00
117 Bob Quick	.60	1.50
118 John Warren	.60	1.50
119 Barry Clemens	.60	1.50
120 Elvin Hayes DP	3.00	8.00
121 Gail Goodrich	2.50	6.00
122 Ed Manning	.75	2.00
123 Herm Gilliam DP	.60	1.50
124 Dennis Awtrey RC	.75	2.00
125 John Hummer DP	.60	1.50
126 Mike Riordan	.75	2.00
127 Mel Counts	.60	1.50
128 Bob Weiss DP	.60	1.50
129 Greg Smith DP	.60	1.50
130 Earl Monroe	3.00	8.00
131 Nate Thurmond DP	1.50	4.00
132 Bill Bridges DP	.75	2.00
133 Playoffs G1	3.00	8.00
Lew Alcindor		
134 NBA Playoffs G2	1.25	3.00
Bucks make it two Straight		
135 Bob Dandridge PO	1.25	3.00
136 Playoffs G4	2.50	6.00
Oscar Robertson		
137 NBA Champs	5.00	12.00
Oscar Robertson		
138 Lew Alcindor	5.00	12.00
Elvin Hayes		
John Havlicek LL		
139 Lew Alcindor	5.00	12.00
John Havlicek		
Elvin Hayes LL		
140 Johnny Green	4.00	10.00
Lew Alcindor		
Wilt Chamberlain LL		
141 Chet Walker	2.00	5.00
Oscar Robertson		
Ron Williams LL		
142 Wilt Chamberlain	8.00	20.00
Elvin Hayes		
Lew Alcindor LL		
143 Norm Van Lier	3.00	8.00
Oscar Robertson		
Jerry West LL		
144A NBA Checklist 1-144	6.00	15.00
(Copyright notation extends up to card 110)		
144B NBA Checklist 1-144	6.00	15.00
(Copyright notation extends up to card 108)		
145 ABA Checklist 145-233	6.00	15.00
146 Dan Issel	2.50	6.00
John Brisker		
Charlie Scott LL		
147 Dan Issel	4.00	10.00
Rick Barry		
John Brisker LL		
148 Zelmo Beaty	1.50	4.00
Bill Paultz		
Roger Brown LL		
149 Rick Barry	3.00	8.00
Darrell Carrier		
Billy Keller LL		
150 Mel Daniels	1.50	4.00
Julius Keye		
Mike Lewis LL		
151 Bill Melchionni	1.50	4.00
Mack Calvin		
Charlie Scott LL		
152 Larry Brown RC	5.00	12.00
153 Bob Bedell	.75	2.00
154 Merv Jackson	.75	2.00
155 Joe Caldwell	1.00	2.50
156 Billy Paultz RC	2.00	5.00
157 Les Hunter	1.00	2.50
158 Charlie Williams	.75	2.00
159 Stew Johnson	.75	2.00
160 Mack Calvin RC	2.00	5.00
161 Don Sidle	.75	2.00
162 Mike Barrett	.75	2.00
163 Tom Workman	.75	2.00
164 Joe Hamilton	1.00	2.50
165 Zelmo Beaty RC	2.50	6.00
166 Dan Hester	.75	2.00
167 Bob Verga	.75	2.00
168 Wilbert Jones	.75	2.00
169 Skeeter Swift	.75	2.00
170 Rick Barry RC	12.50	30.00
171 Billy Keller RC	1.50	4.00
172 Ron Franz	.75	2.00
173 Roland Taylor RC	1.00	2.50
174 Julian Hammond	.75	2.00
175 Steve Jones RC	2.50	6.00
176 Gerald Govan	1.00	2.50
177 Darrell Carrier RC	1.00	2.50
178 Ron Boone RC	2.00	5.00
179 George Peeples	.75	2.00
180 John Brisker	1.00	2.50
181 Doug Moe RC	2.50	6.00
182 Ollie Taylor	.75	2.00
183 Bob Netolicky RC	1.00	2.50
184 Sam Robinson	.75	2.00
185 James Jones	1.00	2.50
186 Julius Keye	1.00	2.50
187 Wayne Hightower	.75	2.00
188 Warren Armstrong RC	1.00	2.50
189 Mike Lewis	.75	2.00
190 Charlie Scott RC	2.50	6.00
191 Jim Ard	.75	2.00
192 George Lehmann	.75	2.00
193 Ira Harge	.75	2.00
194 Willie Wise RC	2.00	5.00
195 Mel Daniels RC	2.50	6.00
196 Larry Cannon	.75	2.00
197 Jim Eakins	1.00	2.50
198 Rich Jones	1.00	2.50
199 Bill Melchionni RC	1.50	4.00
200 Dan Issel RC	8.00	20.00
201 George Stone	.75	2.00
202 George Thompson	.75	2.00
203 Craig Raymond	.75	2.00
204 Freddie Lewis RC	1.00	2.50
205 George Carter	1.00	2.50
206 Lonnie Wright	.75	2.00
207 Cincy Powell	1.00	2.50
208 Larry Miller	1.00	2.50
209 Sonny Dove	.75	2.00
210 Byron Beck RC	1.00	2.50
211 John Beasley	.75	2.00
212 Lee Davis	.75	2.00
213 Rick Mount RC	2.50	6.00
214 Walt Simon	.75	2.00
215 Glen Combs	.75	2.00
216 Neil Johnson	.75	2.00
217 Manny Leaks	.75	2.00
218 Chuck Williams	1.00	2.50
219 Warren Davis	.75	2.00
220 Donnie Freeman RC	1.00	2.50
221 Randy Mahaffey	.75	2.00
222 John Barnhill	.75	2.00
223 Al Cueto	.75	2.00
224 Louie Dampier RC	3.00	8.00
225 Roger Brown RC	2.00	5.00
226 Joe DePre	.75	2.00
227 Ray Scott	.75	2.00
228 Arvesta Kelly	.75	2.00
229 Vann Williford	.75	2.00
230 Larry Jones	1.00	2.50
231 Gene Moore	.75	2.00
232 Ralph Simpson RC	1.25	3.00
233 Red Robbins RC	2.00	5.00

1971-72 Topps Trios

The 1971-72 Topps Trios (insert sticker panels) set contains 26 standard card-sized panels each with three player stickers. There are also three logo sticker panels. Each player sticker has a black border surrounding a color photo with a yellow player's name, and white team name. The NBA players are numbered by the number indicated; stickers of ABA players have the suffix "A" added to their numbers in order to differentiate them. The stickers were printed on a sheet of 77 (7 rows and 11 columns). There are a number of oddities with respect to the distribution on the sheet and hence also to the availability of respective cards in the set. The most difficult cards in the set (34, 37, 40, 43, 1A, 4A, 7A, 10A, 13A, 16A, 19A, 23A, and 24A) appeared on the sheet only twice; they are designated as short prints (SP) in the checklist below. Cards 1, 4, 7, 10, 13, 16, 19, 22, 25, 28, and 31 were all printed three times on the sheet and are hence 50 percent more available than the SP's. The rest of the sheet is comprised of 4 copies of card 22A and 14 copies of card 46; they are referenced as DP and QP respectively. The logo stickers are hard to find in good shape.

COMPLETE SET (26)	200.00	400.00
1 Lou Hudson	4.00	10.00
2 Bob Rule		
3 Calvin Murphy		
1A James Jones SP	10.00	20.00
2A Willie Wise		
3A Dan Issel		
4 Walt Wesley	3.00	8.00
5 JoJo White		
6 Bob Dandridge		
4A Mack Calvin SP	4.00	10.00
5A Roger Brown		
6A Bob Verga		
7 Nate Thurmond	5.00	10.00
8 Earl Monroe		
9 Spencer Haywood		
7A Bill Melchionni SP	4.00	10.00
8A Mel Daniels		
9A Donnie Freeman		
10 Dave DeBusschere	6.00	12.00
11 Bob Lanier		
12 Tom Van Arsdale		
10A Joe Caldwell SP	4.00	10.00
11A Louie Dampier		
12A Mike Lewis		
13 Hal Greer	5.00	10.00
14 Johnny Green		
15 Elvin Hayes		
13A Rick Barry SP	12.50	25.00
14A Larry Jones		
15A Julius Keye		
16 Jimmy Walker	1.50	4.00
17 Don May		
18 Archie Clark		
16A Larry Cannon SP	3.00	8.00
17A Zelmo Beaty		
18A Charlie Scott		
19 Happy Hairston	4.00	10.00
20 Leroy Ellis		
21 Jerry Sloan		
19A Steve Jones SP	4.00	10.00
20A George Carter		
21A John Brisker		
22 Pete Maravich	40.00	80.00
23 Bob Kauffman		
24 John Havlicek		
22A ABA Team DP	1.50	4.00
Logo Stickers		
23A ABA Team SP	20.00	40.00
Logo Stickers		
24A ABA Team SP	20.00	40.00
Logo Stickers		
25 Walt Frazier	7.50	15.00
26 Dick Van Arsdale		
27 Dave Bing		
28 Bob Love	7.50	15.00
29 Ron Williams		
30 Dave Cowens		
31 Jerry West	25.00	50.00
32 Willis Reed		
33 Chet Walker		
34 Oscar Robertson SP	25.00	45.00
35 Wes Unseld		
36 Bobby Smith		
37 Connie Hawkins SP	40.00	80.00
38 Jeff Mullins		
39 Lew Alcindor		
40 Billy Cunningham SP	6.00	15.00
41 Walt Bellamy		
42 Geoff Petrie		
43 Wilt Chamberlain SP	25.00	50.00
44 Gus Johnson		
45 Norm Van Lier		
46 NBA Team QP	1.25	3.00
Logo Stickers		

1972-73 Topps

The 1972-73 Topps set of 264 standard size cards contains NBA players (1-176) and ABA players (177-264). Cards were issued in 10-card packs with 24 packs per box. All-Star selections are depicted for the NBA on cards 161-170 and for the ABA on cards 249-258. Subsets include NBA Playoffs (154-159), NBA Statistical Leaders (171-176), ABA Playoffs (241-247) and ABA Statistical Leaders (259-264). The key Rookie Card is Julius Erving. Other Rookie Cards include Artis Gilmore and Phil Jackson.

COMPLETE SET (264)	400.00	800.00
1 Wilt Chamberlain !	30.00	60.00
2 Stan Love	.40	1.00
3 Geoff Petrie	.60	1.50
4 Curtis Perry RC	.40	1.00
5 Pete Maravich	15.00	40.00
6 Gus Johnson	1.25	3.00
7 Dave Cowens	7.50	15.00
8 Randy Smith RC	1.50	4.00
9 Matt Guokas	.60	1.50
10 Spencer Haywood	1.50	4.00
11 Jerry Sloan	1.25	3.00
12 Dave Sorenson	.40	1.00
13 Howie Komives	.40	1.00
14 Joe Ellis	.40	1.00
15 Jerry Lucas	2.00	5.00
16 Stu Lantz	.60	1.50
17 Bill Bridges	.60	1.50
18 Leroy Ellis	.40	1.00
19 Art Williams	.40	1.00
20 Sidney Wicks RC	3.00	8.00
21 Wes Unseld	2.50	6.00
22 Jim Washington	.40	1.00
23 Fred Hilton	.40	1.00
24 Curtis Rowe RC	.60	1.50
25 Oscar Robertson	10.00	20.00
26 Larry Steele RC	.75	2.00
27 Charlie Davis	.40	1.00
28 Nate Thurmond	2.00	5.00
29 Fred Carter	.60	1.50
30 Connie Hawkins	3.00	8.00
31 Calvin Murphy	2.00	5.00
32 Phil Jackson RC	15.00	40.00
33 Lee Winfield	.40	1.00
34 Jim Fox	.40	1.00
35 Dave Bing	2.50	6.00
36 Gary Gregor	.40	1.00
37 Mike Riordan	.60	1.50
38 George Trapp	.40	1.00
39 Mike Davis	.40	1.00
40 Bob Rule	.60	1.50
41 John Block	.40	1.00
42 Bob Dandridge	.60	1.50
43 John Johnson	.60	1.50
44 Rick Barry	8.00	20.00
45 Jo Jo White	1.50	4.00
46 Cliff Meely	.40	1.00
47 Charlie Scott	1.25	3.00
48 Johnny Green	.60	1.50
49 Pete Cross	.40	1.00
50 Gail Goodrich	2.50	6.00
51 Jim Davis	.40	1.00
52 Dick Barnett	.60	1.50
53 Bob Christian	.40	1.00
54 Jon McGlocklin	.60	1.50
55 Paul Silas	1.25	3.00
56 Hal Greer	1.25	3.00
57 Barry Clemens	.40	1.00
58 Nick Jones	.40	1.00
59 Cornell Warner	.40	1.00
60 Walt Frazier	5.00	10.00
61 Dorie Murrey	.40	1.00
62 Dick Cunningham	.40	1.00
63 Sam Lacey	.60	1.50
64 John Warren	.40	1.00
65 Tom Boerwinkle	.40	1.00
66 Fred Foster	.40	1.00
67 Mel Counts	.40	1.00
68 Toby Kimball	.40	1.00
69 Dale Schlueter	.40	1.00
70 Jack Marin	.60	1.50
71 Jim Barnett	.40	1.00
72 Clem Haskins	1.25	3.00
73 Earl Monroe	2.50	6.00
74 Tom Sanders	.60	1.50
75 Jerry West	12.50	25.00
76 Elmore Smith RC	.60	1.50
77 Don Adams	.40	1.00
78 Wally Jones	.60	1.50
79 Tom Van Arsdale	.60	1.50
80 Bob Lanier	10.00	20.00
81 Len Wilkens	3.00	8.00
82 Neal Walk	.60	1.50
83 Kevin Loughery	.60	1.50
84 Stan McKenzie	.60	1.50
85 Jeff Mullins	.60	1.50
86 Otto Moore	.40	1.00
87 John Tresvant	.40	1.00
88 Dean Meminger RC	.40	1.00
89 Jim McMillian	.60	1.50
90 Austin Carr RC	3.00	8.00
91 Clifford Ray RC	.60	1.50
92 Don Nelson	1.50	4.00
93 Mahdi Abdul-Rahman	.60	1.50
(formerly Walt Hazzard)		
94 Willie Norwood	.40	1.00
95 Dick Van Arsdale	.60	1.50
96 Don May	.40	1.00
97 Walt Bellamy	1.50	4.00
98 Garfield Heard RC	1.50	4.00
99 Dave Wohl	.40	1.00
100 Kareem Abdul-Jabbar	12.50	30.00
101 Ron Knight	.40	1.00
102 Phil Chenier RC	1.50	4.00
103 Rudy Tomjanovich	3.00	8.00
104 Flynn Robinson	.40	1.00
105 Dave DeBusschere	2.50	6.00
106 Dennis Layton	.40	1.00
107 Bill Hewitt	.40	1.00
108 Dick Garrett	.40	1.00
109 Walt Wesley	.40	1.00
110 John Havlicek	12.50	25.00
111 Norm Van Lier	.60	1.50
112 Cazzie Russell	1.25	3.00
113 Herm Gilliam	.40	1.00
114 Greg Smith	.40	1.00
115 Nate Archibald	2.50	6.00
116 Don Kojis	.40	1.00
117 Rick Adelman	.60	1.50
118 Luke Jackson	.60	1.50
119 Lamar Green	.40	1.00
120 Archie Clark	.60	1.50
121 Happy Hairston	1.00	2.50
122 Bill Bradley	10.00	20.00
123 Ron Williams	.40	1.00
124 Jimmy Walker	.60	1.50
125 Bob Kauffman	.40	1.00
126 Rick Roberson	.60	1.50
127 Howard Porter RC	.60	1.50
128 Mike Newlin RC	.60	1.50
129 Willis Reed	3.00	8.00
130 Lou Hudson	1.25	3.00
131 Don Chaney	1.25	3.00
132 Dave Stallworth	.40	1.00
133 Charlie Yelverton	.40	1.00
134 Ken Durrett	.40	1.00
135 John Brisker	.60	1.50
136 Dick Snyder	.40	1.00
137 Jim McDaniels	.40	1.00
138 Clyde Lee	.40	1.00
139 Dennis Awtrey UER	.60	1.50
(Misspelled Awtry on card front)		
140 Keith Erickson	.60	1.50
141 Bob Weiss	.60	1.50
142 Butch Beard RC	1.25	3.00
143 Terry Dischinger	.40	1.00
144 Pat Riley	8.00	20.00
145 Lucius Allen	.60	1.50
146 John Mengelt RC	.40	1.00
147 John Hummer	.40	1.00
148 Bob Love	2.00	5.00
149 Bobby Smith	.60	1.50
150 Elvin Hayes	5.00	10.00
151 Nate Williams	.40	1.00
152 Chet Walker	1.25	3.00
153 Steve Kuberski	.40	1.00
154 Playoffs G1/Earl Monroe	1.25	3.00
155 NBA Playoffs G2	1.00	2.50
Lakers Come Back		
(under the basket)		
156 NBA Playoffs G3	1.00	2.50
Two in a Row		
(under the basket)		
157 Leroy Ellis PO	1.00	2.50
158 Playoffs G5	3.00	8.00
Jerry West		
159 Wilt Chamberlain PO	5.00	10.00
160 NBA Checklist 1-176	6.00	15.00
UER (135 Jim King)		
161 John Havlicek AS	5.00	10.00
162 Spencer Haywood AS	.75	2.00
163 Kareem Abdul-Jabbar AS	12.50	25.00
164 Jerry West AS	8.00	20.00
165 Walt Frazier AS	2.00	5.00
166 Bob Love AS	.75	2.00
167 Billy Cunningham AS	1.50	4.00
168 Wilt Chamberlain AS	10.00	25.00
169 Nate Archibald AS	2.00	5.00
170 Archie Clark AS	.75	2.00
171 Kareem Abdul-Jabbar	6.00	15.00
John Havlicek		
Nate Archibald LL		
172 Kareem Abdul-Jabbar	6.00	15.00
Nate Archibald		
John Havlicek LL		
173 Wilt Chamberlain	6.00	15.00
Kareem Abdul-Jabbar		
Walt Bellamy LL		
174 Jack Marin	1.25	3.00
Calvin Murphy		
Gail Goodrich LL		
175 Wilt Chamberlain	6.00	15.00
Kareem Abdul-Jabbar		
Wes Unseld LL		
176 Len Wilkens	6.00	12.00
Jerry West		
Nate Archibald LL		
177 Roland Taylor	.60	1.50
178 Art Becker	.60	1.50
179 Mack Calvin	.75	2.00
180 Artis Gilmore RC	10.00	20.00
181 Collis Jones	.60	1.50
182 John Roche RC	.75	2.00
183 George McGinnis RC	6.00	15.00
184 Johnny Neumann	.75	2.00
185 Willie Wise	.75	2.00
186 Bernie Williams	.60	1.50
187 Byron Beck	.75	2.00
188 Larry Miller	.75	2.00
189 Cincy Powell	.60	1.50
190 Donnie Freeman	.75	2.00
191 John Baum	.60	1.50
192 Billy Keller	.75	2.00
193 Wilbert Jones	.60	1.50
194 Glen Combs	.60	1.50
195 Julius Erving RC	100.00	200.00
(Forward on front, but Center on back)		
196 Al Smith	.60	1.50
197 George Carter	.60	1.50
198 Louie Dampier	1.25	3.00
199 Rich Jones	.60	1.50
200 Mel Daniels	1.25	3.00
201 Gene Moore	.60	1.50
202 Randy Denton	.60	1.50
203 Larry Jones	.60	1.50
204 Jim Ligon	.60	1.50
205 Warren Jabali	.75	2.00
206 Joe Caldwell	.75	2.00
207 Darrell Carrier	.75	2.00
208 Gene Kennedy	.60	1.50
209 Ollie Taylor	.60	1.50
210 Roger Brown	.75	2.00
211 George Lehmann	.60	1.50
212 Red Robbins	.75	2.00
213 Jim Eakins	.75	2.00
214 Willie Long	.60	1.50
215 Billy Cunningham	3.00	8.00
216 Steve Jones	.75	2.00
217 Les Hunter	.60	1.50
218 Billy Paultz	.75	2.00

219 Freddie Lewis .75 2.00
220 Zelmo Beaty .75 2.00
221 George Thompson .60 1.50
222 Neil Johnson .60 1.50
223 Dave Robisch RC .75 2.00
224 Walt Simon .60 1.50
225 Bill Melchionni .75 2.00
226 Wendell Ladner RC .75 2.00
227 Joe Hamilton .60 1.50
228 Bob Netolicky .75 2.00
229 James Jones .75 2.00
230 Dan Issel 5.00 10.00
231 Charlie Williams .60 1.50
232 Willie Sojourner .60 1.50
233 Merv Jackson .60 1.50
234 Mike Lewis .60 1.50
235 Ralph Simpson .75 2.00
236 Darnell Hillman .75 2.00
237 Rick Mount 1.25 3.00
238 Gerald Govan .60 1.50
239 Ron Boone .75 2.00
240 Tom Washington .60 1.50
241 ABA Playoffs G1 1.00 2.50
Pacers take lead
(under the basket)
242 Playoffs G2 2.00 5.00
Rick Barry
243 Playoffs G3 1.50 4.00
George McGinnis
244 Playoffs G4 2.00 5.00
Rick Barry
245 Billy Keller PO 1.00 2.50
246 ABA Playoffs G6 1.00 2.50
Tight Defense
247 ABA Champs: Pacers 1.25 3.00
248 ABA Checklist 177-264 6.00 15.00
UER (236 John Brisker)
249 Dan Issel AS 2.50 6.00
250 Rick Barry AS 3.00 8.00
251 Artis Gilmore AS 2.50 6.00
252 Donnie Freeman AS 1.00 2.50
253 Bill Melchionni AS 1.00 2.50
254 Willie Wise AS 1.00 2.50
255 Julius Erving AS 25.00 50.00
256 Zelmo Beaty AS 1.00 2.50
257 Ralph Simpson AS 1.00 2.50
258 Charlie Scott AS 1.00 2.50
259 Charlie Scott 3.00 8.00
Rick Barry
Dan Issel LL
260 Artis Gilmore 1.50 4.00
Tom Washington
Larry Jones LL
261 Glen Combs 1.00 2.50
Louie Dampier
Warren Jabali LL
262 Rick Barry 1.50 4.00
Mack Calvin
Steve Jones LL
263 Artis Gilmore 10.00 20.00
Julius Erving
Mel Daniels LL
264 Bill Melchionni 2.50 6.00
Larry Brown
Louie Dampier LL

1973-74 Topps

The 1973-74 Topps set of 264 standard-size cards contains NBA players on cards numbered 1 to 176 and ABA players on cards numbered 177 to 264. Cards were issued in 10-card packs with 24 packs per box. All-Star selections (first and second team) for both leagues are noted on the respective player's regular cards. Card backs are printed in red and green on gray card stock. The backs feature year-by-year ABA and NBA statistics. Subsets include NBA Playoffs (62-68), NBA League Leaders (153-158), ABA Playoffs (202-208) and ABA League Leaders (234-239). The only notable Rookie Cards in this set are Chris Ford, Bob McAdoo, and Paul Westphal.

COMPLETE SET (264) 200.00 325.00
1 Nate Archibald AS1 5.00 10.00
2 Steve Kuberski .20 .50
3 John Mengelt .20 .50
4 Jim McMillian .40 1.00
5 Nate Thurmond 1.50 4.00
6 Dave Wohl .20 .50
7 John Brisker .20 .50
8 Charlie Davis .20 .50
9 Lamar Green .20 .50
10 Walt Frazier AS2 2.50 6.00
11 Bob Christian .20 .50
12 Cornell Warner .20 .50
13 Calvin Murphy 1.50 4.00
14 Dave Sorenson .20 .50
15 Archie Clark .40 1.00
16 Clifford Ray .40 1.00
17 Terry Driscoll .20 .50
18 Matt Guokas .60 1.50
19 Elmore Smith .40 1.00
20 John Havlicek AS1 7.50 15.00
21 Pat Riley 3.00 8.00
22 George Trapp .20 .50
23 Ron Williams .20 .50
24 Jim Fox .20 .50
25 Dick Van Arsdale .40 1.00
26 John Tresvant .20 .50
27 Rick Adelman .40 1.00
28 Eddie Mast .20 .50
29 Jim Cleamons .40 1.00
30 Dave DeBusschere AS2 2.00 5.00
31 Norm Van Lier .40 1.00
32 Stan McKenzie .20 .50
33 Bob Dandridge .40 1.00
34 Leroy Ellis .40 1.00
35 Mike Riordan .40 1.00
36 Fred Hilton .20 .50
37 Toby Kimball .20 .50
38 Jim Price .20 .50
39 Willie Norwood .20 .50
40 Dave Cowens AS2 5.00 10.00
41 Cazzie Russell .40 1.00
42 Lee Winfield .20 .50
43 Connie Hawkins 2.00 5.00
44 Mike Newlin .40 1.00
45 Chet Walker .40 1.00
46 Walt Bellamy 1.50 4.00
47 John Johnson .40 1.00
48 Henry Bibby RC 2.00 5.00
49 Bobby Smith .40 1.00
50 Kareem Abdul-Jabbar AS1 12.50 25.00
51 Mike Price .20 .50
52 John Hummer .20 .50
53 Kevin Porter RC 2.00 5.00
54 Nate Williams .20 .50
55 Gail Goodrich 1.50 4.00
56 Fred Foster .20 .50
57 Don Chaney .40 1.00
58 Bud Stallworth .20 .50
59 Clem Haskins .60 1.50
60 Bob Love AS2 1.25 3.00
61 Jimmy Walker .40 1.00
62 NBA Eastern Semis .40 1.00
Knicks shoot down Bullets in 5
63 NBA Eastern Semis .40 1.00
Celts oust Hawks 2nd Straight Year
64 Western Semis 3.00 8.00
Wilt Chamberlain
65 NBA Western Semis .40 1.00
Warriors overwhelm Milwaukee
66 Eastern Finals 1.25 3.00
Willis Reed
Henry Finkel
67 NBA Western Finals .40 1.00
Lakers Breeze Past Golden State
68 NBA Championship 1.50 4.00
Knicks Do It, Repeat '70 Miracle
(Walt Frazier
Keith Erickson)
69 Larry Steele .40 1.00
70 Oscar Robertson 7.50 15.00
71 Phil Jackson 7.50 15.00
72 John Wetzel .20 .50
73 Steve Patterson RC .40 1.00
74 Manny Leaks .20 .50
75 Jeff Mullins .40 1.00
76 Stan Love .20 .50
77 Dick Garrett .20 .50
78 Don Nelson 1.50 4.00
79 Chris Ford RC 1.25 3.00
80 Wilt Chamberlain 15.00 25.00
81 Dennis Layton .20 .50
82 Bill Bradley 7.50 15.00
83 Jerry Sloan .40 1.00
84 Cliff Meely .20 .50
85 Sam Lacey .20 .50
86 Dick Snyder .20 .50
87 Jim Washington .20 .50
88 Lucius Allen .40 1.00
89 LaRue Martin .20 .50
90 Rick Barry 3.00 8.00
91 Fred Boyd .20 .50
92 Barry Clemens .20 .50
93 Dean Meminger .20 .50
94 Henry Finkel .20 .50
95 Elvin Hayes 2.50 6.00
96 Stu Lantz .40 1.00
97 Bill Hewitt .20 .50
98 Neal Walk .20 .50
99 Garfield Heard .40 1.00
100 Jerry West AS1 10.00 20.00
101 Otto Moore .20 .50
102 Don Kojis .20 .50
103 Fred Brown RC 2.50 6.00
104 Dwight Davis .20 .50
105 Willis Reed 2.50 6.00
106 Herm Gilliam .20 .50
107 Mickey Davis .40 1.00
108 Jim Barnett .20 .50
109 Ollie Johnson .20 .50
110 Bob Lanier 2.50 6.00
111 Fred Carter .40 1.00
112 Paul Silas 1.25 3.00
113 Phil Chenier .40 1.00
114 Dennis Awtrey .20 .50
115 Austin Carr .40 1.00
116 Bob Kauffman .20 .50
117 Keith Erickson .40 1.00
118 Walt Wesley .20 .50
119 Steve Bracey .20 .50
120 Spencer Haywood AS1 1.25 3.00
121 NBA Checklist 1-176 6.00 12.00
122 Jack Marin .40 1.00
123 Jon McGlocklin .20 .50
124 Johnny Green .40 1.00
125 Jerry Lucas 1.25 3.00
126 Paul Westphal RC 10.00 20.00
127 Curtis Rowe .40 1.00
128 Mahdi Abdul-Rahman .40 1.00
(formerly Walt Hazzard)
129 Lloyd Neal RC .40 1.00
130 Pete Maravich AS1 15.00 30.00
131 Don May .20 .50
132 Bob Weiss .40 1.00
133 Dave Stallworth .20 .50
134 Dick Cunningham .20 .50
135 Bob McAdoo RC 10.00 20.00
136 Butch Beard .40 1.00
137 Happy Hairston .40 1.00
138 Bob Rule .60 1.50
139 Don Adams .20 .50
140 Charlie Scott .40 1.00
141 Ron Riley .20 .50
142 Earl Monroe 1.50 4.00
143 Clyde Lee .20 .50
144 Rick Roberson .20 .50
145 Rudy Tomjanovich 2.50 6.00
(Printed without Houston on basket)
146 Tom Van Arsdale .40 1.00
147 Art Williams .20 .50
148 Curtis Perry .20 .50
149 Rich Rinaldi .20 .50
150 Lou Hudson .40 1.00
151 Mel Counts .20 .50
152 Jim McDaniels .20 .50
153 Nate Archibald 3.00 8.00
Kareem Abdul-Jabbar
Spencer Haywood LL
154 Nate Archibald 3.00 8.00
Kareem Abdul-Jabbar
Spencer Haywood LL
155 Wilt Chamberlain 6.00 12.00
Matt Guokas
Kareem Abdul-Jabbar LL
156 Rick Barry 1.50 4.00
Calvin Murphy
Mike Newlin LL
157 Wilt Chamberlain 3.00 8.00
Nate Thurmond
Dave Cowens LL
158 Nate Archibald 1.50 4.00
Len Wilkens
Dave Bing LL
159 Don Smith .20 .50
160 Sidney Wicks 1.25 3.00
161 Howie Komives .20 .50
162 John Gianelli .20 .50
163 Jeff Halliburton .20 .50
164 Kennedy McIntosh .20 .50
165 Len Wilkens 2.50 6.00
166 Corky Calhoun .20 .50
167 Howard Porter .40 1.00
168 Jo Jo White 1.25 3.00
169 John Block .20 .50
170 Dave Bing 1.50 4.00
171 Joe Ellis .20 .50
172 Chuck Terry .20 .50
173 Randy Smith .40 1.00
174 Bill Bridges .40 1.00
175 Geoff Petrie .40 1.00
176 Wes Unseld 1.50 4.00
177 Skeeter Swift .40 1.00
178 Jim Eakins .60 1.50
179 Steve Jones .60 1.50
180 George McGinnis AS1 1.25 3.00
181 Al Smith .40 1.00
182 Tom Washington .40 1.00
183 Louie Dampier .60 1.50
184 Simmie Hill .40 1.00
185 George Thompson .40 1.00
186 Cincy Powell .60 1.50
187 Larry Jones .40 1.00
188 Neil Johnson .40 1.00
189 Tom Owens .40 1.00
190 Ralph Simpson AS2 .60 1.50
191 George Carter .60 1.50
192 Rick Mount .60 1.50
193 Red Robbins .60 1.50
194 George Lehmann .40 1.00
195 Mel Daniels AS2 .60 1.50
196 Bob Warren .40 1.00
197 Gene Kennedy .40 1.00
198 Mike Barr .40 1.00
199 Dave Robisch .40 1.00
200 Billy Cunningham AS1 2.00 5.00
201 John Roche .60 1.50
202 ABA Western Semis .75 2.00
Pacers Outlast Injured Rockets
203 ABA Western Semis .75 2.00
Stars sweep Q's in Four Straight
204 ABA Eastern Semis .75 2.00
Dan Issel PO
205 ABA Eastern Semis .75 2.00
Cougars in strong finish over Nets
206 ABA Western Finals .75 2.00
Pacers nip bitter rival & Stars
207 Eastern Finals 1.25 3.00
Artis Gilmore
208 ABA Championship .75 2.00
George McGinnis
209 Glen Combs .40 1.00
210 Dan Issel AS2 2.50 6.00
211 Randy Denton .40 1.00
212 Freddie Lewis .60 1.50
213 Stew Johnson .40 1.00
214 Roland Taylor .40 1.00
215 Rich Jones .40 1.00
216 Billy Paultz .60 1.50
217 Ron Boone .60 1.50
218 Walt Simon .40 1.00
219 Mike Lewis .40 1.00
220 Warren Jabali AS1 .60 1.50
221 Wilbert Jones .40 1.00
222 Don Buse RC .60 1.50
223 Gene Moore .40 1.00
224 Joe Hamilton .60 1.50
225 Zelmo Beaty .60 1.50
226 Brian Taylor RC .60 1.50
227 Julius Keye .40 1.00
228 Mike Gale RC .40 1.00
229 Warren Davis .40 1.00
230 Mack Calvin AS2 .60 1.50
231 Roger Brown .60 1.50
232 Chuck Williams .60 1.50
233 Gerald Govan .60 1.50
234 Julius Erving 5.00 10.00
George McGinnis
Dan Issel LL
235 Artis Gilmore .75 2.00
Gene Kennedy
Tom Owens LL
236 Glen Combs .75 2.00
Roger Brown
Louie Dampier LL
237 Billy Keller .75 2.00
Ron Boone
Bob Warren LL
238 Artis Gilmore 1.25 3.00
Mel Daniels
Bill Paultz LL
239 Bill Melchionni .75 2.00
Chuck Williams
Warren Jabali LL
240 Julius Erving AS2 25.00 50.00
241 Jimmy O'Brien .40 1.00
242 ABA Checklist 177-264 6.00 12.00
243 Johnny Neumann .40 1.00
244 Darnell Hillman .60 1.50
245 Willie Wise .60 1.50
246 Collis Jones .40 1.00
247 Ted McClain .40 1.00
248 George Irvine RC .40 1.00
249 Bill Melchionni .60 1.50
250 Artis Gilmore AS1 2.50 6.00
251 Willie Long .40 1.00
252 Larry Miller .40 1.00
253 Lee Davis .40 1.00
254 Donnie Freeman .60 1.50
255 Joe Caldwell .60 1.50
256 Bob Netolicky .60 1.50
257 Bernie Williams .40 1.00
258 Byron Beck .60 1.50
259 Jim Chones RC 1.25 3.00
260 James Jones AS1 .60 1.50
261 Wendell Ladner .40 1.00
262 Ollie Taylor .40 1.00
263 Les Hunter .40 1.00
264 Billy Keller ! 1.25 3.00

1973-74 Topps Team Stickers

Measuring 2 1/2" by 3 1/2", these ABA and NBA team stickers were inserted one per wax pack. Two teams are represented on each color sticker. The larger (2 1/2" by 2 1/2") top sticker carries the team logo, while the smaller (1" by 2 1/2") bottom sticker displays only the team name on a banner. Only one of each ABA sticker was produced, while some NBA stickers exhibit two team combinations. The stickers are unnumbered and checklisted below in alphabetical order according to the top sticker for the ABA (1-10) and the NBA (11-33). The team represented on the bottom sticker is listed immediately below each entry.

COMPLETE SET (33) 60.00 125.00
1 Carolina Cougars 2.00 5.00
Stars
2 Denver Rockets 2.00 5.00
Squires
3 Indiana Pacers 2.50 6.00
Squires
4 Kentucky Colonels 2.50 6.00
Tams
5 Memphis Tams 2.50 6.00
Cougars
6 New York Nets 2.50 6.00
Conquistadors
7 San Antonio Spurs 2.00 5.00
Nets
8 San Diego Conquistadors 2.00 5.00
Pacers
9 Utah Stars 2.00 5.00
Colonels
10 Virginia Squires 2.00 5.00
Rockets
11 Atlanta Hawks 1.25 3.00
Celtics
12 Atlanta Hawks 1.25 3.00
Supersonics
13 Boston Celtics 1.50 4.00
Braves
14 Boston Celtics/76ers 1.50 4.00
15 Buffalo Braves 1.50 4.00
Lakers
16 Buffalo Braves 1.50 4.00
Trail Blazers
17 Capitol Bullets 1.25 3.00
Knicks
18 Chicago Bulls 1.25 3.00
Pistons
19 Cleveland Cavaliers 1.25 3.00
Hawks
20 Detroit Pistons 1.25 3.00
Warriors
21 Golden State Warriors 1.25 3.00
Bucks
22 Golden State Warriors 1.25 3.00
Kings
23 Houston Rockets 1.25 3.00
Braves
24 Kansas City Kings 1.25 3.00
Lakers/76ers
25 Los Angeles Lakers 1.50 4.00
Bullets
26 Los Angeles Lakers 1.50 4.00
Celtics
27 Milwaukee Bucks 1.25 3.00
Knicks
28 New York Knicks 1.25 3.00
Bulls
29 New York Knicks 1.25 3.00
Warriors
30 Philadelphia 76ers 1.25 3.00
Hawks
31 Phoenix Suns 1.25 3.00
Cavaliers
32 Portland Trail Blazers 1.25 3.00
Rockets
33 Seattle Supersonics 1.25 3.00
Suns

1974-75 Topps

The 1974-75 Topps set of 264 standard-size cards contains NBA players on cards numbered 1 to 176 and ABA players on cards numbered 177 to 264. For the first time Team Leader (TL) cards are provided for each team. The cards were issued in 10-card packs with 24 packs per box. All-Star selections (first and second team) for both leagues are noted on the respective player's regular cards. The card backs are printed in blue and red on gray card stock. Subsets include NBA Team Leaders (81-98), NBA Statistical Leaders (144-149), NBA Playoffs (161-164), ABA Statistical Leaders (207-212), ABA Team Leaders (221-230) and ABA Playoffs (246-249). The key Rookie Cards in this set are Doug Collins, George Gervin and Bill Walton.

COMPLETE SET (264) 200.00 325.00
1 Kareem Abdul-Jabbar ! 15.00 30.00
2 Don May .20 .50
3 Bernie Fryer RC .40 1.00
4 Don Adams .20 .50
5 Herm Gilliam .20 .50
6 Jim Chones .40 1.00
7 Rick Adelman .40 1.00
8 Randy Smith .40 1.00
9 Paul Silas 1.25 3.00
10 Pete Maravich 12.50 25.00
11 Ron Behagen .20 .50
12 Kevin Porter .40 1.00
13 Bill Bridges .40 1.00
(On back team shown as Los And.& should be Los Ang.)
14 Charles Johnson RC .20 .50
15 Bob Love .40 1.00
16 Henry Bibby .40 1.00
17 Neal Walk .20 .50
18 John Brisker .20 .50
19 Lucius Allen .20 .50
20 Tom Van Arsdale .40 1.00
21 Larry Steele .20 .50
22 Curtis Rowe .40 1.00
23 Dean Meminger .20 .50
24 Steve Patterson .20 .50
25 Earl Monroe 1.25 3.00
26 Jack Marin .20 .50
27 Jo Jo White 1.25 3.00
28 Rudy Tomjanovich 2.50 6.00
29 Otto Moore .20 .50
30 Elvin Hayes AS2 2.00 5.00
31 Pat Riley 3.00 8.00
32 Clyde Lee .20 .50
33 Bob Weiss .20 .50
34 Jim Fox .20 .50
35 Charlie Scott .40 1.00
36 Cliff Meely .20 .50
37 Jon McGlocklin .20 .50
38 Jim McMillian .40 1.00
39 Bill Walton RC 25.00 50.00
40 Dave Bing AS2 1.25 3.00
41 Jim Washington .20 .50
42 Jim Cleamons .40 1.00
43 Mel Davis .20 .50
44 Garfield Heard .40 1.00
45 Jimmy Walker .40 1.00
46 Don Nelson 1.25 3.00
47 Jim Barnett .20 .50
48 Manny Leaks .20 .50
49 Elmore Smith .40 1.00
50 Rick Barry AS1 2.50 6.00
51 Jerry Sloan 1.25 3.00
52 John Hummer .20 .50
53 Keith Erickson .20 .50
54 George E. Johnson .20 .50
55 Oscar Robertson 6.00 12.00
56 Steve Mix RC .40 1.00
57 Rick Roberson .20 .50
58 John Mengelt .20 .50
59 Dwight Jones RC .40 1.00
60 Austin Carr .40 1.00
61 Nick Weatherspoon RC .40 1.00
62 Clem Haskins .40 1.00
63 Don Kojis .20 .50
64 Paul Westphal 1.25 3.00
65 Walt Bellamy 1.50 4.00
66 John Johnson .40 1.00
67 Butch Beard .40 1.00
68 Happy Hairston .40 1.00
69 Tom Boerwinkle .20 .50
70 Spencer Haywood AS2 1.25 3.00
71 Gary Melchionni .20 .50
72 Ed Ratleff RC .40 1.00
73 Mickey Davis .20 .50
74 Dennis Awtrey .20 .50
75 Fred Carter .40 1.00
76 George Trapp .20 .50
77 John Wetzel .20 .50
78 Bobby Smith .40 1.00
79 John Gianelli .20 .50
80 Bob McAdoo AS2 2.50 6.00
81 Pete Maravich 2.50 6.00
Lou Hudson
Walt Bellamy
Pete Maravich TL
82 John Havlicek 2.00 5.00
JoJo White
Dave Cowens
JoJo White TL
83 Bob McAdoo .40 1.00
Ernie DiGregorio
Bob McAdoo
Ernie DiGregorio TL
84 Bob Love 1.25 3.00
Chet Walker
Clifford Ray
Norm Van Lier TL
85 Austin Carr .40 1.00
Austin Carr
Dwight Davis
Len Wilkens TL
86 Bob Lanier .40 1.00
Stu Lantz
Bob Lanier
Dave Bing TL
87 Rick Barry 1.25 3.00
Rick Barry
Nate Thurmond
Rick Barry TL
88 Rudy Tomjanovich .40 1.00
Calvin Murphy
Don Smith
Calvin Murphy TL
89 Jimmy Walker .40 1.00
Jimmy Walker
Sam Lacey
Jimmy Walker TL
90 Gail Goodrich .40 1.00
Gail Goodrich
Happy Hairston
Gail Goodrich TL
91 Kareem Abdul-Jabbar 6.00 12.00
Oscar Robertson
Kareem Abdul-Jabbar
Oscar Robertson TL
92 New Orleans Jazz .40 1.00
Emblem; Expansion
Draft Picks on Back
93 Walt Frazier 2.00 5.00
Bill Bradley
Dave DeBusschere
Walt Frazier TL
94 Fred Carter .40 1.00
Tom Van Arsdale
Leroy Ellis
Fred Carter TL
95 Charlie Scott .40 1.00
Dick Van Arsdale
Neal Walk
Neal Walk TL
96 Geoff Petrie .40 1.00
Geoff Petrie
Rick Roberson
Sidney Wicks TL
97 Spencer Haywood .40 1.00
Dick Snyder
Spencer Haywood
Fred Brown TL
98 Phil Chenier .40 1.00
Phil Chenier
Elvin Hayes
Kevin Porter TL
99 Sam Lacey .20 .50
100 John Havlicek AS1 5.00 10.00
101 Stu Lantz .40 1.00
102 Mike Riordan .20 .50
103 Larry Jones .20 .50
104 Connie Hawkins 1.50 4.00
105 Nate Thurmond 1.25 3.00
106 Dick Gibbs .20 .50
107 Corky Calhoun .20 .50
108 Dave Wohl .20 .50
109 Cornell Warner .20 .50
110 Geoff Petrie UER .40 1.00
(Misspelled Patrie on card front)
111 Leroy Ellis .40 1.00
112 Chris Ford .40 1.00
113 Bill Bradley 5.00 10.00
114 Clifford Ray .20 .50
115 Dick Snyder .20 .50
116 Nate Williams .20 .50
117 Matt Guokas .40 1.00
118 Henry Finkel .20 .50
119 Curtis Perry .20 .50
120 Gail Goodrich AS1 1.25 3.00
121 Wes Unseld 1.25 3.00
122 Howard Porter .40 1.00
123 Jeff Mullins .20 .50
124 Mike Bantom RC .40 1.00
125 Fred Brown .40 1.00
126 Bob Dandridge .40 1.00
127 Mike Newlin .40 1.00
128 Greg Smith .20 .50
129 Doug Collins RC 6.00 15.00
130 Lou Hudson .40 1.00
131 Bob Lanier 2.00 5.00
132 Phil Jackson 5.00 10.00
133 Don Chaney .40 1.00
134 Jim Brewer RC .40 1.00
135 Ernie DiGregorio RC 1.25 3.00
136 Steve Kuberski .20 .50
137 Jim Price .20 .50
138 Mike D'Antoni .20 .50
139 John Brown .20 .50
140 Norm Van Lier AS2 .40 1.00
141 NBA Checklist 1-176 5.00 10.00
142 Slick Watts RC .40 1.00
143 Walt Wesley .20 .50
144 Bob McAdoo 6.00 12.00
Kareem Abdul-Jabbar
Pete Maravich LL
145 Bob McAdoo 6.00 12.00
Pete Maravich
Kareem Abdul-Jabbar LL
146 Bob McAdoo 5.00 10.00
Kareem Abdul-Jabbar
Rudy Tomjanovich LL
147 Ernie DiGregorio .40 1.00
Rick Barry
Jeff Mullins LL
148 Elvin Hayes 1.50 4.00
Dave Cowens
Bob McAdoo LL
149 Ernie DiGregorio .40 1.00
Calvin Murphy
Len Wilkens LL
150 Walt Frazier AS1 2.00 5.00
151 Cazzie Russell .40 1.00
152 Calvin Murphy 1.25 3.00
153 Bob Kauffman .20 .50
154 Fred Boyd .20 .50
155 Dave Cowens 2.50 6.00
156 Willie Norwood .20 .50
157 Lee Winfield .20 .50
158 Dwight Davis .20 .50
159 George T. Johnson .20 .50
160 Dick Van Arsdale .40 1.00
161 NBA Eastern Semis .40 1.00
Celts over Braves
Knicks edge Bullets
162 NBA Western Semis .40 1.00
Bucks over Lakers
Bulls edge Pistons
163 NBA Div. Finals .40 1.00
Celts over Knicks
Bucks sweep Bulls
164 NBA Championship .60 1.50
Celtics over Bucks
165 Phil Chenier .40 1.00
166 Kermit Washington RC .40 1.00
167 Dale Schlueter .20 .50
168 John Block .20 .50
169 Don Smith .20 .50
170 Nate Archibald 1.50 4.00
171 Chet Walker .40 1.00
172 Archie Clark .40 1.00
173 Kennedy McIntosh .20 .50
174 George Thompson .20 .50
175 Sidney Wicks 1.25 3.00
176 Jerry West 10.00 20.00
177 Dwight Lamar .40 1.00
178 George Carter .60 1.50
179 Wil Robinson .40 1.00
180 Artis Gilmore AS1 1.50 4.00
181 Brian Taylor .60 1.50
182 Darnell Hillman .60 1.50
183 Dave Robisch .60 1.50
184 Gene Littles RC .60 1.50
185 Willie Wise AS2 .60 1.50
186 James Silas RC 1.25 3.00
187 Caldwell Jones RC 1.25 3.00
188 Roland Taylor .40 1.00
189 Randy Denton .40 1.00
190 Dan Issel AS2 2.00 5.00
191 Mike Gale .40 1.00
192 Mel Daniels .60 1.50
193 Steve Jones .60 1.50
194 Marv Roberts .40 1.00
195 Ron Boone AS2 .60 1.50
196 George Gervin RC 20.00 40.00
197 Flynn Robinson .40 1.00
198 Cincy Powell .40 1.00
199 Glen Combs .40 1.00
200 Julius Erving AS1 UER 20.00 40.00
(Misspelled Irving on card back)
201 Billy Keller .60 1.50
202 Willie Long .40 1.00
203 ABA Checklist 177-264 5.00 10.00
204 Joe Caldwell .60 1.50
205 Swen Nater RC .60 1.50
206 Rick Mount .60 1.50
207 Julius Erving 5.00 10.00
George McGinnis
Dan Issel LL
208 Swen Nater .75 2.00
James Jones
Tom Owens LL
209 Louie Dampier .75 2.00
Billy Keller
Roger Brown LL
210 James Jones .75 2.00
Mack Calvin
Ron Boone LL
211 Artis Gilmore .75 2.00
George McGinnis
Caldwell Jones LL
212 Al Smith .75 2.00
Chuck Williams
Louie Dampier LL
213 Larry Miller .40 1.00
214 Stew Johnson .40 1.00
215 Larry Finch RC 1.25 3.00
216 Larry Kenon RC 1.25 3.00
217 Joe Hamilton .60 1.50
218 Gerald Govan .60 1.50
219 Ralph Simpson .60 1.50
220 George McGinnis AS1 1.25 3.00
221 Billy Cunningham .75 2.00
Mack Calvin
Tom Owens
Joe Caldwell TL
222 Ralph Simpson .75 2.00
Byron Beck
Dave Robisch
Al Smith TL
223 George McGinnis .75 2.00
Billy Keller
George McGinnis
Freddie Lewis TL
224 Dan Issel 1.25 3.00
Louie Dampier
Artis Gilmore
Louie Dampier TL
225 George Thompson .75 2.00
Larry Finch
Randy Denton
George Thompson TL
226 Julius Erving 5.00 10.00
John Roche
Larry Kenon
Julius Erving TL
227 George Gervin 2.50 6.00
George Gervin
Swen Nater
James Silas TL
228 Dwight Lamar .75 2.00
Stew Johnson
Caldwell Jones
Chuck Williams TL
229 Willie Wise .75 2.00
James Jones
Gerald Govan
James Jones TL
230 George Carter .75 2.00
George Irvine
Jim Eakins
Roland Taylor TL
231 Bird Averitt .40 1.00
232 John Roche .40 1.00
233 George Irvine .40 1.00
234 John Williamson RC .40 1.00
235 Billy Cunningham 1.50 4.00
236 Jimmy O'Brien .40 1.00
237 Wilbert Jones .40 1.00
238 Johnny Neumann .40 1.00
239 Al Smith .40 1.00
240 Roger Brown .60 1.50
241 Chuck Williams .60 1.50
242 Rich Jones .40 1.00
243 Dave Twardzik RC .60 1.50
244 Wendell Ladner .60 1.50
245 Mack Calvin AS1 .60 1.50
246 ABA Eastern Semis .75 2.00
Nets over Squires
Colonels sweep Cougars
247 ABA Western Semis .75 2.00
Stars over Conquistadors
Pacers over Spurs
248 ABA Div. Finals .75 2.00
Nets sweep Colonels
Stars edge Pacers
249 ABA Championships 6.00 12.00
Julius Erving
250 Wilt Chamberlain CO 15.00 40.00
251 Ron Robinson .40 1.00
252 Zelmo Beaty .60 1.50
253 Donnie Freeman .60 1.50
254 Mike Green .40 1.00
255 Louie Dampier AS2 .60 1.50
256 Tom Owens .40 1.00
257 George Karl RC 5.00 10.00
258 Jim Eakins .60 1.50
259 Travis Grant .60 1.50
260 James Jones AS1 .60 1.50
261 Mike Jackson .60 1.50
262 Billy Paultz .60 1.50
263 Freddie Lewis .60 1.50
264 Byron Beck 1.25 3.00
(Back refers to ANA, should be ABA)

1975-76 Topps

The 1975-76 Topps basketball card set of 330 standard-size cards was the largest basketball set ever produced up to that time. Cards were issued in 10-card which cost 15 cents per pack and had 24 packs per box. NBA players are depicted on cards 1-220 and ABA players on cards 221-330. Team Leaders (TL) cards are 116-133 (NBA teams) and 278-287 (ABA). Other subsets include NBA Statistical Leaders (1-6), NBA Playoffs (188-189), NBA Team Checklists (203-220), ABA Statistical Leaders (221-226), ABA Playoffs (309-310) and ABA Team Checklists (321-330). All-Star selections (first and second team) for both leagues are noted on the respective player's regular cards. Card backs are printed in blue and green on gray card stock. The set is particularly hard to sort numerically, as the small card number on the back is printed in blue on a dark green background. The set was printed on three large sheets each containing 110 different cards. Investigation of the second (series) sheet reveals that 22 of the cards were double printed; they are marked DP in the checklist below. Rookie Cards in this set include Bobby Jones, Maurice Lucas, Moses Malone and Keith (Jamaal) Wilkes.

COMPLETE SET (330) 275.00 450.00

Card	Low	High
Bob McAdoo	6.00	12.00
Rick Barry		
Kareem Abdul-Jabbar LL		
Don Nelson	1.50	4.00
Butch Beard		
Rudy Tomjanovich LL		
Rick Barry	2.00	5.00
Calvin Murphy		
Bill Bradley LL		
Wes Unseld	.60	1.50
Dave Cowens		
Sam Lacey LL		
Kevin Porter	.60	1.50
Dave Bing		
Nate Archibald LL		
Rick Barry	1.50	4.00
Walt Frazier		
Larry Steele LL		
Tom Van Arsdale	.50	1.25
Paul Silas	.50	1.25
Jerry Sloan	1.25	3.00
0 Bob McAdoo AS1	2.50	6.00
1 Dwight Davis	.30	.75
2 John Mengelt	.50	1.25
3 George Johnson	.30	.75
4 Ed Ratleff	.30	.75
5 Nate Archibald AS1	1.50	4.00
6 Elmore Smith	.30	.75
7 Bob Dandridge	.50	1.25
8 Louie Nelson RC	.30	.75
9 Neal Walk	.30	.75
20 Billy Cunningham	1.50	4.00
21 Gary Melchionni	.30	.75
22 Barry Clemens	.30	.75
23 Jimmy Jones	.30	.75
24 Tom Burleson RC	.50	1.25
25 Lou Hudson	.50	1.25
26 Henry Finkel	.30	.75
27 Jim McMillian	.50	1.25
28 Matt Guokas	.50	1.25
29 Fred Foster DP	.30	.75
30 Bob Lanier	2.00	5.00
31 Jimmy Walker	.50	1.25
32 Cliff Meely	.30	.75
33 Butch Beard	.75	2.00
34 Cazzie Russell	.50	1.25
35 Jon McGlocklin	.30	.75
36 Bernie Fryer	.30	.75
37 Bill Bradley	5.00	10.00
38 Fred Carter	.50	1.25
39 Dennis Awtrey DP	.30	.75
40 Sidney Wicks	.50	1.25
41 Fred Brown	.50	1.25
42 Rowland Garrett	.30	.75
43 Herm Gilliam	.30	.75
44 Don Nelson	.50	1.25
45 Ernie DiGregorio	.75	2.00
46 Jim Brewer	.30	.75
47 Chris Ford	.75	2.00
48 Nick Weatherspoon	.50	1.25
49 Zaid Abdul-Aziz	.30	.75
(formerly Don Smith)		
50 Keith Wilkes RC	5.00	10.00
51 Ollie Johnson DP	.30	.75
52 Lucius Allen	.50	1.25
53 Mickey Davis	.30	.75
54 Otto Moore	.30	.75
55 Walt Frazier AS1	2.00	5.00
56 Steve Mix	.50	1.25
57 Nate Hawthorne	.30	.75
58 Lloyd Neal	.30	.75
59 Slick Watts	.50	1.25
60 Elvin Hayes	2.00	5.00
61 Checklist 1-110	3.00	8.00
62 Mike Sojourner	.30	.75
63 Randy Smith	.50	1.25
64 John Block DP	.30	.75
65 Charlie Scott	.50	1.25
66 Jim Chones	.50	1.25
67 Rick Adelman	.50	1.25
68 Curtis Rowe	.30	.75
69 Derrek Dickey RC	.50	1.25
70 Rudy Tomjanovich	2.00	5.00
71 Pat Riley	2.50	6.00
72 Cornell Warner	.30	.75
73 Earl Monroe	1.25	3.00
74 Allan Bristow RC	1.25	3.00
75 Pete Maravich DP	12.00	20.00
76 Curtis Perry	.30	.75
77 Bill Walton	12.00	20.00
78 Leonard Gray	.30	.75
79 Kevin Porter	.50	1.25
80 John Havlicek AS2	5.00	10.00
81 Dwight Jones	.30	.75
82 Jack Marin	.30	.75
83 Dick Snyder	.30	.75
84 George Trapp	.30	.75
85 Nate Thurmond	1.25	3.00
86 Charles Johnson	.30	.75
87 Ron Riley	.30	.75
88 Stu Lantz	.50	1.25
89 Scott Wedman RC	.60	1.50
90 Kareem Abdul-Jabbar	10.00	20.00
91 Aaron James	.30	.75
92 Jim Barnett	.30	.75
93 Clyde Lee	.30	.75
94 Larry Steele	.50	1.25
95 Mike Riordan	.30	.75
96 Archie Clark	.50	1.25
97 Mike Bantom	.30	.75
98 Bob Kauffman	.30	.75
99 Kevin Stacom RC	.30	.75
100 Rick Barry AS1	2.50	6.00
101 Ken Charles	.30	.75
102 Tom Boerwinkle	.30	.75
103 Mike Newlin	.50	1.25
104 Leroy Ellis	.50	1.25
105 Austin Carr	.50	1.25
106 Ron Behagen	.30	.75
107 Jim Price	.30	.75
108 Bud Stallworth	.30	.75
109 Earl Williams	.30	.75
110 Gail Goodrich	1.25	3.00
111 Phil Jackson	2.50	6.00
112 Rod Derline	.30	.75
113 Keith Erickson	.30	.75
114 Phil Lumpkin	.30	.75
115 Wes Unseld	1.25	3.00
116 Lou Hudson	.60	1.50
Lou Hudson		
John Drew		
Dean Meminger TL		
117 Dave Cowens	1.25	3.00
Kevin Stacom		
Paul Silas		
JoJo White TL		
118 Bob McAdoo	1.25	3.00
Jack Marin		
Bob McAdoo		
Randy Smith TL		
119 Bob Love	1.25	3.00
Chet Walker		
Nate Thurmond		
Norm Van Lier TL		
120 Bobby Smith	.60	1.50
Dick Snyder		
Jim Chones		
Jim Cleamons TL		
121 Bob Lanier	1.25	3.00
John Mengelt		
Bob Lanier		
Dave Bing TL		
122 Rick Barry	1.25	3.00
Rick Barry		
Clifford Ray		
Rick Barry TL		
123 Rudy Tomjanovich	.75	2.00
Calvin Murphy		
Kevin Kunnert		
Mike Newlin TL		
124 Nate Archibald	.75	2.00
Ollie Johnson		
Sam Lacey UER/(Lacy on front)		
Nate Archibald TL		
125 Gail Goodrich	.60	1.50
Cazzie Russell		
Happy Hairston		
Gail Goodrich TL		
126 Kareem Abdul-Jabbar	3.00	8.00
Mickey Davis		
Kareem Abdul-Jabbar		
Kareem Abdul-Jabbar TL		
127 Pete Maravich	5.00	10.00
Stu Lantz		
E.C. Coleman		
Pete Maravich TL		
128 Walt Frazier	1.25	3.00
Bill Bradley		
John Gianelli		
Walt Frazier TL DP		
129 Fred Carter	.75	2.00
Doug Collins		
Billy Cunningham		
Billy Cunningham TL DP		
130 Charlie Scott	.60	1.50
Keith Erickson		
Curtis Perry		
Dennis Awtrey TL DP		
131 Sidney Wicks	.60	1.50
Geoff Petrie		
Sidney Wicks		
Geoff Petrie TL DP		
132 Spencer Haywood	.75	2.00
Archie Clark		
Spencer Haywood		
Don Watts TL		
133 Elvin Hayes	1.25	3.00
Clem Haskins		
Wes Unseld		
Kevin Porter TL		
134 John Drew RC	.50	1.25
135 Jo Jo White AS2	.75	2.00
136 Garfield Heard	.50	1.25
137 Jim Cleamons	.30	.75
138 Howard Porter	.50	1.25
139 Phil Smith RC	.50	1.25
140 Bob Love	.50	1.25
141 John Gianelli DP	.30	.75
142 Larry McNeill RC	.30	.75
143 Brian Winters RC	1.25	3.00
144 George Thompson	.30	.75
145 Kevin Kunnert	.30	.75
146 Henry Bibby	.50	1.25
147 John Johnson	.30	.75
148 Doug Collins	1.50	4.00
149 John Brisker	.30	.75
150 Dick Van Arsdale	.50	1.25
151 Leonard Robinson RC	1.25	3.00
152 Dean Meminger	.30	.75
153 Phil Hankinson	.30	.75
154 Dale Schlueter	.30	.75
155 Norm Van Lier	.50	1.25
156 Campy Russell RC	1.25	3.00
157 Jeff Mullins	.50	1.25
158 Sam Lacey	.30	.75
159 Happy Hairston	.50	1.25
160 Dave Bing DP	1.25	3.00
161 Kevin Restani RC	.30	.75
162 Dave Wohl	.30	.75
163 E.C. Coleman	.30	.75
164 Jim Fox	.30	.75
165 Geoff Petrie	.50	1.25
166 Hawthorne Wingo DP UER	.30	.75
Misspelled Harthorne on card front		
167 Fred Boyd	.30	.75
168 Willie Norwood	.30	.75
169 Bob Wilson	.30	.75
170 Dave Cowens	2.50	6.00
171 Tom Henderson RC	.30	.75
172 Jim Washington	.30	.75
173 Clem Haskins	.50	1.25
174 Jim Davis	.30	.75
175 Bobby Smith DP	.30	.75
176 Mike D'Antoni	.30	.75
177 Zelmo Beaty	.50	1.25
178 Gary Brokaw RC	.30	.75
179 Mel Davis	.30	.75
180 Calvin Murphy	1.25	3.00
181 Checklist 111-220 DP	3.00	8.00
182 Nate Williams	.30	.75
183 LaRue Martin	.30	.75
184 George McGinnis	1.25	3.00
185 Clifford Ray	.30	.75
186 Paul Westphal	1.50	4.00
187 Talvin Skinner	.30	.75
188 NBA Playoff Semis DP	.60	1.50
Warriors edge Bulls		
Bullets over Celts		
189 NBA Playoff Finals	.60	1.50
Clifford Ray		
190 Phil Chenier AS2 DP	.50	1.25
191 John Brown	.30	.75
192 Lee Winfield	.30	.75
193 Steve Patterson	.30	.75
194 Charles Dudley	.30	.75
195 Connie Hawkins DP	1.25	3.00
196 Leon Benbow	.30	.75
197 Don Kojis	.30	.75
198 Ron Williams	.30	.75
199 Mel Counts	.30	.75
200 Spencer Haywood AS2	1.25	3.00
201 Greg Jackson	.30	.75
202 Tom Kozelko DP	.30	.75
203 Atlanta Hawks CL	.60	1.50
204 Boston Celtics CL	1.25	3.00
205 Buffalo Braves CL	.60	1.50
206 Chicago Bulls CL	1.25	3.00
207 Cleveland Cavs CL	.60	1.50
208 Detroit Pistons CL	.60	1.50
209 Golden State CL	.60	1.50
210 Houston Rockets CL	.60	1.50
211 Kansas City Kings CL DP	.60	1.50
212 Los Angeles Lakers CL DP	.60	1.50
213 Milwaukee Bucks CL	.60	1.50
214 New Orleans Jazz CL	.60	1.50
215 New York Knicks CL	.60	1.50
216 Philadelphia 76ers CL	.60	1.50
217 Phoenix Suns CL DP	.60	1.50
218 Portland Blazers CL	.60	1.50
219 Seattle Sonics CL DP	5.00	10.00
Bill Russell		
220 Washington Bullets CL	.60	1.50
221 George McGinnis	3.00	8.00
Julius Erving		
Ron Boone LL		
222 Bobby Jones	3.00	8.00
Artis Gilmore		
Moses Malone LL		
223 Billy Shepherd	.75	2.00
Louie Dampier		
Al Smith LL		
224 Mack Calvin	.75	2.00
James Silas		
Dave Robisch LL		
225 Swen Nater	.75	2.00
Artis Gilmore		
Marvin Barnes LL		
226 Mack Calvin	.75	2.00
Chuck Williams		
George McGinnis LL		
227 Mack Calvin AS1	.75	2.00
228 Billy Knight RC	1.25	3.00
229 Bird Averitt	.60	1.50
230 George Carter	.60	1.50
231 Swen Nater AS2	.75	2.00
232 Steve Jones	.75	2.00
233 George Gervin	10.00	20.00
234 Lee Davis	.60	1.50
235 Ron Boone AS1	.75	2.00
236 Mike Jackson	.60	1.50
237 Kevin Joyce RC	.60	1.50
238 Marv Roberts	.60	1.50
239 Tom Owens	.60	1.50
240 Ralph Simpson	.75	2.00
241 Gus Gerard	.60	1.50
242 Brian Taylor AS2	.75	2.00
243 Rich Jones	.60	1.50
244 John Roche	.60	1.50
245 Travis Grant	.75	2.00
246 Dave Twardzik	.75	2.00
247 Mike Green	.60	1.50
248 Billy Keller	.75	2.00
249 Stew Johnson	.60	1.50
250 Artis Gilmore AS1	2.00	5.00
251 John Williamson	.75	2.00
252 Marvin Barnes RC	1.50	4.00
253 James Silas AS2	.75	2.00
254 Moses Malone RC	15.00	40.00
255 Willie Wise	.75	2.00
256 Dwight Lamar	.60	1.50
257 Checklist 221-330	3.00	8.00
258 Byron Beck	.75	2.00
259 Len Elmore RC	1.25	3.00
260 Dan Issel	2.00	5.00
261 Rick Mount	.60	1.50
262 Billy Paultz	.75	2.00
263 Donnie Freeman	.60	1.50
264 George Adams	.60	1.50
265 Don Chaney	.75	2.00
266 Randy Denton	.60	1.50
267 Don Washington	.60	1.50
268 Roland Taylor	.60	1.50
269 Charlie Edge	.60	1.50
270 Louie Dampier	.75	2.00
271 Collis Jones	.60	1.50
272 Al Skinner RC	.60	1.50
273 Coby Dietrick	.60	1.50
274 Tim Bassett	.60	1.50
275 Freddie Lewis	.75	2.00
276 Gerald Govan	.60	1.50
277 Ron Thomas	.60	1.50
278 Ralph Simpson	.75	2.00
Mack Calvin		
Mike Green		
Mack Calvin TL		
279 George McGinnis	1.00	2.50
Billy Keller		
George McGinnis		
George McGinnis TL		
280 Artis Gilmore	1.00	2.50
Louie Dampier		
Artis Gilmore		
Louie Dampier TL		
281 George Carter	.75	2.00
Larry Finch		
Tom Owens		
Chuck Williams TL		
282 Julius Erving	6.00	15.00
John Williamson		
Julius Erving		
Julius Erving TL		
283 Marvin Barnes	1.00	2.50
Freddie Lewis		
Marvin Barnes		
Freddie Lewis TL		
284 George Gervin	2.00	5.00
James Silas		
Swen Nater		
James Silas TL		
285 Travis Grant	.75	2.00
Jimmy O'Brien		
Caldwell Jones		
Jimmy O'Brien TL		
286 Ron Boone	3.00	8.00
Ron Boone		
Moses Malone		
Al Smith TL		
287 Willie Wise	.75	2.00
Red Robbins		
Dave Vaughn		
Dave Twardzik TL		
288 Claude Terry	.60	1.50
289 Wilbert Jones	.60	1.50
290 Darnell Hillman	.75	2.00
291 Bill Melchionni	.75	2.00
292 Mel Daniels	.75	2.00
293 Fly Williams RC	.75	2.00
294 Larry Kenon	.75	2.00
295 Red Robbins	.75	2.00
296 Warren Jabali	.75	2.00
297 Jim Eakins	.75	2.00
298 Bobby Jones RC	6.00	12.00
299 Don Buse	.75	2.00
300 Julius Erving AS1	15.00	40.00
301 Billy Shepherd	.60	1.50
302 Maurice Lucas RC	2.50	6.00
303 George Karl	2.00	5.00
304 Jim Bradley	.60	1.50
305 Caldwell Jones	.75	2.00
306 Al Smith	.60	1.50
307 Jan Van Breda Kolff RC	.75	2.00
308 Darrell Elston	.60	1.50
309 ABA Playoff Semifinals	.75	2.00
Colonels over Spirits;		
Pacers edge Nuggets		
310 Artis Gilmore PO	1.00	2.50
311 Ted McClain	.60	1.50
312 Willie Sojourner	.60	1.50
313 Bob Warren	.60	1.50
314 Bob Netolicky	.75	2.00
315 Chuck Williams	.60	1.50
316 Gene Kennedy	.60	1.50
317 Jimmy O'Brien	.60	1.50
318 Dave Robisch	.60	1.50
319 Wali Jones	.60	1.50
320 George Irvine	.60	1.50
321 Denver Nuggets CL	.75	2.00
322 Indiana Pacers CL	.75	2.00
323 Kentucky Colonels CL	.75	2.00
324 Memphis Sounds CL	.75	2.00
325 New York Nets CL	.75	2.00
326 St. Louis Spirits CL	.75	2.00
(Spirits of St. Louis on card back)		
327 San Antonio Spurs CL	.75	2.00
328 San Diego Sails CL	.75	2.00
329 Utah Stars CL	.75	2.00
330 Virginia Squires CL !	1.50	4.00

1975-76 Topps Team Checklist

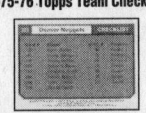

These team checklists were issued in three panels, with nine teams per panel. The panels were available as a complete set via a mail-in offer. Each panel measures approximately 7 1/2" by 10 1/2" and are joined together to form one continuous sheet. The checklists are printed in blue and green on white card stock and list all NBA and ABA teams. They are numbered on the front and listed alphabetically according to the city names. The backs are blank. Since there was only room for 27 teams on the three-part sheet, Topps apparently left off card 324 (Memphis Sounds), which is in the regular set.

Card	Low	High
COMPLETE SET (27)	75.00	150.00
203 Atlanta Hawks	2.50	6.00
204 Boston Celtics	5.00	10.00
205 Buffalo Braves	2.50	6.00
206 Chicago Bulls	2.50	6.00
207 Cleveland Cavaliers	2.50	6.00
208 Detroit Pistons	2.50	6.00
209 Golden State Warriors	2.50	6.00
210 Houston Rockets	2.50	6.00
211 Kansas City Kings	2.50	6.00
212 Los Angeles Lakers	5.00	10.00
213 Milwaukee Bucks	2.50	6.00
214 New Orleans Jazz	2.50	6.00
215 New York Knicks	3.00	8.00
216 Philadelphia 76ers	2.50	6.00
217 Phoenix Suns	2.50	6.00
218 Portland Trail Blazers	3.00	8.00
219 Seattle SuperSonics	2.50	6.00
220 Washington Bullets	2.50	6.00
321 Denver Nuggets	3.00	8.00
322 Indiana Pacers	3.00	8.00
323 Kentucky Colonels	3.00	8.00
325 New York Nets	3.00	8.00
326 Spirits of St. Louis	3.00	8.00
327 San Antonio Spurs	3.00	8.00
328 San Diego Sails	3.00	8.00
329 Utah Stars	3.00	8.00
330 Virginia Squires	2.50	6.00

1976-77 Topps

Perhaps the most popular set of the seventies, the 144-card 1976-77 Topps set witnessed a return to the larger-size at 3 1/8" by 5 1/4". The larger size and excellent photo quality are appealing to collectors. Also, because of the size, they are attractive to autograph collectors. Cards were issued in 10-card packs which cost 15 cents with 24 packs per box. The fronts have a large color photo with the team name vertical on the left border. The player's name and position are at the bottom. Backs have statistical and biographical data. Cards numbered 126-135 are the previous season's NBA All-Star selections. The cards were printed on two large sheets, each with eight rows and nine columns. The checklist card was located in the lower right corner of the second sheet. Card No. 1, Julius Erving, is rarely found centered. Rookie Cards include Alvan Adams, Lloyd Free, Gus Williams and David Thompson.

Card	Low	High
COMPLETE SET (144)	175.00	375.00
1 Julius Erving !	20.00	50.00
2 Dick Snyder	.75	2.00
3 Paul Silas	1.00	2.50
4 Keith Erickson	.75	2.00
5 Wes Unseld	2.00	5.00
6 Butch Beard	1.00	2.50
7 Lloyd Neal	.75	2.00
8 Tom Henderson	.75	2.00
9 Jim McMillian	1.00	2.50
10 Bob Lanier	2.50	6.00
11 Junior Bridgeman RC	1.00	2.50
12 Corky Calhoun	.75	2.00
13 Billy Keller	1.00	2.50
14 Mickey Johnson RC	.75	2.00
15 Fred Brown	1.00	2.50
16 Keith Wilkes	1.00	2.50
17 Louie Nelson	.75	2.00
18 Ed Ratleff	.75	2.00
19 Billy Paultz	1.00	2.50
20 Nate Archibald	2.00	5.00
21 Steve Mix	1.00	2.50
22 Ralph Simpson	.75	2.00
23 Campy Russell	1.00	2.50
24 Charlie Scott	1.00	2.50
25 Artis Gilmore	2.00	5.00
26 Dick Van Arsdale	1.00	2.50
27 Phil Chenier	1.00	2.50
28 Spencer Haywood	2.00	5.00
29 Chris Ford	1.00	2.50
30 Dave Cowens	5.00	10.00
31 Sidney Wicks	1.00	2.50
32 Jim Price	.75	2.00
33 Dwight Jones	.75	2.00
34 Lucius Allen	.75	2.00
35 Marvin Barnes	1.00	2.50
36 Henry Bibby	1.00	2.50
37 Joe Meriweather RC	.75	2.00
38 Doug Collins	2.50	6.00
39 Garfield Heard	1.00	2.50
40 Randy Smith	1.00	2.50
41 Tom Burleson	1.00	2.50
42 Dave Twardzik	1.00	2.50
43 Bill Bradley	6.00	12.00
44 Calvin Murphy	2.00	5.00
45 Bob Love	1.00	2.50
46 Brian Winters	1.00	2.50
47 Glenn McDonald	.75	2.00
48 Checklist 1-144	15.00	30.00
49 Bird Averitt	.75	2.00
50 Rick Barry	5.00	10.00
51 Ticky Burden	.75	2.00
52 Rich Jones	.75	2.00
53 Austin Carr	1.00	2.50
54 Steve Kuberski	.75	2.00
55 Paul Westphal	1.00	2.50
56 Mike Riordan	.75	2.00
57 Bill Walton	15.00	25.00
58 Eric Money RC	.75	2.00
59 John Drew	1.00	2.50
60 Pete Maravich	20.00	40.00
61 John Shumate RC	1.00	2.50
62 Mack Calvin	1.00	2.50
63 Bruce Seals	.75	2.00
64 Walt Frazier	2.50	6.00
65 Elmore Smith	.75	2.00
66 Rudy Tomjanovich	2.50	6.00
67 Sam Lacey	.75	2.00
68 George Gervin	15.00	25.00
69 Gus Williams RC	2.00	5.00
70 George McGinnis	1.00	2.50
71 Len Elmore	.75	2.00
72 Jack Marin	.75	2.00
73 Brian Taylor	.75	2.00
74 Jim Brewer	.75	2.00
75 Alvan Adams RC	2.50	6.00
76 Dave Bing	2.00	5.00
77 Phil Jackson	5.00	10.00
78 Geoff Petrie	1.00	2.50
79 Mike Sojourner	.75	2.00
80 James Silas	1.00	2.50
81 Bob Dandridge	1.00	2.50
82 Ernie DiGregorio	1.00	2.50
83 Cazzie Russell	1.00	2.50
84 Kevin Porter	1.00	2.50
85 Tom Boerwinkle	.75	2.00
86 Darnell Hillman	1.00	2.50
87 Herm Gilliam	.75	2.00
88 Nate Williams	.75	2.00
89 Phil Smith	1.00	2.50
90 John Havlicek	7.50	15.00
91 Kevin Kunnert	.75	2.00
92 Jimmy Walker	1.00	2.50
93 Billy Cunningham	2.00	5.00
94 Dan Issel	2.50	6.00
95 Ron Boone	1.00	2.50
96 Lou Hudson	1.00	2.50
97 Jim Chones	1.00	2.50
98 Earl Monroe	2.00	5.00
99 Tom Van Arsdale	1.00	2.50
100 Kareem Abdul-Jabbar	15.00	40.00
101 Moses Malone	12.50	25.00
102 Ricky Sobers RC	.75	2.00
103 Swen Nater	1.00	2.50
104 Leonard Robinson	1.00	2.50
105 Slick Watts	1.00	2.50
106 Otto Moore	.75	2.00
107 Maurice Lucas	1.00	2.50
108 Norm Van Lier	1.00	2.50
109 Clifford Ray	.75	2.00
110 David Thompson RC	15.00	40.00
111 Fred Carter	1.00	2.50
112 Caldwell Jones	1.00	2.50
113 John Williamson	1.00	2.50
114 Bobby Smith	1.00	2.50
115 Jo Jo White	1.00	2.50
116 Curtis Perry	.75	2.00
117 John Gianelli	.75	2.00
118 Curtis Rowe	.75	2.00
119 Lionel Hollins RC	1.00	2.50
120 Elvin Hayes	2.50	6.00
121 Ken Charles	.75	2.00
122 Dave Meyers RC	1.00	2.50
123 Jerry Sloan	1.00	2.50
124 Billy Knight	1.00	2.50
125 Gail Goodrich	1.00	2.50
126 Kareem Abdul-Jabbar AS	12.00	20.00
127 Julius Erving AS	12.50	25.00
128 George McGinnis AS	1.00	2.50
129 Nate Archibald AS	1.00	2.50
130 Pete Maravich AS	15.00	25.00
131 Dave Cowens AS	2.00	5.00
132 Rick Barry AS	2.00	5.00
133 Elvin Hayes AS	2.00	5.00
134 James Silas AS	.75	2.00
135 Randy Smith AS	.75	2.00
136 Leonard Gray	.75	2.00
137 Charles Johnson	.75	2.00
138 Ron Behagen	.75	2.00
139 Mike Newlin	1.00	2.50
140 Bob McAdoo	2.50	6.00
141 Mike Gale	.75	2.00
142 Scott Wedman	1.00	2.50
143 Lloyd Free RC	2.50	6.00
144 Bobby Jones !	3.00	8.00

1977-78 Topps

The 1977-78 Topps basketball card set consists of 132 standard-size cards. Cards were issued in 10-card packs with 24 packs per box. Fronts feature team and player name at the bottom with the player's position in a basketball at bottom left of the photo. Card backs are printed in green and black on either white or gray card stock. The white card stock is considered more desirable by most collectors and may even be a little tougher to find. However, there is no difference in value for either card stock. Rookie Cards include Adrian Dantley, Darryl Dawkins, John Lucas, Tom McMillen and Robert Parish.

Card	Low	High
COMPLETE SET (132)	50.00	100.00
1 Kareem Abdul-Jabbar !	7.50	15.00
2 Henry Bibby	.15	.40
3 Curtis Rowe	.10	.30
4 Norm Van Lier	.15	.40
5 Darnell Hillman	.15	.40
6 Earl Monroe	.60	1.50
7 Leonard Gray	.10	.30
8 Bird Averitt	.10	.30
9 Jim Brewer	.10	.30
10 Paul Westphal	.40	1.00
11 Bob Gross RC	.15	.40
12 Phil Smith	.10	.30
13 Dan Roundfield RC	.25	.60
14 Brian Taylor	.10	.30
15 Rudy Tomjanovich	.75	2.00
16 Kevin Porter	.15	.40
17 Scott Wedman	.15	.40
18 Lloyd Free	.25	.60
19 Tom Boswell RC	.10	.30
20 Pete Maravich	7.50	15.00
21 Cliff Poindexter	.10	.30
22 Bubbles Hawkins	.15	.40
23 Kevin Grevey RC	.50	1.25
24 Ken Charles	.10	.30
25 Bob Dandridge	.15	.40
26 Lonnie Shelton RC	.15	.40
27 Don Chaney	.15	.40
28 Larry Kenon	.15	.40
29 Checklist 1-132		
30 Fred Brown	.15	.40
31 John Gianelli UER	.10	.30
(Listed as Cavaliers,		
should be Buffalo Braves)		
32 Austin Carr	.15	.40
33 Keith Wilkes	.25	.60
34 Caldwell Jones	.15	.40
35 Jo Jo White	.40	1.00
36 Scott May RC	.60	1.50
37 Mike Newlin	.10	.30
38 Mel Davis	.10	.30
39 Lionel Hollins	.25	.60
40 Elvin Hayes	1.00	2.50
41 Dan Issel	.75	2.00
42 Ricky Sobers	.10	.30
43 Don Ford	.10	.30
44 John Williamson	.10	.30
45 Bob McAdoo	.75	2.00
46 Geoff Petrie	.15	.40
47 M.L. Carr RC	.75	2.00
48 Brian Winters	.20	.60
49 Sam Lacey	.10	.30
50 George McGinnis	.25	.60
51 Slick Watts	.15	.40
52 Sidney Wicks	.25	.60
53 Wilbur Holland	.10	.30
54 Tim Bassett	.15	.40
55 Phil Chenier	.15	.40
56 Adrian Dantley RC	3.00	8.00
57 Jim Chones	.15	.40
58 John Lucas RC	1.00	2.50
59 Cazzie Russell	.15	.40
60 David Thompson	2.00	5.00
61 Bob Lanier	.75	2.00
62 Dave Twardzik	.15	.40
63 Wilbert Jones	.10	.30
64 Clifford Ray	.10	.30
65 Doug Collins	.60	1.50
66 Tom McMillen RC	1.00	2.50
67 Rich Kelley RC	.10	.30
68 Mike Bantom	.10	.30
69 Tom Boerwinkle	.10	.30
70 John Havlicek	2.50	6.00
71 Marvin Webster RC	.15	.40
72 Curtis Perry	.10	.30
73 George Gervin	3.00	8.00
74 Leonard Robinson	.25	.60
75 Wes Unseld	.60	1.50
76 Dave Meyers	.15	.40
77 Gail Goodrich	.25	.60
78 Richard Washington RC	.25	.60
79 Mike Gale	.10	.30
80 Maurice Lucas	.25	.60
81 Harvey Catchings RC	.15	.40
82 Randy Smith	.10	.30
83 Campy Russell	.15	.40
84 Kevin Kunnert	.10	.30
85 Lou Hudson	.15	.40
86 Mickey Johnson	.10	.30
87 Lucius Allen	.10	.30
88 Spencer Haywood	.40	1.00
89 Gus Williams	.25	.60
90 Dave Cowens	1.25	3.00
91 Al Skinner	.10	.30
92 Swen Nater	.10	.30
93 Tom Henderson	.10	.30
94 Don Buse	.15	.40
95 Alvan Adams	.25	.60
96 Mack Calvin	.15	.40
97 Tom Burleson	.10	.30
98 John Drew	.15	.40
99 Mike Green	.10	.30
100 Julius Erving	7.50	15.00
101 John Mengelt	.10	.30
102 Howard Porter	.15	.40
103 Billy Paultz	.15	.40
104 John Shumate	.15	.40
105 Calvin Murphy	.60	1.50
106 Elmore Smith	.10	.30
107 Jim McMillian	.10	.30
108 Kevin Stacom	.10	.30
109 Jan Van Breda Kolff	.10	.30
110 Billy Knight	.15	.40
111 Robert Parish RC	10.00	25.00
112 Larry Wright	.10	.30
113 Bruce Seals	.10	.30
114 Junior Bridgeman	.15	.40
115 Artis Gilmore	.60	1.50
116 Steve Mix	.15	.40
117 Ron Lee	.10	.30
118 Bobby Jones	.25	.60
119 Ron Boone	.15	.40
120 Bill Walton	3.00	8.00
121 Chris Ford	.15	.40
122 Earl Tatum	.10	.30
123 E.C. Coleman	.10	.30
124 Moses Malone	2.50	6.00
125 Charlie Scott	.15	.40
126 Bobby Smith	.10	.30
127 Nate Archibald	.60	1.50
128 Mitch Kupchak RC	.50	1.25
129 Walt Frazier	1.00	2.50
130 Rick Barry	1.25	3.00
131 Ernie DiGregorio	.15	.40
132 Darryl Dawkins RC	5.00	12.00

1978-79 Topps

The 1978-79 Topps basketball card set contains 132 standard-size cards. Cards were issued in 10-card packs with 36 packs per box. Card fronts feature the player and team name down the left border and a small head shot inserted at bottom right. Card backs are printed in orange and brown on gray card stock. The key Rookie Cards in this set inlcude Quinn Buckner, Walter Davis, James "Buddha" Edwards, Dennis Johnson, Marques Johnson, Bernard King, Norm Nixon and Jack Sikma.

Card	Low	High
COMPLETE SET (132)	25.00	60.00
1 Bill Walton !	5.00	10.00
2 Doug Collins	.60	1.50
3 Jamaal Wilkes	.30	.75
4 Wilbur Holland	.10	.30
5 Bob McAdoo	.50	1.25
6 Lucius Allen	.10	.30
7 Wes Unseld	.50	1.25
8 Dave Meyers	.20	.50
9 Austin Carr	.20	.50
10 Walter Davis RC	3.00	8.00
11 John Williamson	.10	.30
12 E.C. Coleman	.10	.30
13 Calvin Murphy	.50	1.25
14 Bobby Jones	.30	.75
15 Chris Ford	.20	.50
16 Kermit Washington	.20	.50
17 Butch Beard	.20	.50
18 Steve Mix	.30	.75
19 Marvin Webster	.20	.50
20 George Gervin	2.50	6.00
21 Steve Hawes	.10	.30
22 Johnny Davis RC	.20	.50
23 Swen Nater	.10	.30
24 Lou Hudson	.20	.50
25 Elvin Hayes	.60	1.50
26 Nate Archibald	.60	1.50
27 James Edwards RC	1.25	3.00
28 Howard Porter	.20	.50
29 Quinn Buckner RC	.50	1.25
30 Leonard Robinson	.20	.50
31 Jim Cleamons	.10	.30
32 Campy Russell	.20	.50
33 Phil Smith	.10	.30
34 Darryl Dawkins	.75	2.00
35 Don Buse	.20	.50
36 Mickey Johnson	.10	.30
37 Mike Gale	.10	.30
38 Moses Malone	1.50	4.00
39 Gus Williams	.30	.75
40 Dave Cowens	.75	2.00
41 Bobby Wilkerson RC	.20	.50
42 Wilbert Jones	.10	.30
43 Charlie Scott	.20	.50
44 John Drew	.20	.50
45 Earl Monroe	.50	1.25
46 John Shumate	.20	.50
47 Earl Tatum	.10	.30
48 Mitch Kupchak	.20	.50
49 Ron Boone	.20	.50
50 Maurice Lucas	.40	1.00
51 Louie Dampier	.20	.50
52 Aaron James	.10	.30
53 John Mengelt	.10	.30
54 Garfield Heard	.20	.50
55 George Johnson	.10	.30
56 Junior Bridgeman	.10	.30
57 Elmore Smith	.10	.30
58 Rudy Tomjanovich	.60	1.50
59 Fred Brown	.20	.50
60 Rick Barry UER	.75	2.00
(reversed negative)		
61 Dave Bing	.50	1.25
62 Anthony Roberts	.20	.50
63 Norm Nixon RC	.75	2.00
64 Leon Douglas RC	.20	.50
65 Henry Bibby	.20	.50
66 Lonnie Shelton	.20	.50
67 Checklist 1-132	.75	2.00
68 Tom Henderson	.10	.30
69 Dan Roundfield	.20	.50
70 Armond Hill RC	.20	.50
71 Larry Kenon	.20	.50
72 Billy Knight	.20	.50
73 Artis Gilmore	.60	1.50
74 Lionel Hollins	.20	.50
75 Bernard King RC	3.00	8.00
76 Brian Winters	.30	.75
77 Alvan Adams	.30	.75
78 Dennis Johnson RC	3.00	8.00
79 Scott Wedman	.10	.30
80 Pete Maravich	5.00	10.00
81 Dan Issel	.60	1.50
82 M.L. Carr	.30	.75
83 Walt Frazier	.60	1.50
84 Dwight Jones	.10	.30
85 Jo Jo White	.30	.75
86 Robert Parish	2.00	5.00
87 Charlie Criss RC	.20	.50
88 Jim McMillian	.10	.30
89 Chuck Williams	.10	.30
90 George McGinnis	.30	.75
91 Billy Paultz	.20	.50
92 Bob Dandridge	.20	.50
93 Ricky Sobers	.10	.30
94 Paul Silas	.20	.50
95 Gail Goodrich	.30	.75
96 Tim Bassett	.20	.50
97 Ron Lee	.10	.30
98 Bob Gross	.20	.50
99 Sam Lacey	.20	.50
100 David Thompson	1.50	4.00
(College North Carolina,		
should be NC State)		

101 John Gianelli .10 .30
102 Norm Van Lier .20 .50
103 Caldwell Jones .20 .50
104 Eric Money .10 .30
105 Jim Chones .20 .50
106 John Lucas .40 1.00
107 Spencer Haywood .30 .75
108 Eddie Johnson RC .10 .30
109 Sidney Wicks .30 .75
110 Kareem Abdul-Jabbar 3.00 8.00
111 Sonny Parker RC .20 .50
112 Randy Smith .10 .30
113 Kevin Grevey .20 .50
114 Rich Kelley .10 .30
115 Scott May .20 .50
116 Lloyd Free .30 .75
117 Jack Sikma RC .75 2.00
118 Kevin Porter .20 .50
119 Darnell Hillman .20 .50
120 Paul Westphal .40 1.00
121 Richard Washington .10 .30
122 Dave Twardzik .20 .50
123 Mike Bantom .10 .30
124 Mike Newlin .10 .30
125 Bob Lanier .60 1.50
126 Marques Johnson RC 1.50 4.00
127 Foots Walker RC .20 .50
128 Cedric Maxwell RC .60 1.50
129 Ray Williams RC .20 .50
130 Julius Erving 5.00 12.00
131 Clifford Ray .10 .30
132 Adrian Dantley ! 1.25 3.00

1979-80 Topps

The 1979-80 Topps basketball set contains 132 standard-size cards. Cards were issued in 12-card packs along with a stick of bubble gum. The player's name, team and position are at the bottom. The team name is wrapped around a basketball. Card backs are printed in red and black on gray card stock. All-Star selections are designated as AS1 for first team selections and AS2 for second team selections and are denoted on the front of the player's regular card. Notable Rookie Cards in this set include Alex English, Reggie Theus, and Mychal Thompson.

COMPLETE SET (132) 40.00 80.00
1 George Gervin ! 2.50 6.00
2 Mitch Kupchak .15 .40
3 Henry Bibby .15 .40
4 Bob Gross .15 .40
5 Dave Cowens .75 2.00
6 Dennis Johnson .60 1.50
7 Scott Wedman .15 .40
8 Earl Monroe .50 1.25
9 Mike Bantom .10 .30
10 Kareem Abdul-Jabbar AS 3.00 8.00
11 Jo Jo White .30 .75
12 Spencer Haywood .25 .60
13 Kevin Porter .15 .40
14 Bernard King .60 1.50
15 Mike Newlin .10 .30
16 Sidney Wicks .25 .60
17 Dan Issel .50 1.25
18 Tom Henderson .10 .30
19 Jim Chones .15 .40
20 Julius Erving 5.00 10.00
21 Brian Winters .25 .60
22 Billy Paultz .15 .40
23 Cedric Maxwell .15 .40
24 Eddie Johnson .10 .30
25 Artis Gilmore .30 .75
26 Maurice Lucas .25 .60
27 Gus Williams .25 .60
28 Sam Lacey .15 .40
29 Toby Knight .10 .30
30 Paul Westphal AS1 .25 .60
31 Alex English RC 4.00 10.00
32 Gail Goodrich .25 .60
33 Caldwell Jones .15 .40
34 Kevin Grevey .15 .40
35 Jamaal Wilkes .25 .60
36 Sonny Parker .10 .30
37 John Gianelli .10 .30
38 John Long RC .15 .40
39 George Johnson .10 .30
40 Lloyd Free AS2 .25 .60
41 Rudy Tomjanovich .50 1.25
42 Foots Walker .15 .40
43 Dan Roundfield .15 .40
44 Reggie Theus RC 1.25 3.00
45 Bill Walton 1.25 3.00
46 Fred Brown .15 .40
47 Darnell Hillman .15 .40
48 Ray Williams .10 .30
49 Larry Kenon .15 .40
50 David Thompson .75 2.00
51 Billy Knight .15 .40
52 Alvan Adams .25 .60
53 Phil Smith .10 .30
54 Adrian Dantley .50 1.25
55 John Williamson .10 .30
56 Campy Russell .15 .40
57 Armond Hill .15 .40
58 Bob Lanier .50 1.25
59 Mickey Johnson .10 .30
60 Pete Maravich 5.00 10.00
61 Nick Weatherspoon .10 .30
62 Robert Reid RC .25 .60
63 Mychal Thompson RC .60 1.50
64 Doug Collins .40 1.00
65 Wes Unseld .50 1.25
66 Jack Sikma .25 .60
67 Bobby Wilkerson .10 .30
68 Bill Robinzine .10 .30
69 Joe Meriweather .10 .30
70 Marques Johnson AS1 .15 .40
71 Ricky Sobers .10 .30
72 Clifford Ray .10 .30
73 Tim Bassett .15 .40
74 James Silas .15 .40
75 Bob McAdoo .30 .75
76 Austin Carr .15 .40
77 Don Ford .10 .30
78 Steve Hawes .10 .30
79 Ron Brewer RC .10 .30
80 Walter Davis .40 1.00
81 Calvin Murphy .40 1.00
82 Tom Boswell .10 .30
83 Lonnie Shelton .10 .30
84 Terry Tyler RC .15 .40
85 Randy Smith .10 .30
86 Rich Kelley .10 .30
87 Otis Birdsong RC .25 .60
88 Marvin Webster .10 .30
89 Eric Money .10 .30
90 Elvin Hayes AS1 .60 1.50
91 Junior Bridgeman .10 .30
92 Johnny Davis .10 .30
93 Robert Parish 1.25 3.00
94 Eddie Jordan .15 .40
95 Leonard Robinson .15 .40
96 Rick Robey RC .15 .40
97 Norm Nixon .25 .60
98 Mark Olberding .10 .30
99 Wilbur Holland .10 .30
100 Moses Malone AS1 1.25 3.00
101 Checklist 1-132 .75 2.00
102 Tom Owens .10 .30
103 Phil Chenier .15 .40
104 John Johnson .10 .30
105 Darryl Dawkins .40 1.00
106 Charlie Scott .15 .40
107 M.L. Carr .25 .60
108 Phil Ford RC 1.00 2.50
109 Swen Nater .10 .30
110 Nate Archibald .60 1.50
111 Aaron James .10 .30
112 Jim Cleamons .10 .30
113 James Edwards .25 .60
114 Don Buse .15 .40
115 Steve Mix .15 .40
116 Charles Johnson .10 .30
117 Elmore Smith .10 .30
118 John Drew .10 .30
119 Lou Hudson .15 .40
120 Rick Barry .75 2.00
121 Kent Benson RC .15 .40
122 Mike Gale .10 .30
123 Jan Van Breda Kolff .10 .30
124 Chris Ford .15 .40
125 George McGinnis .25 .60
126 Leon Douglas .10 .30
127 John Lucas .25 .60
128 Kermit Washington .15 .40
129 Lionel Hollins .15 .40
130 Bob Dandridge AS2 .15 .40
131 James McElroy .10 .30
132 Bobby Jones ! .60 1.50

1980-81 Topps

The 1980-81 Topps basketball card set contains 264 different individual players (1 1/6" by 2 1/2") on 176 different panels of three (2 1/2" by 3 1/2"). This set was issued in packs of eight cards costing 25 cents per pack which came 36 packs per box. The cards come with three individual players per standard card. A perforation line segments each card into three players. In all, there are 176 different complete cards, however, the same player will be on more than one card. The variations stem from the fact that the cards in this set were printed on two separate sheets. In the checklist below, the first 88 cards comprise a complete set of all 264 players. The second 88 cards (89-176) provide a slight rearrangement of players within the card, but still contain the same 264 players. The cards are numbered within each series of 88 by any ordering of the left-hand player's number when the card is viewed from the back. In the checklist below, SD refers to a "Slam Dunk" star card. The letters AS in the checklist refer to an All-Star selection pictured on the front of the checklist card. There are a number of Team Leader (TL) cards which depict the team's leader in assists, scoring or rebounds. Prices given below are for complete panels, as that is the typical way these cards are collected. Cards which have been separated into the three parts are relatively valueless. The key card in this set features Larry Bird, Julius Erving and Magic Johnson. It is the Rookie Card for Bird and Magic. In addition to Bird and Magic, other noteworthy players making their first card appearance in this set include Bill Cartwright, Maurice Cheeks, Michael Cooper, Sidney Moncrief and Tree Rollins. Other lesser-known players making their first card appearance include James Bailey, Greg Ballard, Dudley Bradley, Mike Bratz, Joe Bryant, Kenny Carr, Wayne Cooper, David Greenwood, Phil Hubbard, Geoff Huston, Abdul Jeelani, Greg Kelser, Reggie King, Tom LaGarde, Mark Landsberger, Allen Leavell, Calvin

COMPLETE SET (176) 250.00 450.00
1 3 Dan Roundfield AS 2.00 5.00
181 Julius Erving
258 Ron Brewer SD
2 7 Moses Malone AS .60 1.50
185 Steve Mix
92 Robert Parish TL
3 12 Gus Williams AS .25 .60
67 Geoff Huston
5 John Drew AS
4 24 Steve Hawes .40 1.00
32 Nate Archibald TL
248 Elvin Hayes
5 29 Dan Roundfield .25 .60
73 Dan Issel TL
152 Brian Winters
6 34 Larry Bird RC 100.00 225.00
174 Julius Erving TL
139 Magic Johnson RC
7 36 Dave Cowens .50 1.25
186 Paul Westphal TL
142 Jamaal Wilkes
8 38 Pete Maravich 2.50 6.00
264 Lloyd Free SD
194 Dennis Johnson
9 40 Rick Robey .25 .60
234 Adrian Dantley TL
26 Eddie Johnson
10 47 Scott May .25 .60
196 Kermit Washington TL
177 Henry Bibby
11 55 Don Ford .10 .30
145 Quinn Buckner TL
138 Brad Holland
12 58 Campy Russell .10 .30
247 Kevin Grevey
52 Dave Robisch TL
13 60 Foots Walker .10 .30
113 Mick.Johnson TL
130 Bill Robinzine
14 61 Austin Carr 1.25 3.00
8 Kareem Abdul-Jabbar AS
200 Calvin Natt
15 63 Jim Cleamons .25 .60
256 Robert Reid SD
22 Charlie Criss
16 69 Tom LaGarde .10 .30
215 Swen Nater TL
213 James Silas
17 71 Jerome Whitehead .25 .60
259 Artis Gilmore SD
184 Caldwell Jones
18 74 John Roche TL .10 .30
99 Clifford Ray
235 Ben Poquette TL
19 75 Alex English .50 1.25
2 Marques Johnson AS
68 Jeff Judkins
20 82 Terry Tyler TL .10 .30
21 Armond Hill TL
171 M.R. Richardson
21 84 Kent Benson .25 .60
212 John Shumate
229 Paul Westphal
22 86 Phil Hubbard .60 1.50
93 Robert Parish TL
126 Tom Burleson
23 88 John Long 1.25 3.00
1 Julius Erving AS
49 Ricky Sobers
24 90 Eric Money .10 .30
57 Dave Robisch
254 Rick Robey SD
25 95 Wayne Cooper .10 .30
226 John Johnson TL
45 David Greenwood
26 97 Robert Parish .75 2.00
187 Leon.Robinson TL
46 Dwight Jones
27 98 Sonny Parker .10 .30
197 Dave Twardzik TL
39 Cedric Maxwell
28 105 Rick Barry .40 1.00
122 Otis Birdsong TL
48 John Mengelt
29 106 Allen Leavell .10 .30
53 Foots Walker TL
223 Freeman Williams
30 108 Calvin Murphy .25 .60
176 Maurice Cheeks TL
87 Greg Kelser
31 110 Robert Reid .25 .60
243 Wes Unseld TL
50 Reggie Theus
32 111 Rudy Tomjanovich .25 .60
13 Eddie Johnson AS
179 Doug Collins
33 112 Mickey Johnson TL .10 .30
28 Wayne Rollins
15 M.R.Richardson AS
34 115 Mike Bantom .25 .60
6 Adrian Dantley AS
227 James Bailey
35 116 Dudley Bradley .10 .30
155 Eddie Jordan TL
239 Allan Bristow
36 118 James Edwards .10 .30
153 Mike Newlin TL
182 Lionel Hollins
37 119 Mickey Johnson .10 .30
154 Geo.Johnson TL
193 Leonard Robinson
38 120 Billy Knight .25 .60
16 Paul Westphal AS
59 Randy Smith
39 121 George McGinnis .25 .60
83 Eric Money TL
65 Mike Bratz
40 124 Phil Ford TL .10 .30
101 Phil Smith
224 Gus Williams TL
41 127 Phil Ford .25 .60
19 John Drew TL
209 Larry Kenon
42 131 Scott Wedman .25 .60
164 Bill Cartwright TL
23 John Drew
43 132 K.Abdul-Jabbar TL 1.25 3.00
56 Mike Mitchell
81 Terry Tyler TL
44 135 Kareem Abdul-Jabbar 2.00 5.00
79 David Thompson
216 Brian Taylor TL
45 137 Michael Cooper .60 1.50
103 Moses Malone TL
148 George Johnson
46 140 Mark Landsberger .60 1.50
10 Bob Lanier AS
222 Bill Walton
47 141 Norm Nixon .25 .60
123 Sam Lacey TL
54 Kenny Carr
48 143 Marques Johnson TL 10.00 25.00
30 Larry Bird TL
232 Jack Sikma
49 146 Junior Bridgeman 8.00 20.00
31 Larry Bird TL
198 Ron Brewer
50 147 Quinn Buckner 1.25 3.00
133 Kareem Abdul-Jabbar TL
207 Mike Gale
51 149 Marques Johnson 1.25 3.00
262 Julius Erving SD
62 Abdul Jeelani
52 151 Sidney Moncrief 1.25 3.00
260 Lonnie Shelton SD
220 Paul Silas
53 156 George Johnson .25 .60
9 Bill Cartwright AS
199 Bob Gross
54 158 Maurice Lucas .25 .60
261 James Edwards SD
157 Eddie Jordan
55 159 Mike Newlin .10 .30
134 Norm Nixon TL
180 Darryl Dawkins
56 160 Roger Phegley .10 .30
206 James Silas TL
91 Terry Tyler UER
(First name spelled Jams)
57 161 Cliff Robinson .10 .30
51 Mike Mitchell TL
80 Bobby Wilkerson
58 162 Jan Van Breda Kolff .25 .60
204 George Gervin TL
117 Johnny Davis
59 165 M.R.Richardson TL .10 .30
214 Lloyd Free TL
44 Artis Gilmore
60 166 Bill Cartwright .60 1.50
244 Kevin Porter TL
25 Armond Hill
61 168 Toby Knight .10 .30
14 Lloyd Free AS
240 Adrian Dantley
62 169 Joe Meriweather .25 .60
218 Lloyd Free
42 D.Greenwood TL
63 170 Earl Monroe .25 .60
27 James McElroy
85 Leon Douglas
64 172 Marvin Webster .25 .60
175 Caldwell Jones TL
129 Sam Lacey
65 173 Ray Williams .10 .30
94 John Lucas TL
202 Dave Twardzik
66 178 Maurice Cheeks 6.00 15.00
18 Magic Johnson AS
237 Ron Boone
67 183 Bobby Jones .40 1.00
37 Chris Ford
66 Joe Hassett
68 189 Alvan Adams .40 1.00
163 Bill Cartwright TL
76 Dan Issel
69 190 Don Buse .25 .60
242 Elvin Hayes TL
35 M.L. Carr
70 191 Walter Davis .40 1.00
11 George Gervin AS
136 Jim Chones
71 192 Rich Kelley .40 1.00
102 Moses Malone TL
64 Winford Boynes
72 201 Tom Owens .10 .30
225 Jack Sikma TL
100 Purvis Short
73 208 George Gervin .60 1.50
72 Dan Issel TL
249 Mitch Kupchak
74 217 Joe Bryant .60 1.50
263 Bobby Jones SD
107 Moses Malone
75 219 Swen Nater .25 .60
17 Calvin Murphy AS
70 Richard Washington
76 221 Brian Taylor .10 .30
253 John Shumate SD
167 Larry Demic
77 228 Fred Brown .10 .30
205 Larry Kenon TL
203 Kermit Washington
78 230 John Johnson .40 1.00
4 Walter Davis AS
33 Nate Archibald
79 231 Lonnie Shelton .25 .60
104 Allen Leavell TL
96 John Lucas
80 233 Gus Williams .10 .30
20 Dan Roundfield TL
211 Kevin Restani
81 236 Allan Bristow TL .10 .30
210 Mark Olberding
255 James Bailey SD
82 238 Tom Boswell .40 1.00
109 Billy Paultz
150 Bob Lanier
83 241 Ben Poquette .40 1.00
188 Paul Westphal TL
77 Charlie Scott
84 245 Greg Ballard .10 .30
43 Reggie Theus TL
252 John Williamson
85 246 Bob Dandridge .25 .60
41 Reggie Theus TL
128 Reggie King
86 250 Kevin Porter .10 .30
114 Johnny Davis TL
125 Otis Birdsong
87 251 Wes Unseld .25 .60
195 Tom Owens TL
78 John Roche
88 257 Elvin Hayes SD .25 .60
144 Marques Johnson TL
89 Bob McAdoo
89 3 Dan Roundfield .25 .60
218 Lloyd Free
42 D.Greenwood TL
90 7 Moses Malone .40 1.00
247 Kevin Grevey
52 Dave Robisch TL
91 12 Gus Williams .10 .30
210 Mark Olberding
255 James Bailey SD
92 24 Steve Hawes .10 .30
226 John Johnson TL
45 David Greenwood
93 29 Dan Roundfield .10 .30
113 Mick.Johnson TL
130 Bill Robinzine
94 34 Larry Bird 20.00 50.00
164 Bill Cartwright TL
23 John Drew
95 36 Dave Cowens .40 1.00
16 Paul Westphal AS
59 Randy Smith
96 38 Pete Maravich 3.00 8.00
187 Leonard Robinson TL
46 Dwight Jones
97 40 Rick Robey .25 .60
37 Chris Ford
66 Joe Hassett
98 47 Scott May 8.00 20.00
30 Larry Bird TL
232 Jack Sikma
99 55 Don Ford .40 1.00
144 Marques Johnson TL
89 Bob McAdoo
100 58 Campy Russell .25 .60
21 Armond Hill TL
171 Micheal Ray Richardson
101 60 Foots Walker .10 .30
122 Otis Birdsong TL
48 John Mengelt
102 61 Austin Carr .10 .30
56 Mike Mitchell
81 Terry Tyler TL
103 63 Jim Cleamons .10 .30
261 James Edwards SD
157 Eddie Jordan
104 69 Tom LaGarde .40 1.00
109 Billy Paultz
150 Bob Lanier
105 71 Jerome Whitehead .25 .60
17 Calvin Murphy AS
70 Richard Washington
106 74 John Roche TL .10 .30
28 Wayne Rollins
15 M.R.Richardson AS
107 75 Alex English .60 1.50
102 Moses Malone TL
64 Winford Boynes
108 82 Terry Tyler TL .10 .30
79 David Thompson
216 Brian Taylor TL
109 84 Kent Benson .25 .60
259 Artis Gilmore SD
184 Caldwell Jones
110 86 Phil Hubbard .10 .30
195 Tom Owens TL
78 John Roche
111 88 John Long 6.00 15.00
18 Magic Johnson AS
237 Ron Boone
112 90 Eric Money .10 .30
215 Swen Nater TL
213 James Silas
113 95 Wayne Cooper .10 .30
154 George Johnson TL
193 Leon.Robinson
114 97 Robert Parish .75 2.00
103 Moses Malone TL
148 George Johnson
115 98 Sonny Parker .25 .60
94 John Lucas TL
202 Dave Twardzik
116 105 Rick Barry .40 1.00
123 Sam Lacey TL
54 Kenny Carr
117 106 Allen Leavell .10 .30
197 Dave Twardzik TL
39 Cedric Maxwell
118 108 Calvin Murphy .25 .60
51 Mike Mitchell TL
80 Bobby Wilkerson
119 110 Robert Reid .25 .60
153 Mike Newlin TL
182 Lionel Hollins
120 111 Rudy Tomjanovich .40 1.00
73 Dan Issel TL
152 Brian Winters
121 112 Mick.Johnson TL .40 1.00
264 Lloyd Free SD
194 Dennis Johnson
122 115 Mike Bantom .25 .60
204 George Gervin TL
117 Johnny Davis
123 116 Dudley Bradley .40 1.00
186 Paul Westphal TL
142 Jamaal Wilkes
124 118 James Edwards .50 1.25
32 Nate Archibald TL
248 Elvin Hayes
125 119 Mickey Johnson .40 1.00
72 Dan Issel TL
249 Mitch Kupchak
126 120 Billy Knight .10 .30
104 Allen Leavell TL
96 John Lucas
127 121 George McGinnis .60 1.50
10 Bob Lanier A
222 Bill Walton
128 124 Phil Ford TL .25 .60
234 Adrian Dantley TL
26 Eddie Johnson
129 127 Phil Ford .25 .60
43 Reggie Theus TL
252 John Williamson
130 131 Scott Wedman .10 .30
244 Kevin Porter TL
25 Armond Hill
131 132 Kareem Abdul-Jabbar TL 1.50 4.00
93 Robert Parish TL
126 Tom Burleson
132 135 Kareem Abdul-Jabbar 2.00 5.00
253 John Shumate SD
167 Larry Demic
133 137 Michael Cooper .50 1.25
212 John Shumate
229 Paul Westphal
134 140 Mark Landsberger .25 .60
214 Lloyd Free TL
44 Artis Gilmore
135 141 Norm Nixon .25 .60
242 Elvin Hayes TL
35 M.L. Carr
136 143 Marques Johnson TL .10 .30
57 Dave Robisch
254 Rick Robey SD
137 146 Junior Bridgeman 1.25 3.00
1 Julius Erving AS
49 Ricky Sobers
138 147 Quinn Buckner .25 .60
2 Marques Johnson AS
68 Jeff Judkins
139 149 Marques Johnson .10 .30
83 Eric Money TL
65 Mike Bratz
140 151 Sidney Moncrief 1.50 4.00
133 Kareem Abdul-Jabbar TL
207 Mike Gale
141 156 George Johnson .10 .30
175 Caldwell Jones TL
129 Sam Lacey
142 158 Maurice Lucas 1.25 3.00
262 Julius Erving SD
62 Abdul Jeelani
143 159 Mike Newlin .25 .60
243 Wes Unseld TL
50 Reggie Theus
144 160 Roger Phegley .10 .30
145 Quinn Buckner TL
138 Brad Holland
145 161 Cliff Robinson .10 .30
114 Johnny Davis TL
125 Otis Birdsong
146 162 Jan Van Breda Kolff 15.00 40.00
174 Julius Erving TL
139 Magic Johnson
147 165 Micheal Ray Richardson TL .40 1.00
185 Steve Mix
92 Robert Parish TL
148 166 Bill Cartwright .40 1.00
13 Eddie Johnson AS
179 Doug Collins
149 168 Toby Knight .25 .60
188 Paul Westphal TL
77 Charlie Scott
150 169 Joe Meriweather .10 .30
196 K.Washington TL
177 Henry Bibby
151 170 Earl Monroe .10 .30
206 James Silas TL
91 Terry Tyler
152 172 Marvin Webster .25 .60
155 Eddie Jordan TL
239 Allan Bristow
153 173 Ray Williams .10 .30
225 Jack Sikma TL
100 Purvis Short
154 178 Maurice Cheeks 1.50 4.00
11 George Gervin AS
136 Jim Chones
155 183 Bobby Jones .25 .60
99 Clifford Ray
235 Ben Poquette TL
156 189 Alvan Adams .25 .60
14 Lloyd Free AS
240 Adrian Dantley
157 190 Don Buse .25 .60
6 Adrian Dantley AS
227 James Bailey
158 191 Walter Davis .25 .60
9 Bill Cartwright AS
199 Bob Gross
159 192 Rich Kelley .60 1.50
263 Bobby Jones SD
107 Moses Malone
160 201 Tom Owens .25 .60
134 Norm Nixon TL
180 Darryl Dawkins
161 208 George Gervin .60 1.50
53 Foots Walker TL
223 Freeman Williams
162 217 Joe Bryant 1.25 3.00
8 Kareem Abdul-Jabbar AS
200 Calvin Natt
163 219 Swen Nater .10 .30
101 Phil Smith
224 Gus Williams TL
164 221 Brian Taylor .10 .30
256 Robert Reid SD
22 Charlie Criss
165 228 Fred Brown 7.50 15.00
31 Larry Bird TL
198 Ron Brewer
166 230 John Johnson .40 1.00
163 Bill Cartwright TL
76 Dan Issel
167 231 Lonnie Shelton .10 .30
205 Larry Kenon TL
203 Kermit Washington
168 233 Gus Williams .25 .60
41 Reggie Theus TL
128 Reggie King
169 236 Allan Bristow TL .10 .30
260 Lonnie Shelton SD
220 Paul Silas
170 238 Tom Boswell .10 .30
27 James McElroy
85 Leon Douglas
171 241 Ben Poquette .40 1.00
176 Maurice Cheeks TL
87 Greg Kelser
172 245 Greg Ballard .40 1.00
4 Walter Davis AS
33 Nate Archibald
173 246 Bob Dandridge .10 .30
19 John Drew TL
209 Larry Kenon
174 250 Kevin Porter .10 .30
20 Dan Roundfield TL
211 Kevin Restani
175 251 Wes Unseld .40 1.00
67 Geoff Huston
5 John Drew AS
176 257 Elvin Hayes SD 2.00 5.00
181 Julius Erving
258 Ron Brewer SD

1980-81 Topps Team Posters

This set of 16 numbered team mini-posters was issued as a folded insert (one per pack) in regular wax packs of 1980-81 Topps basketball cards. The small posters feature a full-color posed team picture, with the team name in the frame line. These posters are on thin, white paper stock and measure approximately 4 7/8" by 6 7/8" when unfolded. Since the copies were originally folded by Topps prior to insertion into the packs, they are still considered Mint with fold lines.

COMPLETE SET (16) 8.00 16.00
1 Atlanta Hawks .40 1.00
2 Boston Celtics 3.00 8.00
3 Chicago Bulls .40 1.00
4 Cleveland Cavaliers .40 1.00
5 Detroit Pistons .40 1.00
6 Houston Rockets .40 1.00
7 Indiana Pacers .40 1.00
8 Los Angeles Lakers 2.50 6.00
9 Milwaukee Bucks .40 1.00
10 New Jersey Nets .40 1.00
11 New York Knicks .40 1.00
12 Philadelphia 76ers .75 2.00
13 Phoenix Suns .40 1.00
14 Portland Blazers .40 1.00
15 Seattle Sonics .40 1.00
16 Washington Bullets .40 1.00

1981-82 Topps

The 1981-82 Topps basketball card set contains a total of 198 standard-size cards that were issued in 13-card, 30-cent wax packs with 36 packs per box. These cards are numbered depending upon the regional distribution used in the issue. A 66-card national set was issued to all parts of the country, however, subsets of 44 cards each were issued in the East, Midwest and West. The national set is easier to acquire than any of the regional issues. Card numbers over 66 are prefaced on the card by the region in which they were distributed, e.g., East 96. The cards feature the Topps logo in the frame line and a quarter-round sunburst in the lower left-hand corner which lists the name, position and team of the player depicted. Cards 44-66 are Team Leader (TL) cards picturing each team's statistical leaders. The back, printed in orange and brown on gray stock, features standard Topps biographical data and career statistics. There are a number of Super Action (SA) cards in the set. Rookie Cards include Joe Barry Carroll, Mike Dunleavy, Mike Gminski, Darrell Griffith, Ernie Grunfeld, Vinnie Johnson, Bill Laimbeer, Rick Mahorn, Kevin McHale, Jim Paxson and Larry Smith. The card numbering sequence is alphabetical within team within each series. This was Topps' last basketball card issue until 1992.

COMPLETE SET (198) 25.00 60.00
1 John Drew .07 .20
2 Dan Roundfield .07 .20
3 Nate Archibald .25 .60
4 Larry Bird ! 6.00 15.00
5 Cedric Maxwell .07 .20
6 Robert Parish .60 1.50
7 Artis Gilmore .25 .60
8 Ricky Sobers .02 .10
9 Mike Mitchell .07 .20
10 Tom LaGarde .02 .10
11 Dan Issel .30 .75
12 David Thompson .30 .75
13 Lloyd Free .08 .25
14 Moses Malone .60 1.50
15 Calvin Murphy .08 .25
16 Johnny Davis .02 .10
17 Otis Birdsong .08 .25
18 Phil Ford .07 .20
19 Scott Wedman .02 .10
20 Kareem Abdul-Jabbar 3.00 8.00
21 Magic Johnson ! 4.00 10.00
22 Norm Nixon .08 .25
23 Jamaal Wilkes .08 .25
24 Marques Johnson .08 .25
25 Bob Lanier .30 .75
26 Bill Cartwright .20 .50
27 Michael Ray Richardson .07 .20
28 Ray Williams .07 .20
29 Darryl Dawkins .08 .25
30 Julius Erving 2.00 5.00
31 Lionel Hollins .02 .10
32 Bobby Jones .08 .25
33 Walter Davis .20 .50
34 Dennis Johnson .20 .50
35 Leonard Robinson .08 .25
36 Mychal Thompson .08 .25
37 George Gervin .75 2.00
38 Swen Nater .02 .10
39 Jack Sikma .08 .25
40 Adrian Dantley .25 .60
41 Darrell Griffith RC .40 1.00
42 Elvin Hayes .30 .75
43 Fred Brown .08 .25
44 John Drew .05 .15
Dan Roundfield
Eddie Johnson TL
45 Larry Bird .75 2.00
Larry Bird
Nate Archibald TL
46 Reggie Theus .08 .25
Artis Gilmore
Reggie Theus TL
47 Mike Mitchell .05 .15
Kenny Carr
Mike Bratz TL
48 Jim Spanarkel .05 .15
Tom LaGarde
Brad Davis TL
49 David Thompson .08 .25
Dan Issel
Kenny Higgs TL
50 John Long .05 .15
Phil Hubbard
Ron Lee TL
51 Lloyd Free .08 .25
Larry Smith
John Lucas TL
52 Moses Malone .15 .40
Moses Malone
Allen Leavell TL
53 Billy Knight .08 .25
James Edwards
Johnny Davis TL
54 Otis Birdsong .05 .15
Reggie King
Phil Ford TL
55 Kareem Abdul-Jabbar .50 1.25
Kareem Abdul-Jabbar
Norm Nixon TL
56 Marques Johnson .08 .25
Mickey Johnson
Quinn Buckner TL
57 Mike Newlin .05 .15
Maurice Lucas
Mike Newlin TL
58 Bill Cartwright .08 .25
Bill Cartwright
Micheal Ray Richardson TL
59 Julius Erving .50 1.25
Caldwell Jones
Maurice Cheeks TL
60 Truck Robinson .08 .25
Truck Robinson
Alvan Adams TL
61 Jim Paxson .05 .15
Mychal Thompson
Kermit Washington
Kelvin Ransey TL
62 George Gervin .08 .25
Dave Corzine
Johnny Moore TL
63 Freeman Williams .05 .15
Swen Nater
Brian Taylor TL
64 Jack Sikma .08 .25
Jack Sikma
Vinnie Johnson TL
65 Adrian Dantley .08 .25
Ben Poquette
Allan Bristow TL
66 Elvin Hayes .08 .25
Elvin Hayes
Kevin Porter TL
E67 Charlie Criss .08 .25
E68 Eddie Johnson .05 .15
E69 Wes Matthews .05 .15

E70 Tom McMillen .15 .40
E71 Tree Rollins .15 .40
E72 M.L. Carr .08 .25
E73 Chris Ford .08 .25
E74 Gerald Henderson RC .15 .40
E75 Kevin McHale RC 8.00 20.00
E76 Rick Robey .08 .25
E77 Darwin Cook RC .05 .15
E78 Mike Gminski RC .30 .75
E79 Maurice Lucas .08 .25
E80 Mike Newlin .08 .25
E81 Mike O'Koren RC .08 .25
E82 Steve Hawes .05 .15
E83 Foots Walker .08 .25
E84 Campy Russell .08 .25
E85 DeWayne Scales .05 .15
E86 Randy Smith .08 .25
E87 Marvin Webster .08 .25
E88 Sly Williams .05 .15
E89 Mike Woodson RC .08 .25
E90 Maurice Cheeks .60 1.50
E91 Caldwell Jones .08 .25
E92 Steve Mix .08 .25
E93A Checklist 1-110 ERR .75 2.00
(WEST above card number)
E93B Checklist 1-110 COR .50 1.00
E94 Greg Ballard .05 .15
E95 Don Collins .05 .15
E96 Kevin Grevey .08 .25
E97 Mitch Kupchak .08 .25
E98 Rick Mahorn RC .30 .75
E99 Kevin Porter .08 .25
E100 Nate Archibald SA .08 .25
E101 Larry Bird SA 5.00 12.00
E102 Bill Cartwright SA .05 .15
E103 Darryl Dawkins SA .08 .25
E104 Julius Erving SA .75 2.00
E105 Kevin Porter SA .08 .25
E106 Bobby Jones SA .08 .25
E107 Cedric Maxwell SA .08 .25
E108 Robert Parish SA .40 1.00
E109 M.R.Richardson SA .08 .25
E110 Dan Roundfield SA .08 .25
W67 T.R. Dunn RC .20 .50
W68 Alex English .60 1.50
W69 Billy McKinney RC .08 .25
W70 Dave Robisch .08 .25
W71 Joe Barry Carroll RC .15 .40
W72 Bernard King .40 1.00
W73 Sonny Parker .05 .15
W74 Purvis Short .08. .25
W75 Larry Smith RC .15 .40
W76 Jim Chones .08 .25
W77 Michael Cooper .30 .75
W78 Mark Landsberger .05 .15
W79 Alvan Adams .08 .25
W80 Jeff Cook .05 .15
W81 Rich Kelley .05 .15
W82 Kyle Macy RC .15 .40
W83 Billy Ray Bates RC .20 .50
W84 Bob Gross .08 .25
W85 Calvin Natt .08 .25
W86 Lonnie Shelton .08 .25
W87 Jim Paxson RC .40 1.00
W88 Kelvin Ransey .05 .15
W89 Kermit Washington .08 .25
W90 Henry Bibby .08 .25
W91 Michael Brooks RC .05 .15
W92 Joe Bryant .08 .25
W93 Phil Smith .05 .15
W94 Brian Taylor .05 .15
W95 Freeman Williams .08 .25
W96 James Bailey .05 .15
W97 Checklist 1-110 .50 1.00
W98 John Johnson .05 .15
W99 Vinnie Johnson RC .60 1.50
W100 Wally Walker RC .08 .25
W101 Paul Westphal .08 .25
W102 Allan Bristow .08 .25
W103 Wayne Cooper .05 .15
W104 Carl Nicks .05 .15
W105 Ben Poquette .05 .15
W106 Kareem Abdul-Jabbar SA .75 2.00
W107 Dan Issel SA .20 .50
W108 Dennis Johnson SA .08 .25
W109 Magic Johnson SA ! 3.00 8.00
W110 Jack Sikma SA .08 .25
MW67 David Greenwood .08 .25
MW68 Dwight Jones .05 .15
MW69 Reggie Theus .15 .40
MW70 Bobby Wilkerson .05 .15
MW71 Mike Bratz .05 .15
MW72 Kenny Carr .05 .15
MW73 Geoff Huston .05 .15
MW74 Bill Laimbeer RC 1.25 4.00
MW75 Roger Phegley .05 .15
MW76 Checklist 1-110 .50 1.00
MW77 Abdul Jeelani .05 .15
MW78 Bill Robinzine .05 .15
MW79 Jim Spanarkel .05 .15
MW80 Kent Benson .08 .25
MW81 Keith Herron .05 .15
MW82 Phil Hubbard .05 .15
MW83 John Long .05 .15
MW84 Terry Tyler .05 .15
MW85 Mike Dunleavy RC .30 .75
MW86 Tom Henderson .05 .15
MW87 Billy Paultz .08 .25
MW88 Robert Reid .05 .15
MW89 Mike Bantom .05 .15
MW90 James Edwards .08 .25
MW91 Billy Knight .08 .25
MW92 George McGinnis .08 .25
MW93 Louis Orr .05 .15
MW94 Ernie Grunfeld RC .15 .40
MW95 Reggie King .05 .15
MW96 Sam Lacey .05 .15
MW97 Junior Bridgeman .08 .25
MW98 Mickey Johnson .08 .25
MW99 Sidney Moncrief .30 .75
MW100 Brian Winters .08 .25
MW101 Dave Corzine RC .15 .40
MW102 Paul Griffin .05 .15
MW103 Johnny Moore RC .08 .25
MW104 Mark Olberding .05 .15
MW105 James Silas .08 .25
MW106 George Gervin SA .30 .75
MW107 Artis Gilmore SA .08 .25
MW108 Marques Johnson SA .08 .25
MW109 Bob Lanier SA .20 .50
MW110 Moses Malone SA .40 1.00

1992-93 Topps

The complete 1992-93 Topps basketball set consists of 396 standard-size cards, issued in two 198-card series. Cards were issued in 15-card plastic wrap packs (suggested retail 79 cents, 36 packs per box), 18-card mini-jumbo packs, 45-card retail packs and 41-card magazine jumbo packs. In addition, factory sets were also released. On a white card face, the fronts display color action player photos framed by two-color border stripes. The player's name and team name appear in two different colored bars across the bottom of the picture. In addition to a color close-up photo, the horizontal backs have biography on a light blue panel as well as statistics and brief player profile on a yellow panel. Most Rookie Cards have the a gold-foil "92 Draft Pix" emblem on their card fronts. Topical subsets included are Highlight (2-4), All-Star (100-126), 50 Point Club (199-215), and 20 Assist Club (216-224). Rookie Cards of note include Tom Gugliotta, Robert Horry, Christian Laettner, Alonzo Mourning, Shaquille O'Neal, Latrell Sprewell and Clarence Weatherspoon.

COMPLETE SET (396) 6.00 15.00
COMPLETE FACT. SET (408) 8.00 20.00
COMPLETE SERIES 1 (198) 2.00 4.00
COMPLETE SERIES 2 (198) 5.00 12.00
1 Larry Bird .25 .60
2 Magic Johnson HL .08 .25
Earvin's Magical Moment 2/9/92
3 Michael Jordan HL .40 1.00
Michael Lights It Up 6/3/92
4 David Robinson HL .05 .15
Admiral Ranks High In Five 4/19/92
5 Johnny Newman .02 .10
6 Mike Iuzzolino .02 .10
7 Ken Norman .02 .10
8 Chris Jackson .02 .10
9 Duane Ferrell .02 .10
10 Sean Elliott .02 .10
11 Bernard King .02 .10
12 Armon Gilliam .02 .10
13 Reggie Williams .02 .10
14 Steve Kerr .02 .10
15 Anthony Bowie .02 .10
16 Alton Lister .02 .10
17 Dee Brown .02 .10
18 Tom Chambers .02 .10
19 Otis Thorpe .02 .10
20 Karl Malone .08 .25
21 Kenny Gattison .02 .10
22 Lionel Simmons UER .02 .10
(Misspelled Lionell on card front)
23 Vern Fleming .02 .10
24 John Paxson .02 .10
25 Mitch Richmond .05 .15
26 Danny Schayes .02 .10
27 Derrick McKey .02 .10
28 Mark Randall .02 .10
29 Bill Laimbeer .02 .10
30 Chris Morris .02 .10
31 Alec Kessler .02 .10
32 Vlade Divac .02 .10
33 Rick Fox .02 .10
34 Charles Shackleford .02 .10
35 Dominique Wilkins .05 .15
36 Sleepy Floyd .02 .10
37 Doug West .02 .10
38 Pete Chilcutt .02 .10
39 Orlando Woolridge .02 .10
40 Eric Leckner .02 .10
41 Joe Kleine .02 .10
42 Scott Skiles .02 .10
43 Jerrod Mustaf .02 .10
44 John Starks .02 .10
45 Sedale Threatt .02 .10
46 Doug Smith .02 .10
47 Byron Scott .02 .10
48 Willie Anderson .02 .10
49 David Benoit .02 .10
50 Scott Hastings .02 .10
51 Terry Porter .02 .10
52 Sidney Green .02 .10
53 Danny Young .02 .10
54 Magic Johnson .20 .50
55 Brian Williams .02 .10
56 Randy Wittman .02 .10
57 Kevin McHale .05 .15
58 Dana Barros .02 .10
59 Thurl Bailey .02 .10
60 Kevin Duckworth .02 .10
61 John Williams .02 .10
62 Willie Burton .02 .10
63 Spud Webb .02 .10
64 Detlef Schrempf .02 .10
65 Sherman Douglas .02 .10
66 Patrick Ewing .05 .15
67 Michael Adams .02 .10
68 Vernon Maxwell .02 .10
69 Terrell Brandon .05 .15
70 Terry Catledge .02 .10
71 Mark Eaton .02 .10
72 Tony Smith .02 .10
73 B.J. Armstrong .02 .10
74 Moses Malone .05 .15
75 Anthony Bonner .02 .10
76 George McCloud .02 .10
77 Glen Rice .05 .15
78 Jon Koncak .02 .10
79 Michael Cage .02 .10
80 Ron Harper .02 .10
81 Tom Tolbert .02 .10
82 Brad Sellers .02 .10
83 Winston Garland .02 .10
84 Negele Knight .02 .10
85 Ricky Pierce .02 .10
86 Mark Aguirre .02 .10
87 Ron Anderson .02 .10
88 Loy Vaught .02 .10
89 Luc Longley .02 .10
90 Jerry Reynolds .02 .10
91 Terry Cummings .02 .10
92 Rony Seikaly .02 .10
93 Derek Harper .02 .10
94 Clifford Robinson .02 .10
95 Kenny Anderson .05 .15
96 Chris Gatling .02 .10
97 Stacey Augmon .02 .10
98 Chris Corchiani .02 .10
99 Pervis Ellison .02 .10
100 Larry Bird AS .10 .30
101 John Stockton AS UER .02 .10
(Listed as Center on card back)
102 Clyde Drexler AS .02 .10
103 Scottie Pippen AS .08 .25
104 Reggie Lewis AS .02 .10
105 Hakeem Olajuwon AS .05 .15
106 David Robinson AS .05 .15
107 Charles Barkley AS .05 .15
108 James Worthy AS .02 .10
109 Kevin Willis AS .02 .10
110 Dikembe Mutombo AS .05 .15
111 Joe Dumars AS .02 .10
112 Jeff Hornacek AS UER .02 .10
(5 or 7 shots should be 5 of 7 shots)
113 Mark Price AS .02 .10
114 Michael Adams AS .02 .10
115 Michael Jordan AS .40 1.00
116 Brad Daugherty AS .02 .10
117 Dennis Rodman AS .05 .15
118 Isiah Thomas AS .02 .10
119 Tim Hardaway AS .05 .15
120 Chris Mullin AS .02 .10
121 Patrick Ewing AS .02 .10
122 Dan Majerle AS .02 .10
123 Karl Malone AS .05 .15
124 Otis Thorpe AS .02 .10
125 Dominique Wilkins AS .02 .10
126 Magic Johnson AS .08 .25
127 Charles Oakley .02 .10
128 Robert Pack .02 .10
129 Billy Owens .02 .10
130 Jeff Malone .02 .10
131 Danny Ferry .02 .10
132 Sam Bowie .02 .10
133 Avery Johnson .02 .10
134 Jayson Williams .02 .10
135 Fred Roberts .02 .10
136 Greg Sutton .02 .10
137 Dennis Rodman .10 .30
138 John Williams .02 .10
139 Greg Dreiling .02 .10
140 Rik Smits .02 .10
141 Michael Jordan .75 2.00
142 Nick Anderson .02 .10
143 Jerome Kersey .02 .10
144 Fat Lever .02 .10
145 Tyrone Corbin .02 .10
146 Robert Parish .02 .10
147 Steve Smith .07 .20
148 Chris Dudley .02 .10
149 Antoine Carr .02 .10
150 Elden Campbell .02 .10
151 Randy White .02 .10
152 Felton Spencer .02 .10
153 Cedric Ceballos .02 .10
154 Mark Macon .02 .10
155 Jack Haley .02 .10
156 Bimbo Coles .02 .10
157 A.J. English .02 .10
158 Kendall Gill .02 .10
159 A.C. Green .02 .10
160 Mark West .02 .10
161 Benoit Benjamin .02 .10
162 Tyrone Hill .02 .10
163 Larry Nance .02 .10
164 Gary Grant .02 .10
165 Bill Cartwright .02 .10
166 Greg Anthony .02 .10
167 Jim Les .02 .10
168 Johnny Dawkins .02 .10
169 Alvin Robertson .02 .10
170 Kenny Smith .02 .10
171 Gerald Glass .02 .10
172 Harvey Grant .02 .10
173 Paul Graham .02 .10
174 Sam Perkins .02 .10
175 Manute Bol .02 .10
176 Muggsy Bogues .02 .10
177 Mike Brown .02 .10
178 Donald Hodge .02 .10
179 Dave Jamerson .02 .10
180 Mookie Blaylock .02 .10
181 Randy Brown .02 .10
182 Todd Lichti .02 .10
183 Kevin Gamble .02 .10
184 Gary Payton .10 .30
185 Brian Shaw .02 .10
186 Grant Long .02 .10
187 Frank Brickowski .02 .10
188 Tim Hardaway .07 .20
189 Danny Manning .02 .10
190 Kevin Johnson .05 .15
191 Craig Ehlo .02 .10
192 Dennis Scott .02 .10
193 Reggie Miller .05 .15
194 Darrell Walker .02 .10
195 Anthony Mason .05 .15
196 Buck Williams .02 .10
197 Checklist 1-99 .02 .10
198 Checklist 100-198 .02 .10
199 Karl Malone 50P .05 .15
200 Dominique Wilkins 50P .02 .10
201 Tom Chambers 50P .02 .10
202 Bernard King 50P .02 .10
203 Kiki Vandeweghe 50P .02 .10
204 Dale Ellis 50P .02 .10
205 Michael Jordan 50P .40 1.00
206 Michael Adams 50P .02 .10
207 Charles Smith 50P .02 .10
208 Moses Malone 50P .02 .10
209 Terry Cummings 50P .02 .10
210 Vernon Maxwell 50P .02 .10
211 Patrick Ewing 50P .02 .10
212 Clyde Drexler 50P .02 .10
213 Kevin McHale 50P .02 .10
214 Hakeem Olajuwon 50P .05 .15
215 Reggie Miller 50P .02 .10
216 Gary Grant 20A .02 .10
217 Doc Rivers 20A .02 .10
218 Mark Price 20A .02 .10
219 Isiah Thomas 20A .02 .10
220 Nate McMillan 20A .02 .10
221 Fat Lever 20A .02 .10
222 Kevin Johnson 20A .02 .10
223 John Stockton 20A .02 .10
224 Scott Skiles 20A .02 .10
225 Kevin Brooks .02 .10
226 Bobby Phills RC .05 .15
227 Oliver Miller RC .02 .10
228 John Williams .02 .10
229 Brad Lohaus .02 .10
230 Derrick Coleman .02 .10
231 Ed Pinckney .02 .10
232 Trent Tucker .05 .15
233 Lance Blanks .02 .10
234 Drazen Petrovic .02 .10
235 Mark Bryant .02 .10
236 Lloyd Daniels RC .02 .10
237 Dale Davis .02 .10
238 Jayson Williams .02 .10
239 Mike Sanders .02 .10
240 Mike Gminski .02 .10
241 William Bedford .02 .10
242 Dell Curry .02 .10
243 Gerald Paddio .02 .10
244 Chris Smith RC .02 .10
245 Jud Buechler .02 .10
246 Walter Palmer .02 .10
247 Larry Krystkowiak .02 .10
248 Marcus Liberty .02 .10
249 Sam Mitchell .02 .10
250 Kiki Vandeweghe .02 .10
251 Vincent Askew .02 .10
252 Travis Mays .02 .10
253 Charles Smith .02 .10
254 John Bagley .02 .10
255 James Worthy .05 .15
256 Paul Pressey P/CO .02 .10
257 Rumeal Robinson .02 .10
258 Tom Gugliotta RC .20 .50
259 Eric Anderson RC .02 .10
260 Hersey Hawkins .02 .10
261 Terry Davis .02 .10
262 Rex Chapman .02 .10
263 Chucky Brown .02 .10
264 Danny Young .02 .10
265 Olden Polynice .02 .10
266 Kevin Willis .02 .10
267 Shawn Kemp .10 .30
268 Mookie Blaylock .02 .10
269 Malik Sealy RC .02 .10
270 Charles Barkley .08 .25
271 Corey Williams RC .02 .10
272 Stephen Howard RC .02 .10
(See also card 286)
273 Keith Askins .02 .10
274 Matt Bullard .02 .10
275 John Battle .02 .10
276 Andrew Lang .02 .10
277 David Robinson .08 .25
278 Harold Miner RC .02 .10
279 Tracy Murray RC .02 .10
280 Pooh Richardson .02 .10
281 Dikembe Mutombo .07 .20
282 Wayman Tisdale .02 .10
283 Larry Johnson .07 .20
284 Todd Day RC .02 .10
285 Stanley Roberts .02 .10
286 Randy Woods UER RC .02 .10
(Card misnumbered 272;
run he show should be run the show)
287 Avery Johnson .02 .10
288 Anthony Peeler RC .02 .10
289 Mario Elie .02 .10
290 Doc Rivers .02 .10
291 Blue Edwards .02 .10
292 Sean Rooks RC .02 .10
293 Xavier McDaniel .02 .10
294 C.Weatherspoon RC .05 .15
295 Morlon Wiley .02 .10
296 LaBradford Smith .02 .10
297 Reggie Lewis .02 .10
298 Chris Mullin .05 .15
299 Litterial Green RC .02 .10
300 Elmore Spencer RC .02 .10
301 John Stockton .05 .15
302 Walt Williams RC .05 .15
303 Anthony Pullard RC .02 .10
304 Gundars Vetra RC .02 .10
305 LaSalle Thompson .02 .10
306 Nate McMillan .02 .10
307 Steve Bardo RC .02 .10
308 Robert Horry RC .05 .15
309 Scott Williams . .02 .10
310 Bo Kimble .02 .10
311 Tree Rollins .02 .10
312 Tim Perry .02 .10
313 Isaac Austin RC .02 .10
314 Tate George .02 .10
315 Kevin Lynch .02 .10
316 Victor Alexander .02 .10
317 Doug Overton .02 .10
318 Tom Hammonds .02 .10
319 LaPhonso Ellis RC .05 .15
320 Scott Brooks .02 .10
321 Anthony Avent UER RC .02 .10
(Front photo actually Blue Edwards)
322 Matt Geiger RC .02 .10
323 Duane Causwell .02 .10
324 Horace Grant .02 .10
325 Mark Jackson .02 .10
326 Dan Majerle .02 .10
327 Chuck Person .02 .10
328 Buck Johnson .02 .10
329 Duane Cooper RC .02 .10
330 Rod Strickland .05 .15
331 Isiah Thomas .05 .15
332 Greg Kite .02 .10
(See also card 387)
333 Don MacLean RC .02 .10
334 Christian Laettner RC .10 .30
335 John Crotty RC .02 .10
336 Tracy Moore RC .02 .10
337 Hakeem Olajuwon .08 .25
338 Byron Houston RC .02 .10
339 Walter Bond RC .02 .10
340 Brent Price RC .02 .10
341 Bryant Stith RC .02 .10
342 Will Perdue .02 .10
343 Jeff Hornacek .02 .10
344 Adam Keefe RC .02 .10
345 Rafael Addison .02 .10
346 Marlon Maxey RC .02 .10
347 Joe Dumars .05 .15
348 Jon Barry RC .02 .10
349 Marty Conlon .02 .10
350 Alaa Abdelnaby .02 .10
351 Micheal Williams .02 .10
352 Brad Daugherty .02 .10
353 Tony Bennett RC .02 .10
354 Clyde Drexler .05 .15
355 Rolando Blackman .02 .10
356 Tom Tolbert .02 .10
357 Sarunas Marciulionis .02 .10
358 Jaren Jackson RC .02 .10
359 Stacey King .02 .10
360 Danny Ainge .02 .10
361 Dale Ellis .02 .10
362 Shaquille O'Neal RC 4.00 10.00
363 Bob McCann RC .02 .10
364 Reggie Smith RC .02 .10
365 Vinny Del Negro .02 .10
366 Robert Pack .02 .10
367 David Wood .02 .10
368 Rodney McCray .02 .10
369 Terry Mills .02 .10
370 Eric Murdock UER .02 .10
(Jazz on back spelled Jass)
371 Alex Blackwell RC .02 .10
372 Jay Humphries .02 .10
373 Eddie Lee Wilkins .02 .10
374 James Edwards .02 .10
375 Tim Kempton .02 .10
376 J.R. Reid .02 .10
377 Sam Mack RC .02 .10
378 Donald Royal .02 .10
379 Mark Price .02 .10
380 Mark Acres .02 .10
381 Hubert Davis RC .02 .10
382 Dave Johnson RC .02 .10
383 John Salley .02 .10
384 Eddie Johnson .02 .10
385 Brian Howard RC .02 .10
386 Isaiah Morris RC .02 .10
387 Frank Johnson UER .02 .10
(Card misnumbered 332)
388 Rick Mahorn .02 .10
389 Scottie Pippen .20 .50
390 Lee Mayberry RC .02 .10
391 Tony Campbell .02 .10
392 Latrell Sprewell RC .50 1.25
393 Alonzo Mourning RC .40 1.00
394 Robert Werdann RC .02 .10
395 Checklist 199-297 UER .02 .10
(286 Kennard Winchester;
should be Randy Woods)
396 Checklist 298-396 .04 .10

1992-93 Topps Gold

Gold foil versions of the regular cards were inserted one per 15-card plastic-wrap pack, except if the pack contained a randomly inserted Topps Beam Team card. Gold foil cards were also inserted two per 18-card mini-jumbo pack, three per 45-card retail rack pack, five per 41-card magazine jumbo pack, and 12 per factory set. In addition, complete Gold factory sets were made at the end of the season. These sets include all 396 cards, plus a seven-card Gold Beam Team insert set. The cards are identical in design to the regular issue, except that on the fronts the team color-coded stripes carrying player information are replaced by gold foil stripes. The cards are numbered on the back without a "G" suffix. Reportedly, only 10,000 factory sets were produced. Four different player cards replaced the checklist cards found in the regular 396-card set. Please refer to the pultiplier provided below (coupled with the prices of the corresponding regular issue cards) to ascertain the value.

COMPLETE SET (396) 30.00 70.00
COMPLETE FACTORY SET (403) 37.50 75.00
COMPLETE SERIES 1 (198) 10.00 20.00
COMPLETE SERIES 2 (198) 20.00 50.00
*STARS: 2.5X TO 5X VALUE
*RCs: 1.5X TO 3X VALUE
197G Jeff Sanders .20 .50
198G Elliott Perry UER .20 .50
(Misspelled Elliot on front)
395G David Wingate .20 .50
396G Carl Herrera .20 .50

1992-93 Topps Beam Team

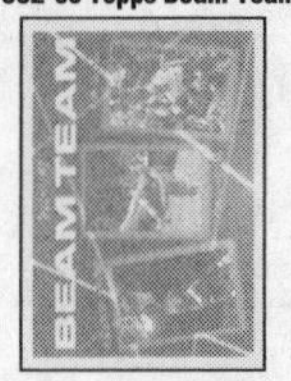

Comprised of some of the NBA's biggest stars, the Topps Beam Team set contains seven standard size cards. Inserted in 15-card second series packs at a ratio of one in 18, these special "Topps Beam Team" bonus cards commemorate Topps' 1993 sponsorship of a six-minute NBA laser animation show. Called Beams Above the Rim, the show premiered at the NBA All-Star Game on Feb. 21. Afterwards, the laser show embarked on a ten-city tour and was featured in either the pre-game or half-time events in ten NBA arenas. Three players are featured on each Topps Beam Team card. The horizontal fronts display three color action player photos on a dark blue background with a grid of brightly colored light beams. The set title "Beam Team" appears in pastel green block lettering across the top. The backs carry three light blue panels, with a close-up color photo, biography, and player profile on each panel.

COMPLETE SET (7) 5.00 10.00
*GOLD: 1.5X TO 3X BASIC
ONE GOLD BT SET PER GOLD FACTORY SET
1 Reggie Miller .40 1.00
Charles Barkley
Clyde Drexler
2 Patrick Ewing .30 .75
Tim Hardaway
Jeff Hornacek
3 Kevin Johnson 2.00 5.00
Michael Jordan
Dennis Rodman
4 Dominique Wilkins .30 .75
John Stockton
Karl Malone
5 Hakeem Olajuwon .50 1.25
Mark Price
Shawn Kemp
6 Scottie Pippen .40 1.00
David Robinson
Jeff Malone
7 Chris Mullin 2.00 5.00
Shaquille O'Neal
Glen Rice

1993-94 Topps

The complete 1993-94 Topps basketball set consists of 396 standard-size cards issued in two 198-card series. Cards were issued in 12, 15 and 29-card packs. Factory sets contain 410 cards including 10 Gold, three Black Gold and one Finest Redemption card. The Finest Redemption card enabled a collector to mail away for two random Finest cards. The redemption deadline was July 31, 1994. The white bordered fronts display color action player photos with a team color coded inner border. The player's name is printed in white script at the lower left corner with the team name appearing on a team color coded bar at the very bottom. The horizontal backs carry a close-up player photo on the right with complete NBA statistics, biography, and career highlights on the left on a beige panel. Subsets featured are Highlights (1-5), 50 Point Club (50, 57, 64), Topps All-Star 1st Team (100-104), Topps All-Star 2nd Team (115-119), Topps All-Star 3rd Team (130-134), Topps All-Rookie 1st Team (150-154), Topps All-Rookie 2nd Team (175-179), Future Playoff MVP's (199-209) and Future Scoring Leaders (384-394). Rookie Cards of note in this set include Vin Baker, Anfernee Hardaway, Allan Houston, Jamal Mashburn, Nick Van Exel and Chris Webber.

COMPLETE SET (396) 10.00 20.00
COMPLETE FACT.SET (410) 12.50 25.00
COMPLETE SERIES 1 (198) 5.00 10.00
COMPLETE SERIES 2 (198) 5.00 10.00
1 Charles Barkley HL .08 .25
2 Hakeem Olajuwon HL .08 .25
3 Shaquille O'Neal HL .20 .50
4 Chris Jackson HL .01 .05
5 Clifford Robinson HL .01 .05
6 Donald Hodge .01 .05
7 Victor Alexander .01 .05
8 Chris Morris .01 .05
9 Muggsy Bogues .02 .10
10 Steve Smith UER .08 .25
(Listed with Kings in '90-91;
was not in NBA that year)
11 Dave Johnson .01 .05
12 Tom Gugliotta .08 .25
13 Doug Edwards RC .01 .05
14 Vlade Divac .02 .10
15 Corie Blount RC .01 .05
16 Derek Harper .02 .10
17 Matt Bullard .01 .05
18 Terry Catledge .01 .05
19 Mark Eaton .01 .05
20 Mark Jackson .02 .10
21 Terry Mills .01 .05
22 Johnny Dawkins .01 .05
23 Michael Jordan UER 1.25 3.00
(Listed as a forward with birthdate
of 1968; he is a guard with
bithdate of 1963)
24 Rick Fox UER .01 .05
(Listed with Kings in '91-92)
25 Charles Oakley .02 .10
26 Derrick McKey .01 .05
27 Christian Laettner .02 .10
28 Todd Day .01 .05
29 Danny Ferry .01 .05
30 Kevin Johnson .02 .10
31 Vinny Del Negro .01 .05
32 Kevin Brooks .01 .05
33 Pete Chilcutt .01 .05
34 Larry Stewart .01 .05
35 Dave Jamerson .01 .05
36 Sidney Green .01 .05
37 J.R. Reid .01 .05
38 Jim Jackson .02 .10
39 Micheal Williams UER .01 .05
(350.2 minutes per game)
40 Rex Walters RC .01 .05
41 Shawn Bradley RC .08 .25
42 Jon Koncak .01 .05
43 Byron Houston .01 .05
44 Brian Shaw .01 .05
45 Bill Cartwright .01 .05
46 Jerome Kersey .01 .05
47 Danny Schayes .01 .05
48 Olden Polynice .01 .05
49 Anthony Peeler .01 .05
50 Nick Anderson 50 .01 .05
51 David Benoit .01 .05
52 David Robinson 50P .08 .25
53 Greg Kite .01 .05
54 Gerald Paddio .01 .05
55 Don MacLean .01 .05
56 Randy Woods .01 .05
57 Reggie Miller 50P .02 .10
58 Kevin Gamble .01 .05
59 Sean Green .01 .05
60 Jeff Hornacek .02 .10
61 John Starks .02 .10
62 Gerald Wilkins .01 .05
63 Jim Les .01 .05
64 Michael Jordan 50P .60 1.50
65 Alvin Robertson .01 .05
66 Tim Kempton .01 .05
67 Bryant Stith .01 .05
68 Jeff Turner .01 .05
69 Malik Sealy .01 .05
70 Dell Curry .01 .05
71 Brent Price .01 .05
72 Kevin Lynch .01 .05
73 Bimbo Coles .01 .05
74 Larry Nance .01 .05
75 Luther Wright RC .01 .05
76 Willie Anderson .01 .05
77 Dennis Rodman .20 .50
78 Anthony Mason .02 .10
79 Chris Gatling .01 .05
80 Antoine Carr .01 .05
81 Kevin Willis .01 .05
82 Thurl Bailey .01 .05
83 Reggie Williams .01 .05
84 Rod Strickland .02 .10
85 Rolando Blackman .01 .05
86 Bobby Hurley RC .02 .10
87 Jeff Malone .01 .05
88 James Worthy .08 .25
89 Alaa Abdelnaby .01 .05
90 Duane Ferrell .01 .05
91 Anthony Avent .01 .05
92 Scottie Pippen .30 .75
93 Ricky Pierce .01 .05
94 P.J. Brown RC .08 .25
95 Jeff Grayer .01 .05
96 Jerrod Mustaf .01 .05
97 Elmore Spencer .01 .05
98 Walt Williams .01 .05
99 Otis Thorpe .02 .10
100 Patrick Ewing AS .02 .10
101 Michael Jordan AS .60 1.50
102 John Stockton AS .02 .10
103 Dominique Wilkins AS .02 .10
104 Charles Barkley AS .08 .25
105 Lee Mayberry .01 .05
106 James Edwards .01 .05
107 Scott Brooks .01 .05
108 John Battle .01 .05
109 Kenny Gattison .01 .05
110 Pooh Richardson .01 .05
111 Rony Seikaly .01 .05
112 Mahmoud Abdul-Rauf .01 .05
113 Nick Anderson .02 .10
114 Gundars Vetra .01 .05
115 Joe Dumars AS .02 .10
116 Hakeem Olajuwon AS .08 .25
117 Scottie Pippen AS .15 .40
118 Mark Price AS .01 .05
119 Karl Malone AS .08 .25
120 Michael Cage .01 .05
121 Ed Pinckney .01 .05
122 Jay Humphries .01 .05
123 Dale Davis .01 .05
124 Sean Rooks .01 .05
125 Mookie Blaylock .02 .10
126 Buck Williams .01 .05
127 John Williams .01 .05
128 Stacey King .01 .05
129 Tim Perry .01 .05
130 Tim Hardaway AS .02 .10
131 Larry Johnson AS .02 .10
132 Detlef Schrempf AS .01 .05
133 Reggie Miller AS .02 .10
134 Shaquille O'Neal AS .20 .50
135 Dale Ellis .01 .05
136 Duane Causwell .01 .05
137 Rumeal Robinson .01 .05
138 Billy Owens .01 .05
139 Malcolm Mackey RC .01 .05
140 Vernon Maxwell .01 .05
141 LaPhonso Ellis .01 .05
142 Robert Parish .02 .10
143 LaBradford Smith .01 .05
144 Charles Smith .01 .05
145 Terry Porter .01 .05
146 Elden Campbell .01 .05
147 Bill Laimbeer .01 .05
148 Chris Mills RC .08 .25
149 Brad Lohaus .01 .05
150 Jim Jackson ART .01 .05
151 Tom Gugliotta ART .02 .10
152 Shaquille O'Neal ART .20 .50
153 Latrell Sprewell ART .08 .25
154 Walt Williams ART .01 .05
155 Gary Payton .15 .40
156 Orlando Woolridge .01 .05
157 Adam Keefe .01 .05
158 Calbert Cheaney RC .02 .10
159 Rick Mahorn .01 .05
160 Robert Horry .02 .10
161 John Salley .01 .05
162 Sam Mitchell .01 .05
163 Stanley Roberts .01 .05
164 Clarence Weatherspoon .01 .05
165 Anthony Bowie .01 .05
166 Derrick Coleman .02 .10
167 Negele Knight .01 .05
168 Marlon Maxey .01 .05
169 Spud Webb UER .02 .10
(Listed as center instead of guard)
170 Alonzo Mourning .15 .40
171 Ervin Johnson RC .02 .10
172 Sedale Threatt .01 .05
173 Mark Macon .01 .05
174 B.J. Armstrong .01 .05
175 Harold Miner ART .01 .05
176 Anthony Peeler ART .01 .05
177 Alonzo Mourning ART .08 .25
178 Christian Laettner ART .01 .05
179 Clarence Weatherspoon ART .01 .05
180 Dee Brown .01 .05
181 Shaquille O'Neal .50 1.25
182 Loy Vaught .01 .05
183 Terrell Brandon .02 .10
184 Lionel Simmons .01 .05
185 Mark Aguirre .01 .05
186 Danny Ainge .02 .10
187 Reggie Miller .08 .25
188 Terry Davis .01 .05
189 Mark Bryant .01 .05
190 Tyrone Corbin .01 .05
191 Chris Mullin .08 .25
192 Johnny Newman .01 .05
193 Doug West .01 .05
194 Keith Askins .01 .05
195 Bo Kimble .01 .05
196 Sean Elliott .02 .10
197 Checklist 1-99 UER .01 .05
(No. 18 listed as Terry Mills
instead of Terry Cummings and
No. 23 listed as Sam Mitchell
instead of Michael Jordan)
198 Checklist 100-198 .01 .05
199 Michael Jordan FPM .60 1.50
200 Patrick Ewing FPM .02 .10
201 John Stockton FPM .02 .10
202 Shawn Kemp FPM .08 .25
203 Mark Price FPM .01 .05
204 Charles Barkley FPM .08 .25
205 Hakeem Olajuwon FPM .08 .25
206 Clyde Drexler FPM .02 .10
207 Kevin Johnson FPM .01 .05
208 John Starks FPM .01 .05
209 Chris Mullin FPM .02 .10
210 Doc Rivers .02 .10
211 Kenny Walker .01 .05
212 Doug Christie .02 .10
213 James Robinson RC .01 .05
214 Larry Krystkowiak .01 .05
215 Manute Bol .01 .05
216 Carl Herrera .01 .05
217 Paul Graham .01 .05
218 Jud Buechler .01 .05
219 Mike Brown .01 .05
220 Tom Chambers .01 .05
221 Kendall Gill .02 .10
222 Kenny Anderson .02 .10
223 Larry Johnson .08 .25
224 Chris Webber RC 1.00 2.50
225 Randy White .01 .05
226 Rik Smits .02 .10
227 A.C. Green .02 .10
228 David Robinson .15 .40
229 Sean Elliott .02 .10
230 Gary Grant .01 .05
231 Dana Barros .01 .05
232 Bobby Hurley .02 .10
233 Blue Edwards .01 .05
234 Tom Hammonds .01 .05
235 Pete Myers UER .01 .05
Card says born in 1993

236 Acie Earl RC .01 .05
237 Tony Smith .01 .05
238 Bill Wennington .01 .05
239 Andrew Lang .01 .05
240 Ervin Johnson .02 .10
241 Byron Scott .02 .10
242 Eddie Johnson .01 .05
243 Anthony Bonner .01 .05
244 Luther Wright .01 .05
245 LaSalle Thompson .01 .05
246 Harold Miner .01 .05
247 Chris Smith .01 .05
248 John Williams .01 .05
249 Clyde Drexler .08 .25
250 Calbert Cheaney .02 .10
251 Avery Johnson .01 .05
252 Steve Kerr .02 .10
253 Warren Kidd RC .01 .05
254 Wayman Tisdale .01 .05
255 Bob Martin RC .01 .05
256 Popeye Jones RC .01 .05
257 Jimmy Oliver .01 .05
258 Kevin Edwards .01 .05
259 Dan Majerle .02 .10
260 Jon Barry .01 .05
261 Allan Houston RC .40 1.00
262 Dikembe Mutombo .08 .25
263 Sleepy Floyd .01 .05
264 George Lynch RC .01 .05
265 Stacey Augmon UER .01 .05
(Listed with Heat in stats)
266 Hakeem Olajuwon .15 .40
267 Scott Skiles .01 .05
268 Detlef Schrempf .02 .10
269 Brian Davis RC .01 .05
270 Tracy Murray .01 .05
271 Gheorghe Muresan RC .08 .25
272 Terry Dehere RC .01 .05
273 Terry Cummings .01 .05
274 Keith Jennings .01 .05
275 Tyrone Hill .01 .05
276 Hersey Hawkins .02 .10
277 Grant Long .01 .05
278 Herb Williams .01 .05
279 Karl Malone .15 .40
280 Mitch Richmond .08 .25
281 Derek Strong RC .01 .05
282 Dino Radja RC .02 .10
283 Jack Haley .01 .05
284 Derek Harper .02 .10
285 Dwayne Schintzius .01 .05
286 Michael Curry RC .01 .05
287 Rodney Rogers RC .08 .25
288 Horace Grant .02 .10
289 Oliver Miller .01 .05
290 Luc Longley .02 .10
291 Walter Bond .01 .05
292 Dominique Wilkins .08 .25
293 Vern Fleming .01 .05
294 Mark Price .01 .05
295 Mark Aguirre .01 .05
296 Shawn Kemp .15 .40
297 Pervis Ellison .01 .05
298 Josh Grant RC .01 .05
299 Scott Burrell RC .08 .25
300 Patrick Ewing .08 .25
301 Sam Cassell RC .40 1.00
302 Nick Van Exel RC .30 .75
303 Clifford Robinson .02 .10
304 Frank Johnson .01 .05
305 Matt Geiger .01 .05
306 Vin Baker RC .25 .60
307 Benoit Benjamin .01 .05
308 Shawn Bradley .08 .25
309 Chris Whitney RC .01 .05
310 Eric Riley RC .01 .05
311 Isiah Thomas .08 .25
312 Jamal Mashburn RC .25 .60
313 Xavier McDaniel .01 .05
314 Mike Peplowski RC .01 .05
315 Darnell Mee RC .01 .05
316 Toni Kukoc RC .40 1.00
317 Felton Spencer .01 .05
318 Sam Bowie .01 .05
319 Mario Elie .01 .05
320 Tim Hardaway .08 .25
321 Ken Norman .01 .05
322 Isaiah Rider RC .20 .50
323 Rex Chapman .01 .05
324 Dennis Rodman .20 .50
325 Derrick McKey .01 .05
326 Corie Blount .01 .05
327 Fat Lever .01 .05
328 Ron Harper .02 .10
329 Eric Anderson .01 .05
330 Armon Gilliam .01 .05
331 Lindsey Hunter RC .08 .25
332 Eric Leckner .01 .05
333 Chris Corchiani .01 .05
334 Anfernee Hardaway RC .75 2.00
335 Randy Brown .01 .05
336 Sam Perkins .02 .10
337 Glen Rice .08 .25
338 Orlando Woolridge .01 .05
339 Mike Gminski .01 .05
340 Latrell Sprewell .25 .60
341 Harvey Grant .01 .05
342 Doug Smith .01 .05
343 Kevin Duckworth .01 .05
344 Cedric Ceballos .02 .10
345 Chuck Person .01 .05
346 Scott Haskin RC .01 .05
347 Frank Brickowski .01 .05
348 Scott Williams .01 .05
349 Brad Daugherty .01 .05
350 Willie Burton .01 .05
351 Joe Dumars .08 .25
352 Craig Ehlo .01 .05
353 Lucious Harris RC .01 .05
354 Danny Manning .02 .10
355 Litterial Green .01 .05
356 John Stockton .08 .25
357 Nate McMillan .01 .05
358 Greg Graham RC .01 .05
359 Rex Walters .01 .05
360 Lloyd Daniels .01 .05
361 Antonio Harvey RC .01 .05
362 Brian Williams .01 .05
363 LeRon Ellis .01 .05
364 Chris Dudley .01 .05
365 Hubert Davis .01 .05
366 Evers Burns RC .01 .05
367 Sherman Douglas .01 .05
368 Sarunas Marciulionis .01 .05
369 Tom Tolbert .01 .05
370 Robert Pack .01 .05
371 Michael Adams .01 .05
372 Negele Knight .01 .05
373 Charles Barkley .15 .40
374 Bryon Russell RC .08 .25
375 Greg Anthony .01 .05
376 Ken Williams .01 .05
377 John Paxson .01 .05
378 Corey Gaines .01 .05
379 Eric Murdock .01 .05
380 Kevin Thompson RC .01 .05
381 Moses Malone .08 .25
382 Kenny Smith .01 .05
383 Dennis Scott .01 .05
384 Michael Jordan FSL .60 1.50
385 Hakeem Olajuwon FSL .08 .25
386 Shaquille O'Neal FSL .20 .50
387 David Robinson FSL .08 .25
388 Derrick Coleman FSL .01 .05
389 Karl Malone FSL .08 .25
390 Patrick Ewing FSL .02 .10
391 Scottie Pippen FSL .15 .40
392 Dominique Wilkins FSL .02 .10
393 Charles Barkley FSL .08 .25
394 Larry Johnson FSL .02 .10
395 Checklist .01 .05
396 Checklist .01 .05
NNO Expired Finest Redemption Card .40 1.00

1993-94 Topps Gold

The cards of this parallel set were distributed through various means. Each pack of '93-94 Topps contained one Gold card with two Gold cards inserted in every fourth pack. Three Gold cards were inserted in every rack pack and 10 in every factory set. Aside from the gold-foil highlights, the 396 standard-size Gold cards are identical to their regular issue counterparts, except the four regular issue checklist cards were replaced by Gold cards featuring the players listed below. Please refer to the multipliers provided below (coupled with the prices of the corresponding regular issue card) to ascertain value.

COMPLETE SET (396) 40.00 70.00
COMPLETE SERIES 1 (198) 15.00 30.00
COMPLETE SERIES 2 (198) 25.00 40.00
*STARS: 2X TO 4X VALUE
*RC's: 1.25X TO 2.5X VALUE
197G Frank Johnson .20 .50
198G David Wingate .20 .50
395G Will Perdue .20 .50
396G Mark West .20 .50

1993-94 Topps Black Gold

Randomly inserted in first and second series packs and three per factory set, this 25-card standard size set features the top five draft picks each year from 1989-1993. Thirteen cards were inserts in series one and 12 in series two. They were inserted at a rate of one in 72 for 12-card packs and one in 18 for 29-card packs. Winner A cards, redeemable for a series 1 set, were randomly inserted into 1 in every 144 series 1 packs. Winner B cards, redeemable for a series 2 set, were randomly inserted into 1 in every 144 series 2 packs. The A/B Winner card (randomly inserted into 1 in every 288 series 2 packs only) was redeemable for a complete set. Each white-bordered front displays a color action player shot with the background tinted in black. Gold prismatic wavy stripes appear above and below the photo with the player's name reversed out of the black bar near the bottom. The white-bordered horizontal backs carry a close-up color cutout on a black background with white concentric stripes. The player's name appears in gold-foil lettering on a wood textured bar with the team name directly to the right in black lettering. Player statistics appear below in an orange background.

COMPLETE SET (25) 12.50 25.00
COMPLETE SERIES 1 (13) 2.00 5.00
COMPLETE SERIES 2 (12) 10.00 20.00
1 Sean Elliott .15 .40
2 Dennis Scott .07 .20
3 Kenny Anderson .15 .40
4 Alonzo Mourning .60 1.50
5 Glen Rice .15 .40
6 Billy Owens .07 .20
7 Jim Jackson .15 .40
8 Derrick Coleman .15 .40
9 Larry Johnson .40 1.00
10 Gary Payton .60 1.50
11 Christian Laettner .15 .40
12 Dikembe Mutombo .40 1.00
13 Mahmoud Abdul-Rauf .07 .20
14 Isaiah Rider .60 1.50
15 Steve Smith .40 1.00
16 LaPhonso Ellis .07 .20
17 Danny Ferry .07 .20
18 Shaquille O'Neal 2.00 5.00
19 Anfernee Hardaway 2.50 6.00
20 J.R. Reid .07 .20
21 Shawn Bradley .40 1.00
22 Pervis Ellison .07 .20
23 Chris Webber 3.00 8.00
24 Jamal Mashburn .75 2.00
25 Kendall Gill .15 .40
A Expired Winner A .30 .75
B Expired Winner B .30 .75
AX Redeemed Winner A .08 .25
BX Redeemed Winner B .08 .25
AB Expired Winner A/B .60 1.50

1994-95 Topps

The 396 standard-size cards that comprise the 1994-95 Topps set were issued in two separate series of 198 cards each. Cards were distributed primarily in 12-card packs that carried a suggested retail price of $1.00 each. Fronts feature full-color action photos framed by a jagged white border. Player's name and team are placed in gold foil along the bottom. The following subsets are included in this set: Eastern All-Star (1-13), Paint Patrol (100-109), and Western All-Star (183-195). In addition, various "From the Roof" subsets cards are intermingled within the set. Rookie Cards of note in this set include Grant Hill, Juwan Howard, Eddie Jones, Jason Kidd and Glenn Robinson.

COMPLETE SET (396) 12.50 25.00
COMPLETE SERIES 1 (198) 5.00 10.00
COMPLETE SERIES 2 (198) 7.50 15.00
1 Patrick Ewing AS .15 .40
2 Mookie Blaylock AS .07 .20
3 Charles Oakley AS .10 .25
4 Mark Price AS .12 .30
5 John Starks AS .10 .25
6 Dominique Wilkins AS .15 .40
7 Horace Grant AS .10 .25
8 Alonzo Mourning AS .15 .40
9 B.J. Armstrong AS .07 .20
10 Kenny Anderson AS .10 .25
11 Scottie Pippen AS .25 .60
12 Derrick Coleman AS .10 .25
13 Shaquille O'Neal AS .30 .75
14 Anfernee Hardaway AS .20 .50
15 Isaiah Rider SPEC .12 .30
16 John Williams .07 .20
17 Todd Day .07 .20
18 Dale Davis .07 .20
19 Sean Rooks .07 .20
20 George Lynch .07 .20
21 Mitchell Butler .07 .20
22 Stacey King .07 .20
23 Sherman Douglas .07 .20
24 Derrick McKey .07 .20
25 Joe Dumars .12 .30
26 Scott Brooks .07 .20
27 Clarence Weatherspoon .07 .20
28 Jayson Williams .07 .20
29 Scottie Pippen .25 .60
30 John Starks .10 .25
31 Robert Pack .07 .20
32 Donald Royal .07 .20
33 Haywoode Workman .07 .20
34 Greg Graham .07 .20
35 Terry Cummings .12 .30
36 Andrew Lang .07 .20
37 Jason Kidd RC .60 1.50
38 Terry Mills .07 .20
39 Alonzo Mourning .15 .40
40 Shawn Kemp .12 .30
41 Kevin Willis FTR .07 .20
42 Kevin Willis .07 .20
43 Armon Gilliam .07 .20
44 Bobby Hurley .12 .30
45 Jerome Kersey .07 .20
46 Xavier McDaniel .07 .20
47 Chris Webber .20 .50
48 Chris Webber FTR .20 .50
49 Jeff Malone .07 .20
50 Dikembe Mutombo SPEC .12 .30
51 Dan Majerle SPEC .12 .30
52 Mookie Blaylock SPEC .07 .20
53 John Stockton SPEC .15 .40
54 Dennis Rodman SPEC .25 .60
55 Eric Murdock SPEC .07 .20
56 Glen Rice .12 .30
57 Glen Rice FTR .12 .30
58 Dino Radja .10 .25
59 Billy Owens .07 .20
60 Doc Rivers .10 .25
61 Don MacLean .07 .20
62 Lindsey Hunter .07 .20
63 Sam Cassell .12 .30
64 James Worthy .15 .40
65 Christian Laettner .10 .25
66 Wesley Person RC .12 .30
67 Rich King .07 .20
68 Jon Koncak .07 .20
69 Muggsy Bogues .10 .25
70 Jamal Mashburn .12 .30
71 Gary Grant .07 .20
72 Eric Murdock .07 .20
73 Scott Burrell .07 .20
74 Scott Burrell FTR .07 .20
75 Anfernee Hardaway .20 .50
76 Anfernee Hardaway FTR .20 .50
77 Yinka Dare RC .07 .20
78 Anthony Avent .07 .20
79 Jon Barry .07 .20
80 Rodney Rogers .07 .20
81 Chris Mills .07 .20
82 Antonio Davis .07 .20
83 Steve Smith .10 .25
84 Buck Williams .07 .20
85 Spud Webb .12 .30
86 Stacey Augmon .10 .25
87 Allan Houston .12 .30
88 Will Perdue .07 .20
89 Chris Gatling .07 .20
90 Danny Ainge .12 .30
91 Rick Mahorn .07 .20
92 Elmore Spencer .07 .20
93 Vin Baker .12 .30
94 Rex Chapman .07 .20
95 Dale Ellis .07 .20
96 Doug Smith .07 .20
97 Tim Perry .07 .20
98 Toni Kukoc .15 .40
99 Terry Dehere .07 .20
100 Shaquille O'Neal PP .30 .75
101 Shawn Kemp PP .12 .30
102 Hakeem Olajuwon PP .15 .40
103 Derrick Coleman PP .07 .20
104 Alonzo Mourning PP .15 .40
105 Dikembe Mutombo PP .12 .30
106 Chris Webber PP .20 .50
107 Dennis Rodman PP .25 .60
108 David Robinson PP .20 .50
109 Charles Barkley PP .20 .50
110 Brad Daugherty .07 .20
111 Derek Harper .10 .25
112 Detlef Schrempf .12 .30
113 Harvey Grant .07 .20
114 Vlade Divac .12 .30
115 Isaiah Rider .12 .30
116 Mitch Richmond .12 .30
117 Tom Chambers .07 .20
118 Kenny Gattison .07 .20
119 Kenny Gattison FTR .07 .20
120 Vernon Maxwell .07 .20
121 Reggie Williams .07 .20
122 Chris Mullin .12 .30
123 Harold Miner .07 .20
124 Harold Miner FTR .07 .20
125 Calbert Cheaney .07 .20
126 Randy Woods .07 .20
127 Mike Gminski .07 .20
128 Willie Anderson .07 .20
129 Mark Macon .07 .20
130 Avery Johnson .10 .25
131 Bimbo Coles .07 .20
132 Kenny Smith .10 .25
133 Dennis Scott .07 .20
134 Lionel Simmons .07 .20
135 Nate McMillan .07 .20
136 Eric Montross RC .12 .30
137 Sedale Threatt .07 .20
138 Kenny Anderson .10 .25
139 Micheal Williams .07 .20
140 Grant Long .07 .20
141 Grant Long FTR .07 .20
142 Tyrone Corbin .07 .20
143 Craig Ehlo .07 .20
144 Gerald Wilkins .07 .20
145 LaPhonso Ellis .07 .20
146 Reggie Miller .15 .40
147 Tracy Murray .07 .20
148 Victor Alexander .07 .20
149 Victor Alexander FTR .07 .20
150 Clifford Robinson .07 .20
151 Anthony Mason FTR .07 .20
152 Anthony Mason .07 .20
153 Jim Jackson .07 .20
154 Jeff Hornacek .10 .25
155 Nick Anderson .07 .20
156 Mike Brown .07 .20
157 Kevin Johnson .12 .30
158 John Paxson .12 .30
159 Loy Vaught .07 .20
160 Carl Herrera .07 .20
161 Shawn Bradley .07 .20
162 Hubert Davis .07 .20
163 David Benoit .07 .20
164 Dell Curry .07 .20
165 Dee Brown .07 .20
166 LaSalle Thompson .07 .20
167 Eddie Jones RC .40 1.00
168 Walt Williams .07 .20
169 A.C. Green .12 .30
170 Kendall Gill .07 .20
171 Kendall Gill FTR .07 .20
172 Danny Ferry .07 .20
173 Bryant Stith .07 .20
174 John Salley .07 .20
175 Cedric Ceballos .07 .20
176 Derrick Coleman .10 .25
177 Tony Bennett .07 .20
178 Kevin Duckworth .07 .20
179 Jay Humphries .07 .20
180 Sean Elliott .12 .30
181 Sam Perkins .10 .25
182 Luc Longley .07 .20
183 Mitch Richmond AS .12 .30
184 Clyde Drexler AS .15 .40
185 Karl Malone AS .15 .40
186 Shawn Kemp AS .12 .30
187 Hakeem Olajuwon AS .15 .40
188 Danny Manning AS .10 .25
189 Kevin Johnson AS .12 .30
190 John Stockton AS .15 .40
191 Latrell Sprewell AS .15 .40
192 Gary Payton AS .12 .30
193 Clifford Robinson AS .07 .20
194 David Robinson AS .20 .50
195 Charles Barkley AS .20 .50
196 Mark Price SPEC .07 .20
197 Checklist 1-99 .07 .20
198 Checklist 100-198 .07 .20
199 Patrick Ewing .15 .40
200 Patrick Ewing FTR .15 .40
201 Tracy Murray PP .07 .20
202 Craig Ehlo PP .07 .20
203 Nick Anderson PP .07 .20
204 John Starks PP .10 .25
205 Rex Chapman PP .07 .20
206 Hersey Hawkins PP .07 .20
207 Glen Rice PP .07 .20
208 Jeff Malone PP .07 .20
209 Dan Majerle PP .07 .20
210 Chris Mullin PP .12 .30
211 Grant Hill RC .60 1.50
212 Bobby Phills .07 .20
213 Dennis Rodman .25 .60
214 Doug West .07 .20
215 Harold Ellis .07 .20
216 Kevin Edwards .07 .20
217 Lorenzo Williams .07 .20
218 Rick Fox .07 .20
219 Mookie Blaylock .07 .20
220 Mookie Blaylock FTR .07 .20
221 John Williams .07 .20
222 Keith Jennings .07 .20
223 Nick Van Exel .12 .30
224 Gary Payton .20 .50
225 John Stockton .15 .40
226 Ron Harper .10 .25
227 Monty Williams RC .12 .30
228 Marty Conlon .07 .20
229 Hersey Hawkins .07 .20
230 Rik Smits .10 .25
231 James Robinson .07 .20
232 Malik Sealy .07 .20
233 Sergei Bazarevich RC .07 .20
234 Brad Lohaus .07 .20
235 Olden Polynice .07 .20
236 Brian Williams .07 .20
237 Tyrone Hill .07 .20
238 Jim McIlvaine RC .07 .20
239 Latrell Sprewell .15 .40
240 Latrell Sprewell FTR .15 .40
241 Popeye Jones .07 .20
242 Scott Williams .07 .20
243 Eddie Jones .20 .50
244 Moses Malone .12 .30
245 B.J. Armstrong .07 .20
246 Jim Les .07 .20
247 Greg Grant .07 .20
248 Lee Mayberry .07 .20
249 Mark Jackson .07 .20
250 Larry Johnson .12 .30
251 Terrell Brandon .12 .30
252 Ledell Eackles .07 .20
253 Yinka Dare .07 .20
254 Dontonio Wingfield RC .07 .20
255 Clyde Drexler .15 .40
256 Andres Guibert .07 .20
257 Gheorghe Muresan .07 .20
258 Tom Hammonds .07 .20
259 Charles Barkley .20 .50
260 Charles Barkley FTR .20 .50
261 Acie Earl .07 .20
262 Lamond Murray RC .12 .30
263 Dana Barros .07 .20
264 Greg Anthony .07 .20
265 Dan Majerle .12 .30
266 Zan Tabak .07 .20
267 Ricky Pierce .07 .20
268 Eric Leckner .07 .20
269 Duane Ferrell .07 .20
270 Mark Price .12 .30
271 Anthony Peeler .07 .20
272 Adam Keefe .07 .20
273 Rex Walters .07 .20
274 Scott Skiles .07 .20
275 Glenn Robinson RC .25 .60
276 Tony Dumas RC .12 .30
277 Elliot Perry .07 .20
278 Bo Outlaw RC .12 .30
279 Karl Malone .15 .40
280 Karl Malone FTR .15 .40
281 Herb Williams .07 .20
282 Vincent Askew .07 .20
283 Askia Jones RC .12 .30
284 Shawn Bradley .07 .20
285 Tim Hardaway .12 .30
286 Mark West .07 .20
287 Chuck Person .10 .25
288 James Edwards .07 .20
289 Antonio Lang RC .12 .30
290 Dominique Wilkins .15 .40
291 Khalid Reeves RC .12 .30
292 Jamie Watson RC .12 .30
293 Darnell Mee .07 .20
294 Brian Grant RC .20 .50
295 Hakeem Olajuwon .15 .40
296 Dickey Simpkins RC .12 .30
297 Tyrone Corbin .07 .20
298 David Wingate .07 .20
299 Shaquille O'Neal .30 .75
300 Shaquille O'Neal FR .30 .75
301 B.J. Armstrong PP .07 .20
302 Mitch Richmond PP .07 .20
303 Jim Jackson PP .07 .20
304 Jeff Hornacek PP .10 .25
305 Mark Price PP .12 .30
306 Kendall Gill PP .07 .20
307 Dale Ellis PP .07 .20
308 Vernon Maxwell PP .07 .20
309 Joe Dumars PP .07 .20
310 Reggie Miller PP .15 .40
311 Geert Hammink .07 .20
312 Charles Smith .07 .20
313 Bill Cartwright .10 .25
314 Aaron McKie RC .12 .30
315 Tom Gugliotta .07 .20
316 P.J. Brown .07 .20
317 David Wesley .07 .20
318 Felton Spencer .07 .20
319 Robert Horry .12 .30
320 Robert Horry FR .12 .30
321 Larry Krystkowiak .07 .20
322 Eric Piatkowski RC .15 .40
323 Anthony Bonner .07 .20
324 Keith Askins .07 .20
325 Mahmoud Abdul-Rauf .07 .20
326 Darrin Hancock RC .12 .30
327 Vern Fleming .07 .20
328 Wayman Tisdale .07 .20
329 Sam Bowie .07 .20
330 Billy Owens .07 .20
331 Donald Hodge .07 .20
332 Derrick Alston RC .12 .30
333 Doug Edwards .07 .20
334 Johnny Newman .07 .20
335 Otis Thorpe .07 .20
336 Bill Curley RC .12 .30
337 Michael Cage .07 .20
338 Chris Smith .07 .20
339 Dikembe Mutombo .12 .30
340 Dikembe Mutombo FTR .12 .30
341 Duane Causwell .07 .20
342 Sean Higgins .07 .20
343 Steve Kerr .10 .25
344 Eric Montross .07 .20
345 Charles Oakley .10 .25
346 Brooks Thompson RC .12 .30
347 Rony Seikaly .07 .20
348 Chris Dudley .07 .20
349 Sharone Wright RC .12 .30
350 Sarunas Marciulionis .07 .20
351 Anthony Miller RC .07 .20
352 Pooh Richardson .07 .20
353 Byron Scott .10 .25
354 Michael Adams .07 .20
355 Ken Norman .07 .20
356 Clifford Rozier RC .12 .30
357 Tim Breaux .07 .20
358 Derek Strong .07 .20
359 David Robinson .20 .50
360 David Robinson FR .20 .50
361 Benoit Benjamin .07 .20
362 Terry Porter .07 .20
363 Ervin Johnson .07 .20
364 Alaa Abdelnaby .07 .20
365 Robert Parish .12 .30
366 Mario Elie .07 .20
367 Antonio Harvey .07 .20
368 Charlie Ward RC .12 .30
369 Kevin Gamble .07 .20
370 Rod Strickland .12 .30
371 Jason Kidd .30 .75
372 Oliver Miller .07 .20
373 Eric Mobley RC .07 .20
374 Brian Shaw .07 .20
375 Horace Grant .10 .25
376 Corie Blount .07 .20
377 Sam Mitchell .07 .20
378 Jalen Rose RC .30 .75
379 Elden Campbell .07 .20
380 Elden Campbell FTR .07 .20
381 Donyell Marshall RC .12 .30
382 Frank Brickowski .07 .20
383 B.J. Tyler RC .07 .20
384 Bryon Russell .07 .20
385 Danny Manning .10 .25
386 Manute Bol .07 .20
387 Brent Price .07 .20
388 J.R. Reid .07 .20
389 Byron Houston .07 .20
390 Blue Edwards .07 .20
391 Adrian Caldwell .07 .20
392 Wesley Person .12 .30
393 Juwan Howard RC .20 .50
394 Chris Morris .07 .20
395 Checklist 199-296 .07 .20
396 Checklist 297-396 .07 .20

1994-95 Topps Spectralight

Randomly inserted into both first and second series packs at a rate of one in four, cards from this standard-size set parallel the basic issue 1994-95 Topps set. Unlike the basic issue cards, fronts feature a full foil-treatment on the pictures. Also, card numbers 197-198 and 395-396 feature players on them (in replacement of the checklist cards that are part of the regular issue set). Please refer to the multipliers provided below (coupled with the prices of the corresponding regular issue card) to ascertain value.

COMPLETE SET (396) 125.00 250.00
COMPLETE SERIES 1 (198) 50.00 100.00
COMPLETE SERIES 2 (198) 75.00 150.00
*SPECT: 2X TO 5X BASE CARD HI
37 Jason Kidd 6.00 15.00
197 Keith Jennings .40 1.00
198 Mark Price .60 1.50
211 Grant Hill 4.00 10.00
371 Jason Kidd 4.00 10.00
395 Chris Webber 15.00 40.00
396 Mitch Richmond 4.00 10.00

1994-95 Topps Franchise/Futures

Randomly inserted into all second series packs at a rate of one in 18, cards from this 20-card set feature a selection of promising youngsters coupled with established stars from the same team. Card fronts feature full-color action shots surrounded by a white border.

COMPLETE SET (20) 8.00 20.00
1 Mookie Blaylock .30 .75
2 Stacey Augmon .40 1.00
3 Dominique Wilkins .60 1.50
4 Eric Montross .50 1.25
5 Dikembe Mutombo .50 1.25
6 Jalen Rose 1.25 3.00
7 Joe Dumars .50 1.25
8 Grant Hill 2.50 6.00
9 Chris Mullin .50 1.25
10 Latrell Sprewell .60 1.50
11 Glen Rice .50 1.25
12 Khalid Reeves .50 1.25
13 Derrick Coleman .40 1.00
14 Yinka Dare .50 1.25
15 Patrick Ewing .60 1.50
16 Monty Williams .50 1.25
17 Shaquille O'Neal 2.00 5.00
18 Anfernee Hardaway .75 2.00
19 Charles Barkley .75 2.00
20 Wesley Person .50 1.25

1994-95 Topps Own the Game

Randomly inserted in all first series packs (12-card packs one in 18, jumbo packs one in 9), cards from this 50-card standard-size unnumbered set featured nine top players in five different statistical categories (Super Passers, Super Rebounders, Super Scorers, Super Stealers and Super Swatters) in addition to five Field Cards. If the player pictured on the card (Field Card represented all other players in the league) led the league in that respective category, it became redeemable for a special 10-card Own the Game redemption set for that category.

COMPLETE SET (50) 15.00 40.00
1 Kenny Anderson PASS .40 1.00
2 Charles Barkley SCORE .75 2.00
3 Mookie Blaylock PASS .30 .75
4 Mookie Blaylock STEAL .30 .75
5 Muggsy Bogues PASS .40 1.00
6 Shawn Bradley SWAT .30 .75
7 Derrick Coleman REB .40 1.00
8 Sherman Douglas PASS .30 .75
9 Patrick Ewing REB .60 1.50
10 Patrick Ewing SCORE .60 1.50
11 Patrick Ewing SWAT .60 1.50
12 Tom Gugliotta STEAL .30 .75
13 Anfernee Hardaway STEAL .75 2.00
14 Mark Jackson PASS .50 1.25
15 Kevin Johnson PASS .50 1.25
16 Karl Malone REB .60 1.50
17 Karl Malone SCORE .60 1.50
18 Nate McMillan STEAL .30 .75
19 Oliver Miller SWAT .30 .75
20 Alonzo Mourning SWAT .60 1.50
21 Eric Murdock STEAL .30 .75
22 Dikembe Mutombo REB .50 1.25
23 Dikembe Mutombo SWAT .50 1.25
24 Charles Oakley REB .40 1.00
25 Hakeem Olajuwon REB .60 1.50
26 Hakeem Olajuwon SCORE .60 1.50
27 Hakeem Olajuwon SWAT .60 1.50
28 Shaquille O'Neal REB 1.25 3.00
29 Shaquille O'Neal SCORE W 1.25 3.00
30 Shaquille O'Neal SWAT 1.25 3.00
31 Gary Payton STEAL .75 2.00
32 Scottie Pippen SCORE 1.00 2.50
33 Scottie Pippen STEAL W 1.00 2.50
34 Mark Price PASS .50 1.25
35 Mitch Richmond SCORE .50 1.25
36 David Robinson SCORE .75 2.00
37 David Robinson SWAT .75 2.00
38 Dennis Rodman REB W 1.00 2.50
39 Latrell Sprewell STEAL .60 1.50
40 John Stockton PASS W .60 1.50
41 John Stockton STEAL .60 1.50
42 Rod Strickland PASS .30 .75
43 Chris Webber SWAT .75 2.00
44 Kevin Willis REB .30 .75
45 Dominique Wilkins SCORE .60 1.50
46 Passers Field Card .30 .75
47 Rebounders Field Card .30 .75
48 Scorers Field Card .30 .75
49 Stealers Field Card .30 .75
50 Swatters Field Card .30 .75

1994-95 Topps Own the Game Redemption

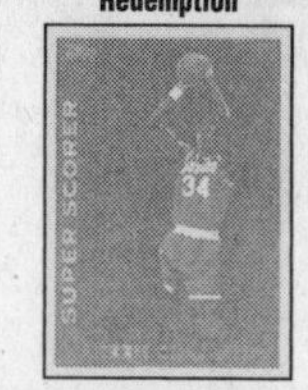

The Own the Game redemption expired on February 7th, 1996 and the exchange cards began shipping in October, 1995. According to Topps, only 8,000 exchange sets were shipped. The 10-card exchange sets consists of the top two players that finished in each category: O'Neal and Olajuwon for Scoring, Stockton and Anderson for Passing, Rodman and Mutombo for Rebounds, Pippen and Blaylock for Steals and Mutombo and Olajuwon for Blocks.

COMPLETE SET (10) 2.50 6.00
1 Shaquille O'Neal 1.25 3.00
2 Hakeem Olajuwon .60 1.50
3 Dennis Rodman 1.00 2.50
4 Patrick Ewing .60 1.50
5 John Stockton .60 1.50
6 Kenny Anderson .40 1.00
7 Scottie Pippen 1.00 2.50
8 Mookie Blaylock .30 .75
9 Dikembe Mutombo .50 1.25
10 Shawn Bradley .30 .75

1994-95 Topps Super Sophomores

Randomly inserted into all second series packs at a rate of one in 36, cards from this 10-card standard-size set spotlight a selection of young phenoms in their second NBA season. Fronts feature full-color player action shots cut out against silver-foil backgrounds.

COMPLETE SET (10) 6.00 15.00
1 Chris Webber 1.50 4.00
2 Anfernee Hardaway 1.50 4.00
3 Vin Baker 1.00 2.50
4 Sam Cassell 1.00 2.50
5 Jamal Mashburn 1.00 2.50
6 Isaiah Rider 1.00 2.50
7 Chris Mills .60 1.50
8 Antonio Davis .60 1.50
9 Nick Van Exel 1.00 2.50
10 Lindsey Hunter .60 1.50

1995-96 Topps

The 1995-96 Topps Basketball set was issued in two separate series of 181 and 110 standard-size cards for a total of 291. Both first and second series cards were issued in 12-card hobby and retail packs (SRP $1.29). The white bordered fronts have a full-color action photo with the player's name in gold set against a black shadow. Horizontal backs have color head-shots with statistics and information. Subsets include Active Leaders (1-5), Scoring Leaders (6-10), Rebound Leaders (11-15), Assist Leaders (16-20), Steal Leaders (21-25) and Block Leaders (26-30). Rookie Cards of note in this set include Michael Finley, Kevin Garnett, Antonio McDyess, Joe Smith, Jerry Stackhouse and Damon Stoudamire.

COMPLETE SET (291) 12.00 30.00
COMPLETE SERIES 1 (181) 6.00 15.00
COMPLETE SERIES 2 (110) 6.00 15.00
1 Michael Jordan AL 1.00 2.50
2 Dennis Rodman AL .25 .60
3 John Stockton AL .15 .40
4 Michael Jordan AL 1.00 2.50
5 David Robinson AL .20 .50
6 Shaquille O'Neal AL .30 .75
7 Hakeem Olajuwon LL .15 .40
8 David Robinson LL .20 .50
9 Karl Malone LL .15 .40
10 Jamal Mashburn LL .12 .30
11 Dennis Rodman LL .25 .60
12 Dikembe Mutombo LL .12 .30
13 Shaquille O'Neal LL .30 .75
14 Patrick Ewing LL .15 .40
15 Tyrone Hill LL .07 .20
16 John Stockton LL .15 .40
17 Kenny Anderson LL .10 .25
18 Tim Hardaway LL .12 .30
19 Rod Strickland LL .07 .20
20 Muggsy Bogues LL .10 .25
21 Scottie Pippen LL .25 .60
22 Mookie Blaylock LL .07 .20
23 Gary Payton LL .20 .50
24 John Stockton LL .15 .40
25 Nate McMillan LL .07 .20
26 Dikembe Mutombo LL .12 .30
27 Hakeem Olajuwon LL .15 .40
28 Shawn Bradley LL .07 .20
29 David Robinson LL .20 .50
30 Alonzo Mourning LL .15 .40
31 Reggie Miller .15 .40
32 Karl Malone .15 .40
33 Grant Hill .20 .50
34 Charles Barkley .20 .50
35 Cedric Ceballos .07 .20
36 Gheorghe Muresan .07 .20
37 Doug West .07 .20
38 Tony Dumas .07 .20

39 Kenny Gattison .07 .20
40 Chris Mullin .12 .30
41 Pervis Ellison .07 .20
42 Vinny Del Negro .07 .20
43 Mario Elie .07 .20
44 Todd Day .07 .20
45 Scottie Pippen .20 .50
46 Buck Williams .07 .20
47 P.J. Brown .07 .20
48 Bimbo Coles .07 .20
49 Terrell Brandon .07 .20
50 Charles Oakley .10 .25
51 Sam Perkins .07 .20
52 Dale Ellis .07 .20
53 Andrew Lang .07 .20
54 Harold Ellis .07 .20
55 Clarence Weatherspoon .07 .20
56 Bill Curley .07 .20
57 Robert Parish .12 .30
58 David Benoit .07 .20
59 Anthony Avent .07 .20
60 Jamal Mashburn .12 .30
61 Duane Ferrell .07 .20
62 Elden Campbell .07 .20
63 Rex Chapman .07 .20
64 Wesley Person .07 .20
65 Mitch Richmond .12 .30
66 Micheal Williams .07 .20
67 Clifford Rozier .07 .20
68 Eric Montross .07 .20
69 Dennis Rodman .25 .60
70 Vin Baker .10 .25
71 Tyrone Hill .07 .20
72 Tyrone Corbin .07 .20
73 Chris Dudley .07 .20
74 Nate McMillan .07 .20
75 Kenny Anderson .10 .25
76 Monty Williams .07 .20
77 Kenny Smith .10 .25
78 Rodney Rogers .07 .20
79 Corie Blount .07 .20
80 Glen Rice .12 .30
81 Walt Williams .07 .20
82 Scott Williams .07 .20
83 Michael Adams .07 .20
84 Terry Mills .07 .20
85 Horace Grant .10 .25
86 Chuck Person .10 .25
87 Adam Keefe .07 .20
88 Scott Brooks .07 .20
89 George Lynch .07 .20
90 Kevin Johnson .12 .30
91 Armon Gilliam .07 .20
92 Greg Minor .07 .20
93 Derrick McKey .07 .20
94 Victor Alexander .07 .20
95 B.J. Armstrong .07 .20
96 Terry Dehere .07 .20
97 Christian Laettner .10 .25
98 Hubert Davis .07 .20
99 Aaron McKie .07 .20
100 Hakeem Olajuwon .15 .40
101 Michael Cage .07 .20
102 Grant Long .07 .20
103 Calbert Cheaney .07 .20
104 Olden Polynice .07 .20
105 Sharone Wright .07 .20
106 Lee Mayberry .07 .20
107 Robert Pack .07 .20
108 Loy Vaught .07 .20
109 Khalid Reeves .07 .20
110 Shawn Kemp .12 .30
111 Lindsey Hunter .07 .20
112 Dell Curry .07 .20
113 Dan Majerle .12 .30
114 Bryon Russell .07 .20
115 John Starks .10 .25
116 Roy Tarpley .07 .20
117 Dale Davis .07 .20
118 Nick Anderson .07 .20
119 Rex Walters .07 .20
120 Dominique Wilkins .15 .40
121 Sam Cassell .12 .30
122 Sean Elliott .12 .30
123 B.J. Tyler .07 .20
124 Eric Mobley .07 .20
125 Toni Kukoc .12 .30
126 Pooh Richardson .07 .20
127 Isaiah Rider .12 .30
128 Steve Smith .10 .25
129 Chris Mills .07 .20
130 Detlef Schrempf .12 .30
131 Donyell Marshall .07 .20
132 Eddie Jones .15 .40
133 Otis Thorpe .07 .20
134 Lionel Simmons .07 .20
135 Jeff Hornacek .10 .25
136 Jalen Rose .15 .40
137 Kevin Willis .07 .20
138 Don MacLean .07 .20
139 Dee Brown .07 .20
140 Glenn Robinson .12 .30
141 Joe Kleine .07 .20
142 Ron Harper .10 .25
143 Antonio Davis .07 .20
144 Jeff Malone .07 .20
145 Joe Dumars .12 .30
146 Jason Kidd .20 .50
147 J.R. Reid .07 .20
148 Lamond Murray .07 .20
149 Derrick Coleman .10 .25
150 Alonzo Mourning .15 .40
151 Clifford Robinson .07 .20
152 Kendall Gill .07 .20
153 Doug Christie .07 .20
154 Stacey Augmon .10 .25
155 Anfernee Hardaway .20 .50
156 Mahmoud Abdul-Rauf .07 .20
157 Latrell Sprewell .12 .30
158 Mark Price .12 .30
159 Brian Grant .10 .25
160 Clyde Drexler .15 .40
161 Juwan Howard .12 .30
162 Tom Gugliotta .07 .20
163 Nick Van Exel .12 .30
164 Billy Owens .07 .20
165 Brooks Thompson .07 .20
166 Acie Earl .07 .20
167 Ed Pinckney .07 .20
168 Oliver Miller .07 .20
169 John Salley .07 .20
170 Jerome Kersey .07 .20
171 Willie Anderson .07 .20
172 Keith Jennings .07 .20
173 Doug Smith .07 .20
174 Gerald Wilkins .07 .20
175 Byron Scott .10 .25
176 Benoit Benjamin .07 .20
177 Blue Edwards .07 .20
178 Greg Anthony .07 .20
179 Trevor Ruffin .07 .20
180 Kenny Gattison .07 .20
181 Checklist 1-181 .07 .20
182 Cherokee Parks RC .12 .30
183 Kurt Thomas RC .12 .30
184 Ervin Johnson .07 .20
185 Chucky Brown .07 .20
186 Luc Longley .07 .20
187 Anthony Miller .07 .20
188 Ed O'Bannon RC .12 .30
189 Bobby Hurley .12 .30
190 Dikembe Mutombo .12 .30
191 Robert Horry .10 .25
192 George Zidek RC .12 .30
193 Rasheed Wallace RC .40 1.00
194 Marty Conlon .07 .20
195 A.C. Green .12 .30
196 Mike Brown .07 .20
197 Oliver Miller .07 .20
198 Charles Smith .07 .20
199 Eric Williams RC .12 .30
200 Rik Smits .10 .25
201 Donald Royal .07 .20
202 Bryant Reeves RC .12 .30
203 Danny Ferry .07 .20
204 Brian Williams .07 .20
205 Joe Smith RC .25 .60
206 Gary Trent RC .12 .30
207 Greg Ostertag RC .12 .30
208 Ken Norman .07 .20
209 Avery Johnson .10 .25
210 Theo Ratliff UER RC .20 .50
Card has no draft pick logo
211 Corie Blount .07 .20
212 Hersey Hawkins .07 .20
213 Loren Meyer RC .12 .30
214 Mario Bennett RC .12 .30
215 Randolph Childress RC .12 .30
216 Spud Webb .12 .30
217 Popeye Jones .07 .20
218 Shawn Respert RC .12 .30
219 Malik Sealy .07 .20
220 Dino Radja .10 .25
221 James Robinson .07 .20
222 David Vaughn .12 .30
223 Michael Smith .07 .20
224 Jamie Watson .07 .20
225 LaPhonso Ellis .07 .20
226 Kevin Gamble .07 .20
227 Dennis Rodman .25 .60
228 B.J. Armstrong .07 .20
229 Jerry Stackhouse RC .40 1.00
230 Muggsy Bogues .10 .25
231 Lawrence Moten RC .12 .30
232 Cory Alexander RC .12 .30
233 Carlos Rogers .07 .20
234 Tyus Edney RC .12 .30
235 Doc Rivers .10 .25
236 Antonio Harvey .07 .20
237 Kevin Garnett RC 1.00 2.50
238 Derek Harper .10 .25
239 Kevin Edwards .07 .20
240 Chris Smith .07 .20
241 Haywoode Workman .07 .20
242 Bobby Phills .07 .20
243 Sherrell Ford RC .12 .30
244 Corliss Williamson RC .12 .30
245 Shawn Bradley .07 .20
246 Jason Caffey RC .12 .30
247 Bryant Stith .07 .20
248 Mark West .07 .20
249 Dennis Scott .07 .20
250 Jim Jackson .07 .20
251 Travis Best RC .12 .30
252 Sean Rooks .07 .20
253 Yinka Dare .07 .20
254 Felton Spencer .07 .20
255 Vlade Divac .12 .30
256 Michael Finley RC .40 1.00
257 Damon Stoudamire RC .30 .75
258 Mark Bryant .07 .20
259 Brent Barry RC .20 .50
260 Rony Seikaly .10 .25
261 Alan Henderson RC .12 .30
262 Kendall Gill .07 .20
263 Rex Chapman .07 .20
264 Eric Murdock .07 .20
265 Rodney Rogers .07 .20
266 Greg Graham .07 .20
267 Jayson Williams .07 .20
268 Antonio McDyess RC .30 .75
269 Sedale Threatt .07 .20
270 Danny Manning .10 .25
271 Pete Chilcutt .07 .20
272 Bob Sura RC .12 .30
273 Dana Barros .07 .20
274 Allan Houston .10 .25
275 Tracy Murray .07 .20
276 Anthony Mason .07 .20
277 Michael Jordan 1.00 2.50
278 Patrick Ewing .15 .40
279 Shaquille O'Neal .30 .75
280 Larry Johnson .12 .30
281 Mark Jackson .12 .30
282 Chris Webber .15 .40
283 David Robinson .20 .50
284 John Stockton .15 .40
285 Mookie Blaylock .07 .20
286 Mark Price .12 .30
287 Tim Hardaway .12 .30
288 Rod Strickland .07 .20
289 Sherman Douglas .07 .20
290 Gary Payton .12 .30
291 Checklist (182-291) .07 .20

1995-96 Topps Draft Redemption

These 29 draft pick cards (covering the entire first round of the 1995 NBA draft) were available exclusively by redeeming one of the Topps Draft Redemption insert cards (randomly inserted in series one packs at a rate of one in 18). These cards feature all foil silver bordered fronts with a full-color action shot of the featured rookie. The first series exchange cards each featured a large number on the card front representing the player that was chosen at that slot in the 1995 NBA draft. Collectors had to then mail the card in to Topps to receive their player card. The redemption deadline for these cards was April 1, 1996.

COMPLETE SET (29) 125.00 225.00
1 Joe Smith 6.00 15.00
2 Antonio McDyess 8.00 20.00
3 Jerry Stackhouse 10.00 25.00
4 Rasheed Wallace 10.00 25.00
5 Kevin Garnett 25.00 60.00
6 Bryant Reeves 3.00 8.00
7 Damon Stoudamire 8.00 20.00
8 Shawn Respert 3.00 8.00
9 Ed O'Bannon 3.00 8.00
10 Kurt Thomas 3.00 8.00
11 Gary Trent 3.00 8.00
12 Cherokee Parks 3.00 8.00
13 Corliss Williamson 3.00 8.00
14 Eric Williams 3.00 8.00
15 Brent Barry 5.00 12.00
16 Alan Henderson 3.00 8.00
17 Bob Sura 3.00 8.00
18 Theo Ratliff 5.00 12.00
19 Randolph Childress 3.00 8.00
20 Jason Caffey 3.00 8.00
21 Michael Finley 10.00 25.00
22 George Zidek 3.00 8.00
23 Travis Best 3.00 8.00
24 Loren Meyer 3.00 8.00
25 David Vaughn 3.00 8.00
26 Sherrell Ford 3.00 8.00
27 Mario Bennett 3.00 8.00
28 Greg Ostertag 3.00 8.00
29 Cory Alexander 3.00 8.00
NNO Expired Exchange Cards .40 1.00

1995-96 Topps Foreign Legion

Featuring foreign players who play in the NBA, this 10-card set was available in retail packs sold in Canada and Australia only. It was randomly inserted in 6-card packs at a rate of one in 36. On a white-bordered metallic background, the fronts feature color player cutouts. The player's name is gold foil stamped across the bottom. The backs carry a color closeup and a player profile, all on a blue background featuring a picture of the earth.

COMPLETE SET (10) 6.00 15.00
FL1 Luc Longley .75 2.00
FL2 Rick Fox .75 2.00
FL3 Dikembe Mutombo 1.25 3.00
FL4 Gheorghe Muresan .75 2.00
FL5 Sarunas Marciulionis .75 2.00
FL6 Dino Radja 1.00 2.50
FL7 Detlef Schrempf 1.25 3.00
FL8 Rony Seikaly 1.00 2.50
FL9 Bill Wennington .75 2.00
FL10 Rik Smits 1.00 2.50

1995-96 Topps Mystery Finest

Randomly inserted into all second series packs at a rate of one in 36, cards from this 22-card standard-size insert set spotlight a selection of top forwards and guards in the league. Each Mystery Finest card was inserted into packs with a black plastic coating on front. Hence, the "mystery" was to peel off the coating to see whether one had a basic card or a parallel refractor. Card fronts featur a silver foil border and a player action photo cut out against a galaxy design background. These cards are often found poorly centered.

COMPLETE SET (22) 50.00 100.00
M1 Michael Jordan 12.50 30.00
M2 Anfernee Hardaway 3.00 8.00
M3 Clyde Drexler 2.50 6.00
M4 Mark Price 2.00 5.00
M5 Steve Smith 1.50 4.00
M6 Jim Jackson 1.25 3.00
M7 Nick Anderson 1.25 3.00
M8 Kenny Anderson 1.50 4.00
M9 Mookie Blaylock 1.25 3.00
M10 Jason Kidd 3.00 8.00
M11 Tim Hardaway 2.00 5.00
M12 Kevin Johnson 2.00 5.00
M13 Gary Payton 2.00 5.00
M14 John Stockton 2.50 6.00
M15 Rod Strickland 1.25 3.00
M16 Jamal Mashburn 2.00 5.00
M17 Danny Manning 1.50 4.00
M18 Billy Owens 1.25 3.00
M19 Grant Hill 3.00 8.00
M20 Scottie Pippen 3.00 8.00
M21 Isaiah Rider 2.00 5.00
M22 Latrell Sprewell 2.00 5.00

1995-96 Topps Mystery Finest Refractors

These twenty-two cards parallel the Topps Mystery Finest inserts. The only difference is the refractive coating on the card fronts. Mystery Finest Refractors are randomly seeded into one in every 36 second series hobby packs and one in every 216 second series retail packs. Many of the cards are found off-center and are considered condition sensitive.

*REF: 2X TO 5X BASE HI
M1 Michael Jordan 100.00 225.00

1995-96 Topps Pan For Gold

Randomly inserted in first series retail packs only at a rate of one in eight, this 15-card standard-size set chronicles the play of NBA stars who came from small colleges and were drafted late. White-bordered fronts feature a full-color player cutout set against a mine shaft background. The player's team name is printed in silver across the top and his name is stamped in gold foil across the bottom. Horizontal backs have a full-color player head shot on the left third of the card with his name, biography and details of his draft and school information on the right. Pieces of gold serve as a background for the back. These cards are numbered with a "PFG" prefix.

COMPLETE SET (15) 20.00 50.00
PFG1 Vin Baker 2.00 5.00
PFG2 John Stockton 3.00 8.00
PFG3 Dan Majerle 2.50 6.00
PFG4 Joe Dumars 2.50 6.00
PFG5 Rik Smits 2.00 5.00
PFG6 Tim Hardaway 2.50 6.00
PFG7 Charles Oakley 2.00 5.00
PFG8 Cedric Ceballos 1.50 4.00
PFG9 Karl Malone 3.00 8.00
PFG10 Scottie Pippen 4.00 10.00
PFG11 David Robinson 4.00 10.00
PFG12 Gary Payton 2.50 6.00
PFG13 Mitch Richmond 2.50 6.00
PFG14 Antonio Davis 1.50 4.00
PFG15 Dennis Rodman 5.00 12.00

1995-96 Topps Power Boosters

This 45-card insert standard-size set is printed on 28-point stock and features the leaders in points, rebounds, assists, steals and blocks paralleling the regular issue subset cards. The first 30 cards in the set (1-30) were seeded into first series packs at a rate of 1 in 36. The last 15 cards in the set (276-290) were seeded into second series packs also at a rate of one in 36. A Power Boosters card replaced two regular cards in every they came in. Full-bleed fronts carry a full-color action player cutout set against diffraction foil background with the player's name stamped in gold foil across the top. The Power Boosters logo appears at the bottom of the card with the individual's category listed above the logo. Borderless backs are one-color background with a full-color player head shot boxed on the right. Player name, team name, profile and biography appear on the back.

COMPLETE SET (45) 140.00 250.00
COMPLETE SERIES 1 (30) 100.00 175.00
COMPLETE SERIES 2 (15) 40.00 75.00
1 Michael Jordan 15.00 40.00
2 Dennis Rodman 4.00 10.00
3 John Stockton 2.50 6.00
4 Michael Jordan 15.00 40.00
5 David Robinson 3.00 8.00
6 Shaquille O'Neal 5.00 12.00
7 Hakeem Olajuwon 2.50 6.00
8 David Robinson 3.00 8.00
9 Karl Malone 2.50 6.00
10 Jamal Mashburn 2.00 5.00
11 Dennis Rodman 4.00 10.00
12 Dikembe Mutombo 2.00 5.00
13 Shaquille O'Neal 5.00 12.00
14 Patrick Ewing 2.50 6.00
15 Tyrone Hill 1.25 3.00
16 John Stockton 2.50 6.00
17 Kenny Anderson 1.50 4.00
18 Tim Hardaway 2.00 5.00
19 Rod Strickland 1.25 3.00
20 Muggsy Bogues 1.50 4.00
21 Scottie Pippen 3.00 8.00
22 Mookie Blaylock 1.25 3.00
23 Gary Payton 2.00 5.00
24 John Stockton 2.50 6.00
25 Nate McMillan 1.25 3.00
26 Dikembe Mutombo 2.00 5.00
27 Hakeem Olajuwon 2.50 6.00
28 Shawn Bradley 1.25 3.00
29 David Robinson 3.00 8.00
30 Alonzo Mourning 2.50 6.00
276 Anthony Mason 1.25 3.00
277 Michael Jordan 15.00 40.00
278 Patrick Ewing 2.50 6.00
279 Shaquille O'Neal 5.00 12.00
280 Larry Johnson 2.00 5.00
281 Mark Jackson 2.00 5.00
282 Chris Webber 2.50 6.00
283 David Robinson 3.00 8.00
284 John Stockton 2.50 6.00
285 Mookie Blaylock 1.25 3.00
286 Mark Price 2.00 5.00
287 Tim Hardaway 2.00 5.00
288 Rod Strickland 1.25 3.00
289 Sherman Douglas 1.25 3.00
290 Gary Payton 2.00 5.00

1995-96 Topps Rattle and Roll

Randomly inserted in second series retail packs only at a rate of one in 12, this 10-card set takes aim at the power mongers of the NBA. Fronts are bordered in silver foil with a blue and red silver swirl pattern for a background. A full-color player cutout appears on the front with his name printed in a copper foil at the bottom. White-bordered backs contain a player head shot and his name printed underneath in red type. The blue and red swirl pattern continues and the player's biography and profile are printed in white type.

COMPLETE SET (10) 5.00 12.00
R1 Juwan Howard 1.00 2.50
R2 Glenn Robinson 1.00 2.50
R3 Grant Hill 1.50 4.00
R4 Sharone Wright .60 1.50
R5 Brian Grant .75 2.00
R6 Antonio McDyess 1.25 3.00
R7 Bryant Reeves .50 1.25
R8 Gary Trent .50 1.25
R9 Jerry Stackhouse 1.50 4.00
R10 Joe Smith 1.00 2.50

1995-96 Topps Show Stoppers

Cards in this set of ten were randomly issued in first series hobby packs only at a rate of one in 24 and feature the top players of the NBA. Fronts are white bordered with silver foil and a full-color player action cutout. The player's name is printed in gold foil at the bottom. Backs have a player head shot with a spotlight description, a game high feature and a show stopper highlight.

COMPLETE SET (10) 20.00 50.00
SS1 Michael Jordan 12.00 30.00
SS2 Grant Hill 2.50 6.00
SS3 Glenn Robinson 1.50 4.00
SS4 Anfernee Hardaway 2.50 6.00
SS5 Charles Barkley 2.50 6.00
SS6 Patrick Ewing 2.00 5.00
SS7 Shaquille O'Neal 4.00 10.00
SS8 Jason Kidd 2.50 6.00
SS9 Glen Rice 1.50 4.00
SS10 Karl Malone 2.00 5.00

1995-96 Topps Spark Plugs

Randomly inserted in all second series retail packs at a rate of one in 8, cards from this 10-card chase set highlight NBA scorers on full-foil fronts. Silver foil serves as a border and a blue and silver foil are background for a full-color action player cutout. A spark plug with sparks flying out and the player's name are printed in silver foil. Horizontal backs are white bordered with a full-color action shot on one side and a player biography and '94-95 season highlights on the other.

COMPLETE SET (10) 10.00 25.00
SP1 Shaquille O'Neal 2.00 5.00
SP2 Michael Jordan 8.00 20.00
SP3 Reggie Miller 1.00 2.50
SP4 Anfernee Hardaway 1.25 3.00
SP5 John Stockton 1.00 2.50
SP6 David Robinson 1.25 3.00
SP7 Hakeem Olajuwon 1.00 2.50
SP8 Tim Hardaway .75 2.00
SP9 Grant Hill 1.25 3.00
SP10 Scottie Pippen 1.25 3.00

1995-96 Topps Sudden Impact

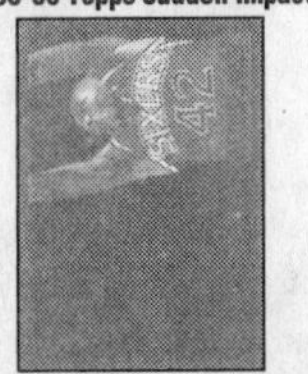

Sudden Impact is a hobby-exclusive insert set of ten rookies that were expected to make a significant impact on their teams. The horizontally designed "all foil" cards were randomly inserted at a rate of 1 in 72 second series hobby packs. The cards are numbered on the back with an "S" prefix.

COMPLETE SET (10) 20.00 50.00
S1 Damon Stoudamire 5.00 12.00
S2 Cherokee Parks 2.00 5.00
S3 Kurt Thomas 2.00 5.00
S4 Gary Trent 2.00 5.00
S5 Bryant Reeves 2.00 5.00
S6 Ed O'Bannon 2.00 5.00
S7 Shawn Respert 2.00 5.00
S8 Antonio McDyess 5.00 12.00
S9 Joe Smith 4.00 10.00
S10 Jerry Stackhouse 6.00 15.00

1995-96 Topps Top Flight

Cards in this 20-piece set feature the high flyers of the NBA and were inserted one per retail pack. The white bordered fronts have a full-color player action cutout set against a background with two fighter jets. The player's name is printed in gold foil near the bottom above a gold foil swooshing jet whose vapor spells out "Top Flight." Backs have a ful-color head shot inset within a sky background of a jet in flight. A biography and special abilities box appear on the back.

COMPLETE SET (20) 20.00 50.00
TF1 Michael Jordan 10.00 25.00
TF2 Isaiah Rider 1.25 3.00
TF3 Harold Miner .75 2.00
TF4 Dominique Wilkins 1.50 4.00
TF5 Clyde Drexler 1.50 4.00
TF6 Scottie Pippen 2.00 5.00
TF7 Shawn Kemp 1.25 3.00
TF8 Chris Webber 1.50 4.00
TF9 Anfernee Hardaway 2.00 5.00
TF10 Grant Hill 2.00 5.00
TF11 Kevin Johnson 1.25 3.00
TF12 John Starks 1.00 2.50
TF13 Dan Majerle 1.25 3.00
TF14 Latrell Sprewell 1.25 3.00
TF15 Dee Brown .75 2.00
TF16 Stacey Augmon 1.00 2.50
TF17 David Benoit .75 2.00
TF18 Sean Elliott 1.25 3.00
TF19 Cedric Ceballos .75 2.00
TF20 Robert Horry 1.00 2.50

1995-96 Topps Whiz Kids

Randomly inserted in all first series packs at a rate of one in 24, this set of 12 standard-size cards highlights the young power of the NBA. Etched silver foil fronts have a basketball court background and a full-color player action cutout. "Whiz Kids" is spelled out in children's letter blocks on the top. The players name is printed in red at the bottom. Borderless backs are numbered with the prefix "WK" and continue with a basketball court background. A full-color player head shot appears inside the key of the court and his name appears underneath the photo in red print on a blue banner. Career stats, biography and a trivia question appear on the lower half and the answer to the question on the preceding card appears at the bottom.

COMPLETE SET (12) 12.50 30.00
WK1 Grant Hill 2.50 6.00
WK2 Nick Van Exel 1.50 4.00
WK3 Juwan Howard 1.50 4.00
WK4 Chris Webber 2.00 5.00
WK5 Brian Grant 1.25 3.00
WK6 Glenn Robinson 1.50 4.00
WK7 Donyell Marshall 1.00 2.50
WK8 Jason Kidd 2.50 6.00
WK9 Anfernee Hardaway 2.50 6.00
WK10 Jamal Mashburn 1.50 4.00
WK11 Vin Baker 1.25 3.00
WK12 Eddie Jones 2.00 5.00

1995-96 Topps World Class

This 10-card standard-size set was randomly inserted approximately one in every 18 second series International packs. These packs were intended for Australia and New Zealand only, but have found their way back to the United States. Card fronts are bordered with a photo of the player and the logo "World Class" clearly written on the front. Card backs are numbered with a "WC" prefix.

COMPLETE SET (10) 15.00 40.00
WC1 Michael Jordan 12.00 30.00
WC2 Karl Malone 1.50 4.00
WC3 Shaquille O'Neal 3.00 8.00
WC4 Reggie Miller 1.50 4.00
WC5 Hakeem Olajuwon 1.50 4.00
WC6 Grant Hill 2.00 5.00
WC7 Anfernee Hardaway 2.00 5.00
WC8 Scottie Pippen 2.00 5.00
WC9 David Robinson 2.00 5.00
WC10 Clyde Drexler 1.50 4.00

1996-97 Topps

The 1996-97 Topps basketball set was issued in two series totaling 222 standard-size cards, although the checklist card from series one (#111) is not considered part of the basic set. Both series cards were issued in 11-card hobby and retail packs carrying a suggested retail price of $1.29. The white-bordered fronts have a full-color action photo with the player's name in gold set against the trail of a moving basketball. Horizontal backs have color head shots with career statistics and information. The checklist card (#111) actually looks more like a premium Finest brand card than a Topps issue. Because it was so much tougher than a normal checklist, it is not considered part of the series one set. Rookie cards include Kobe Bryant, Marcus Camby, Allen Iverson, Stephon Marbury, Shareef Abdur-Rahim and Antoine Walker, among others. Several cards including Shawn Kemp and Damon Stoudamire were used for promotional purposes. The card numbers are identical to the regular issue, but on the front of the card, the Topps logo and the team logo are switched. In addition, Topps released factory sets for both the hobby and retail markets. Each set contained the full 221-card set, 2 of the Season's Best inserts, 1 card from the NBA at 50 parallel and 2 of the Pro File inserts. The hobby factory set also contained one of the 10 autographed cards originally released in the 1996 Topps NBA Stars Reprint Autograph set.

COMPLETE SET (221) 15.00 30.00
COMP.FACT.HOB.SET (227) 15.00 35.00
COMPLETE SERIES 1 (110) 6.00 12.00
COMPLETE SERIES 2 (111) 10.00 20.00
1 Patrick Ewing .20 .50
2 Christian Laettner .12 .30
3 Mahmoud Abdul-Rauf .10 .25
4 Chris Webber .20 .50
5 Jason Kidd .25 .60
6 Clifford Rozier .10 .25
7 Elden Campbell .10 .25
8 Chuck Person .12 .30
9 Jeff Hornacek .12 .30
10 Rik Smits .12 .30
11 Kurt Thomas .10 .25
12 Rod Strickland .10 .25
13 Kendall Gill .10 .25
14 Brian Williams .10 .25
15 Tom Gugliotta .10 .25
16 Ron Harper .12 .30
17 Eric Williams .10 .25
18 A.C. Green .15 .40
19 Scott Williams .10 .25
20 Damon Stoudamire .15 .40
21 Bryant Reeves .10 .25
22 Bob Sura .10 .25
23 Mitch Richmond .15 .40
24 Larry Johnson .15 .40
25 Vin Baker .12 .30
26 Mark Bryant .12 .30
27 Horace Grant .12 .30
28 Allan Houston .12 .30
29 Sam Perkins .10 .25
30 Antonio McDyess .15 .40
31 Rasheed Wallace .20 .50
32 Malik Sealy .10 .25
33 Scottie Pippen .25 .60
34 Charles Barkley .25 .60
35 Hakeem Olajuwon .20 .50
36 John Starks .12 .30
37 Byron Scott .12 .30
38 Arvydas Sabonis .12 .30
39 Vlade Divac .15 .40
40 Joe Dumars .15 .40
41 Danny Ferry .10 .25
42 Jerry Stackhouse .20 .50
43 B.J. Armstrong .10 .25
44 Shawn Bradley .10 .25
45 Kevin Garnett .40 1.00
46 Dee Brown .10 .25
47 Michael Smith .10 .25
48 Doug Christie .10 .25
49 Mark Jackson .15 .40
50 Shawn Kemp .15 .40
51 Sasha Danilovic .10 .25
52 Nick Anderson .10 .25
53 Matt Geiger .10 .25
54 Charles Smith .10 .25
55 Mookie Blaylock .10 .25
56 Johnny Newman .10 .25
57 George McCloud .10 .25
58 Greg Ostertag .10 .25
59 Reggie Williams .10 .25
60 Brent Barry .12 .30
61 Doug West .10 .25
62 Donald Royal .10 .25
63 Randy Brown .10 .25
64 Vincent Askew .10 .25
65 John Stockton .20 .50
66 Joe Kleine .10 .25
67 Keith Askins .10 .25
68 Bobby Phills .10 .25
69 Chris Mullin .15 .40
70 Nick Van Exel .15 .40
71 Rick Fox .10 .25
72 Chicago Bulls - 72 Wins .60 1.50
73 Shawn Respert .10 .25
74 Hubert Davis .10 .25
75 Jim Jackson .10 .25
76 Olden Polynice .10 .25
77 Gheorghe Muresan .10 .25
78 Theo Ratliff .10 .25
79 Khalid Reeves .10 .25
80 David Robinson .25 .60
81 Lawrence Moten .10 .25
82 Sam Cassell .12 .30
83 George Zidek .10 .25
84 Sharone Wright .10 .25
85 Clarence Weatherspoon .10 .25
86 Alan Henderson .10 .25
87 Chris Dudley .10 .25
88 Ed O'Bannon .10 .25
89 Calbert Cheaney .10 .25
90 Cedric Ceballos .10 .25
91 Michael Cage .10 .25
92 Ervin Johnson .10 .25
93 Gary Trent .10 .25
94 Sherman Douglas .10 .25
95 Joe Smith .12 .30
96 Dale Davis .10 .25
97 Tony Dumas .10 .25
98 Muggsy Bogues .12 .30
99 Toni Kukoc .15 .40
100 Grant Hill .25 .60
101 Michael Finley .20 .50
102 Isaiah Rider .12 .30
103 Bryant Stith .10 .25
104 Pooh Richardson .10 .25
105 Karl Malone .20 .50
106 Brian Grant .12 .30
107 Sean Elliott .15 .40
108 Charles Oakley .12 .30
109 Pervis Ellison .10 .25
110 Anfernee Hardaway .25 .60
111 Checklist SP .40 1.00
112 Dikembe Mutombo .15 .40
113 Alonzo Mourning .20 .50
114 Hubert Davis .10 .25
115 Rony Seikaly .12 .30
116 Danny Manning .12 .30
117 Donyell Marshall .10 .25
118 Gerald Wilkins .10 .25
119 Ervin Johnson .10 .25
120 Jalen Rose .12 .30
121 Dino Radja .12 .30
122 Glenn Robinson .15 .40
123 John Stockton .20 .50
124 Matt Maloney RC .15 .40
125 Clifford Robinson .12 .30
126 Steve Kerr .12 .30
127 Nate McMillan .10 .25
128 Shareef Abdur-Rahim RC .30 .75
129 Loy Vaught .10 .25
130 Anthony Mason .10 .25
131 Kevin Garnett .40 1.00
132 Roy Rogers RC .15 .40
133 Erick Dampier RC .15 .40
134 Tyus Edney .10 .25
135 Chris Mills .10 .25
136 Cory Alexander .10 .25
137 Juwan Howard .12 .30
138 Kobe Bryant RC 6.00 15.00
139 Michael Jordan 1.25 3.00
140 Jayson Williams .10 .25
141 Rod Strickland .10 .25
142 Lorenzen Wright RC .15 .40
143 Will Perdue .10 .25
144 Derek Harper .12 .30
145 Billy Owens .10 .25
146 Antoine Walker RC .30 .75
147 P.J. Brown .10 .25
148 Terrell Brandon .15 .40
149 Larry Johnson .15 .40
150 Steve Smith .12 .30
151 Eddie Jones .15 .40
152 Detlef Schrempf .15 .40
153 Dale Ellis .10 .25
154 Isaiah Rider .12 .30
155 Tony Delk RC .15 .40
156 Adrian Caldwell .10 .25
157 Jamal Mashburn .12 .30
158 Dennis Scott .10 .25
159 Dana Barros .10 .25
160 Martin Muursepp RC .15 .40
161 Marcus Camby RC .25 .60
162 Jerome Williams RC .15 .40
163 Wesley Person .10 .25
164 Luc Longley .10 .25
165 Charlie Ward .10 .25
166 Mark Jackson .15 .40
167 Derrick Coleman .12 .30
168 Dell Curry .10 .25
169 Armon Gilliam .10 .25
170 Vlade Divac .15 .40
171 Allen Iverson RC .75 2.00
172 Vitaly Potapenko RC .15 .40
173 Jon Koncak .10 .25
174 Lindsey Hunter .10 .25
175 Kevin Johnson .15 .40
176 Dennis Rodman .30 .75
177 Stephon Marbury RC .40 1.00
178 Karl Malone .20 .50
179 Charles Barkley .25 .60
180 Popeye Jones .10 .25
181 Samaki Walker RC .15 .40
182 Steve Nash RC 1.25 3.00
183 Latrell Sprewell .15 .40
184 Kenny Anderson .12 .30
185 Tyrone Hill .10 .25

186 Robert Pack .10 .25
187 Greg Anthony .10 .25
188 Derrick McKey .10 .25
189 John Wallace RC .15 .40
190 Bryon Russell .10 .25
191 Jermaine O'Neal RC .40 1.00
192 Clyde Drexler .20 .50
193 Mahmoud Abdul-Rauf .10 .25
194 Eric Montross .10 .25
195 Allan Houston .12 .30
196 Harvey Grant .10 .25
197 Rodney Rogers .10 .25
198 Kerry Kittles RC .15 .40
199 Grant Hill .25 .60
200 Lionel Simmons .10 .25
201 Reggie Miller .20 .50
202 Avery Johnson .12 .30
203 LaPhonso Ellis .10 .25
204 Brian Shaw .10 .25
205 Priest Lauderdale RC .15 .40
206 Derek Fisher RC .30 .75
207 Terry Porter .10 .25
208 Todd Fuller RC .15 .40
209 Hersey Hawkins .10 .25
210 Tim Legler .10 .25
211 Terry Dehere .10 .25
212 Gary Payton .15 .40
213 Joe Dumars .15 .40
214 Don MacLean .10 .25
215 Greg Minor .10 .25
216 Tim Hardaway .15 .40
217 Ray Allen RC .60 1.50
218 Mario Elie .10 .25
219 Brooks Thompson .10 .25
220 Shaquille O'Neal .40 1.00

1996-97 Topps NBA at 50

Randomly inserted into both series at a rate of one in every three 11-card packs, these 220 cards parallel the regular issue set. The only difference in design is a silver foil treatment to each card front with a stamp commemorating the NBA at 50. The Factory sets also contained one of these parallel cards. Please refer to the multipliers provided below (coupled with the prices of the corresponding regular issue cards) to ascertain values for individual NBA at 50 cards.
*STARS: 2.5X TO 6X BASE CARD HI
*RCs: 2X TO 5X BASE HI
138 Kobe Bryant 15.00 40.00

1996-97 Topps Draft Redemption

These trade cards were randomly inserted in first series packs at a rate of one in 18. Each trade card has a number printed on front that corresponds to each draft position of the first round of the 1996 NBA draft. Collectors that exchanged their trade card would then receive an exchange card picturing the player selected at that spot in the draft. The Draft Redemption trade deadline was April 1, 1997. Cards number 14 and 23 were not issued as they did not sign NBA contracts during this promotion. Both Stojakovic and Retzias were foreign players who continued playing overseas.
1 Allen Iverson 12.00 30.00
2 Marcus Camby 4.00 10.00
3 Shareef Abdur-Rahim 5.00 12.00
4 Stephon Marbury 6.00 15.00
5 Ray Allen 10.00 25.00
6 Antoine Walker 5.00 12.00
7 Lorenzen Wright 2.50 6.00
8 Kerry Kittles 2.50 6.00
9 Samaki Walker 2.50 6.00
10 Erick Dampier 2.50 6.00
11 Todd Fuller 2.50 6.00
12 Vitaly Potapenko 2.50 6.00
13 Kobe Bryant 50.00 125.00
15 Steve Nash 15.00 40.00
16 Tony Delk 2.50 6.00
17 Jermaine O'Neal 6.00 15.00
18 John Wallace 2.50 6.00
19 Walter McCarty 2.50 6.00
20 Zydrunas Ilgauskas 4.00 10.00
21 Dontae' Jones 2.50 6.00
22 Roy Rogers 2.50 6.00
26 Jerome Williams 2.50 6.00
27 Brian Evans 2.50 6.00
28 Priest Lauderdale 2.50 6.00
29 Travis Knight 2.50 6.00
24 Derek Fisher 5.00 12.00
25 Martin Muursepp 2.50 6.00
NNO Expired Trade Cards .20 .50

1996-97 Topps Finest Reprints

Randomly inserted in series two packs at the rate of one in 36, this 25-card set features reprints of 25 of the 50 greatest NBA players as they appeared on their first Topps, Star Co., or Bowman cards. Cards utilize the Finest technology. The first 25 cards were issued in 1996-97 Stadium Club series one. Card values below refer to unpeeled cards. Peeled cards generally trade for ten to twenty-five percent less.
COMPLETE SERIES 2 (25) 60.00 120.00
*REF: 1.25X TO 3X HI COLUMN
REF: SER.2 STATED ODDS 1:144 HOB/RET
1 Lew Alcindor 4.00 10.00
3 Paul Arizin 1.25 3.00
9 Wilt Chamberlain 5.00 12.00
11 Dave Cowens 1.25 3.00
14 Clyde Drexler 3.00 8.00
16 Patrick Ewing 3.00 8.00
20 John Havlicek 4.00 10.00
21 Elvin Hayes 1.25 3.00
22 Larry Bird 6.00 15.00
Julius Erving
Magic Johnson
23 Sam Jones 1.50 4.00
25 Jerry Lucas 1.25 3.00
27 Moses Malone 1.25 3.00
30 George Mikan 4.00 10.00
31 Earl Monroe 1.25 3.00
32 Shaquille O'Neal 5.00 12.00
33 Hakeem Olajuwon 3.00 8.00
37 Willis Reed 1.25 3.00
38 Oscar Robertson 4.00 10.00
39 David Robinson 3.00 8.00
40 Bill Russell 5.00 12.00
42 Bill Sharman 1.25 3.00
43 John Stockton 4.00 10.00
45 Nate Thurmond 1.25 3.00
46 Wes Unseld 1.25 3.00
47 Bill Walton 2.00 5.00

1996-97 Topps Hobby Masters

Randomly inserted exclusively into both series hobby packs at a rate of one in every 36, these inserts feature a selection of twenty top NBA stars as determined by Topps hobby dealer network. In addition to player selection, the dealers also determined the rate of insertion. Each card features 28 point full diffraction foil stock. Due to the thickness, a Hobby Masters insert replaced two regular issue cards within the packs they were seeded into. The card backs are numbered with an "HM" prefix. The cards are numbered 11-30 due to the fact that they are part of a cross-sport (football, baseball and basketball) insert program by Topps.
COMPLETE SET (20) 50.00 120.00
COMPLETE SERIES 1 (10) 25.00 60.00
COMPLETE SERIES 2 (10) 25.00 60.00
HM11 Shaquille O'Neal 8.00 20.00
HM12 Jerry Stackhouse 4.00 10.00
HM13 Dennis Rodman 6.00 15.00
HM14 Joe Smith 2.50 6.00
HM15 Damon Stoudamire 3.00 8.00
HM16 Gary Payton 3.00 8.00
HM17 Mitch Richmond 3.00 8.00
HM18 Reggie Miller 4.00 10.00
HM19 Chris Webber 4.00 10.00
HM20 Vin Baker 2.50 6.00
HM21 Grant Hill 5.00 12.00
HM22 Scottie Pippen 5.00 12.00
HM23 Karl Malone 4.00 10.00
HM24 Patrick Ewing 4.00 10.00
HM25 Shawn Kemp 3.00 8.00
HM26 Anfernee Hardaway 5.00 12.00
HM27 Charles Barkley 5.00 12.00
HM28 Jason Kidd 5.00 12.00
HM29 Hakeem Olajuwon 4.00 10.00
HM30 Larry Johnson 3.00 8.00

1996-97 Topps Holding Court

Cards in this set of fifteen were randomly inserted in series one hobby and retail packs at a rate of one in 36 and feature the undeniable members of the NBA royalty, crowned "kings of the court" due to their impact on the game. Each card is printed utilizing Topps' exclusive Finest technology. Card backs are numbered with an "HC" prefix. Prices below refer to unpeeled cards. Peeled cards generally trade for ten to twenty-five percent less.
COMPLETE SET (15) 30.00 60.00
*REF: 1X TO 2.5X HI COLUMN
REF: SER.1 ODDS 1:108 H/R, 1:72 JUMBO
HC1 Larry Johnson 1.50 4.00
HC2 Michael Jordan 12.00 30.00
HC3 Cedric Ceballos 1.00 2.50
HC4 Grant Hill 2.50 6.00
HC5 Anfernee Hardaway 2.50 6.00
HC6 Reggie Miller 2.00 5.00
HC7 Glenn Robinson 1.50 4.00
HC8 Patrick Ewing 2.00 5.00
HC9 Chris Webber 2.00 5.00
HC10 Shaquille O'Neal 4.00 10.00
HC11 John Stockton 2.00 5.00
HC12 Mitch Richmond 1.50 4.00
HC13 David Robinson 2.50 6.00
HC14 Gary Payton 1.50 4.00
HC15 Karl Malone 2.00 5.00

1996-97 Topps Mystery Finest

Randomly inserted in all second series packs at a rate of one 36, this 22-card set featues some of the top players from each division. Cards were issued with an opaque protector to keep the player a mystery until peeled. Card backs carry a "M" prefix.
COMPLETE SET (22) 50.00 100.00
*BORDERLESS: .6X TO 1.5X HI COLUMN
BDLS: SER.2 STATED ODDS 1:72 HOB/RET
M1 Scottie Pippen 3.00 8.00
M2 Jason Kidd 3.00 8.00
M3 Anfernee Hardaway 3.00 8.00
M4 Gary Payton 2.00 5.00
M5 Juwan Howard 1.50 4.00
M6 Sean Elliott 2.00 5.00
M7 Dennis Rodman 4.00 10.00
M8 Shawn Kemp 2.00 5.00
M9 David Robinson 3.00 8.00
M10 Alonzo Mourning 2.50 6.00
M11 Dikembe Mutombo 2.00 5.00
M12 Shaquille O'Neal 5.00 12.00
M13 Clyde Drexler 2.50 6.00
M14 Michael Jordan 12.50 30.00
M15 Damon Stoudamire 2.00 5.00
M16 Mitch Richmond 2.00 5.00
M17 Patrick Ewing 2.50 6.00
M18 Vin Baker 1.50 4.00
M19 Hakeem Olajuwon 2.50 6.00
M20 Joe Smith 1.50 4.00
M21 Charles Barkley 3.00 8.00
M22 Reggie Miller 2.50 6.00

1996-97 Topps Mystery Finest Bordered Refractors

Randomly inserted exclusively into second series jumbo packs at a rate of one in 66 packs, these cards parallel the more common Mystery Finest inserts. The refractive sheen on the front of these cards differentiates them. Card backs carry a "M" prefix.
COMPLETE SET (22) 200.00 400.00
*BORDERED REF: 1.25X TO 3X BASE HI
M14 Michael Jordan 50.00 120.00

1996-97 Topps Mystery Finest Borderless Refractors

Randomly inserted in series two packs at a rate of one in 216, this 22-card set is a parallel to the Mystery Finest Borderless set. Card fronts contain the Borderless design with the use of the Refractor technology. Card backs carry a "M" prefix. To ascertain values on individual cards, please refer to the multiplier in the header below, coupled with the value of the base card.
*STARS: 1.5X TO 4X HI COLUMN
M14 Michael Jordan 60.00 150.00

1996-97 Topps Pro Files

Cards in this set of twenty were randomly issued in both series hobby and retail packs at a rate of one in 12. Topps' basketball spokesperson David Robinson was handed the assignment of writing all of the card backs for this insert set. "The Admiral" came through with flying colors as he gets up close and peronal with ten of the NBA's top stars. Card fronts contain a prismatic foil background with an action shot of the player and a head shot of David Robinson in the bottom left corner. Card backs are numbered with a "PF" prefix. In addition, two of these cards were inserted into Factory sets.
COMPLETE SET (20) 8.00 20.00
COMPLETE SERIES 1 (10) 6.00 15.00
COMPLETE SERIES 2 (10) 3.00 8.00
PF1 Grant Hill .75 2.00
PF2 Shawn Kemp .50 1.25
PF3 Michael Jordan 4.00 10.00
PF4 Vin Baker .40 1.00
PF5 Chris Webber .60 1.50
PF6 Joe Smith .40 1.00
PF7 Shaquille O'Neal 1.25 3.00
PF8 Patrick Ewing .60 1.50
PF9 Scottie Pippen .75 2.00
PF10 Damon Stoudamire .50 1.25
PF11 Anfernee Hardaway .75 2.00
PF12 Juwan Howard .40 1.00
PF13 Dikembe Mutombo .50 1.25
PF14 Dennis Rodman 1.00 2.50
PF15 Kevin Garnett 1.25 3.00
PF16 Jerry Stackhouse .60 1.50
PF17 Alonzo Mourning .60 1.50
PF18 Karl Malone .60 1.50
PF19 Hakeem Olajuwon .60 1.50
PF20 Gary Payton .50 1.25

1996-97 Topps Season's Best

Cards in this set of 25 were randomly issued in first series hobby and retail packs at a rate of one in eight and feature five players who have excelled in the five key statistical categories of the game: Points - En Fuego; Rebounds - Board Members; Steals - Sticky Fingers; Assists - Dish Men and Blocks - Swat Team. Card fronts feature a prismatic background with the statistical theme title located around the action shot. Card backs are numbered with a "Season's Best" prefix. In addition, two of these cards were inserted in the Factory sets.
COMPLETE SET (25) 20.00 40.00
SB1 Michael Jordan 6.00 15.00
SB2 Hakeem Olajuwon 1.00 2.50
SB3 Shaquille O'Neal 2.00 5.00
SB4 Karl Malone 1.00 2.50
SB5 David Robinson 1.25 3.00
SB6 Dennis Rodman 1.50 4.00
SB7 David Robinson 1.25 3.00
SB8 Dikembe Mutombo .75 2.00
SB9 Charles Barkley 1.25 3.00
SB10 Shawn Kemp .75 2.00
SB11 John Stockton 1.00 2.50
SB12 Jason Kidd 1.25 3.00
SB13 Avery Johnson .60 1.50
SB14 Rod Strickland .50 1.25
SB15 Damon Stoudamire .75 2.00
SB16 Gary Payton .75 2.00
SB17 Mookie Blaylock .50 1.25
SB18 Michael Jordan 6.00 15.00
SB19 Jason Kidd 1.25 3.00
SB20 Alvin Robertson .50 1.25
SB21 Dikembe Mutombo .75 2.00
SB22 Shawn Bradley .50 1.25
SB23 David Robinson 1.25 3.00
SB24 Hakeem Olajuwon 1.00 2.50
SB25 Alonzo Mourning 1.00 2.50

1996-97 Topps Super Teams

After a one-year hiatus, Topps decided to transfer this insert set concept from their Stadium Club brand which had featured interactive Super Team inserts in 1993-94 and 1994-95. Cards from this set of 29 were randomly issued in first series hobby and retail packs at a rate of one in 36 and featured an action shot or group photo from each team in the league. Cards that feature teams that won either their division, their conference or the NBA finals or was the team selected to have the first draft pick in the 1997 NBA Draft are redeemable for various special Mystery Finest cards. The expiration date for Super Team cards is December 31, 1997.
COMPLETE SET (29) 30.00 60.00
ST1 Atlanta Hawks 1.00 2.50
Stacy Augmon
Grant Long
Ken Norman
ST2 Boston Celtics 1.00 2.50
Dino Radja
Dana Barros
Eric Williams
ST3 Charlotte Hornets 1.00 2.50
Robert Parish
Glen Rice
Kenny Anderson
Larry Johnson
Dell Curry
Muggsy Bogues
ST4 Chicago Bulls WCDF 10.00 25.00
Michael Jordan
Scottie Pippen
Dennis Rodman
Luc Longley
Ron Harper
ST5 Cleveland Cavaliers 1.00 2.50
Bob Sura
Dan Majerle
Donny Marshall
ST6 Dallas Mavericks 1.00 2.50
Jason Kidd
Jamal Mashburn
Jim Jackson
Popeye Jones
ST7 Denver Nuggets 1.00 2.50
Dikembe Mutombo
Bryant Stith
Don MacLean
ST8 Detroit Pistons 1.00 2.50
Mark West
Theo Ratliff
Lindsey Hunter
Joe Dumars
Terry Cummings
Grant Hill
Lou Roe
ST9 Golden State Warriors 1.00 2.50
B.J. Armstrong
Latrell Sprewell
Joe Smith
ST10 Houston Rockets 1.00 2.50
Hakeem Olajuwon
Robert Horry
Chucky Brown
Eldridge Recasner
Clyde Drexler
ST11 Indiana Pacers 1.00 2.50
Rik Smits
Reggie Miller
Dale Davis
Mark Jackson
ST12 Los Angeles Clippers 1.00 2.50
Malik Sealy
Terry Dehere
ST13 Los Angeles Lakers 1.50 4.00
Elden Campbell
Sedale Threatt
Vlade Divac
Anthony Peeler
Eddie Jones
Derek Strong
Frankie King
ST14 Miami Heat WD 1.50 4.00
Voshon Lenard
Alonzo Mourning
Rex Chapman
Keith Askins
Dan Schayes
Jeff Malone
Tony Smith
ST15 Milwaukee Bucks 1.00 2.50
Glenn Robinson
Vin Baker
Benoit Benjamin
Lee Mayberry
Johnny Newman
ST16 Minnesota T'wolves 1.00 2.50
Doug West
Tom Gugliotta
Kevin Garnett
Sam Mitchell
ST17 New Jersey Nets 1.00 2.50
P.J. Brown
Armon Gilliam
Ed O'Bannon
Chris Childs
Vern Fleming
ST18 New York Knicks 1.00 2.50
J.R. Reid
Anthony Mason
Hubert Davis
ST19 Orlando Magic 1.00 2.50
Anfernee Hardaway
Shaquille O'Neal
Dennis Scott
ST20 Philadelphia 76ers 1.00 2.50
Trevor Ruffin
Derrick Alston
LaSalle Thompson
ST21 Phoenix Suns 1.00 2.50
Joe Kleine
Charles Barkley
Wayman Tisdale
Michael Finley
Elliot Perry
ST22 Portland Trail Blazers 1.00 2.50
Arvydas Sabonis
Chris Dudley
Clifford Robinson
James Robinson
Gary Trent
Aaron McKie
ST23 Sacramento Kings 1.00 2.50
Bobby Hurley
Sarunas Marciulionis
Mitch Richmond
Olden Polynice
Brian Grant
ST24 San Antonio Spurs W 5.00 12.00
Vinny Del Negro
David Robinson
Doc Rivers
Dell Demps
ST25 Seattle Supersonics WD 1.00 2.50
Ervin Johnson
Gary Payton
Shawn Kemp
ST26 Toronto Raptors 1.00 2.50
Acie Earl
Carlos Rogers
Alvin Robertson
B.J. Tyler
ST27 Utah Jazz WCD 5.00 12.00
John Stockton
Karl Malone
David Benoit
Felton Spencer
ST28 Vancouver Grizzlies 1.00 2.50
Eric Murdock
Eric Mobley
Lawrence Moten
Blue Edwards
Doug Edwards
Ashraf Amaya
Litterial Green
ST29 Washington Bullets 1.00 2.50
Juwan Howard
Gheorghe Muresan
Chris Webber
Ledell Eackles

1996-97 Topps Super Team Conference Winners

The following teams were eligible for the Conference Winner Super Team cards: Chicago and Utah. If you had one of those cards, you could redeem them for Mystery Finest Borderless Cards from the winners conference. The cards are similar in design to the regular Borderless cards issued in 1996-97 Topps series two. The cards differ by having a "Super Team Champion" logo on the card front. Each card was redeemable for 11 cards from each conference. The Eastern set is comprised of Reggie Miller, Vin Baker, Dennis Rodman, Damon Stoudamire, Michael Jordan, Scottie Pippen, Patrick Ewing, Alonzo Mourning, Juwan Howard, Anfernee Hardaway and Shaquille O'Neal. The Western set is comprised of Joe Smith, Mitch Richmond, Shawn Kemp, Gary Payton, Charles Barkley, Dikembe Mutombo, Hakeem Olajuwon, Clyde Drexler, David Robinson, Sean Elliott and Jason Kidd.
COMPLETE SET (22) 10.00 25.00
M1 Scottie Pippen 1.00 2.50
M2 Jason Kidd 1.00 2.50
M3 Anfernee Hardaway 1.00 2.50
M4 Gary Payton .60 1.50
M5 Juwan Howard .50 1.25
M6 Sean Elliott .60 1.50
M7 Dennis Rodman 1.25 3.00
M8 Shawn Kemp .60 1.50
M9 David Robinson 1.00 2.50
M10 Alonzo Mourning .75 2.00
M11 Dikembe Mutombo .60 1.50
M12 Shaquille O'Neal 1.50 4.00
M13 Clyde Drexler .75 2.00
M14 Michael Jordan 5.00 12.00
M15 Damon Stoudamire .60 1.50
M16 Mitch Richmond .60 1.50
M17 Patrick Ewing .75 2.00
M18 Vin Baker .50 1.25
M19 Hakeem Olajuwon .75 2.00
M20 Joe Smith .50 1.25
M21 Charles Barkley 1.00 2.50
M22 Reggie Miller .75 2.00

1996-97 Topps Super Team Division Winners

The following teams were eligible for the Division Winner Super Team cards: Chicago, Miami, Seattle and Utah. If you had one of those cards, you could redeem them for Mystery Finest Bordered Cards from the winners division. The cards are similar in design to the regular Bordered cards issued in 1996-97 Topps series two. The cards differ by having a "Super Team Champion" logo on the card front. The Bulls Central card returned six (Vin Baker, Michael Jordan, Reggie Miller, Scottie Pippen, Dennis Rodman and Damon Stoudamire), the Heat Atlantic five (Patrick Ewing, Anfernee Hardaway, Juwan Howard, Alonzo Mourning and Shaquille O'Neal), the Sonics Pacific five (Charles Barkley, Shawn Kemp, Gary Payton, Mitch Richmond and Joe Smith) and the Jazz Midwest six (Clyde Drexler, Sean Elliott, Jason Kidd, Dikembe Mutombo, Hakeem Olajuwon and David Robinson.)
COMPLETE SET (22) 8.00 20.00
M1 Scottie Pippen .75 2.00
M2 Jason Kidd .75 2.00
M3 Anfernee Hardaway .75 2.00
M4 Gary Payton .50 1.25
M5 Juwan Howard .40 1.00
M6 Sean Elliott .50 1.25
M7 Dennis Rodman 1.00 2.50
M8 Shawn Kemp .50 1.25
M9 David Robinson .75 2.00
M10 Alonzo Mourning .60 1.50
M11 Dikembe Mutombo .50 1.25
M12 Shaquille O'Neal 1.25 3.00
M13 Clyde Drexler .60 1.50
M14 Michael Jordan 4.00 10.00
M15 Damon Stoudamire .50 1.25
M16 Mitch Richmond .50 1.25
M17 Patrick Ewing .60 1.50
M18 Vin Baker .50 1.25
M19 Hakeem Olajuwon .75 2.00
M20 Joe Smith .50 1.25
M21 Charles Barkley 1.00 2.50
M22 Reggie Miller .75 2.00

1996-97 Topps Super Team NBA Finals

The following teams were eligible for the NBA Finals Super Team cards: Chicago and San Antonio. If you had one of those cards, you could redeem them for a set of Mystery Finest Bordered Refractor Cards - similar in design to the regular Bordered Refractors issued in 1996-97 Topps series two. The cards differ by having a "Super Team Champion" logo on the card front.
COMPLETE SET (22) 40.00 100.00
M1 Scottie Pippen 4.00 10.00
M2 Jason Kidd 4.00 10.00
M3 Anfernee Hardaway 4.00 10.00
M4 Gary Payton 2.50 6.00
M5 Juwan Howard 2.00 5.00
M6 Sean Elliott 2.50 6.00
M7 Dennis Rodman 5.00 12.00
M8 Shawn Kemp 2.50 6.00
M9 David Robinson 4.00 10.00
M10 Alonzo Mourning 3.00 8.00
M11 Dikembe Mutombo 2.50 6.00
M12 Shaquille O'Neal 6.00 15.00
M13 Clyde Drexler 3.00 8.00
M14 Michael Jordan 20.00 50.00
M15 Damon Stoudamire 2.50 6.00
M16 Mitch Richmond 2.50 6.00
M17 Patrick Ewing 3.00 8.00
M18 Vin Baker 2.00 5.00
M19 Hakeem Olajuwon 3.00 8.00
M20 Joe Smith 2.00 5.00
M21 Charles Barkley 4.00 10.00
M22 Reggie Miller 3.00 8.00

1996-97 Topps Youthquake

Randomly inserted into second series retail packs only at a rate of one in 36, this 15-card set features some of the NBA's top young stars. Cards are printed on wood. Card backs carry a "YQ" prefix.
COMPLETE SET (15) 30.00 80.00
YQ1 Allen Iverson 5.00 12.00
YQ2 Samaki Walker 1.00 2.50
YQ3 Stephon Marbury 2.50 6.00
YQ4 Damon Stoudamire 2.00 5.00
YQ5 John Wallace 1.00 2.50
YQ6 Michael Finley 2.50 6.00
YQ7 Marcus Camby 1.50 4.00
YQ8 Kerry Kittles 1.50 4.00
YQ9 Ray Allen 4.00 10.00
YQ10 Jerry Stackhouse 2.50 6.00
YQ11 Shareef Abdur-Rahim 2.00 5.00
YQ12 Antonio McDyess 2.00 5.00
YQ13 Joe Smith 1.50 4.00
YQ14 Brent Barry 1.50 4.00
YQ15 Kobe Bryant 20.00 40.00

1997-98 Topps

The 1997-98 release from Topps contained 220 basic cards, with each series containing 110. The cards were distributed in 11-card packs with a suggested retail price of $1.29. The set features color player photos printed on 16 pt. card stock with foil stamping and spot UV-Coating.
COMPLETE SET (220) 15.00 30.00
COMPLETE SERIES 1 (110) 5.00 10.00
COMPLETE SERIES 2 (110) 10.00 20.00
1 Scottie Pippen .25 .60
2 Nate McMillan .10 .25
3 Byron Scott .12 .30
4 Mark Davis .10 .25
5 Rod Strickland .10 .25
6 Brian Grant .10 .25
7 Damon Stoudamire .10 .25
8 John Stockton .20 .50
9 Grant Long .10 .25
10 Darrell Armstrong .10 .25
11 Anthony Mason .10 .25
12 Travis Best .10 .25
13 Stephon Marbury .20 .50
14 Jamal Mashburn .10 .25
15 Detlef Schrempf .15 .40
16 Terrell Brandon .10 .25
17 Charles Barkley .25 .60
18 Vin Baker .12 .30
19 Gary Trent .10 .25
20 Vinny Del Negro .10 .25
21 Todd Day .10 .25
22 Malik Sealy .10 .25
23 Wesley Person .10 .25
24 Reggie Miller .20 .50
25 Dan Majerle .15 .40
26 Todd Fuller .10 .25
27 Juwan Howard .12 .30
28 Clarence Weatherspoon .10 .25
29 Grant Hill .25 .60
30 John Williams .10 .25
31 Ken Norman .10 .25
32 Patrick Ewing .20 .50
33 Bryon Russell .10 .25
34 Tony Smith .10 .25
35 Andrew Lang .10 .25
36 Rony Seikaly .12 .30
37 Billy Owens .10 .25
38 Dino Radja .10 .25
39 Chris Gatling .10 .25
40 Dale Davis .10 .25
41 Arvydas Sabonis .12 .30
42 Chris Mills .10 .25
43 A.C. Green .15 .40
44 Tyrone Hill .10 .25
45 Tracy Murray .10 .25
46 David Robinson .25 .60
47 Lee Mayberry .10 .25
48 Jayson Williams .10 .25
49 Jason Kidd .25 .60
50 Bryant Stith .10 .25
51 Latrell Sprewell .15 .40
52 Brent Barry .12 .30
53 Henry James .10 .25
54 Allen Iverson .30 .75
55 Shandon Anderson .10 .25
56 Mitch Richmond .15 .40
57 Allan Houston .15 .40
58 Ron Harper .10 .25
59 Gheorghe Muresan .10 .25
60 Vincent Askew .10 .25
61 Ray Allen .20 .50
62 Kenny Anderson .12 .30
63 Dikembe Mutombo .15 .40
64 Sam Perkins .10 .25
65 Walt Williams .10 .25
66 Chris Carr .10 .25
67 Vlade Divac .15 .40
68 LaPhonso Ellis .10 .25
69 B.J. Armstrong .10 .25
70 Jim Jackson .10 .25
71 Clyde Drexler .20 .50
72 Lindsey Hunter .10 .25
73 Sasha Danilovic .10 .25
74 Elden Campbell .10 .25
75 Robert Pack .10 .25
76 Dennis Scott .10 .25
77 Will Perdue .10 .25
78 Anthony Peeler .10 .25
79 Steve Smith .12 .30
80 Steve Kerr .12 .30
81 Buck Williams .10 .25
82 Terry Mills .10 .25
83 Michael Smith .10 .25
84 Adam Keefe .10 .25
85 Kevin Willis .10 .25
86 David Wesley .10 .25
87 Muggsy Bogues .12 .30
88 Bimbo Coles .10 .25
89 Tom Gugliotta .10 .25
90 Jermaine O'Neal .20 .50
91 Cedric Ceballos .10 .25
92 Shawn Kemp .15 .40
93 Horace Grant .12 .30
94 Shareef Abdur-Rahim .15 .40
95 Robert Horry .12 .30
96 Vitaly Potapenko .10 .25
97 Pooh Richardson .10 .25
98 Doug Christie .10 .25
99 Voshon Lenard .10 .25
100 Dominique Wilkins .20 .50
101 Alonzo Mourning .15 .40
102 Sam Cassell .12 .30
103 Sherman Douglas .10 .25
104 Shawn Bradley .10 .25
105 Mark Jackson .15 .40
106 Dennis Rodman .30 .75
107 Charles Oakley .10 .25
108 Matt Maloney .10 .25
109 Shaquille O'Neal .40 1.00
110 Checklist .10 .25
111 Antonio McDyess .12 .30
112 Bob Sura .10 .25
113 Terrell Brandon .10 .25
114 Tim Thomas RC .30 .75
115 Tim Duncan RC 1.00 2.50
116 Antonio Daniels RC .15 .40
117 Bryant Reeves .10 .25
118 Keith Van Horn RC .30 .75
119 Loy Vaught .10 .25
120 Rasheed Wallace .15 .40
121 Bobby Jackson RC .15 .40
122 Kevin Johnson .10 .25
123 Michael Jordan 1.25 3.00
124 Ron Mercer RC .20 .50
125 Tracy McGrady RC .75 2.00
126 Antoine Walker .15 .40
127 Carlos Rogers .10 .25
128 Isaac Austin .10 .25
129 Mookie Blaylock .10 .25
130 Rodrick Rhodes RC .15 .40
131 Dennis Scott .10 .25
132 Chris Mullin .15 .40
133 P.J. Brown .10 .25
134 Rex Chapman .10 .25
135 Sean Elliott .10 .25
136 Alan Henderson .10 .25
137 Austin Croshere RC .15 .40
138 Nick Van Exel .12 .30
139 Derek Strong .10 .25
140 Glenn Robinson .12 .30
141 Avery Johnson .12 .30
142 Calbert Cheaney .10 .25
143 Mahmoud Abdul-Rauf .10 .25
144 Stojko Vrankovic .10 .25
145 Chris Childs .10 .25
146 Danny Manning .10 .25
147 Jeff Hornacek .10 .25
148 Kevin Garnett .30 .75
149 Joe Dumars .15 .40
150 Johnny Taylor RC .15 .40
151 Mark Price .15 .40
152 Toni Kukoc .15 .40
153 Erick Dampier .10 .25
154 Lorenzen Wright .10 .25
155 Matt Geiger .10 .25
156 Tim Hardaway .15 .40
157 Charles Smith RC .15 .40
158 Hersey Hawkins .10 .25
159 Michael Finley .15 .40
160 Tyus Edney .10 .25
161 Christian Laettner .10 .25
162 Doug West .10 .25
163 Jim Jackson .10 .25
164 Larry Johnson .15 .40
165 Vin Baker .10 .25
166 Karl Malone .20 .50
167 Kelvin Cato RC .15 .40
168 Luc Longley .10 .25
169 Dale Davis .10 .25
170 Joe Smith .10 .25
171 Kobe Bryant .75 2.00
172 Scot Pollard RC .15 .40
173 Derek Anderson RC .15 .40
174 Erick Strickland RC .15 .40
175 Olden Polynice .10 .25
176 Chris Whitney .10 .25
177 Anthony Parker RC .15 .40
178 Armon Gilliam .10 .25
179 Gary Payton .15 .40
180 Glen Rice .15 .40
181 Chauncey Billups RC .60 1.50
182 Derek Fisher .15 .40
183 John Starks .12 .30
184 Mario Elie .10 .25
185 Chris Webber .15 .40
186 Shawn Kemp .10 .25
187 Greg Ostertag .10 .25
188 Olivier Saint-Jean RC .15 .40
189 Eric Snow .10 .25
190 Isaiah Rider .10 .25
191 Paul Grant RC .15 .40
192 Samaki Walker .10 .25
193 Cory Alexander .10 .25
194 Eddie Jones .15 .40
195 John Thomas RC .15 .40
196 Otis Thorpe .10 .25
197 Rod Strickland .10 .25
198 David Wesley .10 .25
199 Jacque Vaughn RC .15 .40

200 Rik Smits	.12	.30
201 Brevin Knight RC	.15	.40
202 Clifford Robinson	.10	.25
203 Hakeem Olajuwon	.20	.50
204 Jerry Stackhouse	.15	.40
205 Tyrone Hill	.10	.25
206 Kendall Gill	.10	.25
207 Marcus Camby	.15	.40
208 Tony Battie RC	.20	.50
209 Brent Price	.10	.25
210 Danny Fortson RC	.15	.40
211 Jerome Williams	.10	.25
212 Maurice Taylor RC	.15	.40
213 Brian Williams	.10	.25
214 Keith Booth RC	.15	.40
215 Nick Anderson	.10	.25
216 Travis Knight	.10	.25
217 Adonal Foyle RC	.15	.40
218 Anfernee Hardaway	.25	.60
219 Kerry Kittles	.10	.25
220 Checklist	.10	.25

1997-98 Topps Minted in Springfield

Randomly inserted in first series packs at a rate of one in 6, this 110-card set parallels the basic set. Each card features spot UV-coating and is printed with a "Minted in Springfield" gold foil stamp. To ascertain individual card values, use the multiplier provided below coupled with the single cards in the basic set.
*STARS: 2X TO 5X BASE CARD HI
*RCs: 1.25X TO 3X BASE HI

1997-98 Topps Autographs

Randomly inserted in first series hobby packs at a rate of one in 212, this eight-card set features autographs from some of the NBA's top players. The Hakeem Olajuwon card was available as both a redemption and an actual autograph from packs.

1 John Starks	8.00	20.00
2 Juwan Howard	6.00	15.00
3 Mitch Richmond	8.00	20.00
4 Hakeem Olajuwon	15.00	40.00
5 Glenn Robinson	5.00	12.00
6 Steve Smith	5.00	12.00
7 Antoine Walker	6.00	15.00
8 Clyde Drexler	15.00	40.00

1997-98 Topps Bound for Glory

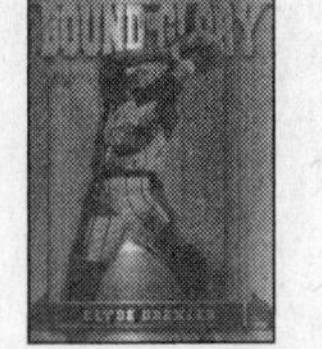

Randomly inserted in series one hobby packs only at a rate of one in 36, this 15-card set is printed on rainbow foilboard stock and features some of the NBA's top players. Card backs carry a "BG" prefix.

COMPLETE SET (15)	25.00	60.00
BG1 Robert Parish	1.25	3.00
BG2 Grant Hill	2.00	5.00
BG3 Chris Mullin	1.25	3.00
BG4 Hakeem Olajuwon	1.50	4.00
BG5 Dennis Rodman	2.50	6.00
BG6 Patrick Ewing	1.50	4.00
BG7 Karl Malone	1.50	4.00
BG8 Charles Barkley	2.00	5.00
BG9 David Robinson	2.00	5.00
BG10 Michael Jordan	10.00	25.00
BG11 Dominique Wilkins	1.50	4.00
BG12 Shaquille O'Neal	3.00	8.00
BG13 Clyde Drexler	1.50	4.00
BG14 John Stockton	1.50	4.00
BG15 Scottie Pippen	2.00	5.00

1997-98 Topps Clutch Time

Randomly inserted into series two hobby packs only at a rate of one in 36, this 20-card set focuses on players who can get it done in the clutch. Card fronts feature a foil background with "Clutch Time" written across the top of the card as if it was a scoreboard. Card backs contain a "CT" prefix.

COMPLETE SET (20)	40.00	80.00
CT1 Michael Jordan	15.00	40.00
CT2 Christian Laettner	1.25	3.00
CT3 Patrick Ewing	2.00	5.00
CT4 Glen Rice	1.50	4.00
CT5 Stephon Marbury	2.00	5.00
CT6 Tim Hardaway	1.50	4.00
CT7 Reggie Miller	2.00	5.00
CT8 Gary Payton	1.50	4.00
CT9 Charles Barkley	2.50	6.00
CT10 Grant Hill	2.50	6.00
CT11 Karl Malone	2.00	5.00
CT12 Dikembe Mutombo	1.50	4.00
CT13 Hakeem Olajuwon	2.00	5.00
CT14 Shawn Kemp	1.50	4.00
CT15 John Stockton	2.00	5.00
CT16 Anfernee Hardaway	2.50	6.00
CT17 Glenn Robinson	1.25	3.00
CT18 Chris Webber	1.50	4.00
CT19 Allen Iverson	3.00	8.00
CT20 Scottie Pippen	2.50	6.00

1997-98 Topps Destiny

Randomly inserted into retail packs only at a rate of one in 18, this 15-card set focuses on players who are destined to become NBA legends. Card fronts feature a full shot of the player surrounded by an embossed circle with the card theme "Destiny" also embossed across the top. Card backs carry a "D" prefix.

COMPLETE SET (15)	20.00	50.00
D1 Grant Hill	2.00	5.00
D2 Kevin Garnett	2.50	6.00
D3 Vin Baker	1.00	2.50
D4 Antoine Walker	1.25	3.00
D5 Kobe Bryant	6.00	15.00
D6 Tracy McGrady	3.00	8.00
D7 Keith Van Horn	1.25	3.00
D8 Tim Duncan	4.00	10.00
D9 Eddie Jones	1.25	3.00
D10 Stephon Marbury	1.50	4.00
D11 Marcus Camby	1.25	3.00
D12 Antonio McDyess	1.00	2.50
D13 Shareef Abdur-Rahim	1.25	3.00
D14 Allen Iverson	2.50	6.00
D15 Shaquille O'Neal	3.00	8.00

1997-98 Topps Draft Redemption

Randomly inserted into series one hobby packs at a rate of 1:12 and retail packs at a rate of 1:18, this 29-card set features trade cards for the first 29 picks of the 1997 NBA Draft. Each redemption card had a number corresponding to each draft position of the first round, and could be exchanged for a special card of the player taken in that draft position once they signed their NBA Contract. The expiration date for the cards was April 1, 1998

DP1 Tim Duncan	12.00	30.00
DP2 Keith Van Horn	4.00	10.00
DP3 Chauncey Billups	8.00	20.00
DP4 Antonio Daniels	2.00	5.00
DP5 Tony Battie	2.50	6.00
DP6 Ron Mercer	2.50	6.00
DP7 Tim Thomas	4.00	10.00
DP8 Adonal Foyle	2.00	5.00
DP9 Tracy McGrady	10.00	25.00
DP10 Danny Fortson	2.00	5.00
DP11 Olivier Saint-Jean	2.00	5.00
DP12 Austin Croshere	2.00	5.00
DP13 Derek Anderson	2.00	5.00
DP14 Maurice Taylor	2.00	5.00
DP15 Kelvin Cato	2.00	5.00
DP16 Brevin Knight	2.00	5.00
DP17 Johnny Taylor	2.00	5.00
DP18 Chris Anstey	2.00	5.00
DP19 Scot Pollard	2.00	5.00
DP20 Paul Grant	2.00	5.00
DP21 Anthony Parker	2.00	5.00
DP22 Ed Gray	2.00	5.00
DP23 Bobby Jackson	2.50	6.00
DP24 Rodrick Rhodes	2.00	5.00
DP25 John Thomas	2.00	5.00
DP26 Charles Smith	2.00	5.00
DP27 Jacque Vaughn	2.00	5.00
DP28 Keith Booth	2.00	5.00
DP29 Serge Zwikker	2.00	5.00

1997-98 Topps Fantastic 15

Randomly inserted in series one retail packs at a rate of one in 36, this 15-card set showcases up-and-comoing greats on holographic cards. Card backs carry a "F" prefix.

COMPLETE SET (15)	20.00	50.00
F1 Antoine Walker	1.50	4.00
F2 Damon Stoudamire	1.50	4.00
F3 Brent Barry	1.25	3.00
F4 Michael Finley	1.50	4.00
F5 Ray Allen	2.00	5.00
F6 Allen Iverson	3.00	8.00
F7 Stephon Marbury	2.00	5.00
F8 Kerry Kittles	1.00	2.50
F9 John Wallace	1.00	2.50
F10 Kevin Garnett	3.00	8.00
F11 Jerry Stackhouse	1.50	4.00
F12 Kobe Bryant	10.00	25.00
F13 Marcus Camby	1.50	4.00
F14 Joe Smith	1.25	3.00
F15 Shareef Abdur-Rahim	1.50	4.00

1997-98 Topps Generations

Randomly inserted into series two packs at a rate of one in 36, this 30-card set features the best rookies from each draft class. The cards are die cut and finished in the Finest technology. Card backs are numbered with a "G" prefix.

COMPLETE SET (30)	75.00	150.00
G1 Clyde Drexler	2.50	6.00
G2 Michael Jordan	15.00	40.00
G3 Charles Barkley	3.00	8.00
G4 Hakeem Olajuwon	2.50	6.00
G5 John Stockton	2.50	6.00
G6 Patrick Ewing	2.50	6.00
G7 Karl Malone	2.50	6.00
G8 Dennis Rodman	4.00	10.00
G9 Scottie Pippen	3.00	8.00
G10 David Robinson	3.00	8.00
G11 Mitch Richmond	2.00	5.00
G12 Glen Rice	2.00	5.00
G13 Shawn Kemp	2.00	5.00
G14 Gary Payton	2.00	5.00
G15 Dikembe Mutombo	2.00	5.00
G16 Steve Smith	1.50	4.00
G17 Christian Laettner	1.50	4.00
G18 Shaquille O'Neal	6.00	15.00
G19 Alonzo Mourning	2.50	6.00
G20 Tom Gugliotta	1.25	3.00
G21 Anfernee Hardaway	3.00	8.00
G22 Grant Hill	3.00	8.00
G23 Kevin Garnett	4.00	10.00
G24 Kobe Bryant	10.00	25.00
G25 Stephon Marbury	2.50	6.00
G26 Antoine Walker	2.00	5.00
G27 Shareef Abdur-Rahim	2.00	5.00
G28 Tim Duncan	6.00	15.00
G29 Keith Van Horn	2.00	5.00
G30 Tracy McGrady	5.00	12.00

1997-98 Topps Generations Refractors

Randomly inserted into series two packs at a rate of one in 144, this 30-card set parallels the basic Generations insert. These cards are finished in the "classic" refractor technology. Card backs are numbered with a "G" prefix. To ascertain values on individual cards, please refer to the multiplier in the header below, coupled with the value of the base card.
*STARS: 1X TO 2.5X HI COLUMN
*RCs: 1.25X TO 3X HI COLUMN

G2 Michael Jordan	50.00	120.00
G8 Dennis Rodman	20.00	50.00
G18 Shaquille O'Neal	12.00	30.00

1997-98 Topps Inside Stuff

Randomly inserted into series two packs at a rate of one in 36, this 10-card set features some of the best plays from the 1997 NBA Playoffs. Card fronts have a foil background and card backs carry an "IS" prefix.

COMPLETE SET (10)	15.00	40.00
IS1 Michael Jordan	10.00	25.00
IS2 Eddie Johnson	.75	2.00
IS3 John Stockton	1.50	4.00
IS4 Patrick Ewing	1.50	4.00
IS5 Shaquille O'Neal	3.00	8.00
IS6 Rex Chapman	.75	2.00
IS7 Shawn Kemp	1.25	3.00
IS8 Scottie Pippen	2.00	5.00
IS9 Kobe Bryant	6.00	15.00
IS10 Anfernee Hardaway	2.00	5.00

1997-98 Topps New School

Randomly inserted in series two hobby packs at a rate of one in 36 and series two retail packs at one in 18, this 15-card set focuses on the key rookies from the 1997 class. Card fronts feature the theme "New School" in a banner and the front is sprinkled in glitter. Card backs contain a "NS" prefix.

COMPLETE SET (15)	15.00	40.00
NS1 Austin Croshere	.75	2.00
NS2 Antonio Daniels	.75	2.00
NS3 Tim Thomas	1.50	4.00
NS4 Keith Van Horn	1.50	4.00
NS5 Bobby Jackson	1.00	2.50
NS6 Derek Anderson	.75	2.00
NS7 Adonal Foyle	.75	2.00
NS8 Johnny Taylor	.75	2.00
NS9 Jacque Vaughn	.75	2.00
NS10 Chauncey Billups	3.00	8.00
NS11 Brevin Knight	.75	2.00
NS12 Tracy McGrady	4.00	10.00
NS13 Tony Battie	1.00	2.50
NS14 Scot Pollard	.75	2.00
NS15 Tim Duncan	5.00	12.00

1997-98 Topps Rock Stars

Randomly inserted in series one packs at a rate of one in 36, this 20-card set features a die-cut borderless Finest design. Card backs carry a "RS" prefix.

COMPLETE SET (20)	50.00	120.00
*REF: 1.25X TO 3X BASE ROCK STARS		
REF: SER.1 STATED ODDS 1:144 H/R		
RS1 Michael Jordan	15.00	40.00
RS2 Jerry Stackhouse	2.00	5.00
RS3 Chris Webber	2.00	5.00
RS4 Charles Barkley	3.00	8.00
RS5 Dennis Rodman	4.00	10.00
RS6 Anfernee Hardaway	3.00	8.00
RS7 Juwan Howard	1.50	4.00
RS8 Tim Hardaway	2.00	5.00
RS9 Gary Payton	2.00	5.00
RS10 Dikembe Mutombo	2.00	5.00
RS11 Tom Gugliotta	1.25	3.00
RS12 Kevin Garnett	4.00	10.00
RS13 Shaquille O'Neal	5.00	12.00
RS14 Hakeem Olajuwon	2.50	6.00
RS15 Grant Hill	3.00	8.00
RS16 Karl Malone	2.50	6.00
RS17 Damon Stoudamire	2.00	5.00
RS18 Shawn Kemp	2.00	5.00
RS19 Alonzo Mourning	2.50	6.00
RS20 Scottie Pippen	3.00	8.00

1997-98 Topps Season's Best

Randomly inserted in series one packs at a rate of one in 16, this 30-card set showcases 25 superstars who have dominated the game in different statistical categories, and five rookies from the 1996 class featured on borderless prismatic illusion foilboard. The groupings used were Key Masters, Power Core, Shooting Stars, Frontcourt Finesse, Pressure Points and Hot Shots. Card backs carry a "SB" prefix.

COMPLETE SET (30)	30.00	60.00
SB1 Gary Payton	1.00	2.50
SB2 Kevin Johnson	1.00	2.50
SB3 Tim Hardaway	1.00	2.50
SB4 John Stockton	1.25	3.00
SB5 Damon Stoudamire	1.00	2.50
SB6 Michael Jordan	12.50	30.00
SB7 Mitch Richmond	1.00	2.50
SB8 Latrell Sprewell	1.00	2.50
SB9 Reggie Miller	1.25	3.00
SB10 Clyde Drexler	1.25	3.00
SB11 Grant Hill	1.50	4.00
SB12 Scottie Pippen	1.50	4.00
SB13 Kendall Gill	.60	1.50
SB14 Glen Rice	1.00	2.50
SB15 LaPhonso Ellis	.60	1.50
SB16 Karl Malone	1.25	3.00
SB17 Charles Barkley	1.50	4.00
SB18 Vin Baker	.75	2.00
SB19 Chris Webber	1.00	2.50
SB20 Tom Gugliotta	.60	1.50
SB21 Shaquille O'Neal	2.50	6.00
SB22 Patrick Ewing	1.25	3.00
SB23 Hakeem Olajuwon	1.25	3.00
SB24 Alonzo Mourning	1.25	3.00
SB25 Dikembe Mutombo	1.00	2.50
SB26 Allen Iverson	2.00	5.00
SB27 Antoine Walker	1.00	2.50
SB28 Shareef Abdur-Rahim	1.00	2.50
SB29 Stephon Marbury	1.25	3.00
SB30 Kerry Kittles	.60	1.50

1997-98 Topps Topps 40

Randomly inserted in both series packs at a rate of one in 12, this set of 40 cards was divided up among both series one and two packs and features 40 of the top players in the NBA as voted on by NBA players, coaches and writers. The cards are printed on foil-stamped mirrorboard cards. Card backs carry a "T40" prefix.

COMPLETE SET (40)	40.00	80.00
COMPLETE SERIES 1 (20)	15.00	40.00
COMPLETE SERIES 2 (20)	15.00	40.00
T1 Glen Rice	1.00	2.50
T2 Patrick Ewing	1.25	3.00
T3 Terrell Brandon	.60	1.50
T4 Jerry Stackhouse	1.00	2.50
T5 Michael Jordan	8.00	20.00
T6 Christian Laettner	.75	2.00
T7 Latrell Sprewell	1.00	2.50
T8 Reggie Miller	1.25	3.00
T9 Gary Payton	1.00	2.50
T10 Detlef Schrempf	1.00	2.50
T11 Kevin Garnett	2.00	5.00
T12 Eddie Jones	1.00	2.50
T13 Clyde Drexler	1.25	3.00
T14 Anfernee Hardaway	1.50	4.00
T15 Chris Webber	1.00	2.50
T16 Jayson Williams	.60	1.50
T17 Joe Smith	.75	2.00
T18 Karl Malone	1.25	3.00
T19 Tim Hardaway	1.00	2.50
T20 Vin Baker	.75	2.00
T21 Tom Gugliotta	.60	1.50
T22 Allen Iverson	2.00	5.00
T23 David Robinson	1.50	4.00
T24 Dikembe Mutombo	1.00	2.50
T25 John Stockton	1.25	3.00
T26 Charles Barkley	1.50	4.00
T27 Mitch Richmond	1.00	2.50
T28 Damon Stoudamire	1.00	2.50
T29 Anthony Mason	.60	1.50
T30 Shaquille O'Neal	2.50	6.00
T31 Glenn Robinson	.75	2.00
T32 Juwan Howard	.75	2.00
T33 Shawn Kemp	1.00	2.50
T34 Dennis Rodman	2.00	5.00
T35 Grant Hill	1.50	4.00
T36 Kevin Johnson	1.00	2.50
T37 Alonzo Mourning	1.25	3.00
T38 Hakeem Olajuwon	1.25	3.00
T39 Joe Dumars	1.00	2.50
T40 Scottie Pippen	1.50	4.00

1998-99 Topps Promos

PP7 Kobe Bryant	3.00	8.00

1998-99 Topps

Both series of Topps was issued in 110-card sets (totalling 220 cards) in 11-card packs with a suggested retail price of $1.29. Each card was produced on a super gloss coated 16-point stock with foil-stamping.

COMPLETE SET (220)	15.00	40.00
COMPLETE SERIES 1 (110)	5.00	12.00
COMPLETE SERIES 2 (110)	10.00	25.00
1 Scottie Pippen	.25	.60
2 Shareef Abdur-Rahim	.15	.40
3 Rod Strickland	.10	.25
4 Keith Van Horn	.15	.40
5 Ray Allen	.20	.50
6 Chris Mullin	.15	.40
7 Anthony Parker	.10	.25
8 Lindsey Hunter	.10	.25
9 Mario Elie	.10	.25
10 Jerry Stackhouse	.15	.40
11 Eldridge Recasner	.10	.25
12 Jeff Hornacek	.12	.30
13 Chris Webber	.15	.40
14 Lee Mayberry	.10	.25
15 Erick Strickland	.10	.25
16 Arvydas Sabonis	.12	.30
17 Tim Thomas	.15	.40
18 Luc Longley	.10	.25
19 Detlef Schrempf	.15	.40
20 Alonzo Mourning	.20	.50
21 Adonal Foyle	.10	.25
22 Tony Battie	.12	.30
23 Robert Horry	.12	.30
24 Derek Harper	.12	.30
25 Jamal Mashburn	.12	.30
26 Elliot Perry	.10	.25
27 Jalen Rose	.12	.30
28 Joe Smith	.12	.30
29 Henry James	.10	.25
30 Travis Knight	.10	.25
31 Tom Gugliotta	.10	.25
32 Chris Anstey	.10	.25
33 Antonio Daniels	.10	.25
34 Elden Campbell	.10	.25
35 Charlie Ward	.10	.25
36 Eddie Johnson	.10	.25
37 John Wallace	.10	.25
38 Antonio Davis	.10	.25
39 Antoine Walker	.15	.40
40 Patrick Ewing	.20	.50
41 Doug Christie	.10	.25
42 Andrew Lang	.10	.25
43 Joe Dumars	.15	.40
44 Jaren Jackson	.10	.25
45 Loy Vaught	.10	.25
46 Allan Houston	.12	.30
47 Mark Jackson	.15	.40
48 Tracy Murray	.10	.25
49 Tim Duncan	.30	.75
50 Micheal Williams	.10	.25
51 Steve Nash	.25	.60
52 Matt Maloney	.10	.25
53 Sam Cassell	.12	.30
54 Voshon Lenard	.10	.25
55 Dikembe Mutombo	.15	.40
56 Malik Sealy	.10	.25
57 Dell Curry	.10	.25
58 Stephon Marbury	.20	.50
59 Tariq Abdul-Wahad	.10	.25
60 Isaiah Rider	.10	.25
61 Kelvin Cato	.10	.25
62 LaPhonso Ellis	.10	.25
63 Jim Jackson	.10	.25
64 Greg Ostertag	.10	.25
65 Glenn Robinson	.12	.30
66 Chris Carr	.10	.25
67 Marcus Camby	.12	.30
68 Kobe Bryant	.75	2.00
69 Bobby Jackson	.12	.30
70 B.J. Armstrong	.10	.25
71 Alan Henderson	.10	.25
72 Terry Davis	.10	.25
73 John Stockton	.20	.50
74 Lamond Murray	.10	.25
75 Mark Price	.15	.40
76 Rex Chapman	.10	.25
77 Michael Jordan	1.25	3.00
78 Terry Cummings	.15	.40
79 Dan Majerle	.15	.40
80 Bo Outlaw	.10	.25
81 Michael Finley	.15	.40
82 Vin Baker	.12	.30
83 Clifford Robinson	.10	.25
84 Greg Anthony	.10	.25
85 Brevin Knight	.10	.25
86 Jacque Vaughn	.10	.25
87 Bobby Phills	.10	.25
88 Sherman Douglas	.10	.25
89 Kevin Johnson	.15	.40
90 Mahmoud Abdul-Rauf	.10	.25
91 Lorenzen Wright	.10	.25
92 Eric Williams	.10	.25
93 Will Perdue	.10	.25
94 Charles Barkley	.25	.60
95 Kendall Gill	.10	.25
96 Wesley Person	.10	.25
97 Buck Williams	.10	.25
98 Erick Dampier	.10	.25
99 Nate McMillan	.10	.25
100 Sean Elliott	.15	.40
101 Rasheed Wallace	.15	.40
102 Zydrunas Ilgauskas	.15	.40
103 Eddie Jones	.15	.40
104 Ron Mercer	.12	.30
105 Horace Grant	.12	.30
106 Corliss Williamson	.10	.25
107 Anthony Mason	.10	.25
108 Mookie Blaylock	.10	.25
109 Dennis Rodman	.30	.75
110 Checklist	.10	.25
111 Steve Smith	.12	.30
112 Cedric Henderson	.10	.25
113 Raef LaFrentz RC	.40	1.00
114 Calbert Cheaney	.10	.25
115 Rik Smits	.12	.30
116 Rony Seikaly	.15	.40
117 Lawrence Funderburke	.10	.25
118 Ricky Davis RC	.50	1.25
119 Howard Eisley	.10	.25
120 Kenny Anderson	.12	.30
121 Corey Benjamin RC	.30	.75
122 Maurice Taylor	.10	.25
123 Eric Murdock	.10	.25
124 Derek Fisher	.15	.40
125 Kevin Garnett	.30	.75
126 Walt Williams	.10	.25
127 Bryce Drew RC	.30	.75
128 A.C. Green	.15	.40
129 Ervin Johnson	.10	.25
130 Christian Laettner	.12	.30
131 Chauncey Billups	.20	.50
132 Hakeem Olajuwon	.20	.50
133 Al Harrington RC	.50	1.25
134 Danny Manning	.12	.30
135 Paul Pierce RC	1.50	4.00
136 Terrell Brandon	.10	.25
137 Bob Sura	.10	.25
138 Chris Gatling	.10	.25
139 Donyell Marshall	.10	.25
140 Marcus Camby	.12	.30
141 Brian Skinner RC	.30	.75
142 Charles Oakley	.12	.30
143 Antawn Jamison RC	.75	2.00
144 Nazr Mohammed RC	.30	.75
145 Karl Malone	.20	.50
146 Chris Mills	.10	.25
147 Bison Dele	.10	.25
148 Gary Payton	.15	.40
149 Terry Porter	.10	.25
150 Tim Hardaway	.15	.40
151 Larry Hughes RC	.60	1.50
152 Derek Anderson	.10	.25
153 Jason Williams RC	.75	2.00
154 Dirk Nowitzki RC	2.00	5.00
155 Juwan Howard	.12	.30
156 Avery Johnson	.12	.30
157 Matt Harpring RC	.40	1.00
158 Reggie Miller	.20	.50
159 Walter McCarty	.10	.25
160 Allen Iverson	.30	.75
161 Felipe Lopez RC	.30	.75
162 Tracy McGrady	.25	.60
163 Damon Stoudamire	.15	.40
164 Antonio McDyess	.12	.30
165 Grant Hill	.25	.60
166 Tyronn Lue RC	.30	.75
167 P.J. Brown	.10	.25
168 Antonio Daniels	.10	.25
169 Mitch Richmond	.15	.40
170 David Robinson	.25	.60
171 Shawn Bradley	.10	.25
172 Shandon Anderson	.10	.25
173 Chris Childs	.10	.25
174 Shawn Kemp	.15	.40
175 Shaquille O'Neal	.40	1.00
176 John Starks	.12	.30
177 Tyrone Hill	.10	.25
178 Jayson Williams	.10	.25
179 Anfernee Hardaway	.25	.60
180 Chris Webber	.15	.40
181 Don Reid	.10	.25
182 Stacey Augmon	.12	.30
183 Hersey Hawkins	.10	.25
184 Sam Mitchell	.10	.25
185 Jason Kidd	.25	.60
186 Nick Van Exel	.12	.30
187 Larry Johnson	.15	.40
188 Bryant Reeves	.10	.25
189 Glen Rice	.15	.40
190 Kerry Kittles	.10	.25
191 Toni Kukoc	.15	.40
192 Ron Harper	.12	.30
193 Bryon Russell	.10	.25
194 Vladimir Stepania RC	.30	.75
195 Michael Olowokandi RC	.40	1.00
196 Mike Bibby RC	.75	2.00
197 Dale Ellis	.10	.25
198 Muggsy Bogues	.12	.30
199 Vince Carter RC	1.50	4.00
200 Robert Traylor RC	.30	.75
201 Peja Stojakovic RC	.75	2.00
202 Aaron McKie	.10	.25
203 Hubert Davis	.10	.25
204 Dana Barros	.10	.25
205 Bonzi Wells RC	.30	.75
206 Michael Doleac RC	.30	.75
207 Keon Clark RC	.30	.75
208 Michael Dickerson RC	.30	.75
209 Nick Anderson	.10	.25
210 Brent Price	.10	.25
211 Cherokee Parks	.10	.25
212 Sam Jacobson RC	.30	.75
213 Pat Garrity RC	.30	.75
214 Tyrone Corbin	.10	.25
215 David Wesley	.10	.25
216 Rodney Rogers	.10	.25
217 Dean Garrett	.10	.25
218 Roshown McLeod RC	.30	.75
219 Dale Davis	.10	.25
220 Checklist	.10	.25

1998-99 Topps Apparitions

Randomly inserted in series one retail packs only at a rate of one in 36, this 15-card set features players whose moves defy the mind's eye. The cards feature micro-dyna etch technology. Card backs are numbered with an "A" prefix.

COMPLETE SET (15)	25.00	60.00
A1 Kobe Bryant	6.00	15.00
A2 Stephon Marbury	1.50	4.00
A3 Brent Barry	1.00	2.50
A4 Karl Malone	1.50	4.00
A5 Shaquille O'Neal	3.00	8.00
A6 Chris Webber	1.25	3.00
A7 Shawn Kemp	1.25	3.00
A8 Hakeem Olajuwon	1.50	4.00
A9 Anfernee Hardaway	2.00	5.00
A10 Michael Finley	1.25	3.00
A11 Keith Van Horn	1.25	3.00
A12 Kevin Garnett	2.50	6.00
A13 Vin Baker	1.00	2.50
A14 Tim Duncan	2.50	6.00
A15 Michael Jordan	12.50	30.00

1998-99 Topps Autographs

Randomly inserted in series one hobby packs at a rate of one in 329 and one in 378 series two hobby packs, this 18-card set features certified autographs of some of the top players in the NBA. AG1-AG8 were included in the first series, while AG9-AG18 were in the second. Each card features a "Topps Certified Autograph Issue" stamp on the front. Card backs feature an "AG" prefix.

AG1 Joe Smith	6.00	15.00
AG2 Kobe Bryant	75.00	150.00
AG3 Stephon Marbury	8.00	20.00
AG4 Dikembe Mutombo	8.00	20.00
AG5 Shareef Abdur-Rahim	6.00	15.00
AG6 Eddie Jones	8.00	20.00
AG7 Keith Van Horn	5.00	12.00
AG8 Glen Rice	6.00	15.00
AG9 Kobe Bryant	75.00	150.00
AG10 Ron Mercer	5.00	12.00
AG11 Glen Rice	6.00	15.00
AG12 Stephon Marbury	8.00	20.00
AG13 Kerry Kittles	5.00	12.00
AG14 Michael Olowokandi	5.00	12.00
AG15 Antawn Jamison	8.00	20.00
AG16 Mike Bibby	8.00	20.00
AG17 Robert Traylor	5.00	12.00
AG18 Paul Pierce	30.00	60.00

1998-99 Topps Chrome Preview

Randomly inserted in series two packs at one in 36, this 10-card set previews the 1998-99 Topps Chrome set. The set is skip-numbered.

COMPLETE SET (10)	30.00	60.00
6 Chris Mullin	3.00	8.00
10 Jerry Stackhouse	3.00	8.00
19 Detlef Schrempf	3.00	8.00
40 Patrick Ewing	4.00	10.00
43 Joe Dumars	3.00	8.00
60 Isaiah Rider	2.00	5.00
73 John Stockton	4.00	10.00
77 Michael Jordan	10.00	25.00
81 Michael Finley	3.00	8.00
100 Sean Elliott	3.00	8.00

1998-99 Topps Chrome Preview Refractors

Randomly inserted in series two hobby collector packs only at a rate of one in 40, this 10-card set parallels the Topps Chrome Preview insert. The cards feature the classic Refractor technology. To ascertain values on individual cards, please refer to the multiplier in the header, coupled with the value of the base insert.
REF: 2.5X TO 6X VALUE

77 Michael Jordan	125.00	250.00

1998-99 Topps Classic Collection

Randomly inserted in series two packs at one in 12, this 10-card set focuses on some of the retired greats of the NBA. The card front features the player in the foreground with a special framed background photo. Card backs are numbered with a "CL" prefix.

COMPLETE SET (10)	5.00	10.00
CL1 Larry Bird	1.25	3.00
CL2 Magic Johnson	1.00	2.50
CL3 Kareem Abdul-Jabbar	.60	1.50
CL4 Julius Erving	.75	2.00
CL5 Bill Russell	.60	1.50
CL6 Wilt Chamberlain	.75	2.00
CL7 Oscar Robertson	.50	1.25
CL8 Jerry West	.50	1.25
CL9 Elgin Baylor	.40	1.00
CL10 Bob Cousy	.60	1.50

1998-99 Topps Coast to Coast

Randomly inserted in series two retail packs only at a rate of one in 36, this 15-card set feature player's that have the ability to take it from one end of the court to the other. Card backs carry a "CC" prefix.

COMPLETE SET (15)	30.00	60.00
CC1 Kobe Bryant	10.00	25.00
CC2 Scottie Pippen	3.00	8.00
CC3 Eddie Jones	2.00	5.00
CC4 Grant Hill	3.00	8.00
CC5 Jason Kidd	3.00	8.00
CC6 Antoine Walker	2.00	5.00
CC7 Michael Finley	2.00	5.00
CC8 Kevin Garnett	4.00	10.00
CC9 Allen Iverson	4.00	10.00
CC10 Shawn Kemp	2.00	5.00
CC11 Glenn Robinson	1.50	4.00
CC12 Anfernee Hardaway	3.00	8.00
CC13 Tim Hardaway	2.00	5.00
CC14 Ron Mercer	1.50	4.00
CC15 Kerry Kittles	1.25	3.00

1998-99 Topps Cornerstones

Randomly inserted in series one hobby packs only at a rate of one in 36, this 15-card set features players that teams would love to build entire teams around. The cards feature uniluster technology. Card backs feature a "C" prefix.

COMPLETE SET (15) 15.00 40.00
C1 Keith Van Horn 1.25 3.00
C2 Kevin Garnett 2.50 6.00
C3 Shareef Abdur-Rahim 1.25 3.00
C4 Antoine Walker 1.25 3.00
C5 Allen Iverson 2.50 6.00
C6 Grant Hill 2.00 5.00
C7 Marcus Camby 1.00 2.50
C8 Stephon Marbury 1.50 4.00
C9 Kobe Bryant 6.00 15.00
C10 Bobby Jackson 1.00 2.50
C11 Kerry Kittles .75 2.00
C12 Ron Mercer 1.00 2.50
C13 Eddie Jones 1.25 3.00
C14 Tim Thomas 1.25 3.00
C15 Tim Duncan 2.50 6.00

1998-99 Topps Draft Redemption

Randomly inserted in series one packs at a rate of one in 18, this 29-card set features a redemption for the players drafted in the first round of the 1998 NBA Draft. Each card number contained a number corresponding to each draft position, and could be redeemed for a special card of that particular player selected. Cards had to be redemmed before April 1, 1999. Cards 17 and 18 do not exist, in redeemed form.

1 Michael Olowokandi 3.00 8.00
2 Mike Bibby 6.00 15.00
3 Raef LaFrentz 3.00 8.00
4 Antawn Jamison 6.00 15.00
5 Vince Carter 12.00 30.00
6 Robert Traylor 2.50 6.00
7 Jason Williams 6.00 15.00
8 Larry Hughes 5.00 12.00
9 Dirk Nowitzki 20.00 50.00
10 Paul Pierce 12.00 30.00
11 Bonzi Wells 2.50 6.00
12 Michael Doleac 2.50 6.00
13 Keon Clark 2.50 6.00
14 Michael Dickerson 2.50 6.00
15 Matt Harpring 3.00 8.00
16 Bryce Drew 2.50 6.00
19 Pat Garrity 2.50 6.00
20 Roshown McLeod 2.50 6.00
21 Ricky Davis 4.00 10.00
22 Brian Skinner 2.50 6.00
23 Tyronn Lue 2.50 6.00
24 Felipe Lopez 2.50 6.00
25 Al Harrington 4.00 10.00
26 Sam Jacobson 2.50 6.00
27 Vladimir Stepania 2.50 6.00
28 Corey Benjamin 2.50 6.00
29 Nazr Mohammed 2.50 6.00

1998-99 Topps East/West

Randomly inserted in series two packs at one in 36, this 20-card double-sided set combines one superstar from the Eastern Conference with one from the Western Conference. The cards feature Finest technology. Card backs are numbered with an "EW" prefix.

COMPLETE SET (20) 40.00 80.00
*REF: 1.25X TO 3X HI COLUMN
REF: SER.2 STATED ODDS 1:144 H/R
EW1 Antoine Walker / Shareef Abdur-Rahim 1.25 3.00
EW2 Alonzo Mourning / Shaquille O'Neal 4.00 10.00
EW3 Tim Hardaway / John Stockton 1.50 4.00
EW4 Scottie Pippen / Kevin Garnett 3.00 8.00
EW5 Michael Jordan / Kobe Bryant 12.00 30.00
EW6 Grant Hill / Michael Finley 1.50 4.00
EW7 Dikembe Mutombo / Hakeem Olajuwon 1.50 4.00
EW8 Keith Van Horn / Tim Duncan 1.50 4.00
EW9 Allen Iverson / Gary Payton 2.00 5.00
EW10 Patrick Ewing / David Robinson 1.50 4.00
EW11 Juwan Howard / Chris Webber 1.25 3.00
EW12 Brevin Knight / Stephon Marbury 1.25 3.00
EW13 Shawn Kemp / Vin Baker 1.25 3.00
EW14 Anthony Mason / Tom Gugliotta 1.00 2.50
EW15 Anfernee Hardaway / Damon Stoudamire 1.50 4.00
EW16 Ron Mercer / Eddie Jones 1.25 3.00
EW17 Rod Strickland / Jason Kidd 2.00 5.00
EW18 Tim Thomas / Antonio McDyess 1.00 2.50
EW19 Jayson Williams / Karl Malone 1.50 4.00
EW20 Reggie Miller / Jim Jackson 1.25 3.00

1998-99 Topps Emissaries

Randomly inserted in series one packs at a rate of one in 24, this 20-card set features players who have represented their country in tough international competition. The cards are produced with mirrorboard technology. Card backs are labeled with an "E" prefix.

COMPLETE SET (20) 25.00 50.00
E1 Scottie Pippen 2.50 6.00
E2 Karl Malone 2.00 5.00
E3 Chris Webber 1.50 4.00
E4 Anfernee Hardaway 2.50 6.00
E5 Detlef Schrempf 1.50 4.00
E6 Mitch Richmond 1.50 4.00
E7 Vlade Divac 1.50 4.00
E8 Shaquille O'Neal 4.00 10.00
E9 Luc Longley 1.00 2.50
E10 Grant Hill 2.50 6.00
E11 Christian Laettner 1.25 3.00
E12 Gary Payton 1.50 4.00
E13 Patrick Ewing 2.00 5.00
E14 Shawn Kemp 1.50 4.00
E15 Toni Kukoc 1.50 4.00
E16 David Robinson 2.50 6.00
E17 Hakeem Olajuwon 2.00 5.00
E18 Charles Barkley 2.50 6.00
E19 John Stockton 2.00 5.00
E20 Arvydas Sabonis 1.25 3.00

1998-99 Topps Gold Label

Randomly inserted in series two packs at one in 12, this 10-card set features players on a Gold Label card. This is not a preview set, since a Gold Label set was not released in 1998-99. Card backs carry a "GL" prefix.

COMPLETE SET (10) 12.00 30.00
*BLACK LABEL: .75X TO 2X HI COLUMN
BLACK: SER.2 STATED ODDS 1:96 H/R
*RED: 10X TO 25X HI
STATED PRINT RUN 100 SERIAL #'d SETS
GL1 Michael Jordan 6.00 15.00
GL2 Shaquille O'Neal 2.00 5.00
GL3 Kobe Bryant 4.00 10.00
GL4 Antoine Walker .75 2.00
GL5 Charles Barkley 1.25 3.00
GL6 Keith Van Horn .75 2.00
GL7 Tim Duncan 1.50 4.00
GL8 Stephon Marbury 1.00 2.50
GL9 Shareef Abdur-Rahim .75 2.00
GL10 Gary Payton .75 2.00

1998-99 Topps Kick Start

Randomly inserted in series two packs at a rate of one in 12, this 15-card set focuses on young players in the NBA who are expected to have a breakout year. The cards feature dot-matrix technology. Card backs carry a "KS" prefix.

COMPLETE SET (15) 10.00 25.00
KS1 Tim Duncan 1.25 3.00
KS2 Kobe Bryant 3.00 8.00
KS3 Antoine Walker .60 1.50
KS4 Stephon Marbury .75 2.00
KS5 Allen Iverson 1.25 3.00
KS6 Shareef Abdur-Rahim .60 1.50
KS7 Keith Van Horn .60 1.50
KS8 Ray Allen .75 2.00
KS9 Vince Carter 2.00 5.00
KS10 Kevin Garnett 1.25 3.00
KS11 Kerry Kittles .40 1.00
KS12 Tim Thomas .60 1.50
KS13 Ron Mercer .50 1.25
KS14 Antawn Jamison 1.00 2.50
KS15 Mike Bibby 1.00 2.50

1998-99 Topps Legacies

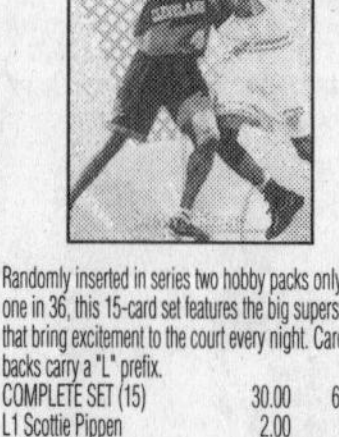

Randomly inserted in series two hobby packs only at one in 36, this 15-card set features the big superstars that bring excitement to the court every night. Card backs carry a "L" prefix.

COMPLETE SET (15) 30.00 60.00
L1 Scottie Pippen 2.00 5.00
L2 Grant Hill 2.00 5.00
L3 Hakeem Olajuwon 1.50 4.00
L4 Alonzo Mourning 1.50 4.00
L5 Shaquille O'Neal 3.00 8.00
L6 Shawn Kemp 1.25 3.00
L7 Gary Payton 1.25 3.00
L8 Karl Malone 1.50 4.00
L9 Patrick Ewing 1.50 4.00
L10 Tim Hardaway 1.25 3.00
L11 Reggie Miller 1.50 4.00
L12 Glen Rice 1.25 3.00
L13 Dikembe Mutombo 1.25 3.00
L14 John Stockton 1.50 4.00
L15 Michael Jordan 15.00 40.00

1998-99 Topps Roundball Royalty

Randomly inserted in series one packs at a rate of one in 36, this 20-card set features the best in the NBA on Finest technology. Card backs are numbered with a "R" prefix.

COMPLETE SET (20) 40.00 100.00
R1 Michael Jordan 15.00 40.00
R2 Kevin Garnett 3.00 8.00
R3 David Robinson 2.50 6.00
R4 Allen Iverson 3.00 8.00
R5 Hakeem Olajuwon 2.00 5.00
R6 Anfernee Hardaway 2.50 6.00
R7 Gary Payton 1.50 4.00
R8 Scottie Pippen 2.50 6.00
R9 Shaquille O'Neal 4.00 10.00
R10 Mitch Richmond 1.50 4.00
R11 John Stockton 2.00 5.00
R12 Grant Hill 2.50 6.00
R13 Charles Barkley 2.50 6.00
R14 Dikembe Mutombo 1.50 4.00
R15 Karl Malone 2.00 5.00
R16 Shawn Kemp 1.50 4.00
R17 Patrick Ewing 2.00 5.00
R18 Kobe Bryant 8.00 20.00
R19 Terrell Brandon 1.00 2.50
R20 Vin Baker 1.25 3.00

1998-99 Topps Roundball Royalty Refractors

Randomly inserted in series one packs at a rate of one in 144, this 20-card set parallels the basic Roundball Royalty insert, but utilizes the "classic" Refractor technology. Card backs are numbered with a "R" prefix. To determine values on individual cards, please refer to the multipliers in the header below, coupled with the value of the base card.

*REF: 1X TO 2.5X VALUE
R1 Michael Jordan 50.00 125.00

1998-99 Topps Season's Best

Randomly inserted in series one packs at a rate of one in 12, this 30-card set features 25 of the top players by position and five of the top rookies from 1997-98. This set is also broken into six themes: Postmen, Rockmen, Bombardiers, Navigators, Soarers and Newcomers. Card backs are numbered with a "SB" prefix.

COMPLETE SET (30) 25.00 60.00
SB1 Rod Strickland .60 1.50
SB2 Gary Payton 1.00 2.50
SB3 Tim Hardaway 1.00 2.50
SB4 Stephon Marbury 1.25 3.00
SB5 Sam Cassell .75 2.00
SB6 Michael Jordan 10.00 25.00
SB7 Mitch Richmond 1.00 2.50
SB8 Steve Smith .75 2.00
SB9 Ray Allen 1.25 3.00
SB10 Isaiah Rider .60 1.50
SB11 Grant Hill 1.50 4.00
SB12 Kevin Garnett 2.00 5.00
SB13 Shareef Abdur-Rahim 1.00 2.50
SB14 Glenn Robinson .75 2.00
SB15 Michael Finley 1.00 2.50
SB16 Karl Malone 1.25 3.00
SB17 Tim Duncan 2.00 5.00
SB18 Antoine Walker 1.00 2.50
SB19 Chris Webber 1.00 2.50
SB20 Vin Baker .75 2.00
SB21 Shaquille O'Neal 2.50 6.00
SB22 David Robinson 1.50 4.00
SB23 Alonzo Mourning 1.25 3.00
SB24 Dikembe Mutombo 1.00 2.50
SB25 Hakeem Olajuwon 1.25 3.00
SB26 Tim Duncan 2.00 5.00
SB27 Keith Van Horn 1.00 2.50
SB28 Zydrunas Ilgauskas 1.00 2.50
SB29 Brevin Knight .60 1.50
SB30 Bobby Jackson .75 2.00

1999-00 Topps

The first series of Topps was released as a 120-card set, while the second series contained 137 cards for a total of 257. The cards were released in 11-card packs that carried a suggested retail price of $1.29. Card fronts featured orange borders with the player's name in gold foil. The set also featured rookie subsets (cards 111-120 and cards 231-248) that were inserted at one in five packs. Series two packs also contained a nine-card Olympic subset that was also inserted at one in five.

COMPLETE SET (257) 30.00 60.00
COMPLETE SERIES 1 (120) 12.50 25.00
COMPLETE SERIES 2 (137) 17.50 35.00
COMP.SERIES 1 w/o SP (110) 6.00 12.00
COMP.SERIES 2 w/o SP (110) 5.00 10.00
1 Steve Smith .12 .30
2 Ron Harper .12 .30
3 Michael Dickerson .12 .30
4 LaPhonso Ellis .12 .30
5 Chris Webber .20 .50
6 Jason Caffey .12 .30
7 Bryon Russell .12 .30
8 Bison Dele .12 .30
9 Isaiah Rider .12 .30
10 Dean Garrett .12 .30
11 Eric Murdock .12 .30
12 Juwan Howard .15 .40
13 Latrell Sprewell .20 .50
14 Jalen Rose .15 .40
15 Larry Johnson .20 .50
16 Eric Williams .12 .30
17 Bryant Reeves .12 .30
18 Tony Battie .15 .40
19 Luc Longley .12 .30
20 Gary Payton .20 .50
21 Tariq Abdul-Wahad .12 .30
22 Armen Gilliam UER should be Armon .12 .30
23 Shaquille O'Neal .50 1.25
24 Gary Trent .12 .30
25 John Stockton .25 .60
26 Mark Jackson .20 .50
27 Cherokee Parks .12 .30
28 Michael Olowokandi .12 .30
29 Raef LaFrentz .15 .40
30 Dell Curry .12 .30
31 Travis Best .12 .30
32 Shawn Kemp .20 .50
33 Voshon Lenard .12 .30
34 Brian Grant .12 .30
35 Alvin Williams .12 .30
36 Derek Fisher .20 .50
37 Allan Houston .15 .40
38 Arvydas Sabonis .15 .40
39 Terry Cummings .12 .30
40 Dale Ellis .12 .30
41 Maurice Taylor .12 .30
42 Grant Hill .25 .60
43 Anthony Mason .12 .30
44 John Wallace .12 .30
45 David Wesley .12 .30
46 Nick Van Exel .15 .40
47 Cuttino Mobley .15 .40
48 Anfernee Hardaway .30 .75
49 Terry Porter .12 .30
50 Brent Barry .15 .40
51 Derek Harper .15 .40
52 Antoine Walker .20 .50
53 Karl Malone .25 .60
54 Ben Wallace .20 .50
55 Vlade Divac .20 .50
56 Sam Mitchell .12 .30
57 Joe Smith .15 .40
58 Shawn Bradley .12 .30
59 Darrell Armstrong .12 .30
60 Kenny Anderson .15 .40
61 Jason Williams .25 .60
62 Alonzo Mourning .25 .60
63 Matt Harpring .15 .40
64 Antonio Davis .12 .30
65 Lindsey Hunter .12 .30
66 Allen Iverson .40 1.00
67 Mookie Blaylock .12 .30
68 Wesley Person .12 .30
69 Bobby Phills .12 .30
70 Theo Ratliff .15 .40
71 Antonio Daniels .12 .30
72 P.J. Brown .12 .30
73 David Robinson .30 .75
74 Sean Elliott .20 .50
75 Zydrunas Ilgauskas .15 .40
76 Kerry Kittles .12 .30
77 Otis Thorpe .12 .30
78 John Starks .20 .50
79 Jaren Jackson .12 .30
80 Hersey Hawkins .12 .30
81 Glenn Robinson .15 .40
82 Paul Pierce .30 .75
83 Glen Rice .20 .50
84 Charlie Ward .12 .30
85 Dee Brown .12 .30
86 Danny Fortson .12 .30
87 Billy Owens .12 .30
88 Jason Kidd .30 .75
89 Brent Price .12 .30
90 Don Reid .12 .30
91 Mark Bryant .12 .30
92 Vinny Del Negro .12 .30
93 Stephon Marbury .15 .40
94 Donyell Marshall .12 .30
95 Jim Jackson .15 .40
96 Horace Grant .15 .40
97 Calbert Cheaney .12 .30
98 Vince Carter .40 1.00
99 Bobby Jackson .15 .40
100 Alan Henderson .12 .30
101 Mike Bibby .20 .50
102 Cedric Henderson .12 .30
103 Lamond Murray .12 .30
104 A.C. Green .20 .50
105 Hakeem Olajuwon .25 .60
106 George Lynch .12 .30
107 Kendall Gill .12 .30
108 Rex Chapman .12 .30
109 Eddie Jones .20 .50
110 Kornel David RC .30 .75
111 Jason Terry RC .75 2.00
112 Corey Maggette RC .60 1.50
113 Ron Artest RC .75 2.00
114 Richard Hamilton RC .75 2.00
115 Elton Brand RC .75 2.00
116 Baron Davis RC 1.00 2.50
117 Wally Szczerbiak RC .60 1.50
118 Steve Francis RC .75 2.00
119 James Posey RC .30 .75
120 Shawn Marion RC .75 2.00
121 Tim Duncan .40 1.00
122 Danny Manning .12 .30
123 Chris Mullin .20 .50
124 Antawn Jamison .20 .50
125 Kobe Bryant 1.00 2.50
126 Matt Geiger .12 .30
127 Rod Strickland .12 .30
128 Howard Eisley .12 .30
129 Steve Nash .30 .75
130 Felipe Lopez .12 .30
131 Ron Mercer .15 .40
132 Ruben Patterson .12 .30
133 Dana Barros .12 .30
134 Dale Davis .12 .30
135 Bo Outlaw .12 .30
136 Shandon Anderson .12 .30
137 Mitch Richmond .20 .50
138 Doug Christie .15 .40
139 Rasheed Wallace .20 .50
140 Chris Childs .12 .30
141 Jamal Mashburn .15 .40
142 Terrell Brandon .12 .30
143 Jamie Feick RC .20 .50
144 Robert Traylor .12 .30
145 Rick Fox .12 .30
146 Charles Barkley .30 .75
147 Tyrone Nesby RC .20 .50
148 Jerry Stackhouse .20 .50
149 Cedric Ceballos .12 .30
150 Dikembe Mutombo .20 .50
151 Anthony Peeler .12 .30
152 Larry Hughes .15 .40
153 Clifford Robinson .12 .30
154 Corliss Williamson .12 .30
155 Olden Polynice .12 .30
156 Avery Johnson .15 .40
157 Tracy Murray .12 .30
158 Tom Gugliotta .12 .30
159 Tim Thomas .15 .40
160 Reggie Miller .20 .50
161 Tim Hardaway .20 .50
162 Dan Majerle .20 .50
163 Will Perdue .12 .30
164 Brevin Knight .12 .30
165 Elden Campbell .12 .30
166 Chris Gatling .12 .30
167 Walter McCarty .12 .30
168 Chauncey Billups .20 .50
169 Chris Mills .12 .30
170 Christian Laettner .15 .40
171 Robert Pack .12 .30
172 Rik Smits .20 .50
173 Tyrone Hill .12 .30
174 Damon Stoudamire .20 .50
175 Nick Anderson .12 .30
176 Peja Stojakovic .20 .50
177 Vladimir Stepania .12 .30
178 Tracy McGrady .30 .75
179 Adam Keefe .12 .30
180 Shareef Abdur-Rahim .15 .40
181 Isaac Austin .12 .30
182 Mario Elie .12 .30
183 Rashard Lewis .20 .50
184 Scott Burrell .12 .30
185 Othella Harrington .12 .30
186 Eric Piatkowski .15 .40
187 Bryant Stith .12 .30
188 Michael Finley .20 .50
189 Chris Crawford .12 .30
190 Toni Kukoc .20 .50
191 Danny Ferry .12 .30
192 Erick Dampier .12 .30
193 Clarence Weatherspoon .12 .30
194 Bob Sura .12 .30
195 Jayson Williams .12 .30
196 Kurt Thomas .12 .30
197 Greg Anthony .12 .30
198 Rodney Rogers .12 .30
199 Detlef Schrempf .15 .40
200 Keith Van Horn .15 .40
201 Robert Horry .20 .50
202 Sam Cassell .15 .40
203 Malik Sealy .12 .30
204 Kelvin Cato .12 .30
205 Antonio McDyess .15 .40
206 Andrew DeClercq .12 .30
207 Ricky Davis .20 .50
208 Vitaly Potapenko .12 .30
209 Loy Vaught .12 .30
210 Kevin Garnett .40 1.00
211 Eric Snow .12 .30
212 Anfernee Hardaway .30 .75
213 Vin Baker .20 .50
214 Lawrence Funderburke .12 .30
215 Jeff Hornacek .15 .40
216 Doug West .12 .30
217 Michael Doleac .12 .30
218 Ray Allen .20 .50
219 Derek Anderson .12 .30
220 Jerome Williams .12 .30
221 Derrick Coleman .15 .40
222 Randy Brown .12 .30
223 Patrick Ewing .25 .60
224 Walt Williams .12 .30
225 Charles Oakley .15 .40
226 Steve Kerr .15 .40
227 Muggsy Bogues .15 .40
228 Kevin Willis .15 .40
229 Marcus Camby .15 .40
230 Scottie Pippen .30 .75
231 Lamar Odom RC 1.00 2.50
232 Jonathan Bender RC .30 .75
233 Andre Miller RC .75 2.00
234 Trajan Langdon RC .30 .75
235 Aleksandar Radojevic RC .30 .75
236 William Avery RC .30 .75
237 Cal Bowdler RC .30 .75
238 Quincy Lewis RC .30 .75
239 Dion Glover RC .30 .75
240 Jeff Foster RC .30 .75
241 Kenny Thomas RC .30 .75
242 Devean George RC .30 .75
243 Tim James RC .30 .75
244 Vonteego Cummings RC .30 .75
245 Jumaine Jones RC .30 .75
246 Scott Padgett RC .30 .75
247 Adrian Griffin RC .30 .75
248 Chris Herren RC .30 .75
249 Allan Houston USA .20 .50
250 Kevin Garnett USA .50 1.25
251 Gary Payton USA .25 .60
252 Steve Smith USA .15 .40
253 Tim Hardaway USA .25 .60
254 Tim Duncan USA .50 1.25
255 Jason Kidd USA .40 1.00
256 Tom Gugliotta USA .15 .40
257 Vin Baker USA .25 .60

1999-00 Topps MVP Promotion

Randomly inserted in series one hobby packs at one in 336 and series two at one in 172, this 248-card set parallels the base set. The USA subset cards were not included in this set. Winner cards could be redeemed for a complete MVP parallel set. To ascertain values on individual cards, please refer to the multiplier in the header, coupled with the value of the base card.

*MVP STARS: 10X TO 25X BASE CARD HI
*MVP RCs: 6X TO 15X BASE HI

1999-00 Topps MVP Promotion Exchange

This set was available by sending in a winner card from the 1999-00 Topps MVP Promotion set. Each card features bronze foil and carries a "MVP" prefix on the back.

COMPLETE SET (22) 25.00 60.00
MVP1 Allen Iverson 2.50 6.00
MVP2 Alonzo Mourning 1.50 4.00
MVP3 Anthony Mason .75 2.00
MVP4 Chris Webber 1.25 3.00
MVP5 Eddie Jones 1.25 3.00
MVP6 Grant Hill 1.50 4.00
MVP7 Jason Kidd 2.00 5.00
MVP8 Karl Malone 1.50 4.00
MVP9 Kevin Garnett 2.50 6.00
MVP10 Kobe Bryant 6.00 15.00
MVP11 Michael Finley 1.25 3.00
MVP12 Sam Cassell 1.00 2.50
MVP13 Shaquille O'Neal 3.00 8.00
MVP14 Stephon Marbury 1.00 2.50
MVP15 Terrell Brandon .75 2.00
MVP16 Tim Duncan 2.50 6.00
MVP17 Vince Carter 2.50 6.00
MVP18 Steve Francis 3.00 8.00
MVP19 Elton Brand / Steve Francis 3.00 8.00
MVP20 Shaquille O'Neal 3.00 8.00
MVP21 Reggie Miller 1.25 3.00
MVP22 Shaquille O'Neal 3.00 8.00

1999-00 Topps 21st Century Topps

Randomly inserted in series two packs at one in 27, this 16-card set focuses on the 1999 NBA Draft Class. The cards are printed with holographic technology. Card backs carry a "C" prefix.

COMPLETE SET (16) 6.00 15.00
C1 Jason Terry .75 2.00
C2 Baron Davis 1.00 2.50
C3 Lamar Odom 1.00 2.50
C4 Jonathan Bender .30 .75
C5 Ron Artest .75 2.00
C6 Richard Hamilton .75 2.00
C7 Andre Miller .75 2.00
C8 Shawn Marion .75 2.00
C9 Steve Francis .75 2.00
C10 Elton Brand .75 2.00
C11 Wally Szczerbiak .60 1.50
C12 Corey Maggette .60 1.50
C13 James Posey .30 .75
C14 Trajan Langdon .30 .75
C15 Tim James .30 .75
C16 Cal Bowdler .30 .75

1999-00 Topps All-Matrix

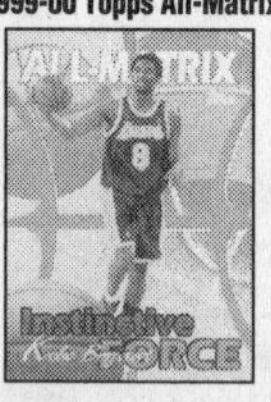

Randomly inserted in series two packs at one in 15, this 30-card set showcases the top players in the league. The insert set was divided into three categories - Feature Force for the veterans, Instinctive Force for the younger stars and Future Force for the league's top rookies. Card backs carry a "AM" prefix.

COMPLETE SET (30) 30.00 80.00
AM1 Karl Malone 1.50 4.00
AM2 Scottie Pippen 2.00 5.00
AM3 Grant Hill 1.50 4.00
AM4 Shawn Kemp 1.25 3.00
AM5 Shaquille O'Neal 3.00 8.00
AM6 Anfernee Hardaway 2.00 5.00
AM7 Chris Webber 1.25 3.00
AM8 Gary Payton 1.25 3.00
AM9 Jason Kidd 2.00 5.00
AM10 John Stockton 1.50 4.00
AM11 Kevin Garnett 2.50 6.00
AM12 Vince Carter 2.50 6.00
AM13 Shareef Abdur-Rahim 1.00 2.50
AM14 Antoine Walker 1.25 3.00
AM15 Kobe Bryant 6.00 15.00
AM16 Tim Duncan 2.50 6.00
AM17 Keith Van Horn 1.00 2.50
AM18 Allen Iverson 2.50 6.00
AM19 Jason Williams 1.50 4.00
AM20 Stephon Marbury 1.00 2.50
AM21 Elton Brand 2.00 5.00
AM22 Jason Terry 2.00 5.00
AM23 Steve Francis 2.00 5.00
AM24 Corey Maggette 1.50 4.00
AM25 Lamar Odom 2.50 6.00
AM26 Ron Artest 2.00 5.00
AM27 Baron Davis 2.50 6.00
AM28 Andre Miller 2.00 5.00
AM29 Shawn Marion 2.00 5.00
AM30 Wally Szczerbiak 1.50 4.00

1999-00 Topps Autographs

Randomly inserted in series one hobby packs only at one in 877 for group A and one in 351 for group B and inserted at one in 196 for series two hobby packs, this 21-card set features autographs of top NBA stars. Card backs are labeled by the player's initials.

AM Antonio McDyess A 4.00 10.00
AM2 Antonio McDyess B 4.00 10.00
AW Antoine Walker A 6.00 15.00
BD Baron Davis A 10.00 25.00
CM Corey Maggette A 6.00 15.00
DS Damon Stoudamire A 5.00 12.00
EB Elton Brand B 6.00 15.00
GP Gary Payton B 15.00 40.00
GP2 Gary Payton A 12.50 30.00
JJ Jumaine Jones A 3.00 8.00
JK Jason Kidd A 20.00 50.00
MR Mitch Richmond A 5.00 12.00
PP Paul Pierce B 15.00 40.00
SF Steve Francis B 6.00 15.00
SP Scottie Pippen B 80.00 160.00
SS Steve Smith B 3.00 8.00
TD Tim Duncan A 100.00 200.00
TG Tom Gugliotta B 3.00 8.00
WA William Avery A 3.00 8.00
WS Wally Szczerbiak A 5.00 12.00
SAR Shareef Abdur-Rahim B 6.00 15.00

1999-00 Topps Highlight Reels

Randomly inserted in series one retail packs only at one in 14, this 15-card set focuses on players with the most heart-pounding, jaw-dropping moves in the NBA. Card backs carry a "HR" prefix.

COMPLETE SET (15) 8.00 20.00
HR1 Stephon Marbury .60 1.50
HR2 Vince Carter 1.50 4.00
HR3 Kevin Garnett 1.50 4.00
HR4 Kobe Bryant 4.00 10.00
HR5 Chris Webber .75 2.00
HR6 Allen Iverson 1.50 4.00
HR7 Grant Hill 1.00 2.50
HR8 Antoine Walker .75 2.00
HR9 Jason Williams 1.00 2.50
HR10 Tim Duncan 1.50 4.00
HR11 Shareef Abdur-Rahim .60 1.50
HR12 Keith Van Horn .60 1.50
HR13 Antonio McDyess .60 1.50
HR14 Jason Kidd 1.25 3.00
HR15 Ron Mercer .60 1.50

1999-00 Topps Impact

Randomly inserted in series two packs at one in 24, this 20-card set was divided into three categories. Initial Impact features members of the 1999 NBA Draft Class, Present Impact highlights young stars and Lasting Impact showcases talented veterans. The cards are printed on Chromium technology. Card backs carry an "I" prefix.

COMPLETE SET (20) 25.00 60.00
*REF: 1X TO 2.5X HI COLUMN
REF: SER.2 STATED ODDS 1:120 H/R
I1 Elton Brand 2.00 5.00
I2 Lamar Odom 2.50 6.00
I3 Wally Szczerbiak 1.50 4.00
I4 Jason Terry 2.00 5.00
I5 Baron Davis 2.50 6.00
I6 Ron Artest 2.00 5.00
I7 Steve Francis 2.00 5.00
I8 Andre Miller 2.00 5.00
I9 Allen Iverson 2.50 6.00
I10 Jason Williams 1.50 4.00
I11 Keith Van Horn 1.00 2.50
I12 Vince Carter 2.50 6.00
I13 Kobe Bryant 6.00 15.00
I14 Tim Duncan 2.50 6.00
I15 Scottie Pippen 2.00 5.00
I16 Kevin Garnett 2.50 6.00
I17 Shaquille O'Neal 3.00 8.00
I18 Gary Payton 1.25 3.00
I19 Karl Malone 1.50 4.00
I20 Grant Hill 1.50 4.00

1999-00 Topps Jumbos

Inserted one per series one hobby box, this eight-card set features a jumbo-sized card of several NBA stars.

COMPLETE SET (8) 2.00 5.00
1 Gary Payton .30 .75
2 Shaquille O'Neal .75 2.00
3 Antoine Walker .30 .75
4 Jason Williams .40 1.00
5 Alonzo Mourning .40 1.00
6 Allen Iverson .60 1.50
7 Stephon Marbury .25 .60
8 Vince Carter .60 1.50

1999-00 Topps Own the Game

ndomly inserted in series two packs at one in 44, 10-card set highlights the statistical leaders from 1998-99 season. Card backs carry an "OTG" prefix.

MPLETE SET (10) 12.50 30.00
G1 Allen Iverson 2.50 6.00
G2 Shaquille O'Neal 3.00 8.00
G3 Jason Kidd 2.00 5.00
G4 Stephon Marbury 1.00 2.50
G5 Dikembe Mutombo 1.25 3.00
G6 Tim Duncan 2.50 6.00
G7 Wally Szczerbiak 2.50 6.00
G8 Quincy Lewis 1.25 3.00
G9 Elton Brand 3.00 8.00
G10 Aleksandar Radojevic 1.25 3.00

1999-00 Topps Patriarchs

ndomly inserted in series one packs at one in 22, s 15-card set. Card backs carry a "P" prefix.

MPLETE SET (15) 10.00 25.00
Patrick Ewing 1.25 3.00
Reggie Miller 1.00 2.50
Hakeem Olajuwon 1.25 3.00
Scottie Pippen 1.50 4.00
Grant Hill 1.25 3.00
Shaquille O'Neal 2.50 6.00
Mitch Richmond 1.00 2.50
Glen Rice 1.00 2.50
Charles Barkley 1.50 4.00
Karl Malone 1.25 3.00
John Stockton 1.25 3.00
Gary Payton 1.00 2.50
David Robinson 1.50 4.00
Tim Hardaway 1.00 2.50
Joe Dumars 1.00 2.50

1999-00 Topps Picture Perfect

ndomly inserted in series one packs at one in eight, 10-card set features NBA stars against cards that not quite correct. Card backs carry a "PIC" prefix.

MPLETE SET (10) 2.00 5.00
C1 Shaquille O'Neal .75 2.00
C2 Alonzo Mourning .40 1.00
C3 Shareef Abdur-Rahim .25 .60
C4 Juwan Howard .25 .60
C5 Keith Van Horn .25 .60
C6 Ron Mercer .25 .60
C7 Tim Hardaway .30 .75
C8 Kevin Garnett .60 1.50
C9 David Robinson .50 1.25
C10 Kerry Kittles .20 .50

1999-00 Topps Prodigy

ndomly inserted in series one packs at one in 36, s 20-card set features the future stars of the NBA. e cards feature a chrome background and a "PR" efix on the back.

MPLETE SET (20) 30.00 80.00
1 Stephon Marbury 1.50 4.00
2 Jason Kidd 3.00 8.00
3 Kevin Garnett 4.00 10.00
4 Kobe Bryant 10.00 25.00
5 Antoine Walker 2.00 5.00
6 Ron Mercer 1.50 4.00
7 Shareef Abdur-Rahim 1.50 4.00
8 Tim Duncan 4.00 10.00
9 Keith Van Horn 1.50 4.00
10 Ray Allen 2.00 5.00
11 Michael Doleac 1.25 3.00
12 Jason Williams 2.50 6.00
13 Michael Dickerson 1.25 3.00
14 Mike Bibby 2.00 5.00
15 Paul Pierce 3.00 8.00
16 Michael Olowokandi 1.25 3.00
17 Vince Carter 4.00 10.00
18 Antawn Jamison 2.00 5.00
19 Felipe Lopez 1.25 3.00
20 Matt Harpring 1.50 4.00

1999-00 Topps Prodigy Refractors

andomly inserted in series one packs at one in 144, is 20-card set parallels the regular Prodigy inserts. e cards feature the classic Refractor technology. ard backs carry a "PR" prefix. To ascertain values on dividual cards, please refer to the multiplier in the eader below, coupled with the value of the base insert.

EF: .6X TO 1.5X HI COLUMN
R4 Kobe Bryant 20.00 50.00

1999-00 Topps Record Numbers

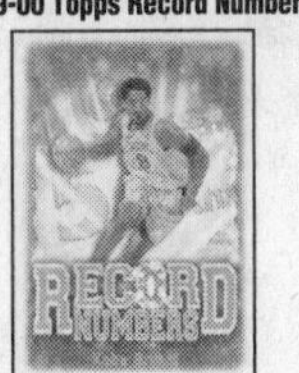

Randomly inserted in series one packs at one in 12, this 10-card set. Card backs carry a "RN" prefix.

COMPLETE SET (10) 2.00 5.00
RN1 Karl Malone .40 1.00
RN2 Kerry Kittles .20 .50
RN3 Reggie Miller .30 .75
RN4 Hakeem Olajuwon .40 1.00
RN5 John Stockton .40 1.00
RN6 Dikembe Mutombo .30 .75
RN7 Kobe Bryant 1.50 4.00
RN8 Tim Duncan .60 1.50
RN9 Allen Iverson .60 1.50
RN10 Patrick Ewing .40 1.00

1999-00 Topps Season's Best

Randomly inserted in packs at one in 12, this 30-card set features some of the top players in different categories from the previous year. Card backs carry a "SB" prefix.

COMPLETE SET (30) 15.00 40.00
SB1 David Robinson 1.25 3.00
SB2 Shaquille O'Neal 2.00 5.00
SB3 Patrick Ewing 1.00 2.50
SB4 Hakeem Olajuwon 1.00 2.50
SB5 Alonzo Mourning 1.00 2.50
SB6 Antonio McDyess .60 1.50
SB7 Tim Duncan 1.50 4.00
SB8 Keith Van Horn .60 1.50
SB9 Karl Malone 1.00 2.50
SB10 Chris Webber .75 2.00
SB11 Kevin Garnett 1.50 4.00
SB12 Juwan Howard .60 1.50
SB13 Shareef Abdur-Rahim .60 1.50
SB14 Glenn Robinson .60 1.50
SB15 Grant Hill 1.00 2.50
SB16 Michael Finley .75 2.00
SB17 Steve Smith .50 1.25
SB18 Mitch Richmond .75 2.00
SB19 Kobe Bryant 4.00 10.00
SB20 Ray Allen .75 2.00
SB21 Allen Iverson 1.50 4.00
SB22 Gary Payton .75 2.00
SB23 Stephon Marbury .60 1.50
SB24 Jason Kidd 1.25 3.00
SB25 Tim Hardaway .75 2.00
SB26 Jason Williams 1.00 2.50
SB27 Vince Carter 1.50 4.00
SB28 Paul Pierce 1.25 3.00
SB29 Mike Bibby .75 2.00
SB30 Michael Dickerson .50 1.25

1999-00 Topps Team Topps

Randomly inserted in series two packs at one in 18, this 24-card set features NBA All-Stars, past and present from both conferences. Card backs carry a "TT" prefix.

COMPLETE SET (24) 25.00 60.00
TT1 Gary Payton 1.25 3.00
TT2 Jason Kidd 2.00 5.00
TT3 Kobe Bryant 6.00 15.00
TT4 Anfernee Hardaway 2.00 5.00
TT5 Kevin Garnett 2.50 6.00
TT6 Patrick Ewing 1.50 4.00
TT7 Tim Duncan 2.50 6.00
TT8 Karl Malone 1.50 4.00
TT9 Shaquille O'Neal 3.00 8.00
TT10 Charles Barkley 2.00 5.00
TT11 John Stockton 1.50 4.00
TT12 Tim Hardaway 1.25 3.00
TT13 Hakeem Olajuwon 1.50 4.00
TT14 Jayson Williams .75 2.00
TT15 Reggie Miller 1.25 3.00
TT16 David Robinson 2.00 5.00
TT17 Grant Hill 1.50 4.00
TT18 Scottie Pippen 2.00 5.00
TT19 Chris Webber 1.25 3.00
TT20 Shawn Kemp 1.25 3.00
TT21 Alonzo Mourning 1.50 4.00
TT22 Mitch Richmond 1.25 3.00
TT23 Antoine Walker 1.25 3.00
TT24 Tom Gugliotta .75 2.00

2000-01 Topps Promos

These two cards were given to hobby dealers and members of the media to promote the 2000-01 Topps product. The set was shipped in a cello wrapper, and featured cards of Elton Brand and Tim Duncan. Card backs carry a "PP" prefix.

COMPLETE SET (2) 1.00 2.50
PP1 Elton Brand .40 1.00
PP2 Tim Duncan .75 2.00

2000-01 Topps

The 2000-01 Topps product was released in early September 2000 for series one and late November 2000 for series two. The sets featured a 295-card base set that is broken into tiers as follows:Base Veterans, Rookies, Season Leaders subset, Second Coming subset and one Team Championship card. Each pack contained 10 cards and carried a suggested retail price of $1.29.

COMPLETE SET (295) 40.00 80.00
COMPLETE SERIES 1 (155) 30.00 60.00
COMP.SERIES 1 w/o RC (130) 7.50 15.00
COMPLETE SERIES 2 (140) 12.50 25.00
COMP.SERIES 2 w/o RC (120) 7.50 15.00
1 Elton Brand .20 .50
2 Marcus Camby .15 .40
3 Jalen Rose .15 .40
4 Jamie Feick .12 .30
5 Toni Kukoc .15 .40
6 Todd MacCulloch .12 .30
7 Mario Elie .12 .30
8 Doug Christie .12 .30
9 Sam Cassell .15 .40
10 Shaquille O'Neal .50 1.25
11 Larry Hughes .15 .40
12 Jerry Stackhouse .15 .40
13 Rick Fox .15 .40
14 Clifford Robinson .12 .30
15 Felipe Lopez .12 .30
16 Dirk Nowitzki .30 .75
17 Cuttino Mobley .15 .40
18 Latrell Sprewell .15 .40
19 Nick Anderson .12 .30
20 Kevin Garnett .40 1.00
21 Rik Smits .12 .30
22 Jerome Williams .12 .30
23 Chris Webber .20 .50
24 Jason Terry .20 .50
25 Elden Campbell .12 .30
26 Kelvin Cato .12 .30
27 Tyrone Nesby .20 .50
28 Jonathan Bender .12 .30
29 Otis Thorpe .15 .40
30 Scottie Pippen .30 .75
31 Radoslav Nesterovic .12 .30
32 P.J. Brown .12 .30
33 Reggie Miller .20 .50
34 Andre Miller .15 .40
35 Tariq Abdul-Wahad .12 .30
36 Michael Doleac .12 .30
37 Rashard Lewis .20 .50
38 Jacque Vaughn .12 .30
39 Larry Johnson .20 .50
40 Steve Francis .20 .50
41 Arvydas Sabonis .15 .40
42 Jaren Jackson .12 .30
43 Howard Eisley .12 .30
44 Rod Strickland .15 .40
45 Tim Thomas .12 .30
46 Robert Horry .15 .40
47 Kenny Thomas .12 .30
48 Anthony Peeler .12 .30
49 Darrell Armstrong .12 .30
50 Vince Carter .40 1.00
51 Othella Harrington .12 .30
52 Derek Anderson .12 .30
53 Anthony Carter .12 .30
54 Scott Burrell .12 .30
55 Ray Allen .20 .50
56 Jason Kidd .30 .75
57 Sean Elliott .15 .40
58 Muggsy Bogues .15 .40
59 LaPhonso Ellis .15 .40
60 Tim Duncan .40 1.00
61 Adrian Griffin .12 .30
62 Wally Szczerbiak .15 .40
63 Austin Croshere .12 .30
64 Wesley Person .12 .30
65 James Posey .12 .30
66 Alan Henderson .12 .30
67 Ruben Patterson .12 .30
68 Jahidi White .12 .30
69 Shawn Marion .20 .50
70 Lamar Odom .20 .50
71 Lindsey Hunter .12 .30
72 Keon Clark .12 .30
73 Gary Trent .12 .30
74 Lamond Murray .12 .30
75 Paul Pierce .25 .60
76 Charlie Ward .12 .30
77 Matt Geiger .12 .30
78 Greg Anthony .12 .30
79 Horace Grant .15 .40
80 John Stockton .25 .60
81 Peja Stojakovic .20 .50
82 William Avery .12 .30
83 Dan Majerle .15 .40
84 Christian Laettner .12 .30
85 Dana Barros .12 .30
86 Corey Benjamin .12 .30
87 Keith Van Horn .15 .40
88 Patrick Ewing .25 .60
89 Steve Smith .15 .40
90 Antonio Davis .12 .30
91 Samaki Walker .12 .30
92 Mitch Richmond .15 .40
93 Michael Olowokandi .12 .30
94 Baron Davis .20 .50
95 Dikembe Mutombo .20 .50
96 Andrew DeClercq .12 .30
97 Raef LaFrentz .12 .30
98 Trajan Langdon .12 .30
99 Ervin Johnson .12 .30
100 Alonzo Mourning .25 .60
101 Kendall Gill .12 .30
102 George Lynch .12 .30
103 Detlef Schrempf .15 .40
104 Donyell Marshall .12 .30
105 Bo Outlaw .12 .30
106 Kenny Anderson .15 .40
107 Eddie Robinson .12 .30
108 Jermaine O'Neal .20 .50
109 John Amaechi .12 .30
110 Glen Rice .15 .40
111 Vlade Divac .15 .40
112 Vin Baker .15 .40
113 Mike Bibby .20 .50
114 Richard Hamilton .15 .40
115 Mookie Blaylock .15 .40
116 Vitaly Potapenko .12 .30
117 Anthony Mason .12 .30
118 Robert Pack .12 .30
119 Vonteego Cummings .12 .30
120 Michael Finley .20 .50
121 Ron Artest .20 .50
122 Tyrone Hill .12 .30
123 Rodney Rogers .12 .30
124 Quincy Lewis .12 .30
125 Kenyon Martin RC 1.00 2.50
126 Stromile Swift RC .40 1.00
127 Darius Miles RC .40 1.00
128 Marcus Fizer RC .40 1.00
129 Mike Miller RC .75 2.00
130 DerMarr Johnson RC .40 1.00
131 Chris Mihm RC .40 1.00
132 Jamal Crawford RC .60 1.50
133 Joel Przybilla RC .40 1.00
134 Keyon Dooling RC .40 1.00
135 Jerome Moiso RC .40 1.00
136 Etan Thomas RC .40 1.00
137 Courtney Alexander RC .40 1.00
138 Mateen Cleaves RC .40 1.00
139 Jason Collier RC .40 1.00
140 Desmond Mason RC .50 1.25
141 Quentin Richardson RC .60 1.50
142 Jamaal Magloire RC .40 1.00
143 Speedy Claxton RC .40 1.00
144 Morris Peterson RC .40 1.00
145 Donnell Harvey RC .40 1.00
146 DeShawn Stevenson RC .50 1.25
147 Mamadou N'Diaye RC .40 1.00
148 Erick Barkley RC .40 1.00
149 Mark Madsen RC .40 1.00
150 Shaquille O'Neal .15 .40
Allen Iverson
Grant Hill SL
151 Jason Kidd .20 .50
Sam Cassell
Nick Van Exel SL
152 Dikembe Mutombo .25 .60
Shaquille O'Neal
Tim Duncan SL
153 Eddie Jones .10 .30
Paul Pierce
Darrell Armstrong SL
154 Alonzo Mourning .20 .50
Dikembe Mutombo
Shaquille O'Neal SL
155 Team Championship SL .30 .75
156 Jason Williams .20 .50
157 David Robinson .30 .75
158 Shammond Williams .12 .30
159 Charles Oakley .15 .40
160 Greg Ostertag .12 .30
161 Juwan Howard .15 .40
162 Antoine Walker .15 .40
163 Alan Henderson .12 .30
164 Eddie Jones .20 .50
165 Allen Iverson .40 1.00
166 Grant Hill .25 .60
167 Terrell Brandon .12 .30
168 Stephon Marbury .15 .40
169 Jason Caffey .12 .30
170 Sam Mitchell .12 .30
171 Jamal Mashburn .15 .40
172 Ron Harper .15 .40
173 Eric Piatkowski .12 .30
174 Sam Perkins .12 .30
175 Walt Williams .12 .30
176 Bob Sura .12 .30
177 Michael Curry .12 .30
178 Nick Van Exel .15 .40
179 Danny Ferry .12 .30
180 Randy Brown .12 .30
181 Danny Fortson .12 .30
182 Jim Jackson .12 .30
183 Brad Miller .20 .50
184 Shawn Bradley .12 .30
185 Voshon Lenard .12 .30
186 Erick Dampier .12 .30
187 Mark Jackson .15 .40
188 Maurice Taylor .12 .30
189 Kobe Bryant 1.00 2.50
190 Clarence Weatherspoon .12 .30
191 Bobby Jackson .12 .30
192 Eric Snow .12 .30
193 Allan Houston .15 .40
194 Kurt Thomas .12 .30
195 Chauncey Billups .20 .50
196 Tom Gugliotta .12 .30
197 Theo Ratliff .12 .30
198 Rasheed Wallace .20 .50
199 Jon Barry .12 .30
200 Malik Rose .12 .30
201 Vernon Maxwell .12 .30
202 Dee Brown .12 .30
203 Bryon Russell .12 .30
204 Brent Barry .12 .30
205 Tracy McGrady .30 .75
206 Bryant Reeves .12 .30
207 Isaac Austin .12 .30
208 Damon Stoudamire .15 .40
209 Anfernee Hardaway .30 .75
210 Aaron McKie .12 .30
211 Johnny Newman .12 .30
212 Scott Williams .12 .30
213 Brian Shaw .12 .30
214 Corey Maggette .15 .40
215 Travis Best .12 .30
216 Hakeem Olajuwon .25 .60
217 Antawn Jamison .20 .50
218 John Starks .12 .30
219 Antonio McDyess .15 .40
220 Cedric Ceballos .12 .30
221 Chris Carr .12 .30
222 Roshown McLeod .12 .30
223 Calbert Cheaney .12 .30
224 Gary Payton .20 .50
225 Karl Malone .25 .60
226 Michael Dickerson .12 .30
227 Tracy Murray .12 .30
228 Chris Childs .12 .30
229 Pat Garrity .12 .30
230 Rex Chapman .12 .30
231 Jumaine Jones .12 .30
232 Fred Hoiberg .12 .30
233 Bimbo Coles .12 .30
234 Shawn Kemp .20 .50
235 David Wesley .12 .30
236 Tony Battie .12 .30
237 Ron Mercer .12 .30
238 John Wallace .12 .30
239 Robert Traylor .12 .30
240 Derrick Coleman .15 .40
241 Steve Nash .30 .75
242 Ben Wallace .20 .50
243 Brian Skinner .12 .30
244 Chris Gatling .12 .30
245 Dale Davis .12 .30
246 Joe Smith .15 .40
247 Glenn Robinson .15 .40
248 Kerry Kittles .12 .30
249 Erick Strickland .12 .30
250 Sam Cassell .15 .40
251 Chucky Atkins .12 .30
252 Brian Grant .12 .30
253 Bonzi Wells .12 .30
254 Corliss Williamson .12 .30
255 Shareef Abdur-Rahim .15 .40
256 Kevin Willis .12 .30
257 Scott Padgett .12 .30
258 Terry Porter .15 .40
259 Tony Delk .12 .30
260 Avery Johnson .15 .40
261 Tim Hardaway .20 .50
262 Derek Fisher .20 .50
263 Isaiah Rider .15 .40
264 Shandon Anderson .12 .30
265 Adonal Foyle .12 .30
266 Hedo Turkoglu RC .75 2.00
267 Brian Cardinal RC .40 1.00
268 Iakovos Tsakalidis RC .40 1.00
269 Dalibor Bagaric RC .40 1.00
270 Marko Jaric RC .40 1.00
271 Dan Langhi RC .40 1.00
272 A.J. Guyton RC .40 1.00
273 Jake Voskuhl RC .40 1.00
274 Khalid El-Amin RC .40 1.00
275 Mike Smith RC .40 1.00
276 Soumaila Samake RC .40 1.00
277 Eddie House RC .40 1.00
278 Eduardo Najera RC .40 1.00
279 Lavor Postell RC .40 1.00
280 Hanno Mottola RC .40 1.00
281 Chris Carrawell RC .40 1.00
282 Olumide Oyedeji RC .40 1.00
283 Michael Redd RC 1.00 2.50
284 Chris Porter RC .40 1.00
285 Mark Karcher RC .40 1.00
286 Steve Francis .20 .50
Gary Payton SC
287 Darius Miles .20 .50
Kevin Garnett SC
288 Lamar Odom .15 .40
Shareef Abdur-Rahim SC
289 Tim Duncan .25 .60
Alonzo Mourning SC
290 Elton Brand .20 .50
Karl Malone SC
291 Larry Hughes .20 .50
Allen Iverson SC
292 Kobe Bryant .50 1.25
Reggie Miller SC
293 Vince Carter .25 .60
Grant Hill SC
294 Tracy McGrady .40 1.00
Scottie Pippen SC
295 Kenyon Martin .60 1.50
Marcus Camby SC

2000-01 Topps MVP Promotion

Randomly inserted into series one packs at one in 253 and series two at one in 179, this 279-card set is a partial parallel of the 2000-01 Topps set. The set features veterans and rookies from the base set, but no subset cards. The cards carry a Topps MVP stamp on the front of the card.

*STARS: 20X TO 50X VALUE
*RCs: 2X TO 5X VALUE

2000-01 Topps Autographs

Randomly inserted into both series packs, this insert features autographed cards of some of the hottest names in basketball. The Tim Duncan autograph was inserted at one in 5,941 packs. Group A autographs were inserted into packs at 1:1009, Group B autographs were inserted at 1:137, Group C autographs were inserted into packs at 1:2511. Overall odds for series one autographs was one in 580, with series two at one in 465. Series Two autographs were inserted at the following rates: Group A 1:664, Group B 1:3113, Group C 1:7783, Group D 1:9398, and the overall odds were 1:465. The Co-Rookie autograph was inserted into packs at 1:11584.

TAAI Allen Iverson A 75.00 150.00
TAAJ Antawn Jamison A 5.00 12.00
TAAM Antonio McDyess B 4.00 10.00
TAAJG A.J. Guyton A 4.00 10.00
TACA Courtney Alexander C 4.00 10.00
TAEB Elton Brand C 5.00 12.00
TAEB Elton Brand B 5.00 12.00
TAEMJ Magic Johnson A 60.00 150.00
TAJC Jamal Crawford A 6.00 15.00
TAJR Jalen Rose D 5.00 12.00
TAKD Keyon Dooling A 4.00 10.00
TALH Larry Hughes A 4.00 10.00
TALS Latrell Sprewell A 40.00 80.00
TAMC Mateen Cleaves B 4.00 10.00
TAMDC Marcus Camby B 5.00 12.00
TARA Ron Artest B 5.00 12.00
TAROY Elton Brand 15.00 40.00
Steve Francis
TASC Sam Cassell B 4.00 10.00
TASE Sean Elliott B 4.00 10.00
TASF Steve Francis B 5.00 12.00
TASO Shaquille O'Neal B 50.00 100.00
TASP Scoonie Penn B 4.00 10.00
TATB Terrell Brandon B 4.00 10.00
TATD Tim Duncan HTA 100.00 175.00
TATM Tracy McGrady B 15.00 40.00

2000-01 Topps Cards That Never Were

Randomly inserted in series two packs at one in 18 (one in six HTA), this 10-card set features new cards of Magic Johnson created with Topps classic designs from the years when Topps did not produced basketball cards. Card backs carry a "MJ" prefix.

COMPLETE SET (10) 15.00 30.00
COMMON CARD (MJ1-MJ10) 1.50 4.00

2000-01 Topps Chrome Previews

Randomly insert into series one packs at one in 18, this 20-card set gives collectors a taste of what the 2000-01 Topps Chrome set will look like. Card backs carry a "TCP" prefix.

COMPLETE SET (20) 15.00 40.00
TCP1 Shaquille O'Neal 2.00 5.00
TCP2 Kevin Garnett 1.50 4.00
TCP3 Vince Carter 1.50 4.00
TCP4 Tim Duncan 1.50 4.00
TCP5 Elton Brand .75 2.00
TCP6 Jason Kidd 1.25 3.00
TCP7 Lamar Odom .75 2.00
TCP8 Marcus Camby .60 1.50
TCP9 Paul Pierce 1.00 2.50
TCP10 Steve Francis .75 2.00
TCP11 Chris Webber .75 2.00
TCP12 Jalen Rose .60 1.50
TCP13 John Stockton 1.00 2.50
TCP14 Larry Hughes .60 1.50
TCP15 Ray Allen .75 2.00
TCP16 Alonzo Mourning 1.00 2.50
TCP17 Keith Van Horn .60 1.50
TCP18 Scottie Pippen 1.25 3.00
TCP19 Jerry Stackhouse .60 1.50
TCP20 Andre Miller .60 1.50

2000-01 Topps Combos 1

Randomly inserted into series one packs at one in 12, this 10-card insert pairs superstar caliber players together on the same card. Card backs carry a "TC" prefix.

COMPLETE SET (10) 6.00 15.00
TC1 Shaquille O'Neal 2.00 5.00
Kobe Bryant
TC2 Stephon Marbury .60 1.50
Allen Iverson
TC3 Chris Webber .60 1.50
Jason Williams
TC4 Patrick Ewing .60 1.50
Dikembe Mutombo
Alonzo Mourning
TC5 Tracy McGrady 2.00 5.00
Vince Carter
TC6 Tim Duncan 1.00 2.50
Grant Hill
TC7 Elton Brand .60 1.50
Lamar Odom
Steve Francis
TC8 Gary Payton .75 2.00
Jason Kidd
TC9 Damon Stoudamire .75 2.00
Scottie Pippen
Steve Smith
Rasheed Wallace
TC10 Tim Duncan 1.25 3.00
Kevin Garnett

2000-01 Topps Combos 2

Randomly inserted in series two packs at one in 12 (one in four HTA), this 10-card set features illustrated cards from NBA superstars and rookies as featured on the cover of Sports Collector's Digest. Card backs carry a "TC" prefix.

COMPLETE SET (10) 4.00 10.00
TC1 Hakeem Olajuwon .40 1.00
TC2 Patrick Ewing .40 1.00
TC3 Karl Malone .40 1.00
TC4 Scottie Pippen .60 1.50
TC5 Reggie Miller .40 1.00
TC6 Shaquille O'Neal 1.50 4.00
Magic Johnson
TC7 Marcus Fizer .40 1.00
Stromile Swift
Kenyon Martin
TC8 Speedy Claxton .40 1.00
Keyon Dooling
Jamal Crawford
TC9 Mike Miller .40 1.00
DerMarr Johnson
Darius Miles
TC10 Magic Johnson .60 1.50
Mateen Cleaves

2000-01 Topps East Meets West Game Jerseys

Randomly inserted in series two HTA packs only at one in 598, this two-card set features jersey swatches of two players who battled in the 2000 NBA Finals. Each card features the Topps "Genuine Issue" sticker. Card backs carry an "EMW" prefix.

EMW1 Shaquille O'Neal 50.00 100.00
Reggie Miller
EMW2 Glen Rice 12.50 30.00
Jalen Rose

2000-01 Topps Final Piece Game Jerseys

Randomly inserted in series two packs at one in 517 (one in 52 HTA), this 23-card set features swatches of game-worn jerseys from the 2000 NBA Finals. Each card features the Topps "Genuine Issue" sticker. Card backs carry a "FP" prefix.

FP1 Shaquille O'Neal A 25.00 60.00
FP2 Glen Rice A 6.00 15.00
FP3 Robert Horry A 8.00 20.00
FP4 Rick Fox A 8.00 20.00
FP5 Brian Shaw A 5.00 12.00
FP6 Ron Harper A 6.00 15.00
FP7 Derek Fisher A 8.00 20.00
FP8 A.C. Green B 6.00 15.00
FP9 John Salley A 5.00 12.00
FP10 Travis Knight A 5.00 12.00
FP11 Devean George A 5.00 12.00
FP12 Reggie Miller A 20.00 50.00
FP13 Jalen Rose A 6.00 15.00
FP14 Dale Davis A 5.00 12.00
FP15 Rik Smits A 5.00 12.00
FP16 Mark Jackson A 8.00 20.00
FP17 Travis Best A 5.00 12.00
FP18 Austin Croshere A 5.00 12.00
FP19 Derrick McKey A 5.00 12.00
FP20 Sam Perkins A 5.00 12.00
FP21 Chris Mullin A 15.00 40.00
FP22 Jonathan Bender A 5.00 12.00
FP23 Zan Tabak A 5.00 12.00

2000-01 Topps Flight Club

Randomly inserted in series two packs at one in 18 (one in six HTA), this 20-card set features players who spend their time above the rim. Card backs carry a "FC" prefix.

COMPLETE SET (20) 15.00 30.00
FC1 Vince Carter 1.50 4.00
FC2 Larry Hughes .60 1.50
FC3 Steve Francis .75 2.00
FC4 Tracy McGrady 1.25 3.00
FC5 Jerry Stackhouse .60 1.50
FC6 Kobe Bryant 4.00 10.00
FC7 Kevin Garnett 1.50 4.00
FC8 Michael Finley .75 2.00
FC9 Latrell Sprewell .60 1.50
FC10 Antonio McDyess .60 1.50
FC11 Lamar Odom .75 2.00
FC12 Shareef Abdur-Rahim .60 1.50
FC13 Chris Webber .75 2.00
FC14 Eddie Jones .75 2.00
FC15 Scottie Pippen 1.25 3.00
FC16 Grant Hill 1.00 2.50
FC17 Paul Pierce 1.00 2.50
FC18 Shawn Marion .75 2.00
FC19 Rasheed Wallace .75 2.00
FC20 Tim Duncan 1.50 4.00

2000-01 Topps Game Jerseys

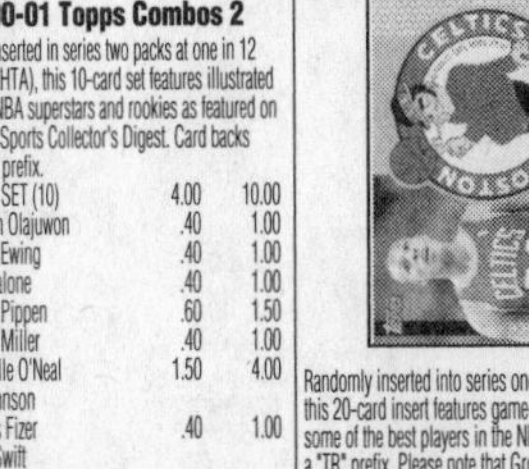

Randomly inserted into series one packs at one in 502, this 20-card insert features game-used jersey cards of some of the best players in the NBA. Card backs carry a "TR" prefix. Please note that Group A were inserted into packs at 1:971 H/R and 1:151 HTA, and Group B were inserted at 1:1946 H/R and 1:302 HTA

TR1 Richard Hamilton A 2.50 6.00
TR2 Tracy Murray A 2.00 5.00
TR3 Chris Whitney B 2.00 5.00
TR4 Jahidi White A 2.00 5.00
TR5 Rod Strickland A 2.50 6.00
TR6 Mitch Richmond B 2.50 6.00
TR7 Juwan Howard B 2.50 6.00

TR8 Isaac Austin B 2.00 5.00
TR9 Michael Smith A 2.00 5.00
TR10 Lorenzo Williams B 2.00 5.00
TR11 Tony Battie B 2.00 5.00
TR12 Antoine Walker A 2.50 6.00
TR13 Adrian Griffin A 2.00 5.00
TR14 Vitaly Potapenko A 2.00 5.00
TR15 Pervis Ellison A 2.00 5.00
TR16 Paul Pierce B 4.00 10.00
TR17 Eric Williams B 2.00 5.00
TR18 Dana Barros B 2.00 5.00
TR19 Walter McCarty A 2.00 5.00
TR20 Danny Fortson B 2.00 5.00

2000-01 Topps Hidden Gems

Randomly inserted into series one packs at one in 11, this 10-card insert features players that quietly put up big numbers every year. Card backs carry a "HG" prefix.

COMPLETE SET (10) 2.50 6.00
HG1 Karl Malone .50 1.25
HG2 Latrell Sprewell .30 .75
HG3 Kobe Bryant 2.00 5.00
HG4 Michael Finley .40 1.00
HG5 Jalen Rose .30 .75
HG6 Reggie Miller .40 1.00
HG7 John Stockton .50 1.25
HG8 Terrell Brandon .25 .60
HG9 Nick Van Exel .30 .75
HG10 Allan Houston .30 .75

2000-01 Topps Hobby Masters

Randomly inserted into series one HTA packs only at one in 5, this 10-card insert features players that are in high demand in the hobby market. Card backs carry a "HM" prefix.

COMPLETE SET (10) 8.00 20.00
HM1 Kevin Garnett 1.25 3.00
HM2 Jason Williams .60 1.50
HM3 Tim Duncan 1.25 3.00
HM4 Tracy McGrady 1.00 2.50
HM5 Kobe Bryant 3.00 8.00
HM6 Allen Iverson 1.25 3.00
HM7 Elton Brand .60 1.50
HM8 Steve Francis .60 1.50
HM9 Vince Carter 1.25 3.00
HM10 Chris Webber .60 1.50

2000-01 Topps Magic Johnson Reprints

Randomly inserted into series one packs, this 14-card set features 7 reprinted Magic Johnson cards (1:508), and 7 autographed Magic Johnson reprint cards (1:7088). According to Topps, less than 75 of each autographs exist.

COMPLETE SET (7) 40.00 70.00
COMMON CARD (1-7) 5.00 12.00
COMMON AU (1-7) 60.00 120.00

2000-01 Topps Jumbos

Inserted as a series one box-topper in hobby boxes, this 10-card jumbo sized set pairs superstar caliber players together on the same card and parallels the Topps Combos insert. Card backs carry a "TC" prefix.

2000-01 Topps No Limit

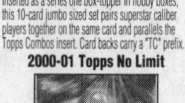

Randomly inserted in series two packs at one in six (one in two HTA), this 20-card set features NBA superstars that have propelled themselves past the competition. Card backs carry a "NL" prefix.

COMPLETE SET (20) 10.00 20.00
NL1 Kobe Bryant 2.00 5.00
NL2 Kevin Garnett .75 2.00
NL3 Vince Carter .75 2.00
NL4 Tracy McGrady .60 1.50
NL5 Tim Duncan .75 2.00
NL6 Elton Brand .40 1.00
NL7 Lamar Odom .40 1.00
NL8 Larry Hughes .30 .75
NL9 Chris Webber .40 1.00
NL10 Shareef Abdur-Rahim .30 .75
NL11 Jason Kidd .60 1.50
NL12 Gary Payton .40 1.00
NL13 Paul Pierce .50 1.25
NL14 Stromile Swift .40 1.00
NL15 Darius Miles .40 1.00
NL16 Mike Miller .75 2.00
NL17 Jason Williams .40 1.00
NL18 Jamal Crawford .60 1.50
NL19 Marcus Fizer .40 1.00
NL20 DerMarr Johnson .40 1.00

2000-01 Topps Quantum Leaps

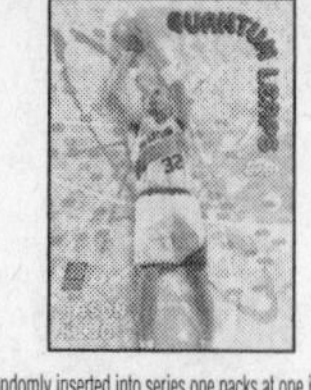

Randomly inserted into series one packs at one in 22, this 10-card insert features players that continue to show improvement everytime they step onto the court. Card backs carry a "QL" prefix.

COMPLETE SET (10) 6.00 15.00
QL1 Chris Webber .60 1.50
QL2 Antonio McDyess .50 1.25
QL3 Stephon Marbury .50 1.25
QL4 Shareef Abdur-Rahim .50 1.25
QL5 Kobe Bryant 3.00 8.00
QL6 Jason Kidd 1.00 2.50
QL7 Elton Brand .60 1.50
QL8 Lamar Odom .60 1.50
QL9 Kevin Garnett 1.25 3.00
QL10 Jerry Stackhouse .50 1.25

2000-01 Topps Rise to Stardom

Randomly inserted in series two packs at one in 36 (one in 12 HTA), this 10-card set depicts Rookie of the Year award winners from the past eight seasons. Card backs carry a "RS" prefix.

COMPLETE SET (10) 8.00 20.00
RS1 Elton Brand .75 2.00
RS2 Steve Francis .75 2.00
RS3 Vince Carter 1.50 4.00
RS4 Tim Duncan 1.50 4.00
RS5 Allen Iverson 1.50 4.00
RS6 Damon Stoudamire .60 1.50
RS7 Grant Hill 1.00 2.50
RS8 Jason Kidd 1.25 3.00
RS9 Chris Webber .75 2.00
RS10 Shaquille O'Neal 2.00 5.00

2001-02 Topps Promos

This two-card cello pack was sent out to dealers and distributors with press material to debut the new Topps set design.

COMPLETE SET (2) 2.00 5.00
PP1 Shaquille O'Neal 1.50 4.00
PP2 Tim Duncan 1.25 3.00

2001-02 Topps

Released in August 2001, this 258-card base set contains 220 veterans and 35 rookies. The set also contains 1 NBA 2001 Championship Team photo card. The cards are standard size and have solid borders on the two vertical sides of the card. The borders on the horizontal sides of the card look as though they are crumbling apart. The cards feature color action shots with the Topps logo in the upper right-hand corner and the player's name in the lower right-hand corner. A special Preseason EXCH card was included in the product, and there was speculation that this would be a limited Michael Jordan card. In the end it was redeemed for a special Pau Gasol card. Topps was packaged in 36-pack boxes with ten cards per pack and packs carrying a suggested retail price of $1.49. HTA packs were packaged in 12-pack boxes with packs containing 38 cards, including one draft pick, and carried a suggested retail price of $5.00.

COMPLETE SET (257) 40.00 80.00
COMP.SET w/o RC (220) 15.00 30.00
1 Shaquille O'Neal .50 1.25
2 Travis Best .12 .30
3 Allen Iverson .40 1.00
4 Shawn Marion .20 .50
5 Rasheed Wallace .20 .50
6 Antonio Daniels .12 .30
7 Rashard Lewis .20 .50
8 John Starks .12 .30
9 Stromile Swift .12 .30
10 Vince Carter .30 .75
11 George Lynch .12 .30
12 Kendall Gill .12 .30
13 Glen Rice .15 .40
14 Glenn Robinson .15 .40
15 Wally Szczerbiak .15 .40
16 Rick Fox .15 .40
17 Darius Miles .12 .30
18 Jermaine O'Neal .20 .50
19 Erick Dampier .12 .30
20 Tracy McGrady .30 .75
21 Kevin Garnett .40 1.00
22 Tim Thomas .12 .30
23 Larry Hughes .15 .40
24 Jerry Stackhouse .15 .40
25 Voshon Lenard .12 .30
26 Howard Eisley .12 .30
27 Clarence Weatherspoon .12 .30
28 Marcus Fizer .12 .30
29 Elden Campbell .12 .30
30 Tim Duncan .40 1.00
31 Doug Christie .12 .30
32 Keon Clark .12 .30
33 Patrick Ewing .25 .60
34 Hakeem Olajuwon .25 .60
35 Stephen Jackson .15 .40
36 Larry Johnson .20 .50
37 Eric Snow .12 .30
38 Tom Gugliotta .12 .30
39 Scottie Pippen .30 .75
40 Chris Webber .20 .50
41 David Robinson .30 .75
42 Elton Brand .20 .50
43 Theo Ratliff .12 .30
44 Paul Pierce .25 .60
45 Jamal Mashburn .15 .40
46 Eric Williams .12 .30
47 DerMarr Johnson .12 .30
48 Andre Miller .15 .40
49 Dirk Nowitzki .30 .75
50 Kobe Bryant 1.00 2.50
51 Keyon Dooling .12 .30
52 Brian Grant .12 .30
53 Ervin Johnson .12 .30
54 Anthony Peeler .12 .30
55 Dikembe Mutombo .20 .50
56 Steve Smith .15 .40
57 Hedo Turkoglu .20 .50
58 Terry Porter .12 .30
59 Lorenzen Wright .12 .30
60 Jason Terry .20 .50
61 Vitaly Potapenko .12 .30
62 Derrick Coleman .15 .40
63 Ron Artest .20 .50
64 Chris Gatling .12 .30
65 Chris Mihm .12 .30
66 Reggie Miller .20 .50
67 Lamar Odom .20 .50
68 Ron Harper .15 .40
69 Baron Davis .20 .50
70 Brad Miller .20 .50
71 Shawn Bradley .12 .30
72 James Posey .12 .30
73 Ben Wallace .20 .50
74 Marc Jackson .12 .30
75 Maurice Taylor .12 .30
76 Aaron McKie .12 .30
77 Grant Hill .25 .60
78 Arvydas Sabonis .15 .40
79 Peja Stojakovic .20 .50
80 Jason Kidd .30 .75
81 Vin Baker .15 .40
82 Morris Peterson .12 .30
83 Bryon Russell .12 .30
84 Michael Dickerson .12 .30
85 Christian Laettner .12 .30
86 Jerome Williams .12 .30
87 Desmond Mason .15 .40
88 Sean Elliott .12 .30
89 Marcus Camby .15 .40
90 Stephon Marbury .15 .40
91 Joel Przybilla .12 .30
92 Alonzo Mourning .25 .60
93 Brian Shaw .12 .30
94 Austin Croshere .12 .30
95 Mookie Blaylock .15 .40
96 Mateen Cleaves .12 .30
97 Nick Van Exel .15 .40
98 Michael Finley .20 .50
99 Jamal Crawford .15 .40
100 Steve Francis .20 .50
101 Tim Hardaway .20 .50
102 Sam Cassell .15 .40
103 Shammond Williams .12 .30
104 DeShawn Stevenson .12 .30
105 Bryant Reeves .12 .30
106 Richard Hamilton .15 .40
107 Antonio Davis .12 .30
108 Brent Barry .12 .30
109 Derek Anderson .12 .30
110 Kenny Anderson .15 .40
111 Brevin Knight .12 .30
112 Tyrone Nesby .12 .30
113 Erick Strickland .12 .30
114 Jacque Vaughn .12 .30
115 John Stockton .25 .60
116 Alvin Williams .12 .30
117 Speedy Claxton .12 .30
118 Bo Outlaw .12 .30
119 Jahidi White .12 .30
120 Karl Malone .25 .60
121 Charles Oakley .15 .40
122 Malik Rose .12 .30
123 Avery Johnson .15 .40
124 Toni Kukoc .15 .40
125 Bryant Stith .12 .30
126 P.J. Brown .12 .30
127 Ron Mercer .12 .30
128 Lamond Murray .12 .30
129 Steve Nash .30 .75
130 Raef LaFrentz .12 .30
131 Corliss Williamson .12 .30
132 Danny Fortson .12 .30
133 Chris Porter .12 .30
134 Shandon Anderson .12 .30
135 Jalen Rose .15 .40
136 Corey Maggette .15 .40
137 Horace Grant .15 .40
138 Eddie Jones .15 .40
139 Chauncey Billups .20 .50
140 Ray Allen .20 .50
141 Terrell Brandon .12 .30
142 Keith Van Horn .15 .40
143 Allan Houston .15 .40
144 Mark Jackson .15 .40
145 Pat Garrity .12 .30
146 Anfernee Hardaway .30 .75
147 Iakovos Tsakalidis .12 .30
148 Damon Stoudamire .15 .40
149 Bobby Jackson .12 .30
150 Antawn Jamison .20 .50
151 Kenny Thomas .12 .30
152 Jonathan Bender .12 .30
153 Jeff McInnis .12 .30
154 Robert Horry .15 .40
155 Anthony Mason .12 .30
156 Lindsey Hunter .12 .30
157 LaPhonso Ellis .15 .40
158 Jamie Feick .12 .30
159 Kurt Thomas .12 .30
160 Gary Payton .20 .50
161 Rod Strickland .15 .40
162 Bonzi Wells .12 .30
163 Scot Pollard .12 .30
164 Raja Bell RC .75 2.00
165 Rodney Rogers .12 .30
166 John Amaechi .12 .30
167 Darrell Armstrong .12 .30
168 Aaron Williams .12 .30
169 Latrell Sprewell .15 .40
170 Radoslav Nesterovic .12 .30
171 Anthony Carter .12 .30
172 Quentin Richardson .15 .40
173 Primoz Brezec RC .60 1.50
174 Michael Olowokandi .12 .30
175 Jason Williams .15 .40
176 Ruben Patterson .12 .30
177 Chris Childs .12 .30
178 Greg Ostertag .12 .30
179 Mike Bibby .20 .50
180 Mitch Richmond .15 .40
181 Donyell Marshall .12 .30
182 Dale Davis .12 .30
183 Tony Delk .12 .30
184 Mike Miller .20 .50
185 Charlie Ward .12 .30
186 Kenyon Martin .20 .50
187 Walt Williams .12 .30
188 Al Harrington .15 .40
189 Chucky Atkins .12 .30
190 Kevin Willis .12 .30
191 Juwan Howard .15 .40
192 Jim Jackson .12 .30
193 Antonio McDyess .15 .40
194 Jamaal Magloire .12 .30
195 Mark Blount .12 .30
196 Fred Hoiberg .12 .30
197 Nazr Mohammed .12 .30
198 Antoine Walker .15 .40
199 Wang Zhizhi .15 .40
200 Shareef Abdur-Rahim .15 .40
201 Chris Whitney .12 .30
202 David Wesley .12 .30
203 Matt Harpring .15 .40
204 George McCloud .12 .30
205 Joe Smith .15 .40
206 Cuttino Mobley .15 .40
207 Tyrone Hill .12 .30
208 Clifford Robinson .12 .30
209 Vlade Divac .15 .40
210 Eddie Robinson .12 .30
211 Michael Curry .12 .30
212 Courtney Alexander .12 .30
213 Grant Long .12 .30
214 Dan Majerle .15 .40
215 Points Leaders .20 .50
Shaquille O'Neal
Kobe Bryant
Chris Webber
Allen Iverson
Jerry Stackhouse
Vince Carter
216 Rebound Leaders .20 .50
Shaquille O'Neal
Tim Duncan
Antonio McDyess
Dikembe Mutombo
Ben Wallace
Antonio Davis
217 Assist Leaders .20 .50
Jason Kidd
John Stockton
Nick Van Exel
Andre Miller
Mark Jackson
Sam Cassell
218 Steals Leaders .20 .50
Mookie Blaylock
Doug Christie
Jason Kidd
Allen Iverson
Baron Davis
Ron Artest
219 Block Leaders .20 .50
Shawn Bradley
Shaquille O'Neal
Adonal Foyle
Theo Ratliff
Jermaine O'Neal
Dikembe Mutombo
220 Team Championship .40 1.00
Los Angeles Lakers
221 Kwame Brown RC .60 1.50
222 Tyson Chandler RC 1.00 2.50
223 Pau Gasol RC 2.00 5.00
224 Eddy Curry RC 1.00 2.50
225 Jason Richardson RC 1.25 3.00
226 Shane Battier RC 1.25 3.00
227 Eddie Griffin RC .60 1.50
228 DeSagana Diop RC .60 1.50
229 Rodney White RC .60 1.50
230 Joe Johnson RC 1.50 4.00
231 Kedrick Brown RC .60 1.50
232 Vladimir Radmanovic RC .60 1.50
233 Richard Jefferson RC 1.25 3.00
234 Troy Murphy RC 1.00 2.50
235 Steven Hunter RC .60 1.50
236 Kirk Haston RC .60 1.50
237 Michael Bradley RC .60 1.50
238 Jason Collins RC .60 1.50
239 Zach Randolph RC 1.50 4.00
240 Brendan Haywood RC .75 2.00
241 Joseph Forte RC .60 1.50
242 Jeryl Sasser RC .60 1.50
243 Brandon Armstrong RC .60 1.50
244 Gerald Wallace RC 1.00 2.50
245 Samuel Dalembert RC .75 2.00
246 Jamaal Tinsley RC .75 2.00
247 Tony Parker RC 2.50 6.00
248 Trenton Hassell RC .60 1.50
249 Gilbert Arenas RC 1.00 2.50
250 Jeff Trepagnier RC .60 1.50
251 Damone Brown RC .60 1.50
252 Loren Woods RC .60 1.50
253 Ousmane Cisse RC .60 1.50
254 Ken Johnson RC .60 1.50
255 Kenny Satterfield RC .60 1.50
256 Alvin Jones RC .60 1.50
257 Pau Gasol Preseason 5.00 12.00
TRSC Shaquille O'Neal JSY 100.00 200.00
Kareem Abdul-Jabbar JSY
NNO Gilbert Arenas SPEC AU 15.00 30.00

2001-02 Topps MVP Promotion

Randomly inserted in hobby packs at the rate of one in 104, Retail packs at the rate of one in 80, and HTA packs at the rate of one in 27, this 250-card set parallels the base Topps set enhanced with the MVP Promotion Stamp. The winning cards from this set offer collectors a complete set of MVP cards or a chance for a trip to the 2002 NBA Finals.

*MVP STARS: 12X TO 30X BASE CARD HI
*MVP RCs: 2X TO 5X BASE CARD HI
EXCHANGE DEADLINE 08/02/02

2001-02 Topps All-Star Remnants

This 21-card insert set is randomly inserted in hobby packs at a rate of 1:160; retail pack at a rate of 1:123; and 1:42 HTA. The set contains swatches of game-worn warm-ups. The cards are standard size, borderless, and printed with a horizontal design. The color action shot of the featured player is set on a background that resembles that of broken glass. The Topps logo is found in the upper right-hand corner with the featured player's team logo in the lower left-hand corner.

TRAH Allan Houston 3.00 8.00
TRAM Andre Miller 3.00 8.00
TRBD Baron Davis 4.00 10.00
TRCW Chris Webber 4.00 10.00
TRDM Darius Miles 2.50 6.00
TRDN Dirk Nowitzki 6.00 15.00
TREB Elton Brand 4.00 10.00
TRJS Jerry Stackhouse 3.00 8.00
TRJT Jason Terry 4.00 10.00
TRJW Jason Williams 3.00 8.00
TRLO Lamar Odom 4.00 10.00
TRMB Mike Bibby 4.00 10.00
TRQR Quentin Richardson 3.00 8.00
TRRA Ray Allen 4.00 10.00
TRRH Richard Hamilton 3.00 8.00
TRRL Raef LaFrentz 2.50 6.00
TRRW Rasheed Wallace 4.00 10.00
TRSF Steve Francis 4.00 10.00
TRSM Shawn Marion 4.00 10.00
TRSO Shaquille O'Neal 10.00 25.00
TRTD Tim Duncan 8.00 20.00

2001-02 Topps All-Star Remnants Autographs

This 10-card insert set is randomly inserted in hobby packs in Groups A thru D. Group A: 1:5848; 1:1514 HTA, Group B: 1:8506; 1:2297 HTA, Group C: 1:17328; 1:4442 HTA, and Group D: 1:77976; 1:22208 HTA. The set contains both swatches of game-worn warm-ups and player autographs. The cards are standard size, borderless, and printed with a horizontal design. The color action shot of the featured player is set on a background that resembles that of broken glass. The Topps Certified Autograph logo is found in the lower right-hand corner.

TREB Elton Brand/42 B 20.00 50.00
TRJT Jason Terry/31 A 20.00 50.00
TRRH Richard Hamilton/32 A 20.00 50.00
TRRL Raef LaFrentz/45 B 10.00 25.00
TRSM Shawn Marion/32 A 50.00 100.00
TRSO Shaquille O'Neal/34 A 150.00 300.00
TRTD Tim Duncan/21 C 200.00 400.00

2001-02 Topps Autographs

This 12-card insert set is randomly inserted in Groups A thru C. Group A: 1:2515 H, 1:1958 R, 1:660 HTA; Group B: 1:1006 H, 1:766 R, 1:264 HTA; Group C: 1:838 H, 1:647 R, 1:221 HTA. The set is standard size and set on borderless cards. The set features players who have signed their Topps cards, including a group of Team Topps stars who exclusively sign with Topps. The cards of Team Topps members feature the "Team Topps" logo.

TAJB Jonathan Bender B 5.00 12.00
TAAJ Antawn Jamison C 5.00 12.00
TABD Baron Davis C 5.00 12.00
TADM Desmond Mason B 5.00 12.00
TAEB Elton Brand B 5.00 12.00
TAJT Jason Terry B 5.00 12.00
TAKAJ Kareem Abdul-Jabbar A 50.00 120.00
TALJ Larry Johnson A 30.00 80.00
TAMJ Magic Johnson A 50.00 120.00
TARH Richard Hamilton C 8.00 20.00
TASM Shawn Marion B 5.00 12.00
TASO Shaquille O'Neal A 40.00 100.00

2001-02 Topps Kareem Abdul-Jabbar Reprints

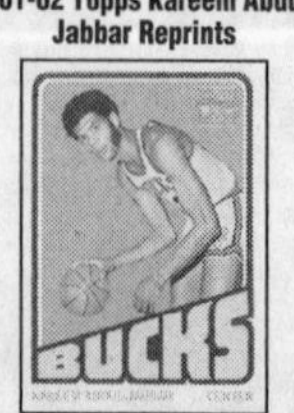

This 13-card insert set is randomly inserted in hobby packs at a rate of 1:14, retail packs at a rate of 1:11, and 1:4 HTA. These cards are reprints of some of Kareem Abdul-Jabbar's original Topps cards.

COMPLETE SET (13) 10.00 25.00
COMMON CARD (1-13) 1.25 3.00

2001-02 Topps Kareem Abdul-Jabbar Reprints Autographs

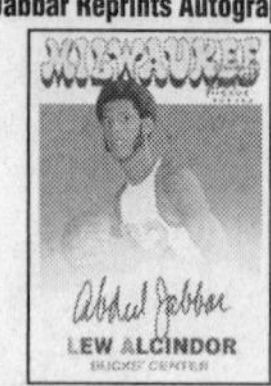

This 13-card insert set is randomly inserted in packs at a rate of 1:9747 and 1:22208 HTA and parallels the base Kareem Abdul-Jabbar Reprints set enhanced with autographs.

COMMON CARD (1-13) 50.00 120.00
1 Lew Alcindor 100.00 200.00

2001-02 Topps Lottery Legends

Randomly inserted in hobby packs at the rate of one in six, retail packs at the rate of one in five, and HTA packs at the rate of one in two, this 13-card set features top draft picks from the past few years on an all foil card with two color player photos and the words "Lottery Legends" and player's draft number centered along the bottom of the card.

COMPLETE SET (13) 5.00 12.00
LL1 Shaquille O'Neal 1.00 2.50
LL2 Steve Francis .40 1.00
LL3 Darius Miles .25 .60
LL4 Stephon Marbury .30 .75
LL5 Vince Carter .60 1.50
LL6 Antoine Walker .30 .75
LL7 Jason Williams .30 .75
LL8 Larry Hughes .30 .75
LL9 Tracy McGrady .60 1.50
LL10 Paul Pierce .50 1.25
LL11 Allan Houston .30 .75
LL12 Austin Croshere .25 .60
LL13 Kobe Bryant 2.00 5.00

2001-02 Topps Mad Game

Randomly inserted in hobby packs at the rate of one in 38, retail packs at the rate of one in 29, and HTA packs at the rate of one in 10, this 10-card set features a full color player action photo on an all foil backdrop where a "shadow" of his photo appears. The top of the card contains the words "Mad Game" which appears to be outlined in gold and filled with diamonds in a true bling-bling display.

COMPLETE SET (10) 10.00 25.00
MG1 Allen Iverson 1.50 4.00
MG2 Shaquille O'Neal 2.00 5.00
MG3 Tim Duncan 1.50 4.00
MG4 Vince Carter 1.25 3.00
MG5 Kevin Garnett 1.50 4.00
MG6 Kobe Bryant 4.00 10.00
MG7 Tracy McGrady 1.25 3.00
MG8 Steve Francis .75 2.00
MG9 Chris Webber .75 2.00
MG10 Darius Miles .50 1.25

2001-02 Topps NBA All-Star Jam Session

Produced by Topps, this set was given away at the All-Star Jam Session show from February 8th-10th exclusively at the Topps booth. These cards utilized the same card stock as the 2001-02 Topps set-blue borders and gold print, but are enhanced with the All-Star game logo in the lower left hand corner on an all holo-foil card stock.

COMPLETE SET (9) 6.00 15.00
1 Shaquille O'Neal 2.00 5.00
2 Tim Duncan 1.50 4.00
3 Allen Iverson 1.50 4.00
4 Tracy McGrady 1.25 3.00
5 Steve Francis .75 2.00
6 Elton Brand .75 2.00
7 Jamaal Tinsley 1.00 2.50
8 Jamaal Tinsley 1.00 2.50
9 Chris Webber .75 2.00

2001-02 Topps Team Topps

Randomly inserted in hobby packs at the rate of one in eight, retail packs at the rate of one in seven, and HTA packs at the rate of one in two, this 10-card set features player's selected by Topps to represent the company as "Team Topps." Each card features an all-foil card stock with full color player action photos and player names printed vertically along the left edge of the card in white.

COMPLETE SET (9) 4.00 10.00
TT1 Shaquille O'Neal 1.25 3.00
TT2 Tim Duncan 1.00 2.50
TT3 Antawn Jamison .50 1
TT4 Jason Terry .50 1
TT5 Baron Davis .50 1
TT6 Elton Brand .50 1
TT7 Peja Stojakovic .50 1
TT8 Richard Hamilton .40 1
TT9 Shawn Marion .50 1
TT10 Team Shot .75 2

2002-03 Topps Promos

This six-card cello pack was distributed with press material to dealers and distributors to debut the new design of 2002-03 Topps.

COMPLETE SET (6) 3.00 8
PP1 Tim Duncan 1.25 3
PP2 Steve Francis .75 2
PP3 Ray Allen .75 2
PP4 Steve Nash 1.00 2
PP5 Kenyon Martin .75 2
PP6 Andre Miller .75 2

2002-03 Topps

Released in late August 2002, Topps boasts a 220-card set divided up into 184 veteran player cards and 35 rookie cards. Card numbers 179-183 showcase six league leaders, Western Conference players on the front and Eastern Conference players on the back, a card number 184 features the NBA Championship winning Lakers from the 2001-02 season. Base card have blue borders, full color player action photos, a silver foil highlights along the bottom for the player' name, team name, and the Topps logo. Topps was packaged in three different ways: Hobby, Retail, and Home Team Advantage packs. Hobby cases contain eight boxes, where boxes contained 36 packs, and packs contained 10 cards and carried a suggested retail price of $1.49. Retail boxes contained 24 pack where packs contained 13 cards and carried a suggested retail price of $1.99, and HTA cases had boxes, where boxes contained six packs, and packs contained 34 cards and carried a suggested retail pr of $5.00. Also included in packs were the Around th World scratch-off cards. These cards had five foil scratch-off circles around a three point arc where th or more "Hits" were winners. The The 10 Grand Priz winners received autographed jersey, one uncut she of Topps Basketball and one copy of the Around the World set. The 1000 First Prize winners received an uncut sheet of Topps basketball and one set of Arou the World, and 5000 third prize winners received the Around the World set.

COMPLETE SET (220) 40.00 80.
1 Shaquille O'Neal .50 1.
2 Pau Gasol .25
3 Allen Iverson .30
4 Tom Gugliotta .12
5 Rasheed Wallace .20
6 Peja Stojakovic .20
7 Jason Richardson .20
8 Rashard Lewis .20
9 Morris Peterson .12
10 Michael Jordan 1.50 4.
11 Matt Harpring .15
12 Shareef Abdur-Rahim .15
13 Antoine Walker .15
14 Stephon Marbury .15
15 Jamal Mashburn .15
16 Eddy Curry .15
17 Jumaine Jones .12
18 Wang Zhizhi .12
19 James Posey .12
20 Jason Kidd .30
21 Jerry Stackhouse .15
22 Kenny Thomas .12
23 Ron Mercer .12
24 Jeff Mcinnis .12
25 Kobe Bryant 1.00 2.
26 Jason Williams .15
27 Eddie Jones .15
28 Anthony Mason .12
29 Kenyon Martin .20
30 Kevin Garnett .40 1.
31 Kurt Thomas .12
32 Karl Malone .25
33 Patrick Ewing .25
34 Antonio McDyess .15
35 Dirk Nowitzki .30
36 Wesley Person .12
37 Theo Ratliff .12
38 Jarron Collins .12
39 Horace Grant .15
40 Vince Carter .30
41 Desmond Mason .15
42 Todd MacCulloch .12
43 Bobby Jackson .12
44 Vlade Divac .15
45 Keith Van Horn .15
46 Bo Outlaw .12
47 Eric Snow .12
48 Grant Hill .25
49 Terrell Brandon .12
50 Tracy Mcgrady .30
51 Tim Thomas .12
52 Loren Woods .12
53 Michael Redd .20
54 Stromile Swift .12
55 Dikembe Mutombo .20
56 Richard Jefferson .20
57 Glenn Robinson .15
58 Samaki Walker .12
59 Quentin Richardson .15
60 Elton Brand .20
61 Reggie Miller .20
62 Eddie Griffin .12
63 Gilbert Arenas .20
64 Zeljko Rebraca .12
65 Donnell Harvey .12
66 Juwan Howard .15
67 Nick Van Exel .15
68 Donyell Marshall .12
69 Tyson Chandler .15
70 Baron Davis .20
71 Nazr Mohammed .12
72 Marcus Camby .15
73 Jamaal Magloire .12

4 Marcus Fizer .12 .30
5 Steve Francis .20 .50
6 Aaron Mckie .12 .30
7 Anfernee Hardaway .30 .75
8 Scottie Pippen .30 .75
9 Mike Bibby .20 .50
0 Paul Pierce .25 .60
1 Tony Delk .12 .30
2 Kwame Brown .12 .30
3 Andrei Kirilenko .20 .50
4 Keon Clark .12 .30
5 Alvin Williams .12 .30
6 Brent Barry .12 .30
7 David Robinson .30 .75
8 Doug Christie .12 .30
9 Derek Anderson .12 .30
0 Chris Webber .20 .50
1 Speedy Claxton .12 .30
2 Robert Horry .15 .40
3 Allan Houston .15 .40
4 Kerry Kittles .12 .30
5 Wally Szczerbiak .15 .40
6 Jonathan Bender .12 .30
7 Sam Cassell .15 .40
8 Rod Strickland .15 .40
9 Shane Battier .20 .50
00 Tim Duncan .40 1.00
01 Jermaine O'Neal .20 .50
02 Cuttino Mobley .15 .40
03 Danny Fortson .12 .30
04 Clifford Robinson .12 .30
05 Tim Hardaway .20 .50
06 Steve Nash .25 .60
07 Zydrunas Ilgauskas .15 .40
08 Travis Best .12 .30
09 Eddie Robinson .12 .30
10 David Wesley .12 .30
11 Kenny Anderson .15 .40
12 DerMarr Johnson .12 .30
13 Courtney Alexander .12 .30
14 Brian Grant .12 .30
15 Lorenzen Wright .12 .30
16 Corliss Williamson .12 .30
17 Malik Rose .12 .30
18 Tony Parker .25 .60
19 Vladimir Radmanovic .12 .30
20 Hedo Turkoglu .20 .50
21 Damon Stoudamire .15 .40
22 Brendan Haywood .12 .30
23 Jalen Rose .15 .40
24 Mike Miller .20 .50
25 Derrick Coleman .15 .40
26 Mark Jackson .15 .40
27 Raef Lafrentz .12 .30
28 Ben Wallace .20 .50
29 Larry Hughes .15 .40
30 Ray Allen .20 .50
31 Gary Payton .20 .50
32 P.J. Brown .12 .30
33 Derek Fisher .15 .40
34 Michael Olowokandi .12 .30
35 Jamaal Tinsley .12 .30
36 Moochie Norris .12 .30
37 Chris Mihm .12 .30
38 Antawn Jamison .20 .50
39 Chucky Atkins .12 .30
40 Mengke Bateer .12 .30
41 Brad Miller .20 .50
42 Michael Finley .20 .50
43 Andre Miller .15 .40
44 Michael Dickerson .12 .30
45 Elden Campbell .12 .30
46 Kedrick Brown .12 .30
47 Jason Terry .15 .40
48 Chris Whitney .12 .30
49 Bryon Russell .12 .30
50 Darius Miles .12 .30
51 Latrell Sprewell .15 .40
52 Darrell Armstrong .12 .30
53 Joe Johnson .20 .50
54 Bonzi Wells .12 .30
55 Jim Jackson .12 .30
56 Steve Smith .15 .40
57 Vin Baker .15 .40
58 Antonio Davis .12 .30
59 John Stockton .25 .60
60 Shawn Marion .20 .50
61 Devean George .12 .30
62 Clarence Weatherspoon .12 .30
63 Rick Fox .15 .40
64 Chauncey Billups .20 .50
65 Joe Smith .15 .40
66 Laphonso Ellis .15 .40
67 Maurice Taylor .12 .30
68 Lamond Murray .12 .30
69 Lamar Odom .20 .50
70 Toni Kukoc .15 .40
71 Alonzo Mourning .25 .60
72 Antonio Daniels .12 .30
73 Troy Murphy .20 .50
74 Hakeem Olajuwon .25 .60
75 Richard Hamilton .15 .40
76 Rodney Rogers .12 .30
77 Ruben Patterson .12 .30
78 Dale Davis .12 .30
79 Shaquille O'Neal .50 1.25
Tim Duncan
Kobe Bryant
Allen Iverson
Paul Pierce
Tracy McGrady
80 Tim Duncan .20 .50
Kevin Garnett
Danny Fortson
Ben Wallace
Dikembe Mutombo
Jermaine O'Neal
81 Gary Payton .20 .50
John Stockton
Stephon Marbury
Andre Miller
Jason Kidd
Baron Davis
82 Doug Christie .20 .50
Karl Malone
John Stockton
Allen Iverson
Ron Artest
Jason Kidd
83 Raef LaFrentz .20 .50
Tim Duncan
Erick Dampier
Ben Wallace
Alonzo Mourning
Dikembe Mutombo
84 Team Championship Card .60 1.50
85 Yao Ming RC 2.50 6.00
86 Jay Williams RC 1.00 2.50
87 Mike Dunleavy RC 1.00 2.50
188 Drew Gooden RC 1.25 3.00
189 Nikoloz Tskitishvili RC .75 2.00
190 DaJuan Wagner RC .75 2.00
191 Nene Hilario RC 1.00 2.50
192 Chris Wilcox RC .75 2.00
193 Amare Stoudemire RC 2.00 5.00
194 Caron Butler RC 1.25 3.00
195 Jared Jeffries RC .75 2.00
196 Melvin Ely RC .75 2.00
197 Marcus Haislip RC .75 2.00
198 Fred Jones RC .75 2.00
199 Bostjan Nachbar RC .75 2.00
200 Jiri Welsch RC .75 2.00
201 Juan Dixon RC 1.00 2.50
202 Curtis Borchardt RC .75 2.00
203 Ryan Humphrey RC .75 2.00
204 Kareem Rush RC .75 2.00
205 Qyntel Woods RC .75 2.00
206 Casey Jacobsen RC .75 2.00
207 Tayshaun Prince RC 1.00 2.50
208 Frank Williams RC .75 2.00
209 John Salmons RC 1.00 2.50
210 Chris Jefferies ERR RC .75 2.00
Photo of Kareem Rush
211 Sam Clancy RC .75 2.00
212 Dan Gadzuric RC .75 2.00
213 Matt Barnes RC 1.00 2.50
214 Robert Archibald RC .75 2.00
215 Vincent Yarbrough RC .75 2.00
216 Dan Dickau RC .75 2.00
217 Carlos Boozer RC 1.50 4.00
218 Tito Maddox RC .75 2.00
219 Chris Owens RC .75 2.00
220 Ronald Murray RC .75 2.00

2002-03 Topps Black

Randomly inserted in Hobby packs at the rate of one in 16, retail packs at the rate of one in 18, and HTA packs at the rate of one in five, this 220-card set parallels the base Topps set with a black border and sequential numbering on the card back in gold foil ink to 500.
*BLACK STARS: 5X TO 12X BASE CARD HI
*BLACK RCs: 1.5X TO 4X BASE CARD HI

2002-03 Topps All-Star Relic Remnants

Randomly inserted in Hobby packs at the rate of one in 149, Retail packs at the rate of one in 540 and HTA packs at the rate of one in 40, this 15-card set places full color player action photos over a "wood court" backdrop featuring the NBA All-Star 2002 logo. The bottom right hand corner showcases an oval swatch of a pice of game worn memorabilia from the 2002 All-Star Game.
TRAI Allen Iverson 6.00 15.00
TRAW Antoine Walker 3.00 8.00
TRCW Chris Webber 4.00 10.00
TREB Elton Brand 4.00 10.00
TRJK Jason Kidd 6.00 15.00
TRJO Jermaine O'Neal 4.00 10.00
TRPS Peja Stojakovic 4.00 10.00
TRRA Ray Allen 4.00 10.00
TRSF Steve Francis 4.00 10.00
TRSN Steve Nash 5.00 12.00
TRTD Tim Duncan 8.00 20.00
TRAEB Elton Brand AU 25.00 60.00
TRATD Tim Duncan AU/25 175.00 350.00

2002-03 Topps Around The World

Here's the information we have on that set in our database of cards, it's cataloged under the name 2002-03 Topps Around the World: This redemption set was available out of regular 2002-03 Topps packs as part of Around the World game pieces. These cards had five foil scratch-off circles around a three point arc where if three or more of they circles were "Hits" the card could be redeemed for a prize. The 10 Grand Prize winners received an autographed jersey, one uncut sheet of Topps basketball and one copy of the Around the World set. The 1000 First Prize winners received an uncut sheet of Topps basketball and one set of Around the World, and 5000 third prize winners received the Around the World set. The set contains 24 cards.
COMPLETE SET (24) 12.00 30.00
AW1 Tim Duncan 1.25 3.00
AW2 Dirk Nowitzki 1.00 2.50
AW3 Pau Gasol .75 2.00
AW4 Steve Nash .75 2.00
AW5 Peja Stojakovic .60 1.50
AW6 Tony Parker .75 2.00
AW7 Hedo Turkoglu .60 1.50
AW8 Andrei Kirilenko .60 1.50
AW9 Dikembe Mutombo .60 1.50
AW10 Wang ZhiZhi .40 1.00
AW11 Michael Olowokandi .40 1.00
AW12 Vladimir Radmanovic .40 1.00
AW13 Nikoloz Tskitishvili .60 1.50
AW14 Shaquille O'Neal 1.50 4.00
AW15 Tracy McGrady 1.00 2.50
AW16 Nene Hilario .75 2.00
AW17 Kevin Garnett 1.25 3.00
AW18 Yao Ming 2.00 5.00
AW19 DaJuan Wagner .60 1.50
AW20 Mike Dunleavy .75 2.00
AW21 Caron Butler 1.00 2.50
AW22 Qyntel Woods .60 1.50
AW23 Drew Gooden 1.00 2.50
AW24 Chris Wilcox .60 1.50

2002-03 Topps Autographs

Randomly seeded in Hobby packs at the rate of one in 303 and HTA packs at the rate of one in 80, this 11-card set places full color player photography against a basketball backdrop. The bottom of the card fades to white where authentic player autographs appear. These cards are garnished with gold foil highlights and the Topps stamp of authenticity.
TAAH Al Harrington 4.00 10.00
TACA Courtney Alexander 4.00 10.00
TACB Chauncey Billups 6.00 15.00
TACM Corey Maggette 4.00 10.00
TADH Donnell Harvey 4.00 10.00
TAEB Erick Barkley 4.00 10.00
TAKA Kareem Abdul-Jabbar 40.00 100.00
TAMD Michael Doleac 4.00 10.00
TAMJ Marc Jackson 4.00 10.00
TARM Roshown McLeod 4.00 10.00
TASO Shaquille O'Neal 40.00 100.00

2002-03 Topps Coast to Coast

Randomly inserted in Hobby packs at the rate of one in 13, retail packs at the rate of one in 10 and HTA packs at the rate of one in two, this 20-card set places top NBA stars on an all holofoil card stock with a street sign background theme.
COMPLETE SET (20) 12.00 30.00
CC1 Tracy McGrady 1.00 2.50
CC2 Jason Kidd 1.00 2.50
CC3 Mike Bibby .60 1.50
CC4 Baron Davis .60 1.50
CC5 Steve Francis .60 1.50
CC6 Vince Carter 1.00 2.50
CC7 Kobe Bryant 3.00 8.00
CC8 Michael Jordan 5.00 12.00
CC9 Paul Pierce .75 2.00
CC10 Stephon Marbury .50 1.25
CC11 Ray Allen .60 1.50
CC12 Gary Payton .60 1.50
CC13 Shawn Marion .60 1.50
CC14 Steve Nash .75 2.00
CC15 Andre Miller .50 1.25
CC16 Jerry Stackhouse .50 1.25
CC17 Latrell Sprewell .50 1.25
CC18 Jason Richardson .60 1.50
CC19 Jamaal Tinsley .40 1.00
CC20 Tony Parker .75 2.00

2002-03 Topps Rookie Autographs

Randomly inserted in packs, this 15-card set features top draft picks at the NBA Rookie Photo Shoot in Jersey City, New Jersey in July 2002. The photos used on these cards were taken on Saturday, they were processed and printed, and the player's autographed the next day, Sunday. There are 50 of each card.
1 Drew Gooden 25.00 60.00
2 Nikoloz Tskitishvili 10.00 25.00
3 Marcus Haislip 10.00 25.00
4 Melvin Ely 10.00 25.00
5 Tayshaun Prince 25.00 60.00
6 Sam Clancy 10.00 25.00
7 Dan Gadzuric 10.00 25.00
8 Ryan Humphrey 10.00 25.00
9 Jared Jeffries 10.00 25.00
10 Fred Jones 20.00 50.00
11 Kareem Rush 20.00 50.00
12 John Salmons 12.00 30.00
13 Amare Stoudemire 125.00 250.00
14 Vincent Yarbrough 10.00 25.00
15 Ronald Murray 10.00 25.00

2002-03 Topps Shaq Attack Relics

Randomly inserted in Hobby packs at the rate of one in 319, Retail packs at the rate of one in 451, and HTA packs at the rate of one in 90, this five card set features Shaquille O'Neal. The cards are horizontally designed with a picture of Shaq on the left and a white break towards the right side. The white side contains a "Shaq Attack" logo in silver foil and a highlight/signifigant place in Shaq's career. The jersey swatch is in the shape of the featured state.
COMPLETE SET (5) 50.00 100.00
COMMON CARD (SA1-SA5) 12.00 30.00

2002-03 Topps Shaq Attack Relics Autographs

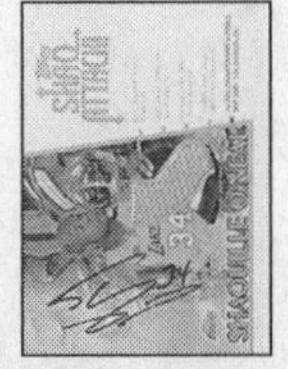

Randomly inserted in HTA packs, this five card set features Shaquille O'Neal. The cards are horizontally designed with a picture of Shaq on the left and a white break towards the right side. The white side contains a "Shaq Attack" logo in silver foil and a highlight/signifigant place in Shaq's career. The jersey swatch is in the shape of the featured state. On the photo, an authentic Shaquille O'Neal autograph appears, and each card is sequentially numbered.
SAA1 Shaquille O'Neal/72 75.00 200.00
SAA2 Shaquille O'Neal/33 150.00 300.00
SAA3 Shaquille O'Neal/92 75.00 200.00
SAA4 Shaquille O'Neal/32 150.00 300.00
SAA5 Shaquille O'Neal/34 150.00 300.00

2002-03 Topps Slam Duncan Relics

Randomly inserted in Hobby packs at the rate of one in 319, Retail packs at the rate of one in 451, and HTA packs at the rate of one in 90, this five card set pays tribute to Tim Duncan. Each card has an action photo of Duncan on the left coupled with a square swatch of a jersey, and a quick blurb about a signifigant event/place in Duncan's career.
COMPLETE SET (5) 30.00 60.00
COMMON CARD (SD1-SD5) 8.00 20.00

2002-03 Topps Slam Duncan Relics Autographs

Randomly inserted in HTA packs, this five card set pays tribute to Tim Duncan. Each card has an action photo of Duncan on the left coupled with a square swatch of a jersey, and a quick blurb about a signifigant event/place in Duncan's career. Autographs are signed along the left edge of the card, and each card is sequentially numbered.
SDA1 Tim Duncan/76 150.00 300.00
SDA2 Tim Duncan/97 100.00 200.00
SDA3 Tim Duncan/21 200.00 400.00
SDA4 Tim Duncan/21 200.00 400.00
SDA5 Tim Duncan/21 200.00 400.00

2002-03 Topps Top Tandems

Randomly inserted in Hobby packs at the rate of one in five, Retail packs at the rate of one in 10, and HTA packs at the rate of one in two, this 10-card set places two players from the same team on the card front. Two photos appear on this all holofoil card with the Topps Tandems logo in the upper left hand corner and the player's names along the right edge in red.
COMPLETE SET (10) 6.00 15.00
TT1 Antoine Walker .75 2.00
Paul Pierce
TT2 Shaquille O'Neal 3.00 8.00
Kobe Bryant
TT3 Derrick Coleman 1.00 2.50
Allen Iverson
TT4 Shawn Marion .60 1.50
Stephon Marbury
TT5 Dirk Nowitzki 1.00 2.50
Michael Finley
TT6 Michael Jordan 5.00 12.00
Richard Hamilton
TT7 Chris Webber .60 1.50
Peja Stojakovic
TT8 Vince Carter 1.00 2.50
Morris Peterson
TT9 Ray Allen .60 1.50
Glenn Robinson
TT10 Steve Francis .60 1.50
Cuttino Mobley

2002-03 Topps Verticality

Randomly seeded in Hobby packs at the rate of one in 10, Retail packs at the rate of one in eight, and HTA packs at the rate of one in three, this 15-card set places full color player action photos on a silver holofoil card stock with gold letter boxes running down both the left and right sides of the card. The left bar contains the player's name, and the right side contains the word, "Verticality" and the Topps logo.
COMPLETE SET (15) 10.00 25.00
V1 Shawn Marion .60 1.50
V2 Darius Miles .40 1.00
V3 Vince Carter 1.00 2.50
V4 Tracy McGrady 1.00 2.50
V5 Kobe Bryant 3.00 8.00
V6 Jason Richardson .60 1.50
V7 Steve Francis .60 1.50
V8 Michael Jordan 5.00 12.00
V9 Jerry Stackhouse .50 1.25
V10 Baron Davis .60 1.50
V11 Pau Gasol .75 2.00
V12 Kevin Garnett 1.25 3.00
V13 Kenyon Martin .60 1.50
V14 Shaquille O'Neal 1.50 4.00
V15 Jermaine O'Neal .60 1.50

2003-04 Topps Promos

Sent out by Topps, this six-card cello pack accompanied press materials to dealers and distributors to debut the new design of 2003-04 Topps.

COMPLETE SET (6) 5.00 12.00
PP1 Shaquille O'Neal 1.50 4.00
PP2 Tracy McGrady .75 2.00
PP3 Chris Webber .60 1.50
PP4 Kevin Garnett 1.25 3.00
PP5 Tim Duncan 1.00 2.50
PP6 Steve Nash .75 2.00

2003-04 Topps

Released in September 2003, Topps boasts a 249-card base set divided up into 220 veterans and 29 rookie cards. Each card places full-color player action photography on a design with silver foil highlights and white borders. Several different packaging was available for the product. Hobby/Retail boxes contain 36 packs of ten cards each with a suggested retail price of $1.59. HTA Jumbo boxes contain 12 packs of 35 cards each and a suggested retail price of $5. HTA First Edition packs were also available to hobby shop account owners, and these were packaged in 20 pack boxes of 10 cards each with a suggested retail price of $1.59.
COMPLETE SET (249) 25.00 60.00
1 Tracy McGrady .25 .60
2 DaJuan Wagner .12 .30
3 Allen Iverson .30 .75
4 Chris Webber .20 .50
5 Jason Kidd .30 .75
6 Stephon Marbury .15 .40
7 Jermaine O'Neal .20 .50
8 Antoine Walker .20 .50
9 Tony Parker .20 .50
10 Mike Bibby .20 .50
11 Yao Ming .40 1.00
12 Walter McCarty .12 .30
13 Steve Nash .25 .60
14 Paul Pierce .25 .60
15 Vince Carter .30 .75
16 Peja Stojakovic .20 .50
17 Kenny Anderson .15 .40
18 Kenyon Martin .20 .50
19 Pau Gasol .20 .50
20 Gary Payton .20 .50
21 Tim Duncan .30 .75
22 Jay Williams .12 .30
23 Jason Richardson .20 .50
24 Andre Miller .15 .40
25 Latrell Sprewell .15 .40
26 Darius Miles .12 .30
27 Richard Jefferson .20 .50
28 Shawn Marion .20 .50
29 Baron Davis .20 .50
30 Ben Wallace .20 .50
31 Reggie Miller .20 .50
32 Karl Malone .25 .60
33 Grant Hill .25 .60
34 Shaquille O'Neal .50 1.25
35 Steve Francis .20 .50
36 Kobe Bryant 1.00 2.50
37 Mike Dunleavy .15 .40
38 Glenn Robinson .15 .40
39 Allan Houston .15 .40
40 Kevin Ollie .12 .30
41 Dirk Nowitzki .30 .75
42 Elton Brand .20 .50
43 Juan Dixon .12 .30
44 Brian Grant .12 .30
45 Jason Terry .15 .40
46 Richard Hamilton .15 .40
47 Morris Peterson .12 .30
48 Ray Allen .20 .50
49 Scottie Pippen .30 .75
50 David Robinson .30 .75
51 Cuttino Mobley .15 .40
52 Jerry Stackhouse .15 .40
53 Marcus Camby .15 .40
54 Jalen Rose .15 .40
55 Dikembe Mutombo .20 .50
56 P.J. Brown .12 .30
57 Jumaine Jones .12 .30
58 Shawn Bradley .12 .30
59 Juwan Howard .15 .40
60 Clifford Robinson .12 .30
61 Antawn Jamison .20 .50
62 Raef LaFrentz .12 .30
63 Kareem Rush .12 .30
64 LaPhonso Ellis .12 .30
65 Toni Kukoc .20 .50
66 Mike Miller .20 .50
67 Aaron McKie .12 .30
68 Tom Gugliotta .12 .30
69 Dale Davis .12 .30
70 Jared Jeffries .12 .30
71 Alvin Williams .12 .30
72 DeShawn Stevenson .12 .30
73 Doug Christie .12 .30
74 Troy Hudson .12 .30
75 Jason Collins .12 .30
76 Eddie Griffin .12 .30
77 Vladimir Radmanovic .12 .30
78 Michael Olowokandi .12 .30
79 Michael Redd .20 .50
80 Tim Thomas .12 .30
81 Ron Mercer .12 .30
82 Shareef Abdur-Rahim .15 .40
83 Eduardo Najera .12 .30
84 Jon Barry .12 .30
85 Erick Dampier .12 .30
86 Derek Fisher .15 .40
87 Drew Gooden .15 .40
88 Dan Gadzuric .12 .30
89 Antonio McDyess .15 .40
90 Derrick Coleman .15 .40
91 Carlos Boozer .20 .50
92 Rasheed Wallace .20 .50
93 Antonio Davis .12 .30
94 Kwame Brown .12 .30
95 Manu Ginobili .25 .60
96 Eric Williams .12 .30
97 Trenton Hassell .12 .30
98 Chris Whitney .12 .30
99 Chauncey Billups .20 .50
100 Kevin Garnett .40 1.00
101 Marko Jaric .12 .30
102 Rasual Butler .12 .30
103 Gilbert Arenas .20 .50
104 Keith Van Horn .15 .40
105 Iakovos Tsakalidis .12 .30
106 Ruben Patterson .12 .30
107 Jarron Collins .12 .30
108 Rodney White .12 .30
109 Rashard Lewis .20 .50
110 Malik Rose .12 .30
111 Bobby Jackson .12 .30
112 Brendan Haywood .12 .30
113 Charlie Ward .12 .30
114 Courtney Alexander .12 .30
115 Kerry Kittles .12 .30
116 Wally Szczerbiak .15 .40
117 Darrell Armstrong .12 .30
118 Anfernee Hardaway .30 .75
119 Qyntel Woods .12 .30
120 Quentin Richardson .15 .40
121 Jonathan Bender .12 .30
122 Robert Horry .15 .40
123 Lorenzen Wright .12 .30
124 Malik Allen .12 .30
125 Sam Cassell .15 .40
126 Joe Smith .15 .40
127 Dion Glover .12 .30
128 Jamal Crawford .15 .40
129 Ricky Davis .15 .40
130 Nikoloz Tskitishvili .12 .30
131 Tyronn Lue .12 .30
132 Scott Padgett .12 .30
133 Jerome James .12 .30
134 Hedo Turkoglu .20 .50
135 Jamal Mashburn .15 .40
136 Pat Burke .12 .30
137 Joe Johnson .20 .50
138 Anthony Peeler .12 .30
139 Ron Artest .20 .50
140 Theo Ratliff .12 .30
141 Caron Butler .20 .50
142 Anthony Mason .12 .30
143 Vin Baker .12 .30
144 Donyell Marshall .12 .30
145 Nene .15 .40
146 Chucky Atkins .12 .30
147 Tyson Chandler .15 .40
148 Jason Williams .15 .40
149 Larry Hughes .15 .40
150 Stephen Jackson .15 .40
151 Kurt Thomas .12 .30
152 Mehmet Okur .15 .40
153 Amare Stoudemire .30 .75
154 Elden Campbell .12 .30
155 Jamaal Tinsley .12 .30
156 Chris Wilcox .12 .30
157 Rick Fox .12 .30
158 Gordan Giricek .12 .30
159 Voshon Lenard .12 .30
160 Brent Barry .12 .30
161 Dan Dickau .12 .30
162 Junior Harrington .12 .30
163 Jiri Welsch .12 .30
164 Vladimir Stepania .12 .30
165 Brad Miller .20 .50
166 Moochie Norris .12 .30
167 Wesley Person .12 .30
168 Greg Buckner .12 .30
169 Bonzi Wells .12 .30
170 Predrag Drobnjak .12 .30
171 Andrei Kirilenko .20 .50
172 Vlade Divac .15 .40
173 Rodney Rogers .12 .30
174 Kendall Gill .12 .30
175 Kenny Thomas .12 .30
176 Derek Anderson .12 .30
177 Steve Smith .12 .30
178 Christian Laettner .12 .30
179 Tony Delk .12 .30
180 Zydrunas Ilgauskas .15 .40
181 James Posey .12 .30
182 Tayshaun Prince .20 .50
183 Devean George .12 .30
184 Eddie Jones .15 .40
185 Corey Maggette .15 .40
186 Ira Newble .12 .30
187 Shane Battier .15 .40
188 Clarence Weatherspoon .12 .30
189 Eric Snow .12 .30
190 Damon Stoudamire .15 .40
191 Keon Clark .12 .30
192 Desmond Mason .15 .40
193 Matt Harpring .15 .40
194 Radoslav Nesterovic .12 .30
195 Jamaal Magloire .12 .30
196 Pat Garrity .12 .30
197 Fred Jones .15 .40
198 Tony Battie .12 .30
199 Tyrone Hill .12 .30
200 Adrian Griffin .12 .30
201 Nick Van Exel .15 .40
202 Shammond Williams .12 .30
203 Corliss Williamson .12 .30
204 Lamar Odom .20 .50
205 Travis Best .12 .30
206 Howard Eisley .12 .30
207 Jerome Williams .12 .30
208 David Wesley .12 .30
209 Bostjan Nachbar .12 .30
210 Marcus Fizer .12 .30
211 Michael Finley .20 .50
212 Troy Murphy .20 .50
213 Adonal Foyle .12 .30
214 Samaki Walker .12 .30
215 Lucious Harris .12 .30
216 Lindsey Hunter .12 .30
217 Stromile Swift .12 .30
218 Eddy Curry .15 .40
219 Kelvin Cato .12 .30
220 Chris Anderson .30 .75
221 LeBron James RC 10.00 25.00
222 Darko Milicic RC 1.00 2.50
223 Carmelo Anthony RC 2.50 6.00
224 Chris Bosh RC 2.00 5.00
225 Dwyane Wade RC 4.00 10.00
226 Chris Kaman RC 1.25 3.00
227 Kirk Hinrich RC 1.25 3.00
228 T.J. Ford RC 1.25 3.00
229 Mike Sweetney RC 1.00 2.50
230 Jarvis Hayes RC 1.00 2.50
231 Mickael Pietrus RC 1.00 2.50
232 Nick Collison RC 1.00 2.50
233 Marcus Banks RC 1.00 2.50
234 Luke Ridnour RC 1.25 3.00
235 Reece Gaines RC 1.00 2.50
236 Troy Bell RC 1.00 2.50
237 Zarko Cabarkapa RC 1.00 2.50
238 David West RC 1.25 3.00
239 Aleksandar Pavlovic RC 1.00 2.50
240 Dahntay Jones RC 1.00 2.50
241 Boris Diaw RC 1.25 3.00
242 Zoran Planinic RC 1.00 2.50
243 Travis Outlaw RC 1.25 3.00
244 Brian Cook RC 1.00 2.50
245 Carlos Delfino RC 1.25 3.00
246 Ndudi Ebi RC 1.00 2.50
247 Kendrick Perkins RC 1.50 4.00
248 Leandro Barbosa RC 1.25 3.00
249 Josh Howard RC 1.00 2.50

2003-04 Topps Black

Randomly inserted in Hobby packs at the rate of one in 29, Retail packs at the rate of one in 26 and HTA packs at the rate of one in nine, this 249-card set parallels the base Topps set enhanced with black borders and sequential numbering to 500.
1-220 SINGLES: 4X TO 10X BASE CARD HI
221-249 RCs: 1.25X TO 3X BASE CARD HI
221 LeBron James 50.00 125.00
223 Carmelo Anthony 10.00 25.00
225 Dwyane Wade 15.00 40.00

2003-04 Topps First Edition

First Edition boxes were distibuted to Home Team Advantage hobby dealers when this product was issued. Each card has a First Edition logo in the upper left hand corner. First Edition boxes contained 20 packs of ten cards each and carried a suggested retail price of $1.59.
1ST ED.SINGLES: 1.5X TO 4X BASE HI
1ST ED.RCs: 1X TO 2.5X BASE CARD HI

2003-04 Topps Gold

Inserted in Hobby packs at the rate of one in 91 and HTA packs at the rate of one in 25, this 249-card set parallels the base Topps set enhanced with gold highlights and sequential numbering to 99.
*1-220 SINGLES: 8X TO 20X BASE CARD HI
*221-249 RCs: 1.5X TO 4X BASE CARD HI

2003-04 Topps Highlight Zone

Inserted in Hobby packs at the rate of one in 16, Retail packs at the rate of one in 18 and HTA packs at the rate of one in six, this 20-card set features an all-foil card stock with full-color player photos set against an irridescent background designed to look like a TV.
COMPLETE SET (20) 12.50 30.00
HZ1 Paul Pierce 1.00 2.50
HZ2 Shaquille O'Neal 2.00 5.00
HZ3 Chris Webber .75 2.00
HZ4 Steve Francis .75 2.00
HZ5 Shawn Marion .75 2.00
HZ6 Elton Brand .75 2.00
HZ7 Peja Stojakovic .75 2.00
HZ8 Vince Carter 1.25 3.00
HZ9 Stephon Marbury .60 1.50
HZ10 Jerry Stackhouse .60 1.50
HZ11 Ray Allen .75 2.00
HZ12 Baron Davis .75 2.00
HZ13 Antoine Walker .75 2.00
HZ14 Jason Kidd 1.25 3.00
HZ15 Antawn Jamison .75 2.00
HZ16 Steve Nash 1.00 2.50
HZ17 Jason Richardson .75 2.00
HZ18 Ricky Davis .60 1.50
HZ19 Latrell Sprewell .60 1.50
HZ20 Kobe Bryant 4.00 10.00

2003-04 Topps Justice of the Court

Inserted in Hobby packs at the rate of one in eight, Retail packs at the rate of one in nine and HTA packs at the rate of one in three, this 20-card set is horzontally designed with a full-color player action photo on a white bordered backdrop.
COMPLETE SET (20) 8.00 20.00
JC1 Ben Wallace .50 1.25
JC2 Gary Payton .50 1.25
JC3 Shaquille O'Neal 1.25 3.00
JC4 Tim Duncan .75 2.00
JC5 Chris Webber .50 1.25
JC6 Dirk Nowitzki .75 2.00
JC7 Kevin Garnett 1.00 2.50
JC8 Shawn Marion .50 1.25
JC9 Karl Malone .60 1.50
JC10 Nene .40 1.00
JC11 Yao Ming 1.00 2.50
JC12 Kobe Bryant 2.50 6.00
JC13 Vince Carter .75 2.00
JC14 Elton Brand .50 1.25
JC15 Kenyon Martin .50 1.25
JC16 Amare Stoudemire .75 2.00
JC17 Pau Gasol .50 1.25

JC18 Derrick Coleman	.40	1.00
JC19 Ron Artest	.50	1.25
JC20 Rasheed Wallace	.50	1.25

2003-04 Topps Love it Live

Inserted in Hobby packs at the rate of one in eight, Retail packs at the rate of one in nine and HTA at the rate of one in three, this 20-card set is horizontally designed with a player action photo on the left and a portrait-style photo on the right.

COMPLETE SET (20)	10.00	25.00
LLAI Allen Iverson	.75	2.00
LLAS Amare Stoudemire	.75	2.00
LLBD Baron Davis	.50	1.25
LLCB Caron Butler	.50	1.25
LLCW Chris Webber	.50	1.25
LLDG Drew Gooden	.40	1.00
LLDN Dirk Nowitzki	.75	2.00
LLDW DaJuan Wagner	.30	.75
LLGP Gary Payton	.50	1.25
LLJO Jermaine O'Neal	.50	1.25
LLJS Jerry Stackhouse	.40	1.00
LLKB Kobe Bryant	2.50	6.00
LLKG Kevin Garnett	1.00	2.50
LLPP Paul Pierce	.60	1.50
LLSF Steve Francis	.50	1.25
LLSO Shaquille O'Neal	1.25	3.00
LLTD Tim Duncan	.75	2.00
LLTM Tracy McGrady	.60	1.50
LLVC Vince Carter	.75	2.00
LLYM Yao Ming	1.00	2.50

2003-04 Topps Love it Live Relics

Insert odds: Group A one in 48614 Hobby, one in 51840 Retail and one in 14090 HTA. Group B one in 2431 Hobby, one in 2142 Retail and one in 733 HTA. Group C one in 10568 Hobby, one in 9425 Retail and one in 3212 HTA. Group D one in 812 Hobby, one in 711 Retail and one in 244 HTA. Group E one in 5675 Hobby, one in 5040 Retail and one in 1712 HTA. This set parallels the design of the Love it Live set enhanced with a square swatch of memorabilia.

AI Allen Iverson B	6.00	15.00
AS Amare Stoudemire D	6.00	15.00
CB Caron Butler B	4.00	10.00
DG Drew Gooden B	3.00	8.00
DN Dirk Nowitzki E	6.00	15.00
DW DaJuan Wagner B	2.50	6.00
GP Gary Payton D	4.00	10.00
JO Jermaine O'Neal D	4.00	10.00
PP Paul Pierce D	5.00	12.00
SF Steve Francis C	4.00	10.00
SO Shaquille O'Neal B	10.00	25.00
TD Tim Duncan D	6.00	15.00
YM Yao Ming D	8.00	20.00

2003-04 Topps Mark of Excellence Autographs

Insert odds: Group A one in 12256 Hobby, one in 10961 Retail, one in 3663 HTA. Group B one in 4051 Hobby, one in 3583 Retail and one in 1221 HTA. Group C one in 1306 Hobby, one in 1144 Retail and one in 391 HTA. Group D one in 1217 Hobby, one in 1069 Retail and one in 366 HTA. Group E one in 522 Hobby, one in 457 Retail and one in 157 HTA. Each card places a full-color player action photo along the top of the card that fades into an area of white on the bottom for player autographs.

BB Brent Barry E	4.00	10.00
CA Carmelo Anthony B	30.00	80.00
EB Elton Brand D	4.00	10.00
FW Frank Williams E	4.00	10.00
JH Jarvis Hayes C	4.00	10.00
JO Jermaine O'Neal	6.00	15.00
JW Jerome Williams B	4.00	10.00
KH Kirk Hinrich D	8.00	20.00
KJ Ken Johnson E	4.00	10.00
LR Luke Ridnour C	5.00	12.00
MB Marcus Banks C	4.00	10.00
MP Morris Peterson E	4.00	10.00
MR Michael Redd B	5.00	12.00
MS Mike Sweetney C	4.00	10.00
NC Nick Collison D	4.00	10.00
RG Reece Gaines A	4.00	10.00
RR Rick Rickert C	4.00	10.00
SO Shaquille O'Neal E	40.00	80.00
TF T.J. Ford D	5.00	12.00
CBO Chris Bosh A	25.00	50.00
DGE Devean George E	4.00	10.00
DWE David West C	6.00	15.00
DWY Dwyane Wade C	50.00	125.00

2003-04 Topps Piece of a Dream Relics

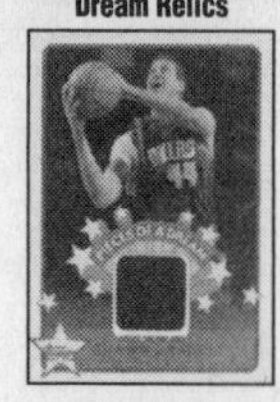

Insert odds: Group A one in 37396 Hobby, one in 34560 Retail and one in 10775 HTA. Group B one in 27518 Hobby, one in 25920 Retail and one in 8326 HTA. Group C one in 4882 Hobby, one in 12960 Retail and one in 4361 HTA. Group De one in 1140 Hobby, one in 1002 Retail and one in 343 HTA. Group E one in 1620 Hobby, one in 1422 Retail and one in 487 HTA. Each card places a full-color player action photo on the top side of the card and a square swatch of memorabilia centered along the bottom.

PDBD Baron Davis C	4.00	10.00
PDCW Chris Webber D	4.00	10.00
PDEB Elton Brand A	4.00	10.00
PDGH Grant Hill C	5.00	12.00
PDJK Jason Kidd A	6.00	15.00
PDJR Jason Richardson C	4.00	10.00
PDMD Mike Dunleavy C	3.00	8.00
PDMP Morris Peterson C	2.50	6.00
PDMR Michael Redd C	4.00	10.00
PDNT Nikoloz Tskitishvili C	2.50	6.00
PDSB Shawn Bradley D	2.50	6.00
PDSM Stephon Marbury D	3.00	8.00
PDSN Steve Nash C	5.00	12.00

2003-04 Topps Rookie Photo Shoot Autographs

Inserted in packs at the rate of one in 458 Hobby and one in 438 HTA, this 27-card set was produced and autographed at the NBA's Rookie Photo Shoot. 56 of each card were inserted into the production run of Topps, however, several more were printed and given to the players themselves.

TABC Brian Cook	15.00	40.00
TACA Carmelo Anthony	175.00	350.00
TACB Chris Bosh	150.00	300.00
TADJ Dahntay Jones	15.00	40.00
TADW1 David West	20.00	50.00
TADW2 Dwyane Wade	400.00	600.00
TAJH1 Jarvis Hayes	15.00	40.00
TAJH2 Josh Howard	15.00	40.00
TAJK Jason Kapono	15.00	40.00
TAKB Keith Bogans	15.00	40.00
TAKH Kirk Hinrich	40.00	100.00
TAKP Kendrick Perkins	40.00	100.00
TALB Leandro Barbosa	20.00	50.00
TALW Luke Walton	15.00	40.00
TAMB1 Marcus Banks	15.00	40.00
TAMB2 Matt Bonner	20.00	50.00
TAMP Mickael Pietrus	15.00	40.00
TAMS Mike Sweetney	15.00	40.00
TAMW Maurice Williams	25.00	60.00
TANE Ndudi Ebi	15.00	40.00
TARG Reece Gaines	15.00	40.00
TASB Steve Blake	20.00	50.00
TASV Slavko Vranes	15.00	40.00
TATB Troy Bell	15.00	40.00
TATF T.J. Ford	20.00	50.00
TATO Travis Outlaw	40.00	80.00
THAT Travis Hansen	15.00	40.00

2003-04 Topps Welcome to Atlanta Dual Relics

Welcome to Atlanta Dual Relics is divided up into two groups, Group A, cards WA1 to WA10, and Group B, WA11 to WA20. Group A was inserted at one in 1460 Hobby, one in 1283 Retail and one in 439 HTA, and Group B was inserted a one in 1042 Hobby, one in 1283 Retail and one in 190 HTA. The set is horizontally designed and places two players and two swatches of memorabilia from the 2003 All-Star Game in Atlanta.

WA1 Allen Iverson	10.00	25.00
DaJuan Wagner		
WA2 Shaquille O'Neal	25.00	50.00
Amare Stoudemire		
WA3 Jason Kidd	10.00	25.00
Tony Parker		
WA4 Tracy McGrady	10.00	25.00
Jason Richardson		
WA5 Jermaine O'Neal	8.00	20.00
Drew Gooden		
WA6 Shawn Marion	8.00	20.00
Richard Jefferson		
WA7 Paul Pierce	10.00	25.00
Caron Butler		
WA8 Stephon Marbury	8.00	20.00
Gilbert Arenas		
WA9 Ben Wallace	8.00	20.00
Carlos Boozer		
WA10 Tim Duncan	10.00	25.00
Nene Hilario		
WA11 Antoine Walker	8.00	20.00
Dirk Nowitzki		
WA12 Nene	8.00	20.00
Andrei Kirilenko		
WA13 Pau Gasol	8.00	20.00
Drew Gooden		
WA14 Jamaal Tinsley	8.00	20.00
DaJuan Wagner		
WA15 Shawn Marion	8.00	20.00
Jamal Mashburn		
WA16 Jason Kidd	10.00	25.00
Gary Payton		
WA17 Yao Ming	30.00	60.00
Shaquille O'Neal		
WA18 Jermaine O'Neal	8.00	20.00
Kevin Garnett		
WA19 Tracy McGrady	10.00	25.00
Allen Iverson		
WA20 Steve Nash	10.00	25.00
Steve Francis		

2004-05 Topps

This 249-card set was released in July/August, 2004. The set was issued in 10-card packs. Cards number 1-220 feature veterans while cards 221-249 feature Rookie Cards.

COMPLETE SET (249)	20.00	50.00
1 Allen Iverson	.30	.75
2 Eddy Curry	.15	.40
3 Stephon Marbury	.15	.40
4 Chris Bosh	.20	.50
5 Jason Kidd	.30	.75
6 Bonzi Wells	.12	.30
7 Fred Jones	.12	.30
8 Kobe Bryant	1.00	2.50
9 Ben Wallace	.20	.50
10 Darrell Armstrong	.12	.30
11 Yao Ming	.40	1.00
12 Udonis Haslem	.15	.40
13 Nene	.15	.40
14 Michael Redd	.20	.50
15 Carmelo Anthony	.40	1.00
16 Gary Trent	.12	.30
17 Larry Hughes	.15	.40
18 Kareem Rush	.12	.30
19 Antonio McDyess	.15	.40
20 Drew Gooden	.15	.40
21 Kevin Garnett	.40	1.00
22 DeShawn Stevenson	.12	.30
23 LeBron James	1.25	3.00
24 Robert Horry	.15	.40
25 Shareef Abdur-Rahim	.15	.40
26 Antonio Daniels	.12	.30
27 Scottie Pippen	.30	.75
28 Mike Dunleavy	.15	.40
29 Joe Smith	.15	.40
30 Vince Carter	.30	.75
31 Reggie Miller	.20	.50
32 Chris Wilcox	.12	.30
33 Rasheed Wallace	.20	.50
34 Paul Pierce	.25	.60
35 Tayshaun Prince	.20	.50
36 Raja Bell	.15	.40
37 Stephen Jackson	.15	.40
38 Eric Snow	.12	.30
39 Zydrunas Ilgauskas	.15	.40
40 Andre Miller	.15	.40
41 Dirk Nowitzki	.30	.75
42 Steve Francis	.20	.50
43 Ray Allen	.20	.50
44 Donyell Marshall	.12	.30
45 Pau Gasol	.20	.50
46 T.J. Ford	.15	.40
47 Andrei Kirilenko	.15	.40
48 Jamaal Tinsley	.12	.30
49 Earl Boykins	.12	.30
50 Tim Duncan	.30	.75
51 Erick Dampier	.12	.30
52 Nazr Mohammed	.12	.30
53 Tim Thomas	.12	.30
54 Keyon Dooling	.12	.30
55 Jason Kapono	.12	.30
56 Kirk Hinrich	.20	.50
57 Aaron McKie	.12	.30
58 Brad Miller	.20	.50
59 Al Harrington	.15	.40
60 Gary Payton	.20	.50
61 Nick Van Exel	.15	.40
62 Cuttino Mobley	.15	.40
63 Marcus Camby	.15	.40
64 Desmond Mason	.15	.40
65 Boris Diaw	.15	.40
66 Kenyon Martin	.20	.50
67 Mike Miller	.20	.50
68 Dwyane Wade	.60	1.50
69 Allan Houston	.15	.40
70 Jermaine O'Neal	.20	.50
71 Travis Hansen	.12	.30
72 Qyntel Woods	.12	.30
73 Jamal Crawford	.15	.40
74 Bobby Jackson	.12	.30
75 Derrick Coleman	.15	.40
76 Brian Skinner	.12	.30
77 Elton Brand	.20	.50
78 Rodney Rogers	.12	.30
79 Zarko Cabarkapa	.12	.30
80 Mike Bibby	.20	.50
81 Jim Jackson	.12	.30
82 Kurt Thomas	.12	.30
83 Vin Baker	.12	.30
84 Rodney White	.12	.30
85 Gordan Giricek	.12	.30
86 Jamal Mashburn	.20	.50
87 Kenny Thomas	.12	.30
88 Antoine Walker	.20	.50
89 Rasho Nesterovic	.12	.30
90 Shawn Marion	.20	.50
91 Shane Battier	.15	.40
92 Marquis Daniels	.12	.30
93 Ruben Patterson	.12	.30
94 Michael Olowokandi	.12	.30
95 Bruce Bowen	.12	.30
96 Caron Butler	.20	.50
97 Corliss Williamson	.12	.30
98 Jeff Foster	.12	.30
99 Carlos Boozer	.20	.50
100 Tracy McGrady	.25	.60
101 Stromile Swift	.12	.30
102 Keith Van Horn	.15	.40
103 Derek Fisher	.15	.40
104 Juwan Howard	.15	.40
105 Tony Parker	.20	.50
106 Jason Terry	.15	.40
107 Vlade Divac	.15	.40
108 Marcus Banks	.12	.30
109 Derek Anderson	.12	.30
110 Karl Malone	.25	.60
111 Baron Davis	.20	.50
112 Chris Crawford	.12	.30
113 Kwame Brown	.12	.30
114 Jiri Welsch	.12	.30
115 Maciej Lampe	.12	.30
116 Josh Howard	.20	.50
117 Luke Walton	.12	.30
118 John Salmons	.20	.50
119 David West	.20	.50
120 Amare Stoudemire	.25	.60
121 Antawn Jamison	.20	.50
122 Clarence Weatherspoon	.12	.30
123 Aleksandar Pavlovic	.12	.30
124 Kerry Kittles	.12	.30
125 Rafer Alston	.12	.30
126 Jarvis Hayes	.12	.30
127 Toni Kukoc	.15	.40
128 Latrell Sprewell	.15	.40
129 Keith Bogans	.12	.30
130 Jason Richardson	.20	.50
131 Brent Barry	.12	.30
132 Darko Milicic	.12	.30
133 Peja Stojakovic	.20	.50
134 Jerome Williams	.12	.30
135 Malik Rose	.12	.30
136 Quentin Richardson	.15	.40
137 Wally Szczerbiak	.15	.40
138 Theo Ratliff	.12	.30
139 Gilbert Arenas	.20	.50
140 Richard Hamilton	.15	.40
141 Rashard Lewis	.20	.50
142 Joe Johnson	.20	.50
143 P.J. Brown	.12	.30
144 Jason Collins	.12	.30
145 Chauncey Billups	.20	.50
146 Raef LaFrentz	.12	.30
147 Mickael Pietrus	.15	.40
148 Lamar Odom	.20	.50
149 Vladimir Radmanovic	.12	.30
150 Chris Webber	.20	.50
151 Tony Delk	.12	.30
152 Troy Hudson	.12	.30
153 David Wesley	.12	.30
154 Juan Dixon	.12	.30
155 Darius Miles	.12	.30
156 Gerald Wallace	.20	.50
157 Jalen Rose	.15	.40
158 Charlie Ward	.12	.30
159 Michael Finley	.20	.50
160 Jonathan Bender	.12	.30
161 Lorenzen Wright	.12	.30
162 George Lynch	.12	.30
163 Leandro Barbosa	.20	.50
164 Dajuan Wagner	.12	.30
165 Francisco Elson	.12	.30
166 Jerry Stackhouse	.15	.40
167 Manu Ginobili	.25	.60
168 Chris Kaman	.20	.50
169 James Posey	.12	.30
170 Doug Christie	.12	.30
171 Zoran Planinic	.12	.30
172 Maurice Taylor	.12	.30
173 Carlos Arroyo	.15	.40
174 Damon Stoudamire	.15	.40
175 Brian Cardinal	.12	.30
176 Devean George	.12	.30
177 Hedo Turkoglu	.20	.50
178 Anfernee Hardaway	.50	1.25
179 Tony Battie	.12	.30
180 Steve Nash	.25	.60
181 Glenn Robinson	.15	.40
182 Morris Peterson	.12	.30
183 Luke Ridnour	.15	.40
184 Mehmet Okur	.15	.40
185 Eddie Jones	.15	.40
186 Tyronn Lue	.12	.30
187 Raul Lopez	.12	.30
188 Lucious Harris	.12	.30
189 Alvin Williams	.12	.30
190 Zach Randolph	.15	.40
191 Steve Blake	.12	.30
192 Marko Jaric	.12	.30
193 Anthony Peeler	.12	.30
194 Troy Murphy	.15	.40
195 Jamaal Magloire	.12	.30
196 Brandon Hunter	.12	.30
197 Jason Williams	.15	.40
198 Corey Maggette	.15	.40
199 Ron Artest	.20	.50
200 Shaquille O'Neal	.50	1.25
201 Richard Jefferson	.20	.50
202 Kelvin Cato	.12	.30
203 Mark Blount	.12	.30
204 Eric Williams	.12	.30
205 Sam Cassell	.15	.40
206 Voshon Lenard	.12	.30
207 Bob Sura	.12	.30
208 Speedy Claxton	.12	.30
209 Samuel Dalembert	.12	.30
210 Tyson Chandler	.15	.40
211 Brian Grant	.12	.30
212 Stanislav Medvedenko	.12	.30
213 Danny Fortson	.12	.30
214 Chucky Atkins	.12	.30
215 Matt Harpring	.15	.40
216 Trenton Hassell	.12	.30
217 Ronald Murray	.12	.30
218 Jeff McInnis	.12	.30
219 Primoz Brezec	.12	.30
220 Ricky Davis	.15	.40
221 Dwight Howard RC	2.50	6.00
222 Emeka Okafor RC	1.25	3.00
223 Ben Gordon RC	1.00	2.50
224 Shaun Livingston RC	.75	2.00
225 Devin Harris RC	1.25	3.00
226 Josh Childress RC	.75	2.00
227 Luol Deng RC	1.25	3.00
228 Rafael Araujo RC	.75	2.00
229 Andre Iguodala RC	1.25	3.00
230 Luke Jackson RC	.75	2.00
231 Andris Biedrins RC	1.00	2.50
232 Robert Swift RC	.75	2.00
233 Sebastian Telfair RC	.75	2.00
234 Kris Humphries RC	.75	2.00
235 Al Jefferson RC	1.25	3.00
236 Kirk Snyder RC	.75	2.00
237 Josh Smith RC	1.25	3.00
238 J.R. Smith RC	1.00	2.50
239 Dorell Wright RC	1.25	3.00
240 Jameer Nelson RC	1.00	2.50
241 Pavel Podkolzine RC	.75	2.00
242 Viktor Khryapa RC	.75	2.00
243 Sergei Monia RC	.75	2.00
244 Delonte West RC	1.00	2.50
245 Tony Allen RC	1.00	2.50
246 Kevin Martin RC	1.00	2.50
247 Sasha Vujacic RC	.75	2.00
248 Beno Udrih RC	.75	2.00
249 David Harrison RC	.75	2.00

2004-05 Topps Black

Randomly inserted into packs, this is a complete parallel of the basic Topps set. Each card has black borders and were issued to a stated print run of 500 serial numbered sets.

*BLACK STARS: 4X TO 10X BASE HI
*BLACK RCs: 1.5X TO 4X BASE HI

2004-05 Topps First Edition

This parallel to the basic set was distributed through Topps network of HTA dealers. The cards, which had special "1st edition" logos on them were issued through 10 card packs with an $1.59 SRP which came 20 packs to a box and two boxes to a case.

*FIRST ED. STARS: 1.5X TO 4X BASE HI
*FIRST ED. RCs: .75X TO 2X BASE HI

2004-05 Topps Gold

Randomly inserted into packs, this is a parallel to the basic set. These cards, with gold borders, were issued to a stated print run of 99 serial numbered sets.

*GOLD STARS: 5X TO 12X BASE HI
*GOLD RCs: 3X TO 8X BASE HI

2004-05 Topps All-Star Support

These cards, of players who were teammates on either All-Star or Rookie Challenge teams, were issued at a stated rate of one in 18.

COMPLETE SET (20)	15.00	40.00
ASAW Ron Artest	1.00	2.50
Ben Wallace		
ASBD Carlos Boozer	1.00	2.50
Mike Dunleavy		
ASBF Kobe Bryant	2.00	5.00
Steve Francis		
ASBW Chris Bosh	2.00	5.00
Dwyane Wade		
ASCA Sam Cassell	1.00	2.50
Ray Allen		
ASCP Vince Carter	1.50	4.00
Paul Pierce		
ASDR Baron Davis	1.00	2.50
Michael Redd		
ASGD Kevin Garnett	1.50	4.00
Tim Duncan		
ASGP Manu Ginobili	1.00	2.50
Tayshaun Prince		
ASHH Kirk Hinrich	1.00	2.50
Jarvis Hayes		
ASIK Allen Iverson	1.50	4.00
Jason Kidd		
ASJA LeBron James	2.50	6.00
Carmelo Anthony		
ASKH Chris Kaman	1.00	2.50
Josh Howard		
ASMJ Ronald Murray	1.00	2.50
Marko Jaric		
ASMK Brad Miller	1.00	2.50
Andrei Kirilenko		
ASMM Jamaal Magloire	1.00	2.50
Kenyon Martin		
ASMO Tracy McGrady	1.25	3.00
Jermaine O'Neal		
ASNS Nene	1.00	2.50
Amare Stoudemire		
ASOM Shaquille O'Neal	1.50	4.00
Yao Ming		
ASSN Peja Stojakovic	1.25	3.00
Dirk Nowitzki		

2004-05 Topps All-Star Support Relics

These cards, featuring game-used relic pieces of players, were issued at a stated rate of one in 200 and issued to a stated print run of 250 serial numbered sets.

ASAW Ron Artest	5.00	12.00
Ben Wallace		
ASBD Carlos Boozer	8.00	20.00
Mike Dunleavy		
ASBF Kobe Bryant (no jsy)	6.00	15.00
Steve Francis		
ASBW Chris Bosh	8.00	20.00
Dwyane Wade		
ASCA Sam Cassell	5.00	12.00
Ray Allen (no jsy)		
ASCP Vince Carter (no jsy)	5.00	12.00
Paul Pierce		
ASDR Baron Davis	5.00	12.00
Michael Redd		
ASGD Kevin Garnett	10.00	25.00
Tim Duncan		
ASGP Manu Ginobili	5.00	12.00
Tayshaun Prince		
ASHH Kirk Hinrich	5.00	12.00
Jarvis Hayes		
ASJA LeBron James (no jsy)	8.00	20.00
Carmelo Anthony		
ASKH Chris Kaman	5.00	12.00
Josh Howard		
ASMJ Ronald Murray	5.00	12.00
Marko Jaric		
ASMK Brad Miller	5.00	12.00
Andrei Kirilenko		
ASMM Jamaal Magloire	5.00	12.00
Kenyon Martin		
ASMO Tracy McGrady	6.00	15.00
Jermaine O'Neal		
ASNS Nene	5.00	12.00
Amare Stoudemire		
ASOM Shaquille O'Neal	10.00	25.00
Yao Ming		
ASSN Peja Stojakovic	5.00	12.00
Dirk Nowitzki		

2004-05 Topps Drive N Thrive Relics

N Nene	2.50	6.00
AI Allen Iverson	5.00	12.00
AK Andrei Kirilenko	2.50	6.00
BD Baron Davis	3.00	8.00
CM Corey Maggette	2.50	6.00
DM Desmond Mason	2.50	6.00
DW Dwyane Wade	8.00	20.00
EG Manu Ginobili	4.00	10.00
GP Gary Payton	3.00	8.00
JC Jamal Crawford	2.50	6.00
JH Jarvis Hayes	2.00	5.00
JR Jason Richardson	3.00	8.00
JS Jerry Stackhouse	2.50	6.00
JT Jason Terry	2.50	6.00
KH Kirk Hinrich	3.00	8.00
KR Kareem Rush	2.00	5.00
MT Maurice Taylor	2.00	5.00
QR Quentin Richardson	2.50	6.00
QW Qyntel Woods	2.00	5.00
RH Richard Hamilton	2.50	6.00
RJ Richard Jefferson	3.00	8.00
RL Rashard Lewis	3.00	8.00
SF Steve Francis	3.00	8.00
SM Shawn Marion	3.00	8.00
SN Steve Nash	4.00	10.00
TM Tracy McGrady	4.00	10.00
CBO Carlos Boozer	3.00	8.00
CBO2 Chris Bosh	3.00	8.00
CBU Caron Butler	3.00	8.00
SMA Stephon Marbury	2.50	6.00

2004-05 Topps Great Expectations

Inserted at a stated rate of one in nine, these 20 cards feature some of the leading young NBA players.

COMPLETE SET (20)	8.00	20.00
AS Amare Stoudemire	.60	1.50
BD Boris Diaw	.40	1.00
CA Carmelo Anthony	1.00	2.50
CB Chris Bosh	.50	1.25
CK Chris Kaman	.50	1.25
DW Dwyane Wade	1.50	4.00
JH Jarvis Hayes	.30	.75
KH Kirk Hinrich	.50	1.25
LJ LeBron James	3.00	8.00
MD Mike Dunleavy	.40	1.00
MG Manu Ginobili	.60	1.50
MS Mike Sweetney	.30	.75
RM Ronald Murray	.30	.75
TP Tayshaun Prince	.50	1.25
YM Yao Ming	1.00	2.50
ZR Zach Randolph	.40	1.00
CAR Carlos Arroyo	.40	1.00
CBZ Carlos Boozer	.50	1.25
JHO Josh Howard	.50	1.25
TJF T.J. Ford	.40	1.00

2004-05 Topps Marks of Excellence

Randomly Inserted into packs at different rates, these 30 cards all feature authentic autographs. Since there were six different groupings of autographs, we have notated the group next to the player's name in our checklist.

BD Baron Davis B	12.00	30.00
BG Ben Gordon D	6.00	15.00
CA Carmelo Anthony D	15.00	40.00
CD Chris Duhon C	5.00	12.00
DH Devin Harris D	8.00	20.00
EO Emeka Okafor E	8.00	20.00
FJ Fred Jones D	5.00	12.00
JC Josh Childress D	5.00	12.00
JK Jason Kidd C	15.00	40.00
JO Jermaine O'Neal B	5.00	12.00
KS Kirk Snyder C	5.00	12.00
LD Luol Deng D	8.00	20.00
LJ Luke Jackson D	5.00	12.00
LO Lamar Odom C	6.00	15.00
PS Peja Stojakovic C	6.00	15.00
RH Richard Hamilton B	10.00	25.00
SL Shaun Livingston D	5.00	12.00
SM Stephon Marbury C	8.00	20.00
SO Shaquille O'Neal B	40.00	80.00
ST Sebastian Telfair D	5.00	12.00
TA Tony Allen C	6.00	15.00
TD Tim Duncan B	40.00	100.00
TM Tracy McGrady B	30.00	80.00
RAL Rafer Alston B	25.00	50.00

2004-05 Topps Peak Performer Relics

Inserted into packs at a stated rate of one in 399, these 24 cards feature game-used relics of the featured player.

AS Amare Stoudemire	4.00	10.00
AW Antoine Walker	3.00	8.00
BW Ben Wallace	3.00	8.00
CA Carmelo Anthony	6.00	15.00
EB Elton Brand	3.00	8.00
GR Glenn Robinson	2.50	6.00
JM Jamal Mashburn	3.00	8.00
KB Kwame Brown	2.00	5.00
KG Kevin Garnett	6.00	15.00
MB Mike Bibby	3.00	8.00
MR Michael Redd	3.00	8.00
PG Pau Gasol	3.00	8.00
PP Paul Pierce	4.00	10.00
PS Peja Stojakovic	3.00	8.00
SO Shaquille O'Neal	8.00	20.00
TD Tim Duncan	5.00	12.00
TP Tony Parker	3.00	8.00
TT Tim Thomas	2.00	5.00
YM Yao Ming	6.00	15.00
ZI Zydrunas Ilgauskas	2.50	6.00
KMA Kenyon Martin	3.00	8.00
RAL Ray Allen	3.00	8.00

2004-05 Topps Rock Rhythm

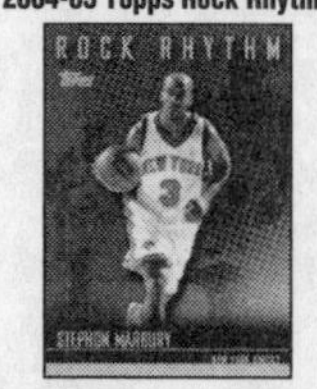

Inserted at a stated rate of one in 12, these cards feature players who can do great things on the basketball court.

COMPLETE SET (15)	12.50	30.00
AI Allen Iverson	1.00	2.50
BD Baron Davis	.60	1.50
BW Ben Wallace	.60	1.50
CA Carmelo Anthony	1.25	3.00
JK Jason Kidd	1.00	2.50
JR Jason Richardson	.60	1.50
KB Kobe Bryant	3.00	8.00
KG Kevin Garnett	1.25	3.00
LJ LeBron James	4.00	10.00
SM Stephon Marbury	.50	1.25
SO Shaquille O'Neal	1.50	4.00
TD Tim Duncan	1.00	2.50
TM Tracy McGrady	.75	2.00
VC Vince Carter	1.00	2.50
YM Yao Ming	1.25	3.00

2004-05 Topps Rookie Photo Shoot Autographs

Inserted at a stated rate of one in 721, these 39 cards feature autographs of players who participated in the Rookie Photo Shoot. Each of these cards were issued to a stated print run of 55 serial numbered sets.

AE Andre Emmett	15.00	40.00
AJ Al Jefferson	60.00	150.00
AV Anderson Varejao	20.00	50.00
BG Ben Gordon	75.00	150.00
BR Bernard Robinson	15.00	40.00
CD Chris Duhon	15.00	40.00
DH Dwight Howard	200.00	400.00
DH2 David Harrison	15.00	40.00
DW Dorell Wright	40.00	100.00
DW Delonte West	40.00	100.00
EO Emeka Okafor	40.00	100.00
JC Josh Childress	15.00	40.00
JN Jameer Nelson	30.00	80.00
JS Josh Smith	50.00	120.00
JV Jackson Vroman	15.00	40.00
KH Kris Humphries	15.00	40.00
KM Kevin Martin	40.00	100.00
KS Kirk Snyder	15.00	40.00
LC Lionel Chalmers	15.00	40.00
LD Luol Deng	60.00	120.00
LJ Luke Jackson	15.00	40.00
RA Rafael Araujo	15.00	40.00
RP Rickey Paulding	15.00	40.00
SL Shaun Livingston	15.00	40.00
ST Sebastian Telfair	15.00	40.00
TA Tony Allen	20.00	50.00
TA2 Trevor Ariza	15.00	40.00
DHA Devin Harris	60.00	120.00
HSJ Ha Seung-Jin	15.00	40.00
JRS J.R. Smith	75.00	150.00

2005-06 Topps

leased in Late August, 2005-06 Topps features a
5-card base set divided up into 220 veteran players,
rookie players and five celebrities. Each card is full
lor with a white border in usual Topps fashion.
pps was packaged in 36-pack boxes with packs
ntaining 10 cards and an SRP of $1.59, and Jumbo
A boxes of 12 packs containing 35 cards and an
P of $5.00.

MPLETE SET (255) 20.00 50.00
NPRICED OVERTIME PRINT RUN ONE SET
Grant Hill .25 .60
Keith Van Horn .15 .40
Quentin Richardson .15 .40
Damon Jones .12 .30
Lamar Odom .20 .50
Jamal Crawford .15 .40
Ben Gordon .20 .50
Zach Randolph .15 .40
Rafer Alston .12 .30
Gilbert Arenas .20 .50
Yao Ming .25 .60
Cuttino Mobley .15 .40
Josh Smith .20 .50
Ray Allen .20 .50
Vince Carter .30 .75
Kenyon Martin .20 .50
Mark Blount .12 .30
Carlos Arroyo .15 .40
Lee Nailon .12 .30
Bobby Simmons .12 .30
Tim Duncan .30 .75
Michael Redd .20 .50
Antawn Jamison .20 .50
Matt Bonner .12 .30
Shane Battier .15 .40
Nick Van Exel .20 .50
Jason Hart .12 .30
Nene .15 .40
Fred Jones .12 .30
Baron Davis .20 .50
Danny Fortson .12 .30
Caron Butler .20 .50
Allen Iverson .30 .75
Eddie Griffin .12 .30
Jameer Nelson .15 .40
Brent Barry .12 .30
Zydrunas Ilgauskas .15 .40
Jason Terry .15 .40
Mike Dunleavy .15 .40
Paul Pierce .25 .60
Reggie Miller .20 .50
Lorenzen Wright .12 .30
Peja Stojakovic .20 .50
Zaza Pachulia .12 .30
Dan Dickau .12 .30
Andre Iguodala .20 .50
Andrei Kirilenko .15 .40
Nenad Krstic .12 .30
Damon Stoudamire .15 .40
Emeka Okafor .20 .50
Jalen Rose .20 .50
Beno Udrih .12 .30
Jared Jeffries .12 .30
Ricky Davis .15 .40
Jason Kidd .30 .75
Eddy Curry .15 .40
Chauncey Billups .20 .50
Eric Snow .12 .30
Derek Fisher .15 .40
Amare Stoudemire .20 .50
Josh Childress .15 .40
Juwan Howard .15 .40
Mehmet Okur .12 .30
Jerome Williams .12 .30
Shaun Livingston .12 .30
Stephen Jackson .15 .40
Alonzo Mourning .25 .60
J.R. Smith .20 .50
Kobe Bryant 1.00 2.50
Dwight Howard .40 1.00
Manu Ginobili .20 .50
Kyle Korver .15 .40
Reggie Evans .12 .30
Shareef Abdur-Rahim .15 .40
Rafael Araujo .12 .30
Kirk Snyder .12 .30
Jermaine O'Neal .20 .50
Melvin Ely .12 .30
Chris Kaman .20 .50
Stephon Marbury .15 .40
Joe Smith .15 .40
Samuel Dalembert .12 .30
Luke Ridnour .15 .40
Sebastian Telfair .15 .40
Larry Hughes .15 .40
Tyson Chandler .15 .40
Michael Finley .20 .50
Drew Gooden .15 .40
Marcus Camby .15 .40
Dwyane Wade .50 1.25
Troy Murphy .15 .40
David Wesley .12 .30
Stromile Swift .12 .30
Clifford Robinson .12 .30
Sam Cassell .20 .50
Joe Johnson .20 .50
Bobby Jackson .12 .30
Derek Anderson .12 .30
Rashard Lewis .20 .50
0 Shaquille O'Neal .40 1.00
1 Keith McLeod .12 .30
2 Keith Bogans .12 .30
3 Al Harrington .15 .40
4 Anderson Varejao .15 .40
5 Al Jefferson .20 .50
6 Jerry Stackhouse .15 .40
7 Chris Duhon .12 .30
8 Earl Boykins .12 .30
9 Tayshaun Prince .20 .50
0 Carlos Boozer .20 .50
1 Rasual Butler .12 .30
2 Bonzi Wells .12 .30
3 Chris Wilcox .12 .30
114 Latrell Sprewell .15 .40
115 Richard Jefferson .20 .50
116 Toni Kukoc .12 .30
117 Doug Christie .12 .30
118 Brad Miller .20 .50
119 Antonio Daniels .12 .30
120 Richard Hamilton .15 .40
121 Kevin Garnett .40 1.00
122 Tony Parker .20 .50
123 Mike Sweetney .12 .30
124 Speedy Claxton .12 .30
125 Udonis Haslem .15 .40
126 Chucky Atkins .12 .30
127 David Harrison .12 .30
128 Jason Collier .12 .30
129 Pau Gasol .20 .50
130 Chris Webber .20 .50
131 Kelvin Cato .12 .30
132 Michael Olowokandi .12 .30
133 Ben Wallace .20 .50
134 Antoine Walker .15 .40
135 Marquis Daniels .12 .30
136 Ira Newble .12 .30
137 Austin Croshere .12 .30
138 Mike James .12 .30
139 Michael Doleac .12 .30
140 Carmelo Anthony .40 1.00
141 Sasha Vujacic .15 .40
142 Brian Cardinal .12 .30
143 Ron Mercer .12 .30
144 Tim Thomas .12 .30
145 Juan Dixon .12 .30
146 Rodney Rogers .12 .30
147 Hedo Turkoglu .20 .50
148 Nazr Mohammed .12 .30
149 Gerald Wallace .20 .50
150 Dirk Nowitzki .30 .75
151 Tony Allen .12 .30
152 Adonal Foyle .12 .30
153 Corey Maggette .15 .40
154 Rasheed Wallace .20 .50
155 Andre Miller .15 .40
156 Luol Deng .20 .50
157 Mike Miller .20 .50
158 Wally Szczerbiak .15 .40
159 Maurice Williams .15 .40
160 Chris Bosh .20 .50
161 Jamaal Magloire .12 .30
162 Leandro Barbosa .15 .40
163 Kevin Martin .20 .50
164 Jeff Foster .12 .30
165 Nick Collison .12 .30
166 Matt Harpring .15 .40
167 Kirk Hinrich .20 .50
168 Antonio McDyess .15 .40
169 Josh Howard .20 .50
170 Elton Brand .20 .50
171 Kurt Thomas .12 .30
172 Tyronn Lue .12 .30
173 Bob Sura .12 .30
174 Chris Mihm .12 .30
175 Jason Williams .15 .40
176 Jim Jackson .12 .30
177 Brevin Knight .12 .30
178 Eduardo Najera .12 .30
179 Jeff McInnis .12 .30
180 Jason Richardson .20 .50
181 Vladimir Radmanovic .12 .30
182 Jamaal Tinsley .12 .30
183 Eddie Jones .15 .40
184 P.J. Brown .12 .30
185 Troy Hudson .12 .30
186 Steve Francis .20 .50
187 Marc Jackson .12 .30
188 Kenny Thomas .12 .30
189 Joel Przybilla .12 .30
190 Steve Nash .25 .60
191 Devin Brown .12 .30
192 Donyell Marshall .12 .30
193 Raja Bell .15 .40
194 Brendan Haywood .12 .30
195 Primoz Brezec .12 .30
196 Gary Payton .20 .50
197 Devin Harris .20 .50
198 Predrag Drobnjak .12 .30
199 Dikembe Mutombo .20 .50
200 LeBron James 1.00 2.50
201 Marko Jaric .12 .30
202 Mike Bibby .20 .50
203 Desmond Mason .12 .30
204 Morris Peterson .12 .30
205 Jarvis Hayes .12 .30
206 Bruce Bowen .12 .30
207 Trevor Ariza .12 .30
208 Raef LaFrentz .12 .30
209 Brian Grant .12 .30
210 Shawn Marion .20 .50
211 Dan Gadzuric .12 .30
212 Andres Nocioni .12 .30
213 Tony Delk .12 .30
214 Darius Miles .12 .30
215 Gordan Giricek .12 .30
216 Rasho Nesterovic .12 .30
217 Jason Collins .12 .30
218 Mickael Pietrus .15 .40
219 Erick Dampier .12 .30
220 Tracy McGrady .25 .60
221 Andrew Bogut RC 1.25 3.00
222 Marvin Williams RC 1.00 2.50
223 Deron Williams RC 2.00 5.00
224 Chris Paul RC 3.00 8.00
225 Raymond Felton RC 1.25 3.00
226 Martell Webster RC .75 2.00
227 Charlie Villanueva RC 1.00 2.50
228 Channing Frye RC 1.00 2.50
229 Ike Diogu RC .75 2.00
230 Andrew Bynum RC 2.50 6.00
231 Fran Vazquez RC .75 2.00
232 Daniel Ewing RC .75 2.00
233 Sean May RC .75 2.00
234 Rashad McCants RC .75 2.00
235 Antoine Wright RC .75 2.00
236 Joey Graham RC .75 2.00
237 Danny Granger RC 1.50 4.00
238 Gerald Green RC 1.00 2.50
239 Hakim Warrick RC 1.00 2.50
240 Julius Hodge RC .75 2.00
241 Nate Robinson RC 1.00 2.50
242 Jarrett Jack RC .75 2.00
243 Francisco Garcia RC 1.00 2.50
244 Luther Head RC .75 2.00
245 Johan Petro RC .75 2.00
246 Jason Maxiell RC .75 2.00
247 Linas Kleiza RC .75 2.00
248 Ryan Gomes RC .75 2.00
249 Wayne Simien RC .75 2.00
250 David Lee RC 1.25 3.00
251 Shannon Elizabeth 1.50 4.00
252 Carmen Electra 1.50 4.00
253 Jenny McCarthy 1.50 4.00
254 Christie Brinkley 1.50 4.00
255 Jay-Z 1.50 4.00

2005-06 Topps Black

Inserted in hobby packs at the rate of one in 34 and sequentially numbered to 500, this 255-card set parallels the base Topps set enhanced with black borders.
*1-220 BLACK: 3X TO 8X BASE HI
*221-250 RC BLACK: 1X TO 2.5X BASE HI
*251-255 BLACK: 1X TO 2.5X BASE HI

2005-06 Topps First Edition

Distributed to Topps Home Team Advantage dealers and distributors, this 255-card set parallels the base Topps set enhanced with a foil first edition stamp. Packaging was the same as the base Topps, aside from the first edition lettering, and SRP upon release was $1.59.
*1-220 1ST ED.: 1.5X TO 4X BASE HI
*221-255 1ST ED.: .75X TO 2X BASE HI

2005-06 Topps Gold

Inserted in hobby packs at the rate of one in 34 and sequentially numbered to 99, this 255-card set parallels the base Topps set enhanced with gold borders.
*1-220 GOLD: 5X TO 12X BASE HI
*221-250 RC GOLD: 2X TO 5X BASE HI
*251-255 GOLD: 1.5X TO 4X BASE HI
69 Kobe Bryant 15.00 40.00

2005-06 Topps All-Star Altitude

Inserted in packs at the rate of one in 10, this 25-card set features players in their All-Star jerseys from the 2005 NBA All-Star Game in Denver. Full color photos are placed agains a sky background.
COMPLETE SET (25) 15.00 30.00
ASAI Allen Iverson 1.00 2.50
ASAJ Antawn Jamison .60 1.50
ASAS Amare Stoudemire .60 1.50
ASBW Ben Wallace .60 1.50
ASDN Dirk Nowitzki 1.00 2.50
ASDW Dwyane Wade 1.50 4.00
ASGA Gilbert Arenas .60 1.50
ASGH Grant Hill .75 2.00
ASJO Jermaine O'Neal .60 1.50
ASKB Kobe Bryant 3.00 8.00
ASKG Kevin Garnett 1.25 3.00
ASLJ LeBron James 3.00 8.00
ASMG Manu Ginobili .60 1.50
ASPP Paul Pierce .75 2.00
ASRA Ray Allen .60 1.50
ASRL Rashard Lewis .60 1.50
ASSM Shawn Marion .60 1.50
ASSN Steve Nash .75 2.00
ASSO Shaquille O'Neal 1.25 3.00
ASTD Tim Duncan 1.00 2.50
ASTM Tracy McGrady .75 2.00
ASVC Vince Carter 1.00 2.50
ASYM Yao Ming .75 2.00
ASZI Zydrunas Ilgauskas .50 1.25

2005-06 Topps All-Star Altitude Relics

Randomly seeded at the rate of one in 488, this set parallels the base All-Star Altitude set enhanced with a star-shaped swatch of All-Star weekend worn memorabilia. The cards are serially numbered out of 250.
BW Ben Wallace 2.50 6.00
DN Dirk Nowitzki 4.00 10.00
GA Gilbert Arenas 2.50 6.00
GH Grant Hill 3.00 8.00
JO Jermaine O'Neal 2.50 6.00
MG Manu Ginobili 2.50 6.00
RA Ray Allen 2.50 6.00
SM Shawn Marion 2.50 6.00
SN Steve Nash 3.00 8.00
SO Shaquille O'Neal 5.00 12.00
TD Tim Duncan 4.00 10.00
TM Tracy McGrady 3.00 8.00
YM Yao Ming 3.00 8.00
ZI Zydrunas Ilgauskas 2.00 5.00
JRS J.R. Smith 2.50 6.00

2005-06 Topps Celebrity Threads

Inserted in packs at the rate of one in 2198, this five card set features various celebritys with their photo on the right and a swatch of worn material on the left set on a yellow and white background.
CB Christie Brinkley 15.00 40.00
JZ Jay-Z 15.00 40.00
SE Shannon Elizabeth 15.00 40.00
CAE Carmen Electra 25.00 60.00
JMC Jenny McCarthy 25.00 60.00

2005-06 Topps Critical Component

Inserted in packs as the rate of one in 17, each card places a full-color photo of the player on the card front, set agains a blue background with the words, "Critical Component" in white along the top.
COMPLETE SET (15) 12.50 25.00
CC1 Ray Allen .75 2.00
CC2 Vince Carter 1.25 3.00
CC3 Tim Duncan 1.25 3.00
CC4 Steve Nash 1.00 2.50
CC5 Gilbert Arenas .75 2.00
CC6 Carmelo Anthony 1.50 4.00
CC7 Chris Bosh .75 2.00
CC8 Richard Hamilton .60 1.50
CC9 Tracy McGrady 1.00 2.50
CC10 Paul Pierce 1.00 2.50
CC11 Dirk Nowitzki 1.25 3.00
CC12 Amare Stoudemire .75 2.00
CC13 Kobe Bryant 4.00 10.00
CC14 Shaquille O'Neal 1.50 4.00
CC15 Mike Bibby .75 2.00

2005-06 Topps Finishing Touch Relics

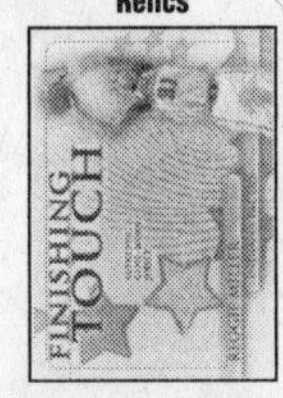

Randomly inserted in packs at the rate of one in 246, this horizintally designed set features a star-shaped jersey swatch on the left and a full color player photo on the right set against a white background.
BG Ben Gordon 2.50 6.00
CA Carmelo Anthony 5.00 12.00
CB Chris Bosh 2.50 6.00
JK Jason Kidd 4.00 10.00
MC Marcus Camby 2.00 5.00
PG Pau Gasol 2.50 6.00
PP Paul Pierce 3.00 8.00
RM Reggie Miller 2.50 6.00
RW Rasheed Wallace 2.50 6.00
SF Steve Francis 2.50 6.00
SM Stephon Marbury 2.00 5.00
SO Shaquille O'Neal 5.00 12.00
TD Tim Duncan 4.00 10.00
WS Wally Szczerbiak 2.00 5.00
YM Yao Ming 3.00 8.00

2005-06 Topps Marks of Excellence

Insertéd at the rate of one in 835 for group A, one in 419 for group B and one in 2016 for group C, this set utilizes oragne and red borders around a full color player photo along with a silver foil autographed sticker.
AI Allen Iverson 40.00 100.00
AS Amare Stoudemire A 20.00 50.00
BD Baron Davis A 8.00 20.00
BU Beno Udrih A 8.00 20.00
CA Carmelo Anthony C 20.00 40.00
DE Daniel Ewing B 5.00 12.00
DG Danny Granger B 10.00 25.00
DW Dorell Wright A 5.00 12.00
EO Emeka Okafor C 10.00 25.00
FV Fran Vazquez B 5.00 12.00
GG Gerald Green B 6.00 15.00
HW Hakim Warrick B 6.00 15.00
JG Joey Graham B 5.00 12.00
JH Julius Hodge B 5.00 12.00
JK Jason Kidd A 12.50 30.00
JM Jason Maxiell B 5.00 12.00
JN Jameer Nelson A 5.00 12.00
JS Josh Smith A 10.00 25.00
LD Luol Deng A 8.00 20.00
LH Luther Head B 5.00 12.00
LO Lamar Odom A 10.00 25.00
PP Pavel Podkolzin A 5.00 12.00
PS Pape Sow A 5.00 12.00
QR Quentin Richardson A 8.00 20.00
RA Rafer Alston A 12.50 30.00
RF Raymond Felton B 10.00 25.00
RH Richard Hamilton A 6.00 15.00
RM Rashad McCants B 5.00 12.00
SL Shaun Livingston A 5.00 12.00
SM Shawn Marion A 10.00 25.00
SO Shaquille O'Neal A 30.00 80.00
TM Tracy McGrady A 12.50 30.00
WS Wayne Simien B 5.00 12.00
ABO Andrew Bogut B 8.00 20.00
CTA Chris Taft B 5.00 12.00
DWI Deron Williams B 15.00 40.00
HSJ Ha Seung-Jin A 5.00 12.00
PST Peja Stojakovic A 6.00 15.00
SMA Stephon Marbury A 8.00 20.00
SMY Sean May B 5.00 12.00

2005-06 Topps Rise to the Occasion Relics

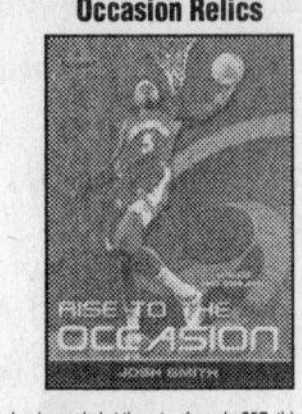

Randomly seeded at the rate of one in 257, this 16-card set features a player action photo on the left, an oval swatch of game-worn memorabilia on the right and is set against a swirling red, purple and green background.
AH Al Harrington 2.00 5.00
AI Andre Iguodala 2.50 6.00
AS Amare Stoudemire 2.50 6.00
CW Chris Webber 2.50 6.00
DF Derek Fisher 2.00 5.00
DG Drew Gooden 2.00 5.00
EB Elton Brand 2.50 6.00
EO Emeka Okafor 2.50 6.00
JC Josh Childress 2.00 5.00
JS Josh Smith 2.50 6.00
KM Kenyon Martin 2.50 6.00
LO Lamar Odom 2.50 6.00
LW Luke Walton 2.00 5.00
RJ Richard Jefferson 2.50 6.00
TM Tracy McGrady 3.00 8.00
JRS J.R. Smith 2.50 6.00

2005-06 Topps Rookie Photo Shoot Autographs

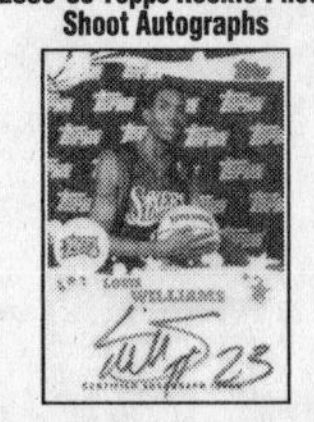

Inserted at the rate of one in 619, this 32-card set features cards made "same day" at the NBA Rookie photo shoot in August. Player photos appear at the top of the card while a white-out design is left on the bottom for the authentic player autographs. Fewer than sixty versions of each card are reported in existance.
UNPRICED TRIPLE STATED ODDS 1:28698
BB Brandon Bass 20.00 50.00
CV Charlie Villanueva 20.00 50.00
DE Daniel Ewing 15.00 40.00
DG Danny Granger 30.00 80.00
DL David Lee 25.00 60.00
DW Deron Williams 100.00 200.00
EI Ersan Ilyasova 20.00 50.00
FG Francisco Garcia 20.00 50.00
GG Gerald Green 20.00 50.00
HW Hakim Warrick 20.00 50.00
JG Joey Graham 15.00 40.00
JH Julius Hodge 15.00 40.00
JJ Jarrett Jack 15.00 40.00
JM Jason Maxiell 15.00 40.00
LH Luther Head 15.00 40.00
LW Louis Williams 25.00 60.00
ME Monta Ellis 60.00 120.00
NR Nate Robinson 20.00 50.00
RF Raymond Felton 25.00 60.00
RG Ryan Gomes 15.00 40.00
RM Rashad McCants 15.00 40.00
SJ Sarunas Jasikevicius 15.00 40.00
SM Sean May 15.00 40.00
WS Wayne Simien 15.00 40.00
ABL Andray Blatche 20.00 50.00
MWE Martell Webster 15.00 40.00

2005-06 Topps Rookie Photo Shoot Autographs Dual

Inserted in packs at the rate of one in 7998, this set parallels the design of the Rookie Photo Shoot Autographs, but is horizontally designed with two NBA rookies.
FM Raymond Felton / Sean May 100.00 200.00
GV Joey Graham / Charlie Villanueva 75.00 150.00
GW Gerald Green / Martell Webster 75.00 150.00
HJ Julius Hodge / Jarrett Jack 20.00 50.00
HW Luther Head / Deron Williams 150.00 300.00
MM Sean May / Rashad McCants 50.00 120.00
WF Deron Williams / Raymond Felton 150.00 300.00
FMC Raymond Felton / Rashad McCants 100.00 200.00
GWI Francisco Garcia / Deron Williams 125.00 250.00

2005-06 Topps Signs of Stardom

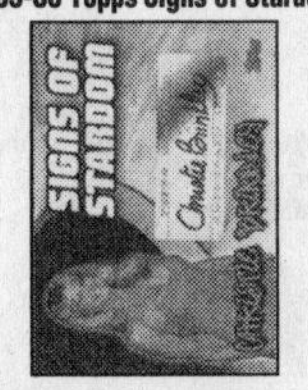

Inserted in packs at the rate of one in 7391, this eight-card set is horizontally designed and features the members of Topps' celebrity lineup. Photos appear on the left of each card while a silver autographed sticker appears on the right.
CB Christie Brinkley 40.00 100.00
JZ Jay-Z 40.00 100.00
SE Shannon Elizabeth 40.00 100.00
CAE Carmen Electra 60.00 150.00
JMC Jenny McCarthy 40.00 100.00

2005-06 Topps Target Hardwood Classics Jerseys

RANDOM INSERTS IN TARGET PACKS
AF Adonal Foyle 1.50 4.00
AI Allen Iverson 4.00 10.00
AJ Antawn Jamison 2.50 6.00
AM Andre Miller 2.00 5.00
AV Anderson Varejao 2.00 5.00
BS Bob Sura 1.50 4.00
CM Chris Mihm 1.50 4.00
DH Devin Harris 2.50 6.00
DM Darko Milicic 1.50 4.00
EB Earl Boykins 1.50 4.00
LW Luke Walton 1.50 4.00
RW Rasheed Wallace 2.50 6.00
SD Samuel Dalembert 1.50 4.00
ST Sebastian Telfair 2.00 5.00
TO Travis Outlaw 2.00 5.00
WG Willie Green 1.50 4.00
DHA David Harrison 1.50 4.00
HSJ Ha Seung-Jin 1.50 4.00

2005-06 Topps Versatile Velocity

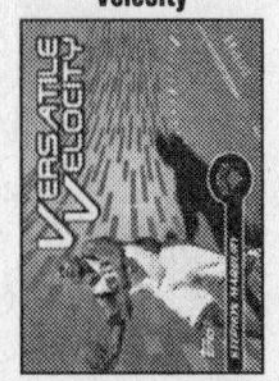

Inserted in packs at the rate of one in 25, this 10-card set is horizontally designed and places player photos on the left of an orange background that features a graphic of an automobile speedometor.
COMPLETE SET (10) 10.00 25.00
VV1 Stephon Marbury .75 2.00
VV2 Kevin Garnett 2.00 5.00
VV3 Dwyane Wade 2.50 6.00
VV4 Shawn Marion 1.00 2.50
VV5 Ben Gordon 1.00 2.50
VV6 Corey Maggette .75 2.00
VV7 LeBron James 5.00 12.00
VV8 Gilbert Arenas 1.00 2.50
VV9 Manu Ginobili 1.00 2.50
VV10 Steve Francis 1.00 2.50

2006-07 Topps

Released in mid September 2006, Topps features a classic design placing full-color player photos on a white-bordered design with silver foil highlights. Veteran players are pictured on cards 1-215 and rookies are picutred on cards 216-155. For several of the first-round draft picks, two versions of each card were issued--one of the player in his college uniform and another of the player in his suit on NBA Draft night. Topps is packaged in 36-pack boxes of 12 cards each and carried an initial suggested retail price of $1.99.

COMPLETE SET (275) 25.00 60.00
COMP.SET w/o SP's (215) 12.50 30.00
UNPRICED PLATINUM PRINT RUN ONE SET
1 Elton Brand .20 .50
2 Tim Duncan .30 .75
3 Chris Paul .40 1.00
4 Joe Johnson .20 .50
5 Chauncey Billups .20 .50
6 Al Harrington .15 .40
7 Andres Nocioni .12 .30
8 Kobe Bryant 1.00 2.50
9 Al Jefferson .20 .50
10 Gerald Wallace .20 .50
11 Jason Terry .15 .40
12 Dwight Howard .30 .75
13 Larry Hughes .15 .40
14 Sebastian Telfair .12 .30
15 Vince Carter .25 .60
16 Mike Bibby .20 .50
17 Ben Gordon .20 .50
18 Desmond Mason .12 .30
19 Eddie Jones .15 .40
20 Raymond Felton .25 .60
21 Paul Pierce .25 .60
22 Eddy Curry .15 .40
23 Jason Richardson .20 .50
24 Rasheed Wallace .20 .50
25 Andrew Bogut .20 .50
26 Stromile Swift .12 .30
27 Peja Stojakovic .20 .50
28 Deron Williams .30 .75
29 Kwame Brown .12 .30
30 Michael Redd .20 .50
31 Shawn Marion .20 .50
32 Shaquille O'Neal .40 1.00
33 Larry Bird 3.00 8.00
34 Ray Allen .20 .50
35 Marko Jaric .12 .30
36 Luther Head .15 .40
37 Robert Horry .15 .40
38 Jason Collins .12 .30
39 Cuttino Mobley .15 .40
40 Donyell Marshall .12 .30
41 Dirk Nowitzki .30 .75
42 Jermaine O'Neal .20 .50
43 Kurt Thomas .12 .30
44 Gerald Green .15 .40
45 Marvin Williams .20 .50
46 Bonzi Wells .12 .30
47 Andrei Kirilenko .15 .40
48 J.R. Smith .20 .50
49 Baron Davis .20 .50
50 Tracy McGrady .25 .60
51 Chris Kaman .15 .40
52 Luol Deng .20 .50
53 Emeka Okafor .20 .50
54 Grant Hill .25 .60
55 Amare Stoudemire .20 .50
56 Lamar Odom .20 .50
57 Eric Snow .12 .30
58 Ike Diogu .12 .30
59 Alonzo Mourning .25 .60
60 Maurice Evans .12 .30
61 Marcus Camby .15 .40
62 Bobby Simmons .12 .30
63 Vladimir Radmanovic .12 .30
64 Ryan Gomes .12 .30
65 Fred Jones .12 .30
66 Kirk Snyder .12 .30
67 Flip Murray .12 .30
68 T.J. Ford .15 .40
69 DeSagana Diop .12 .30
70 Josh Smith .20 .50
71 Lorenzen Wright .12 .30
72 Nate Robinson .20 .50
73 Brendan Haywood .12 .30
74 Darius Miles .12 .30
75 Keith Van Horn .15 .40
76 Johan Petro .12 .30
77 Yao Ming .25 .60
78 Darko Milicic .12 .30
79 Smush Parker .12 .30
80 Sarunas Jasikevicius .15 .40
81 Mike Dunleavy .15 .40
82 Joey Graham .12 .30
83 Jason Williams .15 .40
84 Melvin Ely .12 .30
85 Ricky Davis .15 .40
86 Michael Finley .20 .50
87 Steve Blake .12 .30
88 Nenad Krstic .12 .30
89 Earl Boykins .12 .30
90 Richard Hamilton .15 .40
91 Chris Duhon .12 .30
92 Hakim Warrick .15 .40
93 Wally Szczerbiak .15 .40
94 Corey Maggette .15 .40
95 Leandro Barbosa .15 .40
96 Jamaal Tinsley .12 .30
97 Kenyon Martin .20 .50
98 Kyle Korver .15 .40
99 Jason Kidd .30 .75
100 Dwyane Wade .50 1.25
101 Ben Wallace .20 .50
102 Mike James .12 .30
103 Josh Howard .15 .40
104 Joe Smith .15 .40
105 Josh Childress .15 .40
106 Eddie Griffin .12 .30
107 Richard Jefferson .20 .50
108 Jalen Rose .15 .40
109 Mickael Pietrus .15 .40
110 Steve Nash .25 .60
111 Juwan Howard .15 .40
112 Drew Gooden .15 .40
113 Eduardo Najera .12 .30
114 Chris Mihm .12 .30
115 Jose Calderon .15 .40
116 Kevin Garnett .40 1.00
117 Rafer Alston .12 .30
118 Delonte West .15 .40
119 Jamaal Magloire .12 .30
120 Channing Frye .15 .40
121 Andre Iguodala .20 .50
122 Pau Gasol .20 .50
123 LeBron James 1.00 2.50
124 Antonio Daniels .12 .30
125 James Posey .12 .30
126 Devean George .12 .30
127 Linas Kleiza .12 .30
128 Brian Cook .12 .30
129 Sean May .12 .30
130 Sam Cassell .20 .50
131 Mehmet Okur .12 .30
132 Bruce Bowen .12 .30
133 Kirk Hinrich .20 .50
134 Chris Wilcox .12 .30
135 Brad Miller .20 .50
136 Erick Dampier .12 .30
137 Primoz Brezec .12 .30
138 Derek Fisher .15 .40
139 Antonio McDyess .15 .40
140 Chris Bosh .20 .50
141 Jamal Crawford .15 .40
142 Mike Miller .20 .50
143 Danny Granger .20 .50
144 Quinton Ross .12 .30
145 Manu Ginobili .20 .50
146 Udonis Haslem .15 .40
147 Marquis Daniels .12 .30
148 Maurice Williams .15 .40
149 Viktor Khryapa .12 .30
150 Gilbert Arenas .20 .50
151 Tony Parker .20 .50
152 Carlos Boozer .20 .50
153 Quentin Richardson .15 .40
154 Clifford Robinson .12 .30
155 Speedy Claxton .12 .30
156 Charlie Villanueva .20 .50
157 Rashard Lewis .20 .50
158 DeShawn Stevenson .12 .30
159 Boris Diaw .15 .40
160 Francisco Garcia .15 .40
161 Zaza Pachulia .12 .30
162 Raja Bell .15 .40
163 Juan Dixon .12 .30
164 Shaun Livingston .12 .30
165 Shareef Abdur-Rahim .15 .40
166 Devin Harris .20 .50
167 Brevin Knight .12 .30
168 Troy Murphy .12 .30
169 Antawn Jamison .20 .50
170 Tyson Chandler .15 .40
171 Stephen Jackson .15 .40
172 Shane Battier .15 .40
173 Chris Webber .20 .50
174 Trenton Hassell .12 .30
175 Devin Brown .12 .30
176 Luke Ridnour .15 .40
177 Joel Przybilla .12 .30
178 David West .20 .50
179 John Salmons .20 .50
180 Nazr Mohammed .12 .30
181 Caron Butler .20 .50
182 Troy Hudson .12 .30
183 Zydrunas Ilgauskas .15 .40
184 David Wesley .12 .30
185 Andre Miller .15 .40
186 Nick Collison .12 .30
187 Ron Artest .20 .50
188 Samuel Dalembert .12 .30
189 Tayshaun Prince .20 .50
190 Jameer Nelson .15 .40
191 Zach Randolph .15 .40
192 Stephon Marbury .15 .40
193 Steve Francis .20 .50
194 Matt Harpring .15 .40
195 Kevin Martin .20 .50
196 Rashad McCants .12 .30
197 Carmelo Anthony .25 .60
198 Morris Peterson .12 .30
199 Etan Thomas .12 .30
200 Allen Iverson .25 .60
201 Antoine Walker .15 .40
202 Eddie House .12 .30
203 Adrian Griffin .12 .30
204 Salim Stoudamire .12 .30
205 Raef LaFrentz .12 .30
206 Jared Jeffries .12 .30
207 Rasual Butler .12 .30
208 Damon Jones .12 .30

209 Chuck Hayes .12 .30
210 James Singleton .12 .30
211 Marcus Banks .12 .30
212 P.J. Brown .12 .30
213 Hedo Turkoglu .20 .50
214 Jarrett Jack .15 .40
215 Kendrick Perkins .15 .40
217 Leon Powe RC .75 2.00
219 Alexander Johnson RC .75 2.00
220 Will Blalock RC .75 2.00
221 Steve Novak RC .75 2.00
222 Shawne Williams RC .75 2.00
223 Guillermo Diaz RC .75 2.00
224 Mardy Collins RC .75 2.00
225 Ryan Hollins RC .75 2.00
226 Kyle Lowry RC 1.00 2.50
227 Craig Smith RC .75 2.00
228 Denham Brown RC .75 2.00
229 Dee Brown RC .75 2.00
230 Daniel Gibson RC 1.00 2.50
233 Cedric Simmons RC .75 2.00
234 P.J. Tucker RC .75 2.00
235 Hassan Adams RC .75 2.00
236 Hilton Armstrong RC .75 2.00
237 James Augustine RC .75 2.00
238 Josh Boone RC .75 2.00
239 James White RC .75 2.00
242 Maurice Ager RC .75 2.00
244 Paul Davis RC .75 2.00
245 Jordan Farmar RC .75 2.00
247 Quincy Douby RC .75 2.00
248 Ronnie Brewer RC 1.00 2.50
249 Rodney Carney RC .75 2.00
251 Rajon Rondo RC 3.00 8.00
252 Rudy Gay RC 1.25 3.00
253 Paul Millsap RC 1.25 3.00
254 Saer Sene RC .75 2.00
256 Allan Ray RC .75 2.00
257 Thabo Sefolosha RC 1.00 2.50
258 Darius Washington RC .75 2.00
259 Renaldo Balkman RC .75 2.00
260 Mike Gansey RC .75 2.00
261 Solomon Jones RC .75 2.00
262 Bobby Jones RC .75 2.00
263 David Noel RC .75 2.00
264 Kevin Pittsnogle RC .75 2.00
265 Shannon Brown RC 1.25 3.00
216A Adam Morrison RC 1.00 2.50
216B Adam Morrison Draft RC 1.00 2.50
218A Shelden Williams RC .75 2.00
218B Shelden Williams Draft RC .75 2.00
231A Tyrus Thomas RC 1.00 2.50
231B Tyrus Thomas Draft RC 1.00 2.50
232A Patrick O'Bryant RC .75 2.00
232B Patrick O'Bryant Draft RC .75 2.00
240A J.J. Redick RC 1.00 2.50
240B J.J. Redick Draft RC 1.00 2.50
241A LaMarcus Aldridge RC 2.00 5.00
241B LaMarcus Aldridge Draft RC 2.00 5.00
243A Marcus Williams RC .75 2.00
243B Marcus Williams Draft RC .75 2.00
246A Brandon Roy RC 2.00 5.00
246B Brandon Roy Draft RC 2.00 5.00
250A Randy Foye RC 1.00 2.50
250B Randy Foye Draft RC 1.00 2.50
255A Andrea Bargnani RC 1.25 3.00
255B Andrea Bargnani Draft RC 1.25 3.00

2006-07 Topps Black

*1-215 BLACK: 4X TO 10X BASE HI
*216-275 BLACK: 1.25X TO 3X BASE HI
PRINT RUN 99 SER.#'d SETS
33 Larry Bird 10.00 25.00
251 Rajon Rondo 12.00 30.00

2006-07 Topps Gold

*1-215 GOLD: 1.5X TO 4X BASE HI
*216-275 GOLD: .75X TO 2X BASE HI
PRINT RUN 500 SER.#'d SETS
33 Larry Bird 2.50 6.00

2006-07 Topps 2K7 Promotion

COMPLETE SET (12) 8.00 20.00
APPROXIMATE ODDS 1:12
1 Allen Iverson .75 2.00
2 Dwyane Wade 1.50 4.00
3 Dwight Howard 1.00 2.50
4 LeBron James 3.00 8.00
5 Yao Ming .75 2.00
6 Tim Duncan 1.00 2.50
7 Kobe Bryant 3.00 8.00
8 Steven Nash .75 2.00
9 Kevin Garnett 1.25 3.00
10 Ben Wallace .60 1.50
11 Shaquille O'Neal 1.25 3.00
12 Dirk Nowitzki• 1.00 2.50

2006-07 Topps Clutch City Prospects

COMPLETE SET (18) 6.00 15.00
STATED ODDS 1:9
1 Andrew Bogut .75 2.00
2 Luther Head .60 1.50
3 Channing Frye .60 1.50
4 Danny Granger .75 2.00
5 Chris Paul 1.50 4.00
6 Sarunas Jasikevicius .60 1.50
7 Nate Robinson .75 2.00
8 Charlie Villanueva .75 2.00
9 Deron Williams 1.25 3.00
10 Luol Deng .75 2.00
11 T.J. Ford .60 1.50
12 Ben Gordon .75 2.00
13 Devin Harris .75 2.00
14 Dwight Howard 1.25 3.00
15 Andre Iguodala .75 2.00
16 Nenad Krstic .50 1.25
17 Andres Nocioni .50 1.25
18 Delonte West .60 1.50

2006-07 Topps Clutch City Prospects Relics

GROUP A ODDS 1:1500, GROUP B 1:707
*BLACK: .5X TO 1.25X BASE HI
BLACK PRINT RUN 99 SER.#'d SETS
*GOLD: .6X TO 1.5X BASE HI
GOLD PRINT RUN 25 SER.#'d SETS
UNPRICED AUTO PRINT RUN 5 SETS
AB Andrew Bogut B 3.00 8.00
AN Andres Nocioni B 2.00 5.00
BG Ben Gordon B 3.00 8.00
CF Channing Frye B 2.50 6.00
CP Chris Paul B 6.00 15.00
CV Charlie Villanueva B 3.00 8.00
DH Dwight Howard B 5.00 12.00
DW Deron Williams B 5.00 12.00
HW Hakim Warrick B 2.50 6.00
LD Luol Deng B 3.00 8.00
NK Nenad Krstic B 2.00 5.00
NR Nate Robinson B 3.00 8.00
SJ Sarunas Jasikevicius A 2.50 6.00
DWE Delonte West B 2.50 6.00
TJF T.J. Ford B 2.50 6.00

2006-07 Topps Clutch City Stars

COMPLETE SET (24) 12.50 30.00
STATED ODDS 1:7
1 Allen Iverson .75 2.00
2 Dwyane Wade 1.50 4.00
3 LeBron James 3.00 8.00
4 Vince Carter .75 2.00
5 Shaquille O'Neal 1.25 3.00
6 Ben Wallace .60 1.50
7 Chris Bosh .60 1.50
8 Rasheed Wallace .60 1.50
9 Paul Pierce .75 2.00
10 Richard Hamilton .50 1.25
11 Gilbert Arenas .60 1.50
12 Chauncey Billups .60 1.50
13 Kobe Bryant 3.00 8.00
14 Steve Nash .75 2.00
15 Tim Duncan 1.00 2.50
16 Tracy McGrady .75 2.00
17 Yao Ming .75 2.00
18 Tony Parker .60 1.50
19 Kevin Garnett 1.25 3.00
20 Ray Allen .60 1.50
21 Dirk Nowitzki 1.00 2.50
22 Shawn Marion .60 1.50
23 Elton Brand .60 1.50
24 Pau Gasol .60 1.50

2006-07 Topps Clutch City Stars Relics

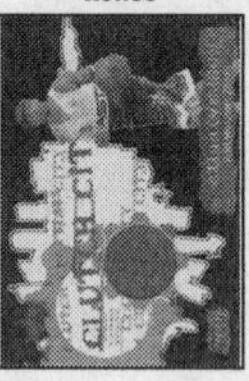

GROUP A ODDS: 1:115000, GROUP B 1:8200
GROUP C ODDS 1:1400
*BLACK: .5X TO 1.25X BASE HI
BLACK PRINT RUN 99 SER.#'d SETS
*GOLD: .6X TO 1.5X BASE HI
GOLD PRINT RUN 25 SER.#'d SETS
UNPRICED AUTO PRINT RUN 5 SETS
AI Allen Iverson C 4.00 10.00
BW Ben Wallace C 3.00 8.00
DN Dirk Nowitzki C 5.00 12.00
DW Dwyane Wade C 6.00 15.00
GA Gilbert Arenas C 3.00 8.00
KB Kobe Bryant C 8.00 20.00
KG Kevin Garnett A 6.00 15.00
PP Paul Pierce B 4.00 10.00
RH Richard Hamilton B 2.50 6.00
SN Steve Nash C 4.00 10.00
SO Shaquille O'Neal B 6.00 15.00
TD Tim Duncan C 5.00 12.00
TP Tony Parker C 3.00 8.00
VC Vince Carter C 4.00 10.00
YM Yao Ming A 4.00 10.00
CBI Chauncey Billups B 3.00 8.00

2006-07 Topps Hobby Masters

COMPLETE SET (20) 12.50 30.00
STATED ODDS 1:8
1 Kobe Bryant 3.00 8.00
2 Shaquille O'Neal 1.25 3.00
3 LeBron James 3.00 8.00
4 Allen Iverson .75 2.00
5 Tracy McGrady .75 2.00
6 Dwyane Wade 1.50 4.00
7 Vince Carter .75 2.00
8 Tim Duncan 1.00 2.50
9 Kevin Garnett 1.25 3.00
10 Yao Ming .75 2.00
11 Steve Nash .75 2.00
12 Carmelo Anthony .75 2.00
13 Jason Kidd 1.00 2.50
14 Jerry West .75 2.00
15 George Gervin .60 1.50
16 Larry Bird 2.00 5.00
17 Pete Maravich 4.00 10.00
18 Wilt Chamberlain 1.25 3.00
19 Oscar Robertson .60 1.50
20 Earl Monroe .60 1.50

2006-07 Topps Larry Bird The Missing Years

COMPLETE SET (10) 20.00 50.00
COMMON CARD (LB82-LB91) 3.00 8.00
STATED ODDS 1:18

2006-07 Topps Marks of Excellence

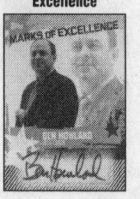

GROUP A ODDS 1:30000, GROUP B 1:1800
GROUP C ODDS 1:1800, GROUP D 1:1144
AI Allen Iverson D 50.00 120.00
AM Adam Morrison D 8.00 20.00
BH Ben Howland C 12.50 30.00
DR DaRoc D 5.00 12.00
DW Dwyane Wade B 30.00 80.00
EO Emeka Okafor D 6.00 15.00
FM Streetballer D 5.00 12.00
FT Future D 5.00 12.00
HS Hops D 5.00 12.00
HW Hakim Warrick B 8.00 20.00
JB Jim Boeheim D 10.00 25.00
JC Jim Calhoun C 8.00 20.00
LB Larry Bird B 50.00 120.00
LR Luke Ridnour D 5.00 12.00
LS Lil Scrappy D 5.00 12.00
RC Rodney Carney B 5.00 12.00
SO Shaquille O'Neal B 40.00 80.00
SW Shelden Williams B 5.00 12.00
TE Too EZ D 5.00 12.00
TW The Wizard D 5.00 12.00
WC White Chocolate D 5.00 12.00
BMA Bird Man D 5.00 12.00
DWE Delonte West D 5.00 12.00
JFK JFK D 5.00 12.00
JJR J.J. Redick D 10.00 25.00
JWO John Wooden C 40.00 100.00
RWI Roy Williams C 20.00 50.00

2006-07 Topps Own the Game

COMPLETE SET (28) 15.00 40.00
STATED ODDS 1:6
1 Kobe Bryant 3.00 8.00
2 Allen Iverson .75 2.00
3 LeBron James 3.00 8.00
4 Gilbert Arenas .60 1.50
5 Dwyane Wade 1.50 4.00
6 Kevin Garnett 1.25 3.00
7 Dwight Howard 1.00 2.50
8 Shawn Marion .60 1.50
9 Ben Wallace .60 1.50
10 Tim Duncan 1.00 2.50
11 Steve Nash .75 2.00
12 Baron Davis .60 1.50
13 Brevin Knight .40 1.00
14 Chauncey Billups .60 1.50
15 Jason Kidd 1.00 2.50
16 Marcus Camby .50 1.25
17 Andrei Kirilenko .50 1.25
18 Alonzo Mourning .75 2.00
19 Josh Smith .60 1.50
20 Elton Brand .60 1.50
21 Gerald Wallace .60 1.50
22 Brevin Knight .40 1.00
23 Chris Paul 1.25 3.00
24 Gilbert Arenas .60 1.50
25 Shawn Marion .60 1.50
26 Chris Paul 1.25 3.00
27 Larry Bird 2.00 5.00
28 Steve Nash .75 2.00

2006-07 Topps Own the Game Relics

GROUP A ODDS 1:35000, GROUP B 1:8200
GROUP C ODDS 1:1202, GROUP D 1:658
*BLACK: .5X TO 1.25X BASE HI
BLACK PRINT RUN 99 SER.#'d SETS
*GOLD: .6X TO 1.5X BASE HI
GOLD PRINT RUN 25 SER.#'d SETS
UNPRICED AUTO PRINT RUN 5 SETS
AI Allen Iverson D 4.00 10.00
CP Chris Paul D 6.00 15.00
DH Dwight Howard C 5.00 12.00
DN Dirk Nowitzki C 5.00 12.00
DW Dwyane Wade D 6.00 15.00
EB Elton Brand A 3.00 8.00
JS Josh Smith B 3.00 8.00
KB Kobe Bryant D 8.00 20.00
KG Kevin Garnett D 6.00 15.00
SN Steve Nash D 4.00 10.00
SO Shaquille O'Neal D 6.00 15.00
TD Tim Duncan D 5.00 12.00
TP Tony Parker D 3.00 8.00

2006-07 Topps Pride of the Program

COMPLETE SET (10) 12.50 30.00
STATED ODDS 1:16
PP1 Rasheed Wallace 2.00 5.00
Chauncey Billups
Richard Hamilton
PP2 LeBron James 3.00 8.00
Zydrunas Ilguaskas
Larry Hughes
PP3 Vince Carter 2.00 5.00
Jason Kidd
Richard Jefferson
PP4 Carmelo Anthony 2.00 5.00
Earl Boykins
Marcus Camby
PP5 Dwyane Wade 3.00 8.00
Antoine Walker
Shaquille O'Neal
PP6 Allen Iverson 2.00 5.00
Samuel Dalembert
Andre Iguodala
PP7 Dirk Nowitzki 2.00 5.00
Jason Terry
Josh Howard
PP8 Tracy McGrady 2.50 6.00
Yao Ming
Luther Head
PP9 Kobe Bryant 2.50 6.00
Lamar Odom
Andrew Bynum
PP10 Tony Parker 2.50 6.00
Manu Ginobili
Tim Duncan

2006-07 Topps Pride of the Program Relics

STATED PRINT RUN 99 SER.#'d SETS
BBW Andrew Bynum 15.00 40.00
Kobe Bryant
James Worthy
JPC Al Jefferson 12.50 30.00
Paul Pierce
Dave Cowens
KBM Andrei Kirilenko 8.00 20.00
Carlos Boozer
Karl Malone
MMD Yao Ming 12.50 30.00
Tracy McGrady
Clyde Drexler
PDG Tony Parker 15.00 40.00
Tim Duncan
George Gervin
RFM Nate Robinson 12.50 30.00
Channing Frye
Earl Monroe

2006-07 Topps Rookie Photo Shoot Autographs

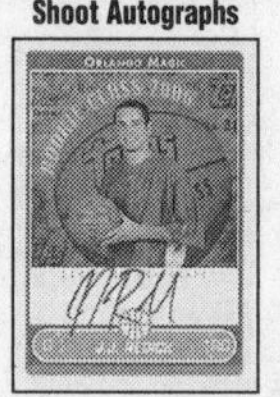

STATED ODDS 1:358
UNPRICED DUAL STATED ODDS 1:9050
UNPRICED TRIPLE STATED ODDS 1:22700
AM Adam Morrison 30.00 80.00
AR Allan Ray 12.00 30.00
CS Craig Smith 12.00 30.00
DN David Noel 12.00 30.00
JB Josh Boone 12.00 30.00
JF Jordan Farmar 12.00 30.00
KL Kyle Lowry 15.00 40.00
MA Maurice Ager 12.00 30.00
MC Mardy Collins 12.00 30.00
MW Marcus Williams 12.00 30.00
PD Paul Davis 12.00 30.00
QD Quincy Douby 12.00 30.00
RB Ronnie Brewer 15.00 40.00
RC Rodney Carney 12.00 30.00
RF Randy Foye 30.00 80.00
RR Rajon Rondo 150.00 300.00
SB Shannon Brown 20.00 50.00
SJ Solomon Jones 12.00 30.00
SN Steve Novak 12.00 30.00
SW Shelden Williams 12.00 30.00
CSI Cedric Simmons 12.00 30.00
DBR Denham Brown 12.00 30.00
DEE Dee Brown 12.00 30.00
HAR Hilton Armstrong 12.00 30.00
JJR J.J. Redick 40.00 100.00
KPI Kevin Pittsnogle 12.00 30.00
RBA Renaldo Balkman 12.00 30.00
SWI Shawne Williams 12.00 30.00

2007-08 Topps

This 135-card set was released in September, 2007. The set was issued into the hobby in nine-card packs with an $1.99 SRP which came 36 packs to a box. Cards numbered 1-110 feature veterans while cards numbered 111-135 feature 2007-08 NBA rookies.

COMPLETE SET (135) 20.00 50.00
UNPRICED SILVER PRINT RUN ONE SET
1 Amare Stoudemire .20 .50
2 Joe Johnson .20 .50
3 Dwyane Wade .50 1.25
4 Chris Bosh .20 .50
5 Jason Kidd .20 .50
6 Bill Russell .30 .75
7 Jermaine O'Neal .20 .50
8 Mike Miller .20 .50
9 Ray Allen .20 .50
10 Elton Brand .20 .50
11 Yao Ming .25 .60
12 Al Harrington .15 .40
13 Steve Nash .25 .60
14 Dwight Howard .30 .75
15 Carmelo Anthony .25 .60
16 Pau Gasol .20 .50
17 Chauncey Billups .20 .50
18 Antawn Jamison .20 .50
19 Shane Battier .15 .40
20 Kevin Garnett .40 1.00
21 Tim Duncan .30 .75
22 Michael Redd .20 .50
23 LeBron James 1.00 2.50
24 Kobe Bryant 1.00 2.50
25 Eddy Curry .12 .30
26 Peja Stojakovic .20 .50
27 Andrew Bogut .20 .50
28 Vince Carter .25 .60
29 Corey Maggette .15 .40
30 Rasheed Wallace .20 .50
31 Shawn Marion .20 .50
32 Shaquille O'Neal .40 1.00
33 Allen Iverson .25 .60
34 Paul Pierce .25 .60
35 Adam Morrison .20 .50
36 Tony Parker .20 .50
37 Mike Bibby .20 .50
38 Andrea Bargnani .25 .60
39 Luol Deng .20 .50
40 Chris Paul .40 1.00
41 Dirk Nowitzki .25 .60
42 David Lee .15 .40
43 Paul Millsap .15 .40
44 Danny Granger .20 .50
45 Al Jefferson .20 .50
46 Rafer Alston .12 .30
47 Andrei Kirilenko .15 .40
48 Shaun Livingston .12 .30
49 Chris Wilcox .12 .30
50 Emeka Okafor .20 .50
51 Zach Randolph .15 .40
52 Devin Harris .20 .50
53 Mo Williams .15 .40
54 Leandro Barbosa .15 .40
55 Smush Parker .12 .30
56 Andre Miller .15 .40
57 Manu Ginobili .20 .50
58 Jason Richardson .20 .50
59 Jason Terry .15 .40
60 Gerald Wallace .20 .50
61 Richard Hamilton .15 .40
62 Ricky Davis .15 .40
63 Boris Diaw .15 .40
64 Carlos Boozer .20 .50
65 Rashard Lewis .15 .40
66 Josh Childress .15 .40
67 Lamar Odom .20 .50
68 Kyle Korver .15 .40
69 Stephon Marbury .15 .40
70 Luke Walton .12 .30
71 Baron Davis .20 .50
72 Larry Hughes .15 .40
73 Jameer Nelson .15 .40
74 Caron Butler .20 .50
75 Udonis Haslem .15 .40
76 Mike Dunleavy .15 .40
77 Ben Gordon .20 .50
78 Andrew Bynum .25 .60
79 Hakim Warrick .15 .40
80 Josh Smith .20 .50
81 Mehmet Okur .12 .30
82 J.R. Smith .20 .50
83 Raymond Felton .25 .60
84 Chris Webber .20 .50
85 Jamal Crawford .15 .40
86 Jarrett Jack .15 .40
87 Anderson Varejao .15 .40
88 Ryan Gomes .12 .30
89 Charlie Villanueva .20 .50
90 Marcus Camby .12 .30
91 Kirk Hinrich .20 .50
92 Tayshaun Prince .20 .50
93 Ron Artest .20 .50
94 T.J. Ford .15 .40
95 Richard Jefferson .20 .50
96 Zydrunas Ilgauskas .15 .40
97 Josh Howard .15 .40
98 Monta Ellis .20 .50
99 Deron Williams .30 .75
100 Gilbert Arenas .20 .50
101 Tracy McGrady .20 .50
102 Steve Blake .12 .30
103 Ben Wallace .20 .50
104 Kevin Martin .20 .50
105 Marcus Williams .12 .30
106 J.J. Redick .20 .50
107 Brandon Roy .25 .60
108 Desmond Mason .12 .30
109 Randy Foye .20 .50
110 Andre Iguodala .20 .50
111 Greg Oden RC 1.00 2.50
112 Kevin Durant RC 6.00 15.00
113 Al Horford RC 1.00 2.50
114 Mike Conley Jr. RC 1.25 3.00
115 Jeff Green RC 1.00 2.50
116 Yi Jianlian RC 1.25 3.00
117 Corey Brewer RC 1.00 2.50
118 Brandan Wright RC .75 2.00
119 Joakim Noah RC 2.00 5.00
120 Spencer Hawes RC .75 2.00
121 Acie Law RC .75 2.00
122 Thaddeus Young RC 1.00 2.50
123 Julian Wright RC .75 2.00
124 Al Thornton RC .75 2.00
125 Rodney Stuckey RC 1.25 3.00
126 Nick Young RC 1.25 3.00
127 Sean Williams RC .75 2.00
128 Marco Belinelli RC .75 2.00
129 Javaris Crittenton RC .75 2.00
130 Jason Smith RC .75 2.00
131 Daequan Cook RC .75 2.00
132 Jared Dudley RC .75 2.00
133 Wilson Chandler RC 1.25 3.00
134 Morris Almond RC .75 2.00
135 Aaron Brooks RC .75 2.00

2007-08 Topps Copper

*1-110 COPPER: 4X TO 10X BASE HI
*111-135 COPPER RC: 2.5X TO 6X BASE HI
COPPER PRINT RUN 50 SER.#'d SETS
112 Kevin Durant 60.00 150.00

2007-08 Topps First Edition

*1-110 1st EDITION: 3X TO 8X BASE HI
*111-135 1st ED.RC: 1.5X TO 4X BASE HI
1st EDITION PRINT RUN 119 SER.#'d SETS

2007-08 Topps Gold

*GOLD STARS: 1.25X TO 3X BASE HI
*GOLD RCs: 1X TO 2.5X BASE HI
PRINT RUN 2007 SER.#'d SETS

2007-08 Topps 1957-58 Variations

COMPLETE SET (50) 20.00 50.00
ONE VARIATION CARD PER PACK
*1-110 COPPER: 1.25X TO 3X BASE HI
*COPPER RC: 2X TO 5X BASE HI
COPPER PRINT RUN 50 SER.#'d SETS
*1-110 1st ED: .6X TO 1.5X BASE HI
*1st ED.RC: 1.5X TO 4X BASE HI
1st EDITION PRINT RUN 119 SER.#'d SETS
*1-110 GOLD: SAME AS BASE
*GOLD RC: .75X TO 2X BASE HI
GOLD PRINT RUN 2007 SER.#'d SETS
UNPRICED SILVER PRINT RUN ONE SET
1 Amare Stoudemire .60 1.50
3 Dwyane Wade 1.50 4.00
4 Chris Bosh .60 1.50
5 Jason Kidd .60 1.50
7 Jermaine O'Neal .60 1.50
11 Yao Ming .75 2.00
13 Steve Nash .75 2.00
14 Dwight Howard 1.00 2.50
15 Carmelo Anthony .75 2.00
17 Chauncey Billups .60 1.50
20 Kevin Garnett 1.25 3.00
21 Tim Duncan 1.00 2.50
23 LeBron James 3.00 8.00
24 Kobe Bryant 3.00 8.00
25 Eddy Curry .40 1.00
28 Vince Carter .75 2.00
31 Shawn Marion .60 1.50
32 Shaquille O'Neal 1.25 3.00
33 Allen Iverson .75 2.00
41 Dirk Nowitzki .75 2.00
100 Gilbert Arenas .60 1.50
101 Tracy McGrady .60 1.50
104 Kevin Martin .60 1.50
107 Brandon Roy .75 2.00
110 Andre Iguodala .60 1.50
111 Greg Oden 1.00 2.50
112 Kevin Durant 6.00 15.00
113 Al Horford 1.00 2.50
114 Mike Conley Jr. 1.25 3.00
115 Jeff Green 1.00 2.50
116 Yi Jianlian 1.25 3.00
117 Corey Brewer 1.00 2.50
118 Brandan Wright .75 2.00
119 Joakim Noah 2.00 5.00
120 Spencer Hawes .75 2.00
121 Acie Law .75 2.00
122 Thaddeus Young 1.00 2.50
123 Julian Wright .75 2.00
124 Al Thornton .75 2.00
125 Rodney Stuckey 1.25 3.00
126 Nick Young 1.25 3.00
127 Sean Williams .75 2.00
128 Marco Belinelli .75 2.00
129 Javaris Crittenton .75 2.00
130 Jason Smith .75 2.00
131 Daequan Cook .75 2.00
132 Jared Dudley .75 2.00
133 Wilson Chandler 1.25 3.00
134 Morris Almond .75 2.00
135 Aaron Brooks .75 2.00

2007-08 Topps 1957-58 Variations Autographs

GROUP A ODDS 1:1700; B ODDS 1:325
GROUP C ODDS 1:299; D ODDS 1:285
3 Dwyane Wade A 25.00 60.00
4 Chris Bosh A 10.00 25.00
9 Ray Allen A 10.00 25.00
12 Al Harrington B 4.00 10.00
17 Chauncey Billups B 8.00 20.00
27 Andrew Bogut C 6.00 15.00
28 Vince Carter A 15.00 40.00
29 Corey Maggette D 4.00 10.00
35 Adam Morrison B 6.00 15.00
42 David Lee D 4.00 10.00
43 Paul Millsap A 4.00 10.00
47 Andrei Kirilenko C 4.00 10.00
54 Leandro Barbosa B 4.00 10.00
55 Smush Parker C 4.00 10.00
63 Boris Diaw D 6.00 15.00
64 Carlos Boozer C 6.00 15.00
70 Luke Walton D 4.00 10.00
73 Jameer Nelson B 4.00 10.00
79 Hakim Warrick D 4.00 10.00
86 Jarrett Jack C 4.00 10.00
89 Charlie Villanueva C 4.00 10.00
91 Kirk Hinrich B 8.00 20.00
97 Josh Howard B 4.00 10.00
106 J.J. Redick C 6.00 15.00
110 Andre Iguodala B 5.00 12.00

2007-08 Topps 1957-58 Variations Relics

STATED ODDS 1:71
1 Amare Stoudemire 3.00 8.0
2 Joe Johnson 3.00 8.0
3 Dwyane Wade 6.00 15.0
4 Chris Bosh 3.00 8.0
5 Jason Kidd 3.00 8.0
7 Jermaine O'Neal 3.00 8.0
11 Yao Ming 4.00 10.0
13 Steve Nash 4.00 10.0
14 Dwight Howard 5.00 12.0
17 Chauncey Billups 3.00 8.0
20 Kevin Garnett 6.00 15.0
21 Tim Duncan 5.00 12.0
24 Kobe Bryant 10.00 25.0
28 Vince Carter 4.00 10.0
31 Shawn Marion 3.00 8.0
32 Shaquille O'Neal 6.00 15.0
33 Allen Iverson 4.00 10.0
35 Adam Morrison 3.00 8.0
41 Dirk Nowitzki 4.00 10.0
61 Richard Hamilton 3.00 8.0
74 Caron Butler 3.00 8.0
91 Kirk Hinrich 3.00 8.0
101 Tracy McGrady 3.00 8.0
104 Kevin Martin 3.00 8.0
107 Brandon Roy 4.00 10.0

2007-08 Topps Bill Russell The Missing Years

COMPLETE SET (11) 10.00 25.0
COMMON CARD (BR58-BR69) 2.00 5.0
STATED ODDS 1:9
AUTOGRAPH ODDS 1:90000
AUTOS NOT PRICED DUE TO SCARCITY

2007-08 Topps Generation Now

COMPLETE SET (30) 8.00 20.0
STATED ODDS 1:3
GN1 LeBron James 2.00 5.0
GN2 Carmelo Anthony .50 1.2
GN3 Dwyane Wade 1.00 2.5
GN4 Chris Bosh .40 1.0
GN5 Josh Howard .30
GN6 Dwight Howard .60 1.5
GN7 Emeka Okafor .40 1.0
GN8 Ben Gordon .40 1.
GN9 Andre Iguodala .40 1.
GN10 Josh Smith .40 1.
GN11 Kevin Martin .40 1.
GN12 Chris Paul .75 2.
GN13 Deron Williams .60 1.5
GN14 Raymond Felton .50 1.2
GN15 Marvin Williams .40 1.0
GN16 David Lee .30
GN17 Andrew Bynum .50 1.2
GN18 Monta Ellis .40 1.0
GN19 Jarrett Jack .30
GN20 Hakim Warrick .30
GN21 Ryan Gomes .25
GN22 Sean May .25
GN23 Charlie Villanueva .40 1.0
GN24 Luke Walton .25
GN25 Boris Diaw .30
GN26 Brandon Roy .50 1.2
GN27 Andrea Bargnani .50 1.2
GN28 Randy Foye .40 1.
GN29 Marcus Williams .25
GN30 Adam Morrison .40 1.

2007-08 Topps Generation Now Relics

STATED ODDS 1:71
GNRAB Andrew Bynum 4.00 10.
GNRAI Andre Iguodala 3.00 8.
GNRAM Adam Morrison 3.00 8.
GNRBD Boris Diaw 2.50 6.
GNRBG Ben Gordon 3.00 8.
GNRBR Brandon Roy 4.00 10.
GNRCA Carmelo Anthony 4.00 10.
GNRCB Chris Bosh 3.00 8.
GNRCP Chris Paul 6.00 15.
GNRCV Charlie Villanueva 3.00 8.
GNRDH Dwight Howard 5.00 12.
GNRDW Dwyane Wade 6.00 15.
GNREO Emeka Okafor 3.00 8.
GNRHW Hakim Warrick 2.50 6.
GNRJH Josh Howard 2.50 6.
GNRJJ Jarrett Jack 2.50 6.
GNRJS Josh Smith 3.00 8.
GNRLW Luke Walton 2.00 5.
GNRME Monta Ellis 3.00 8.
GNRMW Marcus Williams 2.00 5.
GNRRF Raymond Felton 4.00 10.
GNRSM Sean May 2.00 5.
GNRABA Andrea Bargnani 4.00 10.
GNRDWI Deron Williams 5.00 12.
GNRRFO Randy Foye 3.00 8.

2007-08 Topps Mini Exclusives
)NE PER RIP CARD
/IEAI Allen Iverson 4.00 10.00
/IEBR Bill Russell 5.00 12.00
/IEBW Bill Walton 3.00 8.00
/IECA Carmelo Anthony 4.00 10.00
/IECD Clyde Drexler 4.00 10.00
/IECM Chris Mullin 3.00 8.00
/IEDH Dwight Howard 5.00 12.00
/IEDN Dirk Nowitzki 4.00 10.00
/IEDR Dennis Rodman 5.00 12.00
/IEEB Elgin Baylor 3.00 8.00
/IEEM Earl Monroe 3.00 8.00
/IEGA Gilbert Arenas 3.00 8.00
/IEGG George Gervin 3.00 8.00
/IEIT Isiah Thomas 3.00 8.00
/IEJE Julius Erving 6.00 15.00
/IEJH Josh Howard 3.00 8.00
/IEJK Jason Kidd 3.00 8.00
/IEJS John Stockton 5.00 12.00
/IEJW James Worthy 4.00 10.00
/IEKB Kobe Bryant 15.00 40.00
/IEKG Kevin Garnett 6.00 15.00
/IEKM Karl Malone 4.00 10.00
/IELB Larry Bird 10.00 25.00
/IELB Leandro Barbosa 3.00 8.00
/IEOR Oscar Robertson 3.00 8.00
/IERB Rick Barry 3.00 8.00
/IESN Steve Nash 4.00 10.00
/IETD Tim Duncan 5.00 12.00
/IEVC Vince Carter 4.00 10.00
/IEWC Wilt Chamberlain 6.00 15.00
/IEAIG Andre Iguodala 3.00 8.00
/IEDWI Dominique Wilkins 4.00 10.00

2007-08 Topps Mini Exclusives Autographs

OST UNPRICED DUE TO SCARCITY
EDR Dennis Rodman 75.00 150.00
EEB Elgin Baylor 10.00 25.00
EJH Josh Howard 8.00 20.00
EAIG Andre Iguodala 10.00 25.00
EDWI Dominique Wilkins 15.00 40.00

2007-08 Topps Own the Game

OMPLETE SET (9) 6.00 15.00
ATED ODDS 1:11
G1 Mikki Moore .60 1.50
G2 Kyle Korver .75 2.00
G3 Jason Kapono .60 1.50
G4 Kevin Garnett 2.00 5.00
G5 Steve Nash 1.25 3.00
G6 Baron Davis 1.00 2.50
G7 Marcus Camby .60 1.50
G8 Kobe Bryant 5.00 12.00
G9 Jason Kidd 1.00 2.50

2007-08 Topps Rip Card Combinations

IPPED CARDS: HALF VALUE
INT RUN 99 SER.#'d SETS
LUES FOR UNRIPPED CARDS
P1 LeBron James 50.00 125.00
Carmelo Anthony
Dwyane Wade
P2 Gilbert Arenas 20.00 40.00
Allen Iverson
Kobe Bryant
P3 Steve Nash 20.00 50.00
Pete Maravich
Jason Kidd
P4 Dwight Howard 20.00 40.00
Tim Duncan
Kevin Garnett
P5 Dirk Nowitzki 20.00 40.00
Kevin Garnett
Elton Brand
P6 Larry Bird 30.00 60.00
Julius Erving
Magic Johnson
P8 Bill Russell 30.00 80.00
Shaquille O'Neal
Wilt Chamberlain
P9 Dennis Rodman 20.00 40.00
Ron Artest
Ben Wallace
P10 Bill Walton 20.00 40.00
Yao Ming
David Robinson
P11 Dominique Wilkins 20.00 40.00
Vince Carter
Clyde Drexler
P12 Magic Johnson 25.00 50.00
Isiah Thomas
John Stockton
P13 Ray Allen 20.00 40.00
Chris Mullin
Dirk Nowitzki
RIP14 David Robinson 12.50 30.00
Amare Stoudemire
Karl Malone
RIP15 Kobe Bryant 30.00 60.00
Tracy McGrady
LeBron James
RIP16 Earl Monroe 12.50 30.00
Allen Iverson
Oscar Robertson
RIP17 Josh Smith 12.50 30.00
George Gervin
Shawn Marion
RIP18 Jermaine O'Neal 20.00 40.00
James Worthy
Kevin Garnett
RIP19 Shaquille O'Neal 25.00 50.00
Dennis Rodman
Karl Malone
RIP20 Julius Erving 20.00 40.00
Dwyane Wade
Magic Johnson
RIP21 Grant Hill 12.50 30.00
Marvin Williams
Antawn Jamison
RIP22 Chris Paul 25.00 60.00
Ben Gordon
Allen Iverson
RIP23 Larry Bird 25.00 60.00
Magic Johnson
Dwyane Wade
RIP24 Julius Erving 25.00 60.00
Kobe Bryant
Oscar Robertson
RIP25 Jason Kidd 25.00 50.00
John Stockton
Steve Nash
RIP26 Gilbert Arenas 20.00 40.00
Carmelo Anthony
Paul Pierce
RIP27 Chris Mullin 20.00 40.00
Rick Barry
Larry Bird
RIP28 Monta Ellis 12.50 30.00
Raymond Felton
Joe Johnson
RIP30 Marcus Camby 12.50 30.00
Emeka Okafor
Jermaine O'Neal
RIP31 Deron Williams 25.00 50.00
Pete Maravich
John Stockton
RIP32 Julius Erving 30.00 60.00
LeBron James
Dominique Wilkins
RIP34 Michael Redd 20.00 40.00
Ray Allen
Paul Pierce
RIP35 Josh Smith 12.50 30.00
Jason Richardson
Desmond Mason
RIP36 Amare Stoudemire 12.50 30.00
Pau Gasol
Elton Brand
RIP37 Stephon Marbury 20.00 40.00
Dwyane Wade
Jason Kidd
RIP38 LeBron James 30.00 80.00
Shaquille O'Neal
Kobe Bryant

2007-08 Topps Rookie Photo Shoot Autographs

STATED ODDS 1:381
AA Arron Afflalo 12.00 30.00
AB Aaron Brooks 10.00 25.00
AG Aaron Gray 10.00 25.00
AT Al Thornton 10.00 25.00
BW Brandan Wright 10.00 25.00
CL Carl Landry 10.00 25.00
DB Derrick Byars 10.00 25.00
DC Daequan Cook 10.00 25.00
DM Dominic McGuire 10.00 25.00
GD Glen Davis 15.00 40.00
GO Greg Oden 30.00 80.00
GP Gabe Pruitt 10.00 25.00
HH Herbert Hill 10.00 25.00
JC Javaris Crittenton 10.00 25.00
JD Jared Dudley 10.00 25.00
JJ Jared Jordan 10.00 25.00
JM Josh McRoberts 10.00 25.00
JS Jason Smith 10.00 25.00
MA Morris Almond 10.00 25.00
MW Marcus Williams 6.00 15.00
NF Nick Fazekas 10.00 25.00
NY Nick Young 15.00 40.00
RS Rodney Stuckey 15.00 40.00
RT Reyshawn Terry 10.00 25.00
SH Spencer Hawes 10.00 25.00
SL Stephane Lasme 10.00 25.00
SW Sean Williams 10.00 25.00
TG Taurean Green 10.00 25.00
TY Thaddeus Young 12.00 30.00
WC Wilson Chandler 15.00 40.00
AL4 Acie Law 10.00 25.00
ATU Alando Tucker 10.00 25.00
JDA Jermareo Davidson 10.00 25.00

2007-08 Topps Rookie Photo Shoot Autographs Dual

STATED ODDS 1:2500
BL Aaron Brooks 15.00 40.00

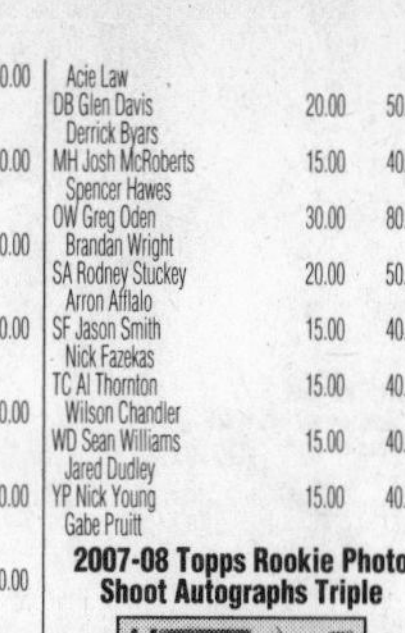

Acie Law
DB Glen Davis 20.00 50.00
Derrick Byars
MH Josh McRoberts 15.00 40.00
Spencer Hawes
OW Greg Oden 30.00 80.00
Brandan Wright
SA Rodney Stuckey 20.00 50.00
Arron Afflalo
SF Jason Smith 15.00 40.00
Nick Fazekas
TC Al Thornton 15.00 40.00
Wilson Chandler
WD Sean Williams 15.00 40.00
Jared Dudley
YP Nick Young 15.00 40.00
Gabe Pruitt

2007-08 Topps Rookie Photo Shoot Autographs Triple

STATED ODDS 1:26000
BCA Aaron Brooks 20.00 50.00
Javaris Crittenton
Arron Afflalo
CLY Daequan Cook 20.00 50.00
Acie Law
Thaddeus Young
HFS Spencer Hawes 20.00 50.00
Nick Fazekas
Jason Smith
OYW Greg Oden 40.00 100.00
Nick Young
Brandan Wright
WTD Sean Williams 25.00 60.00
Al Thornton
Jared Dudley

2007-08 Topps Rookie Set

Issued as a set, this version of the 2007-08 Topps rookie set features white borders and was available in retail outlets for between $9.99 and $14.99.

COMPLETE SET (1-14) 6.00 15.00
1 Greg Oden .60 1.50
2 Kevin Durant 4.00 10.00
3 Al Horford .60 1.50
4 Mike Conley Jr. .75 2.00
5 Jeff Green .60 1.50
6 Yi Jianlian .75 2.00
7 Corey Brewer .60 1.50
8 Brandan Wright .50 1.25
9 Joakim Noah 1.25 3.00
10 Spencer Hawes .50 1.25
11 Acie Law .50 1.25
12 Thaddeus Young .60 1.50
13 Julian Wright .50 1.25
14 Al Thornton .50 1.25

2007-08 Topps Rookie Set Orange

Issued as a set, this version of the 2007-08 Topps rookie set features orange borders and was available at retail outlets.

COMPLETE SET (14) 6.00 15.00
*SAME VALUE AS REGULAR

2008-09 Topps

This set was released on September 11, 2008. The base set consists of 220 cards. Cards 1-195 feature veterans, and cards 196-220 are rookies.

COMPLETE SET (220) 20.00 50.00
ROOKIE STATED ODDS 1:3
UNPRICED PLATINUM PRINT RUN ONE SET
1 Chris Paul .30 .75
2 Joe Johnson .20 .50
3 Allen Iverson .25 .60
4 Luis Scola .15 .40
5 Kevin Garnett .40 1.00
6 Andrew Bogut .20 .50
7 Ben Gordon .20 .50
8 Carlos Boozer .20 .50
9 Tony Parker .20 .50
10 Gilbert Arenas .20 .50
11 Yao Ming .25 .60
12 Dwight Howard .40 1.00
13 Steve Nash .20 .50
14 Daequan Cook .12 .30
15 Carmelo Anthony .25 .60
16 Pau Gasol .20 .50
17 Mike Dunleavy .15 .40
18 Jason Maxiell .12 .30
19 Al Thornton .15 .40
20 Ray Allen .20 .50
21 Tim Duncan .30 .75
22 Michael Redd .20 .50
23 LeBron James 1.00 2.50
24 Kobe Bryant 1.00 2.50
25 Al Jefferson .20 .50
26 Raymond Felton .15 .40
27 LaMarcus Aldridge .20 .50
28 Jose Calderon .15 .40
29 Andris Biedrins .12 .30
30 Rasheed Wallace .20 .50
31 Shawn Marion .20 .50
32 Shaquille O'Neal .40 1.00
33 Mike Miller .20 .50
34 Paul Pierce .25 .60
35 Brad Miller .15 .40
36 Richard Jefferson .20 .50
37 DeShawn Stevenson .12 .30
38 Zach Randolph .15 .40
39 Daniel Gibson .20 .50
40 Nazr Mohammed .12 .30
41 Dirk Nowitzki .25 .60
42 Elton Brand .20 .50
43 Linas Kleiza .12 .30
44 Andrea Bargnani .15 .40
45 Josh Smith .20 .50
46 Luol Deng .20 .50
47 Andrei Kirilenko .15 .40
48 Danny Granger .20 .50
49 Rashad McCants .12 .30
50 Emeka Okafor .20 .50
51 Kyle Korver .15 .40
52 Jamario Moon .12 .30
53 Nick Young .15 .40
54 Rashard Lewis .15 .40
55 Jason Kidd .20 .50
56 Josh Howard .15 .40
57 Desmond Mason .12 .30
58 Andre Miller .15 .40
59 Rafer Alston .12 .30
60 Baron Davis .20 .50
61 Zydrunas Ilgauskas .15 .40
62 Marvin Williams .20 .50
63 Manu Ginobili .20 .50
64 David West .20 .50
65 Rajon Rondo .25 .60
66 Kenyon Martin .20 .50
67 Josh Boone .12 .30
68 Travis Outlaw .15 .40
69 Andre Iguodala .20 .50
70 Yi Jianlian .20 .50
71 Jordan Farmar .12 .30
72 Udonis Haslem .15 .40
73 Caron Butler .20 .50
74 Craig Smith .12 .30
75 Tayshaun Prince .20 .50
76 Rudy Gay .20 .50
77 Jermaine O'Neal .20 .50
78 Devin Harris .20 .50
79 Fabricio Oberto .12 .30
80 Hedo Turkoglu .20 .50
81 Jannero Pargo .12 .30
82 Corey Maggette .15 .40
83 Ricky Davis .15 .40
84 Grant Hill .25 .60
85 Josh Childress .15 .40
86 Jeff Green .15 .40
87 Lamar Odom .20 .50
88 Brandan Wright .15 .40
89 Sean Williams .15 .40
90 Drew Gooden .15 .40
91 Amare Stoudemire .20 .50
92 Charlie Villanueva .20 .50
93 Ron Artest .20 .50
94 Derek Fisher .15 .40
95 Willie Green .12 .30
96 Kirk Hinrich .20 .50
97 Jameer Nelson .15 .40
98 Al Harrington .15 .40
99 Ronnie Brewer .15 .40
100 Dwyane Wade .40 1.00
101 Jamal Crawford .15 .40
102 Ryan Gomes .12 .30
103 Marcus Camby .12 .30
104 Antawn Jamison .20 .50
105 Cuttino Mobley .15 .40
106 Tyson Chandler .15 .40
107 Al Horford .20 .50
108 Chris Wilcox .12 .30
109 Gerald Wallace .20 .50
110 Andrew Bynum .25 .60
111 Tracy McGrady .20 .50
112 Mo Williams .15 .40
113 Nate Robinson .20 .50
114 Wally Szczerbiak .15 .40
115 Vince Carter .25 .60
116 T.J. Ford .12 .30
117 Kevin Martin .20 .50
118 Steve Blake .12 .30
119 Anderson Varejao .15 .40
120 Mike Conley Jr. .15 .40
121 Chris Kaman .15 .40
122 Louis Williams .15 .40
123 Jason Richardson .20 .50
124 John Salmons .20 .50
125 Martell Webster .15 .40
126 Juan Carlos Navarro .15 .40
127 Raja Bell .15 .40
128 Jason Terry .15 .40
129 Corey Brewer .15 .40
130 Bruce Bowen .12 .30
131 Glen Davis .15 .40
132 Richard Hamilton .15 .40
133 Ben Wallace .20 .50
134 Chris Bosh .20 .50
135 Beno Udrih .12 .30
136 Jarrett Jack .15 .40
137 Stephen Jackson .15 .40
138 Damien Wilkins .12 .30
139 Jamaal Tinsley .12 .30
140 Deron Williams .20 .50
141 Andres Nocioni .12 .30
142 David Lee .15 .40
143 Rodney Stuckey .25 .60
144 Luke Walton .12 .30
145 Jerry Stackhouse .15 .40
146 Samuel Dalembert .12 .30
147 Brandon Roy .20 .50
148 Chauncey Billups .20 .50
149 Michael Finley .20 .50
150 Leandro Barbosa .15 .40
151 Keith Bogans .12 .30
152 Mike Bibby .15 .40
153 Troy Murphy .12 .30
154 Eddy Curry .12 .30
155 Anthony Parker .12 .30
156 Kevin Durant .75 2.00
157 Larry Hughes .15 .40
158 Peja Stojakovic .20 .50
159 Shane Battier .15 .40
160 Kendrick Perkins .15 .40
161 Mehmet Okur .12 .30
162 Brendan Haywood .12 .30
163 Monta Ellis .20 .50
164 J.R. Smith .20 .50
165 Greg Oden .20 .50
166 John Stockton .30 .75
167 Tim Hardaway .20 .50
168 Dennis Rodman .30 .75
169 Dominique Wilkins .25 .60
170 David Thompson .25 .60
171 Spencer Haywood .20 .50
172 Larry Bird .60 1.50
173 Isiah Thomas .20 .50
174 Magic Johnson .50 1.25
175 Bill Russell .30 .75
176 Moses Malone .20 .50
177 Sidney Moncrief .20 .50
178 George Gervin .25 .60
179 David Robinson .30 .75
180 Jerry West .25 .60
181 Rick Barry .20 .50
182 Sam Perkins .20 .50
183 Lenny Wilkens .20 .50
184 Jo Jo White .20 .50
185 Elgin Baylor .20 .50
186 Micheal Ray Richardson .20 .50
187 Otis Birdsong .20 .50
188 Derrick Coleman .20 .50
189 Mark Eaton .20 .50
190 Pete Maravich .60 1.50
191 Wilt Chamberlain .40 1.00
192 Alex English .20 .50
193 Patrick Ewing .25 .60
194 Julius Erving .40 1.00
195 Hakeem Olajuwon .25 .60
196 Derrick Rose RC 6.00 15.00
197 Michael Beasley RC 1.00 2.50
198 O.J. Mayo RC 1.00 2.50
199 Russell Westbrook RC 3.00 8.00
200 Kevin Love RC 2.50 6.00
201 Danilo Gallinari RC 1.00 2.50
202 Eric Gordon RC 1.50 4.00
203 Joe Alexander RC .60 1.50
204 D.J. Augustin RC .60 1.50
205 Brook Lopez RC 1.00 2.50
206 Jerryd Bayless RC .60 1.50
207 Jason Thompson RC .60 1.50
208 Brandon Rush RC .60 1.50
209 Anthony Randolph RC .75 2.00
210 Robin Lopez RC .60 1.50
211 Marreese Speights RC .60 1.50
212 Roy Hibbert RC 1.00 2.50
213 George Hill RC 1.00 2.50
214 J.J. Hickson RC .75 2.00
215 Alexis Ajinca RC .60 1.50
216 Ryan Anderson RC 1.00 2.50
217 Courtney Lee RC 1.00 2.50
218 Kosta Koufos RC .60 1.50
219 Darrell Arthur RC .60 1.50
220 Donte Greene RC .60 1.50
BO Barack Obama 20.00 50.00
JM John McCain 6.00 15.00

2008-09 Topps Black

*1-195 BLACK: 6X TO 15X BASE HI
*196-220 RC BLACK: 3X TO 8X BASE HI
PRINT RUN 51 SER.#'d SETS
196 Derrick Rose 125.00 250.00

2008-09 Topps Gold Border

*GOLD BORDER: 1.25X TO 3X BASE HI
1-195 GOLD STATED ODDS 1:7
196-220 GOLD STATED ODDS 1:44

2008-09 Topps Gold Foil

*STARS: .75X TO 2X BASE HI
*RCs: .6X TO 1.5X BASE HI
1-195 GOLD FOIL ODDS 1:2
196-220 GOLD FOIL ODDS 1:11

2008-09 Topps Orange

*ORANGE: 1.25X TO 3X BASE HI
ORANGE PRINT RUN 1199 SETS

2008-09 Topps 1958-59 Variations

STATED ODDS 1:2
*GOLD: 1.25X TO 3X BASE HI
GOLD PRINT RUN 50 SER.#'d SETS
1 Chris Paul 1.25 3.00
5 Kevin Garnett 1.50 4.00
8 Carlos Boozer .75 2.00
10 Gilbert Arenas .75 2.00
12 Dwight Howard 1.50 4.00
15 Carmelo Anthony 1.00 2.50
23 LeBron James 4.00 10.00
24 Kobe Bryant 4.00 10.00
60 Baron Davis .75 2.00
100 Dwyane Wade 1.50 4.00
147 Brandon Roy .75 2.00
166 John Stockton 1.25 3.00
170 David Thompson 1.00 2.50
172 Larry Bird 2.50 6.00
173 Isiah Thomas .75 2.00
174 Magic Johnson 2.00 5.00
175 Bill Russell 1.25 3.00
179 David Robinson 1.25 3.00
180 Jerry West 1.00 2.50
183 Lenny Wilkens .75 2.00
196 Derrick Rose 6.00 15.00
197 Michael Beasley 1.25 3.00
198 O.J. Mayo 1.25 3.00
199 Russell Westbrook 4.00 10.00
200 Kevin Love 3.00 8.00
201 Danilo Gallinari 1.25 3.00
202 Eric Gordon 2.00 5.00
203 Joe Alexander .75 2.00
204 D.J. Augustin .75 2.00
205 Brook Lopez 1.25 3.00

2008-09 Topps 1958-59 Variations Autographs

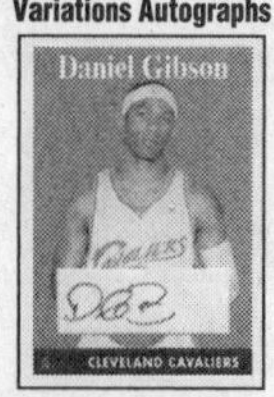

GROUP A ODDS 1:3422; B ODDS 1:1665
GROUP C ODDS 1:846; D ODDS 1:1118
GROUP E ODDS 1:850; F ODDS 1:398
*GOLD: .5X TO 1.25X BASE HI
GOLD PRINT RUN 25 SER.#'d SETS
1 Chris Paul A 25.00 60.00
8 Carlos Boozer C 5.00 12.00
10 Gilbert Arenas C 8.00 20.00
12 Dwight Howard B 12.50 30.00
39 Daniel Gibson D 5.00 12.00
60 Baron Davis C 8.00 20.00
65 Rajon Rondo E 12.00 30.00
100 Dwyane Wade A 25.00 60.00
102 Ryan Gomes E 5.00 12.00
112 Mo Williams D 5.00 12.00
165 Greg Oden A 15.00 40.00
167 Tim Hardaway F 6.00 15.00
170 David Thompson F 5.00 12.00
171 Spencer Haywood B 6.00 15.00
172 Larry Bird A 40.00 100.00
174 Magic Johnson A 30.00 80.00
177 Sidney Moncrief F 5.00 12.00
182 Sam Perkins B 5.00 12.00
183 Lenny Wilkens B 8.00 20.00
184 Jo Jo White B 8.00 20.00
185 Elgin Baylor C 10.00 25.00
186 Micheal Ray Richardson B 5.00 12.00
187 Otis Birdsong B 5.00 12.00
188 Derrick Coleman F 5.00 12.00
189 Mark Eaton B 5.00 12.00

2008-09 Topps 1958-59 Variations Relics

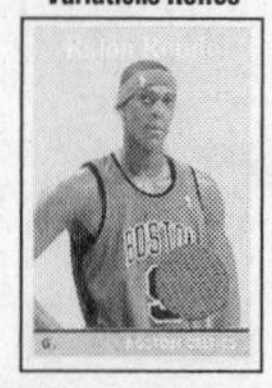

GROUP A ODDS 1:5197; B ODDS 1:437
GROUP C ODDS 1:60
*GOLD: .6X TO 1.5X BASE HI
GOLD PRINT RUN 50 SER.#'d SETS
1 Chris Paul C 4.00 10.00
5 Kevin Garnett C 5.00 12.00
8 Carlos Boozer C 2.50 6.00
10 Gilbert Arenas B 2.50 6.00
12 Dwight Howard C 5.00 12.00
15 Carmelo Anthony C 3.00 8.00
24 Kobe Bryant C 6.00 15.00
39 Daniel Gibson C 2.50 6.00
60 Baron Davis C 2.50 6.00
65 Rajon Rondo C 3.00 8.00
100 Dwyane Wade C 5.00 12.00
102 Ryan Gomes C 2.00 5.00
112 Mo Williams C 2.00 5.00
147 Brandon Roy C 2.50 6.00
165 Greg Oden C 2.50 6.00
166 John Stockton C 4.00 10.00
170 David Thompson B 3.00 8.00
172 Larry Bird B 8.00 20.00
173 Isiah Thomas B 3.00 8.00
174 Magic Johnson C 6.00 15.00
175 Bill Russell A 8.00 20.00
178 George Gervin C 3.00 8.00
179 David Robinson C 4.00 10.00
180 Jerry West A 8.00 20.00
184 Jo Jo White B

2008-09 Topps In the Genes

STATED ODDS 1:9
*GOLD: .75X TO 2X BASE HI
GOLD PRINT RUN 50 SER.#'d SETS
IG1 Kobe Bryant 2.50 6.00
Joe Bryant
IG2 Coby Karl 1.50 4.00
George Karl
IG3 Kevin Love 2.00 5.00
Stan Love
IG4 Mike Dunleavy Jr. 1.50 4.00
Mike Dunleavy Sr.
IG5 Sean May 1.50 4.00
Scott May
IG6 Brent Barry 1.50 4.00
Rick Barry
IG7 Mike Bibby 1.50 4.00
Henry Bibby
IG8 Damien Wilkins 1.50 4.00
Dominique Wilkins
IG9 Luke Walton 2.00 5.00
Bill Walton
IG10 Taurean Green 1.50 4.00
Sidney Green

2008-09 Topps McDonald's All American Autographs

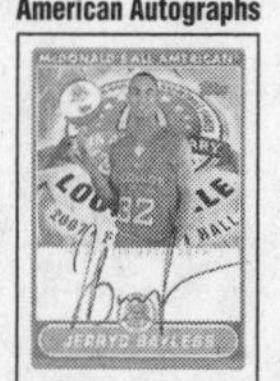

STATED ODDS 1:5908
B13 Darrell Arthur 15.00 40.00
B14 D.J. Augustin 15.00 40.00
B22 Brook Lopez 25.00 60.00
B23 Robin Lopez 15.00 40.00
DG Donte Greene 15.00 40.00
DR Derrick Rose 350.00 700.00
EG Eric Gordon 60.00 150.00
JB Jerryd Bayless 15.00 40.00
JJH J.J. Hickson 20.00 50.00
KK Kosta Koufos 15.00 40.00
KL Kevin Love 125.00 250.00
MB Michael Beasley 50.00 120.00
OJM O.J. Mayo 50.00 120.00

2008-09 Topps Mini Exclusives

MINIS INSERTED IN RIP CARDS
MEAI Allen Iverson 1.25 3.00
MEAJ Al Jefferson 1.00 2.50
MEBG Ben Gordon 1.00 2.50
MEBR Brandon Roy 1.00 2.50
MECA Carmelo Anthony 1.25 3.00
MECB Carlos Boozer 1.00 2.50
MECBI Chauncey Billups 1.00 2.50
MECM Corey Maggette .75 2.00
MECP Chris Paul 1.50 4.00
MEDH Dwight Howard 2.00 5.00
MEDL David Lee .75 2.00
MEDN Dirk Nowitzki 1.25 3.00
MEDR Dennis Rodman 1.50 4.00
MEDW Dwyane Wade 2.00 5.00
MEGA Gilbert Arenas 1.00 2.50
MEGO Greg Oden 1.00 2.50
MEJR Jason Richardson 1.00 2.50
MEJW Jerry West 1.25 3.00
MEKB Kobe Bryant 5.00 12.00
MELB Larry Bird 3.00 8.00
MELJ LeBron James 5.00 12.00
MEMJ Magic Johnson 2.50 6.00
MEMR Michael Redd 1.00 2.50
MENY Nick Young .75 2.00
MERA Ray Allen 1.00 2.50
MESN Steve Nash 1.00 2.50
MESO Shaquille O'Neal 2.00 5.00
METP Tony Parker 1.00 2.50
MEYJ Yi Jianlian 1.00 2.50
MEYM Yao Ming 1.25 3.00

2008-09 Topps Mini Exclusives Autographs

RANDOM INSERTS IN PACKS
MEACP Chris Paul 25.00 50.00

2008-09 Topps Own the Game

COMPLETE SET (20) 8.00 20.00
STATED ODDS 1:5
*GOLD: .75X TO 2X BASE HI
GOLD PRINT RUN 50 SER.#'d SETS
OTG1 Andris Biedrins .50 1.25
OTG2 Tyson Chandler .60 1.50
OTG3 Peja Stojakovic .75 2.00
OTG4 Chauncey Billups .75 2.00
OTG5 Jason Kapono .50 1.25
OTG6 Steve Nash .75 2.00
OTG7 Dwight Howard 1.50 4.00
OTG8 Marcus Camby .50 1.25
OTG9 Chris Paul 1.25 3.00
OTG10 Steve Nash .75 2.00
OTG11 Chris Paul 1.25 3.00
OTG12 Baron Davis .75 2.00
OTG13 Marcus Camby .50 1.25
OTG14 Josh Smith .75 2.00
OTG15 LeBron James 4.00 10.00
OTG16 Kobe Bryant 4.00 10.00
OTG17 Dwight Howard 1.50 4.00
OTG18 Chris Paul 1.25 3.00
OTG19 Allen Iverson 1.00 2.50
OTG20 Joe Johnson .75 2.00

2008-09 Topps Own the Game Relics

STATED ODDS 1:134
*GOLD: .5X TO 1.25X BASE HI
GOLD PRINT RUN 50 SER.#'d SETS
OTGR1 Andris Biedrins 2.00 5.00
OTGR2 Peja Stojakovic 2.50 6.00
OTGR3 Jason Kapono 2.00 5.00
OTGR4 Dwight Howard 5.00 12.00
OTGR5 Chris Paul 4.00 10.00
OTGR6 Baron Davis 2.50 6.00
OTGR7 Marcus Camby 2.00 5.00
OTGR8 Kobe Bryant 6.00 15.00
OTGR9 Dwight Howard 5.00 12.00
OTGR10 Allen Iverson 3.00 8.00

2008-09 Topps Retail Relics

RANDOM INSERTS IN RETAIL PACKS
TBKR1 Daequan Cook 1.50 4.00
TBKR2 Andrea Bargnani 2.00 5.00
TBKR3 LaMarcus Aldridge 2.50 6.00
TBKR4 Andrew Bynum 3.00 8.00
TBKR5 Caron Butler 2.50 6.00
TBKR6 Chris Bosh 2.50 6.00
TBKR7 Corey Brewer 2.00 5.00
TBKR8 Corey Maggette 2.00 5.00
TBKR9 Rashad McCants 2.00 5.00
TBKR10 Zach Randolph 2.00 5.00
TBKR11 Martell Webster 2.00 5.00
TBKR12 Dwight Howard 5.00 12.00
TBKR13 Eddy Curry 2.00 5.00
TBKR14 Gilbert Arenas 2.50 6.00
TBKR15 Greg Oden 2.50 6.00
TBKR16 Jamal Crawford 2.00 5.00
TBKR17 Ronnie Brewer 2.00 5.00
TBKR18 Juan Carlos Navarro 2.00 5.00
TBKR19 Joe Johnson 2.50 6.00
TBKR20 Brandan Wright 2.00 5.00

TBKR21 Kirk Hinrich 2.50 6.00
TBKR22 Lamar Odom 2.50 6.00
TBKR23 Mehmet Okur 2.00 5.00
TBKR24 Glen Davis 2.00 5.00
TBKR25 Monta Ellis 2.50 6.00
TBKR26 Paul Pierce 3.00 8.00
TBKR27 Peja Stojakovic 2.50 6.00
TBKR28 Yao Ming 3.00 8.00
TBKR29 Richard Hamilton 2.00 5.00
TBKR30 Ron Artest 2.50 6.00
TBKR31 Shawn Marion 2.50 6.00
TBKR32 Jarrett Jack 2.00 5.00
TBKR33 Tim Duncan 4.00 10.00
TBKR34 Vince Carter 3.00 8.00
TBKR35 Yi Jianlian 2.50 6.00

2008-09 Topps Rip Cards 99

PRINT RUN 99 SER.#'d SETS
*RIP 25: .5X TO 1.25X BASE HI
RIP 10 UNPRICED DUE TO SCARCITY
1 Chris Paul 8.00 20.00
2 Allen Iverson 6.00 15.00
3 Tony Parker 6.00 15.00
4 LeBron James 15.00 40.00
5 Kobe Bryant 10.00 25.00
6 Shaquille O'Neal 10.00 25.00
7 Larry Bird 15.00 40.00
8 Magic Johnson 10.00 25.00
9 Carlos Boozer 5.00 12.00
10 Jason Kidd 10.00 25.00
11 Chauncey Billups 5.00 12.00
12 Jason Richardson 5.00 12.00
13 Corey Maggette 4.00 10.00
14 David Lee 5.00 12.00
15 Dwyane Wade 10.00 25.00
16 Greg Oden 5.00 12.00
17 Yi Jianlian 5.00 12.00
18 Nick Young 5.00 12.00
19 Dennis Rodman 6.00 15.00
20 Ray Allen 6.00 15.00
21 Steve Nash 6.00 15.00
23 Michael Redd 5.00 12.00
24 Jerry West 6.00 15.00
25 Gilbert Arenas 5.00 12.00
26 Dwight Howard 10.00 25.00
27 Yao Ming 6.00 15.00
28 Carmelo Anthony 6.00 15.00
29 Ben Gordon 5.00 12.00
30 Dirk Nowitzki 6.00 15.00

2008-09 Topps Rookie Medallions

PRINT RUN 15 SER.#'d SETS
14KAR Anthony Randolph 25.00 60.00
14KBL Brook Lopez 30.00 80.00
14KBR Brandon Rush 20.00 50.00
14KDA Darrell Arthur 20.00 50.00
14KDG Danilo Gallinari 30.00 80.00
14KDJA D.J. Augustin 20.00 50.00
14KDR Derrick Rose 150.00 400.00
14KEG Eric Gordon 50.00 120.00
14KJA Joe Alexander 20.00 50.00
14KJB Jerryd Bayless 20.00 50.00
14KKL Kevin Love 80.00 200.00
14KMB Michael Beasley 30.00 80.00
14KOJM O.J. Mayo 30.00 80.00
14KRL Robin Lopez 20.00 50.00
14KRW Russell Westbrook 100.00 250.00

2008-09 Topps Rookie Photo Shoot Autographs

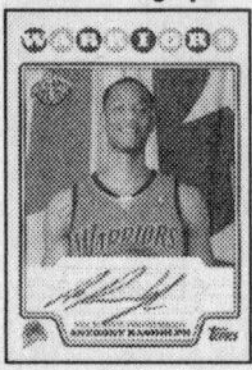

STATED ODDS 1:240 PACKS
*RED INK: .6X TO 1.5X BASE HI
RED INK STATED ODDS 1:243 PACKS
RPAR Anthony Randolph 10.00 25.00
RPBL Brook Lopez 12.00 30.00
RPBR Brandon Rush 8.00 20.00
RPCDR Chris Douglas-Roberts 8.00 20.00
RPCL Courtney Lee 12.00 30.00
RPDA Darrell Arthur 8.00 20.00
RPDGR Donte Greene 8.00 20.00
RPDJ DeAndre Jordan 15.00 40.00
RPDJA D.J. Augustin 8.00 20.00
RPDJW D.J. White 8.00 20.00
RPDR Derrick Rose 175.00 350.00
RPEG Eric Gordon 30.00 80.00
RPGH George Hill 12.00 30.00
RPJA Joe Alexander 8.00 20.00
RPJB Jerryd Bayless 8.00 20.00
RPJD Joey Dorsey 8.00 20.00
RPJJH J.J. Hickson 10.00 25.00
RPJM JaVale McGee 12.00 30.00
RPJRG J.R. Giddens 8.00 20.00
RPJT Jason Thompson 8.00 20.00
RPKK Kosta Koufos 8.00 20.00
RPKL Kevin Love 40.00 100.00
RPKW Kyle Weaver 8.00 20.00
RPMB Michael Beasley 20.00 50.00
RPMC Mario Chalmers 12.00 30.00
RPMS Marreese Speights 8.00 20.00
RPOJM O.J. Mayo 20.00 50.00
RPPE Patrick Ewing Jr. 8.00 20.00
RPRA Ryan Anderson 12.00 30.00
RPRH Roy Hibbert 12.00 30.00
RPRL Robin Lopez 8.00 20.00
RPRW Russell Westbrook 50.00 125.00
RPSW Sonny Weems 8.00 20.00
RPWS Walter Sharpe 8.00 20.00

2008-09 Topps Rookie Photo Shoot Autographs Dual

STATED ODDS 1:1461
RPDAA Ryan Anderson 15.00 40.00
Joe Alexander
RPDBL Michael Beasley 40.00 100.00
Kevin Love
RPDGA Eric Gordon 15.00 40.00
D.J. Augustin
RPDGB Eric Gordon 15.00 40.00
Jerryd Bayless
RPDGW Eric Gordon 15.00 40.00
D.J. White
RPDHK J.J. Hickson 15.00 40.00
Kosta Koufos
RPDLL Brook Lopez 15.00 40.00
Robin Lopez
RPDMB O.J. Mayo 25.00 60.00
Michael Beasley
RPDML O.J. Mayo 30.00 80.00
Kevin Love
RPDRB Derrick Rose 75.00 200.00
Michael Beasley
RPDRC Brandon Rush 15.00 40.00
Mario Chalmers
RPDRL Derrick Rose 200.00 350.00
Kevin Love
RPDRM Derrick Rose 75.00 200.00
O.J. Mayo
RPDTR Jason Thompson 15.00 40.00
Anthony Randolph
RPDWB Russell Westbrook 60.00 150.00
Jerryd Bayless

2008-09 Topps Rookie Photo Shoot Autographs Dual Red

OVERALL STATED ODDS 1:243
SOME UNPRICED DUE TO SCARCITY
RPDAA Ryan Anderson 20.00 50.00
Joe Alexander
RPDGA Eric Gordon 20.00 50.00
D.J. Augustin
RPDGB Eric Gordon 20.00 50.00
Jerryd Bayless
RPDGW Eric Gordon 20.00 50.00
D.J. White
RPDLL Brook Lopez 50.00 100.00
Robin Lopez
RPDMB O.J. Mayo 50.00 120.00
Michael Beasley
RPDML O.J. Mayo 50.00 120.00
Kevin Love
RPDRL Derrick Rose 200.00 350.00
Kevin Love
RPDRM Derrick Rose 75.00 200.00
O.J. Mayo
RPDTR Jason Thompson 30.00 60.00
Anthony Randolph
RPDWB Russell Westbrook 60.00 150.00
Jerryd Bayless

2008-09 Topps Rookie Photo Shoot Autographs Triple

STATED ODDS 1:5908
RPTABS Joe Alexander 30.00 80.00
Kevin Love
Marreese Speights
RPTBLR Michael Beasley 100.00 200.00
Kevin Love
Derrick Rose
RPTDRD Joey Dorsey 60.00 150.00
Derrick Rose
Chris Douglas-Roberts
RPTGBW Eric Gordon 60.00 120.00
Jerryd Bayless
Russell Westbrook
RPTLKL Brook Lopez 20.00 50.00
Kosta Koufos
Robin Lopez
RPTMBA O.J. Mayo 20.00 50.00
Jerryd Bayless
D.J. Augustin
RPTRAC Brandon Rush 40.00 100.00
Darrell Arthur
Mario Chalmers
RPTRBM Derrick Rose 125.00 250.00
Michael Beasley
O.J. Mayo

2008-09 Topps Rookie Photo Shoot Autographs Triple Red

OVERALL STATED ODDS 1:5908
SOME UNPRICED DUE TO SCARCITY
RPTABS Joe Alexander 30.00 80.00
Kevin Love
Marreese Speights
RPTDRD Joey Dorsey 60.00 150.00
Derrick Rose
Chris Douglas-Roberts
RPTRAC Brandon Rush 40.00 100.00
Darrell Arthur
Mario Chalmers
RPTRBM Derrick Rose 125.00 250.00
Michael Beasley
O.J. Mayo

2009-10 Topps

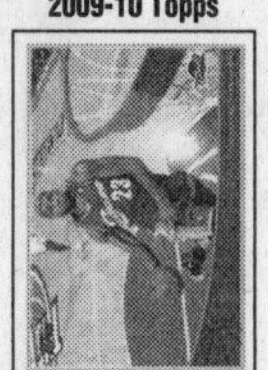

COMP.SET w/o RCs (315) 15.00 40.00
COMPLETE SET (330) 30.00 80.00
UNPRICED TAGS PRINT RUN ONE SET
UNPRICED LOGOMEN PRINT RUN ONE SET
UNPRICED PRESS PLATE PRINT RUN ONE SET
1 Joe Johnson .20 .50
2 Josh Smith .20 .50
3 Mike Bibby .15 .40
4 Marvin Williams .15 .40
5 Al Horford .20 .50
6 Ronald Murray .12 .30
7 Zaza Pachulia .12 .30
8 Acie Law .12 .30
9 Solomon Jones .12 .30
10 Maurice Evans .12 .30
11 Mario West .12 .30
12 Paul Pierce .25 .60
13 Ray Allen .20 .50
14 Kevin Garnett .40 1.00
15 Rajon Rondo .25 .60
16 Eddie House .12 .30
17 Kendrick Perkins .15 .40
18 Tony Allen .12 .30
19 Leon Powe .12 .30
20 Glen Davis .15 .40
21 Brian Scalabrine .12 .30
22 Stephon Marbury .15 .40
23 Gerald Wallace .20 .50
24 Boris Diaw .15 .40
25 Emeka Okafor .20 .50
26 Raymond Felton .15 .40
27 Raja Bell .15 .40
28 D.J. Augustin .15 .40
29 Vladimir Radmanovic .12 .30
30 Sean Singletary .12 .30
31 DeSagana Diop .12 .30
32 Ben Gordon .20 .50
33 Derrick Rose .60 1.50
34 Luol Deng .20 .50
35 John Salmons .12 .30
36 Tim Thomas .12 .30
37 Brad Miller .15 .40
38 Kirk Hinrich .20 .50
39 Tyrus Thomas .15 .40
40 Joakim Noah .20 .50
41 Aaron Gray .12 .30
42 LeBron James 1.00 2.50
43 Mo Williams .15 .40
44 Zydrunas Ilgauskas .15 .40
45 Delonte West .12 .30
46 Anderson Varejao .12 .30
47 Daniel Gibson .15 .40
48 Ben Wallace .20 .50
49 J.J. Hickson .15 .40
50 Wally Szczerbiak .15 .40
51 Aleksandar Pavlovic .12 .30
52 Dirk Nowitzki .25 .60
53 Jason Terry .15 .40
54 Josh Howard .15 .40
55 Jason Kidd .20 .50
56 Brandon Bass .12 .30
57 Jose Barea .25 .60
58 Antoine Wright .12 .30
59 Gerald Green .15 .40
60 Erick Dampier .12 .30
61 Devean George .12 .30
62 Carmelo Anthony .25 .60
63 Chauncey Billups .20 .50
64 Nene .15 .40
65 J.R. Smith .12 .30
66 Kenyon Martin .20 .50
67 Linas Kleiza .12 .30
68 Dahntay Jones .12 .30
69 Chris Andersen .30 .75
70 Renaldo Balkman .12 .30
71 Anthony Carter .12 .30
72 Allen Iverson .25 .60
73 Richard Hamilton .15 .40
74 Tayshaun Prince .20 .50
75 Rodney Stuckey .20 .50
76 Rasheed Wallace .20 .50
77 Antonio McDyess .15 .40
78 Jason Maxiell .12 .30
79 Arron Afflalo .12 .30
80 Amir Johnson .12 .30
81 Walter Herrmann .12 .30
82 Stephen Jackson .12 .30
83 Corey Maggette .15 .40
84 Jamal Crawford .12 .30
85 Kelenna Azubuike .12 .30
86 Monta Ellis .15 .40
87 Andris Biedrins .20 .50
88 Marco Belinelli .12 .30
89 C.J. Watson .12 .30
90 Anthony Morrow .12 .30
91 Brandan Wright .12 .30
92 Anthony Randolph .15 .40
93 Yao Ming .25 .60
94 Ron Artest .20 .50
95 Tracy McGrady .20 .50
96 Luis Scola .15 .40
97 Von Wafer .12 .30
98 Aaron Brooks .12 .30
99 Carl Landry .12 .30
100 Shane Battier .20 .50
101 Kyle Lowry .15 .40
102 Chuck Hayes .12 .30
103 Danny Granger .20 .50
104 Mike Dunleavy .15 .40
105 T.J. Ford .12 .30
106 Marquis Daniels .12 .30
107 Troy Murphy .15 .40
108 Jarrett Jack .15 .40
109 Rasho Nesterovic .12 .30
110 Brandon Rush .15 .40
111 Roy Hibbert .20 .50
112 Jeff Foster .12 .30
113 Zach Randolph .15 .40
114 Al Thornton .15 .40
115 Baron Davis .20 .50
116 Eric Gordon .20 .50
117 Chris Kaman .15 .40
118 Marcus Camby .12 .30
119 Mardy Collins .12 .30
120 Ricky Davis .15 .40
121 DeAndre Jordan .20 .50
122 Steve Novak .12 .30
123 Kobe Bryant 1.00 2.50
124 Pau Gasol .20 .50
125 Andrew Bynum .25 .60
126 Derek Fisher .15 .40
127 Lamar Odom .20 .50
128 Trevor Ariza .12 .30
129 Jordan Farmar .12 .30
130 Adam Morrison .15 .40
131 Sasha Vujacic .12 .30
132 Luke Walton .12 .30
133 D.J. Mbenga .12 .30
134 O.J. Mayo .20 .50
135 Rudy Gay .20 .50
136 Hakim Warrick .15 .40
137 Marc Gasol .15 .40
138 Mike Conley Jr. .15 .40
139 Darko Milicic .12 .30
140 Darrell Arthur .15 .40
141 Hamed Haddadi .20 .50
142 Quinton Ross .12 .30
143 Dwyane Wade .40 1.00
144 Michael Beasley .20 .50
145 Jermaine O'Neal .20 .50
146 Udonis Haslem .15 .40
147 Daequan Cook .12 .30
148 Mario Chalmers .20 .50
149 Chris Quinn .12 .30
150 Jamario Moon .12 .30
151 Joel Anthony RC .20 .50
152 Luther Head .12 .30
153 Michael Redd .20 .50
154 Richard Jefferson .20 .50
155 Charlie Villanueva .15 .40
156 Andrew Bogut .20 .50
157 Luke Ridnour .15 .40
158 Ramon Sessions .15 .40
159 Luc Mbah a Moute .12 .30
160 Joe Alexander .12 .30
161 Charlie Bell .12 .30
162 Keith Bogans .12 .30
163 Shelden Williams .12 .30
164 Al Jefferson .20 .50
165 Randy Foye .12 .30
166 Ryan Gomes .12 .30
167 Kevin Love .30 .75
168 Craig Smith .12 .30
169 Mike Miller .20 .50
170 Sebastian Telfair .12 .30
171 Corey Brewer .12 .30
172 Brian Cardinal .12 .30
173 Rodney Carney .12 .30
174 Devin Harris .20 .50
175 Vince Carter .25 .60
176 Brook Lopez .20 .50
177 Yi Jianlian .15 .40
178 Keyon Dooling .12 .30
179 Jarvis Hayes .12 .30
180 Bobby Simmons .12 .30
181 Ryan Anderson .20 .50
182 Josh Boone .12 .30
183 Chris Douglas-Roberts .12 .30
184 Sean Williams .12 .30
185 Chris Paul .30 .75
186 David West .20 .50
187 Peja Stojakovic .20 .50
188 Rasual Butler .12 .30
189 James Posey .12 .30
190 Tyson Chandler .15 .40
191 Devin Brown .12 .30
192 Morris Peterson .12 .30
193 Hilton Armstrong .12 .30
194 Julian Wright .12 .30
195 Antonio Daniels .12 .30
196 Chris Wilcox .12 .30
197 Al Harrington .15 .40
198 David Lee .15 .40
199 Nate Robinson .20 .50
200 Wilson Chandler .15 .40
201 Chris Duhon .12 .30
202 Quentin Richardson .15 .40
203 Larry Hughes .15 .40
204 Danilo Gallinari .20 .50
205 Jared Jeffries .12 .30
206 Russell Westbrook .30 .75
207 Earl Watson .12 .30
208 Robert Swift .12 .30
209 Joe Smith .15 .40
210 Desmond Mason .12 .30
211 Kevin Durant .60 1.50
212 Jeff Green .15 .40
213 Nick Collison .12 .30
214 Thabo Sefolosha .15 .40
215 Damien Wilkins .12 .30
216 Rafer Alston .12 .30
217 Dwight Howard .30 .75
218 Rashard Lewis .15 .40
219 Hedo Turkoglu .20 .50
220 Jameer Nelson .15 .40
221 Mickael Pietrus .12 .30
222 Courtney Lee .15 .40
223 J.J. Redick .20 .50
224 Tyronn Lue .12 .30
225 Anthony Johnson .12 .30
226 Tony Battie .12 .30
227 Andre Iguodala .20 .50
228 Andre Miller .15 .40
229 Elton Brand .20 .50
230 Thaddeus Young .15 .40
231 Louis Williams .15 .40
232 Willie Green .12 .30
233 Marreese Speights .15 .40
234 Samuel Dalembert .12 .30
235 Reggie Evans .12 .30
236 Donyell Marshall .12 .30
237 Amare Stoudemire .20 .50
238 Shaquille O'Neal .40 1.00
239 Jason Richardson .20 .50
240 Steve Nash .20 .50
241 Leandro Barbosa .15 .40
242 Grant Hill .25 .60
243 Matt Barnes .12 .30
244 Alando Tucker .12 .30
245 Louis Amundson .12 .30
246 Robin Lopez .12 .30
247 Goran Dragic RC .30 .75
248 Jared Dudley .12 .30
249 Brandon Roy .20 .50
250 LaMarcus Aldridge .20 .50
251 Travis Outlaw .15 .40
252 Steve Blake .12 .30
253 Rudy Fernandez .15 .40
254 Greg Oden .15 .40
255 Jerryd Bayless .15 .40
256 Joel Przybilla .12 .30
257 Nicolas Batum .20 .50
258 Sergio Rodriguez .12 .30
259 Martell Webster .15 .40
260 Channing Frye .15 .40
261 Kevin Martin .20 .50
262 Andres Nocioni .12 .30
263 Francisco Garcia .15 .40
264 Beno Udrih .12 .30
265 Jason Thompson .12 .30
266 Spencer Hawes .15 .40
267 Bobby Jackson .12 .30
268 Rashad McCants .12 .30
269 Donte Greene .12 .30
270 Quincy Douby .12 .30
271 Tony Parker .20 .50
272 Tim Duncan .30 .75
273 Manu Ginobili .20 .50
274 Roger Mason .15 .40
275 Michael Finley .20 .50
276 Matt Bonner .12 .30
277 George Hill .20 .50
278 Kurt Thomas .12 .30
279 Bruce Bowen .12 .30
280 Ime Udoka .12 .30
281 Drew Gooden .15 .40
282 Chris Bosh .20 .50
283 Andrea Bargnani .15 .40
284 Shawn Marion .20 .50
285 Jose Calderon .15 .40
286 Anthony Parker .12 .30
287 Jason Kapono .12 .30
288 Marcus Banks .12 .30
289 Joey Graham .12 .30
290 Roko Ukic .12 .30
291 Pops Mensah-Bonsu .12 .30
292 Kris Humphries .12 .30
293 Carlos Boozer .20 .50
294 Deron Williams .20 .50
295 Mehmet Okur .12 .30
296 Paul Millsap .15 .40
297 Ronnie Brewer .15 .40
298 Andrei Kirilenko .20 .50
299 C.J. Miles .12 .30
300 Ronnie Price .12 .30
301 Kyle Korver .15 .40
302 Kosta Koufos .12 .30
303 Matt Harpring .15 .40
304 Brevin Knight .12 .30
305 Antawn Jamison .20 .50
306 Caron Butler .20 .50
307 Nick Young .15 .40
308 Andray Blatche .12 .30
309 DeShawn Stevenson .12 .30
310 JaVale McGee .15 .40
311 Mike James .12 .30
312 Gilbert Arenas .20 .50
313 Juan Dixon .12 .30
314 Dominic McGuire .12 .30
315 Darius Songaila .12 .30
316 Blake Griffin RC 5.00 12.00
317 Ricky Rubio RC 4.00 10.00
318 Hasheem Thabeet RC .75 2.00
319 James Harden RC 2.50 6.00
320 DeMar DeRozan RC 1.25 3.00
321 Stephen Curry RC 2.00 5.00
322 Brandon Jennings RC 1.50 4.00
323 Jordan Hill RC .75 2.00
324 Earl Clark RC .75 2.00
325 Gerald Henderson RC .75 2.00
326 Jonny Flynn RC .75 2.00
327 Tyreke Evans RC 2.00 5.00
328 Tyler Hansbrough RC 1.25 3.00
329 Terrence Williams RC .75 2.00
330 Jrue Holiday RC 1.50 4.00

2009-10 Topps Black

*BLACK: 8X TO 20X BASE HI
*BLACK RC: 5X TO 12X BASE HI
PRINT RUN 50 SER.#'d SETS
33 Derrick Rose 15.00 40.00
247 Goran Dragic 12.00 30.00
316 Blake Griffin 75.00 200.00
317 Ricky Rubio 60.00 150.00

2009-10 Topps Gold

*1-309 GOLD: 2X TO 5X BASE HI
*310-330 GOLD: .75X TO 2X BASE HI
GOLD PRINT RUN 2009 SER.#'d SETS

2009-10 Topps All-Star Relics Dual

STATED PRINT RUN 199 SER.#'d SETS
*QUAD: .6X TO 1.5X BASE HI
QUAD PRINT RUN 100 SER.#'d SETS
ASDAI Allen Iverson 4.00 10.00
ASDAS Amare Stoudemire 3.00 8.00
ASDCB Chris Bosh 3.00 8.00
ASDDW Dwyane Wade 8.00 20.00
ASDGA Gilbert Arenas 3.00 8.00
ASDKB Kobe Bryant 10.00 25.00
ASDKG Kevin Garnett 6.00 15.00
ASDPG Pau Gasol 3.00 8.00
ASDPP Paul Pierce 4.00 10.00
ASDRH Richard Hamilton 2.50 6.00
ASDSM Shawn Marion 3.00 8.00
ASDSN Steve Nash 3.00 8.00
ASDSO Shaquille O'Neal 6.00 15.00
ASDTD Tim Duncan 5.00 12.00
ASDTM Tracy McGrady 3.00 8.00
ASDTP Tony Parker 3.00 8.00
ASDVC Vince Carter 4.00 10.00
ASDYM Yao Ming 4.00 10.00
ASDCBI Chauncey Billups 3.00 8.00

2009-10 Topps Autograph Relics

STATED PRINT RUN 299 SER.#'d SETS
TARAB Andrea Bargnani 6.00 15.00
TARBG Ben Gordon 10.00 25.00
TARBR Brandon Roy 10.00 25.00
TARCB Carlos Boozer 6.00 15.00
TARDG Danny Granger 10.00 25.00
TARGO Greg Oden 6.00 15.00
TARJB Jerryd Bayless 6.00 15.00
TARLW Luke Walton 6.00 15.00
TARNY Nick Young 6.00 15.00
TARRM Rashad McCants 6.00 15.00

2009-10 Topps Championship Materials

GROUP A ODDS 1:94, GROUP B ODDS 1:320
GROUP C ODDS 1:425, GROUP D ODDS 1:235
*PATCHES: .75X TO 2X BASE HI
PATCH PRINT RUN 50 SER.#'d SETS
CMAB Andrew Bynum A 4.00 10.00
CMBB Brent Barry A 2.50 6.00
CMBR Bill Russell D 8.00 20.00
CMBW Ben Wallace A 3.00 8.00
CMCD Clyde Drexler B 5.00 12.00
CMDR David Robinson A 6.00 15.00
CMDW Dwyane Wade C 6.00 15.00
CMEB Elgin Baylor C 4.00 10.00
CMIT Isiah Thomas D 4.00 10.00
CMJE Julius Erving B 8.00 20.00
CMJH John Havlicek C 5.00 12.00
CMKB Kobe Bryant D 8.00 20.00
CMKG Kevin Garnett D 6.00 15.00
CMMG Manu Ginobili D 3.00 8.00
CMMJ Magic Johnson D 6.00 15.00
CMMM Moses Malone B 4.00 10.00
CMPG Pau Gasol D 3.00 8.00
CMPP Paul Pierce A 4.00 10.00
CMRA Ray Allen D 3.00 8.00
CMRH Richard Hamilton C 2.50 6.00
CMRW Rasheed Wallace D 3.00 8.00
CMSC Sam Cassell A 3.00 8.00
CMSO Shaquille O'Neal A 6.00 15.00
CMSP Scottie Pippen D 8.00 20.00
CMTD Tim Duncan A 5.00 12.00
CMTP Tayshaun Prince A 3.00 8.00
CMBWA Bill Walton D 4.00 10.00
CMCBI Chauncey Billups 3.00 8.00
CMDRO Dennis Rodman C 6.00 15.00
CMTPA Tony Parker D 3.00 8.00

2009-10 Topps Draft Snapshot

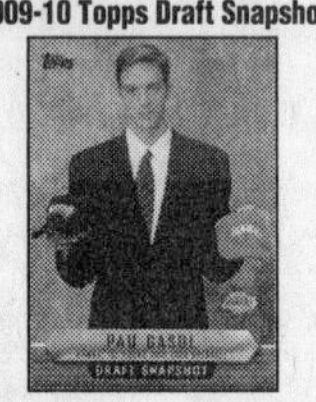

COMPLETE SET (50) 15.00 40.00
STATED ODDS 1:6
DSN Nene .50 1.25
DSAH Allan Houston .60 1.50
DSAI Allen Iverson .75 2.00
DSAS Amare Stoudemire .60 1.50
DSBD Baron Davis .60 1.50
DSBG Ben Gordon .60 1.50
DSCA Carmelo Anthony .75 2.00
DSCB Caron Butler .60 1.50
DSCJ Vince Carter .75 2.00
Antawn Jamison
DSCP Chris Paul 1.00 2.50
DSCW Chris Webber .60 1.50
DSDH Dwight Howard 1.00 2.50
DSDM Dikembe Mutombo .60 1.50
DSDR Derrick Rose 2.00 5.00
DSDW Dwyane Wade 1.25 3.00
DSEB Elton Brand .60 1.50
DSEO Emeka Okafor .60 1.50
DSGH Grant Hill .75 2.00
DSHO Hakeem Olajuwon .75 2.00
DSJJ Joe Johnson .60 1.50
DSJK Jason Kidd .60 1.50
DSJR Jason Richardson .60 1.50
DSJS Joe Smith .50 1.25
DSKA Kenny Anderson .60 1.50
DSKB Kobe Bryant 3.00 8.00
DSKD Kevin Durant 2.00 5.00
DSKG Kevin Garnett 1.25 3.00
DSLJ LeBron James 3.00 8.00
DSMC Marcus Camby .40 1.00
DSMF Michael Finley .60 1.50
DSMM Mike Miller .60 1.50
DSPE Patrick Ewing .75 2.00
DSPG Pau Gasol .60 1.50
DSPH Penny Hardaway 1.50 4.00
DSPP Paul Pierce .75 2.00
DSRA Ray Allen .60 1.50
DSRS Ralph Sampson .60 1.50
DSSN Steve Nash .60 1.50
DSSO Shaquille O'Neal 1.25 3.00
DSSP Scottie Pippen 1.25 3.00
DSTD Tim Duncan 1.00 2.50
DSTM Tracy McGrady .60 1.50
DSYM Yao Ming .75 2.00
DSCBO Chris Bosh .60 1.5
DSDHA Devin Harris .60 1.5
DSDMI Darko Milicic .40 1.0
DSDWI Deron Williams .60 1.5
DSJST Jerry Stackhouse .50 1.2
DSLJO Larry Johnson .60 1.5
DSTJF T.J. Ford .40 1.0

2009-10 Topps Franchise Fabrics Autographs

PRINT RUNS LISTED IN CHECKLIST
SOME UNPRICED DUE TO SCARCITY
FFBG Ben Gordon Number/149 8.00 20.0
FFCB Carlos Boozer Logo/41 8.00 20.0

2009-10 Topps McDonalds All American Game Day Autograph

STATED ODDS 1:670
BG Blake Griffin 400.00 800.0
BJ Brandon Jennings 30.00 80.0
BM B.J. Mullens 12.00 30.0
CB Chase Budinger 12.00 30.0
DR DeMar DeRozan 25.00 60.0
EC Earl Clark 12.00 30.0
GH Gerald Henderson 12.00 30.0
JF Jonny Flynn 12.00 30.0
JH Jrue Holiday 30.00 80.0
JH James Harden 40.00 100.0
MC Mike Conley Jr. 20.00 50.
TE Tyreke Evans 30.00 80.
TL Ty Lawson 20.00 50.
WE Wayne Ellington 12.00 30.

2009-10 Topps Rookie Rewind Jumbo Jersey Autographs

STATED PRINT RUN 99 SER.#'d SETS
JJABL Brook Lopez 10.00 25.0
JJADG Donte Greene 8.00 20.0
JJAEG Eric Gordon 15.00 40.0
JJAGH George Hill 8.00 20.0
JJAKL Kevin Love 20.00 50.0
JJAMS Marreese Speights 10.00 25.0
JJARA Ryan Anderson 8.00 20.0
JJASW Sonny Weems 8.00 20.0
JJACDR Chris Douglas-Roberts 8.00 20.
JJAJJH J.J. Hickson 8.00 20.
JJAOJM O.J. Mayo 12.00 30.

2009-10 Topps Roundball Remnants

GROUP A ODDS 1:65, GROUP B ODDS 1:33
GROUP C ODDS 1:166, GROUP D ODDS 1:955
*PATCHES: .75X TO 2X BASE HI
PATCH PRINT RUN 50 SER.#'d SETS
RRAA Arron Afflalo A 2.00 5.
RRAB Aaron Brooks A 2.00 5.
RRAG Aaron Gray B 2.00 5.
RRAH Al Harrington B 2.50 6.
RRAI Allen Iverson D 4.00 10.
RRAJ Al Jefferson B 3.00 8.0
RRAK Andrei Kirilenko C 2.50 6.0
RRAL Acie Law A 2.00 5.0
RRAM Adam Morrison B 2.50 6.0
RRAS Amare Stoudemire D 3.00 8.0
RRAT Al Thornton B 2.50 6.
RRAV Anderson Varejao D 2.50 6.
RRBD Baron Davis C 3.00 8.
RRBG Ben Gordon D 3.00 8.
RRBM Brad Miller B 2.50 6.
RRBR Brandon Roy D 3.00 8.
RRBU Beno Udrih B 2.00 5.
RRBW Brandan Wright A 2.00 5.
RRCF Channing Frye B 2.50 6.
RRCK Chris Kaman B 2.50 6.
RRCL Carl Landry A 2.00 5.
RRCM Corey Maggette D 2.50 6.
RRCV Charlie Villanueva B 2.50 6.
RRDC Daequan Cook B 2.00 5.
RRDG Danny Granger B 3.00 8.
RRDL David Lee B 2.50 6.
RRDM Darko Milicic B 2.00 5.
RRDW David West B 3.00 8.
RRFG Francisco Garcia B 2.50 6.
RRGD Glen Davis C 2.50 6.
RRJC Jamal Crawford B 2.50 6.

JH Josh Howard D 2.50 6.00
KM Kevin Martin B 3.00 8.00
LA LaMarcus Aldridge D 3.00 8.00
LB Leandro Barbosa B 2.50 6.00
LD Luol Deng B 3.00 8.00
MC Marcus Camby D 2.00 5.00
ME Monta Ellis B 3.00 8.00
PG Pau Gasol D 3.00 8.00
RA Rafer Alston C 2.00 5.00
RB Ronnie Brewer B 2.50 6.00
RG Rudy Gay A 3.00 8.00
SB Shane Battier A 3.00 8.00
SD Samuel Dalembert C 2.00 5.00
SH Spencer Hawes C 2.50 6.00
TA Trevor Ariza B 2.00 5.00
TC Tyson Chandler B 2.50 6.00
TM Tracy McGrady C 3.00 8.00
UH Udonis Haslem A 2.50 6.00
VC Vince Carter C 4.00 10.00
WC Wilson Chandler B 2.50 6.00
YJ Yi Jianlian B 2.50 6.00
ZI Zydrunas Ilgauskas B 2.00 5.00
ABA Andrea Bargnani C 2.50 6.00
ABI Andris Biedrins B 2.00 5.00
ABO Andrew Bogut B 3.00 8.00
ABY Andrew Bynum B 4.00 10.00
AIG Andre Iguodala C 3.00 8.00
AJA Antawn Jamison B 3.00 8.00
AMC Antonio McDyess B 2.50 6.00
AMI Andre Miller B 2.50 6.00
ATU Alando Tucker A 2.00 5.00
BDI Boris Diaw B 2.50 6.00
CBH Chris Bosh C 3.00 8.00
CBO Carlos Boozer B 3.00 8.00
CBR Corey Brewer C 2.00 5.00
CBU Caron Butler B 3.00 8.00
MCO Mike Conley Jr. D 2.50 6.00
RAR Ron Artest C 3.00 8.00
TJF T.J. Ford D 2.00 5.00

2008 Topps All-Star Booklet Cards

A Carmelo Anthony 4.00 10.00
P Chris Paul 4.00 10.00
W Dwyane Wade 6.00 15.00
A Gilbert Arenas 3.00 8.00
Yi Jianlian 3.00 8.00

2006 Topps Allen and Ginter

is 350-card set was release in August, 2006. The set as issued in seven-card hobby packs with an $4 SRP. ose packs came 24 to a box and there were 12 boxes a case. In addition, there were also six-card retail acks issued and those packs came 24 packs to a box d 20 boxes to a case. There were some subsets cluded in this set including Rookies (251-265); etired Greats (266-290); Managers (291-300); odern Personalities (301-314); Reprinted Allen and nters (316-319); Famous People of the Past (326-9).

OMPLETE SET (350) 60.00 120.00
OMP.SET w/o SP's (300) 15.00 40.00
P STATED ODDS 1:2 HOBBY, 1:2 RETAIL
P CL: 5/15/25/35/45/50-59/65/85/105/115
P CL: 125/135/145/150-159/165/175/185
P CL: 205/215/235/245/251/255-256/265
P CL: 285/295/305/315/325/335/345
AMED ORIGINALS ODDS 1:3227 H, 1:3227 R
9 John Wooden .25 .60

2006 Topps Allen and Ginter Mini

MINI 1-350: 1X TO 2.5X BASIC
MINI 1-350: 1X TO 2.5X BASIC RC's
PPX.15 MINIS PER 24-CT SEALED BOX
MINI SP 1-350: .6X TO 1.5X BASIC SP
MINI SP 1-350: .6X TO 1.5X BASIC SP RC's
INI SP ODDS 1:13 H, 1:13 R
OMMON CARD (351-375) 20.00 50.00
EMISTARS 351-375 30.00 60.00
NLISTED STARS 351-375 30.00 60.00
51-375 RANDOM WITHIN RIP CARDS
VERALL PLATE ODDS 1:865 H, 1:865 R
ATE PRINT RUN 1 SET PER COLOR
LACK-CYAN-MAGENTA-YELLOW ISSUED
O PLATE PRICING DUE TO SCARCITY

2006 Topps Allen and Ginter Mini A and G Back

A & G BACK: 2X TO 5X BASIC
A & G BACK: 1.5X TO 4X BASIC RC's
TATED ODDS 1:5 H, 1:5 R
A & G BACK SP: 1X TO 2.5X BASIC SP
A & G BACK SP: 1X TO 2.5X BASIC SP RC's
P STATED ODDS 1:65 H, 1:65 R

2006 Topps Allen and Ginter Mini Black

BLACK: 4X TO 10X BASIC
BLACK: 2.5X TO 6X BASIC RC's
TATED ODDS 1:10 H, 1:10 R
BLACK SP: 1.5X TO 4X BASIC SP
BLACK SP: 1.5X TO 4X BASIC SP RC's
P STATED ODDS 1:130 H, 1:130 R

2006 Topps Allen and Ginter Mini No Card Number

NO NBR: 6X TO 15X BASIC
NO NBR: 4X TO 10X BASIC RC's
NO NBR: 2X TO 5X BASIC SP
NO NBR: 2X TO 5X BASIC SP RC's
TATED ODDS 1:60 H, 1:168 R
TATED PRINT RUN 50 SETS
ARDS ARE NOT SERIAL-NUMBERED
RINT RUN INFO PROVIDED BY TOPPS

2006 Topps Allen and Ginter Autographs

ROUP A ODDS 1:2467 H, 1:3850 R
ROUP B ODDS 1:14,500 H, 1:32,000 R
ROUP C ODDS 1:2200 H, 1:4300 R
ROUP D ODDS 1:548 H, 1:1090 R
ROUP E ODDS 1:473 H, 1:1000 R
ROUP F ODDS 1:250 H, 1:520 R
ROUP G ODDS 1:158 H, 1:299 R
ROUP A PRINT RUN 50 CARDS PER
ROUP A BONDS PRINT RUN 25 CARDS
ROUP B PRINT RUN 75 CARDS PER
ROUP C PRINT RUN 100 CARDS PER
ROUP D PRINT RUN 200 CARDS PER
ROUP A-D ARE NOT SERIAL-NUMBERED
-D PRINT RUNS PROVIDED BY TOPPS
O BONDS PRICING DUE TO SCARCITY
V John Wooden D/200 * 125.00 250.00

2007 Topps Allen and Ginter

is 350-card set was released in August, 2007. The et was issued in both hobby and retail versions. The obby packs, which had an $4 SRP, consisted of eight-ards which came 24 packs to a box and 12 boxes to a ase. Similar to the 2006 set, many non-baseball players were interspersed throughout this set. There were also a group of short-printed cards, which were inserted at a stated rate of one in two hobby or retail packs. In addition, some original 19th century Allen and Ginter cards were repurchased for this product and those original cards (featuring both sports and non-sport subjects) were inserted at a stated rate of one in 17, 072 hobby and one in 34, 654 retail packs.

COMPLETE SET (350) 60.00 120.00
COMP.SET w/o SP's (300) 20.00 50.00
SP STATED ODDS 1:2 HOBBY, 1:2 RETAIL
FRAMED ORIGINALS ODDS 1:17,072 HOBBY
FRAMED ORIGINALS ODDS 1:34,654 RETAIL
331 Dennis Rodman SP 1.25 3.00
339 Jason McElwain SP 1.25 3.00

2007 Topps Allen and Ginter Mini

*MINI 1-350: 1X TO 2.5X BASIC
*MINI 1-350: .6X TO 1.5X BASIC RC's
APPX. ONE MINI PER PACK
*MINI SP 1-350: .6X TO 1.5X BASIC SP
*MINI SP 1-350: .6X TO 1.5X BASIC SP RC's
MINI SP ODDS 1:13 H, 1:13 R
COMMON CARD (351-390) 15.00 40.00
351-390 RANDOM WITHIN RIP CARDS
OVERALL PLATE ODDS 1:788 HOBBY
PLATE PRINT RUN 1 SET PER COLOR
BLACK-CYAN-MAGENTA-YELLOW ISSUED
NO PLATE PRICING DUE TO SCARCITY

2007 Topps Allen and Ginter Mini A and G Back

*A & G BACK: 1.25X TO 3X BASIC
*A & G BACK: .75X TO 2X BASIC RC's
STATED ODDS 1:5 H, 1:5 R
*A & G BACK SP: .75X TO 2X BASIC SP
*A & G BACK SP: .75X TO 2X BASIC SP RC's
SP STATED ODDS 1:65 H, 1:65 R

2007 Topps Allen and Ginter Mini Black

*BLACK: 2X TO 5X BASIC
*BLACK: 1.5X TO 4X BASIC RC's
STATED ODDS 1:10 H, 1:10 R
*BLACK SP: 1.5X TO 4X BASIC SP
*BLACK SP: 1.5X TO 4X BASIC SP RC's
SP STATED ODDS 1:130 H, 1:130 R

2007 Topps Allen and Ginter Mini Black No Number

*BLK NO NBR: 2.5X TO 6X BASIC
*BLK NO NBR: 2X TO 5X BASIC RC's
*BLK NO NBR: 1.5X TO 4X BASIC SP
*BLK NO NBR: 1.5X TO 4X BASIC SP RC's
RANDOM INSERTS IN PACKS

2007 Topps Allen and Ginter Mini No Card Number

*NO NBR: 10X TO 25X BASIC
*NO NBR: 6X TO 15X BASIC RC's
*NO NBR: 2.5X TO 6X BASIC SP
*NO NBR: 2.5X TO 6X BASIC SP RC's
STATED ODDS 1:106 H, 1:108 R
STATED PRINT RUN 50 SETS
CARDS ARE NOT SERIAL-NUMBERED
PRINT RUN INFO PROVIDED BY TOPPS

2007 Topps Allen and Ginter Autographs

GROUP A ODDS 1:64,496 H, 1:122200 R
GROUP B ODDS 1:3261 H, 1:6522 R
GROUP C ODDS 1:13,987 H, 1:27,642 R
GROUP D ODDS 1:288 H, 1:578 R
GROUP E ODDS 1:6789 H, 1:13,578 R
GROUP F ODDS 1:162 H, 1:324 R
GROUP G ODDS 1:680 H, 1:1362 R
GROUP A PRINT RUN 25 CARDS PER
GROUP B PRINT RUN 100 CARDS PER
GROUP C PRINT RUN 120 CARDS PER
GROUP D PRINT RUN 200 CARDS PER
GROUP A-D ARE NOT SERIAL-NUMBERED
A-D PRINT RUNS PROVIDED BY TOPPS
NO PUJOLS PRICING DUE TO SCARCITY
EXCH DEADLINE 7/31/2009
DR Dennis Rodman D/200 * 30.00 60.00
JMC Jason McElwain D/200 * 10.00 25.00

2007 Topps Allen and Ginter National Mini Promos

NCC7 Greg Oden 1.50 4.00

2007 Topps Allen and Ginter National Promos

NCC7 Greg Oden 1.50 4.00

2008 Topps Allen and Ginter

COMP.SET w/o FUKU.(350) 30.00 60.00
COMP.SET w/o SPs (300) 15.00 40.00
COMMON CARD (1-300) .15 .40
COMMON RC (1-300) .40 1.00
COMMON SP (301-350) 1.25 3.00
SP STATED ODDS 1:2 HOBBY
FRAMED ORIG.ODDS 1:26,500 HOBBY
247 Lisa Leslie .40 1.00

2008 Topps Allen and Ginter Mini

*MINI 1-300: .75X TO 2X BASIC
*MINI 1-300 RC: .5X TO 1.2X BASIC RC's
APPX. ONE MINI PER PACK
*MINI SP 300-350: .75X TO 2X BASIC SP
MINI SP ODDS 1:13 HOBBY
351-390 RANDOM WITHIN RIP CARDS
OVERALL PLATE ODDS 1:961 HOBBY
PLATE PRINT RUN 1 SET PER COLOR
BLACK-CYAN-MAGENTA-YELLOW ISSUED
NO PLATE PRICING DUE TO SCARCITY

2008 Topps Allen and Ginter Mini A and G Back

*A & G BACK: 1X TO 2.5X BASIC
*A & G BACK RCs: .6X TO 1.5X BASIC RCs
STATED ODDS 1:5 HOBBY
*A & G BACK SP: 1X TO 2.5X BASIC SP
SP STATED ODDS 1:65 HOBBY

2008 Topps Allen and Ginter Mini Black

*BLACK: 1.5X TO 4X BASIC
*BLACK RCs: .75X TO 2X BASIC RCs
STATED ODDS 1:10 HOBBY
*BLACK SP: 1.2X TO 3X BASIC SP
SP STATED ODDS 1:130 HOBBY

2008 Topps Allen and Ginter Mini No Card Number

*NO NBR: 10X TO 25X BASIC
*NO NBR RCs: 4X TO 10X BASIC RCs
*NO NBR: 1.5X TO 4X BASIC SP
STATED ODDS 1:151 HOBBY
STATED PRINT RUN 50 SETS
CARDS ARE NOT SERIAL-NUMBERED
PRINT RUN INFO PROVIDED BY TOPPS

2008 Topps Allen and Ginter Autographs

GROUP A ODDS 1:277 HOBBY
GROUP B ODDS 1:256 HOBBY
GROUP C ODDS 1:135 HOBBY
GRP A PRINT RUNS B/W 90-240 COPIES PER
CARDS ARE NOT SERIAL-NUMBERED
PRINT RUNS PROVIDED BY TOPPS
EXCHANGE DEADLINE 7/31/2010
LL Lisa Leslie A/190 * 20.00 50.00

2008 Topps Allen and Ginter Relics

GROUP A ODDS 1:280 HOBBY
GROUP B ODDS 1:71 HOBBY
GROUP C ODDS 1:20 HOBBY
RELIC AU ODDS 1:26,431 HOBBY
GROUP A B/W 100-250 COPIES PER
CARDS ARE NOT SERIAL NUMBERED
PRINT RUN INFO PROVIDED BY TOPPS
LL Lisa Leslie A/250 * 12.50 30.00

2009 Topps Allen and Ginter

COMPLETE SET (350) 30.00 60.00
COMP.SET w/o SP's (300) 12.50 30.00
COMMON CARD (1-300) .15 .40
COMMON RC (1-300) .40 1.00
COMMON SP (301-350) 1.25 3.00
SP STATED ODDS 1:2 HOBBY
346 Dominique Wilkins SP 1.25 3.00

2009 Topps Allen and Ginter Mini

COMP.SET w/o EXT (350) 125.00 250.00
*MINI 1-300: .75X TO 2X BASIC
*MINI 1-300 RC: .5X TO 1.2X BASIC RC's
APPX. ONE MINI PER PACK
*MINI SP 301-350: .5X TO 1.2X BASIC SP
MINI SP ODDS 1:13 HOBBY
351-390 RANDOM WITHIN RIP CARDS
OVERALL PLATE ODDS 1:608 HOBBY
PLATE PRINT RUN 1 SET PER COLOR
BLACK-CYAN-MAGENTA-YELLOW ISSUED
NO PLATE PRICING DUE TO SCARCITY

2009 Topps Allen and Ginter Mini A and G Back

*A & G BACK: 1X TO 2.5X BASIC
*A & G BACK RCs: .6X TO 1.5X BASIC RCs
STATED ODDS 1:5 HOBBY
*A & G BACK SP: .6X TO 1.5X BASIC SP
SP STATED ODDS 1:65 HOBBY

2009 Topps Allen and Ginter Mini Bazooka

STATED ODDS 1:191 HOBBY
STATED PRINT RUN 25 SER.#'d SETS
NO PRICING DUE TO SCARCITY

2009 Topps Allen and Ginter Mini Black

*BLACK: 2X TO 5X BASIC
*BLACK RCs: .75X TO 2X BASIC RCs
STATED ODDS 1:10 HOBBY
*BLACK SP: .75X TO 2X BASIC SP
SP STATED ODDS 1:130 HOBBY

2009 Topps Allen and Ginter Mini No Card Number

*NO NBR: 8X TO 20X BASIC
*NO NBR RCs: 3X TO 8X BASIC RCs
*NO NBR SP: 1.2X TO 3X BASIC SP
STATED ODDS 1:95 HOBBY
STATED PRINT RUN 50 SETS

2009 Topps Allen and Ginter Autographs

GROUP A ODDS 1:2730 HOBBY
GROUP B ODDS 1:51 HOBBY
CARDS ARE NOT SERIAL-NUMBERED
PRINT RUNS PROVIDED BY TOPPS
NO PHELPS PRICING DUE TO SCARCITY
EXCHANGE DEADLINE 6/30/2012
DOW Dominique Wilkins/239 * B 15.00 40.00

2009 Topps Allen and Ginter Relics

GROUP A ODDS 1:100 HOBBY
GROUP B ODDS 1:215 HOBBY
GROUP D ODDS 1:17 HOBBY
GROUP C ODDS 1:39 HOBBY
CARDS ARE NOT SERIAL-NUMBERED
PRINT RUNS PROVIDED BY TOPPS
DOW Dominique Wilkins/250 * A 10.00 25.00

2010 Topps Allen and Ginter

COMPLETE SET (350) 60.00 120.00
COMP.SET w/o SPs (300) 15.00 40.00
COMMON CARD (1-300) .15 .40
COMMON RC (1-300) .40 1.00
COMMON SP (301-350) 1.25 3.00
SP STATED ODDS 1:2 HOBBY
148 Anne Donovan .15 .40

2010 Topps Allen and Ginter Mini

*MINI 1-300: .75X TO 2X BASIC
*MINI 1-300 RC: .5X TO 1.2X BASIC RC's
APPX. ONE MINI PER PACK
*MINI SP 301-350: .5X TO 1.2X BASIC SP
MINI SP ODDS 1:13 HOBBY
COMMON CARD (351-400) 6.00 15.00
351-400 RANDOM WITHIN RIP CARDS
STRASBURG 401 ISSUED IN PACKS
OVERALL PLATE ODDS 1:799 HOBBY
PLATE PRINT RUN 1 SET PER COLOR
BLACK-CYAN-MAGENTA-YELLOW ISSUED
NO PLATE PRICING DUE TO SCARCITY

2010 Topps Allen and Ginter Mini A and G Back

*A & G BACK: 1X TO 2.5X BASIC
*A & G BACK RCs: .6X TO 1.5X BASIC RCs
STATED ODDS 1:5 HOBBY
*A & G BACK SP: .6X TO 1.5X BASIC SP
SP STATED ODDS 1:65 HOBBY

2010 Topps Allen and Ginter Mini Black

*BLACK: 2X TO 5X BASIC
*BLACK RCs: .75X TO 2X BASIC RCs
STATED ODDS 1:10 HOBBY
*BLACK SP: .75X TO 2X BASIC SP
SP STATED ODDS 1:130 HOBBY

2010 Topps Allen and Ginter Mini No Card Number

*NO NBR: 8X TO 20X BASIC
*NO NBR RCs: 3X TO 8X BASIC RCs
*NO NBR SP: 1.2X TO 3X BASIC SP
STATED ODDS 1:140 HOBBY

2010 Topps Allen and Ginter Autographs

STATED ODDS 1:HOBBY
ASTERISK EQUALS PARTIAL EXCHANGE
AD Anne Donovan 10.00 25.00

2010 Topps Allen and Ginter Relics

STATED ODDS 1:11 HOBBY
AD Anne Donovan 5.00 12.00

2011 Topps Allen and Ginter

COMPLETE SET (350) 50.00 100.00
COMP.SET w/o SP's (300) 12.50 30.00
COMMON CARD (1-300) .15 .40
COMMON RC (1-300) .40 1.00
COMMON SP (301-350) 1.25 3.00
SP ODDS 1:2 HOBBY
15 Diana Taurasi .15 .40
133 Geno Auriemma .25 .60
136 Dick Vitale .15 .40
190 Sue Bird .15 .40

2011 Topps Allen and Ginter Glossy

ISSUED VIA TOPPS ONLINE STORE
STATED PRINT RUN 999 SER.#'d SETS
15 Diana Taurasi .75 2.00
133 Geno Auriemma 1.25 3.00
136 Dick Vitale .75 2.00
190 Sue Bird .75 2.00

2011 Topps Allen and Ginter Autographs

STATED ODDS 1:68 HOBBY
DUAL AUTO ODDS 1:56,000 HOBBY
EXCHANGE DEADLINE 6/30/2014
DTU Diana Taurasi 12.50 30.00
DVI Dick Vitale 20.00 50.00
GAU Geno Auriemma EXCH 12.50 30.00
SBI Sue Bird 20.00 50.00

2011 Topps Allen and Ginter Code Cards

*MINI 1-300: 1.5X TO 4X BASIC
*MINI 1-300 RC: .75X TO 2X BASIC RC's
OVERALL CODE ODDS 1:8 HOBBY

2011 Topps Allen and Ginter Mini

*MINI 1-300: .75X TO 2X BASIC
*MINI 1-300 RC: .5X TO 1.2X BASIC RC's
*MINI SP 301-350: .5X TO 1.2X BASIC SP
MINI SP ODDS 1:13 HOBBY
COMMON CARD (351-400) 15.00 40.00
351-400 RANDOM WITHIN RIP CARDS
STATED PLATE ODDS 1:751 HOBBY
PLATE PRINT RUN 1 SET PER COLOR
BLACK-CYAN-MAGENTA-YELLOW ISSUED
NO PLATE PRICING DUE TO SCARCITY

2011 Topps Allen and Ginter Mini A and G Back

*A & G BACK: 1X TO 2.5X BASIC
*A & G BACK RCs: .6X TO 1.5X BASIC RCs
A & G BACK ODDS 1:5 HOBBY
*A & G BACK SP: .6X TO 1.5X BASIC SP
A & G BACK SP ODDS 1:65 HOBBY

2011 Topps Allen and Ginter Mini Black

*BLACK: 2X TO 5X BASIC
*BLACK RCs: .75X TO 2X BASIC RCs
BLACK ODDS 1:10 HOBBY
BLACK SP ODDS 1:130 HOBBY
*BLACK SP: .75X TO 2X BASIC SP

2011 Topps Allen and Ginter Mini No Card Number

*NO NBR: 8X TO 20X BASIC
*NO NBR RCs: 3X TO 8X BASIC RCs
*NO NBR SP: 1.2X TO 3X BASIC SP
STATED ODDS 1:142 HOBBY

2011 Topps Allen and Ginter Relics

STATED ODDS 1:10 HOBBY
EXCHANGE DEADLINE 6/30/2014
DTU Diana Taurasi 6.00 15.00
DVA Dick Vitale 6.00 15.00
GAU Geno Auriemma 8.00 20.00
SBI Sue Bird 6.00 15.00

2012 Topps Allen and Ginter

COMPLETE SET (350) 40.00 80.00
COMP.SET w/o SP's (300) 20.00 50.00
SP ODDS 1:2 HOBBY
19 Bob Knight .50 1.25
85 Curly Neal .40 1.00
113 Meadowlark Lemon .40 1.00
154 Bob Hurley Sr. .15 .40
339 Swin Cash SP 1.25 3.00

2012 Topps Allen and Ginter Autographs

STATED ODDS 1:51 HOBBY
EXCHANGE DEADELINE 06/30/2015
BHS Bob Hurley Sr. 8.00 20.00
BKN Bob Knight 40.00 80.00
CNE Curly Neal 20.00 50.00
MLE Meadowlark Lemon 20.00 50.00
SCA Swin Cash 10.00 25.00

2012 Topps Allen and Ginter Mini

COMP.SET w/o EXT (350)
*MINI 1-300: .75X TO 2X BASIC
*MINI 1-300 RC: .5X TO 1.2X BASIC RC's
*MINI SP 301-350: .5X TO 1.2X BASIC SP
MINI SP ODDS 1:13 HOBBY
351-400 RANDOM WITHIN RIP CARDS
STATED PLATE ODDS 1:564 HOBBY

2012 Topps Allen and Ginter Mini A and G Back

*A & G BACK: 1X TO 2.5X BASIC
*A & G BACK RCs: .6X TO 1.5X BASIC RCs
A & G BACK ODDS 1:5 HOBBY
*A & G BACK SP: .6X TO 1.5X BASIC SP
A & G BACK SP ODDS 1:65 HOBBY

2012 Topps Allen and Ginter Mini Black

*BLACK: 1.5X TO 4X BASIC
*BLACK RCs: .6X TO 1.5X BASIC RCs
BLACK ODDS 1:10 HOBBY
*BLACK SP: 1X TO 2.5X BASIC SP
BLACK SP ODDS 1:130 HOBBY

2012 Topps Allen and Ginter Mini Gold Border

*GOLD: .5X TO 1.2X BASIC
*GOLD RCs: .5X TO 1.2X BASIC RCs
COMMON SP (301-350) .40 1.00
SP SEMIS .60 1.50
SP UNLISTED 1.00 2.50
339 Swin Cash .40 1.00

2012 Topps Allen and Ginter Mini No Card Number

*NO NBR: 6X TO 15X BASIC
*NO NBR RCs: 2.5X TO 6X BASIC RCs
*NO NBR SP: 1.2X TO 3X BASIC SP
STATED ODDS 1:111 HOBBY

2012 Topps Allen and Ginter Relics

STATED ODDS 1:10 HOBBY
EXCHANGE DEADELINE 06/30/2015
BH Bob Hurley Sr. 3.00 8.00
BK Bob Knight 5.00 12.00
CN Curly Neal EXCH 6.00 15.00
MLE Meadowlark Lemon 6.00 15.00
SCA Swin Cash 3.00 8.00

2002 Topps All-Star Game

Produced by Topps for distribution at the 2002 NBA All-Star Game Show via wrapper redemption, this nine card set utilizes the base 2001-02 Topps set design enhanced with a holofoil finish on the front and the All-Star Game 2002 Philadelphia logo.

COMPLETE SET (9) 8.00 20.00
1 Shaquille O'Neal 2.00 5.00
2 Tim Duncan 1.50 4.00
3 Allen Iverson 1.25 3.00
4 Tracy McGrady 1.00 2.50
5 Steve Francis .75 2.00
6 Elton Brand .75 2.00
7 Jason Richardson 1.25 3.00
8 Jamaal Tinsley .75 2.00
9 Chris Webber .75 2.00

2003 Topps All-Star Game

Distributed by Topps at the All-Star Jam Session show in Atlanta, this set was available via wrapper redemption at the Topps show booth. Collectors were required to turn in three packs of 2002-03 Topps products in exchange for this eight card set. The set uses the base card design of 2002-03 topps and is enhanced with a gold foil 2003 NBA All-Star Game logo in the lower left hand corner of the card front.

COMPLETE SET (8) 6.00 15.00
1 Shaquille O'Neal 1.50 4.00
2 Mike Dunleavy .75 2.00
3 Glenn Robinson .75 2.00
4 Tracy McGrady 1.50 4.00
5 Stephon Marbury .75 2.00
6 Allen Iverson 1.25 3.00
7 Dirk Nowitzki 1.00 2.50
8 Jason Kidd 1.00 2.50

2009 Topps American Heritage Heroes Heroes of Sport

COMPLETE SET (25) 12.50 25.00
STATED ODDS 1:4
*GOLD/199: 3X TO 8X BASIC INSERTS
*PLATINUM/25: 5X TO 12X BASIC INSERTS
HS5 Larry Bird .60 1.50
HS15 Bill Russell .60 1.50
HS24 Magic Johnson .40 1.00

2009 Topps American Heritage Heroes Heroes of Sport Relics

STATED ODDS 1:234
HSR5 Magic Johnson Jsy 10.00 25.00
HSR8 Larry Bird Jsy 10.00 25.00
HSR14 Bill Russell Jsy 15.00 40.00

1992-93 Topps Archives

Featuring the missing years of Topps basketball from 1981 through 1991, this 150-card set consists of 139 current NBA players and an 11-card subset of the Number One draft picks from 1981 to 1991. Production was limited to 10,000 24-box cases (24 packs per box). Each pack contained 14 cards and one Stadium Club membership card. Since Topps did not produce basketball cards when the photos were taken, the front designs are patterned after the Topps baseball cards issued during the same year. The horizontal backs display a small, square, current action player photo that overlaps a red, yellow, and white box containing biographical information, and statistics from college and the NBA. The set name, player's name, and team are printed in the upper left portion. The background is in varying shades of blue with a light beam design. After opening with a No. 1 Draft Pick (1-11) subset, the player cards are arranged by year in ascending chronological order and alphabetically within each season. The set closes with checklist (149-150) cards.

COMPLETE SET (150) 6.00 15.00
1 Mark Aguirre FDP .08 .15
2 James Worthy FDP .08 .15
3 Ralph Sampson FDP .08 .15
4 Hakeem Olajuwon FDP .10 .30
5 Patrick Ewing FDP .08 .25
6 Brad Daugherty FDP .08 .15
7 David Robinson FDP .10 .30
8 Danny Manning FDP .08 .15
9 Pervis Ellison FDP UER .08 .15
(Text on back: Clippers not Lakers had 2nd pick)
10 Derrick Coleman FDP .08 .15
11 Larry Johnson FDP .08 .15
12 Mark Aguirre .08 .15
13 Danny Ainge .08 .15
14 Rolando Blackman .08 .15
15 Tom Chambers .08 .15
16 Eddie Johnson .08 .15
17 Alton Lister .08 .15
18 Larry Nance .08 .15
19 Kurt Rambis .08 .15
20 Isiah Thomas .10 .30
21 Buck Williams .08 .15
22 Orlando Woolridge .08 .15
23 John Bagley .08 .15
24 Terry Cummings .08 .15
25 Mark Eaton .08 .15
26 Sleepy Floyd .08 .25
27 Fat Lever .08 .15
28 Ricky Pierce .08 .25
29 Trent Tucker .08 .15
30 Dominique Wilkins .10 .30
31 James Worthy .08 .25
32 Thurl Bailey .08 .15
33 Clyde Drexler .10 .30
34 Dale Ellis .08 .15
35 Sidney Green .08 .15
36 Derek Harper .08 .15
37 Jeff Malone .08 .15
38 Rodney McCray .08 .15
39 John Paxson .08 .15
40 Doc Rivers .08 .15
41 Byron Scott .08 .15
42 Sedale Threatt .08 .15
43 Ron Anderson .08 .15
44 Charles Barkley .25 .60
45 Sam Bowie .08 .15
46 Michael Cage .08 .15
47 Tony Campbell .08 .15
48 Antoine Carr .08 .25
49 Craig Ehlo .08 .15
50 Vern Fleming .08 .15
51 Jay Humphries .08 .15
52 Michael Jordan 1.50 5.00
53 Jerome Kersey .08 .15
54 Hakeem Olajuwon .25 .60
55 Sam Perkins .08 .15
56 Alvin Robertson .08 .15
57 John Stockton .15 .40
58 Otis Thorpe .08 .15
59 Kevin Willis .08 .15
60 Michael Adams .08 .15
61 Benoit Benjamin .08 .15
62 Terry Catledge .08 .15
63 Joe Dumars .08 .25
64 Patrick Ewing .15 .40
65 A.C. Green .08 .15
66 Karl Malone .25 .60
67 Reggie Miller .15 .40
68 Chris Mullin .08 .25
69 Xavier McDaniel .08 .15
70 Charles Oakley .08 .15
71 Terry Porter .08 .15
72 Jerry Reynolds .08 .15
73 Detlef Schrempf .08 .15
74 Wayman Tisdale .08 .15
75 Spud Webb .08 .15
76 Gerald Wilkins .08 .15
77 Dell Curry .08 .15
78 Brad Daugherty .08 .15
79 Johnny Dawkins .08 .15
80 Kevin Duckworth .08 .15
81 Ron Harper .08 .15
82 Jeff Hornacek .08 .15
83 Johnny Newman .08 .15
84 Chuck Person .08 .15
85 Mark Price .08 .15
86 Dennis Rodman .25 .60
87 John Salley .08 .15
88 Scott Skiles .08 .15
89 Muggsy Bogues .08 .15
90 Armon Gilliam .08 .15
91 Horace Grant .08 .15
92 Mark Jackson .08 .15
93 Kevin Johnson .08 .15
94 Reggie Lewis .08 .15
95 Derrick McKey .08 .15
96 Ken Norman .08 .15
97 Scottie Pippen .50 1.25
98 Olden Polynice .08 .15
99 Kenny Smith .08 .15
100 John Williams .08 .15
101 Willie Anderson .08 .15
102 Rex Chapman .08 .15
103 Harvey Grant .08 .25
104 Hersey Hawkins .08 .15
105 Dan Majerle .08 .15
106 Danny Manning .08 .15
107 Vernon Maxwell .08 .15
108 Chris Morris .08 .15
109 Mitch Richmond UER .08 .25
(Tim Hardaway pictured on front)
110 Rony Seikaly .08 .15
111 Brian Shaw .08 .15
112 Charles Smith .08 .15
113 Rod Strickland .08 .25
114 Micheal Williams .08 .15
115 Nick Anderson .08 .15
116 B.J. Armstrong .08 .15
117 Mookie Blaylock .08 .15
118 Vlade Divac .08 .15
119 Sherman Douglas .08 .15
120 Blue Edwards .08 .15
121 Sean Elliott .08 .15
122 Pervis Ellison .08 .15
123 Tim Hardaway .10 .30
124 Sarunas Marciulionis .08 .15
125 Drazen Petrovic .08 .15
126 J.R. Reid .08 .15
127 Glen Rice .08 .25
128 Pooh Richardson .08 .15
129 Clifford Robinson .08 .15
130 David Robinson .25 .60
131 Dee Brown .08 .15
132 Cedric Ceballos .08 .15
133 Derrick Coleman .08 .15
134 Kendall Gill .08 .15
135 Chris Jackson .08 .15
136 Shawn Kemp .30 .75
137 Gary Payton .30 .75
138 Dennis Scott .08 .15
139 Lionel Simmons .08 .15
140 Kenny Anderson .08 .25
141 Greg Anthony .08 .15
142 Stacey Augmon .08 .15
143 Rick Fox .08 .15
144 Larry Johnson .08 .25
145 Luc Longley .08 .15
146 Dikembe Mutombo .08 .25
147 Billy Owens .08 .15
148 Steve Smith .08 .25
149 Checklist 1-75 .08 .15
150 Checklist 76-150 .08 .15

1992-93 Topps Archives Gold

10,000 factory sets were made of the 1992-93 Topps Archives Gold. The factory sets were sold to dealers in eight-set cases. The 150 cards comprising this set have identical player selection and numbering as the regular-issue Topps Archives set, except that the checklist cards from the regular Archives set (149 and 150) have been replaced by cards of Rumeal Robinson and Shaquille O'Neal. Like the regular-issue Archive cards, the fronts are designed to mimic the layouts of several Topps' baseball issues of the 1980s; the only differences being that the Topps Archives logo, which doesn't appear on the regular-issue set, and the player's name are stamped in gold foil. The horizontal backs, however, all have the same design, with player action photos displayed in the upper right, the NBA and Topps Archives logos to the left of the picture, and the player's name and team beneath the logos. A brief biography is printed within a red rectangle, a complete college record appears beneath within a yellow rectangle, and the player's record of his NBA rookie year on the bottom rounds out the back. Please refer to the multiplier provided below (coupled with the prices of the corresponding regular issue card) to ascertain value.

COMPLETE FACTORY SET (150) 20.00 50.00
*STARS: 1.5X TO 3X VALUE
149G Rumeal Robinson .30 .40
150G Shaquille O'Neal 20.00 50.00

1992-93 Topps Archives Master Photos

In one out of 24 '92-93 Archives packs, the Stadium Club membership card was replaced by a mini-Master Photo Trade card (2 1/2" by 3 1/2") good for three of these full-size (5" by 7") Master Photos. The expiration date was January 31, 1994. Showcasing the 11 No. 1 NBA draft picks from the missing years of Topps basketball from 1981 through 1991, these 12 oversized cards feature white-bordered color player action shots framed by prismatic silver-foil lines. The player's name, team name and year of his being the No. 1 pick appear in diagonal red, yellow, and blue stripes near the bottom. The words "#1 Draft Pick" followed by a curving comet like prismatic silver-foil tail appear in one of the photo's upper corners. Aside from the Topps and NBA trademarks, the backs are blank. The cards are numbered on the front by year. The mini Master Photo cards are presently valued the same as the large.

COMPLETE SET (12) 4.00 10.00
1981 Mark Aguirre .40 1.00
1982 James Worthy .60 1.50
1983 Ralph Sampson .40 1.00
1984 Hakeem Olajuwon 1.00 2.50
1985 Patrick Ewing .75 2.00
1986 Brad Daugherty .40 1.00
1987 David Robinson 1.00 2.50
1988 Danny Manning .40 1.00
1989 Pervis Ellison .40 1.00
1990 Derrick Coleman .40 1.00
1991 Larry Johnson .60 1.50
NNO First Picks 1981-91 .40 1.06

2005-06 Topps Big Game

Released in October 2005, Big Game features an all-foil all serially numbered set consisting of 146 cards broken down as follows: 1-110 feature veterans and are serially numbered to 179, 111-141 feature rookies and are serially numbered to 529 and 142-146 feature celebrities serially numbered to 529. Base cards have white borders and a stat grid along the bottom with the player's name, position, team and some stats from career-best games. Big Game was packaged in tins containing five cards, a veteran, a rookie, a low-serially numbered parallel, a relic card and an autographed relic card and carried an initial SRP of $75.

UNPRICED BIG GAME 1 PRINT RUN ONE SET
1 Vince Carter 1.50 4.00
2 Mehmet Okur .60 1.50
3 Andre Iguodala 1.00 2.50
4 Baron Davis 1.00 2.50
5 Drew Gooden .75 2.00
6 Yao Ming 1.25 3.00
7 Gary Payton 1.00 2.50
8 Shaun Livingston .60 1.50
9 Marcus Camby .75 2.00
10 Ben Wallace 1.00 2.50
11 Mike Miller 1.00 2.50
12 Steve Francis 1.00 2.50
13 Sam Cassell 1.00 2.50
14 Gilbert Arenas 1.00 2.50
15 Chris Bosh 1.00 2.50
16 Jamaal Magloire .60 1.50
17 Zach Randolph .75 2.00
18 Josh Childress .75 2.00
19 Kirk Hinrich 1.00 2.50
20 Dirk Nowitzki 1.50 4.00
21 Trevor Ariza .60 1.50
22 Primoz Brezec .60 1.50

23 LeBron James	5.00	12.00
24 Vladimir Radmanovic	.60	1.50
25 Tim Duncan	1.50	4.00
26 Damon Jones	.60	1.50
27 Rasheed Wallace	1.00	2.50
28 Corey Maggette	.75	2.00
29 Stephen Jackson	.75	2.00
30 Amare Stoudemire	1.00	2.50
31 Jason Richardson	1.00	2.50
32 Brad Miller	1.00	2.50
33 Kenyon Martin	1.00	2.50
34 Paul Pierce	1.25	3.00
35 Lamar Odom	1.00	2.50
36 Marquis Daniels	.60	1.50
37 Shane Battier	.75	2.00
38 Eddy Curry	.75	2.00
39 Michael Redd	1.00	2.50
40 Ray Allen	1.00	2.50
41 Latrell Sprewell	.75	2.00
42 Rafer Alston	.60	1.50
43 Brendan Haywood	.60	1.50
44 Al Harrington	.75	2.00
45 Udonis Haslem	.75	2.00
46 Chauncey Billups	1.00	2.50
47 Andrei Kirilenko	.75	2.00
48 Chris Webber	1.00	2.50
49 Stephon Marbury	.75	2.00
50 Emeka Okafor	1.00	2.50
51 Cuttino Mobley	.75	2.00
52 Shawn Marion	1.00	2.50
53 Jamaal Tinsley	.60	1.50
54 Nenad Krstic	.60	1.50
55 Bob Sura	.60	1.50
56 Manu Ginobili	1.00	2.50
57 Dan Dickau	.60	1.50
58 Wally Szczerbiak	.75	2.00
59 Mike Dunleavy	.75	2.00
60 Carmelo Anthony	2.00	5.00
61 Zydrunas Ilgauskas	.75	2.00
62 Elton Brand	1.00	2.50
63 Jamal Crawford	.75	2.00
64 Grant Hill	1.25	3.00
65 Ben Gordon	1.00	2.50
66 Rashard Lewis	1.00	2.50
67 Josh Howard	1.00	2.50
68 Jalen Rose	1.00	2.50
69 Pau Gasol	1.00	2.50
70 Steve Nash	1.25	3.00
71 Larry Hughes	.75	2.00
72 J.R. Smith	1.00	2.50
73 Jason Kidd	1.50	4.00
74 Mike Bibby	1.00	2.50
75 Josh Smith	1.00	2.50
76 Richard Hamilton	.75	2.00
77 Caron Butler	1.00	2.50
78 Richard Jefferson	1.00	2.50
79 Mike Sweetney	.60	1.50
80 Shaquille O'Neal	2.00	5.00
81 Dwight Howard	2.00	5.00
82 Allen Iverson	1.50	4.00
83 Luol Deng	1.00	2.50
84 Luke Ridnour	.75	2.00
85 Desmond Mason	.60	1.50
86 Gerald Wallace	1.00	2.50
87 Carlos Boozer	1.00	2.50
88 Antoine Walker	.75	2.00
89 Tony Parker	1.00	2.50
90 Tracy McGrady	1.25	3.00
91 Jermaine O'Neal	1.00	2.50
92 Andre Miller	.75	2.00
93 Quentin Richardson	.75	2.00
94 Dwyane Wade	2.50	6.00
95 Kevin Garnett	2.00	5.00
96 Peja Stojakovic	1.00	2.50
97 Antawn Jamison	1.00	2.50
98 Devin Harris	1.00	2.50
99 Kobe Bryant	5.00	12.00
100 Sebastian Telfair	.75	2.00
101 Samuel Dalembert	.60	1.50
102 Darius Miles	.60	1.50
103 Al Jefferson	1.00	2.50
104 Brevin Knight	.60	1.50
105 Anderson Varejao	.75	2.00
106 Troy Murphy	.75	2.00
107 Mike James	.60	1.50
108 Maurice Williams	.75	2.00
109 Robert Horry	.75	2.00
110 Bobby Simmons	.60	1.50
111 Andrew Bogut RC	3.00	8.00
112 Gerald Green RC	2.50	6.00
113 Raymond Felton RC	3.00	8.00
114 Francisco Garcia RC	2.50	6.00
115 Hakim Warrick RC	2.50	6.00
116 Jarrett Jack RC	2.00	5.00
117 Wayne Simien RC	2.00	5.00
118 Nate Robinson RC	2.50	6.00
119 Julius Hodge RC	2.00	5.00
120 Chris Paul RC	8.00	20.00
121 Rashad McCants RC	2.00	5.00
122 Ike Diogu RC	2.00	5.00
123 Antoine Wright RC	2.00	5.00
124 Luther Head RC	2.00	5.00
125 Ryan Gomes RC	2.00	5.00
126 David Lee RC	3.00	8.00
127 Andrew Bynum RC	6.00	15.00
128 Salim Stoudamire RC	2.00	5.00
129 Sean May RC	2.00	5.00
130 Deron Williams RC	5.00	12.00
131 Joey Graham RC	2.00	5.00
132 Fran Vazquez RC	2.00	5.00
133 Brandon Bass RC	2.50	6.00
134 Jason Maxiell RC	2.00	5.00
135 Charlie Villanueva RC	2.50	6.00
136 Daniel Ewing RC	2.00	5.00
137 Channing Frye RC	2.50	6.00
138 Chris Taft RC	2.00	5.00
139 Marvin Williams RC	2.50	6.00
140 Danny Granger RC	4.00	10.00
141 Travis Diener RC	2.00	5.00
142 Shannon Elizabeth	2.50	6.00
143 Jenny McCarthy	2.50	6.00
144 Christie Brinkley	2.50	6.00
145 Jay-Z	2.50	6.00
146 Carmen Electra	2.50	6.00

2005-06 Topps Big Game 99

Randomly seeded in packs, this 146-card set parallels the base set on cards with red borders and is serially numbered to 99.

*1-110 GAME 99: .6X TO 1.5X BASE HI
*111-141 GAME 99: .75X TO 2X BASE HI
*142-146 GAME 99: .75X TO 2X BASE HI

2005-06 Topps Big Game 33

Randomly seeded in packs, this 146-card set parallels the base set on cards with blue borders and is serially numbered to 33.

*1-110 GAME 33: 1.5X TO 4X BASE HI
*111-141 GAME 33: 1.25X TO 3X BASE HI
*142-146 GAME 33: 1.25X TO 3X BASE HI

2005-06 Topps Big Game All-Star Rally Relics

Randomly seeded in packs, this 20-card set features NBA All-Stars on a horizontally designed card with player images on the left and swatches of memorabilia on the right. Each card is sequentially numbered to 79.

AI Allen Iverson Shirt	5.00	12.00
AJ Al Jefferson RC Chall Shorts	3.00	8.00
AS Amare Stoudemire Warm	3.00	8.00
BW Ben Wallace Warm	3.00	8.00
CA Carmelo Anthony RC Chall JSY	6.00	15.00
CB Chris Bosh Shorts	3.00	8.00
DH Dwight Howard Warm	6.00	15.00
EB Earl Boykins Warm	2.00	5.00
EO Emeka Okafor RC Chall JSY	3.00	8.00
GA Gilbert Arenas Shirt	3.00	8.00
GH Grant Hill Warm	4.00	10.00
MG Manu Ginobili Warm	3.00	8.00
RA Ray Allen JSY	3.00	8.00
RD Ronald Dupree JSY	2.00	5.00
SM Shawn Marion Warm	3.00	8.00
SN Steve Nash Warm	4.00	10.00
SO Shaquille O'Neal Warm	6.00	15.00
TM Tracy McGrady Shirt	4.00	10.00
UH Udonis Haslem RC Chall Shirt	2.50	6.00
YM Yao Ming Warm	4.00	10.00

2005-06 Topps Big Game All-Star Rally Relics Autographs

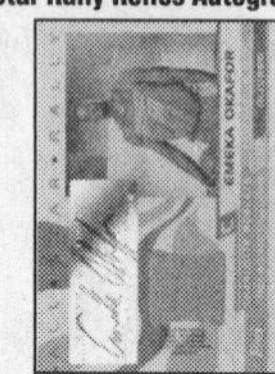

Randomly seeded in packs, this 11-card set parallels the design of the All-Star Rally Relics but is enahnced with sequential numbering and a silver autograph sticker. Cards are numbered to varying amounts. See checklist for details.

AS Amare Stoudemire Shirt/67	20.00	50.00
BW Ben Wallace Pants/20	15.00	40.00
CA Carmelo Anthony RC Chall JSY/199	20.00	50.00
DW Dwyane Wade Pants/199	40.00	100.00
EO Emeka Okafor RC Chall JSY/199	12.50	30.00
QR Quentin Richardson Event Shirt/31	12.50	30.00
SN Steve Nash Pants/199	50.00	100.00
SO Shaquille O'Neal Shirt/199	30.00	80.00
TD Tim Duncan Shirt/111	60.00	120.00
TM Tracy McGrady Shirt/76	20.00	50.00
JRS J.R. Smith Event JSY/32	12.50	30.00

2005-06 Topps Big Game Draft Day Moments Relics

Inserted in packs, this set features 38 rookie players and places a photo of the player on the left and a swatch of memorabilia on the right. Most players have two versions, a draft day ball and a draft day hat, but Andrew Bogut has a jacket version. Cards are serially numbered to varying amounts, see checklist for details.

AB Andrew Bogut Hat/27	10.00	25.00
AB2 Andrew Bogut Ball/75	6.00	15.00
AW Antoine Wright Hat/27	6.00	15.00
AW2 Antoine Wright Ball/75	4.00	10.00
CF Channing Frye Hat/146	8.00	20.00
CF2 Channing Frye Ball/75	5.00	12.00
CP Chris Paul Hat/125	10.00	25.00
CP2 Chris Paul Ball/75	15.00	40.00
CV Charlie Villanueva Hat/33	8.00	20.00
CV2 Charlie Villanueva Ball/75	5.00	12.00
DG Danny Granger Hat/25	12.00	30.00
DG2 Danny Granger Ball/75	8.00	20.00
DW Deron Williams Hat/30	15.00	40.00
DW2 Deron Williams Ball/75	10.00	25.00
FV Fran Vazquez Hat/99	6.00	15.00
GG Gerald Green Hat/21	8.00	20.00
GG2 Gerald Green Ball/75	5.00	12.00
HW Hakim Warrick Hat/26	8.00	20.00
HW2 Hakim Warrick Ball/75	5.00	12.00
IM Ian Mahinmi Hat/124	6.00	15.00
IM2 Ian Mahinmi Ball/75	4.00	10.00
JH2 Julius Hodge Ball/75	4.00	10.00
JP Johan Petro Hat/34	8.00	20.00
JP2 Johan Petro Ball/75	4.00	10.00
RF Raymond Felton Hat/33	10.00	25.00
RF2 Raymond Felton Ball/75	6.00	15.00
RM2 Rashad McCants Ball/75	4.00	10.00
SM Sean May Hat/36	6.00	15.00
YK Yaroslav Korolev Hat/143	6.00	15.00
YK2 Yaroslav Korolev Ball/75	4.00	10.00
ABY Andrew Bynum Hat/30	20.00	50.00
ABY2 Andrew Bynum Ball/75	12.00	30.00
MWE2 Martell Webster Ball/75	4.00	10.00

2005-06 Topps Big Game Draft Day Moments Relics Autographs

Randomly seeded in packs, this set parallels somewhat the design of the Draft Day Moments Relics set and is enhanced with a silver autograph sticker. Players have multiple memorabilia versions, draft day balls which are sequentially numbered to 99 and draft day hats sequentially numbered to 129.

AB Andrew Bogut Hat	10.00	25.00
AB2 Andrew Bogut Ball	10.00	25.00
AW Antoine Wright Hat	6.00	15.00
AW2 Antoine Wright Ball	6.00	15.00
CV Charlie Villanueva Hat	8.00	20.00
CV2 Charlie Villanueva Ball	8.00	20.00
DG Danny Granger Hat	12.00	30.00
DG2 Danny Granger Ball	12.00	30.00
DW Deron Williams Hat	15.00	40.00
DW2 Deron Williams Ball	15.00	40.00
FV Fran Vazquez Hat	6.00	15.00
FV2 Fran Vazquez Ball	6.00	15.00
GG Gerald Green Hat	8.00	20.00
GG2 Gerald Green Ball	8.00	20.00
HW Hakim Warrick Hat	8.00	20.00
HW2 Hakim Warrick Ball	8.00	20.00
JH Julius Hodge Hat	6.00	15.00
JH2 Julius Hodge Ball	6.00	15.00
JP Johan Petro Hat	6.00	15.00
JP2 Johan Petro Ball	6.00	15.00
RF Raymond Felton Hat	10.00	25.00
RF2 Raymond Felton Ball	10.00	25.00
RM Rashad McCants Hat	6.00	15.00
RM2 Rashad McCants Ball	6.00	15.00
SM Sean May Hat	6.00	15.00
SM2 Sean May Ball	6.00	15.00
ABY Andrew Bynum Hat	20.00	50.00
ABY2 Andrew Bynum Ball	20.00	50.00
MWE Martell Webster Hat	6.00	15.00
MWE2 Martell Webster Ball	6.00	15.00

2005-06 Topps Big Game Final Score Relics

Randomly seeded in packs, this 24-card set features a horizontal design with player photos on the left and a circle swatch of memorabilia in the center. Cards are sequentially numbered to 133.

AM Antonio McDyess	2.50	6.00
BB Brent Barry	2.00	5.00
BU Beno Udrih	2.00	5.00
BW Ben Wallace	3.00	8.00
CA Carlos Arroyo	5.00	12.00
CB Chauncey Billups	3.00	8.00
DB Devin Brown	2.00	5.00
DH Darvin Ham	2.00	5.00
DM Darko Milicic	2.00	5.00
EC Elden Campbell	2.00	5.00
GR Glenn Robinson	2.50	6.00
LH Lindsey Hunter	2.00	5.00
MG Manu Ginobili	3.00	8.00
NM Nazr Mohammed	2.00	5.00
RD Ronald Dupree	2.00	5.00
RH Robert Horry	4.00	10.00
RN Rasho Nesterovic	2.00	5.00
RW Rasheed Wallace	3.00	8.00
TD Tim Duncan	5.00	12.00
TM Tony Massenburg	2.00	5.00
TP Tony Parker	3.00	8.00
BBO Bruce Bowen	2.00	5.00
RHA Richard Hamilton	2.50	6.00
TPR Tayshaun Prince	3.00	8.00

2005-06 Topps Big Game Final Score Relics Autographs

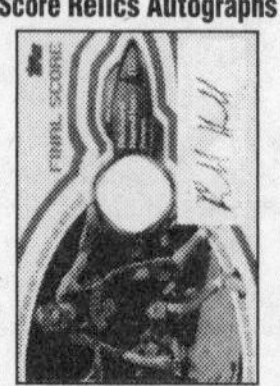

Seeded in packs, this four-card set parallels the design of the Final Score Relics set enhanced with a silver autograph sticker and sequential numbering to the featured player's jersey number.

BU Beno Udrih/50	6.00	15.00
BW Ben Wallace/30	20.00	50.00
RH Richard Hamilton/56	10.00	25.00
TD Tim Duncan/50	100.00	250.00

2005-06 Topps Big Game Picture Perfect Relics

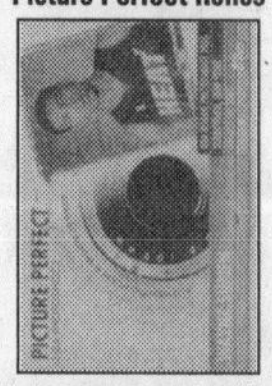

Inserted randomly in packs, this 68-card set features a player photo on the right and a centered circular swatch of memorabilia. Each card is serially numbered to 129, and most players have multiple memorabilia versions. See checklist for details.

AB Andray Blatche JSY	3.00	8.00
AB2 Andray Blatche Shorts	3.00	8.00
AW Antoine Wright JSY	2.50	6.00
AW2 Antoine Wright Shorts	2.50	6.00
BB Brandon Bass JSY	3.00	8.00
BB2 Brandon Bass Shorts	3.00	8.00
CF Channing Frye JSY	3.00	8.00
CF2 Channing Frye Shorts	3.00	8.00
CP Chris Paul JSY	10.00	25.00
CP2 Chris Paul Shorts	10.00	25.00
CV Charlie Villanueva JSY	3.00	8.00
CV2 Charlie Villanueva Shorts	3.00	8.00
DE Daniel Ewing JSY	2.50	6.00
DE2 Daniel Ewing Shorts	2.50	6.00
DG Danny Granger JSY	5.00	12.00
DG2 Danny Granger Shorts	5.00	12.00
DL David Lee JSY	4.00	10.00
DL2 David Lee Shorts	4.00	10.00
DW Deron Williams JSY	6.00	15.00
DW2 Deron Williams Shorts	6.00	15.00
EI Ersan Ilyasova JSY	3.00	8.00
EI2 Ersan Ilyasova Shorts	3.00	8.00
FG Francisco Garcia JSY	3.00	8.00
FG2 Francisco Garcia Shorts	3.00	8.00
GG Gerald Green JSY	3.00	8.00
GG2 Gerald Green Shorts	3.00	8.00
HW Hakim Warrick JSY	3.00	8.00
HW2 Hakim Warrick Shorts	3.00	8.00
JG Joey Graham JSY	2.50	6.00
JG2 Joey Graham Shorts	2.50	6.00
JH Julius Hodge JSY	2.50	6.00
JH2 Julius Hodge Shorts	2.50	6.00
JJ Jarrett Jack JSY	2.50	6.00
JJ2 Jarrett Jack Shorts	2.50	6.00
JM Jason Maxiell JSY	2.50	6.00
JM2 Jason Maxiell Shorts	2.50	6.00
LH Luther Head JSY	2.50	6.00
LH2 Luther Head Shorts	2.50	6.00
LW Louis Williams JSY	4.00	10.00
LW2 Louis Williams Shorts	4.00	10.00
MA Martynas Andriuskevicius JSY	2.50	6.00
MA2 Martynas Andriuskevicius Shorts	2.50	6.00
ME Monta Ellis JSY	5.00	12.00
ME2 Monta Ellis Shorts	5.00	12.00
MW Martell Webster JSY	2.50	6.00
MW2 Martell Webster Shorts	2.50	6.00
NR Nate Robinson JSY	3.00	8.00
NR2 Nate Robinson Shorts	3.00	8.00
RF Raymond Felton JSY	4.00	10.00
RF2 Raymond Felton Shorts	4.00	10.00
RG Ryan Gomes JSY	2.50	6.00
RG2 Ryan Gomes Shorts	2.50	6.00
RM Rashad McCants JSY	2.50	6.00
RM2 Rashad McCants Shorts	2.50	6.00
SJ Sarunas Jasikevicius JSY	2.50	6.00
SJ2 Sarunas Jasikevicius Shorts	2.50	6.00
SM Sean May JSY	2.50	6.00
SM2 Sean May Shorts	2.50	6.00
SS Salim Stoudamire JSY	2.50	6.00
SS2 Salim Stoudamire Shorts	2.50	6.00
TD Travis Diener JSY	2.50	6.00
TD2 Travis Diener Shorts	2.50	6.00
WS Wayne Simien JSY	2.50	6.00
WS2 Wayne Simien Shorts	2.50	6.00
ABO Andrew Bogut JSY	4.00	10.00
ABO2 Andrew Bogut Jacket	4.00	10.00
CJM C.J. Miles JSY	3.00	8.00
CJM2 C.J. Miles Shorts	3.00	8.00

2005-06 Topps Big Game Picture Perfect Relics Autographs

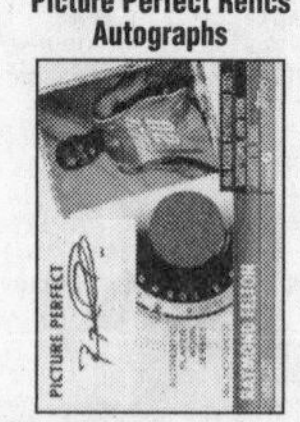

Seeded randomly in packs, this 52-card set parallels the design of the Picture Perfect Relics set enahnced with a silver autograph sticker. Most cards are serially numbered to 199, but there are a few exceptions. See checklist for details.

AB Andray Blatche JSY/129	6.00	15.00
AB2 Andray Blatche Shorts/179	6.00	15.00
AW Antoine Wright JSY	5.00	12.00
AW2 Antoine Wright Shorts	5.00	12.00
BB Brandon Bass JSY	6.00	15.00
BB2 Brandon Bass Shorts	6.00	15.00
CV Charlie Villanueva JSY	6.00	15.00
CV2 Charlie Villanueva Shorts	6.00	15.00
DE Daniel Ewing JSY	5.00	12.00
DE2 Daniel Ewing Shorts	5.00	12.00
DG Danny Granger JSY	10.00	25.00
DG2 Danny Granger Shorts	10.00	25.00
DL David Lee JSY	8.00	20.00
DL2 David Lee Shorts	8.00	20.00
DW Deron Williams JSY	15.00	40.00
DW2 Deron Williams Shorts	15.00	40.00
FG Francisco Garcia JSY	6.00	15.00
FG2 Francisco Garcia Shorts	6.00	15.00
GG Gerald Green JSY	6.00	15.00
GG2 Gerald Green Shorts	6.00	15.00
HW Hakim Warrick JSY	6.00	15.00
HW2 Hakim Warrick Shorts	6.00	15.00
JG Joey Graham JSY	5.00	12.00
JG2 Joey Graham Shorts	5.00	12.00
JH Julius Hodge JSY	5.00	12.00
JH2 Julius Hodge Shorts	5.00	12.00
JJ Jarrett Jack JSY	5.00	12.00
JJ2 Jarrett Jack Shorts	5.00	12.00
JM Jason Maxiell JSY	5.00	12.00
JM2 Jason Maxiell Shorts	5.00	12.00
LH Luther Head JSY	5.00	12.00
LH2 Luther Head Shorts	5.00	12.00
ME Monta Ellis JSY	12.00	30.00
ME2 Monta Ellis Shorts	12.00	30.00
MW Martell Webster JSY	5.00	12.00
MW2 Martell Webster Shorts	5.00	12.00
RF Raymond Felton JSY	8.00	20.00
RF2 Raymond Felton Shorts	8.00	20.00
RG Ryan Gomes JSY	5.00	12.00
RG2 Ryan Gomes Shorts	5.00	12.00
RM Rashad McCants JSY	5.00	12.00
RM2 Rashad McCants Shorts	5.00	12.00
SJ Sarunas Jasikevicius JSY	5.00	12.00
SJ2 Sarunas Jasikevicius Shorts	5.00	12.00
SM Sean May JSY	5.00	12.00
SM2 Sean May Shorts	5.00	12.00
TD Travis Diener JSY	5.00	12.00
TD2 Travis Diener Shorts	5.00	12.00
WS Wayne Simien JSY	5.00	12.00
WS2 Wayne Simien Shorts	5.00	12.00
ABO Andrew Bogut JSY	8.00	20.00
ABO2 Andrew Bogut Jacket	8.00	20.00

2005-06 Topps Big Game Relics

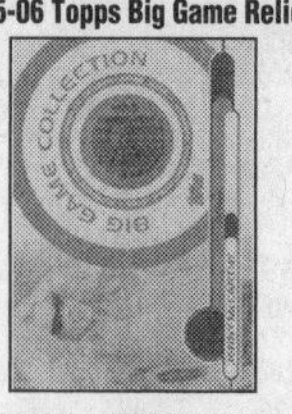

Randomly seeded in packs, this 36-card set showcases both NBA players and celebrities. Photos appear on the left side of the card and a circular swatch of memorabilia appears on the right in a design that resembles a bulls-eye. Each card is serially numbered to 99.

AI Allen Iverson JSY	5.00	12.00
AJ Al Jefferson JSY	3.00	8.00
AN Andres Nocioni JSY	2.00	5.00
AS Amare Stoudemire Shirt	3.00	8.00
BG Ben Gordon JSY	3.00	8.00
BW Ben Wallace Warm	3.00	8.00
CA Carmelo Anthony JSY	6.00	15.00
CB Christie Brinkley Jeans	12.50	30.00
CE Carmen Electra Jeans	12.50	30.00
DH Devin Harris JSY	3.00	8.00
DN Dirk Nowitzki JSY	5.00	12.00
EB Earl Boykins Warm	2.00	5.00
EO Emeka Okafor JSY	3.00	8.00
JM Jenny McCarthy Jeans	10.00	25.00
JO Jermaine O'Neal Warm	3.00	8.00
JS Josh Smith JSY	3.00	8.00
JZ Jay-Z Jeans	20.00	50.00
KB Kobe Bryant JSY	10.00	25.00
KG Kevin Garnett JSY	6.00	15.00
KH Kirk Hinrich JSY	3.00	8.00
KM Kenyon Martin JSY	3.00	8.00
LR Luke Ridnour JSY	2.50	6.00
MG Manu Ginobili Warm	3.00	8.00
NK Nenad Krstic JSY	2.00	5.00
RA Ray Allen JSY	3.00	8.00
RM Reggie Miller Warm	3.00	8.00
RW Rasheed Wallace JSY	3.00	8.00
SE Shannon Elizabeth Jeans	10.00	25.00
SN Steve Nash JSY	4.00	10.00
SO Shaquille O'Neal JSY	6.00	15.00
TD Tim Duncan JSY	5.00	12.00
TM Tracy McGrady JSY	4.00	10.00
YM Yao Ming JSY	4.00	10.00
AJA Antawn Jamison JSY	3.00	8.00
DHO Dwight Howard JSY	6.00	15.00
JRS J.R. Smith JSY	3.00	8.00

2005-06 Topps Big Game Relics Autographs

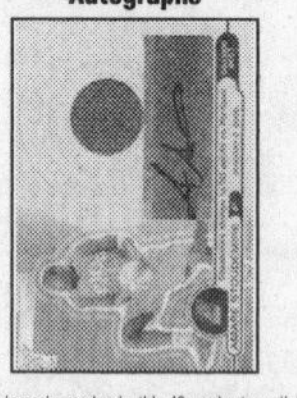

Inserted in packs randomly, this 42-card set parallels the design of the Relics set enhanced with a silver autograph sticker and sequential numbering. Serial numbers vary, see checklist for details.

SOME UNPRICED DUE TO SCARCITY

AI Allen Iverson/129	60.00	150.00
AS Amare Stoudemire Shirt/99	20.00	50.00
BD Baron Davis/128	5.00	12.00
BG Ben Gordon/101	10.00	25.00
BR Bernard Robinson/21	5.00	12.00
BU Beno Udrih Shirt/78	5.00	12.00
BW Ben Wallace Warm/20	20.00	50.00
CA Carmelo Anthony/199	20.00	40.00
CB Christie Brinkley Jeans/50	150.00	275.00
CE Carmen Electra Jeans/50	100.00	250.00
DH Devin Harris/32	8.00	20.00
DW Dwyane Wade/199	40.00	100.00
EO Emeka Okafor/199	10.00	25.00
FJ Fred Jones/199	5.00	12.00
JC Josh Childress/27	8.00	20.00
JK Jason Kidd/199	12.50	30.00
JM Jenny McCarthy Jeans/50	100.00	200.00
JN Jameer Nelson/199	5.00	12.00
JS Josh Smith/86	6.00	15.00
JZ Jay-Z/50	175.00	350.00
KH Kris Humphries/57	5.00	12.00
KM Kevin Martin Event JSY/199	5.00	12.00
KS Kirk Snyder/115	5.00	12.00
LD Luol Deng/147	6.00	15.00
RA Rafael Araujo Event JSY/79	5.00	12.00
RH Richard Hamilton Event Warm/199	5.00	12.00
SE Shannon Elizabeth Jeans/50	100.00	200.00
SL Shaun Livingston/199	5.00	12.00
SM Stephon Marbury/199	6.00	15.00
SN Steve Nash/199	30.00	80.00
SO Shaquille O'Neal/199	40.00	80.00
ST Sebastian Telfair/55	5.00	12.00
TA Trevor Ariza/99	5.00	12.00
TM Tracy McGrady/99	15.00	40.00
DWE Delonte West/23	15.00	40.00
DWR Dorell Wright/199	5.00	12.00

2006-07 Topps Big Game

Issued in December 2006, Topps Big Game employs a basic design with color player images on a white background with silver foil highlights. Card numbers 1-75 picture veteran players and are serially numbered to 269 and card numbers 76-110 picture rookie players are are serially numbered to 579. Big Game is packaged in single packs of five cards each and carried an original suggested retail price of $75.00.

UNPRICED GOLD PRINT RUN ONE SET

1 Dirk Nowitzki	1.25	3.00
2 Tracy McGrady	1.00	2.50
3 Elton Brand	.75	2.00
4 Ricky Davis	.60	1.50
5 Marcus Camby	.60	1.50
6 Gilbert Arenas	.75	2.00
7 Channing Frye	.60	1.50
8 Chauncey Billups	.75	2.00
9 Shaquille O'Neal	1.50	4.00
10 Lamar Odom	.75	2.00
11 Pau Gasol	.75	2.00
12 Charlie Villanueva	.75	2.00
13 Larry Hughes	.60	1.50
14 Peja Stojakovic	.75	2.00
15 Andre Iguodala	.75	2.00
16 Vince Carter	1.00	2.50
17 Jason Terry	.60	1.50
18 Ron Artest	.75	2.00
19 Luke Ridnour	.60	1.50
20 Paul Pierce	1.00	2.50
21 Michael Redd	.75	2.00
22 Rasheed Wallace	.75	2.00
23 Baron Davis	.75	2.00
24 Amare Stoudemire	.75	2.00
25 Zach Randolph	.60	1.50
26 Yao Ming	1.00	2.50
27 Raymond Felton	1.00	2.50
28 Stephon Marbury	.60	1.50
29 Kirk Hinrich	.75	2.00
30 Andre Miller	.60	1.50
31 Jason Kidd	1.25	3.00
32 Tayshaun Prince	.75	2.00
33 Antoine Walker	.60	1.50
34 LeBron James	4.00	10.00
35 Brad Miller	.75	2.00
36 Tim Duncan	1.25	3.00
37 Jermaine O'Neal	.75	2.00
38 Josh Smith	.75	2.00
39 Gerald Wallace	.75	2.00
40 Delonte West	.60	1.50
41 Darius Miles	.50	1.25
42 Chris Paul	1.50	4.00
43 Mike Bibby	.75	2.00
44 Sam Cassell	.75	2.00
45 Josh Howard	.60	1.50
46 Allen Iverson	1.00	2.50
47 Jameer Nelson	.60	1.50
48 Mehmet Okur	.50	1.25
49 Shawn Marion	.75	2.00
50 Ray Allen	.75	2.00
51 Joe Johnson	.75	2.00
52 Richard Hamilton	.60	1.50
53 Richard Jefferson	.75	2.00
54 Kobe Bryant	4.00	10.00
55 Manu Ginobili	.75	2.00
56 Carmelo Anthony	1.00	2.50
57 Ben Gordon	.75	2.00
58 Andrew Bogut	.75	2.00
59 Antawn Jamison	.75	2.00
60 Chris Bosh	.75	2.00
61 David West	.75	2.00
62 Steve Nash	1.00	2.50
63 Ben Wallace	.75	2.00
64 Chris Webber	.75	2.00
65 Caron Butler	.75	2.00
66 Danny Granger	.75	2.00
67 Andrei Kirilenko	.60	1.50
68 Kevin Garnett	1.50	4.00
69 Dwyane Wade	2.00	5.00
70 Tony Parker	.75	2.00
71 Dwight Howard	1.25	3.00
72 Rashard Lewis	.75	2.00
73 Mike Miller	.75	2.00
74 Jason Richardson	.75	2.00
75 T.J. Ford	.60	1.50
76 J.J. Redick RC	2.00	5.00
77 Marcus Williams RC	1.50	4.00
78 Shelden Williams RC	1.50	4.00
79 Tyrus Thomas RC	2.00	5.00
80 LaMarcus Aldridge RC	4.00	10.00
81 Cedric Simmons RC	1.50	4.00
82 Saer Sene RC	1.50	4.00
83 Randy Foye RC	2.00	5.00
84 Patrick O'Bryant RC	1.50	4.00
85 Adam Morrison RC	2.00	5.00
86 Rudy Gay RC	2.50	6.00
87 Ronnie Brewer RC	2.00	5.00
88 Josh Boone RC	1.50	4.00
89 Maurice Ager RC	1.50	4.00
90 Shannon Brown RC	2.50	6.00
91 Renaldo Balkman RC	1.50	4.00
92 Thabo Sefolosha RC	2.00	5.00
93 Shawne Williams RC	1.50	4.00
94 Hilton Armstrong RC	1.50	4.00
95 Brandon Roy RC	4.00	10.00
96 Kyle Lowry RC	2.00	5.00
97 Steve Novak RC	1.50	4.00
98 Paul Davis RC	1.50	4.00
99 Solomon Jones RC	1.50	4.00
100 P.J. Tucker RC	1.50	4.00
101 Rajon Rondo RC	6.00	15.00
102 Dee Brown RC	1.50	4.00
103 Craig Smith RC	1.50	4.00
104 Bobby Jones RC	1.50	4.00
105 James White RC	1.50	4.00
106 Jordan Farmar RC	1.50	4.00
107 Mardy Collins RC	1.50	4.00
108 Quincy Douby RC	1.50	4.00
109 Rodney Carney RC	1.50	4.00
110 Andrea Bargnani RC	2.50	6.00

2006-07 Topps Big Game Blue

*BLUE: 1.25X TO 3X BASE HI
STATED PRINT RUN 59 SER.#'d SETS

2006-07 Topps Big Game Red

*1-75 RED: 1X TO 2.5X BASE HI
*76-110 RED: .5X TO 1.25X BASE HI
STATED PRINT RUN 129 SER.#'d SETS

2006-07 Topps Big Game All-Star Rally Relics Jerseys

PRINT RUN 99 SER.#'d SETS
UNPRICED DUAL PRINT RUN 15 SETS
UNPRICED PATCH PRINT RUN 10 SETS
UNPRICED PATCH AU PRINT RUN 10 SETS

AI Allen Iverson	4.00	10.00
AN Andres Nocioni	2.00	5.00
BW Ben Wallace	3.00	8.00
CB Chauncey Billups	3.00	8.00
CF Channing Frye	2.50	6.00
DN Dirk Nowitzki	5.00	12.00
DW Dwyane Wade	6.00	15.00
KB Kobe Bryant	10.00	25.00
KG Kevin Garnett	6.00	15.00
LH Luther Head	2.50	6.00
NK Nenad Krstic	2.00	5.00
PG Pau Gasol	3.00	8.00
RH Richard Hamilton	2.50	6.00
SM Shawn Marion	3.00	8.00
SN Steve Nash	4.00	10.00
SO Shaquille O'Neal	6.00	15.00
TD Tim Duncan	5.00	12.00
TM Tracy McGrady	4.00	10.00
TP Tony Parker	3.00	8.00
VC Vince Carter	4.00	10.00
AIG Andre Iguodala	3.00	8.00
CBO Chris Bosh	3.00	8.00

2006-07 Topps Big Game All-Star Rally Relics Jerseys Autographs

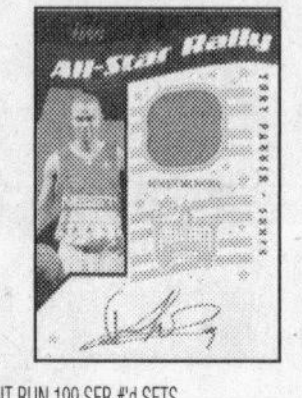

PRINT RUN 199 SER.#'d SETS

AI Allen Iverson	50.00	125.00
DW Dwyane Wade	40.00	100.00
SO Shaquille O'Neal	30.00	80.00
TP Tony Parker	10.00	25.00
VC Vince Carter	15.00	40.00
CBO Chris Bosh	10.00	25.00

2006-07 Topps Big Game All-Star Rally Relics Dual Autographs

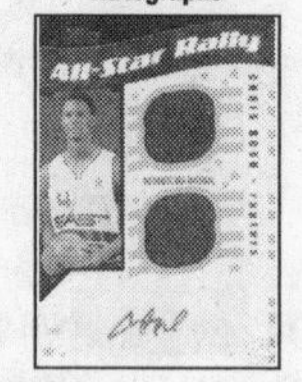

PRINT RUN 25 SER.#'d SETS

AI Allen Iverson	50.00	120.00
DW Dwyane Wade	60.00	120.00
SO Shaquille O'Neal	50.00	100.00
TP Tony Parker	20.00	50.00
VC Vince Carter	30.00	60.00
CBO Chris Bosh	20.00	50.00

2006-07 Topps Big Game Draft Day Moments Jerseys

PRINT RUN 99 SER.#'d SETS
*JUMBO: .6X TO 1.5X BASE HI
JUMBO PRINT RUN 99 SER.#'d SETS
*BALL: 1X TO 2.5X BASE HI
BALL PRINT RUN 25 SER.#'d SETS
UNPRICED BALL AU PRINT RUN 10 SETS
*BALL/HAT: 1X TO 2.5X BASE HI
BALL/HAT PRINT RUN 25 SER.#'d SETS
UNPRICED BALL/HAT AU PRINT RUN 10 SETS
*BALL/JSY: .6X TO 1.5X BASE HI
BALL/JSY PRINT RUN 50 SER.#'d SETS
UNPRICED BALL/JSY AU PRINT RUN 10 SETS
*HAT: .75X TO 2X BASE HI
HAT PRINT RUN 50 SER.#'d SETS
*HAT/JSY: 1X TO 2.5X BASE HI
HAT/JSY PRINT RUN 25 SER.#'d SETS
UNPRICED HAT/JSY AU PRINT RUN 10 SETS
UNPRICED LOGO PRINT RUN ONE SET
*PATCHES: 1X TO 2.5X BASE HI
PATCH PRINT RUN 25 SER.#'d SETS
UNPRICED PATCH JUMBO PRINT RUN 5 SETS
UNPRICED TAG PRINT RUN ONE SET

AB Andrea Bargnani	4.00	10.00
AM Adam Morrison	3.00	8.00
BR Brandon Roy	6.00	15.00
CS Cedric Simmons	2.50	6.00
HA Hilton Armstrong	2.50	6.00
LA LaMarcus Aldridge	6.00	15.00
MA Maurice Ager	2.50	6.00
MW Marcus Williams	2.50	6.00
RB Ronnie Brewer	3.00	8.00
RC Rodney Carney	2.50	6.00
RF Randy Foye	3.00	8.00
RG Rudy Gay	4.00	10.00
SS Saer Sene	2.50	6.00
SW Shelden Williams	2.50	6.00
TS Thabo Sefolosha	3.00	8.00
JJR J.J. Redick	3.00	8.00
POB Patrick O'Bryant	2.50	6.00

2006-07 Topps Big Game Draft Day Moments Jerseys Autographs

RINT RUN 199 SER.#'d SETS
B Andrea Bargnani 12.50 30.00
M Adam Morrison 5.00 12.00
S Cedric Simmons 4.00 10.00
A Hilton Armstrong 4.00 10.00
A Maurice Ager 4.00 10.00
W Marcus Williams 4.00 10.00
B Ronnie Brewer 5.00 12.00
C Rodney Carney 4.00 10.00
F Randy Foye 5.00 12.00
S Saer Sene 4.00 10.00
W Shelden Williams 4.00 10.00
S Thabo Sefolosha 5.00 12.00
R J.J. Redick 5.00 12.00
DB Patrick O'Bryant 4.00 10.00

2006-07 Topps Big Game Draft Day Moments Hat Autographs

RINT RUN 25 SER.#'d SETS
B Andrea Bargnani 25.00 60.00
M Adam Morrison 10.00 25.00
S Cedric Simmons 8.00 20.00
A Hilton Armstrong 8.00 20.00
A Maurice Ager 8.00 20.00
W Marcus Williams 8.00 20.00
B Ronnie Brewer 10.00 25.00
C Rodney Carney 8.00 20.00
F Randy Foye 10.00 25.00
S Saer Sene 8.00 20.00
W Shelden Williams 8.00 20.00
S Thabo Sefolosha 10.00 25.00
R J.J. Redick 10.00 25.00
DB Patrick O'Bryant 8.00 20.00

2006-07 Topps Big Game Draft Day Moments Patches Autographs

RINT RUN 25 SER.#'d SETS
B Andrea Bargnani 25.00 60.00
M Adam Morrison 10.00 25.00
S Cedric Simmons 8.00 20.00
A Hilton Armstrong 8.00 20.00
A Maurice Ager 8.00 20.00
W Marcus Williams 8.00 20.00
B Ronnie Brewer 10.00 25.00
C Rodney Carney 8.00 20.00
F Randy Foye 10.00 25.00
S Saer Sene 8.00 20.00
W Shelden Williams 8.00 20.00
S Thabo Sefolosha 10.00 25.00
JR J.J. Redick 10.00 25.00
OB Patrick O'Bryant 8.00 20.00

2006-07 Topps Big Game Final Score Relics

RINT RUN 99 SER.#'d SETS
PATCHES: .75X TO 2X BASE HI
ATCH PRINT RUN 50 SER.#'d SETS
M Alonzo Mourning 8.00 20.00
W Antoine Walker 2.50 6.00
W Dwyane Wade 6.00 15.00
P Gary Payton 3.00 8.00
K Jason Kapono 2.00 5.00
P James Posey 2.00 5.00
W Jason Williams 2.50 6.00
D Michael Doleac 2.00 5.00
A Shandon Anderson 2.00 5.00
O Shaquille O'Neal 6.00 15.00
H Udonis Haslem 2.50 6.00

2006-07 Topps Big Game Final Score Relics Autographs

RINT RUN 199 SER.#'d SETS
W Dwyane Wade 40.00 100.00
O Shaquille O'Neal 25.00 60.00

2006-07 Topps Big Game Final Score Patches Autographs

RINT RUN 50 SER.#'d SETS
W Dwyane Wade 60.00 120.00
O Shaquille O'Neal 40.00 80.00

2006-07 Topps Big Game Picture Perfect Jerseys

PRINT RUN 99 SER.#'d SETS
*JSY/SHORTS: .5X TO 1.25X BASE HI
JSY/SHRT PRINT RUN 99 SER.#'d SETS
*PATCHES: .75X TO 2X BASE HI
PATCH PRINT RUN 50 SER.#'d SETS
AM Adam Morrison 3.00 8.00
AR Allan Ray 2.50 6.00
BJ Bobby Jones 2.50 6.00
CS Cedric Simmons 2.50 6.00
DB Dee Brown 2.50 6.00
HA Hilton Armstrong 2.50 6.00
JB Josh Boone 2.50 6.00
JF Jordan Farmar 2.50 6.00
JW James White 2.50 6.00
KL Kyle Lowry 3.00 8.00
KP Kevin Pittsnogle 2.50 6.00
LA LaMarcus Aldridge 6.00 15.00
MA Maurice Ager 2.50 6.00
MC Mardy Collins 2.50 6.00
MW Marcus Williams 2.50 6.00
PD Paul Davis 2.50 6.00
PO Patrick O'Bryant 2.50 6.00
QD Quincy Douby 2.50 6.00
RB Renaldo Balkman 2.50 6.00
RC Rodney Carney 2.50 6.00
RF Randy Foye 3.00 8.00
RG Rudy Gay 4.00 10.00
RR Rajon Rondo 10.00 25.00
SB Shannon Brown 4.00 10.00
SN Steve Novak 2.50 6.00
SW Shelden Williams 2.50 6.00
CSM Craig Smith 2.50 6.00
JJR J.J. Redick 3.00 8.00
RBR Ronnie Brewer 3.00 8.00
SWI Shawne Williams 2.50 6.00

2006-07 Topps Big Game Picture Perfect Jerseys Autographs

PRINT RUN 199 SER.#'d SETS
*JSY/SHORTS: .4X TO 1X BASE HI
JSY/SHRT PRINT RUN 199 SER.#'d SETS
*PATCH AU: .6X TO 1.5X BASE HI
PATCH AU PRINT RUN 99 SETS
AM Adam Morrison 5.00 12.00
AR Allan Ray 4.00 10.00
BJ Bobby Jones 4.00 10.00
CS Cedric Simmons 4.00 10.00
DB Dee Brown 4.00 10.00
HA Hilton Armstrong 4.00 10.00
JB Josh Boone 4.00 10.00
JF Jordan Farmar 4.00 10.00
JW James White 4.00 10.00
KL Kyle Lowry 5.00 12.00
MA Maurice Ager 4.00 10.00
MC Mardy Collins 4.00 10.00
MW Marcus Williams 4.00 10.00
PO Patrick O'Bryant 4.00 10.00
QD Quincy Douby 4.00 10.00
RB Renaldo Balkman 4.00 10.00
RC Rodney Carney 4.00 10.00
RF Randy Foye 5.00 12.00
RR Rajon Rondo 20.00 50.00
SB Shannon Brown 6.00 15.00
SW Shelden Williams 4.00 10.00
CSM Craig Smith 4.00 10.00
JJR J.J. Redick 5.00 12.00
RBR Ronnie Brewer 5.00 12.00
SWI Shawne Williams 4.00 10.00

2006-07 Topps Big Game Relics

PRINT RUN 99 SER.#'d SETS
*PATCHES: .75X TO 2X BASE HI
PATCH PRINT RUN 25 SER.#'d SETS
AB Andrew Bogut 3.00 8.00
AI Allen Iverson 4.00 10.00
AM Adam Morrison 4.00 10.00
CA Carmelo Anthony 4.00 10.00
CB Chris Bosh 3.00 8.00
DE Daniel Ewing 2.00 5.00
DW Dwyane Wade 6.00 15.00
EO Emeka Okafor 3.00 8.00
HW Hakim Warrick 2.50 6.00
JC Josh Childress 2.50 6.00
KB Kobe Bryant 10.00 25.00
LD Luol Deng 3.00 8.00
PP Paul Pierce 4.00 10.00
RF Raymond Felton 4.00 10.00
SN Steve Nash 4.00 10.00
SO Shaquille O'Neal 6.00 15.00
TP Tony Parker 3.00 8.00
JJR J.J. Redick 4.00 10.00
TJF T.J. Ford 2.50 6.00

2006-07 Topps Big Game Relics Autographs

PRINT RUN 75 SER.#'d SETS
*PATCH AU: .6X TO 1.5X BASE HI
PATCH AU PRINT RUN 25 SER.#'d SETS
AB Andrew Bogut 8.00 20.00
AI Allen Iverson 40.00 100.00
AM Adam Morrison 8.00 20.00
CB Chris Bosh 10.00 25.00
DE Daniel Ewing 5.00 12.00
DW Dwyane Wade 30.00 80.00
EO Emeka Okafor 5.00 12.00
HW Hakim Warrick 5.00 12.00
JC Josh Childress 5.00 12.00
LD Luol Deng 10.00 25.00
RF Raymond Felton 6.00 15.00
SO Shaquille O'Neal 40.00 80.00
TP Tony Parker 10.00 25.00
JJR J.J. Redick 12.50 30.00
TJF T.J. Ford 5.00 12.00

1996-97 Topps Chrome

The debut 1996-97 Topps Chrome basketball set was issued in one series totaling 220 standard-size cards. The card design is very similar to the 1996-97 Topps issue, but utilizes a Chrome background and silver borders. This product was produced for retail outlets exclusively, but was carried in many hobby stores. The cards were issued in 4-card packs carrying a suggested retail price of $2.99. Rookie cards include Shareef Abdur-Rahim, Kobe Bryant, Marcus Camby, Allen Iverson, Stephon Marbury and Antoine Walker, among others. The set is condition sensitive.

COMPLETE SET (220) 200.00 450.00
1 Patrick Ewing .60 1.50
2 Christian Laettner .40 1.00
3 Mahmoud Abdul-Rauf .30 .75
4 Chris Webber .60 1.50
5 Jason Kidd .75 2.00
6 Clifford Rozier .30 .75
7 Elden Campbell .30 .75
8 Chuck Person .40 1.00
9 Jeff Hornacek .40 1.00
10 Rik Smits .40 1.00
11 Kurt Thomas .30 .75
12 Rod Strickland .30 .75
13 Kendall Gill .30 .75
14 Brian Williams .30 .75
15 Tom Gugliotta .30 .75
16 Ron Harper .40 1.00
17 Eric Williams .30 .75
18 A.C. Green .50 1.25
19 Scott Williams .30 .75
20 Damon Stoudamire .50 1.25
21 Bryant Reeves .30 .75
22 Bob Sura .30 .75
23 Mitch Richmond .50 1.25
24 Larry Johnson .50 1.25
25 Vin Baker .40 1.00
26 Mark Bryant .30 .75
27 Horace Grant .40 1.00
28 Allan Houston .40 1.00
29 Sam Perkins .30 .75
30 Antonio McDyess .50 1.25
31 Rasheed Wallace .60 1.50
32 Malik Sealy .30 .75
33 Scottie Pippen .75 2.00
34 Charles Barkley .75 2.00
35 Hakeem Olajuwon .60 1.50
36 John Starks .40 1.00
37 Byron Scott .40 1.00
38 Arvydas Sabonis .40 1.00
39 Vlade Divac .50 1.25
40 Joe Dumars .50 1.25
41 Danny Ferry .30 .75
42 Jerry Stackhouse .60 1.50
43 B.J. Armstrong .30 .75
44 Shawn Bradley .30 .75
45 Kevin Garnett 1.25 3.00
46 Dee Brown .30 .75
47 Michael Smith .30 .75
48 Doug Christie .30 .75
49 Mark Jackson .50 1.25
50 Shawn Kemp .50 1.25
51 Sasha Danilovic .30 .75
52 Nick Anderson .30 .75
53 Matt Geiger .30 .75
54 Charles Smith .30 .75
55 Mookie Blaylock .30 .75
56 Johnny Newman .30 .75
57 George McCloud .30 .75
58 Greg Ostertag .30 .75
59 Reggie Williams .30 .75
60 Brent Barry .40 1.00
61 Doug West .30 .75
62 Donald Royal .30 .75
63 Randy Brown .30 .75
64 Vincent Askew .30 .75
65 John Stockton .60 1.50
66 Joe Kleine .30 .75
67 Keith Askins .30 .75
68 Bobby Phills .30 .75
69 Chris Mullin .50 1.25
70 Nick Van Exel .50 1.25
71 Rick Fox .30 .75
72 Chicago Bulls - 72 Wins 1.50 4.00
73 Shawn Respert .30 .75
74 Hubert Davis .30 .75
75 Jim Jackson .30 .75
76 Olden Polynice .30 .75
77 Gheorghe Muresan .30 .75
78 Theo Ratliff .30 .75
79 Khalid Reeves .30 .75
80 David Robinson .75 2.00
81 Lawrence Moten .30 .75
82 Sam Cassell .40 1.00
83 George Zidek .30 .75
84 Sharone Wright .30 .75
85 Clarence Weatherspoon .30 .75
86 Alan Henderson .30 .75
87 Chris Dudley .30 .75
88 Ed O'Bannon .30 .75
89 Calbert Cheaney .30 .75
90 Cedric Ceballos .30 .75
91 Michael Cage .30 .75
92 Ervin Johnson .30 .75
93 Gary Trent .30 .75
94 Sherman Douglas .30 .75
95 Joe Smith .40 1.00
96 Dale Davis .30 .75
97 Tony Dumas .30 .75
98 Muggsy Bogues .40 1.00
99 Toni Kukoc .50 1.25
100 Grant Hill .75 2.00
101 Michael Finley .60 1.50
102 Isaiah Rider .40 1.00
103 Bryant Stith .30 .75
104 Pooh Richardson .30 .75
105 Karl Malone .60 1.50
106 Brian Grant .40 1.00
107 Sean Elliott .50 1.25
108 Charles Oakley .40 1.00
109 Pervis Ellison .30 .75
110 Anfernee Hardaway .75 2.00
111 Checklist (1-220) .30 .75
112 Dikembe Mutombo .50 1.25
113 Alonzo Mourning .60 1.50
114 Hubert Davis .30 .75
115 Rony Seikaly .40 1.00
116 Danny Manning .40 1.00
117 Donyell Marshall .30 .75
118 Gerald Wilkins .30 .75
119 Ervin Johnson .30 .75
120 Jalen Rose .40 1.00
121 Dino Radja .40 1.00
122 Glenn Robinson .50 1.25
123 John Stockton .60 1.50
124 Matt Maloney RC 1.50 4.00
125 Clifford Robinson .30 .75
126 Steve Kerr .40 1.00
127 Nate McMillan .30 .75
128 Shareef Abdur-Rahim RC 6.00 15.00
129 Loy Vaught .30 .75
130 Anthony Mason .30 .75
131 Kevin Garnett 1.25 3.00
132 Roy Rogers RC 1.50 4.00
133 Erick Dampier RC 1.50 4.00
134 Tyus Edney .30 .75
135 Chris Mills .30 .75
136 Cory Alexander .30 .75
137 Juwan Howard .40 1.00
138 Kobe Bryant RC 150.00 300.00
139 Michael Jordan 8.00 20.00
140 Jayson Williams .30 .75
141 Rod Strickland .30 .75
142 Lorenzen Wright RC 1.50 4.00
143 Will Perdue .30 .75
144 Derek Harper .40 1.00
145 Billy Owens .30 .75
146 Antoine Walker RC 5.00 12.00
147 P.J. Brown .30 .75
148 Terrell Brandon .30 .75
149 Larry Johnson .50 1.25
150 Steve Smith .40 1.00
151 Eddie Jones .50 1.25
152 Detlef Schrempf .50 1.25
153 Dale Ellis .30 .75
154 Isaiah Rider .40 1.00
155 Tony Delk RC 1.50 4.00
156 Adrian Caldwell .30 .75
157 Jamal Mashburn .40 1.00
158 Dennis Scott .30 .75
159 Dana Barros .30 .75
160 Martin Muursepp RC 1.50 4.00
161 Marcus Camby RC 5.00 12.00
162 Jerome Williams RC 1.50 4.00
163 Wesley Person .30 .75
164 Luc Longley .30 .75
165 Charlie Ward .30 .75
166 Mark Jackson .50 1.25
167 Derrick Coleman .40 1.00
168 Dell Curry .30 .75
169 Armon Gilliam .30 .75
170 Vlade Divac .50 1.25
171 Allen Iverson RC 12.00 30.00
172 Vitaly Potapenko RC 1.50 4.00
173 Jon Koncak .30 .75
174 Lindsey Hunter .30 .75
175 Kevin Johnson .50 1.25
176 Dennis Rodman 1.00 2.50
177 Stephon Marbury RC 8.00 20.00
178 Karl Malone .60 1.50
179 Charles Barkley .75 2.00
180 Popeye Jones .30 .75
181 Samaki Walker RC 1.50 4.00
182 Steve Nash RC 15.00 40.00
183 Latrell Sprewell .50 1.25
184 Kenny Anderson .40 1.00
185 Tyrone Hill .30 .75
186 Robert Pack .30 .75
187 Greg Anthony .30 .75
188 Derrick McKey .30 .75
189 John Wallace RC 1.50 4.00
190 Bryon Russell .30 .75
191 Jermaine O'Neal RC 8.00 20.00
192 Clyde Drexler .60 1.50
193 Mahmoud Abdul-Rauf .30 .75
194 Eric Montross .30 .75
195 Allan Houston .40 1.00
196 Harvey Grant .30 .75
197 Rodney Rogers .30 .75
198 Kerry Kittles RC 1.50 4.00
199 Grant Hill .75 2.00
200 Lionel Simmons .30 .75
201 Reggie Miller .60 1.50
202 Avery Johnson .40 1.00
203 LaPhonso Ellis .30 .75
204 Brian Shaw .30 .75
205 Priest Lauderdale RC 1.50 4.00
206 Derek Fisher RC 8.00 20.00
207 Terry Porter .30 .75
208 Todd Fuller RC 1.50 4.00
209 Hersey Hawkins .30 .75
210 Tim Legler .30 .75
211 Terry Dehere .30 .75
212 Gary Payton .50 1.25
213 Joe Dumars .50 1.25
214 Don MacLean .30 .75
215 Greg Minor .30 .75
216 Tim Hardaway .50 1.25
217 Ray Allen RC 12.00 30.00
218 Mario Elie .30 .75
219 Brooks Thompson .30 .75
220 Shaquille O'Neal 1.25 3.00

1996-97 Topps Chrome Refractors

Randomly inserted into packs at a rate of one in 12, this 220-card set parallels the basic set but utilizes the Refractor technology. Card backs carry a "R" prefix. One card that does not is #72. The set is condition sensitive. To ascertain values on individual cards, please refer to the multiplier in the header below, coupled with the value of the base card.

*STARS: 8X TO 20X HI COLUMN
*RCs: 1.5X TO 4X HI
33 Scottie Pippen 25.00 60.00
72 Chicago Bulls - 72 Wins 75.00 200.00
110 Anfernee Hardaway 20.00 50.00
128 Shareef Abdur-Rahim 50.00 125.00
138 Kobe Bryant 1400.00 1900.00
139 Michael Jordan 350.00 600.00
151 Eddie Jones 12.00 30.00
155 Tony Delk 15.00 40.00
161 Marcus Camby 30.00 80.00
162 Jerome Williams 12.00 30.00
171 Allen Iverson 80.00 200.00
182 Steve Nash 100.00 200.00
206 Derek Fisher 50.00 100.00
220 Shaquille O'Neal 30.00 80.00

1996-97 Topps Chrome Pro Files

Randomly inserted into packs at a rate of one in 8, this 20-card set parallels the Pro Files insert set from the regular 1996-97 Topps issue, but with a Chrome background. Card backs carry a "PF" prefix.

COMPLETE SET (20) 15.00 40.00
PF1 Grant Hill 1.50 4.00
PF2 Shawn Kemp 1.00 2.50
PF3 Michael Jordan 10.00 25.00
PF4 Vin Baker .75 2.00
PF5 Chris Webber 1.25 3.00
PF6 Joe Smith .75 2.00
PF7 Shaquille O'Neal 2.50 6.00
PF8 Patrick Ewing 1.25 3.00
PF9 Scottie Pippen 1.50 4.00
PF10 Damon Stoudamire 1.00 2.50
PF11 Anfernee Hardaway 1.50 4.00
PF12 Juwan Howard .75 2.00
PF13 Dikembe Mutombo 1.00 2.50
PF14 Dennis Rodman 2.00 5.00
PF15 Kevin Garnett 2.50 6.00
PF16 Jerry Stackhouse 1.25 3.00
PF17 Alonzo Mourning 1.25 3.00
PF18 Karl Malone 1.25 3.00
PF19 Hakeem Olajuwon 1.25 3.00
PF20 Gary Payton 1.00 2.50

1996-97 Topps Chrome Season's Best

Randomly inserted into packs at a rate of one in 6, this 25-card set parallels the Season's Best insert set from the regular 1996-97 Topps issue, but with a Chrome background. Card backs carry a "SB" prefix.

COMPLETE SET (25) 20.00 50.00
SB1 Michael Jordan 10.00 25.00
SB2 Hakeem Olajuwon 1.25 3.00
SB3 Shaquille O'Neal 2.50 6.00
SB4 Karl Malone 1.25 3.00
SB5 David Robinson 1.50 4.00
SB6 Dennis Rodman 2.00 5.00
SB7 David Robinson 1.50 4.00
SB8 Dikembe Mutombo 1.00 2.50
SB9 Charles Barkley 1.50 4.00
SB10 Shawn Kemp 1.00 2.50
SB11 John Stockton 1.25 3.00
SB12 Jason Kidd 1.50 4.00
SB13 Avery Johnson .75 2.00
SB14 Rod Strickland .60 1.50
SB15 Damon Stoudamire 1.00 2.50
SB16 Gary Payton 1.00 2.50
SB17 Mookie Blaylock .60 1.50
SB18 Michael Jordan 10.00 25.00
SB19 Jason Kidd 1.50 4.00
SB20 Alvin Robertson .60 1.50
SB21 Dikembe Mutombo 1.00 2.50
SB22 Shawn Bradley .60 1.50
SB23 David Robinson 1.50 4.00
SB24 Hakeem Olajuwon 1.25 3.00
SB25 Alonzo Mourning 1.25 3.00

1996-97 Topps Chrome Youthquake

Randomly inserted into packs at a rate of one in 12, this 15-card set parallels the Youthquake insert set from the regular 1996-97 Topps issue, but with a Chrome background. Card backs carry a "YQ" prefix.

COMPLETE SET (15) 40.00 100.00
YQ1 Allen Iverson 6.00 15.00
YQ2 Samaki Walker 1.00 2.50
YQ3 Stephon Marbury 2.50 6.00
YQ4 Damon Stoudamire 1.50 4.00
YQ5 John Wallace 1.00 2.50
YQ6 Michael Finley 2.00 5.00
YQ7 Marcus Camby 1.50 4.00
YQ8 Kerry Kittles 1.00 2.50
YQ9 Ray Allen 4.00 10.00
YQ10 Jerry Stackhouse 2.00 5.00
YQ11 Shareef Abdur-Rahim 2.00 5.00
YQ12 Antonio McDyess 1.00 2.50
YQ13 Joe Smith .75 2.00
YQ14 Brent Barry .75 2.00
YQ15 Kobe Bryant 30.00 80.00

1997-98 Topps Chrome

The 1997-98 Topps Chrome set was issued in one series totalling 220 cards. The cards are a semi-parallel of the regular Topps set - utilizing the same photography, but released in separate packaging at a suggested retail price of $3 per pack.

COMPLETE SET (220) 60.00 120.00
1 Scottie Pippen 1.00 2.50
2 Nate McMillan .40 1.00
3 Byron Scott .50 1.25
4 Mark Davis .40 1.00
5 Rod Strickland .40 1.00
6 Brian Grant .40 1.00
7 Damon Stoudamire .60 1.50
8 John Stockton .75 2.00
9 Grant Long .40 1.00
10 Darrell Armstrong .40 1.00
11 Anthony Mason .40 1.00
12 Travis Best .40 1.00
13 Stephon Marbury .75 2.00
14 Jamal Mashburn .50 1.25
15 Detlef Schrempf .60 1.50
16 Terrell Brandon .40 1.00
17 Charles Barkley 1.00 2.50
18 Vin Baker .50 1.25
19 Gary Trent .40 1.00
20 Vinny Del Negro .40 1.00
21 Todd Day .40 1.00
22 Malik Sealy .40 1.00
23 Wesley Person .40 1.00
24 Reggie Miller .75 2.00
25 Dan Majerle .60 1.50
26 Todd Fuller .40 1.00
27 Juwan Howard .50 1.25
28 Clarence Weatherspoon .40 1.00
29 Grant Hill 1.00 2.50
30 John Williams .40 1.00
31 Ken Norman .40 1.00
32 Patrick Ewing .75 2.00
33 Bryon Russell .40 1.00
34 Tony Smith .40 1.00
35 Andrew Lang .40 1.00
36 Rony Seikaly .50 1.25
37 Billy Owens .40 1.00
38 Dino Radja .50 1.25
39 Chris Gatling .40 1.00
40 Dale Davis .40 1.00
41 Arvydas Sabonis .50 1.25
42 Chris Mills .40 1.00
43 A.C. Green .60 1.50
44 Tyrone Hill .40 1.00
45 Tracy Murray .40 1.00
46 David Robinson 1.00 2.50
47 Lee Mayberry .40 1.00
48 Jayson Williams .40 1.00
49 Jason Kidd 1.00 2.50
50 Bryant Stith .40 1.00
51 Checklist 1.50 4.00
Bulls - Team of the 90s
Michael Jordan
Scottie Pippen
Dennis Rodman
Ron Harper
52 Brent Barry .50 1.25
53 Henry James .40 1.00
54 Allen Iverson 1.25 3.00
55 Shandon Anderson .40 1.00
56 Mitch Richmond .60 1.50
57 Allan Houston .50 1.25
58 Ron Harper .50 1.25
59 Gheorghe Muresan .40 1.00
60 Vincent Askew .40 1.00
61 Ray Allen .75 2.00
62 Kenny Anderson .50 1.25
63 Dikembe Mutombo .60 1.50
64 Sam Perkins .40 1.00
65 Walt Williams .40 1.00
66 Chris Carr .40 1.00
67 Vlade Divac .60 1.50
68 LaPhonso Ellis .40 1.00
69 B.J. Armstrong .40 1.00
70 Jim Jackson .40 1.00
71 Clyde Drexler .75 2.00
72 Lindsey Hunter .40 1.00
73 Sasha Danilovic .40 1.00
74 Elden Campbell .40 1.00
75 Robert Pack .40 1.00
76 Dennis Scott .40 1.00
77 Will Perdue .40 1.00
78 Anthony Peeler .40 1.00
79 Steve Smith .50 1.25
80 Steve Kerr .50 1.25
81 Buck Williams .40 1.00
82 Terry Mills .40 1.00
83 Michael Smith .40 1.00
84 Adam Keefe .40 1.00
85 Kevin Willis .40 1.00
86 David Wesley .40 1.00
87 Muggsy Bogues .50 1.25
88 Bimbo Coles .40 1.00
89 Tom Gugliotta .40 1.00
90 Jermaine O'Neal .75 2.00
91 Cedric Ceballos .40 1.00
92 Shawn Kemp .60 1.50
93 Horace Grant .50 1.25
94 Shareef Abdur-Rahim .60 1.50
95 Robert Horry .50 1.25
96 Vitaly Potapenko .40 1.00
97 Pooh Richardson .40 1.00
98 Doug Christie .40 1.00
99 Voshon Lenard .40 1.00
100 Dominique Wilkins .75 2.00
101 Alonzo Mourning .75 2.00
102 Sam Cassell .50 1.25
103 Sherman Douglas .40 1.00
104 Shawn Bradley .40 1.00
105 Mark Jackson .60 1.50
106 Dennis Rodman 1.25 3.00
107 Charles Oakley .50 1.25
108 Matt Maloney .40 1.00
109 Shaquille O'Neal 1.50 4.00
110 Checklist .75 2.00
Karl Malone MVP
111 Antonio McDyess .50 1.25
112 Bob Sura .40 1.00
113 Terrell Brandon .40 1.00
114 Tim Thomas RC 2.00 5.00
115 Tim Duncan RC 10.00 25.00
116 Antonio Daniels RC 1.00 2.50
117 Bryant Reeves .40 1.00
118 Keith Van Horn RC 2.00 5.00
119 Loy Vaught .40 1.00
120 Rasheed Wallace .60 1.50
121 Bobby Jackson RC 1.25 3.00
122 Kevin Johnson .60 1.50
123 Michael Jordan 6.00 15.00
124 Ron Mercer RC 1.25 3.00
125 Tracy McGrady RC 6.00 15.00
126 Antoine Walker .60 1.50
127 Carlos Rogers .40 1.00
128 Isaac Austin .40 1.00
129 Mookie Blaylock .40 1.00
130 Rodrick Rhodes RC 1.00 2.50
131 Dennis Scott .40 1.00
132 Chris Mullin .60 1.50
133 P.J. Brown .40 1.00
134 Rex Chapman .40 1.00
135 Sean Elliott .60 1.50
136 Alan Henderson .40 1.00
137 Austin Croshere RC 1.00 2.50
138 Nick Van Exel .50 1.25
139 Derek Strong .40 1.00
140 Glenn Robinson .50 1.25
141 Avery Johnson .50 1.25
142 Calbert Cheaney .40 1.00
143 Mahmoud Abdul-Rauf .40 1.00
144 Stojko Vrankovic .40 1.00
145 Chris Childs .40 1.00
146 Danny Manning .50 1.25
147 Jeff Hornacek .50 1.25
148 Kevin Garnett 1.25 3.00
149 Joe Dumars .60 1.50
150 Johnny Taylor RC 1.00 2.50
151 Mark Price .60 1.50
152 Toni Kukoc .60 1.50
153 Erick Dampier .40 1.00
154 Lorenzen Wright .40 1.00
155 Matt Geiger .40 1.00
156 Tim Hardaway .60 1.50
157 Charles Smith RC 1.00 2.50
158 Hersey Hawkins .40 1.00
159 Michael Finley .60 1.50
160 Tyus Edney .40 1.00
161 Christian Laettner .50 1.25
162 Doug West .40 1.00
163 Jim Jackson .40 1.00
164 Larry Johnson .60 1.50
165 Vin Baker .50 1.25
166 Karl Malone .75 2.00
167 Kelvin Cato RC 1.00 2.50
168 Luc Longley .40 1.00
169 Dale Davis .40 1.00
170 Joe Smith .50 1.25
171 Kobe Bryant 3.00 8.00
172 Scot Pollard RC 1.00 2.50
173 Derek Anderson RC 1.00 2.50
174 Erick Strickland RC 1.00 2.50
175 Olden Polynice .40 1.00
176 Chris Whitney .40 1.00
177 Anthony Parker RC 1.00 2.50
178 Armon Gilliam .40 1.00
179 Gary Payton .60 1.50
180 Glen Rice .60 1.50
181 Chauncey Billups RC 4.00 10.00
182 Derek Fisher .60 1.50
183 John Starks .50 1.25
184 Mario Elie .40 1.00
185 Chris Webber .60 1.50
186 Shawn Kemp .60 1.50
187 Greg Ostertag .40 1.00
188 Olivier Saint-Jean RC 1.00 2.50
189 Eric Snow .40 1.00
190 Isaiah Rider .40 1.00
191 Paul Grant RC 1.00 2.50
192 Samaki Walker .40 1.00
193 Cory Alexander .40 1.00
194 Eddie Jones .60 1.50
195 John Thomas RC 1.00 2.50
196 Otis Thorpe .40 1.00
197 Rod Strickland .40 1.00
198 David Wesley .40 1.00
199 Jacque Vaughn RC 1.00 2.50
200 Rik Smits .50 1.25
201 Brevin Knight RC 1.00 2.50
202 Clifford Robinson .40 1.00
203 Hakeem Olajuwon .75 2.00
204 Jerry Stackhouse .60 1.50
205 Tyrone Hill .40 1.00
206 Kendall Gill .40 1.00
207 Marcus Camby .60 1.50
208 Tony Battie RC 1.25 3.00
209 Brent Price .40 1.00
210 Danny Fortson RC 1.00 2.50
211 Jerome Williams .40 1.00
212 Maurice Taylor RC 1.00 2.50
213 Brian Williams .40 1.00
214 Keith Booth RC 1.00 2.50
215 Nick Anderson .40 1.00
216 Travis Knight .40 1.00
217 Adonal Foyle RC 1.00 2.50
218 Anfernee Hardaway 1.00 2.50
219 Kerry Kittles .40 1.00
220 Dikembe Mutombo CL .60 1.50
Defensive POY

1997-98 Topps Chrome Refractors

Randomly inserted into packs at one in 12, this 220-card set parallels the basic set utilizing the "classic" Refractor technology. To ascertain values on individual cards, please refer to the multiplier in the header below, coupled with the value of the base card.

*STARS: 3X TO 8X BASE CARD HI
*RCs: 2X TO 5X BASE HI
51 Checklist 50.00 125.00
Bulls - Team of the 90s
Michael Jordan
Scottie Pippen
Dennis Rodman
Ron Haper
114 Tim Thomas 20.00 50.00
115 Tim Duncan 80.00 160.00
123 Michael Jordan 60.00 150.00
125 Tracy McGrady 30.00 80.00
171 Kobe Bryant 30.00 80.00

1997-98 Topps Chrome Destiny

Randomly inserted into packs at a rate of one in 12, this 15-card set is a parallel of the regular Topps Destiny utilizing the Chrome technology. Card backs are numbered with a "D" prefix.

COMPLETE SET (15) 12.00 30.00
*REF: 1X TO 2.5X BASE DESTINY
REF: STATED ODDS 1:48
D1 Grant Hill 1.25 3.00
D2 Kevin Garnett 1.50 4.00
D3 Vin Baker .60 1.50
D4 Antoine Walker .75 2.00
D5 Kobe Bryant 4.00 10.00
D6 Tracy McGrady 2.00 5.00
D7 Keith Van Horn .75 2.00
D8 Tim Duncan 2.50 6.00
D9 Eddie Jones .75 2.00
D10 Stephon Marbury 1.00 2.50
D11 Marcus Camby .75 2.00
D12 Antonio McDyess .60 1.50

D13 Shareef Abdur-Rahim .75 2.00
D14 Allen Iverson 1.50 4.00
D15 Shaquille O'Neal 2.00 5.00

1997-98 Topps Chrome Season's Best

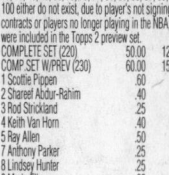

Randomly inserted into packs at a rate of one in eight, this 29-card set is a parallel of the regular Topps Season's Best set utilizing the Chrome technology. The only card not available is SB8, which was not produced. Card backs are numbered with a "SB" prefix.

COMPLETE SET (29) 20.00 50.00
*REF: 1.25X TO 3X BASE SEAS.BEST
REF: STATED ODDS 1:24
SB1 Gary Payton .75 2.00
SB2 Kevin Johnson .75 2.00
SB3 Tim Hardaway .75 2.00
SB4 John Stockton 1.00 2.50
SB5 Damon Stoudamire .75 2.00
SB6 Michael Jordan 6.00 15.00
SB7 Mitch Richmond .75 2.00
SB9 Reggie Miller 1.00 2.50
SB10 Clyde Drexler 1.00 2.50
SB11 Grant Hill 1.25 3.00
SB12 Scottie Pippen 1.25 3.00
SB13 Kendall Gill .50 1.25
SB14 Glen Rice .75 2.00
SB15 LaPhonso Ellis .50 1.25
SB16 Karl Malone 1.00 2.50
SB17 Charles Barkley 1.25 3.00
SB18 Vin Baker .60 1.50
SB19 Chris Webber .75 2.00
SB20 Tom Gugliotta .50 1.25
SB21 Shaquille O'Neal 2.00 5.00
SB22 Patrick Ewing 1.00 2.50
SB23 Hakeem Olajuwon 1.00 2.50
SB24 Alonzo Mourning 1.00 2.50
SB25 Dikembe Mutombo .75 2.00
SB26 Allen Iverson 1.50 4.00
SB27 Antoine Walker .75 2.00
SB28 Shareef Abdur-Rahim .75 2.00
SB29 Stephon Marbury 1.00 2.50
SB30 Kerry Kittles .50 1.25

1997-98 Topps Chrome Topps 40

Randomly inserted into packs at a rate of one in 6, this 39-card set is a parallel of the regular Topps 40 set utilizing the Chrome technology. Card T-40 7 was not produced. Card backs are numbered with a "T40" prefix.

COMPLETE SET (39) 30.00 60.00
*REF: 1.25X TO 3X BASE TOP 40
REF: STATED ODDS 1:18
T1 Glen Rice .75 2.00
T2 Patrick Ewing 1.00 2.50
T3 Terrell Brandon .50 1.25
T4 Jerry Stackhouse .75 2.00
T5 Michael Jordan 6.00 15.00
T6 Christian Laettner .60 1.50
T8 Reggie Miller 1.00 2.50
T9 Gary Payton .75 2.00
T10 Detlef Schrempf .75 2.00
T11 Kevin Garnett 1.50 4.00
T12 Eddie Jones .75 2.00
T13 Clyde Drexler 1.00 2.50
T14 Anfernee Hardaway 1.25 3.00
T15 Chris Webber .75 2.00
T16 Jayson Williams .50 1.25
T17 Joe Smith .60 1.50
T18 Karl Malone 1.00 2.50
T19 Tim Hardaway .75 2.00
T20 Vin Baker .60 1.50
T21 Tom Gugliotta .50 1.25
T22 Allen Iverson 1.50 4.00
T23 David Robinson 1.25 3.00
T24 Dikembe Mutombo .75 2.00
T25 John Stockton 1.00 2.50
T26 Charles Barkley 1.25 3.00
T27 Mitch Richmond .75 2.00
T28 Damon Stoudamire .75 2.00
T29 Anthony Mason .50 1.25
T30 Shaquille O'Neal 2.00 5.00
T31 Glenn Robinson .60 1.50
T32 Juwan Howard .60 1.50
T33 Shawn Kemp .75 2.00
T34 Dennis Rodman 1.50 4.00
T35 Grant Hill 1.25 3.00
T36 Kevin Johnson .75 2.00
T37 Alonzo Mourning 1.00 2.50
T38 Hakeem Olajuwon 1.00 2.50
T39 Joe Dumars 1.00 2.50
T40 Scottie Pippen 1.25 3.00

1998-99 Topps Chrome

Released in four-card packs, this 220-card set is a semi-parallel of the base 1998-99 Topps set. Cards #6, 10, 19, 40, 43, 60, 73, 75, 77, 81, 89, 90, 97, 99, and 100 either do not exist, due to player's not signing contracts or players no longer playing in the NBA, or were included in the Topps 2 preview set.

COMPLETE SET (220) 50.00 120.00
COMP.SET W/PREV (230) 60.00 150.00
1 Scottie Pippen .60 1.50
2 Shareef Abdur-Rahim .40 1.00
3 Rod Strickland .25 .60
4 Keith Van Horn .40 1.00
5 Ray Allen .50 1.25
7 Anthony Parker .25 .60
8 Lindsey Hunter .25 .60
9 Mario Elie .25 .60
11 Eldridge Recasner .25 .60
12 Jeff Hornacek .30 .75
13 Chris Webber .40 1.00
14 Lee Mayberry .25 .60
15 Erick Strickland .25 .60
16 Arvydas Sabonis .30 .75
17 Tim Thomas .40 1.00
18 Luc Longley .25 .60
20 Alonzo Mourning .50 1.25
21 Adonal Foyle .25 .60
22 Tony Battie .30 .75
23 Robert Horry .30 .75
24 Derek Harper .30 .75
25 Jamal Mashburn .30 .75
26 Elliott Perry .25 .60
27 Jalen Rose .30 .75
28 Joe Smith .30 .75
29 Henry James .25 .60
30 Travis Knight .25 .60
31 Tom Gugliotta .25 .60
32 Chris Anstey .25 .60
33 Antonio Daniels .25 .60
34 Elden Campbell .25 .60
35 Charlie Ward .25 .60
36 Eddie Johnson .25 .60
37 John Wallace .25 .60
38 Antonio Davis .25 .60
39 Antoine Walker .40 1.00
41 Doug Christie .25 .60
42 Andrew Lang .25 .60
44 Jaren Jackson .25 .60
45 Loy Vaught .25 .60
46 Allan Houston .30 .75
47 Mark Jackson .40 1.00
48 Tracy Murray .25 .60
49 Tim Duncan .75 2.00
50 Micheal Williams .25 .60
51 Steve Nash .60 1.50
52 Matt Maloney .25 .60
53 Sam Cassell .30 .75
54 Voshon Lenard .25 .60
55 Dikembe Mutombo .40 1.00
56 Malik Sealy .25 .60
57 Dell Curry .25 .60
58 Stephon Marbury .50 1.25
59 Tariq Abdul-Wahad .25 .60
61 Kelvin Cato .25 .60
62 LaPhonso Ellis .25 .60
63 Jim Jackson .25 .60
64 Greg Ostertag .25 .60
65 Glenn Robinson .30 .75
66 Chris Carr .25 .60
67 Marcus Camby .30 .75
68 Kobe Bryant 2.00 5.00
69 Bobby Jackson .30 .75
70 B.J. Armstrong .25 .60
71 Alan Henderson .25 .60
72 Terry Davis .25 .60
74 Lamond Murray .25 .60
76 Rex Chapman .25 .60
78 Terry Cummings .40 1.00
79 Dan Majerle .40 1.00
80 Bo Outlaw .25 .60
82 Vin Baker .30 .75
83 Clifford Robinson .25 .60
84 Greg Anthony .25 .60
85 Brevin Knight .25 .60
86 Jacque Vaughn .25 .60
87 Bobby Phills .25 .60
88 Sherman Douglas .25 .60
91 Lorenzen Wright .25 .60
92 Eric Williams .25 .60
93 Will Perdue .25 .60
94 Charles Barkley .60 1.50
95 Kendall Gill .25 .60
96 Wesley Person .25 .60
98 Erick Dampier .25 .60
101 Rasheed Wallace .40 1.00
102 Zydrunas Ilgauskas .40 1.00
103 Eddie Jones .40 1.00
104 Ron Mercer .30 .75
105 Horace Grant .30 .75
106 Corliss Williamson .25 .60
107 Anthony Mason .25 .60
108 Mookie Blaylock .25 .60
109 Dennis Rodman .75 2.00
110 Checklist .25 .60
111 Steve Smith .30 .75
112 Cedric Henderson .25 .60
113 Raef LaFrentz RC 1.25 3.00
114 Calbert Cheaney .25 .60
115 Rik Smits .30 .75
116 Rony Seikaly .40 1.00
117 Lawrence Funderburke .25 .60
118 Ricky Davis RC 1.50 4.00
119 Howard Eisley .25 .60
120 Kenny Anderson .30 .75
121 Corey Benjamin RC 1.00 2.50
122 Maurice Taylor .25 .60
123 Eric Murdock .25 .60
124 Derek Fisher .40 1.00
125 Kevin Garnett .75 2.00
126 Walt Williams .25 .60
127 Bryce Drew RC 1.00 2.50
128 A.C. Green .40 1.00
129 Ervin Johnson .25 .60
130 Christian Laettner .30 .75
131 Chauncey Billups .50 1.25
132 Hakeem Olajuwon .50 1.25
133 Al Harrington RC 1.50 4.00
134 Danny Manning .25 .60
135 Paul Pierce RC 6.00 15.00
136 Terrell Brandon .25 .60
137 Bob Sura .25 .60
138 Chris Gatling .25 .60
139 Donyell Marshall .25 .60
140 Marcus Camby .30 .75
141 Brian Skinner RC 1.00 2.50
142 Charles Oakley .30 .75
143 Antawn Jamison RC 2.50 6.00
144 Nazr Mohammed RC 1.00 2.50
145 Karl Malone .50 1.25
146 Chris Mills .25 .60
147 Bison Dele .25 .60
148 Gary Payton .40 1.00
149 Terry Porter .25 .60
150 Tim Hardaway .40 1.00
151 Larry Hughes RC 2.00 5.00
152 Derek Anderson .25 .60
153 Jason Williams RC 2.50 6.00
154 Dirk Nowitzki RC 8.00 20.00
155 Juwan Howard .30 .75
156 Avery Johnson .30 .75
157 Matt Harpring RC 1.25 3.00
158 Reggie Miller .50 1.25
159 Walter McCarty .25 .60
160 Allen Iverson .75 2.00
161 Felipe Lopez RC 1.00 2.50
162 Tracy McGrady .60 1.50
163 Damon Stoudamire .40 1.00
164 Antonio McDyess .30 .75
165 Grant Hill .60 1.50
166 Tyronn Lue RC 1.00 2.50
167 P.J. Brown .25 .60
168 Antonio Daniels .25 .60
169 Mitch Richmond .40 1.00
170 David Robinson .60 1.50
171 Shawn Bradley .25 .60
172 Shandon Anderson .25 .60
173 Chris Childs .25 .60
174 Shawn Kemp .40 1.00
175 Shaquille O'Neal 1.00 2.50
176 John Starks .30 .75
177 Tyrone Hill .25 .60
178 Jayson Williams .25 .60
179 Anfernee Hardaway .60 1.50
180 Chris Webber .40 1.00
181 Don Reid .25 .60
182 Stacey Augmon .30 .75
183 Hersey Hawkins .25 .60
184 Sam Mitchell .25 .60
185 Jason Kidd .60 1.50
186 Nick Van Exel .30 .75
187 Larry Johnson .40 1.00
188 Bryant Reeves .25 .60
189 Glen Rice .40 1.00
190 Kerry Kittles .25 .60
191 Toni Kukoc .40 1.00
192 Ron Harper .30 .75
193 Bryon Russell .25 .60
194 Vladimir Stepania RC 1.00 2.50
195 Michael Olowokandi RC 1.25 3.00
196 Mike Bibby RC 2.50 6.00
197 Dale Ellis .25 .60
198 Muggsy Bogues .30 .75
199 Vince Carter RC 6.00 15.00
200 Robert Traylor RC 1.00 2.50
201 Peja Stojakovic RC 2.50 6.00
202 Aaron McKie .25 .60
203 Hubert Davis .25 .60
204 Dana Barros .25 .60
205 Bonzi Wells RC 1.00 2.50
206 Michael Doleac RC 1.00 2.50
207 Keon Clark RC 1.00 2.50
208 Michael Dickerson RC 1.00 2.50
209 Nick Anderson .25 .60
210 Brent Price .25 .60
211 Cherokee Parks .25 .60
212 Sam Jacobson RC 1.00 2.50
213 Pat Garrity RC 1.00 2.50
214 Tyrone Corbin .25 .60
215 David Wesley .25 .60
216 Rodney Rogers .25 .60
217 Dean Garrett .25 .60
218 Roshown McLeod RC 1.00 2.50
219 Dale Davis .25 .60
220 Checklist .25 .60
221 Scottie Pippen MO .60 1.50
222 Antonio McDyess MO .30 .75
223 Stephon Marbury MO .50 1.25
224 Tom Gugliotta MO .25 .60
225 Chris Webber MO .40 1.00
226 Latrell Sprewell MO .40 1.00
227 Mitch Richmond MO .40 1.00
228 Joe Smith MO .30 .75
229 John Starks MO .30 .75
230 Charles Oakley MO .30 .75
231 Dennis Rodman MO .75 2.00
232 Eddie Jones MO .40 1.00
233 Nick Van Exel MO .30 .75
234 Bobby Jackson MO .30 .75
235 Glen Rice MO .40 1.00

1998-99 Topps Chrome Refractors

Randomly inserted into packs at one in 12, this 220-card set parallels the base set. The cards use the "classic" Refractor technology. The following cards were not produced or contained in the Topps 2 preview set: 6, 10, 19, 40, 43, 60, 73, 75, 77, 81, 89, 90, 97, 99 and 100.

*STARS: 4X TO 10X HI COLUMN
*RCs: 1.5X TO 4X HI
133 Al Harrington 8.00 20.00
154 Dirk Nowitzki 40.00 100.00
199 Vince Carter 30.00 80.00
201 Peja Stojakovic 12.00 30.00

1998-99 Topps Chrome Apparitions

Randomly inserted in packs at 1:24, this 14-card set features players that are known for their spectacular moves. Card backs carry an "A" prefix.

COMPLETE SET (14) 12.00 30.00
*REF: 6X TO 15X HI COLUMN
REF: STATED ODDS 1:1,015
REF: PRINT RUN 100 SERIAL #'d SETS
A1 Kobe Bryant 5.00 12.00
A2 Stephon Marbury 1.25 3.00
A3 Brent Barry .75 2.00
A4 Karl Malone 1.25 3.00
A5 Shaquille O'Neal 2.50 6.00
A6 Chris Webber 1.00 2.50
A7 Shawn Kemp 1.00 2.50
A8 Hakeem Olajuwon 1.25 3.00
A9 Anfernee Hardaway 1.50 4.00
A10 Michael Finley 1.00 2.50
A11 Keith Van Horn 1.00 2.50
A12 Kevin Garnett 2.00 5.00
A13 Vin Baker .75 2.00
A14 Tim Duncan 2.00 5.00

1998-99 Topps Chrome Back 2 Back

Randomly inserted in packs at one in 12, this 7-card set features player's who continually produce, resulting in either an individual or team title. Card backs carry a "B" prefix.

COMPLETE SET (7) 7.50 15.00
B1 Michael Jordan 5.00 12.00
B2 Scottie Pippen 1.00 2.50
B3 Dennis Rodman 1.25 3.00
B4 Hakeem Olajuwon .75 2.00
B5 John Stockton .75 2.00
B6 Dikembe Mutombo .60 1.50
B7 Grant Hill 1.00 2.50

1998-99 Topps Chrome Champion Spirit

Randomly inserted at one in 12, this 7-card set features players whose teams, either on the collegiate or professional level, have won team championships. Card backs feature a "CS" prefix.

COMPLETE SET (7) 7.50 15.00
CS1 Michael Jordan 5.00 12.00
CS2 Grant Hill 1.00 2.50
CS3 Ron Mercer .50 1.25
CS4 Mike Bibby 1.50 4.00
CS5 Michael Dickerson .60 1.50
CS6 Patrick Ewing .75 2.00
CS7 Scottie Pippen 1.00 2.50

1998-99 Topps Chrome Coast to Coast

Randomly inserted in packs at one in 24, this 15-card set focuses on player's who can take it "coast to coast" on the floor. Card backs carry a "CC" prefix.

COMPLETE SET (15) 12.00 30.00
*REF: 1.25X TO 3X HI COLUMN
REF: STATED ODDS 1:96
CC1 Kobe Bryant 5.00 12.00
CC2 Scottie Pippen 1.50 4.00
CC3 Eddie Jones 1.00 2.50
CC4 Grant Hill 1.50 4.00
CC5 Jason Kidd 1.50 4.00
CC6 Antoine Walker 1.00 2.50
CC7 Michael Finley 1.00 2.50
CC8 Kevin Garnett 2.00 5.00
CC9 Allen Iverson 2.00 5.00
CC10 Shawn Kemp 1.00 2.50
CC11 Glenn Robinson .75 2.00
CC12 Anfernee Hardaway 1.50 4.00
CC13 Tim Hardaway 1.00 2.50
CC14 Ron Mercer .75 2.00
CC15 Kerry Kittles .60 1.50

1998-99 Topps Chrome Instant Impact

Randomly inserted in packs at one in 36, this 10-card set features player's who make an immediate impact on the court. Card backs carry an "I" prefix.

COMPLETE SET (10) 12.00 30.00
*REF: 1.25X TO 3X HI COLUMN
REF: STATED ODDS 1:144
I1 Tim Duncan 2.50 6.00
I2 Keith Van Horn 1.25 3.00
I3 Stephon Marbury 1.25 3.00
I4 Hakeem Olajuwon 1.50 4.00
I5 Shaquille O'Neal 3.00 8.00
I6 Michael Olowokandi 1.00 2.50
I7 Raef LaFrentz 1.00 2.50
I8 Vince Carter 4.00 10.00
I9 Jason Williams 2.00 5.00
I10 Paul Pierce 4.00 10.00

1998-99 Topps Chrome Season's Best

Randomly inserted in packs at one in six, this 29-card set features player's who perform different "themes" very well. Card backs are numbered with a "SB" prefix. There is no card SB6.

COMPLETE SET (29) 8.00 20.00
*REF: 1.25X TO 3X HI COLUMN
REF: STATED ODDS 1:24
SB1 Rod Strickland .30 .75
SB2 Gary Payton .50 1.25
SB3 Tim Hardaway .50 1.25
SB4 Stephon Marbury .60 1.50
SB5 Sam Cassell .40 1.00
SB7 Mitch Richmond .50 1.25
SB8 Steve Smith .40 1.00
SB9 Ray Allen .60 1.50
SB10 Isaiah Rider .30 .75
SB11 Grant Hill .75 2.00
SB12 Kevin Garnett 1.00 2.50
SB13 Shareef Abdur-Rahim .50 1.25
SB14 Glenn Robinson .40 1.00
SB15 Michael Finley .50 1.25
SB16 Karl Malone .60 1.50
SB17 Tim Duncan 1.00 2.50
SB18 Antoine Walker .50 1.25
SB19 Chris Webber .50 1.25
SB20 Vin Baker .40 1.00
SB21 Shaquille O'Neal 1.25 3.00
SB22 David Robinson .75 2.00
SB23 Alonzo Mourning .60 1.50
SB24 Dikembe Mutombo .50 1.25
SB25 Hakeem Olajuwon .60 1.50
SB26 Tim Duncan 1.00 2.50
SB27 Keith Van Horn .50 1.25
SB28 Zydrunas Ilgauskas .50 1.25
SB29 Brevin Knight .30 .75
SB30 Bobby Jackson .40 1.00

1999-00 Topps Chrome

The 1999-00 Topps Chrome set was released in April 2000. The set contained 257 cards, with 220 veterans, 28 rookies and nine Team USA cards.

COMPLETE SET (257) 60.00 120.00
1 Steve Smith .25 .60
2 Ron Harper .25 .60
3 Michael Dickerson .25 .60
4 LaPhonso Ellis .25 .60
5 Chris Webber .40 1.00
6 Jason Caffey .25 .60
7 Bryon Russell .25 .60
8 Bison Dele .25 .60
9 Isaiah Rider .25 .60
10 Dean Garrett .25 .60
11 Eric Murdock .25 .60
12 Juwan Howard .30 .75
13 Latrell Sprewell .40 1.00
14 Jalen Rose .30 .75
15 Larry Johnson .40 1.00
16 Eric Williams .25 .60
17 Bryant Reeves .25 .60
18 Tony Battie .30 .75
19 Luc Longley .25 .60
20 Gary Payton .40 1.00
21 Tariq Abdul-Wahad .25 .60
22 Armon Gilliam UER .25 .60
mispelled Armen
23 Shaquille O'Neal 1.00 2.50
24 Gary Trent .25 .60
25 John Stockton .50 1.25
26 Mark Jackson .40 1.00
27 Cherokee Parks .25 .60
28 Michael Olowokandi .25 .60
29 Raef LaFrentz .30 .75
30 Dell Curry .25 .60
31 Travis Best .25 .60
32 Shawn Kemp .40 1.00
33 Voshon Lenard .25 .60
34 Brian Grant .30 .75
35 Alvin Williams .25 .60
36 Derek Fisher .40 1.00
37 Allan Houston .30 .75
38 Arvydas Sabonis .30 .75
39 Terry Cummings .25 .60
40 Dale Ellis .25 .60
41 Maurice Taylor .25 .60
42 Grant Hill .50 1.25
43 Anthony Mason .25 .60
44 John Wallace .25 .60
45 David Wesley .25 .60
46 Nick Van Exel .30 .75
47 Cuttino Mobley .30 .75
48 Anfernee Hardaway .60 1.50
49 Terry Porter .25 .60
50 Brent Barry .25 .60
51 Derek Harper .30 .75
52 Antoine Walker .40 1.00
53 Karl Malone .50 1.25
54 Ben Wallace .40 1.00
55 Vlade Divac .40 1.00
56 Sam Mitchell .25 .60
57 Joe Smith .25 .60
58 Shawn Bradley .25 .60
59 Darrell Armstrong .25 .60
60 Kenny Anderson .30 .75
61 Jason Williams .50 1.25
62 Alonzo Mourning .30 .75
63 Matt Harpring .30 .75
64 Antonio Davis .25 .60
65 Lindsey Hunter .25 .60
66 Allen Iverson .75 2.00
67 Mookie Blaylock .25 .60
68 Wesley Person .25 .60
69 Bobby Phills .25 .60
70 Theo Ratliff .30 .75
71 Antonio Daniels .25 .60
72 P.J. Brown .25 .60
73 David Robinson .60 1.50
74 Sean Elliott .40 1.00
75 Zydrunas Ilgauskas .30 .75
76 Kerry Kittles .25 .60
77 Otis Thorpe .25 .60
78 John Starks .40 1.00
79 Jaren Jackson .25 .60
80 Hersey Hawkins .25 .60
81 Glenn Robinson .25 .60
82 Paul Pierce .60 1.50
83 Glen Rice .40 1.00
84 Charlie Ward .25 .60
85 Dee Brown .25 .60
86 Danny Fortson .25 .60
87 Billy Owens .25 .60
88 Jason Kidd .60 1.50
89 Brent Price .25 .60
90 Don Reid .25 .60
91 Mark Bryant .25 .60
92 Vinny Del Negro .25 .60
93 Stephon Marbury .30 .75
94 Donyell Marshall .25 .60
95 Jim Jackson .30 .75
96 Horace Grant .25 .60
97 Calbert Cheaney .30 .75
98 Vince Carter .75 2.00
99 Bobby Jackson .30 .75
100 Alan Henderson .25 .60
101 Mike Bibby .40 1.00
102 Cedric Henderson .25 .60
103 Lamond Murray .25 .60
104 A.C. Green .40 1.00
105 Hakeem Olajuwon .50 1.25
106 George Lynch .25 .60
107 Kendall Gill .25 .60
108 Rex Chapman .25 .60
109 Eddie Jones .40 1.00
110 Kornel David RC .75 2.00
111 Jason Terry RC 2.00 5.00
112 Corey Maggette RC 1.50 4.00
113 Ron Artest RC 2.00 5.00
114 Richard Hamilton RC 2.00 5.00
115 Elton Brand RC 2.00 5.00
116 Baron Davis RC 2.50 6.00
117 Wally Szczerbiak RC 1.50 4.00
118 Steve Francis RC 2.00 5.00
119 James Posey RC .75 2.00
120 Shawn Marion RC 2.00 5.00
121 Tim Duncan .75 2.00
122 Danny Manning .25 .60
123 Chris Mullin .40 1.00
124 Antawn Jamison .40 1.00
125 Kobe Bryant 2.00 5.00
126 Matt Geiger .25 .60
127 Rod Strickland .25 .60
128 Howard Eisley .25 .60
129 Steve Nash .60 1.50
130 Felipe Lopez .25 .60
131 Ron Mercer .30 .75
132 Ruben Patterson .25 .60
133 Dana Barros .25 .60
134 Dale Davis .25 .60
135 Bo Outlaw .25 .60
136 Shandon Anderson .25 .60
137 Mitch Richmond .40 1.00
138 Doug Christie .30 .75
139 Rasheed Wallace .40 1.00
140 Chris Childs .25 .60
141 Jamal Mashburn .30 .75
142 Terrell Brandon .25 .60
143 Jamie Feick RC .75 2.00
144 Robert Traylor .25 .60
145 Rick Fox .25 .60
146 Charles Barkley .60 1.50
147 Tyrone Nesby RC .75 2.00
148 Jerry Stackhouse .40 1.00
149 Cedric Ceballos .25 .60
150 Dikembe Mutombo .40 1.00
151 Anthony Peeler .25 .60
152 Larry Hughes .40 1.00
153 Clifford Robinson .25 .60
154 Corliss Williamson .25 .60
155 Olden Polynice .25 .60
156 Avery Johnson .30 .75
157 Tracy Murray .25 .60
158 Tom Gugliotta .25 .60
159 Tim Thomas .30 .75
160 Reggie Miller .40 1.00
161 Tim Hardaway .40 1.00
162 Dan Majerle .40 1.00
163 Will Perdue .25 .60
164 Brevin Knight .25 .60
165 Elden Campbell .25 .60
166 Chris Gatling .25 .60
167 Walter McCarty .25 .60
168 Chauncey Billups .40 1.00
169 Chris Mills .25 .60
170 Christian Laettner .30 .75
171 Robert Pack .25 .60
172 Rik Smits .40 1.00
173 Tyrone Hill .25 .60
174 Damon Stoudamire .40 1.00
175 Nick Anderson .25 .60
176 Peja Stojakovic .40 1.00
177 Vladimir Stepania .25 .60
178 Tracy McGrady .60 1.50
179 Adam Keefe .25 .60
180 Shareef Abdur-Rahim .40 1.00
181 Isaac Austin .30 .75
182 Mario Elie .25 .60
183 Rashard Lewis .40 1.00
184 Scott Burrell .25 .60
185 Othella Harrington .25 .60
186 Eric Piatkowski .30 .75
187 Bryant Stith .25 .60
188 Michael Finley .40 1.00
189 Chris Crawford .25 .60
190 Toni Kukoc .40 1.00
191 Danny Ferry .25 .60
192 Erick Dampier .25 .60
193 Clarence Weatherspoon .25 .60
194 Bob Sura .25 .60
195 Jayson Williams .25 .60
196 Kurt Thomas .25 .60
197 Greg Anthony .25 .60
198 Rodney Rogers .25 .60
199 Detlef Schrempf .25 .60
200 Keith Van Horn .40 1.00
201 Robert Horry .30 .75
202 Sam Cassell .30 .75
203 Malik Sealy .25 .60
204 Kelvin Cato .25 .60
205 Antonio McDyess .30 .75
206 Andrew DeClercq .25 .60
207 Ricky Davis .40 1.00
208 Vitaly Potapenko .25 .60
209 Loy Vaught .25 .60
210 Kevin Garnett .75 2.00
211 Eric Snow .30 .75
212 Anfernee Hardaway .60 1.50
213 Vin Baker .40 1.00
214 Lawrence Funderburke .25 .60
215 Jeff Hornacek .30 .75
216 Doug West .25 .60
217 Michael Doleac .25 .60
218 Ray Allen .40 1.00
219 Derek Anderson .25 .60
220 Jerome Williams .25 .60
221 Derrick Coleman .30 .75
222 Randy Brown .25 .60
223 Patrick Ewing .50 1.25
224 Walt Williams .25 .60
225 Charles Oakley .30 .75
226 Steve Kerr .30 .75
227 Muggsy Bogues .30 .75
228 Kevin Willis .25 .60
229 Marcus Camby .30 .75
230 Scottie Pippen .60 1.50
231 Lamar Odom RC 2.50 6.00
232 Jonathan Bender RC .75 2.00
233 Andre Miller RC 2.00 5.00
234 Trajan Langdon RC .75 2.00
235 Aleksandar Radojevic RC .75 2.00
236 William Avery RC .75 2.00
237 Cal Bowdler RC .75 2.00
238 Quincy Lewis RC .75 2.00
239 Dion Glover RC .75 2.00
240 Jeff Foster RC .75 2.00
241 Kenny Thomas RC .75 2.00
242 Devean George RC .75 2.00
243 Tim James RC .75 2.00
244 Vonteego Cummings RC .75 2.00
245 Jumaine Jones RC .75 2.00
246 Scott Padgett RC .75 2.00
247 Adrian Griffin RC .75 2.00
248 Chris Herren RC .75 2.00
249 Allan Houston USA .60 1.50
250 Kevin Garnett USA 1.50 4.00
251 Gary Payton USA .75 2.00
252 Steve Smith USA .50 1.25
253 Tim Hardaway USA .75 2.00
254 Tim Duncan USA 1.50 4.00
255 Jason Kidd USA 1.25 3.00
256 Tom Gugliotta USA .50 1.25
257 Vin Baker USA .75 2.00

1999-00 Topps Chrome Refractors

Randomly inserted in packs at one in 12, this 257-card set parallels the base set. Each card features "Refractor" technology. To ascertain values on individual cards, please refer to the multiplier in the header, coupled with the value of the base card.

*STARS: 3X TO 8X BASE CARD HI
*RCs: 2.5X TO 6X BASE HI

1999-00 Topps Chrome All-Etch

Randomly inserted into packs at one in 100, this 30-card insert set features 10 veteran cards, 10 young stars, and 10 draft picks. Card backs carry an "AE" prefix.

COMPLETE SET (30) 25.00 60.00
*REF.STARS: 1.5X TO 4X HI COLUMN
REF: STATED ODDS 1:100
AE1 Karl Malone 1.25 3.00
AE2 Scottie Pippen 1.50 4.00
AE3 Grant Hill 1.25 3.00
AE4 Shawn Kemp 1.00 2.50
AE5 Shaquille O'Neal 2.50 6.00
AE6 Anfernee Hardaway 1.50 4.00
AE7 Chris Webber 1.00 2.50
AE8 Gary Payton 1.00 2.50
AE9 Jason Kidd 1.50 4.00
AE10 John Stockton 1.25 3.00
AE11 Kevin Garnett 2.00 5.00
AE12 Vince Carter 2.00 5.00
AE13 Shareef Abdur-Rahim .75 2.00
AE14 Antoine Walker 1.00 2.50
AE15 Kobe Bryant 5.00 12.00
AE16 Tim Duncan 2.00 5.00
AE17 Keith Van Horn .75 2.00
AE18 Allen Iverson 2.00 5.00
AE19 Jason Williams 1.25 3.00
AE20 Stephon Marbury .75 2.00
AE21 Elton Brand 2.00 5.00
AE22 Jason Terry 2.00 5.00
AE23 Steve Francis 2.00 5.00
AE24 Corey Maggette 1.50 4.00
AE25 Lamar Odom 2.50 6.00
AE26 Ron Artest 2.00 5.00
AE27 Baron Davis 2.50 6.00
AE28 Andre Miller 2.00 5.00
AE29 Shawn Marion 2.00 5.00
AE30 Wally Szczerbiak 1.50 4.00

1999-00 Topps Chrome All-Stars

Randomly inserted in packs at one in 30, this 10-card set focuses on veteran All-Stars in the NBA. Card backs carry an "AS" prefix.

COMPLETE SET (10) 8.00 20.00
*REF: 1.5X TO 4X HI COLUMN
REF: STATED ODDS 1:300
AS1 Patrick Ewing 1.25 3.00
AS2 Karl Malone 1.25 3.00

S3 Hakeem Olajuwon 1.25 3.00
S4 Scottie Pippen 1.50 4.00
S5 Gary Payton 1.00 2.50
S6 John Stockton 1.25 3.00
S7 Shaquille O'Neal 2.50 6.00
S8 Charles Barkley 1.50 4.00
S9 David Robinson 1.50 4.00
S10 Grant Hill 1.25 3.00

1999-00 Topps Chrome Highlight Reels

andomly inserted in packs at one in ten, this 15-card et features some of the most exciting players in the BA. Card backs carry a "HR" prefix.
OMPLETE SET (15) 8.00 20.00
REF: 1.5X TO 4X HI COLUMN
EF: STATED ODDS 1:100
R1 Stephon Marbury .50 1.25
R2 Vince Carter 1.25 3.00
R3 Kevin Garnett 1.25 3.00
R4 Kobe Bryant 3.00 8.00
R5 Chris Webber .60 1.50
R6 Allen Iverson 1.25 3.00
R7 Grant Hill .75 2.00
R8 Antoine Walker .60 1.50
R9 Jason Williams .75 2.00
R10 Tim Duncan 1.25 3.00
R11 Shareef Abdur-Rahim .50 1.25
R12 Keith Van Horn .50 1.25
R13 Antonio McDyess .50 1.25
R14 Jason Kidd 1.00 2.50
R15 Ron Mercer .50 1.25

1999-00 Topps Chrome Instant Impact

andomly inserted in packs at one in 15, this 10-card et focuses on players traded during the 1999/2000 eason. Card backs carry an "II" prefix.
OMPLETE SET (10) 2.50 6.00
REF: 1.5X TO 4X HI COLUMN
EF: STATED ODDS 1:150
1 Scottie Pippen 1.00 2.50
2 Nick Anderson .40 1.00
3 Isaiah Rider .40 1.00
4 Antonio Davis .40 1.00
5 Ron Mercer .50 1.25
6 Anfernee Hardaway 1.00 2.50
7 Isaac Austin .40 1.00
8 Steve Smith .40 1.00
9 Michael Dickerson .40 1.00
10 Horace Grant .50 1.25

1999-00 Topps Chrome Keepers

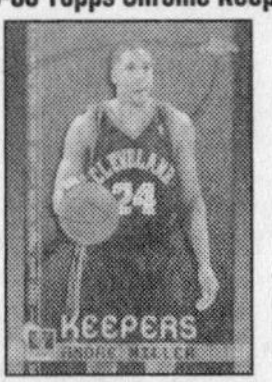

andomly inserted in packs at one in 30, this 10-card et features the top draft picks in the NBA. Card backs arry a "K" prefix.
OMPLETE SET (10) 5.00 12.00
REF: 2X TO 5X HI COLUMN
EF: STATED ODDS 1:300
1 Elton Brand .75 2.00
2 Lamar Odom 1.00 2.50
3 Steve Francis .75 2.00
4 Shawn Marion .75 2.00
5 Wally Szczerbiak .60 1.50
6 Baron Davis 1.00 2.50
7 Andre Miller .75 2.00
8 Corey Maggette .60 1.50
9 Jason Terry .75 2.00
10 Richard Hamilton .75 2.00

2000-01 Topps Chrome

The 2000-01 Topps Chrome product was released in early April, 2001. The product featured a 200-card base set that was broken into tiers as follows:Base Veterans 1-150), and Rookies (151-200) that were inserted at 1:6 and serial numbered to 1999. Each pack contained four cards and carried a suggested retail price of $3.00.

COMPLETE SET (200) 150.00 300.00
COMPLETE SET w/o SP's (150) 15.00 40.00
1 Elton Brand .40 1.00
2 Marcus Camby .30 .75
3 Jalen Rose .30 .75
4 Jamie Feick .25 .60
5 Toni Kukoc .30 .75
6 Doug Christie .25 .60
7 Sam Cassell .30 .75
8 Shaquille O'Neal 1.00 2.50
9 Larry Hughes .30 .75
10 Jerry Stackhouse .30 .75
11 Rick Fox .30 .75
12 Clifford Robinson .25 .60
13 Dirk Nowitzki .60 1.50
14 Cuttino Mobley .30 .75
15 Latrell Sprewell .30 .75
16 Kevin Garnett .75 2.00
17 Jerome Williams .25 .60
18 Chris Webber .40 1.00
19 Jason Terry .40 1.00
20 Elden Campbell .25 .60
21 Jonathan Bender .25 .60
22 Scottie Pippen .60 1.50
23 Radoslav Nesterovic .25 .60
24 Reggie Miller .40 1.00
25 Andre Miller .30 .75
26 Rashard Lewis .40 1.00
27 Larry Johnson .40 1.00
28 Steve Francis .40 1.00
29 Rod Strickland .30 .75
30 Tim Thomas .25 .60
31 Robert Horry .30 .75
32 Darrell Armstrong .25 .60
33 Vince Carter .75 2.00
34 Othella Harrington .25 .60
35 Derek Anderson .25 .60
36 Anthony Carter .25 .60
37 Ray Allen .40 1.00
38 Jason Kidd .60 1.50
39 Sean Elliott .30 .75
40 Tim Duncan .75 2.00
41 Adrian Griffin .25 .60
42 Wally Szczerbiak .30 .75
43 Austin Croshere .25 .60
44 James Posey .25 .60
45 Alan Henderson .25 .60
46 Jahidi White .25 .60
47 Shawn Marion .40 1.00
48 Lamar Odom .40 1.00
49 Keon Clark .25 .60
50 Lamond Murray .25 .60
51 Paul Pierce .50 1.25
52 Charlie Ward .25 .60
53 Horace Grant .30 .75
54 John Stockton .50 1.25
55 Peja Stojakovic .40 1.00
56 Christian Laettner .25 .60
57 Keith Van Horn .30 .75
58 Patrick Ewing .50 1.25
59 Steve Smith .30 .75
60 Antonio Davis .25 .60
61 Mitch Richmond .30 .75
62 Michael Olowokandi .25 .60
63 Baron Davis .40 1.00
64 Dikembe Mutombo .40 1.00
65 Raef LaFrentz .25 .60
66 Ervin Johnson .25 .60
67 Alonzo Mourning .50 1.25
68 Kendall Gill .25 .60
69 George Lynch .25 .60
70 Donyell Marshall .25 .60
71 Bo Outlaw .25 .60
72 Kenny Anderson .30 .75
73 John Amaechi .25 .60
74 Vlade Divac .30 .75
75 Vin Baker .30 .75
76 Mike Bibby .40 1.00
77 Richard Hamilton .30 .75
78 Mookie Blaylock .30 .75
79 Vitaly Potapenko .25 .60
80 Anthony Mason .25 .60
81 Vonteego Cummings .25 .60
82 Michael Finley .40 1.00
83 Ron Artest .40 1.00
84 Rodney Rogers .25 .60
85 Team Championship .75 2.00
86 Jason Williams .40 1.00
87 David Robinson .60 1.50
88 Charles Oakley .30 .75
89 Juwan Howard .30 .75
90 Antoine Walker .30 .75
91 Roshown McLeod .25 .60
92 Eddie Jones .40 1.00
93 Allen Iverson .75 2.00
94 Grant Hill .50 1.25
95 Terrell Brandon .25 .60
96 Stephon Marbury .30 .75
97 Jamal Mashburn .30 .75
98 Ron Harper .30 .75
99 Jermaine O'Neal .40 1.00
100 Nick Van Exel .30 .75
101 Danny Fortson .25 .60
102 Jim Jackson .25 .60
103 Brad Miller .40 1.00
104 Shawn Bradley .25 .60
105 Mark Jackson .30 .75
106 Maurice Taylor .25 .60
107 Kobe Bryant 2.00 5.00
108 Clarence Weatherspoon .25 .60
109 Eric Snow .25 .60
110 Allan Houston .30 .75
111 Chauncey Billups .40 1.00
112 Tom Gugliotta .25 .60
113 Theo Ratliff .25 .60
114 Rasheed Wallace .40 1.00
115 Glen Rice .30 .75
116 Bryon Russell .25 .60
117 Tracy McGrady .60 1.50
118 Bryant Reeves .25 .60
119 Damon Stoudamire .30 .75
120 Anfernee Hardaway .60 1.50
121 Johnny Newman .25 .60
122 Corey Maggette .30 .75
123 Travis Best .25 .60
124 Hakeem Olajuwon .50 1.25
125 Antawn Jamison .40 1.00
126 John Starks .25 .60
127 Antonio McDyess .30 .75
128 Gary Payton .40 1.00
129 Karl Malone .50 1.25
130 Michael Dickerson .25 .60
131 Shawn Kemp .40 1.00
132 David Wesley .25 .60
133 P.J. Brown .25 .60
134 Ron Mercer .25 .60
135 Robert Traylor .25 .60
136 Derrick Coleman .30 .75
137 Steve Nash .60 1.50
138 Ben Wallace .40 1.00
139 Brian Skinner .25 .60
140 Chris Gatling .25 .60
141 Dale Davis .25 .60
142 Glenn Robinson .30 .75
143 Chucky Atkins .25 .60
144 Brian Grant .25 .60
145 Corliss Williamson .25 .60
146 Shareef Abdur-Rahim .30 .75
147 Avery Johnson .30 .75
148 Tim Hardaway .40 1.00
149 Isaiah Rider .30 .75
150 Shandon Anderson .25 .60
151 Kenyon Martin RC 4.00 10.00
152 Stromile Swift RC 1.50 4.00
153 Darius Miles RC 1.50 4.00
154 Marcus Fizer RC 1.50 4.00
155 Mike Miller RC 3.00 8.00
156 DerMarr Johnson RC 1.50 4.00
157 Chris Mihm RC 1.50 4.00
158 Jamal Crawford RC 2.50 6.00
159 Joel Przybilla RC 1.50 4.00
160 Keyon Dooling RC 1.50 4.00
161 Jerome Moiso RC 1.50 4.00
162 Etan Thomas RC 1.50 4.00
163 Courtney Alexander RC 1.50 4.00
164 Mateen Cleaves RC 1.50 4.00
165 Jason Collier RC 1.50 4.00
166 Desmond Mason RC 2.00 5.00
167 Quentin Richardson RC 2.50 6.00
168 Jamaal Magloire RC 1.50 4.00
169 Speedy Claxton RC 1.50 4.00
170 Morris Peterson RC 1.50 4.00
171 Donnell Harvey RC 1.50 4.00
172 DeShawn Stevenson RC 2.00 5.00
173 Mamadou N'Diaye RC 1.50 4.00
174 Erick Barkley RC 1.50 4.00
175 Mark Madsen RC 1.50 4.00
176 Hedo Turkoglu RC 3.00 8.00
177 Brian Cardinal RC 1.50 4.00
178 Iakovos Tsakalidis RC 1.50 4.00
179 Dalibor Bagaric RC 1.50 4.00
180 Dragan Tarlac RC 1.50 4.00
181 Dan Langhi RC 1.50 4.00
182 A.J. Guyton RC 1.50 4.00
183 Jake Voskuhl RC 1.50 4.00
184 Khalid El-Amin RC 1.50 4.00
185 Mike Smith RC 1.50 4.00
186 Soumaila Samake RC 1.50 4.00
187 Eddie House RC 1.50 4.00
188 Eduardo Najera RC 1.50 4.00
189 Lavor Postell RC 1.50 4.00
190 Hanno Mottola RC 1.50 4.00
191 Olumide Oyedeji RC 1.50 4.00
192 Michael Redd RC 4.00 10.00
193 Chris Porter RC 1.50 4.00
194 Jabari Smith RC 1.50 4.00
195 Marc Jackson RC 1.50 4.00
196 Stephen Jackson RC 2.50 6.00
197 Pepe Sanchez RC 1.50 4.00
198 Daniel Santiago RC 2.50 6.00
199 Paul McPherson RC 1.50 4.00
200 Mike Penberthy RC 1.50 4.00

2000-01 Topps Chrome Refractors

Randomly inserted into packs, this 200-card insert set is actually a complete parallel of the Topps Chrome base set. Please note that each of these cards was produced using Topps' patented "Refractor" technology. Cards (1-150) were inserted at 1:12, while cards (151-200) were inserted at 1:118 and serial numbered to 199.
*STARS: 3X TO 8X BASE CARD HI
*ROOKIES 151-200: 2X TO 5X BASE CARD HI

2000-01 Topps Chrome Aptitude for Altitude

Randomly inserted into packs at one in 20, this 10-card set features players that are very capable of dunking over their opponents. Card backs carry a "AA" prefix.
COMPLETE SET (10) 5.00 12.00
*REF: 1.25X TO 3X APTITUDE ALTITUDE HI
REF.STATED ODDS 1:200 PACKS
AA1 Larry Hughes .60 1.50
AA2 Steve Francis .75 2.00
AA3 Shawn Marion .75 2.00
AA4 Michael Finley .75 2.00
AA5 Allen Iverson 1.50 4.00
AA6 Jerry Stackhouse .60 1.50
AA7 Rashard Lewis .75 2.00
AA8 Tim Thomas .50 1.25
AA9 Baron Davis .75 2.00
AA10 Darius Miles .75 2.00

2000-01 Topps Chrome Cards That Never Were

Randomly inserted into packs, this 10-card insert set features cards of Magic Johnson that were never produced. Card backs carry a "MJ" prefix.
COMPLETE SET (10) 15.00 40.00
COMMON CARD (MJ1-MJ10) 2.00 5.00
REF: 1.5X TO 4X HI COLUMN

2000-01 Topps Chrome Combos

Randomly inserted into packs at one in 30, this 20-card insert set features different player combinations . Card backs carry a "TC" prefix.
COMPLETE SET (20) 25.00 60.00
*REF: 1.25X TO 3X COMBOS HI
REF.STATED ODDS 1:300
TC1 Shaquille O'Neal / Kobe Bryant 5.00 12.00
TC2 Stephon Marbury / Allen Iverson 2.00 5.00
TC3 Chris Webber / Jason Williams 1.25 3.00
TC4 Patrick Ewing / Dikembe Mutombo / Alonzo Mourning 1.25 3.00
TC5 Tracy McGrady / Vince Carter 2.50 6.00
TC6 Tim Duncan / Grant Hill 2.00 5.00
TC7 Elton Brand / Lamar Odom / Steve Francis 1.25 3.00
TC8 Gary Payton / Jason Kidd 2.00 5.00
TC9 Damon Stoudamire / Scottie Pippen / Steve Smith / Rasheed Wallace 2.00 5.00
TC10 Tim Duncan / Kevin Garnett 2.50 6.00
TC11 Hakeem Olajuwon 1.25 3.00
TC12 Patrick Ewing 1.25 3.00
TC13 Karl Malone 1.25 3.00
TC14 Scottie Pippen 2.00 5.00
TC15 Reggie Miller 1.25 3.00
TC16 Shaquille O'Neal / Magic Johnson 3.00 8.00
TC17 Marcus Fizer / Stromile Swift / Kenyon Martin 1.25 3.00
TC18 Speedy Claxton / Keyon Dooling / Jamal Crawford 1.25 3.00
TC19 Mike Miller / DerMarr Johnson / Darius Miles 1.25 3.00
TC20 Magic Johnson / Mateen Cleaves 2.00 5.00

2000-01 Topps Chrome Final Piece Game Jerseys

Randomly inserted into packs at one in 2025, this 23-card insert set features swatches of game-used jerseys from the NBA Finals . Card backs carry a "FP" prefix. A refractor version of this set was issued as well. Each of these cards is sequentially numbered to 10.
FP1 Shaquille O'Neal 100.00 250.00
FP2 Glen Rice 30.00 80.00
FP3 Robert Horry 30.00 80.00
FP4 Rick Fox 30.00 80.00
FP5 Brian Shaw 25.00 60.00
FP6 Ron Harper 30.00 80.00
FP7 Derek Fisher 40.00 100.00
FP8 A.C. Green 30.00 80.00
FP9 John Salley 25.00 60.00
FP10 Travis Knight 25.00 60.00
FP11 Devean George 25.00 60.00
FP12 Reggie Miller 75.00 200.00
FP13 Jalen Rose 30.00 80.00
FP14 Dale Davis 25.00 60.00
FP15 Rik Smits 25.00 60.00
FP16 Mark Jackson 30.00 80.00
FP17 Travis Best 25.00 60.00
FP18 Austin Croshere 25.00 60.00
FP19 Derrick McKey 25.00 60.00
FP20 Sam Perkins 25.00 60.00
FP21 Chris Mullin 40.00 100.00
FP22 Jonathan Bender 25.00 60.00
FP23 Zan Tabak 25.00 60.00

2000-01 Topps Chrome Hobby Masters

Randomly inserted into packs at one in 30 hobby, this 10-card insert set features players that are the most popular in the Basketball trading card field. Card backs carry a "HM" prefix.
COMPLETE SET (10) 15.00 40.00
*REF: 2.5X TO 6X HOBBY MASTERS HI
REF.STATED ODDS 1:602 HOBBY
HM1 Kevin Garnett 2.50 6.00
HM2 Jason Williams 1.25 3.00
HM3 Tim Duncan 2.50 6.00
HM4 Tracy McGrady 2.00 5.00
HM5 Kobe Bryant 6.00 15.00
HM6 Allen Iverson 2.50 6.00
HM7 Elton Brand 1.25 3.00
HM8 Steve Francis 1.25 3.00
HM9 Vince Carter 2.50 6.00
HM10 Chris Webber 1.25 3.00

2000-01 Topps Chrome In The Paint

Randomly inserted into packs at one in 60, this 10-card insert set features players that can be found "in the paint" scoring points and grabbing rebounds . Card backs carry an "IP" prefix.
COMPLETE SET (10) 15.00 40.00
*REF: 1.25X TO 3X IN THE PAINT HI
REF.STATED ODDS 1:600
IP1 Elton Brand 2.00 5.00
IP2 Tim Duncan 4.00 10.00
IP3 Antonio McDyess 1.50 4.00
IP4 Karl Malone 2.50 6.00
IP5 Rasheed Wallace 2.00 5.00
IP6 Antoine Walker 1.50 4.00
IP7 Shareef Abdur-Rahim 1.50 4.00
IP8 Lamar Odom 2.00 5.00
IP9 Kenyon Martin 5.00 12.00
IP10 Stromile Swift 2.00 5.00

2000-01 Topps Chrome Magic Johnson Reprints

Randomly inserted into packs at one in 10, this 7-card insert set features reprinted Magic Johnson cards.
COMPLETE SET (7) 12.50 30.00
COMMON CARD (MJ1-MJ7) 2.00 5.00

2000-01 Topps Chrome No Limit

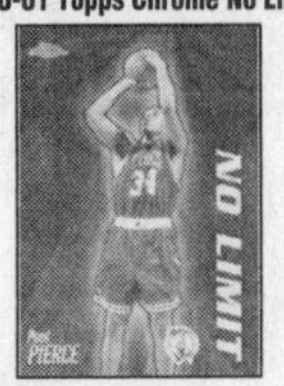

Randomly inserted into packs at one in 15, this 20-card insert set features players whose game has no limits. Card backs carry a "NL" prefix.
COMPLETE SET (20) 20.00 50.00
*REF: 1.25X TO 3X NO LIMIT HI
REF.STATED ODDS 1:150
NL1 Kobe Bryant 5.00 12.00
NL2 Kevin Garnett 2.00 5.00
NL3 Vince Carter 2.00 5.00
NL4 Tracy McGrady 1.50 4.00
NL5 Tim Duncan 2.00 5.00
NL6 Elton Brand 1.00 2.50
NL7 Lamar Odom 1.00 2.50
NL8 Larry Hughes .75 2.00
NL9 Chris Webber 1.00 2.50
NL10 Shareef Abdur-Rahim .75 2.00
NL11 Jason Kidd 1.50 4.00
NL12 Gary Payton 1.00 2.50
NL13 Paul Pierce 1.25 3.00
NL14 Stromile Swift 1.00 2.50
NL15 Darius Miles 1.00 2.50
NL16 Mike Miller 2.00 5.00
NL17 Jason Williams 1.00 2.50
NL18 Jamal Crawford 1.50 4.00
NL19 Marcus Fizer 1.00 2.50
NL20 DerMarr Johnson 1.00 2.50

2001-02 Topps Chrome

This 165 card standard-size set was issued in March, 2002. These cards were issued in four card packs which came 24 packs to a box and 10 boxes to case. Each pack had an SRP of $3.00. Card numbers 1-129 feature veteran players and card numbers 130-165 feature rookies with the respective player's draft pick number. Each card boasts full color player action photos with blue borders on an all chromium card stock.
COMP.SET w/o RC's (129) 12.00 30.00
1 Shaquille O'Neal 1.00 2.50
2 Steve Nash .60 1.50
3 Allen Iverson .75 2.00
4 Shawn Marion .40 1.00
5 Rasheed Wallace .40 1.00
6 Antonio Daniels .25 .60
7 Rashard Lewis .40 1.00
8 Raef LaFrentz .25 .60
9 Stromile Swift .25 .60
10 Vince Carter .60 1.50
11 Danny Fortson .25 .60
12 Jalen Rose .30 .75
13 Glen Rice .30 .75
14 Glenn Robinson .30 .75
15 Wally Szczerbiak .30 .75
16 Rick Fox .30 .75
17 Darius Miles .25 .60
18 Jermaine O'Neal .40 1.00
19 Eddie Jones .30 .75
20 Tracy McGrady .60 1.50
21 Kevin Garnett .75 2.00
22 Tim Thomas .25 .60
23 Larry Hughes .30 .75
24 Jerry Stackhouse .30 .75
25 Ray Allen .40 1.00
26 Terrell Brandon .25 .60
27 Keith Van Horn .30 .75
28 Marcus Fizer .25 .60
29 Elden Campbell .25 .60
30 Tim Duncan .75 2.00
31 Doug Christie .25 .60
32 Allan Houston .30 .75
33 Patrick Ewing .50 1.25
34 Hakeem Olajuwon .50 1.25
35 Anfernee Hardaway .60 1.50
36 Clarence Weatherspoon .25 .60
37 Eric Snow .25 .60
38 Tom Gugliotta .25 .60
39 Scottie Pippen .60 1.50
40 Chris Webber .40 1.00
41 David Robinson .60 1.50
42 Elton Brand .40 1.00
43 Theo Ratliff .25 .60
44 Paul Pierce .50 1.25
45 Jamal Mashburn .30 .75
46 Damon Stoudamire .30 .75
47 DerMarr Johnson .25 .60
48 Andre Miller .30 .75
49 Dirk Nowitzki .60 1.50
50 Kobe Bryant 2.00 5.00
51 Keyon Dooling .25 .60
52 Brian Grant .25 .60
53 Antawn Jamison .40 1.00
54 Jonathan Bender .25 .60
55 Dikembe Mutombo .40 1.00
56 Steve Smith .30 .75
57 Hedo Turkoglu .40 1.00
58 Robert Horry .30 .75
59 Kurt Thomas .25 .60
60 Jason Terry .40 1.00
61 Vitaly Potapenko .25 .60
62 Gary Payton .40 1.00
63 Bonzi Wells .25 .60
64 Raja Bell RC 1.25 3.00
65 Chris Mihm .25 .60
66 Reggie Miller .40 1.00
67 Lamar Odom .40 1.00
68 Darrell Armstrong .25 .60
69 Baron Davis .40 1.00
70 Aaron Williams .25 .60
71 Latrell Sprewell .30 .75
72 James Posey .25 .60
73 Ben Wallace .40 1.00
74 Marc Jackson .25 .60
75 Maurice Taylor .25 .60
76 Aaron McKie .25 .60
77 Grant Hill .50 1.25
78 Anthony Carter .25 .60
79 Peja Stojakovic .40 1.00
80 Jason Kidd .60 1.50
81 Vin Baker .30 .75
82 Morris Peterson .25 .60
83 Bryon Russell .25 .60
84 Michael Dickerson .25 .60
85 Quentin Richardson .30 .75
86 Primoz Brezec RC 1.00 2.50
87 Desmond Mason .30 .75
88 Jason Williams .30 .75
89 Marcus Camby .30 .75
90 Stephon Marbury .30 .75
91 Mike Bibby .40 1.00
92 Alonzo Mourning .50 1.25
93 Mitch Richmond .30 .75
94 Donyell Marshall .25 .60
95 Michael Jordan 5.00 12.00
96 Mike Miller .40 1.00
97 Nick Van Exel .30 .75
98 Michael Finley .40 1.00
99 Jamal Crawford .30 .75
100 Steve Francis .40 1.00
101 Kenyon Martin .40 1.00
102 Sam Cassell .30 .75
103 Chucky Atkins .25 .60
104 Juwan Howard .30 .75
105 Bryant Reeves .25 .60
106 Richard Hamilton .30 .75
107 Antonio Davis .25 .60
108 Antonio McDyess .30 .75
109 Derek Anderson .25 .60
110 Kenny Anderson .30 .75
111 Antoine Walker .30 .75
112 Wang ZhiZhi .30 .75
113 Shareef Abdur-Rahim .30 .75
114 Chris Whitney .25 .60
115 John Stockton .50 1.25
116 Alvin Williams .25 .60
117 David Wesley .25 .60
118 Joe Smith .30 .75
119 Jahidi White .25 .60
120 Karl Malone .50 1.25
121 Cuttino Mobley .30 .75
122 Tyrone Hill .25 .60
123 Clifford Robinson .25 .60
124 Toni Kukoc .30 .75
125 Eddie Robinson .25 .60
126 Courtney Alexander .25 .60
127 Ron Mercer .25 .60
128 Lamond Murray .25 .60
129 Rodney Rogers .25 .60
130 Tyson Chandler RC 1.50 4.00
131 Pau Gasol RC 3.00 8.00
132 Eddy Curry RC 1.50 4.00
133 Jason Richardson RC 2.00 5.00
134 Shane Battier RC 2.00 5.00
135 Eddie Griffin RC 1.00 2.50
136 DeSagana Diop RC 1.00 2.50
137 Rodney White RC 1.00 2.50
138 Joe Johnson RC 2.50 6.00
139 Kedrick Brown RC 1.00 2.50
140 Vladimir Radmanovic RC 1.00 2.50
141 Richard Jefferson RC 2.00 5.00
142 Troy Murphy RC 1.50 4.00
143 Steven Hunter RC 1.00 2.50
144 Kirk Haston RC 1.00 2.50
145 Michael Bradley RC 1.00 2.50
146 Jason Collins RC 1.00 2.50
147 Zach Randolph RC 2.50 6.00
148 Brendan Haywood RC 1.25 3.00
149 Joseph Forte RC 1.00 2.50
150 Jeryl Sasser RC 1.00 2.50
151 Brandon Armstrong RC 1.00 2.50
152 Gerald Wallace RC 1.50 4.00
153 Samuel Dalembert RC 1.25 3.00
154 Jamaal Tinsley RC 1.25 3.00
155 Tony Parker RC 4.00 10.00
156 Trenton Hassell RC 1.00 2.50
157 Gilbert Arenas RC 1.50 4.00
158 Jeff Trepagnier RC 1.00 2.50
159 Damone Brown RC 1.00 2.50
160 Loren Woods RC 1.00 2.50
161 Andrei Kirilenko RC 2.50 6.00
162 Zeljko Rebraca RC 1.00 2.50
163 Kenny Satterfield RC 1.00 2.50
164 Alvin Jones RC 1.00 2.50
165 Kwame Brown RC 1.00 2.50

2001-02 Topps Chrome Refractors

Randomly seeded in packs at the rate of one in four, this 165-card set parallels the base Topps Chrome set enhanced with the rainbow holofoil refractor effect. The word "Refractor" appears on the back of the card next to the card number.
*REF.STARS: 2.5X TO 6X BASE CARD HI
*REF.RCs: 1.5X TO 4X BASE CARD HI
95 Michael Jordan 35.00 70.00

2001-02 Topps Chrome Refractors Black Border

Randomly seeded in packs, this 165-card set parallels the base Topps Chrome set enhanced with black borders and the rainbow holofoil refractor effect. The word "Refractor" appears on the back of the card next to the card number. Each card is sequentially numbered to 50.
*REF.BLK.STRS:12.5X TO 30X BASE CARD HI
*REF.BLK.RCs: 6X TO 15X BASE CARD HI
35 Anfernee Hardaway 25.00 60.00
50 Kobe Bryant 125.00 225.00

2001-02 Topps Chrome Autographs

Randomly inserted in packs at the rate of one in 257, this 10-card set features players signed to Team Topps. Full color player phtos are set against an orange and yellow background which fades to white at the bottom for authentic player autographs. The player names followed with the letter "H" were only available in hobby packs.
CAAD Antonio Daniels H 5.00 12.00
CAAJ Antawn Jamison 5.00 12.00
CABD Baron Davis H 10.00 25.00
CAEB Elton Brand H 5.00 12.00
CAJF Joseph Forte H 5.00 12.00
CAJJ Joe Johnson H 6.00 15.00
CAPS Peja Stojakovic 6.00 15.00
CASB Shane Battier 5.00 12.00
CASM Shawn Marion 5.00 12.00
CAZR Zach Randolph 10.00 25.00

2001-02 Topps Chrome Fast and Furious

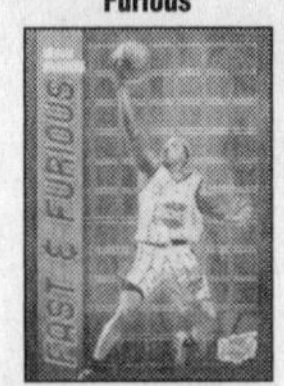

Randomly seeded in packs at the rate of one in six, this 14-card set is printed on an all foil card stock with full color player action photos, colorful backgrounds and the words "Fast and Furious." A refractor version was also produced and was inserted at the rate of one in 30.

COMPLETE SET (14) 20.00 40.00
FF1 Steve Francis .60 1.50
FF2 Allen Iverson 1.25 3.00
FF3 Tracy McGrady 1.00 2.50
FF4 Vince Carter 1.00 2.50
FF5 Michael Jordan 6.00 15.00
FF6 Kobe Bryant 3.00 8.00
FF7 Kevin Garnett 1.25 3.00
FF8 Shaquille O'Neal 1.50 4.00
FF9 Ray Allen .60 1.50
FF10 Paul Pierce .75 2.00
FF11 Jerry Stackhouse .50 1.25
FF12 Antoine Walker .50 1.25
FF13 Chris Webber .60 1.50
FF14 Jason Richardson 1.25 3.00

2001-02 Topps Chrome Fast and Furious Refractors

Randomly seeded in packs at the rate of one in 30, this 14-card set parallels the base Fast and Furious insert set enhanced with the rainbow holofoil refractor effect. The word "Refractor" appears on the back of the card next to the card number.
*REF: 1X TO 2.5X BASE HI
FF5 Michael Jordan 20.00 50.00

2001-02 Topps Chrome Kareem Abdul-Jabbar Reprints

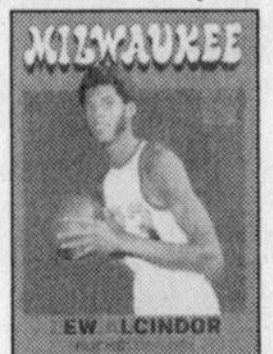

Randomly inserted in packs at the rate of one in 20, this 13-card reprints some of Kareem Abdul-Jabbars original Topps cards. A refractor version of this set was also inserted at the rate of one in 100.
COMPLETE SET (13) 20.00 40.00
COMMON CARD (1-13) 2.50 6.00

2001-02 Topps Chrome Lacing Up

Randomly inserted in packs, this 14-card set is printed on an all-holofoil card stock with full color player action photos centered above a swatch of a shoe lace. The words "Lacing Up" appear along the right side, and each card is sequentially numbered to 50.

Card	Low	High
LUAJ Antawn Jamison	10.00	25.00
LUBD Baron Davis	10.00	25.00
LUEB Elton Brand	10.00	25.00
LUEC Eddy Curry	15.00	40.00
LUJF Joseph Forte	10.00	25.00
LUJT Jason Terry	10.00	25.00
LUKB Kwame Brown	10.00	25.00
LUPS Peja Stojakovic	10.00	25.00
LURH Richard Hamilton	8.00	20.00
LUSB Shane Battier	20.00	50.00
LUSM Shawn Marion	10.00	25.00
LUSO Shaquille O'Neal	25.00	60.00
LUTD Tim Duncan	20.00	50.00
LUVR Vladimir Radmanovic	10.00	25.00

2001-02 Topps Chrome Mad Game

Randomly inserted in packs at the rate of one in 13, this 10-card set features a full color player action photo on an all foil backdrop where a "shadow" of his photo appears. The top of the card contains the words "Mad Game" which appears to be outlined in gold and filled with diamonds. A refractor version was also inserted at the rate of one in 65.

Card	Low	High
COMPLETE SET (10)	12.50	30.00
*REF: 1.25X TO 3X MAD GAME HI		
MG1 Allen Iverson	2.00	5.00
MG2 Shaquille O'Neal	2.50	6.00
MG3 Tim Duncan	2.00	5.00
MG4 Vince Carter	1.50	4.00
MG5 Kevin Garnett	2.00	5.00
MG6 Kobe Bryant	5.00	12.00
MG7 Tracy McGrady	1.50	4.00
MG8 Steve Francis	1.00	2.50
MG9 Chris Webber	1.00	2.50
MG10 Darius Miles	.60	1.50

2001-02 Topps Chrome Shorts Illustrated

Randomly inserted in packs at the rate of one in 180, this 10-card set boasts full color player action photos set against "shadows" of the featured player in the background. The right side contains a black strip from top to bottom with the set name and player's name in gold, and a circular swatch of game used shorts in the bottom corner. A refractor version was also inserted and is sequentially numbered to 50.

Card	Low	High
*REF: 1.25X TO 3X SHORT ILLUSTRATED HI		
SIAH Allan Houston	3.00	8.00
SICM Cuttino Mobley	3.00	8.00
SIDF Derek Fisher	3.00	8.00
SIDN Dirk Nowitzki	6.00	15.00
SIDW David Wesley	2.50	6.00
SIGP Gary Payton	4.00	10.00
SIMF Michael Finley	4.00	10.00
SIRH Richard Hamilton	3.00	8.00
SITD Tim Duncan	8.00	20.00
SIWS Wally Szczerbiak	3.00	8.00

2001-02 Topps Chrome Team Topps

Seeded in packs at the rate of one in 55, this 12-card set showcases the members of Team Topps on an all foil card. A refractor version was also inserted at the rate of one in 55.

Card	Low	High
COMPLETE SET (12)	12.50	30.00
*REF: 1X TO 2.5X TEAM TOPPS HI		
TT1 Shaquille O'Neal	3.00	8.00
TT2 Tim Duncan	2.50	6.00
TT3 Antawn Jamison	1.25	3.00
TT4 Jason Terry	1.25	3.00
TT5 Baron Davis	1.25	3.00
TT6 Elton Brand	1.25	3.00
TT7 Peja Stojakovic	1.25	3.00
TT8 Richard Hamilton	1.00	2.50
TT9 Shawn Marion	1.25	3.00
TT10 Team Photo	1.00	2.50
TT11 Shane Battier	2.50	6.00
TT12 Joseph Forte	1.25	3.00

2001-02 Topps Chrome Team Topps Jerseys

Randomly seeded in packs at the rate of one in 109, this 11-card set features the members of Team Topps on an all foil card with a rainbow colored background. Player portrait photos appear on the left side of the card, and a square jersey swatch appears on the right. A refractor version was also inserted at the rate of one in 682, and each card is sequentially numbered to 50.

Card	Low	High
*REF: 1.25X TO 3X HI		
TTAJ Antawn Jamison	4.00	10.00
TTBD Baron Davis	4.00	10.00
TTEB Elton Brand	4.00	10.00
TTJF Joseph Forte	4.00	10.00
TTJT Jason Terry	4.00	10.00
TTPS Peja Stojakovic	4.00	10.00
TTRH Richard Hamilton	3.00	8.00
TTSB Shane Battier	8.00	20.00
TTSM Shawn Marion	4.00	10.00
TTSO Shaquille O'Neal	10.00	25.00
TTTD Tim Duncan	8.00	20.00

2002-03 Topps Chrome

Released in late February 2003, Topps Chrome consists of 175 total cards but is only numbered consecutively through 165. Ten foreign born rookies have card "B" versions which feature the same photo as their regular card, but all the text is in the player's home language. Ex: Yao Ming has an English and Chinese version. Base cards are printed on an all chrome card stock with blue borders and silver highlights. Topps Chrome was packaged in 24-pack boxes where each pack contained four cards and carried a suggested retail price of $3.00.

Card	Low	High
COMPLETE SET (175)	75.00	180.00
1 Shaquille O'Neal	1.00	2.50
2 Pau Gasol	.50	1.25
3 Allen Iverson	.60	1.50
4 Tom Gugliotta	.25	.60
5 Rasheed Wallace	.40	1.00
6 Peja Stojakovic	.40	1.00
7 Jason Richardson	.40	1.00
8 Rashard Lewis	.40	1.00
9 Morris Peterson	.25	.60
10 Michael Jordan	3.00	8.00
11 Matt Harpring	.30	.75
12 Shareef Abdur-Rahim	.30	.75
13 Antoine Walker	.30	.75
14 Stephon Marbury	.30	.75
15 Jamal Mashburn	.30	.75
16 Eddy Curry	.30	.75
17 Jumaine Jones	.25	.60
18 Jason Kidd	.60	1.50
19 Jerry Stackhouse	.30	.75
20 Kenny Thomas	.25	.60
21 Kobe Bryant	2.00	5.00
22 Jason Williams	.30	.75
23 Eddie Jones	.30	.75
24 Kenyon Martin	.40	1.00
25 Kevin Garnett	.75	2.00
26 Kurt Thomas	.25	.60
27 Karl Malone	.50	1.25
28 Reggie Evans RC	1.50	4.00
29 Dirk Nowitzki	.60	1.50
30 Vince Carter	.60	1.50
31 Desmond Mason	.30	.75
32 Todd MacCulloch	.25	.60
33 Grant Hill	.50	1.25
34 Terrell Brandon	.25	.60
35 Tracy McGrady	.60	1.50
36 Tim Thomas	.25	.60
37 Loren Woods	.25	.60
38 Michael Redd	.40	1.00
39 Stromile Swift	.25	.60
40 Dikembe Mutombo	.40	1.00
41 Richard Jefferson	.40	1.00
42 Glenn Robinson	.30	.75
43 Quentin Richardson	.30	.75
44 Elton Brand	.40	1.00
45 Reggie Miller	.40	1.00
46 Eddie Griffin	.25	.60
47 Gilbert Arenas	.40	1.00
48 Zeljko Rebraca	.25	.60
49 Mark Jackson	.30	.75
50 Juwan Howard	.30	.75
51 Nick Van Exel	.30	.75
52 Donyell Marshall	.25	.60
53 Tyson Chandler	.30	.75
54 Baron Davis	.40	1.00
55 Nate Huffman RC	.40	1.00
56 Jamaal Magloire	.25	.60
57 Marcus Fizer	.25	.60
58 Steve Francis	.40	1.00
59 Aaron McKie	.25	.60
60 Scottie Pippen	.60	1.50
61 Mike Bibby	.40	1.00
62 Paul Pierce	.50	1.25
63 Kwame Brown	.25	.60
64 Andrei Kirilenko	.40	1.00
65 Keon Clark	.25	.60
66 Alvin Williams	.25	.60
67 Brent Barry	.25	.60
68 Doug Christie	.25	.60
69 Chris Webber	.40	1.00
70 Robert Horry	.30	.75
71 Allan Houston	.30	.75
72 Kerry Kittles	.25	.60
73 Wally Szczerbiak	.30	.75
74 Jonathan Bender	.25	.60
75 Sam Cassell	.30	.75
76 Rod Strickland	.30	.75
77 Shane Battier	.40	1.00
78 Tim Duncan	.75	2.00
79 Jermaine O'Neal	.40	1.00
80 Cuttino Mobley	.30	.75
81 Clifford Robinson	.25	.60
82 Steve Nash	.50	1.25
83 Dermarr Johnson	.25	.60
84 Courtney Alexander	.25	.60
85 Corliss Williamson	.25	.60
86 Tony Parker	.50	1.25
87 Damon Stoudamire	.30	.75
88 Jalen Rose	.30	.75
89 Mike Miller	.40	1.00
90 Raef Lafrentz	.25	.60
91 Ben Wallace	.40	1.00
92 Ray Allen	.40	1.00
93 Gary Payton	.40	1.00
94 Derek Fisher	.30	.75
95 Michael Olowokandi	.25	.60
96 Jamaal Tinsley	.25	.60
97 Chris Mihm	.25	.60
98 Antawn Jamison	.40	1.00
99 Mengke Bateer	.25	.60
100 Michael Finley	.40	1.00
101 Andre Miller	.30	.75
102 Elden Campbell	.25	.60
103 Kedrick Brown	.25	.60
104 Jason Terry	.30	.75
105 Kenny Anderson	.30	.75
106 Darius Miles	.25	.60
107 Latrell Sprewell	.30	.75
108 Darrell Armstrong	.25	.60
109 Joe Johnson	.40	1.00
110 Bonzi Wells	.25	.60
111 LaPhonso Ellis	.30	.75
112 Steve Smith	.30	.75
113 Vin Baker	.30	.75
114 Antonio Davis	.25	.60
115 John Stockton	.50	1.25
116 Shawn Marion	.40	1.00
117 Devean George	.25	.60
118 Joe Smith	.30	.75
119 Sean Lampley	.25	.60
120 Lamar Odom	.40	1.00
121 Alonzo Mourning	.50	1.25
122 Antonio Daniels	.25	.60
123 Troy Murphy	.40	1.00
124A Manu Ginobili RC	4.00	10.00
124B Manu Ginobili RC	4.00	10.00
Spanish		
125 Richard Hamilton	.30	.75
126 Amare Stoudemire RC	4.00	10.00
127 Carlos Boozer RC	3.00	8.00
128 Casey Jacobsen RC	1.50	4.00
129 Juaquin Hawkins RC	1.50	4.00
130 Pat Burke RC	1.50	4.00
131 Dan Dickau RC	1.50	4.00
132 Drew Gooden RC	2.50	6.00
133 Fred Jones RC	1.50	4.00
134 Jared Jeffries RC	1.50	4.00
135A Jiri Welsch RC	1.50	4.00
135B Jiri Welsch RC	1.50	4.00
Czech		
136 Juan Dixon RC	2.00	5.00
137 Marcus Haislip RC	1.50	4.00
138 Melvin Ely RC	1.50	4.00
139A Nene Hilario RC	2.00	5.00
139B Nene Hilario RC	2.00	5.00
Spanish		
140 Qyntel Woods RC	1.50	4.00
141 Lonny Baxter RC	1.50	4.00
142 Ryan Humphrey RC	1.50	4.00
143 Smush Parker RC	1.50	4.00
144 Tayshaun Prince RC	2.00	5.00
145 Vincent Yarbrough RC	1.50	4.00
146A Yao Ming RC	5.00	12.00
146B Yao Ming RC	5.00	12.00
Chinese		
147 Pete Mickeal	.25	.60
148 Tamar Slay RC	1.50	4.00
149A Efthimios Rentzias RC	1.50	4.00
149B Efthimios Rentzias RC	1.50	4.00
Greek		
150A Igor Rakocevic RC	1.50	4.00
150B Igor Rakocevic RC	1.50	4.00
Yugoslavian		
151A Gordan Giricek RC	1.50	4.00
151B Gordan Giricek RC	1.50	4.00
Croatian		
152A Nikoloz Tskitishvili RC	1.50	4.00
152B Nikoloz Tskitishvili RC	1.50	4.00
Russian		
153 Mike Dunleavy RC	2.00	5.00
154A Marko Jaric	1.50	4.00
154B Marko Jaric	1.50	4.00
Yugoslavian		
155 Kareem Rush RC	1.50	4.00
156 John Salmons RC	2.00	5.00
157 Jay Williams RC	2.00	5.00
158 J.R. Bremer RC	1.50	4.00
159 Frank Williams RC	1.50	4.00
160 Adam Harrington RC	1.50	4.00
161 DaJuan Wagner RC	1.50	4.00
162 Chris Wilcox RC	1.50	4.00
163 Chris Jefferies RC	1.50	4.00
164 Caron Butler RC	2.50	6.00
165A Bostjan Nachbar RC	1.50	4.00
165B Bostjan Nachbar RC	1.50	4.00
Slovenian		

2002-03 Topps Chrome Refractors

Randomly seeded in packs at the rate of one in four, this 175-card set parallels the base set enhanced with the rainbow holofoil effect that has become the trade mark of refractor cards. These cards are even more easily identified by the word "refractor" appearing on the card back below the number. Note: Both "A" and "B" rookie player versions have refractors.
*STARS: 2.5X TO 6X BASE CARD HI
*RCs: 1X TO 2.5X BASE CARD HI

2002-03 Topps Chrome Refractors Black Border

Randomly inserted, this 175-card set parallels the base Topps Chrome set enhanced with a black border and the trade mark rainbow holofoil refractor effect. Each card is sequentially numbered in gold ink on the back to 99. Both rookie player "A" and "B" versions have black border refractors.

Card	Low	High
*STARS: 8X TO 20X BASE CARD HI		
*RCs: 3X TO 8X BASE CARD HI		
10 Michael Jordan	100.00	250.00
21 Kobe Bryant	50.00	125.00

2002-03 Topps Chrome Refractors White Border

Seeded in packs at the rate of one in 23, this 175-card set parallels the base Topps Chrome set enhanced with a white border and the trade mark rainbow holofoil refractor effect. Cards are sequentially numbered on the back in gold ink to 249. Both rookie player "A" and "B" versions have white border refractors.
*STARS: 5X TO 12X BASE CARD HI
*RCs: 1.5X TO 4X BASE CARD HI

2002-03 Topps Chrome Autographs

Topps Chrome Autographs were inserted in packs for Group A at 1:3796, Yao Ming-also sequentially numbered to 250, Group B at 1:949, Mike Dunleavy and Troy Murphy-also each sequentially numbered to 500, Group C at 1:1130, Shaquille O'Neal-also sequentially numbered to 850, and Group D at 1:862, Tito Maddox-also sequentially numbered to 1100. Each card features an all chrome card stock with a full color player image set agains a basketball background with a fade to white area along the bottom of the card for player autographs. Each card is also stamped in the upper left hand corner with a Topps Chrome Certified Autograph stamp.

Card	Low	High
TCAMD Mike Dunleavy/500	5.00	12.00
TCASO Shaquille O'Neal/850	40.00	100.00
TCATM Troy Murphy/500	5.00	12.00
TCATM Tito Maddox/1100	5.00	12.00
TCAYM Yao Ming/250	40.00	80.00

2002-03 Topps Chrome Coast to Coast

Randomy inserted in packs at the rate of one in eight, this 20-card set places full-color player action photos on a background littered with street signs. Along the top a green sign contains the words, "Coast to Coast," and the player's name appears in a yellow box along the bottom of the card. Refractor versions were inserted at the rate of one in 40 and utilize the rainbow holofoil refractor effect.

Card	Low	High
COMPLETE SET (20)	15.00	40.00
*REF: .75X TO 2X COAST TO COAST HI		
CC1 Tracy McGrady	1.25	3.00
CC2 Jason Kidd	1.25	3.00
CC3 Mike Bibby	.75	2.00
CC4 Baron Davis	.75	2.00
CC5 Steve Francis	.75	2.00
CC6 Vince Carter	1.25	3.00
CC7 Kobe Bryant	4.00	10.00
CC8 Michael Jordan	6.00	15.00
CC9 Paul Pierce	1.00	2.50
CC10 Stephon Marbury	.60	1.50
CC11 Ray Allen	.75	2.00
CC12 Gary Payton	.75	2.00
CC13 Shawn Marion	.75	2.00
CC14 Steve Nash	1.00	2.50
CC15 Andre Miller	.60	1.50
CC16 Jerry Stackhouse	.60	1.50
CC17 Latrell Sprewell	.60	1.50
CC18 Jason Richardson	.75	2.00
CC19 Jamaal Tinsley	.50	1.25
CC20 Tony Parker	1.00	2.50

2002-03 Topps Chrome Destination Relics

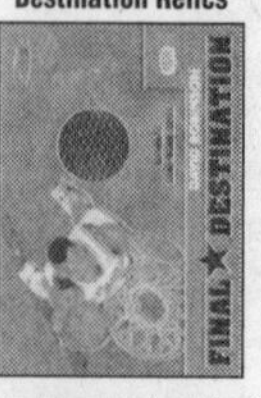

Randomly inserted in packs for Group A at one in 9310, Group B at one in 2373, Group C at one in 1898, Group D at one in 422, and Group E at one in 111. The cards are horizontally designed on an all-foil card stock with a player photo on the left and a circular swatch on the right. Under the swatch, the card tells what piece of clothing the material is from. Refractor versions were also randomly inserted and are sequentially numbered to 25.

Card	Low	High
*REF: 1.25X TO 3X HI		
FDBH Brendan Haywood	2.00	5.00
FDDR David Robinson	6.00	15.00
FDJJ Joe Johnson	3.00	8.00
FDLO Lamar Odom	3.00	8.00
FDMO Michael Olowokandi	2.00	5.00
FDNV Nick Van Exel	2.50	6.00
FDPS Peja Stojakovic	3.00	8.00
FDRW Rasheed Wallace	3.00	8.00
FDSF Steve Francis	3.00	8.00
FDSN Steve Nash	4.00	10.00
FDSS Steve Smith	2.50	6.00
FDWS Wally Szczerbiak	2.50	6.00

2002-03 Topps Chrome Franchise Fabric Relics

Inserted in packs at the rate of one in 11167 for Group A, one in 9099 for Group B, one in 316 for Group C, and one in 135 for Group D, this 13-card set places a full color player action photo on the top with gold borders on an all white background. Below the picture a star-shaped swatch of memorabilia appears. A refractor version of this set was issued and cards are sequentially numbered to 25.

Card	Low	High
*REF: 1.5X TO 4X HI		
FFCW Chris Webber	4.00	10.00
FFDW DaJuan Wagner	3.00	8.00
FFEB Elton Brand	3.00	8.00
FFJO Jermaine O'Neal	3.00	8.00
FFJR Jason Richardson	3.00	8.00
FFKG Kevin Garnett	6.00	15.00
FFKM Kenyon Martin	3.00	8.00
FFMD Mike Dunleavy	4.00	10.00
FFMO Michael Olowokandi	2.00	5.00
FFNH Nene Hilario	4.00	10.00
FFSO Shaquille O'Neal	8.00	20.00
FFTD Tim Duncan	6.00	15.00
FFYM Yao Ming	10.00	25.00

2002-03 Topps Chrome Shaq Attack Relics

Inserted in packs at the rate of one in 474, this five card set highlights Shaquille O'Neal's career from high school to the pros. Cards utilize a horizontal design with a picture of Shaq on the left and a timeline on the right with a white border. The memorabilia featured on the card is centered and in the shape of the state that the highlighted event occurred. A refractor version was also inserted and each card is sequentially numbered to 34.

Card	Low	High
COMMON CARD (1-5)	12.00	30.00
*REF: 1X TO 2.5X BASE HI		

2002-03 Topps Chrome The Move

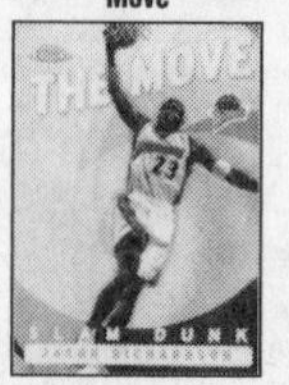

Randomly seeded in packs at the rate of one in 28, this 20-card set places full color player photos on a green background with the words "The Move" along the top of the card. A refractor version of this set was also inserted at the rate of one in 140.

Card	Low	High
COMPLETE SET (20)	30.00	80.00
*REF: 1X TO 2.5X THE MOVE HI		
TM1 Shaquille O'Neal	3.00	8.00
TM2 Reggie Miller	1.25	3.00
TM3 Allen Iverson	2.00	5.00
TM4 Kobe Bryant	6.00	15.00
TM5 Jason Kidd	2.00	5.00
TM6 Michael Jordan	10.00	25.00
TM7 Vince Carter	2.00	5.00
TM8 Ray Allen	1.25	3.00
TM9 Gary Payton	1.25	3.00
TM10 Jason Richardson	1.25	3.00
TM11 Tim Duncan	2.50	6.00
TM12 Scottie Pippen	2.00	5.00
TM13 Paul Pierce	1.50	4.00
TM14 Dikembe Mutombo	1.25	3.00
TM15 Tracy McGrady	2.00	5.00
TM16 Chris Wilcox	1.25	3.00
TM17 Yao Ming	4.00	10.00
TM18 Jay Williams	1.50	4.00
TM19 Mike Dunleavy	1.50	4.00
TM20 DaJuan Wagner	1.25	3.00

2002-03 Topps Chrome Zone Busters

Randomly inserted in packs at the rate of one in 12, this 15-card set places full color player action photos on a blue and yellow background. A white strip runs down the right side of the card containing the words, Zone Busters and the player's name. A refractor version was also inserted at one in 60.

Card	Low	High
COMPLETE SET (15)	12.50	30.00
*REF: .75X TO 2X ZONE BUSTER HI		
ZB1 Shaquille O'Neal	2.00	5.00
ZB2 Kevin Garnett	1.50	4.00
ZB3 Peja Stojakovic	.75	2.00
ZB4 Kenyon Martin	.75	2.00
ZB5 Latrell Sprewell	.60	1.50
ZB6 Michael Finley	.75	2.00
ZB7 Shawn Marion	.75	2.00
ZB8 Kobe Bryant	4.00	10.00
ZB9 Mike Bibby	.75	2.00
ZB10 Tracy McGrady	1.25	3.00
ZB11 Tony Parker	1.00	2.50
ZB12 Vince Carter	1.25	3.00
ZB13 Michael Jordan	6.00	15.00
ZB14 Elton Brand	.75	2.00
ZB15 Jamaal Tinsley	.50	1.25

2003-04 Topps Chrome

Issued in February 2004, Topps Chrome features a 174-card set divided up into 110 veteran player cards and 67 rookie cards (numbers 111-165) where several players have card variations in their native languages. The card design is set to match that of base topps, but is enhanced with an all-foil card stock. Chrome was packaged in 24-pack boxes where packs contained four cards and carried a suggested retail price of $3. Also included in each box was a sealed uncirculated X-Fractor card.

Card	Low	High
COMP.SET w/o RC's (110)	20.00	50.00
B VERSION FOR CARDS 112, 121, 127		
129, 131, 132, 138, 140, 146, 147, 149, 154		
CARD B VERSION FOREIGN, SAME VALUE		
1 Tracy McGrady	.50	1.25
2 Dajuan Wagner	.25	.60
3 Allen Iverson	.60	1.50
4 Chris Webber	.40	1.00
5 Jason Kidd	.60	1.50
6 Stephon Marbury	.30	.75
7 Jermaine O'Neal	.40	1.00
8 Antoine Walker	.40	1.00
9 Tony Parker	.40	1.00
10 Mike Bibby	.40	1.00
11 Yao Ming	.75	2.00
12 Bobby Jackson	.25	.60
13 Steve Nash	.50	1.25
14 Paul Pierce	.50	1.25
15 Vince Carter	.60	1.50
16 Peja Stojakovic	.40	1.00
17 Wally Szczerbiak	.30	.75
18 Kenyon Martin	.40	1.00
19 Pau Gasol	.40	1.00
20 Gary Payton	.40	1.00
21 Tim Duncan	.60	1.50
22 Anfernee Hardaway	.60	1.50
23 Jason Richardson	.40	1.00
24 Andre Miller	.30	.75
25 Latrell Sprewell	.30	.75
26 Darius Miles	.25	.60
27 Richard Jefferson	.40	1.00
28 Shawn Marion	.40	1.00
29 Baron Davis	.40	1.00
30 Ben Wallace	.40	1.00
31 Reggie Miller	.40	1.00
32 Karl Malone	.50	1.25
33 Jonathan Bender	.25	.60
34 Shaquille O'Neal	1.00	2.50
35 Steve Francis	.40	1.00
36 Kobe Bryant	2.00	5.00
37 Mike Dunleavy	.30	.75
38 Glenn Robinson	.30	.75
39 Allan Houston	.30	.75
40 Sam Cassell	.30	.75
41 Dirk Nowitzki	.60	1.50
42 Elton Brand	.40	1.00
43 Joe Smith	.30	.75
44 Brian Grant	.25	.60
45 Jason Terry	.30	.75
46 Richard Hamilton	.30	.75
47 Morris Peterson	.25	.60
48 Ray Allen	.40	1.00
49 Scottie Pippen	.60	1.50
50 Jamal Crawford	.30	.75
51 Cuttino Mobley	.30	.75
52 Jerry Stackhouse	.30	.75
53 Marcus Camby	.30	.75
54 Jalen Rose	.30	.75
55 Ricky Davis	.30	.75
56 Jamal Mashburn	.30	.75
57 Ron Artest	.40	1.00
58 Theo Ratliff	.25	.60
59 Juwan Howard	.30	.75
60 Caron Butler	.40	1.00
61 Antawn Jamison	.40	1.00
62 Nene	.30	.75
63 Tyson Chandler	.30	.75
64 Jason Williams	.30	.75
65 Kurt Thomas	.25	.60
66 Mike Miller	.40	1.00
67 Amare Stoudemire	.60	1.50
68 Jamaal Tinsley	.25	.60
69 Brent Barry	.25	.60
70 Brad Miller	.40	1.00
71 Bonzi Wells	.25	.60
72 Andrei Kirilenko	.40	1.00
73 Kenny Thomas	.25	.60
74 Derek Anderson	.25	.60
75 Zydrunas Ilgauskas	.30	.75
76 Eddie Griffin	.25	.60
77 Tayshaun Prince	.40	1.00
78 Michael Olowokandi	.25	.60
79 Michael Redd	.40	1.00
80 Tim Thomas	.25	.60
81 Eddie Jones	.30	.75
82 Shareef Abdur-Rahim	.30	.75
83 Corey Maggette	.30	.75
84 Eric Snow	.25	.60
85 Keon Clark	.25	.60
86 Desmond Mason	.30	.75
87 Drew Gooden	.30	.75
88 Matt Harpring	.30	.75
89 Antonio McDyess	.30	.75
90 Radoslav Nesterovic	.25	.60
91 Jamaal Magloire	.25	.60
92 Rasheed Wallace	.40	1.00
93 Antonio Davis	.25	.60
94 Kwame Brown	.25	.60
95 Manu Ginobili	.50	1.25
96 Eric Williams	.25	.60
97 Nick Van Exel	.30	.75
98 Lamar Odom	.40	1.00
99 Chauncey Billups	.40	1.00
100 Kevin Garnett	.75	2.00
101 Marko Jaric	.25	.60
102 David Wesley	.25	.60
103 Gilbert Arenas	.40	1.00
104 Keith Van Horn	.30	.75
105 Bostjan Nachbar	.25	.60
106 Michael Finley	.40	1.00
107 Troy Murphy	.40	1.00
108 Eddy Curry	.30	.75
109 Rashard Lewis	.40	1.00
110 Tony Battie	.25	.60
111 LeBron James RC	40.00	100.00
112A Darko Milicic RC	2.50	6.00
112B Darko Milicic	2.50	6.00
113 Carmelo Anthony RC	6.00	15.00
114 Chris Bosh RC	5.00	12.00
115 Dwyane Wade RC	10.00	25.00
116 Chris Kaman RC	3.00	8.00
117 Kirk Hinrich RC	3.00	8.00
118 T.J. Ford RC	3.00	8.00
119 Mike Sweetney RC	2.50	6.00
120 Jarvis Hayes RC	2.50	6.00
121A Mickael Pietrus RC	2.50	6.00
121B Mickael Pietrus	2.50	6.00
122 Nick Collison RC	2.50	6.00
123 Marcus Banks RC	2.50	6.00
124 Luke Ridnour RC	3.00	8.00
125 Reece Gaines RC	2.50	6.00
126 Troy Bell RC	2.50	6.00
127A Zarko Cabarkapa RC	2.50	6.00
127B Zarko Cabarkapa	2.50	6.00
128 David West RC	3.00	8.00
129A Aleksandar Pavlovic RC	2.50	6.00
129B Aleksandar Pavlovic	2.50	6.00
130 Dahntay Jones RC	2.50	6.00
131A Boris Diaw RC	3.00	8.00
131B Boris Diaw RC	3.00	8.00
132A Zoran Planinic RC	2.50	6.00
132B Zoran Planinic	2.50	6.00
133 Travis Outlaw RC	3.00	8.00
134 Brian Cook RC	2.50	6.00
135 Matt Carroll RC	2.50	6.00
136 Ndudi Ebi RC	2.50	6.00
137 Kendrick Perkins RC	4.00	10.00
138A Leandro Barbosa RC	3.00	8.00
138B Leandro Barbosa	3.00	8.00
139 Josh Howard RC	2.50	6.00
140A Maciej Lampe RC	2.50	6.00
140B Maciej Lampe	2.50	6.00
141 Jason Kapono RC	2.50	6.00
142 Luke Walton RC	2.50	6.00
143 Jerome Beasley RC	2.50	6.00
144 Travis Hansen RC	2.50	6.00
145 Steve Blake RC	3.00	8.00
146A Slavko Vranes RC	2.50	6.00
146B Slavko Vranes	2.50	6.00
147A Francisco Elson RC	2.50	6.00
147B Francisco Elson RC	2.50	6.00
148 Willie Green RC	2.50	6.00
149A Zaur Pachulia RC	2.50	6.00
149B Zaur Pachulia	2.50	6.00
150 Keith Bogans RC	2.50	6.00
151 Maurice Williams RC	4.00	10.00
152 James Jones RC	2.50	6.00
153 Kyle Korver RC	3.00	8.00
154A Jon Stefansson RC	2.50	6.00
154B Jon Stefansson	2.50	6.00
155 Brandon Hunter RC	2.50	6.00
156 Josh Moore RC	2.50	6.00
157 Torraye Braggs RC	2.50	6.00
158 Devin Brown RC	2.50	6.00
159 James Lang RC	2.50	6.00
160 Theron Smith RC	2.50	6.00
161 Linton Johnson RC	2.50	6.00
162 Marquis Daniels RC	2.50	6.00
163 Keith McLeod RC	2.50	6.00
164 Udonis Haslem RC	3.00	8.00
165 Ben Handlogten RC	2.50	6.00

2003-04 Topps Chrome Refractors

Inserted in packs at the rate of one in six for cards 1-110 and one in 12 for cards 111-165, this 174-card set parallels the base Topps Chrome set enhanced with Topps' rainbow holofoil refractor effect.

Card	Low	High
*1-110 SINGLES: 2X TO 5X BASE HI		
*111-165 RC SINGLES: 1X TO 2.5X BASE HI		
115 Dwyane Wade	30.00	80.00

2003-04 Topps Chrome Refractors Black

Inserted in packs at the rate of one in 18 for cards 1-110 with cards 111-165 are sequentially numbered to 500, this 174-card set parallels the base Topps Chrome set enhanced with black borders and Topps' rainbow holofoil refractor effect.

Card	Low	High
*1-110 SINGLES: 3X TO 8X BASE HI		
*111-165 RC SINGLES: 1.5X TO 4X BASE HI		
36 Kobe Bryant	20.00	50.00
111 LeBron James	300.00	550.00
115 Dwyane Wade	75.00	150.00

2003-04 Topps Chrome Refractors Gold

Sequentially numbered to 99 for cards 1-110 and 50 for cards 111-165, this 174-card set parallels the base Topps Chrome set enhanced with gold borders and Topps' rainbow holofoil refractor effect.

Card	Low	High
*1-110 SINGLES: 5X TO 12X BASE HI		
*111-165 RC SINGLES: 2.5X TO 6X BASE HI		
36 Kobe Bryant	40.00	100.00
111 LeBron James	700.00	1200.00
113 Carmelo Anthony	100.00	200.00
114 Chris Bosh	75.00	150.00
115 Dwyane Wade	400.00	700.00

2003-04 Topps Chrome X-Fractors

Inserted at one per box as a topper in a separate wrapper, this 174-card set parallels the base set with a holofoil confetti effect and is sequentially numbered to 220.

Card	Low	High
*X-FRAC.SINGLES: 4X TO 10X BASE HI		
*X-FRAC RC SINGLES: 2X TO 5X BASE HI		
111 LeBron James	400.00	700.00
113 Carmelo Anthony	40.00	100.00
115 Dwyane Wade	80.00	200.00

2003-04 Topps Chrome Autographs

serted at the following rates: Group A one in 300, roup B one in 622, Group C one in 2329 and Group one in 595, this 11-card set features full-color player notos on the top of the card and a white space with an itograph at the bottom. The word, Chromograps, eparates the two. A Refractor Parallel was also serted in packs and those cards are sequentially umbered to 25.
REFRACTORS: 1.25X TO 3X BASE HI

ACA Carmelo Anthony A	40.00	80.00
ADW Dwyane Wade A	60.00	150.00
AKB Kwame Brown A	4.00	10.00
AKH Kirk Hinrich B	6.00	15.00
ALR Luke Ridnour A	5.00	12.00
AMR Michael Redd	5.00	12.00
ANC Nick Collison B	4.00	10.00
ARA Ray Allen D	12.50	30.00
ASO Shaquille O'Neal C	30.00	80.00
ASV Slavko Vranes B	4.00	10.00
ATF T.J. Ford D	5.00	12.00

2003-04 Topps Chrome Bonus Coverage Relics

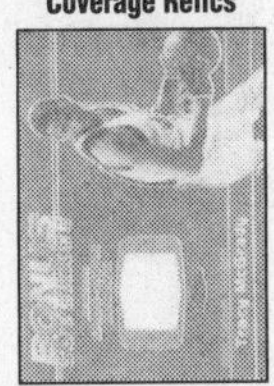

nserted at the following rates, Group A one in 1214, Group B one in 484, Group C one in 242 and Group D ne in 102, this 23-card set is horizontally desiged with a player photo on the right and a swatch of memorabilia on the left. A Refractor parallel set was nserted in packs as well, and the print runs are as ollows: Group A is sequentially numbered to five, Group B is sequentially numbered to 15, Group C is sequentially numbered to 20 and Group D is sequentially numbered to 25.
*REFRACTORS: 1.25X TO 3X BASE HI
SOME REF.NOT PRICED DUE TO SCARCITY

AI Allen Iverson A	5.00	12.00
AW Antoine Walker D	3.00	8.00
BD Baron Davis A	3.00	8.00
CB Caron Butler B	3.00	8.00
CW Chris Webber D	3.00	8.00
DM Darius Miles B	2.00	5.00
DW Dajuan Wagner C	2.00	5.00
JM Jamal Mashburn C	2.50	6.00
JR Jason Richardson A	3.00	8.00
KB Kevin Garnett A	6.00	15.00
MD Mike Dunleavy A	2.50	6.00
MF Michael Finley A	3.00	8.00
PG Pau Gasol D	3.00	8.00
RJ Richard Jefferson C	3.00	8.00
SA Shareef Abdur-Rahim A	2.50	6.00
SM Shawn Marion C	3.00	8.00
SO Shaquille O'Neal D	8.00	20.00
TM Tracy McGrady D	4.00	10.00
SMA Stephon Marbury B	2.50	6.00

2003-04 Topps Chrome Cuts Relics

Inserted in packs at the following rates, Group A one in 1214, Group B one in 484, Group C one in 242 and Group D one in 102, this 23-card set places player photos on the right and memorabilia swatches in the shape of the letter "C" on the left. A Refractor parallel set was inserted in packs as well, and the print runs are as follows: Group A is sequentially numbered to five, Group B is sequentially numbered to 15, Group C is sequentially numbered to 20 and Group D is sequentially numbered to 25.
*REFRACTORS: 1.25X TO 3X BASE HI
SOME REF.NOT PRICED DUE TO SCARCITY

BH Brendan Haywood B	2.00	5.00
BM Brad Miller C	3.00	8.00
BW Ben Wallace D	3.00	8.00
DF Derek Fisher A	2.50	6.00
EC Elden Campbell B	2.00	5.00
EG Manu Ginobili A	4.00	10.00
HT Hedo Turkoglu C	3.00	8.00
JS Jerry Stackhouse B	2.50	6.00
KM Kenyon Martin A	3.00	8.00
MB Mike Bibby B	3.00	8.00
MR Michael Redd B	3.00	8.00
NH Nene C	2.50	6.00
NT Nikoloz Tskitishvili B	2.00	5.00
RW Rasheed Wallace D	3.00	8.00
TC Tyson Chandler D	2.50	6.00
TD Tim Duncan	5.00	12.00
VR Vladimir Radmanovic A	2.00	5.00
ZI Zydrunas Ilgauskas D	2.50	6.00
AHA Anfernee Hardaway A	5.00	12.00

2003-04 Topps Chrome Gametime Gear Relics

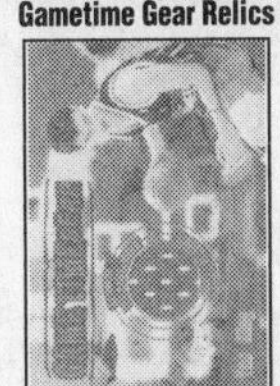

Inserted in packs at the following rates, Group A one in 1214, Group B one in 484, Group C one in 242 and Group D one in 102, this 23-card set places player photos on the right and circular memorabilia swatches on the left. A Refractor parallel set was inserted in packs as well, and the print runs are as follows: Group A is sequentially numbered to five, Group B is sequentially numbered to 15, Group C is sequentially numbered to 20 and Group D is sequentially numbered to 25.
*REFRACTORS: 1.25X TO 3X BASE HI
SOME REF.NOT PRICED DUE TO SCARCITY

AK Andrei Kirilenko A	3.00	8.00
AS Amare Stoudemire C	5.00	12.00
CB Carlos Boozer D	3.00	8.00
CM Cuttino Mobley D	2.50	6.00
DG Devean George A	2.00	5.00
DN Dirk Nowitzki D	5.00	12.00
DW David Wesley D	2.00	5.00
JD Juan Dixon B	2.00	5.00
JK Jason Kidd B	5.00	12.00
JW Jerome Williams D	2.00	5.00
LO Lamar Odom C	3.00	8.00
MP Morris Peterson B	2.00	5.00
PP Paul Pierce C	4.00	10.00
PS Peja Stojakovic D	3.00	8.00
QW Qyntel Woods C	2.00	5.00
RA Ray Allen D	3.00	8.00
TM Troy Murphy A	3.00	8.00
TP Tayshaun Prince A	3.00	8.00
WS Wally Szczerbiak C	2.50	6.00
YM Yao Ming D	6.00	15.00
TPA Tony Parker D	3.00	8.00

2004-05 Topps Chrome

This 220-card was released in February, 2005. The cards were issued in four-card packs with an $3 SRP which came 24 packs to a box and eight boxes to a case. Cards numbered 1-165 feature active veterans while cards 166-220 feature Rookie Cards.

COMPLETE SET (220)	100.00	200.00
COMP.SET w/o RC's (165)	15.00	40.00

UNPRICED SUPERFR.PRINT RUN ONE SET

1 Allen Iverson	.60	1.50
2 Eddy Curry	.30	.75
3 Stephon Marbury	.30	.75
4 Chris Bosh	.40	1.00
5 Jason Kidd	.60	1.50
6 Baron Davis	.40	1.00
7 Kwame Brown	.25	.60
8 Kobe Bryant	2.00	5.00
9 Ben Wallace	.40	1.00
10 Josh Howard	.40	1.00
11 Yao Ming	.75	2.00
12 Luke Walton	.25	.60
13 Nene	.30	.75
14 Michael Redd	.40	1.00
15 Carmelo Anthony	.75	2.00
16 Amare Stoudemire	.50	1.25
17 Jarvis Hayes	.25	.60
18 Toni Kukoc	.30	.75
19 Latrell Sprewell	.30	.75
20 Jason Richardson	.40	1.00
21 Kevin Garnett	.75	2.00
22 Darko Milicic	.25	.60
23 LeBron James	2.50	6.00
24 Peja Stojakovic	.40	1.00
25 Wally Szczerbiak	.30	.75
26 Theo Ratliff	.25	.60
27 Gilbert Arenas	.40	1.00
28 Mike Dunleavy	.30	.75
29 Joe Smith	.30	.75
30 Vince Carter	.60	1.50
31 Reggie Miller	.40	1.00
32 Chris Wilcox	.25	.60
33 Rasheed Wallace	.40	1.00
34 Paul Pierce	.50	1.25
35 Tayshaun Prince	.40	1.00
36 Richard Hamilton	.30	.75
37 Rashard Lewis	.40	1.00
38 Joe Johnson	.40	1.00
39 Zydrunas Ilgauskas	.30	.75
40 Andre Miller	.30	.75
41 Dirk Nowitzki	.60	1.50
42 Chauncey Billups	.40	1.00
43 Ray Allen	.40	1.00
44 Raef LaFrentz	.25	.60
45 Mickael Pietrus	.30	.75
46 T.J. Ford	.30	.75
47 Chris Webber	.40	1.00
48 Jamaal Tinsley	.25	.60
49 Earl Boykins	.25	.60
50 Tim Duncan	.60	1.50
51 Troy Hudson	.25	.60
52 Juan Dixon	.25	.60
53 Tim Thomas	.25	.60
54 Darius Miles	.25	.60
55 Jalen Rose	.30	.75
56 Kirk Hinrich	.40	1.00
57 Michael Finley	.40	1.00
58 Brad Miller	.40	1.00
59 Jonathan Bender	.25	.60
60 Manu Ginobili	.50	1.25
61 Chris Kaman	.40	1.00
62 Doug Christie	.25	.60
63 Marcus Camby	.30	.75
64 Desmond Mason	.30	.75
65 Boris Diaw	.30	.75
66 Maurice Taylor	.25	.60
67 Damon Stoudamire	.30	.75
68 Dwyane Wade	1.25	3.00
69 Allan Houston	.30	.75
70 Jermaine O'Neal	.40	1.00
71 Glenn Robinson	.30	.75
72 Morris Peterson	.25	.60
73 Luke Ridnour	.30	.75
74 Bobby Jackson	.25	.60
75 Eddie Jones	.30	.75
76 Alvin Williams	.25	.60
77 Elton Brand	.40	1.00
78 Zach Randolph	.30	.75
79 Marko Jaric	.25	.60
80 Mike Bibby	.40	1.00
81 Jim Jackson	.25	.60
82 Kurt Thomas	.25	.60
83 Troy Murphy	.30	.75
84 Rodney White	.25	.60
85 Jamaal Magloire	.25	.60
86 Jamal Mashburn	.40	1.00
87 Kenny Thomas	.25	.60
88 Corey Maggette	.30	.75
89 Rasho Nesterovic	.25	.60
90 Shawn Marion	.40	1.00
91 Antonio Daniels	.25	.60
92 Marquis Daniels	.25	.60
93 Richard Jefferson	.40	1.00
94 Michael Olowokandi	.25	.60
95 Bruce Bowen	.25	.60
96 Mark Blount	.25	.60
97 Sam Cassell	.30	.75
98 Voshon Lenard	.25	.60
99 Speedy Claxton	.25	.60
100 Samuel Dalembert	.25	.60
101 Tyson Chandler	.30	.75
102 Keith Van Horn	.30	.75
103 Udonis Haslem	.30	.75
104 Trenton Hassell	.25	.60
105 Tony Parker	.40	1.00
106 Ronald Murray	.25	.60
107 Jeff McInnis	.25	.60
108 Marcus Banks	.25	.60
109 Ricky Davis	.30	.75
110 Karl Malone	.50	1.25
111 Bonzi Wells	.25	.60
112 Antonio McDyess	.30	.75
113 Drew Gooden	.30	.75
114 Stephen Jackson	.30	.75
115 Eric Snow	.25	.60
116 Steve Francis	.40	1.00
117 Pau Gasol	.40	1.00
118 Andrei Kirilenko	.30	.75
119 Erick Dampier	.25	.60
120 Jason Kapono	.25	.60
121 Al Harrington	.30	.75
122 Gary Payton	.40	1.00
123 Nick Van Exel	.30	.75
124 Cuttino Mobley	.30	.75
125 Kenyon Martin	.40	1.00
126 Mike Miller	.40	1.00
127 Jamal Crawford	.30	.75
128 Kerry Kittles	.25	.60
129 Derrick Coleman	.30	.75
130 Gordan Giricek	.25	.60
131 Antoine Walker	.40	1.00
132 Shane Battier	.30	.75
133 Caron Butler	.40	1.00
134 Corliss Williamson	.25	.60
135 Carlos Boozer	.40	1.00
136 Tracy McGrady	.50	1.25
137 Stromile Swift	.25	.60
138 Derek Fisher	.30	.75
139 Juwan Howard	.30	.75
140 Jason Terry	.30	.75
141 Vlade Divac	.30	.75
142 Antawn Jamison	.40	1.00
143 Aleksandar Pavlovic	.25	.60
144 Rafer Alston	.25	.60
145 Brent Barry	.25	.60
146 Quentin Richardson	.30	.75
147 Lamar Odom	.40	1.00
148 Gerald Wallace	.40	1.00
149 Charlie Ward	.25	.60
150 Jerry Stackhouse	.30	.75
151 Carlos Arroyo	.30	.75
152 Hedo Turkoglu	.40	1.00
153 Steve Nash	.50	1.25
154 Mehmet Okur	.30	.75
155 Tyronn Lue	.25	.60
156 Bob Sura	.25	.60
157 Jason Williams	.30	.75
158 Shaquille O'Neal	1.00	2.50
159 Kelvin Cato	.25	.60
160 Eric Williams	.25	.60
161 Brian Grant	.25	.60
162 Danny Fortson	.25	.60
163 Chucky Atkins	.25	.60
164 Matt Harpring	.30	.75
165 Primoz Brezec	.25	.60
166 Dwight Howard RC	8.00	20.00
167 Emeka Okafor RC	2.50	6.00
168 Ben Gordon RC	2.00	5.00
169 Shaun Livingston RC	1.50	4.00
170 Devin Harris RC	2.50	6.00
171 Josh Childress RC	1.50	4.00
172 Luol Deng RC	2.50	6.00
173 Rafael Araujo RC	1.50	4.00
174 Andre Iguodala RC	2.50	6.00
175 Luke Jackson RC	1.50	4.00
176 Andris Biedrins RC	2.00	5.00
177 Robert Swift RC	1.50	4.00
178 Sebastian Telfair RC	1.50	4.00
179 Kris Humphries RC	1.50	4.00
180 Al Jefferson RC	2.50	6.00
181 Kirk Snyder RC	1.50	4.00
182 Josh Smith RC	2.50	6.00
183 J.R. Smith RC	2.00	5.00
184 Dorell Wright RC	2.50	6.00
185 Jameer Nelson RC	2.00	5.00
186 Pavel Podkolzine RC	1.50	4.00
187 Horace Jenkins RC	1.50	4.00
188 Luis Flores RC	1.50	4.00
189 Delonte West RC	2.00	5.00
190 Tony Allen RC	2.00	5.00
191 Kevin Martin RC	2.00	5.00
192 Sasha Vujacic RC	1.50	4.00
193 Beno Udrih RC	1.50	4.00
194 David Harrison RC	1.50	4.00
195 Yuta Tabuse RC	3.00	8.00
196 Peter John Ramos RC	1.50	4.00
197 Chris Duhon RC	1.50	4.00
198 Trevor Ariza RC	1.50	4.00
199 Bernard Robinson RC	1.50	4.00
200 Andre Emmett RC	1.50	4.00
201 Mario Kasun RC	1.50	4.00
202 Matt Freije RC	1.50	4.00
203 Maurice Evans RC	1.50	4.00
204 Erik Daniels RC	1.50	4.00
205 Lionel Chalmers RC	1.50	4.00
206 Jared Reiner RC	1.50	4.00
207 D.J. Mbenga RC	1.50	4.00
208 Antonio Burks RC	1.50	4.00
209 Justin Reed RC	1.50	4.00
210 Pape Sow RC	1.50	4.00
211 Jackson Vroman RC	1.50	4.00
212 Romain Sato RC	1.50	4.00
213 Nenad Kristic RC	1.50	4.00
214 Damien Wilkins RC	1.50	4.00
215 Arthur Johnson RC	1.50	4.00
216 Ibrahim Kutluay RC	1.50	4.00
217 Andres Nocioni RC	1.50	4.00
218 Josh Davis RC	1.50	4.00
219 Donta Smith RC	1.50	4.00
220 Anderson Varejao RC	2.00	5.00

2004-05 Topps Chrome Refractors

Inserted into packs at a stated rate of one in four, this is a parallel to the basic Chrome set. These cards use the Topps refractor technology. There is also a black-bordered refractor parallel which were issued to a stated print run of 500 serial numbered sets.
*1-165 REFRACTORS: 2X TO 5X BASE HI
*166-220 REF.RCs: .75X TO 2X BASE HI

8 Kobe Bryant	15.00	40.00
166 Dwight Howard	20.00	50.00

2004-05 Topps Chrome Refractors Black

Randomly inserted in packs, this 220-card set parallels the base Topps Chrome set with a black border and sequential numbering to 500.
*1-165 SINGLES: 3X TO 8X BASE HI
*166-220 RC SINGLES: 1.5X TO 4X BASE HI

166 Dwight Howard	40.00	100.00

2004-05 Topps Chrome Refractors Gold

Randomly inserted into packs, this is a complete parallel to the base set. These cards use both the Topps refractor process and have gold borders and were issued to a stated print run of 99 serial numbered sets.
*1-165 SINGLES: 6X TO 15X BASE HI
*166-220 RC SINGLES: 2.5X TO 6X BASE HI

8 Kobe Bryant	50.00	125.00
23 LeBron James	50.00	125.00
68 Dwyane Wade	25.00	60.00
166 Dwight Howard	100.00	200.00

2004-05 Topps Chrome X-Fractors

Issued one per hobby box as a box-topper, this is a parallel to the basic set. Each of these cards use the X-fractor technology, come in a protected uncirculated case and were issued to a stated print run of 110 serial numbered sets.
*1-165 SINGLES: 4X TO 10X BASE HI
*166-220 RC SINGLES: 2.5X TO 6X BASE HI

8 Kobe Bryant	25.00	60.00
23 LeBron James	40.00	100.00

2004-05 Topps Chrome Autographs

Randomly inserted into packs, these 22 cards featuring autographs of leading NBA players. Since the players in group A, group B and group C are inserted at different odds, we have notated next to the player's name what group they are a part of. There is also a refractor parallel to this set. Those cards were issued to a stated print run of seven serial numbered sets.
UNPRICED REFRACTOR PRINT RUN 7 SETS

AB Andris Biedrins C	6.00	15.00
AS Amare Stoudemire A	12.50	30.00
AV Anderson Varejao B	6.00	15.00
BG Ben Gordon C	6.00	15.00
CA Carmelo Anthony A	20.00	40.00
DH Devin Harris C	8.00	20.00
EO Emeka Okafor A	8.00	20.00
JC Josh Childress C	5.00	12.00
JK Jason Kidd A	15.00	40.00
JN Jameer Nelson C	6.00	15.00
JO Jermaine O'Neal A	10.00	25.00
JS Josh Smith C	8.00	20.00
LD Luol Deng A	8.00	20.00
LJ Luke Jackson B	5.00	12.00
RH Richard Hamilton A	6.00	15.00
RS Robert Swift B	5.00	12.00
SL Shaun Livingston C	5.00	12.00
SO Shaquille O'Neal A	30.00	80.00
ST Sebastian Telfair C	5.00	12.00
TM Tracy McGrady A	20.00	50.00
JRS J.R. Smith C	6.00	15.00
SMA Shawn Marion A	6.00	15.00

2004-05 Topps Chrome Chrome-Town Heroes

Randomly inserted into packs, these 29 cards featuring game-used swatches of leading veterans. For those players not in Group C, we have listed the stated print runs next to their name. Please note that Corey Maggette and Shaquille O'Neal were issued as exchange cards. There is also a refractor parallel of these cards, which were issued to a stated print run of 25 serial numbered sets.
*REFRACTOR: 1.25X TO 3X BASE HI

AK Andrei Kirilenko/272	2.00	5.00
AS Amare Stoudemire/885	3.00	8.00
BW Ben Wallace/206	2.50	6.00
CA Carmelo Anthony/1000	5.00	12.00
CB Chris Bosh/859	2.50	6.00
CM Corey Maggette	2.00	5.00
CW Chris Webber/500	2.50	6.00
DM Desmond Mason/500	2.00	5.00
DN Dirk Nowitzki/500	4.00	10.00
GA Gilbert Arenas/287	2.50	6.00
GW Gerald Wallace/287	2.50	6.00
JO Jermaine O'Neal/336	2.50	6.00
JT Jason Terry/500	2.00	5.00
KG Kevin Garnett/500	5.00	12.00
KH Kirk Hinrich/1000	2.50	6.00
MD Mike Dunleavy/985	2.00	5.00
PG Pau Gasol/500	2.50	6.00
RJ Richard Jefferson/1000	2.50	6.00
RL Rashard Lewis/500	2.50	6.00
SO Shaquille O'Neal B	6.00	15.00
TP Tony Parker/385	2.50	6.00
YM Yao Ming/467	5.00	12.00
ZR Zach Randolph/364	2.00	5.00
CHB Chauncey Billups/211	2.50	6.00

2004-05 Topps Chrome Refined Remnants

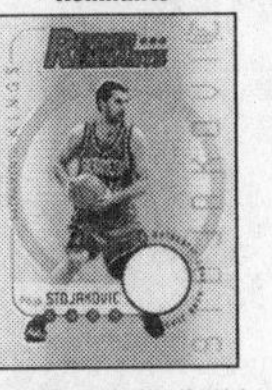

Randomly inserted into packs, these 12 cards featuring game-used swatches of leading veterans. For those players not in Group C, we have listed the stated print runs next to their name. Please note that Gary Payton was issued as exchange cards. There is also a refractor parallel of these cards, which were issued to a stated print run of 25 serial numbered sets.
*REFRACTORS: 1.25X TO 3X BASE HI

BD Baron Davis/780	2.50	6.00
EB Elton Brand/412	2.50	6.00
GP Gary Payton B	2.50	6.00
JK Jason Kidd/782	4.00	10.00
PP Paul Pierce/500	3.00	8.00
PS Peja Stojakovic/1000	2.50	6.00
RA Ray Allen/500	2.50	6.00
RM Reggie Miller/1000	2.50	6.00
SC Sam Cassell/385	2.00	5.00
SM Shawn Marion/332	2.50	6.00
TD Tim Duncan/939	4.00	10.00
TM Tracy McGrady/385	3.00	8.00

2004-05 Topps Chrome Slice of Success

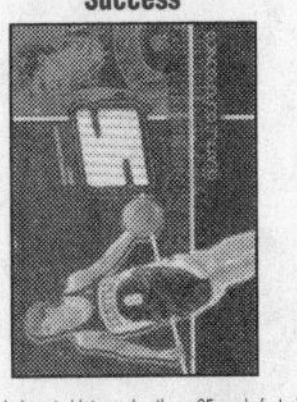

Randomly inserted into packs, these 25 cards featuring game-used swatches of leading veterans. For those players not in Group C, we have listed the stated print runs next to their name. There is also a refractor parallel of these cards, which were issued to a stated print run of 25 serial numbered sets.
*REFRACTORS: 1.25X TO 3X BASE HI

AJ Al Jefferson/976	4.00	10.00
AW Antoine Walker/900	2.50	6.00
BG Ben Gordon/500	3.00	8.00
DH Devin Harris/1000	4.00	10.00
EO Emeka Okafor/1000	4.00	10.00
JC Josh Childress/500	2.50	6.00
JH Jarvis Hayes/200	2.00	5.00
JM Jamaal Magloire/900	2.00	5.00
JT Jamaal Tinsley/500	2.00	5.00
KR Kareem Rush/500	2.00	5.00
KS Kirk Snyder/500	2.50	6.00
LD Luol Deng/307	4.00	10.00
LR Luke Ridnour/249	2.00	5.00
MB Mike Bibby/500	2.50	6.00
MJ Marko Jaric/1000	2.00	5.00
RN Rasho Nesterovic/754	2.00	5.00
SB Shane Battier/332	2.00	5.00
SF Steve Francis/500	2.50	6.00
SL Shaun Livingston/500	2.50	6.00
TA Tony Allen/500	3.00	8.00
TC Tyson Chandler/500	2.00	5.00
TP Tayshaun Prince/500	2.50	6.00
JHO Josh Howard/500	2.50	6.00
SAR Shareef Abdur-Rahim/1000	2.00	5.00

2004-05 Topps Chrome Total Recall

Randomly inserted into packs, these nine cards featuring game-used swatches of a leading rookie paired up with a leading veteran. Each of these cards were issued to a stated print run of 100 serial numbered sets. There is also a refractor parallel of these cards, which were issued to a stated print run of 25 serial numbered sets.
*REFRACTORS: 1X TO 2.5X BASE HI

DD Mike Dunleavy Luol Deng	5.00	12.00
DG Baron Davis Ben Gordon	5.00	12.00
JI Richard Jefferson Andre Iguodala	8.00	20.00
KH Jason Kidd Devin Harris	8.00	20.00
MA Brad Miller Rafael Araujo	5.00	12.00
MC Reggie Miller Josh Childress	8.00	20.00
MT Stephon Marbury Sebastian Telfair	5.00	12.00
PJ Tayshaun Prince Luke Jackson	5.00	12.00
WO Ben Wallace Emeka Okafor	5.00	12.00

2005-06 Topps Chrome

Released in February 2006, this 274-card set pictures veteran players on cards 1-165, rookie players on cards 166-215, celebrities on cards 216-220 and NBA D-League players on cards 221-274. Base cards are printed on an all-foil card stock with white borders. Chrome was packaged in 24 pack boxes where packs contain four cards and carried an initial SRP of $3.00.

COMPLETE SET (274)	60.00	120.00

UNPRICED SUPERFR.PRINT RUN ONE SET

1 Grant Hill	.50	1.25
2 Lamar Odom	.40	1.00
3 Jamal Crawford	.30	.75
4 Ben Gordon	.40	1.00
5 Zach Randolph	.30	.75
6 Chris Duhon	.25	.60
7 Gilbert Arenas	.40	1.00
8 Yao Ming	.50	1.25
9 Josh Smith	.40	1.00
10 Ray Allen	.40	1.00
11 Vince Carter	.60	1.50
12 Kenyon Martin	.40	1.00
13 Tim Duncan	.60	1.50
14 Michael Redd	.40	1.00
15 Antawn Jamison	.40	1.00
16 Shane Battier	.30	.75
17 Baron Davis	.40	1.00
18 Allen Iverson	.60	1.50
19 Jameer Nelson	.30	.75
20 Brent Barry	.25	.60
21 Zydrunas Ilgauskas	.30	.75
22 Jason Terry	.30	.75
23 Mike Dunleavy	.30	.75
24 Paul Pierce	.50	1.25
25 Peja Stojakovic	.40	1.00
26 Andre Iguodala	.40	1.00
27 Andrei Kirilenko	.30	.75
28 Nenad Krstic	.25	.60
29 Emeka Okafor	.40	1.00
30 Jalen Rose	.40	1.00
31 Ricky Davis	.30	.75
32 Jason Kidd	.60	1.50
33 Chauncey Billups	.40	1.00
34 Amare Stoudemire	.40	1.00
35 Josh Childress	.30	.75
36 Mehmet Okur	.25	.60
37 Shaun Livingston	.25	.60
38 Bruce Bowen	.25	.60
39 J.R. Smith	.40	1.00
40 Kobe Bryant	2.00	5.00
41 Dwight Howard	.75	2.00
42 Manu Ginobili	.40	1.00
43 Keith Van Horn	.30	.75
44 Stephon Marbury	.30	.75
45 Samuel Dalembert	.25	.60
46 Luke Ridnour	.30	.75
47 Sebastian Telfair	.30	.75
48 Tyson Chandler	.30	.75
49 Drew Gooden	.30	.75
50 Marcus Camby	.30	.75
51 Dwyane Wade	1.00	2.50
52 Troy Murphy	.30	.75
53 Rashard Lewis	.40	1.00
54 Shaquille O'Neal	.75	2.00
55 Al Harrington	.30	.75
56 Al Jefferson	.40	1.00
57 Earl Boykins	.25	.60
58 Tayshaun Prince	.40	1.00
59 Carlos Boozer	.40	1.00
60 Richard Jefferson	.40	1.00
61 Toni Kukoc	.25	.60
62 Brad Miller	.40	1.00
63 Richard Hamilton	.30	.75
64 Kevin Garnett	.75	2.00
65 Tony Parker	.40	1.00
66 Udonis Haslem	.30	.75
67 Dikembe Mutombo	.40	1.00
68 Pau Gasol	.40	1.00
69 Chris Webber	.40	1.00
70 Ben Wallace	.40	1.00
71 Carmelo Anthony	.75	2.00
72 Dirk Nowitzki	.60	1.50
73 Tony Allen	.25	.60
74 Corey Maggette	.30	.75
75 Rasheed Wallace	.40	1.00
76 Andre Miller	.30	.75
77 Luol Deng	.40	1.00
78 Mike Miller	.40	1.00
79 Wally Szczerbiak	.30	.75
80 Chris Bosh	.40	1.00
81 Marquis Daniels	.25	.60
82 Nick Collison	.25	.60
83 Matt Harpring	.30	.75
84 Kirk Hinrich	.40	1.00
85 Josh Howard	.40	1.00
86 Elton Brand	.40	1.00
87 Tyronn Lue	.25	.60
88 Bob Sura	.25	.60
89 Chris Mihm	.25	.60
90 Brevin Knight	.25	.60
91 Jason Richardson	.40	1.00
92 Vladimir Radmanovic	.25	.60
93 Eddie Griffin	.25	.60
94 P.J. Brown	.25	.60
95 Troy Hudson	.25	.60
96 Steve Francis	.40	1.00
97 Joel Przybilla	.25	.60
98 Steve Nash	.50	1.25
99 Brendan Haywood	.25	.60
100 Primoz Brezec	.25	.60
101 Devin Harris	.40	1.00
102 Lebron James	2.00	5.00
103 Mike Bibby	.40	1.00
104 Jared Jeffries	.25	.60
105 Morris Peterson	.25	.60
106 Trevor Ariza	.25	.60
107 Shawn Marion	.40	1.00
108 Andres Nocioni	.25	.60
109 Darius Miles	.25	.60
110 Tracy Mcgrady	.50	1.25
111 Stephen Jackson	.30	.75
112 Joe Johnson	.40	1.00
113 Bonzi Wells	.25	.60
114 Damon Jones	.25	.60
115 Rafer Alston	.25	.60
116 Cuttino Mobley	.30	.75
117 Nick Van Exel	.40	1.00
118 Jason Hart	.25	.60
119 Fred Jones	.25	.60
120 Dan Dickau	.25	.60
121 Damon Stoudamire	.30	.75
122 Kirk Snyder	.25	.60
123 Larry Hughes	.30	.75
124 Michael Finley	.40	1.00
125 Sam Cassell	.40	1.00
126 Bobby Jackson	.25	.60
127 Austin Croshere	.25	.60
128 Kwame Brown	.25	.60
129 James Posey	.25	.60
130 Antonio Daniels	.25	.60
131 Eddy Curry	.30	.75
132 Mike James	.25	.60
133 Juan Dixon	.25	.60
134 Jason Williams	.30	.75
135 Jeff Mcinnis	.25	.60
136 Jamaal Tinsley	.25	.60
137 Derek Anderson	.25	.60
138 Devin Brown	.25	.60
139 Raja Bell	.30	.75
140 Gary Payton	.40	1.00
141 Marko Jaric	.25	.60
142 Ron Artest	.40	1.00
143 Zaza Pachulia	.25	.60
144 Jermaine O'Neal	.40	1.00
145 Quentin Richardson	.30	.75
146 Lee Nailon	.25	.60
147 Bobby Simmons	.25	.60
148 Caron Butler	.40	1.00
149 Shareef Abdur-Rahim	.30	.75
150 Stromile Swift	.25	.60
151 Rasual Butler	.25	.60
152 Mike Sweetney	.25	.60
153 Antoine Walker	.30	.75
154 Eddie Jones	.30	.75
155 David Harrison	.25	.60
156 Kurt Thomas	.25	.60
157 Donyell Marshall	.25	.60
158 Brian Grant	.25	.60
159 Desmond Mason	.25	.60
160 Tim Thomas	.25	.60
161 Marc Jackson	.25	.60
162 Chucky Atkins	.25	.60
163 Jeff Foster	.25	.60
164 Jamaal Magloire	.25	.60
165 Desagana Diop	.25	.60
166 Danny Granger RC	4.00	10.00
167 Hakim Warrick RC	2.50	6.00
168 Chris Paul RC	8.00	20.00
169 Marvin Williams RC	2.50	6.00
170 Ike Diogu RC	2.00	5.00
171 Wayne Simien RC	2.00	5.00
172 James Singleton RC	2.00	5.00
173 Robert Whaley RC	2.00	5.00
174 Arvydas Macijauskas RC	2.00	5.00
175 Linas Kleiza RC	2.00	5.00
176 Raymond Felton RC	3.00	8.00
177 Ersan Ilyasova RC	2.50	6.00
178 Jarrett Jack RC	2.00	5.00
179 Antoine Wright RC	2.00	5.00
180 David Lee RC	3.00	8.00
181 Esteban Batista RC	2.00	5.00
182 Sarunas Jasikevicius RC	2.00	5.00
183 Francisco Garcia RC	2.50	6.00
184 C.J. Miles RC	2.50	6.00
185 Ryan Gomes RC	2.00	5.00
186 Andrew Bynum RC	6.00	15.00
187 Sean May RC	2.00	5.00
188 Jose Calderon RC	2.00	5.00
189 Rashad McCants RC	2.00	5.00
190 Johan Petro RC	2.00	5.00
191 Jason Maxiell RC	2.00	5.00
192 Martell Webster RC	2.00	5.00
193 Nate Robinson RC	2.50	6.00
194 Daniel Ewing RC	2.00	5.00
195 Fabricio Oberto RC	2.00	5.00
196 Travis Diener RC	2.00	5.00
197 Salim Stoudamire RC	2.00	5.00
198 Charlie Villanueva RC	2.50	6.00
199 Orien Greene RC	2.00	5.00
200 Deron Williams RC	5.00	12.00
201 Bracey Wright RC	2.00	5.00
202 Lawrence Roberts RC	2.00	5.00
203 Eddie Basden RC	2.00	5.00
204 Brandon Bass RC	2.50	6.00
205 Martynas Andriuskevicius RC	2.00	5.00
206 Channing Frye RC	2.50	6.00
207 Julius Hodge RC	2.00	5.00
208 Luther Head RC	2.00	5.00
209 Chris Taft RC	2.00	5.00
210 Andrew Bogut RC	3.00	8.00
211 Gerald Green RC	2.50	6.00
212 Joey Graham RC	2.00	5.00
213 Louis Williams RC	3.00	8.00
214 Yaroslav Korolev RC	2.00	5.00
215 Monta Ellis RC	4.00	10.00
216 Christie Brinkley	1.50	4.00
217 Jay-Z	1.50	4.00
218 Shannon Elizabeth	1.50	4.00
219 Carmen Electra	1.50	4.00
220 Jenny McCarthy Cut Out	25.00	60.00
221 Joe Shipp DL RC	1.00	2.50
222 Dwayne Jones DL RC	1.00	2.50
223 Will Conroy DL RC	1.00	2.50
224 Darnell Miller DL RC	1.00	2.50
225 Will Bynum DL RC	1.00	2.50
226 Jamar Smith DL RC	1.00	2.50
227 Daryl Dorsey DL RC	1.00	2.50
228 Tony Bland DL RC	1.00	2.50
229 Hiram Fuller DL RC	1.00	2.50
230 Tyrone Sally DL RC	1.00	2.50
231 Clay Tucker DL RC	1.00	2.50
232 George Leach DL RC	1.00	2.50
233 Marcus Douthit DL RC	1.00	2.50
234 Carlos Hurt DL RC	1.00	2.50
235 Seamus Boxley DL RC	1.00	2.50
236 Ramel Curry DL RC	1.00	2.50
237 Andreas Glyniadakis DL RC	1.00	2.50
238 Kareem Reid DL RC	1.00	2.50
239 Austin Nichols DL RC	1.00	2.50

240 Chris Shumate DL RC 1.00 2.50
241 Brandon Robinson DL RC 1.00 2.50
242 Harvey Thomas DL RC 1.00 2.50
243 Desmon Farmer DL RC 1.00 2.50
244 Marcus Hill DL RC 1.00 2.50
245 Robb Dryden DL RC 1.00 2.50
246 Nate Daniels DL RC 1.00 2.50
247 James Lang DL RC 1.00 2.50
248 Anthony Terrell DL RC 1.00 2.50
249 Jeff Hagen DL RC 1.00 2.50
250 Kevin Owens DL RC 1.00 2.50
251 Myron Allen DL RC 1.00 2.50
252 Ayudeji Akindele DL RC 1.00 2.50
253 T.J. Cummings DL RC 1.00 2.50
254 Mike King DL RC 1.00 2.50
255 Otis George DL RC 1.00 2.50
256 Ezra Williams DL RC 1.00 2.50
257 Anthony Wilkins DL RC 1.00 2.50
258 Scott Merritt DL RC 1.00 2.50
259 Seth Doliboa DL RC 1.00 2.50
260 Anthony Fuqua DL RC 1.00 2.50
261 Malik Moore DL RC 1.00 2.50
262 Randall Orr DL RC 1.00 2.50
263 Ricky Shields DL RC 1.00 2.50
264 John Lucas III DL RC 2.50 6.00
265 Butter Johnson DL RC 1.00 2.50
266 Isiah Victor DL RC 1.00 2.50
267 Roderick Riley DL RC 1.00 2.50
268 Bernard King DL RC 1.00 2.50
269 E.J. Rowland DL RC 1.00 2.50
270 Anthony Grundy DL RC 1.00 2.50
271 Brian Jackson DL RC 1.00 2.50
272 Keith Langford DL RC 1.00 2.50
273 Chuck Hayes DL RC 1.00 2.50
274 Jonathan Moore DL RC 1.00 2.50

2005-06 Topps Chrome Refractors

Randomly inserted in packs, this 274-card set parallels the base Topps Chrome set enhanced with the rainbow holofoil refractor effect sequentially numbered to 999.
*1-165 REF: 1.5X TO 4X BASE HI
*166-274 REF: .75X TO 2X BASE HI
168 Chris Paul 20.00 50.00
200 Deron Williams 12.00 30.00

2005-06 Topps Chrome Refractors Black

Randomly inserted in packs, this 274-card set parallels the base Topps Chrome set enhanced with the rainbow holofoil refractor effect black borders and sequential numbering to 399.
*1-165 REF.BLACK: 2X TO 5X BASE HI
*166-274 REF.BLACK: 1.25X TO 3X BASE HI
40 Kobe Bryant 20.00 50.00
102 LeBron James 20.00 50.00
168 Chris Paul 30.00 80.00
200 Deron Williams 20.00 50.00

2005-06 Topps Chrome Refractors Gold

Randomly inserted in packs, this 274-card set parallels the base Topps Chrome set enhanced with the rainbow holofoil refractor effect gold borders and sequential numbering to 99.
*REF.GOLD: 6X TO 15X BASE HI
*166-274 REF.GOLD: 2.5X TO 6X BASE HI
40 Kobe Bryant 50.00 125.00
102 LeBron James 50.00 125.00
168 Chris Paul 75.00 200.00

2005-06 Topps Chrome X-Fractors

Randomly inserted in packs, this 274-card set parallels the base Topps Chrome set enhanced with the rainbow holofoil x-fractor effect and sequential numbering to 90.
*1-165 X-FRACTORS: 4X TO 10X BASE HI
*166-274 X-FRAC: 2.5X TO 6X BASE HI
168 Chris Paul 60.00 150.00

2005-06 Topps Chrome Autographs

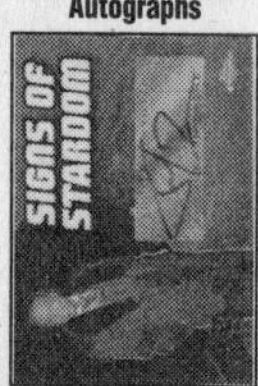

Inserted in packs randomly, this 23-card set actually contains cards from two differently designed sets, Topps Chrome Autographs and Topps Chrome Signs of Stardom. The Autographs cards have orange borders around the player photos with silver autograph stickers and the Signs of Stardom cards are horizontally desinged with a player photo on the left and a silver autograph sticker on the right. Each card is serially numbered, see checklist for details.
*REFRACTORS: .75X TO 2X BASE AU HI
REFRACTOR PRINT RUN 15 TO 25 SETS
UNPRICED REF.GOLD PRINT RUN 3 SETS
UNPRICED REF.SUPER PRINT RUN ONE SET
AI Allen Iverson/162 40.00 100.00
CA Carmelo Anthony/82 20.00 40.00
CB Christie Brinkley/30 40.00 100.00
DE Daniel Ewing/208 6.00 15.00
DG Danny Granger/112 12.50 30.00
EO Emeka Okafor/162 6.00 15.00
GG Gerald Green/208 8.00 20.00
HW Hakim Warrick/162 8.00 20.00
JG Joey Graham/84 6.00 15.00
JH Julius Hodge/84 6.00 15.00
JZ Jay-Z/208 50.00 125.00
LH Luther Head/208 6.00 15.00
OG Orien Greene/162 6.00 15.00
RM Rashad McCants/208 6.00 15.00
SE Shannon Elizabeth/30 60.00 120.00
SL Shaun Livingston/179 6.00 15.00
SM Sean May/208 6.00 15.00
SO Shaquille O'Neal/89 30.00 80.00
ABO Andrew Bogut/162 10.00 25.00
CAE Carmen Electra/30 60.00 120.00
DWA Dwyane Wade/162 40.00 100.00
DWI Deron Williams/162 25.00 60.00
JMC Jenny McCarthy/30 50.00 120.00

2005-06 Topps Chrome Chosen One Relics

Seeded in packs randomly, this 24-card set placed player photos on the right side of the card and a circular swatch of memorabilia in the lower left-hand corner. Every card is on a foil board card stock and serially numbered to 400.
*REFRACTORS: .6X TO 1.5X BASE HI
REF.PRINT RUN 99 SER.#'d SETS
*X-FRACTORS: 1.5X TO 4X BASE HI
X-FRAC.PRINT RUN 25 SER.#'d SETS
UNPRICED REF.GOLD PRINT RUN 9 SETS
UNPRICED SUPERFR.PRINT RUN ONE SET
AB Andrew Bogut 4.00 10.00
AI Allen Iverson 4.00 10.00
CA Carmelo Anthony 5.00 12.00
CB Chauncey Billups 2.50 6.00
CF Channing Frye 3.00 8.00
CP Chris Paul 10.00 25.00
DH Dwight Howard 5.00 12.00
DL David Lee 4.00 10.00
DN Dirk Nowitzki 4.00 10.00
DW Deron Williams 6.00 15.00
EB Elton Brand 2.50 6.00
EO Emeka Okafor 2.50 6.00
GG Gerald Green 3.00 8.00
HW Hakim Warrick 3.00 8.00
JM Jenny McCarthy 6.00 15.00
JO Jermaine O'Neal 2.50 6.00
JZ Jay-Z 6.00 15.00
PG Pau Gasol 2.50 6.00
RF Raymond Felton 4.00 10.00
SO Shaquille O'Neal 5.00 12.00
TD Tim Duncan 4.00 10.00
YM Yao Ming 3.00 8.00
CBR Christie Brinkley 6.00 15.00
DWA Dwyane Wade 6.00 15.00

2005-06 Topps Chrome Hardwood Heroics

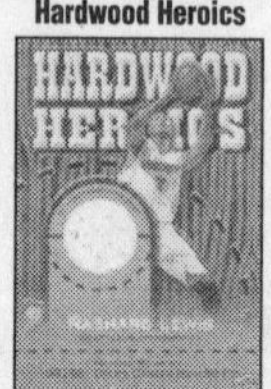

Inserted randomly in packs, this 19-card set features a gray and tan background, player photos and a circular swatch of memorabilia. Each card is serially numbered to 400.
*REFRACTORS: .6X TO 1.5X BASE HI
REF.PRINT RUN 99 SER.#'d SETS
*X-FRACTORS: 1.5X TO 4X BASE HI
X-FRAC.PRINT RUN 25 SER.#'d SETS
UNPRICED REF.GOLD PRINT RUN 9 SETS
UNPRICED REF.SUPER PRINT RUN ONE SET
AS Amare Stoudemire 2.50 6.00
BG Ben Gordon 2.50 6.00
BW Ben Wallace 2.50 6.00
CB Chauncey Billups 2.50 6.00
DW Dwyane Wade 6.00 15.00
EO Emeka Okafor 2.50 6.00
GH Grant Hill 3.00 8.00
JK Jason Kidd 4.00 10.00
JO Jermaine O'Neal 2.50 6.00
KB Kobe Bryant 10.00 25.00
LH Larry Hughes 2.00 5.00
MB Mike Bibby 2.00 5.00
RA Ray Allen 2.50 6.00
RH Robert Horry 4.00 10.00
RL Rashard Lewis 2.50 6.00
SN Steve Nash 3.00 8.00
TD Tim Duncan 4.00 10.00
TM Tracy McGrady 3.00 8.00
VC Vince Carter 4.00 10.00

2005-06 Topps Chrome Premium Performers

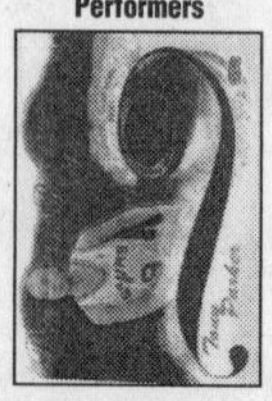

Randomly seeded in packs, this 20-card set is horizontally designed with a player photo on the left and an oval swatch of memorabilia in the lower right hand corner. The background design contains color elements of white, brown, blue and yellow and cards are serially numbered to 400.
*REFRACTORS: .6X TO 1.5X BASE HI
REFRACTOR PRINT RUN 99 SER.#'d SETS
*X-FRACTORS: 1.5X TO 4X BASE HI
X-FRAC.PRINT RUN 25 SER.#'d SETS
UNPRICED REF.GOLD PRINT RUN 9 SETS
UNPRICED REF.SUPER PRINT RUN ONE SET
AB Andrew Bogut 4.00 10.00
CB Chris Bosh 2.50 6.00
CW Chris Webber 2.50 6.00
DN Dirk Nowitzki 4.00 10.00
EB Elton Brand 2.50 6.00
GG Gerald Green 3.00 8.00
JK Jason Kidd 4.00 10.00
JZ Jay-Z 10.00 25.00
KG Kevin Garnett 5.00 12.00
MB Mike Bibby 2.50 6.00
PG Pau Gasol 2.50 6.00
PP Paul Pierce 3.00 8.00
RM Rashad McCants 2.50 6.00
SM Shawn Marion 2.50 6.00
SN Steve Nash 3.00 8.00
SO Shaquille O'Neal 5.00 12.00
ST Sebastian Telfair 2.00 5.00
TD Tim Duncan 4.00 10.00
TM Tracy McGrady 3.00 8.00
TP Tony Parker 2.50 6.00

2005-06 Topps Chrome Second Unit

Randomly inserted in packs, this 25-card set places a player photo on the left, a swatch of memorabilia in the center and a tan-scale portrait photo of the player on the right of a horizontal design. Each card is serially numbered to 400.
*REFRACTORS: .5X TO 1.25X BASE HI
REFRACTOR PRINT RUN 99 SER.#'d SETS
*X-FRACTORS: 1.25X TO 3X BASE HI
X-FRAC.PRINT RUN 25 SER.#'d SETS
UNPRICED REF.GOLD PRINT RUN 9 SETS
UNPRICED REF.SUPER PRINT RUN ONE SET
AJ Al Jefferson 3.00 8.00
AV Anderson Varejao 2.50 6.00
BG Ben Gordon 3.00 8.00
BU Beno Udrih 2.00 5.00
CD Carlos Delfino 2.00 5.00
DF Derek Fisher 2.50 6.00
DH Devin Harris 3.00 8.00
DW Dorell Wright 2.00 5.00
FG Francisco Garcia 4.00 10.00
FJ Fred Jones 2.00 5.00
JH Jarvis Hayes 2.00 5.00
JJ Jim Jackson 2.00 5.00
JK Jason Kapono 2.00 5.00
KK Kyle Korver 2.50 6.00
LW Luke Walton 2.00 5.00
MD Marquis Daniels 2.00 5.00
MJ Marko Jaric 2.00 5.00
MO Mehmet Okur 2.00 5.00
NC Nick Collison 2.00 5.00
RA Rafer Alston 2.00 5.00
SM Sean May 3.00 8.00
WS Wayne Simien 3.00 8.00
JHO Josh Howard 3.00 8.00
JOJ Joe Johnson 3.00 8.00
RAR Rafael Araujo 2.00 5.00

2006-07 Topps Chrome

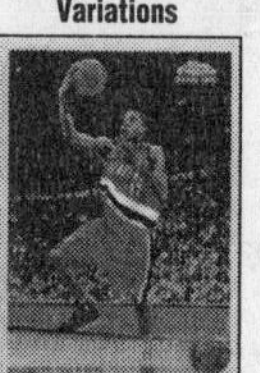

Released in early February 2007, Topps Chrome parallels the design of the base Topps set enhanced with holo-foil card stock. Card numbers 1-160 feature veteran players and retired NBA legends and card numbers 161-210 feature rookie players inserted at the rate of one in two packs. Please note that an alternate version of the rookies using the 1996-97 Topps Chrome card design was also produced for insertion and these cards are not considered the player's actual rookie cards. Topps Chrome is packaged in 24-pack boxes of four cards each and carried an initial suggested retail price of $3.00.
COMPLETE SET (210) 60.00 120.00
COMP.SET w/o SP's (160) 20.00 50.00
UNPRICED SUPERFR.PRINT RUN ONE SET
1 Elton Brand .40 1.00
2 Tim Duncan .60 1.50
3 Chris Paul .75 2.00
4 Joe Johnson .40 1.00
5 Chauncey Billups .40 1.00
6 Andres Nocioni .25 .60
7 Al Jefferson .40 1.00
8 Gerald Wallace .40 1.00
9 Jason Terry .30 .75
10 Dwight Howard .60 1.50
11 Larry Hughes .30 .75
12 Vince Carter .50 1.25
13 Mike Bibby .40 1.00
14 Ben Gordon .40 1.00
15 Desmond Mason .25 .60
16 Raymond Felton .50 1.25
17 Paul Pierce .50 1.25
18 Jason Richardson .40 1.00
19 Rasheed Wallace .40 1.00
20 Leandro Barbosa .30 .75
21 Deron Williams .60 1.50
22 Kwame Brown .25 .60
23 Josh Childress .30 .75
24 Shawn Marion .40 1.00
25 Shaquille O'Neal .75 2.00
26 Ray Allen .40 1.00
27 Cuttino Mobley .30 .75
28 Dirk Nowitzki .60 1.50
29 Jermaine O'Neal .40 1.00
30 Marvin Williams .40 1.00
31 Eddy Curry .30 .75
32 Andrei Kirilenko .30 .75
33 Baron Davis .40 1.00
34 Tracy McGrady .50 1.25
35 Chris Kaman .30 .75
36 Luol Deng .40 1.00
37 Emeka Okafor .40 1.00
38 Lamar Odom .40 1.00
39 Alonzo Mourning .50 1.25
40 Marcus Camby .30 .75
41 Ike Diogu .25 .60
42 Josh Smith .40 1.00
43 Nate Robinson .40 1.00
44 Yao Ming .50 1.25
45 Darko Milicic .25 .60
46 Smush Parker .25 .60
47 Mike Dunleavy .30 .75
48 Ricky Davis .30 .75
49 Michael Finley .40 1.00
50 Nenad Krstic .25 .60
51 Earl Boykins .25 .60
52 Richard Hamilton .30 .75
53 Hakim Warrick .30 .75
54 Corey Maggette .30 .75
55 Kenyon Martin .40 1.00
56 Jason Kidd .60 1.50
57 Dwyane Wade 1.00 2.50
58 Josh Howard .30 .75
59 Richard Jefferson .40 1.00
60 Steve Nash .50 1.25
61 Drew Gooden .30 .75
62 Kevin Garnett .75 2.00
63 Delonte West .30 .75
64 Channing Frye .30 .75
65 Andre Iguodala .40 1.00
66 Pau Gasol .40 1.00
67 LeBron James 2.00 5.00
68 Sam Cassell .40 1.00
69 Mehmet Okur .25 .60
70 Bruce Bowen .25 .60
71 Kirk Hinrich .40 1.00
72 Chris Wilcox .25 .60
73 Brad Miller .40 1.00
74 Chris Bosh .40 1.00
75 Jamal Crawford .30 .75
76 Mike Miller .40 1.00
77 Danny Granger .40 1.00
78 Manu Ginobili .40 1.00
79 Udonis Haslem .30 .75
80 Gilbert Arenas .40 1.00
81 Tony Parker .40 1.00
82 Carlos Boozer .40 1.00
83 Rashard Lewis .40 1.00
84 Boris Diaw .30 .75
85 Shaun Livingston .25 .60
86 Shareef Abdur-Rahim .30 .75
87 Devin Harris .40 1.00
88 Brevin Knight .25 .60
89 Troy Murphy .25 .60
90 Antawn Jamison .40 1.00
91 Stephen Jackson .30 .75
92 Chris Webber .40 1.00
93 Luke Ridnour .30 .75
94 Joel Przybilla .25 .60
95 David West .40 1.00
96 Caron Butler .40 1.00
97 Andre Miller .30 .75
98 Ron Artest .40 1.00
99 Samuel Dalembert .25 .60
100 Tayshaun Prince .40 1.00
101 Jameer Nelson .30 .75
102 Zach Randolph .30 .75
103 Stephon Marbury .30 .75
104 Steve Francis .40 1.00
105 Kevin Martin .40 1.00
106 Carmelo Anthony .50 1.25
107 Morris Peterson .25 .60
108 Allen Iverson .50 1.25
109 Antoine Walker .25 .60
110 Jarrett Jack .25 .60
111 Ben Wallace .40 1.00
112 Vladimir Radmanovic .25 .60
113 Andrew Bogut .40 1.00
114 Nazr Mohammed .25 .60
115 Kirk Snyder .25 .60
116 Marquis Daniels .25 .60
117 T.J. Ford .30 .75
118 Stromile Swift .25 .60
119 Lorenzen Wright .25 .60
120 Mike James .25 .60
121 Amare Stoudemire .40 1.00
122 Raef LaFrentz .25 .60
123 Adrian Griffin .25 .60
124 Maurice Evans .25 .60
125 David Wesley .25 .60
126 J.R. Smith .40 1.00
127 Ronald Murray .25 .60
128 Shane Battier .40 1.00
129 Kobe Bryant 2.00 5.00
130 Jamaal Magloire .25 .60
131 Charlie Villanueva .40 1.00
132 Tyson Chandler .30 .75
133 Eddie House .30 .75
134 Marcus Banks .25 .60
135 Derek Fisher .30 .75
136 Bobby Simmons .25 .60
137 Al Harrington .25 .60
138 Speedy Claxton .25 .60
139 Viktor Khryapa .25 .60
140 Sean May .25 .60
141 Devean George .25 .60
142 Joe Smith .30 .75
143 Peja Stojakovic .40 1.00
144 DeShawn Stevenson .25 .60
145 Fred Jones .25 .60
146 P.J. Brown .25 .60
147 Sebastian Telfair .25 .60
148 Bonzi Wells .25 .60
149 Michael Redd .40 1.00
150 Jared Jeffries .25 .60
151 Larry Bird 1.25 3.00
152 Dominique Wilkins .50 1.25
153 Isiah Thomas .40 1.00
154 Wilt Chamberlain .75 2.00
155 Bill Walton .40 1.00
156 Oscar Robertson .40 1.00
157 Walt Frazier .40 1.00
158 Elgin Baylor .40 1.00
159 George Gervin .40 1.00
160 Moses Malone .40 1.00
161 Solomon Jones RC 1.25 3.00
162 Kyle Lowry RC 1.50 4.00
163 Maurice Ager RC 1.25 3.00
164 Patrick O'Bryant RC 1.25 3.00
165 Marcus Vinicius RC 1.25 3.00
166 Jorge Garbajosa RC 1.25 3.00
167 Josh Boone RC 1.25 3.00
168 Mardy Collins RC 1.25 3.00
169 Rodney Carney RC 1.25 3.00
170 P.J. Tucker RC 1.25 3.00
171 Shelden Williams RC 1.25 3.00
172 Ryan Hollins RC 1.25 3.00
173 Pops Mensah-Bonsu RC 1.25 3.00
174 Steve Novak RC 1.25 3.00
175 Paul Davis RC 1.25 3.00
176 David Noel RC 1.25 3.00
177 Marcus Williams RC 1.25 3.00
178 Renaldo Balkman RC 1.25 3.00
179 Quincy Douby RC 1.25 3.00
180 Andrea Bargnani RC 2.00 5.00
181 Chris Quinn RC 1.25 3.00
182 Thabo Sefolosha RC 1.50 4.00
183 LaMarcus Aldridge RC 3.00 8.00
184 Rudy Gay RC 2.00 5.00
185 Jordan Farmar RC 2.00 5.00
186 Damir Markota RC 1.25 3.00
187 Mile Ilic RC 1.25 3.00
188 James Augustine RC 1.25 3.00
189 Tyrus Thomas RC 1.50 4.00
190 Brandon Roy RC 3.00 8.00
191 Allan Ray RC 1.25 3.00
192 Shannon Brown RC 2.00 5.00
193 Will Blalock RC 1.25 3.00
194 James White RC 1.25 3.00
195 Adam Morrison RC 1.50 4.00
196 Craig Smith RC 1.25 3.00
197 Cedric Simmons RC 1.25 3.00
198 J.J. Redick RC 1.50 4.00
199 Sergio Rodriguez RC 1.25 3.00
200 Ronnie Brewer RC 1.50 4.00
201 Rajon Rondo RC 6.00 15.00
202 Daniel Gibson RC 1.50 4.00
203 Hassan Adams RC 1.25 3.00
204 Shawne Williams RC 1.25 3.00
205 Alexander Johnson RC 1.25 3.00
206 Randy Foye RC 1.50 4.00
207 Hilton Armstrong RC 1.25 3.00
208 Bobby Jones RC 1.25 3.00
209 Saer Sene RC 1.25 3.00
210 Dee Brown RC 1.25 3.00

2006-07 Topps Chrome Refractors

*REF 1-160: 1.25X TO 3X BASE HI
1-160 STATED ODDS 1:4
*REF 161-210: 1.5X TO 4X BASE HI
161-210 REF PRINT RUN 199 SETS
67 LeBron James 10.00 25.00
129 Kobe Bryant 10.00 20.00

2006-07 Topps Chrome Refractors Black

*1-160 REF.BLACK: 5X TO 12X BASE HI
*161-210 REF.BLACK: 2.5X TO 6X BASE HI
REF.BLACK PRINT RUN 99 SER.#'d SETS

2006-07 Topps Chrome Refractors Gold

*1-160 REF.GOLD: 12X TO 30X BASE HI
*161-210 REF.GOLD: 5X TO 12X BASE HI
REF.GOLD PRINT RUN 25 SER.#'d SETS
183 LaMarcus Aldridge 50.00 120.00
190 Brandon Roy 60.00 150.00

2006-07 Topps Chrome 1996-97 Variations

COMPLETE SET (10) 10.00 25.00
STATED ODDS 1:4
*REFRACTORS: 1.25X TO 3X BASE HI
REF.PRINT RUN 199 SER.#'d SETS
*REF.BLACK: 2.5X TO 6X BASE HI
REF.BLACK PRINT RUN 99 SER.#'d SETS
*REF.GOLD: 4X TO 10X BASE HI
REF.GOLD PRINT RUN 25 SER.#'d SETS
UNPRICED SUPERFR.PRINT RUN ONE SET
UNPRICED X-FRAC PRINT RUN 10 SETS
171 Shelden Williams 1.00 2.50
177 Marcus Williams 1.00 2.50
180 Andrea Bargnani 1.50 4.00
183 LaMarcus Aldridge 2.50 6.00
184 Rudy Gay 1.50 4.00
189 Tyrus Thomas 1.25 3.00
190 Brandon Roy 2.50 6.00
195 Adam Morrison 1.25 3.00
198 J.J. Redick 1.25 3.00
200 Ronnie Brewer 1.25 3.00

2006-07 Topps Chrome Autographs Refractors Black

GROUP A ODDS 1:2575, GROUP B 1:590
GROUP C ODDS 1:1191
RC GROUP A ODDS 1:1295, GROUP B 1:1030
RC GROUP C ODDS 1:1192, GROUP D 1:161
RC GROUP E ODDS 1:113, GROUP F 1:73
*REF.GOLD: .75X TO 2X BASE HI
REF.GOLD PRINT RUN 25 SER.#'d SETS
UNPRICED SUPERFR.PRINT RUN ONE SET
UNPRICED X-FRAC PRINT RUN 10 SETS
12 Vince Carter B 20.00 50.00
14 Ben Gordon B 8.00 20.00
25 Shaquille O'Neal A 40.00 100.00
36 Emeka Okafor A 10.00 25.00
46 Smush Parker C 5.00 12.00
57 Dwyane Wade A 60.00 120.00
74 Chris Bosh B 15.00 40.00
108 Allen Iverson A 30.00 80.00
151 Larry Bird A 75.00 150.00
153 Isiah Thomas B 12.50 30.00
161 Solomon Jones D 5.00 12.00
162 Kyle Lowry C 6.00 15.00
163 Maurice Ager D 5.00 12.00
164 Patrick O'Bryant B 5.00 12.00
165 Marcus Vinicius F 5.00 12.00
166 Jorge Garbajosa C 5.00 12.00
167 Josh Boone C 5.00 12.00
168 Mardy Collins C 5.00 12.00
169 Rodney Carney C 5.00 12.00
170 P.J. Tucker D 5.00 12.00
171 Shelden Williams A 5.00 12.00
172 Ryan Hollins E 5.00 12.00
173 Pops Mensah-Bonsu F 5.00 12.00
174 Steve Novak E 5.00 12.00
175 Paul Davis D 5.00 12.00
176 David Noel E 5.00 12.00
177 Marcus Williams A 5.00 12.00
178 Renaldo Balkman B 5.00 12.00
179 Quincy Douby D 5.00 12.00
180 Andrea Bargnani A 30.00 80.00
181 Chris Quinn F 5.00 12.00
182 Thabo Sefolosha E 8.00 20.00
185 Jordan Farmar C 5.00 12.00
186 Damir Markota F 5.00 12.00
187 Mile Ilic F 5.00 12.00
188 James Augustine E 5.00 12.00
191 Allan Ray F 5.00 12.00
192 Shannon Brown C 8.00 20.00
193 Will Blalock F 5.00 12.00
194 James White F 5.00 12.00
195 Adam Morrison A 6.00 15.00
196 Craig Smith E 5.00 12.00
197 Cedric Simmons C 5.00 12.00
198 J.J. Redick A 15.00 40.00
199 Sergio Rodriguez C 5.00 12.00
200 Ronnie Brewer B 6.00 15.00
201 Rajon Rondo C 30.00 80.00
202 Daniel Gibson F 6.00 15.00
203 Hassan Adams F 5.00 12.00
204 Shawne Williams E 5.00 12.00
205 Alexander Johnson F 5.00 12.00
206 Randy Foye B 6.00 15.00
207 Hilton Armstrong B 5.00 12.00
208 Bobby Jones E 5.00 12.00
209 Saer Sene D 5.00 12.00
210 Dee Brown D 5.00 12.00

2007-08 Topps Chrome

This 160-card set was released in January, 2008. The set was issued into the hobby in four-card packs, with a $3 SRP, which came 24 packs to a box and 12 boxes to a case. Cards numbered 1-110 feature a mix of active players and retired greats and cards numbered 101-160 feature 2007-08 NBA rookies.
COMPLETE SET (160) 50.00 100.00
UNPRICED SUPFRACTOR PRINT RUN ONE SET
1 Amare Stoudemire .50 1.25
2 Joe Johnson .50 1.25
3 Dwyane Wade 1.25 3.00
4 Chris Bosh .50 1.25
5 Jason Kidd .50 1.25
6 Bill Russell .75 2.00
7 Jermaine O'Neal .50 1.25
8 Mike Miller .50 1.25
9 Ray Allen .50 1.25
10 Elton Brand .50 1.25
11 Yao Ming .60 1.50
12 Al Harrington .40 1.00
13 Steve Nash .60 1.50
14 Dwight Howard .75 2.00
15 Carmelo Anthony .60 1.50
16 Pau Gasol .50 1.25
17 Chauncey Billups .50 1.25
18 Bob Pettit .60 1.50
19 Jason Kapono .30 .75
20 Kevin Garnett 1.00 2.50
21 Tim Duncan .75 2.00
22 Michael Redd .50 1.25
23 LeBron James 2.50 6.00
24 Kobe Bryant 2.50 6.00
25 Eddy Curry .30 .75
26 Gerald Green .40 1.00
27 Andrew Bogut .50 1.25
28 Vince Carter .60 1.50
29 Corey Maggette .40 1.00
30 Morris Peterson .30 .75
31 Shawn Marion .50 1.25
32 Shaquille O'Neal 1.00 2.50
33 Allen Iverson .60 1.50
34 Paul Pierce .60 1.50
35 Bill Sharman .50 1.25
36 Tony Parker .60 1.50
37 Mike Bibby .50 1.25
38 Andrea Bargnani .60 1.50
39 Luol Deng .60 1.50
40 Chris Paul 1.00 2.50
41 Dirk Nowitzki .60 1.50
42 David Lee .40 1.00
43 Vern Mikkelsen .50 1.25
44 Darko Milicic .30 .75
45 Al Jefferson .50 1.25
46 Bob Cousy .75 2.00
47 Andrei Kirilenko .50 1.25
48 Anfernee Hardaway 1.25 3.00
49 Chris Wilcox .30 .75
50 Dolph Schayes .50 1.25
51 Zach Randolph .50 1.25
52 Grant Hill .60 1.50
53 Jim Loscutoff .50 1.25
54 Leandro Barbosa .50 1.25
55 Smush Parker .30 .75
56 Sam Jones .60 1.50
57 Manu Ginobili .60 1.50
58 Jason Richardson .50 1.25
59 Jason Terry .50 1.25
60 Gerald Wallace .50 1.25
61 Richard Hamilton .40 1.00
62 Cliff Hagan .50 1.25
63 Tom Heinsohn .50 1.25
64 Carlos Boozer .40 1.00
65 Rashard Lewis .50 1.25
66 Josh Childress .30 .75
67 Channing Frye .40 1.00
68 Mike James .30 .75
69 Kurt Thomas .30 .75
70 Mikki Moore .30 .75
71 Baron Davis .50 1.25
72 Reggie Theus .50 1.25
73 Jameer Nelson .30 .75
74 Caron Butler .50 1.25
75 Jamaal Magloire .30 .75
76 Darryl Dawkins .50 1.25
77 Ben Gordon .60 1.50
78 Andrew Bynum .60 1.50
79 Oscar Robertson .50 1.25
80 Josh Smith .50 1.25
81 Spud Webb .60 1.50
82 Chris Mullin .60 1.50
83 Raymond Felton .60 1.50
84 Sebastian Telfair .30 .75
85 Clyde Drexler .60 1.50
86 Jarrett Jack .30 .75
87 Anderson Varejao .30 .75
88 Ryan Gomes .30 .75
89 Bill Walton .50 1.25
90 Marcus Camby .30 .75
91 Kirk Hinrich .50 1.25
92 David Robinson .75 2.0
93 Dennis Rodman .75 2.0
94 Dominique Wilkins .60 1.5
95 Richard Jefferson .50 1.2
96 Isiah Thomas .50 1.2
97 Josh Howard .40 1.0
98 John Stockton .75 2.0
99 Deron Williams .75 2.0
100 Gilbert Arenas .50 1.2
101 Tracy McGrady .50 1.2
102 Steve Blake .30 .7
103 Ben Wallace .50 1.2
104 Kevin Martin .50 1.2
105 Larry Bird 1.50 4.0
106 Magic Johnson 1.25 3.0
107 Brandon Roy .60 1.5
108 Desmond Mason .30 .7
109 Rick Barry .50 1.2
110 Andre Iguodala .50 1.2
111 Mike Conley Jr. RC 2.00 5.0
112 Glen Davis RC 2.00 5.0
113 Julian Wright RC 2.00 5.0
114 Rodney Stuckey RC 2.00 5.0
115 Chris Richard RC 1.25 3.0
116 Coby Karl RC 1.25 3.0
117 Thaddeus Young RC 1.50 4.0
118 Spencer Hawes RC 1.25 3.0
119 Jermareo Davidson RC 1.25 3.0
120 Daequan Cook RC 1.25 3.0
121 Josh McRoberts RC 1.25 3.0
122 Aaron Gray RC 1.25 3.0
123 Wilson Chandler RC 2.00 5.0
124 Herbert Hill RC 1.25 3.0
125 Stephane Lasme RC 1.25 3.0
126 Cheikh Samb RC 1.25 3.0
127 Adam Haluska RC 1.25 3.0
128 Al Thornton RC 1.25 3.0
129 Corey Brewer RC 1.50 4.0
130 Ramon Sessions RC 2.00 5.0
131 Kevin Durant RC 20.00 50.0
132 Alando Tucker RC 1.25 3.0
133 Marco Belinelli RC 1.25 3.0
134 Nick Fazekas RC 1.25 3.0
135 Yi Jianlian RC 2.00 5.0
136 Luis Scola RC 2.00 5.0
137 Jared Dudley RC 1.25 3.0
138 Taurean Green RC 1.25 3.0
139 Kosta Perovic RC 1.25 3.0
140 Kyrylo Fesenko RC 1.25 3.0
141 JamesOn Curry RC 1.25 3.0
142 D.J. Strawberry RC 1.25 3.0
143 Javaris Crittenton RC 1.25 3.0
144 Acie Law RC 1.25 3.0
145 Nick Young RC 2.00 5.0
146 Joakim Noah RC 3.00 8.0
147 Dominic McGuire RC 1.25 3.0
148 Arron Afflalo RC 1.50 4.0
149 Gabe Pruitt RC 1.25 3.0
150 Carl Landry RC 1.25 3.0
151 Jeff Green RC 1.50 4.0
152 Greg Oden RC 1.50 4.0
153 Jason Smith RC 1.25 3.0
154 Morris Almond RC 1.25 3.0
155 Juan Carlos Navarro RC 1.25 3.0
156 Brandon Wallace RC 1.25 3.0
157 Aaron Brooks RC 1.25 3.0
158 Brandan Wright RC 1.25 3.0
159 Sean Williams RC 1.25 3.0
160 Al Horford RC 1.50 4.0

2007-08 Topps Chrome Refractors

1-110 REF.PRINT RUN 999 SER.#'d SETS
111-160 REF.PRINT RUN 1499 SER.#'d SETS
23 LeBron James 12.00 30.00
24 Kobe Bryant 12.00 30.00
131 Kevin Durant 100.00 175.00

2007-08 Topps Chrome Refractors Orange

*1-110 RC REF.ORANGE: 1.5X TO 4X BASE HI
*111-160 RC REF.ORNG: 1.5X TO 4X BASE HI
PRINT RUN 199 SER.#'d SETS
23 LeBron James 15.00 40.00
24 Kobe Bryant 15.00 40.00
131 Kevin Durant 150.00 300.00

2007-08 Topps Chrome Refractors White

*1-110 REF.WHITE: 2X TO 5X BASE HI
*111-160 RC REF.WHT: 2X TO 5X BASE HI
REF.WHITE PRINT RUN 99 SER.#'d SETS
3 Dwyane Wade 8.00 20.00
23 LeBron James 20.00 50.00
24 Kobe Bryant 20.00 50.00
48 Anfernee Hardaway 8.00 20.00
131 Kevin Durant 250.00 450.00

2007-08 Topps Chrome X-Fractors

*1-110 X-FRAC: 4X TO 10X BASE HI
*111-160 RC X-FRAC: 2.5X TO 6X BASE HI
X-FRAC PRINT RUN 50 SER.#'d SETS
23 LeBron James 40.00 100.00
24 Kobe Bryant 40.00 100.00
131 Kevin Durant 350.00 600.00

2007-08 Topps Chrome 1957-58 Variations

COMPLETE SET (50) 40.00 75.00
APPROXIMATE ODDS ONE PER PACK
*X-FRACTORS: 4X TO 10X BASE HI
X-FRAC.PRINT RUN 50 SER.#'d SETS
UNPRICED SUPERFR.PRINT RUN ONE SET
3 Dwyane Wade 1.50 4.00
6 Bill Russell 1.00 2.50
9 Ray Allen .60 1.50
11 Yao Ming .75 2.00
13 Steve Nash .75 2.00
15 Carmelo Anthony .75 2.00
18 Bob Pettit .75 2.00
20 Kevin Garnett 1.25 3.00
21 Tim Duncan 1.00 2.50
23 LeBron James 3.00 8.00
24 Kobe Bryant 3.00 8.00
28 Vince Carter .75 2.00

Shaquille O'Neal 1.25 3.00
Allen Iverson .75 2.00
5 Bill Sharman .60 1.50
Tony Parker .60 1.50
Chris Paul 1.25 3.00
1 Dirk Nowitzki .75 2.00
2 David Lee .50 1.25
Vern Mikkelsen .60 1.50
Bob Cousy 1.00 2.50
Dolph Schayes .60 1.50
Jim Loscutoff .60 1.50
Leandro Barbosa .50 1.25
6 Sam Jones .75 2.00
8 Jason Richardson .60 1.50
0 Gerald Wallace .60 1.50
2 Cliff Hagan .60 1.50
Tom Heinsohn .60 1.50
Carlos Boozer .60 1.50
1 Baron Davis .60 1.50
2 Reggie Theus .60 1.50
6 Darryl Dawkins .60 1.50
9 Oscar Robertson .60 1.50
1 Spud Webb .60 1.50
2 Chris Mullin .60 1.50
5 Clyde Drexler .75 2.00
9 Bill Walton .60 1.50
0 Marcus Camby .40 1.00
2 David Robinson 1.00 2.50
3 Dennis Rodman 1.00 2.50
4 Dominique Wilkins .75 2.00
6 Isiah Thomas .60 1.50
8 John Stockton 1.00 2.50
9 Deron Williams 1.00 2.50
00 Gilbert Arenas .60 1.50
03 Ben Wallace .60 1.50
05 Larry Bird 2.00 5.00
06 Magic Johnson 1.50 4.00
09 Rick Barry .60 1.50

2007-08 Topps Chrome 1957-58 Variations Refractors

REFRACTORS: .75X TO 2X BASE HI
PRINT RUN 999 SER.#'d SETS
3 LeBron James 8.00 20.00
4 Kobe Bryant 8.00 20.00

2007-08 Topps Chrome 1957-58 Variations Refractors Orange

REF.ORANGE: 1.25X TO 3X BASE HI
PRINT RUN 199 SER.#'d SETS
3 LeBron James 12.00 30.00
4 Kobe Bryant 12.00 30.00

2007-08 Topps Chrome 1957-58 Variations Refractors White

REF.WHITE: 1.5X TO 4X BASE HI
PRINT RUN 99 SER.#'d SETS
3 LeBron James 20.00 50.00
4 Kobe Bryant 20.00 50.00

2007-08 Topps Chrome 1957-58 Variations Autographs

PRINT RUN 29 TO 99 SER.#'d SETS
REF.ORANGE: .5X TO 1.25X BASE HI
*REF.ORANGE SP's: SAME VALUE
PRINT RUN 25 SER.#'d SETS
UNPRICED REF.WHITE PRINT RUN 10 SETS
UNPRICED X-FRAC.PRINT RUN 5 SETS
UNPRICED SUPERFR.PRINT RUN ONE SET
EXCH.EXPIRATION DATE 1/31/10
3 Dwyane Wade/29 40.00 100.00
6 Bill Russell/29 100.00 200.00
9 Ray Allen/99 15.00 30.00
28 Vince Carter/99 15.00 40.00
32 Shaquille O'Neal/29 50.00 100.00
42 David Lee/99 6.00 15.00
54 Leandro Barbosa/99 6.00 15.00
60 Gerald Wallace/99 6.00 15.00
64 Carlos Boozer/99 6.00 15.00
71 Baron Davis/99 6.00 15.00
81 Spud Webb/99 8.00 20.00
89 Bill Walton/29 25.00 50.00
92 David Robinson/29 50.00 100.00
93 Dennis Rodman/29 25.00 50.00
94 Dominique Wilkins/99 15.00 30.00
96 Isiah Thomas/29 20.00 40.00
98 John Stockton/29 40.00 80.00
99 Deron Williams/99 20.00 40.00
105 Larry Bird/29 40.00 100.00
109 Rick Barry/99 12.50 30.00

2007-08 Topps Chrome Rookie Autographs

PRINT RUN 149 TO 999 SER.#'d SETS
*REF.ORANGE: .75X TO 2X BASE HI
REF.ORANGE PRINT RUN 25 SER.#'d SETS
UNPRICED REF.WHITE PRINT RUN 10 SETS
UNPRICED X-FRAC PRINT RUN 5 SETS
UNPRICED SUPERFR.PRINT RUN ONE SET
EXCH.EXPIRATION DATE 1/31/10
112 Glen Davis/999 8.00 20.00
114 Rodney Stuckey/999 8.00 20.00
117 Thaddeus Young/149 15.00 30.00
118 Spencer Hawes/149 5.00 12.00
119 Jermareo Davidson/999 5.00 12.00
120 Daequan Cook/539 5.00 12.00
121 Josh McRoberts/999 5.00 12.00
122 Aaron Gray/539 5.00 12.00
123 Wilson Chandler/539 8.00 20.00
124 Herbert Hill/999 5.00 12.00
125 Stephane Lasme/999 5.00 12.00
127 Adam Haluska/999 5.00 12.00
128 Al Thornton/149 5.00 12.00
132 Alando Tucker/539 5.00 12.00
133 Marco Belinelli/539 5.00 12.00
134 Nick Fazekas/999 5.00 12.00
135 Yi Jianlian/149 12.50 30.00
137 Jared Dudley/539 5.00 12.00
138 Taurean Green/999 5.00 12.00
141 JamesOn Curry/999 5.00 12.00
142 D.J. Strawberry/999 5.00 12.00
143 Javaris Crittenton/999 5.00 12.00
144 Acie Law/149 5.00 12.00
145 Nick Young/149 10.00 25.00
147 Dominic McGuire/999 5.00 12.00
148 Arron Afflalo/539 6.00 15.00
149 Gabe Pruitt/999 5.00 12.00
150 Carl Landry/999 5.00 12.00
152 Greg Oden/149 30.00 80.00
153 Jason Smith/149 5.00 12.00
154 Morris Almond/539 5.00 12.00
155 Juan Carlos Navarro/539 5.00 12.00
157 Aaron Brooks/999 5.00 12.00
158 Brandan Wright/999 5.00 12.00
159 Sean Williams/539 5.00 12.00

2008-09 Topps Chrome

This set was released on December 17, 2008. The base set consists of 255 cards. Cards 1-180 feature veterans. and cards 181-220 are rookies.
COMPLETE SET (255) 40.00 80.00
UNPRICED PRESS PLATE PRINT RUN ONE SET
UNPRICED SUPERFR.PRINT RUN ONE SET
1 Chris Paul .75 2.00
2 Joe Johnson .50 1.25
3 Allen Iverson .60 1.50
4 Luis Scola .40 1.00
5 Kevin Garnett 1.00 2.50
6 Andrew Bogut .50 1.25
7 Ben Gordon .50 1.25
8 Carlos Boozer .50 1.25
9 Tony Parker .50 1.25
10 Gilbert Arenas .50 1.25
11 Yao Ming .60 1.50
12 Dwight Howard 1.00 2.50
13 Steve Nash .50 1.25
14 Daequan Cook .30 .75
15 Carmelo Anthony .60 1.50
16 Pau Gasol .50 1.25
17 Mike Dunleavy .40 1.00
18 Jason Maxiell .30 .75
19 Al Thornton .40 1.00
20 Ray Allen .50 1.25
21 Tim Duncan .75 2.00
22 Michael Redd .50 1.25
23 LeBron James 2.50 6.00
24 Kobe Bryant 2.50 6.00
25 Al Jefferson .50 1.25
26 Raymond Felton .40 1.00
27 LaMarcus Aldridge .50 1.25
28 Jose Calderon .40 1.00
29 Andris Biedrins .30 .75
30 Rasheed Wallace .50 1.25
31 Shawn Marion .50 1.25
32 Shaquille O'Neal 1.00 2.50
33 Mike Miller .50 1.25
34 Paul Pierce .60 1.50
35 Brad Miller .40 1.00
36 Richard Jefferson .50 1.25
37 DeShawn Stevenson .30 .75
38 Zach Randolph .40 1.00
39 Daniel Gibson .50 1.25
40 Nazr Mohammed .30 .75
41 Dirk Nowitzki .60 1.50
42 Elton Brand .50 1.25
43 Linas Kleiza .30 .75
44 Andrea Bargnani .40 1.00
45 Josh Smith .50 1.25
46 Luol Deng .50 1.25
47 Andrei Kirilenko .40 1.00
48 Danny Granger .50 1.25
49 Rashad McCants .30 .75
50 Emeka Okafor .50 1.25
51 Kyle Korver .40 1.00
52 Jamario Moon .30 .75
53 Nick Young .40 1.00
54 Rashard Lewis .40 1.00
55 Jason Kidd .50 1.25
56 Josh Howard .40 1.00
57 Desmond Mason .30 .75
58 Andre Miller .40 1.00
59 Rafer Alston .30 .75
60 Baron Davis .50 1.25
61 Zydrunas Ilgauskas .40 1.00
62 Marvin Williams .50 1.25
63 Manu Ginobili .50 1.25
64 David West .50 1.25
65 Rajon Rondo .60 1.50
66 Kenyon Martin .50 1.25
67 Josh Boone .30 .75
68 Travis Outlaw .40 1.00
69 Andre Iguodala .50 1.25
70 Yi Jianlian .50 1.25
71 Jordan Farmar .30 .75
72 Udonis Haslem .40 1.00
73 Caron Butler .50 1.25
74 Craig Smith .30 .75
75 Tayshaun Prince .50 1.25
76 Rudy Gay .50 1.25
77 Jermaine O'Neal .50 1.25
78 Devin Harris .50 1.25
79 Fabricio Oberto .30 .75
80 Hedo Turkoglu .50 1.25
81 James Posey .30 .75
82 Corey Maggette .40 1.00
83 Ricky Davis .40 1.00
84 Grant Hill .60 1.50
85 Eddie House .30 .75
86 Jeff Green .40 1.00
87 Lamar Odom .50 1.25
88 Brandan Wright .40 1.00
89 Sean Williams .40 1.00
90 Drew Gooden .40 1.00
91 Amare Stoudemire .50 1.25
92 Charlie Villanueva .50 1.25
93 Ron Artest .50 1.25
94 Derek Fisher .40 1.00
95 Willie Green .30 .75
96 Kirk Hinrich .50 1.25
97 Jameer Nelson .40 1.00
98 Al Harrington .40 1.00
99 Ronnie Brewer .40 1.00
100 Dwyane Wade 1.00 2.50
101 Jamal Crawford .40 1.00
102 Ryan Gomes .30 .75
103 Marcus Camby .30 .75
104 Antawn Jamison .50 1.25
105 Cuttino Mobley .40 1.00
106 Tyson Chandler .40 1.00
107 Al Horford .50 1.25
108 Chris Wilcox .30 .75
109 Gerald Wallace .50 1.25
110 Andrew Bynum .60 1.50
111 Tracy McGrady .50 1.25
112 Mo Williams .40 1.00
113 Nate Robinson .50 1.25
114 Wally Szczerbiak .40 1.00
115 Vince Carter .60 1.50
116 T.J. Ford .30 .75
117 Kevin Martin .50 1.25
118 Steve Blake .30 .75
119 Anderson Varejao .40 1.00
120 Mike Conley Jr. .40 1.00
121 Chris Kaman .40 1.00
122 Louis Williams .40 1.00
123 Jason Richardson .50 1.25
124 John Salmons .50 1.25
125 Martell Webster .40 1.00
126 Kurt Thomas .30 .75
127 Raja Bell .40 1.00
128 Jason Terry .40 1.00
129 Corey Brewer .40 1.00
130 Bruce Bowen .30 .75
131 Glen Davis .40 1.00
132 Richard Hamilton .40 1.00
133 Ben Wallace .50 1.25
134 Chris Bosh .50 1.25
135 Beno Udrih .30 .75
136 Jarrett Jack .40 1.00
137 Stephen Jackson .40 1.00
138 Damien Wilkins .30 .75
139 Jamaal Tinsley .30 .75
140 Deron Williams .50 1.25
141 Andres Nocioni .30 .75
142 David Lee .40 1.00
143 Rodney Stuckey .60 1.50
144 Luke Walton .30 .75
145 Jerry Stackhouse .40 1.00
146 Samuel Dalembert .30 .75
147 Brandon Roy .50 1.25
148 Chauncey Billups .50 1.25
149 Michael Finley .50 1.25
150 Leandro Barbosa .40 1.00
151 Keith Bogans .30 .75
152 Mike Bibby .40 1.00
153 Troy Murphy .30 .75
154 Eddy Curry .30 .75
155 Anthony Parker .30 .75
156 Kevin Durant 2.00 5.00
157 Larry Hughes .40 1.00
158 Peja Stojakovic .50 1.25
159 Shane Battier .40 1.00
160 Kendrick Perkins .40 1.00
161 Mehmet Okur .30 .75
162 Brendan Haywood .30 .75
163 Monta Ellis .50 1.25
164 J.R. Smith .50 1.25
165 Greg Oden .50 1.25
166 John Stockton .75 2.00
167 Dennis Rodman .75 2.00
168 Dominique Wilkins .60 1.50
169 Larry Bird 1.50 4.00
170 Isiah Thomas .50 1.25
171 Magic Johnson 1.25 3.00
172 Bill Russell .75 2.00
173 David Robinson .75 2.00
174 Jerry West .60 1.50
175 Micheal Ray Richardson .50 1.25
176 Jo Jo White .50 1.25
177 Pete Maravich 1.50 4.00
178 Wilt Chamberlain 1.00 2.50
179 Patrick Ewing .60 1.50
180 Julius Erving 1.00 2.50
181 Derrick Rose RC 25.00 60.00
182 Michael Beasley RC 2.00 5.00
183 O.J. Mayo RC 2.00 5.00
184 Russell Westbrook RC 8.00 20.00
185 Kevin Love RC 6.00 15.00
186 Danilo Gallinari RC 2.00 5.00
187 Eric Gordon RC 3.00 8.00
188 Joe Alexander RC 1.25 3.00
189 D.J. Augustin RC 1.25 3.00
190 Brook Lopez RC 2.00 5.00
191 Jerryd Bayless RC 1.25 3.00
192 Jason Thompson RC 1.25 3.00
193 Anthony Randolph RC 1.50 4.00
194 Robin Lopez RC 1.25 3.00
195 Marreese Speights RC 1.25 3.00
196 Roy Hibbert RC 2.00 5.00
197 JaVale McGee RC 2.00 5.00
198 J.J. Hickson RC 1.50 4.00
199 Alexis Ajinca RC 1.25 3.00
200 Ryan Anderson RC 2.00 5.00
201 Courtney Lee RC 2.00 5.00
202 Kosta Koufos RC 1.25 3.00
203 Donte Greene RC 1.25 3.00
204 George Hill RC 2.00 5.00
205 D.J. White RC 1.25 3.00
206 J.R. Giddens RC 1.25 3.00
207 Joey Dorsey RC 1.25 3.00
208 Mario Chalmers RC 2.00 5.00
209 DeAndre Jordan RC 2.50 6.00
210 Chris Douglas-Roberts RC 1.25 3.00
211 Malik Hairston RC 1.25 3.00
212 Marc Gasol RC 2.00 5.00
213 Kyle Weaver RC 1.25 3.00
214 Patrick Ewing Jr. RC 1.25 3.00
215 Walter Sharpe RC 1.25 3.00
216 Sonny Weems RC 1.25 3.00
217 Trent Plaisted RC 1.25 3.00
218 Nicolas Batum RC 2.00 5.00
219 Brandon Rush RC 1.25 3.00
220 Darrell Arthur RC 1.25 3.00
221 Derrick Rose AU A 350.00 650.00
222 Michael Beasley AU A 25.00 60.00
223 O.J. Mayo AU A 25.00 60.00
224 Russell Westbrook AU A 150.00 300.00
225 Kevin Love AU A 100.00 250.00
226 Danilo Gallinari AU A 15.00 40.00
227 Eric Gordon AU A 50.00 120.00
228 Joe Alexander AU B 6.00 15.00
229 D.J. Augustin AU B 6.00 15.00
230 Brook Lopez AU B 10.00 25.00
231 Jerryd Bayless AU B 6.00 15.00
232 Jason Thompson AU B 6.00 15.00
233 Anthony Randolph AU A 10.00 25.00
234 Robin Lopez AU A 6.00 15.00
235 Marreese Speights AU C 6.00 15.00
236 Roy Hibbert AU B 12.00 30.00
237 JaVale McGee AU C 10.00 25.00
238 J.J. Hickson AU C 8.00 20.00
239 Sonny Weems AU C 6.00 15.00
240 Ryan Anderson AU C 10.00 25.00
241 Courtney Lee AU B 10.00 25.00
242 Kosta Koufos AU C 6.00 15.00
243 Donte Greene AU B 6.00 15.00
244 George Hill AU B 10.00 25.00
245 D.J. White AU C 6.00 15.00
246 J.R. Giddens AU B 6.00 15.00
247 Joey Dorsey AU B 6.00 15.00
248 Mario Chalmers AU B 10.00 25.00
249 DeAndre Jordan AU C 12.00 30.00
250 Chris Douglas-Roberts AU D 6.00 15.00
251 Kyle Weaver AU D 6.00 15.00
252 Patrick Ewing Jr. AU D 6.00 15.00
253 Walter Sharpe AU D 6.00 15.00
254 Brandon Rush AU B 6.00 15.00
255 Darrell Arthur AU B 6.00 15.00

2008-09 Topps Chrome Refractors

*STARS: .75X TO 2X BASE HI
*RCs: 1.25X TO 3X BASE HI
REF.STATED ODDS 1:4
AUTO GRP.A PRINT RUN 145 SETS
AUTO GRP.B PRINT RUN 245 SETS
AUTO GRP.C PRINT RUN 476 SETS
AUTO GRP.D PRINT RUN 795 SETS
23 LeBron James 12.00 30.00
24 Kobe Bryant 12.00 30.00
156 Kevin Durant 8.00 20.00

2008-09 Topps Chrome Refractors Gold

*1-180 REF.GOLD: 8X TO 20X BASE HI
*181-220 REF.GOLD: 4X TO 10X BASE HI
181-220 PRINT RUN 50 SER.#'d SETS
UNPRICED AUTO PRINT RUN 5 SETS
3 Allen Iverson 15.00 40.00
23 LeBron James 75.00 200.00
24 Kobe Bryant 75.00 200.00
32 Shaquille O'Neal 25.00 60.00
100 Dwyane Wade 30.00 80.00
181 Derrick Rose 400.00 800.00
184 Russell Westbrook 200.00 400.00
185 Kevin Love 175.00 350.00
186 Danilo Gallinari 40.00 70.00
187 Eric Gordon 50.00 120.00

2008-09 Topps Chrome Refractors Orange

*ORANGE STARS: 2X TO 5X BASE HI
*ORANGE RCs: 2X TO 5X BASE HI
PRINT RUN 499 SER.#'d SETS
23 LeBron James 25.00 60.00
24 Kobe Bryant 25.00 60.00
156 Kevin Durant 12.00 30.00

2008-09 Topps Chrome X-Fractors

*X-FRACTOR STARS: 1.5X TO 4X BASE HI
*X-FRACTOR RCs: 2X TO 5X BASE HI
PRINT RUN 288 SER.#'d SETS
UNPRICED AUTO PRINT RUN 15 SETS
23 LeBron James 15.00 40.00
24 Kobe Bryant 15.00 40.00
100 Dwyane Wade 6.00 15.00
181 Derrick Rose 175.00 350.00

2008-09 Topps Chrome 1958-59 Variations Autographs Refractors

GROUP A PRINT RUN 20 SETS
GROUP B PRINT RUN 45 SETS
GROUP C PRINT RUN 60 SETS
GROUP D PRINT RUN 360 SETS
UNPRICED GOLD PRINT RUN FIVE SETS
UNPRICED RED PRINT RUN THREE SETS
UNPRICED SUPERFR.PRINT RUN ONE SET
*X-FRAC: .6X TO 1.5X BASE HI
X-FRAC.PRINT RUN 15 SER.#'d SETS
1 Chris Paul A 40.00 80.00
7 Ben Gordon B 8.00 20.00
8 Carlos Boozer B 8.00 20.00
12 Dwight Howard B 25.00 50.00
15 Carmelo Anthony A 25.00 60.00
34 Paul Pierce B 15.00 30.00
46 Luol Deng C 5.00 12.00
48 Danny Granger C 8.00 20.00
60 Baron Davis B 10.00 25.00
76 Rudy Gay D 5.00 12.00
111 Tracy McGrady A 10.00 25.00
147 Brandon Roy B 15.00 30.00
165 Greg Oden A 20.00 50.00
172 Larry Bird A 50.00 120.00

2008-09 Topps Chrome Youthquake Autographs Refractors

STATED PRINT RUN 30 TO 165 SETS
*X-FRACTORS: .75X TO 2X BASE HI
X-FRACTORS PRINT RUN 15 SETS
UNPRICED REF.GOLD PRINT RUN 5 SETS
UNPRICED REF.RED PRINT RUN 3 SETS
UNPRICED SUPERFR.PRINT RUN ONE SET
YQA1 Michael Beasley/30 30.00 80.00
YQA2 Jerryd Bayless/30 15.00 40.00
YQA3 Danilo Gallinari/30 15.00 40.00
YQA4 Eric Gordon/30 40.00 100.00
YQA5 Robin Lopez/165 6.00 15.00
YQA6 Kevin Love/30 100.00 250.00
YQA7 Derrick Rose/30 600.00 1000.00
YQA8 Anthony Randolph/165 10.00 25.00
YQA9 O.J. Mayo/30 30.00 80.00
YQA10 Russell Westbrook/30 175.00 350.00
YQA11 D.J. Augustin/45 10.00 25.00
YQA12 Brook Lopez/45 12.50 30.00
YQA13 Rudy Gay/165 8.00 20.00
YQA14 Al Thornton/45 8.00 20.00
YQA15 Thaddeus Young/30 8.00 20.00

2009-10 Topps Chrome

COMPLETE SET (110) 200.00 400.00
PRINT RUN 999 SER.#'d SETS
UNPRICED SUPERFR.PRINT RUN ONE SET
1 Joe Johnson .60 1.50
2 Josh Smith .60 1.50
3 Mike Bibby .50 1.25
4 Marvin Williams .50 1.25
5 Al Horford .60 1.50
6 Paul Pierce .75 2.00
7 Ray Allen .60 1.50
8 Kevin Garnett 1.25 3.00
9 Rajon Rondo .75 2.00
10 Glen Davis .50 1.25
11 Gerald Wallace .60 1.50
12 Raymond Felton .50 1.25
13 Ben Gordon .60 1.50
14 Derrick Rose 2.00 5.00
15 Luol Deng .60 1.50
16 LeBron James 3.00 8.00
17 Mo Williams .50 1.25
18 Anderson Varejao .50 1.25
19 Daniel Gibson .50 1.25
20 Ben Wallace .60 1.50
21 Dirk Nowitzki .75 2.00
22 Jason Terry .50 1.25
23 Josh Howard .50 1.25
24 Jason Kidd .60 1.50
25 Carmelo Anthony .75 2.00
26 Chauncey Billups .60 1.50
27 J.R. Smith .60 1.50
28 Allen Iverson .75 2.00
29 Richard Hamilton .50 1.25
30 Tayshaun Prince .60 1.50
31 Corey Maggette .50 1.25
32 Monta Ellis .60 1.50
33 Anthony Randolph .50 1.25
34 Yao Ming .75 2.00
35 Ron Artest .60 1.50
36 Tracy McGrady .60 1.50
37 Shane Battier .60 1.50
38 Danny Granger .60 1.50
39 T.J. Ford .40 1.00
40 Troy Murphy .40 1.00
41 Al Thornton .50 1.25
42 Baron Davis .60 1.50
43 Eric Gordon .60 1.50
44 Kobe Bryant 3.00 8.00
45 Pau Gasol .60 1.50
46 Andrew Bynum .75 2.00
47 Lamar Odom .60 1.50
48 O.J. Mayo .60 1.50
49 Rudy Gay .60 1.50
50 Marc Gasol .60 1.50
51 Dwyane Wade 1.25 3.00
52 Michael Beasley .60 1.50
53 Michael Redd .60 1.50
54 Richard Jefferson .60 1.50
55 Andrew Bogut .60 1.50
56 Al Jefferson .60 1.50
57 Kevin Love 1.00 2.50
58 Mike Miller .60 1.50
59 Devin Harris .60 1.50
60 Vince Carter .75 2.00
61 Brook Lopez .60 1.50
62 Yi Jianlian .50 1.25
63 Chris Paul 1.00 2.50
64 David West .60 1.50
65 David Lee .50 1.25
66 Nate Robinson .60 1.50
67 Russell Westbrook 1.00 2.50
68 Kevin Durant 2.00 5.00
69 Dwight Howard 1.00 2.50
70 Rashard Lewis .50 1.25
71 Hedo Turkoglu .60 1.50
72 Jameer Nelson .50 1.25
73 Andre Iguodala .60 1.50
74 Elton Brand .60 1.50
75 Thaddeus Young .40 1.00
76 Amare Stoudemire .60 1.50
77 Shaquille O'Neal 1.25 3.00
78 Jason Richardson .60 1.50
79 Steve Nash .60 1.50
80 Brandon Roy .60 1.50
81 LaMarcus Aldridge .60 1.50
82 Rudy Fernandez .50 1.25
83 Greg Oden .50 1.25
84 Kevin Martin .60 1.50
85 Tony Parker .60 1.50
86 Tim Duncan 1.00 2.50
87 Manu Ginobili .60 1.50
88 Chris Bosh .60 1.50
89 Andrea Bargnani .50 1.25
90 Shawn Marion .60 1.50
91 Jose Calderon .50 1.25
92 Carlos Boozer .60 1.50
93 Deron Williams .60 1.50
94 Antawn Jamison .60 1.50
95 Gilbert Arenas .60 1.50
96 Blake Griffin RC 50.00 125.00
97 Ricky Rubio RC 30.00 80.00
98 Hasheem Thabeet RC 6.00 15.00
99 James Harden RC 20.00 50.00
100 DeMar DeRozan RC 10.00 25.00
101 Stephen Curry RC 15.00 40.00
102 Brandon Jennings RC 12.00 30.00
103 Jordan Hill RC 6.00 15.00
104 Earl Clark RC 6.00 15.00
105 Gerald Henderson RC 6.00 15.00
106 Jonny Flynn RC 6.00 15.00
107 Tyreke Evans RC 15.00 40.00
108 Tyler Hansbrough RC 10.00 25.00
109 Terrence Williams RC 6.00 15.00
110 Jrue Holiday RC 12.00 30.00

2009-10 Topps Chrome Refractors

*REF 1-95: 2.5X TO 6X BASE HI
*REF RC: .6X TO 1.5X BASE HI
REF PRINT RUN 500 SER.#'d SETS
16 LeBron James 20.00 50.00

2009-10 Topps Chrome Refractors Gold

*REF.GOLD 1-95: 6X TO 15X BASE HI
*REF.GOLD RC 96-110: 1.5X TO 4X BASE HI
PRINT RUN 50 SER.#'d SETS
14 Derrick Rose 60.00 150.00
16 LeBron James 60.00 150.00
44 Kobe Bryant 60.00 150.00
96 Blake Griffin 600.00 1200.00
97 Ricky Rubio 200.00 400.00

2003-04 Topps Collection

Released in time for Christmas, Topps Collection parallels the setup and design of the regular Topps set enhanced with gold foil highlights and new photography for some of the veterans and rookies. Initially Topps announced that a special Black Border LeBron James cards would be included in each box set, but this card was never issued. The suggested retail price was $40.
COMP.FACT.SET (265) 40.00 80.00
*SINGLES: .6X TO 1.5X BASE TOPPS HI
*RCs: .5X TO 1.25X BASE TOPPS HI
SOME PLAYERS HAVE PHOTO VARIATIONS

2003-04 Topps Contemporary Collection

Released in April 2004, Topps Contemporary Collection is a 140-card set comprised of 20 rookie cards (numbers 1-20), 10 autographed rookie cards sequentially numbered to 499 (numbers 21-30), 100 veteran cards (numbers 31-130) and 10 autographed veteran cards sequentially numbered to 499 (numbers 131-140). Base cards are bordered and printed on irridescent foil board. Contemporary Collection was packaged in six-pack boxes with four cards per pack and carried a suggested retail price of $50.
1 LeBron James RC 25.00 60.00
2 Darko Milicic RC 2.50 6.00
3 Chris Bosh RC 5.00 12.00
4 Dwyane Wade RC 10.00 25.00
5 Chris Kaman RC 3.00 8.00
6 Kirk Hinrich RC 3.00 8.00
7 Jarvis Hayes RC 2.50 6.00
8 Mickael Pietrus RC 2.50 6.00
9 Luke Ridnour RC 3.00 8.00
10 David West RC 3.00 8.00
11 Aleksandar Pavlovic RC 3.00 8.00
12 Boris Diaw RC 3.00 8.00
13 Zoran Planinic RC 2.50 6.00
14 Francisco Elson RC 2.50 6.00
15 Leandro Barbosa RC 3.00 8.00
16 Josh Howard RC 3.00 8.00
17 Luke Walton RC 2.50 6.00
18 Willie Green RC 2.50 6.00
19 Maurice Williams RC 4.00 10.00
20 Udonis Haslem RC 3.00 8.00
21 Reece Gaines AU RC 5.00 12.00
22 Carmelo Anthony AU RC 40.00 80.00
23 Zarko Cabarkapa AU RC 5.00 12.00
24 Troy Bell AU RC 5.00 12.00
25 Travis Outlaw AU RC 6.00 15.00
26 Marcus Banks AU RC 5.00 12.00
27 Kendrick Perkins AU RC 8.00 20.00
28 Dahntay Jones AU RC 5.00 12.00
29 T.J. Ford AU RC 6.00 15.00
30 Mike Sweetney AU RC 5.00 12.00
31 Jason Terry .75 2.00
32 Theo Ratliff .60 1.50
33 Raef LaFrentz .60 1.50
34 Eddy Curry .75 2.00
35 Ricky Davis .75 2.00
36 Zydrunas Ilgauskas .75 2.00
37 Darius Miles .60 1.50
38 Dirk Nowitzki 1.50 4.00
39 Steve Nash 1.25 3.00
40 Antawn Jamison 1.00 2.50
41 Antoine Walker 1.00 2.50
42 Andre Miller .75 2.00
43 Nene .75 2.00
44 Richard Hamilton .75 2.00
45 Ben Wallace 1.00 2.50
46 Jason Richardson 1.00 2.50
47 Nick Van Exel .75 2.00
48 Troy Murphy 1.00 2.50
49 Yao Ming 2.00 5.00
50 Steve Francis 1.00 2.50
51 Ron Artest 1.00 2.50
52 Jermaine O'Neal 1.00 2.50
53 Al Harrington .75 2.00
54 Marko Jaric .60 1.50
55 Corey Maggette .75 2.00
56 Kobe Bryant 5.00 12.00
57 Shaquille O'Neal 2.50 6.00
58 Devean George .60 1.50
59 Gary Payton 1.00 2.50
60 Pau Gasol 1.00 2.50
61 Stromile Swift .60 1.50
62 Mike Miller 1.00 2.50
63 Lamar Odom 1.00 2.50
64 Caron Butler 1.00 2.50
65 Eddie Jones .75 2.00
66 Brian Grant .60 1.50
67 Desmond Mason .75 2.00
68 Tim Thomas .60 1.50
69 Michael Redd 1.00 2.50
70 Sam Cassell .75 2.00
71 Kevin Garnett 2.00 5.00
72 Latrell Sprewell .75 2.00
73 Michael Olowokandi .60 1.50
74 Wally Szczerbiak .75 2.00
75 Richard Jefferson 1.00 2.50
76 Kenyon Martin 1.00 2.50
77 Alonzo Mourning 1.25 3.00
78 Baron Davis 1.00 2.50
79 Jamal Mashburn .75 2.00
80 Allan Houston .75 2.00
81 Keith Van Horn .75 2.00
82 Kurt Thomas .60 1.50
83 Tracy McGrady 1.25 3.00
84 Juwan Howard .75 2.00
85 Drew Gooden .75 2.00
86 Allen Iverson 1.50 4.00
87 Glenn Robinson .75 2.00
88 Derrick Coleman .75 2.00
89 Stephon Marbury .75 2.00
90 Shawn Marion 1.00 2.50
91 Amare Stoudemire 1.50 4.00
92 Zach Randolph 1.00 2.50
93 Rasheed Wallace 1.00 2.50
94 Bonzi Wells .60 1.50
95 Mike Bibby 1.00 2.50
96 Chris Webber 1.00 2.50
97 Brad Miller 1.00 2.50
98 Tim Duncan 1.50 4.00
99 Rasho Nesterovic .60 1.50
100 Tony Parker 1.00 2.50
101 Manu Ginobili 1.25 3.00
102 Brent Barry .60 1.50
103 Rashard Lewis 1.00 2.50
104 Ray Allen 1.00 2.50
105 Vince Carter 1.50 4.00
106 Jerome Williams .60 1.50
107 Carlos Arroyo .75 2.00
108 Matt Harpring .75 2.00
109 Andrei Kirilenko 1.00 2.50
110 Gilbert Arenas 1.00 2.50
111 Kwame Brown .60 1.50
112 Jerry Stackhouse .75 2.00
113 Darrell Armstrong .60 1.50
114 Alvin Williams .60 1.50
115 Kelvin Cato .60 1.50
116 Stephen Jackson .75 2.00
117 Shareef Abdur-Rahim .75 2.00
118 Eric Williams .60 1.50
119 Tony Battie .60 1.50
120 Tyson Chandler .75 2.00
121 Scottie Pippen 1.50 4.00
122 Nikoloz Tskitishvili .60 1.50
123 Chauncey Billups 1.00 2.50
124 Quentin Richardson .75 2.00
125 Dikembe Mutombo 1.00 2.50
126 Joe Smith .75 2.00
127 Qyntel Woods .60 1.50
128 Dajuan Wagner .60 1.50
129 Robert Horry .75 2.00
130 Cuttino Mobley .75 2.00
131 Bobby Jackson AU 5.00 12.00
132 Elton Brand AU 6.00 15.00
133 Peja Stojakovic AU 6.00 15.00
134 Jamal Crawford AU 6.00 15.00
135 Jalen Rose AU 8.00 20.00
136 Paul Pierce AU 12.50 30.00
137 Jason Kidd AU 12.50 30.00
138 Tayshaun Prince AU 8.00 20.00
139 Morris Peterson AU 5.00 12.00
140 Speedy Claxton AU 5.00 12.00

2003-04 Topps Contemporary Collection Gold

Randomly seeded in packs, this 140-card set parallels the base set enhanced with gold foil highlights. Autographed cards are numbered one of one while the rest of the cards in the set are sequentially numbered to 25.
*1-20 RCs GOLD: 1.25X TO 3X BASE HI
*31-130 STARS GOLD: 2.5X TO 6X BASE HI
1 LeBron James 100.00 250.00
56 Kobe Bryant 40.00 100.00

2003-04 Topps Contemporary Collection Red

Randomly inserted in packs, this 140-card set parallels the base set enhanced with red foil highlights. Autographed cards are sequentially numbered to 50 while the rest of the set is numbered to 225.
*RED: .75X TO 2X BASE HI
56 Kobe Bryant 12.00 30.00

2003-04 Topps Contemporary Collection Caption Autographs

Randomly seeded in packs, this 40-card set features player's autographs along with a caption that has something to do with themselves. Most players have two different caption versions.
BJ1 Bobby Jackson Court Kings 8.00 20.00
BJ2 Bobby Jackson 6th Man 8.00 20.00
CA1 Carmelo Anthony NCAA MVP 03 40.00 100.00
CA2 Carmelo Anthony Mile High 40.00 80.00
DJ1 Dahntay Jones Cameron Crazy 6.00 15.00
DJ2 Dahntay Jones Grizzly Den 6.00 15.00
EB1 Elton Brand ROY 99 6.00 15.00
EB2 Elton Brand Hollywood 6.00 15.00
JC1 Jamal Crawford Go Blue 10.00 25.00
JC2 Jamal Crawford Windy City 10.00 25.00
JK1 Jason Kidd ROY 94 30.00 80.00

JK2 Jason Kidd 30.00 80.00
Jersey Kidd
JR1 Jalen Rose 15.00 30.00
FAB 5
JR2 Jalen Rose 6.00 15.00
Hollywood North
KP1 Kendrick Perkins 8.00 20.00
Ozen Original
KP2 Kendrick Perkins 8.00 20.00
Celtic Pride
MB1 Marcus Banks 8.00 20.00
Runnin Rebel
MB2 Marcus Banks 8.00 20.00
Celtic Pride
MP1 Morris Peterson 6.00 15.00
Runnin Rebel
MP2 Morris Peterson 6.00 15.00
Hollywood North
MS1 Mike Sweetney 6.00 15.00
HOYA 34
MS2 Mike Sweetney 6.00 15.00
Big Apple
PP1 Paul Pierce 15.00 40.00
The Truth
PP2 Paul Pierce 15.00 40.00
Celtic Pride
PS1 Peja Stojakovic 10.00 25.00
Court Kings
PS2 Peja Stojakovic 10.00 25.00
3 Point King
RG1 Reece Gaines 6.00 15.00
Cardinals #1
RG2 Reece Gaines 6.00 15.00
Magic Tricks
SC1 Speedy Claxton 6.00 15.00
Hofstra Pride
SC2 Speedy Claxton 6.00 15.00
Oaktown
TB1 Troy Bell 6.00 15.00
BC Beast
TB2 Troy Bell 6.00 15.00
Grizzly Den
TO1 Travis Outlaw 6.00 15.00
Starkville's Son
TO2 Travis Outlaw 6.00 15.00
City of Roses
TP1 Tayshaun Prince 15.00 40.00
UK Prince
TP2 Tayshaun Prince 15.00 40.00
Motown Prince
ZC1 Zarko Cabarkapa 6.00 15.00
Count of Montenegro
ZC2 Zarko Cabarkapa 6.00 15.00
Valley of the Sun
TJF1 T.J. Ford 12.50 30.00
Longhorn Legend
TJF2 T.J. Ford 12.50 30.00
NCAA POY 03

2003-04 Topps Contemporary Collection Caption Autographs Dual

Randomly seeded, this 20-card set pairs players who have autographed and added a caption to each card.
SOME UNPRICED DUE TO SCARCITY
AF Carmelo Anthony 100.00 200.00
T.J. Ford
BJ Troy Bell 8.00 20.00
Dahntay Jones
BP1 Marcus Banks 10.00 25.00
Kendrick Perkins
BP2 Marcus Banks 8.00 20.00
Morris Peterson
BS Elton Brand 10.00 25.00
Mike Sweetney
CR Jamal Crawford 30.00 80.00
Jalen Rose
GC Reece Gaines 8.00 20.00
Speedy Claxton
OC Travis Outlaw 10.00 25.00
Zarko Cabarkapa
PC Tayshaun Prince 10.00 25.00
Speedy Claxton
PK Paul Pierce 75.00 150.00
Jason Kidd
PP Paul Pierce 40.00 100.00
Morris Peterson
SC Peja Stojakovic 12.50 30.00
Zarko Cabarkapa
SJ Peja Stojakovic 12.50 30.00
Bobby Jackson
SP Mike Sweetney 12.50 30.00
Tayshaun Prince

2003-04 Topps Contemporary Collection Draft 03 Tribute

Randomly seeded in packs, this 23-card set showcases the top rookies from the 2003 NBA draft along with a swatch of memorabilia. Two other parallel version were inserted, a red one sequentially numbered to 50 and a gold one where cards are numbered one of one.
*RED SINGLES: .75X TO 2X BASE DRAFT HI
AP Aleksandar Pavlovic 2.50 6.00
BC Brian Cook 2.50 6.00
BD Boris Diaw 3.00 8.00
CA Carmelo Anthony 6.00 15.00
CB Chris Bosh 5.00 12.00
CK Chris Kaman 3.00 8.00
DJ Dahntay Jones 2.50 6.00
DW Dwyane Wade 10.00 25.00
JH Josh Howard 2.50 6.00
JK Jason Kapono 2.50 6.00
KH Kirk Hinrich 3.00 8.00
LB Leandro Barbosa 3.00 8.00
LR Luke Ridnour 3.00 8.00
LW Luke Walton 2.50 6.00
MB Marcus Banks 2.50 6.00
MP Mickael Pietrus 2.50 6.00
MW Maurice Williams 4.00 10.00
SB Steve Blake 3.00 8.00
TB Troy Bell 2.50 6.00
ZP Zoran Planinic 2.50 6.00
DWE David West 3.00 8.00
JHA Jarvis Hayes 2.50 6.00
TJF T.J. Ford 3.00 8.00

2003-04 Topps Contemporary Collection Lucky Draw

Randomly inserted in packs, this 25-card set is horizontally designed with a player photo on the left and the player's conference logo, Eastern or Western, on the right. Cards are sequentially numbered to 175. Two parallel versions were also issued, one sequentially numbered to 50 and one sequentially numbered to 25.
*50 SINGLES: .6X TO 1.5X BASE HI
*25 SINGLES: 1X TO 2.5X BASE HI
LD1 Carmelo Anthony 10.00 25.00
LD2 Marcus Banks 4.00 10.00
LD3 Chris Bosh 8.00 20.00
LD4 Dwyane Wade 15.00 40.00
LD5 Chris Kaman 5.00 12.00
LD6 Kirk Hinrich 5.00 12.00
LD7 Jarvis Hayes 4.00 10.00
LD8 Mickael Pietrus 4.00 10.00
LD9 Luke Ridnour 5.00 12.00
LD10 David West 5.00 12.00
LD11 Aleksandar Pavlovic 4.00 10.00
LD12 Boris Diaw 5.00 12.00
LD13 Zoran Planinic 4.00 10.00
LD14 Ndudi Ebi 4.00 10.00
LD15 Leandro Barbosa 5.00 12.00
LD16 Josh Howard 4.00 10.00
LD17 Luke Walton 4.00 10.00
LD18 Willie Green 4.00 10.00
LD19 Maurice Williams 6.00 15.00
LD20 Zarko Cabarkapa 4.00 10.00
LD21 Travis Outlaw 5.00 12.00
LD22 Dahntay Jones 4.00 10.00
LD23 Troy Bell 4.00 10.00
LD24 Reece Gaines 4.00 10.00
LD25 Mike Sweetney 4.00 10.00

2003-04 Topps Contemporary Collection Matching Marks Relics

Randomly inserted, this nine-card set pairs players who match in a specific statistical category on a horizontally designed card with two color photos and jersey swatches inside numbers and letters that spell out the stat category. Each card is sequentially numbered to 250. Two parallel versions of this set were issued, a red version sequentially numbered to 50 and a gold version numbered one of one.
*RED SINGLES: .5X TO 1.25X MATCH HI
AH Ray Allen 6.00 15.00
Allan Houston
GD Kevin Garnett 10.00 25.00
Tim Duncan
IM Allen Iverson 8.00 20.00
Tracy McGrady
KM Jason Kidd 6.00 15.00
Andre Miller
MM Karl Malone 6.00 15.00
Alonzo Mourning
OS Shaquille O'Neal 10.00 25.00
Amare Stoudemire
WB Chris Webber 6.00 15.00
Elton Brand
WM Ben Wallace 6.00 15.00
Dikimbe Mutombo
WR Antoine Walker 6.00 15.00
Glenn Robinson

2003-04 Topps Contemporary Collection Memorable Materials

Randomly inserted, this seven-card set places a player photo on the right side of the card and a square shaped swatch of memorabilia on the left. Each card is sequentially numbered to 250. Two parallel versions of this set were issued, a red version sequentially numbered to 50 and a gold version numbered one of one.
*RED SINGLES: .6X TO 1.5X MEM.MAT.HI
AI Allen Iverson 5.00 12.00
JR Jason Richardson 3.00 8.00
KG Kevin Garnett 6.00 15.00
RH Robert Horry 2.50 6.00
RM Reggie Miller 3.00 8.00
SM Stephon Marbury 2.50 6.00
TD Tim Duncan 5.00 12.00

2003-04 Topps Contemporary Collection Milestone Materials

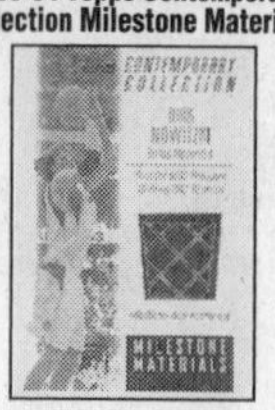

Randomly inserted, this 13-card set places a player photo on the left and a swatch of memorabilia on the right. Each card is sequentially numbered to 250. Two parallel versions of this set were issued, a red version sequentially numbered to 50 and a gold version numbered one of one.
*RED SINGLES: .6X TO 1.5X MILE HI
DM Dikembe Mutombo 3.00 8.00
DN Dirk Nowitzki 5.00 12.00
GP Gary Payton 3.00 8.00
JS Jerry Stackhouse 2.50 6.00
KM Karl Malone 4.00 10.00
MB Mike Bibby 3.00 8.00
RA Ray Allen 3.00 8.00
SC Sam Cassell 2.50 6.00
SF Steve Francis 3.00 8.00
SO Shaquille O'Neal 8.00 20.00
TD Tim Duncan 5.00 12.00
NVE Nick Van Exel 2.50 6.00
RHA Richard Hamilton 2.50 6.00

2003-04 Topps Contemporary Collection Perennial All-Star Relics

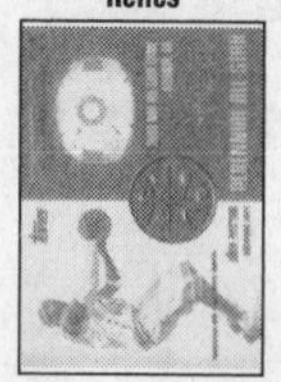

Randomly inserted, this 16-card set showcases NBA All-Stars with a centered swatch of memorabilia. Each card is sequentially numbered to 250 unless noted. Two parallel versions of this set were issued, a red version sequentially numbered to 50 and a gold version numbered one of one.
*RED SINGLES: .6X TO 1.5X ALL-STAR HI
AI Allen Iverson 5.00 12.00
AM Alonzo Mourning 4.00 10.00
CW Chris Webber/175 3.00 8.00
DN Dirk Nowitzki 5.00 12.00
GP Gary Payton 3.00 8.00
JK Jason Kidd 5.00 12.00
KG Kevin Garnett 6.00 15.00
KM Karl Malone 4.00 10.00
PP Paul Pierce 4.00 10.00
RA Ray Allen 3.00 8.00
RM Reggie Miller 3.00 8.00
SF Steve Francis 3.00 8.00
SN Steve Nash 4.00 10.00
SO Shaquille O'Neal 8.00 20.00
TD Tim Duncan 5.00 12.00
TM Tracy McGrady 4.00 10.00

2003-04 Topps Contemporary Collection Performance Tribute Doubles

Randomly seeded in packs, this nine-card set places two players and two swatches of memorabilia on each card. The cards are sequentially numbered to 250. Two parallel versions of this set were issued, a red version sequentially numbered to 50 and a gold version numbered one of one.
*RED SINGLES: .6X TO 1.5X PERF. HI
AM Ron Artest 5.00 12.00
Kenyon Martin
BW Elton Brand 5.00 12.00
Chris Webber
ML Troy Murphy 5.00 12.00
Raef Lafrentz
MW Dikembe Mutombo 5.00 12.00
Ben Wallace
NK Steve Nash 6.00 15.00
Jason Kidd
NS Nene 5.00 12.00
Amare Stoudemire
PB Scottie Pippen 8.00 20.00
Shane Battier
RW Glenn Robinson 5.00 12.00
Rasheed Wallace
WB Jerome Williams 5.00 12.00
Carlos Boozer

2003-04 Topps Contemporary Collection Performance Tribute Triples

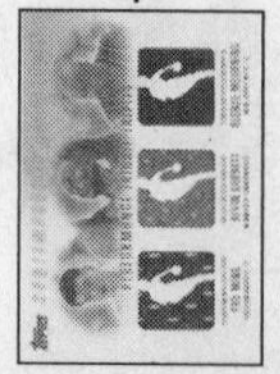

Randomly inserted, this nine-card set places three players and three swatches of memorabilia on each card. Cards are sequentially numbered to 250 unless noted below. Two parallel versions of this set were issued, a red version sequentially numbered to 50 and a gold version numbered one of one.
*RED SINGLES: .5X TO 1.25X PERF.TRIP HI
FDR Steve Francis 8.00 20.00
Baron Davis
Jason Richardson
HJP Richard Hamilton/200 8.00 20.00
Richard Jefferson
Morris Peterson
JAB Marko Jaric 8.00 20.00
Gilbert Arenas
Caron Butler
MGM Yao Ming 10.00 25.00
Kevin Garnett
Alonzo Mourning
MIS Tracy McGrady 12.00 30.00
Allen Iverson
Shaquille O'Neal
OMR Lamar Odom/200 8.00 20.00
Darius Miles
Jalen Rose
PWM Paul Pierce 8.00 20.00
Antoine Walker
Shawn Marion
RWO Theo Ratliff 8.00 20.00
Ben Wallace
Jermaine O'Neal
TMW Jason Terry/200 8.00 20.00
Stephon Marbury
DaJuan Wagner

2003-04 Topps Contemporary Collection Team Tribute Doubles

Randomly inserted, this 13-card set places two players from the same team along with two swatches of memorabilia on the card. Cards are sequentially numbered to 250. Two parallel versions of this set were issued, a red version sequentially numbered to 50 and a gold version numbered one of one.
*RED SINGLES: .6X TO 1.5X DOUBLE HI
AO Ron Artest 5.00 12.00
Jermaine O'Neal
GE Kevin Garnett 6.00 15.00
Ndudi Ebi
HT Robert Horry 5.00 12.00
Hedo Turkoglu
HV Allan Houston 5.00 12.00
Keith Van Horn
IR Allen Iverson 5.00 12.00
Glenn Robinson
KP Jason Kidd 5.00 12.00
Zoran Planinic
MH Reggie Miller 5.00 12.00
Al Harrington
PB Paul Pierce 5.00 12.00
Marcus Banks
PH Tayshaun Prince 6.00 15.00
Richard Hamilton
SH Jerry Stackhouse 5.00 12.00
Jarvis Hayes
TS Kenny Thomas 5.00 12.00
Mike Sweetney
WM Chris Webber 5.00 12.00
Brad Miller
PBO Morris Peterson 5.00 12.00
Chris Bosh

2003-04 Topps Contemporary Collection Team Tribute Triples

Randomly inserted, this 16-card set places three players from the same team along with three swatches of memorabilia on the card. Cards are sequentially numbered to 250. Two parallel versions of this set were issued, a red version sequentially numbered to 50 and a gold version numbered one of one.
*RED SINGLES: .6X TO 1.5X TRIB.TRIP.HI
BMR Elton Brand 6.00 15.00
Corey Maggette
Quentin Richardson
BOW Caron Butler 8.00 20.00
Lamar Odom
Dwyane Wade
BSJ Mike Bibby/200 8.00 20.00
Peja Stojakovic
Bobby Jackson
BSM Leandro Barbosa 6.00 15.00
Amare Stoudemire
Shawn Marion
DMW Baron Davis 6.00 15.00
Jamal Mashburn
David West
DNP Tim Duncan 8.00 20.00
Rasho Nesterovic
Tony Parker
FMR T.J. Ford 6.00 15.00
Desmond Mason
Michael Redd
MAN Andre Miller 8.00 20.00
Carmelo Anthony
Nene
MFM Yao Ming 8.00 20.00
Steve Francis
Cuttino Mobley
MGG Tracy McGrady 6.00 15.00
Reece Gaines
Drew Gooden
NNF Steve Nash 10.00 25.00
Dirk Nowitzki
Michael Finley
PCK Zoran Planinic 6.00 15.00
Keon Clark
Andrei Kirilenko
PMO Gary Payton 12.50 30.00
Karl Malone
Shaquille O'Neal
SOC Latrell Sprewell 6.00 15.00
Michael Olowokandi
Sam Cassell
WMB DaJuan Wagner 6.00 15.00
Darius Miles
Carlos Boozer
WOW Rasheed Wallace 6.00 15.00
Travis Outlaw
Qyntel Woods

2003-04 Topps Contemporary Collection Tribute to the Stars Relics

Randomly inserted in packs, this 22-card set features a centered photo of each player and two star-shaped swatches of memorabilia. Each card is sequentially numbered to 50 unless noted.
UNPRICED GOLD ONE OF ONE'S EXIST
N Nene/50 5.00 12.00
AK Andrei Kirilenko/50 6.00 15.00
AS Amare Stoudemire/50 10.00 25.00
BW Ben Wallace/50 6.00 15.00
CW Chris Webber/50 6.00 15.00
DM Desmond Mason/50 5.00 12.00
EB Elton Brand/50 6.00 15.00
EC Eddy Curry/50 5.00 12.00
JK Jason Kidd/50 10.00 25.00
JO Jermaine O'Neal/50 6.00 15.00
JR Jason Richardson/50 6.00 15.00
JT Jason Terry/50 5.00 12.00
KV Keith Van Horn/50 5.00 12.00
LO Lamar Odom/21 10.00 25.00
PG Pau Gasol/50 6.00 15.00
PP Paul Pierce/50 8.00 20.00
RW Rasheed Wallace/50 6.00 15.00
SM Stephon Marbury/50 5.00 12.00
TM Tracy McGrady/50 8.00 20.00
TP Tony Parker/50 6.00 15.00
YM Yao Ming/50 12.00 30.00

2007-08 Topps Co-Signers

This 100-card set was released in January, 2008. The set was issued into the hobby in six-card packs with an $10 SRP which came 12 packs per box and 24 boxes to a case. Cards numbered 1-30 featured NBA active stars, cards numbered 31-50 featured retired greats and cards numbered 51-100 featured 2007-08 NBA rookies. The Rookie Cards were all issued to a stated print run of 499 serial numbered sets.
COMP.SET w/o SP's (50) 20.00 40.00
1 Dwyane Wade 1.00 2.50
2 Chauncey Billups .40 1.00
3 Allen Iverson .50 1.25
4 Amare Stoudemire .40 1.00
5 Jason Kidd .40 1.00
6 Dirk Nowitzki .50 1.25
7 Jermaine O'Neal .40 1.00
8 Elton Brand .40 1.00
9 Carlos Boozer .40 1.00
10 Ray Allen .40 1.00
11 Yao Ming .50 1.25
12 Dwight Howard .60 1.50
13 Steve Nash .50 1.25
14 Chris Paul .75 2.00
15 Carmelo Anthony .50 1.25
16 Pau Gasol .40 1.00
17 Ben Gordon .40 1.00
18 Andre Iguodala .40 1.00
19 Paul Pierce .50 1.25
20 Tracy McGrady .40 1.00
21 Tim Duncan .60 1.50
22 Josh Smith .40 1.00
23 LeBron James 2.00 5.00
24 Kobe Bryant 2.00 5.00
25 Vince Carter .50 1.25
26 Shaquille O'Neal .75 2.00
27 Kevin Garnett .75 2.00
28 Chris Bosh .40 1.00
29 Baron Davis .40 1.00
30 Gilbert Arenas .40 1.00
31 John Stockton 1.00 2.50
32 Magic Johnson 1.50 4.00
33 Larry Bird 2.00 5.00
34 Rick Barry .60 1.50
35 Isiah Thomas .60 1.50
36 Dominique Wilkins .75 2.00
37 Dennis Rodman 1.00 2.50
38 Wilt Chamberlain 1.25 3.00
39 Pete Maravich 2.00 5.00
40 Bill Russell 1.00 2.50
41 Byron Scott .60 1.50
42 Karl Malone .75 2.00
43 Chris Mullin .60 1.50
44 Kevin McHale .75 2.00
45 Clyde Drexler .75 2.00
46 James Worthy .75 2.00
47 Bill Walton .60 1.50
48 Earl Monroe .60 1.50
49 Elgin Baylor .60 1.50
50 David Robinson 1.00 2.50
51 Nick Young RC 3.00 8.00
52 Greg Oden RC 2.50 6.00
53 Morris Almond RC 2.00 5.00
54 Alando Tucker RC 2.00 5.00
55 Arron Afflalo RC 2.50 6.00
56 Derrick Byars RC 2.00 5.00
57 Adam Haluska RC 2.00 5.00
58 Corey Brewer RC 2.50 6.00
59 Ramon Sessions RC 3.00 8.00
60 Daequan Cook RC 2.00 5.00
61 Mike Conley Jr. RC 3.00 8.00
62 Javaris Crittenton RC 2.00 5.00
63 Jared Jordan RC 2.00 5.00
64 Aaron Brooks RC 2.00 5.00
65 Marco Belinelli RC 2.00 5.00
66 Sammy Mejia RC 2.00 5.00
67 Jared Dudley RC 2.00 5.00
68 Rodney Stuckey RC 3.00 8.00
69 JamesOn Curry RC 2.00 5.00
70 Gabe Pruitt RC 2.00 5.00
71 Acie Law RC 2.00 5.00
72 Dominic McGuire RC 2.00 5.00
73 Herbert Hill RC 2.00 5.00
74 Jeff Green RC 2.50 6.00
75 Wilson Chandler RC 3.00 8.00
76 Marcus Williams RC 2.00 5.00
77 Josh McRoberts RC 2.00 5.00
78 Thaddeus Young RC 2.50 6.00
79 Jared Newson RC 2.00 5.00
80 Stephane Lasme RC 2.00 5.00
81 Demetris Nichols RC 2.00 5.00
82 Julian Wright RC 2.00 5.00
83 Sean Williams RC 2.00 5.00
84 Chris Richard RC 2.00 5.00
85 Yi Jianlian RC 3.00 8.00
86 Al Thornton RC 2.00 5.00
87 Carl Landry RC 2.00 5.00
88 Kevin Durant RC 15.00 40.00
89 Brandan Wright RC 2.00 5.00
90 Nick Fazekas RC 2.00 5.00
91 Joakim Noah RC 5.00 12.00
92 Jermareo Davidson RC 2.00 5.00
93 D.J. Strawberry RC 2.00 5.00
94 Glen Davis RC 3.00 8.00
95 Al Horford RC 2.50 6.00
96 Spencer Hawes RC 2.00 5.00
97 Taurean Green RC 2.00 5.00
98 Jason Smith RC 2.00 5.00
99 Luis Scola RC 3.00 8.00
100 Aaron Gray RC 2.00 5.00

2007-08 Topps Co-Signers Gold Red

PRINT RUN 109 SER.#'d SETS
UNPRICED GOLD RED FOIL PRINT RUN 9 SETS
*GOLD BLUE: .5X TO 1.25X GOLD RED
GOLD BLUE PRINT RUN 89 SETS
UNPRICED GOLD BLUE FOIL PRINT RUN 5 SETS
*GOLD GREEN: .5X TO 1.25X GOLD RED
GOLD GREEN PRINT RUN 59 SETS
*G.GREEN FOIL: 1.5X TO 4X GOLD RED
GOLD GREEN FOIL PRINT RUN 19 SETS
*SILVER BLUE FOIL: 1.25X TO 3X GOLD RED
SILVER BLUE FOIL PRINT RUN 29 SETS
*SILVER GREEN FOIL: 1.5X TO 4X RED GOLD
SILVER GREEN FOIL PRINT RUN 19 SETS
*SILVER RED FOIL: 1.25X TO 3X BASE HI
SILVER RED FOIL PRINT RUN 39 SETS
1 Dwyane Wade 1.50 4.00
Shaquille O'Neal
1A Dwyane Wade 1.25 3.00
Antoine Walker
2 Chauncey Billups 1.25 3.00
Richard Hamilton
2A Chauncey Billups 1.25 3.00
Tayshaun Prince
3 Allen Iverson 1.25 3.00
Carmelo Anthony
3A Allen Iverson 1.25 3.00
Marcus Camby
4 Amare Stoudemire 1.25 3.00
Steve Nash
4A Amare Stoudemire 1.25 3.00
Shawn Marion
5 Jason Kidd 1.25 3.00
Vince Carter
5A Jason Kidd 1.25 3.00
Marcus Williams
6 Dirk Nowitzki 1.25 3.00
Jason Terry
6A Dirk Nowitzki 1.25 3.00
Josh Howard
7 Jermaine O'Neal 1.25 3.00
Danny Granger
7A Jermaine O'Neal 1.25 3.00
Troy Murphy
8 Elton Brand 1.25 3.00
Corey Maggette
8A Elton Brand 1.25 3.00
Shaun Livingston
9 Carlos Boozer 1.25 3.00
Deron Williams
9A Carlos Boozer 1.25 3.00
Andrei Kirilenko
10 Ray Allen 1.25 3.00
Paul Pierce
10A Ray Allen 1.25 3.00
Kevin Garnett
11 Yao Ming 1.25 3.00
Tracy McGrady
11A Yao Ming 1.25 3.00
Shane Battier
12 Dwight Howard 1.25 3.00
Rashard Lewis
12A Dwight Howard 1.25 3.00
Jameer Nelson
13 Steve Nash 1.25 3.00
Shawn Marion
13A Steve Nash 1.25 3.00
Amare Stoudemire
14 Chris Paul 1.25 3.00
Tyson Chandler
14A Chris Paul 1.25 3.00
David West
15 Carmelo Anthony 1.25 3.00
Allen Iverson
15A Carmelo Anthony 1.25 3.00
Marcus Camby
16 Pau Gasol 1.25 3.00
Mike Miller
16A Pau Gasol 1.25 3.00
Rudy Gay
17 Ben Gordon 1.25 3.00
Luol Deng
17A Ben Gordon 1.25 3.00
Ben Wallace
18 Andre Iguodala 1.25 3.00
Kyle Korver
18A Andre Iguodala 1.25 3.00
Andre Miller
19 Paul Pierce 1.25 3.00
Ray Allen
19A Paul Pierce 1.25 3.00
Kevin Garnett
20 Tracy McGrady 1.25 3.00
Yao Ming
20A Tracy McGrady 1.25 3.00
Shane Battier
21 Tim Duncan 1.25 3.00
Tony Parker
21A Tim Duncan 1.25 3.00
Manu Ginobili
22 Josh Smith 1.25 3.00
Marvin Williams
22A Josh Smith 1.25 3.00
Joe Johnson
23 LeBron James 2.50 6.00
Anderson Varejao
23A LeBron James 2.50 6.00
Daniel Gibson
24 Kobe Bryant 2.00 5.00
Andrew Bynum
24A Kobe Bryant 1.50 4.00
Luke Walton
25 Vince Carter 1.25 3.00
Jason Kidd
25A Vince Carter 1.25 3.00
Marcus Williams
26 Shaquille O'Neal 1.50 4.00
Dwyane Wade
26A Shaquille O'Neal 1.25 3.00
Antoine Walker
27 Kevin Garnett 1.25 3.00
Paul Pierce
27A Kevin Garnett 1.25 3.00
Ray Allen
28 Chris Bosh 1.25 3.00
Andrea Bargnani
28A Chris Bosh 1.25 3.00
T.J. Ford
29 Baron Davis 1.25 3.00
Al Harrington
29A Baron Davis 1.25 3.00
Monta Ellis
30 Gilbert Arenas 1.25 3.00
Caron Butler
30A Gilbert Arenas 1.25 3.00
Antawn Jamison
31 John Stockton 1.25 3.00
Deron Williams
31A John Stockton 1.25 3.00
Carlos Boozer
32 Magic Johnson 1.50 4.00
Byron Scott
32A Magic Johnson 2.50 6.00
Kobe Bryant
33 Larry Bird 3.00 8.00
Bill Russell
33A Larry Bird 2.50 6.00
Paul Pierce
34 Rick Barry 1.25 3.00
Baron Davis
34A Rick Barry 1.25 3.00
Chris Mullin
35 Isiah Thomas 1.25 3.00
Chauncey Billups
35A Isiah Thomas 1.50 4.00
Dennis Rodman
36 Dominique Wilkins 1.25 3.00
Josh Smith
36A Dominique Wilkins 1.25 3.00
Joe Johnson
37 Dennis Rodman 1.25 3.00
Ben Wallace
37A Dennis Rodman 1.25 3.00
Luol Deng
38 Wilt Chamberlain 2.00 5.00
Moses Malone
38A Wilt Chamberlain 2.00 5.00
Maurice Cheeks
39 Pete Maravich 4.00 10.00
John Stockton
39A Pete Maravich 3.00 8.00
Deron Williams
40 Bill Russell 3.00 8.00
Larry Bird
40A Bill Russell 3.00 8.00
Kevin Garnett
41 Byron Scott 1.50 4.00
Magic Johnson
41A Byron Scott 2.00 5.00
Kobe Bryant
42 Karl Malone 2.00 5.00
John Stockton
42A Karl Malone 1.25 3.00
Carlos Boozer
43 Chris Mullin 1.25 3.00
Baron Davis
43A Chris Mullin 1.25 3.00
Rick Barry
44 Kevin McHale 1.50 4.00
Larry Bird
44A Kevin McHale 1.50 4.00
John Havlicek
45 Clyde Drexler 1.25 3.00
Tracy McGrady
45A Clyde Drexler 1.25 3.00
Yao Ming
46 James Worthy 1.25 3.00
Kobe Bryant
46A James Worthy 2.00 5.00
Magic Johnson
47 Bill Walton 1.25 3.00
Greg Oden
47A Bill Walton 1.25 3.00
Brandon Roy
48 Earl Monroe 1.25 3.00
Stephon Marbury
48A Earl Monroe 1.25 3.00
Jamal Crawford
49 Elgin Baylor 1.50 4.00
Jerry West
49A Elgin Baylor 2.00 5.00
Kobe Bryant
50 David Robinson 2.00 5.00
Tim Duncan
50A David Robinson 1.50 4.00
Tony Parker
51 Nick Young 1.25 3.00
Gilbert Arenas
51A Nick Young 1.25 3.00
Antawn Jamison
52 Greg Oden 2.50 6.00
Bill Walton
52A Greg Oden 2.50 6.00
Brandon Roy
53 Morris Almond 1.25 3.00
Carlos Boozer

A Morris Almond 1.25 3.00
Deron Williams
Alando Tucker 1.25 3.00
Steve Nash
A Alando Tucker 1.25 3.00
Amare Stoudemire
Arron Afflalo 1.25 3.00
Chauncey Billups
A Arron Afflalo 1.50 4.00
Rodney Stuckey
Derrick Byars 1.25 3.00
Andre Iguodala
A Derrick Byars 1.25 3.00
Jason Smith
Adam Haluska 1.25 3.00
Chris Paul
A Adam Haluska 1.25 3.00
Tyson Chandler
3 Corey Brewer 1.50 4.00
Al Jefferson
3A Corey Brewer 1.25 3.00
Randy Foye
Ramon Sessions 1.25 3.00
Michael Redd
A Ramon Sessions 1.25 3.00
Mo Williams
Daequan Cook 2.00 5.00
Dwyane Wade
0A Daequan Cook 2.00 5.00
Shaquille O'Neal
Mike Conley Jr. 1.25 3.00
Pau Gasol
A Mike Conley Jr. 1.25 3.00
Rudy Gay
2 Javaris Crittenton 2.50 6.00
Kobe Bryant
2A Javaris Crittenton 1.25 3.00
Andrew Bynum
3 Jared Jordan 1.25 3.00
Stephon Marbury
3A Jared Jordan 1.25 3.00
Jamal Crawford
4 Aaron Brooks 1.50 4.00
Tracy McGrady
4A Aaron Brooks 2.00 5.00
Yao Ming
5 Marco Belinelli 1.25 3.00
Baron Davis
5A Marco Belinelli 1.25 3.00
Al Harrington
6 Sammy Mejia 1.25 3.00
Arron Afflalo
6A Sammy Mejia 1.25 3.00
Rodney Stuckey
7 Jared Dudley 1.25 3.00
Emeka Okafor
7A Jared Dudley 1.25 3.00
Raymond Felton
8 Rodney Stuckey 1.25 3.00
Arron Afflalo
8A Rodney Stuckey 1.25 3.00
Chauncey Billups
9 JamesOn Curry 1.25 3.00
Ben Gordon
9A JamesOn Curry 1.25 3.00
Aaron Gray
70 Gabe Pruitt 1.25 3.00
Glen Davis
70A Gabe Pruitt 1.25 3.00
Paul Pierce
71 Acie Law 1.25 3.00
Josh Smith
71A Acie Law 1.25 3.00
Joe Johnson
72 Dominic McGuire 1.25 3.00
Gilbert Arenas
72A Dominic McGuire 1.25 3.00
Nick Young
73 Herbert Hill 1.25 3.00
Derrick Byars
73A Herbert Hill 1.25 3.00
Jason Smith
74 Jeff Green 6.00 15.00
Kevin Durant
74A Jeff Green 1.50 4.00
Chris Wilcox
75 Wilson Chandler 1.25 3.00
Stephon Marbury
75A Wilson Chandler 1.25 3.00
Jamal Crawford
76 Marcus Williams 1.50 4.00
Tim Duncan
76A Marcus Williams 1.25 3.00
Tony Parker
77 Josh McRoberts 2.00 5.00
Greg Oden
77A Josh McRoberts 1.25 3.00
Taurean Green
78 Thaddeus Young 1.25 3.00
Andre Iguodala
78A Thaddeus Young 1.25 3.00
Jason Smith
79 Jared Newson 1.25 3.00
Dirk Nowitzki
79A Jared Newson 1.25 3.00
Jason Terry
80 Stephane Lasme 1.25 3.00
Brandan Wright
80A Stephane Lasme 1.25 3.00
Baron Davis
81 Demetris Nichols 1.25 3.00
Wilson Chandler
81A Demetris Nichols 1.25 3.00
Stephon Marbury
82 Julian Wright 1.50 4.00
Chris Paul
82A Julian Wright 1.25 3.00
David West
83 Sean Williams 1.25 3.00
Jason Kidd
83A Sean Williams 1.50 4.00
Vince Carter
84 Chris Richard 1.25 3.00
Corey Brewer
84A Chris Richard 1.25 3.00
Al Jefferson
85 Yi Jianlian 2.00 5.00
Ramon Sessions
85A Yi Jianlian 2.00 5.00
Michael Redd
86 Al Thornton 1.25 3.00
Elton Brand
86A Al Thornton 1.25 3.00
Corey Maggette
87 Carl Landry 1.50 4.00
Yao Ming
87A Carl Landry 1.50 4.00
Aaron Brooks
88 Kevin Durant 6.00 15.00
Jeff Green
88A Kevin Durant 5.00 12.00
Chris Wilcox
89 Brandan Wright 1.25 3.00
Baron Davis
89A Brandan Wright 1.25 3.00
Chris Mullin
90 Nick Fazekas 1.25 3.00
Dirk Nowitzki
90A Nick Fazekas 1.25 3.00
Jared Newson
91 Joakim Noah 2.50 6.00
Luol Deng
91A Joakim Noah 1.50 4.00
Ben Wallace
92 Jermareo Davidson 1.25 3.00
Jared Dudley
92A Jermareo Davidson 1.25 3.00
Emeka Okafor
93 D.J. Strawberry 1.25 3.00
Steve Nash
93A D.J. Strawberry 1.25 3.00
Alando Tucker
94 Glen Davis 1.50 4.00
Paul Pierce
94A Glen Davis 1.25 3.00
Gabe Pruitt
95 Al Horford 2.00 5.00
Josh Smith
95A Al Horford 1.50 4.00
Acie Law
96 Spencer Hawes 1.25 3.00
Mike Bibby
96A Spencer Hawes 1.25 3.00
Brad Miller
97 Taurean Green 2.50 6.00
Greg Oden
97A Taurean Green 1.25 3.00
Josh McRoberts
98 Jason Smith 1.25 3.00
Derrick Byars
98A Jason Smith 1.25 3.00
Herbert Hill
99 Luis Scola 1.50 4.00
Tracy McGrady
99A Luis Scola 1.50 4.00
Aaron Brooks
100 Aaron Gray 1.25 3.00
Ben Wallace
100A Aaron Gray 1.50 4.00
Joakim Noah

2007-08 Topps Co-Signers Dual Autographs

GROUP A ODDS 1:494, GROUP B 1:191
GROUP C ODDS 1:79, GROUP D 1:327
GROUP E ODDS 1:33, GROUP F 1:122
GROUP G ODDS 1:94
UNPRICED GOLD PRINT RUN 9 SETS
UNPRICED GOLD FOIL PRINT RUN 5 SETS
SILVER FOIL PRINT RUN FIVE SETS
UNPRICED PLATE PRINT RUN ONE SET
EXCH.EXPIRATION DATE 12/31/09
CS1 Dwyane Wade A 50.00 125.00
Carmelo Anthony
CS2 Greg Oden A 40.00 100.00
Bill Walton
CS3 Dennis Rodman A 40.00 80.00
Isiah Thomas
CS4 Bill Russell A 100.00 225.00
John Havlicek
CS5 Ray Allen B 35.00 75.00
Paul Pierce
CS7 Shaquille O'Neal A 50.00 100.00
David Robinson
CS8 Elgin Baylor B 50.00 100.00
John Havlicek
CS9 Rick Barry B 20.00 40.00
Baron Davis
CS10 John Stockton A 50.00 100.00
Deron Williams
CS11 Chris Bosh B 20.00 40.00
Andrea Bargnani
CS12 Luke Walton E 6.00 15.00
Marcus Williams
CS13 David Lee E 6.00 15.00
Taurean Green
CS14 Dominic McGuire E 6.00 15.00
Nick Fazekas
CS15 David Lee E 8.00 20.00
Wilson Chandler
CS16 Herbert Hill E 6.00 15.00
Derrick Byars
CS17 Connie Hawkins C 15.00 30.00
Alando Tucker
CS18 Emeka Okafor D 6.00 15.00
Jared Dudley
CS19 Maurice Cheeks B 20.00 40.00
Moses Malone
CS20 Bob Love F 10.00 25.00
Kirk Hinrich
CS21 Hedo Turkoglu F 8.00 20.00
J.J. Redick
CS22 Andrew Bynum C 15.00 40.00
Javaris Crittenton
CS23 Rudy Tomjanovich G 8.00 20.00
Carl Landry
CS24 Manute Bol D 10.00 25.00
Jason Smith
CS25 Wilson Chandler E 6.00 15.00
Sammy Mejia
CS26 Sergio Rodriguez E 6.00 15.00
Jarrett Jack
CS27 Renaldo Balkman C 6.00 15.00
Wilson Chandler
CS28 Patrick O'Bryant F 6.00 15.00
Stephane Lasme
CS29 Daniel Gibson E 6.00 15.00
Acie Law
CS30 Andre Iguodala B 8.00 20.00
Thaddeus Young
CS31 Marcus Williams C 6.00 15.00
Sean Williams
CS32 Danny Granger G 6.00 15.00
Ike Diogu
CS33 Gabe Pruitt E 6.00 15.00
Glen Davis
CS34 Corey Maggette C 6.00 15.00
Al Thornton
CS35 Aaron Brooks E 8.00 20.00
Carl Landry
CS37 Ben Gordon C 10.00 25.00
Chris Duhon
CS38 Sam Dalembert C 6.00 15.00
Jason Smith
CS39 Raymond Felton C 6.00 15.00
Jermareo Davidson
CS40 Len Elmore G 6.00 15.00
D.J. Strawberry
CS41 Rodney Stuckey E 8.00 20.00
Arron Afflalo
CS42 Carlos Boozer B 6.00 15.00
Morris Almond
CS43 Marco Belinelli E 6.00 15.00
Stephane Lasme
CS44 Jason Smith C 6.00 15.00
Daequan Cook
CS45 Taurean Green E 6.00 15.00
Jarrett Jack
CS46 Sean Williams C 6.00 15.00
Jared Dudley
CS47 Greg Oden A 40.00 100.00
John Havlicek
CS48 Yi Jianlian B 30.00 60.00
Marco Belinelli
CS49 Nick Young C 6.00 15.00
Gabe Pruitt
CS50 Thaddeus Young B 8.00 20.00
Javaris Crittenton

2007-08 Topps Co-Signers Rookie Autographs

GROUP A ODDS 1:112, GROUP B 1:1:16
*GOLD: .5X TO 1.25X BASE HI
GOLD PRINT RUN 25 SER.#'d SETS
UNPRICED GOLD FOIL PRINT RUN 10 SETS
UNPRICED SILVER FOIL PRINT RUN ONE SET
UNPRICED PLATE PRINT RUN ONE SET
51 Nick Young A 6.00 15.00
52 Greg Oden A 25.00 60.00
53 Morris Almond B 4.00 10.00
54 Alando Tucker A 4.00 10.00
55 Arron Afflalo B 5.00 12.00
56 Derrick Byars B 4.00 10.00
57 Adam Haluska B 4.00 10.00
62 Javaris Crittenton B 4.00 10.00
63 Jared Jordan B 4.00 10.00
64 Aaron Brooks B 4.00 10.00
68 Rodney Stuckey B 6.00 15.00
69 JamesOn Curry B 4.00 10.00
71 Acie Law A 4.00 10.00
72 Dominic McGuire B 4.00 10.00
73 Herbert Hill B 4.00 10.00
78 Thaddeus Young A 5.00 12.00
85 Yi Jianlian A 10.00 25.00
86 Al Thornton A 4.00 10.00
89 Brandan Wright A 4.00 10.00
90 Nick Fazekas B 4.00 10.00
92 Jermareo Davidson B 4.00 10.00
94 Glen Davis B 6.00 15.00
96 Spencer Hawes A 4.00 10.00
98 Jason Smith A 4.00 10.00
100 Aaron Gray B 4.00 10.00

2007-08 Topps Co-Signers Triple Autographs

STATED PRINT RUN 9 TO 19 SETS
UNLESS LISTED IN CHECKLIST
PRINT RUNS ANNOUNCED BY TOPPS
UNPRICED GOLD PRINT RUN 5 SER.#'d SETS
UNPRICED GOLD FOIL PRINT RUN 3 SETS
UNPRICED SILVER FOIL PRINT RUN ONE SET
TS3 Dominique Wilkins 30.00 60.00
Josh Smith
Acie Law
TS4 Gerald Wallace 30.00 60.00
Emeka Okafor
Raymond Felton
TS7 Carmelo Anthony 100.00 200.00
Chris Bosh
Dwyane Wade
TS8 Tony Parker 60.00 120.00
Dwyane Wade
Chauncey Billups
TS9 Buck Williams 25.00 50.00
Otis Birdsong
Micheal Ray Richardson
TS10 Isiah Thomas 100.00 200.00
Magic Johnson
John Stockton

2008-09 Topps Co-Signers

This set was released on November 28, 2008. The base set consists of 140 cards. Cards 1-100 feature veterans, and cards 101-140 are rookies serial numbered of 2008.
UNPRICED HYP.PLAT.PRINT RUN ONE SET
UNPRICED PRESS PLATE PRINT RUN ONE SET
1 Tracy McGrady .50 1.25
2 Jason Kidd .50 1.25
3 Allen Iverson .60 1.50
4 Chris Bosh .50 1.25
5 Baron Davis .50 1.25
6 Chauncey Billups .50 1.25
7 Ben Gordon .50 1.25
8 Jermaine O'Neal .50 1.25
9 Jason Richardson .50 1.25
10 Gilbert Arenas .50 1.25
11 Jamal Crawford .40 1.00
12 Dwight Howard 1.00 2.50
13 Steve Nash .50 1.25
14 Vince Carter .60 1.50
15 Carmelo Anthony .60 1.50
16 Pau Gasol .50 1.25
17 Josh Smith .50 1.25
18 Yi Jianlian .50 1.25
19 Andre Iguodala .50 1.25
20 Ray Allen .50 1.25
21 Tim Duncan .75 2.00
22 Tayshaun Prince .50 1.25
23 LeBron James 2.50 6.00
24 Kobe Bryant 2.50 6.00
25 Rudy Gay .50 1.25
26 Caron Butler .50 1.25
27 Al Jefferson .50 1.25
28 Deron Williams .50 1.25
29 Luol Deng .50 1.25
30 Chris Paul .75 2.00
31 Brad Miller .40 1.00
32 Shaquille O'Neal 1.00 2.50
33 Dwyane Wade 1.00 2.50
34 Paul Pierce .60 1.50
35 Kevin Durant 2.00 5.00
36 Anderson Varejao .40 1.00
37 Rashard Lewis .40 1.00
38 Jamario Moon .30 .75
39 Manu Ginobili .50 1.25
40 Mo Williams .40 1.00
41 Dirk Nowitzki .60 1.50
42 David Lee .40 1.00
43 Stephen Jackson .40 1.00
44 Antawn Jamison .50 1.25
45 Mike Dunleavy .40 1.00
46 Devin Harris .50 1.25
47 Andrei Kirilenko .40 1.00
48 Gerald Wallace .50 1.25
49 Mike Miller .50 1.25
50 Corey Maggette .40 1.00
51 Yao Ming .60 1.50
52 Greg Oden .50 1.25
53 Kevin Martin .50 1.25
54 Joe Johnson .50 1.25
55 Kevin Garnett 1.00 2.50
56 Ricky Davis .40 1.00
57 Chris Wilcox .30 .75
58 Rashad McCants .30 .75
59 T.J. Ford .30 .75
60 David West .50 1.25
61 Amare Stoudemire .50 1.25
62 Al Thornton .40 1.00
63 Kirk Hinrich .50 1.25
64 Samuel Dalembert .30 .75
65 Tony Parker .50 1.25
66 Ben Wallace .50 1.25
67 Shawn Marion .50 1.25
68 LaMarcus Aldridge .50 1.25
69 Eddy Curry .30 .75
70 Richard Hamilton .40 1.00
71 Danny Granger .50 1.25
72 Elton Brand .50 1.25
73 Raymond Felton .40 1.00
74 Richard Jefferson .50 1.25
75 Hedo Turkoglu .50 1.25
76 Peja Stojakovic .50 1.25
77 Brandon Roy .50 1.25
78 Ryan Gomes .30 .75
79 Jeff Green .40 1.00
80 Michael Redd .50 1.25
81 Andre Miller .40 1.00
82 Carlos Boozer .50 1.25
83 Marcus Camby .30 .75
84 Hakim Warrick .40 1.00
85 Mike Bibby .40 1.00
86 Josh Howard .40 1.00
87 Andrew Bynum .60 1.50
88 Monta Ellis .50 1.25
89 Shane Battier .40 1.00
90 Ron Artest .50 1.25
91 Dennis Rodman .75 2.00
92 Dominique Wilkins .60 1.50
93 Larry Bird 1.50 4.00
94 John Stockton .75 2.00
95 Moses Malone .50 1.25
96 David Robinson .75 2.00
97 Jerry West .60 1.50
98 Bill Russell .75 2.00
99 George Gervin .60 1.50
100 Magic Johnson 1.25 3.00
101 Derrick Rose RC 8.00 20.00
102 Michael Beasley RC 1.50 4.00
103 O.J. Mayo RC 1.50 4.00
104 Russell Westbrook RC 5.00 12.00
105 Kevin Love RC 4.00 10.00
106 Danilo Gallinari RC 1.50 4.00
107 Eric Gordon RC 2.50 6.00
108 Joe Alexander RC 1.00 2.50
109 D.J. Augustin RC 1.00 2.50
110 Brook Lopez RC 1.50 4.00
111 Jerryd Bayless RC 1.00 2.50
112 Jason Thompson RC 1.00 2.50
113 Anthony Randolph RC 1.25 3.00
114 Robin Lopez RC 1.00 2.50
115 Marreese Speights RC 1.00 2.50
116 Roy Hibbert RC 1.50 4.00
117 JaVale McGee RC 1.50 4.00
118 J.J. Hickson RC 1.25 3.00
119 Alexis Ajinca RC 1.00 2.50
120 Ryan Anderson RC 1.50 4.00
121 Courtney Lee RC 1.50 4.00
122 Kosta Koufos RC 1.00 2.50
123 Donte Greene RC 1.00 2.50
124 George Hill RC 1.50 4.00
125 D.J. White RC 1.00 2.50
126 J.R. Giddens RC 1.00 2.50
127 Joey Dorsey RC 1.00 2.50
128 Mario Chalmers RC 1.50 4.00
129 DeAndre Jordan RC 2.00 5.00
130 Chris Douglas-Roberts RC 1.00 2.50
131 Malik Hairston RC 1.00 2.50
132 Sonny Weems RC 1.00 2.50
133 Kyle Weaver RC 1.00 2.50
134 Patrick Ewing Jr. RC 1.00 2.50
135 Mike Taylor RC 1.00 2.50
136 Walter Sharpe RC 1.00 2.50
137 Rudy Fernandez RC 1.25 3.00
138 Nicolas Batum RC 1.50 4.00
139 Brandon Rush RC 1.00 2.50
140 Darrell Arthur RC 1.00 2.50

2008-09 Topps Co-Signers Bronze

*1-100 BRONZE: .5X TO 1.25 BASE HI
*101-140 BRONZE: SAME AS BASE
BRONZE PRINT RUN 299 SER.#'d SETS
101 Derrick Rose 10.00 25.00

2008-09 Topps Co-Signers Gold

*1-100 GOLD: 1X TO 2.5X BASE HI
*101-140 GOLD: .75X TO 2X BASE HI
STATED PRINT RUN 99 SER.#'d SETS
101 Derrick Rose 20.00 50.00

2008-09 Topps Co-Signers Hyper Bronze

*1-100 HYP.BRNZ: 1.5X TO 4X BASE
*101-140 HYP.BRNZ: 1.25X TO 3X BASE
STATED PRINT RUN 50 SER.#'d SETS

2008-09 Topps Co-Signers Hyper Silver

*1-100 HYP.SILV: 2X TO 5X BASE
*101-140 HYP.SILV: 1.5X TO 4X BASE
STATED PRINT RUN 25 SER.#'d SETS

2008-09 Topps Co-Signers Silver

*SILVER 1-100: .6X TO 1.5X BASE HI
*SILVER 101-140: .5X TO 1.25X BASE HI
STATED PRINT RUN 199 SER.#'d SETS
101 Derrick Rose 12.50 30.00

2008-09 Topps Co-Signers Changing Faces

STATED PRINT RUN 899 SER.#'d SETS
*BRONZE: .5X TO 1.25X BASE HI
BRONZE PRINT RUN 399 SER.#'d SETS
*GOLD: .6X TO 1.5X BASE HI
GOLD PRINT RUN 199 SER.#'d SETS
*SILVER: .75X TO 2X BASE HI
SILVER PRINT RUN 99 SER.#'d SETS
CF1 Tracy McGrady .60 1.50
CF2 Chris Bosh .60 1.50
CF3 Chauncey Billups .60 1.50
CF4 Gilbert Arenas .60 1.50
CF5 Dwight Howard 1.25 3.00
CF6 LeBron James 3.00 8.00
CF7 Kobe Bryant 3.00 8.00
CF8 Chris Paul 1.00 2.50
CF9 Paul Pierce .75 2.00
CF10 Kevin Durant 2.50 6.00
CF11 Dirk Nowitzki .75 2.00
CF12 Greg Oden .60 1.50
CF13 Tony Parker .60 1.50
CF14 Elton Brand .60 1.50
CF15 Brandon Roy .60 1.50
CF16 Carlos Boozer .60 1.50
CF17 Allen Iverson .75 2.00
CF18 Steve Nash .60 1.50
CF19 Vince Carter .75 2.00
CF20 Carmelo Anthony .75 2.00
CF21 Andre Iguodala .60 1.50
CF22 Ray Allen .60 1.50
CF23 Tim Duncan 1.00 2.50
CF24 Shaquille O'Neal 1.25 3.00
CF25 Dwyane Wade 1.25 3.00
CF26 Manu Ginobili .60 1.50
CF27 Yao Ming .75 2.00
CF28 Kevin Garnett 1.25 3.00
CF29 Amare Stoudemire .60 1.50
CF30 Michael Redd .60 1.50
CF31 Jason Kidd .60 1.50
CF32 Deron Williams .60 1.50
CF33 Kevin Martin .60 1.50
CF34 Joe Johnson .60 1.50
CF35 Richard Hamilton .50 1.25
CF36 Magic Johnson 1.50 4.00
CF37 Dominique Wilkins .75 2.00
CF38 Larry Bird 2.00 5.00
CF39 Jerry West .75 2.00
CF40 Bill Russell 1.00 2.50
CF41 Derrick Rose 5.00 12.00
CF42 Michael Beasley 1.00 2.50
CF43 O.J. Mayo 1.00 2.50
CF44 Russell Westbrook 3.00 8.00
CF45 Kevin Love 2.50 6.00
CF46 Brook Lopez 1.00 2.50
CF47 Eric Gordon 1.50 4.00
CF48 Joe Alexander .60 1.50
CF49 D.J. Augustin .60 1.50
CF50 Jerryd Bayless .60 1.50

2008-09 Topps Co-Signers Dual Autographs

GROUP A PRINT RUN 7 SER.#'d SETS
GROUP B PRINT RUN 43 SER.#'d SETS
GROUP C PRINT RUN 240 SER.#'d SETS
SOME UNPRICED DUE TO SCARCITY
UNPRICED GOLD PRINT RUN FIVE SETS
UNPRICED HYP.GOLD PRINT RUN 3 SETS
UNPRICED HYP.PLAT.PRINT RUN ONE SET
UNPRICED PRESS PLATE PRINT RUN ONE SET
CSAC Darrell Arthur 8.00 20.00
Mario Chalmers C
CSBG Andrea Bargnani 10.00 25.00
Danilo Gallinari B
CSBJ Caron Butler 8.00 20.00
Antawn Jamison C
CSBS Elgin Baylor 10.00 25.00
Dolph Schayes C
CSBT Chauncey Billups 15.00 30.00
Isiah Thomas B
CSCB Mario Chalmers 8.00 20.00
Carlos Boozer C
CSDG Baron Davis 15.00 40.00
Eric Gordon B
CSDM Baron Davis 8.00 20.00
Corey Maggette B
CSDRD Chris Douglas-Roberts 6.00 15.00
Joey Dorsey C
CSDT Baron Davis 10.00 25.00
Al Thornton B
CSFA T.J. Ford 6.00 15.00
D.J. Augustin C
CSFG T.J. Ford 8.00 20.00
Danny Granger B
CSFJ T.J. Ford 6.00 15.00
Jarrett Jack C
CSGA Ben Gordon 12.50 30.00
Ray Allen B
CSGM Rudy Gay 6.00 15.00
Jamario Moon C
CSHB Elvin Hayes 12.50 30.00
Rick Barry C
CSHE Roy Hibbert 8.00 20.00
Patrick Ewing Jr. C
CSHT Spencer Hawes 8.00 20.00
Jason Thompson C
CSHW John Havlicek 30.00 60.00
Jo Jo White B
CSHWI Devin Harris 8.00 20.00
Sean Williams B
CSHWS J.J. Hickson 8.00 20.00
John Williams C
CSIY Andre Iguodala 6.00 15.00
Thaddeus Young B
CSJC Yi Jianlian 25.00 50.00
Vince Carter B
CSLC David Lee 6.00 15.00
Wilson Chandler C
CSLD Carl Landry 6.00 15.00
Joey Dorsey C
CSLJ Acie Law 10.00 25.00
DeAndre Jordan C
CSLL Brook Lopez 8.00 20.00
Robin Lopez C
CSLLO Stan Love 10.00 25.00
Kevin Love B
CSLS David Lee 6.00 15.00
Marreese Speights C
CSLW Kevin Love 25.00 60.00
Russell Westbrook B
CSMG O.J. Mayo 15.00 40.00
Rudy Gay B
CSML Mike Miller 15.00 40.00
Kevin Love B
CSMM Pamela McGee 6.00 15.00
JaVale McGee C
CSMS Mike Miller 6.00 15.00
Marreese Speights C
CSMY O.J. Mayo 20.00 40.00
Nick Young B
CSPE Robert Parish 8.00 20.00
Mark Eaton C
CSPW Mickael Pietrus 6.00 15.00
Gerald Wallace C
CSRB Derrick Rose 100.00 200.00
Michael Beasley B
CSRD Derrick Rose 75.00 150.00
Luol Deng B
CSRH Brandon Rush 8.00 20.00
Roy Hibbert C
CSSS Dolph Schayes 6.00 15.00
Danny Schayes C
CSSY Rodney Stuckey 8.00 20.00
Nick Young B
CSTG Al Thornton 10.00 25.00
Eric Gordon B
CSTH Jason Thompson 8.00 20.00
George Hill C
CSWC Dominique Wilkins 25.00 50.00
Vince Carter B
CSWL Spud Webb 8.00 20.00
Fat Lever C

2008-09 Topps Co-Signers Rookie Autographs

GROUP A PRINT RUN 50 SER.#'d SETS
GROUP B PRINT RUN 100 SER.#'d SETS
GROUP C PRINT RUN 350 SER.#'d SETS
*GOLD: .75X TO 2X BASE HI
GOLD PRINT RUN 5 TO 25 SETS
UNPRICED HYP.PLAT PRINT RUN ONE SET
UNPRICED HYP.SIL.PRINT RUN 10 SETS
UNPRICED PRESS PLATE PRINT RUN ONE SET
101 Derrick Rose A 125.00 250.00
102 Michael Beasley A 12.00 30.00
103 O.J. Mayo A 12.00 30.00
104 Russell Westbrook B 40.00 100.00
105 Kevin Love A 25.00 60.00
106 Danilo Gallinari B 6.00 15.00
107 Eric Gordon A 15.00 40.00
108 Joe Alexander B 4.00 10.00
109 D.J. Augustin C 4.00 10.00
110 Brook Lopez B 6.00 15.00
111 Jerryd Bayless B 4.00 10.00
112 Jason Thompson C 4.00 10.00
113 Anthony Randolph C 5.00 12.00
114 Robin Lopez C 4.00 10.00
115 Marreese Speights C 4.00 10.00
116 Roy Hibbert C 6.00 15.00
117 JaVale McGee C 6.00 15.00
118 J.J. Hickson C 5.00 12.00
120 Ryan Anderson C 6.00 15.00
121 Courtney Lee C 6.00 15.00
122 Kosta Koufos C 4.00 10.00
123 Donte Greene C 4.00 10.00
124 George Hill C 6.00 15.00
125 D.J. White C 4.00 10.00
126 J.R. Giddens C 4.00 10.00
127 Joey Dorsey C 4.00 10.00
128 Mario Chalmers C 6.00 15.00
130 Chris Douglas-Roberts C 4.00 10.00
139 Brandon Rush B 5.00 12.00
140 Darrell Arthur C 4.00 10.00

2008-09 Topps Co-Signers Rookie Photo Shoot Quad Autographs

ANNOUNCED PRINT RUN 25 SETS
UNPRICED RED INK EXISTS
RPQABRM D.J. Augustin 100.00 250.00
Jerryd Bayless
Derrick Rose
O.J. Mayo
RPQBLGA Michael Beasley 50.00 120.00
Kevin Love
Brook Lopez
Joe Alexander
RPQBLRM Michael Beasley 100.00 250.00
Kevin Love
Derrick Rose
O.J. Mayo
RPQRARD Brandon Rush 100.00 175.00
Darrell Arthur
Derrick Rose
Chris Douglas-Roberts
RPQRMWG Derrick Rose 200.00 400.00
O.J. Mayo
Russell Westbrook
Eric Gordon

2008-09 Topps Co-Signers Triple Autographs

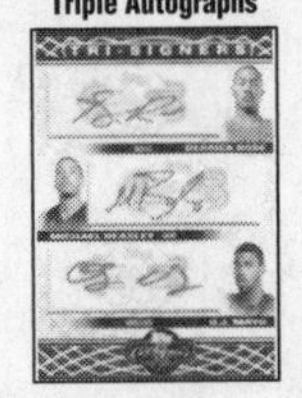

STATED PRINT RUN 36 SER.#'d SETS
UNPRICED HYP.PLAT.PRINT RUN ONE SET
UNPRICED PRESS PLATE PRINT RUN ONE SET
TSBLG Michael Beasley 50.00 100.00
Kevin Love
Danilo Gallinari
TSGAB Eric Gordon 20.00 50.00
D.J. Augustin
Jerryd Bayless
TSGAR Danilo Gallinari 20.00 50.00
Joe Alexander
Anthony Randolph
TSGGA Danilo Gallinari 20.00 50.00
Eric Gordon
Joe Alexander
TSLTR Brook Lopez 20.00 50.00
Jason Thompson
Anthony Randolph
TSMLB O.J. Mayo 40.00 100.00
Kevin Love
Jerryd Bayless
TSRBM Derrick Rose 125.00 300.00
Michael Beasley
O.J. Mayo
TSRGA Derrick Rose 100.00 250.00
Eric Gordon
D.J. Augustin
TSRMB Derrick Rose 100.00 250.00
O.J. Mayo
Jerryd Bayless
TSWLL Russell Westbrook 50.00 120.00
Kevin Love
Brook Lopez

2008 Topps Draft Day Autographs

DDBL Brook Lopez/50 40.00 100.00
DDDR Derrick Rose/100 250.00 500.00
DDEG Eric Gordon/50 50.00 125.00
DDJB Jerryd Bayless/50 30.00 80.00
DDKL Kevin Love/50 75.00 200.00
DDMB Michael Beasley/100 40.00 100.00
DDOM O.J. Mayo/100 40.00 100.00

2007-08 Topps Echelon

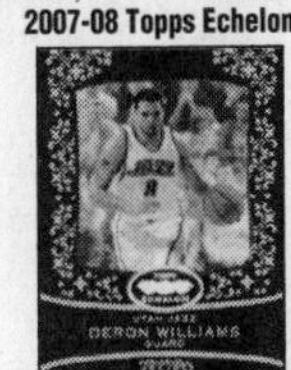

This 85-card set was released in December, 2007. The set was issued into the hobby in four-card packs (mini-boxes) with an $125 SRP which came four to a full box. There were three full boxes to a carton and two cartons to a case. Cards numbered 1-40 feature veterans, while cards numbered 41-50 feature retired greats and cards numbered 51-85 feature NBA rookies. Every card in this set was serial numbered and the serial numbering was done thusly: Cards numbered 1-50 had a stated print run of 999 serial numbered sets, cards 51-54 were issued to a stated print run of 199 serial numbered sets, cards 55-62 had a stated print run of 399 serial numbered sets, cards 63-72 had a stated print run of 499 serial numbered sets and the set concludes with cards 73-85 which had a stated print run of 999 serial numbered sets.
1 Tracy McGrady 1.25 3.00
2 Chris Paul 2.50 6.00
3 Dwyane Wade 3.00 8.00
4 Elton Brand 1.25 3.00
5 Josh Smith 1.25 3.00
6 Brandon Roy 1.50 4.00
7 Andrea Bargnani 1.50 4.00
8 Deron Williams 2.00 5.00
9 Andre Iguodala 1.25 3.00
10 Mike Bibby 1.25 3.00
11 Yao Ming 1.50 4.00
12 Dwight Howard 2.00 5.00
13 Steve Nash 1.50 4.00
14 Randy Foye 1.25 3.00
15 Carmelo Anthony 1.50 4.00
16 Pau Gasol 1.25 3.00
17 Jermaine O'Neal 1.25 3.00
18 Ben Gordon 1.25 3.00
19 Vince Carter 1.50 4.00

20 Tim Duncan	2.00	5.00
21 Kevin Garnett	2.50	6.00
22 Michael Redd	1.25	3.00
23 LeBron James	6.00	15.00
24 Kobe Bryant	6.00	15.00
25 Chris Webber	1.25	3.00
26 Allen Iverson	1.50	4.00
27 Chauncey Billups	1.25	3.00
28 Paul Pierce	1.50	4.00
29 Amare Stoudemire	1.25	3.00
30 Emeka Okafor	1.25	3.00
31 Jason Kidd	1.25	3.00
32 Shaquille O'Neal	2.50	6.00
33 Grant Hill	1.50	4.00
34 Ray Allen	1.25	3.00
35 Adam Morrison	1.25	3.00
36 Gilbert Arenas	1.25	3.00
37 Baron Davis	1.25	3.00
38 Mike Miller	1.25	3.00
39 Chris Bosh	1.25	3.00
40 Dirk Nowitzki	1.50	4.00
41 Bob Pettit	2.00	5.00
42 Bill Russell	2.50	6.00
43 Rick Barry	1.50	4.00
44 Oscar Robertson	1.50	4.00
45 Jerry Lucas	1.50	4.00
46 Magic Johnson	4.00	10.00
47 Larry Bird	5.00	12.00
48 Wes Unseld	1.50	4.00
49 James Worthy	2.00	5.00
50 Bob McAdoo	1.50	4.00
51 Greg Oden RC	6.00	15.00
52 Yi Jianlian RC	8.00	20.00
53 Brandan Wright RC	5.00	12.00
54 Nick Young RC	8.00	20.00
55 Spencer Hawes RC	4.00	10.00
56 Acie Law RC	4.00	10.00
57 Rodney Stuckey RC	6.00	15.00
58 Al Thornton RC	4.00	10.00
59 Arron Afflalo RC	5.00	12.00
60 Marco Belinelli RC	4.00	10.00
61 Gabe Pruitt RC	4.00	10.00
62 Wilson Chandler RC	6.00	15.00
63 Jared Dudley RC	4.00	10.00
64 Marcus Williams RC	4.00	10.00
65 Aaron Brooks RC	4.00	10.00
66 Daequan Cook RC	4.00	10.00
67 Thaddeus Young RC	5.00	12.00
68 Josh McRoberts RC	4.00	10.00
69 Nick Fazekas RC	4.00	10.00
70 Javaris Crittenton RC	4.00	10.00
71 Alando Tucker RC	4.00	10.00
72 Carl Landry RC	4.00	10.00
73 Al Horford RC	4.00	10.00
74 Kevin Durant RC	25.00	60.00
75 Corey Brewer RC	4.00	10.00
76 Jeff Green RC	4.00	10.00
77 Mike Conley Jr. RC	5.00	12.00
78 Joakim Noah RC	8.00	20.00
79 Sean Williams RC	3.00	8.00
80 Julian Wright RC	3.00	8.00
81 Reyshawn Terry RC	3.00	8.00
82 Aaron Gray RC	3.00	8.00
83 Glen Davis RC	5.00	12.00
84 Jermareo Davidson RC	3.00	8.00
85 Taurean Green RC	3.00	8.00

2007-08 Topps Echelon Blue

*1-50 BLUE: 1.25X TO 3X BASE HI
1-50 BLUE PRINT RUN 25 SER.#'d SETS
51-85 BLUE PRINT RUN 10 SER.#'d SETS
51-85 BLUE UNPRICED DUE TO SCARCITY

2007-08 Topps Echelon Red

*1-40 RED: .75X TO 2X BASE HI
*41-50 RED: .6X TO 1.5X BASE HI
1-50 PRINT RUN 50 SER.#'d SETS
*51-85 RC RED: .75X TO 2X BASE HI
51-85 PRINT RUN 25 SER.#'d SETS

74 Kevin Durant	100.00	200.00

2007-08 Topps Echelon Autographs

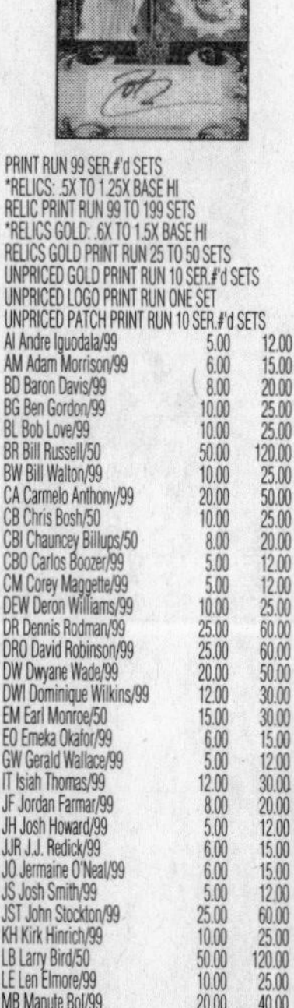

PRINT RUN 99 SER.#'d SETS
*RELICS: .5X TO 1.25X BASE HI
RELIC PRINT RUN 99 TO 199 SETS
*RELICS GOLD: .6X TO 1.5X BASE HI
RELICS GOLD PRINT RUN 25 TO 50 SETS
UNPRICED GOLD PRINT RUN 10 SER.#'d SETS
UNPRICED LOGO PRINT RUN ONE SET
UNPRICED PATCH PRINT RUN 10 SER.#'d SETS

AI Andre Iguodala/99	5.00	12.00
AM Adam Morrison/99	6.00	15.00
BD Baron Davis/99	8.00	20.00
BG Ben Gordon/99	10.00	25.00
BL Bob Love/99	10.00	25.00
BR Bill Russell/50	50.00	120.00
BW Bill Walton/99	10.00	25.00
CA Carmelo Anthony/99	20.00	50.00
CB Chris Bosh/50	10.00	25.00
CBI Chauncey Billups/50	8.00	20.00
CBO Carlos Boozer/99	5.00	12.00
CM Corey Maggette/99	5.00	12.00
DEW Deron Williams/99	10.00	25.00
DR Dennis Rodman/99	25.00	60.00
DRO David Robinson/99	25.00	60.00
DW Dwyane Wade/99	20.00	50.00
DWI Dominique Wilkins/99	12.00	30.00
EM Earl Monroe/50	15.00	30.00
EO Emeka Okafor/99	6.00	15.00
GW Gerald Wallace/99	5.00	12.00
IT Isiah Thomas/99	12.00	30.00
JF Jordan Farmar/99	8.00	20.00
JH Josh Howard/99	5.00	12.00
JJR J.J. Redick/99	6.00	15.00
JO Jermaine O'Neal/99	6.00	15.00
JS Josh Smith/99	5.00	12.00
JST John Stockton/99	25.00	60.00
KH Kirk Hinrich/99	10.00	25.00
LB Larry Bird/50	50.00	120.00
LE Len Elmore/99	10.00	25.00
MB Manute Bol/99	20.00	40.00
MJ Magic Johnson/50	40.00	80.00
RA Ray Allen/99	12.00	30.00
RB Rick Barry/99	10.00	25.00
RF Randy Foye/99	5.00	12.00
RT Rudy Tomjanovich/99	10.00	25.00
SO Shaquille O'Neal/50	40.00	80.00
TJF T.J. Ford/99	5.00	12.00
TP Tony Parker/99	10.00	25.00
VC Vince Carter/50	20.00	40.00

2007-08 Topps Echelon McDonald's All-American Autographs

PRINT RUN 100 SER.#'d SETS

BW Brandan Wright	15.00	40.00
DC Daequan Cook	15.00	40.00
GO Greg Oden	30.00	80.00
JC Javaris Crittenton	15.00	40.00
TY Thaddeus Young	20.00	50.00

2007-08 Topps Echelon McDonald's All-American Autographs Five-Piece Relics

PRINT RUN 75 SER.#'d SETS
GAME/NAME LETTER CARDS #'d ONE OF ONE
GAME/NAME UNPRICED DUE TO SCARCITY

BW Brandan Wright	15.00	40.00
DC Daequan Cook	15.00	40.00
GO Greg Oden	25.00	60.00
JC Javaris Crittenton	15.00	40.00
SH Spencer Hawes	15.00	40.00
TY Thaddeus Young	15.00	40.00

2007-08 Topps Echelon McDonald's All-American Autographs Super Size Patches

PRINT RUN 25 SER.#'d SETS

BW Brandan Wright	30.00	80.00
DC Daequan Cook	30.00	80.00
JC Javaris Crittenton	30.00	80.00
SH Spencer Hawes	30.00	80.00
TY Thaddeus Young	50.00	100.00

2007-08 Topps Echelon Rookie Autographs

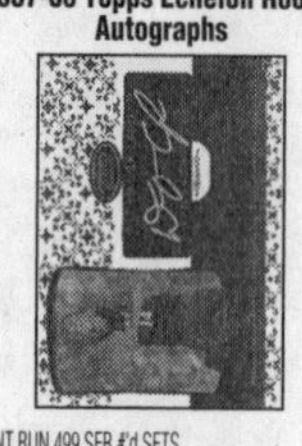

PRINT RUN 499 SER.#'d SETS
*GOLD: .5X TO 1.25X BASE HI
GOLD PRINT RUN 50 SER.#'d SETS

63 Jared Dudley	6.00	15.00
64 Marcus Williams	6.00	15.00
65 Aaron Brooks	6.00	15.00
66 Daequan Cook	6.00	15.00
67 Thaddeus Young	8.00	20.00
68 Josh McRoberts	6.00	15.00
69 Nick Fazekas	6.00	15.00
70 Javaris Crittenton	6.00	15.00
71 Alando Tucker	6.00	15.00
72 Carl Landry	6.00	15.00

2007-08 Topps Echelon Rookie Autographs Dual Relics

PRINT RUN 399 SER.#'d SETS
*GOLD: .6X TO 1.5X BASE HI
GOLD PRINT RUN 50 SER.#'d SETS
PATCHES: .75X TO 2X BASE HI
PATCH PRINT RUN 50 SER.#'d SETS
UNPRICED PATCH GOLD PRINT RUN 5 SETS

55 Spencer Hawes	6.00	15.00
56 Acie Law	6.00	15.00
57 Rodney Stuckey	10.00	25.00
58 Al Thornton	6.00	15.00
59 Arron Afflalo	8.00	20.00
60 Marco Belinelli	6.00	15.00
61 Gabe Pruitt	6.00	15.00
62 Wilson Chandler	10.00	25.00

2007-08 Topps Echelon Rookie Autographs Quad Relics

PRINT RUN 199 SER.#'d SETS
*GOLD: .5X TO 1.25X BASE HI
GOLD PRINT RUN 50 SER.#'d SETS

51 Greg Oden	30.00	80.00
52 Yi Jianlian	20.00	50.00
53 Brandan Wright	12.00	30.00
54 Nick Young	20.00	50.00

2007-08 Topps Echelon Rookie Autographs Quad Patches

PRINT RUN 25 SER.#'d SETS
UNPRICED GOLD PRINT RUN FIVE SETS

51 Greg Oden	150.00	300.00
52 Yi Jianlian	60.00	150.00
53 Brandan Wright	40.00	100.00
54 Nick Young	60.00	150.00

2005-06 Topps First Row

This 150-card set was released in January, 2006. The set was issued in 16-pack boxes which cames six boxes to a case. Each pack had three base cards plus one card which was either a serial numbered autograph, relic, autograph relic, parallel or insert card. Cards numbered 101 through 150 were issued to a stated print run of 549 serial numbered sets. Initial pack SRP was $6.99.

1 Shaquille O'Neal	1.00	2.50
2 Marcus Camby	.40	1.00
3 Caron Butler	.50	1.25
4 Carlos Boozer	.50	1.25
5 Peja Stojakovic	.50	1.25
6 Chris Webber	.50	1.25
7 Vince Carter	.75	2.00
8 Bobby Simmons	.30	.75
9 Pau Gasol	.50	1.25
10 Stromile Swift	.30	.75
11 Carmelo Anthony	1.00	2.50
12 Drew Gooden	.40	1.00
13 Al Harrington	.40	1.00
14 Emeka Okafor	.50	1.25
15 Gilbert Arenas	.50	1.25
16 Tony Parker	.50	1.25
17 Steve Nash	.60	1.50
18 Jamal Crawford	.40	1.00
19 Troy Hudson	.30	.75
20 Kobe Bryant	2.50	6.00
21 Tracy McGrady	.60	1.50
22 Chauncey Billups	.50	1.25
23 Devin Harris	.50	1.25
24 Brevin Knight	.30	.75
25 Joe Johnson	.50	1.25
26 Nenad Krstic	.30	.75
27 Primoz Brezec	.30	.75
28 Mehmet Okur	.30	.75
29 Shareef Abdur-Rahim	.40	1.00
30 Amare Stoudemire	.50	1.25
31 Quentin Richardson	.40	1.00
32 Kevin Garnett	1.00	2.50
33 Shane Battier	.40	1.00
34 Elton Brand	.50	1.25
35 Kenyon Martin	.50	1.25
36 LeBron James	2.50	6.00
37 Al Jefferson	.50	1.25
38 Jermaine O'Neal	.50	1.25
39 Ron Artest	.50	1.25
40 Luke Ridnour	.40	1.00
41 Sebastian Telfair	.40	1.00
42 Steve Francis	.50	1.25
43 Jason Kidd	.75	2.00
44 Ben Wallace	.50	1.25
45 Mike Miller	.50	1.25
46 Jamaal Tinsley	.30	.75
47 Richard Hamilton	.40	1.00
48 Jerry Stackhouse	.40	1.00
49 Kirk Hinrich	.50	1.25
50 Josh Childress	.40	1.00
51 Jamaal Magloire	.30	.75
52 Yao Ming	.60	1.50
53 Tyson Chandler	.40	1.00
54 Andrei Kirilenko	.40	1.00
55 Rashard Lewis	.50	1.25
56 Shawn Marion	.50	1.25
57 Grant Hill	.60	1.50
58 Wally Szczerbiak	.40	1.00
59 Antoine Walker	.40	1.00
60 Corey Maggette	.40	1.00
61 Rasheed Wallace	.50	1.25
62 Dirk Nowitzki	.75	2.00
63 Paul Pierce	.60	1.50
64 Tim Duncan	.75	2.00
65 Desmond Mason	.30	.75
66 Ray Allen	.50	1.25
67 Mike Bibby	.50	1.25
68 Andre Iguodala	.50	1.25
69 J.R. Smith	.50	1.25
70 Dwyane Wade	1.25	3.00
71 Shaun Livingston	.30	.75
72 Jason Richardson	.50	1.25
73 Earl Boykins	.30	.75
74 Ben Gordon	.50	1.25
75 Stephen Jackson	.40	1.00
76 Samuel Dalembert	.30	.75
77 Kwame Brown	.30	.75
78 Zydrunas Ilgauskas	.40	1.00
79 Antawn Jamison	.50	1.25
80 Chris Bosh	.50	1.25
81 Zach Randolph	.40	1.00
82 Dwight Howard	1.00	2.50
83 Richard Jefferson	.50	1.25
84 Udonis Haslem	.40	1.00
85 Lamar Odom	.50	1.25
86 Mike Dunleavy	.40	1.00
87 Josh Howard	.50	1.25
88 Luol Deng	.50	1.25
89 Josh Smith	.50	1.25
90 Jalen Rose	.50	1.25
91 Rafer Alston	.30	.75
92 Manu Ginobili	.50	1.25
93 Allen Iverson	.75	2.00
94 Stephon Marbury	.40	1.00
95 Michael Redd	.50	1.25
96 Sam Cassell	.50	1.25
97 Baron Davis	.50	1.25
98 Andre Miller	.40	1.00
99 Larry Hughes	.40	1.00
100 Ricky Davis	.40	1.00
101 Nate Robinson RC	2.50	6.00
102 Danny Granger RC	4.00	10.00
103 Marvin Williams RC	2.50	6.00
104 Rashad McCants RC	2.50	6.00
105 Jarrett Jack RC	2.00	5.00
106 Andrew Bogut RC	3.00	8.00
107 Ike Diogu RC	2.00	5.00
108 Chris Paul RC	8.00	20.00
109 Julius Hodge RC	2.00	5.00
110 C.J. Miles RC	2.50	6.00
111 Francisco Garcia RC	2.50	6.00
112 Channing Frye RC	2.50	6.00
113 Deron Williams RC	5.00	12.00
114 Hakim Warrick RC	2.50	6.00
115 Salim Stoudamire RC	2.00	5.00
116 Raymond Felton RC	3.00	8.00
117 Joey Graham RC	2.00	5.00
118 Wayne Simien RC	2.00	5.00
119 David Lee RC	3.00	8.00
120 Luther Head RC	2.00	5.00
121 Andrew Bynum RC	6.00	15.00
122 Monta Ellis RC	4.00	10.00
123 Brandon Bass RC	2.50	6.00
124 Antoine Wright RC	2.00	5.00
125 Gerald Green RC	2.50	6.00
126 Charlie Villanueva RC	2.50	6.00
127 Chris Taft RC	2.00	5.00
128 Sarunas Jasikevicius RC	2.00	5.00
129 Sean May RC	2.00	5.00
130 Martell Webster RC	2.00	5.00
131 Yaroslav Korolev RC	2.00	5.00
132 Eddie Basden RC	2.00	5.00
133 Ersan Ilyasova RC	2.50	6.00
134 Martynas Andriuskevicius RC	2.00	5.00
135 Orien Greene RC	2.00	5.00
136 Johan Petro RC	2.00	5.00
137 Linas Kleiza RC	2.00	5.00
138 Daniel Ewing RC	2.00	5.00
139 Fabricio Oberto RC	2.00	5.00
140 Travis Diener RC	2.00	5.00
141 Ryan Gomes RC	2.00	5.00
142 Andray Blatche RC	2.50	6.00
143 Louis Williams RC	3.00	8.00
144 Jose Calderon RC	2.00	5.00
145 Robert Whaley RC	2.00	5.00
146 Jay-Z	4.00	10.00
147 Carmen Electra	4.00	10.00
148 Christie Brinkley	4.00	10.00
149 Shannon Elizabeth	4.00	10.00
150 Jenny McCarthy	4.00	10.00

2005-06 Topps First Row 325

This is a parallel to the First Row set, each of these cards were issued to a stated print run of 325 serial numbered sets.
*1-100: .6X TO 1.5X BASE HI
*101-150: .5X TO 1.25X BASE HI

2005-06 Topps First Row 100

This is a parallel to the basic First Row set, each of these cards were issued to a stated print run of 100 serial numbered sets.
*ROW 100 VETS: 1.5X TO 4X BASE HI
*ROW 100 RCs: .75X TO 2X BASE HI
*ROW 100 CELEBS: .6X TO 1.5X BASE HI

20 Kobe Bryant	15.00	40.00

2005-06 Topps First Row Black and White

This is a parallel to the basic First Row set. These cards were issued in black and white (hence the set name) instead of color and were also issued to a stated print run of 225 serial numbered sets.
*BLACK/WHITE: .6X TO 1.5X BASE HI

2005-06 Topps First Row Sepia

This is a parallel to the basic First Row set. These cards were issued in sepia tone and were also issued to a stated print run of 25 serial numbered sets.
*SEPIA VETS: 5X TO 12X BASE HI
*SEPIA RCs: 1.5X TO 4X BASE HI
*SEPIA CELEB: 1.25X TO 3X BASE HI

2005-06 Topps First Row Alley Oop Dual Relics

These six card, each of which feature two jersey pieces, were issued to a stated print run of 200 serial numbered sets.

AB Carmelo Anthony / Earl Boykins	6.00	15.00
AJ Gilbert Arenas / Antawn Jamison	5.00	12.00
FO Raymond Felton / Emeka Okafor	5.00	12.00
HC Kirk Hinrich / Tyson Chandler	5.00	12.00
NS Steve Nash / Amare Stoudemire	6.00	15.00
PS Chris Paul / J.R. Smith	6.00	15.00

2005-06 Topps First Row Baseline

This set, issued as an insert, was issued to a stated print run of 149 serial numbered sets.
*BASELINE 99: .5X TO 1.25X BASE HI
*BASE.99 PRINT RUN 99 SER.#'d SETS
BASE.10 NOT PRICED DUE TO SCARCITY

1 Baron Davis	1.25	3.00
2 Dwyane Wade	3.00	8.00
3 Allen Iverson	2.00	5.00
4 Ben Gordon	1.25	3.00
5 Andre Miller	1.00	2.50
6 Mike Bibby	1.25	3.00
7 Jason Kidd	2.00	5.00
8 Shaun Livingston	.75	2.00
9 Steve Francis	1.25	3.00
10 Steve Nash	1.50	4.00
11 Luke Ridnour	1.00	2.50
12 T.J. Ford	1.00	2.50
13 Stephon Marbury	1.00	2.50
14 Brevin Knight	.75	2.00
15 Jamaal Tinsley	.75	2.00
16 Rafer Alston	.75	2.00
17 Damon Jones	.75	2.00
18 Chauncey Billups	1.25	3.00
19 Kirk Hinrich	1.25	3.00
20 Devin Harris	1.25	3.00
21 Tony Parker	1.25	3.00
22 Jason Williams	1.00	2.50
23 Troy Hudson	.75	2.00
24 Deron Williams	3.00	8.00
25 Chris Paul	5.00	12.00
26 Tracy McGrady	1.50	4.00
27 Earl Boykins	.75	2.00
28 Marcus Banks	.75	2.00
29 Gilbert Arenas	1.25	3.00
30 Jamal Crawford	1.00	2.50
31 Larry Hughes	1.00	2.50
32 Jarrett Jack	1.25	3.00
33 Kobe Bryant	6.00	15.00
34 Damon Stoudamire	1.00	2.50
35 Jameer Nelson	1.00	2.50
36 Raymond Felton	2.00	5.00
37 Tyronn Lue	.75	2.00
38 Manu Ginobili	1.25	3.00
39 Rashad McCants	1.25	3.00
40 Andre Iguodala	1.25	3.00
41 Carlos Arroyo	1.00	2.50
42 Jason Terry	1.00	2.50
43 Nate Robinson	1.50	4.00
44 Luther Head	1.25	3.00
45 Joe Johnson	1.25	3.00
46 Vince Carter	2.00	5.00
47 Monta Ellis	2.50	6.00
48 Sebastian Telfair	1.00	2.50
49 Cuttino Mobley	1.00	2.50
50 J.R. Smith	1.25	3.00

2005-06 Topps First Row Center Court

Randomly inserted into packs, this is an insert to the First Row set and was issued to a stated print run of 149 serial numbered sets.
*CENTER 99: .5X TO 1.25X BASE HI
CENT.99 PRINT RUN 99 SER.#'d SETS
CENT.10 NOT PRICED DUE TO SCARCITY

1 Jason Kidd	2.00	5.00
2 Richard Hamilton	1.00	2.50
3 Manu Ginobili	1.25	3.00
4 Elton Brand	1.25	3.00
5 Jason Richardson	1.25	3.00
6 Emeka Okafor	1.25	3.00
7 Shawn Marion	1.25	3.00
8 Ben Gordon	1.25	3.00
9 Gilbert Arenas	1.25	3.00
10 Jermaine O'Neal	1.25	3.00
11 Ben Wallace	1.25	3.00
12 LeBron James	6.00	15.00
13 Allen Iverson	2.00	5.00
14 Dirk Nowitzki	2.00	5.00
15 Tracy McGrady	1.50	4.00
16 Steve Nash	1.50	4.00
17 Vince Carter	2.00	5.00
18 Carmelo Anthony	2.50	6.00
19 Kobe Bryant	6.00	15.00
20 Kevin Garnett	2.50	6.00
21 Tim Duncan	2.00	5.00
22 Stephon Marbury	1.00	2.50
23 Kirk Hinrich	1.25	3.00
24 Amare Stoudemire	1.25	3.00
25 Steve Francis	1.25	3.00
26 Yao Ming	1.50	4.00
27 Jamal Crawford	1.00	2.50
28 Ray Allen	1.25	3.00
29 Paul Pierce	1.50	4.00
30 Dwyane Wade	3.00	8.00
31 Corey Maggette	1.00	2.50
32 Rashard Lewis	1.25	3.00
33 Chris Bosh	1.25	3.00
34 Mike Bibby	1.25	3.00
35 Antoine Walker	1.00	2.50
36 Tony Parker	1.25	3.00
37 Kenyon Martin	1.25	3.00
38 Michael Redd	1.25	3.00
39 Baron Davis	1.25	3.00
40 Al Harrington	1.00	2.50
41 Jalen Rose	1.25	3.00
42 Antawn Jamison	1.25	3.00
43 Andre Miller	1.00	2.50
44 Rafer Alston	.75	2.00
45 Jason Terry	1.00	2.50
46 Pau Gasol	1.25	3.00
47 Andrei Kirilenko	1.00	2.50
48 Rasheed Wallace	1.25	3.00
49 Richard Jefferson	1.25	3.00
50 Shaquille O'Neal	2.50	6.00

2005-06 Topps First Row Charity Stripe

Randomly inserted into packs, this is an insert in the First Row product. Each of these cards were issued to a stated print run of 149 serial numbered sets.
*STRIPE 99: .5X TO 1.25X BASE HI
STRIP.99 PRINT RUN 99 SER.#'d SETS
STRIP.10 UNPRICED DUE TO SCARCITY

1 Earl Boykins	.75	2.00
2 Peja Stojakovic	1.25	3.00
3 Damon Stoudamire	1.00	2.50
4 Chauncey Billups	1.25	3.00
5 Steve Nash	1.50	4.00
6 Ray Allen	1.25	3.00
7 Austin Croshere	.75	2.00
8 Dirk Nowitzki	2.00	5.00
9 Sam Cassell	1.25	3.00
10 Ben Gordon	1.25	3.00
11 Caron Butler	1.25	3.00
12 Derek Fisher	1.00	2.50
13 David Wesley	.75	2.00
14 Wally Szczerbiak	1.00	2.50
15 Michael Redd	1.25	3.00
16 Jalen Rose	1.25	3.00
17 Fred Jones	.75	2.00
18 Brian Cardinal	.75	2.00
19 Danny Fortson	.75	2.00
20 Shareef Abdur-Rahim	1.00	2.50
21 Corey Maggette	1.00	2.50
22 Mehmet Okur	.75	2.00
23 Josh Childress	1.00	2.50
24 Shawn Marion	1.25	3.00
25 Hedo Turkoglu	1.25	3.00
26 Jerry Stackhouse	1.00	2.50
27 Bobby Simmons	.75	2.00
28 Jamal Crawford	1.00	2.50
29 Marvin Williams	1.50	4.00
30 Richard Hamilton	1.00	2.50
31 Luke Ridnour	1.00	2.50
32 Julius Hodge	1.25	3.00
33 Danny Granger	2.50	6.00
34 Gerald Green	1.50	4.00
35 Francisco Garcia	1.50	4.00
36 Daniel Ewing	1.25	3.00
37 Antoine Wright	1.25	3.00
38 Martell Webster	1.25	3.00
39 Morris Peterson	.75	2.00
40 Andrew Bogut	2.00	5.00
41 Salim Stoudamire	1.25	3.00
42 Paul Pierce	1.50	4.00
43 Sean May	1.25	3.00
44 Kobe Bryant	6.00	15.00
45 Grant Hill	1.50	4.00
46 P.J. Brown	.75	2.00
47 Dan Dickau	.75	2.00
48 Richard Jefferson	1.25	3.00
49 Stephen Jackson	1.00	2.50
50 Wayne Simien	1.25	3.00

2005-06 Topps First Row Direct Effect Relics

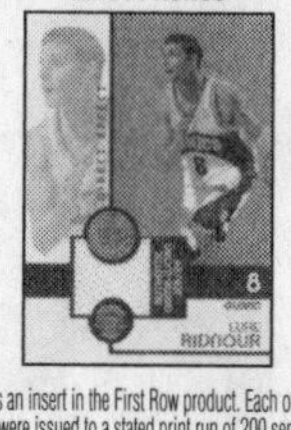

This is an insert in the First Row product. Each of these cards were issued to a stated print run of 200 serial numbered sets.
UNPRICED AUTO PRINT RUN 10 SETS

AI Allen Iverson	4.00	10.00
CP Chris Paul	10.00	25.00
DH Devin Harris	2.50	6.00
DW Dwyane Wade	6.00	15.00
EB Earl Boykins	2.00	5.00
ES Eric Snow	2.00	5.00
GA Gilbert Arenas	2.50	6.00
KH Kirk Hinrich	2.50	6.00
LR Luke Ridnour	2.00	5.00
MB Mike Bibby	2.50	6.00
RA Rafer Alston	2.00	5.00
RF Raymond Felton	4.00	10.00
SF Steve Francis	2.50	6.00
SL Shaun Livingston	2.00	5.00
SN Steve Nash	3.00	8.00
TM Tracy McGrady	3.00	8.00
DWI Deron Williams	6.00	15.00
TJF T.J. Ford	2.00	5.00

2005-06 Topps First Row In The Post

This is an insert to the First Row set. Each of these cards were issued to a stated print run of 149 serial numbered sets.
*POST 99: .5X TO 1.25X BASE HI
POST 99 PRINT RUN 99 SER.#'d SETS
POST 10 NOT PRICED DUE TO SCARCITY

1 Elton Brand	1.25	3.00
2 Emeka Okafor	1.25	3.00
3 Jermaine O'Neal	1.25	3.00
4 Ben Wallace	1.25	3.00
5 Dirk Nowitzki	2.00	5.00
6 Kevin Garnett	2.50	6.00
7 Tim Duncan	2.00	5.00
8 Amare Stoudemire	1.25	3.00
9 Yao Ming	1.50	4.00
10 Chris Bosh	1.25	3.00
11 Andrew Bogut	2.00	5.00
12 Zydrunas Ilgauskas	1.00	2.50
13 Pau Gasol	1.25	3.00
14 Shaquille O'Neal	2.50	6.00
15 Marcus Camby	1.00	2.50
16 Antawn Jamison	1.25	3.00
17 Charlie Villanueva	1.50	4.00
18 Carlos Boozer	1.25	3.00
19 Lamar Odom	1.25	3.00
20 Channing Frye	1.50	4.00
21 Zach Randolph	1.00	2.50
22 Carmelo Anthony	2.50	6.00
23 Ike Diogu	1.25	3.00
24 Chris Webber	1.25	3.00
25 Andrew Bynum	4.00	10.00
26 Sean May	1.25	3.00
27 Wayne Simien	1.25	3.00
28 Drew Gooden	1.00	2.50
29 Rasheed Wallace	1.25	3.00
30 Troy Murphy	1.00	2.50
31 Marvin Williams	1.50	4.00
32 Jason Kidd	2.00	5.00
33 Steve Francis	1.25	3.0
34 Tracy McGrady	1.50	4.0
35 Dwyane Wade	3.00	8.0
36 Quentin Richardson	1.00	2.5
37 Corey Maggette	1.00	2.5
38 Kobe Bryant	6.00	15.0
39 Paul Pierce	1.50	4.0
40 Jalen Rose	1.25	3.0
41 Danny Granger	2.50	6.0
42 Michael Finley	1.25	3.0
43 Tayshaun Prince	1.25	3.0
44 Kenyon Martin	1.25	3.0
45 Brad Miller	1.25	3.0
46 Joey Graham	1.25	3.0
47 Jason Maxiell	1.25	3.0
48 Primoz Brezec	.75	2.0
49 Nenad Krstic	.75	2.0
50 Ron Artest	1.25	3.0

2005-06 Topps First Row Pick n Roll Relics

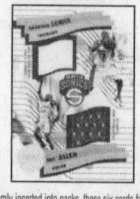

Randomly inserted into packs, these six cards feature game-used jersey swatches from teammates. Each of these cards were issued to a stated print run of 200 serial numbered sets.

AL Ray Allen / Rashard Lewis	5.00	12.00
BL Elton Brand / Shaun Livingston	5.00	12.00
BW Carlos Boozer / Deron Williams	6.00	15.00
GD Manu Ginobili / Tim Duncan	6.00	15.00
MM Tracy McGrady / Yao Ming	6.00	15.00
OW Shaquille O'Neal / Dwyane Wade	12.50	30.00

2005-06 Topps First Row PTP Dual Autographs

Randomly inserted into packs, these five cards feature authentic autographs from the featured players. Each of these cards were issued to a stated print run of 10 serial numbered sets and no pricing is available due to market scarcity.

2005-06 Topps First Row PTP Dual Relics

Randomly inserted into packs, these 32 cards feature two game-used relics from the featured players. Each of these cards were issued to a stated print run of 140 serial numbered sets.
UNPRICED AU PRINT RUNS 10 SETS

AW Carmelo Anthony / Hakeem Warrick	6.00	15.00
BO Kobe Bryant / Shaquille O'Neal	10.00	25.00
DB Tim Duncan / Andrew Bogut	6.00	15.00
IB Alen Iverson / Kobe Bryant	12.50	30.00
IW Allen Iverson / Dwyane Wade	8.00	20.00
MG Tracy McGrady / Gerald Green	5.00	12.00
NW Steve Nash / Deron Williams	6.00	15.00
OI Shaquille O'Neal / Allen Iverson	10.00	25.00
OW Shaquille O'Neal / Dwyane Wade	15.00	40.00
PI Chris Paul / Allen Iverson	12.50	30.00
PM Paul Pierce / Rashad McCants	6.00	15.00
WB Dwyane Wade / Kobe Bryant	15.00	40.00
AB2 Andrew Bogut	5.00	12.00
AI2 Allen Iverson	5.00	12.00
BG2 Ben Gordon	3.00	8.00
CA2 Carmelo Anthony	6.00	15.00
CP2 Chris Paul	12.00	30.00
DN2 Dirk Nowitzki	5.00	12.00
DW1 Dwyane Wade	8.00	20.00
DW2 Deron Williams	8.00	20.00
EO2 Emeka Okafor	3.00	8.00
GA2 Gilbert Arenas	3.00	8.00
JT2 Jason Terry	2.50	6.00
KB2 Kobe Bryant	10.00	25.00
KM2 Kenyon Martin	3.00	8.00
RF2 Raymond Felton	5.00	12.00
SN2 Steve Nash	4.00	10.00
SO2 Shaquille O'Neal	6.00	15.00
TD2 Tim Duncan	5.00	12.00
TM2 Tracy McGrady	4.00	10.00
YM2 Yao Ming	4.00	10.00

2005-06 Topps First Row PTP Dual Relics Autographs

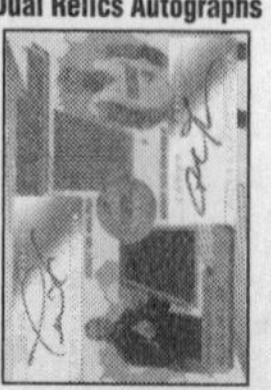

...andomly inserted into packs, these four cards feature ...ith game-used material and authentic signatures from ...e featured players. These cards were issued to a ...ated print run of 10 serial numbered sets and no ...ricing is available due to market scarcity.

2005-06 Topps First Row Range Relics

...andomly inserted into packs, these 15-cards feature ...ayers who can shoot the ball from a long distance. ...ach of these cards were issued to a stated print run of ...0 serial numbered sets.

W Antoine Wright 2.50 6.00
G Ben Gordon 2.50 6.00
N Dirk Nowitzki 4.00 10.00
W Dwyane Wade 6.00 15.00
C Jamal Crawford 2.00 5.00
H Julius Hodge 2.50 6.00
B Kobe Bryant 8.00 20.00
K Kyle Korver 2.00 5.00
G Manu Ginobili 2.50 6.00
P Morris Peterson 1.50 4.00
P Paul Pierce 3.00 8.00
S Peja Stojakovic 2.50 6.00
A Ray Allen 2.50 6.00
J Sarunas Jasikevicius 2.50 6.00
P Tayshaun Prince 2.50 6.00

2005-06 Topps First Row Signature Dish

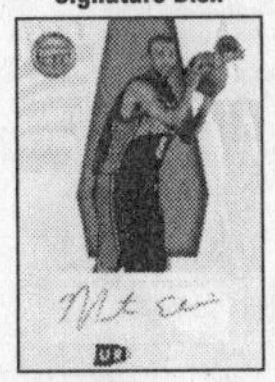

...andomly inserted into packs, these 36 cards feature sticker-signed autographs of the featured players. Most of the players are active but Dave Bing, Earl Monroe and Jo Jo White are vintage players. Since the print run is different for many players, we have put the stated print run next to the player's name in our checklist.

AB Andrew Bogut/190 6.00 15.00
AI Allen Iverson/150 50.00 120.00
AJ Amir Johnson/190 4.00 10.00
AW Antoine Wright/190 4.00 10.00
BW Bracey Wright/190 4.00 10.00
CA Carmelo Anthony/65 20.00 50.00
CV Charlie Villanueva/190 5.00 12.00
DB Dave Bing/67 60.00 120.00
DG Danny Granger/190 8.00 20.00
DL David Lee/190 6.00 15.00
DW Dwyane Wade/190 30.00 80.00
EM Earl Monroe/83 15.00 40.00
FG Francisco Garcia/190 5.00 12.00
GG Gerald Green/190 5.00 12.00
JH Julius Hodge/190 4.00 10.00
JJ Jarrett Jack/190 4.00 10.00
JK Jason Kidd/120 12.50 30.00
JN Jameer Nelson/157 4.00 10.00
JP Johan Petro/190 4.00 10.00
LH Luther Head/190 4.00 10.00
LO Lamar Odom/100 5.00 12.00
LW Louis Williams/190 6.00 15.00
ME Monta Ellis/190 12.50 30.00
MW Martell Webster/190 4.00 10.00
RF Raymond Felton/190 6.00 15.00
RG Ryan Gomes/190 4.00 10.00
RM Rashad McCants/190 4.00 10.00
RS Robert Swift/124 4.00 10.00
RW Robert Whaley/190 4.00 10.00
SJ Sarunas Jasikevicius/190 4.00 10.00
SL Shaun Livingston/190 4.00 10.00
SM Sean May/190 4.00 10.00
TD Travis Diener/110 4.00 10.00
DWI Deron Williams/190 15.00 40.00
JJW Jo Jo White/79 10.00 25.00
PJR Peter John Ramos/190 4.00 10.00

2005-06 Topps First Row Signature Dunk

Randomly inserted into packs, these 37 cards feature sticker-signed autographs of the featured players. Most of the players are active but Dave Cowens, Elgin Baylor and Moses Malone are vintage players. Since the print run is different for many players, we have put the stated print run next to the player's name in our checklist.

AB Andrew Bogut/190 6.00 15.00
AI Allen Iverson/150 50.00 120.00
AW Antoine Wright/190 4.00 10.00
BB Brandon Bass/110 5.00 12.00
BW Bracey Wright/190 4.00 10.00
CA Carmelo Anthony/50 25.00 60.00
CT Chris Taft/190 4.00 10.00
CV Charlie Villanueva/190 5.00 12.00
DC Dave Cowens/83 12.50 30.00
DG Danny Granger/190 8.00 20.00
DL David Lee/190 6.00 15.00
DS Damon Smith/184 4.00 10.00
DW Dwyane Wade/190 30.00 80.00
EB Elgin Baylor/107 10.00 25.00
EO Emeka Okafor/190 8.00 20.00
FG Francisco Garcia/190 5.00 12.00
GG Gerald Green/190 5.00 12.00
ID Ike Diogu/190 4.00 10.00
JH Julius Hodge/190 4.00 10.00
JM Jason Maxiell/190 4.00 10.00
JP Johan Petro/190 4.00 10.00
LH Luther Head/190 4.00 10.00
LW Louis Williams/190 6.00 15.00
ME Mark Eaton/67 12.50 30.00
MM Moses Malone/78 12.50 30.00
MW Martell Webster/190 4.00 10.00
PP Pavel Podkolzin/190 4.00 10.00
RG Ryan Gomes/190 4.00 10.00
RM Rashad McCants/190 4.00 10.00
RW Robert Whaley/190 4.00 10.00
SJ Sarunas Jasikevicius/190 4.00 10.00
SM Sean May/190 4.00 10.00
SO Shaquille O'Neal/115 40.00 80.00
WS Wayne Simien/190 4.00 10.00
ABY Andrew Bynum/190 15.00 40.00
DWI Deron Williams/190 15.00 40.00
PJR Peter John Ramos/190 4.00 10.00

2005-06 Topps First Row Signature Swish

Randomly inserted into packs, these 41 cards feature sticker-signed autographs of the featured players. Most of the players are active but Bill Walton, Rick Barry are vintage players. In addition, celebrities such as Carmen Electra, Shannon Elizabeth, Jay-Z and Christine Brinkley also signed for this product. Since the print run is different for many players, we have put the stated print run next to the player's name in our checklist.

AI Allen Iverson/150 50.00 120.00
AJ Amir Johnson/190 4.00 10.00
AW Antoine Wright/190 4.00 10.00
BW Bill Walton/55 15.00 40.00
CA Carmelo Anthony/75 20.00 50.00
CB Christie Brinkley/50 50.00 120.00
CE Carmen Electra/50 60.00 120.00
CT Chris Taft/37 5.00 12.00
CV Charlie Villanueva/190 5.00 12.00
DE Daniel Ewing/85 4.00 10.00
DG Danny Granger/190 8.00 20.00
DL David Lee/190 6.00 15.00
DS Detlef Schrempf/91 12.50 30.00
DW Dwyane Wade/190 30.00 80.00
EO Emeka Okafor/190 8.00 20.00
FG Francisco Garcia/190 5.00 12.00
JG Joey Graham/190 4.00 10.00
JH Julius Hodge/190 4.00 10.00
JJ Jarrett Jack/190 4.00 10.00
JM Jenny McCarthy/50 60.00 120.00
JP Johan Petro/190 4.00 10.00
KM Kevin Martin/190 4.00 10.00
LH Luther Head/190 4.00 10.00
LO Lamar Odom/75 5.00 12.00
LW Louis Williams/190 6.00 15.00
MW Martell Webster/190 4.00 10.00
OG Orien Greene/190 4.00 10.00
RB Rick Barry/83 15.00 40.00
RG Ryan Gomes/190 4.00 10.00
RM Rashad McCants/190 4.00 10.00
RS Robert Swift/190 4.00 10.00
RW Robert Whaley/190 4.00 10.00
SE Shannon Elizabeth/50 50.00 120.00
SJ Sarunas Jasikevicius/190 4.00 10.00
SM Sean May/190 4.00 10.00
VW Von Wafer/190 4.00 10.00
BWR Bracey Wright/190 4.00 10.00
DWI Deron Williams/190 15.00 40.00
DWR Dorell Wright/190 4.00 10.00
PJR Peter John Ramos/190 4.00 10.00

2005-06 Topps First Row Spokesmen

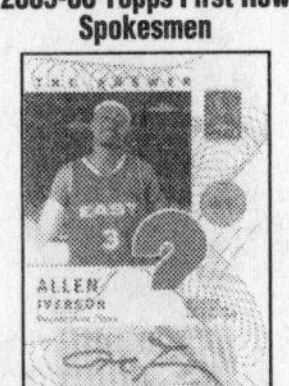

Randomly inserted into packs, these nine cards feature signed cards of people whom Topps uses as spokesmen. Since each card was issued to a different print run, we have put this information next to the player's name in our checklist.

AUTOS UNPRICED DUE TO SCARCITY
SSRAI Allen Iverson JSY/200 5.00 12.00
SSRDW Dwyane Wade JSY/200 6.00 15.00
SSRJZ Jay-Z JSY/200 8.00 20.00

2005-06 Topps First Row Thunder Relics

Randomly inserted into packs, these 22-cards feature game-used relics of players known for their dunking ability. Each of these cards were issued to a stated print run of 200 serial numbered sets.

UNPRICED AUTO PRINT RUN 10 SETS
AI Andre Iguodala 2.50 6.00
AJ Antawn Jamison 2.50 6.00
AS Amare Stoudemire 2.50 6.00
BW Ben Wallace 2.50 6.00
CA Carmelo Anthony 5.00 12.00
CB Chris Bosh 2.50 6.00
DG Drew Gooden 2.00 5.00
DW Dwyane Wade 6.00 15.00
GG Gerald Green 2.50 6.00
HW Hakim Warrick 3.00 8.00
JO Jermaine O'Neal 2.50 6.00
JS Josh Smith 2.50 6.00
KB Kobe Bryant 8.00 20.00
LD Luol Deng 2.50 6.00
PG Pau Gasol 2.50 6.00
RJ Richard Jefferson 2.50 6.00
RL Rashard Lewis 2.50 6.00
SO Shaquille O'Neal 5.00 12.00
TD Tim Duncan 4.00 10.00
VC Vince Carter 4.00 10.00
YM Yao Ming 3.00 8.00
JRS J.R. Smith 2.50 6.00

2006-07 Topps Full Court

Released in mid March 2007, Topps Full Court features full-bleed photo veteran and retired legends cards for card numbers 1-100 and chromium card stock picturing rookies on card numbers 101-150. Full Court is packaged in 18-pack boxes of six cards each and carried an initial suggested retail price of $6.00 per pack.

COMP.SET w/o RC's (100) 12.50 30.00
UNPRICED PLATINUM PRINT RUN ONE SET
UNPRICED PLATES PRINT RUN ONE SET
1 Vince Carter .40 1.00
2 Josh Smith .30 .75
3 Dwyane Wade .75 2.00
4 Lamar Odom .30 .75
5 Jermaine O'Neal .30 .75
6 Andrei Kirilenko .25 .60
7 Rasheed Wallace .30 .75
8 Manu Ginobili .30 .75
9 Richard Hamilton .25 .60
10 Tim Duncan .50 1.25
11 Ricky Davis .25 .60
12 Antoine Walker .25 .60
13 Troy Murphy .20 .50
14 Ray Allen .30 .75
15 Ben Wallace .30 .75
16 Dwight Howard .50 1.25
17 Joe Johnson .30 .75
18 Jason Kidd .50 1.25
19 Michael Redd .30 .75
20 Kobe Bryant 1.50 4.00
21 Al Harrington .25 .60
22 Mehmet Okur .20 .50
23 Danny Granger .30 .75
24 Caron Butler .30 .75
25 Elton Brand .30 .75
26 Gilbert Arenas .30 .75
27 Sam Cassell .30 .75
28 Antawn Jamison .30 .75
29 Carmelo Anthony .40 1.00
30 Zach Randolph .25 .60
31 Ben Gordon .30 .75
32 Andre Iguodala .30 .75
33 Paul Pierce .40 1.00
34 Peja Stojakovic .30 .75
35 Andrew Bogut .30 .75
36 Mike Miller .30 .75
37 Mike James .20 .50
38 Shaquille O'Neal .60 1.50
39 Baron Davis .30 .75
40 Jason Richardson .30 .75
41 Rashard Lewis .30 .75
42 Marcus Camby .25 .60
43 Ron Artest .25 .60
44 Larry Hughes .25 .60
45 Allen Iverson .40 1.00
46 Al Jefferson .30 .75
47 Chris Paul .60 1.50
48 Tony Parker .30 .75
49 Pau Gasol .30 .75
50 Kevin Garnett .60 1.50
51 Richard Jefferson .25 .60
52 Corey Maggette .25 .60
53 Yao Ming .40 1.00
54 T.J. Ford .25 .60
55 Andre Miller .25 .60
56 Mike Bibby .30 .75
57 LeBron James 1.50 4.00
58 Chris Webber .30 .75
59 Emeka Okafor .30 .75
60 Tyson Chandler .25 .60
61 Raymond Felton .40 1.00
62 Channing Frye .25 .60
63 Gerald Wallace .30 .75
64 Stephon Marbury .30 .75
65 Kirk Hinrich .30 .75
66 Jameer Nelson .25 .60
67 Charlie Villanueva .25 .60
68 Smush Parker .20 .50
69 Tracy McGrady .40 1.00
70 Chris Bosh .30 .75
71 Chauncey Billups .30 .75
72 Brad Miller .30 .75
73 Drew Gooden .25 .60
74 Amare Stoudemire .30 .75
75 Dirk Nowitzki .50 1.25
76 Shawn Marion .30 .75
77 Jason Terry .25 .60
78 Steve Nash .40 1.00
79 Josh Howard .30 .75
80 Darius Miles .20 .50
81 John Stockton 1.50 4.00
82 Wilt Chamberlain 2.00 5.00
83 Dennis Rodman 1.50 4.00
84 Karl Malone 1.25 3.00
85 Dominique Wilkins 1.25 3.00
86 Isiah Thomas 1.00 2.50
87 Earl Monroe 1.00 2.50
88 Hakeem Olajuwon 1.25 3.00
89 Clyde Drexler 1.25 3.00
90 George Gervin 1.00 2.50
91 Oscar Robertson 1.00 2.50
92 Rick Barry 1.00 2.50
93 Walt Frazier 1.00 2.50
94 Drazen Petrovic 1.25 3.00
95 Dan Majerle 1.25 3.00
96 Jerry West 1.25 3.00
97 Larry Bird 3.00 8.00
98 Moses Malone 1.00 2.50
99 Kareem Abdul-Jabbar 1.50 4.00
100 Bill Russell 2.00 5.00
101 Shelden Williams RC 1.50 4.00
102 Adam Morrison RC 2.00 5.00
103 Daniel Gibson RC 2.00 5.00
104 Mile Ilic RC 1.50 4.00
105 Jorge Garbajosa RC 2.00 5.00
106 David Noel RC 1.50 4.00
107 Hassan Adams RC 1.50 4.00
108 J.J. Redick RC 2.00 5.00
109 Brandon Roy RC 4.00 10.00
110 Damir Markota RC 1.50 4.00
111 Solomon Jones RC 1.50 4.00
112 Yakhouba Diawara RC 1.50 4.00
113 Maurice Ager RC 1.50 4.00
114 Steve Novak RC 1.50 4.00
115 Jordan Farmar RC 1.50 4.00
116 Randy Foye RC 2.00 5.00
117 Cedric Simmons RC 1.50 4.00
118 James Augustine RC 1.50 4.00
119 Sergio Rodriguez RC 1.50 4.00
120 P.J. Tucker RC 1.50 4.00
121 Rajon Rondo RC 6.00 15.00
122 Tyrus Thomas RC 2.00 5.00
123 Will Blalock RC 1.50 4.00
124 Shawne Williams RC 1.50 4.00
125 Rudy Gay RC 2.50 6.00
126 Craig Smith RC 1.50 4.00
127 Hilton Armstrong RC 1.50 4.00
128 Bobby Jones RC 1.50 4.00
129 Quincy Douby RC 1.50 4.00
130 Andrea Bargnani RC 2.50 6.00
131 Vassilis Spanoulis RC 1.50 4.00
132 Thabo Sefolosha RC 2.00 5.00
133 Pops Mensah-Bonsu RC 1.50 4.00
134 Paul Millsap RC 2.50 6.00
135 Kyle Lowry RC 2.00 5.00
136 Marcus Williams RC 1.50 4.00
137 Renaldo Balkman RC 1.50 4.00
138 Rodney Carney RC 1.50 4.00
139 Marcus Vinicius RC 1.50 4.00
140 Ronnie Brewer RC 2.00 5.00
141 Leon Powe RC 1.50 4.00
142 Shannon Brown RC 2.50 6.00
143 Patrick O'Bryant RC 1.50 4.00
144 Paul Davis RC 1.50 4.00
145 Alexander Johnson RC 1.50 4.00
146 Josh Boone RC 1.50 4.00
147 Mardy Collins RC 1.50 4.00
148 LaMarcus Aldridge RC 4.00 10.00
149 Saer Sene RC 1.50 4.00
150 Dee Brown RC 1.50 4.00

2006-07 Topps Full Court First Day Issue

*1-80 FIRST DAY: .75X TO 2X BASE HI
*81-100 FIRST DAY: .6X TO 1.5X BASE HI
PRINT RUN 429 SER.#'d SETS

2006-07 Topps Full Court Photographer's Proof

*1-80 PROOF: .6X TO 1.5X BASE HI
*81-100 PROOF: .5X TO 1.25X BASE HI
STATED PRINT RUN 1999 SER.#'d SETS

2006-07 Topps Full Court Photographer's Proof Gold

*1-80 PROOF GOLD: 1.25X TO 3X BASE HI
*81-100 PROOF GOLD: .75X TO 2X BASE HI
STATED PRINT RUN 199 SER.#'d SETS

2006-07 Topps Full Court Chrome Rookie Refractors

*REFRACTORS: .6X TO 1.5X BASE HI
PRINT RUN 199 SER.#'d SETS

2006-07 Topps Full Court Chrome Rookie Refractors Gold

*REF.GOLD: 1X TO 2.5X BASE HI
STATED PRINT RUN 50 SER.#'d SETS

2006-07 Topps Full Court Co-Signers

GROUP A ODDS 1:270, GROUP B 1:755
GROUP C ODDS 1:1100, GROUP D 1:375
GROUP E ODDS 1:470, GROUP F 1:218
GROUP G ODDS 1:82, GROUP H 1:36
CS1 Allen Iverson 30.00 80.00
Maurice Cheeks
CS2 Adam Morrison 100.00 200.00
Larry Bird
CS3 Dwyane Wade 150.00 300.00
Shaquille O'Neal
CS4 Bill Walton 60.00 150.00
John Wooden
CS5 Raymond Felton 25.00 60.00
Roy Williams
CS6 Adam Morrison 25.00 60.00
J.J. Redick
CS7 Vince Carter 40.00 80.00
Dominique Wilkins
CS8 Ben Gordon 20.00 40.00
Jim Calhoun
CS9 Tony Parker 10.00 25.00
Boris Diaw
CS10 Charlie Villanueva 8.00 20.00
Emeka Okafor
CS11 Carmelo Anthony 30.00 80.00
Jim Boeheim
CS12 Jermaine O'Neal 8.00 20.00
Len Elmore
CS13 Chris Bosh 15.00 40.00
Connie Hawkins
CS14 T.J. Ford 8.00 20.00
(Speedy Claxton
CS15 Bob Lanier 60.00 120.00
Shaquille O'Neal
CS16 Andrea Bargnani 20.00 40.00
Andrew Bogut
CS17 Luol Deng 12.50 30.00
J.J. Redick
CS18 Daniel Ewing 8.00 20.00
Chris Duhon
CS19 Jordan Farmar 8.00 20.00
Ben Howland
CS20 Bobby Simmons 8.00 20.00
Hedo Turkoglu
CS21 Jameer Nelson 8.00 20.00
Delonte West
CS22 Dee Brown 15.00 40.00
Deron Williams
CS23 Raja Bell 15.00 30.00
Leandro Barbosa
CS24 Mike James 8.00 20.00
Smush Parker
CS25 Manute Bol 20.00 50.00
(Rick Barry
CS26 Allan Ray 10.00 25.00
Randy Foye
CS27 Shannon Brown 8.00 20.00
Maurice Ager
CS28 Hilton Armstrong 8.00 20.00
Josh Boone
CS29 Marcus Williams 20.00 40.00
Vince Carter
CS30 Jordan Farmar 8.00 20.00
Ryan Hollins
CS31 Shawne Williams 8.00 20.00
Rodney Carney
CS32 P.J. Tucker 8.00 20.00
Daniel Gibson
CS33 Earl Monroe 25.00 60.00
Isiah Thomas
CS34 J.J. Redick 12.50 30.00
Shelden Williams
CS35 Josh Howard 10.00 25.00
Devin Harris
CS36 Josh Howard 10.00 25.00
Josh Smith
CS37 Rajon Rondo 12.50 30.00
Quincy Douby
CS38 Renaldo Balkman 8.00 20.00
Mardy Collins
CS39 Patrick O'Bryant 8.00 20.00
Saer Sene
CS40 Ray Allen 75.00 150.00
(Allen Iverson
CS41 Ronnie Brewer 8.00 20.00
Dee Brown
CS42 Craig Smith 8.00 20.00
David Noel
CS43 Dwyane Wade 40.00 100.00
Adam Morrison
CS44 Bobby Jones 8.00 20.00
Solomon Jones
CS45 Allan Ray 8.00 20.00
Kyle Lowry
CS46 Rodney Carney 8.00 20.00
Thabo Sefolosha
CS47 Raymond Felton 10.00 25.00
Ben Gordon
CS48 Bill Walton 30.00 60.00
Luke Walton
CS49 Andre Iguodala 10.00 25.00
(Gerald Wallace
CS50 Magic Johnson 200.00 300.00
Larry Bird

2006-07 Topps Full Court Court Records

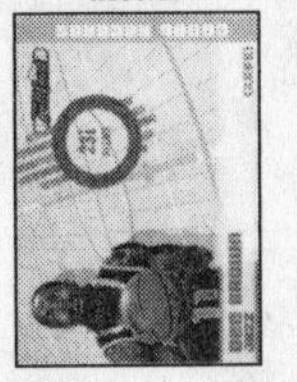

COMPLETE SET (20) 10.00 25.00
PRINT RUN 1499 SER.#'d SETS
CR1 Larry Bird 2.00 5.00
CR2 Dwyane Wade 1.50 4.00
CR3 Adam Morrison .75 2.00
CR4 Allen Iverson .75 2.00
CR5 Shaquille O'Neal 1.25 3.00
CR6 Vince Carter .75 2.00
CR7 Chris Bosh .60 1.50
CR8 Ben Gordon .60 1.50
CR9 J.J. Redick .75 2.00
CR10 Dominique Wilkins .75 2.00
CR11 Isiah Thomas .60 1.50
CR12 Andre Iguodala .60 1.50
CR13 Earl Monroe .60 1.50
CR14 Shelden Williams .60 1.50
CR15 Dee Brown .60 1.50
CR16 Rodney Carney .60 1.50
CR17 Charlie Villanueva .60 1.50
CR18 Quincy Douby .60 1.50
CR19 Raymond Felton .75 2.00
CR20 Randy Foye .75 2.00

2006-07 Topps Full Court Court Records Relics

PRINT RUN 499 SER.#'d SETS
CR1 Larry Bird 8.00 20.00
CR2 Dwyane Wade 5.00 12.00
CR3 Adam Morrison 3.00 8.00
CR4 Allen Iverson 3.00 8.00
CR5 Shaquille O'Neal 5.00 12.00
CR6 Vince Carter 3.00 8.00
CR7 Chris Bosh 2.50 6.00
CR8 Ben Gordon 2.50 6.00
CR9 J.J. Redick 3.00 8.00
CR10 Dominique Wilkins 3.00 8.00
CR11 Isiah Thomas 2.50 6.00
CR12 Andre Iguodala 2.50 6.00
CR13 Earl Monroe 2.50 6.00
CR14 Shelden Williams 2.50 6.00
CR15 Dee Brown 2.50 6.00
CR16 Rodney Carney 2.50 6.00
CR17 Charlie Villanueva 2.50 6.00
CR18 Quincy Douby 2.50 6.00
CR19 Raymond Felton 3.00 8.00
CR20 Randy Foye 3.00 8.00

2006-07 Topps Full Court Court Records Relics Autographs

PRINT RUN 15 TO 50 SER.#'d SETS
CR1 Larry Bird/33 60.00 150.00
CR2 Dwyane Wade/50 30.00 80.00
CR3 Adam Morrison/50 10.00 25.00
CR4 Allen Iverson/50 40.00 80.00
CR5 Shaquille O'Neal/32 60.00 120.00
CR6 Vince Carter/50 20.00 50.00
CR7 Chris Bosh/50 15.00 40.00
CR8 Ben Gordon/50 12.50 30.00
CR9 J.J. Redick/50 12.50 30.00
CR10 Dominique Wilkins/21 60.00 120.00
CR11 Isiah Thomas/50 20.00 40.00
CR12 Andre Iguodala/50 10.00 25.00
CR13 Earl Monroe/15 30.00 60.00
CR14 Shelden Williams/50 10.00 25.00
CR15 Dee Brown/50 10.00 25.00
CR16 Rodney Carney/50 10.00 25.00
CR17 Charlie Villanueva/50 10.00 25.00
CR18 Quincy Douby/50 10.00 25.00

2006-07 Topps Full Court Full Court Press

COMPLETE SET (25) 12.50 30.00
PRINT RUN 1499 SER.#'d SETS
FCP1 Dwyane Wade 2.00 5.00
FCP2 Adam Morrison 1.00 2.50
FCP3 Joe Johnson .75 2.00
FCP4 Ben Gordon .75 2.00
FCP5 Jason Terry .60 1.50
FCP6 Baron Davis .75 2.00
FCP7 Jordan Farmar .75 2.00
FCP8 Randy Foye 1.00 2.50
FCP9 J.J. Redick 1.00 2.50
FCP10 Jason Kidd 1.25 3.00
FCP11 Allen Iverson 1.00 2.50
FCP12 Manu Ginobili .75 2.00
FCP13 Stephon Marbury .60 1.50
FCP14 Caron Butler .75 2.00
FCP15 T.J. Ford .60 1.50
FCP16 Ronnie Brewer 1.00 2.50
FCP17 Mike Bibby .75 2.00
FCP18 Rodney Carney .75 2.00
FCP19 Chauncey Billups .75 2.00
FCP20 Steve Nash 1.00 2.50
FCP21 Rudy Gay 1.25 3.00
FCP22 Rajon Rondo 3.00 8.00
FCP23 Raymond Felton 1.00 2.50
FCP24 Ron Artest .75 2.00
FCP25 Tony Parker .75 2.00

2006-07 Topps Full Court Full Court Press Relics

PRINT RUN 499 SER.#'d SETS
*DUAL: .5X TO 1.25X BASE HI
PRINT RUN 199 SER.#'d SETS
*TRIPLE: .6X TO 1.5X BASE HI
TRIPLE PRINT RUN 50 SER.#'d SETS
FCP1 Dwyane Wade 5.00 12.00
FCP2 Adam Morrison 3.00 8.00
FCP3 Joe Johnson 2.50 6.00
FCP4 Ben Gordon 2.50 6.00
FCP5 Jason Terry 2.00 5.00
FCP6 Baron Davis 2.50 6.00
FCP7 Jordan Farmar 2.50 6.00
FCP8 Randy Foye 3.00 8.00
FCP9 J.J. Redick 3.00 8.00
FCP10 Jason Kidd 4.00 10.00
FCP11 Allen Iverson 3.00 8.00
FCP12 Manu Ginobili 2.50 6.00
FCP13 Stephon Marbury 2.00 5.00
FCP14 Caron Butler 2.50 6.00
FCP15 T.J. Ford 2.00 5.00
FCP16 Ronnie Brewer 3.00 8.00
FCP17 Mike Bibby 2.50 6.00
FCP18 Rodney Carney 2.50 6.00
FCP19 Chauncey Billups 2.50 6.00
FCP20 Steve Nash 3.00 8.00
FCP21 Rudy Gay 4.00 10.00
FCP22 Rajon Rondo 8.00 20.00
FCP23 Raymond Felton 3.00 8.00
FCP24 Ron Artest 2.50 6.00
FCP25 Tony Parker 2.50 6.00

2006-07 Topps Full Court Half Court Press

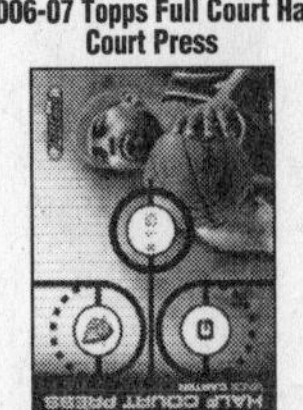

COMPLETE SET (25) 12.50 30.00
PRINT RUN 999 SER.#'d SETS
HCP1 Shaquille O'Neal 1.25 3.00
HCP2 Dirk Nowitzki 1.00 2.50
HCP3 Ben Wallace .60 1.50
HCP4 Carmelo Anthony .75 2.00
HCP5 Jermaine O'Neal .60 1.50
HCP6 Elton Brand .60 1.50
HCP7 J.J. Redick .75 2.00
HCP8 Andrew Bogut .60 1.50
HCP9 Chris Paul 1.25 3.00
HCP10 Dwyane Wade 1.50 4.00
HCP11 Kobe Bryant 3.00 8.00
HCP12 Dwight Howard 1.00 2.50
HCP13 Pau Gasol .60 1.50
HCP14 Tim Duncan 1.00 2.50
HCP15 LaMarcus Aldridge 1.50 4.00
HCP16 Ray Allen .60 1.50
HCP17 Yao Ming .75 2.00
HCP18 Allen Iverson .75 2.00
HCP19 Chris Bosh .60 1.50
HCP20 Adam Morrison .75 2.00
HCP21 Kevin Garnett 1.25 3.00
HCP22 Tracy McGrady .75 2.00
HCP23 Vince Carter .75 2.00
HCP24 Andrea Bargnani 1.00 2.50
HCP25 Gilbert Arenas .60 1.50

2006-07 Topps Full Court Half Court Press Relics

PRINT RUN 249 SER.#'d SETS
*DUAL: .5X TO 1.25X BASE HI
DUAL PRINT RUN 199 SER.#'d SETS
*TRIPLE: .75X TO 2X BASE HI
TRIPLE PRINT RUN 25 SER.#'d SETS
HCP1 Shaquille O'Neal 5.00 12.00
HCP2 Dirk Nowitzki 4.00 10.00
HCP3 Ben Wallace 2.50 6.00
HCP4 Carmelo Anthony 3.00 8.00
HCP5 Jermaine O'Neal 2.50 6.00
HCP6 Elton Brand 2.50 6.00
HCP7 J.J. Redick 3.00 8.00
HCP8 Andrew Bogut 2.50 6.00
HCP9 Chris Paul 5.00 12.00
HCP10 Dwyane Wade 5.00 12.00
HCP11 Kobe Bryant 8.00 20.00
HCP12 Dwight Howard 4.00 10.00
HCP13 Pau Gasol 2.50 6.00
HCP14 Tim Duncan 4.00 10.00
HCP15 LaMarcus Aldridge 6.00 15.00
HCP16 Ray Allen 2.50 6.00
HCP17 Yao Ming 3.00 8.00
HCP18 Allen Iverson 3.00 8.00
HCP19 Chris Bosh 2.50 6.00
HCP20 Adam Morrison 3.00 8.00
HCP21 Kevin Garnett 5.00 12.00
HCP22 Tracy McGrady 3.00 8.00
HCP23 Vince Carter 3.00 8.00
HCP24 Andrea Bargnani 4.00 10.00
HCP25 Gilbert Arenas 2.50 6.00

1995-96 Topps Gallery

The 1995-96 Topps Gallery set was issued in one series of 144 cards. The 8-card packs, offered exclusively to hobby outlets, retailed for $3.00 each. The set features the topical subsets: The Masters (1-18), The Modernists (19-36), New Editions (37-84) and The Classics (85-144). Each card is printed on 24-point stock, covered with an exclusive high-gloss film and etch stamped with one or more foils. Rookie Cards of note in this set include Michael Finley, Kevin Garnett, Antonio McDyess, Jerry Stackhouse and Damon Stoudamire.

COMPLETE SET (144) 15.00 30.00
1 Shaquille O'Neal .60 1.50
2 Shawn Kemp .25 .60
3 Reggie Miller .30 .75
4 Mitch Richmond .25 .60
5 Grant Hill .40 1.00
6 Magic Johnson .60 1.50
7 Vin Baker .20 .50
8 Charles Barkley .40 1.00
9 Hakeem Olajuwon .30 .75
10 Michael Jordan 2.00 5.00
11 Patrick Ewing .30 .75
12 David Robinson .40 1.00
13 Alonzo Mourning .30 .75
14 Karl Malone .30 .75
15 Chris Webber .30 .75
16 Dikembe Mutombo .25 .60
17 Larry Johnson .25 .60
18 Jamal Mashburn .25 .60
19 Anfernee Hardaway .40 1.00
20 Bryant Stith .15 .40
21 Juwan Howard .25 .60
22 Jason Kidd .40 1.00
23 Sharone Wright .15 .40
24 Tom Gugliotta .15 .40
25 Eric Montross .15 .40
26 Allan Houston .20 .50
27 Antonio Davis .15 .40
28 Brian Grant .20 .50
29 Terrell Brandon .15 .40
30 Eddie Jones .30 .75
31 James Robinson .15 .40
32 Wesley Person .15 .40
33 Glenn Robinson .25 .60
34 Donyell Marshall .15 .40
35 Sam Cassell .25 .60
36 Lamond Murray .15 .40
37 Damon Stoudamire RC .60 1.50
38 Tyus Edney RC .15 .40
39 Jerry Stackhouse RC .75 2.00
40 Arvydas Sabonis RC .50 1.25
41 Kevin Garnett RC 2.00 5.00
42 Brent Barry RC .40 1.00
43 Alan Henderson RC .25 .60
44 Bryant Reeves RC .25 .60
45 Shawn Respert RC .25 .60
46 Michael Finley RC .75 2.00
47 Gary Trent RC .15 .40
48 Antonio McDyess RC .60 1.50
49 George Zidek RC .25 .60
50 Joe Smith RC .50 1.25
51 Ed O'Bannon RC .25 .60
52 Rasheed Wallace RC .75 2.00
53 Eric Williams RC .25 .60
54 Kurt Thomas RC .25 .60
55 Mookie Blaylock .15 .40
56 Robert Pack .15 .40
57 Dana Barros .15 .40
58 Eric Murdock .15 .40
59 Glen Rice .25 .60
60 John Stockton .30 .75
61 Scottie Pippen .40 1.00
62 Oliver Miller .15 .40
63 Tyrone Hill .15 .40
64 Gary Payton .25 .60
65 Jim Jackson .15 .40
66 Avery Johnson .20 .50
67 Mahmoud Abdul-Rauf .15 .40
68 Olden Polynice .15 .40
69 Joe Dumars .25 .60
70 Rod Strickland .25 .60
71 Chris Mullin .25 .60
72 Kevin Johnson .25 .60
73 Derrick Coleman .20 .50
74 Clyde Drexler .30 .75
75 Dale Davis .15 .40

76 Horace Grant .20 .50
77 Loy Vaught .15 .40
78 Armon Gilliam .15 .40
79 Nick Van Exel .25 .60
80 Charles Oakley .20 .50
81 Kevin Willis .15 .40
82 Sherman Douglas .15 .40
83 Isaiah Rider .25 .60
84 Steve Smith .20 .50
85 Dee Brown .15 .40
86 Dell Curry .15 .40
87 Calbert Cheaney .15 .40
88 Greg Anthony .15 .40
89 Jeff Hornacek .20 .50
90 Dennis Rodman .50 1.25
91 Willie Anderson .15 .40
92 Chris Mills .15 .40
93 Hersey Hawkins .15 .40
94 Popeye Jones .15 .40
95 Chuck Person .20 .50
96 Reggie Williams .15 .40
97 A.C. Green .25 .60
98 Otis Thorpe .15 .40
99 Walt Williams .15 .40
100 Latrell Sprewell .25 .60
101 Buck Williams .15 .40
102 Robert Horry .20 .50
103 Clarence Weatherspoon .15 .40
104 Dennis Scott .15 .40
105 Rik Smits .20 .50
106 Jayson Williams .15 .40
107 Pooh Richardson .15 .40
108 Anthony Mason .15 .40
109 Cedric Ceballos .15 .40
110 Billy Owens .15 .40
111 Johnny Newman .15 .40
112 Christian Laettner .20 .50
113 Stacey Augmon .20 .50
114 Chris Morris .15 .40
115 Detlef Schrempf .25 .60
116 Dino Radja .20 .50
117 Sean Elliott .25 .60
118 Muggsy Bogues .20 .50
119 Toni Kukoc .25 .60
120 Clifford Robinson .15 .40
121 Bobby Hurley .25 .60
122 Lorenzo Williams .15 .40
123 Wayman Tisdale .15 .40
124 Bobby Phills .15 .40
125 Nick Anderson .15 .40
126 LaPhonso Ellis .15 .40
127 Scott Williams .15 .40
128 Mark West .15 .40
129 P.J. Brown .15 .40
130 Tim Hardaway .25 .60
131 Derek Harper .20 .50
132 Mario Elie .15 .40
133 Benoit Benjamin .15 .40
134 Terry Porter .15 .40
135 Derrick McKey .15 .40
136 Bimbo Coles .15 .40
137 John Salley .15 .40
138 Malik Sealy .15 .40
139 Byron Scott .20 .50
140 Vlade Divac .25 .60
141 Mark Price .25 .60
142 Rony Seikaly .20 .50
143 Mark Jackson .25 .60
144 John Starks .20 .50

1995-96 Topps Gallery Player's Private Issue

Randomly inserted into 1 in every 12 packs, cards from this 126 card set parallel cards 19-144 from the basic Topps Gallery issue. Each Player's Private Issue card is marked with a special holographic silver foil stamp on front, differentiating them from their regular-issue counterparts. According to Topps media literature, half of the cards printed were sent to the actual NBA players featured in the set and the rest were seeded into packs. Quite a hullabaloo was made over the discovery that Topps had never released the first 18 cards in this set (the Masters subset) due to an unannounced production flaw at the printing plant. For many months, it was believed that Private Issue parallels existed for these first eighteen cards (as was stated on Topps media literature) but the cards were simply not turning up on the open market as wholesale dealer buy offers skyrocketed. Topps made good on these 18 cards the following year by producing them and inserting them into series two hobby packs of 1996-97 Stadium Club. To ascertain values on individual cards, please refer to the multiplier in the header, coupled with the value of the base card.

*STARS: 10X TO 25X BASE CARD HI
*RCs: 5X TO 12X BASE HI
10 Michael Jordan 125.00 250.00
61 Scottie Pippen 12.50 30.00
100 Latrell Sprewell 8.00 20.00

1995-96 Topps Gallery Expressionists

Randomly inserted into 1 in every 24 packs, these inserts feature a collection of fifteen NBA team leaders. Each card attempts to capture the intensity and spirit of the featured player incorporating an embossed, textured, brush stroke effect.

COMPLETE SET (15) 30.00 80.00
EX1 Shawn Kemp 2.00 5.00
EX2 Michael Jordan 15.00 40.00
EX3 Reggie Miller 2.50 6.00
EX4 Kevin Willis 1.25 3.00
EX5 Jason Kidd 3.00 8.00
EX6 Larry Johnson 2.00 5.00
EX7 Patrick Ewing 2.50 6.00
EX8 Rasheed Wallace 3.00 8.00
EX9 Karl Malone 2.50 6.00
EX10 Shaquille O'Neal 5.00 12.00
EX11 Joe Smith 2.00 5.00
EX12 Jerry Stackhouse 3.00 8.00
EX13 Glen Rice 2.00 5.00
EX14 Clyde Drexler 2.50 6.00
EX15 Grant Hill 3.00 8.00

1995-96 Topps Gallery Photo Gallery

Randomly inserted into 1 in every 30 packs, this seventeen card set features a selection of premium quality photographs, chronicling classic moments from some of the NBA's biggest stars. Each card is custom-designed to compliment the photography. Multiple foils were also used on each card.

COMPLETE SET (17) 50.00 100.00
PG1 Vin Baker 2.50 6.00
PG2 Brian Grant 2.50 6.00
PG3 George Zidek 1.50 4.00
PG4 Hakeem Olajuwon 4.00 10.00
PG5 Stacey Augmon 2.50 6.00
PG6 Oliver Miller 2.00 5.00
PG7 Kenny Gattison 2.00 5.00
PG8 Dikembe Mutombo 3.00 8.00
PG9 Rony Seikaly 2.50 6.00
PG10 Tom Gugliotta 2.00 5.00
PG11 Scottie Pippen 5.00 12.00
PG12 David Robinson 5.00 12.00
PG13 Anfernee Hardaway 5.00 12.00
PG14 Dennis Rodman 6.00 15.00
PG15 Kevin Garnett 12.00 30.00
PG16 Damon Stoudamire 4.00 10.00
PG17 Charles Barkley 5.00 12.00

1999-00 Topps Gallery Promos

This six-card standard-size set was sent to dealers as a promotional set for the 1999-00 Topps Gallery issue. The cards carry a "PP" prefix.

COMPLETE SET (6) 1.25 3.00
PP1 Jason Williams .25 .60
PP2 Eddie Jones .20 .50
PP3 Allan Houston .15 .40
PP4 Alonzo Mourning .25 .60
PP5 Shareef Abdur-Rahim .15 .40
PP6 Wally Szczerbiak .40 1.00

1999-00 Topps Gallery

Released in May 2000, this set contained 150 base cards which were issued in five-card packs that carried a $3.00 suggested retail price. The base set was composed of 100 veteran cards and three subsets: 12 Masters, focusing on the top veteran players; 12 Artisans, focusing on younger players and 26 Apprentices featuring the top rookies.

COMPLETE SET (150) 30.00 60.00
1 Gary Payton .30 .75
2 Derek Anderson .20 .50
3 Jalen Rose .25 .60
4 Tim Hardaway .30 .75
5 Jerry Stackhouse .30 .75
6 Antonio McDyess .25 .60
7 Paul Pierce .50 1.25
8 Reggie Miller .30 .75
9 Maurice Taylor .20 .50
10 Stephon Marbury .25 .60
11 Terrell Brandon .20 .50
12 Marcus Camby .25 .60
13 Michael Doleac .20 .50
14 Doug Christie .25 .60
15 Brent Barry .25 .60
16 John Stockton .40 1.00
17 Rod Strickland .20 .50
18 Shareef Abdur-Rahim .25 .60
19 Vin Baker .30 .75
20 Jason Kidd .50 1.25
21 Nick Anderson .20 .50
22 Brian Grant .20 .50
23 Chris Webber .30 .75
24 Tariq Abdul-Wahad .20 .50
25 Jason Williams .40 1.00
26 Joe Smith .25 .60
27 Ray Allen .30 .75
28 Glenn Robinson .25 .60
29 Alonzo Mourning .40 1.00
30 Scottie Pippen .50 1.25
31 Mookie Blaylock .20 .50
32 Christian Laettner .25 .60
33 Mark Jackson .30 .75
34 Shawn Kemp .30 .75
35 Anfernee Hardaway .50 1.25
36 Chris Mullin .30 .75
37 Dennis Rodman .60 1.50
38 Lamond Murray .20 .50
39 Jim Jackson .25 .60
40 Shaquille O'Neal .75 2.00
41 Randy Brown .20 .50
42 Nick Van Exel .25 .60
43 Robert Traylor .20 .50
44 Vlade Divac .30 .75
45 Karl Malone .40 1.00
46 Avery Johnson .25 .60
47 Jayson Williams .20 .50
48 Darrell Armstrong .20 .50
49 Michael Olowokandi .20 .50
50 Kevin Garnett .60 1.50
51 Dirk Nowitzki .60 1.50
52 Antawn Jamison .30 .75
53 Latrell Sprewell .30 .75
54 Ruben Patterson .20 .50
55 Vince Carter .60 1.50
56 Michael Dickerson .20 .50
57 Raef LaFrentz .25 .60
58 Keith Van Horn .25 .60
59 Tom Gugliotta .20 .50
60 Allen Iverson .60 1.50
61 Eric Snow .25 .60
62 Kerry Kittles .20 .50
63 Sam Cassell .25 .60
64 Rik Smits .30 .75
65 Isaiah Rider .20 .50
66 Anthony Mason .20 .50
67 Hersey Hawkins .20 .50
68 Cuttino Mobley .25 .60
69 Allan Houston .25 .60
70 Kobe Bryant 1.50 4.00
71 Damon Stoudamire .30 .75
72 Charles Oakley .25 .60
73 Mike Bibby .30 .75
74 David Robinson .50 1.25
75 Eddie Jones .30 .75
76 Juwan Howard .25 .60
77 Antoine Walker .30 .75
78 Michael Finley .30 .75
79 Larry Hughes .25 .60
80 Charles Barkley .50 1.25
81 Tracy McGrady .50 1.25
82 Dikembe Mutombo .30 .75
83 Rasheed Wallace .30 .75
84 Jeff Hornacek .25 .60
85 Patrick Ewing .40 1.00
86 P.J. Brown .20 .50
87 Brevin Knight .20 .50
88 Elden Campbell .20 .50
89 Kenny Anderson .25 .60
90 Grant Hill .40 1.00
91 Mitch Richmond .30 .75
92 Steve Smith .20 .50
93 Jamal Mashburn .25 .60
94 Toni Kukoc .30 .75
95 Hakeem Olajuwon .40 1.00
96 Ron Mercer .25 .60
97 John Starks .30 .75
98 Glen Rice .30 .75
99 Cedric Ceballos .20 .50
100 Tim Duncan .60 1.50
101 Karl Malone MAS .40 1.00
102 Alonzo Mourning MAS .40 1.00
103 Gary Payton MAS .30 .75
104 Scottie Pippen MAS .50 1.25
105 Shaquille O'Neal MAS .75 2.00
106 Charles Barkley MAS .50 1.25
107 Grant Hill MAS .40 1.00
108 John Stockton MAS .40 1.00
109 Jason Kidd MAS .50 1.25
110 Reggie Miller MAS .30 .75
111 Shawn Kemp MAS .30 .75
112 Patrick Ewing MAS .40 1.00
113 Kevin Garnett ART .60 1.50
114 Vince Carter ART .60 1.50
115 Kobe Bryant ART 1.50 4.00
116 Chris Webber ART .30 .75
117 Tracy McGrady ART .50 1.25
118 Shareef Abdur-Rahim ART .25 .60
119 Paul Pierce ART .50 1.25
120 Jason Williams ART .40 1.00
121 Tim Duncan ART .60 1.50
122 Eddie Jones ART .30 .75
123 Allen Iverson ART .60 1.50
124 Stephon Marbury ART .25 .60
125 Elton Brand RC 1.00 2.50
126 Lamar Odom RC 1.25 3.00
127 Steve Francis RC 1.00 2.50
128 Adrian Griffin RC .40 1.00
129 Wally Szczerbiak RC .75 2.00
130 Baron Davis RC 1.25 3.00
131 Richard Hamilton RC 1.00 2.50
132 Jonathan Bender RC .40 1.00
133 Andre Miller RC 1.00 2.50
134 Shawn Marion RC 1.00 2.50
135 Jason Terry RC 1.00 2.50
136 Trajan Langdon RC .40 1.00
137 Corey Maggette RC .75 2.00
138 William Avery RC .40 1.00
139 Ron Artest RC 1.00 2.50
140 Cal Bowdler RC .40 1.00
141 James Posey RC .40 1.00
142 Quincy Lewis RC .40 1.00
143 Kenny Thomas RC .40 1.00
144 Vonteego Cummings RC .40 1.00
145 Todd MacCulloch RC .40 1.00
146 Anthony Carter RC .40 1.00
147 Aleksandar Radojevic RC .40 1.00
148 Devean George RC .40 1.00
149 Scott Padgett RC .40 1.00
150 Jumaine Jones RC .40 1.00

1999-00 Topps Gallery Player's Private Issue

Randomly inserted in packs at one in 17, this 150-card set parallels the base set. The cards feature the Player's Private Issue logo on the front and are serially numbered to 250 on the back. To ascertain values on individual cards, please refer to the multiplier in the header, coupled with the value of the base card.

*STARS: 6X TO 15X BASE CARD HI
*RCs: 3X TO 8X BASE HI

1999-00 Topps Gallery Autographs

Randomly inserted in packs at an overall rate of one in 375, this four-card set features authentic autographs from top NBA players. Group "A" cards were inserted at one in 437, while Group "B" cards were inserted at one in 2,637. Each card is stamped with the Topps Certified Autograph Issue logo and the Topps Authentication sticker. Card backs are numbered by the player's initials.

CM Corey Maggette A 6.00 15.00
EB Elton Brand B 6.00 15.00
TD Tim Duncan B 100.00 200.00
WS Wally Szczerbiak A 5.00 12.00

1999-00 Topps Gallery Exhibits

Randomly inserted in packs at one in 24, this 30-card set traces the history of art and features NBA stars in 10 different themes. Card backs carry a "GE" prefix.

COMPLETE SET (30) 50.00 100.00
GE1 Shaquille O'Neal 4.00 10.00
GE2 Chris Webber 1.50 4.00
GE3 Karl Malone 2.00 5.00
GE4 Hakeem Olajuwon 2.00 5.00
GE5 Scottie Pippen 2.50 6.00
GE6 Patrick Ewing 2.00 5.00
GE7 John Stockton 2.00 5.00
GE8 Tim Duncan 3.00 8.00
GE9 Grant Hill 2.00 5.00
GE10 Dennis Rodman 3.00 8.00
GE11 Reggie Miller 1.50 4.00
GE12 Brian Grant 1.00 2.50
GE13 Antoine Walker 1.50 4.00
GE14 Damon Stoudamire 1.50 4.00
GE15 Tracy McGrady 2.50 6.00
GE16 Alonzo Mourning 2.00 5.00
GE17 Shawn Kemp 1.50 4.00
GE18 Isaiah Rider 1.00 2.50
GE19 Vince Carter 3.00 8.00
GE20 Antonio McDyess 1.25 3.00
GE21 Jason Kidd 2.50 6.00
GE22 Kobe Bryant 10.00 25.00
GE23 Kevin Garnett 3.00 8.00
GE24 Latrell Sprewell 1.50 4.00
GE25 Michael Finley 1.50 4.00
GE26 Nick Van Exel 1.25 3.00
GE27 Anfernee Hardaway 2.50 6.00
GE28 Elton Brand 2.50 6.00
GE29 Lamar Odom 3.00 8.00
GE30 Baron Davis 3.00 8.00

1999-00 Topps Gallery Gallery of Heroes

Randomly inserted in packs at one in 24, this 10-card set features players on card stock that simulates stained glass. Card backs carry a "GH" prefix.

COMPLETE SET (10) 12.00 30.00
GH1 Kevin Garnett 2.00 5.00
GH3 Kobe Bryant 10.00 25.00
GH4 Vince Carter 2.00 5.00
GH5 Tim Duncan 2.00 5.00
GH9 Alonzo Mourning 1.25 3.00
GH10 Karl Malone 1.25 3.00

1999-00 Topps Gallery Heritage

Randomly inserted in packs at one in 12, this 10-card set features players on artwork in the style of the 1956-57 Topps Baseball cards. Card backs carry a "TGH" prefix.

COMPLETE SET (10) 8.00 20.00
*PROOF: .75X TO 2X HI COLUMN
PROOF: STATED ODDS 1:36
TGH1 Tim Duncan 1.50 4.00
TGH2 Elton Brand 2.00 5.00
TGH3 Shaquille O'Neal 2.00 5.00
TGH4 Stephon Marbury .60 1.50
TGH5 Allen Iverson 1.50 4.00
TGH6 Grant Hill 1.00 2.50
TGH7 Charles Barkley 1.25 3.00
TGH8 Jason Williams 1.00 2.50
TGH9 Scottie Pippen 1.25 3.00
TGH10 Allan Houston .60 1.50

1999-00 Topps Gallery Originals

Randomly inserted in packs at one in 87, this 10-card set features swatches of player-worn jerseys from the 1999 NBA Rookie Photo Shoot. Card backs carry a "GO" prefix.

GO1 Elton Brand 5.00 12.00
GO2 Shawn Marion 5.00 12.00
GO3 Corey Maggette 4.00 10.00
GO4 Steve Francis 5.00 12.00
GO5 Wally Szczerbiak 4.00 10.00
GO6 Baron Davis 6.00 15.00
GO7 Jonathan Bender 2.00 5.00
GO8 Jason Terry 5.00 12.00
GO9 Richard Hamilton 5.00 12.00
GO10 Andre Miller 5.00 12.00

1999-00 Topps Gallery Photo Gallery

Randomly inserted in packs at one in 12, this 10-card set features cards that were created in a cross-promotion with NBA.com, where fans chose their favorite photos. Card backs carry a "PG" prefix.

COMPLETE SET (10) 2.00 5.00
PG1 Tim Duncan .50 1.25
PG2 Allen Iverson .50 1.25
PG3 Gary Payton .25 .60
PG4 Elton Brand .60 1.50
PG5 Steve Francis .60 1.50
PG6 Latrell Sprewell .25 .60
PG7 Jason Kidd .40 1.00
PG8 Shawn Marion .60 1.50
PG9 Shareef Abdur-Rahim .20 .50
PG10 Jason Williams .30 .75

2000-01 Topps Gallery

The 2000-01 Topps Gallery product was released in April, 2001 and featured a 150-card base set that was broken into tiers as follows: Base Veterans (1-125) and Rookies (126-150) serial numbered to 999. Each pack contained six cards and carried a suggested retail price of $2.99.

COMP.SET w/o RC's (125) 15.00 40.00
1 Allen Iverson .50 1.25
2 Terrell Brandon .15 .40
3 Tracy McGrady .40 1.00
4 Shawn Marion .25 .60
5 Steve Smith .20 .50
6 Avery Johnson .20 .50
7 Gary Payton .25 .60
8 Mark Jackson .20 .50
9 Mike Bibby .25 .60
10 Karl Malone .30 .75
11 Kevin Garnett .50 1.25
12 Tim Hardaway .25 .60
13 Isaiah Rider .20 .50
14 Corey Maggette .20 .50
15 Vince Carter .50 1.25
16 Vin Baker .20 .50
17 Paul Pierce .30 .75
18 Matt Harpring .20 .50
19 Ron Artest .25 .60
20 Kenny Anderson .20 .50
21 Larry Hughes .20 .50
22 Antonio McDyess .20 .50
23 Shandon Anderson .15 .40
24 Joe Smith .20 .50
25 Jermaine O'Neal .25 .60
26 Horace Grant .20 .50
27 Ray Allen .25 .60
28 Keith Van Horn .20 .50
29 Darrell Armstrong .15 .40
30 Shaquille O'Neal .60 1.50
31 Reggie Miller .25 .60
32 Allan Houston .20 .50
33 Grant Hill .30 .75
34 David Robinson .40 1.00
35 Clifford Robinson .15 .40
36 Theo Ratliff .15 .40
37 Rashard Lewis .25 .60
38 Peja Stojakovic .25 .60
39 Jason Kidd .40 1.00
40 Latrell Sprewell .20 .50
41 Stephon Marbury .20 .50
42 Sam Cassell .20 .50
43 Brian Grant .15 .40
44 Jalen Rose .20 .50
45 Antawn Jamison .25 .60
46 Raef LaFrentz .15 .40
47 Dirk Nowitzki .40 1.00
48 Lamond Murray .15 .40
49 Derrick Coleman .20 .50
50 Steve Francis .25 .60
51 Dikembe Mutombo .25 .60
52 Elton Brand .25 .60
53 Christian Laettner .15 .40
54 Ben Wallace .25 .60
55 Jim Jackson .15 .40
56 Cuttino Mobley .20 .50
57 Jonathan Bender .15 .40
58 Anthony Mason .15 .40
59 Tim Thomas .15 .40
60 Lamar Odom .25 .60
61 Glenn Robinson .20 .50
62 Kendall Gill .15 .40
63 Glen Rice .20 .50
64 Anfernee Hardaway .40 1.00
65 Jason Williams .25 .60
66 Shawn Kemp .25 .60
67 Derek Anderson .15 .40
68 Patrick Ewing .30 .75
69 Shareef Abdur-Rahim .20 .50
70 Tim Duncan .50 1.25
71 Rod Strickland .20 .50
72 Bryon Russell .15 .40
73 Antonio Davis .15 .40
74 Rasheed Wallace .25 .60
75 Wally Szczerbiak .20 .50
76 Eric Snow .15 .40
77 Toni Kukoc .20 .50
78 Michael Olowokandi .15 .40
79 Hakeem Olajuwon .30 .75
80 Kobe Bryant 1.25 3.00
81 Mookie Blaylock .20 .50
82 Michael Finley .25 .60
83 Jerry Stackhouse .20 .50
84 Baron Davis .25 .60
85 Jason Terry .25 .60
86 Andre Miller .20 .50
87 Antoine Walker .20 .50
88 Jamal Mashburn .20 .50
89 Nick Van Exel .20 .50
90 Eddie Jones .25 .60
91 Marcus Camby .20 .50
92 Scottie Pippen .40 1.00
93 John Stockton .30 .75
94 Richard Hamilton .20 .50
95 John Starks .15 .40
96 Juwan Howard .20 .50
97 Michael Dickerson .15 .40
98 Ron Mercer .15 .40
99 Chris Webber .25 .60
100 Magic Johnson .75 2.00
101 Shaquille O'Neal MAS .60 1.50
102 Tim Duncan MAS .50 1.25
103 Chris Webber MAS .25 .60
104 Grant Hill MAS .30 .75
105 Kevin Garnett MAS .50 1.25
106 Vince Carter MAS .50 1.25
107 Gary Payton MAS .25 .60
108 Jason Kidd MAS .40 1.00
109 Kobe Bryant MAS 1.25 3.00
110 Karl Malone MAS .30 .75
111 Scottie Pippen MAS .40 1.00
112 Reggie Miller MAS .25 .60
113 John Stockton MAS .30 .75
114 Elton Brand ART .25 .60
115 Tracy McGrady ART .40 1.00
116 Steve Francis ART .25 .60
117 Lamar Odom ART .25 .60
118 Baron Davis ART .25 .60
119 Andre Miller ART .20 .50
120 Jonathan Bender ART .15 .40
121 Paul Pierce ART .30 .75
122 Jason Williams ART .25 .60
123 Rashard Lewis ART .25 .60
124 Larry Hughes ART .20 .50
125 Shawn Marion ART .25 .60
126 Kenyon Martin RC 3.00 8.00
127 Stromile Swift RC 1.25 3.00
128 Darius Miles RC 1.25 3.00
129 Marcus Fizer RC 1.25 3.00
130 Mike Miller RC 2.50 6.00
131 DerMarr Johnson RC 1.25 3.00
132 Chris Mihm RC 1.25 3.00
133 Jamal Crawford RC 2.00 5.00
134 Joel Przybilla RC 1.25 3.00
135 Keyon Dooling RC 1.25 3.00
136 Jerome Moiso RC 1.25 3.00
137 Etan Thomas RC 1.25 3.00
138 Courtney Alexander RC 1.25 3.00
139 Mateen Cleaves RC 1.25 3.00
140 Jason Collier RC 1.25 3.00
141 Hedo Turkoglu RC 2.50 6.00
142 Desmond Mason RC 1.50 4.00
143 Quentin Richardson RC 2.00 5.00
144 Jamaal Magloire RC 1.25 3.00
145 Speedy Claxton RC 1.25 3.00
146 Morris Peterson RC 1.25 3.00
147 Donnell Harvey RC 1.25 3.00
148 DeShawn Stevenson RC 1.50 4.00
149 Stephen Jackson RC 2.00 5.00
150 Marc Jackson RC 1.25 3.00

2000-01 Topps Gallery Charity Gallery

Randomly inserted into packs at one in 12, this 10-card insert features players that make a difference in the community. Card backs carry a "CG" prefix.

COMPLETE SET (10) 6.00 15.00
CG1 Eddie Jones 1.00 2.50
CG2 Ray Allen 1.00 2.50
CG3 Elton Brand 1.00 2.50
CG4 Jason Kidd 1.50 4.00
CG5 Derek Anderson .60 1.50
CG6 Karl Malone 1.25 3.00
CG7 Brian Grant .60 1.50
CG8 Shareef Abdur-Rahim .75 2.00
CG9 Rasheed Wallace 1.00 2.50
CG10 Marcus Camby .75 2.00

2000-01 Topps Gallery Extremes

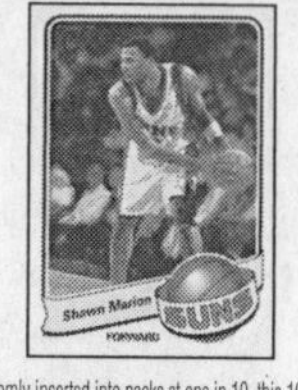

Randomly inserted into packs at one in 18, this 20-card insert features players that have taken their game to the next level. Card backs carry a "E" prefix.

COMPLETE SET (20) 20.00 50.00
E1 Shaquille O'Neal 3.00 8.00
E2 Vince Carter 2.50 6.00
E3 Allen Iverson 2.50 6.00
E4 Kevin Garnett 2.50 6.00
E5 Chris Webber 1.25 3.00
E6 Larry Hughes 1.00 2.50
E7 Jason Williams 1.25 3.00
E8 Steve Francis 1.25 3.00
E9 Antonio McDyess 1.00 2.50
E10 Tim Duncan 2.50 6.00
E11 Gary Payton 1.25 3.00
E12 Lamar Odom 1.25 3.00
E13 Elton Brand 1.25 3.00
E14 Michael Finley 1.25 3.00
E15 Latrell Sprewell 1.00 2.50
E16 Shareef Abdur-Rahim 1.00 2.50
E17 Jerry Stackhouse 1.00 2.50
E18 Rashard Lewis 1.25 3.00
E19 Shawn Marion 1.25 3.00
E20 Darius Miles 1.25 3.00

2000-01 Topps Gallery Gallery of Heroes

Randomly inserted into packs at one in 24, this 10-card insert features players that have a knack for heroics. Card backs carry a "GH" prefix.

COMPLETE SET (10) 20.00 40.00
GH1 Allen Iverson 3.00 8.00
GH2 Tim Duncan 3.00 8.00
GH3 Kobe Bryant 10.00 25.00
GH4 Elton Brand 1.50 4.00
GH5 Ray Allen 1.50 4.00
GH6 Stephon Marbury 1.25 3.00
GH7 Eddie Jones 1.50 4.00
GH8 Gary Payton 1.50 4.00
GH9 Antonio McDyess 1.25 3.00
GH10 Shareef Abdur-Rahim 1.25 3.00

2000-01 Topps Gallery Heritage

Randomly inserted into packs at one in 10, this 10-card insert features some of the hottest players in the league. Card backs carry a "H" prefix. Please note that there is a parallel to this set that was inserted at 1:186.

COMPLETE SET (10) 8.00 20.00
*PROOFS: 1.5X TO 4X BASE CARD HI
PROOFS STATED ODDS 1:186
PROOFS PRINT RUN 250 SERIAL #'d SETS
H1 Tim Duncan 2.00 5.00
H2 Tracy McGrady 1.50 4.00
H3 Steve Francis 1.00 2.50
H4 Elton Brand 1.00 2.50
H5 Rashard Lewis 1.00 2.50
H6 Larry Hughes .75 2.00
H7 Shawn Marion 1.00 2.50
H8 Baron Davis 1.00 2.50
H9 Antawn Jamison 1.00 2.50
H10 Keyon Dooling 1.00 2.50

2000-01 Topps Gallery Originals

Randomly inserted into packs, this 31-card insert features swatches of actual game-used jerseys. Card backs carry a "GO" prefix. Please note that the insert was broken into tiers as follows: Group A was inserted at 1:153, Group B was inserted at one in 1:71, Group C was inserted at 1:255, and Group D at 1:1148.

GO1 Kenyon Martin B 5.00 12.00
GO2 Stromile Swift B 2.00 5.00
GO3 Darius Miles B 2.00 5.00
GO4 Marcus Fizer B 2.00 5.00
GO5 Mike Miller B 4.00 10.00
GO6 DerMarr Johnson B 2.00 5.00
GO7 Chris Mihm B 2.00 5.00
GO8 Joel Przybilla B 2.00 5.00
GO9 Keyon Dooling B 2.00 5.00
GO10 Jerome Moiso B 2.00 5.00
GO11 Etan Thomas B 2.00 5.00
GO12 Courtney Alexander B 2.00 5.00
GO13 Mateen Cleaves B 2.00 5.00
GO14 Jason Collier A 2.00 5.00
GO15 Hedo Turkoglu A 4.00 10.00
GO16 Desmond Mason A 2.50 6.00
GO17 Quentin Richardson A 3.00 8.00
GO18 Jamaal Magloire A 2.00 5.00
GO19 Speedy Claxton A 2.00 5.00
GO20 Morris Peterson A 2.00 5.00
GO21 Donnell Harvey A 2.00 5.00
GO22 DeShawn Stevenson A 2.50 6.00
GO23 Mamadou N'Diaye A 2.00 5.00
GO24 Erick Barkley A 2.00 5.00
GO25 Mark Madsen A 2.00 5.00
GO26 Tracy McGrady C 5.00 12.00
GO27 Shaquille O'Neal D 8.00 20.00
GO28 Grant Hill C 4.00 10.00
GO29 Tim Duncan D 6.00 15.00
GO30 Antoine Walker C 2.50 6.00
GO31 Jason Kidd C 5.00 12.00

2000-01 Topps Gallery Photo Gallery

Randomly inserted into packs at one in 10, this 10-card insert features great photos of some of the great young players in the game. Card backs carry a "PG" prefix.

COMPLETE SET (10) 10.00 25.00
PG1 Kevin Garnett 1.50 4.00

G2 Grant Hill 1.00 2.50
G3 Kobe Bryant 4.00 10.00
G4 Vince Carter 1.50 4.00
G5 Lamar Odom .75 2.00
G6 Stephon Marbury .60 1.50
G7 Baron Davis .75 2.00
G8 Chris Webber .75 2.00
G9 Ray Allen .75 2.00
G10 Kenyon Martin 2.00 5.00

2000-01 Topps Gallery Signatures

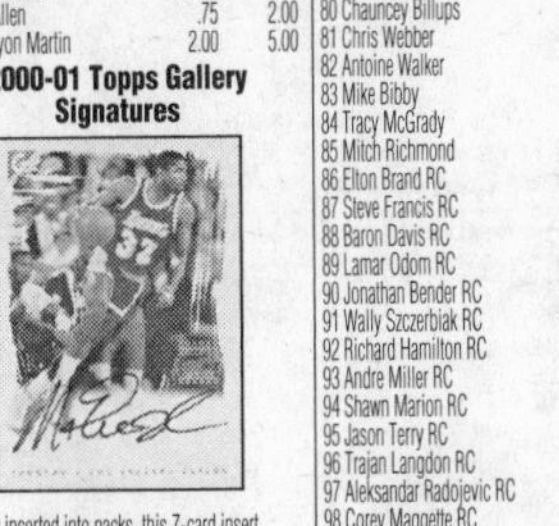

Randomly inserted into packs, this 7-card insert features autographs from some of the hottest young players in the league. Card backs carry a "GS" prefix followed by the players initials. Please note that the insert was broken into tiers as follows: Group A inserted at 1:1836, Group B at 1:765, Group C at 1:574, Group D at 1:918, and Group E at 1:612.

GSEB Elton Brand C 6.00 15.00
GSEJ Eddie Jones A 10.00 25.00
GSGP Gary Payton E 12.50 30.00
GSJC Jamal Crawford B 6.00 15.00
GSMC Mateen Cleaves D 5.00 12.00
GSMJ Magic Johnson B 40.00 100.00

1999-00 Topps Gold Label Class 1

Released for the first time in basketball for the 1999-2000 season, the set contained 100 cards, including 85 veterans and 15 rookies. The cards were available in five-card packs which carried a suggested retail price of $5. The base set, or Class 1, pictured the background photo as dribbling.

COMPLETE SET (100) 25.00 60.00
ONE TO ONE STATED ODDS 1:629
1 Tim Duncan .75 2.00
2 Steve Smith .25 .60
3 Jeff Hornacek .30 .75
4 Kevin Garnett .75 2.00
5 Paul Pierce .60 1.50
6 Doug Christie .30 .75
7 Charles Barkley .60 1.50
8 Nick Van Exel .30 .75
9 Shareef Abdur-Rahim .30 .75
10 Rod Strickland .25 .60
11 Keith Van Horn .30 .75
12 Matt Harpring .30 .75
13 Randy Brown .25 .60
14 Vin Baker .40 1.00
15 Mark Jackson .40 1.00
16 Latrell Sprewell .40 1.00
17 Anthony Mason .25 .60
18 Brian Grant .25 .60
19 Brevin Knight .25 .60
20 Elden Campbell .25 .60
21 Allen Iverson .75 2.00
22 Kobe Bryant 2.00 5.00
23 Antawn Jamison .40 1.00
24 Lindsey Hunter .25 .60
25 Eddie Jones .40 1.00
26 Michael Finley .40 1.00
27 Juwan Howard .30 .75
28 Antonio McDyess .30 .75
29 David Robinson .60 1.50
30 Karl Malone .50 1.25
31 Jason Kidd .60 1.50
32 Zydrunas Ilgauskas .30 .75
33 Vince Carter .75 2.00
34 Maurice Taylor .25 .60
35 Alonzo Mourning .50 1.25
36 Tim Thomas .30 .75
37 Dikembe Mutombo .40 1.00
38 Grant Hill .50 1.25
39 Jason Williams .50 1.25
40 Scottie Pippen .60 1.50
41 Stephon Marbury .30 .75
42 Reggie Miller .40 1.00
43 Tyrone Nesby RC .40 1.00
44 Ron Mercer .30 .75
45 Terrell Brandon .25 .60
46 Darrell Armstrong .25 .60
47 Larry Hughes .30 .75
48 Alan Henderson .25 .60
49 Ray Allen .40 1.00
50 Rasheed Wallace .40 1.00
51 Toni Kukoc .40 1.00
52 Patrick Ewing .50 1.25
53 Tom Gugliotta .25 .60
54 Chris Mills .25 .60
55 Gary Payton .40 1.00
56 Michael Olowokandi .25 .60
57 Chris Mullin .40 1.00
58 Shawn Kemp .40 1.00
59 Joe Smith .30 .75
60 Steve Nash .60 1.50
61 Gary Trent .25 .60
62 Shaquille O'Neal 1.00 2.50
63 Kerry Kittles .25 .60
64 Tim Hardaway .40 1.00
65 Glenn Robinson .30 .75
66 Damon Stoudamire .40 1.00
67 Anfernee Hardaway .60 1.50
68 Vlade Divac .40 1.00
69 John Starks .40 1.00
70 Allan Houston .30 .75
71 Jerry Stackhouse .40 1.00
72 Avery Johnson .30 .75
73 Glen Rice .40 1.00
74 Felipe Lopez .25 .60
75 Clifford Robinson .25 .60
76 Jamal Mashburn .30 .75
77 Hakeem Olajuwon .50 1.25
78 Matt Geiger .25 .60
79 John Stockton .50 1.25
80 Chauncey Billups .40 1.00
81 Chris Webber .40 1.00
82 Antoine Walker .40 1.00
83 Mike Bibby .40 1.00
84 Tracy McGrady .60 1.50
85 Mitch Richmond .40 1.00
86 Elton Brand RC 1.00 2.50
87 Steve Francis RC 1.00 2.50
88 Baron Davis RC 1.25 3.00
89 Lamar Odom RC 1.25 3.00
90 Jonathan Bender RC .40 1.00
91 Wally Szczerbiak RC .75 2.00
92 Richard Hamilton RC 1.00 2.50
93 Andre Miller RC 1.00 2.50
94 Shawn Marion RC 1.00 2.50
95 Jason Terry RC 1.00 2.50
96 Trajan Langdon RC .40 1.00
97 Aleksandar Radojevic RC .40 1.00
98 Corey Maggette RC .75 2.00
99 William Avery RC .40 1.00
100 Cal Bowdler RC .40 1.00

1999-00 Topps Gold Label Class 1 Black Label

Randomly inserted in packs at one in eight, this 100-card set parallels the base Class 1 set. The cards feature a black label instead of the regular gold. The back of the card is also noted as a black label. To ascertain values on individual cards, please refer to the multiplier in the header, coupled with the value of the base card.

*STARS: 1.5X TO 4X BASE HI
*RCs: 1.25X TO 3X BASE HI

1999-00 Topps Gold Label Class 1 Red Label

Randomly inserted in packs at one in 63, this 100-card set parallels the base Class 1 set. The cards feature a red label instead of the regular gold. The back of the card is also noted as a red label. The cards are also serially numbered to 100. To ascertain values on individual cards, please refer to the multiplier in the header, coupled with the value of the base card.

*STARS: 10X TO 25X BASE HI
*RCs: 6X TO 15X BASE HI

1999-00 Topps Gold Label Class 2

Randomly inserted in packs at one in two, this 100-card set is a semi-parallel to the Class 1 set. The background photos on these cards feature the player scoring, rather than dribbling.

COMPLETE SET (100) 40.00 100.00
*STARS: .75X TO 2X CLASS 1 BASE
*RCs: .6X TO 1.5X CLASS 1 BASE

1999-00 Topps Gold Label Class 2 Black Label

Randomly inserted in packs at one in 16, this 100-card set parallels the base Class 2 set. The cards feature a black label instead of the regular gold. The back of the card is also noted as a black label. To ascertain values on individual cards, please refer to the multiplier in the header, coupled with the value of the base card.

*STARS: 3X TO 8X CLASS 1 BASE
*RCs: 2.5X TO 6X CLASS 1 BASE

1999-00 Topps Gold Label Class 2 Red Label

Randomly inserted in packs at one in 126, this 100-card set parallels the base Class 2 set. The cards feature a red label instead of the regular gold. The back of the card is also noted as a red label. The cards are also serially numbered to 50. To ascertain values on individual cards, please refer to the multiplier in the header, coupled with the value of the base card.

*STARS: 15X TO 40X CLASS 1 BASE
*RCs: 8X TO 20X CLASS 1 BASE

1999-00 Topps Gold Label Class 3

Randomly inserted in packs at one in four, this 100-card set is a semi-parallel to the Class 1 base set. The cards feature a portrait shot in the background of the card.

COMPLETE SET (100) 75.00 150.00
*STARS: 1.25X TO 3X CLASS 1 BASE
*RCs: 1X TO 2.5X CLASS 1 BASE

1999-00 Topps Gold Label Class 3 Black Label

Randomly inserted in packs at one in 32, this 100-card set parallels the base Class 3 set. The cards feature a black label instead of the regular gold. The back of the card is also noted as a black label. To ascertain values on individual cards, please refer to the multiplier in the header, coupled with the value of the base card.

*STARS: 5X TO 12X CLASS 1 BASE
*RCs: 4X TO 10X CLASS 1 BASE

1999-00 Topps Gold Label Class 3 Red Label

Randomly inserted in packs at one in 253, this 100-card set parallels the base Class 3 set. The cards feature a red label instead of the regular gold. The back of the card is also noted as a red label. The cards are also serially numbered to 25. To ascertain values on individual cards, please refer to the multiplier in the header, coupled with the value of the base card.

*STARS: 25X TO 60X CLASS 1 BASE
*RCs: 10X TO 25X CLASS 1 BASE

1999-00 Topps Gold Label New Standard

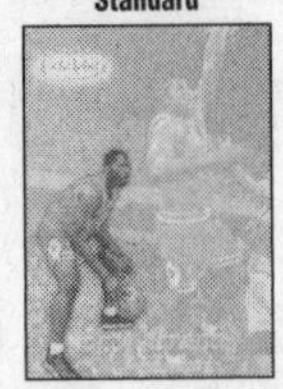

Randomly inserted in packs at one in 12, this 15-card set features current and future stars with less than three years of NBA experience. The cards feature a "NS" prefix on the back.

COMPLETE SET (15) 15.00 40.00
*BLACK: 1X TO 2.5X HI COLUMN
BLACK: STATED ODDS 1:60
*RED STARS: 10X TO 25X HI
RED: PRINT RUN 25 SERIAL #'d SETS
NS1 Vince Carter 1.50 4.00
NS2 Kevin Garnett 1.50 4.00
NS3 Tim Duncan 1.50 4.00
NS4 Kobe Bryant 4.00 10.00
NS5 Allen Iverson 1.50 4.00
NS6 Jason Williams 1.00 2.50
NS7 Keith Van Horn .60 1.50
NS8 Elton Brand 1.50 4.00
NS9 Steve Francis 1.50 4.00
NS10 Baron Davis 2.00 5.00
NS11 Lamar Odom 2.00 5.00
NS12 Jonathan Bender .60 1.50
NS13 Wally Szczerbiak 1.25 3.00
NS14 Jason Terry 1.50 4.00
NS15 Corey Maggette 1.25 3.00

1999-00 Topps Gold Label Prime Gold

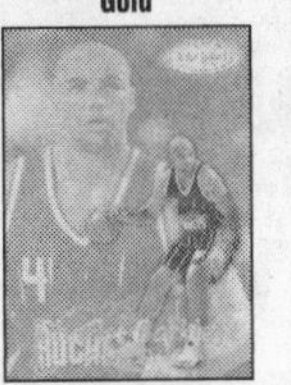

Randomly inserted in packs at one in 18, this 11-card set focuses on veteran players who have set the standard in the NBA. Card backs carry a "PG" prefix.

COMPLETE SET (11) 6.00 15.00
*BLACK: 1X TO 2.5X HI COLUMN
BLACK: STATED ODDS 1:90
*RED: 12X TO 30X HI
RED: PRINT RUN 25 SERIAL #'d SETS
PG1 John Stockton 1.00 2.50
PG2 Hakeem Olajuwon 1.00 2.50
PG3 Charles Barkley 1.25 3.00
PG4 Shaquille O'Neal 2.00 5.00
PG5 Alonzo Mourning 1.00 2.50
PG6 Scottie Pippen 1.25 3.00
PG7 Jason Kidd 1.25 3.00
PG8 David Robinson 1.25 3.00
PG9 Gary Payton .75 2.00
PG10 Karl Malone 1.00 2.50
PG11 Grant Hill 1.00 2.50

1999-00 Topps Gold Label Quest for the Gold

Randomly inserted in packs at one in nine, this nine-card set features players who will participate in the 2000 Summer Olympic Games for the USA Basketball team. Card backs carry a "Q" prefix.

*BLACK: 1X TO 2.5X HI COLUMN
BLACK: STATED ODDS 1:45
*RED: 15X TO 40X HI
RED: PRINT RUN 25 SERIAL #'d SETS
Q1 Allan Houston .50 1.25
Q2 Kevin Garnett 1.25 3.00
Q3 Gary Payton .60 1.50
Q4 Steve Smith .40 1.00
Q5 Tim Hardaway .60 1.50
Q6 Tim Duncan 1.25 3.00
Q7 Jason Kidd 1.00 2.50
Q8 Tom Gugliotta .40 1.00
Q9 Vin Baker .60 1.50

2000-01 Topps Gold Label Class 1

The 2000-01 Topps Gold Label product was released in December,2000. The product features a 100-card base set broken into tiers as follows: 80 Base Veterans (1-80), and 20 Rookies (81-100). Please note that there are four levels of the base set. Class one features the player dribbling, class two features the player shooting, class three features the player defending, and finally, there is a premium parallel that features the player dribbling, shooting, and defending on the same card. Each pack contained five cards and carried a suggested retail price of $5.00. Class 1 rookie cards were inserted at one in 29 and serially numbered to 1499.

COMPLETE SET w/o RC (80) 15.00 30.00
1 Steve Francis .40 1.00
2 Jalen Rose .30 .75
3 Allen Iverson .75 2.00
4 Damon Stoudamire .30 .75
5 David Robinson .60 1.50
6 Bryon Russell .25 .60
7 Toni Kukoc .30 .75
8 Tracy McGrady .60 1.50
9 John Stockton .50 1.25
10 Tim Duncan .75 2.00
11 Hakeem Olajuwon .50 1.25
12 Antoine Walker .30 .75
13 Dikembe Mutombo .40 1.00
14 Shawn Kemp .40 1.00
15 Ron Artest .40 1.00
16 Eddie Jones .40 1.00
17 Dirk Nowitzki .60 1.50
18 Nick Van Exel .30 .75
19 Grant Hill .50 1.25
20 Antawn Jamison .40 1.00
21 Cuttino Mobley .30 .75
22 Jonathan Bender .25 .60
23 Maurice Taylor .25 .60
24 Kobe Bryant 2.00 5.00
25 Tim Hardaway .40 1.00
26 Tim Thomas .25 .60
27 Terrell Brandon .25 .60
28 Marcus Camby .30 .75
29 Keith Van Horn .30 .75
30 Shawn Marion .40 1.00
31 Rasheed Wallace .40 1.00
32 Corey Maggette .30 .75
33 Jason Kidd .60 1.50
34 Shaquille O'Neal 1.00 2.50
35 Rashard Lewis .40 1.00
36 Karl Malone .50 1.25
37 Michael Dickerson .25 .60
38 Richard Hamilton .30 .75
39 Darrell Armstrong .25 .60
40 Wally Szczerbiak .30 .75
41 Glen Rice .30 .75
42 Glenn Robinson .30 .75
43 Reggie Miller .40 1.00
44 Alonzo Mourning .50 1.25
45 Larry Hughes .30 .75
46 Antonio McDyess .30 .75
47 Derrick Coleman .30 .75
48 Brevin Knight .25 .60
49 Jason Terry .40 1.00
50 Elton Brand .40 1.00
51 Latrell Sprewell .30 .75
52 Theo Ratliff .25 .60
53 Scottie Pippen .60 1.50
54 Jason Williams .40 1.00
55 Gary Payton .40 1.00
56 Mitch Richmond .30 .75
57 Vin Baker .30 .75
58 Raef LaFrentz .25 .60
59 Anfernee Hardaway .60 1.50
60 Steve Smith .30 .75
61 Stephon Marbury .30 .75
62 Vlade Divac .30 .75
63 Jamal Mashburn .30 .75
64 Jerome Williams .25 .60
65 Patrick Ewing .50 1.25
66 Lamar Odom .40 1.00
67 Jerry Stackhouse .30 .75
68 Michael Finley .40 1.00
69 Vince Carter .75 2.00
70 Andre Miller .30 .75
71 Paul Pierce .50 1.25
72 Baron Davis .40 1.00
73 Derek Anderson .25 .60
74 Chris Webber .40 1.00
75 Ray Allen .40 1.00
76 Kevin Garnett .75 2.00
77 Allan Houston .30 .75
78 Mike Bibby .40 1.00
79 Shareef Abdur-Rahim .30 .75
80 Juwan Howard .30 .75
81 Kenyon Martin RC 4.00 10.00
82 Stromile Swift RC 1.50 4.00
83 Darius Miles RC 1.50 4.00
84 Marcus Fizer RC 1.50 4.00
85 Mike Miller RC 3.00 8.00
86 DerMarr Johnson RC 1.50 4.00
87 Chris Mihm RC 1.50 4.00
88 Jamal Crawford RC 2.50 6.00
89 Joel Przybilla RC 1.50 4.00
90 Keyon Dooling RC 1.50 4.00
91 Jerome Moiso RC 1.50 4.00
92 Etan Thomas RC 1.50 4.00
93 Courtney Alexander RC 1.50 4.00
94 Mateen Cleaves RC 1.50 4.00
95 Jason Collier RC 1.50 4.00
96 Desmond Mason RC 2.00 5.00
97 Quentin Richardson RC 2.50 6.00
98 Jamaal Magloire RC 1.50 4.00
99 Speedy Claxton RC 1.50 4.00
100 Morris Peterson RC 1.50 4.00

2000-01 Topps Gold Label Class 2

Randomly inserted into packs, this 100-card set is a complete parallel of the Gold Label Class 1 base set. Please note that Class 2 cards feature the players in a shooting motion. These cards were inserted into packs at one in four for veterans and one in 43 for rookies. The rookies were numbered to 999.

*CLASS 2 VETS: .75X TO 2X CLASS 1 HI
*CLASS 2 RCs: .3X TO .8X CLASS 1 HI

2000-01 Topps Gold Label Class 3

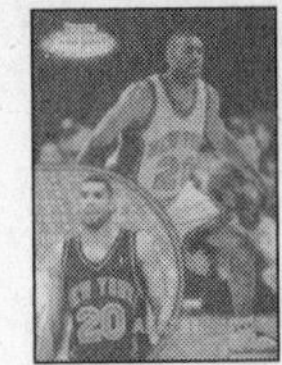

Randomly inserted into packs, this 100-card set is a complete parallel of the Gold Label Class 1 base set. Please note that the Class 3 cards feature the players defending. These cards were inserted into packs at one in 12 for veterans and one in 86 for rookies.

*CLASS 3 VETS: 1.25X TO 3X CLASS 1 HI
*CLASS 3 RCs: .5X TO 1.25X CLASS 1 HI

2000-01 Topps Gold Label Premium

Randomly inserted into packs, this 100-card set is a complete parallel of the Gold Label Class 1 base set. Please note that these cards feature three photos of the players in a defending, dribbling, and shooting motion. Each card is individually serial numbered to 1000. To ascertain values on individual cards, please refer to the multiplier in the header, coupled with the value of the base card.

*STARS: 2.5X TO 6X BASE CARD HI
*RCs: .75X TO 2X BASE CARD HI

2000-01 Topps Gold Label Autographs

Randomly inserted in packs at one in 1718, this two-card set features autographs of Shaquille O'Neal and Jalen Rose. Each card carries the Topps Genuine Issue seal.

TTAJR Jalen Rose 10.00 25.00
TTASO Shaquille O'Neal 125.00 250.00

2000-01 Topps Gold Label Game Jerseys

Randomly inserted into packs at one in 40, this 34-card insert features swatches of game-used jersey. Please note that cards labeled "H" are from Laker home jerseys (yellow), and that cards labeled "A" are from the Lakers away jerseys (purple). Card backs carry a "TT" prefix. A leather version of this set was produced as well where the cards are actually printed on leather and inserted in packs at the rate of one in 1039

*LEATHER: 2X TO 5X BASE JSY HI
TT1A Shaquille O'Neal 15.00 40.00
TT1H Shaquille O'Neal 15.00 40.00
TT2A Glen Rice 10.00 25.00
TT2H Glen Rice 10.00 25.00
TT3A Robert Horry 5.00 12.00
TT3H Robert Horry 5.00 12.00
TT4A Rick Fox 5.00 12.00
TT4H Rick Fox 5.00 12.00
TT5A Brian Shaw 4.00 10.00
TT5H Brian Shaw 4.00 10.00
TT6A Ron Harper 6.00 15.00
TT6H Ron Harper 6.00 15.00
TT7A Derek Fisher 6.00 15.00
TT7H Derek Fisher 6.00 15.00
TT8A A.C. Green 5.00 12.00
TT8H A.C. Green 5.00 12.00
TT9A John Salley 4.00 10.00
TT9H John Salley 4.00 10.00
TT10A Travis Knight 4.00 10.00
TT10H Travis Knight 4.00 10.00
TT11A Devean George 4.00 10.00
TT11H Devean George 4.00 10.00
TT12 Reggie Miller 25.00 60.00
TT13 Jalen Rose 8.00 20.00
TT14 Dale Davis 4.00 10.00
TT15 Rik Smits 5.00 12.00
TT16 Mark Jackson 5.00 12.00
TT17 Travis Best 4.00 10.00
TT18 Austin Croshere 4.00 10.00
TT19 Derrick McKey 4.00 10.00
TT20 Sam Perkins 4.00 10.00
TT21 Chris Mullin 10.00 25.00
TT22 Jonathan Bender 4.00 10.00
TT23 Zan Tabak 4.00 10.00

2000-01 Topps Gold Label Great Expectations

Randomly inserted in packs at one in 32, this 10-card set focuses on some of the younger players in the NBA. Card backs carry a "GE" prefix.

COMPLETE SET (10) 7.50 15.00
GE1 Elton Brand 1.00 2.50
GE2 Shawn Marion 1.00 2.50
GE3 Jason Williams 1.00 2.50
GE4 Baron Davis 1.00 2.50
GE5 Andre Miller .75 2.00
GE6 Paul Pierce 1.25 3.00
GE7 Lamar Odom 1.00 2.50
GE8 Dirk Nowitzki 1.50 4.00
GE9 Kenyon Martin 2.50 6.00
GE10 Marcus Fizer 1.00 2.50

2000-01 Topps Gold Label Home Court Advantage

Randomly inserted in packs at one in 40, this 15-card set focuses players that make it extemely tuff for opposing players to win on their courts. Card backs carry a "HCA" prefix.

COMPLETE SET (15) 15.00 40.00
HCA1 Tim Duncan 3.00 8.00
HCA2 Antoine Walker 1.25 3.00
HCA3 Chris Webber 1.50 4.00
HCA4 Alonzo Mourning 2.00 5.00
HCA5 Karl Malone 2.00 5.00
HCA6 Allen Iverson 3.00 8.00
HCA7 Jason Kidd 2.50 6.00
HCA8 Rasheed Wallace 1.50 4.00
HCA9 Gary Payton 1.50 4.00
HCA10 Shareef Abdur-Rahim 1.25 3.00
HCA11 Eddie Jones 1.50 4.00
HCA12 Stephon Marbury 1.25 3.00
HCA13 Scottie Pippen 2.50 6.00
HCA14 Raef LaFrentz 1.00 2.50
HCA15 Elton Brand 1.50 4.00

2000-01 Topps Gold Label Jam Artists

Randomly inserted in packs at one in 8, this 10-card set focuses players that have helped define the art of dunking in the NBA. Card backs carry a "JA" prefix.

COMPLETE SET (10) 5.00 12.00
JA1 Vince Carter 1.00 2.50
JA2 Tracy McGrady .75 2.00
JA3 Steve Francis .50 1.25
JA4 Jerry Stackhouse .40 1.00
JA5 Kevin Garnett 1.00 2.50
JA6 Michael Finley .50 1.25
JA7 Stromile Swift .50 1.25
JA8 Kobe Bryant 2.50 6.00
JA9 Darius Miles .50 1.25
JA10 Larry Hughes .40 1.00

1998 Topps Golden Greats

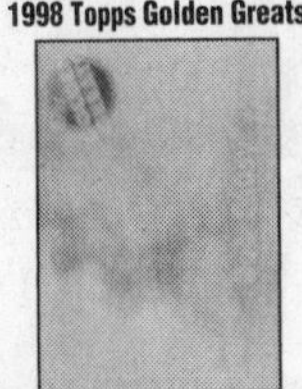

The 1998 Topps Golden Greats set was issued in one series totalling 18 cards. The one card packs retailed for $9.99 each. The cards feature vintage footage on lenticular card technology utilizing Kodamotion technology.

COMPLETE SET (18) 25.00 60.00
1 Kareem Abdul-Jabbar 3.00 8.00
2 Elgin Baylor 2.00 5.00
3 Larry Bird 6.00 15.00
4 Wilt Chamberlain 4.00 10.00
5 Bob Cousy 3.00 8.00
6 Julius Erving 4.00 10.00
7 Walt Frazier 2.00 5.00
8 George Gervin 2.00 5.00
9 John Havlicek 2.50 6.00
10 Magic Johnson 5.00 12.00
11 Kevin McHale 2.50 6.00
12 Earl Monroe 2.00 5.00
13 Willis Reed 2.00 5.00
14 Oscar Robertson 2.50 6.00
15 Bill Russell 3.00 8.00
16 Bill Walton 2.00 5.00
17 Jerry West 2.50 6.00
18 Rick Barry 2.00 5.00

1998 Topps Golden Greats Laser Cuts

Randomly inserted into packs at a rate of one in 36, this 18-card set is a parallel to the basic set. Each card is a laser cut version of the base card.

COMPLETE SET (18) 40.00 100.00
*LASER CUTS: .75X TO 2X BASE HI

2008-09 Topps Hardwood

This set was released on January 21, 2008. The base set consists of 125 cards. Cards 1-100 feature veterans, and cards 101-125 are rookies. Each rookie has two verisons, listed below, with both serially numbered to 2009.

COMP.SET w/o SPs (100) 20.00 40.00
UNPRICED EBONY PRINT RUN ONE SET
UNPRICED PRESS PLATE PRINT RUN ONE SET
1 Paul Pierce .50 1.25
2 Andrew Bogut .40 1.00
3 Greg Oden .40 1.00
4 Monta Ellis .40 1.00
5 Shaquille O'Neal .75 2.00
6 Al Horford .40 1.00
7 Al Thornton .30 .75
8 Anderson Varejao .30 .75
9 Andre Iguodala .40 1.00
10 Carlos Boozer .40 1.00
11 Chris Bosh .40 1.00
12 Corey Maggette .30 .75
13 Craig Smith .25 .60
14 Danny Granger .40 1.00
15 David West .40 1.00
16 Josh Howard .30 .75
17 Kevin Durant 1.50 4.00
18 Kevin Garnett .75 2.00
19 Luis Scola .30 .75
20 Luol Deng .40 1.00
21 Yi Jianlian .40 1.00
22 Pau Gasol .40 1.00
23 Rasheed Wallace .40 1.00
24 Ben Gordon .40 1.00
25 Dwyane Wade .75 2.00
26 Gilbert Arenas .40 1.00
27 Jamal Crawford .30 .75
28 Gerald Wallace .40 1.00
29 Jason Richardson .40 1.00
30 Kevin Martin .40 1.00
31 Mike Conley Jr. .30 .75
32 Richard Hamilton .30 .75
33 Tony Parker .40 1.00
34 Vince Carter .50 1.25
35 Brad Miller .30 .75
36 Al Jefferson .40 1.00
37 Antawn Jamison .40 1.00
38 Carmelo Anthony .50 1.25
39 David Lee .30 .75
40 Dirk Nowitzki .50 1.25
41 Elton Brand .40 1.00
42 Jose Calderon .30 .75
43 Josh Smith .40 1.00
44 LaMarcus Aldridge .40 1.00
45 LeBron James 2.00 5.00
46 Peja Stojakovic .40 1.00
47 Rashard Lewis .30 .75
48 Richard Jefferson .40 1.00
49 Devin Harris .40 1.00
50 Joe Johnson .40 1.00
51 Shawn Marion .40 1.00
52 Stephen Jackson .30 .75
53 Tayshaun Prince .40 1.00
54 Baron Davis .40 1.00
55 Chris Paul .60 1.50
56 Mike Dunleavy .30 .75
57 Deron Williams .40 1.00
58 Kobe Bryant 2.00 5.00
59 Jason Kidd .40 1.00
60 Ray Allen .40 1.00
61 Manu Ginobili .40 1.00
62 Michael Redd .40 1.00
63 Rajon Rondo .50 1.25
64 Raymond Felton .30 .75
65 Steve Nash .40 1.00
66 T.J. Ford .25 .60
67 Tracy McGrady .40 1.00
68 Amare Stoudemire .40 1.00
69 Andrew Bynum .50 1.25
70 Ben Wallace .40 1.00
71 Eddy Curry .25 .60
72 Marcus Camby .25 .60
73 Tyson Chandler .30 .75
74 Yao Ming .50 1.25
75 Andrei Kirilenko .30 .75
76 Andres Nocioni .25 .60
77 Caron Butler .40 1.00
78 Hedo Turkoglu .40 1.00
79 Jeff Green .30 .75
80 Mike Miller .40 1.00
81 Ron Artest .40 1.00
82 Rudy Gay .40 1.00
83 Tim Duncan .60 1.50
84 Udonis Haslem .30 .75
85 Dwight Howard .75 2.00
86 Jermaine O'Neal .40 1.00
87 Allen Iverson .50 1.25
88 Andre Miller .30 .75
89 Brandon Roy .40 1.00
90 Chauncey Billups .40 1.00
91 Dominique Wilkins .50 1.25
92 Isiah Thomas .40 1.00
93 John Stockton .60 1.50
94 Magic Johnson 1.00 2.50
95 George Gervin .50 1.25
96 Bill Russell .60 1.50
97 David Robinson .60 1.50
98 Larry Bird 1.25 3.00
99 Jerry West .50 1.25
100 Dennis Rodman .60 1.50
101 Derrick Rose 1 Ball RC 10.00 25.00
101B Derrick Rose 2 Balls RC 10.00 25.00
102 Michael Beasley Shooting RC 1.50 4.00
102B Michael Beasley Pointing RC 1.50 4.00
103 O.J. Mayo Shooting RC 1.50 4.00
103B O.J. Mayo Standing RC 1.50 4.00
104 Russell Westbrook Shooting RC 5.00 12.00

104B Russell Westbrook Standing RC 5.00 12.00
105 Kevin Love Shooting RC 4.00 10.00
105B Kevin Love Posing RC 4.00 10.00
106 Danilo Gallinari Dribbling RC 1.50 4.00
106B Danilo Gallinari Standing RC 1.50 4.00
107 Eric Gordon Shooting RC 2.50 6.00
107B Eric Gordon Standing RC 2.50 6.00
108 Joe Alexander Shooting RC 1.00 2.50
108B Joe Alexander Passing RC 1.00 2.50
109 D.J. Augustin Shooting RC 1.00 2.50
109B D.J. Augustin Posing RC 1.00 2.50
110 Brook Lopez Shooting RC 1.50 4.00
110B Brook Lopez Posing RC 1.50 4.00
111 Jerryd Bayless Passing RC 1.00 2.50
111B Jerryd Bayless Posing RC 1.00 2.50
112 Jason Thompson Shooting RC 1.00 2.50
112B Jason Thompson Posing RC 1.00 2.50
113 Brandon Rush Action RC 1.00 2.50
113B Brandon Rush Posing RC 1.00 2.50
114 Anthony Randolph Finger RC 1.25 3.00
114B Anthony Randolph Posing RC 1.25 3.00
115 Robin Lopez Shooting RC 1.00 2.50
115B Robin Lopez Posing RC 1.00 2.50
116 Marreese Speights Action RC 1.00 2.50
116B Marreese Speights Posing RC 1.00 2.50
117 Roy Hibbert Shooting RC 1.50 4.00
117B Roy Hibbert Posing RC 1.50 4.00
118 J.J. Hickson Ball in Front RC 1.25 3.00
118B J.J. Hickson Ball on Side RC 1.25 3.00
119 Ryan Anderson Ball RC 1.50 4.00
119B Ryan Anderson Posing RC 1.50 4.00
120 Courtney Lee Face Right RC 1.50 4.00
120B Courtney Lee Face Left RC 1.50 4.00
121 Kosta Koufos Shooting RC 1.00 2.50
121B Kosta Koufos Posing RC 1.00 2.50
122 Darrell Arthur Forward RC 1.00 2.50
122B Darrell Arthur Face Left RC 1.00 2.50
123 Donte Greene Ball Up RC 1.00 2.50
123B Donte Greene Ball Down RC 1.00 2.50
124 Mario Chalmers 2 Balls RC 1.50 4.00
124B Mario Chalmers 1 Ball RC 1.50 4.00
125 Rudy Fernandez 2 Balls RC 1.25 3.00
125B Rudy Fernandez 1 Ball RC 1.25 3.00

2008-09 Topps Hardwood Hardwood

*WOOD: .6X TO 1.5X BASE HI
WOOD PRINT RUN 299 SER.#'d SETS
101 Derrick Rose 1 Ball 20.00 50.00
101B Derrick Rose 2 Balls 20.00 50.00

2008-09 Topps Hardwood Mahogany

*1-100 MAHOGANY: 1.25X TO 3X HI
*101-125 MAHOG: 1X TO 2.5X HI
STATED PRINT RUN 75 SER.#'d SETS

2008-09 Topps Hardwood Maple

*1-100 MAPLE: 1X TO 2.5X BASE HI
*101-125 MAPLE: .75X TO 2X HI
STATED PRINT RUN 175 SER.#'d SETS

2008-09 Topps Hardwood Redwood

*1-100 RED: 6X TO 15X BASE HI
*101-125 RED: 2.5X TO 6X BASE HI
STATED PRINT RUN 15 SER.#'d SETS

2008-09 Topps Hardwood Fabric Signature Patches

STATED PRINT RUN 50 SER.#'d SETS
*MAPLE: .5X TO 1.25X BASE HI
MAPLE PRINT RUN 25 SER.#'d SETS
UNPRICED RED PRINT RUN 5 SER.#'d SETS
UNPRICED ONE OF ONES EXIST
HFSPBL Brook Lopez 15.00 40.00
HFSPBR Brandon Rush 10.00 25.00
HFSPCDR Chris Douglas-Roberts 10.00 25.00
HFSPDGR Donte Greene 10.00 25.00
HFSPEG Eric Gordon 40.00 70.00
HFSPGH George Hill 15.00 40.00
HFSPJJH J.J. Hickson 12.00 30.00
HFSPKL Kevin Love 50.00 125.00
HFSPMS Marreese Speights 10.00 25.00
HFSPOJM O.J. Mayo 15.00 40.00
HFSPRA Ryan Anderson 15.00 40.00
HFSPRH Roy Hibbert 15.00 40.00

2008-09 Topps Hardwood Relics

STATED PRINT RUN 175 SER.#'d SETS
*MAHOGANY: .5X TO 1.25X BASE HI
MAHOG.PRINT RUN 75 SER.#'d SETS
*MAPLE: .6X TO 1.5X BASE HI
MAPLE PRINT RUN 50 SER.#'d SETS
*RED: 1.25X TO 3X BASE HI
RED PRINT RUN 25 SER.#'d SETS
UNPRICED ONE OF ONES EXIST
HRAIG Andre Iguodala 2.50 6.00
HRAS Amare Stoudemire 2.50 6.00
HRBD Baron Davis 2.50 6.00
HRCA Carmelo Anthony 3.00 8.00
HRCB Chauncey Billups 2.50 6.00
HRCBH Chris Bosh 2.50 6.00
HRCBO Carlos Boozer 2.50 6.00
HRCM Corey Maggette 2.00 5.00
HRCP Chris Paul 4.00 10.00
HRDH Dwight Howard 5.00 12.00
HRDN Dirk Nowitzki 3.00 8.00
HRDR Derrick Rose 12.00 30.00
HRDW Dwyane Wade 5.00 12.00
HRDWI Deron Williams 2.50 6.00
HREB Elton Brand 2.50 6.00
HREG Eric Gordon 6.00 15.00
HRGA Gilbert Arenas 2.50 6.00
HRGO Greg Oden 2.50 6.00
HRJJ Joe Johnson 2.50 6.00
HRJO Jermaine O'Neal 2.50 6.00
HRJS Josh Smith 2.50 6.00
HRKB Kobe Bryant 8.00 20.00
HRKG Kevin Garnett 5.00 12.00
HRKL Kevin Love 10.00 25.00
HRKM Kevin Martin 2.50 6.00
HRMB Michael Beasley 4.00 10.00
HROJM O.J. Mayo 4.00 10.00
HRPP Paul Pierce 3.00 8.00
HRSN Steve Nash 2.50 6.00
HRSO Shaquille O'Neal 5.00 12.00
HRTD Tim Duncan 4.00 10.00
HRTM Tracy McGrady 2.50 6.00
HRTP Tony Parker 2.50 6.00
HRVC Vince Carter 3.00 8.00
HRYM Yao Ming 3.00 8.00

2008-09 Topps Hardwood Rookie Autographs

STATED PRINT RUN 69 SER.#'d SETS
MAHOGANY: .6X TO 1.5X BASE HI
MAHOGANY PRINT RUN 19 SER.#'d SETS
UNPRICED MAPLE PRINT RUN 9 SETS
UNPRICED RED PRINT RUN 5 SETS
UNPRICED PRESS PLATES PRINT RUN ONE SET
UNPRICED ONE OF ONES EXIST
101 Derrick Rose 150.00 300.00
102 Michael Beasley 12.00 30.00
103 O.J. Mayo 12.00 30.00
104 Russell Westbrook 50.00 125.00
105 Kevin Love 40.00 100.00
106 Danilo Gallinari 10.00 25.00
107 Eric Gordon 20.00 50.00
108 Joe Alexander 6.00 15.00
110 Brook Lopez 10.00 25.00
111 Jerryd Bayless 6.00 15.00
112 Jason Thompson 6.00 15.00
113 Brandon Rush 6.00 15.00
116 Marreese Speights 6.00 15.00
117 Roy Hibbert 10.00 25.00
118 J.J. Hickson 8.00 20.00
119 Ryan Anderson 10.00 25.00
120 Courtney Lee 10.00 25.00
121 Kosta Koufos 6.00 15.00
123 Donte Greene 6.00 15.00

2008-09 Topps Hardwood Signatures

STATED PRINT RUN 39 SER.#'d SETS
*MAHOGANY:.5X TO 1.25X BASE HI
MAHOGANY PRINT RUN 19 SER.#'d SETS
UNPRICED MAPLE PRINT RUN 9 SER.#'d SETS
UNPRICED RED PRINT RUN 5 SER.#'d SETS
UNPRICED PRESS PLATE PRINT RUN ONE SET
UNPRICED ONE OF ONES EXIST
HSAB Andrea Bargnani 5.00 12.00
HSABY Andrew Bynum 15.00 30.00
HSAJ Antawn Jamison 4.00 10.00
HSBG Ben Gordon 5.00 12.00
HSBR Brandon Roy 10.00 25.00
HSCA Carmelo Anthony 15.00 40.00
HSCB Chauncey Billups 4.00 10.00
HSCP Chris Paul 25.00 50.00
HSDG Danny Granger 8.00 20.00
HSDH Dwight Howard 20.00 50.00
HSDR David Robinson 30.00 60.00
HSDS Dolph Schayes 10.00 25.00
HSDW Dominique Wilkins 15.00 30.00
HSEH Elvin Hayes 5.00 12.00
HSGA Gilbert Arenas 4.00 10.00
HSGG George Gervin 12.50 30.00
HSGO Greg Oden 20.00 40.00
HSIT Isiah Thomas 15.00 30.00
HSJH John Havlicek 15.00 30.00
HSJJW Jo Jo White 6.00 15.00
HSJS John Stockton 30.00 60.00
HSLB Larry Bird 40.00 80.00
HSLW Lenny Wilkens 6.00 15.00
HSMJ Magic Johnson 40.00 80.00
HSPP Paul Pierce 15.00 30.00
HSRB Rick Barry 8.00 20.00
HSRG Rudy Gay 4.00 10.00
HSRP Robert Parish 8.00 20.00
HSRT Reggie Theus 6.00 15.00
HSSO Shaquille O'Neal 40.00 100.00
HSSP Sam Perkins 5.00 12.00
HSTJF T.J. Ford 5.00 12.00
HSTM Tracy McGrady 10.00 25.00
HSTY Thaddeus Young 6.00 15.00

2000-01 Topps Heritage

The 2000-01 Topps Heritage product released in Febuary, 2001. The base set featured 233 cards broken into tiers as follows: Base Veterans (1-24/61-233) and Rookies (25-60) that were inserted at 1:9 and serial numbered to 1972. Each pack contained eight cards, and carried a suggested retail price of $2.99.

COMPLETE SET w/o RC (197) 30.00 60.00
1 Jason Kidd .60 1.50
2 Allen Iverson .75 2.00
3 Tracy McGrady .60 1.50
4 Tim Duncan .75 2.00
5 Michael Finley .40 1.00
6 Jason Williams .40 1.00
7 Kobe Bryant 2.00 5.00
8 Gary Payton .40 1.00
9 Latrell Sprewell .30 .75
10 Antonio McDyess .30 .75
11 Antoine Walker .30 .75
12 Steve Francis .40 1.00
13 Elton Brand .40 1.00
14 Larry Hughes .30 .75
15 Shaquille O'Neal 1.00 2.50
16 Lamar Odom .40 1.00
17 Kevin Garnett .75 2.00
18 Vince Carter .75 2.00
19 Ray Allen .40 1.00
20 Grant Hill .50 1.25
21 Chris Webber .40 1.00
22 Paul Pierce .50 1.25
23 Shareef Abdur-Rahim .30 .75
24 Eddie Jones .40 1.00
25 Kenyon Martin RC 4.00 10.00
26 Stromile Swift RC 1.50 4.00
27 Darius Miles RC 1.50 4.00
28 Marcus Fizer RC 1.50 4.00
29 Mike Miller RC 3.00 8.00
30 DerMarr Johnson RC 1.50 4.00
31 Chris Mihm RC 1.50 4.00
32 Jamal Crawford RC 2.50 6.00
33 Joel Przybilla RC 1.50 4.00
34 Keyon Dooling RC 1.50 4.00
35 Jerome Moiso RC 1.50 4.00
36 Etan Thomas RC 1.50 4.00
37 Courtney Alexander RC 1.50 4.00
38 Mateen Cleaves RC 1.50 4.00
39 Jason Collier RC 1.50 4.00
40 Hedo Turkoglu RC 3.00 8.00
41 Desmond Mason RC 2.00 5.00
42 Quentin Richardson RC 2.50 6.00
43 Jamaal Magloire RC 1.50 4.00
44 Speedy Claxton RC 1.50 4.00
45 Morris Peterson RC 1.50 4.00
46 Donnell Harvey RC 1.50 4.00
47 DeShawn Stevenson RC 2.00 5.00
48 Dalibor Bagaric RC 1.50 4.00
49 Iakovos Tsakalidis RC 1.50 4.00
50 Mamadou N'Diaye RC 1.50 4.00
51 Erick Barkley RC 1.50 4.00
52 Mark Madsen RC 1.50 4.00
53 Dan Langhi RC 1.50 4.00
54 A.J. Guyton RC 1.50 4.00
55 Jake Voskuhl RC 1.50 4.00
56 Khalid El-Amin RC 1.50 4.00
57 Lavor Postell RC 1.50 4.00
58 Eduardo Najera RC 1.50 4.00
59 Michael Redd RC 4.00 10.00
60 Stephen Jackson RC 2.50 6.00
61 Andrew DeClercq .25 .60
62 Darrell Armstrong .25 .60
63 Al Harrington .30 .75
64 Johnny Newman .25 .60
65 Baron Davis .40 1.00
66 Adrian Griffin .25 .60
67 Anthony Mason .25 .60
68 Ron Harper .30 .75
69 Michael Olowokandi .25 .60
70 Maurice Taylor .25 .60
71 Travis Best .25 .60
72 Chucky Atkins .25 .60
73 Bob Sura .25 .60
74 Jason Terry .40 1.00
75 Ervin Johnson .25 .60
76 Eric Snow .25 .60
77 Shawn Bradley .25 .60
78 Christian Laettner .25 .60
79 Keith Van Horn .30 .75
80 Damon Stoudamire .30 .75
81 Peja Stojakovic .40 1.00
82 Clifford Robinson .25 .60
83 Elden Campbell .25 .60
84 Kenny Anderson .30 .75
85 Patrick Ewing .50 1.25
86 Mookie Blaylock .30 .75
87 Brian Skinner .25 .60
88 Rick Fox .30 .75
89 Tim Hardaway .40 1.00
90 Brian Grant .25 .60
91 Joe Smith .30 .75
92 Kerry Kittles .25 .60
93 Scottie Pippen .60 1.50
94 Steve Smith .30 .75
95 Sean Elliott .30 .75
96 Rashard Lewis .40 1.00
97 Michael Dickerson .25 .60
98 Rod Strickland .30 .75
99 Sam Cassell .30 .75
100 Lew Alcindor .60 1.50
101 John Amaechi .25 .60
102 Kendall Gill .25 .60
103 Terrell Brandon .25 .60
104 Dan Majerle .30 .75
105 Mark Jackson .30 .75
106 Hakeem Olajuwon .50 1.25
107 Antawn Jamison .40 1.00
108 Cedric Ceballos .25 .60
109 Shandon Anderson .25 .60
110 Gary Trent .25 .60
111 Wesley Person .25 .60
112 James Posey .25 .60
113 David Wesley .25 .60
114 Vitaly Potapenko .25 .60
115 P.J. Brown .25 .60
116 Alan Henderson .25 .60
117 Terry Porter .30 .75
118 Lindsey Hunter .25 .60
119 Chauncey Billups .40 1.00
120 Doug Christie .25 .60
121 Glen Rice .30 .75
122 Jamie Feick .25 .60
123 Tom Gugliotta .25 .60
124 Arvydas Sabonis .30 .75
125 Toni Kukoc .30 .75
126 Shawn Marion .40 1.00
127 Dale Davis .25 .60
128 Corliss Williamson .25 .60
129 Brent Barry .25 .60
130 Shammond Williams .25 .60
131 Nick Anderson .25 .60
132 Charles Oakley .30 .75
133 Shaquille O'Neal CHAMP .50 1.25
134 Ron Harper CHAMP .30 .75
135 Kobe Bryant CHAMP 1.00 2.50
136 Shaquille O'Neal CHAMP .50 1.25
137 L.A. Lakers CHAMP .40 1.00
138 Vince Carter .50 1.25
  Allen Iverson
  Jerry Stackhouse
139 Allen Iverson .40 1.00
  Grant Hill
  Vince Carter
140 Dikembe Mutombo .40 1.00
  Alonzo Mourning
  Dale Davis
141 Reggie Miller .40 1.00
  Darrell Armstrong
  Ray Allen
142 Dikembe Mutombo .40 1.00
  Elton Brand
  Jerome Williams
143 Sam Cassell .40 1.00
  Mark Jackson
  Eric Snow
144 Checklist .10 .30
145 Checklist .10 .30
146 Shaquille O'Neal .75 2.00
  Karl Malone
  Gary Payton
147 Shaquille O'Neal .60 1.50
  Karl Malone
  Chris Webber
148 Shaquille O'Neal .60 1.50
  Ruben Patterson
  Rasheed Wallace
149 Jeff Hornacek .25 .60
  Terrell Brandon
  Peja Stojakovic
150 Shaquille O'Neal .60 1.50
  Kevin Garnett
  Tim Duncan
151 Gary Payton .40 1.00
  Nick Van Exel
  John Stockton
152 Chris Whitney .25 .60
153 Isaac Austin .25 .60
154 Kevin Willis .25 .60
155 Vin Baker .30 .75
156 Avery Johnson .30 .75
157 Rodney Rogers .25 .60
158 Allan Houston .30 .75
159 Austin Croshere .25 .60
160 George Lynch .25 .60
161 Howard Eisley .25 .60
162 Jerome Williams .25 .60
163 LaPhonso Ellis .30 .75
164 Ron Mercer .25 .60
165 Andre Miller .30 .75
166 Tariq Abdul-Wahad .25 .60
167 Donyell Marshall .25 .60
168 Quincy Lewis .25 .60
169 Mitch Richmond .30 .75
170 Richard Hamilton .30 .75
171 Bryant Reeves .25 .60
172 Jim Jackson .25 .60
173 David Robinson .60 1.50
174 Derrick Coleman .30 .75
175 Anthony Peeler .25 .60
176 Theo Ratliff .25 .60
177 Roshown McLeod .25 .60
178 Ron Artest .40 1.00
179 Bryon Russell .25 .60
180 Othella Harrington .25 .60
181 Juwan Howard .30 .75
182 Antonio Davis .25 .60
183 Ruben Patterson .25 .60
184 Shawn Kemp .40 1.00
185 Larry Johnson .40 1.00
186 Marcus Camby .30 .75
187 Eric Piatkowski .25 .60
188 Reggie Miller .40 1.00
189 Anfernee Hardaway .60 1.50
190 Kelvin Cato .25 .60
191 Erick Dampier .25 .60
192 Keon Clark .25 .60
193 Dirk Nowitzki .60 1.50
194 Robert Traylor .25 .60
195 Lamond Murray .25 .60
196 John Wallace .25 .60
197 Robert Horry .30 .75
198 Robert Pack .25 .60
199 Jamal Mashburn .30 .75
200 Corey Benjamin .25 .60
201 Matt Harpring .30 .75
202 Nick Van Exel .30 .75
203 Vonteego Cummings .25 .60
204 Ben Wallace .40 1.00
205 Karl Malone .50 1.25
206 Jonathan Bender .25 .60
207 Cuttino Mobley .30 .75
208 Isaiah Rider .30 .75
209 Tyrone Nesby .40 1.00
210 Jermaine O'Neal .40 1.00
211 Corey Maggette .30 .75
212 Anthony Carter .25 .60
213 Horace Grant .30 .75
214 Tim Thomas .25 .60
215 Wally Szczerbiak .30 .75
216 Stephon Marbury .30 .75
217 Charlie Ward .25 .60
218 Bo Outlaw .25 .60
219 Matt Geiger .25 .60
220 Vlade Divac .30 .75
221 Rasheed Wallace .40 1.00
222 Derek Anderson .25 .60
223 John Stockton .50 1.25
224 Dikembe Mutombo .40 1.00
225 John Starks .25 .60
226 Mike Bibby .40 1.00
227 Jahidi White .25 .60
228 Jalen Rose .30 .75
229 Glenn Robinson .30 .75
230 Brevin Knight .25 .60
231 Jerry Stackhouse .30 .75
232 Raef LaFrentz .25 .60
233 Brad Miller .40 1.00

2000-01 Topps Heritage Proofs

The original artwork for the Topps Heritage set was auctioned off by Topps. 175 Canvas Proof sets were produced and issued to the first 175 runners up in the bidding. Each card is sequentially numbered to 175 and features the autograph of the original artist, Bill Purdom.

*PROOF VETS: 4X TO 10X BASE HI
*PROOF RCs: .6X TO 1.5X

2000-01 Topps Heritage Retrofractors

Randomly inserted in packs at the rate of one in 95 for veteran players and one in 613 for rookies, this 60-card set parallels the base Topps Heritage set enhanced with an all chrome card stock. The veteran player cards are sequentially numbered to 272 and the rookie player cards are sequentially numbered to 72.

*STARS: 4X TO 10X BASE CARD HI
*RCs: 1.25X TO 3X BASE CARD HI
15 Shaquille O'Neal 12.00 30.00

2000-01 Topps Heritage Authentic Arena

Randomly inserted into packs at one in 87, this 7-card insert set features swatches of actual arena seats. Card backs carry an "AAR" prefix.

AAR1 Shaquille O'Neal 10.00 25.00
AAR2 Gary Payton 4.00 10.00
AAR3 Anfernee Hardaway 6.00 15.00
AAR4 Hakeem Olajuwon 5.00 12.00
AAR5 Toni Kukoc 3.00 8.00
AAR6 Scottie Pippen 6.00 15.00
AAR7 Juwan Howard 3.00 8.00

2000-01 Topps Heritage Autographs

Randomly inserted into packs at one in 90, this 11-card insert set features different player combinations . Card backs carry a "HA" prefix followed by the player's initials. Please note that the Kareem Abdul-Jabbar proof was inserted at 1:25728.

IVERSON WAS NEVER REDEEMED
HACA Courtney Alexander 4.00 10.00
HADM Desmond Mason 4.00 10.00
HAKD Keyon Dooling 4.00 10.00
HALH Larry Hughes 4.00 10.00
HASF Steve Francis 5.00 12.00
HASM Shawn Marion 6.00 15.00
HASO Shaquille O'Neal 30.00 80.00
HATM Tracy McGrady 12.50 30.00
NNO Kareem Abdul-Jabbar Autoproof 200.00 400.00

2000-01 Topps Heritage Back to the Future Game Jerseys

Randomly inserted into packs at one in 113, this 6-card insert set features actual game-used jersey swatches from players like Mark Madsen and Jonathan Bender. Card backs carry a "BF" prefix.

BF1 Joel Przybilla 2.50 6.00
BF2 Jerome Moiso 2.50 6.00
BF3 Mateen Cleaves 2.50 6.00
BF4 Speedy Claxton 2.50 6.00
BF5 Mark Madsen 2.50 6.00
BF6 Jonathan Bender 2.50 6.00

2000-01 Topps Heritage Blast from the Past

Randomly inserted into packs at one in 8, this 15-card insert set features present day players on a retro designed card. Card backs carry a "BP" prefix.

COMPLETE SET (15) 6.00 15.00
BP1 Chris Webber .50 1.25
BP2 Kevin Garnett 1.00 2.50
BP3 Allen Iverson 1.00 2.50
BP4 Rasheed Wallace .50 1.25
BP5 Elton Brand .50 1.25
BP6 Grant Hill .60 1.50
BP7 Ray Allen .50 1.25
BP8 Allan Houston .40 1.00
BP9 Tim Duncan 1.00 2.50
BP10 Eddie Jones .50 1.25
BP11 Tracy McGrady .75 2.00
BP12 Lamar Odom .50 1.25
BP13 Steve Francis .50 1.25
BP14 Jason Williams .50 1.25
BP15 Vince Carter 1.00 2.50

2000-01 Topps Heritage Deja Vu

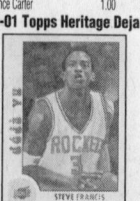

Randomly inserted into packs at one in 5, this 10-card insert set features players that are so consistent on the court, you might believe that they suffer from Deja Vu . Card backs carry a "DV" prefix.

COMPLETE SET (10) 2.50 6.00
DV1 Larry Hughes .25 .60
DV2 Elton Brand .30 .75
DV3 Steve Francis .30 .75
DV4 Paul Pierce .40 1.00
DV5 Allen Iverson .60 1.50
DV6 Gary Payton .30 .75
DV7 Rasheed Wallace .30 .75
DV8 Jason Kidd .50 1.25
DV9 Kobe Bryant 1.50 4.00
DV10 Ray Allen .30 .75

2000-01 Topps Heritage Dynamite Duds Game Jerseys

Randomly inserted into packs at one in 97, this 17-card insert set features actual game-used jersey swatches from players like Stephon Marbury and Darius Miles . Card backs carry a "DD" prefix.

DD1 Dikembe Mutombo 3.00 8.00
DD2 Hanno Mottola 3.00 8.00
DD3 Stephon Marbury 2.50 6.00
DD4 Keith Van Horn 2.50 6.00
DD5 Anfernee Hardaway 5.00 12.00
DD6 Shawn Marion 3.00 8.00
DD7 Shareef Abdur-Rahim 2.50 6.00
DD8 Paul Pierce 4.00 10.00
DD9 Juwan Howard 2.50 6.00
DD10 DerMarr Johnson 2.50 6.00
DD11 Kenyon Martin 6.00 15.00
DD12 Mike Miller 5.00 12.00
DD13 Darius Miles 2.50 6.00
DD14 Keyon Dooling 2.50 6.00
DD15 Quentin Richardson 4.00 10.00
DD16 Iakovos Tsakalidis 2.50 6.00
DD17 Stromile Swift 2.50 6.00

2000-01 Topps Heritage Off the Hook

Randomly inserted into packs at one in 8, this 15-card insert set features players that keep their teams off the hook with their spectacular play on the court. Card backs carry a "OH" prefix.

COMPLETE SET (15) 8.00 20.00
OH1 Kevin Garnett 1.00 2.50
OH2 Vince Carter 1.00 2.50
OH3 Tim Duncan 1.00 2.50
OH4 Allen Iverson 1.00 2.50
OH5 Elton Brand .50 1.25
OH6 Jason Kidd .75 2.00
OH7 Lamar Odom .50 1.25
OH8 Kobe Bryant 2.50 6.00
OH9 Tracy McGrady .75 2.00
OH10 Steve Francis .50 1.25
OH11 Chris Webber .50 1.25
OH12 Larry Hughes .40 1.00
OH13 Jason Williams .50 1.25
OH14 Shareef Abdur-Rahim .40 1.00
OH15 Darius Miles .50 1.25

2001-02 Topps Heritage

Issued in early February 2002, this 264-card set contains veteran players, rookie players, league leader cards, playoff cards, team leader cards, and utilizes the set design for 1974-75 topps. Full color player photos are set against colored backgrounds, white borders, and have the player's team name appearing on the right border of the card. Heritage was packaged in 24-pack boxes where each pack contained eight cards and carried a suggested retail price of $3.00.

COMPLETE SET (264) 100.00 200.00
1 Shaquille O'Neal 1.00 2.50
2 Jalen Rose .30 .75
3 Kwame Brown RC .75 2.00
4 Bryon Russell .25 .60
5 Hakeem Olajuwon .50 1.25
6 Shammond Williams .25 .60
7 Aaron Mckie .25 .60
8 Anfernee Hardaway .60 1.50
9 Dale Davis .25 .60
10 Tracy McGrady .60 1.50
11 Speedy Claxton .25 .60
12 Kurt Thomas .25 .60
13 Keith Van Horn .30 .75
14 Tyson Chandler RC 1.25 3.00
15 Andre Miller .30 .75
16 Dirk Nowitzki .60 1.50
17 Raef Lafrentz .25 .60
18 Mateen Cleaves .25 .60
19 Danny Fortson .25 .60
20 Steve Francis .40 1.00
21 Al Harrington .30 .75
22 Keyon Dooling .25 .60
23 Rick Fox .30 .75
24 Michael Dickerson .25 .60
25 Alonzo Mourning .50 1.25
26 Glenn Robinson .30 .75
27 Wally Szczerbiak .30 .75
28 Todd MacCulloch .25 .60
29 Shandon Anderson .25 .60
30 Kobe Bryant 2.00 5.00
31 Tyrone Hill .25 .60
32 Grant Hill .50 1.25
33 Shawn Marion .40 1.00
34 Derek Anderson .25 .60
35 Hedo Turkoglu .40 1.00
36 David Robinson .60 1.50
37 Gary Payton .40 1.00
38 Alvin Williams .25 .60
39 Pau Gasol RC 2.50 6.00
40 Tim Duncan .75 2.00
41 Rashard Lewis .40 1.00
42 Antonio Davis .25 .60
43 Donyell Marshall .25 .60
44 Jahidi White .25 .60
45 Shareef Abdur-Rahim .30 .75
46 Antoine Walker .30 .75
47 P.J. Brown .25 .60
48 Eddie Robinson .25 .60
49 Chris Mihm .25 .60
50 Kevin Garnett .75 2.00
51 Marcus Camby .30 .75
52 Mike Miller .40 1.00
53 Tony Delk .25 .60
54 Mike Bibby .40 1.00
55 Dikembe Mutombo .40 1.00
56 Eddy Curry RC 1.25 3.00
57 Shawn Bradley .25 .60
58 James Posey .25 .60
59 Jason Richardson RC 1.50 4.00
60 Jason Kidd .60 1.50
61 Eddie Griffin RC .75 2.00
62 Larry Hughes .30 .75
63 Ben Wallace .40 1.00
64 Antonio McDyess .30 .75
65 Tim Hardaway .40 1.00
66 Shawn Kemp .40 1.00
67 Bobby Jackson .25 .60
68 Tom Gugliotta .25 .60
69 Antawn Jamison .40 1.00
70 Lamar Odom .40 1.00
71 Jamaal Tinsley RC 1.00 2.50
72 Moochie Norris .25 .60
73 Marc Jackson .25 .60
74 Andrei Kirilenko RC 2.00 5.00
75 Wang Zhizhi .30 .75
76 Eric Snow .25 .60
77 Rasheed Wallace .40 1.00
78 Antonio Daniels .25 .60
79 Vladimir Radmanovic RC .75 2.00
80 Morris Peterson .25 .60
81 Jason Terry .40 1.00
  Jason Terry/ Dikembe Mutombo
  Jason Terry
82 Paul Pierce .25 .60
  Milt Pallacio
  Antoine Walker
  Antoine Walker
83 Jamal Mashburn .25 .60
  Hersey Hawkins
  P.J.Brown
  Baron Davis
84 Elton Brand .40 1.00
  Fred Hoiberg
  Elton Brnad
  Fred Hoiberg
85 Andre Miller .25 .60
  Trajan Langdon
  Clarence Weatherspoon
  Andre Miller
86 Dirk Nowitzki .40 1.00
  Steve Nash
  Dirk Nowitzki
  Steve Nash
87 Antonio McDyess .25 .60
  George McCloud
  Antonio McDyess
  Nick Van Exel
88 Jerry Stackhouse .40 1.00
  Dana Barros
  Ben Wallace
  Jerry Stackhouse
89 Antawn Jamison .40 1.00
  Marc Jackson
  Antawn Jamison
  Mookie Blaylock
90 Steve Francis .10 .30
  Cuttino Mobley
  Steve Francis
  Steve Francis
91 Jalen Rose .40 1.00
  Reggie Miller
  Jermaine O'Neal
  Travis Best
92 Lamar Odom .40 1.00
  Eric Piatkowski
  Lamar Odom
  Jeff McInnis
93 Shaquille O'Neal .60 1.50
  Mike Penberthy
  Shaquille O'Neal
  Kobe Bryant
94 Shareef Abdur-Rahim .40 1.00
  Shareef Abdur-Rahim
  Shareff Abdur-Rahim
  Mike Bibby
95 Eddie Jones .25 .60
  Eddie Jones
  Anthony Mason
  Tim Hardaway
96 Glenn Robinson .40 1.00
  Ray Allen
  Ervin Johnson
  Sam Cassell
97 Kevin Garnett .50 1.25
  Terrell Brandon
  Kevin Garnett
  Terrell Brandon
98 Stephon Marbury .25 .60
  Johnny Newman
  Aaron Williams
  Stephon Marbury
99 Deshawn Stevenson .25 .60
100 Allen Iverson .75 2.00
101 Jeryl Sasser RC .75 2.00
102 Jason Terry .40 1.00
103 Vitaly Potapenko .25 .60
104 Elden Campbell .25 .60
105 Jamal Crawford .30 .75
106 Michael Finley .40 1.00
107 Earl Watson RC .75 2.00
108 Clifford Robinson .25 .60
109 Chucky Atkins .25 .60
110 Glen Rice .30 .75

11 Jermaine O'Neal .40 1.00
12 Jonathan Bender .25 .60
13 Michael Olowokandi .25 .60
14 Derek Fisher .30 .75
15 Stromile Swift .25 .60
16 Toni Kukoc .30 .75
17 Samuel Dalembert RC 1.00 2.50
18 Paul Pierce .50 1.25
19 Jamal Mashburn .30 .75
20 Ron Mercer .25 .60
21 Lamond Murray .25 .60
22 Steve Nash .60 1.50
23 Nick Van Exel .30 .75
24 Desagana Diop RC .75 2.00
25 Ron Artest .40 1.00
26 Marcus Fizer .25 .60
27 Jumaine Jones .25 .60
28 Corliss Williamson .25 .60
29 Rodney White RC .75 2.00
30 Cuttino Mobley .30 .75
31 Reggie Miller .40 1.00
32 Austin Croshere .25 .60
33 Jeff Mcinnis .25 .60
34 Joe Johnson RC 2.00 5.00
35 Kedrick Brown RC .75 2.00
36 Theo Ratliff .25 .60
37 Laphonso Ellis .30 .75
38 Ervin Johnson .25 .60
39 Terrell Brandon .25 .60
40 Chauncey Billups .40 1.00
41 Kenyon Martin .40 1.00
42 Richard Jefferson RC 1.50 4.00
43 Howard Eisley .25 .60
44 Jerry Stackhouse .50 1.25
Allen Iverson
Shaquille O'Neal
145 Allen Iverson .60 1.50
Jerry Stackhouse
Shaquillle O'Neal
146 Shaquille O'Neal .40 1.00
Bonzi Wells
Marcus Camby
147 Reggie Miller .25 .60
Alllan Houston
Doug Christie
148 Dikembe Mutombo .40 1.00
Ben Wallace
Shaquille O'Neal
149 Jason Kidd .40 1.00
John Stockton
Nick Van Exel
150 Vince Carter .60 1.50
151 Calvin Booth .25 .60
152 Chris Whitney .25 .60
153 John Amaechi .25 .60
154 Keon Clark .25 .60
155 Terry Porter .25 .60
156 Doug Christie .25 .60
157 Gerald Wallace RC 1.25 3.00
158 Zach Randolph RC 2.00 5.00
159 Iakovos Tsakalidis .25 .60
160 Damone Brown RC .75 2.00
161 Allen Iverson .50 1.25
Reggie Miller
Kevin Garnett
Tim Duncan
162 Ray Allen 1.00 2.50
Tracy McGrady
Shaquille O'Neal
Steve Smith
163 Alonzo Mourning .40 1.00
Baron Davis
Chris Webber
Anfernee Hardaway
164 Allan Houston .60 1.50
Vince Carter
Dirk Nowitzki
Karl Malone
165 Christian Laettner .25 .60
166 John Starks .25 .60
167 Jerome Williams .25 .60
168 Brent Barry .25 .60
169 Malik Rose .25 .60
170 Vlade Divac .30 .75
171 Damon Stoudamire .30 .75
172 Rodney Rogers .25 .60
173 Alvin Jones RC .75 2.00
174 Darrell Armstrong .25 .60
175 Mark Jackson .30 .75
176 Kerry Kittles ERR .25 .60
Has Heritage Rookie Logo
177 Radoslav Nesterovic .25 .60
178 Brandon Armstrong RC .75 2.00
179 Joe Smith .30 .75
180 Ray Allen .40 1.00
181 Anthony Mason .25 .60
182 Bryant Reeves .25 .60
183 Jason Williams .30 .75
184 Terence Morris RC .75 2.00
185 Travis Best .25 .60
186 Troy Murphy RC 1.25 3.00
187 Gilbert Arenas RC 1.25 3.00
188 Avery Johnson .30 .75
189 Juwan Howard .30 .75
190 Checklist .10 .30
191 Courtney Alexander .25 .60
192 John Stockton .50 1.25
193 Vin Baker .30 .75
194 Desmond Mason .30 .75
195 Steve Smith .30 .75
196 Steven Hunter RC .75 2.00
197 Stephon Marbury .30 .75
198 Patrick Ewing .50 1.25
199 Allan Houston .30 .75
200 Karl Malone .50 1.25
201 Peja Stojakovic .40 1.00
202 Bonzi Wells .25 .60
203 Latrell Sprewell .30 .75
204 Rafer Alston .25 .60
205 Tony Parker RC 3.00 8.00
206 Michael Bradley RC .75 2.00
207 Richard Hamilton .30 .75
208 Zeljko Rebraca RC .75 2.00
209 Joel Przybilla .25 .60
210 Tim Thomas .25 .60
211 Eddie House .25 .60
212 Brian Grant .25 .60
213 Lindsey Hunter .25 .60
214 Corey Maggette .30 .75
215 Shane Battier RC 1.50 4.00
216 Will Solomon .40 1.00
217 Mitch Richmond .30 .75
218 Eddie Jones .30 .75
219 Elton Brand .40 1.00
220 Quentin Richardson .30 .75
221 Allan Houston .25 .60
Allan Houston
Marcus Camby
Charlie Ward
222 Tracy McGrady .40 1.00
Darrell Armstrong
Bo Outlaw
Darrell Armstrong
223 Allen Iverson .60 1.50
Allen Iverson
Tyrone Hill
Aaron McKie
224 Shawn Marion .40 1.00
Jason Kidd
Shawn Marion
Jason Kidd
225 Rasheed Wallace .25 .60
Steve Smith
Dale Davis
Damon Stoudamire
226 Chris Webber .40 1.00
Doug Christie
Chris Webber
Jason Williams
227 Tim Duncan .40 1.00
Derek Anderson
Tim Duncan
Antonio Daniels
228 Gary Payton .25 .60
Shammond Williams
Patrick Ewing
Gary Payton
229 Vince Carter .40 1.00
Dell Curry
Antonio Davis
Mark Jackson
230 Karl Malone .40 1.00
John Stockton
Karl Malone
John Stockton
231 Juwan Howard .25 .60
Chris Whitney
Jahidi White
Chris Whitney
232 Brendan Haywood RC 1.00 2.50
233 Scottie Pippen .60 1.50
234 Loren Woods RC .75 2.00
235 Sam Cassell .30 .75
236 Anthony Carter .25 .60
237 Raja Bell RC 1.00 2.50
238 Robert Horry .30 .75
239 Maurice Taylor .25 .60
240 Zydrunas Ilgauskas .30 .75
241 Derrick Coleman .30 .75
242 Kenny Anderson .30 .75
243 Joseph Forte RC .75 2.00
244 Baron Davis .40 1.00
245 Nazr Mohammed .25 .60
246 Allen Iverson .50 1.25
Vince Carter
Tim Duncan
Shawn Bradley
247 Ray Allen .75 2.00
Baron Davis
Kobe Bryant
Vlade Divac
248 Dikembe Mutombo .40 1.00
Glenn Robinson
David Robinson
Tyrone Lue
249 Kobe Bryant .50 1.25
Allen Iverson
250 Darius Miles .25 .60
251 Samaki Walker .25 .60
252 Dermarr Johnson .25 .60
253 David Wesley .25 .60
254 Trenton Hassell RC .75 2.00
255 Jeff Trepagnier RC .75 2.00
256 Jacque Vaughn .25 .60
257 Kirk Haston RC .75 2.00
258 Jamaal Magloire .25 .60
259 Jason Collins RC .75 2.00
260 Chris Webber .40 1.00
261 Kenny Satterfield RC .75 2.00
262 Horace Grant .30 .75
263 Jerry Stackhouse .30 .75
264 Michael Jordan 6.00 15.00

2001-02 Topps Heritage Air Alert

Randomly inserted in packs at the rate of one in eight, this 12-card set features high flyers of the NBA in action on white bordered cards and set against colorful backgrounds.

COMPLETE SET (10) 12.50 30.00
1 Shawn Marion .60 1.50
2 Vince Carter 1.00 2.50
3 Tracy McGrady 1.00 2.50
4 Steve Francis .60 1.50
5 Kobe Bryant 3.00 8.00
6 Darius Miles .40 1.00
7 Jerry Stackhouse .50 1.25
8 Baron Davis .60 1.50
9 Kevin Garnett 1.25 3.00
10 Michael Jordan 8.00 20.00
11 Kwame Brown .60 1.50
12 Jason Richardson 1.25 3.00

2001-02 Topps Heritage Articles of the Arena Relics

Inserted in packs at the rate of one in 46, this 20-card set features a horizontal card design with white borders that places full color player action photos on the right side and swatches of memorabilia from The Boston Garden's parquet floor which is die cut in the shape of the letter A.

1 Shaquille O'Neal 10.00 25.00
2 Chris Webber 4.00 10.00
3 Jason Kidd 6.00 15.00
4 Latrell Sprewell 3.00 8.00
5 Jalen Rose 3.00 8.00
6 Grant Hill 5.00 12.00
7 Alonzo Mourning 5.00 12.00
8 Gary Payton 4.00 10.00
9 Anfernee Hardaway 6.00 15.00
10 Scottie Pippen 6.00 15.00
11 Tim Hardaway 4.00 10.00
12 Reggie Miller 4.00 10.00
13 Hakeem Olajuwon 5.00 12.00
14 Patrick Ewing 5.00 12.00
15 Karl Malone 5.00 12.00
16 John Stockton 5.00 12.00
17 Charles Oakley 3.00 8.00
18 Glenn Robinson 3.00 8.00
19 Dikembe Mutombo 4.00 10.00
20 Eddie Jones 3.00 8.00

2001-02 Topps Heritage Autographs

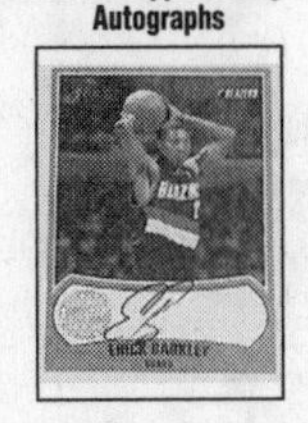

Randomly inserted in packs at the rate of one in 83, this 13-card set places full color player action photos on a white bordered card above a blank white spot set aside for authentic player autographs.

1 Antonio Daniels 5.00 12.00
2 Alvin Jones 5.00 12.00
3 Baron Davis 6.00 15.00
4 Damone Brown 5.00 12.00
5 Erick Barkley 5.00 12.00
6 Elton Brand 6.00 15.00
7 Joseph Forte 5.00 12.00
8 Mike Bibby 6.00 15.00
9 Peja Stojakovic 8.00 20.00
10 Richard Jefferson 6.00 15.00
11 Shane Battier 6.00 15.00
12 Shawn Marion 6.00 15.00
13 Vladimir Radmanovic 5.00 12.00

2001-02 Topps Heritage Ball Basics Relics

Inserted in packs at the rate of one in 627, this 11-card set features photos from the 2001 NBA Rookie Photo Shoot. Each card has a colored background, white borders, and a swatch of a basketball used in that shoot in the lower right hand corner.

1 Courtney Alexander 3.00 8.00
2 Speedy Claxton 3.00 8.00
3 DerMarr Johnson 3.00 8.00
4 Darius Miles 3.00 8.00
5 Desmond Mason 4.00 10.00
6 Hedo Turkoglu 5.00 12.00
7 Kenyon Martin 5.00 12.00
8 Marcus Fizer 3.00 8.00
9 Mike Miller 5.00 12.00
10 Morris Peterson 3.00 8.00
11 Stromile Swift 3.00 8.00

2001-02 Topps Heritage Competitive Threads

Inserted in packs at the rate of one in 61, this 15-card set boasts a horizontal card design with full color player action photos on the left and a swatch of a jersey on the right. The words "COMPETITIVE threads" appear along the right side border of the card.

1 Allan Houston 2.50 6.00
2 Allen Iverson 6.00 15.00
3 Andre Miller 2.50 6.00
4 Baron Davis 3.00 8.00
5 Chris Webber 3.00 8.00
6 Elton Brand 3.00 8.00
7 Jerry Stackhouse 2.50 6.00
8 Karl Malone 4.00 10.00
9 Latrell Sprewell 2.50 6.00
10 Michael Finley 3.00 8.00
11 Ray Allen 3.00 8.00
12 Rasheed Wallace 3.00 8.00
13 Tim Duncan 6.00 15.00
14 Tracy McGrady 5.00 12.00
15 Wally Szczerbiak 2.50 6.00

2001-02 Topps Heritage Competitive Threads Autographs

Randomly inserted in packs at the rate of one in 1862, this five card set parallels the base Competitive Threads set design enhanced with authentic player autographs in a white box below the player photo.

1 Andre Miller 30.00 80.00
3 Elton Brand 30.00 80.00
4 Tim Duncan 150.00 300.00

2001-02 Topps Heritage Crossover

Randomly inserted in packs at the rate of one in 14, this 12-card set showcases some of the NBA's best ball-handlers in full color set against colored backgrounds with white borders.

COMPLETE SET (12) 20.00 40.00
1 Jamaal Tinsley 1.25 3.00
2 Steve Francis 1.00 2.50
3 Vince Carter 1.50 4.00
4 Baron Davis 1.00 2.50
5 Tracy McGrady 1.50 4.00
6 Kobe Bryant 5.00 12.00
7 Jason Terry 1.00 2.50
8 Stephon Marbury .75 2.00
9 Jason Williams .75 2.00
10 Tim Hardaway 1.00 2.50
11 Jason Richardson 2.00 5.00
12 Michael Jordan 10.00 25.00

2001-02 Topps Heritage Out of Bounds

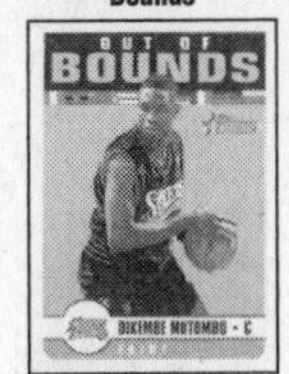

Randomly seeded in packs at the rate of one in 10, this 10-card set showcases some of the NBA's foreign talent in full color with colorful backgrounds and white bordered cards.

COMPELTE SET (10) 8.00 20.00
1 Dirk Nowitzki 1.25 3.00
2 Peja Stojakovic .75 2.00
3 Wang ZhiZhi .60 1.50
4 Dikembe Mutombo .75 2.00
5 Steve Nash 1.25 3.00
6 Hedo Turkoglu .75 2.00
7 Hakeem Olajuwon 1.00 2.50
8 Tony Parker 3.00 8.00
9 Vladimir Radmanovic .75 2.00
10 Pau Gasol 2.50 6.00

2001-02 Topps Heritage Unity

Seeded in packs at the rate of one in 485, this eight card set places full color player action photos of the Charlotte Hornets roster with a swatch of a playoff used headband.

1 Baron Davis 10.00 25.00
2 Derrick Coleman 8.00 20.00
3 David Wesley 6.00 15.00
4 Elden Campbell 6.00 15.00
5 Eddie Robinson 6.00 15.00
6 Jamaal Magloire 6.00 15.00
7 Jamal Mashburn 8.00 20.00
8 P.J. Brown 6.00 15.00

2001-02 Topps High Topps

Released in mid-December 2001, Topps High Topps features a 164-card set divided up as follows: card numbers 1-81 are base veteran cards, card numbers 82-86 are 1st Team All-NBA players, card numbers 87-91 are 2nd Team All-NBA players, card numbers 92-101 are Stat Leaders showcasing top stats grabbers, card numbers 102-105 are Road to the Championship showcasing LA Lakers players, card numbers 106-113 are Super Veteran Autographed cards sequentially numbered to 850, card numbers 114-129 are Super Veteran Relics sequentially numbered to 425, card numbers 130-140 are Rookie Signatures sequentially numbered to 850, card numbers 141-153 are Rookie Relics sequentially numbered to 425, and card numbers 154-164 are rookies sequentially numbered to 1500. All cards feature a jumbo tall-boy design measuring 2 1/2" by 4 11/16" with full color player action photos, white borders and gold foil highlights. High Topps was packaged in six box cases with 24-pack boxes where packs contained eight cards and carried a suggested retail price of $7.00.

COMPLETE SET (164) 350.00 700.00
COMP.SET w/o SP's (105) 30.00 60.00
1 Shaquille O'Neal 1.00 2.50
2 Reggie Miller .40 1.00
3 Steve Francis .40 1.00
4 Jerry Stackhouse .30 .75
5 Nick Van Exel .30 .75
6 Dirk Nowitzki .60 1.50
7 Dikembe Mutombo .40 1.00
8 Terrell Brandon .25 .60
9 Allan Houston .30 .75
10 Kevin Garnett .75 2.00
11 Eric Snow .25 .60
12 Stephon Marbury .30 .75
13 Jalen Rose .30 .75
14 Rick Fox .30 .75
15 Alonzo Mourning .50 1.25
16 Tim Thomas .25 .60
17 Keith Van Horn .30 .75
18 Glen Rice .30 .75
19 Mike Miller .40 1.00
20 Chris Webber .40 1.00
21 Larry Hughes .30 .75
22 Joe Smith .30 .75
23 Ron Mercer .25 .60
24 Jamal Mashburn .30 .75
25 Shareef Abdur-Rahim .30 .75
26 P.J. Brown .25 .60
27 Ben Wallace .40 1.00
28 Wang Zhizhi .30 .75
29 Jermaine O'Neal .40 1.00
30 Lamar Odom .40 1.00
31 Stromile Swift .25 .60
32 Theo Ratliff .25 .60
33 Patrick Ewing .50 1.25
34 Antonio Davis .25 .60
35 John Stockton .50 1.25
36 Courtney Alexander .25 .60
37 Alvin Williams .25 .60
38 Rashard Lewis .40 1.00
39 Mike Bibby .40 1.00
40 Scottie Pippen .60 1.50
41 Anfernee Hardaway .60 1.50
42 Marcus Camby .30 .75
43 Glenn Robinson .30 .75
44 Jason Williams .30 .75
45 Horace Grant .30 .75
46 Chris Mihm .25 .60
47 Paul Pierce .50 1.25
48 DerMarr Johnson .25 .60
49 Steve Nash .60 1.50
50 Vince Carter .60 1.50
51 Michael Jordan 4.00 10.00
52 Donyell Marshall .25 .60
53 Desmond Mason .30 .75
54 Tom Gugliotta .25 .60
55 Hedo Turkoglu .40 1.00
56 Grant Hill .50 1.25
57 Kenyon Martin .40 1.00
58 Wally Szczerbiak .30 .75
59 Eddie Jones .30 .75
60 Kobe Bryant 2.00 5.00
61 Cuttino Mobley .30 .75
62 Michael Dickerson .25 .60
63 Clifford Robinson .25 .60
64 Raef LaFrentz .25 .60
65 Lamond Murray .25 .60
66 Kenny Anderson .30 .75
67 Antonio Daniels .25 .60
68 Hakeem Olajuwon .50 1.25
69 Eddie Robinson .25 .60
70 Karl Malone .50 1.25
71 Richard Hamilton .30 .75
72 Derek Anderson .25 .60
73 Bonzi Wells .25 .60
74 Darrell Armstrong .25 .60
75 Gary Payton .40 1.00
76 Bryon Russell .25 .60
77 Steve Smith .30 .75
78 Sam Cassell .30 .75
79 Brian Grant .25 .60
80 Antoine Walker .30 .75
81 Marcus Fizer .25 .60
82 Tim Duncan AN .75 2.00
83 Chris Webber AN .40 1.00
84 Shaquille O'Neal AN 1.00 2.50
85 Allen Iverson AN .75 2.00
86 Jason Kidd AN .60 1.50
87 Kevin Garnett AN .75 2.00
88 Vince Carter AN .60 1.50
89 Dikembe Mutombo AN .40 1.00
90 Kobe Bryant AN 2.00 5.00
91 Tracy McGrady AN .60 1.50
92 Allen Iverson SL .50 1.25
93 Dikembe Mutombo SL .25 .60
94 Jason Kidd SL .40 1.00
95 Allen Iverson SL .50 1.25
96 Theo Ratliff SL .15 .40
97 Shaquille O'Neal SL .60 1.50
98 Reggie Miller SL .25 .60
99 Antoine Walker SL .20 .50
100 Michael Finley SL .25 .60
101 Jason Kidd SL .40 1.00
102 Shaquille O'Neal RTC .60 1.50
103 Kobe Bryant RTC 1.25 3.00
104 Derek Fisher RTC .20 .50
105 Shaquille O'Neal RTC .60 1.50
106 Shawn Marion AU 6.00 15.00
107 Antawn Jamison AU 8.00 20.00
108 Peja Stojakovic AU 15.00 40.00
109 Jason Terry AU 5.00 12.00
110 Aaron McKie AU 5.00 12.00
111 Keyon Dooling AU 5.00 12.00
112 Al Harrington AU 5.00 12.00
113 Chauncey Billups AU 6.00 15.00
114 Tim Duncan JSY 10.00 25.00
115 Tracy McGrady JSY 8.00 20.00
116 Jason Kidd JSY 8.00 20.00
117 Latrell Sprewell JSY 4.00 10.00
118 David Robinson JSY 8.00 20.00
119 Baron Davis JSY 5.00 12.00
120 Allen Iverson JSY 10.00 25.00
121 Ray Allen JSY 5.00 12.00
122 Rasheed Wallace JSY 5.00 12.00
123 Morris Peterson JSY 3.00 8.00
124 Darius Miles JSY 3.00 8.00
125 Marc Jackson JSY 3.00 8.00
126 Michael Finley JSY 5.00 12.00
127 Elton Brand JSY 5.00 12.00
128 Antonio McDyess JSY 4.00 10.00
129 Andre Miller JSY 4.00 10.00
130 Kwame Brown AU RC 5.00 12.00
131 Eddy Curry AU RC 8.00 20.00
132 Loren Woods AU RC 5.00 12.00
133 Joe Johnson AU RC 10.00 25.00
134 Richard Jefferson AU RC 10.00 25.00
135 Zach Randolph AU RC 15.00 40.00
136 Brendan Haywood AU RC 6.00 15.00
137 Gilbert Arenas AU RC 12.00 30.00
138 Damone Brown AU RC 5.00 12.00
139 Kenny Satterfield AU RC 5.00 12.00
140 Vladimir Radmanovic AU RC 5.00 12.00
141 Eddie Griffin JSY RC 3.00 8.00
142 Shane Battier JSY RC 6.00 15.00
143 Michael Bradley JSY RC 3.00 8.00
144 Gerald Wallace JSY RC 5.00 12.00
145 Samuel Dalembert JSY RC 4.00 10.00
146 Tyson Chandler JSY RC 5.00 12.00
147 Pau Gasol JSY RC 10.00 25.00
148 Steven Hunter JSY RC 3.00 8.00
149 Rodney White JSY RC 3.00 8.00
150 Jeryl Sasser JSY RC 3.00 8.00
151 Brandon Armstrong JSY RC 3.00 8.00
152 Jamaal Tinsley JSY RC 4.00 10.00
153 DeSagana Diop JSY RC 3.00 8.00
154 Jason Richardson RC 2.50 6.00
155 Kirk Haston RC 1.25 3.00
156 Joseph Forte RC 1.25 3.00
157 Jason Collins RC 1.25 3.00
158 Kedrick Brown RC 1.25 3.00
159 Troy Murphy RC 2.00 5.00
160 Tony Parker RC 5.00 12.00
161 Raja Bell RC 1.50 4.00
162 Jeff Trepagnier RC 1.25 3.00
163 Terence Morris RC 1.25 3.00
164 Zeljko Rebraca RC 1.25 3.00

2001-02 Topps High Topps Above and Beyond

Inserted in packs at the rate of one in 10, this seven card 2 1/2" by 4 11/16" design places some of the NBA's shortest stars in action with full color player action photos, white borders, and gold foil highlights.

COMPLETE SET (7) 10.00 25.00
AB1 John Stockton 1.25 3.00
AB2 Shawn Marion 1.00 2.50
AB3 Jason Terry 1.00 2.50
AB4 Alonzo Mourning 1.25 3.00
AB5 Theo Ratliff .60 1.50
AB6 Michael Jordan 8.00 20.00
AB7 Marcus Camby .75 2.00

2001-02 Topps High Topps Dominant Figures

Seeded in packs at the rate of one in nine, this 2 1/2" by 4 11/16" card design features eight perennial NBA All-Stars in action with full color player photos, white borders and gold foil highlights.

COMPLETE SET (8) 20.00 40.00
DF1 Alonzo Mourning 1.50 4.00
DF2 Shaquille O'Neal 3.00 8.00
DF3 Chris Webber 1.25 3.00
DF4 Michael Jordan 10.00 25.00
DF5 Kevin Garnett 2.50 6.00
DF6 Tracy McGrady 2.00 5.00
DF7 Vince Carter 2.00 5.00
DF8 Kobe Bryant 6.00 15.00

2001-02 Topps High Topps Giant Remains

Randomly seeded in packs at the rate of one in 16, this 20-card set measures 2 1/2" by 4 11/16". Full color player photos are separated from the white borders by black along the top and the bottom which are enhanced with gold foil highlights. A swatch of a jersey appears towards the bottom of the card and is die-cut in the shape of the Topps logo.

GRAD Antonio Davis 2.50 6.00
GRAH Allan Houston 3.00 8.00
GRAKM Antonio McDyess 3.00 8.00
GRAM Anthony Mason 2.50 6.00
GRCM Cuttino Mobley 3.00 8.00
GRCW Chris Webber 4.00 10.00
GRGR Glenn Robinson 3.00 8.00
GRJS Jerry Stackhouse 3.00 8.00
GRJT Jason Terry 4.00 10.00
GRKLM Kenyon Martin 4.00 10.00
GRKM Karl Malone 5.00 12.00
GRMM Mike Miller 4.00 10.00
GRRH Richard Hamilton 3.00 8.00
GRSDM Shawn Marion 4.00 10.00
GRSF Steve Francis 4.00 10.00
GRSM Stephon Marbury 3.00 8.00
GRSO Shaquille O'Neal 10.00 25.00
GRTD Tim Duncan 8.00 20.00
GRVD Vlade Divac 3.00 8.00
GRWS Wally Szczerbiak 3.00 8.00

2001-02 Topps High Topps Lofty Lettering

Randomly inserted in packs at the rate of one in 38, this 10-card set measures 2 1/2" by 4 11/16" and places full color player action photos on a white bordered card with gold foil highlights. The bottom of the card fades to white were authentic player autographs appear. These cards also contain a gold foil Topps stamp of authenticity.

LLBD Baron Davis 6.00 15.00
LLBJ Bobby Jackson 5.00 12.00
LLGW Gerald Wallace 12.50 30.00
LLHT Hedo Turkoglu 6.00 15.00
LLJF Joseph Forte 5.00 12.00
LLLP Lavor Postell 5.00 12.00
LLMB Mike Bibby 6.00 15.00
LLSB Shane Battier 6.00 15.00
LLTM Troy Murphy 6.00 15.00
LLTT Tim Thomas 5.00 12.00

2001-02 Topps High Topps Sky's The Limit

Seeded in packs at the rate of one in eight, this 13-card set measures 2 1/2" by 4 11/16". Thirteen players are showcased in full color with black separating the picture from the white borders at the bottom where the player's name appears in gold foil, while the set name appears at the top of the photo in gold foil.

COMPLETE SET (13) 20.00 40.00
SL1 Darius Miles .75 2.00
SL2 Vince Carter 2.00 5.00
SL3 Tracy McGrady 2.00 5.00
SL4 Steve Francis 1.25 3.00
SL5 Baron Davis 1.25 3.00
SL6 Tim Duncan 2.50 6.00
SL7 Shawn Marion 1.25 3.00
SL8 Paul Pierce 1.50 4.00
SL9 Rashard Lewis 1.25 3.00
SL10 Lamar Odom 1.25 3.00
SL11 Antawn Jamison 1.25 3.00
SL12 Dirk Nowitzki 2.00 5.00
SL13 Michael Jordan 10.00 25.00

1983 Topps History's Greatest Olympians

This 99-card boxed set was manufactured under license from the Los Angeles Olympic Organizing Committee. (Sporting a slightly different card design, the 1984 M and M's Olympic Heroes is a subset of this set.) Though widely known to have been produced by Topps, this company name appears nowhere on the cards. On a white card face, the fronts feature either color or black-and-white photos framed by a white inner border and a yellow outer border. The player's name appears in red print across the bottom of the front. On a red panel, the backs carry a headline and news brief. The cards are numbered on the upper left corner.

COMPLETE SET (99) 8.00 20.00
9 Bill Bradley .50 1.25
17 Don Bragg .12 .30
63 Oscar Robertson .60 1.50
91 Jerry West .75 2.00

2002-03 Topps Jersey Edition

Released in April 2003, Topps Jersey Edition consists of 166 cards. Most players have two card versions, a Home Cookin' and a Road Jersey version. Cards that have the "UER" connotation (Uncorrected Error) feature either the Road Jersey or Home Cookin' card stock, however, the opposite swatch was inserted due to the unavailibility of those specific jerseys. Also, a few cards appear with an asterisk, these cards are percieved to be much scarcer than the rest of the cards in the set. Multiple versions were available for the rookie players, so the more abundant version has been tagged as the RC card. Several NNO exchange cards were inserted at the end of the set and these are redeemable for two cards, one of each of the names that appear on the exchange. Note: on the Payton/Dixon EXCH card, Gary Payton was replaced by Jerry Stackhouse.

JEAD Antonio Davis R UER 2.50 6.00
JEAI Allen Iverson R * 6.00 15.00
JEAJ Antawn Jamison R 4.00 10.00
JEAK Andrei Kirilenko R 4.00 10.00
JEAS Amare Stoudemire R RC 10.00 25.00
JEBD Baron Davis R 4.00 10.00
JEBG Brian Grant R 2.50 6.00
JEBW Ben Wallace R 4.00 10.00
JECA Courtney Alexander R UER 2.50 6.00
JECB Carlos Boozer R RC 8.00 20.00
JECJ Chris Jefferies H RC 4.00 10.00
JECM Cuttino Mobley R 3.00 8.00
JECW Chris Wilcox R UER RC 4.00 10.00
JEDD Dan Dickau R RC 4.00 10.00
JEDF Derek Fisher R 3.00 8.00

Card	Low	High
JEDN Dirk Nowitzki R	6.00	15.00
JEDW DaJuan Wagner R RC	4.00	10.00
JEEB Elton Brand R	4.00	10.00
JEEC Eddy Curry R	3.00	8.00
JEEG Eddie Griffin R UER	2.50	6.00
JEEJ Eddie Jones R	3.00	8.00
JEFJ Fred Jones R RC	4.00	10.00
JEGA Gilbert Arenas R UER	4.00	10.00
JEGG Gordan Giricek R RC	4.00	10.00
JEJH Juwan Howard R	3.00	8.00
JEJM Jamal Mashburn R	3.00	8.00
JEJO Jermaine O'Neal R	4.00	10.00
JEJR Jalen Rose R	3.00	8.00
JEJS Joe Smith R	3.00	8.00
JEJT Jamaal Tinsley R	2.50	6.00
JEKG Kevin Garnett R	8.00	20.00
JEKR Kareem Rush R RC	4.00	10.00
JEKS Kenny Satterfield R	2.50	6.00
JEKV Keith Van Horn R	3.00	8.00
JEMD Mike Dunleavy H RC	5.00	12.00
JEMF Michael Finley R	4.00	10.00
JEMO Mehmet Okur R RC	4.00	10.00
JEMP Morris Peterson R UER	2.50	6.00
JENT Nikoloz Tskitishvili R RC	4.00	10.00
JEPG Pau Gasol R	5.00	12.00
JEPP Paul Pierce R	5.00	12.00
JEQR Quentin Richardson R	3.00	8.00
JEQW Qyntel Woods R RC	4.00	10.00
JERA Ray Allen	4.00	10.00
JERB Rasual Butler R RC	4.00	10.00
JERM Reggie Miller R	4.00	10.00
JESA Shareef Abdur-Rahim R	3.00	8.00
JESM Stephon Marbury R	3.00	8.00
JESN Steve Nash R	5.00	12.00
JESO Shaquille O'Neal R	10.00	25.00
JETC Tyson Chandler R	3.00	8.00
JETH Troy Hudson R	2.50	6.00
JEWS Wally Szczerbiak R	3.00	8.00
JEYM Yao Ming R RC	12.00	30.00
JEAFM Aaron McKie R UER	2.50	6.00
JEAHO Allan Houston H	3.00	8.00
JEAIV Allen Iverson H	6.00	15.00
JEALM Andre Miller R	3.00	8.00
JEAMG Drew Gooden R RC	6.00	15.00
JEAMI Andre Miller H	3.00	8.00
JEAST Amare Stoudemire H RC	10.00	25.00
JEBDA Baron Davis H	4.00	10.00
JEBWA Ben Wallace H	4.00	10.00
JECBU Caron Butler H RC	6.00	15.00
JEDAS Damon Stoudamire H	3.00	8.00
JEDDI Dan Dickau H UER RC	4.00	10.00
JEDGO Drew Gooden H RC	6.00	15.00
JEDJG Devean George R	2.50	6.00
JEDLM Darius Miles R	2.50	6.00
JEDMA Donyell Marshall R UER	2.50	6.00
JEDNO Dirk Nowitzki H	6.00	15.00
JEDWA DaJuan Wagner H RC	4.00	10.00
JEEBR Elton Brand H	4.00	10.00
JEECU Eddy Curry H	3.00	8.00
JEECW Elden Campbell R UER	2.50	6.00
JEEGI Manu Ginobili H RC	10.00	25.00
JEGDW Bonzi Wells R	2.50	6.00
JEGRO Glenn Robinson H	3.00	8.00
JEJAR Jason Richardson R	4.00	10.00
JEJAT Jason Terry R	3.00	8.00
JEJCB Caron Butler R RC	6.00	15.00
JEJDM Jamaal Magloire R UER	2.50	6.00
JEJHS John Stockton R	5.00	12.00
JEJKI Jason Kidd H	6.00	15.00
JEJMJ Joe Johnson R	4.00	10.00
JEJON Jermaine O'Neal H	4.00	10.00
JEJOS John Stockton H	5.00	12.00
JEJRI Jason Richardson H	4.00	10.00
JEJRO Jalen Rose H	3.00	8.00
JEJRS John Salmons R RC	5.00	12.00
JEJWL Jerome Williams H	2.50	6.00
JEKAM Karl Malone R	5.00	12.00
JEKGA Kevin Garnett H	8.00	20.00
JEKMA Karl Malone H	5.00	12.00
JEKRU Kareem Rush H RC	4.00	10.00
JEKVH Keith Van Horn H	3.00	8.00
JELSP Latrell Sprewell H	3.00	8.00
JEMAF Marcus Fizer R	2.50	6.00
JEMOK Mehmet Okur H RC	4.00	10.00
JENTS Nikoloz Tskitishvili H RC	4.00	10.00
JEPGA Pau Gasol H	5.00	12.00
JEQRI Quentin Richardson H	3.00	8.00
JEQWO Qyntel Woods H RC	4.00	10.00
JERAO Ron Artest R	4.00	10.00
JERAW Rasheed Wallace R	4.00	10.00
JERBU Rasual Butler H RC	4.00	10.00
JERCH Richard Hamilton R	3.00	8.00
JERHO Robert Horry R	3.00	8.00
JERIH Richard Hamilton H	3.00	8.00
JERWA Rasheed Wallace H	4.00	10.00
JESCB Shane Battier R	4.00	10.00
JESDM Shawn Marion R	4.00	10.00
JESFR Steve Francis H	4.00	10.00
JESMA Shawn Marion H	4.00	10.00
JESNA Steve Nash H *	5.00	12.00
JESON Shaquille O'Neal H	10.00	25.00
JETCH Tyson Chandler H	3.00	8.00
JETDU Tim Duncan H	8.00	20.00
JETDU Tim Duncan R	8.00	20.00
JETLM Tracy McGrady R	6.00	15.00
JETPA Tony Parker H	5.00	12.00
JETPR Tayshaun Prince R RC	5.00	12.00
JEWSZ Wally Szczerbiak H	3.00	8.00

2002-03 Topps Jersey Edition Black

Randomly inserted in packs at the rate of one in seven, this 116-card set parallels the base Topps Jersey Edition set enhanced with a black background and black text along the top of the card. Each card is sequentially numbered to 99 on the back.

*BLACK: .75X TO 2X BASE CARD HI

Card	Low	High
JEAS Amare Stoudemire R	25.00	60.00
JEYM Yao Ming R	40.00	100.00
JEAST Amare Stoudemire H	25.00	60.00

2002-03 Topps Jersey Edition Copper

Randomly inserted in packs at the rate of one in three, this 116-card set parallels the base Topps Jersey Edition set enhanced with a Copper background and Copper text along the top of the card. Each card is sequentially numbered to 299 on the back.

*COPPER: .5X TO 1.25X BASE CARD HI

2003-04 Topps Jersey Edition

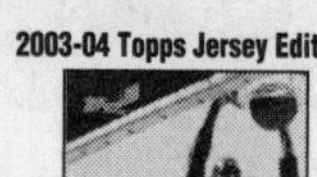

Released in February 2004, Topps Jersey edition boasts 140-cards, all of which have some sort of memorabilia element to them. Several of the rookie cards have jerseys, Standout Selection patches (with the 2003 NBA Draft NY logo on them and inserted at the rate of one in nine) and autographs. Jersey Edition was packaged in 10-pack boxes with packs containing two cards and carried a suggested retail price of $20.

SS RC HAVE NBA DRAFT PATCH

UNPRICED LOGOMAN PRINT RUN ONE SET

Card	Low	High
AD Antonio Davis	2.00	5.00
AH Allan Houston	2.00	5.00
AI Allen Iverson	4.00	10.00
AJ Antawn Jamison	2.50	6.00
AK Andrei Kirilenko	2.50	6.00
AM Andre Miller	2.00	5.00
AP Aleksandar Pavlovic RC	3.00	8.00
AS Amare Stoudemire	4.00	10.00
BB Brent Barry	2.00	5.00
BC Brian Cook RC	3.00	8.00
BD Baron Davis	2.50	6.00
BH Brandon Hunter RC	3.00	8.00
BJ Bobby Jackson	2.00	5.00
BM Brad Miller	2.50	6.00
BW Ben Wallace	2.50	6.00
CA Carmelo Anthony SS RC	8.00	20.00
CB Caron Butler	2.50	6.00
CK Chris Kaman RC	4.00	10.00
CM Corey Maggette	2.00	5.00
CW Chris Webber	2.50	6.00
DC Derrick Coleman	2.00	5.00
DG Drew Gooden	2.00	5.00
DJ Dahntay Jones RC	3.00	8.00
DM Desmond Mason	2.00	5.00
DN Dirk Nowitzki	4.00	10.00
DW Dwyane Wade SS RC	12.00	30.00
EB Elton Brand AU	8.00	20.00
EC Eddy Curry	2.00	5.00
EG Manu Ginobili	3.00	8.00
GA Gilbert Arenas	2.50	6.00
GP Gary Payton	2.50	6.00
GR Glenn Robinson	2.00	5.00
HT Hedo Turkoglu	2.50	6.00
JB Jerome Beasley RC	3.00	8.00
JC Jamal Crawford	2.00	5.00
JH Juwan Howard	2.00	5.00
JJ James Jones RC	3.00	8.00
JK Jason Kidd	4.00	10.00
JM Jamal Mashburn	2.00	5.00
JO Jermaine O'Neal	2.50	6.00
JR Jalen Rose	2.00	5.00
JS Jerry Stackhouse	2.00	5.00
JT Jason Terry	2.00	5.00
JW Jason Williams	2.00	5.00
KB Kwame Brown	2.00	5.00
KC Keon Clark	2.00	5.00
KG Kevin Garnett	5.00	12.00
KH Kirk Hinrich AU RC	12.50	30.00
KM Karl Malone	3.00	8.00
KP Kendrick Perkins RC	5.00	12.00
KR Kareem Rush	2.00	5.00
KT Kurt Thomas	2.00	5.00
LB Leandro Barbosa SS RC	4.00	10.00
LJ LeBron James SS RC	30.00	80.00
LO Lamar Odom	2.50	6.00
LR Luke Ridnour AU RC	6.00	15.00
LS Latrell Sprewell	2.00	5.00
LW Luke Walton SS RC	3.00	8.00
MB Mike Bibby	2.50	6.00
MC Marcus Camby	2.00	5.00
MD Mike Dunleavy	2.00	5.00
MJ Marko Jaric	2.00	5.00
MM Mike Miller	2.50	6.00
MO Michael Olowokandi	2.00	5.00
MP Morris Peterson	1.50	4.00
MR Michael Redd	2.50	6.00
MS Mike Sweetney SS RC	3.00	8.00
MT Maurice Taylor	2.00	5.00
MW Maurice Williams RC	5.00	12.00
NE Ndudi Ebi RC	3.00	8.00
NH Nene	2.00	5.00
PG Pau Gasol	2.50	6.00
PP Paul Pierce	3.00	8.00
PS Peja Stojakovic	2.50	6.00
QR Quentin Richardson	2.00	5.00
QW Qyntel Woods	2.00	5.00
RA Ray Allen	2.50	6.00
RD Ricky Davis	2.00	5.00
RG Reece Gaines SS RC	3.00	8.00
RH Richard Hamilton	2.00	5.00
RJ Richard Jefferson	2.50	6.00
RL Raef LaFrentz	2.00	5.00
RL Rashard Lewis	2.50	6.00
RM Ron Mercer	2.00	5.00
RN Radoslav Nesterovic	2.00	5.00
RW Rasheed Wallace	2.50	6.00
SB Steve Blake RC	4.00	10.00
SC Sam Cassell	2.00	5.00
SF Steve Francis	2.50	6.00
SM Shawn Marion	2.50	6.00
SN Steve Nash	3.00	8.00
SO Shaquille O'Neal AU	30.00	80.00
SP Scottie Pippen	4.00	10.00
TB Troy Bell RC	3.00	8.00
TC Tyson Chandler	2.00	5.00
TD Tim Duncan	4.00	10.00
TM Tracy McGrady	3.00	8.00
TO Travis Outlaw RC	4.00	10.00
TP Tony Parker	2.50	6.00
TR Theo Ratliff	2.00	5.00
TS Theron Smith RC	3.00	8.00
TT Tim Thomas	2.00	5.00
WG Willie Green RC	3.00	8.00
YM Yao Ming	5.00	12.00
ZC Zarko Cabarkapa RC	3.00	8.00
ZI Zydrunas Ilgauskas	2.00	5.00
ZP Zoran Planinic RC	3.00	8.00
ZR Zach Randolph	2.50	6.00
AHA Al Harrington	2.00	5.00
BDR Boris Diaw RC	4.00	10.00
CBI Chauncey Billups	2.50	6.00
CBO Chris Bosh RC	6.00	15.00
CBO Carlos Boozer	2.50	6.00
CMO Cuttino Mobley	2.00	5.00
CWI Corliss Williamson	2.00	5.00
DAM Darko Milicic SS RC	3.00	8.00
DCH Doug Christie	2.00	5.00
DGE Devean George	2.00	5.00
DMI Darius Miles	2.00	5.00
DWA DaJuan Wagner	2.00	5.00
DWE David West SS RC	4.00	10.00
JHA Jarvis Hayes RC	3.00	8.00
JHO Josh Howard RC	3.00	8.00
JKA Jason Kapono SS RC	3.00	8.00
JMA Jamaal Magloire	2.00	5.00
JRI Jason Richardson	2.50	6.00
JSM Joe Smith	2.00	5.00
JWI Jerome Williams	2.00	5.00
KMA Kenyon Martin	2.50	6.00
KVH Keith Van Horn	2.00	5.00
MBA Marcus Banks RC	3.00	8.00
MJA Marc Jackson	2.00	5.00
MPI Mickael Pietrus RC	3.00	8.00
NVE Nick Van Exel	2.00	5.00
RAR Ron Artest	2.50	6.00
RHO Robert Horry	2.00	5.00
RLO Raul Lopez	2.50	6.00
RMI Reggie Miller	2.50	6.00
SAR Shareef Abdur-Rahim	2.00	5.00
SBA Shane Battier	2.00	5.00
SCL Speedy Claxton	2.00	5.00
SMA Stephon Marbury	2.00	5.00
TMU Troy Murphy	2.50	6.00
TPR Tayshaun Prince	2.50	6.00
ZPA Zaur Pachulia RC	3.00	8.00

2003-04 Topps Jersey Edition Black

Randomly inserted in packs, this 140-card set parallels the base set enhanced with black card backs and sequential numbering to 25.

*BLACK SINGLES: 1.25X TO 3X BASE HI
*BLACK AU: 1X TO 2.5X BASE HI
*BLACK RCs: 1X TO 2.5X BASE HI
*BLACK SS RCs: 1.5X TO 4X BASE HI

Card	Low	High
SP Scottie Pippen	25.00	60.00
RMI Reggie Miller	15.00	40.00

2003-04 Topps Jersey Edition Copper

Randomly inserted in packs, this 140-card set parallels the base set enhanced with copper card backs and sequential numbering to 99.

*COPPER SINGLES: .6X TO 1.5X BASE HI
*COPPER AU: .5X TO 1.25X BASE HI
*COPPER RCs: .5X TO 1.25X BASE HI
*COPPER SS RCs: .75X TO 2X BASE HI

2003-04 Topps Jersey Edition Double Team

Inserted in packs at the rate of one in 108, this 15-card set features two players, one on top and one on the bottom and two circular swatches of memorabilia.

Card	Low	High
1 Tracy McGrady	6.00	15.00
Reece Gaines		
2 Paul Pierce	6.00	15.00
Marcus Banks		
3 Steve Nash	8.00	20.00
Dirk Nowitzki		
4 Ben Wallace	6.00	15.00
Richard Hamilton		
5 Jason Richardson	6.00	15.00
Mickael Pietrus		
6 Yao Ming	10.00	25.00
Steve Francis		
8 Jason Kidd	8.00	20.00
Kenyon Martin		
9 Amare Stoudemire	6.00	15.00
Stephon Marbury		
10 Chris Webber	6.00	15.00
Peja Stojakovic		
11 Tim Duncan	15.00	30.00
Tony Parker		
12 Carmelo Anthony	10.00	25.00
Nene		
14 Allen Iverson	6.00	15.00
Glenn Robinson		
15 Kirk Hinrich	8.00	20.00
Tyson Chandler		

2003-04 Topps Jersey Edition Draft Day Hits

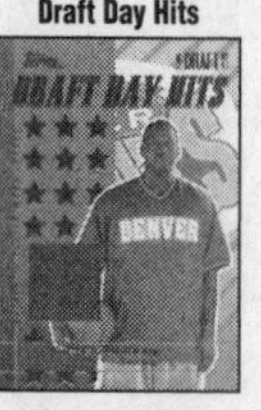

Randomly seeded, this 24-card set features the newest rookies in their warmups on the right of the card and a swatch of memorabilia on the left. Each card is sequentially numbered to 75.

Card	Low	High
BC Brian Cook	4.00	10.00
CA Carmelo Anthony	10.00	25.00
CB Chris Bosh	8.00	20.00
CK Chris Kaman	5.00	12.00
DJ Dahntay Jones	4.00	10.00
DW Dwyane Wade	15.00	40.00
JH Jarvis Hayes	4.00	10.00
JK Jason Kapono	4.00	10.00
KH Kirk Hinrich	5.00	12.00
KP Kendrick Perkins	6.00	15.00
LB Leandro Barbosa	5.00	12.00
LR Luke Ridnour	5.00	12.00
LW Luke Walton	4.00	10.00
MB Marcus Banks	4.00	10.00
MP Mickael Pietrus	4.00	10.00
MS Mike Sweetney	4.00	10.00
NC Nick Collison	4.00	10.00
NE Ndudi Ebi	4.00	10.00
RG Reece Gaines	4.00	10.00
TB Troy Bell	4.00	10.00
TO Travis Outlaw	5.00	12.00
DWE David West	5.00	12.00
JHO Josh Howard	4.00	10.00
TJF T.J. Ford	5.00	12.00

2003-04 Topps Jersey Edition Patch Place

Randomly seeded, this 33-card set features full-color player photos on the left and a circular swatch or memorabilia on the right. Each card is sequentially numbered to 25.

Card	Low	High
1 Paul Pierce	12.00	30.00
2 Baron Davis	10.00	25.00
3 Steve Nash	12.00	30.00
4 Dirk Nowitzki	15.00	40.00
5 Steve Francis	10.00	25.00
6 Yao Ming	20.00	50.00
7 Jason Richardson	10.00	25.00
8 Pau Gasol	10.00	25.00
9 Tracy McGrady	12.00	30.00
10 Ben Wallace	10.00	25.00
11 Zoran Planinic	10.00	25.00
12 Dajuan Wagner	6.00	15.00
13 Darius Miles	6.00	15.00
14 Jermaine O'Neal	10.00	25.00
15 Elton Brand	10.00	25.00
16 Shaquille O'Neal	25.00	60.00
17 Lamar Odom	10.00	25.00
18 Michael Redd	10.00	25.00
19 Kevin Garnett	20.00	50.00
20 Jason Kidd	15.00	40.00
21 Kenyon Martin	10.00	25.00
22 Allen Iverson	15.00	40.00
23 Amare Stoudemire	15.00	40.00
24 Tim Duncan	15.00	40.00
25 Ray Allen	10.00	25.00
26 Carmelo Anthony	25.00	60.00
27 Kirk Hinrich	12.00	30.00
28 T.J. Ford	12.00	30.00
29 Reece Gaines	10.00	25.00
30 Chris Bosh	20.00	50.00
31 Mickael Pietrus	10.00	25.00
32 Mike Sweetney	10.00	25.00
33 Jarvis Hayes	10.00	25.00

2003-04 Topps Jersey Edition Prime Pieces

Randomly inserted, this 34-card set places player photos on the left and a premium swatch of memorabilia on the right. Each card is sequentially numbered to the featured player's jersey number.

STATED PRINT RUN ONE TO 43 SETS

Card	Low	High
11 Richard Hamilton/32	8.00	20.00
12 Allan Houston/20	8.00	20.00
15 Eddie Griffin/33	6.00	15.00
21 David West/30	12.00	30.00
24 Kendrick Perkins/43	15.00	40.00
31 Elton Brand/42	10.00	25.00
32 Shawn Marion/31	10.00	25.00

2003-04 Topps Jersey Edition Triple Threat

Inserted at the rate of one in 217, this 15-card set places three players on each card with a swatch of memorabilia. Players are lined up top to bottom and the swatches starting at the top and going down are shaped like 1, 2 and 3. Each card is sequentially numbered to 25.

Card	Low	High
2 Paul Pierce	10.00	25.00
Tracy McGrady		
Jason Richardson		
4 Carmelo Anthony	30.00	80.00
Dwyane Wade		
Reece Gaines		
10 Kirk Hinrich	10.00	25.00
T.J. Ford		
Mickael Pietrus		

1996 Topps Kellogg's Raptors

This five card set was inserted at the rate of one card per specially marked box of Rice Krispies sold in the Toronto area. The cards are similar to the regular Topps design for this year except all of the printing on the front is in silver foil instead of gold. On the front of each card, there is a small silver foil emblem of the Raptor's logo and the words "Inaugural Season" and "1995-96". The backs have a Kellogg's Logo in red at the top just right of the player's photo.

Card	Low	High
COMPLETE SET (5)	2.50	6.00
1 Willie Anderson	.40	1.00
2 Damon Stoudamire	2.00	5.00
3 Alvin Robertson	.40	1.00
4 Tony Massenburg	.40	1.00
5 Tracy Murray	.40	1.00

2007-08 Topps Letterman

This set was released on September 4, 2008. The base set consists of 75 cards. Cards 1-50 feature veterans, and cards 51-75 are rookies. All cards are serially numbered to 599.

UNPRICED SUPERFR.PRINT RUN ONE SET

Card	Low	High
1 Dwyane Wade	2.50	6.00
2 Kobe Bryant	5.00	12.00
3 Allen Iverson	1.25	3.00
4 Jason Kidd	1.00	2.50
5 Kevin Garnett	2.00	5.00
6 Tony Parker	1.00	2.50
7 Gilbert Arenas	1.00	2.50
8 Dwight Howard	1.50	4.00
9 Steve Nash	1.25	3.00
10 Carmelo Anthony	1.25	3.00
11 Tim Duncan	1.50	4.00
12 Chris Bosh	1.00	2.50
13 LeBron James	5.00	12.00
14 Tracy McGrady	1.00	2.50
15 Vince Carter	1.25	3.00
16 Amare Stoudemire	1.00	2.50
17 Shaquille O'Neal	2.00	5.00
18 Paul Pierce	1.25	3.00
19 Yao Ming	1.25	3.00
20 Dirk Nowitzki	1.25	3.00
21 Pau Gasol	1.00	2.50
22 Michael Redd	1.00	2.50
23 Carlos Boozer	1.00	2.50
24 Baron Davis	1.00	2.50
25 Caron Butler	1.00	2.50
26 Joe Johnson	1.00	2.50
27 Gerald Wallace	1.00	2.50
28 Al Jefferson	1.00	2.50
29 Chris Paul	2.00	5.00
30 Rudy Gay	1.00	2.50
31 Manu Ginobili	1.00	2.50
32 Corey Maggette	.75	2.00
33 Ray Allen	1.00	2.50
34 Ben Gordon	1.00	2.50
35 Jamal Crawford	.75	2.00
36 David West	1.00	2.50
37 Andre Iguodala	1.00	2.50
38 Deron Williams	1.50	4.00
39 Brandon Roy	1.25	3.00
40 Richard Hamilton	.75	2.00
41 Larry Bird	4.00	10.00
42 John Stockton	2.00	5.00
43 Bill Russell	2.00	5.00
44 David Robinson	2.00	5.00
45 Isiah Thomas	1.25	3.00
46 Dennis Rodman	2.00	5.00
47 Jerry West	1.50	4.00
48 Moses Malone	1.25	3.00
49 Dominique Wilkins	1.50	4.00
50 Magic Johnson	3.00	8.00
51 Jamario Moon RC	2.00	5.00
52 Juan Carlos Navarro RC	2.00	5.00
53 Spencer Hawes RC	2.00	5.00
54 Glen Davis RC	3.00	8.00
55 Rodney Stuckey RC	3.00	8.00
56 Kevin Durant RC	20.00	50.00
57 Corey Brewer RC	2.50	6.00
58 Joakim Noah RC	5.00	12.00
59 Mike Conley Jr. RC	3.00	8.00
60 Al Horford RC	2.50	6.00
61 Julian Wright RC	2.00	5.00
62 Jeff Green RC	2.50	6.00
63 Luis Scola RC	3.00	8.00
64 Yi Jianlian RC	3.00	8.00
65 Sean Williams RC	2.00	5.00
66 Arron Afflalo RC	2.50	6.00
67 Al Thornton RC	2.00	5.00
68 Marco Belinelli RC	2.00	5.00
69 Javaris Crittenton RC	2.00	5.00
70 Thaddeus Young RC	2.50	6.00
71 Daequan Cook RC	2.00	5.00
72 Brandan Wright RC	2.00	5.00
73 Acie Law RC	2.00	5.00
74 Nick Young RC	3.00	8.00
75 Greg Oden RC	2.50	6.00
NNO Lottery Exchange	20.00	40.00

2007-08 Topps Letterman Refractors

*REFRACTORS: .75X TO 2X BASE HI
REFRACTOR PRINT RUN 99 SETS

Card	Low	High
56 Kevin Durant	50.00	100.00

2007-08 Topps Letterman Xfractors

*1-50 XFRACTORS: 2X TO 5X BASE HI
*51-75 XFRACTORS: 1.5X TO 4X HI
XFRACTORS PRINT RUN 25 SETS

Card	Low	High
2 Kobe Bryant	30.00	80.00
56 Kevin Durant	400.00	800.00

2007-08 Topps Letterman Authentic Relics Quad Autographs

GROUP A PRINT RUN 9 SETS
GROUP B PRINT RUN 75 SETS
UNPRICED GRP A REF.PRINT RUN 5 SETS
GRP B REF: .5X TO 1.25X BASE HI
GRP B REF.PRINT RUN 19 SETS
UNPRICED SUPERFR.PRINT RUN ONE SET
UNPRICED XFRACTOR PRINT RUN ONE SET

Card	Low	High
ABY Andrew Bynum B	20.00	40.00
AT Al Thornton B	6.00	15.00
ATU Alando Tucker B	6.00	15.00
CB Caron Butler B	8.00	20.00
DH Dwight Howard B	20.00	40.00
DM Darko Milicic B	6.00	15.00
DT David Thompson B	10.00	25.00
IT Isiah Thomas B	15.00	30.00
JJW Jo Jo White B	8.00	20.00
LD Luol Deng B	8.00	20.00
MW Maurice Williams B	6.00	15.00
RG Rudy Gay B	6.00	15.00
RR Rajon Rondo B	20.00	40.00
SM Shawn Marion B	10.00	25.00
YJ Yi Jianlian B	15.00	30.00
ZR Zach Randolph B	6.00	15.00

2007-08 Topps Letterman Booklet Autographs

PRINT RUN 19 SER.#'d SETS
UNPRICED REF.PRINT RUN 5 SETS
UNPRICED XF.PRINT RUN 3 SETS
UNPRICED SUPER PRINT RUN ONE SET

Card	Low	High
AJ Antawn Jamison	20.00	50.00
AL4 Acie Law	20.00	50.00
BWR Brandan Wright	20.00	50.00
CA Carmelo Anthony	40.00	100.00
CB Carlos Boozer	30.00	80.00
CBI Chauncey Billups	30.00	60.00
CP Chris Paul	50.00	100.00
DR Dennis Rodman	75.00	150.00
DW Dwyane Wade	100.00	200.00
DWI Dominique Wilkins	50.00	120.00
GA Gilbert Arenas	40.00	80.00
GO Greg Oden	100.00	200.00
JW Jerry West	75.00	150.00
LB Larry Bird	125.00	250.00
MJ Magic Johnson	75.00	150.00
MM Mike Miller	20.00	50.00
NY Nick Young	25.00	60.00
PP Paul Pierce	100.00	175.00
RA Ray Allen	50.00	100.00
RB Rick Barry	30.00	60.00
RS Rodney Stuckey	40.00	100.00
TY Thaddeus Young	50.00	100.00
VC Vince Carter	50.00	100.00
YJ Yi Jianlian	30.00	80.00

2007-08 Topps Letterman Patches

STATED PRINT RUN NINE SETS
TOTAL PRINT RUNS 36-99
*REFRACTORS: .5X TO 1.25X BASE HI
REFRACTOR PRINT RUN FIVE SETS
FIVE CARDS FOR EACH LETTER
UNPRICED XF.PRINT RUN ONE SET
UNPRICED SUPER PRINT RUN ONE SET

Card	Low	High
LPAA Arron Afflalo/63*	8.00	20.00
LPAH Al Horford/63*	6.00	15.00
LPAI Allen Iverson/63*	20.00	40.00
LPAL4 Acie Law/45*	6.00	15.00
LPAS Amare Stoudemire/90*	15.00	30.00
LPBD Baron Davis/45*	10.00	25.00
LPBG Ben Gordon/54*	6.00	15.00
LPBR Bill Russell/63*	15.00	40.00
LPBWR Brandan Wright/54*	6.00	15.00
LPCA Carmelo Anthony/63*	20.00	50.00
LPCB Corey Brewer/54*	6.00	15.00
LPCBO Carlos Boozer/54*	6.00	15.00
LPCP Chris Paul/36*	20.00	40.00
LPDN Dirk Nowitzki/72*	20.00	40.00
LPDR Dennis Rodman/54*	15.00	30.00
LPDW Dominique Wilkins/63*	8.00	20.00
LPDWA Dwyane Wade/36*	20.00	50.00
LPGA Gilbert Arenas/54*	15.00	30.00
LPGO Greg Oden/36*	20.00	40.00
LPJC Javaris Crittenton/90*	6.00	15.00
LPJG Jeff Green/45*	8.00	20.00
LPJW Julian Wright/54*	6.00	15.00
LPJWE Jerry West/36*	20.00	40.00
LPKB Kobe Bryant/54*	25.00	60.00
LPKD Kevin Durant/54*	20.00	50.00
LPKG Kevin Garnett/63*	15.00	40.00
LPLB Larry Bird/45*	20.00	50.00
LPLJ LeBron James/45*	30.00	80.00
LPMA Morris Almond/54*	6.00	15.00
LPMJ Magic Johnson/63*	20.00	40.00
LPMM Mike Miller/54*	6.00	15.00
LPNY Nick Young/45*	10.00	25.00
LPRS Rodney Stuckey/63*	6.00	15.00
LPSN Steve Nash/45*	15.00	30.00
LPSW Sean Williams/72*	6.00	15.00
LPTD Tim Duncan/54*	25.00	50.00
LPWC Wilt Chamberlain/99*	20.00	40.00
LPWCH Wilson Chandler/72*	8.00	20.00
LPYJ Yi Jianlian/72*	8.00	20.00
LPYM Yao Ming/27*	20.00	40.00

2007-08 Topps Letterman Patches Autographs

UNPRICED GROUP A PRINT RUN 5 SETS
UNPRICED GROUP B PRINT RUN 9 SETS
GROUP C PRINT RUN 33 SETS
UNPRICED GRP.A REF.PRINT RUN 3 SETS
UNPRICED GRP.B REF.PRINT RUN 5 SETS
GRP.C REF: .6X TO 1.5X BASE HI
GRP.C REF.PRINT RUN 15 SETS
UNPRICED X-F.PRINT RUN ONE SET
UNPRICED SUPER PRINT RUN ONE SET

Card	Low	High
AA Arron Afflalo C/231*	8.00	20.00
AL4 Acie Law C/165*	8.00	20.00
BD Baron Davis C/165*	10.00	25.00
BG Ben Gordon C/198*	8.00	20.00
DW Dominique Wilkins C/231*	20.00	40.00
JC Javaris Crittenton C/333*	8.00	20.00
MA Morris Almond C/198*	8.00	20.00
MJ Magic Johnson A/35*	50.00	125.00
MM Mike Miller C/198*	10.00	25.00
NY Nick Young C/165*	10.00	25.00
RS Rodney Stuckey C/231*	12.00	30.00
SW Sean Williams C/264*	8.00	20.00
TY Thaddeus Young C/165*	10.00	25.00
WC Wilson Chandler C/264*	12.00	30.00

2007-08 Topps Letterman Patches Jersey Number Autographs

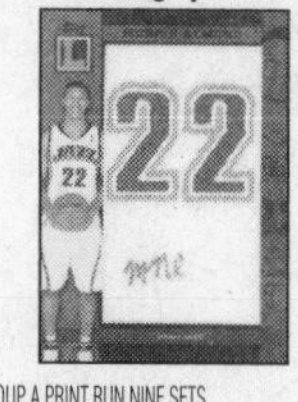

GROUP A PRINT RUN NINE SETS
GROUP B PRINT RUN 75 SETS
*REFRACTORS: .5X TO 1.25X BASE HI
GRP.A REF.PRINT RUN 19 SETS
UNPRICED GRP.B REF.PRINT RUN 5 SETS
UNPRICED SUPER PRINT RUN ONE SET

Card	Low	High
AA Arron Afflalo B	6.00	15.00
AI Andre Iguodala B	8.00	20.00
AJ Antawn Jamison B	6.00	15.00
AL Acie Law B	6.00	15.00
CB Carlos Boozer B	6.00	15.00
CBI Chauncey Billups B	8.00	20.00
CBO Chris Bosh B	15.00	30.00
DC Daequan Cook B	8.00	20.00
DR Dennis Rodman B	25.00	60.00
MA Morris Almond B	6.00	15.00
NY Nick Young B	10.00	25.00
RB Rick Barry B	10.00	25.00
RF Raymond Felton B	6.00	15.00
RS Rodney Stuckey B	12.50	30.00
SW Sean Williams B	6.00	15.00
YJ Yi Jianlian B	15.00	30.00

2007-08 Topps Letterman Patches Team Logo Autographs

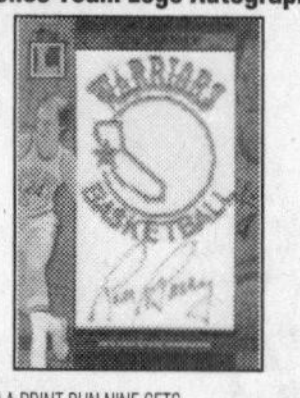

GROUP A PRINT RUN NINE SETS
GROUP B PRINT RUN 75 SETS
*REFRACTORS: .5X TO 1.25X BASE HI
GRP.A REF.PRINT RUN 19 SETS
UNPRICED GRP.B REF.PRINT RUN 5 SETS
UNPRICED SUPER PRINT RUN ONE SET

Card	Low	High
AI Andre Iguodala B	6.00	15.00
AJ Antawn Jamison B	6.00	15.00
AL Acie Law B	6.00	15.00
BD Baron Davis B	10.00	25.00
CB Carlos Boozer B	6.00	15.00
DC Daequan Cook B	8.00	20.00
DW Dominique Wilkins B	15.00	30.00
MA Morris Almond B	6.00	15.00
NY Nick Young B	10.00	25.00
PP Paul Pierce B	20.00	50.00
RA Ray Allen B	20.00	40.00
RB Rick Barry B	10.00	25.00
RS Rodney Stuckey B	10.00	25.00
SH Spencer Hawes B	6.00	15.00
WC Wilson Chandler B	10.00	25.00

2007-08 Topps Letterman Redemptions

These letter patches were available via redemption cards released in 2007-08 Topps Letterman. The cards feature players from the upcoming 2008-09 season. Each card is serially numbered to 25 and the total print run is based on the player's last name.

Card	Low	High
BL Brook Lopez	6.00	15.00
Serial 25, Print Run 125		
BR Brandon Rush	4.00	10.00
Serial 25, Print Run 100		
DR Derrick Rose	30.00	80.00
Serial 25, Print Run 100		
EG Eric Gordon	8.00	20.00
Serial 25, Print Run 150		
JB Jerryd Bayless	4.00	10.00
Serial 25, Print Run 175		
KL Kevin Love	15.00	40.00
Serial 25, Print Run 100		
MB Michael Beasley	6.00	15.00
Serial 25, Print Run 175		
RW Russell Westbrook	20.00	50.00

Serial 25, Print Run 225
DJA D.J. Augustin 4.00 10.00
Serial 25, Print Run 200
OJM O.J. Mayo 6.00 15.00
Serial 25, Print Run 100

2004-05 Topps Luxury Box

Released in March 2005, Luxury Box consists of a 150-card set divided up into 100 veteran players, 30 rookies and 20 retired legends. Cards are horizontally designed with a full-color player action photo and a foil likeness. Each pack of Luxury Box was packaged twice to hide the the inner packaged. Here's how the inner package breaks down: Tier Reserved packs have seven base cards and one season ticket parallel card. Every third Tier Reserved pack contains a sequentially numbered parallel card and each box contains five Tier Reserved packs. Loge Level packs have seven base cards and one sequentially numbered single or dual player relic card. Every third Loge Level pack contains a sequentially numbered single or dual player relic parallel and there are two Loge Level packs in each box. Main Reserved packs have seven base cards and one Sequentially numbered triple or quad-player relic card. Luxury Box packs have six base cards, one Season Ticket parallel and one sequentially numbered autograph card. Every third Luxury Box pack contains a sequentially numbered autograph parallel and each box contains one Luxury Box pack. Full boxes contain 10 mystery packs that carried a suggested retail price of $10.

UNPRICED ONE OF ONE PARALLEL EXISTS
1 Andrei Kirilenko .30 .75
2 Peja Stojakovic .40 1.00
3 Grant Hill .50 1.25
4 Baron Davis .40 1.00
5 Wally Szczerbiak .30 .75
6 Ray Allen .40 1.00
7 Shawn Marion .40 1.00
8 Gilbert Arenas .40 1.00
9 Keith Van Horn .30 .75
10 Eddie Jones .30 .75
11 Lamar Odom .40 1.00
12 Stephen Jackson .30 .75
13 Rasheed Wallace .40 1.00
14 Steve Smith .30 .75
15 Gary Payton .40 1.00
16 Jason Terry .30 .75
17 Eddy Curry .30 .75
18 Yao Ming .75 2.00
19 Kenyon Martin .40 1.00
20 Jason Richardson .40 1.00
21 Bonzi Wells .25 .60
22 Richard Jefferson .40 1.00
23 LeBron James 2.50 6.00
24 Marko Jaric .25 .60
25 Chauncey Billups .40 1.00
26 Jamal Crawford .30 .75
27 Willie Green .25 .60
28 Zach Randolph .30 .75
29 Latrell Sprewell .30 .75
30 Tim Duncan .60 1.50
31 Cuttino Mobley .30 .75
32 Shaquille O'Neal 1.00 2.50
33 Carlos Arroyo .30 .75
34 Jamaal Tinsley .25 .60
35 Luke Ridnour .30 .75
36 Kenny Anderson .30 .75
37 Brad Miller .40 1.00
38 Caron Butler .40 1.00
39 Troy Murphy .30 .75
40 Vince Carter .60 1.50
41 Shane Battier .30 .75
42 Joe Johnson .40 1.00
43 Jason Kapono .25 .60
44 Juwan Howard .30 .75
45 Zydrunas Ilgauskas .30 .75
46 Jerry Stackhouse .30 .75
47 Jamaal Magloire .25 .60
48 Steve Francis .40 1.00
49 Kwame Brown .25 .60
50 Kevin Garnett .75 2.00
51 Shareef Abdur-Rahim .30 .75
52 Tony Parker .40 1.00
53 Marcus Camby .30 .75
54 Morris Peterson .25 .60
55 Antoine Walker .40 1.00
56 Elton Brand .40 1.00
57 Paul Pierce .50 1.25
58 Jason Kidd .60 1.50
59 Gerald Wallace .40 1.00
60 Jason Williams .30 .75
61 Dwyane Wade 1.25 3.00
62 Amare Stoudemire .50 1.25
63 T.J. Ford .30 .75
64 Tyson Chandler .30 .75
65 Alonzo Mourning .50 1.25
66 Dirk Nowitzki .60 1.50
67 Allan Houston .30 .75
68 Andre Miller .30 .75
69 Glenn Robinson .30 .75
70 Richard Hamilton .30 .75
71 Darius Miles .25 .60
72 Mike Dunleavy .30 .75
73 Mike Bibby .40 1.00
74 Tracy McGrady .50 1.25
75 Manu Ginobili .50 1.25
76 Jermaine O'Neal .40 1.00
77 Rashard Lewis .40 1.00
78 Corey Maggette .30 .75
79 Chris Bosh .40 1.00
80 Pau Gasol .40 1.00
81 Carlos Boozer .40 1.00
82 Desmond Mason .30 .75
83 Antawn Jamison .40 1.00
84 Sam Cassell .30 .75
85 Al Harrington .30 .75
86 Steve Nash .50 1.25
87 Ricky Davis .30 .75
88 Chris Andersen .60 1.50
89 Kirk Hinrich .40 1.00
90 Carmelo Anthony .75 2.00
91 Ron Mercer .25 .60
92 Ben Wallace .40 1.00
93 Josh Howard .40 1.00
94 Reggie Miller .40 1.00
95 Chris Webber .40 1.00
96 Drew Gooden .30 .75
97 Michael Redd .40 1.00
98 Allen Iverson .60 1.50
99 Kobe Bryant 2.00 5.00
100 Stephon Marbury .30 .75
101 Dwight Howard RC 3.00 8.00
102 Emeka Okafor RC 1.50 4.00
103 Ben Gordon RC 1.25 3.00
104 Shaun Livingston RC 1.00 2.50
105 Devin Harris RC 1.50 4.00
106 Josh Childress RC 1.00 2.50
107 Luol Deng RC 1.50 4.00
108 Rafael Araujo RC 1.00 2.50
109 Andre Iguodala RC 1.50 4.00
110 Luke Jackson RC 1.00 2.50
111 Andris Biedrins RC 1.25 3.00
112 Robert Swift RC 1.00 2.50
113 Sebastian Telfair RC 1.00 2.50
114 Kris Humphries RC 1.00 2.50
115 Al Jefferson RC 1.50 4.00
116 Kirk Snyder RC 1.00 2.50
117 Josh Smith RC 1.50 4.00
118 J.R. Smith RC 1.25 3.00
119 Dorell Wright RC 1.50 4.00
120 Jameer Nelson RC 1.25 3.00
121 Andres Nocioni RC 1.00 2.50
122 Kevin Martin RC 1.25 3.00
123 Tony Allen RC 1.25 3.00
124 Anderson Varejao RC 1.25 3.00
125 Nenad Krstic RC 1.00 2.50
126 Sasha Vujacic RC 1.00 2.50
127 David Harrison RC 1.00 2.50
128 Pavel Podkolzin RC 1.00 2.50
129 Trevor Ariza RC 1.00 2.50
130 Delonte West RC 1.25 3.00
131 Rick Barry 1.00 2.50
132 Elgin Baylor 1.00 2.50
133 Larry Bird 3.00 8.00
134 Bob Cousy 1.50 4.00
135 Bill Russell 1.50 4.00
136 Walt Frazier 1.00 2.50
137 George Gervin 1.00 2.50
138 John Havlicek 1.00 2.50
139 James Worthy 1.25 3.00
140 Wilt Chamberlain 2.00 5.00
141 Dave Cowens 1.00 2.50
142 Moses Malone 1.00 2.50
143 Kevin McHale 1.25 3.00
144 Earl Monroe 1.00 2.50
145 Pete Maravich 6.00 15.00
146 Willis Reed 1.00 2.50
147 Oscar Robertson 1.00 2.50
148 Isiah Thomas 1.00 2.50
149 Bill Walton 1.00 2.50
150 Kareem Abdul-Jabbar 1.50 4.00

2004-05 Topps Luxury Box Season Tickets

Randomly inserted into packs, this is a parallel to the basic set. Each of these cards, which were much thicker than basic cards. In addition, parallel versions of these were issued to stated print runs of 300, 100, 25 and 1 serial numbered sets.
*SEASON TIX: .6X TO 1.5X BASE HI
*SEASON TIX RC's: .2X TO .5X BASE HI

2004-05 Topps Luxury Box 300

Randomly inserted, this 150-card set parallels the base set enhanced with sequential numbering to 300.
*BOX 300: .75X TO 2X BASE HI
*BOX 300 RC's: .5X TO 1.25X BASE HI

2004-05 Topps Luxury Box 100

Randomly inserted, this 150-card set parallels the base set enhanced with sequential numbering to 100.
*BOX 100: 2X TO 5X BASE HI
*BOX 100 RC's: 1X TO 2X BASE HI
*BOX 100 RET: 1.5X TO 4X BASE HI

2004-05 Topps Luxury Box 25

Randomly inserted, this 150-card set parallels the base set enhanced with sequential numbering to 25.
*BOX 25: 5X TO 12X BASE HI
*BOX 25 RCs: 2.5X TO 6X BASE HI
*BOX 25 RET: 2.5X TO 6X BASE HI

2004-05 Topps Luxury Box and 1

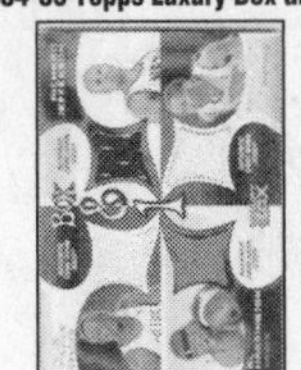

Randomly inserted into packs, these five cards feature four game-used relics on each card. Each of these cards were issued to a stated print run of 450 serial numbered sets. Parallel version of these cards were issued to stated print runs of 200, 75, 30 and 1.
*AND 1 200: .5X TO 1.25X BASE JSY HI
*AND 1 75: .6X TO 1.5X BASE JSY HI
*AND 1 30: .75X TO 2X BASE JSY HI
AMDB Carmelo Anthony 8.00 20.00
Yao Ming
Baron Davis
Elton Brand
MIFK Stephon Marbury 8.00 20.00
Allen Iverson
Steve Francis
Jason Kidd
OHIG Emeka Okafor 8.00 20.00
Dwight Howard
Andre Iguodala
Ben Gordon
OWOO Shaquille O'Neal 8.00 20.00
Ben Wallace
Jermaine O'Neal
Emeka Okafor
PJPH Paul Pierce 8.00 20.00
Richard Jefferson
Tayshaun Prince
Al Harrington

2004-05 Topps Luxury Box Assist Dual Relics

Randomly inserted into packs, these 12 cards feature two game-used relics on each card. Each of these cards were issued to a stated print run of 350 serial numbered sets. Parallel relics were issued to stated print runs of 200, 75 and 30.
PRINT RUN 350 SER.#'d SETS
*ASSIST 200: .5X TO 1.25X BASE JSY HI
*ASSIST 75: .6X TO 1.5X BASE JSY HI
*ASSIST 30: .75X TO 2X BASE JSY HI
UNPRICED AUTO RANDOM INSERTS IN PACKS
ASAP Rafer Alston 3.00 8.00
Morris Peterson
ASDS Baron Davis 3.00 8.00
J.R. Smith
ASGD Ben Gordon 8.00 20.00
Luol Deng
ASID Allen Iverson 4.00 10.00
Samuel Dalembert
ASJA Antawn Jamison 3.00 8.00
Gilbert Arenas
ASKJ Jason Kidd 4.00 10.00
Richard Jefferson
ASLB Shaun Livingston 3.00 8.00
Elton Brand
ASOJ Jermaine O'Neal 3.00 8.00
Fred Jones
ASPP Gary Payton 4.00 10.00
Paul Pierce
ASSN Amare Stoudemire 6.00 15.00
Steve Nash
ASTN Jason Terry 4.00 10.00
Dirk Nowitzki
ASWW Rasheed Wallace 3.00 8.00
Ben Wallace

2004-05 Topps Luxury Box Champagne Toast Autographs

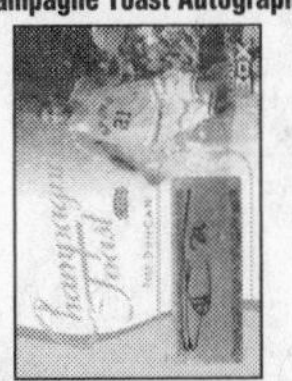

Randomly inserted into packs, these five cards feature autographs of the featured players. Each of these cards were issued to a stated print run of 100 serial numbered sets. Parallel versions of this set was issued to stated print runs of 75, 30 and 10.
*AUTO 75: .5X TO 1.25X BASE AU HI
*AUTO 30: .6X TO 1.5X BASE AU HI
BW Ben Wallace 12.50 30.00
EO Emeka Okafor 15.00 40.00
RH Richard Hamilton 12.50 30.00
SO Shaquille O'Neal 30.00 80.00
TD Tim Duncan 60.00 120.00

2004-05 Topps Luxury Box Lay-Up Relics

Randomly inserted into packs, these 30 cards feature game-used relics on each card. Each of these cards were issued to a stated print run of 500 serial numbered sets. Parallel relics were issued to stated print runs of 200, 75 and 30 and 1.
*LAY UP 200: .4X TO 1X BASE JSY HI
*LAY UP 75: .5X TO 1.25X BASE JSY HI
*LAY UP 30: .6X TO 1.5X BASE JSY HI
AI Andre Iguodala 4.00 10.00
AJ Antawn Jamison 2.50 6.00
AK Andrei Kirilenko 2.00 5.00
AS Amare Stoudemire 3.00 8.00
AW Antoine Walker 2.50 6.00
BD Baron Davis 2.50 6.00
CA Carmelo Anthony 5.00 12.00
DH Dwight Howard 8.00 20.00
EB Elton Brand 2.50 6.00
EO Emeka Okafor 4.00 10.00
GP Gary Payton 2.50 6.00
JO Jermaine O'Neal 2.50 6.00
JS Jerry Stackhouse 2.00 5.00
KG Kevin Garnett 5.00 12.00
KM Kenyon Martin 2.50 6.00
NK Nenad Krstic 2.50 6.00
PG Pau Gasol 2.50 6.00
PP Paul Pierce 3.00 8.00
PS Peja Stojakovic 2.50 6.00
RH Richard Hamilton 2.00 5.00
SF Steve Francis 2.50 6.00
SL Shaun Livingston 2.50 6.00
SM Stephon Marbury 2.00 5.00
SO Shaquille O'Neal 6.00 15.00
ST Sebastian Telfair 2.50 6.00
TD Tim Duncan 4.00 10.00
TM Tracy McGrady 3.00 8.00
YM Yao Ming 5.00 12.00
AIV Allen Iverson 4.00 10.00
JRS J.R. Smith 3.00 8.00

2004-05 Topps Luxury Box Lay-Up Relics Autographs

Randomly inserted in packs, this 7-card set parallels the Lay-Up Relics insert set design enhanced with player autographs and sequential numbering to 15.
SO Shaquille O'Neal 75.00 150.00
TD Tim Duncan 100.00 200.00
TM Tracy McGrady 40.00 100.00

2004-05 Topps Luxury Box Pre-Production

COMPLETE SET (6) 2.00 5.00
PP1 Emeka Okafor .75 2.00
PP2 Sebastian Telfair .50 1.25
PP3 Shaun Livingston .50 1.25
PP4 Shaquille O'Neal 1.25 3.00
PP5 Tracy McGrady .60 1.50
PP6 Carmelo Anthony 1.00 2.50

2004-05 Topps Luxury Box Red Carpet Autographs

Randomly inserted into packs, these 26 cards feature an autograph on each card. Each of these cards were issued to a stated print run of 135 serial numbered sets. Parallel relics were issued to stated print runs of 75 and 30 and 10.
*AUTO 75: .6X TO 1.5X BASE AU HI
*AUTO 30: .75X TO 2X BASE AU HI
AB Andris Biedrins 5.00 12.00
AV Anderson Varejao 5.00 12.00
BG Ben Gordon 5.00 12.00
BU Beno Udrih 4.00 10.00
CD Chris Duhon 4.00 10.00
EO Emeka Okafor 6.00 15.00
JC Josh Childress 4.00 10.00
JN Jameer Nelson 5.00 12.00
JR Justin Reed 4.00 10.00
JS Josh Smith 6.00 15.00
JV Jackson Vroman 4.00 10.00
KH Kris Humphries 4.00 10.00
KM Kevin Martin 5.00 12.00
LC Lionel Chalmers 4.00 10.00
LD Luol Deng 6.00 15.00
PP Pavel Podkolzin 4.00 10.00
RA Rafael Araujo 4.00 10.00
RS Romain Sato 4.00 10.00
SL Shaun Livingston 4.00 10.00
ST Sebastian Telfair 4.00 10.00
TA Tony Allen 5.00 12.00
DEH Devin Harris 6.00 15.00
DHA David Harrison 4.00 10.00
DWE Delonte West 5.00 12.00
DWR Dorell Wright 6.00 15.00
JRS J.R. Smith 5.00 12.00

2004-05 Topps Luxury Box Red Carpet Legends Autographs

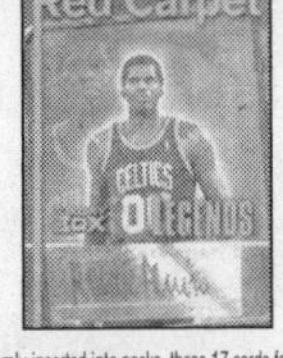
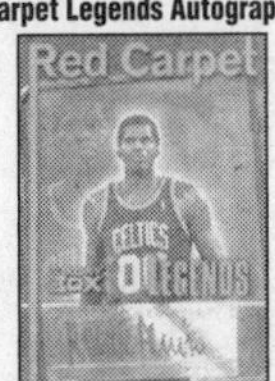

Randomly inserted into packs, these 17 cards feature an autograph of a retired NBA great on each card. Please note that George Karl did not return his cards in time for pack out and was issued as an exchange card. Each of these cards were issued to a stated print run of 30 serial numbered sets. Parallel versions of these cards were issued to stated print runs of 10 and 1 serial numbered copies.
BL Bob Lanier 15.00 40.00
BW Bill Walton 15.00 40.00
CD Clyde Drexler 40.00 80.00
DB Dave Bing 50.00 100.00
DS Detlef Schrempf 15.00 40.00
EB Elgin Baylor 20.00 50.00
GG George Gervin 15.00 40.00
GK George Karl 15.00 40.00
ME Mark Eaton 20.00 50.00
MM Moses Malone 20.00 50.00
RB Rick Barry 25.00 60.00
RP Robert Parish' 30.00 80.00

2004-05 Topps Luxury Box Signs of Luxury

Randomly inserted into packs, these 11 cards feature an autograph on each card. Each of these cards were issued to a stated print run of 100 serial numbered sets. Parallel relics were issued to stated print runs of 75 and 30 and 10.
*SIGS 75: .6X TO 1.5X BASE AU HI
*SIGS 30: .75X TO 2X BASE AU HI
AS Amare Stoudemire 12.50 30.00
BD Baron Davis 6.00 15.00
CA Carmelo Anthony 15.00 40.00
FJ Fred Jones 6.00 15.00
JK Jason Kidd 12.50 30.00
JO Jermaine O'Neal 6.00 15.00
LO Lamar Odom 6.00 15.00
PS Peja Stojakovic 6.00 15.00
RA Rafer Alston 15.00 40.00
TM Tracy McGrady 15.00 40.00
STM Stephon Marbury 6.00 15.00

2004-05 Topps Luxury Box Three-Point Play Relics

Randomly inserted into packs, these 13 cards feature three game-used relics on each card. Each of these cards were issued to a stated print run of 450 serial numbered sets. Parallel versions of these cards were issued to stated print runs of 200, 75 and 30 serial numbered sets.
*RELICS 200: .5X TO 1.25X BASE HI
*RELICS 75: .6X TO 1.5X BASE HI
*RELICS 30: .75X TO 2X BASE HI
AMM Carmelo Anthony 8.00 20.00
Kenyon Martin
Andre Miller
AWJ Tony Allen 4.00 10.00
Delonte West
Al Jefferson
DSM Baron Davis 4.00 10.00
J.R.Smith
Jamaal Magloire
GCS Kevin Garnett 6.00 15.00
Sam Cassell
Latrell Sprewell
HFM Dwight Howard 5.00 12.00
Steve Francis
Cuttino Mobley
IID Andre Iguodala 5.00 12.00
Allen Iverson
Samuel Dalembert
KBA Andrei Kirilenko 4.00 10.00
Carlos Boozer
Carlos Arroyo
KMJ Jason Kidd 6.00 15.00
Alonzo Mourning
Richard Jefferson
OBV Lamar Odom 4.00 10.00
Caron Butler
Sasha Vujacic
OJW Shaquille O'Neal 8.00 20.00
Eddie Jones
Dorell Wright
RAT Zach Randolph 4.00 10.00
Shareef Abdur-Rahim
Sebastian Telfair
WSC Antoine Walker 6.00 15.00
Josh Smith
Josh Childress
WWH Ben Wallace 6.00 15.00
Rasheed Wallace
Richard Hamilton

2004-05 Topps Luxury Box Triple Threat Relics

Randomly inserted into packs, these 12 cards feature three game-used relics on each card. Each of these cards were issued to a stated print run of 450 serial numbered sets. Parallel versions of these cards were issued to stated print runs of 200, 75 and 30 serial numbered sets.
*RELICS 200: .5X TO 1.25X BASE HI
*RELICS 75: .6X TO 1.5X BASE HI
*RELICS 30: .75X TO 2X BASE HI
ALK Shareef Abdur-Rahim 4.00 10.00
Rashard Lewis
Andrei Kirilenko
CJM Josh Childress 4.00 10.00
Eddie Jones
Cuttino Mobley
DJD Luol Deng 4.00 10.00
Luke Jackson
Carlos Delfino
HBF Kirk Hinrich 4.00 10.00
Chauncey Billups
T.J Ford
HES Devin Harris 4.00 10.00
Andre Emmett
J.R. Smith
JBS Al Jefferson 4.00 10.00
Chris Bosh
Mike Sweetney
JIA Al Jefferson 5.00 12.00
Andre Igoudala
Rafael Araujo
KAG Andrei Kirilenko 8.00 20.00
Carmelo Anthony
Kevin Garnett
MCA Andre Miller 4.00 10.00
Sam Cassell
Carlos Arroyo
MND Yao Ming 6.00 15.00
Dirk Nowitzki
Tim Duncan
RMM Jason Richardson 4.00 10.00
Shawn Marion
Corey Maggette
WJH Antoine Walker 4.00 10.00
Antawn Jamison
Grant Hill

2005-06 Topps Luxury Box

This 150-card set was released in March, 2006. The set was issued in six card packs with an $12.50 SRP which came eight packs to a box and 10 boxes to a case. The Rookie Cards numbered 101 through 145 were issued to a stated print run of 999 serial numbered sets.
COMP.SET w/o SP's (100) 20.00 50.00
UNPRICED LUX.BOX 1 PRINT RUN ONE SET
1 Dwyane Wade 1.00 2.50
2 Joe Johnson .40 1.00
3 Larry Hughes .30 .75
4 Michael Finley .40 1.00
5 Josh Howard .40 1.00
6 Kenyon Martin .40 1.00
7 Jermaine O'Neal .40 1.00
8 Luke Ridnour .30 .75
9 Andre Iguodala .40 1.00
10 Wally Szczerbiak .30 .75
11 Yao Ming .50 1.25
12 Dwight Howard .75 2.00
13 Ricky Davis .30 .75
14 Baron Davis .40 1.00
15 Carmelo Anthony .75 2.00
16 Pau Gasol .40 1.00
17 Robert Horry .30 .75
18 Andres Nocioni .25 .60
19 Sam Cassell .40 1.00
20 Shareef Abdur-Rahim .30 .75
21 Gerald Wallace .40 1.00
22 Vince Carter .60 1.50
23 LeBron James 2.00 5.00
24 Richard Hamilton .30 .75
25 Shawn Marion .40 1.00
26 Stephon Marbury .30 .75
27 Chris Bosh .40 1.00
28 Darius Miles .25 .60
29 Jamaal Magloire .25 .60
30 Kevin Garnett .75 2.00
31 Lamar Odom .40 1.00
32 Shaquille O'Neal .75 2.00
33 Allen Iverson .60 1.50
34 Paul Pierce .50 1.25
35 Keith Van Horn .30 .75
36 Damon Stoudamire .30 .75
37 Jason Richardson .40 1.00
38 Ben Gordon .40 1.00
39 J.R. Smith .40 1.00
40 Brad Miller .40 1.00
41 Dirk Nowitzki .60 1.50
42 Bonzi Wells .25 .60
43 Corey Maggette .30 .75
44 Tracy McGrady .50 1.25
45 T.J. Ford .30 .75
46 Steve Francis .40 1.00
47 Bobby Simmons .25 .60
48 Eddy Curry .30 .75
49 Antawn Jamison .40 1.00
50 Emeka Okafor .40 1.00
51 Tim Duncan .60 1.50
52 Chauncey Billups .40 1.00
53 Kwame Brown .25 .60
54 Ray Allen .40 1.00
55 Jason Kidd .60 1.50
56 Marcus Camby .30 .75
57 Stephen Jackson .30 .75
58 Rasheed Wallace .40 1.00
59 Rashard Lewis .40 1.00
60 Sebastian Telfair .30 .75
61 Manu Ginobili .40 1.00
62 Kurt Thomas .25 .60
63 Jamal Crawford .30 .75
64 Jamaal Tinsley .25 .60
65 Donyell Marshall .25 .60
66 Chris Webber .40 1.00
67 Peja Stojakovic .40 1.00
68 P.J. Brown .25 .60
69 Nenad Krstic .25 .60
70 Ben Wallace .40 1.00
71 Grant Hill .50 1.25
72 Elton Brand .40 1.00
73 Zach Randolph .30 .75
74 Josh Smith .40 1.00
75 Samuel Dalembert .25 .60
76 Andre Miller .30 .75
77 Al Jefferson .40 1.00
78 Caron Butler .40 1.00
79 Shaun Livingston .25 .60
80 Richard Jefferson .40 1.00
81 Rafer Alston .25 .60
82 Antoine Walker .30 .75
83 Zydrunas Ilgauskas .30 .75
84 Morris Peterson .25 .60
85 Marko Jaric .25 .60
86 Steve Nash .50 1.25
87 Kirk Hinrich .40 1.00
88 Kobe Bryant 2.00 5.00
89 Eddie Jones .30 .75
90 Luol Deng .40 1.00
91 Ron Artest .40 1.00
92 Desmond Mason .25 .60
93 Jason Terry .30 .75
94 Andrei Kirilenko .30 .75
95 Michael Redd .40 1.00
96 Mehmet Okur .25 .60
97 Mike Dunleavy .30 .75
98 Mike Bibby .40 1.00
99 Amare Stoudemire .40 1.00
100 Gilbert Arenas .40 1.00
101 Daniel Ewing RC 1.25 3.00
102 Andray Blatche RC 1.50 4.00
103 Jose Calderon RC 1.25 3.00
104 Shavlik Randolph RC 1.25 3.00
105 Travis Diener RC 1.25 3.00
106 Brandon Bass RC 1.50 4.00
107 Fabricio Oberto RC 1.25 3.00
108 Ryan Gomes RC 1.25 3.00
109 Gerald Fitch RC 1.25 3.00
110 James Singleton RC 1.25 3.00
111 Deron Williams RC 3.00 8.00
112 Gerald Green RC 1.50 4.00
113 C.J. Miles RC 1.50 4.00
114 Chris Paul RC 5.00 12.00
115 Julius Hodge RC 1.25 3.00
116 Salim Stoudamire RC 1.25 3.00
117 Raymond Felton RC 2.00 5.00
118 Nate Robinson RC 1.50 4.00
119 Sarunas Jasikevicius RC 1.25 3.00
120 Monta Ellis RC 2.50 6.00
121 Jarrett Jack RC 1.25 3.00
122 Orien Greene RC 1.25 3.00
123 Rashad McCants RC 1.25 3.00
124 Francisco Garcia RC 1.50 4.00
125 Antoine Wright RC 1.25 3.00
126 Luther Head RC 1.25 3.00
127 Martell Webster RC 1.25 3.00
128 Eddie Basden RC 1.25 3.00
129 Marvin Williams RC 1.50 4.00
130 Danny Granger RC 2.50 6.00
131 Charlie Villanueva RC 1.50 4.00
132 Hakim Warrick RC 1.50 4.00
133 Ike Diogu RC 1.25 3.00
134 Wayne Simien RC 1.25 3.00
135 Yaroslav Korolev RC 1.25 3.00
136 David Lee RC 2.00 5.00
137 Sean May RC 1.25 3.00
138 Linas Kleiza RC 1.25 3.00
139 Joey Graham RC 1.25 3.00
140 Jason Maxiell RC 1.25 3.00
141 Andrew Bogut RC 2.00 5.00
142 Channing Frye RC 1.50 4.00
143 Andrew Bynum RC 4.00 10.00
144 Martynas Andriuskevicius RC 1.25 3.00
145 Johan Petro RC 1.25 3.00
146 Christie Brinkley 1.50 4.00
147 Jenny McCarthy 1.50 4.00
148 Shannon Elizabeth 1.50 4.00
149 Carmen Electra 1.50 4.00
150 Jay-Z 1.50 4.00

2005-06 Topps Luxury Box Season Ticket

This parallel set was issued one per pack.
*SEASON TICKET: .5X TO 1.25X BASE HI

2005-06 Topps Luxury Box 430

This is a parallel to the basic Luxury Box set. Each of these cards were issued to a stated print run of 430 serial numbered sets.
*BOX 430: .5X TO 1.25X BASE HI

2005-06 Topps Luxury Box 350

This is a parallel to the basic Luxury Box set. Each of these cards were issued to a stated print run of 350 serial numbered sets.
*BOX 350: .6X TO 1.5X BASE HI

2005-06 Topps Luxury Box 200

This is a parallel to the basic Luxury Box set. Each of these cards were issued to a stated print run of 200 serial numbered sets.
*BOX 200: .75X TO 2X BASE HI

2005-06 Topps Luxury Box 100

This is a parallel to the basic Luxury Box set. Each of these cards were issued to a stated print run of 100 serial numbered sets.
*BOX 100 VETS: 1.5X TO 4X BASE HI
*BOX 100 RCs: .75X TO 2X BASE HI

2005-06 Topps Luxury Box 25

This is a parallel to the basic Luxury Box set. Each of these cards were issued to a stated print run of 25 serial numbered sets.
*1-100 BOX 25: 3X TO 8X BASE HI
*101-145 BOX 25: 2X TO 5X BASE HI
*146-150 BOX 25: 4X TO 10X BASE HI

2005-06 Topps Luxury Box 4 on 2 Break 8 Relics

Randomly inserted into packs, these 10-cards feature eight players with game-used relics. Each of these cards were issued to a stated print run of 90 serial numbered sets.
*RELIC 25: .6X TO 1.5X BASE REL.HI
RELICS 1 NOT PRICED DUE TO SCARCITY
1 Dwyane Wade 20.00 50.00
Shaquille O'Neal
Tim Duncan
Jay-Z
Yao Ming
Ben Wallace
Amare Stoudemire
2 Steve Nash 20.00 50.00
Dwyane Wade
Stephon Marbury
Jay-Z
Tracy McGrady
Ray Allen
3 Manu Ginobili 20.00 50.00
Vince Carter
Dwyane Wade
Jay-Z
Grant Hill
Allen Iverson
4 Dirk Nowitzki 25.00 60.00
Gilbert Arenas
Paul Pierce
Dwyane Wade
Allen Iverson
Carmelo Anthony
5 Chris Paul 15.00 40.00
Deron Williams
Rashad McCants
Allen Iverson
Dwyane Wade
Marvin Williams
6 Andrew Bogut 15.00 40.00
Channing Frye
Allen Iverson
Ike Diogu
Jay-Z
Dwyane Wade
7 Steve Francis 15.00 40.00
Allen Iverson
Jason Williams
Ben Gordon
Jay-Z
Kirk Hinrich
8 Allen Iverson 15.00 40.00
Earl Boykins
Chauncey Billups
Baron Davis
Jay-Z
Richard Hamilton
9 Kenyon Martin 20.00 50.00
Dwight Howard
Jermaine O'Neal
Emeka Okafor
Udonis Haslem
10 Antoine Walker 15.00 40.00
Kevin Garnett
Grant Hill

Carmelo Anthony
Rasheed Wallace

2005-06 Topps Luxury Box Box Out Quad Relics

Randomly inserted into packs, these cards feature relics from four people with something in common. Each of these cards were issued to a stated print run of 193 serial numbered sets.

*RELIC 25: .5X TO 1.25X BASE HI
RELICS 1 NOT PRICED DUE TO SCARCITY
1 Josh Smith 5.00 12.00
Josh Childress
Salim Stoudamire
Joe Johnson
2 Gerald Green 8.00 20.00
Al Jefferson
Ryan Gomes
Paul Pierce
3 Ben Gordon 12.50 30.00
Luol Deng
Andres Nocioni
Kirk Hinrich
4 Larry Hughes 6.00 15.00
Anderson Varejao
Luke Jackson
Drew Gooden
5 Dirk Nowitzki 15.00 40.00
Jason Terry
Josh Howard
Jerry Stackhouse
6 Julius Hodge 6.00 15.00
Earl Boykins
Kenyon Martin
Carmelo Anthony
7 Ben Wallace 15.00 40.00
Rasheed Wallace
Tayshaun Prince
Chauncey Billups
8 Ike Diogu 5.00 12.00
Jason Richardson
Baron Davis
Chris Taft
9 Tracy McGrady 8.00 20.00
Stromile Swift
Yao Ming
Luther Head
10 Jermaine O'Neal 6.00 15.00
Danny Granger
Jeff Foster
Sarunas Jasikevicius
11 Elton Brand 6.00 15.00
Corey Maggette
Shaun Livingston
Cuttino Mobley
12 Andrew Bynum 15.00 40.00
Kobe Bryant
Kwame Brown
Lamar Odom
13 Hakim Warrick 6.00 15.00
Pau Gasol
Eddie Jones
Shane Battier
14 Dwyane Wade 20.00 50.00
Shaquille O'Neal
Antoine Walker
Jason Williams
15 Andrew Bogut 5.00 12.00
Michael Redd
Desmond Mason
TJ Ford
16 Kevin Garnett 8.00 20.00
Rashad McCants
Marko Jaric
Wally Szczerbiak
17 Vince Carter 20.00 50.00
Jason Kidd
Nenad Krstic
Richard Jefferson
18 Stephon Marbury 6.00 15.00
Channing Frye
David Lee
Quentin Richardson
19 Chris Paul 6.00 15.00
J.R. Smith
Jamaal Magloire
Brandon Bass
20 Allen Iverson 12.50 30.00
Chris Webber
Andre Iguodala
Samuel Dalembert
21 Steve Nash 10.00 25.00
Kurt Thomas
Amare Stoudemire
Shawn Marion
22 Martell Webster 5.00 12.00
Ha Seung-Jin
Theo Ratliff
Zach Randolph
23 Francisco Garcia 5.00 12.00
Shareef Abdur-Rahim
Mike Bibby
Peja Stojakovic
24 Tony Parker 12.50 30.00
Manu Ginobili
Tim Duncan
Robert Horry
25 Johan Petro 8.00 20.00
Rashard Lewis
Ray Allen
Luke Ridnour
26 Morris Peterson 6.00 15.00
Charlie Villanueva
Joey Graham
Chris Bosh
27 Deron Williams 5.00 12.00
Andrei Kirilenko
Carlos Boozer
Mehmet Okur
28 Antawn Jamison 6.00 15.00
Caron Butler
Gilbert Arenas
Andre Blatche
29 Emeka Okafor 5.00 12.00
Raymond Felton
Sean May
Bernard Robinson
30 Grant Hill 6.00 15.00
Steve Francis
Dwight Howard
Jameer Nelson
31 Jenny McCarthy 20.00 50.00
Carmen Electra
Christie Brinkley
Shannon Elizabeth
32 Jay-Z 12.50 30.00
Shaquille O'Neal
Ben Wallace
Yao Ming
33 Kevin Garnett 6.00 15.00
Shawn Marion
Emeka Okafor
Ben Wallace
34 Andrew Bogut 5.00 12.00
Charlie Villanueva
Channing Frye
Ike Diogu
35 Andrew Bynum 5.00 12.00
Sean May
Hakim Warrick
Gerald Green
36 Jay-Z 12.50 30.00
Allen Iverson
Dwyane Wade
Carmelo Anthony
37 Tim Duncan 12.50 30.00
Shaquille O'Neal
Allen Iverson
Steve Nash
38 Elton Brand 6.00 15.00
Luol Deng
Corey Maggette
Grant Hill
39 Andre Iguodala 5.00 12.00
Channing Frye
Gilbert Arenas
Richard Jefferson
40 Emeka Okafor 6.00 15.00
Richard Hamilton
Ray Allen
Ben Gordon

2005-06 Topps Luxury Box Box Seats Autographs

Randomly inserted into packs, these cards feature sticker-signed autographs of the featured player. For those players whom Topps released print run information on we have published the stated print run next to the player's name in our checklist.

*PARALLEL 25: .6X TO 1.5X BASE HI
PARALLEL PRINT RUN 25 SETS
AB Andrew Bogut/124 10.00 25.00
AI Allen Iverson/224 40.00 100.00
CB Christie Brinkley/74 30.00 80.00
CE Carmen Electra/74 40.00 100.00
DE Daniel Ewing/624 5.00 12.00
DW Dwyane Wade/224 30.00 80.00
EO Emeka Okafor/224 6.00 15.00
JJ Jarrett Jack/44 5.00 12.00
OG Orien Greene/624 5.00 12.00
RF Raymond Felton/424 8.00 20.00
SE Shannon Elizabeth/74 30.00 80.00
SL Shaun Livingston/124 5.00 12.00
SO Shaquille O'Neal/74 30.00 80.00
VC Vince Carter/224 15.00 40.00

2005-06 Topps Luxury Box Divisions 6 Relics

Randomly inserted into packs, these cards feature six players, with something in common, and game-used relics from those players. Each of these cards were issued to a stated print run of 192 serial numbered sets.

*RELIC 25: .5X TO 1.25X BASE REL HI
RELICS 1 NOT PRICED DUE TO SCARCITY
1 Gerald Green 8.00 20.00
Andrew Bogut
Raymond Felton
Deron Williams
Andrew Bynum
Chris Paul
2 Allen Iverson 15.00 40.00
Ben Gordon
Dwyane Wade
Ray Allen
Kobe Bryant
Tracy McGrady
3 Samuel Dalembert 12.50 30.00
Ben Wallace
Shaquille O'Neal
Andrei Kirilenko
Amare Stoudemire
Tim Duncan
4 Vince Carter 12.50 30.00
Tayshaun Prince
Antoine Walker
Kevin Garnett
Lamar Odom
Chris Webber
5 Gerald Green 12.50 30.00
Jermaine O'Neal
Dwight Howard
Kevin Garnett
Kobe Bryant
Tracy McGrady
6 Quentin Richardson 8.00 20.00
Larry Hughes
Joe Johnson
Marko Jaric
Sam Cassell
7 Andre Iguodala 12.50 30.00
Luol Deng
Grant Hill
Carmelo Anthony
Shawn Marion
Hakim Warrick
8 Jason Kidd 12.50 30.00
Kirk Hinrich
Steve Francis
Earl Boykins
Steve Nash
Tony Parker
9 Chris Webber 10.00 25.00
Rasheed Wallace
Dwight Howard
Kenyon Martin
Shareef Abdur-Rahim
10 Morris Peterson 8.00 20.00
Larry Hughes
Joe Johnson
Ray Allen
Peja Stojakovic
Brevin Knight
11 Stephon Marbury 10.00 25.00
Chauncey Billups
Gilbert Arenas
Sebastien Telfair
Baron Davis
12 Nenad Krstic 10.00 25.00
Andres Nocioni
Andray Blatche
Ha Seung-Jin
Peja Stojakovic
13 Charlie Villanueva 6.00 15.00
Anderson Varejao
Sean May
Marcus Camby
Kurt Thomas
14 Chris Bosh 10.00 25.00
Rasheed Wallace
Steve Francis
Julius Hodge
Elton Brand
Chris Paul
15 Channing Frye 8.00 20.00
Drew Gooden
Jared Jeffries
Theo Ratliff
Kwame Brown
16 Joey Graham 8.00 20.00
Danny Granger
Salim Stoudamire
Rashad McCants
Francisco Garcia
17 Richard Jefferson 8.00 20.00
Desmond Mason
Caron Butler
Martell Webster
Corey Maggette
18 Nate Robinson 8.00 20.00
TJ Ford
Steve Francis
Earl Boykins
Baron Davis
Tony Parker
19 Paul Pierce 15.00 40.00
Ben Gordon
Dwyane Wade
Ray Allen
Steve Nash
Tracy McGrady
20 Ryan Gomes 10.00 25.00
Jeff Foster
Al Harrington
Carlos Boozer
Ike Diogu
Keith Van Horn

2005-06 Topps Luxury Box Industry Anchors

Randomly inserted into packs, this set features a few cards of each of these people, who are Topps spokesmen. The print run of each player is the same but each player has a different print run so we have that information in the headers of our checklist.

COMMON IVERSON (1-9) 1.50 4.00
COMMON WADE (1-9) 2.50 6.00
COMMON JAY-Z (1-8) 2.50 6.00
AI/WADE PRINT RUN 599 SER.#'d SETS
JAY-Z PRINT RUN 100 SER.#'d SETS
UNPRICED AUTO PRINT RUN 10 SETS
*RELICS: 1X TO 2.5X BASE HI
RELIC PRINT RUN 279 SER.#'d SETS

2005-06 Topps Luxury Box Industry Anchors Relics Dual

Randomly inserted into packs, these three cards feature two game-used relics from the featured players. Each of these cards were issued to a stated print run of 99 serial numbered sets.

IW Allen Iverson 10.00 25.00
Dwyane Wade
IZ Allen Iverson 10.00 25.00
Jay-Z
WZ Dwyane Wade 10.00 25.00
Jay-Z

2005-06 Topps Luxury Box Industry Anchors Relics Triple

Randomly inserted into packs, this card feature three game-used relics from the featured players. Each of these cards were issued to a stated print run of 25 serial numbered sets.

IWZ Allen Iverson 20.00 50.00
Dwyane Wade
Jay-Z

2005-06 Topps Luxury Box One-on-One Autographs Dual

Randomly inserted into packs, these five cards feature dual-signed cards. Each of these cards were issued to a stated print run of 25 serial numbered sets.

AUTO 1 NOT PRICE DUE TO SCARCITY
UNPRICED AU RELIC PRINT RUN 5 SETS
BO Andrew Bogut 75.00 150.00
Shaquille O'Neal
WI Dwyane Wade 125.00 250.00
Allen Iverson
WW Deron Williams 75.00 150.00
Dwyane Wade

2005-06 Topps Luxury Box One Man Show Autographs

Randomly inserted into packs, these 21 cards feature sticker autographs from the players. For those players Topps released print runs for we have placed that information next to their name in our checklist.

*PARALLEL 25: .6X TO 1.5X BASE HI
PARALLEL PRINT RUN 25 SETS
UNPRICED AUTO RELIC PRINT RUN 10 SETS
AI Allen Iverson/124 40.00 100.00
AJ Amir Johnson/449 4.00 10.00
AW Antoine Wright/426 4.00 10.00
BB Brandon Bass/724 5.00 12.00
DL David Lee/559 6.00 15.00
DW Dwyane Wade/124 30.00 80.00
FG Francisco Garcia/1121 4.00 10.00
FO Fabricio Oberto/724 4.00 10.00
ID Ike Diogu/67 5.00 12.00
JG Joey Graham/724 4.00 10.00
MW Martell Webster/124 4.00 10.00
RW Robert Whaley/167 4.00 10.00
SO Shaquille O'Neal/74 30.00 75.00
VC Vince Carter/124 20.00 40.00
DWI Deron Williams/124 10.00 25.00

2005-06 Topps Luxury Box One Man Show Autographs Relics

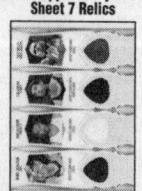

This is a partial parallel to the One Man Show autograph insert set. Each of these cards were issued to a stated print run of 10 serial numbered sets and feature a game-used relic. No pricing is available due to market scarcity.

2005-06 Topps Luxury Box One Man Show Relics

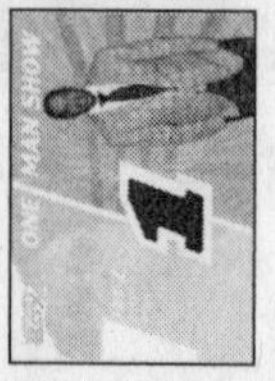

Randomly inserted into packs, this is an insert to the Luxury Box product. Each of these cards were issued to a stated print run of 225 serial numbered sets.

*RELIC 25: .75X TO 2X BASE HI
*RELIC 25 PRINT RUN 25 SETS
RELIC 1 NOT PRICED DUE TO SCARICTY
AI Allen Iverson 4.00 10.00
AK Andrei Kirilenko 2.00 5.00
AS Amare Stoudemire 2.50 6.00
AW Antoine Walker 2.00 5.00
BG Ben Gordon 2.50 6.00
CA Carmelo Anthony 5.00 12.00
CM Corey Maggette 2.00 5.00
CP Chris Paul 8.00 20.00
DM Desmond Mason 2.00 5.00
DN Dirk Nowitzki 4.00 10.00
DW Dwyane Wade 6.00 15.00
GA Gilbert Arenas 2.50 6.00
GG Gerald Green 3.00 8.00
HW Hakim Warrick 2.50 6.00
ID Ike Diogu 2.50 6.00
JC Josh Childress 2.00 5.00
JJ Joe Johnson 2.00 5.00
JS Jerry Stackhouse 2.00 5.00
JT Jamaal Tinsley 2.00 5.00
JZ Jay-Z 4.00 10.00
KB Kobe Bryant 8.00 20.00
KG Kevin Garnett 5.00 12.00
LJ Luke Jackson 2.00 5.00
LR Luke Ridnour 2.00 5.00
MG Manu Ginobili 2.50 6.00
MP Morris Peterson 1.50 4.00
MR Michael Redd 2.50 6.00
MW Martell Webster 2.50 6.00
PP Paul Pierce 3.00 8.00
PS Peja Stojakovic 2.50 6.00
RA Ray Allen 2.50 6.00
RF Raymond Felton 4.00 10.00
RH Robert Horry 3.00 8.00
RJ Richard Jefferson 2.50 6.00
RW Rasheed Wallace 2.50 6.00
SF Steve Francis 2.50 6.00
SL Shaun Livingston 2.00 5.00
SM Stephon Marbury 2.00 5.00
ST Sebastian Telfair 2.00 5.00
TM Tracy McGrady 3.00 8.00
TP Tony Parker 2.50 6.00
VC Vince Carter 4.00 10.00
AIG Andre Iguodala 2.50 6.00
DWI Deron Williams 6.00 15.00
JSM Josh Smith 2.50 6.00
JTE Jason Terry 2.00 5.00
SAR Shareef Abdur-Rahim 2.00 5.00
SMA Shawn Marion 2.50 6.00
J.R. Jason Richardson 2.50 6.00
J.R.S J.R. Smith 2.50 6.00

2005-06 Topps Luxury Box One on One Dual Relics

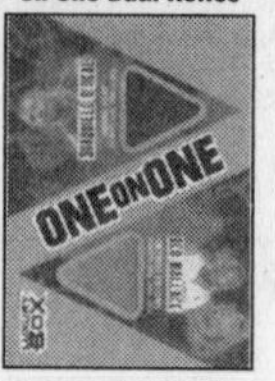

Randomly inserted into packs, these 30-cards feature two game-used relics of the featured players. Each of these cards were issued to a stated print run of 225 serial numbered sets.

*RELIC 25: .5X TO 1.25X HI
RELIC 1 NOT PRICED DUE TO SCARCITY
AP Carmelo Anthony 5.00 12.00
Paul Pierce
AW Ray Allen 4.00 10.00
Bonzi Wells
BB Kobe Bryant 8.00 20.00
Bruce Bowen
BC Earl Boykins 4.00 10.00
Sam Cassell
BS Kwame Brown 4.00 10.00
Stromile Swift
CG Marcus Camby 4.00 10.00
Pau Gasol
DG Luol Deng 4.00 10.00
Francisco Garcia
DM Tim Duncan 5.00 12.00
Yao Ming
FK Channing Frye 4.00 10.00
Nenad Krstic
GB Ben Gordon 5.00 12.00
Chauncey Billups
HF Julius Hodge 4.00 10.00
Raymond Felton
HM Richard Hamilton 4.00 10.00
Rashad McCants
IF Allen Iverson 6.00 15.00
Steve Francis
JB Antawn Jamison 4.00 10.00
Elton Brand
JP Richard Jefferson 4.00 10.00
Tayshaun Prince
LW Rashard Lewis 4.00 10.00
Rasheed Wallace
MG Tracy McGrady 5.00 12.00
Manu Ginobili
MV Jamaal Magloire 4.00 10.00
Anderson Varejao
NW Andres Nocioni 4.00 10.00
Antoine Wright
OH Emeka Okafor 4.00 10.00
Dwight Howard
PC Paul Pierce 5.00 12.00
Vince Carter
PW Chris Paul 6.00 15.00
Deron Williams
RB Quentin Richardson 4.00 10.00
Caron Butler
SG Amare Stoudemire 6.00 15.00
Kevin Garnett
TD Jason Terry 4.00 10.00
Baron Davis
TW Kurt Thomas 4.00 10.00
Hakim Warrick
WI Dwyane Wade 5.00 12.00
Andre Iguodala
WO Ben Wallace 6.00 15.00
Shaquille O'Neal
WT Jason Williams 4.00 10.00
Jamaal Tinsley
WW Antoine Walker 4.00 10.00
Chris Webber

2005-06 Topps Luxury Box Stat Sheet 7 Relics

Randomly inserted into packs, these 20-cards feature seven game-used relics of the featured players. Each of these cards were issued to a stated print run of 140 serial numbered sets.

*RELIC 25: .5X TO 1.25X BASE REL HI
RELIC 1 NOT PRICED DUE TO SCARCITY
1 Allen Iverson 12.50 30.00
Kevin Garnett
Steve Nash
Andrei Kirilenko
Larry Hughes
Gilbert Arenas
Kirk Hinrich
2 Kobe Bryant 20.00 50.00
Ben Wallace
Jason Kidd
Marcus Camby
Allen Iverson
Tracy McGrady
Dwyane Wade
3 Dirk Nowitzki 12.50 30.00
Shawn Marion
Stephon Marbury
Tim Duncan
Gerald Wallace
Amare Stoudemire
Allen Iverson
4 Amare Stoudemire 15.00 40.00
Emeka Okafor
Steve Francis
Theo Ratliff
Gilbert Arenas
Kobe Bryant
Allen Iverson
5 Tracy McGrady 12.50 30.00
Troy Murphy
Allen Iverson
Ben Wallace
Andre Iguodala
Stephon Marbury
6 Gilbert Arenas 12.50 30.00
Shaquille O'Neal
Andre Miller
Zydrunas Ilgauskas
Tracy McGrady
Paul Pierce
7 Vince Carter 20.00 50.00
Kurt Thomas
Mike Bibby
Shaquille O'Neal
Shawn Marion
Ray Allen
Kobe Bryant
8 Dwyane Wade 12.50 30.00
Dwight Howard
Rafer Alston
Elton Brand
Paul Pierce
Shawn Marion
9 Ray Allen 15.00 40.00
Dirk Nowitzki
Dwyane Wade
Yao Ming
Manu Ginobili
Larry Hughes
10 Michael Redd 15.00 40.00
Tyson Chandler
Kirk Hinrich
Josh Smith
Dwyane Wade
Allen Iverson
11 Shaquille O'Neal 12.50 30.00
Elton Brand
Tony Parker
Tyson Chandler
Kirk Hinrich
Carmelo Anthony
12 Allen Iverson 20.00 50.00
Kobe Bryant
Dirk Nowitzki
Amare Stoudemire
Tracy McGrady
Vince Carter
13 Kevin Garnett 15.00 40.00
Ben Wallace
Shawn Marion
Emeka Okafor
Troy Murphy
Shaquille O'Neal
14 Steve Nash 15.00 40.00
Jason Kidd
Stephon Marbury
Allen Iverson
Steve Francis
Andre Miller
15 Andrei Kirilenko 15.00 40.00
Marcus Camby
Tim Duncan
Theo Ratliff
Ben Wallace
Shaquille O'Neal
16 Larry Hughes 12.50 30.00
Allen Iverson
Shawn Marion
Gilbert Arenas
Andre Iguodala
Tracy McGrady
17 Gilbert Arenas 15.00 40.00
Allen Iverson
Tracy McGrady
Kobe Bryant
Stephon Marbury
18 Dirk Nowitzki 20.00 50.00
Allen Iverson
Amare Stoudemire
Dwyane Wade
Corey Maggette
Paul Pierce
Kobe Bryant
19 Chris Paul 20.00 50.00
Andrew Bogut
Deron Williams
Hakim Warrick
Raymond Felton
Channing Frye
20 Martell Webster 20.00 50.00
Charlie Villanueva
Jarrett Jack
Andrew Bynum
Rashad McCants

2005-06 Topps Luxury Box The Machine Autographs

Randomly inserted into packs, these cards feature sticker autographs of the featured players. Since the print run is different for each player, we have put that information next to the player's name in our checklist. Carmelo Anthony did not sign his stickers in time for release and those cards were issued as exchanges.

PARALLEL 25: .6X TO 1.5X BASE HI
PARALLEL PRINT RUN 25 SETS
AB Andrew Bogut/224 8.00 20.00
AI Allen Iverson/224 50.00 120.00
AN Andres Nocioni/349 5.00 12.00
BW Bracey Wright/167 5.00 12.00
CA Carmelo Anthony/74 15.00 40.00
CV Charlie Villanueva/441 6.00 15.00
DW Dwyane Wade/224 40.00 100.00
EO Emeka Okafor/224 6.00 15.00
HW Hakim Warrick/1192 5.00 12.00
JH Julius Hodge/474 5.00 12.00
JM Jason Maxiell/474 5.00 12.00
JP Johan Petro/124 5.00 12.00
NK Nenad Krstic/388 5.00 12.00
SJ Sarunas Jasikevicius/224 5.00 12.00
SM Sean May/474 5.00 12.00
SO Shaquille O'Neal/74 35.00 75.00
VC Vince Carter/124 15.00 40.00
ABY Andrew Bynum/116 20.00 50.00

2005-06 Topps Luxury Box The Machine Relics

Randomly inserted into packs, these 50-cards feature game-used relics of the players. Each of these cards were issued to a stated print run of 225 serial numbered sets.

*RELIC 25: .75X TO 2X BASE REL HI
RELIC 25 PRINT RUN 25 SETS
RELIC 1 NOT PRICED DUE TO SCARCITY
AB Andrew Bogut 4.00 10.00
AH Al Harrington 2.00 5.00
AJ Al Jefferson 2.50 6.00
AN Andres Nocioni 2.00 5.00
AV Anderson Varejao 2.00 5.00
AW Antoine Wright 2.50 6.00
BB Brandon Bass 3.00 8.00
BD Baron Davis 2.50 6.00
BW Ben Wallace 2.50 6.00
CB Carlos Boozer 2.50 6.00
CF Channing Frye 3.00 8.00
CV Charlie Villanueva 3.00 8.00
CW Chris Webber 2.50 6.00
DG Drew Gooden 2.00 5.00
DH Dwight Howard 5.00 12.00
EB Elton Brand 2.50 6.00
EO Emeka Okafor 2.50 6.00
JF Jeff Foster 2.00 5.00
JH Josh Howard 2.50 6.00
JJ Jarrett Jack 2.00 5.00
JK Jason Kidd 4.00 10.00
JM Jamaal Magloire 2.00 5.00
JO Jermaine O'Neal 2.50 6.00
KH Kirk Hinrich 2.50 6.00
KM Kenyon Martin 2.50 6.00
KT Kurt Thomas 2.00 5.00
LO Lamar Odom 2.50 6.00
MB Mike Bibby 2.50 6.00
MC Marcus Camby 2.00 5.00
NR Nate Robinson 3.00 8.00
PG Pau Gasol 2.50 6.00
RH Richard Hamilton 2.00 5.00
RL Rashard Lewis 2.50 6.00
RM Rashad McCants 2.50 6.00
SD Samuel Dalembert 2.00 5.00
SM Sean May 2.50 6.00
SN Steve Nash 3.00 8.00
SO Shaquille O'Neal 5.00 12.00
TD Tim Duncan 4.00 10.00
TR Theo Ratliff 2.00 5.00
YM Yao Ming 3.00 8.00
ABY Andrew Bynum 8.00 20.00
AJA Antawn Jamison 2.50 6.00
BBA Brent Barry 2.00 5.00
BBO Bruce Bowen 2.00 5.00
CBI Chauncey Billups 2.50 6.00
CBO Chris Bosh 2.50 6.00
CBU Caron Butler 2.50 6.00
CDU Chris Duhon 2.00 5.00
KVH Keith Van Horn 2.00 5.00

2005-06 Topps Luxury Box Trinity Triple Relics

Randomly inserted into packs, these 50-cards feature three players and a relic piece from each player. This set was issued to a stated print run of 250 serial numbered sets.

*RELIC 25: .5X TO 1.25X BASE HI
RELIC 25 PRINT RUN 25 SETS
RELIC 1 NOT PRICED DUE TO SCARCITY
ABS Shareef Abdur-Rahim 5.00 12.00
Mike Bibby
Peja Stojakovic
BAM Earl Boykins 6.00 15.00
Carmelo Anthony
Kenyon Martin
BBO Andrew Bynum 10.00 30.00
Kobe Bryant
Lamar Odom
BMI Kobe Bryant 10.00 25.00
Tracy McGrady
Allen Iverson

ML Elton Brand 5.00 12.00
Corey Maggette
Shaun Livingston
MR Andrew Bogut 5.00 12.00
Desmond Mason
Michael Redd
CKJ Vince Carter 8.00 20.00
Jason Kidd
Richard Jefferson
DD Dwyane Wade 15.00 40.00
Dwyane Wade
Dwyane Wade
DKI Samuel Dalembert 6.00 15.00
Kyle Korver
Allen Iverson
DOI Tim Duncan 10.00 25.00
Shaquille O'Neal
Allen Iverson
DRT Baron Davis 6.00 15.00
Jason Richardson
Chris Taft
FMM Raymond Felton 5.00 12.00
Sean May
Rashad McCants
FMR Channing Frye 5.00 12.00
Stephon Marbury
Quentin Richardson
GJM Kevin Garnett 5.00 12.00
Marko Jaric
Rashad McCants
GJP Gerald Green 5.00 12.00
Al Jefferson
Paul Pierce
HBB Robert Horry 5.00 12.00
Bruce Bowen
Brent Barry
HFH Grant Hill 6.00 15.00
Steve Francis
Dwight Howard
HGN Kirk Hinrich 8.00 20.00
Ben Gordon
Andres Nocioni
HIG Larry Hughes 5.00 12.00
Zydrunas Ilgauskas
Drew Gooden
JBA Antawn Jamison 5.00 12.00
Caron Butler
Gilbert Arenas
KPI Jason Kidd 8.00 20.00
Paul Pierce
Allen Iverson
MAI Stephon Marbury 6.00 15.00
Gilbert Arenas
Allen Iverson
MFO Sean May 5.00 12.00
Raymond Felton
Emeka Okafor
MMS Tracy McGrady 6.00 15.00
Yao Ming
Stromile Swift
NSM Steve Nash 8.00 20.00
Amare Stoudemire
Shawn Marion
OBM Shaquille O'Neal 6.00 15.00
Andrew Bogut
Yao Ming
OGA Jermaine O'Neal 5.00 12.00
Danny Granger
Ron Artest
PBS Chris Paul 6.00 15.00
Brandon Bass
J.R. Smith
PGD Tony Parker 10.00 25.00
Manu Ginobili
Tim Duncan
RAL Luke Ridnour 5.00 12.00
Ray Allen
Rashard Lewis
RWT Theo Ratliff 5.00 12.00
Martell Webster
Sebastian Telfair
SCJ Josh Smith 5.00 12.00
Josh Childress
Joe Johnson
TND Jason Terry 8.00 20.00
Dirk Nowitzki
Marquis Daniels
VGB Charlie Villanueva 6.00 15.00
Joey Graham
Chris Bosh
WAB Dwyane Wade 10.00 25.00
Carmelo Anthony
Chris Bosh
WGA Dwyane Wade 6.00 15.00
Ben Gordon
Ray Allen
WGJ Hakim Warrick 5.00 12.00
Pau Gasol
Eddie Jones
WHD Dwyane Wade 8.00 20.00
Richard Hamilton
Baron Davis
WHO Dwyane Wade 12.50 30.00
Shaquille O'Neal
Udonis Haslem
WHT Dwyane Wade 8.00 20.00
Kirk Hinrich
Jason Terry
WIl Chris Webber 6.00 15.00
Andre Iguodala
Allen Iverson
WKO Deron Williams 5.00 12.00
Andrei Kirilenko
Memo Okur
WMB Dwyane Wade 12.50 30.00
Tracy McGrady
Kobe Bryant
WMK Dwyane Wade 10.00 25.00
Stephon Marbury
Jason Kidd
WPF Deron Williams 8.00 20.00
Chris Paul
Raymond Felton
WWF Dwyane Wade 8.00 20.00
Dwyane Wade
Raymond Felton
WWH Ben Wallace 10.00 25.00
Rasheed Wallace
Richard Hamilton
WWP Jason Williams 8.00 20.00
Antoine Walker
James Posey
WWW Dwyane Wade 12.50 30.00
Antoine Walker
Jason Williams
WZI Dwyane Wade 10.00 25.00
Jay-Z
Allen Iverson

2005-06 Topps Luxury Box Trinity Triple Relics Autographs

These cards feature not only game-used relics but also autographs from the featured players. Due to market scarcity, no pricing is provided for these cards.

2005-06 Topps Luxury Box Triple Double 5 Relics

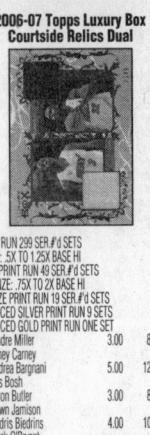

Randomly inserted into packs, these 30-cards feature five game-used pieces from members of the same team. Each of these cards were issued to a stated print run of 193 serial numbered sets.

*RELIC 25: .5X TO 1.25X BASE HI
RELIC 25 PRINT RUN 25 SETS
RELIC 1 NOT PRICED DUE TO SCARCITY
1 Charlie Villanueva 6.00 15.00
Joey Graham
Chris Bosh
Morris Peterson
Rafael Araujo
2 Deron Williams 6.00 15.00
Andrei Kirilenko
Carlos Boozer
Mehmet Okur
Kris Humphries
3 Steve Nash 12.50 30.00
Kurt Thomas
Amare Stoudemire
Shawn Marion
Leandro Barbosa
4 Josh Smith 6.00 15.00
Josh Childress
Salim Stoudamire
Joe Johnson
Al Harrington
5 Ben Gordon 10.00 25.00
Luol Deng
Kirk Hinrich
Andres Nocioni
Chris Duhon
6 Larry Hughes 6.00 15.00
Anderson Varejao
Drew Gooden
Luke Jackson
Martynas Andrius
7 Dirk Nowitzki 10.00 25.00
Josh Howard
Jason Terry
Marquis Daniels
Keith Van Horn
8 Julius Hodge 6.00 15.00
Marcus Camby
Earl Boykins
Kenyon Martin
Carmelo Anthony
9 Ben Wallace 15.00 40.00
Richard Hamilton
Rasheed Wallace
Chauncey Billups
Tayshaun Prince
10 Ike Diogu 6.00 15.00
Baron Davis
Jason Richardson
Monta Ellis
Chris Taft
11 Jermaine O'Neal 6.00 15.00
Danny Granger
Jamaal Tinsley
Jeff Foster
Sarunas Jasike
12 Elton Brand 6.00 15.00
Cuttino Mobley
Sam Cassell
Corey Maggette
Shaun Livingston
13 Dwyane Wade 20.00 50.00
Shaquille O'Neal
Antoine Walker
Jason Williams
Udonis Haslem
14 Andrew Bogut 6.00 15.00
Michael Redd
Ersan Ilyasova
Desmond Mason
TJ Ford
15 Vince Carter 10.00 25.00
Jason Kidd
Antoine Wright
Richard Jefferson
Nenad Krstic
16 Channing Frye 6.00 15.00
Nate Robinson
David Lee
Stephon Marbury
Quentin Richardson
17 Martell Webster 6.00 15.00
Jarrett Jack
Sebastian Telfair
Theo Ratliff
Ha Seung-Jin
18 Francisco Garcia 6.00 15.00
Shareef Abdur-Rahim
Bonzi Wells
Mike Bibby
Peja Stojakovic
19 Tony Parker 10.00 25.00
Manu Ginobili
Tim Duncan
Bruce Bowen
Robert Horry
20 Johan Petro 6.00 15.00
Luke Ridnour
Ray Allen
Rashard Lewis
Robert Swift
21 Antawn Jamison 6.00 15.00
Caron Butler
Gilbert Arenas
Andray Blatche
Jared Jeffries
22 Gerald Green 8.00 20.00
Al Jefferson
Paul Pierce
Ryan Gomes
Kendrick Perkins
23 Emeka Okafor 6.00 15.00
Sean May
Raymond Felton
Bernard Robinson
Jason Kapono
24 Tracy McGrady 10.00 25.00
Yao Ming
Stromile Swift
Luther Head
Dikembe Mutombo
25 Devean George 20.00 50.00
Kobe Bryant
Andrew Bynum
Lamar Odom
Kwame Brown
26 Hakim Warrick 6.00 15.00
Pau Gasol
Eddie Jones
Shane Battier
Mike Miller
27 Kevin Garnett 8.00 20.00
Rashad McCants
Wally Szczerbiak
Marko Jaric
Ndudi Ebi
28 Chris Paul 10.00 25.00
J.R. Smith
Jamaal Magloire
Brandon Bass
David West
29 Grant Hill 8.00 20.00
Steve Francis
Dwight Howard
Travis Diener
Jameer Nelson
30 Allen Iverson 10.00 25.00
Samuel Dalembert
Chris Webber
Andre Iguodala
Kyle Korver

2005-06 Topps Luxury Box Two's Company Dual Relics

Randomly inserted into packs, these cards featuring two players and relics from each one were issued to a stated print run of 193 serial numbered sets.

*RELIC 25: .5X TO 1.25X BASE HI
RELIC 25 PRINT RUN 25 SETS
RELIC 1 NOT PRICED DUE TO SCARCITY
KW Andrei Kirilenko 5.00 12.00
Deron Williams
AJ Gilbert Arenas 5.00 12.00
Antawn Jamison
AW Allen Iverson 10.00 25.00
Chris Webber
BB Kobe Bryant 8.00 25.00
Andrew Bynum
BR Andrew Bogut 6.00 15.00
Michael Redd
BV Chris Bosh 5.00 12.00
Charlie Villanueva
CM Sam Cassell 5.00 12.00
Cuttino Mobley
DG Tim Duncan 6.00 15.00
Manu Ginobili
DR Baron Davis 5.00 12.00
Jason Richardson
HG Kirk Hinrich 5.00 12.00
Ben Gordon
FM Raymond Felton 6.00 15.00
Sean May
AM Carmelo Anthony 5.00 12.00
Kenyon Martin
GH Drew Gooden 5.00 12.00
Larry Hughes
GJ Danny Granger 5.00 12.00
Sarunas Jasikevicius
GM Kevin Garnett 6.00 15.00
Rashad McCants
GW Pau Gasol 5.00 12.00
Hakim Warrick
HF Dwight Howard 5.00 12.00
Steve Francis
JJ Josh Smith 5.00 12.00
Joe Johnson
KC Jason Kidd 6.00 15.00
Vince Carter
LP Rashard Lewis 5.00 12.00
Johan Petro
MF Stephon Marbury 5.00 12.00
Channing Frye
MM Tracy McGrady 8.00 20.00
Yao Ming
ND Dirk Nowitzki 6.00 15.00
Marquis Daniels
NS Steve Nash 6.00 15.00
Amare Stoudemire
PG Paul Pierce 5.00 12.00
Gerald Green
PS Chris Paul 6.00 15.00
J.R. Smith
SA Peja Stojakovic 5.00 12.00
Shareef Abdur-Rahim
TW Sebastian Telfair 5.00 12.00
Martell Webster
WO Dwyane Wade 12.50 30.00
Shaquille O'Neal
WW Ben Wallace 8.00 20.00
Rasheed Wallace

2006-07 Topps Luxury Box

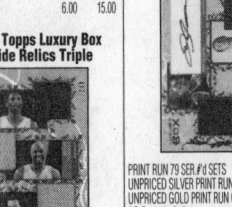

Released in mid May 2007, Topps Luxury Box boasts a 100-card set where veteran players are pictured on card numbers 1-40, retired NBA legends are pictured on card numbers 41-50 and rookies sequentially numbered to 999 are pictured on card numbers 51-100. The base card design places full color player photos on a design-heavy white and blue background showcasing a water-mark portrait of the featured player. Luxury Box is packaged in eight pack boxes of six cards each and originally carried a suggested retail price of $15.00 per pack.

COMP.SET w/o SP's (50) 20.00 50.00
UNPRICED GOLD PRINT RUN ONE SET
UNPRICED SILVER PRINT RUN 9 SETS
1 Chris Bosh .50 1.25
2 Dirk Nowitzki .75 2.00
3 Ben Wallace .50 1.25
4 Mike Bibby .50 1.25
5 Josh Howard .40 1.00
6 Vince Carter .60 1.50
7 Andrei Kirilenko .40 1.00
8 Richard Hamilton .40 1.00
9 Tony Parker .50 1.25
10 Dwyane Wade 1.25 3.00
11 Amare Stoudemire .50 1.25
12 Tim Duncan .75 2.00
13 Steve Nash .60 1.50
14 Dwight Howard .75 2.00
15 Carmelo Anthony .60 1.50
16 Pau Gasol .50 1.25
17 Zach Randolph .40 1.00
18 Kirk Hinrich .50 1.25
19 Stephon Marbury .40 1.00
20 Tracy McGrady .60 1.50
21 Kevin Garnett 1.00 2.50
22 Michael Redd .50 1.25
23 LeBron James 2.50 6.00
24 Kobe Bryant 2.50 6.00
25 Jason Kidd .75 2.00
26 Baron Davis .50 1.25
27 Jermaine O'Neal .50 1.25
28 Ray Allen .50 1.25
29 Joe Johnson .50 1.25
30 Elton Brand .50 1.25
31 Chris Paul 1.00 2.50
32 Shaquille O'Neal 1.00 2.50
33 Allen Iverson .60 1.50
34 Paul Pierce .60 1.50
35 Chauncey Billups .50 1.25
36 Gerald Wallace .50 1.25
37 Jason Richardson .50 1.25
38 Yao Ming .60 1.50
39 Andre Iguodala .50 1.25
40 Gilbert Arenas .50 1.25
41 Larry Bird 2.50 6.00
42 Isiah Thomas .75 2.00
43 Dominique Wilkins 1.00 2.50
44 Moses Malone .75 2.00
45 George Gervin .75 2.00
46 Chris Mullin .75 2.00
47 Karl Malone 1.00 2.50
48 Bob McAdoo .75 2.00
49 James Worthy .75 2.00
50 Walt Frazier .75 2.00
51 J.J. Redick RC 1.50 4.00
52 Tyrus Thomas RC 1.50 4.00
53 Rodney Carney RC 1.25 3.00
54 Jorge Garbajosa RC 1.25 3.00
55 Shawne Williams RC 1.25 3.00
56 Renaldo Balkman RC 1.25 3.00
57 Chris Quinn RC 1.25 3.00
58 Solomon Jones RC 1.25 3.00
59 Maurice Ager RC 1.25 3.00
60 Rudy Gay RC 2.00 5.00
61 Hassan Adams RC 1.25 3.00
62 Sergio Rodriguez RC 1.25 3.00
63 Dee Brown RC 1.25 3.00
64 Saer Sene RC 1.25 3.00
65 Allan Ray RC 1.25 3.00
66 Damir Markota RC 1.25 3.00
67 Bobby Jones RC 1.25 3.00
68 Kyle Lowry RC 1.50 4.00
69 Cedric Simmons RC 1.25 3.00
70 LaMarcus Aldridge RC 3.00 8.00
71 Mardy Collins RC 1.25 3.00
72 Daniel Gibson RC 1.50 4.00
73 Patrick O'Bryant RC 1.25 3.00
74 Josh Boone RC 1.25 3.00
75 Paul Davis RC 1.25 3.00
76 Craig Smith RC 1.25 3.00
77 Andrea Bargnani RC 2.00 5.00
78 Alexander Johnson RC 1.25 3.00
79 James Augustine RC 1.25 3.00
80 Jordan Farmar RC 1.25 3.00
81 Marcus Vinicius RC 1.25 3.00
82 Ryan Hollins RC 1.25 3.00
83 Marcus Williams RC 1.25 3.00
84 Will Blalock RC 1.25 3.00
85 Shannon Brown RC 2.00 5.00
86 Pops Mensah-Bonsu RC 1.25 3.00
87 P.J. Tucker RC 1.25 3.00
88 Steve Novak RC 1.25 3.00
89 Quincy Douby RC 1.25 3.00
90 Rajon Rondo RC 5.00 12.00
91 David Noel RC 1.25 3.00
92 Mile Ilic RC 1.25 3.00
93 Ronnie Brewer RC 1.50 4.00
94 James White RC 1.25 3.00
95 Hilton Armstrong RC 1.25 3.00
96 Randy Foye RC 1.50 4.00
97 Shelden Williams RC 1.25 3.00
98 Thabo Sefolosha RC 1.50 4.00
99 Brandon Roy RC 3.00 8.00
100 Adam Morrison RC 1.50 4.00

2006-07 Topps Luxury Box Blue

*BLUE: 2X TO 5X BASE HI
PRINT RUN 49 SER.#'d SETS

2006-07 Topps Luxury Box Green

*GREEN: .75X TO 2X BASE HI
PRINT RUN 329 SER.#'d SETS

2006-07 Topps Luxury Box Red

*RED: .6X TO 1.5X BASE HI
STATED PRINT RUN 499 SER.#'d SETS

2006-07 Topps Luxury Box Courtside Relics Dual

PRINT RUN 299 SER.#'d SETS
*BLUE: .5X TO 1.25X BASE HI
BLUE PRINT RUN 49 SER.#'d SETS
*BRONZE: .75X TO 2X BASE HI
BRONZE PRINT RUN 19 SER.#'d SETS
UNPRICED SILVER PRINT RUN 9 SETS
UNPRICED GOLD PRINT RUN ONE SET
AM Andre Miller 3.00 8.00
Rodney Carney
BB Andrea Bargnani 5.00 12.00
Chris Bosh
BJ Caron Butler 3.00 8.00
Antawn Jamison
BO Andris Biedrins 4.00 10.00
Patrick O'Bryant
BO Kobe Bryant 5.00 12.00
Lamar Odom
BP Chauncey Billups 4.00 10.00
Tayshaun Prince
DP Tim Duncan 5.00 12.00
Tony Parker
DS Luol Deng 5.00 12.00
Thabo Sefolosha
GB Drew Gooden 3.00 8.00
Shannon Brown
GJ Kevin Garnett 3.00 8.00
Mike James
GM Pau Gasol 3.00 8.00
Mike Miller
HH Devin Harris 3.00 8.00
Josh Howard
HM Dwight Howard 3.00 8.00
Darko Milicic
IA Allen Iverson 5.00 12.00
Carmelo Anthony
II Andre Iguodala 4.00 10.00
Allen Iverson
JK Richard Jefferson 3.00 8.00
Nenad Krstic
KC Jason Kidd 5.00 12.00
Vince Carter
LA Rashard Lewis 3.00 8.00
Ray Allen
LB Shaun Livingston 3.00 8.00
Elton Brand
MAR Brad Miller 3.00 8.00
Ron Artest
MC Corey Maggette 4.00 10.00
Sam Cassell
MF Stephon Marbury 3.00 8.00
Steve Francis
MO Darius Miles 3.00 8.00
Travis Outlaw
MY Tracy McGrady 5.00 12.00
Yao Ming
NT Dirk Nowitzki 4.00 10.00
Jason Terry
OF Emeka Okafor 3.00 8.00
Raymond Felton
OG Jermaine O'Neal 3.00 8.00
Danny Granger
PF Morris Peterson 3.00 8.00
T.J. Ford
PS Chris Paul 4.00 10.00
Peja Stojakovic
PT Paul Pierce 3.00 8.00
Sebastian Telfair
RD Jason Richardson 3.00 8.00
Baron Davis
SJ Josh Smith 3.00 8.00
Joe Johnson
SM Amare Stoudemire 4.00 10.00
Shawn Marion
VR Charlie Villanueva 3.00 8.00
Michael Redd
WB Luke Walton 4.00 10.00
Andrew Bynum
WG Ben Wallace 3.00 8.00
Ben Gordon
WH Rasheed Wallace 4.00 10.00
Richard Hamilton
WK Deron Williams 3.00 8.00
Andrei Kirilenko
WM Gerald Wallace 5.00 12.00
Adam Morrison
WO Dwyane Wade 6.00 15.00
Shaquille O'Neal

2006-07 Topps Luxury Box Courtside Relics Triple

PRINT RUN 249 SER.#'d SETS
*BLUE: .5X TO 1.25X BASE HI
BLUE PRINT RUN 49 SER.#'d SETS
*BRONZE: 1.25X TO 3X BASE HI
BRONZE PRINT RUN 19 SER.#'d SETS
UNPRICED SILVER PRINT RUN 9 SETS
UNPRICED GOLD PRINT RUN ONE SET
ABJ Gilbert Arenas 5.00 12.00
Caron Butler
Antawn Jamison
ACS Ray Allen 4.00 10.00
Nick Collison
Saer Sene
AMB Ron Artest 5.00 12.00
Kevin Martin
Mike Bibby
ANI Carmelo Anthony 8.00 20.00
Nene
Allen Iverson
BDW Chauncey Billups 6.00 15.00
Tim Duncan
Dwyane Wade
BGB Chris Bosh 6.00 15.00
Jorge Garbajosa
Andrea Bargnani
BMM Elton Brand 4.00 10.00
Corey Maggette
Cuttino Mobley
BOF Kobe Bryant 8.00 20.00
Lamar Odom
Jordan Farmar
BRV Andrew Bogut 4.00 10.00
Michael Redd
Charlie Villanueva
CKJ Vince Carter 8.00 20.00
Jason Kidd
Richard Jefferson
CWS Josh Childress 5.00 12.00
Marvin Williams
Josh Smith
DGN Tim Duncan 8.00 20.00
Kevin Garnett
Steve Nash
FOM Raymond Felton 6.00 15.00
Emeka Okafor
Adam Morrison
GDP Manu Ginobili 8.00 20.00
Tim Duncan
Tony Parker
GDW Ben Gordon 4.00 10.00
Chris Duhon
Ben Wallace
GJF Kevin Garnett 4.00 10.00
Marko Jaric
Randy Foye
HHR Grant Hill 8.00 20.00
Dwight Howard
J.J. Redick
IDM Andre Iguodala 4.00 10.00
Samuel Dalembert
Andre Miller
IVH Zydrunas Ilgauskas 5.00 12.00
Anderson Varejao
Larry Hughes
JGM Antawn Jamison 4.00 10.00
Ben Gordon
Mike Miller
KOB Andrei Kirilenko 4.00 10.00
Mehmet Okur
Ronnie Brewer
MAW Dikembe Mutombo 5.00 12.00
Ron Artest
Ben Wallace
MBH Antonio McDyess 6.00 15.00
Chauncey Billups
Richard Hamilton
MFR Stephon Marbury 4.00 10.00
Channing Frye
Nate Robinson
MIB Tracy McGrady 10.00 25.00
Allen Iverson
Kobe Bryant
MJA Darius Miles 4.00 10.00
Jarrett Jack
LaMarcus Aldridge
MOW Alonzo Mourning 10.00 25.00
Shaquille O'Neal
Dwyane Wade
MSD Shawn Marion 5.00 12.00
Amare Stoudemire
Boris Diaw
NHS Dirk Nowitzki 5.00 12.00
Josh Howard
Jerry Stackhouse
OJT Jermaine O'Neal 4.00 10.00
Danny Granger
Jamaal Tinsley
ORB Patrick O'Bryant 5.00 12.00
Jason Richardson
Andris Biedrins
PMA Chris Paul 4.00 10.00
Desmond Mason
Hilton Armstrong
WGS Hakim Warrick 4.00 10.00
Pau Gasol
Damon Stoudamire
WJP Delonte West 4.00 10.00
Al Jefferson
Paul Pierce
YMH Yao Ming 6.00 15.00
Tracy McGrady
Luther Head

2006-07 Topps Luxury Box Courtside Relics Autographs Dual

PRINT RUN 79 SER.#'d SETS
UNPRICED SILVER PRINT RUN 9 SETS
UNPRICED GOLD PRINT RUN ONE SET
AG Carmelo Anthony 25.00 50.00
Ben Gordon
AR Ray Allen 15.00 30.00
J.J. Redick
BC Chris Bosh 30.00 60.00
Vince Carter
BG Andrea Bargnani 30.00 60.00
Jorge Garbajosa
BJ Larry Bird 200.00 300.00
Magic Johnson
DW Boris Diaw 10.00 25.00
Hakim Warrick
FB T.J. Ford 10.00 25.00
Chauncey Billups
FD Jordan Farmar 10.00 25.00
Quincy Douby
HB Devin Harris 10.00 25.00
Leandro Barbosa
JL Mike James 10.00 25.00
Kyle Lowry
KW Andrei Kirilenko 10.00 25.00
Gerald Wallace
MR Adam Morrison 15.00 40.00
J.J. Redick
OI Jermaine O'Neal 10.00 25.00
Andre Iguodala
OM Emeka Okafor 10.00 25.00
Adam Morrison
SD Thabo Sefolosha 10.00 25.00
Chris Duhon
SW Dominique Wilkins 15.00 40.00
Josh Smith
VB Charlie Villanueva 10.00 25.00
Andrew Bogut
WB Dwyane Wade 40.00 80.00
Chauncey Billups
WF Luke Walton 12.50 30.00
Channing Frye
WW Deron Williams 15.00 40.00
Marcus Williams

2006-07 Topps Luxury Box Courtside Relics Autographs Triple

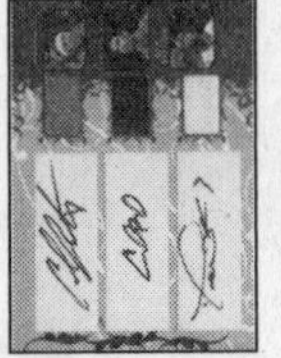

PRINT RUN 29 SER.#'d SETS
UNPRICED SILVER PRINT RUN 9 SETS
UNPRICED GOLD PRINT RUN ONE SET
ABW Carmelo Anthony 100.00 225.00
Chris Bosh
Dwyane Wade
BJW Chauncey Billups 100.00 225.00
Magic Johnson
Dwyane Wade
IFW Andre Iguodala 30.00 60.00
Channing Frye
Luke Walton
WOC Dwyane Wade 75.00 150.00
Jermaine O'Neal
Vince Carter

2006-07 Topps Luxury Box Mezzanine Relics

PRINT RUN 349 SER.#'d SETS
*BLUE: .6X TO 1.5X BASE HI
BLUE PRINT RUN 49 SER.#'d SETS
*BRONZE: .75X TO 2X BASE HI
BRONZE PRINT RUN 19 SER.#'d SETS
UNPRICED SILVER PRINT RUN 9 SETS
UNPRICED GOLD PRINT RUN ONE SET
AB Andrew Bogut 2.50 6.00
ABY Andrew Bynum 4.00 10.00
AJ Antawn Jamison 2.50 6.00
AK Andrei Kirilenko 2.00 5.00
AS Amare Stoudemire 2.50 6.00
BR Brandon Roy 6.00 15.00
BW Ben Wallace 2.50 6.00
CD Chris Duhon 2.00 5.00
CF Channing Frye 2.00 5.00
CP Chris Paul 5.00 12.00
CV Charlie Villanueva 2.50 6.00
CW Chris Webber 2.50 6.00
DH Devin Harris 2.50 6.00
DHO Dwight Howard 4.00 10.00
DM Darko Milicic 2.00 5.00
DN Dirk Nowitzki 4.00 10.00
DW Deron Williams 4.00 10.00
EB Elton Brand 2.50 6.00
EO Emeka Okafor 2.50 6.00
GA Gilbert Arenas 2.50 6.00
GH Grant Hill 4.00 10.00
JF Jordan Farmar 2.50 6.00
JG Jorge Garbajosa 2.50 6.00
JK Jason Kidd 4.00 10.00
JO Jermaine O'Neal 2.50 6.00
JR Jason Richardson 2.50 6.00
JS Josh Smith 2.50 6.00
JT Jason Terry 2.00 5.00
KB Kobe Bryant 8.00 20.00
KG Kevin Garnett 5.00 12.00
KL Kyle Lowry 3.00 8.00
LA LaMarcus Aldridge 6.00 15.00
LH Larry Hughes 2.00 5.00
LO Lamar Odom 2.50 6.00
LW Luke Walton 1.50 4.00
MA Maurice Ager 2.50 6.00
MB Mike Bibby 2.50 6.00
MG Manu Ginobili 2.50 6.00
MJ Mike James 2.00 5.00
MP Morris Peterson 1.50 4.00
MR Michael Redd 2.50 6.00
MW Marcus Williams 2.50 6.00
MWE Martell Webster 2.00 5.00
MWI Marvin Williams 2.50 6.00
PG Pau Gasol 2.50 6.00
PP Paul Pierce 3.00 8.00
PS Peja Stojakovic 2.50 6.00
RA Ron Artest 2.50 6.00
RC Rodney Carney 2.50 6.00
RG Rudy Gay 4.00 10.00
RH Richard Hamilton 2.00 5.00
RJ Richard Jefferson 2.50 6.00
RL Rashard Lewis 2.50 6.00
SM Shawn Marion 2.50 6.00
SMA Stephon Marbury 2.00 5.00
TD Tim Duncan 4.00 10.00
TJF T.J. Ford 2.00 5.00
TM Tracy McGrady 3.00 8.00
TS Thabo Sefolosha 3.00 8.00
YM Yao Ming 3.00 8.00

2006-07 Topps Luxury Box Mezzanine Relics Autographs

STATED PRINT RUN 139 SER.#'d SETS
UNPRICED SILVER PRINT RUN 9 SETS
UNPRICED GOLD PRINT RUN ONE SET
AB Andrew Bogut 6.00 15.00
ABA Andrea Bargnani 10.00 25.00
ABY Andrew Bynum 10.00 25.00
AH Al Harrington 4.00 10.00
AIG Andre Iguodala 6.00 15.00
AK Andrei Kirilenko 4.00 10.00
AM Adam Morrison 5.00 12.00
BD Boris Diaw 4.00 10.00
BG Ben Gordon 10.00 25.00
CA Carmelo Anthony 15.00 40.00
CB Chauncey Billups 6.00 15.00
CD Chris Duhon 4.00 10.00
CF Channing Frye 4.00 10.00
CV Charlie Villanueva 4.00 10.00
DW Dwyane Wade 40.00 80.00
DWI Deron Williams 10.00 25.00
EO Emeka Okafor 4.00 10.00
GW Gerald Wallace 4.00 10.00
HT Hedo Turkoglu 5.00 12.00
HW Hakim Warrick 5.00 12.00
JF Jordan Farmar 4.00 10.00
JG Jorge Garbajosa 4.00 10.00
JH Josh Howard 4.00 10.00
JJ Jarrett Jack 4.00 10.00
JJR J.J. Redick 8.00 20.00
JS Josh Smith 8.00 20.00
KL Kyle Lowry 5.00 12.00
LB Leandro Barbosa 4.00 10.00
LW Luke Walton 4.00 10.00
MA Maurice Ager 4.00 10.00
MW Marcus Williams 4.00 10.00
MWE Martell Webster 4.00 10.00
RA Ray Allen 12.50 30.00
RC Rodney Carney 4.00 10.00
UH Udonis Haslem 5.00 12.00
VC Vince Carter 20.00 40.00

2006-07 Topps Luxury Box Relics Quad

PRINT RUN 199 SER.#'d SETS
*BLUE: .5X TO 1.25X BASE HI
BLUE PRINT RUN 49 SER.#'d SETS
*BRONZE: .6X TO 1.5X BASE HI
BRONZE PRINT RUN 19 SER.#'d SETS
UNPRICED SILVER PRINT RUN 9 SETS
UNPRICED GOLD PRINT RUN ONE SET
1 Shawn Marion 8.00 20.00
Jason Terry
Alonzo Mourning
Chauncey Billups
2 Amare Stoudemire 10.00 25.00
Elton Brand
Tim Duncan
Dirk Nowitzki
3 Dwyane Wade 10.00 25.00
Vince Carter
Larry Hughes
Richard Hamilton
4 Manu Ginobili 15.00 30.00
Mike Bibby
Steve Nash
Kobe Bryant
5 Carmelo Anthony 8.00 20.00
Corey Maggette
Devin Harris
Pau Gasol
6 Rasheed Wallace 15.00 30.00
Michael Redd
Shaquille O'Neal
Ben Gordon
7 Jason Kidd 8.00 20.00
Jermaine O'Neal
Drew Gooden
Antawn Jamison
8 Shaquille O'Neal 30.00 70.00
Dwyane Wade
Dirk Nowitzki
Jason Terry
9 Chris Bosh 8.00 20.00
Stephon Marbury
Emeka Okafor
Martell Webster
10 Josh Smith 8.00 20.00
Kevin Garnett
Paul Pierce
Yao Ming
11 Jason Richardson 8.00 20.00
Ray Allen
Grant Hill
Chris Paul
12 Amare Stoudemire 8.00 20.00
Devin Harris
Jason Williams
Rasheed Wallace
13 Shawn Marion 8.00 20.00
Shaun Livingston
Bruce Bowen
Josh Howard
14 Antoine Walker 8.00 20.00
Richard Jefferson
Anderson Varejao
Antonio McDyess
15 Tony Parker 10.00 25.00
Ron Artest
Steve Nash
Lamar Odom
16 Andre Miller 8.00 20.00
Sam Cassell
Jerry Stackhouse
Mike Miller
17 Chauncey Billups 15.00 30.00
Andrew Bogut
Shaquille O'Neal
Luol Deng
18 Nenad Krstic 8.00 20.00
Danny Granger
Drew Gooden
Gilbert Arenas
19 Andrea Bargnani 6.00 15.00
Steve Francis
Raymond Felton
Darius Miles
20 Marvin Williams 8.00 20.00
Mike James
Andrei Kirilenko
Allen Iverson

2006-07 Topps Luxury Box Relics Five

PRINT RUN 179 SER.#'d SETS
*BLUE: .5X TO 1.25X BASE HI
BLUE PRINT RUN 49 SER.#'d SETS
*BRONZE: .6X TO 1.5X BASE HI
BRONZE PRINT RUN 19 SER.#'d SETS
UNPRICED SILVER PRINT RUN 9 SETS
UNPRICED GOLD PRINT RUN ONE SET
1 Sebastian Telfair 8.00 20.00
Jason Kidd
Allen Iverson
Stephon Marbury
T.J. Ford
2 Chauncey Billups 8.00 20.00
Larry Hughes
Jamaal Tinsley
Chris Duhon
Michael Redd
3 J.J. Redick 8.00 20.00
Gilbert Arenas
Gary Payton
Joe Johnson
Raymond Felton
4 Tony Parker 8.00 20.00
Devin Harris
Tracy McGrady
Chris Paul
Damon Stoudamire
5 Deron Williams 8.00 20.00
Earl Boykins
Mike James
Luke Ridnour
Jarrett Jack
6 Kobe Bryant 12.00 30.00
Steve Nash
Sam Cassell
Baron Davis
Mike Bibby
7 Al Jefferson 8.00 20.00
Richard Jefferson
Chris Webber
Channing Frye
Morris Peterson
8 Tayshaun Prince 8.00 20.00
Drew Gooden
Danny Granger
Luol Deng
Charlie Villanueva
9 Dwight Howard 10.00 25.00
Antawn Jamison
Antoine Walker
Marvin Williams
Adam Morrison
10 Tim Duncan 8.00 20.00
Dirk Nowitzki
Shane Battier
Peja Stojakovic
Rudy Gay
11 Andrei Kirilenko 8.00 20.00
Nene
Kevin Garnett
Rashard Lewis
Darius Miles
12 Lamar Odom 8.00 20.00
Shawn Marion
Elton Brand
Mike Dunleavy
Ron Artest
13 Nenad Krstic 8.00 20.00
Samuel Dalembert
Zydrunas Ilgauskas
Jermaine O'Neal
Ben Wallace
14 Andrew Bogut 8.00 20.00
Shaquille O'Neal
Emeka Okafor
Erick Dampier
Yao Ming
15 Mehmet Okur 8.00 20.00
Saer Sene
LaMarcus Aldridge
Andrew Bynum
Brad Miller

2006-07 Topps Luxury Box Relics Six

PRINT RUN 149 SER.#'d SETS
*BLUE: .5X TO 1.25X BASE HI
BLUE PRINT RUN 49 SER.#'d SETS
*BRONZE: .6X TO 1.5X BASE HI
BRONZE PRINT RUN 19 SER.#'d SETS
UNPRICED SILVER PRINT RUN 9 SETS
UNPRICED GOLD PRINT RUN ONE SET
1 Raymond Felton 8.00 20.00
Rasheed Wallace
Antawn Jamison
Sean May
David Noel
Jerry Stackhouse
2 Shane Battier 10.00 25.00
Elton Brand
Luol Deng
Grant Hill
Corey Maggette
J.J. Redick
3 Ben Gordon 8.00 20.00
Richard Hamilton
Ray Allen
Charlie Villanueva
Emeka Okafor
Rudy Gay
4 Luke Walton 8.00 20.00
Jason Terry
Damon Stoudamire
Mike Bibby
Andre Iguodala
Gilbert Arenas
5 Peja Stojakovic 8.00 20.00
Mehmet Okur
Sergio Rodriguez
Boris Diaw
Jorge Garbajosa
Zydrunas Ilgauskas
6 Dirk Nowitzki 8.00 20.00
Nenad Krstic
Andrea Bargnani
Pau Gasol
Andrei Kirilenko
Tony Parker
7 Baron Davis 8.00 20.00
Brandon Roy
Gary Payton
Jordan Farmar
Nate Robinson
Bill Walton
8 Dwyane Wade 10.00 25.00
Marcus Williams
Allen Iverson
Samuel Dalembert
Carmelo Anthony
Quincy Douby
9 Tim Duncan 10.00 25.00
Stephon Marbury
Sam Cassell
Cedric Simmons
David Noel
J.J. Redick
10 Paul Pierce 8.00 20.00
LaMarcus Aldridge
Tony Battie
Chauncey Billups
Jamaal Tinsley
Antoine Wright
11 Rajon Rondo 10.00 25.00
Antoine Walker
Shaquille O'Neal
Antonio McDyess
Udonis Haslem
Renaldo Balkman
12 Deron Williams 10.00 25.00
Chris Webber
Magic Johnson
Michael Redd
Devin Harris
Jalen Rose
13 Sebastian Telfair 8.00 20.00
Tracy McGrady
Josh Smith
Kwame Brown
Shaun Livingston
Kevin Garnett
14 Kobe Bryant 12.50 30.00
Jermaine O'Neal
Amare Stoudemire
Moses Malone
Dwight Howard
Al Jefferson
15 J.J. Redick 8.00 20.00
Andrew Bogut
Jameer Nelson
T.J. Ford
Shane Battier
Elton Brand

2006-07 Topps Luxury Box Relics Seven

PRINT RUN 99 SER.#'d SETS
*BLUE: .5X TO 1.25X BASE HI
BLUE PRINT RUN 49 SER.#'d SETS
*BRONZE: .6X TO 1.5X BASE HI
BRONZE PRINT RUN 19 SER.#'d SETS
UNPRICED SILVER PRINT RUN 9 SETS
UNPRICED GOLD PRINT RUN ONE SET
1 Chris Paul 12.50 30.00
Charlie Villanueva
Andrew Bogut
Deron Williams
Channing Frye
Danny Granger
Raymond Felton
2 Kobe Bryant 20.00 40.00
Steve Nash
Dirk Nowitzki
Shaquille O'Neal
Chauncey Billups
Dwyane Wade
Tim Duncan
3 Elton Brand 12.50 30.00
Ben Wallace
Allen Iverson
Gilbert Arenas
Shawn Marion
Carmelo Anthony
Yao Ming
4 Bruce Bowen 10.00 25.00
Ben Wallace
Andrei Kirilenko
Ron Artest
Kobe Bryant
Jason Kidd
Tim Duncan
5 Steve Nash 20.00 40.00
Chris Paul
Boris Diaw
Elgin Baylor
Ben Wallace
Mike Miller
Dwyane Wade
6 Kobe Bryant 20.00 40.00
Allen Iverson
Gilbert Arenas
Dwyane Wade
Paul Pierce
Dirk Nowitzki
Carmelo Anthony
7 Kevin Garnett 12.50 30.00
Dwight Howard
Shawn Marion
Ben Wallace
Tim Duncan
Troy Murphy
Elton Brand
8 Steve Nash 12.50 30.00
Baron Davis
Chauncey Billups
Jason Kidd
Andre Miller
Chris Paul
Allen Iverson
9 Richard Hamilton 10.00 25.00
Leandro Barbosa
Mike James
Steve Nash
Ben Gordon
Chauncey Billups
Bruce Bowen
10 Marcus Camby 10.00 25.00
Andrei Kirilenko
Alonzo Mourning
Josh Smith
Elton Brand
Samuel Dalembert
Joel Przybilla

2006-07 Topps Luxury Box Relics Eight

PRINT RUN 79 SER.#'d SETS
*BLUE: .5X TO 1.25X BASE HI
BLUE PRINT RUN 49 SER.#'d SETS
*BRONZE: .6X TO 1.5X BASE HI
BRONZE PRINT RUN 19 SER.#'d SETS
UNPRICED SILVER PRINT RUN 9 SETS
UNPRICED GOLD PRINT RUN ONE SET
1 Andrea Bargnani 15.00 30.00
LaMarcus Aldridge
Adam Morrison
Shelden Williams
Randy Foye
Brandon Roy
Rudy Gay
J.J. Redick
2 Dwyane Wade 15.00 30.00
Dirk Nowitzki
Antoine Walker
Jason Terry
Shaquille O'Neal
Josh Howard
Jason Williams
Jerry Stackhouse
3 Andrea Bargnani 15.00 30.00
Andrew Bogut
Dwight Howard
Yao Ming
Elton Brand
Tim Duncan
Allen Iverson
Shaquille O'Neal
4 Kobe Bryant 20.00 50.00
Kevin Garnett
Tracy McGrady
Shaun Livingston
Dwight Howard
Amare Stoudemire
Jermaine O'Neal
Josh Smith
5 Larry Bird 30.00 60.00
Isiah Thomas
Magic Johnson
Dominique Wilkins
John Stockton
Moses Malone
Clyde Drexler
Karl Malone

2006-07 Topps Luxury Box Rookie Relics Autographs

STATED PRINT RUN 249 SER.#'d SETS
UNPRICED SILVER PRINT RUN 9 SETS
UNPRICED GOLD PRINT RUN ONE SET
AB Andrea Bargnani 10.00 25.00
AM Adam Morrison 5.00 12.00
AR Allan Ray 4.00 10.00
CS Cedric Simmons 4.00 10.00
CSM Craig Smith 4.00 10.00
DB Dee Brown 4.00 10.00
DM Damir Markota 4.00 10.00
DN David Noel 4.00 10.00
HA Hilton Armstrong 4.00 10.00
JB Josh Boone 4.00 10.00
JF Jordan Farmar 4.00 10.00
JG Jorge Garbajosa 4.00 10.00
JJR J.J. Redick 8.00 20.00
JW James White 4.00 10.00
KL Kyle Lowry 5.00 12.00
MA Maurice Ager 4.00 10.00
MC Mardy Collins 4.00 10.00
MW Marcus Williams 4.00 10.00
PD Paul Davis 4.00 10.00
PJT P.J. Tucker 4.00 10.00
PO Patrick O'Bryant 4.00 10.00
QD Quincy Douby 4.00 10.00
RB Renaldo Balkman 4.00 10.00
RBR Ronnie Brewer 5.00 12.00
RC Rodney Carney 4.00 10.00
RF Randy Foye 5.00 12.00
RR Rajon Rondo 20.00 50.00
SB Shannon Brown 6.00 15.00
SEW Shawne Williams 4.00 10.00
SJ Solomon Jones 4.00 10.00
SN Steve Novak 4.00 10.00
SNW Shelden Williams 4.00 10.00
SR Sergio Rodriguez 4.00 10.00
SS Saer Sene 4.00 10.00
TS Thabo Sefolosha 5.00 12.00

2007-08 Topps Luxury Box

Released in April 2008, Topps Luxury Box features a 100-card base set where veterans appear on cards 1-50 and rookies appear on cards 21-100 and are serially numbered to 669. Luxury Box hit the market in 10-pack boxes of four cards each and carried an initial suggested retail price of $16.

COMP.SET w/o SPs (50) 20.00 40.00
UNPRICED GOLD PRINT RUN ONE SET
UNPRICED PLATINUM PRINT RUN ONE SET
1 Kevin Garnett 1.00 2.50
2 Kobe Bryant 2.50 6.00
3 Dwyane Wade 1.25 3.00
4 LeBron James 2.50 6.00
5 Baron Davis .50 1.25
6 Dirk Nowitzki .60 1.50
7 Jermaine O'Neal .50 1.25
8 Jason Richardson .50 1.25
9 Tony Parker .50 1.25
10 Chris Bosh .50 1.25
11 Yao Ming .60 1.50
12 Dwight Howard .75 2.00
13 Steve Nash .60 1.50
14 Luol Deng .50 1.25
15 Carmelo Anthony .60 1.50
16 Pau Gasol .50 1.25
17 Carlos Boozer .50 1.25
18 Vince Carter .60 1.50
19 Chauncey Billups .60 1.50
20 Ray Allen .50 1.25
21 Tim Duncan .75 2.00
22 Amare Stoudemire .50 1.25
23 Kevin Martin .50 1.25
24 Michael Redd .50 1.25
25 Corey Maggette .40 1.00
26 Al Jefferson .50 1.25
27 Brandon Roy .60 1.50
28 Chris Paul 1.00 2.50
29 Andre Iguodala .50 1.25
30 Gilbert Arenas .50 1.25
31 Tracy McGrady .50 1.25
32 Shaquille O'Neal 1.00 2.50
33 Allen Iverson .60 1.50
34 Paul Pierce .60 1.50
35 Jason Kidd .50 1.25
36 John Stockton 1.25 3.00
37 Tim Hardaway .75 2.00
38 Dennis Rodman 1.25 3.00
39 Dominique Wilkins 1.00 2.50
40 David Thompson 1.00 2.50
41 Spencer Haywood .75 2.00
42 Larry Bird 2.50 6.00
43 Isiah Thomas .75 2.00
44 Magic Johnson 2.00 5.00
45 Bill Russell 1.25 3.00
46 Moses Malone .75 2.00
47 Sidney Moncrief .75 2.00
48 Bill Walton .75 2.00
49 David Robinson 1.25 3.00
50 Jerry West 1.00 2.50
51 Thaddeus Young RC 1.50 4.00
52 Javaris Crittenton RC 1.25 3.00
53 Sean Williams RC 1.25 3.00
54 Jared Dudley RC 1.25 3.00
55 Wilson Chandler RC 2.00 5.00
56 Mario West RC 1.25 3.00
57 Chris Richard RC 1.25 3.00
58 Al Horford RC 1.50 4.00
59 Taurean Green RC 1.25 3.00
60 Corey Brewer RC 1.50 4.00
61 Joakim Noah RC 3.00 8.00
62 Al Thornton RC 1.25 3.00
63 Nick Young RC 2.00 5.00
64 Arron Afflalo RC 1.50 4.00
65 Juan Carlos Navarro RC 1.25 3.00
66 Marco Belinelli RC 1.25 3.00
67 Yi Jianlian RC 2.00 5.00
68 Luis Scola RC 2.00 5.00
69 Jeff Green RC 1.50 4.00
70 Herbert Hill RC 1.25 3.00
71 Aaron Gray RC 1.25 3.00
72 Kosta Perovic RC 1.25 3.00
73 Spencer Hawes RC 1.25 3.00
74 Aaron Brooks RC 1.25 3.00
75 Kevin Durant RC 10.00 25.00
76 Alando Tucker RC 1.25 3.00
77 Julian Wright RC 1.25 3.00
78 Carl Landry RC 1.25 3.00
79 Acie Law RC 1.25 3.00
80 Morris Almond RC 1.25 3.00
81 Nick Fazekas RC 1.25 3.00
82 Glen Davis RC 2.00 5.00
83 Jermareo Davidson RC 1.25 3.00
84 Jamario Moon RC 1.25 3.00
85 Jason Smith RC 1.25 3.00
86 Cheikh Samb RC 1.25 3.00
87 Coby Karl RC 1.25 3.00
88 Dominic McGuire RC 1.25 3.00
89 Ramon Sessions RC 2.00 5.00
90 Rodney Stuckey RC 2.00 5.00
91 JamesOn Curry RC 1.25 3.00
92 Gabe Pruitt RC 1.25 3.00
93 Adam Haluska RC 1.25 3.00
94 Kyrylo Fesenko RC 1.25 3.00
95 Josh McRoberts RC 1.25 3.00
96 D.J. Strawberry RC 1.25 3.00
97 Brandon Wright RC 1.25 3.00
98 Mike Conley Jr. RC 2.00 5.00
99 Daequan Cook RC 1.25 3.00
100 Greg Oden RC 1.50 4.00

2007-08 Topps Luxury Box Bronze

*BRONZE 1-50: .75X TO 2X BASE HI
*BRONZE 51-100: .5X TO 1.25X BASE
BRONZE PRINT RUN 249 SER.#'d SETS
75 Kevin Durant 15.00 40.00

2007-08 Topps Luxury Box Silver

*SILVER 1-50: 1X TO 2.5X BASE HI
*SILVER 51-100: .6X TO 1.5X BASE HI
PRINT RUN 75 SER.#'d SETS
75 Kevin Durant 50.00 100.00

2007-08 Topps Luxury Box Courtside Dual Relics

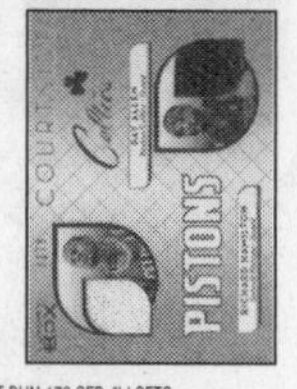

PRINT RUN 179 SER.#'d SETS
*GOLD: .5X TO 1.25X BASE HI
GOLD PRINT RUN 75 SER.#'d SETS
UNPRICED PLATINUM PRINT RUN ONE SET
UNPRICED AUTO PRINT RUN 10 SETS
UNPRICED AUTO GOLD PRINT RUN ONE SET
UNPRICED AUTO PLAT.PRINT RUN ONE SET
AH Ray Allen 4.00 10.00
Richard Hamilton
AM Carmelo Anthony 4.00 10.00
Tracy McGrady
AW Gilbert Arenas 5.00 12.00
Dwyane Wade
CR Vince Carter 5.00 12.00
Jason Richardson
DB Luol Deng 4.00 10.00
Carlos Boozer
DM Tim Duncan 5.00 12.00
Yao Ming
GJ Kevin Garnett 5.00 12.00
Al Jefferson
HB Dwight Howard 5.00 12.00
Chris Bosh
HP Kirk Hinrich 4.00 10.00
Paul Pierce
IM Allen Iverson 4.00 10.00
Stephon Marbury
MD Kevin Martin 4.00 10.00
Baron Davis
NG Dirk Nowitzki 4.00 10.00
Pau Gasol
NP Steve Nash 5.00 12.00
Tony Parker
OB Shaquille O'Neal 10.00 25.00
Kobe Bryant
OH Jermaine O'Neal 4.00 10.00
Al Harrington
RM Michael Redd 4.00 10.00
Mike Miller
RP Brandon Roy 5.00 12.00
Chris Paul
RS Jason Richardson 4.00 10.00
Josh Smith
SK Amare Stoudemire 4.00 10.00
Jason Kidd
WC Ben Wallace 4.00 10.00
Marcus Camby

2007-08 Topps Luxury Box Courtside Triple Relics

PRINT RUN 149 SER.#'d SETS
*GOLD: .5X TO 1.25X BASE HI
GOLD PRINT RUN 49 SER.#'d SETS
UNPRICED PLATINUM PRINT RUN ONE SET
UNPRICED AUTO PRINT RUN 10 SETS
UNPRICED AUTO GOLD PRINT RUN ONE SET
UNPRICED AUTO PLAT.PRINT RUN ONE SET
AAW Carmelo Anthony 6.00 15.00
Gilbert Arenas
Dwyane Wade
AWM Ron Artest 5.00 12.00
Ben Wallace
Shawn Marion
BGN Kobe Bryant 10.00 25.00
Kevin Garnett
Steve Nash
BIW Caron Butler 5.00 12.00
Andre Iguodala
Gerald Wallace
FGT Randy Foye 5.00 12.00
Rudy Gay
Tyrus Thomas
HBC Dwight Howard 5.00 12.00
Carlos Boozer
Marcus Camby
HCG Al Horford 5.00 12.00
Daequan Cook
Taurean Green
IMJ Andre Iguodala 5.00 12.00
Tracy McGrady
Joe Johnson
MOR Yao Ming 8.00 20.00
Shaquille O'Neal
David Robinson
NOB Joakim Noah 8.00 20.00
Greg Oden
Corey Brewer
OGT Mehmet Okur 5.00 12.00
Manu Ginobili
Hedo Turkoglu
OOS Emeka Okafor 5.00 12.00
Jermaine O'Neal
Josh Smith
RAI Michael Redd 5.00 12.00
Ray Allen
Allen Iverson
RMB Brandon Roy 5.00 12.00
Adam Morrison
Andrea Bargnani
SDB Amare Stoudemire 5.00 12.00
Tim Duncan
Chris Bosh
TLD T.J. Ford 5.00 12.00
LaMarcus Aldridge
Daniel Gibson
VFG Charlie Villanueva 5.00 12.00
Channing Frye
Ryan Gomes
WKP Deron Williams 6.00 15.00
Jason Kidd
Chris Paul
YWC Thaddeus Young 5.00 12.00
Brandan Wright
Javaris Crittenton

2007-08 Topps Luxury Box Quad Relics

PRINT RUN 99 SER.#'d SET
*GOLD: .5X TO 1.25X BASE HI
GOLD PRINT RUN 25 SER.#'d SETS
UNPRICED PLATINUM PRINT RUN ONE SET
QR2 Al Horford 8.00 20.00
Taurean Green
Corey Brewer
Joakim Noah
QR3 Tim Duncan 12.50 30.00
Tony Parker
Manu Ginobili
David Robinson
QR4 Gilbert Arenas 6.00 15.00
Caron Butler
Antawn Jamison
Nick Young
QR5 Stephon Marbury 6.00 15.00
David Lee
Zach Randolph
Wilson Chandler
QR7 Larry Bird 20.00 40.00
Magic Johnson
David Robinson
Moses Malone
QR8 Al Jefferson 6.00 15.00
Gerald Green
Randy Foye
Ryan Gomes
QR9 Chauncey Billups 6.00 15.00
Richard Hamilton
Arron Afflalo
Rodney Stuckey
QR10 Baron Davis 6.00 15.00
Al Harrington
Monta Ellis
Marco Belinelli
QR11 Steve Nash 8.00 20.00
Amare Stoudemire
Leandro Barbosa
Shaquille O'Neal
QR12 Devin Harris 8.00 20.00
Dirk Nowitzki
Jason Terry
Josh Howard
QR13 Jason Kidd 6.00 15.00
Richard Jefferson
Vince Carter
Sean Williams
QR14 Kevin Garnett 10.00 25.00
Paul Pierce
Ray Allen
Rajon Rondo
QR15 Tracy McGrady 8.00 20.00
Yao Ming
Aaron Brooks
Carl Landry

2007-08 Topps Luxury Box Five Piece Relics

PRINT RUN 75 SER.#'d SETS
*GOLD: .5X TO 1.25X BASE HI
GOLD PRINT RUN 25 SER.#'d SETS
UNPRICED PLATINUM PRINT RUN ONE SET
R1 Greg Oden 10.00 25.00
Yi Jianlian
Brandan Wright
Nick Young
Thaddeus Young
R2 Joakim Noah 15.00 30.00
Corey Brewer
Al Horford
Julian Wright
Jeff Green
R3 Dirk Nowitzki 10.00 25.00
Tim Duncan
Amare Stoudemire
Steve Nash
Kobe Bryant
R4 Chris Bosh 8.00 20.00
Yao Ming
Gilbert Arenas
Tracy McGrady
Kevin Garnett
R5 Carmelo Anthony 8.00 20.00
Dwight Howard
Dwyane Wade
Chauncey Billups
Carlos Boozer

Marcus Camby	8.00	20.00
ason Kidd		
Ben Wallace		
Tayshaun Prince		
Kirk Hinrich		
Shane Battier	8.00	20.00
Shawn Marion		
Ron Artest		
Gerald Wallace		
Alonzo Mourning		
Dirk Nowitzki	8.00	20.00
Steve Nash		
Kevin Garnett		
Tim Duncan		
Allen Iverson		
Shaquille O'Neal	10.00	25.00
Dwight Howard		
David Robinson		
Moses Malone		
Bill Walton		
0 Brandon Roy	8.00	20.00
Amare Stoudemire		
Chris Paul		
Emeka Okafor		
Pau Gasol		
1 Vince Carter	10.00	25.00
Allen Iverson		
Jason Kidd		
Mike Miller		
Elton Brand		
3 Isiah Thomas	25.00	50.00
Larry Bird		
Dominique Wilkins		
John Stockton		
Spud Webb		
4 Kobe Bryant	20.00	40.00
Allen Iverson		
Shaquille O'Neal		
Kevin Garnett		
Tim Duncan		
5 Greg Oden	20.00	40.00
Andrea Bargnani		
Andrew Bogut		
Dwight Howard		
Yao Ming		

2007-08 Topps Luxury Box Six Piece Relics

RINT RUN 75 SER.#'d SET
GOLD: .5X TO 1.25X BASE HI
OLD PRINT RUN 25 SER.#'d SETS
NPRICED PLATINUM PRINT RUN ONE SET

Tony Parker	10.00	25.00
Tim Duncan		
Manu Ginobili		
Amare Stoudemire		
Steve Nash		
Shaquille O'Neal		
Jason Terry	8.00	20.00
Dirk Nowitzki		
Josh Howard		
Baron Davis		
Al Harrington		
Monta Ellis		
3 Ben Gordon	8.00	20.00
Ben Wallace		
Luol Deng		
Dwyane Wade		
Shawn Marion		
Jason Williams		
Stephon Marbury	8.00	20.00
Eddy Curry		
David Lee		
Jason Kidd		
Vince Carter		
Richard Jefferson		
5 Kevin Garnett	10.00	25.00
Paul Pierce		
Ray Allen		
Andre Iguodala		
Andre Miller		
Thaddeus Young		
LaMarcus Aldridge	8.00	20.00
Brandon Roy		
Jarrett Jack		
Luke Ridnour		
Jeff Green		
Nick Collison		
7 Jameer Nelson	8.00	20.00
Dwight Howard		
Rashard Lewis		
Acie Law		
Joe Johnson		
Al Horford		
3 Allen Iverson	8.00	20.00
Carmelo Anthony		
Marcus Camby		
Carlos Boozer		
Deron Williams		
Mehmet Okur		
9 Tracy McGrady	10.00	25.00
Yao Ming		
Aaron Brooks		
Mike Conley Jr.		
Mike Miller		
Rudy Gay		
10 Chauncey Billups	8.00	20.00
Rasheed Wallace		
Richard Hamilton		
Caron Butler		
Gilbert Arenas		
Antawn Jamison		

2007-08 Topps Luxury Box Seven Piece Relics

RINT RUN 50 SER.#'d SETS
NPRICED GOLD PRINT RUN 10 SETS
NPRICED PLATINUM PRINT RUN ONE SET

1 Jason Kidd	6.00	15.00
T.J. Ford		
Stephon Marbury		
Andre Miller		
Kirk Hinrich		
Chauncey Billups		
Raymond Felton		
2 Vince Carter	8.00	20.00
Chris Bosh		
Kevin Garnett		
Dwyane Wade		
Andre Iguodala		
Luol Deng		
Joe Johnson		
3 Shaquille O'Neal	8.00	20.00
Eddy Curry		
Jermaine O'Neal		
Dwight Howard		
Emeka Okafor		
Sam Dalembert		
Zydrunas Ilgauskas		

R5 Richard Jefferson	6.00	15.00
Andrea Bargnani		
Rashard Lewis		
Tayshaun Prince		
Caron Butler		
Josh Smith		
Zach Randolph		
R7 Kobe Bryant	15.00	30.00
Carmelo Anthony		
Amare Stoudemire		
Tracy McGrady		
Dirk Nowitzki		
Manu Ginobili		
Pau Gasol		
R8 Tim Duncan	8.00	20.00
Carlos Boozer		
Al Jefferson		
Yao Ming		
Elton Brand		
LaMarcus Aldridge		
Marcus Camby		
R9 Shawn Marion	6.00	15.00
Corey Maggette		
Mike Miller		
Kevin Martin		
Al Harrington		
Josh Howard		
Mehmet Okur		
R10 Mike Conley Jr.	8.00	20.00
Nick Young		
Corey Brewer		
Al Horford		
Greg Oden		
Yi Jianlian		
Al Thornton		

2007-08 Topps Luxury Box Eight Piece Relics

PRINT RUN 25 SER.#'d SETS
UNPRICED GOLD PRINT RUN 10 SETS
UNPRICED PLATINUM PRINT RUN ONE SET

R1 Jason Kidd	15.00	30.00
Dwyane Wade		
Kevin Garnett		
Shaquille O'Neal		
Kirk Hinrich		
Joe Johnson		
Chris Bosh		
Andre Iguodala		
R2 Chauncey Billups	10.00	25.00
Gilbert Arenas		
Luol Deng		
Dwight Howard		
Eddy Curry		
Josh Smith		
Raymond Felton		
Richard Jefferson		
R4 Paul Pierce	15.00	30.00
Ben Gordon		
Rashard Lewis		
Jason Richardson		
Ray Allen		
Andrea Bargnani		
Tayshaun Prince		
Stephon Marbury		
R5 Kobe Bryant	20.00	50.00
Allen Iverson		
Tracy McGrady		
Steve Nash		
Dirk Nowitzki		
Tim Duncan		
Pau Gasol		
Carlos Boozer		
R6 Yao Ming	20.00	50.00
Carmelo Anthony		
Amare Stoudemire		
Josh Howard		
Tony Parker		
Chris Paul		
Baron Davis		
Deron Williams		
R7 Manu Ginobili	15.00	30.00
Mike Miller		
Kevin Martin		
Shawn Marion		
Al Jefferson		
Corey Maggette		
Marcus Camby		
LaMarcus Aldridge		
R10 Brandan Wright	20.00	50.00
Joakim Noah		
Thaddeus Young		
Mike Conley Jr.		
Acie Law		
Greg Oden		
Yi Jianlian		
Nick Young		

2007-08 Topps Luxury Box Mezzanine Relics

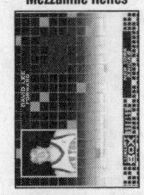

PRINT RUN 199 SER.#'d SETS
*GOLD: .5X TO 1.25X BASE HI
GOLD PRINT RUN 99 SER.#'d SETS
UNPRICED PLATINUM PRINT RUN ONE SET

AB Andrea Bargnani	3.00	8.00
AI Allen Iverson	3.00	8.00
AJ Al Jefferson	2.50	6.00
AJA Antawn Jamison	2.50	6.00
AS Amare Stoudemire	2.50	6.00
BG Ben Gordon	2.50	6.00
BR Brandon Roy	3.00	8.00
BW Buck Williams	2.50	6.00
CA Carmelo Anthony	3.00	8.00
CB Caron Butler	2.50	6.00
CBI Chauncey Billups	2.50	6.00
CBO Chris Bosh	2.50	6.00
CP Chris Paul	5.00	12.00
DL David Lee	2.00	5.00
DN Dirk Nowitzki	3.00	8.00
DW Dwyane Wade	6.00	15.00
EO Emeka Okafor	2.50	6.00
GA Gilbert Arenas	2.50	6.00
GG Gerald Green	2.00	5.00
JJ Joe Johnson	2.50	6.00
JJW Jo Jo White	2.50	6.00
JK Jason Kidd	2.50	6.00
JO Jermaine O'Neal	2.50	6.00
JR Jason Richardson	2.50	6.00
KB Kobe Bryant	8.00	20.00
KG Kevin Garnett	5.00	12.00
KM Kevin Martin	2.50	6.00
LA LaMarcus Aldridge	3.00	8.00
LB Leandro Barbosa	2.00	5.00
LD Luol Deng	2.50	6.00
LO Lamar Odom	2.50	6.00
MC Marcus Camby	2.00	5.00
MM Mike Miller	2.50	6.00
MO Mehmet Okur	2.00	5.00
MP Mickael Pietrus	2.00	5.00
MR Michael Redd	2.50	6.00
PG Pau Gasol	2.50	6.00
PP Paul Pierce	3.00	8.00
RA Ray Allen	2.50	6.00
RAR Ron Artest	2.50	6.00
RF Raymond Felton	3.00	8.00
RG Rudy Gay	2.50	6.00
RGO Ryan Gomes	2.00	5.00
RH Richard Hamilton	2.00	5.00
RJ Richard Jefferson	2.50	6.00
RL Rashard Lewis	2.00	5.00
RW Rasheed Wallace	2.50	6.00
SM Shawn Marion	2.50	6.00
SMA Stephon Marbury	2.00	5.00
SO Shaquille O'Neal	5.00	12.00
SW Spud Webb	2.50	6.00
TD Tim Duncan	4.00	10.00
TJF T.J. Ford	2.00	5.00
TM Tracy McGrady	2.50	6.00
TP Tony Parker	2.50	6.00
VC Vince Carter	3.00	8.00
YM Yao Ming	3.00	8.00
ZR Zach Randolph	2.00	5.00

2007-08 Topps Luxury Box Mezzanine Relics Autographs

PRINT RUN 39 SER.#'d SETS
*AUTO GOLD: .6X TO 1.5X BASE HI
GOLD PRINT RUN 25 SER.#'d SETS
UNPRICED LOGO PRINT RUN ONE SET
UNPRICED PLATINUM PRINT RUN ONE SET

AB Andrea Bargnani	5.00	12.00
AJ Al Jefferson	5.00	12.00
AJA Antawn Jamison	5.00	12.00
BG Ben Gordon	6.00	15.00
BW Buck Williams	6.00	15.00
CB Caron Butler	5.00	12.00
CBI Chauncey Billups	6.00	15.00
CBO Chris Bosh	12.00	30.00
DL David Lee	5.00	12.00
DW Dwyane Wade	25.00	60.00
GA Gilbert Arenas	8.00	20.00
JJW Jo Jo White	6.00	15.00
LB Leandro Barbosa	5.00	12.00
MP Mickael Pietrus	5.00	12.00
PP Paul Pierce	8.00	20.00
RA Ray Allen	15.00	40.00
RF Raymond Felton	5.00	12.00
RGO Ryan Gomes	5.00	12.00
SO Shaquille O'Neal	30.00	80.00
SW Spud Webb	15.00	30.00
TJF T.J. Ford	5.00	12.00
VC Vince Carter	20.00	40.00

2007-08 Topps Luxury Box Rookie Relics

PRINT RUN 499 SER.#'d SETS
*GOLD: .5X TO 1.25X BASE HI
GOLD PRINT RUN 149 SER.#'d SETS
UNPRICED LOGO PRINT RUN ONE SET
UNPRICED PLATINUM PRINT RUN ONE SET

AA Arron Afflalo	3.00	8.00
AB Aaron Brooks	2.50	6.00
AG Aaron Gray	2.50	6.00
AH Al Horford	3.00	8.00
AHA Adam Haluska	2.50	6.00
AL Acie Law	2.50	6.00
AT Al Thornton	2.50	6.00
ATU Alando Tucker	2.50	6.00
BW Brandan Wright	2.50	6.00
CB Corey Brewer	3.00	8.00
CL Carl Landry	2.50	6.00
CR Chris Richard	2.50	6.00
DC Daequan Cook	2.50	6.00
DJS D.J. Strawberry	2.50	6.00
DM Dominic McGuire	2.50	6.00
DN Demetris Nichols	2.50	6.00
GD Glen Davis	4.00	10.00
GO Greg Oden	3.00	8.00
GP Gabe Pruitt	2.50	6.00
HH Herbert Hill	2.50	6.00
JC Javaris Crittenton	2.50	6.00
JD Jared Dudley	2.50	6.00
JDA Jermareo Davidson	2.50	6.00
JG Jeff Green	3.00	8.00
JM Josh McRoberts	2.50	6.00
JN Joakim Noah	6.00	15.00
JS Jason Smith	2.50	6.00
JW Julian Wright	2.50	6.00
MA Morris Almond	2.50	6.00
MB Marco Belinelli	2.50	6.00
MC Mike Conley Jr.	4.00	10.00
NF Nick Fazekas	2.50	6.00
NY Nick Young	4.00	10.00
RS Rodney Stuckey	4.00	10.00
SH Spencer Hawes	2.50	6.00
SW Sean Williams	2.50	6.00
TG Taurean Green	2.50	6.00
TY Thaddeus Young	3.00	8.00
WC Wilson Chandler	4.00	10.00
YJ Yi Jianlian	4.00	10.00

2007-08 Topps Luxury Box Rookie Relics Autographs

PRINT RUN 99 TO 199 SER.#'d SETS
*GOLD: .5X TO 1.25X BASE HI
GOLD PRINT RUN 19 TO 39 SETS
UNPRICED LOGO PRINT RUN ONE SET
UNPRICED PLATINUM PRINT RUN ONE SET

AA Arron Afflalo	5.00	12.00
AB Aaron Brooks	4.00	10.00
AG Aaron Gray	4.00	10.00
AH Adam Haluska	4.00	10.00
AL Acie Law	4.00	10.00
AT Al Thornton	4.00	10.00
ATU Alando Tucker	4.00	10.00
BW Brandan Wright	4.00	10.00
CL Carl Landry	4.00	10.00
DC Daequan Cook	4.00	10.00
DJS D.J. Strawberry	4.00	10.00
DM Dominic McGuire	4.00	10.00
DN Demetris Nichols	4.00	10.00
GD Glen Davis	6.00	15.00
GO Greg Oden	25.00	60.00
GP Gabe Pruitt	4.00	10.00
HH Herbert Hill	4.00	10.00
JC Javaris Crittenton	4.00	10.00
JD Jared Dudley	4.00	10.00
JDA Jermareo Davidson	4.00	10.00
JM Josh McRoberts	4.00	10.00
JS Jason Smith	4.00	10.00
MA Morris Almond	4.00	10.00
MB Marco Belinelli	4.00	10.00
NF Nick Fazekas	4.00	10.00
NY Nick Young	6.00	15.00
RS Rodney Stuckey	6.00	15.00
SH Spencer Hawes	4.00	10.00
SW Sean Williams	4.00	10.00
TG Taurean Green	4.00	10.00
TY Thaddeus Young	5.00	12.00
WC Wilson Chandler	6.00	15.00
YJ Yi Jianlian	6.00	15.00

1983-84 Topps M&M's Olympic Heroes

This 44-card boxed standard-sized set is an abridgment of the 99-card 1983 Topps History's Greatest Olympians set. Though widely known to have been produced by Topps, this company name is found nowhere on the cards. On a white card face, the fronts display either color or black-and-white photos framed by a white inner border and a red outer border. The top of the red outer border carries the olympiad number, year, and city, while the player's name is printed across the bottom of the front. Inside a light blue border, the back carry a headline and news brief in brown ink. The M&M's logo adorns both sides of the cards. The cards are numbered on the back; note that numbering differs completely from that of the larger set.

COMPLETE SET (44)	8.00	20.00
3 Bill Bradley	.50	1.25
33 Oscar Robertson	.60	1.50
42 Jerry West	.75	2.00

1948 Topps Magic Photos

The 1948 Topps Magic Photos set contains 252 small (approximately 7/8" by 1 7/16") individual cards featuring sport and non-sport subjects. They were issued in 19 lettered series with cards numbered within each series. The fronts were developed, much like a photograph, from a "blank" appearance by using moisture and sunlight. Due to varying degrees of photographic sensitivity, the clarity of these cards ranges from fully developed to poorly developed. This set contains Topps' first baseball cards. A premium album holding 126-cards was also issued. The set is sometimes confused with Topps' 1956 Hocus-Focus set, although the cards in this set are slightly smaller than those in the Hocus-Focus set. The checklist below is presented by series. Poorly developed cards are considered in lesser condition and hence have lesser value. The catalog designation for this set is R714-27. Each type of card subject has a letter prefix as follows: Boxing Champions (A), All-American Basketball (B), All-American Football (C), Wrestling Champions (D), Track and Field Champions (E), Stars of Stage and Screen (F), American Dogs (G), General Sports (H), Movie Stars (J), Baseball Hall of Fame (K), Aviation Pioneers (L), Famous Landmarks (M), American Inventors (N), American Military Leaders (O), American Explorers (P), Basketball Thrills (Q), Football Thrills (R), Figures of the Wild West (S), and General Sports (T).

COMPLETE SET (252)	3000.00	5000.00
B1 Ralph Beard	25.00	50.00
B2 Murray Weir	15.00	30.00
B3 Ed Macauley	40.00	80.00
B4 Kevin O'Shea	12.50	25.00
B5 Jim McIntyre	15.00	30.00
B6 Manhattan Beats Dartmouth	12.50	25.00

2006 Topps McDonald's All-American

COMPLETE SET (48)	12.00	30.00
B1 Earl Clark	1.00	2.50
B2 Mike Conley Jr.	1.50	4.00
B3 Jarvaris Crittenton	.75	2.00
B4 Wayne Ellington	.75	2.00
B5 Gerald Henderson	1.50	4.00
B6 Ty Lawson	1.50	4.00
B7 Vernon Macklin	.75	2.00
B8 Greg Oden	2.00	5.00
B9 Scottie Reynolds	.75	2.00
B10 Lance Thomas	.75	2.00
B11 Brandan Wright	.75	2.00
B12 Thaddeus Young	1.25	3.00
B13 Darrell Arthur	.75	2.00
B14 D.J. Augustin	1.00	2.50
B15 Chase Budinger	1.00	2.50
B16 Demond Carter	.75	2.00
B17 Sherron Collins	.75	2.00
B18 Daequan Cook	1.00	2.50
B19 Kevin Durant	5.00	12.00
B20 James Keefe	.75	2.00
B21 Spencer Hawes	1.00	2.50
B22 Brook Lopez	2.00	5.00
B23 Robin Lopez	1.25	3.00
B24 Jon Scheyer	.75	2.00
G1 Jessica Breland	.75	2.00
G2 Tina Charles	1.00	2.50
G3 Joy Cheek	.40	1.00
G4 Amber Harris	.75	2.00
G5 Ashley Houts	.40	1.00
G6 Kaili McLaren	.40	1.00
G7 Bridgette Mitchell	.40	1.00
G8 Porsha Phillips	.40	1.00
G9 Epiphanny Prince	.40	1.00
G10 Amber White	.75	2.00
G11 Danielle Wilson	.40	1.00
G12 Monica Wright	.75	2.00
G13 Jayne Appel	.40	1.00
G14 Jacki Gemelos	.40	1.00
G15 Michelle Harrison	.40	1.00
G16 Allison Hightower	.40	1.00
G17 Dela Quese Jernigan	.40	1.00
G18 Adrian McGowan	.40	1.00
G19 Morghan Medlock	.40	1.00
G20 Jordan Murphee	.40	1.00
G21 Abi Olajuwon	.75	2.00
G22 Brittainey Raven	.40	1.00
G23 Dymond Simon	.40	1.00
G24 Amanda Thompson	.75	2.00

2007 Topps McDonald's All-American

This 48-card set was distributed in box set form and features action photos of both the men's and women's All-American team.

COMPLETE SET (48)	30.00	80.00
AB Angie Bjorklund W	.40	1.00
AC Ashley Cimino W	.40	1.00
AF Austin Freeman	.75	2.00
AJ Alison Jackson W	.40	1.00
AJ2 Amy Jaeschke W	.40	1.00
BG Blake Griffin	10.00	25.00
CA Cole Aldrich	1.25	3.00
CD Cetera DeGraffenrein W	.40	1.00
CS Corey Stokes	.75	2.00
CW Chris Wright	.75	2.00
DG Donte Greene	1.25	3.00
DM Drey Mingo W	.40	1.00
DP Devereaux Peters W	.40	1.00
DR Derrick Rose	10.00	25.00
EG Eric Gordon	2.50	6.00
EM Erica Morrow W	.40	1.00
GL Gani Lawal	.75	2.00
IL Italee Lucas W	.40	1.00
JA James Anderson	1.50	4.00
JB Jerryd Bayless	1.25	3.00
JF Jonny Flynn	2.00	5.00
JH James Harden	2.50	6.00
JJH J.J. Hickson	1.00	2.50
JL Jai Lucas	.75	2.00
JL2 Jantel Lavender W	.40	1.00
JP Jeanette Pohlen W	.40	1.00
JT Jasmine Thomas W	.40	1.00
KC Kelley Cain W	.40	1.00
KK Kosta Koufos	.75	2.00
KL Kevin Love	3.00	8.00
KP Kayla Pedersen W	.50	1.25
KR Khadijah Rushdan W	.40	1.00
KS Kyle Singler	.75	2.00
KT Krystal Thomas W	.40	1.00
LD Lorin Dixon W	.40	1.00
LS Lenita Sanford W	.40	1.00
MB Michael Beasley	4.00	10.00
MM Maya Moore W	2.00	5.00
MS Marah Strickland W	.40	1.00
NC Nick Calathes	.75	2.00
NS Nolan Smith	2.00	5.00
OM O.J. Mayo	3.00	8.00
PP Patrick Patterson	1.50	4.00
SG Stefanie Galbreath W	.40	1.00
TK Taylor King	.75	2.00
TP Ta'Shia Phillips W	.40	1.00
TW Tyra White W	.40	1.00
VB Victoria Baugh W	.40	1.00

2008 Topps McDonald's All-American

This 48-card set was distributed in box set form and features action photos of both the men's and women's All-American team.

COMPLETE SET (48)	25.00	60.00
AB Alyssia Brewer W	.40	1.00
AC Ashley Corral W	.40	1.00
AD Ayana Dunning W	.40	1.00
AFA Al-Farouq Aminu	1.25	3.00
AG Ashley Gayle W	.40	1.00
AG Amber Gray W	.40	1.00
AM Alicia Manning W	.40	1.00
AS April Sykes W	.40	1.00
BG Briana Gilbreath W	.40	1.00
BJ Brandon Jennings	4.00	10.00
BJM B.J. Mullens	.75	2.00
BP Brooklyn Pope W	.40	1.00
CL Chelsea Lee W	.40	1.00
CS Chay Shegog W	.40	1.00
CS Chris Singleton	2.00	5.00
DD DeMar DeRozan	2.00	5.00
DH Destiny Hughes W	.40	1.00
ED Ed Davis	3.00	8.00
EDD Elena Delle Donna W	.40	1.00
EW Elliot Williams	1.25	3.00
GJ Glory Johnson W	.40	1.00
GM Greg Monroe	2.50	6.00
IS Iman Shumpert	2.50	6.00
JD Jasmine Dixon W	.40	1.00
JG JaMychal Green	1.00	2.50
JH Jrue Holiday	3.00	8.00
KW Kemba Walker	6.00	15.00
LB Luke Babbitt	1.25	3.00
LD Larry Drew II	1.00	2.50
LK Lynetta Kizer W	.40	1.00
LSB LaSondra Barrett W	.40	1.00
MD Michael Dunigan	.75	2.00
ML Malcolm Lee	.75	2.00
MR Michael Rosario	.75	2.00
NO Nnemkadi Ogwumike W	.40	1.00
NS Nikki Speed W	.40	1.00
SH Scotty Hopson	1.25	3.00
SJ Shenise Johnson W	.40	1.00
SL Sylven Landesberg	1.25	3.00
SP Samantha Prahalis W	.40	1.00
SS Shekinna Stricklen W	.40	1.00
SS Samardo Samuels	1.25	3.00
SW She'la White W	.40	1.00
TE Tyreke Evans	6.00	15.00
TH Tiffany Hayes W	.40	1.00
TZ Tyler Zeller	.75	2.00
WB William Buford	.75	2.00
WW Willie Warren	.75	2.00

2005-06 Topps NBA Collector Chips

COMPLETE SET (110)	80.00	160.00
1 Al Harrington	.60	1.50
2 Josh Smith	.75	2.00
3 Josh Childress	.60	1.50
4 Paul Pierce	1.00	2.50
5 Al Jefferson	.75	2.00
6 Antoine Walker	.60	1.50
7 Brevin Knight	.50	1.25
8 Primoz Brezec	.50	1.25
9 Emeka Okafor	.75	2.00
10 Luol Deng	.75	2.00
11 Kirk Hinrich	.75	2.00
12 Ben Gordon	.75	2.00
13 Drew Gooden	.60	1.50
14 LeBron James	4.00	10.00
15 Anderson Varejao	.60	1.50
16 Dirk Nowitzki	1.25	3.00
17 Michael Finley	.75	2.00
18 Josh Howard	.75	2.00
19 Carmelo Anthony	1.50	4.00
20 Andre Miller	.60	1.50
21 Kenyon Martin	.75	2.00
22 Ben Wallace	.75	2.00
23 Richard Hamilton	.60	1.50
24 Rasheed Wallace	.75	2.00
25 Troy Murphy	.60	1.50
26 Jason Richardson	.75	2.00
27 Baron Davis	.75	2.00
28 Tracy McGrady	1.00	2.50
29 Yao Ming	1.00	2.50
30 Bob Sura	.50	1.25
31 Jermaine O'Neal	.75	2.00
32 Stephen Jackson	.60	1.50
33 Ron Artest	.75	2.00
34 Elton Brand	.75	2.00
35 Shaun Livingston	.50	1.25
36 Corey Maggette	.60	1.50
37 Kobe Bryant	4.00	10.00
38 Caron Butler	.75	2.00
39 Lamar Odom	.75	2.00
40 Pau Gasol	.75	2.00
41 Shane Battier	.60	1.50
42 Mike Miller	.75	2.00
43 Dwyane Wade	2.00	5.00
44 Shaquille O'Neal	1.50	4.00
45 Udonis Haslem	.60	1.50
46 Maurice Williams	.60	1.50
47 Desmond Mason	.50	1.25
48 Michael Redd	.75	2.00
49 Wally Szczerbiak	.60	1.50
50 Latrell Sprewell	.60	1.50
51 Kevin Garnett	1.50	4.00
52 Vince Carter	1.25	3.00
53 Jason Kidd	1.25	3.00
54 Richard Jefferson	.75	2.00
55 J.R. Smith	.75	2.00
56 Jamaal Magloire	.50	1.25
57 Dan Dickau	.50	1.25
58 Jamal Crawford	.60	1.50
59 Stephon Marbury	.60	1.50
60 Trevor Ariza	.50	1.25
61 Grant Hill	1.00	2.50
62 Steve Francis	.75	2.00
63 Dwight Howard	1.50	4.00
64 Allen Iverson	1.25	3.00
65 Andre Iguodala	.75	2.00
66 Chris Webber	.75	2.00
67 Shawn Marion	.75	2.00
68 Amare Stoudemire	.75	2.00
69 Steve Nash	1.00	2.50
70 Zach Randolph	.60	1.50
71 Sebastian Telfair	.60	1.50
72 Darius Miles	.50	1.25
73 Peja Stojakovic	.75	2.00
74 Brad Miller	.75	2.00
75 Mike Bibby	.75	2.00
76 Tony Parker	.75	2.00
77 Tim Duncan	1.25	3.00
78 Manu Ginobili	.75	2.00
79 Rashard Lewis	.75	2.00
80 Ray Allen	.75	2.00
81 Luke Ridnour	.60	1.50
82 Morris Peterson	.50	1.25
83 Chris Bosh	.75	2.00
84 Jalen Rose	.75	2.00
85 Carlos Boozer	.75	2.00
86 Mehmet Okur	.50	1.25
87 Andrei Kirilenko	.60	1.50
88 Gilbert Arenas	.75	2.00
89 Antawn Jamison	.75	2.00
90 Larry Hughes	.60	1.50
91 Andrew Bogut	1.25	3.00
92 Marvin Williams	1.00	2.50
93 Chris Paul	3.00	8.00
94 Deron Williams	2.00	5.00
95 Gerald Green	1.00	2.50
96 Wayne Simien	.75	2.00
97 Antoine Wright	.75	2.00
98 Martell Webster	.75	2.00
99 Channing Frye	1.00	2.50
100 Charlie Villanueva	1.00	2.50
101 Danny Granger	1.50	4.00
102 Chris Taft	.75	2.00
103 Raymond Felton	1.25	3.00
104 Monta Ellis	1.50	4.00
105 Sean May	.75	2.00
106 Joey Graham	.75	2.00
107 Rashad McCants	.75	2.00
108 Hakim Warrick	1.00	2.50
109 Julius Hodge	.75	2.00
110 Ike Diogu	.75	2.00

2005-06 Topps NBA Collector Chips 599

*1-110 BLUE FOIL: .6X TO 1.5X CHIP 599 HI
*1-10 GREEN FOIL: .75X TO 2X CHIP 599 HI
*1-50 RED FOIL: .5X TO 1.25X CHIP 599 HI

1 Al Jefferson	1.00	2.50
2 Allen Iverson	1.50	4.00
3 Amare Stoudemire	1.00	2.50
4 Andre Iguodala	1.00	2.50
5 Andrei Kirilenko	.75	2.00
6 Andrew Bogut	1.50	4.00
7 Antawn Jamison	1.00	2.50
8 Antoine Walker	.75	2.00
9 Antoine Wright	1.00	2.50
10 Baron Davis	1.00	2.50
11 Ben Wallace	1.00	2.50
12 Bill Walton	1.00	2.50
13 Bob Cousy	1.50	4.00
14 Bob Sura	.60	1.50
15 Brad Miller	1.00	2.50
16 Carlos Boozer	1.00	2.50
17 Carmelo Anthony	2.00	5.00
18 Caron Butler	1.00	2.50
19 Channing Frye	1.25	3.00
20 Charlie Villanueva	1.25	3.00
21 Chris Bosh	1.00	2.50
22 Chris Paul	4.00	10.00
23 Chris Taft	1.00	2.50
24 Chris Webber	1.00	2.50
25 Dan Dickau	.60	1.50
26 Danny Granger	2.00	5.00
27 Darius Miles	.60	1.50
28 Dave Cowens	1.00	2.50
29 Deron Williams	2.50	6.00
30 Dirk Nowitzki	1.50	4.00
31 Drazen Petrovic	1.00	2.50
32 Drew Gooden	.75	2.00
33 Dwight Howard	2.00	5.00
34 Dwyane Wade	2.50	6.00
35 Earl Monroe	1.00	2.50
36 Emeka Okafor	1.00	2.50
37 George Gervin	1.00	2.50
38 Gerald Green	1.25	3.00
39 Gilbert Arenas	1.00	2.50
40 Grant Hill	1.25	3.00
41 Hakim Warrick	1.25	3.00
42 Ike Diogu	1.00	2.50
43 Isiah Thomas	1.00	2.50
44 Jamaal Magloire	.60	1.50
45 Jamal Crawford	.75	2.00
46 Jason Richardson	1.00	2.50
47 Jermaine O'Neal	1.00	2.50
48 Jerry West	1.25	3.00
49 Joey Graham	1.00	2.50
50 John Havlicek	1.00	2.50
51 Josh Howard	1.00	2.50
52 Julius Erving	2.00	5.00
53 Julius Hodge	1.00	2.50
54 Kareem Abdul-Jabbar	1.50	4.00
55 Kevin Garnett	2.00	5.00
56 Kirk Hinrich	1.00	2.50
57 Kobe Bryant	5.00	12.00
58 Lamar Odom	1.00	2.50
59 Larry Bird	3.00	8.00
60 Larry Hughes	.75	2.00
61 Latrell Sprewell	.75	2.00
62 LeBron James	5.00	12.00
63 Luke Ridnour	.75	2.00
64 Luol Deng	1.00	2.50
65 Manu Ginobili	1.00	2.50
66 Martell Webster	1.00	2.50
67 Marvin Williams	1.25	3.00
68 Maurice Williams	.75	2.00
69 Michael Finley	1.00	2.50
70 Michael Redd	1.00	2.50
71 Monta Ellis	2.00	5.00
72 Morris Peterson	.60	1.50
73 Moses Malone	1.00	2.50
74 Oscar Robertson	1.00	2.50
75 Pau Gasol	1.00	2.50
76 Paul Pierce	1.25	3.00
77 Peja Stojakovic	1.00	2.50
78 Pete Maravich	6.00	15.00
79 Primoz Brezec	.60	1.50
80 Quentin Richardson	.75	2.00
81 Rashad McCants	1.00	2.50
82 Rashard Lewis	1.00	2.50
83 Rasheed Wallace	1.00	2.50
84 Ray Allen	1.00	2.50
85 Raymond Felton	1.50	4.00
86 Richard Jefferson	1.00	2.50
87 Richard Hamilton	.75	2.00
88 Rick Barry	1.00	2.50
89 Ron Artest	1.00	2.50
90 Sean May	1.00	2.50
91 Sebastian Telfair	.75	2.00
92 Shane Battier	.75	2.00
93 Shaquille O'Neal	2.00	5.00
94 Shaun Livingston	.60	1.50
95 Shawn Marion	1.00	2.50
96 Steve Francis	1.00	2.50
97 Steve Nash	1.25	3.00
98 Tim Duncan	1.50	4.00
99 Tracy McGrady	1.25	3.00
100 Trevor Ariza	.60	1.50
101 Troy Murphy	.75	2.00
102 Quentin Richardson	.75	2.00
103 Vince Carter	1.50	4.00
104 Walt Frazier	1.00	2.50
105 Wayne Simien	1.00	2.50
106 Willis Reed	1.00	2.50
107 Wilt Chamberlain	2.00	5.00
108 Yao Ming	1.25	3.00
109 Zach Randolph	.75	2.00
110 Zydrunas Ilgauskas	.75	2.00

2005-06 Topps NBA Collector Chips Autographs

PRINT RUN 100 SER.#'d SETS

1 Allen Iverson	60.00	120.00
2 Carmelo Anthony	30.00	60.00
3 Charlie Villanueva	10.00	25.00
4 Chris Taft	8.00	20.00
5 Emeka Okafor	15.00	40.00
6 Gerald Green	8.00	20.00
7 Hakim Warrick	10.00	25.00
8 Joey Graham	8.00	20.00
9 Rashad McCants	10.00	25.00
10 Raymond Felton	15.00	30.00
11 Wayne Simien	8.00	20.00

2005-06 Topps NBA Collector Chips Blue

1 LeBron James	5.00	12.00
2 Dirk Nowitzki	1.50	4.00
3 Carmelo Anthony	2.00	5.00
4 Ben Wallace	1.00	2.50
5 Tracy McGrady	1.25	3.00
6 Yao Ming	1.25	3.00
7 Jermaine O'Neal	1.00	2.50
8 Kobe Bryant	5.00	12.00
9 Dwyane Wade	2.50	6.00
10 Shaquille O'Neal	2.00	5.00
11 Kevin Garnett	2.00	5.00
12 Vince Carter	1.50	4.00
13 Jason Kidd	1.50	4.00
14 Stephon Marbury	.75	2.00

15 Steve Francis	1.00	2.50
16 Allen Iverson	1.50	4.00
17 Amare Stoudemire	1.00	2.50
18 Steve Nash	1.25	3.00
19 Ben Gordon	1.00	2.50
20 Tim Duncan	1.50	4.00
21 Manu Ginobili	1.00	2.50
22 Ray Allen	1.00	2.50
23 Emeka Okafor	1.00	2.50
24 Paul Pierce	1.25	3.00
25 Andrew Bogut	1.50	4.00
26 Marvin Williams	1.25	3.00
27 Chris Paul	4.00	10.00
28 Deron Williams	2.50	6.00
29 Gerald Green	1.25	3.00
30 Raymond Felton	1.50	4.00

2005-06 Topps NBA Collector Chips Green

1 LeBron James	6.00	15.00
2 Tracy McGrady	1.50	4.00
3 Steve Nash	1.50	4.00
4 Shaquille O'Neal	2.50	6.00
5 Tim Duncan	2.00	5.00
6 Dwyane Wade	3.00	8.00
7 Allen Iverson	2.00	5.00
8 Andrew Bogut	2.00	5.00
9 Marvin Williams	1.50	4.00
10 Chris Paul	5.00	12.00

2005-06 Topps NBA Collector Chips Red

1 Bill Russell	2.00	5.00
2 Wilt Chamberlain	2.00	5.00
3 Bob Cousy	1.50	4.00
4 Dave Cowens	1.00	2.50
5 Walt Frazier	1.00	2.50
6 John Havlicek	1.00	2.50
7 Earl Monroe	1.00	2.50
8 Oscar Robertson	1.00	2.50
9 Jerry West	1.25	3.00
10 Kareem Abdul-Jabbar	1.50	4.00
11 Moses Malone	1.00	2.50
12 George Gervin	1.00	2.50
13 Julius Erving	2.00	5.00
14 Drazen Petrovic	1.00	2.50
15 Pete Maravich	6.00	15.00
16 Larry Bird	3.00	8.00
17 Isiah Thomas	1.00	2.50
18 Rick Barry	1.00	2.50
19 Willis Reed	1.00	2.50
20 Bill Walton	1.00	2.50
21 Gilbert Arenas	1.00	2.50
22 Grant Hill	1.25	3.00
23 Zydrunas Ilgauskas	.75	2.00
24 Allen Iverson	1.50	4.00
25 Antawn Jamison	1.00	2.50
26 Jermaine O'Neal	1.00	2.50
27 Shaquille O'Neal	2.00	5.00
28 Paul Pierce	1.25	3.00
29 Dwyane Wade	2.50	6.00
30 Ben Wallace	1.00	2.50
31 Ray Allen	1.00	2.50
32 Tim Duncan	1.50	4.00
33 Kevin Garnett	2.00	5.00
34 Manu Ginobili	1.00	2.50
35 Rashard Lewis	1.00	2.50
36 Shawn Marion	1.00	2.50
37 Tracy McGrady	1.25	3.00
38 Yao Ming	1.25	3.00
39 Steve Nash	1.25	3.00
40 Dirk Nowitzki	1.50	4.00
41 Amare Stoudemire	1.00	2.50
42 LeBron James	5.00	12.00
43 Vince Carter	1.50	4.00
44 Kobe Bryant	5.00	12.00
45 Allen Iverson	1.50	4.00
46 Carmelo Anthony	2.00	5.00
47 Quentin Richardson	.75	2.00
48 Steve Nash	1.25	3.00
49 Josh Smith	1.00	2.50
50 Shawn Marion	1.00	2.50

1997-98 Topps O-Pee-Chee

Randomly inserted at a rate of one in three in Candian packs only, this 220-card set parallels the basic Topps set. The front and the back of the card looks identical, except an O-Pee-Chee logo replaces the normal Topps logo.

COMPLETE SET (220)	125.00	250.00
COMPLETE SERIES 1 (110)	50.00	100.00
COMPLETE SERIES 2 (110)	75.00	150.00
*OPC: 2.5X TO 6X BASE TOPPS HI		
123 Michael Jordan	25.00	60.00

1998-99 Topps O-Pee-Chee

Randomly inserted at a rate of one in three in Candian packs only, this 220-card set parallels the basic Topps set. The front and the back of the card looks identical, except an O-Pee-Chee logo replaces the normal Topps logo.

COMPLETE SET (220)	50.00	120.00
*OPC STARS: 2X TO 5X BASE TOPPS HI		
*OPC RCs: 1X TO 2.5X BASE TOPPS HI		

2001-02 Topps Pristine

Released in Mid April 2002, this 110-card set features 50 Veteran players and 20 different Rookies. Three versions of each rookie player were produced, a base version, an uncommon version, and a rare version. Base cards are standard size with full color player photos set against colored and patterned backgrounds with player name bars along the bottom of the card and the "TP" Topps Pristine circular logo in the upper left-hand corner. Player photos are embossed and printed on an all chromium card stock. SRP for packs was $25, and packs were released in a 3 in 1 format. The outer pack contains one Topps Pristine Refractor card in a sealed protective case. The middle pack conatins one Relic card and the third outer pack. The outer pack conatins four veteran cards plus two base rookie cards. One Jumbo pack is inserted as a box-topper which features playoff-used memorabilia, and the sealed versions were inserted at the rate of one per case.

COMPLETE SET (110)	150.00	300.00
COMP.SET w/o SP's (50)	30.00	80.00
1 Allen Iverson	2.00	5.00
2 Shawn Marion	1.00	2.50
3 Baron Davis	1.00	2.50
4 Peja Stojakovic	1.00	2.50
5 Dirk Nowitzki	1.50	4.00
6 Michael Jordan	8.00	25.00
7 Dikembe Mutombo	1.00	2.50
8 Antoine Walker	.75	2.00
9 David Robinson	1.50	4.00
10 Tracy McGrady	1.50	4.00
11 Rasheed Wallace	1.00	2.50
12 Kenyon Martin	1.00	2.50
13 Glenn Robinson	.75	2.00
14 Shareef Abdur-Rahim	.75	2.00
15 Lamar Odom	1.00	2.50
16 Alonzo Mourning	1.25	3.00
17 Latrell Sprewell	.75	2.00
18 Stephon Marbury	.75	2.00
19 Chris Webber	1.00	2.50
20 Darius Miles	.60	1.50
21 Tim Duncan	2.00	5.00
22 Antawn Jamison	1.00	2.50
23 Jason Kidd	1.50	4.00
24 John Stockton	1.25	3.00
25 Michael Finley	1.00	2.50
26 Eddie Jones	.75	2.00
27 Jamal Mashburn	.75	2.00
28 Paul Pierce	1.25	3.00
29 Jason Terry	1.00	2.50
30 Kobe Bryant	5.00	12.00
31 Reggie Miller	1.00	2.50
32 Elton Brand	1.00	2.50
33 Antonio McDyess	.75	2.00
34 Ray Allen	1.00	2.50
35 Kevin Garnett	2.00	5.00
36 Allan Houston	.75	2.00
37 Grant Hill	1.25	3.00
38 Jalen Rose	.75	2.00
39 Gary Payton	1.00	2.50
40 Vince Carter	1.50	4.00
41 Jerry Stackhouse	.75	2.00
42 Karl Malone	1.25	3.00
43 Wang Zhizhi	.75	2.00
44 Marcus Fizer	.60	1.50
45 Marcus Camby	.75	2.00
46 Andre Miller	.75	2.00
47 Jason Williams	.75	2.00
48 Hakeem Olajuwon	1.25	3.00
49 Shaquille O'Neal	2.50	6.00
50 Steve Francis	1.00	2.50
51 Eddie Griffin C RC	.75	2.00
52 Eddie Griffin U	1.00	2.50
53 Eddie Griffin R	1.50	4.00
54 Kwame Brown C RC	.75	2.00
55 Kwame Brown U	1.00	2.50
56 Kwame Brown R	1.50	4.00
57 Shane Battier C RC	1.50	4.00
58 Shane Battier U	2.00	5.00
59 Shane Battier R	3.00	8.00
60 Eddy Curry C RC	1.25	3.00
61 Eddy Curry U	1.50	4.00
62 Eddy Curry R	2.50	6.00
63 Tyson Chandler C RC	1.25	3.00
64 Tyson Chandler U	1.50	4.00
65 Tyson Chandler R	2.50	6.00
66 Rodney White C RC	.75	2.00
67 Rodney White U	1.00	2.50
68 Rodney White R	1.50	4.00
69 Jason Richardson C RC	1.50	4.00
70 Jason Richardson U	2.00	5.00
71 Jason Richardson R	3.00	8.00
72 Joe Johnson C RC	2.00	5.00
73 Joe Johnson U	2.50	6.00
74 Joe Johnson R	4.00	10.00
75 Pau Gasol C RC	2.50	6.00
76 Pau Gasol U	3.00	8.00
77 Pau Gasol R	5.00	12.00
78 Desagana Diop C RC	.75	2.00
79 Desagana Diop U	1.00	2.50
80 Desagana Diop R	1.50	4.00
81 Vladimir Radmanovic C RC	.75	2.00
82 Vladimir Radmanovic U	1.00	2.50
83 Vladimir Radmanovic R	1.50	4.00
84 Troy Murphy C RC	1.25	3.00
85 Troy Murphy U	1.50	4.00
86 Troy Murphy R	2.50	6.00
87 Zach Randolph C RC	2.00	5.00
88 Zach Randolph U	2.50	6.00
89 Zach Randolph R	4.00	10.00
90 Jamaal Tinsley C RC	1.00	2.50
91 Jamaal Tinsley U	1.25	3.00
92 Jamaal Tinsley R	2.00	5.00
93 Richard Jefferson C RC	1.50	4.00
94 Richard Jefferson U	2.00	5.00
95 Richard Jefferson R	3.00	8.00
96 Loren Woods C RC	.75	2.00
97 Loren Woods U	1.00	2.50
98 Loren Woods R	1.50	4.00
99 Joseph Forte C RC	.75	2.00
100 Joseph Forte U	1.00	2.50
101 Joseph Forte R	1.50	4.00
102 Gerald Wallace C RC	1.25	3.00
103 Gerald Wallace U	1.50	4.00
104 Gerald Wallace R	2.50	6.00
105 Andrei Kirilenko C RC	2.00	5.00
106 Andrei Kirilenko U	2.50	6.00
107 Andrei Kirilenko R	4.00	10.00
108 Tony Parker C RC	3.00	8.00
109 Tony Parker U	4.00	10.00
110 Tony Parker R	6.00	15.00

2001-02 Topps Pristine Refractors

Randomly inserted in packs, this set is divided up into 50 Veteran cards sequentially numbered to 50 and 20 Rookies. The rookie players appear on one card, starting from number 51, then every third card after that, so the set is skip numbered (51, 54, 57, 60, etc). All Refractor cards parallel the base card with a rainbow holofoil effect, and were issued sealed in plastic card holders.

*STARS: 6X TO 15X BASE CARD HI		
*RCs: 1X TO 2.5X BASE CARD HI		
*RC/750: 1.25X TO 3X BASE RC C VERSION		
*RCs/250: 2X TO 5X BASE RC C VERSION		
6 Michael Jordan	250.00	500.00

2001-02 Topps Pristine Autographs

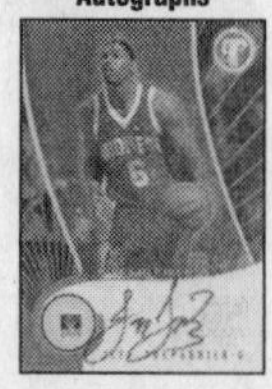

Randomly inserted in packs at the rate of one in four, this 32-card set features player photos on the top half of the card and a white space in the bottom right hand corner for player autographs. These cards also feature the rainbow holofoil refractor effect.

AAD Antonio Daniels	4.00	10.00
AAFM Aaron McKie	4.00	10.00
AAJ Antawn Jamison	6.00	15.00
AAM Andre Miller	5.00	12.00
ABD Baron Davis	8.00	20.00
ABH Brendan Haywood	5.00	12.00
ABJ Bobby Jackson	5.00	12.00
ACB Chauncey Billups	8.00	20.00
ADB Damone Brown	4.00	10.00
ADH Donnell Harvey	4.00	10.00
ADM Desmond Mason	4.00	10.00
AEB Elton Brand	6.00	15.00
AEC Eddy Curry	6.00	15.00
AGA Gilbert Arenas	20.00	50.00
AHT Hedo Turkoglu	6.00	15.00
AIT Iakovos Tsakalidis	4.00	10.00
AJB Jonathan Bender	4.00	10.00
AJF Joseph Forte	4.00	10.00
AJJ Joe Johnson	10.00	25.00
AJO Jermaine O'Neal	8.00	20.00
AJT Jason Terry	5.00	12.00
AJTR Jeff Trepagnier	4.00	10.00
AKAJ Kareem Abdul-Jabbar	50.00	120.00
AKB Kwame Brown	6.00	15.00
AKBR Kedrick Brown	4.00	10.00
AKS Kenny Satterfield	4.00	10.00
ALW Loren Woods	4.00	10.00
AMB Mike Bibby	5.00	12.00
AMJ Marc Jackson	4.00	10.00
APS Peja Stojakovic	8.00	20.00
ARH Richard Hamilton	8.00	20.00
ARJ Richard Jefferson	8.00	20.00
ARL Raef LaFrentz	4.00	10.00
ASB Shane Battier	8.00	20.00
ASM Shawn Marion	6.00	15.00
ASO Shaquille O'Neal	40.00	100.00
ATD Tim Duncan	100.00	225.00
ATMU Troy Murphy	6.00	15.00
AZR Zach Randolph	12.50	30.00

2001-02 Topps Pristine Oversized Relics

Randomly inserted at the rate of one per box, these jumbo cards feature player action photos set against a silver foil background. The cards also contain the NBA logo where "Jerry West" has been replaced with a jersey swatch.

BLAH Allan Houston	4.00	10.00
BLAI Allen Iverson	10.00	25.00
BLAM Alonzo Mourning	6.00	15.00
BLCM Cuttino Mobley	4.00	10.00
BLDM Dikembe Mutombo	5.00	12.00
BLDN Dirk Nowitzki	8.00	20.00
BLDR David Robinson	8.00	20.00
BLDW David Wesley	3.00	8.00
BLGR Glenn Robinson	4.00	10.00
BLJK Jason Kidd	8.00	20.00
BLJS Jerry Stackhouse	4.00	10.00
BLJHS John Stockton	6.00	15.00
BLKM Karl Malone	6.00	15.00
BLLO Lamar Odom	5.00	12.00
BLLS Latrell Sprewell	4.00	10.00
BLRH Richard Hamilton	4.00	10.00
BLRW Rasheed Wallace	5.00	12.00
BLTD Tim Duncan	10.00	25.00

2001-02 Topps Pristine Partners

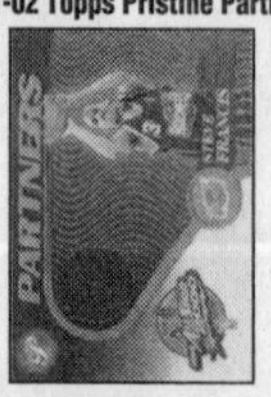

Randomly seeded in packs at the rate of one in 11, this nine card set features full color player photos on the right side, colorful backgrounds, the word "Partners" along the top, and a circular swatch of a warm-up used by the featured player in the NBA All-Star 2-Ball competition.

PAAH Allan Houston	2.50	6.00
PACM Cuttino Mobley	2.50	6.00
PADF Derek Fisher	2.50	6.00
PAGH Grant Hill	4.00	10.00
PAJW Jason Williams	2.50	6.00
PARH Richard Hamilton	2.50	6.00
PASF Steve Francis	3.00	8.00
PATL Trajan Langdon	2.00	5.00
PATM Tracy McGrady	5.00	12.00

2001-02 Topps Pristine Portions

Randomly inserted in packs at the rate of one in three, this 18-card set features a horizontal design where a parobolic line that runs diagonally from the top right hand corner to the bottom left hand corner divides the card between black background on the left and gray background on the right. Full color player photos appear on the left, the word "Portions" appears along the top in white, and a swach of game worn relic in the upper left hand corner.

PPAM Alonzo Mourning	4.00	10.00
PPDM Dikembe Mutombo	3.00	8.00
PPDN Dirk Nowitzki	5.00	12.00
PPEJ Eddie Jones	2.50	6.00
PPGP Gary Payton	3.00	8.00
PPJK Jason Kidd	5.00	12.00
PPJP James Posey	2.00	5.00
PPMB Mike Bibby	3.00	8.00
PPMC Mateen Cleaves	2.00	5.00
PPMD Michael Dickerson	2.00	5.00
PPMO Michael Olowokandi	2.00	5.00
PPRD Ricky Davis	2.50	6.00
PPRH Richard Hamilton	2.50	6.00
PPSJ Stephen Jackson	2.50	6.00
PPSO Shaquille O'Neal	8.00	20.00
PPTD Tim Duncan	6.00	15.00
PPTM Todd MacCulloch	2.00	5.00
PPTP Terry Porter	2.00	5.00

2001-02 Topps Pristine Premier

Seeded in packs at the rate of one in six, this 14-card set features dark backgrounds with player photos on the left, the words Pristine Premier along the bottom, and a star-shaped swatch of a jersey worn in these player's first All-Star game appearances.

PRAD Antonio Davis	2.50	6.00
PRAH Allan Houston	3.00	8.00
PRAI Allen Iverson	8.00	20.00
PRAM Anthony Mason	2.50	6.00
PRAKM Antonio McDyess	3.00	8.00
PRDD Dale Davis	2.50	6.00
PRGR Glenn Robinson	3.00	8.00
PRJS Jerry Stackhouse	3.00	8.00
PRMF Michael Finley	4.00	10.00
PRRA Ray Allen	4.00	10.00
PRRW Rasheed Wallace	4.00	10.00
PRSM Stephon Marbury	3.00	8.00
PRTM Tracy McGrady	6.00	15.00
PRVD Vlade Divac	3.00	8.00

2001-02 Topps Pristine Slice of a Star

Randomly inserted in packs at the rate of one in three, this 18-card set features full color player photos on the left, the words "Slice of a Star" along the top in blue, and a diamond shaped swatch of a game worn relic on the right.

SAI Allen Iverson	6.00	15.00
SAM Alonzo Mourning	4.00	10.00
SBS Bob Sura	2.00	5.00
SCW Chris Webber	3.00	8.00
SDR David Robinson	5.00	12.00
SEJ Eddie Jones	2.50	6.00
SGH Grant Hill	4.00	10.00
SGP Gary Payton	3.00	8.00
SJDS Jerry Stackhouse	2.50	6.00
SJS John Stockton	4.00	10.00
SLH Larry Hughes	2.50	6.00
SLO Lamar Odom	3.00	8.00
SMF Michael Finley	3.00	8.00
SRA Ray Allen	3.00	8.00
SRM Reggie Miller	4.00	10.00
SSO Shaquille O'Neal	8.00	20.00
STD Tim Duncan	6.00	15.00
STP Terry Porter	2.00	5.00

2001-02 Topps Pristine Sweat and Tears

Randomly inserted in packs at the rate of one in eight, this 50-card set features full color player action photos on the right side, colorful backgrounds, and a swatch of a playoff game-used towel which is cut in the shape of the letter S.

CHBD Baron Davis	12.00	30.00
CHDC Derrick Coleman	10.00	25.00
CHDW David Wesley	8.00	20.00
CHEC Elden Campbell	8.00	20.00
CHER Eddie Robinson	8.00	20.00
CHJM Jamal Mashburn	10.00	25.00
CHJDM Jamaal Magloire	8.00	20.00
CHPB P.J. Brown	8.00	20.00
DMCB Calvin Booth	8.00	20.00
DMDN Dirk Nowitzki	20.00	50.00
DMHE Howard Eisley	8.00	20.00
DMJH Juwan Howard	10.00	25.00
DMMF Michael Finley	12.00	30.00
DMSB Shawn Bradley	8.00	20.00
DMSN Steve Nash	15.00	40.00
DMWZ Wang Zhizhi	10.00	25.00
IPAC Austin Croshere	8.00	20.00
IPAH Al Harrington	10.00	25.00
IPJB Jonathan Bender	8.00	20.00
IPJO Jermaine O'Neal	12.00	30.00
IPJR Jalen Rose	10.00	25.00
IPRM Reggie Miller	12.00	30.00
IPTB Travis Best	8.00	20.00
MBEJ Ervin Johnson	8.00	20.00
MBGR Glenn Robinson	10.00	25.00
MBJP Joel Przybilla	8.00	20.00
MBRA Ray Allen	12.00	30.00
MBSC Sam Cassell	10.00	25.00
MBTT Tim Thomas	8.00	20.00
OMAD Andrew DeClercq	8.00	20.00
OMBO Bo Outlaw	8.00	20.00
OMDA Darrell Armstrong	8.00	20.00
OMMM Mike Miller	12.00	30.00
OMPG Pat Garrity	8.00	20.00
OMTM Tracy McGrady	20.00	50.00
PSCR Clifford Robinson	8.00	20.00
PSDS Daniel Santiago	8.00	20.00
PSIT Iakovos Tsakalidis	8.00	20.00
PSJK Jason Kidd	20.00	50.00
PSRR Rodney Rogers	8.00	20.00
PSSM Shawn Marion	12.00	30.00
PSTD Tony Delk	8.00	20.00
PSTG Tom Gugliotta	8.00	20.00
SSAD Antonio Daniels	8.00	20.00
SSAJ Avery Johnson	10.00	25.00
SSDA Derek Anderson	8.00	20.00
SSDR David Robinson	20.00	50.00
SSSE Sean Elliott	8.00	20.00
SSTD Tim Duncan	25.00	60.00
SSTP Terry Porter	8.00	20.00

2001-02 Topps Pristine Team Topps Captain Oversized

Inserted one card per case this is a four by six inch card with a game-used piece of memorabilia.

CLSO Shaquille O'Neal	15.00	40.00
CLTD Tim Duncan	12.00	30.00

2002-03 Topps Pristine

Released in January 2003, Topps Pristine followed in the footsteps of last year's set by once again utilizing the pack-in-a-pack-in-a-pack set up. Each pack conatined the following: Pack #1-one uncirculated refractor or relic refractor encased in plastic with a hologram seal on the end to prevent tampering. Pack #2-one game-used relic card. Pack #3-four veterans, two rookies and randomly inserted autograph cards. Veteran cards comprise the first 50 cards in the set. Rookie players appear on cards 51-125. Three versions of each rookie player were issued, the Common version, which is the actual RC card, an Uncommon version sequentially numbered to 1499 and a Rare version sequentially numbered to 499. Pristine was packaged where each box contained five tri-packs and the packs carried a suggested retail price of $30. Note that an Amare Stoudemire error card was discovered. This card appears to be the same as his base Common RC card but on the back contains the words, "Gold Refractor." It is unknown how many error versions were released, but initial reports place it as a low number.

COMP.SET w/o SP's (50)	20.00	50.00
1 Shaquille O'Neal	1.50	4.00
2 Steve Nash	.75	2.00
3 Vince Carter	1.00	2.50
4 Michael Jordan	5.00	12.00
5 Chris Webber	.60	1.50
6 Tim Duncan	1.25	3.00
7 Vladimir Radmanovic	.40	1.00
8 Kobe Bryant	3.00	8.00
9 Allan Houston	.50	1.25
10 Tracy McGrady	1.00	2.50
11 Allen Iverson	1.00	2.50
12 Scottie Pippen	1.00	2.50
13 Steve Francis	.60	1.50
14 Reggie Miller	.60	1.50
15 Antoine Walker	.50	1.25
16 Shawn Marion	.60	1.50
17 Wally Szczerbiak	.50	1.25
18 Elton Brand	.60	1.50
19 Jerry Stackhouse	.50	1.25
20 Andre Miller	.50	1.25
21 Gary Payton	.60	1.50
22 Richard Hamilton	.50	1.25
23 Pau Gasol	.75	2.00
24 Juwan Howard	.50	1.25
25 Jalen Rose	.50	1.25
26 Eddie Jones	.50	1.25
27 Baron Davis	.60	1.50
28 Darrell Armstrong	.40	1.00
29 John Stockton	.75	2.00
30 Mike Bibby	.60	1.50
31 Eddy Curry	.50	1.25
32 Kevin Garnett	1.25	3.00
33 Dikembe Mutombo	.60	1.50
34 Jason Kidd	1.00	2.50
35 Clifford Robinson	.40	1.00
36 Ray Allen	.60	1.50
37 Paul Pierce	.75	2.00
38 Shane Battier	.60	1.50
39 Kenyon Martin	.60	1.50
40 Rasheed Wallace	.60	1.50
41 Latrell Sprewell	.50	1.25
42 Cuttino Mobley	.50	1.25
43 Karl Malone	.75	2.00
44 Dirk Nowitzki	1.00	2.50
45 Antawn Jamison	.60	1.50
46 Elden Campbell	.40	1.00
47 Lamar Odom	.60	1.50
48 Jason Richardson	.60	1.50
49 Jermaine O'Neal	.60	1.50
50 Shareef Abdur-Rahim	.50	1.25
51 Yao Ming C RC	5.00	12.00
52 Yao Ming U	6.00	15.00
53 Yao Ming R	12.00	30.00
54 Jay Williams C RC	2.00	5.00
55 Jay Williams U	2.50	6.00
56 Jay Williams R	5.00	12.00
57 Mike Dunleavy C RC	2.00	5.00
58 Mike Dunleavy U	2.50	6.00
59 Mike Dunleavy R	5.00	12.00
60 Drew Gooden C RC	2.50	6.00
61 Drew Gooden U	3.00	8.00
62 Drew Gooden R	6.00	15.00
63 Nikoloz Tskitishvili C RC	1.50	4.00
64 Nikoloz Tskitishvili U	2.00	5.00
65 Nikoloz Tskitishvili R	4.00	10.00
66 DaJuan Wagner C RC	1.50	4.00
67 DaJuan Wagner U	2.00	5.00
68 DaJuan Wagner R	4.00	10.00
69 Nene Hilario C RC	2.00	5.00
70 Nene Hilario U	2.50	6.00
71 Nene Hilario R	5.00	12.00
72 Chris Wilcox C RC	1.50	4.00
73 Chris Wilcox U	2.00	5.00
74 Chris Wilcox R	4.00	10.00
75 Amare Stoudemire C RC	4.00	10.00
75A Amare Stoudemire ERR Gold Refractor appears on back		
76 Amare Stoudemire U	5.00	12.00
77 Amare Stoudemire R	10.00	25.00
78 Caron Butler C RC	2.50	6.00
79 Caron Butler U	3.00	8.00
80 Caron Butler R	6.00	15.00
81 Jared Jeffries C RC	1.50	4.00
82 Jared Jeffries U	2.00	5.00
83 Jared Jeffries R	4.00	10.00
84 Melvin Ely C RC	1.50	4.00
85 Melvin Ely U	2.00	5.00
86 Melvin Ely R	4.00	10.00
87 Marcus Haislip C RC	1.50	4.00
88 Marcus Haislip U	2.00	5.00
89 Marcus Haislip R	4.00	10.00
90 Fred Jones C RC	1.50	4.00
91 Fred Jones U	2.00	5.00
92 Fred Jones R	4.00	10.00
93 Casey Jacobsen C RC	1.50	4.00
94 Casey Jacobsen U	2.00	5.00
95 Casey Jacobsen R	4.00	10.00
96 John Salmons C RC	2.00	5.00
97 John Salmons U	2.50	6.00
98 John Salmons R	5.00	12.00
99 Juan Dixon C RC	2.00	5.00
100 Juan Dixon U	2.50	6.00
101 Juan Dixon R	5.00	12.00
102 Chris Jefferies C RC	1.50	4.00
103 Chris Jefferies U	2.00	5.00
104 Chris Jefferies R	4.00	10.00
105 Ryan Humphrey C RC	1.50	4.00
106 Ryan Humphrey U	2.00	5.00
107 Ryan Humphrey R	4.00	10.00
108 Kareem Rush C RC	1.50	4.00
109 Kareem Rush U	2.00	5.00
110 Kareem Rush R	4.00	10.00
111 Qyntel Woods C RC	1.50	4.00
112 Qyntel Woods U	2.00	5.00
113 Qyntel Woods R	4.00	10.00
114 Frank Williams C RC	1.50	4.00
115 Frank Williams U	2.00	5.00
116 Frank Williams R	4.00	10.00
117 Tayshaun Prince C RC	2.00	5.00
118 Tayshaun Prince U	2.50	6.00
119 Tayshaun Prince R	5.00	12.00
120 Carlos Boozer C RC	3.00	8.00
121 Carlos Boozer U	4.00	10.00
122 Carlos Boozer R	8.00	20.00
123 Dan Dickau C RC	1.50	4.00
124 Dan Dickau U	2.00	5.00
125 Dan Dickau R	4.00	10.00

2002-03 Topps Pristine Refractors

Randomly seeded in #1 packs, this 125-card set parallels the base set enhanced with the rainbow holofoil refractor effect. Cards numbers 1-50 are sequentially numbered to 50 and the rookie player cards breakdown as follows: Common rookie refractors are un-numbered, Uncommon rookie refractors are sequentially numbered to 499, and Rare rookie refractors are sequentially numbered to 99. Every refractor is encased and sealed with the hologram Topps sticker.

*STARS: 10X TO 25X BASE CARD HI
*RC's/1899: 1X TO 2X BASE RC C VER. HI
*RC's/499: 1.25X TO 3X BASE RC C VER. HI
*RC's/99: 2.5X TO 6X BASE RC C VER. HI

2002-03 Topps Pristine Refractors Gold

Randomly inserted in Hobby boxes as a topper, this 125-card set parallels the base Topps Pristine set enhanced with gold background and die-cutting. Each card is segentially numbered to 99.

*STARS: 5X TO 12X BASE CARD HI
*C RCs: 2.5X TO 6X BASE CARD HI
*U RCs: 2X TO 5X BASE CARD HI
*R RCs: 1X TO 2.5X BASE CARD HI

2002-03 Topps Pristine Personal Endorsements

Randomly inserted into pack #3, this 235-card set showcases a horizontal design with player photos on the left, a gray-scale portrait photo in the upper right-hand corner and a white-out background in the lower right-hand corner for player autographs. Each card is stamped with the "Topps Certified Autograph Issue" foil.

PEBJ Bobby Jackson	4.00	10.00
PEBN Bostjan Nachbar	4.00	10.00
PECJ Chris Jefferies	4.00	10.00
PECM Corey Maggette	4.00	10.00
PECW Chris Wilcox	4.00	10.00
PEDD Dan Dickau	4.00	10.0
PEDG Drew Gooden	6.00	15.0
PEDW DaJuan Wagner	4.00	10.0
PEFJ Fred Jones	4.00	10.0
PEFW Frank Williams	4.00	10.0
PEGA Gilbert Arenas	10.00	25.0
PEGW Gerald Wallace	6.00	15.0
PEJF Joseph Forte	4.00	10.0
PEJJ Joe Johnson	5.00	12.0
PEKB Kwame Brown	5.00	12.0
PEKD Keyon Dooling	4.00	10.0
PEKR Kareem Rush	4.00	10.0
PELP Lavor Postell	4.00	10.0
PELW Loren Woods	4.00	10.0
PEMD Mike Dunleavy	5.00	12.0
PEME Melvin Ely	4.00	10.0
PERJ Richard Jefferson	6.00	15.0
PESO Shaquille O'Neal	30.00	80.0
PETP Tayshaun Prince	5.00	12.0
PEYM Yao Ming	30.00	60.0

2002-03 Topps Pristine Popula Demand

Randomly inserted in pack #2, this 18-card set is designed horizontally and on a blue and green foil background. Full color player photos are set on the right and a swatch of game worn memorabilia appears on the left. A Refractor version encased in the Topps Uncirculated slab was inserted into #1 packs and card are sequentially numbered to 25.

*REF: 1.5X TO 4X HI		
PDAI Allen Iverson	5.00	12.0
PDBD Baron Davis	3.00	8.0
PDCW Chris Webber	3.00	8.0
PDDM Darius Miles	2.00	5.0
PDDN Dirk Nowitzki	5.00	12.0
PDDR David Robinson	5.00	12.0
PDJK Jason Kidd	5.00	12.0
PDJO Jermaine O'Neal	3.00	8.0
PDKA Kareem Abdul Jabbar	10.00	25.0
PDKG Kevin Garnett	6.00	15.0
PDKM Karl Malone	4.00	10.0
PDMB Mike Bibby	3.00	8.0
PDRA Ray Allen	3.00	8.0
PDSF Steve Francis	3.00	8.0
PDSM Shawn Marion	3.00	8.0
PDSO Shaquille O'Neal	8.00	20.0
PDTD Tim Duncan	6.00	15.0
PDTM Tracy McGrady	5.00	12.0

2002-03 Topps Pristine Patche

Randomly inserted in pack #2, this 19-card set places full-color player action photos on the left side with the background set to look like a quilt on the right side. A hexagonal swatch of a uniform patch appears on the right.

PPAAI Allen Iverson	20.00	50.0
PPADM Darius Miles	8.00	20.0
PPAJO Jermaine O'Neal	12.00	30.0
PPAJR Jason Richardson	12.00	30.0
PPAKM Kenyon Martin	12.00	30.0
PPAMD Mike Dunleavy	15.00	40.0
PPAMM Mike Miller	12.00	30.0
PPAPG Pau Gasol	15.00	40.0
PPAPS Predrag Savovic	12.00	30.0
PPAPS Peja Stojakovic	20.00	50.0
PPAQR Quentin Richardson	10.00	25.0
PPARA Ray Allen	12.00	30.0
PPASB Shane Battier	12.00	30.0
PPASN Steve Nash	15.00	40.0
PPASO Shaquille O'Neal	30.00	80.0
PPASS Steve Smith	10.00	25.0
PPATD Tim Duncan	25.00	60.0

2002-03 Topps Pristine Performance

Randomly seeded in #2 packs, this 14-card set places player action photos to the right of a swatch of game-worn memorabilia. The memorabilia is set and centered on a printed basketball. A Refractor version encased in the Topps Uncirculated slab was inserted into #1 packs and cards are sequentially numbered to 25.

*REF: 1.5X TO 4X HI		
PPEAW Antoine Walker	2.50	6.0
PPEBD Baron Davis	3.00	8.0
PPEBH Brendan Haywood	2.00	5.0
PPECM Cuttino Mobley	2.50	6.0
PPEEN Eduardo Najera	2.00	5.0
PPEGA Gilbert Arenas	3.00	8.0
PPEJM Jamal Mashburn	2.50	6.0
PPEKM Kenyon Martin	3.00	8.0
PPELN Lee Nailon	2.00	5.0
PPENV Nick Van Exel	2.50	6.0
PPEQR Quentin Richardson	2.50	6.0
PPESM Stephon Marbury	2.50	6.0

'ESO Shaquille O'Neal 8.00 20.00
'ETD Tim Duncan 6.00 15.00

002-03 Topps Pristine Portions

serted randomly in #2 packs, this 21-card set utilizes
horizontal design with a centered swatch of game-
ed memorabilia. The words Pristine and Portions run
m the upper left corner down to the lower right and
nnect in the center around the memorabilia swatch.
e backgrounds on these cards are silver, blue and
een, and a full-color player action shot is set on the
ht. A Refractor version encased in the Topps
circulated slab was inserted into #1 packs and cards
e sequentially numbered to 25.

EF: 1.5X TO 4X HI
POAH Allan Houston 2.50 6.00
POCM Cuttino Mobley 2.50 6.00
POCW Chris Webber 3.00 8.00
PODG Devean George 2.00 5.00
PODJ DerMarr Johnson 2.00 5.00
POGR Glenn Robinson 2.50 6.00
POJO Jermaine O'Neal 3.00 8.00
POJT Jason Terry 2.50 6.00
POKM Kenyon Martin 3.00 8.00
POLO Lamar Odom 3.00 8.00
POMM Mike Miller 3.00 8.00
POMO Michael Olowokandi 2.00 5.00
POPS Peja Stojakovic 3.00 8.00
PORL Raef LaFrentz 2.00 5.00
POSB Shawn Bradley 2.00 5.00
POSM Shawn Marion 3.00 8.00
POSS Steve Smith 2.50 6.00
POTD Tim Duncan 6.00 15.00
POTG Tom Gugliotta 2.00 5.00
POVD Vlade Divac 2.50 6.00
POAHA Anfernee Hardaway 5.00 12.00

2002-03 Topps Pristine Rookie Club

ndomly seeded in #2 packs, this 11-card set features
horizontal design with the new rookie player set to a
ckground that features his team's logo and a swatch
memorabilia. A Refractor version encased in the
pps Uncirculated slab was inserted into #1 packs
d cards are sequentially numbered to 25.

EF: 1.25X TO 3X HI
CAS Amare Stoudemire 6.00 15.00
CCB Caron Butler 4.00 10.00
CCW Chris Wilcox 2.50 6.00
CDG Drew Gooden 4.00 10.00
CDW DaJuan Wagner 2.50 6.00
CFJ Fred Jones 2.50 6.00
CKR Kareem Rush 2.50 6.00
CMD Mike Dunleavy 3.00 8.00
CME Melvin Ely 2.50 6.00
CPS Predrag Savovic 2.50 6.00
CYM Yao Ming 8.00 20.00

2003-04 Topps Pristine

eleased in December 2003, Pristine boasts a 199-
rd set divided up into 100 veteran player cards and
rookie player cards. The cards alternate where each
ayer has three cards in a row and the first card is the
mmon, also the rookie card, the second is
common sequentially numbered to 999 and the third
rare and sequentially numbered to 499. Pristine was
ckaged five packs per box where each pack
ntained three individual packs and cards were
serted as follows: Pack one (the outermost pack)
ntains one uncirculated Refractor, Relic Refractor or
old Autograph sealed in a holder. Pack two contains
e relic card plus pack three. Pack three contains four
pps Pristine veteran cards plus two Rookie cards. In
e event that an autographed card is present in the
ird pack, it replaces one of the veteran cards. Also, a
x-topper pack was inserted and those contain one
ini card. Pristine packs (the large one containing the
ree small packs) carried a suggested retail price of
0.

OMP.SET w/o RC's (100) 25.00 60.00
Tracy McGrady .60 1.50
DaJuan Wagner .30 .75
Allen Iverson .75 2.00
Chris Webber .50 1.25
Jason Kidd .75 2.00
Eddie Jones .40 1.00
Jermaine O'Neal .50 1.25
Kobe Bryant 2.50 6.00
Tony Parker .50 1.25
0 Wally Szczerbiak .40 1.00
1 Yao Ming 1.00 2.50
2 Amare Stoudemire .75 2.00
3 Steve Nash .60 1.50
4 Baron Davis .50 1.25
5 Vince Carter .75 2.00
6 Peja Stojakovic .50 1.25
7 Desmond Mason .40 1.00
18 Antoine Walker .50 1.25
19 Steve Francis .50 1.25
20 Gary Payton .50 1.25
21 Tim Duncan .75 2.00
22 Jalen Rose .40 1.00
23 Jason Richardson .50 1.25
24 Andre Miller .40 1.00
25 Allan Houston .40 1.00
26 Ron Artest .50 1.25
27 Andrei Kirilenko .50 1.25
28 Kenyon Martin .50 1.25
29 Kevin Garnett 1.00 2.50
30 Rasheed Wallace .50 1.25
31 Shawn Marion .50 1.25
32 Karl Malone .60 1.50
33 Antawn Jamison .50 1.25
34 Shaquille O'Neal 1.25 3.00
35 Paul Pierce .60 1.50
36 Nene .40 1.00
37 Ray Allen .50 1.25
38 Bonzi Wells .30 .75
39 Ben Wallace .50 1.25
40 Jerry Stackhouse .40 1.00
41 Dirk Nowitzki .75 2.00
42 Elton Brand .50 1.25
43 Pau Gasol .50 1.25
44 Richard Hamilton .40 1.00
45 Shareef Abdur-Rahim .40 1.00
46 Jason Terry .40 1.00
47 Jamal Mashburn .40 1.00
48 Latrell Sprewell .40 1.00
49 Keith Van Horn .40 1.00
50 Mike Miller .50 1.25
51 Theo Ratliff .30 .75
52 Scottie Pippen .75 2.00
53 Nick Van Exel .40 1.00
54 Chauncey Billups .50 1.25
55 Al Harrington .40 1.00
56 Corey Maggette .40 1.00
57 Shane Battier .40 1.00
58 Tim Thomas .30 .75
59 Darius Miles .30 .75
60 Alonzo Mourning .60 1.50
61 Jamaal Magloire .30 .75
62 Antonio McDyess .40 1.00
63 Juwan Howard .40 1.00
64 Eric Snow .30 .75
65 Anfernee Hardaway .75 2.00
66 Tayshaun Prince .50 1.25
67 Derek Anderson .30 .75
68 Mike Bibby .50 1.25
69 Deshawn Stevenson .30 .75
70 Kwame Brown .30 .75
71 Jerome Williams .30 .75
72 Radoslav Nesterovic .30 .75
73 Stephon Marbury .40 1.00
74 P.J. Brown .30 .75
75 Sam Cassell .40 1.00
76 Kenny Thomas .30 .75
77 Jason Williams .40 1.00
78 Jamaal Tinsley .30 .75
79 Nikoloz Tskitishvili .30 .75
80 Michael Finley .50 1.25
81 Jamal Crawford .40 1.00
82 Brent Barry .30 .75
83 Gilbert Arenas .50 1.25
84 Morris Peterson .30 .75
85 Manu Ginobili .60 1.50
86 Dale Davis .30 .75
87 Aaron McKie .30 .75
88 Richard Jefferson .50 1.25
89 Michael Redd .50 1.25
90 Reggie Miller .50 1.25
91 Cuttino Mobley .40 1.00
92 Marcus Camby .40 1.00
93 Tony Delk .30 .75
94 Tyson Chandler .40 1.00
95 Caron Butler .50 1.25
96 Kurt Thomas .30 .75
97 Glenn Robinson .40 1.00
98 Brad Miller .50 1.25
99 Matt Harpring .40 1.00
100 Alvin Williams .30 .75
101 LeBron James C RC 20.00 50.00
102 LeBron James U 25.00 60.00
103 LeBron James R 50.00 100.00
104 Darko Milicic C RC 2.00 5.00
105 Darko Milicic U 2.50 6.00
106 Darko Milicic R 3.00 8.00
107 Carmelo Anthony C RC 5.00 12.00
108 Carmelo Anthony U 6.00 15.00
109 Carmelo Anthony R 8.00 20.00
110 Chris Bosh C RC 4.00 10.00
111 Chris Bosh U 5.00 12.00
112 Chris Bosh R 6.00 15.00
113 Dwyane Wade C RC 8.00 20.00
114 Dwyane Wade U 10.00 25.00
115 Dwyane Wade R 12.00 30.00
116 Chris Kaman C RC 2.50 6.00
117 Chris Kaman U 3.00 8.00
118 Chris Kaman R 4.00 10.00
119 Kirk Hinrich C RC 2.50 6.00
120 Kirk Hinrich U 3.00 8.00
121 Kirk Hinrich R 4.00 10.00
122 T.J. Ford C RC 2.50 6.00
123 T.J. Ford U 3.00 8.00
124 T.J. Ford R 4.00 10.00
125 Mike Sweetney C RC 2.00 5.00
126 Mike Sweetney U 2.50 6.00
127 Mike Sweetney R 3.00 8.00
128 Jarvis Hayes C RC 2.00 5.00
129 Jarvis Hayes U 2.50 6.00
130 Jarvis Hayes R 3.00 8.00
131 Mickael Pietrus C RC 2.00 5.00
132 Mickael Pietrus U 2.50 6.00
133 Mickael Pietrus R 3.00 8.00
134 Nick Collison C RC 2.00 5.00
135 Nick Collison U 2.50 6.00
136 Nick Collison R 3.00 8.00
137 Marcus Banks C RC 2.00 5.00
138 Marcus Banks U 2.50 6.00
139 Marcus Banks R 3.00 8.00
140 Luke Ridnour C RC 2.50 6.00
141 Luke Ridnour U 3.00 8.00
142 Luke Ridnour R 4.00 10.00
143 Reece Gaines C RC 2.00 5.00
144 Reece Gaines U 2.50 6.00
145 Reece Gaines R 3.00 8.00
146 Troy Bell C RC 2.00 5.00
147 Troy Bell U 2.50 6.00
148 Troy Bell R 3.00 8.00
149 Zarko Cabarkapa C RC 2.00 5.00
150 Zarko Cabarkapa U 2.50 6.00
151 Zarko Cabarkapa R 3.00 8.00
152 David West C RC 2.50 6.00
153 David West U 3.00 8.00
154 David West R 4.00 10.00
155 Aleksandar Pavlovic C RC 2.00 5.00
156 Aleksandar Pavlovic U 2.50 6.00
157 Aleksandar Pavlovic R 3.00 8.00
158 Dahntay Jones C RC 2.00 5.00
159 Dahntay Jones U 2.50 6.00
160 Dahntay Jones R 3.00 8.00
161 Boris Diaw C RC 2.50 6.00
162 Boris Diaw U 3.00 8.00
163 Boris Diaw R 4.00 10.00
164 Zoran Planinic C RC 2.00 5.00
165 Zoran Planinic U 2.50 6.00
166 Zoran Planinic R 3.00 8.00
167 Travis Outlaw C RC 2.50 6.00
168 Travis Outlaw U 3.00 8.00
169 Travis Outlaw R 4.00 10.00
170 Brian Cook C RC 2.00 5.00
171 Brian Cook U 2.50 6.00
172 Brian Cook R 3.00 8.00
173 Travis Hansen C RC 2.00 5.00
174 Travis Hansen U 2.50 6.00
175 Travis Hansen R 3.00 8.00
176 Ndudi Ebi C RC 2.00 5.00
177 Ndudi Ebi U 2.50 6.00
178 Ndudi Ebi R 3.00 8.00
179 Kendrick Perkins C RC 3.00 8.00
180 Kendrick Perkins U 4.00 10.00
181 Kendrick Perkins R 5.00 12.00
182 Leandro Barbosa C RC 2.50 6.00
183 Leandro Barbosa U 3.00 8.00
184 Leandro Barbosa R 4.00 10.00
185 Josh Howard C RC 2.00 5.00
186 Josh Howard U 2.50 6.00
187 Josh Howard R 3.00 8.00
188 Maciej Lampe C RC 2.00 5.00
189 Maciej Lampe U 2.50 6.00
190 Maciej Lampe R 3.00 8.00
191 Jason Kapono C RC 2.00 5.00
192 Jason Kapono U 2.50 6.00
193 Jason Kapono R 3.00 8.00
194 Luke Walton C RC 2.00 5.00
195 Luke Walton U 2.50 6.00
196 Luke Walton R 3.00 8.00
197 Jerome Beasley C RC 2.00 5.00
198 Jerome Beasley U 2.50 6.00
199 Jerome Beasley R 3.00 8.00

2003-04 Topps Pristine Refractors

Randomly inserted in #1 packs, this 199-card set parallels the base set in refractor format. Each card is sealed in a case and sequentially numbered to 149.

*1-100 STARS: 3X TO 8X BASE HI
*RC's/1999: .75X TO 2X BASE RC C VER.HI
*RC's/499: 1X TO 2.5X BASE RC U VER.HI
*RC's/149: 1X TO 2.5X BASE RC R VER.HI

2003-04 Topps Pristine Refractors Gold

Randomly inserted in #1 packs, this 199-card set parallels the base set in a gold refractor format. Each card is sealed in a case and sequentially numbered to 99.

*1-100 STARS: 4X TO 10X BASE HI
*RC C VER: 2X TO 5X RC C VER.BASE
*RC U VER: 1.5X TO 4X RC U VER.BASE
*RC R VER:1.25X TO 3X RC R VER.BASE
101 LeBron James C 200.00 400.00
102 LeBron James U 200.00 400.00
103 LeBron James R 200.00 400.00
113 Dwyane Wade C 50.00 120.00
114 Dwyane Wade U 50.00 120.00
115 Dwyane Wade R 50.00 120.00

2003-04 Topps Pristine Borders Relics

Randomly seeded in packs at the following rates in pack #2: Group A one in 4433, Group B one in 41 and no odds given for group E. The cards are horizontally designed and focus on foreign players. Each card has a swatch of memorabilia and the player's home country flag. A sealed refractor parallel was also produced and these cards are sequentially numbered to 25 and were randomly inserted in #1 packs.

*REFRACTORS: 1.25X TO 3X BASE HI
AK Andrei Kirilenko E 3.00 8.00
DN Dirk Nowitzki E 5.00 12.00
EG Manu Ginobili B 4.00 10.00
NH Nene E 2.50 6.00
PG Pau Gasol E 3.00 8.00
PS Peja Stojakovic 3.00 8.00
TD Tim Duncan E 5.00 12.00
TP Tony Parker E 3.00 8.00
YM Yao Ming B 6.00 15.00
ZI Zydrunas Ilgauskas E 2.50 6.00

2003-04 Topps Pristine Challenge Relics

Inserted in packs #2 for Group C at one in 51 and no odds given for Group E, this 14-card set places a circular swatch of memorabilia in the lower right-hand corner. A sealed refractor parallel was also produced and these cards are sequentially numbered to 25 and were randomly inserted in #1 packs.

*REFRACTORS: 1.25X TO 3X BASE HI
AK Andrei Kirilenko E 3.00 8.00
AS Amare Stoudemire E 5.00 12.00
CB Carlos Boozer E 3.00 8.00
DG Drew Gooden E 2.50 6.00
DW Dajuan Wagner E 2.00 5.00
GA Gilbert Arenas E 3.00 8.00
JR Jason Richardson C 3.00 8.00
JT Jamaal Tinsley E 2.00 5.00
MJ Marko Jaric E 2.00 5.00
RJ Richard Jefferson E 3.00 8.00
TC Tyson Chandler E 2.50 6.00
TM Troy Murphy E 3.00 8.00
TP Tony Parker E 3.00 8.00
CBU Caron Butler E 3.00 8.00

2003-04 Topps Pristine Factor Relics

Randomly inserted in pack #2 at the rates of one in 156 for Group B, one in 48 for Group D and no odds given for Group E, this 22-card set places a circular swatch of memorabilia in the lower right-hand corner. A sealed refractor parallel was also produced and these cards are sequentially numbered to 25 and were randomly inserted in #1 packs.

*REFRACTORS: 1.25X TO 3X BASE HI
AI Allen Iverson B 5.00 12.00
BD Baron Davis D 3.00 8.00
DA Darrell Armstrong E 2.00 5.00
DM Darius Miles E 2.00 5.00
EG Eddie Griffin E 2.00 5.00
JK Jason Kidd D 5.00 12.00
JS Jerry Stackhouse E 2.50 6.00
KM Karl Malone E 4.00 10.00
LO Lamar Odom E 3.00 8.00
LS Latrell Sprewell E 2.50 6.00
MB Mike Bibby E 3.00 8.00
MP Morris Peterson E 2.00 5.00
PP Paul Pierce E 4.00 10.00
RL Rashard Lewis E 3.00 8.00
RW Rasheed Wallace B 3.00 8.00
SC Sam Cassell E 2.50 6.00
SF Steve Francis E 3.00 8.00
SM Stephon Marbury D 2.50 6.00
SO Shaquille O'Neal E 8.00 20.00
DMU Dikembe Mutombo E 3.00 8.00

2003-04 Topps Pristine Gems Relics

Randomly inserted in #2 packs at the rates of one in 41 for Group B, one in 51 for Group C, no odds given for Group E, one in nine for Group F and one in three for Group G, this 34-card set is horizontally designed and places a diamond-shaped swatch of memorabilia on the right side of the card. A sealed refractor parallel was also produced and these cards are sequentially numbered to 25 and were randomly inserted in #1 packs.

*REFRACTORS: 1.25X TO 3X BASE HI
AH Allan Houston G 2.50 6.00
BW Ben Wallace G 3.00 8.00
CM Cuttino Mobley G 2.50 6.00
DD Dan Dickau G 2.00 5.00
DF Derek Fisher G 2.50 6.00
DG Drew Gooden F 2.50 6.00
DW David Wesley F 2.00 5.00
EG Eddie Griffin G 2.00 5.00
GH Grant Hill B 4.00 10.00
JJ Jared Jeffries G 2.00 5.00
JK Jason Kidd G 5.00 12.00
JO Jermaine O'Neal G 3.00 8.00
JR Jason Richardson F 3.00 8.00
MB Mike Bibby C 3.00 8.00
MD Mike Dunleavy C 2.50 6.00
MF Michael Finley E 3.00 8.00
MJ Marko Jaric G 2.00 5.00
PG Pat Garrity F 2.00 5.00
PS Peja Stojakovic E 3.00 8.00
RA Ray Allen F 3.00 8.00
RJ Richard Jefferson F 3.00 8.00
SC Sam Cassell G 2.50 6.00
SF Steve Francis F 3.00 8.00
SM Shawn Marion G 3.00 8.00
SN Steve Nash F 4.00 10.00
SO Shaquille O'Neal E 8.00 20.00
TC Tyson Chandler G 2.50 6.00
TD Tim Duncan F 5.00 12.00
TM Tracy McGrady G 4.00 10.00
TP Tayshaun Prince F 3.00 8.00
YM Yao Ming F 6.00 15.00
CBU Caron Butler G 3.00 8.00
PGA Pau Gasol F 3.00 8.00

2003-04 Topps Pristine Generals Relics

Randomly inserted in #2 packs at the rates of one in 41 for Group B, one in 28 for Group C, and no odds given for Group E, this 20-card set has white borders, color photos and a swatch of memorabilia. A sealed refractor parallel was also produced and these cards are sequentially numbered to 25 and were randomly inserted in #1 packs.

*REFRACTORS: 1.25X TO 3X BASE HI
AH Anfernee Hardaway B 5.00 12.00
AI Allen Iverson B 5.00 12.00
AM Anthony Mason B 2.00 5.00
AW Antoine Walker E 3.00 8.00
BW Ben Wallace E 3.00 8.00
CM Cuttino Mobley E 2.50 6.00
DD Dan Dickau E 2.00 5.00
EG Manu Ginobili B 4.00 10.00
GP Gary Payton E 3.00 8.00
JK Jason Kidd C 5.00 12.00
JM Jamal Mashburn E 2.50 6.00
KM Kenyon Martin E 3.00 8.00
MD Mike Dunleavy E 2.50 6.00
MF Michael Finley E 3.00 8.00
RA Ray Allen E 3.00 8.00
SO Shaquille O'Neal E 8.00 20.00
TD Tim Duncan E 5.00 12.00
VR Vladimir Radmanovic E 2.00 5.00
WS Wally Szczerbiak E 2.50 6.00

2003-04 Topps Pristine Minis

Inserted as a box-topper in a pack at one per box, these mini-cards have a black border along the right and photos are full-color portraits.

PM1 Paul Pierce 2.00 5.00
PM2 Dirk Nowitzki 2.50 6.00
PM3 Yao Ming 3.00 8.00
PM4 Steve Francis 1.50 4.00
PM5 Kobe Bryant 8.00 20.00
PM6 Shaquille O'Neal 4.00 10.00
PM7 Gary Payton 1.50 4.00
PM8 Kevin Garnett 3.00 8.00
PM9 Jason Kidd 2.50 6.00
PM10 Tracy Mcgrady 2.00 5.00
PM11 Allen Iverson 2.50 6.00
PM12 Chris Webber 1.50 4.00
PM13 Tim Duncan 2.50 6.00
PM14 Ray Allen 1.50 4.00
PM15 Vince Carter 2.50 6.00
PM16 Antoine Walker 1.50 4.00
PM17 Jermaine O'Neal 1.50 4.00
PM18 Elton Brand 1.50 4.00
PM19 Baron Davis 1.50 4.00
PM20 Shawn Marion 1.50 4.00
PM21 LeBron James 15.00 40.00
PM22 Darko Milicic 1.50 4.00
PM23 Carmelo Anthony 4.00 10.00
PM24 Chris Bosh 3.00 8.00
PM25 Dwyane Wade 6.00 15.00
PM26 Chris Kaman 2.00 5.00
PM27 Kirk Hinrich 2.00 5.00
PM28 T.J. Ford 2.00 5.00
PM29 Mike Sweetney 1.50 4.00
PM30 Jarvis Hayes 1.50 4.00
PM31 Mickael Pietrus 1.50 4.00
PM32 Nick Collison 1.50 4.00
PM33 Marcus Banks 1.50 4.00
PM34 Luke Ridnour 2.00 5.00
PM35 Reece Gaines 1.50 4.00
PM36 Troy Bell 1.50 4.00
PM37 Zarko Cabarkapa 1.50 4.00
PM38 David West 2.00 5.00
PM39 Aleksandar Pavlovic 1.50 4.00
PM40 Dahntay Jones 1.50 4.00
SO Shaquille O'Neal AU/100 50.00 100.00

2003-04 Topps Pristine Personal Endorsements

Randomly seeded in #3 packs at the rates of one in 36 for Group A, one in 156 for Group B, one in 28 for Group C, one in 48 for Group D and one in nine for Group E, this 37-card set places player autographs below a black and white photo. A gold version sequentially numbered to 25 and sealed in a holder was also available in #1 packs.

*GOLD: 1.25X TO 3X BASE HI
BB Bruce Bowen C 5.00 12.00
BC Brian Cook B 4.00 10.00
BW Boris Diaw A 5.00 12.00
CA Carmelo Anthony D 25.00 60.00
CB Chris Bosh C 12.50 30.00
DG Drew Gooden D 4.00 10.00
DJ Dahntay Jones D 4.00 10.00
EB Elton Brand C 4.00 10.00
JK Jason Kapono D 4.00 10.00
KB Keith Bogans A 4.00 10.00
KH Kirk Hinrich D 5.00 12.00
KJ Ken Johnson D 4.00 10.00
KP Kendrick Perkins A 6.00 15.00
LBO Leandro Barbosa A 5.00 12.00
LR Luke Ridnour C 5.00 12.00
LW Luke Walton D 4.00 10.00
ML Maciej Lampe A 4.00 10.00
MP Mickael Pietrus C 4.00 10.00
MR Malik Rose A 4.00 10.00
MS Mike Sweetney D 4.00 10.00
NC Nick Collison E 4.00 10.00
NE Ndudi Ebi A 4.00 10.00
RG Reece Gaines C 4.00 10.00
SB Steve Blake A 5.00 12.00
SO Shaquille O'Neal C 30.00 60.00
TB Troy Bell D 4.00 10.00
TF T.J. Ford B 5.00 12.00
TH Travis Hansen D 4.00 10.00
TO Travis Outlaw D 5.00 12.00
ZC Zarko Cabarkapa A 4.00 10.00
ZP Zaur Pachulia A 4.00 10.00
DWA Dwyane Wade C 50.00 100.00
DWE David West A 5.00 12.00
JHA Jarvis Hayes A 4.00 10.00
JHO Josh Howard E 4.00 10.00
MBA Marcus Banks E 4.00 10.00
ZPL Zoran Planinic D 4.00 10.00

2003-04 Topps Pristine Recruit Relics

Randomly inserted in number two packs at the rate of one in three, this 25-card set is horizontally designed with a red, black and white background and a square swatch of memorabilia. A sealed refractor parallel was also produced and these cards are sequentially numbered to 25 and were randomly inserted in #1 packs.

*REFRACTORS: 1X TO 2.5X BASE HI
BC Brian Cook 3.00 8.00
CA Carmelo Anthony 8.00 20.00
CB Chris Bosh 6.00 15.00
CK Chris Kaman 4.00 10.00
DJ Dahntay Jones 3.00 8.00
DW David West 4.00 10.00
JH Jarvis Hayes 3.00 8.00
KH Kirk Hinrich 4.00 10.00
KP Kendrick Perkins 5.00 12.00
LB Leandro Barbosa 4.00 10.00
LR Luke Ridnour 4.00 10.00
LW Luke Walton 3.00 8.00
MB Marcus Banks 3.00 8.00
MP Mickael Pietrus 3.00 8.00
MS Mike Sweetney 3.00 8.00
NC Nick Collison 3.00 8.00
NE Ndudi Ebi 3.00 8.00
RG Reece Gaines 3.00 8.00
SB Steve Blake 4.00 10.00
SV Slavko Vranes 3.00 8.00
TB Troy Bell 3.00 8.00
TF T.J. Ford 4.00 10.00
TH Travis Hansen 3.00 8.00
TO Travis Outlaw 4.00 10.00
DWY Dwyane Wade 12.00 30.00

2004-05 Topps Pristine

Released in December 2004, Topps Pristine features a 199-card set divided up into 100 veteran players and 33 rookie players who appear on three cards each. The first card, numberwise, each rookie appears on is the common version and is tagged as the rookie card. The second card, Uncommon, is sequentially numbered to 739 and the third card, Rare, is sequentially numbered to 239. Pristine was packaged in its usual triple pack format where the first pack contains an uncirculated refractor card, the second pack contains relic cards and the third pack contains four base veterans and two rookies. One pack per box will contain a bonus fourth pack that holds a mini card. Each box contains five packs and upon release, SRP was $30 per pack.

COMP.SET w/o SP's (100) 25.00 60.00
1 Ben Wallace .50 1.25
2 Michael Redd .50 1.25
3 Dwyane Wade 1.50 4.00
4 Chris Webber .50 1.25
5 Cuttino Mobley .40 1.00
6 Bonzi Wells .30 .75
7 Rashard Lewis .50 1.25
8 Kobe Bryant 2.50 6.00
9 Gilbert Arenas .50 1.25
10 Jeff Foster .30 .75
11 Yao Ming 1.00 2.50
12 Ricky Davis .40 1.00
13 Glenn Robinson .40 1.00
14 Chauncey Billups .50 1.25
15 Carmelo Anthony 1.00 2.50
16 Pau Gasol .50 1.25
17 Erick Dampier .30 .75
18 Jason Terry .40 1.00
19 Corey Maggette .40 1.00
20 Zach Randolph .40 1.00
21 Kevin Garnett 1.00 2.50
22 Steve Nash .60 1.50
23 LeBron James 3.00 8.00
24 Andre Miller .40 1.00
25 Manu Ginobili .60 1.50
26 Gordan Giricek .30 .75
27 Juwan Howard .40 1.00
28 Brad Miller .50 1.25
29 Al Harrington .40 1.00
30 Allen Iverson .75 2.00
31 Shawn Marion .50 1.25
32 Elton Brand .50 1.25
33 Steve Francis .50 1.25
34 Shaquille O'Neal 1.25 3.00
35 Marcus Camby .40 1.00
36 Tyson Chandler .40 1.00
37 Dirk Nowitzki .75 2.00
38 Damon Stoudamire .40 1.00
39 Richard Hamilton .40 1.00
40 Kurt Thomas .30 .75
41 Paul Pierce .60 1.50
42 Jarvis Hayes .30 .75
43 Ray Allen .50 1.25
44 Keith Van Horn .40 1.00
45 Kirk Hinrich .50 1.25
46 Caron Butler .50 1.25
47 Andrei Kirilenko .40 1.00
48 Jamaal Magloire .30 .75
49 Chris Kaman .50 1.25
50 Stephon Marbury .40 1.00
51 Mike Miller .50 1.25
52 Eddy Curry .40 1.00
53 Sam Cassell .40 1.00
54 Vince Carter .75 2.00
55 Jason Kidd .75 2.00
56 Desmond Mason .40 1.00
57 Nene .40 1.00
58 Gerald Wallace .50 1.25
59 Baron Davis .50 1.25
60 Tim Duncan .75 2.00
61 Drew Gooden .40 1.00
62 Jason Williams .40 1.00
63 Eddie Jones .40 1.00
64 Michael Finley .50 1.25
65 Gary Payton .50 1.25
66 Kenyon Martin .50 1.25
67 Mike Bibby .50 1.25
68 Jason Kapono .30 .75
69 Allan Houston .40 1.00
70 Ron Artest .50 1.25
71 Rasho Nesterovic .30 .75
72 Kwame Brown .30 .75
73 Wally Szczerbiak .40 1.00
74 Joe Johnson .50 1.25
75 Jamal Mashburn .50 1.25
76 Peja Stojakovic .50 1.25
77 Lamar Odom .50 1.25
78 Jalen Rose .40 1.00
79 Mike Dunleavy .40 1.00
80 Rasheed Wallace .50 1.25
81 Richard Jefferson .50 1.25
82 Luke Ridnour .40 1.00
83 Samuel Dalembert .30 .75
84 Zydrunas Ilgauskas .40 1.00
85 Carlos Arroyo .40 1.00
86 Primoz Brezec .30 .75
87 Chris Bosh .50 1.25
88 Antoine Walker .50 1.25
89 Boris Diaw .40 1.00
90 Tracy McGrady .60 1.50
91 Amare Stoudemire .60 1.50
92 Karl Malone .60 1.50
93 Jamal Crawford .40 1.00
94 Shareef Abdur-Rahim .40 1.00
95 Jason Richardson .50 1.25
96 Marcus Banks .30 .75
97 Jermaine O'Neal .50 1.25
98 Latrell Sprewell .40 1.00
99 Tony Parker .50 1.25
100 Carlos Boozer .50 1.25
101 Dwight Howard C RC 5.00 12.00
102 Dwight Howard U 8.00 20.00
103 Dwight Howard R 10.00 25.00
104 Ben Gordon C RC 2.00 5.00
105 Ben Gordon U 3.00 8.00
106 Ben Gordon R 4.00 10.00
107 Devin Harris C RC 2.50 6.00
108 Devin Harris U 4.00 10.00
109 Devin Harris R 5.00 12.00
110 Rafael Araujo C RC 1.50 4.00
111 Rafael Araujo U 2.50 6.00
112 Rafael Araujo R 3.00 8.00
113 Luke Jackson C RC 1.50 4.00
114 Luke Jackson U 2.50 6.00
115 Luke Jackson R 3.00 8.00
116 Yuta Tabuse C RC 3.00 8.00
117 Yuta Tabuse U 5.00 12.00
118 Yuta Tabuse R 6.00 15.00
119 Kris Humphries C RC 1.50 4.00
120 Kris Humphries U 2.50 6.00
121 Kris Humphries R 3.00 8.00
122 Josh Smith C RC 2.50 6.00
123 Josh Smith U 4.00 10.00
124 Josh Smith R 5.00 12.00
125 Dorell Wright C RC 2.50 6.00
126 Dorell Wright U 4.00 10.00
127 Dorell Wright R 5.00 12.00
128 Jackson Vroman C RC 1.50 4.00
129 Jackson Vroman U 2.50 6.00
130 Jackson Vroman R 3.00 8.00
131 Sasha Vujacic C RC 1.50 4.00
132 Sasha Vujacic U 2.50 6.00
133 Sasha Vujacic R 3.00 8.00
134 David Harrison C RC 1.50 4.00
135 David Harrison U 2.50 6.00
136 David Harrison R 3.00 8.00
137 Blake Stepp C RC 1.50 4.00
138 Blake Stepp U 2.50 6.00
139 Blake Stepp R 3.00 8.00
140 Lionel Chalmers C RC 1.50 4.00
141 Lionel Chalmers U 2.50 6.00
142 Lionel Chalmers R 3.00 8.00
143 Delonte West C RC 2.00 5.00
144 Delonte West U 3.00 8.00
145 Delonte West R 4.00 10.00
146 Kevin Martin C RC 2.00 5.00
147 Kevin Martin U 3.00 8.00
148 Kevin Martin R 4.00 10.00
149 Robert Swift C RC 1.50 4.00
150 Robert Swift U 2.50 6.00
151 Robert Swift R 3.00 8.00
152 Trevor Ariza C RC 1.50 4.00
153 Trevor Ariza U 2.50 6.00
154 Trevor Ariza R 3.00 8.00
155 Peter John Ramos C RC 1.50 4.00
156 Peter John Ramos U 2.50 6.00
157 Peter John Ramos R 3.00 8.00
158 Anderson Varejao C RC 2.00 5.00
159 Anderson Varejao U 3.00 8.00
160 Anderson Varejao R 4.00 10.00
161 Andre Emmett C RC 1.50 4.00
162 Andre Emmett U 2.50 6.00
163 Andre Emmett R 3.00 8.00
164 Tony Allen C RC 2.00 5.00
165 Tony Allen U 3.00 8.00
166 Tony Allen R 4.00 10.00
167 Jameer Nelson C RC 2.00 5.00
168 Jameer Nelson U 3.00 8.00
169 Jameer Nelson R 4.00 10.00
170 J.R. Smith C RC 2.00 5.00
171 J.R. Smith U 3.00 8.00
172 J.R. Smith R 4.00 10.00
173 Kirk Snyder C RC 1.50 4.00
174 Kirk Snyder U 2.50 6.00
175 Kirk Snyder R 3.00 8.00
176 Al Jefferson C RC 2.50 6.00
177 Al Jefferson U 4.00 10.00
178 Al Jefferson R 5.00 12.00
179 Sebastian Telfair C RC 1.50 4.00
180 Sebastian Telfair U 2.50 6.00
181 Sebastian Telfair R 3.00 8.00
182 Andris Biedrins C RC 2.00 5.00
183 Andris Biedrins U 3.00 8.00
184 Andris Biedrins R 4.00 10.00
185 Andre Iguodala C RC 2.50 6.00
186 Andre Iguodala U 4.00 10.00
187 Andre Iguodala R 5.00 12.00
188 Luol Deng C RC 2.50 6.00
189 Luol Deng U 4.00 10.00
190 Luol Deng R 5.00 12.00
191 Josh Childress C RC 1.50 4.00
192 Josh Childress U 2.50 6.00

193 Josh Childress R 3.00 8.00
194 Shaun Livingston C RC 1.50 4.00
195 Shaun Livingston U 2.50 6.00
196 Shaun Livingston R 3.00 8.00
197 Emeka Okafor C RC 2.50 6.00
198 Emeka Okafor U 4.00 10.00
199 Emeka Okafor R 5.00 12.00

2004-05 Topps Pristine Refractors

Randomly inserted in packs, this 199-card set parallels the base set enhanced with Topps' rainbow holofoil refractor effect. Card numbers 1-100 are sequentially numbered to 25, Common rookies are sequentially numbered to 599, Uncommon rookies are sequentially numbered to 275 and Rare rookies are numbered to 49.

*1-100: 6X TO 15X BASE HI
*COMMON RCs: .75X TO 2X BASE HI
*UNCOMMON RCs: .75X TO 2X BASE HI
*RARE RCs: 1X TO 2.5X BASE HI

2004-05 Topps Pristine Refractors Gold

Randomly inserted into packs, this is a parallel of the basic pristine set. Each of these cards have gold borders and were issued to a stated print run of 27 serial numbered sets.
*1-100: 8X TO 20X BASE HI
*COMMON RCs: 2.5X TO 6X BASE HI
*UNCOMMON RCs: 1.5X TO 4X BASE HI
*RARE RCs: 1.25X TO 3X BASE HI
3 Dwyane Wade 40.00 100.00
8 Kobe Bryant 75.00 200.00
101 Dwight Howard C 40.00 100.00
102 Dwight Howard U 40.00 100.00
103 Dwight Howard R 40.00 100.00

2004-05 Topps Pristine Court Clash

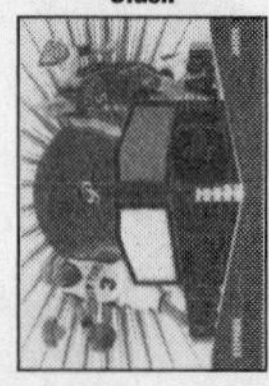

Inserted at stated odds of one in 47, these eight cards feature relics of each of the featured players. There is also a refractor parallel which was issued to a stated print run of 10 sets.
AG Carmelo Anthony 8.00 20.00
Kevin Garnett
AP Ron Artest 5.00 12.00
Paul Pierce
DM Tim Duncan 10.00 25.00
Karl Malone
MK Stephon Marbury 6.00 15.00
Jason Kidd
NW Dirk Nowitzki 8.00 20.00
Chris Webber
OM Shaquille O'Neal 8.00 20.00
Yao Ming
PP Gary Payton 5.00 12.00
Tony Parker
WO Ben Wallace 6.00 15.00
Jermaine O'Neal

2004-05 Topps Pristine Fantasy Favorites

Inserted at a stated rate of one in three, these 54 cards feature game-used relics of the featured player. There was also a refractor version of these cards issued. Those refractors were issued to a stated print run of 25 serial numbered sets.
*REFRACTORS: .75X TO 2X BASE HI
N Nene 2.00 5.00
AK Andrei Kirilenko 2.00 5.00
AS Amare Stoudemire 3.00 8.00
AW Antoine Walker 2.50 6.00
BM Brad Miller 2.50 6.00
CB Chauncey Billups 2.50 6.00
CK Chris Kaman 2.50 6.00
CW Chris Wilcox 2.00 5.00
DD Dan Dickau 2.00 5.00
DF Derek Fisher 2.00 5.00
DM Darko Milicic 2.00 5.00
DW Dajuan Wagner 2.00 5.00
EB Elton Brand 2.50 6.00
FW Frank Williams 2.00 5.00
GA Gilbert Arenas 2.50 6.00
JH Jarvis Hayes 2.00 5.00
JJ Jim Jackson 2.00 5.00
JK Jason Kidd 4.00 10.00
JM Jamaal Magloire 2.00 5.00
JO Jermaine O'Neal 2.50 6.00
JT Jason Terry 2.00 5.00
KG Kevin Garnett 5.00 12.00
KH Kirk Hinrich 2.50 6.00
KR Kareem Rush 2.00 5.00
LB Leandro Barbosa 2.50 6.00
LR Luke Ridnour 2.00 5.00
MB Marcus Banks 2.00 5.00
MD Mike Dunleavy 2.00 5.00
MJ Marko Jaric 2.00 5.00
MO Michael Olowokandi 2.00 5.00
MP Morris Peterson 1.50 4.00
NM Nazr Mohammed 2.00 5.00
PP Paul Pierce 3.00 8.00
PS Peja Stojakovic 2.50 6.00
RA Ron Artest 2.50 6.00
RL Rashard Lewis 2.50 6.00
RM Reggie Miller 2.50 6.00
SF Steve Francis 2.50 6.00
SO Shaquille O'Neal 6.00 15.00
TO Travis Outlaw 2.00 5.00
TP Tayshaun Prince 2.50 6.00
UH Udonis Haslem 2.00 5.00
VR Vladimir Radmanovic 2.00 5.00
WS Wally Szczerbiak 2.00 5.00
YM Yao Ming 5.00 12.00
ZR Zach Randolph 2.00 5.00
CBH Chris Bosh 2.50 6.00
CBO Carlos Boozer 2.50 6.00
CBU Caron Butler 2.50 6.00
DWE David Wesley 2.00 5.00
JAM Jamal Mashburn 2.50 6.00
JHO Josh Howard 2.50 6.00
MPI Mickael Pietrus 2.00 5.00
SAR Shareef Abdur-Rahim 2.00 5.00

2004-05 Topps Pristine Mini

Inserted one per box in #4 packs, these "mini" cards feature some of the leading NBA players.
AI Andre Iguodala 2.00 5.00
AJ Antawn Jamison 1.25 3.00
AK Andrei Kirilenko 1.00 2.50
BD Baron Davis 1.25 3.00
BG Ben Gordon 1.50 4.00
BW Ben Wallace 1.25 3.00
CA Carmelo Anthony 2.50 6.00
DH Dwight Howard 4.00 10.00
DN Dirk Nowitzki 2.00 5.00
DW Dwyane Wade 4.00 10.00
EO Emeka Okafor 2.00 5.00
JC Josh Childress 1.25 3.00
JK Jason Kidd 2.00 5.00
JN Jameer Nelson 1.50 4.00
JO Jermaine O'Neal 1.25 3.00
JR Jason Richardson 1.25 3.00
KB Kobe Bryant 6.00 15.00
KG Kevin Garnett 2.50 6.00
KH Kris Humphries 1.25 3.00
LD Luol Deng 2.00 5.00
LJ LeBron James 8.00 20.00
LJ Luke Jackson 1.25 3.00
PG Pau Gasol 1.25 3.00
PP Paul Pierce 1.50 4.00
PS Peja Stojakovic 1.25 3.00
RA Rafael Araujo 1.25 3.00
SF Steve Francis 1.25 3.00
SL Shaun Livingston 1.25 3.00
SM Stephon Marbury 1.00 2.50
SO Shaquille O'Neal 3.00 8.00
ST Sebastian Telfair 1.25 3.00
TD Tim Duncan 2.00 5.00
TM Tracy McGrady 1.50 4.00
VC Vince Carter 2.00 5.00
YM Yao Ming 2.50 6.00
ALJ Al Jefferson 2.00 5.00
DHA Devin Harris 2.00 5.00
JRS J.R. Smith 1.50 4.00
RAL Ray Allen 1.25 3.00
SMA Shawn Marion 1.25 3.00

2004-05 Topps Pristine Mini Relics

Inserted at a stated rate of one in 47, these eight cards feature game-used relics of the featured player.
AS Amare Stoudemire 3.00 8.00
BW Ben Wallace 2.50 6.00
CA Carmelo Anthony 5.00 12.00
KG Kevin Garnett 5.00 12.00
PS Peja Stojakovic 2.50 6.00
RA Ron Artest 2.50 6.00
SF Steve Francis 2.50 6.00
SM Stephon Marbury 2.00 5.00

2004-05 Topps Pristine Personal Endorsements

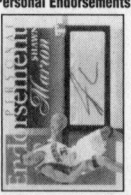

Inserted at different odds depending on what group the player belongs to, these cards feature authentic autographs of the featured player. We have notated which group the player belongs to next to his name in our checklist. In additon, parallel refractor gold cards of these players, issued to stated print runs of 10 or 25 sets were issued.
AB Andris Biedrins C 6.00 15.00
AS Amare Stoudemire A 15.00 40.00
AV Anderson Varejao C 6.00 15.00
BD Baron Davis B 6.00 15.00
BG Ben Gordon C 6.00 15.00
BJ Bobby Jackson A 10.00 25.00
BW Ben Wallace A 12.50 30.00
CA Carmelo Anthony B 35.00 70.00
DH David Harrison C 5.00 12.00
DW Dorell Wright C 8.00 20.00
EB Elton Brand A 8.00 20.00
EO Emeka Okafor C 8.00 20.00
JK Jason Kidd B 12.50 30.00
JO Jermaine O'Neal B 6.00 15.00
JR Jalen Rose A 6.00 15.00
JS Josh Smith C 8.00 20.00
KH Kris Humphries C 5.00 12.00
KS Kirk Snyder C 5.00 12.00
LD Luol Deng C 8.00 20.00
LJ Luke Jackson C 5.00 12.00
PS Peja Stojakovic B 8.00 20.00
RA Rafael Araujo C 5.00 12.00
RH Richard Hamilton B 8.00 20.00
RS Robert Swift C 5.00 12.00
SC Speedy Claxton A 5.00 12.00
SL Shaun Livingston C 5.00 12.00
SM Shawn Marion A 6.00 15.00
SO Shaquille O'Neal A 30.00 80.00
ST Sebastian Telfair C 5.00 12.00
SV Sasha Vujacic C 5.00 12.00
TA Tony Allen C 6.00 15.00
TD Tim Duncan A 60.00 120.00
TM Tracy McGrady A 12.50 30.00
TP Tayshaun Prince A 6.00 15.00
DEH Devin Harris C 8.00 20.00
JOC Josh Childress C 5.00 12.00
JRS J.R. Smith C 6.00 15.00
SMA Stephon Marbury C 8.00 20.00

2004-05 Topps Pristine Rookie Sign In

Inserted at a stated rate of one in eight, these 15 cards feature relics of NBA rookies. There is also a refractor version of each of these cards. Each of these cards were issued to a stated print run of 25 serial numbered sets.
*REFRACTORS: 1X TO 2.5X BASE HI
AI Andre Iguodala 4.00 10.00
AJ Al Jefferson 4.00 10.00
BG Ben Gordon 3.00 8.00
DH Dwight Howard 8.00 20.00
DW Dorell Wright 4.00 10.00
JC Josh Childress 2.50 6.00
JN Jameer Nelson 3.00 8.00
JS Josh Smith 4.00 10.00
LD Luol Deng 4.00 10.00
LJ Luke Jackson 2.50 6.00
RA Rafael Araujo 2.50 6.00
SL Shaun Livingston 2.50 6.00
ST Sebastian Telfair 2.50 6.00
TA Tony Allen 3.00 8.00
DHA Devin Harris 4.00 10.00

2004-05 Topps Pristine Two of a Kind Autographs

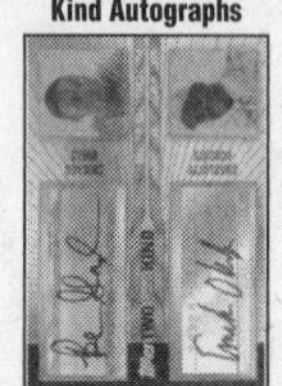

Inserted into packs at a stated rate of one in 305, these 10 cards feature dual autographs of leading NBA players.
MOST NOT PRICED DUE TO SCARCITY
AO Carmelo Anthony 40.00 100.00
Emeka Okafor
DO Tim Duncan 150.00 300.00
Emeka Okafor

2004-05 Topps Pristine Verticality

Inserted into packs at differing rates, these 13-cards feature game-used relic pieces of the featured player. Each of these cards belong to either group A or group B and we have notated that information next to the player's name in our checklist. In addition, each card has a refractor parallel and those cards were issued to a stated print run of 25 serial numbered copies.
*REFRACTORS: .75X TO 2X BASE HI
AK Andrei Kirilenko B 2.00 5.00
AS Amare Stoudemire B 3.00 8.00
CA Chris Anderson B 4.00 10.00
DG Devean George B 2.00 5.00
DM Desmond Mason A 2.00 5.00
DW David West B 2.50 6.00
JR Jason Richardson B 2.50 6.00
RG Reece Gaines B 2.00 5.00
RJ Richard Jefferson B 2.50 6.00
SM Shawn Marion B 2.50 6.00
TC Tyson Chandler B 2.00 5.00
TM Tracy McGrady B 3.00 8.00

2004-05 Topps Pristine Winning Wardrobe

Inserted into packs at differing rates, these 34 cards feature game-used relic pieces of the featured player. Each of these cards belong to either group A or group B and we have notated that information next to the player's name in our checklist. In addition, each card has a refractor parallel and those cards were issued to a stated print run of 25.
*REFRACTORS: 1X TO 2.5X BASE HI
BD Baron Davis B 2.50 6.00
BW Ben Wallace B 2.50 6.00
CA Carmelo Anthony B 5.00 12.00
DF Derek Fisher B 2.00 5.00
DM Desmond Mason A 2.00 5.00
DN Dirk Nowitzki B 4.00 10.00
GP Gary Payton B 2.50 6.00
HT Hedo Turkoglu B 2.50 6.00
JK Jason Kidd B 4.00 10.00
JM Jamaal Magloire B 2.00 5.00
JO Jermaine O'Neal B 2.50 6.00
JT Jamaal Tinsley B 2.00 5.00
KH Kirk Hinrich B 2.50 6.00
KM Karl Malone B 3.00 8.00
MB Mike Bibby B 2.50 6.00
MJ Marko Jaric B 2.00 5.00
MR Michael Redd B 2.50 6.00
PG Pau Gasol B 2.50 6.00
PP Paul Pierce B 3.00 8.00
PS Peja Stojakovic B 2.50 6.00
RA Ray Allen B 2.50 6.00
RH Robert Horry B 2.00 5.00
RJ Richard Jefferson B 2.50 6.00
RM Reggie Miller B 2.50 6.00
RN Rasho Nesterovic B 2.00 5.00
SB Shane Battier B 2.00 5.00
SM Stephon Marbury B 2.00 5.00
SO Shaquille O'Neal B 6.00 15.00
TD Tim Duncan B 4.00 10.00
TM Tracy McGrady B 3.00 8.00
TP Tony Parker B 2.50 6.00
YM Yao Ming B 5.00 12.00
ZP Zoran Planinic B 2.00 5.00
TAP Tayshaun Prince B 2.50 6.00

2005-06 Topps Pristine

Released in December 2005, Pristine boasts a 210 card set where cards 1-100 feature veteran players where color photos are set against a plain white background, cards 101-130 feature rookies, cards 131-180 feature players with memorabilia swatches serially numbered to 500, cards 181-205 feature autographs where most players are serially numbered to 100 (see checklist for details) and cards 206-210 feature memorabilia autograph cards sequentially numbered to 50. Pristine was packaged in five pack boxes where packs contained eight cards, including a format where one of the cards is sealed in an uncirculated case and two more packs where at least one memorabilia cards will be present. SRP upon release was $30 per pack.
COMP.SET w/o SP's 25.00 60.00
1 Ray Allen .40 1.00
2 Cuttino Mobley .30 .75
3 Sebastian Telfair .30 .75
4 Dwight Howard .75 2.00
5 Udonis Haslem .30 .75
6 Luol Deng .40 1.00
7 Lamar Odom .40 1.00
8 Paul Pierce .50 1.25
9 Stephen Jackson .30 .75
10 Mike Dunleavy .30 .75
11 Andre Miller .30 .75
12 Ben Gordon .40 1.00
13 Caron Butler .40 1.00
14 Al Jefferson .40 1.00
15 Jamaal Tinsley .25 .60
16 Josh Childress .30 .75
17 Larry Hughes .30 .75
18 Andrei Kirilenko .30 .75
19 Brad Miller .40 1.00
20 Steve Nash .50 1.25
21 Grant Hill .50 1.25
22 Samuel Dalembert .25 .60
23 Quentin Richardson .30 .75
24 Wally Szczerbiak .30 .75
25 Desmond Mason .25 .60
26 Dwyane Wade 1.00 2.50
27 Richard Hamilton .30 .75
28 Shane Battier .30 .75
29 Chauncey Billups .40 1.00
30 Shawn Marion .40 1.00
31 Kenyon Martin .40 1.00
32 Marquis Daniels .25 .60
33 Al Harrington .30 .75
34 Brendan Haywood .25 .60
35 Mehmet Okur .25 .60
36 Rafer Alston .25 .60
37 Luke Ridnour .30 .75
38 Tim Duncan .60 1.50
39 Mike Miller .40 1.00
40 Allen Iverson .60 1.50
41 Jamal Crawford .30 .75
42 J.R. Smith .40 1.00
43 Kevin Garnett .75 2.00
44 Baron Davis .40 1.00
45 Corey Maggette .30 .75
46 Jermaine O'Neal .40 1.00
47 Yao Ming .50 1.25
48 Pau Gasol .40 1.00
49 Devin Harris .40 1.00
50 Emeka Okafor .40 1.00
51 Zydrunas Ilgauskas .30 .75
52 Vladimir Radmanovic .25 .60
53 Tracy McGrady .50 1.25
54 Steve Francis .40 1.00
55 Stephon Marbury .30 .75
56 Shaun Livingston .25 .60
57 Sam Cassell .40 1.00
58 Rasheed Wallace .40 1.00
59 Primoz Brezec .25 .60
60 Nenad Krstic .25 .60
61 Mike Bibby .40 1.00
62 Marcus Camby .30 .75
63 LeBron James 2.00 5.00
64 Kobe Bryant 2.00 5.00
65 Josh Smith .40 1.00
66 Jason Richardson .40 1.00
67 Jamaal Magloire .25 .60
68 Gilbert Arenas .40 1.00
69 Zach Randolph .30 .75
70 Vince Carter .60 1.50
71 Tony Parker .40 1.00
72 Shaquille O'Neal .75 2.00
73 Richard Jefferson .40 1.00
74 Rashard Lewis .40 1.00
75 Peja Stojakovic .40 1.00
76 Mike Sweetney .25 .60
77 Elton Brand .40 1.00
78 Drew Gooden .30 .75
79 Chris Webber .40 1.00
80 Carmelo Anthony .75 2.00
81 Bobby Simmons .25 .60
82 Bob Sura .25 .60
83 Antoine Walker .30 .75
84 Andre Iguodala .40 1.00
85 Michael Redd .40 1.00
86 Manu Ginobili .40 1.00
87 Latrell Sprewell .30 .75
88 Kirk Hinrich .40 1.00
89 Josh Howard .40 1.00
90 Jason Kidd .60 1.50
91 Jalen Rose .40 1.00
92 Gerald Wallace .40 1.00
93 Eddy Curry .30 .75
94 Dirk Nowitzki .60 1.50
95 Joe Johnson .40 1.00
96 Chris Bosh .40 1.00
97 Carlos Boozer .40 1.00
98 Ben Wallace .40 1.00
99 Antawn Jamison .40 1.00
100 Amare Stoudemire .40 1.00
101 Andrew Bogut RC 3.00 8.00
102 Marvin Williams RC 2.50 6.00
103 Deron Williams RC 5.00 12.00
104 Chris Paul RC 8.00 20.00
105 Raymond Felton RC 3.00 8.00
106 Martell Webster RC 2.00 5.00
107 Charlie Villanueva RC 2.50 6.00
108 Channing Frye RC 2.50 6.00
109 Ike Diogu RC 2.00 5.00
110 Andrew Bynum RC 6.00 15.00
111 Monta Ellis RC 4.00 10.00
112 Yaroslav Korolev RC 2.00 5.00
113 Sean May RC 2.00 5.00
114 Rashad McCants RC 2.00 5.00
115 Antoine Wright RC 2.00 5.00
116 Joey Graham RC 2.00 5.00
117 Danny Granger RC 4.00 10.00
118 Gerald Green RC 2.50 6.00
119 Hakim Warrick RC 2.50 6.00
120 Julius Hodge RC 2.00 5.00
121 Nate Robinson RC 2.50 6.00
122 Jarrett Jack RC 2.00 5.00
123 Francisco Garcia RC 2.50 6.00
124 Luther Head RC 2.00 5.00
125 C.J. Miles RC 2.50 6.00
126 Salim Stoudamire RC 2.00 5.00
127 Sarunas Jasikevicius RC 2.00 5.00
128 Wayne Simien RC 2.00 5.00
129 David Lee RC 3.00 8.00
130 Jay-Z 3.00 8.00
131 Tim Duncan JSY 5.00 12.00
132 Ray Allen JSY 3.00 8.00
133 Grant Hill Warm 4.00 10.00
134 Dwyane Wade Shorts 8.00 20.00
135 Shawn Marion JSY 3.00 8.00
136 Jermaine O'Neal JSY 3.00 8.00
137 Emeka Okafor JSY 3.00 8.00
138 Tracy McGrady JSY 4.00 10.00
139 Chris Bosh Shorts 3.00 8.00
140 Dwight Howard JSY 6.00 15.00
141 Elton Brand JSY 3.00 8.00
142 Manu Ginobili JSY 3.00 8.00
143 Dirk Nowitzki JSY 5.00 12.00
144 Ben Wallace Warm 3.00 8.00
145 Steve Nash Warm 4.00 10.00
146 Allen Iverson Shirt 5.00 12.00
147 Kevin Garnett JSY 6.00 15.00
148 Corey Maggette JSY 2.50 6.00
149 Yao Ming JSY 4.00 10.00
150 Kobe Bryant Shorts 8.00 20.00
151 Rasheed Wallace JSY 3.00 8.00
152 Ben Gordon JSY 3.00 8.00
153 Gilbert Arenas Shirt 3.00 8.00
154 Shaquille O'Neal Warm 6.00 15.00
155 Peja Stojakovic JSY 3.00 8.00
156 Carmelo Anthony JSY 6.00 15.00
157 Kirk Hinrich JSY 3.00 8.00
158 Paul Pierce Shirt 4.00 10.00
159 Antawn Jamison JSY 3.00 8.00
160 Amare Stoudemire Shirt 3.00 8.00
161 Sarunas Jasikevicius Shorts 3.00 8.00
162 Wayne Simien JSY 3.00 8.00
163 Channing Frye JSY 4.00 10.00
164 Antoine Wright JSY 3.00 8.00
165 Sean May JSY 3.00 8.00
166 Rashad McCants JSY 3.00 8.00
167 Julius Hodge JSY 3.00 8.00
168 Nate Robinson JSY 4.00 10.00
169 Jarrett Jack JSY 3.00 8.00
170 Francisco Garcia JSY 4.00 10.00
171 Charlie Villanueva JSY 4.00 10.00
172 Andrew Bogut JSY 5.00 12.00
173 David Lee JSY 5.00 12.00
174 Deron Williams JSY 6.00 15.00
175 Chris Paul JSY 8.00 20.00
176 Raymond Felton JSY 5.00 12.00
177 Martell Webster JSY 3.00 8.00
178 Danny Granger JSY 6.00 15.00
179 Gerald Green JSY 4.00 10.00
180 Hakim Warrick JSY 4.00 10.00
181 Shaun Livingston AU 6.00 15.00
182 Danny Granger AU 12.00 30.00
183 Ryan Gomes AU RC 6.00 15.00
184 Jermaine O'Neal AU/75 10.00 25.00
185 George Gervin AU/60 12.50 30.00
186 Allen Iverson AU 60.00 150.00
187 Sean May AU 6.00 15.00
188 Andrew Bogut AU 10.00 25.00
189 Deron Williams AU 15.00 40.00
190 Stephon Marbury AU 10.00 25.00
191 Jason Kidd AU 12.50 30.00
192 Raymond Felton AU 10.00 25.00
193 Rashad McCants AU 6.00 15.00
194 Gerald Green AU 8.00 20.00
195 Andrew Bynum AU 20.00 50.00
196 Charlie Villanueva AU 8.00 20.00
197 Antoine Wright AU 6.00 15.00
198 Martell Webster AU 6.00 15.00
199 Francisco Garcia AU 8.00 20.00
200 Emeka Okafor AU 8.00 20.00
201 Hakim Warrick AU 8.00 20.00
202 Joey Graham AU 6.00 15.00
203 Julius Hodge AU 6.00 15.00
204 Ike Diogu AU 6.00 15.00
205 Johan Petro AU RC 6.00 15.00
206 Shaquille O'Neal JSY AU 40.00 80.00
208 Andrew Bogut JSY AU 15.00 40.00
209 Deron Williams JSY AU 40.00 80.00
210 Jay-Z Jeans AU 75.00 150.00

2005-06 Topps Pristine Die Cut

Randomly seeded in packs, this 210-card set parallels the base Topps Pristine set enhanced with jagged die-cut edges where cards 1-130 are serially numbered to 50, cards 131-180 are serially numbered to 15, cards 181-205 are serially numbered to seven and cards 206-210 are serially numbered to two.
*1-100 VET DIE CUT: 3X TO 8X BASE HI
*101-130 DIE CUT: 1X TO 2.5X BASE HI
UNPRICED JERSEY PRINT RUN 15 SETS
UNPRICED AU PRINT RUN 7 SETS
UNPRICED JSY AU PRINT RUN 2 SETS

2005-06 Topps Pristine Uncirculated

Randomly inserted in packs, this 210-card set parallels the base set but is sealed in Topps' uncirculated holders. Cards 1-130 are serially numbered to 325, cards 131-180 are serially numbered to 100, cards 181-205 are serially numbered to 20 and cards 206-210 are serially numbered one of one.
*1-100 UNCIR: 1.5X TO 4X BASE HI
*101-130 UNCIR: .6X TO 1.5X BASE HI
*131-180 UNCIR: .5X TO 1.25X BASE HI
*181-205 UNCIR: .6X TO 1.5X BASE HI
UNPRICED JSY AU PRINT RUN ONE SET
185 George Gervin AU/60 12.50 30.00
189 Deron Williams AU 40.00 100.00
195 Andrew Bynum AU 40.00 100.00

2005-06 Topps Pristine Personal Endorsements

Randomly seeded in packs, this 45-card set features a horizontal design with several different serially numbered tiers. Common cards are sequentially numbered to 215, Uncommons are sequentially numbered to 125 (unless noted in checklist), Rare cards are sequentially numbered to 50 and Scarce cards are sequentially numbered to 10.
UNPRICED SCARCE PRINT RUN 10 SETS
UNCIR.COMMON PRINT RUN 7 SETS
UNCIR.UNCOMM.PRINT RUN 5 SETS
UNCIR.RARE PRINT RUN 3 SETS
UNCIR.SCARCE PRINT RUN ONE SET
UNCIR.NOT PRICED DUE TO SCARCITY
CAI Allen Iverson C 30.00 80.00
CBB Brandon Bass C 5.00 12.00
CBW Bracey Wright C 4.00 10.00
CCA Carmelo Anthony C 15.00 30.00
CCT Chris Taft C 4.00 10.00
CDE Daniel Ewing C 4.00 10.00
CDG Danny Granger C 8.00 20.00
CDL David Lee C 6.00 15.00
CDW Dorell Wright C 4.00 10.00
CEO Emeka Okafor C 10.00 25.00
CJJ Jarrett Jack C 4.00 10.00
CJM Jason Maxiell C 4.00 10.00
CJN Jameer Nelson C 4.00 10.00
CLD Luol Deng C 5.00 12.00
CLH Luther Head C 4.00 10.00
CLW Louis Williams C 6.00 15.00
CME Monta Ellis C 8.00 20.00
CRS Robert Swift C 4.00 10.00
CRW Robert Whaley C 4.00 10.00
CSL Shaun Livingston C 4.00 10.00
CTD Travis Diener C 4.00 10.00
CVW Von Wafer C 4.00 10.00
CWS Wayne Simien C 4.00 10.00
RAI Allen Iverson R 50.00 125.00
RCB Christie Brinkley R 40.00 100.00
RCE Carmen Electra R 30.00 80.00
RJM Jenny McCarthy R 40.00 100.00
RSE Shannon Elizabeth R 30.00 80.00
RSN Steve Nash R 40.00 80.00
RSO Shaquille O'Neal R 40.00 80.00
UBD Baron Davis U 5.00 12.00
UBU Beno Udrih U 5.00 12.00
UBW Bill Walton U 10.00 25.00
UCD Clyde Drexler U/105 12.50 30.00
UHW Hakim Warrick U 6.00 15.00
UJS Josh Smith U 5.00 12.00
UKS Kirk Snyder U 5.00 12.00
ULD Luol Deng U 6.00 15.00
URF Raymond Felton U 8.00 20.00
URP Robert Parish U/109 15.00 30.00
USM Stephon Marbury U 6.00 15.00
CDWA Dwyane Wade C 25.00 60.00
USMA Sean May U 5.00 12.00

2005-06 Topps Pristine Personal Pieces

Randomly inserted in packs, this multi-level set is horizontally designed with square swatches of memorabilia in the lower left hand corner. Common cards are serially numbered to 350, Uncommon cards are serially numbered to 175, Rare cards are serially numbered to 75 and Scarce cards are serially numbered to 10.
UNPRICED SCARCE PRINT RUN 10 SETS
UNCIR.COMMON PRINT RUN 7 SETS
UNCIR.UNCOMM.PRINT RUN 5 SETS
UNCIR.RARE PRINT RUN 3 SETS
UNCIR.SCARCE PRINT RUN ONE SET
UNCIR.NOT PRICED DUE TO SCARCITY
CAB Andrew Bogut Warm C 4.00 10.00
CAI Allen Iverson C 4.00 10.00
CAW Antoine Walker Shorts C 2.00 5.00
CBR Bernard Robinson C 2.00 5.00
CCA Carmelo Anthony C 5.00 12.00
CCB Chris Bosh C 2.50 6.00
CCE Carmen Electra Jeans C 8.00 20.00
CCF Channing Frye Warm C 3.00 8.00
CCK Chris Kaman C 2.50 6.00
CCP Chris Paul Warm C 8.00 20.00
CCV Charlie Villanueva Warm C 3.00 8.00
CDG Danny Granger Warm C 5.00 12.00
CDH David Harrison C 2.00 5.00
CDW Deron Williams Warm C 6.00 15.00
CEC Eddy Curry C 2.00 5.00
CEO Emeka Okafor C 2.50 6.00
CES Eric Snow C 2.00 5.00
CGA Gilbert Arenas C 2.50 6.00
CGG Gerald Green Warm C 3.00 8.00
CGP Gary Payton C 2.50 6.00
CHW Hakim Warrick Warm C 3.00 8.00
CJC Josh Childress C 2.00 5.00
CJH Julius Hodge Warm C 2.50 6.00
CJJ Jarrett Jack Warm C 2.50 6.00
CJM Jenny McCarthy Jeans C 8.00 20.00
CJS Josh Smith C 2.50 6.00
CJZ Jay-Z Jeans C 10.00 25.00
CKB Kobe Bryant Shorts C 8.00 20.00
CLR Luke Ridnour C 2.00 5.00
CMC Marcus Camby C 2.00 5.00
CMW Martell Webster Warm C 2.50 6.00
CPB Primoz Brezec C 2.00 5.00
CRF Raymond Felton Warm C 4.00 10.00
CRL Rashard Lewis C 2.50 6.00
CRW Rasheed Wallace C 2.50 6.00
CSD Samuel Dalembert C 2.00 5.00
CSE Shannon Elizabeth Jeans C 8.00 20.00
CSM Shawn Marion C 2.50 6.00
CSO Shaquille O'Neal AS Shorts C 5.00 12.00
CSV Sasha Vujacic C 2.00 5.00
CTA Tony Allen C 2.00 5.00
CTD Tim Duncan AS Shorts C 4.00 10.00
CTM Troy Murphy C 2.00 5.00
CTP Tayshaun Prince C 2.50 6.00
CUH Udonis Haslem C 2.00 5.00
CWS Wally Szczerbiak C 2.00 5.00
CYM Yao Ming C 3.00 8.00
RAI Allen Iverson Shirt R 6.00 15.00
RCA Carmelo Anthony R 8.00 20.00
RDW Dwyane Wade Shorts R 10.00 25.00
REO Emeka Okafor R 4.00 10.00
RJZ Jay-Z Jeans R 15.00 40.00
RKB Kobe Bryant R 12.50 30.00
RMG Manu Ginobili Warm R 4.00 10.00
RSM Sean May R 4.00 10.00
RSO Shaquille O'Neal R 8.00 20.00
RYM Yao Ming R 5.00 12.00
SPP Paul Pierce S 4.00 10.00
UAB Andrew Bogut Shirt U 5.00 12.00
UAI Allen Iverson Shirt U 5.00 12.00
UBW Ben Wallace U 3.00 8.00
UCB Christie Brinkley Jeans U 10.00 25.00
UCE Carmen Electra Jeans U 10.00 25.00
UCP Chris Paul Shirt U 10.00 25.00
UDH Dwight Howard U 6.00 15.00
UDN Dirk Nowitzki U 5.00 12.00
UDW Deron Williams Shirt U 8.00 20.00
UGH Grant Hill U 4.00 10.00
UJM Jenny McCarthy Jeans U 10.00 25.00
UJZ Jay-Z Jeans U 12.50 30.00
UKB Kobe Bryant Warm U 10.00 25.00
UKG Kevin Garnett AS JSY U 6.00 15.00
UKH Kirk Hinrich U 3.00 8.00
UKM Kenyon Martin U 3.00 8.00
ULO Lamar Odom U 3.00 8.00
UMW Martell Webster Shirt U 3.00 8.00
URF Raymond Felton Shirt U 5.00 12.00
URM Rashad McCants Shirt U 3.00 8.00
USE Shannon Elizabeth Jeans U 10.00 25.00
USN Steve Nash Shorts U 4.00 10.00
UST Sebastian Telfair U 2.50 6.00
UTM Tracy McGrady U 4.00 10.00
CAIG Andre Iguodala C 2.50 6.00
CCBR Christie Brinkley Jeans C 8.00 20.00
CDWA Dwyane Wade C 6.00 15.00
UDWA Dwyane Wade Shorts U 8.00 20.00

2008 Topps Red Autographs

NNO Magic Johnson 40.00 80.00
NNO Dwyane Wade 20.00 40.00

2000-01 Topps Reserve

The 2000-01 Topps Reserve product was released in May, 2001 and featured a 134-card base set that was broken into tiers as follows: Base Veterans (1-100), and Rookies (101-134) that were serial numbered to either 499, 999, or 1499. Each pack contained five cards and carried a suggested retail price $115 a box. Please note that each box also contained an autographed 8x10 canvas.
COMPLETE SET (134) 125.00 250.00
COMP.SET w/o SP's (100) 40.00 80.00
1 Tim Duncan 1.00 2.50
2 Clifford Robinson .30 .75
3 Allen Iverson 1.00 2.50
4 Marcus Camby .40 1.00
5 Chauncey Billups .50 1.25
6 Anthony Mason .30 .75
7 Toni Kukoc .40 1.00
8 Tim Thomas .30 .75
9 Corey Maggette .40 1.00
10 Steve Francis .50 1.25
11 Larry Hughes .40 1.00
12 Jerome Williams .30 .75
13 Reggie Miller .50 1.25
14 Chris Gatling .30 .75
15 Ron Artest .50 1.25
16 Derrick Coleman .40 1.00
17 Paul Pierce .60 1.50
18 Dikembe Mutombo .50 1.25
19 Andre Miller .40 1.00
20 Gary Payton .50 1.25
21 Kevin Garnett 1.00 2.50
22 Allan Houston .40 1.00
23 Rasheed Wallace .50 1.25
24 Derek Anderson .30 .75
25 Vin Baker .40 1.00
26 John Stockton .60 1.50
27 Richard Hamilton .40 1.00
28 Mike Bibby .50 1.25
29 Dale Davis .30 .75
30 Vince Carter 1.00 2.50
31 Shawn Marion .50 1.25
32 Karl Malone .60 1.50

Card	Low	High
Patrick Ewing	.60	1.50
Shaquille O'Neal	1.25	3.00
Jermaine O'Neal	.50	1.25
Danny Fortson	.30	.75
Steve Nash	.75	2.00
Antoine Walker	.40	1.00
Jason Terry	.50	1.25
Vlade Divac	.40	1.00
Avery Johnson	.40	1.00
Elton Brand	.50	1.25
Mitch Richmond	.40	1.00
Antonio Davis	.30	.75
Shawn Kemp	.50	1.25
Anfernee Hardaway	.75	2.00
Kendall Gill	.30	.75
Glen Rice	.40	1.00
Tim Hardaway	.50	1.25
Tracy McGrady	.75	2.00
Horace Grant	.40	1.00
Hakeem Olajuwon	.60	1.50
Antawn Jamison	.50	1.25
Dirk Nowitzki	.75	2.00
Antonio McDyess	.40	1.00
Michael Dickerson	.30	.75
Baron Davis	.50	1.25
Nick Van Exel	.40	1.00
Joe Smith	.40	1.00
Kobe Bryant	2.50	6.00
Ray Allen	.50	1.25
Keith Van Horn	.40	1.00
Latrell Sprewell	.40	1.00
Jason Kidd	.75	2.00
Chris Webber	.50	1.25
David Robinson	.75	2.00
Mark Jackson	.40	1.00
Bryon Russell	.30	.75
Lamar Odom	.50	1.25
Maurice Taylor	.30	.75
Jonathan Bender	.30	.75
Raef LaFrentz	.30	.75
Sam Cassell	.40	1.00
Wally Szczerbiak	.40	1.00
Grant Hill	.60	1.50
Theo Ratliff	.30	.75
Rashard Lewis	.50	1.25
Darrell Armstrong	.30	.75
Glenn Robinson	.40	1.00
Stephon Marbury	.40	1.00
Michael Olowokandi	.30	.75
Isaiah Rider	.40	1.00
Jalen Rose	.40	1.00
Cuttino Mobley	.40	1.00
Jerry Stackhouse	.40	1.00
Jamal Mashburn	.40	1.00
Kenny Anderson	.40	1.00
Michael Finley	.50	1.25
Lamond Murray	.30	.75
Eddie Jones	.50	1.25
Eric Snow	.30	.75
Terrell Brandon	.30	.75
Jason Williams	.50	1.25
Scottie Pippen	.75	2.00
Rod Strickland	.40	1.00
Jim Jackson	.30	.75
Ron Mercer	.30	.75
Juwan Howard	.40	1.00
Brian Grant	.30	.75
0 Shareef Abdur-Rahim	.40	1.00
1 Kenyon Martin/499 RC	6.00	15.00
2 Stromile Swift/999 RC	2.00	5.00
3 Darius Miles/1499 RC	1.50	4.00
4 Marcus Fizer/499 RC	2.50	6.00
5 Mike Miller/999 RC	4.00	10.00
6 DerMarr Johnson/1499 RC	1.50	4.00
7 Chris Mihm/499 RC	2.50	6.00
8 Jamal Crawford/999 RC	3.00	8.00
9 Joel Przybilla/1499 RC	1.50	4.00
0 Keyon Dooling/499 RC	2.50	6.00
1 Jerome Moiso/999 RC	2.00	5.00
2 Etan Thomas/1499 RC	1.50	4.00
3 Courtney Alexander/499 RC	2.50	6.00
4 Mateen Cleaves/999 RC	2.00	5.00
5 Jason Collier/1499 RC	1.50	4.00
6 Hedo Turkoglu/499 RC	5.00	12.00
7 Desmond Mason/999 RC	2.50	6.00
8 Quentin Richardson/1499 RC	2.50	6.00
9 Jamaal Magloire/499 RC	2.50	6.00
0 Speedy Claxton/999 RC	2.00	5.00
1 Morris Peterson/1499 RC	1.50	4.00
2 Donnell Harvey/499 RC	2.50	6.00
3 DeShawn Stevenson/999 RC	2.50	6.00
4 Dalibor Bagaric/1499 RC	1.50	4.00
5 Iakovos Tsakalidis/499 RC	2.50	6.00
6 Mamadou N'Diaye/999 RC	2.00	5.00
7 Erick Barkley/1499 RC	1.50	4.00
8 Mark Madsen/499 RC	2.50	6.00
9 A.J. Guyton/999 RC	2.00	5.00
0 Khalid El-Amin/1499 RC	1.50	4.00
1 Lavor Postell/499 RC	2.50	6.00
2 Marc Jackson/999 RC	2.00	5.00
3 Stephen Jackson/1499 RC	2.50	6.00
4 Wang Zhizhi/1499 RC	3.00	8.00

2000-01 Topps Reserve Canvas Autographs

...ndomly inserted into boxes, this 13-canvas insert ...tures autographs from some of the hottest players in ... league. Card backs carry a "TR" prefix followed by ... players initials. Please note that Shaquille O'Neal ...s inserted at 1:68 boxes, while Magic Johnson was ...erted a 1:34 boxes.

Card	Low	High
AJ Antawn Jamison E	6.00	15.00
AM Andre Miller F	6.00	15.00
BD Baron Davis E	6.00	15.00
EB Elton Brand C	6.00	15.00
JO Jermaine O'Neal C	8.00	20.00
KD Keyon Dooling F	6.00	15.00
LH Larry Hughes D	6.00	15.00
MB Mike Bibby E	6.00	15.00
MJ Magic Johnson B	40.00	100.00
MT Maurice Taylor E	6.00	15.00
SM Shawn Marion E	8.00	20.00
SO Shaquille O'Neal A	50.00	120.00
WS Wally Szczerbiak E	6.00	15.00

2000-01 Topps Reserve Game Jerseys

Randomly inserted into packs, this 36-card insert features game-used jersey cards from some of the hottest players in the NBA. Card backs carry a "TAS" prefix.

Card	Low	High
TAS1 Allen Iverson A	6.00	15.00
TAS2 Grant Hill A	4.00	10.00
TAS3 Alonzo Mourning A	4.00	10.00
TAS4 Eddie Jones A	3.00	8.00
TAS5 Allan Houston A	2.50	6.00
TAS6 Dale Davis A	2.00	5.00
TAS7 Reggie Miller A	3.00	8.00
TAS8 Dikembe Mutombo A	3.00	8.00
TAS9 Glenn Robinson A	2.50	6.00
TAS10 Ray Allen A	3.00	8.00
TAS11 Jerry Stackhouse A	2.50	6.00
TAS12 Tim Duncan A	6.00	15.00
TAS13 Shaquille O'Neal A	8.00	20.00
TAS14 Jason Kidd A	5.00	12.00
TAS15 Gary Payton A	3.00	8.00
TAS16 John Stockton A	4.00	10.00
TAS17 Karl Malone A	4.00	10.00
TAS18 David Robinson A	5.00	12.00
TAS19 Rasheed Wallace A	3.00	8.00
TAS20 Michael Finley A	3.00	8.00
TAS21 Chris Webber A	3.00	8.00
TAS22 Mike Bibby B	3.00	8.00
TAS23 Michael Dickerson B	2.00	5.00
TAS24 Cuttino Mobley B	2.50	6.00
TAS25 Raef LaFrentz B	2.00	5.00
TAS26 Dirk Nowitzki B	5.00	12.00
TAS27 Michael Olowokandi B	2.00	5.00
TAS28 Paul Pierce B	4.00	10.00
TAS29 Jason Williams B	3.00	8.00
TAS30 Elton Brand B	3.00	8.00
TAS31 Steve Francis B	3.00	8.00
TAS32 Adrian Griffin B	2.00	5.00
TAS33 Todd MacCulloch B	2.00	5.00
TAS34 Andre Miller B	2.50	6.00
TAS35 James Posey B	2.00	5.00
TAS36 Wally Szczerbiak B	2.50	6.00

2003-04 Topps Rookie Matrix Promos

Card	Low	High
COMPLETE SET (3)	10.00	25.00
PP1 Dwyane Wade	10.00	25.00
Carmelo Anthony		
Chris Bosh		
PP2 T.J. Ford	2.00	5.00
Kirk Hinrich		
Marcus Banks		
PP3 Elton Brand	.40	1.00

2003-04 Topps Rookie Matrix

Released in April 2004, Topps Rookie Matrix boasts a 220-card set broken down into 110 veteran player cards and 110 triple player rookie cards. The rookie cards are not tagged RC's due to lack of space but are widely accepted as such by the Hobby. The cards are numbered by the first letter of each of the three rookies last names from left to right. Card backgrounds are that of streetball courts and the set was designed to appeal to video gamers. Rookie Matrix was packaged in 20-pack boxes where packs contained five veteran cards, two rookie cards, one mini parallel and one checklist and carried a suggested retail price of $4.

Card	Low	High
COMP.SET w/o RC's (110)	12.50	30.00
UNPRICED KEY POINTS PRINT RUN 5 SETS		
1 Allen Iverson	.50	1.25
2 Anfernee Hardaway	.50	1.25
3 Bonzi Wells	.20	.50
4 Bobby Jackson	.20	.50
5 Manu Ginobili	.40	1.00
6 Andrei Kirilenko	.30	.75
7 Ray Allen	.30	.75
8 Kwame Brown	.20	.50
9 Jason Terry	.25	.60
10 Paul Pierce	.40	1.00
11 Tyson Chandler	.25	.60
12 Darius Miles	.20	.50
13 Antoine Walker	.30	.75
14 Antawn Jamison	.30	.75
15 Steve Nash	.40	1.00
16 Marcus Camby	.25	.60
17 Chauncey Billups	.30	.75
18 Jason Richardson	.30	.75
19 Cuttino Mobley	.25	.60
20 Yao Ming	.60	1.50
21 Ron Artest	.30	.75
22 Gary Payton	.30	.75
23 Jason Williams	.25	.60
24 Eddie Jones	.25	.60
25 Kevin Garnett	.60	1.50
26 Wally Szczerbiak	.25	.60
27 Kenyon Martin	.30	.75
28 Jamaal Magloire	.20	.50
29 Keith Van Horn	.25	.60
30 Tracy McGrady	.40	1.00
31 Glenn Robinson	.25	.60
32 Derek Anderson	.20	.50
33 Chris Webber	.30	.75
34 Tony Parker	.30	.75
35 Morris Peterson	.20	.50
36 Jerry Stackhouse	.25	.60
37 Theo Ratliff	.20	.50
38 Jalen Rose	.25	.60
39 Dajuan Wagner	.20	.50
40 Dirk Nowitzki	.50	1.25
41 Nikoloz Tskitishvili	.20	.50
42 Ben Wallace	.30	.75
43 Tayshaun Prince	.30	.75
44 Troy Murphy	.30	.75
45 Jamaal Tinsley	.20	.50
46 Corey Maggette	.25	.60
47 Karl Malone	.40	1.00
48 Mike Miller	.30	.75
49 Lamar Odom	.30	.75
50 Shaquille O'Neal	.75	2.00
51 Michael Redd	.30	.75
52 Sam Cassell	.25	.60
53 Raef LaFrentz	.20	.50
54 Baron Davis	.30	.75
55 Allan Houston	.25	.60
56 Drew Gooden	.25	.60
57 Eric Snow	.20	.50
58 Stephon Marbury	.25	.60
59 Zach Randolph	.30	.75
60 Peja Stojakovic	.30	.75
61 Brent Barry	.20	.50
62 Radoslav Nesterovic	.20	.50
63 Antonio Davis	.20	.50
64 Gilbert Arenas	.30	.75
65 Shareef Abdur-Rahim	.25	.60
66 Scottie Pippen	.50	1.25
67 Ronald Murray	.20	.50
68 Zydrunas Ilgauskas	.25	.60
69 Nene	.25	.60
70 Steve Francis	.30	.75
71 Mike Dunleavy	.25	.60
72 Jermaine O'Neal	.30	.75
73 Elton Brand	.30	.75
74 Caron Butler	.30	.75
75 Kobe Bryant	1.50	4.00
76 Kenny Thomas	.20	.50
77 Joe Smith	.25	.60
78 Jason Kidd	.50	1.25
79 Antonio McDyess	.25	.60
80 Shawn Marion	.30	.75
81 Rasheed Wallace	.30	.75
82 Mike Bibby	.30	.75
83 Tim Thomas	.20	.50
84 Rashard Lewis	.30	.75
85 Vince Carter	.50	1.25
86 Matt Harpring	.25	.60
87 Ricky Davis	.25	.60
88 Michael Finley	.30	.75
89 Andre Miller	.25	.60
90 Pau Gasol	.30	.75
91 Dion Glover	.20	.50
92 Jamal Crawford	.25	.60
93 Richard Hamilton	.25	.60
94 Nick Van Exel	.25	.60
95 Maurice Taylor	.20	.50
96 Reggie Miller	.30	.75
97 Marko Jaric	.20	.50
98 Brian Grant	.20	.50
99 Desmond Mason	.25	.60
100 Tim Duncan	.50	1.25
101 Latrell Sprewell	.25	.60
102 Richard Jefferson	.30	.75
103 David Wesley	.20	.50
104 Kurt Thomas	.20	.50
105 Juwan Howard	.25	.60
106 Amare Stoudemire	.50	1.25
107 Brad Miller	.30	.75
108 Keon Clark	.20	.50
109 Pat Garrity	.20	.50
110 Jamal Mashburn	.25	.60
AJF Carmelo Anthony 113 RC	4.00	10.00
LeBron James 111 RC		
T.J. Ford 118 RC		
AKM Carmelo Anthony 113 RC	2.00	5.00
Chris Kaman 116 RC		
Darko Milicic 112 RC		
AMB Carmelo Anthony 113 RC	3.00	8.00
Darko Milicic 112 RC		
Chris Bosh 114 RC		
AWB Carmelo Anthony 113 RC	6.00	15.00
Dwyane Wade 115 RC		
Chris Bosh 114 RC		
BAH Chris Bosh 114 RC	2.50	6.00
Carmelo Anthony 113 RC		
Kirk Hinrich 117 RC		
BAJ Chris Bosh 114 RC	10.00	25.00
Carmelo Anthony 113 RC		
LeBron James 111 RC		
BBG Leandro Barbosa 137 RC	1.25	3.00
Troy Bell 126 RC		
Reece Gaines 125 RC		
BBR Marcus Banks 125 RC	1.25	3.00
Troy Bell 126 RC		
Luke Ridnour 124 RC		
BCC Troy Bell 126 RC	1.25	3.00
Zarko Cabarkapa 127 RC		
Nick Collison 122 RC		
BCG Troy Bell 126 RC	1.25	3.00
Nick Collison 122 RC		
Reece Gaines 125 RC		
BCP Marcus Banks 125 RC	1.25	3.00
Nick Collison 122 RC		
Mickael Pietrus 121 RC		
BCP Leandro Barbosa 137 RC	1.25	3.00
Zarko Cabarkapa 127 RC		
Aleksandar Pavlovic 129 RC		
BHJ Chris Bosh 114 RC	4.00	10.00
Kirk Hinrich 117 RC		
LeBron James 111 RC		
BJP Troy Bell 126 RC	1.25	3.00
Dahntay Jones 130 RC		
Zoran Planinic 132 RC		
BKC Jerome Beasley 142 RC	1.25	3.00
Jason Kapono 140 RC		
Brian Cook 134 RC		
BKS Marcus Banks 123 RC	1.25	3.00
Chris Kaman 116 RC		
Mike Sweetney 119 RC		
BKW Chris Bosh 114 RC	2.50	6.00
Chris Kaman 116 RC		
Dwyane Wade 115 RC		
BPH Marcus Banks 123 RC	1.25	3.00
Mickael Pietrus 121 RC		
Jarvis Hayes 120 RC		
BPW Leandro Barbosa 137 RC	1.25	3.00
Aleksandar Pavlovic 129 RC		
Maurice Williams 143 RC		
BRG Marcus Banks 123 RC	1.25	3.00
Luke Ridnour 124 RC		
Reece Gaines 125 RC		
BWM Chris Bosh 114 RC	3.00	8.00
Dwyane Wade 115 RC		
Darko Milicic 112 RC		
CEK Brian Cook 134 RC	1.25	3.00
Ndudi Ebi 135 RC		
Jason Kapono 140 RC		
CHB Nick Collison 122 RC	1.25	3.00
Jarvis Hayes 120 RC		
Marcus Banks 123 RC		
CHC Brian Cook 134 RC	1.25	3.00
Josh Howard 138 RC		
Zarko Cabarkapa 127 RC		
CPD Zarko Cabarkapa 127 RC	1.25	3.00
Mickael Pietrus 121 RC		
Boris Diaw 131 RC		
CPS Nick Collison 122 RC	1.25	3.00
Mickael Pietrus 121 RC		
Mike Sweetney 119 RC		
CSH Nick Collison 122 RC	1.25	3.00
Mike Sweetney 119 RC		
Jarvis Hayes 120 RC		
CWC Brian Cook 134 RC	1.25	3.00
David West 128 RC		
Nick Collison 122 RC		
DPP Boris Diaw 131 RC	1.25	3.00
Aleksandar Pavlovic 129 RC		
Zoran Planinic 132 RC		
DPW Boris Diaw 131 RC	1.25	3.00
Aleksandar Pavlovic 129 RC		
David West 128 RC		
EPW Ndudi Ebi 135 RC	1.50	4.00
Kendrick Perkins 136 RC		
David West 128 RC		
EWC Ndudi Ebi 135 RC	1.25	3.00
David West 128 RC		
Brian Cook 134 RC		
FAH T.J. Ford 118 RC	2.00	5.00
Carmelo Anthony 113 RC		
Kirk Hinrich 117 RC		
FBH T.J. Ford 118 RC	1.25	3.00
Marcus Banks 123 RC		
Kirk Hinrich 117 RC		
FBJ T.J. Ford 118 RC	4.00	10.00
Chris Bosh 114 RC		
LeBron James 111 RC		
FBR T.J. Ford 118 RC	1.25	3.00
Marcus Banks 123 RC		
Luke Ridnour 124 RC		
FBW T.J. Ford 118 RC	2.50	6.00
Chris Bosh 114 RC		
Dwyane Wade 115 RC		
FCH T.J. Ford 118 RC	1.25	3.00
Nick Collison 122 RC		
Kirk Hinrich 117 RC		
FGB T.J. Ford 118 RC	1.25	3.00
Reece Gaines 125 RC		
Marcus Banks 123 RC		
FKW T.J. Ford 118 RC	1.50	4.00
Chris Kaman 116 RC		
Dwyane Wade 115 RC		
GBB Reece Gaines 125 RC	1.25	3.00
Marcus Banks 123 RC		
Troy Bell 126 RC		
GBR Reece Gaines 125 RC	1.25	3.00
Troy Bell 126 RC		
Luke Ridnour 124 RC		
HAM Kirk Hinrich 117 RC	2.50	6.00
Carmelo Anthony 113 RC		
Darko Milicic 112 RC		
HBM Kirk Hinrich 117 RC	1.50	4.00
Chris Bosh 114 RC		
Darko Milicic 112 RC		
HBS Jarvis Hayes 120 RC	1.25	3.00
Marcus Banks 123 RC		
Mike Sweetney 119 RC		
HCJ Josh Howard 138 RC	1.25	3.00
Brian Cook 134 RC		
Dahntay Jones 130 RC		
HGP Jarvis Hayes 120 RC	1.25	3.00
Reece Gaines 125 RC		
Mickael Pietrus 121 RC		
HJM Kirk Hinrich 117 RC	3.00	8.00
LeBron James 111 RC		
Darko Milicic 112 RC		
HKC Jarvis Hayes 120 RC	1.25	3.00
Chris Kaman 116 RC		
Nick Collison 122 RC		
HLC Josh Howard 138 RC	1.25	3.00
Maciej Lampe 139 RC		
Brian Cook 134 RC		
HLK Josh Howard 138 RC	1.25	3.00
Maciej Lampe 139 RC		
Jason Kapono 140 RC		
HPR Jarvis Hayes 120 RC	1.25	3.00
Mickael Pietrus 121 RC		
Luke Ridnour 124 RC		
HSL Jarvis Hayes 120 RC	1.25	3.00
Mike Sweetney 119		
Maciej Lampe 139		
HSP Jarvis Hayes 120 RC	1.25	3.00
Mike Sweetney 119 RC		
Mickael Pietrus 121 RC		
HWS Kirk Hinrich 117 RC	1.50	4.00
Dwyane Wade 115 RC		
Mike Sweetney 119 RC		
JAW LeBron James 111 RC	15.00	40.00
Carmelo Anthony 113 RC		
Dwyane Wade 115 RC		
JBM LeBron James 111 RC	4.00	10.00
Chris Bosh 114 RC		
Darko Milicic 112 RC		
JHA LeBron James 111 RC	6.00	15.00
Kirk Hinrich 117 RC		
Carmelo Anthony 113 RC		
JKA LeBron James 111 RC	6.00	15.00
Chris Kaman 116 RC		
Carmelo Anthony 113 RC		
JMA LeBron James 111 RC	8.00	20.00
Darko Milicic 112 RC		
Carmelo Anthony 113 RC		
JMK LeBron James 111 RC	4.00	10.00
Darko Milicic 112 RC		
Chris Kaman 116 RC		
JOB Dahntay Jones 130 RC	1.25	3.00
Travis Outlaw 133 RC		
Leandro Barbosa 137 RC		
JWE Dahntay Jones 130 RC	1.25	3.00
Luke Walton 141 RC		
Ndudi Ebi 135 RC		
KCP Chris Kaman 116 RC	1.25	3.00
Zarko Cabarkapa 127 RC		
Kendrick Perkins 136 RC		
KEW Jason Kapono 140 RC	1.25	3.00
Ndudi Ebi 135 RC		
Maurice Williams 143 RC		
KHW Chris Kaman 116 RC	1.50	4.00
Kirk Hinrich 117 RC		
Dwyane Wade 115 RC		
KPH Chris Kaman 116 RC	1.25	3.00
Mickael Pietrus 121 RC		
Jarvis Hayes 120 RC		
KSC Chris Kaman 116 RC	1.25	3.00
Mike Sweetney 119 RC		
Nick Collison 122 RC		
LBB Maciej Lampe 139 RC	1.25	3.00
Leandro Barbosa 137 RC		
Jerome Beasley 142 RC		
LHC Maciej Lampe 139 RC	1.25	3.00
Josh Howard 138 RC		
Zarko Cabarkapa 127 RC		
LSP Maciej Lampe 139 RC	1.25	3.00
Mike Sweetney 119 RC		
Zoran Planinic 132 RC		
MAF Darko Milicic 112 RC	1.50	4.00
Carmelo Anthony 113 RC		
T.J. Ford 118 RC		
MBF Darko Milicic 112 RC	1.50	4.00
Chris Bosh 114 RC		
T.J. Ford 118 RC		
MFJ Darko Milicic 112 RC	3.00	8.00
T.J. Ford 118 RC		
LeBron James 111 RC		
MJW Darko Milicic 112 RC	5.00	12.00
LeBron James 111 RC		
Dwyane Wade 115 RC		
OBD Travis Outlaw 133 RC	1.25	3.00
Leandro Barbosa 137 RC		
Boris Diaw 131 RC		
OCB Travis Outlaw 133 RC	1.25	3.00
Brian Cook 134 RC		
Jerome Beasley 142 RC		
OEJ Travis Outlaw 133 RC	1.25	3.00
Ndudi Ebi 135 RC		
Dahntay Jones 130 RC		
OPE Travis Outlaw 133 RC	1.25	3.00
Kendrick Perkins 136 RC		
Ndudi Ebi 135 RC		
PBE Kendrick Perkins 136 RC	1.25	3.00
Jerome Beasley 142 RC		
Ndudi Ebi 135 RC		
PBG Kendrick Perkins 136 RC	1.25	3.00
Marcus Banks 123 RC		
Reece Gaines 125 RC		
PBH Mickael Pietrus 121 RC	1.25	3.00
Troy Bell 126 RC		
Jarvis Hayes 120 RC		
PCH Mickael Pietrus 121 RC	1.25	3.00
Nick Collison 122 RC		
Jarvis Hayes 120 RC		
PCR Mickael Pietrus 121 RC	1.25	3.00
Nick Collison 122 RC		
Luke Ridnour 124 RC		
PCW Kendrick Perkins 136 RC	1.50	4.00
Zarko Cabarkapa 127 RC		
David West 128 RC		
PDB Zoran Planinic 132 RC	1.25	3.00
Boris Diaw 131 RC		
Leandro Barbosa 137 RC		
PJD Aleksandar Pavlovic 129 RC	1.25	3.00
Dahntay Jones 130 RC		
Boris Diaw 131 RC		
PLH Kendrick Perkins 136 RC	1.25	3.00
Maciej Lampe 139 RC		
Josh Howard 138 RC		
POP Aleksandar Pavlovic 129 RC	1.25	3.00
Travis Outlaw 133 RC		
Zoran Planinic 132 RC		
PPC Mickael Pietrus 121 RC	1.25	3.00
Aleksandar Pavlovic 129 RC		
Zarko Cabarkapa 127 RC		
PSK Mickael Pietrus 121 RC	1.25	3.00
Aleksandar Pavlovic 119 RC		
Chris Kaman 116 RC		
PWO Zoran Planinic 132 RC	1.25	3.00
David West 128 RC		
Travis Outlaw 133 RC		
RFH Luke Ridnour 124 RC	1.25	3.00
T.J. Ford 118 RC		
Kirk Hinrich 117 RC		
RHC Luke Ridnour 124 RC	1.25	3.00
Jarvis Hayes 120 RC		
Nick Collison 122 RC		
SBC Mike Sweetney 119 RC	1.25	3.00
Marcus Banks 123 RC		
Nick Collison 122 RC		
SHK Mike Sweetney 119 RC	1.25	3.00
Jarvis Hayes 120 RC		
Chris Kaman 116 RC		
SPB Mike Sweetney 119 RC	1.25	3.00
Mickael Pietrus 121 RC		
Marcus Banks 123 RC		
WBH Dwyane Wade 115 RC	2.00	5.00
Chris Bosh 114 RC		
Kirk Hinrich 117 RC		
WBP Maurice Williams 143 RC	1.25	3.00
Leandro Barbosa 137 RC		
Zoran Planinic 132 RC		
WDJ David West 128 RC	1.25	3.00
Boris Diaw 131 RC		
Dahntay Jones 130 RC		
WDP Maurice Williams 143 RC	1.25	3.00
Boris Diaw 131 RC		
Dahntay Jones 130 RC		
WFH Dwyane Wade 115 RC	2.00	5.00
T.J. Ford 118 RC		
Kirk Hinrich 117 RC		
WHL Luke Walton 141 RC	1.25	3.00
Josh Howard 138 RC		
Maciej Lampe 139 RC		
WHO Luke Walton 141 RC	1.25	3.00
Travis Outlaw 133 RC		
Josh Howard 138 RC		
WJB Dwyane Wade 115 RC	30.00	80.00
LeBron James 111 RC		
Chris Bosh 114 RC		
WKP Luke Walton 141 RC	1.25	3.00
Jason Kapono 140 RC		
Kendrick Perkins 136 RC		
WKS Dwyane Wade 115 RC	2.00	5.00
Chris Kaman 116 RC		
Mike Sweetney 119 RC		
WMA Dwyane Wade 115 RC	5.00	12.00
Darko Milicic 112 RC		
Carmelo Anthony 113 RC		
WPJ David West 128 RC	1.25	3.00
Aleksandar Pavlovic 129 RC		
Dahntay Jones 130 RC		
WWB Luke Walton 141 RC	1.25	3.00
Maurice Williams 143 RC		
Jerome Beasley 142 RC		

2003-04 Topps Rookie Matrix Minis

Randomly inserted in packs at the rate of one in one, this 143-card set parallels the base Rookie Matrix set on mini-cards. Several different card backs were issued for each mini: Topps backs are inserted at one in 5, Double Double backs are inserted at one in 13, Triple backs are inserted at one in 203, and Swish backs are inserted at one in 1693.

*DOUBLE: .6X TO 1.5X MINI HI
*SWISH: 5X TO 12X MINI HI
*TOPPS: .5X TO 1.25X MINI HI
*TRIPLE: 1.25X TO 3X MINI HI

Card	Low	High
111 LeBron James	6.00	15.00
112 Darko Milicic	.60	1.50
113 Carmelo Anthony	1.50	4.00
114 Chris Bosh	1.25	3.00
115 Dwyane Wade	2.50	6.00
116 Chris Kaman	.75	2.00
117 Kirk Hinrich	.75	2.00
118 T.J. Ford	.75	2.00
119 Mike Sweetney	.60	1.50
120 Jarvis Hayes	.60	1.50
121 Mickael Pietrus	.60	1.50
122 Nick Collison	.60	1.50
123 Marcus Banks	.60	1.50
124 Luke Ridnour	.75	2.00
125 Reece Gaines	.60	1.50
126 Troy Bell	.60	1.50
127 Zarko Cabarkapa	.60	1.50
128 David West	.75	2.00
129 Aleksandar Pavlovic	.60	1.50
130 Dahntay Jones	.60	1.50
131 Boris Diaw	.75	2.00
132 Zoran Planinic	.60	1.50
133 Travis Outlaw	.75	2.00
134 Brian Cook	.60	1.50
135 Ndudi Ebi	.60	1.50
136 Kendrick Perkins	1.00	2.50
137 Leandro Barbosa	.75	2.00
138 Josh Howard	.60	1.50
139 Maciej Lampe	.60	1.50
140 Jason Kapono	.60	1.50
141 Luke Walton	.60	1.50
142 Jerome Beasley	.60	1.50
143 Maurice Williams	1.00	2.50

2003-04 Topps Rookie Matrix Lottery Draw

Randomly inserted at the rate of one in 371, this 13-card set has a border and encased are small frame photos of each player. There are three different versions per card and features the "A" variation for dribbling, the "B" variation for passing and the "C" variation for shooting. All versions are valued equally.

Card	Low	High
LD1A LeBron James	30.00	80.00
LD2A Darko Milicic	3.00	8.00
LD3A Carmelo Anthony	8.00	20.00
LD4A Chris Bosh	6.00	15.00
LD5A Dwyane Wade	12.00	30.00
LD6A Chris Kaman	4.00	10.00
LD7A Kirk Hinrich	4.00	10.00
LD8A T.J. Ford	4.00	10.00
LD9A Mike Sweetney	3.00	8.00
LD10A Jarvis Hayes	3.00	8.00
LD11A Mickael Pietrus	3.00	8.00
LD12A Nick Collison	3.00	8.00
LD13A Marcus Banks	3.00	8.00

2003-04 Topps Rookie Matrix Mini Autographs

Randomly inserted in packs at the rates of one in 7164 for Group A, one in 3175 for Group B, one in 2039 for Group C, one in 412 for Group D, one in 913 for Group E, one in 148 for group F and one in 49 for Group G, this 25-card set is made up of mini-encased autographed cards.

Card	Low	High
AK Andrei Kirilenko F	5.00	12.00
BM Brad Miller F	5.00	12.00
CA Carmelo Anthony/100 A	30.00	60.00
DW Dwyane Wade D	30.00	80.00
GA Gilbert Arenas D	8.00	20.00
JC Jason Collins G	5.00	12.00
JK Jason Kidd E	12.50	30.00
LW Luke Walton G	5.00	12.00
MC Michael Curry G	5.00	12.00
MR Malik Rose B	5.00	12.00
PP Paul Pierce C	15.00	30.00
RG Reece Gaines F	5.00	12.00
RH Richard Hamilton D	5.00	12.00
TB Troy Bell G	5.00	12.00
TH Travis Hansen G	5.00	12.00
TP Tayshaun Prince G	5.00	12.00
ZC Zarko Cabarkapa G	5.00	12.00
ZP Zoran Planinic G	5.00	12.00
TPA Tony Parker F	10.00	25.00

2003-04 Topps Rookie Matrix Mini Relics

Randomly inserted in packs at the rates of one in 1259 for Group A, one in 372 for Group B, one in 473 for Group C, one in 792 for Group D, one in 219 for Group E, one in 148 for Group F and one in 49 for Group G, this 87-card set is comprised of mini-encased memorabilia cards.

Card	Low	High
AI Allen Iverson F	4.00	10.00
AJ Antawn Jamison/250 C	2.50	6.00
AM Andre Miller G	2.00	5.00
AS Amare Stoudemire G	4.00	10.00
BB Brent Barry/50 A	5.00	12.00
BW Ben Wallace G	2.50	6.00
CA Carmelo Anthony F	6.00	15.00
CB Caron Butler/250 C	2.50	6.00
CK Chris Kaman F	3.00	8.00
CM Corey Maggette A	2.00	5.00
CW Chris Webber/50 A	8.00	20.00
DG Drew Gooden E	2.00	5.00
DM Darius Miles G	2.00	5.00
DN Dirk Nowitzki G	4.00	10.00
DW Dajuan Wagner F	2.00	5.00
EB Elton Brand F	2.50	6.00
GR Glenn Robinson E	2.00	5.00
JH Jarvis Hayes F	2.50	6.00
JK Jason Kidd F	4.00	10.00
JO Jermaine O'Neal G	2.50	6.00
JR Jalen Rose F	2.00	5.00
JT Jason Terry/50 A	6.00	15.00
JW Jason Williams E	2.00	5.00
KB Kwame Brown/150 B	2.50	6.00
KG Kevin Garnett G	5.00	12.00
KH Kirk Hinrich F	3.00	8.00
KT Kurt Thomas/50 A	5.00	12.00
LO Lamar Odom F	2.50	6.00
LR Luke Ridnour F	3.00	8.00
LS Latrell Sprewell G	2.00	5.00
MB Marcus Banks F	2.50	6.00
MD Mike Dunleavy/50 A	5.00	12.00
MM Mike Miller F	2.50	6.00
MO Michael Olowokandi G	1.50	4.00
MP Mickael Pietrus/50 A	5.00	12.00
MS Mike Sweetney F	2.50	6.00
NH Nene G	2.00	5.00
PG Pau Gasol G	2.50	6.00
PP Paul Pierce G	3.00	8.00
QR Quentin Richardson/50 A	5.00	12.00
RA Ray Allen/150 B	5.00	12.00
RG Reece Gaines G	2.50	6.00
RH Richard Hamilton G	2.00	5.00
RJ Richard Jefferson D	2.50	6.00
RL Rashard Lewis/250 C	2.50	6.00
RM Reggie Miller D	2.50	6.00
RW Rasheed Wallace/50 A	6.00	15.00
SF Steve Francis F	2.50	6.00
SM Shawn Marion G	2.50	6.00
SN Steve Nash F	3.00	8.00
SO Shaquille O'Neal G	6.00	15.00
TB Troy Bell F	2.50	6.00
TD Tim Duncan F	4.00	10.00
TM Tracy McGrady G	3.00	8.00
TP Tayshaun Prince/150 B	2.50	6.00
YM Yao Ming F	5.00	12.00
ZC Zarko Cabarkapa/150 B	2.50	6.00
ZI Zydrunas Ilgauskas G	2.00	5.00
CBO Chris Bosh F	5.00	12.00
CMO Cuttino Mobley G	2.00	5.00
DWA Dwyane Wade F	10.00	25.00
JHO Juwan Howard E	2.00	5.00
JRI Jason Richardson/50 A	6.00	15.00
JWI Jerome Williams E	2.00	5.00
KMA Kenyon Martin/50 A	6.00	15.00
MBI Mike Bibby/150 B	2.50	6.00
MPE Morris Peterson F	1.50	4.00
RAR Ron Artest/150 B	2.50	6.00
SMA Stephon Marbury/150 B	2.00	5.00
TMU Troy Murphy E	2.50	6.00
TPA Tony Parker/250 C	2.50	6.00

2003-04 Topps Rookie Matrix Rookie Frames

Randomly inserted, this 33-card set parallels the rookie players with mini-cards encased in a frame. Several different card back versions were inserted: Double Doubles at one in 125, Topps at one in 51, Triple Doubles at one in 2235 and Swish at one in 10348.

*DOUBLE: .6X TO 1.5X BASE FRAME HI
*TOPPS: .5X TO 1.25X BASE FRAME
*TRIPLE: 3X TO 8X BASE FRAME HI
SWISH NOT PRICED DUE TO SCARCITY

Card	Low	High
111 LeBron James	12.00	30.00
112 Darko Milicic	1.25	3.00
113 Carmelo Anthony	3.00	8.00
114 Chris Bosh	2.50	6.00
115 Dwyane Wade	5.00	12.00
116 Chris Kaman	1.50	4.00
117 Kirk Hinrich	1.50	4.00
118 T.J. Ford	1.50	4.00
119 Mike Sweetney	1.25	3.00
120 Jarvis Hayes	1.25	3.00
121 Mickael Pietrus	1.25	3.00
122 Nick Collison	1.25	3.00
123 Marcus Banks	1.25	3.00
124 Luke Ridnour	1.50	4.00
125 Reece Gaines	1.25	3.00
126 Troy Bell	1.25	3.00
127 Zarko Cabarkapa	1.25	3.00
128 David West	1.50	4.00
129 Aleksandar Pavlovic	1.25	3.00
130 Dahntay Jones	1.25	3.00
131 Boris Diaw	1.50	4.00
132 Zoran Planinic	1.25	3.00
133 Travis Outlaw	1.50	4.00
134 Brian Cook	1.25	3.00
135 Ndudi Ebi	1.25	3.00
136 Kendrick Perkins	2.00	5.00
137 Leandro Barbosa	1.50	4.00
138 Josh Howard	1.25	3.00
139 Maciej Lampe	1.25	3.00
140 Jason Kapono	1.25	3.00
141 Luke Walton	1.25	3.00
142 Jerome Beasley	1.25	3.00
143 Maurice Williams	2.00	5.00

2001 Topps Sean Elliott National Kidney Foundation

Given away to the first 10,000 fans on March 14, 2001, this set was issued by Topps in association with the National Kidney Foundation. The two card set commemorates the one year anniversary of Sean Elliott's return to basketball.

COMPLETE SET (2) .75 2.00
SE Sean Elliott .75 2.00
NNO Nation Kidney Foundation .05 .15

2008-09 Topps Signature

COMPLETE SET (85) 75.00 150.00
PRINT RUN 2325 SER.#'d SETS
TSAA Arron Afflalo .60 1.50
TSAT Al Thornton .75 2.00
TSBD Baron Davis 1.00 2.50
TSBR Brandon Roy 1.00 2.50
TSBW Brandan Wright .75 2.00
TSCL Courtney Lee RC 2.00 5.00
TSCP Chris Paul 1.50 4.00
TSDC Daequan Cook .60 1.50
TSDE Dale Ellis 1.00 2.50
TSDH Dwight Howard 2.00 5.00
TSDJ DeAndre Jordan RC 2.50 6.00
TSDR Derrick Rose RC 12.00 30.00
TSDS Dolph Schayes 1.00 2.50
TSEB Elgin Baylor 1.00 2.50
TSEG Eric Gordon RC 3.00 8.00
TSEH Elvin Hayes 1.00 2.50
TSFL Fat Lever 1.00 2.50
TSGA Gilbert Arenas 1.00 2.50
TSGG George Gervin 1.25 3.00
TSGH George Hill RC 2.00 5.00
TSGP Gabe Pruitt .60 1.50
TSGW Gerald Wallace 1.00 2.50
TSIT Isiah Thomas 1.00 2.50
TSJA Joe Alexander RC 1.25 3.00
TSJD Joey Dorsey RC 1.25 3.00
TSJH Josh Howard .75 2.00
TSJM JaVale McGee RC 2.00 5.00
TSJS John Stockton 1.50 4.00
TSJW Jerry West 1.25 3.00
TSKW Kyle Weaver RC 1.25 3.00
TSLB Larry Bird 3.00 8.00
TSLW Lenny Wilkens 1.00 2.50
TSMA Morris Almond .60 1.50
TSME Mark Eaton 1.00 2.50
TSMJ Magic Johnson 2.50 6.00
TSML Maurice Lucas 1.00 2.50
TSMP Mickael Pietrus .60 1.50
TSMW Marcus Williams .60 1.50
TSNY Nick Young .75 2.00
TSOB Otis Birdsong 1.00 2.50
TSPP Paul Pierce 1.25 3.00
TSRA Ryan Anderson RC 2.00 5.00
TSRF Raymond Felton .75 2.00
TSRG Rudy Gay 1.00 2.50
TSRP Robert Parish 1.00 2.50
TSRR Rajon Rondo 1.25 3.00
TSRS Rodney Stuckey 1.00 2.50
TSRT Reggie Theus 1.00 2.50
TSRW Russell Westbrook RC 6.00 15.00
TSSC Speedy Claxton .60 1.50
TSSD Samuel Dalembert .60 1.50
TSSH Spencer Hawes .60 1.50
TSSO Shaquille O'Neal 2.00 5.00
TSSP Sam Perkins 1.00 2.50
TSSS Sean Singletary RC 1.25 3.00
TSSW Sonny Weems RC 1.25 3.00
TSTY Thaddeus Young .75 2.00
TSVC Vince Carter 1.25 3.00
TSWS Walter Sharpe RC 1.25 3.00
TSYJ Yi Jianlian 1.00 2.50
TSZR Zach Randolph .75 2.00
TSABR Aaron Brooks .60 1.50
TSATU Alando Tucker .60 1.50
TSBRU Bill Russell 1.50 4.00
TSBWA Bill Walker RC 1.25 3.00
TSBWI Buck Williams 1.00 2.50
TSCBU Caron Butler 1.00 2.50
TSDGA Danilo Gallinari RC 2.00 5.00
TSDGI Daniel Gibson 1.00 2.50
TSDGR Donte Greene RC 1.25 3.00
TSDRD Dennis Rodman 1.50 4.00
TSDRO David Robinson 1.50 4.00
TSDSC Danny Schayes 1.00 2.50
TSDWA Dwyane Wade 2.00 5.00
TSJHA John Havlicek 1.50 4.00
TSJJH J.J. Hickson RC 1.50 4.00
TSJJW Jo Jo White 1.00 2.50
TSJRG J.R. Giddens RC 1.25 3.00
TSMRR Micheal Ray Richardson 1.00 2.50
TSOJM O.J. Mayo RC 2.00 5.00
TSRAL Ray Allen 1.00 2.50
TSRPI Ricky Pierce 1.00 2.50
TSSHA Spencer Haywood 1.00 2.50
TSSWE Spud Webb 1.00 2.50
TSJHRW John "Hot Rod" Williams 1.00 2.50

2008-09 Topps Signature Facsimile Black

*BLACK: .6X TO 1.5X BASE HI
STATED PRINT RUN 289 SER.#'d SETS
TSDR Derrick Rose 40.00 100.00

2008-09 Topps Signature Facsimile Red

*RED: .5X TO 1.25X BASE HI
STATED PRINT RUN 869 SER.#'d SETS
TSDR Derrick Rose 35.00 70.00

2008-09 Topps Signature Autographs

PRINT RUNS LISTED IN CHECKLIST
TSAAA Arron Afflalo/917 4.00 10.00
TSAAT Al Thornton/1799 4.00 10.00
TSABD Baron Davis/1079 5.00 12.00
TSABR Brandon Roy/649 8.00 20.00
TSABW Brandan Wright/3645 4.00 10.00
TSACL Courtney Lee/149 20.00 50.00
TSACP Chris Paul/649 25.00 60.00
TSADC Daequan Cook/1199 4.00 10.00
TSADE Dale Ellis/999 4.00 10.00
TSADH Dwight Howard/2499 15.00 40.00
TSADJ DeAndre Jordan/149 12.00 30.00
TSADR Derrick Rose/649 100.00 200.00
TSADS Dolph Schayes/425 4.00 10.00
TSAEB Elgin Baylor/1299 10.00 25.00
TSAEG Eric Gordon/275 12.50 30.00
TSAEH Elvin Hayes/625 6.00 15.00
TSAFL Fat Lever/750 4.00 10.00
TSAGA Gilbert Arenas/1199 6.00 15.00
TSAGG George Gervin/875 8.00 20.00
TSAGH George Hill/550 8.00 20.00
TSAGP Gabe Pruitt/1199 4.00 10.00
TSAGW Gerald Wallace/1499 4.00 10.00
TSAIT Isiah Thomas/999 10.00 25.00
TSAJA Joe Alexander/147 10.00 25.00
TSAJD Joey Dorsey/299 4.00 10.00
TSAJH Josh Howard/625 4.00 10.00
TSAJM JaVale McGee/275 5.00 12.00
TSAJS John Stockton/676 25.00 60.00
TSAJW Jerry West/649 20.00 50.00
TSAKW Kyle Weaver/699 4.00 10.00
TSALB Larry Bird/499 30.00 80.00
TSALW Lenny Wilkens/650 6.00 15.00
TSAMA Morris Almond/599 4.00 10.00
TSAME Mark Eaton/1029 4.00 10.00
TSAMJ Magic Johnson/499 30.00 80.00
TSAML Maurice Lucas/999 4.00 10.00
TSAMP Mickael Pietrus/1399 4.00 10.00
TSAMW Marcus Williams/1199 4.00 10.00
TSANY Nick Young/6225 4.00 10.00
TSAOB Otis Birdsong/1199 4.00 10.00
TSAPP Paul Pierce/1999 10.00 25.00
TSARA Ryan Anderson/499 5.00 12.00
TSARF Raymond Felton/1799 4.00 10.00
TSARG Rudy Gay/3640 4.00 10.00
TSARP Robert Parish/650 8.00 20.00
TSARR Rajon Rondo/1299 15.00 40.00
TSARS Rodney Stuckey/450 6.00 15.00
TSART Reggie Theus/940 4.00 10.00
TSARW Russell Westbrook/184 40.00 100.00
TSASC Speedy Claxton/599 4.00 10.00
TSASD Samuel Dalembert/750 4.00 10.00
TSASH Spencer Hawes/999 4.00 10.00
TSASO Shaquille O'Neal/825 25.00 60.00
TSASP Sam Perkins/1199 4.00 10.00
TSASS Sean Singletary/1999 4.00 10.00
TSASW Sonny Weems/799 4.00 10.00
TSATY Thaddeus Young/5775 4.00 10.00
TSAVC Vince Carter/599 10.00 25.00
TSAWS Walter Sharpe/350 4.00 10.00
TSAYJ Yi Jianlian/6225 5.00 12.00
TSAZR Zach Randolph/1799 5.00 12.00
TSAABR Aaron Brooks/492 4.00 10.00
TSAATU Alando Tucker/2999 4.00 10.00
TSABRU Bill Russell/499 40.00 100.00
TSABWA Bill Walker/1999 5.00 12.00
TSABWI Buck Williams/1299 5.00 12.00
TSACBU Caron Butler/1309 4.00 10.00
TSADGA Danilo Gallinari/439 8.00 20.00
TSADGI Daniel Gibson/1799 4.00 10.00
TSADGR Donte Greene/1199 4.00 10.00
TSADRD Dennis Rodman/1299 15.00 40.00
TSADRO David Robinson/899 20.00 40.00
TSADSC Danny Schayes/750 4.00 10.00
TSADWA Dwyane Wade/649 25.00 50.00
TSAJHA John Havlicek/799 15.00 40.00
TSAJJH J.J. Hickson/125 8.00 20.00
TSAJJW Jo Jo White/989 5.00 12.00
TSAJRG J.R. Giddens/625 5.00 12.00
TSAMRR Micheal Ray Richardson/11994.00 10.00
TSAOJM O.J. Mayo/599 8.00 20.00
TSARAL Ray Allen/799 15.00 40.00
TSARPI Ricky Pierce/999 4.00 10.00
TSASHA Spencer Haywood/1179 4.00 10.00
TSASWE Spud Webb/1899 5.00 12.00
TSAJHRW Hot Rod Williams/750 5.00 12.00

2008-09 Topps Signature Autographs Dual

STATED PRINT RUN 49 SER.#'d SETS
TSDBA Chauncey Billups 25.00 50.00
Carmelo Anthony
TSDGM Rudy Gay 15.00 30.00
O.J. Mayo
TSDHW Dwight Howard 50.00 100.00
Dwyane Wade
TSDIG Andre Iguodala 8.00 20.00
Danny Granger
TSDOR Greg Oden 30.00 60.00
Brandon Roy
TSDPR Chris Paul 125.00 250.00
Derrick Rose
TSDRG David Robinson 40.00 100.00
George Gervin
TSDSJ John Stockton 60.00 120.00
Magic Johnson
TSDWC Dominique Wilkins 25.00 50.00
Vince Carter
TSDWR Jerry West 75.00 150.00
Bill Russell

2008-09 Topps Signature Autographs Triple

STATED PRINT RUN 36 SER.#'d SETS
TSTARM Gilbert Arenas 40.00 100.00
Brandon Roy
O.J. Mayo
TSTHOR Dwight Howard 150.00 300.00
Shaquille O'Neal
David Robinson
TSTJWB Magic Johnson 125.00 250.00
Jerry West
Elgin Baylor
TSTWPR Dwyane Wade 300.00 450.00
Chris Paul
Derrick Rose

2005 Topps Special Edition Authentic

AU ISSUED AS REPLACEMENT
EO1 Emeka Okafor/499 5.00 12.00
EO2 Emeka Okafor/99 8.00 20.00
EO3 Emeka Okafor/25 12.00 30.00

1992 Topps Stadium of Stars

This 12-card standard-size set measures the standard size and features stars from different sports and entertainment. The cards have the same design as the regular 1992 Topps cards. The fronts feature color portraits with red and white inner borders and white outer borders. The star's name and the set name appear in two short color stripes respectively at the bottom. The backs carry a short biography and personal information. The cards are unnumbered and checklisted below in alphabetical order.

COMPLETE SET (12) 5.00 12.00
9 Ann Meyers BK .40 1.00
12 John Wooden CO BK 1.00 2.50

1996 Topps Stars

This set was created to commemorate the NBA's announcement of their top 50 players of all time. The set contained 150-cards and was issued in 8-card packs that carried a suggested retail price of $3.00. Each player had three cards - a Golden Season card highlighting their best year and two versions of a Commemorative card, in which the card fronts were the same but one had an all-text back and the other featured all the career statistics showing why each player is among the NBA's top 50. Each player has three different cards, but only one card is priced below. All cards carry the same value. All the cards were full-bleed, double-foil stamped and printed on 20-point stock.

COMPLETE SET (150) 20.00 40.00
CL (NNO) .08 .25
1 Kareem Abdul-Jabbar .25 .60
2 Nate Archibald .15 .40
3 Paul Arizin .15 .40
4 Charles Barkley .25 .60
5 Rick Barry .15 .40
6 Elgin Baylor .15 .40
7 Dave Bing .15 .40
8 Larry Bird .50 1.25
9 Wilt Chamberlain .30 .75
10 Bob Cousy .25 .60
11 Dave Cowens .15 .40
12 Billy Cunningham .15 .40
13 Dave DeBusschere .15 .40
14 Clyde Drexler .20 .50
15 Julius Erving .30 .75
16 Patrick Ewing .20 .50
17 Walt Frazier .15 .40
18 George Gervin .15 .40
19 Hal Greer .15 .40
20 John Havlicek .20 .50
21 Elvin Hayes .15 .40
22 Magic Johnson .40 1.00
23 Sam Jones .20 .50
24 Michael Jordan 1.25 3.00
25 Jerry Lucas .15 .40
26 Karl Malone .20 .50
27 Moses Malone .15 .40
28 Pete Maravich .50 1.25
29 Kevin McHale .20 .50
30 George Mikan .25 .60
31 Earl Monroe .15 .40
32 Shaquille O'Neal .40 1.00
33 Hakeem Olajuwon .20 .50
34 Robert Parish .15 .40
35 Bob Pettit .15 .40
36 Scottie Pippen .25 .60
37 Willis Reed .15 .40
38 Oscar Robertson .20 .50
39 David Robinson .20 .50
40 Bill Russell .25 .60
41 Dolph Schayes .15 .40
42 Bill Sharman .15 .40
43 John Stockton .20 .50
44 Isiah Thomas .15 .40
45 Nate Thurmond .15 .40
46 Wes Unseld .15 .40
47 Bill Walton .15 .40
48 Jerry West .20 .50
49 Lenny Wilkens .15 .40
50 James Worthy .20 .50
51 Kareem Abdul-Jabbar GS .25 .60
52 Nate Archibald GS .15 .40
53 Paul Arizin GS .15 .40
54 Charles Barkley GS .25 .60
55 Rick Barry GS .15 .40
56 Elgin Baylor GS .15 .40
57 Dave Bing GS .15 .40
58 Larry Bird GS .50 1.25
59 Wilt Chamberlain GS .30 .75
60 Bob Cousy GS .25 .60
61 Dave Cowens GS .15 .40
62 Billy Cunningham GS .15 .40
63 Dave DeBusschere GS .15 .40
64 Clyde Drexler GS .20 .50
65 Julius Erving GS .30 .75
66 Patrick Ewing GS .20 .50
67 Walt Frazier GS .15 .40
68 George Gervin GS .15 .40
69 Hal Greer GS .15 .40
70 John Havlicek GS .20 .50
71 Elvin Hayes GS .15 .40
72 Magic Johnson GS .40 1.00
73 Sam Jones GS .20 .50
74 Michael Jordan GS 1.25 3.00
75 Jerry Lucas GS .15 .40
76 Karl Malone GS .20 .50
77 Moses Malone GS .15 .40
78 Pete Maravich GS .50 1.25
79 Kevin McHale GS .20 .50
80 George Mikan GS .25 .60
81 Earl Monroe GS .15 .40
82 Shaquille O'Neal GS .40 1.00
83 Hakeem Olajuwon GS .20 .50
84 Robert Parish GS .15 .40
85 Bob Pettit GS .15 .40
86 Scottie Pippen GS .25 .60
87 Willis Reed GS .15 .40
88 Oscar Robertson GS .20 .50
89 David Robinson GS .25 .60
90 Bill Russell GS .25 .60
91 Dolph Schayes GS .15 .40
92 Bill Sharman GS .15 .40
93 John Stockton GS .20 .50
94 Isiah Thomas GS .15 .40
95 Nate Thurmond GS .15 .40
96 Wes Unseld GS .15 .40
97 Bill Walton GS .15 .40
98 Jerry West GS .20 .50
99 Lenny Wilkens GS .15 .40
100 James Worthy GS .20 .50
101 Kareem Abdul-Jabbar .25 .60
102 Nate Archibald .15 .40
103 Paul Arizin .15 .40
104 Charles Barkley .25 .60
105 Rick Barry .15 .40
106 Elgin Baylor .15 .40
107 Dave Bing .15 .40
108 Larry Bird .50 1.25
109 Wilt Chamberlain .30 .75
110 Bob Cousy .25 .60
111 Dave Cowens .15 .40
112 Billy Cunningham .15 .40
113 Dave DeBusschere .15 .40
114 Clyde Drexler .20 .50
115 Julius Erving .30 .75
116 Patrick Ewing .20 .50
117 Walt Frazier .15 .40
118 George Gervin .15 .40
119 Hal Greer .15 .40
120 John Havlicek .20 .50
121 Elvin Hayes .15 .40
122 Magic Johnson .40 1.00
123 Sam Jones .20 .50
124 Michael Jordan 1.25 3.00
125 Jerry Lucas .15 .40
126 Karl Malone .20 .50
127 Moses Malone .15 .40
128 Pete Maravich .50 1.25
129 Kevin McHale .20 .50
130 George Mikan .25 .60
131 Earl Monroe .15 .40
132 Shaquille O'Neal .40 1.00
133 Hakeem Olajuwon .20 .50
134 Robert Parish .15 .40
135 Bob Pettit .15 .40
136 Scottie Pippen .25 .60
137 Willis Reed .15 .40
138 Oscar Robertson .20 .50
139 David Robinson .25 .60
140 Bill Russell .25 .60
141 Dolph Schayes .15 .40
142 Bill Sharman .15 .40
143 John Stockton .20 .50
144 Isiah Thomas .15 .40
145 Nate Thurmond .15 .40
146 Wes Unseld .15 .40
147 Bill Walton .15 .40
148 Jerry West .20 .50
149 Lenny Wilkens .15 .40
150 James Worthy .20 .50

1996 Topps Stars Finest

Randomly inserted into all packs at a rate of one in six, this 150-card set was a parallel of the basic set. Card fronts on these cards utilized the Finest technology. Please refer to the multipliers in the header coupled with the value of the basic card to ascertain values.

COMPLETE SET (150) 150.00 300.00
*STARS: 2.5X TO 6X BASIC

1996 Topps Stars Finest Atomic Refractors

Randomly inserted into all packs at a rate of one in 96, this 150-card set was a parallel of the basic set. Card fronts on these cards utilized the Finest Atomic Refractor technology. Card backs are marked with the word "Atomic Refractor". To ascertain values on individual cards, please refer to the multiplier below coupled with the base card value.

*ATOMIC: 25X TO 60X BASE HI

1996 Topps Stars Finest Refractors

Randomly inserted into hobby packs at a rate of one in 20 and retail packs at one in 24, this 150-card set was a parallel of the basic set. Card fronts on these cards utilized the Finest Refractor technology. Card backs are marked with the word "Refractor". Each player has three different cards, but only one card is priced below. All cards carry the same value. Please refer to the multipliers in the header coupled with the value of the basic card to ascertain values.

*REFRACTORS: 8X TO 20X BASIC

1996 Topps Stars Imagine

Randomly inserted into all packs at a rate of one in 18, this 25-card dual player set uses computer imagery to pit two players from different eras against one another. Card backs carry an "I" prefix.

COMPLETE SET (25) 65.00 125.00
I1 Shaquille O'Neal 5.00 12.00
Wilt Chamberlain
I2 David Robinson 2.00 5.00
Dave Cowens
I3 Kareem Abdul-Jabbar 4.00 10.00
Bill Russell
I4 Scottie Pippen 4.00 10.00
Julius Erving
I5 Hakeem Olajuwon 2.00 5.00
Elvin Hayes
I6 Michael Jordan 10.00 25.00
Oscar Robertson
I7 Clyde Drexler 1.50 4.00
Earl Monroe
I8 Magic Johnson 4.00 10.00
Jerry West
I9 Larry Bird 3.00 8.00
Rick Barry
I10 Kevin McHale 1.50 4.00
Dave DeBusschere
I11 Moses Malone 1.25 3.00
Jerry Lucas
I12 Robert Parish 1.25 3.00
Nate Thurmond
I13 Pete Maravich 2.00 5.00
Sam Jones
I14 John Stockton 3.00 8.00
Bob Cousy
I15 Isiah Thomas 1.25 3.00
Bill Sharman
I16 Karl Malone 3.00 8.00
Bob Pettit
I17 Bill Walton 2.50 6.00
George Mikan
I18 Patrick Ewing 1.50 4.00
Willis Reed
I19 Billy Cunningham 1.25 3.00
James Worthy
I20 George Gervin 1.25 3.00
Hal Greer
I21 Wes Unseld 1.25 3.00
Dolph Schayes
I22 Nate Archibald 1.25 3.00
Lenny Wilkens
I23 Walt Frazier 1.25 3.00
Paul Arizin
I24 Charles Barkley 2.50 6.00
Elgin Baylor
I25 Dave Bing 2.50 6.00
John Havlicek

1996 Topps Stars Reprints

Randomly inserted into hobby packs at a rate of one in nine and retail at one in six, this 50-card set features reprints of each player's first Topps, Bowman or Star Company cards.

COMPLETE SET (50) 150.00 250.00
1 Lew Alcindor 5.00 12.00
2 Nate Archibald 1.25 3.00
3 Paul Arizin .75 2.00
4 Charles Barkley 5.00 12.00
5 Rick Barry 1.00 2.50
6 Elgin Baylor .75 2.00
7 Dave Bing .75 2.00
8 Larry Bird 10.00 25.00
Julius Erving
Magic Johnson
9 Wilt Chamberlain 5.00 12.00
10 Bob Cousy 3.00 8.00
11 Dave Cowens .75 2.00
12 Billy Cunningham .75 2.00
13 Dave DeBusschere .75 2.00
14 Clyde Drexler 1.50 4.00
15 Julius Erving 5.00 12.00
16 Patrick Ewing 1.50 4.00
17 Walt Frazier 1.25 3.00
18 George Gervin 1.25 3.00
19 Hal Greer .75 2.00
20 John Havlicek 3.00 8.00
21 Elvin Hayes 1.25 3.00
22 Larry Bird 10.00 25.00
Julius Erving
Magic Johnson
23 Sam Jones .75 2.00
24 Michael Jordan 15.00 40.00
25 Jerry Lucas .75 2.00
26 Karl Malone 3.00 8.00
27 Moses Malone 1.50 4.00
28 Pete Maravich 3.00 8.00
29 Kevin McHale 1.25 3.00
30 George Mikan 3.00 8.00
31 Earl Monroe 1.25 3.00
32 Shaquille O'Neal 3.00 8.00
33 Hakeem Olajuwon 4.00 10.00
34 Robert Parish 1.25 3.00
35 Bob Pettit 1.00 2.50
36 Scottie Pippen 4.00 10.00
37 Willis Reed .75 2.00
38 Oscar Robertson 3.00 8.00
39 David Robinson 2.50 6.00
40 Bill Russell 5.00 12.00
41 Dolph Schayes 1.50 4.00
42 Bill Sharman .75 2.00
43 John Stockton 1.50 4.00
44 Isiah Thomas 1.50 4.00
45 Nate Thurmond .75 2.00
46 Wes Unseld .75 2.00
47 Bill Walton 1.25 3.00
48 Jerry West 4.00 10.00
49 Len Wilkens UER .75 2.00
50 James Worthy 1.50 4.00

1996 Topps Stars Reprint Autographs

Inserted one per retail box, 10 of the 50 players from the Topps NBA Stars signed their reprint cards. Each card has a gold seal of authenticity and is signed on the front of the card in black ink. The set is skip-numbered. In addition, one of the ten cards were inserted into 1996-97 Topps Factory Hobby sets.

COMPLETE SET (10) 150.00 300.00
2 Nate Archibald 10.00 25.00
5 Rick Barry 10.00 25.00
17 Walt Frazier 10.00 25.00
18 George Gervin 10.00 25.00
21 Elvin Hayes 10.00 25.00
23 Sam Jones 10.00 25.00
30 George Mikan 80.00 200.00
31 Earl Monroe 10.00 25.00
37 Willis Reed 10.00 25.00
47 Bill Walton 10.00 25.00

1996 Topps Stars Members Only Parallel

COMPLETE SET (150) 300.00 500.00
*MO: 5X TO 12X BASE TOPPS STARS HI

1996 Topps Stars Imagine Members Only Parallel

COMPLETE SET (25) 60.00 150.00
*MO: .6X TO 1.5X BASE IMAGINE HI

1996 Topps Stars Reprints Members Only Parallel

COMPLETE SET (50) 150.00 300.00
*MO: .6X TO 1.5X BASE REPRINT HI

1996 Topps Stars Uncut Sheets

These two sheets were prizes awarded to collector's who received a Fan Favorite ballot card in Topps NBA Stars (around 1:6 packs), filled out their vote for the top five NBA players of all time, and correctly matched them with the overall tally taken from Topps' "blue ribbon media panel". Topps reported that only a small fraction (a total of 1,073 voters) correctly matched the top five players: Kareem Abdul-Jabar, Larry Bird, Wilt Chamberlain, Magic Johnson and Bill Russell. The 33 Basketball Hall of Famers that were in the top 50 NBA list had their Topps reprints on this two-sided, uncut sheet. There are two variations: a Gold bordered sheet awarded to correct entries from hobby packs (a reported 402) and a black bordered sheet awarded to correct entries from retail packs (a reported 671). The sheets were shipped in a round tube, so many of these thick stock sheets are curved as opposed to flat.

COMPLETE SET (2) 20.00 50.00
1 Black Bordered Sheet 10.00 25.00
2 Gold Bordered Sheet 10.00 25.00

2000-01 Topps Stars Promos

These six cards were given to hobby dealers and members of the media to promote the 2000-01 Topps Stars product. The set was shipped in a cello wrapper, and the card backs carry a "PP" prefix.

COMPLETE SET (6) 2.00 5.00
PP1 Allen Iverson 1.00 2.50
PP2 Jason Williams .50 1.25
PP3 Antonio McDyess .40 1.00
PP4 Alonzo Mourning .60 1.50
PP5 Ray Allen .50 1.25
PP6 Larry Hughes .40 1.00

2000-01 Topps Stars

Released in November 2000, the Topps Stars base set was comprised of 150 cards. Cards were available in six-card packs that carried a suggested retail price of $3.00. The base set was broken into the following themes: 100 veterans, 25 rookies, and 25 Spotlight subset cards.

COMPLETE SET (150) 30.00 60.00
1 Elton Brand .25 .60
2 Paul Pierce .30 .75
3 Baron Davis .25 .60
4 Corey Benjamin .15 .40
5 Jason Kidd .40 1.00
6 Stephon Marbury .20 .50
7 Eric Snow .15 .40
8 Joe Smith .20 .50
9 Larry Hughes .20 .50
10 Tim Duncan .50 1.25
11 Theo Ratliff .15 .40
12 Dikembe Mutombo .25 .60
13 Tim Hardaway .25 .60
14 Glenn Robinson .20 .50
15 Grant Hill .30 .75
16 Patrick Ewing .30 .75
17 Ron Mercer .15 .40
18 Ron Artest .25 .60
19 Tom Gugliotta .15 .40
20 Steve Smith .20 .50
21 Vlade Divac .20 .50
22 Rashard Lewis .25 .60
23 Tracy McGrady .40 1.00
24 Bryon Russell .15 .40
25 Michael Dickerson .15 .40
26 Juwan Howard .20 .50
27 Damon Stoudamire .20 .50
28 Hakeem Olajuwon .30 .75
29 Antonio McDyess .20 .50
30 Kobe Bryant 1.25 3.00
31 Lindsey Hunter .15 .40
32 Magic Johnson .75 2.00
33 Alonzo Mourning .30 .75
34 Kenny Anderson .20 .50
35 Allan Houston .20 .50
36 Keith Van Horn .20 .50
37 Shawn Marion .25 .60
38 David Robinson .40 1.00
39 Mitch Richmond .20 .50
40 Shaquille O'Neal .60 1.50
41 Gary Payton .25 .60
42 Sean Elliott .20 .50
43 Sam Cassell .25 .60
44 Dale Davis .15 .40
45 Derek Anderson .15 .40
46 Jonathan Bender .15 .40
47 Shandon Anderson .15 .40
48 Raef LaFrentz .15 .40
49 Michael Finley .25 .60
50 Toni Kukoc .20 .50
51 Anthony Mason .15 .40
52 Jim Jackson .15
53 Glen Rice .20
54 Jalen Rose .20
55 Keon Clark .15
56 Anfernee Hardaway .40 1.
57 Vin Baker .20
58 Shawn Kemp .25
59 John Stockton .30
60 Shareef Abdur-Rahim .20
61 Doug Christie .15
62 Lamond Murray .15
63 Scottie Pippen .40 1.
64 Darrell Armstrong .15
65 Marcus Camby .20
66 Wally Szczerbiak .20
67 Jamal Mashburn .20
68 Antonio Davis .15
69 Kevin Garnett .50 1.
70 Cuttino Mobley .20
71 Jerry Stackhouse .20
72 Cedric Ceballos .15
73 Nick Van Exel .20
74 Latrell Sprewell .20
75 Antoine Walker .20
76 Allen Iverson .50 1.
77 Antawn Jamison .25
78 Derrick Coleman .15
79 Jason Terry .25
80 Steve Francis .25
81 Reggie Miller .25
82 Rasheed Wallace .25
83 Chris Webber .25
84 Donyell Marshall .15
85 Ruben Patterson .15
86 Terrell Brandon .15
87 Mike Bibby .20
88 Richard Hamilton .20
89 Jason Williams .25
90 Corey Maggette .20
91 Kerry Kittles .15
92 Karl Malone .30
93 Rod Strickland .20
94 Eddie Jones .25
95 Maurice Taylor .15
96 Dirk Nowitzki .40 1.
97 Andre Miller .20
98 Lamar Odom .25
99 Ray Allen .25
100 Vince Carter .50 1.
101 Chris Mihm RC .25
102 Kenyon Martin RC .60 1.
103 Stromile Swift RC .25
104 Joel Przybilla RC .25
105 Marcus Fizer RC .25
106 Mike Miller RC .50 1.
107 Darius Miles RC .25
108 Mark Madsen RC .25
109 Courtney Alexander RC .25
110 DeShawn Stevenson RC .30
111 DerMarr Johnson RC .25
112 Mamadou N'Diaye RC .25
113 Mateen Cleaves RC .25
114 Morris Peterson RC .25
115 Etan Thomas RC .25
116 Erick Barkley RC .25
117 Quentin Richardson RC .40 1.
118 Keyon Dooling RC .25
119 Jerome Moiso RC .25
120 Desmond Mason RC .30
121 Speedy Claxton RC .25
122 Jamaal Magloire RC .25
123 Donnell Harvey RC .25
124 Jamal Crawford RC .40 1.
125 Jason Collier RC .25
126 Tim Duncan SPOT .50 1.
127 Shaquille O'Neal SPOT .60 1.
128 Vince Carter SPOT .50 1.
129 Allen Iverson SPOT .50 1.
130 Jason Kidd SPOT .40 1.
131 Kevin Garnett SPOT .50 1.
132 Gary Payton SPOT .25
133 Tracy McGrady SPOT .40 1.
134 Jason Williams SPOT .25
135 Kobe Bryant SPOT 1.25 3.
136 Elton Brand SPOT .25
137 Ray Allen SPOT .25
138 Grant Hill SPOT .30
139 Chris Webber SPOT .25
140 Latrell Sprewell SPOT .25
141 Alonzo Mourning SPOT .30
142 Lamar Odom SPOT .25
143 Shareef Abdur-Rahim SPOT .25
144 Steve Francis SPOT .25
145 Magic Johnson SPOT .75 2.
146 Darius Miles SPOT .25
147 Kenyon Martin SPOT .60 1.
148 Marcus Fizer SPOT .25
149 Mateen Cleaves SPOT .25
150 Stromile Swift SPOT .25

2000-01 Topps Stars Parallel

Randomly inserted in packs at one in 18 for the regu[lar] cards and one in 261 for the Spotlight subset, this 150-card set parallels the base set. The cards from th[e] regular set (1-125) were serially numbered to 299, while the Spotlight subset cards (126-150) were serially numbered to 99. To ascertain values on individual cards, please refer to the multiplier in the header, coupled with the value of the base card.

*BASE STARS: 5X TO 12X BASE CARD HI
*BASE RCs: 2.5X TO 6X BASE CARD HI
*SUB.STARS: 10X TO 25X SUBSET CARD HI
*SUB.RCs: 10X TO 25X SUBSET CARD HI
135 Kobe Bryant SPOT 40.00 100.

2000-01 Topps Stars All-Star Authority

Randomly inserted in packs at one in 12, this 15-card set features All-Star players who continuously demonstrate their dominance of the NBA. Card backs carry an "ASA" prefix.

COMPLETE SET (15) 7.50 15.00
ASA1 John Stockton .75 2.00
ASA2 Shaquille O'Neal 1.50 4.00
ASA3 Patrick Ewing .75 2.00
ASA4 Hakeem Olajuwon .75 2.00
ASA5 Karl Malone .75 2.00
ASA6 Grant Hill .75 2.00
ASA7 Alonzo Mourning .75 2.00
ASA8 Jason Kidd 1.00 2.50
ASA9 Gary Payton .60 1.50
ASA10 Scottie Pippen 1.00 2.50
ASA11 Tim Duncan 1.25 3.00
ASA12 Kevin Garnett 1.25 3.00
ASA13 Reggie Miller .60 1.50
ASA14 David Robinson 1.00 2.50
ASA15 Dikembe Mutombo .60 1.50

2000-01 Topps Stars Autographs

Randomly inserted in packs at an overall rate of one in 316, this 10-card set features autographs of top players in the NBA. Each card features the Topps "Certified Autograph Issue" stamp. The autographs were broken into two levels: Level "A" were inserted at one in 359 packs, while Level "B" were inserted at one in 2,599 packs.

TSAJ Antawn Jamison A 4.00 10.00
TSCA Courtney Alexander A 4.00 10.00
TSEB Elton Brand A 5.00 12.00
TSJC Jamal Crawford A 8.00 20.00
TSJR Jalen Rose A 5.00 12.00
TSMC Mateen Cleaves A 4.00 10.00
TSMJ Magic Johnson A 40.00 100.00
TSSF Steve Francis A 5.00 12.00
TSTD Tim Duncan B 75.00 150.00
TSTM Tracy McGrady A 12.50 30.00

2000-01 Topps Stars Game Jerseys

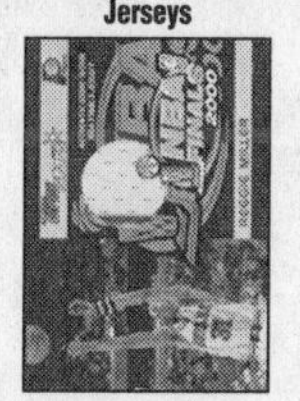

Randomly inserted in packs at an overall rate of one in 71, this 34-card set features swatches of game-worn jersey from players who participated in the 2000 NBA Finals.

TSR1A Shaquille O'Neal 20.00 50.00
TSR1H Shaquille O'Neal 20.00 50.00
TSR2A Glen Rice 5.00 12.00
TSR2H Glen Rice 5.00 12.00
TSR3A Robert Horry 5.00 12.00
TSR3H Robert Horry 5.00 12.00
TSR4A Rick Fox 5.00 12.00
TSR4H Rick Fox 5.00 12.00
TSR5A Brian Shaw 4.00 10.00
TSR5H Brian Shaw 4.00 10.00
TSR6A Ron Harper 5.00 12.00
TSR6H Ron Harper 5.00 12.00
TSR7A Derek Fisher 6.00 15.00
TSR7H Derek Fisher 6.00 15.00
TSR8A A.C. Green 6.00 15.00
TSR8H A.C. Green 5.00 12.00
TSR9A John Salley 4.00 10.00
TSR9H John Salley 4.00 10.00
TSR10A Travis Knight 4.00 10.00
TSR10H Travis Knight 4.00 10.00
TSR11A Devean George 4.00 10.00
TSR11H Devean George 4.00 10.00
TSR12 Reggie Miller 15.00 40.00
TSR13 Jalen Rose 5.00 12.00
TSR14 Dale Davis 4.00 10.00
TSR15 Rik Smits 4.00 10.00
TSR16 Mark Jackson 5.00 12.00
TSR17 Travis Best 4.00 10.00
TSR18 Austin Croshere 4.00 10.00
TSR19 Derrick McKey 4.00 10.00
TSR20 Sam Perkins 4.00 10.00
TSR21 Chris Mullin 15.00 40.00
TSR22 Jonathan Bender 4.00 10.00
TSR23 Zan Tabak 4.00 10.00

2000-01 Topps Stars On the Horizon

Randomly inserted in packs at one in 36, this 10-card set takes a look at young stars ready to explode in the NBA. Card backs carry a "H" prefix.

COMPLETE SET (10) 6.00 15.00
H1 Steve Francis .75 2.00
H2 Elton Brand .75 2.00
H3 Tracy McGrady 1.25 3.00
H4 Stephon Marbury .60 1.50
H5 Lamar Odom .75 2.00
H6 Kenyon Martin 2.00 5.00
H7 Shareef Abdur-Rahim .60 1.50
H8 Marcus Fizer .75 2.00
H9 Larry Hughes .60 1.50
H10 Darius Miles .75 2.00

2000-01 Topps Stars Progression

Randomly inserted in packs at one in 24, this five-card set showcases players from the past, present and future on one card. Card backs carry a "P" prefix.

COMPLETE SET (5) 5.00 12.00
P1 Patrick Ewing .75 2.00
Alonzo Mourning
Chris Mihm
P2 Karl Malone 2.00 5.00
Elton Brand
Kenyon Martin
P3 Scottie Pippen 1.00 2.50
Vince Carter
Darius Miles
P4 Mitch Richmond 1.50 4.00
Kobe Bryant
Courtney Alexander
P5 Magic Johnson 1.25 3.00
John Stockton
Jamal Crawford

2000-01 Topps Stars Walk of Fame

Randomly inserted in packs at one in eight, this 15-card set features current superstars compared against all-time greats at their position. Card backs carry a "WF" prefix.

COMPLETE SET (15) 7.50 15.00
WF1 Grant Hill .60 1.50
WF2 Vince Carter 1.00 2.50
WF3 Kevin Garnett 1.00 2.50
WF4 Jason Kidd .75 2.00
WF5 Gary Payton .50 1.25
WF6 Tim Duncan 1.00 2.50
WF7 Allen Iverson 1.00 2.50
WF8 Kobe Bryant 2.50 6.00
WF9 Ray Allen .50 1.25
WF10 Shareef Abdur-Rahim .40 1.00
WF11 Chris Webber .50 1.25
WF12 Karl Malone .60 1.50
WF13 Reggie Miller .50 1.25
WF14 Jason Williams .50 1.25
WF15 Elton Brand .50 1.25

1997 Topps Stickers

Released in some retail outlets, or through the Topps Stadium Club Members Only catalog, these stickers were issued on five different sheets. Each sheet contained 12 players and had a suggested retail price of $1.49. Boxes were available for $19.95.

COMPLETE SET (5) 3.00 8.00
1 Glen Rice .75 2.00
Dino Radja
Grant Hill
Clifford Robinson
Jerry Stackhouse
Horace Grant
Terrell Brandon
Lorenzen Wright
Sean Elliott
Stephon Marbury
Shaquille O'Neal
Ray Allen
2 Hakeem Olajuwon .75 2.00
Marcus Camby
Kobe Bryant
Chris Webber
Jayson Williams
Kenny Anderson
David Robinson
Joe Dumars
Michael Finley
Reggie Miller
Scottie Pippen
Latrell Sprewell
3 Alonzo Mourning .75 2.00
Bobby Phills
Christian Laettner
Dennis Rodman
Jason Kidd
Joe Smith
John Starks
Juwan Howard
Karl Malone
Kevin Garnett
Bryant Reeves
Mitch Richmond
4 Brent Barry .75 2.00
Anthony Mason
Antonio McDyess
Allen Iverson
Brian Grant
Charles Barkley
Dikembe Mutombo
John Stockton
Kerry Kittles
Rik Smits
Shawn Kemp
Tim Hardaway
5 Derek Harper .75 2.00
Patrick Ewing
Greg Anthony
Gary Payton
Kevin Johnson
Doug Christie
LaPhonso Ellis
Antoine Walker
Damon Stoudamire
Rony Seikaly
Vin Baker
Shareef Abdur-Rahim

2005-06 Topps Style

Released in May 2006, Style boasts a 165-card set where numbers 1-130 feature veteran players, numbers 131-160 feature rookie players and numbers 161-165 feature celebrities. Also printed was card number seven, a special Mickey Mantle basketball card. The set design is that of the 1952 Topps baseball set which utilizes white borders, colorful backgrounds, images that appear as though they were painted and a white-out name box along the bottom with the player's name and a fascimile signature. Style was packaged in 18-pack boxes where packs contain nine cards and carried an initial SRP of $6.00.

COMPLETE SET (165) 30.00 80.00
UNPRICED SUPERFR.PRINT RUN ONE SET
1 Ben Wallace .50 1.25
2 Joe Johnson .50 1.25
3 Luol Deng .50 1.25
4 Morris Peterson .30 .75
5 Jason Terry .40 1.00
6 Carmelo Anthony 1.00 2.50
7 Mickey Mantle 3.00 8.00
8 Ron Artest .50 1.25
9 Elton Brand .50 1.25
10 Chris Mihm .30 .75
11 Shane Battier .40 1.00
12 Speedy Claxton .30 .75
13 Baron Davis .50 1.25
14 Damon Stoudamire .40 1.00
15 Desmond Mason .30 .75
16 Marko Jaric .30 .75
17 Vince Carter .75 2.00
18 Sam Cassell .50 1.25
19 J.R. Smith .50 1.25
20 Trevor Ariza .30 .75
21 Quentin Richardson .40 1.00
22 Jamal Crawford .40 1.00
23 Dwight Howard 1.00 2.50
24 Kyle Korver .40 1.00
25 Steve Nash .60 1.50
26 Amare Stoudemire .50 1.25
27 Zach Randolph .40 1.00
28 Brad Miller .50 1.25
29 Tim Duncan .75 2.00
30 Michael Finley .50 1.25
31 Ray Allen .50 1.25
32 Luke Ridnour .40 1.00
33 Andrei Kirilenko .40 1.00
34 Tony Allen .30 .75
35 Paul Pierce .60 1.50
36 Al Jefferson .50 1.25
37 Emeka Okafor .50 1.25
38 Al Harrington .40 1.00
39 Ben Gordon .50 1.25
40 Andres Nocioni .30 .75
41 Zydrunas Ilgauskas .30 .75
42 Anderson Varejao .40 1.00
43 Keith Van Horn .40 1.00
44 Richard Hamilton .40 1.00
45 Stromile Swift .30 .75
46 Dirk Nowitzki .75 2.00
47 Stephen Jackson .40 1.00
48 Pau Gasol .50 1.25
49 Lamar Odom .50 1.25
50 Kobe Bryant 2.50 6.00
51 Shaquille O'Neal 1.00 2.50
52 Jason Williams .40 1.00
53 Dwyane Wade 1.25 3.00
54 Michael Redd .50 1.25
55 Joe Smith .40 1.00
56 Troy Hudson .30 .75
57 Jameer Nelson .40 1.00
58 Chris Webber .50 1.25
59 Darius Miles .30 .75
60 Chris Wilcox .30 .75
61 Rafer Alston .30 .75
62 Kirk Hinrich .50 1.25
63 Jalen Rose .30 .75
64 Matt Harpring .40 1.00
65 Caron Butler .50 1.25
66 Shareef Abdur-Rahim .40 1.00
67 Josh Childress .40 1.00
68 Delonte West .40 1.00
69 Brevin Knight .30 .75
70 Larry Hughes .40 1.00
71 Dikembe Mutombo .50 1.25
72 Kenyon Martin .50 1.25
73 Earl Boykins .30 .75
74 Tayshaun Prince .50 1.25
75 Chauncey Billups .50 1.25
76 Josh Smith .50 1.25
77 Troy Murphy .40 1.00
78 Jermaine O'Neal .50 1.25
79 Corey Maggette .40 1.00
80 Wally Szczerbiak .40 1.00
81 Richard Jefferson .50 1.25
82 Nenad Krstic .30 .75
83 Jason Kidd .75 2.00
84 Jamaal Magloire .30 .75
85 Stephon Marbury .40 1.00
86 Samuel Dalembert .30 .75
87 Andre Iguodala .50 1.25
88 Yao Ming .60 1.50
89 Kurt Thomas .30 .75
90 Brendan Haywood .30 .75
91 Peja Stojakovic .50 1.25
92 Mike Bibby .50 1.25
93 Tony Parker .50 1.25
94 Manu Ginobili .50 1.25
95 Rashard Lewis .50 1.25
96 Mehmet Okur .30 .75
97 Gilbert Arenas .50 1.25
98 Antawn Jamison .50 1.25
99 Ricky Davis .40 1.00
100 Shawn Marion .50 1.25
101 Melvin Ely .30 .75
102 Tyson Chandler .40 1.00
103 Jason Richardson .50 1.25
104 Drew Gooden .40 1.00
105 Josh Howard .50 1.25
106 Marcus Camby .40 1.00
107 Jerry Stackhouse .40 1.00
108 Andre Miller .40 1.00
109 Rasheed Wallace .50 1.25
110 Mike Dunleavy .40 1.00
111 LeBron James 2.50 6.00
112 Allen Iverson .75 2.00
113 Tracy McGrady .60 1.50
114 Jamaal Tinsley .30 .75
115 Cuttino Mobley .40 1.00
116 Kwame Brown .30 .75
117 Derek Anderson .30 .75
118 Eddie Jones .40 1.00
119 Antoine Walker .40 1.00
120 Alonzo Mourning .60 1.50
121 Bobby Simmons .30 .75
122 Kevin Garnett 1.00 2.50
123 P.J. Brown .30 .75
124 Steve Francis .50 1.25
125 Grant Hill .60 1.50
126 Primoz Brezec .30 .75
127 Mike Miller .50 1.25
128 Sebastian Telfair .40 1.00
129 Chris Bosh .50 1.25
130 Carlos Boozer .50 1.25
131 Andrew Bogut RC 2.00 5.00
132 Raymond Felton RC 2.00 5.00
133 Ike Diogu RC 1.25 3.00
134 Rashad McCants RC 1.25 3.00
135 Gerald Green RC 1.50 4.00
136 Jarrett Jack RC 1.25 3.00
137 Linas Kleiza RC 1.25 3.00
138 Brandon Bass RC 1.50 4.00
139 Marvin Williams RC 1.50 4.00
140 Martell Webster RC 1.25 3.00
141 Sarunas Jasikevicius RC 1.25 3.00
142 Antoine Wright RC 1.25 3.00
143 Hakim Warrick RC 1.50 4.00
144 Francisco Garcia RC 1.50 4.00
145 Wayne Simien RC 1.25 3.00
146 Monta Ellis RC 2.50 6.00
147 Deron Williams RC 3.00 8.00
148 Charlie Villanueva RC 1.50 4.00
149 Chris Taft RC 1.25 3.00
150 Joey Graham RC 1.25 3.00
151 Julius Hodge RC 1.25 3.00
152 Luther Head RC 1.25 3.00
153 David Lee RC 2.00 5.00
154 Chris Paul RC 5.00 12.00
155 Channing Frye RC 1.50 4.00
156 Sean May RC 1.25 3.00
157 Danny Granger RC 2.50 6.00
158 Nate Robinson RC 1.50 4.00
159 Jason Maxiell RC 1.25 3.00
160 Salim Stoudamire RC 1.25 3.00
161 Christie Brinkley 2.00 5.00
162 Carmen Electra 2.00 5.00
163 Shannon Elizabeth 2.00 5.00
164 Jenny McCarthy 2.00 5.00
165 Jay-Z 2.00 5.00

2005-06 Topps Style Chrome

Randomly seeded in packs, this 165-card set parallels the base set enhanced with a chrome foil card stock and sequential numbering to 499.

*1-130 CHROME: .75X TO 2X BASE HI
*131-165 CHROME: .6X TO 1.5X BASE HI

2005-06 Topps Style Chrome Refractors

Randomly seeded in packs, this 165-card set parallels the base set enhanced with a chrome foil card stock, the rainbow holofoil refractor effect and sequential numbering to 299.

*1-130 REF: 1.25X TO 3X BASE HI
*131-165 REF: .75X TO 2X BASE HI

2005-06 Topps Style Chrome Refractors Blue

Randomly seeded in packs, this 165-card set parallels the base set enhanced with a chrome foil card stock, the rainbow holofoil refractor effect, a blue background treatment and sequential numbering to 149.

*1-130 REF.BLUE: 2.5X TO 6X BASE HI
*131-165 REF.BLUE: 1X TO 2.5X BASE HI
50 Kobe Bryant 20.00 50.00
111 LeBron James 20.00 50.00

2005-06 Topps Style Chrome Refractors Gold

Randomly seeded in packs, this 165-card set parallels the base set enhanced with a chrome foil card stock, the rainbow holofoil refractor effect, a gold background treatment and sequential numbering to 25.

*1-130 GOLD: 8X TO 20X BASE HI
*131-160 GOLD: 4X TO 10X BASE HI
*161-165 GOLD: 3X TO 8X BASE HI
7 Mickey Mantle 50.00 120.00
50 Kobe Bryant 100.00 250.00
147 Deron Williams 40.00 100.00
154 Chris Paul 125.00 250.00

2005-06 Topps Style Dwyane Wade Comics

Inserted randomly in packs, this four-card set features comic images of Dwyane Wade on a white background serially numbered to 499.

COMPLETE SET (4) 4.00 10.00
COMMON CARD (1-4) 1.50 4.00
COMMON AUTO (1-4) 40.00 100.00
AUTO STATED ODDS 1:2991
COMMON ART.AU (1-4) 10.00 25.00
ART.AU PRINT RUN 75 SER.#'d SETS
AU DUAL STATED ODDS 1:7704
JSY AU STATED ODDS 1:14124
COMMON RELIC (1-4) 6.00 15.00
RELIC PRINT RUN 99 SER.#'d SETS

2005-06 Topps Style Fan Favorites Autographs

Inserted randomly in packs at the rate of one in 10, this 188-card set uses card designs from both previous year's baseball and basketball sets where each card contains an authentic player autograph. These cards are not serially numbered but print runs were provided by Topps as announced print runs.

UNPRICED CHROME PRINT RUN 8-10 SETS
AA Al Attles/176* 6.00 15.00
AB Andrew Bogut/417* 8.00 20.00
AC Archie Clark/212* 12.00 30.00
AD Adrian Dantley/320* 8.00 20.00
AG A.C. Green/406* 10.00 25.00
AG Artis Gilmore/188* 10.00 25.00
AJ Aaron James/192* 6.00 15.00
AK Albert King/216* 6.00 15.00
BB Bill Bradley/223* 75.00 150.00
BC Billy Cunningham/214* 40.00 100.00
BH Bailey Howell/219* 12.50 30.00
BJ Bobby Jones/220* 15.00 40.00
BK Bernard King/420* 8.00 20.00
BL Bob Lanier/217* 12.00 30.00
BP Billy Paultz/220* 8.00 20.00
BS Bud Stallworth/196* 6.00 15.00
BT Brian Taylor/220* 6.00 15.00
BW Bill Walton/220* 8.00 20.00
CD Chris Dudley/210* 6.00 15.00
CE Craig Ehlo/318* 6.00 15.00
CH Clem Haskins/220* 6.00 15.00
CM Chris Morris/228* 6.00 15.00
CM Calvin Murphy/219* 6.00 15.00
CR Campy Russell/200* 6.00 15.00
CS Charles Smith/199* 6.00 15.00
CW Chuck Williams/220* 6.00 15.00
DA Dan Anderson/194* 6.00 15.00
DB Dee Brown/405* 8.00 20.00
DC Darwin Cook/217* 6.00 15.00
DD Darryl Dawkins/219* 6.00 15.00
DE Dale Ellis/212* 8.00 20.00
DG Danny Granger/410* 8.00 20.00
DI Dan Issel/220* 15.00 40.00
DK Don Kojis/215* 15.00 40.00
DL Dennis Layton/220* 6.00 15.00
DM Dan Majerle/220* 30.00 80.00
DR Dennis Rodman/218* 25.00 60.00
DS Danny Schayes/220* 8.00 20.00
DT David Thompson/220* 12.50 30.00
DW Deron Williams/419* 12.50 30.00
EB Elgin Baylor/417* 10.00 25.00
EJ Eddie Johnson/405* 6.00 15.00
EK Eugene Kennedy/205* 6.00 15.00
EM Earl Monroe/65* 25.00 60.00
EM Eric Money/203* 6.00 15.00
FB Frank Brickowski/213* 6.00 15.00
FC Fred Carter/220* 6.00 15.00
FE Franklin Edwards/219* 6.00 15.00
FL Fat Lever/219* 6.00 15.00
FR Flynn Robinson/209* 6.00 15.00
GG George Gervin/220* 12.00 30.00
GH Gar Heard/420* 6.00 15.00
GM Glenn McDonald/220* 6.00 15.00
GT George Tinsley/218* 6.00 15.00
GW Gerald Wilkens/415* 6.00 15.00
HC Harvey Catchings/219* 6.00 15.00
HG Harry Gallatin/220* 10.00 25.00
HH Hersey Hawkins/320* 6.00 15.00
HP Howard Porter/211* 10.00 25.00
HW Herb Williams/318* 6.00 15.00
JB Junior Bridgeman/220* 6.00 15.00
JE Johnny Egan/214* 6.00 15.00
JG Johnny Green/218* 6.00 15.00
JH Jeff Hornacek/420* 8.00 20.00
JJ J.J. Johnson/413* 6.00 15.00
JL John Lambert/217* 6.00 15.00
JM Jeff Mullins/220* 6.00 15.00
JN Johnny Newman/320* 6.00 15.00
JR Joe Roberts/409* 6.00 15.00
JS Jack Sikma/404* 6.00 15.00
JW Jim Washington/210* 6.00 15.00
KB Kent Benson/217* 6.00 15.00
KC Kenny Charles/215* 6.00 15.00
KE Keith Edmonson/218* 8.00 20.00
KH Keith Herron/220* 6.00 15.00
KT Kelly Tripucka/220* 6.00 15.00
KV Kiki Vandeweghe/420* 6.00 15.00
LC Len Chappell/219* 6.00 15.00
LE Len Elmore/215* 6.00 15.00
LG Lamar Green/199* 6.00 15.00
LH Lou Hudson/401* 6.00 15.00
LM Larue Martin/215* 6.00 15.00
LN Larry Nance/420* 8.00 20.00
LW Lenny Wilkens/405* 10.00 25.00
MB Muggsy Bogues/219* 12.50 30.00
MC Maurice Cheeks/218* 6.00 15.00
MD Mel Davis/215* 6.00 15.00
ME Mark Eaton/209* 6.00 15.00
MG Mike Gale/220* 6.00 15.00
MJ Magic Johnson/220* 40.00 80.00
ML Maurice Lucas/217* 6.00 15.00
MM Moses Malone/212* 12.50 30.00
MW Mark West/221* 6.00 15.00
NA Nate Archibald/220* 8.00 20.00
NN Norm Nixon/219* 8.00 20.00
OB Otis Birdsong/200* 6.00 15.00
OG Orien Greene/420* 6.00 15.00
OR Oscar Robertson/215* 100.00 200.00
OT Ollie Taylor/220* 6.00 15.00
PA Paul Arizin/219* 15.00 40.00
PW Paul Westphal/409* 6.00 15.00
RB Rick Barry/220* 15.00 30.00
RD Rick Darnell/217* 6.00 15.00
RF Raymond Felton/419* 8.00 20.00
RG Richie Guerin/219* 10.00 25.00
RH Roy Hinson/217* 6.00 15.00
RK Rich Kelley/220* 6.00 15.00
RM Rodney McCray/220* 6.00 15.00
RP Ricky Pierce/219* 6.00 15.00
RR Rich Rinaldi/190* 8.00 20.00
RR Robert Reid/220* 6.00 15.00
RS Rik Smits/384* 8.00 20.00
RT Reggie Theus/420* 6.00 15.00
SG Sidney Green/339* 6.00 15.00
SH Spencer Haywood Red/207* 6.00 15.00
SL Sam Lacey/220* 6.00 15.00
SM Sean May/417* 6.00 15.00
ST Sedric Toney/213* 6.00 15.00
SW Samuel Williams/220* 6.00 15.00
TC Terry Cummings/320* 8.00 20.00
TG Tate George/219* 6.00 15.00
TH Tom Hoover/219* 6.00 15.00
TR Tree Rollins/405* 6.00 15.00
TS Tom Sanders/220* 6.00 15.00
TT Thomas Thacker/219* 6.00 15.00
TW Reggie Williams/214* 6.00 15.00
WD Walter Davis/418* 8.00 20.00
WF Walt Frazier/217* 10.00 25.00
WH Walt Hazzard/218* 6.00 15.00
WJ Wali Jones/203* 6.00 15.00
WN Willie Norwood/205* 6.00 15.00
WT Wayman Tisdale/218* 6.00 15.00
WW Walt Wesley/220* 6.00 15.00
XM Xavier McDaniel/208* 8.00 20.00
ZA Zaid Abdul-Aziz/218* 6.00 15.00
AC2 Austin Carr/203* 8.00 20.00
AJ2 Alfonso Buck Johnson/215* 6.00 15.00
BB2 Bob Boozer/220* 8.00 20.00
BH2 Bobby Hansen/406* 6.00 15.00
BL2 Bob Love/208* 10.00 25.00
BS2 Byron Scott/420* 10.00 25.00
BW2 Buck Williams/211* 8.00 20.00
CD2 Clyde Drexler/419* 12.50 30.00
CH2 Cliff Hagan/189* 12.50 30.00
CH3 Connie Hawkins/420* 10.00 25.00
CM2 Cliff Meely/187* 8.00 20.00
DA2 Dennis Awtrey/219* 6.00 15.00
DA3 Don Adams/210* 6.00 15.00
DC2 Dave Cowens/220* 10.00 25.00
DC3 Duane Causwell/220* 6.00 15.00
DD2 Dwight Davis/219* 6.00 15.00
DM2 Dick McGuire/220* 10.00 25.00
DS2 Detlef Schrempf/420* 6.00 15.00
DS3 Dick Schnittker/220* 12.50 30.00
DS4 Dick Snyder/219* 10.00 25.00
DS5 Dolph Schayes/219* 15.00 30.00
DW2 Dominique Wilkins/213* 15.00 40.00
EB2 Em Bryant/217* 6.00 15.00
FB2 Fred Brown/216* 6.00 15.00
FC2 Fred Crawford/201* 6.00 15.00
GH2 Geoff Huston/205* 6.00 15.00
GM2 Greg Minor/210* 6.00 15.00
GW2 Gus Williams/218* 10.00 25.00
JJ2 Jimmy Jones/222* 6.00 15.00
JL2 John Lucas/218* 6.00 15.00
JM2 Jerrod Mustaf/209* 6.00 15.00
JS2 James Silas/206* 10.00 25.00
JS3 John Starks/196* 10.00 25.00
JW2 Jo Jo White/200* 10.00 25.00
KE2 Keith Erickson/218* 6.00 15.00
LG2 Leonard Gray/201* 6.00 15.00
LN2 Louie Nelson/194* 6.00 15.00
MD2 Mike Davis/180* 6.00 15.00
MJ2 Major Jones/204* 6.00 15.00
RB2 Rolando Blackman/218* 8.00 20.00
RB3 Ron Behagen/213* 6.00 15.00
RB4 Ron Boone/213* 6.00 15.00
RP2 Robert Parish/420* 10.00 25.00
RS2 Rory Sparrow/219* 6.00 15.00
SH2 Spencer Haywood/194* 8.00 20.00
SW2 Slick Watts/218* 15.00 30.00
TC2 Tom Chambers/405* 6.00 15.00
TC4 Tyrone Corbin/219* 6.00 15.00
TH2 Tommy Hawkins/220* 8.00 20.00
TT2 Trent Tucker/421* 6.00 15.00
WF2 World B. Free/216* 15.00 30.00

2005-06 Topps Style Hardwood Classics

Inserted in packs at the rate of one in six, this 75-card set is horizontally designed with a player image on the right and an "H" shaped swatch of memorabilia on the left. Though unconfirmed, it appears every swatch of memorabilia was taken from some form of throwback apparel.

N Nene 2.00 5.00
AH Alan Henderson 2.00 5.00
AI Andre Iguodala 2.50 6.00
AJ Anthony Johnson 2.00 5.00
AM Aaron McKie 2.00 5.00
BC Brian Cook 2.00 5.00
BG Brian Grant 2.00 5.00
BR Bryon Russell 2.00 5.00
BW Ben Wallace 2.50 6.00
CA Carmelo Anthony 5.00 12.00
CB Caron Butler 2.50 6.00
CR Cliff Robinson 2.00 5.00
CW Corliss Williamson 2.00 5.00
DA Darrell Armstrong 2.00 5.00
DC Doug Christie 2.00 5.00
DD Dale Davis 2.00 5.00
DG Drew Gooden 2.00 5.00
DJ DerMarr Johnson 2.00 5.00
DW David Wesley 2.00 5.00
ED Erick Dampier 2.00 5.00
EN Eduardo Najera 1.50 4.00
ES Eric Snow 2.00 5.00
ET Etan Thomas 2.00 5.00
GA Gilbert Arenas 2.50 6.00
GO Greg Ostertag 2.00 5.00
HT Hedo Turkoglu 2.50 6.00
IN Ira Newble 2.00 5.00
JF Jeff Foster 2.00 5.00
JH Juwan Howard 2.00 5.00
JJ Jared Jeffries 2.00 5.00
JP Joel Przybilla 2.00 5.00
JS Jerry Stackhouse 2.00 5.00
JT Jamaal Tinsley 2.00 5.00
KB Kobe Bryant 10.00 25.00
KM Kenyon Martin 2.50 6.00
KO Kevin Ollie 2.00 5.00
KT Kurt Thomas 2.00 5.00
LH Lindsey Hunter 2.00 5.00
MB Michael Bradley 2.00 5.00
MD Mike Dunleavy 2.00 5.00
ME Maurice Evans 2.00 5.00
MJ Marc Jackson 2.00 5.00
MN Moochie Norris 2.00 5.00
MT Maurice Taylor 2.00 5.00
PG Pat Garrity 2.00 5.00
RB Ryan Bowen 2.00 5.00
RP Ruben Patterson 2.00 5.00
SA Stacey Augmon 2.00 5.00
SB Steve Blake 2.00 5.00
SJ Stephen Jackson 2.00 5.00
SM Stephon Marbury 2.00 5.00
SP Scott Padgett 2.00 5.00
TA Trevor Ariza 1.50 4.00
TB Tony Battie 2.00 5.00
TM Troy Murphy 2.00 5.00
TR Theo Ratliff 2.00 5.00
TT Tim Thomas 2.00 5.00
CAT Chucky Atkins 2.00 5.00
CWE Clarence Weatherspoon 2.00 5.00
DAN Derek Anderson 1.50 4.00
DST Damon Stoudamire 2.00 5.00
JBA Jon Barry 2.00 5.00
JJO Jumaine Jones 2.00 5.00
JJS James Jones 2.00 5.00
JWI Jerome Williams 2.00 5.00
KBR Kwame Brown 2.00 5.00
KVH Keith Van Horn 2.00 5.00
MDA Marquis Daniels 2.00 5.00
NVE Nick Van Exel 2.50 6.00
SAR Shareef Abdur-Rahim 2.00 5.00
SBR Shawn Bradley 2.00 5.00
SME Slava Medvedenko 2.00 5.00

2008-09 Topps T51 Murad

This set was released on February 26, 2009. The base set consists of 230 cards. Cards 1-170 feature veterans, and cards 171-200 are rookies. Cards 201-230 are short-printed veterans.

COMPLETE SET (230) 100.00 200.00
UNPRICED PRESS PLATE PRINT RUN ONE SET
1 Elton Brand .50 1.25
2 Ray Allen .50 1.25
3 Allen Iverson .60 1.50
4 Luis Scola .40 1.00
5 Jason Kidd .50 1.25
6 Lamar Odom .50 1.25
7 Yi Jianlian .50 1.25
8 Marcus Camby .30 .75
9 Jamal Crawford .40 1.00
10 Steve Nash .50 1.25
11 Al Harrington .40 1.00
12 Carmelo Anthony .60 1.50
13 Peja Stojakovic .50 1.25
14 Mike Dunleavy .40 1.00
15 Larry Hughes .40 1.00
16 Josh Smith .50 1.25
17 Emeka Okafor .40 1.00
18 Ron Artest .50 1.25
19 Vince Carter .60 1.50
20 Jamario Moon .30 .75
21 Mike Miller .50 1.25
22 Brendan Haywood .30 .75
23 Kirk Hinrich .50 1.25
24 Jason Terry .40 1.00
25 Brandan Wright .50 1.25
26 Derek Fisher .50 1.25
27 Desmond Mason .30 .75
28 Tyson Chandler .30 .75
29 Mickael Pietrus .30 .75
30 Ronnie Brewer .40 1.00
31 Gerald Wallace .50 1.25
32 Daniel Gibson .50 1.25
33 J.R. Smith .50 1.25
34 Monta Ellis .50 1.25
35 Kobe Bryant 2.50 6.00
36 Ramon Sessions .40 1.00
37 Zach Randolph .40 1.00
38 Andre Miller .40 1.00
39 Tony Parker .50 1.25
40 Nick Young .40 1.00
41 Kevin Garnett 1.00 2.50
42 Luol Deng .50 1.25
43 Josh Howard .40 1.00
44 Corey Maggette .40 1.00
45 Cuttino Mobley .40 1.00
46 James Posey .30 .75
47 Hedo Turkoglu .50 1.25
48 Brad Miller .40 1.00
49 Andrei Kirilenko .40 1.00
50 Raymond Felton .40 1.00
51 Zydrunas Ilgauskas .40 1.00
52 Jason Maxiell .40 1.00
53 Yao Ming .60 1.50
54 Luke Walton .30 .75
55 Mo Williams .40 1.00
56 David Lee .40 1.00
57 Thaddeus Young .40 1.00
58 Raja Bell .40 1.00
59 Ime Udoka .30 .75
60 Gilbert Arenas .50 1.25
61 Glen Davis .40 1.00
62 Ben Wallace .50 1.25
63 Kenyon Martin .50 1.25
64 Stephen Jackson .40 1.00
65 Andrew Bynum .60 1.50
66 Richard Jefferson .50 1.25
67 Chris Duhon .30 .75
68 John Salmons .50 1.25
69 DeShawn Stevenson .30 .75
70 Zaza Pachulia .30 .75
71 Jason Richardson .50 1.25
72 Anderson Varejao .40 1.00
73 Rasheed Wallace .50 1.25
74 Rafer Alston .30 .75
75 Troy Murphy .30 .75
76 T.J. Ford .30 .75
77 Chris Kaman .40 1.00
78 Hakim Warrick .30 .75
79 Daequan Cook .30 .75
80 Al Jefferson .50 1.25
81 Sean Williams .40 1.00
82 Eddy Curry .30 .75
83 Chris Wilcox .30 .75
84 Willie Green .30 .75
85 Martell Webster .40 1.00
86 Travis Outlaw .40 1.00
87 Bruce Bowen .30 .75

88 Jermaine O'Neal .50 1.25
89 Ben Gordon .50 1.25
90 Antawn Jamison .50 1.25
91 Al Horford .50 1.25
92 Andres Nocioni .30 .75
93 Rodney Stuckey .60 1.50
94 Shane Battier .40 1.00
95 Jarrett Jack .40 1.00
96 Al Thornton .40 1.00
97 Mike Conley Jr. .40 1.00
98 Udonis Haslem .40 1.00
99 Rashad McCants .30 .75
100 Marcus Williams .30 .75
101 Jeff Green .40 1.00
102 Jameer Nelson .40 1.00
103 Shaquille O'Neal 1.00 2.50
104 LaMarcus Aldridge .50 1.25
105 Brandon Roy .50 1.25
106 Manu Ginobili .50 1.25
107 Jose Calderon .40 1.00
108 Jason Kapono .30 .75
109 Mike Bibby .40 1.00
110 Andrea Bargnani .40 1.00
111 Jerry Stackhouse .40 1.00
112 Richard Hamilton .40 1.00
113 Brent Barry .30 .75
114 Baron Davis .50 1.25
115 Darko Milicic .30 .75
116 Ricky Davis .40 1.00
117 Corey Brewer .40 1.00
118 Nick Collison .30 .75
119 Rashard Lewis .40 1.00
120 Amare Stoudemire .50 1.25
121 Steve Blake .30 .75
122 Kevin Martin .50 1.25
123 Fabricio Oberto .30 .75
124 Mehmet Okur .30 .75
125 Wally Szczerbiak .40 1.00
126 Mark Aguirre .75 2.00
127 Danny Ainge .75 2.00
128 Rick Barry .75 2.00
129 Elgin Baylor .75 2.00
130 Dave Bing .75 2.00
131 Otis Birdsong .75 2.00
132 Gail Goodrich .75 2.00
133 Bill Bradley 1.00 2.50
134 Bill Cartwright .75 2.00
135 James Worthy .75 2.00
136 Tom Chambers .75 2.00
137 Maurice Cheeks .75 2.00
138 Archie Clark .75 2.00
139 Michael Cooper .75 2.00
140 Bob Cousy 1.25 3.00
141 Dave Cowens .75 2.00
142 Billy Cunningham .75 2.00
143 Adrian Dantley .75 2.00
144 Darryl Dawkins .75 2.00
145 Clyde Drexler 1.00 2.50
146 Joe Dumars .75 2.00
147 Mario Elie .75 2.00
148 Walt Frazier .75 2.00
149 George Gervin 1.00 2.50
150 Tim Hardaway .75 2.00
151 John Havlicek .75 2.00
152 Bill Russell 1.25 3.00
153 Bill Laimbeer .75 2.00
154 Karl Malone 1.00 2.50
155 Bob McAdoo .75 2.00
156 Larry Bird 2.50 6.00
157 Magic Johnson 2.00 5.00
158 Willis Reed .75 2.00
159 Wilt Chamberlain 1.50 4.00
160 Pete Maravich 2.50 6.00
161 George Mikan 1.50 4.00
162 Hakeem Olajuwon 1.00 2.50
163 Patrick Ewing 1.00 2.50
164 Oscar Robertson .75 2.00
165 Bill Sharman .75 2.00
166 Dennis Rodman 1.25 3.00
167 David Robinson 1.25 3.00
168 Dominique Wilkins 1.00 2.50
169 Isiah Thomas .75 2.00
170 Jerry West 1.00 2.50
171A Derrick Rose Dribbling RC 8.00 20.00
171B Derrick Rose Standing 10.00 25.00
172A Michael Beasley 1BK RC 1.50 4.00
172B Michael Beasley 2BK 2.00 5.00
173A O.J. Mayo Dribbling RC 1.50 4.00
173B O.J. Mayo Standing 2.00 5.00
174A Russell Westbrook Red RC 5.00 12.00
174B Russell Westbrook Blue 6.00 15.00
175A Kevin Love Shooting RC 4.00 10.00
175B Kevin Love Standing 5.00 12.00
176A Danilo Gallinari Standing RC 1.50 4.00
176B Danilo Gallinari Dribbling 2.00 5.00
177A Eric Gordon Dribbling RC 2.50 6.00
177B Eric Gordon Standing 3.00 8.00
178A Joe Alexander Dribbling RC 1.00 2.50
178B Joe Alexander Standing 1.25 3.00
179A D.J. Augustin Dribbling RC 1.00 2.50
179B D.J. Augustin Standing 1.25 3.00
180A Brook Lopez Blue RC 1.50 4.00
180B Brook Lopez Red 2.00 5.00
181A Jerryd Bayless Layup RC 1.00 2.50
181B Jerryd Bayless Standing 1.25 3.00
182 Jason Thompson RC 1.00 2.50
183A Anthony Randolph Crouching RC1.25 3.00
183B Anthony Randolph Standing 1.50 4.00
184A Robin Lopez Standing RC 1.00 2.50
184B Robin Lopez Crouching 1.25 3.00
185 Marreese Speights RC 1.00 2.50
186 Roy Hibbert RC 1.50 4.00
187 JaVale McGee RC 1.50 4.00
188A J.J. Hickson Dribbling RC 1.25 3.00
188B J.J. Hickson Standing 1.50 4.00
189A Brandon Rush Dribbling RC 1.00 2.50
189B Brandon Rush Standing 1.25 3.00
190 Ryan Anderson RC 1.50 4.00
191A Courtney Lee Dribbling RC 1.50 4.00
191B Courtney Lee Standing 2.00 5.00
192A Kosta Koufos Dribbling RC 1.00 2.50
192B Kosta Koufos Standing 1.25 3.00
193 Rudy Fernandez RC 1.25 3.00
194 George Hill RC 1.50 4.00
195 D.J. White RC 1.00 2.50
196 J.R. Giddens RC 1.00 2.50
197A Chris Douglas-Roberts Red RC 1.00 2.50
197B Chris Douglas-Roberts Blue 1.25 3.00
198A Mario Chalmers Dribbling RC 1.50 4.00
198B Mario Chalmers Standing 2.00 5.00
199 DeAndre Jordan RC 2.00 5.00
200A Darrell Arthur Blue RC 1.00 2.50
200B Darrell Arthur Gold 1.25 3.00
201 Joe Johnson SP 1.00 2.50
202 Paul Pierce SP 1.25 3.00
203 LeBron James SP 5.00 12.00
204 Tayshaun Prince SP 1.00 2.50
205 Danny Granger SP 1.00 2.50
206 Pau Gasol SP 1.00 2.50
207 Shawn Marion SP 1.00 2.50
208 Michael Redd SP 1.00 2.50
209 Devin Harris SP 1.00 2.50
210 David West SP 1.00 2.50
211 Kevin Durant SP 4.00 10.00
212 Dwight Howard SP 2.00 5.00
213 Samuel Dalembert SP .75 2.00
214 Greg Oden SP 1.00 2.50
215 Tim Duncan SP 1.50 4.00
216 Carlos Boozer SP 1.00 2.50
217 Caron Butler SP 1.00 2.50
218 Chris Bosh SP 1.00 2.50
219 Leandro Barbosa SP .75 2.00
220 Tracy McGrady SP 1.00 2.50
221 Andrew Bogut SP 1.00 2.50
222 Rudy Gay SP 1.00 2.50
223 Andre Iguodala SP 1.00 2.50
224 Dirk Nowitzki SP 1.25 3.00
225 Deron Williams SP 1.00 2.50
226 Chauncey Billups SP 1.00 2.50
227 Rajon Rondo SP 1.25 3.00
228 Beno Udrih SP .75 2.00
229 Dwyane Wade SP 2.00 5.00
230 Chris Paul SP 1.50 4.00

2008-09 Topps T51 Murad Mini

*1-170 MINI: .75X TO 2X BASE HI
*171-200 RC MINI: .5X TO 1.25X BASE
*201-250 SP MINI: .6X TO 1.5X BASE
ONE MINI PER PACK
171-200 RC STATED ODDS 1:18
201-250 SP ODDS 1:12

2008-09 Topps T51 Murad Mini Black

*1-170 BLACK: 1X TO 2.5X BASE HI
*171-200 RC BLACK: .6X TO 1.5X BASE HI
*201-230 SP BLACK: .75X TO 2X BASE HI

2008-09 Topps T51 Murad Silk

*1-125 SILK: 10X TO 25X BASE HI
*126-170/201-230 SILK: 5X TO 12X BASE HI
*171-200 SILK: 4X TO 10X BASE HI
RC VARIATIONS: SAME VALUE
PRINT RUN 25 SER.#'d SETS
167 David Robinson 20.00 50.00

2008-09 Topps T51 Murad Autographs

*BLACK: .6X TO 1.5X BASE
BLACK PRINT RUN 25 SER.#'d SETS
UNPRICED SILVER PRINT RUN 10 SETS
UNPRICED LEATHER PRINT RUN ONE SET
T51AAB Andrea Bargnani 6.00 15.00
T51AABY Andrew Bynum 15.00 40.00
T51AAIG Andre Iguodala 5.00 12.00
T51AAJ Antawn Jamison 4.00 10.00
T51AAR Anthony Randolph 5.00 12.00
T51ABD Baron Davis 6.00 15.00
T51ABL Brook Lopez 6.00 15.00
T51ABR Brandon Roy 10.00 25.00
T51ABRA Brandon Rush 4.00 10.00
T51ABRL Bill Russell 50.00 100.00
T51ACBI Chauncey Billups 6.00 15.00
T51ACBO Carlos Boozer 4.00 10.00
T51ACM Corey Maggette 4.00 10.00
T51ACP Chris Paul 20.00 50.00
T51ADA Darrell Arthur 4.00 10.00
T51ADG Danny Granger 5.00 12.00
T51ADGA Danilo Gallinari 10.00 25.00
T51ADH Devin Harris 8.00 20.00
T51ADHO Dwight Howard 15.00 40.00
T51ADJA D.J. Augustin 4.00 10.00
T51ADJW D.J. White 4.00 10.00
T51ADL David Lee 5.00 12.00
T51ADR Derrick Rose 125.00 250.00
T51AEG Eric Gordon 20.00 50.00
T51AGO Greg Oden 12.50 30.00
T51AGW Gerald Wallace 4.00 10.00
T51AJA Joe Alexander 4.00 10.00
T51AJB Jerryd Bayless 4.00 10.00
T51AJJ Jarrett Jack 4.00 10.00
T51AJJH J.J. Hickson 5.00 12.00
T51AJRG J.R. Giddens 4.00 10.00
T51AKH Kirk Hinrich 8.00 20.00
T51AKK Kosta Koufos 4.00 10.00
T51AKL Kevin Love 30.00 80.00
T51ALB Larry Bird 50.00 100.00
T51AMB Michael Beasley 15.00 40.00
T51AMC Mario Chalmers 6.00 15.00
T51AMJ Magic Johnson 40.00 80.00
T51AMM Mike Miller 4.00 10.00
T51AMP Mickeal Pietrus 4.00 10.00
T51AOJM O.J. Mayo 12.00 30.00
T51APP Paul Pierce 10.00 25.00
T51ARG Rudy Gay 6.00 15.00
T51ARH Roy Hibbert 6.00 15.00
T51ARL Robin Lopez 4.00 10.00
T51ARM Rashad McCants 4.00 10.00
T51ARWE Russell Westbrook 30.00 80.00
T51ATJF T.J. Ford 4.00 10.00
T51ATM Tracy McGrady 10.00 25.00
T51AVC Vince Carter 20.00 40.00

2008-09 Topps T51 Murad Checklists

COMPLETE SET (30) 6.00 15.00
APPROXIMATE ODDS ONE PER PACK
CL1 Dwyane Wade 1.00 2.50
CL2 Travis Outlaw .40 1.00
CL3 Los Angeles Clippers .50 1.25
CL4 Michael Redd .50 1.25
CL5 Emeka Okafor .50 1.25
Al Jefferson
CL6 Tracy McGrady .50 1.25
CL7 Andre Iguodala .50 1.25
CL8 Kwame Brown .50 1.25
Corey Brewer
Al Jefferson
CL9 Rudy Gay .50 1.25
CL10 Jason Kidd 1.25 3.00
Steve Nash
CL11 Shaquille O'Neal 1.00 2.50
CL12 Carmelo Anthony .60 1.50
CL13 Chris Bosh .50 1.25
CL14 Tony Parker .50 1.25
CL15 Gilbert Arenas .50 1.25
CL16 Mikki Moore .54 1.25
Shelden Williams
Quincy Douby
Francisco Garcia
Reggie Theus
CL17 Mehmet Okur 1.00 2.50
Deron Williams
Kyle Korver
Andrei Kirilenko
Carlos Boozer
CL18 Andris Biedrins .75 1.25
Mikki Moore
CL19 Dwight Howard 1.00 2.50
CL20 Cleveland Cavaliers 1.25 3.00
LeBron James
Anderson Varejao
Delonte West
Sasha Pavlovic
Ben Wallace
CL21 Ray Allen .50 1.25
CL22 Rodney Stuckey 1.25 3.00
Richard Hamilton
Rasheed Wallace
Tayshaun Prince
Jarvis Hayes
Jason Maxiell
Theo Ratliff
CL23 Jason Kidd .75 2.00
Dirk Nowitzki
Malik Allen
Antoine Wright#
CL24 Jamal Crawford .40 1.00
CL25 Danny Granger .50 1.25
CL26 Chauncey Billups .50 1.25
CL27 Al Horford .50 1.25
Joe Johnson
Mike Bibby
CL28 Kevin Garnett 1.00 2.50
CL29 Kobe Bryant 2.50 6.00
CL30 Larry Bird 1.50 4.00

2008-09 Topps T51 Murad Relics

APPROXIMATE ODDS 1:24 PACKS
*GOLD: .5X TO 1.25X BASE
GOLD PRINT RUN 51 SER.#'d SETS
UNPRICED LEATHER PRINT RUN ONE SET
UNPRICED SILVER PRINT RUN 10 SETS
T51RAI Allen Iverson 4.00 10.00
T51RAIG Andre Iguodala 3.00 8.00
T51RAS Amare Stoudemire 3.00 8.00
T51RBK Bernard King 3.00 8.00
T51RBL Bill Laimbeer 3.00 8.00
T51RBR Brandon Roy 3.00 8.00
T51RBW Bill Walton 3.00 8.00
T51RCA Carmelo Anthony 4.00 10.00
T51RCBI Chauncey Billups 3.00 8.00
T51RCBO Chris Bosh 3.00 8.00
T51RCBU Caron Butler 3.00 8.00
T51RCBZ Carlos Boozer 3.00 8.00
T51RCD Clyde Drexler 4.00 10.00
T51RCM Chris Mullin 3.00 8.00
T51RCP Chris Paul 5.00 12.00
T51RDH Dwight Howard 6.00 15.00
T51RDN Dirk Nowitzki 4.00 10.00
T51RDR Dennis Rodman 5.00 12.00
T51RDW Dwyane Wade 6.00 15.00
T51RDWI Deron Williams 3.00 8.00
T51REM Earl Monroe 3.00 8.00
T51RGA Gilbert Arenas 3.00 8.00
T51RGG George Gervin 4.00 10.00
T51RGO Greg Oden 3.00 8.00
T51RIT Isiah Thomas 3.00 8.00
T51RJJ Joe Johnson 3.00 8.00
T51RJK Jason Kidd 3.00 8.00
T51RJS Josh Smith 3.00 8.00
T51RKB Kobe Bryant 8.00 20.00
T51RKG Kevin Garnett 6.00 15.00
T51RKM Kevin Martin 3.00 8.00
T51RLB Larry Bird 10.00 25.00
T51RMC Michael Cooper 3.00 8.00
T51RMG Manu Ginobili 3.00 8.00
T51RMJ Magic Johnson 10.00 25.00
T51RMR Michael Redd 3.00 8.00
T51RMRI Mitch Richmond 3.00 8.00
T51RPG Pau Gasol 3.00 8.00
T51RPM Pete Maravich 30.00 80.00
T51RPP Paul Pierce 4.00 10.00
T51RRG Rudy Gay 3.00 8.00
T51RRR Rajon Rondo 4.00 10.00
T51RSN Steve Nash 3.00 8.00
T51RSO Shaquille O'Neal 6.00 15.00
T51RSP Scottie Pippen 15.00 30.00
T51RTD Tim Duncan 5.00 12.00
T51RTM Tracy McGrady 3.00 8.00
T51RTP Tony Parker 3.00 8.00
T51RVC Vince Carter 4.00 10.00
T51RYM Yao Ming 4.00 10.00

2008-09 Topps T51 Murad T6 Cabinets

ONE CABINET PER BOX
*BLACK: .75X TO 2X BASE HI
BLACK STATED PRINT RUN 51 SETS
UNPRICED SILVER PRINT RUN 10 SETS
T6BR Brandon Roy 1.00 2.50
T6CA Carmelo Anthony 1.25 3.00
T6CP Chris Paul 1.50 4.00
T6DH Dwight Howard 2.00 5.00
T6DR Derrick Rose 10.00 25.00
T6DW Dwyane Wade 2.00 5.00
T6GO Greg Oden 1.00 2.50
T6KB Kobe Bryant 5.00 12.00
T6KG Kevin Garnett 2.00 5.00
T6LB Larry Bird 3.00 8.00
T6LJ LeBron James 5.00 12.00
T6MB Michael Beasley 1.50 4.00
T6MJ Magic Johnson 2.50 6.00
T6OJM O.J. Mayo 1.50 4.00
T6PP Paul Pierce 1.25 3.00
T6YM Yao Ming 1.25 3.00

2001-02 Topps TCC

Released in late April 2002, Topps TCC boasts a 150-card set divided up as follows: card numbers 1-120 feature veterans and are further divided into Playoff Bound, Playoff Hopefuls, Making Strides, and Opportunity knocks; and card numbers 118-150 feature rookie players. Base cards place full color player action photos on a white background with orange trim along the right and bottom of the card, where rookies have this replaced with gold, and gold foil highlights. TCC was released in 10 box cases with 24 packs per box and six card packs which carried a suggested retail price of $2.00. Each pack contained one extra thick insert card which also served to deter collectors from searching packs.

COMPLETE SET (150) 30.00 80.00
1 Shaquille O'Neal .60 1.50
2 Jason Williams .20 .50
3 Eddie Jones .20 .50
4 Anthony Mason .15 .40
5 Joe Smith .20 .50
6 Kenyon Martin .25 .60
7 Tracy McGrady .40 1.00
8 Horace Grant .20 .50
9 Andre Miller .20 .50
10 Allen Iverson .50 1.25
11 Shawn Marion .25 .60
12 Derek Anderson .15 .40
13 Chris Webber .25 .60
14 Bruce Bowen .15 .40
15 Alvin Williams .15 .40
16 Brent Barry .15 .40
17 Donyell Marshall .15 .40
18 Richard Hamilton .20 .50
19 Vlade Divac .20 .50
20 Vince Carter .40 1.00
21 Kevin Garnett .50 1.25
22 Jason Terry .25 .60
23 Antoine Walker .20 .50
24 P.J. Brown .15 .40
25 Baron Davis .25 .60
26 Eddie Robinson .15 .40
27 Chris Mihm .15 .40
28 Michael Finley .25 .60
29 Nick Van Exel .20 .50
30 Steve Francis .25 .60
31 Chucky Atkins .15 .40
32 Raef LaFrentz .15 .40
33 Antawn Jamison .25 .60
34 Jalen Rose .20 .50
35 Lamar Odom .25 .60
36 Elton Brand .25 .60
37 Derek Fisher .20 .50
38 Alonzo Mourning .30 .75
39 Ervin Johnson .15 .40
40 Tim Duncan .50 1.25
41 Kurt Thomas .15 .40
42 Latrell Sprewell .20 .50
43 Darrell Armstrong .15 .40
44 Tom Gugliotta .15 .40
45 Derrick Coleman .20 .50
46 Dale Davis .15 .40
47 David Robinson .40 1.00
48 Scottie Pippen .40 1.00
49 Hakeem Olajuwon .30 .75
50 Darius Miles .15 .40
51 Greg Ostertag .15 .40
52 Karl Malone .30 .75
53 Morris Peterson .15 .40
54 Shareef Abdur-Rahim .20 .50
55 Dikembe Mutombo .25 .60
56 Elden Campbell .15 .40
57 Ron Mercer .15 .40
58 Jumaine Jones .15 .40
59 Wang ZhiZhi .20 .50
60 Ray Allen .25 .60
61 Marcus Camby .20 .50
62 Jermaine O'Neal .25 .60
63 Kenny Thomas .15 .40
64 Danny Fortson .15 .40
65 Ben Wallace .25 .60
66 DeShawn Stevenson .15 .40
67 Antonio Davis .15 .40
68 Doug Christie .15 .40
69 Rasheed Wallace .25 .60
70 Stephon Marbury .20 .50
71 Allan Houston .20 .50
72 Kerry Kittles .15 .40
73 Todd MacCulloch .15 .40
74 Sam Cassell .20 .50
75 Kobe Bryant 1.25 3.00
76 Aaron McKie .15 .40
77 Terrell Brandon .15 .40
78 Brian Grant .15 .40
79 Michael Dickerson .15 .40
80 Jerry Stackhouse .20 .50
81 Antonio McDyess .20 .50
82 Steve Nash .40 1.00
83 Paul Pierce .30 .75
84 Jamal Mashburn .20 .50
85 Toni Kukoc .20 .50
86 James Posey .15 .40
87 Larry Hughes .20 .50
88 Cuttino Mobley .20 .50
89 Jeff Foster .15 .40
90 Jason Kidd .40 1.00
91 Keith Van Horn .20 .50
92 Mike Miller .25 .60
93 Anfernee Hardaway .40 1.00
94 Bonzi Wells .15 .40
95 Mike Bibby .25 .60
96 Steve Smith .20 .50
97 Gary Payton .25 .60
98 John Stockton .30 .75
99 Peja Stojakovic .25 .60
100 Michael Jordan 5.00 12.00
101 Iakovos Tsakalidis .15 .40
102 Mark Jackson .20 .50
103 Wally Szczerbiak .20 .50
104 Rod Strickland .20 .50
105 Rick Fox .20 .50
106 Glenn Robinson .20 .50
107 Michael Olowokandi .15 .40
108 Reggie Miller .25 .60
109 Kelvin Cato .15 .40
110 Clifford Robinson .15 .40
111 Dirk Nowitzki .40 1.00
112 Brad Miller .25 .60
113 David Wesley .15 .40
114 Kenny Anderson .20 .50
115 Theo Ratliff .15 .40
116 Rashard Lewis .25 .60
117 Matt Harpring .20 .50
118 Eddie Griffin RC .40 1.00
119 Brendan Haywood RC .50 1.25
120 Steven Hunter RC .40 1.00
121 Jamaal Tinsley RC .50 1.25
122 Jason Richardson RC .75 2.00
123 Tony Parker RC 1.50 4.00
124 Pau Gasol RC 1.25 3.00
125 Shane Battier RC .75 2.00
126 Joe Johnson RC 1.00 2.50
127 Leon Smith RC .40 1.00
128 Mengke Bateer RC .40 1.00
129 Loren Woods RC .40 1.00
130 Kwame Brown RC .40 1.00
131 Tyson Chandler RC .60 1.50
132 Eddy Curry RC .60 1.50
133 Kedrick Brown RC .40 1.00
134 Joseph Forte RC .40 1.00
135 Troy Murphy RC .60 1.50
136 Richard Jefferson RC .75 2.00
137 DeSagana Diop RC .40 1.00
138 Vladimir Radmanovic RC .40 1.00
139 Zach Randolph RC 1.00 2.50
140 Gerald Wallace RC .60 1.50
141 Brandon Armstrong RC .40 1.00
142 Jeryl Sasser RC .40 1.00
143 Rodney White RC .40 1.00
144 Samuel Dalembert RC .50 1.25
145 Jason Collins RC .40 1.00
146 Michael Bradley RC .40 1.00
147 Oscar Torres RC .40 1.00
148 Zeljko Rebraca RC .40 1.00
149 Andrei Kirilenko RC 1.00 2.50
150 Trenton Hassell RC .40 1.00

2001-02 Topps TCC Red

Randomly inserted in packs at the rate of one in two, this 150-card set parallels the base TCC set on thick cards with a foil shift from the base gold to red.
*STARS: 1.25X TO 3X BASE CARD HI
*RC's: .75X TO 2X BASE CARD HI

2001-02 Topps TCC Autographs

Randomly seeded in packs at the rate of one in 48, this 27-card set features full color player action photos along the top, a gold line with the player's name in the middle, and an authentic autograph on the bottom. Each card is highlighted with gold foil and contains the Topps stamp of authenticity.

CCAAM Andre Miller 5.00 12.00
CCABJ Bobby Jackson 5.00 12.00
CCADB Damone Brown 4.00 10.00
CCADH Donnell Harvey 4.00 10.00
CCADM Desmond Mason 4.00 10.00
CCAGA Gilbert Arenas 10.00 25.00
CCAHT Hedo Turkoglu 5.00 12.00
CCAJF Joseph Forte 4.00 10.00
CCAJJ Joe Johnson 10.00 25.00
CCAJT Jason Terry 5.00 12.00
CCAKB Kedrick Brown 4.00 10.00
CCAKD Keyon Dooling 4.00 10.00
CCAKS Kenny Satterfield 4.00 10.00
CCALP Lavor Postell 4.00 10.00
CCALW Loren Woods 4.00 10.00
CCAMB Mike Bibby 6.00 15.00
CCAMD Michael Doleac 4.00 10.00
CCAPS Peja Stojakovic 8.00 20.00
CCARH Richard Hamilton 5.00 12.00
CCARL Raef LaFrentz 4.00 10.00
CCARM Roshown McLeod 4.00 10.00
CCASB Shane Battier 8.00 20.00
CCASM Shawn Marion 6.00 15.00
CCATM Troy Murphy 6.00 15.00
CCAAJO Alvin Jones 4.00 10.00
CCAJTR Jeff Trepagnier 4.00 10.00

2001-02 Topps TCC Challenging the Champ

Randomly inserted in packs at the rate of one in 32, this 16-card set showcases player's aiming for a shot on the right and a diamond shaped swatch of game memorabilia on the left. All TCC memorabilia swatches are encased with plastic borders to deter replacement or tampering with the swatch.

CCAH Anfernee Hardaway 5.00 12.00
CCBD Baron Davis 3.00 8.00
CCDN Dirk Nowitzki 5.00 12.00
CCEB Elton Brand 3.00 8.00
CCJM Jamal Mashburn 2.50 6.00
CCJT Jason Terry 3.00 8.00
CCMF Michael Finley 3.00 8.00
CCSA Shareef Abdur-Rahim 2.50 6.00
CCSM Stephon Marbury 2.50 6.00
CCSN Steve Nash 5.00 12.00
CCSDM Shawn Marion 3.00 8.00
CCTD Tim Duncan 6.00 15.00
CCTG Tom Gugliotta 2.00 5.00
CCTK Toni Kukoc 2.50 6.00
CCTR Theo Ratliff 2.00 5.00
CCWZ Wang Zhizhi 2.50 6.00

2001-02 Topps TCC Crowning Moment

Seeded in packs at the rate of one in five, this 10-card set features an all foil card stock with a colored background and a player photo as he recieves an award centered and circled with gold foil. All TCC inserts are thicker than standard size cards.

COMPLETE SET (10) 8.00 20.00
CM1 Karl Malone .60 1.50
CM2 Shaquille O'Neal 1.25 3.00
CM3 Tim Duncan 1.00 2.50
CM4 Michael Jordan 4.00 10.00
CM5 Kobe Bryant 2.50 6.00
CM6 Vince Carter .75 2.00
CM7 Dikembe Mutombo .50 1.25
CM8 Elton Brand .50 1.25
CM9 Jason Kidd .75 2.00
CM10 Steve Francis .50 1.25

2001-02 Topps TCC Finals Journey

Inserted in packs at the rate of one in 22, this 23-card set features full color player action phots on the left and a circular swatch of a game worn finals jersey on the right. All TCC memorabilia swatches are encased with plastic borders to deter replacement or tampering with the swatch.

FJAI Allen Iverson 6.00 15.00
FJAM Aaron McKie 2.00 5.00
FJBS Brian Shaw 2.00 5.00
FJDF Derek Fisher 2.50 6.00
FJDG Devean George 2.00 5.00
FJDM Dikembe Mutombo 3.00 8.00
FJES Eric Snow 2.00 5.00
FJGF Greg Foster 2.00 5.00
FJGL George Lynch 2.00 5.00
FJHG Horace Grant 2.50 6.00
FJJJ Jumaine Jones 2.00 5.00
FJKO Kevin Ollie 2.00 5.00
FJMG Matt Geiger 2.00 5.00
FJMM Mark Madsen 2.00 5.00
FJRB Raja Bell 4.00 10.00
FJRF Rick Fox 2.50 6.00
FJRH Robert Horry 2.50 6.00
FJRAB Rodney Buford 2.00 6.00
FJRKH Ron Harper 2.50 6.00
FJSO Shaquille O'Neal 8.00 20.00
FJTH Tyrone Hill 2.00 5.00
FJTL Tyronn Lue 2.00 5.00
FJTM Todd MacCulloch 2.00 5.00

2001-02 Topps TCC First Step Sneakers

Seeded in packs at the rate of one in 222, this 14-card set showcases young stars who have yet to win an NBA Championship. Player color photos appear on the left, and a circular swatch of a game worn sneaker appears in the upper right hand corner. All TCC memorabilia swatches are encased with plastic borders to deter replacement or tampering with the swatch.

FSAJ Antawn Jamison 6.00 15.00
FSBD Baron Davis 6.00 15.00
FSEB Elton Brand 6.00 15.00
FSEC Eddy Curry 10.00 25.00
FSJF Joseph Forte 6.00 15.00
FSJT Jason Terry 6.00 15.00
FSKB Kwame Brown 6.00 15.00
FSPS Peja Stojakovic 6.00 15.00
FSRH Richard Hamilton 5.00 12.00
FSSB Shane Battier 12.00 30.00
FSSM Shawn Marion 6.00 15.00
FSSO Shaquille O'Neal 15.00 40.00
FSTD Tim Duncan 12.00 30.00
FSVR Vladimir Radmanovic 6.00 15.00

2001-02 Topps TCC Heart of a Champion

Inserted in packs at the rate of one in 19, this 10-card set features an all foil card stock with full color player photos centered and surrounded by a border that is shaped like a heart.

COMPLETE SET (10) 25.00 60.00
HC1 Tim Duncan 2.00 5.00
HC2 Shaquille O'Neal 2.50 6.00
HC3 Michael Jordan 12.50 30.00
HC4 Karl Malone 1.25 3.00
HC5 Hakeem Olajuwon 1.25 3.00
HC6 David Robinson 1.50 4.00
HC7 Kobe Bryant 5.00 12.00
HC8 Scottie Pippen 1.50 4.00
HC9 Shane Battier 2.00 5.00
HC10 Jason Richardson 2.00 5.00

2001-02 Topps TCC Heroes Honor

Seeded in packs at the rate of one in five, this six card set features an all foil card stock with full color player photos centered between red white and blue ribbins falling from the words, "Heroes Honor."

COMPLETE SET (6) 3.00 8.00
HH1 Tim Duncan 1.25 3.00
HH2 Vince Carter 1.00 2.50
HH3 Tracy McGrady 1.00 2.50
HH4 Chris Webber .60 1.50
HH5 Baron Davis .60 1.50
HH6 Allan Houston .50 1.25

2001-02 Topps TCC Jump Ball

Randomly seeded in packs at the rate of one in 540, this nine card set showcases full color player action photos set agaist a white background. The right edge of the card has a gold stripe with the words, "Jump Ball" and on the inside of that stripe is a purple stripe with the featured player's name. A swatch of game used basketball appears in the lower right-hand corner.

JBAI Allen Iverson 8.00 20.00
JBBD Baron Davis 4.00 10.00
JBCW Chris Webber 6.00 15.00
JBGR Glenn Robinson 3.00 8.00
JBPS Peja Stojakovic 4.00 10.00
JBRA Ray Allen 4.00 10.00
JBSC Sam Cassell 3.00 8.00
JBSM Shawn Marion 4.00 10.00
JBTM Tracy McGrady 6.00 15.00

2001-02 Topps TCC Setting the Stage

Randomly inserted in packs at the rate of one in 19, this 10-card set showcases some of the NBA's best matchups. Both players are featured on the front of this all foil insert set. The words "Setting the Stage" appear along the bottom of the card which fades to black and places both player's names and team logos.

COMPLETE SET (10) 25.00 60.00
SS1 Tracy McGrady 3.00 8.00
Ray Allen
SS2 Kobe Bryant 4.00 10.00
Allen Iverson
SS3 Shaquille O'Neal 2.50 6.00
Dikembe Mutombo
SS4 Shaquille O'Neal 4.00 10.00
Tim Duncan
SS5 Patrick Ewing 2.50 6.00
Alonzo Mourning
SS6 Latrell Sprewell 2.00 5.00
Vince Carter
SS7 Shaquille O'Neal 3.00 8.00
Hakeem Olajuwon
SS8 Michael Jordan 6.00 15.00
Reggie Miller
SS9 Karl Malone 2.00 5.00
Chris Webber
SS10 John Stockton 2.00 5.00
Gary Payton

2000 Topps Team USA

Released in June 2000, this 96-card set focuses on both the men's and women's Team USA players for the Olympics. The cards were released in seven-card packs that carried a suggested retail price of $1.99. Card number 16 does not exist (Nikki McCray). Instead, two number 40's were produced.

COMPLETE SET (96) 12.50 30.00
1 Tim Duncan ACH .40 1.00
2 Jason Kidd ACH .25 .60
3 Vin Baker ACH .15 .40
4 Steve Smith ACH .07 .20
5 Grant Hill ACH .25 .60
6 Gary Payton ACH .25 .60
7 Vince Carter ACH .50 1.25
8 Ray Allen ACH .25 .60
9 Kevin Garnett ACH .40 1.00
10 Tim Hardaway ACH .25 .60
11 Allan Houston ACH .25 .60
12 Alonzo Mourning ACH .25 .60
13 Lisa Leslie ACH .75 2.00
14 Dawn Staley ACH .40 1.00
15 Katie Smith ACH .40 1.00
16 Nikki McCray ACH UER .40 1.00
numbered as 40
17 Ruthie Bolton-Holifield ACH .40 1.00
18 Chamique Holdsclaw ACH 1.00 2.50
19 Yolanda Griffith ACH .50 1.25
20 Teresa Edwards ACH .30 .75
21 Natalie Williams ACH .50 1.25
22 Delisha Milton ACH .15 .40
23 Kara Wolters ACH .25 .60
24 Gary Payton ST .15 .40
25 Kevin Garnett ST .40 1.00
26 Tim Hardaway ST .15 .40
27 Steve Smith ST .07 .20
28 Ray Allen ST .15 .40
29 Alonzo Mourning ST .15 .40
30 Allan Houston ST .15 .40
31 Vince Carter ST .50 1.25
32 Grant Hill ST .15 .40
33 Tim Duncan ST .40 1.00

4 Jason Kidd ST .25 .60
5 Vin Baker ST .15 .40
6 Ruthie Bolton-Holifield ST .40 1.00
7 Natalie Williams ST .50 1.25
8 Lisa Leslie ST .75 2.00
9 Chamique Holdsclaw ST 1.00 2.50
0 Nikki McCray ST .40 1.00
1 Dawn Staley ST .40 1.00
2 Teresa Edwards ST .30 .75
3 Yolanda Griffith ST .50 1.25
4 Katie Smith ST .40 1.00
5 Delisha Milton ST .15 .40
6 Kara Wolters ST .25 .60
7 Vin Baker PAI .15 .40
8 Jason Kidd PAI .25 .60
9 Allan Houston PAI .15 .40
0 Ray Allen PAI .15 .40
1 Alonzo Mourning PAI .15 .40
2 Kevin Garnett PAI .40 1.00
3 Gary Payton PAI .15 .40
4 Steve Smith PAI .07 .20
5 Vince Carter PAI .50 1.25
6 Grant Hill PAI .15 .40
7 Tim Duncan PAI .40 1.00
8 Tim Hardaway PAI .15 .40
9 Chamique Holdsclaw PAI 1.00 2.50
0 Katie Smith PAI .40 1.00
1 Yolanda Griffith PAI .50 1.25
2 Nikki McCray PAI .40 1.00
3 Lisa Leslie PAI .75 2.00
4 Teresa Edwards PAI .30 .75
5 Dawn Staley PAI .40 1.00
6 Ruthie Bolton-Holifield PAI .40 1.00
7 Natalie Williams PAI .50 1.25
8 Delisha Milton PAI .15 .40
9 Kara Wolters PAI .25 .60
'0 Allan Houston QU .15 .40
'1 Kevin Garnett QU .40 1.00
'2 Tim Duncan QU .40 1.00
'3 Tim Hardaway QU .15 .40
'4 Gary Payton QU .15 .40
'5 Ray Allen QU .15 .40
'6 Vince Carter QU .50 1.25
'7 Grant Hill QU .15 .40
'8 Vin Baker QU .15 .40
'9 Alonzo Mourning QU .15 .40
0 Steve Smith QU .07 .20
1 Jason Kidd QU .25 .60
2 Chamique Holdsclaw QU 1.00 2.50
3 Lisa Leslie QU .75 2.00
4 Dawn Staley QU .40 1.00
5 Natalie Williams QU .50 1.25
6 Nikki McCray QU .40 1.00
7 Katie Smith QU .40 1.00
8 Teresa Edwards QU .30 .75
9 Yolanda Griffith QU .40 1.00
0 Ruthie Bolton-Holifield QU .40 1.00
1 Delisha Milton QU .15 .40
2 Kara Wolters QU .25 .60
3 Team USA Men's .40 1.00
4 Team USA Women's .40 1.00
5 Group Shot .60 1.50
6 Checklist .07 .20

2000 Topps Team USA Gold

nserted one per pack, this 95-card set parallels the base set. All cards are included, except for the checklist (#96). Card number 16 does not exist. Two cards are numbered as 40. To ascertain values on individual cards, please refer to the multiplier listed below, coupled with the value of the base card.
GOLD: 1.25X TO 3X BASE CARD HI

2000 Topps Team USA Autographs

Randomly inserted in packs at one in 291, this 10-card set features autographs from the women of Team USA. Card backs are numbered with the player's initials.

CH Chamique Holdsclaw 100.00 200.00
DM Delisha Milton 25.00 60.00
DS Dawn Staley 25.00 60.00
KS Katie Smith 40.00 80.00
LL Lisa Leslie 50.00 100.00
NM Nikki McCray 40.00 80.00
NW Natalie Williams 25.00 60.00
RH Ruthie Bolton-Holifield 25.00 60.00
TE Teresa Edwards 40.00 80.00
YG Yolanda Griffith 40.00 80.00

2000 Topps Team USA National Spirit

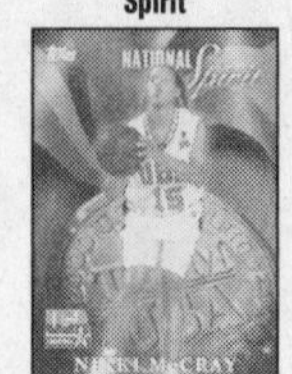

Randomly inserted in packs at one in eight, this 23-card set features every player on Team USA against a billboard technology. Card backs carry a "NS" prefix.

COMPLETE SET (23) 20.00 40.00
NS1 Steve Smith .20 .50
NS2 Ray Allen .60 1.50
NS3 Grant Hill .60 1.50
NS4 Vince Carter 1.50 4.00
NS5 Tim Hardaway .40 1.00
NS6 Jason Kidd 1.00 2.50
NS7 Vin Baker .40 1.00
NS8 Alonzo Mourning .40 1.00
NS9 Tim Duncan 1.25 3.00
NS10 Gary Payton .60 1.50
NS11 Allan Houston .75 2.00
NS12 Kevin Garnett 1.25 3.00
NS13 Nikki McCray 1.25 3.00
NS14 Dawn Staley 1.25 3.00
NS15 Lisa Leslie 2.50 6.00
NS16 Teresa Edwards .75 2.00
NS17 Yolanda Griffith 1.50 4.00
NS18 Chamique Holdsclaw 3.00 8.00
NS19 Katie Smith 1.25 3.00
NS20 Ruthie Bolton-Holifield 1.25 3.00
NS21 Natalie Williams 1.50 4.00
NS22 Delisha Milton .50 1.25
NS23 Kara Wolters .75 2.00

2000 Topps Team USA Side by Side

Randomly inserted in packs at one in 12, this 12-card set highlights a player from both the men's and women's team who share something in common. Prices below are for the Non-Refractor/Refractor technology.

COMPLETE SET (12) 12.00 30.00
RIGHT/LEFT VARIATIONS EQUAL VALUE
*DUAL REF: .75X TO 2X HI COLUMN
DUAL REF: STATED ODDS 1:36
SS1 Tim Duncan 2.50 6.00
Lisa Leslie
SS2 Allan Houston 1.50 4.00
Ruthie Bolton-Holifield
SS3 Kevin Garnett 2.50 6.00
Chamique Holdsclaw
SS4 Jason Kidd 1.50 4.00
Katie Smith
SS5 Vin Baker 1.25 3.00
Natalie Williams
SS6 Gary Payton 1.25 3.00
Dawn Staley
SS7 Vince Carter 1.25 3.00
Theresa Edwards
SS8 Tim Hardaway 1.00 2.50
Dawn Staley
SS9 Steve Smith 1.00 2.50
Kara Wolters
SS10 Alonzo Mourning 1.25 3.00
Yolanda Griffith
SS11 Ray Allen 1.00 2.50
Delisha Milton
SS12 Grant Hill 1.00 2.50
Nikki McCray

2000 Topps Team USA USArchival

Randomly inserted in packs at one in 323, this nine-card set features pieces of game-worn USA jerseys from the 1999 Olympic qualifying tournament in Puerto Rice. Card backs carry a "US" prefix. According to Topps, only 250 sets were produced.

USAR1 Tom Gugliotta 10.00 25.00
USAR2 Allan Houston 15.00 40.00
USAR3 Vin Baker 10.00 25.00
USAR4 Kevin Garnett 20.00 50.00
USAR5 Gary Payton 12.50 30.00
USAR6 Steve Smith 12.50 30.00
USAR7 Tim Duncan 30.00 80.00
USAR8 Jason Kidd 20.00 50.00
USAR9 Tim Hardaway 10.00 25.00

2002-03 Topps Ten

Topps Ten consisted of 150-cards broken down into 120 veteran players and 30 rookie players. Veteran were divided up into 12 different categories: Points Per Game, Points Per 48 Minutes, Rebounds Per Game, Assists Per Game, Blocks Per Game, Steals Per Game, Double-Doubles, Field Goal %, Three-Point FG %, Minutes Per Game, Free Throw %, and Rookie Points Per Game; and Rookies were divided up into: Top 10 Rookie Guards, Top 10 Rookie Small Forwards, and Top 10 Rookie Power Forwards/Centers. Each player is ranked between one and ten. Topps Ten was issue in 24-pack boxes where packs contained eight cards and carried a suggested retail price of $300.

COMPLETE SET (150) 20.00 50.00
1 Allen Iverson .40 1.00
2 Shaquille O'Neal .60 1.50
3 Paul Pierce .30 .75
4 Tracy McGrady .40 1.00
5 Tim Duncan .50 1.25
6 Kobe Bryant 1.25 3.00
7 Dirk Nowitzki .40 1.00
8 Karl Malone .30 .75
9 Antoine Walker .20 .50
10 Gary Payton .25 .60
11 Shaquille O'Neal .60 1.50
12 Allen Iverson .40 1.00
13 Tracy McGrady .40 1.00
14 Kobe Bryant 1.25 3.00
15 Michael Jordan 2.00 5.00
16 Paul Pierce .30 .75
17 Chris Webber .50 1.25
18 Tim Duncan .50 1.25
19 Corliss Williamson .15 .40
20 Dirk Nowitzki .40 1.00
21 Ben Wallace .25 .60
22 Tim Duncan .50 1.25
23 Kevin Garnett .50 1.25
24 Danny Fortson .15 .40
25 Elton Brand .25 .60
26 Dikembe Mutombo .25 .60
27 Jermaine O'Neal .25 .60
28 Dirk Nowitzki .40 1.00
29 Shawn Marion .25 .60
30 P.J. Brown .15 .40
31 Andre Miller .20 .50
32 Jason Kidd .40 1.00
33 Gary Payton .25 .60
34 Baron Davis .25 .60
35 John Stockton .30 .75
36 Stephon Marbury .20 .50
37 Jamaal Tinsley .15 .40
38 Jason Williams .20 .50
39 Steve Nash .30 .75
40 Mark Jackson .20 .50
41 Ben Wallace .25 .60
42 Raef LaFrentz .15 .40
43 Alonzo Mourning .30 .75
44 Tim Duncan .50 1.25
45 Dikembe Mutombo .25 .60
46 Jermaine O'Neal .25 .60
47 Erick Dampier .15 .40
48 Adonal Foyle .15 .40
49 Pau Gasol .30 .75
50 Shaquille O'Neal .60 1.50
51 Allen Iverson .40 1.00
52 Ron Artest .25 .60
53 Jason Kidd .40 1.00
54 Baron Davis .25 .60
55 Doug Christie .15 .40
56 Darrell Armstrong .15 .40
57 Karl Malone .30 .75
58 Paul Pierce .30 .75
59 Kenny Anderson .20 .50
60 John Stockton .30 .75
61 Shaquille O'Neal .60 1.50
62 Elton Brand .25 .60
63 Donyell Marshall .15 .40
64 Pau Gasol .30 .75
65 John Stockton .30 .75
66 Alonzo Mourning .30 .75
67 Ruben Patterson .15 .40
68 Corliss Williamson .15 .40
69 Tim Duncan .50 1.25
70 Brent Barry .15 .40
71 Steve Smith .20 .50
72 Jon Barry .15 .40
73 Eric Piatkowski .15 .40
74 Wally Szczerbiak .20 .50
75 Steve Nash .30 .75
76 Hubert Davis .15 .40
77 Tyronn Lue .15 .40
78 Michael Redd .25 .60
79 Wesley Person .15 .40
80 Ray Allen .25 .60
81 Reggie Miller .25 .60
82 Richard Hamilton .20 .50
83 Darrell Armstrong .15 .40
84 Damon Stoudamire .20 .50
85 Steve Nash .30 .75
86 Chauncey Billups .25 .60
87 Chris Whitney .15 .40
88 Steve Smith .20 .50
89 Peja Stojakovic .25 .60
90 Troy Hudson .15 .40
91 Allen Iverson .40 1.00
92 Cuttino Mobley .20 .50
93 Antoine Walker .20 .50
94 Steve Francis .25 .60
95 Latrell Sprewell .25 .60
96 Tim Duncan .50 1.25
97 Baron Davis .25 .60
98 Paul Pierce .30 .75
99 Gary Payton .25 .60
100 Michael Finley .25 .60
101 Tim Duncan .50 1.25
102 Kevin Garnett .50 1.25
103 Elton Brand .25 .60
104 Jason Kidd .40 1.00
105 Shawn Marion .25 .60
106 Andre Miller .20 .50
107 Shaquille O'Neal .60 1.50
108 Jermaine O'Neal .25 .60
109 Dirk Nowitzki .40 1.00
110 Pau Gasol .30 .75
111 Pau Gasol .30 .75
112 Shane Battier .25 .60
113 Jason Richardson .25 .60
114 Gilbert Arenas .25 .60
115 Andrei Kirilenko .25 .60
116 Richard Jefferson .25 .60
117 Jamaal Tinsley .15 .40
118 Tony Parker .30 .75
119 Eddie Griffin .15 .40
120 Trenton Hassell .15 .40
121 Jay Williams RC 1.00 2.50
122 DaJuan Wagner RC .75 2.00
123 Fred Jones RC .75 2.00
124 Jiri Welsch RC .75 2.00
125 Juan Dixon RC 1.00 2.50
126 Kareem Rush RC .75 2.00
127 Casey Jacobsen RC .75 2.00
128 Frank Williams RC .75 2.00
129 John Salmons RC 1.00 2.50
130 Dan Dickau RC .75 2.00
131 Mike Dunleavy RC 1.00 2.50
132 Nikoloz Tskitishvili RC .75 2.00
133 Caron Butler RC 1.25 3.00
134 Jared Jeffries RC .75 2.00
135 Bostjan Nachbar RC .75 2.00
136 Ryan Humphrey RC .75 2.00
137 Qyntel Woods RC .75 2.00
138 Tayshaun Prince RC 1.00 2.50
139 Chris Jefferies RC .75 2.00
140 Vincent Yarbrough RC .75 2.00
141 Yao Ming RC 2.50 6.00
142 Drew Gooden RC 1.25 3.00
143 Nene Hilario RC 1.00 2.50
144 Chris Wilcox RC .75 2.00
145 Amare Stoudemire RC 2.00 5.00
146 Melvin Ely RC .75 2.00
147 Marcus Haislip RC .75 2.00
148 Curtis Borchardt RC .75 2.00
149 Robert Archibald RC .75 2.00
150 Dan Gadzuric RC .75 2.00

2002-03 Topps Ten Parallel

Randomly inserted in packs at the rate of one in one, this 150-card set parallels the base Topps Ten set enhanced with a noticably thicker card stock. These cards also double as decoys to prevent pack serching and tampering.
*STARS: 1X TO 2.5X BASE CARD HI
*RC's: .75X TO 2X BASE CARD HI

2002-03 Topps Ten Relic Parallel

Randomly inserted in packs at the rate of one in one, this 150-card set parallels the base Topps Ten set enhanced with a noticably thicker card stock and a swatch of game-worn meorabilia.

4 Tracy McGrady/1500 5.00 12.00
7 Dirk Nowitzki/1500 5.00 12.00
8 Karl Malone/1500 4.00 10.00
10 Gary Payton/300 3.00 8.00
11 Shaquille O'Neal/1500 8.00 20.00
17 Chris Webber/1500 3.00 8.00
22 Tim Duncan/1500 6.00 15.00
23 Kevin Garnett/1500 6.00 15.00
31 Andre Miller/300 2.50 6.00
34 Baron Davis/1500 3.00 8.00
51 Allen Iverson/1500 5.00 12.00
62 Elton Brand/750 3.00 8.00
66 Alonzo Mourning/300 4.00 10.00
75 Steve Nash/300 4.00 10.00
80 Ray Allen/1500 3.00 8.00
89 Peja Stojakovic/300 3.00 8.00
92 Cuttino Mobley/1500 2.50 6.00
93 Antoine Walker/1500 2.50 6.00
94 Steve Francis/750 3.00 8.00
95 Latrell Sprewell/300 2.50 6.00
108 Jermaine O'Neal/1500 3.00 8.00
111 Pau Gasol/400 4.00 10.00
114 Gilbert Arenas/750 3.00 8.00
115 Andrei Kirilenko/750 3.00 8.00
118 Tony Parker/300 4.00 10.00

2002-03 Topps Ten Autographs

Topps Ten Autographs consists of 20 cards divided up into five different groups: A, B, C, D, and E; and the inserted odds are as follows: Group A 1:335, Group B 1:679, Group C 1:220, Group D 1:283 and Group E 1:184. Each card places full-color player photography on a white bordered card with a box across the bottom third of the card reserved for autographs.

TAAM Aaron McKie C 4.00 10.00
TABH Brendan Haywood B 5.00 12.00
TACB Chauncey Billups E 6.00 15.00
TAEC Eddy Curry B 5.00 12.00
TAGA Gilbert Arenas B 10.00 25.00
TAJJ Joe Johnson A 6.00 15.00
TAJO Jermaine O'Neal A 8.00 20.00
TAJT Jason Terry D 4.00 10.00
TAKS Kenny Satterfield E 4.00 10.00
TAMB Mike Bibby C 6.00 15.00
TAMD Mike Dunleavy A 6.00 15.00
TAPS Peja Stojakovic E 6.00 15.00
TARJ Richard Jefferson C 6.00 15.00
TARL Raef LaFrentz A 6.00 15.00
TASB Shane Battier D 5.00 12.00
TASM Shawn Marion A 6.00 15.00
TASO Shaquille O'Neal B 50.00 125.00
TATM Troy Murphy C 4.00 10.00
TAVR Vladimir Radmanovic C 4.00 10.00
TAYM Yao Ming 30.00 80.00

2002-03 Topps Ten Team Leader Relics

Randomly inserted in packs, this 28-card set features players who led their teams in a specific statistical category. Each card is sequentially numbered and contains a swatch of game-worn memorabilia.

TLAD Antonio Davis/1000 2.00 5.00
TLAH Allan Houston/1000 2.50 6.00
TLAM Antonio McDyess/290 2.50 6.00
TLAMI Andre Miller/400 2.50 6.00
TLBH Brendan Haywood/400 2.00 5.00
TLCM Cuttino Mobley/1000 2.50 6.00
TLDM Dikembe Mutombo/400 3.00 8.00
TLDMI Darius Miles/1500 2.00 5.00
TLGR Glenn Robinson/1500 2.50 6.00
TLJM Jamal Mashburn/1500 2.50 6.00
TLJS John Stockton/400 4.00 10.00
TLJSH Jerry Stackhouse/1000 2.50 6.00
TLKM Kenyon Martin/1500 3.00 8.00
TLMF Michael Finley/1000 3.00 8.00
TLPG Pat Garrity/400 2.00 5.00
TLPS Peja Stojakovic/1500 3.00 8.00
TLRA Ray Allen/1290 3.00 8.00
TLRH Richard Hamilton/1000 2.50 6.00
TLRM Reggie Miller/400 8.00 20.00
TLRW Rasheed Wallace/125 3.00 8.00
TLSA Shareef Abdur-Rahim/400 2.50 6.00
TLSF Steve Francis/1000 3.00 8.00
TLSM Shawn Marion/400 3.00 8.00
TLSO Shaquille O'Neal/1500 8.00 20.00
TLSS Steve Smith/1000 2.50 6.00
TLTD Tim Duncan/1500 6.00 15.00
TLTM Tracy McGrady/1500 5.00 12.00
TLWS Wally Szczerbiak/1500 2.50 6.00

2005-06 Topps The Finals Promos

COMPLETE SET (4) 2.50 6.00
SCDW Dwyane Wade 1.25 3.00
Stadium Club
SCMJ Magic Johnson 1.25 3.00
Stadium Club
NBAF1 Allen Iverson .75 2.00
Topps
NBAF2 Dwyane Wade 1.25 3.00
Topps

1981 Topps Thirst Break

This 56-card set is actually a set of gum wrappers. These wrappers were issued in Thirst Break Orange Gum, which was reportedly only distributed in Pennsylvania and Ohio. Each of these small gum wrappers has a cartoon-type image of a particular great moment in sports. As the checklist below shows, many different sports are represented in this set. The wrappers each measure approximately 2 9/16" by 1 5/8". The wrappers are numbered in small print at the top. The backs of the wrappers are blank. The "1981 Topps" copyright is at the bottom of each card.

COMPLETE SET (56) 60.00 150.00
16 Wilt Chamberlain 2.00 5.00
100 Points One Game
17 Wilt Chamberlain 2.00 5.00
50.4 Avg Game
18 Wilt Chamberlain 2.00 5.00
No Foulout Record
25 John Havlicek 1.60 4.00
26 Oscar Robertson 1.60 4.00
27 Calvin Murphy .80 2.00

1999-00 Topps Tip-Off

Intended as a retail-only release, this 132-card set is a semi-parallel of the regular Topps set. The cards feature silver foil.

COMPLETE SET (132) 12.50 30.00
1 Steve Smith .12 .30
2 Ron Harper .12 .30
3 Michael Dickerson .12 .30
4 LaPhonso Ellis .12 .30
5 Chris Webber .20 .50
6 Jason Caffey .12 .30
7 Bryon Russell .12 .30
8 Bison Dele .12 .30
9 Isaiah Rider .12 .30
10 Dean Garrett .12 .30
11 Eric Murdock .12 .30
12 Juwan Howard .15 .40
13 Latrell Sprewell .20 .50
14 Jalen Rose .15 .40
15 Larry Johnson .20 .50
16 Eric Williams .12 .30
17 Bryant Reeves .12 .30
18 Tony Battie .15 .40
19 Luc Longley .12 .30
20 Gary Payton .20 .50
21 Tariq Abdul-Wahad .12 .30
22 Armen Gilliam .12 .30
23 Shaquille O'Neal .50 1.25
24 Gary Trent .12 .30
25 John Stockton .25 .60
26 Mark Jackson .20 .50
27 Cherokee Parks .12 .30
28 Michael Olowokandi .12 .30
29 Raef LaFrentz .15 .40
30 Dell Curry .12 .30
31 Travis Best .12 .30
32 Shawn Kemp .20 .50
33 Voshon Lenard .12 .30
34 Brian Grant .12 .30
35 Alvin Williams .12 .30
36 Derek Fisher .20 .50
37 Allan Houston .15 .40
38 Arvydas Sabonis .15 .40
39 Terry Cummings .12 .30
40 Dale Ellis .12 .30
41 Maurice Taylor .12 .30
42 Grant Hill .25 .60
43 Anthony Mason .12 .30
44 John Wallace .12 .30
45 David Wesley .12 .30
46 Nick Van Exel .15 .40
47 Cuttino Mobley .15 .40
48 Anfernee Hardaway .30 .75
49 Terry Porter .12 .30
50 Brent Barry .15 .40
51 Derek Harper .12 .30
52 Antoine Walker .20 .50
53 Karl Malone .25 .60
54 Ben Wallace .25 .60
55 Vlade Divac .20 .50
56 Sam Mitchell .12 .30
57 Joe Smith .12 .30
58 Shawn Bradley .12 .30
59 Darrell Armstrong .12 .30
60 Kenny Anderson .12 .30
61 Jason Williams .25 .60
62 Alonzo Mourning .25 .60
63 Matt Harpring .12 .30
64 Antonio Davis .12 .30
65 Lindsey Hunter .12 .30
66 Allen Iverson .40 1.00
67 Mookie Blaylock .12 .30
68 Wesley Person .12 .30
69 Bobby Phills .12 .30
70 Theo Ratliff .15 .40
71 Antonio Daniels .12 .30
72 P.J. Brown .12 .30
73 David Robinson .30 .75
74 Sean Elliott .20 .50
75 Zydrunas Ilgauskas .15 .40
76 Kerry Kittles .12 .30
77 Otis Thorpe .12 .30
78 John Starks .12 .30
79 Jaren Jackson .12 .30
80 Hersey Hawkins .12 .30
81 Glenn Robinson .15 .40
82 Paul Pierce .30 .75
83 Glen Rice .20 .50
84 Charlie Ward .12 .30
85 Dee Brown .12 .30
86 Danny Fortson .12 .30
87 Billy Owens .12 .30
88 Jason Kidd .30 .75
89 Brent Price .12 .30
90 Don Reid .12 .30
91 Mark Bryant .12 .30
92 Vinny Del Negro .12 .30
93 Stephon Marbury .15 .40
94 Donyell Marshall .12 .30
95 Jim Jackson .12 .30
96 Horace Grant .15 .40
97 Calbert Cheaney .12 .30
98 Vince Carter .40 1.00
99 Bobby Jackson .15 .40
100 Alan Henderson .12 .30
101 Mike Bibby .20 .50
102 Cedric Henderson .12 .30
103 Lamond Murray .12 .30
104 A.C. Green .20 .50
105 Hakeem Olajuwon .25 .60
106 George Lynch .12 .30
107 Kendall Gill .12 .30
108 Rex Chapman .12 .30
109 Eddie Jones .20 .50
110 Kornel David RC .60 1.50
111 Jason Terry RC 1.50 4.00
112 Corey Maggette RC 1.25 3.00
113 Ron Artest RC 1.50 4.00
114 Richard Hamilton RC 1.50 4.00
115 Elton Brand RC 1.50 4.00
116 Baron Davis RC 2.00 5.00
117 Wally Szczerbiak RC 1.25 3.00
118 Steve Francis RC 1.50 4.00
119 James Posey RC .60 1.50
120 Shawn Marion RC 1.50 4.00
121 Tim Duncan .40 1.00
122 Danny Manning .12 .30
123 Chris Mullin .20 .50
124 Antawn Jamison .20 .50
125 Kobe Bryant 1.00 2.50
126 Matt Geiger .12 .30
127 Rod Strickland .12 .30
128 Howard Eisley .12 .30
129 Steve Nash .30 .75
130 Felipe Lopez .12 .30
131 Ron Mercer .15 .40
132 Checklist .05 .15

1999-00 Topps Tip-Off Autographs

Randomly inserted in packs, this three-card set features autographs of some top stars in the NBA. The cards were inserted at different ratios, with Duncan at one in 12,910, Carter at one in 4,303 and Iverson at one in 6,455. Vince Carter did not end up signing the card, thus only the redemption exists. Card backs feature an "AG" prefix.

AG1 Tim Duncan 150.00 325.00

2000-01 Topps Tip-Off

The 2000-01 Topps Tip-Off product was released in late October, 2000. The set includes 124 Veterans, 10 Rookies, 6 Season Highlights, 10 Topps Series 2 Previews, 9 Coming Soon cards, and 1 Checklist. Each pack contained six cards and carried a suggested retail price of $.99.

COMPLETE SET (160) 15.00 40.00
1 Elton Brand .20 .50
2 Marcus Camby .15 .40
3 Jalen Rose .15 .40
4 Jamie Feick .12 .30
5 Toni Kukoc .15 .40
6 Todd MacCulloch .12 .30
7 Mario Elie .12 .30
8 Doug Christie .12 .30
9 Sam Cassell .15 .40
10 Shaquille O'Neal .50 1.25
11 Larry Hughes .15 .40
12 Jerry Stackhouse .15 .40
13 Rick Fox .15 .40
14 Clifford Robinson .12 .30
15 Felipe Lopez .12 .30
16 Dirk Nowitzki .30 .75
17 Cuttino Mobley .15 .40
18 Latrell Sprewell .15 .40
19 Nick Anderson .12 .30
20 Kevin Garnett .40 1.00
21 Rik Smits .12 .30
22 Jerome Williams .12 .30
23 Chris Webber .20 .50
24 Jason Terry .20 .50
25 Elden Campbell .12 .30
26 Kelvin Cato .12 .30
27 Tyrone Nesby .12 .30
28 Jonathan Bender .15 .40
29 Otis Thorpe .12 .30
30 Scottie Pippen .30 .75
31 Radoslav Nesterovic .12 .30
32 P.J. Brown .12 .30
33 Reggie Miller .20 .50
34 Andre Miller .15 .40
35 Tariq Abdul-Wahad .12 .30
36 Michael Doleac .12 .30
37 Rashard Lewis .20 .50
38 Jacque Vaughn .12 .30
39 Larry Johnson .20 .50
40 Steve Francis .20 .50
41 Arvydas Sabonis .15 .40
42 Jaren Jackson .12 .30
43 Howard Eisley .12 .30
44 Rod Strickland .15 .40
45 Tim Thomas .15 .40
46 Robert Horry .15 .40
47 Kenny Thomas .12 .30
48 Anthony Peeler .12 .30
49 Darrell Armstrong .12 .30
50 Vince Carter .40 1.00
51 Othella Harrington .12 .30
52 Derek Anderson .15 .40
53 Anthony Carter .12 .30
54 Scott Burrell .12 .30
55 Ray Allen .20 .50
56 Jason Kidd .30 .75
57 Sean Elliott .15 .40
58 Muggsy Bogues .15 .40
59 LaPhonso Ellis .12 .30
60 Tim Duncan .40 1.00
61 Adrian Griffin .12 .30
62 Wally Szczerbiak .15 .40
63 Austin Croshere .12 .30
64 Wesley Person .12 .30
65 James Posey .12 .30
66 Alan Henderson .12 .30
67 Ruben Patterson .12 .30
68 Jahidi White .12 .30
69 Shawn Marion .20 .50
70 Lamar Odom .20 .50
71 Lindsey Hunter .12 .30
72 Keon Clark .12 .30
73 Gary Trent .12 .30
74 Lamond Murray .12 .30
75 Paul Pierce .25 .60
76 Charlie Ward .12 .30
77 Matt Geiger .12 .30
78 Greg Anthony .12 .30
79 Chris Gatling .15 .40
80 John Stockton .25 .60
81 Peja Stojakovic .20 .50
82 William Avery .12 .30
83 Dan Majerle .15 .40
84 Christian Laettner .15 .40
85 Dana Barros .12 .30
86 Corey Benjamin .12 .30
87 Keith Van Horn .15 .40
88 Patrick Ewing .25 .60
89 Steve Smith .15 .40
90 Antonio Davis .12 .30
91 Samaki Walker .12 .30
92 Mitch Richmond .15 .40
93 Michael Olowokandi .12 .30
94 Baron Davis .20 .50
95 Dikembe Mutombo .20 .50
96 Andrew DeClercq .12 .30
97 Raef LaFrentz .12 .30
98 Trajan Langdon .12 .30
99 Ervin Johnson .12 .30
100 Alonzo Mourning .25 .60
101 Kendall Gill .12 .30
102 George Lynch .12 .30
103 Detlef Schrempf .15 .40
104 Donyell Marshall .12 .30
105 Bo Outlaw .12 .30
106 Kenny Anderson .15 .40
107 Eddie Robinson .12 .30
108 Jermaine O'Neal .20 .50
109 John Amaechi .12 .30
110 Glen Rice .15 .40
111 Vlade Divac .15 .40
112 Vin Baker .15 .40
113 Mike Bibby .20 .50
114 Richard Hamilton .15 .40
115 Mookie Blaylock .15 .40
116 Vitaly Potapenko .12 .30
117 Anthony Mason .12 .30
118 Robert Pack .12 .30
119 Vonteego Cummings .12 .30
120 Michael Finley .20 .50
121 Ron Artest .20 .50
122 Tyrone Hill .12 .30
123 Rodney Rogers .12 .30
124 Quincy Lewis .12 .30
125 Kenyon Martin RC .75 2.00
126 Stromile Swift RC .30 .75
127 Darius Miles RC .30 .75
128 Marcus Fizer RC .30 .75
129 Mike Miller RC .60 1.50
130 DerMarr Johnson RC .30 .75
131 Chris Mihm RC .30 .75
132 Jamal Crawford RC .50 1.25
133 Joel Przybilla RC .30 .75
134 Keyon Dooling RC .30 .75
135 Shaquille O'Neal .15 .40
Allen Iverson
Grant Hill
136 Jason Kidd .20 .50
Nick Van Exel
Sam Cassell
137 Dikembe Mutombo .25 .60
Shaquille O'Neal
Tim Duncan
138 Eddie Jones .10 .30
Paul Pierce
Darrell Armstrong
139 Alonzo Mourning .20 .50
Dikembe Mutombo
Shaquille O'Neal
140 Team Championship SL .30 .75
141 Kobe Bryant 1.00 2.50
142 Stephon Marbury .15 .40
143 Antoine Walker .15 .40
144 Jason Williams .20 .50
145 Shareef Abdur-Rahim .15 .40
146 Gary Payton .20 .50
147 Grant Hill .25 .60
148 Allen Iverson .40 1.00
149 Khalid El-Amin RC .30 .75
150 Chris Carrawell RC .30 .75
151 Shaquille O'Neal CS .50 1.25
152 Allen Iverson CS .40 1.00
153 Kevin Garnett CS .40 1.00
154 Vince Carter CS .40 1.00
155 Tim Duncan CS .40 1.00
156 Karl Malone CS .25 .60
157 Chris Webber CS .25 .60
158 Latrell Sprewell CS .15 .40
159 Alonzo Mourning CS .25 .60
160 Checklist .12 .30

2000-01 Topps Tip-Off Autographs

Randomly inserted in packs at overall odds of one in 1,404, this four-card set features autographs from NBA stars. The autographs were broken into two groups, A and B, and were inserted at one in 1,989 for group A and one in 4,773 for group B. The groupings are marked after the player's name.

TOAEB Elton Brand B 20.00 50.00
TOAEJ Eddie Jones A 20.00 50.00
TOASF Steve Francis A 20.00 50.00
TOATM Tracy McGrady A 40.00 100.00

2008-09 Topps Tip-Off

This set was released on November 26, 2008. The base set consists of 143 cards. Cards 1-110 feature veterans, and cards 111-143 are rookies.

COMPLETE SET (143) 15.00 30.00
UNPRICED PRESS PLATE PRINT RUN ONE SET
1 Kobe Bryant 1.00 2.50
2 Kevin Garnett .40 1.00
3 Chris Paul .30 .75
4 Chris Bosh .20 .50
5 Caron Butler .20 .50
6 Andrew Bogut .20 .50

7 Brandon Roy .20 .50
8 Richard Hamilton .15 .40
9 Tony Parker .20 .50
10 Yao Ming .25 .60
11 Jamal Crawford .15 .40
12 Dwight Howard .40 1.00
13 Steve Nash .20 .50
14 Mike Miller .20 .50
15 Vince Carter .25 .60
16 Pau Gasol .20 .50
17 Mike Dunleavy .15 .40
18 Josh Smith .20 .50
19 Kevin Martin .20 .50
20 Ray Allen .20 .50
21 Tim Duncan .30 .75
22 Michael Redd .20 .50
23 LeBron James 1.00 2.50
24 Richard Jefferson .20 .50
25 Al Jefferson .20 .50
26 Corey Maggette .15 .40
27 Hedo Turkoglu .20 .50
28 Mo Williams .15 .40
29 Andre Iguodala .20 .50
30 David West .20 .50
31 Tracy McGrady .20 .50
32 Shaquille O'Neal .40 1.00
33 Dwyane Wade .40 1.00
34 Paul Pierce .25 .60
35 Kevin Durant .75 2.00
36 Tayshaun Prince .20 .50
37 Shawn Marion .20 .50
38 Anderson Varejao .15 .40
39 Stephen Jackson .15 .40
40 Marcus Camby .12 .30
41 Brad Miller .15 .40
42 David Lee .15 .40
43 Allen Iverson .25 .60
44 Antawn Jamison .20 .50
45 Peja Stojakovic .20 .50
46 Rashad McCants .12 .30
47 Andrei Kirilenko .15 .40
48 Luol Deng .20 .50
49 Hakim Warrick .15 .40
50 Zach Randolph .15 .40
51 Danny Granger .20 .50
52 Greg Oden .20 .50
53 Jason Kidd .20 .50
54 Al Horford .20 .50
55 Carlos Boozer .20 .50
56 Jameer Nelson .15 .40
57 Andre Miller .15 .40
58 Ricky Davis .15 .40
59 Elton Brand .20 .50
60 Kirk Hinrich .20 .50
61 Amare Stoudemire .20 .50
62 Chris Wilcox .12 .30
63 Baron Davis .20 .50
64 Jason Richardson .20 .50
65 Jamario Moon .12 .30
66 LaMarcus Aldridge .20 .50
67 Jermaine O'Neal .20 .50
68 Joe Johnson .20 .50
69 Ben Wallace .20 .50
70 Carmelo Anthony .25 .60
71 T.J. Ford .12 .30
72 Dirk Nowitzki .25 .60
73 Ryan Gomes .12 .30
74 Ben Gordon .20 .50
75 Gerald Wallace .20 .50
76 Rudy Gay .20 .50
77 Lamar Odom .20 .50
78 Jeff Green .15 .40
79 Devin Harris .20 .50
80 Monta Ellis .20 .50
81 Samuel Dalembert .12 .30
82 Raymond Felton .15 .40
83 Ron Artest .20 .50
84 Chauncey Billups .20 .50
85 Josh Howard .15 .40
86 Rafer Alston .12 .30
87 Chris Kaman .15 .40
88 Deron Williams .20 .50
89 Manu Ginobili .20 .50
90 Gilbert Arenas .20 .50
91 Bill Russell .30 .75
92 David Robinson .30 .75
93 Bill Cartwright .20 .50
94 Dominique Wilkins .25 .60
95 Larry Bird .60 1.50
96 Dennis Rodman .30 .75
97 Jerry West .25 .60
98 George Gervin .25 .60
99 Rick Barry .20 .50
100 Bernard King .20 .50
101 Karl Malone .20 .50
102 Gail Goodrich .25 .60
103 Bill Bradley .25 .60
104 Adrian Dantley .20 .50
105 Joe Dumars .20 .50
106 Sam Jones .25 .60
107 John Stockton .30 .75
108 Magic Johnson .50 1.25
109 Larry Nance .20 .50
110 Dave Bing .20 .50
111 Derrick Rose RC 5.00 12.00
112 Michael Beasley RC .60 1.50
113 O.J. Mayo RC .60 1.50
114 Russell Westbrook RC 2.00 5.00
115 Kevin Love RC 1.50 4.00
116 Danilo Gallinari RC .60 1.50
117 Eric Gordon RC 1.00 2.50
118 Joe Alexander RC .40 1.00
119 D.J. Augustin RC .40 1.00
120 Brook Lopez RC .60 1.50
121 Jerryd Bayless RC .40 1.00
122 Jason Thompson RC .40 1.00
123 Brandon Rush RC .40 1.00
124 Anthony Randolph RC .50 1.25
125 Robin Lopez RC .40 1.00
126 Marreese Speights RC .40 1.00
127 Roy Hibbert RC .60 1.50
128 JaVale McGee RC .60 1.50
129 J.J. Hickson RC .50 1.25
130 Alexis Ajinca RC .40 1.00
131 Ryan Anderson RC .60 1.50
132 Courtney Lee RC .60 1.50
133 Kosta Koufos RC .40 1.00
134 Darrell Arthur RC .40 1.00
135 Donte Greene RC .40 1.00
136 Nicolas Batum RC .60 1.50
137 George Hill RC .60 1.50
138 D.J. White RC .40 1.00
139 J.R. Giddens RC .40 1.00
140 Walter Sharpe RC .40 1.00
141 Joey Dorsey RC .40 1.00
142 Mario Chalmers RC .60 1.50
143 Chris Douglas-Roberts RC .40 1.00

2008-09 Topps Tip-Off Gold

*1-110 GOLD: 2.5X TO 6X BASE HI
*111-143 GOLD RC: 2X TO 5X BASE
STATED PRINT RUN 99 SER.#'d SETS

2008-09 Topps Tip-Off Red

*1-110 RED: .75X TO 2X BASE HI
*111-143 RED RC: .6X TO 1.5X BASE
RED PRINT RUN 2008 SER.#'d SETS

2008-09 Topps Tip-Off Rookie Autographs

STATED PRINT RUN 20 SER.#'d SETS
111 Derrick Rose 150.00 300.00
112 Michael Beasley 25.00 50.00
113 O.J. Mayo 25.00 50.00
114 Russell Westbrook 60.00 150.00
116 Danilo Gallinari 15.00 40.00
117 Eric Gordon 25.00 60.00
120 Brook Lopez 15.00 40.00
123 Brandon Rush 10.00 25.00
124 Anthony Randolph 12.00 30.00
125 Robin Lopez 10.00 25.00
126 Marreese Speights 10.00 25.00
127 Roy Hibbert 15.00 40.00
131 Ryan Anderson 15.00 40.00
137 George Hill 15.00 40.00

2008-09 Topps Tip-Off Team Tattoos

COMPLETE SET (30) 6.00 15.00
1 Atlanta Hawks .40 1.00
2 Boston Celtics .75 2.00
3 Charlotte Bobcats .40 1.00
4 Chicago Bulls .75 2.00
5 Cleveland Cavaliers .40 1.00
6 Dallas Mavericks .40 1.00
7 Denver Nuggets .40 1.00
8 Detroit Pistons .40 1.00
9 Golden State Warriors .40 1.00
10 Houston Rockets .40 1.00
11 Indiana Pacers .40 1.00
12 Los Angeles Clippers .40 1.00
13 Los Angeles Lakers .75 2.00
14 Memphis Grizzlies .40 1.00
15 Miami Heat .40 1.00
16 Milwaukee Bucks .40 1.00
17 Minnesota Timberwolves .40 1.00
18 New Jersey Nets .40 1.00
19 New Orleans Hornets .40 1.00
20 New York Knicks .75 2.00
21 Oklahoma City Thunder .40 1.00
22 Orlando Magic .40 1.00
23 Philadelphia 76ers .40 1.00
24 Phoenix Suns .40 1.00
25 Portland Trail Blazers .40 1.00
26 Sacramento Kings .40 1.00
27 San Antonio Spurs .40 1.00
28 Toronto Raptors .40 1.00
29 Utah Jazz .40 1.00
30 Washington Wizards .40 1.00

2004-05 Topps Total

Released in April 2005, Topps Total boasts a large 440-card checklist including most players in the NBA during the 2004-05 season. All cards feature a silver and white bordered design with the Topps Total logo in red. The breaks down as follows: cards 1-311 feature veteran players, cards 312-360 feature rookies, cards 361-420 feature coaches and cards 421-440 feature team mascots. Total was packaged in 36-pack boxes where each pack contained 10 cards.

COMPLETE SET (440) 20.00 50.00
1 Antoine Walker .20 .50
2 Paul Pierce .25 .60
3 Tyson Chandler .15 .40
4 Lebron James 1.25 3.00
5 Dirk Nowitzki .30 .75
6 Carmelo Anthony .20 .50
7 Chauncey Billups .20 .50
8 Juwan Howard .15 .40
9 Eddie Gill .12 .30
10 Elton Brand .20 .50
11 Chucky Atkins .12 .30
12 Shane Battier .15 .40
13 Shaquille O'Neal .50 1.25
14 T.J. Ford .15 .40
15 Sam Cassell .15 .40
16 Rodney Buford .12 .30
17 David West .20 .50
18 Stephon Marbury .15 .40
19 Steve Francis .20 .50
20 Samuel Dalembert .12 .30
21 Steve Nash .20 .50
22 Shareef Abdur-Rahim .15 .40
23 Mike Bibby .20 .50
24 Tim Duncan .30 .75
25 Ray Allen .20 .50
26 Vince Carter .30 .75
27 Carlos Arroyo .15 .40
28 Gilbert Arenas .20 .50
29 Mark Blount .12 .30
30 Primoz Brezec .12 .30
31 Eddy Curry .15 .40
32 Lucious Harris .12 .30
33 Shawn Bradley .12 .30
34 Earl Boykins .12 .30
35 Elden Campbell .12 .30
36 Calbert Cheaney .12 .30
37 Jim Jackson .12 .30
38 Jonathan Bender .12 .30
39 Kobe Bryant 1.00 2.50
40 Malik Allen .12 .30
41 Dan Gadzuric .12 .30
42 Eddie Griffin .12 .30
43 Jason Collins .12 .30
44 Chris Andersen .30 .75
45 Marc Jackson .12 .30
46 Leandro Barbosa .20 .50
47 Derek Anderson .12 .30
48 Doug Christie .12 .30
49 Brent Barry .12 .30
50 Nick Collison .12 .30
51 Carlos Boozer .20 .50
52 Steve Blake .12 .30
53 Al Harrington .15 .40
54 Melvin Ely .12 .30
55 Zydrunas Ilgauskas .15 .40
56 Erick Dampier .12 .30
57 Marcus Camby .12 .30
58 Derrick Coleman .15 .40
59 Speedy Claxton .12 .30
60 Tyronn Lue .12 .30
61 Austin Croshere .12 .30
62 Marko Jaric .12 .30
63 Caron Butler .20 .50
64 Pau Gasol .20 .50
65 Christian Laettner .12 .30
66 Daniel Santiago .12 .30
67 Kevin Garnett .40 1.00
68 Richard Jefferson .20 .50
69 David Wesley .12 .30
70 Vin Baker .12 .30
71 Tony Battie .12 .30
72 Allen Iverson .30 .75
73 Darius Miles .12 .30
74 Bobby Jackson .12 .30
75 Bruce Bowen .12 .30
76 Antonio Daniels .12 .30
77 Chris Bosh .20 .50
78 Gordan Giricek .12 .30
79 Kwame Brown .12 .30
80 Raef Lafrentz .12 .30
81 Jason Hart .12 .30
82 Marquis Daniels .12 .30
83 Francisco Elson .12 .30
84 Carlos Delfino .20 .50
85 Dale Davis .12 .30
86 Tracy McGrady .25 .60
87 Jeff Foster .12 .30
88 Chris Kaman .20 .50
89 Brian Cook .12 .30
90 Mike Miller .20 .50
91 Rasual Butler .12 .30
92 Mike James .12 .30
93 Trenton Hassell .12 .30
94 Jason Kidd .30 .75
95 Lee Nailon .12 .30
96 Jerome Williams .12 .30
97 Stacey Augmon .12 .30
98 Willie Green .12 .30
99 Amare Stoudemire .25 .60
100 Ruben Patterson .12 .30
101 Chris Webber .20 .50
102 Manu Ginobili .25 .60
103 Danny Fortson .12 .30
104 Donyell Marshall .12 .30
105 Matt Harpring .15 .40
106 Juan Dixon .12 .30
107 Boris Diaw .12 .30
108 Ricky Davis .15 .40
109 Kareem Rush .12 .30
110 Kirk Hinrich .20 .50
111 Jeff McInnis .12 .30
112 Michael Finley .20 .50
113 Voshon Lenard .12 .30
114 Darvin Ham .12 .30
115 Mike Dunleavy .12 .30
116 Dikembe Mutombo .20 .50
117 Kerry Kittles .12 .30
118 Vlade Divac .15 .40
119 James Posey .20 .50
120 Michael Doleac .12 .30
121 Toni Kukoc .15 .40
122 Troy Hudson .12 .30
123 Jamal Crawford .15 .40
124 Grant Hill .25 .60
125 Corliss Williamson .12 .30
126 Quentin Richardson .15 .40
127 Zach Randolph .15 .40
128 Peja Stojakovic .20 .50
129 Robert Horry .15 .40
130 Jerome James .12 .30
131 Morris Peterson .12 .30
132 Jarvis Hayes .12 .30
133 Tony Delk .12 .30
134 Jason Kapono .12 .30
135 Adrian Griffin .12 .30
136 Aleksandar Pavlovic .12 .30
137 Kenyon Martin .20 .50
138 Richard Hamilton .12 .30
139 Derek Fisher .15 .40
140 Bob Sura .12 .30
141 Stephen Jackson .15 .40
142 Devean George .12 .30
143 Stromile Swift .12 .30
144 Keyon Dooling .12 .30
145 Desmond Mason .15 .40
146 Michael Olowokandi .12 .30
147 Ron Mercer .12 .30
148 P.J. Brown .12 .30
149 Tim Thomas .12 .30
150 Kelvin Cato .12 .30
151 Kenny Thomas .12 .30
152 Theo Ratliff .12 .30
153 Rasho Nesterovic .12 .30
154 Rashard Lewis .20 .50
155 Jalen Rose .15 .40
156 Brendan Haywood .12 .30
157 Kevin Willis .12 .30
158 Gary Payton .20 .50
159 Brevin Knight .12 .30
160 Othella Harrington .12 .30
161 Eric Snow .12 .30
162 Josh Howard .20 .50
163 Andre Miller .15 .40
164 Lindsey Hunter .12 .30
165 Adonal Foyle .12 .30
166 Maurice Taylor .12 .30
167 Fred Jones .12 .30
168 Corey Maggette .15 .40
169 Brian Grant .12 .30
170 Bonzi Wells .12 .30
171 Michael Redd .20 .50
172 Latrell Sprewell .15 .40
173 Steven Hunter .12 .30
174 Rodney Rogers .12 .30
175 Anfernee Hardaway .50 1.25
176 Pat Garrity .12 .30
177 Brian Skinner .12 .30
178 Zarko Cabarkapa .12 .30
179 Damon Stoudamire .15 .40
180 Tony Parker .20 .50
181 Ronald Murray .12 .30
182 Alvin Williams .12 .30
183 Raul Lopez .12 .30
184 Larry Hughes .15 .40
185 Predrag Drobnjak .12 .30
186 Jiri Welsch .12 .30
187 Robert Traylor .12 .30
188 Nene .15 .40
189 Antonio McDyess .15 .40
190 Troy Murphy .15 .40
191 Charlie Ward .12 .30
192 Reggie Miller .20 .50
193 Bobby Simmons .12 .30
194 Stanislav Medvedenko .12 .30
195 Jason Williams .15 .40
196 Dwyane Wade .60 1.50
197 Joe Smith .15 .40
198 Wally Szczerbiak .15 .40
199 Zoran Planinic .12 .30
200 Baron Davis .20 .50
201 Kurt Thomas .12 .30
202 Deshawn Stevenson .12 .30
203 John Salmons .20 .50
204 Maciej Lampe .12 .30
205 Greg Ostertag .12 .30
206 Malik Rose .12 .30
207 Matt Bonner .12 .30
208 Keith McLeod .12 .30
209 Antawn Jamison .20 .50
210 Marcus Banks .12 .30
211 Keith Bogans .12 .30
212 Antonio Davis .12 .30
213 Jerry Stackhouse .15 .40
214 Nikoloz Tskitishvili .12 .30
215 Darko Milicic .12 .30
216 Eduardo Najera .12 .30
217 Yao Ming .40 1.00
218 Jermaine O'Neal .20 .50
219 Chris Wilcox .12 .30
220 Lamar Odom .20 .50
221 Lorenzen Wright .12 .30
222 Damon Jones .12 .30
223 Keith Van Horn .15 .40
224 Fred Hoiberg .12 .30
225 Brian Scalabrine .12 .30
226 Jamaal Magloire .12 .30
227 Mike Sweetney .12 .30
228 Hedo Turkoglu .20 .50
229 Glenn Robinson .15 .40
230 Casey Jacobsen .12 .30
231 Nick Van Exel .15 .40
232 Matt Barnes .12 .30
233 Luke Ridnour .15 .40
234 Loren Woods .12 .30
235 Raja Bell .15 .40
236 Walter McCarty .12 .30
237 Steve Smith .15 .40
238 Frank Williams .12 .30
239 Dajuan Wagner .12 .30
240 Jason Terry .15 .40
241 Rodney White .12 .30
242 Tayshaun Prince .20 .50
243 Mickael Pietrus .15 .40
244 Reece Gaines .12 .30
245 Jamaal Tinsley .12 .30
246 Zeljko Rebraca .12 .30
247 Chris Mihm .12 .30
248 Eddie Jones .15 .40
249 Zaza Pachulia .12 .30
250 Ervin Johnson .12 .30
251 Jabari Smith .12 .30
252 Nazr Mohammed .12 .30
253 Andrew Declercq .12 .30
254 Kyle Korver .15 .40
255 Jake Voskuhl .12 .30
256 Travis Outlaw .12 .30
257 Vladimir Radmanovic .12 .30
258 Lamond Murray .12 .30
259 Jarron Collins .12 .30
260 Jared Jeffries .12 .30
261 Jason Collier .12 .30
262 Tom Gugliotta .12 .30
263 Gerald Wallace .20 .50
264 Eric Piatkowski .12 .30
265 Desagana Diop .12 .30
266 Alan Henderson .12 .30
267 Greg Buckner .12 .30
268 Ben Wallace .20 .50
269 Jason Richardson .20 .50
270 Ryan Bowen .12 .30
271 Mikki Moore .12 .30
272 Brian Cardinal .12 .30
273 Maurice Williams .12 .30
274 Mark Madsen .12 .30
275 Jacque Vaughn .12 .30
276 George Lynch .12 .30
277 Allan Houston .15 .40
278 Aaron McKie .12 .30
279 Joe Johnson .20 .50
280 Qyntel Woods .12 .30
281 Darius Songaila .12 .30
282 Devin Brown .12 .30
283 Mehmet Okur .15 .40
284 Kenny Anderson .15 .40
285 Jahidi White .12 .30
286 Jon Barry .12 .30
287 Drew Gooden .15 .40
288 Wesley Person .12 .30
289 Rasheed Wallace .20 .50
290 Clifford Robinson .12 .30
291 Bostjan Nachbar .12 .30
292 Scot Pollard .12 .30
293 Quinton Ross .12 .30
294 Luke Walton .15 .40
295 Earl Watson .12 .30
296 Udonis Haslem .15 .40
297 Erick Strickland .12 .30
298 Eric Williams .12 .30
299 Junior Harrington .12 .30
300 Moochie Norris .12 .30
301 Cuttino Mobley .12 .30
302 Shawn Marion .20 .50
303 Richie Frahm .12 .30
304 Brad Miller .20 .50
305 Michael Wilks .12 .30
306 Rafer Alston .12 .30
307 Andrei Kirilenko .15 .40
308 Etan Thomas .12 .30
309 Ndudi Ebi .12 .30
310 Anthony Peeler .12 .30
311 Pavel Podkolzine RC .30 .75
312 Lionel Chalmers RC .30 .75
313 Andre Emmett RC .30 .75
314 Trevor Ariza RC .30 .75
315 Dwight Howard RC 1.00 2.50
316 Rafael Araujo RC .30 .75
317 Tony Allen RC .40 1.00
318 Luol Deng RC .50 1.25
319 Jackson Vroman RC .30 .75
320 Josh Smith RC .50 1.25
321 Ben Gordon RC .40 1.00
322 Luke Jackson RC .30 .75
323 David Harrison RC .30 .75
324 Nenad Krstic RC .30 .75
325 J.R. Smith RC .40 1.00
326 Kris Humphries RC .30 .75
327 Al Jefferson RC .50 1.25
328 Devin Harris RC .50 1.25
329 Shaun Livingston RC .30 .75
330 Kaniel Dickens RC .30 .75
331 Kevin Martin RC .40 1.00
332 Kirk Snyder RC .30 .75
333 Josh Childress RC .30 .75
334 Erik Daniels RC .30 .75
335 Bernard Robinson RC .30 .75
336 Andres Nocioni RC .30 .75
337 D.J. Mbenga RC .30 .75
338 Sebastian Telfair RC .30 .75
339 Robert Swift RC .30 .75
340 Royal Ivey RC .30 .75
341 Anderson Varejao RC .40 1.00
342 Romain Sato RC .30 .75
343 Peter John Ramos RC .30 .75
344 Chris Duhon RC .30 .75
345 Emeka Okafor RC .50 1.25
346 Matt Freije RC .30 .75
347 Maurice Evans RC .30 .75
348 Beno Udrih RC .30 .75
349 John Edwards RC .30 .75
350 Sasha Vujacic RC .30 .75
351 Dorell Wright RC .50 1.25
352 Jameer Nelson RC .40 1.00
353 Damien Wilkins RC .30 .75
354 Pape Sow RC .30 .75
355 Andris Biedrins RC .40 1.00
356 Delonte West RC .40 1.00
357 Arthur Johnson RC .30 .75
358 Antonio Burks RC .30 .75
359 Andre Iguodala RC .50 1.25
360 Ibrahim Kutluay RC .30 .75
361 Mike Woodson CO .20 .50
362 Larry Drew CO .20 .50
363 Doc Rivers CO .40 1.00
364 Tony Brown CO .20 .50
365 Bernie Bickerstaff CO .20 .50
366 Gary Brokaw CO .20 .50
367 Scott Skiles CO .40 1.00
368 Ron Adams CO .20 .50
369 Paul Silas CO .20 .50
370 Brendan Malone CO .20 .50
371 Don Nelson CO .40 1.00
372 Donnie Nelson CO RC .20 .50
373 Jeff Bzdelik CO .20 .50
374 Michael Cooper CO .20 .50
375 Larry Brown CO .50 1.25
376 Dave Hanners CO .20 .50
377 Mike Montgomery CO .40 1.00
378 Terry Stotts CO .20 .50
379 Jeff Van Gundy CO .40 1.00
380 Tom Thibodeau CO .20 .50
381 Rick Carlisle CO .20 .50
382 Mike Brown CO .20 .50
383 Mike Dunleavy Sr. CO .40 1.00
384 Jim Eyen CO .20 .50
385 Rudy Tomjanovich CO .40 1.00
386 Frank Hamblen CO .20 .50
387 Mike Fratello CO .40 1.00
388 Eric Musselman CO .20 .50
389 Stan Van Gundy CO .40 1.00
390 Bob Mcadoo CO .40 1.00
391 Terry Porter CO .20 .50
392 Mike Schuler CO .20 .50
393 Flip Saunders CO .40 1.00
394 Jerry Sichting CO .20 .50
395 Lawrence Frank CO .20 .50
396 Brian Hill CO .20 .50
397 Byron Scott CO .20 .50
398 Darrell Walker CO .20 .50
399 Lenny Wilkens CO .50 1.25
400 Mark Aguirre CO .20 .50
401 Johnny Davis CO .20 .50
402 Paul Westhead CO .20 .50
403 Jim O'Brien CO .40 1.00
404 Lester Conner CO .20 .50
405 Mike D'Antoni CO .40 1.00
406 Marc Iavaroni CO .20 .50
407 Maurice Cheeks CO .40 1.00
408 Jim Lynam CO .20 .50
409 Rick Adelman CO .40 1.00
410 Elston Turner CO .20 .50
411 Gregg Popovich CO .50 1.25
412 P.J. Carlesimo CO .20 .50
413 Nate Mcmillan CO .20 .50
414 Dwane Casey CO .20 .50
415 Sam Mitchell CO .20 .50
416 Alex English CO .40 1.00
417 Jerry Sloan CO .40 1.00
418 Phil Johnson CO .20 .50
419 Eddie Jordan CO .20 .50
420 Mike O'Koren CO .20 .50
421 Harry The Hawk .30 .75
422 Blaze .30 .75
423 Benny Da Bull .30 .75
424 Slamson .30 .75
425 Champ .30 .75
426 Rocky .30 .75
427 Clutch .30 .75
428 Squatch .30 .75
429 Boomer .30 .75
430 The Raptor .30 .75
431 Super Grizz .30 .75
432 G-Wiz .30 .75
433 Crunch .30 .75
434 Sly The Fox .30 .75
435 Hip Hop .30 .75
436 The Gorilla .30 .75
437 Skyhawk .30 .75
438 Turbo .30 .75
439 Bowser .30 .75
440 Da Bull .30 .75

2004-05 Topps Total Parallel

Randomly inserted at one per pack, this 440-card set parallels the base Topps Total set with a full silver border.
*PARALLEL: 1X TO 2.5X BASE HI

2004-05 Topps Total Domination

Inserted at one in nine packs, this 20-card set utilizes a borderless design with a blue bar through the bottom containing the player's name.

COMPLETE SET (20) 4.00 10.00
TD1 Shaquille O'Neal .75 2.00
TD2 Allen Iverson .50 1.25
TD3 Tim Duncan .50 1.25
TD4 Tracy McGrady .40 1.00
TD5 Emeka Okafor .50 1.25
TD6 Vince Carter .50 1.25
TD7 Jermaine O'Neal .30 .75
TD8 Jason Kidd .50 1.25
TD9 Ben Wallace .30 .75
TD10 Dirk Nowitzki .50 1.25
TD11 Peja Stojakovic .30 .75
TD12 Michael Redd .30 .75
TD13 Amare Stoudemire .40 1.00
TD14 Yao Ming .60 1.50
TD15 Lamar Odom .30 .75
TD16 Steve Francis .30 .75
TD17 Sebastian Telfair .30 .75
TD18 Devin Harris .50 1.25
TD19 Luol Deng .50 1.25
TD20 Elton Brand .30 .75

2004-05 Topps Total Package

Inserted at one in nine packs, this 20-card set is gold bordered and places players against colored backgrounds.

COMPLETE SET (20) 6.00 15.00
TP1 Kevin Garnett .60 1.50
TP2 Kobe Bryant 1.50 4.00
TP3 Lebron James 2.00 5.00
TP4 Dwyane Wade 1.00 2.50
TP5 Richard Jefferson .30 .75
TP6 Dwight Howard 1.00 2.50
TP7 Ben Gordon .40 1.00
TP8 Shaun Livingston .30 .75
TP9 Carmelo Anthony .60 1.50
TP10 Paul Pierce .40 1.00
TP11 Baron Davis .30 .75
TP12 Chris Webber .30 .75
TP13 Shawn Marion .30 .75
TP14 Andrei Kirilenko .25 .60
TP15 Ray Allen .30 .75
TP16 Pau Gasol .30 .75
TP17 Richard Hamilton .25 .60
TP18 Stephon Marbury .25 .60
TP19 Jason Richardson .30 .75
TP20 Andre Iguodala .50 1.25

2004-05 Topps Total Signatures

Randomly seeded in packs for Group A at one in 15948, Group B at one in 1492 and Group C at one in 537, this 18-card set is bordered on the top and bottom in gold and has a sticker containing the player's autograph towards the bottom.

CA Carmelo Anthony 20.00 50.00
DH Devin Harris 10.00 25.00
EO Emeka Okafor 10.00 25.00
JR Justin Reed 6.00 15.00
KH Kris Humphries 6.00 15.00
LC Lionel Chalmers 6.00 15.00
LD Luol Deng 10.00 25.00
RS Romain Sato 6.00 15.00
SO Shaquille O'Neal 40.00 80.00
YT Yuta Tabuse 12.00 30.00
RSW Robert Swift 6.00 15.00

2004-05 Topps Total Success

Seeded in packs at one in 18, this 10-card set is printed on foil and places full-color player action photos on a design with a white line through it towards the left.

COMPLETE SET (10) 2.50 6.00
TS1 Carlos Boozer .50 1.25
TS2 Zach Randolph .40 1.00
TS3 Brad Miller .50 1.25
TS4 Ben Wallace .50 1.25
TS5 Cuttino Mobley .40 1.00
TS6 Rashard Lewis .50 1.25
TS7 Rafer Alston .30 .75
TS8 Carlos Arroyo .40 1.00
TS9 Manu Ginobili .60 1.50
TS10 Sam Cassell .40 1.00

2004-05 Topps Total Team Checklists

Inserted in packs at one in 4, this 30-card set showcases one of the team's top players on the front and a listing for all the players who appear on cards on the back.

COMPLETE SET (30) 10.00 25.00
1 Antoine Walker .40 1.00
2 Paul Pierce .50 1.25
3 Emeka Okafor .60 1.50
4 Kirk Hinrich .40 1.00
5 Lebron James 2.50 6.00
6 Dirk Nowitzki .60 1.50
7 Carmelo Anthony .75 2.00
8 Ben Wallace .40 1.00
9 Mike Dunleavy .30 .75
10 Yao Ming .75 2.00
11 Jermaine O'Neal .40 1.00
12 Elton Brand .40 1.00
13 Kobe Bryant 2.00 5.00
14 Pau Gasol .40 1.00
15 Shaquille O'Neal 1.00 2.50
16 Michael Redd .40 1.00
17 Kevin Garnett .75 2.00
18 Richard Jefferson .40 1.00
19 Baron Davis .40 1.00
20 Stephon Marbury .30 .75
21 Dwight Howard 1.25 3.00
22 Allen Iverson .60 1.50
23 Amare Stoudemire .50 1.25
24 Zach Randolph .40 1.00
25 Mike Bibby .40 1.00
26 Tim Duncan .60 1.50
27 Rashard Lewis .40 1.00
28 Vince Carter .60 1.50
29 Andrei Kirilenko .30 .75
30 Antawn Jamison .40 1.00

2005-06 Topps Total

Released in January 2006, This 440-card set is the largest base set issued during the 2005-06 season. Cards 1-360 feature a mix of veteran and rookie players, cards 361-420 feature team coaching staffs, cards 421-435 feature team mascots and cards 436-440 feature Topps celebrities. Base cards have white borders and photos outlined in team colors. Total was packaged in 36-pack boxes where each pack contains 10 cards and carried an initial SRP of $1.00.

COMPLETE SET (440) 20.00 50.00
UNPRICED GOLD PRINT RUN 10 SETS
UNPRICED PRESS PLATES 1/1 EXISTS
1 Josh Childress .15 .40
2 Emeka Okafor .20 .50
3 Luol Deng .20 .50
4 Carmelo Anthony .40 1.00
5 Carlos Arroyo .15 .40
6 Shane Battier .15 .40
7 Vince Carter .30 .75
8 Samuel Dalembert .12 .30
9 Leandro Barbosa .15 .40
10 Mike Bibby .20 .50
11 Brent Barry .12 .30
12 Ray Allen .20 .50
13 Rafer Alston .12 .30
14 Gilbert Arenas .20 .50
15 Al Harrington .15 .40
16 Primoz Brezec .12 .30
17 Antonio Davis .12 .30
18 Earl Boykins .12 .30
19 Chauncey Billups .20 .50
20 Antonio Burks .12 .30
21 Jason Collins .12 .30
22 P.J. Brown .12 .30
23 Andre Iguodala .20 .50
24 Bruce Bowen .12 .30
25 Nick Collison .12 .30
26 Rafael Araujo .12 .30
27 Josh Smith .20 .50
28 Melvin Ely .12 .30
29 Ben Gordon .20 .50
30 Zydrunas Ilgauskas .15 .40
31 Marcus Camby .15 .40
32 Carlos Delfino .12 .30
33 Mike James .12 .30
34 Brian Cardinal .12 .30
35 Udonis Haslem .15 .40
36 Toni Kukoc .12 .30
37 Kevin Garnett .40 1.00
38 Richard Jefferson .20 .50
39 Jamal Crawford .15 .40
40 Allen Iverson .30 .75
41 Tim Duncan .30 .75
42 Danny Fortson .12 .30
43 Chris Bosh .20 .50
44 Ricky Davis .20 .50
45 LeBron James 1.00 2.50
46 Devin Harris .20 .50
47 Tracy McGrady .25 .60
48 Chris Kaman .12 .30
49 Pau Gasol .20 .50
50 Jamaal Magloire .12 .30
51 Trenton Hassell .12 .30
52 Jason Kidd .30 .75
53 Speedy Claxton .12 .30
54 Kevin Martin .20 .50
55 Manu Ginobili .20 .50
56 Rashard Lewis .20 .50
57 Matt Harpring .15 .40
58 Kenyon Martin .20 .50
59 Al Jefferson .20 .50
60 Josh Howard .20 .50
61 Bob Sura .12 .30
62 David Harrison .12 .30
63 Shaun Livingston .12 .30
64 Alonzo Mourning .25 .60
65 Michael Redd .20 .50
66 Mark Madsen .12 .30
67 Brad Miller .20 .50
68 Robert Horry .15 .40
69 Luke Ridnour .15 .40
70 Paul Pierce .25 .60
71 Anderson Varejao .15 .40
72 Dirk Nowitzki .30 .75
73 Stephen Jackson .15 .40
74 Corey Maggette .15 .40
75 Shaquille O'Neal .40 1.00
76 Joe Smith .15 .40

Card	Low	High
7 Troy Hudson	.12	.30
8 Steve Francis	.20	.50
9 Shawn Marion	.20	.50
0 Ruben Patterson	.12	.30
1 Morris Peterson	.12	.30
2 Jarvis Hayes	.12	.30
3 Derek Fisher	.15	.40
4 Fred Jones	.12	.30
5 Chris Mihm	.12	.30
6 Stephon Marbury	.15	.40
7 Grant Hill	.25	.60
8 Steve Nash	.25	.60
9 Joel Przybilla	.12	.30
0 Jalen Rose	.20	.50
1 Brendan Haywood	.12	.30
2 Jerry Stackhouse	.15	.40
3 Adonal Foyle	.12	.30
4 Lamar Odom	.20	.50
5 Dwight Howard	.40	1.00
6 Amare Stoudemire	.20	.50
7 Zach Randolph	.15	.40
8 Peja Stojakovic	.20	.50
9 Mehmet Okur	.12	.30
00 Antawn Jamison	.20	.50
01 Jason Terry	.15	.40
02 Troy Murphy	.15	.40
03 Sasha Vujacic	.15	.40
04 Dwyane Wade	.50	1.25
05 Jameer Nelson	.15	.40
06 Jared Jeffries	.12	.30
07 J.R. Smith	.20	.50
08 Mike Sweetney	.12	.30
09 DeShawn Stevenson	.12	.30
10 Sebastian Telfair	.15	.40
11 Eddie Griffin	.12	.30
12 Tyronn Lue	.12	.30
13 Jon Barry	.12	.30
14 Eric Williams	.12	.30
15 Rasho Nesterovic	.12	.30
16 Keith Van Horn	.15	.40
17 Kenny Thomas	.12	.30
18 Chris Wilcox	.12	.30
19 Chris Webber	.20	.50
20 Nene	.15	.40
21 John Salmons	.20	.50
22 Chris Andersen	.30	.75
23 Lindsey Hunter	.12	.30
24 Matt Bonner	.12	.30
25 Darius Miles	.12	.30
26 Orien Greene RC	.20	.50
27 Jarron Collins	.12	.30
28 Trevor Ariza	.12	.30
29 Dan Gadzuric	.12	.30
30 Loren Woods	.12	.30
31 Jason Richardson	.20	.50
32 Corliss Williamson	.12	.30
33 Zeljko Rebraca	.12	.30
34 Othella Harrington	.12	.30
35 Theo Ratliff	.12	.30
36 David Wesley	.12	.30
37 Bostjan Nachbar	.12	.30
38 Eric Snow	.12	.30
39 Desmond Mason	.12	.30
40 Dahntay Jones	.12	.30
41 Andre Miller	.15	.40
42 Travis Outlaw	.15	.40
43 Jim Jackson	.12	.30
44 Gordan Giricek	.12	.30
45 Kelvin Cato	.12	.30
46 Michael Doleac	.12	.30
47 Lorenzen Wright	.12	.30
48 Vladimir Radmanovic	.12	.30
49 Maurice Evans	.12	.30
50 Hedo Turkoglu	.20	.50
51 Ryan Bowen	.12	.30
52 Brevin Knight	.12	.30
53 Jacque Vaughn	.12	.30
54 Tayshaun Prince	.20	.50
55 Clifford Robinson	.12	.30
56 Delonte West	.15	.40
57 Zoran Planinic	.12	.30
58 Slava Medvedenko	.12	.30
59 Andres Nocioni	.12	.30
60 Kyle Korver	.15	.40
61 Brian Cook	.12	.30
62 Viktor Khryapa	.12	.30
63 Malik Rose	.12	.30
64 Elton Brand	.20	.50
65 Gerald Wallace	.20	.50
66 Michael Bradley	.12	.30
67 DerMarr Johnson	.12	.30
68 Reece Gaines	.12	.30
69 Mickael Pietrus	.15	.40
70 Donta Smith	.12	.30
71 Wally Szczerbiak	.15	.40
72 Aleksandar Pavlovic	.12	.30
73 Michael Olowokandi	.12	.30
74 Jose Calderon RC	.20	.50
75 Jiri Welsch	.12	.30
76 Antonio McDyess	.15	.40
77 Andrei Kirilenko	.15	.40
78 Nenad Krstic	.12	.30
79 Richard Hamilton	.15	.40
80 Stacey Augmon	.12	.30
81 Kobe Bryant	1.00	2.50
82 Erick Dampier	.12	.30
83 Raef LaFrentz	.12	.30
84 Jackie Butler RC	.12	.30
85 Ira Newble	.12	.30
86 Luke Walton	.12	.30
87 Rasheed Wallace	.20	.50
88 Alvin Williams	.12	.30
89 Ben Wallace	.20	.50
90 Chris Duhon	.12	.30
91 Maurice Williams	.15	.40
92 Ronald Murray	.12	.30
93 Yao Ming	.25	.60
94 Eduardo Najera	.12	.30
95 Nazr Mohammed	.12	.30
96 Devean George	.12	.30
97 Kirk Hinrich	.20	.50
98 Baron Davis	.20	.50
99 Juwan Howard	.15	.40
00 Drew Gooden	.15	.40
01 Carlos Boozer	.20	.50
02 Tony Delk	.12	.30
03 David West	.20	.50
04 Keith Bogans	.12	.30
05 Quinton Ross	.12	.30
06 Darrell Armstrong	.12	.30
07 Damien Wilkins	.12	.30
08 Voshon Lenard	.12	.30
09 Vitaly Potapenko	.12	.30
210 Mike Miller	.20	.50
211 Beno Udrih	.12	.30
212 Darko Milicic	.12	.30
213 Tony Parker	.20	.50
214 Brian Skinner	.12	.30
215 Mike Dunleavy	.15	.40
216 Kris Humphries	.12	.30
217 Mark Blount	.12	.30
218 Marquis Daniels	.12	.30
219 Tony Allen	.12	.30
220 Tony Battie	.12	.30
221 Luther Head RC	.20	.50
222 Richie Frahm	.12	.30
223 Arvydas Macijauskas RC	.20	.50
224 Eddie Jones	.15	.40
225 Dan Dickau	.12	.30
226 Marko Jaric	.12	.30
227 Daniel Ewing RC	.20	.50
228 Keyon Dooling	.12	.30
229 James Posey	.12	.30
230 Earl Watson	.12	.30
231 Juan Dixon	.12	.30
232 Rasual Butler	.12	.30
233 Bernard Robinson	.12	.30
234 Joe Johnson	.20	.50
235 Antoine Walker	.15	.40
236 Andris Biedrins	.15	.40
237 Gary Payton	.20	.50
238 Monta Ellis RC	.40	1.00
239 Quentin Richardson	.15	.40
240 Martynas Andriuskevicius RC	.20	.50
241 Kwame Brown	.12	.30
242 Travis Diener RC	.20	.50
243 Stromile Swift	.12	.30
244 Wayne Simien RC	.20	.50
245 Zaza Pachulia	.12	.30
246 Andrew Bogut RC	.30	.75
247 Marvin Williams RC	.25	.60
248 David Lee RC	.30	.75
249 Nate Robinson RC	.25	.60
250 Jason Williams	.15	.40
251 Larry Hughes	.15	.40
252 Ike Diogu RC	.20	.50
253 Marc Jackson	.12	.30
254 Luke Jackson	.12	.30
255 Lee Nailon	.12	.30
256 T.J. Ford	.15	.40
257 Shavlik Randolph RC	.20	.50
258 Eddie Basden RC	.20	.50
259 Yaroslav Korolev RC	.20	.50
260 James Jones	.12	.30
261 Raja Bell	.15	.40
262 Salim Stoudamire RC	.20	.50
263 Cuttino Mobley	.15	.40
264 Kurt Thomas	.12	.30
265 D.J. Mbenga	.12	.30
266 Zarko Cabarkapa	.12	.30
267 Bobby Jackson	.12	.30
268 Rashad McCants RC	.20	.50
269 Antoine Wright RC	.20	.50
270 Josh Powell RC	.20	.50
271 Francisco Garcia RC	.25	.60
272 Robert Swift	.12	.30
273 Gerald Green RC	.25	.60
274 Peter John Ramos	.12	.30
275 Nick Van Exel	.20	.50
276 Jarrett Jack RC	.20	.50
277 Ronnie Price RC	.20	.50
278 Jamaal Tinsley	.12	.30
279 Jake Voskuhl	.12	.30
280 Devin Brown	.12	.30
281 James Singleton RC	.20	.50
282 C.J. Miles RC	.25	.60
283 Charlie Villanueva RC	.25	.60
284 Jeff McInnis	.12	.30
285 Eddie House	.12	.30
286 Rawle Marshall RC	.20	.50
287 Royal Ivey	.12	.30
288 Dikembe Mutombo	.20	.50
289 Fabricio Oberto RC	.20	.50
290 Damon Jones	.12	.30
291 Jason Hart	.12	.30
292 Jumaine Jones	.12	.30
293 Greg Ostertag	.12	.30
294 Ryan Gomes RC	.20	.50
295 Derek Anderson	.12	.30
296 Raymond Felton RC	.30	.75
297 Johan Petro RC	.20	.50
298 Bonzi Wells	.12	.30
299 Tyson Chandler	.15	.40
300 Sarunas Jasikevicius RC	.20	.50
301 Joey Graham RC	.20	.50
302 Alan Anderson RC	.20	.50
303 Steve Blake	.12	.30
304 Nikoloz Tskitishvili	.12	.30
305 Shareef Abdur-Rahim	.15	.40
306 Sean May RC	.20	.50
307 Julius Hodge RC	.20	.50
308 Deron Williams RC	.50	1.25
309 Michael Ruffin	.12	.30
310 Darius Songaila	.12	.30
311 Donyell Marshall	.12	.30
312 Jermaine O'Neal	.20	.50
313 Bracey Wright RC	.20	.50
314 Scot Pollard	.12	.30
315 Linas Kleiza RC	.20	.50
316 Jerome James	.12	.30
317 Brian Scalabrine	.12	.30
318 Tim Thomas	.12	.30
319 Reggie Evans	.12	.30
320 Jason Maxiell RC	.20	.50
321 Jannero Pargo	.12	.30
322 Michael Finley	.20	.50
323 Ersan Ilyasova RC	.25	.60
324 Robert Whaley RC	.20	.50
325 Chris Taft RC	.20	.50
326 Esteban Batista RC	.20	.50
327 Louis Williams RC	.30	.75
328 Austin Croshere	.12	.30
329 Martell Webster RC	.20	.50
330 Etan Thomas	.12	.30
331 Brandon Bass RC	.25	.60
332 Ron Artest	.20	.50
333 Gerald Fitch RC	.20	.50
334 Chucky Atkins	.12	.30
335 Jonathan Bender	.12	.30
336 Boris Diaw	.15	.40
337 Andray Blatche RC	.25	.60
338 Jeff Foster	.12	.30
339 Andrew Bynum RC	.60	1.50
340 Caron Butler	.20	.50
341 Danny Granger RC	.40	1.00
342 Channing Frye RC	.25	.60
343 Antonio Daniels	.12	.30
344 Brian Grant	.12	.30
345 Steven Hunter	.12	.30
346 Chris Paul RC	.75	2.00
347 Lawrence Roberts RC	.20	.50
348 Bobby Simmons	.12	.30
349 Dijon Thompson RC	.20	.50
350 Von Wafer RC	.20	.50
351 Damon Stoudamire	.15	.40
352 Kevin Ollie	.12	.30
353 Kirk Snyder	.12	.30
354 Hakim Warrick RC	.25	.60
355 Eddy Curry	.15	.40
356 Aaron McKie	.12	.30
357 Sam Cassell	.20	.50
358 Dorell Wright	.12	.30
359 Scott Padgett	.12	.30
360 Pat Garrity	.12	.30
361 Mike Woodson	.20	.50
362 Larry Drew	.20	.50
363 Doc Rivers	.20	.50
364 Tony Brown	.12	.30
365 Bernie Bickerstaff	.20	.50
366 Gary Brokaw	.20	.50
367 Scott Skiles	.20	.50
368 Ron Adams	.20	.50
369 Mike Brown	.20	.50
370 Kenny Natt	.20	.50
371 Avery Johnson	.20	.50
372 Del Harris	.20	.50
373 George Karl	.20	.50
374 Scott Brooks	.20	.50
375 Flip Saunders	.20	.50
376 Sid Lowe	.20	.50
377 Mike Montgomery	.20	.50
378 Mario Elie	.20	.50
379 Jeff Van Gundy	.20	.50
380 Tom Thibodeau	.20	.50
381 Rick Carlisle	.20	.50
382 Kevin O'Neill	.20	.50
383 Mike Dunleavy Sr.	.20	.50
384 Jim Eyen	.20	.50
385 Phil Jackson	.25	.60
386 Frank Hamblen	.20	.50
387 Mike Fratello	.25	.60
388 Eric Musselman	.20	.50
389 Pat Riley	.20	.50
390 Bob McAdoo	.20	.50
391 Terry Stotts	.20	.50
392 Lester Conner	.20	.50
393 Dwane Casey	.20	.50
394 Johnny Davis	.20	.50
395 Lawrence Frank	.20	.50
396 Bill Cartwright	.20	.50
397 Byron Scott	.20	.50
398 Darrell Walker	.20	.50
399 Larry Brown	.25	.60
400 Herb Williams	.20	.50
401 Brian Hill	.20	.50
402 Randy Ayers	.20	.50
403 Maurice Cheeks	.20	.50
404 John Kuester	.20	.50
405 Mike D'Antoni	.20	.50
406 Marc Iavaroni	.20	.50
407 Nate McMillan	.20	.50
408 Dean Demopoulos	.20	.50
409 Rick Adelman	.20	.50
410 Elston Turner	.20	.50
411 Gregg Popovich	.25	.60
412 P.J. Carlesimo	.20	.50
413 Bob Weiss	.20	.50
414 Jack Sikma	.20	.50
415 Sam Mitchell	.12	.30
416 Jim Todd	.20	.50
417 Jerry Sloan	.20	.50
418 Phil D. Johnson	.20	.50
419 Eddie Jordan	.20	.50
420 Mike O'Koren	.20	.50
421 The Gorilla	.30	.75
422 Rocky	.30	.75
423 Slamson	.30	.75
424 The Raptor	.30	.75
425 Squatch	.30	.75
426 Blaze	.30	.75
427 Crunch	.30	.75
428 Harry the Hawk	.30	.75
429 Champ	.30	.75
430 Hip Hop	.30	.75
431 Sly the Silver Fox	.30	.75
432 Benny the Bull	.30	.75
433 G-Wiz	.30	.75
434 Clutch	.30	.75
435 Boomer	.30	.75
436 Shannon Elizabeth	.40	1.00
437 Christie Brinkley	.40	1.00
438 Jenny McCarthy	.40	1.00
439 Carmen Electra	.40	1.00
440 Jay-Z	.60	1.50

2005-06 Topps Total Silver

Inserted at one per pack, this 440-card set parallels the base Topps Total set enhanced with silver borders.
*SILVER: .75X TO 2X BASE HI

2005-06 Topps Total Competition

Card	Low	High
COMPLETE SET (10)	3.00	8.00
TC1 Jason Kidd	1.00	2.50
TC2 Richard Hamilton	.50	1.25
TC3 Manu Ginobili	.60	1.50
TC4 Elton Brand	.60	1.50
TC5 Jason Richardson	.60	1.50
TC6 Emeka Okafor	.60	1.50
TC7 Allen Iverson	1.00	2.50
TC8 Shawn Marion	.60	1.50
TC9 Ben Gordon	.60	1.50
TC10 Dwyane Wade	1.50	4.00

2005-06 Topps Total Performance

Card	Low	High
COMPLETE SET (20)	8.00	20.00
STATED ODDS 1:9		
TP1 Shaquille O'Neal	1.00	2.50
TP2 LeBron James	2.50	6.00
TP3 Allen Iverson	.75	2.00
TP4 Dirk Nowitzki	.75	2.00
TP5 Tracy McGrady	.60	1.50
TP6 Steve Nash	.60	1.50
TP7 Vince Carter	.75	2.00
TP8 Carmelo Anthony	1.00	2.50
TP9 Kobe Bryant	2.50	6.00
TP10 Kevin Garnett	1.00	2.50
TP11 Tim Duncan	.75	2.00
TP12 Stephon Marbury	.40	1.00
TP13 Kirk Hinrich	.50	1.25
TP14 Amare Stoudemire	.50	1.25
TP15 Steve Francis	.50	1.25
TP16 Yao Ming	.60	1.50
TP17 Gilbert Arenas	.50	1.25
TP18 Ray Allen	.50	1.25
TP19 Paul Pierce	.60	1.50
TP20 Dwyane Wade	1.25	3.00

2005-06 Topps Total Signatures

Inserted in packs at the rate of one in 1634, this set places player photos on backgrounds set to match team colors along with a silver autograph sticker on each card.

Card	Low	High
TSAB Andrew Bogut	30.00	80.00
TSABY Andrew Bynum	60.00	150.00
TSDWA Dwyane Wade	50.00	120.00
TSJM Jenny McCarthy	50.00	125.00
TSJZ Jay-Z	50.00	125.00
TSSL Shaun Livingston	8.00	20.00
TSSO Shaquille O'Neal	40.00	100.00

2005-06 Topps Total Surprise

Inserted in packs at the rate of one in 18, this 10-card set is printed on an all-foil card stock and places player photos on a colorful background with black borders along the bottom and the words, "Total Surprise" along the top.

Card	Low	High
COMPLETE SET (10)	2.50	6.00
TS1 Chauncey Billups	.60	1.50
TS2 Gilbert Arenas	.60	1.50
TS3 Jermaine O'Neal	.60	1.50
TS4 Marquis Daniels	.40	1.00
TS5 Ben Wallace	.60	1.50
TS6 Michael Redd	.60	1.50
TS7 Earl Boykins	.40	1.00
TS8 Shawn Marion	.60	1.50
TS9 Rafer Alston	.40	1.00
TS10 Manu Ginobili	.60	1.50

2005-06 Topps Total Team Checklists

Card	Low	High
COMPLETE SET (30)	15.00	30.00
RANDOM INSERTS IN PACKS		
1 Josh Smith	.60	1.50
2 Paul Pierce	.75	2.00
3 Emeka Okafor	.60	1.50
4 Kirk Hinrich	.60	1.50
5 LeBron James	3.00	8.00
6 Dirk Nowitzki	1.00	2.50
7 Carmelo Anthony	1.25	3.00
8 Ben Wallace	.60	1.50
9 Baron davis	.60	1.50
10 Yao Ming	.75	2.00
11 Jermaine O'Neal	.60	1.50
12 Elton Brand	.60	1.50
13 Kobe Bryant	3.00	8.00
14 Pau Gasol	.60	1.50
15 Dwyane Wade	1.50	4.00
16 T.J. Ford	.50	1.25
17 Kevin Garnett	1.25	3.00
18 Jason Kidd	1.00	2.50
19 J.R. Smith	.60	1.50
20 Stephon Marbury	.50	1.25
21 Dwight Howard	1.25	3.00
22 Allen Iverson	1.00	2.50
23 Steve Nash	.75	2.00
24 Sebastian Telfair	.50	1.25
25 Mike Bibby	.60	1.50
26 Tim Duncan	1.00	2.50
27 Ray Allen	.60	1.50
28 Chris Bosh	.60	1.50
29 Andrei Kirilenko	.50	1.25
30 Gilbert Arenas	.60	1.50

2005-06 Topps Total Transfer

Randomly seeded in packs at the rate of one in 18, this 10-card set is printed on an all-foil card stock where player photos are framed by a circular border with the setname and player name along with black borders on the top and bottom of the card.

Card	Low	High
COMPLETE SET (10)	2.50	6.00
TT1 Michael Finley	.60	1.50
TT2 Joe Johnson	.60	1.50
TT3 Larry Hughes	.50	1.25
TT4 Caron Butler	.60	1.50
TT5 Quentin Richardson	.50	1.25
TT6 Antoine Walker	.50	1.25
TT7 Sam Cassell	.60	1.50
TT8 Damon Stoudamire	.50	1.25
TT9 Bobby Simmons	.40	1.00
TT10 Shareef Abdur-Rahim	.50	1.25

2006-07 Topps Trademark Moves

Released in early March 2007, Topps Trademark Moves features a 150-card base set with a white background design that places a full-color player photo inside an oval that runs from the top right to the bottom left of the card. Card numbers 1-80 picture veterans, card numbers 81-100 picture retired NBA legends, and card numbers 101-150 picture rookie autographs sequentially numbered to either 149 or 75 (see checklist for details) where rookie autographs are signed on stickers. Trademark Moves is packaged in 18-pack boxes of five cards each and carried an original suggested retail price of $10.00 per pack.

Card	Low	High
COMP.SET w/o SP's (100)	8.00	20.00
1 Dwyane Wade	.75	2.00
2 Richard Jefferson	.30	.75
3 Raymond Felton	.40	1.00
4 Ray Allen	.30	.75
5 Peja Stojakovic	.30	.75
6 Mike Miller	.30	.75
7 Mike Bibby	.30	.75
8 Marcus Camby	.25	.60
9 LeBron James	1.50	4.00
10 Joe Johnson	.30	.75
11 Corey Maggette	.25	.60
12 Charlie Villanueva	.30	.75
13 Caron Butler	.30	.75
14 Amare Stoudemire	.30	.75
15 Vince Carter	.40	1.00
16 Tracy McGrady	.40	1.00
17 Shawn Marion	.30	.75
18 Ron Artest	.30	.75
19 Pau Gasol	.30	.75
20 Smush Parker	.20	.50
21 Josh Smith	.30	.75
22 Gilbert Arenas	.30	.75
23 Elton Brand	.30	.75
24 Dwight Howard	.50	1.25
25 Dirk Nowitzki	.50	1.25
26 Chris Bosh	.30	.75
27 Chauncey Billups	.30	.75
28 Ben Gordon	.30	.75
29 Yao Ming	.40	1.00
30 Tyson Chandler	.25	.60
31 T.J. Ford	.25	.60
32 Steve Nash	.40	1.00
33 Sam Cassell	.30	.75
34 Speedy Claxton	.20	.50
35 Manu Ginobili	.30	.75
36 Kevin Garnett	.60	1.50
37 Jason Terry	.25	.60
38 Jameer Nelson	.25	.60
39 Ben Wallace	.30	.75
40 Antoine Walker	.25	.60
41 Al Jefferson	.30	.75
42 Tim Duncan	.50	1.25
43 Richard Hamilton	.25	.60
44 Paul Pierce	.40	1.00
45 Mike James	.20	.50
46 Martell Webster	.25	.60
47 Kobe Bryant	1.50	4.00
48 Kirk Hinrich	.30	.75
49 Josh Howard	.25	.60
50 Bobby Simmons	.20	.50
51 Channing Frye	.25	.60
52 Andrei Kirilenko	.25	.60
53 Allen Iverson	.40	1.00
54 Al Harrington	.25	.60
55 Zach Randolph	.25	.60
56 Tony Parker	.30	.75
57 Stephon Marbury	.25	.60
58 Shaquille O'Neal	.60	1.50
59 Ricky Davis	.25	.60
60 Lamar Odom	.30	.75
61 Emeka Okafor	.30	.75
62 Raja Bell	.25	.60
63 Deron Williams	.50	1.25
64 Danny Granger	.30	.75
65 Baron Davis	.30	.75
66 Andre Miller	.25	.60
67 Andre Iguodala	.30	.75
68 Michael Redd	.30	.75
69 Rashard Lewis	.30	.75
70 Larry Hughes	.25	.60
71 Jermaine O'Neal	.30	.75
72 Jason Richardson	.30	.75
73 Jason Kidd	.50	1.25
74 Gerald Wallace	.30	.75
75 Leandro Barbosa	.25	.60
76 Chris Paul	.60	1.50
77 Carmelo Anthony	.40	1.00
78 Brad Miller	.30	.75
79 Antawn Jamison	.30	.75
80 Andrew Bogut	.30	.75
81 Dominique Wilkins	.60	1.50
82 Larry Bird	1.50	4.00
83 Clyde Drexler	.60	1.50
84 Dennis Rodman	.75	2.00
85 Isiah Thomas	.50	1.25
86 Rick Barry	.50	1.25
87 Hakeem Olajuwon	.60	1.50
88 George Gervin	.50	1.25
89 Spud Webb	.50	1.25
90 Kareem Abdul-Jabbar	.75	2.00
91 Oscar Robertson	.50	1.25
92 Earl Monroe	.50	1.25
93 Walt Frazier	.50	1.25
94 Moses Malone	.50	1.25
95 Wilt Chamberlain	1.00	2.50
96 Karl Malone	.60	1.50
97 Manute Bol	.50	1.25
98 Bill Walton	.50	1.25
99 Maurice Cheeks	.50	1.25
100 Bob Lanier	.50	1.25
101 Solomon Jones AU/149 RC	3.00	8.00
102 Kyle Lowry AU/149 RC	4.00	10.00
103 Maurice Ager AU/149 RC	3.00	8.00
104 Patrick O'Bryant AU/75 RC	4.00	10.00
105 Pops Mensah-Bonsu AU/149 RC	3.00	8.00
106 Marcus Vinicius AU/149 RC	3.00	8.00
107 Josh Boone AU/149 RC	3.00	8.00
108 Mardy Collins AU/149 RC	3.00	8.00
109 Rodney Carney AU/75 RC	4.00	10.00
110 P.J. Tucker AU/149 RC	3.00	8.00
111 Shelden Williams AU/75 RC	4.00	10.00
112 Ryan Hollins AU/149 RC	3.00	8.00
113 Sergio Rodriguez AU/149 RC	3.00	8.00
114 Steve Novak AU/149 RC	3.00	8.00
115 Paul Davis AU/149 RC	3.00	8.00
116 David Noel AU/149 RC	3.00	8.00
117 Marcus Williams AU/75 RC	4.00	10.00
118 Renaldo Balkman AU/75 RC	4.00	10.00
119 Quincy Douby AU/149 RC	3.00	8.00
120 Andrea Bargnani AU/75 RC	6.00	15.00
121 Chris Quinn AU/149 RC	3.00	8.00
122 Thabo Sefolosha AU/75 RC	5.00	12.00
123 Hassan Adams AU/149 RC	3.00	8.00
124 James White AU/149 RC	3.00	8.00
125 Jordan Farmar AU/75 RC	4.00	10.00
126 Damir Markota AU/149 RC	3.00	8.00
127 Mile Ilic AU/149 RC	3.00	8.00
128 James Augustine AU/149 RC	3.00	8.00
129 Paul Millsap AU/149 RC	5.00	12.00
130 Jorge Garbajosa AU/149 RC	3.00	8.00
131 Allan Ray AU/75 RC	4.00	10.00
132 Shannon Brown AU/149 RC	5.00	12.00
133 Will Blalock AU/149 RC	3.00	8.00
134 Vassilis Spanoulis AU/149 RC	3.00	8.00
135 Adam Morrison AU/75 RC	5.00	12.00
136 Craig Smith AU/149 RC	3.00	8.00
137 Cedric Simmons AU/149 RC	3.00	8.00
138 J.J. Redick AU/75 RC	5.00	12.00
140 Ronnie Brewer AU/75 RC	5.00	12.00
141 Rajon Rondo AU/149 RC	15.00	40.00
142 Daniel Gibson AU/149 RC	4.00	10.00
143 Mickael Gelabale AU/75 RC	4.00	10.00
144 Shawne Williams AU/75 RC	4.00	10.00
145 Alexander Johnson AU/149 RC	3.00	8.00
146 Randy Foye AU/75 RC	5.00	12.00
148 Bobby Jones AU/149 RC	3.00	8.00
149 Saer Sene AU/149 RC	3.00	8.00
150 Dee Brown AU/75 RC	4.00	10.00

2006-07 Topps Trademark Moves Foil

*1-100 FOIL: .75X TO 2X BASE HI
1-100 PRINT RUN 299 SER.#'d SETS
*101-150 AU/75 FOIL: .4X TO 1X BASE HI
*101-150 AU/35 FOIL: .5X TO 1.25X BASE

2006-07 Topps Trademark Moves Rainbow

*1-100 RAINBOW: 1X TO 2.5X BASE
1-100 RAINBOW PRINT RUN 149 SER.#'d SETS
*101-150 AU/35 RAINBOW: .6X TO 1.5X BASE
*101-150 AU/19 RAINBOW: .75 TO 2X BASE

Card	Low	High
47 Kobe Bryant	10.00	25.00

2006-07 Topps Trademark Moves Wood

*1-100 WOOD: 1.5X TO 4X BASE
1-100 WOOD PRINT RUN 75 SETS
*101-150 AU/19 WOOD: .75X TO 3X BASE
101-150 AU/10 WOOD NOT PRICED

Card	Low	High
47 Kobe Bryant	12.00	30.00

2006-07 Topps Trademark Moves Wood Red

*1-80 WOOD RED: 4X TO 10X BASE
*81-100 WOOD RED: 3X TO 8X BASE
1-100 WOOD RED PRINT RUN 35 SETS
101-150 AU PRINT RUN 10 OR 3 SETS
RED WOOD AU NOT PRICED

Card	Low	High
47 Kobe Bryant	25.00	60.00

2006-07 Topps Trademark Moves Autographs

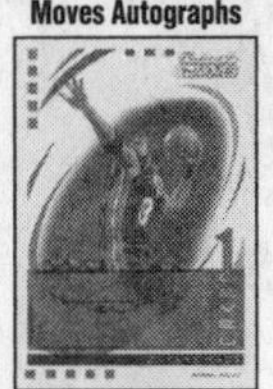

PRINT RUNS 75 TO 149 SER.#'d SETS
*FOIL AU/75: SAME VALUE AS BASE
*FOIL AU/35: .5X TO 1.25X BASE HI
*RAINBOW AU/35: .5X TO 1.25X BASE
*RAINBOW AU/19: .6X TO 1.5X BASE
*WOOD AU/19: .75X TO 2X BASE
WOOD AU/10 NOT PRICED
UNPRICED WOOD RED PRINT RUN 3 TO 10 SETS

Card	Low	High
1 Dwyane Wade/75	25.00	60.00
3 Raymond Felton/149	4.00	10.00
12 Charlie Villanueva/149	3.00	8.00
15 Vince Carter/75	12.50	30.00
20 Smush Parker/149	3.00	8.00
21 Josh Smith/149	4.00	10.00
26 Chris Bosh/149	10.00	25.00
28 Ben Gordon/149	6.00	15.00
31 T.J. Ford/149	3.00	8.00
34 Speedy Claxton/149	3.00	8.00
38 Jameer Nelson/149	3.00	8.00
45 Mike James/149	3.00	8.00
46 Martell Webster/149	3.00	8.00
50 Bobby Simmons/149	3.00	8.00
53 Allen Iverson/75	40.00	80.00
56 Tony Parker/149	6.00	15.00
58 Shaquille O'Neal/75	20.00	50.00
61 Emeka Okafor/149	3.00	8.00
62 Raja Bell/149	6.00	15.00
74 Gerald Wallace/149	3.00	8.00
75 Leandro Barbosa/149	3.00	8.00
80 Andrew Bogut/149	6.00	15.00
81 Dominique Wilkins/75	10.00	25.00
82 Larry Bird/75	40.00	80.00
85 Isiah Thomas/75	12.50	30.00
94 Moses Malone/149	8.00	20.00
98 Bill Walton/75	8.00	20.00
99 Maurice Cheeks/149	3.00	8.00
100 Bob Lanier/75	6.00	15.00

2006-07 Topps Trademark Moves Dish

Card	Low	High
COMPLETE SET (10)	4.00	10.00
*FOIL: .5X TO 1.25X BASE HI		
FOIL PRINT RUN 299 SER.#'d SETS		
*RAINBOW: .6X TO 1.5X BASE HI		
RAINBOW PRINT RUN 149 SER.#'d SETS		
*WOOD: 1X TO 2.5X BASE HI		
WOOD PRINT RUN 75 SER.#'d SETS		
*WOOD RED: 1.25X TO 3X BASE HI		
WOOD RED PRINT RUN 35 SER.#'d SETS		
TDI1 Allen Iverson	1.00	2.50
TDI2 Tony Parker	.75	2.00
TDI3 Jarrett Jack	.60	1.50
TDI4 Delonte West	.60	1.50
TDI5 Chris Duhon	.50	1.25
TDI6 Jameer Nelson	.60	1.50
TDI7 Marcus Williams	.75	2.00
TDI8 Dee Brown	.75	2.00
TDI9 Luke Walton	.50	1.25
TDI10 Jordan Farmar	.75	2.00

2006-07 Topps Trademark Moves Dish Autographs

PRINT RUN 75 TO 149 SER.#'d SETS
*FOIL AU/75: .4X TO 1X BASE HI
*FOIL AU/35: .5X TO 1.25X BASE HI
*RAIN AU/35: .6X TO 1.5X BASE HI
*RAIN AU/19: .75X TO 2X BASE HI
*WOOD AU/19: 1.25X TO 3X BASE HI
WOOD AU/10 NOT PRICED
UNPRICED WOOD RED PRINT RUN 3 TO 10 SETS

Card	Low	High
SDI1 Allen Iverson/75	40.00	80.00
SDI2 Tony Parker/75	6.00	15.00
SDI3 Jarrett Jack/149	3.00	8.00
SDI4 Delonte West/75	4.00	10.00
SDI5 Chris Duhon/149	3.00	8.00
SDI6 Jameer Nelson/75	4.00	10.00
SDI7 Marcus Williams/75	3.00	8.00
SDI8 Dee Brown/149	3.00	8.00
SDI9 Luke Walton/149	3.00	8.00
SDI10 Jordan Farmar/149	4.00	10.00

2006-07 Topps Trademark Moves Dunk

Card	Low	High
COMPLETE SET (20)	10.00	25.00
*FOIL: .5X TO 1.25X BASE HI		
FOIL PRINT RUN 299 SER.#'d SETS		
*RAINBOW: .6X TO 1.5X BASE HI		
RAIN PRINT RUN 149 SER.#'d SETS		
*WOOD: 1X TO 2.5X BASE HI		
WOOD PRINT RUN 75 SER.#'d SETS		
*WOOD RED: 1.25X TO 3X BASE HI		
WOOD RED PRINT RUN 35 SER.#'d SETS		
TDU1 Shaquille O'Neal	2.00	5.00
TDU2 Chris Bosh	1.00	2.50
TDU3 Dwyane Wade	2.50	6.00
TDU4 Hakim Warrick	.75	2.00
TDU5 Josh Smith	1.00	2.50
TDU6 Andrew Bogut	1.00	2.50
TDU7 Ike Diogu	.60	1.50
TDU8 J.R. Smith	1.00	2.50
TDU9 Josh Childress	.75	2.00
TDU10 Emeka Okafor	1.00	2.50
TDU11 Shawne Williams	1.00	2.50
TDU12 Renaldo Balkman	1.00	2.50
TDU13 Gerald Wallace	1.00	2.50
TDU14 Craig Smith	1.00	2.50
TDU15 Andre Iguodala	1.00	2.50
TDU16 Shelden Williams	1.00	2.50
TDU17 Hilton Armstrong	1.00	2.50
TDU18 Vince Carter	1.25	3.00
TDU19 Connie Hawkins	1.00	2.50
TDU20 Dominique Wilkins	1.25	3.00

2006-07 Topps Trademark Moves Dunk Autographs

PRINT RUN 75 TO 149 SER.#'d SETS
*FOIL AU/75: .4X TO 1X BASE HI
*FOIL AU/35: .5X TO 1.25X BASE HI
*RAIN AU/35: .6X TO 1.5X BASE HI
*RAIN AU/19: .75X TO 2X BASE HI
*WOOD AU/19: 1.25X TO 3X BASE HI
WOOD AU/10 NOT PRICED
UNPRICED WOOD RED PRINT RUN 3 TO 10 SETS
SDU1 Shaquille O'Neal/75 20.00 50.00
SDU2 Chris Bosh/75 10.00 25.00
SDU3 Dwyane Wade/75 25.00 60.00
SDU4 Hakim Warrick/149 3.00 8.00
SDU5 Josh Smith/75 5.00 12.00
SDU6 Andrew Bogut/75 5.00 12.00
SDU7 Ike Diogu/149 3.00 8.00
SDU8 J.R. Smith/149 3.00 8.00
SDU9 Josh Childress/75 4.00 10.00
SDU10 Emeka Okafor/75 4.00 10.00
SDU11 Shawne Williams/149 3.00 8.00
SDU12 Renaldo Balkman/149 3.00 8.00
SDU13 Gerald Wallace/149 3.00 8.00
SDU14 Craig Smith/149 3.00 8.00
SDU15 Andre Iguodala/149 3.00 8.00
SDU16 Shelden Williams/75 5.00 12.00
SDU17 Hilton Armstrong/149 3.00 8.00
SDU18 Vince Carter/75 12.50 30.00
SDU19 Connie Hawkins/149 8.00 20.00
SDU20 Dominique Wilkins/75 12.50 30.00

2006-07 Topps Trademark Moves Swish

COMPLETE SET (20) 10.00 25.00
*FOIL: .5X TO 1.25X BASE HI
FOIL PRINT RUN 299 SER.#'d SETS
*RAINBOW: .6X TO 1.5X BASE HI
RAIN PRINT RUN 149 SER.#'d SETS
*WOOD: 1X TO 2.5X BASE HI
WOOD PRINT RUN 75 SER.#'d SETS
*WOOD RED: 1.25X TO 3X BASE HI
WOOD RED PRINT RUN 35 SER.#'d SETS
TSW1 Adam Morrison 1.25 3.00
TSW2 Randy Foye 1.25 3.00
TSW3 Andrea Bargnani 1.50 4.00
TSW4 Thabo Sefolosha 1.25 3.00
TSW5 Maurice Ager 1.00 2.50
TSW6 Mike James .60 1.50
TSW7 J.J. Redick 1.25 3.00
TSW8 Quincy Douby 1.00 2.50
TSW9 Chauncey Billups 1.00 2.50
TSW10 Carmelo Anthony 1.25 3.00
TSW11 Ray Allen 1.00 2.50
TSW12 Rodney Carney 1.00 2.50
TSW13 Rick Barry 1.00 2.50
TSW14 Larry Bird 3.00 8.00
TSW15 Elgin Baylor 1.00 2.50
TSW16 Luol Deng 1.00 2.50
TSW17 Devin Harris 1.00 2.50
TSW18 Rashad McCants .60 1.50
TSW19 Martell Webster .75 2.00
TSW20 Ben Gordon 1.00 2.50

2006-07 Topps Trademark Moves Swish Autographs

PRINT RUN 75 TO 149 SER.#'d SETS
*FOIL AU/75: SAME VALUE AS BASE
*FOIL AU/35: .5X TO 1.25X BASE HI
*RAIN AU/35: .6X TO 1.5X BASE HI
*RAIN AU/19: .75X TO 2X BASE HI
*WOOD AU/19: 1.25X TO 3X BASE HI
WOOD AU/10 NOT PRICED
UNPRICED WOOD RED PRINT RUN 3 TO 10 SETS
SSW1 Adam Morrison/75 5.00 12.00
SSW2 Randy Foye/149 5.00 12.00
SSW3 Andrea Bargnani/75 15.00 30.00
SSW4 Thabo Sefolosha/149 5.00 12.00
SSW5 Maurice Ager/149 3.00 8.00
SSW6 Mike James/149 3.00 8.00
SSW7 J.J. Redick/149 6.00 15.00
SSW8 Quincy Douby/149 3.00 8.00
SSW9 Chauncey Billups/75 4.00 10.00
SSW10 Carmelo Anthony/75 12.50 30.00
SSW11 Ray Allen/75 8.00 20.00
SSW12 Rodney Carney/149 3.00 8.00
SSW13 Rick Barry/75 8.00 20.00
SSW14 Larry Bird/75 40.00 80.00
SSW15 Elgin Baylor/75 15.00 40.00
SSW16 Luol Deng/75 8.00 20.00
SSW17 Devin Harris/149 3.00 8.00
SSW18 Rashad McCants/149 3.00 8.00
SSW19 Martell Webster/149 3.00 8.00
SSW20 Ben Gordon/75 10.00 25.00

2007-08 Topps Trademark Moves

This 100-card set was released in December, 2007. The set was issued into the hobby in five-card packs, with an $30 SRP, which came 12 packs to a box, four boxes to a carton and two cartons per case. Cards numbered 1-40 feature veterans, cards numbered 41-50 feature retired greats and cards numbered 51-100 feature 2007-08 NBA rookies. The Rookie Cards were issued to a stated print run of 1999 serial numbered sets.

COMP.SET w/o SP's (50) 15.00 30.00
1 Amare Stoudemire .50 1.25
2 Elton Brand .50 1.25
3 Dwyane Wade 1.25 3.00
4 Dirk Nowitzki .60 1.50
5 Baron Davis .50 1.25
6 Brandon Roy .60 1.50
7 Ben Gordon .60 1.50
8 Richard Hamilton .40 1.00
9 Andre Iguodala .50 1.25
10 Tim Duncan .75 2.00
11 Yao Ming .60 1.50
12 Jason Kidd .60 1.50
13 Steve Nash .60 1.50
14 Chris Paul 1.00 2.50
15 Carmelo Anthony .60 1.50
16 Pau Gasol .50 1.25
17 Dwight Howard .75 2.00
18 Ray Allen .50 1.25
19 Deron Williams .75 2.00
20 Vince Carter .60 1.50
21 Kevin Garnett 1.00 2.50
22 Michael Redd .50 1.25
23 LeBron James 2.50 6.00
24 Kobe Bryant 2.50 6.00
25 Josh Smith .50 1.25
26 Gilbert Arenas .50 1.25
27 Jermaine O'Neal .50 1.25
28 Kirk Hinrich .50 1.25
29 Eddy Curry .30 .75
30 Chauncey Billups .50 1.25
31 Shawn Marion .50 1.25
32 Shaquille O'Neal 1.00 2.50
33 Allen Iverson .60 1.50
34 Paul Pierce .60 1.50
35 Tony Parker .50 1.25
36 Gerald Wallace .50 1.25
37 Carlos Boozer .50 1.25
38 Chris Bosh .50 1.25
39 Mike Bibby .50 1.25
40 Tracy McGrady .50 1.25
41 Rick Barry .50 1.25
42 David Robinson .75 2.00
43 John Stockton .75 2.00
44 Bill Walton .50 1.25
45 Larry Bird 1.50 4.00
46 Isiah Thomas .75 2.00
47 Magic Johnson 1.25 3.00
48 Dennis Rodman .75 2.00
49 Dominique Wilkins .60 1.50
50 Bill Russell .75 2.00
51 Yi Jianlian RC 1.50 4.00
52 Greg Oden RC 1.25 3.00
53 Mike Conley Jr. RC 1.50 4.00
54 Jeff Green RC 1.50 4.00
55 Corey Brewer RC 1.25 3.00
56 Joakim Noah RC 2.50 6.00
57 Julian Wright RC 1.50 4.00
58 Ramon Sessions RC 1.50 4.00
59 Sammy Mejia RC 1.00 2.50
60 Dominic McGuire RC 1.00 2.50
61 Kevin Durant RC 8.00 20.00
62 Arron Afflalo RC 1.25 3.00
63 Acie Law RC 1.00 2.50
64 Alando Tucker RC 1.00 2.50
65 Gabe Pruitt RC 1.00 2.50
66 Marcus Williams RC 1.00 2.50
67 Spencer Hawes RC 1.00 2.50
68 Carl Landry RC 1.00 2.50
69 Thaddeus Young RC 1.25 3.00
70 Nick Fazekas RC 1.00 2.50
71 Al Thornton RC 1.00 2.50
72 Rodney Stuckey RC 1.50 4.00
73 Nick Young RC 1.50 4.00
74 Glen Davis RC 1.50 4.00
75 Jermareo Davidson RC 1.00 2.50
76 Luis Scola RC 1.50 4.00
77 Jason Smith RC 1.00 2.50
78 Daequan Cook RC 1.00 2.50
79 Jared Dudley RC 1.00 2.50
80 Derrick Byars RC 1.00 2.50
81 Josh McRoberts RC 1.00 2.50
82 Adam Haluska RC 1.00 2.50
83 Juan Carlos Navarro RC 1.00 2.50
84 Aaron Gray RC 1.00 2.50
85 Herbert Hill RC 1.00 2.50
86 Jared Jordan RC 1.00 2.50
87 Wilson Chandler RC 1.50 4.00
88 Morris Almond RC 1.00 2.50
89 Aaron Brooks RC 1.00 2.50
90 Chris Richard RC 1.00 2.50
91 JamesOn Curry RC 1.00 2.50
92 Al Horford RC 1.25 3.00
93 Stephane Lasme RC 1.00 2.50
94 D.J. Strawberry RC 1.00 2.50
95 Sean Williams RC 1.00 2.50
96 Marco Belinelli RC 1.00 2.50
97 Javaris Crittenton RC 1.00 2.50
98 Demetris Nichols RC 1.00 2.50
99 Taurean Green RC 1.00 2.50
100 Brandan Wright RC 1.00 2.50

2007-08 Topps Trademark Moves Blue

*BLUE 1-50: 3X TO 8X BASE HI
BLUE 1-50 PRINT RUN 25 SER.#'d SETS
UNPRICED BLUE RC PRINT RUN 10 SETS

2007-08 Topps Trademark Moves Orange

*1-50 ORANGE: .6X TO 1.5X BASE HI
1-50 ORANGE PRINT RUN 399 SETS
*RC ORANGE: 1.5X TO 4X BASE HI
RC ORANGE PRINT RUN 99 SETS

2007-08 Topps Trademark Moves Red

*1-50 RED: 1.25X TO 3X BASE HI
1-50 RED PRINT RUN 99 SER.#'d SETS
*RC RED: 2X TO 5X BASE HI
RC RED PRINT RUN 50 SER.#'d SETS
61 Kevin Durant 50.00 120.00

2007-08 Topps Trademark Moves Rookies Wood

*WOOD: .5X TO 1.25X BASE HI
PRINT RUN 199 SER.#'d SETS
61 Kevin Durant 12.00 30.00

2007-08 Topps Trademark Moves Ink

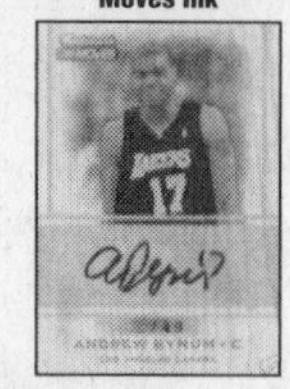

PRINT RUN 49 SER.#'d SETS
UNPRICED BLACK PRINT RUN ONE SET
UNPRICED BLUE PRINT RUN 5 SETS
*ORANGE: .5X TO 1.25X BASE HI
ORANGE PRINT RUN 25 SER.#'d SETS
UNPRICED RED PRINT RUN 10 SETS
AB Andrew Bynum 20.00 40.00
AG Aaron Gray 4.00 10.00
AM Adam Morrison 5.00 12.00
AT Al Thornton 4.00 10.00
ATU Alando Tucker 4.00 10.00
BD Baron Davis 6.00 15.00
BR Bill Russell 75.00 150.00
BW Brandan Wright 4.00 10.00
CA Carmelo Anthony 15.00 40.00
DG Danny Granger 4.00 10.00
DH Devin Harris 6.00 15.00
DJS D.J. Strawberry 4.00 10.00
DL David Lee 4.00 10.00
DM Dominic McGuire 4.00 10.00
DR David Robinson 40.00 80.00
DRO Dennis Rodman 25.00 50.00
DW Dominique Wilkins 15.00 30.00
DWA Dwyane Wade 30.00 60.00
DWI Deron Williams 15.00 30.00
EM Earl Monroe 10.00 25.00
GD Glen Davis 6.00 15.00
GO Greg Oden 25.00 60.00
GW Gerald Wallace 6.00 15.00
HA Hilton Armstrong 4.00 10.00
HT Hedo Turkoglu 4.00 10.00
ID Ike Diogu 4.00 10.00
IT Isiah Thomas 15.00 30.00
JH John Havlicek 20.00 40.00
JS John Stockton 40.00 80.00
KH Kirk Hinrich 8.00 20.00
LB Larry Bird 50.00 100.00
MB Marco Belinelli 4.00 10.00
MJ Magic Johnson 50.00 100.00
MJA Mike James 4.00 10.00
MW Marcus Williams 4.00 10.00
MWE Martell Webster 4.00 10.00
NY Nick Young 6.00 15.00
RB Rick Barry 8.00 20.00
RF Randy Foye 4.00 10.00
RFE Raymond Felton 4.00 10.00
SC Speedy Claxton 4.00 10.00
SD Samuel Dalembert 4.00 10.00
TG Taurean Green 4.00 10.00
TJF T.J. Ford 4.00 10.00
TP Tony Parker 10.00 25.00
TY Thaddeus Young 8.00 20.00
UH Udonis Haslem 4.00 10.00
VC Vince Carter 20.00 40.00
YJ Yi Jianlian 15.00 40.00

2007-08 Topps Trademark Moves Relics

PRINT RUN 299 SER.#'d SETS
UNPRICED BLACK PRINT RUN 10 SETS
*ORANGE: SAME VALUE AS BASE
ORANGE PRINT RUN 199 SER.#'d SETS
*RED: .5X TO 1.25X BASE HI
RED PRINT RUN 50 SER.#'d SETS
AH Al Horford 3.00 8.00
AS Amare Stoudemire 2.50 6.00
CA Carmelo Anthony 3.00 8.00
CB Caron Butler 2.50 6.00
CBI Chauncey Billups 2.50 6.00
CBO Chris Bosh 2.50 6.00
CBR Corey Brewer 3.00 8.00
CBZ Carlos Boozer 2.50 6.00
DH Dwight Howard 3.00 8.00
DN Dirk Nowitzki 3.00 8.00
DW Dwyane Wade 6.00 15.00
GA Gilbert Arenas 2.50 6.00
GO Greg Oden 3.00 8.00
JG Jeff Green 3.00 8.00
JH Josh Howard 2.00 5.00
JJ Joe Johnson 2.50 6.00
JK Jason Kidd 2.50 6.00
JN Joakim Noah 6.00 15.00
JO Jermaine O'Neal 2.50 6.00
JW Julian Wright 2.50 6.00
KB Kobe Bryant 8.00 20.00
KG Kevin Garnett 5.00 12.00
MC Mike Conley Jr. 4.00 10.00
MO Mehmet Okur 2.00 5.00
RA Ray Allen 2.50 6.00
RH Richard Hamilton 2.00 5.00
SM Shawn Marion 2.50 6.00
SN Steve Nash 3.00 8.00
SO Shaquille O'Neal 5.00 12.00
TD Tim Duncan 4.00 10.00
TM Tracy McGrady 2.50 6.00
TP Tony Parker 2.50 6.00
VC Vince Carter 3.00 8.00
YJ Yi Jianlian 4.00 10.00
YM Yao Ming 3.00 8.00

2007-08 Topps Trademark Moves Rookie Relic Ink

PRINT RUN 149 OR 79 SER.#'d SETS
UNPRICED BLACK PRINT RUN ONE SET
UNPRICED BLUE PRINT RUN 10 SETS
*ORANGE: .5X TO 1.25X BASE HI
ORANGE PRINT RUN 50 SER.#'d SETS
*RED: .6X TO 1.5X BASE HI
RED PRINT RUN 25 SER.#'d SETS
EXCH.EXPIRATION DATE 11/30/09
51 Yi Jianlian/79 12.50 30.00
52 Greg Oden/139 15.00 40.00
60 Dominic McGuire/139 5.00 12.00
62 Arron Afflalo/139 6.00 15.00
63 Acie Law/79 5.00 12.00
65 Gabe Pruitt/139 5.00 12.00
66 Marcus Williams/139 5.00 12.00
67 Spencer Hawes/79 5.00 12.00
68 Carl Landry/139 5.00 12.00
69 Thaddeus Young/79 6.00 15.00
70 Nick Fazekas/139 5.00 12.00
72 Rodney Stuckey/79 8.00 20.00
73 Nick Young/79 8.00 20.00
74 Glen Davis/139 8.00 20.00
75 Jermareo Davidson/139 5.00 12.00
77 Jason Smith/79 5.00 12.00
78 Daequan Cook/139 5.00 12.00
79 Jared Dudley/79 5.00 12.00
80 Derrick Byars/139 5.00 12.00
81 Josh McRoberts/139 5.00 12.00
82 Adam Haluska/139 5.00 12.00
84 Aaron Gray/139 5.00 12.00
87 Wilson Chandler/139 8.00 20.00
88 Morris Almond/79 5.00 12.00
89 Aaron Brooks/139 5.00 12.00
93 Stephane Lasme/139 5.00 12.00
97 Javaris Crittenton/79 5.00 12.00
99 Taurean Green/139 5.00 12.00
100 Brandan Wright/79 5.00 12.00

2007-08 Topps Trademark Moves Triple Ink

PRINT RUN 39 SER.#'d SETS
UNPRICED BLACK PRINT RUN ONE SET
UNPRICED BLUE PRINT RUN 3 SETS
UNPRICED ORANGE PRINT RUN 10 SETS
UNPRICED RED PRINT RUN 5 SETS
APD Ray Allen 12.50 30.00
Gabe Pruitt
Glen Davis
ASY Ray Allen 25.00 50.00
Rodney Stuckey
Nick Young
AYT Carmelo Anthony 25.00 50.00
Thaddeus Young
Al Thornton
BBF Chris Bosh 25.00 50.00
Andrea Bargnani
T.J. Ford
BLC Chauncey Billups 10.00 25.00
Acie Law
Javaris Crittenton
BSA Chauncey Billups 25.00 50.00
Rodney Stuckey
Arron Afflalo
BTS Leandro Barbosa 20.00 40.00
Alando Tucker
D.J. Strawberry
BWA Carlos Boozer 25.00 60.00
Deron Williams
Morris Almond
BWB Rick Barry 15.00 30.00
Brandan Wright
Marco Belinelli
BYC Chris Bosh 20.00 40.00
Thaddeus Young
Javaris Crittenton
CAA Daequan Cook 10.00 25.00
Morris Almond
Arron Afflalo
CAW Vince Carter 50.00 120.00
Carmelo Anthony
Dwyane Wade
CWW Vince Carter 15.00 40.00
Marcus Williams
Sean Williams
CYA Vince Carter 15.00 40.00
Nick Young
Morris Almond
DPL Baron Davis 25.00 60.00
Tony Parker
Acie Law
FBP T.J. Ford 15.00 30.00
Aaron Brooks
Gabe Pruitt
GGC Ben Gordon 10.00 25.00
Aaron Gray
JamesOn Curry
HFM Spencer Hawes 10.00 25.00
Nick Fazekas
Josh McRoberts
HSG Spencer Hawes 10.00 25.00
Jason Smith
Aaron Gray
JBL Mike James 10.00 25.00
Aaron Brooks
Carl Landry
JBT Magic Johnson 100.00 225.00
Larry Bird
Isiah Thomas
LCB Acie Law 15.00 30.00
Javaris Crittenton
Aaron Brooks
LCN David Lee 10.00 25.00
Wilson Chandler
Demetris Nichols
OMF Emeka Okafor 15.00 30.00
Adam Morrison
Raymond Felton
OOY Jermaine O'Neal 12.50 30.00
Emeka Okafor
Yi Jianlian
OWD Emeka Okafor 10.00 25.00
Gerald Wallace
Jared Dudley
OWY Greg Oden 75.00 150.00
Brandan Wright
Nick Young
PBF Tony Parker 20.00 40.00
Chauncey Billups
T.J. Ford
PBY Tony Parker 30.00 60.00
Marco Belinelli
Yi Jianlian
RBH Bill Russell 75.00 150.00
Elgin Baylor
John Havlicek
ROO David Robinson 100.00 225.00
Shaquille O'Neal
Greg Oden
RRO Bill Russell 100.00 225.00
David Robinson
Shaquille O'Neal
RWD Dennis Rodman 20.00 50.00
Sean Williams
Jared Dudley
SBH Jason Smith 10.00 25.00
Derrick Byars
Herbert Hill
SBW John Stockton 60.00 120.00
Carlos Boozer
Deron Williams
SYB Rodney Stuckey 20.00 40.00
Nick Young
Marco Belinelli
TCM Al Thornton 15.00 30.00
Javaris Crittenton
Corey Maggette
TWS Alando Tucker 15.00 30.00
Marcus Williams
D.J. Strawberry
WDA Bill Walton 30.00 60.00
Baron Davis
Arron Afflalo
WGM Gerald Wallace 10.00 25.00
Danny Granger
Corey Maggette
WSR Dominique Wilkins 60.00 120.00
John Stockton
Dennis Rodman
WTD Sean Williams 10.00 25.00
Al Thornton
Jared Dudley
WTY Dominique Wilkins 25.00 50.00
Al Thornton
Thaddeus Young
YBL Yi Jianlian 30.00 60.00
Marco Belinelli
Stephane Lasme
YSB Thaddeus Young 10.00 25.00
Jason Smith
Derrick Byars
YTD Thaddeus Young 10.00 25.00
Al Thornton
Jared Dudley

2007-08 Topps Trademark Moves Triple Relics

PRINT RUN 199 SER.#'d SETS
UNPRICED BLACK PRINT RUN 10 SETS
*BLUE: 1.25X TO 3X BASE HI
BLUE PRINT RUN 25 SER.#'d SETS
*ORANGE: .5X TO 1.25X BASE HI
ORANGE PRINT RUN 99 SER.#'d SETS
*RED: .6X TO 1.5X BASE HI
RED PRINT RUN 50 SER.#'d SETS
ABB Gilbert Arenas 4.00 10.00
Caron Butler
Chris Bosh
AHM Carmelo Anthony 6.00 15.00
Josh Howard
Tracy McGrady
BEF Andrew Bogut 4.00 10.00
Monta Ellis
Raymond Felton
BFF Andrea Bargnani 4.00 10.00
Jordan Farmar
Randy Foye
BGH Andrew Bynum 4.00 10.00
Danny Granger
Luther Head
BGP Chauncey Billups 5.00 12.00
Ben Gordon
Tony Parker
BSG Kobe Bryant 10.00 25.00
Amare Stoudemire
Kevin Garnett
BSY Corey Brewer 4.00 10.00
Rodney Stuckey
Nick Young
CHW Vince Carter 6.00 15.00
Dwight Howard
Dwyane Wade
CLC Mike Conley Jr. 4.00 10.00
Acie Law
Javaris Crittenton
GDN Kevin Garnett 8.00 20.00
Tim Duncan
Dirk Nowitzki
GGM Jorge Garbajosa 4.00 10.00
Rudy Gay
Paul Millsap
GRH Gerald Green 4.00 10.00
Nate Robinson
Dwight Howard
GYW Jeff Green 4.00 10.00
Thaddeus Young
Julian Wright
HBB Richard Hamilton 4.00 10.00
Chauncey Billups
Chris Bosh
HBN Al Horford 6.00 15.00
Corey Brewer
Joakim Noah
HWW Al Horford 4.00 10.00
Brandan Wright
Sean Williams
KAN Jason Kapono 4.00 10.00
Gilbert Arenas
Dirk Nowitzki
KNB Jason Kidd 6.00 15.00
Steve Nash
Carlos Boozer
LPW David Lee 4.00 10.00
Chris Paul
Deron Williams
MJT Mike Miller 4.00 10.00
Damon Jones
Jason Terry
MRW Adam Morrison 4.00 10.00
Brandon Roy
Marcus Williams
NSM Steve Nash 5.00 12.00
Amare Stoudemire
Shawn Marion
OCC Greg Oden 5.00 12.00
Mike Conley Jr.
Daequan Cook
OGM Mehmet Okur 4.00 10.00
Kevin Garnett
Tracy McGrady
OHA Shaquille O'Neal 5.00 12.00
Dwight Howard
Gilbert Arenas
OHS Greg Oden 4.00 10.00
Spencer Hawes
Jason Smith
PDA Tony Parker 6.00 15.00
Tim Duncan
Carmelo Anthony
WBP Dwyane Wade 12.00 30.00
Kobe Bryant
Chris Paul
WOO Dwyane Wade 6.00 15.00
Shaquille O'Neal
Jermaine O'Neal

2008-09 Topps Treasury

This set was released on October 1, 2008. The base set consists of 120 cards. Cards 1-100 feature veterans, and cards 101-120 are rookies.

COMPLETE SET (120) 30.00 60.00
UNPRICED X-FRCT PRINT RUN ONE SET
1 Kobe Bryant 2.50 6.00
2 Ray Allen .50 1.25
3 Chris Paul .75 2.00
4 Tim Duncan .75 2.00
5 Josh Smith .50 1.25
6 Luis Scola .40 1.00
7 Rashad McCants .30 .75
8 Vince Carter .60 1.50
9 LeBron James 2.50 6.00
10 Mike Dunleavy .40 1.00
11 Chauncey Billups .50 1.25
12 Dwight Howard 1.00 2.50
13 Steve Nash .50 1.25
14 Monta Ellis .50 1.25
15 Carmelo Anthony .60 1.50
16 Pau Gasol .50 1.25
17 Anderson Varejao .40 1.00
18 Yi Jianlian .50 1.25
19 Deron Williams .50 1.25
20 Joe Johnson .50 1.25
21 Yao Ming .60 1.50
22 Rudy Gay .50 1.25
23 Jason Richardson .50 1.25
24 Andrew Bogut .50 1.25
25 Kevin Garnett 1.00 2.50
26 Chris Wilcox .30 .75
27 Zach Randolph .40 1.00
28 Kirk Hinrich .50 1.25
29 Tony Parker .50 1.25
30 Allen Iverson .60 1.50
31 David West .50 1.25
32 Shaquille O'Neal 1.00 2.50
33 Dwyane Wade 1.00 2.50
34 Paul Pierce .60 1.50
35 Mike Miller .50 1.25
36 Hedo Turkoglu .50 1.25
37 LaMarcus Aldridge .50 1.25
38 Kevin Martin .50 1.25
39 Jamal Crawford .40 1.00
40 Gilbert Arenas .50 1.25
41 Dirk Nowitzki .60 1.50
42 Amare Stoudemire .50 1.25
43 Danny Granger .50 1.25
44 Chris Bosh .50 1.25
45 Luol Deng .50 1.25
46 Al Thornton .40 1.00
47 Andrei Kirilenko .40 1.00
48 Tayshaun Prince .50 1.25
49 Gerald Wallace .50 1.25
50 Corey Maggette .40 1.00
51 Andre Iguodala .50 1.25
52 Greg Oden .50 1.25
53 Al Jefferson .50 1.25
54 Devin Harris .50 1.25
55 Baron Davis .50 1.25
56 Marcus Camby .30 .75
57 Udonis Haslem .40 1.00
58 Ron Artest .50 1.25
59 Jeff Green .40 1.00
60 Richard Hamilton .40 1.00
61 Samuel Dalembert .30 .75
62 Antawn Jamison .50 1.25
63 Mike Conley Jr. .40 1.00
64 Raymond Felton .40 1.00
65 Carlos Boozer .50 1.25
66 Ben Gordon .50 1.25
67 Jermaine O'Neal .50 1.25
68 Peja Stojakovic .50 1.25
69 Ryan Gomes .30 .75
70 Michael Redd .50 1.25
71 Manu Ginobili .50 1.25
72 Elton Brand .50 1.25
73 Josh Howard .40 1.00
74 Stephen Jackson .40 1.00
75 Richard Jefferson .40 1.00
76 Andrew Bynum .60 1.50
77 Shawn Marion .50 1.25
78 David Lee .40 1.00
79 Jamario Moon .30 .75
80 Caron Butler .50 1.25
81 Tracy McGrady .50 1.25
82 Al Horford .50 1.25
83 Brandon Roy .50 1.25
84 Ben Wallace .50 1.25
85 Andre Miller .40 1.00
86 Brad Miller .40 1.00
87 Jameer Nelson .40 1.00
88 Andrea Bargnani .40 1.00
89 Kevin Durant 2.00 5.00
90 Jason Kidd .50 1.25
91 Dennis Rodman .75 2.00
92 Larry Bird 1.50 4.00
93 Moses Malone .50 1.25
94 Jerry West .60 1.50
95 Bill Russell .75 2.00
96 David Robinson .75 2.00
97 John Stockton .75 2.00
98 Magic Johnson 1.25 3.00
99 George Gervin .60 1.50
100 Dominique Wilkins .60 1.50
101 Derrick Rose RC 5.00 12.00
102 Michael Beasley RC 1.00 2.50
103 O.J. Mayo RC 1.00 2.50
104 Russell Westbrook RC 3.00 8.00
105 Kevin Love RC 2.50 6.00
106 Danilo Gallinari RC 1.00 2.50
107 Eric Gordon RC 1.50 4.00
108 Joe Alexander RC .60 1.50
109 D.J. Augustin RC .60 1.50
110 Brook Lopez RC 1.00 2.50
111 Jerryd Bayless RC .60 1.50
112 Brandon Rush RC .60 1.50
113 Anthony Randolph RC .75 2.00
114 Robin Lopez RC .60 1.50
115 Courtney Lee RC 1.00 2.50
116 Darrell Arthur RC .60 1.50
117 Joey Dorsey RC .60 1.50
118 Mario Chalmers RC 1.00 2.50
119 DeAndre Jordan RC 1.25 3.00
120 Kosta Koufos RC .60 1.50

2008-09 Topps Treasury Refractors Bronze

*BRONZE: .6X TO 1.5X BASE HI
*BRONZE 101-120: 1X TO 2.5X BASE HI
1-100 PRINT RUN 999 SER.#'d SETS
101-120 PRINT RUN 2008 SER.#'d SETS
1 Kobe Bryant 5.00 12.00
101 Derrick Rose 20.00 50.00

2008-09 Topps Treasury Refractors Gold

*GOLD 1-100: 3X TO 8X BASE HI
*GOLD 101-120: 3X TO 5X BASE HI
STATED PRINT RUN 50 SER.#'d SETS
101 Derrick Rose 60.00 150.00

2008-09 Topps Treasury Refractors Silver

*SILVER 1-100: 1X TO 2.5X BASE HI
*SILVER 101-120: 2X TO 5X BASE HI
STATED PRINT RUN 199 SER.#'d SETS
1 Kobe Bryant 8.00 20.00
9 LeBron James 8.00 20.00
101 Derrick Rose 30.00 80.00

2008-09 Topps Treasury Bird's All Rookie Team Autographs Dual

STATED PRINT RUN 39 SER.#'d SETS
UNPRICED GREEN PRINT RUN ONE SET
UNPRICED RED PRINT RUN 5 SETS
BA Larry Bird 40.00 80.00
Joe Alexander
BAU Larry Bird 40.00 80.00
D.J. Augustin
BB Larry Bird 40.00 100.00
Michael Beasley
BBA Larry Bird 40.00 80.00
Jerryd Bayless
BG Larry Bird 40.00 80.00
Brandon Rush
BGO Larry Bird 50.00 120.00
Eric Gordon
BL Larry Bird 50.00 120.00
Kevin Love
BM Larry Bird 50.00 120.00
O.J. Mayo
BR Larry Bird 125.00 300.00
Derrick Rose
BW Larry Bird 50.00 125.00
Russell Westbrook

2008-09 Topps Treasury Magic's All Rookie Team Autographs Dual

STATED PRINT RUN 39 SER.#'d SETS
UNPRICED GREEN PRINT RUN ONE SET
UNPRICED RED PRINT RUN FIVE SETS
A Magic Johnson 40.00 80.00
Joe Alexander
AU Magic Johnson 40.00 80.00
D.J. Augustin
B Magic Johnson 40.00 100.00
Michael Beasley
BA Magic Johnson 40.00 80.00
Jerryd Bayless
G Magic Johnson 50.00 120.00
Eric Gordon
L Magic Johnson 50.00 120.00
Kevin Love
LO Magic Johnson 40.00 80.00
Brook Lopez
M Magic Johnson 50.00 120.00
O.J. Mayo
R Magic Johnson 125.00 300.00
Derrick Rose
W Magic Johnson 50.00 125.00
Russell Westbrook

2008-09 Topps Treasury Mini Exclusives

COMPLETE SET (50) 30.00 60.00
STATED PRINT RUN 278 SER.#'d SETS
ONE MINI CARD PER RIP CARD
*BRONZE: .5X TO 1.25X BASE HI
BRONZE PRINT RUN 99 SER.#'d SETS
*SILVER: 1.5X TO 4X BASE HI
SILVER PRINT RUN 25 SER.#'d SETS
UNPRICED GOLD PRINT RUN ONE SET
UNPRICED LOGOMAN PRINT RUN ONE SET
MEAH Al Horford .75 2.00
MEAI Allen Iverson 1.00 2.50
MEAIG Andre Iguodala .75 2.00
MEAK Andrei Kirilenko .60 1.50
MEAS Amare Stoudemire .75 2.00
MEAT Al Thornton .60 1.50
MEBD Baron Davis .75 2.00
MEBG Ben Gordon .75 2.00
MEBR Bill Russell 1.25 3.00
MEBRO Brandon Roy .75 2.00
MECA Carmelo Anthony 1.00 2.50
MECB Chris Bosh .75 2.00
MECBO Carlos Boozer .75 2.00
MECBU Caron Butler .75 2.00
MECM Corey Maggette .60 1.50
MECP Chris Paul 1.25 3.00
MEDH Dwight Howard 1.50 4.00
MEDN Dirk Nowitzki 1.00 2.50
MEDR Dennis Rodman 1.25 3.00
MEDW Deron Williams .75 2.00
MEDWA Dwyane Wade 1.50 4.00
MEDWE David West .75 2.00
MEDWI Dominique Wilkins 1.00 2.50
MEGA Gilbert Arenas .75 2.00
MEGO Greg Oden .75 2.00
MEJJ Joe Johnson .75 2.00
MEJK Jason Kidd .75 2.00
MEJW Jerry West 1.00 2.50
MEKB Kobe Bryant 4.00 10.00
MEKD Kevin Durant 3.00 8.00
MEKG Kevin Garnett 1.50 4.00
MEKM Kevin Martin .75 2.00
MELA LaMarcus Aldridge .75 2.00
MELB Larry Bird 2.50 6.00
MELJ LeBron James 4.00 10.00
MEMG Manu Ginobili .75 2.00
MEMJ Magic Johnson 2.00 5.00
MEMM Mike Miller .75 2.00
MEMR Michael Redd .75 2.00
MEPG Pau Gasol .75 2.00
MEPP Paul Pierce 1.00 2.50
MERG Rudy Gay .75 2.00
MESN Steve Nash .75 2.00
MESO Shaquille O'Neal 1.50 4.00
METD Tim Duncan 1.25 3.00
METM Tracy McGrady .75 2.00
METP Tony Parker .75 2.00
MEVC Vince Carter 1.00 2.50
MEYJ Yi Jianlian .75 2.00
MEYM Yao Ming 1.00 2.50

2008-09 Topps Treasury Mini Exclusives Autographs

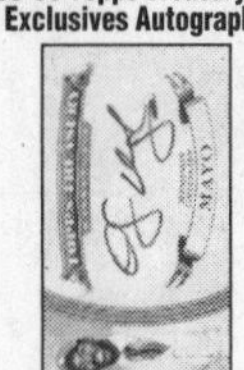

ONE MINI CARD PER RIP CARD
RANDOM INSERTS IN PACKS
BD Baron Davis 10.00 25.00
BL Brook Lopez 12.00 30.00
CA Carmelo Anthony 30.00 80.00
CB Chris Bosh 25.00 50.00
CBO Carlos Boozer 8.00 20.00
CP Chris Paul 25.00 60.00
DJA D.J. Augustin 8.00 20.00
DR Derrick Rose 100.00 200.00
DW Dwyane Wade 40.00 80.00
EG Eric Gordon 20.00 50.00
GO Greg Oden 15.00 40.00
JB Jerryd Bayless 8.00 20.00
JJH J.J. Hickson 10.00 25.00
KL Kevin Love 30.00 80.00
MB Michael Beasley 15.00 40.00
MM Mike Miller 8.00 20.00
OJM O.J. Mayo 15.00 40.00
RL Robin Lopez 8.00 20.00
YJ Yi Jianlian 10.00 25.00

2008-09 Topps Treasury Relics

RANDOM INSERTS IN RETAIL PACKS
AB Andrea Bargnani 2.00 5.00
AH Al Horford 2.50 6.00
AT Al Thornton 2.00 5.00
CB Corey Brewer 2.00 5.00
CF Channing Frye 2.00 5.00
DW Dwyane Wade 5.00 12.00
GO Greg Oden 2.50 6.00
JC Javaris Crittenton 2.00 5.00
JH Josh Howard 2.00 5.00
JJ Jarrett Jack 2.00 5.00
JT Jason Terry 2.00 5.00
PG Pau Gasol 2.50 6.00
RJ Richard Jefferson 2.50 6.00
SC Sam Cassell 2.50 6.00
SO Shaquille O'Neal 5.00 12.00
TY Thaddeus Young 2.00 5.00
DWI Deron Williams 2.50 6.00
JTI Jamaal Tinsley 2.00 5.00

2008-09 Topps Treasury Rip Cards

PRINT RUN 299 SER.#'d SETS
*BRONZE: .5X TO 1.25X BASE HI
BRONZE PRINT RUN 99 SER.#'d SETS
*SILVER: .6X TO 1.5X BASE HI
SILVER PRINT RUN 25 SETS
UNPRICED GOLD PRINT RUN 10 SETS
UNPRICED PLATINUM PRINT RUN ONE SET
1 Kobe Bryant 20.00 50.00
2 Chris Paul 10.00 25.00
3 Tim Duncan 10.00 25.00
4 Vince Carter 8.00 20.00
5 LeBron James 20.00 50.00
6 Dwight Howard 10.00 25.00
7 Steve Nash 10.00 25.00
8 Carmelo Anthony 10.00 25.00
9 Pau Gasol 6.00 15.00
10 Yi Jianlian 8.00 20.00
11 Deron Williams 10.00 25.00
12 Joe Johnson 6.00 15.00
13 Yao Ming 10.00 25.00
14 Rudy Gay 6.00 15.00
15 Kevin Garnett 10.00 25.00
16 Tony Parker 8.00 20.00
17 Allen Iverson 8.00 20.00
18 David West 6.00 15.00
19 Shaquille O'Neal 12.00 30.00
20 Dwyane Wade 10.00 25.00
21 Paul Pierce 10.00 25.00
22 Mike Miller 6.00 15.00
23 Kevin Martin 8.00 20.00
24 Gilbert Arenas 10.00 25.00
25 Dirk Nowitzki 10.00 25.00
26 Amare Stoudemire 8.00 20.00
27 Chris Bosh 10.00 25.00
28 Corey Maggette 6.00 15.00
29 Andre Iguodala 6.00 15.00
30 Greg Oden 6.00 15.00
31 Baron Davis 8.00 20.00
32 Carlos Boozer 6.00 15.00
33 Ben Gordon 8.00 20.00
34 Michael Redd 8.00 20.00
35 Manu Ginobili 8.00 20.00
36 Caron Butler 6.00 15.00
37 Tracy McGrady 8.00 20.00
38 Al Horford 6.00 15.00
39 Brandon Roy 8.00 20.00
40 Kevin Durant 20.00 50.00
41 Jason Kidd 8.00 20.00
42 LaMarcus Aldridge 6.00 15.00
43 Al Thornton 6.00 15.00
44 Andrei Kirilenko 6.00 15.00
45 Jerry West 8.00 20.00
46 Bill Russell 8.00 20.00
47 Dennis Rodman 8.00 20.00
48 Dominique Wilkins 6.00 15.00
49 Larry Bird 15.00 40.00
50 Magic Johnson 12.00 30.00

2008-09 Topps Treasury Rookie Autographs

STATED ODDS 1:23 PACKS
*BRONZE: .5X TO 1.25X BASE HI
BRONZE PRINT RUN 50 SETS
*SILVER: .6X TO 1.5X BASE HI
SILVER PRINT RUN 25 SER.#'d SETS
UNPRICED GOLD PRINT RUN 10 SETS
UNPRICED X-FRAC PRINT RUN ONE SET
121 Derrick Rose 125.00 250.00
122 Michael Beasley 15.00 40.00
123 O.J. Mayo 15.00 40.00
124 Russell Westbrook 40.00 100.00
125 Kevin Love 40.00 100.00
126 Danilo Gallinari 10.00 25.00
127 Eric Gordon 20.00 50.00
128 Joe Alexander 5.00 12.00
129 D.J. Augustin 5.00 12.00
130 Brook Lopez 8.00 20.00
131 Jerryd Bayless 5.00 12.00
132 Brandon Rush 5.00 12.00
133 Anthony Randolph 6.00 15.00
134 Robin Lopez 5.00 12.00
135 Courtney Lee 8.00 20.00
136 Darrell Arthur 5.00 12.00
137 Joey Dorsey 5.00 12.00
138 Mario Chalmers 8.00 20.00
139 DeAndre Jordan 10.00 25.00
140 Kosta Koufos 5.00 12.00

2008-09 Topps Treasury Rookie Medallions

STATED PRINT RUN 19 SER.#'d SETS
UNPRICED GOLD PRINT RUN ONE SET
AR Anthony Randolph 25.00 60.00
BL Brook Lopez 30.00 80.00
BR Brandon Rush 20.00 50.00
DA Darrell Arthur 20.00 50.00
DG Danilo Gallinari 30.00 80.00
DJA D.J. Augustin 20.00 50.00
DR Derrick Rose 100.00 200.00
EG Eric Gordon 50.00 120.00
JA Joe Alexander 20.00 50.00
JB Jerryd Bayless 20.00 50.00
KL Kevin Love 80.00 200.00
MB Michael Beasley 30.00 80.00
OJM O.J. Mayo 30.00 80.00
RL Robin Lopez 20.00 50.00
RW Russell Westbrook 100.00 250.00

2008-09 Topps Treasury They're Money Rip Cards

STATED PRINT RUN 42 SER.#'d SETS
1 Kobe Bryant 75.00 200.00
2 LeBron James 75.00 200.00
3 Carmelo Anthony 60.00 120.00
4 Kevin Garnett 50.00 100.00
5 Allen Iverson 50.00 100.00
8 Dirk Nowitzki 40.00 80.00
10 Chris Paul 75.00 150.00

2006-07 Topps Triple Threads

Released in late April 2007, Triple Threads is Topps' premium 2006-07 basketball product. With a 130-card set, Triple Threads pictures veteran players on cards 1-86, rookie players on cards 87-90 and retired players on cards 91-100 which are serially numbered to 899. Cards 1-100 share the same design which utilizes a white background with a centered grey-ish/blue oval framing a full-color player action photo. Card numbers 101-130 showcase a horizontal design which places a framed autograph sticker between two premium swatches of jersey. 101-130 are rookie cards and are sequentially numbered to 99. Triple Threads is packaged in two-pack boxes of six cards each and carried an initial suggested retail price of $100.00 per pack. Each pack contains three base cards, two parallels and one triple memorabilia card. In each box, one of the two packs contains a triple memorabilia autographs card.

UNPRICED PLATINUM PRINT RUN ONE SET
1 Amare Stoudemire 1.00 2.50
2 Dirk Nowitzki 1.50 4.00
3 Dwyane Wade 2.50 6.00
4 Allen Iverson 1.25 3.00
5 LeBron James 5.00 12.00
6 Tracy McGrady 1.25 3.00
7 Ben Wallace 1.00 2.50
8 Jason Richardson 1.00 2.50
9 Vince Carter 1.25 3.00
10 Joe Johnson 1.00 2.50
11 Paul Pierce 1.25 3.00
12 Gerald Wallace 1.00 2.50
13 Elton Brand 1.00 2.50
14 Gilbert Arenas 1.00 2.50
15 Marcus Camby .75 2.00
16 Andrew Bogut 1.00 2.50
17 Stephon Marbury .75 2.00
18 Kevin Garnett 2.00 5.00
19 Al Harrington .75 2.00
20 Tim Duncan 1.50 4.00
21 Pau Gasol 1.00 2.50
22 Kobe Bryant 5.00 12.00
23 Dwight Howard 1.50 4.00
24 Jarrett Jack .75 2.00
25 T.J. Ford .75 2.00
26 Ron Artest 1.00 2.50
27 Deron Williams 1.50 4.00
28 Rasheed Wallace 1.00 2.50
29 Shaquille O'Neal 2.00 5.00
30 Ray Allen 1.00 2.50
31 Peja Stojakovic 1.00 2.50
32 Jermaine O'Neal 1.00 2.50
33 Larry Hughes .75 2.00
34 Brad Miller 1.00 2.50
35 Caron Butler 1.00 2.50
36 Andre Miller .75 2.00
37 Kirk Hinrich 1.00 2.50
38 Andrei Kirilenko .75 2.00
39 Charlie Villanueva 1.00 2.50
40 Sebastian Telfair .60 1.50
41 Josh Howard .75 2.00
42 Emeka Okafor 1.00 2.50
43 Danny Granger 1.00 2.50
44 Tony Parker 1.00 2.50
45 Zach Randolph .75 2.00
46 Ricky Davis .75 2.00
47 Chris Webber 1.00 2.50
48 Mike Bibby 1.00 2.50
49 Troy Murphy .60 1.50
50 Josh Smith 1.00 2.50
51 Steve Nash 1.25 3.00
52 Chris Paul 2.00 5.00
53 Rashard Lewis 1.00 2.50
54 Ben Gordon 1.00 2.50
55 Mehmet Okur .60 1.50
56 Chris Bosh 1.00 2.50
57 Drew Gooden .75 2.00
58 Corey Maggette .75 2.00
59 Eddy Curry .75 2.00
60 Yao Ming 1.25 3.00
61 Al Jefferson 1.00 2.50
62 Smush Parker .60 1.50
63 Jason Kidd 1.50 4.00
64 Hakim Warrick .75 2.00
65 Richard Hamilton .75 2.00
66 Luke Ridnour .75 2.00
67 Raymond Felton 1.25 3.00
68 Andre Iguodala 1.00 2.50
69 Jason Terry .75 2.00
70 Richard Jefferson 1.00 2.50
71 Lamar Odom 1.00 2.50
72 Jameer Nelson .75 2.00
73 Mike James .60 1.50
74 Antawn Jamison 1.00 2.50
75 Shaun Livingston .60 1.50
76 Manu Ginobili 1.00 2.50
77 Antoine Walker .75 2.00
78 Desmond Mason .60 1.50
79 Channing Frye .75 2.00
80 Morris Peterson .60 1.50
81 Michael Redd 1.00 2.50
82 Shawn Marion 1.00 2.50
83 Bonzi Wells .60 1.50
84 Chauncey Billups 1.00 2.50
85 Baron Davis 1.00 2.50
86 Carmelo Anthony 1.25 3.00
87 Brandon Roy RC 4.00 10.00
88 Rudy Gay RC 2.50 6.00
89 Tyrus Thomas RC 2.00 5.00
90 LaMarcus Aldridge RC 4.00 10.00
91 Wilt Chamberlain 3.00 8.00
92 Larry Bird 5.00 12.00
93 Isiah Thomas 1.50 4.00
94 Bernard King 1.50 4.00
95 Elgin Baylor 1.50 4.00
96 Oscar Robertson 1.50 4.00
97 Walt Frazier 1.50 4.00
98 Chris Mullin 1.50 4.00
99 Bill Laimbeer 1.50 4.00
100 George Gervin 1.50 4.00
101 Dee Brown JSY AU RC 6.00 15.00
102 Renaldo Balkman JSY AU RC 6.00 15.00
103 Maurice Ager JSY AU RC 6.00 15.00
104 Shelden Williams JSY AU RC 6.00 15.00
105 Rodney Carney JSY AU RC 6.00 15.00
106 J.J. Redick JSY AU RC 8.00 20.00
107 Hilton Armstrong JSY AU RC 6.00 15.00
108 Craig Smith JSY AU RC 6.00 15.00
109 Kyle Lowry JSY AU RC 8.00 20.00
110 Josh Boone JSY AU RC 6.00 15.00
111 Saer Sene JSY AU RC 6.00 15.00
112 Jorge Garbajosa JSY AU RC 6.00 15.00
113 Paul Davis JSY AU RC 6.00 15.00
114 Thabo Sefolosha JSY AU RC 8.00 20.00
115 Shannon Brown JSY AU RC 10.00 25.00
116 Bobby Jones JSY AU RC 6.00 15.00
117 Jordan Farmar JSY AU RC 6.00 15.00
118 Allan Ray JSY AU RC 6.00 15.00
119 Randy Foye JSY AU RC 8.00 20.00
120 Marcus Williams JSY AU RC 6.00 15.00
121 Adam Morrison JSY AU RC 8.00 20.00
122 Cedric Simmons JSY AU RC 6.00 15.00
123 Rajon Rondo JSY AU RC 30.00 80.00
124 Patrick O'Bryant JSY AU RC 6.00 15.00
125 Shawne Williams JSY AU RC 6.00 15.00
126 Mardy Collins JSY AU RC 6.00 15.00
127 Steve Novak JSY AU RC 6.00 15.00
128 Ronnie Brewer JSY AU RC 8.00 20.00
129 Quincy Douby JSY AU RC 6.00 15.00
130 Andrea Bargnani JSY AU RC 10.00 25.00

2006-07 Topps Triple Threads Emerald

*EMERALD: .5X TO 1.25X BASE HI
1-100 EMERALD PRINT RUN 199 SER.#'d SETS
101-130 EMERALD PRINT RUN 50 SER.#'d SETS

2006-07 Topps Triple Threads Gold

*GOLD: .75X TO 2X BASE HI
1-100 PRINT RUN 99 SER.#'d SETS
101-130 PRINT RUN 25 SER.#'d SETS

2006-07 Topps Triple Threads Sapphire

*1-100 SAPPH: 1.25X TO 3X BASE HI
1-100 PRINT RUN 25 SER.#'d SETS
101-130 PRINT RUN 10 SER.#'d SETS
101-130 NOT PRICED DUE TO SCARCITY

2006-07 Topps Triple Threads Sepia

SEPIA: .4X TO 1X BASE HI
STATED PRINT RUN 299 SER.#'d SETS

2006-07 Topps Triple Threads Relics

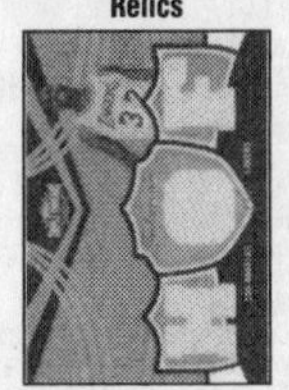

PRINT RUN 36 SER.#'d SETS
EACH PLAYER HAS THREE VERSIONS
ALL VERSIONS SAME VALUE
*EMERALD: .6X TO 1.5X BASE HI
EMERALD PRINT RUN 18 SER.#'d SETS
UNPRICED GOLD PRINT RUN 9 SETS
UNPRICED PLATINUM PRINT RUN ONE SET
UNPRICED SAPPHIRE PRINT RUN 3 SETS
*SEPIA: .5X TO 1.25X BASE HI
SEPIA PRINT RUN 27 SER.#'d SETS
1 Adam Morrison NBA 6.00 15.00
4 Amare Stoudemire NBA 5.00 12.00
7 Andrea Bargnani NBA 8.00 20.00
10 Andrei Kirilenko AK47 4.00 10.00
13 Antawn Jamison NBA 5.00 12.00
16 Ben Wallace NBA 5.00 12.00
19 Brandon Roy NBA 12.00 30.00
22 Carmelo Anthony Nuggets 6.00 15.00
25 Charlie Villanueva NBA 5.00 12.00
28 Chauncey Billups NBA 5.00 12.00
31 Chris Paul NBA 10.00 25.00
34 Dirk Nowitzki Symbol 8.00 20.00
37 Dominique Wilkins HOF 6.00 15.00
40 Dwight Howard NBA 8.00 20.00
43 Dwyane Wade NBA 12.00 30.00
46 Isiah Thomas HOF 6.00 15.00
49 J.J. Redick NBA 6.00 15.00
52 Jason Kidd Symbol 8.00 20.00
55 Josh Smith NBA 5.00 12.00
58 Kevin Garnett KG 10.00 25.00
61 Kobe Bryant NBA 20.00 40.00
64 LaMarcus Aldridge Blazers 12.00 30.00
67 Larry Bird #33 20.00 50.00
70 Magic Johnson #32 12.00 30.00
73 Manu Ginobili Spurs 5.00 12.00
76 Pau Gasol #16 5.00 12.00
79 Paul Pierce #34 6.00 15.00
82 Rudy Gay NBA 8.00 20.00
85 Shaquille O'Neal MVP 10.00 25.00
88 Shawn Marion NBA 5.00 12.00
91 Steve Nash #13 6.00 15.00
94 Tim Duncan #21 8.00 20.00
97 Tracy McGrady NBA 6.00 15.00
100 Vince Carter NBA 6.00 15.00
103 Yao Ming Rockets 6.00 15.00

2006-07 Topps Triple Threads Relics Autographs

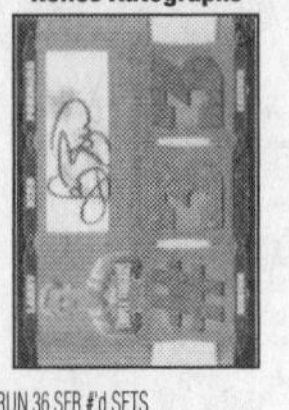

PRINT RUN 36 SER.#'d SETS
EACH PLAYER HAS THREE VERSIONS
ALL VERSIONS SAME VALUE
*EMERALD: .6X TO 1.5X BASE HI
EMERALD PRINT RUN 18 SER.#'d SETS
UNPRICED GOLD PRINT RUN 9 SETS
UNPRICED PLATINUM PRINT RUN ONE SET
UNPRICED PR.PLATE PRINT RUN ONE SET
UNPRICED SAPPHIRE PRINT RUN 3 SETS
1 Adam Morrison #35 12.50 30.00
4 Chauncey Billups NBA 10.00 25.00
7 Andre Iguodala NBA 10.00 25.00
10 Andrea Bargnani Raptors 15.00 40.00
13 Andrew Bogut NBA 10.00 25.00
16 Ben Gordon Bulls 12.50 30.00
19 Bill Walton NBA 15.00 40.00
22 Bob Lanier NBA 12.50 30.00
25 Channing Frye NBA 10.00 25.00
28 Charlie Villanueva NBA 10.00 25.00
31 Chris Bosh Raptors 15.00 40.00
34 Chris Duhon NBA 10.00 25.00
37 Devin Harris NBA 10.00 25.00
40 Dominique Wilkins HOF 25.00 50.00
43 Dwyane Wade NBA 40.00 100.00
46 Earl Monroe #15 15.00 40.00
49 Emeka Okafor #50 10.00 25.00
52 Gerald Wallace NBA 10.00 25.00
55 Hakim Warrick NBA 10.00 25.00
58 John Stockton #12 40.00 100.00
61 Isiah Thomas HOF 15.00 40.00
64 J.J. Redick Magic 12.50 30.00
67 Jameer Nelson NBA 10.00 25.00
70 Jarrett Jack NBA 10.00 25.00
73 Josh Smith Dunking 10.00 25.00
76 Larry Bird Legend 75.00 150.00
77 Larry Bird BOS 75.00 150.00
78 Larry Bird #33 75.00 150.00
79 Luol Deng NBA 10.00 25.00
82 Magic Johnson #32 60.00 120.00
85 Dennis Rodman #91 30.00 75.00
88 Martell Webster Blazers 10.00 25.00
91 Randy Foye NBA 10.00 25.00
94 Ray Allen NBA 25.00 50.00
97 Luke Walton NBA 10.00 25.00
100 Ronnie Brewer NBA 10.00 25.00
103 Andrei Kirilenko AK47 10.00 25.00
106 Jermaine O'Neal NBA 10.00 25.00
109 Carmelo Anthony Nuggets 20.00 50.00
112 Shelden Williams #33 10.00 25.00
115 T.J. Ford NBA 10.00 25.00
118 Vince Carter NBA 20.00 40.00

2006-07 Topps Triple Threads Relics Combos

PRINT RUN 36 SER.#'d SETS
*EMERALD: .5X TO 1.25X BASE HI
EMERALD PRINT RUN 18 SER.#'d SETS
UNPRICED GOLD PRINT RUN 9 SETS
UNPRICED SAPPHIRE PRINT RUN 3 SETS
*SEPIA: .4X TO 1X BASE HI
SEPIA PRINT RUN 27 SER.#'d SETS
1 Adam Morrison 12.00 30.00
Dwyane Wade
J.J. Redick
2 Amare Stoudemire 15.00 40.00
Steve Nash
Shawn Marion
3 Shawn Marion 10.00 25.00
Steve Nash
Leandro Barbosa
4 Yao Ming 12.50 30.00
Tracy McGrady
Steve Novak
5 Andrea Bargnani 10.00 25.00
Andrew Bogut
Dwight Howard
6 Dwyane Wade 30.00 80.00
Shaquille O'Neal
Alonzo Mourning
7 Dwyane Wade 15.00 40.00
Chris Bosh
Carmelo Anthony
8 Tracy McGrady 30.00 60.00
Vince Carter
Kobe Bryant
9 Kobe Bryant 25.00 50.00
Lamar Odom
Magic Johnson
10 Ray Allen 10.00 25.00
Rashard Lewis
Luke Ridnour
11 Tim Duncan 15.00 40.00
Manu Ginobili
Tony Parker
12 Cedric Simmons 10.00 25.00
J.J. Redick
Shelden Williams
13 Rudy Gay 10.00 25.00
Adam Morrison
Rodney Carney
14 Randy Foye 10.00 25.00
Allan Ray
Kyle Lowry
15 Ray Allen 10.00 25.00
Ben Gordon
Emeka Okafor
16 Rick Barry 15.00 40.00
Ray Allen
Larry Bird
17 Larry Bird 30.00 80.00
Magic Johnson
Isiah Thomas
18 Isiah Thomas 10.00 25.00
Richard Hamilton
Chauncey Billups
19 Kevin Garnett 12.50 30.00
Tim Duncan
Amare Stoudemire
20 Adam Morrison 15.00 50.00
Larry Bird
J.J. Redick
21 Dirk Nowitzki 10.00 25.00
Andrea Bargnani
Andrei Kirilenko
22 Dwight Howard 10.00 25.00
Emeka Okafor
Ben Gordon
23 Dominique Wilkins 12.50 30.00
Josh Smith
Josh Childress
24 Andre Iguodala 12.50 30.00
Dominique Wilkins
Vince Carter
26 Dwight Howard 25.00 50.00
Jameer Nelson
Grant Hill
27 Vince Carter 10.00 25.00
Rasheed Wallace
Antawn Jamison
28 Adam Morrison 10.00 25.00
Andrew Bogut
Emeka Okafor
29 Steve Nash 20.00 50.00
Magic Johnson
Jason Kidd
30 Chris Paul 10.00 25.00
Emeka Okafor
Amare Stoudemire
31 Pau Gasol 10.00 25.00
Elton Brand
Vince Carter
32 Tim Duncan 15.00 40.00
Allen Iverson
Jason Kidd
33 Grant Hill 15.00 30.00
Mitch Richmond
Shaquille O'Neal
34 Rudy Gay 10.00 25.00
LaMarcus Aldridge
Randy Foye
35 James Worthy 15.00 40.00
Shaquille O'Neal
Tim Duncan
36 Larry Bird 30.00 80.00
Magic Johnson
Isiah Thomas
37 Rick Barry 12.50 30.00
Moses Malone
Dwyane Wade
38 Tony Parker 10.00 25.00
Gilbert Arenas
Chauncey Billups
39 Michael Redd 10.00 25.00
Manu Ginobili
Gilbert Arenas
40 Allen Iverson 30.00 60.00
Kobe Bryant
Tracy McGrady
41 Isiah Thomas 30.00 80.00
Magic Johnson
Larry Bird
42 Kevin Garnett 20.00 50.00
Amare Stoudemire
Kobe Bryant
43 Tim Duncan 15.00 40.00
Shaquille O'Neal
Kevin Garnett
44 Kobe Bryant 15.00 40.00
Allen Iverson
Karl Malone
45 Dominique Wilkins 50.00 100.00
Clyde Drexler
Julius Erving
46 Tim Duncan 12.50 30.00
George Gervin
Tony Parker
47 Moses Malone 15.00 40.00
Andre Iguodala
Julius Erving
48 Jerry West 25.00 50.00
Magic Johnson
Elgin Baylor
49 Stephon Marbury 10.00 25.00
Earl Monroe
Channing Frye
50 Magic Johnson 25.00 50.00
Kobe Bryant
Elgin Baylor
51 Bob Lanier 15.00 40.00
Isiah Thomas
Dennis Rodman
52 Yao Ming 15.00 40.00
Tim Duncan
Allen Iverson
53 Larry Bird 25.00 60.00
Dave Cowens
Bill Walton
54 Chris Bosh 10.00 25.00
J.J. Redick
Raymond Felton
55 Chris Webber 20.00 50.00
Jalen Rose
Juwan Howard

2006-07 Topps Triple Threads Relics Combos Autographs

PRINT RUN 36 SER.#'d SETS
*EMERALD: .5X TO 1.25X BASE HI
EMERALD PRINT RUN 18 SER.#'d SETS
UNPRICED GOLD PRINT RUN 9 SETS
UNPRICED PR.PLATE PRINT RUNS ONE SET
UNPRICED SAPPHIRE PRINT RUN 3 SETS
1 Dwyane Wade 50.00 120.00
Adam Morrison
Carmelo Anthony
2 Larry Bird 125.00 250.00
Magic Johnson
Rick Barry
3 Dominique Wilkins 40.00 100.00
Josh Smith
Vince Carter
4 Elgin Baylor 40.00 100.00
Earl Monroe
Isiah Thomas
5 Larry Bird 100.00 200.00
Adam Morrison
John Stockton
6 Bill Walton 125.00 250.00
Magic Johnson
Larry Bird
7 Bob Lanier 40.00 100.00
Moses Malone
Bill Walton
8 Dwyane Wade 150.00 300.00
Magic Johnson
Larry Bird
9 Larry Bird 125.00 250.00
Magic Johnson
Isiah Thomas
10 Andrea Bargnani 25.00 60.00
Adam Morrison
Randy Foye

2007-08 Topps Triple Threads

Released in February 2008, Topps Triple Threads boasts a 150-card set where cards 1-90 feature NBA veterans serially numbered to 33, cards 91-100 feature retired NBA legends serially numbered to 333 and cards 101-150 feature NBA rookies serially numbered to 99. Triple Threads released in two-pack boxes of three cards each and packs carried an initial suggested retail price of $150.

UNPRICED PLATINUM PRINT RUN ONE SET
UNPRICED SAPPHIRE PRINT RUN ONE SET
1 Yao Ming 1.00 2.50
2 Michael Redd .75 2.00
3 Dwyane Wade 2.00 5.00
4 Chris Bosh .75 2.00
5 Kevin Garnett 1.50 4.00
6 Sam Cassell .75 2.00
7 Ben Gordon .75 2.00
8 Deron Williams 1.25 3.00
9 Andre Iguodala .75 2.00
10 Mike Bibby .75 2.00
11 Chauncey Billups .75 2.00
12 Dwight Howard 1.25 3.00
13 Steve Nash 1.00 2.50
14 Raymond Felton 1.00 2.50
15 Carmelo Anthony 1.00 2.50
16 Pau Gasol .75 2.00
17 Brandon Roy 1.00 2.50
18 Chris Wilcox .50 1.25
19 Josh Howard .60 1.50
20 Ray Allen .75 2.00
21 Tim Duncan 1.25 3.00
22 Tayshaun Prince .75 2.00
23 LeBron James 4.00 10.00
24 Kobe Bryant 4.00 10.00
25 Al Jefferson .75 2.00
26 Stephon Marbury .60 1.50
27 Mike Miller .75 2.00
28 Jason Terry .60 1.50
29 Corey Maggette .60 1.50
30 Allen Iverson 1.00 2.50
31 Tracy McGrady .75 2.00
32 Shaquille O'Neal 1.50 4.00
33 Ben Wallace .75 2.00
34 Paul Pierce 1.00 2.50
35 Vince Carter 1.00 2.50
36 Chris Paul 1.50 4.00
37 Kyle Korver .60 1.50
38 LaMarcus Aldridge 1.00 2.50
39 Al Harrington .60 1.50
40 Gilbert Arenas .75 2.00
41 Dirk Nowitzki 1.00 2.50
42 David Lee .60 1.50
43 Gerald Wallace .75 2.00
44 Luke Walton .50 1.25
45 Manu Ginobili .75 2.00
46 Charlie Villanueva .75 2.00
47 Andrei Kirilenko .60 1.50
48 Richard Jefferson .75 2.00
49 Joe Johnson .75 2.00
50 Zach Randolph .60 1.50
51 Andrea Bargnani 1.00 2.50
52 Elton Brand .75 2.00
53 Anderson Varejao .60 1.50
54 Kirk Hinrich .75 2.00
55 Baron Davis .75 2.00
56 Shane Battier .60 1.50
57 Jameer Nelson .60 1.50
58 Antawn Jamison .75 2.00
59 Andrew Bynum 1.00 2.50
60 Kevin Martin .75 2.00
61 Amare Stoudemire .75 2.00
62 Randy Foye .75 2.00
63 Marcus Camby .50 1.25
64 Larry Hughes .60 1.50
65 Luol Deng .75 2.00
66 Danny Granger .75 2.00

67 Eddy Curry .50 1.25
68 David West .75 2.00
69 Tony Parker .75 2.00
70 Jason Kidd .75 2.00
71 Monta Ellis .75 2.00
72 Richard Hamilton .60 1.50
73 Udonis Haslem .60 1.50
74 Rudy Gay .75 2.00
75 Carlos Boozer .75 2.00
76 Luke Ridnour .60 1.50
77 Jermaine O'Neal .75 2.00
78 Ricky Davis .60 1.50
79 Desmond Mason .50 1.25
80 Lamar Odom .75 2.00
81 T.J. Ford .60 1.50
82 Jarrett Jack .60 1.50
83 Ron Artest .75 2.00
84 Sam Dalembert .50 1.25
85 Josh Smith .75 2.00
86 Tyson Chandler .60 1.50
87 Shawn Marion .75 2.00
88 Caron Butler .75 2.00
89 Jason Richardson .75 2.00
90 Rashard Lewis .60 1.50
91 Larry Bird 2.50 6.00
92 Isiah Thomas .75 2.00
93 Magic Johnson 2.00 5.00
94 John Stockton 1.25 3.00
95 Bill Russell 1.25 3.00
96 Dennis Rodman 1.25 3.00
97 Dominique Wilkins 1.00 2.50
98 David Robinson 1.25 3.00
99 Bill Walton .75 2.00
100 Jerry West 1.00 2.50
101 Greg Oden RC 3.00 8.00
102 Daequan Cook RC 2.50 6.00
103 Morris Almond RC 2.50 6.00
104 Sean Williams RC 2.50 6.00
105 Arron Afflalo RC 3.00 8.00
106 Coby Karl RC 2.50 6.00
107 Adam Haluska RC 2.50 6.00
108 Corey Brewer RC 3.00 8.00
109 Herbert Hill RC 2.50 6.00
110 Nick Young RC 4.00 10.00
111 Joakim Noah RC 6.00 15.00
112 Mike Conley Jr. RC 4.00 10.00
113 Kyrylo Fesenko RC 2.50 6.00
114 Aaron Brooks RC 2.50 6.00
115 Marco Belinelli RC 2.50 6.00
116 Juan Carlos Navarro RC 2.50 6.00
117 Jared Dudley RC 2.50 6.00
118 Rodney Stuckey RC 4.00 10.00
119 JamesOn Curry RC 2.50 6.00
120 Gabe Pruitt RC 2.50 6.00
121 Acie Law RC 2.50 6.00
122 Dominic McGuire RC 2.50 6.00
123 Ramon Sessions RC 4.00 10.00
124 Jeff Green RC 3.00 8.00
125 Wilson Chandler RC 4.00 10.00
126 Kosta Perovic RC 2.50 6.00
127 Josh McRoberts RC 2.50 6.00
128 Jason Smith RC 2.50 6.00
129 Cheik Samb RC 2.50 6.00
130 Stephane Lasme RC 2.50 6.00
131 Brandon Wallace RC 2.50 6.00
132 Alando Tucker RC 2.50 6.00
133 Javaris Crittenton RC 2.50 6.00
134 Chris Richard RC 2.50 6.00
135 Kevin Durant RC 40.00 80.00
136 Al Thornton RC 2.50 6.00
137 Carl Landry RC 2.50 6.00
138 Yi Jianlian RC 4.00 10.00
139 Brandan Wright RC 2.50 6.00
140 Nick Fazekas RC 2.50 6.00
141 Al Horford RC 3.00 8.00
142 Jermareo Davidson RC 2.50 6.00
143 D.J. Strawberry RC 2.50 6.00
144 Glen Davis RC 4.00 10.00
145 Julian Wright RC 2.50 6.00
146 Spencer Hawes RC 2.50 6.00
147 Taurean Green RC 2.50 6.00
148 Luis Scola RC 4.00 10.00
149 Aaron Gray RC 2.50 6.00
150 Thaddeus Young RC 3.00 8.00

2007-08 Topps Triple Threads Emerald

*1-100 EMERALD: 1X TO 2.5X BASE HI
*101-150 EMERALD RCs: 1X TO 2.5X BASE HI
1-100 EMERALD PRINT RUN 66 SER.#'d SETS
101-150 EMERALD RC PRINT RUN 33 SETS

2007-08 Topps Triple Threads Gold

*1-100 GOLD: 1.5X TO 4X BASE HI
1-100 PRINT RUN 33 SER.#'d SETS
101-150 PRINT RUN 3 SER.#'d SET
101-150 UNPRICED DUE TO SCARCITY

2007-08 Topps Triple Threads Sepia

*1-100 SEPIA: .75X TO 2X BASE HI
*101-150 SEPIA RCs: .6X TO 1.5X BASE HI
1-100 SEPIA PRINT RUN 99 SET.#'d SETS
101-150 SEPIA RC PRINT RUN 66 SETS

2007-08 Topps Triple Threads Relics

PRINT RUN 18 SER.#'d SETS
THREE VERSIONS OF EACH EXIST
ALL VERSIONS SAME VALUE
UNPRICED EMERALD PRINT RUN 5 SETS
UNPRICED GOLD PRINT RUN ONE SET
UNPRICED PLATINUM PRINT RUN ONE SET
UNPRICED SAPPHIRE PRINT RUN ONE SET
*SEPIA: .75X TO 2X BASE HI
SEPIA PRINT RUN NINE SETS
1 Kobe Bryant KB24 25.00 50.00
2 Kobe Bryant Ball 25.00 50.00
3 Kobe Bryant 81 Points 25.00 50.00
4 Allen Iverson Nuggets 15.00 30.00
5 Allen Iverson Answer 15.00 30.00
6 Allen Iverson MVP 15.00 30.00
7 Gilbert Arenas Ball 6.00 15.00
8 Gilbert Arenas Hibachi 6.00 15.00
9 Gilbert Arenas WAS 6.00 15.00
10 Kevin Garnett #5 20.00 40.00
11 Kevin Garnett Shamrock 20.00 40.00
12 Kevin Garnett Big Ticket 20.00 40.00
13 Dwight Howard 10.00 25.00
14 Dwight Howard Dunk 10.00 25.00
15 Dwight Howard Magic 10.00 25.00
16 Chris Paul ROY 20.00 40.00
17 Chris Paul Shoot 20.00 40.00
18 Chris Paul Hornets 20.00 40.00
19 Steve Nash APG 10.00 25.00
20 Steve Nash Floor General 10.00 25.00
21 Steve Nash Captain Canada 10.00 25.00
22 Tim Duncan Slam Duncan 10.00 25.00
23 Tim Duncan Spurs 10.00 25.00
24 Tim Duncan MVP 10.00 25.00
25 Jason Kidd JK5 10.00 25.00
26 Jason Kidd Trip.Double 10.00 25.00
27 Jason Kidd APG 10.00 25.00
28 Tracy McGrady Tmac 10.00 25.00
29 Tracy McGrady #1 10.00 25.00
30 Tracy McGrady Ball 10.00 25.00
31 Dirk Nowitzki MVP 15.00 30.00
32 Dirk Nowitzki All-Star 15.00 30.00
33 Dirk Nowitzki 3PT 15.00 30.00
34 Amare Stoudemire ROY 10.00 25.00
35 Amare Stoudemire Double 10.00 25.00
36 Amare Stoudemire Dunk 10.00 25.00
37 Joe Johnson NBA 6.00 15.00
38 Joe Johnson ATL 6.00 15.00
39 Joe Johnson Ball 6.00 15.00
40 Pau Gasol ROY 6.00 15.00
41 Pau Gasol Grizzlies 6.00 15.00
42 Pau Gasol Dunk 6.00 15.00
43 Baron Davis GSW 10.00 25.00
44 Baron Davis #5 10.00 25.00
45 Baron Davis Shoot 10.00 25.00
46 Richard Hamilton DET 6.00 15.00
47 Richard Hamilton RIP 6.00 15.00
48 Richard Hamilton Ball 6.00 15.00
49 Manu Ginobili Argentina 10.00 25.00
50 Manu Ginobili Ball 10.00 25.00
51 Manu Ginobili Manu 10.00 25.00
52 Lamar Odom LAL 6.00 15.00
53 Lamar Odom #7 6.00 15.00
54 Lamar Odom Shoot 6.00 15.00
55 Josh Smith #5 6.00 15.00
56 Josh Smith Jsmooth 6.00 15.00
57 Josh Smith Dunk 6.00 15.00
58 Yao Ming Chinese 10.00 25.00
59 Yao Ming #1 Pick 10.00 25.00
60 Yao Ming Ball 10.00 25.00
61 Jermaine O'Neal Pacers 6.00 15.00
62 Jermaine O'Neal #7 6.00 15.00
63 Jermaine O'Neal Double 6.00 15.00
64 Michael Redd PTS 6.00 15.00
65 Michael Redd 3PT 6.00 15.00
66 Michael Redd Ball 6.00 15.00
67 Shawn Marion Suns 6.00 15.00
68 Shawn Marion Dunk 6.00 15.00
69 Shawn Marion All-Star 6.00 15.00
70 Josh Howard DAL 6.00 15.00
71 Josh Howard #5 6.00 15.00
72 Josh Howard NBA 6.00 15.00
73 Ben Wallace Big Ben 6.00 15.00
74 Ben Wallace Bulls 6.00 15.00
75 Ben Wallace Defense 6.00 15.00
76 Kevin Martin #23 6.00 15.00
77 Kevin Martin SAC 6.00 15.00
78 Kevin Martin NBA 6.00 15.00
79 Carmelo Anthony Ball 10.00 25.00
80 Carmelo Anthony Melo 10.00 25.00
81 Carmelo Anthony PTS 10.00 25.00
82 Mike Conley Jr. MEM 6.00 15.00
83 Mike Conley Jr. #11 6.00 15.00
84 Mike Conley Jr. NBA 6.00 15.00
85 Al Horford ATL 10.00 25.00
86 Al Horford #15 10.00 25.00
87 Al Horford NBA 10.00 25.00
88 Corey Brewer MIN 8.00 20.00
89 Corey Brewer #22 8.00 20.00
90 Corey Brewer NBA 8.00 20.00
91 Joakim Noah CHI 8.00 20.00
92 Joakim Noah NBA 8.00 20.00
93 Joakim Noah #13 8.00 20.00
94 Greg Oden #52 12.50 30.00
95 Greg Oden #1 Pick 12.50 30.00
96 Greg Oden POR 12.50 30.00
97 Eddy Curry NYK 6.00 15.00
98 Eddy Curry #34 6.00 15.00
99 Eddy Curry NBA 6.00 15.00
100 Mike Miller #33 6.00 15.00
101 Mike Miller MEM 6.00 15.00
102 Mike Miller Ball 6.00 15.00
103 Dwyane Wade Heat 15.00 30.00
104 Dwyane Wade Flash 15.00 30.00
105 Dwyane Wade DW3 15.00 30.00

2007-08 Topps Triple Threads Relics Autographs

PRINT RUN NINE SETS
THREE VERSIONS OF EACH CARD EXIST
ALL VERSIONS SAME VALUE
UNPRICED EMERALD PRINT RUN ONE SET
UNPRICED GOLD PRINT RUN ONE SET
UNPRICED PLATINUM PRINT RUN ONE SET
UNPRICED SAPPHIRE PRINT RUN ONE SET
1 Dwyane Wade Heat 40.00 80.00
2 Dwyane Wade Flash 40.00 80.00
3 Dwyane Wade DW3 40.00 80.00
7 Nick Young NY1 30.00 60.00
8 Nick Young WAS 30.00 60.00
9 Nick Young Ball 30.00 60.00
10 Brandan Wright #32 20.00 50.00
11 Brandan Wright GSW 20.00 50.00
12 Brandan Wright Ball 20.00 50.00
13 Yi Jianlian YI 40.00 80.00
14 Yi Jianlian MIL 40.00 80.00
15 Yi Jianlian Chinese 40.00 80.00
19 Paul Pierce #34 40.00 80.00
20 Paul Pierce Ball 40.00 80.00
21 Paul Pierce Shamrock 40.00 80.00
22 Vince Carter Nets 25.00 60.00
23 Vince Carter Dunk 25.00 60.00
24 Vince Carter Vinsanity 25.00 60.00
25 Andre Iguodala 73ers 20.00 40.00
26 Andre Iguodala Dunk 20.00 40.00
27 Andre Iguodala AI9 20.00 40.00
28 Corey Maggette LAC 15.00 30.00
29 Corey Maggette #50 15.00 30.00
30 Corey Maggette NBA 15.00 30.00
31 Mickael Pietrus MP2 15.00 30.00
32 Mickael Pietrus GSW 15.00 30.00
33 Mickael Pietrus Shoot 15.00 30.00
34 Raymond Felton CHA 15.00 30.00
35 Raymond Felton Floor Gen. 15.00 30.00
36 Raymond Felton #20 15.00 30.00
37 Rajon Rondo Bean Town 30.00 80.00
38 Rajon Rondo BOS 30.00 80.00
39 Rajon Rondo Ball 30.00 80.00
46 Craig Smith MIN 15.00 30.00
47 Craig Smith Dunk 15.00 30.00
48 Craig Smith #5 15.00 30.00
49 Magic Johnson Ball 100.00 200.00
50 Magic Johnson MVP 100.00 200.00
51 Magic Johnson Champ 100.00 200.00
52 Larry Bird MVP 125.00 225.00
53 Larry Bird Ball 125.00 225.00
54 Larry Bird All-Star 125.00 225.00
55 Rick Barry GSW 30.00 60.00
56 Rick Barry Under Hand 30.00 60.00
57 Rick Barry FT% 30.00 60.00
58 Dominique Wilkins HHFilm 30.00 60.00
59 Dominique Wilkins Dunk 30.00 60.00
60 Dominique Wilkins 23 FTs 30.00 60.00
61 David Robinson Admiral 100.00 200.00
62 David Robinson #50 100.00 200.00
63 David Robinson MVP 100.00 200.00
67 John Stockton APG 60.00 120.00
68 John Stockton Double 60.00 120.00
69 John Stockton SPG 60.00 120.00
70 Dennis Rodman Worm 50.00 100.00
71 Dennis Rodman RPG 50.00 100.00
72 Dennis Rodman Defense 50.00 100.00
73 Isiah Thomas ZEKE 25.00 50.00
74 Isiah Thomas MVP 25.00 50.00
75 Isiah Thomas Shoot 25.00 50.00
76 Ray Allen #20 40.00 80.00
77 Ray Allen Bean Town 40.00 80.00
78 Ray Allen 3PT 40.00 80.00
82 David Lee #42 15.00 30.00
83 David Lee NYK 15.00 30.00
84 David Lee Lee 15.00 30.00
85 Bill Walton Bean Town 25.00 50.00
86 Bill Walton Shamrock 25.00 50.00
87 Bill Walton Red Head 25.00 50.00
88 Chauncey Billups Big Shot 25.00 50.00
89 Chauncey Billups Pistons 25.00 50.00
90 Chauncey Billups MVP 25.00 50.00
91 Al Jefferson MIN 20.00 40.00
92 Al Jefferson #25 20.00 40.00
93 Al Jefferson Dunk 20.00 40.00
94 Luke Walton Shoot 15.00 30.00
95 Luke Walton #4 15.00 30.00
96 Luke Walton Walton 15.00 30.00
97 Ben Gordon #7 15.00 30.00
98 Ben Gordon 3PT 15.00 30.00
99 Ben Gordon 6th Man 15.00 30.00
100 Shaquille O'Neal Double 75.00 200.00
101 Shaquille O'Neal Dunk 75.00 200.00
102 Shaquille O'Neal MVP 75.00 200.00
103 Carmelo Anthony Ball 30.00 60.00
104 Carmelo Anthony Melo 30.00 60.00
105 Carmelo Anthony PTS 30.00 60.00
106 Chris Paul ROY 50.00 100.00
107 Chris Paul Shoot 50.00 100.00
108 Chris Paul Hornets 50.00 100.00
109 Deron Williams Jazz 30.00 60.00
110 Deron Williams UTA 30.00 60.00
111 Deron Williams Ball 30.00 60.00
112 Antawn Jamison WAS 15.00 30.00
113 Antawn Jamison 6th Man 15.00 30.00
114 Antawn Jamison PTS 15.00 30.00
118 Ryan Gomes Wolves #8 15.00 30.00
119 Ryan Gomes Shoot 15.00 30.00
120 Ryan Gomes MIN 15.00 30.00
121 David Thompson #33 20.00 40.00
122 David Thompson All-Star 20.00 40.00
123 David Thompson DEN 20.00 40.00
124 Moses Malone HOF 20.00 40.00
125 Moses Malone PTS 20.00 40.00
126 Moses Malone MVP 20.00 40.00
127 Dwight Howard Magic 12 50.00 100.00
128 Dwight Howard Dunk 50.00 100.00
129 Dwight Howard REB 50.00 100.00
130 Thaddeus Young PHI 30.00 80.00
131 Thaddeus Young #21 30.00 80.00
132 Thaddeus Young Shoot 30.00 80.00
133 Adam Morrison Cats 35 15.00 30.00
134 Adam Morrison Ball 15.00 30.00
135 Adam Morrison 3PT 15.00 30.00

2007-08 Topps Triple Threads Relics Autographs Sepia

PRINT RUN FIVE SETS
THREE VERSIONS OF EACH CARD
UNLISTED VERSIONS SAME VALUE
1 Dwyane Wade Heat 40.00 80.00
2 Dwyane Wade Flash 40.00 80.00
3 Dwyane Wade DW3 40.00 80.00
4 Greg Oden #52 60.00 150.00
5 Greg Oden #1Pick 60.00 150.00
6 Greg Oden POR 60.00 150.00
13 Yi Jianlian YI 50.00 100.00
14 Yi Jianlian MIL 50.00 100.00
15 Yi Jianlian Chinese 50.00 100.00
16 Chris Bosh CB4 30.00 60.00
17 Chris Bosh TOR 30.00 60.00
18 Chris Bosh All-Star 30.00 60.00
19 Paul Pierce #34 60.00 120.00
20 Paul Pierce Ball 60.00 120.00
21 Paul Pierce Shamrock 60.00 120.00
22 Vince Carter Nets 30.00 80.00
23 Vince Carter Dunk 30.00 80.00
24 Vince Carter Vinsanity 30.00 80.00
25 Andre Iguodala 73ers 25.00 50.00
26 Andre Iguodala Dunk 25.00 50.00
27 Andre Iguodala AI9 25.00 50.00
28 Corey Maggette LAC 20.00 40.00
29 Corey Maggette #50 20.00 40.00
30 Corey Maggette NBA 20.00 40.00
31 Mickael Pietrus MP2 20.00 40.00
32 Mickael Pietrus GSW 20.00 40.00
33 Mickael Pietrus Shoot 20.00 40.00
34 Raymond Felton CHA 20.00 40.00
35 Raymond Felton Floor Gen. 20.00 40.00
36 Raymond Felton #20 20.00 40.00
37 Rajon Rondo Bean Town 40.00 100.00
38 Rajon Rondo BOS 40.00 100.00
39 Rajon Rondo Ball 40.00 100.00
40 Jarrett Jack POR 20.00 40.00
41 Jarrett Jack NBA 20.00 40.00
42 Jarrett Jack Ball 20.00 40.00
46 Craig Smith MIN 20.00 40.00
47 Craig Smith Dunk 20.00 40.00
48 Craig Smith #5 20.00 40.00
49 Magic Johnson Ball 100.00 200.00
50 Magic Johnson MVP 100.00 200.00
51 Magic Johnson Champ 100.00 200.00
52 Larry Bird MVP 125.00 225.00
53 Larry Bird Ball 125.00 225.00
54 Larry Bird All-Star 125.00 225.00
55 Rick Barry GSW 50.00 100.00
56 Rick Barry Under Hand 50.00 100.00
57 Rick Barry FT 50.00 100.00
58 Dominique Wilkins HHFilm 40.00 80.00
59 Dominique Wilkins Dunk 40.00 80.00
60 Dominique Wilkins 23 FTs 40.00 80.00
64 Mike Miller MEM 20.00 40.00
65 Mike Miller #33 20.00 40.00
66 Mike Miller Ball 20.00 40.00
67 John Stockton APG 80.00 160.00
68 John Stockton Double 80.00 160.00
69 John Stockton SPG 80.00 160.00
73 Isiah Thomas ZEKE 25.00 50.00
74 Isiah Thomas MVP 25.00 50.00
75 Isiah Thomas Shoot 25.00 50.00
76 Ray Allen #20 60.00 120.00
77 Ray Allen Bean Town 60.00 120.00
78 Ray Allen 3PT 60.00 120.00
79 Gilbert Arenas Ball 40.00 100.00
80 Gilbert Arenas Hibachi 40.00 100.00
81 Gilbert Arenas WAS 40.00 100.00
85 Bill Walton Bean Town 30.00 75.00
86 Bill Walton Shamrock 30.00 75.00
87 Bill Walton Red Head 30.00 75.00
88 Chauncey Billups Big Shot 30.00 75.00
89 Chauncey Billups Pistons 30.00 75.00
90 Chauncey Billups MVP 30.00 75.00
94 Luke Walton Shoot 20.00 40.00
95 Luke Walton #4 20.00 40.00
96 Luke Walton Walton 20.00 40.00
97 Ben Gordon #7 20.00 40.00
98 Ben Gordon 3PT 20.00 40.00
99 Ben Gordon 6th Man 20.00 40.00
100 Shaquille O'Neal Double 80.00 160.00
101 Shaquille O'Neal Dunk 80.00 160.00
102 Shaquille O'Neal MVP 80.00 160.00
103 Carmelo Anthony Ball 50.00 100.00
104 Carmelo Anthony Melo 50.00 100.00
105 Carmelo Anthony PTS 50.00 100.00
106 Chris Paul ROY 100.00 200.00
107 Chris Paul Shoot 100.00 200.00
108 Chris Paul Hornets 100.00 200.00
109 Deron Williams Jazz 40.00 80.00
110 Deron Williams UTA 40.00 80.00
111 Deron Williams Ball 40.00 80.00
112 Antawn Jamison WAS 25.00 50.00
113 Antawn Jamison 6th Man 25.00 50.00
114 Antawn Jamison PTS 25.00 50.00
115 Joe Johnson ATL 20.00 40.00
116 Joe Johnson Ball 20.00 40.00
117 Joe Johnson Hawks #2 20.00 40.00
118 Ryan Gomes Wolves #8 20.00 40.00
119 Ryan Gomes Shoot 20.00 40.00
120 Ryan Gomes MIN 20.00 40.00
121 David Thompson #33 25.00 50.00
122 David Thompson All-Star 25.00 50.00
123 David Thompson DEN 25.00 50.00
124 Moses Malone HOF 30.00 60.00
125 Moses Malone PTS 30.00 60.00
126 Moses Malone MVP 30.00 60.00
127 Dwight Howard Magic 12 75.00 150.00
128 Dwight Howard Dunk 75.00 150.00
129 Dwight Howard REB 75.00 150.00
130 Thaddeus Young PHI 40.00 80.00
131 Thaddeus Young #21 40.00 80.00
132 Thaddeus Young Shoot 40.00 80.00
133 Adam Morrison Cats 35 15.00 30.00
134 Adam Morrison Ball 15.00 30.00
135 Adam Morrison 3PT 15.00 30.00

2007-08 Topps Triple Threads Relics Combos

PRINT RUN 18 SER.#'d SETS
UNPRICED EMERALD PRINT RUN 3 SETS
UNPRICED GOLD PRINT RUN ONE SET
UNPRICED PLATINUM PRINT RUN ONE SET
UNPRICED SEPIA PRINT RUN 9 SETS
1 Paul Pierce 40.00 80.00
Ray Allen
Kevin Garnett
2 Allen Iverson 25.00 50.00
Marcus Camby
Carmelo Anthony
3 Greg Oden 50.00 100.00
Brandon Roy
LaMarcus Aldridge
4 Ben Wallace 20.00 40.00
Joakim Noah
Ben Gordon
5 Mike Conley Jr. 10.00 25.00
Pau Gasol
Mike Miller
6 Josh Smith 25.00 50.00
Al Horford
Joe Johnson
7 Al Jefferson 10.00 25.00
Corey Brewer
Randy Foye
8 Yi Jianlian 12.50 30.00
Dirk Nowitzki
Yao Ming
9 Dirk Nowitzki 20.00 40.00
Steve Nash
Tim Duncan
10 Shaquille O'Neal 30.00 60.00
Karl Malone
David Robinson
11 Larry Bird 40.00 80.00
Kevin Garnett
Bill Walton
12 Dwyane Wade 20.00 40.00
Isiah Thomas
Tony Parker
13 Kobe Bryant 25.00 50.00
Gilbert Arenas
Carmelo Anthony
14 Michael Redd 25.00 50.00
Ray Allen
Allen Iverson
15 Baron Davis 10.00 25.00
Brandan Wright
Monta Ellis
16 Antawn Jamison 10.00 25.00
Nick Young
Caron Butler
17 Thaddeus Young 10.00 25.00
Andre Iguodala
Samuel Dalembert
18 Larry Bird 40.00 80.00
David Robinson
Shaquille O'Neal
19 Brandon Roy 20.00 40.00
Chris Paul
Vince Carter
20 John Stockton 25.00 50.00
Magic Johnson
Isiah Thomas
21 Jason Kidd 20.00 40.00
Stephon Marbury
Steve Nash
22 Bill Russell 25.00 50.00
Elgin Baylor
Dennis Rodman
23 Shaquille O'Neal 20.00 40.00
Tim Duncan
Ben Wallace
24 Ray Allen 10.00 25.00
Eddie Jones
Antoine Walker
25 Allen Iverson 20.00 40.00
Tracy McGrady
Vince Carter
26 Dominique Wilkins 25.00 50.00
Clyde Drexler
Magic Johnson
27 Tim Hardaway 25.00 50.00
Mitch Richmond
Chris Mullin
29 Tracy McGrady 15.00 30.00
Shane Battier
Yao Ming
30 Shawn Marion 10.00 25.00
Andre Iguodala
Ron Artest
31 Nick Young 15.00 30.00
Dwyane Wade
Thaddeus Young
32 Marcus Camby 10.00 25.00
Tayshaun Prince
Ben Wallace
33 Leandro Barbosa 10.00 25.00
Mike Miller
Ben Gordon
35 Gilbert Arenas 10.00 25.00
Jermaine O'Neal
Tracy McGrady
36 Yao Ming 20.00 40.00
Amare Stoudemire
Carlos Boozer
37 Kirk Hinrich 10.00 25.00
T.J. Ford
Josh Howard
38 Jason Richardson 10.00 25.00
Raymond Felton
Gerald Wallace
39 Arron Afflalo 10.00 25.00
Chauncey Billups
Rodney Stuckey
42 Chris Bosh 15.00 30.00
Tracy McGrady
Carmelo Anthony
43 Kevin Garnett 20.00 40.00
Dwight Howard
Dwyane Wade
44 Luke Ridnour 10.00 25.00
Jeff Green
Delonte West
46 Richard Jefferson 10.00 25.00
Sean Williams
Jason Kidd
47 Al Horford 20.00 40.00
Corey Brewer
Joakim Noah
48 Rick Barry 25.00 50.00
Elgin Baylor
Larry Bird
49 Magic Johnson 40.00 80.00
Shaquille O'Neal
Karl Malone
50 John Stockton 20.00 40.00
Bill Walton
Isiah Thomas

2007-08 Topps Triple Threads Rookie Relics Autographs

SKIP-NUMBERED SET
PRINT RUN 50 SER.#'d SETS
UNPRICED EMERALD PRINT RUN ONE SET
UNPRICED GOLD PRINT RUN ONE SET
UNPRICED PLATINUM PRINT RUN ONE SET
UNPRICED SAPPHIRE PRINT RUN ONE SET
*SEPIA: .5X TO 1.25X BASE HI
SEPIA PRINT RUN 23 SER.#'d SETS
101 Greg Oden 40.00 100.00
102 Daequan Cook 10.00 25.00
103 Morris Almond 10.00 25.00
104 Sean Williams 10.00 25.00
105 Arron Afflalo 12.00 30.00
107 Adam Haluska 10.00 25.00
109 Herbert Hill 10.00 25.00
110 Nick Young 15.00 40.00
113 Jared Jordan 10.00 25.00
114 Aaron Brooks 10.00 25.00
115 Marco Belinelli 10.00 25.00
117 Jared Dudley 10.00 25.00
118 Rodney Stuckey 15.00 40.00
120 Gabe Pruitt 10.00 25.00
121 Acie Law 10.00 25.00
122 Dominic McGuire 10.00 25.00
125 Wilson Chandler 15.00 40.00
126 Marcus Williams 10.00 25.00
127 Josh McRoberts 10.00 25.00
128 Jason Smith 10.00 25.00
130 Stephane Lasme 10.00 25.00
132 Alando Tucker 10.00 25.00
133 Javaris Crittenton 10.00 25.00
136 Al Thornton 10.00 25.00
137 Carl Landry 10.00 25.00
138 Yi Jianlian 15.00 40.00
139 Brandan Wright 10.00 25.00
140 Nick Fazekas 10.00 25.00
142 Jermareo Davidson 10.00 25.00
143 D.J. Strawberry 10.00 25.00
144 Glen Davis 15.00 40.00
146 Spencer Hawes 10.00 25.00
147 Taurean Green 10.00 25.00
149 Aaron Gray 10.00 25.00
150 Thaddeus Young 12.00 30.00

2006-07 Topps Turkey Red

Released in early February 2007, Turkey Red employs an old-school design which resembles a framed portrait of each player painted on a textured card stock. The 275-card base set pictures veteran players on cards 1-175 where short prints are labeled as "SP" (inserted at the rate of one in four packs), rookies are pictured on cards 176-225, retired NBA legends are pictured on cards 226-250 and cards 251-260 are checklist cards. Also inserted were a series of advertisement-back variations. These are noted in the checklist with "Ad." Turkey Red is packaged in 24-pack boxes of eight cards each and carried an original suggested retail price of $4.00 per pack.

COMPLETE SET (275) 60.00 120.00
COMP.SET w/o RC's (175) 15.00 40.00
UNPRICED GOLD PRINT RUN 5 SETS
UNPRICED SUEDE PRINT RUN 3 SETS
UNPRICED WOOD PRINT RUN ONE SET
1 Dwyane Wade SP 1.50 4.00
2 LeBron James 2.00 5.00
3 Allen Iverson SP .75 2.00
4 Sebastian Telfair .25 .60
5 Bonzi Wells .25 .60
6 Antawn Jamison .40 1.00
7 Joe Johnson .40 1.00
8 DeSagana Diop .25 .60
9 Stromile Swift .25 .60
10 Shaun Livingston .25 .60
11 Baron Davis .40 1.00
12 Richard Hamilton .30 .75
13 Andrei Kirilenko SP .50 1.25
14 Richard Jefferson .40 1.00
15 T.J. Ford .30 .75
16 Luke Ridnour .30 .75
17 Carlos Boozer .40 1.00
18 Al Jefferson .40 1.00
19 Andrew Bogut SP .60 1.50
20 Kobe Bryant 2.00 5.00
21 Tim Duncan .60 1.50
22B Ben Gordon Ad .60 1.50
22 Ben Gordon .40 1.00
23 Stephen Jackson .30 .75
24 Peja Stojakovic .40 1.00
25 Mike Miller .40 1.00
26 Ricky Davis SP .50 1.25
27 Boris Diaw SP .50 1.25
28 Shareef Abdur-Rahim .30 .75
29 Caron Butler .40 1.00
30 Al Harrington .30 .75
31 Ben Wallace SP .60 1.50
32 Jason Richardson .40 1.00
33 Channing Frye .30 .75
34 Paul Pierce .50 1.25
35 Andre Iguodala .40 1.00
35B Andre Iguodala Ad .60 1.50
36 Joey Graham .25 .60
37 Corey Maggette .30 .75
38 Sarunas Jasikevicius .30 .75
39 Lamar Odom .40 1.00
40 Shaquille O'Neal .75 2.00
40B Shaquille O'Neal Ad 1.25 3.00
41 Larry Hughes SP .50 1.25
42 Darko Milicic SP .40 1.00
43 Jerry Stackhouse .30 .75
44 Raymond Felton .50 1.25
45 Nenad Krstic SP .40 1.00
46 Michael Redd .40 1.00
47 Shane Battier .30 .75
48 Kevin Garnett .75 2.00
49 Deron Williams .60 1.50
50 Chris Paul SP 1.25 3.00
51 Rashard Lewis .40 1.00
52 Kevin Martin SP .60 1.50
53 Zach Randolph .30 .75
54 Jared Jeffries .25 .60
55 Donyell Marshall .25 .60
56 Josh Howard SP .50 1.25
57 Stephon Marbury .30 .75
58 Raja Bell .30 .75
59 Tony Parker .40 1.00
60 Dwight Howard .60 1.50
61 Kirk Hinrich .40 1.00
62 Emeka Okafor .40 1.00
63 Zaza Pachulia .25 .60
64 Troy Murphy .25 .60
65 Chris Duhon .25 .60
65B Chris Duhon Ad .40 1.00
66 Earl Boykins SP .40 1.00
67 Tracy McGrady .50 1.25
68 Hakim Warrick .30 .75
69 Charlie Villanueva SP .60 1.50
70 Jason Kidd .60 1.50
71 Joel Przybilla SP .40 1.00
72 Antonio Daniels .25 .60
73 Wally Szczerbiak .30 .75
74 Drew Gooden .30 .75
75 Antonio McDyess .30 .75
76 Ray Allen SP .60 1.50
77 Rashad McCants .25 .60
78 Eddy Curry .30 .75
79 Chris Webber .40 1.00
80 Yao Ming SP .75 2.00
81 Tyson Chandler .30 .75
82 Bobby Simmons .25 .60
83 Jarrett Jack .30 .75
84 Jameer Nelson SP .50 1.25
85 Luol Deng .40 1.00
86 Kurt Thomas .25 .60
87 Mickael Pietrus .30 .75
88 Chris Bosh SP .60 1.50
89 Devin Harris .40 1.00
90 Jermaine O'Neal .40 1.00
91 Luther Head .30 .75
92 Elton Brand SP .60 1.50
93 Antoine Walker .30 .75
94 Smush Parker .25 .60
95 Nate Robinson SP .60 1.50
96 Marvin Williams SP .60 1.50
97 Primoz Brezec .25 .60
98 Desmond Mason .25 .60
99 Ron Artest SP .60 1.50
100 Jason Terry .30 .75
101 Mehmet Okur .25 .60
102 Kenyon Martin .40 1.00
103 Ike Diogu SP .40 1.00
104 Eddie Griffin .25 .60
105 Amare Stoudemire .40 1.00
106 Kwame Brown SP .40 1.00
107 Hedo Turkoglu .40 1.00
108 Chauncey Billups .40 1.00
108B Chauncey Billups Ad .60 1.50
109 Rafer Alston .25 .60
110 Dirk Nowitzki SP 1.00 2.50
111 Steve Francis .40 1.00
112 Mike Bibby .40 1.00
113 Kirk Snyder .25 .60
114 Luke Walton .25 .60
114B Luke Walton Ad .40 1.00
115 Maurice Williams .30 .75
116 Nick Collison .25 .60
117 Brendan Haywood .25 .60
118 Delonte West SP .50 1.25
119 Mike Dunleavy .30 .75
120 Vince Carter .50 1.25
120B Vince Carter Ad .75 2.00
121 Juwan Howard .30 .75
122 J.R. Smith .40 1.00
123 Gerald Wallace SP .60 1.50
124 Cuttino Mobley .30 .75
125 James Posey .25 .60
126 Tayshaun Prince SP .60 1.50
127 Anderson Varejao .30 .75
128 Trenton Hassell .25 .60
129 Matt Harpring .30 .75
130 Gilbert Arenas SP .60 1.50
131 Leandro Barbosa .30 .75
132 Bruce Bowen .25 .60
133 Morris Peterson .25 .60
134 David West SP .60 1.50
135 Joe Smith .30 .75
136 Rasheed Wallace .40 1.00
137 Nene .30 .75
138 Alonzo Mourning .50 1.25
139 Jamal Crawford .30 .75
140 Carmelo Anthony SP .75 2.00
141 Brad Miller .40 1.00
142 Tim Thomas .25 .60
143 Jose Calderon .30 .75
144 Sean May .25 .60
145 Andres Nocioni SP .40 1.00
146 Samuel Dalembert .25 .60
147 Chris Wilcox .25 .60
148 Jason Williams .30 .75
149 DeShawn Stevenson .25 .60
150 Josh Smith SP .60 1.50
151 Andre Miller .30 .75
152 Michael Finley .40 1.00
153 Marquis Daniels .25 .60
154 Martell Webster .30 .75
155 Brevin Knight .25 .60
156 Steve Nash SP .75 2.00
157 Vladimir Radmanovic .25 .60
158B Speedy Claxton Ad .40 1.00
158 Speedy Claxton .25 .60
159 Darius Miles .25 .60
160 Pau Gasol SP .60 1.50
161 Sam Cassell .40 1.00
162 Nazr Mohammed .25 .60
163 Shawn Marion .40 1.00
164 Francisco Garcia .30 .75
165 Kyle Korver .30 .75
166 Udonis Haslem .30 .75
167 Manu Ginobili SP .60 1.50
168 Zydrunas Ilgauskas .30 .75
169 Eddie Jones .30 .75
170 Danny Granger SP .60 1.50
171 Mike James .25 .60
172 Ryan Gomes .25 .60
173 Josh Childress .30 .75
174 Marcus Camby .30 .75
175 Chris Kaman SP .50 1.25
176 Brandon Roy RC 2.50 6.00
177 Kyle Lowry RC 1.25 3.00
178 Tyrus Thomas RC 1.25 3.00
179 Hilton Armstrong RC 1.00 2.50
180 LaMarcus Aldridge RC 2.50 6.00
181 Ronnie Brewer RC 1.25 3.00
182 Rajon Rondo RC 4.00 10.00
183 Marcus Vinicius RC 1.00 2.50
184 Solomon Jones RC 1.00 2.50
185 Leon Powe RC 1.00 2.50
186 Shawne Williams RC 1.00 2.50
187 Craig Smith RC 1.00 2.50
187B Craig Smith Ad RC 1.00 2.50
188 Patrick O'Bryant RC 1.00 2.50
189 James Augustine RC 1.00 2.50
190 Maurice Ager RC 1.00 2.50
191 Quincy Douby RC 1.00 2.50
192 Rudy Gay RC 1.50 4.00
193 Thabo Sefolosha RC 1.25 3.00
194 Bobby Jones RC 1.00 2.50
195 Shelden Williams RC 1.00 2.50
195B Shelden Williams Ad RC 1.00 2.50
196 Mile Ilic RC 1.00 2.50
197 Jorge Garbajosa RC 1.00 2.50

Cedric Simmons RC 1.00 2.50
Josh Boone RC 1.00 2.50
Adam Morrison RC 1.25 3.00
B Adam Morrison Ad RC 1.25 3.00
Marcus Williams RC 1.00 2.50
B Marcus Williams Ad RC 1.00 2.50
2 Steve Novak RC 1.00 2.50
3 Vassilis Spanoulis RC 1.00 2.50
4 Allan Ray RC 1.00 2.50
5 David Noel RC 1.00 2.50
5 Alexander Johnson RC 1.00 2.50
Mardy Collins RC 1.00 2.50
3 Dee Brown RC 1.00 2.50
3 P.J. Tucker RC 1.00 2.50
) Paul Millsap RC 1.50 4.00
Paul Davis RC 1.00 2.50
2B Rodney Carney Ad RC 1.00 2.50
2 Rodney Carney RC 1.00 2.50
3 Saer Sene RC 1.00 2.50
Renaldo Balkman RC 1.00 2.50
5 Ryan Hollins RC 1.00 2.50
5 Will Blalock RC 1.00 2.50
Mickael Gelabale RC 1.00 2.50
3 Daniel Gibson RC 1.25 3.00
3 Hassan Adams RC 1.00 2.50
) J.J. Redick RC 1.25 3.00
Jordan Farmar RC 1.00 2.50
B Jordan Farmar Ad RC 1.00 2.50
2 Randy Foye RC 1.25 3.00
3 Shannon Brown RC 1.50 4.00
4 Sergio Rodriguez RC 1.00 2.50
5 Andrea Bargnani RC 1.50 4.00
5B Andrea Bargnani Ad RC 1.50 4.00
6 Larry Bird 3.00 8.00
7 George Gervin 1.00 2.50
3 Earl Monroe 1.00 2.50
3 Kareem Abdul-Jabbar 1.50 4.00
) Wilt Chamberlain 2.00 5.00
1 Bill Walton 1.00 2.50
2 Isiah Thomas 1.00 2.50
3 Oscar Robertson 1.00 2.50
4 Pete Maravich 6.00 15.00
5 Bill Russell 2.00 5.00
5 James Worthy 1.00 2.50
7 Rick Barry 1.00 2.50
3 Walt Frazier 1.00 2.50
3 Elgin Baylor 1.00 2.50
0 Karl Malone 1.25 3.00
1 Connie Hawkins 1.00 2.50
2 Dennis Rodman 1.50 4.00
3 John Stockton 1.50 4.00
4 Jerry West 1.25 3.00
5 Bob Cousy 1.50 4.00
6 Hakeem Olajuwon 1.25 3.00
7 John Havlicek 1.00 2.50
8 Spencer Haywood 1.00 2.50
9 Moses Malone 1.00 2.50
0 Willis Reed 1.00 2.50
1 LeBron James CL 1.25 3.00
2 Shaquille O'Neal CL .50 1.25
3 Dwyane Wade CL .60 1.50
4 Yao Ming .60 1.50
Tracy McGrady CL
5 Carmelo Anthony CL .30 .75
6 Kevin Garnett .75 2.00
Dwight Howard CL
7 Nate Robinson CL .25 .60
8 Kobe Bryant 1.00 2.50
Lakers Team CL
9 Larry Bird CL 2.00 5.00
0 Steve Nash .60 1.50
Kurt Thomas CL

2006-07 Topps Turkey Red Black

-175 BLACK: .75X TO 2X BASE HI
76-225 BLACK RC: .4X TO 1X BASE HI
26-260 BLACK: .75X TO 2X BASE HI
TATED ODDS 1:4

2006-07 Topps Turkey Red Red

ED: .4X TO 1X BASE HI
TATED ODDS ONE PER PACK

2006-07 Topps Turkey Red White

-175 WHITE: .5X TO 1.25X BASE HI
76-225 WHITE RC: .3X TO .75X BASE HI
26-260 WHITE: .5X TO 1.25X BASE HI
TATED ODDS 1:4

2006-07 Topps Turkey Red Autographs

ROUP A ODDS 1:505, GROUP B ODDS 1:186
NPRICED BLACK PRINT RUN 10 SETS
NPRICED GOLD PRINT RUN 5 SETS
NPRICED SUEDE PRINT RUN 3 SETS
3 Andrea Bargnani A 12.50 30.00
Allen Iverson A 30.00 80.00
M Adam Morrison A 6.00 15.00
G Ben Gordon A 8.00 20.00
) Chris Bosh A 15.00 40.00
) Chris Duhon B 4.00 10.00
S Cedric Simmons B 4.00 10.00
V Charlie Villanueva A 4.00 10.00
I Devin Harris A 5.00 12.00
W Dwyane Wade A 25.00 60.00
) Emeka Okafor A 5.00 12.00
A Hilton Armstrong B 4.00 10.00
W Hakim Warrick B 4.00 10.00
3 Josh Boone B 4.00 10.00
Jordan Farmar B 8.00 20.00
) Jermaine O'Neal A 5.00 12.00
Kyle Lowry B 4.00 10.00
B Larry Bird A 50.00 120.00
) Luol Deng A 5.00 12.00
R Luke Ridnour B 4.00 10.00
A Maurice Ager B 4.00 10.00
C Mardy Collins B 4.00 10.00
W Marcus Williams A 4.00 10.00
D Quincy Douby B 4.00 10.00
B Ronnie Brewer B 5.00 12.00
RC Rodney Carney B 4.00 10.00
RF Randy Foye B 6.00 15.00
RR Rajon Rondo B 20.00 50.00
SO Shaquille O'Neal A 40.00 80.00
ST Sebastian Telfair A 4.00 10.00
SW Shelden Williams A 5.00 12.00
TP Vince Carter A 15.00 40.00
ABO Andrew Bogut A 6.00 15.00
JJR J.J. Redick A 12.50 30.00
POB Patrick O'Bryant B 4.00 10.00
RBA Renaldo Balkman B 4.00 10.00
RFE Raymond Felton A 6.00 15.00
SWI Shawne Williams B 4.00 10.00
TJF T.J. Ford B 4.00 10.00
TPA Tony Parker A 8.00 20.00

2006-07 Topps Turkey Red Autographs Red

*WHITE: .5X TO 1.25X BASE HI
WHITE PRINT RUN 15 TO 50 SER.#'d SETS
AB Andrea Bargnani/25 15.00 40.00
AI Allen Iverson/25 40.00 100.00
AM Adam Morrison/25 8.00 20.00
BG Ben Gordon/25 10.00 25.00
CB Chris Bosh/25 20.00 50.00
CD Chris Duhon/99 5.00 12.00
CS Cedric Simmons/99 5.00 12.00
CV Charlie Villanueva/25 5.00 12.00
DH Devin Harris/25 6.00 15.00
DW Dwyane Wade/25 30.00 80.00
EO Emeka Okafor/25 6.00 15.00
HA Hilton Armstrong/99 5.00 12.00
HW Hakim Warrick/99 5.00 12.00
JB Josh Boone/99 5.00 12.00
JF Jordan Farmar/99 10.00 25.00
JO Jermaine O'Neal/25 6.00 15.00
KL Kyle Lowry/99 6.00 15.00
LB Larry Bird/25 60.00 150.00
LD Luol Deng/25 6.00 15.00
LR Luke Ridnour/99 5.00 12.00
MA Maurice Ager/99 5.00 12.00
MC Mardy Collins/99 5.00 12.00
MW Marcus Williams/25 5.00 12.00
QD Quincy Douby/99 5.00 12.00
RB Ronnie Brewer/99 6.00 15.00
RC Rodney Carney/99 5.00 12.00
RF Randy Foye/99 8.00 20.00
RR Rajon Rondo/99 25.00 60.00
SO Shaquille O'Neal/25 50.00 120.00
ST Sebastian Telfair/25 5.00 12.00
SW Shelden Williams/25 6.00 15.00
TP Vince Carter/25 20.00 50.00
ABO Andrew Bogut/25 8.00 20.00
JJR J.J. Redick/25 15.00 40.00
POB Patrick O'Bryant/99 5.00 12.00
RBA Renaldo Balkman/99 5.00 12.00
RFE Raymond Felton/25 8.00 20.00
SWI Shawne Williams/99 5.00 12.00
TJF T.J. Ford/99 5.00 12.00
TPA Tony Parker/25 10.00 25.00

2006-07 Topps Turkey Red Cabinet Jumbos

*GOLD: .5X TO 1.25X BASE HI
ONE PER BOX AS TOPPER
GOLD PRINT RUN 50 SER.#'d SET
UNPRICED SUEDE PRINT RUN 3 SETS
UNPRICED AUTO PRINT RUN 10 SETS
UNPRICED AUTO GOLD PRINT RUN 5 SETS
UNPRICED AUTO SUEDE PRINT RUN ONE SET
UNPRICED AUTO DUAL PRINT RUN 10 SETS
UNPRICED AUTO DUAL GOLD PRINT RUN 5 SETS
UNPRICED AUTO DUAL SUEDE PRINT RUN ONE SET
1 Chris Paul 3.00 8.00
2 Gilbert Arenas 1.50 4.00
3 Dwyane Wade 4.00 10.00
4 Joe Johnson 1.50 4.00
5 Carmelo Anthony 2.00 5.00
6 Shane Battier 1.25 3.00
7 Bruce Bowen 1.00 2.50
8 LeBron James 8.00 20.00
9 Elton Brand 1.50 4.00
10 Antawn Jamison 1.50 4.00
11 Chris Bosh 1.50 4.00
12 Dwight Howard 2.50 6.00
13 Brad Miller 1.50 4.00
14 Kirk Hinrich 1.50 4.00
15 Amare Stoudemire 1.50 4.00
16 Andrea Bargnani 2.50 6.00
17 LaMarcus Aldridge 4.00 10.00
18 Adam Morrison 2.00 5.00
19 Tyrus Thomas 2.00 5.00
20 Shelden Williams 1.50 4.00
21 Brandon Roy 4.00 10.00
22 Randy Foye 2.00 5.00
23 Rudy Gay 2.50 6.00
24 Patrick O'Bryant 1.50 4.00
25 Saer Sene 1.50 4.00
26 J.J. Redick 2.00 5.00
27 Hilton Armstrong 1.50 4.00
28 Thabo Sefolosha 2.00 5.00
29 Ronnie Brewer 2.00 5.00
30 Cedric Simmons 1.50 4.00

2006-07 Topps Turkey Red Relics

GROUP A ODDS 1:88, GROUP B ODDS 1:23
UNPRICED BLACK PRINT RUN 10 SETS
UNPRICED GOLD PRINT RUN 5 SETS
*RED: .5X TO 1.25X BASE HI
RED PRINT RUN 99 SER.#'d SETS
*WHITE: .6X TO 1.5X BASE HI
WHITE PRINT RUN 50 SER.#'d SETS
AI Allen Iverson B 3.00 8.00
AM Adam Morrison A 3.00 8.00
BG Ben Gordon B 2.50 6.00
BR Brandon Roy A 6.00 15.00
CB Chris Bosh A 2.50 6.00
CP Chris Paul A 5.00 12.00
CS Cedric Simmons B 2.50 6.00
DH Dwight Howard B 4.00 10.00
DW Dwyane Wade B 6.00 15.00
GA Gilbert Arenas B 2.50 6.00
GW Gerald Wallace A 2.50 6.00
HA Hilton Armstrong B 2.50 6.00
JB Josh Boone B 2.50 6.00
JF Jordan Farmar B 2.50 6.00
JR Jason Richardson A 2.50 6.00
JT Jason Terry A 2.00 5.00
KB Kobe Bryant B 6.00 15.00
KG Kevin Garnett A 5.00 12.00
KL Kyle Lowry B 3.00 8.00
LA LaMarcus Aldridge B 6.00 15.00
MA Maurice Ager A 2.50 6.00
MW Marcus Williams A 2.50 6.00
PP Paul Pierce A 3.00 8.00
QD Quincy Douby B 2.50 6.00
RA Ray Allen B 2.50 6.00
RB Ronnie Brewer B 3.00 8.00
RC Rodney Carney B 2.50 6.00
RF Randy Foye B 3.00 8.00
RG Rudy Gay B 4.00 10.00
RR Rajon Rondo A 8.00 20.00
SM Shawn Marion B 2.50 6.00
SO Shaquille O'Neal B 5.00 12.00
SW Shelden Williams B 2.50 6.00
TD Tim Duncan B 4.00 10.00
TM Tracy McGrady A 3.00 8.00
VC Vince Carter A 3.00 8.00
AIG Andre Iguodala A 2.50 6.00
JJR J.J. Redick B 3.00 8.00
POB Patrick O'Bryant B 2.50 6.00
SWI Shawne Williams B 2.50 6.00

2012 Topps U.S. Olympic Team

COMPLETE SET (100) 10.00 25.00
20 Sue Bird .40 1.00
46 Candace Parker .25 .60
60 Maya Moore .50 1.25
91 Seimone Augustus .25 .60

2012 Topps U.S. Olympic Team Bronze

*BRONZE: .5X TO 1.2X BASIC CARDS
STATED ODDS 1:1

2012 Topps U.S. Olympic Team Gold

*GOLD: .8X TO 2X BASIC CARDS
STATED ODDS 1:3

2012 Topps U.S. Olympic Team Silver

*SILVER: .6X TO 1.5X BASIC CARDS
STATED ODDS 1:2

2012 Topps U.S. Olympic Team Autographs

STATED ODDS 1:23
20 Sue Bird 15.00 40.00
60 Maya Moore 25.00 50.00

2012 Topps U.S. Olympic Team Autographs Bronze

*BRONZE: SAME AS BASIC AUTO
STATED ODDS 1:202
STATED PRINT RUN 50 SER.#'d SETS

2012 Topps U.S. Olympic Team Autographs Gold

*GOLD: .6X TO 1.5X BASIC CARDS
STATED ODDS 1:577
STATED PRINT RUN 15 SER.#'d SETS

2012 Topps U.S. Olympic Team Autographs Silver

*SILVER: .5X TO 1.2X BASIC CARDS
STATED ODDS 1:286
STATED PRINT RUN 30 SER.#'d SETS

2012 Topps U.S. Olympic Team Event Pins

ELPCP Candace Parker 5.00 12.00
ELPMM Maya Moore 10.00 25.00
ELPSA Seimone Augustus 5.00 12.00
ELPSB Sue Bird 8.00 20.00

2012 Topps U.S. Olympic Team Games of the XXX Olympiad

COMPLETE SET (25) 12.00 30.00
STATED ODDS 1:4
OLY3 Maya Moore 2.00 5.00

2012 Topps U.S. Olympic Team Olympic Team Patch

STATED ODDS 1:131
ULPCP Candace Parker 5.00 12.00
ULPMM Maya Moore 10.00 25.00
ULPSA Seimone Augustus 5.00 12.00
ULPSB Sue Bird 8.00 20.00

2012 Topps U.S. Olympic Team Relics

STATED ODDS 1:31
ORMM Maya Moore 8.00 20.00
ORSB Sue Bird 8.00 20.00

2012 Topps U.S. Olympic Team Relics Bronze

*BRONZE: SAME PRICE AS BASIC CARDS
STATED ODDS 1:222
STATED PRINT RUN 75 SER. #'d SETS

2012 Topps U.S. Olympic Team Relics Gold

*GOLD: .6X TO 1.5X BASIC CARDS
STATED ODDS 1:666
STATED PRINT RUN 25 SER. #'d SETS

2012 Topps U.S. Olympic Team Relics Silver

*SILVER: .5X TO 1.2X BASIC CARDS
STATED ODDS 1:333
STATED PRINT RUN 50 SER. #'d SETS

2012 Topps U.S. Olympic Team U.S. Flag Patch

STATED ODDS 1:131
FLPCP Candace Parker 5.00 12.00
FLPMM Maya Moore 10.00 25.00
FLPSA Seimone Augustus 5.00 12.00
FLPSB Sue Bird 8.00 20.00

2012 Topps U.S. Olympic Team USOC Pins

STATED ODDS 1:92
PINCP Candace Parker 5.00 12.00
PINMM Maya Moore 10.00 25.00
PINSA Seimone Augustus 5.00 12.00
PINSB Sue Bird 8.00 20.00

1996 Topps USA Women's National Team

Topps, a corporate sponsor of the USA Women's National team, issued this 24-card set featuring the core of the team that represented the United States at the Olympic Games in Atlanta. The cards were available in 8-card packs. The set consists of two cards each (a regular card [1-11] and a "Profiles" card [13-23]) of the 11 players on the team, a coach card, and a team photo card listing a complete pre-Olympics tour schedule. The cards were sold in 10-card packs for a suggested retail price of $1.29. Against a background featuring an American flag, the fronts of the regular cards display a color action cutout of each athlete in her U.S.A. Basketball uniform. The backs provide complete biographical information and collegiate statistics. The horizontal fronts of the "Profiles" cards have a color closeup and a gold foil-stamped facsimile autograph. The backs list a variety of questions and answers that provide a glimpse into the players' personal lives.

COMPLETE SET (24) 10.00 25.00
1 Jennifer Azzi 1.25 3.00
2 Ruthie Bolton 1.00 2.50
3 Teresa Edwards .75 2.00
4 Lisa Leslie 1.50 4.00
5 Rebecca Lobo 1.25 3.00
6 Katrina McClain .20 .50
7 Nikki McCray 1.25 3.00
8 Carla McGhee .20 .50
9 Dawn Staley 1.25 3.00
10 Katy Steding .20 .50
11 Sheryl Swoopes 2.00 5.00
12 Tara VanDerveer CO .20 .50
13 Jennifer Azzi PRO .60 1.50
14 Ruthie Bolton PRO .50 1.25
15 Teresa Edwards PRO .40 1.00
16 Lisa Leslie PRO .75 2.00
17 Rebecca Lobo PRO .60 1.50
18 Katrina McClain PRO .08 .25
19 Nikki McCray PRO .60 1.50
20 Carla McGhee PRO .08 .25
21 Dawn Staley PRO .60 1.50
22 Katy Steding PRO .08 .25
23 Sheryl Swoopes PRO 1.00 2.50
24 Team Photo 1.25 3.00

2001 Topps Wilkins Oversized

This oversized card was given to each fan coming through the turnstile for the 2000-01 Hawks-Clippers game. This exclusive-issued Topps card, lists Wilkins' Atlanta Hawks career stats on the back.

NNO Dominique Wilkins 2.00 5.00

2001-02 Topps Xpectations Promos

Released with the press material, this six card promo set debuts the future design of the Topps Xpectations set which was to be released in November 2001.

COMPLETE SET (6) .75 2.00
P1 Antawn Jamison .30 .75
P2 Paul Pierce .40 1.00
P3 Larry Hughes .25 .60
P4 Derek Anderson .20 .50
P5 Bonzi Wells .20 .50
P6 Wally Szczerbiak .25 .60

2001-02 Topps Xpectations

Released in November of 2001, this 151-card base set includes 101 veterans and 50 rookies. The 100 veteran cards were selected by NBA Drafts (1997-2000) and NBA Drafts (before 1997). The 50 rookie cards feature reel game footage and carry the Xpectations "Rookie Card" logo. Cards of six of the rookies have been selected to be sequentially numbered to 250. The cards are standard size and are set on borderless cards. Xpectations was issued in 10 box cases with 20 packs per box and six cards per pack which carried a suggested retail price of $6.00.

COMP.SET w/o SP's (141) 50.00 120.00
1 Baron Davis .30 .75
2 Jason Terry .30 .75
3 Paul Pierce .40 1.00
4 Ron Mercer .20 .50
5 Dirk Nowitzki .50 1.25
6 Marc Jackson .20 .50
7 Cuttino Mobley .25 .60
8 Al Harrington .25 .60
9 Keyon Dooling .20 .50
10 Mark Madsen .20 .50
11 Jumaine Jones .20 .50
12 Shawn Marion .30 .75
13 Mike Bibby .30 .75
14 Antonio Daniels .20 .50
15 Vince Carter .50 1.25
16 Stromile Swift .25 .60
17 Courtney Alexander .20 .50
18 Desmond Mason .25 .60
19 Hedo Turkoglu .30 .75
20 Speedy Claxton .20 .50
21 Lavor Postell .20 .50
22 Chauncey Billups .30 .75
23 Eddie House .20 .50
24 Maurice Taylor .20 .50
25 Lamar Odom .30 .75
26 Antawn Jamison .30 .75
27 Raef LaFrentz .20 .50
28 Marcus Fizer .20 .50
29 Chris Mihm .20 .50
30 Eddie Robinson .20 .50
31 Mark Blount .20 .50
32 DerMarr Johnson .20 .50
33 Wang Zhizhi .25 .60
34 Danny Fortson .20 .50
35 Elton Brand .30 .75
36 Anthony Carter .20 .50
37 Wally Szczerbiak .25 .60
38 Mike Miller .30 .75
39 Bonzi Wells .20 .50
40 Tim Duncan .60 1.50
41 Ruben Patterson .20 .50
42 Keon Clark .20 .50
43 Jason Williams .25 .60
44 Richard Hamilton .25 .60
45 Scott Padgett .20 .50
46 Derek Anderson .20 .50
47 Keith Van Horn .20 .50
48 Tim Thomas .20 .50
49 Jonathan Bender .20 .50
50 Tracy McGrady .50 1.25
51 Tyronn Lue .20 .50
52 Austin Croshere .20 .50
53 James Posey .20 .50
54 Mateen Cleaves .20 .50
55 Matt Harpring .25 .60
56 Calvin Booth .20 .50
57 Quentin Richardson .25 .60
58 Joel Przybilla .20 .50
59 Kenyon Martin .30 .75
60 Iakovos Tsakalidis .20 .50
61 Peja Stojakovic .30 .75
62 Shammond Williams .20 .50
63 Alvin Williams .20 .50
64 Jahidi White .20 .50
65 Morris Peterson .20 .50
66 Larry Hughes .25 .60
67 Andre Miller .25 .60
68 Jamaal Magloire .20 .50
69 Steve Francis .30 .75
70 Todd MacCulloch .20 .50
71 Rashard Lewis .30 .75
72 Michael Dickerson .20 .50
73 Nazr Mohammed .20 .50
74 Jamal Crawford .25 .60
75 Darius Miles .30 .75
76 Allen Iverson .60 1.50
77 Shaquille O'Neal .75 2.00
78 Michael Finley .30 .75
79 Antonio McDyess .25 .60
80 Jerry Stackhouse .25 .60
81 Chris Webber .30 .75
82 Eddie Jones .25 .60
83 Reggie Miller .30 .75
84 Antoine Walker .25 .60
85 Latrell Sprewell .25 .60
86 Alonzo Mourning .40 1.00
87 Jalen Rose .25 .60
88 Ray Allen .30 .75
89 Gary Payton .30 .75
90 Jason Kidd .50 1.25
91 Stephon Marbury .25 .60
92 Kobe Bryant 1.50 4.00
93 Grant Hill .40 1.00
94 Karl Malone .40 1.00
95 John Stockton .40 1.00
96 Anfernee Hardaway .50 1.25
97 Rasheed Wallace .30 .75
98 Hakeem Olajuwon .40 1.00
99 Shareef Abdur-Rahim .25 .60
100 Kevin Garnett .60 1.50
101 Kwame Brown/250 RC 6.00 15.00
102 Tyson Chandler RC 1.25 3.00
103 Pau Gasol RC 2.50 6.00
104 Eddy Curry RC 1.25 3.00
105 Jason Richardson/250 RC 12.00 30.00
106 Shane Battier/250 RC 12.00 30.00
107 Eddie Griffin RC .75 2.00
108 DeSagana Diop RC .75 2.00
109 Rodney White RC .75 2.00
110 Joe Johnson/250 RC 15.00 40.00
111 Kedrick Brown RC .75 2.00
112 Vladimir Radmanovic RC .75 2.00
113 Richard Jefferson RC 1.50 4.00
114 Troy Murphy/250 RC 10.00 25.00
115 Steven Hunter RC .75 2.00
116 Kirk Haston RC .75 2.00
117 Michael Bradley RC .75 2.00
118 Jason Collins RC .75 2.00
119 Zach Randolph/250 RC 15.00 40.00
120 Brendan Haywood RC 1.00 2.50
121 Joseph Forte RC .75 2.00
122 Jeryl Sasser RC .75 2.00
123 Brandon Armstrong RC .75 2.00
124 Gerald Wallace RC 1.25 3.00
125 Samuel Dalembert RC 1.00 2.50
126 Jamaal Tinsley RC 1.00 2.50
127 Tony Parker RC 3.00 8.00
128 Trenton Hassell RC .75 2.00
129 Gilbert Arenas RC 1.25 3.00
130 Raja Bell RC 1.00 2.50
131 Will Solomon RC .75 2.00
132 Terence Morris RC .75 2.00
133 Brian Scalabrine RC .75 2.00
134 Jeff Trepagnier RC .75 2.00
135 Damone Brown RC .75 2.00
136 Carlos Arroyo RC 6.00 15.00
137 Earl Watson RC .75 2.00
138 Jamison Brewer RC .75 2.00
139 Bobby Simmons RC .75 2.00
140 Andrei Kirilenko RC 2.00 5.00
141 Zeljko Rebraca RC .75 2.00
142 Sean Lampley RC .75 2.00
143 Loren Woods RC .75 2.00
144 Alton Ford RC .75 2.00
145 Antonis Fotsis RC .75 2.00
146 Charlie Bell RC .75 2.00
147 Ruben Boumtje-Boumtje RC .75 2.00
148 Jarron Collins RC .75 2.00
149 Kenny Satterfield RC .75 2.00
150 Alvin Jones RC .75 2.00
151 Michael Jordan 4.00 10.00

2001-02 Topps Xpectations Autographs

This 42-card insert set is randomly inserted in packs at a rate of 1:13. The set features signed cards of NBA athletes who are quickly on their way to becoming elite ranked all-stars. The cards are standard size and have solid black borders on two of its four sides. There is a color action shot in the center. The Certified Autograph Issue logo is in the lower right-hand corner and the featured player's name and team name is in the lower left-hand corner.

TXAAD Antonio Daniels 4.00 10.00
TXAAJ Antawn Jamison 5.00 12.00
TXAAM Andre Miller 4.00 10.00
TXABD Baron Davis 6.00 15.00
TXABH Brendan Haywood 5.00 12.00
TXABJ Bobby Jackson 4.00 10.00
TXACA Courtney Alexander 4.00 10.00
TXACB Chauncey Billups 6.00 15.00
TXADB Damone Brown 4.00 10.00
TXADH Donnell Harvey 4.00 10.00
TXAEB Erick Barkley 4.00 10.00
TXAEC Eddy Curry 6.00 15.00
TXAGA Gilbert Arenas 12.00 30.00
TXAGW Gerald Wallace 6.00 15.00
TXAHT Hedo Turkoglu 6.00 15.00
TXAIT Iakovos Tsakalidis 4.00 10.00
TXAJB Jonathan Bender 4.00 10.00
TXAJF Joseph Forte 4.00 10.00
TXAJO Jermaine O'Neal 6.00 15.00
TXAJT Jason Terry 5.00 12.00
TXAKB Kwame Brown 4.00 10.00
TXAKD Keyon Dooling 4.00 10.00
TXALP Lavor Postell 4.00 10.00
TXALW Loren Woods 4.00 10.00
TXAMB Mike Bibby 5.00 12.00
TXAMD Michael Doleac 4.00 10.00
TXAMJ Marc Jackson 4.00 10.00
TXAPS Peja Stojakovic 6.00 15.00
TXARH Richard Hamilton 5.00 12.00
TXARL Raef LaFrentz 4.00 10.00
TXARM Roshown McLeod 4.00 10.00
TXASB Shane Battier 8.00 20.00
TXASM Shawn Marion 5.00 12.00
TXATT Tim Thomas 4.00 10.00
TXAVR Vladimir Radmanovic 4.00 10.00
TXAZR Zach Randolph 12.50 30.00
TXAAJO Alvin Jones 4.00 10.00
TXADTM Desmond Mason 4.00 10.00
TXAETB Elton Brand 5.00 12.00
TXAJTR Jeff Trepagnier 4.00 10.00
TXAKBR Kedrick Brown 4.00 10.00

2001-02 Topps Xpectations Bowman's Best

With the cancellation of the Bowman's best brand in 2001-02, Topps inserted some of the better inserts that were slated for the Bowman's Best set. This nine card set features both jersey and autograph cards of Magic Johnson, Shaquille O'Neal, and Kareem Abdul-Jabbar.

FF1 Magic Johnson JSY 25.00 60.00
FF2 Kareem Abdul-Jabbar JSY 15.00 40.00
FF3 Shaquille O'Neal JSY 15.00 40.00
FF4 Kareem Abdul-Jabbar JSY 40.00 100.00
Magic Johnson JSY
FF5 Shaquille O'Neal JSY 30.00 80.00
Kareem Abdul-Jabbar JSY
FF6 Shaquille O'Neal JSY 60.00 120.00
Magic Johnson JSY
FF7 Kareem Abdul-Jabbar JSY 125.00 300.00
Shaquille O'Neal JSY
Magic Johnson JSY/50
FFA1 Kareem Abdul-Jabbar JSY AU/50 100.00 200.00
FFA1A Magic Johnson JSY AU/50 75.00 150.00
FFA3 Shaquille O'Neal JSY AU/50 75.00 150.00
FFA4 Kareem Abdul-Jabbar 125.00 250.00
Magic Johnson
JSY AU/25

2001-02 Topps Xpectations Changing of the Guard

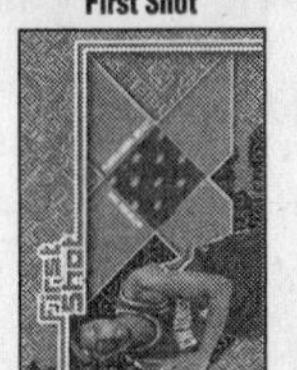

Randomly inserted in packs at a rate of 1:10, this 10-card insert set features the top 10 guards in the NBA.

COMPLETE SET (10) 8.00 20.00
CG1 Allen Iverson 1.50 4.00
CG2 Kobe Bryant 4.00 10.00
CG3 Vince Carter 1.25 3.00
CG4 Tracy McGrady 1.25 3.00
CG5 Jason Kidd 1.25 3.00
CG6 Steve Francis .75 2.00
CG7 Stephon Marbury .60 1.50
CG8 Gary Payton .75 2.00
CG9 Michael Finley .75 2.00
CG10 Baron Davis .75 2.00

2001-02 Topps Xpectations Class Challenge

Randomly inserted in packs at a rate of 1:9, this 28-card insert set is horizontally designed and measures standard size. The cards feature swatches of game-worn warm-ups from the 2000/01 NBA Rookie Challenge All-Star Weekends. The card fronts carry an "X" design with the player's name running across one arm of the "X". The Topps logo is found in the upper left-hand corner. A color action shot of the player is also featured.

CCAG Adrian Griffin 2.00 5.00
CCAM Andre Miller 2.50 6.00
CCBD Baron Davis 3.00 8.00
CCCM Cuttino Mobley 2.50 6.00
CCDM Darius Miles 2.00 5.00
CCDN Dirk Nowitzki 5.00 12.00
CCEB Elton Brand 3.00 8.00
CCJP James Posey 2.00 5.00
CCJT Jason Terry 3.00 8.00
CCJW Jason Williams 2.50 6.00
CCKM Kenyon Martin 3.00 8.00
CCLO Lamar Odom 3.00 8.00
CCMB Mike Bibby 3.00 8.00
CCMC Mateen Cleaves 2.00 5.00
CCMD Michael Dickerson 2.00 5.00
CCMJ Marc Jackson 2.00 5.00
CCMM Mike Miller 3.00 8.00
CCMO Michael Olowokandi 2.00 5.00
CCMP Morris Peterson 2.00 5.00
CCPP Paul Pierce 4.00 10.00
CCQR Quentin Richardson 2.50 6.00
CCRH Richard Hamilton 2.50 6.00
CCRL Raef LaFrentz 2.00 5.00
CCSF Steve Francis 3.00 8.00
CCSJ Stephen Jackson 2.50 6.00
CCSM Shawn Marion 3.00 8.00
CCTM Todd MacCulloch 2.00 5.00
CCWS Wally Szczerbiak 2.50 6.00

2001-02 Topps Xpectations Class Challenge Autographs

Randomly inserted in packs, this seven card set parallels the base insert set design of the Class Challenge set enhanced with authentic player autographs. Each card is sequentially numbered.

CCAEB Elton Brand/43 25.00 60.00
CCAJT Jason Terry/31 25.00 60.00
CCARH Richard Hamilton/32 25.00 60.00
CCARL Raef LaFrentz/45 8.00 20.00
CCASM Shawn Marion/31 30.00 80.00

2001-02 Topps Xpectations First Shot

Randomly inserted in packs at a rate of 1:17, this 25-card insert set features top draft picks from the 2001 NBA draft, a photo of each in their respective team's jersey, and a swatch of jersey.

FS1 Kwame Brown 2.00 5.00
FS2 Tyson Chandler 3.00 8.00
FS3 Pau Gasol 6.00 15.00
FS4 Eddy Curry 3.00 8.00
FS5 Jason Richardson 4.00 10.00
FS6 Shane Battier 4.00 10.00
FS7 Eddie Griffin 2.00 5.00
FS8 DeSagana Diop 2.00 5.00
FS9 Rodney White 2.00 5.00
FS10 Joe Johnson 5.00 12.00
FS11 Kedrick Brown 2.00 5.00
FS12 Vladimir Radmanovic 2.00 5.00
FS13 Richard Jefferson 4.00 10.00
FS14 Troy Murphy 3.00 8.00
FS15 Steven Hunter 2.00 5.00
FS16 Kirk Haston 2.00 5.00
FS17 Michael Bradley 2.00 5.00
FS18 Zach Randolph 5.00 12.00
FS19 Brendan Haywood 2.50 6.00
FS20 Joseph Forte 2.00 5.00
FS21 Jeryl Sasser 2.00 5.00
FS22 Brandon Armstrong 2.00 5.00
FS23 Primoz Brezec 2.00 5.00
FS24 Jamaal Tinsley 2.50 6.00
FS25 Tony Parker 8.00 20.00

2001-02 Topps Xpectations Forward Thinking

Randomly inserted in packs at a rate of 1:10, this 10-card insert set honors the integral position of the NBA Forward. The set is borderless and comes on standard size cards. The card design is a color action shot of the featured player with a multiple linear background. The set name, team logo, and player name are all found at the bottom of the card. The Topps logo is found in the upper left-hand corner.

COMPLETE SET (10) 8.00 20.00
FT1 Chris Webber 1.00 2.50
FT2 Kevin Garnett 2.00 5.00
FT3 Lamar Odom 1.00 2.50
FT4 Tim Duncan 2.00 5.00
FT5 Dirk Nowitzki 1.50 4.00
FT6 Karl Malone 1.25 3.00
FT7 Paul Pierce 1.25 3.00
FT8 Shawn Marion 1.00 2.50
FT9 Scottie Pippen 1.50 4.00
FT10 Darius Miles .60 1.50

2001-02 Topps Xpectations Future Features

Randomly inserted in packs at a rate of 1:31, this 10-card insert set is horizontally designed and measures standard size. The cards feature swatches of authentic NBA All-Star game-worn shooting shirts. The card fronts carry an "X" design. The Topps logo is found in the upper left-hand corner. A color action shot of the player is also featured along with his name and team logo.

FFAM Andre Miller 3.00 8.00
FFDM Darius Miles 2.50 6.00
FFDN Dirk Nowitzki 6.00 15.00
FFEB Elton Brand 4.00 10.00
FFJT Jason Terry 4.00 10.00
FFPP Paul Pierce 5.00 12.00
FFRH Richard Hamilton 3.00 8.00
FFRW Rasheed Wallace 4.00 10.00
FFSF Steve Francis 4.00 10.00
FFSM Shawn Marion 4.00 10.00

2001-02 Topps Xpectations Future Features Autographs

Randomly inserted in packs at a rate of 1:812, this 5-card autographed parallel insert set is horizontally designed and measures standard size. The cards feature swatches of authentic NBA All-Star game-worn shooting shirts. The card fronts carry an "X" design. The Topps logo is found in the upper left-hand corner. A color action shot of the player is also featured along with his name and team logo. Each card is sequentially numbered.

FFAEB Elton Brand/42 20.00 50.00
FFAJT Jason Terry/31 20.00 50.00
FFARH Richard Hamilton/32 25.00 60.00
FFASM Shawn Marion/31 40.00 80.00

2001-02 Topps Xpectations In The Center

This six-card insert set is randomly inserted in packs at a rate of 1:17. The standard size cards are borderless and pay tribute to legendary NBA centers. The cards feature a center court design with a color action shot of the featured player "In the Center". The player name and team name are found at the bottom and the Topps logo is found in the upper left-hand corner.

COMPLETE SET (6) 4.00 10.00
IC1 Shaquille O'Neal 2.50 6.00
IC2 Alonzo Mourning 1.25 3.00
IC3 Jermaine O'Neal 1.00 2.50
IC4 Hakeem Olajuwon 1.25 3.00
IC5 David Robinson 1.50 4.00
IC6 Dikembe Mutombo 1.00 2.50

2002-03 Topps Xpectations

Released in November 2002, Topps Xpectations was issued as a 178-card set divided up into 100 base cards, 53 Rookie cards, where card numbers 134-153 are sequentially numbered to 500, and 24 Xceeding Xpectations cards (154-178) which were inserted one in 14 packs and are sequentially numbered to 750. All base cards feature a colored background with an "X" behind the player photo and are highlighted with gold foil. The Xceeding Xpectations cards have a true life background inside the "X" and white around it. Xpectations was packaged in 20-pack boxes where each pack contained five cards and carried a suggested retail price of $6.00.

COMPLETE SET (178) 125.00 300.00
COMP.SET w/o SP's (100) 10.00 25.00
1 Darius Miles .15 .40
2 Jason Williams .20 .50
3 Speedy Claxton .15 .40
4 Eduardo Najera .15 .40
5 Chris Mihm .15 .40
6 Eddie Robinson .15 .40
7 Lee Nailon .15 .40
8 Joseph Forte .15 .40
9 Jason Terry .20 .50
10 Vince Carter .40 1.00
11 Matt Harpring .20 .50
12 Bonzi Wells .15 .40
13 Mike Bibby .25 .60
14 Jerome James .15 .40
15 Morris Peterson .15 .40
16 Jarron Collins .15 .40
17 Brendan Haywood .15 .40
18 Dermarr Johnson .15 .40
19 Kirk Haston .15 .40
20 Paul Pierce .30 .75
21 Eddy Curry .20 .50
22 Ricky Davis .20 .50
23 James Posey .15 .40
24 Zeljko Rebraca .15 .40
25 Jason Richardson .25 .60
26 Ron Artest .25 .60
27 Jonathan Bender .15 .40
28 Elton Brand .25 .60
29 Stromile Swift .15 .40
30 Steve Francis .25 .60
31 Devean George .15 .40
32 Eddie House .15 .40
33 Loren Woods .15 .40
34 Richard Jefferson .25 .60
35 Mike Miller .25 .60
36 Joe Johnson .25 .60
37 Zach Randolph .25 .60
38 Peja Stojakovic .25 .60
39 Predrag Drobnjak .15 .40
40 Kwame Brown .15 .40
41 DeShawn Stevenson .15 .40
42 Desmond Mason .20 .50
43 Stephen Jackson .20 .50
44 Ruben Patterson .15 .40
45 Samuel Dalembert .15 .40
46 Pat Garrity .15 .40
47 Jason Collins .15 .40
48 Marc Jackson .15 .40
49 Rafer Alston .15 .40
50 Shawn Marion .25 .60
51 Joel Przybilla .15 .40
52 Shane Battier .25 .60
53 Quentin Richardson .20 .50
54 Jamaal Tinsley .15 .40
55 Cuttino Mobley .20 .50
56 Antawn Jamison .25 .60
57 Chucky Atkins .15 .40
58 Raef Lafrentz .15 .40
59 Jumaine Jones .15 .40
60 Dirk Nowitzki .40 1.00
61 Marcus Fizer .15 .40
62 Kedrick Brown .15 .40
63 Nazr Mohammed .15 .40
64 Jamaal Magloire .15 .40
65 Tyson Chandler .20 .50
66 Andre Miller .20 .50
67 Wang Zhizhi .15 .40
68 Mengke Bateer .15 .40
69 Gilbert Arenas .25 .60
70 Baron Davis .25 .60
71 Lamar Odom .25 .60
72 Mark Madsen .15 .40
73 Pau Gasol .30 .75
74 Anthony Carter .15 .40
75 Wally Szczerbiak .20 .50
76 Todd MacCulloch .15 .40
77 Steven Hunter .15 .40
78 Iakovos Tsakalidis .15 .40
79 Ruben Boumtje-Boumtje .15 .40
80 Gerald Wallace .25 .60
81 Vladimir Radmanovic .15 .40
82 Keon Clark .15 .40
83 Andrei Kirilenko .25 .60
84 Richard Hamilton .20 .50
85 Trenton Hassell .15 .40
86 Donnell Harvey .15 .40
87 Rodney White .15 .40
88 Troy Murphy .25 .60
89 Terence Morris .15 .40
90 Al Harrington .20 .50
91 Michael Redd .25 .60
92 Kenyon Martin .25 .60
93 Lavor Postell .15 .40
94 Jeryl Sasser .15 .40
95 Hedo Turkoglu .25 .60
96 Tony Parker .30 .75
97 Rashard Lewis .25 .60
98 Michael Bradley .15 .40
99 Courtney Alexander .15 .40
100 Eddie Griffin .15 .40
101 Yao Ming RC 2.50 6.00
102 Dan Gadzuric RC .75 2.00
103 Mike Dunleavy RC 1.00 2.50
104 Drew Gooden RC 1.25 3.00
105 Nikoloz Tskitishvili RC .75 2.00
106 Roger Mason RC .75 2.00
107 Nene Hilario RC 1.00 2.50
108 Chris Wilcox RC .75 2.00
109 Rod Grizzard RC .75 2.00
110 Chris Owens RC .75 2.00
111 Jared Jeffries RC .75 2.00
112 Efthimios Rentzias RC .75 2.00
113 Marcus Haislip RC .75 2.00
114 Fred Jones RC .75 2.00
115 Bostjan Nachbar RC .75 2.00
116 Jiri Welsch RC .75 2.00
117 Jannero Pargo RC .75 2.00
118 Curtis Borchardt RC .75 2.00
119 Ryan Humphrey RC .75 2.00
120 Raul Lopez RC .75 2.00
121 Cezary Trybanski RC .75 2.00
122 Predrag Savovic RC .75 2.00
123 Tayshaun Prince RC 1.00 2.50
124 Frank Williams RC .75 2.00
125 John Salmons RC 1.00 2.50
126 Chris Jefferies RC .75 2.00
127 Luke Recker RC .75 2.00
128 Tamar Slay RC .75 2.00
129 Matt Barnes RC 1.00 2.50
130 Rasual Butler RC .75 2.00
131 Vincent Yarbrough RC .75 2.00
132 Junior Harrington RC .75 2.00
133 Carlos Boozer RC 1.50 4.00
134 DaJuan Wagner/500 RC 2.50 6.00
135 Jay Williams/500 RC 3.00 8.00
136 Amare Stoudemire/500 RC 6.00 15.00
137 Caron Butler/500 RC 4.00 10.00
138 Melvin Ely/500 RC 2.50 6.00
139 Juan Dixon/500 RC 3.00 8.00
140 Kareem Rush/500 RC 2.50 6.00
141 Qyntel Woods/500 RC 2.50 6.00
142 Casey Jacobsen/500 RC 2.50 6.00
143 Robert Archibald/500 RC 2.50 6.00
144 Tito Maddox/500 RC 2.50 6.00
145 Ronald Murray/500 RC 2.50 6.00
146 Sam Clancy/500 RC 2.50 6.00
147 Dan Dickau/500 RC 2.50 6.00
148 Mehmet Okur/500 RC 2.50 6.00
149 Marko Jaric/500 2.50 6.00
150 Gordan Giricek/500 RC 2.50 6.00
151 Manu Ginobili/500 RC 6.00 15.00
152 J.R. Bremer/500 RC 2.50 6.00
153 Corsley Edwards/500 RC 2.50 6.00
154 Michael Jordan XX 10.00 25.00
155 Allen Iverson XX 1.50 4.00
156 Shaquille O'Neal XX 2.50 6.00
157 Tim Duncan XX 2.00 5.00
158 Tracy McGrady XX 1.50 4.00
159 Kevin Garnett XX 2.00 5.00
160 Chris Webber XX 1.00 2.50
161 Alonzo Mourning XX 1.25 3.00
162 Antoine Walker XX .75 2.00
163 Latrell Sprewell XX .75 2.00
164 Eddie Jones XX .75 2.00
165 Kobe Bryant XX 5.00 12.00
166 Allan Houston XX .75 2.00
167 Ray Allen XX 1.00 2.50
168 Gary Payton XX 1.00 2.50
169 Antonio McDyess XX .75 2.00
170 Jason Kidd XX 1.50 4.00
171 Jerry Stackhouse XX .75 2.00
172 Stephon Marbury XX .75 2.00
173 Karl Malone XX 1.25 3.00
174 Reggie Miller XX 1.00 2.50
175 Shareef Abdur-Rahim XX .75 2.00
176 Rasheed Wallace XX 1.00 2.50
177 John Stockton XX 1.25 3.00
178 Grant Hill XX 1.25 3.00

2002-03 Topps Xpectations Parallel

Randomly inserted at the rate of one per pack, this 178-card set parallels the base set enhanced with a thicker-point card stock. These cards are noticably thicker by three times over the base cards. These cards also act as a decoy to prevent the searching of packs for memorabilia cards.

*1-100 STARS: .6X TO 1.5X BASE CARD HI
*101-133 RCs: .6X TO 1.5X BASE CARD HI
*134-153 RCs: .2X TO .5X BASE CARD HI
*154-178 STARS: .15X TO .4X BASE CARD HI

2002-03 Topps Xpectations Parallel Xtra

Randomly inserted in packs, this 178-card set parallels the base set enhanced with a silver background instead of the base card bronze. Each card is thicker than the base card and is sequentially numbered to 99 on the back.

*1-100 STARS: 6X TO 15X BASE CARD HI
*RC's: 1.5X TO 4X BASE CARD HI
*134-153 RCs: .75X TO 2X BASE CARD HI
*154-178 STARS: 1.5X TO 4X BASE CARD HI

2002-03 Topps Xpectations Autographs

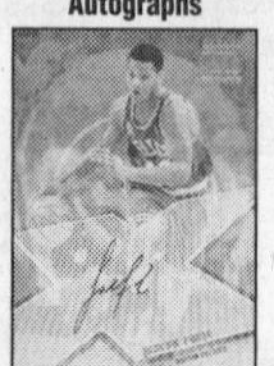

Xpectations autographs were divided up into five different groups and were inserted at the following rates: Group A at one in 177 packs, Group B at one in 312 packs, Group C at one in 42 packs, Group D at one in 412 packs and Group E at one in 332 packs. Each card places a full color player action photo in the background with the lower half of the card faded in an X shape so the autograph stands out. All cards are enahanced with the Topps Certified Autograph Issue stamp and gold foil highlights.

XAAH Al Harrington C 4.00 10.00
XACM Corey Maggette E 4.00 10.00
XACBC Curtis Borchardt E 4.00 10.00
XACBO Carlos Boozer C 8.00 20.00
XADB Damone Brown A 4.00 10.00
XADG Drew Gooden A 6.00 15.00
XADH Donnell Harvey A 4.00 10.00
XADW DaJuan Wagner C 4.00 10.00
XAEC Eddy Curry C 4.00 10.00
XAFW Frank Williams B 4.00 10.00
XAHT Hedo Turkoglu E 5.00 12.00
XAJB Jonathan Bender B 4.00 10.00
XAJF Joseph Forte E 4.00 10.00
XAJJ Joe Johnson A 8.00 20.00
XAJT Iakovos Tsakalidis A 4.00 10.00
XAJJE Jared Jeffries C 4.00 10.00
XAJTR Jeff Trepagnier A 4.00 10.00
XAKBR Kedrick Brown C 4.00 10.00
XALW Loren Woods A 4.00 10.00
XAMD Mike Dunleavy C 5.00 12.00
XAMJ Marc Jackson A 4.00 10.00
XANT Nikoloz Tskitishvili C 4.00 10.00
XASB Shane Battier C 5.00 12.00
XASM Shawn Marion A 6.00 15.00
XATD Tim Duncan B 75.00 150.00
XATM Troy Murphy C 4.00 10.00
XATT Tim Thomas A 4.00 10.00
XAVY Vincent Yarbrough C 4.00 10.00
XAYM Yao Ming C 12.50 30.00
XAZR Zach Randolph D 5.00 12.00

2002-03 Topps Xpectations Class Challenge Relics

Xpectations Class Challenge Relics was divided up into four different groups and inserted as follows: Group A at one in 298 packs, Group B at one in 30 packs and group C and D combined at one per box. The set showcases young NBA talent and places a portrait style photograph on the left and a swatch of game-worn memorabilia on the right. Brandon Haywood and Shane Battier signed versions of these cards that were inserted at the rate of one in 3804.

AUTO's NOT PRICED DUE TO SCARCITY
CCAK Andrei Kirilenko D 3.00 8.00
CCBH Brendan Haywood D 2.00 5.00
CCCM Chris Mihm D 2.00 5.00
CCDM Darius Miles D 2.00 5.00
CCJR Jason Richardson D 3.00 8.00
CCKM Kenyon Martin D 3.00 8.00
CCLN Lee Nailon D 2.00 5.00
CCMF Marcus Fizer D 2.00 5.00
CCMM Mike Miller D 3.00 8.00
CCPG Pau Gasol C 4.00 10.00
CCQR Quentin Richardson C 2.50 6.00
CCSB Shane Battier A 3.00 8.00
CCTP Tony Parker B 4.00 10.00
CCZR Zeljko Rebraca D 2.00 5.00

2002-03 Topps Xpectations First Shot Relics

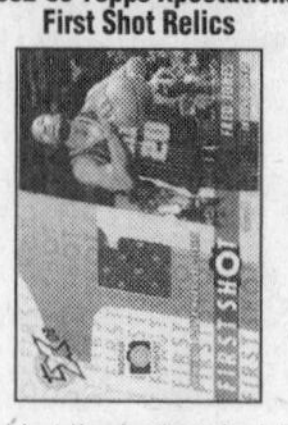

Randomly inserted in packs at the rate of one in 10, this 25-card set places a full-color action photo of the player on the right and a swatch of jersey worn at the NBA Photo Shoot on the left. Background colors on the left side of the card are white and gold.

FSAS Amare Stoudemire 8.00 20.00
FSCB Carlos Boozer 6.00 15.00
FSCB Caron Butler 5.00 12.00
FSCW Chris Wilcox 3.00 8.00
FSCJA Casey Jacobsen 3.00 8.00
FSCJE Chris Jefferies 3.00 8.00
FSDW DaJuan Wagner 3.00 8.00
FSDGO Drew Gooden 5.00 12.00
FSFJ Fred Jones 3.00 8.00
FSJD Juan Dixon 4.00 10.00
FSJJ Jared Jeffries 3.00 8.00
FSJS John Salmons 4.00 10.00
FSKR Kareem Rush 3.00 8.00
FSMD Mike Dunleavy 4.00 10.00
FSME Melvin Ely 3.00 8.00
FSMH Marcus Haislip 3.00 8.00
FSNH Nene Hilario 4.00 10.00
FSNT Nikoloz Tskitishvili 3.00 8.00
FSPS Predrag Savovic 3.00 8.00
FSQW Qyntel Woods 3.00 8.00
FSRH Ryan Humphrey 3.00 8.00
FSSC Sam Clancy 3.00 8.00
FSSL Steve Logan 3.00 8.00
FSTP Tayshaun Prince 4.00 10.00
FSVY Vincent Yarbrough 3.00 8.00

2002-03 Topps Xpectations Future Features Relics

Inserted overall at the rate of one in 40, this 15-card set places a full-color player photo on the right of the card and a swatch of game-worn material on the left. The background is composed of different color circles coming from around the player photo.

FFAM Andre Miller C 2.50 6.00
FFBH Brendan Haywood C 2.00 5.00
FFDN Dirk Nowitzki A 5.00 12.00
FFGW Gerald Wallace C 3.00 8.00
FFJJ Joe Johnson A 3.00 8.00
FFMM Mike Miller C 3.00 8.00
FFPP Paul Pierce C 4.00 10.00
FFPS Peja Stojakovic C 3.00 8.00
FFQR Quentin Richardson B 2.50 6.00
FFRL Raef LaFrentz A 2.00 5.00
FFSF Steve Francis A 3.00 8.00
FFSM Stephon Marbury C 2.50 6.00
FFSN Steve Nash A 4.00 10.00
FFSDM Shawn Marion C 3.00 8.00
FFWS Wally Szczerbiak C 2.50 6.00

2002-03 Topps Xpectations Future Features Relics Autographs

Inserted in packs at the rate of one in 1259, this five card set parallels the design of the Xpectations Future Features Relics set enhanced with authentic player autographs.

FFAGW Gerald Wallace 10.00 25.00
FFAJJ Joe Johnson 10.00 25.00
FFAPS Peja Stojakovic 30.00 60.00

2002-03 Topps Xpectations Xtra Threads Relics

Inserted in packs overall at the rate of one in 25, this 16-card set places full color player action photography on the right side of the card and an "X" shaped swatch of memorabilia on the left. Background colors are set to match the featured player's team colors.

XTAH Anfernee Hardaway C 5.00 12.00
XTAI Allen Iverson C 5.00 12.00
XTAHO Allan Houston A 2.50 6.00
XTCW Chris Webber C 3.00 8.00
XTGR Glenn Robinson C 2.50 6.00
XTJK Jason Kidd C 5.00 12.00
XTJO Jermaine O'Neal C 3.00 8.00
XTMJ Michael Finley C 3.00 8.00
XTMO Michael Olowokandi C 2.00 5.00
XTNV Nick Van Exel C 2.50 6.00
XTRA Ray Allen C 3.00 8.00
XTSN Steve Nash C 4.00 10.00
XTSO Shaquille O'Neal C 8.00 20.00
XTTD Tim Duncan C 6.00 15.00
XTTG Tom Gugliotta C 2.00 5.00
XTTM Tracy McGrady B 5.00 12.00

2010-11 Totally Certified

COMP.SET w/o RCs (150) 40.00 100.00
1-150 PRINT RUN 1849 SER.#'d SETS
JSY AU RC PRINT RUN 575 TO 599 SETS
UNPRICED BLACK PRINT RUN ONE SET
UNPRICED GREEN PRINT RUN 5 SETS
1 Andre Iguodala .75 2.00
2 Elton Brand .75 2.00
3 Jrue Holiday .75 2.00
4 Thaddeus Young .50 1.25
5 D.J. Augustin .60 1.50
6 Boris Diaw .60 1.50
7 Gerald Henderson .50 1.25
8 Stephen Jackson .60 1.50
9 Brandon Jennings .75 2.00
10 Andrew Bogut .75 2.00
11 John Salmons .75 2.00
12 Corey Maggette .60 1.50
13 Luc Mbah a Moute .50 1.25
14 Derrick Rose 2.50 6.00
15 Carlos Boozer .75 2.00
16 Luol Deng .75 2.00
17 Joakim Noah .75 2.00
18 Taj Gibson .60 1.50
19 Antawn Jamison .75 2.00
20 Daniel Gibson .60 1.50
21 Baron Davis .75 2.00
22 Anderson Varejao .60 1.50
23 Paul Pierce 1.00 2.50
24 Rajon Rondo 1.00 2.50
25 Kevin Garnett 1.50 4.00
26 Shaquille O'Neal 1.50 4.00
27 Ray Allen .75 2.00
28 Troy Murphy .50 1.25
29 Blake Griffin 2.00 5.00
30 DeAndre Jordan .75 2.00
31 Eric Gordon .75 2.00
32 Ryan Gomes .50 1.25
33 Chris Kaman .60 1.50
34 Shane Battier .60 1.50
35 Marc Gasol .75 2.00
36 Zach Randolph .60 1.50
37 Rudy Gay .75 2.00
38 O.J. Mayo .75 2.00
39 Joe Johnson .75 2.00
40 Josh Smith .75 2.00
41 Al Horford .60 1.50
42 Jamal Crawford .60 1.50
43 Kirk Hinrich .75 2.00
44 Dwyane Wade 1.50 4.00
45 LeBron James 4.00 10.00
46 Chris Bosh .75 2.00
47 Eddie House .50 1.25
48 Mike Bibby .60 1.50
49 Chris Paul 1.25 3.00
50 David West .75 2.00
51 Trevor Ariza .50 1.25
52 Emeka Okafor .75 2.00
53 Jarrett Jack .60 1.50
54 Al Jefferson .75 2.00
55 Devin Harris .75 2.00
56 Andrei Kirilenko .60 1.50
57 Paul Millsap .60 1.50
58 Mehmet Okur .50 1.25
59 Tyreke Evans 1.00 2.50
60 Omri Casspi .50 1.25
61 Samuel Dalembert .50 1.25
62 Marcus Thornton .75 2.00
63 Beno Udrih .50 1.25
64 Amare Stoudemire .75 2.00
65 Carmelo Anthony 1.00 2.50
66 Chauncey Billups .75 2.00
67 Toney Douglas .50 1.25
68 Ronny Turiaf .50 1.25
69 Kobe Bryant 4.00 10.00
70 Pau Gasol .75 2.00
71 Ron Artest .75 2.00
72 Lamar Odom .75 2.00
73 Derek Fisher .60 1.50
74 Matt Barnes .50 1.25
75 Dwight Howard 1.25 3.00
76 Jameer Nelson .60 1.50
77 Gilbert Arenas .75 2.00
78 J.J. Redick .75 2.00
79 Hedo Turkoglu .75 2.00
80 Dirk Nowitzki 1.00 2.50
81 Caron Butler .75 2.00
82 Shawn Marion .75 2.00
83 Jason Terry .60 1.50
84 Tyson Chandler .60 1.50
85 Jason Kidd .75 2.00
86 Deron Williams .75 2.00
87 Brook Lopez .75 2.00
88 Anthony Morrow .50 1.25
89 Sasha Vujacic .50 1.25
90 Travis Outlaw .60 1.50
91 Nene .60 1.50
92 Raymond Felton .60 1.50
93 Chris Andersen .75 2.00
94 Danilo Gallinari .75 2.00
95 Al Harrington .60 1.50
96 Danny Granger .75 2.00
97 Darren Collison .75 2.00
98 Mike Dunleavy .50 1.25
99 T.J. Ford .50 1.25
100 Jeff Foster .50 1.25
101 Ben Gordon .75 2.00
102 Richard Hamilton .60 1.50
103 Tracy McGrady .75 2.00
104 Tayshaun Prince .75 2.00
105 Rodney Stuckey .75 2.00
106 DeMar DeRozan .75 2.00
107 Jose Calderon .60 1.50
108 Andrea Bargnani .60 1.50
109 Leandro Barbosa .60 1.50
110 Linas Kleiza .50 1.25
111 Kevin Martin .75 2.00
112 Luis Scola .60 1.50
113 Goran Dragic .75 2.00
114 Chase Budinger .50 1.25
115 Kyle Lowry .60 1.50
116 Tim Duncan 1.25 3.00
117 Tony Parker .75 2.00
118 Manu Ginobili .75 2.00
119 Richard Jefferson .75 2.00
120 DeJuan Blair .60 1.50
121 Steve Nash .75 2.00
122 Grant Hill 1.00 2.50
123 Channing Frye .60 1.50
124 Aaron Brooks .50 1.25
125 Vince Carter 1.00 2.50
126 Kevin Durant 2.50 6.00
127 Russell Westbrook 1.00 2.50
128 Serge Ibaka 1.00 2.50
129 James Harden 1.00 2.50
130 Kendrick Perkins .60 1.50
131 Kevin Love 1.00 2.50
132 Michael Beasley .75 2.00
133 Jonny Flynn .50 1.25
134 Anthony Randolph .60 1.50
135 Darko Milicic .50 1.25
136 LaMarcus Aldridge .75 2.00
137 Brandon Roy .75 2.00
138 Andre Miller .60 1.50
139 Rudy Fernandez .60 1.50
140 Marcus Camby .50 1.25
141 Monta Ellis .75 2.00
142 Stephen Curry 1.00 2.50
143 David Lee .60 1.50
144 Al Thornton .60 1.50
145 Dorell Wright .50 1.25
146 Josh Howard .60 1.50
147 Nick Young .60 1.50
148 JaVale McGee .60 1.50
149 Rashard Lewis .60 1.50
150 Yi Jianlian .60 1.50
151 John Wall/599 JSY AU RC 50.00 125.00
152 DeMarcus Cousins/593 JSY AU RC15.00 40.00
153 Quincy Pondexter/585 JSY AU RC5.00 12.00
154 Gordon Hayward/579 JSY AU RC10.00 25.00
155 Al-Farouq Aminu/596 JSY AU RC5.00 12.00
156 Ed Davis/599 JSY AU RC 6.00 15.00
157 Greivis Vasquez/599 JSY AU RC 6.00 15.00
158 Ekpe Udoh/599 JSY AU RC 5.00 12.00
159 Damion James/599 JSY AU RC 5.00 12.00
160 Landry Fields/599 JSY AU RC 8.00 20.00
161 Greg Monroe/599 JSY AU RC 10.00 25.00
162 Cole Aldrich/599 JSY AU RC 5.00 12.00
163 Evan Turner/599 JSY AU RC 10.00 25.00
164 Luke Babbitt/597 JSY AU RC 5.00 12.00
165 Derrick Favors/599 JSY AU RC 10.00 25.00
166 Xavier Henry/599 JSY AU RC 6.00 15.00
167 Jordan Crawford/595 JSY AU RC8.00 20.00
168 Larry Sanders/583 JSY AU RC 5.00 12.00
169 Wesley Johnson/599 JSY AU RC8.00 20.00
170 Eric Bledsoe/599 JSY AU RC 8.00 20.00
171 Avery Bradley/575 JSY AU RC 10.00 25.00
172 Daniel Orton/599 JSY AU RC 5.00 12.00
173 Paul George/599 JSY AU RC 12.00 30.00
174 James Anderson/599 JSY AU RC5.00 12.00
175 Elliot Williams/599 JSY AU RC 5.00 12.00
176 Dominique Jones/599 JSY AU RC5.00 12.00
177 Dexter Pittman/599 JSY AU RC 5.00 12.00
178 Lazar Hayward/599 JSY AU RC 5.00 12.00
179 Trevor Booker/599 JSY AU RC 5.00 12.00
180 Luke Harangody/599 JSY AU RC 5.00 12.00
181 Patrick Patterson/599 JSY AU RC8.00 20.00
182 Hassan Whiteside/565 JSY AU RC5.00 12.00
183 Willie Warren/599 JSY AU RC 5.00 12.00
184 Terrico White/599 JSY AU RC 5.00 12.00
185 Andy Rautins/599 JSY AU RC 5.00 12.00

2010-11 Totally Certified Blue

*BLUE: .75X TO 2X BASE HI
STATED PRINT RUN 299 SER.#'d SETS
122 Grant Hill 4.00 10.00

2010-11 Totally Certified Blue Autographs

*BLUE RC AUTOGRAPHS: .5X TO 1.25X BASE HI
STATED PRINT RUN 32 TO 49 SER.#'d SETS
151 John Wall JSY AU/49 75.00 200.00
152 DeMarcus Cousins JSY AU/49 25.00 60.00
163 Evan Turner JSY AU/49 15.00 40.00
167 Jordan Crawford JSY AU/49 12.00 30.00

2010-11 Totally Certified Blue Materials

*BLUE MATERIALS: 2X TO 5X BASE HI
STATED PRINT RUN 49 TO 99 SER.#'d SETS
45 LeBron James/99 12.00 30.00
69 Kobe Bryant/99 12.00 30.00
122 Grant Hill/99 10.00 25.00
126 Kevin Durant/99 10.00 25.00

2010-11 Totally Certified Gold

*GOLD: 6X TO 15X BASE HI
STATED PRINT RUN 25 SER.#'d SETS
14 Derrick Rose 50.00 125.00
26 Shaquille O'Neal 30.00 80.00
29 Blake Griffin 40.00 100.00
45 LeBron James 75.00 200.00
69 Kobe Bryant 100.00 225.00
122 Grant Hill 20.00 50.00
126 Kevin Durant 50.00 125.00
127 Russell Westbrook 20.00 50.00

2010-11 Totally Certified Gold Autographs

*GOLD RC AUTOGRAPHS: 1.25X TO 3X BASE HI
STATED PRINT RUN 10 TO 25 SER.#'d SETS
SOME UNPRICED DUE TO SCARCITY
1 Andre Iguodala/25 6.00 15.00
3 Jrue Holiday/25 10.00 25.00
5 D.J. Augustin/25 6.00 15.00
6 Boris Diaw/25 6.00 15.00
7 Gerald Henderson/25 6.00 15.00
8 Stephen Jackson/25 6.00 15.00
9 Brandon Jennings/25 12.50 30.00
10 Andrew Bogut/25 15.00 40.00
15 Carlos Boozer/25 10.00 25.00
17 Joakim Noah/25 15.00 40.00
18 Taj Gibson/25 10.00 25.00
19 Antawn Jamison/25 6.00 15.00
20 Daniel Gibson/25 6.00 15.00
21 Baron Davis/25 6.00 15.00
23 Paul Pierce/25 40.00 100.0
24 Rajon Rondo/25 20.00 50.0
27 Ray Allen/25 50.00 120.0
29 Blake Griffin/25 125.00 250.0
31 Eric Gordon/25 10.00 25.0
32 Ryan Gomes/25 6.00 15.0
34 Shane Battier/25 6.00 15.0
35 Marc Gasol/25 12.00 30.0
36 Zach Randolph/25 12.00 30.0
39 Joe Johnson/25 10.00 25.0
40 Josh Smith/25 8.00 20.0
41 Al Horford/25 6.00 15.0
46 Chris Bosh/25 20.00 50.0
48 Mike Bibby/25 10.00 25.0
51 Trevor Ariza/25 6.00 15.0
52 Emeka Okafor/25 6.00 15.0
54 Al Jefferson/25 6.00 15.0
55 Devin Harris/25 6.00 15.0
56 Andrei Kirilenko/25 6.00 15.0
59 Tyreke Evans/25 15.00 40.0
60 Omri Casspi/25 6.00 15.0
61 Samuel Dalembert/25 6.00 15.0
62 Marcus Thornton/25 6.00 15.0
63 Beno Udrih/25 6.00 15.0
66 Chauncey Billups/25 10.00 25.0
67 Toney Douglas/25 6.00 15.0
69 Kobe Bryant/25 250.00 450.0
72 Lamar Odom/25 12.00 30.0
73 Derek Fisher/25 15.00 40.0
78 J.J. Redick/25 10.00 25.0
79 Hedo Turkoglu/25 6.00 15.0
81 Caron Butler/25 8.00 20.0
85 Jason Kidd/25 30.00 80.0
86 Deron Williams/25 12.50 30.0
87 Brook Lopez/25 10.00 25.0
93 Chris Andersen/25 30.00 80.0
94 Danilo Gallinari/25 12.50 30.0
96 Danny Granger/25 8.00 20.0
97 Darren Collison/25 6.00 15.0
98 Mike Dunleavy/25 6.00 15.0
99 T.J. Ford/25 6.00 15.0
101 Ben Gordon/25 10.00 25.0
102 Richard Hamilton/25 12.50 30.0
106 DeMar DeRozan/25 8.00 20.0
108 Andrea Bargnani/25 8.00 20.0
113 Goran Dragic/25 15.00 40.0
114 Chase Budinger/25 6.00 15.0
117 Tony Parker/25 10.00 25.0
120 DeJuan Blair/25 6.00 15.0
122 Grant Hill/25 150.00 300.0
123 Channing Frye/25 6.00 15.0
124 Aaron Brooks/25 6.00 15.0
125 Vince Carter/25 25.00 60.0
127 Russell Westbrook/25 25.00 60.0
128 Serge Ibaka/25 12.50 30.0
129 James Harden/25 15.00 40.0
130 Kendrick Perkins/25 8.00 20.0
131 Kevin Love/25 15.00 40.0
132 Michael Beasley/25 10.00 25.0
133 Jonny Flynn/25 6.00 15.0
135 Darko Milicic/25 6.00 15.0
136 LaMarcus Aldridge/25 12.00 30.0
137 Brandon Roy/25 10.00 25.0
138 Andre Miller/25 8.00 20.0
139 Rudy Fernandez/25 6.00 15.0
140 Marcus Camby/25 10.00 25.0
141 Monta Ellis/25 15.00 40.0
142 Stephen Curry/25 20.00 50.0
143 David Lee/25 6.00 15.0
144 Al Thornton/25 6.00 15.0
146 Josh Howard/25 6.00 15.0
148 JaVale McGee/25 6.00 15.0
152 DeMarcus Cousins JSY AU/25 100.00 250.0
154 Gordon Hayward JSY AU/25 30.00 80.0
155 Al-Farouq Aminu JSY AU/25 30.00 80.0
161 Greg Monroe JSY AU/25 40.00 100.0
163 Evan Turner JSY AU/25 60.00 150.0
165 Derrick Favors JSY AU/25 40.00 100.0
167 Jordan Crawford JSY AU/25 40.00 100.0
173 Paul George JSY AU/25 60.00 150.0

2010-11 Totally Certified Gold Materials Prime

*GOLD MATERIALS: 6X TO 15X BASE HI
STATED PRINT RUN 3 TO 25 SER.#'d SETS
SOME UNPRICED DUE TO SCARCITY
14 Derrick Rose/25 60.00 150.0
44 Dwyane Wade/25 40.00 100.0
49 Chris Paul/25 25.00 60.0
93 Chris Andersen/25 15.00 40.0
122 Grant Hill/25 50.00 125.0
126 Kevin Durant/25 40.00 100.0

2010-11 Totally Certified Red

*RED: .5X TO 1.25X BASE HI
STATED PRINT RUN 499 SER.#'d SETS

2010-11 Totally Certified Red Autographs

*RED RC AUTOGRAPHS: .4X TO 1X BASE HI
STATED PRINT RUN 3 TO 99 SER.#'d SETS
SOME UNPRICED DUE TO SCARCITY
1 Andre Iguodala/25 6.00 15.0
3 Jrue Holiday/49 10.00 25.0
5 D.J. Augustin/49 4.00 10.0
6 Boris Diaw/49 4.00 10.0
7 Gerald Henderson/99 4.00 10.0
8 Stephen Jackson/49 4.00 10.0

9 Brandon Jennings/25 15.00 40.00
10 Andrew Bogut/49 10.00 25.00
15 Carlos Boozer/49 8.00 20.00
17 Joakim Noah/49 10.00 25.00
18 Taj Gibson/99 6.00 15.00
19 Antawn Jamison/49 4.00 10.00
20 Daniel Gibson/49 4.00 10.00
21 Baron Davis/25 8.00 20.00
24 Rajon Rondo/25 20.00 50.00
31 Eric Gordon/99 6.00 15.00
32 Ryan Gomes/99 4.00 10.00
33 Chris Kaman/25 4.00 10.00
34 Shane Battier/25 6.00 15.00
35 Marc Gasol/25 12.00 30.00
36 Zach Randolph/25 10.00 25.00
38 O.J. Mayo/20 6.00 15.00
39 Joe Johnson/25 10.00 25.00
40 Josh Smith/25 8.00 20.00
41 Al Horford/25 6.00 15.00
48 Mike Bibby/25 10.00 25.00
51 Trevor Ariza/25 6.00 15.00
52 Emeka Okafor/25 6.00 15.00
54 Al Jefferson/25 6.00 15.00
55 Devin Harris/25 6.00 15.00
56 Andrei Kirilenko/25 6.00 15.00
59 Tyreke Evans/49 12.50 30.00
60 Omri Casspi/99 4.00 10.00
61 Samuel Dalembert/49 4.00 10.00
62 Marcus Thornton/99 4.00 10.00
63 Beno Udrih/99 4.00 10.00
66 Chauncey Billups/25 10.00 25.00
67 Toney Douglas/49 4.00 10.00
69 Kobe Bryant/49 125.00 250.00
70 Pau Gasol/15 25.00 60.00
73 Derek Fisher/49 10.00 25.00
78 J.J. Redick/49 6.00 15.00
79 Hedo Turkoglu/49 4.00 10.00
81 Caron Butler/49 5.00 12.00
87 Brook Lopez/25 10.00 25.00
93 Chris Andersen/25 20.00 50.00
94 Danilo Gallinari/49 10.00 25.00
97 Darren Collison/49 4.00 10.00
98 Mike Dunleavy/49 4.00 10.00
99 T.J. Ford/99 4.00 10.00
101 Ben Gordon/25 10.00 25.00
102 Richard Hamilton/25 10.00 25.00
106 DeMar DeRozan/25 8.00 20.00
108 Andrea Bargnani/25 6.00 15.00
113 Goran Dragic/99 8.00 20.00
114 Chase Budinger/99 4.00 10.00
117 Tony Parker/25 10.00 25.00
120 DeJuan Blair/99 4.00 10.00
123 Channing Frye/49 4.00 10.00
124 Aaron Brooks/49 4.00 10.00
127 Russell Westbrook/25 25.00 60.00
128 Serge Ibaka/99 10.00 25.00
129 James Harden/25 12.50 30.00
130 Kendrick Perkins/49 6.00 15.00
131 Kevin Love/25 12.50 30.00
133 Jonny Flynn/99 4.00 10.00
134 Anthony Randolph/25 5.00 12.00
135 Darko Milicic/99 4.00 10.00
136 LaMarcus Aldridge/49 10.00 25.00
137 Brandon Roy/25 12.50 30.00
138 Andre Miller/49 4.00 10.00
139 Rudy Fernandez/99 4.00 10.00
140 Marcus Camby/25 10.00 25.00
141 Monta Ellis/25 15.00 40.00
142 Stephen Curry/99 12.00 30.00
143 David Lee/25 6.00 15.00
144 Al Thornton/99 4.00 10.00
146 Josh Howard/25 6.00 15.00
148 JaVale McGee/49 4.00 10.00
151 John Wall JSY AU/99 50.00 125.00
152 DeMarcus Cousins JSY AU/99 20.00 50.00
153 Quincy Pondexter JSY AU/99 5.00 12.00
154 Gordon Hayward JSY AU/99 10.00 25.00
155 Al-Farouq Aminu JSY AU/98 5.00 12.00
156 Ed Davis JSY AU/99 6.00 15.00
157 Greivis Vasquez JSY AU/99 6.00 15.00
158 Ekpe Udoh JSY AU/99 5.00 12.00
159 Damion James JSY AU/99 5.00 12.00
160 Landry Fields JSY AU/98 8.00 20.00
161 Greg Monroe JSY AU/99 10.00 25.00
162 Cole Aldrich JSY AU/99 5.00 12.00
163 Evan Turner JSY AU/99 12.00 30.00
164 Luke Babbitt JSY AU/99 5.00 12.00
165 Derrick Favors JSY AU/88 12.00 30.00
166 Xavier Henry JSY AU/99 6.00 15.00
167 Jordan Crawford JSY AU/99 10.00 25.00
168 Larry Sanders JSY AU/99 5.00 12.00
169 Wesley Johnson JSY AU/99 8.00 20.00
170 Eric Bledsoe JSY AU/99 8.00 20.00
171 Avery Bradley JSY AU/99 10.00 25.00
172 Daniel Orton JSY AU/99 5.00 12.00
173 Paul George JSY AU/99 12.00 30.00
174 James Anderson JSY AU/99 5.00 12.00
175 Elliot Williams JSY AU/99 5.00 12.00
176 Dominique Jones JSY AU/99 5.00 12.00
177 Dexter Pittman JSY AU/99 5.00 12.00
178 Lazar Hayward JSY AU/99 5.00 12.00
179 Trevor Booker JSY AU/99 5.00 12.00
180 Luke Harangody JSY AU/99 5.00 12.00
181 Patrick Patterson JSY AU/99 8.00 20.00
182 Hassan Whiteside JSY AU/91 5.00 12.00
183 Willie Warren JSY AU/99 5.00 12.00
184 Terrico White JSY AU/99 5.00 12.00
185 Andy Rautins JSY AU/99 5.00 12.00

2010-11 Totally Certified Red Materials

*RED MATERIALS: 1.5X TO 4X BASE HI
STATED PRINT RUN 199 TO 249 SER.#'d SETS
45 LeBron James/249 10.00 25.00
69 Kobe Bryant/249 10.00 25.00
122 Grant Hill/249 8.00 20.00
126 Kevin Durant/249 8.00 20.00

2010-11 Totally Certified Fabric of the Game Jumbo Jersey Number

STATED PRINT RUN ONE TO 299 SETS
1 Patrick Ewing/99 8.00 20.00
2 Dirk Nowitzki/299 4.00 10.00
3 Chris Andersen/299 3.00 8.00
4 Dwyane Wade/299 6.00 15.00
5 Chris Paul/299 5.00. 12.00
6 Dwight Howard/299 5.00 12.00
7 Elton Brand/299 3.00 8.00
8 Grant Hill/299 5.00 12.00
9 Rudy Fernandez/299 2.50 6.00
10 LeBron James/299 10.00 25.00
11 Manu Ginobili/99 3.00 8.00
12 Karl Malone/299 4.00 10.00
13 Al Horford/299 2.50 6.00
14 Kevin McHale/99 3.00 8.00
15 Andres Nocioni/299 2.00 5.00
16 Larry Johnson/99 8.00 20.00
17 Scottie Pippen/299 8.00 20.00
18 Jason Terry/299 2.50 6.00
19 Tim Duncan/299 5.00 12.00
20 Dikembe Mutombo/99 5.00 12.00
21 Omri Casspi/299 2.00 5.00
22 Luis Scola/299 2.50 6.00
23 Chris Kaman/299 2.50 6.00
24 Ron Artest/299 3.00 8.00
25 O.J. Mayo/299 3.00 8.00
26 Andrew Bogut/299 3.00 8.00
27 Brook Lopez/299 3.00 8.00
28 Shawn Marion/299 3.00 8.00
30 Jonny Flynn/299 2.00 5.00
31 James Harden/299 4.00 10.00
32 Toni Kukoc/299 3.00 8.00
33 Udonis Haslem/299 2.50 6.00
34 LaMarcus Aldridge/299 3.00 8.00
35 Shawn Kemp/99 20.00 50.00
36 John Stockton/299 5.00 12.00
37 Josh Smith/299 3.00 8.00
38 Paul Pierce/299 4.00 10.00
39 Luol Deng/299 3.00 8.00
40 Ty Lawson/299 3.00 8.00
41 Joe Dumars/99 3.00 8.00
42 Nick Van Exel/99 4.00 10.00
43 Charles Oakley/99 6.00 15.00
44 Maurice Cheeks/99 3.00 8.00
45 David West/299 3.00 8.00
46 Andre Iguodala/299 3.00 8.00
47 Rasheed Wallace/299 3.00 8.00
48 Boris Diaw/299 2.50 6.00
49 Arron Afflalo/299 2.00 5.00
50 Andre Miller/299 2.50 6.00

2010-11 Totally Certified Fabric of the Game Jumbo Jersey Number Prime

*PRIME: 1X TO 2.5X BASE HI
STATED PRINT RUN ONE TO 25 SER.#'d SETS
1 Patrick Ewing/25 25.00 60.00
2 Dirk Nowitzki/25 12.00 30.00
4 Dwyane Wade/20 20.00 50.00
8 Grant Hill/25 20.00 50.00
10 LeBron James/25 30.00 80.00
16 Larry Johnson/25 15.00 40.00
29 Hakeem Olajuwon/25 10.00 25.00
32 Toni Kukoc/25 10.00 25.00
42 Nick Van Exel/25 12.00 30.00
43 Charles Oakley/25 10.00 25.00

2010-11 Totally Certified Fabric of the Game Jumbo Team

STATED PRINT RUN 5 TO 299 SER.#'d SETS
1 Ray Allen/5
2 Brook Lopez/99 3.00 8.00
3 Amare Stoudemire/49 3.00 8.00
4 Elton Brand/299 3.00 8.00
5 DeMar DeRozan/299 3.00 8.00
6 Derrick Rose/299 10.00 25.00
7 Antawn Jamison/299 3.00 8.00
8 Ben Gordon/299 3.00 8.00
9 Danny Granger/299 3.00 8.00
10 Brandon Jennings/299 3.00 8.00
11 Joe Johnson/299 3.00 8.00
12 Stephen Jackson/299 2.50 6.00
13 LeBron James/299 10.00 25.00
14 Dwight Howard/299 5.00 12.00
15 Jason Kidd/299 3.00 8.00
16 Luis Scola/299 2.50 6.00
17 Marc Gasol/299 3.00 8.00
18 Chris Paul/299 5.00 12.00
19 Tony Parker/25 6.00 15.00
20 Nene/99 2.50 6.00
21 Michael Beasley/299 3.00 8.00
22 Brandon Roy/299 3.00 8.00
23 Kevin Durant/299 8.00 20.00
24 Al Jefferson/49 3.00 8.00
25 Monta Ellis/299 3.00 8.00
26 Blake Griffin/49 8.00 20.00
27 Kobe Bryant/299 10.00 25.00
28 Steve Nash/299 3.00 8.00
29 Tyreke Evans/299 4.00 10.00
30 JaVale McGee/299 2.50 6.00
31 Shaquille O'Neal/299 6.00 15.00
32 Andre Iguodala/190 3.00 8.00
33 Andrea Bargnani/299 2.50 6.00
34 Carlos Boozer/299 3.00 8.00
35 Andrew Bogut/299 3.00 8.00
36 Dwyane Wade/299 6.00 15.00
37 Caron Butler/299 3.00 8.00
38 LaMarcus Aldridge/299 3.00 8.00
39 Stephen Curry/99 4.00 10.00
40 Eric Gordon/299 3.00 8.00
41 Pau Gasol/299 3.00 8.00
42 Tim Duncan/299 5.00 12.00
43 Kevin Love/299 4.00 10.00
44 Russell Westbrook/299 4.00 10.00
45 Joakim Noah/199 3.00 8.00
46 Chris Bosh/99 3.00 8.00
47 Chris Kaman/299 2.50 6.00
48 Manu Ginobili/99 3.00 8.00
49 Andrei Kirilenko/99 2.50 6.00
50 Tyson Chandler/299 2.50 6.00

2010-11 Totally Certified Fabric of the Game Jumbo Team Prime

*PRIME: 1X TO 2.5X BASE HI
STATED PRINT RUN ONE TO 25 SER.#'d SETS
1 Ray Allen/25 12.00 30.00
13 LeBron James/25 30.00 80.00
19 Tony Parker/25 8.00 20.00
23 Kevin Durant/25 25.00 60.00
28 Steve Nash/25 12.00 30.00
31 Shaquille O'Neal/25 25.00 60.00
36 Dwyane Wade/20 25.00 60.00
48 Manu Ginobili/25 12.00 30.00

2010-11 Totally Certified HRX Video Cards

STATED PRINT RUN 40 SER.#'d SETS
UNPRICED AUTO PRINT RUN 10 SETS
UNPRICED AUTO GOLD PRINT RUN ONE SET
1 Kobe Bryant 250.00 600.00
2 Kevin Durant 200.00 500.00
3 Blake Griffin 200.00 500.00
4 John Wall 250.00 500.00

2010-11 Totally Certified Potential

STATED PRINT RUN 249 SER.#'d SETS
*BLUE: .75X TO 2X BASE HI
BLUE PRINT RUN 49 SER.#'d SETS
*GOLD: 2X TO 5X BASE HI
GOLD PRINT RUN 25 SER.#'d SETS
*RED: .6X TO 1.5X BASE HI
RED PRINT RUN 99 SER.#'d SETS
UNPRICED BLACK PRINT RUN ONE SET
UNPRICED GREEN PRINT RUN 5 SETS
1 Blake Griffin 3.00 8.00
2 Derrick Rose 4.00 10.00
3 Stephen Curry 1.50 4.00
4 Tyreke Evans 1.50 4.00
5 DeJuan Blair 1.00 2.50
6 Eric Gordon 1.25 3.00
7 Brandon Jennings 1.25 3.00
8 Kevin Love 1.50 4.00
9 Michael Beasley 1.25 3.00
10 Wesley Matthews 1.25 3.00
11 Zach Randolph 1.00 2.50
12 Russell Westbrook 1.50 4.00
13 Taj Gibson 1.00 2.50
14 James Harden 1.50 4.00
15 JaVale McGee 1.00 2.50

2010-11 Totally Certified Potential Autographs Gold

STATED PRINT RUN 25 SER.#'d SETS
UNPRICED BLACK PRINT RUN ONE SET
UNPRICED GREEN PRINT RUN 5 SETS
1 Blake Griffin 75.00 150.00
2 Derrick Rose 100.00 200.00
3 Stephen Curry 15.00 40.00
4 Tyreke Evans 15.00 40.00
5 DeJuan Blair 6.00 15.00
6 Eric Gordon 8.00 20.00
7 Brandon Jennings 15.00 40.00
8 Kevin Love 15.00 40.00
9 Michael Beasley 12.50 30.00
10 Wesley Matthews 15.00 40.00
11 Zach Randolph 10.00 25.00
12 Russell Westbrook 20.00 50.00
13 Taj Gibson 10.00 25.00
14 James Harden 12.50 30.00
15 JaVale McGee 6.00 15.00

2010-11 Totally Certified Potential Jerseys Prime Gold

*GOLD PRIME: 3X TO 8X BASE HI
STATED PRINT RUN 15 TO 25 SER.#'d SETS
UNPRICED BLACK PRINT RUN ONE SET
UNPRICED GREEN PRINT RUN 5 SETS

1984-85 Trail Blazers Ball Boy

This one card set features Trail Blazer star Kiki Vandewedge posing with a Trail Blazer ball boy.
1 Kiki Vandeweghe 4.00 10.00

1990-91 Trail Blazers British Petroleum

These large (approximately 8 1/2" by 11") high-gloss action player photos were taken by Bryan Drake. The photos are printed on thin paper and have white, red, and white borders (in that order), on a black background. The player's name appears below the picture, between the team and the sponsor's logos. The backs are blank. The set features members of the Portland Trail Blazers. These unnumbered cards were ordered alphabetically by player in the checklist below.

COMPLETE SET (6) 6.00 15.00
1 Danny Ainge 1.50 4.00
2 Clyde Drexler 3.00 8.00
3 Kevin Duckworth .75 2.00
4 Jerome Kersey .75 2.00
5 Terry Porter .75 2.00
6 Buck Williams .75 2.00

1991-92 Trail Blazers Dairy Queen Glasses

Dairy Queen produced this six-glass set to commemorate the Portland Trail Blazers. These glasses show the players in their uniforms. The glasses are not numbered and are checklisted below in alphabetical order.
COMPLETE SET (6) 6.00 15.00
1 Clyde Drexler 2.00 5.00
2 Kevin Duckworth .75 2.00
3 Jerome Kersey .75 2.00
4 Terry Porter .75 2.00
5 Clifford Robinson 1.25 3.00
6 Buck Williams .75 2.00

1992-93 Trail Blazers Dairy Queen Glasses

Dairy Queen produced this six-glass set to commemorate the Portland Trail Blazers. These glasses show the players in casual settings - doing their hobbies. The glasses are not numbered and are checklisted below in alphabetical order.
COMPLETE SET (6) 6.00 15.00
1 Clyde Drexler 2.00 5.00
2 Kevin Duckworth .75 2.00
3 Jerome Kersey .75 2.00
4 Terry Porter .75 2.00
5 Clifford Robinson 1.25 3.00
6 Buck Williams .75 2.00

1984-85 Trail Blazers Franz/Star

This 13-card standard-size set was produced for the Franz Bakery in Portland, Oregon by the Star Company. One card was placed in each loaf of Franz Bread as a promotional giveaway. Cards were printed with FDA approved vegetable ink. The cards have a red border around the fronts of the cards and red printing on the backs. Cards feature the Franz logo on the fronts. These numbered cards were ordered alphabetically by player. The set features one of the first professional cards of Jerome Kersey.
COMPLETE SET (13) 20.00 50.00
1 Jack Ramsay CO 1.50 4.00
2 Sam Bowie 2.50 6.00
3 Kenny Carr .75 2.00
4 Steve Colter .75 2.00
5 Clyde Drexler 12.50 30.00
6 Jerome Kersey 2.50 6.00
7 Audie Norris .75 2.00
8 Jim Paxson 1.25 3.00
9 Tom Scheffler 1.00 2.50
10 Bernard Thompson .75 2.00
11 Mychal Thompson 1.25 3.00
12 Darnell Valentine 1.00 2.50
13 Kiki Vandeweghe 1.50 4.00

1985-86 Trail Blazers Franz/Star

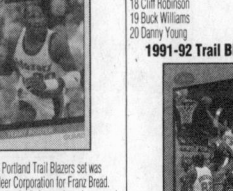

The 1985-86 Franz Portland Trail Blazers standard-size set was produced by The Star Company for Franz Bread. There are 12 player cards and one coach card. The front borders are reddish orange, and the backs feature statistics and biographical information. The set features the first professional card of Terry Porter.
COMPLETE SET (13) 15.00 40.00
1 Jack Ramsay CO 1.25 3.00
2 Sam Bowie 1.25 3.00
3 Kenny Carr .75 2.00
4 Steve Colter .75 2.00
5 Clyde Drexler 6.00 15.00
6 Ken Johnson .75 2.00
7 Caldwell Jones .75 2.00
8 Jerome Kersey 1.25 3.00
9 Jim Paxson 1.25 3.00
10 Terry Porter 4.00 10.00
11 Mychal Thompson 1.25 3.00
12 Darnell Valentine .75 2.00
13 Kiki Vandeweghe 1.25 3.00

1986-87 Trail Blazers Franz

The 1986-87 Franz Portland Trail Blazers set was produced by Fleer for Franz Bread. There are 12 player standard-size cards and one coach card. The front borders are reddish-orange, and the backs feature statistics and biographical information. Card backs are printed in pink and red on white card stock. These numbered cards were ordered alphabetically by player.
COMPLETE SET (13) 30.00 60.00
1 Walter Berry 1.25 3.00
2 Sam Bowie 2.00 5.00
3 Kenny Carr 1.25 3.00
4 Clyde Drexler 12.50 30.00
5 Michael Holton 1.25 3.00
6 Steve Johnson 1.25 3.00
7 Caldwell Jones 1.25 3.00
8 Jerome Kersey 1.50 4.00
9 Fernando Martin 1.25 3.00
10 Jim Paxson 1.50 4.00
11 Terry Porter 2.50 6.00
12 Kiki Vandeweghe 2.50 6.00
13 Mike Schuler CO 1.25 3.00

1987-88 Trail Blazers Franz

This 13 card standard-size card set was produced by Fleer as a promotion for Franz Bread. The cards were distributed in loaves of Franz Bread. The backs have biographical and statistical information. The cards are numbered on the back and are ordered alphabetically by player. The set includes Kevin Duckworth's first professional card.
COMPLETE SET (13) 40.00 70.00
1 Clyde Drexler 15.00 40.00
2 Kevin Duckworth 2.00 5.00
3 Michael Holton 1.50 4.00
4 Steve Johnson 1.25 3.00
5 Caldwell Jones 1.50 4.00
6 Jerome Kersey 2.50 6.00
7 Maurice Lucas 3.00 7.00
8 Jim Paxson 2.00 5.00
9 Terry Porter 3.00 7.00
10 Mike Schuler CO 1.25 3.00
11 Kiki Vandeweghe 2.50 6.00
12 Steve Johnson 1.25 3.00
13 Kiki Vandeweghe 3.00 7.00

1988-89 Trail Blazers Franz

The 1988-89 Franz Portland Trail Blazers set was produced by The Fleer Corporation for Franz Bread. There are 12 player standard-size cards and one coach card. The front borders are white with red bars and the backs feature statistics and biographical information. Card backs are printed in pink and red on white card stock. These numbered cards were ordered alphabetically by player.
COMPLETE SET (13) 25.00 55.00
1 Richard Anderson 1.25 3.00
2 Sam Bowie 1.50 4.00
3 Mark Bryant 1.25 3.00
4 Clyde Drexler 12.50 30.00
5 Kevin Duckworth 1.25 3.00
6 Rolando Ferreira .75 2.00
7 Steve Johnson .75 2.00
8 Caldwell Jones 1.25 3.00
9 Jerome Kersey 1.25 3.00
10 Terry Porter 2.00 5.00
11 Mike Schuler CO .75 2.00
12 Jerry Sichting 1.25 3.00
13 Kiki Vandeweghe 2.00 5.00

1989-90 Trail Blazers Franz

This 20-card standard-size set was produced by the Fleer Corporation for Franz Bread. The set commemorates the 20th anniversary season of the Trail Blazers and showcases current players as well as some "Blazer Greats" from past teams. The front features color action photos on white card stock, with orange border stripes on the left side and black border stripes on the right side and bottom of the picture. The Franz Bread logo appears in the upper right corner. The horizontally oriented back has biographical and statistical information, printed in pink and red on white card stock. The cards are numbered on the back. The set ordering is alphabetical within each group of current (1-11) and past (12-20) Trail Blazers. The set features the first professional card of Drazen Petrovic and Cliff Robinson.
COMPLETE SET (20) 20.00 50.00
1 Rick Adelman CO .75 2.00
2 Mark Bryant .60 1.50
3 Wayne Cooper .60 1.50
4 Kevin Duckworth .60 1.50
5 Clyde Drexler 6.00 15.00
6 Byron Irvin .60 1.50
7 Jerome Kersey .75 2.00
8 Drazen Petrovic 5.00 12.00
9 Terry Porter 1.00 2.50
10 Cliff Robinson 3.00 8.00
11 Buck Williams 1.50 4.00
12 Lionel Hollins .75 2.00
13 Maurice Lucas .75 2.00
14 Calvin Natt .60 1.50
15 Lloyd Neal .60 1.50
16 Jim Paxson .75 2.00
17 Geoff Petrie .75 2.00
18 Larry Steele .60 1.50
19 Mychal Thompson .75 2.00
20 Bill Walton 3.00 8.00

1990-91 Trail Blazers Franz

This 20-card standard-size set was produced by the Fleer Corporation for Franz Bread for distribution in the Portland area. The fronts feature color action player photos on a white card face, with black borders on the left side and red borders on the right. The Franz logo appears in a blue oval in the upper left corner, with the words "1991 Collector's Issue" to the right. The player's name, position, and team name appear below the picture. The back has biographical information and player statistics printed in pink and red on white. The team card can be found with and without the notation, 1989-90 Western Conference Champions, at the bottom of the (horizontally oriented) obverse. The set features an early professional card of Cliff Robinson.
COMPLETE SET (20) 15.00 30.00
1 Team Card .75 2.00
2 1989-90 Playoffs .30 .75
3 1989-90 Playoffs .30 .75
4 1989-90 Playoffs .30 .75
5 1989-90 Playoffs 2.50 6.00
Clyde Drexler
6 Bill Walton 2.00 5.00
7 Rick Adelman CO .40 1.00
8 John Schalow ACO and .30 .75
John Wetzel ACO
9 Alaa Abdelnaby .30 .75
10 Danny Ainge 1.25 3.00
11 Mark Bryant .30 .75
12 Wayne Cooper .30 .75
13 Clyde Drexler 5.00 12.00
14 Kevin Duckworth .40 1.00
15 Jerome Kersey .40 1.00
16 Drazen Petrovic 2.00 5.00
17 Terry Porter .75 2.00
18 Cliff Robinson 2.00 5.00
19 Buck Williams .75 2.00
20 Danny Young .30 .75

1991-92 Trail Blazers Franz

This 17-card standard size set was produced by Hoops for Franz Bread. The print run was 150,000 of each card. Beginning in November, one card per week was issued in a plastic sleeve in loaves of Franz Premium White Bread and Franz 100 Percent Wheat Bread. Robert Pack made the roster in October, and his card (17) was added to the rotation for distribution in February. After the 17-week promotion, Franz repeated each card statewide for one day each to allow collectors who might have missed one or more cards to complete their sets. The front features a full-bleed gold border with a color action photo at a slight angle within a three-sided black border and a red border at the bottom. The player's name appears in a black border beneath the picture. The horizontally oriented backs display a head shot, biography, statistics (by season and career), and career highlights. The cards are numbered in a basketball icon at the upper right corner. The set features the first professional card of Robert Pack.
COMPLETE SET (17) 10.00 25.00
1 Team Photo .75 2.00
2 Blazers All-Star Weekend .40 1.00
3 Buck Williams .60 1.50
4 Rick Adelman CO .40 1.00
5 Alaa Abdelnaby .30 .75
6 Danny Ainge 1.25 3.00
7 Mark Bryant .30 .75
8 Wayne Cooper .30 .75
9 Walter Davis 1.25 3.00
10 Clyde Drexler 5.00 12.00
11 Kevin Duckworth .40 1.00
12 Jerome Kersey .40 1.00
13 Terry Porter .75 2.00
14 Cliff Robinson 1.50 4.00
15 Buck Williams .75 2.00
16 Danny Young .30 .75
17 Robert Pack 1.25 3.00

1992-93 Trail Blazers Franz

This 20-card standard-size set was manufactured by SkyBox for the Trailblazers and distributed by Franz Bread. One card per week was inserted into loaves of Franz Premium White and Roman Meal Sandwich breads, with each card repeated for one day at the end of 20 weeks. The first card was in stores Monday, December 7, and the final card was issued the week of April 19th. Production was limited to 165,000 of each card. The set features color player photos that are full-bleed except at the bottom where a royal blue border stripe carries the player's name. The horizontal backs display close-up color player photos on a white background. A black stripe at the top stretches from the photo to a basketball icon that holds the card number. The black stripe also contains the player's name. Below are statistics and season highlights. The team logo and sponsor logo appear at the bottom.
COMPLETE SET (20) 10.00 25.00
1 Team Photo .75 2.00
2 Buck Williams .75 2.00
1991-92 NBA Playoffs
3 Clifford Robinson .75 2.00
1991-92 NBA Playoffs
4 Terry Porter .40 1.00
1991-92 NBA Playoffs
5 Jerome Kersey 1.25 3.00
Clyde Drexler
1991-92 NBA Playoffs
6 Clyde Drexler AS 1.50 4.00
7 Rick Adelman CO .40 1.00
8 Mark Bryant .20 .50
9 Clyde Drexler 3.00 8.00
10 Kevin Duckworth .30 .75
11 Jerome Kersey UER .40 1.00
(Card back has bio and stats for Tracy Murray)
12 Terry Porter .60 1.50
13 Cliff Robinson .75 2.00
14 Rod Strickland .60 1.50
15 Buck Williams .75 2.00
16 Mario Elie .40 1.00
17 Lamont Strothers .20 .50
18 Dave Johnson .20 .50
19 Tracy Murray .60 1.50
20 Reggie Smith .20 .50

1993-94 Trail Blazers Franz

As with the previous year's set, this 20-card standard-size set was produced by SkyBox. Beginning on December 6, one card per week was inserted in loaves of Franz and Williams Premium White and 100 Percent Wheat Bread. Based in Portland, United States Bakery owns both Franz and Williams. In 1993, the Oregon territory was divided into two regions, with Franz supplying the northern half of the state and Williams (which is based in Eugene) the southern half. As a result of this extended distribution, the production run was increased to 250,000 of each card. The fronts display color action player photos inside a silver frame with a black outer border. The horizontal backs carry a color head shot, biography, statistics, and career summary. Also this is the first year that the set includes Trail Blazers Walk of Fame Charter Member cards, which honor past players and other important individuals; these cards sport black-and-white portraits by S. Katagiri.
COMPLETE SET (20) 10.00 25.00
1 Team Photo .75 2.00
2 Jack Schalow ACO .40 1.00
Rick Adelman CO
John Wetzel ACO
3 Harry Glickman .40 1.00
Trail Blazers Walk of
Fame Charter Member
4 Mark Bryant .20 .50
5 Clyde Drexler 4.00 10.00
6 Maurice Lucas .75 2.00
Trail Blazers Walk of
Fame Charter Member
7 Chris Dudley .20 .50
8 Harvey Grant .20 .50
9 Geoff Petrie .40 1.00
Trail Blazers Walk of
Fame Charter Member
10 Reggie Smith .20 .50
11 Jerome Kersey UER .40 1.00
(Bio& stats& and career
summary are Murray's)
12 Jack Ramsay CO .60 1.50
Trail Blazers Walk of
Fame Charter Member
13 Tracy Murray .40 1.00
14 Terry Porter .60 1.50
15 Bill Walton 2.00 5.00
Trail Blazers Walk of
Fame Charter Member
16 Cliff Robinson 1.25 3.00
17 James Robinson .40 1.00
18 Larry Weinberg .40 1.00
Trail Blazers Walk of
Fame Charter Member
19 Rod Strickland .60 1.50
20 Buck Williams .75 2.00

1994-95 Trail Blazers Franz

Produced by SkyBox, this 20-card standard-size set commemorates the Trail Blazers 25th anniversary as an NBA franchise. One card per week was inserted in loaves of Franz and Williams Premium White and 100% White Bread. Both Franz and Williams are owned by United States Bakery, a family-owned business based in Portland. Distribution began on December 5, with the final card being issued the week of April 17th. Following the weekly release of the individual cards, the cards were repeated chronologically over a four- week period, beginning Monday, April 24. This year's set includes a 5-card subset honoring Blazers president emeritus Harry Glickman and the team's first 25 years. Glickman chose an all-time Blazer squad of the players who had the greatest influence on the franchise. The fronts feature full-bleed color action player photos, with the player's name printed in a black bar at the bottom. The backs carry a small color player portrait, along with biography, season highlights and stats.

COMPLETE SET (20)	10.00	25.00
1 Team Photo	.75	2.00
2 P.J. Carlesimo CO	.75	2.00
3 Bill Walton	1.50	4.00
Glickman's All-Time Team		
4 Mark Bryant	.20	.50
5 Clyde Drexler	2.50	6.00
6 Chris Dudley	.20	.50
7 Buck Williams	.75	2.00
Glickman's All-Time Team		
8 James Edwards	.20	.50
9 Harvey Grant	.30	.75
10 Jerome Kersey	.30	.75
11 Clyde Drexler	1.50	4.00
Glickman's All-Time Team		
12 Aaron McKie	.50	1.25
13 Tracy Murray	.20	.50
14 Terry Porter	.40	1.00
15 Geoff Petrie	.40	1.00
Glickman's All-Time Team		
16 Clifford Robinson	.75	2.00
17 James Robinson	.20	.50
18 Rod Strickland	.50	1.25
19 Maurice Lucas	.60	1.50
Glickman's All-Time Team		
20 Buck Williams	.75	2.00

1995-96 Trail Blazers Franz

Produced by SkyBox, this 13-card standard-size set continues the long run of regional team sets from the Franz bread company. One card per week was inserted in loaves of Franz and Williams bread. The promotion ran from late 1995 through Spring, 1996. Unlike previous years, the 1995-96 set contained no extraneous playoff or commemorative cards.

COMPLETE SET (13)	4.00	10.00
1 Clifford Robinson	.60	1.50
2 Randolph Childress	.20	.50
3 Chris Dudley	.20	.50
4 Aaron McKie	.40	1.00
5 Harvey Grant	.30	.75
6 Gary Trent	.60	1.50
7 P.J. Carlesimo CO	.20	.50
8 Dontonio Wingfield	.20	.50
9 Arvydas Sabonis	1.50	4.00
10 James Robinson	.20	.50
11 Rod Strickland	.40	1.00
12 Bill Curley	.20	.50
13 Buck Williams	.60	1.50

1996-97 Trail Blazers Franz

Produced by SkyBox, this 7-card standard-size set replicates the cards from the 1996-97 SkyBox set. Cards are numbered "x of 7" on the back. Franz and the Blazers also issued a 6-card sticker/tatoo set. Those were not numbered. The only tatoos with a player photo is Arvydas Sabonis, who is pictured on two of them.

COMPLETE SET (7)	6.00	15.00
1 Jermaine O'Neal	3.00	8.00
2 Clifford Robinson	.40	1.00
3 Gary Trent	.20	.50
4 Kenny Anderson	.20	.50
5 Arvydas Sabonis	.75	2.00
6 Isaiah Rider	.50	1.25
7 Rasheed Wallace	2.00	5.00
NNO Arvydas Sabonis Tatoo	2.00	5.00
Passing behind back		
NNO Arvydas Sabonis Tatoo	2.00	5.00
In Black Uniform		

1975-76 Trail Blazers Iron Ons

Sponsored by PayLess Drug Store, this is a set of seven iron ons. Printed on very thin paper and measuring 5" by 7 7/8", they feature black-and-white player portraits. The players' jerseys are outlined in red. A facsimile autograph, also in red, is printed on the bottom. The iron ons are unnumbered and checklisted below in alphabetical order.

COMPLETE SET (7)	20.00	40.00
1 Dan Anderson	1.25	3.00
2 Barry Clemens	1.25	3.00
3 Bob Gross	1.50	4.00
4 LaRue Martin	1.25	3.00
5 Larry Steele	1.50	4.00
6 Bill Walton	12.50	25.00
7 Sidney Wicks	3.00	8.00

1984 Trail Blazers Mr. Z's/Star

This five-card set was produced by Star Co. as a promotion for Mr. Z's frozen pizzas. Reportedly 10,000 cards of each player were produced. The cards were issued beginning in January 1984. The cards measure approximately 5" by 7" and feature on the fronts glossy color action player photos, with rounded corners as well as white and black borders on a dark red background. The team logo is superimposed over the picture at the intersection of the left side and bottom borders. The sponsor logo "Mr. Z's" appears in the upper right corner of the front, and player information is given below the picture. The backs have an advertisement for Blazer merchandise. The cards are unnumbered and are checklisted below in alphabetical order. Originally the set was planned to feature the whole team (12 players) but only five players were issued. Individual cards were given out in Mr. Z's frozen pizzas.

COMPLETE SET (5)	100.00	200.00
1 Kenny Carr	8.00	20.00
2 Clyde Drexler	60.00	120.00
3 Audie Norris	20.00	40.00
4 Mychal Thompson	8.00	20.00
5 Darnell Valentine	8.00	20.00

1981-82 Trail Blazers Playoff Tickets

These tickets are the actual tickets used in the Portland Trailblazers playoff games for the 1981-82 season. Each ticket was produced with different color backgrounds with black lettering. In addition, some other NBA stars were also featured on these tickets. They are listed after the Trail Blazers.

COMPLETE SET	40.00	100.00
1A Billy Ray Bates	1.50	4.00
White		
1B Billy Ray Bates	1.50	4.00
Blue		
2A Bob Gross	2.00	5.00
Orange		
2B Bob Gross	2.00	5.00
Yellow		
3A Michael Harper	1.50	4.00
Orange		
3B Michael Harper	1.50	4.00
Yellow		
4A Kevin Kunnert	1.50	4.00
Yellow		
4B Kevin Kunnert	1.50	4.00
Orange		
4C Kevin Kunnert	1.50	4.00
Pink		
5A Calvin Natt	1.50	4.00
Yellow		
5B Calvin Natt	1.50	4.00
Blue		
6A Jim Paxson	2.00	5.00
Orange		
6B Jim Paxson	2.00	5.00
Yellow		
7A Kelvin Ransey	1.50	4.00
Blue		
7B Kelvin Ransey	1.50	4.00
Pink		
8A Larry Steele	1.50	4.00
Pink		
8B Larry Steele	1.50	4.00
Yellow		
9 Mychal Thompson	2.00	5.00
Yellow		
10 Dave Twardzik	1.50	4.00
11A Marvin Webster	1.50	4.00
Yellow		
11B Marvin Webster	1.50	4.00
White		
12 George Gervin	3.00	8.00
13 Julius Erving	6.00	15.00
14 Moses Malone	3.00	8.00

1982-83 Trail Blazers Playoff Tickets

These tickets are the actual tickets used in the Portland Trailblazers playoff games for the 1981-82 season. Each ticket was produced with different color backgrounds with black lettering.

COMPLETE SET (10)	30.00	75.00
1 Wayne Cooper	1.50	4.00
White		
1 Wayne Cooper	1.50	4.00
Blue		
2 Jeff Judkins	1.50	4.00
Blue		
2 Jeff Judkins	1.50	4.00
White		
3 Jeff Lamp	1.50	4.00
Blue		
3 Jeff Lamp	1.50	4.00
White		
4 Lafayette Lever	2.00	5.00
Blue		
4 Lafayette Lever	2.00	5.00
White		
5 Audie Norris	1.50	4.00
Blue		
5 Audie Norris	1.50	4.00
White		
6 Larry Steele	1.50	4.00
Blue		
6 Larry Steele	1.50	4.00
White		
7 Linton Townes	1.50	4.00
Blue		
7 Linton Townes	1.50	4.00
White		
8 Dave Twardzik	1.50	4.00
Blue UER		
Spelled Twarzik		
8 Dave Twardzik	1.50	4.00
White UER		
Spelled Twarzik		
9 Darnell Valentine	1.50	4.00
White		
9 Darnell Valentine	1.50	4.00
Blue		
10 Pete Verhoeven	1.50	4.00
White		
10 Pete Verhoeven	1.50	4.00
Blue		

1983-84 Trail Blazers Playoff Tickets

These tickets are the actual tickets used in the Portland Trailblazers playoff games for the 1981-82 season. Each ticket was produced with different color backgrounds with black lettering.

COMPLETE SET (2)	4.00	10.00
1 Jim Paxson	2.00	5.00
Blue		
2 Mychal Thompson	2.00	5.00
White		

1984-85 Trail Blazers Playoff Tickets

These tickets are the actual tickets used in the Portland Trailblazers playoff games for the 1981-82 season. Each ticket was produced with different color backgrounds with black lettering.

COMPLETE SET (7)	15.00	30.00
1 Rick Adelman ACO	2.00	5.00
2 Bucky Buckwalter ACO	1.50	4.00
3 Audie Norris	1.50	4.00
4 Jim Paxson	2.00	5.00
5 Jack Ramsay CO	3.00	8.00
6 Tom Scheffler	1.50	4.00
7 Kiki Vandeweghe	3.00	8.00

1977-78 Trail Blazers Police

This set contains 14 cards measuring approximately 2 5/8" by 4 1/8" featuring the Portland Trail Blazers. The cards are unnumbered except for uniform number. Backs contain safety tips ("Tips from the Blazers") and are written in black ink with red accent. The set was sponsored by the Kiwanis and the Police Department. According to informed sources, 26, 000 sets were produced.

COMPLETE SET (14)	25.00	50.00
10 Corky Calhoun	1.25	3.00
13 Dave Twardzik	2.00	5.00
14 Lionel Hollins	2.00	5.00
15 Larry Steele	2.00	5.00
16 Johnny Davis	1.50	4.00
20 Maurice Lucas	3.00	8.00
23 T.R. Dunn	1.50	4.00
25 Tom Owens	1.25	3.00
30 Bob Gross	1.50	4.00
32 Bill Walton	10.00	20.00
36 Lloyd Neal	1.25	3.00
NNO Jack Ramsay CO	2.50	6.00
NNO Jack McKinney ACO	2.00	5.00
NNO Ron Culp TR	1.25	3.00

1979-80 Trail Blazers Police

This set contains 16 cards measuring 2 5/8" by 4 1/8" featuring the Portland Trail Blazers. Backs contain safety tips and are available with either light red or maroon printing on the backs. The year of issue and a facsimile autograph are printed on the front of the cards. The set was sponsored by 7-Up, Safeway, Kiwanis, KEX-1190AM, and the Police Departments. The cards are ordered below according to uniform number. The set features an early professional card of Mychal Thompson.

COMPLETE SET (16)	4.00	10.00
4 Jim Paxson	.75	2.00
9 Lionel Hollins	.60	1.50
10 Ron Brewer	.30	.75
11 Abdul Jeelani	.30	.75
13 Dave Twardzik	.60	1.50
15 Larry Steele	.50	1.25
20 Maurice Lucas	.75	2.00
23 T.R. Dunn	.40	1.00
25 Tom Owens	.30	.75
30 Bob Gross	.40	1.00
42 Kermit Washington	.50	1.25
43 Mychal Thompson	.75	2.00
44 Kevin Kunnert	.30	.75
xx Jack Ramsay CO	.60	1.50
xx Bucky Buckwalter ACO	.30	.75
xx Bill Schonely ANN	.30	.75

1981-82 Trail Blazers Police

This set contains 16 cards measuring 2 5/8" by 4 1/8" featuring the Portland Trail Blazers. Backs contain safety tips and are written in black ink with red accent. Cards are unnumbered except for uniform number. The year of issue is indicated on the card front. The set was produced courtesy of Kiwanis, the Trail Blazers, the NBA, and the Portland Police Bureau.

COMPLETE SET (16)	4.00	10.00
3 Jeff Lamp	.75	2.00
4 Jim Paxson	.60	1.50
10 Darnell Valentine	.40	1.00
12 Billy Ray Bates	.40	1.00
14 Kelvin Ransey	.30	.75
30 Bob Gross	.40	1.00
31 Peter Verhoeven	.40	1.00
32 Mike Harper	.30	.75
33 Calvin Natt	.40	1.00
40 Petur Gudmundsson	.40	1.00
42 Kermit Washington	.40	1.00
43 Mychal Thompson	.60	1.50
44 Kevin Kunnert	.40	1.00
NNO Jack Ramsay CO	.60	1.50
NNO Bucky Buckwalter ACO	.30	.75
NNO Jimmy Lynam ACO	.40	1.00

1982-83 Trail Blazers Police

This set contains 16 cards measuring approximately 2 5/8" by 4 1/8" featuring the Portland Trail Blazers. Backs contain safety tips and are written in black ink with red accent. The year of issue and a facsimile autograph are given on the front. The cards are ordered below according to uniform number. The set features the first professional card of Lafayette "Fat" Lever.

COMPLETE SET (16)	4.00	10.00
2 Linton Townes	.30	.75
3 Jeff Lamp	.40	1.00
4 Jim Paxson	.40	1.00
12 Lafayette Lever	.75	2.00
14 Darnell Valentine	.40	1.00
22 Jeff Judkins	.30	.75
24 Audie Norris	.30	.75
31 Peter Verhoeven	.30	.75
33 Calvin Natt	.40	1.00
34 Kenny Carr	.40	1.00
42 Wayne Cooper	.40	1.00
43 Mychal Thompson	.60	1.50
NNO Jack Ramsay CO	.75	2.00
NNO Bucky Buckwalter ACO	.30	.75
NNO Jim Lynam ACO	.40	1.00

1983-84 Trail Blazers Police

This set contains 16 cards measuring approximately 2 5/8" by 4 1/8" featuring the Portland Trail Blazers. Backs contain safety tips ("Blazer Tips") and are written in black ink with red accent. Drexler and the coaches are the only cards without a small inset photo. The year of issue is indicated on the front of the card. A facsimile autograph is printed on the back of the card. The cards are ordered below according to uniform number. This set features one of Clyde Drexler's first cards.

COMPLETE SET (16)	10.00	25.00
3 Jeff Lamp	.40	1.00
4 Jim Paxson	.40	1.00
12 Lafayette Lever	.40	1.00
14 Darnell Valentine	.40	1.00
22 Clyde Drexler	6.00	15.00
24 Audie Norris	.30	.75
31 Peter Verhoeven	.30	.75
33 Calvin Natt	.40	1.00
34 Kenny Carr	.30	.75
42 Wayne Cooper	.30	.75
43 Mychal Thompson	.60	1.50
54 Tom Piotrowski	.30	.75
NNO Jack Ramsay CO	.60	1.50
NNO Morris Buckwalter ACO	.50	1.25
Rick Adelman ACO		
NNO Ron Culp TR	.30	.75
NNO Dave Twardzik ANN	.30	.75
and Bill Schonely ANN		

1984-85 Trail Blazers Police

This set contains 16 cards measuring approximately 2 5/8" by 4 1/8" featuring the Portland Trail Blazers. Backs contain safety tips ("Blazer Tips") and are written in black ink with red accent. The cards are numbered in the upper left corner of the obverse; the year of issue is indicated in the lower right corner. The set features one of the first professional cards of Jerome Kersey.

COMPLETE SET (16)	6.00	15.00
1 Portland Team	.75	2.00
2 Jim Paxson	.40	1.00
3 Bernard Thompson	.30	.75
4 Darnell Valentine	.30	.75
5 Jack Ramsay CO	.75	2.00
Rick Adelman ACO		
Bucky Buckwalter ACO		
6 Steve Colter	.30	.75
7 Clyde Drexler	3.00	8.00
8 Audie Norris	.30	.75
9 Jerome Kersey	1.25	3.00
10 Sam Bowie	1.25	3.00
11 Kenny Carr	.30	.75
12 Lloyd Neal	.30	.75
13 Mychal Thompson	.40	1.00
14 Geoff Petrie	.40	1.00
15 Tom Scheffler	.30	.75
16 Kiki Vandeweghe	.75	2.00

1978-79 Trail Blazers Portfolio

These collector prints of Portland Trail Blazers were sponsored by The Benj. Franklin Federal Savings and Loan Association in Portland as a special gift to Blazer-Savers. They were produced by artist Michael Lundy and measure approximately 11" by 14". The Lucas print is in color, while the rest of the prints are in black and white. Two Trail Blazers are depicted together on two of the prints. The backs are blank. The prints are unnumbered and checklisted below in alphabetical order.

COMPLETE SET (10)	20.00	40.00
1 Kim Anderson and	1.25	3.00
Clemon Johnson		
2 T.R. Dunn	1.50	4.00
3 Bob Gross	1.50	4.00
4 Lionel Hollins	2.50	6.00
5 Maurice Lucas	3.00	8.00
6 Lloyd Neal	1.25	3.00
7 Tom Owens	1.25	3.00
8 Willie Smith and	1.25	3.00
Ron Brewer		
9 Larry Steele	2.50	6.00
10 Dave Twardzik	2.50	6.00

1991-92 Trail Blazers Posters

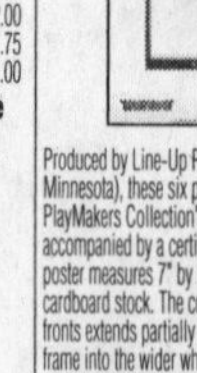

Produced by Line-Up Productions Inc. (Minnetonka, Minnesota), these six posters are part of "The PlayMakers Collection" print series. Each set was accompanied by a certificate of authenticity. Each poster measures 7" by 18" and is printed on slick cardboard stock. The color action painting on the fronts extends partially outside the inner black picture frame into the wider white border. The player's name is reversed out at the bottom of the picture frame. Various logos are printed across the bottom of the front. The backs are blank. The posters are unnumbered and checklisted below in alphabetical order.

COMPLETE SET (5)	8.00	20.00
1 Clyde Drexler	6.00	15.00
2 Kevin Duckworth	1.25	3.00
3 Jerome Kersey	1.25	3.00
4 Terry Porter	1.50	4.00
5 Buck Williams	1.50	4.00

1977-78 Trail Blazers RC Glasses

These appoximately 6 3/8" tall glasses were produced to celebrate the Portland Trailblazers 1976-77 NBA Championship. The glasses have a head shot with the players name, height and position, a facsimile signature, and other personal data below the player. The back of the glass has the "Me and my RC" slogan, and the glass is ringed with "RC Salutes the Champs-Portland Players" in black type over the blue ring. The checklist below may be incomplete, and any additions would be welcomed.

COMPLETE SET (8)	50.00	100.00
1 Johnny Davis	5.00	10.00
2 Bob Gross	5.00	10.00
3 Lionel Hollins	5.00	10.00
4 Maurice Lucas	7.50	15.00
5 Lloyd Neal	5.00	10.00
6 Larry Steele	5.00	10.00
7 Dave Twardzik	5.00	10.00
8 Bill Walton	20.00	40.00

1972-73 Trail Blazers Team Issue

Measuring 8" x 10", this 25-photo set features members from the 1972-73 Portland Trail Blazers. Each photo features either a close-up posed shot and an in action shot of each player in black and white. The player's name, height and college are listed on the front, as well as the team logo. The backs are blank. The photos are not numbered and listed below alphabetically.

COMPLETE SET (25)	65.00	125.00
1 Rick Adelman	3.00	8.00
2 Rick Adelman IA	2.50	6.00
3 Bob Davis	2.00	5.00
4 Bob Davis IA	2.00	5.00
5 Bobby Fields	2.00	5.00
6 Bobby Fields IA	2.00	5.00
7 Stu Inman VP	2.00	5.00
8 Neil Johnston ACO	3.00	8.00
9 Ollie Johnson	2.00	5.00
10 Ollie Johnson IA	2.00	5.00
11 LaRue Martin	2.00	5.00
12 LaRue Martin IA	2.00	5.00
13 Leo Marty TR	2.00	5.00
14 Jack McCloskey CO	2.00	5.00
15 Stan McKenzie	2.00	5.00
16 Stan McKenzie IA	2.00	5.00
17 Lloyd Neal	2.00	5.00
18 Lloyd Neal IA	2.00	5.00
19 Geoffrey Petrie	5.00	10.00
20 Geoffrey Petrie IA	3.00	8.00
21 Dale Schlueter	2.00	5.00
22 Dale Schlueter IA	2.00	5.00
23 Larry Steele	3.00	8.00
24 Larry Steele IA	2.50	6.00
25 Sidney Wicks IA	7.50	15.00

1976-77 Trail Blazers Team Issue

This 8" x10" set was produced for the Portland Trailblazers during the 1976-77 season. The set features 15 black and white cards of the team's players and coaches.

COMPLETE SET (15)	20.00	40.00
1 Dan Anderson	1.25	3.00
2 Barry Clemens	1.25	3.00
3 Bob Gross	1.25	3.00
4 Steve Hawes	1.25	3.00
5 Lionel Hollins	1.50	4.00
6 Maurice Lucas	2.50	6.00
7 Lloyd Neal	1.25	3.00
8 Larry Steele	1.25	3.00
9 Dave Twardzik	1.25	3.00
10 Wally Walker	1.25	3.00
11 Stu Inman VP	1.25	3.00
12 Ron Culp TR	1.25	3.00
13 Jack McKinney CO	1.25	3.00
14 Harry Glickman EVP	1.25	3.00
15 Larry Weinberg PRES	1.25	3.00

1977-78 Trail Blazers Team Issue

These color photos, which measure 5 7/8" by 9" and are blank-backed, feature members of the Portland Trail Blazers who were the defending NBA champs. Since these photos are unnumbered, we have sequenced them in alphabetical order.

COMPLETE SET (13)	17.50	35.00
1 Corky Calhoun	.75	2.00
2 Johnny Davis	.75	2.00
3 T.R. Dunn	.75	2.00
4 Bob Gross	.75	2.00
5 Lionel Hollins	.75	2.00
6 Maurice Lucas	1.50	4.00
7 Lloyd Neal	.75	2.00
8 Tom Owens	.75	2.00
9 Jack Ramsey CO	1.50	4.00
10 Larry Steele	.75	2.00
11 Dave Twardzik	.75	2.00
12 Bill Walton	3.00	8.00
13 Portland Trail Blazers	1.50	4.00
Team Composite		

1971-72 Trail Blazers Texaco

This 12-card set was sponsored by Texaco. The cards measure approximately 8" by 9 5/8" and feature full-bleed, posed player photos. The player's name is printed in white script lettering in the upper right corner. The card backs have biographical information and career statistics. The Texaco logo is printed at the bottom of the card. The cards are unnumbered and checklisted below in alphabetical order.

COMPLETE SET (12)	30.00	60.00
1 Rick Adelman	5.00	12.00
2 Gary Gregor	3.00	8.00
3 Ron Knight	3.00	8.00
4 Jim Marsh	3.00	8.00
5 Willie McCarter	3.00	8.00
6 Stan McKenzie	3.00	8.00
7 Geoff Petrie	5.00	12.00
8 Dale Schlueter	3.00	8.00
9 Bill Smith	3.00	8.00
10 Larry Steele	3.00	8.00
11 Sidney Wicks	6.00	15.00
12 Charles Yelverton	3.00	8.00

2010 TRISTAR Obak

COMMON CARD (1-109)	.20	.50
COMMON VAR (1-109)	.40	1.00
COMMON SP (110-120)	1.50	4.00
THREE SPs PER BOX		
102 Dave Debusschere	.20	.50

2010 TRISTAR Obak Black

*BLACK: 2.5X TO 6X BASIC
*BLACK VAR: 1.2X TO 3X BASIC VAR
*BLACK SP: .5X TO 1.2X BASIC SP
OVERALL PARALLEL ODDS 1:10
STATED PRINT RUN 50 SER.#'d SETS

1996-97 UD3

The 1996-97 Upper Deck UD3 set was issued in one series totalling 60 cards. The set breaks down into three different technologies: Light F/X, Cel Chrome and Electric Wood-Cel. The Hardwood prospect cards (1-20) use the Wood-Cel technology, the NBA StarFocus cards (21-40) use the Cel Chrome technology and the Aerial Artists (41-60) use the Light F/X technology. Cards were issued in 3-card packs with a suggested retail price of $3.99.

COMPLETE SET (60)	12.00	30.00
1 Kerry Kittles RC	.25	.60
2 Stephon Marbury RC	.60	1.50
3 Jermaine O'Neal RC	.60	1.50
4 Shareef Abdur-Rahim RC	.50	1.25
5 Ray Allen RC	1.00	2.50
6 Antoine Walker RC	.50	1.25
7 Erick Dampier RC	.25	.60
8 Walter McCarty RC	.25	.60
9 Todd Fuller RC	.25	.60
10 Tony Delk RC	.25	.60
11 Marcus Camby RC	.40	1.00
12 John Wallace RC	.25	.60
13 Vitaly Potapenko RC	.25	.60
14 Allen Iverson RC	1.25	3.00
15 Steve Nash RC	2.50	6.00
16 Derek Fisher RC	.50	1.25
17 Samaki Walker RC	.25	.60
18 Roy Rogers RC	.25	.60
19 Kobe Bryant RC	5.00	12.00
20 Lorenzen Wright RC	.25	.60
21 Kevin Garnett	1.00	2.50
22 Hakeem Olajuwon	.50	1.25
23 Michael Jordan	3.00	8.00
24 John Stockton	.50	1.25
25 Terrell Brandon	.25	.60
26 Damon Stoudamire	.40	1.00
27 Charles Barkley	.60	1.50
28 Dikembe Mutombo	.40	1.00
29 Gary Payton	.40	1.00
30 Patrick Ewing	.50	1.25
31 Dennis Rodman	.75	2.00
32 Joe Smith	.30	.75
33 Grant Hill	.60	1.50
34 Shaquille O'Neal	1.00	2.50
35 Kevin Johnson	.40	1.00
36 David Robinson	.60	1.50
37 Juwan Howard	.30	.75
38 Mitch Richmond	.40	1.00
39 Alonzo Mourning	.50	1.25
40 Reggie Miller	.50	1.25
41 Shawn Kemp	.40	1.00
42 Scottie Pippen	.60	1.50
43 Kobe Bryant	3.00	8.00
44 Anfernee Hardaway	.60	1.50
45 Brent Barry	.30	.75
46 Glenn Robinson	.40	1.00
47 Karl Malone	.50	1.25
48 Chris Webber	.50	1.25
49 Danny Manning	.30	.75
50 Antonio McDyess	.40	1.00
51 Dominique Wilkins	.50	1.25
52 Vin Baker	.30	.75
53 Isaiah Rider	.30	.75
54 Eddie Jones	.40	1.00
55 Glen Rice	.40	1.00
56 Larry Johnson	.40	1.00
57 Latrell Sprewell	.40	1.00
58 Sean Elliott	.40	1.00
59 Clyde Drexler	.50	1.25
60 Jerry Stackhouse	.50	1.25

1996-97 UD3 Court Commemorative Autographs

Randomly inserted in packs at a rate of one in 1500, this four-card set features autographed cards of the Upper Deck spokesmen.

C1 Michael Jordan	1250.00	2000.00
C2 Damon Stoudamire	20.00	50.00
C3 Anfernee Hardaway	125.00	250.00
C4 Shawn Kemp	125.00	250.00

1996-97 UD3 Superstar Spotlight

Randomly inserted in packs at a rate of one in 144, this 10-card set utilizes Cel-Chrome technology and focuses on NBA All-Stars.

COMPLETE SET (10)	50.00	100.00
S1 Shaquille O'Neal	10.00	25.00
S2 Alonzo Mourning	5.00	12.00
S3 Anfernee Hardaway	6.00	15.00
S4 Karl Malone	5.00	12.00
S5 Michael Jordan	30.00	80.00
S6 Hakeem Olajuwon	5.00	12.00
S7 Shawn Kemp	4.00	10.00
S8 Allen Iverson	10.00	25.00
S9 Dennis Rodman	8.00	20.00
S10 Charles Barkley	6.00	15.00

1996-97 UD3 The Winning Edge

Randomly inserted in packs at a rate of one in 11, this 20-card set utilizes the Light F/X technology, and each card focuses on a specific trait that makes these players a success in the NBA.

COMPLETE SET (20)	30.00	80.00
W1 Michael Jordan	10.00	25.00
W2 Charles Barkley	2.50	6.00
W3 Reggie Miller	2.00	5.00
W4 Grant Hill	2.50	6.00
W5 Larry Johnson	1.50	4.00
W6 Hakeem Olajuwon	2.00	5.00
W7 Anfernee Hardaway	2.50	6.00
W8 Shaquille O'Neal	4.00	10.00
W9 Vin Baker	1.25	3.00
W10 Kevin Garnett	4.00	10.00
W11 Juwan Howard	1.25	3.00
W12 John Stockton	2.00	5.00
W13 Mookie Blaylock	1.00	2.50
W14 Shawn Kemp	1.50	4.00
W15 David Robinson	2.50	6.00
W16 Kevin Johnson	1.50	4.00
W17 Joe Dumars	1.50	4.00
W18 Marcus Camby	1.25	3.00
W19 Clyde Drexler	2.00	5.00
W20 Chris Webber	2.00	5.00

1997-98 UD3

Released in three-card packs that carried a suggested retail price of $3.99, this 60 card set is broken up into three different "subset" themes. The first 20 cards are Jam Masters, the next 20 are All-Stars and the final 20 are The Big Picture. A Michael Jordan promo card was also released with the word "Sample" in white letters on the card front. Since the card is numbered the same as the basic Jordan card (#45), the promo is listed as a "NNO" at the end of the set.

COMPLETE SET (60)	15.00	40.00
1 Anfernee Hardaway JM	.50	1.25
2 Alonzo Mourning JM	.40	1.00
3 Grant Hill JM	.50	1.25
4 Kerry Kittles JM	.20	.50
5 Latrell Sprewell JM	.30	.75
6 Rasheed Wallace JM	.30	.75
7 Jerry Stackhouse JM	.30	.75
8 Glen Rice JM	.30	.75
9 Marcus Camby JM	.30	.75
10 Scottie Pippen JM	.50	1.25
11 Patrick Ewing JM	.40	1.00
12 Michael Finley JM	.30	.75
13 Karl Malone JM	.40	1.00
14 Antonio McDyess JM	.25	.60
15 Michael Jordan JM	3.00	8.00
16 Clyde Drexler JM	.40	1.00
17 Brent Barry JM	.25	.60
18 Glenn Robinson JM	.25	.60
19 Kobe Bryant JM	1.50	4.00
20 Reggie Miller JM	.40	1.00
21 John Stockton AS	.40	1.00
22 Gary Payton AS	.30	.75
23 Michael Jordan AS	3.00	8.00
24 Vin Baker AS	.25	.60
25 Karl Malone AS	.40	1.00
26 Juwan Howard AS	.25	.60
27 Charles Barkley AS	.50	1.25
28 Jason Kidd AS	.50	1.25
29 Joe Dumars AS	.30	.75
30 Anfernee Hardaway AS	.50	1.25
31 Mitch Richmond AS	.30	.75
32 Alonzo Mourning AS	.40	1.00
33 Grant Hill AS	.50	1.25
34 Shaquille O'Neal AS	.75	2.00
35 Scottie Pippen AS	.50	1.25
36 Reggie Miller AS	.40	1.00
37 Hakeem Olajuwon AS	.40	1.00
38 Tim Hardaway AS	.30	.75
39 David Robinson AS	.50	1.25
40 Shawn Kemp AS	.30	.75
41 Allen Iverson BP	.60	1.50
42 Stephon Marbury BP	.40	1.00
43 Dennis Rodman BP	.60	1.50
44 Terrell Brandon BP	.20	.50
45 Michael Jordan BP	3.00	8.00
46 Kerry Kittles BP	.20	.50
47 Hakeem Olajuwon BP	.40	1.00
48 Loy Vaught BP	.20	.50
49 Antoine Walker BP	.30	.75
50 Gary Payton BP	.30	.75
51 Kevin Johnson BP	.30	.75
52 Kevin Garnett BP	.60	1.50
53 Shareef Abdur-Rahim BP	.30	.75
54 Larry Johnson BP	.30	.75
55 Dikembe Mutombo BP	.30	.75
56 Chris Webber BP	.30	.75
57 Joe Smith BP	.25	.60
58 Kendall Gill BP	.20	.50
59 Kenny Anderson BP	.25	.60
60 Damon Stoudamire BP	.30	.75
NNO Michael Jordan PROMO	2.00	5.00

1997-98 UD3 Awesome Action

Randomly inserted in packs at one in 11, this 20-card set features great action shots of the NBA's best. Card backs carry an "A" prefix.

COMPLETE SET (20)	50.00	120.00
A1 Michael Jordan	15.00	40.00
A2 Nick Van Exel	1.50	4.00
A3 Jerry Stackhouse	2.00	5.00
A4 Shawn Kemp	2.00	5.00
A5 Hakeem Olajuwon	2.50	6.00
A6 Grant Hill	3.00	8.00
A7 Scottie Pippen	3.00	8.00
A8 Alonzo Mourning	2.50	6.00
A9 Damon Stoudamire	2.00	5.00
A10 Kevin Garnett	4.00	10.00
A11 Anfernee Hardaway	3.00	8.00
A12 Shareef Abdur-Rahim	2.00	5.00
A13 Allen Iverson	4.00	10.00
A14 Dennis Rodman	4.00	10.00
A15 Shaquille O'Neal	5.00	12.00
A16 Jason Kidd	3.00	8.00
A17 Gary Payton	2.00	5.00
A18 Dikembe Mutombo	2.00	5.00
A19 Karl Malone	2.50	6.00
A20 Stephon Marbury	2.50	6.00

1997-98 UD3 MJ3

Randomly inserted into packs, this three-card set features a three time tribute to Michael Jordan. The first card was inserted at one in 45, the second at one in 119 and the last at one in 167. When put together, the three cards from one big card. Card backs carry a "MJ3" prefix.

MJ31 Michael Jordan	8.00	20.00
MJ32 Michael Jordan	10.00	25.00
MJ33 Michael Jordan	15.00	40.00

1997-98 UD3 Rookie Portfolio

Randomly inserted into packs at one in 144, this 10-card set features a still shot of some of the top rookies from the 1997 class. The cards feature a portrait front against a see-through back. Card backs carry a "R" prefix.

COMPLETE SET (10)	50.00	100.00
R1 Tim Duncan	15.00	40.00
R2 Keith Van Horn	5.00	12.00
R3 Chauncey Billups	10.00	25.00
R4 Antonio Daniels	2.50	6.00
R5 Tony Battie	3.00	8.00
R6 Ron Mercer	3.00	8.00
R7 Tim Thomas	5.00	12.00
R8 Adonal Foyle	2.50	6.00
R9 Tracy McGrady	12.00	30.00
R10 Danny Fortson	2.50	6.00

1997-98 UD3 Season Ticket Autographs

Randomly inserted in packs at a rate of one in 1,800, this 4-card set features autographs against a facsimile ticket stub. Card backs carry a congratulatory message from Upper Deck.

AH Anfernee Hardaway	100.00	200.00
JH Juwan Howard	30.00	80.00
MJ Michael Jordan	1250.00	2000.00
TH Tim Hardaway	40.00	100.00

1997-98 UD3 Season Ticket Trade

These cards are the original trade cards for the Season Ticket Autographs. These cards are still traded on the secondary market due to both the player photo on the card and the toughness of the original trade cards. The checklist also includes some players that were not actually made for the autograph set.

AMT Alonzo Mourning	100.00	200.00
JHT Juwan Howard	4.00	10.00
MJT Michael Jordan	300.00	500.00

2000 UDA The Jordan Experience Printer's Proofs

This 12-proof set was released by UDA in 2000, the set features 22kt gold cards that highlight Michael Jordan's career. There were 23,000 of each proof produced. Each proofed was sold exclusively through UDA's direct marketing channel, and carried a suggested retail price of $29.95.

2002-03 UD Authentics

Issued in November 2002, UD Authentics boasts a 132-card set divided up into 90 veteran player cards and 42 rookie player cards. The base cards borrow their design from 1989 Upper Deck Basebaeball. Cards have full color player photos with white borders and the trademark Upper Deck hologram on the back of the card. Rookie players have red borders instead of the base white and are serially numbered as follows: Cards 91-123 are numbered to 799, and cards 124-132 are numbered to 499. Also inserted within the product were Upper Deck Authenticated redemption cards which were good for autographs, photos, jerseys and other memorabilia-inserted at the rate of one in 216. As with all of UD's new exchange cards, these items were redeemable via UD's website as an e-redemption. UD Authentics was packaged in 18-pack boxes where packs contained five cards and carried a suggested retail price of $6.99.

COMPLETE SET (132)	150.00	300.00
COMP.SET w/o SP's (90)	15.00	40.00
1 Shareef Abdur-Rahim	.25	.60
2 Jason Terry	.25	.60
3 Glenn Robinson	.25	.60
4 Paul Pierce	.40	1.00
5 Antoine Walker	.25	.60
6 Eric Williams	.20	.50
7 Kedrick Brown	.20	.50
8 Jalen Rose	.25	.60
9 Tyson Chandler	.25	.60
10 Eddy Curry	.25	.60
11 Darius Miles	.20	.50
12 Lamond Murray	.20	.50
13 Chris Mihm	.20	.50
14 Dirk Nowitzki	.50	1.25
15 Steve Nash	.40	1.00
16 Michael Finley	.30	.75
17 Raef LaFrentz	.20	.50
18 James Posey	.20	.50
19 Juwan Howard	.25	.60
20 Jerry Stackhouse	.25	.60
21 Ben Wallace	.30	.75
22 Clifford Robinson	.20	.50
23 Jason Richardson	.30	.75
24 Antawn Jamison	.30	.75
25 Gilbert Arenas	.30	.75
26 Steve Francis	.30	.75
27 Eddie Griffin	.20	.50
28 Cuttino Mobley	.25	.60
29 Reggie Miller	.30	.75
30 Jamaal Tinsley	.20	.50
31 Jermaine O'Neal	.30	.75
32 Elton Brand	.30	.75
33 Lamar Odom	.30	.75
34 Andre Miller	.25	.60
35 Kobe Bryant	1.50	4.00
36 Shaquille O'Neal	.75	2.00
37 Derek Fisher	.25	.60
38 Devean George	.20	.50
39 Pau Gasol	.40	1.00
40 Shane Battier	.30	.75
41 Alonzo Mourning	.40	1.00
42 Brian Grant	.20	.50
43 Eddie Jones	.25	.60
44 Ray Allen	.30	.75
45 Tim Thomas	.20	.50
46 Kevin Garnett	.60	1.50
47 Wally Szczerbiak	.25	.60
48 Terrell Brandon	.20	.50
49 Jason Kidd	.50	1.25
50 Dikembe Mutombo	.30	.75
51 Richard Jefferson	.30	.75
52 Baron Davis	.30	.75
53 Jamal Mashburn	.25	.60
54 David Wesley	.20	.50
55 P.J. Brown	.20	.50
56 Latrell Sprewell	.25	.60
57 Allan Houston	.25	.60
58 Antonio McDyess	.25	.60
59 Tracy McGrady	.50	1.25
60 Mike Miller	.30	.75
61 Darrell Armstrong	.20	.50
62 Allen Iverson	.50	1.25
63 Keith Van Horn	.25	.60
64 Stephon Marbury	.25	.60
65 Shawn Marion	.30	.75
66 Anfernee Hardaway	.50	1.25
67 Rasheed Wallace	.30	.75
68 Bonzi Wells	.20	.50
69 Scottie Pippen	.50	1.25
70 Chris Webber	.30	.75
71 Peja Stojakovic	.30	.75
72 Mike Bibby	.30	.75
73 Hedo Turkoglu	.30	.75
74 Tim Duncan	.60	1.50
75 David Robinson	.50	1.25
76 Tony Parker	.40	1.00
77 Malik Rose	.20	.50
78 Gary Payton	.30	.75
79 Rashard Lewis	.30	.75
80 Desmond Mason	.25	.60
81 Brent Barry	.20	.50
82 Vince Carter	.50	1.25
83 Morris Peterson	.20	.50
84 Antonio Davis	.20	.50
85 Karl Malone	.40	1.00
86 John Stockton	.40	1.00
87 Andrei Kirilenko	.30	.75
88 Michael Jordan	2.50	6.00
89 Richard Hamilton	.25	.60
90 Kwame Brown	.20	.50
91 Efthimios Rentzias RC	2.00	5.00
92 Darius Songaila RC	2.00	5.00
93 Matt Barnes RC	2.50	6.00
94 Sam Clancy RC	2.00	5.00
95 Lonny Baxter RC	2.00	5.00
96 Manu Ginobili RC	5.00	12.00
97 Rod Grizzard RC	2.00	5.00
98 Tito Maddox RC	2.00	5.00
99 Predrag Savovic RC	2.00	5.00
100 Carlos Boozer RC	4.00	10.00
101 Dan Gadzuric RC	2.00	5.00
102 Vincent Yarbrough RC	2.00	5.00
103 Robert Archibald RC	2.00	5.00
104 Roger Mason RC	2.00	5.00
105 Steve Logan RC	2.00	5.00
106 Dan Dickau RC	2.00	5.00
107 Chris Jefferies RC	2.00	5.00
108 John Salmons RC	2.50	6.00
109 Frank Williams RC	2.00	5.00
110 Tayshaun Prince RC	2.50	6.00
111 Casey Jacobsen RC	2.00	5.00
112 Qyntel Woods RC	2.00	5.00
113 Kareem Rush RC	2.00	5.00
114 Ryan Humphrey RC	2.00	5.00
115 Curtis Borchardt RC	2.00	5.00
116 Juan Dixon RC	2.50	6.00
117 Jiri Welsch RC	2.00	5.00
118 Bostjan Nachbar RC	2.00	5.00
119 Fred Jones RC	2.00	5.00
120 Marcus Haislip RC	2.00	5.00
121 Melvin Ely RC	2.00	5.00
122 Jared Jeffries RC	2.00	5.00
123 Caron Butler RC	3.00	8.00
124 Amare Stoudemire RC	6.00	15.00
125 Chris Wilcox RC	2.50	6.00
126 Nene Hilario RC	3.00	8.00
127 DaJuan Wagner RC	2.50	6.00
128 Nikoloz Tskitishvili RC	2.50	6.00
129 Drew Gooden RC	4.00	10.00
130 Mike Dunleavy RC	3.00	8.00
131 Jay Williams RC	3.00	8.00
132 Yao Ming RC	8.00	20.00

2002-03 UD Authentics Gold

Randomly inserted in packs, this 132-card set parallels the base set enhanced with gold borders on the card front. Veteran players, numbers 1-90, are sequentially numbered to 250 and rookie players, numbers 91-132, are sequentially numbered to 100. Several of the rookie players also have jersey swatches, these cards are denoted with JSY tags.

*1-90 STARS: 4X TO 10X BASE CARD HI
*91-123 RCs: 1.25X TO 3X BASE RC HI
*124-132 RCs: 1X TO 2.5X BASE HI

88 Michael Jordan	30.00	80.00

2002-03 UD Authentics Rainbow

Randomly inserted in packs, this 132-card set parallels the base UD Authentics set enhanced with silver borders. Veteran players, numbers 1-90, are sequentially numbered to 50 and rookie players, numbers 91-132, are sequentially numbered to 25.

*STARS: 10X TO 25X BASE CARD HI
*RCs 91-123: 3X TO 8X HI
*RCs 124-132: 2.5X TO 6X HI

88 Michael Jordan	75.00	200.00

2002-03 UD Authentics 100% Amazing

Randomly inserted in packs, this eight card set features some of the NBA's brightest stars. The cards are horizontally designed with a full color player action photo on the left and a swatch of game used memorabilia on the right. Orange borders are present along the top and bottom of the card and the words 100% Amazing make the border along the left side of the card.

AI Allen Iverson	8.00	20.00
AM Alonzo Mourning	6.00	15.00
CW Chris Webber	5.00	12.00
JK Jason Kidd	8.00	20.00
KB Kobe Bryant	25.00	60.00
KG Kevin Garnett	10.00	25.00
MJ Michael Jordan	75.00	150.00
TM Tracy McGrady	8.00	20.00

2002-03 UD Authentics Awesome Authentics

Randomly seeded in packs, this 16-card set places full-color player action photography on a colored background on the right and an "A" shaped swatch of game worn memorabilia on the left set against a different colored background. The background colors are set to match the featured player's team colors. Each card is sequentially numbered to 250.

AWA Antoine Walker	2.50	6.00
CWA Chris Webber	3.00	8.00
DMA Darius Miles	2.00	5.00
DNA Dirk Nowitzki	5.00	12.00
EBA Elton Brand	3.00	8.00
JMA Jamal Mashburn	2.50	6.00
KBA Kobe Bryant	15.00	40.00
KGA Kevin Garnett	6.00	15.00
MJA Michael Jordan	50.00	120.00
MPA Morris Peterson	2.00	5.00
QRA Quentin Richardson	2.50	6.00
RWA Rasheed Wallace	3.00	8.00
SFA Steve Francis	3.00	8.00
SMA Stephon Marbury	2.50	6.00
SSA Stromile Swift	2.00	5.00
WSA Wally Szczerbiak	2.50	6.00

2002-03 UD Authentics Court Quality

Randomly inserted in packs, this 15-card set features a horizontal design with player photos on the left and a square swatch of game-worn memorabilia on the right. Each card is sequentially numbered to 300.

AMQ Alonzo Mourning	4.00	10.00
CMQ Chris Mihm	2.00	5.00
DJQ DerMarr Johnson	2.00	5.00
DMQ Darius Miles	2.00	5.00
DWQ David Wesley	2.00	5.00
ECQ Eddy Curry	2.50	6.00
GHQ Grant Hill	4.00	10.00
GRQ Glenn Robinson	2.50	6.00
KBQ Kobe Bryant	15.00	40.00
KGQ Kevin Garnett	6.00	15.00
KMQ Kenyon Martin	3.00	8.00
KVQ Keith Van Horn	2.50	6.00
PEQ Patrick Ewing	4.00	10.00
TBQ Terrell Brandon	2.00	5.00
TCQ Tyson Chandler	2.50	6.00

2002-03 UD Authentics Kevin Garnett Heroes of Basketball

Randomly inserted in packs, this 10-card set pays tribute to Kevin Garnett. Cards are white bordered with full-color player action photos. Each card is sequentially numbered to 1989. An Autographed parallel of this set was also inserted with cards sequentially numbered to 10.

COMPLETE SET (10)	15.00	40.00
COMMON CARD (KG1-KG10)	2.50	6.00

2002-03 UD Authentics Kobe Bryant Heroes of Basketball

Randomly inserted in packs, this 10-card set pays tribute to Kobe Bryant. Cards are white bordered with full-color player action photos. Each card is sequentially numbered to 989. An Autographed parallel of this set was also inserted with each card sequentially numbered to eight.

COMPLETE SET (10)	25.00	60.00
COMMON CARD (KB1-KB10)	5.00	12.00

2002-03 UD Authentics Michael Jordan Heroes of Basketball

Randomly inserted in packs, this 10-card set pays tribute to Michael Jordan. Cards are white bordered with full-color player action photos. Each card is sequentially numbered to 198. An Autographed parallel of this set was also inserted where each card is a one of one.

COMPLETE SET (10)	175.00	350.00
COMMON CARD (1-10)	20.00	50.00

2002-03 UD Authentics Signatures

Seeded in packs at the rate of one in 108, this 23-card set places full color player photographs at the top of the card and an authentic player autograph above the player's printed name on the bottom.

BA Brandon Armstrong	4.00	10.00
BR Brian Scalabrine	4.00	10.00
CM Corey Maggette	4.00	10.00
EC Eddy Curry	5.00	12.00
EG Eddie Griffin	4.00	10.00
EW Earl Watson	4.00	10.00
JA Jarron Collins	4.00	10.00
JC Jason Collins	4.00	10.00
JR Jason Richardson	6.00	15.00
JS Jeryl Sasser	4.00	10.00
KE Kedrick Brown	4.00	10.00
KH Kirk Haston	4.00	10.00
KS Kenny Satterfield	4.00	10.00
KW Kwame Brown	5.00	12.00
MB Michael Bradley	4.00	10.00
RB Ruben Boumtje-Boumtje	4.00	10.00
RJ Richard Jefferson	5.00	12.00
RW Rodney White	4.00	10.00
SD Samuel Dalembert	4.00	10.00
SH Steven Hunter	4.00	10.00
TC Tyson Chandler	6.00	15.00
TM Troy Murphy	4.00	10.00
ZR Zeljko Rebraca	4.00	10.00

2002-03 UD Authentics Stat Patterns

Inserted in packs, this 18-card set features a horzontal design with a blue background. Swatches of game-worn memorabilia appear on the right side of the card and full color player photos appear on the left. Each card is sequentially numbered to 500.

AIS Allen Iverson	5.00	12.00
AMS Andre Miller	2.50	6.00
CMS Corey Maggette	2.50	6.00
CWS Chris Webber	3.00	8.00
DMS Dikembe Mutombo	3.00	8.00
EBS Elton Brand	3.00	8.00
ESS Eric Snow	2.00	5.00
GPS Gary Payton	3.00	8.00
JOS Jermaine O'Neal	3.00	8.00
KAS Kenny Anderson	2.50	6.00
KBS Kobe Bryant	12.50	30.00
KGS Kevin Garnett	6.00	15.00
MOS Michael Olowokandi	2.00	5.00
PSS Peja Stojakovic	3.00	8.00
RLS Rashard Lewis	3.00	8.00
SMS Joe Smith	2.50	6.00
TMS Tracy McGrady	5.00	12.00
WSS Wally Szczerbiak	2.50	6.00

2002-03 UD Authentics Uniform Greatness

Inserted in packs at the rate of one in ten, this 21-card set utilizes a horizontal design with full-color player action photographs on the right side of the card and a star swatch of game-used memorabilia on the left side. Background colors on the right are set to match the featured player's team jersey while the background on the left is white with a peach-colored stripe through the middle.

AHU Anfernee Hardaway	5.00	12.00
ALU Allan Houston	2.50	6.00
BRU Bryon Russell	2.00	5.00
DFU Derek Fisher	2.50	6.00
DGU Devean George	2.00	5.00
DMU Desmond Mason	2.50	6.00
JSU Joe Smith	2.50	6.00
JTU Jason Terry	2.50	6.00
KBU Kobe Bryant	10.00	25.00
KGU Kevin Garnett	6.00	15.00
LSU Latrell Sprewell	2.50	6.00
MAU Marcus Fizer	2.00	5.00
MJU Michael Jordan	40.00	100.00
RHU Robert Horry	2.50	6.00
SHU Shawn Marion	3.00	8.00
SMU Stephon Marbury	2.50	6.00
SNU Steve Nash	4.00	10.00
SSU Stromile Swift	2.00	5.00
TBU Terrell Brandon	2.00	5.00
TGU Tom Gugliotta	2.00	5.00
WSU Wally Szczerbiak	2.50	6.00

2006-07 UD Black

STATED PRINT RUN 99 SER.#'d SETS

2 Jerry West	10.00	25.00
3 Michael Jordan	60.00	150.00
4 Kevin McHale	10.00	25.00
5 Ben Wallace	8.00	20.00
6 Antawn Jamison	8.00	20.00
7 Andrei Kirilenko	6.00	15.00
8 Ray Allen	8.00	20.00
9 Tony Parker	8.00	20.00
12 Chris Webber	8.00	20.00
15 Antoine Walker	6.00	15.00
16 Gary Payton	8.00	20.00
19 Josh Smith	8.00	20.00
20 Peja Stojakovic	8.00	20.00

2006-07 UD Black 25

*BLACK: .75X TO 2X BASE HI
STATED PRINT RUN 25 SER.#'d SETS

2006-07 UD Black Autographs Dual

STATED PRINT RUN 25 SER.#'d SETS
UNPRICED DUAL PRINT RUN 10 SETS

CI Rodney Carney	15.00	40.00
Andre Iguodala		
GG Pau Gasol	12.00	30.00
Rudy Gay		
JH LeBron James	150.00	300.00
Dwight Howard		
JR Michael Jordan	300.00	500.00
Dennis Rodman		
KA B.J. Armstrong	25.00	60.00
Steve Kerr		
NW Paul Westphal	25.00	60.00
Steve Nash		
PS Chris Paul	25.00	60.00
Cedric Simmons		
RF Walt Frazier	25.00	60.00
Nate Robinson		
WJ Shelden Williams	10.00	25.00
Solomon Jones		

2006-07 UD Black Autographs Flags

STATED PRINT RUN 25 SER.#'d SETS

AB Andrea Bargnani	15.00	40.00
AI Andre Iguodala	20.00	50.00
EH Elvin Hayes	10.00	25.00
LA LaMarcus Aldridge	20.00	50.00
RG Rudy Gay	15.00	40.00
RO Brandon Roy	20.00	50.00
TT Tyrus Thomas	12.00	30.00
YM Yao Ming	50.00	120.00

2006-07 UD Black Autographs Legends

STATED PRINT RUN 25 SER.#'d SETS
UNPRICED PARALLEL PRINT RUN 5 SETS

AD Adrian Dantley	10.00	25.00
BD Brad Daugherty	10.00	25.00
BL Bill Laimbeer	10.00	25.00
WF Walt Frazier	10.00	25.00

2006-07 UD Black Autographs Nameplates

STATED PRINT RUN 50 SER.#'d SETS
UNPRICED PARALLEL PRINT RUN 5 SETS

BR Brandon Roy	25.00	60.00
JB Josh Boone	10.00	25.00
JF Jordan Farmar	10.00	25.00
KL Kyle Lowry	12.00	30.00
LA LaMarcus Aldridge	25.00	60.00
LJ LeBron James	125.00	250.00
QD Quincy Douby	10.00	25.00
RC Rodney Carney	10.00	25.00
RF Randy Foye	12.00	30.00
RG Rudy Gay	15.00	40.00
RR Rajon Rondo	50.00	120.00
SW Shawne Williams	10.00	25.00
TT Tyrus Thomas	12.00	30.00

2006-07 UD Black Autographs Rookie Materials

STATED PRINT RUN 50 SER.#'d SETS
UNPRICED PARALLEL PRINT RUN 15 SETS

BR Brandon Roy	25.00	60.00
HA Hilton Armstrong	10.00	25.00
JF Jordan Farmar	10.00	25.00
KL Kyle Lowry	12.00	30.00
KP Kevin Pittsnogle	10.00	25.00
LA LaMarcus Aldridge	25.00	60.00
MC Mardy Collins	10.00	25.00
PT P.J. Tucker	10.00	25.00
RG Rudy Gay	15.00	40.00
RR Rajon Rondo	50.00	120.00
TT Tyrus Thomas	12.00	30.00

2006-07 UD Black Autographs Rookies

STATED PRINT RUN 99 SER.#'d SETS
UNPRICED PARALLEL PRINT RUN 15 SETS

AB Andrea Bargnani	12.00	30.00
BA Renaldo Balkman	8.00	20.00
BR Brandon Roy	20.00	50.00
CS Cedric Simmons	8.00	20.00
HA Hilton Armstrong	8.00	20.00
JB Josh Boone	8.00	20.00
JF Jordan Farmar	8.00	20.00
KL Kyle Lowry	10.00	25.00
MW Marcus Williams	8.00	20.00
PO Patrick O'Bryant	8.00	20.00
RB Ronnie Brewer	10.00	25.00
RC Rodney Carney	8.00	20.00
RR Rajon Rondo	40.00	100.00
SB Shannon Brown	12.00	30.00
SW Shelden Williams	8.00	20.00
TS Thabo Sefolosha	10.00	25.00

2006-07 UD Black Autographs Tickets

STATED PRINT RUN 50 SER.#'d SETS
UNPRICED PARALLEL PRINT RUN 10 SETS

DN David Noel	8.00	20.00
FO Randy Foye	10.00	25.00
JF Jordan Farmar	8.00	20.00
JS J.R. Smith	8.00	20.00
LA LaMarcus Aldridge	20.00	50.00
LB Leandro Barbosa	8.00	20.00
LJ LeBron James	200.00	400.00
MA Maurice Ager	8.00	20.00
NR Nate Robinson	15.00	40.00
RF Raymond Felton	10.00	25.00
SN Steve Novak	8.00	20.00
TT Tyrus Thomas	10.00	25.00

2006-07 UD Black Autographs Veteran Materials

STATED PRINT RUN 25 SER.#'d SETS
UNPRICED PARALLEL PRINT RUN 5 SETS

BD Baron Davis	10.00	25.00
BG Ben Gordon	12.50	30.00
CF Channing Frye	10.00	25.00
CM Corey Maggette	12.50	30.00
DH Dwight Howard	30.00	80.00
PP Paul Pierce	25.00	60.00
PS Peja Stojakovic	20.00	50.00
RF Raymond Felton	10.00	25.00
VC Vince Carter	20.00	50.00

2006-07 UD Black Autographs Veterans

UNPRICED PARALLEL PRINT RUN 15 SETS

CV Charlie Villanueva	8.00	20.00
NR Nate Robinson	8.00	20.00
RM Rashad McCants/99	8.00	20.00
RT Ronny Turiaf/99	10.00	25.00
TF T.J. Ford/89	8.00	20.00

2006-07 UD Black Dual Materials

STATED PRINT RUN 99 SER.#'d SETS
*DUAL 25: .5X TO 1.25X BASE HI
DUAL PRINT RUN 25 SER.#'d SETS

AI Allen Iverson	10.00	25.00
CA Carmelo Anthony	10.00	25.00
CM Corey Maggette	6.00	15.00
CP Chris Paul	15.00	40.00
DG Drew Gooden	6.00	15.00
DR David Robinson	12.00	30.00
JE Julius Erving	15.00	40.00
JR Jason Richardson	8.00	20.00
KK Kyle Korver	6.00	15.00
LA LaMarcus Aldridge	20.00	50.00

LD Luol Deng 8.00 20.00
LJ LeBron James 25.00 60.00
MG Manu Ginobili 8.00 20.00
MJ Michael Jordan 60.00 150.00
RA Ray Allen 8.00 20.00
RE J.J. Redick 10.00 25.00
RF Randy Foye 10.00 25.00
RH Richard Hamilton 6.00 15.00
RO Brandon Roy 20.00 50.00
RW Rasheed Wallace 8.00 20.00
SM Shawn Marion 8.00 20.00
SW Shelden Williams 8.00 20.00
TD Tim Duncan 12.00 30.00
TM Tracy McGrady 10.00 25.00
TP Tony Parker 8.00 20.00
WC Wilt Chamberlain 50.00 120.00
WF Walt Frazier 10.00 25.00

2006-07 UD Black Dual Materials Autographs

STATED PRINT RUN 25 SER.#'d SETS
UNPRICED PARALLEL PRINT RUN 15 SETS
BR Brandon Roy 40.00 100.00
CD Clyde Drexler 25.00 60.00
CP Chris Paul 40.00 100.00
EB Elton Brand 8.00 20.00
LA LaMarcus Aldridge 40.00 100.00
LJ LeBron James 200.00 450.00
NR Nate Robinson 15.00 40.00
PP Paul Pierce 25.00 60.00
PS Peja Stojakovic 20.00 50.00
RB Renaldo Balkman 8.00 20.00
RF Raymond Felton 10.00 25.00
RG Rudy Gay 25.00 60.00
RR Rajon Rondo 75.00 150.00

2006-07 UD Black Jerseys Autographs

STATED PRINT RUN 50 SER.#'d SETS
UNPRICED PARALLEL PRINT RUN 10 SETS
AI Andre Iguodala 6.00 15.00
BM Brad Miller 6.00 15.00
DH Dwight Howard 30.00 80.00
DR Dennis Rodman 40.00 100.00
FO Randy Foye 6.00 15.00
JF Jordan Farmar 8.00 20.00
KK Kyle Korver 6.00 15.00
LA LaMarcus Aldridge 20.00 50.00
PG Pau Gasol 10.00 25.00
TC Tyson Chandler 6.00 15.00
TT Tyrus Thomas 10.00 25.00

2006-07 UD Black Jerseys Dual

STATED PRINT RUN 50 SER.#'d SETS
UNPRICED PARALLEL PRINT RUN 15 SETS
BJ Kobe Bryant 30.00 80.00
Magic Johnson
BM Larry Bird 15.00 40.00
Kevin McHale
BT Isiah Thomas 10.00 25.00
Chauncey Billups
CA Tyson Chandler 6.00 15.00
Hilton Armstrong
DM Paul Davis 6.00 15.00
Corey Maggette
GJ Kevin Garnett 10.00 25.00
Mike James
GL Pau Gasol 10.00 25.00
Kyle Lowry
JB LeBron James 40.00 100.00
Shannon Brown
KW Jason Kidd 10.00 25.00
Marcus Williams
OW Shaquille O'Neal 12.50 30.00
Antoine Walker

2006-07 UD Black Jerseys Dual Autographs

STATED PRINT RUN 25 SER.#'d SETS
AM Shareef Abdur-Rahim 30.00 80.00
Tracy McGrady
CJ LeBron James 175.00 350.00
Vince Carter
EC Mark Eaton 10.00 25.00
Tom Chambers
MY Brad Miller 50.00 125.00
Yao Ming

2006-07 UD Black Legends Materials Autographs

STATED PRINT RUN 25 SER.#'d SETS
UNPRICED PARALLEL PRINT RUN 5 SETS
BW Bill Walton 12.50 30.00
MJ Michael Jordan 350.00 650.00

2006-07 UD Black Patches

STATED PRINT RUN 50 SER.#'d SETS
*PATCH 25: .5X TO 1.25X BASE HI
PATCH 25 PRINT RUN 25 SETS
UNPRICED PARALLEL PRINT RUN 15 SETS
AI Allen Iverson 50.00 125.00
AM Alonzo Mourning 100.00 200.00
AS Amare Stoudemire 10.00 25.00
DH Devin Harris 8.00 20.00
JN Jameer Nelson 8.00 20.00
JO Jermaine O'Neal 8.00 20.00
JR Jason Richardson 8.00 20.00
KB Kobe Bryant 100.00 200.00
KG Kevin Garnett 25.00 60.00
KM Kevin McHale 20.00 50.00
LJ LeBron James 100.00 200.00
MK Karl Malone 25.00 60.00
MM Moses Malone 20.00 50.00
MR Michael Redd 8.00 20.00
MW Marvin Williams 8.00 20.00
RL Rashard Lewis 8.00 20.00
RW Rasheed Wallace 10.00 25.00
SO Shaquille O'Neal 25.00 60.00
TD Tim Duncan 25.00 60.00
ZI Zydrunas Ilgauskas 8.00 20.00

2006-07 UD Black Patches Autographs

STATED PRINT RUN 25 SER.#'d SETS
UNPRICED PARALLEL PRINT RUN 10 SETS
CS Cedric Simmons 8.00 20.00
DE Dee Brown 8.00 20.00
DN David Noel 8.00 20.00
PD Paul Davis 8.00 20.00
RB Renaldo Balkman 8.00 20.00
RF Randy Foye 10.00 25.00
RR Rajon Rondo 75.00 150.00
SB Shannon Brown 25.00 60.00
SW Shawne Williams 8.00 20.00

2006-07 UD Black Patches Dual

STATED PRINT RUN 25 SER.#'d SETS
UNPRICED COLLEGE PRINT RUN 10 SETS
JM Antawn Jamison 8.00 20.00
Sean May
OA Emeka Okafor 8.00 20.00
Ray Allen
OT Shaquille O'Neal 20.00 50.00
Tyrus Thomas
PH Paul Pierce 12.00 30.00
Kirk Hinrich

2006-07 UD Black Patches Numbers

STATED PRINT RUN 25 SER.#'d SETS
BD Baron Davis 12.00 30.00
BW Ben Wallace 15.00 40.00
JR Jason Richardson 12.00 30.00
KB Kobe Bryant 60.00 150.00
TP Tayshaun Prince 8.00 20.00

2007-08 UD Black

Released in March 2008, UD Black was packaged in two-pack boxes with one card per pack where the intial pack SRP was $125. The complete 126-card set is divided up as follows: cards 1-84 are sequentially numbered to 25 and feature a horizontal design which places a player photo on the right next to four swatches of jersey patch, cards 85-120 are sequentially numbered to 99 and feature rookies along with both autographs and jersey swatches, and cards 121-126 feature rookie players sequentially numbered to 99.
UNPRICED GOLD PRINT RUN 5 TO 10 SETS
UNPRICED WHITE PRINT RUN ONE SET
1 Clyde Drexler JSY 35.00 75.00
2 Al Jefferson JSY 10.00 25.00
3 Allen Iverson JSY 25.00 60.00
4 Alonzo Mourning JSY 25.00 50.00
5 Amare Stoudemire JSY 15.00 40.00
6 Andre Iguodala JSY 10.00 25.00
7 Andrea Bargnani JSY 12.00 30.00
8 Andrew Bogut JSY 10.00 25.00
9 Antawn Jamison JSY 10.00 25.00
10 Baron Davis JSY 10.00 25.00
11 Ben Gordon JSY 10.00 25.00
12 Bernard King JSY 10.00 25.00
13 Bill Laimbeer JSY 10.00 25.00
14 Bill Russell JSY 20.00 50.00
15 Dwyane Wade JSY 25.00 60.00
16 Brandon Roy JSY 15.00 40.00
17 Carlos Arroyo JSY 10.00 25.00
18 Carlos Boozer JSY 10.00 25.00
19 Carmelo Anthony JSY 20.00 50.00
20 Chris Bosh JSY 20.00 50.00
21 Chris Mullin JSY 20.00 40.00
22 Chris Paul JSY 40.00 75.00
23 Corey Maggette JSY 10.00 25.00
24 Adrian Dantley JSY 10.00 25.00
25 Dennis Rodman JSY 25.00 60.00
26 Deron Williams JSY 20.00 40.00
27 Dirk Nowitzki JSY 20.00 50.00
28 Dominique Wilkins JSY 20.00 40.00
29 Dwight Howard JSY 20.00 50.00
30 Eddy Curry JSY 10.00 25.00
31 Elton Brand JSY 10.00 25.00
32 Emeka Okafor JSY 10.00 25.00
33 George Gervin JSY 12.50 30.00
34 Gilbert Arenas JSY 12.50 30.00
35 Hakeem Olajuwon JSY 20.00 40.00
36 Jamaal Tinsley JSY 10.00 25.00
37 James Worthy JSY 20.00 40.00
38 Jason Kidd JSY 15.00 40.00
39 Jason Richardson JSY 10.00 25.00
40 Jermaine O'Neal JSY 10.00 25.00
41 Jerry West JSY 40.00 75.00
42 Joe Dumars JSY 15.00 40.00
43 John Stockton JSY 20.00 40.00
44 Josh Howard JSY 10.00 25.00
45 Julius Erving JSY 20.00 50.00
46 Kareem Abdul-Jabbar JSY 30.00 60.00
47 Karl Malone JSY 20.00 40.00
48 Kevin Garnett JSY 40.00 70.00
49 Kevin McHale JSY 12.00 30.00
50 Kirk Hinrich JSY 10.00 25.00
51 Kobe Bryant JSY 100.00 200.00
52 Kyle Korver JSY 10.00 25.00
53 Lamar Odom JSY 10.00 25.00
54 LaMarcus Aldridge JSY 12.00 30.00
55 Larry Bird JSY 30.00 80.00
56 Larry Hughes JSY 10.00 25.00
57 LeBron James JSY 125.00 225.00
58 Magic Johnson JSY 40.00 75.00
59 Marvin Williams JSY 10.00 25.00
60 Michael Jordan JSY 300.00 600.00
61 Michael Redd JSY 10.00 25.00
62 Mike Bibby JSY 10.00 25.00
63 Oscar Robertson JSY 35.00 70.00
64 Pau Gasol JSY 10.00 25.00
65 Paul Pierce JSY 12.00 30.00
66 Pete Maravich JSY 60.00 120.00
67 Randy Foye JSY 10.00 25.00
68 Rashard Lewis JSY 10.00 25.00
69 Rasheed Wallace JSY 12.50 30.00
70 Ray Allen JSY 15.00 40.00
71 Ron Artest JSY 10.00 25.00
72 Rudy Gay JSY 10.00 25.00
73 Shaquille O'Neal JSY 20.00 50.00
74 Shelden Williams JSY 10.00 25.00
75 Stephon Marbury JSY 10.00 25.00
76 Steve Nash JSY 20.00 40.00
77 Tayshaun Prince JSY 10.00 25.00
78 Tim Duncan JSY 30.00 60.00
79 Tony Parker JSY 10.00 25.00
80 Tracy McGrady JSY 10.00 25.00
81 Vince Carter JSY 25.00 50.00
82 Walt Frazier JSY 10.00 25.00
83 Wilt Chamberlain JSY 50.00 120.00
84 Yao Ming JSY 20.00 40.00
85 Carl Landry JSY AU RC 10.00 25.00
86 Gabe Pruitt JSY AU RC 10.00 25.00
87 Marcus Williams JSY AU RC 10.00 25.00
88 Nick Fazekas JSY AU RC 10.00 25.00
89 Glen Davis JSY AU RC 15.00 40.00
90 Jermareo Davidson JSY AU RC 10.00 25.00
91 Josh McRoberts JSY AU RC 10.00 25.00
92 Chris Richard JSY AU RC 10.00 25.00
93 Derrick Byars JSY AU RC 10.00 25.00
94 Adam Haluska JSY AU RC 10.00 25.00
95 Reyshawn Terry JSY AU RC 10.00 25.00
96 Jared Jordan JSY AU RC 10.00 25.00
97 Stephane Lasme JSY AU RC 10.00 25.00
98 Dominic McGuire JSY AU RC 10.00 25.00
99 Al Horford JSY AU RC 12.00 30.00
100 Mike Conley Jr. JSY AU RC 15.00 40.00
101 Jeff Green JSY AU RC 12.00 30.00
102 Corey Brewer JSY AU RC 12.00 30.00
103 Joakim Noah JSY AU RC 25.00 60.00
104 Spencer Hawes JSY AU RC 10.00 25.00
105 Acie Law JSY AU RC 10.00 25.00
106 Kevin Durant JSY AU RC 400.00 800.00
107 Julian Wright JSY AU RC 10.00 25.00
108 Al Thornton JSY AU RC 10.00 25.00
109 Rodney Stuckey JSY AU RC 15.00 40.00
110 Sean Williams JSY AU RC 10.00 25.00
111 Marco Belinelli JSY AU RC 10.00 25.00
112 Javaris Crittenton JSY AU RC 10.00 25.00
113 Jason Smith JSY AU RC 10.00 25.00
114 Daequan Cook JSY AU RC 10.00 25.00
115 Aaron Brooks JSY AU RC 10.00 25.00
116 Arron Afflalo JSY AU RC 12.00 30.00
117 Alando Tucker JSY AU RC 10.00 25.00
118 Jared Dudley JSY AU RC 10.00 25.00
119 Wilson Chandler JSY AU RC 15.00 40.00
120 Morris Almond JSY AU RC 10.00 25.00
121 Greg Oden RC 10.00 25.00
122 Nick Young RC 12.00 30.00
123 Yi Jianlian RC 12.00 30.00
124 Brandan Wright RC 8.00 20.00
125 Sun Yue RC 8.00 20.00
126 Thaddeus Young RC 10.00 25.00

2007-08 UD Black 50th Anniversary Autographs

PRINT RUN 50 SER.#'d SETS
UNPRICED GOLD PRINT RUN 10 SER.#'d SETS
UNPRICED WHITE PRINT RUN ONE SET
BR Bill Russell 125.00 250.00
BS Bill Sharman 25.00 60.00
BW Bill Walton 30.00 70.00
CD Clyde Drexler 125.00 225.00
DC Dave Cowens 25.00 60.00
DR David Robinson 100.00 200.00
DS Dolph Schayes 25.00 60.00
EB Elgin Baylor 35.00 70.00
HG Hal Greer 35.00 70.00
HO Hakeem Olajuwon 40.00 75.00
JE Julius Erving 100.00 200.00
JH John Havlicek 40.00 80.00
JL Jerry Lucas 25.00 60.00
JO Michael Jordan 500.00 750.00
JS John Stockton 75.00 150.00
JW Jerry West 100.00 200.00
KA Kareem Abdul-Jabbar 100.00 200.00
LB Larry Bird 100.00 200.00
LW Lenny Wilkens 30.00 80.00
MJ Magic Johnson 80.00 200.00
NA Nate Tiny Archibald 25.00 60.00
NT Nate Thurmond 25.00 60.00
RB Rick Barry 25.00 60.00
RP Robert Parish 25.00 60.00
SJ Sam Jones 30.00 80.00
WF Walt Frazier 25.00 60.00
WO James Worthy 40.00 100.00
WU Wes Unseld 35.00 70.00

2007-08 UD Black All-Star Autographs

PRINT RUN 25 SER.#'d SETS
*GOLD: .5X TO 1.25X BASE HI
GOLD PRINT RUN 15 SER.#'d SETS
UNPRICED WHITE PRINT RUN ONE SET
UAJ Antawn Jamison 20.00 40.00
UBD Brad Daugherty 20.00 40.00
UCD Clyde Drexler 50.00 125.00
UDR David Robinson 75.00 150.00
UDT David Thompson 20.00 40.00
UDW Dominique Wilkins 40.00 80.00
UGR Glen Rice 20.00 40.00
UHG Horace Grant 20.00 40.00
UJE Julius Erving 100.00 200.00
UJK Jason Kidd 40.00 80.00
UJS John Stockton 75.00 150.00
UKB Kobe Bryant 400.00 600.00
UKG Kevin Garnett 75.00 150.00
ULJ LeBron James 300.00 500.00
UMJ Michael Jordan 500.00 1000.00
UNA Nate Archibald 20.00 40.00
UPP Paul Pierce 20.00 40.00
URB Rick Barry 30.00 60.00

2007-08 UD Black Autographs

PRINT RUN 25 OR 50 SER.#'d SETS
*GOLD/25: .5X TO 1.25X BASE HI
GOLD/10 UNPRICED DUE TO SCARCITY
UNPRICED WHITE PRINT RUN ONE SET
AUAD Adrian Dantley/50 10.00 25.00
AUAH Al Horford/25 25.00 50.00
AUAJ Antawn Jamison/50 10.00 25.00
AUAL Acie Law/50 10.00 25.00
AUAM Alonzo Mourning/25 40.00 100.00
AUAT Al Thornton/50 10.00 25.00
AUBA Leandro Barbosa/50 10.00 25.00
AUBE Marco Belinelli/50 10.00 25.00
AUBG Ben Gordon/50 10.00 25.00
AUBL Bill Laimbeer/50 10.00 25.00
AUBR Brandon Roy/50 12.50 30.00
AUBW Bill Walton/25 15.00 30.00
AUCA Carmelo Anthony/25 30.00 80.00
AUCB Chris Bosh/25 30.00 60.00
AUCD Chuck Daly/50 10.00 25.00
AUCH Connie Hawkins/25 10.00 25.00
AUCR Javaris Crittenton/50 10.00 25.00
AUCY Corey Brewer/25 10.00 25.00
AUDC Daequan Cook/50 10.00 25.00
AUDH Dwight Howard/25 25.00 60.00
AUDT David Thompson/50 12.50 30.00
AUDW Dominique Wilkins/25 20.00 40.00
AUHO Hakeem Olajuwon/25 20.00 40.00
AUJA James Worthy/25 25.00 50.00
AUJG Jeff Green/50 10.00 25.00
AUJK Jason Kidd/25 30.00 60.00
AUJM Josh McRoberts/50 10.00 25.00
AUJN Joakim Noah/25 40.00 75.00
AUJO Michael Jordan/25 400.00 700.00
AUJS Jason Smith/50 10.00 25.00
AUJS John Stockton/25 40.00 80.00
AUJW Julian Wright/25 10.00 25.00
AUKH Kirk Hinrich/25 10.00 25.00
AULA LaMarcus Aldridge/25 10.00 25.00
AULJ LeBron James/25 125.00 250.00
AUMB Mike Bibby/25 10.00 25.00
AUMC Mike Conley Jr./25 15.00 40.00
AUMJ Magic Johnson/25 50.00 120.00
AUPP Pat Riley/50 12.50 30.00
AUPP Paul Pierce/25 20.00 50.00
AUPR Pat Riley/25 15.00 40.00
AURB Rick Barry/25 15.00 30.00
AURG Rudy Gay/50 12.00 30.00
AURR Rajon Rondo/50 25.00 60.00
AURS Rodney Stuckey/50 15.00 40.00
AUSP Sam Perkins/50 10.00 25.00
AUSW Sean Williams/25 10.00 25.00
AUTP Tayshaun Prince/25 10.00 25.00
AUWF Walt Frazier/50 15.00 40.00
AUWI Deron Williams/50 20.00 40.00
AUWU Wes Unseld/50 10.00 25.00
AUYM Yao Ming/25 20.00 40.00

2007-08 UD Black Autographs Dual

PRINT RUN 25 SER.#'d SETS
*GOLD: .5X TO 1.25X BASE HI
GOLD PRINT RUN 15 SER.#'d SETS
UNPRICED WHITE PRINT RUN ONE SET
BL Ernie Banks 15.00 40.00
Acie Law
BW Kobe Bryant 225.00 325.00
Jerry West
CB Mike Conley Jr. 15.00 40.00
Corey Brewer
CC Mike Conley Jr. 15.00 40.00
Mike Conley Sr.
CM Vince Carter 40.00 80.00
Tracy McGrady
DA Kevin Durant 150.00 250.00
LaMarcus Aldridge
DC Daequan Cook 15.00 40.00
Mike Conley Jr.
GB Corey Brewer 15.00 40.00
Taurean Green
GN Ben Gordon 35.00 75.00
Joakim Noah
HH Alfredo Tito Horford 25.00 50.00
Al Horford
HR Spencer Hawes 15.00 40.00
Brandon Roy
JA Carmelo Anthony 200.00 350.00
LeBron James
JB Magic Johnson 150.00 250.00
Larry Bird
JJ LeBron James 500.00 900.00
Michael Jordan
JR Michael Jordan 400.00 600.00
Dennis Rodman
LD Bill Laimbeer 15.00 40.00
Adrian Dantley
NK Steve Nash 60.00 120.00
Jason Kidd
OD Hakeem Olajuwon 30.00 60.00
Clyde Drexler
OG Emeka Okafor 15.00 40.00
Ben Gordon
PM Pat Riley 60.00 120.00
Magic Johnson
RH Bill Russell 75.00 150.00
Tom Heinsohn
RJ Sam Jones 100.00 200.00
Bill Russell
WS Deron Williams 60.00 120.00
John Stockton
WW Dominique Wilkins 25.00 50.00
Spud Webb
YD Kevin Durant 150.00 300.00
Vince Young

2007-08 UD Black Autographs Triple

PRINT RUN 15 SER.#'d SETS
UNPRICED GOLD PRINT RUN TEN SETS
UNPRICED WHITE PRINT RUN ONE SET
ECW Julius Erving 75.00 150.00
Dominique Wilkins
Vince Carter
GBM Kevin Garnett 200.00 350.00
Kobe Bryant
Moses Malone
HBN Al Horford 50.00 100.00
Corey Brewer
Joakim Noah
JBJ Kobe Bryant 1500.00 2500.00
LeBron James
Michael Jordan
NKS John Stockton 200.00 400.00
Steve Nash
Jason Kidd
OSM Ralph Sampson 100.00 200.00
Hakeem Olajuwon
Yao Ming
PRB Bill Russell 300.00 450.00
Larry Bird
Paul Pierce
WJA Kareem Abdul-Jabbar 200.00 300.00
Magic Johnson
James Worthy

2007-08 UD Black Flags Autographs

PRINT RUN 25 SER.#'d SETS
UNPRICED GOLD PRINT RUN 10 SER.#'d SETS
UNPRICED WHITE PRINT RUN ONE SET
FAAB Andrea Bargnani 25.00 60.00
FAAH Al Horford 20.00 40.00
FABG Ben Gordon 20.00 40.00
FACB Corey Brewer 20.00 40.00
FADW Dominique Wilkins 30.00 60.00
FAGR Jeff Green 25.00 50.00
FAHO Hakeem Olajuwon 40.00 80.00
FAJN Joakim Noah 40.00 75.00
FAJW Julian Wright 30.00 60.00
FAKB Kobe Bryant 350.00 500.00
FAKD Kevin Durant 250.00 450.00
FALB Leandro Barbosa 20.00 40.00
FARB Rolando Blackman 20.00 40.00
FASK Steve Kerr 25.00 60.00
FASN Steve Nash 60.00 120.00
FATP Tony Parker 25.00 50.00

2007-08 UD Black Framed Autographs

PRINT RUN 25 SER.#'d SETS
UNPRICED GOLD PRINT RUN 5 SETS
UNPRICED WHITE PRINT RUN ONE SET
AD Adrian Dantley 10.00 25.00
AH Al Horford 25.00 50.00
AL Acie Law 10.00 25.00
BR Brandon Roy 15.00 40.00
CB Corey Brewer 12.50 30.00
CP Chris Paul 40.00 100.00
JG Jeff Green 15.00 30.00
JL Jerry Lucas 10.00 25.00
JN Joakim Noah 40.00 75.00
JO Magic Johnson 40.00 80.00
JS John Stockton 40.00 80.00
JW Julian Wright 15.00 30.00
LA LaMarcus Aldridge 15.00 40.00
MC Mike Conley Jr. 15.00 30.00
PP Paul Pierce 15.00 40.00
RG Rudy Gay 15.00 30.00
SN Steve Nash 40.00 100.00
TT Tyrus Thomas 10.00 25.00
VC Vince Carter 25.00 60.00
WI Deron Williams 20.00 40.00
WO James Worthy 25.00 50.00

2007-08 UD Black Letters Autographs

PRINT RUN 25 SER.#'d SETS
UNPRICED GOLD PRINT RUN 10 SETS
UNPRICED WHITE PRINT RUN ONE SET
LAAD Adrian Dantley 20.00 40.00
LAAE Alex English 20.00 40.00
LAAI Andre Iguodala 20.00 40.00
LAAJ Antawn Jamison 20.00 40.00
LAAM Alonzo Mourning 50.00 100.00
LAAR Arnie Risen 20.00 40.00
LABG Ben Gordon 20.00 40.00
LABL Bill Laimbeer 20.00 40.00
LABS Bill Sharman 25.00 50.00
LABW Bill Walton 20.00 40.00
LADH Dwight Howard 30.00 60.00
LADM Danny Manning 20.00 40.00
LADR David Robinson 50.00 100.00
LADS Dolph Schayes 20.00 40.00
LADW Deron Williams 40.00 75.00
LAJE Julius Erving 100.00 200.00
LAJK Jason Kidd 50.00 100.00
LAJS John Stockton 40.00 80.00
LAKB Kobe Bryant 250.00 400.00
LAPP Paul Pierce 25.00 50.00
LARO Dennis Rodman 50.00 100.00
LASN Steve Nash 60.00 120.00
LASP Sam Perkins 20.00 40.00
LATP Tony Parker 30.00 60.00
LAWE Jerry West 75.00 150.00

2007-08 UD Black Numbers Autographs

PRINT RUNS LISTED IN CHECKLIST
UNPRICED GOLD PRINT RUN 10 SER.#'d SETS
UNPRICED WHITE PRINT RUN ONE SET
NAAA Al Attles/16 25.00 50.00
NAAJ Al Jefferson/25 25.00 60.00
NABW Bill Walton/32 20.00 50.00
NACD Clyde Drexler/22 40.00 75.00
NACH Connie Hawkins/42 15.00 40.00
NADC Dave Cowens/18 30.00 60.00
NADH Dwight Howard/12 50.00 120.00
NADN Don Nelson/19 20.00 40.00
NAEB Elgin Baylor/22 25.00 50.00
NAEO Emeka Okafor/50 10.00 25.00
NAHG Hal Greer/15 20.00 40.00
NAHO Hakeem Olajuwon/34 30.00 80.00
NAJS Jack Sikma/43 10.00 25.00
NAKB Kobe Bryant/24 400.00 550.00
NAKD Kevin Durant/35 150.00 300.00
NAKV Kiki Vandeweghe/55 10.00 25.00
NALA LaMarcus Aldridge/12 25.00 50.00
NALB Larry Bird/33 100.00 200.00
NANT Nate Thurmond/42 15.00 40.00
NARG Rudy Gay/22 20.00 40.00
NART Rudy Tomjanovich/45 20.00 40.00
NASN Steve Nash/13 75.00 150.00
NAVC Vince Carter/15 30.00 60.00

2007-08 UD Black Patch Material Autographs

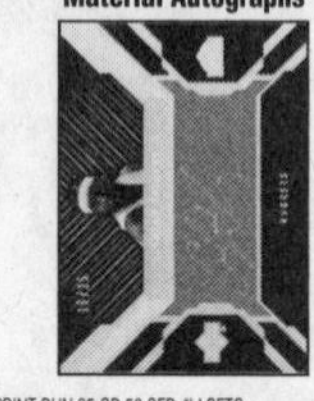

PRINT RUN 25 OR 50 SER.#'d SETS
UNPRICED GOLD PRINT RUN 10 SER.#'d SETS
UNPRICED BLUE PRINT RUN ONE SET
AA Al Attles/50 10.00 25.00
AC Al Cervi/50 10.00 25.00
AE Alex English/50 10.00 25.00
AH Al Horford/25 10.00 25.00
AM Alonzo Mourning/25 40.00 80.00
AR Arnie Risen/50 10.00 25.00
AT Al Thornton/50 10.00 25.00
BD Baron Davis/50 12.50 30.00
BG Ben Gordon/50 10.00 25.00
BL Bill Laimbeer/50 10.00 25.00
BR Brandon Roy/50 20.00 40.00
CB Chris Bosh/25 30.00 60.00
CD Clyde Drexler/50 25.00 50.00
CL Walt Frazier/50 10.00 25.00
CO Corey Brewer/25 10.00 25.00
CP Chris Paul/25 50.00 100.00
DC Daequan Cook/50 10.00 25.00
DL David Lee/50 12.50 30.00
DO Dominique Wilkins/25 25.00 60.00
DR Dennis Rodman/25 40.00 80.00
DW Deron Williams/50 20.00 50.00
EB Elgin Baylor/50 12.00 30.00
GG Gail Goodrich/50 15.00 40.00
GR Jeff Green/25 20.00 40.00
HG Hal Greer/25 20.00 40.00
JC Javaris Crittenton/50 10.00 25.00
JE Julius Erving/25 75.00 150.00
JL Jerry Lucas/25 30.00 80.00
JN Joakim Noah/25 35.00 70.00
JO Magic Johnson/25 75.00 150.00
JS John Stockton/25 60.00 120.00
JW Julian Wright/25 12.50 30.00
KB Kobe Bryant/25 200.00 400.00
KD Kevin Durant/50 200.00 400.00
KH Kirk Hinrich/25 12.50 30.00
LA LaMarcus Aldridge/50 10.00 25.00
LB Larry Bird/25 75.00 150.00
LJ LeBron James/25 125.00 250.00
MC Dick McGuire/50 10.00 25.00
MI Mike Conley Jr./25 20.00 40.00
MJ Michael Jordan/25 400.00 600.00
PP Paul Pierce/50 20.00 40.00
RB Renaldo Balkman/50 10.00 25.00
RG Rudy Gay/50 12.00 30.00
RI Rick Barry/25 20.00 40.00
RO David Robinson/25 60.00 120.00
RP Robert Parish/50 15.00 30.00
SH Spencer Hawes/50 10.00 25.00
SN Steve Nash/25 40.00 100.00
TG Taurean Green/50 10.00 25.00
TH Tom Heinsohn/50 10.00 25.00
TY Acie Law/50 10.00 25.00
VC Vince Carter/25 15.00 40.00
WO James Worthy/25 30.00 60.00

2007-08 UD Black Patch Material Autographs Dual

PRINT RUN 15 SER.#'d SETS
UNPRICED GOLD PRINT RUN 5 SETS
UNPRICED WHITE PRINT RUN ONE SET
AE Carmelo Anthony 30.00 80.00
Alex English
BG Elgin Baylor 30.00 60.00
Gail Goodrich
BN Kobe Bryant 300.00 500.00
Steve Nash
DA Baron Davis 30.00 60.00
Al Attles
EW Julius Erving 100.00 200.00
Dominique Wilkins
FD Walt Frazier 60.00 120.00
Clyde Drexler
JB Michael Jordan 500.00 800.00
Larry Bird
JD Kevin Durant 400.00 800.00
LeBron James
LC Acie Law 30.00 60.00
Javaris Crittenton
LM Jerry Lucas 30.00 60.00
Dick McGuire
LR Bill Laimbeer 50.00 100.00
Dennis Rodman
MR Alonzo Mourning 100.00 200.00
David Robinson
NG Joakim Noah 40.00 80.00
Taurean Green
OG Rudy Gay 30.00 60.00
Emeka Okafor
WJ Magic Johnson 200.00 300.00
James Worthy
WS John Stockton 75.00 150.00
Deron Williams

2007-08 UD Black Patches Dual

PRINT RUN 15 SER.#'d SETS
UNPRICED GOLD PRINT RUN 10 SER.#'d SETS
UNPRICED WHITE PRINT RUN ONE SET
DPAJ Gilbert Arenas 12.00 40.00
Antawn Jamison
DPAR LaMarcus Aldridge 12.00 30.00
Brandon Roy
DPBO Kobe Bryant 40.00 80.00
Lamar Odom
DPBP Chauncey Billups 12.00 30.00
Tayshaun Prince
DPDG Kevin Durant 30.00 80.00
Jeff Green
DPDR Tim Duncan 25.00 50.00
David Robinson
DPHR Dwight Howard 12.00 30.00
J.J. Redick
DPIA Allen Iverson 40.00 70.00
Carmelo Anthony
DPJF Al Jefferson 12.00 30.00
Randy Foye
DPJR Michael Jordan 75.00 150.00
Dennis Rodman
DPKC Vince Carter 20.00 40.00
Jason Kidd
DPMB Larry Bird 25.00 50.00
Kevin McHale
DPMM Yao Ming 12.00 30.00
Tracy McGrady
DPMS Karl Malone 25.00 50.00
John Stockton
DPNS Steve Nash 20.00 40.00
Amare Stoudemire
DPOD Hakeem Olajuwon 25.00 50.00
Clyde Drexler
DPPG Manu Ginobili 20.00 40.00
Tony Parker
DPRF Walt Frazier 12.00 30.00
Willis Reed
DPSP Chris Paul 12.00 30.00
Peja Stojakovic

2007-08 UD Black Ticket Autographs

PRINT RUN 50 SER.#'d SETS
*GOLD: .5X TO 1.25X BASE HI
GOLD PRINT RUN 15 SER.#'d SETS
UNPRICED WHITE PRINT RUN ONE SET
TAAB Aaron Brooks 8.00 20.00
TAAH Al Horford 15.00 40.00
TAAI Andre Iguodala 8.00 20.00

TAAJ Antawn Jamison 8.00 20.00
TAAL Acie Law 8.00 20.00
TAAM Alonzo Mourning 20.00 50.00
TAAT Al Thornton 8.00 20.00
TABD Baron Davis 10.00 25.00
TABG Ben Gordon 8.00 20.00
TABI Mike Bibby 8.00 20.00
TABR Brandon Roy 20.00 40.00
TACA Carmelo Anthony 25.00 60.00
TACB Corey Brewer 10.00 25.00
TACH Chris Mihm 8.00 20.00
TACL Carl Landry 8.00 20.00
TACM Corey Maggette 8.00 20.00
TACP Chris Paul 30.00 60.00
TADC Daequan Cook 10.00 25.00
TADG Danny Granger 8.00 20.00
TADH Dwight Howard 20.00 50.00
TADL David Lee 10.00 25.00
TADW Deron Williams 20.00 40.00
TAEO Emeka Okafor 8.00 20.00
TAGD Glen Davis 20.00 40.00
TAGP Gabe Pruitt 8.00 20.00
TAJC Javaris Crittenton 8.00 20.00
TAJD Jared Dudley 8.00 20.00
TAJG Jeff Green 12.00 30.00
TAJM Josh McRoberts 8.00 20.00
TAJN Joakim Noah 20.00 50.00
TAJS Jason Smith 8.00 20.00
TAJW Julian Wright 8.00 20.00
TAKB Kobe Bryant 200.00 400.00
TAKD Kevin Durant 200.00 400.00
TAKG Kevin Garnett 40.00 100.00
TALA LaMarcus Aldridge 10.00 25.00
TALJ LeBron James 200.00 300.00
TAMA Morris Almond 8.00 20.00
TAMB Marco Belinelli 8.00 20.00
TAMC Mike Conley Jr. 10.00 25.00
TANF Nick Fazekas 8.00 20.00
TAPP Paul Pierce 15.00 30.00
TAPR Tayshaun Prince 8.00 20.00
TARF Randy Foye 8.00 20.00
TARG Rudy Gay 10.00 25.00
TARS Rodney Stuckey 12.50 30.00
TASE Shawne Williams 8.00 20.00
TASH Spencer Hawes 8.00 20.00
TASN Steve Nash 40.00 75.00
TASW Sean Williams 8.00 20.00
TATP Tony Parker 10.00 25.00
TATU Alando Tucker 8.00 20.00
TAVC Vince Carter 20.00 50.00
TAWC Wilson Chandler 12.50 30.00
TAWS Shelden Williams 8.00 20.00
TAYM Yao Ming 25.00 50.00

2007-08 UD Black Ticket Autographs Dual

PRINT RUN 15 SER.#'d SETS
UNPRICED GOLD PRINT RUN 5 SETS
UNPRICED WHITE PRINT RUN ONE SET
AD Kevin Durant 150.00 300.00
Carmelo Anthony
BH Mike Bibby 20.00 40.00
Spencer Hawes
BM Yao Ming 400.00 600.00
Kobe Bryant
BP Mike Bibby 40.00 80.00
Chris Paul
DG Kevin Durant 125.00 250.00
Jeff Green
DW Deron Williams 30.00 60.00
Baron Davis
FB Corey Brewer 25.00 50.00
Randy Foye
GC Mike Conley Jr. 25.00 50.00
Rudy Gay
GN Ben Gordon 30.00 60.00
Joakim Noah
HL Acie Law 20.00 40.00
Al Horford
HW Spencer Hawes 20.00 40.00
Julian Wright
JG Antawn Jamison 20.00 40.00
Danny Granger
MP Tayshaun Prince 25.00 60.00
Alonzo Mourning
MT Al Thornton 20.00 40.00
Corey Maggette
NT Steve Nash 40.00 80.00
Alando Tucker
NW Joakim Noah 25.00 50.00
Sean Williams
OD Emeka Okafor 20.00 40.00
Jared Dudley
PD Glen Davis 25.00 50.00
Gabe Pruitt
PG Paul Pierce 200.00 300.00
Kevin Garnett
PR Brandon Roy 30.00 60.00
Tony Parker
PW Chris Paul 40.00 80.00
Julian Wright
RM Brandon Roy 30.00 60.00
Josh McRoberts
SC Rodney Stuckey 25.00 50.00
Daequan Cook

2007-08 UD Black Trophy Autographs

PRINT RUN 25 SER.#'d SETS
UNPRICED GOLD PRINT RUN ONE TO 11 SETS
UNPRICED WHITE PRINT RUN ONE SET
BL Bill Laimbeer 25.00 50.00
BR Bill Russell 250.00 500.00
BW Bill Walton 40.00 80.00
DR Dennis Rodman 100.00 200.00
GR Hal Greer 25.00 50.00
HO Hakeem Olajuwon 50.00 100.00
JO Michael Jordan 700.00 1200.00
JS Jack Sikma 25.00 50.00
JW James Worthy 50.00 100.00
KA Kareem Abdul-Jabbar 100.00 200.00
KB Kobe Bryant 500.00 800.00
LB Larry Bird 150.00 300.00
MJ Magic Johnson 150.00 300.00
TH Tom Heinsohn 30.00 60.00
TP Tony Parker 50.00 120.00
VM Vern Mikkelsen 30.00 60.00
WF Walt Frazier 30.00 60.00

2008-09 UD Black

1-42 PRINT RUN 25 SER.#'d SETS
JSY AU RC PRINT RUN 99 SER.#'d SETS
UNPRICED WHITE PRINT RUN ONE SET
1 Al Horford 12.00 30.00
2 Allen Iverson 25.00 60.00
3 Amare Stoudemire 12.00 30.00
4 Baron Davis 12.00 30.00
5 Kirk Hinrich 12.00 30.00
6 Brandon Roy 12.00 30.00
7 Carmelo Anthony 30.00 80.00
8 Chauncey Billups 12.00 30.00
9 Chris Bosh 12.00 30.00
10 Peja Stojakovic 12.00 30.00
11 Corey Maggette 10.00 25.00
12 Danny Granger 12.00 30.00
13 Andrei Kirilenko 10.00 25.00
14 Dirk Nowitzki 15.00 40.00
15 Dwight Howard 25.00 60.00
16 Elton Brand 12.00 30.00
17 Gerald Wallace 12.00 30.00
18 Gilbert Arenas 12.00 30.00
19 Jason Kidd 12.00 30.00
20 Kevin Durant 50.00 125.00
21 Kevin Garnett 40.00 100.00
22 Kevin Martin 12.00 30.00
23 Kobe Bryant 60.00 150.00
24 LeBron James 60.00 150.00
25 Michael Redd 12.00 30.00
26 Mike Miller 12.00 30.00
27 Pau Gasol 12.00 30.00
28 Paul Pierce 15.00 40.00
29 Rudy Gay 12.00 30.00
30 Shawn Marion 12.00 30.00
31 Steve Nash 12.00 30.00
32 Tim Duncan 20.00 50.00
33 Tracy McGrady 12.00 30.00
34 Vince Carter 15.00 40.00
35 Yao Ming 30.00 80.00
36 Zach Randolph 10.00 25.00
37 Julius Erving 25.00 60.00
38 Larry Bird 40.00 100.00
39 Magic Johnson 30.00 80.00
40 Michael Jordan 300.00 600.00
41 Oscar Robertson 25.00 50.00
42 Patrick Ewing 30.00 80.00
43 Derrick Rose JSY AU RC 250.00 500.00
44 Michael Beasley JSY AU RC 20.00 50.00
45 O.J. Mayo JSY AU RC 50.00 100.00
46 Russell Westbrook JSY AU RC 100.00 200.00
47 Kevin Love JSY AU RC 100.00 200.00
48 Eric Gordon JSY AU RC 40.00 100.00
49 Joe Alexander JSY AU RC 8.00 20.00
50 D.J. Augustin JSY AU RC 10.00 25.00
51 Brook Lopez JSY AU RC 12.00 30.00
52 Jerryd Bayless JSY AU RC 8.00 20.00
53 Jason Thompson JSY AU RC 8.00 20.00
54 Brandon Rush JSY AU RC 8.00 20.00
55 Anthony Randolph JSY AU RC 10.00 25.00
56 Robin Lopez JSY AU RC 8.00 20.00
57 Marreese Speights JSY AU RC 8.00 20.00
58 Roy Hibbert JSY AU RC 15.00 40.00
59 Javale McGee JSY AU RC 15.00 40.00
60 J.J. Hickson JSY AU RC 10.00 25.00
61 Ryan Anderson JSY AU RC 12.00 30.00
62 Kosta Koufos JSY AU RC 8.00 20.00
63 George Hill JSY AU RC 12.00 30.00
64 Darrell Arthur JSY AU RC 8.00 20.00
65 Donte Greene JSY AU RC 8.00 20.00
66 J.R. Giddens JSY AU RC 8.00 20.00
67 Walter Sharpe JSY AU RC 8.00 20.00
68 Joey Dorsey JSY AU RC 8.00 20.00
69 Mario Chalmers JSY AU RC 12.00 30.00
70 Sonny Weems JSY AU RC 8.00 20.00
71 Rudy Fernandez JSY AU RC 10.00 25.00
72 Patrick Ewing Jr. JSY AU RC 8.00 20.00

2008-09 UD Black Gold

*GOLD 1-42: .5X TO 1.25X BASE HI
STATED PRINT RUN 15 SER.#'d SETS
*GOLD 43-72: 1X TO 2.5X BASE HI
STATED PRINT RUN 30 SER.#'d SETS
28 Paul Pierce 25.00 60.00
51 Brook Lopez JSY AU 40.00 100.00
52 Jerryd Bayless JSY AU 30.00 80.00
61 Ryan Anderson JSY AU 40.00 100.00
63 George Hill JSY AU 40.00 100.00

2008-09 UD Black 50 Greatest Autographs

PRINT RUN 50 SER.#'d SETS
*GOLD: .5X TO 1.25X BASE HI
GOLD PRINT RUN 15 SER.#'d SETS
50AUBP Bob Pettit 30.00 60.00
50AUBR Bill Russell 80.00 200.00
50AUBS Bill Sharman 20.00 50.00
50AUBW Bill Walton 20.00 50.00
50AUCD Clyde Drexler 30.00 80.00
50AUDC Dave Cowens 20.00 50.00
50AUDR David Robinson 40.00 80.00
50AUDS Dolph Schayes 20.00 50.00
50AUHO Hakeem Olajuwon 30.00 80.00
50AUJE Julius Erving 50.00 125.00
50AUJH John Havlicek 25.00 60.00
50AUJO Michael Jordan 500.00 800.00
50AUJS John Stockton 30.00 60.00
50AUJW Jerry West 40.00 100.00
50AUKA Kareem Abdul-Jabbar 50.00 120.00
50AULB Larry Bird 60.00 150.00
50AULW Lenny Wilkens 20.00 50.00
50AUMJ Magic Johnson 50.00 120.00
50AUNT Nate Thurmond 30.00 60.00
50AUOR Oscar Robertson 50.00 100.00
50AURB Rick Barry 20.00 50.00
50AURP Robert Parish 20.00 50.00
50AUWF Walt Frazier 20.00 50.00
50AUWO James Worthy 30.00 60.00

2008-09 UD Black ABA Autographs

STATED PRINT RUN 25 SER.#'d SETS
*GOLD: .5X TO 1.25X BASE HI
GOLD PRINT RUN 10 SER.#'d SETS
UNPRICED WHITE PRINT RUN ONE SET
ABAAG Artis Gilmore 8.00 20.00
ABACS Charlie Scott 15.00 30.00
ABADB Don Buse 8.00 20.00
ABAFL Freddie Lewis 8.00 20.00
ABAJE Julius Erving 60.00 120.00
ABALD Louie Dampier 8.00 20.00

2008-09 UD Black ABA/NBA 30th Anniversary Autographs

PRINT RUN 20 TO 30 SER.#'d SETS
UNPRICED GOLD PRINT RUN 5 SER.#'d SETS
UNPRICED WHITE PRINT RUN ONE SET
30DB Don Buse/30 15.00 30.00
30DT David Thompson/30 8.00 20.00
30FL Freddie Lewis/30 8.00 20.00
30GK George Karl/29 10.00 25.00
30GM George McGinnis/20 8.00 20.00
30JE Julius Erving/30 60.00 120.00
30JS James Silas/30 8.00 20.00
30RB Rick Barry/30 15.00 30.00

2008-09 UD Black All-Star Autographs

STATED PRINT RUN 24 TO 25 SER.#'d SETS
UNPRICED GOLD PRINT RUN ONE TO 11 SETS
UNPRICED WHITE PRINT RUN ONE SET
ASAJ Antawn Jamison/25 15.00 30.00
ASAS Amare Stoudemire/25 20.00 40.00
ASBM Brad Miller/25 8.00 20.00
ASCP Chris Paul/25 30.00 60.00
ASDW David West/25 8.00 20.00
ASJK Jason Kidd/24 25.00 60.00
ASKB Kobe Bryant/25 200.00 350.00
ASKG Kevin Garnett/25 50.00 100.00
ASLJ LeBron James/25 200.00 350.00
ASPP Paul Pierce/25 20.00 40.00
ASRA Ray Allen/25 30.00 80.00
ASTM Tracy McGrady/24 15.00 30.00
ASYM Yao Ming/25 40.00 80.00

2008-09 UD Black Autographs

STATED PRINT RUN 23 TO 50 SER.#'d SETS
UNPRICED AUTO OCTO PRINT RUN 5 SETS
UNPRICED AUTO OCTO GOLD PRINT RUN 3 SETS
UNPRICED AUTO OCTO WHITE PRINT RUN ONE SET
UNPRICED AUTO SIX PRINT RUN 5 SETS
UNPRICED AUTO SIX GOLD PRINT RUN 3 SETS
UNPRICED AUTO SIX WHITE PRINT RUN ONE SET
A1AJ Antawn Jamison/35 10.00 25.00
A1AM Alonzo Mourning/35 30.00 80.00
A1BL Bob Lanier/35 8.00 20.00
A1BR Brandon Roy/35 20.00 40.00
A1BW Bill Walton/35 12.50 30.00
A1CP Chris Paul/35 40.00 75.00
A1HO Hakeem Olajuwon/35 25.00 60.00
A1JE Julius Erving/32 40.00 80.00
A1JO Magic Johnson/32 40.00 100.00
A1JS J.R. Smith/35 10.00 25.00
A1KA Kareem Abdul-Jabbar/33 50.00 100.00
A1KD Kevin Durant/35 75.00 150.00
A1KG Kevin Garnett/35 50.00 100.00
A1LB Larry Bird/33 40.00 80.00
A1LJ LeBron James/23 250.00 350.00
A1MJ Michael Jordan/23 400.00 700.00
A1MP Mark Price/35 20.00 50.00
A1PP Paul Pierce/35 25.00 60.00
A1RA Ray Allen/35 25.00 60.00
A1ST John Stockton/35 30.00 80.00
A1TM Tracy McGrady/35 15.00 40.00
A2AB Andrew Bynum/50 25.00 50.00
A2AE Alex English/50 8.00 20.00
A2AJ Al Jefferson/50 8.00 20.00
A2AT Al Thornton/50 8.00 20.00
A2BB Bruce Bowen/50 8.00 20.00
A2BD Brad Daugherty/50 10.00 25.00
A2BS Bill Sharman/50 8.00 20.00
A2CL Carl Landry/50 8.00 20.00
A2FL Freddie Lewis/50 8.00 20.00
A2RR Rajon Rondo/50 15.00 40.00

2008-09 UD Black Autographs Jerseys Quad

STATED PRINT RUN 10 SER.#'d SETS
UNPRICED JERSEY SIX PRINT RUN 5 SETS
UNPRICED PATCH QUAD GOLD PRINT RUN 5 SETS
UNPRICED PATCH QUAD WHITE PRINT RUN 1 SET
UNPRICED PATCH SIX GOLD PRINT RUN 5 SETS
UNPRICED PATCH SIX WHITE PRINT RUN 1 SET
QAJ08RK Michael Beasley 200.00 450.00
O.J. Mayo
Kevin Love
Derrick Rose
QAJBSTN Robert Parish 150.00 325.00
Larry Bird
Paul Pierce
Kevin Garnett
QAJBULL Dennis Rodman 150.00 300.00
Ben Gordon
Derrick Rose
Joakim Noah
QAJCAVS J.J. Hickson 150.00 300.00
LeBron James
Mark Price
Daniel Gibson
QAJEVSW Larry Bird 350.00 600.00
Kevin Garnett
Kobe Bryant
Magic Johnson
QAJHAWK Spud Webb 50.00 120.00
Mike Bibby
Dominique Wilkins
Al Horford
QAJLAKR Kobe Bryant 300.00 550.00
Magic Johnson
Andrew Bynum
Kareem Abdul-Jabbar
QAJROCK Yao Ming 50.00 120.00
Carl Landry
Luis Scola
Joey Dorsey
QAJROOK Jerryd Bayless 50.00 120.00
Eric Gordon
Joe Alexander
D.J. Augustin
QAJUDEX LeBron James 1000.00 1500.00
Kobe Bryant
Michael Jordan
Kevin Garnett

2008-09 UD Black Commemorative Logo Autographs

STATED PRINT RUN 19 TO 25 SER.#'d SETS
*GOLD: .5X TO 1.25X BASE HI
GOLD PRINT RUN 10 SER.#'d SETS
UNPRICED WHITE PRINT RUN ONE SET
CBB Bruce Bowen/25 8.00 20.00
CBG Ben Gordon/25 15.00 40.00
CBR Bill Russell/20 60.00 150.00
CBS Bill Sharman/25 10.00 25.00
CCH Chuck Daly/25 30.00 60.00
CDH Dwight Howard/23 50.00 100.00
CHO Hakeem Olajuwon/25 20.00 50.00
CJO Michael Jordan Finals/19 350.00 650.00
CJW Jerry West/25 30.00 60.00
CKB Kobe Bryant/24 225.00 350.00
CKG Kevin Garnett/25 60.00 120.00
CKV Kiki Vandeweghe/25 8.00 20.00
CLO Lamar Odom/25 20.00 50.00
CMI Michael Jordan/23 350.00 700.00
CMJ Magic Johnson/25 40.00 100.00
CPP Paul Pierce/25 40.00 80.00
CPR Tayshaun Prince/25 8.00 20.00
CRA Ray Allen/25 40.00 100.00
CRR Rajon Rondo/24 20.00 40.00
CRS Rodney Stuckey/25 12.50 30.00
CSK Steve Kerr/25 10.00 25.00
CST John Stockton/25 40.00 100.00
CTP Tony Parker/25 15.00 30.00
CYM Yao Ming/24 20.00 40.00

2008-09 UD Black Dual Autographs

STATED PRINT RUN 15 SER.#'d SETS
UNPRICED GOLD PRINT RUN 5 SETS
UNPRICED WHITE PRINT RUN ONE SET
DABG Kobe Bryant 200.00 350.00
Kevin Garnett
DABL Shane Battier 25.00 60.00
Carl Landry
DABW Carlos Boozer 40.00 80.00
Deron Williams
DACW Vince Carter 40.00 80.00
Dominique Wilkins
DADH Kevin Durant 75.00 150.00
Al Horford
DAEJ Julius Erving 250.00 400.00
LeBron James
DAJA Kareem Abdul-Jabbar 100.00 200.00
Magic Johnson
DAJB Kobe Bryant 1000.00 1400.00
Michael Jordan
DALT Bill Laimbeer 40.00 100.00
Isiah Thomas
DAMS Yao Ming 30.00 80.00
Luis Scola
DAPG Kevin Garnett 50.00 125.00
Paul Pierce
DAPR Chris Paul 50.00 125.00
Rajon Rondo
DAPS Tayshaun Prince 25.00 60.00
Rodney Stuckey
DARA Kareem Abdul-Jabbar 100.00 200.00
Oscar Robertson
DARJ Bill Russell 100.00 200.00
Sam Jones
DAVF Jordan Farmar 25.00 60.00
Sasha Vujacic
DAWP Chris Paul 40.00 80.00
David West
DAWW Luke Walton 25.00 60.00
Bill Walton

2008-09 UD Black Dual Inscriptions

STATED PRINT RUN 10 SER.#'d SETS
UNPRICED GOLD PRINT RUN 5 SER.#'d SETS
DIDG Kevin Durant 125.00 225.00
Jeff Green
DIMB Shane Battier 60.00 120.00
Tracy McGrady
DIPG Paul Pierce 60.00 150.00
Kevin Garnett
DIRA Kareem Abdul-Jabbar 250.00 350.00
David Robinson
DIWR Jamaal Wilkes 100.00 200.00
Dennis Rodman

2008-09 UD Black Dual Patch Autographs

STATED PRINT RUN 15 SER.#'d SETS
UNPRICED GOLD PRINT RUN 5 SETS
UNPRICED WHITE PRINT RUN ONE SET
DPAAF Rudy Fernandez 40.00 80.00
LaMarcus Aldridge
DPABC Michael Beasley 40.00 80.00
Daequan Cook
DPABF Jordan Farmar 30.00 60.00
Andrew Bynum
DPABH Mike Bibby 40.00 80.00
Al Horford
DPABJ Kobe Bryant 500.00 750.00
LeBron James
DPADG Kevin Durant 125.00 250.00
Jeff Green
DPAGC Mike Conley Jr. 30.00 60.00
Rudy Gay
DPAJB Andrew Bogut 30.00 60.00
Richard Jefferson
DPAJJ Michael Jordan 1500.00 2200.00
LeBron James
DPALB Corey Brewer 50.00 125.00
Kevin Love
DPAMB Tracy McGrady 40.00 100.00
Shane Battier
DPAMH Al Harrington 30.00 60.00
Corey Maggette
DPAMS Yao Ming 40.00 100.00
Amare Stoudemire
DPANK Jason Kidd 30.00 60.00
Steve Nash
DPAOF Emeka Okafor 30.00 60.00
Raymond Felton
DPAPG Paul Pierce 100.00 200.00
Kevin Garnett
DPAPS Tayshaun Prince 30.00 60.00
Rodney Stuckey
DPATN Tyrus Thomas 40.00 80.00
Joakim Noah

2008-09 UD Black Dual Rookie Autographs

STATED PRINT RUN 10 SER.#'d SETS
UNPRICED GOLD PRINT RUN 5 SETS
DRAAB D.J. Augustin 25.00 50.00
Jerryd Bayless
DRABR Derrick Rose 150.00 300.00
Michael Beasley
DRAFG Danilo Gallinari 40.00 80.00
Rudy Fernandez
DRAGL Courtney Lee 40.00 80.00
Eric Gordon
DRAHS J.J. Hickson 25.00 50.00
Marreese Speights
DRALG Kevin Love 40.00 80.00
Marc Gasol
DRALL Robin Lopez 25.00 50.00
Brook Lopez
DRAMW Russell Westbrook 60.00 150.00
O.J. Mayo
DRART Anthony Randolph 25.00 50.00
Jason Thompson

2008-09 UD Black Dual Rookie Jersey Autographs

STATED PRINT RUN 25 SER.#'d SETS
*GOLD: .75X TO 2X BASE HI
GOLD PRINT RUN 10 SER.#'d SETS
UNPRICED WHITE PRINT RUN ONE SET
DRBR Michael Beasley 125.00 250.00
Derrick Rose
DRDE Patrick Ewing Jr. 10.00 25.00
Joey Dorsey
DRGL Eric Gordon 50.00 125.00
Kevin Love
DRGS Walter Sharpe 10.00 25.00
J.R. Giddens
DRHM Javale McGee 20.00 50.00
Roy Hibbert
DRHS J.J. Hickson 12.50 30.00
Marreese Speights
DRLL Robin Lopez 20.00 50.00
Brook Lopez
DRMW Russell Westbrook 50.00 120.00
O.J. Mayo
DRRB Brandon Rush 15.00 30.00
Jerryd Bayless
DRRT Jason Thompson 20.00 40.00
Anthony Randolph

2008-09 UD Black Flag Autographs

STATED PRINT RUN 23 TO 50 SER.#'d SETS
*GOLD: .5X TO 1.25X BASE HI
GOLD PRINT RUN 10 TO 25 SER.#'d SETS
UNPRICED WHITE PRINT RUN ONE SET
USAA Arron Afflalo/50 10.00 25.00
USAG Artis Gilmore/50 10.00 25.00
USAJ Al Jefferson/50 10.00 25.00
USAM Alonzo Mourning/50 30.00 80.00
USAT Al Thornton/50 10.00 25.00
USAU D.J. Augustin/50 10.00 25.00
USBL Bill Laimbeer/50 15.00 30.00
USBM Brad Miller/50 10.00 25.00
USBR Brandon Roy/50 20.00 50.00
USBW Bill Walton/50 15.00 40.00
USCB Corey Brewer/50 10.00 25.00
USCH Tom Chambers/50 10.00 25.00
USCL Carl Landry/50 10.00 25.00
USCP Chris Paul/50 40.00 100.00
USDT David Thompson/50 10.00 25.00
USDW David West/50 10.00 25.00
USGI Daniel Gibson/50 10.00 25.00
USGR Donte Greene/50 10.00 25.00
USJB Jerryd Bayless/50 10.00 25.00
USJF Jordan Farmar/50 10.00 25.00
USJG Joey Graham/50 10.00 25.00
USJJ Jarrett Jack/50 10.00 25.00
USJK Jason Kidd/50 30.00 80.00
USKB Kobe Bryant/24 200.00 400.00
USKD Kevin Durant/50 50.00 125.00
USKG Kevin Garnett/25 50.00 100.00
USLB Larry Bird/33 100.00 175.00
USLJ LeBron James/23 300.00 500.00
USMJ Michael Jordan/23 400.00 800.00
USMP Mark Price/50 20.00 40.00
USRP Robert Parish/50 10.00 25.00
USSB Shane Battier/50 15.00 30.00
USTC Tyson Chandler/50 10.00 25.00

2008-09 UD Black Flag Autographs Dual

STATED PRINT RUN 10 SER.#'d SETS
UNPRICED GOLD PRINT RUN 5 SER.#'d SETS
UNPRICED WHITE PRINT RUN ONE SET
DUSBR Andrew Bynum 100.00 200.00
Dennis Rodman
DUSDD Adrian Dantley 100.00 200.00
Kevin Durant
DUSGE Kevin Garnett 75.00 150.00
Alex English
DUSGJ Magic Johnson 100.00 200.00
George Gervin
DUSHF Walt Frazier 50.00 100.00
Dwight Howard
DUSJE Julius Erving 500.00 800.00
Michael Jordan
DUSRH Oscar Robertson 50.00 100.00
Bailey Howell
DUSRP Robert Parish 100.00 175.00
Bill Russell
DUSSR David Robinson 100.00 200.00
Amare Stoudemire
DUSTP Chris Paul 50.00 100.00
David Thompson
DUSWW Jerry West 100.00 200.00
Deron Williams

2008-09 UD Black HOF Letters Autographs

TOTAL PRINT RUNS LISTED IN CHECKLIST
HOFAD Adrian Dantley 15.00 40.00
Serial 6, Print Run 84
HOFAE Alex English 15.00 40.00
Serial 7, Print Run 98
HOFAR Arnie Risen 15.00 40.00
Serial 7, Print Run 98
HOFBH Bailey Howell 15.00 40.00
Serial 7, Print Run 98
HOFBI Larry Bird 75.00 150.00
Serial 4, Print Run 56
HOFBL Bob Lanier 15.00 40.00
Serial 5, Print Run 70
HOFBR Bill Russell 75.00 150.00
Serial 4, Print Run 56
HOFBS Bill Sharman 15.00 40.00
Serial 5, Print Run 70
HOFBW Bill Walton 15.00 40.00
Serial 6, Print Run 84
HOFCD Clyde Drexler 40.00 80.00
Serial 5, Print Run 70
HOFDC Dave Cowens 15.00 40.00
Serial 5, Print Run 70
HOFDT David Thompson 15.00 40.00
Serial 6, Print Run 84
HOFDW Dominique Wilkins 30.00 80.00
Serial 5, Print Run 70
HOFEB Elgin Baylor 20.00 50.00
Serial 5, Print Run 70
HOFGO Gail Goodrich 15.00 40.00
Serial 5, Print Run 70
HOFHG Hal Greer 15.00 40.00
Serial 5, Print Run 70
HOFHO Hakeem Olajuwon 40.00 100.00
Serial 5, Print Run 70
HOFJH John Havlicek 25.00 60.00
Serial 5, Print Run 70
HOFJW James Worthy 25.00 60.00
Serial 5, Print Run 70
HOFKA Kareem Abdul-Jabbar 50.00 125.00
Serial 5, Print Run 70
HOFLW Lenny Wilkens 15.00 40.00
Serial 6, Print Run 84
HOFMJ Magic Johnson 60.00 150.00
Serial 4, Print Run 56
HOFOR Oscar Robertson 40.00 80.00
Serial 5, Print Run 70
HOFPR Pat Riley 20.00 50.00
Serial 5, Print Run 70
HOFRB Rick Barry 15.00 40.00
Serial 5, Print Run 70
HOFRP Robert Parish 25.00 60.00
Serial 7, Print Run 98
HOFWE Jerry West 40.00 80.00
Serial 5, Print Run 70
HOFWF Walt Frazier 15.00 40.00
Serial 6, Print Run 84

2008-09 UD Black Inscriptions Autographs

STATED PRINT RUN 25 SER.#'d SETS
*GOLD: .5X TO 1.25X BASE HI
GOLD PRINT RUN 10 SER.#'d SETS
AIJO Larry Johnson Grandmama 100.00 200.00
AICB3 Corey Brewer C-Brew 8.00 20.00
AIDH1 Dwight Howard Manchild 60.00 120.00
AIDR1 Dennis Rodman Worm 75.00 150.00
AIDW1 Deron Williams Slick 50.00 100.00
AIKD1 Kevin Durant 100.00 250.00
AIKG1 Kevin Garnett None 75.00 150.00
AILJ1 LeBron James None 200.00 400.00
AIPP1 Paul Pierce Go Jayhawks 75.00 150.00

2008-09 UD Black Legend Signed Jersey Pieces

STATED PRINT RUN 23 TO 25 SER.#'d SETS
UNPRICED GOLD PRINT RUN 5 SER.#'d SETS
UNPRICED WHITE PRINT RUN ONE SET
SPLBK Bernard King/25 10.00 25.00
SPLDR David Robinson/25 50.00 100.00
SPLJO Magic Johnson/25 50.00 120.00
SPLJS John Stockton/25 40.00 80.00
SPLLB Larry Bird/25 50.00 120.00
SPLMJ Michael Jordan/23 400.00 600.00
SPLRO Dennis Rodman/25 60.00 120.00
SPLSA Stacey Augmon/25 10.00 25.00
SPLSK Steve Kerr/25 20.00 50.00

2008-09 UD Black Legend Signed Jersey Pieces Dual

STATED PRINT RUN 10 SER.#'d SETS
UNPRICED GOLD PRINT RUN 5 SER.#'d SETS
UNPRICED WHITE PRINT RUN ONE SET
DJLEG Julius Erving 60.00 120.00
George Gervin
DJLJB Magic Johnson 125.00 250.00
Larry Bird
DJLJJ Magic Johnson 400.00 700.00
Michael Jordan
DJLKR Steve Kerr 80.00 160.00
Dennis Rodman
DJLOR Hakeem Olajuwon 60.00 120.00
David Robinson
DJLSK John Stockton 60.00 120.00
Steve Kerr

2008-09 UD Black Michael Jordan Signed Floor

STATED PRINT RUN 23 SER.#'d SETS
UNPRICED GOLD PRINT RUN 5 SER.#'d SETS
UNPRICED WHITE PRINT RUN ONE SET
MJ Michael Jordan/23 500.00 800.00

2008-09 UD Black MJ Induction

MJHOF Michael Jordan 25.00 60.00
MJHOFG Michael Jordan Gold/23 75.00 200.00

2008-09 UD Black Quad Autographs

STATED PRINT RUN 10 SER.#'d SETS
UNPRICED GOLD PRINT RUN 5 SER.#'d SETS
UNPRICED WHITE PRINT RUN ONE SET
QA2007 Al Thornton 50.00 100.00
Al Horford
Jeff Green
Luis Scola
QA2008 O.J. Mayo 200.00 500.00
Derrick Rose
Michael Beasley
Russell Westbrook
QADUNK Dwight Howard 100.00 200.00
Spud Webb
Vince Carter
Dominique Wilkins
QAPGDS John Stockton 125.00 250.00
Isiah Thomas
Deron Williams
Chris Paul
QAROOK Kevin Love 75.00 150.00
Joe Alexander
Eric Gordon
Danilo Gallinari
QASTUD LeBron James 900.00 1500.00
Kevin Garnett
Kobe Bryant
Michael Jordan

2008-09 UD Black Rookie Signed Jersey Pieces

STATED PRINT RUN 50 SER.#'d SETS
*GOLD: .75X TO 2X BASE HI
GOLD PRINT RUN 10 SER.#'d SETS
UNPRICED WHITE PRINT RUN ONE SET
SJRAR Anthony Randolph 10.00 25.00
SJRBL Brook Lopez 12.00 30.00
SJRBR Brandon Rush 8.00 20.00
SJRCD Chris Douglas-Roberts 8.00 20.00
SJRCL Courtney Lee 12.00 30.00
SJRDA D.J. Augustin 8.00 20.00
SJRDG Donte Greene 8.00 20.00
SJRDR Derrick Rose 175.00 350.00
SJRDW D.J. White 8.00 20.00
SJREG Eric Gordon 30.00 80.00
SJRGH George Hill 12.00 30.00
SJRJA Joe Alexander 8.00 20.00
SJRJB Jerryd Bayless 10.00 25.00
SJRJD Joey Dorsey 8.00 20.00
SJRJG J.R. Giddens 8.00 20.00
SJRJH J.J. Hickson 10.00 25.00
SJRJM Javale McGee 12.00 30.00
SJRJT Jason Thompson 8.00 20.00
SJRKK Kosta Koufos 8.00 20.00
SJRKL Kevin Love 40.00 100.00
SJRMB Michael Beasley 15.00 40.00
SJRMC Mario Chalmers 12.00 30.00
SJRMS Marreese Speights 8.00 20.00
SJROM O.J. Mayo 15.00 40.00
SJRRA Ryan Anderson 12.00 30.00
SJRRF Rudy Fernandez 10.00 25.00
SJRRH Roy Hibbert 12.00 30.00
SJRRL Robin Lopez 8.00 20.00
SJRRW Russell Westbrook 50.00 120.00
SJRSW Sonny Weems 8.00 20.00
SJRWS Walter Sharpe 8.00 20.00

2008-09 UD Black Rookie Signed Jersey Pieces Dual

STATED PRINT RUN 10 SER.#'d SETS
UNPRICED GOLD PRINT RUN 5 SER.#'d SETS
UNPRICED WHITE PRINT RUN ONE SET
DJRAL Ryan Anderson 20.00 40.00
Brook Lopez
DJRAM Darrell Arthur 25.00 50.00
O.J. Mayo
DJRAR Brandon Rush 20.00 40.00
D.J. Augustin
DJRBC Mario Chalmers 30.00 80.00
Michael Beasley
DJRBR Michael Beasley 300.00 600.00
Derrick Rose
DJRDD Chris Douglas-Roberts 10.00 25.00
Joey Dorsey
DJRDH George Hill 20.00 40.00
Chris Douglas-Roberts
DJRGB Eric Gordon 25.00 50.00
Jerryd Bayless
DJRGJ DeAndre Jordan 40.00 100.00
Eric Gordon
DJRGS J.R. Giddens 10.00 25.00
Walter Sharpe
DJRGW Sonny Weems 10.00 25.00
J.R. Giddens
DJRHR Roy Hibbert 15.00 40.00
Brandon Rush
DJRHS J.J. Hickson 15.00 30.00
Walter Sharpe
DJRLA Joe Alexander 25.00 60.00
Kevin Love
DJRLL Robin Lopez 15.00 30.00
Brook Lopez
DJRML Robin Lopez 12.50 30.00
Javale McGee
DJRRA Anthony Randolph 20.00 40.00
Joe Alexander
DJRRH Anthony Randolph 10.00 25.00
J.J. Hickson
DJRSK Kosta Koufos 10.00 25.00
Marreese Speights
DJRTL Kevin Love 25.00 60.00
Jason Thompson
DJRTS Jason Thompson 10.00 25.00
Marreese Speights
DJRWG Sonny Weems 10.00 25.00
Donte Greene
DJRWW Russell Westbrook 30.00 80.00
D.J. White

2008-09 UD Black Team Logo Autographs

STATED PRINT RUN 21 TO 49 SER.#'d SETS
*GOLD: .6X TO 1.5X BASE HI
GOLD PRINT RUN 9 TO 20 SETS
UNPRICED WHITE PRINT RUN ONE SET
TLAH Al Horford/25 6.00 15.00
TLAJ Antawn Jamison/24 6.00 15.00
TLAT Al Thornton/21 6.00 15.00
TLBG Ben Gordon/25 10.00 25.00
TLBR Brandon Roy/25 25.00 60.00
TLCB Corey Brewer/25 6.00 15.00
TLCP Chris Paul/25 40.00 80.00
TLDC Daequan Cook/49 8.00 20.00
TLDH Dwight Howard/25 40.00 100.00
TLDL David Lee/25 6.00 15.00
TLJC Javaris Crittenton/24 6.00 15.00
TLJD Jared Dudley/25 6.00 15.00
TLJK Jason Kidd/25 20.00 50.00
TLJS Jason Smith/25 6.00 15.00
TLKG Kevin Garnett/25 50.00 120.00
TLLJ LeBron James/25 200.00 400.00
TLRA Ramon Sessions/25 6.00 15.00
TLRJ Richard Jefferson/25 6.00 15.00
TLRS Rodney Stuckey/25 10.00 25.00
TLSM J.R. Smith/25 10.00 25.00

2008-09 UD Black Trophy Patch Autographs

STATED PRINT RUN 5 TO 25 SER.#'d SETS
UNPRICED GOLD PRINT RUN ONE TO 6 SETS
UNPRICED WHITE PRINT RUN ONE SET
TPDR David Robinson/25 100.00 200.00
TPJO Michael Jordan/25 500.00 800.00
TPKG Kevin Garnett/25 60.00 150.00
TPLB Larry Bird/25 60.00 150.00
TPMJ Magic Johnson/25 100.00 200.00
TPOR Oscar Robertson/25 125.00 250.00

2008-09 UD Black Veteran Signed Jersey Pieces

STATED PRINT RUN 5 TO 50 SER.#'d SETS
UNPRICED GOLD PRINT RUN 4 TO 15 SETS
UNPRICED WHITE PRINT RUN ONE SET
SPVAB Andrew Bynum/50 20.00 50.00
SPVAH Al Horford/50 8.00 20.00
SPVAM Alonzo Mourning/50 25.00 50.00
SPVAS Amare Stoudemire/50 15.00 40.00
SPVBE Marco Belinelli/50 8.00 20.00
SPVDH Dwight Howard/50 25.00 60.00
SPVGI Daniel Gibson/50 10.00 25.00
SPVJF Jordan Farmar/50 10.00 25.00
SPVJJ Jarrett Jack/50 8.00 20.00
SPVKB Kobe Bryant/50 150.00 300.00
SPVKD Kevin Durant/50 75.00 150.00

SPVKG Kevin Garnett/50 50.00 100.00
SPVLJ LeBron James/50 175.00 300.00
SPVMB Mike Bibby/50 10.00 25.00
SPVMC Mike Conley Jr./50 8.00 20.00
SPVPP Paul Pierce/50 20.00 50.00
SPVRF Randy Foye/50 8.00 20.00
SPVRJ Richard Jefferson/50 8.00 20.00
SPVSN Steve Nash/50 25.00 50.00
SPVTC Tyson Chandler/50 8.00 20.00
SPVYM Yao Ming/50 25.00 60.00

2008-09 UD Black Veteran Signed Jersey Pieces Dual

STATED PRINT RUN 10 SER.#'d SETS
DJVAP Ray Allen / Paul Pierce 125.00 250.00
DJVBG Kevin Garnett / Kobe Bryant 300.00 450.00
DJVBJ Mike Bibby / Jarrett Jack 25.00 50.00
DJVBP Mike Bibby / Chris Paul 40.00 80.00
DJVGJ Richard Jefferson / Rudy Gay 20.00 40.00
DJVGS Daniel Gibson / Rodney Stuckey 20.00 40.00
DJVHC Dwight Howard / Tyson Chandler 30.00 60.00
DJVJD LeBron James / Kevin Durant 250.00 500.00
DJVNS Amare Stoudemire / Steve Nash 75.00 150.00
DJVPJ LeBron James / Paul Pierce 200.00 350.00

2008-09 UD Black Veteran Signed Patch Pieces

STATED PRINT RUN 15 SER.#'d SETS
UNPRICED GOLD PRINT RUN 4 TO 12 SETS
UNPRICED WHITE PRINT RUN ONE SET
AB Andrew Bynum 30.00 60.00
DC Daequan Cook 12.50 30.00
DG Danny Granger 20.00 50.00
JF Jordan Farmar 15.00 40.00
KD Kevin Durant 100.00 200.00
KG Kevin Garnett 75.00 200.00
LJ LeBron James 300.00 500.00
MB Mike Bibby 15.00 40.00
PP Paul Pierce 40.00 80.00
RF Randy Foye 12.50 30.00
RJ Richard Jefferson 12.50 30.00
SN Steve Nash 50.00 120.00
TC Tyson Chandler 12.50 30.00
YM Yao Ming 50.00 120.00
AH2 Al Harrington 12.50 30.00

1998-99 UD Choice Preview

The 1998-99 Upper Deck UD Choice Preview set was issued in one series totalling 55 cards. The 6-card packs retail for $.88 each. The set is skip-numbered and features the word "Preview" in gold foil letters across the front of the card. The set previews the upcoming 1998-99 Upper Deck UD Choice release.

COMPLETE SET (55) 3.00 8.00
1 Dikembe Mutombo .10 .25
3 Mookie Blaylock .05 .15
7 Ron Mercer .07 .20
9 Walter McCarty .05 .15
13 Anthony Mason .05 .15
14 Glen Rice .10 .25
18 Toni Kukoc .10 .25
23 Michael Jordan .75 2.00
26 Zydrunas Ilgauskas .10 .25
27 Cedric Henderson .05 .15
29 Michael Finley .10 .25
32 Hubert Davis .05 .15
34 Bobby Jackson .07 .20
37 Danny Fortson .05 .15
41 Grant Hill .15 .40
43 Jerome Williams .05 .15
45 Erick Dampier .05 .15
48 Donyell Marshall .05 .15
50 Charles Barkley .15 .40
51 Hakeem Olajuwon .12 .30
56 Reggie Miller .12 .30
60 Chris Mullin .10 .25
64 Eric Piatkowski .07 .20
65 Maurice Taylor .05 .15
68 Shaquille O'Neal .25 .60
69 Kobe Bryant .50 1.25
74 Alonzo Mourning .10 .25
75 Tim Hardaway .10 .25
79 Ray Allen .12 .30
80 Terrell Brandon .05 .15
84 Stephon Marbury .12 .30
85 Kevin Garnett .20 .50
89 Keith Van Horn .10 .25
90 Sam Cassell .07 .20
95 Patrick Ewing .12 .30
97 John Starks .07 .20
100 Anfernee Hardaway .15 .40
101 Nick Anderson .05 .15
105 Allen Iverson .20 .50
110 Jason Kidd .15 .40
117 Isaiah Rider .05 .15
118 Rasheed Wallace .10 .25
121 Corliss Williamson .05 .15
123 Billy Owens .05 .15
126 Tim Duncan .20 .50
127 Sean Elliott .10 .25
131 Vin Baker .07 .20
135 Gary Payton .10 .25
137 Chauncey Billups .12 .30
142 John Stockton .12 .30
143 Karl Malone .12 .30
148 Bryant Reeves .05 .15
149 Shareef Abdur-Rahim .10 .25
152 Harvey Grant .05 .15
153 Juwan Howard .07 .20

1998-99 UD Choice Preview Michael Jordan NBA Finals Shots

Inserted one per special retail pack or tin, this 10-card set features memorable shots from Michael Jordan during the 1998 NBA Finals. The card fronts feature a red and black background with "Michael Jordan" in gold foil. The card backs remember a moment from the NBA Finals.

COMMON CARD (1-10) 2.50 5.00

1998-99 UD Choice

The 1998-99 Upper Deck UD Choice Series One was issued with a total of 200 cards. Each pack contained 12 cards with a suggested retail price of $1.29. The fronts feature a color action photo surrounded by a white border. The series two release was cancelled due to the NBA lockout.

COMPLETE SET (200) 8.00 20.00
1 Dikembe Mutombo .12 .30
2 Alan Henderson .07 .20
3 Mookie Blaylock .07 .20
4 Ed Gray .07 .20
5 Eldridge Recasner .07 .20
6 Kenny Anderson .10 .25
7 Ron Mercer .10 .25
8 Dana Barros .07 .20
9 Walter McCarty .07 .20
10 Travis Knight .07 .20
11 Andrew DeClercq .07 .20
12 David Wesley .07 .20
13 Anthony Mason .07 .20
14 Glen Rice .12 .30
15 J.R. Reid .07 .20
16 Bobby Phills .07 .20
17 Dell Curry .07 .20
18 Toni Kukoc .12 .30
19 Randy Brown .07 .20
20 Ron Harper .10 .25
21 Keith Booth .07 .20
22 Scott Burrell .07 .20
23 Michael Jordan 1.00 2.50
24 Derek Anderson .07 .20
25 Brevin Knight .07 .20
26 Zydrunas Ilgauskas .12 .30
27 Cedric Henderson .07 .20
28 Vitaly Potapenko .07 .20
29 Michael Finley .12 .30
30 Erick Strickland .07 .20
31 Shawn Bradley .07 .20
32 Hubert Davis .07 .20
33 Khalid Reeves .07 .20
34 Bobby Jackson .10 .25
35 Tony Battie .10 .25
36 Bryant Stith .07 .20
37 Danny Fortson .07 .20
38 Dean Garrett .07 .20
39 Eric Williams .07 .20
40 Brian Williams .07 .20
41 Grant Hill .20 .50
42 Lindsey Hunter .07 .20
43 Jerome Williams .07 .20
44 Eric Montross .07 .20
45 Erick Dampier .07 .20
46 Muggsy Bogues .10 .25
47 Tony Delk .07 .20
48 Donyell Marshall .07 .20
49 Bimbo Coles .07 .20
50 Charles Barkley .20 .50
51 Hakeem Olajuwon .15 .40
52 Brent Price .07 .20
53 Mario Elie .07 .20
54 Rodrick Rhodes .07 .20
55 Kevin Willis .07 .20
56 Reggie Miller .15 .40
57 Jalen Rose .10 .25
58 Mark Jackson .12 .30
59 Dale Davis .07 .20
60 Chris Mullin .12 .30
61 Derrick McKey .07 .20
62 Lorenzen Wright .07 .20
63 Rodney Rogers .07 .20
64 Eric Piatkowski .10 .25
65 Maurice Taylor .07 .20
66 Isaac Austin .07 .20
67 Corie Blount .07 .20
68 Shaquille O'Neal .30 .75
69 Kobe Bryant .60 1.50
70 Robert Horry .10 .25
71 Sean Rooks .07 .20
72 Derek Fisher .12 .30
73 P.J. Brown .07 .20
74 Alonzo Mourning .15 .40
75 Tim Hardaway .12 .30
76 Voshon Lenard .07 .20
77 Dan Majerle .12 .30
78 Ervin Johnson .07 .20
79 Ray Allen .15 .40
80 Terrell Brandon .07 .20
81 Tyrone Hill .07 .20
82 Elliot Perry .07 .20
83 Anthony Peeler .07 .20
84 Stephon Marbury .15 .40
85 Kevin Garnett .25 .60
86 Paul Grant .07 .20
87 Chris Carr .07 .20
88 Micheal Williams UER .07 .20
spelled Michael
89 Keith Van Horn .12 .30
90 Sam Cassell .10 .25
91 Kendall Gill .07 .20
92 Chris Gatling .07 .20
93 Kerry Kittles .07 .20
94 Allan Houston .10 .25
95 Patrick Ewing UER .15 .40
back Ewing Ewing
96 Charles Oakley .10 .25
97 John Starks .10 .25
98 Charlie Ward .07 .20
99 Chris Mills .07 .20
100 Anfernee Hardaway .20 .50
101 Nick Anderson .07 .20
102 Mark Price .12 .30
103 Horace Grant .10 .25
104 David Benoit .07 .20
105 Allen Iverson .25 .60
106 Joe Smith .10 .25
107 Tim Thomas .12 .30
108 Brian Shaw .07 .20
109 Aaron McKie .07 .20
110 Jason Kidd .20 .50
111 Danny Manning .10 .25
112 Steve Nash .20 .50
113 Rex Chapman .07 .20
114 Dennis Scott .07 .20
115 Antonio McDyess .10 .25
116 Damon Stoudamire .12 .30
117 Isaiah Rider .07 .20
118 Rasheed Wallace .12 .30
119 Kelvin Cato .07 .20
120 Jermaine O'Neal .12 .30
121 Corliss Williamson .07 .20
122 Olden Polynice .07 .20
123 Billy Owens .07 .20
124 Lawrence Funderburke .07 .20
125 Anthony Johnson .07 .20
126 Tim Duncan .25 .60
127 Sean Elliott .12 .30
128 Avery Johnson .10 .25
129 Vinny Del Negro .07 .20
130 Monty Williams .07 .20
131 Vin Baker .07 .20
132 Hersey Hawkins .07 .20
133 Nate McMillan .07 .20
134 Detlef Schrempf .12 .30
135 Gary Payton .12 .30
136 Jim McIlvaine .07 .20
137 Chauncey Billups .15 .40
138 Doug Christie .07 .20
139 John Wallace .07 .20
140 Tracy McGrady .20 .50
141 Dee Brown .07 .20
142 John Stockton .15 .40
143 Karl Malone .15 .40
144 Shandon Anderson .07 .20
145 Jacque Vaughn .07 .20
146 Bryon Russell .07 .20
147 Lee Mayberry .07 .20
148 Bryant Reeves .07 .20
149 Shareef Abdur-Rahim .12 .30
150 Michael Smith .07 .20
151 Pete Chilcutt .07 .20
152 Harvey Grant .07 .20
153 Juwan Howard .10 .25
154 Calbert Cheaney .07 .20
155 Tracy Murray .07 .20
156 Dikembe Mutombo FS .12 .30
157 Antoine Walker FS .12 .30
158 Glen Rice FS .12 .30
159 Michael Jordan FS 1.00 2.50
160 Wesley Person FS .07 .20
161 Shawn Bradley FS .07 .20
162 Dean Garrett FS .07 .20
163 Jerry Stackhouse FS .12 .30
164 Donyell Marshall FS .07 .20
165 Hakeem Olajuwon FS .15 .40
166 Chris Mullin FS .12 .30
167 Isaac Austin FS .07 .20
168 Shaquille O'Neal FS .30 .75
169 Tim Hardaway FS .12 .30
170 Glenn Robinson FS .10 .25
171 Kevin Garnett FS .25 .60
172 Keith Van Horn FS .12 .30
173 Larry Johnson FS .12 .30
174 Horace Grant FS .10 .25
175 Derrick Coleman FS .10 .25
176 Steve Nash FS .20 .50
177 Arvydas Sabonis FS UER .10 .25
spelled Arvadas
178 Corliss Williamson FS .07 .20
179 David Robinson FS .20 .50
180 Vin Baker FS .07 .20
181 Marcus Camby FS .10 .25
182 John Stockton FS .15 .40
183 Antonio Daniels FS .07 .20
184 Rod Strickland FS .07 .20
185 Michael Jordan FS 1.00 2.50
186 Kobe Bryant YIR .60 1.50
187 Clyde Drexler YIR .15 .40
188 Gary Payton YIR .12 .30
189 Michael Jordan YIR 1.00 2.50
190 David Robinson .25 .60
Tim Duncan YIR
191 Attendance Record YIR .07 .20
192 Karl Malone YIR .15 .40
193 Dikembe Mutombo YIR .12 .30
194 Keith Van Horn .12 .30
Kerry Kittles
Jayson Williams
Kendall Gill
Sam Cassell
195 Ray Allen YIR .15 .40
196 Michael Jordan YIR 1.00 2.50
197 Kobe Bryant .60 1.50
Eddie Jones
Shaquille O'Neal
Nick Van Exel
198 Michael Jordan YIR 1.00 2.50
199 Michael Jordan CL .40 1.00
200 Michael Jordan CL .40 1.00

1998-99 UD Choice Reserve

Randomly inserted in packs at a rate of one in six, this 200-card set parallels the basic set. The front of the cards carry a "Choice Reserve" logo in foil. To ascertain values, please refer to the multiplier in the header, coupled with the value of the base card.

*STARS: 2.5X TO 6X BASE CARD HI

1998-99 UD Choice Premium Choice Reserve

Randomly inserted in packs, this 200-card set parallels the basic set. The card fronts feature a foil-treatment to differentiate the cards. They are also serially numbered to 100 on the back. To ascertain values on individual cards, please refer to the multipliers, coupled with the value of the base card.

*STARS: 40X TO 100X BASE CARD HI
23 Michael Jordan 250.00 350.00

1998-99 UD Choice Mini Bobbing Heads

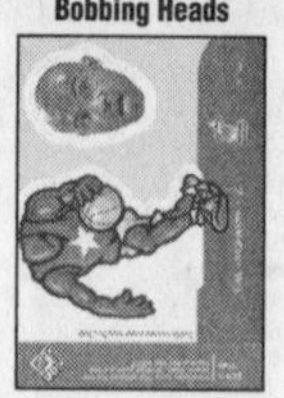

Randomly inserted into packs at a rate of one in four, this 30-card set features cards that can be popped-up and displayed similar to a "bobbing" head.

COMPLETE SET (30) 4.00 10.00
1 Dikembe Mutombo .15 .40
2 Antoine Walker .15 .40
3 Anthony Mason .10 .25
4 Toni Kukoc .15 .40
5 Shawn Kemp .15 .40
6 Shawn Bradley .10 .25
7 Danny Fortson .10 .25
8 Brian Williams .10 .25
9 Muggsy Bogues .12 .30
10 Charles Barkley .25 .60
11 Mark Jackson .15 .40
12 Rodney Rogers .10 .25
13 Kobe Bryant .75 2.00
14 Tim Hardaway .15 .40
15 Ray Allen .20 .50
16 Kevin Garnett .30 .75
17 Sam Cassell .12 .30
18 John Starks .12 .30
19 Anfernee Hardaway .25 .60
20 Allen Iverson .30 .75
21 Danny Manning .12 .30
22 Rasheed Wallace .15 .40
23 Chris Webber .15 .40
24 David Robinson .25 .60
25 Gary Payton .15 .40
26 Marcus Camby .12 .30
27 John Stockton .20 .50
28 Bryant Reeves .10 .25
29 Juwan Howard .12 .30
30 Michael Jordan 1.25 3.00

1998-99 UD Choice StarQuest Blue

Randomly inserted into packs at a rate of one per pack, this 30-card set features some of the best players in the NBA. The card front features blue borders with a photo of the player in the middle. The card backs feature one star to denote the first tier of the insert. Card backs are also numbered with a "SQ" prefix.

*GREEN STARS: 1.25X TO 3X HI COLUMN
GREEN: STATED ODDS 1:8 H/R
*RED STARS: 3X TO 8X HI COLUMN
RED: STATED ODDS 1:23 H/R
SQ1 Steve Smith .15 .40
SQ2 Kenny Anderson .15 .40
SQ3 Glen Rice .20 .50
SQ4 Toni Kukoc .20 .50
SQ5 Shawn Kemp .20 .50
SQ6 Michael Finley .20 .50
SQ7 Bobby Jackson .15 .40
SQ8 Grant Hill .30 .75
SQ9 Donyell Marshall .12 .30
SQ10 Hakeem Olajuwon .25 .60
SQ11 Reggie Miller .25 .60
SQ12 Maurice Taylor .12 .30
SQ13 Kobe Bryant 1.00 2.50
SQ14 Alonzo Mourning .25 .60
SQ15 Terrell Brandon .12 .30
SQ16 Stephon Marbury .25 .60
SQ17 Keith Van Horn .20 .50
SQ18 Patrick Ewing .25 .60
SQ19 Anfernee Hardaway .30 .75
SQ20 Allen Iverson .40 1.00
SQ21 Jason Kidd .30 .75
SQ22 Damon Stoudamire .20 .50
SQ23 Corliss Williamson .12 .30
SQ24 Tim Duncan .40 1.00
SQ25 Gary Payton .20 .50
SQ26 Chauncey Billups .25 .60
SQ27 Karl Malone .25 .60
SQ28 Shareef Abdur-Rahim .20 .50
SQ29 Juwan Howard .15 .40
SQ30 Michael Jordan 1.50 4.00

1998-99 UD Choice StarQuest Gold

Randomly inserted into packs, this 30-card set features some of the best players in the NBA. The card front features gold borders with a photo of the player in the middle. The card backs feature four stars to denote the final tier of the insert and are sequentially numbered to 100. Card backs are also numbered with a "SQ" prefix.

*STARS: 60X TO 150X BASE INSERT
SQ8 Grant Hill 100.00 200.00
SQ13 Kobe Bryant 250.00 500.00
SQ19 Anfernee Hardaway 100.00 200.00
SQ30 Michael Jordan 1000.00 2000.00

2002-03 UD Glass

Released in April 2003, UD Glass consists of 150 cards and is divided up as follows: Cards 1-90 feature veteran player base cards, 91-110 are Clear Winner subset cards printed on Upper Deck's Plexi-Glass card stock (1/8" thick clear plastic) inserted at 1:15 packs, 111-120 are also printed on the Plexi-Glass but feature rookies and are sequentially numbered to 250, 121-130 on glass with rookies and sequentially numbered to 500, and 131-150 on glass with rookies and sequentially numbered to 900. Every glass card's face is covered with a masking tape like peel so cards are priced in out-of-pack unpeeled condition. Peeled Glass cards sell for up to 25% less than unpeeled. UD Glass boxes also had one Magnifying Jumbo Glass box-topper. Packaging was three mini-boxes per box which contained eight packs of five cards and packs carried a suggested retail price of $5.99.

COMP.SET w/o SP's (90) 15.00 40.00
1 Shareef Abdur-Rahim .30 .75
2 Glenn Robinson .30 .75
3 Jason Terry .30 .75
4 Paul Pierce .50 1.25
5 Antoine Walker .30 .75
6 Vin Baker .30 .75
7 Jalen Rose .30 .75
8 Eddy Curry .30 .75
9 Tyson Chandler .30 .75
10 Darius Miles .25 .60
11 Ricky Davis .30 .75
12 Zydrunas Ilgauskas .30 .75
13 Dirk Nowitzki .60 1.50
14 Michael Finley .40 1.00
15 Steve Nash .50 1.25
16 Raef LaFrentz .25 .60
17 Rodney White .25 .60
18 Marcus Camby .30 .75
19 Juwan Howard .30 .75
20 Richard Hamilton .30 .75
21 Ben Wallace .40 1.00
22 Chauncey Billups .40 1.00
23 Jason Richardson .40 1.00
24 Antawn Jamison .40 1.00
25 Steve Francis .40 1.00
26 Cuttino Mobley .30 .75
27 Eddie Griffin .25 .60
28 Jermaine O'Neal .40 1.00
29 Reggie Miller .40 1.00
30 Jamaal Tinsley .25 .60
31 Andre Miller .30 .75
32 Elton Brand .40 1.00
33 Quentin Richardson .30 .75
34 Kobe Bryant 2.00 5.00
35 Shaquille O'Neal 1.00 2.50
36 Robert Horry .30 .75
37 Pau Gasol .50 1.25
38 Shane Battier .40 1.00
39 Jason Williams .30 .75
40 Eddie Jones .30 .75
41 Brian Grant .25 .60
42 Malik Allen .25 .60
43 Ray Allen .40 1.00
44 Tim Thomas .25 .60
45 Sam Cassell .30 .75
46 Kevin Garnett .75 2.00
47 Wally Szczerbiak .25 .60
48 Troy Hudson .25 .60
49 Loren Woods .25 .60
50 Jason Kidd .60 1.50
51 Richard Jefferson .40 1.00
52 Kenyon Martin .40 1.00
53 Baron Davis .40 1.00
54 Jamal Mashburn .30 .75
55 David Wesley .25 .60
56 P.J. Brown .25 .60
57 Allan Houston .30 .75
58 Kurt Thomas .25 .60
59 Latrell Sprewell .30 .75
60 Tracy McGrady .60 1.50
61 Mike Miller .40 1.00
62 Grant Hill .50 1.25
63 Allen Iverson .60 1.50
64 Keith Van Horn .30 .75
65 Aaron McKie .25 .60
66 Stephon Marbury .30 .75
67 Shawn Marion .40 1.00
68 Anfernee Hardaway .60 1.50
69 Rasheed Wallace .40 1.00
70 Damon Stoudamire .30 .75
71 Bonzi Wells .25 .60
72 Chris Webber .40 1.00
73 Mike Bibby .40 1.00
74 Peja Stojakovic .40 1.00
75 Hedo Turkoglu .40 1.00
76 Tim Duncan .75 2.00
77 David Robinson .60 1.50
78 Tony Parker .50 1.25
79 Gary Payton .40 1.00
80 Rashard Lewis .40 1.00
81 Desmond Mason .30 .75
82 Vince Carter .60 1.50
83 Antonio Davis .25 .60
84 Morris Peterson .25 .60
85 John Stockton .50 1.25
86 Karl Malone .50 1.25
87 Andrei Kirilenko .40 1.00
88 Jerry Stackhouse .30 .75
89 Larry Hughes .30 .75
90 Michael Jordan 3.00 8.00
91 Kobe Bryant CW 12.00 30.00
92 Paul Pierce CW 3.00 8.00
93 Chris Webber CW 2.50 6.00
94 Vince Carter CW 4.00 10.00
95 Tracy McGrady CW 4.00 10.00
96 Allen Iverson CW 4.00 10.00
97 Pau Gasol CW 3.00 8.00
98 Steve Francis CW 2.50 6.00
99 Jason Kidd CW 4.00 10.00
100 Dirk Nowitzki CW 4.00 10.00
101 Antoine Walker CW 2.00 5.00
102 Jason Richardson CW 2.50 6.00
103 Baron Davis CW 2.50 6.00
104 Elton Brand CW 2.50 6.00
105 Stephon Marbury CW 2.00 5.00
106 Ray Allen CW 2.50 6.00
107 Shaquille O'Neal CW 6.00 15.00
108 Kevin Garnett CW 5.00 12.00
109 Tim Duncan CW 5.00 12.00
110 Mike Bibby CW 2.50 6.00
111 Jay Williams RC 8.00 20.00
112 Yao Ming RC 20.00 50.00
113 Mike Dunleavy RC 8.00 20.00
114 Drew Gooden RC 10.00 25.00
115 Nikoloz Tskitishvili RC 6.00 15.00
116 DaJuan Wagner RC 6.00 15.00
117 Nene Hilario RC 8.00 20.00
118 Amare Stoudemire RC 15.00 40.00
119 Caron Butler RC 10.00 25.00
120 Manu Ginobili RC 15.00 40.00
121 Juaquin Hawkins RC 4.00 10.00
122 Kareem Rush RC 4.00 10.00
123 Jiri Welsch RC 4.00 10.00
124 Chris Wilcox RC 4.00 10.00
125 Tayshaun Prince RC 5.00 12.00
126 Qyntel Woods RC 4.00 10.00
127 Jared Jeffries RC 4.00 10.00
128 Gordan Giricek RC 4.00 10.00
129 Ryan Humphrey RC 4.00 10.00
130 Marko Jaric 4.00 10.00
131 Casey Jacobsen RC 2.50 6.00
132 Dan Dickau RC 2.50 6.00
133 Juan Dixon RC 3.00 8.00
134 Melvin Ely RC 2.50 6.00
135 Fred Jones RC 2.50 6.00
136 John Salmons RC 3.00 8.00
137 Marcus Haislip RC 2.50 6.00
138 Carlos Boozer RC 5.00 12.00
139 Chris Jefferies RC 2.50 6.00
140 Smush Parker RC 2.50 6.00
141 Vincent Yarbrough RC 2.50 6.00
142 Pat Burke RC 2.50 6.00
143 Lonny Baxter RC 2.50 6.00
144 Bostjan Nachbar RC 2.50 6.00
145 Rasual Butler RC 2.50 6.00
146 Ronald Murray RC 2.50 6.00
147 J.R. Bremer RC 2.50 6.00
148 Reggie Evans RC 2.50 6.00
149 Sam Clancy RC 2.50 6.00
150 Tamar Slay RC 2.50 6.00
NNO Kobe Bryant AF PROMO 4.00 10.00

2002-03 UD Glass Auto Focus

Inserted in packs at the rate of one in 72, this 20-card set is printed on Upper Deck's Plexi-Glass and uses a horizontal design. Player photos appear on the left and player autographs appear on the right. Jamaal Magloire was issued with some live versions and some EXCH versions.

AW Antoine Walker 6.00 15.00
CB Chauncey Billups 8.00 20.00
DS DeShawn Stevenson 4.00 10.00
DW Dominique Wilkins 15.00 40.00
ET Etan Thomas 4.00 10.00
GW Gerald Wallace 6.00 15.00
JK Jason Kidd 20.00 50.00
JM Jamaal Magloire 4.00 10.00
JO Jermaine O'Neal 10.00 25.00
JR Jason Richardson 6.00 15.00
JW Jay Williams 6.00 15.00
KA Kareem Abdul-Jabbar/20 75.00 150.00
KB Kobe Bryant/50 125.00 250.00
KG Kevin Garnett/50 50.00 120.00
MB Mike Bibby 10.00 25.00
MJ Michael Jordan/23 400.00 700.00
MM Mike Miller 6.00 15.00
PP Paul Pierce 12.50 30.00
TC Tyson Chandler 6.00 15.00
YM Yao Ming 25.00 50.00

2002-03 UD Glass One Two Combo Jerseys

Randomly inserted in packs, this 13-card set is horizontally designed with a white area in the middle separating full-bleed full-color player action photos on each side. Within each photo is a swatch of game-worn memorabilia. Cards are sequentially numbered to 125. An autographed parallel of this set was also inserted with cards sequentially numbered to 25.

ASCJ Amare Stoudemire 10.00 25.00
Casey Jacobsen
CWME Chris Wilcox 6.00 15.00
Melvin Ely
DWCB Dajuan Wagner 6.00 15.00
Carlos Boozer
JJDC Jared Jeffries 6.00 15.00
Juan Dixon
JOFJ Jermaine O'Neal 6.00 15.00
Fred Jones
JWJR Jay Williams 6.00 15.00
Jason Richardson
JWTC Jay Williams 6.00 15.00
Tyson Chandler
KBKR Kobe Bryant 15.00 40.00
Kareem Rush
MJKB Michael Jordan 60.00 150.00
Kobe Bryant
MMRH Mike Miller 6.00 15.00
Ryan Humphrey
MPCJ Morris Peterson 6.00 15.00
Chris Jefferies
NHNT Nene Hilario 6.00 15.00
Nikoloz Tskitishvili
SMAS Shawn Marion 12.50 30.00
Amare Stoudemire

2002-03 UD Glass One Two Combo Jerseys Autographs

Randomly seeded, this 14-card set parallels the design of the base One Two Combo Jerseys set enhanced with authentic player autographs. Each card is sequentially numbered to 25.

ASCJ Amare Stoudemire 75.00 150.00
Casey Jacobsen
CWME Chris Wilcox 15.00 40.00
Melvin Ely
DWCB DaJuan Wagner 60.00 120.00
Carlos Boozer
JJJD Jared Jeffries 15.00 40.00
Juan Dixon
JWTC Jay Williams 15.00 40.00
Tyson Chandler
KBKR Kobe Bryant 200.00 400.00
Kareem Rush
MBGW Mike Bibby 50.00 100.00
Gerald Wallace
MJKB Michael Jordan 700.00 1200.00
Kobe Bryant
MPCJ Morris Peterson 15.00 40.00
Chris Jefferies
NHNT Nene Hilario 40.00 100.00
Nikoloz Tskitishvili
SMAS Shawn Marion 80.00 200.00
Amare Stoudemire

2002-03 UD Glass 2 Exciting Dual Jersey

Randomly inserted in packs, this seven card set utilizes a horizontal design with one player photo on the left and one on the right. Each player is coupled with a swatch of game worn memorabilia. The swatch on the left is in the shape of the number two and the swatch on the right is in the shape of the letter X. Each card is sequentially numbered to 50. An Autographed parallel of this set was also inserted with cards sequentially numbered to 10.

JKKM Jason Kidd 20.00 50.00
Kenyon Martin
KBJK Kobe Bryant 30.00 80.00
Jason Kidd
KBKG Kobe Bryant 40.00 100.00
Kevin Garnett
MJKB Michael Jordan 100.00 250.00
Kobe Bryant
PPAW Paul Pierce 20.00 40.00
Antoine Walker
SMAS Shawn Marion 12.50 30.00
Amare Stoudemire
YMJW Yao Ming 15.00 40.00
Jay Williams

2002-03 UD Glass Game Gear

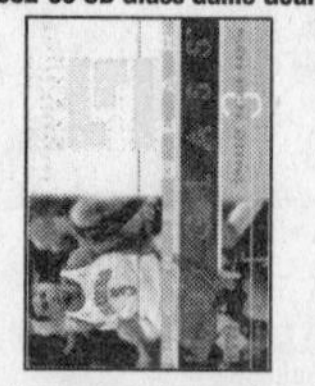

Inserted in packs at the rate of one in 24, this 14-card set is horizontally designed with full-color player action photos on the left and a swatch of game-worn memorabilia on the right.

DMGG Darius Miles 2.00 5.00
DNGG Dirk Nowitzki 5.00 12.00
DWGG David Wesley 2.00 5.00
EBGG Elton Brand 3.00 8.00
JMGG Jamal Mashburn 2.50 6.00
JTGG Jamaal Tinsley 2.00 5.00
LSGG Latrell Sprewell 2.50 6.00
RAGG Ray Allen 3.00 8.00
RLGG Rashard Lewis 3.00 8.00
RWGG Rasheed Wallace 3.00 8.00
SAGG Shareef Abdur-Rahim 2.50 6.00
SBGG Shane Battier 3.00 8.00
SMGG Shawn Marion 3.00 8.00
WZGG Wang Zhizhi 2.00 5.00

2002-03 UD Glass Get Real Jersey

Seeded in packs randomly at the rate of one in 48, this six-card set places full color player action photos on a white card with a colored V-shape behind them. Below the photo is a swatch of game-worn memorabilia in the

hape of an exclamation point.
KR Jason Kidd 6.00 15.00
BR Kobe Bryant SP 15.00 40.00
GR Kevin Garnett 8.00 20.00
MBR Mike Bibby 4.00 10.00
PR Paul Pierce 5.00 12.00
PR Scottie Pippen 6.00 15.00

2002-03 UD Glass Magnifying Glass

nserted as a box-topper at the rate of one per box, these jumbo cards are printed on Upper Deck's Plexi-Glass. The Magnifying Glass cards are horizontally designed with a color player photo on the left and a red stripe running through the middle from left to right.
AIM Allen Iverson 3.00 8.00
BDM Baron Davis 2.00 5.00
CWM Chris Webber 2.00 5.00
DGM Drew Gooden 3.00 8.00
DMM Darius Miles 1.25 3.00
JRM Jason Richardson 2.00 5.00
JSM Jerry Stackhouse 1.50 4.00
JWM Jay Williams 2.50 6.00
KBM Kobe Bryant 10.00 25.00
KMM Karl Malone 2.50 6.00
MJM Michael Jordan 15.00 40.00
PSM Peja Stojakovic 2.00 5.00
RAM Ray Allen 2.00 5.00
RLM Rashard Lewis 2.00 5.00
SAM Shareef Abdur-Rahim 1.50 4.00
SBM Shane Battier 2.00 5.00
SFM Steve Francis 2.00 5.00
SHM Shawn Marion 2.00 5.00
SMM Stephon Marbury 1.50 4.00
YMM Yao Ming 6.00 15.00

2002-03 UD Glass Magnifying Glass Autographs

Randomly inserted as a box-topper at the rate of one in six boxes, this 20-card set parallels the design of the base Magnifying Glass insert. Each card is enhanced with an authentic player autograph.
AWA Antoine Walker/84 12.50 30.00
CBA Chauncey Billups 10.00 25.00
DSA DeShawn Stevenson 5.00 12.00
ETA Etan Thomas 5.00 12.00
GWA Gerald Wallace 10.00 25.00
JKA Jason Kidd 25.00 60.00
JMA Jamaal Magloire 5.00 12.00
JOA Jermaine O'Neal 12.50 30.00
JRA Jason Richardson 10.00 25.00
JWA Jay Williams 8.00 20.00
KBA Kobe Bryant/50 200.00 400.00
KGA Kevin Garnett/21 75.00 150.00
KMA Kenyon Martin 6.00 15.00
MBA Mike Bibby 12.50 30.00
MFA Marcus Fizer 5.00 12.00
MJA Michael Jordan/23 400.00 700.00
MMA Mike Miller 10.00 25.00
PPA Paul Pierce 15.00 40.00
TCA Tyson Chandler 10.00 25.00
YMA Yao Ming 25.00 60.00

2002-03 UD Glass Premiere Issues Jersey

Inserted in packs at the rate of one in 48, this six card set features rookie players in posed portrait-style photos. The top of the card is white and the bottom of the card contains a jersey swatch with a background set to match the player's jersey colors.
CBP Carlos Boozer 6.00 15.00
CJP Chris Jefferies 3.00 8.00
JDP Juan Dixon 4.00 10.00
JWP Jay Williams SP 4.00 10.00
SCP Sam Clancy 3.00 8.00
VYP Vincent Yarbrough 3.00 8.00

2002-03 UD Glass Superlative Swatch

Inserted in packs at the rate of one in 36, this 10-card set uses a horizontal design with full-color player photos on the right and a circular swatch of game-worn memorabilia on the left.
AMS Andre Miller 2.50 6.00
AWS Antoine Walker 2.50 6.00
BDS Baron Davis 3.00 8.00
CWS Chris Webber 3.00 8.00
DMS Darius Miles 2.00 5.00
KBS Kobe Bryant SP 15.00 40.00
KMS Karl Malone 4.00 10.00
MFS Michael Finley 3.00 8.00
PGS Pau Gasol 4.00 10.00
SMS Stephon Marbury 2.50 6.00

2002-03 UD Glass VIP Access Jersey

Seeded in packs at the rate of one in 72, this six card set has white borders around a rectangular centered portrait-style photo of the featured player. Under this photo there is a swatch of game-worn memorabilia in the shape of the letter V.
AI Allen Iverson 6.00 15.00
JW Jay Williams 5.00 12.00
KB Kobe Bryant SP 15.00 40.00
MJ Michael Jordan SP 40.00 100.00
SF Steve Francis 4.00 10.00
TM Tracy McGrady 6.00 15.00

2003-04 UD Glass

Released in January 2004, UD Glass is a 100-card set comprised of 60 base veteran cards with centered full color player action photos on a white background with color highlights to match the player's jersey. Level Three Rookies (cards 61-80) sequentially numbered to 1100, Level Two Rookies (cards 81-90) sequentially numbered to 750 and Level One Rookies (cards 91-100) sequentially numbered to 250. UD Glass was packaged in eight-pack mini boxes where packs contained five cards and carried a suggested retail price of $5.99.
COMP.SET w/o SP's (60) 17.50 35.00
1 Shareef Abdur-Rahim .40 1.00
2 Jason Terry .40 1.00
3 Paul Pierce .60 1.50
4 Antoine Walker .50 1.25
5 Scottie Pippen .75 2.00
6 Jalen Rose .40 1.00
7 Darius Miles .30 .75
8 Dajuan Wagner .30 .75
9 Dirk Nowitzki .75 2.00
10 Steve Nash .60 1.50
11 Michael Finley .50 1.25
12 Andre Miller .40 1.00
13 Nene .40 1.00
14 Richard Hamilton .40 1.00
15 Ben Wallace .50 1.25
16 Jason Richardson .50 1.25
17 Nick Van Exel .40 1.00
18 Steve Francis .50 1.25
19 Yao Ming 1.00 2.50
20 Jermaine O'Neal .50 1.25
21 Reggie Miller .50 1.25
22 Elton Brand .50 1.25
23 Corey Maggette .40 1.00
24 Kobe Bryant 2.50 6.00
25 Shaquille O'Neal 1.25 3.00
26 Gary Payton .50 1.25
27 Pau Gasol .50 1.25
28 Shane Battier .40 1.00
29 Caron Butler .50 1.25
30 Eddie Jones .40 1.00
31 Desmond Mason .40 1.00
32 Michael Redd .50 1.25
33 Kevin Garnett 1.00 2.50
34 Latrell Sprewell .40 1.00
35 Jason Kidd .75 2.00
36 Richard Jefferson .50 1.25
37 Baron Davis .50 1.25
38 Jamal Mashburn .40 1.00
39 Allan Houston .40 1.00
40 Keith Van Horn .40 1.00
41 Tracy McGrady .60 1.50
42 Juwan Howard .40 1.00
43 Allen Iverson .75 2.00
44 Glenn Robinson .40 1.00
45 Amare Stoudemire .75 2.00
46 Stephon Marbury .40 1.00
47 Rasheed Wallace .50 1.25
48 Bonzi Wells .30 .75
49 Chris Webber .50 1.25
50 Mike Bibby .50 1.25
51 Tim Duncan .75 2.00
52 Tony Parker .50 1.25
53 Ray Allen .50 1.25
54 Rashard Lewis .50 1.25
55 Vince Carter .75 2.00
56 Antonio Davis .30 .75
57 Andrei Kirilenko .50 1.25
58 Jarron Collins .30 .75
59 Gilbert Arenas .50 1.25
60 Jerry Stackhouse .40 1.00
61 Kyle Korver RC 2.50 6.00
62 Travis Hansen RC 2.00 5.00
63 Willie Green RC 2.00 5.00
64 Keith Bogans RC 2.00 5.00
65 Theron Smith RC 2.00 5.00
66 Zaur Pachulia RC 2.00 5.00
67 Derrick Zimmerman RC 2.00 5.00
68 Jason Kapono RC 2.00 5.00
69 Steve Blake RC 2.50 6.00
70 Slavko Vranes RC 2.00 5.00
71 Jerome Beasley RC 2.00 5.00
72 Aleksandar Pavlovic RC 2.00 5.00
73 Boris Diaw RC 2.50 6.00
74 Kendrick Perkins RC 3.00 8.00
75 Leandro Barbosa RC 2.50 6.00
76 Josh Howard RC 2.00 5.00
77 Luke Walton RC 2.00 5.00
78 Maciej Lampe RC 2.00 5.00
79 Brian Cook RC 2.00 5.00
80 Zarko Cabarkapa RC 2.00 5.00
81 Travis Outlaw RC 4.00 10.00
82 Ndudi Ebi RC 3.00 8.00
83 David West RC 4.00 10.00
84 Reece Gaines RC 3.00 8.00
85 Dahntay Jones RC 3.00 8.00
86 Marcus Banks RC 3.00 8.00
87 Troy Bell RC 3.00 8.00
88 Luke Ridnour RC 4.00 10.00
89 Mickael Pietrus RC 3.00 8.00
90 Chris Kaman RC 4.00 10.00
91 Nick Collison RC 8.00 20.00
92 Mike Sweetney RC 8.00 20.00
93 Jarvis Hayes RC 8.00 20.00
94 T.J. Ford RC 10.00 25.00
95 Kirk Hinrich RC 10.00 25.00
96 Chris Bosh RC 15.00 40.00
97 Dwyane Wade RC 40.00 100.00
98 Carmelo Anthony RC 20.00 50.00
99 Darko Milicic RC 8.00 20.00
100 LeBron James RC 150.00 300.00

2003-04 UD Glass Crystal

Randomly inserted in packs, this 100-card set parallels the set order of the base UD Glass set enhanced with a new design and the cards are printed on UD's plexi-glass clear card stock. Each card is sequentially numbered to 25 and came from packs with a protective coating.
*1-60 SINGLES: 4X TO 10X BASE HI
*61-80 RCs: 2X TO 5X BASE HI
*81-90 RCs: 1.25X TO 3X BASE HI
*91-100 RCs: .5X TO 1.25X BASE HI
96 Chris Bosh 25.00 60.00
97 Dwyane Wade 150.00 300.00
98 Carmelo Anthony 75.00 150.00
100 LeBron James 300.00 600.00

2003-04 UD Glass Gold

Randomly seeded, this 60-card set is a partial parallel of the base UD Glass set enhanced with gold foil highlights and sequential numbering to 100.
*1-60 SINGLES: 2.5X TO 6X BASE HI

2003-04 UD Glass Plexi-Glass

Randomly inserted in packs at the rate of one in 20, this 60-card set parallels the veteran portion of the UD Glass base set with a new design on UD's plexi-glass clear card stock. Each card comes out of the pack with a protective coating.
*GLASS SINGLES: 1.5X TO 4X BASE HI

2003-04 UD Glass Auto Focus

Randomly seeded at one in 48, this 22-card set is printed on UD's plexi-glass clear cards with player photos on the left and the set logo and autograph on the right. A crystal parallel of this set was also issued and is sequentially numbered to 25.
BC Brian Cook 5.00 12.00
CA Carmelo Anthony 30.00 80.00
CB Caron Butler 5.00 12.00
CK Chris Kaman 6.00 15.00
DA Darius Miles 5.00 12.00
DJ DerMarr Johnson 5.00 12.00
DM Darko Milicic 5.00 12.00
GA Gilbert Arenas 6.00 15.00
GG Gordan Giricek 5.00 12.00
GP Gary Payton 12.50 30.00
KB Kobe Bryant SP 100.00 200.00
LJ LeBron James/100 350.00 650.00
MC Antonio McDyess 5.00 12.00
MJ Michael Jordan SP 300.00 550.00
PI Mickael Pietrus 5.00 12.00
PS Peja Stojakovic 8.00 20.00
RG Reece Gaines 5.00 12.00
SB Shane Battier 5.00 12.00
TB Troy Bell 5.00 12.00
TM Tracy McGrady 15.00 40.00
YM Yao Ming 15.00 40.00

2003-04 UD Glass Auto Focus Crystal

This 22-card set parallels the base Auto Foucs insert set enhanced with sequential numbering to 25.
*CRYSTAL: 1X TO 2.5X BASE HI
LJ LeBron James 700.00 1000.00
MJ Michael Jordan 400.00 700.00

2003-04 UD Glass Clear Cut Winners Jerseys

Randomly inserted in packs, this 14-card set places a full-color player photo on the left side of the card and a "W" shaped swatch of jersey on the right. Each card is sequentially numbered to 350.
CWAH Allan Houston 2.00 5.00
CWAJ Antawn Jamison 2.50 6.00
CWDN Dirk Nowitzki 4.00 10.00
CWDR David Robinson 6.00 15.00
CWJK Jason Kidd 4.00 10.00
CWKB Kobe Bryant 12.00 30.00
CWKG Kevin Garnett 5.00 12.00
CWKM Kenyon Martin 2.50 6.00
CWLJ LeBron James 50.00 120.00
CWMJ Michael Jordan 30.00 80.00
CWSF Steve Francis 2.50 6.00
CWSM Stephon Marbury 2.00 5.00
CWSO Shaquille O'Neal 6.00 15.00
CWTD Tim Duncan 4.00 10.00

2003-04 UD Glass Cutting Edge Jerseys

Randomly inserted in packs, this 14-card set places full-color player action photos on a white background with colored highlights and a semi-circle swatch of jersey towards the bottom. Each card is sequentially numbered to 100.
CEAS Amare Stoudemire 6.00 15.00
CEDR David Robinson 10.00 25.00
CEDW Dajuan Wagner 2.50 6.00
CEGH Grant Hill 5.00 12.00
CEJK Jason Kidd 6.00 15.00
CEKB Kobe Bryant 25.00 60.00
CEKG Kevin Garnett 8.00 20.00
CELJ LeBron James 60.00 150.00
CELS Latrell Sprewell 3.00 8.00
CEMJ Michael Jordan 60.00 150.00
CERW Rasheed Wallace 4.00 10.00
CESF Steve Francis 4.00 10.00
CESN Steve Nash 5.00 12.00
CESO Shaquille O'Neal 10.00 25.00

2003-04 UD Glass Game Gear

Inserted in packs at the rate of one in 24, this 30-card set places full-color player action photos on the left and a semi-circle white border on the right. A swatch of game worn memorabilia appears in the lower right-hand corner of the card.
GGAI Allen Iverson 4.00 10.00
GGAM Alonzo Mourning 4.00 10.00
GGAN Andre Miller 2.00 5.00
GGAS Amare Stoudemire 4.00 10.00
GGAW Antoine Walker 2.50 6.00
GGCB Caron Butler SP 2.50 6.00
GGCW Chris Webber 2.50 6.00
GGDM Darius Miles 2.00 5.00
GGDN Dirk Nowitzki 4.00 10.00
GGDW Dajuan Wagner 2.00 5.00
GGEB Elton Brand 2.50 6.00
GGEG Manu Ginobili 3.00 8.00
GGGH Grant Hill 4.00 10.00
GGKB Kobe Bryant SP 10.00 25.00
GGKG Kevin Garnett 5.00 12.00
GGLJ LeBron James SP 50.00 120.00
GGLO Lamar Odom 2.50 6.00
GGLS Latrell Sprewell 2.00 5.00
GGMB Mike Bibby 2.50 6.00
GGMJ Michael Jordan SP 30.00 80.00
GGPP Paul Pierce 3.00 8.00
GGSA Shareef Abdur-Rahim 2.00 5.00
GGSF Steve Francis 2.50 6.00
GGSM Stephon Marbury SP 2.00 5.00
GGSN Steve Nash 3.00 8.00
GGTD Tim Duncan 4.00 10.00
GGTM Tracy McGrady 3.00 8.00
GGTP Tony Parker 2.50 6.00
GGWS Wally Szczerbiak 2.00 5.00
GGYM Yao Ming 5.00 12.00

2003-04 UD Glass Monumental Marks

Randomly seeded at the rate of one in 144, this 20-card set places a full-color player head shot in the upper left hand corner of the card with an "M" shaped swatch of jersey below it. The right side of the card contains an authentic player autograph.
AMJ Andre Miller 6.00 15.00
DAJ Darius Miles 6.00 15.00
DMJ Darko Milicic 6.00 15.00
JKJ Jason Kidd 20.00 50.00
JRJ Jason Richardson 6.00 15.00
KBJ Kobe Bryant/100 125.00 250.00
LJJ LeBron James/100 500.00 900.00
LOJ Lamar Odom 10.00 25.00
LRJ Luke Ridnour 8.00 20.00
MBJ Mike Bibby 6.00 15.00
MJJ Michael Jordan/50 700.00 1200.00
MPJ Morris Peterson 6.00 15.00
MSJ Mike Sweetney 6.00 15.00
PIJ Mickael Pietrus 6.00 15.00
PPJ Paul Pierce 15.00 40.00
PSJ Peja Stojakovic 10.00 25.00
RHJ Richard Hamilton 8.00 20.00
RJJ Richard Jefferson 8.00 20.00
RMJ Reggie Miller 60.00 150.00
SFJ Steve Francis 8.00 20.00

2003-04 UD Glass Premier Issue Jerseys

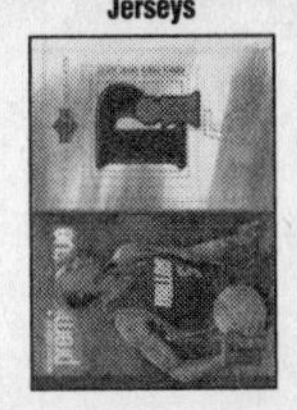

Seeded in packs at the rate of one in 96, this 21-card set is horizontally designed where full-color player photos appear on the left side and jersey swatches in the shape of a "P" appear on the right. The focus of the set is this year's new rookies.
PIBC Brian Cook 2.50 6.00
PICA Carmelo Anthony 6.00 15.00
PICB Chris Bosh 5.00 12.00
PICK Chris Kaman 3.00 8.00
PIDE David West 3.00 8.00
PIDJ Dahntay Jones 2.50 6.00
PIDM Darko Milicic 2.50 6.00
PIDY Dwyane Wade 10.00 25.00
PIHO Josh Howard 2.50 6.00
PIJH Jarvis Hayes 2.50 6.00
PILJ LeBron James SP 60.00 120.00
PILR Luke Ridnour 3.00 8.00
PILW Luke Walton 2.50 6.00
PIMB Marcus Banks 2.50 6.00
PIMP Mickael Pietrus 2.50 6.00
PIMS Mike Sweetney 2.50 6.00
PIRG Reece Gaines 2.50 6.00
PISB Steve Blake 3.00 8.00
PITB Troy Bell 2.50 6.00
PITO Travis Outlaw 3.00 8.00
PIZC Zarko Cabarkapa 2.50 6.00

2003-04 UD Glass Superlative Swatches

Inserted at the rate of one in 24, this 21-card set is horizontally designed and player photos on the left of the card appear in black and white while an "S" shaped swatch of memorabilia appears on the right.
SSAH Allan Houston 2.00 5.00
SSAI Allen Iverson 4.00 10.00
SSCB Caron Butler 2.50 6.00
SSCW Charlie Ward 2.00 5.00
SSDN Dirk Nowitzki 4.00 10.00
SSEC Eddy Curry 2.00 5.00
SSGA Gilbert Arenas 2.50 6.00
SSJJ Joe Johnson 2.50 6.00
SSJK Jason Kidd 4.00 10.00
SSJR Jason Richardson 2.50 6.00
SSKB Kobe Bryant SP 10.00 25.00
SSLO Lamar Odom 2.50 6.00
SSMJ Michael Jordan SP 40.00 100.00
SSMM Mark Madsen 2.00 5.00
SSRS Radoslav Nesterovic 2.00 5.00
SSTB Terrell Brandon 2.00 5.00
SSTC Tyson Chandler 2.00 5.00
SSTD Tim Duncan 4.00 10.00
SSTM Tracy McGrady 3.00 8.00
SSWS Wally Szczerbiak 2.00 5.00
SSYM Yao Ming 5.00 12.00

2003-04 UD Glass Swatch of Class

Inserted in packs at the rate of one in 96, this 21-card set is horizontally designed with full-color player photos appearing on the left, a blue-scale light photo centered in the background and a swatch of memorabilia on the right.
SCAJ Antawn Jamison 2.50 6.00
SCEB Elton Brand 2.50 6.00
SCJO Jermaine O'Neal 2.50 6.00
SCJS Jerry Stackhouse 2.00 5.00
SCKB Kobe Bryant SP 20.00 50.00
SCKE Kenyon Martin 2.50 6.00
SCKM Karl Malone 3.00 8.00
SCLJ LeBron James SP 60.00 150.00
SCLO Lamar Odom 2.50 6.00
SCMC Marcus Camby 2.00 5.00
SCMF Michael Finley 2.50 6.00
SCMJ Michael Jordan SP 75.00 150.00
SCPG Pau Gasol 2.50 6.00
SCPP Paul Pierce 3.00 8.00
SCPS Peja Stojakovic 2.50 6.00
SCRA Ray Allen 2.50 6.00
SCRL Rashard Lewis 2.50 6.00
SCRM Reggie Miller 2.50 6.00
SCSH Shawn Marion 2.50 6.00
SCSM Stephon Marbury 2.00 5.00
SCTP Tony Parker 2.50 6.00

2003-04 UD Glass VIP Access Jerseys

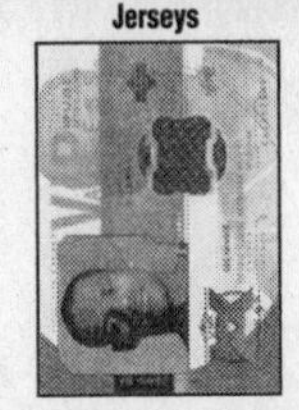

Sequentially numbered to 25, this 14-card set is horizontally designed with a player portrait style photo to the left of the card and a memorabilia swatch to the lower right.
AI Allen Iverson 15.00 40.00
BW Ben Wallace 10.00 25.00
CA Carmelo Anthony 25.00 60.00
CW Chris Webber 10.00 25.00
DM Darko Milicic 10.00 25.00
DW Dajuan Wagner 6.00 15.00
JO Jermaine O'Neal 10.00 25.00
KB Kobe Bryant 50.00 125.00
LJ LeBron James 200.00 400.00
MJ Michael Jordan 80.00 200.00
PP Paul Pierce 12.00 30.00
SO Shaquille O'Neal 25.00 60.00
TM Tracy McGrady 12.00 30.00
YM Yao Ming 20.00 50.00

2002-03 UD Glass Beckett.com Samples

Randomly inserted in Beckett Basketball Collector issue #154, this 90-card set parallels the base UD Glass set enhanced with a silver foil "UD PROMO" stamp along the bottom of the card.
*SINGLES: .75X TO 2X BASE UD GLASS HI

1998-99 UD Ionix

This 80-card set was issued in four card packs that carried a suggested retail price of $4.99. It was the debut issue for Ionix. The rookie card subset, Electrix, was inserted at one in four packs and featured 20 of the top rookies from the 1998 NBA Draft.
COMPLETE SET (80) 25.00 60.00
COMPLETE SET w/o RC (60) 10.00 25.00
1 Michael Jordan 1.50 4.00
2 Michael Jordan 1.50 4.00
3 Michael Jordan 1.50 4.00
4 Michael Jordan 1.50 4.00
5 Michael Jordan 1.50 4.00
6 Michael Jordan 1.50 4.00
7 Steve Smith .20 .50
8 Dikembe Mutombo .25 .60
9 Ron Mercer .20 .50
10 Antoine Walker .25 .60
11 Derrick Coleman .20 .50
12 Glen Rice .25 .60
13 Michael Jordan 1.50 4.00
14 Toni Kukoc .25 .60
15 Derek Anderson .15 .40
16 Shawn Kemp .25 .60
17 Michael Finley .25 .60
18 Steve Nash .40 1.00
19 Antonio McDyess .20 .50
20 Nick Van Exel .20 .50
21 Grant Hill .40 1.00
22 Jerry Stackhouse .25 .60
23 Donyell Marshall .15 .40
24 John Starks .20 .50
25 Charles Barkley .40 1.00
26 Hakeem Olajuwon .30 .75
27 Scottie Pippen .40 1.00
28 Reggie Miller .30 .75
29 Rik Smits .20 .50
30 Maurice Taylor .15 .40
31 Kobe Bryant 1.25 3.00
32 Shaquille O'Neal .60 1.50
33 Tim Hardaway .25 .60
34 Alonzo Mourning .30 .75
35 Ray Allen .30 .75
36 Glenn Robinson .20 .50
37 Stephon Marbury .30 .75
38 Kevin Garnett .50 1.25
39 Jayson Williams .15 .40
40 Keith Van Horn .25 .60
41 Patrick Ewing .30 .75
42 Allan Houston .20 .50
43 Anfernee Hardaway .40 1.00
44 Isaac Austin .15 .40
45 Tim Thomas .25 .60
46 Allen Iverson .50 1.25
47 Tom Gugliotta .15 .40
48 Jason Kidd .40 1.00
49 Damon Stoudamire .25 .60
50 Chris Webber .25 .60
51 Tim Duncan .50 1.25
52 David Robinson .40 1.00
53 Gary Payton .25 .60
54 Vin Baker .20 .50
55 Tracy McGrady .40 1.00
56 John Stockton .30 .75
57 Karl Malone .30 .75
58 Shareef Abdur-Rahim .25 .60
59 Juwan Howard .20 .50
60 Mitch Richmond .25 .60
61 Michael Olowokandi RC .75 2.00
62 Mike Bibby RC 1.50 4.00
63 Raef LaFrentz RC .75 2.00
64 Antawn Jamison RC 1.50 4.00
65 Vince Carter RC 3.00 8.00
66 Robert Traylor RC .60 1.50
67 Jason Williams RC 1.50 4.00
68 Larry Hughes RC 1.25 3.00
69 Dirk Nowitzki RC 4.00 10.00
70 Paul Pierce RC 3.00 8.00
71 Cuttino Mobley RC 1.25 3.00
72 Corey Benjamin RC .60 1.50
73 Peja Stojakovic RC 1.50 4.00
74 Michael Dickerson RC .60 1.50
75 Matt Harpring RC .75 2.00
76 Rashard Lewis RC 1.50 4.00
77 Pat Garrity RC .60 1.50
78 Roshown McLeod RC .60 1.50
79 Ricky Davis RC 1.00 2.50
80 Felipe Lopez RC .60 1.50
J1A Michael Jordan AU/23 2500.00 4500.00

1998-99 UD Ionix Reciprocal

Randomly inserted into packs, this 80-card set parallels the base set. The cards actually switch the photo from the back of the card and puts it on the front. The veterans (cards 1-60) were serially numbered to 750, and the rookies (cards 61-80) were serially numbered to 100. To ascertain values for individual cards, please use the multipliers in the header below, coupled with the value of the base card.
COMMON MJ (1-6/13) 15.00 40.00
*STARS: 5X TO 12X BASE CARD HI
*RCs: 4X TO 10X BASE HI
65 Vince Carter 75.00 150.00
69 Dirk Nowitzki 100.00 200.00

1998-99 UD Ionix Area 23

Randomly inserted in packs at one in 18, this 10-card set features Michael Jordan on cards using rainbow Ionix technology. Card backs carry an "A" prefix.
COMPLETE SET (10) 30.00 80.00
COMMON CARD (A1-A10) 4.00 10.00

1998-99 UD Ionix Kinetix

Randomly inserted into packs at one in nine, this 20-card set focuses on players with lightning quick moves. The card backs carry a "K" prefix.
COMPLETE SET (20) 20.00 50.00
K1 Michael Jordan 6.00 15.00
K2 Michael Olowokandi .60 1.50
K3 Keith Van Horn .75 2.00
K4 Grant Hill 1.25 3.00
K5 Stephon Marbury 1.00 2.50
K6 Larry Hughes 1.00 2.50
K7 Vince Carter 2.50 6.00
K8 Jason Kidd 1.25 3.00
K9 Robert Traylor .50 1.25
K10 Ron Mercer .60 1.50
K11 Dirk Nowitzki 3.00 8.00
K12 Antawn Jamison 1.25 3.00
K13 Kobe Bryant 4.00 10.00
K14 Jason Williams 1.25 3.00
K15 Raef LaFrentz .60 1.50
K16 Gary Payton .75 2.00
K17 Tim Duncan 1.50 4.00
K18 Paul Pierce 2.50 6.00
K19 Mike Bibby 1.25 3.00
K20 Scottie Pippen 1.25 3.00

1998-99 UD Ionix MJ HoloGrFX

Randomly inserted in packs at one in 1500, this 10-card set features new technology - and takes trading cards to a new level. Card backs carry a "MJ" prefix.
COMMON CARD (MJ1-10) 80.00 200.00

1998-99 UD Ionix Skyonix

Randomly inserted in packs at one in 53, this 25-card set features players who can fly through the air like no others. Card backs carry a "S" prefix.
COMPLETE SET (25) 100.00 200.00
S1 Michael Jordan 25.00 60.00
S2 Scottie Pippen 5.00 12.00
S3 Derek Anderson 2.00 5.00
S4 Jason Kidd 5.00 12.00
S5 Damon Stoudamire 3.00 8.00
S6 Antoine Walker 3.00 8.00
S7 Shaquille O'Neal 8.00 20.00
S8 Tim Thomas 3.00 8.00
S9 Reggie Miller 4.00 10.00
S10 Allen Iverson 6.00 15.00
S11 Antonio McDyess 2.50 6.00
S12 Michael Finley 3.00 8.00
S13 Charles Barkley 5.00 12.00
S14 Shareef Abdur-Rahim 3.00 8.00
S15 Gary Payton 3.00 8.00

S16 David Robinson 5.00 12.00
S17 Anfernee Hardaway 5.00 12.00
S18 Ray Allen 4.00 10.00
S19 Ron Mercer 2.50 6.00
S20 Tim Hardaway 3.00 8.00
S21 Chris Webber 3.00 8.00
S22 Kevin Garnett 6.00 15.00
S23 Juwan Howard 2.50 6.00
S24 Karl Malone 4.00 10.00
S25 Keith Van Horn 3.00 8.00

1998-99 UD Ionix UD Authentics

Randomly inserted in packs, this 5-card set features autographs from rookies. Each card is serially numbered out of 475. The card are numbered by the player's initials.
CB Corey Benjamin 4.00 10.00
DO Michael Doleac 4.00 10.00
JW Jason Williams 25.00 60.00
RL Raef LaFrentz 5.00 12.00
RM Roshown McLeod 4.00 10.00

1998-99 UD Ionix Warp Zone

Randomly inserted in packs at one in 216, this 15-card set utilizes a special holographic foil enhancement. Card backs carry a "Z" prefix.
COMPLETE SET (15) 200.00 400.00
Z1 Michael Jordan 75.00 150.00
Z2 Tim Duncan 12.00 30.00
Z3 Robert Traylor 2.50 6.00
Z4 Michael Olowokandi 3.00 8.00
Z5 Vince Carter 12.00 30.00
Z6 Dirk Nowitzki 15.00 40.00
Z7 Antawn Jamison 6.00 15.00
Z8 Jason Williams 8.00 20.00
Z9 Larry Hughes 5.00 12.00
Z10 Raef LaFrentz 3.00 8.00
Z11 Allen Iverson 12.00 30.00
Z12 Kobe Bryant 40.00 100.00
Z13 Grant Hill 12.00 30.00
Z14 Mike Bibby 6.00 15.00
Z15 Paul Pierce 12.00 30.00

1999-00 UD Ionix

The 1999-00 UD Ionix set was released in March,2000 as a 90-card set, containing 60 veterans and 30 rookies. The rookie subset was inserted at one in six packs. Each pack contained 4-cards and carried a suggested retail price of 3.99.
COMPLETE SET (90) 30.00 80.00
COMPLETE SET w/o SP (60) 10.00 25.00
1 Dikembe Mutombo .30 .75
2 Isaiah Rider .20 .50
3 Antoine Walker .30 .75
4 Paul Pierce .50 1.25
5 Eddie Jones .30 .75
6 Anthony Mason .20 .50
7 Toni Kukoc .30 .75
8 Hersey Hawkins .20 .50
9 Shawn Kemp .30 .75
10 Lamond Murray .20 .50
11 Michael Finley .30 .75
12 Cedric Ceballos .20 .50
13 Antonio McDyess .25 .60
14 Ron Mercer .25 .60
15 Grant Hill .40 1.00
16 Jerry Stackhouse .30 .75
17 Antawn Jamison .50 1.25
18 Mookie Blaylock .20 .50
19 Charles Barkley .50 1.25
20 Hakeem Olajuwon .40 1.00
21 Reggie Miller .30 .75
22 Rik Smits .30 .75
23 Maurice Taylor .20 .50
24 Derek Anderson .20 .50
25 Kobe Bryant 1.50 4.00
26 Shaquille Oâ€™Neal .75 2.00
27 Tim Hardaway .30 .75
28 Alonzo Mourning .40 1.00
29 Ray Allen .30 .75
30 Glenn Robinson .25 .60
31 Kevin Garnett .60 1.50
32 Terrell Brandon .20 .50
33 Stephon Marbury .25 .60
34 Keith Van Horn .25 .60
35 Allan Houston .25 .60
36 Latrell Sprewell .30 .75
37 Darrell Armstrong .20 .50
38 Tariq Abdul-Wahad .20 .50
39 Allen Iverson .60 1.50
40 Larry Hughes .25 .60
41 Anfernee Hardaway .50 1.25
42 Jason Kidd .50 1.25
43 Tom Gugliotta .20 .50
44 Scottie Pippen .50 1.25
45 Damon Stoudamire .30 .75
46 Rasheed Wallace .30 .75
47 Jason Williams .40 1.00
48 Chris Webber .30 .75
49 Tim Duncan .60 1.50
50 David Robinson .50 1.25
51 Gary Payton .30 .75
52 Vin Baker .30 .75
53 Vince Carter .60 1.50
54 Tracy McGrady .50 1.25
55 Karl Malone .40 1.00
56 John Stockton .40 1.00
57 Mike Bibby .30 .75
58 Shareef Abdur-Rahim .25 .60
59 Mitch Richmond .30 .75
60 Juwan Howard .25 .60
61 Elton Brand RC 2.00 5.00
62 Steve Francis RC 2.00 5.00
63 Baron Davis RC 2.50 6.00
64 Lamar Odom RC 2.50 6.00
65 Jonathan Bender RC .75 2.00
66 Wally Szczerbiak RC 1.50 4.00
67 Richard Hamilton RC 2.00 5.00
68 Andre Miller RC 2.00 5.00
69 Shawn Marion RC 2.00 5.00
70 Jason Terry RC 2.00 5.00
71 Trajan Langdon RC .75 2.00
72 Aleksandar Radojevic RC .75 2.00
73 Corey Maggette RC 1.50 4.00
74 William Avery RC .75 2.00
75 Ron Artest RC 2.00 5.00
76 Cal Bowdler RC .75 2.00
77 James Posey RC .75 2.00
78 Quincy Lewis RC .75 2.00
79 Dion Glover RC .75 2.00
80 Jeff Foster RC .75 2.00
81 Kenny Thomas RC .75 2.00
82 Devean George RC .75 2.00
83 Tim James RC .75 2.00
84 Vonteego Cummings RC .75 2.00
85 Jumaine Jones RC .75 2.00
86 Scott Padgett RC .75 2.00
87 Chucky Atkins RC .75 2.00
88 Adrian Griffin RC .75 2.00
89 Todd MacCulloch RC .75 2.00
90 Anthony Carter RC .75 2.00

1999-00 UD Ionix Reciprocal

Randomly inserted in packs at one in four for veterans and one in 11 for the rookie's subset, this 90-card set parallels the base set. To ascertain values on individual cards, please refer to the multiplier in the header, coupled with the value of the base card.
*STARS: 1.5X TO 4X BASE CARD HI
*RCs: 1.25X TO 3X BASE HI

1999-00 UD Ionix Awesome Powers

Randomly inserted in packs at one in 23, this 15-card set takes a look at the league's greatest powers. Card backs carry an "AP" prefix.
COMPLETE SET (15) 6.00 15.00
AP1 Elton Brand 1.00 2.50
AP2 Corey Maggette .75 2.00
AP3 Wally Szczerbiak .75 2.00
AP4 Charles Barkley 1.25 3.00
AP5 Shawn Marion 1.00 2.50
AP6 Jason Terry 1.00 2.50
AP7 Keith Van Horn .60 1.50
AP8 Steve Francis 1.00 2.50
AP9 Trajan Langdon .40 1.00
AP10 Reggie Miller .75 2.00
AP11 Richard Hamilton 1.00 2.50
AP12 Jonathan Bender .40 1.00
AP13 Baron Davis 1.25 3.00
AP14 Paul Pierce 1.25 3.00
AP15 Andre Miller 1.00 2.50

1999-00 UD Ionix BIOrhythm

Randomly inserted in packs at one in seven, this 15-card set features key stats and facts on the most thrilling players in the game. Card backs carry a "B" prefix.
COMPLETE SET (15) 5.00 12.00
B1 Grant Hill .75 2.00
B2 Antawn Jamison .60 1.50
B3 Shaquille O'Neal 1.50 4.00
B4 Stephon Marbury .50 1.25
B5 Michael Finley .60 1.50
B6 Hakeem Olajuwon .75 2.00
B7 Ron Mercer .50 1.25
B8 Tim Hardaway .60 1.50
B9 Jason Kidd 1.00 2.50
B10 Allan Houston .50 1.25
B11 Ray Allen .60 1.50
B12 Shawn Kemp .60 1.50
B13 Alonzo Mourning .75 2.00
B14 Tim Duncan 1.25 3.00
B15 Eddie Jones .60 1.50

1999-00 UD Ionix Pyrotechnics

Randomly inserted in packs at one in 72, this 15-card set focuses on the NBA's most electrifying performers. Card backs carry a "P" prefix.
COMPLETE SET (15) 40.00 80.00
P1 Kevin Garnett 5.00 12.00
P2 Shareef Abdur-Rahim 2.00 5.00
P3 Jason Kidd 4.00 10.00
P4 Antonio McDyess 2.00 5.00
P5 Karl Malone 3.00 8.00
P6 Eddie Jones 2.50 6.00
P7 Antoine Walker 2.50 6.00
P8 Kobe Bryant 12.00 30.00
P9 Anfernee Hardaway 4.00 10.00
P10 Antawn Jamison 2.50 6.00
P11 Keith Van Horn 2.00 5.00
P12 Grant Hill 3.00 8.00
P13 Gary Payton 2.50 6.00
P14 Allen Iverson 5.00 12.00
P15 Vince Carter 5.00 12.00

1999-00 UD Ionix UD Authentics

Randomly inserted in packs at one in 144, this 22-card set features autographs of top NBA stars and rookies. Card backs carry the player's initials.
AH Anfernee Hardaway 40.00 80.00
AJ Antawn Jamison 5.00 12.00
AM Andre Miller 5.00 12.00
BD Baron Davis 10.00 25.00
BG Brian Grant 3.00 8.00
CM Corey Maggette 5.00 12.00
JB Jonathan Bender 3.00 8.00
JP James Posey 3.00 8.00
JT Jason Terry 5.00 12.00
KB Kobe Bryant 125.00 225.00
MJ Michael Jordan/23 750.00 1500.00
MT Maurice Taylor 3.00 8.00
RA Ron Artest 8.00 20.00
RH Richard Hamilton 8.00 20.00
RT Robert Traylor 3.00 8.00
SF Steve Francis 8.00 20.00
SM Shawn Marion 8.00 20.00
TG Tom Gugliotta 3.00 8.00
TL Trajan Langdon 3.00 8.00
WA William Avery 3.00 8.00
WS Wally Szczerbiak 4.00 10.00

1999-00 UD Ionix Warp Zone

Randomly inserted in packs at one in 144, this 15-card set features the hottest players in the NBA on rainbow foil. Card backs carry a "WZ" prefix.
COMPLETE SET (15) 150.00 300.00
WZ1 Kobe Bryant 40.00 100.00
WZ2 Kevin Garnett 12.00 30.00
WZ3 Tim Duncan 12.00 30.00
WZ4 Elton Brand 10.00 25.00
WZ5 Wally Szczerbiak 8.00 20.00
WZ6 Stephon Marbury 5.00 12.00
WZ7 Allen Iverson 12.00 30.00
WZ8 Anfernee Hardaway 10.00 25.00
WZ9 Shaquille O'Neal 15.00 40.00
WZ10 Baron Davis 12.00 30.00
WZ11 Scottie Pippen 10.00 25.00
WZ12 Jason Williams 8.00 20.00
WZ13 Steve Francis 10.00 25.00
WZ14 Vince Carter 12.00 30.00
WZ15 Lamar Odom 12.00 30.00

2005-06 UD Portraits

Released in January 2006, this 142-card set features 100 cards where cards 1-100 picture veterans, cards 101-136 picture rookies serially numbered to 399 and cards 137-142 picture rookies serially numbered to 99. Base cards have borders along the bottom with player names, positions and logos and full color player action shots. Portraits was packaged in boxes which contain six cards, one 8x10 autograph and carried a SRP of $125.
COMP.SET w/o SP's (100) 50.00 125.00
UNPRICED PARALLEL PRINT RUN 10 SETS
1 Al Harrington .60 1.50
2 Al Jefferson .75 2.00
3 Allen Iverson 1.25 3.00
4 Amare Stoudemire .75 2.00
5 Andre Iguodala .75 2.00
6 Andre Miller .60 1.50
7 Andrei Kirilenko .60 1.50
8 Antawn Jamison .75 2.00
9 Antoine Walker .60 1.50
10 Baron Davis .75 2.00
11 Ben Gordon .75 2.00
12 Ben Wallace .75 2.00
13 Bob Sura .50 1.25
14 Brevin Knight .50 1.25
15 Carlos Boozer .75 2.00
16 Carmelo Anthony 1.50 4.00
17 Caron Butler .75 2.00
18 Chauncey Billups .75 2.00
19 Chris Bosh .75 2.00
20 Chris Webber .75 2.00
21 Corey Maggette .60 1.50
22 Cuttino Mobley .60 1.50
23 Damon Jones .50 1.25
24 Dan Dickau .50 1.25
25 Desmond Mason .50 1.25
26 Dirk Nowitzki 1.25 3.00
27 Donyell Marshall .50 1.25
28 Drew Gooden .60 1.50
29 Dwight Howard 1.50 4.00
30 Dwyane Wade 2.00 5.00
31 Elton Brand .75 2.00
32 Emeka Okafor .75 2.00
33 Gary Payton .75 2.00
34 Gerald Wallace .75 2.00
35 Gilbert Arenas .75 2.00
36 Grant Hill 1.00 2.50
37 J.R. Smith .75 2.00
38 Jalen Rose .75 2.00
39 Jamaal Magloire .50 1.25
40 Jamaal Tinsley .50 1.25
41 Jamal Crawford .60 1.50
42 Jameer Nelson .60 1.50
43 Jason Kidd 1.25 3.00
44 Jason Richardson .75 2.00
45 Jason Terry .60 1.50
46 Jason Williams .60 1.50
47 Jermaine O'Neal .60 1.50
48 Joe Johnson .75 2.00
49 Josh Childress .60 1.50
50 Josh Howard .75 2.00
51 Josh Smith .75 2.00
52 Kenyon Martin .75 2.00
53 Kevin Garnett 1.50 4.00
54 Kirk Hinrich .75 2.00
55 Kobe Bryant 4.00 10.00
56 Kurt Thomas .50 1.25
57 Kyle Korver .60 1.50
58 Lamar Odom .75 2.00
59 Larry Hughes .60 1.50
60 Eddie Griffin .50 1.25
61 LeBron James 4.00 10.00
62 Luke Ridnour .60 1.50
63 Luol Deng .75 2.00
64 Manu Ginobili .75 2.00
65 Marcus Camby .60 1.50
66 Maurice Williams .60 1.50
67 Michael Finley .75 2.00
68 Michael Jordan 6.00 15.00
69 Michael Redd .75 2.00
70 Mike Bibby .75 2.00
71 Pau Gasol .75 2.00
72 Paul Pierce 1.00 2.50
73 Peja Stojakovic .75 2.00
74 Raja Bell .60 1.50
75 Rashard Lewis .75 2.00
76 Rasheed Wallace .75 2.00
77 Ray Allen .75 2.00
78 Richard Hamilton .60 1.50
79 Richard Jefferson .75 2.00
80 Ron Artest .75 2.00
81 Sam Cassell .75 2.00
82 Sebastian Telfair .60 1.50
83 Shaquille O'Neal 1.50 4.00
84 Shareef Abdur-Rahim .60 1.50
85 Shaun Livingston .50 1.25
86 Shawn Marion .75 2.00
87 Stephon Marbury .60 1.50
88 Steve Francis .75 2.00
89 Steve Nash 1.00 2.50
90 Stromile Swift .50 1.25
91 Tim Duncan 1.25 3.00
92 Tony Parker 1.00 2.50
93 Tracy McGrady 1.00 2.50
94 Troy Murphy .60 1.50
95 Tyronn Lue .50 1.25
96 Vince Carter 1.25 3.00
97 Vladimir Radmanovic .50 1.25
98 Yao Ming 1.00 2.50
99 Zach Randolph .60 1.50
100 Zydrunas Ilgauskas .60 1.50
101 Andray Blatche RC 2.50 6.00
102 Andrew Bynum RC 6.00 15.00
103 Antoine Wright RC 2.00 5.00
104 Brandon Bass RC 2.50 6.00
105 C.J. Miles RC 2.50 6.00
106 Channing Frye RC 2.50 6.00
107 Charlie Villanueva RC 2.50 6.00
108 Chris Taft RC 2.00 5.00
109 Daniel Ewing RC 2.00 5.00
110 Danny Granger RC 4.00 10.00
111 David Lee RC 3.00 8.00
112 Dijon Thompson RC 2.00 5.00
113 Ersan Ilyasova RC 2.00 5.00
114 Sarunas Jasikevicius RC 2.50 6.00
115 Francisco Garcia RC 2.50 6.00
116 Gerald Green RC 2.50 6.00
117 Hakim Warrick RC 2.50 6.00
118 Jose Calderon RC 2.50 6.00
119 Ike Diogu RC 2.00 5.00
120 Jarrett Jack RC 2.00 5.00
121 Jason Maxiell RC 2.00 5.00
122 Joey Graham RC 2.00 5.00
123 Julius Hodge RC 2.00 5.00
124 Linas Kleiza RC 2.00 5.00
125 Louis Williams RC 3.00 8.00
126 Luther Head RC 2.00 5.00
127 Martell Webster RC 2.00 5.00
128 Monta Ellis RC 4.00 10.00
129 Nate Robinson RC 2.50 6.00
130 Rashad McCants RC 2.00 5.00
131 James Singleton RC 2.00 5.00
132 Ryan Gomes RC 2.00 5.00
133 Salim Stoudamire RC 2.00 5.00
134 Travis Diener RC 2.00 5.00
135 Wayne Simien RC 2.00 5.00
136 Yaroslav Korolev RC 2.00 5.00
137 Andrew Bogut RC 5.00 12.00
138 Chris Paul RC 12.00 30.00
139 Deron Williams RC 8.00 20.00
140 Raymond Felton RC 6.00 15.00
141 Marvin Williams RC 4.00 10.00
142 Sean May RC 3.00 8.00

2005-06 UD Portraits 75

Randomly seeded in packs, this 142-card set parallels the base set enhanced with silver highlights and sequenial numbering to 75.
*1-100 PORT.75: .75X TO 2X BASE HI
*101-136 PORT.75: .5X TO 1.5X BASE HI
*137-142 PORT.75: .4X TO 1X BASE HI

2005-06 UD Portraits 30

Randomly seeded in packs, this 142-card set parallels the base set enhanced with gold highlights and sequential numbering to 30.
*1-100 PORT.30: 1.5X TO 4X BASE HI
*101-136 PORT.30: 1X TO 2.5X BASE HI
*137-142 PORT.30: .6X TO 1.5X BASE HI
68 Michael Jordan 30.00 80.00

2005-06 UD Portraits Material Moments

Inserted at the rate of one per pack, this 42-card set features framed color photos along the top of the card and a square swatch of memorabilia along the bottom. Borders are brown along the sides and top with a red strip through the middle and white along the bottom.
AB Andrew Bogut 4.00 10.00
AM Aaron McKie 2.00 5.00
AS Amare Stoudemire 2.50 6.00
AW Antoine Wright 2.50 6.00
CB Caron Butler 2.50 6.00
CF Channing Frye 3.00 8.00
CM C.J. Miles 3.00 8.00
CP Chris Paul 8.00 20.00
CW Chris Webber 2.50 6.00
DA David Wesley 2.00 5.00
DE Deron Williams 6.00 15.00
DF Derek Fisher 2.00 5.00
DG Danny Granger 5.00 12.00
DH Dwight Howard 5.00 12.00
DN Dirk Nowitzki 4.00 10.00
EB Elton Brand 2.50 6.00
ES Eric Snow 2.00 5.00
GG Gerald Green 3.00 8.00
HW Hakim Warrick 3.00 8.00
JA Jason Terry 2.00 5.00
JK Jason Kidd 4.00 10.00
JM Jamaal Magloire 2.00 5.00
JO Jermaine O'Neal 2.50 6.00
JR Jason Richardson 2.50 6.00
JT Jamaal Tinsley 2.00 5.00
KB Kobe Bryant 10.00 25.00
KD Keyon Dooling 2.00 5.00
KG Kevin Garnett 5.00 12.00
KM Kenyon Martin 2.50 6.00
LJ LeBron James 12.50 30.00
LW Luke Walton 2.00 5.00
MA Marvin Williams 3.00 8.00
MJ Michael Jordan SP 40.00 80.00
MW Martell Webster 2.50 6.00
QR Quentin Richardson 2.00 5.00
RF Raymond Felton 4.00 10.00
RW Rasheed Wallace 2.50 6.00
SH Shawn Marion 2.50 6.00
SM Sean May 2.50 6.00
SO Shaquille O'Neal 5.00 12.00
TD Tim Duncan 4.00 10.00
YM Yao Ming 3.00 8.00

2005-06 UD Portraits Scrapbook Signatures

Inserted randomly in packs, this 37-card set features framed player photos with brown borders and player autographs. Each card is sequentially numbered to 25.
AB Andrew Bogut 12.00 30.00
AN Andrew Bynum 25.00 60.00
BB Brandon Bass 10.00 25.00
CA Carmelo Anthony 30.00 80.00
CJ C.J. Miles 10.00 25.00
CP Chris Paul 80.00 200.00
DE Daniel Ewing 8.00 20.00
DG Danny Granger 15.00 40.00
DH Dwight Howard 25.00 60.00
DL David Lee 12.00 30.00
DT Dijon Thompson 8.00 20.00
DW Deron Williams 20.00 50.00
EI Ersan Ilyasova 10.00 25.00
FG Francisco Garcia 10.00 25.00
GA Gilbert Arenas 12.50 30.00
GG Gerald Green 10.00 25.00
ID Ike Diogu 8.00 20.00
JG Joey Graham 8.00 20.00
JH Julius Hodge 8.00 20.00
JM Jason Maxiell 8.00 20.00
JP Johan Petro 8.00 20.00
LH Luther Head 8.00 20.00
LJ LeBron James 200.00 400.00
LW Louis Williams 12.00 30.00
MA Marvin Williams 12.00 30.00
MB Mike Bibby 15.00 40.00
MJ Michael Jordan 400.00 600.00
PP Paul Pierce 20.00 50.00
RF Raymond Felton 12.00 30.00
RJ Richard Jefferson 8.00 20.00
SM Sean May 8.00 20.00
SN Steve Nash 50.00 120.00
ST Stephon Marbury 12.50 30.00
WS Wayne Simien 8.00 20.00

2005-06 UD Portraits Scrapbook Swatches

Inserted at the rate of one per pack, this 42-card set is horizontally designed with framed player photos on the left side of the card and a square swatch of memorabilia on the right.
AB Andrew Bogut 4.00 10.00
AI Andre Iguodala 2.50 6.00
AW Antoine Wright 2.50 6.00
BG Ben Gordon 2.50 6.00
CA Carmelo Anthony 5.00 12.00
CF Channing Frye 3.00 8.00
CM Corey Maggette 2.00 5.00
CP Chris Paul 8.00 20.00
CT Chris Taft 2.50 6.00
CV Charlie Villanueva 3.00 8.00
DE Daniel Ewing 2.50 6.00
DG Danny Granger 5.00 12.00
DH Dwight Howard 5.00 12.00
DW Deron Williams 6.00 15.00
FG Francisco Garcia 3.00 8.00
GA Gilbert Arenas 2.50 6.00
GG Gerald Green 3.00 8.00
GP Gary Payton 2.50 6.00
HK Hakim Warrick 3.00 8.00
JA Jason Maxiell 2.50 6.00
JC Josh Childress 2.00 5.00
JG Joey Graham 2.50 6.00
JH Julius Hodge 2.50 6.00
JJ Jarrett Jack 2.50 6.00
JK Jason Kidd 4.00 10.00
JM Jamaal Magloire 2.00 5.00
JR J.R. Smith 2.50 6.00
LJ LeBron James 12.50 30.00
LW Louis Williams 4.00 10.00
MA Marvin Williams 3.00 8.00
ME Monta Ellis 5.00 12.00
MJ Michael Jordan SP 40.00 80.00
MW Martell Webster 2.50 6.00
QR Quentin Richardson 2.00 5.00
RF Raymond Felton 4.00 10.00
RM Rashad McCants 2.50 6.00
SH Shawn Marion 2.50 6.00
SM Sean May 2.50 6.00
TM Tracy McGrady 3.00 8.00
UH Udonis Haslem 2.00 5.00
WS Wayne Simien 2.50 6.00
YM Yao Ming 3.00 8.00

2005-06 UD Portraits Scrapbook Swatches Autographs

This 31-card set parallels the design of the Scrapbook Swatches set enhanced with authentic player autographs. Most cards are serially numbered to either 40 or 10, but there are a few exceptions in the set. See checklist for details.
SOME UNPRICED DUE TO SCARCITY
CM Corey Maggette/49 8.00 20.00
DE Daniel Ewing/40 8.00 20.00
DG Danny Granger/40 15.00 40.00
FG Francisco Garcia/40 10.00 25.00
GA Gilbert Arenas/40 12.50 30.00
GG Gerald Green/40 10.00 25.00
GP Gary Payton/40 12.50 30.00
JA Jason Maxiell/40 8.00 20.00
JG Joey Graham/40 8.00 20.00
JH Julius Hodge/40 8.00 20.00
JJ Jarrett Jack/40 8.00 20.00
JR J.R. Smith/40 10.00 25.00
LW Louis Williams/40 12.00 30.00
MW Martell Webster/40 8.00 20.00
RF Raymond Felton/40 12.00 30.00
RM Rashad McCants/40 8.00 20.00
SH Shawn Marion/40 12.50 30.00
WS Wayne Simien/40 8.00 20.00

2005-06 UD Portraits Signature Portraits 8x10

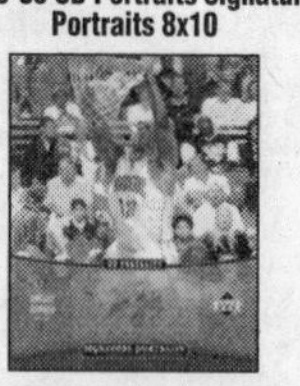

Inserted at about one per box (unless a parallel or other 8x10 autograph is present), this 47-card set places full color player photos at the top of the card and a coloring strip along the bottom to match player team colors along with a large autograph sticker.
*BLACK/WHITE: .5X TO 1.25X BASE HI
AB Andrew Bogut 10.00 25.00
AI Andre Iguodala 12.50 30.00
AN Andrew Bynum 20.00 50.00
BK Bernard King 8.00 20.00
CA Carmelo Anthony SP 25.00 50.00
CB Chauncey Billups 12.50 30.00
CP Chris Paul 40.00 100.00
DE Dennis Rodman SP 40.00 100.00
DG Danny Granger 12.00 30.00
DH Dwight Howard 15.00 40.00
DR David Robinson SP 40.00 80.00
DW Deron Williams 15.00 40.00
EH Elvin Hayes 10.00 25.00
HO Hakeem Olajuwon SP 20.00 50.00
ID Ike Diogu 6.00 15.00
IT Isiah Thomas SP 20.00 50.00
JC Josh Childress 6.00 15.00
JG Joey Graham 6.00 15.00
JH Julius Hodge 6.00 15.00
JJ Jarrett Jack 6.00 15.00
JK Jason Kidd SP 20.00 50.00
JN Jameer Nelson 8.00 20.00
JS John Stockton SP 75.00 150.00
JW John Wooden SP 50.00 120.00
KA Kareem Abdul-Jabbar 40.00 100.00
KN Bob Knight SP 30.00 75.00
LJ1 LeBron James 125.00 250.00
LJ2 LeBron James 125.00 250.00
MJ1 Michael Jordan SP 300.00 500.00
MJ2 Michael Jordan SP 300.00 500.00
MW Martell Webster 6.00 15.00
PP Paul Pierce 15.00 40.00
RF Raymond Felton 10.00 25.00
RH Richard Hamilton 8.00 20.00
RJ Richard Jefferson 6.00 15.00
RM Rashad McCants 6.00 15.00
SE Sebastian Telfair 6.00 15.00
SH Shawn Marion 15.00 40.00
SM Sean May 6.00 15.00
SN Steve Nash SP 40.00 100.00
SP Scottie Pippen SP 80.00 200.00
ST Stephon Marbury SP 15.00 40.00
WF Walt Frazier 15.00 40.00
WI Marvin Williams SP 8.00 20.00
WR Willis Reed 15.00 40.00
YM Yao Ming SP 15.00 40.00

2005-06 UD Portraits Signature Portraits 8x10 Dual

Inserted in packs randomly, this 22-card set is horizontally designed with two players and/or coaches, side by side, and two large autograph stickers. Each card is serially numbered to 40.
DSP1 Michael Jordan / LeBron James 600.00 1000.00
DSP2 LeBron James / Dwight Howard 200.00 350.00
DSP3 Larry Bird / Michael Jordan 350.00 600.00
DSP4 Marvin Williams / Chris Paul 50.00 100.00
DSP5 Dwight Howard / Andrew Bogut 30.00 80.00
DSP6 Tracy McGrady / Gerald Green 25.00 60.00
DSP7 Raymond Felton / Rashad McCants 25.00 60.00
DSP9 Magic Johnson / John Stockton 125.00 250.00
DSP10 Carmelo Anthony / Hakim Warrick 30.00 80.00
DSP11 Sean May / Antawn Jamison 20.00 50.00
DSP12 Walt Frazier / Willis Reed 40.00 100.00
DSP14 Kirk Hinrich / Wayne Simien 20.00 50.00
DSP16 Yao Ming / Andrew Bogut 40.00 80.00
DSP17 Bob Knight / John Wooden 75.00 150.00
DSP19 Jarrett Jack / Martell Webster 20.00 50.00
DSP20 Elvin Hayes / Gilbert Arenas 20.00 50.00
DSP21 Hakeem Olajuwon / Yao Ming 50.00 120.00
DSP22 J.R. Smith / Martell Webster 20.00 50.00
DSP23 Deron Williams / Luther Head 40.00 75.00
DSP24 Mike Bibby / Salim Stoudamire 20.00 50.00
DSP26 Scottie Pippen / Dennis Rodman 175.00 350.00

2005-06 UD Portraits Signature Portraits 8x10 Triple

Randomly seeded in packs and limited to 20 copies, this six card set features a horizontal design with three player photos and three sticker autographs.
UNPRICED TEN PRINT RUN 3 SETS
TSP2 LeBron James / Carmelo Anthony / Chris Bosh 200.00 350.00
TSP3 Andrew Bogut / Marvin Williams / Chris Paul 75.00 150.00
TSP4 Sean May / Raymond Felton / Rashad McCants 40.00 80.00
TSP6 Paul Pierce / Al Jefferson / Gerald Green 40.00 80.00
TSP7 Steve Nash / Shawn Marion / Dijon Thompson 60.00 120.00
TSP8 Gilbert Arenas / Mike Bibby / Salim Stoudamire 60.00 120.00

2000-01 UD Reserve

COMP.SET w/o SP's (90) 8.00 20.00
1 Dikembe Mutombo .30 .75
2 Jason Terry .30 .75
3 Alan Henderson .20 .50

Paul Pierce .40 1.00
Antoine Walker .25 .60
Kenny Anderson .25 .60
Derrick Coleman .25 .60
Baron Davis .30 .75
Jamal Mashburn .25 .60
Elton Brand .30 .75
Ron Mercer .20 .50
Ron Artest .30 .75
Lamond Murray .20 .50
Andre Miller .25 .60
Matt Harpring .25 .60
Michael Finley .30 .75
Dirk Nowitzki .50 1.25
Steve Nash .50 1.25
Antonio McDyess .25 .60
James Posey .20 .50
Nick Van Exel .25 .60
Jerry Stackhouse .25 .60
Jerome Williams .20 .50
Chucky Atkins .20 .50
Antawn Jamison .30 .75
Larry Hughes .25 .60
Chris Mills .20 .50
Steve Francis .30 .75
Hakeem Olajuwon .40 1.00
Cuttino Mobley .25 .60
Reggie Miller .30 .75
Jalen Rose .25 .60
Austin Croshere .20 .50
Lamar Odom .30 .75
Jeff McInnis .20 .50
Corey Maggette .25 .60
Shaquille Oâ•™Neal .75 2.00
Kobe Bryant 1.50 4.00
Isaiah Rider .25 .60
Horace Grant .25 .60
Eddie Jones .30 .75
Tim Hardaway .30 .75
Brian Grant .20 .50
Ray Allen .30 .75
Tim Thomas .20 .50
Glenn Robinson .25 .60
Sam Cassell .25 .60
Kevin Garnett .60 1.50
Wally Szczerbiak .25 .60
Terrell Brandon .20 .50
Chauncey Billups .30 .75
Stephon Marbury .25 .60
Keith Van Horn .25 .60
Kendall Gill .20 .50
Latrell Sprewell .25 .60
Marcus Camby .25 .60
Allan Houston .25 .60
Grant Hill .40 1.00
Tracy McGrady .50 1.25
Darrell Armstrong .20 .50
Allen Iverson .60 1.50
Theo Ratliff .20 .50
Toni Kukoc .25 .60
Jason Kidd .50 1.25
Clifford Robinson .20 .50
Shawn Marion .30 .75
Rasheed Wallace .30 .75
Scottie Pippen .50 1.25
Damon Stoudamire .25 .60
70 Chris Webber .30 .75
71 Jason Williams .30 .75
72 Vlade Divac .25 .60
73 Tim Duncan .60 1.50
74 David Robinson .50 1.25
75 Derek Anderson .20 .50
76 Gary Payton .30 .75
77 Patrick Ewing .40 1.00
78 Rashard Lewis .30 .75
79 Vince Carter .60 1.50
80 Mark Jackson .25 .60
81 Antonio Davis .20 .50
82 Karl Malone .40 1.00
83 John Stockton .40 1.00
84 John Starks .20 .50
85 Shareef Abdur-Rahim .25 .60
86 Mike Bibby .30 .75
87 Michael Dickerson .20 .50
88 Mitch Richmond .25 .60
89 Richard Hamilton .25 .60
90 Juwan Howard .25 .60
91 Kenyon Martin RC 1.00 2.50
92 Stromile Swift RC .40 1.00
93 Darius Miles RC .40 1.00
94 Marcus Fizer RC .40 1.00
95 Mike Miller RC .75 2.00
96 DerMarr Johnson RC .40 1.00
97 Chris Mihm RC .40 1.00
98 Jamal Crawford RC .60 1.50
99 Joel Przybilla RC .40 1.00
100 Keyon Dooling RC .40 1.00
101 Jerome Moiso RC .40 1.00
102 Etan Thomas RC .40 1.00
103 Courtney Alexander RC .40 1.00
104 Mateen Cleaves RC .40 1.00
105 Hedo Turkoglu RC .75 2.00
106 Desmond Mason RC .50 1.25
107 Quentin Richardson RC .60 1.50
108 Jamaal Magloire RC .40 1.00
109 Speedy Claxton RC .40 1.00
110 Morris Peterson RC .40 1.00
111 Donnell Harvey RC .40 1.00
112 DeShawn Stevenson RC .50 1.25
113 Mamadou N'Diaye RC .40 1.00
114 Erick Barkley RC .40 1.00
115 Mark Madsen RC .40 1.00
116 Eduardo Najera RC .40 1.00
117 Lavor Postell RC .40 1.00
118 Hanno Mottola RC .40 1.00
119 Stephen Jackson RC .60 1.50
120 Marc Jackson RC .40 1.00

2000-01 UD Reserve Bank Shots

COMPLETE SET (10) 4.00 10.00
BK1 Kevin Garnett 1.00 2.50
BK2 Lamar Odom .50 1.25
BK3 Grant Hill .60 1.50
BK4 Rashard Lewis .50 1.25
BK5 Reggie Miller .50 1.25
BK6 Ray Allen .50 1.25
BK7 Eddie Jones .50 1.25
BK8 Kobe Bryant 2.50 6.00
BK9 Michael Finley .50 1.25
BK10 Jerry Stackhouse .40 1.00

2000-01 UD Reserve BuyBacks

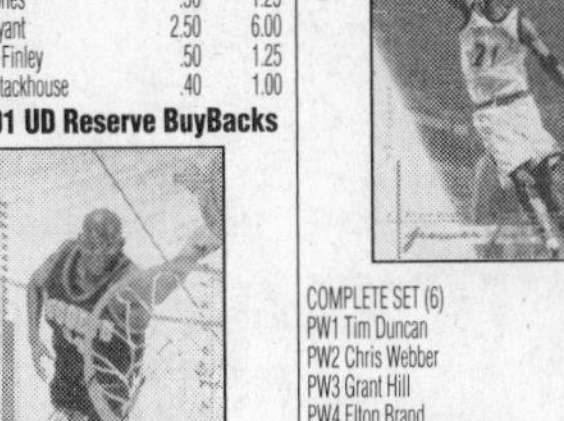

SOME AU's NOT PRICED DUE TO SCARCITY
1 Courtney Alexander 00-1P&PPM/9810.00 25.00
6 Speedy Claxton 00-1UD/190 10.00 25.00
7 Mateen Cleaves 00-1UD/74 10.00 25.00
8 Mateen Cleaves 00-1P&PSF/25 12.50 30.00
9 Jamal Crawford 00-1UD/120 15.00 40.00
10 Khalid El-Amin 00-1UD/95 10.00 25.00
11 Marcus Fizer 00-1UD/50 10.00 25.00
12 Marcus Fizer 00-1P&PPM/48 10.00 25.00
13 Marcus Fizer 00-1P&PSF/100 10.00 25.00
15 Kevin Garnett 95-96UD/21 100.00 200.00
16 Donnell Harvey 00-1UD/98 10.00 25.00
17 DerMarr Johnson 00-1P&PPM/4810.00 25.00
18 DerMarr Johnson 00-1P&PSF/9510.00 25.00
22 Mark Madsen 00-1UD/95 10.00 25.00
23 Jamaal Magloire 00-1UD/98 10.00 25.00
24 Kenyon Martin P&PPM/50 20.00 40.00
25 Chris Mihm 00-1UD/95 10.00 25.00
26 Darius Miles 00-1UD/50 15.00 40.00
27 Darius Miles 00-1P&PM/48 15.00 40.00
28 Darius Miles 00-1P&PSF/48 15.00 40.00
29 Mike Miller 00-1P&PPM/24 30.00 80.00
30 Mike Miller 00-1P&PSF/23 30.00 80.00
31 Mike Miller 99-0UD/48 20.00 50.00
32 Jerome Moiso 00-1UD/95 10.00 25.00
33 Hanno Mottola 00-1UD/95 10.00 25.00
34 Mamadou N'diaye 00-1UD/95 10.00 25.00
35 Morris Peterson 00-1UD/95 12.50 30.00
36 Joel Przybilla 00-1UD/238 10.00 25.00
37 Quentin Richardson 00-1UD/95 20.00 50.00
38 DeShawn Stevenson 00-1UD/95 12.50 30.00
39 Stromile Swift 00-1UD/50 10.00 25.00
40 Stromile Swift 00-1P&PPM/50 10.00 25.00
41 Stromile Swift 00-1P&PSF/50 10.00 25.00

2000-01 UD Reserve Fast Company

COMPLETE SET (10) 4.00 10.00
FC1 Steve Francis .50 1.25
FC2 Kobe Bryant 2.50 6.00
FC3 Allen Iverson 1.00 2.50
FC4 Jason Kidd .75 2.00
FC5 Larry Hughes .40 1.00
FC6 Stephon Marbury .40 1.00
FC7 Jason Williams .50 1.25
FC8 Andre Miller .40 1.00
FC9 Gary Payton .50 1.25
FC10 Paul Pierce .60 1.50

2000-01 UD Reserve NBA Start-Ups

DA Darius Miles 2.50 6.00
DJ DerMarr Johnson 2.50 6.00
JC Jamal Crawford 4.00 10.00
KB Kobe Bryant 15.00 40.00
KG Kevin Garnett 5.00 12.00
KM Kenyon Martin 6.00 15.00
MC Mateen Cleaves 2.50 6.00
MF Marcus Fizer 2.50 6.00
QR Quentin Richardson 4.00 10.00

2000-01 UD Reserve NBA Start-Ups Autographs

DAA Darius Miles 4.00 10.00
DJA DerMarr Johnson 4.00 10.00
JCA Jamal Crawford 8.00 20.00
KGA Kevin Garnett/21 75.00 150.00
KMA Kenyon Martin 10.00 25.00
MFA Marcus Fizer 4.00 10.00
QRA Quentin Richardson 6.00 15.00

2000-01 UD Reserve Power Portfolios

COMPLETE SET (6) 3.00 8.00
PW1 Tim Duncan 1.00 2.50
PW2 Chris Webber .50 1.25
PW3 Grant Hill .60 1.50
PW4 Elton Brand .50 1.25
PW5 Kevin Garnett 1.00 2.50
PW6 Kobe Bryant 2.50 6.00

2000-01 UD Reserve Principal Powers

COMPLETE SET (10) 6.00 15.00
PP1 Shaquille O'Neal 1.25 3.00
PP2 Tim Duncan 1.00 2.50
PP3 Vince Carter 1.00 2.50
PP4 Elton Brand .50 1.25
PP5 Kevin Garnett 1.00 2.50
PP6 Tracy McGrady .75 2.00
PP7 Karl Malone .60 1.50
PP8 Kobe Bryant 2.50 6.00
PP9 Shareef Abdur-Rahim .40 1.00
PP10 Antonio McDyess .40 1.00

2000-01 UD Reserve Setting the Standard

COMPLETE SET (6) 4.00 10.00
SS1 Steve Francis .50 1.25
SS2 Vince Carter 1.00 2.50
SS3 Kobe Bryant 2.50 6.00
SS4 Kevin Garnett 1.00 2.50
SS5 Allen Iverson 1.00 2.50
SS6 Shaquille O'Neal 1.25 3.00

2006-07 UD Reserve

Released in mid May 2007, UD Reserve features a chromium card stock-enhanced version of the base Upper Deck set design. The 240 card-set pictures veteran players on cards 1-200 and rookies, inserted at the approximate rate of one in four packs, on cards 201-240. UD Reserve is packaged in 10-pack boxes of four cards each and carried an initial suggested retail price of $10.00 per pack.

COMP.SET w/o SP's (200) 30.00 60.00
1 Josh Childress .50 1.25
2 Al Harrington .50 1.25
3 Joe Johnson .60 1.50
4 Josh Smith .60 1.50
5 Salim Stoudamire .40 1.00
6 Marvin Williams .60 1.50
7 Tony Allen .40 1.00
8 Dan Dickau .40 1.00
9 Al Jefferson .60 1.50
10 Raef LaFrentz .40 1.00
11 Michael Olowokandi .40 1.00
12 Paul Pierce .75 2.00
13 Wally Szczerbiak .50 1.25
14 Brevin Knight .40 1.00
15 Raymond Felton .75 2.00
16 Othella Harrington .40 1.00
17 Sean May .40 1.00
18 Emeka Okafor .60 1.50
19 Primoz Brezec .40 1.00
20 Gerald Wallace .60 1.50
21 Tyson Chandler .50 1.25
22 Michael Jordan 5.00 12.00
23 Luol Deng .60 1.50
24 Chris Duhon .40 1.00
25 Ben Gordon .60 1.50
26 Kirk Hinrich .60 1.50
27 Mike Sweetney .40 1.00
28 Drew Gooden .50 1.25
29 Larry Hughes .50 1.25
30 Zydrunas Ilgauskas .50 1.25
31 LeBron James 3.00 8.00
32 Damon Jones .40 1.00
33 Donyell Marshall .40 1.00
34 Anderson Varejao .50 1.25
35 Erick Dampier .40 1.00
36 Marquis Daniels .40 1.00
37 Devin Harris .60 1.50
38 Josh Howard .50 1.25
39 Dirk Nowitzki 1.00 2.50
40 Jerry Stackhouse .50 1.25
41 Jason Terry .50 1.25
42 Carmelo Anthony .75 2.00
43 Earl Boykins .40 1.00
44 Marcus Camby .50 1.25
45 Kenyon Martin .60 1.50
46 Andre Miller .50 1.25
47 Eduardo Najera .40 1.00
48 Nene .50 1.25
49 Chauncey Billups .60 1.50
50 Richard Hamilton .50 1.25
51 Lindsey Hunter .40 1.00
52 Antonio McDyess .50 1.25
53 Tayshaun Prince .60 1.50
54 Ben Wallace .60 1.50
55 Rasheed Wallace .60 1.50
56 Baron Davis .60 1.50
57 Ike Diogu .40 1.00
58 Mike Dunleavy .50 1.25
59 Derek Fisher .50 1.25
60 Troy Murphy .40 1.00
61 Mickael Pietrus .50 1.25
62 Jason Richardson .60 1.50
63 Rafer Alston .40 1.00
64 Luther Head .50 1.25
65 Juwan Howard .50 1.25
66 Tracy McGrady .75 2.00
67 Dikembe Mutombo .60 1.50
68 Stromile Swift .40 1.00
69 Yao Ming .75 2.00
70 Austin Croshere .40 1.00
71 Stephen Jackson .50 1.25
72 Sarunas Jasikevicius .50 1.25
73 Jermaine O'Neal .60 1.50
74 Peja Stojakovic .60 1.50
75 Jamaal Tinsley .40 1.00
76 Elton Brand .60 1.50
77 Sam Cassell .60 1.50
78 Chris Kaman .50 1.25
79 Shaun Livingston .40 1.00
80 Corey Maggette .50 1.25
81 Cuttino Mobley .50 1.25
82 Vladimir Radmanovic .40 1.00
83 Kwame Brown .40 1.00
84 Kobe Bryant 3.00 8.00
85 Devean George .40 1.00
86 Lamar Odom .60 1.50
87 Ronny Turiaf .50 1.25
88 Sasha Vujacic .40 1.00
89 Luke Walton .40 1.00
90 Shane Battier .50 1.25
91 Pau Gasol .60 1.50
92 Bobby Jackson .40 1.00
93 Eddie Jones .50 1.25
94 Mike Miller .60 1.50
95 Damon Stoudamire .50 1.25
96 Hakim Warrick .50 1.25
97 Alonzo Mourning .75 2.00
98 Shaquille O'Neal 1.25 3.00
99 Gary Payton .60 1.50
100 Wayne Simien .40 1.00
101 Dwyane Wade 1.50 4.00
102 Antoine Walker .50 1.25
103 Jason Williams .50 1.25
104 Andrew Bogut .60 1.50
105 T.J. Ford .50 1.25
106 Jamaal Magloire .40 1.00
107 Michael Redd .60 1.50
108 Bobby Simmons .40 1.00
109 Maurice Williams .50 1.25
110 Ricky Davis .50 1.25
111 Kevin Garnett 1.25 3.00
112 Kelenna Azubuike .75 2.00
113 Trenton Hassell .40 1.00
114 Troy Hudson .40 1.00
115 Rashad McCants .40 1.00
116 Vince Carter .75 2.00
117 Jason Collins .40 1.00
118 Richard Jefferson .60 1.50
119 Jason Kidd 1.00 2.50
120 Nenad Krstic .40 1.00
121 Jeff McInnis .40 1.00
122 Antoine Wright .40 1.00
123 P.J. Brown .40 1.00
124 Speedy Claxton .40 1.00
125 Desmond Mason .40 1.00
126 Chris Paul 1.25 3.00
127 J.R. Smith .60 1.50
128 Kirk Snyder .40 1.00
129 David West .60 1.50
130 Jamal Crawford .50 1.25
131 Eddy Curry .50 1.25
132 Channing Frye .50 1.25
133 Stephon Marbury .50 1.25
134 Quentin Richardson .50 1.25
135 Nate Robinson .60 1.50
136 David Lee .50 1.25
137 Carlos Arroyo .50 1.25
138 Tony Battie .40 1.00
139 Keyon Dooling .40 1.00
140 Grant Hill .75 2.00
141 Dwight Howard 1.00 2.50
142 Darko Milicic .40 1.00
143 Jameer Nelson .50 1.25
144 Samuel Dalembert .40 1.00
145 Steven Hunter .40 1.00
146 Andre Iguodala .60 1.50
147 Allen Iverson .75 2.00
148 Kyle Korver .50 1.25
149 Shavlik Randolph .40 1.00
150 Chris Webber .60 1.50
151 Raja Bell .50 1.25
152 Boris Diaw .50 1.25
153 Shawn Marion .60 1.50
154 Steve Nash .75 2.00
155 Amare Stoudemire .60 1.50
156 Kurt Thomas .40 1.00
157 Tim Thomas .40 1.00
158 Steve Blake .40 1.00
159 Juan Dixon .40 1.00
160 Zach Randolph .50 1.25
161 Joel Przybilla .40 1.00
162 Sebastian Telfair .40 1.00
163 Martell Webster .50 1.25
164 Shareef Abdur-Rahim .50 1.25
165 Ron Artest .60 1.50
166 Mike Bibby .60 1.50
167 Brad Miller .60 1.50
168 Kenny Thomas .40 1.00
169 Bonzi Wells .40 1.00
170 Bruce Bowen .40 1.00
171 Tim Duncan 1.00 2.50
172 Michael Finley .60 1.50
173 Manu Ginobili .60 1.50
174 Nazr Mohammed .40 1.00
175 Tony Parker .60 1.50
176 Ray Allen .60 1.50
177 Danny Fortson .40 1.00
178 Rashard Lewis .60 1.50
179 Luke Ridnour .50 1.25
180 Earl Watson .40 1.00
181 Chris Wilcox .40 1.00
182 Rafael Araujo .40 1.00
183 Chris Bosh .60 1.50
184 Joey Graham .40 1.00
185 Mike James .40 1.00
186 Morris Peterson .40 1.00
187 Charlie Villanueva .60 1.50
188 Carlos Boozer .60 1.50
189 Matt Harpring .50 1.25
190 Kris Humphries .40 1.00
191 Andrei Kirilenko .50 1.25
192 C.J. Miles .40 1.00
193 Paul Millsap 1.00 2.50
194 Deron Williams 1.00 2.50
195 Gilbert Arenas .60 1.50
196 Andray Blatche .40 1.00
197 Caron Butler .60 1.50
198 Antonio Daniels .40 1.00
199 Brendan Haywood .40 1.00
200 Antawn Jamison .60 1.50
201 Andrea Bargnani RC 2.00 5.00
202 LaMarcus Aldridge RC 3.00 8.00
203 Adam Morrison RC 1.50 4.00
204 Tyrus Thomas RC 1.50 4.00
205 Shelden Williams RC 1.25 3.00
206 Brandon Roy RC 3.00 8.00
207 Randy Foye RC 1.50 4.00
208 Rudy Gay RC 2.00 5.00
209 Patrick O'Bryant RC 1.25 3.00
210 Saer Sene RC 1.25 3.00
211 J.J. Redick RC 1.50 4.00
212 Hilton Armstrong RC 1.25 3.00
213 Thabo Sefolosha RC 1.50 4.00
214 Ronnie Brewer RC 1.50 4.00
215 Cedric Simmons RC 1.25 3.00
216 Rodney Carney RC 1.25 3.00
217 Shawne Williams RC 1.25 3.00
218 Quincy Douby RC 1.25 3.00
219 Renaldo Balkman RC 1.25 3.00
220 Rajon Rondo RC 5.00 12.00
221 Marcus Williams RC 1.25 3.00
222 Josh Boone RC 1.25 3.00
223 Kyle Lowry RC 1.50 4.00
224 Shannon Brown RC 2.00 5.00
225 Jordan Farmar RC 1.25 3.00
226 Maurice Ager RC 1.25 3.00
227 Mardy Collins RC 1.25 3.00
228 Jorge Garbajosa RC 1.25 3.00
229 James White RC 1.25 3.00
230 Steve Novak RC 1.25 3.00
231 Solomon Jones RC 1.25 3.00
232 Paul Davis RC 1.25 3.00
233 P.J. Tucker RC 1.25 3.00
234 Craig Smith RC 1.25 3.00
235 Bobby Jones RC 1.25 3.00
236 David Noel RC 1.25 3.00
237 Vassilis Spanoulis RC 1.25 3.00
238 James Augustine RC 1.25 3.00
239 Daniel Gibson RC 1.50 4.00
240 Alexander Johnson RC 1.25 3.00

2006-07 UD Reserve Gold

GOLD: 1.25X TO 3X BASE HI
APPROXIMATE ODDS ONE PER BOX

2006-07 UD Reserve Flight Team

COMPLETE SET (30) 15.00 40.00
APPROXIMATE ODDS 1:4
*GOLD: .75X TO 2X BASE HI
APPROXIMATE GOLD ODDS 1:20
AI Andre Iguodala 1.00 2.50
AS Amare Stoudemire 1.00 2.50
BB Brent Barry .60 1.50
BD Boris Diaw .75 2.00
CA Carmelo Anthony 1.25 3.00
CB Chris Bosh 1.00 2.50
CM Corey Maggette .75 2.00
DH Dwight Howard 1.50 4.00
DM Desmond Mason .60 1.50
DW Dwyane Wade 2.50 6.00
EJ Eddie Jones .75 2.00
FJ Fred Jones .60 1.50
GA Gilbert Arenas 1.00 2.50
JR Jason Richardson 1.00 2.50
JS J.R. Smith 1.00 2.50
KB Kobe Bryant 5.00 12.00
KM Kenyon Martin 1.00 2.50
LJ LeBron James 5.00 12.00
MA Shawn Marion 1.00 2.50
MG Manu Ginobili 1.00 2.50
MI Darius Miles .60 1.50
MJ Michael Jordan 8.00 20.00
NR Nate Robinson 1.00 2.50
RD Ricky Davis .75 2.00
RJ Richard Jefferson 1.00 2.50
SM Josh Smith 1.00 2.50
SS Stromile Swift .60 1.50
TM Tracy McGrady 1.25 3.00
TP Tayshaun Prince 1.00 2.50
VC Vince Carter 1.25 3.00

2006-07 UD Reserve Game Jerseys

APPROXIMATE ODDS ONE PER BOX
*PATCHES: .75X TO 2X BASE HI
APPROXIMATE ODDS 1:12
AB Andrew Bogut 3.00 8.00
AC Carlos Arroyo 2.50 6.00
AI Allen Iverson 4.00 10.00
AJ Al Jefferson 3.00 8.00
AK Andrei Kirilenko 2.50 6.00
AL Rafer Alston 2.50 6.00
AN Antawn Jamison 3.00 8.00
AR Ron Artest 3.00 8.00
AS Amare Stoudemire 3.00 8.00
AW Antoine Walker 2.50 6.00
BB Bruce Bowen 2.50 6.00
BD Baron Davis 3.00 8.00
BG Ben Gordon 3.00 8.00
BM Brad Miller 3.00 8.00
BW Ben Wallace 3.00 8.00
CB Chauncey Billups 3.00 8.00
CF Channing Frye 2.50 6.00
CM Corey Maggette 2.50 6.00
CP Chris Paul 6.00 15.00
CW Chris Webber 3.00 8.00
DG Drew Gooden 2.50 6.00
DH Devin Harris 3.00 8.00
DM Donyell Marshall 2.50 6.00
DN Dirk Nowitzki 5.00 12.00
DW Deron Williams 5.00 12.00
EO Emeka Okafor 3.00 8.00
GA Gilbert Arenas 3.00 8.00
GE Devean George 2.50 6.00
GH Grant Hill 6.00 15.00
HE Luther Head 2.50 6.00
HO Dwight Howard 5.00 12.00
ID Ike Diogu 2.00 5.00
IG Andre Iguodala 3.00 8.00
JC Jamal Crawford 2.50 6.00
JD Juan Dixon 2.50 6.00
JH Josh Howard 2.50 6.00
JJ Joe Johnson 3.00 8.00
JK Jason Kidd 5.00 12.00
JN Jameer Nelson 2.50 6.00
JO Jermaine O'Neal 3.00 8.00
JR Jason Richardson 3.00 8.00
JS J.R. Smith 3.00 8.00
JT Jason Terry 2.50 6.00
JW Jason Williams 2.50 6.00
KB Kwame Brown 2.50 6.00
KG Kevin Garnett 6.00 15.00
KH Kirk Hinrich 3.00 8.00
KK Kyle Korver 2.50 6.00
KM Kenyon Martin 3.00 8.00
LB Leandro Barbosa 2.50 6.00
LD Luol Deng 3.00 8.00
LH Larry Hughes 2.50 6.00
LJ LeBron James 10.00 25.00
LO Lamar Odom 3.00 8.00
LW Luke Walton 2.00 5.00
MA Stephon Marbury 2.50 6.00
MB Mike Bibby 3.00 8.00
MD Marquis Daniels 2.50 6.00
MG Manu Ginobili 3.00 8.00
MJ Michael Jordan 25.00 60.00
MR Michael Redd 3.00 8.00
MW Marvin Williams 3.00 8.00
NR Nate Robinson 3.00 8.00
PA Tony Parker 3.00 8.00
PG Pau Gasol 3.00 8.00
PS Peja Stojakovic 3.00 8.00
QR Quentin Richardson 2.50 6.00
RA Ray Allen 3.00 8.00
RF Raymond Felton 4.00 10.00
RH Richard Hamilton 2.50 6.00
RL Rashard Lewis 3.00 8.00
RM Rashad McCants 2.00 5.00
RW Rasheed Wallace 3.00 8.00
SD Samuel Dalembert 2.50 6.00
SF Steve Francis 3.00 8.00
SH Shawn Marion 3.00 8.00
SJ Sarunas Jasikevicius 2.50 6.00
SL Shaun Livingston 2.50 6.00
SM Sean May 2.00 5.00
SO Shaquille O'Neal 6.00 15.00
ST Sebastian Telfair 2.00 5.00
TC Tyson Chandler 2.50 6.00
TF T.J. Ford 2.50 6.00
TP Tayshaun Prince 3.00 8.00
VC Vince Carter 4.00 10.00
WE Martell Webster 2.50 6.00
WS Wally Szczerbiak 2.50 6.00
ZI Zydrunas Ilgauskas 2.50 6.00

2006-07 UD Reserve Legendary Signatures

APPROXIMATE ODDS ONE PER BOX
BK Bernard King 8.00 20.00
BM Bob McAdoo 8.00 20.00
CD Clyde Drexler 12.50 30.00
CH Connie Hawkins 10.00 25.00
CM Cedric Maxwell 8.00 20.00
DD Darryl Dawkins 8.00 20.00
DR David Robinson 40.00 80.00
HO Hakeem Olajuwon 12.50 30.00
JE Julius Erving 40.00 80.00
JO Michael Jordan 300.00 550.00
JS John Stockton 60.00 120.00
KV Kiki Vandeweghe 8.00 20.00
LB Larry Bird 75.00 150.00
MC Maurice Cheeks 8.00 20.00
MJ Magic Johnson 60.00 120.00
ML Maurice Lucas 10.00 25.00
NA Nate Archibald 8.00 20.00
RO Dennis Rodman 40.00 75.00
SP Sam Perkins 8.00 20.00
SW Spud Webb 8.00 20.00

2006-07 UD Reserve Materials

STATED PRINT RUN 100 SER.#'d SETS
*PATCHES: .75X TO 2X BASE HI
PRINT RUN 35 SER.#'d SETS
AB Andray Blatche 3.00 8.00
AI Allen Iverson 5.00 12.00
AJ Antawn Jamison 4.00 10.00
AK Andrei Kirilenko 3.00 8.00
BD Baron Davis 4.00 10.00
BG Ben Gordon 4.00 10.00
BM Brad Miller 4.00 10.00
BO Chris Bosh 4.00 10.00
BW Ben Wallace 4.00 10.00
CA Carmelo Anthony 5.00 12.00
CB Carlos Boozer 4.00 10.00
CM Corey Maggette 3.00 8.00
CP Chris Paul 8.00 20.00
DG Danny Granger 4.00 10.00
DH Dwight Howard 6.00 15.00
DN Dirk Nowitzki 6.00 15.00
DW David West 4.00 10.00
EB Elton Brand 4.00 10.00
EO Emeka Okafor 4.00 10.00
GH Grant Hill 8.00 20.00
HW Hakim Warrick 3.00 8.00
JC Josh Childress 3.00 8.00
JG Joey Graham 2.50 6.00
JK Jason Kidd 6.00 15.00
JN Jameer Nelson 3.00 8.00
JO Jermaine O'Neal 4.00 10.00
JS Josh Smith 4.00 10.00
KB Kobe Bryant 12.50 30.00
KG Kevin Garnett 8.00 20.00
LH Luther Head 3.00 8.00
LJ LeBron James 12.50 30.00
LW Luke Walton 2.50 6.00
MB Mike Bibby 4.00 10.00
MG Manu Ginobili 4.00 10.00
MJ Michael Jordan 30.00 80.00
MR Michael Redd 4.00 10.00
MW Marvin Williams 4.00 10.00
NE Nene 3.00 8.00
PP Paul Pierce 5.00 12.00
PS Peja Stojakovic 4.00 10.00
RA Ray Allen 4.00 10.00
RB Raja Bell 3.00 8.00
RF Raymond Felton 5.00 12.00
RH Richard Hamilton 3.00 8.00
RJ Richard Jefferson 4.00 10.00
RM Rashad McCants 2.50 6.00
RW Rasheed Wallace 4.00 10.00
SM Stephon Marbury 3.00 8.00
SN Steve Nash 5.00 12.00
TD Tim Duncan 6.00 15.00
TP Tony Parker 4.00 10.00
WI Deron Williams 6.00 15.00
WS Wally Szczerbiak 3.00 8.00
YM Yao Ming 5.00 12.00
ZI Zydrunas Ilgauskas 3.00 8.00

2006-07 UD Reserve Materials Dual

PRINT RUN 50 SER.#'d SETS
*PATCHES: .75X TO 2X BASE HI
PATCH PRINT RUN 15 SER.#'d SETS
AR LaMarcus Aldridge 10.00 25.00
Brandon Roy
BG Chris Bosh 6.00 15.00
Joey Graham
BM Elton Brand 5.00 12.00
Corey Maggette
BO Kwame Brown 5.00 12.00
Lamar Odom
CJ Josh Childress 5.00 12.00
Joe Johnson
FM Randy Foye 5.00 12.00
Rashad McCants
GW Pau Gasol 5.00 12.00
Hakim Warrick
HB Richard Hamilton 8.00 20.00
Chauncey Billups
HH Devin Harris 5.00 12.00
Josh Howard
HN Grant Hill 6.00 15.00
Jameer Nelson
JB Antawn Jamison 5.00 12.00
Andray Blatche
JJ LeBron James 60.00 150.00
Michael Jordan
KB Andrei Kirilenko 5.00 12.00
Carlos Boozer
MB Brad Miller 5.00 12.00
Mike Bibby
MF Channing Frye 5.00 12.00
Stephon Marbury
MM Yao Ming 10.00 25.00
Tracy McGrady
MO Yao Ming 20.00 40.00
Shaquille O'Neal
OG Jermaine O'Neal 5.00 12.00
Danny Granger
PD Tony Parker 10.00 25.00

Tim Duncan
PJ Paul Pierce 5.00 12.00
Al Jefferson
PW Chris Paul 6.00 15.00
David West
RD Jason Richardson 5.00 12.00
Baron Davis
VR Charlie Villanueva 5.00 12.00
Michael Redd
WB Marcus Williams 5.00 12.00
Josh Boone
PAN Carmelo Anthony 6.00 15.00
Nene

2006-07 UD Reserve Materials Triple

PRINT RUN 25 SER.#'d SETS
UNPRICED PATCH PRINT RUN 5 SETS
ARW LaMarcus Aldridge 20.00 40.00
Brandon Roy
Martell Webster
BSS Andrea Bargnani 10.00 25.00
Saer Sene
Thabo Sefolosha
CWS Josh Childress 8.00 20.00
Marvin Williams
Josh Smith
GST Ben Gordon 8.00 20.00
Thabo Sefolosha
Tyrus Thomas
GWB Rudy Gay 8.00 20.00
Marcus Williams
Josh Boone
GWG Pau Gasol 8.00 20.00
Hakim Warrick
Rudy Gay
ICK Andre Iguodala 8.00 20.00
Rodney Carney
Kyle Korver
KCJ Jason Kidd 20.00 40.00
Vince Carter
Richard Jefferson
SNM Amare Stoudemire 20.00 40.00
Steve Nash
Shawn Marion
SRR Wally Szczerbiak 8.00 20.00
Rajon Rondo
Allan Ray

2006-07 UD Reserve MVP Watch

COMPLETE SET (15) 15.00 40.00
APPROXIMATE ODDS 1:6
*GOLD: .75X TO 2X BASE HI
APPROXIMATE GOLD ODDS 1:24
AI Allen Iverson 1.25 3.00
BW Ben Wallace 1.00 2.50
CB Chauncey Billups 1.00 2.50
DN Dirk Nowitzki 1.50 4.00
DW Dwyane Wade 2.50 6.00
EB Elton Brand 1.00 2.50
GA Gilbert Arenas 1.00 2.50
KB Kobe Bryant 5.00 12.00
KG Kevin Garnett 2.00 5.00
LJ LeBron James 5.00 12.00
PP Paul Pierce 1.25 3.00
SN Steve Nash 1.25 3.00
SO Shaquille O'Neal 2.00 5.00
TD Tim Duncan 1.50 4.00
TM Tracy McGrady 1.25 3.00

2006-07 UD Reserve Signatures

APPROXIMATE ODDS ONE PER BOX
AI Andre Iguodala 5.00 12.00
AJ Al Jefferson 5.00 12.00
AN Antawn Jamison 5.00 12.00
AR Hilton Armstrong 5.00 12.00
BA Andrea Bargnani 10.00 25.00
BB Brent Barry 5.00 12.00
BD Baron Davis 5.00 12.00
BE Raja Bell 6.00 15.00
BG Ben Gordon 8.00 20.00
BJ Bobby Jackson 5.00 12.00
BO Bruce Bowen 5.00 12.00
BS Bobby Simmons 5.00 12.00
CA Carmelo Anthony 20.00 40.00
CB Chauncey Billups 8.00 20.00
CD Chris Duhon 5.00 12.00
CH Charlie Bell 5.00 12.00
CM Corey Maggette 5.00 12.00
CS Cedric Simmons 5.00 12.00
DB Dee Brown 5.00 12.00
DE Daniel Ewing 5.00 12.00
DG Danny Granger 5.00 12.00
DI Boris Diaw 5.00 12.00
DM Damir Markota 5.00 12.00
DN David Noel 5.00 12.00
DW Deron Williams 15.00 30.00
EC Eddy Curry 5.00 12.00
EO Emeka Okafor 5.00 12.00
FE Raymond Felton 5.00 12.00
GG Gerald Green 5.00 12.00
GI Daniel Gibson 10.00 25.00
GR Joey Graham 5.00 12.00
HA Hassan Adams 5.00 12.00
HW Hakim Warrick 5.00 12.00
IU Ime Udoka 5.00 12.00
JA James Augustine 5.00 12.00
JB Josh Boone 5.00 12.00
JC Josh Childress 5.00 12.00
JF Jordan Farmar 5.00 12.00
JG Jorge Garbajosa 5.00 12.00
JJ Jarrett Jack 5.00 12.00
JO Bobby Jones 5.00 12.00
JS J.R. Smith 5.00 12.00
KD Keyon Dooling 5.00 12.00
KH Kirk Hinrich 10.00 25.00
KK Kyle Korver 5.00 12.00
KL Kyle Lowry 6.00 15.00
LA LaMarcus Aldridge 10.00 25.00
LB Leandro Barbosa 5.00 12.00
LH Larry Hughes 5.00 12.00
LJ LeBron James 125.00 250.00
LR Luke Ridnour 5.00 12.00
MA Maurice Ager 5.00 12.00
MC Mardy Collins 5.00 12.00
MI Mile Ilic 5.00 12.00
MM Chris Mihm 5.00 12.00
MO Cuttino Mobley 5.00 12.00
MW Marvin Williams 5.00 12.00
NO Steve Novak 5.00 12.00
PD Paul Davis 5.00 12.00
PM Paul Millsap 5.00 12.00
PO Patrick O'Bryant 5.00 12.00
PP Paul Pierce 8.00 20.00
PS Peja Stojakovic 5.00 12.00
PT P.J. Tucker 5.00 12.00
QD Quincy Douby 5.00 12.00
QR Quentin Richardson 5.00 12.00
RB Ronnie Brewer 5.00 12.00
RC Rodney Carney 5.00 12.00
RE Renaldo Balkman 5.00 12.00
RF Randy Foye 6.00 15.00
RG Rudy Gay 6.00 15.00
RH Ryan Hollins 5.00 12.00
RM Rashad McCants 5.00 12.00
RO Brandon Roy 10.00 25.00
RR Rajon Rondo 15.00 40.00
SA Shareef Abdur-Rahim 5.00 12.00
SB Shannon Brown 6.00 15.00
SH Shawne Williams 5.00 12.00
SJ Solomon Jones 5.00 12.00
SM Craig Smith 5.00 12.00
SN Steve Nash 25.00 60.00
SR Sergio Rodriguez 5.00 12.00
SS Saer Sene 5.00 12.00
ST Sebastian Telfair 5.00 12.00
SW Shelden Williams 5.00 12.00
TA Tony Allen 5.00 12.00
TF T.J. Ford 5.00 12.00
TM Tracy McGrady 12.50 30.00
TS Thabo Sefolosha 5.00 12.00
TT Tyrus Thomas 8.00 20.00
VC Vince Carter 30.00 60.00
VS Vassilis Spanoulis 5.00 12.00
WB Will Blalock 5.00 12.00
WE Martell Webster 5.00 12.00
WH James White 5.00 12.00
WM Marcus Williams 5.00 12.00
YM Yao Ming 15.00 40.00

2006-07 UD Reserve Signatures Dual

PRINT RUN 50 SER.#'d SETS
AB Hilton Armstrong 6.00 15.00
Josh Boone
AM Carmelo Anthony 25.00 60.00
Tracy McGrady
AP Maurice Ager 6.00 15.00
Sam Perkins
AR LaMarcus Aldridge 40.00 100.00
Brandon Roy
AW James Augustine 15.00 40.00
Deron Williams
BB Chauncey Billups 8.00 20.00
Will Blalock
BG Shannon Brown 8.00 20.00
Daniel Gibson
CB Renaldo Balkman 6.00 15.00
Mardy Collins
CW Rodney Carney 6.00 15.00
Shawne Williams
DA Quincy Douby 6.00 15.00
Shareef Abdur-Rahim
DO Baron Davis 8.00 20.00
Patrick O'Bryant
FS Randy Foye 8.00 20.00
Craig Smith
GF T.J. Ford 6.00 15.00
Joey Graham
HD Kirk Hinrich 12.50 30.00
Chris Duhon
HF Raymond Felton 6.00 15.00
Ryan Hollins
IK Andre Iguodala 8.00 20.00
Kyle Korver
JD James Augustine 6.00 15.00
Dee Brown
JJ LeBron James 400.00 700.00
Michael Jordan
LR David Lee 6.00 15.00
Quentin Richardson
MD Corey Maggette 6.00 15.00
Paul Davis
OF Emeka Okafor 15.00 30.00
Raymond Felton
OM Hakeem Olajuwon 40.00 80.00
Yao Ming
RB David Robinson 40.00 80.00
Brent Barry
RD Ronnie Brewer 6.00 15.00
Dee Brown
RF Allan Ray 10.00 25.00
Randy Foye
SM Shelden Williams 6.00 15.00
Marvin Williams
TJ Sebastian Telfair 6.00 15.00
Al Jefferson
TR Tony Allen 15.00 40.00
Rajon Rondo
TS Tyrus Thomas 15.00 40.00
Thabo Sefolosha
VS Kiki Vandeweghe 6.00 15.00
J.R. Smith
WC Josh Childress 6.00 15.00
Spud Webb
WG Shawne Williams 6.00 15.00
Danny Granger
WS Damien Wilkins 6.00 15.00
Saer Sene
WW James White 6.00 15.00
Brent Barry

2006-07 UD Reserve Signatures Triple

UNPRICED QUAD PRINT RUN 5 SETS
AWB Hassan Adams 15.00 40.00
Marcus Williams
Josh Boone
BAT Andrea Bargnani 25.00 60.00
LaMarcus Aldridge
Tyrus Thomas
BCR Renaldo Balkman 15.00 40.00
Mardy Collins
Quentin Richardson
FSM Randy Foye 15.00 40.00
Craig Smith
Rashad McCants
GBH Daniel Gibson 30.00 60.00
Shannon Brown
Larry Hughes
RGR Rajon Rondo 25.00 60.00
Gerald Green
Allan Ray
RWS Luke Ridnour 15.00 40.00
Damien Wilkins
Saer Sene
SSA Peja Stojakovic 15.00 40.00
Cedric Simmons
Hilton Armstrong
WLG Hakim Warrick 25.00 50.00
Kyle Lowry
Rudy Gay

2006-07 UD Reserve The LeBrons

COMPLETE SET (15) 20.00 50.00
APPROXIMATE ODDS 1:12
COMMON GOLD 15.00 30.00
COMMON MEMORABILIA 12.00 30.00
COMMON DUAL/TRIP.MEM. 20.00 50.00

2002-03 UD SuperStars

This 300 card set was released in March, 2003. This set was issued in five card packs with an $3 SRP. The packs were issued in 24 pack boxes which came 12 boxes to a case. The final 50 cards of the set featured two rookies from different sports.

COMPLETE SET (300) 30.00 80.00
12 Stephon Marbury .30 .75
13 Shawn Marion .25 .60
20 Shareef Abdur-Rahim .25 .60
34 Paul Pierce .50 1.25
35 Antoine Walker .30 .75
97 Ray Allen .30 .75
103 Steve Francis .40 1.00
104 Reggie Miller .40 1.00
119 Kobe Bryant 1.25 3.00
120 Shaquille O'Neal .60 1.50
121 Wilt Chamberlain .60 1.50
122 Andre Miller .25 .60
124 Pau Gasol .30 .75
132 Kevin Garnett .60 1.50
139 Baron Davis .40 1.00
143 Jason Kidd .50 1.25
178 Jason Richardson .40 1.00
179 Grant Hill .40 1.00
180 Tracy McGrady .60 1.50
187 Allen Iverson .60 1.50
188 Julius Erving .60 1.50
198 Rasheed Wallace .30 .75
199 Chris Webber .40 1.00
200 Mike Bibby .30 .75
201 Tim Duncan .60 1.50
222 Rashard Lewis .15 .40
223 Gary Payton .40 1.00
243 Vince Carter .50 1.25
245 Karl Malone .40 1.00
246 Jerry Stackhouse .25 .60
247 Michael Jordan 2.00 5.00
254 Stanislav Chistov .40 1.00
Melvin Ely
258 Jay Williams .50 1.25
Francis Beltran
262 Dajuan Wagner .60 1.50
William Green
264 Chad Hutchinson .50 1.25
Casey Jacobsen
266 Nene Hilario .40 1.00
Nick Rolovich
267 Joey Harrington 1.25 3.00
Tayshaun Prince
269 Jay Bouwmeester 1.00 2.50
Caron Butler
270 Mike Dunleavy .40 1.00
Phillip Buchanon
272 Bostjan Nachbar .20 .50
Jonathan Wells
273 David Carr 4.00 10.00
Yao Ming
276 Drew Gooden .75 2.00
Scottie Upshall
278 Marcus Haislip .60 1.50
Javon Walker
283 Pierre-Marc Bouchard .20 .50
Igor Rakocevic
284 Anderson Machado .40 1.00
John Salmons
285 Amare Stoudemire 1.50 4.00
Jeremy Ward
295 Reed Johnson .20 .50
Chris Jefferies
296 Patrick Ramsey .60 1.50
Juan Dixon
297 Jared Jeffries .20 .50
Steve Bechler

2002-03 UD SuperStars Gold

Randomly inserted in packs, this is a parallel to the UD SuperStars set. These cards were issued to a stated print run of 250 serial numbered sets.

*GOLD 1-250: 2.5X TO 6X BASIC
*GOLD MATSUI: 6X TO 12X BASIC
*GOLD 251-300: 2X TO 5X BASIC

2002-03 UD SuperStars Benchmarks

Inserted at a stated rate of one in 20, these 10 cards feature two athletes from different sports with something in common. It could be being a legendary figure in the sport or playing in the same city.

B4 Bill Russell 4.00 10.00
Mickey Mantle
B5 Allen Iverson 1.00 2.50
Donovan McNabb
B7 Kevin Garnett 1.50 4.00
Randy Moss
B10 Kobe Bryant 3.00 8.00
Derek Jeter

2002-03 UD SuperStars City All-Stars Dual Jersey

Inserted at a stated rate of one in 32, these 43 cards featured two jersey swatches from star athletes from the same city. Some cards were issued in smaller quantities and we have notated that information with an SP in our database.

ABBD Aaron Brooks 6.00 15.00
Baron Davis
ADDM Antoine Davis 5.00 12.00
Darius Miles
EJJO Edgerrin James 5.00 12.00
Jermaine O'Neal
GSSA Gary Sheffield 4.00 10.00
Shareef Abdur-Rahim
IRMF Ivan Rodriguez 6.00 15.00
Michael Finley
MRPP Manny Ramirez 6.00 15.00
Paul Pierce
RJSM Randy Johnson 6.00 15.00
Stephon Marbury
SDJS Stephen Davis 6.00 15.00
Jerry Stackhouse SP
SMPG Steve McNair 10.00 25.00
Pau Gasol
SSAW Sergei Samsonov 5.00 12.00
Antoine Walker
TCMO Tyson Chandler 6.00 15.00
Magglio Ordonez
WSMB Wally Szczerbiak 5.00 12.00
Michael Bennett

2002-03 UD SuperStars City All-Stars Triple Jersey

Randomly inserted in packs, these cards featured three game-used jersey swatches from all-stars from the same city. These cards were issued to a stated print run of 250 serial numbered sets.

CVT Chipper Jones 15.00 40.00
Michael Vick
Jason Terry
DPE Darin Erstad 10.00 25.00
Paul Kariya
Elton Brand
IGS Ichiro Suzuki 30.00 60.00
Gary Payton
Shaun Alexander
IMD Ivan Rodriguez 15.00 40.00
Mike Modano
Dirk Nowitzki
JCK Ken Griffey Jr. 10.00 25.00
Corey Dillon
Kenyon Martin
JDW Jacque Jones 10.00 25.00
Daunte Culpepper
Wally Szczerbiak
JDY Jeff Bagwell 40.00 80.00
David Carr
Yao Ming
JLP Jason Giambi 6.00 15.00
Latrell Sprewell
Pavel Bure
JSB Joey Harrington 25.00 50.00
Steve Yzerman
Ben Wallace
MJA Mark Prior 5.00 12.00
Jay Williams
Anthony Thomas
MJC Mike Piazza 10.00 25.00
Jason Kidd
Curtis Martin
MJJ Miguel Tejada 10.00 25.00
Jason Richardson
Jerry Rice
OTD Omar Vizquel 10.00 25.00
Tim Couch
Dajuan Wagner
PTP Pedro Martinez 20.00 50.00
Tom Brady
Paul Pierce
REA Roger Clemens 15.00 30.00
Eric Lindros
Allan Houston
RSS Randy Johnson 6.00 15.00
Shawn Marion
Shane Doan
SWK Shawn Green 40.00 80.00
Wayne Gretzky
Kobe Bryant

2002-03 UD SuperStars Keys to the City

Inserted at a stated rate of one in six. These 10 cards feature two star athletes from the same city.

COMPLETE SET (10) 10.00 25.00
K1 Carlos Delgado .75 2.00
Vince Carter
K2 Kobe Bryant 2.00 5.00
Kazuhisa Ishii

2002-03 UD SuperStars Legendary Leaders Dual Jersey

Inserted at a stated rate of one in 96, these 20 cards feature game-worn jersey pieces from two star athletes from the same city.

AIDM Allen Iverson 10.00 25.00
Donovan McNabb
EJJO Edgerrin James 6.00 15.00
Jermaine O'Neal
JKCP Jason Kidd 8.00 20.00
Chad Pennington
JRJR Jerry Rice 10.00 25.00
Jason Richardson
JWAT Jay Williams 6.00 15.00
Anthony Thomas
KGRM Kevin Garnett 15.00 30.00
Randy Moss
RMPM Reggie Miller 15.00 30.00
Peyton Manning
SMRJ Shawn Marion 6.00 15.00
Randy Johnson

2002-03 UD SuperStars Legendary Leaders Triple Jersey

Randomly inserted in packs, these 18 cards feature game-used jersey swatches from three athletes. This set is significant by the usage of game-worn swatches of soccer great David Beckham. Each card was issued to a stated print run of 250 serial numbered sets.

ADJ Allen Iverson 20.00 50.00
Donovan McNabb
Jeremy Roenick
GMS Greg Maddux 12.50 30.00
Michael Vick
Shareef Abdur-Rahim
IDK Ichiro Suzuki 75.00 150.00
David Beckham
Kobe Bryant
IKD Ichiro Suzuki 40.00 80.00
Kevin Garnett
David Beckham
JWL Joe DiMaggio 60.00 120.00
Wayne Gretzky
Larry Bird
KJT Karl Malone 20.00 50.00
Jerry Rice
Tony Gwynn
PPT Pedro Martinez 20.00 50.00
Paul Pierce
Tom Brady
SKM Sammy Sosa 25.00 60.00
Kobe Bryant
Marshall Faulk
SWK Shawn Green 40.00 80.00
Wayne Gretzky
Kobe Bryant

2002-03 UD SuperStars Magic Moments

Inserted at a stated rate of one in five, this 20 card set featured a mix of active and retired players along with history about key moments in their career.

COMPLETE SET (20) 10.00 25.00
MM14 Michael Jordan 2.50 6.00
MM15 Kobe Bryant 1.50 4.00
MM16 Jay Williams .50 1.25

2002-03 UD SuperStars Rookie Review

Inserted at a stated rate of one in 20, these 10 cards feature two athletes who made their American professional debut in the same year.

R3 Josh Beckett 1.00 2.50
Steve Francis
R4 Vince Carter 1.25 3.00
Peyton Manning
R7 Jason Kidd 1.00 2.50
Alex Rodriguez
R8 Alfonso Soriano 1.00 2.50
Shawn Marion
R9 Ken Griffey Jr. 1.25 3.00
David Robinson

2002-03 UD SuperStars Spokesmen

Issued as a three-card pack topper, these 30 cards feature a mix of players who were also serving as spokesmen for Upper Deck.

*BLACK: 1.25X TO 3X BASIC SPOKESMEN
BLACK/GOLD INSERTS IN SPOKESMEN PACKS
BLACK PRINT RUN 250 SERIAL #'d SETS
*GOLD/25: 3X TO 8X BASIC INSERTS
GOLD PRINT RUN 25 SERIAL #'d SETS
UD8 Michael Jordan 4.00 10.00
UD9 Kobe Bryant 2.00 5.00
UD10 Jay Williams 1.25 3.00
UD23 Michael Jordan 4.00 10.00
UD24 Kobe Bryant 2.00 5.00
UD25 Jay Williams 1.25 3.00

1996 UDA 22kt Gold Michael Jordan Slam Dunk Champion

NNO Michael Jordan 75.00 150.00

2003 UDA LeBron James

Released by Upper Deck Authenticated during the 2003-04, this one-card set commemorates LBJ's first NBA game-October 29th, 2003. The cards have a gold border along the left side, a UDA authentication hologram on the front of the card below which, the words, "first game" are printed. The Upper Deck Collectibles logo appears in the upper right-hand corner of the card and each card is accompanied by a UDA tri-fold certificate of authenticity. Also, Released was a LeBron James Rookie of the Month card. This release has a red border along the left side of the card and is also signed and limited to 23 copies.

NNO LeBron James 4.00 10.00
First Game/2323
NNO LeBron James 200.00 500.00
First Game AU/23
NNO LeBron James 200.00 500.00
ROM AU/23
NNO LeBron James 3.00 8.00
Youngest to 1000/5000

1995-98 UDA Michael Jordan Commemorative Cards

NH1 1996 National Hero/5000 10.00 25.00
NNO 1996 Magic Memories MTS 8.00 20.00
NNO 1996 Space Jam w/ball/5000 10.00 25.00
NNO 1996 25,000 Points (no serial #)8.00 20.00
NNO 1995 UNC 1st Champ.blue foil/500010.00 25.00
NNO Celebration of Excellence 8.00 20.00
NNO 1997 9-Time Scoring Champ/500010.00 25.00
NNO 1996 10-Time All-Star/5000 10.00 25.00
NNO 1996 8-Time Scoring Champ/500010.00 25.00
NNO 1997 5-Time NBA Finals MVP/500010.00 25.00
NNO 1997 4-Time Champs AU/50
NNO 1997 11-Time All-Star/5000 10.00 25.00
NNO 1996 All-Star First Team/2500 12.50 30.00
NNO 1996 Reg.season MVP/2500 12.50 30.00
NNO 1996 25,000 Career Point 8.00 20.00
NNO 1996 Space Jam w/Porky/500010.00 25.00
NNO 1995 UNC 1st Champ.gold foil/500010.00 25.00
NNO 1996 Space Jam w/Bugs/5000 10.00 25.00
NNO Olympic Gold '84 and '92 8.00 20.00
NNO 1996 4-Time Finals MVP/2500 12.50 30.00

2000 UDA Michael Jordan Final Shot

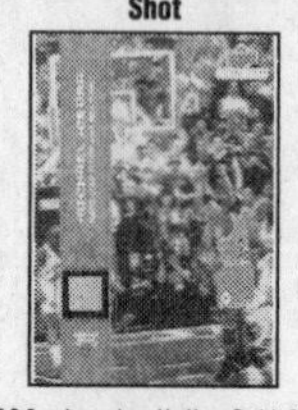

This 3.5x5 card was released by Upper Deck in 2000, and features a piece of the Delta Center floor upon which Michael Jordan took his final shot. There were 1000 total cards produced, and Michael Jordan signed the first 100. These cards were sold exclusively through Upper Deck's direct marketing channel. The unsigned version retailed at $395, while the signed version retailed at $3999.95.

1A Michael Jordan 2000.00 4000.00
Floor AU/100
1B Michael Jordan 150.00 400.00
Floor/900

1996 UDA SPx Record Breaker Michael Jordan

Released as a special product through Upper Deck Authenticated, this card is serially numbered to 250 and features a UDA Authentication hologram with the lettered prefix BAD.

R1 Michael Jordan AU/250 400.00 750.00

2000-01 Ultimate Collection

The 2000-01 Upper Deck Ultimate Collection product shipped in February, 2001 and featured a 60-card base veteran set. The full set was broken into tiers as follows: 60 Veterans, and 14 Rookies and 6 Autographed Rookies - the rookies are listed seperately since they were graded. Each pack contained four cards, and carried a suggested retail price of $100 per pack.

1 Dikembe Mutombo 2.50 6.00
2 Hanno Mottola RC 3.00 8.00
3 Paul Pierce 3.00 8.00
4 Antoine Walker 2.00 5.00
5 Derrick Coleman 2.00 5.00
6 Baron Davis 2.50 6.00
7 Elton Brand 2.50 6.00
8 Michael Jordan 20.00 50.00
9 Andre Miller 2.00 5.00
10 Chris Mihm RC 3.00 8.00
11 Michael Finley 2.50 6.00
12 Donnell Harvey RC 3.00 8.00
13 Antonio McDyess 2.00 5.00
14 Nick Van Exel 2.00 5.00
15 Jerry Stackhouse 2.00 5.00
16 Jerome Williams 1.50 4.00
17 Larry Hughes 2.00 5.00
18 Antawn Jamison 2.50 6.00
19 Steve Francis 2.50 6.00
20 Hakeem Olajuwon 3.00 8.00
21 Reggie Miller 2.50 6.00
22 Jalen Rose 2.50 6.00
23 Lamar Odom 2.50 6.00
24 Michael Olowokandi 1.50 4.00
25 Shaquille O'Neal 6.00 15.00
26 Kobe Bryant 12.00 30.00
27 Ron Harper 2.00 5.00
28 Alonzo Mourning 3.00 8.00
29 Eddie House RC 3.00 8.00
30 Glenn Robinson 2.00 5.00
31 Ray Allen 2.50 6.00
32 Kevin Garnett 5.00 12.00
33 Wally Szczerbiak 2.50 6.00
34 Terrell Brandon 1.50 4.00
35 Stephon Marbury 2.00 5.00
36 Keith Van Horn 2.00 5.00
37 Allan Houston 2.00 5.00
38 Latrell Sprewell 2.00 5.00
39 Grant Hill 3.00 8.00
40 Tracy McGrady 4.00 10.00
41 Allen Iverson 5.00 12.00
42 Toni Kukoc 2.00 5.00
43 Jason Kidd 4.00 10.00
44 Anfernee Hardaway 4.00 10.00
45 Scottie Pippen 4.00 10.00
46 Rasheed Wallace 2.50 6.00
47 Chris Webber 2.50 6.00
48 Jason Williams 2.50 6.00
49 Tim Duncan 5.00 12.00
50 David Robinson 4.00 10.00
51 Gary Payton 2.50 6.00
52 Rashard Lewis 2.50 6.00
53 Vince Carter 5.00 12.00
54 Morris Peterson RC 3.00 8.00
55 Karl Malone 3.00 8.00
56 John Stockton 3.00 8.00
57 Shareef Abdur-Rahim 2.00 5.00
58 Mike Bibby 2.50 6.00
59 Mike Smith RC 3.00 8.00
60 Richard Hamilton 2.00 5.00
P1 Kenyon Martin SAMPLE 1.00 2.50

2000-01 Ultimate Collection Rookies

Randomly inserted into packs, this 20-card set features the rookies from the 2000-01 season. Please note that there were only 250 of each card produced.

STATED PRINT RUN 250 SERIAL #'d SETS
61 Mamadou N'Diaye RC 6.00 15.00
62 Erick Barkley RC 6.00 15.00
63 Desmond Mason RC 8.00 20.00
64 Speedy Claxton RC 6.00 15.00
65 Jamaal Magloire RC 6.00 15.00
66 DeShawn Stevenson RC 8.00 20.00
67 Etan Thomas RC 6.00 15.00
68 Jamal Crawford RC 10.00 25.00
69 Joel Przybilla RC 6.00 15.00
70 Keyon Dooling RC 6.00 15.00
71 Jerome Moiso RC 6.00 15.00
72 Quentin Richardson RC 10.00 25.00
73 Courtney Alexander RC 6.00 15.00
74 Mateen Cleaves RC 6.00 15.00
75 Mike Miller AU RC 20.00 50.00
76 DerMarr Johnson AU RC 10.00 25.00
77 Darius Miles AU RC 10.00 25.00
78 Marcus Fizer AU RC 10.00 25.00
79 Kenyon Martin AU RC 25.00 60.00
80 Stromile Swift AU RC 10.00 25.00

2000-01 Ultimate Collection BuyBacks

Representatives at Upper Deck purchased back a selection of vintage Upper Deck cards, featuring 10 different players. The "vintage" cards were all purchased in 2000-01 through hobby dealers. Each card was then hand-numbered in blue ink sharpie on front (please see listings for print runs), affixed with a serial numbered UDA hologram on back and packaged with a 2 1/2" by 3 1/2" UDA Certificate of Authenticity (of which had a hologram with a matching serial number of the signed card). The Certificate of Authenticity and the signed card were placed together in a soft plastic "penny" sleeve and then randomly seeded into 2000-01 Upper Deck Ultimate Collection packs.

2000-01 Ultimate Collection Game Jerseys Bronze

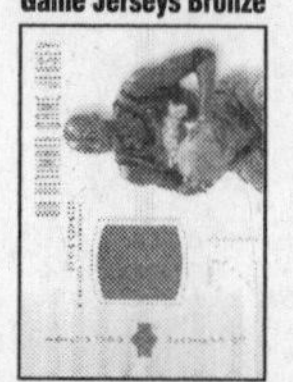

Randomly inserted into packs at one in three, this nine-card insert features swatches from actual game-used NBA jerseys. Please note that there are three different tiers (Gold, Silver, and Bronze). Card backs carry the players initials as numbering followed by a "J".

*SILVER: .5X TO 1.25X BRONZE HI
SILVER STATED ODDS 1:6
DSJ Damon Stoudamire 4.00 10.00
JKJ Jason Kidd 8.00 20.00
JSJ John Stockton 12.50 30.00
KBJ Kobe Bryant 25.00 60.00
KGJ Kevin Garnett 10.00 25.00
KMJ Kenyon Martin 12.50 30.00
MFJ Marcus Fizer 5.00 12.00
MJJ Michael Jordan 50.00 120.00
WSJ Wally Szczerbiak 4.00 10.00

2000-01 Ultimate Collection Game Jerseys Gold

Randomly inserted into packs at one in 17, this 10-card insert features swatches from actual game-used NBA jerseys. Card backs carry the players initials as numbering followed by a "J".

*GOLD: .5X TO 1.5X HI COLUMN
MJJ Michael Jordan 100.00 250.00
SFJ Steve Francis 8.00 20.00

2000-01 Ultimate Collection Game Jerseys Patches

Randomly inserted into packs at one in 11, this 25-card insert features swatches from actual game-used NBA jersey patches. Card backs carry the players initials as numbering followed by a "P".

AHP Anfernee Hardaway/75 50.00 120.00
AIP Allen Iverson/75 80.00 200.00
AMP Alonzo Mourning/100 30.00 80.00
DRP David Robinson/100 40.00 100.00
DSP Damon Stoudamire/75 20.00 50.00
GPP Gary Payton/100 25.00 60.00
JKP Jason Kidd/75 50.00 120.00
JSP John Stockton/100 50.00 120.00
JWP Jason Williams/25 50.00 100.00
KGA Kevin Garnett AU/21 150.00 300.00
KGP Kevin Garnett/21 75.00 150.00

KMP Karl Malone/100 40.00 100.00
KVP Keith Van Horn/100 20.00 50.00
MFP Michael Finley/75 25.00 60.00
MJA Michael Jordan AU/23 1500.00 2500.00
PPP Paul Pierce/50 40.00 100.00
RAP Ray Allen/100 40.00 100.00
RMP Reggie Miller/100 50.00 120.00
SAP Shareef Abdur-Rahim/100 20.00 50.00
SHP Shawn Marion/25 40.00 100.00
SMP Stephon Marbury/75 20.00 50.00
SOP Shaquille O'Neal/75 60.00 150.00
WSP Wally Szczerbiak/100 20.00 50.00

2000-01 Ultimate Collection Signatures Bronze

Randomly inserted into packs, this 15-card insert features authenticated autographs of some of the NBA's top players. The checklist includes Kobe Bryant, Kevin Garnett and Michael Jordan. Please note that there were only 200 serial numbered sets produced. Card backs carry the player's initials as numbering followed by a "B". A gold version was also produced and is sequentially numbered to 25.

UNPRICED SUPER PRINT RUN ONE SET
AHB Anfernee Hardaway 30.00 80.00
AJB Antawn Jamison 6.00 15.00
AMB Andre Miller 6.00 15.00
CAB Courtney Alexander 6.00 15.00
DJB DerMarr Johnson 6.00 15.00
JMB Jerome Moiso 6.00 15.00
JRB Jalen Rose 6.00 15.00
KBB Kobe Bryant 80.00 160.00
KGB Kevin Garnett 25.00 60.00
LHB Larry Hughes 6.00 15.00
MFB Marcus Fizer 6.00 15.00
QRB Quentin Richardson 10.00 25.00
SAB Shareef Abdur-Rahim 6.00 15.00
SMB Shawn Marion 6.00 15.00
TMB Tracy McGrady 20.00 50.00

2000-01 Ultimate Collection Signatures Gold

Randomly inserted into packs, this 15-card insert features authenticated autographs of some of the NBA's top players. The checklist includes Kobe Bryant, Kevin Garnett and Michael Jordan. Please note that there were only 25 serial numbered sets produced. Card backs carry the player's initials as numbering followed by a "G".

AHG Anfernee Hardaway 75.00 200.00
BRG Bill Russell 150.00 300.00
DMG Darius Miles 15.00 40.00
GPG Gary Payton 30.00 80.00
JRG Jalen Rose 40.00 100.00
KBG Kobe Bryant 200.00 400.00
KGG Kevin Garnett 75.00 200.00
KMG Kenyon Martin 30.00 80.00
LHG Larry Hughes 15.00 40.00
MJG Michael Jordan 600.00 1200.00
SAG Shareef Abdur-Rahim 15.00 40.00
SFG Steve Francis 15.00 40.00
SSG Stromile Swift 15.00 40.00
TMG Tracy McGrady 40.00 100.00

2000-01 Ultimate Collection Signatures Silver

Randomly inserted into packs, this 15-card insert features authenticated autographs of some of the NBA's top players. The checklist includes Kobe Bryant, Kevin Garnett and Michael Jordan. Please note that there were only 75 serial numbered sets produced. Card backs carry the player's initials as numbering followed by a "SI".

AHSI Anfernee Hardaway 50.00 120.00
AMSI Antonio McDyess 8.00 20.00
DSSI DeShawn Stevenson 8.00 20.00
GPSI Gary Payton 20.00 50.00
JCSI Jamal Crawford 10.00 25.00
KBSI Kobe Bryant 100.00 200.00
KGSI Kevin Garnett 40.00 100.00
MCSI Mateen Cleaves 8.00 20.00
MMSI Mike Miller 15.00 40.00
MPSI Morris Peterson 8.00 20.00
PPSI Paul Pierce 15.00 40.00
SFSI Steve Francis 8.00 20.00
SMSI Shawn Marion 8.00 20.00
THSI Tim Hardaway 10.00 25.00

2001-02 Ultimate Collection

Released in January of 2002, Upper Deck Ultimate Collection boasts a 90-card set broken down into 60 veteran cards and 30 rookie cards. Base cards feature full color player action photos with silver foil and block highlights. Each card is sequentially numbered to 750. The rookies are divided up as follows: card numbers 61-70 have a full color player photo with a bronze stripe centered across the card horizontally and white both above and below this line. These cards have silver foil highlights are are sequentially numbered to 750. Card numbers 71-84 feature the same design except the bronze line is shifted to a silver line and these cards are sequentially numbered to 250. Card numbers 85-90 feature authentic player autographs are sequentailly numbered to 250 as well. Upper Deck Ultimate Collection was packaged in four box cases where boxes contained four packs each, and packs contained four cards and carried a suggested retail price of $100.

COMP.SET w/o SP's (60) 200.00 400.00
1 Jason Terry 2.50 6.00
2 Shareef Abdur-Rahim 2.00 5.00
3 Paul Pierce 3.00 8.00
4 Antoine Walker 2.00 5.00
5 Baron Davis 2.50 6.00
6 Jamal Mashburn 2.00 5.00
7 Ron Mercer 1.50 4.00
8 Marcus Fizer 1.50 4.00
9 Andre Miller 2.00 5.00
10 Lamond Murray 1.50 4.00
11 Dirk Nowitzki 4.00 10.00
12 Michael Finley 2.50 6.00
13 Antonio McDyess 2.00 5.00
14 Nick Van Exel 2.00 5.00
15 Jerry Stackhouse 2.00 5.00
16 Zeljko Rebraca RC 3.00 8.00
17 Antawn Jamison 2.50 6.00
18 Larry Hughes 2.00 5.00
19 Steve Francis 2.50 6.00
20 Cuttino Mobley 2.00 5.00
21 Reggie Miller 2.50 6.00
22 Jalen Rose 2.00 5.00
23 Darius Miles 1.50 4.00
24 Quentin Richardson 2.00 5.00
25 Kobe Bryant 12.00 30.00
26 Shaquille O'Neal 6.00 15.00
27 Mitch Richmond 2.00 5.00
28 Stromile Swift 1.50 4.00
29 Jason Williams 2.00 5.00
30 Alonzo Mourning 3.00 8.00
31 Eddie Jones 2.00 5.00
32 Ray Allen 2.50 6.00
33 Glenn Robinson 2.00 5.00
34 Kevin Garnett 5.00 12.00
35 Terrell Brandon 1.50 4.00
36 Wally Szczerbiak 2.00 5.00
37 Jason Kidd 4.00 10.00
38 Kenyon Martin 2.50 6.00
39 Latrell Sprewell 2.00 5.00
40 Allan Houston 2.00 5.00
41 Tracy McGrady 4.00 10.00
42 Grant Hill 3.00 8.00
43 Allen Iverson 5.00 12.00
44 Dikembe Mutombo 2.50 6.00
45 Stephon Marbury 2.00 5.00
46 Anfernee Hardaway 4.00 10.00
47 Rasheed Wallace 2.50 6.00
48 Derek Anderson 1.50 4.00
49 Chris Webber 2.50 6.00
50 Peja Stojakovic 2.50 6.00
51 Tim Duncan 5.00 12.00
52 David Robinson 4.00 10.00
53 Rashard Lewis 2.50 6.00
54 Desmond Mason 2.00 5.00
55 Vince Carter 4.00 10.00
56 Morris Peterson 1.50 4.00
57 Karl Malone 3.00 8.00
58 John Stockton 3.00 8.00
59 Richard Hamilton 2.00 5.00
60 Michael Jordan 25.00 60.00
61 Andrei Kirilenko RC 8.00 20.00
62 Gilbert Arenas RC 8.00 20.00
63 Trenton Hassell RC 3.00 8.00
64 Tony Parker RC 12.00 30.00
65 Jamaal Tinsley RC 4.00 10.00
66 Samuel Dalembert RC 4.00 10.00
67 Gerald Wallace RC 5.00 12.00
68 Brandon Armstrong RC 3.00 8.00
69 Jeryl Sasser RC 3.00 8.00
70 Joseph Forte RC 3.00 8.00
71 Pau Gasol RC 25.00 60.00
72 Brendan Haywood RC 10.00 25.00
73 Zach Randolph RC 20.00 50.00
74 Jason Collins RC 8.00 20.00
75 Michael Bradley RC 8.00 20.00
76 Kirk Haston RC 8.00 20.00
77 Steven Hunter RC 8.00 20.00
78 Troy Murphy RC 12.00 30.00
79 Richard Jefferson RC 15.00 40.00
80 Vladimir Radmanovic RC 8.00 20.00
81 Kedrick Brown RC 8.00 20.00
82 Joe Johnson RC 20.00 50.00
83 DeSagana Diop RC 8.00 20.00
84 Shane Battier RC 15.00 40.00
85 Rodney White AU RC 8.00 20.00
86 Eddie Griffin AU RC 8.00 20.00
87 Jason Richardson AU RC 15.00 40.00
88 Eddy Curry AU RC 12.00 30.00
89 Tyson Chandler AU RC 12.00 30.00
90 Kwame Brown AU RC 8.00 20.00

2001-02 Ultimate Collection Platinum

Randomly inserted in packs, this 88-card set parallels the base Upper Deck Ultimate Collection set enhanced with platinum backdrops, and sequential numbering to 25. Card numbers 62 and 63 do not have platinum versions.

*STARS: 4X TO 10X BASE CARD HI
*ROOKIES 16/61-70: 4X TO 10X HI
*ROOKIES 71-84: 1.5X TO 4X HI
*ROOKIES 85-90: 2X TO 5X HI
60 Michael Jordan 200.00 500.00

2001-02 Ultimate Collection BuyBacks

Randomly inserted in packs at the rate of one in 16, this set features cards from some of Upper Decks's past releases enhanced with authentic player autographs and hand numbering. Each card was accompanied in the pack with a certificate of authenticity which like the card itself, contained a UDA hologram of authenticity. These holograms carried an "AAA" prefix before the rest of the serial number.

MOST UNPRICED DUE TO SCARCITY
4 Antoine Walker 98-9SPA/18 25.00 60.00
7 Antoine Walker 00-1BlaDia/26 25.00 60.00
12 Courtney Alexander 00-1SPGamF/30 10.00 25.00
35 Jason Kidd 00-1UltColJsyBrnz/31 75.00 150.00
45 Kobe Bryant 00-1BlaDiaDia/40 150.00 300.00
47 Kobe Bryant 00-1SPA/31 200.00 400.00
52 Kobe Bryant 00-1SPGameFlr/24 200.00 400.00
56 Kobe Bryant 00-1UltColJsyBrz/27 300.00 600.00
59 Kobe Bryant 00-1UltVic/15 200.00 400.00
75 Kevin Garnett 00-1SPxWM#KG1/32 100.00 200.00
81 Kevin Garnett 00-1UltColJsyBz/21 125.00 250.00
84 Kenyon Martin 00-1SPGFlrAFlr/39 40.00 100.00
86 Kenyon Martin 00-1UppDeck/97 25.00 60.00
90 Kenyon Martin 00-1UltColJsyBrz/19 75.00 150.00
108 Lamar Odom 99-0UD/37 40.00 80.00
110 Lamar Odom 99-0UDOvat/48 30.00 80.00
120 Michael Jordan 98-9SPA#7/25 600.00 1000.00
138 Michael Jordan 00-1UltColJsyB/20 700.00 1200.00
156 Wally Szczerbiak 00-1UltColJsySilv/22 25.00 60.00

2001-02 Ultimate Collection BuyBacks Unsigned

Randomly inserted in packs, this 16-card set features unsigned buyback cards from previously released Upper Deck products. Each card is sequentially numbered.

MOST UNPRICED DUE TO SCARCITY
4 Shaquille O'Neal 92-3UD#1B/38 40.00 100.00

2001-02 Ultimate Collection Jerseys

Randomly seeded in packs, this 30-card set features several different block backgrounds in blue, one containing a full color player photo, one containing a blue-scale player portrait photo, the player's initials, the set name, and a swatch of a game worn jersey. Each card is sequentially numbered to 250.

*GOLD: 1X TO 2.5X BASE HI
GOLD PRINT RUN 50 SER.#'d SETS
*SILVER: .6X TO 1.5X BASE HI
SILVER PRINT RUN 125 SER.#'d SETS
AI Allen Iverson 10.00 25.00
BR Kedrick Brown 5.00 12.00
CW Chris Webber 5.00 12.00
DM Darius Miles 3.00 8.00
EC Eddy Curry 8.00 20.00
EG Eddie Griffin 5.00 12.00
JJ Joe Johnson 12.00 30.00
JR Jason Richardson 10.00 25.00
JS John Stockton 6.00 15.00
JT Jamaal Tinsley 6.00 15.00
KB Kobe Bryant 25.00 60.00
KB2 Kobe Bryant 25.00 60.00
KE Kenyon Martin 5.00 12.00
KG Kevin Garnett 10.00 25.00
KG2 Kevin Garnett 10.00 25.00
KM Karl Malone 6.00 15.00
KW Kwame Brown 5.00 12.00
MF Michael Finley 5.00 12.00
MJ Michael Jordan 50.00 120.00
MJ2 Michael Jordan 50.00 120.00
MM Mike Miller 5.00 12.00
NO Dirk Nowitzki 8.00 20.00
PP Paul Pierce 6.00 15.00
RA Ray Allen 5.00 12.00
RJ Richard Jefferson 10.00 25.00
RW Rodney White 5.00 12.00
SF Steve Francis 5.00 12.00
TC Tyson Chandler 8.00 20.00
TM Tracy McGrady 8.00 20.00
TP Tony Parker 20.00 50.00

2001-02 Ultimate Collection Jerseys Patches

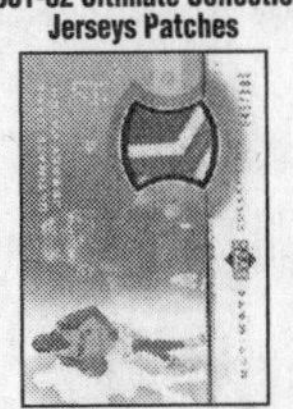

Randomly inserted in packs, this 30-card set features a horizontal card design with a full color player photo, and orange background, and an orange-scale player portrait photo. Premium jersey patch swatches appear in the lower right hand corner of the card, and each card is sequentially numbered to 100. Gold and Silver Patch versions were also issued numbered to 10 and 25 respectively.

*SILVER: .75X TO 2X HI
KB2P Kobe Bryant 100.00 250.00
KG2P Kevin Garnett 30.00 80.00
MJ2P Michael Jordan 250.00 500.00
AIP Allen Iverson 30.00 80.00
BDP Baron Davis 15.00 40.00
BRP Kedrick Brown 12.00 30.00
CWP Chris Webber 15.00 40.00
DMP Darius Miles 10.00 25.00
ECP Eddy Curry 20.00 50.00
EGP Eddie Griffin 12.00 30.00
JJP Joe Johnson 30.00 80.00
JRP Jason Richardson 25.00 60.00
JSP John Stockton 25.00 60.00
JTP Jason Terry 15.00 40.00
JTP Jamaal Tinsley 15.00 40.00
KBP Kobe Bryant 75.00 200.00
KEP Kenyon Martin 15.00 40.00
KGP Kevin Garnett 30.00 80.00
KMP Karl Malone 20.00 50.00
KWP Kwame Brown 12.00 30.00
MFP Michael Finley 15.00 40.00
MJP Michael Jordan 250.00 500.00
MMP Mike Miller 15.00 40.00
NOP Dirk Nowitzki 25.00 60.00
PPP Paul Pierce 20.00 50.00
RWP Rodney White 12.00 30.00
SFP Steve Francis 15.00 40.00
TCP Tyson Chandler 20.00 50.00
TMP Tracy McGrady 25.00 60.00
TPP Tony Parker 30.00 80.00

2001-02 Ultimate Collection Signatures

Randomly inserted in packs at the rate of one in four, this 15-card set features centered full color player action photo, a gray-scale portrait photo on the left, and an open area with white background on the right for authentic player autographs.

DMA Darius Miles 6.00 15.00
DRA Julius Erving 50.00 120.00
ECA Eddy Curry 8.00 20.00
EGA Eddie Griffin 8.00 20.00
JJA Joe Johnson 10.00 25.00
JKA Jason Kidd 20.00 40.00
JRA Jason Richardson 12.00 30.00
KBA Kobe Bryant 125.00 225.00
KGA Kevin Garnett 25.00 60.00
KWA Kwame Brown 6.00 15.00
LBA Larry Bird 75.00 150.00
MGA Magic Johnson 60.00 120.00
MJA Michael Jordan 400.00 800.00
RWA Rodney White 6.00 15.00
TCA Tyson Chandler 8.00 20.00

2001-02 Ultimate Collection Signatures Gold

Randomly inserted in packs, this 15-card set parallels the base Ultimate Collection Signatures with a background color shift to gold. Each card is sequentially numbered to the featured player's jersey number.

DMA Darius Miles/21 25.00 60.00
EGA Eddie Griffin/33 15.00 40.00
JJA Joe Johnson/31 30.00 80.00
JRA Jason Richardson/23 40.00 100.00
KGA Kevin Garnett/21 150.00 300.00
LBA Larry Bird/33 150.00 300.00
MGA Magic Johnson/32 100.00 200.00
MJA Michael Jordan/23 500.00 1000.00

2002-03 Ultimate Collection

Issued in March 2003, this 120-card set is divided up into four tiers as follows: cards 1-67 feature veteran players and are sequentially numbered to 750, cards 68-79 feature rookies and autographs and are sequentially numbered to 250, cards 80-103 feature rookies and are sequentially numbered to 250, and cards 104-120 feature rookies and are sequentially numbered to 750. Base cards have a white border along the left side and the right side contains a full-color player action photo with background to match the player's team colors and the team name along the right edge. Ultimate Collection was packaged in four pack boxes with four cards per pack and carried a suggested retail price of $100 per pack.

COMP.SET w/o SP's (67) 150.00 300.00
1 Shareef Abdur-Rahim 1.50 4.00
2 Glenn Robinson 1.50 4.00
3 Jason Terry 1.50 4.00
4 Paul Pierce 2.50 6.00
5 Antoine Walker 1.50 4.00
6 Vin Baker 1.50 4.00
7 Jalen Rose 1.50 4.00
8 Darius Miles 1.25 3.00
9 Dirk Nowitzki 3.00 8.00
10 Michael Finley 2.00 5.00
11 Steve Nash 2.50 6.00
12 Raef LaFrentz 1.25 3.00
13 Juwan Howard 1.50 4.00
14 Richard Hamilton 1.50 4.00
15 Chauncey Billups 2.00 5.00
16 Ben Wallace 2.00 5.00
17 Jason Richardson 2.00 5.00
18 Gilbert Arenas 2.00 5.00
19 Antawn Jamison 2.00 5.00
20 Steve Francis 2.00 5.00
21 Reggie Miller 2.00 5.00
22 Jamaal Tinsley 1.25 3.00
23 Jermaine O'Neal 2.00 5.00
24 Elton Brand 2.00 5.00
25 Andre Miller 1.50 4.00
26 Kobe Bryant 10.00 25.00
27 Shaquille O'Neal 5.00 12.00
28 Pau Gasol 2.50 6.00
29 Shane Battier 2.00 5.00
30 Eddie Jones 1.50 4.00
31 Brian Grant 1.25 3.00
32 Ray Allen 2.00 5.00
33 Kevin Garnett 4.00 10.00
34 Wally Szczerbiak 1.50 4.00
35 Troy Hudson 1.25 3.00
36 Jason Kidd 3.00 8.00
37 Richard Jefferson 2.00 5.00
38 Kenyon Martin 2.00 5.00
39 Baron Davis 2.00 5.00
40 Jamal Mashburn 1.50 4.00
41 David Wesley 1.25 3.00
42 P.J. Brown 1.25 3.00
43 Allan Houston 1.50 4.00
44 Latrell Sprewell 1.50 4.00
45 Kurt Thomas 1.25 3.00
46 Tracy McGrady 3.00 8.00
47 Grant Hill 2.50 6.00
48 Allen Iverson 3.00 8.00
49 Stephon Marbury 1.50 4.00
50 Shawn Marion 2.00 5.00
51 Rasheed Wallace 2.00 5.00
52 Derek Anderson 1.25 3.00
53 Bonzi Wells 1.25 3.00
54 Chris Webber 2.00 5.00
55 Mike Bibby 2.00 5.00
56 Peja Stojakovic 2.00 5.00
57 Tim Duncan 4.00 10.00
58 David Robinson 3.00 8.00
59 Tony Parker 2.50 6.00
60 Gary Payton 2.00 5.00
61 Rashard Lewis 2.00 5.00
62 Desmond Mason 1.50 4.00
63 Vince Carter 3.00 8.00
64 Morris Peterson 1.25 3.00
65 Karl Malone 2.50 6.00
66 John Stockton 2.50 6.00
67 Michael Jordan 15.00 40.00
68 Chris Wilcox AU RC 6.00 15.00
69 Drew Gooden AU RC 10.00 25.00
70 Marcus Haislip AU RC 6.00 15.00
71 Melvin Ely AU RC 6.00 15.00
72 Jared Jeffries AU RC 6.00 15.00
73 Caron Butler AU RC 10.00 25.00
74 Amare Stoudemire AU RC 50.00 120.00
75 Nene Hilario AU RC 8.00 20.00
76 DaJuan Wagner AU RC 6.00 15.00
77 Nikoloz Tskitishvili AU RC 6.00 15.00
78 Jay Williams AU RC 8.00 20.00
79 Yao Ming AU RC 60.00 120.00
80 Predrag Savovic RC 5.00 12.00
81 Igor Rakocevic RC 5.00 12.00
82 Sam Clancy RC 5.00 12.00
83 Ronald Murray RC 5.00 12.00
84 Tito Maddox RC 5.00 12.00
85 Carlos Boozer RC 10.00 25.00
86 Dan Gadzuric RC 5.00 12.00
87 Vincent Yarbrough RC 5.00 12.00
88 Robert Archibald RC 5.00 12.00
89 Roger Mason RC 5.00 12.00
90 Juaquin Hawkins RC 5.00 12.00
91 Chris Jefferies RC 5.00 12.00
92 John Salmons RC 6.00 15.00
93 Manu Ginobili RC 12.00 30.00
94 Tayshaun Prince RC 6.00 15.00
95 Casey Jacobsen RC 5.00 12.00
96 Qyntel Woods RC 5.00 12.00
97 Kareem Rush RC 5.00 12.00
98 Ryan Humphrey RC 5.00 12.00
99 Juan Dixon RC 6.00 15.00
100 Fred Jones RC 5.00 12.00
101 Jiri Welsch RC 5.00 12.00
102 Bostjan Nachbar RC 5.00 12.00
103 Marko Jaric 5.00 12.00
104 Gordan Giricek RC 3.00 8.00
105 Frank Williams RC 3.00 8.00
106 Pat Burke RC 3.00 8.00
107 Junior Harrington RC 3.00 8.00
108 Rasual Butler RC 3.00 8.00
109 Raul Lopez RC 3.00 8.00
110 Cezary Trybanski RC 3.00 8.00
111 Dan Dickau RC 3.00 8.00
112 Efthimios Rentzias RC 3.00 8.00
113 Mehmet Okur RC 3.00 8.00
114 Curtis Borchardt RC 3.00 8.00
115 J.R. Bremer RC 3.00 8.00
116 Lonny Baxter RC 3.00 8.00
117 Jamal Sampson RC 3.00 8.00
118 Tamar Slay RC 3.00 8.00
119 Jannero Pargo RC 3.00 8.00
120 Smush Parker RC 3.00 8.00

2002-03 Ultimate Collection Ultimate Parallel

Inserted in packs, this 120-card set parallels the base set enhanced with gold foil highlights. Each card is sequentially numbered to 25.

*STARS: 3X TO 8X BASE CARD HI
*RCs 68-79: 1.5X TO 4X HI
*RCs 80-103: 1.5X TO 4X HI
*RCs 104-120: 2X TO 5X HI
68 Chris Wilcox JSY AU 30.00 80.00
74 Amare Stoudemire JSY AU 300.00 600.00
75 Nene Hilario JSY AU 40.00 100.00
79 Yao Ming JSY AU 400.00 800.00

2002-03 Ultimate Collection Buybacks

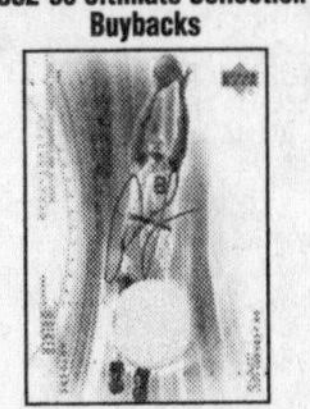

Randomly inserted in packs, this set features older upper deck issues re-inserted with player autographs. Most cards are hand numbered and the UDA authenticity hologram sticker begins with an AAA prefix for the registration number.

MOST UNPRICED DUE TO SCARCITY
17 Kobe Bryant 01-2SPAuth/38 150.00 300.00
18 Kobe Bryant 01-2SPx/32 150.00 300.00
21 Kobe Bryant 01-2UDFlightTm/24 150.00 300.00
27 Kevin Garnett 95-6SPAuth/24 75.00 150.00
32 Kevin Garnett 01-2SPAuth/23 75.00 150.00
34 Kevin Garnett 01-2SPx/46 75.00 150.00
35 Kevin Garnett 00-1SPGFAF#KG2/18 75.00 150.00
36 Kevin Garnett 01-2UDFlightTm/18 75.00 150.00
42 Michael Jordan 00-1UDMJMater#MJ1/24 500.00 800.00
47 Jason Kidd 01-2 UDLegLFloor/22 25.00 60.00
54 Kenyon Martin 00-1UD/97 15.00 40.00
70 Tony Parker 01-2UD#185/155 20.00 50.00
72 Paul Pierce 01-2UDGJPatch/20 75.00 150.00
78 Peja Stojakovic 01-2SPAuth/23 30.00 60.00
79 Peja Stojakovic 01-2SPx/17 40.00 100.00
80 Peja Stojakovic 01-2UDInspir/26 30.00 60.00
84 Antoine Walker 00-1UDHardGF/54 20.00 50.00
87 Antoine Walker 01-2UDOvSSWU/26 20.00 50.00

2002-03 Ultimate Collection Jerseys

Randomly inserted in packs, this 30-card set places a full color player action photo on the card with a swatch of game worn jersey. Each card is sequentially numbered to 250.

AI Allen Iverson 10.00 25.00
AM Andre Miller 3.00 8.00
AW Antoine Walker 3.00 8.00
BD Baron Davis 4.00 10.00
CB Caron Butler 6.00 15.00
CW Chris Webber 4.00 10.00
DG Drew Gooden 6.00 15.00
DM Darius Miles 2.50 6.00
DN Dirk Nowitzki 6.00 15.00
DW DaJuan Wagner 4.00 10.00
JK Jason Kidd 6.00 15.00
JR Jason Richardson 4.00 10.00
JW Jay Williams 5.00 12.00
KB Kobe Bryant 20.00 50.00
KG Kevin Garnett 8.00 20.00
KR Kareem Rush 4.00 10.00
MB Mike Bibby 4.00 10.00
MJ Michael Jordan 50.00 120.00
NH Nene Hilario 5.00 12.00
PG Pau Gasol 5.00 12.00
PP Paul Pierce 5.00 12.00
PS Peja Stojakovic 4.00 10.00
RJ Richard Jefferson 4.00 10.00
RL Rashard Lewis 4.00 10.00
SB Shane Battier 4.00 10.00
SF Steve Francis 4.00 10.00
SM Stephon Marbury 3.00 8.00
TM Tracy McGrady 6.00 15.00
WI Chris Wilcox 4.00 10.00
YM Yao Ming 12.00 30.00

2002-03 Ultimate Collection Jerseys Gold

Randomly inserted, this 12-card set parallels the Game Jerseys insert set enhanced with gold highlights and sequential numbering to 50.

AI Allen Iverson 20.00 50.00
BD Baron Davis 8.00 20.00
CW Chris Webber 8.00 20.00
DN Dirk Nowitzki 12.00 30.00
DW DaJuan Wagner 8.00 20.00
JK Jason Kidd 12.00 30.00
JR Jason Richardson 8.00 20.00
JW Jay Williams 10.00 25.00
KB Kobe Bryant 40.00 100.00
KG Kevin Garnett 15.00 40.00
MJ Michael Jordan 80.00 200.00
PP Paul Pierce 10.00 25.00
SF Steve Francis 8.00 20.00
TM Tracy McGrady 12.00 30.00
YM Yao Ming 25.00 60.00

2002-03 Ultimate Collection Jerseys Silver

Randomly inserted, this 12-card set parallels the Game Jerseys insert set enhanced with silver highlights and sequential numbering to 125.

AM Andre Miller 4.00 10.00
AW Antoine Walker 4.00 10.00
CB Caron Butler 8.00 20.00
DG Drew Gooden 8.00 20.00
DM Darius Miles 3.00 8.00
KR Kareem Rush 5.00 12.00
MB Mike Bibby 5.00 12.00
NH Nene Hilario 6.00 15.00
PG Pau Gasol 6.00 15.00
PS Peja Stojakovic 5.00 12.00
RJ Richard Jefferson 5.00 12.00
RL Rashard Lewis 5.00 12.00
SB Shane Battier 5.00 12.00
SM Stephon Marbury 4.00 10.00
WI Chris Wilcox 5.00 12.00

2002-03 Ultimate Collection Jerseys Dual

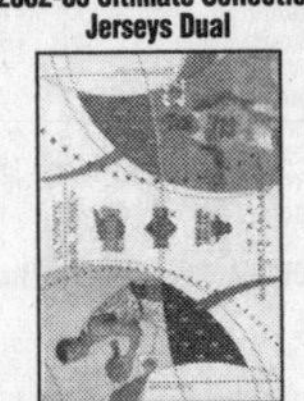

Inserted in packs, this 12-card set places two players and two swatches of game worn jersey on each card. Cards are sequentially numbered to 125. Gold and Siiver Parallel versions were also inserted and are sequentially numbered to 10 and 25 respectively.

*SILVER: .75X TO 2X BASE HI
AISF Allen Iverson / Steve Francis 12.50 30.00
AMEB Andre Miller / Elton Brand 10.00 25.00
CWMB Chris Webber / Mike Bibby 10.00 25.00
DNSN Dirk Nowitzki / Steve Nash 10.00 25.00
JKBD Jason Kidd / Baron Davis 10.00 25.00
KBJW Kobe Bryant / Jay Williams 15.00 40.00
MJKB Michael Jordan / Kobe Bryant 75.00 200.00
PPAW Paul Pierce / Antoine Walker 10.00 25.00
SBPG Shane Battier / Pau Gasol 10.00 25.00
SMSM Stephon Marbury / Shawn Marion 10.00 25.00
TMKG Tracy McGrady / Kevin Garnett 12.50 30.00
YMJW Yao Ming / Jay Williams 20.00 50.00

2002-03 Ultimate Collection Jerseys Patches

Inserted in packs, this 30-card set places a player and a patch from a game worn jersey on each card. Cards are sequentially numbered to 50. Gold and Silver parallels were also inserted in packs and are sequentially numbered to 10 and 25 respectively.

ASP Amare Stoudemire 60.00 120.00
AWP Antoine Walker 10.00 25.00
BZP Carlos Boozer 25.00 60.00
CAP Casey Jacobsen 12.00 30.00
CBP Caron Butler 20.00 50.00
CJP Chris Jefferies 12.00 30.00
CWP Chris Wilcox 12.00 30.00
DGP Drew Gooden 20.00 50.00
FJP Fred Jones 12.00 30.00
GAP Dan Gadzuric 12.00 30.00
JJP Jared Jeffries 12.00 30.00
JRP Jason Richardson 12.00 30.00
JSP John Salmons 15.00 40.00
JWP Jay Williams 15.00 40.00
KBP Kobe Bryant 100.00 250.00
KMP Karl Malone 15.00 40.00
KRP Kareem Rush 12.00 30.00
MEP Melvin Ely 12.00 30.00
MHP Marcus Haislip 12.00 30.00
NHP Nene Hilario 15.00 40.00
NTP Nikoloz Tskitishvili 12.00 30.00
PPP Paul Pierce 15.00 40.00
QWP Qyntel Woods 12.00 30.00
RHP Ryan Humphrey 12.00 30.00
RLP Rashard Lewis 12.00 30.00
RMP Roger Mason 12.00 30.00
SHP Shareef Abdur-Rahim 10.00 25.00
TPP Tayshaun Prince 15.00 40.00
VYP Vincent Yarbrough 12.00 30.00
YMP Yao Ming 60.00 120.00

2002-03 Ultimate Collection Jerseys Patches Dual

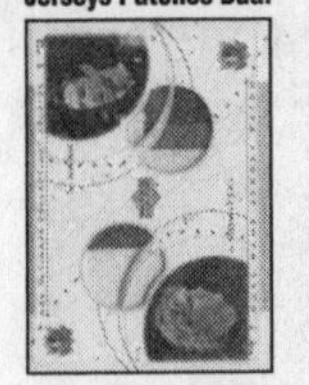

Inserted randomly, this 12-card set pairs up players with premium swatches of each of their jerseys (one player on the left and one on the right). Cards are sequentially numbered to 25. A Platinum version was also inserted where cards are sequentially numbered to five.

BDJMP Baron Davis / Jamal Mashburn 25.00 60.00
CWMBP Chris Webber / Mike Bibby 50.00 120.00
DMDWP Darius Miles / DaJuan Wagner 25.00 60.00
DNSNP Dirk Nowitzki / Steve Nash 60.00 150.00
KBAIP Kobe Bryant / Allen Iverson 150.00 300.00
KBJWP Kobe Bryant / Jay Williams 125.00 250.00
MJKBP Michael Jordan / Kobe Bryant 400.00 700.00
PGDGP Pau Gasol / Drew Gooden 30.00 80.00
SFJDP Steve Francis / Juan Dixon 25.00 60.00
SMSMP Stephon Marbury / Shawn Marion 40.00 100.00
TMJKP Tracy McGrady / Jason Kidd 60.00 150.00
YMJWP Yao Ming / Jay Williams 150.00 300.00

2002-03 Ultimate Collection Signatures

Randomly seeded in packs, this 15-card set places a small circular portrait photo of a player towards the top and leaves the bottom of the card open for authentic player autographs.

ASS Amare Stoudemire 30.00 80.00
BRS Bill Russell 100.00 200.00
CBS Caron Butler 10.00 25.00
DRS Julius Erving 60.00 120.00
DWS DaJuan Wagner 8.00 20.00
JKS Jason Kidd 15.00 40.00
JWS Jay Williams 10.00 25.00
KAS Kareem Abdul-Jabbar 50.00 120.00
KBS Kobe Bryant 100.00 200.00
KGS Kevin Garnett 30.00 80.00
KRS Kareem Rush 8.00 20.00
LBS Larry Bird 75.00 150.00

MJS Michael Jordan 300.00 600.00
NTS Nikoloz Tskitishvili 8.00 20.00
YMS Yao Ming 40.00 80.00

2002-03 Ultimate Collection Signatures Gold

Randomly inserted in packs, this 15-card set parallels the base Signatures insert set enhanced with gold highlights and sequential numbering to the featured player's jersey number.
MOST UNPRICED DUE TO SCARCITY

ASS Amare Stoudemire/32 125.00 250.00
JWS Jay Williams/22 30.00 80.00
KAS Kareem Abdul-Jabbar/33 150.00 300.00
KGS Kevin Garnett/21 75.00 150.00
KRS Kareem Rush/21 20.00 50.00
LBS Larry Bird/33 125.00 300.00
MJS Michael Jordan/23 500.00 800.00
NTS Nikoloz Tskitishvili/22 20.00 50.00

2003-04 Ultimate Collection

Released in April 2004, Ultimate Collection is a 190-card set comprised of 116 base cards of mixed veterans and retired players sequentially numbered to 750, 10 base rookie cards (numbers 117-126) sequentially numbered to 750, 37 autographed rookie cards (numbers 127-164) sequentially numbered to 250, and 25 Ultimate Stars cards (numbers 165-190) sequentially numbered to 500. A Limited Parallel set was also inserted into packs and these cards are sequentialy numbered to 25; and a Limited Black set where cards are serially numbered one of one. Ultimate Collection was packaged in four-pack boxes where packs contained four cards and carried a suggested retail price of $100.
UNPRICED LIMITED BLACK PRINT RUN ONE SET

1 Dominique Wilkins 2.50 6.00
2 Jason Terry 1.50 4.00
3 Dion Glover 1.25 3.00
4 Stephen Jackson 1.50 4.00
5 Bill Russell 3.00 8.00
6 Paul Pierce 2.50 6.00
7 Larry Bird 6.00 15.00
8 Ricky Davis 1.50 4.00
9 Antonio Davis 1.25 3.00
10 Michael Jordan 15.00 40.00
11 Scottie Pippen 3.00 8.00
12 Tyson Chandler 1.50 4.00
13 Jeff McInnis 1.25 3.00
14 Dajuan Wagner 1.25 3.00
15 Carlos Boozer 2.00 5.00
16 Zydrunas Ilgauskas 1.50 4.00
17 Dirk Nowitzki 3.00 8.00
18 Steve Nash 2.50 6.00
19 Antoine Walker 2.00 5.00
20 Michael Finley 2.00 5.00
21 Andre Miller 1.50 4.00
22 Nene 1.50 4.00
23 Nikoloz Tskitishvili 1.25 3.00
24 Marcus Camby 1.50 4.00
25 Richard Hamilton 1.50 4.00
26 Ben Wallace 2.00 5.00
27 Chauncey Billups 2.00 5.00
28 Rasheed Wallace 2.00 5.00
29 Jason Richardson 2.00 5.00
30 Nick Van Exel 1.50 4.00
31 Speedy Claxton 1.25 3.00
32 Mike Dunleavy 1.50 4.00
33 Yao Ming 4.00 10.00
34 Steve Francis 2.00 5.00
35 Cuttino Mobley 1.50 4.00
36 Jim Jackson 1.25 3.00
37 Reggie Miller 2.00 5.00
38 Jermaine O'Neal 2.00 5.00
39 Ron Artest 2.00 5.00
40 Al Harrington 1.50 4.00
41 Elton Brand 2.00 5.00
42 Corey Maggette 1.50 4.00
43 Quentin Richardson 1.50 4.00
44 Chris Wilcox 1.25 3.00
45 Kobe Bryant 10.00 25.00
46 Shaquille O'Neal 5.00 12.00
47 Gary Payton 2.00 5.00
48 Karl Malone 2.50 6.00
49 Pau Gasol 2.00 5.00
50 Bonzi Wells 1.25 3.00
51 Mike Miller 2.00 5.00
52 Jason Williams 1.50 4.00
53 Caron Butler 2.00 5.00
54 Lamar Odom 2.00 5.00
55 Eddie Jones 1.50 4.00
56 Brian Grant 1.25 3.00
57 Desmond Mason 1.50 4.00
58 Oscar Robertson 2.00 5.00
59 Michael Redd 2.00 5.00
60 Toni Kukoc 2.00 5.00
61 Latrell Sprewell 1.50 4.00
62 Kevin Garnett 4.00 10.00
63 Wally Szczerbiak 1.50 4.00
64 Sam Cassell 1.50 4.00
65 Kenyon Martin 2.00 5.00
66 Jason Kidd 3.00 8.00
67 Richard Jefferson 2.00 5.00
68 Alonzo Mourning 2.50 6.00
69 Jamal Mashburn 1.50 4.00
70 David Wesley 1.25 3.00
71 Baron Davis 2.00 5.00
72 Jamaal Magloire 1.25 3.00
73 Allan Houston 1.50 4.00
74 Patrick Ewing 2.50 6.00
75 Stephon Marbury 1.50 4.00
76 Dikembe Mutombo 2.00 5.00
77 Tracy McGrady 2.50 6.00
78 Drew Gooden 1.50 4.00
79 Juwan Howard 1.50 4.00
80 DeShawn Stevenson 1.25 3.00
81 Julius Erving 4.00 10.00
82 Allen Iverson 3.00 8.00
83 Glenn Robinson 1.50 4.00
84 Eric Snow 1.25 3.00
85 Amare Stoudemire 3.00 8.00
86 Shawn Marion 2.00 5.00
87 Antonio McDyess 1.50 4.00
88 Joe Johnson 2.00 5.00
89 Shareef Abdur-Rahim 1.50 4.00
90 Derek Anderson 1.25 3.00
91 Damon Stoudamire 1.50 4.00
92 Zach Randolph 2.00 5.00
93 Mike Bibby 2.00 5.00
94 Chris Webber 2.00 5.00
95 Peja Stojakovic 2.00 5.00
96 Bobby Jackson 1.25 3.00
97 Manu Ginobili 2.50 6.00
98 Tim Duncan 3.00 8.00
99 Tony Parker 2.00 5.00
100 Radoslav Nesterovic 1.25 3.00
101 Rashard Lewis 2.00 5.00
102 Ray Allen 2.00 5.00
103 Vladimir Radmanovic 1.25 3.00
104 Brent Barry 1.25 3.00
105 Vince Carter 3.00 8.00
106 Morris Peterson 1.25 3.00
107 Jalen Rose 1.50 4.00
108 Donyell Marshall 1.25 3.00
109 John Stockton 2.50 6.00
110 Andrei Kirilenko 2.00 5.00
111 Matt Harpring 1.50 4.00
112 Carlos Arroyo 1.50 4.00
113 Gilbert Arenas 2.00 5.00
114 Jerry Stackhouse 1.50 4.00
115 Kwame Brown 1.25 3.00
116 Larry Hughes 1.50 4.00
117 T.J. Ford RC 5.00 12.00
118 Kirk Hinrich RC 5.00 12.00
119 Nick Collison RC 4.00 10.00
120 James Jones RC 4.00 10.00
121 Travis Hansen RC 4.00 10.00
122 Alex Garcia RC 4.00 10.00
123 Theron Smith RC 4.00 10.00
124 Francisco Elson RC 4.00 10.00
125 Jon Stefansson RC 4.00 10.00
126 Ronald Dupree RC 4.00 10.00
127 LeBron James AU RC 800.00 1100.00
128 Darko Milicic AU RC 6.00 15.00
129 Carmelo Anthony AU RC 150.00 300.00
130 Chris Bosh AU RC 60.00 150.00
131 Dwyane Wade AU RC 200.00 400.00
132 Chris Kaman AU RC 8.00 20.00
133 Jarvis Hayes AU RC 6.00 15.00
134 Mickael Pietrus AU RC 6.00 15.00
135 Dahntay Jones AU RC 6.00 15.00
136 Marcus Banks AU RC 6.00 15.00
137 Luke Ridnour AU RC 8.00 20.00
138 Reece Gaines AU RC 6.00 15.00
139 Troy Bell AU RC 6.00 15.00
140 Mike Sweetney AU RC 6.00 15.00
141 David West AU RC 8.00 20.00
142 Aleksandar Pavlovic AU RC 6.00 15.00
143 Steve Blake AU RC 8.00 20.00
144 Boris Diaw AU RC 8.00 20.00
145 Zoran Planinic AU RC 6.00 15.00
146 Travis Outlaw AU RC 8.00 20.00
147 Brian Cook AU RC 6.00 15.00
148 Jerome Beasley AU RC 6.00 15.00
149 Ndudi Ebi AU RC 6.00 15.00
150 Kendrick Perkins AU RC 10.00 25.00
151 Leandro Barbosa AU RC 8.00 20.00
152 Josh Howard AU RC 6.00 15.00
153 Maciej Lampe AU RC 6.00 15.00
154 Jason Kapono AU RC 6.00 15.00
155 Luke Walton AU RC 6.00 15.00
156 Kyle Korver AU RC 8.00 20.00
157 Zarko Cabarkapa AU RC 6.00 15.00
158 Zaur Pachulia AU RC 6.00 15.00
159 Maurice Williams AU RC 10.00 25.00
160 Brandon Hunter AU RC 6.00 15.00
161 Keith Bogans AU RC 6.00 15.00
162 Marquis Daniels AU RC 6.00 15.00
163 Willie Green AU RC 6.00 15.00
164 Udonis Haslem AU RC 8.00 20.00
165 Larry Bird US 10.00 25.00
166 Bill Russell US 5.00 12.00
167 Michael Jordan US 25.00 60.00
168 Steve Nash US 4.00 10.00
169 Michael Finley US 3.00 8.00
170 Ben Wallace US 3.00 8.00
171 Jason Richardson US 3.00 8.00
172 Yao Ming US 6.00 15.00
173 Reggie Miller US 3.00 8.00
174 Kobe Bryant US 15.00 40.00
175 Shaquille O'Neal US 8.00 20.00
176 Gary Payton US 3.00 8.00
177 Magic Johnson US 10.00 25.00
178 Pau Gasol US 3.00 8.00
179 Lamar Odom US 3.00 8.00
180 Oscar Robertson US 3.00 8.00
181 Kenyon Martin US 3.00 8.00
182 Baron Davis US 3.00 8.00
183 Julius Erving US 6.00 15.00
184 Amare Stoudemire US 5.00 12.00
185 Mike Bibby US 3.00 8.00
186 Tony Parker US 3.00 8.00
187 Rashard Lewis US 3.00 8.00
188 Vince Carter US 5.00 12.00
189 Andrei Kirilenko US 3.00 8.00
190 Gilbert Arenas US 3.00 8.00

2003-04 Ultimate Collection Limited

Randomly inserted in packs, this 190-card set parallels the base Ultimate Collection set enhanced with sequential numbering to 25. Cards 127-158 contain both a jersey and an autograph.
*SINGLES 1-116: 2X TO 5X BASE HI
*RCs 117-126: .75X TO 2X BASE HI
*AUTO RCs: 2X TO 5X BASE HI
*US 165-190: 1.25X TO 3X BASE HI

11 Scottie Pippen 25.00 60.00
127 LeBron James JSY AU 2000.00 3000.00
129 Carmelo Anthony JSY AU 500.00 1000.00

2003-04 Ultimate Collection BuyBacks

Randomly seeded, this set is made up of cards from previous year's products that are signed and numbered by the featured player. Each card comes with a certificate of authenticity and UD's Authenticated Hologram. The serial number on the holograms for this set begins with an AAA prefix
SOME UNPRICED DUE TO SCARCITY

5 Shane Battier 12.50 30.00
02-3UDSwtSht/33
6 Mike Bibby 20.00 50.00
02-3SPGameUse/19
9 Mike Bibby 20.00 50.00
02-3MVPMatShirt/17
10 Mike Bibby 20.00 50.00
02-3UDSwtSht/35
12 Chauncey Billups 12.50 30.00
02-3UDSwtSht/27
21 Kobe Bryant 125.00 250.00
02-3UDSwtShtGlass/15
23 Patrick Ewing 150.00 300.00
01-2UD15000Jsy/32
25 Kevin Garnett 50.00 120.00
02-3SPxWinMat/33
29 Kevin Garnett 50.00 120.00
02-3UDSwtSht/22
30 Kevin Garnett 50.00 120.00
02-3UDSwtShtJsy/21
33 Richard Hamilton 15.00 40.00
02-3SPxWinMat/32
34 Richard Hamilton 20.00 50.00
02-3UDSeaPrmJsy/19
35 Richard Hamilton 15.00 40.00
02-3UDSwtSht/39
36 Richard Hamilton 20.00 50.00
02-3UDSwtShtJsy/18
37 Antawn Jamison 15.00 40.00
02-3UDAll-AccJsy/18
38 Antawn Jamison 12.50 30.00
02-3UDSwtSht/28
39 Antawn Jamison 15.00 40.00
02-3UDSwtShtJsy/16
40 Richard Jefferson 15.00 40.00
02-3SPxWinMat/17
41 Richard Jefferson 12.50 30.00
02-3UDSwtSht/31
43 Michael Jordan 600.00 1000.00
03-4UDSEDieCut/24
44 Michael Jordan 400.00 800.00
03-4UDHardcourt/21
45 Jason Kidd 30.00 80.00
02-3SPGU#60 SP/16
46 Jason Kidd 30.00 80.00
SPxWinMat/16
48 Jason Kidd 20.00 50.00
02-3UDSwtSht/40
49 Jason Kidd 30.00 80.00
02-3UDSwtShtGlass/15
50 Corey Maggette 12.50 30.00
02-3UDAll-AccJsy/16
51 Shawn Marion 20.00 50.00
02-3SPx/31
52 Shawn Marion 20.00 50.00
02-3SPxWinMat/20
55 Shawn Marion 15.00 40.00
02-3UDSweetShot/36
56 Shawn Marion 20.00 50.00
02-3UDSwtShtSwSw/20
57 Antonio McDyess 20.00 50.00
02-3SPxWinMat/19
58 Antonio McDyess 20.00 50.00
02-3MVPMatWarm/15
62 Tracy McGrady 60.00 150.00
02-3UDGenRTJsy/19
63 Tracy McGrady 60.00 150.00
02-3SwtSht/26
64 Tracy McGrady 60.00 150.00
02-3SwtShtSwSw/20
65 Darius Miles 15.00 40.00
02-3SPGU/21
66 Darius Miles 15.00 40.00
02-3UDAirAppJsy/17
67 Darius Miles 12.50 30.00
02-3UDSwtSht/34
68 Darius Miles 15.00 40.00
02-3UDSwtShtSwSw/19
70 Andre Miller 12.50 30.00
02-3SPGU/19
71 Andre Miller 12.50 30.00
02-3UDSwtSht/38
72 Andre Miller 12.50 30.00
02-3UDSwtShtSSw/20
75 Cuttino Mobley 12.50 30.00
02-3UDSwtSht/30
77 Lamar Odom 15.00 40.00
02-3MVPMatComb/17
78 Lamar Odom 15.00 40.00
02-3UDAirAppJsy/19
79 Lamar Odom 15.00 40.00
02-3UDSwtShot/20
80 Lamar Odom 12.50 30.00
02-3UDSwtShtSSw/32
81 Tony Parker 40.00 100.00
02-3SPGU/18
82 Tony Parker 40.00 100.00
02-3UDAll-SAShort/19
84 Tony Parker 40.00 100.00
02-3UDSwtSht/22
85 Gary Payton 50.00 120.00
02-3SPGUA-Sapp/19
86 Paul Pierce 40.00 80.00
02-3SPxWinMat/27
90 Paul Pierce 40.00 80.00
02-3UDSwtSht/37
91 Paul Pierce 40.00 80.00
02-3UDSwtShtGlass/16
92 David Robinson 100.00 200.00
02-3SPxWinMat/16
93 David Robinson 75.00 150.00
02-3UDSwtSht/24
94 Jalen Rose 20.00 50.00
02-3UDSwtSht/20
95 Jerry Stackhouse 20.00 50.00
02-3UDAll-AuthJsy/16
96 Jerry Stackhouse 20.00 50.00
02-3UDGmJsy2/14
97 Jerry Stackhouse 15.00 40.00
02-3UDSwtSht/37
100 John Stockton 125.00 250.00
02-3UDSwtSht/32
102 Peja Stojakovic 25.00 60.00
02-3UDAll-StAuth/16
103 Peja Stojakovic 20.00 50.00
02-3UDInspirations/26
104 Peja Stojakovic 20.00 50.00
02-3UDSwtSht/37

2003-04 Ultimate Collection Jerseys

Randomly inserted, this 42-card set features a black and white photo of the player along with a swatch (divided into two swatches by design) on the right side of the card. Each card is sequentially numbered to 200. Jerseys Dual and Jerseys Triple parallels of this set were also inserted. Dual jerseys are sequentially numbered to 100, while triple jerseys are sequentially numbered to 25.
*DUAL: .6X TO 1.5X BASE JSY HI
*TRIPLE: 1.25X TO 3X BASE HI

AI Allen Iverson 6.00 15.00
AS Amare Stoudemire 6.00 15.00
AW Antoine Walker 4.00 10.00
BR Bill Russell 15.00 40.00
BW Ben Wallace 4.00 10.00
CA Carmelo Anthony 10.00 25.00
CB Caron Butler 4.00 10.00
CH Chris Bosh 8.00 20.00
CW Chris Webber 4.00 10.00
DM Darko Milicic 4.00 10.00
DN Dirk Nowitzki 6.00 15.00
DR David Robinson 6.00 15.00
DW Dajuan Wagner 2.50 6.00
DY Dwyane Wade 15.00 40.00
EB Elton Brand 4.00 10.00
EG Manu Ginobili 5.00 12.00
GP Gary Payton 4.00 10.00
JE Julius Erving 8.00 20.00
JK Jason Kidd 6.00 15.00
JO Jermaine O'Neal 4.00 10.00
JR Jason Richardson 4.00 10.00
JS John Stockton 5.00 12.00
KB Kobe Bryant 25.00 60.00
KG Kevin Garnett 8.00 20.00
KM Karl Malone 5.00 12.00
LB Larry Bird 12.00 30.00
LJ LeBron James 75.00 150.00
MA Magic Johnson 10.00 25.00
MJ Michael Jordan 40.00 100.00
OR Oscar Robertson 8.00 20.00
PE Patrick Ewing 8.00 20.00
PP Paul Pierce 5.00 12.00
RA Ray Allen 4.00 10.00
RJ Richard Jefferson 4.00 10.00
SF Steve Francis 4.00 10.00
SH Shawn Marion 4.00 10.00
SM Stephon Marbury 3.00 8.00
SN Steve Nash 5.00 12.00
SO Shaquille O'Neal 10.00 25.00
TD Tim Duncan 6.00 15.00
TM Tracy McGrady 5.00 12.00
YM Yao Ming 8.00 20.00

2003-04 Ultimate Collection Patches

Randomly seeded, this 72-card set parallels the design of the Jerseys set enhanced with premium patch swatches. Each card is squentially numbered to 100. Patches Dual and Patches Triple versions were also inserted and are numbered to 50 and 15 respectively.

AH Allan Houston 6.00 15.00
AI Allen Iverson 12.00 30.00
AJ Antawn Jamison 8.00 20.00
AK Andrei Kirilenko 8.00 20.00
AL Alonzo Mourning 15.00 40.00
AM Andre Miller 6.00 15.00
AP Aleksandar Pavlovic 8.00 20.00
AS Amare Stoudemire 12.00 30.00
BD Baron Davis 8.00 20.00
BG Keith Bogans 8.00 20.00
BO Boris Diaw 10.00 25.00
CA Carmelo Anthony 40.00 80.00
CH Chris Bosh 15.00 40.00
CK Chris Kaman 10.00 25.00
CM Corey Maggette 6.00 15.00
CW Chris Webber 8.00 20.00
DA Darius Miles 5.00 12.00
DE Desmond Mason 6.00 15.00
DJ Dahntay Jones 8.00 20.00
DM Darko Milicic 8.00 20.00
DN Dirk Nowitzki 12.00 30.00
DR David Robinson 12.00 30.00
DW David West 10.00 25.00
DY Dwyane Wade 50.00 120.00
EB Elton Brand 8.00 20.00
GA Gilbert Arenas 8.00 20.00
GH Grant Hill 10.00 25.00
GP Gary Payton 8.00 20.00
JA Jalen Rose 6.00 15.00
JD Josh Howard 8.00 20.00
JE Jerry Stackhouse 6.00 15.00
JH Jarvis Hayes 8.00 20.00
JK Jason Kidd 12.00 30.00
JM Jamal Mashburn 6.00 15.00
JO Jermaine O'Neal 8.00 20.00
JR Jason Richardson 8.00 20.00
JS John Stockton 10.00 25.00
JT Jason Terry 6.00 15.00
KE Kenyon Martin 8.00 20.00
KG Kevin Garnett 15.00 40.00
KM Karl Malone 12.00 30.00
LJ LeBron James 125.00 300.00
LO Lamar Odom 8.00 20.00
LR Luke Ridnour 10.00 25.00
LS Latrell Sprewell 8.00 20.00
MB Mike Bibby 8.00 20.00
MF Michael Finley 8.00 20.00
MO Morris Peterson 5.00 12.00
MP Mickael Pietrus 8.00 20.00
MR Marcus Banks 8.00 20.00
MS Mike Sweetney 8.00 20.00
PG Pau Gasol 8.00 20.00
PP Paul Pierce 10.00 25.00
PS Peja Stojakovic 8.00 20.00
QR Quentin Richardson 6.00 15.00
RA Ray Allen 12.50 30.00
RG Reece Gaines 8.00 20.00
RJ Richard Jefferson 8.00 20.00
RM Reggie Miller 12.50 30.00
SA Shareef Abdur-Rahim 6.00 15.00
SB Steve Blake 10.00 25.00
SF Steve Francis 8.00 20.00
SH Shawn Marion 8.00 20.00
SM Stephon Marbury 6.00 15.00
SN Steve Nash 10.00 25.00
SO Shaquille O'Neal 20.00 50.00
SP Scottie Pippen 40.00 100.00
TB Troy Bell 8.00 20.00
TD Tim Duncan 12.00 30.00
TM Tracy McGrady 10.00 25.00
TP Tony Parker 8.00 20.00
YM Yao Ming 15.00 40.00

2003-04 Ultimate Collection Patches Dual

Randomly inserted, this 42-card set is a partial parallel of the the Patches insert set with two swatches and each card is sequentially numbered to 50.
*DUAL: .75X TO 2X BASE PATCH HI

AW Antoine Walker 15.00 40.00
JS John Stockton 25.00 60.00
KB Kobe Bryant 100.00 200.00
MJ Michael Jordan 300.00 600.00
PE Patrick Ewing 30.00 80.00

2003-04 Ultimate Collection Patches Triple

Randomly inserted, this 42-card set is a partial parallel the the Patches insert set with three swatches and each card is sequentially numbered to 15.

AI3 Allen Iverson 125.00 250.00
CA3 Carmelo Anthony 150.00 300.00
DM3 Darko Milicic 30.00 80.00
DU3 Dajuan Wagner 20.00 50.00
DY3 Dwyane Wade 200.00 400.00
KB3 Kobe Bryant 150.00 300.00
LB3 Larry Bird 100.00 250.00
LJ3 LeBron James 300.00 800.00
MJ3 Michael Jordan 400.00 700.00
TD3 Tim Duncan 50.00 125.00

2003-04 Ultimate Collection Signatures

Inserted in packs at the overall rate of one in four for autographs, this 21-card set places a full color player portrait style photo in the upper left hand corner of the card and an autograph in the lower right.

AS Amare Stoudemire 12.50 30.00
CA Carmelo Anthony 40.00 80.00
DM Darko Milicic 6.00 15.00
DY Dwyane Wade 60.00 120.00
GP Gary Payton 15.00 40.00
JE Julius Erving 30.00 80.00
JH Jarvis Hayes 6.00 15.00
JK Jason Kidd 15.00 40.00
JS John Stockton 60.00 150.00
KB Kobe Bryant 100.00 200.00
KG Kevin Garnett SP 50.00 120.00
LB Larry Bird SP 50.00 120.00
LJ LeBron James 350.00 600.00
MA Magic Johnson SP 50.00 120.00
MJ Michael Jordan 400.00 800.00
MS Mike Sweetney 6.00 15.00
PE Patrick Ewing 100.00 225.00
RM Reggie Miller 40.00 100.00
RO Dennis Rodman 50.00 120.00
TM Tracy McGrady 12.50 30.00
YM Yao Ming 20.00 50.00

2003-04 Ultimate Collection Signatures Gold

Randomly inserted, this 21-card set parallels the base signatures set enhanced with sequential numbering to the featured player's jersey number. A Logos signature set was also produced with an autograph, the NBA logo swatch from a jersey and serial one of one numbering.
SOME NOT PRICED DUE TO SCARCITY
UNPRICED LOGOS SER.#'d TO ONE

AS Amare Stoudemire/32 30.00 80.00
CA Carmelo Anthony/15 150.00 300.00
DM Darko Milicic/31 20.00 50.00
GP Gary Payton/20 30.00 80.00
JH Jarvis Hayes/24 15.00 40.00
KG Kevin Garnett/21 75.00 150.00
LB Larry Bird/33 150.00 300.00
LJ LeBron James/23 700.00 1200.00
MA Magic Johnson/32 100.00 200.00
MJ Michael Jordan/23 600.00 1000.00
MS Mike Sweetney/50 15.00 40.00
PE Patrick Ewing/33 150.00 300.00
RM Reggie Miller/31 125.00 250.00
RO Dennis Rodman/91 60.00 150.00

2004-05 Ultimate Collection

Released in June 2005, Ultimate Collection boasts a 168-card set divided up to where cards 1-116 feature veteran players serially numbered to 750, cards 117-126 feature rookies serially numbered to 750 and cards 127-168 feature autographed rookies serially numbered to 250. Ultimate Collection was packaged in four-pack boxes that contained four cards each that carried a SRP of $100.
UNPRICED SPECTRUM PRINT RUN ONE SET

1 Tyronn Lue 1.00 2.50
2 Tony Delk 1.00 2.50
3 Al Harrington 1.25 3.00
4 Paul Pierce 2.00 5.00
5 Antoine Walker 1.50 4.00
6 Bill Russell 2.50 6.00
7 Larry Bird 5.00 12.00
8 Gerald Wallace 1.50 4.00
9 Jason Kapono 1.00 2.50
10 Primoz Brezec 1.00 2.50
11 Kirk Hinrich 1.50 4.00
12 Eddy Curry 1.25 3.00
13 Tyson Chandler 1.25 3.00
14 Michael Jordan 12.00 30.00
15 LeBron James 10.00 25.00
16 Drew Gooden 1.25 3.00
17 Jeff McInnis 1.00 2.50
18 Zydrunas Ilgauskas 1.25 3.00
19 Dirk Nowitzki 2.50 6.00
20 Michael Finley 1.50 4.00
21 Josh Howard 1.50 4.00
22 Marquis Daniels 1.00 2.50
23 Carmelo Anthony 3.00 8.00
24 Kenyon Martin 1.50 4.00
25 Andre Miller 1.25 3.00
26 Nene 1.25 3.00
27 Ben Wallace 1.50 4.00
28 Richard Hamilton 1.25 3.00
29 Isiah Thomas 1.50 4.00
30 Chauncey Billups 1.50 4.00
31 Jason Richardson 1.50 4.00
32 Baron Davis 1.50 4.00
33 Derek Fisher 1.25 3.00
34 Tracy McGrady 2.00 5.00
35 Yao Ming 3.00 8.00
36 Hakeem Olajuwon 2.00 5.00
37 Jermaine O'Neal 1.50 4.00
38 Reggie Miller 1.50 4.00
39 Ron Artest 1.50 4.00
40 Stephen Jackson 1.25 3.00
41 Elton Brand 1.50 4.00
42 Chris Kaman 1.50 4.00
43 Corey Maggette 1.25 3.00
44 Bobby Simmons 1.00 2.50
45 Kobe Bryant 8.00 20.00
46 Magic Johnson 4.00 10.00
47 Wilt Chamberlain 3.00 8.00
48 Lamar Odom 1.50 4.00
49 Pau Gasol 1.50 4.00
50 Bonzi Wells 1.00 2.50
51 Jason Williams 1.25 3.00
52 Mike Miller 1.50 4.00
53 Shaquille O'Neal 4.00 10.00
54 Dwyane Wade 5.00 12.00
55 Eddie Jones 1.25 3.00
56 Udonis Haslem 1.25 3.00
57 Oscar Robertson 1.50 4.00
58 Michael Redd 1.50 4.00
59 Desmond Mason 1.25 3.00
60 T.J. Ford 1.25 3.00
61 Kevin Garnett 3.00 8.00
62 Latrell Sprewell 1.25 3.00
63 Sam Cassell 1.25 3.00
64 Michael Olowokandi 1.00 2.50
65 Jason Kidd 2.50 6.00
66 Richard Jefferson 1.50 4.00
67 Vince Carter 2.50 6.00
68 Ron Mercer 1.00 2.50
69 Dan Dickau 1.00 2.50
70 Jamaal Magloire 1.00 2.50
71 P.J. Brown 1.00 2.50
72 Lee Nailon 1.00 2.50
73 Stephon Marbury 1.25 3.00
74 Allan Houston 1.25 3.00
75 Jamal Crawford 1.25 3.00
76 Bernard King 1.50 4.00
77 Steve Francis 1.50 4.00
78 Doug Christie 1.00 2.50
79 Grant Hill 2.00 5.00
80 Hedo Turkoglu 1.50 4.00
81 Allen Iverson 2.50 6.00
82 Julius Erving 3.00 8.00
83 Chris Webber 1.50 4.00
84 Kyle Korver 1.25 3.00
85 Amare Stoudemire 2.00 5.00
86 Steve Nash 2.00 5.00
87 Shawn Marion 1.50 4.00
88 Quentin Richardson 1.25 3.00
89 Shareef Abdur-Rahim 1.25 3.00
90 Darius Miles 1.00 2.50
91 Zach Randolph 1.25 3.00
92 Damon Stoudamire 1.25 3.00
93 Peja Stojakovic 1.50 4.00
94 Mike Bibby 1.50 4.00
95 Cuttino Mobley 1.25 3.00
96 Brad Miller 1.50 4.00
97 Tim Duncan 2.50 6.00
98 Manu Ginobili 2.00 5.00
99 Tony Parker 1.50 4.00
100 David Robinson 2.50 6.00
101 Ray Allen 1.50 4.00
102 Rashard Lewis 1.50 4.00
103 Ronald Murray 1.00 2.50
104 Luke Ridnour 1.25 3.00
105 Rafer Alston 1.00 2.50
106 Jalen Rose 1.25 3.00
107 Chris Bosh 1.50 4.00
108 Morris Peterson 1.00 2.50
109 Andrei Kirilenko 1.25 3.00
110 Carlos Boozer 1.50 4.00
111 John Stockton 2.50 6.00
112 Matt Harpring 1.25 3.00
113 Gilbert Arenas 1.50 4.00
114 Antawn Jamison 1.50 4.00
115 Jarvis Hayes 1.00 2.50
116 Larry Hughes 1.25 3.00
117 D.J. Mbenga RC 3.00 8.00
118 Damien Wilkins RC 3.00 8.00
119 Billy Thomas RC 3.00 8.00
120 Andre Barrett RC 3.00 8.00
121 Erik Daniels RC 3.00 8.00
122 Justin Reed RC 3.00 8.00
123 Viktor Khryapa RC 3.00 8.00
124 Mario Kasun RC 3.00 8.00
125 Luis Flores RC 3.00 8.00
126 Emeka Okafor RC 5.00 12.00
127 Dwight Howard AU RC 125.00 250.00
128 Ben Gordon AU RC 12.50 30.00
129 Shaun Livingston AU RC 6.00 15.00
130 Devin Harris AU RC 10.00 25.00
131 Josh Childress AU RC 6.00 15.00
132 Luol Deng AU RC 10.00 25.00
133 Rafael Araujo AU RC 6.00 15.00
134 Andre Iguodala AU RC 10.00 25.00
135 Luke Jackson AU RC 6.00 15.00
136 Andris Biedrins AU RC 8.00 20.00
137 Robert Swift AU RC 6.00 15.00
138 Sebastian Telfair AU RC 6.00 15.00
139 Kris Humphries AU RC 6.00 15.00
140 Al Jefferson AU RC 15.00 40.00
141 Kirk Snyder AU RC 6.00 15.00
142 Josh Smith AU RC 10.00 25.00
143 J.R. Smith AU RC 10.00 25.00
144 Dorell Wright AU RC 10.00 25.00
145 Jameer Nelson AU RC 8.00 20.00
146 Pavel Podkolzin AU RC 6.00 15.00
147 Delonte West AU RC 10.00 25.00
148 Tony Allen AU RC 8.00 20.00
149 Kevin Martin AU RC 10.00 25.00
150 Sasha Vujacic AU RC 6.00 15.00
151 Beno Udrih AU RC 6.00 15.00
152 David Harrison AU RC 6.00 15.00
153 Anderson Varejao AU RC 8.00 20.00
154 Jackson Vroman AU RC 6.00 15.00
155 Peter John Ramos AU RC 6.00 15.00
156 Lionel Chalmers AU RC 6.00 15.00
157 Donta Smith AU RC 6.00 15.00
158 Andre Emmett AU RC 6.00 15.00
159 Antonio Burks AU RC 6.00 15.00
160 Royal Ivey AU RC 6.00 15.00
161 Chris Duhon AU RC 6.00 15.00
162 Nenad Krstic AU RC 6.00 15.00
163 Trevor Ariza AU RC 6.00 15.00
164 Matt Freije AU RC 6.00 15.00
165 Bernard Robinson AU RC 6.00 15.00
166 Andres Nocioni AU RC 6.00 15.00
167 Pape Sow AU RC 6.00 15.00
168 Ha Seung-Jin AU RC 8.00 20.00

2004-05 Ultimate Collection Limited

Randomly seeded in packs, this 163-card set parallels the base Ultimate Collection set enhanced with sequential numbering to 25. A Spectrum one of one parallel set was also produced and inserted.
*1-116: 1.5X TO 4X BASE HI
*117-126: 1X TO 2.5X BASE HI
*127-168: 1.25X TO 3X BASE HI

14 Michael Jordan 60.00 150.00
45 Kobe Bryant 40.00 100.00
127 Dwight Howard JSY AU 200.00 500.00
128 Ben Gordon JSY AU 75.00 150.00
130 Devin Harris JSY AU 40.00 100.00
132 Luol Deng JSY AU 75.00 150.00
134 Andre Iguodala JSY AU 100.00 200.00
136 Andris Biedrins JSY AU 40.00 100.00
140 Al Jefferson JSY AU 75.00 200.00
142 Josh Smith JSY AU 75.00 150.00
143 J.R. Smith JSY AU 60.00 150.00
145 Jameer Nelson JSY AU 30.00 80.00
147 Delonte West JSY AU 40.00 100.00
149 Kevin Martin JSY AU 40.00 100.00

2004-05 Ultimate Collection Achievements Signatures

Randomly seeded in packs, this 13-card set is horizontally designed with a player photo on the right and an autograph on the left. Each card is sequentially numbered, see checklist for print runs.

BK Bernard King/60 12.50 30.00
CA Carmelo Anthony/41 30.00 80.00
CD Clyde Drexler/50 40.00 80.00
DR David Robinson/71 60.00 120.00
HO Hakeem Olajuwon/52 40.00 100.00
JS John Stockton/28 125.00 250.00
KB Kobe Bryant/56 125.00 250.00
KG Kevin Garnett/40 75.00 150.00
LB Larry Bird/60 75.00 150.00
LJ LeBron James/43 150.00 300.00
MA Magic Johnson/24 75.00 150.00
MJ Michael Jordan/69 350.00 600.00
TM Tracy McGrady/62 30.00 80.00

2004-05 Ultimate Collection Buybacks

Randomly seeded in packs, this 163-card set features autographed cards and COA's from previous year's Upper Deck products.
MOST UNPRICED DUE TO SCARCITY

1 Shareef Abdur-Rahim 15.00 40.00
03-4SPGUFab/18
2 Ray Allen EXCH 15.00 40.00
3 Carmelo Anthony 40.00 100.00
03-4FntElmJsy/16
6 Gilbert Arenas 15.00 40.00
SwtShJsy/18
7 Mike Bibby 15.00 40.00
02-3OvatShtSht/14
8 Mike Bibby 15.00 40.00
02-3OvatWrmUp/21
10 Mike Bibby 20.00 50.00
03-4GlasGamGr/15
13 Chauncey Billups 15.00 40.00
04-5ASLUWkTh/28
14 Chauncey Billups 20.00 50.00
03-4SPGUAtFab/17
15 Kobe Bryant 100.00 200.00
02-3HardCrtGmFlr/14
16 Kobe Bryant 100.00 200.00
02-3HrdCrtGmFlrFm/17
22 Baron Davis 15.00 40.00
03-4SwtShtJsy/20
23 Baron Davis 15.00 40.00
01-2FltTmPtrn/34
24 Baron Davis 15.00 40.00
01-2UDAirApp/17
25 Baron Davis 15.00 40.00
02-3FinteEleJsy/20
26 Baron Davis 15.00 40.00
02-3OvatAthUni/20
27 Baron Davis 15.00 40.00
02-3SPxWinMat/19

8 Baron Davis 15.00 40.00
02-3SwtShtSS/19
9 Baron Davis 15.00 40.00
02-3UDGamPlnJsy/19
0 Baron Davis 15.00 40.00
03-4SPGUAuthFab/19
1 Baron Davis 15.00 40.00
03-4SPxWinMat/22
2 Clyde Drexler 75.00 150.00
02-3GenATAth/18
3 Julius Erving 75.00 150.00
02-3GenAllTmAth/15
5 Kevin Garnett 50.00 120.00
02-3OvtAthWU/15
6 Kevin Garnett 50.00 120.00
03-4SPxWinMat/18
7 Kevin Garnett 50.00 120.00
03-4SwtShtJsy/20
9 Pau Gasol 15.00 40.00
02-3ChpDrvPropJsy/14
1 Pau Gasol 15.00 40.00
03-4SPxWinMat/22
2 Pau Gasol 15.00 40.00
03-4UDAllStWkAth/18
5 Richard Hamilton 15.00 40.00
03-4UDSPGUAthFb/18
6 Al Harrngton 15.00 40.00
01-2UDAirApp/26
7 Devin Harris 40.00 100.00
04-5SwtShtJsy/16
8 Kirk Hinrich 40.00 80.00
03-4UpperDeck/28
9 Dwight Howard 50.00 120.00
04-5SwtShtJsy/18
0 LeBron James 175.00 350.00
03-4FinElemJsy/19
3 Antawn Jamison 15.00 40.00
02-3UDPractJsy/24
5 Antawn Jamison 15.00 40.00
03-4SPxWinMat/23
7 Richard Jefferson 15.00 40.00
03-4SPxWinMat/15
8 Magic Johnson 75.00 150.00
02-3GenATAWht/16
9 Magic Johnson 75.00 150.00
02-3GenATAYel/19
0 Jason Kidd 25.00 60.00
02-3HardFlr/15
1 Jason Kidd 25.00 60.00
02-3HardFtrFilm/14
2 Jason Kidd 25.00 60.00
02-3OvatWarUp/16
4 Jason Kidd 25.00 60.00
03-4SPxWinMat/21
5 Jason Kidd 25.00 60.00
03-4SwtShtJsy/19
6 Jason Kidd 25.00 60.00
03-4UDGlsSupSw/20
7 Andrei Kirilenko 15.00 40.00
02-3UDASAuth/21
8 Andrei Kirilenko 15.00 40.00
03-4UDASWkAth/18
9 Andrei Kirilenko 15.00 40.00
04-5HardMat/21
70 Andrei Kirilenko 15.00 40.00
04-5HardMatCom/21
71 Andrei Kirilenko 15.00 40.00
04-5SwtShtSwt/14
72 Andrei Kirilenko 15.00 40.00
04-5UDASWkAth/17
73 Corey Maggette 15.00 40.00
01-2FltTmPatrn/28
74 Corey Maggette 15.00 40.00
02-3UDGamPln/19
76 Corey Maggette 15.00 40.00
04-5SPGUAthFab/19
77 Corey Maggette 15.00 40.00
04-5SwtShtSw/17
78 Stephon Marbury 15.00 40.00
01-2FltTmJmJsy/22
81 Stephon Marbury 15.00 40.00
02-3SPxWinMat/17
82 Stephon Marbury 15.00 40.00
03-4FinEleWU/20
83 Shawn Marion 15.00 40.00
02-3SwtShot/36
84 Shawn Marion 15.00 40.00
02-3UDPractice/16
86 Shawn Marion 15.00 40.00
03-4SwtShtJsy/18
89 Desmond Mason 15.00 40.00
02-3UDAllStrAuth/15
95 Tracy McGrady 40.00 100.00
03-4SPxWinMat/23
96 Tracy McGrady 40.00 100.00
Amare Stoudemire
03-4SPxWMC/18
98 Andre Miller 15.00 40.00
02-3SwtSht/38
99 Andre Miller 15.00 40.00
03-4SPxWinMat/22
100 Andre Miller 15.00 40.00
04-5SPGUAuthFab/20
103 Yao Ming 40.00 100.00
03-4FiniteElemJsy/15
104 Yao Ming 40.00 100.00
03-4GlasSupSw/18
109 Alonzo Mourning 100.00 200.00
03-4GlasGamGr/17
110 Alonzo Mourning 100.00 200.00
03-4SPGUAuthFab/15
111 Steve Nash 50.00 120.00
03-4SPGUAuthFab/20
112 Steve Nash 50.00 120.00
03-4SPxWinMat/20
113 Steve Nash 50.00 120.00
03-4UDSwtShtJsy/15
114 Steve Nash 50.00 120.00
04-5HardMat/19
115 Steve Nash 50.00 120.00
04-5HardMatCom/21
116 Lamar Odom 15.00 40.00
02-3MVPMatComb/17
117 Lamar Odom 15.00 40.00
03-4GlasGamGr/19
118 Lamar Odom 15.00 40.00
04-5HardMatCom/21
119 Lamar Odom 15.00 40.00
04-5HrdMatCom/21
120 Lamar Odom 15.00 40.00
04-5SPGUAthFab/23
123 Tony Parker 25.00 60.00
03-4SPxWinMat/21
124 Tony Parker 25.00 60.00
04-5HardMat/19
125 Tony Parker 25.00 60.00
04-5HardMatCom/21
126 Tony Parker 25.00 60.00
04-5SwtShtSwt/14
127 Gary Payton 25.00 60.00
02-3GenATAth/20
128 Gary Payton 20.00 50.00
03-4HardFloor/14
129 Gary Payton 20.00 50.00
03-4SPxWinMat/21
130 Gary Payton 20.00 50.00
04-5SwtShtSwt/18
131 Paul Pierce Jsy/17 15.00 40.00
132 Scottie Pippen Jsy/19 150.00 300.00
135 Jason Richardson 15.00 40.00
03-4SwtShtSwt/17
138 David Robinson 100.00 200.00
03-4SPGUAthFab/18
139 David Robinson 100.00 200.00
03-4SPxWinMat/17
141 John Stockton 100.00 200.00
02-3OvatAthShrt/14
142 John Stockton 100.00 200.00
03-4SwtShtSwt/20
145 Peja Stojakovic 20.00 50.00
03-4BlkDiamJsy/14
147 Peja Stojakovic 20.00 50.00
03-4SPGUAuthFab/16
148 Peja Stojakovic 20.00 50.00
03-4UDAllStWkAth/14
149 Amare Stoudemire 25.00 60.00
03-4GlasGamGr/17
150 Amare Stoudemire 25.00 60.00
03-4SPxWinMat/20
151 Amare Stoudemire 25.00 60.00
03-4SwtShtJsy/20
152 Amare Stoudemire 25.00 60.00
03-4SwtShtSwt/17
153 Amare Stoudemire 25.00 60.00
04-5HardMatCom/21
154 Amare Stoudemire 25.00 60.00
04-5HardMatr/20
155 Amare Stoudemire 25.00 60.00
04-5SPGUAuthFab/16
156 Amare Stoudemire 25.00 60.00
04-5SwtShtSwt/16
159 Ben Wallace 25.00 60.00
03-4BlaDiaJsy/14
160 Ben Wallace 25.00 60.00
03-4SPGUFab/20
161 Ben Wallace 25.00 60.00
03-4UDAsWAth/21
163 Jason Kidd 40.00 100.00
Richard Jefferson
03-4SPxWinMat/18

2004-05 Ultimate Collection Debuts

Serially numbered to 350, this 30-card set focuses on rookies and places them on colored backgrounds set to match their team's colors.

UD1 Dwight Howard 8.00 20.00
UD2 Emeka Okafor 4.00 10.00
UD3 Ben Gordon 3.00 8.00
UD4 Shaun Livingston 2.50 6.00
UD5 Devin Harris 4.00 10.00
UD6 Josh Childress 2.50 6.00
UD7 Luol Deng 4.00 10.00
UD8 Rafael Araujo 2.50 6.00
UD9 Andre Iguodala 4.00 10.00
UD10 Luke Jackson 2.50 6.00
UD11 Andris Biedrins 3.00 8.00
UD12 Robert Swift 2.50 6.00
UD13 Sebastian Telfair 2.50 6.00
UD14 Kris Humphries 2.50 6.00
UD15 Al Jefferson 4.00 10.00
UD16 Kirk Snyder 2.50 6.00
UD17 Josh Smith 4.00 10.00
UD18 J.R. Smith 3.00 8.00
UD19 Dorell Wright 4.00 10.00
UD20 Jameer Nelson 3.00 8.00
UD21 Nenad Krstic 2.50 6.00
UD22 Anderson Varejao 3.00 8.00
UD23 Jackson Vroman 2.50 6.00
UD24 Delonte West 3.00 8.00
UD25 Tony Allen 3.00 8.00
UD26 Kevin Martin 3.00 8.00
UD27 Sasha Vujacic 2.50 6.00
UD28 Beno Udrih 2.50 6.00
UD29 Ha Seung-Jin 2.50 6.00
UD30 Andres Nocioni 2.50 6.00

2004-05 Ultimate Collection Game Jerseys

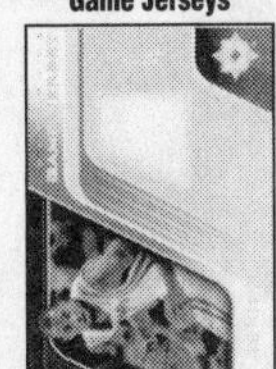

Randomly seeded in packs and serially numbered to 175 copies, this 42-card set places a player photo on the left and a swatch of game jersey on the right. A Limited parallel serially numbered to 75 and a Limited Extra parallel serially numbered to 25 were also produced.
*EXTRA: 1X TO 2.5X BASE HI
*LIMITED: .5X TO 1.25X BASE JSY HI

AI Allen Iverson 5.00 12.00
AK Andrei Kirilenko 2.50 6.00
AS Amare Stoudemire 4.00 10.00
BD Baron Davis 3.00 8.00
BG Ben Gordon 4.00 10.00
BK Bernard King 3.00 8.00
BW Ben Wallace 3.00 8.00
CA Carmelo Anthony 6.00 15.00
CD Clyde Drexler 4.00 10.00
DE Dennis Rodman 8.00 20.00
DH Dwight Howard 10.00 25.00
DN Dirk Nowitzki 6.00 15.00
DR David Robinson 5.00 12.00
EG Manu Ginobili 4.00 10.00
HO Hakeem Olajuwon 4.00 10.00
IT Isiah Thomas 3.00 8.00
JE Julius Erving 6.00 15.00
JK Jason Kidd 5.00 12.00
JO Jermaine O'Neal 3.00 8.00
JR Jason Richardson 3.00 8.00
JS John Stockton 5.00 12.00
KB Kobe Bryant 10.00 25.00
KG Kevin Garnett 6.00 15.00
LB Larry Bird 10.00 25.00
LD Luol Deng 5.00 12.00
LJ LeBron James 12.50 30.00
MA Magic Johnson 8.00 20.00
MB Mike Bibby 3.00 8.00
MJ Michael Jordan 40.00 100.00
OR Oscar Robertson 8.00 20.00
PG Pau Gasol 3.00 8.00
PP Paul Pierce 4.00 10.00
PS Peja Stojakovic 3.00 8.00
RM Reggie Miller 6.00 15.00
SF Steve Francis 3.00 8.00
SM Stephon Marbury 2.50 6.00
SN Steve Nash 4.00 10.00
SO Shaquille O'Neal 8.00 20.00
TD Tim Duncan 5.00 12.00
TM Tracy McGrady 4.00 10.00
WC Wilt Chamberlain 15.00 40.00
YM Yao Ming 6.00 15.00

2004-05 Ultimate Collection Game Patches

Randomly seeded in packs, this 42-card set parallels the Game Jerseys insert enhanced with a patch swatch and sequential numbering to 100. A Patches Limited parallel sequentially numbered to 25 and a Patches Limited Extra parallel sequentially numbered to 10 were also produced and inserted.
*LIMITED: .5X TO 1.25X BASE JSY HI

AI Allen Iverson/100 25.00 60.00
AK Andrei Kirilenko/100 6.00 15.00
AS Amare Stoudemire/100 10.00 25.00
BD Baron Davis/100 8.00 20.00
BG Ben Gordon/100 10.00 25.00
BK Bernard King/100 8.00 20.00
BW Ben Wallace/100 8.00 20.00
CA Carmelo Anthony/100 15.00 40.00
CD Clyde Drexler/100 15.00 40.00
DE Dennis Rodman/100 25.00 60.00
DH Dwight Howard/100 20.00 50.00
DN Dirk Nowitzki/100 12.00 30.00
DR David Robinson/100 12.00 30.00
EG Manu Ginobili/100 10.00 25.00
HO Hakeem Olajuwon/100 10.00 25.00
IT Isiah Thomas/100 8.00 20.00
JE Julius Erving/100 15.00 40.00
JK Jason Kidd/100 12.00 30.00
JO Jermaine O'Neal/100 8.00 20.00
JR Jason Richardson/100 8.00 20.00
JS John Stockton/100 20.00 50.00
KB Kobe Bryant/100 30.00 80.00
KG Kevin Garnett/100 15.00 40.00
LB Larry Bird/50 40.00 100.00
LD Luol Deng/100 12.00 30.00
LJ LeBron James/100 40.00 100.00
MA Magic Johnson/100 20.00 50.00
MB Mike Bibby/100 8.00 20.00
MJ Michael Jordan/100 100.00 225.00
OR Oscar Robertson/50 20.00 50.00
PG Pau Gasol/100 8.00 20.00
PP Paul Pierce/100 10.00 25.00
PS Peja Stojakovic/100 8.00 20.00
RM Reggie Miller/100 12.50 30.00
SF Steve Francis/100 8.00 20.00
SM Stephon Marbury/100 6.00 15.00
SN Steve Nash/100 15.00 40.00
SO Shaquille O'Neal/100 20.00 50.00
TD Tim Duncan/100 12.00 30.00
TM Tracy McGrady/100 10.00 25.00
WC Wilt Chamberlain/100 50.00 120.00
YM Yao Ming/100 15.00 40.00

2004-05 Ultimate Collection MVP Autographs

Randomly seeded, this seven card set is horizontally designed with a photo on the left and an autograph on the right. Cards are sequentially numbered to either total number of league MVP's won or the year the player received the award.
MOST NOT PRICED DUE TO SCARCITY

HO Hakeem Olajuwon/94 25.00 60.00
JE Julius Erving/81 40.00 80.00

2004-05 Ultimate Collection Premium Patches

Randomly seeded, this 42-card set is horizontally designed and places player photos on the left of the card and an oversized patch swatch on the right. Each card is sequentially numbered to 75.

AI Allen Iverson/75 60.00 150.00
AK Andrei Kirilenko/75 25.00 60.00
AS Amare Stoudemire/50 30.00 80.00
BD Baron Davis/75 25.00 60.00
BG Ben Gordon/75 25.00 60.00
BW Ben Wallace/75 25.00 60.00
CA Carmelo Anthony/75 50.00 125.00
CW Chris Webber/75 25.00 60.00
DE Devin Harris/75 30.00 80.00
DH Dwight Howard/50 100.00 250.00
DN Dirk Nowitzki/75 40.00 100.00
EB Elton Brand/75 25.00 60.00
JC Josh Childress/75 20.00 50.00
JK Jason Kidd/75 40.00 100.00
JN Jameer Nelson/75 25.00 60.00
JO Jermaine O'Neal/75 25.00 60.00
JR Jason Richardson/75 25.00 60.00
KB Kobe Bryant/75 175.00 350.00
KG Kevin Garnett/75 50.00 125.00
LD Luol Deng/75 30.00 80.00
LJ LeBron James/50 150.00 400.00
LO Lamar Odom/75 25.00 60.00
MJ Michael Jordan/25 350.00 650.00
PG Pau Gasol/75 25.00 60.00
PP Paul Pierce/75 40.00 100.00
PS Peja Stojakovic/50 25.00 60.00
RA Ray Allen/75 30.00 80.00
RH Richard Hamilton/75 20.00 50.00
RJ Richard Jefferson/75 25.00 60.00
RM Reggie Miller/75 40.00 100.00
SA Shareef Abdur-Rahim/75 20.00 50.00
SF Steve Francis/75 25.00 60.00
SH Shawn Marion/75 20.00 50.00
SL Shaun Livingston/75 20.00 50.00
SM Stephon Marbury/50 25.00 60.00
SN Steve Nash/75 30.00 80.00
SO Shaquille O'Neal/75 60.00 150.00
ST Sebastian Telfair/75 20.00 50.00
TD Tim Duncan/75 50.00 125.00
TM Tracy McGrady/50 30.00 80.00
TP Tony Parker/75 25.00 60.00
YM Yao Ming/75 50.00 125.00

2004-05 Ultimate Collection Rookie Jerseys

Limited to 275 serially numbered copies, this 29-card set places rookie player photos on the left and a swatch of jersey on the right. A Parallel version of this set was also produced and is sequentially numbered to 75.
*PARALLEL: .5X TO 1.25X BASE HI

AB Andris Biedrins 4.00 10.00
AE Andre Emmett 3.00 8.00
AI Andre Iguodala 5.00 12.00
AJ Al Jefferson 5.00 12.00
AV Anderson Varejao 4.00 10.00
BG Ben Gordon 4.00 10.00
DA David Harrison 3.00 8.00
DE Devin Harris 5.00 12.00
DH Dwight Howard 10.00 25.00
DW Dorell Wright 5.00 12.00
HS Ha Seung-Jin 3.00 8.00
JC Josh Childress 3.00 8.00
JN Jameer Nelson 4.00 10.00
JR J.R. Smith 4.00 10.00
JS Josh Smith 5.00 12.00
JV Jackson Vroman 3.00 8.00
KH Kris Humphries 3.00 8.00
KM Kevin Martin 4.00 10.00
KS Kirk Snyder 3.00 8.00
LC Lionel Chalmers 3.00 8.00
LD Luol Deng 5.00 12.00
LU Luke Jackson 3.00 8.00
PR Peter John Ramos 3.00 8.00
RA Rafael Araujo 3.00 8.00
SL Shaun Livingston 3.00 8.00
ST Sebastian Telfair 3.00 8.00
SV Sasha Vujacic 3.00 8.00
TA Tony Allen 4.00 10.00
WE Delonte West 4.00 10.00

2004-05 Ultimate Collection Signature Patches

Inserted randomly and limited to 25 copies, this 27-card set features a player photo and an autographed jersey patch.

AI Andre Iguodala 60.00 150.00
AS Amare Stoudemire 100.00 200.00
BG Ben Gordon 40.00 100.00
BK Bernard King 40.00 100.00
BW Ben Wallace 50.00 120.00
CA Carmelo Anthony 100.00 200.00
CD Clyde Drexler 100.00 200.00
DE Dennis Rodman 150.00 300.00
DH Dwight Howard 250.00 450.00
DR David Robinson 100.00 200.00
IT Isiah Thomas 30.00 80.00
JC Josh Childress 25.00 60.00
JE Julius Erving 100.00 200.00
JK Jason Kidd 75.00 150.00
JS John Stockton 150.00 300.00
KB Kobe Bryant 400.00 700.00
KG Kevin Garnett 125.00 250.00
LB Larry Bird 150.00 300.00
LD Luol Deng 50.00 120.00
LJ LeBron James 400.00 800.00
MA Magic Johnson 125.00 250.00
MJ Michael Jordan 600.00 1000.00
PG Pau Gasol 30.00 80.00
PP Paul Pierce 50.00 100.00
PS Peja Stojakovic 50.00 100.00
TM Tracy McGrady 100.00 200.00
YM Yao Ming 100.00 200.00

2004-05 Ultimate Collection Signatures

Randomly inserted in packs as no odds are given, this 31-card set is horizontally designed with player photos on the left and autographs on the right.

AM Alonzo Mourning 25.00 60.00
AS Amare Stoudemire 12.50 30.00
BG Ben Gordon 8.00 20.00
BK Bernard King 10.00 25.00
BR Bill Russell 75.00 150.00
BW Ben Wallace 10.00 25.00
CA Carmelo Anthony 20.00 50.00
CD Clyde Drexler 15.00 40.00
DE Devin Harris 10.00 25.00
DH Dwight Howard 25.00 60.00
DR David Robinson 40.00 70.00
HO Hakeem Olajuwon 15.00 40.00
IT Isiah Thomas 20.00 50.00
JE Julius Erving 40.00 100.00
JK Jason Kidd 12.50 30.00
JS John Stockton 50.00 120.00
KB Kobe Bryant SP 100.00 200.00
KG Kevin Garnett SP 25.00 60.00
KH Kirk Hinrich 12.50 30.00
LB Larry Bird 75.00 150.00
LD Luol Deng 12.00 30.00
LJ LeBron James 150.00 300.00
MA Magic Johnson 40.00 100.00
MJ Michael Jordan 350.00 600.00
PS Peja Stojakovic 10.00 25.00
RA Ray Allen 15.00 40.00
RO Dennis Rodman 40.00 100.00
SL Shaun Livingston 8.00 20.00
SM Stephon Marbury 10.00 25.00
TM Tracy McGrady 15.00 40.00
YM Yao Ming 20.00 50.00

2004-05 Ultimate Collection Signatures Gold

Randomly seeded, this 31-card set parallels the Signatures set enhanced with gold foil and sequential numbering to the featured player's jersey number.
SOME UNPRICED DUE TO SCARCITY

AM Alonzo Mourning/33 150.00 250.00
AS Amare Stoudemire/32 30.00 80.00
BK Bernard King/30 15.00 40.00
CA Carmelo Anthony/15 75.00 150.00
CD Clyde Drexler/22 50.00 120.00
DE Devin Harris/34 20.00 50.00
DR David Robinson/50 40.00 100.00
HO Hakeem Olajuwon/34 40.00 80.00
KG Kevin Garnett/21 75.00 150.00
KH Kirk Hinrich/31 25.00 60.00
LB Larry Bird/33 100.00 200.00
LJ LeBron James/23 200.00 400.00
MA Magic Johnson/32 60.00 150.00
MJ Michael Jordan/23 350.00 650.00
RA Ray Allen/34 20.00 50.00
RO Dennis Rodman/91 40.00 100.00

2005-06 Ultimate Collection

Released in April 2006, Ultimate Collection boasts a 183-card set where cards 1-130 feature veteran players serially numbered to 750, cards 131-142 feature rookie players serially numbered to 750, cards 143-183 feature rookie autographs serially numbered to 250. Base veteran cards have black backgrounds and white borders on the left and right side of the cards. Ultimate was packaged in four-pack boxes where packs contain four cards and carried an initial suggested retail price of $100.

1 Josh Smith 1.00 2.50
2 Josh Childress .75 2.00
3 Joe Johnson 1.00 2.50
4 Al Harrington .75 2.00
5 Tony Allen .60 1.50
6 Ricky Davis .75 2.00
7 Al Jefferson 1.00 2.50
8 Paul Pierce 1.25 3.00
9 Delonte West .75 2.00
10 Brevin Knight .60 1.50
11 Emeka Okafor 1.00 2.50
12 Kareem Rush .60 1.50
13 Gerald Wallace 1.00 2.50
14 Tyson Chandler .75 2.00
15 Luol Deng 1.00 2.50
16 Michael Jordan 12.00 30.00
17 Ben Gordon 1.00 2.50
18 Kirk Hinrich .75 2.00
19 LeBron James 5.00 12.00
20 Drew Gooden .75 2.00
21 Larry Hughes .75 2.00
22 Donyell Marshall .60 1.50
23 Zydrunas Ilgauskas .75 2.00
24 Marquis Daniels .60 1.50
25 Josh Howard .75 2.00
26 Dirk Nowitzki 1.50 4.00
27 Jason Terry .75 2.00
28 Devin Harris .75 2.00
29 Carmelo Anthony 2.00 5.00
30 Marcus Camby .75 2.00
31 Nene .75 2.00
32 Kenyon Martin 1.00 2.50
33 Andre Miller .75 2.00
34 Ben Wallace 1.00 2.50
35 Richard Hamilton .75 2.00
36 Tayshaun Prince 1.00 2.50
37 Chauncey Billups 1.00 2.50
38 Rasheed Wallace 1.00 2.50
39 Baron Davis 1.00 2.50
40 Mike Dunleavy .75 2.00
41 Troy Murphy .75 2.00
42 Jason Richardson 1.00 2.50
43 Tracy McGrady 1.25 3.00
44 Yao Ming 1.25 3.00
45 Stromile Swift .60 1.50
46 Juwan Howard .75 2.00
47 Bob Sura .60 1.50
48 Ron Artest 1.00 2.50
49 Stephen Jackson .75 2.00
50 Jermaine O'Neal 1.00 2.50
51 Jamaal Tinsley .60 1.50
52 Elton Brand 1.00 2.50
53 Corey Maggette .75 2.00
54 Sam Cassell 1.00 2.50
55 Shaun Livingston .60 1.50
56 Cuttino Mobley .75 2.00
57 Kobe Bryant 5.00 12.00
58 Kwame Brown .60 1.50
59 Lamar Odom 1.00 2.50
60 Devean George .60 1.50
61 Pau Gasol 1.00 2.50
62 Damon Stoudamire .75 2.00
63 Eddie Jones .75 2.00
64 Bobby Jackson .60 1.50
65 Shaquille O'Neal 2.00 5.00
66 Gary Payton 1.00 2.50
67 Antoine Walker .75 2.00
68 Dwyane Wade 2.50 6.00
69 Jason Williams .75 2.00
70 Jamaal Magloire .60 1.50
71 Michael Redd 1.00 2.50
72 Bobby Simmons .60 1.50
73 Maurice Williams .75 2.00
74 Kevin Garnett 2.00 5.00
75 Marko Jaric .60 1.50
76 Wally Szczerbiak .75 2.00
77 Michael Olowokandi .60 1.50
78 Vince Carter 1.50 4.00
79 Richard Jefferson 1.00 2.50
80 Jason Kidd 1.50 4.00
81 Jeff McInnis .60 1.50
82 J.R. Smith 1.00 2.50
83 Desmond Mason .60 1.50
84 Speedy Claxton .60 1.50
85 David West 1.00 2.50
86 Stephon Marbury .75 2.00
87 Jamal Crawford .75 2.00
88 Quentin Richardson .75 2.00
89 Eddy Curry .75 2.00
90 Steve Francis 1.00 2.50
91 Grant Hill 1.25 3.00
92 Dwight Howard 2.00 5.00
93 Jameer Nelson .75 2.00
94 Hedo Turkoglu 1.00 2.50
95 Allen Iverson 1.50 4.00
96 Andre Iguodala 1.00 2.50
97 Kyle Korver 1.00 2.50
98 Chris Webber 1.00 2.50
99 Steve Nash 1.25 3.00
100 Shawn Marion 1.00 2.50
101 Amare Stoudemire 1.50 4.00
102 Kurt Thomas .60 1.50
103 Juan Dixon .60 1.50
104 Darius Miles .60 1.50
105 Zach Randolph .75 2.00
106 Sebastian Telfair .75 2.00
107 Shareef Abdur-Rahim .75 2.00
108 Mike Bibby 1.00 2.50
109 Brad Miller 1.00 2.50
110 Peja Stojakovic 1.00 2.50
111 Tim Duncan 1.50 4.00
112 Manu Ginobili 1.00 2.50
113 Tony Parker 1.00 2.50
114 Michael Finley 1.00 2.50
115 Ray Allen 1.00 2.50
116 Rashard Lewis 1.00 2.50
117 Vladimir Radmanovic .60 1.50
118 Luke Ridnour .75 2.00
119 Chris Bosh 1.00 2.50
120 Morris Peterson .60 1.50
121 Jalen Rose 1.00 2.50
122 Alvin Williams .60 1.50
123 Carlos Boozer 1.00 2.50
124 Matt Harpring .75 2.00
125 Andrei Kirilenko .75 2.00
126 Mehmet Okur .60 1.50
127 Gilbert Arenas 1.00 2.50
128 Caron Butler 1.00 2.50
129 Antawn Jamison 1.00 2.50
130 Brendan Haywood .60 1.50
131 Von Wafer RC 2.50 6.00
132 Bracey Wright RC 2.50 6.00
133 Ryan Gomes RC 2.50 6.00
134 Robert Whaley RC 2.50 6.00
135 Orien Greene RC 2.50 6.00
136 Dijon Thompson RC 2.50 6.00
137 Lawrence Roberts RC 2.50 6.00
138 Amir Johnson RC 2.50 6.00
139 John Lucas III RC 6.00 15.00
140 Chuck Hayes RC 2.50 6.00
141 Alex Acker RC 2.50 6.00
142 Fabricio Oberto RC 2.50 6.00
143 Andrew Bogut AU RC 10.00 25.00
144 Marvin Williams AU RC 30.00 80.00
145 Deron Williams AU RC 30.00 80.00
146 Chris Paul AU RC 75.00 150.00
147 Raymond Felton AU RC 10.00 25.00
148 Martell Webster AU RC 5.00 12.00
149 Charlie Villanueva AU RC 6.00 15.00
150 Channing Frye AU RC 6.00 15.00
151 Ike Diogu AU RC 5.00 12.00
152 Andrew Bynum AU RC 30.00 80.00
153 Yaroslav Korolev AU RC 5.00 12.00
154 Sean May AU RC 5.00 12.00
155 Rashad McCants AU RC 5.00 12.00
156 Antoine Wright AU RC 5.00 12.00
157 Joey Graham AU RC 5.00 12.00
158 Danny Granger AU RC 10.00 25.00
159 Gerald Green AU RC 6.00 15.00
160 Hakim Warrick AU RC 6.00 15.00
161 Julius Hodge AU RC 5.00 12.00
162 Nate Robinson AU RC 8.00 20.00
163 Jarrett Jack AU RC 5.00 12.00
164 Francisco Garcia AU RC 6.00 15.00
165 Luther Head AU RC 5.00 12.00
166 Johan Petro AU RC 5.00 12.00
167 Jason Maxiell AU RC 5.00 12.00
168 Linas Kleiza AU RC 5.00 12.00
169 Wayne Simien AU RC 5.00 12.00
170 David Lee AU RC 8.00 20.00
171 Salim Stoudamire AU RC 5.00 12.00
172 Daniel Ewing AU RC 5.00 12.00
173 Brandon Bass AU RC 6.00 15.00
174 C.J. Miles AU RC 6.00 15.00
175 Ersan Ilyasova AU RC 6.00 15.00
176 Travis Diener AU RC 5.00 12.00
177 Chris Taft AU RC 5.00 12.00
178 M.Andriuskevicius AU RC 5.00 12.00
179 Louis Williams AU RC 8.00 20.00
180 Monta Ellis AU RC 25.00 50.00
181 Andray Blatche AU RC 6.00 15.00
182 Sarunas Jasikevicius AU RC 5.00 12.00
183 James Singleton AU RC 5.00 12.00

2005-06 Ultimate Collection Blue

Limited to 125 serially numbered copies, this set parallels the base Ultimate Collection set with blue highlights.
*1-130 BLUE: .75X TO 2X BASE HI
*131-142 RC BLUE: .6X TO 1.5X BASE HI

2005-06 Ultimate Collection Red

Randomly seeded in packs, this 142-card set parallels the base set enhanced with red highlights and sequential numbering to 50.
*1-130 RED: 1.25X TO 3X BASE HI
*131-142 RC RED: .75X TO 2X BASE HI

2005-06 Ultimate Collection Silver

Limited to 25 copies, this 142-card set parallels the base Ultimate Collection set enhanced with silver foil highlights and sequential numbering to 25.
*1-130 SILV: 2.5X TO 6X BASE HI
*131-142 SILV.RC: 1X TO 2.5X BASE HI

68 Dwyane Wade 20.00 50.00

2005-06 Ultimate Collection Achievements Signatures

Randomly seeded in packs, this 20-card set is horizontally designed with a player image on the left, a tan stripe through the midde, white borders along the top and bottom and a centered player autograph. Each card is serially numbered to an achievement significant to the player on the card.

UABG Ben Gordon/35 15.00 40.00
UABK Bernard King/85 10.00 25.00
UADH Dwight Howard/20 40.00 80.00
UADR Dennis Rodman/34 40.00 100.00
UAEB Elton Brand/44 12.50 30.00
UAHO Hakeem Olajuwon/89 20.00 50.00
UAKA Kareem Abdul-Jabbar/76 40.00 80.00
UAKG Kevin Garnett/47 40.00 80.00
UALB Larry Bird/84 60.00 120.00
UALJ LeBron James/56 150.00 300.00
UAMA Magic Johnson/46 60.00 120.00
UAMJ Michael Jordan/63 350.00 550.00
UAPG Pau Gasol/37 10.00 25.00
UAPP Paul Pierce/48 20.00 50.00
UASM Stephon Marbury/50 10.00 25.00
UASN Steve Nash/19 75.00 150.00
UATM Tracy McGrady/17 30.00 60.00
UAVC Vince Carter/51 25.00 60.00
UAYM Yao Ming/41 35.00 75.00

2005-06 Ultimate Collection All-Stars Signatures

Randomly seeded in packs, this 20-card set is horizontally designed with a player image on the left, a tan stripe through the midde, white borders along the top and bottom and a centered player autograph. Cards are serially numbered to the total All-Star Game appearances by player.
MOST NOT PRICED DUE TO SCARCITY

ASBR Bill Russell/12 125.00 250.00
ASGG George Gervin/12 50.00 100.00
ASHO Hakeem Olajuwon/12 50.00 100.00
ASKA Kareem Abdul-Jabbar/19 60.00 120.00
ASLB Larry Bird/12 150.00 250.00
ASMJ Michael Jordan/14 450.00 650.00

2005-06 Ultimate Collection Honors Signatures

Randomly seeded in packs, this 20-card set is horizontally designed with a player image on the left, a tan stripe through the midde, white borders along the top and bottom and a centered player autograph. Cards are serially numbered to a significant statistic in the featured player's career.
MOST NOT PRICED DUE TO SCARCITY

HSHO Hakeem Olajuwon/93 20.00 50.00
HSJK Jason Kidd/95 20.00 50.00
HSPP Paul Pierce/99 12.50 30.00
HSWF Walt Frazier/68 12.50 30.00

2005-06 Ultimate Collection Jerseys

Randomly seeded in packs, this 60-card set is horizontally designed with a player photo on the right and a jersey swatch on the left. Each card is serially numbered to 99.
*GOLD: .75X TO 2X BASE JSY HI

UJAB Andrew Bogut 5.00 12.00
UJAN Andrew Bynum 10.00 25.00

UJAS Amare Stoudemire 3.00 8.00
UJAW Antoine Wright 3.00 8.00
UJBG Ben Gordon 3.00 8.00
UJBK Bernard King 3.00 8.00
UJCA Carmelo Anthony 6.00 15.00
UJCB Chauncey Billups 3.00 8.00
UJCD Clyde Drexler 4.00 10.00
UJCF Channing Frye 4.00 10.00
UJCP Chris Paul 12.00 30.00
UJCV Charlie Villanueva 4.00 10.00
UJDA David Robinson 5.00 12.00
UJDG Danny Granger 6.00 15.00
UJDH Dwight Howard 6.00 15.00
UJDN Dirk Nowitzki 5.00 12.00
UJDR Dennis Rodman 5.00 12.00
UJDW Deron Williams 8.00 20.00
UJEO Emeka Okafor 3.00 8.00
UJFG Francisco Garcia 4.00 10.00
UJGG Gerald Green 4.00 10.00
UJHO Hakeem Olajuwon 4.00 10.00
UJHW Hakim Warrick 4.00 10.00
UJID Ike Diogu 3.00 8.00
UJIT Isiah Thomas 3.00 8.00
UJJA Jason Richardson 3.00 8.00
UJJG Joey Graham 3.00 8.00
UJJH Julius Hodge 3.00 8.00
UJJJ Jarrett Jack 3.00 8.00
UJJR J.R. Smith 3.00 8.00
UJJS John Stockton 6.00 15.00
UJJW James Worthy 3.00 8.00
UJKB Kobe Bryant 12.50 30.00
UJKE Kevin McHale 4.00 10.00
UJKG Kevin Garnett 6.00 15.00
UJKM Karl Malone 4.00 10.00
UJLB Larry Bird 10.00 25.00
UJLJ LeBron James 12.50 30.00
UJMA Magic Johnson 8.00 20.00
UJMG Manu Ginobili 3.00 8.00
UJMJ Michael Jordan 35.00 75.00
UJMR Martell Webster 3.00 8.00
UJMW Marvin Williams 4.00 10.00
UJNR Nate Robinson 4.00 10.00
UJOR Oscar Robertson/35 20.00 50.00
UJPP Paul Pierce 4.00 10.00
UJRA Ray Allen 3.00 8.00
UJRF Raymond Felton 5.00 12.00
UJRM Rashad McCants 3.00 8.00
UJSE Sean May 3.00 8.00
UJSF Steve Francis 3.00 8.00
UJSM Shawn Marion 3.00 8.00
UJSN Steve Nash 4.00 10.00
UJSO Shaquille O'Neal 8.00 20.00
UJST Stephon Marbury 2.50 6.00
UJTD Tim Duncan 5.00 12.00
UJTM Tracy McGrady 4.00 10.00
UJTP Tony Parker 3.00 8.00
UJVC Vince Carter 5.00 12.00
UJYM Yao Ming 4.00 10.00

2005-06 Ultimate Collection Jerseys Dual

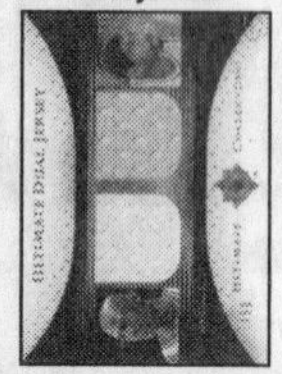

Randomly inserted in packs, this 40-card set is horizontally designed with player photos on the right and left side and centered swatches of jersey. Cards are serially numbered to 50.
UNPRICED DUAL GOLD PRINT RUN 10 SETS
DJAO Ron Artest 6.00 15.00
Jermaine O'Neal
DJAS Amare Stoudemire 6.00 15.00
Shawn Marion
DJBA Chris Bosh 10.00 25.00
Carmelo Anthony
DJBS Mike Bibby 6.00 15.00
Peja Stojakovic
DJBW Andrew Bogut 6.00 15.00
Marvin Williams
DJCL Carmelo Anthony 25.00 60.00
LeBron James
DJDG Tim Duncan 8.00 20.00
Manu Ginobili
DJDL Deron Williams 8.00 20.00
Luther Head
DJFB Channing Frye 8.00 20.00
Andrew Bynum
DJGV Joey Graham 6.00 15.00
Charlie Villanueva
DJGW Gerald Green 6.00 15.00
Martel Webster
DJHF Dwight Howard 6.00 15.00
Steve Francis
DJJB Magic Johnson 50.00 100.00
Larry Bird
DJJJ Michael Jordan 75.00 200.00
LeBron James
DJKJ Andrei Kirilenko 6.00 15.00
Antawn Jamison
DJLK LeBron James 40.00 100.00
Kobe Bryant
DJMF Rashad McCants 6.00 15.00
Raymond Felton
DJMG Tracy McGrady 10.00 25.00
Kevin Garnett
DJMK Stephon Marbury 8.00 20.00
Jason Kidd
DJMM Michael Jordan 50.00 120.00
Magic Johnson
DJNH Dirk Nowitzki 8.00 20.00
Josh Howard
DJNK Steve Nash 12.50 30.00
Jason Kidd
DJOG Emeka Okafor 6.00 15.00
Ben Gordon
DJOM Shaquille O'Neal 12.50 30.00
Yao Ming
DJPG Tony Parker 8.00 20.00
Manu Ginobili
DJPW Chris Paul 8.00 20.00
Deron Williams
DJRA Michael Redd 6.00 15.00
Ray Allen
DJRD Jason Richardon 6.00 15.00
Baron Davis
DJRJ Nate Robinson 6.00 15.00
Jarrett Jack
DJRO David Robinson 12.50 30.00
Hakeem Olajuwon
DJSM John Stockton 12.50 30.00
Karl Malone
DJSR Sean May 6.00 15.00
Raymond Felton
DJSS J.R. Smith 6.00 15.00
Josh Smith
DJTL Sebastian Telfair 6.00 15.00
Shaun Livingston
DJTS Isiah Thomas 12.50 30.00
John Stockton
DJWD Hakim Warrick 6.00 15.00
Ike Diogu
DJWH Ben Wallace 8.00 20.00
Richard Hamilton
DJWS Marvin Williams 6.00 15.00
Salim Stoudamire
DJWW Martell Webster 6.00 15.00
Antoine Wright

2005-06 Ultimate Collection Loyalty Signatures

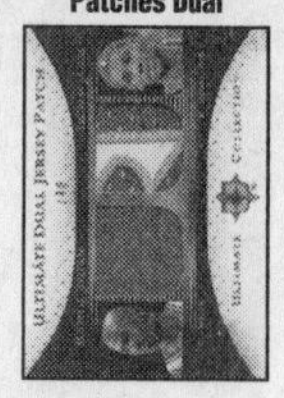

Randomly seeded in packs, this 20-card set is horizontally designed with a player image on the left, a tan stripe through the midde, white borders along the top and bottom and a centered player autograph. Cards are serially numbered to the number of years each player spent with a single team.
SOME NOT PRICED DUE TO SCARCITY
UNPRICED MVP SIG PRINT RUN ONE TO 6 SETS
LSBL Bill Laimbeer/13 60.00 120.00
LSBR Bill Russell/13 125.00 250.00
LSDR David Robinson/14 75.00 150.00
LSGG George Gervin/11 25.00 60.00
LSHO Hakeem Olajuwon/17 25.00 60.00
LSJE Julius Erving/11 75.00 200.00
LSJS John Stockton/19 100.00 250.00
LSKA Kareem Abdul-Jabbar/14 75.00 150.00
LSLB Larry Bird/13 125.00 250.00
LSMA Magic Johnson/13 100.00 200.00
LSMJ Michael Jordan/13 500.00 700.00

2005-06 Ultimate Collection Patches

Randomly inserted, this 59-card set parallels the design of the jerseys set enhanced with a premium swatch of patch and sequential numbering to 75.
GOLD: .75X TO 2X BASE PAT.HI
UJPAB Andrew Bogut 10.00 25.00
UJPAN Andrew Bynum 20.00 50.00
UJPAS Amare Stoudemire 6.00 15.00
UJPAW Antoine Wright 6.00 15.00
UJPBG Ben Gordon 6.00 15.00
UJPBK Bernard King 6.00 15.00
UJPCA Carmelo Anthony 12.00 30.00
UJPCB Chauncey Billups 6.00 15.00
UJPCD Clyde Drexler 10.00 25.00
UJPCF Channing Frye 8.00 20.00
UJPCP Chris Paul 20.00 50.00
UJPCV Charlie Villanueva 8.00 20.00
UJPDA David Robinson 10.00 25.00
UJPDG Danny Granger 10.00 25.00
UJPDH Dwight Howard 12.00 30.00
UJPDN Dirk Nowitzki 10.00 25.00
UJPDR Dennis Rodman 12.50 30.00
UJPDW Deron Williams 10.00 25.00
UJPEO Emeka Okafor 6.00 15.00
UJPFG Francisco Garcia 8.00 20.00
UJPGG Gerald Green 8.00 20.00
UJPHO Hakeem Olajuwon 8.00 20.00
UJPHW Hakim Warrick 8.00 20.00
UJPID Ike Diogu 6.00 15.00
UJPIT Isiah Thomas 6.00 15.00
UJPJA Jason Richardson 6.00 15.00
UJPJG Joey Graham 6.00 15.00
UJPJH Julius Hodge 6.00 15.00
UJPJJ Jarrett Jack 6.00 15.00
UJPJR J.R. Smith 6.00 15.00
UJPJS John Stockton 12.00 30.00
UJPJW James Worthy 12.00 30.00
UJPKB Kobe Bryant 40.00 100.00
UJPKE Kevin McHale 8.00 20.00
UJPKG Kevin Garnett 12.00 30.00
UJPKM Karl Malone 12.50 30.00
UJPLB Larry Bird 20.00 50.00
UJPLJ LeBron James 40.00 100.00
UJPMA Magic Johnson 15.00 40.00
UJPMG Manu Ginobili 6.00 15.00
UJPMJ Michael Jordan 100.00 200.00
UJPMR Martell Webster 6.00 15.00
UJPMW Marvin Williams 8.00 20.00
UJPNR Nate Robinson 8.00 20.00
UJPOR Oscar Robertson/20 25.00 60.00
UJPPP Paul Pierce 8.00 20.00
UJPRA Ray Allen 6.00 15.00
UJPRF Raymond Felton 10.00 25.00
UJPRM Rashad McCants 6.00 15.00
UJPSE Sean May 6.00 15.00
UJPSF Steve Francis 6.00 15.00
UJPSM Shawn Marion 6.00 15.00
UJPSO Shaquille O'Neal 12.00 30.00
UJPST Stephon Marbury 5.00 12.00
UJPTD Tim Duncan 10.00 25.00
UJPTM Tracy McGrady 8.00 20.00
UJPTP Tony Parker 6.00 15.00
UJPVC Vince Carter 10.00 25.00
UJPYM Yao Ming 12.00 30.00

2005-06 Ultimate Collection Patches Dual

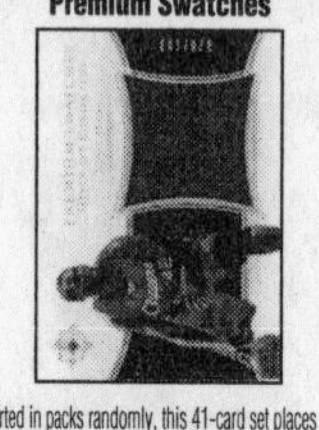

Randomly seeded, this 39-card set parallels the design of the Jerseys Dual set enhanced with premium patch swatches and sequential numbering to 40.
UNPRICED GOLD PRINT RUN 10 SETS
DPAO Ron Artest 12.50 30.00
Jermaine O'Neal
DPAS Amare Stoudemire 12.50 30.00
Shawn Marion
DPBA Chris Bosh 20.00 50.00
Carmelo Anthony
DPBS Mike Bibby 12.50 30.00
Peja Stojakovic
DPBW Andrew Bogut 12.50 30.00
Marvin Williams
DPCL Carmelo Anthony 60.00 150.00
LeBron James
DPDG Tim Duncan 25.00 60.00
Manu Ginobili
DPDL Deron Williams 15.00 40.00
Luther Head
DPFB Channing Frye 25.00 50.00
Andrew Bynum
DPGV Joey Graham 12.50 30.00
Charlie Villanueva
DPGW Gerald Green 12.50 30.00
Martell Webster
DPHF Dwight Howard 12.50 30.00
Steve Francis
DPJB Magic Johnson 60.00 120.00
Larry Bird
DPJJ Michael Jordan 200.00 350.00
LeBron James
DPKJ Andrei Kirilenko 15.00 40.00
Antawn Jamison
DPLK LeBron James 125.00 250.00
Kobe Bryant
DPMF Rashad McCants 12.50 30.00
Raymond Felton
DPMG Tracy McGrady 15.00 40.00
Kevin Garnett
DPMK Stephon Marbury 25.00 60.00
Jason Kidd
DPMM Michael Jordan 80.00 160.00
Magic Johnson
DPNH Dirk Nowitzki 15.00 40.00
Josh Howard
DPOG Emeka Okafor 15.00 40.00
Ben Gordon
DPOM Shaquille O'Neal 40.00 80.00
Yao Ming
DPPG Tony Parker 20.00 50.00
Manu Ginobili
DPPW Chris Paul 40.00 80.00
Deron Williams
DPRA Michael Redd 12.50 30.00
Ray Allen
DPRD Jason Richardson 12.50 30.00
Baron Davis
DPRJ Nate Robinson 12.50 30.00
Jarrett Jack
DPRO David Robinson 20.00 50.00
Hakeem Olajuwon
DPSM John Stockton 40.00 80.00
Karl Malone
DPSR Sean May 12.50 30.00
Raymond Felton
DPSS J.R. Smith 12.50 30.00
Josh Smith
DPTL Sebastian Telfair 12.50 30.00
Shaun Livingston
DPTS Isiah Thomas 35.00 75.00
John Stockton
DPVJ Vince Carter 15.00 40.00
Richard Jefferson
DPWD Hakim Warrick 12.50 30.00
Ike Diogu
DPWH Ben Wallace 20.00 50.00
Richard Hamilton
DPWS Marvin Williams 12.50 30.00
Salim Stoudamire
DPWW Martell Webster 12.50 30.00
Antoine Wright

2005-06 Ultimate Collection Premium Patches

Seeded randomly in packs, this 42-card set places player photos on the left side of the card and premium patch swatches on the right side of the card. Cards are serially numbered to either 25 or 50.
PPAB Andrew Bogut/50 20.00 50.00
PPAK Andrei Kirilenko/50 10.00 25.00
PPAS Amare Stoudemire/50 12.00 30.00
PPBD Baron Davis/50 12.00 30.00
PPBG Ben Gordon/50 12.00 30.00
PPCB Chris Bosh/50 12.00 30.00
PPCF Channing Frye/50 15.00 40.00
PPCM Corey Maggette/50 10.00 25.00
PPCP Chris Paul/50 50.00 125.00
PPCV Charlie Villanueva/50 15.00 40.00
PPDH Dwight Howard/25 25.00 60.00
PPDN Dirk Nowitzki/25 25.00 60.00
PPDW Deron Williams/50 30.00 80.00
PPEB Elton Brand/50 12.00 30.00
PPEO Emeka Okafor/50 12.00 30.00
PPID Ike Diogu/50 12.00 30.00
PPJK Jason Kidd/50 20.00 50.00
PPJR Jason Richardson/50 12.00 30.00
PPJS J.R. Smith/50 12.00 30.00
PPKB Kobe Bryant/25 100.00 225.00
PPKG Kevin Garnett/25 25.00 60.00
PPLJ LeBron James/25 125.00 300.00
PPMA Marvin Williams/50 15.00 40.00
PPMB Mike Bibby/50 12.00 30.00
PPMJ Michael Jordan/25 300.00 600.00
PPMR Michael Redd/50 12.00 30.00
PPMW Martell Webster/50 12.00 30.00
PPPP Paul Pierce/50 15.00 40.00
PPPP Peja Stojakovic/50 12.00 30.00
PPRF Raymond Felton/50 20.00 50.00
PPRM Rashad McCants/50 12.00 30.00
PPSE Sean May/50 12.00 30.00
PPSF Steve Francis/50 12.00 30.00
PPSH Shawn Marion/50 12.00 30.00
PPSM Stephon Marbury/50 10.00 25.00
PPSN Steve Nash/25 25.00 60.00
PPSO Shaquille O'Neal/25 40.00 80.00
PPTD Tim Duncan/25 40.00 80.00
PPTM Tracy McGrady/25 25.00 60.00
PPTP Tony Parker/50 12.00 30.00
PPVC Vince Carter/25 40.00 100.00
PPYM Yao Ming/25 25.00 60.00

2005-06 Ultimate Collection Premium Swatches

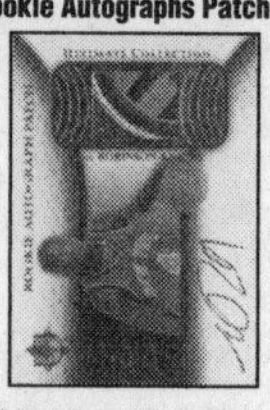

Inserted in packs randomly, this 41-card set places player photos on the left and large jersey swatches on the right. Cards are serially numbered to 100.
PSAB Andrew Bogut 6.00 15.00
PSAK Andrei Kirilenko 3.00 8.00
PSAS Amare Stoudemire 4.00 10.00
PSBD Baron Davis 4.00 10.00
PSBG Ben Gordon 4.00 10.00
PSCB Chris Bosh 4.00 10.00
PSCF Channing Frye 5.00 12.00
PSCM Corey Maggette 3.00 8.00
PSCP Chris Paul 15.00 40.00
PSCV Charlie Villanueva 5.00 12.00
PSDH Dwight Howard 8.00 20.00
PSDN Dirk Nowitzki 6.00 15.00
PSDW Deron Williams 10.00 25.00
PSEB Elton Brand 4.00 10.00
PSEO Emeka Okafor 4.00 10.00
PSID Ike Diogu 4.00 10.00
PSJK Jason Kidd 6.00 15.00
PSJR Jason Richardson 4.00 10.00
PSJS J.R. Smith 4.00 10.00
PSKB Kobe Bryant 20.00 50.00
PSKG Kevin Garnett 8.00 20.00
PSLJ LeBron James 25.00 60.00
PSMA Marvin Williams 5.00 12.00
PSMB Mike Bibby 4.00 10.00
PSMJ Michael Jordan 100.00 200.00
PSMR Michael Redd 4.00 10.00
PSMW Martell Webster 4.00 10.00
PSPP Paul Pierce 5.00 12.00
PSPS Peja Stojakovic 4.00 10.00
PSRF Raymond Felton 6.00 15.00
PSRM Rashad McCants 4.00 10.00
PSSE Sean May 4.00 10.00
PSSF Steve Francis 4.00 10.00
PSSH Shawn Marion 4.00 10.00
PSSM Stephon Marbury 3.00 8.00
PSSO Shaquille O'Neal 8.00 20.00
PSTD Tim Duncan 6.00 15.00
PSTM Tracy McGrady 5.00 12.00
PSTP Tony Parker 4.00 10.00
PSVC Vince Carter 6.00 15.00
PSYM Yao Ming 5.00 12.00

2005-06 Ultimate Collection Rookie Autographs Gold

Randomly inserted in packs, this 41-card set parallels the rookie subset from the base Ultimate Collection enhanced with gold foil highlights and sequential numbering to 25.
143 Andrew Bogut 40.00 100.00
144 Marvin Williams 20.00 50.00
145 Deron Williams 100.00 200.00
146 Chris Paul 250.00 400.00
147 Raymond Felton 25.00 60.00
148 Martell Webster 15.00 40.00
149 Charlie Villanueva 20.00 50.00
150 Channing Frye 20.00 50.00
151 Ike Diogu 15.00 40.00
152 Andrew Bynum 100.00 200.00
153 Yaroslav Korolev 15.00 40.00
154 Sean May 15.00 40.00
155 Rashad McCants 15.00 40.00
156 Antoine Wright 15.00 40.00
157 Joey Graham 15.00 40.00
158 Danny Granger 30.00 80.00
159 Gerald Green 20.00 50.00
160 Hakim Warrick 20.00 50.00
161 Julius Hodge 15.00 40.00
162 Nate Robinson 20.00 50.00
163 Jarrett Jack 15.00 40.00
164 Francisco Garcia 20.00 50.00
165 Luther Head 15.00 40.00
166 Johan Petro 15.00 40.00
167 Jason Maxiell 15.00 40.00
168 Linas Kleiza 15.00 40.00
169 Wayne Simien 15.00 40.00
170 David Lee 25.00 60.00
171 Salim Stoudamire 15.00 40.00
172 Daniel Ewing 15.00 40.00
173 Brandon Bass 20.00 50.00
174 C.J. Miles 20.00 50.00
175 Ersan Ilyasova 20.00 50.00
176 Travis Diener 15.00 40.00
177 Chris Taft 15.00 40.00
178 Martynas Andriuskevicius 15.00 40.00
179 Louis Williams 25.00 60.00
180 Monta Ellis 60.00 120.00
181 Andray Blatche 20.00 50.00
182 Sarunas Jasikevicius 15.00 40.00
183 James Singleton 15.00 40.00

2005-06 Ultimate Collection Rookie Autographs Patches

Randomly inserted in packs, this 40-card set is horizontally designed with player photos on the left and a premium patch swatch on the right. Each card is serially numbered to 25.
UNPRICED LOGO PRINT RUN ONE SET
RPAB Andrew Bogut 100.00 200.00
RPAN Andrew Bynum 125.00 250.00
RPAW Antoine Wright 20.00 50.00
RPBB Brandon Bass 25.00 60.00
RPBL Andray Blatche 25.00 60.00
RPCF Channing Frye 25.00 60.00
RPCJ C.J. Miles 25.00 60.00
RPCP Chris Paul 300.00 550.00
RPCT Chris Taft 20.00 50.00
RPCV Charlie Villanueva 25.00 60.00
RPDE Daniel Ewing 20.00 50.00
RPDG Danny Granger 40.00 100.00
RPDL David Lee 30.00 80.00
RPDW Deron Williams 125.00 250.00
RPEI Ersan Ilyasova 25.00 60.00
RPFG Francisco Garcia 25.00 60.00
RPGG Gerald Green 25.00 60.00
RPHW Hakim Warrick 25.00 60.00
RPID Ike Diogu 20.00 50.00
RPJG Joey Graham 20.00 50.00
RPJH Julius Hodge 20.00 50.00
RPJJ Jarrett Jack 20.00 50.00
RPJM Jason Maxiell 20.00 50.00
RPJP Johan Petro 20.00 50.00
RPLH Luther Head 20.00 50.00
RPLK Linas Kleiza 20.00 50.00
RPLW Louis Williams 30.00 80.00
RPMA Martynas Andriuskevicius 20.00 50.00
RPME Monta Ellis 100.00 200.00
RPMW Marvin Williams 25.00 60.00
RPNR Nate Robinson 25.00 60.00
RPRF Raymond Felton 30.00 80.00
RPRG Ryan Gomes 20.00 50.00
RPRM Rashad McCants 20.00 50.00
RPSJ Sarunas Jasikevicius 20.00 50.00
RPSM Sean May 20.00 50.00
RPSS Salim Stoudamire 20.00 50.00
RPTD Travis Diener 20.00 50.00
RPWE Martell Webster 20.00 50.00
RPWS Wayne Simien 20.00 50.00

2005-06 Ultimate Collection Signatures

Found in packs at random, this 42-card set is horizontally designed with player photos on the left, white borders along the top and the bottom, a gray stripe through the midde and a player autograph on the right.
USAB Andrew Bogut 8.00 20.00
USAN Andrew Bynum 20.00 50.00
USBD Baron Davis 5.00 12.00
USBK Bernard King 5.00 12.00
USBR Bill Russell SP 75.00 200.00
USCA Carmelo Anthony SP 20.00 50.00
USCF Channing Frye 6.00 15.00
USCP Chris Paul 40.00 100.00
USCV Charlie Villanueva 6.00 15.00
USDE Dennis Rodman 25.00 60.00
USDG Danny Granger 10.00 25.00
USDH Dwight Howard 15.00 40.00
USDR David Robinson 25.00 60.00
USDW Deron Williams 12.00 30.00
USEB Elton Brand 6.00 15.00
USEO Emeka Okafor 6.00 15.00
USGG Gerald Green 6.00 15.00
USHO Hakeem Olajuwon 15.00 40.00
USHW Hakim Warrick 6.00 15.00
USID Ike Diogu 5.00 12.00
USJE Julius Erving SP 50.00 120.00
USJK Jason Kidd 10.00 25.00
USKA Kareem Abdul-Jabbar SP 40.00 80.00
USKG Kevin Garnett 25.00 60.00
USLB Larry Bird SP 60.00 120.00
USLH Larry Hughes 5.00 12.00
USLJ LeBron James 200.00 350.00
USLR Luke Ridnour 5.00 12.00
USMA Magic Johnson SP 50.00 100.00
USMJ Michael Jordan SP 300.00 450.00
USMR Martell Webster 5.00 12.00
USMW Marvin Williams 6.00 15.00
USRF Raymond Felton 8.00 20.00
USRM Rashad McCants 5.00 12.00
USSM Sean May 5.00 12.00
USSN Steve Nash 30.00 75.00
USSP Scottie Pippen 100.00 200.00
USST Stephon Marbury 6.00 15.00
USTM Tracy McGrady 15.00 40.00
USTP Tayshaun Prince 5.00 12.00
USVC Vince Carter 15.00 40.00
USYM Yao Ming 20.00 50.00

2005-06 Ultimate Collection Signatures Dual

Inserted in packs, this 30-card set utilizes the design of the base Signatures set but with two players. Each card is serially numbered to 25.
UNPRICED TRIPLE PRINT RUN 10 SETS
UNPRICED QUAD PRINT RUN 5 SETS
DSAR Ron Artest 75.00 150.00
Dennis Rodman
DSAW Carmelo Anthony 30.00 80.00
Hakim Warrick
DSBF Andrew Bogut 25.00 60.00
Channing Frye
DSBJ Larry Bird 200.00 400.00
Magic Johnson
DSBR Andrew Bogut 25.00 60.00
Michael Redd
DSCK Vince Carter 75.00 150.00
Jason Kidd
DSDD Baron Davis 20.00 50.00
Ike Diogu
DSFO Raymond Felton 20.00 50.00
Emeka Okafor
DSGM Kevin Garnett 40.00 80.00
Rashad McCanis
DSGV Joey Graham 20.00 50.00
Charlie Villanueva
DSHB Richard Hamilton 50.00 100.00
Chauncey Billups
DSHM Dwight Howard 30.00 80.00
Tracy McGrady
DSHO Dwight Howard 40.00 80.00
Emeka Okafor
DSJA Magic Johnson 200.00 350.00
Kareem Abdul-Jabbar
DSJG Al Jefferson 20.00 50.00
Gerald Green
DSJH LeBron James 200.00 400.00
Dwight Howard
DSJJ LeBron James 600.00 1100.00
Michael Jordan
DSJP Michael Jordan 900.00 1400.00
Scottie Pippen
DSLB Larry Bird 200.00 300.00
Bill Russell
DSMF Stephon Marbury 20.00 50.00
Channing Frye
DSMH Yao Ming 40.00 80.00
Dwight Howard
DSMM Sean May 20.00 50.00
Rashad McCants
DSMS Tracy McGrady 25.00 60.00
Stromile Swift
DSPS Chris Paul 60.00 150.00
J.R. Smith
DSWF Marvin Williams 20.00 50.00
Raymond Felton
DSWJ Marvin Williams 20.00 50.00
Joe Johnson
DSWM Deron Williams 30.00 80.00
C.J. Miles
DSWP Deron Williams 100.00 200.00
Chris Paul
DSWT Martell Webster 20.00 50.00
Sebastian Telfair

2006-07 Ultimate Collection

Released in late June 2007, Ultimate Collection features a 243-card set where cards 1-140 picture NBA veterans sequentially numbered to 499, cards 141-180 picture retired NBA stars sequentially numbered to 99, cards 181-228 picture NBA rookies, which are sequentially numbered to 350 and contain an on-card player autograph, and cards 236-243 picture NBA rookies sequentially numbered to 499. Ultimate Collection is packaged in four-pack boxes of four packs each and carried an initial suggested retail price of $100.00 per pack.
1 Josh Childress 1.25 3.00
2 Joe Johnson 1.50 4.00
3 Salim Stoudamire 1.00 2.50
4 Marvin Williams 1.50 4.00
5 Tony Allen 1.00 2.50
6 Al Jefferson 1.50 4.00
7 Paul Pierce 2.00 5.00
8 Wally Szczerbiak 1.25 3.00
9 Sebastian Telfair 1.00 2.50
10 Raymond Felton 2.00 5.00
11 Sean May 1.00 2.50
12 Emeka Okafor 1.50 4.00
13 Gerald Wallace 1.50 4.00
14 Luol Deng 1.50 4.00
15 Chris Duhon 1.00 2.50
16 Ben Gordon 1.50 4.00
17 Kirk Hinrich 1.50 4.00
18 Ben Wallace 1.50 4.00
19 Drew Gooden 1.25 3.00
20 Larry Hughes 1.25 3.00
21 Zydrunas Ilgauskas 1.25 3.00
22 LeBron James 8.00 20.00
23 Donyell Marshall 1.00 2.50
24 Devin Harris 1.50 4.00
25 Josh Howard 1.25 3.00
26 Dirk Nowitzki 2.50 6.00
27 Jerry Stackhouse 1.25 3.00
28 Jason Terry 1.25 3.00
29 Carmelo Anthony 2.00 5.00
30 Marcus Camby 1.25 3.00
31 Kenyon Martin 1.50 4.00
32 Andre Miller 1.25 3.00
33 J.R. Smith 1.50 4.00
34 Chauncey Billups 1.50 4.00
35 Richard Hamilton 1.25 3.00
36 Antonio McDyess 1.25 3.00
37 Tayshaun Prince 1.50 4.00
38 Rasheed Wallace 1.50 4.00
39 Baron Davis 1.50 4.00
40 Mike Dunleavy 1.25 3.00
41 Troy Murphy 1.00 2.50
42 Jason Richardson 1.50 4.00
43 Rafer Alston 1.00 2.50
44 Shane Battier 1.25 3.00
45 Tracy McGrady 2.00 5.00
46 Bonzi Wells 1.00 2.50
47 Yao Ming 2.00 5.00
48 Marquis Daniels 1.00 2.50
49 Al Harrington 1.25 3.00
50 Sarunas Jasikevicius 1.25 3.00
51 Jermaine O'Neal 1.50 4.00
52 Elton Brand 1.50 4.00
53 Sam Cassell 1.50 4.00
54 Chris Kaman 1.25 3.00
55 Shaun Livingston 1.00 2.50
56 Corey Maggette 1.25 3.00
57 Kobe Bryant 8.00 20.00
58 Andrew Bynum 2.50 6.00
59 Lamar Odom 1.50 4.00
60 Vladimir Radmanovic 1.00 2.50
61 Kwame Brown 1.00 2.50
62 Eddie Jones 1.25 3.00
63 Mike Miller 1.50 4.00
64 Hakim Warrick 1.25 3.00
65 Pau Gasol 1.50 4.00
66 Stromile Swift 1.00 2.50
67 Alonzo Mourning 2.00 5.00
68 Shaquille O'Neal 3.00 8.00
69 Gary Payton 1.50 4.00
70 Dwyane Wade 4.00 10.00
71 Jason Williams 1.25 3.00
72 Andrew Bogut 1.50 4.00
73 Michael Redd 1.50 4.00
74 Charlie Villanueva 1.50 4.00
75 Bobby Simmons 1.00 2.50
76 Ricky Davis 1.25 3.00
77 Kevin Garnett 3.00 8.00
78 Troy Hudson 1.00 2.50
79 Mike James 1.00 2.50
80 Rashad McCants 1.00 2.50
81 Vince Carter 2.00 5.00
82 Richard Jefferson 1.50 4.00
83 Jason Kidd 2.50 6.00
84 Nenad Krstic 1.00 2.50
85 Tyson Chandler 1.25 3.00
86 Bobby Jackson 1.00 2.50
87 Desmond Mason 1.00 2.50
88 Chris Paul 3.00 8.00
89 Peja Stojakovic 1.50 4.00
90 Steve Francis 1.50 4.00
91 Channing Frye 1.25 3.00
92 Stephon Marbury 1.25 3.00
93 Quentin Richardson 1.25 3.00
94 Nate Robinson 1.50 4.00
95 Carlos Arroyo 1.25 3.00
96 Grant Hill 2.00 5.00
97 Dwight Howard 2.50 6.00
98 Darko Milicic 1.00 2.50
99 Jameer Nelson 1.25 3.00
100 Samuel Dalembert 1.00 2.50
101 Andre Iguodala 1.50 4.00
102 Allen Iverson 2.00 5.00
103 Kyle Korver 1.25 3.00
104 Chris Webber 1.50 4.00
105 Leandro Barbosa 1.25 3.00
106 Boris Diaw 1.25 3.00
107 Shawn Marion 1.50 4.00
108 Steve Nash 2.00 5.00
109 Amare Stoudemire 1.50 4.00
110 Juan Dixon 1.00 2.50
111 Jarrett Jack 1.25 3.00
112 Jamaal Magloire 1.00 2.50
113 Zach Randolph 1.25 3.00
114 Martell Webster 1.25 3.00
115 Shareef Abdur-Rahim 1.25 3.00
116 Ron Artest 1.50 4.00
117 Brad Miller 1.50 4.00
118 Mike Bibby 1.50 4.00
119 Tim Duncan 2.50 6.00
120 Michael Finley 1.50 4.00
121 Manu Ginobili 1.50 4.00
122 Robert Horry 1.25 3.00
123 Tony Parker 1.50 4.00
124 Ray Allen 1.50 4.00
125 Rashard Lewis 1.50 4.00
126 Luke Ridnour 1.25 3.00
127 Chris Wilcox 1.00 2.50
128 Chris Bosh 1.50 4.00
129 T.J. Ford 1.25 3.00
130 Joey Graham 1.00 2.50
131 Morris Peterson 1.00 2.50
132 Carlos Boozer 1.50 4.00
133 Andrei Kirilenko 1.25 3.00
134 C.J. Miles 1.00 2.50
135 Mehmet Okur 1.00 2.50
136 Deron Williams 2.50 6.00
137 Gilbert Arenas 1.50 4.00
138 Caron Butler 1.50 4.00
139 Antonio Daniels 1.00 2.50
140 Antawn Jamison 1.50 4.00
141 David Robinson 6.00 15.00
142 Hakeem Olajuwon 5.00 12.00
143 Bill Russell 8.00 20.00
144 Walt Frazier 4.00 10.00
145 Nate Archibald 4.00 10.00
146 Spud Webb 4.00 10.00
147 Larry Bird 12.00 30.00
148 Michael Jordan 40.00 100.00
149 Magic Johnson 10.00 25.00
150 Julius Erving 8.00 20.00
151 Alvin Robertson 4.00 10.00
152 Bill Laimbeer 4.00 10.00
153 Bill Walton 4.00 10.00
154 Bob McAdoo 4.00 10.00
155 Clyde Drexler 5.00 12.00
156 Connie Hawkins 4.00 10.00
157 Dennis Rodman 6.00 15.00
158 Earl Monroe 4.00 10.00
159 Elvin Hayes 4.00 10.00
160 George Gervin 4.00 10.00
161 Kareem Abdul-Jabbar 6.00 15.00
162 Elgin Baylor 4.00 10.00

163 Rolando Blackman 4.00 10.00
164 Maurice Cheeks 4.00 10.00
165 Adrian Dantley 4.00 10.00
166 Joe Dumars 4.00 10.00
167 World B. Free 4.00 10.00
168 Robert Parish 4.00 10.00
169 Kevin McHale 5.00 12.00
170 Kevin Johnson 4.00 10.00
171 Bernard King 4.00 10.00
172 Moses Malone 4.00 10.00
173 Chris Mullin 4.00 10.00
174 Calvin Murphy 4.00 10.00
175 Oscar Robertson 4.00 10.00
176 Isiah Thomas 4.00 10.00
177 Reggie Theus 4.00 10.00
178 Rudy Tomjanovich 4.00 10.00
179 Wes Unseld 4.00 10.00
180 John Starks 4.00 10.00
181 Allan Ray AU RC 5.00 12.00
182 Andrea Bargnani AU RC 10.00 25.00
183 Bobby Jones AU RC 5.00 12.00
184 Brandon Roy AU RC 15.00 40.00
185 Cedric Simmons AU RC 5.00 12.00
186 Craig Smith AU RC 5.00 12.00
187 Damir Markota AU RC 5.00 12.00
188 Daniel Gibson AU RC 6.00 15.00
189 David Noel AU RC 5.00 12.00
190 Dee Brown AU RC 5.00 12.00
191 Hassan Adams AU RC 5.00 12.00
192 Hilton Armstrong AU RC 5.00 12.00
193 James Augustine AU RC 5.00 12.00
194 James White AU RC 5.00 12.00
195 Jordan Farmar AU RC 5.00 12.00
196 Jorge Garbajosa AU RC 5.00 12.00
197 Josh Boone AU RC 5.00 12.00
198 Kyle Lowry AU RC 6.00 15.00
199 LaMarcus Aldridge AU RC 15.00 40.00
200 Marcus Williams AU RC 5.00 12.00
201 Mardy Collins AU RC 5.00 12.00
202 Maurice Ager AU RC 5.00 12.00
203 Patrick O'Bryant AU RC 5.00 12.00
204 Paul Davis AU RC 5.00 12.00
205 Paul Millsap AU RC 8.00 20.00
206 P.J. Tucker AU RC 5.00 12.00
207 Pops Mensah-Bonsu AU RC 5.00 12.00
208 Quincy Douby AU RC 5.00 12.00
209 Rajon Rondo AU RC 30.00 60.00
210 Randy Foye AU RC 6.00 15.00
211 Renaldo Balkman AU RC 5.00 12.00
212 Rodney Carney AU RC 5.00 12.00
213 Ronnie Brewer AU RC 6.00 15.00
214 Rudy Gay AU RC 10.00 25.00
215 Yakhouba Diawara AU 5.00 12.00
216 Saer Sene AU RC 5.00 12.00
217 Sergio Rodriguez AU RC 5.00 12.00
218 Shannon Brown AU RC 8.00 20.00
219 Shawne Williams AU RC 5.00 12.00
220 Shelden Williams AU RC 5.00 12.00
221 Solomon Jones AU RC 5.00 12.00
222 Steve Novak AU RC 5.00 12.00
223 Thabo Sefolosha AU RC 6.00 15.00
224 Tyrus Thomas AU RC 8.00 20.00
225 Will Blalock AU RC 5.00 12.00
226 Robert Hite AU RC 5.00 12.00
227 Vassilis Spanoulis AU RC 5.00 12.00
236 Adam Morrison RC 4.00 10.00
237 Alexander Johnson RC 3.00 8.00
238 J.J. Redick RC 4.00 10.00
239 Kelenna Azubuike RC 4.00 10.00
240 Chris Quinn RC 3.00 8.00
241 Tarence Kinsey RC 3.00 8.00
242 Vassilis Spanoulis RC 3.00 8.00
243 Yakhouba Diawara RC 3.00 8.00
244 Mike Hall RC 3.00 8.00
245 Randolph Morris RC 3.00 8.00
246 Walter Herrmann RC 3.00 8.00
247 Mickael Gelabale RC 3.00 8.00
248 Andre Brown RC 3.00 8.00
249 Justin Williams RC 3.00 8.00
250 Lynn Greer RC 3.00 8.00

2006-07 Ultimate Collection Achievements Signatures

STATED PRINT RUN ONE TO 51 SER.#'d SETS
SOME UNPRICED DUE TO SCARCITY
UAAI Andre Iguodala/27 12.00 30.00
UAAJ Antawn Jamison/51 10.00 25.00
UABG Ben Gordon/39 15.00 40.00
UABJ Bobby Jackson/31 10.00 25.00
UABL Bill Laimbeer/14 100.00 200.00
UABM Bob McAdoo/14 100.00 200.00
UABO Chris Bosh/22 30.00 60.00
UABS Byron Scott/14 50.00 100.00
UACK Chris Kaman/23 10.00 25.00
UACM Corey Maggette/13 20.00 40.00
UACS Cedric Simmons/15 10.00 25.00
UADM Desmond Mason/17 10.00 25.00
UADO Dennis Rodman/34 50.00 125.00
UADU Chris Duhon/38 10.00 25.00
UAGG George Gervin/33 30.00 60.00
UAHO Hakeem Olajuwon/18 40.00 70.00
UAHW Hakim Warrick/19 12.50 30.00
UAJJ Jarrett Jack/22 10.00 25.00
UAJS J.R. Smith/33 10.00 25.00
UALE Leandro Barbosa/28 10.00 25.00
UAMA Magic Johnson/13 80.00 160.00
UAMO Cuttino Mobley/41 10.00 25.00
UAPS Peja Stojakovic/41 10.00 25.00
UARP Robert Parish/21 20.00 40.00
UASE Sean Elliott/12 75.00 150.00
UASK Steve Kerr/15 30.00 60.00
UASN Steve Nash/22 100.00 175.00
UASW Spud Webb/12 30.00 60.00
UATE Sebastian Telfair/13 10.00 25.00

2006-07 Ultimate Collection Autographs Jerseys

PRINT RUN 75 SER.#'d SETS
AUAH Al Harrington 6.00 15.00
AUAI Andre Iguodala 8.00 20.00
AUAJ Al Jefferson 6.00 15.00
AUAM Andre Miller 6.00 15.00
AUBD Baron Davis 8.00 20.00
AUBG Ben Gordon 10.00 25.00
AUBJ Bobby Jackson 6.00 15.00
AUBM Brad Miller 6.00 15.00
AUBO Chris Bosh 20.00 50.00
AUCA Carmelo Anthony 30.00 60.00
AUCB Chauncey Billups 8.00 20.00
AUCD Chris Duhon 6.00 15.00
AUCF Channing Frye 6.00 15.00
AUCM Corey Maggette 6.00 15.00
AUCP Chris Paul 35.00 75.00
AUDM Donyell Marshall 6.00 15.00
AUDR Clyde Drexler 25.00 50.00
AUDW Deron Williams 20.00 50.00
AUEO Emeka Okafor 6.00 15.00
AUHO Hakeem Olajuwon 25.00 60.00
AUID Ike Diogu 6.00 15.00
AUJA Antawn Jamison 6.00 15.00
AUJC Josh Childress 6.00 15.00
AUJG Joey Graham 6.00 15.00
AUJJ Jarrett Jack 6.00 15.00
AUJM Jamaal Magloire 6.00 15.00
AUJO Jermaine O'Neal 10.00 25.00
AUJS J.R. Smith 6.00 15.00
AUKB Kobe Bryant 125.00 250.00
AUKH Kirk Hinrich 12.50 30.00
AUKK Kyle Korver 8.00 20.00
AULB Larry Bird 50.00 120.00
AULH Larry Hughes 8.00 20.00
AULJ LeBron James 150.00 300.00
AULR Luke Ridnour 6.00 15.00
AUMA Magic Johnson 60.00 120.00
AUMB Mike Bibby 6.00 15.00
AUMD Marquis Daniels 6.00 15.00
AUMJ Michael Jordan 350.00 600.00
AUMO Alonzo Mourning 60.00 150.00
AUMR Michael Ray Richardson 8.00 20.00
AUMW Marvin Williams 6.00 15.00
AUPP Paul Pierce 12.50 30.00
AUQR Quentin Richardson 6.00 15.00
AURF Raymond Felton 8.00 20.00
AURJ Richard Jefferson 6.00 15.00
AURM Rashad McCants 6.00 15.00
AURO David Robinson 40.00 80.00
AUSK Steve Kerr 12.50 30.00
AUSL Shaun Livingston 6.00 15.00
AUSS Stromile Swift 6.00 15.00
AUST Sebastian Telfair 6.00 15.00
AUTC Tyson Chandler 8.00 20.00
AUTM Tracy McGrady 15.00 40.00
AUTP Tony Parker 20.00 40.00
AUVC Vince Carter 20.00 50.00
AUWF Walt Frazier 15.00 40.00
AUYM Yao Ming 20.00 50.00

2006-07 Ultimate Collection Autographs Patches

*PATCHES: .75X TO 2X BASE HI
PRINT RUN 15 SER.#'d SETS
AULB Larry Bird 100.00 250.00
AULJ LeBron James 300.00 500.00
AUMA Magic Johnson 100.00 200.00

2006-07 Ultimate Collection Combos Jerseys Dual

PRINT RUN 75 SER.#'d SETS
*PATCHES: .75X TO 2X BASE HI
PATCH PRINT RUN 25 SER.#'d SETS
AB Shannon Brown 4.00 10.00
Maurice Ager
AN Jameer Nelson 4.00 10.00
Carlos Arroyo
AR LaMarcus Aldridge 8.00 20.00
Brandon Roy
BB Leandro Barbosa 4.00 10.00
Raja Bell
BD Mike Bibby 4.00 10.00
Quincy Douby
BV Charlie Villanueva 5.00 12.00
Andrew Bogut
CB Renaldo Balkman 4.00 10.00
Mardy Collins
CS Tyson Chandler 4.00 10.00
Cedric Simmons
CW Shawne Williams 4.00 10.00
Rodney Carney
DO Ike Diogu 4.00 10.00
Jermaine O'Neal
DR Baron Davis 4.00 10.00
Jason Richardson
GH Ben Gordon 4.00 10.00
Kirk Hinrich
GW Pau Gasol 4.00 10.00
Hakim Warrick
HB Chauncey Billups 5.00 12.00
Richard Hamilton
HG Drew Gooden 4.00 10.00
Larry Hughes
IK Zydrunas Ilgauskas 4.00 10.00
Chris Kaman
JC Rodney Carney 4.00 10.00
Bobby Jones
JJ Michael Jordan 50.00 100.00
LeBron James
JL Alexander Johnson 4.00 10.00
Kyle Lowry
JR Al Jefferson 4.00 10.00
Allan Ray
JW Solomon Jones 4.00 10.00
Marvin Williams
MJ Desmond Mason 4.00 10.00
Bobby Jackson
ML Shaun Livingston 4.00 10.00
Corey Maggette
MO Shaquille O'Neal 25.00 60.00
Alonzo Mourning
MS Rashad McCants 4.00 10.00
Craig Smith
OH Emeka Okafor 6.00 15.00
Dwight Howard
OS Patrick O'Bryant 4.00 10.00
Saer Sene
PA Paul Pierce 8.00 20.00
Carmelo Anthony
PW Gary Payton 8.00 20.00
Jason Williams
RM Jamaal Magloire 4.00 10.00
Zach Randolph
RN Michael Redd 4.00 10.00
David Noel
SN Peja Stojakovic 5.00 12.00
Steve Novak
TG P.J. Tucker 4.00 10.00
Jorge Garbajosa
TH Devin Harris 4.00 10.00
Jason Terry
TR Allan Ray 4.00 10.00
Sebastian Telfair
TS Tyrus Thomas 6.00 15.00
Thabo Sefolosha
WB Marcus Williams 4.00 10.00
Josh Boone
WI Chris Webber 10.00 25.00
Allen Iverson
WP Rasheed Wallace 4.00 10.00
Tayshaun Prince
WR J.J. Redick 4.00 10.00
Shelden Williams

2006-07 Ultimate Collection Combos Jerseys Triple

PRINT RUN 25 SER.#'d SETS
UNPRICED QUAD PRINT RUN 5 SETS
UNPRICED TRIPLE PATCH PRINT RUN 10 SETS
UNPRICED QUAD PATCH PRINT RUN ONE SET
ADB Shannon Brown 8.00 20.00
Maurice Ager
Paul Davis
AKS Ray Allen 12.50 30.00
Peja Stojakovic
Kyle Korver
BBB Elton Brand 8.00 20.00
Carlos Boozer
Shane Battier
BBS Chris Bosh 12.50 30.00
Carlos Boozer
Amare Stoudemire
DPG Tim Duncan 25.00 50.00
Manu Ginobili
Tony Parker
FMR Stephon Marbury 12.50 30.00
Steve Francis
Nate Robinson
FRF Quentin Richardson 8.00 20.00
Channing Frye
Steve Francis
GDF Kevin Garnett 25.00 50.00
Randy Foye
Ricky Davis
LRS Rashard Lewis 8.00 20.00
Luke Ridnour
Saer Sene
NKB Andrei Kirilenko 15.00 30.00
Andrea Bargnani
Dirk Nowitzki
WBB Deron Williams 8.00 20.00
Ronnie Brewer
Dee Brown

2006-07 Ultimate Collection Debut Jerseys

PRINT RUN 50 SER.#'d SETS
*PATCHES: .75X TO 2X BASE HI
PATCH PRINT RUN 25 SER.#'d SETS
UDAB Andrea Bargnani 5.00 12.00
UDAR Allan Ray 3.00 8.00
UDBA Renaldo Balkman 3.00 8.00
UDBJ Bobby Jones 3.00 8.00
UDBR Brandon Roy 8.00 20.00
UDCS Cedric Simmons 3.00 8.00
UDDB Dee Brown 3.00 8.00
UDDG Daniel Gibson 4.00 10.00
UDDN David Noel 3.00 8.00
UDHA Hilton Armstrong 3.00 8.00
UDJB Josh Boone 3.00 8.00
UDJF Jordan Farmar 3.00 8.00
UDJG Jorge Garbajosa 3.00 8.00
UDJR J.J. Redick 4.00 10.00
UDJW James White 3.00 8.00
UDKL Kyle Lowry 4.00 10.00
UDLA LaMarcus Aldridge 8.00 20.00
UDMA Maurice Ager 3.00 8.00
UDMC Mardy Collins 3.00 8.00
UDMW Marcus Williams 3.00 8.00
UDPD Paul Davis 3.00 8.00
UDPO Patrick O'Bryant 3.00 8.00
UDPT P.J. Tucker 3.00 8.00
UDQD Quincy Douby 3.00 8.00
UDRB Ronnie Brewer 4.00 10.00
UDRC Rodney Carney 3.00 8.00
UDRF Randy Foye 4.00 10.00
UDRG Rudy Gay 5.00 12.00
UDRR Rajon Rondo 12.00 30.00
UDSB Shannon Brown 5.00 12.00
UDSJ Solomon Jones 3.00 8.00
UDSM Craig Smith 3.00 8.00
UDSN Steve Novak 3.00 8.00
UDSS Saer Sene 3.00 8.00
UDSW Shelden Williams 3.00 8.00
UDTS Thabo Sefolosha 4.00 10.00
UDTT Tyrus Thomas 4.00 10.00
UDWB Will Blalock 3.00 8.00
UDWI Shawne Williams 3.00 8.00

2006-07 Ultimate Collection Debut Jerseys Autographs

PRINT RUN 35 SER.#'d SETS
UNPRICED PATCH AUTO PRINT RUN 10 SETS
UDAB Andrea Bargnani 12.00 30.00
UDAR Allan Ray 8.00 20.00
UDBA Renaldo Balkman 8.00 20.00
UDBJ Bobby Jones 8.00 20.00
UDBR Brandon Roy 20.00 50.00
UDCS Cedric Simmons 8.00 20.00
UDDB Dee Brown 8.00 20.00
UDDN David Noel 8.00 20.00
UDHA Hilton Armstrong 8.00 20.00
UDJB Josh Boone 8.00 20.00
UDJF Jordan Farmar 8.00 20.00
UDJG Jorge Garbajosa 8.00 20.00
UDJW James White 8.00 20.00
UDKL Kyle Lowry 10.00 25.00
UDLA LaMarcus Aldridge 20.00 50.00
UDMA Maurice Ager 8.00 20.00
UDMC Mardy Collins 8.00 20.00
UDMW Marcus Williams 8.00 20.00
UDPO Patrick O'Bryant 8.00 20.00
UDPT P.J. Tucker 8.00 20.00
UDQD Quincy Douby 8.00 20.00
UDRB Ronnie Brewer 10.00 25.00
UDRF Randy Foye 10.00 25.00
UDRG Rudy Gay 12.00 30.00
UDRR Rajon Rondo 30.00 80.00
UDSB Shannon Brown 12.00 30.00
UDSJ Solomon Jones 8.00 20.00
UDSM Craig Smith 8.00 20.00
UDSN Steve Novak 8.00 20.00
UDSS Saer Sene 8.00 20.00
UDSW Shelden Williams 8.00 20.00
UDTS Thabo Sefolosha 10.00 25.00
UDTT Tyrus Thomas 10.00 25.00
UDWB Will Blalock 8.00 20.00
UDWI Shawne Williams 8.00 20.00

2006-07 Ultimate Collection Jerseys Dual

PRINT RUN 25 SER.#'d SETS
*PATCH DUAL: 1X TO 2.5X BASE HI
PATCH DUAL PRINT RUN 25 SETS
UNPRICED TRIPLE PRINT RUN 10 SETS
UNPRICED PAT.TRIPLE PRINT RUN TEN SETS
UJAB Andrea Bargnani 8.00 20.00
UJAI Andre Iguodala 5.00 12.00
UJAS Amare Stoudemire 5.00 12.00
UJBC Carlos Boozer 5.00 12.00
UJBD Baron Davis 5.00 12.00
UJBJ Bobby Jones 5.00 12.00
UJBO Chris Bosh 5.00 12.00
UJBW Ben Wallace 5.00 12.00
UJCA Carmelo Anthony 6.00 15.00
UJCB Chauncey Billups 5.00 12.00
UJCP Chris Paul 10.00 25.00
UJCW Chris Webber 5.00 12.00
UJDB Dee Brown 5.00 12.00
UJDG Drew Gooden 4.00 10.00
UJDH Dwight Howard 8.00 20.00
UJDN Dirk Nowitzki 8.00 20.00
UJDW Deron Williams 8.00 20.00
UJEB Elton Brand 5.00 12.00
UJEO Emeka Okafor 5.00 12.00
UJFE Raymond Felton 6.00 15.00
UJHA Hilton Armstrong 5.00 12.00
UJJF Jordan Farmar 5.00 12.00
UJJK Jason Kidd 6.00 15.00
UJJO Jermaine O'Neal 5.00 12.00
UJJR J.J. Redick 5.00 12.00
UJKB Kobe Bryant 25.00 60.00
UJKG Kevin Garnett 10.00 25.00
UJKH Kirk Hinrich 5.00 12.00
UJKL Kyle Lowry 6.00 15.00
UJLA LaMarcus Aldridge 12.00 30.00
UJLD Luol Deng 5.00 12.00
UJLJ LeBron James 20.00 50.00
UJLO Lamar Odom 5.00 12.00
UJMA Shawn Marion 5.00 12.00
UJMJ Michael Jordan 100.00 200.00
UJMR Michael Redd 5.00 12.00
UJMW Marvin Williams 5.00 12.00
UJNA Steve Nash 6.00 15.00
UJPG Pau Gasol 5.00 12.00
UJPO Patrick O'Bryant 5.00 12.00
UJPP Paul Pierce 6.00 15.00
UJRB Ronnie Brewer 6.00 15.00
UJRC Rodney Carney 5.00 12.00
UJRF Randy Foye 6.00 15.00
UJRG Rudy Gay 8.00 20.00
UJRH Richard Hamilton 4.00 10.00
UJRO Brandon Roy 12.00 30.00
UJSJ Solomon Jones 5.00 12.00
UJSM Stephon Marbury 4.00 10.00
UJSN Steve Novak 5.00 12.00
UJSO Shaquille O'Neal 10.00 25.00
UJSW Shelden Williams 5.00 12.00
UJTD Tim Duncan 8.00 20.00
UJTM Tracy McGrady 6.00 15.00
UJTP Tony Parker 5.00 12.00
UJTT Tyrus Thomas 6.00 15.00
UJVC Vince Carter 6.00 15.00
UJWI Shawne Williams 5.00 12.00
UJYM Yao Ming 6.00 15.00
UJZI Zydrunas Ilgauskas 4.00 10.00

2006-07 Ultimate Collection Numbers

STATED PRINT RUN ONE TO 40 SER.#'d SETS
SOME UNPRICED DUE TO SCARCITY
UNBL Bill Laimbeer/40 15.00 40.00
UNCA Carmelo Anthony/15 50.00 120.00
UNCD Clyde Drexler/22 50.00 120.00
UNDM Desmond Mason/24 10.00 25.00
UNGO Sebastian Telfair/30 10.00 25.00
UNMW Marvin Williams/24 12.50 30.00
UNPP Paul Pierce/34 20.00 50.00
UNPS Peja Stojakovic/16 15.00 40.00
UNRJ Richard Jefferson/24 10.00 25.00
UNST John Stockton/12 100.00 200.00
UNVC Vince Carter/15 60.00 120.00
UNWI Maurice Williams/25 10.00 25.00
UNYM Yao Ming/11 50.00 100.00

2006-07 Ultimate Collection Premium Swatches

PRINT RUN 75 SER.#'d SETS
PRAB Andrea Bargnani 6.00 15.00
PRAI Allen Iverson 8.00 20.00
PRAJ Antawn Jamison 6.00 15.00
PRBA Renaldo Balkman 4.00 10.00
PRBD Baron Davis 6.00 15.00
PRBG Ben Gordon 6.00 15.00
PRBJ Bobby Jones 4.00 10.00
PRBR Brandon Roy 10.00 25.00
PRCA Carlos Arroyo 5.00 12.00
PRCP Chris Paul 12.00 30.00
PRCS Cedric Simmons 4.00 10.00
PRDB Dee Brown 4.00 10.00
PRDG Drew Gooden 5.00 12.00
PRDH Dwight Howard 10.00 25.00
PRDN Dirk Nowitzki 10.00 25.00
PRDW Deron Williams 10.00 25.00
PREB Elton Brand 6.00 15.00
PRHA Hilton Armstrong 4.00 10.00
PRJB Josh Boone 4.00 10.00
PRJF Jordan Farmar 4.00 10.00
PRJK Jason Kidd 10.00 25.00
PRJN Jameer Nelson 5.00 12.00
PRKB Kobe Bryant 20.00 50.00
PRKG Kevin Garnett 12.00 30.00
PRKL Kyle Lowry 5.00 12.00
PRLA LaMarcus Aldridge 10.00 25.00
PRLB Leandro Barbosa 5.00 12.00
PRLJ LeBron James 25.00 60.00
PRMA Maurice Ager 4.00 10.00
PRMB Mike Bibby 6.00 15.00
PRMC Mardy Collins 4.00 10.00
PRMG Manu Ginobili 6.00 15.00
PRMR Michael Redd 6.00 15.00
PRMW Marcus Williams 4.00 10.00
PRNA Steve Nash 8.00 20.00
PRPD Paul Davis 4.00 10.00
PRPG Pau Gasol 6.00 15.00
PRPO Patrick O'Bryant 4.00 10.00
PRPP Paul Pierce 8.00 20.00
PRPT P.J. Tucker 4.00 10.00
PRQD Quincy Douby 4.00 10.00
PRRA Rafer Alston 4.00 10.00
PRRB Ronnie Brewer 5.00 12.00
PRRF Randy Foye 5.00 12.00
PRRG Rudy Gay 6.00 15.00
PRRR Rajon Rondo 10.00 25.00
PRSB Shannon Brown 6.00 15.00
PRSJ Solomon Jones 4.00 10.00
PRSM Craig Smith 4.00 10.00
PRSN Steve Novak 4.00 10.00
PRSO Shaquille O'Neal 12.00 30.00
PRSS Saer Sene 4.00 10.00
PRST Stephon Marbury 5.00 12.00
PRSW Shelden Williams 4.00 10.00
PRTM Tracy McGrady 8.00 20.00
PRTP Tayshaun Prince 6.00 15.00
PRTT Tyrus Thomas 8.00 20.00
PRVC Vince Carter 8.00 20.00
PRWI Shawne Williams 4.00 10.00
PRZI Zydrunas Ilgauskas 5.00 12.00

2006-07 Ultimate Collection Premium Swatches Patch

PRINT RUN 50 SER.#'d SETS
PRAB Andrea Bargnani 12.00 30.00
PRAI Allen Iverson 50.00 100.00
PRAJ Antawn Jamison 10.00 25.00
PRBA Renaldo Balkman 8.00 20.00
PRBD Baron Davis 10.00 25.00
PRBG Ben Gordon 10.00 25.00
PRBJ Bobby Jones 8.00 20.00
PRBR Brandon Roy 25.00 60.00
PRCA Carlos Arroyo 15.00 40.00
PRCP Chris Paul 20.00 50.00
PRCS Cedric Simmons 8.00 20.00
PRDB Dee Brown 8.00 20.00
PRDG Drew Gooden 8.00 20.00
PRDH Dwight Howard 40.00 80.00
PRDN Dirk Nowitzki 40.00 100.00
PREB Elton Brand 10.00 25.00
PRHA Hilton Armstrong 8.00 20.00
PRJB Josh Boone 8.00 20.00
PRJK Jason Kidd 35.00 75.00
PRJN Jameer Nelson 8.00 20.00
PRKB Kobe Bryant 125.00 250.00
PRKG Kevin Garnett 40.00 100.00
PRKL Kyle Lowry 10.00 25.00
PRLA LaMarcus Aldridge 25.00 60.00
PRLJ LeBron James 125.00 250.00
PRMA Maurice Ager 8.00 20.00
PRMB Mike Bibby 10.00 25.00
PRMC Mardy Collins 8.00 20.00
PRMG Manu Ginobili 30.00 60.00
PRMR Michael Redd 10.00 25.00
PRMW Marcus Williams 8.00 20.00
PRPD Paul Davis 8.00 20.00
PRPG Pau Gasol 10.00 25.00
PRPO Patrick O'Bryant 8.00 20.00
PRQD Quincy Douby 8.00 20.00
PRRA Rafer Alston 15.00 30.00
PRRB Ronnie Brewer 10.00 25.00
PRRF Randy Foye 10.00 25.00
PRRG Rudy Gay 12.00 30.00
PRRR Rajon Rondo 40.00 100.00
PRSB Shannon Brown 20.00 50.00
PRSJ Solomon Jones 8.00 20.00
PRSM Craig Smith 8.00 20.00
PRSN Steve Novak 8.00 20.00
PRSO Shaquille O'Neal 50.00 120.00
PRSS Saer Sene 8.00 20.00
PRST Stephon Marbury 12.50 30.00
PRSW Shelden Williams 8.00 20.00
PRTM Tracy McGrady 25.00 60.00
PRTP Tayshaun Prince 10.00 25.00
PRTT Tyrus Thomas 10.00 25.00
PRVC Vince Carter 50.00 100.00
PRWI Shawne Williams 8.00 20.00
PRZI Zydrunas Ilgauskas 12.50 30.00

2006-07 Ultimate Collection Rookie Patches Autographs

PRINT RUN 25 SER.#'d SETS
UNPRICED LOGOMAN PRINT RUN ONE SET
AB Andrea Bargnani 75.00 200.00
AR Allan Ray 15.00 40.00
BJ Bobby Jones 15.00 40.00
BR Brandon Roy 100.00 250.00
CS Cedric Simmons 15.00 40.00
DB Dee Brown 15.00 40.00
DN David Noel 15.00 40.00
HA Hilton Armstrong 15.00 40.00
JB Josh Boone 15.00 40.00
JF Jordan Farmar 15.00 40.00
JG Jorge Garbajosa 15.00 40.00
JW James White 15.00 40.00
KL Kyle Lowry 40.00 100.00
LA LaMarcus Aldridge 100.00 250.00
MA Maurice Ager 15.00 40.00
MC Mardy Collins 15.00 40.00
MW Marcus Williams 15.00 40.00
PT P.J. Tucker 15.00 40.00
QD Quincy Douby 15.00 40.00
RB Renaldo Balkman 15.00 40.00
RC Rodney Carney 15.00 40.00
RF Randy Foye 40.00 80.00
RG Rudy Gay 75.00 150.00
RO Ronnie Brewer 20.00 50.00
RR Rajon Rondo 200.00 400.00
SB Shannon Brown 25.00 60.00
SJ Solomon Jones 15.00 40.00
SM Craig Smith 15.00 40.00
SN Steve Novak 15.00 40.00
SW Shawne Williams 15.00 40.00
TS Thabo Sefolosha 20.00 50.00
TT Tyrus Thomas 40.00 100.00
WB Will Blalock 15.00 40.00
WI Shelden Williams 15.00 40.00

2006-07 Ultimate Collection Signatures

APPROXIMATE ODDS ONE PER BOX
USAB Andrea Bargnani 10.00 25.00
USBL Bill Laimbeer 10.00 25.00
USBO Chris Bosh 12.50 30.00
USBR Brandon Roy 15.00 40.00
USCA Carmelo Anthony 20.00 50.00
USCP Chris Paul 30.00 80.00
USDW Deron Williams 10.00 25.00
USHO Hakeem Olajuwon 20.00 50.00
USHW Hakim Warrick 8.00 20.00
USJE Julius Erving 50.00 120.00
USJF Jordan Farmar 8.00 20.00
USJK Jason Kidd 12.50 30.00
USJO Jermaine O'Neal 8.00 20.00
USJS J.R. Smith 8.00 20.00
USKB Kobe Bryant 125.00 250.00
USLJ LeBron James 125.00 250.00
USMB Mike Bibby 8.00 20.00
USMG Magic Johnson 60.00 120.00
USMJ Michael Jordan 350.00 650.00
USNA Steve Nash 30.00 80.00
USRG Rudy Gay 10.00 25.00
USRO Dennis Rodman 30.00 80.00
USRU Bill Russell 80.00 160.00
USSW Shelden Williams 8.00 20.00

2007-08 Ultimate Collection

This set was released on May 14, 2008. The base set consists of 150 cards. Cards 1-100 feature veterans serial numbered of 199, and cards 101-144 are autographed rookies serial numbered of either 99 or 150. Cards 145-150 are non-autographed rookies serial numbered of 99. Ultimate Collection is packaged in four-pack boxes of four cards each and packs carried an initial SRP of $125.

1 LaMarcus Aldridge 1.50 4.00
2 Ray Allen 1.25 3.00
3 Carmelo Anthony 1.50 4.00
4 Gilbert Arenas 1.25 3.00
5 Ron Artest 1.25 3.00
6 Andrea Bargnani 1.50 4.00
7 Mike Bibby 1.25 3.00
8 Chauncey Billups 1.25 3.00
9 Andrew Bogut 1.25 3.00
10 Carlos Boozer 1.25 3.00
11 Chris Bosh 1.25 3.00
12 Elton Brand 1.25 3.00
13 Kobe Bryant 6.00 15.00
14 Caron Butler 1.25 3.00
15 Jorge Garbajosa 1.00 2.50
16 Marcus Camby .75 2.00
17 Rodney Carney .75 2.00
18 Vince Carter 1.50 4.00
19 Tyson Chandler 1.00 2.50
20 Damien Wilkins .75 2.00
21 Eddy Curry .75 2.00
22 Baron Davis 1.25 3.00
23 Ricky Davis 1.00 2.50
24 Luol Deng 1.25 3.00
25 Tim Duncan 2.00 5.00
26 Shawne Williams .75 2.00
27 Monta Ellis 1.25 3.00
28 Jordan Farmar .75 2.00
29 T.J. Ford 1.00 2.50
30 Randy Foye 1.00 2.50
31 Channing Frye 1.00 2.50
32 Al Jefferson 1.25 3.00
33 Pau Gasol 1.25 3.00
34 Rudy Gay 1.25 3.00
35 Manu Ginobili 1.25 3.00
36 Ben Gordon 1.25 3.00
37 Richard Hamilton 1.00 2.50
38 Luther Head 1.00 2.50
39 Grant Hill 1.50 4.00
40 Kirk Hinrich 1.25 3.00
41 Dwight Howard 2.00 5.00
42 Josh Howard 1.25 3.00
43 Larry Hughes 1.00 2.50
44 Andre Iguodala 1.25 3.00
45 Daniel Gibson 1.25 3.00
46 Allen Iverson 1.50 4.00
47 Morris Peterson .75 2.00
48 Stephen Jackson 1.00 2.50
49 LeBron James 6.00 15.00
50 Antawn Jamison 1.25 3.00
51 Kevin Garnett 2.50 6.00
52 Richard Jefferson 1.25 3.00
53 Joe Johnson 1.25 3.00
54 Jason Kidd 1.25 3.00
55 Andrei Kirilenko 1.00 2.50
56 David Lee 1.00 2.50
57 Rashard Lewis 1.00 2.50
58 Corey Maggette 1.00 2.50
59 Stephon Marbury 1.00 2.50
60 Shawn Marion 1.25 3.00
61 Kevin Martin 1.25 3.00
62 Tracy McGrady 1.25 3.00
63 Al Harrington 1.00 2.50
64 Andre Miller 1.00 2.50
65 Francisco Garcia 1.00 2.50
66 Yao Ming 1.50 4.00
67 Cuttino Mobley 1.00 2.50
68 Alonzo Mourning 1.50 4.00
69 Steve Nash 1.50 4.00
70 Dirk Nowitzki 1.50 4.00
71 Jermaine O'Neal 1.25 3.00
72 Shaquille O'Neal 2.50 6.00
73 Lamar Odom 1.25 3.00
74 Adam Morrison 1.25 3.00
75 Mehmet Okur .75 2.00
76 Tony Parker 1.25 3.00
77 Chris Paul 2.50 6.00
78 Johan Petro .75 2.00
79 Paul Pierce 1.50 4.00
80 Tayshaun Prince 1.25 3.00
81 Zach Randolph 1.00 2.50
82 Michael Redd 1.25 3.00
83 Jason Richardson 1.25 3.00
84 Brandon Roy 1.50 4.00
85 Josh Smith 1.25 3.00
86 Amare Stoudemire 1.50 4.00
87 Jason Terry 1.00 2.50
88 Jamaal Tinsley .75 2.00
89 Hedo Turkoglu 1.25 3.00
90 Desmond Mason .75 2.00
91 Dwyane Wade 3.00 8.00
92 Ben Wallace 1.25 3.00
93 Gerald Wallace 1.25 3.00
94 Rasheed Wallace 1.25 3.00
95 Mike Miller 1.25 3.00
96 David West 1.25 3.00
97 Delonte West 1.00 2.50
98 Deron Williams 2.00 5.00
99 Marvin Williams 1.25 3.00
100 Raymond Felton 1.50 4.00
101 Arron Afflalo AU/99 RC 8.00 20.00
102 Morris Almond AU/99 RC 6.00 15.00
103 Marco Belinelli AU/99 RC 6.00 15.00
104 Corey Brewer AU/150 RC 8.00 20.00

105 Aaron Brooks AU/99 RC 6.00 15.00
106 Julian Wright AU/150 RC 6.00 15.00
107 Wilson Chandler AU/99 RC 10.00 25.00
108 Mike Conley Jr. AU/150 RC 10.00 25.00
109 Daequan Cook AU/99 RC 6.00 15.00
110 Javaris Crittenton AU/150 RC 6.00 15.00
111 JamesOn Curry AU/99 RC 6.00 15.00
112 Jermareo Davidson AU/99 RC 6.00 15.00
113 Glen Davis AU/150 RC 10.00 25.00
114 Jared Dudley AU/99 RC 6.00 15.00
115 Kevin Durant AU/150 RC 175.00 350.00
116 Nick Fazekas AU/99 RC 6.00 15.00
117 Aaron Gray AU/99 RC 6.00 15.00
118 Jeff Green AU/150 RC 8.00 20.00
119 Taurean Green AU/99 RC 6.00 15.00
120 Adam Haluska AU/99 RC 6.00 15.00
121 Spencer Hawes AU/99 RC 6.00 15.00
122 Herbert Hill AU/99 RC 6.00 15.00
123 Al Horford AU/150 RC 8.00 20.00
124 Louis Amundson AU/99 RC 6.00 15.00
125 Carl Landry AU/99 RC 6.00 15.00
126 Jamario Moon AU/150 RC 6.00 15.00
127 Acie Law AU/150 RC 6.00 15.00
128 Dominic McGuire AU/99 RC 6.00 15.00
129 Josh McRoberts AU/99 RC 6.00 15.00
130 Oleksiy Pecherov AU/99 RC 6.00 15.00
131 Coby Karl AU/99 RC 6.00 15.00
132 Joakim Noah AU/150 RC 15.00 40.00
133 Gabe Pruitt AU/99 RC 6.00 15.00
134 Chris Richard AU/99 RC 6.00 15.00
135 Juan Navarro AU/150 RC 6.00 15.00
136 Ramon Sessions AU/99 RC 10.00 25.00
137 Jason Smith AU/99 RC 6.00 15.00
138 D.J. Strawberry AU/99 RC 6.00 15.00
139 Rodney Stuckey AU/150 RC 10.00 25.00
140 Luis Scola AU/150 RC 10.00 25.00
141 Al Thornton AU/150 RC 6.00 15.00
142 Alando Tucker AU/99 RC 6.00 15.00
143 Sean Williams AU/99 RC 6.00 15.00
144 Cheikh Samb AU/99 RC 6.00 15.00
145 Yi Jianlian RC 6.00 15.00
146 Thaddeus Young RC 5.00 12.00
147 Nick Young RC 6.00 15.00
148 Kyrylo Fesenko RC 4.00 10.00
149 Greg Oden RC 5.00 12.00
150 Brandan Wright RC 4.00 10.00

2007-08 Ultimate Collection Foil

*1-100 FOIL: 2.5X TO 6X BASE HI
101-144 UNPRICED DUE TO SCARCITY
PRINT RUN 10 SER.#'d SETS

2007-08 Ultimate Collection Rookies Gold

*GOLD: .4X TO 1X BASE HI
PRINT RUN 50 SER.#'d SETS
UNPRICED LOGO PRINT RUN ONE SET
115 Kevin Durant AU 300.00 500.00

2007-08 Ultimate Collection Rookies Signature Patches

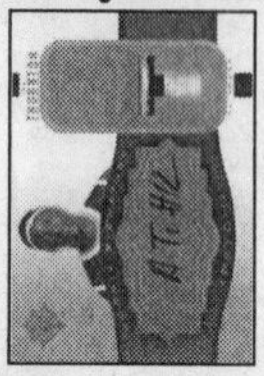

PRINT RUN 25 SER.#'d SETS
AL Acie Law 20.00 50.00
AT Al Thornton 20.00 50.00
CB Corey Brewer 25.00 60.00
DC Daequan Cook 20.00 50.00
DS D.J. Strawberry 20.00 50.00
GD Glen Davis 30.00 80.00
HO Al Horford 25.00 60.00
JC Javaris Crittenton 20.00 50.00
JG Jeff Green 30.00 80.00
JN Joakim Noah 50.00 125.00
JS Jason Smith 20.00 50.00
JW Julian Wright 20.00 50.00
KD Kevin Durant 400.00 700.00
MC Mike Conley Jr. 30.00 80.00
RS Rodney Stuckey 30.00 80.00
SW Sean Williams 20.00 50.00

2007-08 Ultimate Collection Archetypal Autographs

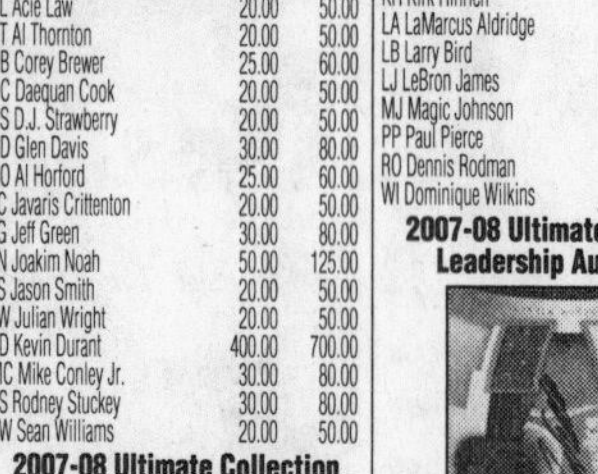

PRINT RUN 25 SER.#'d SETS
AD Adrian Dantley 10.00 25.00
BL Bill Laimbeer 15.00 30.00
DH Dwight Howard 35.00 75.00
HO Hakeem Olajuwon 20.00 40.00
JW Jerry West 30.00 60.00
LB Larry Bird 75.00 150.00
RB Rick Barry 10.00 25.00
RP Robert Parish 10.00 25.00
TC Tom Chambers 8.00 20.00
TY Tyson Chandler 8.00 20.00
WF Walt Frazier 15.00 30.00
XM Xavier McDaniel 8.00 20.00

2007-08 Ultimate Collection Commitment

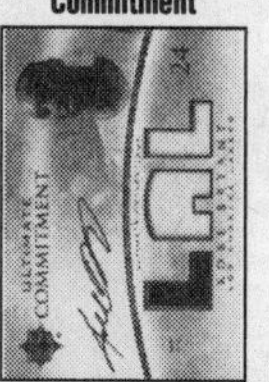

PRINT RUN 25 SER.#'d SETS
UNPRICED PATCH PRINT RUN 10 SETS
CA Carmelo Anthony 20.00 50.00
CD Clyde Drexler 25.00 60.00
CH Chris Mullin 25.00 60.00
DH Dwight Howard 30.00 60.00
DR David Robinson 40.00 80.00
DW Deron Williams 20.00 40.00
JE Julius Erving 60.00 120.00
JS John Stockton 50.00 100.00
KB Kobe Bryant 200.00 300.00
LJ LeBron James 200.00 300.00
MJ Michael Jordan 500.00 800.00
SN Steve Nash 30.00 60.00
VC Vince Carter 25.00 50.00
YM Yao Ming 25.00 50.00

2007-08 Ultimate Collection Leadership

PRINT RUN 99 SER.#'d SETS
*GOLD: .5X TO 1.25X BASE HI
GOLD PRINT RUN 50 SER.#'d SETS
BO Chris Bosh 4.00 10.00
BR Brandon Roy 5.00 12.00
CA Carmelo Anthony 5.00 12.00
CB Chauncey Billups 4.00 10.00
CP Chris Paul 5.00 12.00
DH Dwight Howard 5.00 12.00
DR David Robinson 6.00 15.00
DW Deron Williams 5.00 12.00
JE Julius Erving 8.00 20.00
JK Jason Kidd 4.00 10.00
JO Michael Jordan 50.00 125.00
JS John Stockton 5.00 12.00
KA Kareem Abdul-Jabbar 8.00 20.00
KB Kobe Bryant 20.00 50.00
KG Kevin Garnett 6.00 15.00
KH Kirk Hinrich 4.00 10.00
LA LaMarcus Aldridge 4.00 10.00
LB Larry Bird 10.00 25.00
LJ LeBron James 25.00 50.00
MJ Magic Johnson 10.00 25.00
PP Paul Pierce 5.00 12.00
RO Dennis Rodman 5.00 12.00
SN Steve Nash 5.00 12.00
TM Tracy McGrady 4.00 10.00
TP Tony Parker 4.00 10.00
VC Vince Carter 5.00 12.00
WI Dominique Wilkins 6.00 15.00

2007-08 Ultimate Collection Leadership Patches

PRINT RUN 25 SER.#'d SETS
BR Brandon Roy 6.00 15.00
CA Carmelo Anthony 15.00 30.00
CP Chris Paul 15.00 30.00
DR David Robinson 15.00 30.00
JE Julius Erving 20.00 50.00
JK Jason Kidd 10.00 25.00
KA Kareem Abdul-Jabbar 10.00 25.00
KB Kobe Bryant 40.00 75.00
KG Kevin Garnett 15.00 40.00
KH Kirk Hinrich 6.00 15.00
LA LaMarcus Aldridge 6.00 15.00
LB Larry Bird 20.00 40.00
LJ LeBron James 40.00 75.00
MJ Magic Johnson 20.00 40.00
PP Paul Pierce 15.00 30.00
RO Dennis Rodman 15.00 40.00
WI Dominique Wilkins 15.00 40.00

2007-08 Ultimate Collection Leadership Autographs

PRINT RUN 25 SER.#'d SETS
CA Carmelo Anthony 30.00 60.00
CP Chris Paul 40.00 80.00
DR David Robinson 50.00 100.00
JE Julius Erving 40.00 100.00
JK Jason Kidd 25.00 60.00
JO Michael Jordan 500.00 750.00
JS John Stockton 30.00 80.00
KA Kareem Abdul-Jabbar 40.00 80.00
KB Kobe Bryant 175.00 350.00
KG Kevin Garnett 75.00 150.00
KH Kirk Hinrich 20.00 50.00
LA LaMarcus Aldridge 20.00 50.00
LB Larry Bird 50.00 100.00
LJ LeBron James 200.00 400.00
MJ Magic Johnson 100.00 200.00
PP Paul Pierce 30.00 80.00
RO Dennis Rodman 60.00 120.00
VC Vince Carter 20.00 50.00

2007-08 Ultimate Collection Matchups

PRINT RUN 99 SER.#'d SETS
*GOLD: .5X TO 1.25X BASE HI
GOLD PRINT RUN 50 SER.#'d SETS
BG Kobe Bryant 10.00 25.00
George Gervin
CM Vince Carter 5.00 12.00
Tracy McGrady
DA LaMarcus Aldridge 12.00 30.00
Kevin Durant
DR Donyell Marshall 5.00 12.00
Ronnie Brewer
EA Julius Erving 8.00 20.00
Carmelo Anthony
FF Raymond Felton 5.00 12.00
Randy Foye
GH Horace Grant 5.00 12.00
Dwight Howard
GI Ben Gordon 5.00 12.00
Andre Iguodala
GR Kevin Garnett 10.00 25.00
Dennis Rodman
HG Kirk Hinrich 5.00 12.00
Daniel Gibson
JB Magic Johnson 20.00 50.00
Larry Bird
JJ Michael Jordan 40.00 100.00
LeBron James
JP Paul Pierce 6.00 15.00
Richard Jefferson
MR Yao Ming 6.00 15.00
David Robinson
OM Hakeem Olajuwon 15.00 40.00
Alonzo Mourning
PJ Tayshaun Prince 5.00 12.00
Al Jefferson
PR Chris Paul 6.00 15.00
Brandon Roy
PW Tony Parker 5.00 12.00
Deron Williams

2007-08 Ultimate Collection Matchups Patches

PRINT RUN 25 SER.#'d SETS
BG Kobe Bryant 40.00 100.00
George Gervin
CM Vince Carter 15.00 40.00
Tracy McGrady
DA LaMarcus Aldridge 40.00 80.00
Kevin Durant
EA Julius Erving 25.00 60.00
Carmelo Anthony
GH Horace Grant 25.00 50.00
Dwight Howard
GR Kevin Garnett 30.00 80.00
Dennis Rodman
JB Magic Johnson 30.00 80.00
Larry Bird
JJ Michael Jordan 125.00 250.00
LeBron James
MR Yao Ming 20.00 50.00
David Robinson
OM Hakeem Olajuwon 30.00 60.00
Alonzo Mourning
PR Chris Paul 15.00 40.00
Brandon Roy
PW Tony Parker 15.00 40.00
Deron Williams

2007-08 Ultimate Collection Matchups Autographs

PRINT RUN 25 SER.#'d SETS
BG Kobe Bryant 175.00 275.00
George Gervin
CM Vince Carter 40.00 80.00
Tracy McGrady
DA LaMarcus Aldridge 150.00 300.00
Kevin Durant
EA Julius Erving 60.00 120.00
Carmelo Anthony
GR Kevin Garnett 50.00 120.00
Dennis Rodman
JB Magic Johnson 175.00 275.00
Larry Bird
JJ Michael Jordan 600.00 1000.00
LeBron James
MR Yao Ming 60.00 120.00
David Robinson
OM Hakeem Olajuwon 40.00 80.00
Alonzo Mourning
PR Chris Paul 50.00 100.00
Brandon Roy

2007-08 Ultimate Collection Materials

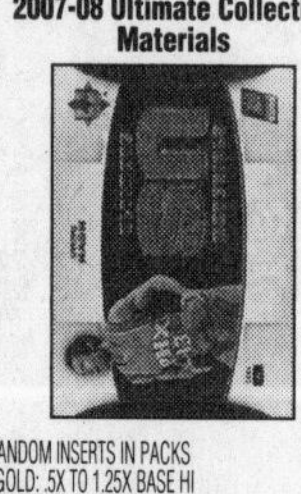

RANDOM INSERTS IN PACKS
*GOLD: .5X TO 1.25X BASE HI
GOLD PRINT RUN 50 SER.#'d SETS
AL Al Jefferson 2.50 6.00
BD Baron Davis 2.50 6.00
BG Ben Gordon 2.50 6.00
BR Brandon Roy 3.00 8.00
CA Carmelo Anthony 3.00 8.00
CP Chris Paul 5.00 12.00
DR David Robinson 4.00 10.00
DW Deron Williams 4.00 10.00
GG George Gervin 2.50 6.00
HG Horace Grant 2.50 6.00
HO Hakeem Olajuwon 3.00 8.00
JE Julius Erving 5.00 12.00
JK Jason Kidd 2.50 6.00
KA Kareem Abdul-Jabbar 4.00 10.00
KB Kobe Bryant 10.00 25.00
KG Kevin Garnett 5.00 12.00
KH Kirk Hinrich 2.50 6.00
LA LaMarcus Aldridge 3.00 8.00
LB Larry Bird 8.00 20.00
LD Luol Deng 2.50 6.00
LE LeBron James 8.00 20.00
LJ LeBron James 8.00 20.00
MJ Magic Johnson 6.00 15.00
MW Marvin Williams 2.50 6.00
PA Tony Parker 2.50 6.00
PG Pau Gasol 2.50 6.00
PP Paul Pierce 3.00 8.00
RG Rudy Gay 2.50 6.00
RH Richard Hamilton 2.00 5.00
RJ Richard Jefferson 2.50 6.00
RO Dennis Rodman 4.00 10.00
RR Rajon Rondo 4.00 10.00
SN Steve Nash 3.00 8.00
ST John Stockton 4.00 10.00
TM Tracy McGrady 2.50 6.00
TT Tyrus Thomas 2.50 6.00
VC Vince Carter 3.00 8.00
WF Walt Frazier 2.50 6.00
YM Yao Ming 3.00 8.00

2007-08 Ultimate Collection Materials Autographs

RANDOM INSERTS IN PACKS
AL Al Jefferson 8.00 20.00
BD Baron Davis 8.00 20.00
BG Ben Gordon 8.00 20.00
BR Brandon Roy 10.00 25.00
CA Carmelo Anthony 20.00 40.00
CP Chris Paul 30.00 60.00
DR David Robinson 30.00 60.00
DW Deron Williams 10.00 25.00
GG George Gervin 15.00 30.00
HG Horace Grant 25.00 60.00
HO Hakeem Olajuwon 30.00 60.00
JE Julius Erving 40.00 80.00
JW Julian Wright 8.00 20.00
KA Kareem Abdul-Jabbar 40.00 80.00
KB Kobe Bryant 125.00 250.00
KH Kirk Hinrich 10.00 25.00
LA LaMarcus Aldridge 10.00 25.00
LJ LeBron James 125.00 225.00
PA Tony Parker 10.00 25.00
PP Paul Pierce 15.00 30.00
RG Rudy Gay 8.00 20.00
RJ Richard Jefferson 8.00 20.00
RO Dennis Rodman 30.00 80.00
RR Rajon Rondo 20.00 50.00
SN Steve Nash 30.00 60.00
ST John Stockton 30.00 80.00
TM Tracy McGrady 10.00 25.00
TT Tyrus Thomas 8.00 20.00
VC Vince Carter 15.00 40.00
WF Walt Frazier 20.00 40.00

2007-08 Ultimate Collection Materials Patches

PRINT RUN 25 SER.#'d SETS
AL Al Jefferson 6.00 15.00
BG Ben Gordon 6.00 15.00
BR Brandon Roy 8.00 20.00
CA Carmelo Anthony 10.00 25.00
CP Chris Paul 15.00 30.00
DR David Robinson 15.00 40.00
DW Deron Williams 6.00 15.00
GG George Gervin 6.00 15.00
HO Hakeem Olajuwon 8.00 20.00
JE Julius Erving 10.00 25.00
JK Jason Kidd 6.00 15.00
KA Kareem Abdul-Jabbar 20.00 40.00
KB Kobe Bryant 30.00 60.00
KG Kevin Garnett 20.00 40.00
KH Kirk Hinrich 8.00 20.00
LA LaMarcus Aldridge 8.00 20.00
LB Larry Bird 20.00 50.00
LD Luol Deng 6.00 15.00
LJ LeBron James 25.00 50.00
MJ Magic Johnson 15.00 30.00
MW Marvin Williams 6.00 15.00
PA Tony Parker 6.00 15.00
PG Pau Gasol 6.00 15.00
PP Paul Pierce 8.00 20.00
RG Rudy Gay 8.00 20.00
RH Richard Hamilton 6.00 15.00
RJ Richard Jefferson 6.00 15.00
RO Dennis Rodman 10.00 25.00
SN Steve Nash 10.00 25.00
ST John Stockton 15.00 30.00
TM Tracy McGrady 8.00 20.00
TT Tyrus Thomas 6.00 15.00
VC Vince Carter 10.00 25.00
WF Walt Frazier 10.00 25.00
YM Yao Ming 10.00 25.00

2007-08 Ultimate Collection Materials Dual

PRINT RUN 99 SER#'d SETS
DBJ Kobe Bryant 25.00 60.00
LeBron James
DDP Tim Duncan 5.00 12.00
Tony Parker
DGB Kobe Bryant 15.00 30.00
Kevin Garnett
DGJ Kevin Garnett 15.00 30.00
LeBron James
DHB Richard Hamilton 5.00 12.00
Chauncey Billups
DIA Allen Iverson 6.00 15.00
Carmelo Anthony
DJW LeBron James 15.00 30.00
Dwyane Wade
DKW Andrei Kirilenko 5.00 12.00
Deron Williams
DMD Tim Duncan 6.00 15.00
Yao Ming
DMM Tracy McGrady 5.00 12.00
Yao Ming
DNH Dirk Nowitzki 5.00 12.00
Josh Howard
DNS Steve Nash 5.00 12.00
Amare Stoudemire
DSH Amare Stoudemire 6.00 15.00
Dwight Howard

2007-08 Ultimate Collection Materials Dual Patches

PRINT RUN 25 SER.#'d SETS
DBJ Kobe Bryant 50.00 125.00
LeBron James
DDS Tim Duncan 15.00 30.00
Amare Stoudemire
DGB Kobe Bryant 30.00 60.00
Kevin Garnett
DGJ Kevin Garnett 30.00 60.00
LeBron James
DHB Richard Hamilton 8.00 20.00
Chauncey Billups
DIA Allen Iverson 20.00 40.00
Carmelo Anthony
DJW LeBron James 30.00 80.00
Dwyane Wade
DMD Tim Duncan 15.00 30.00
Yao Ming
DNH Dirk Nowitzki 12.00 30.00
Josh Howard
DNS Steve Nash 15.00 30.00
Amare Stoudemire
DSH Amare Stoudemire 20.00 40.00
Dwight Howard

2007-08 Ultimate Collection Materials Triple

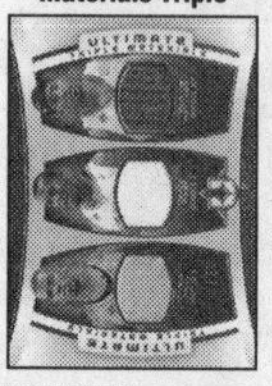

PRINT RUN 50 SER.#'d SETS
UNPRICED PATCH PRINT RUN 10 SETS
TCCM Darko Milicic 4.00 10.00
Javaris Crittenton
Mike Conley Jr.
TDGT Luol Deng 4.00 10.00
Ben Gordon
Tyrus Thomas
TDPG Tim Duncan 5.00 12.00
Tony Parker
Manu Ginobili
TDRG Luke Ridnour 8.00 20.00
Kevin Durant
Jeff Green
THSB DeShawn Stevenson 4.00 10.00
Brendan Haywood
Caron Butler
THWP Richard Hamilton 5.00 12.00
Rasheed Wallace
Tayshaun Prince
TJMF Al Jefferson 5.00 12.00
Rashad McCants
Randy Foye
TLHN Rashard Lewis 4.00 10.00
Dwight Howard
Jameer Nelson
TMBM Tracy McGrady 4.00 10.00
Shane Battier
Yao Ming
TMRB Desmond Mason 4.00 10.00
Michael Redd
Andrew Bogut
TMRR Stephon Marbury 4.00 10.00
Quentin Richardson
Zach Randolph
TPAG Paul Pierce 20.00 40.00
Ray Allen
Kevin Garnett
TPWP Morris Peterson 8.00 20.00
David West
Chris Paul
TWRM Shawn Marion 5.00 12.00
Ricky Davis
Dwyane Wade

2007-08 Ultimate Collection Materials Quad

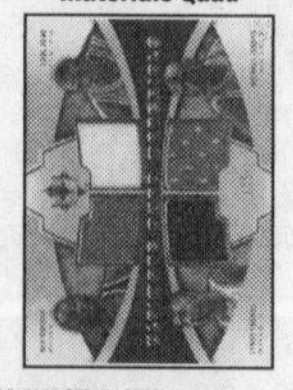

PRINT RUN 25 SER.#'d SETS
UNPRICED PATCH PRINT RUN FIVE SETS
BGJW Kobe Bryant 40.00 80.00
Kevin Garnett
LeBron James
Dwyane Wade
BPPW Mike Bibby 15.00 30.00
Tony Parker
Chris Paul
Deron Williams
BRJA Kobe Bryant 40.00 80.00
Michael Redd
LeBron James
Carmelo Anthony
CGBH Marcus Camby 15.00 30.00
Kevin Garnett
Carlos Boozer
Dwight Howard
DPGR Tim Duncan 25.00 50.00
Tony Parker
Manu Ginobili
David Robinson
DSHJ Tim Duncan 10.00 25.00
Amare Stoudemire
Dwight Howard
Al Jefferson
GMMW Kevin Garnett 10.00 25.00
Tracy McGrady
Shawn Marion
Gerald Wallace
HRSG Richard Hamilton 10.00 25.00
Michael Redd
Peja Stojakovic
Daniel Gibson
HWBP Richard Hamilton 10.00 25.00
Rasheed Wallace
Chauncey Billups
Tayshaun Prince
JDGT Michael Jordan 60.00 120.00
Luol Deng
Ben Gordon
Tyrus Thomas
JEJB Michael Jordan 100.00 200.00
Julius Erving
Magic Johnson
Larry Bird
JIPG LeBron James 30.00 60.00
Andre Iguodala
Chris Paul
Gerald Green
JWHR LeBron James 25.00 50.00
Dwyane Wade
Dwight Howard
Brandon Roy
NKPW Steve Nash 15.00 30.00
Jason Kidd
Chris Paul
Deron Williams
OMMO Hakeem Olajuwon 30.00 60.00
Alonzo Mourning
Yao Ming
Shaquille O'Neal
PAGB Paul Pierce 40.00 80.00
Ray Allen
Kevin Garnett
Larry Bird

2007-08 Ultimate Collection Materials Rookies

RANDOM INSERTS IN PACKS
*GOLD: .5X TO 1.25X BASE HI
GOLD PRINT RUN 99 SER.#'d SETS
*PATCH: .75X TO 2X BASE HI
PATCH PRINT RUN 25 SER.#'d SETS
AA Arron Afflalo 2.50 6.00
AB Aaron Brooks 2.00 5.00
AG Aaron Gray 2.00 5.00
AH Al Horford 2.50 6.00
AL Acie Law 2.00 5.00
AT Al Thornton 2.00 5.00
CB Corey Brewer 2.50 6.00
CL Carl Landry 2.00 5.00
DA Jermareo Davidson 2.00 5.00
DC Daequan Cook 2.00 5.00
DM Dominic McGuire 2.00 5.00
GD Glen Davis 3.00 8.00
GP Gabe Pruitt 2.00 5.00
HA Adam Haluska 2.00 5.00
HH Herbert Hill 2.00 5.00
JC Javaris Crittenton 2.00 5.00
JD Jared Dudley 2.00 5.00
JG Jeff Green 2.50 6.00
JN Joakim Noah 5.00 12.00
JS Jason Smith 2.00 5.00
JW Julian Wright 2.00 5.00
KD Kevin Durant 15.00 40.00
MA Morris Almond 2.00 5.00
MC Mike Conley Jr. 3.00 8.00
NF Nick Fazekas 2.00 5.00
RS Rodney Stuckey 3.00 8.00
SH Spencer Hawes 2.00 5.00
SW Sean Williams 2.00 5.00
TU Alando Tucker 2.00 5.00
WC Wilson Chandler 3.00 8.00

2007-08 Ultimate Collection Materials Rookies Autographs

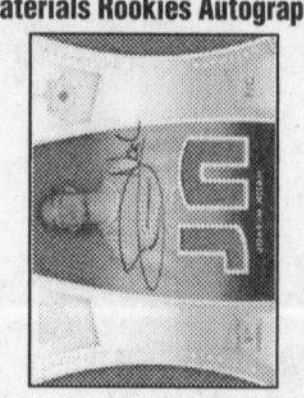

RANDOM INSERTS IN PACKS
AA Arron Afflalo 5.00 12.00
AB Aaron Brooks 4.00 10.00
AH Al Horford 5.00 12.00
AL Acie Law 4.00 10.00
AT Al Thornton 4.00 10.00
CB Corey Brewer 5.00 12.00
CL Carl Landry 4.00 10.00
DC Daequan Cook 4.00 10.00
GD Glen Davis 6.00 15.00
JC Javaris Crittenton 4.00 10.00
JD Jared Dudley 4.00 10.00
JG Jeff Green 5.00 12.00
JN Joakim Noah 12.50 30.00
JS Jason Smith 4.00 10.00
JW Julian Wright 4.00 10.00
KD Kevin Durant 150.00 300.00
MC Mike Conley Jr. 6.00 15.00
RS Rodney Stuckey 6.00 15.00
SH Spencer Hawes 4.00 10.00
SW Sean Williams 4.00 10.00

2007-08 Ultimate Collection Rookie Matchups

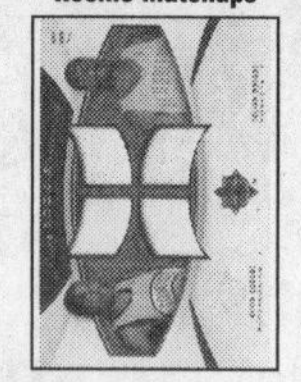

PRINT RUN 99 SER.#'d SETS
*GOLD: .5X TO 1.25X HI COLUMN
GOLD PRINT RUN 50 SER.#'d SETS
BC Corey Brewer 3.00 8.00
Mike Conley Jr.
CD Glen Davis 4.00 10.00
Wilson Chandler
DC Jared Dudley 3.00 8.00
Wilson Chandler
DH Kevin Durant 10.00 25.00
Al Horford
DW Kevin Durant 10.00 25.00
Julian Wright
GS Taurean Green 3.00 8.00
D.J. Strawberry
GW Jeff Green 3.00 8.00
Julian Wright
HD Glen Davis 3.00 8.00
Spencer Hawes
HN Joakim Noah 5.00 12.00
Al Horford
LA Morris Almond 3.00 8.00
Acie Law
SC Rodney Stuckey 3.00 8.00
Daequan Cook
ST Alando Tucker 3.00 8.00
D.J. Strawberry
TC Al Thornton 3.00 8.00
Javaris Crittenton
TL Alando Tucker 3.00 8.00
Carl Landry

2007-08 Ultimate Collection Rookie Matchups Patches

PRINT RUN 25 SER.#'d SETS
BC Corey Brewer 8.00 20.00
Mike Conley Jr.
CD Glen Davis 10.00 25.00
Wilson Chandler
DH Kevin Durant 40.00 80.00
Al Horford
DW Kevin Durant 40.00 80.00
Julian Wright
GS Taurean Green 20.00 40.00
D.J. Strawberry
GW Jeff Green 10.00 25.00
Julian Wright
HN Joakim Noah 12.50 30.00
Al Horford
LA Morris Almond 8.00 20.00
Acie Law
SC Rodney Stuckey 8.00 20.00
Daequan Cook
TC Al Thornton 8.00 20.00
Javaris Crittenton

2007-08 Ultimate Collection Rookie Matchups Autographs

PRINT RUN 25 SER.#'d SETS
BC Corey Brewer 20.00 40.00
Mike Conley Jr.
CD Glen Davis 15.00 40.00
Wilson Chandler
DH Kevin Durant 150.00 300.00
Al Horford
DW Kevin Durant 75.00 200.00
Julian Wright
GW Jeff Green 12.50 30.00
Julian Wright
LA Morris Almond 12.50 30.00
Acie Law

2007-08 Ultimate Collection Signatures

STATED PRINT RUN 20 TO 75 SER.#'d SETS
UNPRICED GOLD PRINT RUN 10 SETS
UNPRICED QUAD PRINT RUN 10 SETS
UNPRICED SIX PRINT RUN 5 SETS
AD Adrian Dantley/50 6.00 15.00
AM Alonzo Mourning/50 25.00 60.00
BA B.J. Armstrong/75 10.00 25.00
BD Baron Davis/75 8.00 20.00
BR Brandon Roy/50 8.00 20.00
BW Bill Walton/25 15.00 30.00
CA Carmelo Anthony/20 20.00 40.00
DA Brad Daugherty/75 6.00 15.00

DF Derek Fisher/50 6.00 15.00
DG Daniel Gibson/75 6.00 15.00
DH Dwight Howard/50 15.00 40.00
DM Donyell Marshall/75 6.00 15.00
DO Dominique Wilkins/50 15.00 40.00
DR David Robinson/20 50.00 100.00
DY Danny Manning/25 15.00 30.00
EC Eddy Curry/25 6.00 15.00
GG George Gervin/50 10.00 25.00
GH Horace Grant/25 20.00 40.00
HA Hilton Armstrong/75 6.00 15.00
HE Luther Head/75 6.00 15.00
HO Hakeem Olajuwon/20 20.00 50.00
JE Al Jefferson/50 6.00 15.00
JJ Jarrett Jack/75 6.00 15.00
JK Jason Kidd/20 20.00 40.00
JW James Worthy/20 30.00 60.00
KH Kirk Hinrich/50 6.00 15.00
KV Kiki Vandeweghe/75 8.00 20.00
LA LaMarcus Aldridge/25 10.00 25.00
LJ LeBron James/20 100.00 200.00
MJ Magic Johnson/20 50.00 100.00
PA Tony Parker/25 12.00 30.00
PR Pat Riley/25 15.00 30.00
RA Randolph Morris/75 6.00 15.00
RF Randy Foye/50 6.00 15.00
RG Rudy Gay/50 6.00 15.00
RO Dennis Rodman/25 30.00 60.00
SJ Solomon Jones/75 6.00 15.00
SM Craig Smith/75 6.00 15.00
SP Sam Perkins/50 6.00 15.00
TC Terry Cummings/75 6.00 15.00
TM Tracy McGrady/20 15.00 40.00
TO Tom Chambers/50 10.00 25.00
TT Tyrus Thomas/25 6.00 15.00
TY Tyson Chandler/75 6.00 15.00
VC Vince Carter/20 25.00 50.00
WE Jerry West/20 30.00 80.00
WF Walt Frazier/50 15.00 30.00
WI Deron Williams/50 10.00 25.00

2007-08 Ultimate Collection Signatures Dual

PRINT RUN 25 SER.#'d SETS
AM Hilton Armstrong 10.00 25.00
Paul Millsap
BD Baron Davis 10.00 25.00
Marco Belinelli
BH Chris Bosh 40.00 80.00
Dwight Howard
BJ Richard Jefferson 30.00 60.00
Bruce Bowen
CJ Vince Carter 20.00 50.00
Antawn Jamison
CL Kyle Lowry 10.00 25.00
Mike Conley Jr.
CM Vince Carter 25.00 50.00
Tracy McGrady
CP Tyson Chandler 15.00 30.00
Tayshaun Prince
CS Rodney Carney 10.00 25.00
Craig Smith
CW Tyson Chandler 10.00 25.00
Julian Wright
DB Boris Diaw 10.00 25.00
Leandro Barbosa
DL Keyon Dooling 10.00 25.00
Kyle Lowry
FR Randy Foye 15.00 30.00
Rajon Rondo
FS Derek Fisher 40.00 80.00
John Stockton
GA Ben Gordon 10.00 25.00
Maurice Ager
GB Daniel Gibson 10.00 25.00
Shannon Brown
GD Kevin Garnett 150.00 300.00
Kevin Durant
GH Horace Grant 30.00 60.00
Dwight Howard
GP Artis Gilmore 15.00 30.00
Robert Parish
HP Al Harrington 10.00 25.00
Leon Powe
HW Al Harrington 10.00 25.00
Marvin Williams
JG Al Jefferson 10.00 25.00
Rudy Gay
JP Richard Jefferson 10.00 25.00
Tayshaun Prince
KA Steve Kerr 20.00 40.00
B.J. Armstrong
LC David Lee 10.00 25.00
Rodney Carney
LG David Lee 10.00 25.00
Rudy Gay
MB Rick Barry 40.00 75.00
Chris Mullin
MJ Paul Millsap 10.00 25.00
Solomon Jones
MW Yao Ming 25.00 50.00
Bill Walton
OM Patrick O'Bryant 10.00 25.00
Paul Millsap
OR Hakeem Olajuwon 50.00 100.00
David Robinson
PD Paul Pierce 20.00 40.00
Adrian Dantley
PW Chris Paul 50.00 100.00
Deron Williams
RF Randy Foye 15.00 30.00
Brandon Roy
RP Rajon Rondo 15.00 40.00
Gabe Pruitt
WH Dominique Wilkins 30.00 60.00
Al Horford

2007-08 Ultimate Collection Signatures Triple

PRINT RUN 15 SER.#'d SETS
BMG Mike Bibby 25.00 50.00
Brad Miller
Francisco Garcia
CPW Tyson Chandler 60.00 120.00
Chris Paul
Julian Wright
DAE Walter Davis 25.00 50.00
Carmelo Anthony
Alex English
DAR Clyde Drexler 60.00 120.00
LaMarcus Aldridge
Brandon Roy
DHB Baron Davis 20.00 40.00
Al Harrington
Marco Belinelli
FSB Randy Foye 15.00 30.00
Craig Smith
Corey Brewer
GLC Rudy Gay 15.00 30.00
Kyle Lowry
Mike Conley Jr.
GTN Ben Gordon 40.00 80.00
Tyrus Thomas
Joakim Noah
KCJ Jason Kidd 40.00 80.00
Vince Carter
Richard Jefferson
LPR Bill Laimbeer 60.00 120.00
Tayshaun Prince
Dennis Rodman
MLT Corey Maggette 15.00 30.00
Shaun Livingston
Al Thornton
OMM Hakeem Olajuwon 60.00 120.00
Tracy McGrady
Yao Ming
PRB Bruce Bowen 50.00 100.00
Tony Parker
David Robinson
WDG Damien Wilkins 75.00 150.00
Kevin Durant
Jeff Green
WHL Dominique Wilkins 30.00 60.00
Al Horford
Acie Law

2007-08 Ultimate Collection Virtuoso

PRINT RUN 25 SER.#'d SETS
UNPRICED PATCH PRINT RUN 10 SETS
AM Alonzo Mourning 40.00 80.00
BG Ben Gordon 10.00 25.00
CB Carlos Boozer 10.00 25.00
CM Chris Mullin 20.00 50.00
CP Chris Paul 40.00 100.00
DH Dwight Howard 25.00 60.00
GG George Gervin 20.00 40.00
KB Kobe Bryant 150.00 250.00
KH Kirk Hinrich 10.00 25.00
LA LaMarcus Aldridge 15.00 40.00
LJ LeBron James 150.00 250.00
YM Yao Ming 25.00 50.00

2007-08 Ultimate Collection Write of Passage Autographs Dual

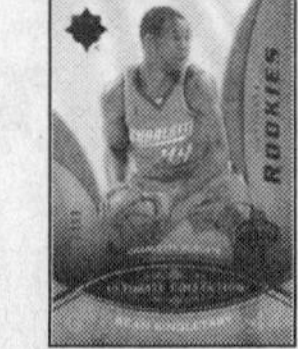

PRINT RUN 25 SER.#'d SETS
CC Daequan Cook 12.50 30.00
Mike Conley Jr.
DG Kevin Durant 100.00 225.00
Jeff Green
DH Kevin Durant 100.00 225.00
Al Horford
HL Al Horford 20.00 40.00
Acie Law
PD Gabe Pruitt 12.50 30.00
Glen Davis
SC Javaris Crittenton 12.50 30.00
Luis Scola

2008-09 Ultimate Collection

1-80 PRINT RUN 499 SER.#'d SETS
81-100 PRINT RUN 499 SER.#'d SETS
101-120 PRINT RUN 499 SER.#'d SETS
121-141 PRINT RUN 150 SER.#'d SETS
1 LaMarcus Aldridge 2.00 5.00
2 Ray Allen 2.00 5.00
3 Carmelo Anthony 2.50 6.00
4 Gilbert Arenas 2.00 5.00
5 Ron Artest 2.00 5.00
6 Chauncey Billups 2.00 5.00
7 Carlos Boozer 2.00 5.00
8 Chris Bosh 2.00 5.00
9 Elton Brand 2.00 5.00
10 Kobe Bryant 10.00 25.00
11 Caron Butler 2.00 5.00
12 Andrew Bynum 2.50 6.00
13 Jose Calderon 1.50 4.00
14 Vince Carter 2.50 6.00
15 Tyson Chandler 1.50 4.00
16 Mike Conley Jr. 1.50 4.00
17 Jamal Crawford 1.50 4.00
18 Baron Davis 2.00 5.00
19 Luol Deng 2.00 5.00
20 Chris Duhon 1.25 3.00
21 Tim Duncan 3.00 8.00
22 Kevin Durant 8.00 20.00
23 Raymond Felton 1.50 4.00
24 T.J. Ford 1.25 3.00
25 Kevin Garnett 4.00 10.00
26 Pau Gasol 2.00 5.00
27 Rudy Gay 2.00 5.00
28 Manu Ginobili 2.00 5.00
29 Ben Gordon 2.00 5.00
30 Danny Granger 2.00 5.00
31 Jeff Green 1.50 4.00
32 Al Harrington 1.50 4.00
33 Devin Harris 2.00 5.00
34 Kirk Hinrich 2.00 5.00
35 Al Horford 2.00 5.00
36 Dwight Howard 4.00 10.00
37 Josh Howard 1.50 4.00
38 Andre Iguodala 2.00 5.00
39 Allen Iverson 2.50 6.00
40 Stephen Jackson 1.50 4.00
41 LeBron James 10.00 25.00
42 Antawn Jamison 2.00 5.00
43 Al Jefferson 2.00 5.00
44 Richard Jefferson 2.00 5.00
45 Yi Jianlian 2.00 5.00
46 Joe Johnson 2.00 5.00
47 Jason Kidd 2.00 5.00
48 David Lee 1.50 4.00
49 Rashard Lewis 1.50 4.00
50 Corey Maggette 1.50 4.00
51 Shawn Marion 2.00 5.00
52 Kevin Martin 2.00 5.00
53 Tracy McGrady 2.00 5.00
54 Andre Miller 1.50 4.00
55 Mike Miller 2.00 5.00
56 Paul Millsap 1.50 4.00
57 Yao Ming 2.50 6.00
58 Steve Nash 2.00 5.00
59 Jameer Nelson 1.50 4.00
60 Dirk Nowitzki 2.50 6.00
61 Greg Oden 2.00 5.00
62 Tony Parker 2.00 5.00
63 Chris Paul 3.00 8.00
64 Paul Pierce 2.50 6.00
65 Tayshaun Prince 2.00 5.00
66 Zach Randolph 1.50 4.00
67 Michael Redd 2.00 5.00
68 Jason Richardson 2.00 5.00
69 Brandon Roy 2.00 5.00
70 John Salmons 2.00 5.00
71 Josh Smith 2.00 5.00
72 Amare Stoudemire 2.00 5.00
73 Rodney Stuckey 2.50 6.00
74 Al Thornton 1.50 4.00
75 Dwyane Wade 4.00 10.00
76 Gerald Wallace 2.00 5.00
77 David West 2.00 5.00
78 Deron Williams 2.00 5.00
79 Mo Williams 1.50 4.00
80 Thaddeus Young 1.50 4.00
81 Sean Singletary RC 2.50 6.00
82 Luc Mbah A Moute RC 2.50 6.00
83 Darnell Jackson/491 RC 2.50 6.00
84 Nathan Jawai RC 2.50 6.00
85 Jawad Williams RC 2.50 6.00
86 Joey Dorsey RC 2.50 6.00
87 Alexis Ajinca RC 2.50 6.00
88 DeAndre Jordan/491 RC 5.00 12.00
89 Javale McGee RC 4.00 10.00
90 Hamed Haddadi RC 2.50 6.00
91 Roko Ukic RC 2.50 6.00
92 Kosta Koufos RC 2.50 6.00
93 Nicolas Batum RC 4.00 10.00
94 Ryan Anderson/491 RC 4.00 10.00
95 Joe Alexander RC 2.50 6.00
96 Chris Douglas-Roberts RC 2.50 6.00
97 Anthony Morrow RC 6.00 15.00
98 Darrell Arthur RC 2.50 6.00
99 Danilo Gallinari RC 4.00 10.00
100 Marc Gasol RC 4.00 10.00
101 Michael Jordan 20.00 50.00
102 Larry Bird 6.00 15.00
103 Magic Johnson 5.00 12.00
104 Oscar Robertson 2.00 5.00
105 John Stockton 3.00 8.00
106 Julius Erving 4.00 10.00
107 Manute Bol 2.00 5.00
108 Dee Brown 2.00 5.00
109 Joe Dumars 2.00 5.00
110 James Edwards 2.00 5.00
111 A.C. Green 2.00 5.00
112 Tim Hardaway 2.00 5.00
113 Kevin Johnson 2.00 5.00
114 Karl Malone 2.50 6.00
115 Danny Ainge 2.00 5.00
116 Kurt Rambis 2.50 6.00
117 Willis Reed 2.00 5.00
118 Scottie Pippen 3.00 8.00
119 Wilt Chamberlain 4.00 10.00
120 Drazen Petrovic 3.00 8.00
121 Kevin Love JSY AU RC 50.00 125.00
122 Michael Beasley JSY AU RC 15.00 40.00
123 Rudy Fernandez JSY AU RC 10.00 25.00
124 O.J. Mayo JSY AU RC 15.00 40.00
125 Derrick Rose JSY AU RC 250.00 450.00
126 Brook Lopez JSY AU RC 12.00 30.00
127 Russell Westbrook JSY AU RC 75.00 150.00
128 Courtney Lee JSY AU RC 12.00 30.00
129 Jerryd Bayless JSY AU RC 8.00 20.00
130 Marreese Speights JSY AU RC 8.00 20.00
131 Donte Greene JSY AU RC 8.00 20.00
132 J.J. Hickson JSY AU RC 10.00 25.00
133 D.J. Augustin JSY AU RC 8.00 20.00
134 Jason Thompson JSY AU RC 8.00 20.00
135 Robin Lopez JSY AU RC 8.00 20.00
136 Anthony Randolph JSY AU RC 10.00 25.00
137 Eric Gordon JSY AU RC 25.00 60.00
138 Brandon Rush JSY AU RC 8.00 20.00
139 Roy Hibbert JSY AU RC 12.00 30.00
140 Mario Chalmers JSY AU RC 12.00 30.00
141 George Hill JSY AU RC 12.00 30.00

2008-09 Ultimate Collection Rookies Patches

STATED PRINT RUN 10 SER.#'d SETS
121 Kevin Love JSY AU 300.00 600.00
122 Michael Beasley JSY AU 75.00 200.00
123 Rudy Fernandez JSY AU 40.00 100.00
124 O.J. Mayo JSY AU 75.00 200.00
125 Derrick Rose JSY AU 2000.00 3000.00
126 Brook Lopez JSY AU 50.00 125.00
127 Russell Westbrook JSY AU 400.00 700.00
128 Courtney Lee JSY AU 50.00 125.00
129 Jerryd Bayless JSY AU 50.00 125.00
130 Marreese Speights JSY AU 30.00 80.00
131 Donte Greene JSY AU 30.00 80.00
132 J.J. Hickson JSY AU 40.00 100.00
133 D.J. Augustin JSY AU 30.00 80.00
134 Jason Thompson JSY AU 30.00 80.00
135 Robin Lopez JSY AU 30.00 80.00
136 Anthony Randolph JSY AU 60.00 150.00
137 Eric Gordon JSY AU 100.00 250.00
138 Brandon Rush JSY AU 30.00 80.00
139 Roy Hibbert JSY AU 50.00 125.00
140 Mario Chalmers JSY AU 50.00 125.00
141 George Hill JSY AU 50.00 125.00

2008-09 Ultimate Collection Rookies Silver

*SILVER: .5X TO 1.25X BASE HI
SILVER PRINT RUN 60 SER.#'d SETS

2008-09 Ultimate Collection Century Legends Epic Signature Update

COMBINED AUTO ODDS 1:3
CLAA Adrian Dantley 8.00 20.00
CLAG Artis Gilmore 8.00 20.00
CLAM Alonzo Mourning 30.00 60.00
CLBK Bernard King 8.00 20.00
CLBL Bill Laimbeer 8.00 20.00
CLBM Bob McAdoo 15.00 30.00
CLBR Brandon Roy 15.00 30.00
CLBS Bill Sharman 8.00 20.00
CLCP Chris Paul SP 200.00 400.00
CLDE Derrick Rose 175.00 325.00
CLDF Derek Fisher 10.00 25.00
CLDG Darrell Griffith 8.00 20.00
CLDH Dwight Howard 40.00 80.00
CLDR David Robinson 60.00 120.00
CLDW Deron Williams 25.00 50.00
CLHG Horace Grant 25.00 60.00
CLJK Jason Kidd 40.00 80.00
CLJS John Stockton 50.00 125.00
CLKB Kobe Bryant 200.00 300.00
CLKD Kevin Durant 50.00 125.00
CLLJ LeBron James 200.00 300.00
CLLW Lenny Wilkens 15.00 30.00
CLMB Michael Beasley 25.00 60.00
CLMJ Magic Johnson 100.00 200.00
CLOJ O.J. Mayo 25.00 60.00
CLPP Paul Pierce 25.00 60.00
CLRB Rick Barry 15.00 30.00
CLRO Dennis Rodman 50.00 100.00
CLRP Robert Parish 8.00 20.00
CLRS Ralph Sampson 8.00 20.00
CLSJ Sam Jones 15.00 40.00
CLSN Steve Nash 60.00 120.00
CLSW Spud Webb 8.00 20.00
CLTM Tracy McGrady 30.00 60.00
CLVC Vince Carter 25.00 50.00

2008-09 Ultimate Collection Entry

STATED PRINT RUN 10 SER.#'d SETS
UEAD Adrian Dantley 15.00 30.00
UEAE Alex English 15.00 30.00
UEBD Brad Daugherty 15.00 30.00
UEBL Bob Lanier 15.00 30.00
UEBS Bill Sharman 15.00 30.00
UEBW Bill Walton 25.00 50.00
UECL Clyde Lovellette 15.00 30.00
UEDC Dave Cowens 25.00 50.00
UEDW Dominique Wilkins 25.00 50.00
UEGE George Gervin 20.00 50.00
UEGG Gail Goodrich 20.00 40.00
UEHG Hal Greer 20.00 40.00
UEJH John Havlicek 25.00 50.00
UEJK Jason Kidd 40.00 80.00
UEJS Jack Sikma 15.00 30.00
UEKG Kevin Garnett 50.00 100.00
UELW Lenny Wilkens 15.00 30.00
UEMJ Michael Jordan 600.00 1000.00
UENT Nate Thurmond 20.00 40.00
UERB Rick Barry 20.00 40.00
UERP Robert Parish 20.00 40.00
UESJ Sam Jones 30.00 60.00
UEVC Vince Carter 40.00 100.00

2008-09 Ultimate Collection Initiation Writes

STATED PRINT RUN 25 SER.#'d SETS
IWAA Alexis Ajinca 6.00 15.00
IWAR Anthony Randolph 12.00 30.00
IWBL Brook Lopez 10.00 25.00
IWBR Brandon Rush 6.00 15.00
IWCL Courtney Lee 15.00 40.00
IWDA D.J. Augustin 10.00 25.00
IWDG Danilo Gallinari 10.00 25.00
IWDR Derrick Rose 250.00 450.00
IWDW D.J. White 6.00 15.00
IWEG Eric Gordon 20.00 50.00
IWGH George Hill 10.00 25.00
IWJA Joe Alexander 6.00 15.00
IWJB Jerryd Bayless 10.00 25.00
IWJH J.J. Hickson 8.00 20.00
IWJM Javale McGee 10.00 25.00
IWJT Jason Thompson 10.00 25.00
IWKK Kosta Koufos 6.00 15.00
IWKL Kevin Love 25.00 60.00
IWMB Michael Beasley 15.00 40.00
IWMG Marc Gasol 10.00 25.00
IWMS Marreese Speights 6.00 15.00
IWNB Nicolas Batum 30.00 80.00
IWOM O.J. Mayo 15.00 40.00
IWRA Ryan Anderson 10.00 25.00
IWRF Rudy Fernandez 8.00 20.00
IWRH Roy Hibbert 10.00 25.00
IWRL Robin Lopez 6.00 15.00
IWRW Russell Westbrook 30.00 80.00

2008-09 Ultimate Collection Jerseys Eight

STATED PRINT RUN 25 SER.#'d SETS
UNPRICED PATCH PRINT RUN 6 SER.#'d SETS
76ERS Andre Miller 30.00 60.00
Marreese Speights
Thaddeus Young
Elton Brand
Julius Erving
Samuel Dalembert
Donyell Marshall
Andre Iguodala
BULLS Dennis Rodman 40.00 80.00
Derrick Rose
Joakim Noah
Tyrus Thomas
Scottie Pippen
Luol Deng
Larry Hughes
Ben Gordon
HAWKS Marvin Williams 20.00 40.00
Al Horford
Acie Law
Joe Johnson
Spud Webb
Dominique Wilkins
Mike Bibby
Josh Smith
KNICK Willis Reed 30.00 80.00
John Starks
Patrick Ewing
Eddy Curry
Chris Duhon
Nate Robinson
Micheal Ray Richardson
David Lee
SPURS David Robinson 50.00 100.00
Steve Kerr
Bruce Bowen
Tony Parker
Manu Ginobili
Tim Duncan
George Gervin
Michael Finley
CELTIC Larry Bird 60.00 120.00
Robert Parish
Bill Russell
Glen Davis
Kevin McHale
Ray Allen
Kevin Garnett
Paul Pierce
LACLIP Baron Davis 20.00 40.00
Marcus Camby
Chris Kaman
Zach Randolph
Eric Gordon
DeAndre Jordan
Al Thornton
Bill Walton
LAKERS Jordan Farmar 60.00 120.00
Magic Johnson
Lamar Odom
Luke Walton
Michael Cooper
Sasha Vujacic
Jerry West
Kobe Bryant
PISTON Richard Hamilton 40.00 100.00
Allen Iverson
Rasheed Wallace
Tayshaun Prince
Antonio McDyess
Bill Laimbeer
Rodney Stuckey
Isiah Thomas
ROCKET Luther Head 20.00 50.00
Shane Battier
Hakeem Olajuwon
Dikembe Mutombo
Yao Ming
Joey Dorsey
Clyde Drexler
Tracy McGrady
UTAHJZ John Stockton 40.00 80.00
C.J. Miles
Darrell Griffith
Jeff Hornacek
Karl Malone
Carlos Boozer
Andrei Kirilenko
Deron Williams
ROOKIE08 Jason Thompson 25.00 50.00
Eric Gordon
Kevin Love
Joe Alexander
Derrick Rose
Michael Beasley
Russell Westbrook
O.J. Mayo

2008-09 Ultimate Collection Jerseys Foursome Combos

STATED PRINT RUN 35 SER.#'d SETS
*PATCHES: .75X TO 2X BASE HI
PATCH PRINT RUN 10 SER.#'d SETS
UFCOKC Kevin Durant 10.00 25.00
Jeff Green
Russell Westbrook
Damien Wilkins
UFC3PTS Donyell Marshall 15.00 30.00
Ray Allen
Steve Kerr
Dan Majerle
UFC76ER Marreese Speights 10.00 25.00
Julius Erving
Elton Brand
Andre Iguodala
UFCBLAZ Jerryd Bayless 20.00 50.00
Clyde Drexler
Rudy Fernandez
Brandon Roy
UFCBSTN Kevin McHale 25.00 60.00
Kevin Garnett
Paul Pierce
J.R. Giddens
UFCBULL Derrick Rose 30.00 60.00
Scottie Pippen
Dennis Rodman
Ben Gordon
UFCCHMP Isiah Thomas 15.00 30.00
Joe Dumars
Richard Hamilton
Chauncey Billups
UFCCLIP Marcus Camby 8.00 20.00
Baron Davis
Eric Gordon
Mardy Collins
UFCDETP Richard Hamilton 10.00 25.00
Rasheed Wallace
Walter Sharpe
Arron Afflalo
UFCEVSW Magic Johnson 40.00 80.00
Kobe Bryant
Kevin Garnett
Larry Bird
UFCGRDS Jason Kidd 20.00 40.00
Deron Williams
John Stockton
Chris Paul
UFCGRIZ Darrell Arthur 8.00 20.00
Mike Conley Jr.
O.J. Mayo
Hakim Warrick
UFCHAWK Mike Bibby 8.00 20.00
Josh Smith
Joe Johnson
Al Horford
UFCHEAT Michael Beasley 20.00 40.00
Udonis Haslem
Dorell Wright
Alonzo Mourning
UFCJAZG Ronnie Brewer 10.00 25.00
John Stockton
Deron Williams
Kyle Korver
UFCJAZZ Mark Eaton 10.00 25.00
Andrei Kirilenko
Karl Malone
Kosta Koufos
UFCKNIC Al Harrington 8.00 20.00
Earl Monroe
Wilson Chandler
Quentin Richardson
UFCLAKR Andrew Bynum 30.00 60.00
Jerry West
Kareem Abdul-Jabbar
Kobe Bryant
UFCLEGS Robert Parish 20.00 40.00
Bill Russell
Willis Reed
Kareem Abdul-Jabbar
UFCLGND Pat Riley 15.00 30.00
Adrian Dantley
Hakeem Olajuwon
Patrick Ewing
UFCNETS Brook Lopez 8.00 20.00
Chris Douglas-Roberts
Devin Harris
Vince Carter
UFCNICK Willis Reed 10.00 25.00
Earl Monroe
Patrick Ewing
Eddy Curry
UFCPSTN Isiah Thomas 8.00 20.00
Rodney Stuckey
Joe Dumars
Richard Hamilton
UFCROCK Hakeem Olajuwon 10.00 25.00
Yao Ming
Luis Scola
Joey Dorsey
UFCSCOR Kareem Abdul-Jabbar 30.00 80.00
Kobe Bryant
Wilt Chamberlain
George Gervin
UFCSGRD Kobe Bryant 40.00 80.00
Earl Monroe
Allen Iverson
Pete Maravich
UFCTWLV Kevin Love 8.00 20.00
Rashad McCants
Corey Brewer
Craig Smith
UFCUDEX LeBron James 75.00 200.00
Kobe Bryant
Kevin Garnett
Michael Jordan
UFCWARS Jo Jo White 10.00 25.00
Anthony Randolph
Jamal Crawford
Corey Maggette

2008-09 Ultimate Collection Jerseys Foursome Legends

STATED PRINT RUN 25 SER.#'d SETS
*PATCHES: 1X TO 2.5X BASE HI
PATCH PRINT RUN 10 SER.#'d SETS
UFL76ER Julius Erving 30.00 60.00
Moses Malone
Wilt Chamberlain
Maurice Cheeks
UFLBIGS Willis Reed 30.00 60.00
Hakeem Olajuwon
Bill Russell
David Robinson
UFLBULL Scottie Pippen 80.00 200.00
Dennis Rodman
Michael Jordan
Steve Kerr
UFLCELT Bill Russell 40.00 80.00
Larry Bird
Kevin McHale
Robert Parish
UFLCLSC Robert Parish 30.00 80.00
Wilt Chamberlain
Jo Jo White
Pete Maravich
UFLDUNK Darrell Griffith 20.00 40.00
Dominique Wilkins
Moses Malone
George Gervin
UFLEGRD Maurice Cheeks 10.00 25.00
Spud Webb
John Starks
Isiah Thomas
UFLGRDS Michael Cooper 15.00 30.00
Jerry West
Stacey Augmon
Adrian Dantley
UFLGSTB Jo Jo White 30.00 60.00
Chris Mullin
Clyde Drexler
Scottie Pippen
UFLHRSA Hakeem Olajuwon 30.00 60.00
Clyde Drexler
David Robinson
George Gervin
UFLJAZZ Jeff Hornacek 30.00 60.00
Karl Malone
Mark Eaton
John Stockton
UFLLABC Kevin McHale 30.00 80.00
Larry Bird
Magic Johnson
Kareem Abdul-Jabbar
UFLLAKR Wilt Chamberlain 50.00 120.00
Dennis Rodman
Karl Malone
Horace Grant
UFLLGND Magic Johnson 60.00 150.00
Larry Bird
Bill Russell
Michael Jordan
UFLMBBC Kevin McHale 20.00 40.00
Robert Parish
Oscar Robertson
Kareem Abdul-Jabbar
UFLNYKK Willis Reed 15.00 30.00
Earl Monroe
Bernard King
Walt Frazier
UFLNYUJ Patrick Ewing 20.00 50.00
John Starks
John Stockton
Karl Malone
UFLUJCB Karl Malone 75.00 150.00
John Stockton
Michael Jordan
Scottie Pippen
UFLWGRD Steve Kerr 20.00 50.00
Magic Johnson
John Stockton
Clyde Drexler

2008-09 Ultimate Collection Jerseys Foursome Rookies

STATED PRINT RUN 50 SER.#'d SETS
*PATCHES: 1X TO 2.5X BASE HI
PATCH PRINT RUN 15 SER.#'d SETS
UFR1234 Derrick Rose 12.50 30.00
Michael Beasley
O.J. Mayo
Russell Westbrook
UFRBGEA Javale McGee 6.00 15.00
Donte Greene
Joe Alexander
Roy Hibbert
UFRCNTR Roy Hibbert 6.00 15.00
Robin Lopez
Jason Thompson
Brook Lopez
UFRCUSA Chris Douglas-Roberts 10.00 25.00

Joey Dorsey
Walter Sharpe
Derrick Rose
UFREACE Walter Sharpe 6.00 15.00
Roy Hibbert
Joe Alexander
J.J. Hickson
UFREASE Mario Chalmers 8.00 20.00
Courtney Lee
Javale McGee
D.J. Augustin
UFRLASK Eric Gordon 6.00 15.00
DeAndre Jordan
Jason Thompson
Donte Greene
UFRMGOC Russell Westbrook 6.00 15.00
D.J. White
O.J. Mayo
Darrell Arthur
UFRMHIP Brandon Rush 6.00 15.00
Roy Hibbert
Mario Chalmers
Michael Beasley
UFRNCAA Mario Chalmers 12.50 30.00
Derrick Rose
Chris Douglas-Roberts
Darrell Arthur
UFRPC10 Jerryd Bayless 8.00 20.00
Kyle Weaver
Ryan Anderson
Robin Lopez
UFRPFWD Kevin Love 8.00 20.00
J.J. Hickson
Marreese Speights
Michael Beasley
UFRPGRD Derrick Rose 15.00 40.00
Russell Westbrook
D.J. Augustin
Jerryd Bayless
UFRROOK Rudy Fernandez 8.00 20.00
Joe Alexander
Kevin Love
Eric Gordon
UFRSGRD Eric Gordon 6.00 15.00
Courtney Lee
Rudy Fernandez
O.J. Mayo
UFRWEAT J.R. Giddens 6.00 15.00
Marreese Speights
Chris Douglas-Roberts
Brook Lopez
UFRWENW Kosta Koufos 6.00 15.00
Sonny Weems
Jerryd Bayless
Kyle Weaver
UFRWEPA Donte Greene 8.00 20.00
Anthony Randolph
DeAndre Jordan
Robin Lopez
UFRWESW Joey Dorsey 6.00 15.00
George Hill
O.J. Mayo
Darrell Arthur

2008-09 Ultimate Collection Jerseys Foursome Veterans

PRINT RUN 50 SER.#'d SETS
UFV05AS Amare Stoudemire 10.00 25.00
Shaquille O'Neal
Yao Ming
Dwight Howard
UFV06AS Pau Gasol 10.00 25.00
Richard Hamilton
Rasheed Wallace
Gilbert Arenas
UFV07AS Vince Carter 15.00 30.00
Josh Howard
Joe Johnson
Carmelo Anthony
UFV76ER Thaddeus Young 6.00 15.00
Andre Miller
Andre Iguodala
Samuel Dalembert
UFVA06S Tony Parker 12.50 30.00
Paul Pierce
Ray Allen
LeBron James
UFVA07S Steve Nash 12.50 30.00
Ray Allen
Tony Parker
Chauncey Billups
UFVAS03 Allen Iverson 15.00 30.00
Tim Duncan
Paul Pierce
Jason Kidd
UFVAS05 Kobe Bryant 35.00 75.00
Steve Nash
LeBron James
Tracy McGrady
UFVAS06 Yao Ming 10.00 25.00
Rasheed Wallace
Dirk Nowitzki
Elton Brand
UFVAS07 Carmelo Anthony 10.00 25.00
Jermaine O'Neal
Mehmet Okur
Carlos Boozer
UFVBUCK Charlie Villanueva 6.00 15.00
Richard Jefferson
Andrew Bogut
Michael Redd
UFVBULL Luol Deng 8.00 20.00
Ben Gordon
Kirk Hinrich
Thabo Sefolosha
UFVCAVS Ben Wallace 20.00 40.00
Zydrunas Ilgauskas
LeBron James
Daniel Gibson
UFVCBOB Boris Diaw 6.00 15.00
Emeka Okafor
Gerald Wallace
Raja Bell
UFVCELT Paul Pierce 15.00 40.00
Ray Allen
Kevin Garnett
Rajon Rondo
UFVDETP Rodney Stuckey 10.00 25.00
Tayshaun Prince
Rasheed Wallace
Richard Hamilton
UFVDNUG Carmelo Anthony 8.00 20.00
Chauncey Billups
Nene
Linas Kleiza
UFVHAWK Joe Johnson 6.00 15.00
Josh Smith
Al Horford
Marvin Williams
UFVKING Francisco Garcia 10.00 25.00
Kenny Thomas
Kevin Martin
Beno Udrih
UFVLACP Baron Davis 6.00 15.00
Zach Randolph
Chris Kaman
Al Thornton
UFVMAVS Jason Kidd 8.00 20.00
Dirk Nowitzki
Jason Terry
Josh Howard
UFVNOHO Chris Paul 8.00 20.00
Peja Stojakovic
Morris Peterson
Julian Wright
UFVNYKK Stephon Marbury 6.00 15.00
David Lee
Wilson Chandler
Nate Robinson
UFVOMAG J.J. Redick 8.00 20.00
Dwight Howard
Jameer Nelson
Rashard Lewis
UFVRG03 Pau Gasol 6.00 15.00
Tony Parker
Richard Jefferson
Jamaal Tinsley
UFVRG04 Mike Dunleavy 6.00 15.00
Jarvis Hayes
Nene
Udonis Haslem
UFVRG05 Luol Deng 8.00 20.00
Josh Smith
Josh Howard
Devin Harris
UFVSPUR Tim Duncan 10.00 25.00
Michael Finley
Bruce Bowen
Manu Ginobili
UFVSUNS Amare Stoudemire 10.00 25.00
Jason Richardson
Shaquille O'Neal
Jared Dudley
UFVUDEX LeBron James 60.00 150.00
Kobe Bryant
Kevin Garnett
Kevin Durant

2008-09 Ultimate Collection Jerseys Six

STATED PRINT RUN 35 SER.#'d SETS
US05AS Yao Ming 10.00 25.00
Amare Stoudemire
Manu Ginobili
Tim Duncan
Shawn Marion
Rashard Lewis
US06AS Paul Pierce 25.00 50.00
Chauncey Billups
Shaquille O'Neal
LeBron James
Rasheed Wallace
Gilbert Arenas
US76ER Julius Erving 10.00 25.00
Elton Brand
Andre Iguodala
Samuel Dalembert
Andre Miller
Thaddeus Young
USBLAZ Rudy Fernandez 20.00 40.00
Clyde Drexler
Jerryd Bayless
Martell Webster
LaMarcus Aldridge
Brandon Roy
USBULL Derrick Rose 40.00 100.00
Dennis Rodman
Scottie Pippen
Luol Deng
Ben Gordon
Tyrus Thomas
USCAVS J.J. Hickson 40.00 80.00
Daniel Gibson
Mark Price
Dan Majerle
LeBron James
Zydrunas Ilgauskas
USCELT Paul Pierce 40.00 80.00
Kevin Garnett
Ray Allen
Kevin McHale
Bill Russell
Larry Bird
USCLIP Al Thornton 10.00 25.00
Eric Gordon
Zach Randolph
Chris Kaman
Baron Davis
Bill Walton
USDNUG Chauncey Billups 10.00 25.00
Kenyon Martin
J.R. Smith
Carmelo Anthony
Nene
Sonny Weems
USGSWR Marco Belinelli 10.00 25.00
Corey Maggette
Jamal Crawford
Chris Mullin
Andris Biedrins
Brandan Wright
USHAWK Mike Bibby 10.00 25.00
Dominique Wilkins
Spud Webb
Joe Johnson
Al Horford
Marvin Williams
USHEAT Mario Chalmers 10.00 25.00
Michael Beasley
Udonis Haslem
Daequan Cook
Jermaine O'Neal
Alonzo Mourning
USJAZZ Deron Williams 30.00 50.00
Andrei Kirilenko
Carlos Boozer
Jeff Hornacek
Karl Malone
John Stockton
USLSHO Kobe Bryant 40.00 80.00
Jerry West
Michael Cooper
Lamar Odom
Magic Johnson
Jordan Farmar
USNETS Vince Carter 15.00 30.00
Devin Harris
Keyon Dooling
Brook Lopez
Ryan Anderson
Chris Douglas-Roberts
USNICK Patrick Ewing 15.00 30.00
Al Harrington
John Starks
Micheal Ray Richardson
David Lee
Eddy Curry
USPSTN Richard Hamilton 15.00 30.00
Allen Iverson
Arron Afflalo
Isiah Thomas
Rodney Stuckey
Joe Dumars
USROCK Tracy McGrady 15.00 30.00
Clyde Drexler
Yao Ming
Dikembe Mutombo
Hakeem Olajuwon
Luther Head
USSPUR David Robinson 15.00 30.00
Steve Kerr
Tim Duncan
George Gervin
Manu Ginobili
Bruce Bowen
USSUNS Shaquille O'Neal 15.00 30.00
Louis Amundson
Robin Lopez
Amare Stoudemire
Steve Nash
Jason Richardson

2008-09 Ultimate Collection Jerseys Ten

STATED PRINT RUN 15 SER.#'d SETS
UNPRICED PATCH PRINT RUN 3 SER.#'d SETS
UTAH Darrell Griffith 25.00 60.00
Adrian Dantley
C.J. Miles
John Stockton
Kosta Koufos
Deron Williams
Andrei Kirilenko
Carlos Boozer
Karl Malone
Jeff Hornacek
PHILY Julius Erving 40.00 80.00
Elton Brand
Andre Iguodala
Samuel Dalembert
Marreese Speights
Andre Miller
Maurice Cheeks
Thaddeus Young
Jason Smith
Moses Malone
SPURS Steve Kerr 75.00 150.00
Michael Finley
Tim Duncan
George Gervin
Manu Ginobili
Tony Parker
Bruce Bowen
David Robinson
Dennis Rodman
George Hill
08ROOKIE J.J. Hickson 25.00 60.00
Brandon Rush
Roy Hibbert
Robin Lopez
Anthony Randolph
Jason Thompson
Ryan Anderson
Marreese Speights
Jerryd Bayless
Javale McGee
BOSTON Paul Pierce 75.00 150.00
Kevin Garnett
Ray Allen
Kevin McHale
Glen Davis
Bill Russell
Rajon Rondo
Robert Parish
Bill Walton
Larry Bird
LAKERS Kobe Bryant 75.00 150.00
Jerry West
Sasha Vujacic
Michael Cooper
Pat Riley
Lamar Odom
Luke Walton
Magic Johnson
Jordan Farmar
Wilt Chamberlain
CHICAGO Thabo Sefolosha 60.00 150.00
Scottie Pippen
Joakim Noah
Dennis Rodman
Derrick Rose
Ben Gordon
Kirk Hinrich
Tyrus Thomas
Larry Hughes
Luol Deng
DETROIT Allen Iverson 50.00 100.00
Richard Hamilton
Rodney Stuckey
Isiah Thomas
Bill Laimbeer
Walter Sharpe
Antonio McDyess
Tayshaun Prince
Rasheed Wallace
Joe Dumars
NEW YORK Micheal Ray Richardson 40.00 80.00
David Lee
Nate Robinson
Chris Duhon
Eddy Curry
Quentin Richardson
Patrick Ewing
Bernard King
John Starks
Willis Reed
ROOKIE08 Brook Lopez 50.00 100.00
Kevin Love
Joe Alexander
Eric Gordon
Derrick Rose
Michael Beasley
Mario Chalmers
O.J. Mayo
Russell Westbrook
D.J. Augustin

2008-09 Ultimate Collection Legendary Signatures

STATED PRINT RUN 10 SER.#'d SETS
LSAD Adrian Dantley 15.00 30.00
LSAG Artis Gilmore 15.00 30.00
LSBA B.J. Armstrong 25.00 50.00
LSBD Brad Daugherty 15.00 30.00
LSBK Bernard King 15.00 40.00
LSBL Bill Laimbeer 15.00 30.00
LSBR Bill Russell 100.00 200.00
LSCD Clyde Drexler 40.00 80.00
LSDW Dominique Wilkins 25.00 50.00
LSGG George Gervin 25.00 50.00
LSHO Hakeem Olajuwon 30.00 80.00
LSJE Julius Erving 75.00 150.00
LSJO Magic Johnson 100.00 200.00
LSKV Kiki Vandeweghe 15.00 30.00
LSLB Larry Bird 100.00 200.00
LSLJ Larry Johnson 100.00 200.00
LSMJ Michael Jordan 500.00 700.00
LSMP Mark Price 40.00 80.00
LSRO Dennis Rodman 50.00 120.00
LSRP Robert Parish 30.00 60.00
LSRS Ralph Sampson 25.00 50.00
LSSI Jack Sikma 15.00 30.00
LSSJ Sam Jones 30.00 80.00
LSTC Tom Chambers 15.00 30.00

2008-09 Ultimate Collection Memories

STATED PRINT RUN 10 SER.#'d SETS
UMDF Derek Fisher Draft Day 225.00 325.00
UMDW Dominique Wilkins GM7 100.00 200.00
UMJP John Paxson 20.00 50.00
UMJS John Stockton 50.00 100.00
UMJW Jerry West Gold Medal 225.00 325.00
UMKG Kevin Garnett 75.00 150.00
UMMJ Magic Johnson AS MVP 300.00 500.00

2008-09 Ultimate Collection Patches Foursome Veterans

*PATCHES: 1X TO 2.5X BASE HI
PATCH PRINT RUN 20 SER.#'d SETS
UFVAS05 Kobe Bryant 125.00 300.00
Steve Nash
LeBron James
Tracy McGrady

2008-09 Ultimate Collection Patches Six

STATED PRINT RUN 10 SER.#'d SETS
US05AS Shawn Marion 60.00 120.00
Manu Ginobili
Tim Duncan
Rashard Lewis
Amare Stoudemire
Yao Ming
US76ER Elton Brand 40.00 80.00
Julius Erving
Samuel Dalembert
Andre Miller
Andre Iguodala
Thaddeus Young
USBLAZ Rudy Fernandez 50.00 100.00
Jerryd Bayless
Clyde Drexler
Brandon Roy
LaMarcus Aldridge
Martell Webster
USBULL Derrick Rose 100.00 200.00
Dennis Rodman
Scottie Pippen
Luol Deng
Tyrus Thomas
Ben Gordon
USCAVS J.J. Hickson 80.00 160.00
Daniel Gibson
Dan Majerle
Mark Price
LeBron James
Zydrunas Ilgauskas
USCELT Paul Pierce 100.00 200.00
Larry Bird
Bill Russell
Kevin McHale
Ray Allen
Kevin Garnett
USCLIP Al Thornton 20.00 40.00
Eric Gordon
Baron Davis
Chris Kaman
Zach Randolph
Bill Walton
USGSWR Marco Belinelli 20.00 40.00
Brandan Wright
Andris Biedrins
Chris Mullin
Jamal Crawford
Corey Maggette
USHAWK Mike Bibby 40.00 80.00
Dominique Wilkins
Spud Webb
Joe Johnson
Marvin Williams
Al Horford
USHEAT Mario Chalmers 60.00 120.00
Udonis Haslem
Jermaine O'Neal
Michael Beasley
Daequan Cook
Alonzo Mourning
USJAZZ Jeff Hornacek 50.00 120.00
Karl Malone
Carlos Boozer
Andrei Kirilenko
Deron Williams
John Stockton
USLSHO Kobe Bryant 150.00 300.00
Magic Johnson
Jordan Farmar
Jerry West
Lamar Odom
Michael Cooper
USNETS Keyon Dooling 50.00 100.00
Devin Harris
Vince Carter
Brook Lopez
Ryan Anderson
Chris Douglas-Roberts
USNICK John Starks 75.00 150.00
Patrick Ewing
Al Harrington
Eddy Curry
David Lee
Micheal Ray Richardson
USPSTN Richard Hamilton 60.00 120.00
Allen Iverson
Arron Afflalo
Rodney Stuckey
Isiah Thomas
Joe Dumars
USROCK Tracy McGrady 60.00 120.00
Clyde Drexler
Yao Ming
Hakeem Olajuwon
Dikembe Mutombo
Luther Head
USSPUR David Robinson 75.00 150.00
Steve Kerr
Tim Duncan
George Gervin
Manu Ginobili
Bruce Bowen

2008-09 Ultimate Collection Prototypical Portraits

STATED PRINT RUN 25 SER.#'d SETS
PPBL Bill Laimbeer 10.00 25.00
PPBM Bob McAdoo 20.00 40.00
PPCD Chris Douglas-Roberts 10.00 25.00
PPCK Chris Kaman 10.00 25.00
PPCM Corey Maggette 10.00 25.00
PPDF Derek Fisher 15.00 30.00
PPDJ DeAndre Jordan 20.00 50.00
PPDR Dennis Rodman 25.00 60.00
PPFE Rudy Fernandez 10.00 25.00
PPJD Joey Dorsey 10.00 25.00
PPJK Jason Kidd 25.00 50.00
PPJS Jack Sikma 10.00 25.00
PPLJ LeBron James 200.00 400.00
PPMJ Michael Jordan 400.00 700.00
PPRF Raymond Felton 10.00 25.00
PPRS Ramon Sessions 12.00 30.00
PPSA Ralph Sampson 12.00 30.00
PPTC Tom Chambers 10.00 25.00

2008-09 Ultimate Collection Signature Materials Combos

STATED PRINT RUN 10 SER.#'d SETS
UNPRICED PATCH PRINT RUN 5 SER.#'d SETS
UMCBJ LeBron James 500.00 800.00
Kobe Bryant
UMCBR Michael Beasley 150.00 300.00
Derrick Rose
UMCFM O.J. Mayo 60.00 120.00
Rudy Fernandez
UMCGL Kevin Love 75.00 150.00
Kevin Garnett
UMCHH Al Horford 40.00 80.00
Dwight Howard

2008-09 Ultimate Collection Signature Materials Legends

STATED PRINT RUN 10 SER.#'d SETS
UNPRICED PATCH PRINT RUN 5 SER.#'d SETS
UMLBK Bernard King 30.00 60.00
UMLDR David Robinson 60.00 120.00
UMLGG George Gervin 30.00 60.00
UMLIT Isiah Thomas 40.00 80.00
UMLLB Larry Bird 75.00 150.00
UMLMJ Michael Jordan 500.00 650.00
UMLSK Steve Kerr 30.00 60.00

2008-09 Ultimate Collection Signature Materials Rookies

STATED PRINT RUN 25 SER.#'d SETS
UNPRICED PATCH PRINT RUN 5 SER.#'d SETS
UMRCD Chris Douglas-Roberts 8.00 20.00
UMRDA Darrell Arthur 8.00 20.00
UMRDJ DeAndre Jordan 15.00 40.00
UMRDR Derrick Rose 250.00 500.00
UMRGH George Hill 25.00 50.00
UMRJA Joe Alexander 8.00 20.00
UMRJB Jerryd Bayless 25.00 50.00
UMRJD Joey Dorsey 8.00 20.00
UMRJG J.R. Giddens 8.00 20.00
UMRJM Javale McGee 12.00 30.00
UMRKK Kosta Koufos 8.00 20.00
UMRKL Kevin Love 50.00 125.00
UMRMB Michael Beasley 25.00 60.00
UMROM O.J. Mayo 25.00 60.00
UMRRA Ryan Anderson 12.00 30.00
UMRRF Rudy Fernandez 10.00 25.00
UMRWS Walter Sharpe 8.00 20.00

2008-09 Ultimate Collection Signature Materials Veterans

STATED PRINT RUN 10 SER.#'d SETS
UNPRICED PATCH PRINT RUN 5 SER.#'d SETS
UMVAM Alonzo Mourning 75.00 150.00
UMVAS Amare Stoudemire 25.00 50.00
UMVBD Baron Davis 15.00 30.00
UMVJJ Jarrett Jack 15.00 30.00
UMVJO Jermaine O'Neal 15.00 30.00
UMVKB Kobe Bryant 300.00 400.00
UMVKG Kevin Garnett 100.00 200.00
UMVMB Mike Bibby 15.00 30.00
UMVYM Yao Ming 25.00 60.00

2008-09 Ultimate Collection Signatures

STATED PRINT RUN 23 TO 25 SER.#'d SETS
UNPRICED OCTO PRINT RUN 4 SER.#'d SETS
UNPRICED QUAD PRINT RUN 8 SER.#'d SETS
UNPRICED SIX PRINT RUN 6 SER.#'d SETS
UAB Aaron Brooks/25 6.00 15.00
UAT Al Thornton/25 6.00 15.00
UBB Bobby Brown/25 6.00 15.00
UBO Josh Boone/25 6.00 15.00
UBR Brandon Roy/25 15.00 30.00
UCB Corey Brewer/25 6.00 15.00
UCL Carl Landry/25 10.00 25.00
UDC Daequan Cook/25 6.00 15.00
UDF Derek Fisher/25 20.00 40.00
UDW Deron Williams/25 20.00 40.00
UEC Eddy Curry/25 6.00 15.00
UGD Glen Davis/25 8.00 20.00
UJB Jose Barea/25 25.00 60.00
UJF Jordan Farmar/25 6.00 15.00
UJG Jeff Green/25 8.00 20.00
UJN Joakim Noah/25 15.00 30.00
UJW Julian Wright/25 6.00 15.00
UKG Kevin Garnett/25 50.00 100.00
ULJ LeBron James/23 125.00 250.00
ULO Lamar Odom/25 8.00 20.00
UMC Mike Conley Jr./25 6.00 15.00
URR Rajon Rondo/25 10.00 25.00
URS Rodney Stuckey/25 6.00 15.00

2008-09 Ultimate Collection Signatures Dual

STATED PRINT RUN 25 SER.#'d SETS
SD76 Andre Iguodala 10.00 25.00
Andre Miller
SDAH Mike Bibby 15.00 30.00
Al Horford
SDBC Paul Pierce 75.00 150.00
Kevin Garnett
SDCB Raymond Felton 10.00 25.00
Sean Singletary
SDCC LeBron James 125.00 225.00
Mo Williams
SDCH Joakim Noah 15.00 30.00
Tyrus Thomas
SDDM Jose Barea 30.00 80.00
Jason Kidd
SDDN Carmelo Anthony 40.00 80.00
J.R. Smith
SDDP Rodney Stuckey 10.00 25.00
Tayshaun Prince
SDGS Marco Belinelli 10.00 25.00
Corey Maggette
SDHR Joey Dorsey 10.00 25.00
Carl Landry
SDIP T.J. Ford 10.00 25.00
Danny Granger
SDLA Derek Fisher 20.00 40.00
Jordan Farmar
SDLC Al Thornton 12.00 30.00
DeAndre Jordan
SDMB Ramon Sessions 10.00 25.00
Richard Jefferson
SDMG Mike Conley Jr. 10.00 25.00
Rudy Gay
SDMH Daequan Cook 10.00 25.00
Shaun Livingston
SDMT Randy Foye 10.00 25.00
Corey Brewer
SDNJ Josh Boone 10.00 25.00
Ryan Anderson
SDNO David West 10.00 25.00
Julian Wright
SDNY Wilson Chandler 10.00 25.00
Quentin Richardson
SDOC Jeff Green 40.00 100.00
Kevin Durant
SDOM Courtney Lee 30.00 80.00
Dwight Howard
SDPS Jared Dudley 10.00 25.00
Robin Lopez
SDSA Bruce Bowen 20.00 40.00
Tony Parker
SDTB LaMarcus Aldridge 25.00 50.00
Brandon Roy
SDUJ Deron Williams 15.00 30.00
Carlos Boozer

2008-09 Ultimate Collection Signatures Rookie

STATED PRINT RUN 25 SER.#'d SETS
URAR Anthony Randolph 10.00 25.00
URBR Brandon Rush 8.00 20.00
URCD Chris Douglas-Roberts 8.00 20.00
URDA D.J. Augustin 8.00 20.00
URDG Danilo Gallinari 12.00 30.00
URDR Derrick Rose 200.00 400.00
UREG Eric Gordon 25.00 60.00
URGH George Hill 20.00 40.00
URGR Donte Greene 8.00 20.00
URJA Joe Alexander 8.00 20.00
URJB Jerryd Bayless 8.00 20.00
URJJ J.J. Hickson 10.00 25.00
URKL Kevin Love 30.00 80.00
URMB Michael Beasley 25.00 60.00
URMC Mario Chalmers 12.00 30.00
URMS Marreese Speights 8.00 20.00
UROM O.J. Mayo 25.00 60.00
URRF Rudy Fernandez 10.00 25.00
URRW Russell Westbrook 40.00 100.00

2008-09 Ultimate Collection Signatures Triple

STATED PRINT RUN 10 SER.#'d SETS
STBOS J.R. Giddens 25.00 50.00
Ray Allen
Rajon Rondo
STCAV Brad Daugherty 125.00 250.00
LeBron James
J.J. Hickson
STCHI Derrick Rose 100.00 225.00
Ben Gordon
B.J. Armstrong
STHOU Carl Landry 30.00 60.00
Joey Dorsey
Shane Battier
STLAL Jordan Farmar 30.00 60.00
Lamar Odom
Michael Cooper
STMIA Daequan Cook 75.00 150.00
Michael Beasley
Alonzo Mourning
STMIN Kevin Love 30.00 60.00
Al Jefferson
Corey Brewer
STNJN Vince Carter 40.00 80.00
Sean Williams
Brook Lopez
STNYK Quentin Richardson 20.00 40.00
Danilo Gallinari
Micheal Ray Richardson
STPTB Brandon Roy 50.00 100.00
Clyde Drexler
Jerryd Bayless
STSAS George Hill 40.00 80.00
Tony Parker
George Gervin
STUTA Adrian Dantley 20.00 40.00
Carlos Boozer
Kosta Koufos

2008-09 Ultimate Collection Validation

STATED PRINT RUN 25 SER.#'d SETS
VAI Andre Iguodala 6.00 15.00
VAM Alonzo Mourning 50.00 100.00
VBK Bernard King 10.00 25.00
VCB Carlos Boozer 10.00 25.00
VCD Chris Duhon 6.00 15.00
VCL Carl Landry 20.00 40.00
VGW Gerald Wallace 8.00 20.00
VMR Micheal Ray Richardson 6.00 15.00
VPW Paul Westphal 6.00 15.00
VRR Rajon Rondo 12.00 30.00
VRS Ramon Sessions 10.00 25.00
VSK Steve Kerr 10.00 25.00
VSV Sasha Vujacic 10.00 25.00
VSW Spud Webb 10.00 25.00

2010-11 Ultimate Collection

COMP.SET w/o AUs (60) 25.00 50.00
AU PRINT RUN 99 SER.#'d SETS
1 Michael Jordan 6.00 15.00
2 James Harden 1.00 2.50
3 Bill Russell 1.25 3.00
4 Larry Bird 2.50 6.00
5 Magic Johnson 2.00 5.00
6 Jerry West 1.00 2.50
7 Hakeem Olajuwon 1.00 2.50
8 David Robinson 1.25 3.00
9 Dennis Rodman 1.25 3.00
10 Rick Fox .75 2.00
11 LeBron James 3.00 8.00
12 Julius Erving 1.50 4.00
13 Roy Williams .75 2.00
14 Clyde Drexler 1.00 2.50
15 George Gervin .75 2.00
16 Dominique Wilkins 1.00 2.50
17 Tracy McGrady .75 2.00
18 Hal Greer .75 2.00
19 Cazzie Russell .75 2.00
20 George Lynch .75 2.00
21 Alonzo Mourning 1.00 2.50
22 Adrian Dantley .75 2.00
23 John Stockton 1.25 3.00
24 Tim Hardaway .75 2.00
25 James Worthy 1.00 2.50
26 Rudy Tomjanovich .75 2.00
27 Gail Goodrich .75 2.00
28 Jack Sikma .75 2.00
29 Hubert Davis .75 2.00
30 David Thompson 1.00 2.50
31 Bill Walton .75 2.00
32 Sam Cassell .75 2.00
33 Walter Davis .75 2.00
34 Jerry Sloan .75 2.00
35 Yao Ming 1.00 2.50
36 Bill Laimbeer .75 2.00
37 Glen Rice .75 2.00
38 Anfernee Hardaway 2.00 5.00
39 B.J. Armstrong .75 2.00
40 Robert Horry 1.00 2.50
41 Mike Krzyzewski 1.00 2.50
42 Michael Cooper .75 2.00
43 Elgin Baylor .75 2.00
44 Tom Izzo 1.00 2.50
45 Brandon Roy .75 2.00
46 Christian Laettner 1.00 2.50
47 Larry Johnson 1.00 2.50
48 Mark Jackson .75 2.00
49 Ricky Rubio 2.00 5.00
50 Darrell Griffith .75 2.00
51 John Calipari 1.00 2.50
52 Sam Perkins .75 2.00
53 Bobby Hurley .75 2.00
54 Mateen Cleaves .75 2.00
55 Derrick Rose 2.50 6.00
56 Steve Alford .75 2.00
57 Kenny Smith .75 2.00
58 Avery Johnson .75 2.00
59 Danny Manning .75 2.00
60 Calbert Cheaney .75 2.00
61 Paul George AU 15.00 40.00
62 Deon Thompson AU 8.00 20.00
63 Derrick Favors AU 12.00 30.00
64 DeMarcus Cousins AU 30.00 80.00
65 Jordan Crawford AU 10.00 25.00
66 Cole Aldrich AU 12.50 30.00
67 Ed Davis AU 10.00 25.00
68 Al-Farouq Aminu AU 6.00 15.00
69 Greg Monroe AU 15.00 40.00
70 Ekpe Udoh AU 6.00 15.00
71 Daniel Orton AU 6.00 15.00
72 Gani Lawal AU 6.00 15.00

Hassan Whiteside AU	6.00	15.00
Xavier Henry AU	10.00	25.00
James Anderson AU	10.00	25.00
Eric Bledsoe AU EXCH	30.00	60.00
Damion James AU	6.00	15.00
Solomon Alabi AU	6.00	15.00
Gordon Hayward AU	15.00	40.00
Quincy Pondexter AU	6.00	15.00
Patrick Patterson AU	25.00	60.00

2010-11 Ultimate Collection 1997 Legends Autographs

NDOM INSERTS IN PACKS

1 Michael Jordan	400.00	700.00
2 LeBron James	150.00	300.00
3 Magic Johnson	80.00	200.00
4 Larry Bird	60.00	150.00
5 Julius Erving	50.00	100.00
6 Yao Ming	15.00	40.00
7 Brandon Roy	12.50	30.00
8 Derrick Rose	50.00	120.00
9 Tracy McGrady	30.00	80.00
11 Gail Goodrich	8.00	20.00
12 Dominique Wilkins	20.00	50.00
13 George Gervin	8.00	20.00
15 David Robinson	75.00	200.00
16 Alonzo Mourning	25.00	60.00
17 Bill Walton	12.50	30.00
18 Mark Jackson	8.00	20.00
19 Bobby Hurley	8.00	20.00
20 Jerry West	40.00	100.00
21 Christian Laettner	10.00	25.00

2010-11 Ultimate Collection All-Time Draft Signatures Gold

ATED PRINT RUN 25 TO 75 SER.#'d SETS
PRICED SILVER PRINT RUN 5 SETS

Michael Jordan/25	400.00	700.00
LeBron James/25	175.00	350.00
Bill Russell/25	50.00	120.00
Julius Erving/25	40.00	100.00
Magic Johnson/25	40.00	100.00
Jerry West/25	30.00	80.00
Larry Bird/25	50.00	100.00
Chris Mullin/25	15.00	40.00
Bill Walton/75	10.00	25.00
Bob Lanier/25	10.00	25.00
David Robinson/25	40.00	100.00
Elgin Baylor/75	8.00	20.00
George Gervin/25	12.50	30.00
Hakeem Olajuwon/25	20.00	50.00
Moses Malone/75	10.00	25.00
Yao Ming/25	15.00	40.00
Alonzo Mourning/25	30.00	80.00
Bobby Hurley/75	6.00	15.00
Bill Sharman/75	6.00	15.00
Calbert Cheaney/75	6.00	15.00
Christian Laettner/75	10.00	25.00
Cazzie Russell/75	6.00	15.00
Derrick Rose/75	50.00	120.00
Danny Ferry/75	6.00	15.00
Darrell Griffith/75	6.00	15.00
Danny Manning/75	8.00	20.00
David Thompson/75	6.00	15.00
Gail Goodrich/75	6.00	15.00
Hal Greer/75	6.00	15.00
Lennie Rosenbluth/75	12.00	30.00
Mateen Cleaves/75	6.00	15.00
Phil Ford/75	8.00	20.00
Brandon Roy/75	8.00	20.00
Steve Alford/75	6.00	15.00
Tim Hardaway/75	6.00	15.00
Tracy McGrady/75	10.00	25.00
Adrian Dantley/75	6.00	15.00

2010-11 Ultimate Collection All-Time Team Signatures Gold

TATED PRINT RUN 23 TO 25 SER.#'d SETS
NPRICED SILVER PRINT RUN 5SETS

TAH Anfernee Hardaway/25	50.00	125.00
TAM Alonzo Mourning/25	30.00	80.00
TBR Brandon Roy/25	12.50	30.00
TBW Bill Walton/25	10.00	25.00
TCC Calbert Cheaney/25	8.00	20.00
TCL Christian Laettner/25	25.00	60.00
TDF Danny Ferry/25	12.00	30.00
TDR Derrick Rose/25	60.00	150.00
THO Hakeem Olajuwon/25	20.00	50.00
TKS Kenny Smith/25	12.50	30.00
TLB Larry Bird/25	50.00	120.00
TLJ Larry Johnson/25	30.00	80.00
TMC Mateen Cleaves/25	8.00	20.00
TMJ Michael Jordan/23	400.00	700.00
TRO David Robinson/25	40.00	100.00
TRU Bill Russell/25	50.00	100.00
TSA Steve Alford/25	8.00	20.00

2010-11 Ultimate Collection Base Autographs

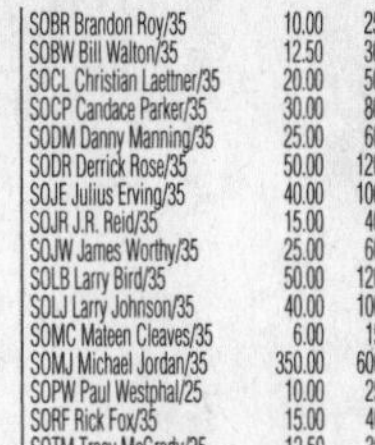

STATED PRINT RUN 25 TO 99 SER.#'d SETS

1 Michael Jordan/25	400.00	700.00
2 James Harden/99	8.00	20.00
3 Bill Russell/25	75.00	150.00
4 Larry Bird/25	50.00	100.00
5 Magic Johnson/25	40.00	100.00
6 Jerry West/25	30.00	80.00
7 Hakeem Olajuwon/75	15.00	40.00
8 David Robinson/75	25.00	60.00
9 Dennis Rodman/75	20.00	50.00
10 Rick Fox/99	10.00	25.00
11 LeBron James/25	150.00	300.00
14 Clyde Drexler/25	25.00	60.00
15 George Gervin/99	8.00	20.00
16 Dominique Wilkins/25	12.50	30.00
17 Tracy McGrady/25	15.00	40.00
18 Hal Greer/75	4.00	10.00
19 Cazzie Russell/25	6.00	15.00
20 George Lynch/75	15.00	40.00
21 Alonzo Mourning/25	30.00	80.00
22 Adrian Dantley/99	6.00	15.00
24 Tim Hardaway/99	6.00	15.00
25 James Worthy/75	15.00	40.00
26 Rudy Tomjanovich/99	6.00	15.00
27 Gail Goodrich/75	4.00	10.00
28 Jack Sikma/75	4.00	10.00
29 Hubert Davis/75	10.00	25.00
30 David Thompson/99	4.00	10.00
31 Bill Walton/99	6.00	15.00
32 Sam Cassell/99	6.00	15.00
33 Walter Davis/75	10.00	25.00
34 Jerry Sloan/99	6.00	15.00
35 Yao Ming/75	15.00	40.00
36 Bill Laimbeer/75	6.00	15.00
37 Glen Rice/75	6.00	15.00
38 Anfernee Hardaway/99	30.00	80.00
39 B.J. Armstrong/99	4.00	10.00
40 Robert Horry/75	10.00	25.00
42 Michael Cooper/75	4.00	10.00
43 Elgin Baylor/75	6.00	15.00
45 Brandon Roy/99	8.00	20.00
46 Christian Laettner/75	10.00	25.00
47 Larry Johnson/25	30.00	80.00
48 Mark Jackson/99	4.00	10.00
49 Ricky Rubio/75	75.00	150.00
50 Darrell Griffith/99	4.00	10.00
52 Sam Perkins/75	10.00	25.00
53 Bobby Hurley/75	6.00	15.00
54 Mateen Cleaves/99	4.00	10.00
55 Derrick Rose/99	40.00	100.00
56 Steve Alford/99	4.00	10.00
57 Kenny Smith/99	6.00	15.00
58 Avery Johnson/99	6.00	15.00
59 Danny Manning/75	8.00	20.00
60 Calbert Cheaney/75	6.00	15.00

2010-11 Ultimate Collection Big Game Signatures Gold

STATED PRINT RUN 23 TO 75 SER.#'d SETS
SILVER UNPRICED SILVER PRINT RUN 5 SETS

BGAJ Avery Johnson/75	4.00	10.00
BGAL Al-Farouq Aminu/75	6.00	15.00
BGAW Al Wood/75	12.50	30.00
BGBH Bobby Hurley/75	6.00	15.00
BGBR Bill Russell/25	50.00	120.00
BGBW Bill Walton/75	8.00	20.00
BGCL Christian Laettner/75	12.50	30.00
BGCS Charlie Scott/75	15.00	40.00
BGDF Derrick Favors/75	20.00	50.00
BGDG Darrell Griffith/75	4.00	10.00
BGDM Danny Manning/75	8.00	20.00
BGDR Derrick Rose/75	50.00	120.00
BGDT David Thompson/75	4.00	10.00
BGEB Elgin Baylor/75	8.00	20.00
BGGR Glen Rice/75	6.00	15.00
BGHO Hakeem Olajuwon/25	15.00	40.00
BGJE Julius Erving/25	40.00	100.00
BGJH James Harden/25	12.00	30.00
BGJO Magic Johnson/25	40.00	100.00
BGJW James Worthy/25	25.00	60.00
BGLB Larry Bird/25	50.00	100.00
BGMC Mateen Cleaves/75	6.00	15.00
BGMJ Michael Jordan/23	400.00	700.00
BGRO Brandon Roy/75	8.00	20.00
BGSA Steve Alford/75	8.00	20.00
BGWD Walter Davis/75	15.00	40.00
BGWE Jerry West/75	25.00	60.00
BGYM Yao Ming/75	12.50	30.00

2010-11 Ultimate Collection College Shout Out Signatures

STATED PRINT RUN 25 TO 35 SER.#'d SETS

SOBA B.J. Armstrong/35	12.50	30.00
SOBL Bill Laimbeer/35	6.00	15.00
SOBR Brandon Roy/35	10.00	25.00
SOBW Bill Walton/35	12.50	30.00
SOCL Christian Laettner/35	20.00	50.00
SOCP Candace Parker/35	30.00	80.00
SODM Danny Manning/35	25.00	60.00
SODR Derrick Rose/35	50.00	120.00
SOJE Julius Erving/35	40.00	100.00
SOJR J.R. Reid/35	15.00	40.00
SOJW James Worthy/35	25.00	60.00
SOLB Larry Bird/35	50.00	120.00
SOLJ Larry Johnson/35	40.00	100.00
SOMC Mateen Cleaves/35	6.00	15.00
SOMJ Michael Jordan/35	350.00	600.00
SOPW Paul Westphal/25	10.00	25.00
SORF Rick Fox/35	15.00	40.00
SOTM Tracy McGrady/35	12.50	30.00

2010-11 Ultimate Collection Personal Touch Hero Autographs

STATED PRINT RUN 25 SER.#'d SETS

HAH Anfernee Hardaway	75.00	200.00
HAM Alonzo Mourning	25.00	60.00
HBR Brandon Roy	15.00	40.00
HCD Clyde Drexler	25.00	60.00
HCL Christian Laettner	25.00	60.00
HDR David Robinson	60.00	150.00
HDW Dominique Wilkins	20.00	50.00
HFA Derrick Favors	40.00	100.00
HHO Hakeem Olajuwon/25	25.00	60.00
HJE Julius Erving	40.00	80.00
HJR J.R. Reid	15.00	40.00
HLB Larry Brown	20.00	50.00
HLJ LeBron James	200.00	400.00
HMA Mark Jackson	6.00	15.00
HMJ Magic Johnson	50.00	125.00
HPP Patrick Patterson	25.00	60.00
HPR Pat Riley	20.00	50.00
HPW Paul Westphal	10.00	25.00
HRF Rick Fox	20.00	50.00
HRH Robert Horry	60.00	120.00
HRR Ricky Rubio	100.00	250.00
HRT Rudy Tomjanovich	10.00	25.00
HSL Jerry Sloan	10.00	25.00
HTM Tracy McGrady	15.00	40.00
HYM Yao Ming	40.00	100.00

2010-11 Ultimate Collection Personal Touch Movie Autographs

STATED PRINT RUN 25 SER.#'d SETS

MAF Al-Farouq Aminu	12.50	30.00
MAH Anfernee Hardaway	100.00	200.00
MAM Alonzo Mourning	25.00	60.00
MBR Brandon Roy	12.50	30.00
MBW Bill Walton	10.00	25.00
MCL Christian Laettner	20.00	50.00
MDO Donald Williams	10.00	25.00
MDR Derrick Rose	75.00	150.00
MDW Dominique Wilkins	20.00	50.00
MED Ed Davis	25.00	60.00
MFA Derrick Favors	30.00	80.00
MGL George Lynch	30.00	80.00
MJC Jordan Crawford	25.00	60.00
MJE Julius Erving	40.00	100.00
MJR J.R. Reid	20.00	40.00
MKS Kenny Smith	15.00	40.00
MLJ LeBron James	200.00	400.00
MMJ Magic Johnson	50.00	120.00
MRH Robert Horry	40.00	100.00
MRO David Robinson	50.00	100.00
MRR Ricky Rubio	100.00	250.00
MRT Rudy Tomjanovich	10.00	25.00
MTM Tracy McGrady	15.00	40.00
MYM Yao Ming	40.00	100.00

2010-11 Ultimate Collection Rivalries Signatures

STATED PRINT RUN 25 SER.#'d SETS

RAS Steve Alford	10.00	25.00
Kenny Smith		
RBJ Magic Johnson	100.00	200.00
Larry Bird		
RCR Calbert Cheaney	20.00	40.00
Glen Rice		
RFA Derrick Favors	30.00	80.00
Al-Farouq Aminu		
RFJ Walt Frazier	125.00	300.00
LeBron James		
RHH Anfernee Hardaway	100.00	200.00
Tim Hardaway		
RHW Bobby Hurley	10.00	25.00
Donald Williams		
RJB Michael Jordan	300.00	600.00
Larry Bird		
RJE Michael Jordan	300.00	500.00
Julius Erving		
RJG Mark Jackson	10.00	25.00
Darrell Griffith		
RJR Michael Jordan	450.00	750.00
Bill Russell		
RJU Damion James	15.00	30.00
Ekpe Udoh		
RLD Christian Laettner	25.00	60.00
Ed Davis		
RLJ Christian Laettner	30.00	80.00
Larry Johnson		
RMJ LeBron James	100.00	200.00
Tracy McGrady		
RRC Mateen Cleaves	30.00	80.00
Glen Rice		
RRM Danny Manning	50.00	120.00
Derrick Rose		
RRR Brandon Roy	40.00	80.00
Derrick Rose		
RTW David Thompson	20.00	40.00
Bill Walton		
RWG Paul Westphal	10.00	25.00
Gail Goodrich		

2010-11 Ultimate Collection Signatures

STATED PRINT RUN 23 TO 99 SER.#'d SETS

SAF Al-Farouq Aminu/99	6.00	15.00
SAH Anfernee Hardaway/99	25.00	60.00
SAM Alonzo Mourning/99	12.00	30.00
SBL Bob Lanier/99	6.00	15.00
SBR Brandon Roy/99	6.00	15.00
SCL Christian Laettner/99	10.00	25.00
SDC DeMarcus Cousins/99	25.00	60.00
SDF Derrick Favors/99	15.00	40.00
SDR Derrick Rose/99	50.00	120.00
SDW Dominique Wilkins/99	10.00	25.00
SFL Freddie Lewis/99	5.00	12.00
SGL George Lynch/99	12.50	30.00
SGO Gail Goodrich/99	5.00	12.00
SHW Hassan Whiteside/99	5.00	12.00
SJA James Anderson/99	8.00	20.00
SJC Jordan Crawford/99	10.00	25.00
SJE Julius Erving/25	40.00	80.00
SLA Larry Johnson/99	15.00	40.00
SLB Larry Bird/25	50.00	100.00
SLJ LeBron James/23	200.00	350.00
SMA Mark Jackson/99	5.00	12.00
SMJ Michael Jordan/23	400.00	700.00
SMM Moses Malone/99	10.00	25.00
SRF Rick Fox/25	15.00	40.00
SRR Ricky Rubio/99	75.00	150.00
STH Tim Hardaway/99	6.00	15.00
STM Tracy McGrady/99	10.00	25.00
SXH Xavier Henry/99	10.00	25.00
SYM Yao Ming/99	12.50	30.00

2010-11 Ultimate Collection Signatures Dual

STATED PRINT RUN 10 TO 50 SER.#'d SETS
SOME UNPRICED DUE TO SCARCITY

DBJ Michael Jordan	350.00	600.00
Larry Bird		
DBM Larry Bird	60.00	150.00
Chris Mullin		
DEM Julius Erving	40.00	80.00
Tracy McGrady		
DHH Anfernee Hardaway	50.00	120.00
Tim Hardaway		
DJB Magic Johnson	150.00	300.00
Larry Bird		
DJR Michael Jordan	400.00	700.00
Bill Russell		
DKD Bobby Knight	30.00	60.00
Billy Donovan		
DKJ Shawn Kemp	100.00	250.00
Larry Johnson		
DLD LeBron James	200.00	400.00
Derrick Rose		
DMH Tim Hardaway	30.00	80.00
Alonzo Mourning		
DMJ Larry Johnson	40.00	100.00
Alonzo Mourning		
DML Freddie Lewis	10.00	25.00
Chris Mullin		
DOB Daniel Orton	20.00	50.00
Eric Bledsoe		
DOM Hakeem Olajuwon	50.00	100.00
Yao Ming		
DOR David Robinson	40.00	100.00
Hakeem Olajuwon		
DPP DeMarcus Cousins	40.00	100.00
Patrick Patterson		
DRJ LeBron James	175.00	350.00
Ricky Rubio		
DRR Brandon Roy	50.00	120.00
Derrick Rose		

2010-11 Ultimate Collection Signatures Quad

STATED PRINT RUN 15 SER.#'d SETS

UNC Sam Perkins	40.00	100.00
Phil Ford		
George Lynch		
Eric Montross		
1987 David Robinson	75.00	150.00
Kenny Smith		
Mark A. Jackson		
Billy Donovan		
1993 George Lynch	75.00	200.00
Anfernee Hardaway		
Sam Cassell		
Calbert Cheaney		
2010 Ed Davis	75.00	150.00
Gordon Hayward		
Derrick Favors		
DeMarcus Cousins		
9192 Christian Laettner	100.00	200.00
Alonzo Mourning		
Larry Johnson		
Hubert Davis		
09HOF Michael Jordan	600.00	1000.00
David Robinson		
John Stockton		
Jerry Sloan		
JHRR LeBron James	250.00	500.00
Anfernee Hardaway		
Ricky Rubio		
Derrick Rose		
JJJB Julius Erving	300.00	600.00
LeBron James		
Magic Johnson		
Larry Bird		
JREA Michael Jordan	600.00	1000.00
Bill Russell		
Julius Erving		
Larry Bird		
ROCK Yao Ming	75.00	150.00
Hakeem Olajuwon		
Tracy McGrady		
Kenny Smith		
RRBE Brandon Roy	175.00	350.00
Derrick Rose		
Larry Bird		
Julius Erving		
RRRM Derrick Rose	150.00	300.00
Ricky Rubio		
Tracy McGrady		
Brandon Roy		
TSRS Rudy Tomjanovich	40.00	100.00
Jerry Sloan		
Pat Riley		
Bill Sharman		

2010-11 Ultimate Collection Signatures Triple

STATED PRINT RUN 25 SER.#'d SETS

TDET Bill Laimbeer	40.00	100.00
Adrian Dantley		
Dennis Rodman		
TEML Freddie Lewis	50.00	100.00
Julius Erving		
Moses Malone		
THOU Clyde Drexler	50.00	120.00
Kenny Smith		
Hakeem Olajuwon		
TJBE Larry Bird	200.00	400.00
Julius Erving		
Magic Johnson		
TJJJ Michael Jordan	500.00	800.00
Julius Erving		
Magic Johnson		
TJRB Larry Bird	250.00	400.00
Bill Russell		
LeBron James		
TJRR Derrick Rose	150.00	300.00
LeBron James		
Brandon Roy		
TLAL Gail Goodrich	75.00	200.00
Magic Johnson		
Jerry West		
TLCH Calbert Cheaney	15.00	40.00
Bobby Hurley		
George Lynch		
TMHL George Lynch	75.00	200.00
Anfernee Hardaway		
Tracy McGrady		
TNYK Walt Frazier	60.00	150.00
Mark Jackson		
Larry Johnson		
TSAS Avery Johnson	60.00	150.00
David Robinson		
Dominique Wilkins		
TUOM Glen Rice	40.00	100.00
Rudy Tomjanovich		
Cazzie Russell		

2010-11 Ultimate Collection Ultimate Inscriptions

STATED PRINT RUN 25 SER.#'d SETS

NAH Anfernee Hardaway	100.00	250.00
NBR Brandon Roy	15.00	40.00
NBW Bill Walton	15.00	30.00
NCD Clyde Drexler	50.00	100.00
NDR Derrick Rose	75.00	200.00
NDT David Thompson	10.00	25.00
NHO Hakeem Olajuwon	25.00	60.00
NJA LeBron James	175.00	350.00
NJE Julius Erving	40.00	80.00
NJS Jerry Sloan	10.00	25.00
NLJ Larry Johnson	40.00	100.00
NMA Mark Jackson	5.00	12.00
NSP Sam Perkins	20.00	40.00
NYM Yao Ming	50.00	120.00

1992-93 Ultimate USBL Promo Sheet

The United States Basketball League in conjunction with The Ultimate Trading Card Company released this approximately 7 1/2" by 10 1/2" sheet as a promotion for the planned 1992-93 USBL set. The sheet features nine standard size cards with action color player photos. The upper right corners of the picture appears to be peeled back to reveal The Ultimate Trading Card Company logo. Yellow-orange stripes across the bottom of each photo contain the players' names. The USBL logo overlaps the stripe and photo at the lower right corner. The cards have white borders. The backs display biographies, career highlights, statistics, and a small player photo against a medium gray and white pinstriped background. The card backs are shown on just the two outside columns of cards on the sheet. The center column is printed with promotional information. The players pictured are checklisted below as they appear on the sheet, beginning in the upper left corner and moving toward the lower right.

NNO USBL Promo Sheet	2.00	5.00
Norris Coleman		
Dallas Comegys		
Kermit Holmes		
Anthony Mason		
Anthony Pullard		
Lloyd Daniels		
Michael Anderson		
Darrell Armstrong		
Roy Tarpley		

1999-00 Ultimate Victory

Released in one series as a 150 card set each pack contained five cards and carried a suggested retail price of $2.99. The set breakdown includes 90 regular player cards, 30 MJ's Greatest Hits subset cards (inserted one in two) and 30 Ultimate Rookie cards (inserted one in four).

COMPLETE SET (150)	50.00	100.00
COMP. SET w/o RC (120)	20.00	50.00
1 Dikembe Mutombo	.40	1.00
2 Alan Henderson	.25	.60
3 LaPhonso Ellis	.25	.60
4 Kenny Anderson	.30	.75
5 Antoine Walker	.40	1.00
6 Paul Pierce	.60	1.50
7 Elden Campbell	.25	.60
8 Eddie Jones	.40	1.00
9 David Wesley	.25	.60
10 Michael Jordan	3.00	8.00
11 Kornell David RC	.40	1.00
12 Toni Kukoc	.40	1.00
13 Shawn Kemp	.40	1.00
14 Brevin Knight	.25	.60
15 Zydrunas Ilgauskas	.30	.75
16 Michael Finley	.40	1.00
17 Shawn Bradley	.25	.60
18 Dirk Nowitzki	.75	2.00
19 Antonio McDyess	.30	.75
20 Nick Van Exel	.30	.75
21 Ron Mercer	.30	.75
22 Grant Hill	.50	1.25
23 Lindsey Hunter	.25	.60
24 Jerry Stackhouse	.40	1.00
25 John Starks	.40	1.00
26 Antawn Jamison	.40	1.00
27 Mookie Blaylock	.25	.60
28 Hakeem Olajuwon	.50	1.25
29 Cuttino Mobley	.30	.75
30 Charles Barkley	.60	1.50
31 Reggie Miller	.40	1.00
32 Rik Smits	.40	1.00
33 Jalen Rose	.30	.75
34 Maurice Taylor	.25	.60
35 Tyrone Nesby RC	.40	1.00
36 Michael Olowokandi	.25	.60
37 Kobe Bryant	2.00	5.00
38 Shaquille O'Neal	1.00	2.50
39 Glen Rice	.40	1.00
40 Robert Horry	.40	1.00
41 Tim Hardaway	.40	1.00
42 Alonzo Mourning	.50	1.25
43 Jamal Mashburn	.30	.75
44 Ray Allen	.40	1.00
45 Glenn Robinson	.30	.75
46 Robert Traylor	.25	.60
47 Kevin Garnett	.75	2.00
48 Joe Smith	.30	.75
49 Bobby Jackson	.30	.75
50 Keith Van Horn	.30	.75
51 Stephon Marbury	.30	.75
52 Jayson Williams	.25	.60
53 Patrick Ewing	.50	1.25
54 Allan Houston	.30	.75
55 Latrell Sprewell	.40	1.00
56 Marcus Camby	.30	.75
57 Darrell Armstrong	.25	.60
58 Matt Harpring	.30	.75
59 Bo Outlaw	.25	.60
60 Allen Iverson	.75	2.00
61 Theo Ratliff	.30	.75
62 Larry Hughes	.30	.75
63 Jason Kidd	.60	1.50
64 Tom Gugliotta	.25	.60
65 Anfernee Hardaway	.60	1.50
66 Scottie Pippen	.60	1.50
67 Damon Stoudamire	.40	1.00
68 Brian Grant	.25	.60
69 Jason Williams	.50	1.25
70 Vlade Divac	.40	1.00
71 Chris Webber	.40	1.00
72 Tim Duncan	.75	2.00
73 Sean Elliott	.40	1.00
74 David Robinson	.60	1.50
75 Avery Johnson	.30	.75
76 Gary Payton	.40	1.00
77 Vin Baker	.40	1.00
78 Brent Barry	.30	.75
79 Vince Carter	.75	2.00
80 Doug Christie	.30	.75
81 Tracy McGrady	.60	1.50
82 Karl Malone	.50	1.25
83 John Stockton	.50	1.25
84 Bryon Russell	.25	.60
85 Shareef Abdur-Rahim	.30	.75
86 Mike Bibby	.40	1.00
87 Felipe Lopez	.25	.60
88 Juwan Howard	.30	.75
89 Rod Strickland	.25	.60
90 Mitch Richmond	.40	1.00
121 Elton Brand RC	1.50	4.00
122 Steve Francis RC	1.50	4.00
123 Baron Davis RC	2.00	5.00
124 Lamar Odom RC	2.00	5.00
125 Jonathan Bender RC	.60	1.50
126 Wally Szczerbiak RC	1.25	3.00
127 Richard Hamilton RC	1.50	4.00
128 Andre Miller RC	1.50	4.00
129 Shawn Marion RC	1.50	4.00
130 Jason Terry RC	1.50	4.00
131 Trajan Langdon RC	.60	1.50
132 Aleksandar Radojevic RC	.60	1.50
133 Corey Maggette RC	1.25	3.00
134 William Avery RC	.60	1.50
135 Ron Artest RC	1.50	4.00
136 Cal Bowdler RC	.60	1.50
137 James Posey RC	.60	1.50
138 Quincy Lewis RC	.60	1.50
139 Dion Glover RC	.60	1.50
140 Jeff Foster RC	.60	1.50
141 Kenny Thomas RC	.60	1.50
142 Devean George RC	.60	1.50
143 Tim James RC	.60	1.50
144 Vonteego Cummings RC	.60	1.50
145 Jumaine Jones RC	.60	1.50
146 Scott Padgett RC	.60	1.50
147 John Celestand RC	.60	1.50
148 Adrian Griffin RC	.60	1.50
149 Chris Herren RC	.60	1.50
150 Anthony Carter RC	.60	1.50

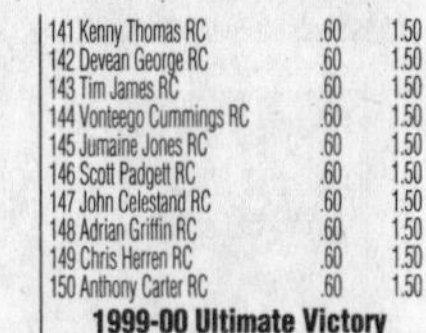

1999-00 Ultimate Victory Victory Collection

Randomly inserted in packs at one in 12 for base cards and one in 24 for rookies, this 150-card set parallels the base set. To ascertain values on individual cards, please refer to the multiplier in the header, coupled with the value of the base card.

COMMON MJ GH (91-120)	2.00	5.00

*STARS: 1.25X TO 3X BASE CARD HI
*RCs: .6X TO 1.5X BASE HI

1999-00 Ultimate Victory 1 of 1

Randomly inserted in packs, this 150-card set parallels the base set. Each card is serially numbered to one.

1999-00 Ultimate Victory Parallel 100

Randomly inserted in packs, this 150-card set parallels the base set. The cards are serially numbered to 100. To ascertain values on individual cards, please refer to the multiplier in the header, coupled with the value of the base card.

COMMON MJ GH (91-120)	25.00	60.00

*STARS: 8X TO 20X BASE CARD HI
*RCs: 2.5X TO 6X BASE HI

1999-00 Ultimate Victory Court Impact

Randomly inserted in packs at one in 24, this 10-card set contains players who draw the biggest crowds in the league. Card backs carry a "C" prefix.

COMPLETE SET (10)	15.00	40.00
C1 Michael Jordan	10.00	25.00
C2 Vince Carter	2.50	6.00
C3 Kobe Bryant	6.00	15.00
C4 Kevin Garnett	2.50	6.00
C5 Tim Duncan	2.50	6.00
C6 Jason Williams	1.50	4.00
C7 Grant Hill	1.50	4.00
C8 Keith Van Horn	1.00	2.50
C9 Allen Iverson	2.50	6.00
C10 Karl Malone	1.50	4.00

1999-00 Ultimate Victory Dr. J Glory Days

Randomly inserted in packs at one in 24, this eight-card set revisits some of the most memorable moments in NBA history from Dr. J. Card backs carry a "DR" prefix.

COMPLETE SET (8)	12.50	30.00
COMMON CARD (DR1-DR8)	2.00	5.00

1999-00 Ultimate Victory Got Skills?

Randomly inserted in packs at one in 24, this eight-card set highlights the game's flashiest performers. Card backs carry a "GS" prefix.

COMPLETE SET (8)	4.00	10.00
GS1 Kevin Garnett	1.50	4.00
GS2 Tim Hardaway	.75	2.00
GS3 Mike Bibby	.75	2.00
GS4 Stephon Marbury	.60	1.50
GS5 Reggie Miller	.75	2.00
GS6 Jason Williams	1.00	2.50
GS7 Antoine Walker	.75	2.00
GS8 Jason Kidd	1.25	3.00

1999-00 Ultimate Victory MJ's World Famous

Randomly inserted in packs at one in 24, this 12-card set focuses on some of Jordan's most spectacular feats. Card backs carry a "MJ" prefix.

COMPLETE SET (12)	25.00	50.00
COMMON CARD (MJ1-MJ12)	2.50	6.00

1999-00 Ultimate Victory Scorin' Legion

Randomly inserted in packs at one in 12, this 10-card set features the NBA's top scorers. Card backs carry a "SL" prefix.

COMPLETE SET (10)	4.00	10.00
SL1 Tim Duncan	1.25	3.00
SL2 Karl Malone	.75	2.00
SL3 Stephon Marbury	.50	1.25
SL4 Shaquille O'Neal	1.50	4.00
SL5 Antonio McDyess	.50	1.25
SL6 Gary Payton	.60	1.50
SL7 Allen Iverson	1.25	3.00
SL8 Keith Van Horn	.50	1.25
SL9 Shareef Abdur-Rahim	.50	1.25
SL10 Grant Hill	.75	2.00

1999-00 Ultimate Victory Surface to Air

Randomly inserted in packs at one in six, this 12-card set features some of the most dynamic aerial performers. Card backs carry a "SA" prefix.

COMPLETE SET (12)	5.00	12.00
SA1 Vince Carter	1.00	2.50
SA2 Antawn Jamison	.50	1.25
SA3 Eddie Jones	.50	1.25
SA4 Anfernee Hardaway	.75	2.00
SA5 Latrell Sprewell	.50	1.25
SA6 Antonio McDyess	.40	1.00
SA7 Michael Finley	.50	1.25
SA8 Kobe Bryant	2.50	6.00
SA9 Chris Webber	.50	1.25
SA10 Shawn Kemp	.50	1.25
SA11 Ray Allen	.50	1.25
SA12 Shaquille O'Neal	1.25	3.00

1999-00 Ultimate Victory Ultimate Fabrics

Randomly inserted in packs, this three-card set features a swatch of a game-used jersey card. The cards were serially numbered with Erving numbered to 300, Chamberlain to 100, Erving/Kobe to 25 and the special Erving autographed jersey to six.

UF1 Julius Erving/300	30.00	80.00
UF2 Wilt Chamberlain/100	200.00	500.00
UF3 Julius Erving/25 Kobe Bryant	125.00	250.00

2000-01 Ultimate Victory

The 2000-01 Upper Deck Ultimate Victory product was released in February, 2001 and features a 120-card base set. The base set was broken into tiers as follows: 60 Base Veterans (1-60), 30 FLY cards featuring Kobe Bryant and Kevin Garnett, and finally 30 Rookie Cards (individually serial numbered to 1500). Each pack contained 5 cards, and carried a suggested retail price of $2.99.

COMP.SET w/o SP (60)	10.00	25.00
1 Dikembe Mutombo	.30	.75
2 Jim Jackson	.20	.50
3 Paul Pierce	.40	1.00
4 Antoine Walker	.25	.60
5 Jamal Mashburn	.25	.60
6 Baron Davis	.30	.75
7 Elton Brand	.30	.75
8 Ron Artest	.30	.75
9 Lamond Murray	.20	.50
10 Andre Miller	.25	.60
11 Michael Finley	.30	.75
12 Dirk Nowitzki	.50	1.25
13 Antonio McDyess	.25	.60
14 Nick Van Exel	.25	.60
15 Jerry Stackhouse	.25	.60
16 Chucky Atkins	.20	.50
17 Antawn Jamison	.30	.75
18 Larry Hughes	.25	.60
19 Steve Francis	.30	.75
20 Hakeem Olajuwon	.40	1.00
21 Reggie Miller	.30	.75
22 Jalen Rose	.25	.60
23 Lamar Odom	.30	.75
24 Corey Maggette	.25	.60
25 Shaquille O'Neal	.75	2.00
26 Kobe Bryant	1.50	4.00
27 Ron Harper	.25	.60
28 Tim Hardaway	.30	.75
29 Eddie Jones	.30	.75
30 Ray Allen	.30	.75
31 Tim Thomas	.20	.50
32 Kevin Garnett	.60	1.50
33 Wally Szczerbiak	.25	.60
34 Terrell Brandon	.20	.50
35 Stephon Marbury	.25	.60
36 Keith Van Horn	.25	.60
37 Allan Houston	.25	.60
38 Latrell Sprewell	.25	.60
39 Grant Hill	.40	1.00
40 Tracy McGrady	.50	1.25
41 Allen Iverson	.60	1.50
42 Toni Kukoc	.25	.60
43 Jason Kidd	.50	1.25
44 Anfernee Hardaway	.50	1.25
45 Scottie Pippen	.50	1.25
46 Rasheed Wallace	.30	.75
47 Jason Williams	.30	.75
48 Chris Webber	.30	.75
49 Tim Duncan	.60	1.50
50 David Robinson	.50	1.25
51 Gary Payton	.30	.75
52 Rashard Lewis	.30	.75
53 Vince Carter	.60	1.50
54 Mark Jackson	.25	.60
55 Karl Malone	.40	1.00
56 John Stockton	.40	1.00
57 Shareef Abdur-Rahim	.25	.60
58 Mike Bibby	.30	.75
59 Mitch Richmond	.25	.60
60 Richard Hamilton	.25	.60
61 Kobe Bryant FLY	1.50	4.00
62 Kobe Bryant FLY	1.50	4.00
63 Kobe Bryant FLY	1.50	4.00
64 Kobe Bryant FLY	1.50	4.00
65 Kobe Bryant FLY	1.50	4.00
66 Kobe Bryant FLY	1.50	4.00
67 Kobe Bryant FLY	1.50	4.00
68 Kobe Bryant FLY	1.50	4.00
69 Kobe Bryant FLY	1.50	4.00
70 Kobe Bryant FLY	1.50	4.00
71 Kobe Bryant FLY	1.50	4.00
72 Kobe Bryant FLY	1.50	4.00
73 Kobe Bryant FLY	1.50	4.00
74 Kobe Bryant FLY	1.50	4.00
75 Kobe Bryant FLY	1.50	4.00
76 Kevin Garnett FLY	1.00	2.50
77 Kevin Garnett FLY	1.00	2.50
78 Kevin Garnett FLY	1.00	2.50
79 Kevin Garnett FLY	1.00	2.50
80 Kevin Garnett FLY	1.00	2.50
81 Kevin Garnett FLY	1.00	2.50
82 Kevin Garnett FLY	1.00	2.50
83 Kevin Garnett FLY	1.00	2.50
84 Kevin Garnett FLY	1.00	2.50
85 Kevin Garnett FLY	1.00	2.50
86 Kevin Garnett FLY	1.00	2.50
87 Kevin Garnett FLY	1.00	2.50
88 Kevin Garnett FLY	1.00	2.50
89 Kevin Garnett FLY	1.00	2.50
90 Kevin Garnett FLY	1.00	2.50
91 Kenyon Martin RC	3.00	8.00
92 Stromile Swift RC	1.25	3.00
93 Darius Miles RC	1.25	3.00
94 Marcus Fizer RC	1.25	3.00
95 Mike Miller RC	2.50	6.00
96 DerMarr Johnson RC	1.25	3.00
97 Chris Mihm RC	1.25	3.00
98 Jamal Crawford RC	2.00	5.00
99 Joel Przybilla RC	1.25	3.00
100 Keyon Dooling RC	1.25	3.00
101 Jerome Moiso RC	1.25	3.00
102 Etan Thomas RC	1.25	3.00
103 Courtney Alexander RC	1.25	3.00
104 Mateen Cleaves RC	1.25	3.00
105 Jason Collier RC	1.25	3.00
106 Hedo Turkoglu RC	2.50	6.00
107 Desmond Mason RC	1.50	4.00
108 Quentin Richardson RC	2.00	5.00
109 Jamaal Magloire RC	1.25	3.00
110 Speedy Claxton RC	1.25	3.00
111 Morris Peterson RC	1.25	3.00
112 Donnell Harvey RC	1.25	3.00
113 DeShawn Stevenson RC	1.50	4.00
114 Mamadou N'Diaye RC	1.25	3.00
115 Erick Barkley RC	1.25	3.00
116 Mike Smith RC	1.25	3.00
117 Eddie House RC	1.25	3.00
118 Eduardo Najera RC	1.25	3.00
119 Jason Hart RC	1.25	3.00
120 Chris Porter RC	1.25	3.00

2000-01 Ultimate Victory Victory Collection

Randomly inserted into packs, this 120-card insert is a complete parallel of the 120-card base set. This parallel features a red refractor-like card front, and each card is individually serial numbered to 350.

COMMON KOBE (61-75)	8.00	20.00
COMMON KG (76-90)	5.00	12.00

*STARS: 2.5X TO 6X BASE CARD HI
*RCs: .6X TO 1.5X BASE CARD HI

2000-01 Ultimate Victory Ultimate Collection

Randomly inserted into packs, this 120-card insert is a complete parallel of the 120-card base set. This parallel features a silver refractor-like card front, and each card is individually serial numbered to 100.

COMMON KOBE (61-75)	15.00	40.00
COMMON KG (76-90)	12.50	30.00

*STARS: 6X TO 15X BASE CARD HI
*RCs: 1X TO 2.5X BASE CARD HI

2000-01 Ultimate Victory Ultimate Victory

Randomly inserted into packs, this 120-card insert is a complete parallel of the 120-card base set. This parallel features a golden refractor-like card front, and each card is individually serial numbered to 25.

COMMON KOBE (61-75)	75.00	200.00
COMMON KG (76-90)	30.00	80.00

*STARS: 30X TO 80X BASE CARD HI
*RCs: 3X TO 8X BASE HI

2000-01 Ultimate Victory Championship Fabrics

Randomly inserted into packs at one in 480, this 8-card insert set features swatches of actual game-used jerseys. Card backs carry a "CF" prefix.

CF1 Kobe Bryant	20.00	50.00
CF2 Shaquille O'Neal	12.50	30.00
CF3 Michael Jordan	60.00	150.00
CF4 Julius Erving	15.00	40.00
CF5 Larry Bird	25.00	60.00
CF6 Isiah Thomas	10.00	25.00
CFC1 Kobe Bryant/25 Larry Bird	80.00	160.00

2000-01 Ultimate Victory Starstruck

Randomly inserted into packs at one in 11, this 10-card insert set features NBA players that have been starstruck from their abilities to play the game. Card backs carry a "S" prefix.

COMPLETE SET (10)	5.00	12.00
S1 Kobe Bryant	2.50	6.00
S2 Gary Payton	.50	1.25
S3 Chris Webber	.50	1.25
S4 Kevin Garnett	1.00	2.50
S5 Stephon Marbury	.40	1.00
S6 Shareef Abdur-Rahim	.40	1.00
S7 Steve Francis	.50	1.25
S8 Tim Duncan	1.00	2.50
S9 Anfernee Hardaway	.75	2.00
S10 Vince Carter	1.00	2.50

2000-01 Ultimate Victory The Reel World

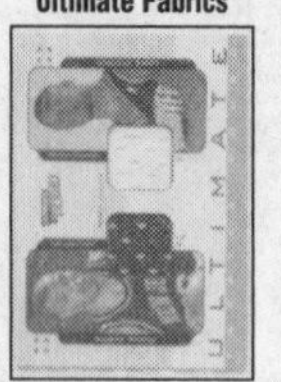

Randomly inserted into packs at one in 11, this 10-card insert features players that make the highlight reels night in night out. Card backs carry a "RW" prefix.

COMPLETE SET (10)	7.50	15.00
RW1 Kobe Bryant	2.50	6.00
RW2 Vince Carter	1.00	2.50
RW3 Tim Duncan	1.00	2.50
RW4 Allen Iverson	1.00	2.50
RW5 Elton Brand	.50	1.25
RW6 Jason Kidd	.75	2.00
RW7 Kevin Garnett	1.00	2.50
RW8 Lamar Odom	.50	1.25
RW9 Scottie Pippen	.75	2.00
RW10 Karl Malone	.60	1.50

2000-01 Ultimate Victory Ultimate Fabrics

Randomly inserted into packs at one in 240, this 5-card insert set features swatches of actual game-used jerseys. Card backs carry a "UFC" prefix. Please note that there is also an autographed version of the Martin/Swift card that is serial numbered to 25.

UFC1 Kenyon Martin Stromile Swift	5.00	12.00
UFC2 Kenyon Martin Darius Miles	5.00	12.00
UFC3 Kenyon Martin DerMarr Johnson	5.00	12.00
UFC4 Kenyon Martin Marcus Fizer AU	5.00	12.00
UFCA1 Kenyon Martin/25 Stromile Swift AU	20.00	40.00

2000-01 Ultimate Victory Ultimate Powers

Randomly inserted into packs at one in 23, this 10-card insert set features players that have incredible skills. Card backs carry a "U" prefix.

COMPLETE SET (10)	12.50	25.00
U1 Shaquille O'Neal	2.00	5.00
U2 Grant Hill	1.00	2.50
U3 Vince Carter	1.50	4.00
U4 Allen Iverson	1.50	4.00
U5 Kevin Garnett	1.50	4.00
U6 Tim Duncan	1.50	4.00
U7 Gary Payton	.75	2.00
U8 Kobe Bryant	4.00	10.00
U9 Steve Francis	.75	2.00
U10 Elton Brand	.75	2.00

1992-93 Ultra Promo Sheet

Measuring approximately 11" by 11 1/2", this promo sheet displays ten cards on one side and nine on the other. Both sides combine to present the top 20 dunkers in the NBA, with the exception that number 16 is omitted. The glossy 2 1/2" by 3 1/2" action photos sport the characteristic Ultra design, with a gold foil stripe separating the bottom of the picture from a black marbleized border. The player's name appears in a gray bar, while his team name and position are printed in a jade bar. Though the cards are unnumbered, they are listed below according to their dunk ranking.

NNO Ultra Panel David Robinson Dikembe Mutombo Otis Thorpe Hakeem Olajuwon Shawn Kemp Charles Barkley Pervis Ellison Chris Morris	2.00	5.00

1992-93 Ultra

The complete premier 1992-93 Ultra basketball set (made by Fleer) consists of 375 standard-size cards. The set was released in two series of 200 and 175 cards, respectively. Both series packs contained 14 cards each with 36 packs to a box. Suggested retail pack price was 1.79. The glossy color action player photos on the fronts are full-bleed except at the bottom where a diagonal gold-foil stripe edges a pale green variegated border. The player's name and team appear on two team color-coded bars that overlay the bottom border. The horizontal backs display action and close-up cut-out player photos against a basketball court background. The team logo and biographical information appear in a pale green bar like that on the front that edges the right side, while the player's name and statistics are given in bars running across the card bottom. The cards are numbered on the back and grouped alphabetically within team order. The first series closes with an NBA Draft Picks subset (193-198) and both series close with checklists (199-200/373-375). The second series contains more than 40 rookies, 30 trade cards, free agent signings, and other veterans omitted from the first series. The second series opens with an NBA Jam Session (201-220) subset. Three players from this Jam Session subset, Duane Causwell, Pervis Ellison, and Stacey Augmon, autographed a total of more than 2,500 cards that were randomly inserted in second series foil packs. These cards were embossed with Fleer logos for authenticity. On each series two pack, a mail-in offer provided the opportunity to acquire two more exclusive Jam Session cards, showing all 20 players in the set, for ten wrappers and 1.00 for postage and handling. According to Fleer, they anticipated about 100,000 requests. Key Rookie Cards include Tom Gugliotta, Robert Horry, Christian Laettner, Alonzo Mourning, Shaquille O'Neal, Latrell Sprewell and Clarence Weatherspoon.

COMPLETE SET (375)	15.00	30.00
COMPLETE SERIES 1 (200)	7.50	15.00
COMPLETE SERIES 2 (175)	7.50	15.00
1 Stacey Augmon	.08	.25
2 Duane Ferrell	.02	.10
3 Paul Graham	.02	.10
4 Blair Rasmussen	.02	.10
5 Rumeal Robinson	.02	.10
6 Dominique Wilkins	.20	.50
7 Kevin Willis	.02	.10
8 John Bagley	.02	.10
9 Dee Brown	.02	.10
10 Rick Fox	.08	.25
11 Kevin Gamble	.02	.10
12 Joe Kleine	.02	.10
13 Reggie Lewis	.08	.25
14 Kevin McHale	.20	.50
15 Robert Parish	.08	.25
16 Ed Pinckney	.02	.10
17 Muggsy Bogues	.08	.25
18 Dell Curry	.02	.10
19 Kenny Gattison	.02	.10
20 Kendall Gill	.08	.25
21 Larry Johnson	.25	.60
22 Johnny Newman	.02	.10
23 J.R. Reid	.02	.10
24 B.J. Armstrong	.02	.10
25 Bill Cartwright	.02	.10
26 Horace Grant	.08	.25
27 Michael Jordan	2.50	6.00
28 Stacey King	.02	.10
29 John Paxson	.02	.10
30 Will Perdue	.02	.10
31 Scottie Pippen	.60	1.50
32 Scott Williams	.02	.10
33 John Battle	.02	.10
34 Terrell Brandon	.20	.50
35 Brad Daugherty	.02	.10
36 Craig Ehlo	.02	.10
37 Larry Nance	.02	.10
38 Mark Price	.02	.10
39 Mike Sanders	.02	.10
40 John Williams	.02	.10
41 Terry Davis	.02	.10
42 Derek Harper	.08	.25
43 Donald Hodge	.02	.10
44 Mike Iuzzolino	.02	.10
45 Fat Lever	.02	.10
46 Doug Smith	.02	.10
47 Randy White	.02	.10
48 Winston Garland	.02	.10
49 Chris Jackson	.02	.10
50 Marcus Liberty	.02	.10
51 Todd Lichti	.02	.10
52 Mark Macon	.02	.10
53 Dikembe Mutombo	.25	.60
54 Reggie Williams	.02	.10
55 Mark Aguirre	.02	.10
56 Joe Dumars	.20	.50
57 Bill Laimbeer	.08	.25
58 Dennis Rodman	.40	1.00
59 Isiah Thomas	.20	.50
60 Darrell Walker	.02	.10
61 Orlando Woolridge	.02	.10
62 Victor Alexander	.02	.10
63 Chris Gatling	.02	.10
64 Tim Hardaway	.25	.60
65 Tyrone Hill	.02	.10
66 Sarunas Marciulionis	.02	.10
67 Chris Mullin	.20	.50
68 Billy Owens	.08	.25
69 Sleepy Floyd	.02	.10
70 Avery Johnson	.02	.10
71 Vernon Maxwell	.02	.10
72 Hakeem Olajuwon	.30	.75
73 Kenny Smith	.02	.10
74 Otis Thorpe	.08	.25
75 Dale Davis	.02	.10
76 Vern Fleming	.02	.10
77 George McCloud	.02	.10
78 Reggie Miller	.20	.50
79 Detlef Schrempf	.08	.25
80 Rik Smits	.08	.25
81 LaSalle Thompson	.02	.10
82 Gary Grant	.02	.10
83 Ron Harper	.08	.25
84 Mark Jackson	.08	.25
85 Danny Manning	.08	.25
86 Ken Norman	.02	.10
87 Stanley Roberts	.02	.10
88 Loy Vaught	.02	.10
89 Elden Campbell	.08	.25
90 Vlade Divac	.08	.25
91 A.C. Green	.08	.25
92 Sam Perkins	.08	.25
93 Byron Scott	.08	.25
94 Tony Smith	.02	.10
95 Sedale Threatt	.02	.10
96 James Worthy	.20	.50
97 Willie Burton	.02	.10
98 Bimbo Coles	.02	.10
99 Kevin Edwards	.02	.10
100 Grant Long	.02	.10
101 Glen Rice	.20	.50
102 Rony Seikaly	.02	.10
103 Brian Shaw	.02	.10
104 Steve Smith	.25	.60
105 Frank Brickowski	.02	.10
106 Moses Malone	.20	.50
107 Fred Roberts	.02	.10
108 Alvin Robertson	.02	.10
109 Thurl Bailey	.02	.10
110 Gerald Glass	.02	.10
111 Luc Longley	.08	.25
112 Felton Spencer	.02	.10
113 Doug West	.02	.10
114 Kenny Anderson	.20	.50
115 Mookie Blaylock	.08	.25
116 Sam Bowie	.02	.10
117 Derrick Coleman	.08	.25
118 Chris Dudley	.02	.10
119 Chris Morris	.02	.10
120 Drazen Petrovic	.02	.10
121 Greg Anthony	.02	.10
122 Patrick Ewing	.20	.50
123 Anthony Mason	.20	.50
124 Charles Oakley	.08	.25
125 Doc Rivers	.08	.25
126 Charles Smith	.02	.10
127 John Starks	.08	.25
128 Nick Anderson	.08	.25
129 Anthony Bowie	.02	.10
130 Terry Catledge	.02	.10
131 Jerry Reynolds	.02	.10
132 Dennis Scott	.08	.25
133 Scott Skiles	.02	.10
134 Brian Williams	.02	.10
135 Ron Anderson	.02	.10
136 Manute Bol	.02	.10
137 Johnny Dawkins	.02	.10
138 Armon Gilliam	.02	.10
139 Hersey Hawkins	.08	.25
140 Jeff Ruland	.02	.10
141 Charles Shackleford	.02	.10
142 Cedric Ceballos	.08	.25
143 Tom Chambers	.02	.10
144 Kevin Johnson	.20	.50
145 Negele Knight	.02	.10
146 Dan Majerle	.08	.25
147 Mark West	.02	.10
148 Mark Bryant	.02	.10
149 Clyde Drexler	.20	.50
150 Kevin Duckworth	.02	.10
151 Jerome Kersey	.02	.10
152 Robert Pack	.02	.10
153 Terry Porter	.02	.10
154 Clifford Robinson	.08	.25
155 Buck Williams	.08	.25
156 Anthony Bonner	.02	.10
157 Duane Causwell	.02	.10
158 Mitch Richmond	.20	.50
159 Lionel Simmons	.02	.10
160 Wayman Tisdale	.02	.10
161 Spud Webb	.08	.25
162 Willie Anderson	.02	.10
163 Antoine Carr	.02	.10
164 Terry Cummings	.08	.25
165 Sean Elliott	.08	.25
166 Sidney Green	.02	.10
167 David Robinson	.30	.75
168 Dana Barros	.02	.10
169 Benoit Benjamin	.02	.10
170 Michael Cage	.02	.10
171 Eddie Johnson	.02	.10
172 Shawn Kemp	.40	1.00
173 Derrick McKey	.02	.10
174 Nate McMillan	.02	.10
175 Gary Payton	.40	1.00
176 Ricky Pierce	.02	.10
177 David Benoit	.02	.10
178 Mike Brown	.02	.10
179 Tyrone Corbin	.02	.10
180 Mark Eaton	.02	.10
181 Jeff Malone	.02	.10
182 Karl Malone	.30	.75
183 John Stockton	.20	.50
184 Michael Adams	.02	.10
185 Ledell Eackles	.02	.10
186 Pervis Ellison	.02	.10
187 A.J. English	.02	.10
188 Harvey Grant	.02	.10
189 Buck Johnson	.02	.10
190 LaBradford Smith	.02	.10
191 Larry Stewart	.02	.10
192 David Wingate	.02	.10
193 Alonzo Mourning RC	.75	2.00
194 Adam Keefe RC	.02	.10
195 Robert Horry RC	.20	.50
196 Anthony Peeler RC	.08	.25
197 Tracy Murray RC	.08	.25
198 Dave Johnson RC	.02	.10
199 Checklist 1-104	.02	.10
200 Checklist 105-200	.02	.10
201 David Robinson JS	.10	.30
202 Dikembe Mutombo JS	.10	.30
203 Otis Thorpe JS	.01	.05
204 Hakeem Olajuwon JS	.10	.30
205 Shawn Kemp JS	.20	.50
206 Charles Barkley JS	.10	.30
207 Pervis Ellison JS	.01	.05
208 Chris Morris JS	.01	.05
209 Brad Daugherty JS	.01	.05
210 Derrick Coleman JS	.01	.05
211 Tim Perry JS	.01	.05
212 Duane Causwell JS	.01	.05
213 Scottie Pippen JS	.20	.50
214 Robert Parish JS	.01	.05
215 Stacey Augmon JS	.01	.05
216 Michael Jordan JS	.75	2.00
217 Karl Malone JS	.10	.30
218 John Williams JS	.01	.05
219 Horace Grant JS	.01	.05
220 Orlando Woolridge JS	.01	.05
221 Mookie Blaylock	.05	.15
222 Greg Foster	.01	.05
223 Steve Henson	.01	.05
224 Adam Keefe	.01	.05
225 Jon Koncak	.01	.05
226 Travis Mays	.01	.05
227 Alaa Abdelnaby	.01	.05
228 Sherman Douglas	.01	.05
229 Xavier McDaniel	.01	.05
230 Marcus Webb RC	.01	.05
231 Tony Bennett RC	.01	.05
232 Mike Gminski	.01	.05
233 Kevin Lynch	.01	.05
234 Alonzo Mourning	.30	.75
235 David Wingate	.01	.05
236 Rodney McCray	.01	.05
237 Trent Tucker	.01	.05
238 Corey Williams RC	.01	.05
239 Danny Ferry	.01	.05
240 Jay Guidinger RC	.01	.05
241 Jerome Lane	.01	.05
242 Bobby Phills RC	.10	.30
243 Gerald Wilkins	.01	.05
244 Walter Bond RC	.01	.05
245 Dexter Cambridge RC	.01	.05
246 Radisav Curcic UER RC (Misspelled Radislav on card front)	.01	.05
247 Brian Howard RC	.01	.05
248 Tracy Moore RC	.01	.05
249 Sean Rooks RC	.01	.05
250 Kevin Brooks	.01	.05
251 LaPhonso Ellis RC	.10	.30
252 Scott Hastings	.01	.05
253 Robert Pack	.01	.05
254 Gary Plummer RC	.01	.05
255 Bryant Stith RC	.05	.15
256 Robert Werdann RC	.01	.05
257 Gerald Glass	.01	.05
258 Terry Mills	.01	.05
259 Olden Polynice	.01	.05
260 Danny Young	.01	.05
261 Jud Buechler	.01	.05
262 Jeff Grayer	.01	.05
263 Byron Houston RC	.01	.05
264 Keith Jennings RC	.01	.05
265 Ed Nealy	.01	.05
266 Latrell Sprewell RC	1.00	2.50
267 Scott Brooks	.01	.05
268 Matt Bullard	.01	.05
269 Winston Garland	.01	.05
270 Carl Herrera	.01	.05
271 Robert Horry	.10	.30
272 Tree Rollins	.01	.05
273 Greg Dreiling	.01	.05
274 Sean Green	.01	.05
275 Sam Mitchell	.01	.05
276 Pooh Richardson	.01	.05
277 Malik Sealy RC	.05	.15
278 Kenny Williams	.01	.05
279 Mark Jackson	.05	.15
280 Stanley Roberts	.01	.05
281 Elmore Spencer RC	.01	.05
282 Kiki Vandeweghe	.01	.05
283 John S. Williams	.01	.05
284 Randy Woods RC	.01	.05
285 Alex Blackwell RC	.01	.05
286 Duane Cooper RC	.01	.05
287 James Edwards	.01	.05
288 Jack Haley	.01	.05
289 Anthony Peeler	.05	.15
290 Keith Askins	.01	.05
291 Matt Geiger RC	.05	.15
292 Alec Kessler	.01	.05
293 Harold Miner RC with Michael Jordan	.10	.30
294 John Salley	.01	.05
295 Anthony Avent RC	.01	.05
296 Jon Barry RC	.05	.15
297 Todd Day RC	.05	.15
298 Blue Edwards	.01	.05
299 Brad Lohaus	.01	.05
300 Lee Mayberry RC	.01	.05
301 Eric Murdock	.01	.05
302 Danny Schayes	.01	.05
303 Lance Blanks	.01	.05
304 Christian Laettner RC	.25	.60
305 Marlon Maxey RC	.01	.05
306 Bob McCann RC	.01	.05
307 Chuck Person	.01	.05
308 Brad Sellers	.01	.05
309 Chris Smith RC	.01	.05
310 Gundars Vetra RC	.01	.05
311 Micheal Williams	.01	.05
312 Rafael Addison	.01	.05
313 Chucky Brown	.01	.05
314 Maurice Cheeks	.01	.05
315 Tate George	.01	.05
316 Rick Mahorn	.01	.05
317 Rumeal Robinson	.01	.05
318 Eric Anderson RC	.01	.05
319 Rolando Blackman	.01	.05
320 Tony Campbell	.01	.05
321 Hubert Davis RC	.05	.15
322 Doc Rivers	.05	.15
323 Charles Smith	.01	.05
324 Herb Williams	.01	.05
325 Litterial Green RC	.01	.05
326 Steve Kerr	.05	.15
327 Greg Kite	.01	.05
328 Shaquille O'Neal RC	4.00	10.00
329 Tom Tolbert	.01	.05
330 Jeff Turner	.01	.05
331 Greg Grant	.01	.05
332 Jeff Hornacek	.05	.15
333 Andrew Lang	.01	.05
334 Tim Perry	.01	.05
335 C.Weatherspoon RC	.10	.30
336 Danny Ainge	.05	.15
337 Charles Barkley	.20	.50
338 Richard Dumas RC	.01	.05
339 Frank Johnson	.01	.05
340 Tim Kempton	.01	.05
341 Oliver Miller RC	.05	.15
342 Jerrod Mustaf	.01	.05
343 Mario Elie	.05	.15
344 Dave Johnson	.01	.05
345 Tracy Murray	.05	.15
346 Rod Strickland	.10	.30
347 Randy Brown	.01	.05
348 Pete Chilcutt	.01	.05
349 Marty Conlon	.01	.05
350 Jim Les	.01	.05
351 Kurt Rambis	.01	.05
352 Walt Williams RC	.10	.30
353 Lloyd Daniels RC	.01	.05
354 Vinny Del Negro	.01	.05
355 Dale Ellis	.01	.05
356 Avery Johnson	.01	.05
357 Sam Mack RC	.05	.15
358 J.R. Reid	.01	.05
359 David Wood	.01	.05
360 Vincent Askew	.01	.05
361 Isaac Austin RC	.05	.15
362 John Crotty RC	.01	.05
363 Stephen Howard RC	.01	.05
364 Jay Humphries	.01	.05
365 Larry Krystkowiak	.01	.05
366 Rex Chapman	.01	.05
367 Tom Gugliotta RC	.40	1.00
368 Buck Johnson	.01	.05
369 Charles Jones	.01	.05
370 Don MacLean RC	.01	.05
371 Doug Overton	.01	.05
372 Brent Price RC	.05	.15
373 Checklist 201-266	.01	.05
374 Checklist 267-330	.01	.05
375 Checklist 331-375	.01	.05
JS207 Pervis Ellison AU	10.00	25.00
JS212 Duane Causwell AU	10.00	25.00
JS215 Stacey Augmon AU	15.00	30.00
NNO Jam Session Rank 1-10 David Robinson Dikembe Mutombo Otis Thorpe Hakeem Olajuwon Shawn Kemp Charles Barkley Pervis Ellison Chris Morris Brad Daugherty Derrick Coleman	1.00	2.50
NNO Jam Session 11-20 Tim Perry Duane Causwell Scottie Pippen Robert Parish Stacey Augmon Michael Jordan Karl Malone John Williams Horace Grant Orlando Woolridge	1.00	2.50

1992-93 Ultra All-NBA

This set features 15 standard-size cards, one for each All-NBA first, second, and third-team player. The cards were randomly inserted into approximately one out of every 14 first series foil packs. The fronts feature color action player photos which are full-bleed except at the bottom, where a gold foil stripe separates a marbleized diagonal bottom border. A crest showing which All-NBA team the player was on overlaps the border and picture. The player's name is gold-foil stamped at the bottom. The horizontal backs carry a cut-out player close-up and career highlights on a marbleized background.

COMPLETE SET (15)	20.00	40.00
1 Karl Malone	1.25	3.00
2 Chris Mullin	.75	2.00
3 David Robinson	1.25	3.00
4 Michael Jordan	8.00	20.00
5 Clyde Drexler	.75	2.00
6 Scottie Pippen	2.50	6.00
7 Charles Barkley	1.25	3.00
8 Patrick Ewing	.75	2.00
9 Tim Hardaway	1.00	2.50

John Stockton	.75	2.00
Dennis Rodman	1.50	4.00
Kevin Willis	.20	.50
Brad Daugherty	.20	.50
Mark Price	.20	.50
Kevin Johnson	.75	2.00

1992-93 Ultra All-Rookies

ndomly inserted in second series foil packs at a ported rate of approximately one card per nine packs, s ten-card standard-size set focuses on the 1992-93 ass of outstanding rookies. A color action shot on the nt has been cut out and superimposed on grid of entical close-up shots of the player, which resemble e effect produced by a wall of TV sets displaying the me image. The "All-Rookie" logo and the player's me are gold-foil stamped across the bottom of the cture. On the backs, a wheat-colored panel carrying a ayer profile overlays a second full-bleed color action oto. The set is sequenced in alphabetical order.

OMPLETE SET (10)	8.00	20.00
LaPhonso Ellis	.30	.75
Tom Gugliotta	1.00	2.50
Robert Horry	.50	1.25
Christian Laettner	.60	1.50
Harold Miner	.15	.40
Alonzo Mourning	2.00	5.00
Shaquille O'Neal	8.00	20.00
Latrell Sprewell	2.50	6.00
Clarence Weatherspoon	.30	.75
Walt Williams	.30	.75

1992-93 Ultra Award Winners

is five-card standard-size Ultra Award Winners insert t spotlights the 1991-92 MVP, Rookie of the Year, efensive Player of the Year, top "6th Man" and Most proved Player. These cards were randomly inserted to first series packs at a rate of one card in every 42 acks according to information printed on the rappers. Card fronts feature an action photo with the ayer's name and Award Winners logo at the bottom. acks have career highlights and a photo.

OMPLETE SET (5)	12.50	25.00
Michael Jordan	10.00	25.00
David Robinson	1.00	2.50
Larry Johnson	.75	2.00
Detlef Schrempf	.30	.75
Pervis Ellison	.10	.30

1992-93 Ultra Scottie Pippen

is 12-card standard-size "Career Highlights" set ronicles Scottie Pippen's rise to NBA stardom. The rds were inserted at a rate of one card per 21 first eries packs according to information printed on the rappers. Pippen autographed more than 2,000 of ese cards for random insertion in first series packs. ese autograph cards have embossed Fleer logos for thenticity. Through a special mail-in offer only, two dditional Pippen cards were made available to llectors who sent in ten wrappers and 1.00 for stage and handling. On the front, the cards feature lor action player photos with brownish-green arbleized borders. The player's name and the words Career Highlights" are stamped in gold foil below the cture. On the same marbleized background, the backs rry a color head shot as well as biography and career ummary.

OMPLETE SET (10)	7.50	15.00
OMMON PIPPEN (1-10)	.60	1.50
ERTIFIED AUTOGRAPH (AU)	60.00	150.00
OMMON SEND-OFF (11-12)	.60	1.50

1992-93 Ultra Playmakers

andomly inserted in second series foil packs at a ported rate of one card per 13 packs, this ten-card andard-size set features the NBA's top point guards. e glossy color action photos on the fronts are full-eed except at the bottom where a lavender stripe lges the picture. The "Playmaker" logo and the ayer's name are gold-foil stamped across the bottom the picture. On the backs, a wheat-colored panel rrying a player profile overlays a second full-bleed lor action photo. The cards are numbered in the wer left corner of the panel.

COMPLETE SET (10)	2.00	4.00
1 Kenny Anderson	.60	1.50
2 Muggsy Bogues	.30	.75
3 Tim Hardaway	.75	2.00
4 Mark Jackson	.30	.75
5 Kevin Johnson	.60	1.50
6 Mark Price	.15	.40
7 Terry Porter	.15	.40
8 Scott Skiles	.15	.40
9 John Stockton	.60	1.50
10 Isiah Thomas	.60	1.50

1992-93 Ultra Rejectors

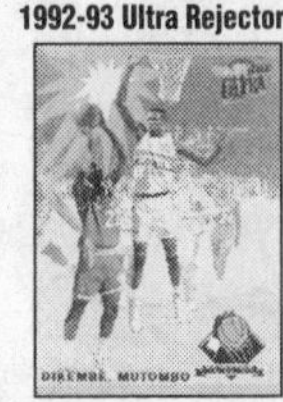

Randomly inserted in second series foil packs at a reported rate of one in 26, this five-card standard-size set showcases defensive big men who are aptly dubbed "Rejectors." The glossy color action photos on the fronts are full-bleed except at the bottom where a gold stripe edges the picture. The player's name and the "Rejector" logo are gold-foil stamped across the bottom of the picture. On a black panel inside gold borders, the horizontal backs carry text describing the player's defensive accomplishments and a color close-up photo. The set is sequenced in alphabetical order.

COMPLETE SET (5)	4.00	10.00
1 Alonzo Mourning	.50	1.25
2 Dikembe Mutombo	.40	1.00
3 Hakeem Olajuwon	.50	1.25
4 Shaquille O'Neal	3.00	8.00
5 David Robinson	.50	1.25

1993-94 Ultra

The complete 1993-94 Ultra basketball set consists of 375 standard-size cards that were issued in series of 200 and 175 respectively. Cards were issued in 14 and 19-card packs. There are 36 packs per box. The glossy color action player photos on the fronts are full-bleed except at the bottom. The bottom of the front consists of player name, team name and a peach colored border. The horizontal backs feature a player photos against a basketball court background. The team logo and biographical information appear a pale peach bar, while the player's name and statistics are printed in team color-coded bars running across the card bottom. The cards are alphabetically arranged by team and are numbered alphabetically within team order. A USA Basketball subset contains cards 361-372. Ten second series wrappers and $1.50 could be redeemed for USA cards of Reggie Miller (M1), Shaquille O'Neal (M2) and a team photo (M3). The offer was good through June 10, 1994. These cards are not considered part of the basic set. Rookie Cards of note in this set include Vin Baker, Anfernee Hardaway, Allan Houston, Toni Kukoc, Jamal Mashburn, Nick Van Exel and Chris Webber.

COMPLETE SET (375)	15.00	30.00
COMPLETE SERIES 1 (200)	7.50	15.00
COMPLETE SERIES 2 (175)	7.50	15.00
1 Stacey Augmon	.01	.05
2 Mookie Blaylock	.05	.15
3 Doug Edwards RC	.01	.05
4 Duane Ferrell	.01	.05
5 Paul Graham	.01	.05
6 Adam Keefe	.01	.05
7 Dominique Wilkins	.10	.30
8 Kevin Willis	.01	.05
9 Alaa Abdelnaby	.01	.05
10 Dee Brown	.01	.05
11 Sherman Douglas	.01	.05
12 Rick Fox	.01	.05
13 Kevin Gamble	.01	.05
14 Xavier McDaniel	.01	.05
15 Robert Parish	.05	.15
16 Muggsy Bogues	.05	.15
17 Scott Burrell RC	.10	.30
18 Dell Curry	.01	.05
19 Kenny Gattison	.01	.05
20 Hersey Hawkins	.05	.15
21 Eddie Johnson	.01	.05
22 Larry Johnson	.10	.30
23 Alonzo Mourning	.20	.50
24 Johnny Newman	.01	.05
25 David Wingate	.01	.05
26 B.J. Armstrong	.01	.05
27 Corie Blount RC	.01	.05
28 Bill Cartwright	.01	.05
29 Horace Grant	.05	.15
30 Michael Jordan	1.50	4.00
31 Stacey King	.01	.05
32 John Paxson	.01	.05
33 Will Perdue	.01	.05
34 Scottie Pippen	.40	1.00
35 Terrell Brandon	.05	.15
36 Brad Daugherty	.01	.05
37 Danny Ferry	.01	.05
38 Chris Mills RC	.10	.30
39 Larry Nance	.01	.05
40 Mark Price	.01	.05
41 Gerald Wilkins	.01	.05
42 John Williams	.01	.05
43 Terry Davis	.01	.05
44 Derek Harper	.05	.15
45 Donald Hodge	.01	.05
46 Jim Jackson	.05	.15
47 Sean Rooks	.01	.05
48 Doug Smith	.01	.05
49 Mahmoud Abdul-Rauf	.01	.05
50 LaPhonso Ellis	.01	.05
51 Mark Macon	.01	.05
52 Dikembe Mutombo	.10	.30
53 Bryant Stith	.01	.05
54 Reggie Williams	.01	.05
55 Mark Aguirre	.01	.05
56 Joe Dumars	.10	.30
57 Bill Laimbeer	.01	.05
58 Terry Mills	.01	.05
59 Olden Polynice	.01	.05
60 Alvin Robertson	.01	.05
61 Sean Elliott	.05	.15
62 Isiah Thomas	.10	.30
63 Victor Alexander	.01	.05
64 Chris Gatling	.01	.05
65 Tim Hardaway	.10	.30
66 Byron Houston	.01	.05
67 Sarunas Marciulionis	.01	.05
68 Chris Mullin	.10	.30
69 Billy Owens	.01	.05
70 Latrell Sprewell	.30	.75
71 Matt Bullard	.01	.05
72 Sam Cassell RC	.50	1.25
73 Carl Herrera	.01	.05
74 Robert Horry	.05	.15
75 Vernon Maxwell	.01	.05
76 Hakeem Olajuwon	.20	.50
77 Kenny Smith	.01	.05
78 Otis Thorpe	.05	.15
79 Dale Davis	.01	.05
80 Vern Fleming	.01	.05
81 Reggie Miller	.10	.30
82 Sam Mitchell	.01	.05
83 Pooh Richardson	.01	.05
84 Detlef Schrempf	.05	.15
85 Rik Smits	.05	.15
86 Ron Harper	.05	.15
87 Mark Jackson	.05	.15
88 Danny Manning	.05	.15
89 Stanley Roberts	.01	.05
90 Loy Vaught	.01	.05
91 John Williams	.01	.05
92 Sam Bowie	.01	.05
93 Doug Christie	.05	.15
94 Vlade Divac	.05	.15
95 George Lynch RC	.01	.05
96 Anthony Peeler	.01	.05
97 James Worthy	.10	.30
98 Bimbo Coles	.01	.05
99 Grant Long	.01	.05
100 Harold Miner	.01	.05
101 Glen Rice	.05	.15
102 Rony Seikaly	.01	.05
103 Brian Shaw	.01	.05
104 Steve Smith	.10	.30
105 Anthony Avent	.01	.05
106 Vin Baker RC	.30	.75
107 Frank Brickowski	.01	.05
108 Todd Day	.01	.05
109 Blue Edwards	.01	.05
110 Lee Mayberry	.01	.05
111 Eric Murdock	.01	.05
112 Orlando Woolridge	.01	.05
113 Thurl Bailey	.01	.05
114 Christian Laettner	.05	.15
115 Chuck Person	.01	.05
116 Doug West	.01	.05
117 Micheal Williams	.01	.05
118 Kenny Anderson	.05	.15
119 Derrick Coleman	.05	.15
120 Rick Mahorn	.01	.05
121 Chris Morris	.01	.05
122 Rumeal Robinson	.01	.05
123 Rex Walters RC	.01	.05
124 Greg Anthony	.01	.05
125 Rolando Blackman	.01	.05
126 Hubert Davis	.01	.05
127 Patrick Ewing	.10	.30
128 Anthony Mason	.05	.15
129 Charles Oakley	.05	.15
130 Doc Rivers	.05	.15
131 Charles Smith	.01	.05
132 John Starks	.05	.15
133 Nick Anderson	.05	.15
134 Anthony Bowie	.01	.05
135 Shaquille O'Neal	.60	1.50
136 Dennis Scott	.01	.05
137 Scott Skiles	.01	.05
138 Jeff Turner	.01	.05
139 Shawn Bradley RC	.10	.30
140 Johnny Dawkins	.01	.05
141 Jeff Hornacek	.05	.15
142 Tim Perry	.01	.05
143 Clarence Weatherspoon	.01	.05
144 Danny Ainge	.05	.15
145 Charles Barkley	.20	.50
146 Cedric Ceballos	.05	.15
147 Kevin Johnson	.05	.15
148 Negele Knight	.01	.05
149 Malcolm Mackey RC	.01	.05
150 Dan Majerle	.05	.15
151 Oliver Miller	.01	.05
152 Mark West	.01	.05
153 Mark Bryant	.01	.05
154 Clyde Drexler	.10	.30
155 Jerome Kersey	.01	.05
156 Terry Porter	.01	.05
157 Clifford Robinson	.05	.15
158 Rod Strickland	.05	.15
159 Buck Williams	.01	.05
160 Duane Causwell	.01	.05
161 Bobby Hurley RC	.05	.15
162 Mitch Richmond	.10	.30
163 Lionel Simmons	.01	.05
164 Wayman Tisdale	.01	.05
165 Spud Webb	.05	.15
166 Walt Williams	.01	.05
167 Willie Anderson	.01	.05
168 Antoine Carr	.01	.05
169 Lloyd Daniels	.01	.05
170 Dennis Rodman	.25	.60
171 Dale Ellis	.01	.05
172 Avery Johnson	.01	.05
173 J.R. Reid	.01	.05
174 David Robinson	.20	.50
175 Michael Cage	.01	.05
176 Kendall Gill	.05	.15
177 Ervin Johnson RC	.05	.15
178 Shawn Kemp	.20	.50
179 Derrick McKey	.01	.05
180 Nate McMillan	.01	.05
181 Gary Payton	.20	.50
182 Sam Perkins	.05	.15
183 Ricky Pierce	.01	.05
184 David Benoit	.01	.05
185 Tyrone Corbin	.01	.05
186 Mark Eaton	.01	.05
187 Jay Humphries	.01	.05
188 Jeff Malone	.01	.05
189 Karl Malone	.20	.50
190 John Stockton	.10	.30
191 Luther Wright RC	.01	.05
192 Michael Adams	.01	.05
193 Calbert Cheaney RC	.05	.15
194 Pervis Ellison	.01	.05
195 Tom Gugliotta	.10	.30
196 Buck Johnson	.01	.05
197 LaBradford Smith	.01	.05
198 Larry Stewart	.01	.05
199 Checklist	.01	.05
200 Checklist	.01	.05
201 Doug Edwards	.01	.05
202 Craig Ehlo	.01	.05
203 Jon Koncak	.01	.05
204 Andrew Lang	.01	.05
205 Ennis Whatley	.01	.05
206 Chris Corchiani	.01	.05
207 Acie Earl RC	.01	.05
208 Jimmy Oliver	.01	.05
209 Ed Pinckney	.01	.05
210 Dino Radja RC	.01	.05
211 Matt Wenstrom RC	.01	.05
212 Tony Bennett	.01	.05
213 Scott Burrell	.10	.30
214 LeRon Ellis	.01	.05
215 Hersey Hawkins	.05	.15
216 Eddie Johnson	.01	.05
217 Rumeal Robinson	.01	.05
218 Corie Blount	.01	.05
219 Dave Johnson	.01	.05
220 Steve Kerr	.05	.15
221 Toni Kukoc RC	.50	1.25
222 Pete Myers	.01	.05
223 Bill Wennington	.01	.05
224 Scott Williams	.01	.05
225 John Battle	.01	.05
226 Tyrone Hill	.01	.05
227 Gerald Madkins RC	.01	.05
228 Chris Mills	.10	.30
229 Bobby Phills	.01	.05
230 Greg Dreiling	.01	.05
231 Lucious Harris RC	.01	.05
232 Popeye Jones RC	.01	.05
233 Tim Legler RC	.01	.05
234 Fat Lever	.01	.05
235 Jamal Mashburn RC	.30	.75
236 Tom Hammonds	.01	.05
237 Darnell Mee RC	.01	.05
238 Robert Pack	.01	.05
239 Rodney Rogers RC	.10	.30
240 Brian Williams	.01	.05
241 Greg Anderson	.01	.05
242 Sean Elliott	.05	.15
243 Allan Houston RC	.50	1.25
244 Lindsey Hunter RC	.10	.30
245 Mark Macon	.01	.05
246 David Wood -	.01	.05
247 Jud Buechler	.01	.05
248 Josh Grant RC	.01	.05
249 Jeff Grayer	.01	.05
250 Keith Jennings	.01	.05
251 Avery Johnson	.01	.05
252 Chris Webber RC	1.25	3.00
253 Scott Brooks	.01	.05
254 Sam Cassell	.10	.30
255 Mario Elie	.01	.05
256 Richard Petruska RC	.01	.05
257 Eric Riley RC	.01	.05
258 Antonio Davis RC	.15	.40
259 Scott Haskin RC	.01	.05
260 Derrick McKey	.01	.05
261 Byron Scott	.05	.15
262 Malik Sealy	.01	.05
263 Kenny Williams	.01	.05
264 Haywoode Workman	.01	.05
265 Mark Aguirre	.01	.05
266 Terry Dehere RC	.01	.05
267 Harold Ellis RC	.01	.05
268 Gary Grant	.01	.05
269 Bob Martin RC	.01	.05
270 Elmore Spencer	.01	.05
271 Tom Tolbert	.01	.05
272 Sam Bowie	.01	.05
273 Elden Campbell	.01	.05
274 Antonio Harvey RC	.01	.05
275 George Lynch	.01	.05
276 Tony Smith	.01	.05
277 Sedale Threatt	.01	.05
278 Nick Van Exel RC	.40	1.00
279 Willie Burton	.01	.05
280 Matt Geiger	.01	.05
281 John Salley	.01	.05
282 Vin Baker	.15	.40
283 Jon Barry	.01	.05
284 Brad Lohaus	.01	.05
285 Ken Norman	.01	.05
286 Derek Strong RC	.01	.05
287 Mike Brown	.01	.05
288 Brian Davis RC	.01	.05
289 Tellis Frank	.01	.05
290 Luc Longley	.05	.15
291 Marlon Maxey	.01	.05
292 Isaiah Rider RC	.25	.60
293 Chris Smith	.01	.05
294 P.J. Brown RC	.10	.30
295 Kevin Edwards	.01	.05
296 Armon Gilliam	.01	.05
297 Johnny Newman	.01	.05
298 Rex Walters	.01	.05
299 David Wesley RC	.10	.30
300 Jayson Williams	.05	.15
301 Anthony Bonner	.01	.05
302 Derek Harper	.05	.15
303 Herb Williams	.01	.05
304 Litterial Green	.01	.05
305 Anfernee Hardaway RC	1.00	2.50
306 Greg Kite	.01	.05
307 Larry Krystkowiak	.01	.05
308 Keith Tower RC	.01	.05
309 Dana Barros	.01	.05
310 Shawn Bradley	.10	.30
311 Greg Graham RC	.01	.05
312 Sean Green	.01	.05
313 Warren Kidd RC	.01	.05
314 Eric Leckner	.01	.05
315 Moses Malone	.10	.30
316 Orlando Woolridge	.01	.05
317 Duane Cooper	.01	.05
318 Joe Courtney RC	.01	.05
319 A.C. Green	.05	.15
320 Frank Johnson	.01	.05
321 Joe Kleine	.01	.05
322 Chris Dudley	.01	.05
323 Harvey Grant	.01	.05
324 Jaren Jackson	.01	.05
325 Tracy Murray	.01	.05
326 James Robinson RC	.01	.05
327 Reggie Smith	.01	.05
328 Kevin Thompson RC	.01	.05
329 Randy Brown	.01	.05
330 Evers Burns RC	.01	.05
331 Pete Chilcutt	.01	.05
332 Bobby Hurley	.05	.15
333 Mike Peplowski RC	.01	.05
334 LaBradford Smith	.01	.05
335 Trevor Wilson	.01	.05
336 Terry Cummings	.01	.05
337 Vinny Del Negro	.01	.05
338 Sleepy Floyd	.01	.05
339 Negele Knight	.01	.05
340 Dennis Rodman	.25	.60
341 Chris Whitney RC	.01	.05
342 Vincent Askew	.01	.05
343 Kendall Gill	.05	.15
344 Ervin Johnson	.05	.15
345 Chris King RC	.01	.05
346 Detlef Schrempf	.05	.15
347 Walter Bond	.01	.05
348 Tom Chambers	.01	.05
349 John Crotty	.01	.05
350 Bryon Russell RC	.10	.30
351 Felton Spencer	.01	.05
352 Mitchell Butler RC	.01	.05
353 Rex Chapman	.01	.05
354 Calbert Cheaney	.05	.15
355 Kevin Duckworth	.01	.05
356 Don MacLean	.01	.05
357 Gheorghe Muresan RC	.10	.30
358 Doug Overton	.01	.05
359 Brent Price	.01	.05
360 Kenny Walker	.01	.05
361 Derrick Coleman USA	.01	.05
362 Joe Dumars USA	.05	.15
363 Tim Hardaway USA	.05	.15
364 Larry Johnson USA	.05	.15
365 Shawn Kemp USA	.15	.40
366 Dan Majerle USA	.01	.05
367 Alonzo Mourning USA	.10	.30
368 Mark Price USA	.01	.05
369 Steve Smith USA	.05	.15
370 Isiah Thomas USA	.05	.15
371 Dominique Wilkins USA	.05	.15
372 Don Nelson Don Chaney	.05	.15
373 Jamal Mashburn CL	.10	.30
374 Checklist	.01	.05
375 Checklist	.01	.05
M1 Reggie Miller USA	.30	.75
M2 Shaquille O'Neal USA	2.50	6.00
M3 Team Checklist USA	.75	2.00

1993-94 Ultra All-Defensive

Randomly inserted in 1 of 24 first series 19-card jumbo packs, this standard-size ten-card set features members of the first (1-5) and second (6-10) All-NBA defensive teams. The design features a borderless front and color player action cutout set against a background of an enlarged and ghosted version of the same photo. The player's name appears in gold-foil lettering at the bottom. The back features a color player photo at the lower left, along with his career highlights set against the same ghosted photo background. The cards are numbered on the back as "X of 10."

COMPLETE SET (10)	60.00	120.00
1 Joe Dumars	1.25	3.00
2 Michael Jordan	35.00	70.00
3 Hakeem Olajuwon	4.00	10.00
4 Scottie Pippen	10.00	20.00
5 Dennis Rodman	5.00	12.00
6 Horace Grant	1.25	3.00
7 Dan Majerle	1.25	3.00
8 Larry Nance	.75	2.00
9 David Robinson	4.00	10.00
10 John Starks	1.25	3.00

1993-94 Ultra All-NBA

Randomly inserted in 14-card first series packs at a rate of approximately one in 16, this 14-card standard-size set features one card for each All-NBA first (1-5), second (6-10) and third (11-14) team player from the 1992-93 season. Drazen Petrovic was named to the third team. Due to his death following the '92-93 season, a card was not produced. The fronts display full-bleed glossy color action photos with a series of three smaller photos along the left side. The player's name appears in gold-foil lettering at the lower right. The back carries a hardwood floor-design background with three small photos along the left side that progressively zoom in on the player. Career highlights appear alongside. The cards are numbered on the back as "X of 14."

COMPLETE SET (14)	25.00	50.00
1 Charles Barkley	1.50	4.00
2 Michael Jordan	10.00	25.00
3 Karl Malone	1.50	4.00
4 Hakeem Olajuwon	1.50	4.00
5 Mark Price	.15	.40
6 Joe Dumars	1.00	2.50
7 Patrick Ewing	1.00	2.50
8 Larry Johnson	1.00	2.50
9 John Stockton	1.00	2.50
10 Dominique Wilkins	1.00	2.50
11 Derrick Coleman	.50	1.25
12 Tim Hardaway	1.00	2.50
13 Scottie Pippen	3.00	8.00
14 David Robinson	1.50	4.00

1993-94 Ultra All-Rookie Series

Randomly inserted in 14-card second series packs at an approximate rate of one in seven, this 15-card standard-size set features some of the NBA's top draft picks of 1993-94. Each borderless front features a color action photo. The player's name appears in silver foil near the bottom. The horizontal borderless back carries a color player action shot on one side and career highlights on the other. The cards are numbered on the back as "X of 15" and are sequenced in alphabetical order.

COMPLETE SET (15)	12.00	30.00
1 Vin Baker	1.25	3.00
2 Shawn Bradley	.50	1.25
3 Calbert Cheaney	.25	.60
4 Anfernee Hardaway	4.00	10.00
5 Lindsey Hunter	.50	1.25
6 Bobby Hurley	.25	.60
7 Popeye Jones	.07	.20
8 Toni Kukoc	2.00	5.00
9 Jamal Mashburn	1.25	3.00
10 Chris Mills	.50	1.25
11 Dino Radja	.07	.20
12 Isaiah Rider	1.00	2.50
13 Rodney Rogers	.50	1.25
14 Nick Van Exel	1.50	4.00
15 Chris Webber	4.00	10.00

1993-94 Ultra All-Rookie Team

Randomly inserted in series one 14-card packs at an approximate rate of one in 24, this five-card standard-size set features the NBA's 1992-93 All-Rookie Team. Fronts feature borderless fronts with color player action cutouts breaking out of hardwood floor backgrounds. The player's name appears in gold-foil lettering at the bottom. The horizontal borderless back carries a color player cutout and career highlights on a hardwood floor background. The cards are numbered on the back as "X of 5" and are sequenced in alphabetical order.

COMPLETE SET (5)	5.00	10.00
1 LaPhonso Ellis	.08	.25
2 Tom Gugliotta (with Michael Jordan)	.60	1.50
3 Christian Laettner	.30	.75
4 Alonzo Mourning	1.00	2.50
5 Shaquille O'Neal	3.00	8.00

1993-94 Ultra Award Winners

Randomly inserted in first series 19-card jumbo packs at a rate of one in 36, this five-card standard-size set features NBA award winners from the 1992-93 season. Borderless fronts feature color player action cutouts on metallic backgrounds. The player's name appears in silver-foil lettering at the bottom. The back carries a color player close-up and career highlights. The cards are numbered on the back as "X of 5." and are sequenced in alphabetical order.

COMPLETE SET (5)	7.50	15.00
1 Mahmoud Abdul-Rauf	.15	.40
2 Charles Barkley	1.50	4.00
3 Hakeem Olajuwon	1.50	4.00
4 Shaquille O'Neal	5.00	12.00
5 Clifford Robinson	.50	1.25

1993-94 Ultra Famous Nicknames

Randomly inserted into 14-card second series packs at a rate of one in five, this 15-card standard-size set features popular nicknames of today's stars. Borderless fronts feature color action cutouts on hardwood-floor and basket-net backgrounds. The player's nickname appears in silver-foil lettering on the right. The borderless back carries a color player photo on one side. On the other, the shot's game background blends into a hardwood-floor background for the player's name in vertical silver-foil lettering and his career highlights. The cards are numbered on the back as "X of 15" and are sequenced in alphabetical order.

COMPLETE SET (15)	15.00	40.00
1 Charles Barkley	1.25	3.00
2 Muggsy Bogues	.40	1.00
3 Derrick Coleman	.40	1.00
4 Clyde Drexler	.75	2.00
5 Anfernee Hardaway	6.00	15.00
6 Larry Johnson	.75	2.00
7 Michael Jordan	8.00	20.00
8 Toni Kukoc	3.00	8.00
9 Karl Malone	1.25	3.00
10 Harold Miner	.20	.50
11 Alonzo Mourning	1.25	3.00
12 Hakeem Olajuwon	1.25	3.00
13 Shaquille O'Neal	4.00	10.00
14 David Robinson	1.25	3.00
15 Dominique Wilkins	.75	2.00

1993-94 Ultra Inside/Outside

Randomly inserted in 14-card second series packs, this 10-card standard-size set features on each borderless front a color player action cutout over a shot of a comet like basketball going through the basket, all on a black background. The player's name appears in gold foil near the bottom. This design, but with a different action cutout, is mirrored somewhat on the borderless back, which also carries to the left of the player photo his career highlights within a ghosted box framed by a purple line. The cards are numbered on the back as "X of 10" and are sequenced in alphabetical order.

COMPLETE SET (10)	4.00	10.00
1 Patrick Ewing	.25	.60
2 Jim Jackson	.10	.30
3 Larry Johnson	.25	.60
4 Michael Jordan	3.00	8.00
5 Dan Majerle	.10	.30
6 Hakeem Olajuwon	.40	1.00
7 Scottie Pippen	.75	2.00
8 Latrell Sprewell	.60	1.50
9 John Starks	.10	.30
10 Walt Williams	.02	.10

1993-94 Ultra Jam City

Randomly inserted in 19-card second series jumbo packs at a rate of one in 37, this 9-card standard-size set features borderless fronts with color player action cutouts on black and purple metallic cityscape backgrounds. The player's name appears in gold foil in a lower corner. The borderless back carries a color player action cutout on a non-metallic cityscape background otherwise similar to the front. The player's name and career highlights appear in a ghosted box to the left of the photo. The cards are numbered on the back as "X of 10" and are sequenced in alphabetical order.

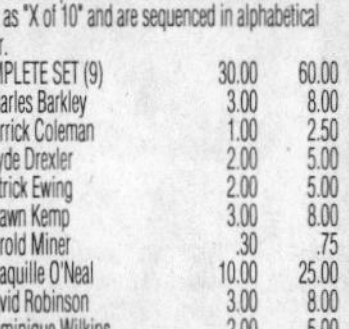

COMPLETE SET (9)	30.00	60.00
1 Charles Barkley	3.00	8.00
2 Derrick Coleman	1.00	2.50
3 Clyde Drexler	2.00	5.00
4 Patrick Ewing	2.00	5.00
5 Shawn Kemp	3.00	8.00
6 Harold Miner	.30	.75
7 Shaquille O'Neal	10.00	25.00
8 David Robinson	3.00	8.00
9 Dominique Wilkins	2.00	5.00

1993-94 Ultra Karl Malone

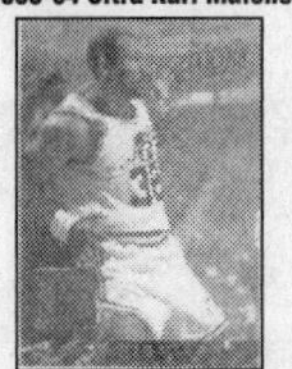

This ten-card standard-size set of Career Highlights spotlights Utah Jazz forward Karl Malone. The cards were randomly inserted in 14-card first series packs at a rate of approximately one in 16. The full-bleed color fronts have purple tinted ghosted backgrounds with Malone portrayed in normal color action and posed photos. Across the bottom edge is a marbleized border with the subset title "Career Highlights", above the lower border is a silver and black box containing Malone's name. The backs carry information about Malone within a purple tinted ghosted box that is superimposed over a color photo. More than 2,000 autographed cards were randomly inserted in packs. These card have embossed Fleer logos for authenticity. An additional two cards (Nos.11 and 12) were available through a mail-in offer. Prior to June 10, 1994, collectors had to send 10 first series Ultra wrappers and $1.50 to receive the cards. The set is considered complete without these cards.

COMPLETE SET (10)	5.00	10.00
COMMON MALONE (1-10)	.50	1.25
CERTIFIED AUTOGRAPH (AU)	40.00	100.00
COMMON SEND-OFF (11-12)	.75	2.00

1993-94 Ultra Power In The Key

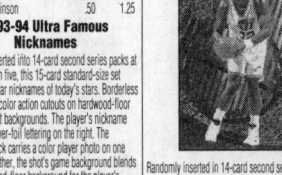

Randomly inserted in 14-card second series packs at a rate of one in 37, this nine-card standard-size features some of the NBA's top power players. Card fronts feature borderless color player action cutouts on multicolored metallic court illustration backgrounds. The player's name appears in gold-foil lettering at the lower right. The borderless horizontal back carries on its right side a color player close-up on a nonmetallic background otherwise similar to the front. The player's name and career highlights appear in a ghosted box to the left of the photo. The cards are numbered on the back as "X of 9" and are sequenced in alphabetical order.

COMPLETE SET (9)	25.00	50.00
1 Larry Johnson	1.00	2.50
2 Michael Jordan	10.00	25.00
3 Karl Malone	1.50	4.00
4 Oliver Miller	.15	.40
5 Alonzo Mourning	1.50	4.00
6 Hakeem Olajuwon	1.50	4.00
7 Shaquille O'Neal	5.00	12.00

8 Otis Thorpe	.50	1.25
9 Chris Webber	10.00	25.00

1993-94 Ultra Rebound Kings

Randomly inserted in 14-card second series packs at a rate of one in four, this 10-card standard-size set features some of the NBA's top rebounders. Borderless fronts feature color player action shots on backgrounds that blend from the actual action background at the bottom to a ghosted and color-screened player close-up at the top. The player's name appears vertically in gold foil on one side. The borderless horizontal back carries a color player cutout on one side and the player's name in gold foil and career highlights on the other, all on a ghosted and color-screened background. The cards are numbered on the back as "X of 10" and are sequenced in alphabetical order.

COMPLETE SET (10)	2.50	6.00
1 Charles Barkley	.40	1.00
2 Derrick Coleman	.10	.30
3 Shawn Kemp	.40	1.00
4 Karl Malone	.40	1.00
5 Alonzo Mourning	.40	1.00
6 Dikembe Mutombo	.25	.60
7 Charles Oakley	.10	.30
8 Hakeem Olajuwon	.40	1.00
9 Shaquille O'Neal	1.25	3.00
10 Dennis Rodman	.50	1.25

1993-94 Ultra Scoring Kings

Randomly inserted in first series hobby packs at a rate of one in 36, this 10-card standard-size set features some of the NBA's top scorers. Card fronts feature color player action cutouts on borderless metallic backgrounds highlighted by lightning filaments. The player's name appears in silver-foil lettering in a lower corner. The horizontal back carries a color player close-up on the right, with the player's name appearing in silver-foil lettering at the upper left, followed below by career highlights, all on a dark borderless background again highlighted by lightning filaments. The cards are numbered on the back as "X of 10" and are sequenced in alphabetical order.

COMPLETE SET (10)	75.00	150.00
1 Charles Barkley	5.00	12.00
2 Joe Dumars	4.00	10.00
3 Patrick Ewing	5.00	12.00
4 Larry Johnson	5.00	12.00
5 Michael Jordan	50.00	120.00
6 Karl Malone	5.00	12.00
7 Alonzo Mourning	5.00	12.00
8 Shaquille O'Neal	10.00	25.00
9 David Robinson	5.00	12.00
10 Dominique Wilkins	5.00	12.00

1994-95 Ultra

The 350 standard-size cards comprising the 1994-95 Ultra set were issued in two separate series of 200 and 150 cards each. Cards were distributed in 14-card ($1.99) and 17-card ($2.69) retail packs. Borderless fronts feature color player action shots. The player's name, team name, and position appear in vertical silver-foil lettering in an upper corner. The borderless back carries multiple player images, with the player's name and team logo appearing in gold foil, followed by biography and statistics near the bottom. The cards are numbered on the back and grouped alphabetically within team order. Unlike previous years, there are no subset cards in this set. Rookie Cards of note include Grant Hill, Juwan Howard, Jason Kidd, Eddie Jones, and Glenn Robinson. There is an insert in every pack. Every 72nd pack is a Hot Pack that contains inserts only.

COMPLETE SET (350)	17.50	35.00
COMPLETE SERIES 1 (200)	10.00	20.00
COMPLETE SERIES 2 (150)	7.50	15.00
1 Stacey Augmon	.15	.40
2 Mookie Blaylock	.12	.30
3 Craig Ehlo	.12	.30
4 Adam Keefe	.12	.30
5 Andrew Lang	.12	.30
6 Ken Norman	.12	.30
7 Kevin Willis	.12	.30
8 Dee Brown	.12	.30
9 Sherman Douglas	.12	.30
10 Acie Earl	.12	.30
11 Pervis Ellison	.12	.30
12 Rick Fox	.12	.30
13 Xavier McDaniel	.12	.30
14 Eric Montross RC	.20	.50
15 Dino Radja	.15	.40
16 Dominique Wilkins	.25	.60
17 Michael Adams	.12	.30
18 Muggsy Bogues	.15	.40
19 Dell Curry	.12	.30
20 Kenny Gattison	.12	.30
21 Hersey Hawkins	.12	.30
22 Larry Johnson	.20	.50
23 Alonzo Mourning	.25	.60
24 Robert Parish	.20	.50
25 B.J. Armstrong	.12	.30
26 Steve Kerr	.15	.40
27 Toni Kukoc	.25	.60
28 Luc Longley	.12	.30
29 Pete Myers	.12	.30
30 Will Perdue	.12	.30
31 Scottie Pippen	.40	1.00
32 Terrell Brandon	.12	.30
33 Brad Daugherty	.15	.40
34 Tyrone Hill	.12	.30
35 Chris Mills	.12	.30
36 Bobby Phills	.12	.30
37 Mark Price	.20	.50
38 Gerald Wilkins	.12	.30
39 John Williams	.12	.30
40 Terry Davis	.12	.30
41 Jim Jackson	.12	.30
42 Popeye Jones	.12	.30
43 Jason Kidd RC	1.00	2.50
44 Jamal Mashburn	.20	.50
45 Sean Rooks	.12	.30
46 Doug Smith	.12	.30
47 Mahmoud Abdul-Rauf	.12	.30
48 LaPhonso Ellis	.12	.30
49 Dikembe Mutombo	.20	.50
50 Robert Pack	.12	.30
51 Rodney Rogers	.12	.30
52 Bryant Stith	.12	.30
53 Brian Williams	.12	.30
54 Reggie Williams	.12	.30
55 Greg Anderson	.12	.30
56 Joe Dumars	.20	.50
57 Allan Houston	.20	.50
58 Lindsey Hunter	.12	.30
59 Terry Mills	.12	.30
60 Tim Hardaway	.20	.50
61 Chris Mullin	.20	.50
62 Billy Owens	.12	.30
63 Latrell Sprewell	.25	.60
64 Chris Webber	.30	.75
65 Sam Cassell	.20	.50
66 Carl Herrera	.12	.30
67 Robert Horry	.20	.50
68 Vernon Maxwell	.12	.30
69 Hakeem Olajuwon	.25	.60
70 Kenny Smith	.15	.40
71 Otis Thorpe	.12	.30
72 Antonio Davis	.12	.30
73 Dale Davis	.12	.30
74 Mark Jackson	.20	.50
75 Derrick McKey	.12	.30
76 Reggie Miller	.25	.60
77 Byron Scott	.15	.40
78 Rik Smits	.15	.40
79 Haywoode Workman	.12	.30
80 Gary Grant	.12	.30
81 Ron Harper	.15	.40
82 Elmore Spencer	.12	.30
83 Loy Vaught	.12	.30
84 Elden Campbell	.12	.30
85 Doug Christie	.12	.30
86 Vlade Divac	.20	.50
87 Eddie Jones RC	.60	1.50
88 George Lynch	.12	.30
89 Anthony Peeler	.12	.30
90 Sedale Threatt	.12	.30
91 Nick Van Exel	.20	.50
92 James Worthy	.25	.60
93 Bimbo Coles	.12	.30
94 Matt Geiger	.12	.30
95 Grant Long	.12	.30
96 Harold Miner	.12	.30
97 Glen Rice	.20	.50
98 John Salley	.12	.30
99 Rony Seikaly	.15	.40
100 Brian Shaw	.12	.30
101 Steve Smith	.15	.40
102 Vin Baker	.20	.50
103 Jon Barry	.12	.30
104 Todd Day	.12	.30
105 Lee Mayberry	.12	.30
106 Eric Murdock	.12	.30
107 Thurl Bailey	.12	.30
108 Stacey King	.12	.30
109 Christian Laettner	.15	.40
110 Isaiah Rider	.20	.50
111 Chris Smith	.12	.30
112 Doug West	.12	.30
113 Micheal Williams	.12	.30
114 Kenny Anderson	.15	.40
115 Benoit Benjamin	.12	.30
116 P.J. Brown	.12	.30
117 Derrick Coleman	.15	.40
118 Yinka Dare RC	.20	.50
119 Kevin Edwards	.12	.30
120 Armon Gilliam	.12	.30
121 Chris Morris	.12	.30
122 Greg Anthony	.12	.30
123 Anthony Bonner	.12	.30
124 Hubert Davis	.12	.30
125 Patrick Ewing	.25	.60
126 Derek Harper	.15	.40
127 Anthony Mason	.12	.30
128 Charles Oakley	.15	.40
129 Doc Rivers	.15	.40
130 John Starks	.15	.40
131 Nick Anderson	.12	.30
132 Anthony Avent	.12	.30
133 Anthony Bowie	.12	.30
134 Anfernee Hardaway	.30	.75
135 Shaquille O'Neal	.50	1.25
136 Dennis Scott	.12	.30
137 Jeff Turner	.12	.30
138 Dana Barros	.12	.30
139 Shawn Bradley	.12	.30
140 Greg Graham	.12	.30
141 Jeff Malone	.12	.30
142 Tim Perry	.12	.30
143 Clarence Weatherspoon	.12	.30
144 Scott Williams	.12	.30
145 Danny Ainge	.20	.50
146 Charles Barkley	.30	.75
147 Cedric Ceballos	.12	.30
148 A.C. Green	.20	.50
149 Frank Johnson	.12	.30
150 Kevin Johnson	.20	.50
151 Dan Majerle	.20	.50
152 Oliver Miller	.12	.30
153 Wesley Person RC	.20	.50
154 Mark Bryant	.12	.30
155 Clyde Drexler	.25	.60
156 Harvey Grant	.12	.30
157 Jerome Kersey	.12	.30
158 Tracy Murray	.12	.30
159 Terry Porter	.12	.30
160 Clifford Robinson	.12	.30
161 James Robinson	.12	.30
162 Rod Strickland	.12	.30
163 Buck Williams	.12	.30
164 Duane Causwell	.12	.30
165 Olden Polynice	.12	.30
166 Mitch Richmond	.20	.50
167 Lionel Simmons	.12	.30
168 Walt Williams	.12	.30
169 Willie Anderson	.12	.30
170 Terry Cummings	.20	.50
171 Sean Elliott	.20	.50
172 Avery Johnson	.15	.40
173 J.R. Reid	.12	.30
174 David Robinson	.30	.75
175 Dennis Rodman	.40	1.00
176 Kendall Gill	.12	.30
177 Shawn Kemp	.20	.50
178 Nate McMillan	.12	.30
179 Gary Payton	.20	.50
180 Sam Perkins	.12	.30
181 Detlef Schrempf	.20	.50
182 David Benoit	.12	.30
183 Tyrone Corbin	.12	.30
184 Jeff Hornacek	.15	.40
185 Jay Humphries	.12	.30
186 Karl Malone	.25	.60
187 Bryon Russell	.12	.30
188 Felton Spencer	.12	.30
189 John Stockton	.25	.60
190 Mitchell Butler	.12	.30
191 Rex Chapman	.12	.30
192 Calbert Cheaney	.12	.30
193 Kevin Duckworth	.12	.30
194 Tom Gugliotta	.12	.30
195 Don MacLean	.12	.30
196 Gheorghe Muresan	.12	.30
197 Scott Skiles	.12	.30
198 Checklist	.12	.30
199 Checklist	.12	.30
200 Checklist	.12	.30
201 Tyrone Corbin	.12	.30
202 Doug Edwards	.12	.30
203 Jim Les	.12	.30
204 Grant Long	.12	.30
205 Ken Norman	.12	.30
206 Steve Smith	.15	.40
207 Blue Edwards	.12	.30
208 Greg Minor RC	.20	.50
209 Eric Montross	.12	.30
210 Derek Strong	.12	.30
211 David Wesley	.12	.30
212 Tony Bennett	.12	.30
213 Scott Burrell	.12	.30
214 Darrin Hancock	.20	.50
215 Greg Sutton	.12	.30
216 Corie Blount	.12	.30
217 Jud Buechler	.12	.30
218 Ron Harper	.15	.40
219 Larry Krystkowiak	.12	.30
220 Dickey Simpkins RC	.20	.50
221 Bill Wennington	.12	.30
222 Michael Cage	.12	.30
223 Tony Campbell	.12	.30
224 Steve Colter	.12	.30
225 Greg Dreiling	.12	.30
226 Danny Ferry	.12	.30
227 Tony Dumas RC	.20	.50
228 Lucious Harris	.12	.30
229 Donald Hodge	.12	.30
230 Jason Kidd	.60	1.50
231 Lorenzo Williams	.12	.30
232 Dale Ellis	.12	.30
233 Tom Hammonds	.12	.30
234 Jalen Rose RC	.50	1.25
235 Reggie Slater	.12	.30
236 Rafael Addison	.12	.30
237 Bill Curley RC	.20	.50
238 Johnny Dawkins	.12	.30
239 Grant Hill RC	1.00	2.50
240 Eric Leckner	.12	.30
241 Mark Macon	.12	.30
242 Oliver Miller	.12	.30
243 Mark West	.12	.30
244 Victor Alexander	.12	.30
245 Chris Gatling	.12	.30
246 Tom Gugliotta	.12	.30
247 Keith Jennings	.12	.30
248 Ricky Pierce	.12	.30
249 Carlos Rogers RC	.20	.50
250 Clifford Rozier RC	.20	.50
251 Rony Seikaly	.15	.40
252 David Wood	.12	.30
253 Tim Breaux	.12	.30
254 Scott Brooks	.12	.30
255 Zan Tabak	.12	.30
256 Duane Ferrell	.12	.30
257 Mark Jackson	.20	.50
258 Sam Mitchell	.12	.30
259 John Williams	.12	.30
260 Terry Dehere	.12	.30
261 Harold Ellis	.12	.30
262 Matt Fish	.12	.30
263 Tony Massenburg	.12	.30
264 Lamond Murray RC	.20	.50
265 Bo Outlaw RC	.20	.50
266 Eric Piatkowski RC	.25	.60
267 Pooh Richardson	.12	.30
268 Malik Sealy	.12	.30
269 Randy Woods	.12	.30
270 Sam Bowie	.12	.30
271 Cedric Ceballos	.12	.30
272 Antonio Harvey	.12	.30
273 Eddie Jones	.40	1.00
274 Anthony Miller RC	.20	.50
275 Tony Smith	.12	.30
276 Ledell Eackles	.12	.30
277 Kevin Gamble	.12	.30
278 Brad Lohaus	.12	.30
279 Billy Owens	.12	.30
280 Khalid Reeves RC	.20	.50
281 Kevin Willis	.12	.30
282 Marty Conlon	.12	.30
283 Alton Lister	.12	.30
284 Eric Mobley RC	.20	.50
285 Johnny Newman	.12	.30
286 Ed Pinckney	.12	.30
287 Glenn Robinson RC	.40	1.00
288 Howard Eisley	.20	.50
289 Winston Garland	.12	.30
290 Andres Guibert	.12	.30
291 Donyell Marshall RC	.20	.50
292 Sean Rooks	.12	.30
293 Yinka Dare	.12	.30
294 Sleepy Floyd	.12	.30
295 Sean Higgins	.12	.30
296 Rex Walters	.12	.30
297 Jayson Williams	.12	.30
298 Charles Smith	.12	.30
299 Charlie Ward RC	.20	.50
300 Herb Williams	.12	.30
301 Monty Williams RC	.20	.50
302 Horace Grant	.15	.40
303 Geert Hammink	.12	.30
304 Tree Rollins	.12	.30
305 Donald Royal	.12	.30
306 Brian Shaw	.12	.30
307 Brooks Thompson RC	.20	.50
308 Derrick Alston RC	.20	.50
309 Willie Burton	.12	.30
310 Jaren Jackson	.12	.30
311 B.J. Tyler RC	.20	.50
312 Scott Williams	.12	.30
313 Sharone Wright RC	.20	.50
314 Joe Kleine	.12	.30
315 Danny Manning	.15	.40
316 Elliot Perry	.12	.30
317 Wesley Person	.12	.30
318 Trevor Ruffin RC	.20	.50
319 Danny Schayes	.12	.30
320 Wayman Tisdale	.12	.30
321 Chris Dudley	.12	.30
322 James Edwards	.12	.30
323 Alaa Abdelnaby	.12	.30
324 Randy Brown	.12	.30
325 Brian Grant RC	.30	.75
326 Bobby Hurley	.20	.50
327 Michael Smith RC	.20	.50
328 Henry Turner	.12	.30
329 Trevor Wilson	.12	.30
330 Vinny Del Negro	.12	.30
331 Moses Malone	.20	.50
332 Julius Nwosu	.12	.30
333 Chuck Person	.15	.40
334 Chris Whitney	.12	.30
335 Vincent Askew	.12	.30
336 Bill Cartwright	.15	.40
337 Ervin Johnson	.12	.30
338 Sarunas Marciulionis	.12	.30
339 Antoine Carr	.12	.30
340 Tom Chambers	.20	.50
341 John Crotty	.12	.30
342 Jamie Watson RC	.20	.50
343 Juwan Howard RC	.30	.75
344 Jim McIlvaine RC	.20	.50
345 Doug Overton	.12	.30
346 Scott Skiles	.12	.30
347 Anthony Tucker RC	.20	.50
348 Chris Webber	.30	.75
349 Checklist	.12	.30
350 Checklist	.12	.30

1994-95 Ultra All-NBA

Randomly inserted into approximately one in every three first series packs, cards from this 15-card standard-size set feature members of the All-NBA first (1-5), second (6-10), and third (11-15) teams. The fronts are laid out horizontally and have a color action photo and three photos that look like they were taken in a room with a black light. On the right side is the player's first name in white behind his last name in the color of his team. At the bottom in gold-foil are the words "ALL-NBA" and the corresponding team he made. On the backs are a color photo in front of the same photo with the black light look. Their is also player information and the cards are numbered "X of 15."

COMPLETE SET (15)	4.00	10.00
1 Karl Malone	.50	1.25
2 Hakeem Olajuwon	.50	1.25
3 Scottie Pippen	.75	2.00
4 Latrell Sprewell	.50	1.25
5 John Stockton	.50	1.25
6 Charles Barkley	.60	1.50
7 Kevin Johnson	.40	1.00
8 Shawn Kemp	.40	1.00
9 Mitch Richmond	.40	1.00
10 David Robinson	.60	1.50
11 Derrick Coleman	.30	.75
12 Shaquille O'Neal	1.00	2.50
13 Gary Payton	.40	1.00
14 Mark Price	.40	1.00
15 Dominique Wilkins	.50	1.25

1994-95 Ultra All-Rookie Team

Randomly inserted exclusively into first series jumbo packs at a rate of one in 36, cards from this 10-card standard-size set feature some of the top rookies from the 1993-94 season. Fronts feature a full-color action shot aside a bold, gold-foil All-Rookie logo with the player's name.

COMPLETE SET (10)	20.00	50.00
1 Vin Baker	2.50	6.00
2 Anfernee Hardaway	8.00	20.00
3 Jamal Mashburn	2.50	6.00
4 Isaiah Rider	2.50	6.00
5 Chris Webber	8.00	20.00
6 Shawn Bradley	1.50	4.00
7 Lindsey Hunter	1.50	4.00
8 Toni Kukoc	3.00	8.00
9 Dino Radja	2.00	5.00
10 Nick Van Exel	2.50	6.00

1994-95 Ultra All-Rookies

Randomly inserted at a rate of one in every five second series packs, this 15-card standard-size set captures the best first-year players from the 1994-95 season. The fronts have a full-color photo with a hardwood floor background. The words "All-Rookie" and the player's name are on the left side in gold-foil. The backs a full-color photo with his name and a hardwood floor in the background. There is also player information and the cards are numbered "X of 15." The set is sequenced in alphabetical order.

COMPLETE SET (15)	5.00	12.00
1 Brian Grant	.50	1.25
2 Grant Hill	1.50	4.00
3 Juwan Howard	.50	1.25
4 Eddie Jones	1.00	2.50
5 Jason Kidd	1.50	4.00
6 Donyell Marshall	.30	.75
7 Eric Montross	.30	.75
8 Lamond Murray	.30	.75
9 Wesley Person	.30	.75
10 Khalid Reeves	.30	.75
11 Glenn Robinson	.60	1.50
12 Carlos Rogers	.30	.75
13 Jalen Rose	.75	2.00
14 B.J. Tyler	.30	.75
15 Sharone Wright	.30	.75

1994-95 Ultra Award Winners

Randomly inserted into approximately one in every four first series packs, cards from this four-card standard-size set feature players who won individual awards during the 1993-94 season. The fronts are laid out horizontally and have a color-action photo with the backgrounds having a black and white head shot with horizontal white lines across the card. At on of the bottom corners are the words "NBA Award Winner" with a basketball in gold-foil. The backs have a color photo from the chest up with a similar background to the front. There is also player information and the cards are numbered "X of 4." The set is sequenced in alphabetical order.

COMPLETE SET (4)	.60	1.50
1 Dell Curry	.12	.30
2 Don MacLean	.12	.30
3 Hakeem Olajuwon	.25	.60
4 Chris Webber	.30	.75

1994-95 Ultra Defensive Gems

Randomly inserted at a rate of one in every 37 second-series packs, this 6-card standard-size set focuses on six NBA stars who play standout defense. The borderless fronts feature 100% etched-foil backgrounds. The player's name is located at the bottom while the words "Defensive Gems" surrounding a diamond are in the lower right. The backs are split between another player photo and some information about the player's defensive prowess. The cards are numbered in the lower left as "X" of 6. The set is sequenced in alphabetical order.

COMPLETE SET (6)	6.00	15.00
1 Mookie Blaylock	1.00	2.50
2 Hakeem Olajuwon	2.00	5.00
3 Gary Payton	1.50	4.00
4 Scottie Pippen	3.00	8.00
5 David Robinson	2.50	6.00
6 Latrell Sprewell	2.00	5.00

1994-95 Ultra Double Trouble

Randomly inserted into approximately one in every five first series packs, cards from this 10-card standard-size set feature a selection of multi-skilled NBA stars. The fronts feature two photos of the player in a split player design. The words "Double Trouble" and player's name are printed in silver foil on the bottom. The borderless backs are split between an explanation of the the player's skills as well as a photo. The cards are numbered "X" of 10 in the lower left corner. The set is sequenced in alphabetical order.

COMPLETE SET (10)	2.00	5.00
1 Derrick Coleman	.25	.60
2 Patrick Ewing	.40	1.00
3 Anfernee Hardaway	.50	1.25
4 Jamal Mashburn	.30	.75
5 Reggie Miller	.40	1.00
6 Alonzo Mourning	.40	1.00
7 Scottie Pippen	.60	1.50
8 David Robinson	.50	1.25
9 Latrell Sprewell	.40	1.00
10 John Stockton	.40	1.00

1994-95 Ultra Inside/Outside

Randomly inserted exclusively into one in every seven second series hobby packs, cards from this 10-card standard-size set focus on players who can score from anywhere on the court. The borderless fronts feature dual player photos against a gray background. The player's name is in the lower left corner while the words "Inside/Outside" are in the lower right corner. The backs describe the player's shooting ability and have a small photo as well. The cards are numbered in the lower right as "X" of 10. The set is sequenced in alphabetical order.

COMPLETE SET (10)	2.00	5.00
1 Sam Cassell	.40	1.00
2 Cedric Ceballos	.25	.60
3 Calbert Cheaney	.25	.60
4 Anfernee Hardaway	.60	1.50
5 Jim Jackson	.25	.60
6 Dan Majerle	.40	1.00
7 Robert Pack	.25	.60
8 Scottie Pippen	.75	2.00
9 Mitch Richmond	.40	1.00
10 Latrell Sprewell	.50	1.25

1994-95 Ultra Jam City

Randomly inserted exclusively into one in every seven second series jumbo packs, cards from this 10-card standard size set spotlight ten well known dunkers. The borderless fronts feature color player action cutouts on a multi colored metallic cityscape background. The words "Jam City" and the player's name are printed in gold foil on the bottom of the card. The back features another cutout photo against a different skyscraper background with the player's name in the middle in gold foil. A brief blurb about the player is inset at the bottom. The cards are numbered "X" of 10 in the bottom right. The set is sequenced in alphabetical order.

COMPLETE SET (10)	8.00	20.00
1 Vin Baker	.75	2.00
2 Grant Hill	4.00	10.00
3 Robert Horry	.75	2.00
4 Shawn Kemp	.75	2.00
5 Jamal Mashburn	.75	2.00
6 Alonzo Mourning	1.00	2.50
7 Dikembe Mutombo	.75	2.00
8 Shaquille O'Neal	2.00	5.00
9 Glenn Robinson	1.50	4.00
10 Dominique Wilkins	1.00	2.50

1994-95 Ultra Power

Randomly inserted in all first series packs at an approximate rate of one in three, cards from this 10-card standard-size set feature a selection of the NBA's most powerful stars. This set features color player action cutouts set on a colorful and sparkly starburst background design. The player's name appears in vertical gold lettering in a lower corner. The colorful starburst design continues on the borderless horizontal back, which carries a color player head shot on one side, and career highlights on the other. The cards are numbered on the back as "X of 10." The set is sequenced in alphabetical order.

COMPLETE SET (10)	2.00	5.00
1 Charles Barkley	.50	1.25
2 Derrick Coleman	.25	.60
3 Larry Johnson	.30	.75
4 Shawn Kemp	.30	.75
5 Karl Malone	.40	1.00
6 Dikembe Mutombo	.30	.75
7 Charles Oakley	.25	.60
8 Shaquille O'Neal	.75	2.00
9 Dennis Rodman	.60	1.50
10 Chris Webber	.50	1.25

1994-95 Ultra Power In The Key

Randomly inserted exclusively into one in every seven second series retail packs, cards from this 10-card standard-size set feature ten players who are effective playing near the basket. The front feature a player cutout against a multicolored basketball court design. The words "Power in the Key" are on either side, with the player's name directly underneath those words. The backs contain biographical information along with an inset photo of the player. The cards are numbered in the lower right as "X" of 10. The set is sequenced in alphabetical order.

COMPLETE SET (10)	5.00	12.00
1 Charles Barkley	.60	1.50
2 Patrick Ewing	.50	1.25
3 Horace Grant	.30	.75
4 Larry Johnson	.40	1.00
5 Karl Malone	.50	1.25
6 Hakeem Olajuwon	.50	1.25
7 Shaquille O'Neal	1.00	2.50
8 David Robinson	.60	1.50
9 Chris Webber	.60	1.50
10 Kevin Willis	.25	.60

1994-95 Ultra Rebound Kings

Randomly inserted at a rate of one in every two second-series packs, cards from this 10-card standard-size set focus on league's top rebounders. The fronts have a color-action photo and a color picture of his head at the bottom along with a gold-foil crown. The words "Rebound King" are at the top and side with rebound behind king at the top and vice-versa on the side, each card uses different colors for the words. The backs have a color photo with his name in gold-foil and information on why he is a top rebounder. The cards are numbered "X of 10." The set is sequenced in alphabetical order.

COMPLETE SET (10)	1.25	3.00
1 Derrick Coleman	.15	.40
2 A.C. Green	.20	.50
3 Alonzo Mourning	.25	.60
4 Dikembe Mutombo	.20	.50
5 Charles Oakley	.15	.40
6 Hakeem Olajuwon	.25	.60
7 Shaquille O'Neal	.50	1.25
8 David Robinson	.30	.75
9 Chris Webber	.30	.75
10 Kevin Willis	.12	.30

1994-95 Ultra Scoring Kings

Randomly inserted exclusively into one in every 37 first series hobby packs, cards from this 10-card standard-size set feature a selection of perennial NBA scoring leaders. Fronts feature full-color player action shots cut out against 100% etched-foil backgrounds. The set is sequenced in alphabetical order.

COMPLETE SET (10)	15.00	40.00
1 Charles Barkley	3.00	8.00
2 Patrick Ewing	2.50	6.00
3 Karl Malone	2.50	6.00
4 Hakeem Olajuwon	2.50	6.00
5 Shaquille O'Neal	5.00	12.00
6 Scottie Pippen	4.00	10.00
7 Mitch Richmond	2.00	5.00
8 David Robinson	3.00	8.00
9 Latrell Sprewell	2.50	6.00
10 Dominique Wilkins	2.50	6.00

1995-96 Ultra Promo Sheet

Measuring 10" by 10", this promo sheet was issued to preview the second series of the 1995-96 Ultra set. The sheet consists of six cards, with an advertisement at the top of the sheet. The cards, unfortunately, are identical their regular issue counterparts with card numbers being left the same. Some people went on to cut out cards like the Antonio McDyess and Damon Stoudamire All-Rookie cards, which caused a fluctuation in price of their regular issue insert cards.

COMPLETE SET (6)	2.00	5.00
4 Antonio McDyess	2.50	6.00
8 Damon Stoudamire	2.50	6.00
202 Mookie Blaylock	.15	.40
219 Hakeem Olajuwon	.30	.75
344 Nick Van Exel	.25	.60
S3 Jerry Stackhouse	1.25	3.00

1995-96 Ultra

The 1995-96 Ultra set was issued in two series of 200 and 150 for a total of 350 standard-size cards. They were issued in 12-card hobby and retail packs (SRP $2.49) in addition to 17-card pre-priced packs (SRP $2.99). Each 12-card pack contains two insert cards and one in every 72 packs contains nothing but insert cards (referred to as a "Hot Pack"). Fleer upgraded the stock of the 1995-96 cards by making them 40% thicker than the previous year's Ultra release. The fronts have a full-color action photo with the player's name and team at the bottom in gold-foil. The backs have two-color photos and one full black-and-white with statistics at the bottom. The basic issue cards are grouped alphabetically within teams and checklisted below alphabetically according to city. Subsets featured are Rookies (263-298) and Encore (299-348). Rookie Cards of note in this set include Michael Finley, Kevin Garnett, Antonio McDyess, Joe Smith, Jerry

tackhouse and Damon Stoudamire.
OMPLETE SET (350) 20.00 40.00
OMPLETE SERIES 1 (200) 10.00 20.00
OMPLETE SERIES 2 (150) 10.00 20.00
Stacey Augmon .20 .50
Mookie Blaylock .15 .40
Craig Ehlo .15 .40
Andrew Lang .15 .40
Grant Long .15 .40
Ken Norman .15 .40
Steve Smith .20 .50
Spud Webb .25 .60
Dee Brown .15 .40
0 Sherman Douglas .15 .40
1 Pervis Ellison .15 .40
2 Rick Fox .15 .40
3 Eric Montross .15 .40
4 Dino Radja .20 .50
5 David Wesley .15 .40
6 Dominique Wilkins .30 .75
7 Muggsy Bogues .20 .50
8 Scott Burrell .15 .40
9 Dell Curry .15 .40
0 Kendall Gill .15 .40
1 Larry Johnson .25 .60
2 Alonzo Mourning .30 .75
3 Robert Parish .25 .60
4 Ron Harper .20 .50
5 Michael Jordan 2.00 5.00
6 Toni Kukoc .25 .60
7 Will Perdue .15 .40
8 Scottie Pippen .40 1.00
9 Terrell Brandon .15 .40
0 Michael Cage .15 .40
1 Tyrone Hill .15 .40
2 Chris Mills .15 .40
3 Bobby Phills .15 .40
4 Mark Price .25 .60
5 John Williams .15 .40
6 Lucious Harris .15 .40
7 Jim Jackson .15 .40
8 Popeye Jones .15 .40
9 Jason Kidd .40 1.00
0 Jamal Mashburn .25 .60
1 George McCloud .15 .40
2 Roy Tarpley .15 .40
3 Lorenzo Williams .15 .40
4 Mahmoud Abdul-Rauf .15 .40
5 Dikembe Mutombo .25 .60
6 Robert Pack .15 .40
7 Jalen Rose .30 .75
8 Bryant Stith .15 .40
9 Brian Williams .15 .40
0 Reggie Williams .15 .40
1 Joe Dumars .25 .60
2 Grant Hill .40 1.00
3 Allan Houston .20 .50
4 Lindsey Hunter .15 .40
5 Terry Mills .15 .40
6 Mark West .15 .40
7 Chris Gatling .15 .40
8 Tim Hardaway .25 .60
9 Donyell Marshall .15 .40
0 Chris Mullin .25 .60
1 Carlos Rogers .15 .40
2 Clifford Rozier .15 .40
3 Rony Seikaly .20 .50
4 Latrell Sprewell .25 .60
5 Sam Cassell .25 .60
6 Clyde Drexler .30 .75
7 Mario Elie .15 .40
8 Carl Herrera .15 .40
9 Robert Horry .20 .50
0 Hakeem Olajuwon .30 .75
1 Kenny Smith .20 .50
2 Antonio Davis .15 .40
3 Dale Davis .15 .40
4 Mark Jackson .25 .60
5 Derrick McKey .15 .40
6 Reggie Miller .30 .75
7 Rik Smits .20 .50
8 Terry Dehere .15 .40
9 Lamond Murray .15 .40
0 Bo Outlaw .15 .40
Pooh Richardson .15 .40
2 Rodney Rogers .15 .40
3 Malik Sealy .15 .40
4 Loy Vaught .15 .40
5 Sam Bowie .15 .40
6 Elden Campbell .15 .40
7 Cedric Ceballos .15 .40
8 Vlade Divac .25 .60
9 Eddie Jones .30 .75
0 Anthony Peeler .15 .40
Sedale Threatt .15 .40
Nick Van Exel .25 .60
Rex Chapman .15 .40
Bimbo Coles .15 .40
Matt Geiger .15 .40
Billy Owens .15 .40
Khalid Reeves .15 .40
Glen Rice .25 .60
Kevin Willis .15 .40
00 Vin Baker .20 .50
01 Marty Conlon .15 .40
02 Todd Day .15 .40
03 Eric Murdock .15 .40
04 Glenn Robinson .25 .60
05 Winston Garland .15 .40
06 Tom Gugliotta .15 .40
07 Christian Laettner .20 .50
8 Isaiah Rider .25 .60
09 Sean Rooks .15 .40
10 Doug West .15 .40
11 Kenny Anderson .20 .50
12 P.J. Brown .15 .40
13 Derrick Coleman .20 .50
14 Armon Gilliam .15 .40
15 Chris Morris .15 .40
16 Anthony Bonner .15 .40
17 Patrick Ewing .30 .75
18 Derek Harper .20 .50
19 Anthony Mason .15 .40
20 Charles Oakley .20 .50
21 Charles Smith .15 .40
22 John Starks .20 .50
23 Nick Anderson .15 .40
24 Horace Grant .20 .50
25 Anfernee Hardaway .40 1.00
26 Shaquille O'Neal .60 1.50
27 Donald Royal .15 .40
28 Dennis Scott .15 .40
29 Brian Shaw .15 .40
30 Derrick Alston .15 .40
31 Dana Barros .15 .40
132 Shawn Bradley .15 .40
133 Willie Burton .15 .40
134 Jeff Malone .15 .40
135 Clarence Weatherspoon .15 .40
136 Scott Williams .15 .40
137 Sharone Wright .15 .40
138 Danny Ainge .25 .60
139 Charles Barkley .40 1.00
140 A.C. Green .25 .60
141 Kevin Johnson .25 .60
142 Dan Majerle .25 .60
143 Danny Manning .20 .50
144 Elliot Perry .15 .40
145 Wesley Person .15 .40
146 Wayman Tisdale .15 .40
147 Chris Dudley .15 .40
148 Harvey Grant .15 .40
149 Aaron McKie .15 .40
150 Terry Porter .15 .40
151 Clifford Robinson .15 .40
152 Rod Strickland .15 .40
153 Otis Thorpe .15 .40
154 Buck Williams .15 .40
155 Brian Grant .20 .50
156 Bobby Hurley .25 .60
157 Olden Polynice .15 .40
158 Mitch Richmond .25 .60
159 Michael Smith .15 .40
160 Walt Williams .15 .40
161 Vinny Del Negro .15 .40
162 Sean Elliott .25 .60
163 Avery Johnson .20 .50
164 Chuck Person .20 .50
165 J.R. Reid .15 .40
166 Doc Rivers .20 .50
167 David Robinson .40 1.00
168 Dennis Rodman .50 1.25
169 Vincent Askew .15 .40
170 Hersey Hawkins .15 .40
171 Shawn Kemp .25 .60
172 Sarunas Marciulionis .15 .40
173 Nate McMillan .15 .40
174 Gary Payton .25 .60
175 Sam Perkins .15 .40
176 Detlef Schrempf .25 .60
177 B.J. Armstrong .15 .40
178 Jerome Kersey .15 .40
179 Tony Massenburg .15 .40
180 Oliver Miller .15 .40
181 John Salley .15 .40
182 David Benoit .15 .40
183 Antoine Carr .15 .40
184 Jeff Hornacek .20 .50
185 Karl Malone .30 .75
186 Felton Spencer .15 .40
187 John Stockton .30 .75
188 Greg Anthony .15 .40
189 Benoit Benjamin .15 .40
190 Byron Scott .20 .50
191 Calbert Cheaney .15 .40
192 Juwan Howard .25 .60
193 Don MacLean .15 .40
194 Gheorghe Muresan .15 .40
195 Doug Overton .15 .40
196 Scott Skiles .15 .40
197 Chris Webber .30 .75
198 Checklist (1-94) .15 .40
199 Checklist (95-190) .15 .40
200 Checklist (191-200) .15 .40
201 Stacey Augmon .20 .50
202 Mookie Blaylock .15 .40
203 Grant Long .15 .40
204 Steve Smith .20 .50
205 Dana Barros .15 .40
206 Kendall Gill .15 .40
207 Khalid Reeves .15 .40
208 Glen Rice .25 .60
209 Luc Longley .15 .40
210 Dennis Rodman .50 1.25
211 Dan Majerle .25 .60
212 Tony Dumas .15 .40
213 Elmore Spencer .15 .40
214 Otis Thorpe .15 .40
215 B.J. Armstrong .15 .40
216 Sam Cassell .25 .60
217 Clyde Drexler .30 .75
218 Robert Horry .20 .50
219 Hakeem Olajuwon .30 .75
220 Eddie Johnson .15 .40
221 Ricky Pierce .15 .40
222 Eric Piatkowski .20 .50
223 Rodney Rogers .15 .40
224 Brian Williams .15 .40
225 George Lynch .15 .40
226 Alonzo Mourning .30 .75
227 Benoit Benjamin .15 .40
228 Terry Porter .15 .40
229 Shawn Bradley .15 .40
230 Kevin Edwards .15 .40
231 Jayson Williams .15 .40
232 Charlie Ward .15 .40
233 Jon Koncak .15 .40
234 Derrick Coleman .20 .50
235 Richard Dumas .15 .40
236 Vernon Maxwell .15 .40
237 John Williams .15 .40
238 Dontonio Wingfield .15 .40
239 Tyrone Corbin .15 .40
240 Will Perdue .15 .40
241 Shawn Kemp .25 .60
242 Gary Payton .25 .60
243 Sam Perkins .15 .40
244 Detlef Schrempf .25 .60
245 Chris Morris .15 .40
246 Robert Pack .15 .40
247 Willie Anderson EXP .15 .40
248 Oliver Miller EXP .15 .40
249 Tracy Murray EXP .15 .40
250 Alvin Robertson EXP .15 .40
251 Carlos Rogers EXP .15 .40
252 John Salley EXP .15 .40
253 Damon Stoudamire EXP .40 1.00
254 Zan Tabak EXP .15 .40
255 Greg Anthony EXP .15 .40
256 Blue Edwards EXP .15 .40
257 Kenny Gattison EXP .15 .40
258 Chris King EXP .15 .40
259 Lawrence Moten EXP .15 .40
260 Eric Murdock EXP .15 .40
261 Bryant Reeves EXP .15 .40
262 Byron Scott EXP .20 .50
263 Cory Alexander RC .25 .60
264 Brent Barry RC .40 1.00
265 Mario Bennett RC .25 .60
266 Travis Best RC .25 .60
267 Junior Burrough RC .25 .60
268 Jason Caffey RC .25 .60
269 Randolph Childress RC .25 .60
270 Sasha Danilovic RC .25 .60
271 Tyus Edney RC .25 .60
272 Michael Finley RC .75 2.00
273 Sherrell Ford RC .25 .60
274 Kevin Garnett RC 2.00 5.00
275 Alan Henderson RC .25 .60
276 Donny Marshall RC .25 .60
277 Antonio McDyess RC .60 1.50
278 Loren Meyer RC .25 .60
279 Lawrence Moten RC .25 .60
280 Ed O'Bannon RC .25 .60
281 Greg Ostertag RC .25 .60
282 Cherokee Parks RC .25 .60
283 Theo Ratliff RC .40 1.00
284 Bryant Reeves RC .25 .60
285 Shawn Respert RC .25 .60
286 Lou Roe RC .25 .60
287 Arvydas Sabonis RC .50 1.25
288 Joe Smith RC .50 1.25
289 Jerry Stackhouse RC .75 2.00
290 Damon Stoudamire RC .60 1.50
291 Bob Sura RC .25 .60
292 Kurt Thomas RC .25 .60
293 Gary Trent RC .25 .60
294 David Vaughn RC .25 .60
295 Rasheed Wallace RC .75 2.00
296 Eric Williams RC .25 .60
297 Corliss Williamson RC .25 .60
298 George Zidek RC .25 .60
299 Mahmoud Abdul-Rauf ENC .15 .40
300 Kenny Anderson ENC .20 .50
301 Vin Baker ENC .20 .50
302 Charles Barkley ENC .40 1.00
303 Mookie Blaylock ENC .15 .40
304 Cedric Ceballos ENC .15 .40
305 Vlade Divac ENC .25 .60
306 Clyde Drexler ENC .30 .75
307 Joe Dumars ENC .25 .60
308 Sean Elliott ENC .25 .60
309 Patrick Ewing ENC .30 .75
310 Anfernee Hardaway ENC .40 1.00
311 Tim Hardaway ENC .25 .60
312 Grant Hill ENC .40 1.00
313 Tyrone Hill ENC .15 .40
314 Robert Horry ENC .20 .50
315 Juwan Howard ENC .25 .60
316 Jim Jackson ENC .15 .40
317 Kevin Johnson ENC .25 .60
318 Larry Johnson ENC .25 .60
319 Eddie Jones ENC .30 .75
320 Shawn Kemp ENC .25 .60
321 Jason Kidd ENC .40 1.00
322 Christian Laettner ENC .20 .50
323 Karl Malone ENC .30 .75
324 Jamal Mashburn ENC .25 .60
325 Reggie Miller ENC .30 .75
326 Alonzo Mourning ENC .30 .75
327 Dikembe Mutombo ENC .25 .60
328 Hakeem Olajuwon ENC .30 .75
329 Gary Payton ENC .25 .60
330 Scottie Pippen ENC .40 1.00
331 Dino Radja ENC .20 .50
332 Glen Rice ENC .25 .60
333 Mitch Richmond ENC .25 .60
334 Clifford Robinson ENC .15 .40
335 David Robinson ENC .40 1.00
336 Glenn Robinson ENC .25 .60
337 Dennis Rodman ENC .50 1.25
338 Carlos Rogers ENC .15 .40
339 Detlef Schrempf ENC .25 .60
340 Byron Scott ENC .20 .50
341 Rik Smits ENC .20 .50
342 Latrell Sprewell ENC .25 .60
343 John Stockton ENC .30 .75
344 Nick Van Exel ENC .25 .60
345 Loy Vaught ENC .15 .40
346 Clarence Weatherspoon ENC .15 .40
347 Chris Webber ENC .30 .75
348 Kevin Willis ENC .15 .40
349 Checklist (201-298) .15 .40
350 Checklist (299-350/inserts) .15 .40

1995-96 Ultra Gold Medallion

One card from this 200-card parallel set was inserted in every first series pack. Due to lack of collector reponse the set was discontinued for the second series, and is thus considered complete at 200 cards. The attractive fronts feature borderless, full gold foil backgrounds with a full-color player cutout. Backs are identical to the regular cards. Please refer to the multipliers provided in the header to ascertain values for singles.

COMPLETE SET (200) 60.00 120.00
*STARS: 2.5X TO 6X BASE CARD HI

1995-96 Ultra All-NBA

Randomly inserted in all series one packs at a rate of one in five, this 15-card set features the league's best and is divided into three standard-size sets of five (first, second and third team NBA All-Stars). Borderless fronts picture the player in a full-color action cutout with a black and gold metallic streak background. The "All NBA" box is printed in reverse-type metallic foil on the bottom left with the player's name printed in gold foil across the bottom right. Full-bleed backs continue with the black and gold metallic streaks and another full-color action player cutout. A screened box highlights the player's accomplishments and includes his name in gold foil.

COMPLETE SET (15) 6.00 15.00
*GOLD MEDALLION: 1.25X TO 3X HI COLUMN
GOLD: SER.1 STATED ODDS 1:50 HOB/RET
1 Anfernee Hardaway 1.00 2.50
2 Karl Malone .75 2.00
3 Scottie Pippen 1.00 2.50
4 David Robinson 1.00 2.50
5 John Stockton .75 2.00
6 Charles Barkley 1.00 2.50
7 Shawn Kemp .60 1.50
8 Shaquille O'Neal 1.50 4.00
9 Gary Payton .60 1.50
10 Mitch Richmond .60 1.50
11 Clyde Drexler .75 2.00
12 Reggie Miller .75 2.00
13 Hakeem Olajuwon .75 2.00
14 Dennis Rodman 1.25 3.00
15 Detlef Schrempf .60 1.50

1995-96 Ultra All-Rookie Team

Randomly inserted in first series retail cello packs at a rate of one in seven, this 10-card set is divided into first team rookies (1-5) and second team rookies (6-10). Borderless fronts feature a full-color action player cutout set against a dark background with multicolored basketballs. All-Rookie team and the player's name are printed in gold foil across the bottom. Borderless backs continue with the multicolored basketball backgrounds and a full-color cutout of the player. A tan-screened box profiles the player and his name is printed in gold foil script across the top of the screen.

COMPLETE SET (10) 12.00 30.00
*GOLD MEDALLION: 1.5X TO 4X HI COLUMN
GOLD: SER.1 STATED ODDS 1:70 RETAIL
1 Brian Grant 1.50 4.00
2 Grant Hill 3.00 8.00
3 Eddie Jones 2.50 6.00
4 Jason Kidd 3.00 8.00
5 Glenn Robinson 2.00 5.00
6 Juwan Howard 2.00 5.00
7 Donyell Marshall 1.25 3.00
Sharone Wright
8 Eric Montross 1.25 3.00
9 Wesley Person 1.25 3.00
10 Jalen Rose 2.50 6.00

1995-96 Ultra All-Rookies

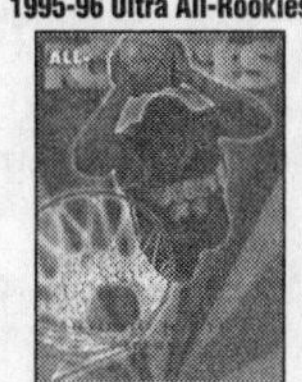

Randomly inserted in all second series packs at a rate of one in 30, this set of 10 standard-size cards focuses on the play of the hot rookies of the '95 draft. Borderless fronts have a team color spectrum background with a full-color action cutout. The player's name and position are printed in gold foil near the bottom and "All Rookies" appears at the top. Backs have another full-color action cutout set against a color spectrum background. A screened box holds the player's name and a player profile. Card #'s 4 and 8 (McDyess and Stoudamire) were featured on an unperforated promo sheet of Ultra cards saluting card stores across America. The sheets were distributed to shop owners nationwide. Unfortunately, some unscrupulous parties cut up a number of the sheets and distributed the cut cards into the hobby market under false pretenses. The cut up cards are identical to the real inserts, thus supply has been altered and we've applied a "DP" designation to signify a double-print on this card.

COMPLETE SET (10) 15.00 40.00
1 Tyus Edney 1.00 2.50
2 Michael Finley 3.00 8.00
3 Kevin Garnett 8.00 20.00
4 Antonio McDyess DP 2.50 6.00
5 Ed O'Bannon 1.00 2.50
6 Joe Smith 2.00 5.00
7 Jerry Stackhouse 3.00 8.00
8 Damon Stoudamire DP 2.50 6.00
9 Rasheed Wallace 3.00 8.00
10 Eric Williams 1.00 2.50

1995-96 Ultra Double Trouble

Randomly inserted in all first series packs at a rate of one in five, this 10-card standard-size set celebrates the players who perform well in more than one category. Full-bleed fronts feature a full-color action player cutout and a one-color action shot that serves as a background. "Double Trouble" is repeatedly printed in the background with a shadow effect. The player's name and "Double Trouble" are printed in alternating black and gold foil at the bottom. Another full-color action cutout appears on the back against the repeating "Double Trouble" colored background. A light screened box appears on the back with the player's abilities and accomplishments printed in black type. The player's name is printed in gold foil above the screened box. The set is sequenced in alphabetical order.

COMPLETE SET (10) 5.00 12.00
*GOLD MEDALLION: 1.25X TO 3X HI COLUMN
GOLD: SER.1 STATED ODDS 1:50 HOB/RET
1 Charles Barkley .60 1.50
2 Anfernee Hardaway .60 1.50
3 Michael Jordan 3.00 8.00
4 Alonzo Mourning .50 1.25
5 Hakeem Olajuwon .50 1.25
6 Shaquille O'Neal 1.00 2.50
7 Gary Payton .40 1.00
8 Scottie Pippen .60 1.50
9 David Robinson .60 1.50
10 John Stockton .50 1.25

1995-96 Ultra Fabulous Fifties

Randomly inserted in first series hobby packs at a rate of one in 12, this seven-card standard-size set spotlights players who scored 50 or more points in a 94/95 NBA single game. The horizontal fronts feature a full-color action player cutout set against a two-color background with basketball nets and "Fabulous 50's" printed in alternating red boxes. Player's name and "Fabulous 50's" are printed in silver foil across the bottom left. A one-color picture of a basketball net serves as a backdrop on the back with the player's name and team printed in silver foil on the top. A full-color action cutout appears with a story of how and when the player reached his 50-point scoring mark. The set is sequenced in alphabetical order.

COMPLETE SET (7) 6.00 15.00
*GOLD MEDALLION: 1.25X TO 3X HI COLUMN
GOLD: SER.1 STATED ODDS 1:120 HOBBY
1 Dana Barros .50 1.25
2 Willie Burton .50 1.25
3 Cedric Ceballos .50 1.25
4 Jim Jackson .50 1.25
5 Michael Jordan 6.00 15.00
6 Jamal Mashburn .75 2.00
7 Glen Rice .75 2.00

1995-96 Ultra Jam City

Randomly inserted exclusively in second series retail packs at a rate of one in 12, cards from this 12-card standard-size set focus on the NBA's most powerful dunkers. Borderless fronts have full-color action cutouts set against a one-color etched foil background. "Jam City" is printed in gold foil vertically along one side and the player's name is printed in silver foil vertically. Borderless backs feature a full-color player cutout with a halo effect set against a skyline background and a player profile. The set is sequenced in alphabetical order.

COMPLETE SET (12) 20.00 50.00
HP CARDS: .10X TO .30X HI COLUMN
HP: SER.2 STATED ODDS 1:72 RETAIL
1 Grant Hill 2.50 6.00
2 Robert Horry 1.25 3.00
3 Michael Jordan 12.00 30.00
4 Shawn Kemp 1.50 4.00
5 Jamal Mashburn 1.50 4.00
6 Antonio McDyess 2.00 5.00
7 Alonzo Mourning 2.00 5.00
8 Hakeem Olajuwon 2.00 5.00
9 Shaquille O'Neal 4.00 10.00
10 David Robinson 2.50 6.00
11 Joe Smith 1.50 4.00
12 Jerry Stackhouse 2.50 6.00

1995-96 Ultra Power

Randomly inserted in all first series packs at a rate of one in four, this 10-card standard-size set features the big rebounders and strong inside men of the NBA. A multicolored kaleidoscopic front serves as a background for a full-color action shot. The "Ultra Power" logo and player's name are stamped at the bottom left in gold foil. Backs continue with the kaleidoscopic background and another full-color action cutout. A screened box holds the player's name in gold foil along with a synopsis of the player's abilities and accomplishments. Gold Medallion editions were seeded in packs at 10 percent the rate of regular cards. Backs are identical to regular inserts.

COMPLETE SET (10) 2.00 5.00
*GOLD MEDALLION: 1.25X TO 3X HI COLUMN
GOLD: SER.1 STATED ODDS 1:40 HOB/RET
1 Charles Barkley .60 1.50
2 Patrick Ewing .50 1.25
3 Larry Johnson .40 1.00
4 Shawn Kemp .40 1.00
5 Karl Malone .50 1.25
6 Alonzo Mourning .50 1.25
7 Dikembe Mutombo .40 1.00
8 Hakeem Olajuwon .50 1.25
9 Shaquille O'Neal 1.00 2.50
10 David Robinson .60 1.50

1995-96 Ultra Rising Stars

Randomly inserted in all first series packs at a rate of one in 37, this nine-card standard-size set features promising youngsters of the NBA. Etched foil fronts feature multicolored basketballs and a full-color action cutout. The "Rising Star" logo and player's name are printed in silver foil on the fronts. Backs include a screened player information box and a full-color action cutout set against a multicolored basketball background. The set is sequenced in alphabetical order.

COMPLETE SET (9) 20.00 50.00
*GOLD MEDALLION: 1.5X TO 4X HI COLUMN
GOLD: SER.1 STATED ODDS 1:370 HOB/RET
1 Vin Baker 2.00 5.00
2 Anfernee Hardaway 4.00 10.00
3 Grant Hill 4.00 10.00
4 Jason Kidd 4.00 10.00
5 Jamal Mashburn 2.50 6.00
6 Shaquille O'Neal 6.00 15.00
7 Glenn Robinson 2.50 6.00
8 Nick Van Exel 2.50 6.00
9 Chris Webber 3.00 8.00

1995-96 Ultra Scoring Kings

Randomly inserted at a rate of one in 24 hobby packs only, this 12-card standard-size set spotlights the number crunchers of the NBA. Borderless fronts have full color player action shots and are stamped with gold foil. Backs have another full-color action shot and include a player profile. The set is sequenced in alphabetical order.

COMPLETE SET (12) 30.00 80.00
1 Patrick Ewing 3.00 8.00
2 Grant Hill 4.00 10.00
3 Jim Jackson 1.50 4.00
4 Michael Jordan 20.00 50.00
5 Karl Malone 3.00 8.00
6 Reggie Miller 3.00 8.00
7 Hakeem Olajuwon 3.00 8.00
8 Shaquille O'Neal 6.00 15.00
9 Scottie Pippen 4.00 10.00
10 David Robinson 4.00 10.00
11 Glenn Robinson 2.50 6.00
12 Jerry Stackhouse 4.00 10.00

1995-96 Ultra Scoring Kings Hot Pack

This full parallel Hot Pack set could be found in one of every 72 packs (known appropriately as "Hot Packs"). These Hot Pack parallels are four times easier to obtain than corresponding regular issue Jam City inserts. To ascertain values on individual cards, please refer to the multiplier in the header below, coupled with the value of the base insert.

COMPLETE SET (12) 12.00 30.00
*HOT PACK CARDS: .15X TO .4X HI COLUMN
4 Michael Jordan 10.00 25.00

1995-96 Ultra Stackhouse's Scrapbook

Randomly inserted into one in every 24 second series packs, these two cards continue the eight-card, cross-brand set devoted to Fleer spokesperson Jerry Stackhouse. Card #S3 was featured on an unperforated promo sheet of Ultra cards saluting card stores across America. The sheets were distributed to shop owners nationwide. Unfortunately, some unscrupulous parties cut up a number of the sheets and distributed the cut cards into the hobby market which are identical to the real inserts, thus supply has been altered and we've applied a "DP" designation to signify a double-print on this card.

COMPLETE SET (2) 1.50 4.00
COMMON CARD (S3-S4) 1.00 2.50

1995-96 Ultra USA Basketball

Randomly inserted into all second series packs at a rate of one in 54, cards from this 10-card standard-size set capture the first 10 members named to the USA Olympic team in their new red, white and blue jerseys. Borderless fronts feature the player in full-color action set against an American flag backdrop. The player's name, position and the USA basketball logo are stamped in gold foil at the bottom. Backs have a full-color action shot on one side and a player profile set against a red and white stripe background with blue stars on the other side. The set is sequenced in alphabetical order.

COMPLETE SET (10) 25.00 60.00
1 Anfernee Hardaway 4.00 10.00
2 Grant Hill 4.00 10.00
3 Karl Malone 3.00 8.00
4 Reggie Miller 3.00 8.00
5 Hakeem Olajuwon 3.00 8.00
6 Shaquille O'Neal 6.00 15.00
7 Scottie Pippen 4.00 10.00
8 David Robinson 4.00 10.00
9 Glenn Robinson 2.50 6.00
10 John Stockton 3.00 8.00

1996-97 Ultra

The 300-card Ultra set from Fleer/SkyBox was issued in two series in 12-card packs with a suggested retail price of $2.49. Each basic player card front features full-bleed photography with the player's name written in script at the bottom of the card in silver holofoil, with the team name printed on the "tail" of the script. Card backs contain two photos of the player with biographical information and career statistics. Subsets include On the Block, Ultra Effort, Maximum Effort, Rookie Encore, Step It Up and Play of the Game. Rookie cards include Shareef Abdur-Rahim, Ray Allen, Kobe Bryant, Marcus Camby, Allen Iverson, Stephon Marbury and Antoine Walker, among others. A Jerry Stackhouse promo was released before the cards went live. It looks exactly like the regular issue card except it does not bear a card number. It is listed below at the end of the set.

COMPLETE SET (300) 25.00 50.00
COMPLETE SERIES 1 (150) 17.50 35.00
COMPLETE SERIES 2 (150) 7.50 15.00
1 Mookie Blaylock .15 .40
2 Alan Henderson .15 .40
3 Christian Laettner .20 .50
4 Dikembe Mutombo .25 .60
5 Steve Smith .20 .50
6 Dana Barros .15 .40
7 Rick Fox .15 .40
8 Dino Radja .20 .50
9 Antoine Walker RC .50 1.25
10 Eric Williams .15 .40
11 Dell Curry .15 .40
12 Tony Delk RC .25 .60
13 Matt Geiger .15 .40
14 Glen Rice .25 .60
15 Ron Harper .20 .50
16 Michael Jordan 2.00 5.00
17 Toni Kukoc .25 .60
18 Scottie Pippen .40 1.00
19 Dennis Rodman .50 1.25
20 Terrell Brandon .15 .40
21 Chris Mills .15 .40
22 Bobby Phills .15 .40
23 Bob Sura .15 .40
24 Jim Jackson .15 .40
25 Jason Kidd .40 1.00
26 Jamal Mashburn .20 .50
27 George McCloud .15 .40
28 Samaki Walker RC .25 .60
29 LaPhonso Ellis .15 .40
30 Antonio McDyess .25 .60
31 Bryant Stith .15 .40
32 Joe Dumars .25 .60
33 Grant Hill .40 1.00
34 Theo Ratliff .15 .40
35 Otis Thorpe .15 .40
36 Chris Mullin .25 .60
37 Joe Smith .20 .50
38 Latrell Sprewell .25 .60
39 Charles Barkley .40 1.00
40 Clyde Drexler .30 .75
41 Mario Elie .15 .40
42 Hakeem Olajuwon .30 .75
43 Erick Dampier RC .25 .60
44 Dale Davis .15 .40
45 Derrick McKey .15 .40
46 Reggie Miller .30 .75
47 Rik Smits .20 .50
48 Brent Barry .20 .50
49 Malik Sealy .15 .40
50 Loy Vaught .15 .40
51 Lorenzen Wright RC .25 .60
52 Kobe Bryant RC 6.00 15.00
53 Cedric Ceballos .15 .40
54 Eddie Jones .25 .60
55 Shaquille O'Neal .60 1.50
56 Nick Van Exel .25 .60
57 Tim Hardaway .25 .60
58 Alonzo Mourning .30 .75
59 Kurt Thomas .15 .40
60 Ray Allen RC 1.00 2.50
61 Vin Baker .20 .50
62 Sherman Douglas .15 .40
63 Glenn Robinson .25 .60
64 Kevin Garnett .60 1.50
65 Tom Gugliotta .15 .40
66 Stephon Marbury RC .60 1.50
67 Doug West .15 .40
68 Shawn Bradley .15 .40
69 Kendall Gill .15 .40
70 Kerry Kittles RC .25 .60
71 Ed O'Bannon .15 .40
72 Patrick Ewing .30 .75
73 Larry Johnson .25 .60
74 Charles Oakley .20 .50
75 John Starks .20 .50
76 John Wallace RC .25 .60
77 Nick Anderson .15 .40
78 Horace Grant .20 .50
79 Anfernee Hardaway .40 1.00
80 Dennis Scott .15 .40
81 Derrick Coleman .20 .50
82 Allen Iverson RC 2.00 5.00
83 Jerry Stackhouse .30 .75
84 Clarence Weatherspoon .15 .40
85 Michael Finley .30 .75
86 Kevin Johnson .25 .60
87 Steve Nash RC 2.00 5.00
88 Wesley Person .15 .40
89 Jermaine O'Neal RC .60 1.50
90 Clifford Robinson .15 .40
91 Arvydas Sabonis .20 .50
92 Gary Trent .15 .40
93 Tyus Edney .15 .40
94 Brian Grant .20 .50
95 Olden Polynice .15 .40
96 Mitch Richmond .25 .60
97 Corliss Williamson .15 .40
98 Vinny Del Negro .15 .40
99 Sean Elliott .25 .60

100 Avery Johnson .20 .50
101 David Robinson .40 1.00
102 Hersey Hawkins .15 .40
103 Shawn Kemp .25 .60
104 Gary Payton .25 .60
105 Sam Perkins .15 .40
106 Detlef Schrempf .25 .60
107 Marcus Camby RC .40 1.00
108 Doug Christie .15 .40
109 Damon Stoudamire .25 .60
110 Sharone Wright .15 .40
111 Jeff Hornacek .20 .50
112 Karl Malone .30 .75
113 Chris Morris .15 .40
114 Bryon Russell .15 .40
115 John Stockton .30 .75
116 Shareef Abdur-Rahim RC .50 1.25
117 Greg Anthony .15 .40
118 Blue Edwards .15 .40
119 Bryant Reeves .15 .40
120 Calbert Cheaney .15 .40
121 Juwan Howard .20 .50
122 Gheorghe Muresan .15 .40
123 Chris Webber .30 .75
124 Vin Baker OTB .20 .50
125 Charles Barkley OTB .40 1.00
126 Kevin Garnett OTB .60 1.50
127 Juwan Howard OTB .20 .50
128 Larry Johnson OTB .25 .60
129 Shawn Kemp OTB .25 .60
130 Karl Malone OTB .30 .75
131 Anthony Mason OTB .15 .40
132 Antonio McDyess OTB .25 .60
133 Alonzo Mourning OTB .30 .75
134 Hakeem Olajuwon OTB .30 .75
135 Shaquille O'Neal OTB .60 1.50
136 David Robinson OTB .40 1.00
137 Dennis Rodman OTB .50 1.25
138 Joe Smith OTB .20 .50
139 Mookie Blaylock UE .15 .40
140 Terrell Brandon UE .15 .40
141 Anfernee Hardaway UE .40 1.00
142 Grant Hill UE .40 1.00
143 Michael Jordan UE 2.00 5.00
144 Jason Kidd UE .40 1.00
145 Gary Payton UE .25 .60
146 Jerry Stackhouse UE .30 .75
147 Damon Stoudamire UE .25 .60
148 Hakeem Olajuwon .40 1.00
David Robinson
Robert Horry
Oliver Miller
Clarence Weatherspoon
149 Checklist .15 .40
150 Checklist .15 .40
151 Tyrone Corbin .08 .25
152 Priest Lauderdale RC .25 .60
153 Dikembe Mutombo .25 .60
154 Eldridge Recasner RC .25 .60
155 Todd Day .15 .40
156 Greg Minor .15 .40
157 David Wesley .15 .40
158 Vlade Divac .25 .60
159 Anthony Mason .15 .40
160 Malik Rose RC .30 .75
161 Jason Caffey .15 .40
162 Steve Kerr .20 .50
163 Luc Longley .15 .40
164 Danny Ferry .15 .40
165 Tyrone Hill .15 .40
166 Vitaly Potapenko RC .25 .60
167 Sam Cassell .20 .50
168 Michael Finley .30 .75
169 Chris Gatling .15 .40
170 A.C. Green .25 .60
171 Oliver Miller .15 .40
172 Eric Montross .15 .40
173 Dale Ellis .15 .40
174 Mark Jackson .25 .60
175 Ervin Johnson .15 .40
176 Sarunas Marciulionis .15 .40
177 Stacey Augmon .20 .50
178 Joe Dumars .25 .60
179 Grant Hill .40 1.00
180 Lindsey Hunter .15 .40
181 Grant Long .15 .40
182 Terry Mills .15 .40
183 Otis Thorpe .15 .40
184 Jerome Williams RC .25 .60
185 Todd Fuller RC .25 .60
186 Ray Owes RC .25 .60
187 Mark Price .25 .60
188 Felton Spencer .15 .40
189 Charles Barkley .40 1.00
190 Emanual Davis RC .25 .60
191 Othella Harrington RC .25 .60
192 Matt Maloney RC .25 .60
193 Brent Price .15 .40
194 Kevin Willis .15 .40
195 Travis Best .15 .40
196 Antonio Davis .15 .40
197 Jalen Rose .20 .50
198 Pooh Richardson .15 .40
199 Stanley Roberts .15 .40
200 Rodney Rogers .15 .40
201 Elden Campbell .15 .40
202 Derek Fisher RC .50 1.25
203 Travis Knight RC .25 .60
204 Shaquille O'Neal .60 1.50
205 Byron Scott .20 .50
206 Sasha Danilovic .15 .40
207 Dan Majerle .25 .60
208 Martin Muursepp RC .25 .60
209 Armon Gilliam .15 .40
210 Andrew Lang .15 .40
211 Johnny Newman .15 .40
212 Kevin Garnett .60 1.50
213 Tom Gugliotta .15 .40
214 Shane Heal RC .25 .60
215 Stojko Vrankovic .15 .40
216 Robert Pack .15 .40
217 Khalid Reeves .15 .40
218 Jayson Williams .15 .40
219 Chris Childs .15 .40
220 Allan Houston .20 .50
221 Larry Johnson .25 .60
222 Walter McCarty RC .25 .60
223 Charlie Ward .15 .40
224 Brian Evans RC .25 .60
225 Amal McCaskill RC .25 .60
226 Rony Seikaly .20 .50
227 Gerald Wilkins .15 .40
228 Mark Davis .15 .40
229 Lucious Harris .15 .40
230 Don MacLean .15 .40
231 Cedric Ceballos .15 .40
232 Rex Chapman .15 .40
233 Jason Kidd .40 1.00
234 Danny Manning .20 .50
235 Kenny Anderson .20 .50
236 Aaron McKie .15 .40
237 Isaiah Rider .20 .50
238 Rasheed Wallace .30 .75
239 Mahmoud Abdul-Rauf .15 .40
240 Billy Owens .15 .40
241 Michael Smith .15 .40
242 Vernon Maxwell .15 .40
243 Charles Smith .15 .40
244 Dominique Wilkins .30 .75
245 Craig Ehlo .15 .40
246 Jim McIlvaine .15 .40
247 Nate McMillan .15 .40
248 Hubert Davis .15 .40
249 Carlos Rogers .15 .40
250 Zan Tabak .15 .40
251 Walt Williams .15 .40
252 Jeff Hornacek .20 .50
253 Karl Malone .30 .75
254 Greg Ostertag .15 .40
255 Bryon Russell .15 .40
256 John Stockton .30 .75
257 George Lynch .15 .40
258 Lawrence Moten .15 .40
259 Anthony Peeler .15 .40
260 Roy Rogers RC .25 .60
261 Tracy Murray .15 .40
262 Rod Strickland .15 .40
263 Ben Wallace RC 1.50 4.00
264 Shareef Abdur-Rahim RE .25 .60
265 Ray Allen RE .50 1.25
266 Kobe Bryant RE 3.00 8.00
267 Marcus Camby RE .20 .50
268 Erick Dampier RE .12 .30
269 Tony Delk RE .12 .30
270 Allen Iverson RE 1.00 2.50
271 Kerry Kittles RE .12 .30
272 Stephon Marbury RE .30 .75
273 Steve Nash RE 1.00 2.50
274 Jermaine O'Neal RE .30 .75
275 Antoine Walker RE .25 .60
276 Samaki Walker RE .12 .30
277 John Wallace RE .12 .30
278 Lorenzen Wright RE .12 .30
279 Anfernee Hardaway SU .40 1.00
280 Michael Jordan SU 2.00 5.00
281 Jason Kidd SU .40 1.00
282 Hakeem Olajuwon SU .30 .75
283 Gary Payton SU .25 .60
284 Mitch Richmond SU .25 .60
285 David Robinson SU .40 1.00
286 John Stockton SU .30 .75
287 Damon Stoudamire SU .25 .60
288 Chris Webber SU .30 .75
289 Clyde Drexler PG .30 .75
290 Kevin Garnett PG .60 1.50
291 Grant Hill PG .40 1.00
292 Shawn Kemp PG .25 .60
293 Karl Malone PG .30 .75
294 Antonio McDyess PG .25 .60
295 Alonzo Mourning PG .30 .75
296 Shaquille O'Neal PG .60 1.50
297 Scottie Pippen PG .40 1.00
298 Jerry Stackhouse PG .30 .75
299 Checklist (151-263) .15 .40
300 Checklist (264-300/inserts) .15 .40
NNO Jerry Stackhouse Promo 1.25 3.00

1996-97 Ultra Gold Medallion

This 296-card semi-parallel was randomly inserted into boxes at a rate of one in twelve packs for series one and one per pack for series two. The foil on the card fronts differ from the regular silver holofoil. Instead, the player and team names are printed in gold holofoil. Card backs are also numbered with a "G" prefix for the regular set. The subsets: On the Block, Ultra Effort and Maximum effort do not contain the "G" prefix. The series two subsets do contain the "G" prefix. Please refer to the multipliers below (coupled with the individual values) to ascertain values for individual singles.

*SER.1 STARS: 2X TO 5X BASE CARD HI
*SER.1 RCs: 1.5X TO 4X BASE HI
*SER.2 STARS: .6X TO 1.5X BASE HI
*SER.2 RCs: .5X TO 1.25X BASE HI
*SER.2 SUBSET: .4X TO 1X BASE HI
G52 Kobe Bryant 20.00 50.00
G266 Kobe Bryant RE 10.00 25.00

1996-97 Ultra Platinum Medallion

This 296-card parallel was randomly inserted into boxes at a rate of one in 180 packs for series one and one in 100 packs for series two. The foil on the card fronts differ from the regular silver holofoil. Instead, the player and team names are printed in platinum holofoil. Card backs are also numbered with a "P" prefix for the basic set. The subsets: On The Block, Ultra Effort and Maximum Effort do not have the "P" prefix. The series two subsets do contain the "P" prefix. Reportedly, less than 250 sets exist. To ascertain values on individual cards, please refer to the multiplier in the header below, coupled with the value of the base card.

*STARS: 15X TO 40X BASE CARD HI
*RCs: 10X TO 25X BASE HI
P16 Michael Jordan 300.00 600.00
P18 Scottie Pippen 20.00 50.00
P52 Kobe Bryant 400.00 800.00
P266 Kobe Bryant RE 125.00 250.00

1996-97 Ultra All-Rookies

Randomly inserted in series two packs at a rate of one in 4, this 15-card set focuses on some of the top players from the 1996-97 rookie class. The cards feature gold foil-stamping, glossy UV coating and embossing of the spotlight in the background.

COMPLETE SET (15) 12.00 30.00
1 Shareef Abdur-Rahim 1.25 3.00
2 Ray Allen 2.50 6.00
3 Kobe Bryant 8.00 20.00
4 Marcus Camby 1.00 2.50
5 Tony Delk .60 1.50
6 Derek Fisher 1.25 3.00
7 Allen Iverson 3.00 8.00
8 Kerry Kittles .60 1.50
9 Matt Maloney .60 1.50
10 Stephon Marbury 1.50 4.00
11 Vitaly Potapenko .60 1.50
12 Roy Rogers .60 1.50
13 Antoine Walker 1.25 3.00
14 Samaki Walker .60 1.50
15 John Wallace .60 1.50

1996-97 Ultra Board Game

Randomly inserted in series two packs at a rate of one in 9, this 20-card set features some of the top rebounders in the NBA featured against a "checkerboard" pattern on the front of the cards.

COMPLETE SET (20) 15.00 40.00
1 Vin Baker .75 2.00
2 Charles Barkley 1.50 4.00
3 Dale Davis .60 1.50
4 Clyde Drexler 1.25 3.00
5 Patrick Ewing 1.25 3.00
6 Grant Hill 1.50 4.00
7 Michael Jordan 8.00 20.00
8 Shawn Kemp 1.00 2.50
9 Jason Kidd 1.50 4.00
10 Karl Malone 1.25 3.00
11 Alonzo Mourning 1.25 3.00
12 Dikembe Mutombo 1.00 2.50
13 Hakeem Olajuwon 1.25 3.00
14 Shaquille O'Neal 2.50 6.00
15 Scottie Pippen 1.50 4.00
16 David Robinson 1.50 4.00
17 Dennis Rodman 2.00 5.00
18 Loy Vaught .60 1.50
19 Chris Webber 1.25 3.00
20 Jayson Williams .60 1.50

1996-97 Ultra Court Masters

This 15-card set was randomly inserted into series one retail packs only at a rate of one in 180. The cards are made with a plastic stock and features members of the 1st, 2nd and 3rd 1995-96 All-NBA teams.

COMPLETE SET (15) 300.00 600.00
1 Anfernee Hardaway 20.00 50.00
2 Michael Jordan 125.00 250.00
3 Karl Malone 15.00 40.00
4 Scottie Pippen 20.00 50.00
5 David Robinson 20.00 50.00
6 Grant Hill 20.00 50.00
7 Shawn Kemp 20.00 50.00
8 Hakeem Olajuwon 15.00 40.00
9 Gary Payton 12.00 30.00
10 John Stockton 20.00 50.00
11 Charles Barkley 20.00 50.00
12 Juwan Howard 10.00 25.00
13 Reggie Miller 15.00 40.00
14 Shaquille O'Neal 30.00 80.00
15 Mitch Richmond 12.00 30.00

1996-97 Ultra Decade of Excellence

Randomly inserted in both series packs at a rate of one in 100, this 20-card set salutes twenty of the players who were included in the 1986-87 Fleer set. Each card features the 1986-87 design, with gold-foil trim and the words "Ultra Decade 1986-1996" in gold foil. Card backs are numbered with a "U" prefix.

COMPLETE SET (20) 25.00 60.00
COMPLETE SERIES 1 (10) 15.00 40.00
COMPLETE SERIES 2 (10) 12.50 25.00
U1 Clyde Drexler 2.50 6.00
U2 Joe Dumars 2.00 5.00
U3 Derek Harper 1.50 4.00
U4 Michael Jordan 12.50 30.00
U5 Karl Malone 2.50 6.00
U6 Chris Mullin 2.00 5.00
U7 Charles Oakley 1.50 4.00
U8 Sam Perkins 1.25 3.00
U9 Ricky Pierce 1.25 3.00
U10 Buck Williams 1.25 3.00
U11 Charles Barkley 5.00 12.00
U12 Patrick Ewing 2.50 6.00
U13 Eddie Johnson 1.25 3.00
U14 Hakeem Olajuwon 2.50 6.00
U15 Robert Parish 2.00 5.00
U16 Byron Scott 1.50 4.00
U17 Wayman Tisdale 1.25 3.00
U18 Gerald Wilkins 1.25 3.00
U19 Herb Williams 1.25 3.00
U20 Kevin Willis 1.25 3.00

1996-97 Ultra Fresh Faces

Randomly inserted in series one packs at a rate of one in 72, this 9-card set focuses on top players from the 1996 NBA Draft. Each card is die cut featuring an action photo of the player printed against a backdrop of a die cut team jersey. The design was submitted by Shinto Imai, who submitted the winning entry in the 1995-96 Fleer "Design Your Own NBA Card" contest.

COMPLETE SET (9) 40.00 80.00
1 Shareef Abdur-Rahim 3.00 8.00
2 Ray Allen 6.00 15.00
3 Kobe Bryant 20.00 50.00
4 Marcus Camby 2.50 6.00
5 Allen Iverson 10.00 25.00
6 Kerry Kittles 1.50 4.00
7 Stephon Marbury 4.00 10.00
8 Steve Nash 8.00 20.00
9 Antoine Walker 3.00 8.00

1996-97 Ultra Full Court Trap

Randomly inserted in series one packs at a rate of one in 15, this 10-card set showcases the players selected to the NBA 1st and 2nd All-Defensive Teams. Card fronts have a foil-etched colored background.

COMPLETE SET (10) 10.00 25.00
*GOLD: 2.5X TO 6X HI COLUMN
GOLD: SER.1 STATED ODDS 1:180 HOB/RET
1 Michael Jordan 8.00 20.00
2 Gary Payton 1.00 2.50
3 Scottie Pippen 1.50 4.00
4 David Robinson 1.50 4.00
5 Dennis Rodman 2.00 5.00
6 Mookie Blaylock .60 1.50
7 Horace Grant .75 2.00
8 Derrick McKey .60 1.50
9 Hakeem Olajuwon 1.25 3.00
10 Bobby Phills .60 1.50

1996-97 Ultra Give and Take

Randomly inserted in series two retail packs only at a rate of one in 18, this 10-card set focuses on players who can not only dish out the assist, but make the key steals. The cards have a full foil background that is divided into a gold and silver tone split equally from top to bottom.

COMPLETE SET (10) 20.00 50.00
1 Mookie Blaylock 1.00 2.50
2 Anfernee Hardaway 2.50 6.00
3 Tim Hardaway 1.50 4.00
4 Allen Iverson 5.00 12.00
5 Michael Jordan 12.00 30.00
6 Jason Kidd 2.50 6.00
7 Gary Payton 1.50 4.00
8 Scottie Pippen 2.50 6.00
9 John Stockton 2.00 5.00
10 Damon Stoudamire 1.50 4.00

1996-97 Ultra Rising Stars

Randomly inserted in series one hobby packs only at a rate of one in 180, this 10-card set focuses on young stars and rookies. Each card front features a full photo shot of the player against a matted background.

COMPLETE SET (10) 40.00 100.00
1 Shareef Abdur-Rahim 3.00 8.00
2 Kobe Bryant 40.00 70.00
3 Anfernee Hardaway 8.00 20.00
4 Grant Hill 8.00 20.00
5 Juwan Howard 4.00 10.00
6 Allen Iverson 8.00 20.00
7 Jason Kidd 8.00 20.00
8 Stephon Marbury 4.00 10.00
9 Joe Smith 4.00 10.00
10 Damon Stoudamire 5.00 12.00

1996-97 Ultra Rookie Flashback

Randomly inserted in series one packs at a rate of one in 45, this 11-card set features the members of the 1995-96 NBA All-Rookie Team, printed against an etched-foil design.

COMPLETE SET (11) 20.00 40.00
1 Michael Finley 3.00 8.00
2 Antonio McDyess 2.50 6.00
3 Arvydas Sabonis 2.00 5.00
4 Joe Smith 2.00 5.00
5 Jerry Stackhouse 3.00 8.00
6 Damon Stoudamire 2.50 6.00
7 Brent Barry 2.00 5.00
8 Tyus Edney 1.50 4.00
9 Kevin Garnett 6.00 15.00
10 Bryant Reeves 1.50 4.00
11 Rasheed Wallace 3.00 8.00

1996-97 Ultra Scoring Kings

Randomly inserted in series two hobby packs only at a rate of one in 24, this 29-card set returns for the fourth straight year focusing on some of the NBA's top scoreres. The cards feature a metallic ink background.

COMPLETE SET (29) 60.00 150.00
*PLUS STARS: 1.25X TO 3X HI COLUMN
PLUS: SER.2 STATED ODDS 1:96 HOBBY
1 Steve Smith 2.00 5.00
2 Dino Radja 2.00 5.00
3 Glen Rice 2.50 6.00
4 Michael Jordan 30.00 80.00
5 Terrell Brandon 1.50 4.00
6 Jim Jackson - 1.50 4.00
7 Antonio McDyess 2.50 6.00
8 Grant Hill 4.00 10.00
9 Latrell Sprewell 2.50 6.00
10 Hakeem Olajuwon 3.00 8.00
11 Reggie Miller 3.00 8.00
12 Loy Vaught 1.50 4.00
13 Shaquille O'Neal 6.00 15.00
14 Alonzo Mourning 3.00 8.00
15 Vin Baker 2.00 5.00
16 Tom Gugliotta 1.50 4.00
17 Kendall Gill 1.50 4.00
18 Patrick Ewing 3.00 8.00
19 Anfernee Hardaway 4.00 10.00
20 Allen Iverson 6.00 15.00
21 Danny Manning 2.00 5.00
22 Kenny Anderson 2.00 5.00
23 Mitch Richmond 2.50 6.00
24 David Robinson 4.00 10.00
25 Shawn Kemp 2.50 6.00
26 Damon Stoudamire 2.50 6.00
27 Karl Malone 3.00 8.00
28 Shareef Abdur-Rahim 2.50 6.00
29 Chris Webber 3.00 8.00

1996-97 Ultra Starring Role

Randomly inserted in series two packs at a rate of one in 288, this 10-card set focuses on players who are spotlighted on their teams. The card design is plastic with silver foil.

COMPLETE SET (10) 175.00 350.00
1 Kevin Garnett 15.00 40.00
2 Anfernee Hardaway 10.00 25.00
3 Grant Hill 10.00 25.00
4 Michael Jordan 175.00 300.00
5 Shawn Kemp 8.00 20.00
6 Karl Malone 8.00 20.00
7 Hakeem Olajuwon 8.00 20.00
8 Shaquille O'Neal 15.00 40.00
9 David Robinson 10.00 25.00
10 Damon Stoudamire 6.00 15.00

1997-98 Ultra

The 1997-98 Ultra set, produced by Fleer/SkyBox, was issued in two series with the first containing 150 cards and the second 125 and were packaged in 10-card packs that carried a suggested retail price of $2.49. The first series feature most of the 1997-98 rookie class including Derek Anderson, Tony Battie, Chauncey Billups, Antonio Daniels, Tim Duncan, Brevin Knight, Ron Mercer, Tim Thomas and Keith Van Horn. Those cards were seeded into packs at a rate of one in four. The second series featured the subset "98 Greats" and were inserted at a rate of one in four. A Jerry Stackhouse promo card was also issued. Since that card shares the same number as the regular Stackhouse in the base set (#105), we have made it a "NNO" and listed it at the bottom of the set.

COMPLETE SET (275) 50.00 100.00
COMPLETE SERIES 1 (150) 25.00 50.00
COMPLETE SERIES 2 (125) 25.00 50.00
1 Kobe Bryant 1.25 3.00
2 Charles Barkley .40 1.00
3 Joe Dumars .25 .60
4 Wesley Person .15 .40
5 Walt Williams .15 .40
6 Vlade Divac .25 .60
7 Mookie Blaylock .15 .40
8 Jason Kidd .40 1.00
9 Ron Harper .20 .50
10 Sherman Douglas .15 .40
11 Cedric Ceballos .15 .40
12 Karl Malone .30 .75
13 Antonio McDyess .20 .50
14 Steve Kerr .20 .50
15 Matt Maloney .15 .40
16 Glenn Robinson .20 .50
17 Rony Seikaly .20 .50
18 Derrick Coleman .20 .50
19 Jermaine O'Neal .30 .75
20 Scott Burrell .15 .40
21 Glen Rice .25 .60
22 Dale Ellis .15 .40
23 Michael Jordan 2.00 5.00
24 Anfernee Hardaway .40 1.00
25 Bryon Russell .15 .40
26 Toni Kukoc .25 .60
27 Theo Ratliff .20 .50
28 Tom Gugliotta .15 .40
29 Dennis Rodman .50 1.25
30 John Stockton .30 .75
31 Priest Lauderdale .15 .40
32 Luc Longley .15 .40
33 Grant Hill .40 1.00
34 Antonio Davis .15 .40
35 Eddie Jones .25 .60
36 Nick Anderson .15 .40
37 Shareef Abdur-Rahim .25 .60
38 Stephon Marbury .30 .75
39 Todd Day .15 .40
40 Tim Hardaway .25 .60
41 Larry Johnson .25 .60
42 Sam Perkins .15 .40
43 Dikembe Mutombo .25 .60
44 Bo Outlaw .15 .40
45 Mitch Richmond .25 .60
46 Bryant Reeves .15 .40
47 P.J. Brown .15 .40
48 Steve Smith .20 .50
49 Martin Muursepp .15 .40
50 Jamal Mashburn .20 .50
51 Kendall Gill .15 .40
52 Vinny Del Negro .15 .40
53 Roy Rogers .15 .40
54 Khalid Reeves .15 .40
55 Scottie Pippen .40 1.00
56 Joe Smith .20 .50
57 Mark Jackson .25 .60
58 Voshon Lenard .15 .40
59 Dan Majerle .25 .60
60 Alonzo Mourning .30 .75
61 Kerry Kittles .15 .40
62 Chris Childs .15 .40
63 Patrick Ewing .30 .75
64 Allan Houston .20 .50
65 Marcus Camby .25 .60
66 Christian Laettner .20 .50
67 Loy Vaught .15 .40
68 Jayson Williams .15 .40
69 Avery Johnson .20 .50
70 Damon Stoudamire .25 .60
71 Kevin Johnson .25 .60
72 Gheorghe Muresan .15 .40
73 Reggie Miller .30 .75
74 John Wallace .15 .40
75 Terrell Brandon .15 .40
76 Dale Davis .15 .40
77 Latrell Sprewell .25 .60
78 Lorenzen Wright .15 .40
79 Rod Strickland .15 .40
80 Kenny Anderson .20 .50
81 Anthony Mason .15 .40
82 Hakeem Olajuwon .30 .75
83 Kevin Garnett .50 1.25
84 Isaiah Rider .15 .40
85 Mark Price .25 .60
86 Shawn Bradley .15 .40
87 Vin Baker .20 .50
88 Steve Nash .50 1.25
89 Jeff Hornacek .20 .50
90 Tony Delk .15 .40
91 Horace Grant .20 .50
92 Othella Harrington .15 .40
93 Arvydas Sabonis .20 .50
94 Antoine Walker .25 .60
95 Todd Fuller .15 .40
96 John Starks .20 .50
97 Olden Polynice .15 .40
98 Sean Elliott .25 .60
99 Travis Best .15 .40
100 Chris Gatling .15 .40
101 Derek Harper .20 .50
102 LaPhonso Ellis .15 .40
103 Dean Garrett .15 .40
104 Hersey Hawkins .15 .40
105 Jerry Stackhouse .25 .60
106 Ray Allen .30 .75
107 Allen Iverson .50 1.25
108 Chris Webber .25 .60
109 Robert Pack .15 .40
110 Gary Payton .25 .60
111 Mario Elie .15 .40
112 Dell Curry .15 .40
113 Lindsey Hunter .15 .40
114 Robert Horry .20 .50
115 David Robinson .40 1.00
116 Kevin Willis .15 .40
117 Tyrone Hill .15 .40
118 Vitaly Potapenko .15 .40
119 Clyde Drexler .30 .75
120 Derek Fisher .25 .60
121 Detlef Schrempf .25 .60
122 Gary Trent .15 .40
123 Danny Ferry .15 .40
124 Derek Anderson RC .75 2.00
125 Chris Anstey RC .75 2.00
126 Tony Battie RC 1.00 2.50
127 Chauncey Billups RC 3.00 8.00
128 Kelvin Cato RC .75 2.00
129 Austin Croshere RC .75 2.00
130 Antonio Daniels RC .75 2.00
131 Tim Duncan RC 5.00 12.00
132 Danny Fortson RC .75 2.00
133 Adonal Foyle RC .75 2.00
134 Paul Grant RC .75 2.00
135 Ed Gray RC .75 2.00
136 Bobby Jackson RC 1.00 2.50
137 Brevin Knight RC .75 2.00
138 Tracy McGrady RC 4.00 10.00
139 Ron Mercer RC 1.00 2.50
140 Anthony Parker RC .75 2.00
141 Scot Pollard RC .75 2.00
142 Rodrick Rhodes RC .75 2.00
143 Olivier Saint-Jean RC .75 2.00
144 Maurice Taylor RC .75 2.00
145 Johnny Taylor RC .75 2.00
146 Tim Thomas RC 1.50 4.00
147 Keith Van Horn RC 1.50 4.00
148 Jacque Vaughn RC .75 2.00
149 Checklist .15 .40
150 Checklist .15 .40
151 Scott Burrell .15 .40
152 Brian Williams .15 .40
153 Terry Mills .15 .40
154 Jim Jackson .15 .40
155 Michael Finley .25 .60
156 Jeff Nordgaard RC .25 .60
157 Carl Herrera .15 .40
158 Otis Thorpe .15 .40
159 Wesley Person .15 .40
160 Tyrone Hill .15 .40
161 Charles O'Bannon RC .25 .60
162 Greg Anthony .15 .40
163 Rusty LaRue RC .25 .60
164 David Wesley .15 .40
165 Chris Garner RC .25 .60
166 George McCloud .15 .40
167 Mark Price .25 .60
168 God Shammgod RC .25 .60
169 Isaac Austin .15 .40
170 Alan Henderson .15 .40
171 Eric Washington RC .25 .60
172 Darrell Armstrong .15 .40
173 Calbert Cheaney .15 .40
174 Cedric Henderson RC .25 .60
175 Bryant Stith .15 .40
176 Sean Rooks .15 .40
177 Chris Mills .15 .40
178 Eldridge Recasner .15 .40
179 Priest Lauderdale .15 .40
180 Rick Fox .15 .40
181 Keith Closs RC .25 .60
182 Chris Dudley .15 .40
183 Lawrence Funderburke RC .25 .60
184 Michael Stewart RC .25 .60
185 Alvin Williams RC .25 .60
186 Adam Keefe .15 .40
187 Chauncey Billups 1.00 2.50
188 Jon Barry .15 .40
189 Bobby Jackson .30 .75
190 Sam Cassell .20 .50
191 Dee Brown .15 .40
192 Travis Knight .15 .40
193 Dean Garrett .15 .40
194 David Benoit .15 .40
195 Chris Morris .15 .40
196 Bubba Wells RC .25 .60
197 James Robinson .15 .40
198 Anthony Johnson RC .25 .60
199 Dennis Scott .15 .40
200 DeJuan Wheat RC .25 .60
201 Rodney Rogers .15 .40
202 Tariq Abdul-Wahad .25 .60
203 Cherokee Parks .15 .40
204 Jacque Vaughn .25 .60
205 Cory Alexander .15 .40
206 Kevin Ollie RC .25 .60
207 George Lynch .15 .40
208 Lamond Murray .15 .40
209 Jud Buechler .15 .40
210 Erick Dampier .15 .40
211 Malcolm Huckaby RC .25 .60
212 Chris Webber .25 .60
213 Chris Crawford RC .25 .60
214 J.R. Reid .15 .40
215 Eddie Johnson .15 .40
216 Nick Van Exel .20 .50
217 Antonio McDyess .20 .50
218 David Wingate .15 .40
219 Malik Sealy .15 .40
220 Bo Outlaw .15 .40
221 Serge Zwikker RC .25 .60
222 Bobby Phills .15 .40
223 Shea Seals RC .25 .60
224 Clifford Robinson .15 .40
225 Zydrunas Ilgauskas .25 .60
226 John Thomas RC .25 .60
227 Rik Smits .20 .50
228 Rasheed Wallace .25 .60
229 John Wallace .15 .40
230 Bob Sura .15 .40
231 Ervin Johnson .15 .40
232 Keith Booth RC .25 .60
233 Chuck Person .20 .50
234 Brian Shaw .15 .40
235 Todd Day .15 .40
236 Clarence Weatherspoon .15 .40
237 Charlie Ward .15 .40
238 Rod Strickland .15 .40
239 Shawn Kemp .25 .60
240 Terrell Brandon .15 .40
241 Corey Beck RC .25 .60
242 Vin Baker .20 .50
243 Fred Hoiberg .15 .40
244 Chris Mullin .25 .60
245 Brian Grant .15 .40
246 Derek Anderson .25 .60
247 Zan Tabak .15 .40
248 Charles Smith RC .25 .60
249 Shareef Abdur-Rahim GRE .50 1.25
250 Ray Allen GRE .60 1.50
251 Charles Barkley GRE .75 2.00
252 Kobe Bryant GRE 2.50 6.00
253 Marcus Camby GRE .50 1.25
254 Kevin Garnett GRE 1.00 2.5
255 Anfernee Hardaway GRE .75 2.0
256 Grant Hill GRE .75 2.0
257 Juwan Howard GRE .40 1.0
258 Allen Iverson GRE 1.00 2.5
259 Michael Jordan GRE 4.00 10.0
260 Shawn Kemp GRE .50 1.2
261 Kerry Kittles GRE .30 .7
262 Karl Malone GRE .60 1.5
263 Stephon Marbury GRE .60 1.5
264 Hakeem Olajuwon GRE .60 1.5
265 Shaquille O'Neal GRE 1.25 3.0
266 Gary Payton GRE .50 1.2
267 Scottie Pippen GRE .75 2.0
268 David Robinson GRE .75 2.0
269 Dennis Rodman GRE 1.00 2.5
270 Joe Smith GRE .40 1.0
271 Jerry Stackhouse GRE .50 1.2
272 Damon Stoudamire GRE .50 1.2
273 Antoine Walker GRE .50 1.2
274 Checklist .15 .4
275 Checklist .15 .4
NNO Jerry Stackhouse PROMO .75 2.0

1997-98 Ultra Gold Medallion

Seeded on per both series hobby packs, this 271-carc set parallels the basic set, minus the checklists. Card backs have a gold tinted background and the player's name is in gold foil rather than the regular color. The card backs are numbered with a "G" suffix. To ascerta individual card values, please refer to the multiplier in the header below coupled with the value of the basic card.

*SER.1 STARS: 1X TO 2.5X BASE CARD HI
*SER.1 RCs: .4X TO 1X BASE HI
*SER.2 STARS/RCs: 1X TO 2.5X BASE HI
*SER.2 98 GREATS: .5X TO 1.25X BASE HI

1997-98 Ultra Masterpieces

Randomly inserted in hobby packs only, this set is parallel to the base set. Only one of each card was produced and is numbered "The Only One of One Masterpiece" with purple foil highlights.

1997-98 Ultra Platinum Medallion

Randomly inserted into both series hobby packs, this 271-card set parallels the basic set. Each card is seria numbered on the back to 100 sets. The last ten sets were available via redemption cards randomly inserte into packs. Each card was good for a complete Platinum Medallion set.

*STARS: 30X TO 80X BASE CARD HI
*RCs: 4X TO 10X BASE HI
*GREATS: SAME VALUE AS BASE PLATINUM
*SER.2 RCs: 8X TO 20X BASE HI
1 Kobe Bryant 200.00 350.0
8 Jason Kidd 75.00 150.0
23 Michael Jordan 800.00 1300.0
24 Anfernee Hardaway 75.00 150.0
29 Dennis Rodman 125.00 250.0
33 Grant Hill 75.00 150.0
55 Scottie Pippen 40.00 100.0
60 Alonzo Mourning 40.00 100.0
73 Reggie Miller 30.00 80.0
88 Steve Nash 50.00 125.0
131 Tim Duncan 150.00 300.0
138 Tracy McGrady 75.00 150.0

1997-98 Ultra All-Rookies

Randomly inserted into series two packs at one in fou this 15-card set features the top players from the 199 Draft. Card backs carry an "AR" prefix.

COMPLETE SET (15) 5.00 12.0
AR1 Tim Duncan 2.50 6.0
AR2 Tony Battie .50 1.2
AR3 Keith Van Horn .75 2.0
AR4 Antonio Daniels .40 1.0
AR5 Chauncey Billups 1.50 4.0
AR6 Ron Mercer .50 1.2
AR7 Tracy McGrady 2.00 5.0
AR8 Danny Fortson .40 1.0
AR9 Brevin Knight .40 1.0
AR10 Derek Anderson .40 1.0
AR11 Cedric Henderson .40 1.0
AR12 Jacque Vaughn .40 1.0
AR13 Tim Thomas .75 2.0
AR14 Austin Croshere .40 1.0
AR15 Kelvin Cato .40 1.0

1997-98 Ultra Big Shots

Randomly inserted into series one packs at a rate of one in four, this 15-card set focuses on some of the best clutch shots from the 1996-97 season.

COMPLETE SET (15) 6.00 15.0
1 Michael Jordan 3.00 8.0
2 Allen Iverson .75 2.0
3 Shaquille O'Neal 1.00 2.5
4 Anfernee Hardaway .60 1.5
5 Dennis Rodman .75 2.0
6 Grant Hill .60 1.5
7 Juwan Howard .30 .7
8 David Robinson .60 1.5
9 Gary Payton .40 1.0
10 Joe Smith .30 .7
11 Charles Barkley .60 1.5
12 Terrell Brandon .25 .6
13 John Stockton .50 1.2
14 Mitch Richmond .40 1.0
15 Vin Baker .30 .7

1997-98 Ultra Court Masters

andomly inserted into series two packs at one in 144, is 20-card set features double images of players who ve mastered the game. Each player is shown in both s home and away uniform. The background of the rd fronts mimic a hardwood court. Card backs carry "CM" prefix.

OMPLETE SET (20) 400.00 700.00
M1 Michael Jordan 175.00 350.00
M2 Allen Iverson 20.00 50.00
M3 Kobe Bryant 80.00 160.00
M4 Shaquille O'Neal 25.00 60.00
M5 Stephon Marbury 12.00 30.00
M6 Shawn Kemp 10.00 25.00
M7 Anfernee Hardaway 15.00 40.00
M8 Kevin Garnett 20.00 50.00
M9 Shareef Abdur-Rahim 10.00 25.00
M10 Dennis Rodman 25.00 60.00
M11 Grant Hill 15.00 40.00
M12 Kerry Kittles 6.00 15.00
M13 Antoine Walker 10.00 25.00
M14 Scottie Pippen 15.00 40.00
M15 Damon Stoudamire 10.00 25.00
M16 Marcus Camby 10.00 25.00
M17 Hakeem Olajuwon 12.00 30.00
M18 Tim Duncan 20.00 50.00
M19 Keith Van Horn 8.00 20.00
M20 Chauncey Billups 12.00 30.00

997-98 Ultra Heir to the Throne

andomly inserted in series one packs at a rate of one 18, this 15-card set focuses on some of the best okies from the 1997-98 class. The cards feature each okie sitting in a chair that is made up of basketballs.

OMPLETE SET (15) 12.00 30.00
Derek Anderson .60 1.50
Tony Battie .75 2.00
Chauncey Billups 2.50 6.00
Kelvin Cato .60 1.50
Austin Croshere .60 1.50
Antonio Daniels .60 1.50
Tim Duncan 4.00 10.00
Danny Fortson .60 1.50
Jacque Vaughn .60 1.50
) Tracy McGrady 3.00 8.00
Ron Mercer .75 2.00
2 Olivier Saint-Jean .60 1.50
3 Maurice Taylor .60 1.50
Tim Thomas 1.25 3.00
Keith Van Horn 1.25 3.00

1997-98 Ultra Inside/Outside

andomly inserted in series one packs at a rate of one six, this 15-card set focuses on players who can get e job done with both their inside and outside games.

OMPLETE SET (15) 3.00 8.00
Shareef Abdur-Rahim .50 1.25
Juwan Howard .40 1.00
David Robinson .75 2.00
Joe Smith .40 1.00
Charles Barkley .75 2.00
Tom Gugliotta .30 .75
Glenn Robinson .40 1.00
Patrick Ewing .60 1.50
Chris Webber .50 1.25
) Glen Rice .50 1.25
Shawn Kemp .50 1.25
2 Antonio McDyess .40 1.00
3 Clyde Drexler .60 1.50
Eddie Jones .50 1.25
Jason Kidd .75 2.00

1997-98 Ultra Jam City

andomly inserted in series one packs at a rate of one eight, this 18-card set features some of the NBA's gh flying players.

OMPLETE SET (18) 10.00 20.00
Kevin Garnett 1.25 3.00
Antoine Walker .60 1.50
Scottie Pippen 1.00 2.50
Shawn Kemp .60 1.50
Hakeem Olajuwon .75 2.00
Jerry Stackhouse .60 1.50
7 Karl Malone .75 2.00
8 Shaquille O'Neal 1.50 4.00
9 John Wallace .40 1.00
10 Marcus Camby .60 1.50
11 Juwan Howard .50 1.25
12 David Robinson 1.00 2.50
13 Gary Payton .60 1.50
14 Dennis Rodman 1.25 3.00
15 Joe Smith .50 1.25
16 Charles Barkley 1.00 2.50
17 Terrell Brandon .40 1.00
18 Kobe Bryant 4.00 10.00

1997-98 Ultra Neat Feats

Randomly inserted into series two packs at one in eight, this 18-card set focuses on player's career highlights. The card fronts features UV coated player photos on a matte finish background. Card backs are numbered with a "NF" prefix.

COMPLETE SET (18) 5.00 12.00
NF1 Michael Finley .60 1.50
NF2 Jason Kidd 1.00 2.50
NF3 Rasheed Wallace .60 1.50
NF4 Shaquille O'Neal 1.50 4.00
NF5 Tom Gugliotta .40 1.00
NF6 Marcus Camby .60 1.50
NF7 Jerry Stackhouse .60 1.50
NF8 John Wallace .40 1.00
NF9 Juwan Howard .50 1.25
NF10 David Robinson 1.00 2.50
NF11 Gary Payton .60 1.50
NF12 Joe Smith .50 1.25
NF13 Charles Barkley 1.00 2.50
NF14 Terrell Brandon .40 1.00
NF15 John Stockton .75 2.00
NF16 Vin Baker .50 1.25
NF17 Antonio McDyess .50 1.25
NF18 Antonio Daniels .60 1.50

1997-98 Ultra Quick Picks

Randomly inserted in series one packs at a rate of one in eight, this 12-card set focuses on the young defensive wizards of the NBA.

COMPLETE SET (12) 3.00 8.00
1 Stephon Marbury .75 2.00
2 Ray Allen .75 2.00
3 Damon Stoudamire .60 1.50
4 Kerry Kittles .40 1.00
5 Gary Payton .60 1.50
6 Terrell Brandon .40 1.00
7 John Stockton .75 2.00
8 Mookie Blaylock .40 1.00
9 Eddie Jones .60 1.50
10 Nick Van Exel .50 1.25
11 Kenny Anderson .50 1.25
12 Tim Hardaway .60 1.50

1997-98 Ultra Rim Rocker

Randomly inserted into series two packs at one in eight, this 12-card set features color photos of some of the best dunkers in the game printed on custom die-cut silver holofoil cards. Card backs are numbered with a "RR" prefix.

COMPLETE SET (12) 3.00 8.00
RR1 Ron Mercer .50 1.25
RR2 Juwan Howard .50 1.25
RR3 David Robinson 1.00 2.50
RR4 Gary Payton .60 1.50
RR5 Joe Smith .50 1.25
RR6 Charles Barkley 1.00 2.50
RR7 Terrell Brandon .40 1.00
RR8 John Stockton .75 2.00
RR9 Adonal Foyle .40 1.00
RR10 Tim Thomas .75 2.00
RR11 Tony Battie .50 1.25
RR12 Antonio McDyess .50 1.25

1997-98 Ultra Star Power

Randomly inserted into series two packs at one in four, this 20-card set chronicles the path of some notable NBA players. These cards in particular focus on early to mid-career highlights. Card backs carry a "SP" prefix.

COMPLETE SET (20) 12.00 30.00
*PLUS: 2X TO 5X BASE STAR POWER
PLUS: SER.2 STATED ODDS 1:36 H/R
SP1 Michael Jordan 4.00 10.00
SP2 Allen Iverson 1.00 2.50
SP3 Kobe Bryant 2.50 6.00
SP4 Shaquille O'Neal 1.25 3.00
SP5 Stephon Marbury .60 1.50
SP6 Shawn Kemp .50 1.25
SP7 Anfernee Hardaway .75 2.00
SP8 Kevin Garnett 1.00 2.50
SP9 Shareef Abdur-Rahim .50 1.25
SP10 Dennis Rodman 1.00 2.50
SP11 Grant Hill .75 2.00
SP12 Gary Payton .50 1.25
SP13 Antoine Walker .50 1.25
SP14 Scottie Pippen .75 2.00
SP15 Damon Stoudamire .50 1.25
SP16 Marcus Camby .50 1.25
SP17 Hakeem Olajuwon .60 1.50
SP18 Tim Duncan 1.50 4.00
SP19 Keith Van Horn .50 1.25
SP20 Jerry Stackhouse .50 1.25

1997-98 Ultra Star Power Supreme

Randomly inserted into series two packs at one in 288, this 20-card set chronicles the path of some notable NBA players. The cards parallel both of the "Star Power" and "Star Power Plus" inserts and are printed on silver holofoil stamped die-cut cards. These cards in particular capture the brilliance of these NBA greats. Card backs carry a "SP" prefix. To ascertain values on individual cards, please refer to the multiplier in the header below, coupled with the value of the base card.

*SUPREME: 15X TO 40X VALUE
SPS1 Michael Jordan 300.00 600.00
SPS3 Kobe Bryant 125.00 300.00
SPS10 Dennis Rodman 50.00 120.00

1997-98 Ultra Stars

Randomly inserted in series one packs at a rate of one in 288, this 20-card set features some of the NBA's top stars. Ten percent of the print run was done in gold foil as opposed to the more common silver foil.

1 Michael Jordan 150.00 300.00
2 Allen Iverson 20.00 50.00
3 Kobe Bryant 50.00 125.00
4 Shaquille O'Neal 25.00 60.00
5 Stephon Marbury 12.00 30.00
6 Marcus Camby 10.00 25.00
7 Anfernee Hardaway 15.00 40.00
8 Kevin Garnett 20.00 50.00
9 Shareef Abdur-Rahim 10.00 25.00
10 Dennis Rodman 20.00 50.00
11 Ray Allen 12.00 30.00
12 Grant Hill 15.00 40.00
13 Kerry Kittles 6.00 15.00
14 Antoine Walker 10.00 25.00
15 Scottie Pippen 15.00 40.00
16 Damon Stoudamire 10.00 25.00
17 Shawn Kemp 10.00 25.00
18 Hakeem Olajuwon 12.00 30.00
19 Jerry Stackhouse 10.00 25.00
20 John Wallace 6.00 15.00

1997-98 Ultra Stars Gold

Randomly inserted into series one packs, this 20-card set represents the first 10 percent of the press run of the Ultra Stars insert. The cards are treated with gold foil on the card front as opposed to the more common silver. To ascertain values on individual cards, please refer to the multiplier in the header below, coupled with the value of the base card.

*GOLD: 2X TO 5X HI COLUMN
1 Michael Jordan 1800.00 2600.00
3 Kobe Bryant 900.00 1500.00
10 Dennis Rodman 150.00 300.00
15 Scottie Pippen 125.00 250.00

1997-98 Ultra Sweet Deal

Randomly inserted into series two packs at one in six, this 12-card set gives insight to some of the best players in the game. Card backs carry a "SD" prefix.

COMPLETE SET (12) 2.50 6.00
SD1 Ray Allen .50 1.25
SD2 Chauncey Billups 1.50 4.00
SD3 Ron Mercer .50 1.25
SD4 Hakeem Olajuwon .50 1.25
SD5 Jerry Stackhouse .40 1.00
SD6 John Wallace .25 .60
SD7 Juwan Howard .30 .75
SD8 David Robinson .60 1.50
SD9 Bobby Jackson .50 1.25
SD10 Joe Smith .30 .75
SD11 Charles Barkley .60 1.50
SD12 Terrell Brandon .25 .60

1997-98 Ultra Ultrabilities

Randomly inserted in series one packs at a rate of one in four, this 20-card set features NBA players that have many different abilities.

COMPLETE SET (20) 12.00 30.00
*ALL-STAR: 2X TO 5X BASE ULTRABIL.
ALL-STAR: SER.1 STATED ODDS 1:36 H/R
1 Michael Jordan 4.00 10.00
2 Allen Iverson 1.00 2.50
3 Kobe Bryant 2.50 6.00
4 Shaquille O'Neal 1.25 3.00
5 Stephon Marbury .60 1.50
6 Gary Payton .50 1.25
7 Anfernee Hardaway .75 2.00
8 Kevin Garnett 1.00 2.50
9 Scottie Pippen .75 2.00
10 Grant Hill .75 2.00
11 Marcus Camby .50 1.25
12 Ray Allen .60 1.50
13 Kerry Kittles .30 .75
14 Antoine Walker .50 1.25
15 Shareef Abdur-Rahim .50 1.25
16 Damon Stoudamire .50 1.25
17 Shawn Kemp .50 1.25
18 Hakeem Olajuwon .60 1.50
19 Jerry Stackhouse .50 1.25
20 Juwan Howard .40 1.00

1997-98 Ultra Ultrabilities Superstar

Randomly inserted into series one packs at a rate of one in 288, this 20-card set parallels the the Ultrabilities All-Star set. These cards feature a gold background against a die cut card. To ascertain values on individual cards, please refer to the multiplier in the header below, coupled with the value of the base card.

*SUPERSTAR: 12X TO 30X VALUE
1 Michael Jordan 200.00 400.00

1997-98 Ultra View to a Thrill

Randomly inserted into series two packs at one in 18, this 15-card set features colorful profiles of players that make the game a thrill to watch. Card backs carry a "VT" prefix.

COMPLETE SET (15) 20.00 50.00
VT1 Michael Jordan 8.00 20.00
VT2 Allen Iverson 2.00 5.00
VT3 Kobe Bryant 5.00 12.00
VT4 Tracy McGrady 2.50 6.00
VT5 Stephon Marbury 1.25 3.00
VT6 Shawn Kemp 1.00 2.50
VT7 Anfernee Hardaway 1.50 4.00
VT8 Kevin Garnett 2.00 5.00
VT9 Shareef Abdur-Rahim 1.00 2.50
VT10 Dennis Rodman 2.00 5.00
VT11 Grant Hill 1.50 4.00
VT12 Kerry Kittles .60 1.50
VT13 Antoine Walker 1.00 2.50
VT14 Scottie Pippen 1.50 4.00
VT15 Damon Stoudamire 1.00 2.50

1998-99 Ultra

Due to the NBA lockout early in the season, the 1998-99 Ultra product was released in early 1999, and featured a 125-card base set. The set features 100 Veterans (1-100), and 25 Rookies (101-125). Each pack contained 10 cards and carried a suggested retail price of $2.69.

COMPLETE SET (125) 50.00 100.00
COMPLETE SET w/o SP (100) 12.50 25.00
1 Keith Van Horn .25 .60
1B Keith Van Horn PROMO .40 1.00
2 Antonio Daniels .15 .40
3 Patrick Ewing .30 .75
4 Alonzo Mourning .30 .75
5 Isaac Austin .15 .40
6 Bryant Reeves .15 .40
7 Dennis Scott .15 .40
8 Damon Stoudamire .25 .60
9 Kenny Anderson .20 .50
10 Mookie Blaylock .15 .40
11 Mitch Richmond .25 .60
12 Jalen Rose .20 .50
13 Vin Baker .20 .50
14 Donyell Marshall .15 .40
15 Bryon Russell .15 .40
16 Rasheed Wallace .25 .60
17 Allan Houston .20 .50
18 Shawn Kemp .25 .60
19 Nick Van Exel .20 .50
20 Theo Ratliff .20 .50
21 Jayson Williams .15 .40
22 Chauncey Billups .30 .75
23 Brent Barry .20 .50
24 David Wesley .15 .40
25 Joe Dumars .25 .60
26 Marcus Camby .20 .50
27 Juwan Howard .20 .50
28 Brevin Knight .15 .40
29 Reggie Miller .30 .75
30 Ray Allen .30 .75
31 Michael Finley .25 .60
32 Tom Gugliotta .15 .40
33 Allen Iverson .50 1.25
34 Toni Kukoc .25 .60
35 Tim Thomas .25 .60
36 Jeff Hornacek .20 .50
37 Bobby Jackson .20 .50
38 Bo Outlaw .15 .40
39 Steve Smith .20 .50
40 Terrell Brandon .15 .40
41 Glen Rice .25 .60
42 Rik Smits .20 .50
43 Calbert Cheaney .15 .40
44 Stephon Marbury .30 .75
45 Glenn Robinson .20 .50
46 Corliss Williamson .15 .40
47 Larry Johnson .25 .60
48 Antonio McDyess .20 .50
49 Detlef Schrempf .25 .60
50 Jerry Stackhouse .25 .60
51 Doug Christie .15 .40
52 Eddie Jones .25 .60
53 Karl Malone .30 .75
54 Anthony Mason .15 .40
55 Tim Duncan .50 1.25
56 Christian Laettner .20 .50
57 Isaiah Rider .15 .40
58 Shawn Bradley .15 .40
59 Jim Jackson .15 .40
60 Mark Jackson .25 .60
61 Kobe Bryant 1.25 3.00
62 Zydrunas Ilgauskas .25 .60
63 Ron Mercer .20 .50
64 Hersey Hawkins .15 .40
65 John Wallace .15 .40
66 Avery Johnson .20 .50
67 Dikembe Mutombo .25 .60
68 Hakeem Olajuwon .30 .75
69 Tony Battie .20 .50
70 Jason Kidd .40 1.00
71 Latrell Sprewell .25 .60
72 Kevin Garnett .50 1.25
73 Voshon Lenard .15 .40
74 Gary Payton .25 .60
75 Cherokee Parks .15 .40
76 Antoine Walker .25 .60
77 Anthony Johnson .15 .40
78 Danny Fortson .15 .40
79 Grant Hill .40 1.00
80 Dennis Rodman .50 1.25
81 Arvydas Sabonis .20 .50
82 Tracy McGrady .40 1.00
83 David Robinson .40 1.00
84 Tariq Abdul-Wahad .15 .40
85 Michael Jordan 2.00 5.00
86 Kerry Kittles .15 .40
87 Maurice Taylor .15 .40
88 Cedric Ceballos .15 .40
89 Anfernee Hardaway .40 1.00
90 John Stockton .30 .75
91 Shareef Abdur-Rahim .25 .60
92 Tim Hardaway .25 .60
93 Shaquille O'Neal .60 1.50
94 Rodney Rogers .15 .40
95 Derek Anderson .15 .40
96 Kendall Gill .15 .40
97 Rod Strickland .15 .40
98 Charles Barkley .40 1.00
99 Chris Webber .25 .60
100 Scottie Pippen .40 1.00
101 Raef LaFrentz RC .75 2.00
102 Ricky Davis RC 1.00 2.50
103 Robert Traylor RC .60 1.50
104 Roshown McLeod RC .60 1.50
105 Tyronn Lue RC .60 1.50
106 Vince Carter RC 3.00 8.00
107 Miles Simon RC .60 1.50
108 Paul Pierce RC 3.00 8.00
109 Pat Garrity RC .60 1.50
110 Nazr Mohammed RC .60 1.50
111 Mike Bibby RC 1.50 4.00
112 Michael Dickerson RC .60 1.50
113 Michael Doleac RC .60 1.50
114 Matt Harpring RC .75 2.00
115 Larry Hughes RC 1.25 3.00
116 Keon Clark RC .60 1.50
117 Felipe Lopez RC .60 1.50
118 Dirk Nowitzki RC 5.00 12.00
119 Corey Benjamin RC .60 1.50
120 Bryce Drew RC .60 1.50
121 Brian Skinner RC .60 1.50
122 Bonzi Wells RC .60 1.50
123 Antawn Jamison RC 1.50 4.00
124 Al Harrington RC 1.00 2.50
125 Michael Olowokandi RC .75 2.00

1998-99 Ultra Gold Medallion

Inserted one per hobby pack for veterans and one in 35 for rookies, this 125-card set parallels the basic Ultra set. The cards feature a gold background on the card front. To ascertain prices, please use the base card value, coupled with the mutipler in the header below.

*STARS: 1X TO 2.5X BASE CARD HI
*RCs: .6X TO 1.5X BASE HI

1998-99 Ultra Masterpieces

Randomly inserted in hobby packs only, this 125-card set parallels the base set. There is only one card for each player produced.

1998-99 Ultra Platinum Medallion

Randomly inserted in hobby packs only, this 125-card set parallels the basic Ultra set. The cards feature a black and white background on the front and serial numbering on the back to differentiate. Veteran stars are serial numbered to 99, while the rookies are serial numbered to 66. To ascertain values on individual cards, please refer to the multiplier in the header below, coupled with the value of the base card.

*STARS: 20X TO 50X BASE CARD HI
*RCs: 8X TO 20X HI
18 Shawn Kemp 25.00 60.00
61 Kobe Bryant 150.00 300.00
79 Grant Hill 40.00 100.00
80 Dennis Rodman 75.00 200.00
85 Michael Jordan 500.00 1000.00
89 Anfernee Hardaway 30.00 80.00
106 Vince Carter 150.00 300.00
108 Paul Pierce 125.00 250.00
118 Dirk Nowitzki 150.00 300.00

1998-99 Ultra Exclamation Points

Randomly inserted into packs at one in 288, this 15-card set features players that have a knack for slam-dunking the basketball.

COMPLETE SET (15) 300.00 500.00
1 Vince Carter 12.00 30.00
2 Tim Duncan 12.00 30.00
3 Shawn Kemp 8.00 20.00
4 Shaquille O'Neal 15.00 40.00
5 Mike Bibby 6.00 15.00
6 Michael Jordan 250.00 500.00
7 Michael Olowokandi 3.00 8.00
8 Larry Hughes 5.00 12.00
9 Kobe Bryant 50.00 125.00
10 Kevin Garnett 12.00 30.00
11 Keith Van Horn 6.00 15.00
12 Grant Hill 10.00 25.00
13 Gary Payton 6.00 15.00
14 Antoine Walker 6.00 15.00
15 Antawn Jamison 6.00 15.00

1998-99 Ultra Give and Take

Randomly inserted into retail packs at one in 18, this 10-card set features players that have a knack for stealing the ball.

COMPLETE SET (10) 6.00 15.00
1 Gary Payton 1.00 2.50
2 Shawn Kemp 1.00 2.50
3 Kerry Kittles .60 1.50
4 Ron Mercer .75 2.00
5 Scottie Pippen 1.50 4.00
6 Ray Allen 1.25 3.00
7 Anfernee Hardaway 1.50 4.00
8 Maurice Taylor .60 1.50
9 Brevin Knight .60 1.50
10 Karl Malone 1.25 3.00

1998-99 Ultra Leading Performers

Randomly inserted into packs at one in 72, this 15-card insert features players that are always among the league leaders in the NBA.

COMPLETE SET (15) 60.00 120.00
1 Allen Iverson 4.00 10.00
2 Anfernee Hardaway 3.00 8.00
3 Kobe Bryant 10.00 25.00
4 Michael Jordan 25.00 60.00
5 Ron Mercer 1.50 4.00
6 Stephon Marbury 2.50 6.00
7 Tim Duncan 4.00 10.00
8 Shareef Abdur-Rahim 2.00 5.00
9 Kevin Garnett 4.00 10.00
10 Grant Hill 3.00 8.00
11 Damon Stoudamire 2.00 5.00
12 Dennis Rodman 4.00 10.00
13 Keith Van Horn 2.00 5.00
14 Scottie Pippen 3.00 8.00
15 Shaquille O'Neal 5.00 12.00

1998-99 Ultra NBAttitude

Randomly inserted into packs at one in six, this 20-card insert features NBA players that have award-winning attitudes.

COMPLETE SET (20) 3.00 8.00
1 Allen Iverson .75 2.00
2 Chauncey Billups .50 1.25
3 Keith Van Horn .40 1.00
4 Ray Allen .50 1.25
5 Shareef Abdur-Rahim .40 1.00
6 Stephon Marbury .50 1.25
7 Kerry Kittles .25 .60
8 Tim Thomas .40 1.00
9 Damon Stoudamire .40 1.00
10 Antoine Walker .40 1.00
11 Brevin Knight .25 .60
12 Maurice Taylor .25 .60
13 Ron Mercer .30 .75
14 Tim Duncan .75 2.00
15 Zydrunas Ilgauskas .40 1.00
16 Michael Finley .40 1.00
17 Bobby Jackson .30 .75
18 Tim Hardaway .40 1.00
19 David Robinson .60 1.50
20 Vin Baker .30 .75

1998-99 Ultra Unstoppable

Randomly inserted into packs at one in 36, this 15-card set features players that are purely unstoppable on the court.

COMPLETE SET (15) 25.00 60.00
1 Michael Jordan 10.00 25.00
2 Scottie Pippen 2.00 5.00
3 Grant Hill 2.00 5.00
4 Dennis Rodman 2.50 6.00
5 Stephon Marbury 1.50 4.00
6 Antoine Walker 1.25 3.00
7 Shareef Abdur-Rahim 1.25 3.00
8 Shaquille O'Neal 3.00 8.00
9 Damon Stoudamire 1.25 3.00
10 Kerry Kittles .75 2.00
11 Maurice Taylor .75 2.00
12 Kobe Bryant 6.00 15.00
13 Kevin Garnett 2.50 6.00
14 Anfernee Hardaway 2.00 5.00
15 Allen Iverson 2.50 6.00

1998-99 Ultra World Premiere

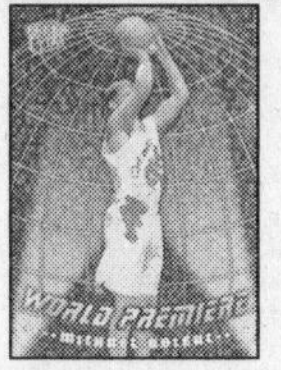

Randomly inserted into packs at one in 20, this 15-card set features players that have come from all over the world to play in the NBA.

COMPLETE SET (15) 10.00 25.00
1 Robert Traylor .60 1.50
2 Paul Pierce 3.00 8.00
3 Michael Olowokandi .75 2.00
4 Felipe Lopez .60 1.50
5 Raef LaFrentz .75 2.00
6 Antawn Jamison 1.50 4.00
7 Larry Hughes 1.25 3.00
8 Al Harrington 1.00 2.50
9 Pat Garrity .60 1.50
10 Bryce Drew .60 1.50
11 Michael Doleac .60 1.50
12 Michael Dickerson .60 1.50
13 Keon Clark .60 1.50
14 Vince Carter 3.00 8.00
15 Mike Bibby 1.50 4.00

1999-00 Ultra

Produced by Fleer/SkyBox, the 1999-00 Ultra set contained 150 cards, featuring 125 veterans and 25 rookies. Each pack contained 10 cards and carried a suggested retail price of $2.69. The rookie subset was inserted at one in four packs. Two checklist were also inserted in packs at one in six.

COMPLETE SET (150) 30.00 80.00
COMPLETE SET w/o RC (125) 12.50 25.00
UNPRICED MASTERPIECES SERIAL #'d TO 1
1 Vince Carter .60 1.50
2 Randell Jackson .20 .50
3 Ray Allen .30 .75
4 Corliss Williamson .20 .50
5 Darrell Armstrong .20 .50
6 Charles Oakley .25 .60
7 Tyrone Nesby RC .30 .75
8 Eddie Jones .30 .75
9 Kerry Kittles .20 .50
10 Jason Williams .40 1.00
11 Elden Campbell .20 .50
12 Mookie Blaylock .20 .50
13 Brent Barry .25 .60
14 Mark Jackson .30 .75
15 Tim Hardaway .30 .75
16 Kendall Gill .20 .50
17 Larry Johnson .30 .75
18 Eric Snow .25 .60
19 Raef LaFrentz .25 .60
20 Allen Iverson .60 1.50
21 Kenny Anderson .25 .60
22 John Starks .30 .75
23 Isaiah Rider .20 .50
24 Tariq Abdul-Wahad .20 .50
25 Vitaly Potapenko .20 .50
26 Patrick Ewing .40 1.00
27 Mitch Richmond .30 .75
28 Steve Nash .50 1.25
29 Dickey Simpkins .20 .50
30 Grant Hill .40 1.00
31 Matt Geiger .20 .50
32 John Stockton .40 1.00
33 Jayson Williams .20 .50
34 Reggie Miller .30 .75
35 Eric Piatkowski .25 .60
36 Jason Kidd .50 1.25
37 Allan Houston .25 .60
38 Christian Laettner .25 .60
39 Marcus Camby .25 .60
40 Shaquille O'Neal .75 2.00
41 Derek Anderson .20 .50
42 Gary Trent .20 .50
43 Vin Baker .30 .75
44 Alonzo Mourning .40 1.00
45 Latrell Sprewell .30 .75
46 Rod Strickland .20 .50
47 Bobby Jackson .25 .60
48 Karl Malone .40 1.00
49 Mario Elie .20 .50
50 Kobe Bryant 1.50 4.00
51 Clifford Robinson .20 .50
52 Jamal Mashburn .25 .60
53 Dirk Nowitzki .60 1.50
54 Rik Smits .30 .75
55 Doug Christie .25 .60
56 Ricky Davis .30 .75
57 Jalen Rose .25 .60
58 Michael Olowokandi .20 .50
59 Cedric Ceballos .20 .50

60 Ron Mercer .25 .60
61 Brevin Knight .20 .50
62 Rashard Lewis .30 .75
63 Detlef Schrempf .25 .60
64 Keith Van Horn .25 .60
64B Keith Van Horn PROMO .25 .60
65 Nick Anderson .20 .50
66 Larry Hughes .25 .60
67 Antonio McDyess .25 .60
68 Terrell Brandon .20 .50
69 Felipe Lopez .20 .50
70 Scottie Pippen .50 1.25
71 Erick Dampier .20 .50
72 Arvydas Sabonis .25 .60
73 Brian Grant .20 .50
74 Nick Van Exel .25 .60
75 Bryon Russell .20 .50
76 Danny Fortson .20 .50
77 Avery Johnson .25 .60
78 Jerry Stackhouse .30 .75
79 Robert Traylor .20 .50
80 Tim Duncan .60 1.50
81 Lindsey Hunter .20 .50
82 Tyronn Lue .20 .50
83 Michael Finley .30 .75
84 Dikembe Mutombo .30 .75
85 Zydrunas Ilgauskas .25 .60
86 Pat Garrity .20 .50
87 Damon Stoudamire .30 .75
88 Shareef Abdur-Rahim .25 .60
89 Matt Harpring .25 .60
90 Michael Dickerson .20 .50
91 Steve Smith .20 .50
92 Bison Dele .20 .50
93 Glenn Robinson .25 .60
94 Antawn Jamison .30 .75
95 Glen Rice .30 .75
96 Vlade Divac .30 .75
97 Vladimir Stepania .20 .50
98 Kornell David RC .30 .75
99 Shawn Kemp .30 .75
100 Kevin Garnett .60 1.50
101 Tim Thomas .25 .60
102 Mike Bibby .30 .75
103 Maurice Taylor .20 .50
104 Gary Payton .30 .75
105 Voshon Lenard .20 .50
106 Theo Ratliff .25 .60
107 Hakeem Olajuwon .40 1.00
108 Joe Smith .25 .60
109 Toni Kukoc .30 .75
110 Stephon Marbury .25 .60
111 Anthony Mason .20 .50
112 Anfernee Hardaway .50 1.25
113 Juwan Howard .25 .60
114 Charles Barkley .50 1.25
115 Antoine Walker .30 .75
116 Donyell Marshall .20 .50
117 Tom Gugliotta .20 .50
118 Rasheed Wallace .30 .75
119 Tracy McGrady .50 1.25
120 Paul Pierce .50 1.25
121 Sean Elliott .30 .75
122 Bryant Reeves .20 .50
123 Michael Doleac .20 .50
124 Chris Webber .30 .75
125 David Robinson .50 1.25
126 Steve Francis RC 1.50 4.00
127 Elton Brand RC 1.50 4.00
128 Wally Szczerbiak RC 1.25 3.00
129 Richard Hamilton RC 1.50 4.00
130 Shawn Marion RC 1.50 4.00
131 Trajan Langdon RC .60 1.50
132 Corey Maggette RC 1.25 3.00
133 Dion Glover RC .60 1.50
134 James Posey RC .60 1.50
135 Lamar Odom RC 2.00 5.00
136 Aleksandar Radojevic RC .60 1.50
137 Cal Bowdler RC .60 1.50
138 Scott Padgett RC .60 1.50
139 Jumaine Jones RC .60 1.50
140 Jonathan Bender RC .60 1.50
141 Tim James RC .60 1.50
142 Jason Terry RC 1.50 4.00
143 Quincy Lewis RC .60 1.50
144 William Avery RC .60 1.50
145 Galen Young RC .60 1.50
146 Ron Artest RC 1.50 4.00
147 Kenny Thomas RC .60 1.50
148 Devean George RC .60 1.50
149 Andre Miller RC 1.50 4.00
150 Baron Davis RC 2.00 5.00

1999-00 Ultra Gold Medallion

Randomly inserted in hobby packs only at one per pack for veterans and one in 35 for rookies, this 150-card set parallels the base set. The cards feature gold foil. To ascertain values on individual cards, please refer to the multiplier in the header, coupled with the value of the base card.
*STARS: .75X TO 2X BASE CARD HI
*RCs: .6X TO 1.5X BASE HI

1999-00 Ultra Masterpieces

Randomly inserted in hobby packs, this 150-card set parallels the base set. There were only one card of each player produced.

1999-00 Ultra Platinum Medallion

Randomly inserted in hobby packs, this 150-card set parallels the base set. The veterans were serially numbered to 50, while the rookies were serially numbered to just 25. To ascertain values on individual cards, please refer to the multiplier in the header, coupled with the value of the base card.
*STARS: 20X TO 50X BASE CARD HI
*RCs: 10X TO 25X BASE HI
40 Shaquille O'Neal 75.00 150.00
50 Kobe Bryant 150.00 300.00

1999-00 Ultra Feel the Game

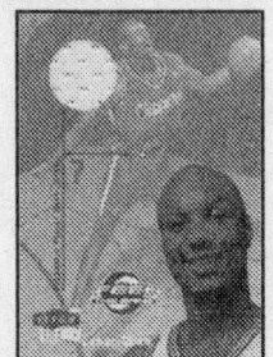

Randomly inserted in packs, this 15-card set featues cards with pieces of player worn memorabilia from the top rookies in the NBA. The cards are not numbered and listed below in alphabetical order. Each player contains a different print run and those are noted below next to the player's name.
1 Steve Francis 4.00 10.00
2 Richard Hamilton 4.00 10.00
3 Jonathan Bender 2.00 5.00
4 Baron Davis 5.00 12.00
5 Wally Szczerbiak 3.00 8.00
6 Lamar Odom 5.00 12.00
7 Andre Miller 4.00 10.00
8 Jason Terry 4.00 10.00
9 Trajan Langdon 2.00 5.00
10 Corey Maggette 3.00 8.00
11 Cal Bowdler 2.00 5.00
12 James Posey 2.00 5.00
13 Tim James 2.00 5.00
14 Scott Padgett 2.00 5.00
15 Jumaine Jones 2.00 5.00

1999-00 Ultra Fresh Ink

Randomly inserted in packs, this 56-card set features autographs from top NBA stars and rookies. The cards are not numbered, so they are listed below alphabetically. Individual print runs are listed after each card.
1 Ray Allen/300 20.00 50.00
2 Ron Artest/1000 6.00 15.00
3 William Avery/1000 2.50 6.00
4 Jonathan Bender/500 2.50 6.00
5 Mike Bibby/550 5.00 12.00
6 Calvin Booth/975 2.50 6.00
7 Cal Bowdler/1000 2.50 6.00
8 Bruce Bowen/1000 4.00 10.00
9 Marcus Camby/750 5.00 12.00
10 John Celestand/1000 2.50 6.00
11 Baron Davis/475 8.00 20.00
12 Michael Dickerson/975 2.50 6.00
13 Michael Doleac/1000 2.50 6.00
14 Bryce Drew/1000 2.50 6.00
15 Evan Eschmeyer/1000 2.50 6.00
16 Steve Francis/500 6.00 15.00
17 Pat Garrity/600 2.50 6.00
18 Devean George/1000 2.50 6.00
19 Dion Glover/875 2.50 6.00
20 Brian Grant/500 2.50 6.00
21 Richard Hamilton/750 6.00 15.00
22 Juwan Howard/225 6.00 15.00
23 Larry Hughes/750 5.00 12.00
24 Jumaine Jones/1000 2.50 6.00
25 Eddie Jones/250 10.00 25.00
26 Raef LaFrentz/500 2.50 6.00
27 Quincy Lewis/1000 2.50 6.00
28 Felipe Lopez/1000 2.50 6.00
29 Corey Maggette/250 8.00 20.00
30 Stephon Marbury/400 5.00 12.00
31 Shawn Marion/1000 6.00 15.00
32 Lamar Odom/350 8.00 20.00
33 Shaquille O'Neal/200 75.00 150.00
34 Scottie Pippen/130 100.00 200.00
35 James Posey/1000 2.50 6.00
36 Aleksandar Radojevic/1000 2.50 6.00
37 David Robinson/155 40.00 100.00
38 Jalen Rose/500 8.00 20.00
39 Wally Szczerbiak/500 5.00 12.00
40 Jerry Stackhouse/650 6.00 15.00
41 Maurice Taylor/400 2.50 6.00
42 Jason Terry/1000 6.00 15.00
43 Robert Traylor/1000 2.50 6.00
44 Keith Van Horn/500 6.00 15.00
45 Antoine Walker/245 8.00 20.00
46 Chris Webber/200 100.00 200.00

1999-00 Ultra Good Looks

Randomly inserted in packs at one in six, this 15-card set feature players who put themselves in a position to take over the game at any time. Card fronts feature all-foil.
COMPLETE SET (15) 6.00 15.00
1 Grant Hill .60 1.50
2 Kevin Garnett 1.00 2.50
3 Richard Hamilton .75 2.00
4 Larry Hughes .40 1.00
5 Shaquille O'Neal 1.25 3.00
6 Kobe Bryant 2.50 6.00
7 Antoine Walker .50 1.25
8 Lamar Odom 1.00 2.50
9 Allen Iverson 1.00 2.50
10 Scottie Pippen .75 2.00
11 Ron Mercer .40 1.00
12 Anfernee Hardaway .75 2.00
13 Chris Webber .50 1.25
14 Jason Williams .60 1.50
15 Baron Davis 1.00 2.50

1999-00 Ultra Heir to the Throne

Randomly inserted in packs at one in 24, this 10-card set features the best young players in the NBA on a clear holo-pattern crown background with silver foil stamping.
COMPLETE SET (10) 6.00 15.00
1 Allen Iverson 1.50 4.00
2 Keith Van Horn .60 1.50
3 Paul Pierce 1.25 3.00
4 Stephon Marbury .60 1.50
5 Vince Carter 1.50 4.00
6 Tim Duncan 1.50 4.00
7 Ron Mercer .60 1.50
8 Antawn Jamison .75 2.00
9 Shaquille O'Neal 2.00 5.00
10 Grant Hill 1.00 2.50

1999-00 Ultra Millennium Men

Randomly inserted in hobby packs, this 15-card set features young stars who will take the league to new levels in the next millennium. Card fronts feature a translucent lenticular patterned plastic with silver foil stamping. The cards are serially numbered to 100.
1 Allen Iverson 50.00 125.00
2 Paul Pierce 40.00 100.00
3 Steve Francis 40.00 100.00
4 Kobe Bryant 250.00 500.00
5 Vince Carter 60.00 150.00
6 Ron Mercer 20.00 50.00
7 Jason Williams 30.00 80.00
8 Elton Brand 40.00 100.00
9 Grant Hill 30.00 80.00
10 Tim Duncan 50.00 125.00
11 Stephon Marbury 20.00 50.00
12 Keith Van Horn 20.00 50.00
13 Kevin Garnett 50.00 125.00
14 Antawn Jamison 25.00 60.00
15 Antoine Walker 25.00 60.00

1999-00 Ultra Parquet Players

Randomly inserted in packs at one in 72, this 15-card set features players you want on the court when the game is on the line. The fronts feature a debossed parquet pattern floor background with gold foil stamping.
COMPLETE SET (15) 50.00 100.00
1 Kobe Bryant 12.00 30.00
2 Keith Van Horn 2.00 5.00
3 Tim Duncan 5.00 12.00
4 Shaquille O'Neal 6.00 15.00
5 Kevin Garnett 5.00 12.00
6 Jason Williams 3.00 8.00
7 Vince Carter 5.00 12.00
8 Stephon Marbury 2.00 5.00
9 Paul Pierce 4.00 10.00
10 Scottie Pippen 4.00 10.00
11 Baron Davis 5.00 12.00
12 Antoine Walker 2.50 6.00
13 Larry Hughes 2.00 5.00
14 Antawn Jamison 2.50 6.00
15 Elton Brand 4.00 10.00

1999-00 Ultra World Premiere

Randomly inserted in packs at one in 12, this 10-card set highlights the top rookies from the 99-00 season. The cards feature die cutting and foil etching.
COMPLETE SET (10) 4.00 10.00
1 Elton Brand .75 2.00
2 Andre Miller .75 2.00
3 Baron Davis 1.00 2.50
4 Steve Francis .75 2.00
5 Richard Hamilton .75 2.00
6 Jason Terry .75 2.00
7 Jonathan Bender .30 .75
8 Trajan Langdon .30 .75
9 Wally Szczerbiak .60 1.50
10 Lamar Odom 1.00 2.50

2000-01 Ultra

The 2000-01 Ultra product was released in November,2000 as a 225-card set. The set features 200 veterans, and 25 rookies (serial numbered to 2999). Each pack contained ten cards and carried a suggested retail price of $2.99.
COMPLETE SET w/o RC (200) 15.00 40.00
1 Vince Carter .60 1.50
2 Antawn Jamison .30 .75
3 Shaquille O'Neal .75 2.00
4 Paul Pierce .40 1.00
5 Antonio McDyess .25 .60
6 Scott Burrell .20 .50
7 Elton Brand .30 .75
8 Lamar Odom .30 .75
9 Nick Van Exel .25 .60
10 Kobe Bryant 1.50 4.00
11 Reggie Miller .30 .75
12 Sam Cassell .25 .60
13 Darrell Armstrong .20 .50
14 Rasheed Wallace .30 .75
15 Charles Oakley .25 .60
16 David Wesley .20 .50
17 Al Harrington .25 .60
18 Latrell Sprewell .25 .60
19 Rick Brunson .20 .50
20 Steve Smith .25 .60
21 Antonio Davis .20 .50
22 Michael Finley .30 .75
23 Shandon Anderson .20 .50
24 Danny Fortson .20 .50
25 Kerry Kittles .20 .50
26 Anfernee Hardaway .50 1.25
27 Vin Baker .25 .60
28 Calvin Booth .20 .50
29 Haywoode Workman .20 .50
30 Dickey Simpkins .20 .50
31 Jerome Williams .20 .50
32 Ron Artest .30 .75
33 Dennis Scott .20 .50
34 Ron Mercer .20 .50
35 Chris Webber .30 .75
36 Bryon Russell .20 .50
37 Dale Davis .20 .50
38 Dirk Nowitzki .50 1.25
39 Steve Francis .30 .75
40 Glen Rice .25 .60
41 Stephon Marbury .25 .60
42 Jason Kidd .50 1.25
43 Brent Barry .20 .50
44 Richard Hamilton .25 .60
45 Antoine Walker .25 .60
46 Gary Trent .20 .50
47 Cuttino Mobley .25 .60
48 P.J. Brown .20 .50
49 Elliot Perry .20 .50
50 Shawn Marion .30 .75
51 Horace Grant .25 .60
52 Juwan Howard .25 .60
53 Elden Campbell .20 .50
54 Erick Strickland .20 .50
55 Hakeem Olajuwon .40 1.00
56 Anthony Carter .20 .50
57 Keith Van Horn .25 .60
58 Clifford Robinson .20 .50
59 Ruben Patterson .20 .50
60 Mitch Richmond .25 .60
61 Jason Terry .30 .75
62 Andre Miller .25 .60
63 Vonteego Cummings .20 .50
64 Joe Smith .25 .60
65 Toni Kukoc .25 .60
66 Sean Elliott .25 .60
67 Michael Dickerson .20 .50
68 Derrick Coleman .25 .60
69 Shawn Bradley .20 .50
70 Kenny Thomas .20 .50
71 Tim Hardaway .30 .75
72 Rex Chapman .20 .50
73 Gary Payton .30 .75
74 Jahidi White .20 .50
75 Baron Davis .30 .75
76 Chauncey Billups .30 .75
77 Moochie Norris .20 .50
78 Dan Majerle .25 .60
79 Marcus Camby .25 .60
80 Rodney Rogers .20 .50
81 Rashard Lewis .30 .75
82 Laron Profit .20 .50
83 Ricky Davis .25 .60
84 Keon Clark .20 .50
85 Anthony Miller .20 .50
86 Jamal Mashburn .25 .60
87 Chris Childs .20 .50
88 Brian Grant .20 .50
89 Muggsy Bogues .25 .60
90 Randy Brown .20 .50
91 Tariq Abdul-Wahad .20 .50
92 Lindsey Hunter .20 .50
93 Rik Smits .20 .50
94 Glenn Robinson .25 .60
95 Michael Doleac .20 .50
96 Quincy Lewis .20 .50
97 Grant Hill .40 1.00
98 Jalen Rose .25 .60
99 Ervin Johnson .20 .50
100 Chucky Atkins .20 .50
101 Jermaine O'Neal .30 .75
102 Howard Eisley .20 .50
103 Kenny Anderson .25 .60
104 Lamond Murray .20 .50
105 Adonal Foyle .20 .50
106 Derek Fisher .30 .75
107 Wally Szczerbiak .25 .60
108 Todd MacCulloch .20 .50
109 Avery Johnson .25 .60
110 Othella Harrington .20 .50
111 Tony Battie .20 .50
112 Bob Sura .20 .50
113 Larry Hughes .25 .60
114 Rick Fox .25 .60
115 Travis Best .20 .50
116 Theo Ratliff .20 .50
117 David Robinson .50 1.25
118 Felipe Lopez .20 .50
119 John Amaechi .20 .50
120 George Lynch .20 .50
121 Christian Laettner .20 .50
122 Derek Anderson .20 .50
123 Tim Thomas .20 .50
124 Matt Harpring .25 .60
125 Nick Anderson .20 .50
126 Karl Malone .40 1.00
127 Dion Glover .20 .50
128 Wesley Person .20 .50
129 Mikki Moore RC .30 .75
130 Michael Olowokandi .20 .50
131 William Avery .20 .50
132 Bo Outlaw .20 .50
133 Jason Williams .30 .75
134 John Stockton .40 1.00
135 Adrian Griffin .20 .50
136 Hubert Davis .20 .50
137 Donyell Marshall .20 .50
138 Travis Knight .20 .50
139 Kendall Gill .20 .50
140 Tom Gugliotta .20 .50
141 Malik Rose .20 .50
142 Isaac Austin .20 .50
143 Alan Henderson .20 .50
144 Shawn Kemp .30 .75
145 Terry Mills .20 .50
146 Maurice Taylor .20 .50
147 Terrell Brandon .20 .50
148 Matt Geiger .20 .50
149 Corliss Williamson .20 .50
150 Jacque Vaughn .20 .50
151 Dikembe Mutombo .30 .75
152 Trajan Langdon .20 .50
153 Jason Caffey .20 .50
154 Tyrone Nesby .30 .75
155 Bobby Jackson .20 .50
156 Allen Iverson .60 1.50
157 Mario Elie .20 .50
158 Mike Bibby .30 .75
159 Robert Horry .25 .60
160 James Posey .20 .50
161 Mark Jackson .25 .60
162 Ray Allen .30 .75
163 Charlie Ward .20 .50
164 Damon Stoudamire .25 .60
165 Tracy McGrady .50 1.25
166 Bimbo Coles .20 .50
167 Chucky Brown .20 .50
168 Jerry Stackhouse .25 .60
169 Greg Ostertag .20 .50
170 Radoslav Nesterovic .20 .50
171 Corey Maggette .25 .60
172 Vlade Divac .25 .60
173 Scott Padgett .20 .50
174 Anthony Mason .20 .50
175 Raef LaFrentz .20 .50
176 Austin Croshere .20 .50
177 Mark Strickland .20 .50
178 Allan Houston .25 .60
179 Arvydas Sabonis .25 .60
180 Doug Christie .20 .50
181 Jim Jackson .20 .50
182 Brevin Knight .20 .50
183 Mookie Blaylock .25 .60
184 Chris Herren .20 .50
185 Kevin Garnett .60 1.50
186 Tyrone Hill .20 .50
187 Tim Duncan .60 1.50
188 Shareef Abdur-Rahim .25 .60
189 Eddie Jones .30 .75
190 Jonathan Bender .20 .50
191 Alonzo Mourning .40 1.00
192 Patrick Ewing .40 1.00
193 Scottie Pippen .50 1.25
194 Scot Pollard .20 .50
195 Cedric Ceballos .20 .50
196 Clarence Weatherspoon .20 .50
197 Jamie Feick .20 .50
198 Eric Snow .20 .50
199 Ron Harper .25 .60
200 Bryant Reeves .20 .50
201 Chris Mihm RC .75 2.00
202 Joel Przybilla RC .75 2.00
203 Kenyon Martin RC 2.00 5.00
204 Stromile Swift RC .75 2.00
205 Etan Thomas RC .75 2.00
206 Jason Collier RC .75 2.00
207 Marcus Fizer RC .75 2.00
208 Mateen Cleaves RC .75 2.00
209 Dan Langhi RC .75 2.00
210 Mike Miller RC 1.50 4.00
211 Jabari Smith RC .75 2.00
212 Hanno Mottola RC .75 2.00
213 Chris Porter RC .75 2.00
214 Desmond Mason RC 1.00 2.50
215 Erick Barkley RC .75 2.00
216 Donnell Harvey RC .75 2.00
217 DerMarr Johnson RC .75 2.00
218 Jerome Moiso RC .75 2.00
219 Quentin Richardson RC 1.25 3.00
220 Courtney Alexander RC .75 2.00
221 Michael Redd RC 2.00 5.00
222 Morris Peterson RC .75 2.00
223 Darius Miles RC .75 2.00
224 Jamal Crawford RC 1.25 3.00
225 Keyon Dooling RC .75 2.00

2000-01 Ultra Gold Medallion

Randomly inserted in packs at one per pack for veterans and one in 24 for rookies, this 225-card set parallels the base set. The cards feature gold foil. To ascertain values on individual cards, please refer to the multiplier in the header, coupled with the value of the base card.

2000-01 Ultra Platinum Medallion

Randomly inserted in packs, this 225-card set parallels the base set. The cards feature a planium background. Veteran cards (1-200) were serially numbered to 50, while rookie cards (201-225) were serially numbered to 25. To ascertain values on individual cards, please refer to the multipliers in the header below, coupled with the value of the base card.
*STARS: 20X TO 50X BASE CARD HI
10 Kobe Bryant 150.00 350.00
35 Chris Webber 20.00 50.00

2000-01 Ultra Air Club for Men

Randomly inserted in packs at one in six, this 15-card set features aeriel artists whose play changes the game. Card backs carry an "AC" prefix.
COMPLETE SET (15) 7.50 15.00
*PLATINUM: 8X TO 20X AIR CLUB HI
PLATINUM: PRINT RUN 100 SERIAL #'d SETS
AC1 Kobe Bryant 2.50 6.00
AC2 Lamar Odom .40 1.00
AC3 Vince Carter .75 2.00
AC4 Tim Duncan .75 2.00
AC5 Grant Hill .50 1.25
AC6 Tracy McGrady .60 1.50
AC7 Kevin Garnett .75 2.00
AC8 Steve Francis .40 1.00
AC9 Allen Iverson .75 2.00
AC10 Jason Williams .40 1.00
AC11 Shaquille O'Neal 1.00 2.50
AC12 Jason Kidd .60 1.50
AC13 Elton Brand .40 1.00
AC14 Eddie Jones .40 1.00
AC15 Stephon Marbury .30 .75

2000-01 Ultra Vince Carter Rookie Remnants

This three-card insert was randomly inserted into 2000-01 Fleer products. The set includes a Vince Carter floor card (numbered to 100), a Vince Carter floor/jersey card (numbered to 15), and finally an autographed Vince Carter floor/jersey card (numbered 1/1).
NNO Vince Carter FLR/100 12.50 30.00

2000-01 Ultra Slam Show

Randomly inserted in packs at one in 24, this 10-card set features shots from the 1999-2000 NBA Slam Dunk contest. Card backs carry a "SS" prefix.
COMPLETE SET (10) 7.50 15.00
*PLATINUM: 3X TO 8X SLAM SHOW HI
PLATINUM: PRINT RUN 100 SERIAL #'d SETS
SS1 Steve Francis .75 2.00
SS2 Tracy McGrady 1.25 3.00
SS3 Jerry Stackhouse .60 1.50
SS4 Larry Hughes .60 1.50
SS5 Ricky Davis .60 1.50
SS6 Vince Carter 1.50 4.00
SS7 Vince Carter 1.50 4.00
SS8 Vince Carter 1.50 4.00
SS9 Vince Carter 1.50 4.00
SS10 Vince Carter 1.50 4.00

2000-01 Ultra Thrillinium

Randomly inserted in packs at one in 48 packs, this 10-card set features players leading the NBA in the new millennium. Card backs carry a "T" prefix.
COMPLETE SET (10) 25.00 50.00
*PLATINUM: 2.5X TO 6X THRILLINIUM HI
PLATINUM: PRINT RUN 100 SERIAL #'d SETS
T1 Vince Carter 3.00 8.00
T2 Kobe Bryant 10.00 25.00
T3 Tim Duncan 3.00 8.00
T4 Kevin Garnett 3.00 8.00
T5 Allen Iverson 3.00 8.00
T6 Jason Williams 1.50 4.00
T7 Shaquille O'Neal 4.00 10.00
T8 Lamar Odom 1.50 4.00
T9 Eddie Jones 1.50 4.00
T10 Stephon Marbury 1.25 3.00

2000-01 Ultra Two Ball

Randomly inserted in packs at one in three, this 15-card set focuses on second year players. Card backs carry a "TB" prefix.
COMPLETE SET (15) 2.00 5.00
*PLATINUM: 8X TO 20X TWO BALL HI
PLATINUM: PRINT RUN 100 SERIAL #'d SETS
TB1 Lamar Odom .30 .75
TB2 Elton Brand .30 .75
TB3 Steve Francis .30 .75
TB4 Adrian Griffin .20 .50
TB5 Todd MacCulloch .20 .50
TB6 Andre Miller .25 .60
TB7 James Posey .20 .50
TB8 Wally Szczerbiak .25 .60
TB9 Ron Artest .30 .75
TB10 Corey Maggette .25 .60
TB11 Shawn Marion .30 .75
TB12 Chucky Atkins .20 .50
TB13 Vonteego Cummings .20 .50
TB14 Kenny Thomas .20 .50
TB15 Richard Hamilton .25 .60

2000-01 Ultra Year 3

Randomly inserted in packs at one in 12, this 10-card set showcases players in their third year, from the class of 1998-99. Card backs carry a "YT" prefix.
COMPLETE SET (10) 2.50 6.00
*PLATINUM: 5X TO 12X YEAR 3 HI
PLATINUM: PRINT RUN 100 SERIAL #'d SETS
YT1 Mike Bibby .50 1.25
YT2 Michael Dickerson .30 .75
YT3 Larry Hughes .40 1.00
YT4 Raef LaFrentz .30 .75
YT5 Dirk Nowitzki .75 2.00
YT6 Michael Olowokandi .30 .75
YT7 Paul Pierce .60 1.50
YT8 Jason Williams .50 1.25
YT9 Vince Carter 1.00 2.50
YT10 Antawn Jamison .50 1.25

2001-02 Ultra

Issued in mid-November of 2001, Ultra boasts a 181-card base set divided up into 150 base veteran cards and 31 short printed rookie cards sequentially numbered to 2222. The last six cards in the set were inserted in Fleer Focus as Ultra update and are numbered 1U to 6U-these cards are also sequentially numbered to 2222. The card design places full color player action photos on a borderless card design with a foil box centered at the bottom containing the player's name and team logo in silver foil. Ultra was issued in both 16 and six box cases where boxes contained 24 packs of ten cards each.
COMP.SET w/o SP's (150) 10.00 25.00
COMP.UPDATE SET (6) 8.00 20.00
1 Vince Carter .50 1.25
2 Allen Iverson .60 1.50
3 Jerry Stackhouse .25 .60
4 Travis Best .20 .50
5 Eddie Jones .25 .60
6 Felipe Lopez .20 .50
7 Antonio Daniels .20 .50
8 A.J. Guyton .20 .50
9 Quentin Richardson .25 .60
10 Charlie Ward .20 .50
11 Ron Mercer .20 .50
12 Shandon Anderson .20 .50
13 Antawn Jamison .30 .75
14 Darius Miles .20 .50
15 Anthony Mason .20 .50
16 Latrell Sprewell .25 .60
17 Scottie Pippen .50 1.25
18 Shammond Williams .20 .50
19 P.J. Brown .20 .50
20 Dirk Nowitzki .50 1.25
21 Mateen Cleaves .20 .50
22 Tim Hardaway .30 .75
23 Christian Laettner .20 .50
24 Toni Kukoc .25 .60
25 Bob Sura .20 .50
26 Kobe Bryant 1.50 4.00
27 Wally Szczerbiak .25 .60
28 Darrell Armstrong .20 .50
29 Chris Webber .30 .75
30 David Wesley .20 .50
31 Michael Finley .30 .75
32 Jermaine O'Neal .30 .75
33 Jason Kidd .50 1.25
34 Tony Delk .20 .50
35 Avery Johnson .25 .60
36 Elden Campbell .20 .50
37 Lamond Murray .20 .50
38 Ben Wallace .30 .75
39 Jalen Rose .25 .60
40 Michael Dickerson .20 .50
41 Shawn Marion .30 .75
42 Jahidi White .20 .50
43 Jamal Mashburn .25 .60
44 Trajan Langdon .20 .50
45 Reggie Miller .30 .75
46 Stromile Swift .20 .50
47 Keith Van Horn .25 .60
48 Tom Gugliotta .20 .50
49 Brent Barry .20 .50
50 Courtney Alexander .20 .50
51 Antonio McDyess .25 .60
52 Robert Horry .25 .60
53 Ervin Johnson .20 .50
54 Speedy Claxton .20 .50
55 Bryon Russell .20 .50
56 Baron Davis .30 .75
57 Robert Traylor .20 .50
58 Chucky Atkins .20 .50
59 Stephon Marbury .25 .60
60 Desmond Mason .25 .60
61 Tyrone Nesby .20 .50
62 Brevin Knight .20 .50
63 Kenyon Martin .30 .75
64 Jumaine Jones .20 .50
65 Rashard Lewis .30 .75
66 Kenny Anderson .25 .60
67 Andre Miller .25 .60
68 Joe Smith .25 .60
69 Kelvin Cato .20 .50
70 Jason Williams .25 .60
71 Marcus Camby .25 .60
72 Eric Snow .20 .50
73 Gary Payton .30 .75
74 Robert Pack .20 .50
75 Brian Cardinal .20 .50
76 Sam Cassell .25 .60
77 Allan Houston .25 .60
78 Anfernee Hardaway .50 1.25
79 Morris Peterson .20 .50
80 Chris Mihm .20 .50
81 Elton Brand .30 .75
82 Glenn Robinson .25 .60
83 Damon Stoudamire .25 .60
84 Alvin Williams .20 .50
85 Paul Pierce .40 1.00
86 James Posey .20 .50
87 Cuttino Mobley .25 .60
88 Tim Thomas .20 .50
89 Dikembe Mutombo .30 .75
90 Tim Duncan .60 1.50
91 John Starks .20 .50

Antoine Walker .25 .60
Moochie Norris .20 .50
Dalibor Bagaric .20 .50
Ray Allen .30 .75
David Robinson .50 1.25
Shareef Abdur-Rahim .25 .60
Wang Zhizhi .25 .60
Chris Porter .20 .50
) Chauncey Billups .30 .75
1 Tracy McGrady .50 1.25
2 Michael Jordan 5.00 12.00
3 Jerome Williams .20 .50
4 Jason Terry .30 .75
5 Calvin Booth .20 .50
6 Shaquille O'Neal .75 2.00
7 Kevin Garnett .60 1.50
8 Doug Christie .20 .50
9 Karl Malone .40 1.00
0 Steve Nash .50 1.25
1 Austin Croshere .20 .50
2 Alonzo Mourning .40 1.00
3 Dan Majerle .25 .60
4 Malik Rose .20 .50
5 Richard Hamilton .25 .60
6 DerMarr Johnson .20 .50
7 Raef LaFrentz .20 .50
8 Derek Fisher .25 .60
9 Vlade Divac .25 .60
0 John Stockton .40 1.00
1 Dion Glover .20 .50
2 Voshon Lenard .20 .50
3 Steve Francis .30 .75
4 Darvin Ham .20 .50
5 Aaron McKie .20 .50
6 Peja Stojakovic .30 .75
7 Ron Artest .30 .75
8 Keyon Dooling .20 .50
9 Anthony Carter .20 .50
0 Kurt Thomas .20 .50
1 Rasheed Wallace .30 .75
2 Theo Ratliff .20 .50
3 Eric Piatkowski .20 .50
4 Terrell Brandon .20 .50
5 Mike Miller .30 .75
6 Mike Bibby .30 .75
7 Antonio Davis .20 .50
8 Lamar Odom .30 .75
9 Eddie House .20 .50
0 Nick Van Exel .25 .60
1 Rick Fox .25 .60
2 Juwan Howard .25 .60
3 Hedo Turkoglu .30 .75
4 Donyell Marshall .20 .50
5 Marcus Fizer .20 .50
6 Larry Hughes .25 .60
7 Steve Smith .25 .60
8 Brian Grant .20 .50
9 Grant Hill .40 1.00
0 Derek Anderson .20 .50
1 Kwame Brown RC 1.25 3.00
2 Eddie Griffin RC 1.25 3.00
3 Eddy Curry RC 2.00 5.00
4 Jamaal Tinsley RC 1.50 4.00
5 Jason Richardson RC 2.50 6.00
6 Shane Battier RC 2.50 6.00
7 Troy Murphy RC 2.00 5.00
8 Richard Jefferson RC 2.50 6.00
9 DeSagana Diop RC 1.25 3.00
0 Tyson Chandler RC 2.00 5.00
1 Joe Johnson RC 3.00 8.00
2 Zach Randolph RC 3.00 8.00
3 Andrei Kirilenko RC 3.00 8.00
4 Loren Woods RC 1.25 3.00
5 Jason Collins RC 1.25 3.00
6 Rodney White RC 1.25 3.00
7 Jeryl Sasser RC 1.25 3.00
8 Kirk Haston RC 1.25 3.00
9 Pau Gasol RC 4.00 10.00
0 Kedrick Brown RC 1.25 3.00
1 Steven Hunter RC 1.25 3.00
2 Michael Bradley RC 1.25 3.00
3 Joseph Forte RC 1.25 3.00
4 Brandon Armstrong RC 1.25 3.00
5 Primoz Brezec RC 1.25 3.00
6U Gerald Wallace RC 2.00 5.00
7U Tony Parker RC 5.00 12.00
8U Vladimir Radmanovic RC 1.25 3.00
9U Trenton Hassell RC 1.25 3.00
0U Zeljko Rebraca RC 1.25 3.00
1U Oscar Torres RC 1.25 3.00

2001-02 Ultra Gold Medallion

andomly inserted in packs at the rate of one in one, is 175-card set parallels the base Ultra set enhanced th an all gold background.
GOLD STARS: .6X TO 1.5X BASE CARD HI
GOLD RC's: 1.5X TO 4X BASE CARD HI

2001-02 Ultra 02 Good

serted in packs at the rate of one in 20, this 20-card t places player action photos on the left side of the rd with a colored background that extends two thirds the way across the card. The right side features "02 ood" in bronze foil.
OMPLETE SET (20) 10.00 20.00
Vince Carter 1.25 3.00
A Vince Carter AU 25.00 50.00
Allen Iverson 1.50 4.00
Shawn Marion .75 2.00
Jalen Rose .60 1.50
Steve Francis .75 2.00
Kenyon Martin .75 2.00
Sam Cassell .60 1.50
Darius Miles .50 1.25
Mike Miller .75 2.00
0 Jason Terry .75 2.00
1 Baron Davis .75 2.00
2 Lamar Odom .75 2.00
3 Latrell Sprewell .60 1.50
4 Morris Peterson .50 1.25
15 Antonio Davis .50 1.25
16 Ray Allen .75 2.00
17 Rashard Lewis .75 2.00
18 Desmond Mason .60 1.50
19 Antonio McDyess .60 1.50
20 Keith Van Horn .60 1.50

2001-02 Ultra 02 Good Game Worn

Inserted in packs at the rate of one in 157, this 20-card set parallels the set design of the base 02 Good set enhanced with a swatch of player worn jersey.
1 Vince Carter 6.00 15.00
2 Allen Iverson 8.00 20.00
3 Shawn Marion 4.00 10.00
4 Jalen Rose 3.00 8.00
5 Steve Francis 4.00 10.00
6 Kenyon Martin 4.00 10.00
7 Sam Cassell 3.00 8.00
8 Darius Miles 2.50 6.00
9 Mike Miller 4.00 10.00
10 Jason Terry 4.00 10.00
11 Baron Davis 4.00 10.00
12 Lamar Odom 4.00 10.00
13 Latrell Sprewell 3.00 8.00
14 Morris Peterson 2.50 6.00
15 Antonio Davis 2.50 6.00
16 Ray Allen 4.00 10.00
17 Rashard Lewis 4.00 10.00
18 Desmond Mason 3.00 8.00
19 Antonio McDyess 3.00 8.00
20 Keith Van Horn 3.00 8.00

2001-02 Ultra League Leaders

Randomly seeded in packs at the rate of one in 20, this 20-card set places two photos of each player on the card. The photo on the right is a full color action photo, and the photo of the left is a portrait style photo of the player's head. The cards have each player's team logo centered towards the left and bronze foil highlights. A Platinum medallion versions sequentially numbered to 25 was also inserted in packs.
COMPLETE SET (20) 10.00 20.00
*PLATINUM: 12X TO 30X HI
1 Vince Carter 1.25 3.00
2 Allen Iverson 1.50 4.00
3 Ray Allen .75 2.00
4 Reggie Miller .75 2.00
5 Karl Malone 1.00 2.50
6 Jalen Rose .60 1.50
7 Baron Davis .75 2.00
8 Tracy McGrady 1.25 3.00
9 Chris Webber .75 2.00
10 John Stockton 1.00 2.50
11 Dikembe Mutombo .75 2.00
12 Steve Francis .75 2.00
13 Andre Miller .60 1.50
14 Kenyon Martin .75 2.00
15 Mike Miller .75 2.00
16 Antonio Davis .50 1.25
17 Darius Miles .50 1.25
18 Latrell Sprewell .60 1.50
19 Cuttino Mobley .60 1.50
20 Lamar Odom .75 2.00

2001-02 Ultra League Leaders Game Worn

Inserted in packs, this 20-card set parallels the set design of the base League Leaders set enhanced with a swatch of player worn jersey. Each card is sequentially numbered to 450.
1 Vince Carter 6.00 15.00
2 Allen Iverson 8.00 20.00
3 Ray Allen 4.00 10.00
4 Reggie Miller 4.00 10.00
5 Karl Malone 5.00 12.00
6 Jalen Rose 3.00 8.00
7 Baron Davis 4.00 10.00
8 Tracy McGrady 6.00 15.00
9 Chris Webber 4.00 10.00
10 John Stockton 5.00 12.00
11 Dikembe Mutombo 4.00 10.00
12 Steve Francis 4.00 10.00
13 Andre Miller 3.00 8.00
14 Kenyon Martin 4.00 10.00
15 Mike Miller 4.00 10.00
16 Antonio Davis 2.50 6.00
17 Darius Miles 2.50 6.00
18 Latrell Sprewell 3.00 8.00
19 Cuttino Mobley 3.00 8.00
20 Lamar Odom 4.00 10.00

2001-02 Ultra On the Road Game Worn

Inserted in packs at the rate of one in 156, this 20-card set parallels the set design of the base On the Road set enhanced with a swatch of player worn jersey. A Platinum medallion versions sequentially numbered to 25 was also inserted in packs.
*PLATINUM: 2.5X TO 6X HI
1 Vince Carter 6.00 15.00
2 Morris Peterson 2.50 6.00
3 Rashard Lewis 4.00 10.00
4 Keith Van Horn 3.00 8.00
5 Cuttino Mobley 3.00 8.00
6 Tracy McGrady 6.00 15.00
7 Tom Gugliotta 2.50 6.00
8 Dikembe Mutombo 4.00 10.00
9 Stromile Swift 2.50 6.00
10 Mike Miller 4.00 10.00

2001-02 Ultra Triple Double Trouble

Randomly seeded in packs at the rate of one in 72, this 15-card set places a full color player action phot on the right of this horizontal design and the set name and player's name on the left in silver foil. A Platinum medallion versions sequentially numbered to 25 was also inserted in packs.
COMPLETE SET (15) 25.00 60.00
*PLATINUM: 4X TO 10X HI
1 Vince Carter 4.00 10.00
2 Steve Francis 2.50 6.00
3 Ray Allen 2.50 6.00
4 Chris Webber 2.50 6.00
5 Kobe Bryant 12.00 30.00
6 Kenyon Martin 2.50 6.00
7 Shaquille O'Neal 6.00 15.00
8 Kevin Garnett 5.00 12.00
9 Tracy McGrady 4.00 10.00
10 Baron Davis 2.50 6.00
11 Lamar Odom 2.50 6.00
12 Allen Iverson 5.00 12.00
13 Antoine Walker 2.00 5.00
14 Reggie Miller 2.50 6.00
15 Terrell Brandon 1.50 4.00

2001-02 Ultra Triple Double Trouble Game Worn

Inserted in packs at the rate of one in 157, this 12-card set parallels the set design of the base Triple Double Trouble set enhanced with a swatch of player worn jersey. Kobe Bryant, Shaquille O'Neal and Kevin Garnett do not have game worn versions.
1 Vince Carter 8.00 20.00
2 Steve Francis 5.00 12.00
3 Ray Allen 5.00 12.00
4 Chris Webber 5.00 12.00
6 Kenyon Martin 5.00 12.00
9 Tracy McGrady 8.00 20.00
10 Baron Davis 5.00 12.00
11 Lamar Odom 5.00 12.00
12 Allen Iverson 10.00 25.00
13 Antoine Walker 4.00 10.00
14 Reggie Miller 5.00 12.00
15 Terrell Brandon 3.00 8.00

2002-03 Ultra

Released in late August 2002, Ultra was packaged in 24-pack boxes with 10 cards per pack and carried a suggested retail price of $2.99. Base cards are borderless with the Fleer Ultra logo in the upper right hand corner and silver foil highlights at the bottom of the card including the player's name, position, team name and jersey number.
COMPLETE SET (210) 75.00 150.00
COMP.SET w/o RC's (180) 20.00 50.00
1 Vince Carter .50 1.25
2 Ben Wallace .30 .75
3 Tim Thomas .20 .50
4 Eric Snow .20 .50
5 Peja Stojakovic .30 .75
6 Andrei Kirilenko .30 .75
7 Dion Glover .20 .50
8 James Posey .20 .50
9 Kenny Thomas .20 .50
10 Michael Dickerson .20 .50
11 Charlie Ward .20 .50
12 Gary Payton .30 .75
13 Eddy Curry .25 .60
14 Rick Fox .25 .60
15 Joel Przybilla .20 .50
16 Aaron McKie .20 .50
17 Hedo Turkoglu .30 .75
18 Jarron Collins .20 .50
19 Jason Collins .20 .50
20 Nick Van Exel .25 .60
21 Reggie Miller .30 .75
22 Devean George .20 .50
23 Michael Jordan 2.50 6.00
24 Tony Parker .40 1.00
25 Robert Horry .25 .60
26 Wally Szczerbiak .25 .60
27 Dikembe Mutombo .30 .75
28 Scot Pollard .20 .50
29 Darrell Armstrong .20 .50
30 Jalen Rose .25 .60
31 Antawn Jamison .30 .75
32 Anfernee Hardaway .50 1.25
33 Paul Pierce .40 1.00
34 Juwan Howard .25 .60
35 Eddie Griffin .20 .50
36 Shane Battier .30 .75
37 Shandon Anderson .20 .50
38 Vladimir Radmanovic .20 .50
39 DerMarr Johnson .20 .50
40 Antonio McDyess .25 .60
41 Cuttino Mobley .25 .60
42 Stromile Swift .20 .50
43 Tracy McGrady .50 1.25
44 Charles Smith .20 .50
45 Shawn Marion .30 .75
46 P.J. Brown .20 .50
47 Wang Zhizhi .20 .50
48 Austin Croshere .20 .50
49 Ervin Johnson .20 .50
50 Jason Kidd .50 1.25
51 Tom Gugliotta .20 .50
52 Jamal Crawford .25 .60
53 Toni Kukoc .25 .60
54 Mengke Bateer .20 .50
55 Moochie Norris .20 .50
56 Jason Williams .25 .60
57 Mike Miller .30 .75
58 Steve Smith .25 .60
59 Shareef Abdur-Rahim .25 .60
60 Michael Finley .30 .75
61 Jermaine O'Neal .30 .75
62 Mark Madsen .20 .50
63 Troy Hudson .20 .50
64 David Robinson .50 1.25
65 Corliss Williamson .20 .50
66 Rodney Rogers .20 .50
67 Derek Fisher .25 .60
68 Anthony Carter .20 .50
69 Allan Houston .25 .60
70 Desmond Mason .25 .60
71 Brendan Haywood .20 .50
72 Tony Delk .20 .50
73 Ryan Bowen .20 .50
74 Danny Fortson .20 .50
75 Alonzo Mourning .40 1.00
76 Latrell Sprewell .25 .60
77 Rashard Lewis .30 .75
78 Courtney Alexander .20 .50
79 Marcus Fizer .20 .50
80 Jason Richardson .30 .75
81 Terrell Brandon .20 .50
82 Allen Iverson .50 1.25
83 Vlade Divac .25 .60
84 Jahidi White .20 .50
85 Eric Piatkowski .20 .50
86 Marc Jackson .20 .50
87 Pat Garrity .20 .50
88 Tim Duncan .60 1.50
89 Kwame Brown .20 .50
90 Andre Miller .25 .60
91 Troy Murphy .30 .75
92 John Stockton .40 1.00
93 Kenny Anderson .25 .60
94 Chris Mihm .20 .50
95 Larry Hughes .25 .60
96 Lamar Odom .30 .75
97 Brian Grant .20 .50
98 Marcus Camby .25 .60
99 Mike Bibby .30 .75
100 Joseph Forte .20 .50
101 Lamond Murray .20 .50
102 Darius Miles .20 .50
103 Eddie Jones .25 .60
104 Aaron Williams .20 .50
105 Derek Anderson .20 .50
106 Karl Malone .40 1.00
107 Jon Barry .20 .50
108 Tony Battie .20 .50
109 Jumaine Jones .20 .50
110 Corey Maggette .25 .60
111 Eddie House .20 .50
112 Theo Ratliff .20 .50
113 Scottie Pippen .50 1.25
114 Hakeem Olajuwon .40 1.00
115 Antoine Walker .25 .60
116 Tim Hardaway .30 .75
117 Steve Francis .30 .75
118 Lorenzen Wright .20 .50
119 Howard Eisley .20 .50
120 Brent Barry .20 .50
121 Baron Davis .30 .75
122 Michael Doleac .20 .50
123 Quentin Richardson .25 .60
124 LaPhonso Ellis .25 .60
125 Richard Jefferson .30 .75
126 Damon Stoudamire .25 .60
127 Alvin Williams .20 .50
128 Chucky Atkins .20 .50
129 Jamal Mashburn .25 .60
130 Wesley Person .20 .50
131 Elton Brand .30 .75
132 Ray Allen .30 .75
133 Kerry Kittles .20 .50
134 Rasheed Wallace .30 .75
135 Antonio Davis .20 .50
136 David Wesley .20 .50
137 Dirk Nowitzki .50 1.25
138 Rodney White .20 .50
139 Jamaal Tinsley .20 .50
140 Sam Cassell .25 .60
141 Keith Van Horn .25 .60
142 Ruben Patterson .20 .50
143 Jerome Williams .20 .50
144 Jason Terry .25 .60
145 Eduardo Najera .20 .50
146 Maurice Taylor .20 .50
147 Pau Gasol .40 1.00
148 Grant Hill .40 1.00
149 Antonio Daniels .20 .50
150 George Lynch .20 .50
151 Steve Nash .40 1.00
152 Al Harrington .25 .60
153 Anthony Mason .20 .50
154 Kenyon Martin .30 .75
155 Bonzi Wells .20 .50
156 Morris Peterson .20 .50
157 Eddie Robinson .20 .50
158 Kevin Garnett .60 1.50
159 Chris Webber .30 .75
160 John Amaechi .20 .50
161 Kobe Bryant 1.50 4.00
162 Joe Smith .25 .60
163 Speedy Claxton .20 .50
164 Doug Christie .20 .50
165 Richard Hamilton .25 .60
166 Tyson Chandler .25 .60
167 Gilbert Arenas .30 .75
168 Stephon Marbury .25 .60
169 Jamaal Magloire .20 .50
170 Raef LaFrentz .20 .50
171 Ron Mercer .20 .50
172 Glenn Robinson .25 .60
173 Chauncey Billups .30 .75
174 Iakovos Tsakalidis .20 .50
175 Vin Baker .25 .60
176 Joe Johnson .30 .75
177 Jerry Stackhouse .25 .60
178 Shaquille O'Neal .75 2.00
179 Derrick Coleman .25 .60
180 Bryon Russell .20 .50
181 Yao Ming RC 4.00 10.00
182 Jay Williams RC 1.50 4.00
183 Drew Gooden RC 2.00 5.00
184 DaJuan Wagner RC 1.25 3.00
185 Qyntel Woods RC 1.25 3.00
186 Chris Wilcox RC 1.25 3.00
187 Curtis Borchardt RC 1.25 3.00
188 Nikoloz Tskitishvili RC 1.25 3.00
189 Caron Butler RC 2.00 5.00
190 Nene Hilario RC 1.50 4.00
191 Jared Jeffries RC 1.25 3.00
192 Mike Dunleavy RC 1.50 4.00
193 Kareem Rush RC 1.25 3.00
194 Amare Stoudemire RC 3.00 8.00
195 Melvin Ely RC 1.25 3.00
196 Marcus Haislip RC 1.25 3.00
197 Jiri Welsch RC 1.25 3.00
198 Frank Williams RC 1.25 3.00
199 John Salmons RC 1.50 4.00
200 Gordan Giricek RC 1.25 3.00
201 Ryan Humphrey RC 1.25 3.00
202 Casey Jacobsen RC 1.25 3.00
203 Carlos Boozer RC 2.50 6.00
204 Manu Ginobili RC 3.00 8.00
205 Bostjan Nachbar RC 1.25 3.00
206 Fred Jones RC 1.25 3.00
207 Dan Dickau RC 1.25 3.00
208 Tayshaun Prince RC 1.50 4.00
209 Memo Okur RC 1.25 3.00
210 Juan Dixon RC 1.50 4.00

2002-03 Ultra Gold Medallion

Card numbers 1-180 were inserted in packs at the rate of one in one, and 181-210 were randomly inserted and are sequentially numbered to 100. This 210-card set parallels the base Ultra set enhanced with gold foil highlights and die cut top and bottom of the card.
*GOLD STARS: .6X TO 1.5X BASE CARD HI
*GOLD RCs: 1.5X TO 4X BASE CARD HI

2002-03 Ultra Back 2 Back

Randomly inserted in packs, this 18-card set features full color player action photography and borderless cards. The left side of the card has a box that runs from top to bottom and contains the player's name, and the bottom left hand corner of the card has the Back 2 Back logo. Each card is sequentially numbered to 1000. Game Used and Game Used Gold parallels were inserted and are numbered to 500 and 50 respectively.
COMPLETE SET (18) 20.00 50.00
1 Vince Carter 2.50 6.00
2 Tracy McGrady 2.50 6.00
3 Allen Iverson 2.50 6.00
4 Baron Davis 1.50 4.00
5 Chris Webber 1.50 4.00
6 Michael Finley 1.50 4.00
7 Steve Francis 1.50 4.00
8 Elton Brand 1.50 4.00
9 Mike Miller 1.50 4.00
10 Morris Peterson 1.00 2.50
11 Dikembe Mutombo 1.50 4.00
12 Alonzo Mourning 2.00 5.00
13 Darius Miles 1.00 2.50
14 Quentin Richardson 1.25 3.00
15 John Stockton 2.00 5.00
16 Karl Malone 2.00 5.00
17 Stephon Marbury 1.25 3.00
18 Jerry Stackhouse 1.25 3.00

2002-03 Ultra Back 2 Back Game Used

Randomly seeded in packs, this 18-card set parallels the base Back 2 Back insert set enhanced with a swatch of game used memorabilia. Each card is sequentially numbered to 500.
*GOLD: 1X TO 2.5X BASE HI
GOLD PRINT RUN 50 SER.#'d SETS
1 Vince Carter 5.00 12.00
2 Tracy McGrady 5.00 12.00
3 Allen Iverson 5.00 12.00
4 Baron Davis 3.00 8.00
5 Chris Webber 3.00 8.00
6 Michael Finley 3.00 8.00
7 Steve Francis 3.00 8.00
8 Elton Brand 3.00 8.00
9 Mike Miller 3.00 8.00
10 Morris Peterson 2.00 5.00
11 Dikembe Mutombo 3.00 8.00
12 Alonzo Mourning 4.00 10.00
13 Darius Miles 2.00 5.00
14 Quentin Richardson 2.50 6.00
15 John Stockton 4.00 10.00
16 Karl Malone 4.00 10.00
17 Stephon Marbury 2.50 6.00
18 Jerry Stackhouse 2.50 6.00

2002-03 Ultra O!

Inserted in packs at the rate of one in 12, this 20-card set places full color player action photos on a borderless card with a box running from top to bottom on the right side. This box contains the players name and team name. The O! logo appears in the upper right hand corner.
COMPLETE SET (20) 8.00 20.00
1 Vince Carter 1.00 2.50
2 Shareef Abdur-Rahim .50 1.25
3 Baron Davis .60 1.50
4 Quentin Richardson .50 1.25
5 John Stockton .75 2.00
6 Morris Peterson .40 1.00
7 Elton Brand .60 1.50
8 Glenn Robinson .50 1.25
9 Latrell Sprewell .50 1.25
10 Darius Miles .40 1.00
11 Jason Terry .50 1.25
12 Keith Van Horn .50 1.25
13 Karl Malone .75 2.00
14 Antoine Walker .50 1.25
15 Jason Williams .50 1.25
16 Rasheed Wallace .60 1.50
17 Gary Payton .60 1.50
18 Lamar Odom .60 1.50
19 Cuttino Mobley .50 1.25
20 Desmond Mason .50 1.25

2002-03 Ultra O! Game Used

Randomly inserted in packs at the rate of one in 30, this 19-card set parallels the base O! insert set enhanced with a circular swatch of game used memorabilia in the lower right hand corner.
1 Vince Carter 5.00 12.00
2 Shareef Abdur-Rahim 2.50 6.00
3 Baron Davis 3.00 8.00
4 Quentin Richardson 2.50 6.00
5 John Stockton 4.00 10.00
6 Morris Peterson 2.00 5.00
7 Elton Brand 3.00 8.00
8 Glenn Robinson 2.50 6.00
9 Latrell Sprewell 2.50 6.00
10 Darius Miles 2.00 5.00
11 Jason Terry 2.50 6.00
12 Keith Van Horn 2.50 6.00
13 Karl Malone 4.00 10.00
14 Antoine Walker 2.50 6.00
15 Jason Williams 2.50 6.00
16 Rasheed Wallace 3.00 8.00
17 Gary Payton 3.00 8.00
18 Lamar Odom 3.00 8.00
19 Cuttino Mobley 2.50 6.00

2002-03 Ultra One on One

Randomly seeded in packs at the rate of one in eight, this 10-card set places a player on the front and a player on the back. The right side of the card has "One on One" running from top to bottom, and the left side has a white box from top to bottom which contains the player's name in silver foil and his team logo.
COMPLETE SET (10) 10.00 25.00
1 Vince Carter / Tracy McGrady 3.00 8.00
2 Allen Iverson / Baron Davis 1.25 3.00
3 Chris Webber / Michael Finley 1.25 3.00
4 Steve Francis / Elton Brand 1.25 3.00
5 Mike Miller / Morris Peterson 1.25 3.00
6 Dikembe Mutombo / Alonzo Mourning 1.25 3.00
7 Darius Miles / Quentin Richardson 1.25 3.00
8 John Stockton / Karl Malone 1.25 3.00
9 Stephon Marbury / Jason Kidd 1.25 3.00
10 Vince Carter / Jerry Stackhouse 1.50 4.00

2002-03 Ultra One on One Game Used

Randomly inserted in packs, this 10-card set parallels the base One on One insert set enhanced with two swatches of game jersey, one on each side. Each card is sequentially numbered to 100.
1 Vince Carter / Tracy McGrady 30.00 80.00
2 Allen Iverson / Baron Davis 20.00 50.00
3 Chris Webber / Michael Finley 12.50 30.00
4 Steve Francis / Elton Brand 12.50 30.00
5 Mike Miller / Morris Peterson 12.50 30.00
6 Dikembe Mutombo / Alonzo Mourning 15.00 40.00
7 Darius Miles / Quentin Richardson 12.50 30.00
8 John Stockton / Karl Malone 20.00 50.00
9 Stephon Marbury / Jason Kidd 20.00 50.00
10 Vince Carter / Jerry Stackhouse 25.00 60.00

2002-03 Ultra Photo Effex

Randomly inserted in packs at the rate of one in 12, this 20-card set is white bordered and features a portrait style photograph of the featured player. The Fleer Ultra logo appears in the upper left hand corner of the card, and the player's name, team name, and "Photo Effex" appear along the bottom. A Masterpiece version sequentially numbered to 25 was also produced.
COMPLETE SET (20) 12.50 30.00
*MASTERPIECE: 8X TO 20X BASE HI
1 Vince Carter 1.00 2.50
2 Kobe Bryant 3.00 8.00
3 Michael Jordan 5.00 12.00
4 Peja Stojakovic .60 1.50
5 Allen Iverson 1.00 2.50
6 Shaquille O'Neal 1.50 4.00
7 Tracy McGrady 1.00 2.50
8 Mike Bibby .60 1.50
9 Dirk Nowitzki 1.00 2.50
10 Pau Gasol .75 2.00
11 Jason Kidd 1.00 2.50
12 Ben Wallace .60 1.50
13 Andrei Kirilenko .60 1.50
14 Paul Pierce .75 2.00
15 Antoine Walker .50 1.25
16 Kevin Garnett 1.25 3.00
17 Tony Parker .75 2.00
18 Ray Allen .60 1.50
19 Kenyon Martin .60 1.50
20 Tim Duncan 1.25 3.00

2003-04 Ultra

Released in August 2003, this 195-card set is the first to feature a live out-of-pack LeBron James RC. Base cards are borderless with a player name box along the bottom and as with recent years, the photography is incredible. Ultra was divided up into three different parts, veteran player cards 1-170, Lucky 13 Rookie Cards 171-183 sequentially numbered to 500, and Rookie Cards 184-195 inserted at one in four packs. Ultra was packaged in 24-pack boxes where packs contained eight cards and carried a suggested retail price of $2.99.
COMP. SET w/o SP's 12.50 30.00
1 Yao Ming .75 2.00
2 DeShawn Stevenson .25 .60
3 Malik Rose .25 .60
4 DaJuan Wagner .25 .60
5 Troy Murphy .40 1.00
6 Caron Butler .40 1.00
7 Radoslav Nesterovic .25 .60
8 Joe Johnson .40 1.00
9 Al Harrington .30 .75
10 Carlos Boozer .40 1.00
11 Morris Peterson .25 .60
12 Malik Allen .25 .60
13 Kurt Thomas .25 .60
14 Derek Anderson .25 .60
15 Zydrunas Ilgauskas .30 .75
16 Jason Richardson .40 1.00

17 Brian Grant .25 .60
18 Allan Houston .30 .75
19 Bonzi Wells .25 .60
20 Stephen Jackson .30 .75
21 Eddy Curry .30 .75
22 Tayshaun Prince .40 1.00
23 Brad Miller .40 1.00
24 Stromile Swift .25 .60
25 Kendall Gill .25 .60
26 Vladimir Radmanovic .25 .60
27 Theo Ratliff .25 .60
28 Nick Van Exel .30 .75
29 Marko Jaric .25 .60
30 Jason Collins .25 .60
31 Darrell Armstrong .25 .60
32 Vlade Divac .30 .75
33 Juan Dixon .25 .60
34 Calbert Cheaney .25 .60
35 Tyson Chandler .30 .75
36 Chauncey Billups .40 1.00
37 Reggie Miller .40 1.00
38 Mike Miller .40 1.00
39 Marc Jackson .25 .60
40 Casey Jacobsen .25 .60
41 Ray Allen .40 1.00
42 Mehmet Okur .30 .75
43 Jermaine O'Neal .40 1.00
44 Lorenzen Wright .25 .60
45 Wally Szczerbiak .30 .75
46 Anfernee Hardaway .60 1.50
47 Matt Harpring .30 .75
48 Jay Williams .25 .60
49 Corliss Williamson .25 .60
50 Jamaal Tinsley .25 .60
51 Shane Battier .30 .75
52 Kevin Garnett .75 2.00
53 Shawn Marion .40 1.00
54 Alvin Williams .25 .60
55 Juwan Howard .30 .75
56 Shaquille O'Neal 1.00 2.50
57 Jamal Mashburn .30 .75
58 Kenny Thomas .25 .60
59 Tim Duncan .60 1.50
60 Predrag Drobnjak .25 .60
61 Jalen Rose .30 .75
62 Ben Wallace .40 1.00
63 James Posey .25 .60
64 Pau Gasol .40 1.00
65 Michael Redd .40 1.00
66 Amare Stoudemire .60 1.50
67 Karl Malone .50 1.25
68 Richard Hamilton .30 .75
69 Eddie Griffin .25 .60
70 Robert Horry .30 .75
71 Tim Thomas .25 .60
72 Eric Snow .25 .60
73 Brent Barry .25 .60
74 Jamal Crawford .30 .75
75 Nikoloz Tskitishvili .25 .60
76 Bostjan Nachbar .25 .60
77 Devean George .25 .60
78 Dan Gadzuric .25 .60
79 Brian Skinner .25 .60
80 Cuttino Mobley .30 .75
81 Desmond Mason .30 .75
82 Othella Harrington .25 .60
83 Chris Webber .40 1.00
84 Dirk Nowitzki .60 1.50
85 Steve Francis .40 1.00
86 Gary Payton .40 1.00
87 Howard Eisley .25 .60
88 Zach Randolph .40 1.00
89 Sam Cassell .30 .75
90 Tony Battie .25 .60
91 Shammond Williams .25 .60
92 Rick Fox .25 .60
93 David Wesley .25 .60
94 Frank Williams .25 .60
95 Tony Delk .25 .60
96 Troy Hudson .25 .60
97 Donnell Harvey .25 .60
98 Derek Fisher .30 .75
99 Jamaal Magloire .25 .60
100 Keith Van Horn .30 .75
101 Tony Parker .40 1.00
102 Rashard Lewis .40 1.00
103 Shareef Abdur-Rahim .30 .75
104 Michael Finley .40 1.00
105 Jason Kidd .60 1.50
106 Drew Gooden .30 .75
107 Mike Bibby .40 1.00
108 Jerry Stackhouse .30 .75
109 Chris Jefferies .25 .60
110 Glenn Robinson .30 .75
111 Shawn Bradley .25 .60
112 Corey Maggette .30 .75
113 Richard Jefferson .40 1.00
114 Gordan Giricek .25 .60
115 Bobby Jackson .25 .60
116 Larry Hughes .30 .75
117 Scott Padgett .25 .60
118 Gilbert Arenas .40 1.00
119 Ron Artest .40 1.00
120 Jason Williams .30 .75
121 Eric Williams .25 .60
122 Stephon Marbury .30 .75
123 Vince Carter .60 1.50
124 Jason Terry .30 .75
125 Raef LaFrentz .25 .60
126 Michael Olowokandi .25 .60
127 Kerry Kittles .25 .60
128 Pat Garrity .25 .60
129 Peja Stojakovic .40 1.00
130 Jared Jeffries .25 .60
131 Antonio Davis .25 .60
132 Rodney White .25 .60
133 Kobe Bryant 2.00 5.00
134 Baron Davis .40 1.00
135 Derrick Coleman .30 .75
136 Walter McCarty .25 .60
137 Bruce Bowen .25 .60
138 Mike Dunleavy .30 .75
139 Rasual Butler .25 .60
140 Latrell Sprewell .30 .75
141 Rasheed Wallace .40 1.00
142 Andrei Kirilenko .40 1.00
143 Dan Dickau .25 .60
144 Steve Nash .50 1.25
145 Elton Brand .40 1.00
146 Kenyon Martin .40 1.00
147 Jeryl Sasser .25 .60
148 Doug Christie .25 .60
149 Kwame Brown .25 .60
150 Ricky Davis .30 .75
151 Antawn Jamison .40 1.00
152 Travis Best .25 .60
153 Courtney Alexander .25 .60
154 Scottie Pippen .60 1.50
155 Jerome Williams .25 .60
156 Quentin Richardson .30 .75
157 Lucious Harris .25 .60
158 Allen Iverson .60 1.50
159 Manu Ginobili .50 1.25
160 Bryon Russell .25 .60
161 Paul Pierce .50 1.25
162 Nene .30 .75
163 Darius Miles .25 .60
164 Earl Boykins .25 .60
165 Eddie Jones .30 .75
166 P.J. Brown .25 .60
167 Qyntel Woods .25 .60
168 Andre Miller .30 .75
169 Tracy McGrady .50 1.25
170 Antoine Walker .40 1.00
171 LeBron James L13 RC 60.00 150.00
172 Darko Milicic L13 RC 3.00 8.00
173 Carmelo Anthony L13 RC 8.00 20.00
174 Chris Bosh L13 RC 6.00 15.00
175 Dwyane Wade L13 RC 12.00 30.00
176 Chris Kaman L13 RC 4.00 10.00
177 Kirk Hinrich L13 RC 4.00 10.00
178 T.J. Ford L13 RC 4.00 10.00
179 Mike Sweetney L13 RC 3.00 8.00
180 Jarvis Hayes L13 RC 3.00 8.00
181 Mickael Pietrus L13 RC 3.00 8.00
182 Nick Collison L13 RC 3.00 8.00
183 Marcus Banks L13 RC 3.00 8.00
184 Luke Ridnour RC 1.50 4.00
185 Troy Bell RC 1.25 3.00
186 Zarko Cabarkapa RC 1.25 3.00
187 David West RC 1.50 4.00
188 Sofoklis Schortsanitis RC 1.25 3.00
189 Travis Outlaw RC 1.50 4.00
190 Leandro Barbosa RC 1.50 4.00
191 Josh Howard RC 1.25 3.00
192 Maciej Lampe RC 1.25 3.00
193 Luke Walton RC 1.25 3.00
194 Travis Hansen RC 1.25 3.00
195 Rick Rickert RC 1.25 3.00

2003-04 Ultra Gold Medallion

Randomly inserted in packs at the rate of one in one with rookies inserted at the rate of one in eight, this 194-card set parallels the base Ultra set enhanced with a gold background and one corner circular die-cutting.

*STARS: .6X TO 1.5X BASE CARD HI
*171-182 L13s: .25X TO .6X BASE CARD HI
*183-195 RCs: .6X TO 1.5X BASE CARD HI
171 LeBron James L13 30.00 80.00

2003-04 Ultra Platinum Medallion

Randomly inserted in packs, this 195-card set parallels the base Ultra set enhanced with platinum background, a circular die-cut corner and sequential numbering to 100.

*1-170 STARS: 4X TO 10X BASE CARD HI
*171-182 L13s: 1X TO 2.5X BASE CARD HI
*183-195 RCs: 2.5X TO 6X BASE CARD HI
41 Ray Allen 6.00 15.00
133 Kobe Bryant 75.00 200.00

2003-04 Ultra Leaps and Bounds

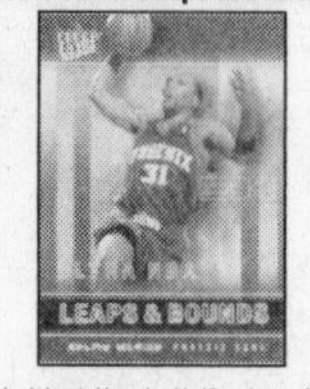

Randomly inserted in packs, this 15-card set profiles dominating scorers and defenders who use their hops to get above the rim. Each card is bordered on the top and the bottom and is sequentially numbered to 500.

COMPLETE SET (15) 15.00 30.00
1 Ben Wallace 1.00 2.50
2 Amare Stoudemire 1.50 4.00
3 Tracy McGrady 1.25 3.00
4 Dirk Nowitzki 1.50 4.00
5 Vince Carter 1.50 4.00
6 Ricky Davis .75 2.00
7 Shawn Marion 1.00 2.50
8 Steve Francis 1.00 2.50
9 Jason Richardson 1.00 2.50
10 Nene .75 2.00
11 Richard Jefferson 1.00 2.50
12 Yao Ming 2.00 5.00
13 Tim Duncan 1.50 4.00
14 Kobe Bryant 5.00 12.00
15 Kevin Garnett 2.00 5.00

2003-04 Ultra Leaps and Bounds Game Used

Randomly inserted in packs at the rate of one in 36, this 10-card set parallels the design of the Leaps and Bounds set enhanced with a square swatch of game used memorabilia.

LBN Nene 2.00 5.00
LBAS Amare Stoudemire 4.00 10.00
LBBW Ben Wallace 2.50 6.00
LBDN Dirk Nowitzki 4.00 10.00
LBJR Jason Richardson 2.50 6.00
LBKG Kevin Garnett 5.00 12.00
LBRJ Richard Jefferson 2.50 6.00
LBSF Steve Francis 2.50 6.00
LBSM Shawn Marion 2.50 6.00
LBTM Tracy McGrady 3.00 8.00
LBVC Vince Carter 4.00 10.00
LBYM Yao Ming 5.00 12.00

2003-04 Ultra Leaps and Bounds Ultra Swatch

Inserted in packs, this 11-card set parallels the look of the Leaps and Bounds Game Used set enhanced with a larger swatch of game used memorabilia and sequential numbering to the featured player's jersey number.

MOST UNPRICED DUE TO SCARCITY
LBN Nene/31 8.00 20.00
LBAS Amare Stoudemire/32 15.00 40.00
LBDN Dirk Nowitzki/41 15.00 40.00
LBJR Jason Richardson/23 10.00 25.00
LBKG Kevin Garnett/21 20.00 50.00
LBSM Shawn Marion/31 10.00 25.00

2003-04 Ultra Roundball Discs

Randomly inserted in packs at the rate of one in eight, this 36-Disc set is circular and about the width of a normal sized card. Player portrait photos are set against a white background with a dark border color.

COMPLETE SET (36) 25.00 50.00
1 Vince Carter 1.00 2.50
2 Tracy McGrady .75 2.00
3 Allen Iverson 1.00 2.50
4 Yao Ming 1.25 3.00
5 Dirk Nowitzki 1.00 2.50
6 Ben Wallace .60 1.50
7 Paul Pierce .75 2.00
8 Jason Kidd 1.00 2.50
9 Baron Davis .60 1.50
10 Gilbert Arenas .60 1.50
11 DaJuan Wagner .40 1.00
12 Pau Gasol .60 1.50
13 Chris Webber .60 1.50
14 Jermaine O'Neal .60 1.50
15 Steve Francis .60 1.50
16 Ray Allen .60 1.50
17 Steve Nash .75 2.00
18 Gary Payton .60 1.50
19 Caron Butler .60 1.50
20 Karl Malone .75 2.00
21 Mike Bibby .60 1.50
22 Allan Houston .50 1.25
23 Amare Stoudemire 1.00 2.50
24 Scottie Pippen 1.00 2.50
25 Kevin Garnett 1.25 3.00
26 Michael Finley .60 1.50
27 Richard Hamilton .50 1.25
28 Shaquille O'Neal 1.50 4.00
29 Tim Duncan 1.00 2.50
30 Kobe Bryant 3.00 8.00
31 LeBron James 6.00 15.00
32 Mike Sweetney .60 1.50
33 Carmelo Anthony 1.50 4.00
34 Chris Bosh 1.25 3.00
35 Dwyane Wade 2.50 6.00
36 Chris Kaman .75 2.00

2003-04 Ultra Roundball Discs Game Used

Randomly inserted in packs at the rate of one in 24, this 26-card set parallels the design of the base Roundball Discs insert set enhanced with a swatch of game used memorabilia.

RDAH Allan Houston 2.00 5.00
RDAI Allen Iverson 4.00 10.00
RDAS Amare Stoudemire 4.00 10.00
RDBD Baron Davis 2.50 6.00
RDBW Ben Wallace 2.50 6.00
RDCB Caron Butler 2.50 6.00
RDCW Chris Webber 2.50 6.00
RDDN Dirk Nowitzki 4.00 10.00
RDDWO DaJuan Wagner 2.00 5.00
RDGP Gary Payton 2.50 6.00
RDJK Jason Kidd 4.00 10.00
RDJO Jermaine O'Neal 2.50 6.00
RDKG Kevin Garnett 5.00 12.00
RDKG Karl Malone 3.00 8.00
RDMB Mike Bibby 2.50 6.00
RDMF Michael Finley 2.50 6.00
RDPG Pau Gasol 2.50 6.00
RDPP Paul Pierce 3.00 8.00
RDRA Ray Allen 2.50 6.00
RDRH Richard Hamilton 2.00 5.00
RDSF Steve Francis 2.50 6.00
RDSN Steve Nash 3.00 8.00
RDSP Scottie Pippen 4.00 10.00
RDTM Tracy McGrady 3.00 8.00
RDVC Vince Carter 4.00 10.00
RDYM Yao Ming 5.00 12.00

2003-04 Ultra Roundball Discs Ultra Swatch

Randomly seeded in packs, this 26-card set parallels the design of the Ultra Swatch Game Used discs enhanced with a second swatch of game worn memorabilia and sequential numbering to the player's jersey number.

MOST UNPRICED DUE TO SCARCITY
RDAH Allan Houston/20 8.00 20.00
RDAS Amare Stoudemire/32 15.00 40.00
RDDN Dirk Nowitzki/41 15.00 40.00
RDKG Kevin Garnett/21 20.00 50.00
RDKG Karl Malone/32 12.00 30.00
RDPG Pau Gasol/16 12.50 30.00
RDPP Paul Pierce/34 12.00 30.00
RDRA Ray Allen/34 15.00 40.00
RDRH Richard Hamilton/32 8.00 20.00
RDSP Scottie Pippen/33 30.00 80.00

2003-04 Ultra Scoring Kings

Randomly inserted in packs at the rate of one in 24, this 10-card set places player action photos on the top of the card with a gray-scale background on the bottom.

COMPLETE SET (10) 6.00 15.00
1 Vince Carter 1.25 3.00
2 Allen Iverson 1.25 3.00
3 Tracy McGrady 1.00 2.50
4 Dirk Nowitzki 1.25 3.00
5 Kevin Garnett 1.50 4.00
6 Steve Francis .75 2.00
7 Chris Webber .75 2.00
8 Ray Allen .75 2.00
9 Paul Pierce 1.00 2.50
10 Yao Ming 1.50 4.00

2003-04 Ultra Scoring Kings Game Used

Randomly inserted in packs at the rate of one in 100, this 10-card set parallels the look of the base Scoring Kings insert set enhanced with a swatch of game worn memorabilia.

1 Vince Carter 5.00 12.00
2 Allen Iverson 5.00 12.00
3 Tracy McGrady 4.00 10.00
4 Dirk Nowitzki 5.00 12.00
5 Kevin Garnett 6.00 15.00
6 Steve Francis 3.00 8.00
7 Chris Webber 3.00 8.00
8 Ray Allen 3.00 8.00
9 Paul Pierce 4.00 10.00
10 Yao Ming 6.00 15.00

2003-04 Ultra Scoring Kings PPG

Randomly inserted in packs, this eight card set parallels the design of the base Scoring Kings insert set enhanced with a swatch of game worn memorabilia and sequential numbering to the player's point per game average from the 2002-03 season.

SOME NOT PRICED DUE TO SCARCITY
AI Allen Iverson/27 15.00 40.00
DN Dirk Nowitzki/25 15.00 40.00
KG Kevin Garnett/25 20.00 50.00
RA Ray Allen/22 10.00 25.00
SF Steve Francis/21 10.00 25.00
TM Tracy McGrady/32 12.00 30.00

2003-04 Ultra Scoring Kings Ultra Swatch

Randomly inserted in packs, this 10-card set parallels the base Scoring Kings Game Used set enhanced with larger jersey swatches and sequential numbering to the featured player's jersey number.

MOST UNPRICED DUE TO SCARCITY
4 Dirk Nowitzki/41 15.00 40.00
5 Kevin Garnett/21 20.00 50.00
8 Ray Allen/34 15.00 40.00

2003-04 Ultra Signatures

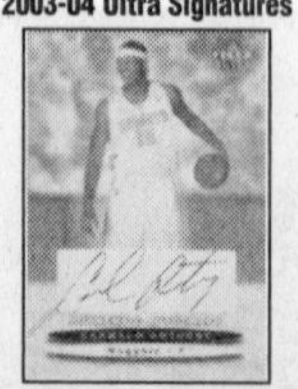
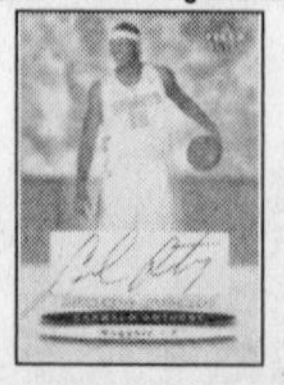

Randomly inserted in packs, this 20-card set features the base card with an embedded cut signature. Each card is sequentially numbered to 350.

1 Carmelo Anthony 25.00 60.00
2 Leandro Barbosa 5.00 12.00
3 Mike Bibby 4.00 10.00
4 Chris Bosh 15.00 40.00
5 Earl Boykins 4.00 10.00
6 Vince Carter 12.00 30.00
7 Manu Ginobili 8.00 20.00
8 Richard Jefferson 4.00 10.00
9 Mike Sweetney 4.00 10.00
11 Jermaine O'Neal 6.00 15.00
12 Tracy McGrady 15.00 40.00
13 Tayshaun Prince 5.00 12.00
14 Luke Ridnour 5.00 12.00
15 Amare Stoudemire 15.00 40.00
16A Dwyane Wade 40.00 100.00
16B Dwyane Wade/250 60.00 150.00
17 DaJuan Wagner 4.00 10.00
18 Ben Wallace 8.00 20.00
19 Luke Walton 4.00 10.00
20 David West 5.00 12.00

2004-05 Ultra

Released in August 2004, Ultra consists of a 219-card set where cards 1-175 feature veteran players, cards 176-188 feature the first 13 lottery picks on a Lucky 13 rookie card sequentially numbered to 500, 189-199 feature rookies inserted at the rate of one in four and cards 200-219 feature Update rookies that were inserted at two per box in Fleer Tradition. Ultra was offered in both Hobby and Retail formats where both contained 24 packs of eight cards each, but Hobby carried a $2.99 SRP and Retail carried a $1.99 SRP.

COMP.SET w/o RC's (175) 15.00 40.00
1 Ben Wallace .30 .75
2 Chris Kaman .30 .75
3 Steve Nash .40 1.00
4 Al Harrington .25 .60
5 T.J. Ford .25 .60
6 Jason Collins .20 .50
7 Theo Ratliff .20 .50
8 Kobe Bryant 1.50 4.00
9 Kirk Hinrich .30 .75
10 Darko Milicic .20 .50
11 Karl Malone .40 1.00
12 Michael Olowokandi .20 .50
13 Frank Williams .20 .50
14 Vlade Divac .25 .60
15 Vince Carter .50 1.25
16 Eddy Curry .25 .60
17 Keith Van Horn .25 .60
18 Chris Wilcox .20 .50
19 Tim Thomas .20 .50
20 Shareef Abdur-Rahim .25 .60
21 Carlos Arroyo .25 .60
22 Jason Collier .20 .50
23 Voshon Lenard .20 .50
24 Reggie Miller .30 .75
25 Dan Gadzuric .20 .50
26 David Wesley .20 .50
27 Vladimir Radmanovic .20 .50
28 Derek Anderson .20 .50
29 Zydrunas Ilgauskas .25 .60
30 Nick Van Exel .25 .60
31 Stromile Swift .20 .50
32 Kerry Kittles .20 .50
33 Zaza Pachulia .20 .50
34 Brad Miller .30 .75
35 Jerry Stackhouse .25 .60
36 Jason Terry .25 .60
37 Earl Boykins .20 .50
38 Jermaine O'Neal .30 .75
39 Joe Smith .25 .60
40 Jamaal Magloire .20 .50
41 Zarko Cabarkapa .20 .50
42 Ronald Murray .20 .50
43 Bob Sura .20 .50
44 Andre Miller .25 .60
45 Jamaal Tinsley .20 .50
46 Michael Redd .30 .75
47 Baron Davis .30 .75
48 Amare Stoudemire .40 1.00
49 Rashard Lewis .30 .75
50 Jiri Welsch .20 .50
51 Marcus Camby .25 .60
52 Ron Artest .30 .75
53 Eddie Jones .25 .60
54 Darrell Armstrong .20 .50
55 Shawn Marion .30 .75
56 Brent Barry .20 .50
57 Michael Finley .30 .75
58 Jim Jackson .20 .50
59 Jason Williams .25 .60
60 Kenyon Martin .30 .75
61 Kyle Korver .25 .60
62 Marquis Daniels .20 .50
63 Chucky Atkins .20 .50
64 Nene .25 .60
65 Marko Jaric .20 .50
66 Dwyane Wade 1.00 2.50
67 P.J. Brown .20 .50
68 Casey Jacobsen .20 .50
69 Morris Peterson .20 .50
70 Ricky Davis .25 .60
71 Tayshaun Prince .30 .75
72 Corey Maggette .25 .60
73 Udonis Haslem .25 .60
74 Kurt Thomas .20 .50
75 Leandro Barbosa .30 .75
76 Alvin Williams .20 .50
77 Mark Blount .20 .50
78 Chauncey Billups .30 .75
79 Boris Diaw .25 .60
80 Brian Grant .20 .50
81 Allan Houston .25 .60
82 Joe Johnson .30 .75
83 Donyell Marshall .20 .50
84 Jamal Crawford .25 .60
85 Jason Richardson .30 .75
86 Gary Payton .30 .75
87 Nazr Mohammed .20 .50
88 Mike Bibby .30 .75
89 Jalen Rose .25 .60
90 Scottie Pippen .50 1.25
91 Speedy Claxton .20 .50
92 Devean George .20 .50
93 Sam Cassell .25 .60
94 Mike Sweetney .20 .50
95 Chris Webber .30 .75
96 Chris Bosh .30 .75
97 Antoine Walker .30 .75
98 Cuttino Mobley .25 .60
99 Caron Butler .30 .75
100 John Salmons .30 .75
101 Bruce Bowen .20 .50
102 Josh Howard .30 .75
103 Steve Francis .30 .75
104 Lamar Odom .30 .75
105 Troy Hudson .20 .50
106 Allen Iverson .50 1.25
107 Dajuan Wagner .20 .50
108 Erick Dampier .20 .50
109 Luke Walton .20 .50
110 Aaron Williams .20 .50
111 Juwan Howard .25 .60
112 Bobby Jackson .20 .50
113 Andrei Kirilenko .25 .60
114 LeBron James 2.00 5.00
115 Brian Cardinal .20 .50
116 Mike Miller .30 .75
117 Tracy McGrady .40 1.00
118 Doug Christie .20 .50
119 Larry Hughes .25 .60
120 Stephen Jackson .25 .60
121 Carmelo Anthony .60 1.50
122 Fred Jones .20 .50
123 Desmond Mason .25 .60
124 Jamal Mashburn .30 .75
125 Ray Allen .30 .75
126 Jeff McInnis .20 .50
127 Yao Ming .60 1.50
128 Bonzi Wells .20 .50
129 Richard Jefferson .30 .75
130 Kenny Thomas .20 .50
131 Hedo Turkoglu .30 .75
132 Kwame Brown .20 .50
133 Dirk Nowitzki .50 1.25
134 Maurice Taylor .20 .50
135 Pau Gasol .30 .75
136 Jason Kidd .50 1.25
137 Samuel Dalembert .20 .50
138 Tim Duncan .50 1.25
139 Gilbert Arenas .30 .75
140 Tony Parker .30 .75
141 Tyson Chandler .25 .60
142 Richard Hamilton .25 .60
143 Shaquille O'Neal .75 2.00
144 Stephon Marbury .25 .60
145 Damon Stoudamire .25 .60
146 Gordan Giricek .20 .50
147 Latrell Sprewell .25 .60
148 Carlos Boozer .30 .75
149 Mike Dunleavy .25 .60
150 Luke Ridnour .25 .60
151 Reece Gaines .20 .50
152 Peja Stojakovic .30 .75
153 Juan Dixon .20 .50
154 Marcus Banks .20 .50
155 Rasheed Wallace .30 .75
156 Quentin Richardson .25 .60
157 Wally Szczerbiak .25 .60
158 Keith Bogans .20 .50
159 Darius Miles .20 .50
160 Matt Harpring .25 .60
161 Antawn Jamison .30 .75
162 Kelvin Cato .20 .50
163 James Posey .20 .50
164 Willie Green .20 .50
165 Rasho Nesterovic .20 .50
166 Jarvis Hayes .20 .50
167 Paul Pierce .40 1.00
168 Mehmet Okur .25 .60
169 Elton Brand .30 .75
170 Kevin Garnett .60 1.50
171 Drew Gooden .25 .60
172 Zach Randolph .25 .60
173 Raul Lopez .20 .50
174 Manu Ginobili .40 1.00
175 Raja Bell .25 .60
176 Dwight Howard L13 RC 10.00 25.00
177 Emeka Okafor L13 RC 5.00 12.00
178 Ben Gordon L13 RC 4.00 10.00
179 Shaun Livingston L13 RC 3.00 8.00
180 Devin Harris L13 RC 5.00 12.00
181 Josh Childress L13 RC 3.00 8.00
182 Luol Deng L13 RC 5.00 12.00
183 Rafael Araujo L13 RC 3.00 8.00
184 Andre Iguodala L13 RC 5.00 12.00
185 Luke Jackson L13 RC 3.00 8.00
186 Andris Biedrins L13 RC 4.00 10.00
187 Robert Swift L13 RC 3.00 8.00
188 Sebastian Telfair L13 RC 3.00 8.00
189 Kris Humphries RC 1.50 4.00
190 Al Jefferson RC 2.50 6.00
191 Kirk Snyder RC 1.50 4.00
192 Josh Smith RC 2.50 6.00
193 J.R. Smith RC 2.00 5.00
194 Dorell Wright RC 2.50 6.00
195 Jameer Nelson RC 2.00 5.00
196 Pavel Podkolzine RC 1.50 4.00
197 Ha Seung-Jin RC 1.50 4.00
198 Sasha Vujacic RC 1.50 4.00
199 Anderson Varejao RC 2.00 5.00
200U Bernard Robinson RC 2.00 5.00
201U Andres Nocioni RC 2.00 5.00
202U Delonte West RC 2.50 6.00
203U Tony Allen RC 2.50 6.00
204U Kevin Martin RC 2.50 6.00
205U Beno Udrih RC 2.00 5.00
206U David Harrison RC 2.00 5.00
207U Jackson Vroman RC 2.00 5.00
208U Peter John Ramos RC 2.00 5.00
209U Lionel Chalmers RC 2.00 5.00
210U Donta Smith RC 2.00 5.00
211U Andre Emmett RC 2.00 5.00
212U Antonio Burks RC 2.00 5.00
213U Royal Ivey RC 2.00 5.00
214U Chris Duhon RC 2.00 5.00
215U Damien Wilkins RC 2.00 5.00
216U Justin Reed RC 2.00 5.00
217U Trevor Ariza RC 2.00 5.00
218U Tim Pickett RC 2.00 5.00
219U Yuta Tabuse RC 4.00 10.00

2004-05 Ultra Gold Medallion

Inserted in packs at the rate of one in one for cards 1-175 and one in eight for cards 176-199, this 199-card set parallels the base Ultra set enhanced with gold backgrounds and a rounded corner.

*1-175 GOLD: .6X TO 1.5X BASE HI
*176-188 GOLD: .25X TO .6X BASE HI
*189-199 GOLD: .5X TO 1.25X BASE HI

2004-05 Ultra Platinum Medallion

Randomy seeded in packs, this 199-card set parallels the base set with a platinum background and a die cut corner. Cards 1-175 and 189-199 are sequentially numbered to 100 and cards 176-188 are sequentially numbered to 13.

*1-175 SINGLES: 5X TO 12X BASE HI
*189-199 SINGLES: 2X TO 5X BASE HI
8 Kobe Bryant 75.00 150.00
114 LeBron James 30.00 80.00
125 Ray Allen 6.00 15.00

2004-05 Ultra Hoop Nation

Randomly inserted in Excel/MVP Retail boxes as three per, this 15-card set features borders along the top and the bottom to match team colors and player photos.

COMPLETE SET (15) 6.00 15.00
1 LeBron James 2.00 5.00
2 Kobe Bryant 1.50 4.00
3 Tim Duncan .50 1.25
4 Vince Carter .50 1.25
5 Allen Iverson .50 1.25
6 Shaquille O'Neal .75 2.00
7 Tracy McGrady .40 1.00
8 Carmelo Anthony .60 1.50
9 Yao Ming .60 1.50
10 Dwyane Wade 1.00 2.50
11 Dirk Nowitzki .50 1.25
12 Jason Kidd .50 1.25
13 Kevin Garnett .60 1.50
14 Jermaine O'Neal .30 .75
15 Paul Pierce .40 1.00

2004-05 Ultra Point Gods

Inserted in packs at the rate of one in 36, this 15-card set features the league's premier point guards on a tan background.

COMPLETE SET (15) 10.00 25.00
1 Jason Kidd 1.25 3.00
2 Stephon Marbury .60 1.50
3 Allen Iverson 1.25 3.00
4 Chauncey Billups .75 2.00
5 Vince Carter 1.25 3.00
6 Steve Nash 1.00 2.50
7 Michael Redd .75 2.00
8 Baron Davis .75 2.00
9 Mike Bibby .75 2.00
10 Reggie Miller .75 2.00
11 LeBron James 5.00 12.00
12 Tracy McGrady 1.00 2.50
13 Kirk Hinrich .75 2.00
14 Kobe Bryant 4.00 10.00
15 Dwyane Wade 2.50 6.00

2004-05 Ultra Point Gods Game Used

Randomly inserted in packs, this 12-card set parallels the design of the Point Gods insert set but is enhanced with a swatch of memorabilia and is sequentially numbered to 250. A Ultra Swatch version was also issued and features premium patch swatches and sequential numbering to 25.

*ULTRA SWATCH: 1X TO 2.5X BASE HI
AI Allen Iverson 4.00 10.00
BD Baron Davis 2.50 6.00
CB Chauncey Billups 2.50 6.00
DW Dwyane Wade 8.00 20.00
JK Jason Kidd 4.00 10.00
MB Mike Bibby 2.50 6.00
SM Stephon Marbury 2.00 5.00
TM Tracy McGrady 3.00 8.00
VC Vince Carter 4.00 10.00

2004-05 Ultra Scoring Kings

Inserted in packs at the rate of one in six, this 25-card set places full color player photos on a gray background with a profile of the players face.

COMPLETE SET (25) 12.50 30.00
1 Vince Carter .75 2.00
2 Tracy McGrady .60 1.50
3 Peja Stojakovic .50 1.25
4 Kevin Garnett 1.00 2.50
5 Paul Pierce .60 1.50
6 Baron Davis .50 1.25
7 Tim Duncan .75 2.00
8 Dirk Nowitzki .75 2.00
9 Michael Redd .50 1.25
10 Shaquille O'Neal 1.25 3.00
11 Carmelo Anthony 1.00 2.50
12 Stephon Marbury .40 1.00
13 Corey Maggette .40 1.00
14 Zach Randolph .40 1.00
15 Jermaine O'Neal .50 1.25

16 Yao Ming 1.00 2.50
17 Andrei Kirilenko .40 1.00
18 Rashard Lewis .50 1.25
19 Latrell Sprewell .40 1.00
20 Pau Gasol .50 1.25
21 Kobe Bryant 2.50 6.00
22 LeBron James 3.00 8.00
23 Michael Finley .50 1.25
24 Jason Richardson .50 1.25
25 Richard Hamilton .40 1.00

2004-05 Ultra Scoring Kings Game Used

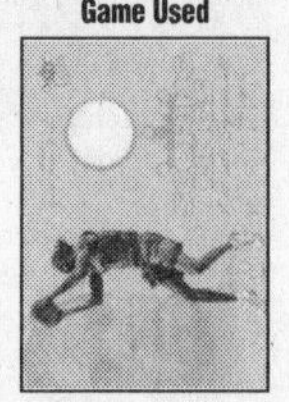

Randomly inserted in packs at the rate of one in 72, this 23-card set parallels the design of the Scoring Kings insert set but is enhanced with a swatch of memorabilia.. A Ultra Swatch version was also issued and features premium patch swatches and sequential numbering to 50.

*ULTRA SWATCH: .75X TO 2X BASE HI
AK Andrei Kirilenko 2.00 5.00
BD Baron Davis 2.50 6.00
CA Carmelo Anthony 5.00 12.00
CM Corey Maggette 2.00 5.00
JO Jermaine O'Neal 2.50 6.00
JR Jason Richardson 2.50 6.00
KG Kevin Garnett 5.00 12.00
LS Latrell Sprewell 2.00 5.00
MR Michael Redd 2.50 6.00
PG Pau Gasol 2.50 6.00
PP Paul Pierce 3.00 8.00
PS Peja Stojakovic 2.50 6.00
RH Richard Hamilton 2.00 5.00
SM Stephon Marbury 2.00 5.00
SO Shaquille O'Neal 6.00 15.00
TD Tim Duncan 4.00 10.00
TM Tracy McGrady 3.00 8.00
VC Vince Carter 4.00 10.00
YM Yao Ming 5.00 12.00
ZR Zach Randolph 2.00 5.00

2004-05 Ultra Season Crowns Autographs

Inserted in packs at the rate of one in 75, this 33-card set is horizontally designed with a player photo on the left and an autograph on the right.

AK Andrei Kirilenko/74 10.00 25.00
AS Amare Stoudemire/238 8.00 20.00
BG Ben Gordon 6.00 15.00
DM Darius Miles/386 4.00 10.00
DW Dwyane Wade 40.00 100.00
EC Eddy Curry/86 4.00 10.00
GA Gilbert Arenas/86 6.00 15.00
JJ Joe Johnson/222 4.00 10.00
JN Jameer Nelson 6.00 15.00
JS J.R. Smith 6.00 15.00
KB Kwame Brown/86 4.00 10.00
KK Kyle Korver 5.00 12.00
KM Kenyon Martin/50 6.00 15.00
MS Mike Sweetney/86 4.00 10.00
PP Paul Pierce 10.00 25.00
PS Peja Stojakovic/390 6.00 15.00
RG Reece Gaines/386 4.00 10.00
RM Ronald Murray/286 4.00 10.00
SM Shawn Marion/86 8.00 20.00
ST Sebastian Telfair/182 6.00 15.00
TM Tracy McGrady/278 12.50 30.00
VC Vince Carter/286 15.00 40.00

2004-05 Ultra Season Crowns Autographs Gold

Randomly inserted in packs, this set parallels the design of the Season Crowns Autographs insert set but is enhanced with gold highlights and sequential numbering to 15.

N Nene 12.00 30.00
AS Amare Stoudemire 20.00 50.00
DW Dwyane Wade 75.00 200.00
EC Eddy Curry 12.00 30.00
JN Jameer Nelson 15.00 40.00
KM Kenyon Martin 12.00 30.00
RM Ronald Murray 12.00 30.00
ST Sebastian Telfair 12.00 30.00
TM Tracy McGrady 30.00 80.00

2004-05 Ultra Season Crowns Autographs Silver

Randomly inserted in packs, this 24-card set semi-parallels the base Season Crowns Autographs insert with a silver background and sequential numbering to 99.

PRINT RUN 99 SER.#'d SETS
N Nene 6.00 15.00
AK Andrei Kirilenko 10.00 25.00
AS Amare Stoudemire 10.00 25.00
AW Antoine Walker 6.00 15.00
BG Ben Gordon 8.00 20.00
DM Darius Miles 6.00 15.00
DW Dwyane Wade 40.00 100.00
EC Eddy Curry 6.00 15.00
GA Gilbert Arenas 6.00 15.00
JJ Joe Johnson 6.00 15.00
JS J.R. Smith 8.00 20.00
JW Jason Williams 15.00 40.00
KB Kwame Brown 6.00 15.00
KK Kyle Korver 6.00 15.00

KM Kenyon Martin 6.00 15.00
MS Mike Sweetney 6.00 15.00
PP Paul Pierce 10.00 25.00
PS Peja Stojakovic 10.00 25.00
RG Reece Gaines 6.00 15.00
RM Ronald Murray 6.00 15.00
SM Shawn Marion 8.00 20.00
ST Sebastian Telfair 6.00 15.00
TM Tracy McGrady 15.00 40.00
VC Vince Carter 25.00 50.00

2004-05 Ultra Season Crowns Game Used

Inserted in packs randomly, this 40-card set utilizes the design from the Season Crowns Autographs but replaced the auto with a swatch of memorabilia. Several parallel versions of this set were inserted and they are numbered to 149, 99 and 29.

*149 JSY SINGLES: .5X TO 1.25X BASE JSY HI
*99 JSY SINGLES: .6X TO 1.5X BASE JSY HI
*29 JSY SINGLES: 1.25X TO 3X BASE JSY HI
N Nene 2.00 5.00
AI Allen Iverson 4.00 10.00
AK Andrei Kirilenko 2.00 5.00
AS Amare Stoudemire 3.00 8.00
BD Boris Diaw 2.00 5.00
BW Ben Wallace 2.50 6.00
CA Carmelo Anthony 5.00 12.00
CB Carlos Boozer 2.50 6.00
CB Chris Bosh 2.50 6.00
CK Chris Kaman 2.50 6.00
CM Corey Maggette 2.00 5.00
DM Darius Miles 2.00 5.00
DW Dwyane Wade 8.00 20.00
EB Elton Brand 2.50 6.00
EC Eddy Curry 2.00 5.00
GP Gary Payton 2.50 6.00
JC Jamal Crawford 2.00 5.00
JJ Joe Johnson 2.50 6.00
JK Jason Kidd 4.00 10.00
JO Jermaine O'Neal 2.50 6.00
JW Jason Williams 2.00 5.00
KM Kenyon Martin 2.50 6.00
LO Lamar Odom 2.50 6.00
MG Manu Ginobili 3.00 8.00
MS Mike Sweetney 2.00 5.00
RA Ron Artest 2.50 6.00
RA Ray Allen 2.50 6.00
RJ Richard Jefferson 2.50 6.00
RL Rashard Lewis 2.50 6.00
RM Reggie Miller 2.50 6.00
SM Stephon Marbury 2.00 5.00
SM Shawn Marion 2.50 6.00
SN Steve Nash 3.00 8.00
SP Scottie Pippen 4.00 10.00
TD Tim Duncan 4.00 10.00
TM Tracy McGrady 3.00 8.00
TP Tayshaun Prince 2.50 6.00
TP Tony Parker 2.50 6.00
VC Vince Carter 4.00 10.00
YM Yao Ming 5.00 12.00

2004-05 Ultra Ten for Ten

Inserted in packs at the rate of one in 100, this 10-card set places player images on the right and a portrait photo on the left.

COMPLETE SET (10) 15.00 35.00
1 Kevin Garnett 2.50 6.00
2 Vince Carter 2.00 5.00
3 Shaquille O'Neal 3.00 8.00
4 Tim Duncan 2.00 5.00
5 Dirk Nowitzki 2.00 5.00
6 Yao Ming 2.50 6.00
7 Carmelo Anthony 2.50 6.00
8 Allen Iverson 2.00 5.00
9 Tracy McGrady 1.50 4.00
10 Ben Wallace 1.25 3.00

2004-05 Ultra Ten for Ten Game Used

Randomly seeded in packs, this 10-card set paralells the Ten for Ten set enhanced with a swatch of memorabilia and sequential numbering to 100. An Ultra Swatch parallel set was also issued and is sequentially numbered to 10.

UNPRICED ULTRA SWATCH PRINT RUN 10 SETS
AI Allen Iverson 6.00 15.00
BW Ben Wallace 4.00 10.00
DA Carmelo Anthony 8.00 20.00
DN Dirk Nowitzki 6.00 15.00
KG Kevin Garnett 8.00 20.00
SO Shaquille O'Neal 10.00 25.00
TD Tim Duncan 6.00 15.00
TM Tracy McGrady 5.00 12.00
VC Vince Carter 6.00 15.00
YM Yao Ming 8.00 20.00

2006-07 Ultra

Released in mid September 2006, Ultra employs a slightly tweaked version of previous year's minimally designed full-bleed photo card fronts. The 244-card set pictures veteran players on cards 1-170, 2005-06 rookie players in a Lucky 14 Retro subset on cards 171-184 (since no Fleer or Ultra products were issued during the 2005-06 season), 2005-06 rookie players in a World Premier Retro subset on cards 185-200, Lucky 14 rookies serially numbered to 500 on cards 201-214 and World Premier rookies on cards 215-244. Ultra is packaged in 24-pack boxes of eight cards each and carried an initial suggested retail price of $2.99.

COMP.SET w/o SP's (170) 20.00 50.00
1 Josh Childress .25 .60
2 Al Harrington .25 .60
3 Joe Johnson .30 .75
4 Tyronn Lue .20 .50
5 Josh Smith .30 .75
6 Tony Allen .20 .50
7 Dan Dickau .20 .50
8 Al Jefferson .30 .75
9 Paul Pierce .40 1.00
10 Wally Szczerbiak .25 .60
11 Raef LaFrentz .20 .50
12 Primoz Brezec .20 .50
13 Brevin Knight .20 .50
14 Emeka Okafor .30 .75
15 Kareem Rush .20 .50
16 Gerald Wallace .30 .75
17 Bernard Robinson .20 .50
18 Tyson Chandler .25 .60
19 Luol Deng .30 .75
20 Chris Duhon .20 .50
21 Ben Gordon .30 .75
22 Kirk Hinrich .30 .75
23 Drew Gooden .25 .60
24 Larry Hughes .25 .60
25 Zydrunas Ilgauskas .25 .60
26 LeBron James 1.50 4.00
27 Luke Jackson .20 .50
28 Anderson Varejao .25 .60
29 Erick Dampier .20 .50
30 Marquis Daniels .20 .50
31 Devin Harris .30 .75
32 Josh Howard .25 .60
33 Dirk Nowitzki .50 1.25
34 Jason Terry .25 .60
35 Carmelo Anthony .40 1.00
36 Earl Boykins .20 .50
37 Marcus Camby .25 .60
38 Kenyon Martin .30 .75
39 Andre Miller .25 .60
40 Eduardo Najera .20 .50
41 Chauncey Billups .30 .75
42 Richard Hamilton .25 .60
43 Antonio McDyess .25 .60
44 Tayshaun Prince .30 .75
45 Ben Wallace .30 .75
46 Rasheed Wallace .30 .75
47 Baron Davis .30 .75
48 Mike Dunleavy .25 .60
49 Derek Fisher .25 .60
50 Troy Murphy .20 .50
51 Jason Richardson .30 .75
52 Rafer Alston .20 .50
53 Juwan Howard .25 .60
54 Tracy McGrady .40 1.00
55 Stromile Swift .20 .50
56 David Wesley .20 .50
57 Yao Ming .40 1.00
58 Austin Croshere .20 .50
59 Stephen Jackson .25 .60
60 Jermaine O'Neal .30 .75
61 Peja Stojakovic .30 .75
62 Jamaal Tinsley .20 .50
63 Elton Brand .30 .75
64 Sam Cassell .30 .75
65 Chris Kaman .25 .60
66 Shaun Livingston .20 .50
67 Corey Maggette .25 .60
68 Cuttino Mobley .25 .60
69 Kwame Brown .20 .50
70 Kobe Bryant 1.50 4.00
71 Devean George .20 .50
72 Lamar Odom .30 .75
73 Smush Parker .20 .50
74 Luke Walton .20 .50
75 Shane Battier .25 .60
76 Pau Gasol .30 .75
77 Bobby Jackson .20 .50
78 Mike Miller .30 .75
79 Damon Stoudamire .25 .60
80 Alonzo Mourning .40 1.00
81 Shaquille O'Neal .60 1.50
82 Gary Payton .30 .75
83 Dwyane Wade .75 2.00
84 Antoine Walker .25 .60
85 Jason Williams .25 .60
86 T.J. Ford .25 .60
87 Jamaal Magloire .20 .50
88 Michael Redd .30 .75
89 Bobby Simmons .20 .50
90 Maurice Williams .25 .60
91 Mark Blount .20 .50
92 Ricky Davis .25 .60
93 Kevin Garnett .60 1.50
94 Eddie Griffin .20 .50
95 Trenton Hassell .20 .50
96 Troy Hudson .20 .50
97 Vince Carter .40 1.00
98 Jason Collins .20 .50
99 Richard Jefferson .30 .75
100 Jason Kidd .50 1.25
101 Jeff McInnis .20 .50
102 Antoine Wright .20 .50
103 P.J. Brown .20 .50
104 Speedy Claxton .20 .50
105 Marc Jackson .20 .50
106 Desmond Mason .20 .50
107 J.R. Smith .30 .75
108 Eddy Curry .25 .60
109 Steve Francis .30 .75
110 Stephon Marbury .25 .60
111 Quentin Richardson .25 .60
112 Jalen Rose .25 .60
113 Maurice Taylor .20 .50
114 Carlos Arroyo .25 .60
115 Grant Hill .40 1.00
116 Dwight Howard .50 1.25
117 Darko Milicic .20 .50
118 Jameer Nelson .25 .60
119 DeShawn Stevenson .20 .50
120 Samuel Dalembert .20 .50
121 Steven Hunter .20 .50
122 Andre Iguodala .30 .75
123 Allen Iverson .40 1.00
124 Kyle Korver .25 .60
125 Chris Webber .30 .75
126 Raja Bell .25 .60
127 Boris Diaw .25 .60
128 Shawn Marion .30 .75
129 Steve Nash .40 1.00
130 Amare Stoudemire .30 .75
131 Kurt Thomas .20 .50
132 Darius Miles .20 .50
133 Joel Przybilla .20 .50
134 Zach Randolph .25 .60
135 Ha Seung-Jin .20 .50
136 Sebastian Telfair .20 .50
137 Shareef Abdur-Rahim .25 .60
138 Ron Artest .30 .75
139 Mike Bibby .30 .75
140 Brad Miller .30 .75
141 Vitaly Potapenko .20 .50
142 Bruce Bowen .20 .50
143 Tim Duncan .50 1.25
144 Michael Finley .30 .75
145 Manu Ginobili .30 .75
146 Robert Horry .25 .60
147 Tony Parker .30 .75
148 Ray Allen .30 .75
149 Rashard Lewis .30 .75
150 Luke Ridnour .25 .60
151 Robert Swift .20 .50
152 Earl Watson .20 .50
153 Chris Wilcox .20 .50
154 Rafael Araujo .20 .50
155 Chris Bosh .30 .75
156 Jose Calderon .25 .60
157 Mike James .20 .50
158 Morris Peterson .20 .50
159 Pape Sow .20 .50
160 Carlos Boozer .30 .75
161 Gordan Giricek .20 .50
162 Kris Humphries .20 .50
163 Andrei Kirilenko .25 .60
164 Mehmet Okur .20 .50
165 Greg Ostertag .20 .50
166 Gilbert Arenas .30 .75
167 Calvin Booth .20 .50
168 Caron Butler .30 .75
169 Antonio Daniels .20 .50
170 Antawn Jamison .30 .75
171 Andrew Bogut L14 Ret 1.25 3.00
172 Marvin Williams L14 Ret 1.25 3.00
173 Deron Williams L14 Ret 2.00 5.00
174 Chris Paul L14 Ret 2.50 6.00
175 Raymond Felton L14 Ret 1.50 4.00
176 Martell Webster L14 Ret 1.00 2.50
177 Charlie Villanueva L14 Ret 1.25 3.00
178 Channing Frye L14 Ret 1.00 2.50
179 Ike Diogu L14 Ret .75 2.00
180 Andrew Bynum L14 Ret 2.00 5.00
181 Yaroslav Korolev L14 Ret .75 2.00
182 Sean May L14 Ret .75 2.00
183 Rashad McCants L14 Ret .75 2.00
184 Antoine Wright L14 Ret .75 2.00
185 Nate Robinson WP Ret 1.25 3.00
186 Luther Head WP Ret 1.00 2.50
187 Joey Graham WP Ret .75 2.00
188 Johan Petro WP Ret .75 2.00
189 Wayne Simien WP Ret .75 2.00
190 David Lee WP Ret 1.00 2.50
191 Salim Stoudamire WP Ret .75 2.00
192 Travis Diener WP Ret .75 2.00
193 Monta Ellis WP Ret 1.25 3.00
194 Martynas Andriuskevicius WP Ret .75 2.00
195 Chuck Hayes WP Ret .75 2.00
196 Danny Granger WP Ret 1.25 3.00
197 Sarunas Jasikevicius WP Ret 1.00 2.50
198 Francisco Garcia WP Ret 1.00 2.50
199 Jarrett Jack WP Ret 1.00 2.50
200 Jose Calderon WP Ret 1.00 2.50
201 Andrea Bargnani L14/500 RC 6.00 15.00
202 LaMarcus Aldridge L14/500 RC 10.00 25.00
203 Adam Morrison L14/500 RC 5.00 12.00
204 Tyrus Thomas L14/500 RC 5.00 12.00
205 Shelden Williams L14/500 RC 4.00 10.00
206 Brandon Roy L14/500 RC 10.00 25.00
207 Randy Foye L14/500 RC 5.00 12.00
208 Rudy Gay L14/500 RC 6.00 15.00
209 Patrick O'Bryant L14/500 RC 4.00 10.00
210 Saer Sene L14/500 RC 4.00 10.00
211 J.J. Redick L14/500 RC 5.00 12.00
212 Hilton Armstrong L14/500 RC 4.00 10.00
213 Thabo Sefolosha L14/500 RC 5.00 12.00
214 Ronnie Brewer L14/500 RC 5.00 12.00
215 Allan Ray WP RC 1.00 2.50
216 Leon Powe WP RC 1.00 2.50
217 Joel Freeland WP RC 1.00 2.50
218 Shawne Williams WP RC 1.00 2.50
219 Kevin Pittsnogle WP RC 1.00 2.50
220 Shannon Brown WP RC 1.50 4.00
221 Kyle Lowry WP RC 1.25 3.00
222 Mardy Collins WP RC 1.00 2.50
223 Rodney Carney WP RC 1.00 2.50
224 Maurice Ager WP RC 1.00 2.50
225 Quincy Douby WP RC 1.00 2.50
226 Rajon Rondo WP RC 4.00 10.00
227 Jordan Farmar WP RC 1.00 2.50
228 Marcus Williams WP RC 1.00 2.50
229 Josh Boone WP RC 1.00 2.50
230 Solomon Jones WP RC 1.00 2.50
231 Denham Brown WP RC 1.00 2.50
232 Renaldo Balkman WP RC 1.00 2.50
233 Will Blalock WP RC 1.00 2.50
234 Bobby Jones WP RC 1.00 2.50
235 Steve Novak WP RC 1.00 2.50
236 James Augustine WP RC 1.00 2.50
237 Dee Brown WP RC 1.00 2.50
238 Hassan Adams WP RC 1.00 2.50
239 Alexander Johnson WP RC 1.00 2.50
240 Cedric Simmons WP RC 1.00 2.50
241 James White WP RC 1.00 2.50
242 Paul Davis WP RC 1.00 2.50
243 P.J. Tucker WP RC 1.00 2.50
244 Ryan Hollins WP RC 1.00 2.50

2006-07 Ultra Gold Medallion

*1-200 GOLD: .75X TO 2X BASE HI
*201-214 GOLD: HALF VALUE OF BASE
*215-244 GOLD: .75X TO 2X BASE HI
ONE PER PACK

2006-07 Ultra Platinum Medallion

*1-170 PLATINUM: 5X TO 12X BASE HI
*171-200 PLATINUM: 1X TO 2.5X BASE HI
1-200 PLAT.PRINT RUN 100 SER.#'d SETS
201-214 NOT PRICED DUE TO SCARCITY
201-214 PRINT RUN 14 SER.#'d SETS
*215-244 PLATINUM: 4X TO 10X BASE HI
215-244 PLAT.PRINT RUN 25 SER.#'d SETS
26 LeBron James 30.00 80.00
70 Kobe Bryant 125.00 225.00

2006-07 Ultra Red

*201-214 RED: .3X TO .75X BASE HI
*215-244 RED: 1.25X TO 3X BASE HI
RED APPROXIMATELY ONE PER BOX

2006-07 Ultra Fresh Ink

RANDOM INSERTS IN PACKS
FIBB Brent Barry 6.00 15.00
FIDH Dwight Howard 10.00 25.00
FIHW Hakim Warrick 6.00 15.00
FIKM Kevin Martin 5.00 12.00
FILJ LeBron James SP 75.00 150.00
FIRF Raymond Felton 6.00 15.00
FIRT Ronny Turiaf 6.00 15.00

2006-07 Ultra Kings of the Court

APPROXIMATE ODDS 1:24
KKAI Andre Iguodala 3.00 8.00
KKAJ Antawn Jamison 3.00 8.00
KKAL Al Jefferson 3.00 8.00
KKBD Baron Davis 3.00 8.00
KKBH Brendan Haywood 2.00 5.00
KKBW Ben Wallace 3.00 8.00
KKCM Corey Maggette 2.50 6.00
KKDG Drew Gooden 2.50 6.00
KKDN Dirk Nowitzki 5.00 12.00
KKJM Jeff McInnis 2.00 5.00
KKJO Jermaine O'Neal 3.00 8.00
KKJR Jason Richardson 3.00 8.00
KKKB Kobe Bryant 8.00 20.00
KKKG Kevin Garnett 6.00 15.00
KKLD Luol Deng 3.00 8.00
KKLJ LeBron James 8.00 20.00
KKMG Manu Ginobili 3.00 8.00
KKPS Peja Stojakovic 3.00 8.00
KKSM Stephon Marbury 2.50 6.00
KKYM Yao Ming 4.00 10.00

2006-07 Ultra One on One

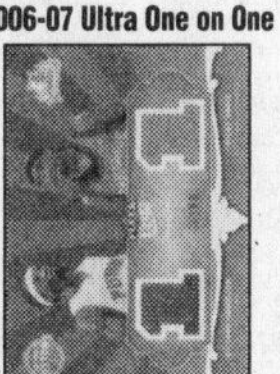

PRINT RUN 100 SER.#'d SETS
OOBN Chauncey Billups 6.00 15.00
Steve Nash
OOFM Steve Francis 5.00 12.00
Stephon Marbury
OOHD Richard Hamilton 5.00 12.00
Ricky Davis
OOMB Shawn Marion 6.00 15.00
Chris Bosh
OOMO Yao Ming 10.00 25.00
Shaquille O'Neal
OOMP Kenyon Martin 5.00 12.00
Tayshaun Prince
OOSH Amare Stoudemire 6.00 15.00
Dwight Howard

2006-07 Ultra Scoring Kings

COMPLETE SET 10.00 25.00
APPROXIMATE ODDS 1:6
SKAI Allen Iverson .75 2.00
SKCA Carmelo Anthony .75 2.00
SKDN Dirk Nowitzki 1.00 2.50
SKDW Dwyane Wade 1.50 4.00
SKEB Elton Brand .60 1.50
SKGA Gilbert Arenas .60 1.50
SKJR Jason Richardson .60 1.50
SKKB Kobe Bryant 3.00 8.00
SKKG Kevin Garnett 1.25 3.00
SKLJ LeBron James 3.00 8.00
SKPP Paul Pierce .75 2.00
SKRA Ray Allen .60 1.50
SKRH Richard Hamilton .50 1.25
SKRJ Richard Jefferson .60 1.50
SKSM Shawn Marion .60 1.50
SKSN Steve Nash .75 2.00
SKTD Tim Duncan 1.00 2.50
SKTM Tracy McGrady .75 2.00
SKTP Tony Parker .60 1.50
SKVC Vince Carter .75 2.00

2006-07 Ultra Season Crowns

COMPLETE SET 8.00 20.00
APPROXIMATE ODDS 1:12
SCAI Allen Iverson 1.00 2.50
SCAS Amare Stoudemire .75 2.00
SCCP Chris Paul 1.50 4.00
SCGA Gilbert Arenas .75 2.00
SCJK Jason Kidd 1.25 3.00
SCKG Kevin Garnett 1.50 4.00
SCSO Shaquille O'Neal 1.50 4.00
SCTD Tim Duncan 1.25 3.00
SCTP Tony Parker .75 2.00
SCVC Vince Carter 1.00 2.50

2006-07 Ultra Three Kings

PRINT RUN 50 SER.#'d SETS
TKBMJ Kobe Bryant 30.00 80.00
Tracy McGrady
LeBron James
TKDMO Tim Duncan 15.00 40.00
Yao Ming
Shaquille O'Neal
TKJHB LeBron James 15.00 40.00
Dwight Howard
Andrew Bogut
TKJWD Antawn Jamison 6.00 15.00
Rasheed Wallace
Luol Deng
TKKMN Jason Kidd 12.50 30.00
Stephon Marbury
Steve Nash
TKPFV Chris Paul 12.50 30.00
Channing Frye
Charlie Villanueva

2007-08 Ultra SE

This 273-card set was released in September, 2007. The set was issued into the hobby in five-card packs with an $20 SRP which came 15 packs to a box. Cards numbered 1-200 feature veterans in team alphabetical order while cards numbered 201-243 feature 2007-08 NBA rookies. The set concludes with retired greats from cards 244-256. The final 13 cards in the rookie subset and the retired greats were all issued as Lucky 13 cards. A few of the players from 201-256 were released in a blank back version. We have notated those cards with an BB notation in our data base.

COMP.SET w/o SP's (200) 25.00 50.00
1 Joe Johnson .40 1.00
2 Josh Smith .40 1.00
3 Josh Childress .30 .75
4 Marvin Williams .40 1.00
5 Anthony Johnson .25 .60
6 Shelden Williams .25 .60
7 Tyronn Lue .25 .60
8 Al Jefferson .40 1.00
9 Paul Pierce .50 1.25
10 Wally Szczerbiak .30 .75
11 Sebastian Telfair .25 .60
12 Gerald Green .30 .75
13 Rajon Rondo .60 1.50
14 Delonte West .30 .75
15 Adam Morrison .40 1.00
16 Emeka Okafor .40 1.00
17 Gerald Wallace .40 1.00
18 Raymond Felton .50 1.25
19 Sean May .25 .60
20 Matt Carroll .25 .60
21 Ben Wallace .40 1.00
22 Ben Gordon .40 1.00
23 Tyrus Thomas .40 1.00
24 Luol Deng .40 1.00
25 Kirk Hinrich .40 1.00
26 Andres Nocioni .25 .60
27 Thabo Sefolosha .40 1.00
28 LeBron James 2.00 5.00
29 Larry Hughes .30 .75
30 Zydrunas Ilgauskas .30 .75
31 Drew Gooden .30 .75
32 Daniel Gibson .40 1.00
33 Shannon Brown .40 1.00
34 Dirk Nowitzki .50 1.25
35 Josh Howard .30 .75
36 Jason Terry .30 .75
37 Jerry Stackhouse .30 .75
38 Devin Harris .40 1.00
39 Erick Dampier .25 .60
40 Jose Barea .60 1.50
41 Carmelo Anthony .50 1.25
42 Allen Iverson .50 1.25
43 J.R. Smith .40 1.00
44 Yakhouba Diawara .25 .60
45 Marcus Camby .25 .60
46 Eduardo Najera .25 .60
47 Chauncey Billups .40 1.00
48 Richard Hamilton .30 .75
49 Tayshaun Prince .40 1.00
50 Chris Webber .40 1.00
51 Rasheed Wallace .40 1.00
52 Will Blalock .25 .60
53 Nazr Mohammed .25 .60
54 Baron Davis .40 1.00
55 Al Harrington .30 .75
56 Stephen Jackson .30 .75
57 Jason Richardson .40 1.00
58 Monta Ellis .40 1.00
59 Mickael Pietrus .25 .60
60 Kelenna Azubuike .25 .60
61 Yao Ming .50 1.25
62 Tracy McGrady .40 1.00
63 Rafer Alston .25 .60
64 Luther Head .30 .75
65 Shane Battier .30 .75
66 Juwan Howard .30 .75
67 Bonzi Wells .25 .60
68 Jermaine O'Neal .40 1.00
69 Danny Granger .40 1.00
70 Jamaal Tinsley .25 .60
71 Mike Dunleavy .30 .75
72 Troy Murphy .25 .60
73 Shawne Williams .25 .60
74 Elton Brand .40 1.00
75 Corey Maggette .30 .75
76 Sam Cassell .40 1.00
77 Cuttino Mobley .30 .75
78 Tim Thomas .25 .60
79 Chris Kaman .30 .75
80 Kobe Bryant 2.00 5.00
81 Jordan Farmar .25 .60
82 Lamar Odom .40 1.00
83 Andrew Bynum .50 1.25
84 Smush Parker .25 .60
85 Luke Walton .25 .60
86 Maurice Evans .25 .60
87 Rudy Gay .40 1.00
88 Pau Gasol .40 1.00
89 Mike Miller .40 1.00
90 Hakim Warrick .30 .75
91 Kyle Lowry .40 1.00
92 Damon Stoudamire .30 .75
93 Shaquille O'Neal .75 2.00
94 Dwyane Wade 1.00 2.50
95 Jason Williams .30 .75
96 Jason Kapono .25 .60
97 Alonzo Mourning .50 1.25
98 Udonis Haslem .30 .75
99 Gary Payton .40 1.00
100 Michael Redd .40 1.00
101 Maurice Williams .30 .75
102 Andrew Bogut .40 1.00
103 Charlie Villanueva .40 1.00
104 Ruben Patterson .25 .60
105 Charlie Bell .25 .60
106 Kevin Garnett .75 2.00
107 Rashad McCants .25 .60
108 Ricky Davis .30 .75
109 Randy Foye .40 1.00
110 Craig Smith .25 .60
111 Mike James .25 .60
112 Jason Kidd .40 1.00
113 Vince Carter .50 1.25
114 Richard Jefferson .40 1.00
115 Nenad Krstic .25 .60
116 Bernard Robinson .25 .60
117 Marcus Williams .25 .60
118 Josh Boone .25 .60
119 Chris Paul .75 2.00
120 Peja Stojakovic .40 1.00
121 David West .40 1.00
122 Desmond Mason .25 .60
123 Cedric Simmons .30 .75
124 Hilton Armstrong .25 .60
125 Devin Brown .25 .60
126 Nate Robinson .40 1.00
127 Eddy Curry .25 .60
128 Jamal Crawford .30 .75
129 Stephon Marbury .30 .75
130 Quentin Richardson .30 .75
131 David Lee .30 .75
132 Channing Frye .30 .75
133 Dwight Howard .60 1.50
134 J.J. Redick .40 1.00
135 Grant Hill .50 1.25
136 Jameer Nelson .30 .75
137 Hedo Turkoglu .40 1.00
138 Tony Battie .25 .60
139 Darko Milicic .25 .60
140 Carlos Arroyo .30 .75
141 Andre Iguodala .40 1.00
142 Kyle Korver .30 .75
143 Samuel Dalembert .25 .60
144 Rodney Carney .25 .60
145 Willie Green .25 .60
146 Andre Miller .30 .75
147 Bobby Jones .25 .60
148 Steve Nash .50 1.25
149 Amare Stoudemire .40 1.00
150 Shawn Marion .40 1.00
151 Leandro Barbosa .30 .75
152 Raja Bell .30 .75
153 Boris Diaw .30 .75
154 LaMarcus Aldridge .50 1.25
155 Zach Randolph .30 .75
156 Brandon Roy .50 1.25
157 Jarrett Jack .30 .75
158 Ime Udoka .25 .60
159 Martell Webster .30 .75
160 Sergio Rodriguez .25 .60
161 Fred Jones .25 .60
162 Kevin Martin .40 1.00
163 Ron Artest .40 1.00

164 Mike Bibby .40 1.00
165 Brad Miller .30 .75
166 Quincy Douby .25 .60
167 Shareef Abdur-Rahim .30 .75
168 Radoslav Nesterovic .25 .60
169 Tony Parker .40 1.00
170 Tim Duncan .60 1.50
171 Manu Ginobili .40 1.00
172 Michael Finley .40 1.00
173 Brent Barry .25 .60
174 Bruce Bowen .25 .60
175 Ray Allen .40 1.00
176 Rashard Lewis .30 .75
177 Chris Wilcox .25 .60
178 Luke Ridnour .30 .75
179 Nick Collison .25 .60
180 Earl Watson .25 .60
181 Mickael Gelabale .25 .60
182 Chris Bosh .40 1.00
183 Andrea Bargnani .50 1.25
184 T.J. Ford .30 .75
185 Anthony Parker .25 .60
186 Jorge Garbajosa .30 .75
187 Morris Peterson .25 .60
188 Jose Calderon .30 .75
189 Carlos Boozer .40 1.00
190 Mehmet Okur .25 .60
191 Deron Williams .60 1.50
192 Paul Millsap .30 .75
193 Ronnie Brewer .30 .75
194 Andrei Kirilenko .30 .75
195 Gilbert Arenas .40 1.00
196 Caron Butler .40 1.00
197 Antawn Jamison .40 1.00
198 DeShawn Stevenson .25 .60
199 Brendan Haywood .25 .60
200 Etan Thomas .25 .60
201 Al Thornton RC 2.00 5.00
201B Al Thornton BB 2.00 5.00
202 Rodney Stuckey RC 3.00 8.00
203 Nick Young RC 3.00 8.00
204 Sean Williams RC 2.00 5.00
205 Marco Belinelli RC 2.00 5.00
206 Javaris Crittenton RC 2.00 5.00
206B Javaris Crittenton BB 2.00 5.00
207 Jason Smith RC 2.00 5.00
208 Daequan Cook RC 2.00 5.00
209 Jared Dudley RC 2.00 5.00
210 Wilson Chandler RC 3.00 8.00
211 Morris Almond RC 2.00 5.00
212 Aaron Brooks RC 2.00 5.00
213 Arron Afflalo RC 2.50 6.00
214 Alando Tucker RC 2.00 5.00
215 Petteri Koponen RC 2.00 5.00
216 Carl Landry RC 2.00 5.00
217 Gabe Pruitt RC 2.00 5.00
217B Gabe Pruitt BB 2.00 5.00
218 Marcus Williams RC 2.00 5.00
219 Nick Fazekas RC 2.00 5.00
220 Glen Davis RC 3.00 8.00
220B Glen Davis BB 3.00 8.00
221 Jermareo Davidson RC 2.00 5.00
222 Josh McRoberts RC 2.00 5.00
223 Kyrylo Fesenko RC 2.00 5.00
224 Stanko Barac RC 2.00 5.00
225 Sun Yue RC 2.00 5.00
225B Sun Yue BB 2.00 5.00
226 Chris Richard RC 2.00 5.00
227 Derrick Byars RC 2.00 5.00
227B Derrick Byars BB 2.00 5.00
228 Adam Haluska RC 2.00 5.00
229 Reyshawn Terry RC 2.00 5.00
230 Taurean Green RC 2.00 5.00
231 Greg Oden L13 RC 3.00 8.00
231B Greg Oden BB 3.00 8.00
232 Kevin Durant L13 RC 15.00 40.00
233 Al Horford L13 RC 3.00 8.00
233B Al Horford BB 3.00 8.00
234 Mike Conley Jr. L13 RC 4.00 10.00
235 Jeff Green L13 RC 3.00 8.00
236 Yi Jianlian L13 RC 4.00 10.00
236B Yi Jianlian BB 4.00 10.00
237 Corey Brewer L13 RC 3.00 8.00
238 Brandan Wright L13 RC 2.50 6.00
239 Joakim Noah L13 RC 6.00 15.00
239B Joakim Noah BB 6.00 15.00
240 Spencer Hawes L13 RC 2.50 6.00
241 Acie Law L13 RC 2.50 6.00
242 Thaddeus Young L13 RC 3.00 8.00
242B Thaddeus Young BB 3.00 8.00
243 Julian Wright L13 RC 2.50 6.00
243B Julian Wright BB 2.50 6.00
244 Michael Jordan L13 12.00 30.00
244B Michael Jordan BB 12.00 30.00
245 Larry Bird L13 5.00 12.00
246 Magic Johnson L13 4.00 10.00
246B Magic Johnson BB 4.00 10.00
247 Bill Russell L13 2.50 6.00
248 Dennis Rodman L13 2.50 6.00
248B Dennis Rodman BB 2.50 6.00
249 Kareem Abdul-Jabbar L13 2.50 6.00
249B Kareem Abdul-Jabbar BB 2.50 6.00
250 Clyde Drexler L13 2.00 5.00
251 Hakeem Olajuwon L13 2.00 5.00
252 John Havlicek L13 1.50 4.00
253 David Robinson L13 2.50 6.00
254 John Stockton L13 2.50 6.00
254B John Stockton BB 2.50 6.00
255 Jerry West L13 2.00 5.00
256 Julius Erving L13 3.00 8.00

2007-08 Ultra SE Gold Medallion

*1-200 GOLD: .75X TO 2X BASE HI
*201-230 GOLD: .6X TO 1.5X BASE HI
*231-243 GOLD: .5X TO 1.25X BASE HI
*243-256 GOLD: .6X TO 1.5X BASE HI
GOLD ODDS ONE PER PACK
232 Kevin Durant L13 25.00 60.00

2007-08 Ultra SE Platinum Medallion

*1-200 PLAT: 6X TO 15X BASE HI
*201-230 PLAT: 2X TO 5X BASE
*231-243 PLAT: 1.5X TO 4X BASE
*244-256 PLAT: 2X TO 5X BASE HI
PRINT RUN 25 SER.#'d SETS
80 Kobe Bryant 150.00 300.00
232 Kevin Durant L13 150.00 300.00
244 Michael Jordan L13 250.00 400.00

2007-08 Ultra SE Autographics Black

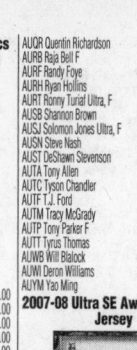

ONE AUTO CARD PER HOBBY BOX
CARDS WITH (F) INSERTED IN FLEER
AUAB Andrea Bargnani 6.00 15.00
AUAH Al Harrington 3.00 8.00
AUAI Andre Iguodala 6.00 15.00
AUAJ Antawn Jamison 4.00 10.00
AUAR Allan Ray 3.00 8.00
AUAU James Augustine 3.00 8.00
AUBB Bruce Bowen Ultra, F 3.00 8.00
AUBD Boris Diaw F 3.00 8.00
AUBJ Bobby Jackson 3.00 8.00
AUBJ2 Bobby Jones 3.00 8.00
AUBM Brad Miller F 3.00 8.00
AUBR Ronnie Brewer 3.00 8.00
AUCB Charlie Bell 3.00 8.00
AUCM Chris Mihm 3.00 8.00
AUCS Cedric Simmons 3.00 8.00
AUDB Dee Brown 3.00 8.00
AUDE Daniel Ewing 3.00 8.00
AUDL David Lee F 4.00 10.00
AUDM Donyell Marshall 3.00 8.00
AUDN David Noel 3.00 8.00
AUDW Damien Wilkens F 3.00 8.00
AUFE Raymond Felton Ultra, F 3.00 8.00
AUGK George Karl 8.00 20.00
AUHW Hakim Warrick 3.00 8.00
AUJB Josh Boone 3.00 8.00
AUJJ Jarrett Jack 3.00 8.00
AUJK Jason Kapono 3.00 8.00
AUJO Bobby Jones 4.00 10.00
AUJS J.R. Smith 3.00 8.00
AUJW James White 3.00 8.00
AUKD Keyon Dooling 3.00 8.00
AUKH Kirk Hinrich 8.00 20.00
AUKK Kyle Korver 3.00 8.00
AULA Larry Hughes 5.00 12.00
AULP Leon Powe 3.00 8.00
AUMA Mardy Collins 3.00 8.00
AUMD Marquis Daniels Ultra, F 3.00 8.00
AUMG Corey Maggette 3.00 8.00
AUMI Andre Miller 4.00 10.00
AUMP Morris Peterson 3.00 8.00
AUPD Paul Davis 3.00 8.00
AUPM Paul Millsap 3.00 8.00
AUQR Quentin Richardson 3.00 8.00
AURB Raja Bell F 5.00 12.00
AURC Rodney Carney Ultra, F 3.00 8.00
AURF Randy Foye 4.00 10.00
AURH Ryan Hollins Ultra, F 3.00 8.00
AURM Rashad McCants 3.00 8.00
AURR Rajon Rondo 12.00 30.00
AURT Ronny Turiaf F 6.00 15.00
AUSA Shareef Abdur-Rahim F 3.00 8.00
AUSB Shannon Brown Ultra, F 3.00 8.00
AUSE Sean May F 3.00 8.00
AUSI James Singleton 3.00 8.00
AUSJ Solomon Jones 3.00 8.00
AUSM Craig Smith 3.00 8.00
AUSN Steve Novak 3.00 8.00
AUST DeShawn Stevenson 3.00 8.00
AUTA Tony Allen 3.00 8.00
AUTC Tyson Chandler 3.00 8.00
AUTF T.J. Ford 3.00 8.00
AUWB Will Blalock 3.00 8.00
AUWI Deron Williams F 10.00 25.00

2007-08 Ultra SE Autographics Blue

ONE AUTO CARD PER HOBBY BOX
CARDS WITH (F) INSERTED IN FLEER
RED AU UNPRICED DUE TO SCARCITY
AUAB Andrea Bargnani 6.00 15.00
AUAH Al Harrington 3.00 8.00
AUAI Andre Iguodala 10.00 25.00
AUAJ Antawn Jamison 6.00 15.00
AUAM Alonzo Mourning 50.00 100.00
AUAU James Augustine 3.00 8.00
AUBB Bruce Bowen Ultra, F 3.00 8.00
AUBG Ben Gordon 8.00 20.00
AUBJ Bobby Jackson 6.00 15.00
AUCA Carmelo Anthony Ultra, F 30.00 80.00
AUCB Charlie Bell 3.00 8.00
AUCM Chris Mihm 3.00 8.00
AUCP Chris Paul 15.00 40.00
AUCS Cedric Simmons 3.00 8.00
AUDB Dee Brown 3.00 8.00
AUDE Daniel Ewing 3.00 8.00
AUDM Donyell Marshall 3.00 8.00
AUDN David Noel 3.00 8.00
AUDS Dean Smith 30.00 80.00
AUEO Emeka Okafor 4.00 10.00
AUHW Hakim Warrick 3.00 8.00
AUJB Josh Boone 3.00 8.00
AUJE Julius Erving Ultra, F 30.00 80.00
AUJG Joey Graham 3.00 8.00
AUJJ Jarrett Jack 3.00 8.00
AUJK Jason Kapono 3.00 8.00
AUJO Bobby Jones 3.00 8.00
AUJW James White 3.00 8.00
AUKB Kobe Bryant 100.00 200.00
AUKH Kirk Hinrich 8.00 20.00
AUKI Jason Kidd 12.50 30.00
AUKK Kyle Korver 4.00 10.00
AULA LaMarcus Aldridge Ultra, F 15.00 40.00
AULB Larry Bird 60.00 120.00
AULH Larry Hughes 6.00 15.00
AULJ LeBron James 125.00 250.00
AULP Leon Powe 3.00 8.00
AUMA Magic Johnson 60.00 120.00
AUMC Mardy Collins 3.00 8.00
AUMD Marquis Daniels Ultra, F 3.00 8.00
AUMG Corey Maggette 3.00 8.00
AUMI Andre Miller 3.00 8.00
AUMJ Michael Jordan 400.00 600.00
AUMP Morris Peterson 3.00 8.00
AUNO Steve Novak 3.00 8.00
AUON Jermaine O'Neal 6.00 15.00
AUPM Paul Millsap 5.00 12.00
AUPP Paul Pierce 10.00 25.00
AUPR Pat Riley 15.00 30.00
AUQR Quentin Richardson 3.00 8.00
AURB Raja Bell F 6.00 15.00
AURF Randy Foye 4.00 10.00
AURH Ryan Hollins 3.00 8.00
AURT Ronny Turiaf Ultra, F 5.00 12.00
AUSB Shannon Brown 3.00 8.00
AUSJ Solomon Jones Ultra, F 3.00 8.00
AUSN Steve Nash 50.00 100.00
AUST DeShawn Stevenson 3.00 8.00
AUTA Tony Allen 3.00 8.00
AUTC Tyson Chandler 3.00 8.00
AUTF T.J. Ford 3.00 8.00
AUTM Tracy McGrady 15.00 30.00
AUTP Tony Parker F 10.00 25.00
AUTT Tyrus Thomas 10.00 25.00
AUWB Will Blalock 3.00 8.00
AUWI Deron Williams 10.00 25.00
AUYM Yao Ming 20.00 40.00

2007-08 Ultra SE Award Winners Jersey

PRINT RUN 199 SER.#'d SETS
*PATCH: 1.25X TO 3X BASE HI
PATCH PRINT RUN 25 SER.#'d SETS
AWAI Allen Iverson 4.00 10.00
AWAJ Antawn Jamison 3.00 8.00
AWAM Alonzo Mourning 4.00 10.00
AWAS Amare Stoudemire 3.00 8.00
AWBD Boris Diaw 2.50 6.00
AWBR Brandon Roy 4.00 10.00
AWBW Ben Wallace 3.00 8.00
AWCB Chauncey Billups 3.00 8.00
AWCW Chris Webber 3.00 8.00
AWDM Dikembe Mutombo 3.00 8.00
AWDN Dirk Nowitzki 4.00 10.00
AWDS Damon Stoudamire 2.50 6.00
AWEB Elton Brand 3.00 8.00
AWEO Emeka Okafor 3.00 8.00
AWGA Gilbert Arenas 3.00 8.00
AWGH Grant Hill 4.00 10.00
AWGP Gary Payton 3.00 8.00
AWJK Jason Kidd 3.00 8.00
AWJN Jameer Nelson 2.50 6.00
AWJO Jermaine O'Neal 3.00 8.00
AWKB Kobe Bryant 8.00 20.00
AWKG Kevin Garnett 6.00 15.00
AWLJ LeBron James 8.00 20.00
AWMC Marcus Camby 2.00 5.00
AWNR Nate Robinson 3.00 8.00
AWPG Pau Gasol 3.00 8.00
AWRA Ron Artest 3.00 8.00
AWSN Steve Nash 4.00 10.00
AWTD Tim Duncan 5.00 12.00
AWVC Vince Carter 4.00 10.00

2007-08 Ultra SE Call to the Hall

COMPLETE SET (10) 8.00 20.00
RANDOM INSERTS IN PACKS
CH1 Kobe Bryant 3.00 8.00
CH2 LeBron James 3.00 8.00
CH3 Paul Pierce .75 2.00
CH4 Shaquille O'Neal 1.25 3.00
CH5 Kevin Garnett 1.25 3.00
CH6 Yao Ming .75 2.00
CH7 Michael Jordan 5.00 12.00
CH8 Gary Payton .60 1.50
CH9 Tim Duncan 1.00 2.50
CH10 Allen Iverson .75 2.00

2007-08 Ultra SE Call to the Hall Memorabilia

RANDOM INSERTS IN PACKS
CHAI Allen Iverson 3.00 8.00
CHGP Gary Payton 2.50 6.00
CHKB Kobe Bryant 8.00 20.00
CHKG Kevin Garnett 5.00 12.00
CHLJ LeBron James 8.00 20.00
CHMJ Michael Jordan 25.00 60.00
CHPP Paul Pierce 3.00 8.00
CHSO Shaquille O'Neal 5.00 12.00
CHTD Tim Duncan 4.00 10.00
CHYM Yao Ming 3.00 8.00

2007-08 Ultra SE Court Masters

COMPLETE SET (15) 10.00 25.00
RANDOM INSERTS IN PACKS
CM1 Steve Nash 1.25 3.00
CM2 Jason Williams .75 2.00
CM3 John Stockton 1.50 4.00
CM4 Gary Payton 1.00 2.50
CM5 Stephon Marbury .75 2.00
CM6 Damon Stoudamire .75 2.00
CM7 Jason Kidd 1.00 2.50
CM8 Deron Williams 1.50 4.00
CM9 Chris Paul 2.00 5.00
CM10 Baron Davis 1.00 2.50
CM11 Kevin Garnett 2.00 5.00
CM12 Chauncey Billups 1.00 2.50
CM13 Jamaal Tinsley .60 1.50
CM14 Grant Hill 1.25 3.00
CM15 Jarrett Jack .75 2.00

2007-08 Ultra SE Court Masters Memorabilia

RANDOM INSERTS IN PACKS
CMBD Baron Davis 2.50 6.00
CMCB Chauncey Billups 2.50 6.00
CMCP Chris Paul 5.00 12.00
CMDS Damon Stoudamire 2.00 5.00
CMDW Deron Williams 4.00 10.00
CMGH Grant Hill 3.00 8.00
CMGP Gary Payton 2.50 6.00
CMJJ Jarrett Jack 2.00 5.00
CMJK Jason Kidd 2.50 6.00
CMJS John Stockton 4.00 10.00
CMJT Jamaal Tinsley 2.00 5.00
CMJW Jason Williams 2.00 5.00
CMKG Kevin Garnett 5.00 12.00
CMSM Stephon Marbury 2.00 5.00
CMSN Steve Nash 3.00 8.00

2007-08 Ultra SE Heir to the Throne Jersey

PRINT RUN 199 SER.#'d SETS
*PATCHES: 1.25X TO 3X BASE HI
PATCH PRINT RUN 25 SER.#'d SETS
HTAB Andrea Bargnani 4.00 10.00
HTAI Andre Iguodala 3.00 8.00
HTAJ Al Jefferson 3.00 8.00
HTAS Amare Stoudemire 3.00 8.00
HTBL Andray Blatche 2.00 5.00
HTBO Andrew Bogut 3.00 8.00
HTBR Brandon Roy 4.00 10.00
HTCA Carmelo Anthony 4.00 10.00
HTCB Caron Butler 3.00 8.00
HTCP Chris Paul 6.00 15.00
HTDH Dwight Howard 5.00 12.00
HTDW David West 3.00 8.00
HTEO Emeka Okafor 3.00 8.00
HTFE Raymond Felton 4.00 10.00
HTGW Gerald Wallace 2.50 6.00
HTHW Hakim Warrick 2.50 6.00
HTJC Josh Childress 2.50 6.00
HTJF Jordan Farmar 2.00 5.00
HTJH Josh Howard 2.50 6.00
HTJR J.J. Redick 3.00 8.00
HTJS J.R. Smith 3.00 8.00
HTKH Kirk Hinrich 3.00 8.00
HTLA LaMarcus Aldridge 4.00 10.00
HTLD Luol Deng 3.00 8.00
HTLH Luther Head 2.50 6.00
HTLJ LeBron James 8.00 20.00
HTMW Marvin Williams 3.00 8.00
HTPA Tony Parker 3.00 8.00
HTPD Paul Davis 2.00 5.00
HTQD Quincy Douby 2.00 5.00
HTRF Randy Foye 3.00 8.00
HTRG Rudy Gay 3.00 8.00
HTRJ Richard Jefferson 3.00 8.00
HTRM Rashad McCants 2.00 5.00
HTSB Shannon Brown 3.00 8.00
HTSJ Josh Smith 3.00 8.00
HTSM Sean May 2.00 5.00
HTTP Tayshaun Prince 3.00 8.00
HTTS Thabo Sefolosha 3.00 8.00
HTWI Deron Williams 5.00 12.00

2007-08 Ultra SE Jam City

RANDOM INSERTS IN PACKS
JC1 Baron Davis 1.00 2.50
JC2 Clyde Drexler 1.25 3.00
JC3 Dee Brown .60 1.50
JC4 Dwight Howard 1.50 4.00
JC5 Desmond Mason .60 1.50
JC6 DeShawn Stevenson .60 1.50
JC7 Fred Jones .60 1.50
JC8 Gerald Green .75 2.00
JC9 Julius Erving 2.00 5.00
JC10 Michael Jordan 10.00 25.00
JC11 Jason Richardson 1.00 2.50
JC12 Josh Smith 1.00 2.50
JC13 Kobe Bryant 5.00 12.00
JC14 Larry Nance 1.00 2.50
JC15 Michael Finley 1.00 2.50
JC16 Michael Jordan 10.00 25.00
JC17 Nate Robinson 1.00 2.50
JC18 Tom Chambers 1.00 2.50
JC19 Tyrus Thomas 1.00 2.50
JC20 Vince Carter 1.25 3.00

2007-08 Ultra SE Jersey

PRINT RUN 50 SER.#'d SETS
UJAJ Al Jefferson 4.00 10.00
UJBJ Bobby Jones 2.50 6.00
UJCF Channing Frye 3.00 8.00
UJCM Corey Maggette 3.00 8.00
UJCS Cedric Simmons 3.00 8.00
UJDS DeShawn Stevenson 2.50 6.00
UJGW Gerald Wallace 4.00 10.00
UJHA Hilton Armstrong 2.50 6.00
UJJC Jose Calderon 3.00 8.00
UJJO Jermaine O'Neal 4.00 10.00
UJJT Jamaal Tinsley 2.50 6.00
UJKB Kwame Brown 2.50 6.00
UJLJ LeBron James 12.50 30.00
UJMA Maurice Ager 2.50 6.00
UJMB Mike Bibby 4.00 10.00
UJMD Mike Dunleavy 3.00 8.00
UJMP Morris Peterson 2.50 6.00
UJQR Quentin Richardson 3.00 8.00
UJRA Ray Allen 4.00 10.00
UJRD Ricky Davis 3.00 8.00
UJRH Richard Hamilton 3.00 8.00
UJRW Rasheed Wallace 4.00 10.00
UJSD Samuel Dalembert 2.50 6.00
UJSF Steve Francis 4.00 10.00
UJSN Steve Novak 2.50 6.00
UJTP Tayshaun Prince 4.00 10.00
UJUH Udonis Haslem 3.00 8.00
UJWB Will Blalock 2.50 6.00
UJWS Wally Szczerbiak 3.00 8.00
UJZI Zydrunas Ilgauskas 3.00 8.00

2007-08 Ultra SE Mini Jerseys

RANDOM INSERTS IN PACKS
1 LeBron James 6.00 15.00
2 Kobe Bryant 6.00 15.00
3 Allen Iverson 4.00 10.00
4 Shaquille O'Neal 5.00 12.00
5 Paul Pierce 4.00 10.00
6 Dirk Nowitzki 4.00 10.00
7 Tim Duncan 4.00 10.00
8 Kevin Garnett 4.00 10.00
9 Dwight Howard 4.00 10.00
10 Yao Ming 4.00 10.00
11 Steve Nash 4.00 10.00
12 Chris Bosh 4.00 10.00
13 Michael Jordan 10.00 25.00

2007-08 Ultra SE Mini Jerseys Autographs

MOST UNPRICED DUE TO SCARCITY
13 Michael Jordan 400.00 650.00

2007-08 Ultra SE One on One Jersey

PRINT RUN 99 SER.#'d SETS
*PATCHES: 1.25X TO 3X BASE HI
PATCH PRINT RUN 25 SER.#'d SETS
OOAH Ray Allen / Richard Hamilton 4.00 10.00
OOBA Mike Bibby / Gilbert Arenas 4.00 10.00
OOBB Carlos Boozer / Shane Battier 4.00 10.00
OOBH Elton Brand / Grant Hill 6.00 15.00
OOBJ Kobe Bryant / LeBron James 15.00 30.00
OOCB Caron Butler / Chris Bosh 4.00 10.00
OOCC Jason Collins / Jarron Collins 4.00 10.00
OOCM Antawn Jamison / Sean May 4.00 10.00
OOGO Ben Gordon / Emeka Okafor 4.00 10.00
OOGS Pau Gasol / Wally Szczerbiak 4.00 10.00
OOHC Luther Head / Brian Cook 4.00 10.00
OOHP Kirk Hinrich / Paul Pierce 5.00 12.00
OOHW Juwan Howard / Chris Webber 5.00 12.00
OOIW Andre Iguodala / Luke Walton 4.00 10.00
OOJC Bobby Jones / Mardy Collins 4.00 10.00
OOJJ Michael Jordan / LeBron James 30.00 60.00
OOJR Fred Jones / Luke Ridnour 4.00 10.00
OOJW Jamaal Magloire / Antoine Walker 4.00 10.00
OOKF Jason Kapono / Jordan Farmar 4.00 10.00
OOMB Yao Ming / Andrea Bargnani 5.00 12.00
OOMD Corey Maggette / Luol Deng 4.00 10.00
OOMK Darko Milicic / Nenad Krstic 4.00 10.00
OOML Larry Bird / Magic Johnson 10.00 25.00
OOMW Jameer Nelson / Jeff McInnis 4.00 10.00
OOOL Lamar Odom / Shaun Livingston 4.00 10.00
OOOM Shaquille O'Neal / Dikembe Mutombo 5.00 12.00
OORR Zach Randolph / Jason Richardson 4.00 10.00
OOSR Josh Smith / Nate Robinson 4.00 10.00
OOWT Jason Williams / Jason Terry 4.00 10.00
OOWW Ben Wallace / Rasheed Wallace 4.00 10.00

2007-08 Ultra SE Rising Stars

COMPLETE SET (19) 15.00 40.00
RANDOM INSERTS IN PACKS
RS1 Kevin Durant 8.00 20.00
RS2 Al Horford 1.25 3.00
RS3 Mike Conley Jr. 1.50 4.00
RS4 Jeff Green 1.25 3.00
RS5 Corey Brewer 1.25 3.00
RS6 Greg Oden 1.25 3.00
RS8 Brandan Wright 1.00 2.50
RS9 Joakim Noah 2.50 6.00
RS10 Spencer Hawes 1.00 2.50
RS11 Acie Law 1.00 2.50
RS12 Thaddeus Young 1.25 3.00
RS13 Julian Wright 1.00 2.50
RS14 Al Thornton 1.00 2.50
RS15 Rodney Stuckey 1.50 4.00
RS16 Nick Young 1.50 4.00
RS17 Sean Williams 1.00 2.50
RS18 Marco Belinelli 1.00 2.50
RS19 Javaris Crittenton 1.00 2.50
RS20 Jason Smith 1.00 2.50

2007-08 Ultra SE Scoring Kings

COMPLETE SET (20) 8.00 20.00
RANDOM INSERTS IN PACKS
SK1 Carmelo Anthony .75 2.00
SK2 Gilbert Arenas .60 1.50
SK3 LeBron James 3.00 8.00
SK4 Mehmet Okur .40 1.00
SK5 Michael Redd .60 1.50
SK6 Joe Johnson .60 1.50
SK7 Ray Allen .60 1.50
SK8 Vince Carter .75 2.00
SK9 Tracy McGrady .60 1.50
SK10 Carlos Boozer .60 1.50
SK11 Kevin Martin .60 1.50
SK12 Ben Gordon .60 1.50
SK13 Elton Brand .60 1.50
SK14 Jermaine O'Neal .60 1.50
SK15 Josh Howard .50 1.25
SK16 Zach Randolph .50 1.25
SK17 Luol Deng .60 1.50
SK18 Ron Artest .60 1.50
SK19 Shawn Marion .60 1.50
SK20 Peja Stojakovic .60 1.50

2007-08 Ultra SE Scoring Kings Memorabilia

RANDOM INSERTS IN PACKS
SKAR Ron Artest 2.50 6.00
SKBG Ben Gordon 2.50 6.00
SKCA Carmelo Anthony 3.00 8.00
SKCB Carlos Boozer 2.50 6.00
SKEB Elton Brand 2.50 6.00
SKGA Gilbert Arenas 2.50 6.00
SKJH Josh Howard 2.00 5.00
SKJJ Joe Johnson 2.50 6.00
SKJO Jermaine O'Neal 2.50 6.00
SKKM Kevin Martin 2.50 6.00
SKLD Luol Deng 2.50 6.00
SKLJ LeBron James 8.00 20.00
SKME Mehmet Okur 2.00 5.00
SKMR Michael Redd 2.50 6.00
SKPS Peja Stojakovic 2.50 6.00
SKRA Ray Allen 2.50 6.00
SKSM Shawn Marion 2.50 6.00
SKTM Tracy McGrady 2.50 6.00
SKVC Vince Carter 3.00 8.00
SKZR Zach Randolph 2.00 5.00

2007-08 Ultra SE Season Crowns

COMPLETE SET (25) 20.00 40.00
RANDOM INSERTS IN PACKS
SC1 Tim Duncan 1.00 2.50
SC2 Michael Jordan 5.00 12.00
SC3 Chauncey Billups .60 1.50
SC4 Shaquille O'Neal 1.25 3.00
SC5 Kareem Abdul-Jabbar 1.00 2.50
SC6 Hakeem Olajuwon .75 2.00
SC7 Alonzo Mourning .75 2.00
SC8 Horace Grant .60 1.50
SC9 Tony Parker .60 1.50
SC10 Manu Ginobili .60 1.50
SC11 David Robinson 1.00 2.50
SC12 Richard Hamilton .50 1.25
SC13 Tayshaun Prince .60 1.50
SC14 Clyde Drexler .75 2.00
SC15 Dennis Rodman 1.00 2.50
SC16 Larry Bird 2.00 5.00
SC17 Julius Erving 1.25 3.00
SC18 Magic Johnson 1.50 4.00
SC19 Sean Elliott .60 1.50
SC20 Jason Williams .50 1.25
SC21 Ben Wallace .60 1.50
SC22 Michael Jordan 6.00 15.00
SC23 Bruce Bowen .40 1.00
SC24 Devean George .40 1.00
SC25 Bill Laimbeer .60 1.50

2007-08 Ultra SE Season Crowns Memorabilia

RANDOM INSERTS IN PACKS
SCAM Alonzo Mourning 3.00 8.00
SCBB Bruce Bowen 2.00 5.00
SCBL Bill Laimbeer 2.50 6.00
SCBW Ben Wallace 2.50 6.00
SCCB Chauncey Billups 2.50 6.00
SCCD Clyde Drexler 3.00 8.00
SCDG Devean George 1.50 4.00
SCDR David Robinson 4.00 10.00
SCHG Horace Grant 2.50 6.00
SCHO Hakeem Olajuwon 3.00 8.00
SCJE Julius Erving 5.00 12.00
SCJO Magic Johnson 6.00 15.00
SCJW Jason Williams 2.00 5.00
SCKA Kareem Abdul-Jabbar 4.00 10.00
SCLB Larry Bird 8.00 20.00
SCMG Manu Ginobili 2.50 6.00
SCMI Michael Jordan 20.00 50.00
SCMJ Michael Jordan 20.00 50.00
SCPR Tayshaun Prince 2.50 6.00
SCRH Richard Hamilton 2.00 5.00
SCRO Dennis Rodman 4.00 10.00
SCSE Sean Elliott 2.50 6.00
SCSO Shaquille O'Neal 5.00 12.00
SCTD Tim Duncan 4.00 10.00
SCTP Tony Parker 2.50 6.00

2007-08 Ultra SE Signature Class

PRINT RUN 50 SER.#'d SETS
SCAA Arron Afflalo 8.00 20.00
SCAG Aaron Gray
SCAH Al Horford 8.00 20.00
SCAL Acie Law 6.00 15.00
SCAT Al Thornton
SCCB Corey Brewer 8.00 20.00
SCCL Carl Landry 6.00 15.00
SCDA Jermareo Davidson 6.00 15.00
SCDJ D.J. Strawberry 6.00 15.00
SCGD Glen Davis 10.00 25.00
SCGP Gabe Pruitt 6.00 15.00
SCHH Herbert Hill 6.00 15.00
SCJC Javaris Crittenton 6.00 15.00
SCJD Jared Dudley 6.00 15.00
SCJG Jeff Green 8.00 20.00
SCJJ Jared Jordan 6.00 15.00
SCJN Joakim Noah 30.00 80.00
SCJO JamesOn Curry 6.00 15.00
SCJS Jason Smith 6.00 15.00
SCKD Kevin Durant 250.00 450.00
SCMC Mike Conley Jr. 10.00 25.00
SCMW Marcus Williams 6.00 15.00
SCNF Nick Fazekas 6.00 15.00
SCRT Reyshawn Terry 6.00 15.00
SCSB Stanko Barac 6.00 15.00
SCSH Spencer Hawes 6.00 15.00
SCSL Stephane Lasme 6.00 15.00
SCSM Sammy Mejia 6.00 15.00
SCSW Sean Williams 6.00 15.00

CTG Taurean Green 6.00 15.00
CWC Wilson Chandler 10.00 25.00

2007-08 Ultra SE Snap Shots

OMPLETE SET (40) 30.00 60.00
ANDOM INSERTS IN PACKS
S1 Marvin Williams .75 2.00
S2 Larry Bird 2.50 6.00
S3 John Havlicek .75 2.00
S4 Bill Russell 1.25 3.00
S5 Adam Morrison .75 2.00
S6 Raymond Felton 1.00 2.50
S7 Michael Jordan 6.00 15.00
S8 Ben Gordon .75 2.00
S9 Dennis Rodman 1.25 3.00
S10 LeBron James 4.00 10.00
S11 Dirk Nowitzki 1.00 2.50
S12 Carmelo Anthony 1.00 2.50
S13 Allen Iverson 1.00 2.50
S14 Tracy McGrady .75 2.00
S15 Stephon Marbury .60 1.50
S16 Clyde Drexler 1.00 2.50
S17 Hakeem Olajuwon 1.00 2.50
S18 Kobe Bryant 4.00 10.00
S19 Magic Johnson 2.00 5.00
S20 Kareem Abdul-Jabbar 1.25 3.00
S21 Shaquille O'Neal 1.50 4.00
S22 Dwyane Wade 2.00 5.00
S23 Andrew Bogut .75 2.00
S24 Kevin Garnett 1.50 4.00
S25 Peja Stojakovic .75 2.00
S26 Jason Kidd .75 2.00
S27 Chris Paul 1.50 4.00
S28 Dwight Howard 1.25 3.00
S29 J.J. Redick .75 2.00
S30 Julius Erving 1.50 4.00
S31 Andre Iguodala .75 2.00
S32 Steve Nash 1.00 2.50
S33 LaMarcus Aldridge 1.00 2.50
S34 Brandon Roy 1.00 2.50
S35 Paul Pierce 1.00 2.50
S36 David Robinson 1.25 3.00
S37 Lenny Wilkens .75 2.00
S38 Kevin Martin .75 2.00
S39 Lamar Odom .75 2.00
S40 John Stockton 1.25 3.00

2007-08 Ultra SE Stars

COMPLETE SET (30) 10.00 25.00
RANDOM INSERTS IN PACKS
JS1 LeBron James 2.50 6.00
JS2 Kevin Martin .50 1.25
JS3 Kobe Bryant 2.50 6.00
JS4 Jason Richardson .50 1.25
JS5 Alonzo Mourning .60 1.50
JS6 Brad Miller .40 1.00
JS7 Carlos Boozer .50 1.25
JS8 Amare Stoudemire .50 1.25
JS9 Andrei Kirilenko .40 1.00
JS10 Baron Davis .50 1.25
JS11 Corey Maggette .40 1.00
JS12 Brandon Roy .60 1.50
JS13 Lamar Odom .50 1.25
JS14 Larry Hughes .40 1.00
JS15 Chris Bosh .50 1.25
JS16 Tracy McGrady .50 1.25
JS17 Yao Ming .60 1.50
JS18 Richard Jefferson .50 1.25
JS19 Andrea Bargnani .60 1.50
JS20 Jordan Farmar .30 .75
JS21 Raymond Felton .60 1.50
JS22 Drew Gooden .40 1.00
JS23 Dirk Nowitzki .60 1.50
JS24 Pau Gasol .50 1.25
JS25 Mike Bibby .50 1.25
JS26 Zach Randolph .40 1.00
JS27 Michael Redd .50 1.25
JS28 Marvin Williams .50 1.25
JS29 Deron Williams .75 2.00
JS30 Antoine Walker .40 1.00

2007-08 Ultra SE Stars Memorabilia

RANDOM INSERTS IN PACKS
USAB Andrea Bargnani 3.00 8.00
USAK Andrei Kirilenko 2.00 5.00
USAM Alonzo Mourning 3.00 8.00
USAS Amare Stoudemire 2.50 6.00
USAW Antoine Walker 2.00 5.00
USBD Baron Davis 2.50 6.00
USBM Brad Miller 2.00 5.00
USBO Chris Bosh 2.50 6.00
USBR Brandon Roy 3.00 8.00
USCB Carlos Boozer 2.50 6.00
USCM Corey Maggette 2.00 5.00
USDG Drew Gooden 2.00 5.00
USDN Dirk Nowitzki 3.00 8.00
USDW Deron Williams 4.00 10.00
USJF Jordan Farmar 1.50 4.00
USJR Jason Richardson 2.50 6.00
USKB Kobe Bryant 6.00 15.00
USKM Kevin Martin 2.50 6.00
USLH Larry Hughes 2.00 5.00
USLJ LeBron James 8.00 20.00
USLO Lamar Odom 2.50 6.00
USMB Mike Bibby 2.50 6.00
USMR Michael Redd 2.50 6.00
USMW Marvin Williams 2.50 6.00
USPG Pau Gasol 2.50 6.00
USRF Raymond Felton 3.00 8.00
USRJ Richard Jefferson 2.50 6.00
USTM Tracy McGrady 2.50 6.00
USYM Yao Ming 3.00 8.00
USZR Zach Randolph 2.00 5.00

1992-93 Ultra Jam Session Cassette Insert

Measuring the standard size, this card was included in NBA Jam Session "Gangsta Rap" cassette. On a gray marbleized background, this card display small color action photos of the top five NBA jammers. Their "dunk rank" (from one to five) is reflected in the listing below.

1 David Robinson 1.25 3.00
Dikembe Mutombo
Otis Thorpe
Hakeem Olajuwon
Shawn Kemp

1999 Ultra WNBA

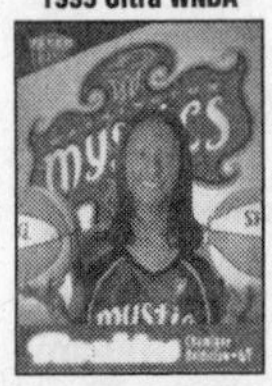

The debut issue of Ultra WNBA, produced by Fleer/SkyBox, was issued as a 125 card set. The packs contained 10 cards that carried a suggested retail price of $2.49. The rookie subset, cards 101-125, was shortprinted at one in two packs.

COMPLETE SET (125) 40.00 100.00
COMP.SET w/o SP (100) 8.00 20.00
UNPRICED MASTERPIECES SERIAL #'d TO 1
1 Sheryl Swoopes 1.25 3.00
2 Christy Smith .20 .50
3 Nikki McCray .60 1.50
4 Coquese Washington RC .40 1.00
5 Vickie Johnson .30 .75
6 Toni Foster .30 .75
7 Allison Feaster RC .50 1.25
8 Penny Toler .30 .75
9 Brandy Reed RC .60 1.50
10 Yolanda Moore .20 .50
11 Lisa Leslie 1.00 2.50
12 Kisha Ford .20 .50
13 Merlakia Jones .30 .75
14 Umeki Webb .20 .50
15 Tora Suber .30 .75
16 Octavia Blue RC .20 .50
17 Bridget Pettis .20 .50
18 LaTonya Johnson RC .30 .75
19 Alessandra Santos de Oliveria RC .30 .75
20 Tia Paschal RC .20 .50
21 Jennifer Gillom .50 1.25
22 Wanda Guyton .20 .50
23 Franthea Price RC .20 .50
24 Andrea Kuklova .20 .50
25 Vicky Bullett .30 .75
26 Dena Head .20 .50
27 Isabelle Fijalkowski .20 .50
28 Michelle Edwards .40 1.00
29 Pamela McGee .30 .75
30 Elisabeth Cebrian RC .20 .50
31 Olympia Scott-Richardson .20 .50
32 Murriel Page .30 .75
33 Korie Hlede RC .60 1.50
34 Andrea Stinson .40 1.00
35 Kristie Harrower RC .30 .75
36 Kym Hampton .30 .75
37 Gergana Branzova RC .20 .50
38 Teresa Weatherspoon .75 2.00
39 Rebecca Lobo .60 1.50
40 Michele Timms .60 1.50
41 Tamecka Dixon .30 .75
42 Tina Thompson .75 2.00
43 Janice Braxton .20 .50
44 Elena Baranova .50 1.25
45 Adrienne Johnson RC .60 1.50
46 Adia Barnes RC .30 .75
47 Elaine Powell RC .30 .75
48 Lady Hardmon .20 .50
49 Kim Perrot .60 1.50
50 Marlies Askamp RC .30 .75
51 Deborah Carter .20 .50
52 Sandy Brondello RC .75 2.00
53 Heidi Burge .20 .50
54 Janeth Arcain .20 .50
55 Rushia Brown .20 .50
56 Suzie McConnell-Serio .50 1.25
57 Penny Moore .30 .75
58 Margo Dydek RC .75 2.00
59 Angie Potthoff RC .20 .50
60 Monica Lamb RC .30 .75
61 Jamila Wideman .30 .75
62 Ticha Penicheiro RC 1.00 2.50
63 Andrea Congreaves .20 .50
64 Rachael Sporn RC .30 .75
65 Chantel Tremitiere .20 .50
66 Carla McGhee RC .30 .75
67 Kim Williams .20 .50
68 Tangela Smith .20 .50
69 Quacy Barnes .20 .50
70 Sue Wicks .30 .75
71 Tracy Reid RC .40 1.00
72 Linda Burgess .20 .50
73 Razija Brcaninovic RC .30 .75
74 Sharon Manning .20 .50
75 Tammy Jackson .20 .50
76 Rita Williams .25 .60
77 Carla Porter RC .30 .75
78 Michelle Griffiths RC .40 1.00
79 Eva Nemcova .30 .75
80 Sophia Witherspoon .30 .75
81 Sonja Tate RC .30 .75
82 Cynthia Cooper 1.25 3.00
83 Wendy Palmer .50 1.25
84 Ruthie Bolton-Holifield .60 1.50
85 Tammi Reiss .30 .75
86 Katrina Colleton RC .20 .50
87 Cindy Brown .40 1.00
88 Latasha Byears .30 .75
89 Mwadi Mabika .20 .50
90 Rhonda Mapp .25 .60
91 Tina Thompson AW .40 1.00
92 Sheryl Swoopes AW .60 1.50
93 Jennifer Gillom AW .25 .60
94 Cynthia Cooper AW .60 1.50
95 Suzie McConnell Serio AW .25 .60
96 Cindy Brown AW .20 .50
97 Eva Nemcova AW .15 .40
98 Lisa Leslie AW .50 1.25
99 Andrea Stinson AW .20 .50
100 Teresa Weatherspoon AW .40 1.00
101 Dawn Staley RC 2.50 6.00
102 Chamique Holdsclaw RC 6.00 15.00
103 Kristin Folkl RC 1.50 4.00
104 Nykesha Sales RC 2.00 5.00
105 Natalie Williams RC 2.00 5.00
106 Yolanda Griffith RC 4.00 10.00
107 Crystal Robinson RC 1.25 3.00
108 Edna Campbell RC 1.50 4.00
109 Tari Phillips RC 1.25 3.00
110 Tonya Edwards RC 1.00 2.50
111 Debbie Black RC 1.50 4.00
112 Kate Starbird RC 1.50 4.00
113 Adrienne Goodson RC 1.25 3.00
114 Sheri Sam RC 1.00 2.50
115 DeLisha Milton RC 1.00 2.50
116 Shannon Johnson RC 1.00 2.50
117 Katie Smith RC 2.50 6.00
118 Kara Wolters RC 1.50 4.00
119 Jennifer Azzi RC 2.50 6.00
120 Michele VanGorp RC 1.25 3.00
121 Stephanie White-McCarty RC 1.50 4.00
122 Ukari Figgs RC 1.25 3.00
123 Val Whiting RC 1.00 2.50
124 Mery Andrade RC 1.00 2.50
125 Charlotte Smith RC 1.00 2.50

1999 Ultra WNBA Gold Medallion

Inserted at one per hobby pack, this 125-card set parallels the base Ultra WNBA set. The cards feature gold foil on the front. To ascertain values for individual cards, please refer to the multiplier in the header, coupled with the value of the base card.

COMPLETE SET (125) 75.00 150.00
*GOLD 1-100: .75X TO 2X BASE HI

1999 Ultra WNBA Platinum Medallion

Randomly inserted in packs, this 125-card set parallels the base set. The cards feature a platinum front and are serially numbered out of 99 on the back for cards 1-100, and numbered to 66 for cards 101-125.

*PLATINUM 1-100: 10X TO 25X HI COL.
*PLATINUM 101-125: 6X TO 15X HI COL.

1999 Ultra WNBA Fresh Ink

Randomly inserted in packs, this 13-card set features autographs from the WNBA. The cards feature the Fleer/SkyBox authentication logo in the center with a certificate as the card back. The cards were hand-numbered to 400. They are not numbered and listed below alphabetically.

COMPLETE SET (13) 175.00 350.00
1 Elena Baranova 12.00 30.00
2 Cynthia Cooper 30.00 80.00
3 Kristin Folkl 10.00 25.00
4 Lisa Leslie 25.00 60.00
5 Suzie McConnell-Serio 12.00 30.00
6 Nikki McCray 15.00 40.00
7 Nykesha Sales 12.00 30.00
8 Dawn Staley 15.00 40.00
9 Andrea Stinson 10.00 25.00
10 Sheryl Swoopes 30.00 80.00
11 Michele Timms 15.00 40.00
12 Penny Toler 8.00 20.00
13 Teresa Weatherspoon 20.00 50.00

1999 Ultra WNBA Rock Talk

Randomly inserted in packs at one in 24, this set features players who leave opponents talking to themselves.

COMPLETE SET (10) 15.00 40.00
1 Eva Nemcova 1.25 3.00
2 Cynthia Cooper 5.00 12.00
3 Ruthie Bolton-Holifield 2.50 6.00
4 Michele Timms 2.50 6.00
5 Jennifer Gillom 2.00 5.00
6 Cindy Brown 1.50 4.00
7 Lisa Leslie 4.00 10.00
8 Andrea Stinson 1.50 4.00
9 Teresa Weatherspoon 3.00 8.00
10 Rebecca Lobo 2.50 6.00

1999 Ultra WNBA WNBAttitude

Randomly inserted in packs at one in six, this 10-card set features some of the league's most high profile personalities.

COMPLETE SET (10) 5.00 12.00
1 Lisa Leslie 1.25 3.00
2 Cynthia Cooper 1.50 4.00
3 Ruthie Bolton-Holifield .75 2.00
4 Rebecca Lobo .75 2.00
5 Sheryl Swoopes 1.50 4.00
6 Nikki McCray .75 2.00
7 Cindy Brown .50 1.25
8 Jennifer Gillom .60 1.50
9 Wendy Palmer .60 1.50
10 Michele Timms .75 2.00

1999 Ultra WNBA World Premiere

Randomly inserted at one in 12, this 10-card set features the newcomers to the WNBA.

COMPLETE SET (10) 8.00 20.00
1 Chamique Holdsclaw 4.00 10.00
2 Dawn Staley 1.50 4.00
3 Nykesha Sales 1.25 3.00
4 Kristin Folkl 1.00 2.50
5 Natalie Williams 1.25 3.00
6 Yolanda Griffith 2.50 6.00
7 Crystal Robinson .75 2.00
8 Edna Campbell 1.00 2.50
9 DeLisha Milton .60 1.50
10 Debbie Black 1.00 2.50

2000 Ultra WNBA Promo

This card was sent out to dealers for promotional purposes. It features Cynthia Cooper.

1 Cynthia Cooper 1.50 4.00

2000 Ultra WNBA

Released in August 2000, this 150-card set features players from the WNBA. The cards came in 10-card packs that carried a suggested retail price of $2.99. The set features 125 regular player cards (with rookies) and a special 25 card rookie subset, inserted at one in two.

COMPLETE SET (150) 35.00 70.00
COMP.SET w/o SP (125) 15.00 40.00
UNPRICED MASTERPIECES SERIAL #'d TO 1
1 Cynthia Cooper 1.50 4.00
2 Chamique Holdsclaw 1.50 4.00
3 Lisa Leslie 1.25 3.00
4 Anna DeForge RC .25 .60
5 Stephanie McCarty .50 1.25
6 Katrina Colleton .25 .60
7 Clarisse Machanguana RC .25 .60
8 Adrienne Goodson .25 .60
9 Charlotte Smith .25 .60
10 DeLisha Milton .25 .60
11 Janeth Arcain .25 .60
12 Donna Harrington RC .25 .60
13 Michele Timms .75 2.00
14 Charmin Smith RC .60 1.50
15 Tricia Bader RC .25 .60
16 Vickie Johnson .40 1.00
17 Monica Lamb .25 .60
18 Dawn Staley .60 1.50
19 Ruthie Bolton-Holifield .75 2.00
20 Jennifer Azzi .75 2.00
21 Becky Hammon RC 3.00 8.00
22 Latasha Byears .40 1.00
23 Lisa Harrison RC .60 1.50
24 Jennifer Rizzotti RC 1.25 3.00
25 Yolanda Griffith .75 2.00
26 Tracy Henderson RC .25 .60
27 Sophia Witherspoon .40 1.00
28 Sheryl Swoopes 1.50 4.00
29 Korie Hlede .40 1.00
30 Shannon Johnson .25 .60
31 Chasity Melvin RC .25 .60
32 Tamika Whitmore RC .40 1.00
33 Tina Thompson .75 2.00
34 Kedra Holland-Corn RC .40 1.00
35 Markita Aldridge RC .25 .60
36 Dalma Ivanyi RC .25 .60
37 Ticha Penicheiro .60 1.50
38 Quacy Barnes .25 .60
39 Ukari Figgs .25 .60
40 Andrea Lloyd Curry RC .40 1.00
41 Tammy Jackson .25 .60
42 Nikki McCray .60 1.50
43 Kate Starbird .40 1.00
44 Andrea Nagy RC .60 1.50
45 Bridget Pettis .25 .60
46 Eva Nemcova .40 1.00
47 Tangela Smith .25 .60
48 Astou Ndiaye-Diatta RC .75 2.00
49 Tamecka Dixon .40 1.00
50 Taj McWilliams RC .40 1.00
51 Kristin Folkl .40 1.00
52 Amanda Wilson RC .75 2.00
53 Chantel Tremitiere .25 .60
54 Dominique Canty RC .75 2.00
55 Allison Feaster .30 .75
56 Angie Potthoff .25 .60
57 Nykesha Sales .40 1.00
58 Rhonda Mapp .30 .75
59 Murriel Page .30 .75
60 Maria Stepanova .25 .60
61 Katie Smith .75 2.00
62 Michelle Edwards .50 1.25
63 Venus Lacy RC .25 .60
64 Adrienne Johnson .40 1.00
65 Rita Williams .30 .75
66 Andrea Stinson .50 1.25
67 La'Keshia Frett RC .25 .60
68 Jennifer Gillom .60 1.50
69 LaTonya Johnson .25 .60
70 Joy Holmes-Harris RC .25 .60
71 Rushia Brown .25 .60
72 Michelle Campbell RC .25 .60
73 Angie Braziel RC .50 1.25
74 Crystal Robinson .25 .60
75 Alicia Thompson .25 .60
76 Suzie McConnell-Serio .50 1.25
77 Tanja Kostic RC .25 .60
78 Amaya Valdemoro RC .40 1.00
79 Sue Wicks .40 1.00
80 Sonja Tate .25 .60
81 Natalie Williams .50 1.25
82 Mery Andrade .25 .60
83 Tracy Reid .40 1.00
84 Olympia Scott-Richardson .25 .60
85 Rebecca Lobo .75 2.00
86 Margo Dydek .50 1.25
87 Sonja Henning RC .40 1.00
88 Vicky Bullett .40 1.00
89 Mwadi Mabika .25 .60
90 Linda Burgess .25 .60
91 Merlakia Jones .40 1.00
92 Umeki Webb .25 .60
93 Niesa Johnson RC .25 .60
94 Texlan Quinney RC .25 .60
95 Teresa Weatherspoon 1.00 2.50
96 Wendy Palmer .60 1.50
97 Brandy Reed .40 1.00
98 Oksana Zakaluzhnaya RC .25 .60
99 Sharon Manning .25 .60
100 Kara Wolters .30 .75
101 Keisha Anderson RC .40 1.00
102 Edna Campbell .30 .75
103 DeMya Walker RC .25 .60
104 Michele VanGorp .30 .75
105 Coquese Washington .25 .60
106 Marlies Askamp .25 .60
107 Michelle Marciniak RC .60 1.50
108 Angela Aycock RC .40 1.00
109 Tari Phillips .25 .60
110 Sylvia Crawley RC .40 1.00
111 Tonya Edwards .25 .60
112 Monica Maxwell RC .25 .60
113 Beth Cunningham RC .25 .60
114 Debbie Black .40 1.00
115 Shalonda Enis RC .25 .60
116 Naomi Mulitauaopele RC .40 1.00
117 Jamila Wideman .40 1.00
118 Shanele Stires RC .40 1.00
119 Alisa Burras RC .40 1.00
120 Gordana Grubin RC .25 .60
121 Elaine Powell .25 .60
122 Tausha Mills RC .40 1.00
123 Katy Steding RC .25 .60
124 Jannon Roland RC .25 .60
125 Jessie Hicks .25 .60
126 Ann Wauters RC 1.00 2.50
127 Edwina Brown RC 1.00 2.50
128 Grace Daley RC 1.00 2.50
129 Helen Darling RC 1.00 2.50
130 Summer Erb RC 1.00 2.50
131 Kamila Vodichkova RC 1.00 2.50
132 Tamicha Jackson RC 1.00 2.50
133 Betty Lennox RC 4.00 10.00
134 Maylana Martin RC 1.00 2.50
135 Lynn Pride RC 1.00 2.50
136 Paige Sauer RC 1.00 2.50
137 Madinah Slaise RC 1.00 2.50
138 Stacey Thomas RC 1.00 2.50
139 Cintia Dos Santos RC 1.00 2.50
140 Milena Flores RC 1.00 2.50
141 Rhonda Banchero RC 1.00 2.50
142 Jameka Jones RC 1.00 2.50
143 Jessica Bibby RC 1.00 2.50
144 Adrain Williams RC 1.00 2.50
145 Olga Firsova RC 1.00 2.50
146 Usha Gilmore RC 1.00 2.50
147 Shantia Owens RC 1.00 2.50
148 Jurgita Streimikyte RC 1.00 2.50
149 Katrina Hibbert RC 1.00 2.50
150 Tonya Washington RC 1.00 2.50

2000 Ultra WNBA Gold Medallion

Randomly inserted at one per pack for cards 1-125 and at one in 24 for cards 126-150, this 150-card set parallels the base set. The cards feature gold foil. To ascertain values on individual cards, please refer to the multipliers in the headers below, coupled with the value of the base card.

COMPLETE SET (150) 80.00 200.00
*GOLD 1-125: .75X TO 2X BASE CARD HI
*GOLD 126-150: 1.25X TO 3X BASE HI

2000 Ultra WNBA Platinum Medallion

Randomly inserted in packs, this 150-card set parallels the base set. The cards feature platinum, or silver foil. Cards 1-125 featured serial numbering to 50, while cards 126-150 featured serial numbering to 25.

*PLAT 1-125: 12X TO 30X BASE CARD HI
*PLAT 126-150: 8X TO 20X HI COL.

2000 Ultra WNBA Feel the Game

Randomly inserted in packs at one in 144, this 16-card set features swatches of game-worn sneakers. The cards are not numbered and listed below in alphabetical order. Two of the cards also feature numbered autographs: Cynthia Cooper to 14 and Sheryl Swoopes to 22. Those cards are not included in the set price.

1 Debbie Black 10.00 25.00
2 Ruthie Bolton-Holifield 20.00 50.00
3 Cynthia Cooper 40.00 100.00
3A Cynthia Cooper AU/14 400.00 600.00
4 Tonya Edwards 6.00 15.00
5 Jennifer Gillom 15.00 40.00
6 Yolanda Griffith 20.00 50.00
7 Kedra Holland-Corn 10.00 25.00
8 Lisa Leslie 30.00 80.00
9 Suzie McConnell-Serio 12.00 30.00
10 Taj McWilliams 10.00 25.00
11 DeLisha Milton 6.00 15.00
12 Ticha Penicheiro 15.00 40.00
13 Dawn Staley 15.00 40.00
14 Kate Starbird 12.00 30.00
15 Sheryl Swoopes 40.00 100.00
15A Sheryl Swoopes AU/22 300.00 500.00
16 Natalie Williams 12.00 30.00

2000 Ultra WNBA Feminine Adrenaline

Randomly inserted in packs at one in four, this 10-card set features players who always provide a jump-start for their team.

COMPLETE SET (10) 6.00 15.00
1 Nikki McCray 1.00 2.50
2 Ticha Penicheiro 1.00 2.50
3 Teresa Weatherspoon 1.50 4.00
4 Jennifer Azzi 1.25 3.00
5 Lisa Leslie 2.00 5.00
6 Sheryl Swoopes 2.50 6.00
7 Tina Thompson 1.25 3.00
8 Jennifer Gillom 1.00 2.50
9 Suzie McConnell-Serio .75 2.00
10 Dawn Staley 1.00 2.50

2000 Ultra WNBA Fresh Ink

Randomly inserted in packs at one in 72, this 18-card set features autographs from some of the top players in the WNBA. The cards are not numbered on the back, and listed below alphabetically.

COMPLETE SET (18) 150.00 300.00
*GOLD: 1.25X TO 3X BASE HI
GOLD PRINT RUN 50 SER.#'d SETS
1 Debbie Black 5.00 12.00
2 Ruthie Bolton-Holifield 10.00 25.00
3 Cynthia Cooper 20.00 50.00
4 Tonya Edwards 3.00 8.00
5 Jennifer Gillom 8.00 20.00
6 Yolanda Griffith 10.00 25.00
7 Vickie Johnson 5.00 12.00
8 Carolyn Jones-Young 5.00 12.00
9 Lisa Leslie 15.00 40.00
10 Suzie McConnell-Serio 6.00 15.00
11 DeLisha Milton 3.00 8.00
12 Eva Nemcova 5.00 12.00
13 Ticha Penicheiro 8.00 20.00
14 Nykesha Sales 5.00 12.00
15 Dawn Staley 8.00 20.00
16 Sheryl Swoopes 20.00 50.00
17 Teresa Weatherspoon/500 12.00 30.00
18 Natalie Williams 6.00 15.00

2000 Ultra WNBA Trophy Case

Randomly inserted in packs at one in 12, this 10-card set features players named to the WNBA's First or Second All-WNBA team in 1999. The cards feature a die cut design in the shape of a court.

COMPLETE SET (10) 15.00 40.00
1 Sheryl Swoopes 4.00 10.00
2 Natalie Williams 1.25 3.00
3 Yolanda Griffith 2.00 5.00
4 Cynthia Cooper 4.00 10.00
5 Ticha Penicheiro 1.50 4.00
6 Chamique Holdsclaw 4.00 10.00
7 Tina Thompson 2.00 5.00
8 Lisa Leslie 3.00 8.00
9 Teresa Weatherspoon 2.50 6.00
10 Shannon Johnson .60 1.50

2000 Ultra WNBA WNBAttitude

Randomly inserted in packs at one in eight, this 10-card set features the players who play with extreme emotion every night.

COMPLETE SET (10) 8.00 20.00
1 Andrea Stinson 1.00 2.50
2 Eva Nemcova .75 2.00
3 Wendy Palmer 1.25 3.00
4 Shannon Johnson .50 1.25
5 Jennifer Gillom 1.25 3.00
6 Yolanda Griffith 1.50 4.00
7 Natalie Williams 1.00 2.50
8 Chamique Holdsclaw 3.00 8.00
9 Cynthia Cooper 3.00 8.00
10 Vickie Johnson .75 2.00

2001 Ultra WNBA

Released in late August 2001, this 150-card set features a full color borderless card design with a floating box towards the bottom with the player's name and her team logo. A coach subset was printed for cards 110-123, and rookies 124-150 were inserted at 1:2 packs. A special Cynthia Cooper autograph was also inserted with the set and is sequentially numbered to 350. Ultra WNBA was packaged in 24-pack boxes where packs contained eight cards each.

COMPLETE SET (150) 80.00 160.00
1 Betty Lennox .75 2.00
2 Ukari Figgs .25 .60
3 Tangela Smith .25 .60
4 Sue Wicks .40 1.00
5 Marla Brumfield RC .25 .60
6 Maria Stepanova .25 .60
7 Murriel Page .30 .75
8 Michele Timms .75 2.00
9 Janeth Arcain .25 .60
10 Lisa Harrison .40 1.00
11 Tausha Mills .25 .60
12 Sheri Sam .25 .60
13 Sonja Henning .25 .60
14 Adrienne Johnson .40 1.00
15 Mwadi Mabika .25 .60
16 Chasity Melvin .25 .60
17 Allison Feaster .30 .75
18 Monica Maxwell .25 .60
19 Katie Smith .75 2.00
20 Stacey Thomas .25 .60
21 Robin Threatt-Elliott RC .25 .60
22 Jennifer Azzi .75 2.00
23 Shannon Johnson .25 .60
24 Rhonda Mapp .30 .75
25 Eva Nemcova .40 1.00
26 Edwina Brown .30 .75
27 Margo Dydek .40 1.00
28 Ann Wauters .30 .75
29 Nicky McCrimmon RC .25 .60
30 Dominique Canty .40 1.00
31 Adrienne Goodson .25 .60
32 Taj McWilliams-Franklin .25 .60
33 DeLisha Milton .25 .60
34 Mery Andrade .25 .60
35 Yolanda Griffith .75 2.00
36 Tari Phillips .25 .60
37 Rita Williams .30 .75
38 Marlies Askamp .25 .60
39 Korie Hlede .40 1.00
40 Tamicha Jackson .25 .60
41 Elaine Powell .25 .60
42 Elena Baranova .60 1.50
43 Astou Ndiaye-Diatta .40 1.00
44 Nykesha Sales .40 1.00
45 Natalie Williams .50 1.25
46 Debbie Black .40 1.00
47 Vicky Bullett .40 1.00
48 Michelle Cleary RC .25 .60
49 Wendy Palmer .60 1.50
50 Tully Bevilaqua RC .40 1.00
51 Helen Darling .30 .75
52 Katy Steding .25 .60
53 Sheryl Swoopes 1.50 4.00
54 Kristin Folkl .40 1.00
55 Lady Hardmon .25 .60
56 Jennifer Rizzotti .60 1.50
57 Adrain Williams .25 .60
58 Tricia Bader Binford .25 .60
59 Kedra Holland-Corn .25 .60
60 Crystal Robinson .25 .60
61 Kara Wolters .30 .75
62 Rushia Brown .25 .60
63 Tamecka Dixon .40 1.00
64 Ticha Penicheiro .60 1.50
65 Teresa Weatherspoon 1.00 2.50
66 Edna Campbell .30 .75
67 Sylvia Crawley .25 .60
68 Shalonda Enis .25 .60
69 Andrea Lloyd-Curry .25 .60
70 Tina Thompson .75 2.00
71 Michelle Edwards .50 1.25
72 Stephanie McCarty .50 1.25
73 Shantia Owens .25 .60
74 Shanele Stires .25 .60
75 DeMya Walker .25 .60
76 Quacy Barnes .25 .60
77 Cintia Dos Santos .25 .60
78 Merlakia Jones .40 1.00
79 Lisa Leslie 1.25 3.00
80 Grace Daley .25 .60
81 Jamie Redd RC .25 .60
82 Charlotte Smith .25 .60
83 Jurgita Streimikyte .25 .60
84 Sophia Witherspoon .40 1.00
85 Ruthie Bolton-Holifield .75 2.00
86 Vickie Johnson .40 1.00
87 Andrea Stinson .50 1.25
88 Texlan Quinney .25 .60
89 Tammy Jackson .25 .60
90 Andrea Nagy .40 1.00
91 Brandy Reed .40 1.00
92 Umeki Webb .25 .60
93 Andrea Garner RC .25 .60
94 Maylana Martin .30 .75
95 Vanessa Nygaard RC .25 .60
96 Kamila Vodichkova .25 .60
97 Coquese Washington .25 .60
98 Jennifer Gillom .60 1.50
99 Nikki McCray .60 1.50
100 Tracy Reid .40 1.00
101 Elena Tornikidou RC .25 .60
102 Becky Hammon 1.50 4.00
103 Dawn Staley .60 1.50
104 Alicia Thompson .25 .60
105 Tiffany Travis RC .40 1.00
106 Sandy Brondello .60 1.50
107 Tonya Edwards .25 .60
108 Chamique Holdsclaw 1.50 4.00
109 Olympia Scott-Richardson .25 .60
110 Anne Donovan CO .75 2.00
111 Brian Alger CO .75 2.00
112 Lin Dunn CO .75 2.00
113 Van Chancellor CO .75 2.00
114 Nell Fortner CO .75 2.00
115 Michael Cooper CO .75 2.00
116 Ron Rothstein CO .75 2.00
117 Richie Adubato CO .75 2.00
118 Cynthia Cooper CO 1.50 4.00
119 Linda Hargrove CO .75 2.00
120 Fred Williams CO .75 2.00
121 Dan Hughes CO .75 2.00
122 Carolyn Peck CO .75 2.00
123 Sonny Allen CO .75 2.00
124 Brooke Wyckoff RC 6.00 15.00
125 Jackie Stiles RC 10.00 25.00
126 Svetlana Abrosimova RC 2.50 6.00
127 Tamika Catchings RC 5.00 12.00
128 Katie Douglas RC 4.00 10.00
129 Lauren Jackson RC 10.00 25.00
130 Shea Ralph RC 2.50 6.00
131 Ruth Riley RC 3.00 8.00
132 Kelly Miller RC 2.50 6.00
133 Marie Ferdinand RC 2.50 6.00
134 Tammy Sutton-Brown RC 2.50 6.00
135 Camille Cooper RC 2.50 6.00
136 Janell Burse RC 2.50 6.00
137 LaQuanda Barksdale RC 2.50 6.00
138 Niele Ivey RC 2.50 6.00
139 Coco Miller RC 2.50 6.00
140 Deanna Nolan RC 2.50 6.00
141 Penny Taylor RC 3.00 8.00
142 Kristen Veal RC 2.50 6.00

143 Kelly Schumacher RC 2.50 6.00
144 Amanda Lassiter RC 2.50 6.00
145 Semeka Randall RC 2.50 6.00
146 Jenny Mowe RC 2.50 6.00
147 Georgia Schweitzer RC 2.50 6.00
148 Jae Kingi RC 2.50 6.00
149 Erin Buescher RC 2.50 6.00
150 Michaela Pavlickova RC 2.50 6.00
NNO Cynthia Cooper AU/350 20.00 50.00

2001 Ultra WNBA Autographics

Randomly inserted in packs, this two card set features Cynthia Cooper and Ticha Penicheire. Each card contains an authentic player autograph.

1 Cynthia Cooper 15.00 40.00
2 Ticha Penicheiro 8.00 20.00

2001 Ultra WNBA Feel the Game

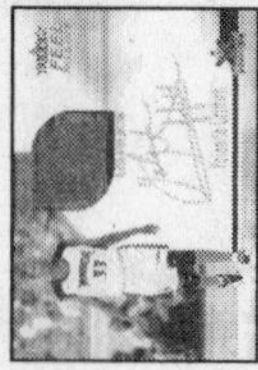

Randomly inserted in packs at the rate of one in six, this six card set features player photos, a facsimile autograph, and a swatch of a game worn jersey.

COMPLETE SET (6) 20.00 50.00
1 Jennifer Azzi 6.00 15.00
2 Cynthia Cooper 6.00 15.00
3 Yolanda Griffith 3.00 8.00
4 Chamique Holdsclaw 6.00 15.00
5 Lisa Leslie 5.00 12.00
6 Natalie Williams 2.00 5.00

2002 Ultra WNBA

Released in April 2002, this 120-card set is divided up into 100 veteran player cards and 20 Rookie exchange cards. Base cards are borderless and feature full color player action photos with a foil name box towards the bottom. Ultra WNBA was packaged in 24 pack boxes where packs contained eight cards each.

COMPLETE SET (120) 75.00 200.00
COMP.SET w/o SP's (100) 15.00 40.00
1 Jackie Stiles 1.00 2.50
2 Sheryl Swoopes 1.50 4.00
3 Katie Smith .75 2.00
4 Sophia Witherspoon .40 1.00
5 Natalie Williams .50 1.25
6 Trisha Stafford-Odom .25 .60
7 Lynn Pride .25 .60
8 Ruthie Bolton-Holifield .75 2.00
9 Coquese Washington .25 .60
10 Erin Buescher .25 .60
11 Tully Bevilaqua .25 .60
12 Deanna Nolan .25 .60
13 Kristen Rasmussen .25 .60
14 Bridget Pettis .25 .60
15 Marie Ferdinand .25 .60
16 Andrea Stinson .50 1.25
17 Olympia Scott-Richardson .25 .60
18 Teresa Weatherspoon 1.00 2.50
19 Edna Campbell .30 .75
20 Elena Tornikidou .25 .60
21 Elena Baranova .60 1.50
22 Kristen Veal .25 .60
23 Margo Dydek .40 1.00
24 Wendy Palmer .60 1.50
25 Sandy Brondello .60 1.50
26 Lisa Harrison .40 1.00
27 Korie Hlede .40 1.00
28 Astou Ndiaye-Diatta .40 1.00
29 Sheri Sam .25 .60
30 Trisha Fallon RC .25 .60
31 Chamique Holdsclaw 1.50 4.00
32 Chasity Melvin .25 .60
33 Mwadi Mabika .25 .60
34 Shannon Johnson .25 .60
35 Kamila Vodichkova .25 .60
36 Edwina Brown .30 .75
37 Ruth Riley .40 1.00
38 Maria Stepanova .25 .60
39 Coco Miller .25 .60
40 Eva Nemcova .40 1.00
41 DeLisha Milton .25 .60
42 Jennifer Gillom .60 1.50
43 Vicky Bullett .40 1.00
44 Penny Taylor .40 1.00
45 Rhonda Mapp .30 .75
46 Tawona Alehaleem .25 .60
47 Murriel Page .30 .75
48 Tamika Catchings .60 1.50
49 Sue Wicks .40 1.00
50 Ticha Penicheiro .60 1.50
51 Tammy Jackson .25 .60
52 Rebecca Lobo .75 2.00
53 Yolanda Griffith .75 2.00
54 Ann Wauters .30 .75
55 Latasha Byears .40 1.00
56 Katie Douglas .40 1.00
57 Sonja Henning .25 .60
58 Rushia Brown .25 .60
59 Ukari Figgs .25 .60
60 Elaine Powell .25 .60
61 Jennifer Azzi .75 2.00
62 Allison Feaster .30 .75
63 Rita Williams .30 .75
64 Tangela Smith .25 .60
65 Tari Phillips .25 .60
66 Shalonda Enis .25 .60
67 Alicia Thompson .25 .60
68 Crystal Robinson .25 .60
69 Lauren Jackson 1.25 3.00
70 Jae Kingi .25 .60
71 Marla Brumfield .25 .60
72 Dawn Staley .60 1.50
73 Adrienne Goodson .25 .60
74 Clarisse Machanguana .25 .60
75 Nikki McCray .60 1.50
76 Becky Hammon 1.25 3.00
77 Semeka Randall .25 .60
78 Merlakia Jones .40 1.00
79 Tamecka Dixon .40 1.00
80 Taj McWilliams-Franklin .25 .60
81 Jamie Redd .25 .60
82 Amanda Lassiter .25 .60
83 Maylana Martin .30 .75
84 Tamicha Jackson .25 .60
85 Tammy Sutton-Brown .25 .60
86 Jurgita Streimikyte .25 .60
87 Vickie Johnson .40 1.00
88 Kedra Holland-Corn .25 .60
89 Janeth Arcain .25 .60
90 Betty Lennox .60 1.50
91 Kristin Folkl .40 1.00
92 Helen Luz .25 .60
93 Kelly Miller .25 .60
94 Lisa Leslie 1.25 3.00
95 Nykesha Sales .40 1.00
96 Simone Edwards RC .25 .60
97 Tina Thompson .75 2.00
98 Svetlana Abrosimova .25 .60
99 Sylvia Crawley .25 .60
100 Annie Burgess RC .25 .60
101 Sue Bird RC 20.00 50.00
102 Swin Cash RC 5.00 12.00
103 Stacey Dales-Schuman RC 3.00 8.00
104 Asjha Jones RC 3.00 8.00
105 Nikki Teasley RC 2.00 5.00
106 Tamika Williams RC 3.00 8.00
107 Shiela Lambert RC 2.00 5.00
108 Lindsay Yamasaki RC 2.00 5.00
109 Shaunzinski Gortman RC 2.00 5.00
110 Michelle Snow RC 4.00 10.00
111 Danielle Crockrom RC 2.50 6.00
112 Hamchetou Maiga RC 2.00 5.00
113 Towana McDonald RC 2.00 5.00
114 Laneisha Caufield RC 2.00 5.00
115 Tamara Moore RC 2.00 5.00
116 Rosalind Ross RC 2.00 5.00
117 Zuzi Klimesova RC 2.00 5.00
118 Lanae Williams RC 2.00 5.00
119 Iziane Castro-Marques RC 2.00 5.00
120 Ayana Walker RC 2.50 6.00

2002 Ultra WNBA Gold Medallion

Inserted in packs at the rate of one in one, this 120-card set parallels the base Ultra set with full gold backgrounds.

*STARS: .6X TO 1.5X BASE CARD HI
101-120 PRINT RUN 25 SER.#'d SETS
101-120 NOT PRICED DUE TO SCARCITY

2002 Ultra WNBA House of Stiles

Randomly seeded in packs at the rate of one in 24, this five card set pays homage to rookie of the year Jackie Stiles. Also inserted with this set is an autographed jersey card sequentially numbered to 50 and a jersey card numbered to 110.

COMPLETE SET (5) 6.00 15.00
COMMON CARD (HS1-HS5) 2.50 6.00
NNO Jackie Stiles JSY AU/50 100.00 200.00
NNO Jackie Stiles JSY/110 40.00 100.00

2002 Ultra WNBA Summer Love

Inserted in packs at the rate of one in six, this 18-card set showcases a retro-seventies design that places full color action player photos on the left side of the card and a yellow and pink design with gold foil highlights on the right side.

COMPLETE SET (18) 15.00 40.00
SL1 Sheryl Swoopes 3.00 8.00
SL2 Ruthie Bolton-Holifield 1.50 4.00
SL3 Natalie Williams 1.00 2.50
SL4 Jennifer Gillom 1.25 3.00
SL5 Becky Hammon 2.50 6.00
SL6 Dawn Staley 1.25 3.00
SL7 Nikki McCray 1.25 3.00
SL8 Eva Nemcova .75 2.00
SL9 Nykesha Sales .75 2.00
SL10 Jennifer Azzi 1.50 4.00
SL11 Chamique Holdsclaw 3.00 8.00
SL12 Yolanda Griffith 1.50 4.00
SL13 Lisa Leslie 2.50 6.00
SL14 Jackie Stiles 2.00 5.00
SL15 Lauren Jackson 2.50 6.00
SL16 Katie Smith 1.50 4.00
SL17 Deanna Nolan .50 1.25
SL18 Ruth Riley .75 2.00

2002 Ultra WNBA Summer Love Memorabilia

Inserted in packs at the rate of one in 12, this 14-card set parallels the base Summer Love set enhanced with a circular swatch of game worn memorabilia.

SL1 Sheryl Swoopes 6.00 15.00
SL2 Ruthie Bolton-Holifield 4.00 10.00
SL3 Natalie Williams 2.50 6.00
SL4 Jennifer Gillom 3.00 8.00
SL5 Becky Hammon 6.00 15.00
SL6 Dawn Staley 3.00 8.00
SL7 Nikki McCray 3.00 8.00
SL8 Eva Nemcova 2.00 5.00
SL9 Nykesha Sales 2.00 5.00
SL10 Jennifer Azzi 4.00 10.00
SL11 Chamique Holdsclaw 8.00 20.00
SL12 Yolanda Griffith 4.00 10.00
SL13 Lisa Leslie 6.00 15.00
SL14 Jackie Stiles 5.00 12.00

2003 Ultra WNBA

Released in August 2003, Ultra WNBA boasts a 120-card base set divided up into 105 veteran player cards and 15 rookie cards inserted at the rate of one in three. Base cards are borderless with the Ultra logo in the upper right hand corner and player's names along the bottom. Ultra WNBA was packaged in 24-pack boxes where packs contained eight cards and carried a suggested retail price of $2.99.

COMP.SET w/o SP's (105) 12.50 30.00
1 Sue Bird 2.00 5.00
2 Kelly Schumacher .25 .60
3 Tamika Williams .30 .75
4 Rebecca Lobo .75 2.00
5 Stacey Thomas .25 .60
6 Lisa Leslie 1.25 3.00
7 Adrain Williams .25 .60
8 Helen Luz .25 .60
9 Rushia Brown .25 .60
10 Bridget Pettis .25 .60
11 Annie Burgess .25 .60
12 Allison Feaster .30 .75
13 Sylvia Crawley .25 .60
14 Svetlana Abrosimova .25 .60
15 Jessie Hicks .25 .60
16 Dominique Canty .40 1.00
17 Michele VanGorp .25 .60
18 Yolanda Griffith .75 2.00
19 Dawn Staley .60 1.50
20 Shalonda Enis .25 .60
21 Katie Smith .75 2.00
22 Brooke Wyckoff .40 1.00
23 Adrienne Goodson .25 .60
24 Erin Buescher .25 .60
25 Sonja Henning .25 .60
26 Betty Lennox .50 1.25
27 Wendy Palmer .60 1.50
28 Semeka Randall .25 .60
29 Charlotte Smith-Taylor .25 .60
30 Tully Bevilaqua .25 .60
31 DeLisha Milton .25 .60
32 Katie Douglas .40 1.00
33 Natalie Williams .50 1.25
34 Kayte Christensen RC .40 1.00
35 Janeth Arcain .25 .60
36 Vickie Johnson .40 1.00
37 Kamila Vodichkova .25 .60
38 Kelly Miller .25 .60
39 Grace Daley .25 .60
40 Nicky McCrimmon .25 .60
41 Taj McWilliams-Franklin .25 .60
42 LaTonya Johnson .25 .60
43 Jackie Stiles 1.00 2.50
44 Rita Williams .30 .75
45 Tamecka Dixon .40 1.00
46 Nykesha Sales .40 1.00
47 Murriel Page .30 .75
48 Marie Ferdinand .25 .60
49 Penny Taylor .40 1.00
50 Tina Thompson .75 2.00
51 Anna DeForge .25 .60
52 Ruth Riley .40 1.00
53 Stacey Dales-Schuman .40 1.00
54 Merlakia Jones .40 1.00
55 Nikki Teasley .25 .60
56 Ticha Penicheiro .60 1.50
57 Lindsey Yamasaki .25 .60
58 Chasity Melvin .25 .60
59 Mwadi Mabika .25 .60
60 Alisa Burras .25 .60
61 Tonya Washington .25 .60
62 Michelle Snow .30 .75
63 Tari Phillips .25 .60
64 Simone Edwards .25 .60
65 Sheryl Swoopes 1.50 4.00
66 Crystal Robinson .25 .60
67 Adia Barnes .25 .60
68 DeMya Walker .25 .60
69 Lynn Pride .25 .60
70 Ruthie Bolton-Holifield .75 2.00
71 Sandy Brondello .60 1.50
72 Debbie Black .40 1.00
73 Sheri Sam .25 .60
74 Kedra Holland-Corn .25 .60
75 Andrea Stinson .50 1.25
76 Tamika Catchings .60 1.50
77 Georgia Schweitzer .25 .60
78 Shannon Johnson .25 .60
79 Jennifer Azzi .75 2.00
80 Deanna Nolan .25 .60
81 Teresa Weatherspoon 1.00 2.50
82 Tangela Smith .25 .60
83 Ukari Figgs .25 .60
84 Becky Hammon 1.25 3.00
85 Lauren Jackson 1.25 3.00
86 LaQuanda Quick RC .25 .60
87 Jennifer Rizzotti .60 1.50
88 Tamicha Jackson .25 .60
89 Asjha Jones .30 .75
90 Margo Dydek .40 1.00
91 Swintayla Cash .50 1.25
92 Kristi Harrower .25 .60
93 Edna Campbell .30 .75
94 Deanna Jackson RC .25 .60
95 Nikki McCray .60 1.50
96 Cynthia Cooper 1.50 4.00
97 Jennifer Gillom .60 1.50
98 Coco Miller .25 .60
99 Ayana Walker .25 .60
100 Tamika Whitmore .25 .60
101 Tammy Sutton-Brown .25 .60
102 Edwina Brown .25 .60
103 Coquese Washington .25 .60
104 Lisa Harrison .40 1.00
105 Chamique Holdsclaw 1.50 4.00
106 LaToya Thomas RC 2.00 5.00
107 Plenette Pierson RC 2.00 5.00
108 Coretta Brown RC 2.00 5.00
109 Sun-Min Jung RC 2.00 5.00
110 Kara Lawson RC 6.00 15.00
111 Gwen Jackson RC 2.00 5.00
112 Cheryl Ford RC 5.00 12.00
113 Courtney Coleman RC 2.00 5.00
114 Chantelle Anderson RC 2.00 5.00
115 Shaquala Williams RC 2.50 6.00
116 Tamara Bowie RC 2.00 5.00
117 Teresa Edwards RC 6.00 15.00
118 Aiysha Smith RC 2.50 6.00
119 Petra Ujhelyi RC 2.00 5.00
120 Allison Curtin RC 2.50 6.00

2003 Ultra WNBA Gold Medallion

Randomly inserted in packs at the rate of one in one for card numbers 1-105 and sequentially numbered to 25 for card numbers 106-120, this 120-card set parallels the base Ultra set enhanced with a gold background and one die-cut rounded corner.

*1-105: .6X TO 1.5X BASE CARD HI
*106-120: 5X TO 12X BASE HI

2003 Ultra WNBA All-Star Review

Inserted in packs at the rate of one in 12, this 20-card set utilizes a horizontal design with white borders a yellow and orage background and full-color player photos on the left side.

COMPLETE SET (20) 12.00 30.00
1 Tamecka Dixon .60 1.50
2 Katie Smith 1.25 3.00
3 Ticha Penicheiro 1.00 2.50
4 Tari Phillips .40 1.00
5 Teresa Weatherspoon 1.50 4.00
6 Andrea Stinson .75 2.00
7 Lauren Jackson 2.00 5.00
8 Nykesha Sales .60 1.50
9 Tina Thompson 1.25 3.00
10 Lisa Leslie 2.00 5.00
11 Yolanda Griffith 1.25 3.00
12 Janeth Arcain .40 1.00
13 Vickie Johnson .60 1.50
14 Mwadi Mabika .40 1.00
15 Chamique Holdsclaw 2.50 6.00
16 Tamika Catchings 1.00 2.50
17 Sheryl Swoopes 2.50 6.00
18 Penny Taylor .60 1.50
19 Stacey Dales-Schuman .60 1.50
20 Sue Bird 3.00 8.00

2003 Ultra WNBA All-Star Review Material

Inserted in packs at the rate of one in 18, this 20-card set parallels the base All-Star Review set enhnanced with a circular swatch of game worn memorabilia on the right side of the card.

COMMON CARD 2.00 5.00
*PATCHES: 1.5X TO 4X BASE HI
PATCH PRINT RUN 100 SER.#'d SETS
1 Tamecka Dixon 2.00 5.00
2 Katie Smith 4.00 10.00
3 Ticha Penicheiro 3.00 8.00
4 Tari Phillips 2.00 5.00
5 Teresa Weatherspoon 5.00 12.00
6 Andrea Stinson 2.50 6.00
7 Lauren Jackson 6.00 15.00
8 Nykesha Sales 2.00 5.00
9 Tina Thompson 4.00 10.00
10 Lisa Leslie 6.00 15.00
11 Yolanda Griffith 4.00 10.00
12 Janeth Arcain 2.00 5.00
13 Vickie Johnson 2.00 5.00
14 Mwadi Mabika 2.00 5.00
15 Chamique Holdsclaw 6.00 15.00
16 Tamika Catchings 3.00 8.00
17 Sheryl Swoopes 6.00 15.00
18 Penny Taylor 2.00 5.00
19 Stacey Dales-Schuman 2.00 5.00
20 Sue Bird 10.00 25.00

2003 Ultra WNBA Nameplates

Randomly inserted in packs, this 20-card set places player's on a license plate-shaped card where a full-color player action photo appears on the left and a premium swatch of game-worn memorabilia appears on the right. Each card is sequentially numbered to 50.

1 Tamecka Dixon 30.00 80.00
3 Ticha Penicheiro 50.00 125.00
4 Tari Phillips 30.00 80.00
5 Teresa Weatherspoon 80.00 200.00
7 Lauren Jackson 100.00 250.00
8 Nykesha Sales 30.00 80.00
9 Tina Thompson 60.00 150.00
10 Lisa Leslie 100.00 250.00
13 Vickie Johnson 30.00 80.00
14 Mwadi Mabika 30.00 80.00
15 Chamique Holdsclaw 100.00 250.00
16 Tamika Catchings 50.00 125.00
17 Sheryl Swoopes 75.00 200.00
18 Penny Taylor 30.00 80.00
19 Stacey Dales-Schuman 30.00 80.00
20 Sue Bird 150.00 400.00

2003 Ultra WNBA Who I AM

Inserted in packs at the rate of one in eight, this 14-card set shows the ladies of the WNBA in their home scene and home lives.

COMPLETE SET (14) 8.00 20.00
1 Chamique Holdsclaw 1.50 4.00
2 Tamika Catchings .60 1.50
3 Tina Thompson .75 2.00
4 Dawn Staley .60 1.50
5 Nykesha Sales .40 1.00
6 Teresa Weatherspoon 1.00 2.50
7 Lisa Leslie 1.25 3.00
8 Sheryl Swoopes 1.50 4.00
9 Swintayla Cash .50 1.25
10 Tamika Williams .30 .75
11 Jennifer Azzi .75 2.00
12 Ticha Penicheiro .60 1.50
13 Sue Bird 2.00 5.00
14 Lisa Harrison .40 1.00

2003 Ultra WNBA Who I AM Game Used

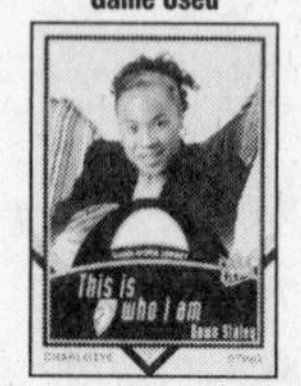

Randomly seeded in packs at the rate of one in nine, this 10-card set parallels the base Who I AM set enhanced with a swatch of game used memorabilia.

1 Chamique Holdsclaw 6.00 15.00
2 Tamika Catchings 3.00 8.00
3 Tina Thompson 4.00 10.00
4 Dawn Staley 3.00 8.00
5 Nykesha Sales 2.00 5.00
6 Teresa Weatherspoon 5.00 12.00
7 Lisa Leslie 6.00 15.00
8 Sheryl Swoopes 6.00 15.00
9 Ticha Penicheiro 3.00 8.00
10 Sue Bird 10.00 25.00

2004 Ultra WNBA

Released in late July 2004, Ultra WNBA consists of a 110-card set where cards 1-90 feature veteran players and cards 91-110 feature rookies inserted at the rate of one in four packs. All cards are borderless with the Ultra logo in the upper right hand corner and the player's name centered along the bottom. Rookie cards feature a bronze background and full color player images. Ultra was packaged in 24-pack boxes with packs containing eight cards and an SRP of $2.99.

COMPLETE SET (110) 25.00 60.00
COMP.SET w/o SP's (90) 8.00 20.00
1 Tamika Catchings .50 1.25
2 Sheri Sam .20 .50
3 Ruthie Bolton .60 1.50
4 Chamique Holdsclaw 1.25 3.00
5 Michelle Snow .25 .60
6 Crystal Robinson .20 .50
7 Betty Lennox .40 1.00
8 Dominique Canty .30 .75
9 Vickie Johnson .30 .75
10 Margo Dydek .30 .75
11 Charlotte Smith-Taylor .20 .50
12 Katie Smith .60 1.50
13 Shannon Johnson .20 .50
14 Teresa Weatherspoon .75 2.00
15 Natalie Williams .40 1.00
16 Yolanda Griffith .60 1.50
17 Adia Barnes .20 .50
18 Andrea Stinson .40 1.00
19 Michele VanGorp .20 .50
20 Kara Lawson .50 1.25
21 Tammy Sutton-Brown .20 .50
22 Svetlana Abrosimova .20 .50
23 Chantelle Anderson .20 .50
24 Tynesha Lewis .20 .50
25 Tamika Williams .25 .60
26 LaToya Thomas .20 .50
27 Edna Campbell .25 .60
28 Lisa Leslie 1.00 2.50
29 Kayte Christensen .20 .50
30 Stacey Dales-Schuman .30 .75
31 Wendy Palmer .50 1.25
32 Swin Cash .40 1.00
33 Jessie Hicks .20 .50
34 Katie Douglas .30 .75
35 Mwadi Mabika .20 .50
36 Adrienne Goodson .20 .50
37 Taj McWilliams-Franklin .20 .50
38 Slobodanka Tuvic RC .30 .75
39 Semeka Randall .20 .50
40 Kelly Miller .20 .50
41 Tamika Whitmore .20 .50
42 Tully Bevilaqua .20 .50
43 Sheryl Swoopes 1.25 3.00
44 Becky Hammon 1.00 2.50
45 Sue Bird 1.50 4.00
46 Debbie Black .30 .75
47 DeLisha Milton-Jones .20 .50
48 Adrain Williams .20 .50
49 Asjha Jones .25 .60
50 Janell Burse .20 .50
51 Tamecka Dixon .30 .75
52 Penny Taylor .30 .75
53 Coco Miller .20 .50
54 Cheryl Ford .40 1.00
55 Deanna Jackson .20 .50
56 DeMya Walker .20 .50
57 Kamila Vodichkova .20 .50
58 Deanna Nolan .20 .50
59 Allison Feaster .25 .60
60 Plenette Pierson .20 .50
61 Lauren Jackson 1.00 2.50
62 Dawn Staley .50 1.25
63 Nykesha Sales .30 .75
64 Tangela Smith .20 .50
65 Aiysha Smith .20 .50
66 Ruth Riley .30 .75
67 Nikki McCray .50 1.25
68 Nikki Teasley .20 .50
69 Chasity Melvin .20 .50
70 Merlakia Jones .30 .75
71 Coretta Brown .20 .50
72 Anna DeForge .20 .50
73 Murriel Page .25 .60
74 Tina Thompson .60 1.50
75 Tari Phillips .20 .50
76 Gwen Jackson .20 .50
77 Ayana Walker .20 .50
78 Kelly Schumacher .20 .50
79 Ticha Penicheiro .50 1.25
80 Simone Edwards .20 .50
81 Kedra Holland-Corn .20 .50
82 K.B. Sharp RC .30 .75
83 LaQuanda Quick .20 .50
84 Barbara Farris RC .30 .75
85 Stephanie White .40 1.00
86 Tamicha Jackson .20 .50
87 Elena Baranova .50 1.25
88 Elaine Powell .20 .50
89 Teresa Edwards .50 1.25
90 Marie Ferdinand .20 .50
91 Diana Taurasi RC 8.00 20.00
92 Alana Beard RC 4.00 10.00
93 Nicole Powell RC 2.50 6.00
94 Lindsay Whalen RC 6.00 15.00
95 Shameka Christon RC 2.00 5.00
96 Nicole Ohlde RC 2.00 5.00
97 Vanessa Hayden RC 2.00 5.00
98 Chandi Jones RC 1.50 4.00
99 Ebony Hoffman RC 2.50 6.00
100 Rebekkah Brunson RC 1.50 4.00
101 Iciss Tillis RC 1.50 4.00
102 Christi Thomas RC 1.50 4.00
103 Shereka Wright RC 1.50 4.00
104 Ashley Robinson RC 1.50 4.00
105 Kaayla Chones RC 1.50 4.00
106 Jessica Brungo RC 1.50 4.00
107 Kelly Mazzante RC 2.50 6.00
108 Catrina Frierson RC 1.50 4.00
109 Bethany Donaphin RC 1.50 4.00
110 Agnieszka Bibrzycka RC 1.50 4.00

2004 Ultra WNBA Gold Medallion

Inserted in packs at the rate of one in one, this 110-card set parallels the base Ultra WNBA set enhanced with a gold background and a die-cut upper left corner. Card numbers 91-100 are sequentially numbered to 100. A platinum version exists as well, these feature a platinum background and sequential numbering to 25.

*1-90 GOLD SINGLES: .75X TO 2X BASE HI
*91-110 GOLD RC: 1.5X TO 4X BASE HI

2004 Ultra WNBA Platinum Medallion

Randomly inserted, this 110-card set parallels the base Ultra WNBA set enhanced with a platinum background and sequential numbering to 25.

*PLATINUM 1-90: 10X TO 25X HI
*PLATINUM 91-110: 4X TO 10X HI
45 Sue Bird 50.00 125.00

2004 Ultra WNBA All-Star Review

Inserted in packs at the rate of one in six, this 20-card set showcases WNBA all-stars on a horizontal card design with a player photo on the left and a facsimile signature on the right. All the wording on the card is printed in red and blue and the background is white.

COMPLETE SET (20) 12.50 30.00
1 Lauren Jackson 2.00 5.00
2 Chamique Holdsclaw 2.50 6.00
3 Tamika Catchings 1.00 2.50
4 Lisa Leslie 2.00 5.00
5 Katie Smith 1.25 3.00
6 Nikki Teasley .40 1.00
7 Swin Cash .75 2.00
8 Tari Phillips .40 1.00
9 Sheryl Swoopes 2.50 6.00
10 Marie Ferdinand .40 1.00
11 Yolanda Griffith 1.25 3.00
12 Tamecka Dixon .60 1.50
13 Natalie Williams .75 2.00
14 Deanna Nolan .40 1.00
15 Sue Bird 3.00 8.00
16 Dawn Staley 1.00 2.50
17 Cheryl Ford .75 2.00
18 Margo Dydek .60 1.50
19 Adrain Williams .40 1.00
20 Teresa Weatherspoon 1.50 4.00

2004 Ultra WNBA All-Star Review Jerseys

Seeded in packs at the rate of one in 24, this 20-card set parallels the base All-Star Review set enhanced with a square swatch of game-worn jersey. There is also a parallel version available with patch swatches that is sequentially numbered to 100.

*PATCHES: 2X TO 5X BASE JSY HI
1 Lauren Jackson 5.00 12.00
2 Chamique Holdsclaw 6.00 15.00
3 Tamika Catchings 2.50 6.00
4 Lisa Leslie 5.00 12.00
5 Katie Smith 3.00 8.00
6 Nikki Teasley 1.50 4.00
7 Swin Cash 2.00 5.00
8 Tari Phillips 1.50 4.00
9 Sheryl Swoopes 6.00 15.00
10 Marie Ferdinand 1.50 4.00
11 Yolanda Griffith 3.00 8.00
12 Tamecka Dixon 1.50 4.00
13 Natalie Williams 2.00 5.00
14 Deanna Nolan 1.50 4.00
15 Sue Bird 8.00 20.00
16 Dawn Staley 2.50 6.00
17 Cheryl Ford 2.00 5.00
18 Margo Dydek 2.00 5.00
19 Adrain Williams 1.50 4.00
20 Teresa Weatherspoon 4.00 10.00

2004 Ultra WNBA Scoring Stars

Inserted in packs at the rate of one in three, this 15-card set is horizontally designed with a full silver background. On the left side a gray-scale portrait is set behind an action photo of the player and on the right, lettering appears in bronze ink.

COMPLETE SET (15) 8.00 20.00
1 Lauren Jackson 1.25 3.00
2 Chamique Holdsclaw 1.50 4.00
3 Tamika Catchings .60 1.50
4 Lisa Leslie 1.25 3.00
5 Katie Smith .75 2.00
6 Tina Thompson .75 2.00
7 Swin Cash .50 1.25
8 Cheryl Ford .50 1.25
9 Sheryl Swoopes 1.50 4.00
10 Marie Ferdinand .25 .60
11 Yolanda Griffith .75 2.00
12 Tamecka Dixon .40 1.00
13 Natalie Williams .50 1.25
14 Deanna Nolan .25 .60
15 Sue Bird 2.00 5.00

2004 Ultra WNBA Scoring Stars Jerseys

Inserted in packs at one in 24, this set parallels the Scoring Stars set enhanced with a circular swatch of jersey on the right.

1 Lauren Jackson 5.00 12.00
2 Chamique Holdsclaw 6.00 15.00
3 Tamika Catchings 2.50 6.00
4 Lisa Leslie 5.00 12.00
5 Katie Smith 3.00 8.00
6 Tina Thompson 3.00 8.00
7 Swin Cash 2.00 5.00
8 Cheryl Ford 2.00 5.00
9 Sheryl Swoopes 6.00 15.00
10 Marie Ferdinand 1.50 4.00
11 Yolanda Griffith 3.00 8.00
12 Tamecka Dixon 1.50 4.00
13 Natalie Williams 2.00 5.00

Deanna Nolan 1.50 4.00
Sue Bird 8.00 20.00

2004 Ultra WNBA Season Crowns Autographs

equentially numbered to 100, this 13-card set nploys a horizontal design with player action photos n the left and an embedded cut signature on the right.

Tamika Catchings 60.00 150.00
Chamique Holdsclaw 20.00 50.00
Swin Cash 10.00 25.00
Alana Beard 20.00 50.00
Becky Hammon 40.00 100.00
Cheryl Ford 10.00 25.00
Tangela Smith 5.00 12.00
Delisha Milton-Jones 5.00 12.00
Deanna Nolan 5.00 12.00
0 Elaine Powell 5.00 12.00
Taj McWilliams-Franklin 5.00 12.00
2 Vanessa Hayden 10.00 25.00
3 Ruth Riley 8.00 20.00

2004 Ultra WNBA Season Crowns Rookie Jerseys

equentially numbered to 500, this two card set utilizes he same Season Crowns design with a swatch of ame-worn jersey.

Alana Beard 10.00 25.00
Diana Taurasi 20.00 50.00

1957-59 Union Oil Booklets

hese booklets were distributed by Union Oil. The front over of each booklet features a drawing of the subject layer. The booklets are numbered and were issued ver several years beginning in 1957. These are 12-age pamphlets and are approximately 4" by 5 1/2". he set is subtitled "Family Sports Fun." This was pparently primarily a Southern California promotion.

COMPLETE SET (44) 200.00 400.00
Bill Russell BK 57 20.00 40.00
Forrest Twogood BK57 6.00 12.00
Phil Woolpert BK 58 6.00 12.00
Bill Sharman BK 58 10.00 20.00
1 George Yardley BK 58 7.50 15.00
2 John Wooden BK 58 20.00 40.00
4 Bob Cousy BK 59 17.50 35.00
6 Slats Gill BK 59 7.50 15.00

1961 Union Oil Chiefs

The 1961 Union Oil basketball card set contains 10 oversized (3" by 3 15/16"), attractive, brown-tinted cards. The cards feature players from the Hawaii Chiefs of the American Basketball League. The backs, printed in dark blue ink, feature a short biography of the player, an ad for KGU radio and the Union Oil circle 76 logo. The catalog number for this set is UO-17. These unnumbered cards are ordered alphabetically by player in the checklist below. Rick Herrscher would go on to have a short career with the 1962 New York Mets baseball team.

COMPLETE SET (10) 125.00 250.00
1 Frank Burgess 12.50 25.00
2 Jeff Cohen 12.50 25.00
3 Lee Harman 12.50 25.00
4 Rick Herrscher 15.00 40.00
5 Lowery Kirk 12.50 25.00
6 Dave Mills 12.50 25.00
7 Max Perry 12.50 25.00
8 George Price 12.50 25.00
9 Fred Sawyer 12.50 25.00
10 Dale Wise 12.50 25.00

1990-91 Upper Deck Prototypes

These standard-size promo cards were issued when Upper Deck applied for a basketball card license with the NBA. The card numbers on the back correspond to the the players' uniform numbers.

COMPLETE SET (2) 700.00 1000.00
32 Magic Johnson 250.00 500.00
33 Larry Bird 300.00 600.00

1991-92 Upper Deck Promos

These standard-size promo cards displayed different pictures of each player from their regular series cards.

COMPLETE SET (2) 8.00 20.00
1 Michael Jordan 6.00 15.00
400 David Robinson 2.00 5.00

1991-92 Upper Deck

The 1991-92 set marks Upper Deck's debut in the basketball card industry. The set contains 500 standard-size cards. The set was released in two series of 400 and 100 cards, respectively. High series cards are in relatively shorter supply because high series packs contained a mix of both high and low series cards. High series lockers contained seven 12-card packs of cards 1-500 and a special "Rookie Standouts" card. Both low and high series were offered in a 500-card factory set. The fronts feature glossy color player photos, bordered below and on the right by a hardwood basketball floor design. The player's name appears beneath the picture, while the team name is printed vertically alongside the picture. The backs display a second color player photo as well as biographical and statistical information. Special subsets featured include Draft Choices (1-21), Classic Confrontations (30-34), All-Rookie Team (35-39), All-Stars (49-72), and Team Checklists (73-99). The fronts feature glossy color player photos, bordered below and on the right by a hardwood basketball floor design. The player's name appears beneath the picture, while the team name is printed vertically alongside the picture. The backs display a second color player photo as well as biographical and statistical information. In addition to rookie and traded players, the high series includes the following topical subsets: Top Prospects (438-448), All-Star Skills (476-484), capturing players who participated in the slam dunk competition as well as the three-point shootout winner, Eastern All-Star Team (449, 451-462), and Western All-Star Team (450, 463-475). Rookie Cards of note include Kenny Anderson, Stacey Augmon, Terrell Brandon, Larry Johnson, Anthony Mason, Dikembe Mutombo, Steve Smith, and John Starks.

COMPLETE SET (500) 10.00 20.00
COMPLETE FACT.SET (500) 10.00 20.00
COMPLETE SERIES 1 (400) 6.00 12.00
COMPLETE SERIES 2 (100) 4.00 8.00
1 Stacey Augmon CL .02 .10
Rodney Monroe
2 Larry Johnson UER RC .40 1.00
(Career FG Percentage is .643 not .648)
3 Dikembe Mutombo RC .40 1.00
4 Steve Smith RC .40 1.00
5 Stacey Augmon RC .08 .25
6 Terrell Brandon RC .30 .75
7 Greg Anthony RC .08 .25
8 Rich King RC .02 .10
9 Chris Gatling RC .08 .25
10 Victor Alexander RC .02 .10
11 John Turner RC .02 .10
12 Eric Murdock RC .02 .10
13 Mark Randall RC .02 .10
14 Rodney Monroe RC .02 .10
15 Myron Brown RC .02 .10
16 Mike Iuzzolino RC .02 .10
17 Chris Corchiani RC .02 .10
18 Elliot Perry RC .02 .10
19 Jimmy Oliver RC .02 .10
20 Doug Overton RC .02 .10
21 Steve Hood UER RC .02 .10
(Card has NBA record, but he's a rookie)
22 Michael Jordan SCHOOL .30 .75
23 Kevin Johnson SCHOOL .02 .10
24 Kurk Lee .02 .10
25 Sean Higgins RC .02 .10
26 Morlon Wiley .02 .10
27 Derek Smith .02 .10
28 Kenny Payne .02 .10
29 Magic Johnson .15 .40
Assist Record
30 Larry Bird CC .08 .25
Chuck Person
31 Karl Malone CC .08 .25
Charles Barkley
32 Kevin Johnson CC .02 .10
John Stockton
33 Hakeem Olajuwon CC .08 .25
Patrick Ewing
34 Magic Johnson CC .40 1.00
Michael Jordan
35 Derrick Coleman ART .02 .10
36 Lionel Simmons ART .02 .10
37 Dee Brown ART .02 .10
38 Dennis Scott ART .02 .10
39 Kendall Gill ART .02 .10
40 Winston Garland .02 .10
41 Danny Young .02 .10
42 Rick Mahorn .02 .10
43 Michael Adams .02 .10
44 Michael Jordan 1.25 3.00
45 Magic Johnson .30 .75
46 Doc Rivers .02 .10
47 Moses Malone .08 .25
48 Michael Jordan AS CL .60 1.50
49 James Worthy AS .02 .10
50 Tim Hardaway AS .08 .25
51 Karl Malone AS .08 .25
52 John Stockton AS .02 .10
53 Clyde Drexler AS .02 .10
54 Terry Porter AS .02 .10
55 Kevin Duckworth AS .02 .10
56 Tom Chambers AS .02 .10
57 Magic Johnson AS .15 .40
58 David Robinson AS .08 .25
59 Kevin Johnson AS .02 .10
60 Chris Mullin AS .02 .10
61 Joe Dumars AS .02 .10
62 Kevin McHale AS .02 .10
63 Brad Daugherty AS .02 .10
64 Alvin Robertson AS .02 .10
65 Bernard King AS .02 .10
66 Dominique Wilkins AS .02 .10
67 Ricky Pierce AS .02 .10
68 Patrick Ewing AS .02 .10
69 Michael Jordan AS .60 1.50
70 Charles Barkley AS .08 .25
71 Hersey Hawkins AS .02 .10
72 Robert Parish AS .02 .10
73 Alvin Robertson TC .02 .10
74 Bernard King TC .02 .10
75 Michael Jordan TC .60 1.50
76 Brad Daugherty TC .02 .10
77 Larry Bird TC .20 .50
78 Ron Harper TC .02 .10
79 Dominique Wilkins TC .02 .10
80 Rony Seikaly TC .02 .10
81 Rex Chapman TC .02 .10
82 Mark Eaton TC .02 .10
83 Lionel Simmons TC .02 .10
84 Gerald Wilkins TC .02 .10
85 James Worthy TC .02 .10
86 Scott Skiles TC .02 .10
87 Rolando Blackman TC .02 .10
88 Derrick Coleman TC .02 .10
89 Chris Jackson TC .02 .10
90 Reggie Miller TC .02 .10
91 Isiah Thomas TC .02 .10
92 Hakeem Olajuwon TC .08 .25
93 Hersey Hawkins TC .02 .10
94 David Robinson TC .08 .25
95 Tom Chambers TC .02 .10
96 Shawn Kemp TC .08 .25
97 Pooh Richardson TC .02 .10
98 Clyde Drexler TC .02 .10
99 Chris Mullin TC .02 .10
100 Checklist 1-100 .02 .10
101 John Shasky .02 .10
102 Dana Barros .02 .10
103 Stojko Vrankovic .02 .10
104 Larry Drew .02 .10
105 Randy White .02 .10
106 Dave Corzine .02 .10
107 Joe Kleine .02 .10
108 Lance Blanks .02 .10
109 Rodney McCray .02 .10
110 Sedale Threatt .02 .10
111 Ken Norman .02 .10
112 Rickey Green .02 .10
113 Andy Toolson .02 .10
114 Bo Kimble .02 .10
115 Mark West .02 .10
116 Mark Eaton .02 .10
117 John Paxson .02 .10
118 Mike Brown .02 .10
119 Brian Oliver .02 .10
120 Will Perdue .02 .10
121 Michael Smith .02 .10
122 Sherman Douglas .02 .10
123 Reggie Lewis .02 .10
124 James Donaldson .02 .10
125 Scottie Pippen .30 .75
126 Elden Campbell .02 .10
127 Michael Cage .02 .10
128 Tony Smith .02 .10
129 Ed Pinckney .02 .10
130 Keith Askins RC .02 .10
131 Darrell Griffith .02 .10
132 Vinnie Johnson .02 .10
133 Ron Harper .02 .10
134 Andre Turner .02 .10
135 Jeff Hornacek .02 .10
136 John Stockton .08 .25
137 Derek Harper .02 .10
138 Loy Vaught .02 .10
139 Thurl Bailey .02 .10
140 Olden Polynice .02 .10
141 Kevin Edwards .02 .10
142 Byron Scott .02 .10
143 Dee Brown .02 .10
144 Sam Perkins .02 .10
145 Rony Seikaly .02 .10
146 James Worthy .08 .25
147 Glen Rice .08 .25
148 Craig Hodges .02 .10
149 Bimbo Coles .02 .10
150 Mychal Thompson .02 .10
151 Xavier McDaniel .02 .10
152 Roy Tarpley .02 .10
153 Gary Payton .25 .60
154 Rolando Blackman .02 .10
155 Hersey Hawkins .02 .10
156 Ricky Pierce .02 .10
157 Fat Lever .02 .10
158 Andrew Lang .02 .10
159 Benoit Benjamin .02 .10
160 Cedric Ceballos .02 .10
161 Charles Smith .02 .10
162 Jeff Martin .02 .10
163 Robert Parish .02 .10
164 Danny Manning .02 .10
165 Mark Aguirre .02 .10
166 Jeff Malone .02 .10
167 Bill Laimbeer .02 .10
168 Willie Burton .02 .10
169 Dennis Hopson .02 .10
170 Kevin Gamble .02 .10
171 Terry Teagle .02 .10
172 Dan Majerle .02 .10
173 Shawn Kemp .25 .60
174 Tom Chambers .02 .10
175 Vlade Divac .02 .10
176 Johnny Dawkins .02 .10
177 A.C. Green .02 .10
178 Manute Bol .02 .10
179 Terry Davis .02 .10
180 Ron Anderson .02 .10
181 Horace Grant .02 .10
182 Stacey King .02 .10
183 William Bedford .02 .10
184 B.J. Armstrong .02 .10
185 Dennis Rodman .20 .50
186 Nate McMillan .02 .10
187 Cliff Levingston .02 .10
188 Quintin Dailey .02 .10
189 Bill Cartwright .02 .10
190 John Salley .02 .10
191 Jayson Williams .08 .25
192 Grant Long .02 .10
193 Negele Knight .02 .10
194 Alec Kessler .02 .10
195 Gary Grant .02 .10
196 Billy Thompson .02 .10
197 Delaney Rudd .02 .10
198 Alan Ogg .02 .10
199 Blue Edwards .02 .10
200 Checklist 101-200 .02 .10
201 Mark Acres .02 .10
202 Craig Ehlo .02 .10
203 Anthony Cook .02 .10
204 Eric Leckner .02 .10
205 Terry Catledge .02 .10
206 Reggie Williams .02 .10
207 Greg Kite .02 .10
208 Steve Kerr .02 .10
209 Kenny Battle .02 .10
210 John Morton .02 .10
211 Kenny Williams .02 .10
212 Mark Jackson .02 .10
213 Alaa Abdelnaby .02 .10
214 Rod Strickland .08 .25
215 Micheal Williams .02 .10
216 Kevin Duckworth .02 .10
217 David Wingate .02 .10
218 LaSalle Thompson .02 .10
219 John Starks RC .08 .25
220 Clifford Robinson .02 .10
221 Jeff Grayer .02 .10
222 Marcus Liberty .02 .10
223 Larry Nance .02 .10
224 Michael Ansley .02 .10
225 Kevin McHale .02 .10
226 Scott Skiles .02 .10
227 Darnell Valentine .02 .10
228 Nick Anderson .02 .10
229 Brad Davis .02 .10
230 Gerald Paddio .02 .10
231 Sam Bowie .02 .10
232 Sam Vincent .02 .10
233 George McCloud .02 .10
234 Gerald Wilkins .02 .10
235 Mookie Blaylock .02 .10
236 Jon Koncak .02 .10
237 Danny Ferry .02 .10
238 Vern Fleming .02 .10
239 Mark Price .02 .10
240 Sidney Moncrief .02 .10
241 Jay Humphries .02 .10
242 Muggsy Bogues .02 .10
243 Tim Hardaway .15 .40
244 Alvin Robertson .02 .10
245 Chris Mullin .08 .25
246 Pooh Richardson .02 .10
247 Winston Bennett .02 .10
248 Kelvin Upshaw .02 .10
249 John Williams .02 .10
250 Steve Alford .02 .10
251 Spud Webb .02 .10
252 Sleepy Floyd .02 .10
253 Chuck Person .02 .10
254 Hakeem Olajuwon .15 .40
255 Dominique Wilkins .08 .25
256 Reggie Miller .08 .25
257 Dennis Scott .02 .10
258 Charles Oakley .02 .10
259 Sidney Green .02 .10
260 Detlef Schrempf .02 .10
261 Rod Higgins .02 .10
262 J.R. Reid .02 .10
263 Tyrone Hill .02 .10
264 Reggie Theus .02 .10
265 Mitch Richmond .08 .25
266 Dale Ellis .02 .10
267 Terry Cummings .02 .10
268 Johnny Newman .02 .10
269 Doug West .02 .10
270 Jim Petersen .02 .10
271 Otis Thorpe .02 .10
272 John Williams .02 .10
273 Kennard Winchester RC .02 .10
274 Duane Ferrell .02 .10
275 Vernon Maxwell .02 .10
276 Kenny Smith .02 .10
277 Jerome Kersey .02 .10
278 Kevin Willis .02 .10
279 Danny Ainge .02 .10
280 Larry Smith .02 .10
281 Maurice Cheeks .02 .10
282 Willie Anderson .02 .10
283 Tom Tolbert .02 .10
284 Jerrod Mustaf .02 .10
285 Randolph Keys .02 .10
286 Jerry Reynolds .02 .10
287 Sean Elliott .02 .10
288 Otis Smith .02 .10
289 Terry Mills RC .08 .25
290 Kelly Tripucka .02 .10
291 Jon Sundvold .02 .10
292 Rumeal Robinson .02 .10
293 Fred Roberts .02 .10
294 Rik Smits .02 .10
295 Jerome Lane .02 .10
296 Dave Jamerson .02 .10
297 Joe Wolf .02 .10
298 David Wood RC .02 .10
299 Todd Lichti .02 .10
300 Checklist 201-300 .02 .10
301 Randy Breuer .02 .10
302 Buck Johnson .02 .10
303 Scott Brooks .02 .10
304 Jeff Turner .02 .10
305 Felton Spencer .02 .10
306 Greg Dreiling .02 .10
307 Gerald Glass .02 .10
308 Tony Brown .02 .10
309 Sam Mitchell .02 .10
310 Adrian Caldwell .02 .10
311 Chris Dudley .02 .10
312 Blair Rasmussen .02 .10
313 Antoine Carr .02 .10
314 Greg Anderson .02 .10
315 Drazen Petrovic .02 .10
316 Alton Lister .02 .10
317 Jack Haley .02 .10
318 Bobby Hansen .02 .10
319 Chris Jackson .02 .10
320 Herb Williams .02 .10
321 Kendall Gill .02 .10
322 Tyrone Corbin .02 .10
323 Kiki Vandeweghe .02 .10
324 David Robinson .20 .50
325 Rex Chapman .02 .10
326 Tony Campbell .02 .10
327 Dell Curry .02 .10
328 Charles Jones .02 .10
329 Kenny Gattison .02 .10
330 Haywoode Workman RC .02 .10
331 Travis Mays .02 .10
332 Derrick Coleman .02 .10
333 Isiah Thomas .08 .25
334 Jud Buechler .02 .10
335 Joe Dumars .08 .25
336 Tate George .02 .10
337 Mike Sanders .02 .10
338 James Edwards .02 .10
339 Chris Morris .02 .10
340 Scott Hastings .02 .10
341 Trent Tucker .02 .10
342 Harvey Grant .02 .10
343 Patrick Ewing .08 .25
344 Larry Bird .40 1.00
345 Charles Barkley .15 .40
346 Brian Shaw .02 .10
347 Kenny Walker .02 .10
348 Danny Schayes .02 .10
349 Tom Hammonds .02 .10
350 Frank Brickowski .02 .10
351 Terry Porter .02 .10
352 Orlando Woolridge .02 .10
353 Buck Williams .02 .10
354 Sarunas Marciulionis .02 .10
355 Karl Malone .15 .40
356 Kevin Johnson .08 .25
357 Clyde Drexler .08 .25
358 Duane Causwell .02 .10
359 Paul Pressey .02 .10
360 Jim Les RC .02 .10
361 Derrick McKey .02 .10
362 Scott Williams RC .02 .10
363 Mark Alarie .02 .10
364 Brad Daugherty .02 .10
365 Bernard King .02 .10
366 Steve Henson .02 .10
367 Darrell Walker .02 .10
368 Larry Krystkowiak .02 .10
369 Henry James UER .02 .10
(Scored 20 points vs. Pistons, not Jazz)
370 Jack Sikma .02 .10
371 Eddie Johnson .02 .10
372 Wayman Tisdale .02 .10
373 Joe Barry Carroll .02 .10
374 David Greenwood .02 .10
375 Lionel Simmons .02 .10
376 Dwayne Schintzius .02 .10
377 Tod Murphy .02 .10
378 Wayne Cooper .02 .10
379 Anthony Bonner .02 .10
380 Walter Davis .02 .10
381 Lester Conner .02 .10
382 Ledell Eackles .02 .10
383 Brad Lohaus .02 .10
384 Derrick Gervin .02 .10
385 Pervis Ellison .02 .10
386 Tim McCormick .02 .10
387 A.J. English .02 .10
388 John Battle .02 .10
389 Roy Hinson .02 .10
390 Armon Gilliam .02 .10
391 Kurt Rambis .02 .10
392 Mark Bryant .02 .10
393 Chucky Brown .02 .10
394 Avery Johnson .02 .10
395 Rory Sparrow .02 .10
396 Mario Elie RC .08 .25
397 Ralph Sampson .02 .10
398 Mike Gminski .02 .10
399 Bill Wennington .02 .10
400 Checklist 301-400 .02 .10
401 David Wingate .02 .10
402 Moses Malone .20 .50
403 Darrell Walker .02 .10
404 Antoine Carr .02 .10
405 Charles Shackleford .02 .10
406 Orlando Woolridge .02 .10
407 Robert Pack RC .08 .25
408 Bobby Hansen .02 .10
409 Dale Davis RC .20 .50
410 Vincent Askew RC .02 .10
411 Alexander Volkov .02 .10
412 Dwayne Schintzius .02 .10
413 Tim Perry .02 .10
414 Tyrone Corbin .02 .10
415 Pete Chilcutt RC .02 .10
416 James Edwards .02 .10
417 Jerrod Mustaf .02 .10
418 Thurl Bailey .02 .10
419 Spud Webb .08 .25
420 Doc Rivers .08 .25
421 Sean Green RC .02 .10
422 Walter Davis .02 .10
423 Terry Davis .02 .10
424 John Battle .02 .10
425 Vinnie Johnson .02 .10
426 Sherman Douglas .02 .10
427 Kevin Brooks RC .02 .10
428 Greg Sutton RC .02 .10
429 Rafael Addison RC .02 .10
430 Anthony Mason RC .40 1.00
431 Paul Graham RC .02 .10
432 Anthony Frederick RC .02 .10
433 Dennis Hopson .02 .10
434 Rory Sparrow .02 .10
435 Michael Adams .02 .10
436 Kevin Lynch RC .02 .10
437 Randy Brown RC .02 .10
438 Larry Johnson CL .08 .25
Billy Owens
439 Stacey Augmon TP .02 .10
440 Larry Stewart TP RC .02 .10
441 Terrell Brandon TP .20 .50
442 Billy Owens TP RC .02 .10
443 Rick Fox TP RC .08 .25
444 Kenny Anderson TP RC .40 1.00
445 Larry Johnson TP .20 .50
446 Dikembe Mutombo TP .20 .50
447 Steve Smith TP .20 .50
448 Greg Anthony TP .08 .25
449 East All-Star CL .08 .25
450 West All-Star CL .08 .25
451 Isiah Thomas AS .20 .50
(Magic Johnson also shown)
452 Michael Jordan AS 1.25 3.00
453 Scottie Pippen AS .30 .75
454 Charles Barkley AS .20 .50
455 Patrick Ewing AS .08 .25
456 Michael Adams AS .02 .10
457 Dennis Rodman AS .20 .50
458 Reggie Lewis AS .02 .10
459 Joe Dumars AS .08 .25
460 Mark Price AS .02 .10
461 Brad Daugherty AS .02 .10
462 Kevin Willis AS .02 .10
463 Clyde Drexler AS .08 .25
464 Magic Johnson AS .30 .75
465 Chris Mullin AS .08 .25
466 Karl Malone AS .20 .50
467 David Robinson AS .20 .50
468 Tim Hardaway AS .20 .50
469 Jeff Hornacek AS .02 .10
470 John Stockton AS .08 .25
471 Dikembe Mutombo AS UER .08 .25
Drafted in 1992, should be 1991
472 Hakeem Olajuwon AS .20 .50
473 James Worthy AS .08 .25
474 Otis Thorpe AS .02 .10
475 Dan Majerle AS .02 .10
476 Cedric Ceballos SD CL .02 .10
477 Nick Anderson SD .02 .10
478 Stacey Augmon SD .08 .25
479 Cedric Ceballos SD .02 .10
480 Larry Johnson SD .20 .50
481 Shawn Kemp SD .25 .60
482 John Starks SD .08 .25
483 Doug West SD .02 .10
484 Craig Hodges LD .02 .10
485 LaBradford Smith RC .02 .10
486 Winston Garland .02 .10
487 David Benoit RC .08 .25
488 John Bagley .02 .10
489 Mark Macon RC .02 .10
490 Mitch Richmond .08 .25
491 Luc Longley RC .08 .25
492 Sedale Threatt .02 .10
493 Doug Smith RC .02 .10
494 Travis Mays .02 .10
495 Xavier McDaniel .02 .10
496 Brian Shaw .02 .10
497 Stanley Roberts RC .02 .10
498 Blair Rasmussen .02 .10
499 Brian Williams RC .20 .50
500 Checklist Card .02 .10

1991-92 Upper Deck Award Winner Holograms

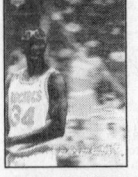

These holograms feature NBA statistical leaders in nine different categories. The first six holograms were random inserts in 1991-92 Upper Deck low series foil and jumbo packs, while the last three were inserted in high series foil and jumbo packs. The standard-size holograms have the player's name and award received in the lower right corner on the front. The back has a color player photo and a summary of the player's performance. The cards are numbered on the back with an "AW" prefix before the number.

COMPLETE SET (9) 5.00 12.00
AW1 Michael Jordan 3.00 8.00
Scoring Leader
AW2 Alvin Robertson .10 .25
Steals Leader
AW3 John Stockton .30 .75
Assists Leader
AW4 Michael Jordan 3.00 8.00
MVP
AW5 Detlef Schrempf .15 .40
Sixth Man
AW6 David Robinson .60 1.50
Rebounds Leader
AW7 Derrick Coleman .15 .40
Rookie of the Year
AW8 Hakeem Olajuwon .50 1.25
Blocked Shots Leader
AW9 Dennis Rodman .60 1.50
Defensive POY

1991-92 Upper Deck Rookie Standouts

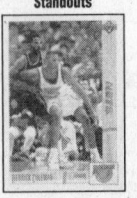

Inserted one per jumbo and locker pack in both the low and high series, fronts of this standard-size 40-card set feature color action player photos, bordered on the right and below by a hardwood basketball court and with the "91-92 Rookie Standouts" emblem in the lower right corner. The back features a second color player photo and player profile.

COMPLETE SET (40) 7.50 15.00
COMPLETE SERIES 1 (20) 2.50 5.00
COMPLETE SERIES 2 (20) 5.00 10.00
R1 Gary Payton 1.00 2.50
R2 Dennis Scott .15 .40
R3 Kendall Gill .25 .60
R4 Felton Spencer .08 .25
R5 Bo Kimble .08 .25
R6 Willie Burton .08 .25
R7 Tyrone Hill .15 .40
R8 Loy Vaught .15 .40
R9 Travis Mays .08 .25
R10 Derrick Coleman .25 .60
R11 Duane Causwell .08 .25
R12 Dee Brown .08 .25
R13 Gerald Glass .08 .25
R14 Jayson Williams .25 .60
R15 Elden Campbell .15 .40
R16 Negele Knight .08 .25
R17 Chris Jackson .08 .25
R18 Danny Ferry .08 .25
R19 Tony Smith .08 .25
R20 Cedric Ceballos .25 .60
R21 Victor Alexander .08 .25
R22 Terrell Brandon .75 2.00
R23 Rick Fox .25 .60
R24 Stacey Augmon .25 .60
R25 Mark Macon .08 .25
R26 Larry Johnson 1.00 2.50
R27 Paul Graham .08 .25
R28 Stanley Roberts UER .08 .25
(Not the Magic's 1st pick in 1991)
R29 Dikembe Mutombo 1.00 2.50
R30 Robert Pack .08 .25
R31 Doug Smith .08 .25
R32 Steve Smith 1.00 2.50
R33 Billy Owens .25 .60
R34 David Benoit .15 .40
R35 Brian Williams .25 .60
R36 Kenny Anderson .50 1.25
R37 Greg Anthony .25 .60
R38 Dale Davis .25 .60
R39 Larry Stewart .08 .25
R40 Mike Iuzzolino .08 .25

1991-92 Upper Deck Jerry West Heroes

This ten-card insert set was randomly inserted in Upper Deck's high series basketball foil packs. Also included in the packs were 2,500 checklist cards autographed by West. The fronts of the standard-size cards capture memorable moments from his college and professional career. The player photos are cut out and superimposed over a jump ball circle on a hardwood basketball floor design. The card backs present commentary.

COMMON WEST (1-9) .50 1.25
AU Jerry West AU/2500 30.00 80.00
NNO Jerry West Cover .75 2.00

1991-92 Upper Deck Jerry West Box Bottoms

These oversized cards, measuring approximately 5" by 7", are actually the bottom panel of the 1991-92 Upper Deck high number series basketball wax/foil boxes. Except for the size and the blank backs, these waxbox bottoms are identical to the first-eight cards in the Jerry West Basketball Heroes insert set.

COMPLETE SET (8) 2.00 5.00
COMMON CARD (1-8) .30 .75

1992-93 Upper Deck

The complete 1992-93 Upper Deck basketball set consists of 510 standard-size cards issued in two series of 310 and 200 cards, respectively. High series cards are slightly tougher to find (compared to the low numbers) because high series packs contained a mix of high and low series cards. For both series, cards were issued in 15-card hobby and retail foil packs, 27-card locker packs and 27-card jumbo packs. No factory sets were produced by Upper Deck for this issue. Both series were also distributed through 27-card Locker packs. Card number 1A (available only in low series packs) is a "Trade Upper Deck" card that the collector could trade to Upper Deck for a Shaquille O'Neal mail-away trade card beginning on Jan. 1, 1993. The offer expired June 30, 1993. The fronts feature color action player photos with white borders. The team name is gold-foil stamped across the top of the picture. The border design at the bottom consists of a team colored stripe that shades from one team color to the other with diagonal stripes within the larger stripe that add texture. The entire design is edged in gold foil. The right end is off-set slightly by the Upper Deck logo. The backs show an action player photo that runs down the left side of the card. The right side displays statistics printed on a ghosted NBA logo. Topical subsets featured include NBA Draft (2-21), Team Checklists (35-61), and Scoring Threats (62-66). The set also includes two art cards (67-68) and one Stay in School card (69). Second series subsets featured are Team Fact Cards (350-376), NBA East All-Star Game (421-433), NBA West All-Star Game (434-445), In Your Face (446-454), Top Prospects (455-482), NBA Game Faces (483-497), Scoring Threats (498-505), and Fanimation (506-510). The cards are numbered on the back. Rookie Cards of note include Doug Christie (second series SP), Tom Gugliotta, Jim Jackson (second series SP), Christian Laettner, Alonzo Mourning, Shaquille O'Neal (second series SP), Latrell Sprewell and Clarence Weatherspoon. A card commemorating the retirement of Larry Bird and Magic Johnson (SP1) and the 20,000th point scored by Dominique Wilkins and Michael Jordan (SP2) were first and second series inserts, respectively. There were inserted at a rate of one in 72 packs. The basic card numbers of Jordan (23), Magic (32) and Bird (33) represent their uniform numbers.

COMPLETE SET (514) 40.00 80.00
COMPLETE LO SERIES (311) 10.00 20.00
COMPLETE HI SERIES (203) 30.00 60.00
1 Shaquille O'Neal SP RC 10.00 25.00
NBA First Draft Pick
1A 1992 NBA Draft Trade .10 .30
Card SP
1B Shaquille O'Neal TRADE 6.00 15.00
1AX 1992 NBA Draft Trade .10 .30
Card (Stamped)
2 Alonzo Mourning RC .75 2.00
3 Christian Laettner RC .25 .60
4 LaPhonso Ellis RC .10 .30
5 Clarence Weatherspoon RC .10 .30
6 Adam Keefe RC .02 .10
7 Robert Horry RC .15 .40
8 Harold Miner RC .10 .30
9 Bryant Stith RC .05 .15
10 Malik Sealy RC .05 .15
11 Anthony Peeler RC .05 .15
12 Randy Woods RC .02 .10
13 Tracy Murray RC .05 .15
14 Tom Gugliotta RC .40 1.00
15 Hubert Davis RC .05 .15
16 Don MacLean RC .02 .10
17 Lee Mayberry RC .02 .10
18 Corey Williams RC .02 .10
19 Sean Rooks RC .02 .10

20 Todd Day RC .05 .15
21 Bryant Stith CL .10 .30
LaPhonso Ellis
22 Jeff Hornacek .05 .15
23 Michael Jordan 1.50 4.00
24 John Salley .02 .10
25 Andre Turner .02 .10
26 Charles Barkley .20 .50
27 Anthony Frederick .02 .10
28 Mario Elie .05 .15
29 Olden Polynice .02 .10
30 Rodney Monroe .02 .10
31 Tim Perry .02 .10
32 Doug Christie SP RC .40 1.00
32A Magic Johnson SP .75 2.00
33 Jim Jackson SP RC 1.00 2.50
33A Larry Bird SP 1.00 2.50
34 Randy White .02 .10
35 Frank Brickowski TC .02 .10
36 Michael Adams TC .02 .10
37 Scottie Pippen TC .20 .50
38 Mark Price TC .02 .10
39 Robert Parish TC .02 .10
40 Danny Manning TC .02 .10
41 Kevin Willis TC .02 .10
42 Glen Rice TC .05 .15
43 Kendall Gill TC .02 .10
44 Karl Malone TC .10 .30
45 Mitch Richmond TC .10 .30
46 Patrick Ewing TC .10 .30
47 Sam Perkins TC .02 .10
48 Dennis Scott TC .02 .10
49 Derek Harper TC .02 .10
50 Drazen Petrovic TC .02 .10
51 Reggie Williams TC .02 .10
52 Rik Smits TC .02 .10
53 Joe Dumars TC .05 .15
54 Otis Thorpe TC .02 .10
55 Johnny Dawkins TC .02 .10
56 Sean Elliott TC .02 .10
57 Kevin Johnson TC .05 .15
58 Ricky Pierce TC .02 .10
59 Doug West TC .02 .10
60 Terry Porter TC .02 .10
61 Tim Hardaway TC .10 .30
62 Michael Jordan ST .40 1.00
Scottie Pippen
63 Kendall Gill ST .10 .30
Larry Johnson
64 Tom Chambers ST .05 .15
Kevin Johnson
65 Tim Hardaway ST .05 .15
Chris Mullin
66 Karl Malone ST .10 .30
John Stockton
67 Michael Jordan MVP .75 2.00
68 Stacey Augmon .02 .10
Six Million Point Man
69 Bob Lanier .05 .15
Stay in School
70 Alaa Abdelnaby .02 .10
71 Andrew Lang .02 .10
72 Larry Krystkowiak .02 .10
73 Gerald Wilkins .02 .10
74 Rod Strickland .10 .30
75 Danny Ainge .05 .15
76 Chris Corchiani .02 .10
77 Jeff Grayer .02 .10
78 Eric Murdock .02 .10
79 Rex Chapman .02 .10
80 LaBradford Smith .02 .10
81 Jay Humphries .02 .10
82 David Robinson .20 .50
83 William Bedford .02 .10
84 James Edwards .02 .10
85 Danny Schayes .02 .10
86 Lloyd Daniels RC .02 .10
87 Blue Edwards .02 .10
88 Dale Ellis .02 .10
89 Rolando Blackman .02 .10
90 Michael Jordan CL .10 .30
91 Rik Smits .05 .15
92 Terry Davis .02 .10
93 Bill Cartwright .02 .10
94 Avery Johnson .02 .10
95 Micheal Williams .02 .10
96 Spud Webb .05 .15
97 Benoit Benjamin .02 .10
98 Derek Harper .05 .15
99 Matt Bullard .02 .10
100A Tyrone Corbin ERR .40 1.00
(Heat on front)
100B Tyrone Corbin COR .02 .10
101 Doc Rivers .05 .15
102 Tony Smith .02 .10
103 Doug West .02 .10
104 Kevin Duckworth .02 .10
105 Luc Longley .05 .15
106 Antoine Carr .02 .10
107 Clifford Robinson .05 .15
108 Grant Long .02 .10
109 Terry Porter .02 .10
110A Steve Smith ERR 4.00 10.00
(Jazz on front)
110B Steve Smith COR .15 .40
111 Brian Williams .02 .10
112 Karl Malone .20 .50
113 Reggie Williams .02 .10
114 Tom Chambers .02 .10
115 Winston Garland .02 .10
116 John Stockton .10 .30
117 Chris Jackson .02 .10
118 Mike Brown .02 .10
119 Kevin Johnson .10 .30
120 Reggie Lewis .05 .15
121 Bimbo Coles .02 .10
122 Drazen Petrovic .02 .10
123 Reggie Miller .10 .30
124 Derrick Coleman .05 .15
125 Chuck Person .02 .10
126 Glen Rice .10 .30
127 Kenny Anderson .10 .30
128 Willie Burton .02 .10
129 Chris Morris .02 .10
130 Patrick Ewing .10 .30
131 Sean Elliott .05 .15
132 Clyde Drexler .10 .30
133 Scottie Pippen .40 1.00
134 Pooh Richardson .02 .10
135 Horace Grant .05 .15
136 Hakeem Olajuwon .20 .50
137 John Paxson .02 .10
138 Kendall Gill .05 .15
139 Michael Adams .02 .10
140 Otis Thorpe .05 .15
141 Dennis Scott .05 .15
142 Stacey Augmon .05 .15
143 Robert Pack .02 .10
144 Kevin Willis .02 .10
145 Jerome Kersey .02 .10
146 Paul Graham .02 .10
147 Stanley Roberts .02 .10
148 Dominique Wilkins .10 .30
149 Scott Skiles .02 .10
150 Rumeal Robinson .02 .10
151 Mookie Blaylock .05 .15
152 Elden Campbell .05 .15
153 Chris Dudley .02 .10
154 Sedale Threatt .02 .10
155 Tate George .02 .10
156 James Worthy .10 .30
157 B.J. Armstrong .02 .10
158 Gary Payton .25 .60
159 Ledell Eackles .02 .10
160 Sam Perkins .05 .15
161 Nick Anderson .05 .15
162 Mitch Richmond .10 .30
163 Buck Williams .05 .15
164 Blair Rasmussen .02 .10
165 Vern Fleming .02 .10
166 Duane Ferrell .02 .10
167 George McCloud .02 .10
168 Terry Cummings .05 .15
169 Detlef Schrempf .05 .15
170 Willie Anderson .02 .10
171 Scott Williams .02 .10
172 Vernon Maxwell .02 .10
173 Todd Lichti .02 .10
174 David Benoit .02 .10
175 Marcus Liberty .02 .10
176 Kenny Smith .02 .10
177 Dan Majerle .05 .15
178 Jeff Malone .02 .10
179 Robert Parish .05 .15
180 Mark Eaton .02 .10
181 Rony Seikaly .02 .10
182 Tony Campbell .02 .10
183 Kevin McHale .10 .30
184 Thurl Bailey .02 .10
185 Kevin Edwards .02 .10
186 Gerald Glass .02 .10
187 Hersey Hawkins .05 .15
188 Sam Mitchell .02 .10
189 Brian Shaw .02 .10
190 Felton Spencer .02 .10
191 Mark Macon .02 .10
192 Jerry Reynolds .02 .10
193 Dale Davis .02 .10
194 Sleepy Floyd .02 .10
195 A.C. Green .05 .15
196 Terry Catledge .02 .10
197 Byron Scott .05 .15
198 Sam Bowie .02 .10
199 Vlade Divac .05 .15
200 Michael Jordan CL .10 .30
201 Brad Lohaus .02 .10
202 Johnny Newman .02 .10
203 Gary Grant .02 .10
204 Sidney Green .02 .10
205 Frank Brickowski .02 .10
206 Anthony Bowie .02 .10
207 Duane Causwell .02 .10
208 A.J. English .02 .10
209 Mark Aguirre .02 .10
210 Jon Koncak .02 .10
211 Kevin Gamble .02 .10
212 Craig Ehlo .02 .10
213 Herb Williams .05 .15
214 Cedric Ceballos .05 .15
215 Mark Jackson .05 .15
216 John Bagley .02 .10
217 Ron Anderson .02 .10
218 John Battle .02 .10
219 Kevin Lynch .02 .10
220 Donald Hodge .02 .10
221 Chris Gatling .02 .10
222 Muggsy Bogues .05 .15
223 Bill Laimbeer .05 .15
224 Anthony Bonner .02 .10
225 Fred Roberts .02 .10
226 Larry Stewart .02 .10
227 Darrell Walker .02 .10
228 Larry Smith .02 .10
229 Billy Owens .05 .15
230 Vinnie Johnson .02 .10
231 Johnny Dawkins .02 .10
232 Rick Fox .05 .15
233 Travis Mays .02 .10
234 Mark Price .02 .10
235 Derrick McKey .02 .10
236 Greg Anthony .02 .10
237 Doug Smith .02 .10
238 Alec Kessler .02 .10
239 Anthony Mason .10 .30
240 Shawn Kemp .25 .60
241 Jim Les .02 .10
242 Dennis Rodman .25 .60
243 Lionel Simmons .02 .10
244 Pervis Ellison .02 .10
245 Terrell Brandon .10 .30
246 Mark Bryant .02 .10
247 Brad Daugherty .02 .10
248 Scott Brooks .02 .10
249 Sarunas Marciulionis .02 .10
250 Danny Ferry .02 .10
251 Loy Vaught .02 .10
252 Dee Brown .02 .10
253 Alvin Robertson .02 .10
254 Charles Smith .02 .10
255 Dikembe Mutombo .15 .40
256 Greg Kite .02 .10
257 Ed Pinckney .02 .10
258 Ron Harper .05 .15
259 Elliot Perry .02 .10
260 Rafael Addison .02 .10
261 Tim Hardaway .15 .40
262 Randy Brown .02 .10
263 Isiah Thomas .10 .30
264 Victor Alexander .02 .10
265 Wayman Tisdale .02 .10
266 Harvey Grant .02 .10
267 Mike Iuzzolino .02 .10
268 Joe Dumars .10 .30
Michael Jordan
269 Xavier McDaniel .02 .10
270 Jeff Sanders .02 .10
271 Danny Manning .05 .15
272 Jayson Williams .05 .15
273 Ricky Pierce .02 .10
274 Will Perdue .02 .10
275 Dana Barros .02 .10
276 Randy Breuer .02 .10
277 Manute Bol .02 .10
278 Negele Knight .02 .10
279 Rodney McCray .02 .10
280 Greg Sutton .02 .10
281 Larry Nance .02 .10
Michael Jordan
282 John Starks .05 .15
283 Pete Chilcutt .02 .10
284 Kenny Gattison .02 .10
285 Stacey King .02 .10
Michael Jordan
286 Bernard King .02 .10
287 Larry Johnson .15 .40
288 John Williams .02 .10
289 Dell Curry .02 .10
290 Orlando Woolridge .02 .10
291 Nate McMillan .02 .10
292 Terry Mills .02 .10
293 Sherman Douglas .02 .10
294 Charles Shackleford .02 .10
295 Ken Norman .02 .10
296 LaSalle Thompson .02 .10
297 Chris Mullin .10 .30
298 Eddie Johnson .02 .10
299 Armon Gilliam .02 .10
300 Michael Cage .02 .10
301 Moses Malone .10 .30
302 Charles Oakley .05 .15
303 David Wingate .02 .10
304 Steve Kerr .05 .15
305 Tyrone Hill .02 .10
306 Mark West .02 .10
307 Fat Lever .02 .10
308 J.R. Reid .02 .10
309 Ed Nealy .02 .10
310 Michael Jordan CL .10 .30
311 Alaa Abdelnaby .02 .10
312 Stacey Augmon .05 .15
313 Anthony Avent RC .02 .10
314 Walter Bond RC .02 .10
315 Byron Houston RC .02 .10
316 Rick Mahorn .02 .10
317 Sam Mitchell .02 .10
318 Mookie Blaylock .05 .15
319 Lance Blanks .02 .10
320 John Williams .02 .10
321 Rolando Blackman .02 .10
322 Danny Ainge .05 .15
323 Gerald Glass .02 .10
324 Robert Pack .02 .10
325 Oliver Miller RC .05 .15
326 Charles Smith .02 .10
327 Duane Ferrell .02 .10
328 Pooh Richardson .02 .10
329 Scott Brooks .02 .10
330 Walt Williams RC .10 .30
331 Andrew Lang .02 .10
332 Eric Murdock .02 .10
333 Vinny Del Negro .02 .10
334 Charles Barkley .20 .50
335 James Edwards .02 .10
336 Xavier McDaniel .02 .10
337 Paul Graham .02 .10
338 David Wingate .02 .10
339 Richard Dumas RC .02 .10
340 Jay Humphries .02 .10
341 Mark Jackson .05 .15
342 John Salley .02 .10
343 Jon Koncak .02 .10
344 Rodney McCray .02 .10
345 Chuck Person .02 .10
346 Mario Elie .05 .15
347 Frank Johnson .02 .10
348 Rumeal Robinson .02 .10
349 Terry Mills .02 .10
350 Kevin Willis TFC .02 .10
351 Dee Brown TFC .02 .10
352 Muggsy Bogues TFC .02 .10
353 B.J. Armstrong TFC .02 .10
354 Larry Nance TFC .02 .10
355 Doug Smith TFC .02 .10
356 Robert Pack TFC .02 .10
357 Joe Dumars TFC .05 .15
358 Sarunas Marciulionis TFC .02 .10
359 Kenny Smith TFC .02 .10
360 Pooh Richardson TFC .02 .10
361 Mark Jackson TFC .02 .10
362 Sedale Threatt TFC .02 .10
363 Grant Long TFC .02 .10
364 Eric Murdock TFC .02 .10
365 Doug West TFC .02 .10
366 Kenny Anderson TFC .05 .15
367 Anthony Mason TFC .05 .15
368 Nick Anderson TFC .02 .10
369 Jeff Hornacek TFC .02 .10
370 Dan Majerle TFC .02 .10
371 Clifford Robinson TFC .02 .10
372 Lionel Simmons TFC .02 .10
373 Dale Ellis TFC .02 .10
374 Gary Payton TFC .10 .30
375 David Benoit TFC .02 .10
376 Harvey Grant TFC .02 .10
377 Buck Johnson .02 .10
378 Brian Howard RC .02 .10
379 Travis Mays .02 .10
380 Jud Buechler .02 .10
381 Matt Geiger RC .05 .15
382 Bob McCann RC .02 .10
383 Cedric Ceballos .05 .15
384 Rod Strickland .10 .30
385 Kiki Vandeweghe .02 .10
386 Latrell Sprewell RC 1.00 2.50
387 Larry Krystkowiak .02 .10
388 Dale Ellis .02 .10
389 Trent Tucker .02 .10
390 Negele Knight .02 .10
391 Stanley Roberts .02 .10
392 Tony Campbell .02 .10
393 Tim Perry .02 .10
394 Doug Overton .02 .10
395 Dan Majerle .05 .15
396 Duane Cooper RC .02 .10
397 Kevin Willis .02 .10
398 Micheal Williams .02 .10
399 Avery Johnson .02 .10
400 Dominique Wilkins .10 .30
401 Chris Smith RC .02 .10
402 Blair Rasmussen .02 .10
403 Jeff Hornacek .05 .15
404 Blue Edwards .02 .10
405 Olden Polynice .02 .10
406 Jeff Grayer .02 .10
407 Tony Bennett RC .02 .10
408 Don MacLean .02 .10
409 Tom Chambers .02 .10
410 Keith Jennings RC .02 .10
411 Gerald Wilkins .02 .10
412 Kennard Winchester .02 .10
413 Doc Rivers .05 .15
414 Brent Price RC .05 .15
415 Mark West .02 .10
416 J.R. Reid .02 .10
417 Jon Barry RC .05 .15
418 Kevin Johnson .10 .30
419 Michael Jordan CL .10 .30
420 Michael Jordan CL .10 .30
421 Brad Daugherty CL .02 .10
Mark Price
Larry Nance
422 Scottie Pippen AS .20 .50
423 Larry Johnson AS .10 .30
424 Shaquille O'Neal AS 1.00 2.50
425 Michael Jordan AS .75 2.00
426 Isiah Thomas AS .05 .15
427 Brad Daugherty AS .02 .10
428 Joe Dumars AS .05 .15
429 Patrick Ewing AS .05 .15
430 Larry Nance AS .02 .10
431 Mark Price AS .02 .10
432 Detlef Schrempf AS .02 .10
433 Dominique Wilkins AS .05 .15
434 Karl Malone AS .10 .30
435 Charles Barkley AS .10 .30
436 David Robinson AS .10 .30
437 John Stockton AS .05 .15
438 Clyde Drexler AS .05 .15
439 Sean Elliott AS .02 .10
440 Tim Hardaway AS .10 .30
441 Shawn Kemp AS .10 .30
442 Dan Majerle AS .02 .10
443 Danny Manning AS .02 .10
444 Hakeem Olajuwon AS .10 .30
445 Terry Porter AS .02 .10
446 Harold Miner FACE .05 .15
447 David Benoit FACE .02 .10
448 Cedric Ceballos FACE .02 .10
449 Chris Jackson FACE .02 .10
450 Tim Perry FACE .02 .10
451 Kenny Smith FACE .02 .10
452 Clarence Weatherspoon FACE .10 .30
453A Michael Jordan 6.00 15.00
FACE ERR (Slam Dunk Champ
in 1985 and 1990)
453B Michael Jordan .75 2.00
FACE COR (Slam Dunk Champ
in 1987 and 1988)
454A Dominique Wilkins 1.00 2.50
FACE ERR (Slam Dunk Champ
in 1987 and 1988)
454B Dominique Wilkins .10 .30
FACE COR (Slam Dunk Champ
in 1985 and 1990)
455 Anthony Peeler .02 .10
Duane Cooper CL
456 Adam Keefe TP .02 .10
457 Alonzo Mourning TP .20 .50
458 Jim Jackson TP .10 .30
459 Sean Rooks TP .02 .10
460 LaPhonso Ellis TP .05 .15
461 Bryant Stith TP .02 .10
462 Byron Houston TP .02 .10
463 Latrell Sprewell TP .10 .30
464 Robert Horry TP .05 .15
465 Malik Sealy TP .02 .10
466 Doug Christie TP .10 .30
467 Duane Cooper TP .02 .10
468 Anthony Peeler TP .02 .10
469 Harold Miner TP .02 .10
470 Todd Day TP .02 .10
471 Lee Mayberry TP .02 .10
472 Christian Laettner TP .10 .30
473 Hubert Davis TP .02 .10
474 Shaquille O'Neal TP 1.00 2.50
475 Clarence Weatherspoon TP .10 .30
476 Richard Dumas TP .02 .10
477 Oliver Miller TP .02 .10
478 Tracy Murray TP .02 .10
479 Walt Williams TP .05 .15
480 Lloyd Daniels TP .02 .10
481 Tom Gugliotta TP .10 .30
482 Brent Price TP .02 .10
483 Mark Aguirre GF .02 .10
484 Frank Brickowski GF .02 .10
485 Derrick Coleman GF .02 .10
486 Clyde Drexler GF .05 .15
487 Harvey Grant GF .02 .10
488 Michael Jordan GF .75 2.00
489 Karl Malone GF .10 .30
490 Xavier McDaniel GF .02 .10
491 Drazen Petrovic GF .02 .10
492 John Starks GF .02 .10
493 Robert Parish GF .02 .10
494 Christian Laettner GF .10 .30
495 Ron Harper GF .02 .10
496 David Robinson GF .10 .30
497 John Salley GF .02 .10
498 Brad Daugherty ST .02 .10
Mark Price
499 Dikembe Mutombo ST .10 .30
Chris Jackson
500 Isiah Thomas ST .10 .30
Joe Dumars
501 Hakeem Olajuwon .10 .30
Otis Thorpe ST
502 Derrick Coleman ST .05 .15
Drazen Petrovic
503 Terry Porter ST .10 .30
Clyde Drexler
504 Lionel Simmons ST .05 .15
Mitch Richmond
505 David Robinson ST .10 .30
Sean Elliott
506 Michael Jordan FAN .75 2.00
507 Larry Bird FAN .25 .60
508 Karl Malone FAN .10 .30
509 Dikembe Mutombo FAN .10 .30
510 Larry Bird FAN .40 1.00
Michael Jordan
SP1 Larry Bird 1.25 3.00
Magic Johnson Retirement
SP2 20,000 Points 2.50 6.00
Dominique Wilkins Nov. 6, 1992
Michael Jordan Jan. 8, 1993

1992-93 Upper Deck All-Division

Inserted one per second series red or gray jumbo pack, this 20-card standard-size set consists of Upper Deck's selection of the top five players in each of the NBA's four divisions. There is a special logo representing each division. The cards are arranged according to division as follows: Atlantic (1-5), Central (6-10), Midwest (11-15), and Pacific (16-20). The cards are numbered with an "AD" prefix. The fronts feature full-bleed, color, action player photos. A black and team color-coded bar outlined with gold foil carries the player's name and position. These cards can be distinguished by an All-Division Team icon in the lower left corner above the player's name. The backs display career highlights against a light blue panel. A U.S. map shows the player's division.

COMPLETE SET (20) 10.00 20.00
AD1 Shaquille O'Neal 3.00 8.00
AD2 Derrick Coleman .15 .40
AD3 Glen Rice .30 .75
AD4 Reggie Lewis .15 .40
AD5 Kenny Anderson .30 .75
AD6 Brad Daugherty .08 .20
AD7 Dominique Wilkins .30 .75
AD8 Larry Johnson .40 1.00
AD9 Michael Jordan 4.00 10.00
AD10 Mark Price .08 .20
AD11 David Robinson .50 1.25
AD12 Karl Malone .50 1.25
AD13 Sean Elliott .15 .40
AD14 John Stockton .30 .75
AD15 Derek Harper .15 .40
AD16 Kevin Duckworth .08 .20
AD17 Chris Mullin .30 .75
AD18 Charles Barkley .50 1.25
AD19 Tim Hardaway .40 1.00
AD20 Clyde Drexler .30 .75

1992-93 Upper Deck All-NBA

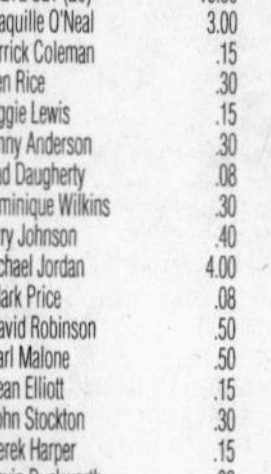

This ten-card standard-size set featuring the 1991-92 All-NBA team was issued one per 27-card low series Locker pack. Each plastic locker box contained four specially wrapped. The fronts feature full-bleed color action player photos with black bottom borders. The player's name is foil-stamped in the border, and the words "All-NBA Team" are foil-stamped at the top. Gold and silver foil stamping are used to designate the First (1-5) and Second Teams (6-10) respectively. The backs carry a close-up player photo and career summary. The cards are numbered on the back with an "AN" prefix.

COMPLETE SET (10) 25.00 50.00
AN1 Michael Jordan ! 10.00 25.00
AN2 Clyde Drexler 1.00 2.50
AN3 David Robinson 1.50 4.00
AN4 Karl Malone 1.50 4.00
AN5 Chris Mullin 1.00 2.50
AN6 John Stockton 1.00 2.50
AN7 Tim Hardaway 1.25 3.00
AN8 Patrick Ewing 1.00 2.50
AN9 Scottie Pippen 3.00 8.00
AN10 Charles Barkley 1.50 4.00

1992-93 Upper Deck All-Rookies

Randomly inserted in low series 15-card retail foil packs at a reported rate of one card for every twelve packs, this ten-card standard-size insert set features the top first-year players of the 1991-92 season. Card numbers 1-5 present the first team and card numbers 6-10 the second team. The cards are numbered with an "AR" prefix. The fronts feature full-bleed, color, action player photos. A gold and red bottom border design carries the player's name, position, the number team (first or second), and an NBA All-Rookie Team icon. The backs carry player profiles.

COMPLETE SET (10) 5.00 10.00
AR1 Larry Johnson 1.00 2.50
AR2 Dikembe Mutombo 1.00 2.50
AR3 Billy Owens .40 1.00
AR4 Steve Smith 1.00 2.50
AR5 Stacey Augmon .40 1.00
AR6 Rick Fox .40 1.00
AR7 Terrell Brandon .75 2.00
AR8 Larry Stewart .10 .30
AR9 Stanley Roberts .10 .30
AR10 Mark Macon .10 .30

1992-93 Upper Deck Award Winner Holograms

The 1992-93 Upper Deck Award Winner Holograms set features nine holograms depicting league leaders in various statistical categories. The set also honors 1991-92 award winners such as top Sixth Man, Rookie of the Year, Defensive Player of the Year and Most Valuable Player. Card numbers 1-6 were randomly inserted in all forms of low series packs while card numbers 7-9 were included in all forms of high series packs. The card numbers have an "AW" prefix. The fronts feature holographic cut-out images of the player against a game-action photo of the player. The player's name and award are displayed at the bottom. The backs carry vertical, color player photos. A light blue plaque-style panel contains information about the player and the award won.

COMPLETE SET (9) 8.00 20.00
COMPLETE LO SERIES (6) 5.00 12.00
COMPLETE HI SERIES (3) 3.00 8.00
AW1 Michael Jordan 4.00 10.00
Scoring
AW2 John Stockton .30 .75
Steals
AW3 Dennis Rodman .60 1.50
Rebounds
AW4 Detlef Schrempf .20 .50
Sixth Man
AW5 Larry Johnson .40 1.00
Rookie of the Year
AW6 David Robinson .50 1.25
Blocked Shots
AW7 David Robinson .50 1.25
Def. Player of Year
AW8 John Stockton .30 .75
Assists
AW9 Michael Jordan 4.00 10.00
Most Valuable Player

1992-93 Upper Deck Larry Bird Heroes

Randomly inserted into all forms of high series packs, this ten-card standard-size set chronicles the career of Larry Bird from his college days at Indiana State University to pro stardom with the Boston Celtics. The color action player photos on the fronts are bordered on the left and bottom by black borders that carry the card subtitle and "Basketball Heroes, Larry Bird" respectively. On a background shading from white to green, brief summaries of Bird's career are presented on a center panel. The cards are numbered on the back in continuation of the Upper Deck Basketball Heroes.

COMMON BIRD (19-27) .30 .75
NNO Larry Bird .75 2.00
Title Header Card

1992-93 Upper Deck Wilt Chamberlain Heroes

Randomly inserted in all types of low series packs, this ten-card standard-size set honors Wilt Chamberlain by highlighting various points in his career. Circular photos on the fronts depict Wilt from college, to the Globetrotter's to pro basketball. Information on the back corresponds to the portion of his career that is represented on front. The set is numbered in continuation of Upper Deck's Hero series.

COMMON CHAMBER. (10-18) .30 .75
NNO Wilt Chamberlain .50 1.25
(Header card)

1992-93 Upper Deck Wilt Chamberlain Box Bottom

Measuring approximately 5" by 7", this box bottom displays a color painting by artist Alan Studt. Four different images of Chamberlain are presented, each showing Wilt at a different stage of his career according to uniform (Kansas, Harlem Globetrotters, Philadelphia 76ers, and Los Angeles Lakers). The back is blank. The box bottom is unnumbered.

NNO Wilt Chamberlain .30 .75

1992-93 Upper Deck 15000 Point Club

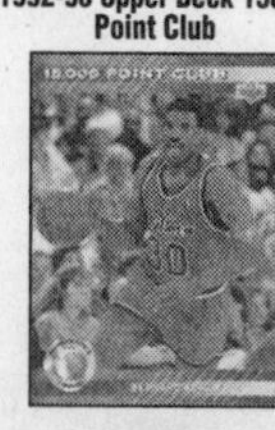

Randomly inserted in 15-card high series hobby packs at a reported rate of one card per nine packs, this 20-card standard-size set spotlights then-active NBA players who had scored more than 15,000 points in their career. The fronts feature full-bleed color action player photos accented at the top and bottom by team color-coded stripes carrying the phrase "15,000 Point Club" and the player's name respectively. A gold 15,000-Point club logo at the lower left corner carries the season the player joined this elite club. The backs display a small player photo and year-by-year scoring totals. The cards are numbered with an "PC" prefix.

COMPLETE SET (20) 20.00 50.00
PC1 Dominique Wilkins 1.00 2.50
PC2 Kevin McHale 1.00 2.50
PC3 Robert Parish .50 1.25
PC4 Michael Jordan 12.50 30.00
PC5 Isiah Thomas 1.00 2.50
PC6 Mark Aguirre .30 .75
PC7 Kiki Vandeweghe .30 .75
PC8 James Worthy 1.00 2.50
PC9 Rolando Blackman .30 .75
PC10 Moses Malone 1.00 2.50
PC11 Charles Barkley 1.50 4.00
PC12 Tom Chambers .30 .75
PC13 Clyde Drexler 1.00 2.50
PC14 Terry Cummings .50 1.25
PC15 Eddie Johnson .30 .75
PC16 Karl Malone 1.50 4.00
PC17 Bernard King .30 .75
PC18 Larry Nance .30 .75
PC19 Jeff Malone .30 .75
PC20 Hakeem Olajuwon 1.50 4.00

1992-93 Upper Deck Foreign Exchange

Inserted one card per pack in second series 4-pack locker boxes, this ten-card standard-size set showcases foreign born players who are stars in the NBA. Each card uses the colors of the flag from the player's homeland as well as a "Foreign Exchange" logo. The cards are numbered with an "FE" prefix. The fronts carry full-bleed, color, action player photos. The player's name, position, and place of birth appear in border stripes at the bottom. The backs display either an action or close-up player photo on a pale beige panel along with a player profile. A small representation of the player's home flag appears at the lower right corner of the picture. The set is sequenced in alphabetical order.

COMPLETE SET (10) 7.50 15.00
FE1 Manute Bol .25 .60
FE2 Vlade Divac .75 2.00
FE3 Patrick Ewing 1.50 4.00
FE4 Sarunas Marciulionis .25 .60
FE5 Dikembe Mutombo 2.00 5.00
FE6 Hakeem Olajuwon 2.50 6.00
FE7 Drazen Petrovic .75 2.00
FE8 Detlef Schrempf .75 2.00
FE9 Rik Smits .75 2.00
FE10 Dominique Wilkins 1.50 4.00

1992-93 Upper Deck Rookie Standouts

Randomly inserted in high series retail and high series red jumbo packs at a reported rate of one card per nine packs, this 20-card standard-size set honors top rookies who made the most impact during the 1992-93 NBA season. The cards are numbered on the back with an "RS" prefix. The fronts feature full-bleed, color, action player photos. The player's name and position appear in a teal stripe across the bottom. A "Rookie Standouts" icon overlaps the stripe and the picture at the lower right corner. The backs have a vertical action photo and career highlights within a gold box. A red banner over a gold basketball icon accent the top of the box.

COMPLETE SET (20) 10.00 25.00
RS1 Adam Keefe .05 .15
RS2 Alonzo Mourning 2.00 5.00
RS3 Sean Rooks .05 .15
RS4 LaPhonso Ellis .30 .75
RS5 Latrell Sprewell 2.50 6.00
RS6 Robert Horry .30 .75
RS7 Malik Sealy .15 .40
RS8 Anthony Peeler .15 .40
RS9 Harold Miner .15 .40
RS10 Anthony Avent .05 .15
RS11 Todd Day .15 .40
RS12 Lee Mayberry .05 .15
RS13 Christian Laettner .60 1.50
RS14 Hubert Davis .15 .40
RS15 Shaquille O'Neal 6.00 15.00
RS16 Clarence Weatherspoon .30 .75
RS17 Richard Dumas .05 .15
RS18 Walt Williams .30 .75
RS19 Lloyd Daniels .05 .15
RS20 Tom Gugliotta 1.00 2.50

1992-93 Upper Deck Team MVPs

This 28-card standard-size set honors a top player from each NBA team. One "Team MVP" card was inserted into each 1992-93 Upper Deck low series 27-card jumbo pack. Card fronts feature a photo that takes up most of the front. The only other feature on front is the player's name within a bottom border. Backs contain a photo with highlights. These cards are numbered on the back with a "TM" prefix.

COMPLETE SET (28) 20.00 50.00
TM1 Michael Jordan CL 10.00 25.00
TM2 Dominique Wilkins .75 2.00
TM3 Reggie Lewis .40 1.00
TM4 Kendall Gill .40 1.00
TM5 Michael Jordan 10.00 25.00
TM6 Brad Daugherty .10 .30
TM7 Derek Harper .40 1.00
TM8 Dikembe Mutombo 1.00 2.50
TM9 Isiah Thomas .75 2.00
TM10 Chris Mullin .75 2.00
TM11 Hakeem Olajuwon 1.25 3.00
TM12 Reggie Miller .75 2.00
TM13 Ron Harper .40 1.00
TM14 James Worthy .75 2.00
TM15 Rony Seikaly .10 .30
TM16 Alvin Robertson .10 .30
TM17 Pooh Richardson .10 .30
TM18 Derrick Coleman .40 1.00
TM19 Patrick Ewing .75 2.00
TM20 Scott Skiles .10 .30
TM21 Hersey Hawkins .40 1.00
TM22 Kevin Johnson .75 2.00
TM23 Clyde Drexler .75 2.00
TM24 Mitch Richmond .75 2.00
TM25 David Robinson 1.25 3.00
TM26 Ricky Pierce .10 .30
TM27 John Stockton .75 2.00
TM28 Pervis Ellison .10 .30

1992-93 Upper Deck Jerry West Selects

Randomly inserted in 15-card low series hobby packs at a reported rate of one card per nine packs, this 20-card standard-size set pays tribute to Jerry West's selection of NBA players who are the most dominant (or projected to be) in ten different basketball skills. The cards feature color action player photos bordered on the right edge by a white stripe containing the player's name. Two stripes border the bottom of the cards, a black stripe containing a gold foil facsimile autograph of Jerry West and the word "Select," and a gradated team-colored stripe. This second stripe contains the player's specific achievement. The backs show a smaller color action shot of the player above a pale gray panel containing comments by West. The right edge of the card has a 1/2" white border containing the player's name. A small cut-out action image of Jerry West appears at the lower right corner. Card numbers 1-10 feature his present selections for best in ten different categories while card numbers 11-20 are his future selections. The cards are numbered on the back with a "JW" prefix. The set includes four cards of Michael Jordan.

COMPLETE SET (20) 30.00 80.00
JW1 Michael Jordan 10.00 25.00
Best Shooter
JW2 Dennis Rodman 1.50 4.00
Best Rebounder
JW3 David Robinson 1.25 3.00
Best Shot Blocker
JW4 Michael Jordan 10.00 25.00
Best Defender
JW5 Magic Johnson 5.00 12.00
Best Point Guard
JW6 Detlef Schrempf .40 1.00
Best Sixth Man
JW7 Magic Johnson 5.00 12.00
Most Inspirational Player
JW8 Michael Jordan 10.00 25.00
Best All-Around Player
JW9 Michael Jordan 10.00 25.00
Best Clutch Player
JW10 Magic Johnson 5.00 12.00
Best Court Leader
JW11 Glen Rice .75 2.00
Best Shooter
JW12 Dikembe Mutombo 1.00 2.50
Best Rebounder
JW13 Dikembe Mutombo 1.00 2.50
Best Shot Blocker
JW14 Stacey Augmon .40 1.00
Best Defender
JW15 Tim Hardaway 1.00 2.50
Best Point Guard
JW16 Shawn Kemp 1.50 4.00
Best Sixth Man
JW17 Danny Manning .40 1.00
Most Inspirational Player
JW18 Larry Johnson 1.00 2.50
Best All-Around Player
JW19 Reggie Lewis .40 1.00
Best Clutch Player
JW20 Tim Hardaway 1.00 2.50
Best Court Leader

1993-94 Upper Deck

This 510-card standard-size UV-coated set was issued in two series of 255. The cards were issued in 12-card hobby and retail packs (36 per box), 22-card green and blue retail jumbo packs (first series only), 22-card red and purple retail jumbo packs (second series only) and 22-card hobby locker packs for both series. Card fronts feature glossy color player action photos on the fronts. The left and bottom borders (team colors) contain the team and player's name respectively. The backs feature another color action player photo at the top. At bottom, player stats are shaded in team colors. Topical subsets featured are the following: Season Leaders (166-177), NBA Playoffs Highlights (178-197), NBA Finals Highlights (198-209), Schedules (210-236), Signature Moves (237-251), Executive Board (421-435), Breakaway Threats (436-455), Game Images (456-465), Skylights (467-480), Top Prospects (482-497) and McDonald's Open (498-507). The cards are numbered on the back. The SP3 card was inserted randomly in all forms of first series packaging with the SP4 in the second series. Both cards were inserted at a rate of 1 in 72 packs. Rookie Cards of note include Vin Baker, Anfernee Hardaway, Allan Houston, Toni Kukoc, Jamal Mashburn, Nick Van Exel and Chris Webber.

COMPLETE SET (510) 15.00 30.00
COMPLETE SERIES 1 (255) 7.50 15.00
COMPLETE SERIES 2 (255) 7.50 15.00
1 Muggsy Bogues .05 .15
2 Kenny Anderson .05 .15
3 Dell Curry .01 .05
4 Charles Smith .01 .05
5 Chuck Person .01 .05
6 Chucky Brown .01 .05
7 Kevin Johnson .05 .15
8 Winston Garland .01 .05
9 John Salley .01 .05
10 Dale Ellis .01 .05
11 Otis Thorpe .05 .15
12 John Stockton .10 .30
13 Kendall Gill .05 .15
14 Randy White .01 .05
15 Mark Jackson .05 .15
16 Vlade Divac .05 .15
17 Scott Skiles .01 .05
18 Xavier McDaniel .01 .05
19 Jeff Hornacek .05 .15
20 Stanley Roberts .01 .05
21 Harold Miner .01 .05
22 Terrell Brandon .05 .15
23 Michael Jordan 1.50 4.00
24 Jim Jackson .05 .15
25 Keith Askins .01 .05
26 Corey Williams .01 .05
27 David Benoit .01 .05
28 Charles Oakley .05 .15
29 Michael Adams .01 .05
30 Clarence Weatherspoon .01 .05
31 Jon Koncak .01 .05
32 Gerald Wilkins .01 .05
33 Anthony Bowie .01 .05
34 Willie Burton .01 .05
35 Stacey Augmon .01 .05
36 Doc Rivers .05 .15
37 Luc Longley .05 .15
38 Dee Brown .01 .05
39 Litterial Green .01 .05
40 Dan Majerle .05 .15
41 Doug West .01 .05
42 Joe Dumars .10 .30
43 Dennis Scott .01 .05
44 Mahmoud Abdul-Rauf .01 .05
45 Mark Eaton .01 .05
46 Danny Ferry .01 .05
47 Kenny Smith .01 .05
48 Ron Harper .05 .15
49 Adam Keefe .01 .05
50 David Robinson .20 .50
51 John Starks .05 .15
52 Jeff Malone .01 .05
53 Vern Fleming .01 .05
54 Olden Polynice .01 .05
55 Dikembe Mutombo .10 .30
56 Chris Morris .01 .05
57 Paul Graham .01 .05
58 Richard Dumas .01 .05
59 J.R. Reid .01 .05
60 Brad Daugherty .01 .05
61 Blue Edwards .01 .05
62 Mark Macon .01 .05
63 Latrell Sprewell .30 .75
64 Mitch Richmond .10 .30
65 David Wingate .01 .05
66 LaSalle Thompson .01 .05
67 Sedale Threatt .01 .05
68 Larry Krystkowiak .01 .05
69 John Paxson .01 .05
70 Frank Brickowski .01 .05
71 Duane Causwell .01 .05
72 Fred Roberts .01 .05
73 Rod Strickland .05 .15
74 Willie Anderson .01 .05
75 Thurl Bailey .01 .05
76 Ricky Pierce .01 .05
77 Todd Day .01 .05
78 Hot Rod Williams .01 .05
79 Danny Ainge .05 .15
80 Mark West .01 .05
81 Marcus Liberty .01 .05
82 Keith Jennings .01 .05
83 Derrick Coleman .05 .15
84 Larry Stewart .01 .05
85 Tracy Murray .01 .05
86 Robert Horry .05 .15
87 Derek Harper .05 .15
88 Scott Hastings .01 .05
89 Sam Perkins .05 .15
90 Clyde Drexler .10 .30
91 Brent Price .01 .05
92 Chris Mullin .10 .30
93 Rafael Addison .01 .05
94 Tyrone Corbin .01 .05
95 Sarunas Marciulionis .01 .05
96 Antoine Carr .01 .05
97 Tony Bennett .01 .05
98 Sam Mitchell .01 .05
99 Lionel Simmons .01 .05
100 Tim Perry .01 .05
101 Horace Grant .05 .15
102 Tom Hammonds .01 .05
103 Walter Bond .01 .05
104 Detlef Schrempf .05 .15
105 Terry Porter .01 .05
106 Danny Schayes .01 .05
107 Rumeal Robinson .01 .05
108 Gerald Glass .01 .05
109 Mike Gminski .01 .05
110 Terry Mills .01 .05
111 Loy Vaught .01 .05
112 Jim Les .01 .05
113 Byron Houston .01 .05
114 Randy Brown .01 .05
115 Anthony Avent .01 .05
116 Donald Hodge .01 .05
117 Kevin Willis .01 .05
118 Robert Pack .01 .05
119 Dale Davis .01 .05
120 Grant Long .01 .05
121 Anthony Bonner .01 .05
122 Chris Smith .01 .05
123 Elden Campbell .01 .05
124 Clifford Robinson .05 .15
125 Sherman Douglas .01 .05
126 Alvin Robertson .01 .05
127 Rolando Blackman .01 .05
128 Malik Sealy .01 .05
129 Ed Pinckney .01 .05
130 Anthony Peeler .01 .05
131 Scott Brooks .01 .05
132 Rik Smits .05 .15
133 Derrick McKey .01 .05
134 Alaa Abdelnaby .01 .05
135 Rex Chapman .01 .05
136 Tony Campbell .01 .05
137 John Williams .01 .05
138 Vincent Askew .01 .05
139 LaBradford Smith .01 .05
140 Vinny Del Negro .01 .05
141 Darrell Walker .01 .05
142 James Worthy .10 .30
143 Jeff Turner .01 .05
144 Duane Ferrell .01 .05
145 Larry Smith .01 .05
146 Eddie Johnson .01 .05
147 Chris Gatling .01 .05
148 Buck Williams .01 .05
149 Donald Royal .01 .05
150 Dino Radja RC .01 .05
151 Johnny Dawkins .01 .05
152 Tim Legler RC .01 .05
153 Bill Laimbeer .01 .05
154 Glen Rice .05 .15
155 Bill Cartwright .01 .05
156 Luther Wright RC .01 .05
157 Rex Walters RC .01 .05
158 Doug Edwards RC .01 .05
159 George Lynch RC .01 .05
160 Chris Mills RC .10 .30
161 Sam Cassell RC .50 1.25
162 Nick Van Exel RC .40 1.00
163 Shawn Bradley RC .10 .30
164 Calbert Cheaney RC .05 .15
165 Corie Blount RC .01 .05
166 Michael Jordan SL .75 2.00
167 Dennis Rodman SL .10 .30
168 John Stockton SL .05 .15
169 B.J. Armstrong SL .01 .05
170 Hakeem Olajuwon SL .10 .30
171 Michael Jordan SL .75 2.00
172 Cedric Ceballos SL .01 .05
173 Mark Price SL .01 .05
174 Charles Barkley SL .10 .30
175 Clifford Robinson SL .01 .05
176 Hakeem Olajuwon SL .10 .30
177 Shaquille O'Neal SL .25 .60
178 Reggie Miller .05 .15
Charles Oakley PO
179 Rick Fox .01 .05
Kenny Gattison PO
180 Michael Jordan .40 1.00
Stacey Augmon PO
181 Brad Daugherty PO .01 .05
182 Oliver Miller .01 .05
Byron Scott PO
183 David Robinson .10 .30
Sean Elliott PO
184 Kenny Smith .01 .05
Mark Jackson PO
185 Eddie Johnson PO .01 .05
186 Anthony Mason .10 .30
Patrick Ewing
Alonzo Mourning PO
187 Michael Jordan .40 1.00
Gerald Wilkins PO
188 Oliver Miller PO .01 .05
189 Sam Perkins .10 .30
Hakeem Olajuwon PO
190 Bill Cartwright PO .01 .05
191 Kevin Johnson PO .05 .15
192 Dan Majerle PO .01 .05
193 Michael Jordan PO .75 2.00
194 Larry Johnson .01 .05
Muggsy Bogues PO
195 Reggie Miller PO .05 .15
196 John Starks .10 .30
Scottie Pippen PO
197 Charles Barkley PO .10 .30
198 Michael Jordan FIN .75 2.00
199 Scottie Pippen FIN .20 .50
200 Kevin Johnson FIN .01 .05
201 Michael Jordan FIN .75 2.00
202 Richard Dumas FIN .01 .05
203 Horace Grant FIN .01 .05
204 Michael Jordan FIN .75 2.00
205 Scottie Pippen FIN .10 .30
Charles Barkley
206 John Paxson FIN .01 .05
207 B.J. Armstrong FIN .01 .05
208 1992-93 Bulls FIN .10 .30
209 1992-93 Suns FIN .01 .05
210 Atlanta Hawks Sked .01 .05
Kevin Willis
211 Boston Celtics Sked .01 .05
Brian Shaw
212 Charlotte Hornets SKED .01 .05
213 Chicago Bulls Sked .40 1.00
Michael Jordan
214 Cleveland Cavaliers Sked .01 .05
Mark Price
215 Dallas Mavericks Sked .01 .05
Jim Jackson
Sean Rooks
216 Denver Nuggets Sked .05 .15
Dikembe Mutombo
217 Detroit Pistons Sked .05 .15
Isiah Thomas
Bill Laimbeer
Terry Mills
218 Golden State Warriors SKED .01 .05
219 Houston Rockets Sked .10 .30
Hakeem Olajuwon
220 Indiana Pacers Sked .01 .05
Rik Smits
Detlef Schrempf
221 L.A. Clippers Sked .01 .05
Ron Harper
Danny Manning
Mark Jackson
222 L.A. Lakers SKED .01 .05
223 Miami Heat Sked .05 .15
Steve Smith
Harold Miner
Rony Seikaly
224 Milwaukee Bucks SKED .01 .05
225 Minnesota Timberwolves SKED .01 .05
226 New Jersey Nets Sked .01 .05
Kenny Anderson
227 New York Knicks Sked .01 .05
Rolando Blackmon
228 Orlando Magic Sked .15 .40
Shaquille O'Neal
229 Philadelphia 76ers Sked .01 .05
Hersey Hawkins
Jeff Hornacek
230 Phoenix Suns Sked .10 .30
Charles Barkley
231 Portland Trail Blazers .01 .05
Buck Williams
Jerome Kersey
Terry Porter)
232 Sacramento Kings SKED .01 .05
233 San Antonio Spurs Sked .10 .30
David Robinson
Avery Johnson
Sean Elliott
234 Seattle Supersonics Sked .05 .15
Gary Payton
Shawn Kemp
235 Utah Jazz SKED .01 .05
236 Washington Bullets .05 .15
Tom Gugliotta
Michael Adams
237 Michael Jordan SM .75 2.00
238 Clyde Drexler SM .05 .15
239 Tim Hardaway SM .05 .15
240 Dominique Wilkins SM .05 .15
241 Brad Daugherty SM .01 .05
242 Chris Mullin SM .05 .15
243 Kenny Anderson SM .01 .05
244 Patrick Ewing SM .05 .15
245 Isiah Thomas SM .05 .15
246 Dikembe Mutombo SM .05 .15
247 Danny Manning SM .01 .05
248 David Robinson SM .10 .30
249 Karl Malone SM .10 .30
250 James Worthy SM .05 .15
251 Shawn Kemp SM .10 .30
252 Checklist 1-64 .01 .05
253 Checklist 65-128 .01 .05
254 Checklist 129-192 .01 .05
255 Checklist 193-255 .01 .05
256 Patrick Ewing .10 .30
257 B.J. Armstrong .01 .05
258 Oliver Miller .01 .05
259 Jud Buechler .01 .05
260 Pooh Richardson .01 .05
261 Victor Alexander .01 .05
262 Kevin Gamble .01 .05
263 Doug Smith .01 .05
264 Isiah Thomas .10 .30
265 Doug Christie .05 .15
266 Mark Bryant .01 .05
267 Lloyd Daniels .01 .05
268 Micheal Williams .01 .05
269 Nick Anderson .05 .15
270 Tom Gugliotta .10 .30
271 Kenny Gattison .01 .05
272 Vernon Maxwell .01 .05
273 Terry Cummings .01 .05
274 Karl Malone .20 .50
275 Rick Fox .01 .05
276 Matt Bullard .01 .05
277 Johnny Newman .01 .05
278 Mark Price .01 .05
279 Mookie Blaylock .05 .15
280 Charles Barkley .20 .50
281 Larry Nance .01 .05
282 Walt Williams .01 .05
283 Brian Shaw .01 .05
284 Robert Parish .05 .15
285 Pervis Ellison .01 .05
286 Spud Webb .05 .15
287 Hakeem Olajuwon .20 .50
288 Jerome Kersey .01 .05
289 Carl Herrera .01 .05
290 Dominique Wilkins .10 .30
291 Billy Owens .01 .05
292 Greg Anthony .01 .05
293 Nate McMillan .01 .05
294 Christian Laettner .05 .15
295 Gary Payton .20 .50
296 Steve Smith .10 .30
297 Anthony Mason .05 .15
298 Sean Rooks .01 .05
299 Toni Kukoc RC .50 1.25
300 Shaquille O'Neal .60 1.50
301 Jay Humphries .01 .05
302 Sleepy Floyd .01 .05
303 Bimbo Coles .01 .05
304 John Battle .01 .05
305 Shawn Kemp .20 .50
306 Scott Williams .01 .05
307 Wayman Tisdale .01 .05
308 Rony Seikaly .01 .05
309 Reggie Miller .10 .30
310 Scottie Pippen .40 1.00
311 Chris Webber RC 1.25 3.00
312 Trevor Wilson .01 .05
313 Derek Strong RC .01 .05
314 Bobby Hurley RC .05 .15
315 Herb Williams .01 .05
316 Rex Walters .01 .05
317 Doug Edwards .01 .05
318 Ken Williams .01 .05
319 Jon Barry .01 .05
320 Joe Courtney RC .01 .05
321 Ervin Johnson RC .05 .15
322 Sam Cassell .10 .30
323 Tim Hardaway .10 .30
324 Steve Kerr .01 .05
325 Pete Chilcutt .05 .15
326 Doug Overton .01 .05
327 Reggie Williams .01 .05
328 Avery Johnson .01 .05
329 Stacey King .01 .05
330 Vin Baker RC .30 .75
331 Greg Kite .01 .05
332 Michael Cage .01 .05
333 Alonzo Mourning .20 .50
334 Acie Earl RC .01 .05
335 Terry Dehere RC .01 .05
336 Negele Knight .01 .05
337 Gerald Madkins RC .01 .05
338 Lindsey Hunter RC .10 .30
339 Luther Wright .01 .05
340 Mike Peplowski RC .01 .05
341 Dino Radja .01 .05
342 Danny Manning .05 .15
343 Chris Mills .10 .30
344 Hubert Davis .01 .05
345 Shawn Bradley .10 .30
346 Evers Burns RC .01 .05
347 Rodney Rogers RC .10 .30
348 Cedric Ceballos .05 .15
349 Warren Kidd RC .01 .05
350 Darnell Mee RC .01 .05
351 Matt Geiger .01 .05
352 Jamal Mashburn RC .30 .75
353 Antonio Davis RC .15 .40
354 Calbert Cheaney .05 .15
355 George Lynch .01 .05
356 Derrick McKey .01 .05
357 Jerry Reynolds .01 .05
358 Don MacLean .01 .05
359 Scott Haskin RC .01 .05
360 Malcolm Mackey RC .01 .05
361 Isaiah Rider RC .25 .60
362 Detlef Schrempf .05 .15
363 Josh Grant RC .01 .05
364 Kurt Rambis .01 .05
365 Larry Johnson .10 .30
366 Richard Petruska RC .01 .05
367 Ken Norman .01 .05
368 Kenny Walker .01 .05
369 James Robinson RC .01 .05
370 Kevin Duckworth .01 .05
371 Chris Whitney RC .01 .05
372 Moses Malone .10 .30
373 Nick Van Exel .20 .50
374 Scott Burrell RC .10 .30
375 Harvey Grant .01 .05
376 Benoit Benjamin .01 .05
377 Henry James .01 .05
378 Pete Myers .01 .05
379 Dwayne Schintzius .01 .05
380 Sean Green .01 .05
381 Eric Murdock .01 .05
382 Anfernee Hardaway RC 1.00 2.50
383 Gheorghe Muresan RC .10 .30
384 Kendall Gill .05 .15
385 David Wood .01 .05
386 Mario Elie .01 .05
387 Chris Corchiani .01 .05
388 Greg Graham RC .01 .05
389 Hersey Hawkins .05 .15
390 Mark Aguirre .01 .05
391 LaPhonso Ellis .01 .05
392 Anthony Bonner .01 .05
393 Lucious Harris RC .01 .05
394 Andrew Lang .01 .05
395 Chris Dudley .01 .05
396 Dennis Rodman .25 .60
397 Larry Krystkowiak .01 .05
398 A.C. Green .05 .15
399 Eddie Johnson .01 .05
400 Kevin Edwards .01 .05
401 Tyrone Hill .01 .05
402 Greg Anderson .01 .05
403 P.J. Brown RC .25 .60
404 Dana Barros .01 .05
405 Allan Houston RC .50 1.25
406 Mike Brown .01 .05
407 Lee Mayberry .01 .05
408 Fat Lever .01 .05
409 Tony Smith .01 .05
410 Tom Chambers .01 .05
411 Manute Bol .01 .05
412 Joe Kleine .01 .05
413 Bryant Stith .01 .05
414 Chuck Nevitt .01 .05
415 Jo Jo English RC .01 .05
416 Sean Elliott .05 .15
417 Sam Bowie .01 .05
418 Armon Gilliam .01 .05
419 Brian Williams .01 .05
420 Popeye Jones RC .01 .05
421 Dennis Rodman EB .10 .30
422 Karl Malone EB .10 .30
423 Tom Gugliotta EB .05 .15
424 Kevin Willis EB .01 .05
425 Hakeem Olajuwon EB .10 .30
426 Charles Oakley EB .01 .05
427 Clarence Weatherspoon EB .01 .05
428 Derrick Coleman EB .01 .05
429 Buck Williams EB .01 .05
430 Christian Laettner EB .01 .05
431 Dikembe Mutombo EB .05 .15
432 Rony Seikaly EB .01 .05
433 Brad Daugherty EB .01 .05
434 Horace Grant EB .01 .05
435 Larry Johnson EB .05 .15
436 Dee Brown BT .01 .05
437 Muggsy Bogues BT .01 .05
438 Michael Jordan BT .75 2.00
439 Tim Hardaway BT .05 .15
440 Micheal Williams BT .01 .05
441 Gary Payton BT .10 .30
442 Mookie Blaylock BT .01 .05
443 Doc Rivers BT .01 .05
444 Kenny Smith BT .01 .05
445 John Stockton BT .05 .15
446 Alvin Robertson BT .01 .05
447 Mark Jackson BT .01 .05
448 Kenny Anderson BT .01 .05
449 Scottie Pippen BT .20 .50
450 Isiah Thomas BT .05 .15
451 Mark Price BT .01 .05
452 Latrell Sprewell BT .10 .30
453 Sedale Threatt BT .01 .05
454 Nick Anderson BT .01 .05
455 Rod Strickland BT .01 .05
456 Oliver Miller GI .01 .05
457 James Worthy .01 .05
Vlade Divac GI
458 Robert Horry GI .01 .05
459 Rockets Shoot-Around GI .01 .05
460 Sean Rooks .01 .05
Jim Jackson
Tim Legler GI
461 Mitch Richmond GI .05 .15
462 Chris Morris GI .01 .05
463 Mark Jackson .01 .05
Gary Grant GI
464 David Robinson GI .10 .30
465 Danny Ainge GI .01 .05
466 Michael Jordan SKL .75 2.00
467 Dominique Wilkins SKL .05 .15
468 Alonzo Mourning SKL .10 .30
469 Shaquille O'Neal SKL .25 .60
470 Tim Hardaway SL .05 .15
471 Patrick Ewing SKL .05 .15
472 Kevin Johnson SL .01 .05
473 Clyde Drexler SKL .05 .15
474 David Robinson SKL .10 .30
475 Shawn Kemp SKL .10 .30
476 Dee Brown SL .01 .05
477 Jim Jackson SKL .01 .05
478 John Stockton SKL .05 .15
479 Robert Horry SL .01 .05
480 Glen Rice SL .01 .05
481 Micheal Williams SIS .01 .05
482 George Lynch .01 .05
Terry Dehere CL
483 Chris Webber TP .60 1.50
484 Anfernee Hardaway TP .50 1.25
485 Shawn Bradley TP .05 .15
486 Jamal Mashburn TP .10 .30
487 Calbert Cheaney TP .01 .05
488 Isaiah Rider TP .10 .30
489 Bobby Hurley TP .01 .05
490 Vin Baker TP .10 .30
491 Rodney Rogers TP .05 .15
492 Lindsey Hunter TP .05 .15
493 Allan Houston TP .10 .30
494 Terry Dehere TP .01 .05
495 George Lynch TP .01 .05
496 Toni Kukoc TP .10 .30
497 Nick Van Exel TP .10 .30
498 Charles Barkley MO .10 .30
499 A.C. Green MO .01 .05
500 Dan Majerle MO .01 .05
501 Jerrod Mustaf MO .01 .05
502 Kevin Johnson MO .01 .05
503 Joe Kleine MO .01 .05
504 Danny Ainge MO .01 .05
505 Oliver Miller MO .01 .05
506 Joe Courtney MO .01 .05
507 Checklist .01 .05
508 Checklist .01 .05
509 Checklist .01 .05
510 Checklist .01 .05
SP3 Michael Jordan 3.00 8.00
Wilt Chamberlain
SP4 Chicago Bulls Third 3.00 8.00
NBA Championship

1993-94 Upper Deck All-NBA

Inserted one per blue and green first series retail 22-card jumbo packs, this 15-card standard-size set spotlights All-NBA first, second and third teams. The cards feature a borderless front with a color action photo set against a game-crowd background. The player's name appears in a red vertical stripe along the right side. The All NBA Team appears in a blue vertical stripe along the right side. The back features a color action photo along the left side with player's statistics along the right side.

COMPLETE SET (15) 6.00 12.00
AN1 Charles Barkley .40 1.00
AN2 Karl Malone .40 1.00
AN3 Hakeem Olajuwon .40 1.00
AN4 Michael Jordan 3.00 8.00
AN5 Mark Price .02 .10
AN6 Dominique Wilkins .25 .60
AN7 Larry Johnson .25 .60
AN8 Patrick Ewing .25 .60
AN9 John Stockton .25 .60
AN10 Joe Dumars .25 .60
AN11 Scottie Pippen .60 1.50
AN12 Derrick Coleman .10 .30
AN13 David Robinson .40 1.00
AN14 Tim Hardaway .25 .60
AN15 Michael Jordan CL 3.00 8.00

1993-94 Upper Deck All-Rookies

Randomly inserted in first series 12-card retail packs at a rate of one in 30, this 10-card standard-size set features the NBA All-Rookie first (1-5) and second (6-10) teams from 1992-93. The cards feature color game-action player photos on their fronts. They are borderless, except at the top, where a red stripe edges the cards of the first team and a blue one edges those of the second. The player's name appears in white lettering within a red or blue stripe near the bottom. The back carries a color player action photo on the left and career highlights on the right.

COMPLETE SET (10) 7.50 15.00
AR1 Shaquille O'Neal 4.00 10.00
AR2 Alonzo Mourning 1.25 3.00
AR3 Christian Laettner .40 1.00
AR4 Tom Gugliotta .75 2.00
AR5 LaPhonso Ellis .10 .30
AR6 Walt Williams .10 .30
AR7 Robert Horry .40 1.00
AR8 Latrell Sprewell 2.00 5.00
AR9 Clarence Weatherspoon .10 .30
AR10 Richard Dumas .10 .30

1993-94 Upper Deck Box Bottoms

Measuring approximately 5" by 7", these box bottoms display enlarged versions of the fronts of regular series cards. The backs are blank. The box bottoms are unnumbered and checklisted below in alphabetical order.

COMPLETE SET (2) .75 2.00
1 Bobby Hurley .08 .25
2 Michael Jordan .75 2.00

1993-94 Upper Deck Flight Team

Michael Jordan selected the league's best dunkers for this 20-card insert set. The cards are randomly inserted in first series 12-card hobby packs at a rate of one in 30. The standard-size cards feature on their fronts full-bleed color action player photos. The words "Michael Jordan's Flight Team" appear in ghosted block lettering over the background. The player's name is gold-foil stamped at the bottom, with the Flight Team insignia displayed immediately above carrying his team's city name and the his uniform number. On a background consisting of blue sky and clouds, the back carries a color player action cutout and an evaluative quote by Jordan. The set is sequenced in alphabetical order.

COMPLETE SET (20) 40.00 80.00
FT1 Stacey Augmon .40 1.00
FT2 Charles Barkley 4.00 10.00
FT3 David Benoit .40 1.00
FT4 Dee Brown .40 1.00
FT5 Cedric Ceballos 1.25 3.00
FT6 Derrick Coleman 1.25 3.00
FT7 Clyde Drexler 2.50 6.00
FT8 Sean Elliott 1.25 3.00
FT9 LaPhonso Ellis .40 1.00
FT10 Kendall Gill 1.25 3.00
FT11 Larry Johnson 2.50 6.00
FT12 Shawn Kemp 4.00 10.00
FT13 Karl Malone 4.00 10.00
FT14 Harold Miner .40 1.00
FT15 Alonzo Mourning 4.00 10.00
FT16 Shaquille O'Neal 10.00 25.00
FT17 Scottie Pippen 8.00 20.00
FT18 Clarence Weatherspoon .40 1.00
FT19 Spud Webb 1.25 3.00
FT20 Dominique Wilkins 2.50 6.00

1993-94 Upper Deck Future Heroes

Inserted one per first series locker pack, this set continues Upper Deck's year-by-year basketball Heroes program. Unlike previous sets devoted to individual players, the 1993-94 set features a selection of young phenoms destined to be stars. This 10-card standard-size set features color player action shots on its fronts. The photos are bordered on the left and bottom by gray and team color-coded stripes. The player's name and position appear in white lettering in the color-coded stripe at the bottom. An embossed silver-foil basketball appears at the lower left. The white back carries the player's career highlights. The set is numbered in continuation of Upper Deck's Hero Series and is sequenced in alphabetical order.

COMPLETE SET (10) 10.00 20.00
28 Derrick Coleman .50 1.25
29 LaPhonso Ellis .15 .40
30 Jim Jackson .50 1.25
31 Larry Johnson 1.00 2.50
32 Shawn Kemp 1.50 4.00
33 Christian Laettner .50 1.25
34 Alonzo Mourning 1.50 4.00
35 Shaquille O'Neal 5.00 12.00
36 Walt Williams .15 .40
NNO LaPhonso Ellis CL .50 1.25
Christian Laettner

1993-94 Upper Deck Locker Talk

Inserted one per Series II locker pack, this 15-card standard-size set features color player action photos on their fronts. The player's name appears in white lettering within the gold stripe that edges the left side. A personal player quote appears in white lettering within the photo's "torn" lower right corner. The back carries the same quote at the upper right, within a shot of a locker that has a print of the front's action shot taped to the door. Another player photo and more personal player quotes round out the back.

COMPLETE SET (15) 15.00 40.00
LT1 Michael Jordan 8.00 20.00
LT2 Stacey Augmon .20 .50
LT3 Shaquille O'Neal 6.00 15.00
LT4 Alonzo Mourning 2.00 5.00
LT5 Harold Miner .20 .50
LT6 Clarence Weatherspoon .20 .50
LT7 Derrick Coleman .60 1.50
LT8 Charles Barkley 2.00 5.00
LT9 David Robinson 2.00 5.00
LT10 Chuck Person .20 .50
LT11 Karl Malone 2.00 5.00
LT12 Muggsy Bogues .60 1.50
LT13 Latrell Sprewell 3.00 8.00
LT14 John Starks .60 1.50
LT15 Jim Jackson .60 1.50

1993-94 Upper Deck Mr. June

Randomly inserted in series two 12-card hobby packs at a rate of one in 30, this 10-card standard-size set focuses on Michael Jordan's performance while leading his team to three consecutive NBA Championships. The front features a color action shot of Michael Jordan with his name, accomplishment, and year thereof printed in the team-colored (Chicago Bulls) stripe at bottom. The back features a color action photo at the upper right with a description of his accomplishments printed alongside and below.

COMPLETE SET (10)	40.00	100.00
COMMON JORDAN (1-10)	6.00	15.00

1993-94 Upper Deck Rookie Exchange

This 10-card standard-size set features the top ten players from the 1993 NBA Draft. The set could only be obtained by mail in exchange for the Silver Trade card that was randomly inserted in first series 12-card packs at a rate of one in 72. The Silver Exchange expiration date was 12/31/93. The borderless front features a color player action photo with the his name printed in white lettering within a red stripe near the bottom. The word "Exchange" runs vertically along the left side in silver-foil lettering. The white and gray back carries a color player photo at the upper left and career highlights and statistics alongside and below. The set is sequenced in draft order.

COMPLETE SILVER SET (10)	4.00	8.00
*GOLD CARDS: 1X TO 2X BASIC		
RE1 Chris Webber	1.25	3.00
RE2 Shawn Bradley	.10	.30
RE3 Anfernee Hardaway	1.00	2.50
RE4 Jamal Mashburn	.30	.75
RE5 Isaiah Rider	.25	.60
RE6 Calbert Cheaney	.05	.15
RE7 Bobby Hurley	.05	.15
RE8 Vin Baker	.30	.75
RE9 Rodney Rogers	.10	.30
RE10 Lindsey Hunter	.10	.30
TC2 Expired Silver Trade	.08	.25
TC2 Redeemed Silver Trade	.02	.10

1993-94 Upper Deck Rookie Standouts

Randomly inserted at a rate of one in 30 second series 12-card retail packs and inserted one per second series 22-card purple jumbo pack, this 20-card standard-size set showcases top rookies of the 1993-94 NBA season. The borderless front features a color player action photo with his name printed in a gold-foil banner beneath the silver-foil set logo in a lower corner. The gray back carries a color player photo on one side and career highlights on the other.

COMPLETE SET (20)	12.00	30.00
RS1 Chris Webber	5.00	12.00
RS2 Bobby Hurley	.25	.60
RS3 Isaiah Rider	1.00	2.50
RS4 Terry Dehere	.07	.20
RS5 Toni Kukoc	2.00	5.00
RS6 Shawn Bradley	.50	1.25
RS7 Allan Houston	2.00	5.00
RS8 Chris Mills	.50	1.25
RS9 Jamal Mashburn	1.25	3.00
RS10 Acie Earl	.07	.20
RS11 George Lynch	.07	.20
RS12 Scott Burrell	.50	1.25
RS13 Calbert Cheaney	.25	.60
RS14 Lindsey Hunter	.50	1.25
RS15 Nick Van Exel	1.50	4.00
RS16 Rex Walters	.07	.20
RS17 Anfernee Hardaway	4.00	10.00
RS18 Sam Cassell	2.00	5.00
RS19 Vin Baker	1.25	3.00
RS20 Rodney Rogers	.50	1.25

1993-94 Upper Deck Team MVPs

Cards from this 27-card standard-size set were issued one per second series red and purple 22-card jumbo packs. The set highlights one key "Team MVP" from each of the 27 NBA teams. The white and prismatic team-colored foil-bordered front features a color player action shot, with the player's name printed vertically in the foil border at the upper right. The horizontal back is bordered in white and a team color and carries a color action shot on the left with career highlights appearing in a gray panel alongside on the right. The set is sequenced in team alphabetical order.

COMPLETE SET (27)	6.00	12.00
TM1 Dominique Wilkins	.30	.75
TM2 Robert Parish	.15	.40
TM3 Larry Johnson	.30	.75
TM4 Scottie Pippen	1.00	2.50
TM5 Mark Price	.05	.15
TM6 Jim Jackson	.15	.40
TM7 Mahmoud Abdul-Rauf	.05	.15
TM8 Joe Dumars	.30	.75
TM9 Chris Mullin	.30	.75
TM10 Hakeem Olajuwon	.50	1.25
TM11 Reggie Miller	.30	.75
TM12 Danny Manning	.15	.40
TM13 James Worthy	.30	.75
TM14 Glen Rice	.15	.40
TM15 Blue Edwards	.05	.15
TM16 Christian Laettner	.15	.40
TM17 Derrick Coleman	.15	.40
TM18 Patrick Ewing	.30	.75
TM19 Shaquille O'Neal	1.50	4.00
TM20 Clarence Weatherspoon	.05	.15
TM21 Charles Barkley	.50	1.25
TM22 Clyde Drexler	.30	.75
TM23 Mitch Richmond	.30	.75
TM24 David Robinson	.50	1.25
TM25 Shawn Kemp	.50	1.25
TM26 John Stockton	.30	.75
TM27 Tom Gugliotta	.30	.75

1993-94 Upper Deck Triple Double

This 10-card standard-size set features the NBA leaders in triple-doubles from the 1992-93 season. Cards were randomly inserted at a rate of 1 in 20 first series 12-card hobby and retail packs, 1 in 20 first series 22-card blue jumbo packs, one per first series 22-card green jumbo pack and approximately 1 in every 11 first series 22-card locker packs. The standard-size horizontal hologram cards feature one color player action cutout and two hologram action shots on their fronts. Each of the three images show the player performing three different skills (scoring, rebounding, passing or blocking) necessary to achieve a triple-double. The words "Triple Double" appear vertically on the left. The player's name appears at the upper right of the hologram. The horizontal back displays another color player action shot on the left, with a story of the player's triple-double feat on the right. The player's name appears in a team-colored bar at the bottom.

COMPLETE SET (10)	10.00	20.00
TD1 Charles Barkley	.75	2.00
TD2 Michael Jordan	8.00	20.00
TD3 Scottie Pippen	1.50	4.00
TD4 Detlef Schrempf	.25	.60
TD5 Mark Jackson	.25	.60
TD6 Kenny Anderson	.25	.60
TD7 Larry Johnson	.50	1.25
TD8 Dikembe Mutombo	.50	1.25
TD9 Rumeal Robinson	.07	.20
TD10 Micheal Williams	.07	.20

1994-95 Upper Deck

The 1994-95 Upper Deck basketball set consists of 360 standard-size cards, released in two separate 180-card series. Cards were primarily distributed in 12-card packs, each of which carried a suggested retail price of $1.99. Fronts feature full-color action photos with player's name and team running in color-coded bars along the side. Topical subsets featured are All-Rookie Team (1-10), All-NBA (11-25), USA Basketball (167-180), Draft Analysis (181-198), and Then and Now (352-360). Rookie Cards of note include Grant Hill, Juwan Howard, Eddie Jones, Jason Kidd and Glenn Robinson.

COMPLETE SET (360)	17.50	35.00
COMPLETE SERIES 1 (180)	10.00	20.00
COMPLETE SERIES 2 (180)	7.50	15.00
1 Chris Webber ART	.25	.60
2 Anfernee Hardaway ART	.25	.60
3 Vin Baker ART	.15	.40
4 Jamal Mashburn ART	.15	.40
5 Isaiah Rider ART	.15	.40
6 Dino Radja ART	.12	.30
7 Nick Van Exel ART	.15	.40
8 Shawn Bradley ART	.10	.25
9 Toni Kukoc ART	.20	.50
10 Lindsey Hunter ART	.10	.25
11 Scottie Pippen AN	.30	.75
12 Karl Malone AN	.20	.50
13 Hakeem Olajuwon AN	.20	.50
14 John Stockton AN	.20	.50
15 Latrell Sprewell AN	.20	.50
16 Shawn Kemp AN	.15	.40
17 Charles Barkley AN	.25	.60
18 David Robinson AN	.25	.60
19 Mitch Richmond AN	.15	.40
20 Kevin Johnson AN	.15	.40
21 Derrick Coleman AN	.12	.30
22 Dominique Wilkins AN	.20	.50
23 Shaquille O'Neal AN	.40	1.00
24 Mark Price AN	.15	.40
25 Gary Payton AN	.15	.40
26 Dan Majerle	.15	.40
27 Vernon Maxwell	.10	.25
28 Matt Geiger	.10	.25
29 Jeff Turner	.10	.25
30 Vinny Del Negro	.10	.25
31 B.J. Armstrong	.10	.25
32 Chris Gatling	.10	.25
33 Tony Smith	.10	.25
34 Doug West	.10	.25
35 Clyde Drexler	.20	.50
36 Keith Jennings	.10	.25
37 Steve Smith	.12	.30
38 Kendall Gill	.10	.25
39 Bob Martin	.10	.25
40 Calbert Cheaney	.10	.25
41 Terrell Brandon	.10	.25
42 Pete Chilcutt	.10	.25
43 Avery Johnson	.12	.30
44 Tom Gugliotta	.10	.25
45 LaBradford Smith	.10	.25
46 Sedale Threatt	.10	.25
47 Chris Smith	.10	.25
48 Kevin Edwards	.10	.25
49 Lucious Harris	.10	.25
50 Tim Perry	.10	.25
51 Lloyd Daniels	.10	.25
52 Dee Brown	.10	.25
53 Sean Elliott	.15	.40
54 Tim Hardaway	.15	.40
55 Christian Laettner	.12	.30
56 Bo Outlaw RC	.20	.50
57 Kevin Johnson	.15	.40
58 Duane Ferrell	.10	.25
59 Jo Jo English	.10	.25
60 Stanley Roberts	.10	.25
61 Kevin Willis	.10	.25
62 Dana Barros	.10	.25
63 Gheorghe Muresan	.10	.25
64 Vern Fleming	.10	.25
65 Anthony Peeler	.10	.25
66 Negele Knight	.10	.25
67 Harold Ellis	.10	.25
68 Vincent Askew	.10	.25
69 Ennis Whatley	.10	.25
70 Elden Campbell	.10	.25
71 Sherman Douglas	.10	.25
72 Luc Longley	.10	.25
73 Lorenzo Williams	.10	.25
74 Jay Humphries	.10	.25
75 Chris King	.10	.25
76 Tyrone Corbin	.10	.25
77 Bobby Hurley	.15	.40
78 Dell Curry	.10	.25
79 Dino Radja	.12	.30
80 A.C. Green	.15	.40
81 Craig Ehlo	.10	.25
82 Gary Payton	.15	.40
83 Sleepy Floyd	.10	.25
84 Rodney Rogers	.10	.25
85 Brian Shaw	.10	.25
86 Kevin Gamble	.10	.25
87 John Stockton	.20	.50
88 Hersey Hawkins	.10	.25
89 Johnny Newman	.10	.25
90 Larry Johnson	.15	.40
91 Robert Pack	.10	.25
92 Willie Burton	.10	.25
93 Bobby Phills	.10	.25
94 David Benoit	.10	.25
95 Harold Miner	.10	.25
96 David Robinson	.25	.60
97 Nate McMillan	.10	.25
98 Chris Mills	.10	.25
99 Hubert Davis	.10	.25
100 Shaquille O'Neal	.40	1.00
101 Loy Vaught	.10	.25
102 Kenny Smith	.12	.30
103 Terry Dehere	.10	.25
104 Carl Herrera	.10	.25
105 LaPhonso Ellis	.10	.25
106 Armon Gilliam	.10	.25
107 Greg Graham	.10	.25
108 Eric Murdock	.10	.25
109 Ron Harper	.12	.30
110 Andrew Lang	.10	.25
111 Johnny Dawkins	.10	.25
112 David Wingate	.10	.25
113 Tom Hammonds	.10	.25
114 Brad Daugherty	.12	.30
115 Charles Smith	.10	.25
116 Dale Ellis	.10	.25
117 Bryant Stith	.10	.25
118 Lindsey Hunter	.10	.25
119 Patrick Ewing	.20	.50
120 Kenny Anderson	.12	.30
121 Charles Barkley	.25	.60
122 Harvey Grant	.10	.25
123 Anthony Bowie	.10	.25
124 Shawn Kemp	.15	.40
125 Lee Mayberry	.10	.25
126 Reggie Miller	.20	.50
127 Scottie Pippen	.30	.75
128 Spud Webb	.15	.40
129 Antonio Davis	.10	.25
130 Greg Anderson	.10	.25
131 Jim Jackson	.10	.25
132 Dikembe Mutombo	.15	.40
133 Terry Porter	.10	.25
134 Mario Elie	.10	.25
135 Vlade Divac	.15	.40
136 Robert Horry	.15	.40
137 Popeye Jones	.10	.25
138 Brad Lohaus	.10	.25
139 Anthony Bonner	.10	.25
140 Doug Christie	.10	.25
141 Rony Seikaly	.12	.30
142 Allan Houston	.15	.40
143 Tyrone Hill	.10	.25
144 Latrell Sprewell	.20	.50
145 Andres Guibert	.10	.25
146 Dominique Wilkins	.20	.50
147 Jon Barry	.10	.25
148 Tracy Murray	.10	.25
149 Mike Peplowski	.10	.25
150 Mike Brown	.10	.25
151 Cedric Ceballos	.10	.25
152 Stacey King	.10	.25
153 Trevor Wilson	.10	.25
154 Anthony Avent	.10	.25
155 Horace Grant	.12	.30
156 Bill Curley RC	.20	.50
157 Grant Hill RC	1.00	2.50
158 Charlie Ward RC	.20	.50
159 Jalen Rose RC	.50	1.25
160 Jason Kidd RC	1.00	2.50
161 Yinka Dare RC	.20	.50
162 Eric Montross RC	.20	.50
163 Donyell Marshall RC	.20	.50
164 Tony Dumas RC	.20	.50
165 Wesley Person RC	.20	.50
166 Eddie Jones RC	.60	1.50
167 Tim Hardaway USA	.15	.40
168 Isiah Thomas USA	.15	.40
169 Joe Dumars USA	.15	.40
170 Mark Price USA	.15	.40
171 Derrick Coleman USA	.12	.30
172 Shawn Kemp USA	.15	.40
173 Steve Smith USA	.12	.30
174 Dan Majerle USA	.15	.40
175 Reggie Miller USA	.20	.50
176 Kevin Johnson USA	.15	.40
177 Dominique Wilkins USA	.20	.50
178 Shaquille O'Neal USA	.40	1.00
179 Alonzo Mourning USA	.20	.50
180 Larry Johnson USA	.15	.40
181 Brian Grant DA	.15	.40
182 Darrin Hancock DA	.10	.25
183 Grant Hill DA	.50	1.25
184 Jalen Rose DA	.25	.60
185 Lamond Murray DA	.10	.25
186 Jason Kidd DA	.50	1.25
187 Donyell Marshall DA	.10	.25
188 Eddie Jones DA	.30	.75
189 Eric Montross DA	.10	.25
190 Khalid Reeves DA	.10	.25
191 Sharone Wright DA	.10	.25
192 Wesley Person DA	.10	.25
193 Glenn Robinson DA	.20	.50
194 Carlos Rogers DA	.10	.25
195 Aaron McKie DA	.10	.25
196 Juwan Howard DA	.25	.60
197 Charlie Ward DA	.10	.25
198 Brooks Thompson DA	.10	.25
199 Tony Massenburg	.10	.25
200 James Robinson	.10	.25
201 Dickey Simpkins RC	.20	.50
202 Johnny Dawkins	.10	.25
203 Joe Kleine	.10	.25
204 Bill Wennington	.10	.25
205 Sean Higgins	.10	.25
206 Larry Krystkowiak	.10	.25
207 Winston Garland	.10	.25
208 Muggsy Bogues	.12	.30
209 Charles Oakley	.12	.30
210 Vin Baker	.15	.40
211 Malik Sealy	.10	.25
212 Willie Anderson	.10	.25
213 Dale Davis	.10	.25
214 Grant Long	.10	.25
215 Danny Ainge	.15	.40
216 Toni Kukoc	.20	.50
217 Doug Smith	.10	.25
218 Danny Manning	.12	.30
219 Otis Thorpe	.10	.25
220 Mark Price	.15	.40
221 Victor Alexander	.10	.25
222 Brent Price	.10	.25
223 Howard Eisley RC	.20	.50
224 Chris Mullin	.15	.40
225 Nick Van Exel	.15	.40
226 Xavier McDaniel	.10	.25
227 Khalid Reeves RC	.20	.50
228 Anfernee Hardaway	.25	.60
229 B.J. Tyler RC	.20	.50
230 Elmore Spencer	.10	.25
231 Rick Fox	.10	.25
232 Alonzo Mourning	.20	.50
233 Hakeem Olajuwon	.20	.50
234 Blue Edwards	.10	.25
235 P.J. Brown	.10	.25
236 Ron Harper	.12	.30
237 Isaiah Rider	.15	.40
238 Eric Mobley RC	.20	.50
239 Brian Williams	.10	.25
240 Eric Piatkowski RC	.25	.60
241 Karl Malone	.20	.50
242 Wayman Tisdale	.10	.25
243 Sarunas Marciulionis	.10	.25
244 Sean Rooks	.10	.25
245 Ricky Pierce	.10	.25
246 Don MacLean	.10	.25
247 Aaron McKie RC	.20	.50
248 Kenny Gattison	.10	.25
249 Derek Harper	.12	.30
250 Michael Smith RC	.20	.50
251 John Williams	.10	.25
252 Pooh Richardson	.10	.25
253 Sergei Bazarevich RC	.20	.50
254 Brian Grant RC	.30	.75
255 Ed Pinckney	.10	.25
256 Ken Norman	.10	.25
257 Marty Conlon	.10	.25
258 Matt Fish	.10	.25
259 Darrin Hancock RC	.20	.50
260 Mahmoud Abdul-Rauf	.10	.25
261 Roy Tarpley	.10	.25
262 Chris Morris	.10	.25
263 Sharone Wright RC	.20	.50
264 Jamal Mashburn	.15	.40
265 John Starks	.12	.30
266 Rod Strickland	.10	.25
267 Adam Keefe	.10	.25
268 Scott Burrell	.10	.25
269 Eric Riley	.10	.25
270 Sam Perkins	.10	.25
271 Stacey Augmon	.12	.30
272 Kevin Willis	.10	.25
273 Lamond Murray RC	.20	.50
274 Derrick Coleman	.12	.30
275 Scott Skiles	.10	.25
276 Buck Williams	.10	.25
277 Sam Cassell	.15	.40
278 Rik Smits	.12	.30
279 Dennis Rodman	.30	.75
280 Olden Polynice	.10	.25
281 Glenn Robinson RC	.40	1.00
282 Clarence Weatherspoon	.10	.25
283 Monty Williams RC	.20	.50
284 Terry Mills	.10	.25
285 Oliver Miller	.10	.25
286 Dennis Scott	.10	.25
287 Micheal Williams	.10	.25
288 Moses Malone	.15	.40
289 Donald Royal	.10	.25
290 Mark Jackson	.15	.40
291 Walt Williams	.10	.25
292 Bimbo Coles	.10	.25
293 Derrick Alston RC	.20	.50
294 Scott Williams	.10	.25
295 Acie Earl	.10	.25
296 Jeff Hornacek	.12	.30
297 Kevin Duckworth	.10	.25
298 Dontonio Wingfield RC	.20	.50
299 Danny Ferry	.10	.25
300 Mark West	.10	.25
301 Jayson Williams	.10	.25
302 David Wesley	.10	.25
303 Jim McIlvaine RC	.20	.50
304 Michael Adams	.10	.25
305 Greg Minor RC	.20	.50
306 Jeff Malone	.10	.25
307 Pervis Ellison	.10	.25
308 Clifford Rozier RC	.20	.50
309 Billy Owens	.10	.25
310 Duane Causwell	.10	.25
311 Rex Chapman	.10	.25
312 Detlef Schrempf	.15	.40
313 Mitch Richmond	.15	.40
314 Carlos Rogers RC	.20	.50
315 Byron Scott	.12	.30
316 Dwayne Morton	.10	.25
317 Bill Cartwright	.12	.30
318 J.R. Reid	.10	.25
319 Derrick McKey	.10	.25
320 Jamie Watson RC	.20	.50
321 Mookie Blaylock	.10	.25
322 Chris Webber	.25	.60
323 Joe Dumars	.15	.40
324 Shawn Bradley	.10	.25
325 Chuck Person	.12	.30
326 Haywoode Workman	.10	.25
327 Benoit Benjamin	.10	.25
328 Will Perdue	.10	.25
329 Sam Mitchell	.10	.25
330 George Lynch	.10	.25
331 Juwan Howard RC	.30	.75
332 Robert Parish	.15	.40
333 Glen Rice	.15	.40
334 Michael Cage	.10	.25
335 Brooks Thompson RC	.20	.50
336 Rony Seikaly	.12	.30
337 Steve Kerr	.12	.30
338 Anthony Miller RC	.20	.50
339 Nick Anderson	.10	.25
340 Clifford Robinson	.10	.25
341 Todd Day	.10	.25
342 Jon Koncak	.10	.25
343 Felton Spencer	.10	.25
344 Willie Burton	.10	.25
345 Ledell Eackles	.10	.25
346 Anthony Mason	.10	.25
347 Derek Strong	.10	.25
348 Reggie Williams	.10	.25
349 Johnny Newman	.10	.25
350 Terry Cummings	.15	.40
351 Anthony Tucker RC	.20	.50
352 Junior Bridgeman TN	.15	.40
353 Jerry West TN	.20	.50
354 Harvey Catchings TN	.15	.40
355 John Lucas TN	.15	.40
356 Bill Bradley TN	.20	.50
357 Bill Walton TN	.15	.40
358 Don Nelson TN	.15	.40
359 Michael Jordan TN	1.25	3.00
360 Tom (Satch) Sanders TN	.15	.40

1994-95 Upper Deck Draft Trade

This set was available exclusively by redeeming the Upper Deck Draft Trade card before the June 30th, 1995 deadline. Draft Trade cards were randomly seeded into one in every 240 first series Upper Deck packs. The first ten players selected in the 1994 NBA Draft are featured within this set. The fronts feature the words NBA Draft Lottery Picks 1994 on the top of the card with the player vertically identified on the front left. The NBA draft logo is in the lower left corner. All of this surrounds a playerr cutout photo against a shaded background. The backs contain player information as well as a player photo. The cards are numbered with a "D" prefix in the upper left corner.

COMPLETE SET (10)	4.00	10.00
D1 Glenn Robinson	.60	1.50
D2 Jason Kidd	1.50	4.00
D3 Grant Hill	1.50	4.00
D4 Donyell Marshall	.30	.75
D5 Juwan Howard	.50	1.25
D6 Sharone Wright	.30	.75
D7 Lamond Murray	.30	.75
D8 Brian Grant	.50	1.25
D9 Eric Montross	.30	.75
D10 Eddie Jones	1.00	2.50
NNO Expired Exchange Card	.07	.20

1994-95 Upper Deck Jordan He's Back Reprints

The nine standard-size cards were reissued to celebrate the return of Michael Jordan. These cards parallel earlier Upper Deck Michael Jordan cards, the difference being that each is stamped with a foil "He's Back" logo on front. The cards were distributed one per second series rack pack. Jumbo versions of these cards were also released. They are priced in the header.

COMPLETE SET (9)	6.00	12.00
COMMON CARD (1-9)	.60	1.50
COMPLETE JUMBO SET (3)	5.00	12.00
COMMON JUMBO (1-3)	2.00	5.00

1994-95 Upper Deck Jordan Heroes

Randomly inserted in 12-card first series hobby and retail packs at a rate of one in 30, these 10 (nine numbered cards and one unnumbered header card) standard-size cards spotlight Michael Jordan's outstanding career. The fronts feature color action shots of Jordan from different stages in his career. His name appears in gold-foil lettering in the bottom margin and also as a facsimile autograph in gold foil in the upper margin. The card's subtitle appears in vertical gold-foil lettering in the left margin. The right side is full-bleed. The back carries a color action shot of Jordan on a ghosted background. A small color action shot appears at the lower left. Career highlights appear in a colored panel set off to one side. The cards are numbered on the back 37-45, a continuation of previous Heroes sets which included Jerry West, Wilt Chamberlain, Larry Bird, and Future Heroes. A 3" by 5" jumbo version of the entire set was also issued one card per blister pack sold at retail outlets. These cards are valued at approximately 50% of the values of the standard-size cards.

COMPLETE SET (10)	20.00	50.00
COMMON JORDAN	3.00	8.00

1994-95 Upper Deck Predictor Award Winners

Randomly inserted exclusively into one in every 25 first and second series hobby packs, cards from this 40-card standard-size set are subdivided into All-Star MVP (H1-H10), Defensive Player of the Year (H11-H20), MVP (H21-H30) and ROY (H31-H40) subsets. If the featured player placed first or second in his respective category, the card was redeemable before the June 30th, 1995 deadline for a special Predictors exchange set (of which mailing was delayed until late October, 1995). Winner cards have been designated below with a "W1" (good for a 20-card exchange set) or "W2" (good for a 10-card exchange set) listing. The fronts feature the player photo for most of the card. The award that the card is good for is vertically on the left side of the card. The player's name, team and position is in the lower right corner and is printed in white. The backs of the card contain contest information. The cards are numbered with an "H" prefix.

COMPLETE SET (40)	25.00	60.00
COMPLETE SERIES 1 (20)	12.00	30.00
COMPLETE SERIES 2 (20)	12.00	30.00
*RED.CARDS: .2X TO .5X HI COLUMN		
TWO RED.SETS PER W1 CARD BY MAIL		
ONE RED.SET PER W2 CARD BY MAIL		
H1 Charles Barkley	1.25	3.00
H2 Hakeem Olajuwon	1.00	2.50
H3 Shaquille O'Neal	2.00	5.00
H4 Scottie Pippen	1.50	4.00
H5 David Robinson	1.25	3.00
H6 Shawn Kemp W2	.75	2.00
H7 Alonzo Mourning	1.00	2.50
H8 Larry Johnson	.75	2.00
H9 Patrick Ewing	1.00	2.50
H10 AS-MVP Wild Card W1	.50	1.25
H11 Hakeem Olajuwon	1.00	2.50
H12 Dikembe Mutombo W1	.75	2.00
H13 Nate McMillan	.50	1.25
H14 Dennis Rodman	1.50	4.00
H15 Alonzo Mourning	1.00	2.50
H16 Patrick Ewing	1.00	2.50
H17 Charles Barkley	1.25	3.00
H18 David Robinson	1.25	3.00
H19 John Stockton	1.00	2.50
H20 DEF-POY Wild Card W2	.50	1.25
H21 Shaquille O'Neal W2	2.00	5.00
H22 Hakeem Olajuwon	1.00	2.50
H23 David Robinson W1	1.25	3.00
H24 Scottie Pippen	1.50	4.00
H25 Alonzo Mourning	1.00	2.50
H26 Shawn Kemp	.75	2.00
H27 Charles Barkley	1.25	3.00
H28 Patrick Ewing	1.00	2.50
H29 Larry Johnson	.75	2.00
H30 MVP Wild Card	.50	1.25
H31 Jason Kidd W1	2.50	6.00
H32 Grant Hill W1	2.50	6.00
H33 Glenn Robinson	1.00	2.50
H34 Eddie Jones	1.50	4.00
H35 Donyell Marshall	.50	1.25
H36 Eric Montross	.50	1.25
H37 Sharone Wright	.50	1.25
H38 Juwan Howard	.75	2.00
H39 Carlos Rogers	.50	1.25
H40 ROY Wild Card W1	.50	1.25

1994-95 Upper Deck Predictor League Leaders

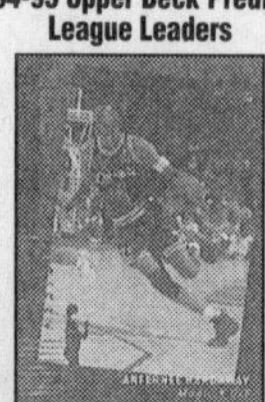

Randomly inserted exclusively into one in every 25 first and second series retail packs, cards from this 40-card standard-size set are subdivided into Scoring (R1-R10), Assists (R11-R20), Rebounds (R21-R30) and Blocks (R31-R40) subsets. If the featured player placed first or second in his respective category, the card was redeemable before the June 30th, 1995 deadline for a special Predictors exchange set (of which mailing was delayed until late October, 1995).. Winner cards have been designated below with a "W1" (good for a 20-card exchange set) or "W2" (good for a 10-card exchange set) listing.

COMPLETE SET (40)	20.00	50.00
COMPLETE SERIES 1 (20)	10.00	25.00
COMPLETE SERIES 2 (20)	10.00	25.00
*RED.CARDS: .2X TO .5X HI COLUMN		
TWO RED.SETS PER W1 CARD BY MAIL		
ONE EXCH.SET PER W2 CARD BY MAIL		
R1 David Robinson	1.25	3.00
R2 Shaquille O'Neal W1	2.00	5.00
R3 Hakeem Olajuwon W2	1.00	2.50
R4 Scottie Pippen	1.50	4.00
R5 Chris Webber	1.25	3.00
R6 Karl Malone	1.00	2.50
R7 Patrick Ewing	1.00	2.50
R8 Mitch Richmond	.75	2.00
R9 Charles Barkley	1.25	3.00
R10 Scorers Wild Card	.50	1.25
R11 John Stockton W1	1.00	2.50
R12 Mookie Blaylock	.50	1.25
R13 Kenny Anderson W2	.60	1.50
R14 Kevin Johnson	.75	2.00
R15 Muggsy Bogues	.60	1.50
R16 Tim Hardaway	.75	2.00
R17 Anfernee Hardaway	1.25	3.00
R18 Rod Strickland	.50	1.25
R19 Sherman Douglas	.50	1.25
R20 Assists Wild Card	.50	1.25
R21 Shaquille O'Neal	2.00	5.00
R22 Hakeem Olajuwon	1.00	2.50
R23 Dennis Rodman W1	1.50	4.00
R24 Dikembe Mutombo W2	.75	2.00
R25 Karl Malone	1.00	2.50
R26 Kevin Willis	.50	1.25
R27 Chris Webber	1.25	3.00
R28 Alonzo Mourning	1.00	2.50
R29 Derrick Coleman	.60	1.50
R30 Rebounds Wild Card	.50	1.25
R31 Dikembe Mutombo W1	.75	2.00
R32 Hakeem Olajuwon W2	1.00	2.50
R33 David Robinson	1.25	3.00
R34 Shawn Bradley	.50	1.25
R35 Shaquille O'Neal	2.00	5.00
R36 Patrick Ewing	1.00	2.50
R37 Alonzo Mourning	1.00	2.50
R38 Shawn Kemp	.75	2.00
R39 Derrick Coleman	.60	1.50
R40 Blocks Wild Card	.50	1.25

1994-95 Upper Deck Rookie Standouts

Randomly inserted into one in every 30 second series packs, cards from this 20-card standard size set feature a selection of the top rookies from the 1994-95 season. The borderless fronts feature a color photo in the middle. The words "Rookie Standouts" are in gold foil in the bottom left corner. The hard to read player's names are in the upper left corner. The backs have player information and are numbered with a RS prefix in the upper left corner. The set is sequenced in 1994 NBA draft order.

COMPLETE SET (20)	20.00	50.00
RS1 Glenn Robinson	2.00	5.00
RS2 Jason Kidd	5.00	12.00
RS3 Grant Hill	5.00	12.00
RS4 Donyell Marshall	1.00	2.50
RS5 Juwan Howard	1.50	4.00
RS6 Sharone Wright	1.00	2.50
RS7 Lamond Murray	1.00	2.50
RS8 Brian Grant	1.50	4.00
RS9 Eric Montross	1.00	2.50
RS10 Eddie Jones	3.00	8.00
RS11 Carlos Rogers	1.00	2.50
RS12 Khalid Reeves	1.00	2.50
RS13 Jalen Rose	2.50	6.00
RS14 Michael Smith	1.00	2.50
RS15 Eric Piatkowski	1.25	3.00
RS16 Clifford Rozier	1.00	2.50
RS17 Aaron McKie	1.00	2.50
RS18 Eric Mobley	1.00	2.50
RS19 Bill Curley	1.00	2.50
RS20 Wesley Person	1.00	2.50

1994-95 Upper Deck Slam Dunk Stars

Randomly inserted into one in every 30 second series packs, cards from this 20-card standard-size set feature Upper Deck spokesperson Shawn Kemp's selections of the top dunkers. The fronts feature the words "Kemp Slam Dunk Stars" as well as a sculpture of Kemp in gold foil on the left. The rest of the card is dedicated to a photo of the player dunking. The back has Kemp's opinion of each player. There is also a small inset photo of Kemp as well as a cutout of the featured player. The set is sequenced in alphabetical order.

COMPLETE SET (20)	20.00	50.00
S1 Vin Baker	1.50	4.00
S2 Charles Barkley	2.50	6.00
S3 Derrick Coleman	1.25	3.00
S4 Clyde Drexler	2.00	5.00
S5 LaPhonso Ellis	1.00	2.50
S6 Larry Johnson	1.50	4.00
S7 Shawn Kemp	1.50	4.00
S8 Donyell Marshall	1.50	4.00
S9 Jamal Mashburn	1.50	4.00
S10 Gheorghe Muresan	1.00	2.50
S11 Alonzo Mourning	2.00	5.00
S12 Shaquille O'Neal	4.00	10.00
S13 Hakeem Olajuwon	2.00	5.00
S14 Scottie Pippen	3.00	8.00
S15 Isaiah Rider	1.50	4.00
S16 David Robinson	2.50	6.00

17 Clarence Weatherspoon 1.00 2.50
18 Chris Webber 2.50 6.00
19 Dominique Wilkins 2.00 5.00
20 Rik Smits 1.25 3.00

1994-95 Upper Deck Special Edition

Inserted one per pack into both first and second series 12-card packs and four per second series rack pack, cards from this 180-card standard-size set (issued in two separate 90-card series) are comprised of a wide selection of the top stars and prospects in the NBA. Fronts feature full-color player action shots against silver-foil backgrounds. Cards are numbered with an SE prefix on back.

COMPLETE SET (180) 20.00 40.00
COMPLETE SERIES 1 (90) 7.50 15.00
COMPLETE SERIES 2 (90) 15.00 30.00
1 Stacey Augmon .25 .60
2 Kevin Willis .20 .50
3 Mookie Blaylock .20 .50
4 Rick Fox .20 .50
5 Xavier McDaniel .20 .50
6 Dee Brown .20 .50
7 Muggsy Bogues .25 .60
8 Kenny Gattison .20 .50
9 Alonzo Mourning .40 1.00
10 B.J. Armstrong .20 .50
11 Bill Cartwright .25 .60
12 Toni Kukoc .40 1.00
13 Mark Price .30 .75
14 Gerald Wilkins .20 .50
15 John Williams .20 .50
16 Jamal Mashburn .30 .75
17 Sean Rooks .20 .50
18 Doug Smith .20 .50
19 Jim Jackson .20 .50
20 Mahmoud Abdul-Rauf .20 .50
21 Rodney Rogers .20 .50
22 Reggie Williams .20 .50
23 LaPhonso Ellis .20 .50
24 Allan Houston .30 .75
25 Terry Mills .20 .50
26 Joe Dumars .30 .75
27 Chris Mullin .30 .75
28 Billy Owens .20 .50
29 Latrell Sprewell .40 1.00
30 Chris Webber .50 1.25
31 Sam Cassell .30 .75
32 Vernon Maxwell .20 .50
33 Hakeem Olajuwon .40 1.00
34 Otis Thorpe .20 .50
35 Rik Smits .25 .60
36 Derrick McKey .20 .50
37 Haywoode Workman .20 .50
38 Bo Outlaw .30 .75
39 Elmore Spencer .20 .50
40 Loy Vaught .20 .50
41 George Lynch .20 .50
42 Nick Van Exel .30 .75
43 James Worthy .40 1.00
44 Elden Campbell .20 .50
45 Grant Long .20 .50
46 Harold Miner .20 .50
47 Glen Rice .30 .75
48 Steve Smith .25 .60
49 Todd Day .20 .50
50 Eric Murdock .20 .50
51 Vin Baker .30 .75
52 Christian Laettner .25 .60
53 Isaiah Rider .30 .75
54 Micheal Williams .20 .50
55 Benoit Benjamin .20 .50
56 Derrick Coleman .25 .60
57 Chris Morris .20 .50
58 Charles Smith .20 .50
59 Greg Anthony .20 .50
60 Doc Rivers .25 .60
61 Derek Harper .25 .60
62 John Starks .25 .60
63 Anfernee Hardaway .50 1.25
64 Dennis Scott .20 .50
65 Nick Anderson .20 .50
66 Shawn Bradley .20 .50
67 Clarence Weatherspoon .20 .50
68 Jeff Malone .20 .50
69 Cedric Ceballos .20 .50
70 Kevin Johnson .30 .75
71 Oliver Miller .20 .50
72 Clifford Robinson .20 .50
73 Rod Strickland .20 .50
74 Buck Williams .20 .50
75 Mitch Richmond .30 .75
76 Walt Williams .20 .50
77 Lionel Simmons .20 .50
78 Willie Anderson .20 .50
79 Terry Cummings .30 .75
80 J.R. Reid .20 .50
81 Dennis Rodman .60 1.50
82 Kendall Gill .20 .50
83 Sam Perkins .20 .50
84 Detlef Schrempf .30 .75
85 Jeff Hornacek .25 .60
86 Karl Malone .40 1.00
87 Felton Spencer .20 .50
88 Calbert Cheaney .20 .50
89 Don MacLean .20 .50
90 Brent Price .20 .50
91 Tyrone Corbin .20 .50
92 Rex Chapman .20 .50
93 Ken Norman .20 .50
94 Steve Smith .25 .60
95 Eric Montross .30 .75
96 Dino Radja .25 .60
97 Dominique Wilkins .40 1.00
98 Scott Burrell .20 .50
99 Hersey Hawkins .20 .50
100 Larry Johnson .30 .75
101 Ron Harper .25 .60
102 Scottie Pippen .60 1.50
103 Dickey Simpkins .30 .75
104 Tyrone Hill .20 .50
105 Chris Mills .20 .50
106 Bobby Phills .20 .50
107 Lorenzo Williams .20 .50
108 Popeye Jones .20 .50
109 Jason Kidd 1.50 4.00
110 Dikembe Mutombo .30 .75
111 Robert Pack .20 .50
112 Jalen Rose .75 2.00
113 Bill Curley .30 .75
114 Grant Hill 1.50 4.00
115 Lindsey Hunter .20 .50
116 Roy Tarpley .20 .50
117 Tim Hardaway .30 .75
118 Ricky Pierce .20 .50
119 Carlos Rogers .30 .75
120 Clifford Rozier .30 .75
121 Rony Seikaly .25 .60
122 Mario Elie .20 .50
123 Robert Horry .30 .75
124 Kenny Smith .25 .60
125 Antonio Davis .20 .50
126 Dale Davis .20 .50
127 Reggie Miller .40 1.00
128 Lamond Murray .30 .75
129 Eric Piatkowski .40 1.00
130 Pooh Richardson .20 .50
131 Cedric Ceballos .20 .50
132 Vlade Divac .30 .75
133 Eddie Jones 1.00 2.50
134 Mark Jackson .30 .75
135 Matt Geiger .20 .50
136 Khalid Reeves .30 .75
137 Kevin Willis .20 .50
138 Lee Mayberry .20 .50
139 Eric Mobley .30 .75
140 Glenn Robinson .60 1.50
141 Doug West .20 .50
142 Donyell Marshall .30 .75
143 Chris Smith .20 .50
144 Kenny Anderson .25 .60
145 Chris Morris .20 .50
146 Armon Gilliam .20 .50
147 Dana Barros .20 .50
148 Patrick Ewing .40 1.00
149 Charles Oakley .25 .60
150 Charlie Ward .30 .75
151 Horace Grant .25 .60
152 Shaquille O'Neal .75 2.00
153 Brian Shaw .20 .50
154 Brooks Thompson .30 .75
155 B.J. Tyler .30 .75
156 Scott Williams .20 .50
157 Sharone Wright .30 .75
158 Charles Barkley .50 1.25
159 Dan Majerle .30 .75
160 Danny Manning .25 .60
161 Wesley Person .30 .75
162 Clyde Drexler .40 1.00
163 Harvey Grant .20 .50
164 Terry Porter .20 .50
165 Brian Grant .50 1.25
166 Bobby Hurley .30 .75
167 Olden Polynice .20 .50
168 Sean Elliott .30 .75
169 Chuck Person .25 .60
170 David Robinson .50 1.25
171 Shawn Kemp .30 .75
172 Nate McMillan .20 .50
173 Gary Payton .30 .75
174 Michael Smith .30 .75
175 David Benoit .20 .50
176 Jay Humphries .20 .50
177 John Stockton .40 1.00
178 Juwan Howard .50 1.25
179 Chris Webber .50 1.25
180 Scott Skiles .20 .50

1994-95 Upper Deck Special Edition Gold

Randomly inserted at the rate of one per 35 first and second series packs, these 180 standard-size cards are similar in design to their regular Special Edition counterparts, except that their fronts are gold foil instead of silver foil, and their backs have a gold-hued background for the area that carries the team logo. Cards are numbered with an SE prefix on back. To ascertain values on individual cards, please refer to the multiplier in the header, coupled with the value of the base insert.

*STARS: 3X TO 8X HI COLUMN
*RCs: 2.5X TO 6X HI

1994-95 Upper Deck Special Edition Jumbos

One of these twenty-seven different over-sized Special Edition Jumbo cards was inserted into each Upper Deck second series hobby box. The cards parallel their corresponding basic Special Edition inserts except for their size and numbering.

COMPLETE SET (27) 15.00 40.00
1 Steve Smith .60 1.50
2 Dominique Wilkins 1.00 2.50
3 Larry Johnson .75 2.00
4 Scottie Pippen 1.50 4.00
5 Chris Mills .50 1.25
6 Jason Kidd 4.00 10.00
7 Jalen Rose 2.00 5.00
8 Lindsey Hunter .50 1.25
9 Tim Hardaway .75 2.00
10 Kenny Smith .60 1.50
11 Mark Jackson .75 2.00
12 Lamond Murray .75 2.00
13 Cedric Ceballos .50 1.25
14 Kevin Willis .50 1.25
15 Glenn Robinson 1.50 4.00
16 Doug West .50 1.25
17 Kenny Anderson .60 1.50
18 Patrick Ewing 1.00 2.50
19 Horace Grant .60 1.50
20 Sharone Wright .75 2.00
21 Charles Barkley 1.25 3.00
22 Clyde Drexler 1.00 2.50
23 Brian Grant 1.25 3.00
24 Sean Elliott .75 2.00
25 Shawn Kemp .75 2.00
26 John Stockton 1.00 2.50
27 Juwan Howard 1.25 3.00

1995 Upper Deck

Issued in two series over the first half of 1995, Upper Deck released both products through 10-card packs with 36-packs per box. Both series included several insert sets including the popular Predictor redemption cards and one Silver or Gold parallel card in every pack. Series one hobby packs featured a Jeff Gordon Salute card randomly inserted (1:108 packs) and the retail version a Sterling Marlin Salute (1:108 packs). A special Sterling Marlin Back-to-Back Salute card was randomly seeded in series two retail packs (1:108). As with most Upper Deck issues, subsets abound. Series one included Championship Pit Crew, Star Rookies, Images of '95 and Next in Line. Series two featured New for '95, Did You Know, Speedway Legends and more Star Rookies.

COMPLETE SET (300) 12.50 30.00
COMP.SERIES 1 SET (150) 8.00 20.00
COMP.SERIES 2 SET (150) 6.00 15.00
WAX BOX HOBBY SER.1 20.00 50.00
WAX BOX HOBBY SER.2 20.00 50.00
133 Michael Jordan CPC 2.50 6.00

1995 Upper Deck Gold Signature/Electric Gold

Gold parallel cards were produced for both series of 1995 Upper Deck -- Gold Signature for series one and Electric Gold for series two. The parallel versions look very similar to the regular issue Upper Deck cards with the addition of either a gold foil facsimile signature or the word "Electric" in gold foil on the card fronts. The Gold cards were randomly inserted at the wrapper stated rate of 1:35 packs for either series.

COMPLETE GOLD SET (300) 350.00 700.00
COMP.GOLD SIG.SET (150) 200.00 400.00
COMP. ELE.GOLD SET (150) 150.00 300.00
*GOLD STARS: 8X TO 20X BASE CARDS

1995-96 Upper Deck

The 1995-96 Upper Deck set was issued in two separate series of 180 cards each, for a total of 360 cards. Twelve-card packs carried a suggested retail price of $1.99. The fronts are borderless full-color player action shots with the player's name printed in gold foil at the bottom. The backs feature another player color action shot with a graph of the player's career stats. The player's name and biography are printed vertically on the left side of the back in white type. The set features the following topical subsets: The Rookie Years (136-154), All-Rookie team (155-165), All NBA Team (166-180), USA '96 (316-325), Images of '95 (326-335), Major Attractions (336-346) and Slams and Jams (347-360). Rookie Cards of note include Michael Finley, Kevin Garnett, Antonio McDyess, Jerry Stackhouse and Damon Stoudamire.

COMPLETE SET (360) 25.00 50.00
COMPLETE SERIES 1 (180) 10.00 20.00
COMPLETE SERIES 2 (180) 15.00 30.00
1 Eddie Jones .30 .75
2 Hubert Davis .15 .40
3 Latrell Sprewell .25 .60
4 Stacey Augmon .20 .50
5 Mario Elie .15 .40
6 Tyrone Hill .15 .40
7 Dikembe Mutombo .25 .60
8 Antonio Davis .15 .40
9 Horace Grant .20 .50
10 Ken Norman .15 .40
11 Aaron McKie .15 .40
12 Vinny Del Negro .15 .40
13 Glenn Robinson .25 .60
14 Allan Houston .20 .50
15 Bryon Russell .15 .40
16 Tony Dumas .15 .40
17 Gary Payton .25 .60
18 Rik Smits .20 .50
19 Dino Radja .20 .50
20 Robert Pack .15 .40
21 Calbert Cheaney .15 .40
22 Clarence Weatherspoon .15 .40
23 Michael Jordan 2.00 5.00
24 Felton Spencer .15 .40
25 J.R. Reid .15 .40
26 Cedric Ceballos .15 .40
27 Dan Majerle .25 .60
28 Donald Hodge .15 .40
29 Nate McMillan .15 .40
30 Bimbo Coles .15 .40
31 Mitch Richmond .25 .60
32 Scott Brooks .15 .40
33 Patrick Ewing .30 .75
34 Carl Herrera .15 .40
35 Rick Fox .15 .40
36 James Robinson .15 .40
37 Donald Royal .15 .40
38 Joe Dumars .25 .60
39 Rony Seikaly .20 .50
40 Dennis Rodman .50 1.25
41 Muggsy Bogues .20 .50
42 Gheorghe Muresan .15 .40
43 Ervin Johnson .15 .40
44 Todd Day .15 .40
45 Rex Walters .15 .40
46 Terrell Brandon .15 .40
47 Wesley Person .15 .40
48 Terry Dehere .15 .40
49 Steve Smith .20 .50
50 Brian Grant .20 .50
51 Eric Piatkowski .20 .50
52 Lindsey Hunter .15 .40
53 Chris Webber .30 .75
54 Antoine Carr .15 .40
55 Chris Dudley .15 .40
56 Clyde Drexler .30 .75
57 P.J. Brown .15 .40
58 Kevin Willis .15 .40
59 Jeff Turner .15 .40
60 Sean Elliott .25 .60
61 Kevin Johnson .25 .60
62 Scott Skiles .15 .40
63 Charles Smith .15 .40
64 Derrick McKey .15 .40
65 Danny Ferry .15 .40
66 Detlef Schrempf .25 .60
67 Shawn Bradley .15 .40
68 Isaiah Rider .25 .60
69 Karl Malone .30 .75
70 Will Perdue .15 .40
71 Terry Mills .15 .40
72 Glen Rice .25 .60
73 Tim Breaux .15 .40
74 Malik Sealy .15 .40
75 Walt Williams .15 .40
76 Bobby Phills .15 .40
77 Anthony Avent .15 .40
78 Jamal Mashburn UER .25 .60
Career FG percentage is wrong
79 Vlade Divac .25 .60
80 Reggie Williams .15 .40
81 Xavier McDaniel .15 .40
82 Avery Johnson .20 .50
83 Derek Harper .20 .50
84 Don MacLean .15 .40
85 Tom Gugliotta .15 .40
86 Craig Ehlo .15 .40
87 Robert Horry .20 .50
88 Kevin Edwards .15 .40
89 Chuck Person .20 .50
90 Sharone Wright .15 .40
91 Steve Kerr .20 .50
92 Marty Conlon .15 .40
93 Jalen Rose .30 .75
94 Bryant Reeves RC .25 .60
95 Shaquille O'Neal .60 1.50
96 David Wesley .15 .40
97 Chris Mills .15 .40
98 Rod Strickland .15 .40
99 Pooh Richardson .15 .40
100 Sam Perkins .15 .40
101 Dell Curry .15 .40
102 David Benoit .15 .40
103 Christian Laettner .20 .50
104 Duane Causwell .15 .40
105 Jason Kidd .40 1.00
106 Mark West .15 .40
107 Lee Mayberry .15 .40
108 John Salley .15 .40
109 Jeff Malone .15 .40
110 George Zidek RC .25 .60
111 Kenny Smith .20 .50
112 George Lynch .15 .40
113 Toni Kukoc .25 .60
114 A.C. Green .25 .60
115 Kenny Anderson .20 .50
116 Robert Parish .25 .60
117 Chris Mullin .25 .60
118 Loy Vaught .15 .40
119 Olden Polynice .15 .40
120 Clifford Robinson .15 .40
121 Eric Mobley .15 .40
122 Doug West .15 .40
123 Sam Cassell .25 .60
124 Nick Anderson .15 .40
125 Matt Geiger .15 .40
126 Elden Campbell .15 .40
127 Alonzo Mourning .30 .75
128 Bryant Stith .15 .40
129 Mark Jackson .25 .60
130 Cherokee Parks RC .25 .60
131 Shawn Respert RC .25 .60
132 Alan Henderson RC .25 .60
133 Jerry Stackhouse RC .75 2.00
134 Rasheed Wallace RC .75 2.00
135 Antonio McDyess RC .60 1.50
136 Charles Barkley ROO .40 1.00
137 Michael Jordan ROO 1.00 2.50
138 Hakeem Olajuwon ROO .30 .75
139 Joe Dumars ROO .25 .60
140 Patrick Ewing ROO .30 .75
141 A.C. Green ROO .25 .60
142 Karl Malone ROO .30 .75
143 Detlef Schrempf ROO .25 .60
144 Chuck Person ROO .20 .50
145 Muggsy Bogues ROO .20 .50
146 Horace Grant ROO .20 .50
147 Mark Jackson ROO .25 .60
148 Kevin Johnson ROO .25 .60
149 Mitch Richmond ROO .25 .60
150 Rik Smits ROO .20 .50
151 Nick Anderson ROO .15 .40
152 Tim Hardaway ROO .25 .60
153 Shawn Kemp ROO .25 .60
154 David Robinson ROO .40 1.00
155 Jason Kidd ART .40 1.00
156 Grant Hill ART .40 1.00
157 Glenn Robinson ART .25 .60
158 Eddie Jones ART .30 .75
159 Brian Grant ART .20 .50
160 Juwan Howard ART .25 .60
161 Eric Montross ART .15 .40
162 Wesley Person ART .15 .40
163 Jalen Rose ART .30 .75
164 Donyell Marshall ART .15 .40
165 Sharone Wright ART .15 .40
166 Karl Malone AN .30 .75
167 Scottie Pippen AN .40 1.00
168 David Robinson AN .40 1.00
169 John Stockton AN .30 .75
170 Anfernee Hardaway AN .40 1.00
171 Charles Barkley AN .40 1.00
172 Shawn Kemp AN .25 .60
173 Shaquille O'Neal AN .60 1.50
174 Gary Payton AN .25 .60
175 Mitch Richmond AN .25 .60
176 Dennis Rodman AN .50 1.25
177 Detlef Schrempf AN .25 .60
178 Hakeem Olajuwon AN .30 .75
179 Reggie Miller AN .30 .75
180 Clyde Drexler AN .30 .75
181 Hakeem Olajuwon .30 .75
182 Vin Baker .20 .50
183 Jeff Hornacek .20 .50
184 Popeye Jones .15 .40
185 Sedale Threatt .15 .40
186 Scottie Pippen .40 1.00
187 Terry Porter .15 .40
188 Dan Majerle .25 .60
189 Clifford Rozier .15 .40
190 Greg Minor .15 .40
191 Dennis Scott .15 .40
192 Hersey Hawkins .15 .40
193 Chris Gatling .15 .40
194 Charles Oakley .20 .50
195 Dale Davis .15 .40
196 Robert Pack .15 .40
197 Lamond Murray .15 .40
198 Mookie Blaylock .15 .40
199 Dickey Simpkins .15 .40
200 Kevin Gamble .15 .40
201 Lorenzo Williams .15 .40
202 Scott Burrell .15 .40
203 Armon Gilliam .15 .40
204 Doc Rivers .20 .50
205 Blue Edwards .15 .40
206 Billy Owens .15 .40
207 Juwan Howard .25 .60
208 Harvey Grant .15 .40
209 Richard Dumas .15 .40
210 Anthony Peeler .15 .40
211 Matt Geiger .15 .40
212 Lucious Harris .15 .40
213 Grant Long .15 .40
214 Sasha Danilovic RC .25 .60
215 Chris Morris .15 .40
216 Donyell Marshall .15 .40
217 Alonzo Mourning .30 .75
218 John Stockton .30 .75
219 Khalid Reeves .15 .40
220 Mahmoud Abdul-Rauf .15 .40
221 Sean Rooks .15 .40
222 Shawn Kemp .25 .60
223 John Williams .15 .40
224 Dee Brown .15 .40
225 Jim Jackson .15 .40
226 Harold Miner .15 .40
227 B.J. Armstrong .15 .40
228 Elliot Perry .15 .40
229 Anthony Miller .15 .40
230 Donny Marshall RC .25 .60
231 Tyrone Corbin .15 .40
232 Anthony Mason .15 .40
233 Grant Hill .40 1.00
234 Buck Williams .15 .40
235 Brian Shaw .15 .40
236 Dale Ellis .15 .40
237 Magic Johnson .60 1.50
238 Eric Montross .15 .40
239 Rex Chapman .15 .40
240 Otis Thorpe .15 .40
241 Tracy Murray .15 .40
242 Sarunas Marciulionis .15 .40
243 Luc Longley .15 .40
244 Elmore Spencer .15 .40
245 Terry Cummings .25 .60
246 Sam Mitchell .15 .40
247 Terrence Rencher RC .25 .60
248 Byron Houston .15 .40
249 Pervis Ellison .15 .40
250 Carlos Rogers .15 .40
251 Kendall Gill .15 .40
252 Sherrell Ford RC .25 .60
253 Michael Finley RC .75 2.00
254 Kurt Thomas RC .25 .60
255 Joe Smith RC .50 1.25
256 Bobby Hurley .25 .60
257 Greg Anthony .15 .40
258 Willie Anderson .15 .40
259 Theo Ratliff RC .40 1.00
260 Duane Ferrell .15 .40
261 Antonio Harvey .15 .40
262 Gary Grant .15 .40
263 Brian Williams .15 .40
264 Danny Manning .20 .50
265 Micheal Williams .15 .40
266 Dennis Rodman .50 1.25
267 Arvydas Sabonis RC .50 1.25
268 Don MacLean .15 .40
269 Keith Askins .15 .40
270 Reggie Miller .30 .75
271 Ed Pinckney .15 .40
272 Bob Sura RC .25 .60
273 Kevin Garnett RC 2.50 6.00
274 Byron Scott .20 .50
275 Mario Bennett RC .25 .60
276 Junior Burrough RC .25 .60
277 Anfernee Hardaway .40 1.00
278 George McCloud .15 .40
279 Loren Meyer RC .25 .60
280 Ed O'Bannon RC .25 .60
281 Lawrence Moten RC .25 .60
282 Dana Barros .15 .40
283 Damon Stoudamire RC .60 1.50
284 Eric Williams RC .25 .60
285 Wayman Tisdale .15 .40
286 Rodney Rogers .15 .40
287 Sherman Douglas .15 .40
288 Greg Ostertag RC .25 .60
289 Alvin Robertson .15 .40
290 Tim Legler .15 .40
291 Zan Tabak .15 .40
292 Gary Trent RC .25 .60
293 Haywoode Workman .15 .40
294 Charles Barkley .40 1.00
295 Derrick Coleman .20 .50
296 Ricky Pierce .15 .40
297 Benoit Benjamin .15 .40
298 Larry Johnson .25 .60
299 Travis Best RC .25 .60
300 Jason Caffey RC .25 .60
301 Cory Alexander RC .25 .60
302 Nick Van Exel .25 .60
303 Corliss Williamson RC .25 .60
304 Eric Murdock .15 .40
305 Tyus Edney RC .25 .60
306 Lou Roe RC .25 .60
307 John Salley .15 .40
308 Spud Webb .25 .60
309 Brent Barry RC .40 1.00
310 David Robinson .40 1.00
311 Glen Rice .25 .60
312 Chris King .15 .40
313 David Vaughn RC .25 .60
314 Kenny Gattison .15 .40
315 Randolph Childress RC .25 .60
316 Anfernee Hardaway USA .40 1.00
317 Grant Hill USA .40 1.00
318 Karl Malone USA .30 .75
319 Reggie Miller USA .30 .75
320 Hakeem Olajuwon USA .30 .75
321 Shaquille O'Neal USA .60 1.50
322 Scottie Pippen USA .40 1.00
323 David Robinson USA .40 1.00
324 Glenn Robinson USA .25 .60
325 John Stockton USA .30 .75
326 Cedric Ceballos I95 .15 .40
327 Shaquille O'Neal I95 .60 1.50
328 Glenn Robinson I95 .25 .60
329 Shawn Kemp I95 .25 .60
330 Nick Anderson I95 .15 .40
331 Shawn Bradley I95 .15 .40
332 Horace Grant I95 .20 .50
Brooks Thompson
333 Robert Horry I95 .20 .50
334 NBA Expansion I95 .15 .40
Grizzlies/Raptors
335 Michael Jordan I95 1.00 2.50
336 Nick Van Exel .25 .60
Dyan Cannon MA
337 Michael Jordan 1.00 2.50
David Hanson MA
338 Scottie Pippen .40 1.00
Jenna Von Oy MA
339 Michael Jordan 1.00 2.50
Charlie Sheen MA
340 Jason Kidd .40 1.00
Christopher Kid Reid MA
341 Michael Jordan 1.00 2.50
Queen Latifah MA
342 Charles Barkley .40 1.00
Don Johnson MA
343 Hakeem Olajuwon .30 .75
Corbin Bernsen MA
344 Ahmad Rashad MA .15 .40
345 Willow Bay MA .15 .40
346 Gary Payton .25 .60
Mark Curry MA
347 Horace Grant SJ .20 .50
348 Juwan Howard SJ .25 .60
349 David Robinson SJ .40 1.00
350 Reggie Miller SJ .30 .75
351 Brian Grant SJ .20 .50
352 Michael Jordan SJ 1.00 2.50
353 Cedric Ceballos SJ .15 .40
354 Blue Edwards SJ .15 .40
355 Acie Earl SJ .15 .40
356 Dennis Rodman SJ .50 1.25
357 Shawn Kemp SJ .25 .60
358 Jerry Stackhouse SJ .50 1.25
359 Jamal Mashburn SJ .25 .60
360 Antonio McDyess SJ .40 1.00

1995-96 Upper Deck Electric Court

One card from this 360-card parallel set was inserted into each retail pack. The cards are distinguished from their regular issue counterparts by a thicker card stock, a new logo, and special foil treatment. Please refer to the multipliers in the header to ascertain values.

COMPLETE SET (360) 50.00 100.00
COMPLETE SERIES 1 (180) 25.00 50.00
COMPLETE SERIES 2 (180) 25.00 50.00
*STARS: 1X TO 2.5X BASE CARD HI
*SUBSETS/RCs: .75X TO 2X BASE HI

1995-96 Upper Deck Electric Court Gold

Parallel to the basic set, Electric Court Gold differs in design with their refractive "Electric Court" logo on each card front. The cards were randomly seeded in both series retail packs at an approximate rate of one in 35. To ascertain values on indivdual cards, please refer to the multiplier in the header, coupled with the value of the base card.

*STARS: 8X TO 20X BASE CARD HI
*SUBSETS/RCs: 5X TO 12X BASE HI
23 Michael Jordan 50.00 120.00
137 Michael Jordan ROO 25.00 60.00
335 Michael Jordan I95 25.00 60.00
337 Michael Jordan 25.00 60.00
David Hansen MA
339 Micheal Jordan 25.00 60.00
Charlie Sheen MA
341 Michael Jordan 25.00 60.00
Queen Latifah MA
352 Michael Jordan SJ 25.00 60.00

1995-96 Upper Deck All Star Class

Randomly inserted in first series packs at a rate of one in 17, this 25-card standard-size set highlights the play of the NBA's best in the 1995 All Star Game. Borderless foil fronts feature the player in full-color action and include the Upper Deck logo stamped in blue foil on the upper right. "1995 NBA All Star Class" is printed in blue foil and centered at the bottom. On either side of the logo are gold pyramids which feature the player's name, team and position printed in black type. Blue backs have a copper bordered posed player shot with game highlights. The Phoenix All Star Weekend logo is printed at the top of the picture and the player's name, team and position are printed over the logo.

COMPLETE SET (25) 60.00 120.00
AS1 Anfernee Hardaway 5.00 12.00
AS2 Reggie Miller 4.00 10.00
AS3 Grant Hill 5.00 12.00
AS4 Scottie Pippen 5.00 12.00
AS5 Shaquille O'Neal 8.00 20.00
AS6 Larry Johnson 3.00 8.00
AS7 Dana Barros 2.00 5.00
AS8 Vin Baker 2.50 6.00
AS9 Alonzo Mourning 4.00 10.00
AS10 Joe Dumars 3.00 8.00
AS11 Patrick Ewing 4.00 10.00
AS12 Tyrone Hill 2.00 5.00
AS13 Latrell Sprewell 3.00 8.00
AS14 Dan Majerle 3.00 8.00
AS15 Shawn Kemp 3.00 8.00
AS16 Karl Malone 4.00 10.00
AS17 Hakeem Olajuwon 4.00 10.00
AS18 Gary Payton 3.00 8.00
AS19 Mitch Richmond 3.00 8.00
AS20 David Robinson 5.00 12.00
AS21 Detlef Schrempf 3.00 8.00
AS22 Cedric Ceballos 2.00 5.00
AS23 John Stockton 4.00 10.00
AS24 Dikembe Mutombo 3.00 8.00
AS25 Charles Barkley 5.00 12.00

1995-96 Upper Deck Jordan Collection

Upper Deck spokesperson and NBA legend Michael Jordan is featured on these eight, multi-series insert cards. Cards JC5-JC8 were randomly inserted into one in every 29 first series packs. Cards JC13-JC16 were randomly inserted into one in every 29 second series packs. The eight cards actually represent two segments of a twenty-four card set issued in six different series across all of Upper Deck's 1995-96 products (except SPx). Full-bleed, silver-foil fronts feature Jordan in full color in both posed and action shots. Backs feature Jordan in a spectacular action shot with alternating boxes of separated colors. A "Jordan Collection" box appears at the mid-left of the card with an explanation of the award that was featured on the front.

COMPLETE SER.1 (4) 12.00 30.00
COMPLETE SER.2 (4) 12.00 30.00
COMMON UD 1 (JC5-JC8) 4.00 10.00
COMMON UD 2 (JC13-JC16) 4.00 10.00

1995-96 Upper Deck Jordan Collection Jumbos

COMPLETE SET (24) 25.00 60.00
COMMON CARD 2.00 5.00

1995-96 Upper Deck Predictor MVP

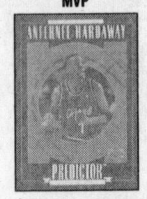

Randomly inserted exclusively into second series retail packs at a rate of one in 30, this 10-card standard-size set features five Michael Jordan cards, four top NBA stars and a Long Shot card (representing all other NBA players). In addition, Upper Deck offered dealers a 5-card Predictor pack with the purchase of one case (20 boxes) of second series product. Dealers were given all 20 second series Predictor cards (retail MVP and hobby Scoring) with the purchase of two cases. Black and red basketball court fronts frame a full-color action player cutout. A black border surrounds the player's name, team and the month of the predicted award, all of which are stamped in gold foil. The outer border of the front is a black marble texture. Numbered backs are printed on white, have the prefix "R" and explain the rules of the game. Those holding a winning Predictor card redeemed the cards through a mail-in offer for a full set of the Predictor MVP cards. The expiration date to redeem winning cards was July 8, 1996.

COMPLETE SET (10) 10.00 25.00
*RED.CARDS: .20X TO .50X HI COLUMN
ONE RED.SET PER "W" CARD BY MAIL
R1 Michael Jordan MVP W 3.00 8.00
R2 Michael Jordan All-NBA W 3.00 8.00
R3 Michael Jordan Def. POY L 3.00 8.00
R4 Michael Jordan All-Defensive W 3.00 8.00
R5 Michael Jordan Finals MVP W 3.00 8.00
R6 Hakeem Olajuwon L 1.00 2.50
R7 Charles Barkley L 1.25 3.00
R8 Karl Malone L 1.00 2.50
R9 Anfernee Hardaway L 1.25 3.00
R10 Long Shot Card L .75 2.00

1995-96 Upper Deck Predictor Player of the Month

Randomly inserted exclusively into first series retail packs at a rate of one in 30, this 10-card standard-size set features five Michael Jordan cards, four top NBA stars and a Long Shot card (representing all other NBA players). In addition, Upper Deck offered dealers a 5-card Predictor pack with the purchase of one case (20 boxes) of first series product. Dealers were given all 20 first series Predictor cards (retail Player of the Month and hobby Player of the Week) with the purchase of two cases. Each card lists months that the featured player might win Player of the Month honors. Black and red basketball court fronts frame a full-color action player cutout. A black border surrounds the player's name, team and the month of the predicted award, all of which are stamped in gold foil. The outer border of the front is a black marble texture. Numbered backs are printed on white, have the prefix "R" and explain the rules of the game. Those holding a winning Predictor card redeemed the cards through a mail-in offer for a full set of the Predictor Player of the Month cards. The expiration date to redeem winning cards was July 1, 1996.

COMPLETE SET (10) 10.00 25.00
*RED.CARDS: .20X TO .50X HI COLUMN
ONE RED.SET PER "W" CARD BY MAIL
R1 Michael Jordan Nov./Dec. L 3.00 8.00
R2 Michael Jordan Jan. W 3.00 8.00
R3 Michael Jordan Feb. L 3.00 8.00
R4 Michael Jordan March L 3.00 8.00
R5 Michael Jordan April L 3.00 8.00
R6 Jamal Mashburn L .75 2.00
R7 David Robinson W 1.25 3.00
R8 Latrell Sprewell L .75 2.00
R9 Chris Webber L 1.00 2.50
R10 Long Shot Card W .75 2.00

1995-96 Upper Deck Predictor Player of the Week

Randomly inserted exclusively into first series hobby packs at a rate of one in 30, this 10-card standard-sized set features five Michael Jordan cards, four top NBA stars and a Long Shot card (representing all other NBA players). In addition, Upper Deck offered dealers a 5-card Predictor pack with the purchase of one case (20 boxes) of first series product. Dealers were given all 20 first series Predictor cards (retail Player of the Month and hobby Player of the Week) with the purchase of two cases. Each card lists weeks that the featured player might win Player of the Week honors. The fronts feature the player in a full color cutout set against a red court background and a black border surrounding the red. The player's name, team name and predictor category are printed in gold foil. Card edges are trimmed with a black marble texture. Those holding a winning Predictor card redeemed the cards through a mail-in offer for a full set of the Predictor Player of the Week cards. The expiration date to redeem winning cards was July 1, 1996.

*RED.CARDS: .20X TO .50X HI COLUMN
ONE RED.SET PER "W" CARD BY MAIL
H1 Michael Jordan Nov./Dec. W 3.00 8.00
H2 Michael Jordan Jan. W 3.00 8.00
H3 Michael Jordan Feb. L 3.00 8.00
H4 Michael Jordan March L 3.00 8.00
H5 Michael Jordan April L 3.00 8.00
H6 Anfernee Hardaway W 1.25 3.00
H7 Hakeem Olajuwon W 1.00 2.50
H8 Scottie Pippen W 1.25 3.00
H9 Glenn Robinson L .75 2.00
H10 Long Shot Card W .75 2.00

1995-96 Upper Deck Predictor Scoring

Randomly inserted in second series hobby packs at a rate of one in 30, cards from this 10-card insert set feature five Michael Jordan cards, four top NBA stars and a Long Shot card (representing all other NBA players). In addition, Upper Deck offered dealers a 5-

card Predictor pack with the purchase of one case (20 boxes) of second series product. Dealers were given all 20 second series Predictor cards (retail MVP and hobby Scoring) with the purchase of two cases. Card fronts feature the player in a full color cutout set against a red court background and a black border surrounding the red. The player's name, team name and predictor category are printed in gold foil. Card edges are trimmed with a black marble texture. If the player pictured won the NBA scoring title, the card was redeemable for a special version of the hobby Predictor Scoring set. The expiration date to redeem winning cards was July 8, 1996.
*RED.CARDS: .20X TO .50X HI COLUMN
ONE RED.SET PER "W" CARD BY MAIL

H1 Michael Jordan Scoring W	3.00	8.00
H2 Michael Jordan Assists L	3.00	8.00
H3 Michael Jordan Steals L	3.00	8.00
H4 Michael Jordan 3-pt. L	3.00	8.00
H5 Michael Jordan Playoff W	3.00	8.00
H6 David Robinson L	1.25	3.00
H7 Scottie Pippen L	1.25	3.00
H8 Jerry Stackhouse L	1.25	3.00
H9 Glenn Robinson L	.75	2.00
H10 Long Shot Card L	.75	2.00

1995-96 Upper Deck Special Edition

These 180 standard-size cards were inserted at a rate of one per hobby pack only and were printed on a silver foil front. The cards were issued in two separate series of 90 (1-90 in first series packs and 91-180 in second series). Only the top veterans and rookies were selected for inclusion in this set. The player is featured in an action shot but only he is singled out for color. The rest of the shot is faded out to black and white. The player's name is stamped in silver foil at the bottom and the Special Edition logo is stamped in silver foil at the top right. "SE" is stamped in silver foil and runs vertically down the left side of the front. Backs are printed on a white and gray background and include a player biography, career statistics and player highlights. A color player action shot appears on the upper left side and includes the card number.

COMPLETE SET (180)	40.00	80.00
COMPLETE SERIES 1 (90)	15.00	30.00
COMPLETE SERIES 2 (90)	20.00	50.00
1 Mookie Blaylock	.40	1.00
2 Tyrone Corbin	.40	1.00
3 Grant Long	.40	1.00
4 Dee Brown	.40	1.00
5 Sherman Douglas	.40	1.00
6 Eric Montross	.40	1.00
7 Scott Burrell	.40	1.00
8 Dell Curry	.40	1.00
9 Larry Johnson	.60	1.50
10 Will Perdue	.40	1.00
11 Scottie Pippen	1.00	2.50
12 Dickey Simpkins	.40	1.00
13 Michael Cage	.40	1.00
14 Mark Price	.60	1.50
15 John Williams	.40	1.00
16 Lucious Harris	.40	1.00
17 Jim Jackson	.40	1.00
18 Popeye Jones	.40	1.00
19 Mahmoud Abdul-Rauf	.40	1.00
20 LaPhonso Ellis	.40	1.00
21 Robert Pack	.40	1.00
22 Bill Curley	.40	1.00
23 Grant Hill	1.00	2.50
24 Allan Houston	.50	1.25
25 Chris Gatling	.40	1.00
26 Tim Hardaway	.60	1.50
27 Donyell Marshall	.40	1.00
28 Clifford Rozier	.40	1.00
29 Mario Elie	.40	1.00
30 Robert Horry	.50	1.25
31 Hakeem Olajuwon	.75	2.00
32 Kenny Smith	.50	1.25
33 Dale Davis	.40	1.00
34 Duane Ferrell	.40	1.00
35 Derrick McKey	.40	1.00
36 Reggie Miller	.75	2.00
37 Lamond Murray	.40	1.00
38 Bo Outlaw	.40	1.00
39 Eric Piatkowski	.50	1.25
40 Anthony Peeler	.40	1.00
41 Sedale Threatt	.40	1.00
42 Nick Van Exel	.60	1.50
43 Kevin Gamble	.40	1.00
44 Matt Geiger	.40	1.00
45 Billy Owens	.40	1.00
46 Khalid Reeves	.40	1.00
47 Vin Baker	.50	1.25
48 Eric Murdock	.40	1.00
49 Lee Mayberry	.40	1.00
50 Christian Laettner	.50	1.25
51 Sean Rooks	.40	1.00
52 Doug West	.40	1.00
53 P.J. Brown	.40	1.00
54 Derrick Coleman	.50	1.25
55 Armon Gilliam	.40	1.00
56 Hubert Davis	.40	1.00
57 Charles Oakley	.50	1.25
58 John Starks	.50	1.25
59 Monty Williams	.40	1.00
60 Anfernee Hardaway	1.00	2.50
61 Donald Royal	.40	1.00
62 Dennis Scott	.40	1.00
63 Jeff Turner	.40	1.00
64 Clarence Weatherspoon	.40	1.00
65 Jeff Malone	.40	1.00
66 Scott Williams	.40	1.00
67 A.C. Green	.60	1.50
68 Kevin Johnson	.60	1.50
69 Elliot Perry	.40	1.00
70 Wesley Person	.40	1.00
71 Harvey Grant	.40	1.00
72 Aaron McKie	.40	1.00
73 Rod Strickland	.40	1.00
74 Buck Williams	.40	1.00
75 Randy Brown	.40	1.00
76 Bobby Hurley	.60	1.50
77 Lionel Simmons	.40	1.00
78 Terry Cummings	.60	1.50
79 Vinny Del Negro	.40	1.00
80 Avery Johnson	.50	1.25
81 David Robinson	1.00	2.50
82 Vincent Askew	.40	1.00
83 Shawn Kemp	.60	1.50
84 Nate McMillan	.40	1.00
85 David Benoit	.40	1.00
86 Jeff Hornacek	.50	1.25
87 John Stockton	.75	2.00
88 Juwan Howard	.60	1.50
89 Gheorghe Muresan	.40	1.00
90 Doug Overton	.40	1.00
91 Stacey Augmon	.50	1.25
92 Alan Henderson	.60	1.50
93 Steve Smith	.50	1.25
94 Rick Fox	.40	1.00
95 Dino Radja	.50	1.25
96 Eric Williams	.60	1.50
97 Muggsy Bogues	.50	1.25
98 Kendall Gill	.40	1.00
99 Glen Rice	.60	1.50
100 Michael Jordan	5.00	12.00
101 Toni Kukoc	.60	1.50
102 Dennis Rodman	1.25	3.00
103 Terrell Brandon	.40	1.00
104 Tyrone Hill	.40	1.00
105 Dan Majerle	.60	1.50
106 Jason Kidd	1.00	2.50
107 Jamal Mashburn	.60	1.50
108 Cherokee Parks	.60	1.50
109 Antonio McDyess	1.50	4.00
110 Dikembe Mutombo	.60	1.50
111 Reggie Williams	.40	1.00
112 Joe Dumars	.60	1.50
113 Lindsey Hunter	.40	1.00
114 Otis Thorpe	.40	1.00
115 Chris Mullin	.60	1.50
116 Joe Smith	1.25	3.00
117 Latrell Sprewell	.60	1.50
118 Chucky Brown	.40	1.00
119 Sam Cassell	.60	1.50
120 Clyde Drexler	.75	2.00
121 Travis Best	.60	1.50
122 Mark Jackson	.60	1.50
123 Rik Smits	.50	1.25
124 Brent Barry	1.00	2.50
125 Rodney Rogers	.40	1.00
126 Loy Vaught	.40	1.00
127 Cedric Ceballos	.40	1.00
128 Magic Johnson	1.50	4.00
129 Eddie Jones	.75	2.00
130 Alonzo Mourning	.75	2.00
131 Kurt Thomas	.60	1.50
132 Kevin Willis	.40	1.00
133 Sherman Douglas	.40	1.00
134 Shawn Respert	.60	1.50
135 Glenn Robinson	.60	1.50
136 Kevin Garnett	5.00	12.00
137 Tom Gugliotta	.40	1.00
138 Isaiah Rider	.60	1.50
139 Kenny Anderson	.50	1.25
140 Ed O'Bannon	.60	1.50
141 Jayson Williams	.40	1.00
142 Patrick Ewing	.75	2.00
143 Derek Harper	.50	1.25
144 Charles Smith	.40	1.00
145 Nick Anderson	.40	1.00
146 Horace Grant	.50	1.25
147 Shaquille O'Neal	1.50	4.00
148 Vernon Maxwell	.40	1.00
149 Jerry Stackhouse	2.00	5.00
150 Sharone Wright	.40	1.00
151 Charles Barkley	1.00	2.50
152 Michael Finley	2.00	5.00
153 Danny Manning	.50	1.25
154 John Williams	.40	1.00
155 Clifford Robinson	.40	1.00
156 Arvydas Sabonis	1.25	3.00
157 Gary Trent	.60	1.50
158 Brian Grant	.50	1.25
159 Mitch Richmond	.60	1.50
160 Corliss Williamson	.60	1.50
161 Sean Elliott	.60	1.50
162 Will Perdue	.40	1.00
163 Doc Rivers	.50	1.25
164 Gary Payton	.60	1.50
165 Sam Perkins	.40	1.00
166 Detlef Schrempf	.60	1.50
167 Tracy Murray	.40	1.00
168 Ed Pinckney	.40	1.00
169 Carlos Rogers	.40	1.00
170 Damon Stoudamire	1.50	4.00
171 Karl Malone	.75	2.00
172 Chris Morris	.40	1.00
173 Greg Ostertag	.60	1.50
174 Greg Anthony	.40	1.00
175 Lawrence Moten	.60	1.50
176 Bryant Reeves	.60	1.50
177 Byron Scott	.50	1.25
178 Calbert Cheaney	.40	1.00
179 Rasheed Wallace	2.00	5.00
180 Chris Webber	.75	2.00

1995-96 Upper Deck Special Edition Gold

Randomly inserted in hobby packs only at a rate of one in 35, this 180-card set parallels the more common Special Edition insert set. The Gold foil wording on the front of each card (instead of silver) differentiate them. Each card contains a "SE" prefix. To ascertain values on individual cards, please refer to the multiplier in the header, coupled with the values of the base insert.
*STARS: 2.5X TO 6X HI COLUMN
*RCs: 1.5X TO 4X HI

1996-97 Upper Deck

This 360-card Upper Deck set was distributed in two series with packs of 12 cards each at the suggested retail price of $2.49. The fronts feature color action player photos with the date stamped in foil indicating the actual game of the photo featured on each card. The backs carry player information. Rookies from both series include Kobe Bryant, Marcus Camby, Allen Iverson, Stephon Marbury, Shareef Abdur-Rahim and Antoine Walker, among others. Randomly inserted in packs at the rate of one in three were "Meet the Stars" trivia game cards which gave the collector a chance to answer questions for prizes including a chance to meet a star player. Inserted one in 56 packs were instant win cards which entitled the holder to prizes without answering questions. One in seven series one packs contained "NBA Pick Up Game" cards which featured stickers representing players' jersey numbers in which the collector affixed to a "3-in-a-Row" game board and sent in for a chance to win a trip to All-Star Weekend.

COMPLETE SET (360)	25.00	50.00
COMPLETE SERIES 1 (180)	15.00	30.00
COMPLETE SERIES 2 (180)	10.00	20.00
1 Mookie Blaylock	.15	.40
2 Alan Henderson	.15	.40
3 Christian Laettner	.20	.50
4 Ken Norman	.15	.40
5 Dee Brown	.15	.40
6 Todd Day	.15	.40
7 Rick Fox	.15	.40
8 Dino Radja	.20	.50
9 Dana Barros	.15	.40
10 Eric Williams	.15	.40
11 Scott Burrell	.15	.40
12 Dell Curry	.15	.40
13 Matt Geiger	.15	.40
14 Glen Rice	.25	.60
15 Ron Harper	.20	.50
16 Michael Jordan	2.00	5.00
17 Luc Longley	.15	.40
18 Toni Kukoc	.25	.60
19 Dennis Rodman	.50	1.25
20 Danny Ferry	.15	.40
21 Tyrone Hill	.15	.40
22 Bobby Phills	.15	.40
23 Bob Sura	.15	.40
24 Tony Dumas	.15	.40
25 George McCloud	.15	.40
26 Jim Jackson	.15	.40
27 Jamal Mashburn	.20	.50
28 Loren Meyer	.15	.40
29 Dale Ellis	.15	.40
30 LaPhonso Ellis	.15	.40
31 Tom Hammonds	.15	.40
32 Antonio McDyess	.25	.60
33 Joe Dumars	.25	.60
34 Grant Hill	.40	1.00
35 Lindsey Hunter	.15	.40
36 Terry Mills	.15	.40
37 Theo Ratliff	.15	.40
38 B.J. Armstrong	.15	.40
39 Donyell Marshall	.15	.40
40 Chris Mullin	.25	.60
41 Rony Seikaly	.20	.50
42 Joe Smith	.20	.50
43 Sam Cassell	.20	.50
44 Clyde Drexler	.30	.75
45 Mario Elie	.15	.40
46 Robert Horry	.20	.50
47 Travis Best	.15	.40
48 Antonio Davis	.15	.40
49 Dale Davis	.15	.40
50 Eddie Johnson	.15	.40
51 Derrick McKey	.15	.40
52 Reggie Miller	.30	.75
53 Brent Barry	.20	.50
54 Lamond Murray	.15	.40
55 Eric Piatkowski	.20	.50
56 Rodney Rogers	.15	.40
57 Loy Vaught	.15	.40
58 Kobe Bryant RC	6.00	15.00
59 Eddie Jones	.25	.60
60 Elden Campbell	.15	.40
61 Shaquille O'Neal	.60	1.50
62 Nick Van Exel	.25	.60
63 Keith Askins	.15	.40
64 Rex Chapman	.15	.40
65 Sasha Danilovic	.15	.40
66 Alonzo Mourning	.30	.75
67 Kurt Thomas	.15	.40
68 Tim Hardaway	.25	.60
69 Ray Allen RC	1.00	2.50
70 Johnny Newman	.15	.40
71 Shawn Respert	.15	.40
72 Glenn Robinson	.25	.60
73 Tom Gugliotta	.15	.40
74 Stephon Marbury RC	.60	1.50
75 Terry Porter	.15	.40
76 Doug West	.15	.40
77 Shawn Bradley	.15	.40
78 Kevin Edwards	.15	.40
79 Vern Fleming	.15	.40
80 Ed O'Bannon	.15	.40
81 Jayson Williams	.15	.40
82 John Starks	.20	.50
83 Patrick Ewing	.30	.75
84 Charlie Ward	.15	.40
85 Nick Anderson	.15	.40
86 Anfernee Hardaway	.40	1.00
87 Jon Koncak	.15	.40
88 Donald Royal	.15	.40
89 Brian Shaw	.15	.40
90 Derrick Coleman	.20	.50
91 Allen Iverson RC	1.25	3.00
92 Jerry Stackhouse	.30	.75
93 Clarence Weatherspoon	.15	.40
94 Charles Barkley	.40	1.00
95 Kevin Johnson	.25	.60
96 Danny Manning	.20	.50
97 Elliot Perry	.15	.40
98 Wayman Tisdale	.15	.40
99 Randolph Childress	.15	.40
100 Aaron McKie	.15	.40
101 Arvydas Sabonis	.20	.50
102 Gary Trent	.15	.40
103 Chris Dudley	.15	.40
104 Tyus Edney	.15	.40
105 Brian Grant	.20	.50
106 Bobby Hurley	.25	.60
107 Olden Polynice	.15	.40
108 Corliss Williamson	.15	.40
109 Vinny Del Negro	.15	.40
110 Avery Johnson	.20	.50
111 Will Perdue	.15	.40
112 David Robinson	.40	1.00
113 Hersey Hawkins	.15	.40
114 Shawn Kemp	.25	.60
115 Nate McMillan	.15	.40
116 Detlef Schrempf	.25	.60
117 Gary Payton	.25	.60
118 Marcus Camby RC	.40	1.00
119 Zan Tabak	.15	.40
120 Damon Stoudamire	.25	.60
121 Carlos Rogers	.15	.40
122 Sharone Wright	.15	.40
123 Antoine Carr	.15	.40
124 Jeff Hornacek	.20	.50
125 Adam Keefe	.15	.40
126 Chris Morris	.15	.40
127 John Stockton	.30	.75
128 Blue Edwards	.15	.40
129 Shareef Abdur-Rahim RC	.50	1.25
130 Bryant Reeves	.15	.40
131 Roy Rogers RC	.25	.60
132 Calbert Cheaney	.15	.40
133 Tim Legler	.15	.40
134 Gheorghe Muresan	.15	.40
135 Chris Webber	.30	.75
136 Dikembe Mutombo	.25	.60
Mookie Blaylock		
Steve Smith		
Christian Laettner		
Alan Henderson		
137 Dana Barros	.20	.50
Dino Radja		
Eric Williams		
Dee Brown		
Pervis Ellison		
138 Glen Rice	.25	.60
Matt Geiger		
Vlade Divac		
Scott Burrell		
George Zidek		
139 Michael Jordan	1.00	2.50
Scottie Pippen		
Dennis Rodman		
Toni Kukoc		
Ron Harper		
140 Terrell Brandon	.15	.40
Danny Ferry		
Tyrone Hill		
Bobby Phills		
Bobby Sura		
141 Jason Kidd	.40	1.00
Jamal Mashburn		
Jim Jackson		
Tony Dumas		
Loren Meyer		
142 LaPhonso Ellis	.25	.60
Antonio McDyess		
Mark Jackson		
Dale Ellis		
Bryant Stith		
143 Joe Dumars	.40	1.00
Grant Hill		
Stacey Augmon		
Lindsey Hunter		
Theo Ratliff		
144 Joe Smith	.25	.60
Latrell Sprewell		
Chris Mullin		
Rony Seikaly		
BJ Armstrong		
145 Hakeem Olajuwon	.40	1.00
Clyde Drexler		
Charles Barkley		
Brent Price		
Mario Elie		
146 Reggie Miller	.30	.75
Travis Best		
Rik Smits		
Dale Davis		
Antonio Davis		
147 Brent Barry	.20	.50
Lamond Murray		
Rodney Rogers		
Terry Dehere		
Eric Piatkowski		
148 Shaquille O'Neal	1.25	3.00
Eddie Jones		
Kobe Bryant		
Cedric Ceballos		
Nick Van Exel		
149 Alonzo Mourning	.30	.75
Tim Hardaway		
Sasha Danilovic		
Kurt Thomas		
Keith Askins		
150 Vin Baker	.25	.60
Glenn Robinson		
Sherman Douglas		
Shawn Respert		
Johnnie Newman		
151 Kevin Garnett	.60	1.50
Tom Gugliotta		
Cherokee Parks		
Terry Porter		
Doug West		
152 Shawn Bradley	.15	.40
Kendall Gill		
Ed O'Bannon		
Jayson Williams		
Robert Pack		
153 Patrick Ewing	.30	.75
Allan Houston		
Larry Johnson		
Charles Oakley		
John Starks		
154 Anfernee Hardaway	.40	1.00
Dennis Scott		
Horace Grant		
Nick Anderson		
Brian Shaw		
155 Jerry Stackhouse	.30	.75
Clarence Weatherspoon		
Derrick Coleman		
Scott Williams		
Rex Walters		
156 Kevin Johnson	.30	.75
Danny Manning		
Michael Finley		
Wesley Person		
A.C. Green		
157 Clifford Robinson	.30	.75
Isaiah Rider		
Arvydas Sabonis		
Rasheed Wallace		
Kenny Anderson		
158 Mitch Richmond	.25	.60
Brian Grant		
Billy Owens		
Tyus Edney		
Michael Smith		
159 David Robinson	.40	1.00
Sean Elliott		
Avery Johnson		
Vinny Del Negro		
Chuck Person		
160 Shawn Kemp	.25	.60
Gary Payton		
Detlef Schrempf		
Hersey Hawkins		
Sam Perkins		
161 Damon Stoudamire	.25	.60
Zan Tabak		
Sharone Wright		
Doug Christie		
Carlos Rogers		
162 John Stockton	.30	.75
Karl Malone		
Jeff Hornacek		
Bryon Russell		
Antoine Carr		
163 Bryant Reeves	.50	1.25
Shareef Abdur-Rahim		
Greg Anthony		
Blue Edwards		
Lawrence Moten		
164 Juwan Howard	.30	.75
Gheorge Muresan		
Chris Webber		
Calbert Cheaney		
Tim Legler		
165 Michael Jordan GP	2.00	5.00
166 Corliss Williamson GP	.15	.40
167 Dell Curry GP	.15	.40
168 John Starks GP	.20	.50
169 Dennis Rodman GP	.50	1.25
170 Chris Webber	.30	.75
Latrell Sprewell GP		
171 Cedric Ceballos GP	.15	.40
172 Theo Ratliff GP	.15	.40
173 Anfernee Hardaway GP	.40	1.00
174 Grant Hill GP	.40	1.00
175 Alonzo Mourning GP	.30	.75
176 Shawn Kemp GP	.25	.60
177 Jason Kidd GP	.40	1.00
178 Avery Johnson GP	.20	.50
179 Gary Payton GP	.25	.60
180 Michael Jordan CL	1.00	2.50
181 Priest Lauderdale RC	.25	.60
182 Dikembe Mutombo	.25	.60
183 Eldridge Recasner RC	.25	.60
184 Steve Smith	.20	.50
185 Pervis Ellison	.15	.40
186 Greg Minor	.15	.40
187 Antoine Walker RC	.50	1.25
188 David Wesley	.15	.40
189 Muggsy Bogues	.20	.50
190 Tony Delk RC	.25	.60
191 Vlade Divac	.25	.60
192 Anthony Mason	.15	.40
193 George Zidek	.15	.40
194 Jason Caffey	.15	.40
195 Steve Kerr	.20	.50
196 Robert Parish	.25	.60
197 Scottie Pippen	.40	1.00
198 Terrell Brandon	.15	.40
199 Antonio Lang	.15	.40
200 Chris Mills	.15	.40
201 Vitaly Potapenko RC	.25	.60
202 Mark West	.15	.40
203 Chris Gatling	.15	.40
204 Derek Harper	.20	.50
205 Sam Cassell	.20	.50
206 Eric Montross	.15	.40
207 Samaki Walker RC	.25	.60
208 Mark Jackson	.25	.60
209 Ervin Johnson	.15	.40
210 Sarunas Marciulionis	.15	.40
211 Ricky Pierce	.15	.40
212 Bryant Stith	.15	.40
213 Stacey Augmon	.20	.50
214 Grant Long	.15	.40
215 Rick Mahorn	.15	.40
216 Otis Thorpe	.15	.40
217 Jerome Williams RC	.25	.60
218 Bimbo Coles	.15	.40
219 Todd Fuller RC	.25	.60
220 Mark Price	.25	.60
221 Felton Spencer	.15	.40
222 Latrell Sprewell	.25	.60
223 Charles Barkley	.40	1.00
224 Othella Harrington RC	.25	.60
225 Hakeem Olajuwon	.30	.75
226 Matt Maloney RC	.25	.60
227 Kevin Willis	.15	.40
228 Erick Dampier RC	.25	.60
229 Duane Ferrell	.15	.40
230 Jalen Rose	.20	.50
231 Rik Smits	.20	.50
232 Terry Dehere	.15	.40
233 Bo Outlaw	.15	.40
234 Pooh Richardson	.15	.40
235 Malik Sealy	.15	.40
236 Lorenzen Wright RC	.25	.60
237 Cedric Ceballos	.15	.40
238 Derek Fisher RC	.50	1.25
239 Travis Knight RC	.25	.60
240 Sean Rooks	.15	.40
241 Byron Scott	.20	.50
242 P.J. Brown	.15	.40
243 Voshon Lenard RC	.25	.60
244 Dan Majerle	.25	.60
245 Martin Muursepp RC	.25	.60
246 Gary Grant	.15	.40
247 Vin Baker	.20	.50
248 Armon Gilliam	.15	.40
249 Andrew Lang	.15	.40
250 Elliot Perry	.15	.40
251 Kevin Garnett	.60	1.50
252 Shane Heal RC	.25	.60
253 Cherokee Parks	.15	.40
254 Stojko Vrankovic	.15	.40
255 Kendall Gill	.15	.40
256 Kerry Kittles RC	.25	.60
257 Xavier McDaniel	.15	.40
258 Robert Pack	.15	.40
259 Chris Childs	.15	.40
260 Allan Houston	.20	.50
261 Larry Johnson	.25	.60
262 Dontae' Jones RC	.25	.60
263 Walter McCarty RC	.25	.60
264 Charles Oakley	.20	.50
265 John Wallace RC	.25	.60
266 Buck Williams	.15	.40
267 Brian Evans RC	.25	.60
268 Horace Grant	.20	.50
269 Dennis Scott	.15	.40
270 Rony Seikaly	.20	.50
271 David Vaughn	.15	.40
272 Michael Cage	.15	.40
273 Lucious Harris	.15	.40
274 Don MacLean	.15	.40
275 Mark Davis	.15	.40
276 Jason Kidd	.40	1.00
277 Michael Finley	.30	.75
278 A.C. Green	.25	.60
279 Robert Horry	.20	.50
280 Steve Nash RC	2.00	5.00
281 Wesley Person	.15	.40
282 Kenny Anderson	.20	.50
283 Aleksandar Djordjevic RC	.25	.60
284 Jermaine O'Neal RC	.60	1.50
285 Isaiah Rider	.20	.50
286 Clifford Robinson	.15	.40
287 Rasheed Wallace	.30	.75
288 Mahmoud Abdul-Rauf	.15	.40
289 Billy Owens	.15	.40
290 Mitch Richmond	.25	.60
291 Michael Smith	.15	.40
292 Cory Alexander	.15	.40
293 Sean Elliott	.25	.60
294 Vernon Maxwell	.15	.40
295 Dominique Wilkins	.30	.75
296 Craig Ehlo	.15	.40
297 Jim McIlvaine	.15	.40
298 Sam Perkins	.15	.40
299 Steve Scheffler RC	.25	.60
300 Hubert Davis	.15	.40
301 Popeye Jones	.15	.40
302 Donald Whiteside RC	.25	.60
303 Walt Williams	.15	.40
304 Karl Malone	.30	.75
305 Greg Ostertag	.15	.40
306 Bryon Russell	.15	.40
307 Jamie Watson	.15	.40
308 Greg Anthony	.15	.40
309 George Lynch	.15	.40
310 Lawrence Moten	.15	.40
311 Anthony Peeler	.15	.40
312 Juwan Howard	.20	.50
313 Tracy Murray	.15	.40
314 Rod Strickland	.15	.40
315 Harvey Grant	.15	.40
316 Charles Barkley DN	.40	1.00
317 Clyde Drexler DN	.30	.75
318 Dikembe Mutombo DN	.25	.60
319 Larry Johnson DN	.25	.60
320 Shaquille O'Neal DN	.60	1.50
321 Mookie Blaylock DN	.15	.40
322 Tim Hardaway DN	.25	.60
323 Dennis Rodman DN	.50	1.25
324 Dan Majerle DN	.25	.60
325 Stacey Augmon DN	.20	.50
326 Anthony Mason DN	.15	.40
327 Kenny Anderson DN	.20	.50
328 Mahmoud Abdul-Rauf DN	.15	.40
329 Chris Webber DN	.30	.75
330 Dominique Wilkins DN	.30	.75
331 Dikembe Mutombo WD	.25	.60
332 Dana Barros WD	.15	.40
333 Glen Rice WD	.25	.60
334 Dennis Rodman WD	.50	1.25
335 Terrell Brandon WD	.15	.40
336 Jason Kidd WD	.40	1.00
337 Antonio McDyess WD	.25	.60
338 Grant Hill WD	.40	1.00
339 Joe Smith WD	.20	.50
340 Charles Barkley WD	.40	1.00
341 Reggie Miller WD	.30	.75
342 Brent Barry WD	.20	.50
343 Shaquille O'Neal WD	.60	1.50
344 Alonzo Mourning WD	.30	.75
345 Glenn Robinson WD	.25	.60
346 Stephon Marbury WD	.30	.75
347 Kerry Kittles WD	.12	.30
348 Patrick Ewing WD	.30	.75
349 Anfernee Hardaway WD	.40	1.00
350 Allen Iverson WD	.60	1.50
351 Danny Manning WD	.20	.50
352 Arvydas Sabonis WD	.20	.50
353 Mitch Richmond WD	.25	.60
354 David Robinson WD	.40	1.00
355 Shawn Kemp WD	.25	.60
356 Marcus Camby WD	.20	.50
357 Karl Malone WD	.30	.75
358 Shareef Abdur-Rahim WD	.25	.60
359 Gheorghe Muresan WD	.15	.40
360 Checklist 181-360	.15	.40

1996-97 Upper Deck Autographs

Hand-numbered to 500, these autographed cards were randomly inserted into packs of series 2 Upper Deck. The cards feature the autograph on the card front, with a congratulatory message on the back. The backs are also numbered with an "A" prefix.

A1 Anfernee Hardaway	50.00	120.00
A2 Shawn Kemp	40.00	100.00
A3 Antonio McDyess	20.00	50.00
A4 Damon Stoudamire	20.00	50.00

1996-97 Upper Deck Fast Break Connections

Randomly inserted in series one packs at a rate of one in eight, this set features color photos of 30 players. Each card features three different players from the same team on special die-cut designs that are combined into one over-sized card. Each card is numbered with a "FB" prefix.

COMPLETE SET (30)	25.00	60.00
FB1 Jim Jackson	.75	2.00
FB2 Jason Kidd	2.00	5.00
FB3 Jamal Mashburn	1.00	2.50
FB4 Mario Elie	.75	2.00
FB5 Hakeem Olajuwon	1.50	4.00
FB6 Clyde Drexler	1.50	4.00
FB7 Cedric Ceballos	.75	2.00
FB8 Nick Van Exel	1.25	3.00
FB9 Eddie Jones	1.25	3.00
FB10 Danny Manning	1.00	2.50
FB11 Michael Finley	1.50	4.00
FB12 Kevin Johnson	1.25	3.00
FB13 Tyus Edney	.75	2.00
FB14 Brian Grant	1.00	2.50
FB15 Mitch Richmond	1.25	3.00
FB16 Sean Elliott	1.25	3.00
FB17 David Robinson	2.00	5.00
FB18 Avery Johnson	1.00	2.50
FB19 Shawn Kemp	1.25	3.00
FB20 Gary Payton	1.25	3.00
FB21 Detlef Schrempf	1.25	3.00
FB22 Scottie Pippen	2.00	5.00
FB23 Michael Jordan	10.00	25.00
FB24 Toni Kukoc	1.25	3.00
FB25 Sherman Douglas	.75	2.00
FB26 Glenn Robinson	1.25	3.00
FB27 Vin Baker	1.00	2.50
FB28 Jeff Hornacek	1.00	2.50
FB29 John Stockton	1.50	4.00
FB30 Karl Malone	1.50	4.00

1996-97 Upper Deck Generation Excitement

Randomly inserted in series one packs at a rate of one in 33, this 30-card set features some of the biggest young stars of the 1990's who willl take the game into the next century. The fronts display color action player images on a background with a head photo of the player on a unique die cut card. Each card is numbered with a "G" prefix.

COMPLETE SET (20)	30.00	80.00
G1 Steve Smith	2.00	5.00
G2 Eric Williams	1.50	4.00
G3 Jason Kidd	4.00	10.00
G4 Antonio McDyess	2.50	6.00
G5 Grant Hill	4.00	10.00
G6 Joe Smith	2.00	5.00
G7 Brent Barry	2.00	5.00
G8 Eddie Jones	2.50	6.00
G9 Vin Baker	2.00	5.00
G10 Kevin Garnett	6.00	15.00
G11 Ed O'Bannon	1.50	4.00
G12 Anfernee Hardaway	4.00	10.00
G13 Jerry Stackhouse	3.00	8.00
G14 Michael Finley	3.00	8.00
G15 Gary Trent	1.50	4.00
G16 Tyus Edney	1.50	4.00
G17 Sean Elliott	2.50	6.00
G18 Shawn Kemp	2.50	6.00
G19 Damon Stoudamire	2.50	6.00
G20 Gheorghe Muresan	1.50	4.00

1996-97 Upper Deck Jordan Greater Heights

Randomly inserted in series one packs at a rate of one in 71, this 10-card set features highlights of Michael Jordan's many trips to the basket. Each card focuses on an area of the game including shooting, dunking, rebounding and defense. Each card is numbered with a "GH" prefix.

COMPLETE SET (10)	40.00	100.00
COMMON JORDAN (1-10)	6.00	15.00

1996-97 Upper Deck Jordan Greater Heights Jumbos

Sold as a box set in retail outlets, this 10-card set is a jumbo parallel to the Jordan Greater Heights inserted in series one 96-97 Upper Deck packs.

COMPLETE SET (10)	10.00	25.00
COMMON CARD (GH1-GH10)	1.25	3.00

1996-97 Upper Deck Jordan's Viewpoints

Randomly inserted in series two packs at a rate of one in 34, this 10-card die cut set focuses on Michael Jordan's preparation for a full game. Some of the card themes include practice, talking to the media and winning. Each card is numbered with a "VP" prefix.

COMPLETE SET (10)	40.00	100.00
COMMON JORDAN (1-10)	6.00	15.00

1996-97 Upper Deck Michael's Viewpoints Jumbos

Available as a set through retail outlets for around $10, this 10-card set is a jumbo parallel to the same set that was issued in 1996-97 Upper Deck focusing on Michael Jordan's preparation for a full game. Measuring 3 1/2" x 5", some of the card themes include practice, talking to the media and winning. These cards do not have the shadow of MJ cut-out nor is their any foil treatment on the card fronts like its standard-sized counterparts. Each card is numbered with a "VP" prefix.

COMPLETE SET (10)	10.00	25.00
COMMON CARD (VP1-VP10)	1.25	3.00

1996-97 Upper Deck Predictor Scoring 1

Randomly inserted in series one packs at a rate of one in 23, this 30-card set featured interactive cards based

on the above-average game output of 30 players in the scoring category. If the player reached the performance goal printed on the front of the card, the card could be traded for a SP-quality replacement. Each card is numbered with a "P" prefix.
COMPLETE SET (20) 20.00 50.00
*TV CEL RED.CARDS: .6X TO 1.5X HI COL.
P1 Mookie Blaylock 30 PTS. W .75 2.00
P2 Dino Radja 35 PTS. L 1.00 2.50
P3 Michael Jordan 35 PTS. W 10.00 25.00
P4 Terrell Brandon 35 PTS. L .75 2.00
P5 Jason Kidd 30 PTS. W 2.00 5.00
P6 Joe Dumars 25 PTS. W 1.25 3.00
P7 Joe Smith 30 PTS. W 1.00 2.50
P8 Hakeem Olajuwon 35 PTS. W 1.50 4.00
P9 Rik Smits 35 PTS. W 1.00 2.50
P10 Brent Barry 25 PTS. L 1.00 2.50
P11 Kurt Thomas 25 PTS. L .75 2.00
P12 Anfernee Hardaway 35 PTS. W 2.00 5.00
P13 Clarence Weatherspoon 35 PTS. L .75 2.00
P14 Clifford Robinson 35 PTS. L .75 2.00
P15 Mitch Richmond 35 PTS. W 1.25 3.00
P16 David Robinson 35 PTS. L 2.00 5.00
P17 Shawn Kemp 35 PTS. L 1.25 3.00
P18 Damon Stoudamire 35 PTS. W 1.25 3.00
P19 Karl Malone 35 PTS. W 1.50 4.00
P20 Bryant Reeves 30 PTS. W .75 2.00

1996-97 Upper Deck Predictor Scoring 2

Randomly inserted in series two packs at a rate of one in 23, this 20-card set featured interactive cards based on the above-average game output of 30 players in the scoring category. If the player reached the performance goal printed on the front of the card, the card could be traded for a SP-quality replacement. Each card is numbered with a "P" prefix.
COMPLETE SET (20) 25.00 60.00
*TV CEL RED.CARDS: .6X TO 1.5X HI COL.
P1 Glen Rice 35 PTS. W 1.25 3.00
P2 Michael Jordan 35 PTS. W 10.00 25.00
P3 Jamal Mashburn 30 PTS. L 1.00 2.50
P4 Antonio McDyess 30 PTS. W 1.25 3.00
P5 Charles Barkley 35 PTS. W 2.00 5.00
P6 Reggie Miller 35 PTS. W 1.50 4.00
P7 Shaquille O'Neal 35 PTS. W 3.00 8.00
P8 Alonzo Mourning 35 PTS. W 1.50 4.00
P9 Vin Baker 30 PTS. W 1.00 2.50
P10 Kevin Garnett 30 PTS. W 3.00 8.00
P11 Kerry Kittles 25 PTS. W .60 1.50
P12 Patrick Ewing 30 PTS. W 1.50 4.00
P13 Anfernee Hardaway 35 PTS. W 2.00 5.00
P14 Allen Iverson 25 PTS. W 3.00 8.00
P15 Robert Horry 30 PTS. L 1.00 2.50
P16 Shawn Kemp 35 PTS. L 1.25 3.00
P17 Marcus Camby 25 PTS. W 1.00 2.50
P18 John Stockton 25 PTS. W 1.50 4.00
P19 Shareef Abdur-Rahim 25 PTS. W 1.25 3.00
P20 Juwan Howard 30 PTS. W 1.00 2.50

1996-97 Upper Deck Rookie Exclusives

Randomly inserted in series two packs at a rate of one in 4, this 20-card set focuses on the 1996-97 rookie class and features quotes from selected NBA stars on each rookie. Card fronts have a basketball textured background. Each card is numbered with a "R" prefix.
COMPLETE SET (20) 15.00 40.00
R1 Allen Iverson 3.00 8.00
R2 John Wallace .60 1.50
R3 Kerry Kittles .60 1.50
R4 Roy Rogers .60 1.50
R5 Marcus Camby 1.00 2.50
R6 Antoine Walker 1.25 3.00
R7 Ray Allen 2.50 6.00
R8 Samaki Walker .60 1.50
R9 Walter McCarty .60 1.50
R10 Kobe Bryant 6.00 15.00
R11 Shareef Abdur-Rahim 1.25 3.00
R12 Dontae' Jones .60 1.50
R13 Todd Fuller .60 1.50
R14 Lorenzen Wright .60 1.50
R15 Stephon Marbury 1.50 4.00
R16 Vitaly Potapenko .60 1.50
R17 Tony Delk .60 1.50
R18 Steve Nash 3.00 8.00
R19 Jermaine O'Neal 1.50 4.00
R20 Erick Dampier .60 1.50
R1P Allen Iverson PROMO 1.00 2.50
R10P Kobe Bryant PROMO 2.00 5.00

1996-97 Upper Deck Rookie of the Year Collection

Randomly inserted in series two packs at a rate of one in 138, this 14-card set spotlight current NBA players who have been named NBA Rookie of the Year. Each card is die cut and features a shot of the player in a rectangle in the middle of the card. Card backs are numbered with a "RC" prefix.
COMPLETE SET (14) 75.00 150.00
RC1 Damon Stoudamire 5.00 12.00
RC2 Grant Hill 8.00 20.00
RC3 Jason Kidd 8.00 20.00
RC4 Chris Webber 6.00 15.00
RC5 Shaquille O'Neal 12.00 30.00
RC6 Larry Johnson 5.00 12.00
RC7 Derrick Coleman 4.00 10.00
RC8 David Robinson 8.00 20.00
RC9 Mitch Richmond 5.00 12.00
RC10 Mark Jackson 5.00 12.00
RC11 Chuck Person 4.00 10.00
RC12 Patrick Ewing 6.00 15.00
RC13 Michael Jordan 40.00 100.00
RC14 Buck Williams 3.00 8.00

1996-97 Upper Deck Smooth Grooves

Randomly inserted in series two packs at a rate of one in 72, the 15-card set focuses on players whose slick moves are reminiscent of the great players of the 60's and 70's. Card fronts are full-bleed and feature a shot of the player "swirled" in the background. Card backs are numbered with a "SG" prefix.
COMPLETE SET (15) 50.00 120.00
SG1 Dennis Rodman 5.00 12.00
SG2 Jason Kidd 4.00 10.00
SG3 Grant Hill 4.00 10.00
SG4 Damon Stoudamire 2.50 6.00
SG5 Shaquille O'Neal 6.00 15.00
SG6 Clyde Drexler 3.00 8.00
SG7 Shareef Abdur-Rahim 3.00 8.00
SG8 Michael Jordan 20.00 50.00
SG9 Alonzo Mourning 3.00 8.00
SG10 Allen Iverson 8.00 20.00
SG11 Vin Baker 2.00 5.00
SG12 Kevin Garnett 6.00 15.00
SG13 Anfernee Hardaway 4.00 10.00
SG14 Jerry Stackhouse 3.00 8.00
SG15 Shawn Kemp 2.50 6.00

1997-98 Upper Deck

The 1997-98 Upper Deck set was issued in two series totaling 360 cards and was distributed in 12-card packs with a suggested retail price of $2.49. The fronts feature color action player photos while the backs carry player information. The set contains the topical subsets: Jams '97 (136-164), Court Perspectives (165-179), Overtime (316-330) and Defining Moments (331-359).
COMPLETE SET (360) 25.00 50.00
COMPLETE SERIES 1 (180) 12.50 25.00
COMPLETE SERIES 2 (180) 12.50 25.00
BLACK POWER AUDIO 1:23 HOBBY
RED POWER AUDIO 1:72 HOBBY
1 Steve Smith .20 .50
2 Christian Laettner .20 .50
3 Alan Henderson .15 .40
4 Dikembe Mutombo .25 .60
5 Dana Barros .15 .40
6 Antoine Walker .25 .60
7 Dee Brown .15 .40
8 Eric Williams .15 .40
9 Muggsy Bogues .20 .50
10 Dell Curry .15 .40
11 Vlade Divac .25 .60
12 Anthony Mason .15 .40
13 Glen Rice .25 .60
14 Jason Caffey .15 .40
15 Steve Kerr .20 .50
16 Toni Kukoc .25 .60
17 Luc Longley .15 .40
18 Michael Jordan 2.00 5.00
19 Terrell Brandon .15 .40
20 Danny Ferry .15 .40
21 Tyrone Hill .15 .40
22 Derek Anderson RC .25 .60
23 Bob Sura .15 .40
24 Shawn Bradley .15 .40
25 Michael Finley .25 .60
26 Ed O'Bannon .15 .40
27 Robert Pack .15 .40
28 Samaki Walker .15 .40
29 LaPhonso Ellis .15 .40
30 Tony Battie RC .30 .75
31 Antonio McDyess .20 .50
32 Bryant Stith .15 .40
33 Randolph Childress .15 .40
34 Grant Hill .40 1.00
35 Lindsey Hunter .15 .40
36 Grant Long .15 .40
37 Theo Ratliff .20 .50
38 B.J. Armstrong .15 .40
39 Adonal Foyle RC .25 .60
40 Mark Price .25 .60
41 Felton Spencer .15 .40
42 Latrell Sprewell .25 .60
43 Clyde Drexler .30 .75
44 Mario Elie .15 .40
45 Hakeem Olajuwon .30 .75
46 Brent Price .15 .40
47 Kevin Willis .15 .40
48 Erick Dampier .15 .40
49 Antonio Davis .15 .40
50 Dale Davis .15 .40
51 Mark Jackson .25 .60
52 Rik Smits .20 .50
53 Brent Barry .20 .50
54 Lamond Murray .15 .40
55 Eric Piatkowski .20 .50
56 Loy Vaught .15 .40
57 Lorenzen Wright .15 .40
58 Kobe Bryant 1.25 3.00
59 Elden Campbell .15 .40
60 Derek Fisher .25 .60
61 Eddie Jones .25 .60
62 Nick Van Exel .20 .50
63 Keith Askins .15 .40
64 Isaac Austin .15 .40
65 P.J. Brown .15 .40
66 Tim Hardaway .25 .60
67 Alonzo Mourning .30 .75
68 Ray Allen .30 .75
69 Vin Baker .20 .50
70 Sherman Douglas .15 .40
71 Armon Gilliam .15 .40
72 Elliot Perry .15 .40
73 Chris Carr .15 .40
74 Tom Gugliotta .15 .40
75 Kevin Garnett .50 1.25
76 Doug West .15 .40
77 Keith Van Horn RC .50 1.25
78 Chris Gatling .15 .40
79 Kendall Gill .15 .40
80 Kerry Kittles .15 .40
81 Jayson Williams .15 .40
82 Chris Childs .15 .40
83 Allan Houston .20 .50
84 Larry Johnson .25 .60
85 Charles Oakley .20 .50
86 John Starks .20 .50
87 Horace Grant .20 .50
88 Anfernee Hardaway .40 1.00
89 Dennis Scott .15 .40
90 Rony Seikaly .20 .50
91 Brian Shaw .15 .40
92 Derrick Coleman .20 .50
93 Allen Iverson .50 1.25
94 Tim Thomas RC .50 1.25
95 Scott Williams .15 .40
96 Cedric Ceballos .15 .40
97 Kevin Johnson .25 .60
98 Loren Meyer .15 .40
99 Steve Nash .50 1.25
100 Wesley Person .15 .40
101 Kenny Anderson .20 .50
102 Jermaine O'Neal .30 .75
103 Isaiah Rider .15 .40
104 Arvydas Sabonis .20 .50
105 Gary Trent .15 .40
106 Mahmoud Abdul-Rauf .15 .40
107 Billy Owens .15 .40
108 Olden Polynice .15 .40
109 Mitch Richmond .25 .60
110 Michael Smith .15 .40
111 Cory Alexander .15 .40
112 Vinny Del Negro .15 .40
113 Carl Herrera .15 .40
114 Tim Duncan RC 1.50 4.00
115 Hersey Hawkins .15 .40
116 Shawn Kemp .25 .60
117 Nate McMillan .15 .40
118 Sam Perkins .15 .40
119 Detlef Schrempf .25 .60
120 Doug Christie .15 .40
121 Popeye Jones .15 .40
122 Carlos Rogers .15 .40
123 Damon Stoudamire .25 .60
124 Adam Keefe .15 .40
125 Chris Morris .15 .40
126 Greg Ostertag .15 .40
127 John Stockton .30 .75
128 Shareef Abdur-Rahim .25 .60
129 George Lynch .15 .40
130 Lee Mayberry .15 .40
131 Anthony Peeler .15 .40
132 Calbert Cheaney .15 .40
133 Tracy Murray .15 .40
134 Rod Strickland .15 .40
135 Chris Webber .25 .60
136 Christian Laettner JAM .20 .50
137 Eric Williams JAM .15 .40
138 Vlade Divac JAM .25 .60
139 Michael Jordan JAM 2.00 5.00
140 Tyrone Hill JAM .15 .40
141 Michael Finley JAM .25 .60
142 Tom Hammonds JAM .15 .40
143 Theo Ratliff JAM .20 .50
144 Latrell Sprewell JAM .25 .60
145 Hakeem Olajuwon JAM .30 .75
146 Reggie Miller JAM .30 .75
147 Rodney Rogers JAM .15 .40
148 Eddie Jones JAM .25 .60
149 Jamal Mashburn JAM .20 .50
150 Glenn Robinson JAM .20 .50
151 Chris Carr JAM .15 .40
152 Kendall Gill JAM .15 .40
153 John Starks JAM .20 .50
154 Anfernee Hardaway JAM .40 1.00
155 Derrick Coleman JAM .20 .50
156 Cedric Ceballos JAM .15 .40
157 Rasheed Wallace JAM .25 .60
158 Corliss Williamson JAM .20 .50
159 Sean Elliott JAM .20 .50
160 Shawn Kemp JAM .20 .50
161 Doug Christie JAM .15 .40
162 Karl Malone JAM .30 .75
163 Bryant Reeves JAM .15 .40
164 Gheorghe Muresan JAM .15 .40
165 Michael Jordan CP 2.00 5.00
166 Dikembe Mutombo CP .25 .60
167 Glen Rice CP .25 .60
168 Mitch Richmond CP .25 .60
169 Juwan Howard CP .20 .50
170 Clyde Drexler CP .30 .75
171 Terrell Brandon CP .15 .40
172 Jerry Stackhouse CP .25 .60
173 Damon Stoudamire CP .25 .60
174 Jayson Williams CP .15 .40
175 P.J. Brown CP .15 .40
176 Anfernee Hardaway CP .40 1.00
177 Vin Baker CP .20 .50
178 LaPhonso Ellis CP .15 .40
179 Shawn Kemp CP .20 .50
180 Checklist .15 .40
181 Mookie Blaylock .15 .40
182 Tyrone Corbin .15 .40
183 Chucky Brown .15 .40
184 Ed Gray RC .25 .60
185 Chauncey Billups RC 1.00 2.50
186 Tyus Edney .15 .40
187 Travis Knight .15 .40
188 Ron Mercer RC .30 .75
189 Walter McCarty .15 .40
190 B.J. Armstrong .15 .40
191 Matt Geiger .15 .40
192 Bobby Phills .15 .40
193 David Wesley .15 .40
194 Keith Booth RC .25 .60
195 Randy Brown .15 .40
196 Ron Harper .20 .50
197 Scottie Pippen .40 1.00
198 Dennis Rodman .50 1.25
199 Zydrunas Ilgauskas .25 .60
200 Brevin Knight RC .25 .60
201 Shawn Kemp .25 .60
202 Vitaly Potapenko .15 .40
203 Wesley Person .15 .40
204 Erick Strickland RC .25 .60
205 A.C. Green .25 .60
206 Khalid Reeves .15 .40
207 Hubert Davis .15 .40
208 Dennis Scott .15 .40
209 Danny Fortson RC .25 .60
210 Bobby Jackson RC .30 .75
211 Eric Williams .15 .40
212 Dean Garrett .15 .40
213 Priest Lauderdale .15 .40
214 Joe Dumars .25 .60
215 Aaron McKie .15 .40
216 Scot Pollard RC .25 .60
217 Brian Williams .15 .40
218 Malik Sealy .15 .40
219 Duane Ferrell .15 .40
220 Erick Dampier .15 .40
221 Todd Fuller .15 .40
222 Donyell Marshall .15 .40
223 Joe Smith .20 .50
224 Charles Barkley .40 1.00
225 Matt Bullard .15 .40
226 Othella Harrington .15 .40
227 Rodrick Rhodes RC .25 .60
228 Eddie Johnson .15 .40
229 Matt Maloney .15 .40
230 Travis Best .15 .40
231 Reggie Miller .30 .75
232 Chris Mullin .25 .60
233 Fred Hoiberg .15 .40
234 Austin Croshere RC .25 .60
235 Keith Closs RC .25 .60
236 Darrick Martin .15 .40
237 Pooh Richardson .15 .40
238 Rodney Rogers .15 .40
239 Maurice Taylor RC .25 .60
240 Robert Horry .20 .50
241 Rick Fox .15 .40
242 Shaquille O'Neal .60 1.50
243 Corie Blount .15 .40
244 Charles Smith RC .25 .60
245 Voshon Lenard .15 .40
246 Eric Murdock .15 .40
247 Dan Majerle .25 .60
248 Terry Mills .15 .40
249 Terrell Brandon .15 .40
250 Tyrone Hill .15 .40
251 Ervin Johnson .15 .40
252 Glenn Robinson .20 .50
253 Terry Porter .15 .40
254 Paul Grant RC .25 .60
255 Stephon Marbury .30 .75
256 Sam Mitchell .15 .40
257 Cherokee Parks .15 .40
258 Sam Cassell .20 .50
259 David Benoit .15 .40
260 Kevin Edwards .15 .40
261 Don MacLean .15 .40
262 Patrick Ewing .30 .75
263 Herb Williams .15 .40
264 John Starks .20 .50
265 Chris Mills .15 .40
266 Chris Dudley .15 .40
267 Darrell Armstrong .15 .40
268 Nick Anderson .15 .40
269 Derek Harper .20 .50
270 Johnny Taylor RC .25 .60
271 Mark Price .25 .60
272 Clarence Weatherspoon .15 .40
273 Jerry Stackhouse .25 .60
274 Eric Montross .15 .40
275 Anthony Parker RC .25 .60
276 Antonio McDyess .20 .50
277 Clifford Robinson .15 .40
278 Jason Kidd .40 1.00
279 Danny Manning .20 .50
280 Rex Chapman .15 .40
281 Stacey Augmon .15 .40
282 Kelvin Cato RC .25 .60
283 Brian Grant .15 .40
284 Rasheed Wallace .25 .60
285 Lawrence Funderburke RC .25 .60
286 Anthony Johnson .25 .60
287 Tariq Abdul-Wahad RC .25 .60
288 Corliss Williamson .15 .40
289 Sean Elliott .20 .50
290 Avery Johnson .20 .50
291 David Robinson .40 1.00
292 Will Perdue .15 .40
293 Greg Anthony .15 .40
294 Jim McIlvaine .15 .40
295 Dale Ellis .15 .40
296 Gary Payton .25 .60
297 Aaron Williams .15 .40
298 Marcus Camby .25 .60
299 John Wallace .15 .40
300 Tracy McGrady RC 1.25 3.00
301 Walt Williams .15 .40
302 Shandon Anderson .15 .40
303 Antoine Carr .15 .40
304 Jeff Hornacek .20 .50
305 Karl Malone .30 .75
306 Bryon Russell .15 .40
307 Jacque Vaughn RC .25 .60
308 Antonio Daniels RC .25 .60
309 Blue Edwards .15 .40
310 Bryant Reeves .15 .40
311 Otis Thorpe .15 .40
312 Harvey Grant .15 .40
313 Terry Davis .15 .40
314 Juwan Howard .20 .50
315 Gheorghe Muresan .15 .40
316 Michael Jordan OT 2.00 5.00
317 Allen Iverson OT .50 1.25
318 Karl Malone OT .30 .75
319 Glen Rice OT .25 .60
320 Dikembe Mutombo OT .25 .60
321 Grant Hill OT .40 1.00
322 Hakeem Olajuwon OT .30 .75
323 Stephon Marbury OT .30 .75
324 Anfernee Hardaway OT .40 1.00
325 Shawn Kemp OT .25 .60
326 Mitch Richmond OT .25 .60
327 Damon Stoudamire OT .25 .60
328 Kevin Garnett OT .50 1.25
329 Shareef Abdur-Rahim OT .25 .60
330 Damon Stoudamire OT .25 .60
331 Dikembe Mutombo .20 .50
Christian Laettner
Mookie Blaylock
Steve Smith
332 Antoine Walker .20 .50
Ron Mercer
Chauncey Billups
Dana Barros
333 Glen Rice .20 .50
Larry Johnson
Alonzo Mourning
Vlade Divac
Anthony Mason
334 Michael Jordan .40 1.00
Scottie Pippen
Dennis Rodman
Toni Kukoc
335 Shawn Kemp .20 .50
Brevin Knight
Terrell Brandon
Mark Price
336 A.C. Green .20 .50
Michael Finley
Derek Harper
Detlef Schrempf
337 Bobby Jackson .25 .60
Tony Battie
Dikembe Mutombo
LaPhonso Ellis
338 Joe Dumars .25 .60
Grant Hill
Dennis Rodman
Lindsey Hunter
339 Joe Smith .25 .60
Chris Mullin
Chris Webber
Tim Hardaway
340 Hakeem Olajuwon .30 .75
Charles Barkley
Clyde Drexler
Sam Cassell
Otis Thorpe
341 Chris Mullin .20 .50
Reggie Miller
Antonio Davis
Dale Davis
Rik Smits
342 Brent Barry .20 .50
Loy Vaught
Danny Manning
Ron Harper
343 Shaquille O'Neal .40 1.00
Kobe Bryant
Eddie Jones
Nick Van Exel
344 Tim Hardaway .25 .60
Alonzo Mourning
P.J. Brown
Rony Seikaly
Glen Rice
345 Terrell Brandon .20 .50
Glenn Robinson
Vin Baker
Terry Cummings
346 Kevin Garnett .20 .50
Stephon Marbury
Tom Gugliotta
Sam Mitchell
Isaiah Rider
347 Keith Van Horn .20 .50
Jayson Williams
Buck Williams
Kenny Anderson
348 Patrick Ewing .20 .50
Larry Johnson
John Starks
Charles Oakley
349 Anfernee Hardaway .25 .60
Rony Seikaly
Shaquille O'Neal
Nick Anderson
350 Allen Iverson .20 .50
Jerry Stackhouse
Charles Barkley
Clarence Weatherspoon
351 Antonio McDyess .20 .50
Jason Kidd
Charles Barkley
Kevin Johnson
352 Kenny Anderson .20 .50
Isaiah Rider
Clyde Drexler
Terry Porter
353 Mitch Richmond .20 .50
Corliss Williamson
Lionel Simmons
Billy Owens
354 Tim Duncan .40 1.00
David Robinson
Sean Elliott
Dennis Rodman
355 Gary Payton .25 .60
Vin Baker
Nate McMillan
Shawn Kemp
356 Damon Stoudamire .40 1.00
Tracy McGrady
Marcus Camby
Walt Williams
357 John Stockton .25 .60
Karl Malone
Jeff Hornacek
358 Bryant Reeves .20 .50
Shareef Abdur-Rahim
Antonio Daniels
Greg Anthony
359 Chris Webber .20 .50
Juwan Howard
Gheorghe Muresan
Rod Strickland
360 Checklist .15 .40
NNO Michael Jordan Red Audio 10.00 25.00
NNO Michael Jordan Black Audio 4.00 10.00

1997-98 Upper Deck Game Dated Memorable Moments

Randomly inserted in series one packs at the rate of one in 1,500, this 30-card set features color photos of memorable moments of the NBA season printed on stunning Light F/X cards. The date of the game and the significance of the moment is found in a bar at the bottom.
*STARS: 12.5X TO 30X BASE CARD HI
18 Michael Jordan 175.00 350.00
61 Eddie Jones 10.00 25.00

1997-98 Upper Deck AIRlines

Randomly inserted in series two packs at a rate of one in 230 packs, this 12-card die cut set chronicles each year in Michael Jordan's career. Card backs are numbered with an "AL" prefix.
COMPLETE SET (12) 250.00 450.00
COMMON JORDAN (AL1-AL12) 15.00 40.00

1997-98 Upper Deck Game Jerseys

Randomly inserted in both series packs at the rate of one in 2,500, this 22-card set features color player images on a jersey print background with an actual piece of an NBA game worn jersey embedded in the card. Series two packs also contained a special Michael Jordan autographed Game Jersey, which was hand-numbered to 23.
GJ1 Charles Barkley 175.00 350.00
GJ2 Clyde Drexler 100.00 250.00
GJ3 Kevin Garnett 150.00 300.00
GJ4 Anfernee Hardaway HOME 200.00 400.00
GJ5 Grant Hill HOME 125.00 250.00
GJ6 Allen Iverson 200.00 400.00
GJ7 Kerry Kittles 25.00 60.00
GJ8 Toni Kukoc 75.00 150.00
GJ9 Reggie Miller 100.00 200.00
GJ10 Hakeem Olajuwon 100.00 200.00
GJ11 Glen Rice 50.00 120.00
GJ12 David Robinson 75.00 150.00
GJ13 Michael Jordan 1500.00 2500.00
GJ14 Alonzo Mourning 50.00 125.00
GJ15 Tim Hardaway 50.00 100.00
GJ16 Marcus Camby 100.00 200.00
GJ17 Antoine Walker 40.00 70.00
GJ18 Kevin Johnson 50.00 120.00
GJ19 Glenn Robinson 25.00 60.00
GJ20 Patrick Ewing 50.00 120.00
GJ21 Anfernee Hardaway AWAY 250.00 500.00
GJ22 Grant Hill AWAY 125.00 250.00

1997-98 Upper Deck Great Eight

Randomly inserted into series two packs, this 8-card set features eight of the best veterans in the NBA. The card backs are serially numbered to 800 and carry a "G" prefix.
G1 Charles Barkley 15.00 40.00
G2 Clyde Drexler 12.00 30.00
G3 Joe Dumars 10.00 25.00
G4 Patrick Ewing 12.00 30.00
G5 Michael Jordan 80.00 200.00
G6 Karl Malone 12.00 30.00
G7 Hakeem Olajuwon 12.00 30.00
G8 John Stockton 12.00 30.00

1997-98 Upper Deck High Dimensions

Randomly inserted in series one packs, this 30-card set is parallel to the Diamond Dimensions insert set. Only 2,000 of each card was produced and are sequentially numbered.
D1 Anfernee Hardaway 8.00 20.00
D2 Gary Payton 5.00 12.00
D3 Marcus Camby 5.00 12.00
D4 Charles Barkley 8.00 20.00
D5 Jason Kidd 8.00 20.00
D6 Alonzo Mourning 6.00 15.00
D7 Kenny Anderson 4.00 10.00
D8 Kobe Bryant 25.00 60.00
D9 Dennis Rodman 10.00 25.00
D10 Kerry Kittles 3.00 8.00
D11 Dikembe Mutombo 5.00 12.00
D12 Shaquille O'Neal 12.00 30.00
D13 Glenn Robinson 4.00 10.00
D14 Tony Delk 3.00 8.00
D15 Larry Johnson 5.00 12.00
D16 Brent Barry 4.00 10.00
D17 Scottie Pippen 8.00 20.00
D18 Shareef Abdur-Rahim 5.00 12.00
D19 Sean Elliott 5.00 12.00
D20 Damon Stoudamire 5.00 12.00
D21 Kevin Garnett 10.00 25.00
D22 Bob Sura 3.00 8.00
D23 Michael Jordan 40.00 100.00
D24 Latrell Sprewell 5.00 12.00
D25 Karl Malone 6.00 15.00
D26 Antonio McDyess 4.00 10.00
D27 Allen Iverson 10.00 25.00
D28 Dale Davis 3.00 8.00
D29 Antoine Walker 5.00 12.00
D30 Chris Webber 5.00 12.00

1997-98 Upper Deck Diamond Dimensions

Randomly inserted in first series packs, this 30-card parallel of the High Dimension set features color images of the most versatile players of the NBA printed on die cut cards. Only 100 of each card was produced and are sequentially numbered.
*STARS: 4X TO 10X HIGH DIMEN. HI
D1 Anfernee Hardaway 125.00 250.00
D9 Dennis Rodman 175.00 350.00
D12 Shaquille O'Neal 200.00 400.00
D23 Michael Jordan 700.00 1200.00
D24 Latrell Sprewell 60.00 150.00
D25 Karl Malone 75.00 200.00

1997-98 Upper Deck Jordan Air Time

Randomly inserted in series one packs at a rate of one in 12, this 10-card set features color action photos of Michael Jordan printed on double-front style cards. The set is comprised of three different fronts, or "Departures," and three different backs, or "Arrivals." The first nine cards combine to create a Jordan "Flight" to the basket. The tenth card features front and back photos and is tougher to find than the first nine, thus commanding a premium.
COMPLETE SET (10) 50.00 120.00
COMMON JORDAN (AT1-AT9) 4.00 10.00
COMMON JORDAN (AT10) 25.00 60.00

1997-98 Upper Deck Records Collection

Randomly inserted into series two packs at a rate of one in 23, this 30-card set features a special look at the outstanding achievements of great NBA performers. The card fronts are similar to a record with a black etched background. Card backs carry a "RC" prefix.
COMPLETE SET (30) 40.00 100.00
RC1 Dikembe Mutombo 1.50 4.00
RC2 Dana Barros 1.00 2.50
RC3 Glen Rice 1.50 4.00
RC4 Dennis Rodman 3.00 8.00
RC5 Shawn Kemp 1.50 4.00
RC6 A.C. Green 1.50 4.00
RC7 LaPhonso Ellis 1.00 2.50
RC8 Grant Hill 2.50 6.00
RC9 Joe Smith 1.25 3.00
RC10 Charles Barkley 2.50 6.00
RC11 Reggie Miller 2.00 5.00
RC12 Loy Vaught 1.00 2.50
RC13 Shaquille O'Neal 4.00 10.00
RC14 Tim Hardaway 1.50 4.00
RC15 Glenn Robinson 1.25 3.00
RC16 Stephon Marbury 2.00 5.00
RC17 Sam Cassell 1.25 3.00
RC18 Patrick Ewing 2.00 5.00
RC19 Anfernee Hardaway 2.50 6.00
RC20 Allen Iverson 3.00 8.00
RC21 Kevin Johnson 1.50 4.00
RC22 Kenny Anderson 1.50 4.00
RC23 Mitch Richmond 1.50 4.00
RC24 David Robinson 2.50 6.00
RC25 Gary Payton 1.50 4.00
RC26 Damon Stoudamire 1.50 4.00
RC27 John Stockton 2.00 5.00
RC28 Bryant Reeves 1.00 2.50
RC29 Chris Webber 1.50 4.00
RC30 Michael Jordan 12.00 30.00

1997-98 Upper Deck Rookie Discovery 1

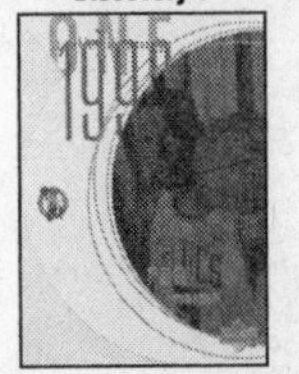

Randomly inserted into packs at a rate of one in four, this 15-card set focuses on the 1997 Rookie Class, and their thoughts and secrets on the game. Card backs are numbered with a "R" prefix.
COMPLETE SET (15) 6.00 15.00
*RD2: 2.5X TO 6X HI COLUMN
RD2: SER.2 STATED ODDS 1:108
R1 Tim Duncan 2.00 5.00
R2 Keith Van Horn .60 1.50
R3 Chauncey Billups 1.25 3.00
R4 Antonio Daniels .30 .75
R5 Tony Battie .40 1.00

Card	Low	High
R6 Ron Mercer	.40	1.00
R7 Tim Thomas	.60	1.50
R8 Adonal Foyle	.30	.75
R9 Tracy McGrady	1.50	4.00
R10 Danny Fortson	.30	.75
R11 Tariq Abdul-Wahad	.30	.75
R12 Austin Croshere	.30	.75
R13 Derek Anderson	.30	.75
R14 Maurice Taylor	.30	.75
R15 Kelvin Cato	.30	.75

1997-98 Upper Deck Teammates

Randomly inserted in series one packs at the rate of one in four, this 60-card set features color action photos of players who are the top tandems for each team in the league printed on die-cut, embossed cards.. When the teammates are placed together, the cards spell out the team name.

Card	Low	High
COMPLETE SET (60)	25.00	60.00
T1 Mookie Blaylock	.30	.75
T2 Steve Smith	.40	1.00
T3 Antoine Walker	.50	1.25
T4 Dana Barros	.30	.75
T5 Anthony Mason	.30	.75
T6 Glen Rice	.50	1.25
T7 Michael Jordan	4.00	10.00
T8 Scottie Pippen	.75	2.00
T9 Terrell Brandon	.30	.75
T10 Tyrone Hill	.30	.75
T11 Shawn Bradley	.30	.75
T12 Robert Pack	.30	.75
T13 LaPhonso Ellis	.30	.75
T14 Antonio McDyess	.40	1.00
T15 Grant Hill	.75	2.00
T16 Lindsey Hunter	.30	.75
T17 Latrell Sprewell	.50	1.25
T18 Joe Smith	.40	1.00
T19 Hakeem Olajuwon	.60	1.50
T20 Charles Barkley	.75	2.00
T21 Mark Jackson	.50	1.25
T22 Reggie Miller	.60	1.50
T23 Brent Barry	.40	1.00
T24 Loy Vaught	.30	.75
T25 Shaquille O'Neal	1.25	3.00
T26 Nick Van Exel	.40	1.00
T27 Tim Hardaway	.50	1.25
T28 Alonzo Mourning	.60	1.50
T29 Vin Baker	.40	1.00
T30 Glenn Robinson	.40	1.00
T31 Kevin Garnett	1.00	2.50
T32 Stephon Marbury	.60	1.50
T33 Kendall Gill	.30	.75
T34 Kerry Kittles	.30	.75
T35 Patrick Ewing	.60	1.50
T36 John Starks	.40	1.00
T37 Horace Grant	.40	1.00
T38 Anfernee Hardaway	.75	2.00
T39 Allen Iverson	1.00	2.50
T40 Jerry Stackhouse	.50	1.25
T41 Jason Kidd	.75	2.00
T42 Kevin Johnson	.50	1.25
T43 Kenny Anderson	.40	1.00
T44 Isaiah Rider	.30	.75
T45 Billy Owens	.30	.75
T46 Mitch Richmond	.50	1.25
T47 Sean Elliott	.50	1.25
T48 David Robinson	.75	2.00
T49 Gary Payton	.50	1.25
T50 Shawn Kemp	.50	1.25
T51 Marcus Camby	.50	1.25
T52 Damon Stoudamire	.50	1.25
T53 John Stockton	.60	1.50
T54 Karl Malone	.60	1.50
T55 Shareef Abdur-Rahim	.50	1.25
T56 Bryant Reeves	.30	.75
T57 Juwan Howard	.40	1.00
T58 Chris Webber	.50	1.25
T59 Michael Jordan	4.00	10.00
T60 Anfernee Hardaway	.75	2.00

1997-98 Upper Deck Ultimates

Randomly inserted in series one packs at the rate of one in 23, this 30-card set features color action player images on Light F/X cards with some of the player's abilities printed across the background.

Card	Low	High
COMPLETE SET (30)	50.00	100.00
U1 Michael Jordan	12.00	30.00
U2 Grant Hill	2.50	6.00
U3 Charles Barkley	2.50	6.00
U4 Tom Gugliotta	1.00	2.50
U5 Dennis Rodman	3.00	8.00
U6 Reggie Miller	2.00	5.00
U7 Jason Kidd	2.50	6.00
U8 Loy Vaught	1.00	2.50
U9 Mookie Blaylock	1.00	2.50
U10 Tim Hardaway	1.50	4.00
U11 Juwan Howard	1.25	3.00
U12 Shawn Kemp	1.50	4.00
U13 Mitch Richmond	1.50	4.00
U14 Patrick Ewing	2.00	5.00
U15 Marcus Camby	1.50	4.00
U16 Bryant Stith	1.00	2.50
U17 Bryant Reeves	1.00	2.50
U18 Joe Smith	1.25	3.00
U19 Jerry Stackhouse	1.50	4.00
U20 Arvydas Sabonis	1.25	3.00
U21 John Stockton	2.00	5.00
U22 Eddie Jones	1.50	4.00
U23 Anfernee Hardaway	2.50	6.00
U24 Ray Allen	2.00	5.00
U25 Terrell Brandon	1.00	2.50
U26 David Robinson	2.50	6.00
U27 Anthony Mason	1.00	2.50
U28 Robert Pack	1.00	2.50
U29 Dana Barros	1.00	2.50
U30 Kendall Gill	1.00	2.50

1998-99 Upper Deck

The 1998 Upper Deck series one product contained 175 cards featuring two inserted subsets: Heart and Soul (1:4) and To the Net (1:9). The ten card packs carried a suggested retail price of $3.00. The fronts feature color game-action photography. The series two set (also known as MJ Access) features 180 cards with two subsets - Michael Jordan (1:4) and Rookies (1:4). A special card commemorating Michael Jordan's retirement was inserted at one in 11 packs. That card is numbered "UDX".

Card	Low	High
COMPLETE SET (355)	60.00	150.00
COMPLETE SERIES 1 (175)	30.00	75.00
COMPLETE SERIES 2 (180)	30.00	75.00
1 Mookie Blaylock	.15	.40
2 Ed Gray	.15	.40
3 Dikembe Mutombo	.25	.60
4 Steve Smith	.20	.50
5 Dikembe Mutombo	.40	1.00
Steve Smith HS		
6 Kenny Anderson	.20	.50
7 Dana Barros	.15	.40
8 Travis Knight	.15	.40
9 Walter McCarty	.15	.40
10 Ron Mercer	.20	.50
11 Greg Minor	.15	.40
12 Antoine Walker	.40	1.00
Ron Mercer HS		
13 B.J. Armstrong	.15	.40
14 David Wesley	.15	.40
15 Anthony Mason	.15	.40
16 Glen Rice	.25	.60
17 J.R. Reid	.15	.40
18 Bobby Phills	.15	.40
19 Glen Rice	.40	1.00
Anthony Mason HS		
20 Ron Harper	.20	.50
21 Toni Kukoc	.25	.60
22 Scottie Pippen	.40	1.00
23 Michael Jordan	2.00	5.00
24 Dennis Rodman	.50	1.25
25 Michael Jordan	3.00	8.00
Scottie Pippen HS		
26 Michael Jordan	4.00	10.00
Michael Jordan HS		
27 Shawn Kemp	.25	.60
28 Zydrunas Ilgauskas	.25	.60
29 Cedric Henderson	.15	.40
30 Vitaly Potapenko	.15	.40
31 Derek Anderson	.15	.40
32 Shawn Kemp	.40	1.00
Zydrunas Ilgauskas HS		
33 Shawn Bradley	.15	.40
34 Khalid Reeves	.15	.40
35 Robert Pack	.15	.40
36 Michael Finley	.25	.60
37 Erick Strickland	.15	.40
38 Michael Finley	.40	1.00
Shawn Bradley HS		
39 Bryant Stith	.15	.40
40 Dean Garrett	.15	.40
41 Eric Williams	.15	.40
42 Bobby Jackson	.20	.50
43 Danny Fortson	.15	.40
44 LaPhonso Ellis	.25	.60
Bryant Stith HS		
45 Grant Hill	.40	1.00
46 Lindsey Hunter	.15	.40
47 Brian Williams	.15	.40
48 Scot Pollard	.15	.40
49 Grant Hill	.60	1.50
Brian Williams HS		
50 Donyell Marshall	.15	.40
51 Tony Delk	.15	.40
52 Erick Dampier	.15	.40
53 Felton Spencer	.15	.40
54 Bimbo Coles	.15	.40
55 Muggsy Bogues	.20	.50
56 Donyell Marshall	.30	.75
Muggsy Bogues HS		
57 Charles Barkley	.40	1.00
58 Brent Price	.15	.40
59 Hakeem Olajuwon	.30	.75
60 Rodrick Rhodes	.15	.40
61 Charles Barkley	.60	1.50
Hakeem Olajuwon HS		
62 Dale Davis	.15	.40
63 Antonio Davis	.15	.40
64 Chris Mullin	.25	.60
65 Jalen Rose	.20	.50
66 Reggie Miller	.30	.75
67 Mark Jackson	.25	.60
68 Reggie Miller	.50	1.25
Mark Jackson HS		
69 Rodney Rogers	.15	.40
70 Lamond Murray	.15	.40
71 Eric Piatkowski	.20	.50
72 Lorenzen Wright	.15	.40
73 Maurice Taylor	.15	.40
74 Maurice Taylor	.25	.60
Lamond Murray HS		
75 Kobe Bryant	1.25	3.00
76 Shaquille O'Neal	.60	1.50
77 Derek Fisher	.25	.60
78 Elden Campbell	.15	.40
79 Corie Blount	.15	.40
80 Shaquille O'Neal	2.00	5.00
Kobe Bryant HS		
81 Jamal Mashburn	.20	.50
82 Alonzo Mourning	.30	.75
83 Tim Hardaway	.25	.60
84 Voshon Lenard	.15	.40
85 Alonzo Mourning	.50	1.25
Tim Hardaway HS		
86 Ray Allen	.30	.75
87 Terrell Brandon	.15	.40
88 Elliot Perry	.15	.40
89 Ervin Johnson	.15	.40
90 Ray Allen	.50	1.25
Glenn Robinson HS		
91 Micheal Williams	.15	.40
92 Anthony Peeler	.15	.40
93 Chris Carr	.15	.40
94 Kevin Garnett	.50	1.25
95 Kevin Garnett	.75	2.00
Stephon Marbury HS		
96 Keith Van Horn	.25	.60
97 Kerry Kittles	.15	.40
98 Kendall Gill	.15	.40
99 Sam Cassell	.20	.50
100 Chris Gatling	.15	.40
101 Keith Van Horn	.40	1.00
Sam Cassell HS		
102 Patrick Ewing	.30	.75
103 John Starks	.20	.50
104 Allan Houston	.20	.50
105 Chris Mills	.15	.40
106 Chris Childs	.15	.40
107 Charlie Ward	.15	.40
108 Patrick Ewing	.50	1.25
John Starks HS		
109 Anfernee Hardaway	.40	1.00
110 Horace Grant	.20	.50
111 Nick Anderson	.15	.40
112 Johnny Taylor	.15	.40
113 Anfernee Hardaway	.60	1.50
Horace Grant HS		
114 Allen Iverson	.50	1.25
115 Scott Williams	.15	.40
116 Tim Thomas	.25	.60
117 Brian Shaw	.15	.40
118 Anthony Parker	.15	.40
119 Allen Iverson	.75	2.00
Tim Thomas HS		
120 Jason Kidd	.40	1.00
121 Rex Chapman	.15	.40
122 Danny Manning	.20	.50
123 Jason Kidd	.60	1.50
Danny Manning HS		
124 Rasheed Wallace	.25	.60
125 Walt Williams	.15	.40
126 Kelvin Cato	.15	.40
127 Arvydas Sabonis	.20	.50
128 Brian Grant	.15	.40
129 Rasheed Wallace	.40	1.00
Isaiah Rider HS		
130 Tariq Abdul-Wahad	.15	.40
131 Corliss Williamson	.15	.40
132 Olden Polynice	.15	.40
133 Chris Robinson	.15	.40
134 Tariq Abdul-Wahad	.25	.60
Olden Polynice HS		
135 Tim Duncan	.50	1.25
136 Avery Johnson	.20	.50
137 David Robinson	.40	1.00
138 Monty Williams	.15	.40
139 Tim Duncan	.75	2.00
David Robinson HS		
140 Vin Baker	.20	.50
141 Hersey Hawkins	.15	.40
142 Detlef Schrempf	.25	.60
143 Jim McIlvaine	.15	.40
144 Gary Payton	.40	1.00
Vin Baker HS		
145 Chauncey Billups	.30	.75
146 Tracy McGrady	.40	1.00
147 John Wallace	.15	.40
148 Doug Christie	.15	.40
149 Dee Brown	.15	.40
150 Tracy McGrady	.60	1.50
Chauncey Billups HS		
151 Karl Malone	.30	.75
152 John Stockton	.30	.75
153 Adam Keefe	.15	.40
154 Howard Eisley	.15	.40
155 Karl Malone	.50	1.25
John Stockton HS		
156 Bryant Reeves	.15	.40
157 Lee Mayberry	.15	.40
158 Michael Smith	.15	.40
159 Shareef Abdur-Rahim	.40	1.00
Bryant Reeves HS		
160 Juwan Howard	.20	.50
161 Calbert Cheaney	.15	.40
162 Tracy Murray	.15	.40
163 Juwan Howard	.30	.75
Calbert Cheaney HS		
164 Shaquille O'Neal TN	1.25	3.00
165 Maurice Taylor TN	.30	.75
166 Stephon Marbury TN	.60	1.50
167 Tracy McGrady TN	.75	2.00
168 Antoine Walker TN	.50	1.25
169 Michael Jordan TN	4.00	10.00
170 Keith Van Horn TN	.50	1.25
171 Shareef Abdur-Rahim TN	.50	1.25
172 Kobe Bryant TN	2.50	6.00
173 Gary Payton TN	.50	1.25
174 Michael Jordan CL	.40	1.00
175 Michael Jordan CL	.40	1.00
176 Kevin Johnson	.25	.60
177 Glenn Robinson	.20	.50
178 Antoine Walker	.25	.60
179 Jerry Stackhouse	.25	.60
180 Mark Price	.25	.60
181 Stephon Marbury	.30	.75
182 Shareef Abdur-Rahim	.25	.60
183 Wesley Person	.15	.40
184 Keith Booth	.15	.40
185 Sean Elliott	.25	.60
186 Alan Henderson	.15	.40
187 Bryon Russell	.15	.40
188 Jermaine O'Neal	.25	.60
189 Steve Nash	.40	1.00
190 Eldridge Recasner	.15	.40
191 Damon Stoudamire	.25	.60
192 Dell Curry	.15	.40
193 Michael Stewart	.15	.40
194 Bruce Bowen RC	.30	.75
195 Steve Kerr	.20	.50
196 Dale Ellis	.15	.40
197 Shandon Anderson	.15	.40
198 Larry Johnson	.25	.60
199 Chris Webber	.25	.60
200 Matt Geiger	.15	.40
201 Chris Anstey	.15	.40
202 Loy Vaught	.15	.40
203 Aaron McKie	.15	.40
204 A.C. Green	.25	.60
205 Bo Outlaw	.15	.40
206 Antonio McDyess	.20	.50
207 Priest Lauderdale	.15	.40
208 Greg Ostertag	.15	.40
209 Dan Majerle	.25	.60
210 Johnny Newman	.15	.40
211 Tyrone Corbin	.15	.40
212 Pervis Ellison	.15	.40
213 Shawnelle Scott	.15	.40
214 Travis Best	.15	.40
215 Stacey Augmon	.20	.50
216 Brevin Knight	.15	.40
217 Jerome Williams	.15	.40
218 Terry Mills	.15	.40
219 Matt Maloney	.15	.40
220 Dennis Scott	.15	.40
221 John Thomas	.15	.40
222 Nick Van Exel	.20	.50
223 Duane Ferrell	.15	.40
224 Chris Whitney	.15	.40
225 Luc Longley	.15	.40
226 Robert Horry	.20	.50
227 Clifford Robinson	.15	.40
228 Samaki Walker	.15	.40
229 Derrick McKey	.15	.40
230A Michael Jordan	1.25	3.00
230B Michael Jordan	1.25	3.00
230C Michael Jordan	1.25	3.00
230D Michael Jordan	1.25	3.00
230E Michael Jordan	1.25	3.00
230F Michael Jordan	1.25	3.00
230G Michael Jordan	1.25	3.00
230H Michael Jordan	1.25	3.00
230I Michael Jordan	1.25	3.00
230J Michael Jordan	1.25	3.00
230K Michael Jordan	1.25	3.00
230L Michael Jordan	1.25	3.00
230M Michael Jordan	1.25	3.00
230N Michael Jordan	1.25	3.00
230O Michael Jordan	1.25	3.00
230P Michael Jordan	1.25	3.00
230Q Michael Jordan	1.25	3.00
230R Michael Jordan	1.25	3.00
230S Michael Jordan	1.25	3.00
230T Michael Jordan	1.25	3.00
230U Michael Jordan	1.25	3.00
230V Michael Jordan	1.25	3.00
230W Michael Jordan	1.25	3.00
231 Armon Gilliam	.15	.40
232 Andrew DeClercq	.15	.40
233 Stojko Vrankovic	.15	.40
234 Jayson Williams	.15	.40
235 Vinny Del Negro	.15	.40
236 Theo Ratliff	.20	.50
237 Othella Harrington	.15	.40
238 Mitch Richmond	.25	.60
239 Vlade Divac	.25	.60
240 Duane Causwell	.15	.40
241 Todd Fuller	.15	.40
242 Tom Gugliotta	.15	.40
243 LaPhonso Ellis	.15	.40
244 Brian Evans	.15	.40
245 Jason Caffey	.15	.40
246 Pooh Richardson	.15	.40
247 George Lynch	.15	.40
248 Bill Wennington	.15	.40
249 Rik Smits	.20	.50
250 Kevin Willis	.15	.40
251 Mario Elie	.15	.40
252 Austin Croshere	.15	.40
253 Sharone Wright	.15	.40
254 Danny Ferry	.15	.40
255 Jacque Vaughn	.15	.40
256 Adonal Foyle	.15	.40
257 Billy Owens	.15	.40
258 Randy Brown	.15	.40
259 Joe Smith	.20	.50
260 Joe Dumars	.25	.60
261 Sean Rooks	.15	.40
262 Eric Montross	.15	.40
263 Hubert Davis	.15	.40
264 Gary Payton	.25	.60
265 Tyrone Hill	.15	.40
266 John Crotty	.15	.40
267 P.J. Brown	.15	.40
268 Michael Cage	.15	.40
269 Scott Burrell	.15	.40
270 Marcus Camby	.20	.50
271 Rod Strickland	.15	.40
272 Jim Jackson	.15	.40
273 Corey Beck	.15	.40
274 James Robinson	.15	.40
275 Cedric Ceballos	.15	.40
276 Charles Oakley	.20	.50
277 Anthony Johnson	.15	.40
278 Bob Sura	.15	.40
279 Isaiah Rider	.15	.40
280 Jeff Hornacek	.20	.50
281 Rony Seikaly	.25	.60
282 Charles Smith	.15	.40
283 Eddie Jones	.25	.60
284 Lucious Harris	.15	.40
285 Andrew Lang	.15	.40
286 Terry Cummings	.25	.60
287 Keith Closs	.15	.40
288 Chris Anstey	.15	.40
289 Clarence Weatherspoon	.15	.40
290 Michael Jordan H99	2.00	5.00
291 Shawn Kemp H99	.25	.60
292 Tracy McGrady H99	.40	1.00
293 Glen Rice H99	.25	.60
294 David Robinson H99	.40	1.00
295 Antonio McDyess H99	.20	.50
296 Vin Baker H99	.20	.50
297 Juwan Howard H99	.20	.50
298 Ron Mercer H99	.20	.50
299 Michael Finley H99	.25	.60
300 Scottie Pippen H99	.40	1.00
301 Tim Thomas H99	.25	.60
302 Rasheed Wallace H99	.25	.60
303 Alonzo Mourning H99	.30	.75
304 Dikembe Mutombo H99	.25	.60
305 Derek Anderson H99	.15	.40
306 Ray Allen H99	.30	.75
307 Patrick Ewing H99	.30	.75
308 Sean Elliott H99	.25	.60
309 Shaquille O'Neal H99	.60	1.50
310 Michael Jordan CL	.40	1.00
311 Michael Jordan CL	.40	1.00
312 Michael Olowokandi RC	1.00	2.50
313 Mike Bibby RC	2.00	5.00
314 Raef LaFrentz RC	1.00	2.50
315 Antawn Jamison RC	2.00	5.00
316 Vince Carter RC	4.00	10.00
317 Robert Traylor RC	.75	2.00
318 Jason Williams RC	2.00	5.00
319 Larry Hughes RC	1.50	4.00
320 Dirk Nowitzki RC	6.00	15.00
321 Paul Pierce RC	4.00	10.00
322 Bonzi Wells RC	.75	2.00
323 Michael Doleac RC	.75	2.00
324 Keon Clark RC	.75	2.00
325 Michael Dickerson RC	.75	2.00
326 Matt Harpring RC	1.00	2.50
327 Bryce Drew RC	.75	2.00
328 Pat Garrity RC	.75	2.00
329 Roshown McLeod RC	.75	2.00
330 Ricky Davis RC	1.25	3.00
331 Peja Stojakovic RC	2.00	5.00
332 Felipe Lopez RC	.75	2.00
333 Al Harrington RC	1.25	3.00
UDX Michael Jordan Retires	1.00	2.50
P123 Michael Jordan PROMO	2.00	5.00

1998-99 Upper Deck Bronze

Randomly inserted in hobby packs, this 355-card set parallels the basic set, but the foil borders on the card front are silver, rather than gold. The cards are serially numbered to 100 on the back. To ascertain values on individual cards, please refer to the multiplier in the header, coupled with the value of the base card.

Card	Low	High
COMMON MJ (230A-230W)	25.00	60.00
*STARS: 20X TO 50X BASE CARD HI		
*HS SUBSET: 12X TO 30X BASE HI		
*TN SUBSET: 10X TO 25X BASE HI		
*RCs: 3X TO 8X BASE HI		
24 Dennis Rodman	30.00	80.00
26 Michael Jordan	125.00	300.00
Michael Jordan HS		
174 Michael Jordan CL	30.00	80.00
175 Michael Jordan CL	30.00	80.00
310 Michael Jordan CL	30.00	80.00
311 Michael Jordan CL	30.00	80.00
316 Vince Carter	80.00	160.00
320 Dirk Nowitzki	60.00	150.00

1998-99 Upper Deck Gold

Randomly inserted in hobby packs, this 355-card set parallels the base set. The only difference is the borders are gold rather than silver. The cards are serially numbered to one on the back.

1998-99 Upper Deck AeroDynamics

Randomly inserted in series one packs at a rate of seven, this 30-set features the hottest athletes who's talents are best displayed above the rim. The card backs are numbered with an "A" prefix.

Card	Low	High
COMPLETE SET (30)	15.00	40.00
*BRONZE: 1.25X TO 3X HI COLUMN		
STATED PRINT RUN 2000 SERIAL #'d SETS		
*SILVER: 10X TO 25X HI		
STATED PRINT RUN 100 SERIAL #'d SETS		
A1 Michael Jordan	5.00	12.00
A2 Shawn Kemp	.60	1.50
A3 Anfernee Hardaway	1.00	2.50
A4 Tracy McGrady	1.00	2.50
A5 Glen Rice	.60	1.50
A6 Maurice Taylor	.40	1.00
A7 Kevin Garnett	1.25	3.00
A8 Jason Kidd	1.00	2.50
A9 Grant Hill	1.00	2.50
A10 Kendall Gill	.40	1.00
A11 Hakeem Olajuwon	.75	2.00
A12 Mookie Blaylock	.40	1.00
A13 Toni Kukoc	.60	1.50
A14 Kobe Bryant	3.00	8.00
A15 Corliss Williamson	.40	1.00
A16 Ray Allen	.75	2.00
A17 Vin Baker	.50	1.25
A18 Reggie Miller	.75	2.00
A19 Allan Houston	.50	1.25
A20 Shareef Abdur-Rahim	.60	1.50
A21 Tim Duncan	1.25	3.00
A22 Michael Finley	.60	1.50
A23 Damon Stoudamire	.60	1.50
A24 Juwan Howard	.50	1.25
A25 Antoine Walker	.60	1.50
A26 Donyell Marshall	.40	1.00
A27 Allen Iverson	1.25	3.00
A28 Karl Malone	.75	2.00
A29 Bobby Jackson	.50	1.25
A30 Tim Hardaway	.60	1.50

1998-99 Upper Deck AeroDynamics Gold

Randomly inserted in series one packs, this 30-card set parallels the AeroDynamics insert. The cards feature gold die cuts and are serially numbered to 25.

Card	Low	High
*STARS: 30X TO 80X BASE INSERT		
A1 Michael Jordan	900.00	1500.00
A14 Kobe Bryant	500.00	900.00

1998-99 Upper Deck Forces

Randomly inserted in series one packs at a rate of one in 23, this 30-card set features high-impact players who dominate the court. The card backs are numbered with a "F" prefix.

Card	Low	High
COMPLETE SET (30)	30.00	80.00
*BRONZE: 1X TO 2.5X HI COLUMN		
STATED PRINT RUN 1000 SERIAL #'d SETS		
*GOLD: 15X TO 40X HI		
STATED PRINT RUN 25 SER.#'d SETS		
*SILVER: 6X TO 15X HI		
STATED PRINT RUN 50 SERIAL #'d SETS		
F1 Michael Jordan	10.00	25.00
F2 Shareef Abdur-Rahim	1.25	3.00
F3 Shaquille O'Neal	3.00	8.00
F4 Gary Payton	1.25	3.00
F5 Allen Iverson	2.50	6.00
F6 Allan Houston	1.00	2.50
F7 LaPhonso Ellis	.75	2.00
F8 Kevin Garnett	2.50	6.00
F9 Chauncey Billups	1.50	4.00
F10 Tim Hardaway	1.25	3.00
F11 Reggie Miller	1.50	4.00
F12 Glen Rice	1.25	3.00
F13 Damon Stoudamire	1.25	3.00
F14 Lamond Murray	.75	2.00
F15 Shawn Kemp	1.25	3.00
F16 Steve Smith	1.00	2.50
F17 Tim Duncan	2.50	6.00
F18 Hakeem Olajuwon	1.50	4.00
F19 Karl Malone	1.50	4.00
F20 Donyell Marshall	.75	2.00
F21 Anfernee Hardaway	2.00	5.00
F22 Grant Hill	2.00	5.00
F23 Antoine Walker	1.25	3.00
F24 Toni Kukoc	1.25	3.00
F25 Corliss Williamson	.75	2.00
F26 Glenn Robinson	1.00	2.50
F27 Keith Van Horn	1.25	3.00
F28 Jason Kidd	2.00	5.00
F29 Juwan Howard	1.00	2.50
F30 Michael Finley	1.25	3.00

1998-99 Upper Deck Game Jerseys

Randomly inserted into packs, this 49-card set features cards with pieces cut from actual game-worn jerseys. The 49-card set is divided into several tiers: GJ1-GJ10 and GJ21-30 were inserted in both hobby and retail packs at a rate of one in 2500. GJ11-GJ20 and GJ31-40 were inserted in hobby packs only at a rate of one in 288. Rookie Game Jerseys were also added in the series two product (GJ41-50) and inserted in both hobby and retail packs at one in 2500. Card GJ38 was not produced.

Card	Low	High
GJ1 Glen Rice	25.00	60.00
GJ2 Shawn Kemp	50.00	125.00
GJ3 Reggie Miller	25.00	60.00
GJ4 Shaquille O'Neal	60.00	150.00
GJ5 Ray Allen	40.00	100.00
GJ6 Keith Van Horn	10.00	25.00
GJ7 Allen Iverson	40.00	100.00
GJ8 David Robinson	25.00	60.00
GJ9 Karl Malone	25.00	60.00
GJ10 Shareef Abdur-Rahim	12.50	30.00
GJ11 Grant Hill	40.00	100.00
GJ12 Hakeem Olajuwon	20.00	50.00
GJ13 Kevin Garnett	40.00	100.00
GJ14 Jayson Williams	10.00	25.00
GJ15 Tim Duncan	40.00	100.00
GJ16 Gary Payton	25.00	60.00
GJ17 John Stockton	20.00	50.00
GJ18 Bryant Reeves	10.00	25.00
GJ19 Kobe Bryant	125.00	300.00
GJ20 Michael Jordan	400.00	800.00
GJ21 Kobe Bryant	150.00	350.00
GJ22 Grant Hill	40.00	100.00
GJ23 Anfernee Hardaway	100.00	200.00
GJ24 Tim Thomas	25.00	50.00
GJ25 Hakeem Olajuwon	20.00	50.00
GJ26 Damon Stoudamire	30.00	80.00
GJ27 Gary Payton	25.00	60.00
GJ28 Jason Kidd	30.00	80.00
GJ29 Reggie Miller	25.00	60.00
GJ30 Kevin Garnett	40.00	100.00
GJ31 Tim Duncan	40.00	100.00
GJ32 Keith Van Horn	10.00	25.00
GJ33 Stephon Marbury	15.00	40.00
GJ34 Shaquille O'Neal	40.00	100.00
GJ35 Allen Iverson	40.00	100.00
GJ36 Antoine Walker	12.00	30.00
GJ37 Karl Malone	25.00	60.00
GJ39 Shareef Abdur-Rahim	12.50	30.00
GJ40 David Robinson	25.00	60.00
GJ41 Corey Benjamin	10.00	25.00
GJ42 Mike Bibby	30.00	80.00
GJ43 Vince Carter	300.00	600.00
GJ44 Michael Doleac	10.00	25.00
GJ45 Larry Hughes	25.00	60.00
GJ46 Antawn Jamison	30.00	60.00
GJ47 Raef LaFrentz	10.00	25.00
GJ48 Robert Traylor	15.00	40.00
GJ49 Bonzi Wells	15.00	40.00
GJ50 Jason Williams	40.00	100.00

1998-99 Upper Deck Intensity

Randomly inserted in series one packs at a rate of one in 12, this 30-card set features the NBA's most emotionally intense players. The card backs are numbered with an "I" prefix.

Card	Low	High
COMPLETE SET (30)	15.00	40.00
*BRONZE: 1X TO 2.5X HI COLUMN		
STATED PRINT RUN 1500 SERIAL #'d SETS		
*GOLD: 20X TO 50X HI		
STATED PRINT RUN 25 SER.#'d SETS		
*SILVER: 6X TO 15X HI		
STATED PRINT RUN 75 SERIAL #'d SETS		
I1 Michael Jordan	8.00	20.00
I2 Tracy Murray	.60	1.50
I3 Ron Mercer	.75	2.00
I4 Terrell Brandon	.60	1.50
I5 Brevin Knight	.60	1.50
I6 Rasheed Wallace	1.00	2.50
I7 Sam Cassell	.75	2.00
I8 Erick Dampier	.60	1.50
I9 LaPhonso Ellis	.60	1.50
I10 Tim Thomas	1.00	2.50
I11 Anfernee Hardaway	1.50	4.00
I12 Tariq Abdul-Wahad	.60	1.50
I13 Lorenzen Wright	.60	1.50
I14 Bryant Reeves	.60	1.50
I15 Charles Barkley	1.50	4.00
I16 Chauncey Billups	1.25	3.00
I17 John Starks	.75	2.00
I18 Jerry Stackhouse	1.00	2.50
I19 Vlade Divac	1.00	2.50
I20 Detlef Schrempf	1.00	2.50
I21 John Stockton	1.25	3.00
I22 Nick Anderson	.60	1.50
I23 Alonzo Mourning	1.25	3.00
I24 Dikembe Mutombo	1.00	2.50
I25 Jalen Rose	.75	2.00
I26 Robert Pack	.60	1.50
I27 Antonio McDyess	.75	2.00
I28 Eddie Jones	1.00	2.50
I29 Stephon Marbury	1.25	3.00
I30 David Robinson	1.50	4.00

1998-99 Upper Deck MJ23

Randomly inserted in series two packs at a rate of one in 23, this 30-card set focuses on Michael Jordan and is a tribute to his mastery of the game. Card backs feature a "M" prefix.

Card	Low	High
COMMON CARD (M1-M30)	3.00	8.00
*BRONZE: .5X TO 1.25X HI COLUMN		
BRONZE PRINT RUN 2300 SETS		
*SILVER: 12X TO 30X HI COLUMN		
SILVER PRINT RUN 23 SETS		
UNPRICED GOLD PARALLEL SERIAL #'d TO 1		

1998-99 Upper Deck Michael Jordan Game Jersey Autographs

This six-card set was randomly inserted into packs of series one SPx Finite, Michael Jordan - Living Legend, series one Upper Deck, series two Upper Deck, Ovation, and MJx. Each product had 23 of these cards available. The cards feature an actual swatch from a Michael Jordan game worn red Bulls jersey. Each card is autographed by Jordan and hand numbered to 23.

Card	Low	High
COMMON CARD	3000.00	4500.00

1998-99 Upper Deck Next Wave

Randomly inserted in series two packs at a rate of one in 11, this 30-card set takes a look at some of the likely candidates who may carry the NBA's torch into the next millennium. Card backs carry a "NW" prefix.

Card	Low	High
*BRONZE: 1X TO 2.5X HI COLUMN		
STATED PRINT RUN 1500 SERIAL #'d SETS		
*GOLD: 6X TO 15X HI		
STATED PRINT RUN 75 SERIAL #'d SETS		
*SILVER: 4X TO 10X HI		
STATED PRINT RUN 200 SERIAL #'d SETS		
NW1 Kobe Bryant	5.00	12.00
NW2 John Wallace	.60	1.50
NW3 Kerry Kittles	.60	1.50
NW4 Tim Thomas	1.00	2.50
NW5 Maurice Taylor	.60	1.50
NW6 Antonio McDyess	.75	2.00
NW7 Jermaine O'Neal	1.00	2.50
NW8 Zydrunas Ilgauskas	1.00	2.50
NW9 Danny Fortson	.60	1.50
NW10 Tim Duncan	2.00	5.00
NW11 Derek Anderson	.60	1.50
NW12 Ron Mercer	.75	2.00
NW13 Joe Smith	.75	2.00
NW14 Eddie Jones	1.00	2.50
NW15 Rodrick Rhodes	.60	1.50
NW16 Kevin Garnett	2.00	5.00
NW17 Ed Gray	.60	1.50
NW18 Bobby Jackson	.75	2.00
NW19 Allan Houston	.75	2.00
NW20 Chauncey Billups	1.25	3.00
NW21 Keith Booth	.60	1.50
NW22 Brevin Knight	.60	1.50
NW23 Othella Harrington	.60	1.50
NW24 Keith Van Horn	1.00	2.50
NW25 Michael Finley	1.00	2.50
NW26 Tracy McGrady	1.50	4.00
NW27 Derek Fisher	1.00	2.50
NW28 Ray Allen	1.25	3.00
NW29 Anthony Johnson	.60	1.50
NW30 Vin Baker	.75	2.00

1998-99 Upper Deck Super Powers

Randomly inserted in series two packs at one in five, this 30-card set focuses on NBA players who are considered franchise players. Card backs carry a "PS" prefix.

Card	Low	High
COMPLETE SET (30)	15.00	40.00
*BRONZE: 2X TO 5X HI COLUMN		
STATED PRINT RUN 1000 SERIAL #'d SETS		
*GOLD: 15X TO 40X HI		

STATED PRINT RUN 50 SERIAL #'d SETS
*SILVER: 10X TO 25X HI
STATED PRINT RUN 100 SERIAL #'d SETS
PS1 Dikembe Mutombo .60 1.50
PS2 Ron Mercer .50 1.25
PS3 Glen Rice .60 1.50
PS4 Scottie Pippen 1.00 2.50
PS5 Shawn Kemp .60 1.50
PS6 Michael Finley .60 1.50
PS7 Bobby Jackson .50 1.25
PS8 Grant Hill 1.00 2.50
PS9 Jim Jackson .40 1.00
PS10 Hakeem Olajuwon .75 2.00
PS11 Reggie Miller .75 2.00
PS12 Maurice Taylor .40 1.00
PS13 Kobe Bryant 3.00 8.00
PS14 Tim Hardaway .60 1.50
PS15 Ray Allen .75 2.00
PS16 Stephon Marbury .75 2.00
PS17 Keith Van Horn .60 1.50
PS18 Allan Houston .50 1.25
PS19 Anfernee Hardaway 1.00 2.50
PS20 Allen Iverson 1.25 3.00
PS21 Jason Kidd 1.00 2.50
PS22 Damon Stoudamire .60 1.50
PS23 Corliss Williamson .40 1.00
PS24 Tim Duncan 1.25 3.00
PS25 Gary Payton .60 1.50
PS26 Tracy McGrady 1.00 2.50
PS27 Karl Malone .75 2.00
PS28 Shareef Abdur-Rahim .60 1.50
PS29 Juwan Howard .50 1.25
PS30 Michael Jordan 5.00 12.00

1999-00 Upper Deck

The 1999-00 Upper Deck set was released in two series, with both containing 180 cards. Each pack contained 10 cards and carried a suggested retail price of $2.99. The base set was made up of 266 regular cards and three subsets: Air of Greatness (20 cards focusing on Michael Jordan), Rookie Class, which features rookie cards inserted one in four series one packs and Rookie Action, which features first year players and rookies inserted one in four series two packs. Also availble in packs, but unpriced, were five redemption cards for the Michael Jordan Master Collection set.

COMPLETE SET (360) 60.00 150.00
COMPLETE SERIES 1 (180) 40.00 100.00
COMPLETE SERIES 2 (180) 20.00 50.00
COMP.SERIES 1 w/o RC (155) 15.00 40.00
COMP.SERIES 2 w/o SP (133) 4.00 10.00
1 Roshown McLeod .20 .50
2 Dikembe Mutombo .30 .75
3 Alan Henderson .20 .50
4 LaPhonso Ellis .20 .50
5 Chris Crawford .20 .50
6 Kenny Anderson .25 .60
7 Antoine Walker .30 .75
8 Paul Pierce .50 1.25
9 Vitaly Potapenko .20 .50
10 Dana Barros .20 .50
11 Elden Campbell .20 .50
12 Eddie Jones .30 .75
13 David Wesley .20 .50
14 Derrick Coleman .25 .60
15 Ricky Davis .30 .75
16 Corey Benjamin .20 .50
17 Randy Brown .20 .50
18 Kornel David RC .30 .75
19 Toni Kukoc .30 .75
20 Keith Booth .20 .50
21 Shawn Kemp .20 .50
22 Wesley Person .20 .50
23 Brevin Knight .20 .50
24 Bob Sura .20 .50
25 Zydrunas Ilgauskas .25 .60
26 Michael Finley .30 .75
27 Shawn Bradley .20 .50
28 Dirk Nowitzki .60 1.50
29 Steve Nash .50 1.25
30 Antonio McDyess .25 .60
31 Nick Van Exel .25 .60
32 Chauncey Billups .30 .75
33 Bryant Stith .20 .50
34 Raef LaFrentz .25 .60
35 Grant Hill .40 1.00
36 Lindsey Hunter .20 .50
37 Bison Dele .20 .50
38 Jerry Stackhouse .30 .75
39 John Starks .30 .75
40 Antawn Jamison .30 .75
41 Erick Dampier .20 .50
42 Jason Caffey .20 .50
43 Hakeem Olajuwon .40 1.00
44 Scottie Pippen .50 1.25
45 Cuttino Mobley .25 .60
46 Charles Barkley .50 1.25
47 Bryce Drew .20 .50
48 Reggie Miller .30 .75
49 Jalen Rose .25 .60
50 Mark Jackson .30 .75
51 Dale Davis .20 .50
52 Chris Mullin .30 .75
53 Maurice Taylor .20 .50
54 Tyrone Nesby RC .20 .50
55 Michael Olowokandi .20 .50
56 Eric Piatkowski .25 .60
57 Troy Hudson RC .30 .75
58 Kobe Bryant 1.50 4.00
59 Shaquille O'Neal .75 2.00
60 Glen Rice .30 .75
61 Robert Horry .30 .75
62 Tim Hardaway .30 .75
63 Alonzo Mourning .40 1.00
64 P.J. Brown .20 .50
65 Dan Majerle .30 .75
66 Ray Allen .30 .75
67 Glenn Robinson .25 .60
68 Sam Cassell .25 .60
69 Robert Traylor .20 .50
70 Kevin Garnett .60 1.50
71 Sam Mitchell .20 .50
72 Dean Garrett .20 .50
73 Bobby Jackson .25 .60
74 Radoslav Nesterovic RC .30 .75
75 Keith Van Horn .25 .60
76 Stephon Marbury .25 .60
77 Kendall Gill .20 .50
78 Scott Burrell .20 .50
79 Patrick Ewing .40 1.00
80 Allan Houston .25 .60
81 Latrell Sprewell .30 .75
82 Larry Johnson .30 .75
83 Marcus Camby .25 .60
84 Darrell Armstrong .20 .50
85 Derek Strong .20 .50
86 Matt Harpring .25 .60
87 Michael Doleac .20 .50
88 Bo Outlaw .20 .50
89 Allen Iverson .60 1.50
90 Theo Ratliff .25 .60
91 Larry Hughes .25 .60
92 Eric Snow .25 .60
93 Jason Kidd .50 1.25
94 Clifford Robinson .20 .50
95 Tom Gugliotta .20 .50
96 Luc Longley .20 .50
97 Rasheed Wallace .30 .75
98 Arvydas Sabonis .25 .60
99 Damon Stoudamire .25 .60
100 Brian Grant .20 .50
101 Jason Williams .40 1.00
102 Vlade Divac .30 .75
103 Peja Stojakovic .30 .75
104 Lawrence Funderburke .20 .50
105 Tim Duncan .60 1.50
106 Sean Elliott .30 .75
107 David Robinson .50 1.25
108 Mario Elie .20 .50
109 Avery Johnson .25 .60
110 Gary Payton .30 .75
111 Vin Baker .30 .75
112 Rashard Lewis .30 .75
113 Jelani McCoy .20 .50
114 Vladimir Stepania .20 .50
115 Vince Carter .60 1.50
116 Doug Christie .25 .60
117 Kevin Willis .20 .50
118 Dee Brown .20 .50
119 John Thomas .20 .50
120 Karl Malone .40 1.00
121 John Stockton .40 1.00
122 Howard Eisley .20 .50
123 Bryon Russell .20 .50
124 Greg Ostertag .20 .50
125 Shareef Abdur-Rahim .25 .60
126 Mike Bibby .30 .75
127 Felipe Lopez .20 .50
128 Cherokee Parks .20 .50
129 Juwan Howard .25 .60
130 Rod Strickland .20 .50
131 Chris Whitney .20 .50
132 Tracy Murray .20 .50
133 Jahidi White .20 .50
134 Michael Jordan AIR 1.25 3.00
135 Michael Jordan AIR 1.25 3.00
136 Michael Jordan AIR 1.25 3.00
137 Michael Jordan AIR 1.25 3.00
138 Michael Jordan AIR 1.25 3.00
139 Michael Jordan AIR 1.25 3.00
140 Michael Jordan AIR 1.25 3.00
141 Michael Jordan AIR 1.25 3.00
142 Michael Jordan AIR 1.25 3.00
143 Michael Jordan AIR 1.25 3.00
144 Michael Jordan AIR 1.25 3.00
145 Michael Jordan AIR 1.25 3.00
146 Michael Jordan AIR 1.25 3.00
147 Michael Jordan AIR 1.25 3.00
148 Michael Jordan AIR 1.25 3.00
149 Michael Jordan AIR 1.25 3.00
150 Michael Jordan AIR 1.25 3.00
151 Michael Jordan AIR 1.25 3.00
152 Michael Jordan AIR 1.25 3.00
153 Michael Jordan AIR 1.25 3.00
154 Michael Jordan CL .75 2.00
155 Michael Jordan CL .75 2.00
156 Elton Brand RC 1.50 4.00
157 Steve Francis RC 1.50 4.00
158 Baron Davis RC 2.00 5.00
159 Lamar Odom RC 2.00 5.00
160 Jonathan Bender RC .60 1.50
161 Wally Szczerbiak RC 1.25 3.00
162 Richard Hamilton RC 1.50 4.00
163 Andre Miller RC 1.50 4.00
164 Shawn Marion RC 1.50 4.00
165 Jason Terry RC 1.50 4.00
166 Trajan Langdon RC .60 1.50
167 Kenny Thomas RC .60 1.50
168 Corey Maggette RC 1.25 3.00
169 William Avery RC .60 1.50
170 Jumaine Jones RC .60 1.50
171 Ron Artest RC 1.50 4.00
172 Cal Bowdler RC .60 1.50
173 James Posey RC .60 1.50
174 Quincy Lewis RC .60 1.50
175 Vonteego Cummings RC .60 1.50
176 Jeff Foster RC .60 1.50
177 Dion Glover RC .60 1.50
178 Devean George RC .60 1.50
179 Evan Eschmeyer RC .60 1.50
180 Tim James RC .60 1.50
181 Jim Jackson .25 .60
182 Isaiah Rider .20 .50
183 Lorenzen Wright .20 .50
184 Bimbo Coles .20 .50
185 Anthony Johnson .20 .50
186 Calbert Cheaney .20 .50
187 Pervis Ellison .20 .50
188 Walter McCarty .20 .50
189 Eric Williams .20 .50
190 Tony Battie .25 .60
191 Anthony Mason .20 .50
192 Bobby Phills .20 .50
193 Todd Fuller .20 .50
194 Brad Miller .30 .75
195 Eldridge Recasner .20 .50
196 Chris Anstey .20 .50
197 Fred Hoiberg .20 .50
198 Hersey Hawkins .20 .50
199 Will Perdue .20 .50
200 Mark Bryant .20 .50
201 Lamond Murray .20 .50
202 Cedric Henderson .20 .50
203 Andrew DeClercq .20 .50
204 Danny Ferry .20 .50
205 Erick Strickland .20 .50
206 Cedric Ceballos .20 .50
207 Hubert Davis .20 .50
208 Robert Pack .20 .50
209 Gary Trent .20 .50
210 Ron Mercer .25 .60
211 George McCloud .20 .50
212 Roy Rogers .20 .50
213 Keon Clark .20 .50
214 Terry Mills .20 .50
215 Michael Curry .20 .50
216 Christian Laettner .25 .60
217 Jerome Williams .20 .50
218 Loy Vaught .20 .50
219 Jud Buechler .20 .50
220 Mookie Blaylock .20 .50
221 Terry Cummings .20 .50
222 Donyell Marshall .20 .50
223 Chris Mills .20 .50
224 Adonal Foyle .20 .50
225 Shandon Anderson .20 .50
226 Kelvin Cato .20 .50
227 Walt Williams .20 .50
228 Al Harrington .30 .75
229 Rik Smits .20 .50
230 Derrick McKey .20 .50
231 Sam Perkins .20 .50
232 Austin Croshere .30 .75
233 Derek Anderson .25 .60
234 Keith Closs .20 .50
235 Eric Murdock .20 .50
236 Brian Skinner .20 .50
237 Charles Jones .20 .50
238 Ron Harper .20 .50
239 Derek Fisher .30 .75
240 Rick Fox .20 .50
241 A.C. Green .30 .75
242 Jamal Mashburn .25 .60
243 Mark Strickland .20 .50
244 Rex Walters .20 .50
245 Clarence Weatherspoon .20 .50
246 Ervin Johnson .20 .50
247 J.R. Reid .20 .50
248 Dale Ellis .20 .50
249 Danny Manning .20 .50
250 Tim Thomas .25 .60
251 Terrell Brandon .20 .50
252 Malik Sealy .20 .50
253 Joe Smith .25 .60
254 Anthony Peeler .20 .50
255 Jayson Williams .20 .50
256 Jamie Feick RC .30 .75
257 Kerry Kittles .20 .50
258 Johnny Newman .20 .50
259 Chris Childs .20 .50
260 Kurt Thomas .25 .60
261 Charlie Ward .20 .50
262 Chris Dudley .20 .50
263 John Wallace .20 .50
264 Tariq Abdul-Wahad .20 .50
265 John Amaechi RC .30 .75
266 Chris Gatling .20 .50
267 Monty Williams .20 .50
268 Ben Wallace .30 .75
269 George Lynch .20 .50
270 Tyrone Hill .20 .50
271 Billy Owens .20 .50
272 Anfernee Hardaway .50 1.25
273 Rex Chapman .20 .50
274 Oliver Miller .20 .50
275 Rodney Rogers .20 .50
276 Randy Livingston .20 .50
277 Scottie Pippen .50 1.25
278 Detlef Schrempf .25 .60
279 Steve Smith .25 .60
280 Jermaine O'Neal .30 .75
281 Bonzi Wells .30 .75
282 Chris Webber .30 .75
283 Nick Anderson .20 .50
284 Darrick Martin .20 .50
285 Corliss Williamson .20 .50
286 Samaki Walker .20 .50
287 Terry Porter .20 .50
288 Malik Rose .20 .50
289 Jaren Jackson .20 .50
290 Antonio Daniels .20 .50
291 Steve Kerr .25 .60
292 Brent Barry .25 .60
293 Horace Grant .25 .60
294 Vernon Maxwell .20 .50
295 Ruben Patterson .25 .60
296 Shammond Williams .20 .50
297 Antonio Davis .20 .50
298 Tracy McGrady .50 1.25
299 Dell Curry .20 .50
300 Charles Oakley .25 .60
301 Muggsy Bogues .25 .60
302 Jeff Hornacek .25 .60
303 Adam Keefe .20 .50
304 Olden Polynice .20 .50
305 Doug West .20 .50
306 Michael Dickerson .20 .50
307 Othella Harrington .20 .50
308 Bryant Reeves .20 .50
309 Brent Price .20 .50
310 Mitch Richmond .30 .75
311 Aaron Williams .20 .50
312 Isaac Austin .20 .50
313 Michael Smith .20 .50
314 Michael Jordan CL .75 2.00
315 Kevin Garnett CL .30 .75
316 Elton Brand .75 2.00
317 Steve Francis .75 2.00
318 Baron Davis 1.00 2.50
319 Lamar Odom 1.00 2.50
320 Jonathan Bender .30 .75
321 Wally Szczerbiak .60 1.50
322 Richard Hamilton .75 2.00
323 Andre Miller .75 2.00
324 Shawn Marion .75 2.00
325 Jason Terry .75 2.00
326 Trajan Langdon .30 .75
327 Aleksandar Radojevic RC .60 1.50
328 Corey Maggette .60 1.50
329 William Avery .30 .75
330 Ron Artest .75 2.00
331 Cal Bowdler .30 .75
332 James Posey .30 .75
333 Quincy Lewis .30 .75
334 Dion Glover .30 .75
335 Jeff Foster .30 .75
336 Kenny Thomas .30 .75
337 Devean George .30 .75
338 Tim James .30 .75
339 Vonteego Cummings .30 .75
340 Jumaine Jones .30 .75
341 Scott Padgett RC .60 1.50
342 John Celestand RC .60 1.50
343 Adrian Griffin RC .60 1.50
344 Michael Ruffin RC .60 1.50
345 Chris Herren RC .60 1.50
346 Evan Eschmeyer .60 1.50
347 Eddie Robinson RC .60 1.50
348 Obinna Ekezie RC .60 1.50
349 Laron Profit RC .60 1.50
350 Jermaine Jackson RC .60 1.50
351 Lazaro Borrell RC .60 1.50
352 Chucky Atkins RC .60 1.50
353 Ryan Robertson RC .60 1.50
354 Todd MacCulloch RC .60 1.50
355 Rafer Alston RC .75 2.00
356 Mirsad Turkcan RC .60 1.50
357 Anthony Carter RC .60 1.50
358 Ryan Bowen RC .60 1.50
359 Rodney Buford RC .60 1.50
360 Tim Young RC .60 1.50

1999-00 Upper Deck Bronze

Randomly inserted in packs, this 360-card set parallels the base set featuring bronze foil. The card are also serially numbered to 100. To ascertain values on individual cards, please refer to the multiplier in the header below, coupled with the value of the base card.

COMMON MJ (134-153) 30.00 80.00
*STARS: 12.5X TO 30X BASE CARD HI
*RCs: 2.5X TO 6X BASE HI
*SER.2 DRAFT PICKS: 5X TO 12X BASE HI

1999-00 Upper Deck Gold

Randomly inserted in packs, this 360-card set parallels the base set featuring gold foil. The card are also serially numbered to 1. To ascertain values on individual cards, please refer to the multiplier in the header below, coupled with the value of the base card.

1999-00 Upper Deck BioGraphics

Randomly inserted in series two packs at one in four, this 30-card set focuses on NBA stars and their on the court achievements. Card backs carry a "B" prefix.

COMPLETE SET (30) 10.00 25.00
*LEVEL 1: 6X TO 15X VALUE
LEVEL 1: PRINT RUN 100 SERIAL #'d SETS
*LEVEL 2: 15X TO 40X VALUE
LEVEL 2: PRINT RUN 25 SERIAL #'d SETS
B1 Antawn Jamison .60 1.50
B2 Mike Bibby .60 1.50
B3 Antoine Walker .60 1.50
B4 Ray Allen .60 1.50
B5 Anfernee Hardaway 1.00 2.50
B6 Hakeem Olajuwon .75 2.00
B7 Jason Williams .75 2.00
B8 Keith Van Horn .50 1.25
B9 Jason Kidd 1.00 2.50
B10 Reggie Miller .60 1.50
B11 Eddie Jones .60 1.50
B12 Jim Jackson .50 1.25
B13 Jerry Stackhouse .60 1.50
B14 Tim Duncan 1.25 3.00
B15 Kevin Garnett 1.25 3.00
B16 Mitch Richmond .60 1.50
B17 Steve Smith .40 1.00
B18 Charles Barkley 1.00 2.50
B19 Glen Rice .60 1.50
B20 Paul Pierce 1.00 2.50
B21 Alonzo Mourning .75 2.00
B22 Karl Malone .75 2.00
B23 Stephon Marbury .50 1.25
B24 Chris Webber .60 1.50
B25 Brent Barry .60 1.50
B26 Shawn Kemp .60 1.50
B27 John Stockton .75 2.00
B28 Ron Mercer .50 1.25
B29 Tim Hardaway .60 1.50
B30 Allan Houston .50 1.25

1999-00 Upper Deck Cool Air

Randomly inserted in packs at one in 72, this eight-card set focuses on Michael Jordan's "cool" moves on the court. Card backs carry a "MJ" prefix.

COMPLETE SET (8) 35.00 70.00
COMMON CARD (MJ1-MJ8) 4.00 10.00
*LEVEL 1: 2.5X TO 6X HI
LEVEL 1: PRINT RUN 100 SERIAL #'d SETS
UNPRICED LEVEL 2 SERIAL #'d TO 1

1999-00 Upper Deck Julius Erving Heroes

Randomly inserted in series one packs at one in 23, this 10-card set relives the career of Dr. J. Card backs feature a "H" prefix. The cards are numbered 46-55, which is a continuation of the Basketball Heroes series from earlier Upper Deck releases.

COMMON CARD (H46-H55) 2.00 5.00
*LEVEL 1: 2X TO 5X HI COLUMN
LEVEL 1: PRINT RUN 100 SERIAL #'d SETS

1999-00 Upper Deck Future Charge

Randomly inserted in series one packs at one in eight, this 15-card set highlights the current youth movement in the NBA. Card backs carry a "FC" prefix.

COMPLETE SET (15) 4.00 10.00
*LEVEL 1: 6X TO 15X HI COLUMN
LEVEL 1: PRINT RUN 100 SERIAL #'d SETS
*LEVEL 2: 15X TO 40X HI
LEVEL 2: PRINT RUN 25 SERIAL #'d SETS
FC1 Antawn Jamison .50 1.25
FC2 Mike Bibby .50 1.25
FC3 Antoine Walker .50 1.25
FC4 Baron Davis 1.00 2.50
FC5 Jason Terry .75 2.00
FC6 Andre Miller .75 2.00
FC7 Ray Allen .50 1.25
FC8 Wally Szczerbiak .60 1.50
FC9 Raef LaFrentz .40 1.00
FC10 William Avery .30 .75
FC11 Jason Williams .60 1.50
FC12 Michael Olowokandi .30 .75
FC13 Stephon Marbury .40 1.00
FC14 Quincy Lewis .30 .75
FC15 Shawn Marion .75 2.00

1999-00 Upper Deck Game Jerseys

These cards were inserted at different ratios in both series packs. Cards GJ1-GJ10 and GJ21-GJ42 were inserted at 1:2500 in both hobby and retail packs. Cards GJ11-GJ20 were inserted at one in 287 hobby packs and cards GJ43-GJ64 were inserted at one in 288 hobby packs. Also inserted were Game Jersey autographs. For the hobby and retail market, Charles Barkley (numbered to four), Kevin Garnett (numbered to 21), Michael Jordan (numbered to 23) and Kobe Bryant (numbered to 8) were inserted. For the hobby only market, Karl Malone (numbered to 32) and Baron Davis (numbered to 1) was inserted. Card backs carry a "GJ" prefix.

*CENT.CLUB: .6X TO 1.5X HI COLUMN
CENT.CLUB: PRINT RUN 100 SERIAL #'d SETS
GJ1 Jason Kidd 35.00 70.00
GJ2 Shaquille O'Neal 30.00 80.00
GJ3 Tim Duncan 30.00 80.00
GJ4 Charles Barkley 75.00 150.00
GJ5 Kevin Garnett 25.00 60.00
GJ5A Kevin Garnett AU/21 250.00 500.00
GJ6 John Stockton 25.00 60.00
GJ7 Keith Van Horn 8.00 20.00
GJ8 Hakeem Olajuwon 15.00 40.00
GJ9 Paul Pierce 20.00 40.00
GJ10 Michael Jordan 250.00 500.00
GJ10A Michael Jordan AU/23 2500.00 4000.00
GJ11 Kobe Bryant 60.00 150.00
GJ12 Scottie Pippen 20.00 50.00
GJ13 Grant Hill 20.00 50.00
GJ14 Gary Payton 15.00 40.00
GJ15 Vince Carter 50.00 120.00
GJ16 Reggie Miller 25.00 60.00
GJ17 Allen Iverson 25.00 60.00
GJ18 David Robinson 30.00 80.00
GJ19 Antoine Walker 8.00 20.00
GJ20 Karl Malone 15.00 40.00
GJ20A Karl Malone AU/32 300.00 500.00
GJ21 Kobe Bryant 60.00 150.00
GJ22 Wally Szczerbiak 8.00 20.00
GJ23 Richard Hamilton 8.00 20.00
GJ24 Shawn Marion 10.00 25.00
GJ25 Trajan Langdon 8.00 20.00
GJ26 Aleksandar Radojevic 8.00 20.00
GJ27 Corey Maggette 8.00 20.00
GJ28 William Avery 8.00 20.00
GJ29 Quincy Lewis 8.00 20.00
GJ30 Dion Glover 8.00 20.00
GJ31 Jeff Foster 8.00 20.00
GJ32 Devean George 8.00 20.00
GJ33 Shareef Abdur-Rahim 12.50 30.00
GJ34 John Stockton 25.00 60.00
GJ35 Allen Iverson 25.00 60.00
GJ36 Kevin Garnett 25.00 60.00
GJ36A Kevin Garnett AU/21 250.00 500.00
GJ37 Grant Hill 8.00 20.00
GJ38 Vin Baker 8.00 20.00
GJ39 Keith Van Horn 8.00 20.00
GJ40 Reggie Miller 25.00 60.00
GJ41 Tim Hardaway 10.00 25.00
GJ42 Hakeem Olajuwon 15.00 40.00
GJ43 Steve Francis 20.00 50.00
GJ44 Jonathan Bender 8.00 20.00
GJ45 Andre Miller 10.00 25.00
GJ46 Jason Terry 8.00 20.00
GJ47 Alonzo Mourning 12.00 30.00
GJ48 Cal Bowdler 8.00 20.00
GJ49 James Posey 8.00 20.00
GJ50 Kenny Thomas 8.00 20.00
GJ51 Tim James 8.00 20.00
GJ52 Vonteego Cummings 8.00 20.00
GJ53 Jumaine Jones 8.00 20.00
GJ54 Scott Padgett 8.00 20.00
GJ55 Baron Davis 15.00 40.00
GJ56 Karl Malone 15.00 40.00
GJ56A Karl Malone AU/32 300.00 500.00
GJ57 Gary Payton 15.00 40.00
GJ58 Michael Finley 8.00 20.00
GJ59 Bryon Russell 10.00 25.00
GJ60 Antoine Walker 8.00 20.00
GJ61 Shaquille O'Neal 30.00 80.00
GJ62 Jason Kidd 35.00 70.00
GJ63 Jason Williams 20.00 50.00
GJ64 Antonio McDyess 8.00 20.00

1999-00 Upper Deck Game Jerseys Patch

Randomly inserted in both series packs at one in 7,000, this 30-card set features a higher level of Game Jersey cards by featuring swatches from the names, numbers and team patches from the player's actual game-worn jerseys. Card backs carry a "GJP" prefix.

GJP1 Jason Kidd 150.00 300.00
GJP2 Shaquille O'Neal 150.00 300.00
GJP3 Tim Duncan 200.00 400.00
GJP4 Charles Barkley 200.00 400.00
GJP5 Kevin Garnett 150.00 300.00
GJP6 John Stockton 200.00 400.00
GJP7 Keith Van Horn 75.00 150.00
GJP8 Hakeem Olajuwon 150.00 300.00
GJP9 Paul Pierce 150.00 300.00
GJP10 Michael Jordan 700.00 1200.00
GJP11 Kobe Bryant 300.00 600.00
GJP12 Scottie Pippen 150.00 300.00
GJP13 Grant Hill 150.00 300.00
GJP14 Gary Payton 200.00 400.00
GJP15 Vince Carter 200.00 400.00
GJP16 Reggie Miller 200.00 400.00
GJP17 Allen Iverson 150.00 300.00
GJP18 David Robinson 150.00 300.00
GJP19 Antoine Walker 100.00 200.00
GJP20 Karl Malone 150.00 300.00
GJP21 Baron Davis 150.00 300.00
GJP22 Shaquille O'Neal 150.00 300.00
GJP23 Grant Hill 150.00 300.00
GJP24 Allen Iverson 150.00 300.00
GJP25 Steve Francis 100.00 200.00
GJP26 Jonathan Bender 75.00 150.00
GJP27 Kobe Bryant 300.00 600.00
GJP28 Kevin Garnett 150.00 300.00
GJP29 Jason Williams 100.00 200.00
GJP30 Jason Kidd 125.00 250.00

1999-00 Upper Deck Game Jerseys Patch Super

Randomly inserted in both series packs, this 20-card set is a parallel of the base insert. The cards are serially numbered to 25. Card backs are numbered by the player's initials.

AI Allen Iverson 1 250.00 500.00
AI Allen Iverson 2 250.00 500.00
AW Antoine Walker 125.00 250.00
BD Baron Davis 150.00 300.00
GH Grant Hill 1 300.00 600.00
GH Grant Hill 2 300.00 600.00
JB Jonathan Bender 125.00 250.00
JK Jason Kidd 250.00 500.00
JW Jason Williams 200.00 400.00
KB Kobe Bryant 1 600.00 1200.00
KB Kobe Bryant 2 600.00 1200.00
KG Kevin Garnett 1 175.00 350.00
KG Kevin Garnett 2 175.00 350.00
KV Keith Van Horn 100.00 200.00
MJ Michael Jordan 1400.00 2200.00
SF Steve Francis 125.00 250.00
SO Shaquille O'Neal 1 300.00 600.00
SO Shaquille O'Neal 2 300.00 600.00
TD Tim Duncan 350.00 650.00
VC Vince Carter 350.00 650.00

1999-00 Upper Deck High Definition

Randomly inserted in series two packs at one in 11, this 20-card set features spectacular dunk shots. Card backs carry a "HD" prefix.

COMPLETE SET (20) 15.00 40.00
*LEVEL 1: 4X TO 10X HI COLUMN
LEVEL 1: PRINT RUN 100 SERIAL #'d SETS
*LEVEL 2: 10X TO 25X HI
LEVEL 2: PRINT RUN 25 SERIAL #'d SETS
HD1 Antonio McDyess .75 2.00
HD2 Kevin Garnett 2.00 5.00
HD3 Vince Carter 2.00 5.00
HD4 Shareef Abdur-Rahim .75 2.00
HD5 Patrick Ewing 1.25 3.00
HD6 Gary Payton 1.00 2.50
HD7 Glenn Robinson .75 2.00
HD8 Kobe Bryant 5.00 12.00
HD9 Antawn Jamison 1.00 2.50
HD10 Chris Webber 1.00 2.50
HD11 Corey Maggette 2.00 5.00
HD12 Shawn Kemp 1.00 2.50
HD13 Derek Anderson .60 1.50
HD14 Michael Finley 1.00 2.50
HD15 Allan Houston .75 2.00
HD16 Anfernee Hardaway 1.50 4.00
HD17 Grant Hill 1.25 3.00
HD18 Shaquille O'Neal 2.50 6.00
HD19 Paul Pierce 1.50 4.00
HD20 Scottie Pippen 1.50 4.00

1999-00 Upper Deck History Class

Randomly inserted in series one packs at one in 11, this 20-card set features some of the NBA's top legends using Rainbow Light F/X technology. Card backs carry a "HC" prefix.

COMPLETE SET (20) 15.00 40.00
*LEVEL 1: 5X TO 12X HI COLUMN
LEVEL 1: PRINT RUN 100 SER.#'d SETS
*LEVEL 2: 10X TO 25X HI COLUMN
LEVEL 2: PRINT RUN 25 SER.#'d SETS
HC1 Michael Jordan 8.00 20.00
HC2 Julius Erving 1.50 4.00
HC3 Jamaal Wilkes .75 2.00
HC4 John Havlicek 1.00 2.50
HC5 Moses Malone .75 2.00
HC6 Nate Archibald .75 2.00
HC7 Jerry West 1.00 2.50
HC8 Dave DeBusschere .75 2.00
HC9 Bob Cousy 1.25 3.00
HC10 Kevin McHale 1.00 2.50
HC11 Dave Bing .75 2.00
HC12 Walt Frazier .75 2.00
HC13 Bob Lanier .75 2.00
HC14 George Gervin .75 2.00
HC15 Hal Greer .75 2.00
HC16 Earl Monroe .75 2.00
HC17 David Thompson 1.00 2.50
HC18 Wes Unseld .75 2.00
HC19 Bill Walton .75 2.00
HC20 Larry Bird 2.50 6.00

1999-00 Upper Deck Jamboree

Randomly inserted in series one packs at one in 11, this 15-card set features some of the most electrifying slam-dunkers in the business. Card backs carry a "J" prefix.

COMPLETE SET (15) 8.00 20.00
*LEVEL 1: 6X TO 15X HI COLUMN
LEVEL 1: PRINT RUN 100 SERIAL #'d SETS
*LEVEL 2: 15X TO 40X VALUE
LEVEL 2: PRINT RUN 25 SERIAL #'d SETS
J1 Michael Jordan 5.00 12.00
J2 Karl Malone .75 2.00
J3 Kevin Garnett 1.25 3.00
J4 Antonio McDyess .50 1.25
J5 Shareef Abdur-Rahim .50 1.25
J6 David Robinson 1.00 2.50
J7 Marcus Camby .50 1.25
J8 Kobe Bryant 3.00 8.00
J9 Jason Kidd 1.00 2.50
J10 Scottie Pippen 1.00 2.50
J11 Keith Van Horn .50 1.25
J12 Glenn Robinson .50 1.25
J13 Grant Hill .75 2.00
J14 Michael Finley .60 1.50
J15 Alonzo Mourning .75 2.00

1999-00 Upper Deck MJ - A Higher Power

Randomly inserted in series one packs at one in 23, this 12-card set relives Jordan's high-flying career. Card backs carry a "MJ" prefix.

COMPLETE SET (12) 25.00 60.00
COMMON CARD (MJ1-MJ12) 2.50 6.00

1999-00 Upper Deck MJ Final Floor

Randomly inserted in the following Upper Deck products: SPx, Hardcourt, Ovation, Black Diamond, SP Authentic, UD Ionix, Upper Deck Encore, Upper Deck HoloGrFX, 2000 Century Legends, 2000/01 Upper Deck MVP and Upper Deck 2, this set features pieces of the floor from MJ's final game. The base card is just a piece of the floor and was inserted at one in 2500 packs in each product. The second level features an autograph and those were hand numbered to 23. The final tier features a hand-built wood card that includes the Jordan auto. Only one of these cards were available in each product.

COMMON CARD (FF1-FF12) 12.00 30.00
COMMON AU (FF1A-FF12A) 400.00 800.00

1999-00 Upper Deck Now Showing

Randomly inserted in series one packs at one in four, this 30-card set captures the top NBA talent. Card backs carry a "NS" prefix.

COMPLETE SET (30) 12.50 30.00
*LEVEL 1: 6X TO 15X HI COLUMN

LEVEL 1: PRINT RUN 100 SERIAL #'d SETS
*LEVEL 2: 15X TO 40X VALUE
LEVEL 2: PRINT RUN 25 SERIAL #'d SETS
NS1 Dikembe Mutombo .60 1.50
NS2 Antoine Walker .60 1.50
NS3 Eddie Jones .60 1.50
NS4 Toni Kukoc .60 1.50
NS5 Shawn Kemp .60 1.50
NS6 Michael Finley .60 1.50
NS7 Antonio McDyess .50 1.25
NS8 Grant Hill .75 2.00
NS9 Antawn Jamison .60 1.50
NS10 Scottie Pippen 1.00 2.50
NS11 Reggie Miller .60 1.50
NS12 Maurice Taylor .40 1.00
NS13 Shaquille O'Neal 1.50 4.00
NS14 Tim Hardaway .60 1.50
NS15 Ray Allen .60 1.50
NS16 Kevin Garnett 1.25 3.00
NS17 Stephon Marbury .50 1.25
NS18 Marcus Camby .50 1.25
NS19 Darrell Armstrong .40 1.00
NS20 Allen Iverson 1.25 3.00
NS21 Jason Kidd 1.00 2.50
NS22 Damon Stoudamire .60 1.50
NS23 Jason Williams .75 2.00
NS24 Tim Duncan 1.25 3.00
NS25 Gary Payton .60 1.50
NS26 Vince Carter 1.25 3.00
NS27 Karl Malone .75 2.00
NS28 Shareef Abdur-Rahim .50 1.25
NS29 Juwan Howard .50 1.25
NS30 Michael Jordan 5.00 12.00

1999-00 Upper Deck PowerDeck

Randomly inserted in both series hobby packs, this 14-card set features Upper Deck's interactive digital technology that focus on one retired NBA star and other current standouts. The series one cards were inserted at one in 23 hobby packs, while the series two cards were inserted at one in 72 hobby packs. Also, randomly inserted in series one packs at one in 288, were two additional Jordan cards - MJPD1 and MJPD2. Each of the three Jordan series one cards were offered as one of ones. In series two, two additonal cards were inserted at one in 2500 packs - PDX1 (Michael Jordan) and PDX2 (Kevin Garnett). None of the special cards are included in the set price.
PD1 Michael Jordan 8.00 20.00
PD2 Kobe Bryant 5.00 12.00
PD3 Tim Duncan 2.00 5.00
PD4 Allen Iverson 2.00 5.00
PD5 Vince Carter 2.00 5.00
PD6 Jason Kidd 1.50 4.00
PD7 Scottie Pippen 1.50 4.00
PD8 Elton Brand 2.50 6.00
PD9 Steve Francis 2.50 6.00
PD10 Baron Davis 3.00 8.00
PD11 Lamar Odom 3.00 8.00
PD12 Wally Szczerbiak 2.00 5.00
PD13 Richard Hamilton 2.50 6.00
PD14 Shawn Marion 2.50 6.00
PDX1 Michael Jordan 30.00 80.00
PDX2 Kevin Garnett 8.00 20.00
MJPD1 Michael Jordan 8.00 20.00
MJPD2 Michael Jordan 8.00 20.00

1999-00 Upper Deck Rookies Illustrated

Randomly inserted in series two packs at one in 11, this 10-card set focuses on the top ten rookies from the 1999 Draft Class. Card backs carry a "RI" prefix.
COMPLETE SET (10) 4.00 10.00
*LEVEL 1: 6X TO 15X HI COLUMN
LEVEL 1: PRINT RUN 100 SERIAL #'d SETS
*LEVEL 2: 15X TO 40X HI
LEVEL 2: PRINT RUN 25 SERIAL #'d SETS
RI1 Elton Brand .75 2.00
RI2 Shawn Marion .75 2.00
RI3 Trajan Langdon .30 .75
RI4 Adrian Griffin .30 .75
RI5 Baron Davis 1.00 2.50
RI6 Richard Hamilton .75 2.00
RI7 Lamar Odom 1.00 2.50
RI8 Corey Maggette .60 1.50
RI9 Steve Francis .75 2.00
RI10 Wally Szczerbiak .60 1.50

1999-00 Upper Deck Star Surge

Randomly inserted in series two packs at one in 23, this 15-card set salutes the most skilled players in the NBA. Card backs carry a "S" prefix.
COMPLETE SET (15) 15.00 40.00
*LEVEL 1: 3X TO 8X HI COLUMN
LEVEL 1: PRINT RUN 100 SERIAL #'d SETS
*LEVEL 2: 8X TO 20X HI
LEVEL 2: PRINT RUN 25 SERIAL #'d SETS
S1 Michael Jordan 10.00 25.00
S2 Kevin Garnett 2.50 6.00
S3 Allen Iverson 2.50 6.00
S4 Vince Carter 2.50 6.00
S5 Karl Malone 1.50 4.00
S6 Tim Duncan 2.50 6.00
S7 Grant Hill 1.50 4.00
S8 Scottie Pippen 2.00 5.00
S9 Shaquille O'Neal 3.00 8.00
S10 Antoine Walker 1.25 3.00
S11 Shareef Abdur-Rahim 1.00 2.50
S12 Keith Van Horn 1.00 2.50
S13 Gary Payton 1.25 3.00
S14 John Stockton 1.50 4.00
S15 Stephon Marbury 1.00 2.50

1999-00 Upper Deck Wild!

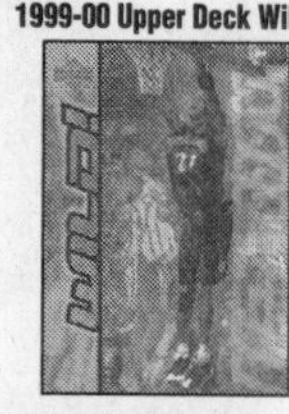

Randomly inserted in packs at one in 23, this 19-card set features some of the NBA's most entertaining talent. Card backs carry a "W" prefix.
COMPLETE SET (19) 20.00 50.00
*LEVEL 1: 3X TO 8X HI COLUMN
LEVEL 1: PRINT RUN 100 SERIAL #'d SETS
*LEVEL 2: 8X TO 20X HI
LEVEL 2: PRINT RUN 25 SERIAL #'d SETS
W1 Kobe Bryant 6.00 15.00
W2 Kevin Garnett 2.50 6.00
W3 Shareef Abdur-Rahim 1.00 2.50
W4 Tim Hardaway 1.25 3.00
W5 Jason Williams 1.50 4.00
W6 Grant Hill 1.50 4.00
W7 Vince Carter 2.50 6.00
W8 Ron Mercer 1.00 2.50
W9 Charles Barkley 2.00 5.00
W10 Eddie Jones 1.25 3.00
W11 Tim Duncan 2.50 6.00
W12 Antonio McDyess 1.00 2.50
W13 Allen Iverson 2.50 6.00
W14 Anfernee Hardaway 2.00 5.00
W15 Michael Jordan 10.00 25.00
W16 Stephon Marbury 1.00 2.50
W17 Paul Pierce 2.00 5.00
W18 Elton Brand 2.00 5.00
W19 Jason Terry 2.00 5.00

2000-01 Upper Deck

The 2000-01 Upper Deck product was released in late November,2000. The product features a 245-card base set that is broken into tiers as follows: 200 veterans (1-200), and 45 Rookies (201-245) that are seeded at one in four packs. Each pack contained 10 cards, and carried a suggested retail price of 2.99. Series two cards all say "Game Jersey Edition" below the Upper Deck logo in the top right hand corner.
COMPLETE SET (445) 100.00 200.00
COMPLETE SERIES 1 (245) 60.00 120.00
COMPLETE SER.1 w/o RC (200) 20.00 40.00
COMPLETE SERIES 2 (200) 40.00 80.00
1 Dikembe Mutombo .30 .75
2 Jim Jackson .20 .50
3 Alan Henderson .20 .50
4 Jason Terry .30 .75
5 Roshown McLeod .20 .50
6 Lorenzen Wright .20 .50
7 Paul Pierce .40 1.00
8 Antoine Walker .25 .60
9 Vitaly Potapenko .20 .50
10 Kenny Anderson .25 .60
11 Tony Battie .20 .50
12 Adrian Griffin .20 .50
13 Eric Williams .20 .50
14 Derrick Coleman .25 .60
15 David Wesley .20 .50
16 Baron Davis .30 .75
17 Elden Campbell .20 .50
18 Jamal Mashburn .25 .60
19 Eddie Robinson .20 .50
20 Elton Brand .30 .75
21 Chris Carr .20 .50
22 Ron Artest .30 .75
23 Michael Ruffin .20 .50
24 Fred Hoiberg .20 .50
25 Corey Benjamin .20 .50
26 Shawn Kemp .30 .75
27 Lamond Murray .20 .50
28 Andre Miller .25 .60
29 Cedric Henderson .20 .50
30 Wesley Person .20 .50
31 Brevin Knight .20 .50
32 Mark Bryant .20 .50
33 Michael Finley .30 .75
34 Cedric Ceballos .20 .50
35 Dirk Nowitzki .50 1.25
36 Hubert Davis .20 .50
37 Steve Nash .50 1.25
38 Gary Trent .20 .50
39 Antonio McDyess .25 .60
40 James Posey .20 .50
41 Nick Van Exel .25 .60
42 Raef LaFrentz .20 .50
43 George McCloud .20 .50
44 Keon Clark .20 .50
45 Jerry Stackhouse .25 .60
46 Christian Laettner .20 .50
47 Loy Vaught .20 .50
48 Jerome Williams .20 .50
49 Michael Curry .20 .50
50 Lindsey Hunter .20 .50
51 Antawn Jamison .30 .75
52 Larry Hughes .25 .60
53 Chris Mills .20 .50
54 Donyell Marshall .20 .50
55 Mookie Blaylock .25 .60
56 Vonteego Cummings .20 .50
57 Erick Dampier .20 .50
58 Steve Francis .30 .75
59 Shandon Anderson .20 .50
60 Hakeem Olajuwon .40 1.00
61 Walt Williams .20 .50
62 Kenny Thomas .20 .50
63 Kelvin Cato .20 .50
64 Cuttino Mobley .25 .60
65 Reggie Miller .30 .75
66 Jalen Rose .25 .60
67 Austin Croshere .20 .50
68 Dale Davis .20 .50
69 Travis Best .20 .50
70 Jonathan Bender .20 .50
71 Al Harrington .25 .60
72 Lamar Odom .30 .75
73 Tyrone Nesby .30 .75
74 Michael Olowokandi .20 .50
75 Brian Skinner .20 .50
76 Eric Piatkowski .20 .50
77 Keith Closs .20 .50
78 Shaquille O'Neal .75 2.00
79 Ron Harper .25 .60
80 Kobe Bryant 1.50 4.00
81 Rick Fox .25 .60
82 Robert Horry .25 .60
83 Derek Fisher .30 .75
84 Devean George .20 .50
85 Alonzo Mourning .40 1.00
86 Eddie Jones .30 .75
87 Anthony Carter .20 .50
88 Bruce Bowen .20 .50
89 Clarence Weatherspoon .20 .50
90 Tim Hardaway .30 .75
91 Ray Allen .30 .75
92 Tim Thomas .20 .50
93 Glenn Robinson .25 .60
94 Scott Williams .20 .50
95 Sam Cassell .25 .60
96 Ervin Johnson .20 .50
97 Darvin Ham .20 .50
98 Kevin Garnett .60 1.50
99 Wally Szczerbiak .25 .60
100 Terrell Brandon .20 .50
101 Joe Smith .25 .60
102 Radoslav Nesterovic .20 .50
103 William Avery .20 .50
104 Stephon Marbury .25 .60
105 Kerry Kittles .20 .50
106 Keith Van Horn .25 .60
107 Lucious Harris .20 .50
108 Jamie Feick .20 .50
109 Johnny Newman .20 .50
110 Patrick Ewing .40 1.00
111 Latrell Sprewell .25 .60
112 Marcus Camby .25 .60
113 Larry Johnson .30 .75
114 Charlie Ward .20 .50
115 Allan Houston .25 .60
116 Chris Childs .20 .50
117 Grant Hill .40 1.00
118 John Amaechi .20 .50
119 Tracy McGrady .50 1.25
120 Michael Doleac .20 .50
121 Darrell Armstrong .20 .50
122 Bo Outlaw .20 .50
123 Allen Iverson .60 1.50
124 Theo Ratliff .20 .50
125 Matt Geiger .20 .50
126 Tyrone Hill .20 .50
127 George Lynch .20 .50
128 Toni Kukoc .25 .60
129 Jason Kidd .50 1.25
130 Rodney Rogers .20 .50
131 Anfernee Hardaway .50 1.25
132 Clifford Robinson .20 .50
133 Tom Gugliotta .20 .50
134 Shawn Marion .30 .75
135 Luc Longley .20 .50
136 Rasheed Wallace .30 .75
137 Scottie Pippen .50 1.25
138 Arvydas Sabonis .25 .60
139 Steve Smith .25 .60
140 Damon Stoudamire .25 .60
141 Bonzi Wells .20 .50
142 Jermaine O'Neal .30 .75
143 Chris Webber .30 .75
144 Jason Williams .30 .75
145 Nick Anderson .20 .50
146 Vlade Divac .25 .60
147 Peja Stojakovic .30 .75
148 Jon Barry .20 .50
149 Corliss Williamson .20 .50
150 Tim Duncan .60 1.50
151 David Robinson .50 1.25
152 Terry Porter .25 .60
153 Malik Rose .20 .50
154 Steve Kerr .20 .50
155 Avery Johnson .25 .60
156 Gary Payton .30 .75
157 Brent Barry .20 .50
158 Vin Baker .25 .60
159 Rashard Lewis .30 .75
160 Ruben Patterson .20 .50
161 Shammond Williams .20 .50
162 Vince Carter .60 1.50
163 Dell Curry .20 .50
164 Doug Christie .20 .50
165 Antonio Davis .20 .50
166 Kevin Willis .20 .50
167 Charles Oakley .25 .60
168 Karl Malone .40 1.00
169 John Stockton .40 1.00
170 Bryon Russell .20 .50
171 Olden Polynice .20 .50
172 Quincy Lewis .20 .50
173 Scott Padgett .20 .50
174 Shareef Abdur-Rahim .25 .60
175 Mike Bibby .30 .75
176 Michael Dickerson .20 .50
177 Bryant Reeves .20 .50
178 Othella Harrington .20 .50
179 Grant Long .20 .50
180 Mitch Richmond .25 .60
181 Richard Hamilton .25 .60
182 Juwan Howard .25 .60
183 Rod Strickland .25 .60
184 Tracy Murray .20 .50
185 Chris Whitney .20 .50
186 Kobe Bryant Y3K .50 1.25
187 Kobe Bryant Y3K .50 1.25
188 Kobe Bryant Y3K .50 1.25
189 Kobe Bryant Y3K .50 1.25
190 Kobe Bryant Y3K .50 1.25
191 Kevin Garnett Y3K .20 .50
192 Kevin Garnett Y3K .20 .50
193 Kevin Garnett Y3K .20 .50
194 Kevin Garnett Y3K .20 .50
195 Kevin Garnett Y3K .20 .50
196 Kenyon Martin Y3K .25 .60
197 Kenyon Martin Y3K .25 .60
198 Kenyon Martin Y3K .25 .60
199 Kenyon Martin Y3K .25 .60
200 Kenyon Martin Y3K .25 .60
201 Kenyon Martin RC 1.00 2.50
202 Stromile Swift RC .40 1.00
203 Chris Mihm RC .40 1.00
204 Marcus Fizer RC .40 1.00
205 Darius Miles RC .40 1.00
206 Joel Przybilla RC .40 1.00
207 Mike Miller RC .75 2.00
208 Courtney Alexander RC .40 1.00
209 DerMarr Johnson RC .40 1.00
210 Iakovos Tsakalidis RC .40 1.00
211 Jerome Moiso RC .40 1.00
212 Keyon Dooling RC .40 1.00
213 Erick Barkley RC .40 1.00
214 Jason Collier RC .40 1.00
215 Jamaal Magloire RC .40 1.00
216 DeShawn Stevenson RC .50 1.25
217 Hedo Turkoglu RC .75 2.00
218 Morris Peterson RC .40 1.00
219 Jamal Crawford RC .60 1.50
220 Etan Thomas RC .40 1.00
221 Quentin Richardson RC .60 1.50
222 Mateen Cleaves RC .40 1.00
223 Chris Carrawell RC .40 1.00
224 Corey Hightower RC .40 1.00
225 Donnell Harvey RC .40 1.00
226 Mark Madsen RC .40 1.00
227 Jake Voskuhl RC .40 1.00
228 Soumaila Samake RC .40 1.00
229 Mamadou N'Diaye RC .40 1.00
230 Dan Langhi RC .40 1.00
231 Hanno Mottola RC .40 1.00
232 Olumide Oyedeji RC .40 1.00
233 Jason Hart RC .40 1.00
234 Mike Smith RC .40 1.00
235 Chris Porter RC .40 1.00
236 Jabari Smith RC .40 1.00
237 Desmond Mason RC .50 1.25
238 Eddie House RC .40 1.00
239 A.J. Guyton RC .40 1.00
240 Speedy Claxton RC .40 1.00
241 Lavor Postell RC .40 1.00
242 Khalid El-Amin RC .40 1.00
243 Pepe Sanchez RC .40 1.00
244 Eduardo Najera RC .40 1.00
245 Michael Redd RC 1.00 2.50
246 DerMarr Johnson .30 .75
247 Hanno Mottola .30 .75
248 Dion Glover .20 .50
249 Matt Maloney .20 .50
250 Jason Terry .30 .75
251 Jerome Moiso .30 .75
252 Bryant Stith .20 .50
253 Randy Brown .20 .50
254 Mark Blount .30 .75
255 Chris Herren .20 .50
256 Jamal Mashburn .25 .60
257 P.J. Brown .20 .50
258 Lee Nailon .30 .75
259 Jamaal Magloire .30 .75
260 Otis Thorpe .25 .60
261 Ron Mercer .20 .50
262 Marcus Fizer .30 .75
263 Jamal Crawford .50 1.25
264 A.J. Guyton .30 .75
265 Dalibor Bagaric RC .40 1.00
266 Chris Mihm .30 .75
267 Robert Traylor .20 .50
268 Matt Harpring .25 .60
269 Clarence Weatherspoon .20 .50
270 Bimbo Coles .20 .50
271 Etan Thomas .30 .75
272 Courtney Alexander .30 .75
273 Donnell Harvey .30 .75
274 Eduardo Najera .30 .75
275 Christian Laettner .20 .50
276 Mamadou N'Diaye .30 .75
277 Tariq Abdul-Wahad .20 .50
278 Voshon Lenard .20 .50
279 Robert Pack .20 .50
280 Tracy Murray .20 .50
281 Mateen Cleaves .30 .75
282 Ben Wallace .30 .75
283 Chucky Atkins .20 .50
284 Billy Owens .20 .50
285 Brian Cardinal RC .40 1.00
286 Chris Porter .30 .75
287 Bob Sura .20 .50
288 Vinny Del Negro .20 .50
289 Marc Jackson RC .40 1.00
290 Danny Fortson .20 .50
291 Jason Collier .30 .75
292 Maurice Taylor .20 .50
293 Dan Langhi .30 .75
294 Carlos Rogers .20 .50
295 Moochie Norris .20 .50
296 Jermaine O'Neal .30 .75
297 Derrick McKey .20 .50
298 Sam Perkins .20 .50
299 Zan Tabak .20 .50
300 Jeff Foster .20 .50
301 Corey Maggette .25 .60
302 Darius Miles .30 .75
303 Keyon Dooling .30 .75
304 Quentin Richardson .50 1.25
305 Jeff McInnis .20 .50
306 Isaiah Rider .25 .60
307 Mark Madsen .30 .75
308 Mike Penberthy RC .40 1.00
309 Brian Shaw .20 .50
310 Horace Grant .25 .60
311 Eddie Jones .30 .75
312 Brian Grant .20 .50
313 Anthony Mason .20 .50
314 Duane Causwell .20 .50
315 Eddie House .30 .75
316 Lindsey Hunter .20 .50
317 Jason Caffey .20 .50
318 Joel Przybilla .30 .75
319 Michael Redd .75 2.00
320 Rafer Alston .20 .50
321 Chauncey Billups .30 .75
322 LaPhonso Ellis .25 .60
323 Sam Mitchell .20 .50
324 Dean Garrett .20 .50
325 Tom Hammonds .20 .50
326 Kenyon Martin .75 2.00
327 Soumaila Samake .30 .75
328 Aaron Williams .20 .50
329 Kendall Gill .20 .50
330 Stephen Jackson RC .60 1.50
331 Lavor Postell .30 .75
332 Pete Mickeal RC .40 1.00
333 Kurt Thomas .20 .50
334 Erick Strickland .20 .50
335 Glen Rice .25 .60
336 Grant Hill .40 1.00
337 Tracy McGrady .50 1.25
338 Pat Garrity .20 .50
339 Troy Hudson .20 .50
340 Mike Miller .60 1.50
341 Speedy Claxton .30 .75
342 Eric Snow .20 .50
343 Pepe Sanchez .30 .75
344 Aaron McKie .20 .50
345 Nazr Mohammed .20 .50
346 Ruben Garces RC .40 1.00
347 Daniel Santiago RC .60 1.50
348 Tony Delk .20 .50
349 Paul McPherson RC .40 1.00
350 Iakovos Tsakalidis .30 .75
351 Dale Davis .20 .50
352 Shawn Kemp .30 .75
353 Erick Barkley .30 .75
354 Greg Anthony .20 .50
355 Stacey Augmon .20 .50
356 Bobby Jackson .20 .50
357 Hedo Turkoglu .60 1.50
358 Jabari Smith .30 .75
359 Doug Christie .20 .50
360 Darrick Martin .20 .50
361 Sean Elliott .25 .60
362 Jaren Jackson .20 .50
363 Samaki Walker .20 .50
364 Derek Anderson .20 .50
365 Antonio Daniels .20 .50
366 Patrick Ewing .40 1.00
367 Desmond Mason .40 1.00
368 Jelani McCoy .20 .50
369 Ruben Wolkowyski RC .40 1.00
370 Emanual Davis .20 .50
371 Mark Jackson .25 .60
372 Morris Peterson .30 .75
373 Muggsy Bogues .25 .60
374 Alvin Williams .20 .50
375 Corliss Williamson .20 .50
376 John Starks .20 .50
377 Danny Manning .20 .50
378 DeShawn Stevenson .40 1.00
379 Donyell Marshall .20 .50
380 David Benoit .20 .50
381 Isaac Austin .20 .50
382 Mahmoud Abdul-Rauf .20 .50
383 Stromile Swift .30 .75
384 Kevin Edwards .20 .50
385 Brent Price .20 .50
386 Popeye Jones .20 .50
387 Mike Smith .30 .75
388 Jahidi White .20 .50
389 Laron Profit .20 .50
390 Felipe Lopez .20 .50
391 Dikembe Mutombo MVP .30 .75
392 Paul Pierce MVP .40 1.00
393 Derrick Coleman MVP .25 .60
394 Elton Brand MVP .30 .75
395 Andre Miller MVP .25 .60
396 Michael Finley MVP .30 .75
397 Antonio McDyess MVP .25 .60
398 Jerry Stackhouse MVP .25 .60
399 Larry Hughes MVP .25 .60
400 Steve Francis MVP .30 .75
401 Reggie Miller MVP .30 .75
402 Lamar Odom MVP .30 .75
403 Shaquille O'Neal MVP .75 2.00
404 Tim Hardaway MVP .30 .75
405 Ray Allen MVP .30 .75
406 Kevin Garnett MVP .60 1.50
407 Stephon Marbury MVP .25 .60
408 Allan Houston MVP .25 .60
409 Grant Hill MVP .40 1.00
410 Allen Iverson MVP .60 1.50
411 Jason Kidd MVP .50 1.25
412 Rasheed Wallace MVP .30 .75
413 Chris Webber MVP .30 .75
414 Tim Duncan MVP .60 1.50
415 Gary Payton MVP .30 .75
416 Vince Carter MVP .60 1.50
417 Karl Malone MVP .40 1.00
418 Shareef Abdur-Rahim MVP .25 .60
419 Mitch Richmond MVP .25 .60
420 Kobe Bryant MVP 1.50 4.00
421 Mateen Cleaves ROC .30 .75
422 Speedy Claxton ROC .30 .75
423 Courtney Alexander ROC .30 .75
424 Desmond Mason ROC .40 1.00
425 Mike Miller ROC .60 1.50
426 DerMarr Johnson ROC .30 .75
427 Chris Mihm ROC .30 .75
428 Jamal Crawford ROC .50 1.25
429 Joel Przybilla ROC .30 .75
430 Keyon Dooling ROC .30 .75
431 Kobe Bryant PR .50 1.25
432 Kobe Bryant PR .50 1.25
433 Kobe Bryant PR .50 1.25
434 Kobe Bryant PR .50 1.25
435 Kobe Bryant PR .50 1.25
436 Kobe Bryant PR .50 1.25
437 Kobe Bryant PR .50 1.25
438 Kobe Bryant PR .50 1.25
439 Kobe Bryant PR .50 1.25
440 Kobe Bryant PR .50 1.25
441 Kobe Bryant PR .50 1.25
442 Kobe Bryant PR .50 1.25
443 Kobe Bryant PR .50 1.25
444 Kobe Bryant PR .50 1.25
445 Kobe Bryant PR .50 1.25
CL1 Checklist .08 .25
CL1 Checklist .08 .25
CL2 Checklist .08 .25
CL2 Checklist .08 .25
CL3 Checklist .08 .25
CL3 Checklist .08 .25

2000-01 Upper Deck Gold

Randomly inserted in packs, this 245-card set parallels the base set featuring gold foil. Cards 1-200 are serially numbered to 100, while cards 201-245 are serial numbered to 25. To ascertain values on individual cards, please refer to the multiplier in the header below, coupled with the value of the base card.
*SER.1 STARS: 6X TO 15X BASE CARD HI
*SER.2 STARS: 12X TO 30X BASE CARD HI
*RCs: 10X TO 25X BASE CARD HI
*SER.2 DP: 12X TO 30X BASE CARD HI

2000-01 Upper Deck Silver

Randomly inserted in packs, this 245-card set parallels the base set featuring silver foil. Cards 1-200 are serially numbered to 500, while cards 201-245 are serial numbered to 100. To ascertain values on individual cards, please refer to the multiplier in the header below, coupled with the value of the base card.
*SER.1 STARS: 2.5X TO 6X BASE CARD HI
*SER.2 STARS: 8X TO 20X BASE CARD HI
*RCs: 2X TO 5X BASE CARD HI
*SER.2 DP: 6X TO 15X BASE CARD HI

2000-01 Upper Deck All Star Class

Randomly inserted into series 2 packs at one in 23 hobby/retail, this 10-card insert features players that are usually among the top vote-getters in the All-Star game. Card backs carry a "AS" prefix.
COMPLETE SET (10) 12.50 25.00
AS1 Tim Duncan 1.50 4.00
AS2 Shaquille O'Neal 2.00 5.00
AS3 Chris Webber .75 2.00
AS4 Allan Houston .60 1.50
AS5 Kobe Bryant 4.00 10.00
AS6 Ray Allen .75 2.00
AS7 Karl Malone 1.00 2.50
AS8 Rasheed Wallace .75 2.00
AS9 Kevin Garnett 1.50 4.00
AS10 Vince Carter 1.50 4.00

2000-01 Upper Deck Combo Materials

Randomly inserted into series two packs at one in 144, this 7-card insert features patch swatches from actual game-used materials. Card backs are numbered using the players' initials.
AMCM Andre Miller 3.00 8.00
DMCM Darius Miles 4.00 10.00
JKCM Jason Kidd 6.00 15.00
JSCM Jerry Stackhouse 3.00 8.00
MCCM Mateen Cleaves 4.00 10.00
QRCM Quentin Richardson 6.00 15.00
SMCM Shawn Marion 4.00 10.00

2000-01 Upper Deck e-Card 1

Inserted as a two-pack box-topper in Upper Deck Series one, this six-card insert features cards that can be viewed over the Upper Deck website. Cards feature a serial number that is to be typed in at the Upper Deck website to reveal that card. Card backs carry an "EC" prefix.
COMPLETE SET (6) 4.00 10.00
EC1 Kobe Bryant 3.00 8.00
EC1A Kobe Bryant JSY AU/50 125.00 250.00
EC1J Kobe Bryant JSY/300 20.00 50.00
EC1S Kobe Bryant AU/200 100.00 200.00
EC2 Kevin Garnett 1.25 3.00
EC2A Kevin Garnett JSY AU/50 40.00 100.00
EC2J Kevin Garnett JSY/300 10.00 25.00
EC2S Kevin Garnett AU/200 25.00 60.00
EC3 Anfernee Hardaway 1.00 2.50
EC3A Anfernee Hardaway JSY AU/5040.00 100.00
EC3J Anfernee Hardaway JSY/300 10.00 25.00
EC3S Anfernee Hardaway AU/200 30.00 60.00
EC4 Shareef Abdur-Rahim .50 1.25
EC4J Shareef Abdur-Rahim JSY/300 8.00 20.00
EC5 Reggie Miller .60 1.50
EC5A Reggie Miller JSY AU/50 75.00 150.00
EC5J Reggie Miller JSY/300 15.00 40.00
EC5S Reggie Miller AU/200 60.00 120.00
EC6 Karl Malone .75 2.00
EC6A Karl Malone JSY AU/50 125.00 225.00
EC6J Karl Malone JSY/300 10.00 25.00
EC6S Karl Malone AU/200 75.00 150.00

2000-01 Upper Deck e-Card 2

Inserted as a two-pack box-topper in Upper Deck Series two, this six-card insert features cards that can be viewed over the Upper Deck website. Cards feature a serial number that is to be typed in at the Upper Deck website to reveal that card. Card backs carry an "EC" prefix.
COMPLETE SET (6) 5.00 12.00
EC1 Kobe Bryant 3.00 8.00
EC1A Kobe Bryant JSY AU/50 125.00 250.00
EC1J Kobe Bryant JSY/300 20.00 50.00
EC1S Kobe Bryant AU/200 100.00 200.00
EC2 Kevin Garnett 1.25 3.00
EC2A Kevin Garnett JSY AU/50 40.00 100.00
EC2J Kevin Garnett JSY/300 10.00 25.00
EC2S Kevin Garnett AU/200 25.00 60.00
EC3 Kenyon Martin 1.50 4.00
EC3A Kenyon Martin JSY AU/50 15.00 40.00
EC3J Kenyon Martin JSY/300 8.00 20.00
EC3S Kenyon Martin AU/200 10.00 25.00
EC4 Stromile Swift .60 1.50
EC4J Stromile Swift JSY/300 5.00 12.00
EC4S Stromile Swift AU/200 8.00 20.00
EC5 Darius Miles .60 1.50
EC5J Darius Miles JSY/300 8.00 20.00
EC5S Darius Miles AU/200 12.50 30.00
EC6 Marcus Fizer .60 1.50
EC6J Marcus Fizer JSY/300 6.00 15.00
EC6S Marcus Fizer AU/200 8.00 20.00

2000-01 Upper Deck Game Jerseys 1

Randomly inserted into series one hobby/retail packs at one in 287, this 20-card insert features swatches from actual game-worn jerseys. Card backs are numbered using the players initials. Please note that autographed game-jerseys were only inserted into hobby packs.
AGH Adrian Griffin AU 5.00 12.00
AHH Anfernee Hardaway AU 30.00 80.00
AIC Allen Iverson 8.00 20.00
AMC Alonzo Mourning 8.00 20.00
AWC Antoine Walker 3.00 8.00
BDH Baron Davis AU 15.00 40.00
DRC David Robinson 10.00 25.00
EJH Eddie Jones AU 10.00 25.00
GPC Gary Payton 4.00 10.00
GRH Glenn Robinson AU 12.50 30.00
JKC Jason Kidd 6.00 15.00
JSC Joe Smith 3.00 8.00
KBC Kobe Bryant 20.00 50.00
KBH Kobe Bryant AU 100.00 200.00
KGA Kevin Garnett AU/21 100.00 200.00
KGC Kevin Garnett 8.00 20.00
KGH Kevin Garnett AU 40.00 70.00
KVC Keith Van Horn 3.00 8.00
MBH Mike Bibby AU 12.50 30.00
PPH Paul Pierce AU 12.50 30.00
RMA Reggie Miller AU/31 125.00 250.00
RMC Reggie Miller 4.00 10.00
SAC Shareef Abdur-Rahim 3.00 8.00
SMC Stephon Marbury 3.00 8.00
SOC Shaquille O'Neal 10.00 25.00
STC John Stockton 8.00 20.00
TBH Terrell Brandon AU 8.00 20.00
VBA Vin Baker AU/42 8.00 20.00
VBC Vin Baker 3.00 8.00
WAH William Avery AU 5.00 12.00
WSH Wally Szczerbiak AU 8.00 20.00

2000-01 Upper Deck Game Jerseys 2

Randomly inserted into series two hobby/retail packs at one in 287, this 43-card insert features swatches from actual game-worn jerseys. Card backs carry an "AH" prefix followed by the players initials. Please note that autographed game-jerseys were only inserted into hobby packs.
AAG Adrian Griffin AU 5.00 12.00
AAH Anfernee Hardaway AU 30.00 80.00
ACM Chris Mihm AU 5.00 12.00
ADM Darius Miles AU 8.00 20.00
AJC Jamal Crawford AU 8.00 20.00
AJM Jamaal Magloire AU 5.00 12.00
AKB Kobe Bryant AU 100.00 200.00
AKG Kevin Garnett AU 25.00 60.00
ASS Stromile Swift AU 8.00 20.00
AHC Allan Houston 3.00 8.00
AHH Anfernee Hardaway 8.00 20.00
AMC Andre Miller 3.00 8.00
CMH Chris Mihm 4.00 10.00
DAH Darrell Armstrong 2.50 6.00
DBC Dalibor Bagaric 4.00 10.00
DMH Darius Miles 4.00 10.00
GHH Grant Hill 8.00 20.00
JCH Jamal Crawford 6.00 15.00
JKC Jason Kidd 6.00 15.00
JKH Jason Kidd 6.00 15.00
JMH Jamaal Magloire 4.00 10.00
JSC Jerry Stackhouse 3.00 8.00
KBC Kobe Bryant 20.00 50.00
KBH Kobe Bryant 20.00 50.00
KDC Keyon Dooling 4.00 10.00
KDH Keyon Dooling 4.00 10.00
KGA Kevin Garnett AU/21 100.00 200.00
KGC Kevin Garnett 8.00 20.00
KGH Kevin Garnett 8.00 20.00
KMC Kenyon Martin 10.00 25.00
LSC Latrell Sprewell 3.00 8.00
LSH Latrell Sprewell 3.00 8.00
MAH Marcus Camby 3.00 8.00
MCC Mateen Cleaves 4.00 10.00
MFC Marcus Fizer 4.00 10.00
QRC Quentin Richardson 6.00 15.00
SMC Shawn Marion 4.00 10.00
SMH Shawn Marion 4.00 10.00
SSH Stromile Swift 4.00 10.00
TGC Tom Gugliotta 2.50 6.00
TMH Tracy McGrady 6.00 15.00

2000-01 Upper Deck Game Jerseys Combo 1

Randomly inserted into series one hobby/retail packs, this 10-card insert features combo swatches from actual game-worn jerseys. Card backs are numbered using the players' initials. Each card is serial numbered to 50. Please note that the two autographed combo game-jerseys were only inserted into hobby packs, and are serial numbered to 10.

Card	Low	High
DRLB Julius Erving Larry Bird/50	75.00	150.00
JKAH Jason Kidd Anfernee Hardaway/50	40.00	80.00
KBDR Kobe Bryant Julius Erving/50	50.00	100.00
KBKG Kobe Bryant Kevin Garnett/50	40.00	80.00
KBSO Kobe Bryant Shaquille O'Neal/50	75.00	150.00
KMJS Karl Malone John Stockton/50	40.00	80.00
MJLB Magic Johnson Larry Bird/50	75.00	150.00
WCBR Wilt Chamberlain Bill Russell/50	200.00	400.00

2000-01 Upper Deck Game Jerseys Combo 2

Randomly inserted into series two hobby/retail packs, this 12-card insert features combo swatches from actual game-worn jerseys. Card backs are numbered using the players' initials. Each card is serial numbered to 50. Please note that the autographed combo game-jerseys were only inserted into hobby packs, and are serial numbered to 10.

Card	Low	High
AHLS Allan Houston Latrell Sprewell/50	25.00	60.00
KBDM Kobe Bryant Darius Miles/50	25.00	60.00
KBKG Kobe Bryant Kevin Garnett/50	30.00	80.00
KBKM Kobe Bryant Kenyon Martin/50	25.00	60.00
KBSO Kobe Bryant Shaquille O'Neal/50	75.00	150.00
MJKB Michael Jordan Kobe Bryant/50	100.00	225.00
SASS Shareef Abdur-Rahim Stromile Swift/50	25.00	60.00

2000-01 Upper Deck Game Jerseys Patch 1

Randomly inserted into series one packs at one in 7500, this 17-card insert features patch swatches from actual game-worn jerseys. Card backs are numbered using the players' initials. Please note that the five autographed patch cards are serial numbered to the player's jersey number.

Card	Low	High
AHP Anfernee Hardaway	50.00	120.00
AIP Allen Iverson	50.00	125.00
GPP Gary Payton	40.00	100.00
GPPA Gary Payton AU/20	75.00	150.00
JKP Jason Kidd	40.00	100.00
KBP Kobe Bryant	100.00	200.00
KGP Kevin Garnett	50.00	125.00
KGPA Kevin Garnett AU/21	200.00	400.00
MJP Michael Jordan	200.00	400.00
MJPA Michael Jordan AU/23	1500.00	2200.00
RMP Reggie Miller	75.00	150.00
SAP Shareef Abdur-Rahim	20.00	50.00
SMP Stephon Marbury	20.00	50.00
SOP Shaquille O'Neal	60.00	150.00
STP John Stockton	40.00	100.00

2000-01 Upper Deck Game Jerseys Patch 2

Randomly inserted into series two packs at one in 5000, this 18-card insert features patch swatches from actual game-worn jerseys. Card backs are numbered using the players' initials. Please note that the five autographed patch cards are serial numbered to the player's jersey number.

Card	Low	High
AIP Allen Iverson	50.00	125.00
DJP DerMarr Johnson	12.00	30.00
DMP Darius Miles	12.00	30.00
DMPA Darius Miles AU/21	75.00	150.00
JCP Jamal Crawford	20.00	50.00
KBP Kobe Bryant	100.00	200.00
KDP Keyon Dooling	12.00	30.00
KGP Kevin Garnett	50.00	125.00
KGPA Kevin Garnett AU/21	200.00	400.00
KMP Kenyon Martin	30.00	80.00
MFP Marcus Fizer	12.00	30.00
MJP Michael Jordan	200.00	400.00
MJPA Michael Jordan AU/23	1500.00	2200.00
MMP Mike Miller	25.00	60.00
SOP Shaquille O'Neal	60.00	150.00
SSP Stromile Swift	12.00	30.00

2000-01 Upper Deck Game Jerseys Patch Gold 1

Randomly inserted into series one packs, this 10-card insert features patch swatches from actual game-worn jerseys. Card backs are numbered using the players' initials. Please note that these cards are serial numbered to 25.

*GOLD: .75X TO 2X BASE HI

Card	Low	High
AIG Allen Iverson	200.00	400.00
GHG Grant Hill	200.00	400.00
KBG Kobe Bryant	250.00	500.00
KGG Kevin Garnett	100.00	200.00

2000-01 Upper Deck Game Jerseys Patch Gold 2

Randomly inserted into series two packs, this 10-card insert features patch swatches from actual game-worn jerseys. Card backs are numbered using the players' initials. Please note that these cards are serial numbered to 25.

*GOLD: .75X TO 2X BASE HI

Card	Low	High
AIG Allen Iverson	200.00	400.00
KBG Kobe Bryant	250.00	500.00
MJG Michael Jordan	300.00	600.00
SOG Shaquille O'Neal	150.00	300.00

2000-01 Upper Deck Graphic Jam

Randomly inserted into series one packs at one in 14, this 12-card insert features players that have mastered the slam dunk. Card backs carry a "G" prefix.

Card	Low	High
COMPLETE SET (12)	6.00	15.00
G1 Kobe Bryant	3.00	8.00
G2 Kevin Garnett	1.25	3.00
G3 Chris Webber	.60	1.50
G4 Larry Hughes	.50	1.25
G5 Tim Duncan	1.25	3.00
G6 Latrell Sprewell	.50	1.25
G7 Vince Carter	1.25	3.00
G8 Shareef Abdur-Rahim	.50	1.25
G9 Elton Brand	.60	1.50
G10 Antonio McDyess	.50	1.25
G11 Lamar Odom	.60	1.50
G12 Rasheed Wallace	.60	1.50

2000-01 Upper Deck Highlight Zone

Randomly inserted into series 2 packs at one in 23 hobby/retail, this 10-card insert features players that usually make the nightly highlight reels. Card backs carry a "HZ" prefix.

Card	Low	High
COMPLETE SET (10)	8.00	20.00
HZ1 Kobe Bryant	4.00	10.00
HZ2 Eddie Jones	.75	2.00
HZ3 Lamar Odom	.75	2.00
HZ4 Steve Francis	.75	2.00
HZ5 Stephon Marbury	.60	1.50
HZ6 Scottie Pippen	1.25	3.00
HZ7 Kevin Garnett	1.50	4.00
HZ8 Chris Webber	.75	2.00
HZ9 Anfernee Hardaway	1.25	3.00
HZ10 Shareef Abdur-Rahim	.60	1.50

2000-01 Upper Deck Lightning Strikes

Randomly inserted into series one packs at one in 12, this 15-card insert features players that light it up on the court. Card backs carry a "LS" prefix.

Card	Low	High
COMPLETE SET (15)	7.50	15.00
LS1 Allen Iverson	1.00	2.50
LS2 Stephon Marbury	.40	1.00
LS3 Ray Allen	.50	1.25
LS4 Allan Houston	.40	1.00
LS5 Kevin Garnett	1.00	2.50
LS6 Gary Payton	.50	1.25
LS7 Shawn Marion	.50	1.25
LS8 Kobe Bryant	2.50	6.00
LS9 Tim Duncan	1.00	2.50
LS10 Scottie Pippen	.75	2.00
LS11 Andre Miller	.40	1.00
LS12 Steve Francis	.50	1.25
LS13 Jalen Rose	.40	1.00
LS14 Jason Williams	.50	1.25
LS15 Larry Hughes	.40	1.00

2000-01 Upper Deck Live Action

Randomly inserted into series 2 packs at one in 12 hobby/retail, this 8-card insert features players that supply plenty of action on the court. Card backs carry a "LA" prefix.

Card	Low	High
COMPLETE SET (8)	2.50	6.00
LA1 Kevin Garnett	.75	2.00
LA2 Lamar Odom	.40	1.00
LA3 Jalen Rose	.30	.75
LA4 Larry Hughes	.30	.75
LA5 Tim Thomas	.25	.60
LA6 Kobe Bryant	2.00	5.00
LA7 Wally Szczerbiak	.30	.75
LA8 Anfernee Hardaway	.60	1.50

2000-01 Upper Deck Masters of Arts

Randomly inserted into series one packs at one in six, this 10-card insert features players that have mastered life in the NBA. Card backs carry a "MA" prefix.

Card	Low	High
COMPLETE SET (10)	2.50	6.00
MA1 Vince Carter	.60	1.50
MA2 Ray Allen	.30	.75
MA3 Larry Hughes	.25	.60
MA4 Kevin Garnett	.60	1.50
MA5 Antonio McDyess	.25	.60
MA6 Steve Francis	.30	.75
MA7 Stephon Marbury	.25	.60
MA8 Kobe Bryant	1.50	4.00
MA9 Paul Pierce	.40	1.00
MA10 Reggie Miller	.30	.75

2000-01 Upper Deck MJ Materials

Randomly inserted into series one packs, this seven-card insert features memorabilia cards of Michael Jordan. Card backs carry a "MJ" prefix. Cards in the set include game-used jerseys,shoes,shorts, and even a suit that Jordan wore.

Card	Low	High
MJ1 Michael Jordan Suit	15.00	40.00
MJ2 Michael Jordan Jersey	50.00	120.00
MJ3 Michael Jordan Shoe	100.00	200.00
MJ4 Michael Jordan/250 Suit-Jersey	150.00	300.00
MJ5 Michael Jordan/100 Shorts-Shoe	175.00	350.00
MJ6 Michael Jordan/100 Jersey-Shorts	250.00	500.00
MJ7 Michael Jordan/23 Suit-Jersey-Shorts-Patch	900.00	1500.00

2000-01 Upper Deck Pure Basketball

Randomly inserted into series 2 packs at one in 12 hobby/retail, this 8-card insert features only the purest of basketball players. Card backs carry a "PB" prefix.

Card	Low	High
COMPLETE SET (8)	2.50	6.00
PB1 Elton Brand	.40	1.00
PB2 Andre Miller	.30	.75
PB3 Mitch Richmond	.30	.75
PB4 Kobe Bryant	2.00	5.00
PB5 John Stockton	.50	1.25
PB6 Antawn Jamison	.40	1.00
PB7 Kevin Garnett	.75	2.00
PB8 Reggie Miller	.40	1.00

2000-01 Upper Deck Rookie Focus

Randomly inserted into series 2 packs at one in 10 hobby/retail, this 9-card insert set focuses on this year's rookie crop. Card backs carry a "RF" prefix.

Card	Low	High
COMPLETE SET (9)	2.00	5.00
RF1 Kenyon Martin	.75	2.00
RF2 Jamal Crawford	.50	1.25
RF3 Keyon Dooling	.30	.75
RF4 Mike Miller	.60	1.50
RF5 Morris Peterson	.30	.75
RF6 DerMarr Johnson	.30	.75
RF7 Marcus Fizer	.30	.75
RF8 DeShawn Stevenson	.40	1.00
RF9 Chris Mihm	.30	.75

2000-01 Upper Deck Super Powers

Randomly inserted into series 2 packs at one in 72 hobby/retail, this 10-card insert features players that have super powers. Card backs carry a "SP" prefix.

Card	Low	High
COMPLETE SET (10)	25.00	50.00
SP1 Kobe Bryant	8.00	20.00
SP2 Vince Carter	3.00	8.00
SP3 Tim Duncan	3.00	8.00
SP4 Steve Francis	1.50	4.00
SP5 Gary Payton	1.50	4.00
SP6 Chris Webber	1.50	4.00
SP7 Kevin Garnett	3.00	8.00
SP8 Allen Iverson	3.00	8.00
SP9 Jason Kidd	2.50	6.00
SP10 Elton Brand	1.50	4.00

2000-01 Upper Deck Total Dominance

Randomly inserted into series one packs at one in 12, this 15-card insert features players that are truly dominanting on the court. Card backs carry a "TD" prefix.

Card	Low	High
COMPLETE SET (15)	10.00	25.00
TD1 Shaquille O'Neal	1.50	4.00
TD2 Gary Payton	.60	1.50
TD3 Kevin Garnett	1.25	3.00
TD4 Elton Brand	.60	1.50
TD5 Jalen Rose	.50	1.25
TD6 Allen Iverson	1.25	3.00
TD7 Vince Carter	1.25	3.00
TD8 Kobe Bryant	3.00	8.00
TD9 Lamar Odom	.60	1.50
TD10 Jason Kidd	1.00	2.50
TD11 Rasheed Wallace	.60	1.50
TD12 Chris Webber	.60	1.50
TD13 Ray Allen	.60	1.50
TD14 Alonzo Mourning	.75	2.00
TD15 Tim Duncan	1.25	3.00

2000-01 Upper Deck Touch the Sky

Randomly inserted into series 2 packs at one in 10 hobby/retail, this 9-card insert features players that can jump so high, you might believe that they could touch the sky. Card backs carry a "T" prefix.

Card	Low	High
COMPLETE SET (9)	3.00	8.00
T1 Kobe Bryant	2.00	5.00
T2 Kevin Garnett	.75	2.00
T3 Michael Finley	.40	1.00
T4 Anfernee Hardaway	.60	1.50
T5 Scottie Pippen	.60	1.50
T6 Antonio McDyess	.30	.75
T7 Larry Hughes	.30	.75
T8 Latrell Sprewell	.30	.75
T9 Rashard Lewis	.40	1.00

2000-01 Upper Deck True Talents

Randomly inserted into series one packs at one in three, this 20-card insert features players that are the true talents of the NBA. Card backs carry a "TT" prefix.

Card	Low	High
COMPLETE SET (20)	4.00	10.00
TT1 Kobe Bryant	1.50	4.00
TT2 Jalen Rose	.25	.60
TT3 Chris Webber	.30	.75
TT4 Alonzo Mourning	.40	1.00
TT5 Paul Pierce	.40	1.00
TT6 Allan Houston	.25	.60
TT7 Keith Van Horn	.25	.60
TT8 Andre Miller	.25	.60
TT9 Dirk Nowitzki	.50	1.25
TT10 Richard Hamilton	.25	.60
TT11 Jason Williams	.30	.75
TT12 Antonio McDyess	.25	.60
TT13 Antoine Walker	.25	.60
TT14 Antawn Jamison	.30	.75
TT15 Glenn Robinson	.25	.60
TT16 Lamar Odom	.30	.75
TT17 Scottie Pippen	.50	1.25
TT18 Mike Bibby	.30	.75
TT19 Elton Brand	.30	.75
TT20 Kevin Garnett	.60	1.50

2000-01 Upper Deck Unleashed

Randomly inserted into series 2 packs at one in 12 hobby/retail, this 8-card insert features players that unleash their extreme talent on a daily basis. Card backs carry a "U" prefix.

Card	Low	High
COMPLETE SET (8)	3.00	8.00
U1 Vince Carter	.75	2.00
U2 Lamar Odom	.40	1.00
U3 Jason Williams	.40	1.00
U4 Kevin Garnett	.75	2.00
U5 Paul Pierce	.50	1.25
U6 Shareef Abdur-Rahim	.30	.75
U7 Elton Brand	.40	1.00
U8 Kobe Bryant	2.00	5.00

2001-02 Upper Deck

This 450-card base set includes both Series 1 and Series 2. Each series includes 180 veterans and 45 rookies. This commemorative set celebrates Upper Deck Basketball's 10th anniversary! The cards are standard sized and borderless. The card fronts feature the type of quality action shots that have made Upper Deck Basketball so successful. The recurring theme in this product is the blonde court-wood design found in either the background of the cards or somewhere else on the card, as in this case, it acts as borders on two sides of the player's photo. One border carries the player's name and the other carries his team name. The Upper Deck logo is found in the upper right-hand corner with the featured player's team logo and position found in the lower right-hand corner. Cards 406-450 feature two versions - one inserted into Hobby (A) and one inserted into Retail (B). The difference is in the photos, but both are valued equally and were inserted 1:4 packs.

Card	Low	High
COMP.SET w/o SP's (360)	45.00	90.00
COMPLETE SER.1 (225)	75.00	150.00
COMP.SER 1 w/o SP's (180)	12.00	30.00
COMPLETE SER.2 (225)	75.00	150.00
COMP.SER 2 w/o SP's (180)	30.00	60.00
406B-450B NOT INCLUDED IN SET PRICES		
1 Jason Terry	.30	.75
2 Toni Kukoc	.25	.60
3 Alan Henderson	.20	.50
4 Theo Ratliff	.20	.50
5 Shareef Abdur-Rahim	.25	.60
6 DerMarr Johnson	.20	.50
7 Paul Pierce	.40	1.00
8 Antoine Walker	.25	.60
9 Kenny Anderson	.25	.60
10 Vitaly Potapenko	.20	.50
11 Eric Williams	.20	.50
12 Jamal Mashburn	.25	.60
13 Baron Davis	.30	.75
14 David Wesley	.20	.50
15 P.J. Brown	.20	.50
16 Elden Campbell	.20	.50
17 Jamaal Magloire	.20	.50
18 Lee Nailon	.20	.50
19 A.J. Guyton	.20	.50
20 Ron Mercer	.20	.50
21 Jamal Crawford	.25	.60
22 Fred Hoiberg	.20	.50
23 Marcus Fizer	.20	.50
24 Ron Artest	.30	.75
25 Lamond Murray	.20	.50
26 Andre Miller	.25	.60
27 Jim Jackson	.20	.50
28 Chris Mihm	.20	.50
29 Trajan Langdon	.20	.50
30 Chris Gatling	.20	.50
31 Michael Finley	.30	.75
32 Dirk Nowitzki	.50	1.25
33 Steve Nash	.50	1.25
34 Juwan Howard	.25	.60
35 Wang Zhizhi	.25	.60
36 Eduardo Najera	.20	.50
37 Shawn Bradley	.20	.50
38 Antonio McDyess	.25	.60
39 Nick Van Exel	.25	.60
40 Raef LaFrentz	.20	.50
41 James Posey	.20	.50
42 Voshon Lenard	.20	.50
43 Ben Wallace	.30	.75
44 Jerry Stackhouse	.25	.60
45 Corliss Williamson	.20	.50
46 Chucky Atkins	.20	.50
47 Michael Curry	.20	.50
48 Dana Barros	.20	.50
49 Antawn Jamison	.30	.75
50 Larry Hughes	.25	.60
51 Bob Sura	.20	.50
52 Marc Jackson	.20	.50
53 Chris Porter	.20	.50
54 Vonteego Cummings	.20	.50
55 Steve Francis	.30	.75
56 Cuttino Mobley	.25	.60
57 Maurice Taylor	.20	.50
58 Kenny Thomas	.20	.50
59 Moochie Norris	.20	.50
60 Walt Williams	.20	.50
61 Reggie Miller	.30	.75
62 Jalen Rose	.25	.60
63 Jermaine Oâ•™Neal	.30	.75
64 Austin Croshere	.20	.50
65 Travis Best	.20	.50
66 Jonathan Bender	.20	.50
67 Eric Piatkowski	.20	.50
68 Darius Miles	.20	.50
69 Lamar Odom	.30	.75
70 Quentin Richardson	.25	.60
71 Corey Maggette	.25	.60
72 Elton Brand	.30	.75
73 Jeff McInnis	.20	.50
74 Kobe Bryant	1.50	4.00
75 Shaquille O'Neal	.75	2.00
76 Derek Fisher	.25	.60
77 Rick Fox	.25	.60
78 Mitch Richmond	.25	.60
79 Ron Harper	.25	.60
80 Brian Shaw	.20	.50
81 Stromile Swift	.20	.50
82 Michael Dickerson	.20	.50
83 Jason Williams	.25	.60
84 Grant Long	.20	.50
85 Bryant Reeves	.20	.50
86 Alonzo Mourning	.40	1.00
87 Eddie Jones	.25	.60
88 Brian Grant	.20	.50
89 Anthony Mason	.20	.50
90 LaPhonso Ellis	.25	.60
91 Anthony Carter	.20	.50
92 Jason Caffey	.20	.50
93 Ray Allen	.30	.75
94 Glenn Robinson	.25	.60
95 Sam Cassell	.25	.60
96 Tim Thomas	.20	.50
97 Ervin Johnson	.20	.50
98 Joel Przybilla	.20	.50
99 Kevin Garnett	.60	1.50
100 Terrell Brandon	.20	.50
101 Wally Szczerbiak	.25	.60
102 Felipe Lopez	.20	.50
103 Chauncey Billups	.30	.75
104 Anthony Peeler	.20	.50
105 Kenyon Martin	.30	.75
106 Keith Van Horn	.25	.60
107 Jamie Feick	.20	.50
108 Aaron Williams	.20	.50
109 Lucious Harris	.20	.50
110 Jason Kidd	.50	1.25
111 Latrell Sprewell	.25	.60
112 Allan Houston	.25	.60
113 Marcus Camby	.25	.60
114 Mark Jackson	.25	.60
115 Othella Harrington	.20	.50
116 Kurt Thomas	.20	.50
117 Tracy McGrady	.50	1.25
118 Mike Miller	.30	.75
119 Darrell Armstrong	.20	.50
120 Grant Hill	.40	1.00
121 Pat Garrity	.20	.50
122 Bo Outlaw	.20	.50
123 Allen Iverson	.60	1.50
124 Dikembe Mutombo	.30	.75
125 Aaron McKie	.20	.50
126 Matt Geiger	.20	.50
127 Eric Snow	.20	.50
128 George Lynch	.20	.50
129 Raja Bell RC	.75	2.00
130 Shawn Marion	.30	.75
131 Tom Gugliotta	.20	.50
132 Rodney Rogers	.20	.50
133 Anfernee Hardaway	.50	1.25
134 Tony Delk	.20	.50
135 Stephon Marbury	.25	.60
136 Rasheed Wallace	.30	.75
137 Damon Stoudamire	.25	.60
138 Rod Strickland	.25	.60
139 Dale Davis	.20	.50
140 Scottie Pippen	.50	1.25
141 Bonzi Wells	.20	.50
142 Peja Stojakovic	.30	.75
143 Chris Webber	.30	.75
144 Doug Christie	.20	.50
145 Mike Bibby	.30	.75
146 Hedo Turkoglu	.30	.75
147 Scot Pollard	.20	.50
148 Vlade Divac	.25	.60
149 Tim Duncan	.60	1.50
150 David Robinson	.50	1.25
151 Antonio Daniels	.20	.50
152 Danny Ferry	.20	.50
153 Malik Rose	.20	.50
154 Terry Porter	.20	.50
155 Rashard Lewis	.30	.75
156 Gary Payton	.30	.75
157 Brent Barry	.20	.50
158 Vin Baker	.25	.60
159 Desmond Mason	.25	.60
160 Shammond Williams	.20	.50
161 Vince Carter	.50	1.25
162 Antonio Davis	.20	.50
163 Morris Peterson	.20	.50
164 Keon Clark	.20	.50
165 Chris Childs	.20	.50
166 Alvin Williams	.20	.50
167 Karl Malone	.40	1.00
168 John Stockton	.40	1.00
169 Donyell Marshall	.20	.50
170 John Starks	.20	.50
171 Bryon Russell	.20	.50
172 David Benoit	.20	.50
173 DeShawn Stevenson	.20	.50
174 Richard Hamilton	.25	.60
175 Jahidi White	.20	.50
176 Courtney Alexander	.20	.50
177 Chris Whitney	.20	.50
178 Michael Jordan	4.00	10.00
179 Kobe Bryant CL	.75	2.00
180 Kevin Garnett CL	.30	.75
181 Sean Lampley RC	1.00	2.50
182 Andrei Kirilenko RC	2.50	6.00
183 Brandon Armstrong RC	1.00	2.50
184 Gerald Wallace RC	1.50	4.00
185 Tony Parker RC	4.00	10.00
186 Jeryl Sasser RC	1.00	2.50
187 Alton Ford RC	1.00	2.50
188 Kenny Satterfield RC	1.00	2.50
189 Will Solomon RC	1.00	2.50
190 Earl Watson RC	1.00	2.50
191 Michael Wright RC	1.00	2.50
192 Samuel Dalembert RC	1.25	3.00
193 Ousmane Cisse RC	1.00	2.50
194 Ruben Boumtje-Boumtje RC	1.00	2.50
195 Damone Brown RC	1.00	2.50
196 Jarron Collins RC	1.00	2.50
197 Terence Morris RC	1.00	2.50
198 Pau Gasol RC	3.00	8.00
199 Trenton Hassell RC	1.00	2.50
200 Kirk Haston RC	1.00	2.50
201 Brian Scalabrine RC	1.00	2.50
202 Gilbert Arenas RC	1.50	4.00
203 Jeff Trepagnier RC	1.00	2.50
204 Joseph Forte RC	1.00	2.50
205 Steven Hunter RC	1.00	2.50
206 Omar Cook RC	1.00	2.50
207 Jason Collins RC	1.00	2.50
208 Kedrick Brown RC	1.00	2.50
209 Michael Bradley RC	1.00	2.50
210 Zach Randolph RC	2.50	6.00
211 Richard Jefferson RC	2.00	5.00
212 Jamaal Tinsley RC	1.25	3.00
213 Vladimir Radmanovic RC	1.00	2.50
214 Brendan Haywood RC	1.25	3.00
215 Troy Murphy RC	1.50	4.00
216 DeSagana Diop RC	1.00	2.50
217 Jason Richardson RC	2.00	5.00
218 Joe Johnson RC	2.50	6.00
219 Rodney White RC	1.00	2.50
220 Loren Woods RC	1.00	2.50
221 Tyson Chandler RC	1.50	4.00
222 Eddy Curry RC	1.50	4.00
223 Shane Battier RC	2.00	5.00
224 Eddie Griffin RC	1.00	2.50
225 Kwame Brown RC	1.00	2.50
226 Shareef Abdur-Rahim	.25	.60
227 Nazr Mohammed	.20	.50
228 Hanno Mottola	.20	.50
229 Emanual Davis	.20	.50
230 Dion Glover	.20	.50
231 Chris Crawford	.20	.50
232 Mark Blount	.20	.50
233 Joe Johnson	1.25	3.00
234 Milt Palacio	.20	.50
235 Kedrick Brown	.50	1.25
236 Tony Battie	.20	.50
237 Erick Strickland	.20	.50
238 Kirk Haston	.50	1.25
239 Stacey Augmon	.20	.50
240 Matt Bullard	.20	.50
241 Bryce Drew	.20	.50
242 Jerome Moiso	.20	.50
243 Robert Traylor	.20	.50
244 Tyson Chandler	.75	2.00
245 Eddy Curry	.75	2.00
246 Charles Oakley	.25	.60
247 Brad Miller	.30	.75
248 Kevin Ollie	.20	.50
249 Trenton Hassell	.50	1.25
250 Ricky Davis	.25	.60
251 Jumaine Jones	.20	.50
252 DeSagana Diop	.50	1.25
253 Bryant Stith	.20	.50
254 Jeff Trepagnier	.50	1.25
255 Michael Doleac	.20	.50
256 Tim Hardaway	.30	.75
257 Danny Manning	.20	.50
258 Johnny Newman	.20	.50
259 Adrian Griffin	.20	.50
260 Greg Buckner	.20	.50
261 Donnell Harvey	.20	.50
262 Evan Eschmeyer	.20	.50
263 Avery Johnson	.25	.60
264 Kenny Satterfield	.50	1.25
265 Scott Williams	.20	.50
266 Tariq Abdul-Wahad	.20	.50
267 George McCloud	.20	.50
268 Clifford Robinson	.20	.50
269 Jon Barry	.20	.50
270 Brian Cardinal	.20	.50
271 Rodney White	.50	1.25
272 Mikki Moore	.20	.50
273 Victor Alexander	.20	.50
274 Jason Richardson	1.00	2.50
275 Adonal Foyle	.20	.50
276 Troy Murphy	.75	2.00
277 Chris Mills	.20	.50
278 Gilbert Arenas	.75	2.00
279 Erick Dampier	.20	.50
280 Glen Rice	.25	.60
281 Eddie Griffin	.50	1.25
282 Kevin Willis	.20	.50
283 Terence Morris	.50	1.25
284 Kelvin Cato	.20	.50
285 Dan Langhi	.20	.50
286 Jason Collier	.20	.50
287 Jamaal Tinsley	.60	1.50
288 Carlos Rogers	.20	.50
289 Jeff Foster	.20	.50
290 Al Harrington	.25	.60
291 Bruno Sundov	.20	.50
292 Elton Brand	.30	.75
293 Keyon Dooling	.20	.50
294 Michael Olowokandi	.20	.50
295 Obinna Ekezie	.20	.50
296 Earl Boykins	.25	.60
297 Harold Jamison	.20	.50
298 Sean Rooks	.20	.50
299 Lindsey Hunter	.20	.50
300 Samaki Walker	.20	.50
301 Mitch Richmond	.25	.60
302 Stanislav Medvedenko	.20	.50
303 Devean George	.20	.50
304 Robert Horry	.25	.60
305 Jelani McCoy	.20	.50
306 Pau Gasol	1.50	4.00
307 Shane Battier	1.00	2.50
308 Jason Williams	.25	.60
309 Isaac Austin	.20	.50
310 Will Solomon	.50	1.25
311 Lorenzen Wright	.20	.50
312 Kendall Gill	.20	.50
313 LaPhonso Ellis	.25	.60
314 Sean Marks	.20	.50
315 Rod Strickland	.25	.60
316 Jim Jackson	.20	.50
317 Eddie House	.20	.50
318 Jason Caffey	.20	.50
319 Rafer Alston	.20	.50
320 Anthony Mason	.20	.50
321 Mark Pope	.20	.50
322 Michael Redd	.30	.75
323 Darvin Ham	.20	.50
324 Joe Smith	.25	.60
325 William Avery	.20	.50
326 Sam Mitchell	.20	.50
327 Loren Woods	.50	1.25
328 Dean Garrett	.20	.50
329 Gary Trent	.20	.50
330 Jason Kidd	.50	1.25
331 Todd MacCulloch	.20	.50
332 Richard Jefferson	1.00	2.50
333 Brandon Armstrong	.50	1.25
334 Jason Collins	.50	1.25
335 Kerry Kittles	.20	.50
336 Shandon Anderson	.20	.50
337 Howard Eisley	.20	.50
338 Charlie Ward	.20	.50
339 Lavor Postell	.20	.50
340 Clarence Weatherspoon	.20	.50
341 Travis Knight	.20	.50
342 Horace Grant	.25	.60
343 Steven Hunter	.50	1.25
344 Patrick Ewing	.40	1.00
345 Jeryl Sasser	.50	1.25
346 Don Reid	.20	.50
347 Troy Hudson	.20	.50
348 Speedy Claxton	.20	.50
349 Derrick Coleman	.25	.60
350 Damone Brown	.50	1.25
351 Samuel Dalembert	.60	1.50
352 Vonteego Cummings	.20	.50
353 Matt Harpring	.25	.60

Card	Low	High
354 Corie Blount	.20	.50
355 Stephon Marbury	.25	.60
356 Dan Majerle	.25	.60
357 Jake Voskuhl	.20	.50
358 Alton Ford	.50	1.25
359 Iakovos Tsakalidis	.20	.50
360 John Wallace	.20	.50
361 Derek Anderson	.20	.50
362 Erick Barkley	.20	.50
363 Ruben Boumtje-Boumtje	.50	1.25
364 Zach Randolph	1.25	3.00
365 Steve Kerr	.20	.50
366 Shawn Kemp	.30	.75
367 Mateen Cleaves	.20	.50
368 Bobby Jackson	.20	.50
369 Mike Bibby	.30	.75
370 Gerald Wallace	.75	2.00
371 Jabari Smith	.20	.50
372 Lawrence Funderburke	.20	.50
373 Brent Price	.20	.50
374 Bruce Bowen	.20	.50
375 Stephen Jackson	.25	.60
376 Tony Parker	2.00	5.00
377 Steve Smith	.25	.60
378 Cherokee Parks	.20	.50
379 Mark Bryant	.20	.50
380 Jerome James	.20	.50
381 Earl Watson	.30	.75
382 Vladimir Radmanovic	.50	1.25
383 Art Long	.20	.50
384 Calvin Booth	.20	.50
385 Olumide Oyedeji	.20	.50
386 Jerome Williams	.20	.50
387 Hakeem Olajuwon	.40	1.00
388 Dell Curry	.20	.50
389 Michael Bradley	.50	1.25
390 Tracy Murray	.20	.50
391 Eric Montross	.20	.50
392 John Amaechi	.20	.50
393 John Crotty	.20	.50
394 Scott Padgett	.20	.50
395 Andrei Kirilenko	1.25	3.00
396 Jarron Collins	.50	1.25
397 Quincy Lewis	.20	.50
398 Kwame Brown	.50	1.25
399 Christian Laettner	.20	.50
400 Tyrone Nesby	.20	.50
401 Brendan Haywood	.60	1.50
402 Tyronn Lue	.20	.50
403 Michael Jordan	4.00	10.00
404 Kobe Bryant CL	.75	2.00
405 Michael Jordan CL	2.00	5.00
406A Zeljko Rebraca RC	1.00	2.50
406B Zeljko Rebraca RC	1.00	2.50
407A Jamison Brewer RC	1.00	2.50
407B Jamison Brewer RC	1.00	2.50
408A Shawn Marion	.60	1.50
408B Shawn Marion	.60	1.50
409A Primoz Brezec RC	1.00	2.50
409B Primoz Brezec RC	1.00	2.50
410A Antonis Fotsis RC	1.00	2.50
410B Antonis Fotsis RC	1.00	2.50
411A Bobby Simmons RC	1.00	2.50
411B Bobby Simmons RC	1.00	2.50
412A Malik Allen RC	1.00	2.50
412B Malik Allen RC	1.00	2.50
413A Ratko Varda RC	1.00	2.50
413B Ratko Varda RC	1.00	2.50
414A Tierre Brown RC	1.00	2.50
414B Tierre Brown RC	1.00	2.50
415A Norm Richardson RC	1.00	2.50
415B Norm Richardson RC	1.00	2.50
416A Oscar Torres RC	1.00	2.50
416B Oscar Torres RC	1.00	2.50
417A Chris Andersen RC	5.00	12.00
417B Chris Andersen RC	5.00	12.00
418A Predrag Drobnjak RC	1.00	2.50
418B Predrag Drobnjak RC	1.00	2.50
419A Dirk Nowitzki	1.00	2.50
419B Dirk Nowitzki	1.00	2.50
420A Shareef Abdur-Rahim	.50	1.25
420B Shareef Abdur-Rahim	.50	1.25
421A Kenny Anderson	.50	1.25
421B Kenny Anderson	.50	1.25
422A Jamal Mashburn	.50	1.25
422B Jamal Mashburn	.50	1.25
423A Charles Oakley	.50	1.25
423B Charles Oakley	.50	1.25
424A Andre Miller	.50	1.25
424B Andre Miller	.50	1.25
425A Michael Finley	.60	1.50
425B Michael Finley	.60	1.50
426A Tim Hardaway	.60	1.50
426B Tim Hardaway	.60	1.50
427A Nick Van Exel	.50	1.25
427B Nick Van Exel	.50	1.25
428A Jerry Stackhouse	.50	1.25
428B Jerry Stackhouse	.50	1.25
429A Mookie Blaylock	.50	1.25
429B Mookie Blaylock	.50	1.25
430A Glen Rice	.50	1.25
430B Glen Rice	.50	1.25
431A Reggie Miller	.60	1.50
431B Reggie Miller	.60	1.50
432A Elton Brand	.60	1.50
432B Elton Brand	.60	1.50
433A Kobe Bryant	3.00	8.00
433B Kobe Bryant	3.00	8.00
434A Jason Williams	.50	1.25
434B Jason Williams	.50	1.25
435A Eddie Jones	.50	1.25
435B Eddie Jones	.50	1.25
436A Alonzo Mourning	.75	2.00
436B Alonzo Mourning	.75	2.00
437A Glenn Robinson	.50	1.25
437B Glenn Robinson	.50	1.25
438A Kevin Garnett	1.25	3.00
438B Kevin Garnett	1.25	3.00
439A Jason Kidd	1.00	2.50
439B Jason Kidd	1.00	2.50
440A Latrell Sprewell	.50	1.25
440B Latrell Sprewell	.50	1.25
441A Grant Hill	.75	2.00
441B Grant Hill	.75	2.00
442A Dikembe Mutombo	.60	1.50
442B Dikembe Mutombo	.60	1.50
443A Anfernee Hardaway	1.00	2.50
443B Anfernee Hardaway	1.00	2.50
444A Scottie Pippen	1.00	2.50
444B Scottie Pippen	1.00	2.50
445A Mike Bibby	.60	1.50
445B Mike Bibby	.60	1.50
446A David Robinson	1.00	2.50
446B David Robinson	1.00	2.50
447A Gary Payton	.60	1.50
447B Gary Payton	.60	1.50
448A Vince Carter	1.00	2.50
448B Vince Carter	1.00	2.50
449A John Stockton	.75	2.00
449B John Stockton	.75	2.00
450A Michael Jordan Bulls	6.00	15.00
450B Michael Jordan Wizards	6.00	15.00

2001-02 Upper Deck UDX

This set is a 225-card partial parallel insert to the Upper Deck base set. It is randomly inserted in packs only at a rate of 1:4. The set includes 180 veterans and 45 rookies. This commemorative set celebrates Upper Deck Basketball's 10th anniversary. It features a special 10th anniversary logo and sequential numbering. The rookies are numbered to 50; the remainder of the cards are numbered to 100. The cards are standard sized and borderless. The card fronts feature the type of quality action shots that have made Upper Deck Basketball so successful. The recurring theme in this product is the blonde court-wood design found in either the background of the cards or somewhere else on the card, as in this case, it acts as borders on two sides of the player's photo. One border carries the player's name and the other carries his team name.

*UDX STARS: 6X TO 15X BASE CARD HI
*UDX RCs: 3X TO 8X BASE CARD HI
*UDX CLs: 12X TO 30X BASE CARD HI

2001-02 Upper Deck 10th Power Game Jerseys

Randomly inserted in series one packs at a rate of 1:144, this 11-card insert set celebrates the brand's 10th anniversary with a game jersey set. The standard sized cards are borderless and feature swatches of the featured player's game worn jerseys. They also offer a UD Decade Milestone written in the lower right-hand corner of each card. The player's name is in the lower left-hand corner.

Card	Low	High
AWX Antoine Walker	3.00	8.00
DRX David Robinson	6.00	15.00
KBX Kobe Bryant	20.00	50.00
KGX Kevin Garnett	8.00	20.00
KVX Keith Van Horn	3.00	8.00
MJX Michael Jordan	60.00	120.00
MTX Dikembe Mutombo	4.00	10.00
NVX Nick Van Exel	3.00	8.00
RAX Ray Allen	4.00	10.00
RHH Richard Hamilton	3.00	8.00
WSX Wally Szczerbiak	3.00	8.00

2001-02 Upper Deck 15000 Point Club Jerseys

Randomly inserted in series 2 packs at the rate of one in 120, this nine card set showcases the elite members of the NBA's 15000 point club with a swatch of game worn jersey.

Card	Low	High
GR15K Glen Rice	4.00	10.00
IT15K Isiah Thomas	8.00	20.00
JH15K John Havlicek	8.00	20.00
JW15K Jerry West	10.00	25.00
KM15K Karl Malone	6.00	15.00
LB15K Larry Bird	15.00	40.00
MJ15K Michael Jordan	60.00	120.00
MM15K Moses Malone	5.00	12.00
PE15K Patrick Ewing	6.00	15.00

2001-02 Upper Deck Breakout Performers

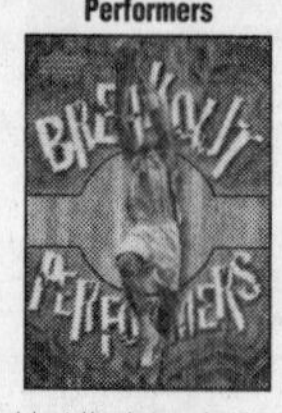

Randomly inserted in series two packs at the rate of one in 12, this 15-card set showcases players that came straight out into the league and proved they belong. Full color player action photos are surrounded on both the top and the bottom by the words "Breakout Performers" and look as if they're jumping straight out of the card.

Card	Low	High
COMPLETE SET (15)	7.50	15.00
BP1 Kenyon Martin	.60	1.50
BP2 Steve Francis	.60	1.50
BP3 Stromile Swift	.40	1.00
BP4 Baron Davis	.60	1.50
BP5 Rashard Lewis	.60	1.50
BP6 Vince Carter	1.00	2.50
BP7 Richard Hamilton	.50	1.25
BP8 Kobe Bryant	3.00	8.00
BP9 DerMarr Johnson	.40	1.00
BP10 Andre Miller	.50	1.25
BP11 Kevin Garnett	1.25	3.00
BP12 Morris Peterson	.40	1.00
BP13 Dirk Nowitzki	1.00	2.50
BP14 Mike Miller	.60	1.50
BP15 Shawn Marion	.60	1.50

2001-02 Upper Deck BuyBacks

PRINT RUNS LISTED BELOW
MOST UNPRICED DUE TO SCARCITY

Card	Low	High
2 Kobe Bryant	100.00	200.00
00-1UD/80/88		
12 Jerry Stackhouse	25.00	60.00
00-1 SPA/21		

2001-02 Upper Deck Class

Randomly inserted in series one packs at a rate of 1:24, this 7-card insert celebrates the best photos from Upper Deck's first ten years in basketball. Player photos appear on the right side of the card, and an irredescent strip with gold foil highlights appears on the left.

Card	Low	High
COMPLETE SET (7)	8.00	20.00
C1 Michael Jordan	6.00	15.00
C2 Shaquille O'Neal	2.00	5.00
C3 Alonzo Mourning	1.00	2.50
C4 Steve Francis	.75	2.00
C5 Kobe Bryant	4.00	10.00
C6 Tim Duncan	1.50	4.00
C7 Kevin Garnett	1.50	4.00

2001-02 Upper Deck Classic Duals Jerseys

Seeded in series two packs at the rate of one in 240, this nine card set pairs two players together on the card front of this horizontal design. Player action photos are set on both the left and the right side, and semi-circular swatch of jerseys appear below.

Card	Low	High
JS/GP John Stockton	8.00	20.00
Gary Payton		
JT/TP Jamaal Tinsley	8.00	20.00
Tony Parker		
KB/AI Kobe Bryant	20.00	50.00
Allen Iverson		
KB/DM Kobe Bryant	15.00	40.00
Darius Miles		
KB/TM Kobe Bryant	20.00	50.00
Tracy McGrady		
KM/KG Karl Malone	8.00	20.00
Kevin Garnett		

2001-02 Upper Deck Cool Cats Jerseys

Randomly inserted in series two packs at the rate of one in 288, this eight card set showcases some of the University of Kentucky Wildcats best players. Car backgrounds are blue on the top and black on the bottom. The top of the card has a swatch in the shape of a Wildcat paw, and the bottom has a portrait style photo of the featured player.

Card	Low	High
AWC Antoine Walker	4.00	10.00
BRC Michael Bradley	5.00	12.00
DJC DerMarr Johnson	3.00	8.00
JMC Jamal Mashburn	4.00	10.00
KMC Kenyon Martin	5.00	12.00
RJC Richard Jefferson	10.00	25.00
RMC Ron Mercer	3.00	8.00
TDC Tony Delk	3.00	8.00

2001-02 Upper Deck Game Jerseys

Randomly inserted in series one packs at a rate of 1:144, this 10-card insert features full color player photos on the right and a rectangular swatch of a game jersey in the lower right hand corner.

Card	Low	High
BR Bryon Russell	2.50	6.00
CM Cuttino Mobley	3.00	8.00
GP Gary Payton	4.00	10.00
JS Joe Smith	3.00	8.00
JT Jason Terry	4.00	10.00
KB Kobe Bryant	20.00	50.00
KG Kevin Garnett	8.00	20.00
KM Karl Malone	5.00	12.00
MC Marc Jackson	2.50	6.00
RA Ron Artest	4.00	10.00

2001-02 Upper Deck Game Jerseys Autographs 1

Randomly inserted in series one hobby packs, this 11-card set features both a swatch of a game worn jersey as well as an authentic player autographs.

Card	Low	High
CHA Chris Mihm	6.00	15.00
KBA Kobe Bryant	150.00	300.00
KGA Kevin Garnett	40.00	80.00
KMA Kenyon Martin	15.00	40.00
LHA Larry Hughes	20.00	50.00
MAA Marcus Fizer	10.00	25.00
MMA Mike Miller	20.00	50.00
MPA Morris Peterson	10.00	25.00
WZA Wang Zhizhi	20.00	50.00

2001-02 Upper Deck Game Jerseys Autographs 2

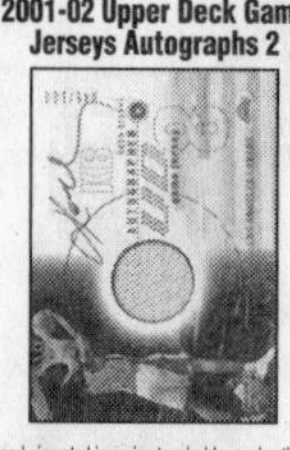

Randomly inserted in series two hobby packs, this 11-card set features both a swatch of a game worn jersey as well as an authentic player autographs.

Card	Low	High
DJA DerMarr Johnson	12.00	30.00
DMA Desmond Mason	12.00	30.00
EGA Eddie Griffin	12.00	30.00
JRA Jason Richardson	30.00	80.00
KBA Kobe Bryant	150.00	300.00
KGA Kevin Garnett	40.00	80.00
RMA Ron Mercer	12.00	30.00
RWA Rodney White	12.00	30.00

2001-02 Upper Deck Game Jerseys Combos

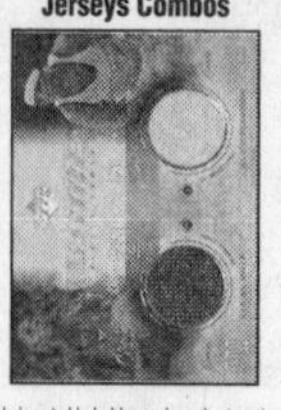

Randomly inserted in hobby packs only at a rate of 1:144, this 10-card insert set includes two swatches of a game-worn jersey from two different players on one card.

Card	Low	High
AJLH Antawn Jamison	6.00	15.00
Larry Hughes		
AMLM Andre Miller	6.00	15.00
Lamond Murray		
DMCM Darius Miles	6.00	15.00
Corey Maggette		
DMQR Darius Miles	6.00	15.00
Quentin Richardson		
JCRM Jamal Crawford	6.00	15.00
Ron Mercer		
JMBD Jamal Mashburn	6.00	15.00
Baron Davis		
JTTK Jason Terry	6.00	15.00
Toni Kukoc		
KBKG Kobe Bryant	20.00	50.00
Kevin Garnett		
KMJS Karl Malone	12.50	30.00
John Stockton		
MFDN Michael Finley	8.00	20.00
Dirk Nowitzki		

2001-02 Upper Deck Game Jerseys Logos

Randomly seeded in series two packs at the rate of one in 5000, this nine card set utilizes the same design as the Game Jerseys insert set enhanced with premium jersey swatches from uniform logos.

Card	Low	High
AHPL Allan Houston	20.00	50.00
KBPL Kobe Bryant	125.00	300.00
MMPL Mike Miller	25.00	60.00

2001-02 Upper Deck Game Jerseys Names

Randomly seeded in series two packs at the rate of one in 7500, this nine card set utilizes the same design as the Game Jerseys insert set enhanced with premium jersey swatches from uniform names.

Card	Low	High
MJ2PN Michael Jordan	300.00	600.00
KGPN Kevin Garnett	60.00	150.00

2001-02 Upper Deck Game Jerseys Numbers

Randomly seeded in series two packs at the rate of one in 2500, this nine card set utilizes the same design as the Game Jerseys insert set enhanced with premium jersey swatches from uniform numbers.

Card	Low	High
AMP Antonio McDyess	15.00	40.00
JMP Jamal Mashburn	15.00	40.00
KBP Kobe Bryant	100.00	250.00
KMP Karl Malone	25.00	60.00
MFP Michael Finley	20.00	50.00

2001-02 Upper Deck Game Jerseys Patches

Randomly seeded in series one packs at the rate of one in 2500, this nine card set utilizes the same design as the Game Jerseys insert set enhanced with premium jersey swatches from uniform patches.

Card	Low	High
AIP Allen Iverson	40.00	100.00
AMP Andre Miller	15.00	40.00
JMP Jamal Mashburn	15.00	40.00
JTP Jason Terry	20.00	50.00
KBP Kobe Bryant	100.00	250.00
KGP Kevin Garnett	40.00	100.00
KMP Kenyon Martin	20.00	50.00
MAP Marc Jackson	12.00	30.00
MFP Michael Finley	20.00	50.00
MMP Mike Miller	20.00	50.00
QRP Quentin Richardson	15.00	40.00
RAP Ray Allen	20.00	50.00
RWP Rasheed Wallace	20.00	50.00
SMP Shawn Marion	20.00	50.00

2001-02 Upper Deck Higher Ground

Randomly inserted in series one packs at the rate of one in 18, this 10-card set places full color player action photos on a white background with a colored strip to match the player jersey and irridescent foil highlights throught the center of the card. The top and bottom of the card are colored to resemble the three point arc on a basketball court.

Card	Low	High
COMPLETE SET (10)	7.50	15.00
HG1 Vince Carter	1.25	3.00
HG2 Kevin Garnett	1.50	4.00
HG3 Paul Pierce	1.00	2.50
HG4 Mike Miller	.75	2.00
HG5 Jamal Mashburn	.60	1.50
HG6 Steve Francis	.75	2.00
HG7 Jerry Stackhouse	.60	1.50
HG8 Kobe Bryant	4.00	10.00
HG9 Eddie Jones	.60	1.50
HG10 Shawn Marion	.75	2.00

2001-02 Upper Deck MJ Jersey Collection

Randomly inserted in packs of Upper Deck, this 19 card set features Michael Jordan with different swatches from the different jerseys he's worn throughout the years. Cards MJC1-MJC10 were inserted in series one packs, and cards MJC11-MJC19 were inserted in series two packs. The jerseys are cut in the shape of the letter "M," and each card is sequentially numbered to 50.

Card	Low	High
COMMON CARD	150.00	300.00

2001-02 Upper Deck Motion Pictures

Randomly seeded in series two packs at the rate of one in 18, this 10-card set pictures players in action set on a "film strip" backdrop on the right side of the card. The left side contains the set name and the player's name in gold foil.

Card	Low	High
COMPLETE SET (10)	12.50	25.00
MP1 Kobe Bryant	4.00	10.00
MP2 Tim Duncan	1.50	4.00
MP3 Michael Jordan	6.00	15.00
MP4 Elton Brand	.75	2.00
MP5 Vince Carter	1.25	3.00
MP6 Eddie Jones	.60	1.50
MP7 Kevin Garnett	1.50	4.00
MP8 Michael Finley	.75	2.00
MP9 Paul Pierce	1.00	2.50
MP10 Shaquille O'Neal	2.00	5.00

2001-02 Upper Deck NBA All-Star Authentics

Randomly inserted in series one packs at the rate of one in 96, this five card set features NBA All-Stars in full color action coupled with a swatch of game worn memorabilia.

Card	Low	High
BDAS Baron Davis	5.00	12.00
DMAS Desmond Mason	4.00	10.00
PSAS Peja Stojakovic	5.00	12.00
RLAS Rashard Lewis	5.00	12.00
SSAS Stromile Swift	3.00	8.00

2001-02 Upper Deck NBA Finals Fabrics

Randomly inserted in series two packs at the rate of one in 120, this 20-card set features players from the 2000-01 finals in action and swatches of the jerseys they wore in those games.

Card	Low	High
AIF Allen Iverson	12.00	30.00
AMF Aaron McKie	4.00	10.00
BSF Brian Shaw	4.00	10.00
DFF Derek Fisher	5.00	12.00
DGF Devean George	4.00	10.00
DMF Dikembe Mutombo	6.00	15.00
ESF Eric Snow	4.00	10.00
GFF Greg Foster	4.00	10.00
HGF Horace Grant	5.00	12.00
JJF Jumaine Jones	4.00	10.00
KBF Kobe Bryant	100.00	200.00
KOF Kevin Ollie	4.00	10.00
MMF Mark Madsen	4.00	10.00
RBF Rodney Buford	4.00	10.00
RFF Rick Fox	5.00	12.00
RJF Raja Bell	8.00	20.00
ROF Robert Horry	8.00	20.00
THF Tyrone Hill	4.00	10.00
TLF Tyronn Lue	4.00	10.00
TMF Todd MacCulloch	4.00	10.00

2001-02 Upper Deck Rookie Threads

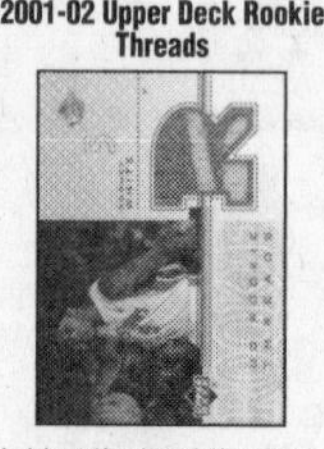

Randomly inserted in series two hobby packs at the rate of one in 144, this 10-card set features full color photos of rookie players on the right side of this horizontal card design with a swatch of a jersey that is cut in the shape of the letter R.

Card	Low	High
ECT Eddy Curry	4.00	10.00
EGT Eddie Griffin	2.50	6.00
GWT Gerald Wallace	4.00	10.00
JJT Joe Johnson	6.00	15.00
JRT Jason Richardson	5.00	12.00
KET Kedrick Brown	2.50	6.00
KWT Kwame Brown	2.50	6.00
RJT Richard Jefferson	5.00	12.00
RWT Rodney White	2.50	6.00
TCT Tyson Chandler	4.00	10.00

2001-02 Upper Deck Sky High

Randomly inserted in series two packs at the rate of one in 24, this seven card set showcases high flyers of the NBA with full color action photos. The photos are centered on the card and along the right side, each of the letters in the words, "Sky High" are surrounded with a gold foil circle.

Card	Low	High
COMPLETE SET (7)	7.50	15.00
SH1 Kobe Bryant	4.00	10.00
SH2 Kevin Garnett	1.50	4.00
SH3 Darius Miles	.50	1.25
SH4 Tracy McGrady	1.25	3.00
SH5 Kwame Brown	.75	2.00
SH6 Eddy Curry	1.25	3.00
SH7 Tyson Chandler	1.25	3.00

2001-02 Upper Deck SlamCenter

Randomly inserted in series one packs at the rate of one in 12, this 15-card set features in action player photos set on a square irridescent background with white borders. Cards are highlighted with gold foil and the word Slam along the right side and the word Center across the player photo.

Card	Low	High
COMPLETE SET (15)	7.50	15.00
SC1 Kobe Bryant	3.00	8.00
SC2 Desmond Mason	.50	1.25
SC3 Vince Carter	1.00	2.50
SC4 Antonio McDyess	.50	1.25
SC5 Lamar Odom	.60	1.50
SC6 Rashard Lewis	.60	1.50
SC7 Chris Webber	.60	1.50
SC8 Latrell Sprewell	.50	1.25
SC9 Antoine Walker	.50	1.25
SC10 Stromile Swift	.40	1.00
SC11 Glenn Robinson	.50	1.25
SC12 Kevin Garnett	1.25	3.00
SC13 Antawn Jamison	.60	1.50
SC14 Jerry Stackhouse	.50	1.25
SC15 Shaquille O'Neal	1.50	4.00

2001-02 Upper Deck Superstar Summit

Inserted in series two packs at the rate of one in 18, this 10-card set places full color player action photos on an all foil backdrop. The background is shaped like the letter "X" and has gold foil highlights.

Card	Low	High
COMPLETE SET (10)	12.50	25.00
SS1 Kobe Bryant	4.00	10.00
SS2 Vince Carter	1.25	3.00
SS3 Kevin Garnett	1.50	4.00
SS4 Chris Webber	.75	2.00
SS5 Shaquille O'Neal	2.00	5.00
SS6 Tim Duncan	1.50	4.00
SS7 Allen Iverson	1.50	4.00
SS8 Ray Allen	.75	2.00
SS9 Steve Francis	.75	2.00
SS10 Michael Jordan	6.00	15.00

2001-02 Upper Deck Triple Jump Jerseys

Inserted in hobby packs, this 10-card set featues three small in action photos of the showcased players on the right set against a white background and three swatches of game jersey on the left. Each card is sequentially numbered to 25.

Card	Low	High
JTJRTP Jamaal Tinsley	30.00	80.00
Jason Richardson		
Tony Parker		
KBTMCW Kobe Bryant	75.00	150.00
Tracy McGrady		
Chris Webber		
MJDRKB Michael Jordan	250.00	500.00
Julius Erving		
Kobe Bryant		
MJKBKG Michael Jordan	200.00	400.00
Kobe Bryant		
Kevin Garnett		
MJMJMJ Michael Jordan	300.00	600.00
Michael Jordan		
Michael Jordan		

2001-02 Upper Deck UD Originals Jerseys

Seeded in series two packs at the rate of one in 120, this 10-card set focuses on some of the younger players of the NBA. The card design resembles that of the base Upper Deck cards with a swatch of jersey in the lower right hand corner.

Card	Low	High
BDO Baron Davis	5.00	12.00
CWO Chris Webber	5.00	12.00
DMO Darius Miles	3.00	8.00
KBO Kobe Bryant	25.00	60.00
KGO Kevin Garnett	10.00	25.00
MMO Mike Miller	5.00	12.00
RAO Ray Allen	5.00	12.00
SHO Shawn Marion	5.00	12.00
SMO Stephon Marbury	4.00	10.00
SSO Stromile Swift	3.00	8.00

2001-02 Upper Deck Upper Decade Team

Seeded in series one packs at the rate of one in 18, this 10-card set features a colored border on the left side of the card, a full color player action photo in the center on a white background, and an irridescent player portrait style photo along the right side.

Card	Low	High
COMPLETE SET (10)	12.50	30.00
UD1 Michael Jordan	6.00	15.00
UD2 Kobe Bryant	4.00	10.00
UD3 Vince Carter	1.25	3.00
UD4 Kevin Garnett	1.50	4.00
UD5 Shaquille O'Neal	2.00	5.00
UD6 Tim Hardaway	.75	2.00
UD7 Gary Payton	.75	2.00
UD8 Scottie Pippen	1.25	3.00
UD9 Tim Duncan	1.50	4.00
UD10 David Robinson	1.25	3.00

2001-02 Upper Deck Winning Touch Game Jerseys

Seeded in series one packs at the rate of one in 144, this 11-card set places players in action along the right side of the card, a colored border on the left side, and a "wood grain" center with a swatch of a game jersey.

Card	Low	High
AIWT Allen Iverson	8.00	20.00
DRWT David Robinson	6.00	15.00
JSWT John Stockton	5.00	12.00
KMWT Karl Malone	5.00	12.00
PEWT Patrick Ewing	5.00	12.00
RFWT Rick Fox	3.00	8.00
RPWT Robert Parish	4.00	10.00
SEWT Sean Elliott	2.50	6.00
SKWT Steve Kerr	5.00	12.00

2001-02 Upper Deck World Piece Game Jerseys

Inserted in series one hobby packs at the rate of one in 288, this 10-card set features some of the NBA's most prominent foreign players and a swatch of a game worn jersey.

Card	Low	High
DBWP Dalibor Bagaric	2.50	6.00
DNWP Dirk Nowitzki	6.00	15.00
FLWP Felipe Lopez	2.50	6.00
HMWP Hanno Mottola	2.50	6.00
MOWP Michael Olowokandi	2.50	6.00
MTWP Dikembe Mutombo	4.00	10.00
SNWP Steve Nash	6.00	15.00
TKWP Toni Kukoc	3.00	8.00
VLWP Vlade Divac	3.00	8.00
ZWWP Wang Zhizhi	3.00	8.00

2002-03 Upper Deck

Upper Deck was issued as a 420-card set divided up into two series. Series one contains 210 cards and was released in November 2002, and Series two contains 220 cards and was released in February 2003. Base cards are borderless with a name box at the bottom and silver foil highlights. The breakdown is as follows: Numbers 1-180 feature veteran players, numbers 181-210 feature rookies, numbers 211-390 feature both veterans and rookies, however, the rookie players in this section have rookie cards in series one so these are not RC cards, and numbers 391-419 again feature rookies. The last card in the set features Michael Jordan. Upper Deck was packaged in 24-pack boxes where packs contained eight cards and carried a suggested retail price of $2.99.

Card	Low	High
COMPLETE SER.1 (210)	80.00	160.00
COMPLETE SER. 2 (210)	20.00	40.00
COMP.SER.1 w/o SP's (180)	15.00	40.00
1 Shareef Abdur-Rahim	.25	.60
2 Jason Terry	.25	.60
3 Glenn Robinson	.25	.60
4 Nazr Mohammed	.20	.50
5 DerMarr Johnson	.20	.50
6 Dion Glover	.20	.50
7 Paul Pierce	.40	1.00
8 Antoine Walker	.25	.60
9 Vin Baker	.25	.60
10 Eric Williams	.20	.50
11 Tony Delk	.20	.50
12 Kedrick Brown	.20	.50
13 Jalen Rose	.25	.60
14 Eddy Curry	.25	.60
15 Tyson Chandler	.25	.60
16 Jamal Crawford	.25	.60
17 Marcus Fizer	.20	.50
18 Trenton Hassell	.20	.50
19 Zydrunas Ilgauskas	.25	.60
20 Tyrone Hill	.20	.50
21 Darius Miles	.20	.50
22 Chris Mihm	.20	.50
23 Ricky Davis	.25	.60
24 Jumaine Jones	.20	.50
25 Dirk Nowitzki	.50	1.25
26 Michael Finley	.30	.75
27 Steve Nash	.40	1.00
28 Raef LaFrentz	.20	.50
29 Nick Van Exel	.25	.60
30 Adrian Griffin	.20	.50
31 Wang Zhizhi	.20	.50
32 Marcus Camby	.25	.60
33 Juwan Howard	.25	.60
34 James Posey	.20	.50
35 Donnell Harvey	.20	.50
36 Ryan Bowen	.20	.50
37 Zeljko Rebraca	.20	.50
38 Ben Wallace	.30	.75
39 Clifford Robinson	.20	.50
40 Corliss Williamson	.20	.50
41 Chucky Atkins	.20	.50
42 Michael Curry	.20	.50
43 Jason Richardson	.30	.75
44 Antawn Jamison	.30	.75
45 Troy Murphy	.30	.75
46 Gilbert Arenas	.30	.75
47 Danny Fortson	.20	.50
48 Steve Francis	.30	.75
49 Eddie Griffin	.20	.50
50 Cuttino Mobley	.25	.60
51 Kenny Thomas	.20	.50
52 Moochie Norris	.20	.50
53 Kelvin Cato	.20	.50
54 Reggie Miller	.30	.75
55 Jermaine O'Neal	.30	.75
56 Ron Mercer	.20	.50
57 Austin Croshere	.20	.50
58 Ron Artest	.30	.75
59 Jamaal Tinsley	.20	.50
60 Elton Brand	.30	.75
61 Andre Miller	.25	.60
62 Lamar Odom	.30	.75
63 Michael Olowokandi	.20	.50
64 Quentin Richardson	.25	.60
65 Corey Maggette	.25	.60
66 Kobe Bryant	1.50	4.00
67 Shaquille O'Neal	.75	2.00
68 Rick Fox	.25	.60
69 Robert Horry	.25	.60
70 Devean George	.20	.50
71 Samaki Walker	.20	.50
72 Brian Shaw	.20	.50
73 Pau Gasol	.40	1.00
74 Jason Williams	.25	.60
75 Shane Battier	.30	.75
76 Stromile Swift	.20	.50
77 Lorenzen Wright	.20	.50
78 LaPhonso Ellis	.25	.60
79 Eddie Jones	.25	.60
80 Brian Grant	.20	.50
81 Vladimir Stepania	.20	.50
82 Eddie House	.20	.50
83 Anthony Carter	.20	.50
84 Ray Allen	.30	.75
85 Sam Cassell	.25	.60
86 Tim Thomas	.20	.50
87 Toni Kukoc	.25	.60
88 Jason Caffey	.20	.50
89 Anthony Mason	.20	.50
90 Joel Przybilla	.20	.50
91 Kevin Garnett	.60	1.50
92 Wally Szczerbiak	.25	.60
93 Terrell Brandon	.20	.50
94 Joe Smith	.25	.60
95 Felipe Lopez	.20	.50
96 Anthony Peeler	.20	.50
97 Radoslav Nesterovic	.20	.50
98 Jason Kidd	.50	1.25
99 Kenyon Martin	.30	.75
100 Dikembe Mutombo	.30	.75
101 Richard Jefferson	.30	.75
102 Kerry Kittles	.20	.50
103 Lucious Harris	.20	.50
104 Jason Collins	.20	.50
105 Baron Davis	.30	.75
106 Jamal Mashburn	.25	.60
107 Elden Campbell	.20	.50
108 David Wesley	.20	.50
109 P.J. Brown	.20	.50
110 Lee Nailon	.20	.50
111 Latrell Sprewell	.25	.60
112 Allan Houston	.25	.60
113 Kurt Thomas	.20	.50
114 Antonio McDyess	.25	.60
115 Othella Harrington	.20	.50
116 Clarence Weatherspoon	.20	.50
117 Tracy McGrady	.50	1.25
118 Mike Miller	.30	.75
119 Darrell Armstrong	.20	.50
120 Grant Hill	.40	1.00
121 Pat Garrity	.20	.50
122 Steven Hunter	.20	.50
123 Allen Iverson	.50	1.25
124 Keith Van Horn	.25	.60
125 Aaron McKie	.20	.50
126 Eric Snow	.20	.50
127 Derrick Coleman	.25	.60
128 Samuel Dalembert	.20	.50
129 Stephon Marbury	.25	.60
130 Shawn Marion	.30	.75
131 Joe Johnson	.30	.75
132 Tom Gugliotta	.20	.50
133 Anfernee Hardaway	.50	1.25
134 Iakovos Tsakalidis	.20	.50
135 Rasheed Wallace	.30	.75
136 Bonzi Wells	.20	.50
137 Damon Stoudamire	.25	.60
138 Scottie Pippen	.50	1.25
139 Derek Anderson	.20	.50
140 Ruben Patterson	.20	.50
141 Dale Davis	.20	.50
142 Mike Bibby	.30	.75
143 Chris Webber	.30	.75
144 Peja Stojakovic	.30	.75
145 Doug Christie	.20	.50
146 Hedo Turkoglu	.30	.75
147 Vlade Divac	.25	.60
148 Scot Pollard	.20	.50
149 Tim Duncan	.60	1.50
150 David Robinson	.50	1.25
151 Tony Parker	.40	1.00
152 Malik Rose	.20	.50
153 Steve Smith	.25	.60
154 Bruce Bowen	.20	.50
155 Danny Ferry	.20	.50
156 Gary Payton	.30	.75
157 Rashard Lewis	.30	.75
158 Brent Barry	.20	.50
159 Kenny Anderson	.25	.60
160 Desmond Mason	.25	.60
161 Predrag Drobnjak	.20	.50
162 Vince Carter	.50	1.25
163 Morris Peterson	.20	.50
164 Antonio Davis	.20	.50
165 Alvin Williams	.20	.50
166 Jerome Williams	.20	.50
167 Michael Bradley	.20	.50
168 Karl Malone	.40	1.00
169 John Stockton	.40	1.00
170 John Amaechi	.20	.50
171 Andrei Kirilenko	.30	.75
172 Greg Ostertag	.20	.50
173 Jarron Collins	.20	.50
174 DeShawn Stevenson	.20	.50
175 Christian Laettner	.20	.50
176 Brendan Haywood	.20	.50
177 Chris Whitney	.20	.50
178 Tyronn Lue	.20	.50
179 Kwame Brown	.20	.50
180 Michael Jordan	2.50	6.00
181 Jay Williams RC	1.50	4.00
182 Juan Dixon RC	1.50	4.00
183 Vincent Yarbrough RC	1.25	3.00
184 Casey Jacobsen RC	1.25	3.00
185 Chris Wilcox RC	1.25	3.00
186 John Salmons RC	1.50	4.00
187 Marcus Haislip RC	1.25	3.00
188 Robert Archibald RC	1.25	3.00
189 Jared Jeffries RC	1.25	3.00
190 Nikoloz Tskitishvili RC	1.25	3.00
191 Kareem Rush RC	1.25	3.00
192 Fred Jones RC	1.25	3.00
193 Caron Butler RC	2.00	5.00
194 Chris Jefferies RC	1.25	3.00
195 Ryan Humphrey RC	1.25	3.00
196 Frank Williams RC	1.25	3.00
197 DaJuan Wagner RC	1.25	3.00
198 Bostjan Nachbar RC	1.25	3.00
199 Mike Dunleavy RC	1.50	4.00
200 Roger Mason RC	1.25	3.00
201 Nene Hilario RC	1.50	4.00
202 Melvin Ely RC	1.25	3.00
203 Tayshaun Prince RC	1.50	4.00
204 Jiri Welsch RC	1.25	3.00
205 Dan Dickau RC	1.25	3.00
206 Qyntel Woods RC	1.25	3.00
207 Curtis Borchardt RC	1.25	3.00
208 Amare Stoudemire RC	3.00	8.00
209 Drew Gooden RC	2.00	5.00
210 Yao Ming RC	4.00	10.00
211 Glenn Robinson	.25	.60
212 Theo Ratliff	.20	.50
213 Emanual Davis	.20	.50
214 Dan Dickau	.60	1.50
215 Alan Henderson	.20	.50
216 Chris Crawford	.20	.50
217 Darvin Ham	.20	.50
218 Ira Newble	.20	.50
219 Vin Baker	.25	.60
220 Shammond Williams	.20	.50
221 Tony Battie	.20	.50
222 Walter McCarty	.20	.50
223 Bruno Sundov	.20	.50
224 Ruben Wolkowyski	.20	.50
225 Eddie Robinson	.20	.50
226 Jay Williams	.75	2.00
227 Fred Hoiberg	.20	.50
228 Donyell Marshall	.20	.50
229 Roger Mason	.60	1.50
230 Darius Miles	.20	.50
231 Michael Stewart	.20	.50
232 Tyrone Hill	.20	.50
233 DaJuan Wagner	.60	1.50
234 DeSagana Diop	.20	.50
235 Bimbo Coles	.20	.50
236 Milt Palacio	.20	.50
237 Avery Johnson	.25	.60
238 Evan Eschmeyer	.20	.50
239 Raja Bell	.25	.60
240 Shawn Bradley	.20	.50
241 Walt Williams	.20	.50
242 Eduardo Najera	.20	.50
243 Marcus Camby	.25	.60
244 Chris Whitney	.20	.50
245 Nikoloz Tskitishvili	.60	1.50
246 Kenny Satterfield	.20	.50
247 Nene Hilario	.75	2.00
248 Mark Blount	.20	.50
249 Richard Hamilton	.25	.60
250 Chauncey Billups	.30	.75
251 Tayshaun Prince	.75	2.00
252 Don Reid	.20	.50
253 Jon Barry	.20	.50
254 Hubert Davis	.20	.50
255 Pepe Sanchez	.20	.50
256 Chris Mills	.20	.50
257 Bob Sura	.20	.50
258 Mike Dunleavy	.75	2.00
259 Jiri Welsch	.60	1.50
260 Adonal Foyle	.20	.50
261 Erick Dampier	.20	.50
262 Maurice Taylor	.20	.50
263 Glen Rice	.25	.60
264 Yao Ming	2.00	5.00
265 Bostjan Nachbar	.60	1.50
266 Jason Collier	.20	.50
267 Terence Morris	.20	.50
268 Jonathan Bender	.20	.50
269 Jeff Foster	.20	.50
270 Fred Jones	.60	1.50
271 Al Harrington	.25	.60
272 Brad Miller	.30	.75
273 Jamison Brewer	.20	.50
274 Erick Strickland	.20	.50
275 Andre Miller	.25	.60
276 Melvin Ely	.60	1.50
277 Keyon Dooling	.20	.50
278 Chris Wilcox	.60	1.50
279 Eric Piatkowski	.20	.50
280 Sean Rooks	.20	.50
281 Wang Zhi Zhi	.20	.50
282 Mark Madsen	.20	.50
283 Kareem Rush	.60	1.50
284 Stanislav Medvedenko	.20	.50
285 Derek Fisher	.25	.60
286 Tracy Murray	.20	.50
287 Michael Dickerson	.20	.50
288 Wesley Person	.20	.50
289 Drew Gooden	1.00	2.50
290 Robert Archibald	.60	1.50
291 Brevin Knight	.20	.50
292 Mike James	.20	.50
293 LaPhonso Ellis	.25	.60
294 Caron Butler	1.00	2.50
295 Malik Allen	.20	.50
296 Travis Best	.20	.50
297 Alonzo Mourning	.40	1.00
298 Toni Kukoc	.25	.60
299 Michael Redd	.30	.75
300 Marcus Haislip	.60	1.50
301 Ervin Johnson	.20	.50
302 Kevin Ollie	.20	.50
303 Troy Hudson	.20	.50
304 Marc Jackson	.20	.50
305 Gary Trent	.20	.50
306 Kendall Gill	.20	.50
307 Loren Woods	.20	.50
308 Dikembe Mutombo	.30	.75
309 Anthony Johnson	.20	.50
310 Rodney Rogers	.20	.50
311 Brandon Armstrong	.20	.50
312 Brian Scalabrine	.20	.50
313 Aaron Williams	.20	.50
314 Courtney Alexander	.20	.50
315 Kirk Haston	.20	.50
316 George Lynch	.20	.50
317 Stacey Augmon	.20	.50
318 Robert Traylor	.20	.50
319 Jamaal Magloire	.20	.50
320 Lee Nailon	.20	.50
321 Frank Williams	.60	1.50
322 Michael Doleac	.20	.50
323 Shandon Anderson	.20	.50
324 Howard Eisley	.20	.50
325 Travis Knight	.20	.50
326 Lavor Postell	.20	.50
327 Charlie Ward	.20	.50
328 Mark Pope	.20	.50
329 Olumide Oyedeji	.20	.50
330 Shawn Kemp	.30	.75
331 Jacque Vaughn	.20	.50
332 Ryan Humphrey	.60	1.50
333 Andrew DeClercq	.20	.50
334 Jeryl Sasser	.20	.50
335 Keith Van Horn	.25	.60
336 Todd MacCulloch	.20	.50
337 Monty Williams	.20	.50
338 John Salmons	.75	2.00
339 Brian Skinner	.20	.50
340 Mark Bryant	.20	.50
341 Greg Buckner	.20	.50
342 Bo Outlaw	.20	.50
343 Amare Stoudemire	1.50	4.00
344 Casey Jacobsen	.60	1.50
345 Alton Ford	.20	.50
346 Scott Williams	.20	.50
347 Dan Langhi	.20	.50
348 Arvydas Sabonis	.25	.60
349 Antonio Daniels	.20	.50
350 Jeff McInnis	.20	.50
351 Qyntel Woods	.60	1.50
352 Zach Randolph	.30	.75
353 Ruben Boumtje-Boumtje	.20	.50
354 Chris Dudley	.20	.50
355 Charles Smith	.20	.50
356 Keon Clark	.20	.50
357 Bobby Jackson	.20	.50
358 Mateen Cleaves	.20	.50
359 Gerald Wallace	.30	.75
360 Lawrence Funderburke	.20	.50
361 Speedy Claxton	.20	.50
362 Stephen Jackson	.25	.60
363 Kevin Willis	.20	.50
364 Steve Kerr	.20	.50
365 Mengke Bateer	.20	.50
366 Kenny Anderson	.25	.60
367 Vladimir Radmanovic	.20	.50
368 Joseph Forte	.20	.50
369 Jerome James	.20	.50
370 Vitaly Potapenko	.20	.50
371 Calvin Booth	.20	.50
372 Ansu Sesay	.20	.50
373 Voshon Lenard	.20	.50
374 Lindsey Hunter	.20	.50
375 Mamadou N'Diaye	.20	.50
376 Chris Jefferies	.60	1.50
377 Jelani McCoy	.20	.50
378 Lamond Murray	.20	.50
379 Eric Montross	.20	.50
380 Matt Harpring	.25	.60
381 Calbert Cheaney	.20	.50
382 Curtis Borchardt	.60	1.50
383 Mark Jackson	.25	.60
384 Scott Padgett	.20	.50
385 Jerry Stackhouse	.25	.60
386 Jared Jeffries	.60	1.50
387 Larry Hughes	.25	.60
388 Juan Dixon	.75	2.00
389 Bryon Russell	.20	.50
390 Etan Thomas	.20	.50
391 Elthimios Rentzias RC	1.25	3.00
392 Manu Ginobili RC	3.00	8.00
393 Juaquin Hawkins RC	1.25	3.00
394 Rasual Butler RC	1.25	3.00
395 Ronald Murray RC	1.25	3.00
396 Igor Rakocevic RC	1.25	3.00
397 Tito Maddox RC	1.25	3.00
398 Mike Batiste RC	1.25	3.00
399 Sam Clancy RC	1.25	3.00
400 Tamar Slay RC	1.25	3.00
401 Lonny Baxter RC	1.25	3.00
402 Marko Jaric	1.25	3.00
403 Dan Gadzuric RC	1.25	3.00
404 Jannero Pargo RC	1.25	3.00
405 Pat Burke RC	1.25	3.00
406 Smush Parker RC	1.25	3.00
407 Reggie Evans RC	1.25	3.00
408 Gordan Giricek RC	1.25	3.00
409 Mehmet Okur RC	1.25	3.00
410 Jamal Sampson RC	1.25	3.00
411 Raul Lopez RC	1.25	3.00
412 Predrag Savovic RC	1.25	3.00
413 Carlos Boozer RC	2.50	6.00
414 Ken Johnson RC	1.25	3.00
415 Cezary Trybanski RC	1.25	3.00
416 Mike Wilks RC	1.25	3.00
417 J.R. Bremer RC	1.25	3.00
418 Junior Harrington RC	1.25	3.00
419 Nate Huffman RC	1.25	3.00
420 Michael Jordan	2.50	6.00

2002-03 Upper Deck Exclusives

Randomly inserted in packs, this 420-card set parallels the base Upper Deck set enhanced with gold foil highlights and sequentialy numbering. Base veteran cards are numbered to 100 and RC cards are numbered to 50.

*STARS: 5X TO 12X BASE CARD HI
*RCs: 2.5X TO 6X BASE CARD HI
*NON RC ROOKIES: 4X TO 10X BASE CARD HI

2002-03 Upper Deck Air Apparel

Randomly inserted in Series One packs at the rate of one in 72, this 12-card set places full color player photos on the right of a blue and white background. The left side of the card has a swatch of game-worn memorabilia and the words, Air Apparel appear along the bottom.

Card	Low	High
BDAA Baron Davis	3.00	8.00
DJAA DerMarr Johnson	2.00	5.00
DMAA Darius Miles	2.00	5.00
JMAA Jamal Mashburn	2.50	6.00
JPAA James Posey	2.00	5.00
KMAA Kenyon Martin	3.00	8.00
KWAA Kwame Brown	2.00	5.00
LOAA Lamar Odom	3.00	8.00
LSAA Latrell Sprewell	2.50	6.00
RHAA Richard Hamilton	2.50	6.00
SAAA Shareef Abdur-Rahim SP	2.50	6.00
TCAA Tyson Chandler	2.50	6.00

2002-03 Upper Deck All-ACCess Jerseys

Randomly inserted in Series Two packs at the rate of one in 96, this 12-card set utilizes a horizontal design where color player action photos are on the right and a swatch of game-worn jersey is on the left. The backgrounds are different shades of blue and the shape of the background on the left side of the card is the same shape as the jersey swatch.

Card	Low	High
AAJ Antawn Jamison	3.00	8.00
ABH Brendan Haywood	2.00	5.00
ACM Corey Maggette	2.50	6.00
AEB Elton Brand	3.00	8.00
AJS Joe Smith	2.50	6.00
AMJ Michael Jordan SP	75.00	150.00
ARF Rick Fox	2.50	6.00
ARM Roger Mason	3.00	8.00
ASB Shane Battier	3.00	8.00
ASF Steve Francis SP	3.00	8.00
ASM Stephon Marbury	2.50	6.00
AST Jerry Stackhouse	2.50	6.00

2002-03 Upper Deck All-Star Authentics Jerseys

Randomly inserted in Series One packs, this 13-card set is designed horizontally with a full color player action photo on the left side and a star-shaped swatch of game-used jersey. Some cards were issued as short prints and some of a known limited quantity-those numbers appear below.

Card	Low	High
AIAJ Allen Iverson	8.00	20.00
AMAJ Alonzo Mourning SP	6.00	15.00
BHAJ Brendan Haywood SP	3.00	8.00
CWAJ Chris Webber	5.00	12.00
GAAJ Gilbert Arenas SP	5.00	12.00
KMAJ Kenyon Martin/61*	6.00	15.00
MFAJ Marcus Fizer SP	3.00	8.00
PGAJ Pau Gasol/80*	6.00	15.00
PPAJ Paul Pierce	6.00	15.00
PSAJ Peja Stojakovic	5.00	12.00

2002-03 Upper Deck All-Star Authentics Jerseys Autographs

Randomly inserted in Series one packs, this six-card set parallels the base design of the All-Star Authentics Jerseys set enhanced with player autographs. Each card is sequentially numbered to 25.

Card	Low	High
KMAAA Kenyon Martin	12.50	30.00
PPAAJ Paul Pierce	20.00	50.00

2002-03 Upper Deck All-Star Authentics Shorts

Inserted in Series one packs at the rate of one in 96, this 14-card set parallels the design of the All-Star Authentics Jerseys set with a swatch of game-used shorts.

Card	Low	High
AKAS Andrei Kirilenko	3.00	8.00
BHAS Brendan Haywood	2.00	5.00
CMAS Chris Mihm	2.00	5.00
DMAS Desmond Mason	2.50	6.00
DNAS Dirk Nowitzki	5.00	12.00
KBAS Kobe Bryant	12.50	30.00
LNAS Lee Nailon	2.00	5.00
MJAS Michael Jordan SP	60.00	150.00
QRAS Quentin Richardson	2.50	6.00
SNAS Steve Nash	4.00	10.00
SSAS Steve Smith	2.50	6.00
TPAS Tony Parker	4.00	10.00
WSAS Wally Szczerbiak SP	2.50	6.00
ZRAS Zeljko Rebraca	2.00	5.00

2002-03 Upper Deck All-Star Authentics Warm-Ups

Inserted in Series one packs at the rate of one in 48, this 14-card set parallels the design of the All-Star Authentics Jerseys set with a swatch of game-used warmups.

Card	Low	High
AKAW Andrei Kirilenko	2.50	6.00
AMAW Alonzo Mourning	3.00	8.00
CMAW Chris Mihm	2.00	5.00
DFAW Derek Fisher	2.00	5.00
DMAW Desmond Mason	2.00	5.00
KBAW Kobe Bryant	10.00	25.00
KGAW Kevin Garnett	5.00	12.00
MFAW Marcus Fizer	2.00	5.00
MJAW Michael Jordan SP	40.00	100.00
RAAW Ray Allen	2.50	6.00
SBAW Shane Battier	2.50	6.00
TMAW Tracy McGrady	4.00	10.00
WPAW Wesley Person	2.00	5.00
ZRAW Zeljko Rebraca	2.00	5.00

2002-03 Upper Deck BuyBacks

Randomly inserted in Series two packs, this set is made up of previous year's Upper Deck cards with player autographs. Each card was accompanied out of the pack with a certificate of authenticity.

Card	Low	High
2 Mike Bibby 01-2UD#369/29	30.00	80.00
13 Tyson Chandler 01-2UD#244/54	25.00	60.00
14 Marcus Fizer 00-1UDEncWup/28	20.00	50.00
29 Kenyon Martin 01-2UDHnRoll/50	40.00	100.00
31 Mike Miller 01-2UD#207/95	25.00	60.00
33 Mike Miller 01-2UDHRoll/26	40.00	100.00
36 Jerome Moiso 01-2UD#242/113	8.00	20.00
38 Tony Parker 01-2UD#376/155	25.00	60.00
39 Tony Parker 01-2UDHRollFFR/46	30.00	80.00
41 Jason Richardson 01-2UDHRFFR/41	60.00	120.00
42 DeShawn Stevenson 00-1SPGFAFlr/35	25.00	60.00
45 Etan Thomas 00-1UD#220/84	8.00	20.00
46 Gerald Wallace 01-2UD#370/63	20.00	50.00

2002-03 Upper Deck Combo All-Star Authentics

Randomly inserted in Series one packs, this ten card set teams up players along with swatches of game-worn memorabilia and authentic autographs. Each card is sequentially numbered to 300.

Card	Low	High
DNSN Dirk Nowitzki Steve Nash	10.00	25.00
EBQR Elton Brand Quentin Richardson	6.00	15.00
JRGA Jason Richardson Gilbert Arenas	6.00	15.00
JTMF Jamaal Tinsley Marcus Fizer	6.00	15.00
KBKG Kevin Garnett Kobe Bryant Kevin Garnett	20.00	50.00
KGWS Kevin Garnett Wally Szczerbiak	10.00	25.00
MJKB Michael Jordan Kobe Bryant Kobe Bryant	40.00	100.00
RATM Tracy McGrady Ray Allen Tracy McGrady	12.50	30.00
SAJK Shareef Abdur-Rahim Jason Kidd Jason Kidd	10.00	25.00
WPSB Wesley Person Shane Battier	6.00	15.00

2002-03 Upper Deck Double Team Dual Jerseys

Inserted in Series Two Retail packs at the rate of one in 960, this six-card set pairs up teammates with one guy on the left and one on the right and two swatches of game-worn jersey. The jersey swatches are flat on one side and rounded on the other with one on the top of the card and another on the bottom.

Card	Low	High
CWMBD Chris Webber Mike Bibby	15.00	40.00
JWJRD Jay Williams Jalen Rose	6.00	15.00
PGDGD Pau Gasol Drew Gooden	6.00	15.00
PPAWD Paul Pierce Antoine Walker	15.00	40.00
TMRHD Tracy McGrady Ryan Humphrey	12.50	30.00

2002-03 Upper Deck Dual Shooting Shirts

Randomly seeded in Series two packs at the rate of one in 288, this nine card set pairs up players, one on the top and one on the bottom, with a small square portrait style photo and an hour-glass shaped shooting shirt swatch. The borders along the top and bottom are made to look like wood and the background is white.

Card	Low	High
BDDWS Baron Davis David Wesley	4.00	10.00
CWPJS Chris Webber Peja Stojakovic	6.00	15.00
DRTPS David Robinson Tony Parker	8.00	20.00
ECJCS Eddy Curry Jamal Crawford	4.00	10.00
JPJHS James Posey Juwan Howard	4.00	10.00
KBJWS Kobe Bryant Jay Williams	15.00	40.00
MJKBS Michael Jordan Kobe Bryant SP	60.00	150.00
SBDGS Shane Battier Drew Gooden	4.00	10.00
SMSMS Stephon Marbury Shawn Marion	4.00	10.00

2002-03 Upper Deck Dunkvision

Randomly inserted in Series one packs at the rate of one in 24, this seven card set places full color player action photos on a blue background set to look like a television.

Card	Low	High
COMPLETE SET (7)	10.00	25.00
DV1 Michael Jordan	6.00	15.00
DV2 Kobe Bryant	4.00	10.00
DV3 Tim Duncan	1.50	4.00
DV4 Vince Carter	1.25	3.00
DV5 Shaquille O'Neal	2.00	5.00
DV6 Jason Richardson	.75	2.00
DV7 Steve Francis	.75	2.00

2002-03 Upper Deck Electric Company

Randomly inserted in Series two packs at the rate of one in 24, this seven card set places a full color player action photo on a greenish blue background with gray lines coming out from the center.

Card	Low	High
COMPLETE SET (7)	6.00	15.00
EC1 Jay Williams	1.00	2.50
EC2 Paul Pierce	1.00	2.50
EC3 Tracy McGrady	1.25	3.00
EC4 Nene Hilario	1.00	2.50
EC5 Caron Butler	1.25	3.00
EC6 Kareem Rush	.75	2.00
EC7 Kobe Bryant	4.00	10.00

2002-03 Upper Deck Electric Company Jerseys

Randomly inserted in Series two Retail packs at the rate of one in 480, this six-card set parallels the design of the base Electric Company insert set enhanced with an "E" shaped swatch of game-worn memorabilia and player photos are slightly smaller.

Card	Low	High
ECCB Caron Butler	6.00	15.00
ECJW Jay Williams	5.00	12.00
ECKR Kareem Rush	4.00	10.00
ECNH Nene Hilario	5.00	12.00
ECPP Paul Pierce	5.00	12.00
ECTM Tracy McGrady	6.00	15.00

2002-03 Upper Deck Game Night

Randomly inserted in Series two packs at the rate of one in 12, this 14-card set uses a horizontal design which places a full color player action photo on the left and a dark colored scale photo of the player's team city on the right.

COMPLETE SET (14) 10.00 25.00
GN1 Kobe Bryant 3.00 8.00
GN2 Ray Allen .60 1.50
GN3 Michael Finley .60 1.50
GN4 Karl Malone .75 2.00
GN5 Kevin Garnett 1.25 3.00
GN6 Jason Richardson .60 1.50
GN7 Shawn Marion .60 1.50
GN8 Mike Miller .60 1.50
GN9 Jamaal Tinsley .40 1.00
GN10 Jay Williams .75 2.00
GN11 Rashard Lewis .60 1.50
GN12 Michael Jordan 5.00 12.00
GN13 Tim Duncan 1.25 3.00
GN14 Vince Carter 1.00 2.50

2002-03 Upper Deck Game Night Jerseys

Randomly inserted in Series two Hobby packs, this nine-card set parallels the design of the Game Night Jerseys set enhanced with a circular swatch of game-worn Jersey in between the two photos.

GNJR Jason Richardson 3.00 8.00
GNJT Jamaal Tinsley 2.00 5.00
GNKB Kobe Bryant SP 15.00 40.00
GNKG Kevin Garnett 6.00 15.00
GNKM Karl Malone 4.00 10.00
GNMF Michael Finley 3.00 8.00
GNMM Mike Miller 3.00 8.00
GNRA Ray Allen 3.00 8.00
GNSM Shawn Marion 3.00 8.00

2002-03 Upper Deck Game Plan Jerseys

Randomly inserted in series one packs at the rate of one in 144, this seven card set features full color player action photography on the left side, white borders on a horizontal design, and a swatch of game-worn jersey on the right.

BDGP Baron Davis 3.00 8.00
CMGP Corey Maggette 2.50 6.00
EBGP Elton Brand 3.00 8.00
ECGP Eddy Curry 2.50 6.00
GHGP Grant Hill 4.00 10.00
KMGP Karl Malone 4.00 10.00
SAGP Shareef Abdur-Rahim 2.50 6.00

2002-03 Upper Deck I Love L.A.

Randomly inserted in Series one packs at the rate of one in 12, this 14-card set features members of the 2002 NBA Championship winning Lakers. Each card showcases full-color player photos and yellow and purple borders.

COMPLETE SET (14) 15.00 40.00
LA1 Kobe Bryant 3.00 8.00
LA2 Shaquille O'Neal 2.00 5.00
LA3 Rick Fox 1.25 3.00
LA4 Robert Horry 1.25 3.00
LA5 Brian Shaw 1.25 3.00
LA6 Derek Fisher 1.25 3.00
LA7 Devean George 1.25 3.00
LA8 Stanislav Medvedenko 1.25 3.00
LA9 Mark Madsen 1.25 3.00
LA10 Samaki Walker 1.25 3.00
LA11 Shaquille O'Neal 2.00 5.00
LA12 Mitch Richmond 1.25 3.00
LA13 Kobe Bryant 3.00 8.00
LA14 Kobe Bryant 3.00 8.00

2002-03 Upper Deck MJ The Comeback

Randomly inserted in Series one packs, this seven card set pays tribute to Michael Jordan's second comeback to the NBA. The cards are horizontally desiged with full-color photos on the left and a black box on the right with silver foil highlights.

COMPLETE SET (7) 20.00 50.00
COMMON CARD (J1-J7) 4.00 10.00

2002-03 Upper Deck New Wave

Randomly seeded in Series one packs at the rate of one in 12, this 14-card set places emerging young stars on a green, purple and blue foil background with silver foil highlights.

COMPLETE SET (14) 6.00 15.00
NW1 Dirk Nowitzki 1.25 3.00
NW2 Wally Szczerbiak .60 1.50
NW3 Richard Jefferson .75 2.00
NW4 Mike Miller .75 2.00
NW5 Shawn Marion .75 2.00
NW6 Tyson Chandler .60 1.50
NW7 Baron Davis .75 2.00
NW8 Jamaal Tinsley .50 1.25
NW9 Rashard Lewis .75 2.00
NW10 Eddy Curry .60 1.50
NW11 Vince Carter 1.25 3.00
NW12 Shane Battier .75 2.00
NW13 Tony Parker 1.00 2.50
NW14 Eddie Griffin .50 1.25

2002-03 Upper Deck Practice Session Jerseys

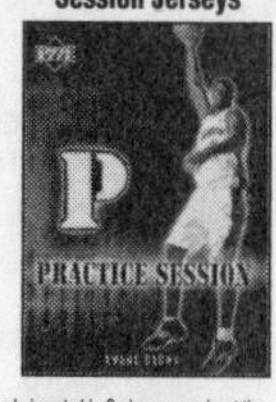

Randomly inserted in Series one packs at the rate of one in 72, this seven card set places full color player photos on a black and gray background with a swatch of a practice jersey.

AJPS Antawn Jamison 3.00 8.00
AWPS Antoine Walker 2.50 6.00
CAPS Courtney Alexander 2.00 5.00
DAPS Darrell Armstrong 2.00 5.00
JTPS Jason Terry 2.50 6.00
KWPS Kwame Brown 2.00 5.00
SMPS Shawn Marion 3.00 8.00

2002-03 Upper Deck Rated PG

Randomly inserted in Series two packs at the rate of one in 24, this seven card set is designed to look like a move poster. Full color player photos are accented with silver foil highlights.

COMPLETE SET (7) 5.00 12.00
PG1 Jay Williams 1.00 2.50
PG2 Tony Parker 1.00 2.50
PG3 Jason Kidd 1.25 3.00
PG4 Baron Davis .75 2.00
PG5 DaJuan Wagner .75 2.00
PG6 Steve Francis .75 2.00
PG7 Allen Iverson 1.25 3.00

2002-03 Upper Deck Rated PG Jerseys

Randomly inserted in Series two Retail packs, this six-card set parallels the design of the base Rated PG insert set enhanced with a swatch of jersey.

PGBD Baron Davis 4.00 10.00
PGDW DaJuan Wagner 4.00 10.00
PGJK Jason Kidd 6.00 15.00
PGJW Jay Williams 5.00 12.00
PGSM Stephon Marbury 3.00 8.00
PGTP Tony Parker 5.00 12.00

2002-03 Upper Deck Rookie Portfolio Jerseys

Inserted in Series two packs at the rate of one in 72, this 16-card set uses a horizontal design where two color portrait style photos appear on the left and right of the card with a centered swatch of a jersey.

RPAS Amare Stoudemire 8.00 20.00
RPCA Carlos Boozer 6.00 15.00
RPCB Caron Butler SP 5.00 12.00
RPCW Chris Wilcox 3.00 8.00
RPDG Drew Gooden 5.00 12.00
RPDW DaJuan Wagner 3.00 8.00
RPJD Juan Dixon 4.00 10.00
RPJJ Jared Jeffries 3.00 8.00
RPKR Kareem Rush 3.00 8.00
RPMH Marcus Haislip 3.00 8.00
RPNH Nene Hilario 4.00 10.00
RPNT Nikoloz Tskitishvili 3.00 8.00
RPPS Peja Stojakovic 3.00 8.00
RPQW Qyntel Woods 3.00 8.00
RPRH Ryan Humphrey 3.00 8.00
RPYM Yao Ming SP 10.00 25.00

2002-03 Upper Deck Scoring Threads

Randomly inserted in Series one Hobby and Retail packs at the rate of one in 288, this 13-card set is horizontally desiged with a white background on the right side of the card and a swatch of memorabilia and a photo of the player on the left side with border's to match team colors.

AHST Allan Houston H 2.50 6.00
AWST Antoine Walker H 2.50 6.00
CWST Chris Webber H 3.00 8.00
SCAM Andre Miller R SP 2.50 6.00
SCJM Jamal Mashburn R 2.50 6.00
SCKB Kobe Bryant R SP 12.50 30.00
SCPP Paul Pierce R SP 4.00 10.00
SCRM Ron Mercer R 2.00 5.00
SCSM Shawn Marion R 3.00 8.00
SCTP Tony Parker R 4.00 10.00
SMST Stephon Marbury H 2.50 6.00

2002-03 Upper Deck Season Premier Jerseys

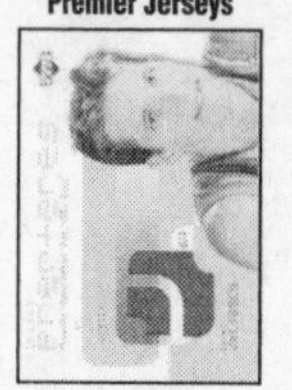

Randomly inserted in Series two packs at the rate of one in 144, this seven card set places close up player mug shots on the right side of the card with a white border and a swatch of jersey on the left.

CAP Caron Butler 5.00 12.00
CJP Casey Jacobsen 3.00 8.00
JEP Chris Jefferies 3.00 8.00
MTP Dikembe Mutombo 3.00 8.00
NTP Nikoloz Tskitishvili 3.00 8.00
RHP Richard Hamilton 2.50 6.00
TPP Tayshaun Prince 4.00 10.00

2002-03 Upper Deck Star Imports

Randomly inserted in Series two packs at the rate of one in 12, this 14-card set showcases foreign NBA player photos set against a globe, a blue and white background, and the player's home country flag in the upper right hand corner.

COMPLETE SET (14) 10.00 25.00
SI1 Yao Ming 2.50 6.00
SI2 Dirk Nowitzki 1.25 3.00
SI3 Pau Gasol 1.00 2.50
SI4 Peja Stojakovic .75 2.00
SI5 Nene Hilario 1.00 2.50
SI6 Tony Parker 1.00 2.50
SI7 Hedo Turkoglu .75 2.00
SI8 Nikoloz Tskitishvili .75 2.00
SI9 Andrei Kirilenko .75 2.00
SI10 Manu Ginobili 2.00 5.00
SI11 Steve Nash 1.00 2.50
SI12 Dikembe Mutombo .75 2.00
SI13 Marko Jaric .75 2.00
SI14 Tim Duncan 1.50 4.00

2002-03 Upper Deck Star Imports Jerseys

Randomly inserted in Series two Hobby packs at the rate of one in 72, this nine card set parallels the Star Imports insert set enhanced with a star shaped swatch of jersey on the left side of the card.

AKSI Andrei Kirilenko 3.00 8.00
DNSI Dirk Nowitzki 5.00 12.00
NHSI Nene Hilario 4.00 10.00
NTSI Nikoloz Tskitishvili 3.00 8.00
PGSI Pau Gasol 4.00 10.00
RFSI Rick Fox 2.50 6.00
TPSI Tony Parker SP 4.00 10.00
VDSI Vlade Divac 2.50 6.00
YMSI Yao Ming SP 10.00 25.00

2002-03 Upper Deck Super Swatches Jerseys

Randomly inserted in Series two packs, this 16-card set places a full color player photo on the left side of the card and and oversized swatch of jersey on the right in the shape of the letter S.

AIS Allen Iverson 12.00 30.00
ASS Amare Stoudemire 20.00 50.00
AWS Antoine Walker 6.00 15.00
CJS Casey Jacobsen 8.00 20.00
DWS DaJuan Wagner 8.00 20.00
FJS Fred Jones 8.00 20.00
JJS Jared Jeffries 8.00 20.00
JWS Jay Williams 10.00 25.00
KBS Kobe Bryant 40.00 100.00
KGS Kevin Garnett 15.00 40.00
MES Melvin Ely 8.00 20.00
MHS Marcus Haislip 8.00 20.00
QWS Qyntel Woods 8.00 20.00
RHS Ryan Humphrey 8.00 20.00
TMS Tracy McGrady 12.00 30.00
TPS Tayshaun Prince 10.00 25.00

2002-03 Upper Deck Three-Point Play Jerseys

AKKMJS Andrei Kirilenko
John Stockton
Karl Malone
AMEBLO Andre Miller
Elton Brand
Lamar Odom
AWPPVB Antoine Walker
Paul Pierce
Vin Baker
KBMJJW Jay Williams
Kobe Bryant
Michael Jordan
KMJKRJ Jason Kidd
Kenyon Martin
Richard Jefferson
PSCWMB Chris Webber
Mike Bibby
Peja Stojakovic

2002-03 Upper Deck Triple Shooting Shirts

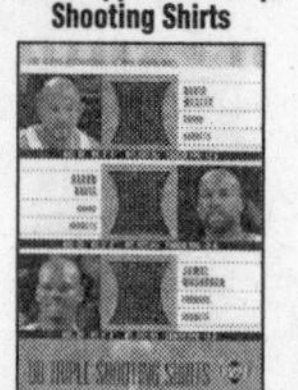

Inserted in Series two packs, this six-card set ties three players together from top to bottom, each with a small square mug shot and a swatch of a shooting shirt. Each card is sequentially numbered to 25.

1 Kobe Bryant 125.00 250.00
Michael Jordan
Jay Wiliams
4 David Wesley 20.00 50.00
Baron Davis
Jamal Mashburn

2002-03 Upper Deck UD Game Jerseys 1

Randomly inserted in Series one Hobby and Retail packs, this twelve-card set places full color player photos on the left, a jersey swatch in the middle and silver background on the right. Patch Logo 1 and Patch Names 1 parallels exist and were inserted at the rate of one in 5000 and one in 7500 respectively.

AH Allan Houston H 2.50 6.00
KB Kobe Bryant H SP 15.00 40.00
MB Mike Bibby H 3.00 8.00
MC Antonio McDyess H 2.50 6.00
PG Pau Gasol H 4.00 10.00
RA Ron Artest H 3.00 8.00
AMRJ Aaron McKie R 2.00 5.00
JSRJ Joe Smith R 2.50 6.00
KBRJ Kobe Bryant R SP 20.00 50.00
MJRJ Michael Jordan R SP 100.00 200.00
RFRJ Rick Fox R 2.50 6.00
TBRJ Terrell Brandon R 2.00 5.00

2002-03 Upper Deck UD Game Jerseys 2

Randomly inserted in Series two packs, this seven-card set places full color player photos on the left, a jersey swatch in the middle and silver background on the right. Patch Logo 1 and Patch Names 1 parallels exist and were inserted at the rate of one in 5000 and one in 7500 respectively.

GJAW Antoine Walker 2.50 6.00
GJCW Chris Wilcox 3.00 8.00
GJJR Jason Richardson 3.00 8.00
GJJS Jerry Stackhouse 2.50 6.00
GJJW Jay Williams SP 4.00 10.00
GJKB Kobe Bryant SP 15.00 40.00
GJWS Wally Szczerbiak 2.50 6.00

2002-03 Upper Deck UD Game Jerseys Autographs 1

Randomly inserted in Series one packs, this 11-card set parallels the design of the UD Game Jerseys set enhanced with player autographs. Each card is sequentially numbered to 275.

AUCB Chauncey Billups 8.00 20.00
AUDS DeShawn Stevenson 6.00 15.00
AUJR Jason Richardson 10.00 25.00
AUKM Kenyon Martin 12.50 30.00
AUMB Mike Bibby 10.00 25.00
AUMB2 Mike Bibby 10.00 25.00
AUMM Mike Miller 12.50 30.00
AUPP Paul Pierce 15.00 40.00
AUQR Quentin Richardson 6.00 15.00
AURM Ron Mercer 6.00 15.00
AUTB Terrell Brandon 8.00 20.00
AUTC Tyson Chandler 12.50 30.00

2002-03 Upper Deck UD Game Jerseys Autographs 2

Randomly inserted in Series two packs, this 16-card set parallels the design of the UD Game Jerseys set enhanced with player autographs. Each card is sequentially numbered to 100.

AUAW Antoine Walker 10.00 25.00
AUDG Drew Gooden 15.00 40.00
AUDS DeShawn Stevenson 10.00 25.00
AUDW DaJuan Wagner 10.00 25.00
AUET Etan Thomas 10.00 25.00
AUJK Jason Kidd 30.00 80.00
AUJM Jerome Moiso 10.00 25.00
AUJW Jay Williams 12.50 30.00
AUKB Kobe Bryant 100.00 250.00
AUKG Kevin Garnett 50.00 120.00
AUKM Kenyon Martin 15.00 40.00
AUMB Mike Bibby 12.50 30.00
AUMF Marcus Fizer 10.00 25.00
AUMM Mike Miller 15.00 40.00
AUPP Paul Pierce 25.00 60.00
AUTC Tyson Chandler 15.00 40.00

2002-03 Upper Deck UD Game Jerseys Combos 2

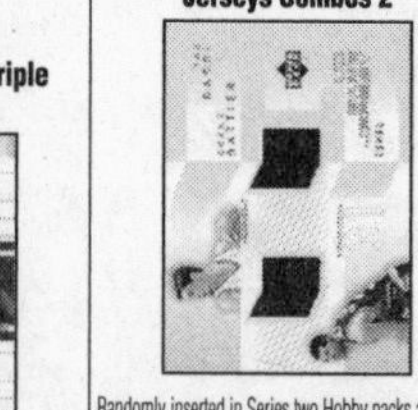

Randomly inserted in Series two Hobby packs at the rate of one in 72, this nine-card set features two player photos and two swatches of game worn jersey. An Autographed parallel was also inserted and is sequentially numbered to 10.

AIJR Allen Iverson 8.00 20.00
Jalen Rose
BDJM Baron Davis 5.00 12.00
Jamal Mashburn
DNSN Dirk Nowitzki 8.00 20.00
Steve Nash
JWTC Jay Williams 5.00 12.00
Tyson Chandler
KBJW Kobe Bryant 12.50 30.00
Jay Williams
MBPS Mike Bibby 6.00 15.00
Peja Stojakovic
PGSB Pau Gasol 5.00 12.00
Shane Battier
PPAW Paul Pierce 6.00 15.00
Antoine Walker
SMSM Stephon Marbury 5.00 12.00
Shawn Marion

2002-03 Upper Deck UD Game Jerseys Patch Logos 1

Randomly inserted in Series one packs at the rate of one in 5000, this 10-card set features both player photos and a swatch from the logo on the player's uniform.

AIPL Allen Iverson 50.00 120.00
JKPL Jason Kidd 40.00 100.00
JRPL Jason Richardson 25.00 60.00
KBPL Kobe Bryant 100.00 200.00
KGPL Kevin Garnett 50.00 120.00
MMPL Mike Miller 25.00 60.00
PSPL Peja Stojakovic 25.00 60.00
TMPL Tracy McGrady 50.00 120.00

2002-03 Upper Deck UD Game Jerseys Patch Logos 2

Randomly inserted in Series two packs at the rate of one in 5000, this 10-card set features both player photos and a swatch from the logo on the player's uniform.

AIPL Allen Iverson 50.00 120.00
JKPL Jason Kidd 40.00 100.00
KBPL Kobe Bryant 100.00 200.00
KGPL Kevin Garnett 50.00 120.00
TMPL Tracy McGrady 50.00 120.00

2002-03 Upper Deck UD Game Jerseys Patch Names 1

Randomly inserted in Series one packs at the rate of one in 7500, this 10-card set features both player photos and a swatch from the name on the player's uniform.

AIPN Allen Iverson 60.00 150.00
KBPN Kobe Bryant 125.00 300.00
KGPN Kevin Garnett 50.00 120.00
MMPN Mike Miller 30.00 80.00
SFPN Steve Francis 30.00 80.00
TMPN Tracy McGrady 75.00 150.00

2002-03 Upper Deck UD Game Jerseys Patch Names 2

Randomly inserted in Series two packs at the rate of one in 7500, this 10-card set features both player photos and a swatch from the name on the player's uniform.

AIPN Allen Iverson 60.00 150.00
CWPN Chris Webber 50.00 120.00
DNPN Dirk Nowitzki 75.00 150.00
KBPN Kobe Bryant 125.00 300.00
MJPN Michael Jordan 300.00 500.00
SFPN Steve Francis 40.00 100.00

2002-03 Upper Deck UD Game Jerseys Patch Numbers 1

Randomly inserted in Series one packs at the rate of one in 2500, this 10-card set features both player photos and a swatch from the logo on the player's uniform.

AIP Allen Iverson 40.00 100.00
JKP Jason Kidd 40.00 100.00
JRP Jason Richardson 20.00 50.00
KBP Kobe Bryant 75.00 150.00
KGP Kevin Garnett 40.00 100.00
MJP Michael Jordan 150.00 300.00
MMP Mike Miller 20.00 50.00
PSP Peja Stojakovic 20.00 50.00
SFP Steve Francis 20.00 50.00
TMP Tracy McGrady 40.00 100.00

2002-03 Upper Deck UD Game Jerseys Patch Numbers 2

Randomly inserted in Series two packs at the rate of one in 2500, this 10-card set features both player photos and a swatch from the number on the player's uniform.

AIP Allen Iverson 40.00 100.00
CWP Chris Webber 40.00 80.00
DNP Dirk Nowitzki 50.00 120.00
JKP Jason Kidd 40.00 100.00
JWP Jay Williams 20.00 50.00
KBP Kobe Bryant SP 75.00 150.00
KGP Kevin Garnett 40.00 100.00
SFP Steve Francis 20.00 50.00
TMP Tracy McGrady 40.00 100.00

2002-03 Upper Deck UD Playbook Jerseys

Randomly inserted in Series one Hobby packs, this six player set is actually composed of sealed mini-books that open up to reveal a player photo and a swatch of jersey. Only 100 total books were issued and currently actual player print runs are unknown.

JWH Jay Williams Gold 10.00 25.00
JWR Jay Williams Silver 10.00 25.00
KBH Kobe Bryant Gold 30.00 80.00
KBR Kobe Bryant Silver 30.00 80.00
MJH Michael Jordan Gold 125.00 250.00
MJR Michael Jordan Silver 125.00 250.00

2002-03 Upper Deck UD Playbook Jerseys Combos

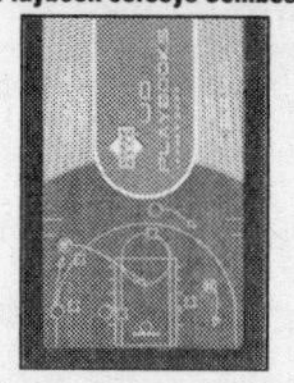

Inserted in both hobby and retail packs, this set parallels the design of the base Playbook Jerseys insert set with two players.

KBJWH Kobe Bryant 40.00 100.00
Jay Williams
MJJWH Michael Jordan 100.00 250.00
Jay Williams
MJKBH Michael Jordan 200.00 400.00
Kobe Bryant

2002-03 Upper Deck Beckett.com Samples

Randomly inserted in Beckett Basketball Collector issue #153, this 210-card set parallels the base Upper Deck Series 2 set enhanced with a "UD PROMO" stamp along the right side of the card.
*SINGLES: .75X TO 2X BASE UD HI
*NON RC ROOKIES: .4X TO 1X BASE UD HI

2003-04 Upper Deck

Released in late November 2003, Upper Deck is a 342-card set divided up into 300 veteran cards and 42 rookie cards inserted at the rate of one in four. Base cards are borderless on three sides with the bottom colored to match the featured player's team colors. Upper Deck was packaged in 24-pack boxes where packs contained eight cards and carried a suggested retail price of $2.99.

COMP.SET w/o SP's (300) 25.00 50.00
1 Shareef Abdur-Rahim .25 .60
2 Alan Henderson .20 .50
3 Dan Dickau .20 .50
4 Theo Ratliff .20 .50
5 Terrell Brandon .20 .50
6 Darvin Ham .20 .50
7 Nazr Mohammed .20 .50
8 Jason Terry .25 .60
9 Dion Glover .20 .50
10 Chris Crawford .20 .50
11 Paul Pierce .40 1.00
12 Antoine Walker .30 .75
13 Eric Williams .20 .50
14 Kedrick Brown .20 .50
15 Tony Battie .20 .50
16 Vin Baker .20 .50
17 Mark Blount .20 .50
18 Tony Delk .20 .50
19 Walter McCarty .20 .50
20 Jumaine Jones .20 .50
21 Jalen Rose .25 .60
22 Marcus Fizer .20 .50
23 Jamal Crawford .25 .60
24 Donyell Marshall .20 .50
25 Eddy Curry .25 .60
26 Trenton Hassell .20 .50
27 Michael Jordan 2.50 6.00
28 Tyson Chandler .25 .60
29 Jay Williams .20 .50
30 Scottie Pippen .50 1.25
31 Eddie Robinson .20 .50
32 Lonny Baxter .20 .50
33 Darius Miles .20 .50
34 DeSagana Diop .20 .50
35 Ricky Davis .25 .60
36 Chris Mihm .20 .50
37 Carlos Boozer .30 .75
38 Michael Stewart .20 .50
39 Zydrunas Ilgauskas .25 .60
40 Dajuan Wagner .20 .50
41 J.R. Bremer .20 .50
42 Kevin Ollie .20 .50
43 Dirk Nowitzki .50 1.25
44 Antawn Jamison .30 .75
45 Shawn Bradley .20 .50
46 Raef LaFrentz .20 .50
47 Eduardo Najera .20 .50
48 Travis Best .20 .50
49 Danny Fortson .20 .50
50 Michael Finley .30 .75
51 Jiri Welsch .20 .50
52 Steve Nash .40 1.00
53 Marcus Camby .25 .60
54 Chris Anderson .50 1.25
55 Rodney White .20 .50
56 Vincent Yarbrough .20 .50
57 Nikoloz Tskitishvili .20 .50
58 Nene .25 .60
59 Andre Miller .25 .60
60 Earl Boykins .20 .50
61 Ryan Bowen .20 .50
62 Ben Wallace .30 .75
63 Tayshaun Prince .30 .75
64 Richard Hamilton .25 .60
65 Mehmet Okur .25 .60
66 Bob Sura .20 .50
67 Chucky Atkins .20 .50
68 Chauncey Billups .30 .75
69 Elden Campbell .20 .50
70 Corliss Williamson .20 .50
71 Zeljko Rebraca .20 .50
72 Jason Richardson .30 .75
73 Popeye Jones .20 .50

74 Clifford Robinson .20 .50
75 Mike Dunleavy .25 .60
76 Troy Murphy .30 .75
77 Speedy Claxton .20 .50
78 Erick Dampier .20 .50
79 Nick Van Exel .25 .60
80 Avery Johnson .25 .60
81 Adonal Foyle .20 .50
82 Pepe Sanchez .20 .50
83 Steve Francis .30 .75
84 Glen Rice .20 .50
85 Eddie Griffin .20 .50
86 Moochie Norris .20 .50
87 Maurice Taylor .20 .50
88 Kelvin Cato .20 .50
89 Jason Collier .20 .50
90 Cuttino Mobley .25 .60
91 Yao Ming .60 1.50
92 Eric Piatkowski .20 .50
93 Bostjan Nachbar .20 .50
94 Adrian Griffin .20 .50
95 Reggie Miller .30 .75
96 Fred Jones .25 .60
97 Scot Pollard .20 .50
98 Jamaal Tinsley .20 .50
99 Al Harrington .25 .60
100 Jonathan Bender .20 .50
101 Primoz Brezec .20 .50
102 Ron Artest .30 .75
103 Jermaine O'Neal .30 .75
104 Kenny Anderson .25 .60
105 Jeff Foster .20 .50
106 Austin Croshere .20 .50
107 Elton Brand .30 .75
108 Tremaine Fowlkes .20 .50
109 Quentin Richardson .25 .60
110 Melvin Ely .20 .50
111 Marko Jaric .20 .50
112 Chris Wilcox .20 .50
113 Wang Zhizhi .25 .60
114 Corey Maggette .25 .60
115 Keyon Dooling .20 .50
116 Kobe Bryant 1.50 4.00
117 Shaquille O'Neal .75 2.00
118 Slava Medvedenko .20 .50
119 Gary Payton .30 .75
120 Jannero Pargo .20 .50
121 Kareem Rush .20 .50
122 Karl Malone .40 1.00
123 Derek Fisher .25 .60
124 Rick Fox .25 .60
125 Devean George .20 .50
126 Pau Gasol .30 .75
127 Jason Williams .25 .60
128 Stromile Swift .20 .50
129 Wesley Person .20 .50
130 Michael Dickerson .20 .50
131 Lorenzen Wright .20 .50
132 Earl Watson .20 .50
133 Mike Miller .30 .75
134 Shane Battier .25 .60
135 Eddie Jones .25 .60
136 Rasual Butler .20 .50
137 Caron Butler .30 .75
138 Brian Grant .20 .50
139 Lamar Odom .30 .75
140 Malik Allen .20 .50
141 Ken Johnson .20 .50
142 Samaki Walker .20 .50
143 Sean Lampley .20 .50
144 Vladimir Stepania .20 .50
145 Erick Strickland .20 .50
146 Toni Kukoc .30 .75
147 Joel Przybilla .20 .50
148 Tim Thomas .20 .50
149 Dan Gadzuric .20 .50
150 Joe Smith .25 .60
151 Michael Redd .30 .75
152 Desmond Mason .25 .60
153 Brian Skinner .20 .50
154 Kevin Garnett .60 1.50
155 Michael Olowokandi .20 .50
156 Troy Hudson .20 .50
157 Latrell Sprewell .25 .60
158 Wally Szczerbiak .25 .60
159 Sam Cassell .25 .60
160 Fred Hoiberg .20 .50
161 Ervin Johnson .20 .50
162 Mark Madsen .20 .50
163 Gary Trent .20 .50
164 Jason Kidd .50 1.25
165 Dikembe Mutombo .30 .75
166 Lucious Harris .20 .50
167 Kerry Kittles .20 .50
168 Brandon Armstrong .20 .50
169 Jason Collins .20 .50
170 Alonzo Mourning .40 1.00
171 Kenyon Martin .30 .75
172 Richard Jefferson .30 .75
173 Rodney Rogers .20 .50
174 Aaron Williams .20 .50
175 Jamal Mashburn .25 .60
176 David Wesley .20 .50
177 Kirk Haston .20 .50
178 Courtney Alexander .20 .50
179 Darrell Armstrong .20 .50
180 Robert Traylor .20 .50
181 George Lynch .20 .50
182 Jamaal Magloire .20 .50
183 Baron Davis .30 .75
184 P.J. Brown .20 .50
185 Sean Rooks .20 .50
186 Stacey Augmon .20 .50
187 Allan Houston .25 .60
188 Antonio McDyess .25 .60
189 Clarence Weatherspoon .20 .50
190 Kurt Thomas .20 .50
191 Shandon Anderson .20 .50
192 Keith Van Horn .25 .60
193 Michael Doleac .20 .50
194 Othella Harrington .20 .50
195 Charlie Ward .20 .50
196 Lee Nailon .20 .50
197 Tracy McGrady .40 1.00
198 Pat Garrity .20 .50
199 Grant Hill .40 1.00
200 Gordan Giricek .20 .50
201 Steven Hunter .20 .50
202 Jeryl Sasser .20 .50
203 Andrew DeClercq .20 .50
204 Juwan Howard .25 .60
205 Tyronn Lue .20 .50
206 Drew Gooden .25 .60
207 Marc Jackson .20 .50
208 Aaron McKie .20 .50
209 Derrick Coleman .25 .60
210 Eric Snow .20 .50
211 Glenn Robinson .25 .60
212 Greg Buckner .20 .50
213 Allen Iverson .50 1.25
214 Kenny Thomas .20 .50
215 Sam Clancy .20 .50
216 Monty Williams .20 .50
217 Stephon Marbury .30 .75
218 Shawn Marion .30 .75
219 Joe Johnson .30 .75
220 Bo Outlaw .20 .50
221 Amare Stoudemire .50 1.25
222 Casey Jacobsen .20 .50
223 Tom Gugliotta .20 .50
224 Scott Williams .20 .50
225 Jake Tsakalidis .20 .50
226 Damon Stoudamire .25 .60
227 Arvydas Sabonis .25 .60
228 Zach Randolph .30 .75
229 Ruben Patterson .25 .60
230 Derek Anderson .20 .50
231 Dale Davis .20 .50
232 Bonzi Wells .20 .50
233 Rasheed Wallace .30 .75
234 Jeff McInnis .20 .50
235 Qyntel Woods .20 .50
236 Chris Webber .30 .75
237 Doug Christie .25 .60
238 Vlade Divac .25 .60
239 Bobby Jackson .20 .50
240 Lawrence Funderburke .20 .50
241 Peja Stojakovic .30 .75
242 Gerald Wallace .30 .75
243 Brad Miller .30 .75
244 Mike Bibby .30 .75
245 Anthony Peeler .20 .50
246 Jim Jackson .20 .50
247 David Robinson .50 1.25
248 Ron Mercer .20 .50
249 Tony Parker .30 .75
250 Malik Rose .20 .50
251 Kevin Willis .20 .50
252 Manu Ginobili .40 1.00
253 Bruce Bowen .20 .50
254 Hedo Turkoglu .20 .50
255 Tim Duncan .50 1.25
256 Robert Horry .25 .60
257 Radoslav Nesterovic .20 .50
258 Ray Allen .30 .75
259 Rashard Lewis .30 .75
260 Reggie Evans .20 .50
261 Brent Barry .20 .50
262 Ronald Murray .20 .50
263 Vladimir Radmanovic .20 .50
264 Predrag Drobnjak .20 .50
265 Antonio Daniels .20 .50
266 Vitaly Potapenko .20 .50
267 Calvin Booth .20 .50
268 Vince Carter .50 1.25
269 Chris Jefferies .20 .50
270 Mengke Bateer .20 .50
271 Alvin Williams .20 .50
272 Jerome Williams .20 .50
273 Michael Bradley .20 .50
274 Lamond Murray .20 .50
275 Antonio Davis .20 .50
276 Morris Peterson .20 .50
277 Jerome Moiso .20 .50
278 Carlos Arroyo .25 .60
279 Matt Harpring .25 .60
280 Andrei Kirilenko .30 .75
281 Jarron Collins .20 .50
282 Greg Ostertag .20 .50
283 Curtis Borchardt .25 .60
284 DeShawn Stevenson .20 .50
285 Keon Clark .25 .60
286 John Amaechi .20 .50
287 Raul Lopez .30 .75
288 Jerry Stackhouse .30 .75
289 Kwame Brown .20 .50
290 Larry Hughes .25 .60
291 Brendan Haywood .20 .50
292 Juan Dixon .25 .60
293 Bryon Russell .20 .50
294 Christian Laettner .20 .50
295 Jahidi White .20 .50
296 Jared Jeffries .20 .50
297 Gilbert Arenas .30 .75
298 Kobe Bryant CL .75 2.00
299 Michael Jordan CL 1.25 3.00
300 Michael Jordan CL 1.25 3.00
301 LeBron James RC 12.00 30.00
302 Darko Milicic RC 1.25 3.00
303 Carmelo Anthony RC 3.00 8.00
304 Chris Bosh RC 2.50 6.00
305 Dwyane Wade RC 5.00 12.00
306 Chris Kaman RC 1.50 4.00
307 Kirk Hinrich RC 1.50 4.00
308 T.J. Ford RC 1.50 4.00
309 Mike Sweetney RC 1.25 3.00
310 Jarvis Hayes RC 1.25 3.00
311 Mickael Pietrus RC 1.25 3.00
312 Nick Collison RC 1.25 3.00
313 Marcus Banks RC 1.25 3.00
314 Luke Ridnour RC 1.50 4.00
315 Reece Gaines RC 1.25 3.00
316 Troy Bell RC 1.25 3.00
317 Zarko Cabarkapa RC 1.25 3.00
318 David West RC 1.50 4.00
319 Aleksandar Pavlovic RC 1.25 3.00
320 Dahntay Jones RC 1.25 3.00
321 Boris Diaw RC 1.50 4.00
322 Zoran Planinic RC 1.25 3.00
323 Travis Outlaw RC 1.50 4.00
324 Brian Cook RC 1.25 3.00
325 Kirk Penney RC 1.25 3.00
326 Ndudi Ebi RC 1.25 3.00
327 Kendrick Perkins RC 2.00 5.00
328 Leandro Barbosa RC 2.00 5.00
329 Josh Howard RC 1.25 3.00
330 Maciej Lampe RC 1.25 3.00
331 Jason Kapono RC 1.25 3.00
332 Luke Walton RC 1.25 3.00
333 Jerome Beasley RC 1.25 3.00
334 Brandon Hunter RC 1.25 3.00
335 Kyle Korver RC 1.50 4.00
336 Travis Hansen RC 1.25 3.00
337 Steve Blake RC 1.50 4.00
338 Slavko Vranes RC 1.25 3.00
339 Zaur Pachulia RC 1.25 3.00
340 Keith Bogans RC 1.25 3.00
341 Willie Green RC 1.25 3.00
342 Maurice Williams RC 2.00 5.00

2003-04 Upper Deck Gold

Randomly inserted, this 342-card set parallels the base Upper Deck set enhanced with gold foil highlights and sequential numbering to 100. A Rainbow parallel was also produced and enhances cards with holofoil highlights and sequential numbering to 25.
*1-297 GOLD SINGLES: 5X TO 12X BASE HI
*298-300 GOLD CL: 10X TO 25X BASE HI
*301-342 GOLD RCs: 2X TO 5X BASE HI
301 LeBron James 75.00 200.00
305 Dwyane Wade 30.00 80.00

2003-04 Upper Deck Rainbow

This 342-card set parallels the base Upper Deck set enhanced with holofoil highlights and sequential numbering to 25.
*1-297 RAINBOW: 8X TO 20X BASE HI
*298-300 RAINBOW: 15X TO 40X BASE HI
*301-342 RAINBOW: 3X TO 8X BASE CARD HI
27 Michael Jordan 75.00 150.00
301 LeBron James 200.00 400.00
305 Dwyane Wade 100.00 200.00

2003-04 Upper Deck Air Academy

Inserted at the rate of one in four, this 42-card set centers action photos of players on a white and blue background.
COMPLETE SET (42) 20.00 40.00
AA1 Michael Jordan 3.00 8.00
AA2 Kobe Bryant 2.00 5.00
AA3 LeBron James 4.00 10.00
AA4 Vince Carter .60 1.50
AA5 Shaquille O'Neal 1.00 2.50
AA6 Richard Jefferson .40 1.00
AA7 Jason Richardson .40 1.00
AA8 Paul Pierce .50 1.25
AA9 Michael Finley .40 1.00
AA10 Steve Francis .40 1.00
AA11 Shareef Abdur-Rahim .30 .75
AA12 Desmond Mason .30 .75
AA13 Latrell Sprewell .30 .75
AA14 Baron Davis .40 1.00
AA15 Glenn Robinson .30 .75
AA16 Joe Johnson .40 1.00
AA17 Rasheed Wallace .40 1.00
AA18 Gerald Wallace .40 1.00
AA19 Rashard Lewis .40 1.00
AA20 Jamaal Tinsley .25 .60
AA21 Karl Malone .50 1.25
AA22 Jerry Stackhouse .30 .75
AA23 Gilbert Arenas .40 1.00
AA24 Boris Diaw .50 1.25
AA25 Josh Howard .40 1.00
AA26 Antoine Walker .40 1.00
AA27 Darius Miles .25 .60
AA28 Darko Milicic .40 1.00
AA29 Carmelo Anthony 1.00 2.50
AA30 Chris Bosh .75 2.00
AA31 Dwyane Wade 1.50 4.00
AA32 Mike Sweetney .40 1.00
AA33 Jarvis Hayes .40 1.00
AA34 Mickael Pietrus .40 1.00
AA35 Nick Collison .40 1.00
AA36 Elton Brand .40 1.00
AA37 David West .50 1.25
AA38 Aleksandar Pavlovic .40 1.00
AA39 Zarko Cabarkapa .40 1.00
AA40 Travis Outlaw .50 1.25
AA41 Brian Cook .40 1.00
AA42 Ndudi Ebi .40 1.00

2003-04 Upper Deck All-Star Weekend Authentics

Horizontally designed, this 29-card set places a gray-scale portrait photo of the player on the left side and a swatch of memorabilia worn on all-star weekend on the right. The set was inserted in packs at the rate of one in 144.
ASAK Andrei Kirilenko 2.50 6.00
ASBM Brad Miller 2.50 6.00
ASBW Ben Wallace 2.50 6.00
ASCB Carlos Boozer 2.50 6.00
ASCB Caron Butler 2.50 6.00
ASDG Drew Gooden 2.00 5.00
ASDN Dirk Nowitzki 4.00 10.00
ASGG Gordan Giricek 2.00 5.00
ASGP Gary Payton 2.50 6.00
ASJA Marko Jaric 2.00 5.00
ASJK Jason Kidd 4.00 10.00
ASJM Jamal Mashburn 2.00 5.00
ASJO Jermaine O'Neal 2.50 6.00
ASJT Jamaal Tinsley 2.00 5.00
ASJW Jay Williams 2.00 5.00
ASKB Kobe Bryant 10.00 25.00
ASKG Kevin Garnett 5.00 12.00
ASNH Nene 2.00 5.00
ASPG Pau Gasol 2.50 6.00
ASPS Peja Stojakovic 2.50 6.00
ASSF Steve Francis 2.50 6.00
ASSM Stephon Marbury 2.00 5.00
ASSN Steve Nash 3.00 8.00
ASTC Tyson Chandler 2.00 5.00
ASTD Tim Duncan 4.00 10.00
ASTM Tracy McGrady 3.00 8.00
ASTP Tony Parker 2.50 6.00
ASYM Yao Ming 5.00 12.00
ASZI Zydrunas Ilgauskas 2.00 5.00

2003-04 Upper Deck All-Star Weekend Authentics Dual

Inserted at the rate of one in 144, this 12-card set utilizes the same basic design as the All-Star Weekend Authentics set with two players and two swatches of All-Star Weekend worn memorabilia.
BMBW Brad Miller / Ben Wallace 4.00 10.00
CBDW Carlos Boozer / DaJuan Wagner 4.00 10.00
DGGG Drew Gooden / Gordan Giricek 4.00 10.00
DMJR Desmond Mason / Jason Richardson 4.00 10.00
JWTC Jay Williams / Tyson Chandler 4.00 10.00
KBKG Kobe Bryant / Kevin Garnett 15.00 40.00
KBMJ Kobe Bryant / Michael Jordan 30.00 80.00
NHAK Nene / Andrei Kirilenko 4.00 10.00
PPAW Paul Pierce / Antoine Walker 4.00 10.00
SFYM Steve Francis / Yao Ming 5.00 12.00
SMSM Shawn Marion / Stephon Marbury 4.00 10.00
TMJO Tracy McGrady / Jermaine O'Neal 5.00 12.00

2003-04 Upper Deck Black Diamond Rookies F/X

Inserted at the rate of one in 288, this set places full-color action photos of the 2003-04 draft class with colored borders along the left side and bottom. These cards have a completely different design from the Black Diamond set.
BD1 LeBron James 75.00 200.00
BD2 Darko Milicic 6.00 15.00
BD3 Carmelo Anthony 15.00 40.00
BD4 Chris Bosh 12.00 30.00
BD5 Dwyane Wade 25.00 60.00
BD6 Chris Kaman 8.00 20.00
BD7 Kirk Hinrich 8.00 20.00
BD8 T.J. Ford 8.00 20.00
BD9 Mike Sweetney 6.00 15.00
BD10 Jarvis Hayes 6.00 15.00
BD11 Mickael Pietrus 6.00 15.00
BD12 Nick Collison 6.00 15.00
BD13 Marcus Banks 6.00 15.00
BD14 Luke Ridnour 8.00 20.00
BD15 Reece Gaines 6.00 15.00
BD16 Troy Bell 6.00 15.00
BD17 Zarko Cabarkapa 6.00 15.00
BD18 David West 8.00 20.00
BD19 Aleksandar Pavlovic 6.00 15.00
BD20 Dahntay Jones 6.00 15.00
BD21 Boris Diaw 8.00 20.00
BD22 Zoran Planinic 6.00 15.00
BD23 Travis Outlaw 8.00 20.00
BD24 Brian Cook 6.00 15.00
BD25 Kirk Penney 6.00 15.00
BD26 Ndudi Ebi 6.00 15.00
BD27 Kendrick Perkins 10.00 25.00
BD28 Leandro Barbosa 8.00 20.00
BD29 Josh Howard 6.00 15.00
BD30 Maciej Lampe 6.00 15.00
BD31 Jason Kapono 6.00 15.00
BD32 Luke Walton 6.00 15.00
BD33 Jerome Beasley 6.00 15.00
BD34 Brandon Hunter 6.00 15.00
BD35 Kyle Korver 8.00 20.00
BD36 Travis Hansen 6.00 15.00
BD37 Steve Blake 8.00 20.00
BD38 Slavko Vranes 6.00 15.00
BD39 Zaur Pachulia 6.00 15.00
BD40 Keith Bogans 6.00 15.00
BD41 Willie Green 6.00 15.00
BD42 Maurice Williams 10.00 25.00

2003-04 Upper Deck East Coast/West Coast Jerseys

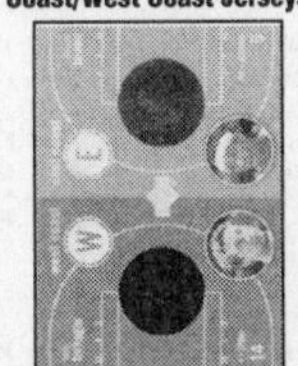

Inserted in hobby packs at the rate of one in 36, this 14-card set pairs players from the eastern and western conference on each card with a half red/half blue background and two circular swatches of jersey.
BATB Marcus Banks / Troy Bell 4.00 10.00
BLAJ Steve Blake / Antawn Jamison 4.00 10.00
DEMF Desmond Mason / Michael Finley 4.00 10.00
JOMC Jermaine O'Neal / Michael Olowokandi 4.00 10.00
JTMB Jason Terry / Mike Bibby 4.00 10.00
KPNE Kendrick Perkins / Ndudi Ebi 4.00 10.00
KVLW Keith Van Horn / Luke Walton 4.00 10.00
KWHT Kwame Brown / Hedo Turkoglu 4.00 10.00
MJKB Michael Jordan / Kobe Bryant 40.00 100.00
MPJR Morris Peterson / Jason Richardson 4.00 10.00
RGCO Reece Gaines / Brian Cook 4.00 10.00
RHDJ Richard Hamilton / Dahntay Jones 4.00 10.00
SAPG Shareef Abdur-Rahim / Pau Gasol 4.00 10.00
TISB Jamaal Tinsley / Shane Battier 4.00 10.00

2003-04 Upper Deck LeBron's Diary

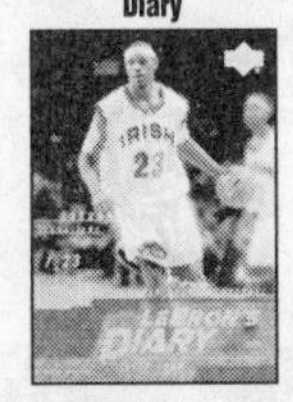

Inserted at the rate of one per pack in retail packs only, this 15-card set showcases highlights from young LeBron's High School and brief NBA career.
COMPLETE SET (15) 12.50 30.00
COMMON LEBRON (1-15) 1.25 3.00

2003-04 Upper Deck Rookie Review Jerseys

Inserted in hobby packs at the rate of one in 96, this 14-card set features the rookies from the 2002-03 season in full color on the right with a swatch of jersey in the lower left hand corner.
RRAS Amare Stoudemire 4.00 10.00
RRCB Caron Butler 2.50 6.00
RRCJ Casey Jacobsen 2.00 5.00
RRCW Chris Wilcox 2.00 5.00
RRDG Dan Gadzuric 2.00 5.00
RRDG Drew Gooden 2.00 5.00
RRDW DaJuan Wagner 2.00 5.00
RRJD Juan Dixon 2.00 5.00
RRJJ Jared Jeffries 2.00 5.00
RRJS John Salmons 2.50 6.00
RRKR Kareem Rush 2.00 5.00
RRQW Qyntel Woods 2.00 5.00
RRRA Robert Archibald 2.00 5.00
RRYM Yao Ming 5.00 12.00

2003-04 Upper Deck SE Die Cut All-Stars

Inserted in hobby packs at the rate of one in 288, this 15-card set parallels the design of the popular 1993-94 Upper Deck SE Die-Cut All-Stars set. Base cards place a full-color player photo on a card die-cut in the shape of the key on a basketball court. A Black parallel was also inserted with cards sequentially numbered to 25.
COMPLETE SET (15) 250.00 500.00
*BLACK: .6X TO 1.5X BASE HI
SE1 Michael Jordan 400.00 700.00
SE2 Kobe Bryant 80.00 200.00
SE3 Shaquille O'Neal 40.00 100.00
SE4 Vince Carter 25.00 60.00
SE5 Ray Allen 15.00 40.00
SE6 Kevin Garnett 30.00 80.00
SE7 Jason Kidd 25.00 60.00
SE8 Paul Pierce 20.00 50.00
SE9 Dirk Nowitzki 25.00 60.00
SE10 Ben Wallace 15.00 40.00
SE11 Tracy McGrady 20.00 50.00
SE12 Allen Iverson 25.00 60.00
SE13 Gary Payton 15.00 40.00
SE14 Elton Brand 15.00 40.00
SE15 Tim Duncan 25.00 60.00

2003-04 Upper Deck SE Die Cut Future All-Stars

Inserted in hobby packs at the rate of one in 24, this 15-card set uses the design for the SE Die Cut All-Stars set but features this year's rookie crop. A black version of the set was also produced with cards sequentially numbered to 25.
COMPLETE SET (15) 100.00 200.00
*BLACK: 1X TO 2.5X BASE HI
E1 Nick Collison 3.00 8.00
E2 Dahntay Jones 3.00 8.00
E3 Zarko Cabarkapa 3.00 8.00
E4 Marcus Banks 3.00 8.00
E5 Mickael Pietrus 3.00 8.00
E6 Jarvis Hayes 3.00 8.00
E7 Mike Sweetney 3.00 8.00
E8 T.J. Ford 4.00 10.00
E9 Kirk Hinrich 4.00 10.00
E10 Chris Kaman 4.00 10.00
E11 Dwyane Wade 12.00 30.00
E12 Chris Bosh 6.00 15.00
E13 Carmelo Anthony 8.00 20.00
E14 Darko Milicic 3.00 8.00
E15 LeBron James 30.00 80.00

2003-04 Upper Deck Shooting Stars Jerseys

Inserted in packs at the rate of one in 96, this 14-card set places some of the NBA's best shooters on a horizontally designed card with full-color player photos and a swatch of jersey.
SSDW David Wesley 2.00 5.00
SSGG Gordan Giricek 2.00 5.00
SSJA Jamaal Magloire 2.00 5.00
SSJT Jason Terry 2.00 5.00
SSKV Keith Van Horn 2.00 5.00
SSMM Mike Miller 2.50 6.00
SSPS Peja Stojakovic 2.50 6.00
SSRH Richard Hamilton 2.00 5.00
SSRM Reggie Miller 2.50 6.00
SSSS Steve Smith 2.00 5.00
SSTB Terrell Brandon 2.00 5.00
SSTK Toni Kukoc 2.50 6.00
SSWP Wesley Person 2.00 5.00
SSWS Wally Szczerbiak 2.00 5.00

2003-04 Upper Deck Super Swatches

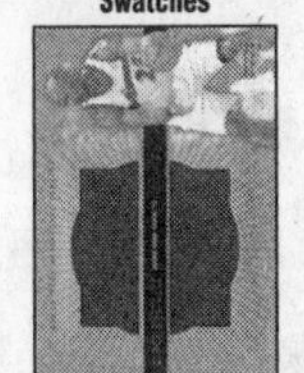

Randomly seeded in hobby packs, this 18-card set is horizontally designed with a full-color player photo on the right and an oversized swatch of memorabilia on the left.
AISS Allen Iverson 10.00 25.00
AMSS Antonio McDyess 5.00 12.00
ASSS Amare Stoudemire 10.00 25.00
BDSS Baron Davis 6.00 15.00
CMSS Corey Maggette 5.00 12.00
DMSS Darius Miles 4.00 10.00
DWSS Dajuan Wagner 4.00 10.00
EBSS Elton Brand 6.00 15.00
ECSS Eddy Curry 5.00 12.00
GHSS Grant Hill 8.00 20.00
JMSS Jamal Mashburn 5.00 12.00
JOSS Joe Smith 5.00 12.00
JPSS James Posey 4.00 10.00
KBSS Kobe Bryant 20.00 50.00
LOSS Lamar Odom 6.00 15.00
MJSS Michael Jordan 75.00 150.00
SPSS Scottie Pippen 10.00 25.00
TESS Jason Terry 5.00 12.00

2003-04 Upper Deck UD Game Jerseys

Inserted in packs at the rate of one in 288, this 21-card set places full-color player photos and a swatch of jersey cut to resemble the stitching design of a basketball.
GJ1 Caron Butler 2.50 6.00
GJ2 Gilbert Arenas 2.50 6.00
GJ3 Mike Bibby 2.50 6.00
GJ4 Tony Parker 2.50 6.00
GJ5 Manu Ginobili 3.00 8.00
GJ6 Darius Miles 2.00 5.00
GJ7 David Robinson 4.00 10.00
GJ8 Allen Iverson 4.00 10.00
GJ9 Kenyon Martin 2.50 6.00
GJ10 Eddie Jones 2.00 5.00
GJ11 Eddy Curry 2.00 5.00
GJ12 Jalen Rose 2.00 5.00
GJ13 Antawn Jamison 2.50 6.00
GJ14 Lamar Odom 2.50 6.00
GJ15 Karl Malone 3.00 8.00
GJ16 Jamal Mashburn 2.00 5.00
GJ17 Richard Jefferson 2.50 6.00
GJ18 Shaquille O'Neal 6.00 15.00
GJ19 LeBron James 50.00 120.00
GJ20 Kobe Bryant 12.50 30.00
GJ21 Michael Jordan 60.00 150.00

2003-04 Upper Deck UD Game Jerseys Autographs

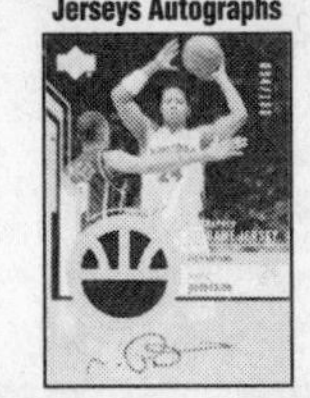

Randomly inserted, this set parallels the design of the UD Game Jerseys set enhanced with an authentic player autograph. Each card is sequentially numbered to 100. Card 39, Rashard Lewis, was not produced.
1 Kobe Bryant 125.00 225.00
2 Paul Pierce 25.00 60.00
3 Jason Kidd 25.00 60.00
4 Etan Thomas 8.00 20.00
5 Jerome Moiso 8.00 20.00
6 Shawn Marion 12.50 30.00
7 Mike Bibby 12.50 30.00
8 Peja Stojakovic 15.00 30.00
9 Chauncey Billups 10.00 25.00
10 Richard Hamilton 8.00 20.00
11 Richard Jefferson 8.00 20.00
12 Jason Richardson 8.00 20.00
13 Tony Parker 20.00 50.00
14 David Robinson 40.00 100.00
15 Jalen Rose 8.00 20.00
16 Corey Maggette 8.00 20.00
17 Jamaal Tinsley 8.00 20.00
18 Yao Ming 25.00 60.00
19 Drew Gooden 8.00 20.00
20 Caron Butler 8.00 20.00
21 Manu Ginobili 15.00 40.00
22 Marko Jaric 8.00 20.00
23 Wang Zhizhi 15.00 40.00
24 Tracy McGrady 30.00 60.00
25 Morris Peterson 8.00 20.00
27 Amare Stoudemire 15.00 40.00
30 Steve Francis 15.00 40.00
31 Andre Miller 10.00 25.00
32 Shane Battier 8.00 20.00
34 Dan Dickau 8.00 20.00
35 Earl Boykins 10.00 25.00
36 Jerry Stackhouse 8.00 20.00
37 Gilbert Arenas 8.00 20.00
38 Lamar Odom 8.00 20.00
40 Antawn Jamison 8.00 20.00
41 Kevin Garnett 30.00 80.00

2003-04 Upper Deck UD Game Jerseys Patches Logo

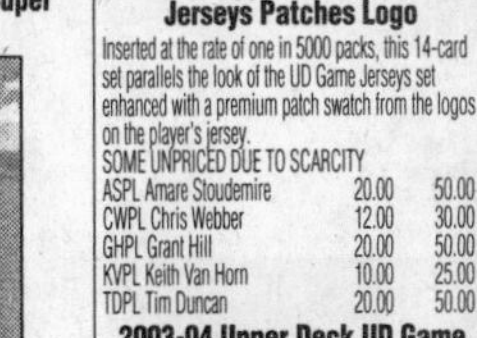

Inserted at the rate of one in 5000 packs, this 14-card set parallels the look of the UD Game Jerseys set enhanced with a premium patch swatch from the logos on the player's jersey.
SOME UNPRICED DUE TO SCARCITY
ASPL Amare Stoudemire 20.00 50.00
CWPL Chris Webber 12.00 30.00
GHPL Grant Hill 20.00 50.00
KVPL Keith Van Horn 10.00 25.00
TDPL Tim Duncan 20.00 50.00

2003-04 Upper Deck UD Game Jerseys Patches Name

Inserted at the rate of one in 7500 packs, this 14-card set parallels the look of the UD Game Jerseys set enhanced with a premium patch swatch from the name on the player's jersey.
SOME UNPRICED DUE TO SCARCITY
AJPN Antawn Jamison 15.00 40.00
DRPN David Robinson 25.00 60.00
KBPN Kobe Bryant 125.00 300.00
KVPN Keith Van Horn 12.00 30.00
MJPN Michael Jordan 250.00 500.00

2003-04 Upper Deck UD Game Jerseys Patches Numbers

Inserted at the rate of one in 2500 packs, this 14-card set parallels the look of the UD Game Jerseys set enhanced with a premium patch swatch from the numbers on the player's jersey.
SOME UNPRICED DUE TO SCARCITY
AWPN Antoine Walker 10.00 25.00
KMPN Kenyon Martin 10.00 25.00
KVPN Keith Van Horn 8.00 20.00
MJPN Michael Jordan 200.00 350.00
SNPN Steve Nash 12.00 30.00
TDPN Tim Duncan 15.00 40.00

2004-05 Upper Deck

Released in February 2005, Upper Deck features a 230-card set divided up into 200 veteran cards and 20 rookie cards inserted at one in four (cards 201-220) and ten rookie cards inserted at one in 20 (cards 221-230). Upper Deck was packaged for both Hobby and Retail where both boxes contained 24 packs but Hobby packs had eight cards per pack and Retail had nine and packs carried a SRP of $2.99.
COMPLETE SET (230) 60.00 120.00
COMP.SET w/o SP's (200) 20.00 40.00
IMMACULATE UNPRICED DUE TO SCARCITY
1 Antoine Walker .30 .75
2 Boris Diaw .25 .60

3 Al Harrington	.25	.60
4 Tony Delk	.20	.50
5 Jason Collier	.20	.50
6 Chris Crawford	.20	.50
7 Ricky Davis	.25	.60
8 Paul Pierce	.40	1.00
9 Jiri Welsch	.20	.50
10 Gary Payton	.30	.75
11 Rick Fox	.25	.60
12 Mark Blount	.20	.50
13 Adrian Griffin	.20	.50
14 Tyson Chandler	.25	.60
15 Eddy Curry	.25	.60
16 Kirk Hinrich	.30	.75
17 Scottie Pippen	.50	1.25
18 Jannero Pargo	.20	.50
19 Antonio Davis	.20	.50
20 Gerald Wallace	.30	.75
21 Eddie House	.20	.50
22 Steve Smith	.25	.60
23 Brandon Hunter	.20	.50
24 Theron Smith	.20	.50
25 Jahidi White	.20	.50
26 LeBron James	2.00	5.00
27 DeSagana Diop	.20	.50
28 Zydrunas Ilgauskas	.25	.60
29 Dajuan Wagner	.25	.60
30 Jeff McInnis	.20	.50
31 Eric Snow	.20	.50
32 Dirk Nowitzki	.50	1.25
33 Jason Terry	.25	.60
34 Michael Finley	.30	.75
35 Jerry Stackhouse	.30	.75
36 Erick Dampier	.20	.50
37 Josh Howard	.30	.75
38 Marquis Daniels	.20	.50
39 Carmelo Anthony	.60	1.50
40 Nene	.25	.60
41 Andre Miller	.25	.60
42 Earl Boykins	.20	.50
43 Marcus Camby	.25	.60
44 Voshon Lenard	.20	.50
45 Kenyon Martin	.30	.75
46 Richard Hamilton	.25	.60
47 Chauncey Billups	.30	.75
48 Rasheed Wallace	.30	.75
49 Tayshaun Prince	.30	.75
50 Ben Wallace	.30	.75
51 Antonio McDyess	.25	.60
52 Carlos Delfino	.30	.75
53 Jason Richardson	.30	.75
54 Dale Davis	.20	.50
55 Adonal Foyle	.20	.50
56 Mickael Pietrus	.25	.60
57 Mike Dunleavy	.25	.60
58 Speedy Claxton	.20	.50
59 Derek Fisher	.25	.60
60 Yao Ming	.60	1.50
61 Jim Jackson	.20	.50
62 Tracy McGrady	.40	1.00
63 Maurice Taylor	.20	.50
64 Juwan Howard	.25	.60
65 Tyronn Lue	.20	.50
66 Dikembe Mutombo	.30	.75
67 Reggie Miller	.30	.75
68 Stephen Jackson	.25	.60
69 Jermaine O'Neal	.25	.60
70 Jamaal Tinsley	.20	.50
71 Ron Artest	.30	.75
72 Fred Jones	.20	.50
73 Jonathan Bender	.20	.50
74 Kerry Kittles	.20	.50
75 Chris Kaman	.30	.75
76 Elton Brand	.30	.75
77 Marko Jaric	.20	.50
78 Corey Maggette	.25	.60
79 Bobby Simmons	.20	.50
80 Chris Wilcox	.20	.50
81 Lamar Odom	.30	.75
82 Karl Malone	.40	1.00
83 Kobe Bryant	1.50	4.00
84 Kareem Rush	.20	.50
85 Caron Butler	.30	.75
86 Devean George	.20	.50
87 Vlade Divac	.25	.60
88 Pau Gasol	.25	.60
89 Bonzi Wells	.20	.50
90 Mike Miller	.30	.75
91 Jason Williams	.25	.60
92 Shane Battier	.25	.60
93 James Posey	.20	.50
94 Stromile Swift	.20	.50
95 Shaquille O'Neal	.75	2.00
96 Dwyane Wade	1.00	2.50
97 Eddie Jones	.25	.60
98 Wang Zhizhi	.20	.50
99 Rasual Butler	.20	.50
100 Malik Allen	.20	.50
101 Udonis Haslem	.25	.60
102 Michael Redd	.30	.75
103 T.J. Ford	.25	.60
104 Keith Van Horn	.25	.60
105 Toni Kukoc	.20	.50
106 Desmond Mason	.20	.50
107 Mike James	.20	.50
108 Joe Smith	.25	.60
109 Kevin Garnett	.60	1.50
110 Michael Olowokandi	.20	.50
111 Sam Cassell	.25	.60
112 Troy Hudson	.20	.50
113 Latrell Sprewell	.25	.60
114 Fred Hoiberg	.20	.50
115 Wally Szczerbiak	.25	.60
116 Richard Jefferson	.30	.75
117 Alonzo Mourning	.40	1.00
118 Jason Kidd	.50	1.25
119 Jacque Vaughn	.20	.50
120 Jason Collins	.20	.50
121 Aaron Williams	.20	.50
122 Zoran Planinic	.20	.50
123 Jamaal Magloire	.20	.50
124 P.J. Brown	.20	.50
125 Baron Davis	.30	.75
126 Darrell Armstrong	.20	.50
127 Jamal Mashburn	.30	.75
128 Rodney Rogers	.20	.50
129 David Wesley	.20	.50
130 Allan Houston	.25	.60
131 Jamal Crawford	.25	.60
132 Stephon Marbury	.25	.60
133 Tim Thomas	.20	.50
134 Anfernee Hardaway	.75	2.00
135 Kurt Thomas	.20	.50
136 Mike Sweetney	.20	.50
137 Tony Battie	.20	.50
138 DeShawn Stevenson	.20	.50
139 Steve Francis	.30	.75
140 Cuttino Mobley	.25	.60
141 Hedo Turkoglu	.30	.75
142 Keith Bogans	.20	.50
143 Samuel Dalembert	.20	.50
144 Kenny Thomas	.20	.50
145 Allen Iverson	.50	1.25
146 Aaron McKie	.20	.50
147 Glenn Robinson	.25	.60
148 Willie Green	.20	.50
149 Corliss Williamson	.20	.50
150 Shawn Marion	.30	.75
151 Leandro Barbosa	.30	.75
152 Amare Stoudemire	.40	1.00
153 Quentin Richardson	.25	.60
154 Joe Johnson	.20	.50
155 Steve Nash	.40	1.00
156 Damon Stoudamire	.25	.60
157 Theo Ratliff	.25	.60
158 Shareef Abdur-Rahim	.25	.60
159 Derek Anderson	.20	.50
160 Zach Randolph	.20	.50
161 Nick Van Exel	.25	.60
162 Darius Miles	.20	.50
163 Mike Bibby	.30	.75
164 Brad Miller	.30	.75
165 Peja Stojakovic	.30	.75
166 Bobby Jackson	.20	.50
167 Chris Webber	.30	.75
168 Darius Songaila	.20	.50
169 Doug Christie	.20	.50
170 Manu Ginobili	.40	1.00
171 Brent Barry	.25	.60
172 Tony Parker	.30	.75
173 Malik Rose	.20	.50
174 Tim Duncan	.50	1.25
175 Radoslav Nesterovic	.20	.50
176 Bruce Bowen	.20	.50
177 Rashard Lewis	.30	.75
178 Vladimir Radmanovic	.30	.75
179 Ray Allen	.30	.75
180 Antonio Daniels	.20	.50
181 Ronald Murray	.20	.50
182 Luke Ridnour	.25	.60
183 Vince Carter	.50	1.25
184 Donyell Marshall	.30	.75
185 Chris Bosh	.30	.75
186 Morris Peterson	.20	.50
187 Jalen Rose	.25	.60
188 Rafer Alston	.20	.50
189 Carlos Arroyo	.25	.60
190 Matt Harpring	.25	.60
191 Andrei Kirilenko	.25	.60
192 Carlos Boozer	.30	.75
193 Gordan Giricek	.25	.60
194 Mehmet Okur	.20	.50
195 Antawn Jamison	.30	.75
196 Larry Hughes	.25	.60
197 Gilbert Arenas	.30	.75
198 Kwame Brown	.20	.50
199 Jarvis Hayes	.20	.50
200 Juan Dixon	.20	.50
201 Rafael Araujo RC	1.25	3.00
202 Luke Jackson RC	1.25	3.00
203 Andris Biedrins RC	1.50	4.00
204 Robert Swift RC	1.25	3.00
205 Kris Humphries RC	1.25	3.00
206 Al Jefferson RC	2.00	5.00
207 Kirk Snyder RC	1.25	3.00
208 J.R. Smith RC	1.50	4.00
209 Dorell Wright RC	2.00	5.00
210 Jameer Nelson RC	1.50	4.00
211 Pavel Podkolzine RC	1.25	3.00
212 Viktor Khryapa RC	1.25	3.00
213 Sergei Monia RC	1.25	3.00
214 Delonte West RC	1.50	4.00
215 Tony Allen RC	1.50	4.00
216 Kevin Martin RC	1.50	4.00
217 Sasha Vujacic RC	1.25	3.00
218 Beno Udrih RC	1.25	3.00
219 David Harrison RC	1.25	3.00
220 Chris Duhon RC	1.25	3.00
221 Josh Smith SP RC	2.50	6.00
222 Sebastian Telfair SP RC	1.50	4.00
223 Andre Iguodala SP RC	2.50	6.00
224 Dwight Howard SP RC	5.00	12.00
225 Emeka Okafor SP RC	2.50	6.00
226 Ben Gordon SP RC	2.00	5.00
227 Shaun Livingston SP RC	1.50	4.00
228 Devin Harris SP RC	2.50	6.00
229 Josh Childress SP RC	1.50	4.00
230 Luol Deng SP RC	2.50	6.00

2004-05 Upper Deck Exclusives

Randomly seeded in Hobby packs, this 230-card set parallels the base set enhanced with sequential numbering to 100. A Spectrum parallel and an Immaculate parallel were also produced and inserted. Spectrum is sequentially numbered to 25 and no odds were given for the Immaculate.

*1-200: 4X TO 10X BASE HI
*201-220: 1.25X TO 3X BASE HI
*221-230: 1X TO 2.5X BASE HI

2004-05 Upper Deck Exclusives Spectrum

Randomly seeded in packs, this 230-card set parallels the base set enhanced with sequential numbering to 25.

*1-200: 10X TO 25X BASE HI
*201-220: 2.5X TO 6X BASE HI
*221-230: 2X TO 5X BASE HI

2004-05 Upper Deck All-Star Weekend Authentics

AK Andrei Kirilenko	2.00	5.00
AL Ray Allen	2.50	6.00
AS Amare Stoudemire	3.00	8.00
BD Baron Davis	2.50	6.00
BM Brad Miller	2.50	6.00
BW Ben Wallace	2.50	6.00
CA Carlos Boozer	2.50	6.00
CB Chauncey Billups SP	4.00	10.00
CH Chris Bosh SP	5.00	12.00
CK Chris Kaman	2.50	6.00
CM Cuttino Mobley	2.00	5.00
DF Derek Fisher	2.00	5.00
EB Earl Boykins	2.00	5.00
EG Manu Ginobili	3.00	8.00
FJ Fred Jones	2.00	5.00
JH Jarvis Hayes	2.00	5.00
JM Jamaal Magloire	2.00	5.00
JO Josh Howard	2.50	6.00
JR Jason Richardson	2.50	6.00
KB Kobe Bryant	12.50	30.00
KK Kyle Korver	2.00	5.00
KM Kenyon Martin	2.50	6.00
LJ LeBron James SP	25.00	60.00
MD Mike Dunleavy	2.00	5.00
MJ Marko Jaric SP	2.00	5.00
NH Nene	2.00	5.00
PP Paul Pierce	3.00	8.00
PS Peja Stojakovic	2.50	6.00
RA Ron Artest	2.50	6.00
RL Rashard Lewis	2.50	6.00
RM Ronald Murray	2.00	5.00
SC Sam Cassell	2.00	5.00
SF Steve Francis	2.50	6.00
SM Stephon Marbury	2.00	5.00
TD Tim Duncan	4.00	10.00
UH Udonis Haslem	2.00	5.00
VL Voshon Lenard	2.00	5.00
YM Yao Ming	5.00	12.00

2004-05 Upper Deck All-Star Weekend Authentics Dual

AC Ray Allen / Sam Cassell	6.00	15.00
FB Derek Fisher / Chauncey Billups	5.00	12.00
GN Manu Ginobili / Nene	5.00	12.00
HH Udonis Haslem / Josh Howard	5.00	12.00
JR Fred Jones / Jason Richardson	5.00	12.00
KH Kyle Korver / Jarvis Hayes	5.00	12.00
LB Voshon Lenard / Earl Boykins	5.00	12.00
ML Ronald Murray / Rashard Lewis	5.00	12.00
NL Nene / Voshon Lenard	5.00	12.00

2004-05 Upper Deck All-Star Weekend Authentics Triple

AI Allen Iverson	8.00	20.00
DN Dirk Nowitzki	8.00	20.00
JK Jason Kidd	8.00	20.00
KB Kobe Bryant	25.00	60.00
KG Kevin Garnett	10.00	25.00
KK Kyle Korver	4.00	10.00
LJ LeBron James SP	30.00	80.00
MD Mike Dunleavy	4.00	10.00
RL Rashard Lewis	5.00	12.00
SO Shaquille O'Neal SP	12.00	30.00
TM Tracy McGrady	6.00	15.00

2004-05 Upper Deck East Coast West Coast

Inserted in Hobby packs at the rate of one in 288, this 12-card set features a horizontal design with a player from the Eastern Conference on the left, a player from the Western Conference on the right and two swatches of jersey between them.

BN Chauncey Billups / Steve Nash	6.00	15.00
CR Eddy Curry / Zach Randolph	5.00	12.00
JM Richard Jefferson / Corey Maggette	5.00	12.00
MB Reggie Miller / Mike Bibby	6.00	15.00
MG Desmond Mason / Manu Ginobili	5.00	12.00
MR Kenyon Martin / Quentin Richardson	5.00	12.00
PB Paul Pierce / Elton Brand	6.00	15.00
WA Rasheed Wallace / Shareef Abdur-Rahim	5.00	12.00

2004-05 Upper Deck Flight Team

Randomly inserted at the rate of one in four, this 50-card set is printed on foil and places player photos against a blue background.

COMPLETE SET (50) 15.00 40.00
*RAINBOW: 12X TO 30X BASE HI
RAINBOW STATED ODDS 1:1000 PACKS

FT1 Scottie Pippen	.60	1.50
FT2 Lamar Odom	.40	1.00
FT3 Andrei Kirilenko	.30	.75
FT4 Dirk Nowitzki	.60	1.50
FT5 Michael Redd	.40	1.00
FT6 Kobe Bryant	2.00	5.00
FT7 Jermaine O'Neal	.40	1.00
FT8 Shawn Marion	.40	1.00
FT9 Antawn Jamison	.40	1.00
FT10 Kevin Garnett	.75	2.00
FT11 Michael Finley	.40	1.00
FT12 Latrell Sprewell	.30	.75
FT13 Richard Hamilton	.30	.75
FT14 Al Harrington	.30	.75
FT15 Dwyane Wade	1.25	3.00
FT16 Shaquille O'Neal	1.00	2.50
FT17 Chris Webber	.40	1.00
FT18 Rasheed Wallace	.40	1.00
FT19 Kenyon Martin	.40	1.00
FT20 Ben Wallace	.40	1.00
FT21 Baron Davis	.40	1.00
FT22 Mickael Pietrus	.30	.75
FT23 Stephon Marbury	.30	.75
FT24 Ricky Davis	.30	.75
FT25 Pau Gasol	.40	1.00
FT26 Tim Duncan	.60	1.50
FT27 Gilbert Arenas	.40	1.00
FT28 Bonzi Wells	.25	.60
FT29 Chris Bosh	.40	1.00
FT30 Carmelo Anthony	.75	2.00
FT31 Yao Ming	.75	2.00
FT32 Tracy McGrady	.50	1.25
FT33 Michael Jordan	3.00	8.00
FT34 Fred Jones	.25	.60
FT35 Amare Stoudemire	.50	1.25
FT36 Dajuan Wagner	.25	.60
FT37 Desmond Mason	.30	.75
FT38 Jerry Stackhouse	.30	.75
FT39 Caron Butler	.40	1.00
FT40 Quentin Richardson	.30	.75
FT41 Shareef Abdur-Rahim	.30	.75
FT42 Vince Carter	.60	1.50
FT43 Corey Maggette	.30	.75
FT44 Peja Stojakovic	.40	1.00
FT45 LeBron James	2.50	6.00
FT46 Steve Francis	.40	1.00
FT47 Allen Iverson	.60	1.50
FT48 Ray Allen	.40	1.00
FT49 Elton Brand	.40	1.00
FT50 Darius Miles	.25	.60

2004-05 Upper Deck Flight Team Onyx

Seeded in packs randomly, this 50-card set parallels the Flight Team insert enhanced with sequential numbering to the player's jersey number. A Rainbow parallel was also inserted at one in 1000 packs.

CARDS #'d TO PLAYER JERSEY
SOME NOT PRICED DUE TO SCARCITY

FT1 Scottie Pippen/33	15.00	40.00
FT4 Dirk Nowitzki/41	25.00	60.00
FT5 Michael Redd/22	10.00	25.00
FT38 Jerry Stackhouse/42	8.00	20.00
FT44 Peja Stojakovic/16	10.00	25.00
FT48 Ray Allen/34	10.00	25.00

2004-05 Upper Deck Majestic Materials

Inserted in Hobby packs at the rate of one in 288, this 41-card set is horizontally designed with a player image on the right and a large swatch of memorabilia on the left in the shape of the letter "M."

AH Al Harrington	5.00	12.00
AL Allan Houston	5.00	12.00
AN Anfernee Hardaway	15.00	40.00
BM Brad Miller	6.00	15.00
BW Bonzi Wells	4.00	10.00
CB Caron Butler	6.00	15.00
CM Corey Maggette	5.00	12.00
CU Cuttino Mobley	5.00	12.00
DA Darko Milicic	4.00	10.00
DM Darius Miles	4.00	10.00
DW Dajuan Wagner	4.00	10.00
ES Eric Snow	4.00	10.00
GA Gilbert Arenas	6.00	15.00
GG Gordan Giricek	4.00	10.00
JC Jamal Crawford	5.00	12.00
JH Juwan Howard	5.00	12.00
JJ Joe Johnson	6.00	15.00
JM Jamaal Magloire	4.00	10.00
JP James Posey	4.00	10.00
JS Joe Smith	5.00	12.00
JT Jason Terry	5.00	12.00
KK Kerry Kittles	4.00	10.00
KV Keith Van Horn	5.00	12.00
KW Kwame Brown	4.00	10.00
LO Lamar Odom	6.00	15.00
LS Latrell Sprewell	5.00	12.00
MO Michael Olowokandi	4.00	10.00
MP Morris Peterson	4.00	10.00
QR Quentin Richardson	5.00	12.00
RH Richard Hamilton	5.00	12.00
SB Shane Battier	5.00	12.00
SD Samuel Dalembert	4.00	10.00
SF Steve Francis	6.00	15.00
SM Shawn Marion	6.00	15.00
TC Tyson Chandler	5.00	12.00
TT Tim Thomas	4.00	10.00
WS Wally Szczerbiak	5.00	12.00
ZI Zydrunas Ilgauskas	5.00	12.00
ZR Zach Randolph	5.00	12.00

2004-05 Upper Deck March Memories

Inserted in Hobby packs at the rate of one in 72, this 18-card set features players along with a circular swatch of jersey in honor of the NCAA accomplishments.

AW Antoine Walker	3.00	8.00
BG Ben Gordon	4.00	10.00
CB Carlos Boozer	3.00	8.00
CW Chris Wilcox	2.00	5.00
GH Grant Hill	4.00	10.00
JD Juan Dixon	2.00	5.00
JM Jamaal Magloire	2.00	5.00
JR Jason Richardson	3.00	8.00
JT Jason Terry	2.50	6.00
MA Magic Johnson SP	40.00	100.00
MB Mike Bibby	3.00	8.00
MD Mike Dunleavy	2.50	6.00
MP Morris Peterson	2.00	5.00
RH Richard Hamilton	2.50	6.00
SB Shane Battier	2.50	6.00

2004-05 Upper Deck Rookie Academy

Inserted in packs at the rate of one in 24, this 30-card set is printed on foil, has a gold box along the bottom and shows the 2004-05 rookies in action.

COMPLETE SET (30) 25.00 60.00
UNPRICED RAINBOW STATED ODDS 1:288

RA1 Rafael Araujo	1.00	2.50
RA2 Luke Jackson	1.00	2.50
RA3 Andris Biedrins	1.25	3.00
RA4 Robert Swift	1.00	2.50
RA5 Kris Humphries	1.00	2.50
RA6 Al Jefferson	1.50	4.00
RA7 Kirk Snyder	1.00	2.50
RA8 J.R. Smith	1.25	3.00
RA9 Dorell Wright	1.50	4.00
RA10 Jameer Nelson	1.25	3.00
RA11 Pavel Podkolzine	1.00	2.50
RA12 Viktor Khryapa	1.00	2.50
RA13 Nenad Krstic	1.00	2.50
RA14 Delonte West	1.25	3.00
RA15 Tony Allen	1.25	3.00
RA16 Kevin Martin	1.25	3.00
RA17 Sasha Vujacic	1.00	2.50
RA18 Beno Udrih	1.00	2.50
RA19 David Harrison	1.00	2.50
RA20 Andre Emmett	1.00	2.50
RA21 Josh Smith	1.50	4.00
RA22 Sebastian Telfair	1.00	2.50
RA23 Andre Iguodala	1.50	4.00
RA24 Dwight Howard	3.00	8.00
RA25 Emeka Okafor	1.50	4.00
RA26 Ben Gordon	1.25	3.00
RA27 Shaun Livingston	1.00	2.50
RA28 Devin Harris	1.50	4.00
RA29 Josh Childress	1.00	2.50
RA30 Luol Deng	1.50	4.00

2004-05 Upper Deck Rookie Academy Onyx

Seeded in packs randomly, this 30-card set parallels the Rookie Academy insert enhanced with sequential numbering to the player's jersey number. A Rainbow parallel was also inserted at the rate of one in 288.

CARDS #'d TO PLAYER JERSEY
MOST NOT PRICED DUE TO SCARCITY

RA3 Andris Biedrins/15	6.00	15.00
RA16 Kevin Martin/23	6.00	15.00
RA27 Shaun Livingston/14	5.00	12.00

2004-05 Upper Deck Rookie Review

Inserted in packs at the rate of one in 48, this 20-card set features the newest rookie crop in action along with a jersey swatch in the shape of an "R."

BD Boris Diaw	2.00	5.00
CA Carmelo Anthony SP	8.00	20.00
CB Chris Bosh	2.50	6.00
CK Chris Kaman	2.50	6.00
DA David West	2.50	6.00
DJ Dahntay Jones	2.00	5.00
DM Darko Milicic	2.00	5.00
JH Jarvis Hayes	2.00	5.00
JO Josh Howard	2.50	6.00
KB Keith Bogans	2.00	5.00
LB Leandro Barbosa SP	2.50	6.00
LJ LeBron James SP	15.00	40.00
LR Luke Ridnour	2.00	5.00
LW Luke Walton	1.50	4.00
MB Marcus Banks	2.00	5.00
MP Mickael Pietrus	2.00	5.00
MS Mike Sweetney	2.00	5.00
NE Ndudi Ebi	2.00	5.00
RG Reece Gaines	2.00	5.00
SB Steve Blake	2.00	5.00

2004-05 Upper Deck Rookie Scrapbook

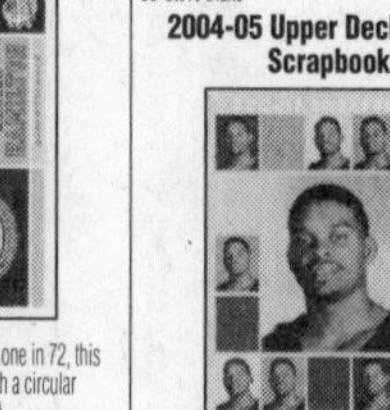

Inserted in Retail packs at the rate of one in one, this 30-card set places a rookie portrait photo in the middle of the card and then frames it with the same portrait on all sided.

COMPLETE SET (30) 6.00 15.00

RS1 Rafael Araujo	.30	.75
RS2 Luke Jackson	.30	.75
RS3 Andris Biedrins	.40	1.00
RS4 Robert Swift	.30	.75
RS5 Kris Humphries	.30	.75
RS6 Al Jefferson	.50	1.25
RS7 Kirk Snyder	.30	.75
RS8 J.R. Smith	.40	1.00
RS9 Dorell Wright	.50	1.25
RS10 Jameer Nelson	.40	1.00
RS11 Pavel Podkolzine	.30	.75
RS12 Viktor Khryapa	.30	.75
RS13 Nenad Krstic	.30	.75
RS14 Delonte West	.40	1.00
RS15 Tony Allen	.40	1.00
RS16 Kevin Martin	.40	1.00
RS17 Sasha Vujacic	.30	.75
RS18 Beno Udrih	.30	.75
RS19 David Harrison	.30	.75
RS20 Andre Emmett	.30	.75
RS21 Josh Smith	.50	1.25
RS22 Sebastian Telfair	.30	.75
RS23 Andre Iguodala	.50	1.25
RS24 Dwight Howard	1.00	2.50
RS25 Emeka Okafor	.50	1.25
RS26 Ben Gordon	.40	1.00
RS27 Shaun Livingston	.30	.75
RS28 Devin Harris	.50	1.25
RS29 Josh Childress	.30	.75
RS30 Luol Deng	.50	1.25

2004-05 Upper Deck UD Game Jerseys

Inserted in Hobby packs at the rate of one in 288, this 42-card set is borderless and centers a swatch of jersey along the bottom of the card.

AH Allan Houston	2.50	6.00
AJ Antawn Jamison	3.00	8.00
AK Andrei Kirilenko	2.50	6.00
AM Andre Miller	2.50	6.00
BA Marcus Banks	2.00	5.00
BD Baron Davis	3.00	8.00
BW Ben Wallace	3.00	8.00
CB Caron Butler	3.00	8.00
CW Chris Webber	3.00	8.00
DA Darko Milicic	2.00	5.00
DE Desmond Mason	2.50	6.00
DM Darius Miles	2.00	5.00
DS Damon Stoudamire	2.50	6.00
DW Dajuan Wagner	2.00	5.00
EB Elton Brand	3.00	8.00
GA Gilbert Arenas	3.00	8.00
GP Gary Payton	3.00	8.00
JO Jermaine O'Neal	3.00	8.00
JS Jerry Stackhouse	2.50	6.00
JT Jason Terry	2.50	6.00
KM Karl Malone	4.00	10.00
LO Lamar Odom	3.00	8.00
LS Latrell Sprewell	2.50	6.00
MB Mike Bibby	3.00	8.00
MF Michael Finley	3.00	8.00
MR Michael Redd	3.00	8.00
PG Pau Gasol	3.00	8.00
PS Peja Stojakovic	3.00	8.00
RJ Richard Jefferson	3.00	8.00
RM Reggie Miller	3.00	8.00
RW Rasheed Wallace	3.00	8.00
SA Shareef Abdur-Rahim	2.50	6.00
SM Shawn Marion	3.00	8.00
SN Steve Nash	4.00	10.00
SP Scottie Pippen	8.00	20.00
TP Tony Parker	3.00	8.00
VD Vlade Divac	2.50	6.00
YM Yao Ming	6.00	15.00

2004-05 Upper Deck UD Game Jerseys Autographs

Randomly seeded in Hobby packs, this 39-card set parallels the look of the UD Game Jerseys set enhanced with player autographs. Each card is sequentially numbered to 100 unless noted in the checklist.

UNPRICED PROOF AUTO PRINT RUN ONE SET

AJ Antawn Jamison/100	10.00	25.00
BD Baron Davis/100	10.00	25.00
BM Brad Miller/100	8.00	20.00
DF Derek Fisher/100	12.00	30.00
DM Darko Milicic/100	8.00	20.00
JS Jerry Stackhouse/100	10.00	25.00
LJ LeBron James/25	250.00	600.00
MB Mike Bibby/100	8.00	20.00
MJ Michael Jordan/25	400.00	800.00
MR Michael Redd/100	10.00	25.00
PPO Paul Pierce/25	20.00	50.00
RM Reggie Miller/100	40.00	100.00
SC Sam Cassell/100	10.00	25.00
SM Stephon Marbury/25	15.00	40.00
TM Tracy McGrady/25	40.00	100.00
ZR Zach Randolph/100	10.00	25.00

2004-05 Upper Deck UD Game Jerseys Patches Logos

Inserted in packs at the rate of one in 5000, this 14-card set parallels the design of the UD Game Jerseys set but is enhanced with a patch swatch from the jersey's logo.

SOME UNPRICED DUE TO SCARCITY

JK Jason Kidd	20.00	50.00
KB Kobe Bryant	60.00	150.00
KG Kevin Garnett	25.00	60.00
SO Shaquille O'Neal	30.00	80.00

2004-05 Upper Deck UD Game Jerseys Patches Names

Inserted in packs at the rate of one in 7500, this 14-card set parallels the design of the UD Game Jerseys set but is enhanced with a patch swatch from the jersey's name.

SOME UNPRICED DUE TO SCARCITY

CA Carmelo Anthony	30.00	80.00
JK Jason Kidd	25.00	60.00
MJ Michael Jordan	300.00	500.00
PP Paul Pierce	20.00	50.00
TD Tim Duncan	25.00	60.00
TM Tracy McGrady	20.00	50.00

2004-05 Upper Deck UD Game Jerseys Patches Numbers

Inserted in packs at the rate of one in 2500, this 14-card set parallels the design of the UD Game Jerseys set but is enhanced with a patch swatch from the jersey's numbers.

SOME UNPRICED DUE TO SCARCITY

AI Allen Iverson	15.00	40.00
JK Jason Kidd	15.00	40.00
KB Kobe Bryant	40.00	100.00
KG Kevin Garnett	20.00	50.00
MJ Michael Jordan SP	150.00	300.00
SO Shaquille O'Neal	25.00	60.00
TD Tim Duncan	15.00	40.00

2005-06 Upper Deck

Released in November 2005, Upper Deck boasts a 230-card set where the first 200 cards in the set picture veterans and cards 201-230 feature rookies inserted at the rate of one in every four packs. Base cards feature a borderless design with a name and position bar along the bottom of the card. Upper Deck was packaged in 24 pack boxes where packs contained eight cards and carry a suggested retail price of $2.99.

COMP.SET w/o SP's (200)	20.00	40.00
1 Josh Childress	.25	.60
2 Josh Smith	.30	.75
3 Al Harrington	.25	.60
4 Tyronn Lue	.20	.50
5 Boris Diaw	.25	.60
6 Tony Delk	.20	.50
7 Paul Pierce	.40	1.00
8 Antoine Walker	.25	.60
9 Gary Payton	.30	.75
10 Al Jefferson	.30	.75
11 Tony Allen	.20	.50
12 Ricky Davis	.25	.60
13 Delonte West	.20	.50
14 Emeka Okafor	.30	.75
15 Primoz Brezec	.20	.50
16 Kareem Rush	.20	.50
17 Gerald Wallace	.30	.75
18 Brevin Knight	.20	.50
19 Jason Kapono	.20	.50
20 Kirk Hinrich	.30	.75
21 Ben Gordon	.50	1.25
22 Eddy Curry	.25	.60
23 Michael Jordan	2.50	6.00
24 Andres Nocioni	.20	.50
25 Chris Duhon	.20	.50
26 Luol Deng	.30	.75

27 LeBron James 1.50 4.00
28 Zydrunas Ilgauskas .25 .60
29 Drew Gooden .25 .60
30 Jeff McInnis .20 .50
31 Dajuan Wagner .20 .50
32 Larry Hughes .25 .60
33 Robert Traylor .20 .50
34 Dirk Nowitzki .50 1.25
35 Michael Finley .30 .75
36 Jerry Stackhouse .25 .60
37 Josh Howard .30 .75
38 Marquis Daniels .20 .50
39 Devin Harris .30 .75
40 Jason Terry .25 .60
41 Carmelo Anthony .60 1.50
42 Kenyon Martin .30 .75
43 Andre Miller .25 .60
44 Earl Boykins .20 .50
45 Nene .25 .60
46 Marcus Camby .25 .60
47 Ben Wallace .30 .75
48 Richard Hamilton .25 .60
49 Chauncey Billups .30 .75
50 Rasheed Wallace .30 .75
51 Tayshaun Prince .30 .75
52 Carlos Arroyo .25 .60
53 Antonio McDyess .25 .60
54 Jason Richardson .30 .75
55 Baron Davis .30 .75
56 Troy Murphy .25 .60
57 Mickael Pietrus .25 .60
58 Derek Fisher .25 .60
59 Mike Dunleavy .25 .60
60 Yao Ming .40 1.00
61 Tracy McGrady .40 1.00
62 David Wesley .20 .50
63 Bob Sura .20 .50
64 Mike James .20 .50
65 Jon Barry .20 .50
66 Jermaine O'Neal .30 .75
67 Ron Artest .30 .75
68 Stephen Jackson .25 .60
69 Jamaal Tinsley .20 .50
70 Dale Davis .20 .50
71 Anthony Johnson .20 .50
72 Elton Brand .30 .75
73 Corey Maggette .25 .60
74 Bobby Simmons .20 .50
75 Marko Jaric .20 .50
76 Shaun Livingston .20 .50
77 Chris Kaman .30 .75
78 Chris Wilcox .20 .50
79 Kobe Bryant 1.50 4.00
80 Caron Butler .30 .75
81 Lamar Odom .30 .75
82 Chucky Atkins .20 .50
83 Brian Cook .20 .50
84 Devean George .20 .50
85 Sasha Vujacic .25 .60
86 Pau Gasol .30 .75
87 Mike Miller .30 .75
88 Jason Williams .25 .60
89 Shane Battier .25 .60
90 Bonzi Wells .20 .50
91 James Posey .20 .50
92 Stromile Swift .20 .50
93 Shaquille O'Neal .60 1.50
94 Dwyane Wade .75 2.00
95 Eddie Jones .25 .60
96 Udonis Haslem .25 .60
97 Damon Jones .20 .50
98 Alonzo Mourning .40 1.00
99 Keyon Dooling .20 .50
100 Michael Redd .30 .75
101 Desmond Mason .20 .50
102 Maurice Williams .25 .60
103 Joe Smith .25 .60
104 Toni Kukoc .20 .50
105 Dan Gadzuric .20 .50
106 T.J. Ford .25 .60
107 Kevin Garnett .60 1.50
108 Sam Cassell .30 .75
109 Latrell Sprewell .25 .60
110 Wally Szczerbiak .25 .60
111 Troy Hudson .20 .50
112 Eddie Griffin .20 .50
113 Jason Kidd .50 1.25
114 Richard Jefferson .30 .75
115 Vince Carter .50 1.25
116 Nenad Krstic .20 .50
117 Scott Padgett .20 .50
118 Jason Collins .20 .50
119 Jamaal Magloire .20 .50
120 J.R. Smith .30 .75
121 Speedy Claxton .20 .50
122 Lee Nailon .20 .50
123 P.J. Brown .20 .50
124 Chris Andersen .50 1.25
125 Stephon Marbury .25 .60
126 Jamal Crawford .25 .60
127 Allan Houston .20 .50
128 Trevor Ariza .20 .50
129 Quentin Richardson .25 .60
130 Tim Thomas .20 .50
131 Michael Sweetney .20 .50
132 Dwight Howard .60 1.50
133 Steve Francis .30 .75
134 Grant Hill .40 1.00
135 Jameer Nelson .25 .60
136 Hedo Turkoglu .30 .75
137 Doug Christie .20 .50
138 DeShawn Stevenson .20 .50
139 Allen Iverson .50 1.25
140 Chris Webber .30 .75
141 Andre Iguodala .30 .75
142 Samuel Dalembert .20 .50
143 Kyle Korver .25 .60
144 Willie Green .20 .50
145 Marc Jackson .20 .50
146 Steve Nash .40 1.00
147 Amare Stoudemire .30 .75
148 Joe Johnson .30 .75
149 Shawn Marion .30 .75
150 Kurt Thomas .20 .50
151 Jim Jackson .20 .50
152 Leandro Barbosa .25 .60
153 Damon Stoudamire .25 .60
154 Shareef Abdur-Rahim .25 .60
155 Zach Randolph .25 .60
156 Darius Miles .20 .50
157 Sebastian Telfair .25 .60
158 Theo Ratliff .20 .50
159 Nick Van Exel .30 .75
160 Peja Stojakovic .30 .75
161 Mike Bibby .30 .75
162 Brad Miller .30 .75
163 Cuttino Mobley .25 .60
164 Bobby Jackson .20 .50
165 Kenny Thomas .20 .50
166 Corliss Williamson .20 .50
167 Tim Duncan .50 1.25
168 Tony Parker .30 .75
169 Manu Ginobili .30 .75
170 Robert Horry .25 .60
171 Beno Udrih .20 .50
172 Nazr Mohammed .20 .50
173 Brent Barry .20 .50
174 Ray Allen .30 .75
175 Rashard Lewis .30 .75
176 Ronald Murray .20 .50
177 Luke Ridnour .25 .60
178 Vladimir Radmanovic .20 .50
179 Antonio Daniels .20 .50
180 Danny Fortson .20 .50
181 Chris Bosh .30 .75
182 Donyell Marshall .20 .50
183 Jalen Rose .30 .75
184 Morris Peterson .20 .50
185 Rafer Alston .20 .50
186 Matt Bonner .20 .50
187 Aaron Williams .20 .50
188 Andrei Kirilenko .25 .60
189 Carlos Boozer .30 .75
190 Matt Harpring .25 .60
191 Keith McLeod .20 .50
192 Raja Bell .25 .60
193 Raul Lopez .20 .50
194 Gordan Giricek .20 .50
195 Gilbert Arenas .30 .75
196 Antawn Jamison .30 .75
197 Jarvis Hayes .20 .50
198 Brendan Haywood .20 .50
199 Juan Dixon .20 .50
200 Etan Thomas .20 .50
201 Daniel Ewing RC 1.25 3.00
202 Nate Robinson RC 1.50 4.00
203 C.J. Miles RC 1.50 4.00
204 Salim Stoudamire RC 1.25 3.00
205 Francisco Garcia RC 1.50 4.00
206 Julius Hodge RC 1.25 3.00
207 Andrew Bynum RC 4.00 10.00
208 Joey Graham RC 1.25 3.00
209 Johan Petro RC 1.25 3.00
210 Luther Head RC 1.25 3.00
211 Channing Frye RC 1.50 4.00
212 Sean May RC 1.25 3.00
213 Wayne Simien RC 1.25 3.00
214 Antoine Wright RC 1.25 3.00
215 Ike Diogu RC 1.25 3.00
216 Jarrett Jack RC 1.25 3.00
217 Jason Maxiell RC 1.25 3.00
218 David Lee RC 2.00 5.00
219 Travis Diener RC 1.25 3.00
220 Danny Granger RC 2.50 6.00
221 Charlie Villanueva SP RC 2.50 6.00
222 Hakim Warrick SP RC 2.50 6.00
223 Rashad McCants SP RC 2.00 5.00
224 Raymond Felton SP RC 3.00 8.00
225 Martell Webster SP RC 2.00 5.00
226 Gerald Green SP RC 2.50 6.00
227 Deron Williams SP RC 5.00 12.00
228 Andrew Bogut SP RC 3.00 8.00
229 Marvin Williams SP RC 2.50 6.00
230 Chris Paul SP RC 8.00 20.00

2005-06 Upper Deck Gold

Randomly seeded in packs, this 230-card set parallels the base Upper Deck set enhanced with gold foil highlights and sequential numbering to 50.
*1-200 GOLD: 4X TO 10X BASE HI
201-220 RC GOLD: 1.25X TO 3X BASE HI
221-230 RC GOLD: .75X TO 2X BASE HI

2005-06 Upper Deck Silver

Randomly seeded in packs, this 230-card set parallels the base set enhanced with silver foil highlights and sequential numbering to 100.
*1-200 SILVER: 2.5X TO 6X BASE HI
201-220 RC SILVER: .75X TO 2X BASE HI
221-230 RC SILVER: .5X TO 1.25X BASE HI

2005-06 Upper Deck All-Star Weekend Authentics

Inserted at approximately one per box, this 40-card set features swatches of memorabilia worn by players at All-Star Weekend. Each card has a full-color player photo, the Denver All-Star Game logo and a swatch of memorabilia.
AJ Antawn Jamison 3.00 8.00
AL Al Jefferson 3.00 8.00
AM Andre Miller 2.50 6.00
AN Andre Iguodala 3.00 8.00
AS Amare Stoudemire 3.00 8.00
BG Ben Gordon 3.00 8.00
BU Beno Udrih 2.00 5.00
BW Ben Wallace 3.00 8.00
CA Carmelo Anthony 6.00 15.00
CB Chris Bosh 3.00 8.00
DE Devin Harris 3.00 8.00
DN Dirk Nowitzki 5.00 12.00
GA Gilbert Arenas 3.00 8.00
GH Grant Hill 4.00 10.00
JH Josh Howard 3.00 8.00
JJ Joe Johnson 3.00 8.00
JO Jermaine O'Neal 3.00 8.00
JR J.R. Smith 3.00 8.00
JS Josh Smith 3.00 8.00
KB Kobe Bryant 8.00 20.00
KG Kevin Garnett 6.00 15.00
KH Kirk Hinrich 3.00 8.00
KK Kyle Korver 2.50 6.00
LD Luol Deng 3.00 8.00
LJ LeBron James 12.50 30.00
LR Luke Ridnour 2.50 6.00
MG Manu Ginobili 3.00 8.00
PP Paul Pierce 4.00 10.00
QR Quentin Richardson 2.50 6.00
RA Ray Allen 3.00 8.00
RL Rashard Lewis 3.00 8.00
SM Shawn Marion 3.00 8.00
SN Steve Nash 4.00 10.00
SO Shaquille O'Neal 6.00 15.00
TA Tony Allen 2.00 5.00
TD Tim Duncan 5.00 12.00
TM Tracy McGrady 4.00 10.00
UH Udonis Haslem 2.50 6.00
YM Yao Ming 4.00 10.00
ZI Zydrunas Ilgauskas 2.50 6.00

2005-06 Upper Deck Game Jerseys

Inserted at the rate of approximately one per box, this 102-card set is horizontally designed with a player photo on the right and a square swatch of memorabilia on the left. The tops and bottoms have gray borders and the middle is colored to match the featured players team colors.
AD Antonio Davis 2.00 5.00
AH Allan Houston 2.00 5.00
AJ Antawn Jamison 2.50 6.00
AK Andrei Kirilenko 2.00 5.00
AM Andre Miller 2.00 5.00
AN Antoine Walker 2.00 5.00
AS Amare Stoudemire 2.50 6.00
AW Aaron Williams 2.00 5.00
BB Bruce Bowen 2.00 5.00
BD Baron Davis 2.50 6.00
BG Ben Gordon 2.50 6.00
BH Brendan Haywood 2.00 5.00
BN Bostjan Nachbar 2.00 5.00
BO Boris Diaw 2.00 5.00
BR Bryon Russell 2.00 5.00
BW Ben Wallace 2.50 6.00
BZ Carlos Boozer 2.50 6.00
CA Carmelo Anthony 5.00 12.00
CA Chris Anderson 4.00 10.00
CB Caron Butler 2.50 6.00
CH Chauncey Billups 2.50 6.00
CJ Andris Biedrins 2.00 5.00
CM Chris Mihm 2.00 5.00
CO Corey Maggette 2.00 5.00
CU Cuttino Mobley 2.00 5.00
CW Charlie Ward 2.00 5.00
DA David Wesley 2.00 5.00
DF Derek Fisher 2.00 5.00
DG Drew Gooden 2.00 5.00
DH Dwight Howard 5.00 12.00
DM Darius Miles 2.00 5.00
DN Dirk Nowitzki 4.00 10.00
DO Donyell Marshall 2.00 5.00
DS DeShawn Stevenson 2.00 5.00
DW Dajuan Wagner 2.00 5.00
EB Elton Brand 2.50 6.00
ES Eric Snow 2.00 5.00
GA Gilbert Arenas 2.50 6.00
GE Devean George 2.00 5.00
GH Grant Hill 3.00 8.00
GP Gary Payton 2.50 6.00
HA Devin Harris 2.50 6.00
JA Jamal Crawford 2.00 5.00
JC Jason Collins 2.00 5.00
JK Jason Kidd 4.00 10.00
JL Jalen Rose 2.50 6.00
JM Jeff McInnis 2.00 5.00
JO Jermaine O'Neal 2.50 6.00
JR Jason Richardson 2.50 6.00
JT Jason Terry 2.00 5.00
KB Kobe Bryant 8.00 20.00
KD Keyon Dooling 2.00 5.00
KG Kevin Garnett 5.00 12.00
KH Kirk Hinrich 2.50 6.00
KK Kerry Kittles 1.50 4.00
KM Kenyon Martin 2.50 6.00
KP Kendrick Perkins 2.00 5.00
KR Kareem Rush 2.00 5.00
KT Kurt Thomas 2.00 5.00
LD Luol Deng 2.50 6.00
LF Luis Flores 2.00 5.00
LJ LeBron James 8.00 20.00
LO Lamar Odom 2.50 6.00
LU Luke Jackson 2.00 5.00
LW Luke Walton 2.00 5.00
LZ Raul Lopez 2.00 5.00
MA Mark Blount 2.00 5.00
MB Mike Bibby 2.50 6.00
MG Manu Ginobili 2.50 6.00
MI Michael Finley 2.50 6.00
MJ Michael Jordan 30.00 80.00
MP Mickael Pietrus 2.00 5.00
MU Troy Murphy 2.00 5.00
NH Nene 2.00 5.00
PG Pau Gasol 2.50 6.00
PP Paul Pierce 3.00 8.00
PS Peja Stojakovic 2.50 6.00
QR Quentin Richardson 2.00 5.00
RA Ray Allen 2.50 6.00
RB Ryan Bowen 2.00 5.00
RH Richard Hamilton 2.00 5.00
RJ Richard Jefferson 2.50 6.00
RL Rashard Lewis 2.50 6.00
RO Ron Artest 2.50 6.00
RW Rasheed Wallace 2.50 6.00
SA Shareef Abdur-Rahim 2.00 5.00
SC Sam Cassell 2.50 6.00
SF Steve Francis 2.50 6.00
SM Shawn Marion 2.50 6.00
SN Steve Nash 3.00 8.00
SO Shaquille O'Neal 5.00 12.00
ST Stephon Marbury 2.00 5.00
TD Tim Duncan 4.00 10.00
TM Tracy McGrady 3.00 8.00
TP Tony Parker 2.50 6.00
TR Theo Ratliff 2.00 5.00
TT Tim Thomas 2.00 5.00
VB Vin Baker 2.00 5.00
WE Chris Webber 2.50 6.00
WI Chris Wilcox 2.00 5.00
YM Yao Ming 3.00 8.00
ZI Zydrunas Ilgauskas 2.00 5.00

2005-06 Upper Deck Game Jerseys Patches

Limited to 25 serially numbered copies, this 102-card set parallels the base Game Jerseys set enhanced with premium patch swatches.
*PATCHES: 1.25X TO 3X BASE HI
WE Chris Webber 12.00 30.00

2005-06 Upper Deck LeBron James

COMPLETE SET (45) 15.00 40.00
COMMON CARD (LJ1-LJ45) 1.25 3.00

2005-06 Upper Deck LeBron James Gold

*GOLD: 6X TO 15X BASE
STATED PRINT RUN 23 SER.#'d SETS
UNPRICED SILVER PRINT RUN 5 SETS

2005-06 Upper Deck Michael Jordan

COMPLETE SET (45) 25.00 60.00
COMMON CARD (MJ1-MJ45) 1.50 4.00

2005-06 Upper Deck Michael Jordan Silver

*SILVER: 6X TO 15X BASE JORDAN HI

2005-06 Upper Deck Michael Jordan/LeBron James

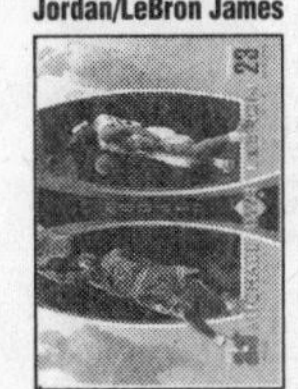

COMPLETE SET (10) 15.00 40.00
COMMON CARD 3.00 8.00

2005-06 Upper Deck Michael Jordan/LeBron James Silver

*SILVER: 3X TO 8X BASE MJ/LJ HI

2005-06 Upper Deck Performance Clause Jerseys

STATED PRINT RUN 250 SER.#'d SETS
AK Andrei Kirilenko 2.00 5.00
AN Andre Iguodala 2.50 6.00
BG Ben Gordon 2.50 6.00
BO Carlos Boozer 2.50 6.00
CA Carmelo Anthony 5.00 12.00
CF Channing Frye 3.00 8.00
CP Chris Paul 10.00 25.00
DG Danny Granger 5.00 12.00
DH Dwight Howard 5.00 12.00
DN Dirk Nowitzki 4.00 10.00
DW Deron Williams 6.00 15.00
FG Francisco Garcia 3.00 8.00
GA Gilbert Arenas 2.50 6.00
JJ Jarrett Jack 2.50 6.00
JO Josh Childress 2.00 5.00
JR J.R. Smith 2.50 6.00
KB Kobe Bryant 10.00 25.00
KG Kevin Garnett 5.00 12.00
KK Kyle Korver 2.00 5.00
LH Luther Head 2.50 6.00
LO Lamar Odom 2.50 6.00
MA Marvin Williams 3.00 8.00
MB Mike Bibby 2.50 6.00
MR Michael Redd 2.50 6.00
PG Pau Gasol 2.50 6.00
RF Raymond Felton 4.00 10.00
RG Ryan Gomes 2.50 6.00
RM Rashad McCants 2.50 6.00
SB Shane Battier 2.00 5.00
SF Steve Francis 2.50 6.00
SL Shaun Livingston 2.00 5.00
SM Sean May 2.50 6.00
SO Shaquille O'Neal 5.00 12.00
SS Salim Stoudamire 2.50 6.00
TD Tim Duncan 4.00 10.00
TR Trevor Ariza 2.00 5.00
WE Delonte West 2.00 5.00
YM Yao Ming 3.00 8.00

2005-06 Upper Deck Performance Clause Jerseys Autographs

STATED PRINT RUN 50 SER.#'d SETS
MOST UNPRICED DUE TO SCARCITY
CP Chris Paul 40.00 100.00
KB Kobe Bryant 100.00 200.00

2005-06 Upper Deck Rookie Review Materials

Inserted at approximately one per box, this set features a full-color player image towards the top, a bar along the bottom with the player's name and the set name and an "R" shaped swatch of memorabilia in the lower right-hand corner.
AB Andris Biedrins 2.00 5.00
AE Andre Emmett 2.00 5.00
AI Andre Iguodala 2.50 6.00
AJ Al Jefferson 2.50 6.00
AV Anderson Varejao 2.00 5.00
BU Beno Udrih 2.00 5.00
CD Chris Duhon 1.50 4.00
DE Devin Harris 2.50 6.00
DH Dwight Howard 5.00 12.00
DO Dorell Wright 2.00 5.00
DW Delonte West 2.00 5.00
HA David Harrison 2.00 5.00
HS Ha Seung-Jin 2.00 5.00
JC Josh Childress 2.00 5.00
JN Jameer Nelson 2.00 5.00
JR J.R. Smith 2.50 6.00
JS Josh Smith 2.50 6.00
JV Jackson Vroman 2.00 5.00
KH Kris Humphries 2.00 5.00
KM Kevin Martin 2.50 6.00
KS Kirk Snyder 2.00 5.00
LC Lionel Chalmers 2.00 5.00
LD Luol Deng 2.50 6.00
NK Nenad Krstic 2.00 5.00
RA Rafael Araujo 2.00 5.00
SL Shaun Livingston 2.00 5.00
ST Sebastian Telfair 2.00 5.00
SV Sasha Vujacic 2.00 5.00
TA Tony Allen 2.00 5.00
TR Trevor Ariza 2.00 5.00

2005-06 Upper Deck Rookie Scrapbook

Inserted in Retail packs at the rate of one in one, this 30-card set showcases the 2005-06 rookie class with black and white photography and design elements that make the card look like the pages of a spiral notebook.
COMPLETE SET (30) 12.50 30.00
1 Andrew Bogut .75 2.00
2 Andrew Bynum 1.50 4.00
3 Antoine Wright .50 1.25
4 Channing Frye .60 1.50
5 Charlie Villanueva .60 1.50
6 Chris Paul 2.00 5.00
7 Daniel Ewing .50 1.25
8 Danny Granger 1.00 2.50
9 David Lee .75 2.00
10 Deron Williams 1.25 3.00
11 Travis Diener .50 1.25
12 Francisco Garcia .60 1.50
13 Gerald Green .60 1.50
14 Hakim Warrick .60 1.50
15 Ike Diogu .50 1.25
16 Jarrett Jack .50 1.25
17 Jason Maxiell .50 1.25
18 Joey Graham .50 1.25
19 Julius Hodge .50 1.25
20 Luther Head .50 1.25
21 Martell Webster .50 1.25
22 Marvin Williams .60 1.50
23 Monta Ellis 1.00 2.50
24 Nate Robinson .60 1.50
25 Rashad McCants .50 1.25
26 Raymond Felton .75 2.00
27 C.J. Miles .60 1.50
28 Salim Stoudamire .50 1.25
29 Sean May .50 1.25
30 Wayne Simien .50 1.25

2005-06 Upper Deck Signature Sensations

Randomly seeded in packs, this 96-card set features player photos on the top of the card and player autographs at the bottom. Each card is sequentially numbered to 25.
AL Al Jefferson 8.00 20.00
BG Ben Gordon 12.50 30.00
BW Ben Wallace 12.50 30.00
CA Carmelo Anthony 25.00 60.00
CB Chris Bosh 15.00 40.00
CF Channing Frye 10.00 25.00
CJ C.J. Miles 10.00 25.00
CV Charlie Villanueva 10.00 25.00
DE Devin Harris 8.00 20.00
DF Derek Fisher 12.50 30.00
DH Dwight Howard 20.00 50.00
DT Dijon Thompson 8.00 20.00
ID Ike Diogu 8.00 20.00
LH Luther Head 8.00 20.00
LJ LeBron James 175.00 300.00
MD Marquis Daniels 8.00 20.00
ME Monta Ellis 50.00 120.00
MJ Michael Jordan 300.00 500.00
MP Morris Peterson 8.00 20.00
PP Paul Pierce 20.00 50.00
RI Royal Ivey 8.00 20.00
TM Tracy McGrady 12.00 30.00
WI Deron Williams 50.00 120.00
YM Yao Ming 25.00 60.00

2005-06 Upper Deck UD Materials

Inserted in Upper Deck at the rate of approximately one per box, this 30-card set is horizontally designed with full color player photos on the left side of the card and diamond shaped swatches of memorabilia on the right.
AK Andrei Kirilenko 2.00 5.00
AW Antoine Walker 2.00 5.00
BD Baron Davis 2.50 6.00
BO Carlos Boozer 2.50 6.00
CB Caron Butler 2.50 6.00
CH Chris Anderson 4.00 10.00
CM Corey Maggette 2.00 5.00
CW Chris Webber 2.50 6.00
DA David Wesley 2.00 5.00
DW Dajuan Wagner 2.00 5.00
EB Earl Boykins 2.00 5.00
EC Eddy Curry 2.00 5.00
GP Gary Payton 2.50 6.00
JJ Joe Johnson 2.50 6.00
JK Jason Kidd 4.00 10.00
JM Jamaal Magloire 2.00 5.00
JO Jermaine O'Neal 2.50 6.00
JT Jason Terry 2.00 5.00
KB Kobe Bryant 10.00 25.00
KM Kenyon Martin 2.50 6.00
LJ LeBron James 10.00 25.00
MJ Michael Jordan 30.00 80.00
RD Ronald Dupree 2.00 5.00
RJ Richard Jefferson 2.50 6.00
SD Samuel Dalembert 2.00 5.00
SF Steve Francis 2.50 6.00
TP Tony Parker 2.50 6.00
UH Udonis Haslem 2.00 5.00
VL Voshon Lenard 2.00 5.00
VR Vladimir Radmanovic 2.00 5.00

2006-07 Upper Deck

Released in mid November 2006, Upper Deck boasts a 240-card base set where cards 1-200 picture veteran players and cards 201-240 picture rookies inserted at the rate of one in three packs. Base card design consists of full-bleed photos and a box along the bottom containing the player's name, position and team. Upper Deck is packaged in 24-pack boxes of eight cards each and carried an original suggested retail price of $3.00.
COMP.SET w/o SP's (200) 15.00 40.00
1 Josh Childress .25 .60
2 Al Harrington .25 .60
3 Joe Johnson .30 .75
4 Josh Smith .30 .75
5 Salim Stoudamire .20 .50
6 Marvin Williams .30 .75
7 Tony Allen .20 .50
8 Dan Dickau .20 .50
9 Al Jefferson .30 .75
10 Raef LaFrentz .20 .50
11 Michael Olowokandi .20 .50
12 Paul Pierce .40 1.00
13 Wally Szczerbiak .25 .60
14 Alan Anderson .20 .50
15 Raymond Felton .40 1.00
16 Othella Harrington .20 .50
17 Sean May .20 .50
18 Emeka Okafor .30 .75
19 Primoz Brezec .20 .50
20 Gerald Wallace .30 .75
21 Tyson Chandler .25 .60
22 Michael Jordan 2.50 6.00
23 Luol Deng .30 .75
24 Chris Duhon .20 .50
25 Ben Gordon .30 .75
26 Kirk Hinrich .30 .75
27 Mike Sweetney .20 .50
28 Drew Gooden .25 .60
29 Larry Hughes .25 .60
30 Zydrunas Ilgauskas .25 .60
31 LeBron James 1.50 4.00
32 Damon Jones .20 .50
33 Donyell Marshall .20 .50
34 Anderson Varejao .25 .60
35 Erick Dampier .20 .50
36 Marquis Daniels .20 .50
37 Devin Harris .30 .75
38 Josh Howard .25 .60
39 Dirk Nowitzki .50 1.25
40 Jerry Stackhouse .25 .60
41 Jason Terry .25 .60
42 Carmelo Anthony .40 1.00
43 Earl Boykins .20 .50
44 Marcus Camby .25 .60
45 Kenyon Martin .30 .75
46 Andre Miller .25 .60
47 Eduardo Najera .20 .50
48 Nene .25 .60
49 Chauncey Billups .30 .75
50 Richard Hamilton .25 .60
51 Lindsey Hunter .20 .50
52 Antonio McDyess .25 .60
53 Tayshaun Prince .30 .75
54 Ben Wallace .30 .75
55 Rasheed Wallace .30 .75
56 Baron Davis .30 .75
57 Ike Diogu .20 .50
58 Mike Dunleavy .25 .60
59 Derek Fisher .25 .60
60 Troy Murphy .20 .50
61 Mickael Pietrus .25 .60
62 Jason Richardson .30 .75
63 Rafer Alston .20 .50
64 Luther Head .25 .60
65 Juwan Howard .25 .60
66 Tracy McGrady .40 1.00
67 Dikembe Mutombo .30 .75
68 Stromile Swift .20 .50
69 Yao Ming .40 1.00
70 Austin Croshere .20 .50
71 Stephen Jackson .25 .60
72 Sarunas Jasikevicius .25 .60
73 Jermaine O'Neal .30 .75
74 Peja Stojakovic .30 .75
75 Jamaal Tinsley .20 .50
76 Elton Brand .30 .75
77 Sam Cassell .30 .75
78 Chris Kaman .25 .60
79 Shaun Livingston .20 .50
80 Corey Maggette .25 .60
81 Cuttino Mobley .25 .60
82 Vladimir Radmanovic .20 .50
83 Kwame Brown .20 .50
84 Kobe Bryant 1.50 4.00
85 Devean George .20 .50
86 Lamar Odom .30 .75
87 Ronny Turiaf .25 .60
88 Sasha Vujacic .20 .50
89 Luke Walton .20 .50
90 Shane Battier .25 .60
91 Pau Gasol .30 .75
92 Bobby Jackson .20 .50
93 Eddie Jones .25 .60
94 Mike Miller .30 .75
95 Damon Stoudamire .25 .60
96 Hakim Warrick .25 .60
97 Alonzo Mourning .40 1.00
98 Shaquille O'Neal .60 1.50
99 Gary Payton .30 .75
100 Wayne Simien .20 .50
101 Dwyane Wade .75 2.00
102 Antoine Walker .25 .60
103 Jason Williams .25 .60
104 Andrew Bogut .30 .75
105 T.J. Ford .25 .60
106 Jamaal Magloire .20 .50
107 Michael Redd .30 .75
108 Bobby Simmons .20 .50
109 Maurice Williams .25 .60
110 Ricky Davis .25 .60
111 Kevin Garnett .60 1.50
112 Eddie Griffin .20 .50
113 Trenton Hassell .20 .50
114 Troy Hudson .20 .50
115 Rashad McCants .20 .50
116 Vince Carter .40 1.00
117 Jason Collins .20 .50
118 Richard Jefferson .30 .75
119 Jason Kidd .50 1.25
120 Nenad Krstic .20 .50
121 Jeff McInnis .20 .50
122 Antoine Wright .20 .50
123 P.J. Brown .20 .50
124 Speedy Claxton .20 .50
125 Desmond Mason .20 .50
126 Chris Paul .60 1.50
127 J.R. Smith .30 .75
128 Kirk Snyder .20 .50
129 David West .30 .75
130 Jamal Crawford .25 .60
131 Steve Francis .30 .75
132 Channing Frye .25 .60
133 Stephon Marbury .25 .60
134 Quentin Richardson .25 .60
135 Nate Robinson .30 .75
136 Maurice Taylor .20 .50
137 Carlos Arroyo .25 .60
138 Tony Battie .20 .50
139 Keyon Dooling .20 .50
140 Grant Hill .40 1.00
141 Dwight Howard .50 1.25
142 Darko Milicic .20 .50
143 Jameer Nelson .25 .60
144 Samuel Dalembert .20 .50
145 Steven Hunter .20 .50
146 Andre Iguodala .30 .75
147 Allen Iverson .40 1.00
148 Kyle Korver .25 .60
149 Shavlik Randolph .20 .50
150 Chris Webber .30 .75
151 Raja Bell .25 .60

152 Boris Diaw	.25	.60
153 Shawn Marion	.30	.75
154 Steve Nash	.40	1.00
155 Amare Stoudemire	.30	.75
156 Kurt Thomas	.20	.50
157 Tim Thomas	.20	.50
158 Steve Blake	.20	.50
159 Juan Dixon	.20	.50
160 Zach Randolph	.25	.60
161 Ha Seung-Jin	.20	.50
162 Sebastian Telfair	.20	.50
163 Martell Webster	.25	.60
164 Shareef Abdur-Rahim	.25	.60
165 Ron Artest	.30	.75
166 Mike Bibby	.30	.75
167 Brad Miller	.30	.75
168 Kenny Thomas	.20	.50
169 Bonzi Wells	.20	.50
170 Bruce Bowen	.20	.50
171 Tim Duncan	.50	1.25
172 Michael Finley	.30	.75
173 Manu Ginobili	.30	.75
174 Nazr Mohammed	.20	.50
175 Tony Parker	.30	.75
176 Ray Allen	.30	.75
177 Danny Fortson	.20	.50
178 Rashard Lewis	.30	.75
179 Luke Ridnour	.25	.60
180 Earl Watson	.20	.50
181 Chris Wilcox	.20	.50
182 Rafael Araujo	.20	.50
183 Chris Bosh	.30	.75
184 Joey Graham	.20	.50
185 Mike James	.20	.50
186 Morris Peterson	.20	.50
187 Charlie Villanueva	.30	.75
188 Carlos Boozer	.30	.75
189 Matt Harpring	.25	.60
190 Kris Humphries	.20	.50
191 Andrei Kirilenko	.25	.60
192 C.J. Miles	.20	.50
193 Chris Taft	.20	.50
194 Deron Williams	.50	1.25
195 Gilbert Arenas	.30	.75
196 Andray Blatche	.20	.50
197 Caron Butler	.30	.75
198 Antonio Daniels	.20	.50
199 Brendan Haywood	.20	.50
200 Antawn Jamison	.30	.75
201 Andrea Bargnani RC	1.50	4.00
202 LaMarcus Aldridge RC	2.50	6.00
203 Adam Morrison RC	1.25	3.00
204 Tyrus Thomas RC	1.25	3.00
205 Shelden Williams RC	1.00	2.50
206 Brandon Roy RC	2.50	6.00
207 Randy Foye RC	1.25	3.00
208 Rudy Gay RC	1.50	4.00
209 Patrick O'Bryant RC	1.00	2.50
210 Saer Sene RC	1.00	2.50
211 J.J. Redick RC	1.25	3.00
212 Hilton Armstrong RC	1.00	2.50
213 Thabo Sefolosha RC	1.25	3.00
214 Ronnie Brewer RC	1.25	3.00
215 Cedric Simmons RC	1.00	2.50
216 Rodney Carney RC	1.00	2.50
217 Shawne Williams RC	1.00	2.50
218 Quincy Douby RC	1.00	2.50
219 Renaldo Balkman RC	1.00	2.50
220 Rajon Rondo RC	4.00	10.00
221 Marcus Williams RC	1.00	2.50
222 Josh Boone RC	1.00	2.50
223 Kyle Lowry RC	1.25	3.00
224 Shannon Brown RC	1.50	4.00
225 Jordan Farmar RC	1.00	2.50
226 Maurice Ager RC	1.00	2.50
227 Mardy Collins RC	1.00	2.50
228 Jorge Garbajosa RC	1.00	2.50
229 James White RC	1.00	2.50
230 Steve Novak RC	1.00	2.50
231 Solomon Jones RC	1.00	2.50
232 Paul Davis RC	1.00	2.50
233 P.J. Tucker RC	1.00	2.50
234 Craig Smith RC	1.00	2.50
235 Bobby Jones RC	1.00	2.50
236 David Noel RC	1.00	2.50
237 Denham Brown RC	1.00	2.50
238 James Augustine RC	1.00	2.50
239 Daniel Gibson RC	1.25	3.00
240 Alexander Johnson RC	1.00	2.50

2006-07 Upper Deck Star Rookies Hot Pack

*HOT PACK: .5X TO 1.25X BASE HI
ONE HOT PACK PER BOX

2006-07 Upper Deck Flight Team

COMPLETE SET (30)	12.50	30.00
*HOT PACK SILVER: .5X TO 1.25X BASE HI		
APPROXIMATE ODDS 1:12		
ONE HOT PACK PER BOX		
AI Andre Iguodala	.75	2.00
AS Amare Stoudemire	.75	2.00
BB Brent Barry	.50	1.25
CA Carmelo Anthony	1.00	2.50
CB Chris Bosh	.75	2.00
CM Corey Maggette	.60	1.50
DH Dwight Howard	1.25	3.00
DM Desmond Mason	.50	1.25
DW Dwyane Wade	2.00	5.00
FJ Fred Jones	.50	1.25
GA Gilbert Arenas	.75	2.00
JR Jason Richardson	.75	2.00
JS J.R. Smith	.75	2.00
KB Kobe Bryant	4.00	10.00
KG Kevin Garnett	1.50	4.00
KM Kenyon Martin	.75	2.00
LJ LeBron James	4.00	10.00
MA Shawn Marion	.75	2.00
MG Manu Ginobili	.75	2.00
MI Darius Miles	.50	1.25
MJ Michael Jordan	6.00	15.00
NR Nate Robinson	.75	2.00
RJ Richard Jefferson	.75	2.00
SF Steve Francis	.75	2.00
SM Josh Smith	.75	2.00
SO Shaquille O'Neal	1.50	4.00
SS Stromile Swift	.50	1.25
TM Tracy McGrady	1.00	2.50
TP Tayshaun Prince	.75	2.00
VC Vince Carter	1.00	2.50

2006-07 Upper Deck MVP Watch

COMPLETE SET (15)	8.00	20.00
APPROXIMATE ODDS 1:12		
*HOT PACK: .5X TO 1.25X BASE HI		
ONE HOT PACK PER BOX		
AI Allen Iverson	.75	2.00
CB Chauncey Billups	.60	1.50
DN Dirk Nowitzki	1.00	2.50
DW Dwyane Wade	1.50	4.00
EB Elton Brand	.60	1.50
GA Gilbert Arenas	.60	1.50
KB Kobe Bryant	3.00	8.00
KG Kevin Garnett	1.25	3.00
LJ LeBron James	3.00	8.00
PP Paul Pierce	.75	2.00
SM Shawn Marion	.60	1.50
SN Steve Nash	.75	2.00
SO Shaquille O'Neal	1.25	3.00
TD Tim Duncan	1.00	2.50
TM Tracy McGrady	.75	2.00

2006-07 Upper Deck Signature Sensations

PRINT RUN 25 SER.#'d SETS		
AB Andrew Bogut	8.00	20.00
AI Andre Iguodala	10.00	25.00
BB Bruce Bowen	6.00	15.00
BD Dee Brown	6.00	15.00
CA Carmelo Anthony	30.00	80.00
CP Chris Paul	25.00	60.00
DB Denham Brown	6.00	15.00
DM Donyell Marshall	6.00	15.00
DN David Noel	6.00	15.00
HA Hassan Adams	6.00	15.00
ID Ike Diogu	6.00	15.00
JK Jason Kapono	6.00	15.00
KB Kwame Brown	6.00	15.00
LA LaMarcus Aldridge	20.00	50.00
NR Nate Robinson	8.00	20.00
RH Ryan Hollins	6.00	15.00
RT Ronny Turiaf	8.00	20.00
VW Von Wafer	6.00	15.00
WM Maurice Williams	6.00	15.00
YK Yaroslav Korolev	6.00	15.00

2006-07 Upper Deck Signature Sensations Dual

GG Joey Graham / Stephen Graham	10.00	25.00
JJ Michael Jordan / LeBron James	500.00	800.00
LP Shaun Livingston / Chris Paul	25.00	60.00
PC Paul Pierce / Vince Carter	40.00	100.00

2006-07 Upper Deck The LeBrons

COMPLETE SET (15)	10.00	25.00
COMMON LEBRON (1-12)	2.50	6.00
*HOT PACK: .5X TO 1.25X BASE HI		
ONE HOT PACK PER BOX		
APPROXIMATE ODDS 1:3		
COMMON MEMORABILIA	12.50	30.00
COMMON DUAL MEM.	40.00	100.00
QUAD UNPRICED DUE TO SCARCITY		
RANDOM INSERTS IN PACKS		
13 LeBron James Dual	3.00	8.00
14 LeBron James Dual	3.00	8.00
15 LeBron James Triple	3.00	8.00

2006-07 Upper Deck UD Game Jersey

APPROXIMATE ODDS ONE PER BOX		
AB Andrew Bogut	3.00	8.00
AI Allen Iverson	4.00	10.00
AJ Al Jefferson	3.00	8.00
AK Andrei Kirilenko	2.50	6.00
AL Ray Allen	3.00	8.00
AS Amare Stoudemire	3.00	8.00
AW Antoine Walker	2.50	6.00
BB Bruce Bowen	2.00	5.00
BD Baron Davis	3.00	8.00
BG Ben Gordon	3.00	8.00
BK Kwame Brown	2.00	5.00
BM Brad Miller	3.00	8.00
BW Ben Wallace	3.00	8.00
CA Carmelo Anthony	4.00	10.00
CB Chauncey Billups	3.00	8.00
CF Channing Frye	2.50	6.00
CM Corey Maggette	2.50	6.00
CP Chris Paul	6.00	15.00
CW Chris Webber	3.00	8.00
DG Drew Gooden	2.50	6.00
DH Devin Harris	3.00	8.00
DM Donyell Marshall	2.00	5.00
DN Dirk Nowitzki	5.00	12.00
EB Elton Brand	3.00	8.00
EO Emeka Okafor	3.00	8.00
GA Gilbert Arenas	3.00	8.00
GE Devean George	2.00	5.00
GH Grant Hill	4.00	10.00
HD Dwight Howard	5.00	12.00
HU Larry Hughes	2.50	6.00
IA Andre Iguodala	3.00	8.00
ID Ike Diogu	2.00	5.00
JC Jamal Crawford	2.50	6.00
JD Juan Dixon	2.00	5.00
JH Josh Howard	2.50	6.00
JJ Joe Johnson	3.00	8.00
JK Jason Kidd	5.00	12.00
JM Jeff McInnis	2.00	5.00
JO Jermaine O'Neal	3.00	8.00
JR Jason Richardson	3.00	8.00
JS J.R. Smith	3.00	8.00
JT Jason Terry	2.50	6.00
KB Kobe Bryant	8.00	20.00
KG Kevin Garnett	6.00	15.00
KH Kirk Hinrich	3.00	8.00
KK Kyle Korver	2.50	6.00
LD Luol Deng	3.00	8.00
LH Luther Head	2.50	6.00
LJ LeBron James	8.00	20.00
LO Lamar Odom	3.00	8.00
LW Luke Walton	2.00	5.00
MA Sean May	2.00	5.00
MB Mike Bibby	3.00	8.00
MD Marquis Daniels	2.00	5.00
MG Manu Ginobili	3.00	8.00
MJ Michael Jordan SP	25.00	60.00
MS Stephon Marbury	2.50	6.00
MW Marvin Williams	3.00	8.00
NR Nate Robinson	3.00	8.00
PG Pau Gasol	3.00	8.00
PP Paul Pierce	4.00	10.00
PS Peja Stojakovic	3.00	8.00
PT Tayshaun Prince	3.00	8.00
QR Quentin Richardson	2.50	6.00
RA Ron Artest	3.00	8.00
RF Raymond Felton	4.00	10.00
RH Richard Hamilton	2.50	6.00
RJ Richard Jefferson	3.00	8.00
RL Rashard Lewis	3.00	8.00
RM Rashad McCants	2.00	5.00
RW Rasheed Wallace	3.00	8.00
SD Samuel Dalembert	2.00	5.00
SJ Sarunas Jasikevicius	2.50	6.00
SL Shaun Livingston	2.00	5.00
SM Shawn Marion	3.00	8.00
SN Steve Nash	4.00	10.00
SO Shaquille O'Neal	6.00	15.00
ST Sebastian Telfair	2.00	5.00
TC Tyson Chandler	2.50	6.00
TD Tim Duncan	5.00	12.00
TF T.J. Ford	2.50	6.00
TM Tracy McGrady	4.00	10.00
TP Tony Parker	3.00	8.00
VC Vince Carter	4.00	10.00
WM Martell Webster	2.50	6.00
WS Wally Szczerbiak	2.50	6.00
YM Yao Ming	4.00	10.00
ZI Zydrunas Ilgauskas	2.50	6.00

2006-07 Upper Deck UD Game Patch

*PATCH: .75X TO 2X BASE HI		
PRINT RUN 25 SER.#'d SETS		
LJ LeBron James	25.00	60.00

2007-08 Upper Deck

This 242-card set was released in October, 2007. The set was issued into the hobby in two versions (West and East) both versions of which had 15 cards in the pack with 16 packs to a box and 12 boxes to a case and packs carried an initial SRP of $9.99. Cards numbered 1-200 feature NBA veterans while cards numbered 201-242 feature 2007-08 NBA rookies.

COMPLETE SET (242)	75.00	150.00
COMP.SET w/o SP's (200)	15.00	30.00
1 Austin Croshere	.20	.50
2 Devean George	.20	.50
3 Devin Harris	.30	.75
4 Josh Howard	.25	.60
5 Jerry Stackhouse	.25	.60
6 Jason Terry	.25	.60
7 Rafer Alston	.20	.50
8 Shane Battier	.25	.60
9 Luther Head	.25	.60
10 Juwan Howard	.25	.60
11 Tracy McGrady	.30	.75
12 Steve Novak	.20	.50
13 Rudy Gay	.30	.75
14 Eddie Jones	.25	.60
15 Kyle Lowry	.30	.75
16 Mike Miller	.30	.75
17 Damon Stoudamire	.25	.60
18 Hakim Warrick	.25	.60
19 Brandon Bass	.20	.50
20 Tyson Chandler	.25	.60
21 Bobby Jackson	.20	.50
22 Desmond Mason	.20	.50
23 Cedric Simmons	.25	.60
24 Peja Stojakovic	.30	.75
25 Bruce Bowen	.20	.50
26 Michael Finley	.30	.75
27 Manu Ginobili	.30	.75
28 Tony Parker	.30	.75
29 Beno Udrih	.20	.50
30 Monta Ellis	.30	.75
31 Al Harrington	.25	.60
32 Sarunas Jasikevicius	.20	.50
33 Stephen Jackson	.25	.60
34 Jason Richardson	.30	.75
35 Sam Cassell	.30	.75
36 Chris Kaman	.25	.60
37 Shaun Livingston	.20	.50
38 Corey Maggette	.25	.60
39 Cuttino Mobley	.25	.60
40 Tim Thomas	.20	.50
41 Kwame Brown	.20	.50
42 Andrew Bynum	.40	1.00
43 Jordan Farmar	.20	.50
44 Lamar Odom	.30	.75
45 Ronny Turiaf	.25	.60
46 Luke Walton	.20	.50
47 Leandro Barbosa	.25	.60
48 Raja Bell	.25	.60
49 Boris Diaw	.25	.60
50 Shawn Marion	.30	.75
51 Amare Stoudemire	.30	.75
52 Shareef Abdur-Rahim	.25	.60
53 Ron Artest	.30	.75
54 Quincy Douby	.20	.50
55 Kevin Martin	.30	.75
56 Brad Miller	.25	.60
57 Allen Iverson	.40	1.00
58 Kenyon Martin	.30	.75
59 Eduardo Najera	.20	.50
60 Nene	.25	.60
61 J.R. Smith	.30	.75
62 Ricky Davis	.25	.60
63 Randy Foye	.30	.75
64 Troy Hudson	.20	.50
65 Mike James	.20	.50
66 Rashad McCants	.20	.50
67 Craig Smith	.20	.50
68 LaMarcus Aldridge	.40	1.00
69 Jarrett Jack	.25	.60
70 Jamaal Magloire	.20	.50
71 Sergio Rodriguez	.20	.50
72 Brandon Roy	.40	1.00
73 Martell Webster	.25	.60
74 Rashard Lewis	.25	.60
75 Luke Ridnour	.25	.60
76 Danny Fortson	.20	.50
77 Chris Wilcox	.20	.50
78 Damien Wilkins	.20	.50
79 Ronnie Brewer	.25	.60
80 Derek Fisher	.25	.60
81 Matt Harpring	.25	.60
82 Andrei Kirilenko	.25	.60
83 Paul Millsap	.25	.60
84 Deron Williams	.50	1.25
85 Tony Allen	.20	.50
86 Gerald Green	.25	.60
87 Al Jefferson	.30	.75
88 Wally Szczerbiak	.25	.60
89 Allan Ray	.20	.50
90 Delonte West	.25	.60
91 Hassan Adams	.20	.50
92 Richard Jefferson	.30	.75
93 Jason Kidd	.30	.75
94 Nenad Krstic	.20	.50
95 Marcus Williams	.20	.50
96 Renaldo Balkman	.20	.50
97 Jamal Crawford	.25	.60
98 Eddy Curry	.20	.50
99 Channing Frye	.25	.60
100 Quentin Richardson	.25	.60
101 Nate Robinson	.30	.75
102 Rodney Carney	.20	.50
103 Samuel Dalembert	.20	.50
104 Steven Hunter	.20	.50
105 Kyle Korver	.25	.60
106 Andre Miller	.25	.60
107 Shavlik Randolph	.20	.50
108 Andrea Bargnani	.40	1.00
109 Jose Calderon	.25	.60
110 T.J. Ford	.25	.60
111 Jorge Garbajosa	.25	.60
112 Joey Graham	.20	.50
113 Morris Peterson	.20	.50
114 Luol Deng	.30	.75
115 Ben Gordon	.30	.75
116 Kirk Hinrich	.30	.75
117 Thabo Sefolosha	.30	.75
118 Tyrus Thomas	.30	.75
119 Ben Wallace	.30	.75
120 Shannon Brown	.30	.75
121 Drew Gooden	.25	.60
122 Larry Hughes	.25	.60
123 Zydrunas Ilgauskas	.25	.60
124 Donyell Marshall	.20	.50
125 Richard Hamilton	.25	.60
126 Amir Johnson	.20	.50
127 Antonio McDyess	.25	.60
128 Tayshaun Prince	.30	.75
129 Rasheed Wallace	.30	.75
130 Chris Webber	.30	.75
131 Marquis Daniels	.20	.50
132 Ike Diogu	.20	.50
133 Mike Dunleavy	.25	.60
134 Jeff Foster	.20	.50
135 Troy Murphy	.20	.50
136 Jamaal Tinsley	.20	.50
137 Charlie Bell	.20	.50
138 Andrew Bogut	.30	.75
139 Earl Boykins	.20	.50
140 Bobby Simmons	.20	.50
141 Charlie Villanueva	.30	.75
142 Maurice Williams	.25	.60
143 Speedy Claxton	.20	.50
144 Solomon Jones	.20	.50
145 Tyronn Lue	.20	.50
146 Marvin Williams	.30	.75
147 Shelden Williams	.20	.50
148 Raymond Felton	.40	1.00
149 Othella Harrington	.20	.50
150 Sean May	.20	.50
151 Adam Morrison	.30	.75
152 Gerald Wallace	.30	.75
153 Udonis Haslem	.25	.60
154 Alonzo Mourning	.40	1.00
155 Shaquille O'Neal	.60	1.50
156 Gary Payton	.30	.75
157 Antoine Walker	.25	.60
158 Jason Williams	.25	.60
159 Carlos Arroyo	.25	.60
160 Travis Diener	.20	.50
161 Grant Hill	.40	1.00
162 Darko Milicic	.20	.50
163 Jameer Nelson	.25	.60
164 J.J. Redick	.30	.75
165 Andray Blatche	.20	.50
166 Caron Butler	.30	.75
167 Antonio Daniels	.20	.50
168 Brendan Haywood	.20	.50
169 Antawn Jamison	.30	.75
170 DeShawn Stevenson	.20	.50
171 Dirk Nowitzki	.40	1.00
172 Yao Ming	.40	1.00
173 Pau Gasol	.30	.75
174 Chris Paul	.60	1.50
175 Tim Duncan	.50	1.25
176 Baron Davis	.30	.75
177 Elton Brand	.30	.75
178 Kobe Bryant	1.50	4.00
179 Steve Nash	.40	1.00
180 Mike Bibby	.30	.75
181 Carmelo Anthony	.40	1.00
182 Kevin Garnett	.60	1.50
183 Zach Randolph	.25	.60
184 Ray Allen	.30	.75
185 Carlos Boozer	.30	.75
186 Paul Pierce	.40	1.00
187 Vince Carter	.40	1.00
188 Stephon Marbury	.25	.60
189 Andre Iguodala	.30	.75
190 Chris Bosh	.30	.75
191 Michael Jordan	2.50	6.00
192 LeBron James	1.50	4.00
193 Chauncey Billups	.30	.75
194 Jermaine O'Neal	.30	.75
195 Michael Redd	.30	.75
196 Joe Johnson	.30	.75
197 Emeka Okafor	.30	.75
198 Dwyane Wade	.75	2.00
199 Dwight Howard	.50	1.25
200 Gilbert Arenas	.30	.75
201 Acie Law RC	1.00	2.50
202 Thaddeus Young RC	1.25	3.00
203 Julian Wright RC	1.00	2.50
204 Al Thornton RC	1.00	2.50
205 Rodney Stuckey RC	1.50	4.00
206 Nick Young RC	1.50	4.00
207 Sean Williams RC	1.00	2.50
208 Marco Belinelli RC	1.00	2.50
209 Javaris Crittenton RC	1.00	2.50
210 Jason Smith RC	1.00	2.50
211 Daequan Cook RC	1.00	2.50
212 Jared Dudley RC	1.00	2.50
213 Wilson Chandler RC	1.50	4.00
214 Morris Almond RC	1.00	2.50
215 Aaron Brooks RC	1.00	2.50
216 Arron Afflalo RC	1.25	3.00
217 Alando Tucker RC	1.00	2.50
218 Petteri Koponen RC	1.00	2.50
219 Carl Landry RC	1.00	2.50
220 Gabe Pruitt RC	1.00	2.50
221 Marcus Williams RC	1.00	2.50
222 Nick Fazekas RC	1.00	2.50
223 Glen Davis RC	1.50	4.00
224 Jermareo Davidson RC	1.00	2.50
225 Josh McRoberts RC	1.00	2.50
226 Chris Richard RC	1.00	2.50
227 Derrick Byars RC	1.00	2.50
228 Adam Haluska RC	1.00	2.50
229 Reyshawn Terry RC	1.00	2.50
230 Jared Jordan RC	1.00	2.50
231 Stephane Lasme RC	1.00	2.50
232 Dominic McGuire RC	1.00	2.50
233 Greg Oden SP RC	1.50	4.00
234 Kevin Durant SP RC	10.00	25.00
235 Al Horford SP RC	1.50	4.00
236 Mike Conley Jr. SP RC	2.00	5.00
237 Jeff Green SP RC	1.50	4.00
238 Taurean Green SP RC	1.25	3.00
239 Corey Brewer SP RC	1.50	4.00
240 Brandan Wright SP RC	1.25	3.00
241 Joakim Noah SP RC	3.00	8.00
242 Spencer Hawes SP RC	1.25	3.00

2007-08 Upper Deck Championship Court Stamp

These cards were available via redemption through the 2007-08 Upper Deck Championship Predictor insert. Collectors holding the winning Predictor card could exchange it for this complete set. Card fronts have a holographic "Championship Court" logo.
*COURT STAMP: 4X TO 10X BASE HI

2007-08 Upper Deck Electric Court Gold

*1-200 GOLD: 1.25X TO 3X BASE HI
*200-242 GOLD RC: .5X TO 1.25X HI
APPROXIMATE ODDS 1:4

2007-08 Upper Deck All-NBA

COMPLETE SET (15)	8.00	20.00
RANDOM INSERTS IN PACKS		
1 Dirk Nowitzki	.75	2.00
2 Tim Duncan	1.00	2.50
3 Amare Stoudemire	.60	1.50
4 Steve Nash	.75	2.00
5 Kobe Bryant	3.00	8.00
6 LeBron James	3.00	8.00
7 Chris Bosh	.60	1.50
8 Yao Ming	.75	2.00
9 Gilbert Arenas	.60	1.50
10 Tracy McGrady	.60	1.50
11 Kevin Garnett	1.25	3.00
12 Carmelo Anthony	.75	2.00
13 Dwight Howard	1.00	2.50
14 Dwyane Wade	1.50	4.00
15 Chauncey Billups	.60	1.50

2007-08 Upper Deck All-Star Die Cuts

RANDOM INSERTS IN PACKS		
AS1 Antawn Jamison	8.00	20.00
AS2 Ben Wallace	8.00	20.00
AS3 Bill Russell	12.00	30.00
AS4 Chauncey Billups	8.00	20.00
AS5 Jason Kidd	10.00	25.00
AS6 Jermaine O'Neal	8.00	20.00
AS7 John Havlicek	8.00	20.00
AS8 Larry Bird	15.00	40.00
AS9 LeBron James	30.00	80.00
AS10 Michael Jordan	200.00	400.00
AS11 Michael Redd	8.00	20.00
AS12 Paul Pierce	10.00	25.00
AS13 Richard Hamilton	6.00	15.00
AS14 Robert Parish	8.00	20.00
AS15 Walt Frazier	8.00	20.00
AS16 Amare Stoudemire	8.00	20.00
AS17 Bill Walton	8.00	20.00
AS18 Carmelo Anthony	10.00	25.00
AS19 David Robinson	12.00	30.00
AS20 Elton Brand	8.00	20.00
AS21 Hakeem Olajuwon	10.00	25.00
AS22 James Worthy	10.00	25.00
AS23 Jerry West	10.00	25.00
AS24 John Stockton	12.00	30.00
AS25 Josh Howard	6.00	15.00
AS26 Magic Johnson	12.00	30.00
AS27 Manu Ginobili	8.00	20.00
AS28 Yao Ming	10.00	25.00
AS29 Rick Barry	8.00	20.00
AS30 Tony Parker	8.00	20.00

2007-08 Upper Deck Behind the Glass

COMPLETE SET (25)	20.00	40.00
RANDOM INSERTS IN PACKS		
AI Allen Iverson	1.00	2.50
AS Amare Stoudemire	.75	2.00
BO Carlos Boozer	.75	2.00
BW Ben Wallace	.75	2.00
CA Carmelo Anthony	1.00	2.50
CB Chris Bosh	.75	2.00
CP Chris Paul	1.50	4.00
DH Dwight Howard	1.25	3.00
DN Dirk Nowitzki	1.00	2.50
DW Dwyane Wade	2.00	5.00
GA Gilbert Arenas	.75	2.00
JR Jason Richardson	.75	2.00
KB Kobe Bryant	4.00	10.00
KG Kevin Garnett	1.50	4.00
LJ LeBron James	4.00	10.00
MA Shawn Marion	.75	2.00
MG Manu Ginobili	.75	2.00
MJ Michael Jordan	6.00	15.00
PP Paul Pierce	1.00	2.50
SM Stephon Marbury	.60	1.50
SN Steve Nash	1.00	2.50
SO Shaquille O'Neal	1.50	4.00
TD Tim Duncan	1.25	3.00
TM Tracy McGrady	.75	2.00
YM Yao Ming	1.00	2.50

2007-08 Upper Deck Champions of the Court

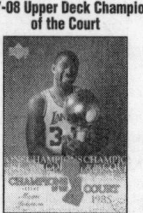

COMPLETE SET (25)	15.00	40.00
RANDOM INSERTS IN PACKS		
BR Bill Russell	1.25	3.00
BW Bill Walton	.75	2.00
CB Chauncey Billups	.75	2.00
DR Dennis Rodman	1.25	3.00
DW Dwyane Wade	2.00	5.00
GM George Mikan	1.50	4.00
HO Hakeem Olajuwon	1.00	2.50
JD Joe Dumars	.75	2.00
JE Julius Erving	1.50	4.00
JH John Havlicek	.75	2.00
JO Magic Johnson	2.00	5.00
JW James Worthy	1.00	2.50
KA Kareem Abdul-Jabbar	1.25	3.00
KB Kobe Bryant	4.00	10.00
LB Larry Bird	2.50	6.00
MG Manu Ginobili	.75	2.00
MJ Michael Jordan	6.00	15.00
MM Moses Malone	.75	2.00
RH Robert Horry	.60	1.50
RO David Robinson	1.25	3.00
SK Steve Kerr	.75	2.00
SO Shaquille O'Neal	1.50	4.00
TD Tim Duncan	1.25	3.00
TP Tony Parker	.75	2.00
WC Wilt Chamberlain	1.50	4.00

2007-08 Upper Deck Championship Predictor

RANDOM INSERTS IN PACKS		
CP1 Atlanta Hawks	2.00	5.00
CP2 Boston Celtics	4.00	10.00
CP3 Charlotte Bobcats	2.00	5.00
CP4 Chicago Bulls	2.00	5.00
CP5 Cleveland Cavaliers	4.00	10.00
CP6 Dallas Mavericks	2.00	5.00
CP7 Denver Nuggets	2.00	5.00
CP8 Detroit Pistons	2.00	5.00
CP9 Golden State Warriors	2.00	5.00
CP10 Houston Rockets	2.00	5.00
CP11 Indiana Pacers	2.00	5.00
CP12 Los Angeles Clippers	2.00	5.00
CP13 Los Angeles Lakers	4.00	10.00
CP14 Memphis Grizzlies	2.00	5.00
CP15 Miami Heat	2.00	5.00
CP16 Milwaukee Bucks	2.00	5.00
CP17 Minnesota Timberwolves	2.00	5.00
CP18 New Jersey Nets	2.00	5.00
CP19 New Orleans Hornets	2.00	5.00
CP20 New York Knicks	2.00	5.00
CP21 Orlando Magic	2.00	5.00
CP22 Philadelphia 76ers	2.00	5.00
CP23 Phoenix Suns	2.00	5.00
CP24 Portland Trail Blazers	2.00	5.00
CP25 Sacramento Kings	2.00	5.00
CP26 San Antonio Spurs	2.00	5.00
CP27 Seattle Supersonics	2.00	5.00
CP28 Toronto Raptors	2.00	5.00
CP29 Utah Jazz	2.00	5.00
CP30 Washington Wizards	2.00	5.00

2007-08 Upper Deck Draft Notices

COMPLETE SET (25)	10.00	25.00
RANDOM INSERTS IN PACKS		
DN1 Greg Oden	.75	2.00
DN2 Kevin Durant	5.00	12.00
DN3 Al Horford	.75	2.00
DN4 Mike Conley Jr.	1.00	2.50
DN5 Jeff Green	.75	2.00
DN6 Alando Tucker	.60	1.50
DN7 Corey Brewer	.75	2.00
DN8 Brandan Wright	.60	1.50
DN9 Joakim Noah	1.50	4.00
DN10 Spencer Hawes	.60	1.50
DN11 Acie Law	.60	1.50
DN12 Thaddeus Young	.75	2.00
DN13 Julian Wright	.60	1.50
DN14 Al Thornton	.60	1.50
DN15 Rodney Stuckey	1.00	2.50
DN16 Nick Young	1.00	2.50
DN17 Sean Williams	.60	1.50
DN18 Javaris Crittenton	.60	1.50
DN19 Jason Smith	.60	1.50
DN20 Daequan Cook	.60	1.50
DN21 Jared Dudley	.60	1.50
DN22 Wilson Chandler	1.00	2.50
DN23 Morris Almond	.60	1.50
DN24 Aaron Brooks	.60	1.50
DN25 Arron Afflalo	.75	2.00

2007-08 Upper Deck Jordan Chronicles

COMPLETE SET (20)	40.00	80.00
COMMON JORDAN	4.00	10.00
RANDOM INSERTS IN PACKS		
AUTOS UNPRICED DUE TO SCARCITY		

2007-08 Upper Deck Legendary All-Stars

COMPLETE SET (20)	15.00	40.00
RANDOM INSERTS IN PACKS		
AUTOS NOT PRICED DUE TO SCARCITY		
LA1 Michael Jordan	10.00	25.00
LA2 Bill Laimbeer	1.25	3.00
LA3 Isiah Thomas	1.25	3.00
LA4 Larry Bird	4.00	10.00

LA5 Magic Johnson 3.00 8.00
LA6 Bill Russell 2.00 5.00
LA7 Kareem Abdul-Jabbar 2.00 5.00
LA8 David Robinson 2.00 5.00
LA9 Hakeem Olajuwon 1.50 4.00
LA10 James Worthy 1.50 4.00
LA11 Robert Parish 1.25 3.00
LA12 Jerry West 1.50 4.00
LA13 Bill Walton 1.25 3.00
LA14 John Havlicek 1.25 3.00
LA15 Rick Barry 1.25 3.00
LA16 Walt Frazier 1.25 3.00
LA17 Bernard King 1.25 3.00
LA18 Clyde Drexler 1.50 4.00
LA19 Elgin Baylor 1.25 3.00
LA20 Maurice Cheeks 1.25 3.00

2007-08 Upper Deck Mini Jersey

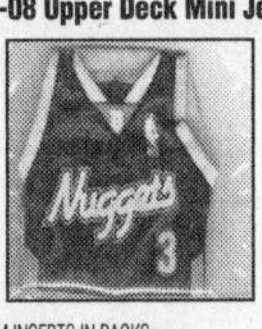

RANDOM INSERTS IN PACKS
1 LeBron James 5.00 12.00
2 Kobe Bryant 5.00 12.00
3 Allen Iverson 2.50 6.00
4 Shaquille O'Neal 3.00 8.00
5 Paul Pierce 2.50 6.00
6 Dirk Nowitzki 2.50 6.00
7 Tim Duncan 2.50 6.00
8 Kevin Garnett 3.00 8.00
9 Dwight Howard 2.50 6.00
10 Yao Ming 3.00 8.00
11 Steve Nash 3.00 8.00
12 Chris Bosh 2.50 6.00
13 Michael Jordan 8.00 20.00

2007-08 Upper Deck MVP Predictor

RANDOM INSERTS IN PACKS
1 Allen Iverson 1.00 2.50
2 Amare Stoudemire .75 2.00
3 Andre Iguodala .75 2.00
4 Baron Davis .75 2.00
5 Ben Gordon .75 2.00
6 Carlos Boozer .75 2.00
7 Carmelo Anthony 1.00 2.50
8 Chauncey Billups .75 2.00
9 Chris Bosh .75 2.00
10 Chris Paul 1.50 4.00
11 Dirk Nowitzki 1.00 2.50
12 Dwight Howard 1.25 3.00
13 Dwyane Wade 2.00 5.00
14 Eddy Curry .50 1.25
15 Elton Brand .75 2.00
16 Emeka Okafor .75 2.00
17 Gilbert Arenas .75 2.00
18 Jason Kidd .75 2.00
19 Jermaine O'Neal .75 2.00
20 Joe Johnson .75 2.00
21 Kevin Garnett 1.50 4.00
22 Kobe Bryant 4.00 10.00
23 LeBron James 4.00 10.00
24 Michael Redd .75 2.00
25 Mike Bibby .75 2.00
26 Pau Gasol .75 2.00
27 Paul Pierce 1.00 2.50
28 Ray Allen .75 2.00
29 Tim Duncan 1.25 3.00
30 Tony Parker .75 2.00
31 Tracy McGrady .75 2.00
32 Vince Carter 1.00 2.50
33 Yao Ming 1.00 2.50
34 Zach Randolph .60 1.50
35 Wild Card .60 1.50

2007-08 Upper Deck NBA Heroes

COMMON DURANT 2.50 6.00
COMMON LEBRON 3.00 8.00
COMMON JORDAN 3.00 8.00
APPROXIMATELY TWO PER BOX
UNPRICED AUTO PRINT RUN 5 SETS

2007-08 Upper Deck Rookie Debut Signatures

RANDOM INSERTS IN PACKS
AA Arron Afflalo 10.00 25.00
AB Aaron Brooks 8.00 20.00
AG Aaron Gray 8.00 20.00
AH Al Horford 10.00 25.00
AL Acie Law 8.00 20.00
AT Al Thornton 8.00 20.00
CB Corey Brewer 10.00 25.00
CL Carl Landry 8.00 20.00
CR Chris Richard 8.00 20.00
DB Derrick Byars 8.00 20.00
DC Daequan Cook 8.00 20.00
DM Dominic McGuire 8.00 20.00
DN Demetris Nichols 8.00 20.00
DS D.J. Strawberry 8.00 20.00
DU Jared Dudley 8.00 20.00
GD Glen Davis 12.00 30.00
GP Gabe Pruitt 8.00 20.00
HA Adam Haluska 8.00 20.00
JC Javaris Crittenton 8.00 20.00
JD Jermareo Davidson 8.00 20.00
JJ Jared Jordan 8.00 20.00
JM Josh McRoberts 8.00 20.00
JN Joakim Noah 25.00 60.00
JS Jason Smith 8.00 20.00
JW Julian Wright 8.00 20.00
KD Kevin Durant 250.00 500.00
MA Morris Almond 8.00 20.00
MC Mike Conley Jr. 12.00 30.00
MW Marcus Williams 5.00 12.00
NF Nick Fazekas 8.00 20.00
RS Rodney Stuckey 12.00 30.00
RT Reyshawn Terry 8.00 20.00
SH Spencer Hawes 8.00 20.00
SL Stephane Lasme 8.00 20.00
SW Sean Williams 8.00 20.00
TG Taurean Green 8.00 20.00
TU Alando Tucker 8.00 20.00
TY Thaddeus Young 10.00 25.00
WC Wilson Chandler 12.00 30.00

2007-08 Upper Deck ROY Predictor

RANDOM INSERTS IN PACKS
1 Greg Oden 2.50 6.00
2 Kevin Durant 15.00 40.00
3 Al Horford 2.50 6.00
4 Mike Conley Jr. 3.00 8.00
5 Jeff Green 2.50 6.00
6 Derrick Byars 2.00 5.00
7 Corey Brewer 2.50 6.00
8 Brandan Wright 2.00 5.00
9 Joakim Noah 5.00 12.00
10 Spencer Hawes 2.00 5.00
11 Acie Law 2.00 5.00
12 Thaddeus Young 2.50 6.00
13 Julian Wright 2.00 5.00
14 Al Thornton 2.00 5.00
15 Rodney Stuckey 3.00 8.00
16 Nick Young 2.00 5.00
17 Sean Williams 2.00 5.00
18 Marco Belinelli 2.00 5.00
19 Javaris Crittenton 2.00 5.00
20 Jason Smith 2.00 5.00
21 Daequan Cook 2.00 5.00
22 Jared Dudley 2.00 5.00
23 Wilson Chandler 3.00 8.00
24 Morris Almond 2.00 5.00
25 Aaron Brooks 2.00 5.00
26 Arron Afflalo 2.50 6.00
27 Alando Tucker 2.00 5.00
28 Reyshawn Terry 2.00 5.00
29 Carl Landry 2.00 5.00
30 Gabe Pruitt 2.00 5.00
31 Marcus Williams 1.25 3.00
32 Nick Fazekas 2.00 5.00
33 Glen Davis 3.00 8.00
34 Jermareo Davidson 2.00 5.00
35 Josh McRoberts 2.00 5.00

2007-08 Upper Deck Santa Hat Rookies

*HAT RCs: .5X TO 1.25X BASE HI
*HAT SP RCs: .4X TO 1X BASE HI
RANDOM INSERTS IN RACK PACKS

2007-08 Upper Deck Star Signings

APPROXIMATELY ONE PER BOX
UNPRICED GOLD PRINT RUN 5 TO 20 SETS
AB Andrea Bargnani 8.00 20.00
AI Andre Iguodala 4.00 10.00
AJ Antawn Jamison 4.00 10.00
BB Bruce Bowen 4.00 10.00
BG Ben Gordon 6.00 15.00
BM Brad Miller 4.00 10.00
BR Brandon Roy 6.00 15.00
BW Bill Walton 8.00 20.00
CD Chris Duhon 4.00 10.00
CP Chris Paul 15.00 40.00
CS Cedric Simmons 4.00 10.00
DG Daniel Gibson 4.00 10.00
DL David Lee 4.00 10.00
DM Damir Markota 4.00 10.00
DO Keyon Dooling 4.00 10.00
DS DeShawn Stevenson 4.00 10.00
DW Deron Williams 8.00 20.00
FE Raymond Felton 4.00 10.00
GA Jorge Garbajosa 4.00 10.00
GG George Gervin 8.00 20.00
IU Ime Udoka 4.00 10.00
JA James Augustine 4.00 10.00
JG Joey Graham 4.00 10.00
JJ Jarrett Jack 4.00 10.00
JW Julian Wright 6.00 15.00
KB Kobe Bryant 75.00 150.00
KD Kevin Durant 100.00 200.00
KK Kyle Korver 4.00 10.00
LA LaMarcus Aldridge 6.00 15.00
LB Larry Bird 50.00 100.00
LH Larry Hughes 4.00 10.00
LJ LeBron James 100.00 200.00
LL Donyell Marshall 4.00 10.00
MC Mardy Collins 4.00 10.00
MJ Michael Jordan 200.00 400.00
MW Marcus Williams 4.00 10.00
NO Steve Novak 4.00 10.00
PM Paul Millsap 4.00 10.00
PO Patrick O'Bryant 4.00 10.00
RF Randy Foye 4.00 10.00
RG Rudy Gay 4.00 10.00
RJ Richard Jefferson 4.00 10.00
RR Rajon Rondo 15.00 40.00
SB Shannon Brown 4.00 10.00
SJ Solomon Jones 4.00 10.00
SW Shawne Williams 4.00 10.00
TA Tony Allen 4.00 10.00
TC Tyson Chandler 4.00 10.00
TF T.J. Ford 4.00 10.00
TM Tracy McGrady 15.00 40.00
TP Tayshaun Prince 4.00 10.00
TT Tyrus Thomas 8.00 20.00
VC Vince Carter 15.00 30.00
WS Wayne Simien 4.00 10.00

2007-08 Upper Deck UD Game Jersey

APPROXIMATELY TWO PER BOX
*PATCHES: 1.25X TO 3X BASE HI
PATCHES RANDOM INSERTS IN PACKS
AB Andrew Bogut 2.50 6.00
AI Allen Iverson 3.00 8.00
AJ Al Jefferson 2.50 6.00
AK Andrei Kirilenko 2.00 5.00
AM Alonzo Mourning 3.00 8.00
AW Antoine Walker 2.00 5.00
BC Brian Cook 2.00 5.00
BG Ben Gordon 2.50 6.00
BH Brendan Haywood 2.00 5.00
BO Chris Bosh 2.50 6.00
BR Brandon Roy 3.00 8.00
BW Ben Wallace 2.50 6.00
BY Andrew Bynum 3.00 8.00
CA Carmelo Anthony 3.00 8.00
CB Caron Butler 2.50 6.00
CM Corey Maggette 2.00 5.00
CV Charlie Villanueva 2.50 6.00
DG Danny Granger 2.50 6.00
DH Devin Harris 2.50 6.00
DM Darko Milicic 2.00 5.00
DN Dirk Nowitzki 3.00 8.00
DR Dennis Rodman 4.00 10.00
EB Elton Brand 2.50 6.00
EO Emeka Okafor 2.00 5.00
FG Francisco Garcia 2.00 5.00
GA Gilbert Arenas 2.50 6.00
GH Grant Hill 3.00 8.00
GO Drew Gooden 2.00 5.00
GP Gary Payton 2.50 6.00
HE Luther Head 2.00 5.00
HO Dwight Howard 4.00 10.00
IG Andre Iguodala 2.50 6.00
JA Antawn Jamison 2.50 6.00
JC Josh Childress 2.00 5.00
JE Julius Erving 5.00 12.00
JH Josh Howard 2.50 6.00
JK Jason Kidd 3.00 8.00
JM Michael Jordan 20.00 50.00
JN Jameer Nelson 2.00 5.00
JO Jermaine O'Neal 2.50 6.00
JP Johan Petro 2.00 5.00
JR J.J. Redick 2.50 6.00
JS John Stockton 4.00 10.00
JU Juwan Howard 2.00 5.00
JW Jason Williams 2.00 5.00
KB Kobe Bryant 8.00 20.00
KG Kevin Garnett 5.00 12.00
KH Kirk Hinrich 2.50 6.00
KM Kenyon Martin 2.50 6.00
KT Kevin Garnett 5.00 12.00
KW Kwame Brown 2.00 5.00
LB Larry Bird 10.00 25.00
LD Luol Deng 2.50 6.00
LH Larry Hughes 2.00 5.00
LJ LeBron James 10.00 25.00
LK Linas Kleiza 2.00 5.00
LO Lamar Odom 2.50 6.00
MA Donyell Marshall 2.00 5.00
MB Mike Bibby 2.50 6.00
MD Mike Dunleavy 2.00 5.00
MG Manu Ginobili 2.50 6.00
MI Andre Miller 2.00 5.00
MJ Magic Johnson 8.00 20.00
MO Mehmet Okur 2.00 5.00
MR Michael Redd 2.50 6.00
MW Martell Webster 2.00 5.00
NH Nene 2.00 5.00
PG Pau Gasol 2.50 6.00
PP Paul Pierce 3.00 8.00
RA Ray Allen 3.00 8.00
RI Jason Richardson 2.50 6.00
RJ Richard Jefferson 2.50 6.00
RL Rashard Lewis 2.00 5.00
RO David Robinson 5.00 12.00
RP Robert Parish 2.50 6.00
RW Rasheed Wallace 2.50 6.00
SB Shannon Brown 2.50 6.00
SD Samuel Dalembert 2.00 5.00
SH Shawn Marion 2.50 6.00
SJ Josh Smith 2.50 6.00
SM Sean May 2.00 5.00
SN Steve Nash 3.00 8.00
SO Shaquille O'Neal 5.00 12.00
TD Tim Duncan 4.00 10.00
TM Tracy McGrady 2.50 6.00
TP Tony Parker 2.50 6.00
VC Vince Carter 3.00 8.00
WI Marvin Williams 2.50 6.00
YM Yao Ming 3.00 8.00
ZR Zach Randolph 2.00 5.00

2007-08 Upper Deck UD Top 30

COMPLETE SET (30) 12.50 30.00
RANDOM INSERTS IN PACKS
AUTOS NOT PRICED DUE TO SCARCITY
UT1 Al Jefferson .75 2.00
UT2 Baron Davis .75 2.00
UT3 Ben Gordon .75 2.00
UT4 Brandon Roy 1.00 2.50
UT5 Carlos Boozer .75 2.00
UT6 Chris Paul 1.50 4.00
UT7 Corey Maggette .60 1.50
UT8 Deron Williams 1.25 3.00
UT9 Dwyane Wade 2.00 5.00
UT10 Eddy Curry .50 1.25
UT11 Emeka Okafor .75 2.00
UT12 Gerald Wallace .75 2.00
UT13 Grant Hill 1.00 2.50
UT14 Jason Richardson .75 2.00
UT15 Jason Terry .60 1.50
UT16 Joe Johnson .75 2.00
UT17 Josh Howard .60 1.50
UT18 Kirk Hinrich .60 1.50
UT19 LeBron James 4.00 10.00
UT20 Luol Deng .75 2.00
UT21 Mike Bibby .75 2.00
UT22 Rashard Lewis .60 1.50
UT23 Raymond Felton 1.00 2.50
UT24 Richard Hamilton .60 1.50
UT25 Richard Jefferson .60 1.50
UT26 Shaquille O'Neal 1.50 4.00
UT27 Shawn Marion .75 2.00
UT28 Stephon Marbury .60 1.50
UT29 Steve Nash 1.00 2.50
UT30 Tayshaun Prince .75 2.00

2008-09 Upper Deck

This set was released on September 9, 2008. The base set consists of 266 cards. Cards 1-224 feature veterans, and cards 225-266 are rookies. The Legends were inserted at one in two packs and the rookies at one in 4.5.

COMP.SET w/o SPs (200) 25.00 50.00
1 Mike Bibby .25 .60
2 Al Horford .30 .75
3 Joe Johnson .30 .75
4 Josh Childress .25 .60
5 Josh Smith .30 .75
6 Marvin Williams .30 .75
7 Eddie House .20 .50
8 Glen Davis .25 .60
9 Sam Cassell .30 .75
10 Kevin Garnett .60 1.50
11 Rajon Rondo .40 1.00
12 Ray Allen .30 .75
13 Paul Pierce .40 1.00
14 Adam Morrison .30 .75
15 Emeka Okafor .30 .75
16 Gerald Wallace .30 .75
17 Jared Dudley .25 .60
18 Jason Richardson .30 .75
19 Nazr Mohammed .20 .50
20 Raymond Felton .25 .60
21 Andres Nocioni .20 .50
22 Ben Gordon .30 .75
23 Larry Hughes .25 .60
24 Joakim Noah .30 .75
25 Kirk Hinrich .30 .75
26 Luol Deng .30 .75
27 Tyrus Thomas .25 .60
28 Aleksandar Pavlovic .20 .50
29 Anderson Varejao .25 .60
30 Daniel Gibson .30 .75
31 Wally Szczerbiak .25 .60
32 Ben Wallace .30 .75
33 LeBron James 1.50 4.00
34 Zydrunas Ilgauskas .25 .60
35 Jason Kidd .30 .75
36 Dirk Nowitzki .40 1.00
37 Jason Terry .25 .60
38 Jerry Stackhouse .25 .60
39 Jose Barea .40 1.00
40 Josh Howard .25 .60
41 Allen Iverson .40 1.00
42 Carmelo Anthony .40 1.00
43 J.R. Smith .30 .75
44 Kenyon Martin .30 .75
45 Linas Kleiza .20 .50
46 Marcus Camby .20 .50
47 Antonio McDyess .25 .60
48 Chauncey Billups .30 .75
49 Jason Maxiell .20 .50
50 Rasheed Wallace .30 .75
51 Richard Hamilton .25 .60
52 Rodney Stuckey .40 1.00
53 Tayshaun Prince .30 .75
54 Al Harrington .25 .60
55 Baron Davis .30 .75
56 Kelenna Azubuike .20 .50
57 Matt Barnes .20 .50
58 Monta Ellis .30 .75
59 Stephen Jackson .25 .60
60 Luis Scola .25 .60
61 Luther Head .20 .50
62 Rafer Alston .20 .50
63 Shane Battier .25 .60
64 Tracy McGrady .30 .75
65 Yao Ming .40 1.00
66 Andre Owens .20 .50
67 Danny Granger .30 .75
68 Jamaal Tinsley .20 .50
69 Jermaine O'Neal .30 .75
70 Kareem Rush .20 .50
71 Mike Dunleavy .25 .60
72 Troy Murphy .20 .50
73 Al Thornton .25 .60
74 Chris Kaman .25 .60
75 Corey Maggette .25 .60
76 Cuttino Mobley .25 .60
77 Elton Brand .30 .75
78 Tim Thomas .20 .50
79 Andrew Bynum .40 1.00
80 Derek Fisher .25 .60
81 Jordan Farmar .20 .50
82 Kobe Bryant 1.50 4.00
83 Pau Gasol .30 .75
84 Lamar Odom .30 .75
85 Luke Walton .20 .50
86 Darko Milicic .20 .50
87 Javaris Crittenton .20 .50
88 Kyle Lowry .30 .75
89 Mike Conley Jr. .25 .60
90 Mike Miller .30 .75
91 Kwame Brown .20 .50
92 Rudy Gay .30 .75
93 Daequan Cook .20 .50
94 Dorell Wright .20 .50
95 Dwyane Wade .60 1.50
96 Jason Williams .25 .60
97 Ricky Davis .25 .60
98 Shawn Marion .30 .75
99 Udonis Haslem .25 .60
100 Andrew Bogut .30 .75
101 Charlie Villanueva .30 .75
102 Desmond Mason .20 .50
103 Michael Redd .30 .75
104 Mo Williams .25 .60
105 Yi Jianlian .30 .75
106 Al Jefferson .30 .75
107 Corey Brewer .25 .60
108 Craig Smith .20 .50
109 Randy Foye .30 .75
110 Rashad McCants .20 .50
111 Ryan Gomes .20 .50
112 Sebastian Telfair .20 .50
113 Bostjan Nachbar .20 .50
114 Devin Harris .30 .75
115 Josh Boone .20 .50
116 Nenad Krstic .20 .50
117 Richard Jefferson .30 .75
118 Sean Williams .25 .60
119 Vince Carter .40 1.00
120 David Lee .25 .60
121 Eddy Curry .20 .50
122 Jamal Crawford .25 .60
123 Nate Robinson .30 .75
124 Quentin Richardson .25 .60
125 Stephon Marbury .25 .60
126 Zach Randolph .25 .60
127 Chris Paul .50 1.25
128 David West .30 .75
129 Julian Wright .25 .60
130 Morris Peterson .20 .50
131 Peja Stojakovic .30 .75
132 Tyson Chandler .25 .60
133 Carlos Arroyo .25 .60
134 Dwight Howard .60 1.50
135 Hedo Turkoglu .30 .75
136 J.J. Redick .30 .75
137 Jameer Nelson .25 .60
138 Maurice Evans .20 .50
139 Rashard Lewis .25 .60
140 Andre Iguodala .30 .75
141 Andre Miller .25 .60
142 Jason Smith .20 .50
143 Louis Williams .25 .60
144 Samuel Dalembert .20 .50
145 Thaddeus Young .25 .60
146 Willie Green .20 .50
147 Amare Stoudemire .30 .75
148 Boris Diaw .20 .50
149 Grant Hill .40 1.00
150 Leandro Barbosa .25 .60
151 Raja Bell .25 .60
152 Shaquille O'Neal .60 1.50
153 Steve Nash .30 .75
154 Brandon Roy .30 .75
155 Channing Frye .25 .60
156 Greg Oden .30 .75
157 LaMarcus Aldridge .30 .75
158 Martell Webster .25 .60
159 Steve Blake .20 .50
160 Beno Udrih .20 .50
161 Brad Miller .25 .60
162 Francisco Garcia .25 .60
163 John Salmons .30 .75
164 Kevin Martin .30 .75
165 Mikki Moore .20 .50
166 Ron Artest .30 .75
167 Brent Barry .20 .50
168 Bruce Bowen .20 .50
169 Manu Ginobili .30 .75
170 Michael Finley .30 .75
171 Robert Horry .25 .60
172 Tim Duncan .50 1.25
173 Tony Parker .30 .75
174 Chris Wilcox .20 .50
175 Damien Wilkins .20 .50
176 Jeff Green .25 .60
177 Kevin Durant 1.25 3.00
178 Nick Collison .20 .50
179 Earl Watson .20 .50
180 Andrea Bargnani .25 .60
181 Anthony Parker .20 .50
182 Carlos Delfino .20 .50
183 Chris Bosh .30 .75
184 Jamario Moon .20 .50
185 Jose Calderon .25 .60
186 T.J. Ford .20 .50
187 Andrei Kirilenko .25 .60
188 Carlos Boozer .30 .75
189 Deron Williams .30 .75
190 Kyle Korver .25 .60
191 Mehmet Okur .20 .50
192 Paul Millsap .25 .60
193 Ronnie Brewer .25 .60
194 Antawn Jamison .30 .75
195 Antonio Daniels .20 .50
196 Brendan Haywood .20 .50
197 Caron Butler .30 .75
198 DeShawn Stevenson .20 .50
199 Gilbert Arenas .30 .75
200 Nick Young .25 .60
201 Spud Webb .50 1.25
202 Bob Cousy .75 2.00
203 Kevin McHale .60 1.50
204 Larry Bird 1.50 4.00
205 Dennis Rodman .75 2.00
206 Michael Jordan 4.00 10.00
207 Isiah Thomas .50 1.25
208 Joe Dumars .50 1.25
209 Nate Thurmond .50 1.25
210 Hakeem Olajuwon .60 1.50
211 Calvin Murphy .50 1.25
212 Kareem Abdul-Jabbar .75 2.00
213 Magic Johnson 1.25 3.00
214 Oscar Robertson .50 1.25
215 Bill Bradley .60 1.50
216 Earl Monroe .50 1.25
217 Willis Reed .50 1.25
218 Julius Erving 1.00 2.50
219 Clyde Drexler .60 1.50
220 Bill Walton .50 1.25
221 Maurice Lucas .50 1.25
222 David Robinson .75 2.00
223 John Stockton .75 2.00
224 Karl Malone .60 1.50
225 D.J. Augustin RC 1.00 2.50
226 Brook Lopez RC 1.50 4.00
227 Jerryd Bayless RC 1.00 2.50
228 Jason Thompson RC 1.00 2.50
229 Brandon Rush RC 1.00 2.50
230 Anthony Randolph RC 1.25 3.00
231 Robin Lopez RC 1.00 2.50
232 Marreese Speights RC 1.00 2.50
233 Roy Hibbert RC 1.50 4.00
234 Courtney Lee RC 1.50 4.00
235 J.J. Hickson RC 1.25 3.00
236 Ryan Anderson RC 1.50 4.00
237 Kosta Koufos RC 1.00 2.50
238 James Gist RC 1.00 2.50
239 Darrell Arthur RC 1.00 2.50
240 Donte Greene RC 1.00 2.50
241 D.J. White RC 1.00 2.50
242 J.R. Giddens RC 1.00 2.50
243 Deron Washington RC 1.00 2.50
244 Joey Dorsey RC 1.00 2.50
245 Mario Chalmers RC 1.50 4.00
246 DeAndre Jordan RC 2.00 5.00
247 Luc Richard Mbah A Moute RC 1.00 2.50
248 Kyle Weaver RC 1.00 2.50
249 Sonny Weems RC 1.00 2.50
250 Chris Douglas-Roberts RC 1.00 2.50
251 Sean Singletary RC 1.00 2.50
252 Patrick Ewing Jr. RC 1.00 2.50
253 Shan Foster RC 1.00 2.50
254 Bill Walker RC 1.00 2.50
255 Malik Hairston RC 1.00 2.50
256 Richard Hendrix RC 1.00 2.50
257 DeVon Hardin RC 1.00 2.50
258 Darnell Jackson RC 1.00 2.50
259 Derrick Rose RC 8.00 20.00
260 Michael Beasley RC 1.50 4.00
261 O.J. Mayo RC 1.50 4.00
262 Russell Westbrook RC 5.00 12.00
263 Kevin Love RC 4.00 10.00
264 Danilo Gallinari RC 1.50 4.00
265 Eric Gordon RC 2.50 6.00
266 Joe Alexander RC 1.00 2.50

2008-09 Upper Deck Electric Court Gold

*GOLD: .6X TO 1.5X BASE HI
GOLD STATED ODDS 1:5
206 Michael Jordan 10.00 25.00

2008-09 Upper Deck All Star Class

COMPLETE SET (30) 30.00 60.00
RANDOM INSERTS IN PACKS
AUTOS UNPRICED DUE TO SCARCITY
ASAI Allen Iverson 1.25 3.00
ASBL Bill Laimbeer 1.00 2.50
ASBO Chris Bosh 1.00 2.50
ASCB Chauncey Billups 1.00 2.50
ASDN Dirk Nowitzki 1.25 3.00
ASDR David Robinson 1.50 4.00
ASDW Dominique Wilkins 1.25 3.00
ASGG George Gervin 1.25 3.00
ASJE Julius Erving 2.00 5.00
ASJK Jason Kidd 1.00 2.50
ASJO Magic Johnson 2.50 6.00
ASKA Kareem Abdul-Jabbar 1.50 4.00
ASKB Kobe Bryant 5.00 12.00
ASKG Kevin Garnett 2.00 5.00
ASKM Karl Malone 1.25 3.00
ASLJ LeBron James 5.00 12.00
ASMJ Michael Jordan 8.00 20.00
ASNA Nate Archibald 1.00 2.50
ASRA Ray Allen 1.00 2.50
ASRB Rick Barry 1.00 2.50
ASSM Shawn Marion 1.00 2.50
ASSN Steve Nash 1.00 2.50
ASSO Shaquille O'Neal 2.00 5.00
ASTD Tim Duncan 1.50 4.00
ASTM Tracy McGrady 1.00 2.50
ASTP Tony Parker 1.00 2.50
ASVC Vince Carter 1.25 3.00
ASWA Dwyane Wade 2.00 5.00
ASWF Walt Frazier 1.00 2.50
ASYM Yao Ming 1.25 3.00

2008-09 Upper Deck Bulls Dynasty

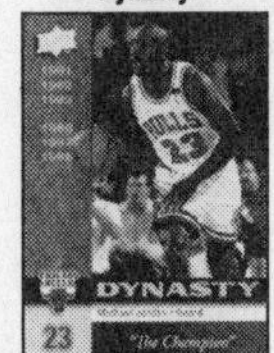

COMPLETE SET (30) 25.00 50.00
STATED ODDS 1:8
CHI1 Dennis Rodman 1.25 3.00
CHI2 Horace Grant .75 2.00
CHI3 Toni Kukoc .75 2.00
CHI4 Horace Grant .75 2.00
CHI5 Toni Kukoc .75 2.00
CHI6 Steve Kerr .75 2.00
CHI7 John Paxson .75 2.00
CHI8 Michael Jordan 6.00 15.00
CHI9 Michael Jordan 6.00 15.00
CHI10 Michael Jordan 6.00 15.00
CHI11 Michael Jordan 6.00 15.00
CHI12 Michael Jordan 6.00 15.00
CHI13 Michael Jordan 6.00 15.00
CHI14 Michael Jordan 6.00 15.00
CHI15 Michael Jordan 6.00 15.00
CHI16 Dennis Rodman 1.25 3.00
CHI17 Bill Wennington .75 2.00
CHI18 Bill Cartwright .75 2.00
CHI19 Bill Cartwright .75 2.00
CHI20 Will Perdue .75 2.00
CHI21 Will Perdue .75 2.00
CHI22 Dennis Rodman 1.25 3.00
CHI23 B.J. Armstrong .75 2.00
CHI24 Ron Harper .75 2.00
CHI25 Ron Harper .75 2.00
CHI26 Scottie Pippen 1.25 3.00
CHI27 B.J. Armstrong .75 2.00
CHI28 John Paxson .75 2.00
CHI29 Steve Kerr .75 2.00
CHI30 Scottie Pippen 1.25 3.00

2008-09 Upper Deck Celtics Dynasty

COMPLETE SET (30) 10.00 25.00
STATED ODDS 1:8
BOS1 John Havlicek .75 2.00
BOS2 John Havlicek .75 2.00
BOS3 John Havlicek .75 2.00
BOS4 Sam Jones 1.00 2.50
BOS5 Sam Jones 1.00 2.50
BOS6 Sam Jones 1.00 2.50
BOS7 Bob Cousy 1.25 3.00
BOS8 Don Nelson .75 2.00
BOS9 Don Nelson .75 2.00
BOS10 Tom Sanders .75 2.00
BOS11 Tom Sanders .75 2.00
BOS12 Tom Sanders .75 2.00
BOS13 Gene Conley .75 2.00
BOS14 Bill Russell 1.25 3.00
BOS15 Bill Russell 1.25 3.00
BOS16 Tom Heinsohn .75 2.00
BOS17 Tom Heinsohn .75 2.00
BOS18 Tom Heinsohn .75 2.00
BOS19 Bill Sharman .75 2.00
BOS20 Bill Sharman .75 2.00
BOS21 Bill Sharman .75 2.00
BOS22 Em Bryant .75 2.00
BOS23 Bailey Howell .75 2.00
BOS24 K.C. Jones .75 2.00
BOS25 Clyde Lovellette .75 2.00
BOS26 Bob Cousy 1.25 3.00
BOS27 Wayne Embry .75 2.00
BOS28 Jim Loscutoff .75 2.00
BOS29 Frank Ramsey .75 2.00
BOS30 K.C. Jones .75 2.00

2008-09 Upper Deck Emulation Memorabilia Dual

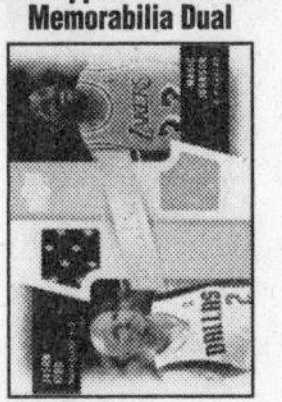

STATED ODDS 1:32
*PATCHES: 1.25X TO 3X BASE HI
PATCH STATED ODDS 1:600
EAB Ray Allen 6.00 15.00
Larry Bird
EBW Kobe Bryant 8.00 20.00
Dominique Wilkins
EDR Tim Duncan 6.00 15.00
David Robinson
EEJ Julius Erving 10.00 25.00
LeBron James
EGB Kevin Garnett 5.00 12.00
Andrew Bynum
EGM George Gervin 6.00 15.00
Tracy McGrady
EHO Dwight Howard 8.00 20.00
Shaquille O'Neal
EIP Chris Paul 6.00 15.00
Allen Iverson
EKJ Jason Kidd 6.00 15.00
Magic Johnson
EWR Ben Wallace 5.00 12.00
Dennis Rodman

2008-09 Upper Deck Game Jerseys

STATED ODDS 1:7
*PATCHES: 1.25X TO 3X BASE HI
PATCH STATED ODDS 1:250

Card	Low	High
GAAB Andrea Bargnani	2.00	5.00
GAAI Allen Iverson	3.00	8.00
GAAJ Al Jefferson	2.50	6.00
GAAK Andrei Kirilenko	2.00	5.00
GAAS Amare Stoudemire	2.50	6.00
GABG Ben Gordon	2.50	6.00
GABI Chauncey Billups	2.50	6.00
GABO Chris Bosh	2.50	6.00
GABU Caron Butler	2.50	6.00
GABW Ben Wallace	2.50	6.00
GACA Carmelo Anthony	3.00	8.00
GACB Carlos Boozer	2.50	6.00
GACP Chris Paul	4.00	10.00
GADG Danny Granger	2.50	6.00
GADH Dwight Howard	5.00	12.00
GADN Dirk Nowitzki	3.00	8.00
GADW Deron Williams	2.50	6.00
GAEB Elton Brand	2.50	6.00
GAEO Emeka Okafor	2.50	6.00
GAIG Andre Iguodala	2.50	6.00
GAJA Antawn Jamison	2.50	6.00
GAJH Josh Howard	2.00	5.00
GAJJ Joe Johnson	2.50	6.00
GAJK Jason Kidd	2.50	6.00
GAJO Jermaine O'Neal	2.50	6.00
GAJR Jason Richardson	2.50	6.00
GAJS Josh Smith	2.50	6.00
GAKB Kobe Bryant	6.00	15.00
GAKG Kevin Garnett	5.00	12.00
GAKH Kirk Hinrich	2.50	6.00
GALJ LeBron James	8.00	20.00
GAMB Mike Bibby	2.00	5.00
GAMG Manu Ginobili	2.50	6.00
GAMR Michael Redd	2.50	6.00
GAMW Marvin Williams	2.50	6.00
GAPA Tony Parker	2.50	6.00
GAPG Pau Gasol	2.50	6.00
GAPP Paul Pierce	3.00	8.00
GARH Richard Hamilton	2.00	5.00
GARJ Richard Jefferson	2.50	6.00
GARL Rashard Lewis	2.00	5.00
GARW Rasheed Wallace	2.50	6.00
GASM Shawn Marion	2.50	6.00
GASO Shaquille O'Neal	5.00	12.00
GATD Tim Duncan	4.00	10.00
GATM Tracy McGrady	2.50	6.00
GATP Tayshaun Prince	2.50	6.00
GAVC Vince Carter	3.00	8.00
GAYM Yao Ming	3.00	8.00
GAZR Zach Randolph	2.00	5.00

2008-09 Upper Deck Kobe Bryant Heroes

Card	Low	High
COMPLETE SET (10)	15.00	40.00
COMMON CARD (KB1-KB10)	2.50	6.00

STATED ODDS 1:25
UNPRICED AUTO PRINT RUN 5 SER.#'d SETS

2008-09 Upper Deck Lakers Dynasty

Card	Low	High
COMPLETE SET (30)	15.00	30.00
STATED ODDS 1:8		
LAL1 Kobe Bryant	4.00	10.00
LAL2 Kobe Bryant	4.00	10.00
LAL3 Kobe Bryant	4.00	10.00
LAL4 Derek Fisher	.60	1.50
LAL5 Derek Fisher	.60	1.50
LAL6 Horace Grant	.75	2.00
LAL7 Horace Grant	.75	2.00
LAL8 A.C. Green	.75	2.00
LAL9 A.C. Green	.75	2.00
LAL10 Byron Scott	.75	2.00
LAL11 James Worthy	.75	2.00
LAL12 James Worthy	.75	2.00
LAL13 Magic Johnson	2.00	5.00
LAL14 Magic Johnson	2.00	5.00
LAL15 Magic Johnson	2.00	5.00
LAL16 Kareem Abdul-Jabbar	1.25	3.00
LAL17 Kareem Abdul-Jabbar	1.25	3.00
LAL18 Kareem Abdul-Jabbar	1.25	3.00
LAL19 Michael Cooper	.75	2.00
LAL20 Michael Cooper	.75	2.00
LAL21 Jamaal Wilkes	.75	2.00
LAL22 Jamaal Wilkes	.75	2.00
LAL23 Norm Nixon	.75	2.00
LAL24 Slater Martin	.75	2.00
LAL25 Mitch Richmond	.75	2.00
LAL26 Ron Harper	.75	2.00
LAL27 George Mikan	1.50	4.00
LAL28 Clyde Lovellette	.75	2.00
LAL29 Mitch Kupchak	.75	2.00
LAL30 Kurt Rambis	1.00	2.50

2008-09 Upper Deck Same Day Signatures

RANDOM INSERTS IN PACKS

Card	Low	High
RPSBR Brandon Rush	15.00	40.00
RPSCD Chris Douglas-Roberts	10.00	25.00
RPSCL Courtney Lee	15.00	40.00
RPSDJ DeAndre Jordan	20.00	50.00
RPSDW D.J. White	10.00	25.00
RPSEG Eric Gordon	25.00	60.00
RPSGH George Hill	15.00	40.00
RPSGR Donte Greene	10.00	25.00
RPSHE Patrick Ewing Jr.	10.00	25.00
RPSJB Jerryd Bayless	10.00	25.00
RPSJG J.R. Giddens	10.00	25.00
RPSJH J.J. Hickson	12.00	30.00
RPSJT Jason Thompson	10.00	25.00
RPSKK Kosta Koufos	10.00	25.00
RPSKL Kevin Love	40.00	100.00
RPSKW Kyle Weaver	10.00	25.00
RPSMC Mario Chalmers	15.00	40.00
RPSMS Marreese Speights	10.00	25.00
RPSOM O.J. Mayo	25.00	60.00
RPSRA Ryan Anderson	15.00	40.00
RPSRH Roy Hibbert	15.00	40.00
RPSSW Sonny Weems	10.00	25.00
RPSWS Walter Sharpe	10.00	25.00

2008-09 Upper Deck Star Signings

STATED ODDS 1:28
GOLD: .6X TO 1.5X BASE HI
GOLD PRINT RUN 25 SER.#'d SETS

Card	Low	High
SSAH Al Harrington	3.00	8.00
SSAI Andre Iguodala	5.00	12.00
SSAJ Antawn Jamison	3.00	8.00
SSBB Bruce Bowen	3.00	8.00
SSBD Baron Davis	4.00	10.00
SSBG Ben Gordon	5.00	12.00
SSBK Coby Karl	3.00	8.00
SSBM Brad Miller	3.00	8.00
SSBR Brandon Roy	10.00	25.00
SSCA Carmelo Anthony	20.00	40.00
SSCB Corey Brewer	3.00	8.00
SSCM Corey Maggette	3.00	8.00
SSCP Chris Paul	30.00	60.00
SSCS Cedric Simmons	3.00	8.00
SSDA Danny Granger	5.00	12.00
SSDC Daequan Cook	3.00	8.00
SSDG Daniel Gibson	3.00	8.00
SSDM Donyell Marshall	3.00	8.00
SSDO Keyon Dooling	3.00	8.00
SSDS DeShawn Stevenson	3.00	8.00
SSDW Deron Williams	10.00	25.00
SSGD Glen Davis	5.00	12.00
SSGR Jeff Green	4.00	10.00
SSHO Al Horford	5.00	12.00
SSID Ike Diogu	3.00	8.00
SSJB Josh Boone	3.00	8.00
SSJG Joey Graham	3.00	8.00
SSJK Jason Kidd	6.00	15.00
SSJM Jamario Moon	3.00	8.00
SSJO Joakim Noah	10.00	25.00
SSKA Kelenna Azubuike	4.00	10.00
SSKD Kevin Durant	100.00	175.00
SSLH Larry Hughes	4.00	10.00
SSLJ LeBron James	125.00	225.00
SSLP Leon Powe	3.00	8.00
SSLS Luis Scola	3.00	8.00
SSMB Mike Bibby	3.00	8.00
SSMC Mike Conley Jr.	4.00	10.00
SSMW Mo Williams	3.00	8.00
SSNO Steve Novak	3.00	8.00
SSOP Oleksiy Pecherov	3.00	8.00
SSRB Renaldo Balkman	3.00	8.00
SSRF Randy Foye	3.00	8.00
SSRG Rudy Gay	6.00	15.00
SSRJ Richard Jefferson	3.00	8.00
SSSM Craig Smith	3.00	8.00
SSTC Tyson Chandler	3.00	8.00
SSTF T.J. Ford	3.00	8.00
SSTM Tracy McGrady	20.00	40.00
SSTP Tayshaun Prince	3.00	8.00
SSTT Tyrus Thomas	3.00	8.00
SSVC Vince Carter	20.00	50.00
SSWI Marvin Williams	3.00	8.00

2008-09 Upper Deck Starquest

Card	Low	High
COMPLETE SET (30)	20.00	50.00

APPROXIMATE ODDS 1:8
*BLACK: 1.5X TO 4X BASE HI
BLACK STATED ODDS 1:16
*BLUE: 1X TO 2.5X BASE HI
BLUE: RANDOM INSERTS IN PACKS
*COPPER: .6X TO 1.5X BASE HI
COPPER: RANDOM INSERTS IN PACKS
*CYAN: 1X TO 2.5X BASE HI
CYAN: RANDOM INSERTS IN PACKS
*GOLD: 1X TO 2.5X BASE HI
GOLD: RANDOM INSERTS IN PACKS

Card	Low	High
SQ1 Carmelo Anthony	.75	2.00
SQ2 Chauncey Billups	.60	1.50
SQ3 Larry Bird	2.00	5.00
SQ4 Chris Bosh	.60	1.50
SQ5 Kobe Bryant	3.00	8.00
SQ6 Vince Carter	.75	2.00
SQ7 Baron Davis	.60	1.50
SQ8 Tim Duncan	1.00	2.50
SQ9 Kevin Durant	2.50	6.00
SQ10 Julius Erving	1.25	3.00
SQ11 Walt Frazier	.60	1.50
SQ12 Kevin Garnett	1.25	3.00
SQ13 Rudy Gay	.60	1.50
SQ14 Artis Gilmore	.60	1.50
SQ15 Dwight Howard	1.25	3.00
SQ16 Allen Iverson	.75	2.00
SQ17 LeBron James	3.00	8.00
SQ18 Al Jefferson	.60	1.50
SQ19 Magic Johnson	1.50	4.00
SQ20 Michael Jordan	5.00	12.00
SQ21 Shawn Marion	.60	1.50
SQ22 Tracy McGrady	.60	1.50
SQ23 Yao Ming	.75	2.00
SQ24 Dirk Nowitzki	.75	2.00
SQ25 Shaquille O'Neal	1.25	3.00
SQ26 Greg Oden	.60	1.50
SQ27 Chris Paul	1.00	2.50
SQ28 Brandon Roy	.60	1.50
SQ29 Dwyane Wade	1.25	3.00
SQ30 Deron Williams	.60	1.50

2008-09 Upper Deck Team MVPs

Card	Low	High
COMPLETE SET (30)	10.00	25.00
THREE PER RACK PACK		
MVP1 Josh Smith	.60	1.50
MVP2 Kevin Garnett	1.25	3.00
MVP3 Gerald Wallace	.60	1.50
MVP4 Luol Deng	.60	1.50
MVP5 LeBron James	3.00	8.00
MVP6 Dirk Nowitzki	.75	2.00
MVP7 Carmelo Anthony	.75	2.00
MVP8 Chauncey Billups	.60	1.50
MVP9 Baron Davis	.60	1.50
MVP10 Yao Ming	.75	2.00
MVP11 Jermaine O'Neal	.60	1.50
MVP12 Chris Kaman	.60	1.50
MVP13 Kobe Bryant	3.00	8.00
MVP14 Rudy Gay	.60	1.50
MVP15 Dwyane Wade	1.25	3.00
MVP16 Michael Redd	.60	1.50
MVP17 Al Jefferson	.60	1.50
MVP18 Jason Kidd	.60	1.50
MVP19 Chris Paul	1.00	2.50
MVP20 Zach Randolph	.50	1.25
MVP21 Dwight Howard	1.25	3.00
MVP22 Andre Iguodala	.60	1.50
MVP23 Steve Nash	.60	1.50
MVP24 Brandon Roy	.60	1.50
MVP25 Kevin Martin	.60	1.50
MVP26 Tony Parker	.60	1.50
MVP27 Kevin Durant	2.50	6.00
MVP28 Chris Bosh	.60	1.50
MVP29 Deron Williams	.60	1.50
MVP30 Caron Butler	.60	1.50

2008-09 Upper Deck True Talents

Card	Low	High
COMPLETE SET (30)	8.00	20.00
TWO PER RETAIL VALUE PACK		
TT1 Thaddeus Young	.50	1.25
TT2 Julian Wright	.50	1.25
TT3 Sean Williams	.50	1.25
TT4 David West	.60	1.50
TT5 Luke Walton	.40	1.00
TT6 Al Thornton	.50	1.25
TT7 Rodney Stuckey	.75	2.00
TT8 J.R. Smith	.60	1.50
TT9 Luis Scola	.50	1.25
TT10 Greg Oden	.60	1.50
TT11 Joakim Noah	.60	1.50
TT12 Mike Conley Jr.	.50	1.25
TT13 Jamario Moon	.40	1.00
TT14 Jason Maxiell	.40	1.00
TT15 Chris Kaman	.50	1.25
TT16 Yi Jianlian	.60	1.50
TT17 Al Horford	.60	1.50
TT18 Jeff Green	.50	1.25
TT19 Daniel Gibson	.60	1.50
TT20 Rudy Gay	.60	1.50
TT21 Francisco Garcia	.50	1.25
TT22 Jordan Farmar	.40	1.00
TT23 Monta Ellis	.60	1.50
TT24 Kevin Durant	2.50	6.00
TT25 Luol Deng	.60	1.50
TT26 Daequan Cook	.40	1.00
TT27 Andrew Bynum	.75	2.00
TT28 Ronnie Brewer	.50	1.25
TT29 Corey Brewer	.50	1.25
TT30 Jose Barea	.75	2.00

2008-09 Upper Deck Ultimates

Card	Low	High
COMPLETE SET (30)	25.00	50.00

RANDOM INSERTS IN RETAIL PACKS
UNPRICED AUTOS RANDOM INSERTS IN PACKS

Card	Low	High
U1 Danny Ainge	1.00	2.50
U2 Dave Bing	1.00	2.50
U3 Larry Bird	3.00	8.00
U4 Muggsy Bogues	1.00	2.50
U5 Manute Bol	1.00	2.50
U6 Bill Bradley	1.25	3.00
U7 Wilt Chamberlain	2.00	5.00
U8 Vlade Divac	1.00	2.50
U9 Clyde Drexler	1.25	3.00
U10 Joe Dumars	1.00	2.50
U11 Julius Erving	2.00	5.00
U12 Patrick Ewing	1.25	3.00
U13 Kevin Johnson	1.00	2.50
U14 Larry Johnson	1.00	2.50
U15 Magic Johnson	2.50	6.00
U16 Michael Jordan	8.00	20.00
U17 Karl Malone	1.25	3.00
U18 Pete Maravich	3.00	8.00
U19 Gheorghe Muresan	1.00	2.50
U20 Hakeem Olajuwon	1.25	3.00
U21 Scottie Pippen	1.50	4.00
U22 Oscar Robertson	1.00	2.50
U23 David Robinson	1.50	4.00
U24 Bill Russell	1.50	4.00
U25 John Salley	1.00	2.50
U26 Kenny Smith	1.00	2.50
U27 John Stockton	1.50	4.00
U28 Isiah Thomas	1.00	2.50
U29 Jerry West	1.25	3.00
U30 Dominique Wilkins	1.25	3.00

2009-10 Upper Deck

Card	Low	High
COMPLETE SET (295)	40.00	100.00
COMP.SET w/o RCs (200)	15.00	30.00
1 Josh Smith	.30	.75
2 Al Horford	.30	.75
3 Mike Bibby	.25	.60
4 Joe Johnson	.30	.75
5 Marvin Williams	.25	.60
6 Maurice Evans	.20	.50
7 Kevin Garnett	.60	1.50
8 Paul Pierce	.40	1.00
9 Ray Allen	.30	.75
10 Rajon Rondo	.40	1.00
11 Kendrick Perkins	.25	.60
12 Bill Walker	.20	.50
13 Leon Powe	.20	.50
14 Raymond Felton	.25	.60
15 Raja Bell	.25	.60
16 D.J. Augustin	.25	.60
17 Gerald Wallace	.30	.75
18 Boris Diaw	.25	.60
19 Emeka Okafor	.30	.75
20 Vladimir Radmanovic	.20	.50
21 Derrick Rose	1.00	2.50
22 Luol Deng	.30	.75
23 Michael Jordan	2.50	6.00
24 John Salmons	.30	.75
25 Joakim Noah	.30	.75
26 Tyrus Thomas	.25	.60
27 Ben Gordon	.30	.75
28 LeBron James	1.50	4.00
29 Mo Williams	.25	.60
30 Ben Wallace	.30	.75
31 Delonte West	.20	.50
32 Zydrunas Ilgauskas	.20	.50
33 Daniel Gibson	.25	.60
34 Wally Szczerbiak	.25	.60
35 Josh Howard	.25	.60
36 Dirk Nowitzki	.40	1.00
37 Jason Kidd	.30	.75
38 Antoine Wright	.20	.50
39 Erick Dampier	.20	.50
40 Jason Terry	.25	.60
41 Chauncey Billups	.30	.75
42 Carmelo Anthony	.40	1.00
43 Kenyon Martin	.30	.75
44 Dahntay Jones	.20	.50
45 Nene	.25	.60
46 J.R. Smith	.30	.75
47 Allen Iverson	.40	1.00
48 Richard Hamilton	.25	.60
49 Tayshaun Prince	.30	.75
50 Rodney Stuckey	.30	.75
51 Amir Johnson	.20	.50
52 Rasheed Wallace	.30	.75
53 Monta Ellis	.30	.75
54 Stephen Jackson	.25	.60
55 Jamal Crawford	.25	.60
56 Kelenna Azubuike	.20	.50
57 Andris Biedrins	.20	.50
58 Anthony Morrow	.20	.50
59 Corey Maggette	.25	.60
60 Luis Scola	.25	.60
61 Tracy McGrady	.30	.75
62 Yao Ming	.40	1.00
63 Ron Artest	.30	.75
64 Aaron Brooks	.20	.50
65 Shane Battier	.30	.75
66 Von Wafer	.20	.50
67 T.J. Ford	.20	.50
68 Danny Granger	.30	.75
69 Mike Dunleavy	.20	.50
70 Troy Murphy	.20	.50
71 Jeff Foster	.20	.50
72 Jarrett Jack	.25	.60
73 Eric Gordon	.30	.75
74 Baron Davis	.30	.75
75 Al Thornton	.25	.60
76 Zach Randolph	.25	.60
77 Chris Kaman	.25	.60
78 Mardy Collins	.20	.50
79 Kobe Bryant	1.50	4.00
80 Pau Gasol	.30	.75
81 Lamar Odom	.30	.75
82 Derek Fisher	.25	.60
83 Adam Morrison	.25	.60
84 Andrew Bynum	.40	1.00
85 Sasha Vujacic	.20	.50
86 Trevor Ariza	.20	.50
87 O.J. Mayo	.30	.75
88 Marc Gasol	.30	.75
89 Rudy Gay	.30	.75
90 Darrell Arthur	.25	.60
91 Marko Jaric	.20	.50
92 Mike Conley Jr.	.25	.60
93 Michael Beasley	.30	.75
94 Mario Chalmers	.30	.75
95 Dwyane Wade	.60	1.50
96 Jermaine O'Neal	.30	.75
97 Udonis Haslem	.25	.60
98 Chris Quinn	.20	.50
99 Daequan Cook	.20	.50
100 Luke Ridnour	.25	.60
101 Michael Redd	.30	.75
102 Richard Jefferson	.30	.75
103 Charlie Villanueva	.25	.60
104 Andrew Bogut	.30	.75
105 Ramon Sessions	.25	.60
106 Joe Alexander	.20	.50
107 Kevin Love	.50	1.25
108 Sebastian Telfair	.20	.50
109 Al Jefferson	.30	.75
110 Randy Foye	.20	.50
111 Ryan Gomes	.20	.50
112 Craig Smith	.20	.50
113 Mike Miller	.30	.75
114 Devin Harris	.30	.75
115 Vince Carter	.40	1.00
116 Yi Jianlian	.25	.60
117 Bobby Simmons	.20	.50
118 Brook Lopez	.30	.75
119 Chris Douglas-Roberts	.20	.50
120 Eduardo Najera	.20	.50
121 Chris Paul	.50	1.25
122 Peja Stojakovic	.30	.75
123 David West	.30	.75
124 Tyson Chandler	.25	.60
125 Rasual Butler	.20	.50
126 James Posey	.20	.50
127 Al Harrington	.25	.60
128 Chris Duhon	.20	.50
129 Quentin Richardson	.25	.60
130 David Lee	.25	.60
131 Jared Jeffries	.20	.50
132 Wilson Chandler	.25	.60
133 Danilo Gallinari	.30	.75
134 Russell Westbrook	.50	1.25
135 Kevin Durant	1.00	2.50
136 Jeff Green	.25	.60
137 Desmond Mason	.20	.50
138 Nick Collison	.20	.50
139 Earl Watson	.20	.50
140 Dwight Howard	.50	1.25
141 Courtney Lee	.25	.60
142 Hedo Turkoglu	.30	.75
143 Jameer Nelson	.25	.60
144 Rashard Lewis	.25	.60
145 Mickael Pietrus	.20	.50
146 Elton Brand	.30	.75
147 Andre Miller	.25	.60
148 Andre Iguodala	.30	.75
149 Thaddeus Young	.20	.50
150 Willie Green	.20	.50
151 Samuel Dalembert	.20	.50
152 Jason Richardson	.30	.75
153 Shaquille O'Neal	.60	1.50
154 Steve Nash	.30	.75
155 Grant Hill	.40	1.00
156 Amare Stoudemire	.30	.75
157 Leandro Barbosa	.25	.60
158 Robin Lopez	.20	.50
159 Brandon Roy	.30	.75
160 LaMarcus Aldridge	.30	.75
161 Jerryd Bayless	.25	.60
162 Rudy Fernandez	.25	.60
163 Steve Blake	.20	.50
164 Martell Webster	.25	.60
165 Greg Oden	.25	.60
166 Spencer Hawes	.25	.60
167 Kevin Martin	.30	.75
168 Beno Udrih	.20	.50
169 Andres Nocioni	.20	.50
170 Jason Thompson	.20	.50
171 Rashad McCants	.20	.50
172 Francisco Garcia	.25	.60
173 Tim Duncan	.50	1.25
174 Tony Parker	.30	.75
175 Manu Ginobili	.30	.75
176 Roger Mason	.20	.50
177 Michael Finley	.30	.75
178 Matt Bonner	.20	.50
179 George Hill	.30	.75
180 Chris Bosh	.30	.75
181 Jose Calderon	.25	.60
182 Andrea Bargnani	.25	.60
183 Shawn Marion	.30	.75
184 Anthony Parker	.20	.50
185 Jason Kapono	.20	.50
186 Roko Leni Ukic	.20	.50
187 Deron Williams	.30	.75
188 Carlos Boozer	.30	.75
189 Ronnie Brewer	.25	.60
190 C.J. Miles	.20	.50
191 Mehmet Okur	.20	.50
192 Kyle Korver	.25	.60
193 Andrei Kirilenko	.25	.60
194 Gilbert Arenas	.30	.75
195 Antawn Jamison	.30	.75
196 DeShawn Stevenson	.20	.50
197 Caron Butler	.30	.75
198 Brendan Haywood	.20	.50
199 Nick Young	.25	.60
200 Dominic McGuire	.20	.50
201 Toney Douglas RC	1.00	2.50
202 Taylor Griffin RC	1.00	2.50
203 DeJuan Blair RC	1.25	3.00
204 Darren Collison RC	1.50	4.00
205 Patrick Mills RC	1.25	3.00
206 DaJuan Summers RC	1.00	2.50
207 Austin Daye RC	1.00	2.50
208 Eric Maynor RC	1.00	2.50
209 DeMarre Carroll RC	1.00	2.50
210 Taj Gibson RC	1.25	3.00
211 Patrick Beverley RC	1.00	2.50
212 Dante Cunningham RC	1.00	2.50
213 Sam Young RC	1.00	2.50
214 Terrence Williams RC	1.00	2.50
215 Omri Casspi RC	1.00	2.50
216 Jeff Pendergraph RC	1.00	2.50
217 Jrue Holiday RC	2.00	5.00
218 Jeff Teague RC	1.25	3.00
219 James Johnson RC	1.00	2.50
220 B.J. Mullens RC	1.00	2.50
221 Nick Calathes RC	1.00	2.50
222 A.J. Price RC	1.00	2.50
223 Danny Green RC	1.50	4.00
224 Marcus Thornton RC	1.50	4.00
225 Chase Budinger RC	1.00	2.50
226 Blake Griffin SP RC	8.00	20.00
227 James Harden SP RC	4.00	10.00
228 Tyler Hansbrough SP RC	2.00	5.00
229 Gerald Henderson SP RC	1.25	3.00
230 Jordan Hill SP RC	1.25	3.00
231 Hasheem Thabeet SP RC	1.25	3.00
232 Earl Clark SP RC	1.25	3.00
233 Brandon Jennings SP RC	2.50	6.00
234 Stephen Curry SP RC	3.00	8.00
235 Ty Lawson SP RC	2.00	5.00
236 Wayne Ellington SP RC	1.25	3.00
237 Ricky Rubio SP RC	6.00	15.00
238 DeMar DeRozan SP RC	2.00	5.00
239 Jonny Flynn SP RC	1.25	3.00
240 Tyreke Evans SP RC	3.00	8.00
241 Michael Jordan	5.00	12.00
242 Larry Bird	2.00	5.00
243 Horace Grant	.60	1.50
244 Kiki Vandeweghe	.60	1.50
245 Michael Cooper	.60	1.50
246 Magic Johnson	1.50	4.00
247 Kareem Abdul-Jabbar	1.00	2.50
248 Julius Erving	1.25	3.00
249 Oscar Robertson	.60	1.50
250 Isiah Thomas	.60	1.50
251 Patrick Ewing	.75	2.00
252 A.C. Green	.60	1.50
253 Adrian Dantley	.60	1.50
254 Alex English	.60	1.50
255 Jerry West	.75	2.00
256 Bernard King	.60	1.50
257 Bill Laimbeer	.60	1.50
258 Bob McAdoo	.60	1.50
259 Byron Scott	.60	1.50
260 Calvin Murphy	.60	1.50
261 Clyde Drexler	.75	2.00
262 David Robinson	1.00	2.50
263 Dominique Wilkins	.75	2.00
264 Glen Rice	.60	1.50
265 Hakeem Olajuwon	.75	2.00
266 John Stockton	1.00	2.50
267 Robert Parish	.60	1.50
268 Scottie Pippen	1.25	3.00
269 Sean Elliott	.60	1.50
270 Bill Walton	.60	1.50
271 Chris Mullin	.60	1.50
272 Dee Brown	.60	1.50
273 Dennis Rodman	1.00	2.50
274 Joe Dumars	.60	1.50
275 John Paxson	.60	1.50
276 Mark Price	.60	1.50
277 Maurice Cheeks	.60	1.50
278 Moses Malone	.60	1.50
279 Spud Webb	.60	1.50
280 Terry Porter	.60	1.50
281 Darryl Dawkins	.60	1.50
282 Dino Radja	.60	1.50
283 Jamaal Wilkes	.60	1.50
284 John Salley	.60	1.50
285 Larry Johnson	.60	1.50
286 Larry Nance	.60	1.50
287 Pooh Richardson	.60	1.50
288 Reggie Theus	.60	1.50
289 Rick Mahorn	.60	1.50
290 Rick Barry	.60	1.50
291 Ron Harper	.60	1.50
292 Steve Kerr	.60	1.50
293 Tom Chambers	.60	1.50
294 Spencer Haywood	.60	1.50
295 Walt Frazier	.60	1.50

2009-10 Upper Deck Star Rookies Gold

Card	Low	High
COMPLETE SET (25)	7.50	15.00
GOLD FOIL RETAIL BLASTER INSERT		
201 Toney Douglas	.60	1.50
202 Taylor Griffin	.60	1.50
203 DeJuan Blair	.75	2.00
204 Darren Collison	1.00	2.50
205 Patrick Mills	.75	2.00
206 DaJuan Summers	.60	1.50
207 Austin Daye	.60	1.50
208 Eric Maynor	.60	1.50
209 DeMarre Carroll	.60	1.50
210 Taj Gibson	.75	2.00
211 Patrick Beverley	.60	1.50
212 Dante Cunningham	.60	1.50
213 Sam Young	.60	1.50
214 Terrence Williams	.60	1.50
215 Omri Casspi	.60	1.50
216 Jeff Pendergraph	.60	1.50
217 Jrue Holiday	1.25	3.00
218 Jeff Teague	.75	2.00
219 James Johnson	.60	1.50
220 B.J. Mullens	.60	1.50
221 Nick Calathes	.60	1.50
222 A.J. Price	.60	1.50
223 Danny Green	1.00	2.50
224 Marcus Thornton	1.00	2.50
225 Chase Budinger	.60	1.50

2009-10 Upper Deck 3D NBA Stars

Card	Low	High
COMPLETE SET (50)	60.00	120.00
STATED ODDS 1:8		
3DAI Allen Iverson	1.50	4.00
3DAR Brandon Roy	1.25	3.00
LaMarcus Aldridge		
3DAS DeShawn Stevenson	1.25	3.00
Gilbert Arenas		
3DAT Rafer Alston	.75	2.00
Sebastian Telfair		
3DBA Carmelo Anthony	1.50	4.00
Chauncey Billups		
3DBD Baron Davis	1.25	3.00
3DBJ Kobe Bryant	6.00	15.00
LeBron James		
3DBR Derrick Rose	4.00	10.00
Michael Beasley		
3DBW Carlos Boozer	1.25	3.00
Deron Williams		
3DCA Carmelo Anthony	1.50	4.00
3DCH Devin Harris	1.50	4.00
Vince Carter		
3DCP Chris Paul	2.00	5.00
Tyson Chandler		
3DDE Deron Williams	1.25	3.00
3DDG Baron Davis	1.25	3.00
Eric Gordon		
3DDH Dwight Howard	2.00	5.00
3DDK Dwight Howard	2.50	6.00
Kevin Garnett		
3DDP Tim Duncan	2.00	5.00
Tony Parker		
3DDR Derrick Rose	4.00	10.00
Luol Deng		
3DDW Kevin Durant	4.00	10.00
Russell Westbrook		
3DGA Gilbert Arenas	1.25	3.00
3DGG Marc Gasol	1.25	3.00
Pau Gasol		
3DHN Dwight Howard	2.00	5.00
Jameer Nelson		
3DIB Allen Iverson	1.50	4.00
Chauncey Billups		
3DIS Allen Iverson	1.50	4.00
Rodney Stuckey		
3DJB Kobe Bryant	10.00	25.00
Michael Jordan		
3DJJ LeBron James	10.00	25.00
Michael Jordan		
3DJR Michael Redd	1.25	3.00
Richard Jefferson		
3DJS Joe Johnson	1.25	3.00
Josh Smith		
3DJW LeBron James	6.00	15.00
Mo Williams		
3DKB Kobe Bryant	6.00	15.00
3DKD Kevin Durant	4.00	10.00
3DKN Dirk Nowitzki	1.50	4.00
Jason Kidd		
3DLJ LeBron James	6.00	15.00
3DMI Andre Iguodala	1.25	3.00
Andre Miller		
3DMJ Michael Jordan	10.00	25.00
3DMM Tracy McGrady	1.50	4.00
Yao Ming		
3DNK Jason Kidd	1.25	3.00
Steve Nash		
3DNR Nate Robinson	1.25	3.00
3DNS Amare Stoudemire	1.25	3.00
Steve Nash		
3DPA Chris Paul	2.00	5.00
3DPG Kevin Garnett	2.50	6.00
Paul Pierce		
3DPW Chris Paul	2.00	5.00
Deron Williams		
3DRF Rudy Fernandez	1.00	2.50
3DRO Brandon Roy	1.25	3.00
3DSM Josh Smith	1.25	3.00
3DSN Steve Nash	1.25	3.00
3DTP Tayshaun Prince	1.25	3.00
3DVC Vince Carter	1.50	4.00
3DWA Dwyane Wade	2.50	6.00
3DWC Dwyane Wade	2.50	6.00
Mario Chalmers		

2009-10 Upper Deck Game Materials

COMBINED MEM ODDS 3:16
*GOLD: .5X TO 1.25X BASE HI
GOLD PRINT RUN 150 SER.#'d SETS

Card	Low	High
GJAA Arron Afflalo/550	2.00	5.00
GJAB Andray Blatche/545	2.00	5.00
GJAH Al Harrington/550	2.50	6.00
GJAI Andre Iguodala/550	3.00	8.00
GJAJ Antawn Jamison/550	3.00	8.00
GJAL Acie Law/550	2.00	5.00
GJAM Alonzo Mourning/400	4.00	10.00
GJAW Antoine Wright/305	2.00	5.00
GJBA Andrea Bargnani/550	2.50	6.00
GJBD Baron Davis/550	3.00	8.00
GJBG Ben Gordon/400	3.00	8.00
GJBH Brendan Haywood/550	2.00	5.00
GJBI Chauncey Billups/550	3.00	8.00
GJBO Andrew Bogut/550	3.00	8.00
GJBR Brandon Roy/400	3.00	8.00
GJBU Beno Udrih/487	2.00	5.00
GJBW Ben Wallace/550	3.00	8.00
GJCA Carmelo Anthony/550	4.00	10.00
GJCB Carlos Boozer/550	3.00	8.00
GJCF Channing Frye/550	2.50	6.00
GJCH Chris Bosh/400	3.00	8.00
GJCK Chris Kaman/550	2.50	6.00
GJCM Chris Mullin/550	4.00	10.00
GJCP Chris Paul/400	5.00	12.00
GJCS Craig Smith/550	2.00	5.00
GJCV Charlie Villanueva/550	2.50	6.00
GJDA Dan Majerle/550	3.00	8.00
GJDG Daniel Gibson/600	2.50	6.00
GJDH Dwight Howard/545	5.00	12.00
GJDI Boris Diaw/545	2.50	6.00
GJDL David Lee/550	2.50	6.00
GJDM Desmond Mason/550	2.00	5.00
GJDN Dirk Nowitzki/400	4.00	10.00
GJDR David Robinson/400	5.00	12.00
GJDS DeShawn Stevenson/550	2.00	5.00
GJDW Dorell Wright/550	2.00	5.00
GJEB Elton Brand/400	3.00	8.00
GJEH Eddie House/400	2.00	5.00
GJEO Emeka Okafor/550	3.00	8.00
GJFE Raymond Felton/550	2.50	6.00
GJGW Gerald Wallace/400	3.00	8.00
GJHE Luther Head	2.00	5.00
GJHO Juwan Howard/550	2.50	6.00
GJJC Jarron Collins/550	2.00	5.00
GJJF Jordan Farmar/400	2.00	5.00
GJJH Josh Howard/550	2.50	6.00
GJJK Jason Kapono/550	2.00	5.00
GJJN Joakim Noah/238	3.00	8.00
GJJO Jermaine O'Neal/545	3.00	8.00
GJJS J.R. Smith/481	3.00	8.00
GJJU Julian Wright/550	2.00	5.00
GJKA Kelenna Azubuike/550	2.00	5.00
GJKB Keith Bogans/400	2.00	5.00
GJKG Kevin Garnett/550	6.00	15.00
GJKO Kobe Bryant/550	8.00	20.00
GJLA LaMarcus Aldridge/550	3.00	8.00
GJLD Luol Deng/550	3.00	8.00
GJLH Larry Hughes/508	2.50	6.00
GJLJ LeBron James/545	8.00	20.00
GJLO Lamar Odom/550	3.00	8.00
GJLS Luis Scola/550	2.50	6.00
GJLU Luke Walton/550	2.00	5.00
GJLW Lorenzen Wright/400	2.00	5.00
GJMA Maurice Ager/550	2.00	5.00
GJMC Mike Conley Jr./397	2.50	6.00
GJMD Marquis Daniels/479	2.00	5.00
GJMJ Mike James/400	2.00	5.00
GJMM Mikki Moore/550	2.00	5.00
GJMO Mehmet Okur/400	2.00	5.00
GJPE Patrick Ewing/400	6.00	15.00
GJPG Pau Gasol/400	3.00	8.00
GJPP Paul Pierce/508	4.00	10.00
GJQD Quincy Douby/550	2.00	5.00
GJRA Ron Artest/550	3.00	8.00
GJRF Randy Foye/545	2.00	5.00
GJRG Rudy Gay/545	3.00	8.00
GJRS Robert Swift/550	2.00	5.00
GJRW Rasheed Wallace/550	3.00	8.00
GJSB Shannon Brown/550	3.00	8.00
GJSI James Singleton/400	2.00	5.00
GJSM Sean May/550	3.00	8.00
GJSN Steve Novak/545	2.00	5.00
GJSO Shaquille O'Neal/550	6.00	15.00
GJSR Sergio Rodriguez/250	2.00	5.00
GJST Stephon Marbury/545	2.50	6.00
GJSW Shawne Williams/550	2.00	5.00
GJTC Tyson Chandler/400	2.50	6.00
GJTF T.J. Ford/550	2.00	5.00
GJTM Tracy McGrady/550	3.00	8.00
GJTP Tayshaun Prince/550	3.00	8.00
GJTT Tyrus Thomas/550	2.50	6.00
GJUH Udonis Haslem/563	2.50	6.00

GJVC Vince Carter/550 4.00 10.00
GJWA Dwyane Wade/550 6.00 15.00
GJWC Wilson Chandler/545 2.50 6.00
GJWE Martell Webster/550 2.50 6.00
GJWI Shelden Williams/563 2.00 5.00
GJWR Brandan Wright/550 2.00 5.00
GJYM Yao Ming/550 4.00 10.00
GJZR Zach Randolph/400 2.50 6.00

2009-10 Upper Deck Game Materials Dual

COMBINED MEM ODDS 3:16
*GOLD: .5X TO 1.25X BASE HI
GOLD PRINT RUN 150 SER.#'d SETS
DGAB Larry Bird 8.00 20.00
Ray Allen
DGAD Glen Davis 4.00 10.00
Ray Allen
DGAG Andre Iguodala 4.00 10.00
Gilbert Arenas
DGAJ Gilbert Arenas 8.00 20.00
LeBron James
DGAP Mark Price 5.00 12.00
Nate Archibald
DGAT Carmelo Anthony 5.00 12.00
Tracy McGrady
DGBB Andrea Bargnani 4.00 10.00
Chris Bosh
DGBF Chauncey Billups 4.00 10.00
T.J. Ford
DGBH Andrew Bynum 6.00 15.00
Dwight Howard
DGBI Andre Iguodala 5.00 12.00
Elton Brand
DGBJ Chauncey Billups 4.00 10.00
Joe Johnson
DGBO Carlos Boozer 4.00 10.00
Mehmet Okur
DGBP Larry Bird 10.00 25.00
Robert Parish
DGBR Brandon Roy 4.00 10.00
Chauncey Billups
DGCB Chris Bosh 5.00 12.00
Vince Carter
DGCK Chris Bosh 5.00 12.00
Kevin Garnett
DGCM Sean May 4.00 10.00
Vince Carter
DGCN Dirk Nowitzki 5.00 12.00
Vince Carter
DGCT Clyde Drexler 6.00 15.00
Tracy McGrady
DGDA Carmelo Anthony 5.00 12.00
Tim Duncan
DGDL Bill Laimbeer 5.00 12.00
Joe Dumars
DGDO Shaquille O'Neal 6.00 15.00
Tim Duncan
DGDS Daniel Gibson 4.00 10.00
Shannon Brown
DGEM Julius Erving 6.00 15.00
Moses Malone
DGGH Daniel Gibson 4.00 10.00
Kirk Hinrich
DGFB Randy Foye 4.00 10.00
Shannon Brown
DGFC Mike Conley Jr. 4.00 10.00
Raymond Felton
DGFD Clyde Drexler 5.00 12.00
Raymond Felton
DGFF Jordan Farmar 4.00 10.00
T.J. Ford
DGFG Daniel Gibson 4.00 10.00
Jordan Farmar
DGFJ Al Jefferson 6.00 15.00
Randy Foye
DGGA Carmelo Anthony 5.00 12.00
George Gervin
DGGD Baron Davis 5.00 12.00
Ben Gordon
DGGG Kevin Garnett 5.00 12.00
Pau Gasol
DGGJ Kevin Garnett 10.00 25.00
LeBron James
DGGM Kevin Garnett 5.00 12.00
Tracy McGrady
DGGN Dirk Nowitzki 5.00 12.00
Kevin Garnett
DGGO Jermaine O'Neal 5.00 12.00
Kevin Garnett
DGGS Amare Stoudemire 6.00 15.00
Kevin Garnett
DGHB Josh Howard 4.00 10.00
Shannon Brown
DGHC Richard Hamilton 5.00 12.00
Vince Carter
DGHG Ben Gordon 4.00 10.00
Richard Hamilton
DGHH Josh Howard 4.00 10.00
Larry Hughes
DGHT Larry Hughes 4.00 10.00
Tyrus Thomas
DGIB Allen Iverson 4.00 10.00
Chauncey Billups
DGIP Allen Iverson 6.00 15.00
Chris Paul
DGJA Carmelo Anthony 10.00 25.00
LeBron James
DGJD Clyde Drexler 8.00 20.00
LeBron James
DGJE Julius Erving 25.00 60.00
Michael Jordan
DGJG Ben Gordon 4.00 10.00
Joe Johnson
DGJH Al Horford 4.00 10.00
Joe Johnson
DGJJ LeBron James 12.00 30.00
Magic Johnson
DGJP Chris Paul 8.00 20.00
Magic Johnson
DGJR Brandon Roy 4.00 10.00
Joe Johnson
DGJW Dwyane Wade 12.00 30.00
LeBron James
DGKL Kevin Durant 6.00 15.00
LaMarcus Aldridge
DGKM Kareem Abdul-Jabbar 35.00 70.00
Michael Jordan
DGLG Kevin Garnett 15.00 40.00
Larry Bird
DGLK Kevin Garnett 12.00 30.00
LeBron James
DGLR Bill Laimbeer 8.00 20.00
Dennis Rodman
DGMA Carmelo Anthony 5.00 12.00
Shawn Marion
DGMB Chris Bosh 4.00 10.00
Corey Maggette
DGMD Clyde Drexler 6.00 15.00
Tracy McGrady
DGMK Kareem Abdul-Jabbar 15.00 40.00
Magic Johnson
DGML LeBron James 25.00 60.00
Michael Jordan
DGMM Alonzo Mourning 8.00 20.00
Moses Malone
DGMN Corey Maggette 5.00 12.00
Dirk Nowitzki
DGMP Tayshaun Prince 5.00 12.00
Tracy McGrady
DGMS Amare Stoudemire 4.00 10.00
Shawn Marion
DGMW Corey Maggette 4.00 10.00
Shelden Williams
DGNB Dirk Nowitzki 10.00 25.00
Larry Bird
DGNH Dirk Nowitzki 4.00 10.00
Josh Howard
DGNK Carmelo Anthony 20.00 50.00
Michael Jordan
DGNP Chris Paul 8.00 20.00
Steve Nash
DGNS Amare Stoudemire 6.00 15.00
Dirk Nowitzki
DGOD Clyde Drexler 8.00 20.00
Hakeem Olajuwon
DGOM Emeka Okafor 4.00 10.00
Sean May
DGON Jermaine O'Neal 4.00 10.00
Lamar Odom
DGOO Hakeem Olajuwon 10.00 25.00
Shaquille O'Neal
DGOR David Robinson 10.00 25.00
Hakeem Olajuwon
DGPS Chris Paul 10.00 25.00
John Stockton
DGRF Walt Frazier 8.00 20.00
Willis Reed
DGRG David Robinson 10.00 25.00
Manu Ginobili
DGRT Dennis Rodman 5.00 12.00
Tyrus Thomas
DGRW Dennis Rodman 4.00 10.00
Shelden Williams
DGSB Amare Stoudemire 4.00 10.00
Chris Bosh
DGSM Shawn Marion 5.00 12.00
Tracy McGrady
DGST Shelden Williams 4.00 10.00
Tracy McGrady
DGSW Deron Williams 6.00 15.00
John Stockton
DGTB Brandon Roy 5.00 12.00
Tony Parker
DGTD David Robinson 6.00 15.00
Tony Parker
DGVT Tracy McGrady 5.00 12.00
Vince Carter
DGWA Jerry West 15.00 30.00
Kareem Abdul-Jabbar
DGWB Marvin Williams 4.00 10.00
Mike Bibby
DGWJ James Worthy 10.00 25.00
Magic Johnson
DGWO Emeka Okafor 5.00 12.00
Rasheed Wallace
DGWS Amare Stoudemire 5.00 12.00
Rasheed Wallace
DGYH Hakeem Olajuwon 10.00 25.00
Yao Ming
DGYM Moses Malone 5.00 12.00
Yao Ming
DGYS Luis Scola 5.00 12.00
Yao Ming

2009-10 Upper Deck Jordan Brand Classic

RANDOM INSERTS IN PACKS
JCBJ Brandon Jennings 6.00 15.00
JCBM B.J. Mullens 3.00 8.00
JCBR Brandon Jennings 6.00 15.00
JCBS B.J. Mullens 3.00 8.00
JCDD DeMar DeRozan 5.00 12.00
JCDM DeMar DeRozan 5.00 12.00
JCDZ DeMar DeRozan 5.00 12.00
JCEV Tyreke Evans 8.00 20.00
JCJE Brandon Jennings 6.00 15.00
JCJH Jrue Holiday 6.00 15.00
JCJR Jrue Holiday 6.00 15.00
JCMU B.J. Mullens 3.00 8.00
JCTE Tyreke Evans 8.00 20.00

2009-10 Upper Deck Masterpieces

COMPLETE SET (35) 25.00 50.00
STATED ODDS 1:8
MAAR Anthony Randolph .75 2.00
MABL Brook Lopez 1.00 2.50
MABR Brandon Rush .75 2.00
MACL Courtney Lee .75 2.00
MACP Chris Paul 1.50 4.00
MADE Deron Williams 1.00 2.50
MADG Danilo Gallinari 1.00 2.50
MADH Dwight Howard 1.50 4.00
MADR Derrick Rose 3.00 8.00
MADW Dwyane Wade 2.00 5.00
MAGR Donte Greene .60 1.50
MAHI J.J. Hickson .60 1.50
MAJB Jerryd Bayless .75 2.00
MAJE Julius Erving 2.00 5.00
MAJG J.R. Giddens .60 1.50
MAJH John Havlicek 1.00 2.50
MAJO Michael Jordan 8.00 20.00
MAKA Kareem Abdul-Jabbar 1.50 4.00
MAKB Kobe Bryant 5.00 12.00
MAKG Kevin Garnett 2.00 5.00
MAKL Kevin Love 1.50 4.00
MALB Larry Bird 3.00 8.00
MALJ LeBron James 5.00 12.00
MAMB Michael Beasley 1.00 2.50
MAMJ Michael Jordan 8.00 20.00
MAMS Marreese Speights .75 2.00
MAOM O.J. Mayo 1.00 2.50
MAPP Paul Pierce 1.25 3.00
MARA Ryan Anderson 1.00 2.50
MARH Roy Hibbert 1.00 2.50
MARL Robin Lopez .60 1.50
MASN Steve Nash 1.00 2.50
MATP Tony Parker 1.00 2.50
MAWI Dominique Wilkins 1.25 3.00

2009-10 Upper Deck Now Appearing

COMPLETE SET (20) 8.00 20.00
STATED ODDS 1:8
NA1 Derrick Rose 2.50 6.00
NA2 Michael Beasley .75 2.00
NA3 O.J. Mayo .75 2.00
NA4 Russell Westbrook 1.25 3.00
NA5 Kevin Love 1.25 3.00
NA6 Michael Jordan 6.00 15.00
NA7 Kevin Durant 2.50 6.00
NA8 LeBron James 4.00 10.00
NA9 Kobe Bryant 4.00 10.00
NA10 Kevin Garnett 1.50 4.00
NA11 Rasheed Wallace .75 2.00
NA12 Tim Duncan 1.25 3.00
NA13 Shaquille O'Neal 1.50 4.00
NA14 Dwight Howard 1.25 3.00
NA15 Tracy McGrady .75 2.00
NA16 Chris Paul 1.25 3.00
NA17 Dwyane Wade 1.50 4.00
NA18 Dirk Nowitzki 1.00 2.50
NA19 Paul Pierce 1.00 2.50
NA20 Baron Davis .75 2.00

2009-10 Upper Deck Signature Collection

COMBINED AUTO ODDS 1:19
1 Alexis Ajinca 5.00 12.00
2 Joe Alexander 5.00 12.00
3 Steve Nash 40.00 70.00
4 Clyde Drexler 10.00 25.00
5 Ryan Anderson 5.00 12.00
6 T.J. Ford SP 5.00 12.00
7 D.J. Augustin 5.00 12.00
8 Rajon Rondo 20.00 50.00
9 Chris Paul 20.00 50.00
10 Jerryd Bayless 5.00 12.00
12 Michael Beasley 6.00 15.00
13 Von Wafer 5.00 12.00
14 Stephen Graham 5.00 12.00
15 Josh Boone 5.00 12.00
16 David Robinson 40.00 100.00
17 Bruce Bowen 12.50 30.00
18 Corey Brewer 6.00 15.00
19 Kirk Hinrich 6.00 15.00
20 Bobby Brown 5.00 12.00
21 Hilton Armstrong 5.00 12.00
22 Andrew Bynum 12.00 30.00
23 Louie Dampier 20.00 50.00
25 Mike Conley Jr. 6.00 15.00
26 DaJuan Summers 5.00 12.00
27 Ricky Rubio 50.00 120.00
30 Joey Dorsey 5.00 12.00
31 Jared Dudley 5.00 12.00
32 Hakeem Olajuwon 25.00 60.00
34 Oscar Robertson 50.00 125.00
35 Danilo Gallinari 5.00 12.00
36 Spud Webb 8.00 20.00
37 Kevin Garnett 30.00 80.00
39 Eric Gordon 8.00 20.00
40 Aaron Gray 5.00 12.00
41 Jeff Green 8.00 20.00
42 Spencer Hawes 5.00 12.00
43 Richard Hendrix 5.00 12.00
44 J.J. Hickson 5.00 12.00
46 Darnell Jackson 5.00 12.00
47 Antawn Jamison 6.00 15.00
48 Al Jefferson 6.00 15.00
49 Bobby Jackson 5.00 12.00
50 DeAndre Jordan 8.00 20.00
51 Kosta Koufos 5.00 12.00
52 Andre Iguodala 8.00 20.00
53 Glen Davis 8.00 20.00
54 Courtney Lee 6.00 15.00
55 Brook Lopez 6.00 15.00
56 Kyle Korver 6.00 15.00
57 Robin Lopez 5.00 12.00
58 Kevin Love 12.00 30.00
59 Walter Herrmann 5.00 12.00
60 Moses Malone 15.00 40.00
61 O.J. Mayo 8.00 20.00
62 Luc Mbah A Moute 5.00 12.00
63 Rashad McCants 5.00 12.00
64 Javale McGee 6.00 15.00
65 Josh McRoberts 5.00 12.00
66 Jerry West 25.00 60.00
67 Larry Hughes 6.00 15.00
68 Yao Ming 20.00 50.00
69 Shannon Brown 8.00 20.00
70 Joakim Noah 8.00 20.00
71 Donte Greene 5.00 12.00
75 Darren Collison 8.00 20.00
76 Tayshaun Prince 6.00 15.00
77 Quentin Richardson 5.00 12.00
78 Derrick Rose 75.00 150.00
79 Brandon Rush 5.00 12.00
82 Sean Singletary 5.00 12.00
83 Jason Smith 5.00 12.00
84 J.R. Giddens 5.00 12.00
85 Marreese Speights 6.00 15.00
86 A.J. Price 5.00 12.00
87 Rodney Stuckey 6.00 15.00
88 Mike Taylor 5.00 12.00
89 Jason Thompson 6.00 15.00
90 Al Thornton 5.00 12.00
91 Alando Tucker 5.00 12.00
92 Ike Diogu 10.00 25.00
94 Kyle Weaver 5.00 12.00
95 Russell Westbrook 15.00 40.00
97 Deron Williams 10.00 25.00
98 Mo Williams 10.00 25.00
99 Sean Williams 5.00 12.00
100 Shelden Williams 5.00 12.00
101 Kareem Abdul-Jabbar 50.00 120.00
102 Arron Afflalo 5.00 12.00
103 Shane Battier 6.00 15.00
104 LaMarcus Aldridge 12.50 30.00
105 Andre Miller 6.00 15.00
106 Chase Budinger 6.00 15.00
107 James Harden 12.00 30.00
108 Al Harrington 6.00 15.00
109 Alonzo Mourning 50.00 120.00
110 Jack Sikma 6.00 15.00
111 Anthony Randolph 5.00 12.00
112 Patrick Beverley 5.00 12.00
114 Brad Daugherty 10.00 25.00
115 Bailey Howell SP 25.00 60.00
116 Patrick O'Bryant 5.00 12.00
117 James Johnson 5.00 12.00
118 Earl Clark 8.00 20.00
119 Brandon Roy 10.00 25.00
120 Bill Sharman 10.00 25.00
121 Bill Walton 10.00 25.00
122 Jeff Adrien 5.00 12.00
123 Gerald Henderson 6.00 15.00
125 Corey Maggette 5.00 12.00
127 Wayne Ellington 6.00 15.00
128 B.J. Mullens 6.00 15.00
129 Danny Green 8.00 20.00
130 Jonny Flynn 8.00 20.00
131 Joe Crawford 8.00 20.00
132 David Lee 6.00 15.00
133 Donyell Marshall 5.00 12.00
134 Chris Douglas-Roberts 5.00 12.00
135 Damon Stoudamire 10.00 25.00
136 David West 6.00 15.00
137 Eddy Curry 5.00 12.00
138 D.J. White 5.00 12.00
139 Francisco Garcia 6.00 15.00
140 Gail Goodrich 12.00 30.00
141 George Hill 6.00 15.00
142 George Karl 10.00 25.00
143 Gabe Pruitt 5.00 12.00
144 Will Bynum 5.00 12.00
145 Derek Fisher 10.00 25.00
146 Hal Greer 10.00 25.00
147 Horace Grant 15.00 40.00
148 Isiah Thomas 15.00 40.00
149 LeBron James 100.00 200.00
150 Julius Erving SP 75.00 150.00
151 Magic Johnson 40.00 100.00
152 Jason Kidd 20.00 50.00
153 Sonny Weems 5.00 12.00
154 Jeff Pendergraph 5.00 12.00
155 J.R. Smith 6.00 15.00
156 Taj Gibson 6.00 15.00
157 Maurice Ager 5.00 12.00
158 Mike Bibby 5.00 12.00
159 Ronnie Brewer 8.00 20.00
160 Larry Bird SP 100.00 200.00
161 Larry Johnson 25.00 50.00
162 Carmelo Anthony 50.00 120.00
164 Mario Chalmers 6.00 15.00
165 Michael Jordan 300.00 500.00
166 Randy Foye 5.00 12.00
168 Cedric Simmons SP 10.00 25.00
170 Marvin Williams 5.00 12.00
171 Nicolas Batum 6.00 15.00
172 Jrue Holiday 10.00 25.00
174 Pat Riley 20.00 50.00
175 Stephen Curry 20.00 50.00
176 Ben Gordon 6.00 15.00
177 Joey Graham 5.00 12.00
178 Dionte Christmas 5.00 12.00
179 Raymond Felton 8.00 20.00
180 Rudy Gay 5.00 12.00
181 Roy Hibbert 6.00 15.00
182 George Gervin 12.50 30.00
183 Dennis Rodman SP 40.00 100.00
184 Aaron Brooks 5.00 12.00
185 Robert Parish 8.00 20.00
187 David Noel 6.00 15.00
188 Jamario Moon 5.00 12.00
189 John Stockton SP 50.00 120.00
190 Solomon Jones 5.00 12.00
191 Jermaine Taylor 5.00 12.00
192 Carlos Boozer 6.00 15.00
193 Tracy McGrady 20.00 40.00
194 Tyrus Thomas 5.00 12.00
195 Vince Carter 20.00 50.00
196 Paul Pierce 15.00 40.00
198 Ty Lawson 10.00 25.00
199 Luis Scola 6.00 15.00
200 Julian Wright 5.00 12.00

2009-10 Upper Deck Sophomore Sensations

COMPLETE SET (30) 10.00 25.00
RANDOM INSERTS IN PACKS
SSAA Alexis Ajinca .60 1.50
SSAR Darrell Arthur .75 2.00
SSBB Bobby Brown .60 1.50
SSBL Brook Lopez 1.00 2.50
SSBR Brandon Rush .75 2.00
SSBW Bill Walker .60 1.50
SSCL Courtney Lee .75 2.00
SSDA D.J. Augustin .75 2.00
SSDG Danilo Gallinari 1.00 2.50
SSDJ Darnell Jackson .60 1.50
SSDR Derrick Rose 3.00 8.00
SSEG Eric Gordon 1.00 2.50
SSJB Jerryd Bayless .75 2.00
SSJM Javale McGee .75 2.00
SSJO DeAndre Jordan 1.00 2.50
SSJT Jason Thompson .60 1.50
SSKK Kosta Koufos .60 1.50
SSKL Kevin Love 1.50 4.00
SSLM Luc Mbah A Moute .60 1.50
SSMB Michael Beasley 1.00 2.50
SSMS Marreese Speights .75 2.00
SSMT Mike Taylor .60 1.50
SSOM O.J. Mayo 1.00 2.50
SSRA Ryan Anderson .60 1.50
SSRF Rudy Fernandez .75 2.00
SSRH Richard Hendrix .60 1.50
SSRL Robin Lopez .60 1.50
SSRW Russell Westbrook 1.50 4.00
SSSS Sean Singletary .60 1.50
SSWS Walter Sharpe .60 1.50

2009-10 Upper Deck Sophomore Sensations Autographs

COMBINED AUTO ODDS 1:16
STATED PRINT RUN 199 SER.#'d SETS
SSAA Alexis Ajinca 5.00 12.00
SSBB Bobby Brown 5.00 12.00
SSBL Brook Lopez 10.00 25.00
SSBR Brandon Rush 6.00 15.00
SSBW Bill Walker 5.00 12.00
SSCL Courtney Lee 8.00 20.00
SSDA D.J. Augustin 5.00 12.00
SSDG Danilo Gallinari 6.00 15.00
SSDJ Darnell Jackson 5.00 12.00
SSDR Derrick Rose 50.00 125.00
SSEG Eric Gordon 10.00 25.00
SSJB Jerryd Bayless 5.00 12.00
SSJM Javale McGee 8.00 20.00
SSJO DeAndre Jordan 10.00 25.00
SSJT Jason Thompson 5.00 12.00
SSKK Kosta Koufos 5.00 12.00
SSKL Kevin Love 12.50 30.00
SSLM Luc Mbah A Moute 5.00 12.00
SSMB Michael Beasley 10.00 25.00
SSMS Marreese Speights 5.00 12.00
SSMT Mike Taylor 5.00 12.00
SSOM O.J. Mayo 10.00 25.00
SSRA Ryan Anderson 5.00 12.00
SSRH Richard Hendrix 5.00 12.00
SSRL Robin Lopez 5.00 12.00
SSRW Russell Westbrook 12.50 30.00
SSSS Sean Singletary 5.00 12.00
SSWS Walter Sharpe 5.00 12.00

2009-10 Upper Deck Spokesman Signatures

RANDOM INSERTS IN PACKS
SSAH Al Horford 5.00 12.00
SSKG Kevin Garnett 40.00 100.00
SSLJ LeBron James 125.00 250.00

2009-10 Upper Deck VS Dual Materials

COMBINED MEM ODDS 3:16
STATED PRINT RUN 40 TO 795 SETS
*BRONZE: .5X TO 1.25X BASE HI
BRONZE PRINT RUN 150 SER.#'d SETS
VSAA Carmelo Anthony 5.00 12.00
Ron Artest
VSAB Chauncey Billups 5.00 12.00
Ray Allen
VSAC Amare Stoudemire 4.00 10.00
Chris Bosh
VSAM Corey Maggette 5.00 12.00
Ray Allen
VSAO Andrea Bargnani 5.00 12.00
Shaquille O'Neal
VSAR Nate Robinson 4.00 10.00
Rafer Alston
VSAS Carmelo Anthony 5.00 12.00
Thabo Sefolosha
VSAW Al Horford 4.00 10.00
Marvin Williams
VSBA Kobe Bryant 8.00 20.00
Ron Artest
VSBB Kobe Bryant 6.00 15.00
Raja Bell
VSBJ Kobe Bryant 15.00 40.00
LeBron James
VSBK Bernard King 4.00 10.00
Bill Walton
VSBL Carl Landry 4.00 10.00
Kwame Brown
VSBM Elton Brand 5.00 12.00
Yao Ming
VSBN Kobe Bryant 8.00 20.00
Steve Nash
VSBR Michael Redd 4.00 10.00
Mike Bibby
VSBS Carlos Boozer 4.00 10.00
Luis Scola
VSBT Alando Tucker/570 4.00 10.00
Shannon Brown
VSCA Carmelo Anthony 5.00 12.00
Vince Carter
VSCD Eddy Curry 4.00 10.00
Samuel Dalembert
VSCF Jordan Farmar 4.00 10.00
Jose Calderon
VSCK Andrei Kirilenko 4.00 10.00
Marcus Camby
VSCM Shawn Marion 5.00 12.00
Vince Carter
VSCO Eddy Curry 4.00 10.00
Jermaine O'Neal
VSCS Josh Smith 5.00 12.00
Vince Carter
VSCW Marvin Williams 5.00 12.00
Vince Carter
VSDB Chris Duhon 4.00 10.00
Corey Brewer
VSDC Glen Davis 4.00 10.00
Wilson Chandler
VSDF Channing Frye 4.00 10.00
Darko Milicic
VSDJ Deron Williams 6.00 15.00
Jason Kidd
VSDL Kyle Lowry 4.00 10.00
Marquis Daniels
VSDS Baron Davis 4.00 10.00
DeShawn Stevenson
VSEB Julius Erving 10.00 25.00
Larry Bird
VSEC Chris Bosh 4.00 10.00
Elton Brand
VSEE Mark Eaton/400 5.00 12.00
Patrick Ewing
VSER David Robinson/570 5.00 12.00
Mark Eaton
VSFG Daniel Gibson 4.00 10.00
Raymond Felton
VSFM Michael Finley/570 4.00 10.00
Tracy McGrady
VSFW Brandan Wright/570 4.00 10.00
Channing Frye
VSGA Gilbert Arenas/570 5.00 12.00
Kevin Garnett
VSGL Kevin Garnett 5.00 12.00
Rashard Lewis
VSGN Dirk Nowitzki/570 5.00 12.00
Kevin Garnett
VSGO Kevin Garnett/570 6.00 15.00
Shaquille O'Neal
VSGR David Robinson/570 6.00 15.00
Kevin Garnett
VSGW Chris Webber/570 6.00 15.00
Kevin Garnett
VSHB Corey Brewer/795 4.00 10.00
Larry Hughes
VSHI Andre Iguodala/570 4.00 10.00
Josh Howard
VSHW Al Horford/570 4.00 10.00
Julian Wright
VSIB Andrew Bogut 4.00 10.00
Zydrunas Ilgauskas
VSIH Dwight Howard 4.00 10.00
Zydrunas Ilgauskas
VSJS Jordan Farmar/776 4.00 10.00
Stephon Marbury
VSJW Al Jefferson/570 4.00 10.00
Shelden Williams
VSKA Antawn Jamison 5.00 12.00
Kobe Bryant
VSKD Jason Kidd 5.00 12.00
Kevin Durant
VSKH Jason Kidd 4.00 10.00
Kirk Hinrich
VSKT Kevin Martin 4.00 10.00
Trevor Ariza
VSKU Beno Udrih 4.00 10.00
Jason Kidd
VSKW Chris Kaman 4.00 10.00
Sean Williams
VSLA Carmelo Anthony 4.00 10.00
Rashard Lewis
VSLL Acie Law 4.00 10.00
Kyle Lowry
VSMA Carmelo Anthony/776 5.00 12.00
Shawn Marion
VSMB Chris Bosh 5.00 12.00
Yao Ming
VSMF Desmond Mason 4.00 10.00
Randy Foye
VSMK Bernard King/551 5.00 12.00
Kevin McHale
VSMM Brad Miller/570 4.00 10.00
Sean May
VSMO Shaquille O'Neal/570 6.00 15.00
Yao Ming
VSMP Karl Malone/570 8.00 20.00
Scottie Pippen
VSMR Corey Maggette 4.00 10.00
J.J. Redick
VSMT Corey Maggette/570 4.00 10.00
Tyrus Thomas
VSMW Donyell Marshall 4.00 10.00
Luke Walton
VSNB Chauncey Billups 5.00 12.00
Steve Nash
VSNK Andrei Kirilenko/570 4.00 10.00
Dirk Nowitzki
VSNR David Robinson/570 6.00 15.00
Dirk Nowitzki
VSOB Andrew Bogut/570 4.00 10.00
Emeka Okafor
VSOD Emeka Okafor 4.00 10.00
Ike Diogu
VSOE Hakeem Olajuwon/570 5.00 12.00
Patrick Ewing
VSOO Hakeem Olajuwon 6.00 15.00
Shaquille O'Neal
VSOP Lamar Odom/551 4.00 10.00
Tayshaun Prince
VSOW Emeka Okafor/570 4.00 10.00
Hakim Warrick
VSPA Paul Pierce/570 4.00 10.00
Trevor Ariza
VSPG Danny Granger 4.00 10.00
Tayshaun Prince
VSPH Morris Peterson 4.00 10.00
Udonis Haslem
VSPJ LeBron James 5.00 12.00
Tayshaun Prince
VSPK Gary Payton 4.00 10.00
Steve Kerr
VSRS J.R. Smith 4.00 10.00
Luke Ridnour
VSSB Cedric Simmons 4.00 10.00
Shannon Brown
VSSJ John Starks 6.00 15.00
Magic Johnson
VSST Ramon Sessions 4.00 10.00
Sebastian Telfair
VSTC Chris Paul 4.00 10.00
Tracy McGrady
VSTG Daniel Gibson/570 4.00 10.00
Sebastian Telfair
VSTM Martell Webster/570 4.00 10.00
Thabo Sefolosha
VSVA Antawn Jamison 4.00 10.00
Vince Carter
VSVJ Jarrett Jack/570 4.00 10.00
Sasha Vujacic
VSVW Charlie Villanueva 4.00 10.00
Marvin Williams
VSWH Ben Wallace 4.00 10.00
Dwight Howard
VSWN Marvin Williams 4.00 10.00
Nene
VSWS Cedric Simmons 4.00 10.00
Hakim Warrick
VSWY Marvin Williams 4.00 10.00
Thaddeus Young
VSYA Andrea Bargnani 4.00 10.00
Yao Ming
VSYD Dikembe Mutombo 6.00 15.00
Yao Ming

2008 Upper Deck 20th Anniversary

Upper Deck produced this 80-card set featuring past and present athletes from baseball, football, basketball and hockey and issued them through their Certified Diamond Dealers program. Eight cards were released every month from March through December 2008. By entering in all 80 unique codes from the back of the cards on the company's website by December 31, 2008, collectors had a chance to win a trip to four major sporting events.

UD1 Michael Jordan 2.00 5.00
UD2 LeBron James 1.25 3.00
UD3 Kobe Bryant 1.25 3.00
UD4 Dennis Rodman .75 2.00
UD5 Kevin Durant .60 1.50
UD6 Larry Bird 1.50 4.00
UD7 Magic Johnson 1.50 4.00
UD8 Julius Erving .75 2.00
UD9 Bill Russell .75 2.00
UD10 Al Horford .50 1.25
UD11 David Robinson .75 2.00
UD12 Kareem Abdul-Jabbar .75 2.00
UD13 Jeff Green .30 .75
UD14 Mike Conley Jr. .30 .75
UD15 Steve Nash .60 1.50
UD61 Derrick Rose 1.50 4.00
UD62 O.J. Mayo 1.25 3.00
UD63 Kevin Love .75 2.00
UD64 Michael Beasley 1.25 3.00
UD65 Jerryd Bayless .50 1.25

2009 Upper Deck 20th Anniversary

CARDS ISSUED IN FIVE CARD RUNS
EACH PRICED EQUALLY WITHIN RUNS
36 Michael Jordan 2.50 6.00
37 Michael Jordan 2.50 6.00
38 Michael Jordan 2.50 6.00
39 Michael Jordan 2.50 6.00
40 Michael Jordan 2.50 6.00
56 Kareem Abdul-Jabbar .75 2.00
57 Kareem Abdul-Jabbar .75 2.00
58 Kareem Abdul-Jabbar .75 2.00
59 Kareem Abdul-Jabbar .75 2.00
60 Kareem Abdul-Jabbar .75 2.00
91 Minnesota Timberwolves .20 .50
92 Minnesota Timberwolves .20 .50
93 Minnesota Timberwolves .20 .50
94 Minnesota Timberwolves .20 .50
95 Minnesota Timberwolves .20 .50
96 Orlando Magic .20 .50
97 Orlando Magic .20 .50
98 Orlando Magic .20 .50
99 Orlando Magic .20 .50
100 Orlando Magic .20 .50
176 Michael Jordan 2.50 6.00
177 Michael Jordan 2.50 6.00
178 Michael Jordan 2.50 6.00
179 Michael Jordan 2.50 6.00
180 Michael Jordan 2.50 6.00
216 Detroit Pistons .20 .50
Isiah Thomas
217 Detroit Pistons .20 .50
218 Detroit Pistons .20 .50
219 Detroit Pistons .20 .50
220 Detroit Pistons .20 .50
251 David Robinson .75 2.00
252 David Robinson .75 2.00
253 David Robinson .75 2.00
254 David Robinson .75 2.00
255 David Robinson .75 2.00
276 Magic Johnson .75 2.00
277 Magic Johnson .75 2.00
278 Magic Johnson .75 2.00
279 Magic Johnson .75 2.00
280 Magic Johnson .75 2.00
291 Michael Jordan 2.50 6.00
292 Michael Jordan 2.50 6.00
293 Michael Jordan 2.50 6.00
294 Michael Jordan 2.50 6.00
295 Michael Jordan 2.50 6.00
306 Chicago Bulls 1.00 2.50
Michael Jordan
307 Chicago Bulls .20 .50
308 Chicago Bulls .20 .50
309 Chicago Bulls .20 .50
310 Chicago Bulls .20 .50
336 Michael Jordan 2.50 6.00
337 Michael Jordan 2.50 6.00
338 Michael Jordan 2.50 6.00
339 Michael Jordan 2.50 6.00
340 Michael Jordan 2.50 6.00
376 Magic Johnson .75 2.00
377 Magic Johnson .75 2.00
378 Magic Johnson .75 2.00
379 Magic Johnson .75 2.00
380 Magic Johnson .75 2.00
421 Chicago Bulls .20 .50
422 Chicago Bulls .20 .50
423 Chicago Bulls .20 .50
424 Chicago Bulls 1.00 2.50
Michael Jordan
425 Chicago Bulls .20 .50
426 Michael Jordan 2.50 6.00
427 Michael Jordan 2.50 6.00
428 Michael Jordan 2.50 6.00
429 Michael Jordan 2.50 6.00
430 Michael Jordan 2.50 6.00
521 John Paxson .20 .50
522 John Paxson .20 .50
523 John Paxson .20 .50
524 John Paxson .20 .50
525 John Paxson .20 .50
536 Chicago Bulls .20 .50
537 Chicago Bulls .20 .50
538 Chicago Bulls .20 .50
539 Chicago Bulls .20 .50
540 Chicago Bulls .20 .50
541 Michael Jordan 2.50 6.00
542 Michael Jordan 2.50 6.00
543 Michael Jordan 2.50 6.00
544 Michael Jordan 2.50 6.00
545 Michael Jordan 2.50 6.00
561 Julius Erving .75 2.00
562 Julius Erving .75 2.00
563 Julius Erving .75 2.00
564 Julius Erving .75 2.00
565 Julius Erving .75 2.00
606 Shaquille O'Neal 1.25 3.00
607 Shaquille O'Neal 1.25 3.00
608 Shaquille O'Neal 1.25 3.00
609 Shaquille O'Neal 1.25 3.00
610 Shaquille O'Neal 1.25 3.00
656 Houston Rockets .20 .50
657 Houston Rockets .20 .50
658 Houston Rockets .20 .50
659 Houston Rockets .20 .50
660 Houston Rockets .20 .50
686 John Stockton .60 1.50
687 John Stockton .60 1.50
688 John Stockton .60 1.50
689 John Stockton .60 1.50
690 John Stockton .60 1.50
691 Jason Kidd .40 1.00
692 Jason Kidd .40 1.00
693 Jason Kidd .40 1.00
694 Jason Kidd .40 1.00
695 Jason Kidd .40 1.00
696 NCAA National Champions .20 .50
Arizona Razorbacks
697 NCAA National Champions .20 .50
Arizona Razorbacks
698 NCAA National Champions .20 .50
Arizona Razorbacks
699 NCAA National Champions .20 .50
Arizona Razorbacks
700 NCAA National Champions .20 .50
Arizona Razorbacks

726 Hakeem Olajuwon .60 1.50
727 Hakeem Olajuwon .60 1.50
728 Hakeem Olajuwon .60 1.50
729 Hakeem Olajuwon .60 1.50
730 Hakeem Olajuwon .60 1.50
751 Michael Jordan 2.50 6.00
752 Michael Jordan 2.50 6.00
753 Michael Jordan 2.50 6.00
754 Michael Jordan 2.50 6.00
755 Michael Jordan 2.50 6.00
771 NCAA National Champions .20 .50
UCLA Bruins
772 NCAA National Champions .20 .50
UCLA Bruins
773 NCAA National Champions .20 .50
UCLA Bruins
774 NCAA National Champions .20 .50
UCLA Bruins
775 NCAA National Champions .20 .50
UCLA Bruins
781 Final Game at Boston Garden .75 2.00
Larry Bird
782 Final Game at Boston Garden .20 .50
783 Final Game at Boston Garden .60 1.50
784 Final Game at Boston Garden .60 1.50
785 Final Game at Boston Garden .60 1.50
786 Houston Rockets .40 1.00
Hakeem Olajuwon
Shaquille O'Neal
787 Houston Rockets .20 .50
788 Houston Rockets .20 .50
789 Houston Rockets .20 .50
790 Houston Rockets .20 .50
851 Kareem Abdul-Jabbar .75 2.00
852 Kareem Abdul-Jabbar .75 2.00
853 Kareem Abdul-Jabbar .75 2.00
854 Kareem Abdul-Jabbar .75 2.00
855 Kareem Abdul-Jabbar .75 2.00
881 Chicago Bulls .20 .50
882 Chicago Bulls .20 .50
883 Chicago Bulls .20 .50
884 Chicago Bulls .20 .50
885 Chicago Bulls .20 .50
886 Michael Jordan 2.50 6.00
887 Michael Jordan 2.50 6.00
888 Michael Jordan 2.50 6.00
889 Michael Jordan 2.50 6.00
890 Michael Jordan 2.50 6.00
916 NCAA National Champions .20 .50
Kentucky Wildcats
917 NCAA National Champions .20 .50
Kentucky Wildcats
918 NCAA National Champions .20 .50
Kentucky Wildcats
919 NCAA National Champions .20 .50
Kentucky Wildcats
920 NCAA National Champions .20 .50
Kentucky Wildcats
931 Bill Russell .75 2.00
932 Bill Russell .75 2.00
933 Bill Russell .75 2.00
934 Bill Russell .75 2.00
935 Bill Russell .75 2.00
981 Tim Duncan .60 1.50
982 Tim Duncan .60 1.50
983 Tim Duncan .60 1.50
984 Tim Duncan .60 1.50
985 Tim Duncan .60 1.50
1006 Michael Jordan 2.50 6.00
1007 Michael Jordan 2.50 6.00
1008 Michael Jordan 2.50 6.00
1009 Michael Jordan 2.50 6.00
1010 Michael Jordan 2.50 6.00
1021 NCAA National Champions .20 .50
1022 NCAA National Champions .20 .50
1023 NCAA National Champions .20 .50
1024 NCAA National Champions .20 .50
1025 NCAA National Champions .20 .50
1106 Julius Erving .75 2.00
1107 Julius Erving .75 2.00
1108 Julius Erving .75 2.00
1109 Julius Erving .75 2.00
1110 Julius Erving .75 2.00
1126 Chicago Bulls .20 .50
1127 Chicago Bulls .20 .50
1128 Chicago Bulls .20 .50
1129 Chicago Bulls .20 .50
1130 Chicago Bulls .20 .50
1131 Michael Jordan 2.50 6.00
1132 Michael Jordan 2.50 6.00
1133 Michael Jordan 2.50 6.00
1134 Michael Jordan 2.50 6.00
1135 Michael Jordan 2.50 6.00
1186 Larry Bird 1.25 3.00
1187 Larry Bird 1.25 3.00
1188 Larry Bird 1.25 3.00
1189 Larry Bird 1.25 3.00
1190 Larry Bird 1.25 3.00
1271 San Antonio Spurs .20 .50
1272 San Antonio Spurs .20 .50
1273 San Antonio Spurs .20 .50
1274 San Antonio Spurs .20 .50
1275 San Antonio Spurs .20 .50
1406 Los Angeles Lakers .30 .75
1407 Los Angeles Lakers .30 .75
1408 Los Angeles Lakers .30 .75
1409 Los Angeles Lakers .30 .75
1410 Los Angeles Lakers .30 .75
1466 Shaquille O'Neal 1.25 3.00
1467 Shaquille O'Neal 1.25 3.00
1468 Shaquille O'Neal 1.25 3.00
1469 Shaquille O'Neal 1.25 3.00
1470 Shaquille O'Neal 1.25 3.00
1526 Los Angeles Lakers .30 .75
1527 Los Angeles Lakers .30 .75
1528 Los Angeles Lakers .30 .75
1529 Los Angeles Lakers .30 .75
1530 Los Angeles Lakers .30 .75
1616 Tony Parker .20 .50
1617 Tony Parker .20 .50
1618 Tony Parker .20 .50
1619 Tony Parker .20 .50
1620 Tony Parker .20 .50
1631 Los Angeles Lakers .30 .75
1632 Los Angeles Lakers .30 .75
1633 Los Angeles Lakers .30 .75
1634 Los Angeles Lakers .30 .75
1635 Los Angeles Lakers .30 .75
1651 Magic Johnson .75 2.00
1652 Magic Johnson .75 2.00
1653 Magic Johnson .75 2.00
1654 Magic Johnson .75 2.00
1655 Magic Johnson .75 2.00
1666 Yao Ming .25 .60
1667 Yao Ming .25 .60
1668 Yao Ming .25 .60
1669 Yao Ming .25 .60
1670 Yao Ming .25 .60
1701 Tim Duncan .60 1.50
1702 Tim Duncan .60 1.50
1703 Tim Duncan .60 1.50
1704 Tim Duncan .60 1.50
1705 Tim Duncan .60 1.50
1741 Kobe Bryant 1.50 4.00
1742 Kobe Bryant 1.50 4.00
1743 Kobe Bryant 1.50 4.00
1744 Kobe Bryant 1.50 4.00
1745 Kobe Bryant 1.50 4.00
1786 San Antonio Spurs .20 .50
1787 San Antonio Spurs .20 .50
1788 San Antonio Spurs .20 .50
1789 San Antonio Spurs .20 .50
1790 San Antonio Spurs .20 .50
1796 Dwyane Wade .60 1.50
1797 Dwyane Wade .60 1.50
1798 Dwyane Wade .60 1.50
1799 Dwyane Wade .60 1.50
1800 Dwyane Wade .60 1.50
1821 LeBron James 2.00 5.00
1822 LeBron James 2.00 5.00
1823 LeBron James 2.00 5.00
1824 LeBron James 2.00 5.00
1825 LeBron James 2.00 5.00
1826 Tim Duncan .60 1.50
1827 Tim Duncan .60 1.50
1828 Tim Duncan .60 1.50
1829 Tim Duncan .60 1.50
1830 Tim Duncan .60 1.50
1871 Chris Bosh .20 .50
1872 Chris Bosh .20 .50
1873 Chris Bosh .20 .50
1874 Chris Bosh .20 .50
1875 Chris Bosh .20 .50
1906 LeBron James 2.00 5.00
1907 LeBron James 2.00 5.00
1908 LeBron James 2.00 5.00
1909 LeBron James 2.00 5.00
1910 LeBron James 2.00 5.00
1926 Detroit Pistons .20 .50
1927 Detroit Pistons .20 .50
1928 Detroit Pistons .20 .50
1929 Detroit Pistons .20 .50
1930 Detroit Pistons .20 .50
1976 Dwight Howard .60 1.50
1977 Dwight Howard .60 1.50
1978 Dwight Howard .60 1.50
1979 Dwight Howard .60 1.50
1980 Dwight Howard .60 1.50
1996 Clyde Drexler .50 1.25
1997 Clyde Drexler .50 1.25
1998 Clyde Drexler .50 1.25
1999 Clyde Drexler .50 1.25
2000 Clyde Drexler .50 1.25
2091 San Antonio Spurs .20 .50
2092 San Antonio Spurs .20 .50
2093 San Antonio Spurs .20 .50
2094 San Antonio Spurs .20 .50
2095 San Antonio Spurs .20 .50
2111 Steve Nash .40 1.00
2112 Steve Nash .40 1.00
2113 Steve Nash .40 1.00
2114 Steve Nash .40 1.00
2115 Steve Nash .40 1.00
2146 Chris Paul .60 1.50
2147 Chris Paul .60 1.50
2148 Chris Paul .60 1.50
2149 Chris Paul .60 1.50
2150 Chris Paul .60 1.50
2166 Kobe Bryant 1.50 4.00
2167 Kobe Bryant 1.50 4.00
2168 Kobe Bryant 1.50 4.00
2169 Kobe Bryant 1.50 4.00
2170 Kobe Bryant 1.50 4.00
2171 Miami Heat .20 .50
2172 Miami Heat .20 .50
2173 Miami Heat .20 .50
2174 Miami Heat .20 .50
2175 Miami Heat .20 .50
2196 Steve Nash .40 1.00
2197 Steve Nash .40 1.00
2198 Steve Nash .40 1.00
2199 Steve Nash .40 1.00
2200 Steve Nash .40 1.00
2211 Dominique Wilkins .50 1.25
2212 Dominique Wilkins .50 1.25
2213 Dominique Wilkins .50 1.25
2214 Dominique Wilkins .50 1.25
2215 Dominique Wilkins .50 1.25
2336 San Antonio Spurs .20 .50
2337 San Antonio Spurs .20 .50
2338 San Antonio Spurs .20 .50
2339 San Antonio Spurs .20 .50
2340 San Antonio Spurs .20 .50
2356 Kevin Durant 1.25 3.00
2357 Kevin Durant 1.25 3.00
2358 Kevin Durant 1.25 3.00
2359 Kevin Durant 1.25 3.00
2360 Kevin Durant 1.25 3.00
2361 Dirk Nowitzki .40 1.00
2362 Dirk Nowitzki .40 1.00
2363 Dirk Nowitzki .40 1.00
2364 Dirk Nowitzki .40 1.00
2365 Dirk Nowitzki .40 1.00
2426 Boston Celtics .40 1.00
2427 Boston Celtics .40 1.00
2428 Boston Celtics .40 1.00
2429 Boston Celtics .40 1.00
2430 Boston Celtics .40 1.00
2436 Kobe Bryant 1.50 4.00
2437 Kobe Bryant 1.50 4.00
2438 Kobe Bryant 1.50 4.00
2439 Kobe Bryant 1.50 4.00
2440 Kobe Bryant 1.50 4.00
2441 Hakeem Olajuwon .60 1.50
2442 Hakeem Olajuwon .60 1.50
2443 Hakeem Olajuwon .60 1.50
2444 Hakeem Olajuwon .60 1.50
2445 Hakeem Olajuwon .60 1.50
2456 Derrick Rose 1.50 4.00
2457 Derrick Rose 1.50 4.00
2458 Derrick Rose 1.50 4.00
2459 Derrick Rose 1.50 4.00
2460 Derrick Rose 1.50 4.00
2471 Michael Beasley 1.25 3.00
2472 Michael Beasley 1.25 3.00
2473 Michael Beasley 1.25 3.00
2474 Michael Beasley 1.25 3.00
2475 Michael Beasley 1.25 3.00

2009 Upper Deck 20th Anniversary Memorabilia

NBABI Chauncey Billups 4.00 10.00
NBACA Carmelo Anthony 4.00 10.00
NBACB Chris Bosh 3.00 8.00
NBACP Chris Paul 3.00 8.00
NBAEO Emeka Okafor 4.00 10.00
NBAKB Kobe Bryant 20.00 40.00
NBAKG Kevin Garnett 4.00 10.00
NBALJ LeBron James 12.50 30.00
NBAMJ Michael Jordan 40.00 80.00
NBASO Shaquille O'Neal 12.50 30.00
NBATD Tim Duncan 5.00 12.00
NBATM Tracy McGrady 4.00 10.00
NBAVC Vince Carter 4.00 10.00
NBAYM Yao Ming 5.00 12.00

1996 Upper Deck 22K Gold Michael Jordan

NNO Michael Jordan 40.00 100.00
ROY/1985
NNO Michael Jordan 30.00 80.00
He's Back
NNO Michael Jordan 30.00 80.00
First Championship

1998 Upper Deck 22K Gold Michael Jordan

COMMON CARD 8.00 20.00

1999 Upper Deck 22K Gold Michael Jordan

Released through Upper Deck and Upper Deck Authenticated, these 5-cards commemorate the retirement of Michael Jordan. Each card is not numbered, but is serially numbered to 9923 on the back.

2000 Upper Deck 22K Gold Michael Jordan

This 2.5x3.5 sized card was released by Upper Deck in 2000, and features a solid gold card with an actual piece of the Delta Center floor upon which Jordan took his final shot. This card was sold through Upper Deck's direct marketing channel, and carried a suggested retail price of $79.99.

1 Michael Jordan 100.00 200.00

1996 Upper Deck 23 Nights Jordan Experience

Available as both a complete set with or without the interview compact disc, this 23-card set carried a suggested retail price of $19.99. Each set included the oversized (3 1/2" by 5") cards and a circular commemorative card. Each card is specifically dated commemorating each event.

COMPLETE SET w/CD (23) 12.00 30.00
COMPLETE SET (23) 10.00 25.00
COMMON CARD (1-23) .60 1.50
NNO Cardboard Disk .40 1.00
(Michael Jordan)
NNO Compact Disc 2.00 5.00
The Jordan Interview

1993 Upper Deck Adventures in Toon World

NNO Joe Montana 1.00 2.50
Wayne Gretzky
Reggie Jackson
Michael Jordan

2002 Upper Deck All-Star Game Jordan

Available to collectors at the 2001-02 NBA All-Star game, this 3-card set features Michael Jordan with the Bulls and the Wizards. Each card has and All-Star game stamping on the front, and the card backs are sequentally numbered to 2002.

COMPLETE SET (3) 8.00 20.00
COMMON CARD 3.00 8.00

2003 Upper Deck All-Star Game

Distributed by Upper Deck at the All-Star Jam Session Show in Atlanta, this 4-card set features some of the games greatest slam dunk champion with a full color action photo on a grey background with gold foil highlights. Each card is sequentially numbered to the corresponding year the player won the slam dunk competition.

COMPLETE SET (4) 10.00 25.00
DW1 Dominique Wilkins/1985 1.50 4.00
KB1 Kobe Bryant/1997 4.00 10.00
MJ1 Michael Jordan/1987 6.00 15.00
MJ2 Michael Jordan/1988 6.00 15.00

2004 Upper Deck All-Star Game

Given out by Upper Deck at the 2004 NBA All-Star Jam Session in Los Angeles, this 10-card set was available at the Upper Deck booth as a redemption with 10 packages of any 2003-04 Upper Deck Basketball Product. Cards place players on a purple background with orange trim and holographic highlights. Each card is sequentially numbered to 2004 and the players were available on days as follows: LJ1 LeBron James and Gary Payton on Feb. 12th, LJ2 LeBron James and Carmelo Anthony on Feb. 13th, LJ3 LeBron James and Kobe Bryant on Feb. 14th, LJ4 LeBron James and Michael Jordan on Feb. 15th, and LJ5 LeBron James and Chris Bosh on Feb. 16th. The Star Zone Michael Jordan Sample was also handed out and was not included in the original press material as the set. Rumor has it that these cards were handed out when the initial players with print runs of 2004 ran out.

COMPLETE SET (10) 75.00 150.00
BO Chris Bosh 3.00 8.00
LJ1 LeBron James 12.50 30.00
LJ2 LeBron James 12.50 30.00
LJ3 LeBron James 12.50 30.00
LJ4 LeBron James 12.50 30.00
LJ5 LeBron James 12.50 30.00
CA Carmelo Anthony 4.00 10.00
GP Gary Payton 3.00 8.00
KB Kobe Bryant 5.00 12.00
MJ Michael Jordan 6.00 15.00
SZMJ Michael Jordan 6.00 15.00
Star Zone SAMPLE

2005 Upper Deck All-Star Game

COMPLETE SET 8.00 20.00
LJ LeBron James 4.00 10.00
MJ Michael Jordan 5.00 12.00
KB Kobe Bryant 3.00 8.00

2006-07 Upper Deck All-Star Game

COMPLETE SET (13) 8.00 20.00
AS1 Yao Ming .60 1.50
AS2 Julius Erving 1.00 2.50
AS3 Larry Bird 1.50 4.00
AS4 Magic Johnson 1.25 3.00
AS5 Steve Nash .60 1.50
AS6 LaMarcus Aldridge 1.25 3.00
AS7 Rudy Gay .75 2.00
AS8 Brandon Roy 1.25 3.00
AS9 Tyrus Thomas .60 1.50
AS10 Jerry Tarkanian .50 1.25
AS11 LeBron James 2.50 6.00
AS12 Michael Jordan 4.00 10.00
AS13 Kobe Bryant 2.50 6.00

2004-05 Upper Deck All-Star Lineup

Released in February 2005, this 132-card set features veteran players on cards 1-90 and rookies on cards 91-132. All-Star Lineup was packaged in 24-pack boxes were packs contained six cards and carried a SRP of $2.99.

COMP.SET w/o SP's (90) 12.50 30.00
1 Jason Terry .25 .60
2 Al Harrington .25 .60
3 Boris Diaw .25 .60
4 Paul Pierce .40 1.00
5 Ricky Davis .25 .60
6 Jiri Welsch .20 .50
7 Marcus Fizer .20 .50
8 Gerald Wallace .30 .75
9 Jahidi White .20 .50
10 Eddy Curry .25 .60
11 Kirk Hinrich .30 .75
12 Jamal Crawford .25 .60
13 LeBron James 2.00 5.00
14 Dajuan Wagner .20 .50
15 Jeff McInnis .20 .50
16 Dirk Nowitzki .50 1.25
17 Antoine Walker .30 .75
18 Michael Finley .30 .75
19 Carmelo Anthony .60 1.50
20 Andre Miller .25 .60
21 Kenyon Martin .30 .75
22 Chauncey Billups .30 .75
23 Rasheed Wallace .30 .75
24 Ben Wallace .30 .75
25 Erick Dampier .20 .50
26 Jason Richardson .30 .75
27 Mike Dunleavy .25 .60
28 Yao Ming .60 1.50
29 Tracy McGrady .40 1.00
30 Juwan Howard .25 .60
31 Jermaine O'Neal .30 .75
32 Reggie Miller .30 .75
33 Ron Artest .30 .75
34 Elton Brand .30 .75
35 Corey Maggette .25 .60
36 Quentin Richardson .25 .60
37 Kobe Bryant 1.50 4.00
38 Gary Payton .30 .75
39 Lamar Odom .30 .75
40 Pau Gasol .30 .75
41 Jason Williams .25 .60
42 Bonzi Wells .20 .50
43 Shaquille O'Neal .75 2.00
44 Dwyane Wade 1.00 2.50
45 Eddie Jones .25 .60
46 Michael Redd .30 .75
47 Desmond Mason .25 .60
48 T.J. Ford .25 .60
49 Latrell Sprewell .25 .60
50 Kevin Garnett .60 1.50
51 Sam Cassell .25 .60
52 Richard Jefferson .30 .75
53 Kerry Kittles .20 .50
54 Jason Kidd .50 1.25
55 Jamal Mashburn .30 .75
56 Baron Davis .30 .75
57 Jamaal Magloire .20 .50
58 Allan Houston .25 .60
59 Kurt Thomas .20 .50
60 Stephon Marbury .25 .60
61 Cuttino Mobley .25 .60
62 Drew Gooden .25 .60
63 Steve Francis .30 .75
64 Glenn Robinson .25 .60
65 Allen Iverson .50 1.25
66 Samuel Dalembert .20 .50
67 Amare Stoudemire .40 1.00
68 Steve Nash .40 1.00
69 Shawn Marion .30 .75
70 Shareef Abdur-Rahim .25 .60
71 Damon Stoudamire .25 .60
72 Zach Randolph .25 .60
73 Peja Stojakovic .30 .75
74 Chris Webber .30 .75
75 Mike Bibby .30 .75
76 Tony Parker .30 .75
77 Tim Duncan .50 1.25
78 Manu Ginobili .40 1.00
79 Ronald Murray .20 .50
80 Ray Allen .30 .75
81 Rashard Lewis .30 .75
82 Chris Bosh .30 .75
83 Vince Carter .50 1.25
84 Jalen Rose .25 .60
85 Andrei Kirilenko .25 .60
86 Carlos Boozer .30 .75
87 Carlos Arroyo .25 .60
88 Gilbert Arenas .30 .75
89 Jarvis Hayes .20 .50
90 Antawn Jamison .30 .75
91 Emeka Okafor RC 1.25 3.00
92 Dwight Howard RC 2.50 6.00
93 Shaun Livingston RC .75 2.00
94 Luol Deng RC 1.25 3.00
95 Ben Gordon RC 1.00 2.50
96 Devin Harris RC 1.25 3.00
97 Andre Iguodala RC 1.25 3.00
98 Andris Biedrins RC 1.00 2.50
99 Josh Childress RC .75 2.00
100 Josh Smith RC 1.25 3.00
101 Jameer Nelson RC 1.00 2.50
102 J.R. Smith RC 1.00 2.50
103 Sergei Monia RC .75 2.00
104 Sebastian Telfair RC .75 2.00
105 Pavel Podkolzine RC .75 2.00
106 Luke Jackson RC .75 2.00
107 Dorell Wright RC 1.25 3.00
108 Robert Swift RC .75 2.00
109 Anderson Varejao RC 1.00 2.50
110 Sasha Vujacic RC .75 2.00
111 Rafael Araujo RC .75 2.00
112 Al Jefferson RC 1.25 3.00
113 Kris Humphries RC .75 2.00
114 Kirk Snyder RC .75 2.00
115 Darius Rice RC .75 2.00
116 Beno Udrih RC .75 2.00
117 Viktor Khryapa RC .75 2.00
118 David Harrison RC .75 2.00
119 Trevor Ariza RC .75 2.00
120 Ha Seung-Jin RC .75 2.00
121 Kevin Martin RC 1.00 2.50
122 Delonte West RC 1.00 2.50
123 Rickey Paulding RC .75 2.00
124 Chris Duhon RC .75 2.00
125 Tony Allen RC 1.00 2.50
126 Donta Smith RC .75 2.00
127 Andre Emmett RC .75 2.00
128 Royal Ivey RC .75 2.00
129 Matt Freije RC .75 2.00
130 Romain Sato RC .75 2.00
131 Antonio Burks RC .75 2.00
132 Lionel Chalmers RC .75 2.00

2004-05 Upper Deck All-Star Lineup Gold

Randomly seeded, this 132-card set parallels the base All-Star Lineup enhanced with gold foil highlights. Cards 1-90 are sequentially numbered to 100, while cards 91-132 are numbered to 25.

*1-90 GOLD: 3X TO 8X BASE HI
*91-132 GOLD RCs: 2X TO 5X BASE HI

2004-05 Upper Deck All-Star Lineup All-Star Staples

Inserted randomly in packs at the rate of one in three, this 14-card set is horizontally designed on gray background with player images on the right and their jersey number on the left. A parallel version serially numbered to 10 was also issued for this set.

COMPLETE SET (14) 6.00 15.00
AI Allen Iverson .75 2.00
BW Ben Wallace .50 1.25
DN Dirk Nowitzki .75 2.00
JK Jason Kidd .75 2.00
JO Jermaine O'Neal .50 1.25
KB Kobe Bryant 2.50 6.00
KG Kevin Garnett 1.00 2.50
KM Kenyon Martin .50 1.25
PP Paul Pierce .60 1.50
SF Steve Francis .50 1.25
SO Shaquille O'Neal 1.25 3.00
TD Tim Duncan .75 2.00
TM Tracy McGrady .60 1.50
YM Yao Ming 1.00 2.50

2004-05 Upper Deck All-Star Lineup All-Star Staples Threads

Randomly seeded in packs at the rate of one in 12, this 14-card set parallels the base All-Star Staples insert enhanced with a swatch of jersey.

AI Allen Iverson 4.00 10.00
BW Ben Wallace 2.50 6.00
DN Dirk Nowitzki 4.00 10.00
JK Jason Kidd 4.00 10.00
JO Jermaine O'Neal 2.50 6.00
KB Kobe Bryant 6.00 15.00
KG Kevin Garnett 5.00 12.00
KM Kenyon Martin 2.50 6.00
PP Paul Pierce 3.00 8.00
SF Steve Francis 2.50 6.00
SO Shaquille O'Neal 6.00 15.00
TD Tim Duncan 4.00 10.00
TM Tracy McGrady 3.00 8.00
YM Yao Ming 5.00 12.00

2004-05 Upper Deck All-Star Lineup Prominent Futures

Inserted in packs at the rate of one in three, this 14-card set is horizontally designed with a two players, one on each side and gray borders. A parallel version of this set was also inserted in packs and those are sereially numbered to 50.

COMPLETE SET (15) 6.00 15.00
*PARALLEL: 1.5X TO 4X BASE HI
BD Carlos Boozer .60 1.50
Mike Dunleavy
HH Josh Howard .60 1.50
Jarvis Hayes
HK Udonis Haslem .60 1.50
Chris Kaman
JA LeBron James 2.00 5.00
Carmelo Anthony
JB Marko Jaric .60 1.50
Chris Bosh
JS LeBron James 1.50 4.00
Amare Stoudemire
KD Chris Kaman .60 1.50
Mike Dunleavy
MH Ronald Murray .60 1.50
Jarvis Hayes
MN Yao Ming 1.00 2.50
Nene
NH Nene .60 1.50
Udonis Haslem
PH Tayshaun Prince .60 1.50
Josh Howard
PM Tayshaun Prince .60 1.50
Ronald Murray
SG Amare Stoudemire 1.00 2.50
Manu Ginobili
WG Dwyane Wade 1.25 3.00
Manu Ginobili

2004-05 Upper Deck All-Star Lineup Prominent Futures Threads

Randomly seeded in packs at the rate of one in 12, this 14-card set parallels the base All-Star Staples insert enhanced with two swatches of memorabilia.

BD Carlos Boozer 4.00 10.00
Mike Dunleavy
HH Josh Howard 4.00 10.00
Jarvis Hayes
HK Udonis Haslem 4.00 10.00
Chris Kaman
JA LeBron James 20.00 50.00
Carmelo Anthony
JB Marko Jaric 4.00 10.00
Chris Bosh
JS LeBron James 12.00 30.00
Amare Stoudemire
KD Chris Kaman 4.00 10.00
Mike Dunleavy
MH Ronald Murray 4.00 10.00
Jarvis Hayes
MN Yao Ming 5.00 12.00
Nene
NH Nene 4.00 10.00
Udonis Haslem
PH Tayshaun Prince 4.00 10.00
Josh Howard
PM Tayshaun Prince 4.00 10.00
Ronald Murray
SG Amare Stoudemire 5.00 12.00
Manu Ginobili
WG Dwyane Wade 8.00 20.00
Manu Ginobili

2004-05 Upper Deck All-Star Lineup Promos/eCards

Inserted in packs at the rate of one in six for the eCards and two per pack on the Promos, these cards were designed to send people to Upper Deck's website and possibly redeem for cool prizes.

AS1 Kobe Bryant EC 2.50 6.00
AS2 LeBron James EC 3.00 8.00
AS3 Kevin Garnett EC 1.00 2.50
AS4 Tracy McGrady EC .60 1.50
AS5 Shaquille O'Neal EC 1.25 3.00
AS6 Allen Iverson EC .75 2.00
AS7 Tim Duncan EC .75 2.00
AS8 Jason Kidd EC .75 2.00
AS9 Paul Pierce .40 1.00
AS10 Carmelo Anthony .60 1.50
AS11 Ben Wallace .30 .75
AS12 Yao Ming .60 1.50
AS13 Jermaine O'Neal .30 .75
AS14 Dirk Nowitzki .50 1.25
AS15 Dwyane Wade 1.00 2.50
AS16 Brad Miller .30 .75
AS17 Kenyon Martin .30 .75
AS18 Jason Richardson .30 .75
AS19 Stephon Marbury .25 .60
AS20 Amare Stoudemire .40 1.00
AS21 Baron Davis .30 .75
AS22 Ray Allen .30 .75
AS23 Vince Carter .50 1.25
AS24 Andrei Kirilenko .25 .60
AS25 Jamal Mashburn .30 .75
AS26 Chris Webber .30 .75
AS27 Chris Bosh .30 .75
AS28 Shareef Abdur-Rahim .25 .60
AS29 Michael Redd .30 .75
AS30 Zach Randolph .25 .60
AS31 Rasheed Wallace .30 .75
AS32 Peja Stojakovic .30 .75
AS33 Pau Gasol .30 .75
AS34 Shawn Marion .30 .75
AS35 Jamaal Magloire .20 .50
AS36 Tony Parker .30 .75
AS37 Ron Artest .30 .75
AS38 Elton Brand .30 .75
AS39 Wild Card EC .40 1.00

2004-05 Upper Deck All-Star Lineup Rookie Review

Inserted as a topper in each box, this 30-card set follows LeBron James's rookie season on cards RR-RR21 and some of the more impressive rookies from the class on cards RR22-RR30.

COMPLETE SET (30) 15.00 40.00
RR1 LeBron James 1.50 4.00
RR2 LeBron James 1.50 4.00
RR3 LeBron James 1.50 4.00
RR4 LeBron James 1.50 4.00
RR5 LeBron James 1.50 4.00
RR6 LeBron James 1.50 4.00
RR7 LeBron James 1.50 4.00
RR8 LeBron James 1.50 4.00
RR9 LeBron James 1.50 4.00
RR10 LeBron James 1.50 4.00
RR11 LeBron James 1.50 4.00
RR12 LeBron James 1.50 4.00
RR13 LeBron James 1.50 4.00
RR14 LeBron James 1.50 4.00
RR15 LeBron James 1.50 4.00
RR16 LeBron James 1.50 4.00
RR17 LeBron James 1.50 4.00
RR18 LeBron James 1.50 4.00
RR19 LeBron James 1.50 4.00
RR20 LeBron James 1.50 4.00
RR21 LeBron James 1.50 4.00
RR22 Udonis Haslem .40 1.00
RR23 T.J. Ford .40 1.00
RR24 Marquis Daniels .30 .75
RR25 Josh Howard .50 1.25
RR26 Kirk Hinrich .50 1.25
RR27 Jarvis Hayes .30 .75
RR28 Carmelo Anthony 1.00 2.50
RR29 Chris Bosh .50 1.25
RR30 Dwyane Wade 1.50 4.00

2004-05 Upper Deck All-Star Lineup Signature Class

Inserted in packs at the rate of one in 240, this 21-card set is horizontally designed and places player photos on the right and autographs on the left.

COMMON CARD 8.00 20.00
JD Juan Dixon 8.00 20.00
KB Kobe Bryant 100.00 200.00
KG Kevin Garnett 30.00 60.00
LJ LeBron James 150.00 300.00
RM Reggie Miller 40.00 100.00

2004-05 Upper Deck All-Star Lineup Weekend Highlights

Inserted at the rate of one in three, this 14-card set features a full-color image surrounded by red, then gray borders. A parallel version set was printed where cards denoted as L1 are serially numbered to 100 and cards denoted as L2 are serially numbered to 250.

COMPLETE SET (14) 3.00 8.00
STATED ODDS 1:3
*L1 PARALLEL: 2.5X TO 6X BASE HI
*L2 PARALLEL: 1.5X TO 4X BASE HI
AN Chris Anderson L1 .75 2.00
BD Baron Davis L2 .50 1.25

CB Chauncey Billups L2 .50 1.25
CM Cuttino Mobley L2 .40 1.00
DF Derek Fisher L1 .40 1.00
EB Earl Boykins L1 .30 .75
FJ Fred Jones L1 .30 .75
JA Marko Jaric L1 .30 .75
JR Jason Richardson L2 .50 1.25
KK Kyle Korver L1 .40 1.00
PS Peja Stojakovic L2 .50 1.25
RD Ricky Davis L2 .40 1.00
SM Stephon Marbury L2 .40 1.00
VL Voshon Lenard L1 .30 .75

2004-05 Upper Deck All-Star Lineup Weekend Highlights Threads

Randomly seeded in packs at the rate of one in 12, this 14-card set parallels the Weekend Highlights insert enhanced with a swatch of memorabilia.
AN Chris Anderson 4.00 10.00
BD Baron Davis 2.50 6.00
CB Chauncey Billups 2.50 6.00
CM Cuttino Mobley 2.00 5.00
DF Derek Fisher 2.00 5.00
EB Earl Boykins 2.00 5.00
FJ Fred Jones 2.00 5.00
JA Marko Jaric 2.00 5.00
JR Jason Richardson 2.50 6.00
KK Kyle Korver 2.00 5.00
PS Peja Stojakovic SP 2.50 6.00
RD Ricky Davis 2.00 5.00
SM Stephon Marbury 2.00 5.00
VL Voshon Lenard 2.00 5.00

1992-93 Upper Deck All-Star Weekend

This 40-card boxed set was originally available only to hobby dealers and to dealers at The Upper Deck Trading Card and Memorabilia Show at the Salt Palace in Salt Lake City, Utah, during February 18-21, 1993. The set captures NBA All-Stars from the past, present, and future, as well as memories of previous NBA All-Star Games. The standard-size cards display full-bleed photos with silver foil highlights on their fronts. At least one set in each case had gold (rather than silver) foil highlights valued at two to four times the prices listed below. The set is comprised of three subsets: NBA All-Star Heroes (1-25), NBA All-Star Recruits (26-35), and NBA All-Star Flashbacks (36-40).
COMP. FACT SET (40) 5.00 12.00
*GOLD: 1.5X TO 4X BASE HI
1 Nate Archibald .08 .25
2 Elgin Baylor .15 .40
3 Wilt Chamberlain .40 1.00
4 Dave Cowens .08 .25
5 Walt Frazier .08 .25
6 George Gervin .15 .40
7 John Havlicek .25 .60
8 Elvin Hayes .10 .30
9 Oscar Robertson .25 .60
10 Jerry West .30 .75
11 Charles Barkley .25 .60
12 Brad Daugherty .08 .25
13 Clyde Drexler .20 .50
14 Patrick Ewing .20 .50
15 Michael Jordan 1.25 3.00
16 Karl Malone .20 .50
17 Moses Malone .08 .25
18 Chris Mullin .08 .25
19 Hakeem Olajuwon .20 .50
20 Robert Parish .08 .25
21 David Robinson .20 .50
22 John Stockton .20 .50
23 Isiah Thomas .08 .25
24 Dominique Wilkins .08 .25
25 James Worthy .10 .30
26 Kenny Anderson .08 .25
27 Stacey Augmon .08 .25
28 Derrick Coleman .08 .25
29 Larry Johnson .10 .30
30 Christian Laettner .25 .60
31 Harold Miner .08 .25
32 Alonzo Mourning .50 1.25
33 Dikembe Mutombo .08 .25
34 Shaquille O'Neal 1.25 3.00
35 Steve Smith .08 .25
36 Larry Nance .08 .25
37 Larry Bird .40 1.00
38 Tom Chambers MVP .08 .25
39 Karl Malone .15 .40
John Stockton
40 Charles Barkley MVP .25 .60

2011 Upper Deck All Time Greats

STATED PRINT RUN 50 TO 80 SER.#'d SETS
UNPRICED GOLD PRINT RUN 5 SETS
1 Michael Jordan/80 12.00 30.00
2 Michael Jordan/80 12.00 30.00
3 Michael Jordan/80 12.00 30.00
4 Michael Jordan/80 12.00 30.00
5 Michael Jordan/80 12.00 30.00
6 Michael Jordan/80 12.00 30.00
7 Michael Jordan/80 12.00 30.00
8 Michael Jordan/80 12.00 30.00
9 Michael Jordan/80 12.00 30.00
10 Michael Jordan/80 12.00 30.00
11 Michael Jordan/80 12.00 30.00
12 Michael Jordan/80 12.00 30.00
13 Michael Jordan/80 12.00 30.00
14 Michael Jordan/80 12.00 30.00
15 Michael Jordan/80 12.00 30.00
16 Michael Jordan/80 12.00 30.00
17 Michael Jordan/80 12.00 30.00
18 Michael Jordan/80 12.00 30.00
19 Michael Jordan/80 12.00 30.00
20 Michael Jordan/80 12.00 30.00
21 Michael Jordan/80 12.00 30.00
22 Michael Jordan/80 12.00 30.00
23 Michael Jordan/80 12.00 30.00
24 Michael Jordan/80 12.00 30.00
25 LeBron James/50 10.00 25.00
26 LeBron James/50 10.00 25.00
27 LeBron James/50 10.00 25.00
28 LeBron James/50 10.00 25.00
29 LeBron James/50 10.00 25.00
30 LeBron James/50 10.00 25.00
31 LeBron James/50 10.00 25.00
32 LeBron James/50 10.00 25.00
33 LeBron James/50 10.00 25.00
34 LeBron James/50 10.00 25.00
35 LeBron James/50 10.00 25.00
36 LeBron James/50 10.00 25.00
37 LeBron James/50 10.00 25.00
38 LeBron James/50 10.00 25.00
39 LeBron James/50 10.00 25.00
40 LeBron James/50 10.00 25.00
41 LeBron James/50 10.00 25.00
42 LeBron James/50 10.00 25.00
43 LeBron James/50 10.00 25.00
44 LeBron James/50 10.00 25.00
45 Steve Nash/50 2.50 6.00
46 Steve Nash/50 2.50 6.00
47 Steve Nash/50 2.50 6.00
48 Steve Nash/50 2.50 6.00
49 James Worthy/50 4.00 10.00
50 James Worthy/50 4.00 10.00
51 James Worthy/50 4.00 10.00
52 James Worthy/50 4.00 10.00
53 James Worthy/50 4.00 10.00
54 James Worthy/50 4.00 10.00
55 James Worthy/50 4.00 10.00
56 James Worthy/50 4.00 10.00
57 James Worthy/50 4.00 10.00
58 James Worthy/50 4.00 10.00
59 John Havlicek/50 2.50 6.00
60 John Havlicek/50 2.50 6.00
61 John Havlicek/50 2.50 6.00
62 David Robinson/50 4.00 10.00
63 David Robinson/50 4.00 10.00
64 David Robinson/50 4.00 10.00
65 David Robinson/50 4.00 10.00
66 David Robinson/50 4.00 10.00
67 David Robinson/50 4.00 10.00
68 David Robinson/50 4.00 10.00
69 David Robinson/50 4.00 10.00
70 David Robinson/50 4.00 10.00
71 David Robinson/50 4.00 10.00
72 Bill Russell/50 5.00 12.00
73 Bill Russell/50 5.00 12.00
74 Bill Russell/50 5.00 12.00
75 Bill Russell/50 5.00 12.00
76 Bill Russell/50 5.00 12.00
77 Alonzo Mourning/50 5.00 12.00
78 Alonzo Mourning/50 5.00 12.00
79 Alonzo Mourning/50 5.00 12.00
80 Alonzo Mourning/50 5.00 12.00
81 Alonzo Mourning/50 5.00 12.00
82 Alonzo Mourning/50 5.00 12.00
83 Alonzo Mourning/50 5.00 12.00
84 Alonzo Mourning/50 5.00 12.00
85 Alonzo Mourning/50 5.00 12.00
86 Alonzo Mourning/50 5.00 12.00
87 Alonzo Mourning/50 5.00 12.00
88 Alonzo Mourning/50 5.00 12.00
89 Alonzo Mourning/50 5.00 12.00
90 Alonzo Mourning/50 5.00 12.00
91 Alonzo Mourning/50 5.00 12.00
92 Hakeem Olajuwon/50 4.00 10.00
93 Hakeem Olajuwon/50 4.00 10.00
94 Hakeem Olajuwon/50 4.00 10.00
95 Hakeem Olajuwon/50 4.00 10.00
96 Hakeem Olajuwon/50 4.00 10.00
97 Hakeem Olajuwon/50 4.00 10.00
98 Hakeem Olajuwon/50 4.00 10.00
99 Walt Frazier/50 2.50 6.00
100 Walt Frazier/50 2.50 6.00
101 Walt Frazier/50 2.50 6.00
102 Walt Frazier/50 2.50 6.00
103 Walt Frazier/50 2.50 6.00
104 Julius Erving/50 4.00 10.00
105 Julius Erving/50 4.00 10.00
106 Julius Erving/50 4.00 10.00
107 Julius Erving/50 4.00 10.00
108 Julius Erving/50 4.00 10.00
109 Larry Bird/50 5.00 12.00
110 Larry Bird/50 5.00 12.00
111 Larry Bird/50 5.00 12.00
112 Larry Bird/50 5.00 12.00
113 Larry Bird/50 5.00 12.00
114 Larry Bird/50 5.00 12.00
115 Larry Bird/50 5.00 12.00
116 Larry Bird/50 5.00 12.00
117 Larry Bird/50 5.00 12.00
118 Larry Bird/50 5.00 12.00
119 Larry Bird/50 5.00 12.00
120 Larry Bird/50 5.00 12.00
121 Larry Bird/50 5.00 12.00
122 Larry Bird/50 5.00 12.00
123 Larry Bird/50 5.00 12.00
124 Derrick Rose/50 6.00 15.00
125 Derrick Rose/50 6.00 15.00
126 Derrick Rose/50 6.00 15.00
127 Derrick Rose/50 6.00 15.00
128 Derrick Rose/50 6.00 15.00
129 Clyde Drexler/50 4.00 10.00
130 Clyde Drexler/50 4.00 10.00
131 Clyde Drexler/50 4.00 10.00
132 Clyde Drexler/50 4.00 10.00
133 Clyde Drexler/50 4.00 10.00
134 Clyde Drexler/50 4.00 10.00
135 Clyde Drexler/50 4.00 10.00
136 Clyde Drexler/50 4.00 10.00
137 Magic Johnson/50 5.00 12.00
138 Magic Johnson/50 5.00 12.00
139 Magic Johnson/50 5.00 12.00
140 Magic Johnson/50 5.00 12.00
141 Magic Johnson/50 5.00 12.00
142 Magic Johnson/50 5.00 12.00
143 Magic Johnson/50 5.00 12.00
144 Magic Johnson/50 5.00 12.00
145 Magic Johnson/50 5.00 12.00
146 Magic Johnson/50 5.00 12.00
147 Magic Johnson/50 5.00 12.00
148 Magic Johnson/50 5.00 12.00
149 Magic Johnson/50 5.00 12.00
150 Magic Johnson/50 5.00 12.00
151 Magic Johnson/50 5.00 12.00
152 Larry Johnson/50 4.00 10.00
153 Larry Johnson/50 4.00 10.00
154 Larry Johnson/50 4.00 10.00
155 Larry Johnson/50 4.00 10.00
156 Larry Johnson/50 4.00 10.00
157 Larry Johnson/50 4.00 10.00
158 Larry Johnson/50 4.00 10.00
159 Larry Johnson/50 4.00 10.00
160 Larry Johnson/50 4.00 10.00
161 Larry Johnson/50 4.00 10.00
162 Grant Hill/50 10.00 25.00
163 Grant Hill/50 10.00 25.00
164 Grant Hill/50 10.00 25.00
165 Grant Hill/50 10.00 25.00
166 Grant Hill/50 10.00 25.00
167 Grant Hill/50 10.00 25.00
168 Grant Hill/50 10.00 25.00
169 Grant Hill/50 10.00 25.00
170 Grant Hill/50 10.00 25.00
171 Grant Hill/50 10.00 25.00
172 Chris Paul/50 2.50 6.00
173 Chris Paul/50 2.50 6.00
174 Chris Paul/50 2.50 6.00
175 Chris Paul/50 2.50 6.00
176 Chris Paul/50 2.50 6.00
177 Chris Paul/50 2.50 6.00
178 Chris Paul/50 2.50 6.00
179 Chris Paul/50 2.50 6.00
180 Chris Paul/50 2.50 6.00
181 Chris Paul/50 2.50 6.00
182 Chris Paul/50 2.50 6.00
183 Chris Paul/50 2.50 6.00
184 Chris Paul/50 2.50 6.00
185 Chris Paul/50 2.50 6.00
186 Chris Paul/50 2.50 6.00
187 Jerry West/50 4.00 10.00
188 Jerry West/50 4.00 10.00
189 Jerry West/50 4.00 10.00
190 Anfernee Hardaway/50 10.00 25.00
191 Anfernee Hardaway/50 10.00 25.00
192 Anfernee Hardaway/50 10.00 25.00
193 Anfernee Hardaway/50 10.00 25.00
194 Anfernee Hardaway/50 10.00 25.00
195 Anfernee Hardaway/50 10.00 25.00
196 Anfernee Hardaway/50 10.00 25.00
197 Anfernee Hardaway/50 10.00 25.00
198 Anfernee Hardaway/50 10.00 25.00
199 Anfernee Hardaway/50 10.00 25.00
200 Anfernee Hardaway/50 10.00 25.00

2011 Upper Deck All Time Greats Career Book Card Autographs

STATED PRINT RUN ONE TO 15 SER.#'d SETS
SOME UNPRICED DUE TO SCARCITY
SCCP1 Chris Paul/15 40.00 100.00
SCCP2 Chris Paul/15 40.00 100.00
SCMJ1 Michael Jordan/15 400.00 700.00
SCMJ2 Michael Jordan/15 400.00 700.00
SCMJ3 Michael Jordan/15 400.00 700.00
SCRO1 Derrick Rose/15 150.00 350.00

2011 Upper Deck All Time Greats Illustrious Signatures

STATED PRINT RUN 3 TO 15 SER.#'d SETS
SOME UNPRICED DUE TO SCARCITY
UNPRICED PARALLEL PRINT RUN ONE SET
ISAM1 Alonzo Mourning/15 40.00 100.00
ISAM2 Alonzo Mourning/15 40.00 100.00
ISAM3 Alonzo Mourning/15 40.00 100.00
ISAM4 Alonzo Mourning/15 40.00 100.00
ISCD1 Clyde Drexler/10 50.00 120.00
ISCD2 Clyde Drexler/10 50.00 120.00
ISCD3 Clyde Drexler/10 50.00 120.00
ISCD4 Clyde Drexler/10 50.00 120.00
ISCD5 Clyde Drexler/10 50.00 120.00
ISCD6 Clyde Drexler/10 50.00 120.00
ISCP1 Chris Paul/10 30.00 80.00
ISCP2 Chris Paul/10 30.00 80.00
ISCP3 Chris Paul/10 30.00 80.00
ISCP4 Chris Paul/10 30.00 80.00
ISCP5 Chris Paul/10 30.00 80.00
ISCP6 Chris Paul/10 30.00 80.00
ISCP7 Chris Paul/10 30.00 80.00
ISDR1 David Robinson/10 40.00 100.00
ISDR2 David Robinson/10 40.00 100.00
ISDR3 David Robinson/10 40.00 100.00
ISDR4 David Robinson/10 40.00 100.00
ISDR5 David Robinson/10 40.00 100.00
ISDR6 David Robinson/10 40.00 100.00
ISGH1 Grant Hill/10 100.00 250.00
ISGH2 Grant Hill/10 100.00 250.00
ISGH3 Grant Hill/10 100.00 250.00
ISGH4 Grant Hill/10 100.00 250.00
ISGH5 Grant Hill/10 100.00 250.00
ISJA1 LeBron James/15 125.00 225.00
ISJA2 LeBron James/15 125.00 225.00
ISJA3 LeBron James/15 125.00 225.00
ISJA4 LeBron James/15 125.00 225.00
ISJA5 LeBron James/15 125.00 225.00
ISJA6 LeBron James/15 125.00 225.00
ISJA7 LeBron James/15 125.00 225.00
ISJA8 LeBron James/15 125.00 225.00
ISJO1 Magic Johnson/15 50.00 120.00
ISJO2 Magic Johnson/15 50.00 120.00
ISJO3 Magic Johnson/15 50.00 120.00
ISJO4 Magic Johnson/15 50.00 120.00
ISJO5 Magic Johnson/15 50.00 120.00
ISJW1 James Worthy/10 30.00 80.00
ISJW2 James Worthy/10 30.00 80.00
ISJW3 James Worthy/10 30.00 80.00
ISJW4 James Worthy/10 30.00 80.00
ISJW5 James Worthy/10 30.00 80.00
ISJW6 James Worthy/10 30.00 80.00
ISLB1 Larry Bird/15 50.00 120.00
ISLB2 Larry Bird/15 50.00 120.00
ISLB3 Larry Bird/15 50.00 120.00
ISLB4 Larry Bird/15 50.00 120.00
ISLB5 Larry Bird/15 50.00 120.00
ISLB6 Larry Bird/15 50.00 120.00
ISLJ1 Larry Johnson/10 30.00 80.00
ISLJ2 Larry Johnson/10 30.00 80.00
ISLJ3 Larry Johnson/10 30.00 80.00
ISLJ4 Larry Johnson/10 30.00 80.00
ISLJ5 Larry Johnson/10 30.00 80.00
ISMJ1 Michael Jordan/15 300.00 600.00
ISMJ2 Michael Jordan/15 300.00 600.00
ISMJ3 Michael Jordan/15 300.00 600.00
ISMJ4 Michael Jordan/15 300.00 600.00
ISMJ5 Michael Jordan/15 300.00 600.00
ISMJ6 Michael Jordan/15 300.00 600.00
ISMJ7 Michael Jordan/15 300.00 600.00
ISMJ8 Michael Jordan/15 300.00 600.00
ISMJ9 Michael Jordan/15 300.00 600.00
ISMJ10 Michael Jordan/15 300.00 600.00

2011 Upper Deck All Time Greats Lettermen Autographs

STATED PRINT RUN 12 TO 80 SER.#'d SETS
PRINT RUNS BASED ON LAST NAME
TOTAL PRINT RUN LISTED WITH ASTERISK
LAH Anfernee Hardaway 75.00 200.00
Serial 10, Print Run 80
LAM Alonzo Mourning 60.00 150.00
Serial 10, Print Run 80
LBR Bill Russell 100.00 200.00
Serial 3, Print Run 21
LCD Clyde Drexler 75.00 150.00
Serial 3, Print Run 21
LCP Chris Paul 75.00 150.00
Serial 5, Print Run 20
LDR David Robinson 75.00 200.00
Serial 3, Print Run 24
LGH Grant Hill 175.00 350.00
Serial 3, Print Run 12
LHO Hakeem Olajuwon 75.00 150.00
Serial 4, Print Run 32
LJA LeBron James 200.00 400.00
Serial 5, Print Run 25
LJE Julius Erving 80.00 200.00
Serial 3, Print Run 18
LJH John Havlicek 30.00 80.00
Serial 3, Print Run 24
LJO Magic Johnson 75.00 200.00
Serial 3, Print Run 21
LJW James Worthy 50.00 125.00
Serial 4, Print Run 24
LLB Larry Bird 75.00 200.00
Serial 10, Print Run 40
LLJ Larry Johnson 75.00 200.00
Serial 5, Print Run 35
LMJ Michael Jordan 600.00 1000.00
Serial 5, Print Run 30
LRO Derrick Rose 100.00 200.00
Serial 5, Print Run 20
LSN Steve Nash 50.00 120.00
Serial 5, Print Run 20
LWE Jerry West 50.00 120.00
Serial 3, Print Run 12
LWF Walt Frazier 60.00 150.00
Serial 3, Print Run 21

2011 Upper Deck All Time Greats Signatures

STATED PRINT RUN 5 TO 25 SER.#'d SETS
SOME UNPRICED DUE TO SCARCITY
UNPRICED GOLD PRINT RUN ONE SET
UNPRICED SILVER PRINT RUN 3 TO 10 SETS
AGSAH1 Anfernee Hardaway/15 50.00 120.00
AGSAH2 Anfernee Hardaway/15 50.00 120.00
AGSAH3 Anfernee Hardaway/15 50.00 120.00
AGSAH4 Anfernee Hardaway/15 50.00 120.00
AGSAM1 Alonzo Mourning/10 60.00 150.00
AGSAM2 Alonzo Mourning/10 60.00 150.00
AGSAM3 Alonzo Mourning/10 60.00 150.00
AGSAM4 Alonzo Mourning/10 60.00 150.00
AGSAM5 Alonzo Mourning/10 60.00 150.00
AGSAM6 Alonzo Mourning/10 60.00 150.00
AGSCP1 Chris Paul/10 40.00 100.00
AGSCP2 Chris Paul/10 40.00 100.00
AGSCP3 Chris Paul/10 40.00 100.00
AGSCP4 Chris Paul/10 40.00 100.00
AGSCP5 Chris Paul/10 40.00 100.00
AGSCP6 Chris Paul/10 40.00 100.00
AGSCP7 Chris Paul/10 40.00 100.00
AGSDR1 David Robinson/15 50.00 120.00
AGSDR2 David Robinson/15 50.00 120.00
AGSDR3 David Robinson/15 50.00 120.00
AGSDR4 David Robinson/15 50.00 120.00
AGSGH1 Grant Hill/10 100.00 225.00
AGSGH2 Grant Hill/10 100.00 225.00
AGSGH3 Grant Hill/10 100.00 225.00
AGSGH4 Grant Hill/10 100.00 225.00
AGSGH5 Grant Hill/10 100.00 225.00
AGSHO1 Hakeem Olajuwon/10 40.00 100.00
AGSHO2 Hakeem Olajuwon/10 40.00 100.00
AGSHO3 Hakeem Olajuwon/10 40.00 100.00
AGSHO4 Hakeem Olajuwon/10 40.00 100.00
AGSJA1 LeBron James/15 125.00 225.00
AGSJA2 LeBron James/15 125.00 225.00
AGSJA3 LeBron James/15 125.00 225.00
AGSJA4 LeBron James/15 125.00 225.00
AGSJA5 LeBron James/15 125.00 225.00
AGSJA6 LeBron James/15 125.00 225.00
AGSJA7 LeBron James/15 125.00 225.00
AGSJA8 LeBron James/15 125.00 225.00
AGSJA9 LeBron James/15 125.00 225.00
AGSJO1 Magic Johnson/15 50.00 120.00
AGSJO2 Magic Johnson/15 50.00 120.00
AGSJO3 Magic Johnson/15 50.00 120.00
AGSJO4 Magic Johnson/15 50.00 120.00
AGSJO5 Magic Johnson/15 50.00 120.00
AGSJO6 Magic Johnson/15 50.00 120.00
AGSJO7 Magic Johnson/15 50.00 120.00
AGSJW1 James Worthy/10 30.00 80.00
AGSJW2 James Worthy/10 30.00 80.00
AGSJW3 James Worthy/10 30.00 80.00
AGSJW4 James Worthy/10 30.00 80.00
AGSLB1 Larry Bird/15 60.00 150.00
AGSLB2 Larry Bird/15 60.00 150.00
AGSLB3 Larry Bird/15 60.00 150.00
AGSLB4 Larry Bird/15 60.00 150.00
AGSLB5 Larry Bird/15 60.00 150.00
AGSLJ1 Larry Johnson/10 40.00 100.00
AGSLJ2 Larry Johnson/10 40.00 100.00
AGSLJ3 Larry Johnson/10 40.00 100.00
AGSLJ4 Larry Johnson/10 40.00 100.00
AGSMJ1 Michael Jordan/25 300.00 550.00
AGSMJ2 Michael Jordan/25 300.00 550.00
AGSMJ3 Michael Jordan/25 300.00 550.00
AGSMJ4 Michael Jordan/25 300.00 550.00
AGSMJ5 Michael Jordan/25 300.00 550.00
AGSMJ6 Michael Jordan/25 300.00 550.00
AGSMJ7 Michael Jordan/25 300.00 550.00
AGSMJ8 Michael Jordan/25 300.00 550.00
AGSMJ9 Michael Jordan/25 300.00 550.00
AGSJA10 LeBron James/15 125.00 225.00
AGSMJ10 Michael Jordan/25 300.00 550.00
AGSMJ11 Michael Jordan/25 300.00 550.00
AGSMJ12 Michael Jordan/25 300.00 550.00

1996 Upper Deck Authenticated Space Jam Celcards

Released in two separate matching collections, these celcards were produced by Upper Deck Authenticated and feature pieces from the 1996 Space Jam movie. Set number one contains four-cards with matching numbers 1-5,000. Set number two contains two-cards with matching numbers 5,001-10,000. The cels are not numbered, but listed in order of the sets, with the first four cards representing set one, and the final two representing set two.
COMPLETE SET 1 (4) 30.00 80.00
COMPLETE SET 2 (2) 15.00 40.00
NNO Michael Jordan 8.00 20.00
Bugs Bunny
NNO Michael Jordan 8.00 20.00
Bugs Bunny #2
NNO Michael Jordan 8.00 20.00
Monstar
NNO Michael Jordan 8.00 20.00
The Tune Squad
NNO Michael Jordan 8.00 20.00
Bugs Bunny
NNO Michael Jordan 8.00 20.00
Porky Pig

1995-96 Upper Deck Ball Park Jordan

This 5-card standard size set was available as a mail-in offer from Ball Park hot dogs by sending in two UPCs and one dollar. The card fronts have color action photos (with jersey number and logos airbrushed out) within a U.S. flag border. Michael Jordan's name is below the photo in a transparent font. Ball Park and Upper Deck logos adorn the top. The backs have the same U.S. flag background with some biographical information below the same, but smaller, color action photo. His name appears again in the same font vertically on the left side. The traditional Upper Deck hologram resides in the bottom right corner. The cards are numbered with the prefix BP.
COMPLETE SET (5) 15.00 40.00
COMMON CARD (1-5) 4.00 10.00

1995-96 Upper Deck Ball Park Jordan Gold

This 5-card standard size set was available as a mail-in offer from Ball Park hot dogs by sending in four UPCs and one dollar. The offer was only made available once you received the base set redemption. The card fronts have color action photos (with jersey number and logos airbrushed out) within a gold, foil-etched border. Michael Jordan's name is embossed in the gold border below the photo. Ball Park and Upper Deck logos adorn the top. The traditional Upper Deck hologram resides in the bottom right corner. The cards are numbered with the prefix BP.
COMPLETE SET (5) 24.00 60.00
COMMON CARD (1-5) 6.00 15.00

1996-97 Upper Deck Ball Park Jordan

These Michael Jordan tribute cards were available one per limited edition Ball Park hot dog package. The fronts have color action shots or close-ups of Jordan, a Ball Park logo in the top left corner and "Michael" written in large block letters vertically on the right side. The backs contain half of the same photo as the front and a small blurb describing the indescribable player. The Upper Deck logo and hologram are found at the bottom. A gold version, listed separately, was also available as a redemption offer with 4 UPC codes.
COMPLETE SET (5) 10.00 25.00
COMMON CARD (1-5) 2.50 6.00

1996-97 Upper Deck Ball Park Jordan Gold

This set is a gold bordered version of the base set from the same year. The set was available by sending in four UPC's from Ball Park hot dogs. The five Michael Jordan cards are numbered "x/5" on the back.
COMPLETE SET (5) 12.00 30.00
COMMON CARD (1-5) 3.00 8.00

1999 Upper Deck Century Legends

Released as a 89-card set, this set focuses on the best basketball athletes of the century. The cards were released in 5-card packs with a suggested retail price of $4.99. The set featues the top 50 players by The Sporting News, 30 21st Century Phenom cards and 10 Michael Jordan Player of the Century cards. Card number six does not exist. Please note that card "S1" was given out to dealers and members of the hobby press as a promotional card.
COMPLETE SET (89) 20.00 40.00
1 Michael Jordan 2.00 5.00
2 Bill Russell .40 1.00
3 Wilt Chamberlain .50 1.25
4 George Mikan .40 1.00
5 Oscar Robertson .30 .75
7 Larry Bird .75 2.00
8 Karl Malone .30 .75
9 Elgin Baylor .25 .60
10 Kareem Abdul-Jabbar .40 1.00
11 Jerry West .30 .75
12 Bob Cousy .40 1.00
13 Julius Erving .50 1.25
14 Hakeem Olajuwon .30 .75
15 John Havlicek .30 .75
16 John Stockton .30 .75
17 Rick Barry .25 .60
18 Moses Malone .25 .60
19 Nate Thurmond .25 .60
20 Bob Pettit .25 .60
21 Pete Maravich .75 2.00
22 Willis Reed .25 .60
23 Isiah Thomas .25 .60
24 Dolph Schayes .25 .60
25 Walt Frazier .25 .60
26 Wes Unseld .25 .60
27 Bill Sharman .25 .60
28 George Gervin .25 .60
29 Hal Greer .25 .60
30 Dave DeBusschere .25 .60
31 Earl Monroe .25 .60
32 Kevin McHale .30 .75
33 Charles Barkley .30 .75
34 Elvin Hayes .25 .60
35 Scottie Pippen .40 1.00
36 Jerry Lucas .25 .60
37 Dave Bing .25 .60
38 Lenny Wilkens .25 .60
39 Paul Arizin .25 .60
40 Nate Archibald .25 .60
41 James Worthy .30 .75
42 Patrick Ewing .30 .75
43 Billy Cunningham .25 .60
44 Sam Jones .30 .75
45 Dave Cowens .25 .60
46 Robert Parish .25 .60
47 Bill Walton .25 .60
48 Shaquille O'Neal .60 1.50
49 David Robinson .40 1.00
50 Dominique Wilkins .30 .75
51 Kobe Bryant 1.25 3.00
52 Vince Carter .50 1.25
53 Paul Pierce .40 1.00
54 Allen Iverson .50 1.25
55 Stephon Marbury .20 .50
56 Mike Bibby .25 .60
57 Jason Williams .30 .75
58 Kevin Garnett .50 1.25
59 Tim Duncan .50 1.25
60 Antawn Jamison .25 .60
61 Antoine Walker .25 .60
62 Shareef Abdur-Rahim .20 .50
63 Michael Olowokandi .15 .40
64 Robert Traylor .15 .40
65 Keith Van Horn .20 .50
66 Shaquille O'Neal .60 1.50
67 Ray Allen .25 .60
68 Gary Payton .25 .60
69 Raef LaFrentz .15 .40
70 Grant Hill .30 .75
71 Anfernee Hardaway .40 1.00
72 Maurice Taylor .15 .40
73 Ron Mercer .20 .50
74 Michael Finley .25 .60
75 Jason Kidd .40 1.00
76 Allan Houston .20 .50
77 Damon Stoudamire .20 .50
78 Antonio McDyess .20 .50
79 Eddie Jones .25 .60
80 Michael Dickerson .15 .40
81 Michael Jordan 1.25 3.00
82 Michael Jordan 1.25 3.00
83 Michael Jordan 1.25 3.00
84 Michael Jordan 1.25 3.00
85 Michael Jordan 1.25 3.00
86 Michael Jordan 1.25 3.00
87 Michael Jordan 1.25 3.00
88 Michael Jordan 1.25 3.00
89 Michael Jordan 1.25 3.00
90 Michael Jordan 1.25 3.00
S1 Michael Jordan PROMO 2.00 5.00

1999 Upper Deck Century Legends Century Collection

Randomly inserted in packs, this 89-card set parallels the base set. The cards feature a die cut design and sequential numbering to 100. Card number six does not exist.
COMMON MJ (81-90) 60.00 150.00
*STARS: 15X TO 40X BASE CARD HI
1 Michael Jordan 200.00 400.00
51 Kobe Bryant 200.00 400.00

1999 Upper Deck Century Legends All-Century Team

Randomly inserted in packs at one in 11, this set features the top ten player's of all time as selected by Upper Deck. Card backs carry an "A" prefix.
COMPLETE SET (12) 20.00 40.00
A1 Michael Jordan 8.00 20.00
A2 Oscar Robertson 1.25 3.00
A3 Wilt Chamberlain 2.00 5.00
A4 Larry Bird 3.00 8.00
A5 Julius Erving 2.00 5.00
A6 Jerry West 1.25 3.00
A7 Charles Barkley 1.25 3.00
A8 John Stockton 1.25 3.00
A9 Hakeem Olajuwon 1.25 3.00
A10 Karl Malone 1.25 3.00
A11 Scottie Pippen 1.50 4.00
A12 David Robinson 1.50 4.00

1999 Upper Deck Century Legends Epic Milestones

Randomly inserted in packs at one in 11, this 12-card set showcases ten of the most impressive milestones ever achieved in pro basketball history. Card backs carry an "EM" prefix.
COMPLETE SET (12) 20.00 40.00
EM1 Michael Jordan 8.00 20.00
EM2 Jerry West 1.25 3.00
EM3 John Stockton 1.25 3.00
EM4 Wilt Chamberlain 2.00 5.00
EM5 Julius Erving 2.00 5.00
EM6 Reggie Miller 1.00 2.50
EM7 Hakeem Olajuwon 1.25 3.00
EM8 Robert Parish 1.00 2.50
EM9 Kobe Bryant 5.00 12.00
EM10 Rick Barry 1.00 2.50
EM11 Patrick Ewing 1.25 3.00
EM12 Charles Barkley 1.25 3.00

1999 Upper Deck Century Legends Epic Signatures

Randomly inserted in packs at one in 23, this 32-card set features autographs from some of the greatest stars of the 20th century. The cards are numbered by the player's name initials. Hakeem Olajuwon was issued a trade card, but did not end up signing for the set. Upper Deck sent Allen Iverson cards for Olajuwon.
AE Alex English 8.00 20.00
AI Allen Iverson 125.00 250.00
BC Bob Cousy 25.00 60.00
BL Bob Lanier 10.00 25.00
BP Bob Pettit 15.00 40.00
BR Bill Russell 350.00 650.00
BS Bill Sharman 10.00 25.00
BW Bill Walton 15.00 40.00
CD Clyde Drexler 20.00 50.00
DC Dave Cowens 10.00 25.00
DR Julius Erving 200.00 400.00
DT David Thompson 8.00 20.00
EB Elgin Baylor 12.50 30.00
EH Elvin Hayes 10.00 25.00
EM Earl Monroe 15.00 40.00
GG George Gervin 15.00 30.00
JL Jerry Lucas 8.00 20.00
JW Jerry West 25.00 60.00
KA Kareem Abdul-Jabbar 75.00 150.00
LB Larry Bird 250.00 500.00
MB Mike Bibby 8.00 20.00
MM Moses Malone 12.50 30.00
MO Michael Olowokandi 8.00 20.00
NA Nate Archibald 8.00 20.00
OR Oscar Robertson 40.00 100.00
TH Tim Hardaway 12.00 30.00
WC Wilt Chamberlain 1500.00 2200.00
WF Walt Frazier 10.00 25.00
WR Willis Reed 12.50 30.00
WU Wes Unseld 8.00 20.00
JH John Havlicek 15.00 40.00

1999 Upper Deck Century Legends Epic Signatures Century

Randomly inserted in packs, this 33-card set parallels the Epic Signatures insert set. The cards are serially numbered to 100 with the following exceptions: Bill Russell (6), Julius Erving (6), Larry Bird (33) and Michael Jordan (23).
*CENTURY: .75X TO 2X HI COLUMN
AI Allen Iverson/100 400.00 700.00
BC Bob Cousy/100 40.00 100.00
BL Bob Lanier/100 25.00 60.00
BW Bill Walton/100 40.00 100.00
LB Larry Bird/33 400.00 800.00
MJ Michael Jordan/23 1500.00 3000.00
WC Wilt Chamberlain/100 2500.00 3800.00

1999 Upper Deck Century Legends Generations

Randomly inserted in packs at one in four, this 12-card set features double-sided cards of a modern NBA star coupled with an NBA legend. The cards carry a "G" prefix.
COMPLETE SET (12) 12.50 30.00
G1 Michael Jordan 5.00 12.00
Julius Erving
G2 Kobe Bryant 5.00 12.00
Michael Jordan
G3 Shaquille O'Neal 1.50 4.00
Wilt Chamberlain
G4 Jason Williams 2.00 5.00
Pete Maravich
G5 Stephon Marbury .60 1.50
Nate Archibald
G6 Antoine Walker .75 2.00
Karl Malone
G7 Grant Hill .75 2.00
George Gervin
G8 Gary Payton .60 1.50
Isiah Thomas
G9 Kevin Garnett 1.25 3.00
Dominique Wilkins
G10 Hakeem Olajuwon .75 2.00
Moses Malone
G11 Keith Van Horn 2.00 5.00
Larry Bird
G12 Vince Carter 1.25 3.00
Oscar Robertson

1999 Upper Deck Century Legends Jerseys of the Century

Randomly inserted in packs at one in 475, this eight-card set features authentic jersey swatches from current and legendary NBA players. In addition, two autographed Game Jersey cards were available, Julius Erving and Kareem Abdul-Jabbar. Those cards are priced at the end of the set.
CD Clyde Drexler 20.00 50.00
DR Julius Erving 40.00 100.00
JS John Stockton 20.00 50.00
KA Kareem Abdul-Jabbar 40.00 80.00
KM Karl Malone 15.00 40.00
LB Larry Bird 30.00 80.00
MJ Michael Jordan 350.00 700.00
SO Shaquille O'Neal 30.00 80.00
KAA Kareem Abdul-Jabbar AU/33 150.00 300.00

1999 Upper Deck Century Legends MJ's Most Memorable Shots

Randomly inserted in packs at one in 23, this six-card set features highlights of the most unforgettable shots of Jordan's career. Card backs feature a "MJ" prefix.
COMPLETE SET (6) 20.00 50.00
COMMON CARD (MJ1-MJ6) 4.00 10.00

2000 Upper Deck Century Legends

Released in June 2000, this 90-card set was issued in five-card packs that carried a suggested retail price of $4.99. The base card consisted of 50 regular players plus three subsets that include: History of the Dunk (20 cards), All Upper Deck Team (10 cards) and Jordan - The Best (10 cards).
COMPLETE SET (90) 10.00 25.00
1 Michael Jordan 2.00 5.00
2 Magic Johnson .75 2.00
3 Larry Bird .75 2.00
4 Bob Cousy .40 1.00
5 Bill Russell .40 1.00
6 Julius Erving .50 1.25
7 Nate Archibald .25 .60
8 Oscar Robertson .30 .75
9 Elgin Baylor .25 .60
10 Jo Jo White .25 .60
11 Hal Greer .25 .60
12 Clyde Drexler .30 .75
13 Wilt Chamberlain .50 1.25
14 Walt Bellamy .25 .60
15 Walt Frazier .25 .60
16 Earl Monroe .25 .60
17 John Havlicek .30 .75
18 George Mikan .50 1.25
19 George Karl .25 .60
20 Tom Heinsohn .25 .60
21 Kareem Abdul-Jabbar .40 1.00
22 Bill Sharman .25 .60
23 Elvin Hayes .25 .60
24 Rick Barry .25 .60
25 Paul Silas .25 .60
26 Mitch Kupchak .25 .60
27 Dave Cowens .25 .60
28 Nate Thurmond .25 .60
29 Dave DeBusschere .25 .60
30 Jerry Lucas .25 .60
31 Bill Walton .25 .60
32 Jerry West .30 .75
33 David Thompson .25 .60
34 Spencer Haywood .25 .60
35 Moses Malone .25 .60
36 Alex English .25 .60
37 Willis Reed .25 .60
38 George Gervin .25 .60
39 Dolph Schayes .25 .60
40 Wes Unseld .25 .60
41 Bob Lanier .25 .60
42 James Worthy .30 .75
43 Maurice Lucas .25 .60
44 Pete Maravich .75 2.00
45 Isiah Thomas .25 .60
46 Robert Parish .25 .60
47 Dominique Wilkins .30 .75
48 Walter Davis .25 .60
49 Bob Pettit .25 .60
50 Kevin McHale .30 .75
51 Julius Erving HD .25 .60
52 Dominique Wilkins HD .15 .40
53 George Gervin HD .12 .30
54 Kareem Abdul-Jabbar HD .20 .50
55 Clyde Drexler HD .15 .40
56 David Thompson HD .12 .30
57 Walter Davis HD .12 .30
58 James Worthy HD .15 .40
59 Moses Malone HD .12 .30
60 Bob Lanier HD .12 .30
61 Robert Parish HD .12 .30
62 Maurice Lucas HD .12 .30
63 Wes Unseld HD .12 .30
64 Ron Boone HD .12 .30
65 Larry Nance HD .12 .30
66 Michael Jordan HD 1.00 2.50
67 Michael Jordan HD 1.00 2.50
68 Michael Jordan HD 1.00 2.50
69 Michael Jordan HD 1.00 2.50
70 Michael Jordan HD 1.00 2.50
71 Michael Jordan UDT 1.00 2.50
72 Wilt Chamberlain UDT .25 .60
73 Magic Johnson UDT .40 1.00
74 Julius Erving UDT .25 .60
75 Larry Bird UDT .40 1.00
76 Bill Russell UDT .20 .50
77 Jerry West UDT .15 .40
78 Oscar Robertson UDT .15 .40
79 John Havlicek UDT .15 .40
80 Elgin Baylor UDT .12 .30
81 Michael Jordan TB 1.00 2.50
82 Michael Jordan TB 1.00 2.50
83 Michael Jordan TB 1.00 2.50
84 Michael Jordan TB 1.00 2.50
85 Michael Jordan TB 1.00 2.50
86 Michael Jordan TB 1.00 2.50
87 Michael Jordan TB 1.00 2.50
88 Michael Jordan TB 1.00 2.50
89 Michael Jordan TB 1.00 2.50
90 Michael Jordan TB 1.00 2.50

2000 Upper Deck Century Legends Commemorative Collection

Randomly inserted in packs, this 90-card set parallels the base set. The cards are serially numbered to 50. To ascertain values on individual cards, please refer to the multiplier in the header, coupled with the value of the base card.
*STARS: 12.5X TO 30X BASE CARD HI
*SUBSETS: 25X TO 60X BASE HI

2000 Upper Deck Century Legends History's Heroes

Randomly inserted in packs at one in 12, this nine-card set features some of the greatest heroes in NBA history. Card backs carry a "HH" prefix.
COMPLETE SET (9) 6.00 15.00
HH1 Michael Jordan 5.00 12.00
HH2 Julius Erving 1.25 3.00
HH3 Larry Bird 2.00 5.00
HH4 Clyde Drexler .75 2.00
HH5 Elgin Baylor .60 1.50
HH6 George Gervin .60 1.50
HH7 Oscar Robertson .75 2.00
HH8 Jerry West .75 2.00
HH9 Alex English .60 1.50

2000 Upper Deck Century Legends Legendary Jerseys

Randomly inserted in packs at one in 288, this 10-card set features swatches of game-used jerseys from NBA Legends. Card backs carry the player's initials. Two jerseys were also autographed, Larry Bird to 33 and Michael Jordan to 23.
*GOLD: 1.5X TO 4X HI
GOLD PRINT RUN 25 SER.#'d SETS
BCJ Bob Cousy 12.00 30.00
CDJ Clyde Drexler 10.00 25.00
DRJ Julius Erving 15.00 40.00
DWJ Dominique Wilkins 10.00 25.00
ITJ Isiah Thomas 8.00 20.00
KAJ Kareem Abdul-Jabbar 12.00 30.00
LBA Larry Bird AU/33 300.00 600.00
LBJ Larry Bird 25.00 60.00
MJA Michael Jordan AU/23 2000.00 3000.00
MJJ Michael Jordan 60.00 150.00
MMJ Moses Malone 8.00 20.00
WCJ Wilt Chamberlain 30.00 80.00

2000 Upper Deck Century Legends Legendary Signatures

Randomly inserted in packs at one in 24, this 41-card set features autographs of vintage players. Card backs are numbered with the player's initials.
AE Alex English 8.00 20.00
BC Bob Cousy 30.00 80.00
BL Bob Lanier 8.00 20.00
BP Bob Pettit 15.00 40.00
BR Bill Russell 150.00 300.00
BS Bill Sharman 8.00 20.00
BW Bill Walton 12.50 30.00
CD Clyde Drexler 30.00 80.00
DC Dave Cowens 10.00 25.00
DD Dave DeBusschere 75.00 150.00
DR Julius Erving 125.00 225.00
DS Dolph Schayes 8.00 20.00
DT David Thompson 8.00 20.00
DW Dominique Wilkins 10.00 25.00
EB Elgin Baylor 10.00 25.00
EH Elvin Hayes 8.00 20.00
EM Earl Monroe 8.00 20.00
GA Gail Goodrich 10.00 25.00
GG George Gervin 8.00 20.00
HG Hal Greer 8.00 20.00
IT Isiah Thomas 20.00 50.00
JA Jamaal Wilkes 8.00 20.00
JH John Havlicek 15.00 40.00
JJ Jo Jo White 10.00 25.00
JL Jerry Lucas 10.00 25.00
JW Jerry West 25.00 60.00
KA Kareem Abdul-Jabbar 40.00 100.00
LB Larry Bird 125.00 250.00
MG Magic Johnson 125.00 250.00
MM Moses Malone 12.50 30.00
NA Nate Archibald 8.00 20.00
NT Nate Thurmond 12.50 30.00
OR Oscar Robertson 50.00 100.00
PA Paul Arizin 10.00 25.00
PS Paul Silas 10.00 25.00
RB Rick Barry 12.50 30.00
SH Spencer Haywood 8.00 20.00
WB Walt Bellamy 10.00 25.00
WF Walt Frazier 10.00 25.00
WR Willis Reed 8.00 20.00
WU Wes Unseld 8.00 20.00

2000 Upper Deck Century Legends Legendary Signatures Gold

Randomly inserted in packs, this 42-card set is a parallel to the Legendary Signatures insert. Each card was serially numbered to 25. To ascertain values on unlisted cards, please refer to the multiplier in the header, coupled with the value of the base insert.
*GOLD: 1.25X TO 3X HI COLUMN
BL Bob Lanier 30.00 80.00
BR Bill Russell 250.00 500.00
DD Dave DeBusschere 125.00 250.00
DR Julius Erving 250.00 500.00
KA Kareem Abdul-Jabbar 150.00 400.00
MG Magic Johnson 250.00 600.00
MJ Michael Jordan 2000.00 3000.00
OR Oscar Robertson 100.00 250.00

2000 Upper Deck Century Legends MJ Final Floor Jumbos

Inserted one per box, this 12-card set features 3" by 5" enlargements of MJ's Final Floor.
COMPLETE SET (12) 150.00 300.00
COMMON CARD (FF1-FF12) 12.00 30.00

2000 Upper Deck Century Legends NBA Originals

Randomly inserted in packs at one in 12, this six-card set features the NBA groundbreakers who invented trademark moves. Card backs carry an "O" prefix.
COMPLETE SET (6) 5.00 12.00
O1 Magic Johnson 1.50 4.00
O2 Julius Erving 1.00 2.50
O3 Michael Jordan 4.00 10.00
O4 David Thompson .50 1.25
O5 Kareem Abdul-Jabbar .75 2.00
O6 Clyde Drexler .60 1.50

2000 Upper Deck Century Legends Players of the Century

Randomly inserted in packs at one in four, this 20-card set featues the some of the finest NBA performances of the past century. Card backs carry a "P" prefix.
COMPLETE SET (20) 10.00 25.00
P1 Michael Jordan 5.00 12.00
P2 Wilt Chamberlain 1.25 3.00
P3 Magic Johnson 2.00 5.00
P4 Larry Bird 2.00 5.00
P5 Bill Russell 1.00 2.50
P6 Jerry West .75 2.00
P7 Oscar Robertson .75 2.00
P8 John Havlicek .75 2.00
P9 Kareem Abdul-Jabbar 1.00 2.50
P10 Pete Maravich 2.00 5.00
P11 Willis Reed .60 1.50
P12 Bob Lanier .60 1.50
P13 George Gervin .60 1.50
P14 Bill Walton .60 1.50
P15 Elvin Hayes .60 1.50
P16 Julius Erving 1.25 3.00
P17 Rick Barry .60 1.50
P18 Walt Frazier .60 1.50
P19 Nate Thurmond .60 1.50
P20 Moses Malone .60 1.50

2000 Upper Deck Century Legends Recollections

Randomly inserted in packs at one in 24, this seven-card set features memorable moments from former NBA stars. Card backs carry a "R" prefix.
COMPLETE SET (7) 8.00 20.00
R1 Michael Jordan 6.00 15.00
R2 Isiah Thomas .75 2.00
R3 Julius Erving 1.50 4.00
R4 Wilt Chamberlain 1.50 4.00
R5 Clyde Drexler 1.00 2.50
R6 Bill Walton .75 2.00
R7 Dominique Wilkins 1.00 2.50

2002-03 Upper Deck Championship Drive

Released in late January 2003, this 155-card set divided up as follows: Numbers 1-100 are base veteran cards, numbers 101-130 are jersey rookie cards sequentially numbered to 400, and numbers 131-155 are rookies sequentially numbered to 500. Championship drive was packaged in 18-pack boxes with five cards per pack and carried a suggested retail price of $4.99. Also inserted at one per box as it's own mini-box were small gold replica NBA Championship trophies. One version was done for each team and another for each of the NBA Champs from 1978-2002.
COMP.SET w/o SP's (100) 15.00 40.00
1 Shareef Abdur-Rahim .30 .75
2 Glenn Robinson .30 .75
3 Jason Terry .30 .75
4 Dion Glover .25 .60
5 Antoine Walker .30 .75
6 Paul Pierce .50 1.25
7 Vin Baker .30 .75
8 Kedrick Brown .25 .60
9 Jalen Rose .30 .75
10 Tyson Chandler .30 .75
11 Eddy Curry .30 .75
12 Darius Miles .25 .60
13 Ricky Davis .30 .75
14 Zydrunas Ilgauskas .30 .75
15 Dirk Nowitzki .60 1.50
16 Michael Finley .40 1.00
17 Steve Nash .50 1.25
18 Raef LaFrentz .25 .60
19 Nick Van Exel .30 .75
20 James Posey .25 .60
21 Juwan Howard .30 .75
22 Chauncey Billups .40 1.00
23 Ben Wallace .40 1.00
24 Richard Hamilton .30 .75
25 Jason Richardson .40 1.00
26 Antawn Jamison .40 1.00
27 Gilbert Arenas .40 1.00
28 Steve Francis .40 1.00
29 Cuttino Mobley .30 .75
30 Eddie Griffin .25 .60
31 Reggie Miller .40 1.00
32 Jermaine O'Neal .40 1.00
33 Jamaal Tinsley .25 .60
34 Ron Mercer .25 .60
35 Elton Brand .40 1.00
36 Andre Miller .30 .75
37 Kobe Bryant 2.00 5.00
38 Shaquille O'Neal 1.00 2.50
39 Rick Fox .30 .75
40 Devean George .25 .60
41 Pau Gasol .50 1.25
42 Shane Battier .40 1.00
43 Jason Williams .30 .75
44 Eddie Jones .30 .75
45 Brian Grant .25 .60
46 Anthony Carter .25 .60
47 Ray Allen .40 1.00
48 Tim Thomas .25 .60
49 Kevin Garnett .75 2.00
50 Terrell Brandon .25 .60
51 Wally Szczerbiak .30 .75
52 Joe Smith .30 .75
53 Jason Kidd .60 1.50
54 Richard Jefferson .40 1.00
55 Dikembe Mutombo .40 1.00
56 Kenyon Martin .40 1.00
57 Baron Davis .40 1.00
58 Jamal Mashburn .30 .75
59 David Wesley .25 .60
60 P.J. Brown .25 .60
61 Courtney Alexander .25 .60
62 Latrell Sprewell .30 .75
63 Allan Houston .30 .75
64 Kurt Thomas .25 .60
65 Antonio McDyess .30 .75
66 Tracy McGrady .60 1.50
67 Mike Miller .40 1.00
68 Grant Hill .50 1.25
69 Allen Iverson .60 1.50
70 Keith Van Horn .30 .75
71 Shawn Marion .40 1.00
72 Stephon Marbury .30 .75
73 Anfernee Hardaway .60 1.50
74 Rasheed Wallace .40 1.00
75 Bonzi Wells .25 .60
76 Scottie Pippen .60 1.50
77 Mike Bibby .40 1.00
78 Peja Stojakovic .40 1.00
79 Chris Webber .40 1.00
80 Hedo Turkoglu .40 1.00
81 Vlade Divac .30 .75
82 Tim Duncan .75 2.00
83 David Robinson .60 1.50
84 Tony Parker .50 1.25
85 Malik Rose .25 .60
86 Gary Payton .40 1.00
87 Rashard Lewis .40 1.00
88 Brent Barry .25 .60
89 Desmond Mason .30 .75
90 Vladimir Radmanovic .25 .60
91 Vince Carter .60 1.50
92 Morris Peterson .25 .60
93 Antonio Davis .25 .60
94 Karl Malone .50 1.25
95 John Stockton .50 1.25
96 Andrei Kirilenko .40 1.00
97 Matt Harpring .30 .75
98 Jerry Stackhouse .30 .75
99 Larry Hughes .30 .75
100 Michael Jordan 3.00 8.00
101 Juan Dixon JSY RC 5.00 12.00
102 Carlos Boozer JSY RC 8.00 20.00
103 Dan Gadzuric JSY RC 4.00 10.00
104 Vincent Yarbrough JSY RC 4.00 10.00
105 Robert Archibald JSY RC 4.00 10.00
106 Roger Mason JSY RC 4.00 10.00
107 Ronald Murray JSY RC 4.00 10.00
108 Chris Jefferies JSY RC 4.00 10.00
109 John Salmons JSY RC 5.00 12.00
110 Predrag Savovic JSY RC 4.00 10.00
111 Tayshaun Prince JSY RC 5.00 12.00
112 Casey Jacobsen JSY RC 4.00 10.00
113 Qyntel Woods JSY RC 4.00 10.00
114 Kareem Rush JSY RC 4.00 10.00
115 Ryan Humphrey JSY RC 4.00 10.00
116 Sam Clancy JSY RC 4.00 10.00
117 Lonny Baxter JSY RC 4.00 10.00
118 Fred Jones JSY RC 4.00 10.00
119 Marcus Haislip JSY RC 4.00 10.00
120 Melvin Ely JSY RC 4.00 10.00
121 Jared Jeffries JSY RC 4.00 10.00
122 Caron Butler JSY RC 6.00 15.00
123 Amare Stoudemire JSY RC 10.00 25.00
124 Chris Wilcox JSY RC 4.00 10.00
125 Nene Hilario JSY RC 5.00 12.00
126 DaJuan Wagner JSY RC 4.00 10.00
127 Nikoloz Tskitishvili JSY RC 4.00 10.00
128 Drew Gooden JSY RC 6.00 15.00
129 Jay Williams JSY RC 5.00 12.00
130 Yao Ming JSY RC 12.00 30.00
131 Manu Ginobili RC 5.00 12.00
132 Efthimios Rentzias RC 2.00 5.00
133 Juaquin Hawkins RC 2.00 5.00
134 Marko Jaric 2.00 5.00
135 Dan Dickau RC 2.00 5.00
136 Frank Williams RC 2.00 5.00
137 Curtis Borchardt RC 2.00 5.00
138 Mike Dunleavy RC 2.50 6.00
139 Smush Parker RC 2.00 5.00
140 Tito Maddox RC 2.00 5.00
141 Jannero Pargo RC 2.00 5.00
142 Jiri Welsch RC 2.00 5.00
143 Bostjan Nachbar RC 2.00 5.00
144 Rasual Butler RC 2.00 5.00
145 Gordan Giricek RC 2.00 5.00
146 Igor Rakocevic RC 2.00 5.00
147 Tamar Slay RC 2.00 5.00
148 Junior Harrington RC 2.00 5.00
149 Nate Huffman RC 2.00 5.00
150 Jamal Sampson RC 2.00 5.00
151 Reggie Evans RC 2.00 5.00
152 Cezary Trybanski RC 2.00 5.00
153 Pat Burke RC 2.00 5.00
154 J.R. Bremer RC 2.00 5.00
155 Mehmet Okur RC 2.00 5.00

2002-03 Upper Deck Championship Drive Parallel

Randomly inserted in packs, this 155-card set parallels the base set enhanced with gold foil highlights where veteran cards are numbered to 125 and rookie cards are numbered to 25.
*STARS: 3X TO 8X BASE CARD HI
*RCs 101-130: 1.5X TO 4X HI
*RCs 131-155: 2.5X TO 6X HI

2002-03 Upper Deck Championship Drive 2 Amazing Jerseys

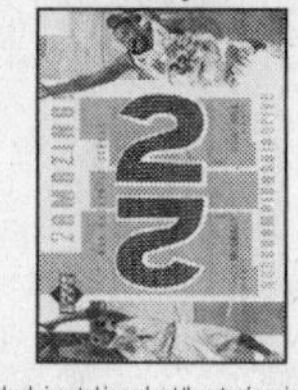

Randomly inserted in packs at the rate of one in 144, this eight card set features a horizontal design with one player on each side and two jerseys in the middle in the shape of the number two.
AIJKJ Allen Iverson 10.00 25.00
Jason Kidd
CWMBJ Chris Webber 8.00 20.00
Mike Bibby
KBJRJ Kobe Bryant 15.00 40.00
Jason Richardson
KGWSJ Kevin Garnett 10.00 25.00
Wally Szczerbiak
MJKBM Michael Jordan 60.00 150.00
Kobe Bryant SP
PPAWJ Paul Pierce 8.00 20.00
Antoine Walker
SMSFJ Stephon Marbury 8.00 20.00
Steve Francis
TMGHJ Tracy McGrady 10.00 25.00
Grant Hill

2002-03 Upper Deck Championship Drive Best of Seven Jersey

Randomly seeded in packs, this seven card set also features a horizontal design with full color player photos on the right set against a white background and a swatch of a game worn jersey on the left. Each card is sequentially numbered to 50.
AIB Allen Iverson 15.00 40.00
JKB Jason Kidd 15.00 40.00
JWB Jay Williams 12.00 30.00
KBB Kobe Bryant 50.00 120.00
MJB Michael Jordan 150.00 300.00
PPB Paul Pierce 12.00 30.00
YMB Yao Ming 30.00 80.00

2002-03 Upper Deck Championship Drive Key Pieces Jersey

Inserted in packs at the rate of one in 96, this 12-card set places a color-scale portrait photo of the player on the far right set to match team colors, a full-color action photo to the left of that and a jersey swatch on the right.
BDKP Baron Davis 3.00 8.00
DNKP Dirk Nowitzki 5.00 12.00
JSKP Jerry Stackhouse 2.50 6.00
KBKP Kobe Bryant SP 12.00 30.00
KGKP Kevin Garnett 6.00 15.00
KMKP Karl Malone 4.00 10.00
MBKP Michael Jordan SP 60.00 150.00
MBKP Mike Bibby 3.00 8.00
PPKP Paul Pierce 4.00 10.00
RAKP Ray Allen 3.00 8.00
SBKP Shane Battier 3.00 8.00
SMKP Stephon Marbury 2.50 6.00

2002-03 Upper Deck Championship Drive Prized Properties Jersey

Inserted in packs at the rate of one in 36, this 12-card set is horizontally designed with player color photos on the left on a colored background to match team colors and a swatch of jersey on the right set to look like the letters PP.
AHPP Allan Houston 2.50 6.00
AWPP Antoine Walker 2.50 6.00
BDPP Baron Davis 3.00 8.00
CWPP Chris Webber 3.00 8.00
EBPP Elton Brand 3.00 8.00
JRPP Jason Richardson 3.00 8.00
KBPP Kobe Bryant 15.00 40.00
KMPP Karl Malone 4.00 10.00
MJPP Michael Jordan 80.00 160.00
PGPP Pau Gasol 4.00 10.00
SAPP Shareef Abdur-Rahim 2.50 6.00
TMPP Tracy McGrady 5.00 12.00

2002-03 Upper Deck Championship Drive Signs of Success Dual Jersey

Randomly seeded in packs, this nine card set centers two small photos of the two featured players, two jersey swatches on the outside of this, and two authentic autographs below the pictures and swatches. Each card is sequentially numbered to 25.
CBDG Caron Butler 25.00 60.00
Drew Gooden
CWME Chris Wilcox 25.00 60.00
Melvin Ely
KBKG Kobe Bryant 250.00 500.00
Kevin Garnett
MJKB Michael Jordan 400.00 700.00
Kobe Bryant
PPAW Paul Pierce 40.00 100.00
Antoine Walker
YMJW Yao Ming 100.00 200.00
Jay Williams

2002-03 Upper Deck Championship Drive Signs of Success Jersey

Randomly inserted in packs, this set features a swatch of a jersey and an authentic player autograph. Each card is sequentially numbered to 225.
AWA Antoine Walker 12.50 30.00
JKA Jason Kidd 25.00 60.00
JWA Jay Williams 12.50 30.00
KMA Kenyon Martin 15.00 40.00
MFA Marcus Fizer 12.50 30.00
YMA Yao Ming 50.00 120.00

2002-03 Upper Deck Championship Drive Superstar Material Jersey

Randomly inserted in packs, this 14-card set places full color player photos on the left side of the card and a swatch of jersey on the right. Each card is sequentially numbered to 100.
AIM Allen Iverson 8.00 20.00
AWM Antoine Walker 4.00 10.00
BDM Baron Davis 5.00 12.00
CWM Chris Webber 5.00 12.00
DNM Dirk Nowitzki 8.00 20.00
JRM Jason Richardson 5.00 12.00
JWM Jay Williams 6.00 15.00
KGM Kevin Garnett 10.00 25.00
KMB Kobe Bryant 25.00 60.00
MJM Michael Jordan 100.00 200.00
PGM Pau Gasol 6.00 15.00
RAM Ray Allen 5.00 12.00
SFM Steve Francis 5.00 12.00
YMM Yao Ming 15.00 40.00

2002-03 Upper Deck Championship Drive Then and Now Jersey

Inserted in packs at the rate of one in 108, this nine card set photos recently traded players in their old jerseys on the left and new jerseys on the right. There are also two swatches, one from each of the team's jersey.
TNAM Andre Miller 4.00 10.00
TNJH Juwan Howard 4.00 10.00
TNJK Jason Kidd 8.00 20.00
TNJM Jamal Mashburn 4.00 10.00
TNMB Mike Bibby 5.00 12.00
TNMJ Michael Jordan SP 125.00 250.00
TNSA Shareef Abdur-Rahim 4.00 10.00
TNSM Stephon Marbury 4.00 10.00
TNTM Tracy McGrady 8.00 20.00

2009-10 Upper Deck Champ's Hall of Legends Memorabilia

STATED ODDS 1:160
HLCB Chris Bosh 8.00 20.00
HLJE Julius Erving 12.00 30.00
HLKB Kobe Bryant 25.00 60.00
HLLB Larry Bird 20.00 50.00
HLLJ LeBron James 40.00 80.00
HLMG Magic Johnson 15.00 40.00

LMJ Michael Jordan 50.00 100.00
LSN Steve Nash 8.00 20.00

2009-10 Upper Deck Champ's Signatures

STATED ODDS 1:15
CSDR Derrick Rose 50.00 125.00
CSJE Julius Erving SP 200.00 350.00
CSLB Larry Bird 60.00 120.00
CSMJ Michael Jordan 400.00 700.00
CSTM Tracy McGrady 10.00 25.00
CSYM Yao Ming 40.00 80.00

2005 Upper Deck Chicago National

Given away at the 2005 National Sports Collector's Convention, this set featured some of the brightest young stars in the game. Each day, in exchange for wrappers from previously released products, Upper Deck handed out a different card. Card fronts feature borders along the left and the bottom, gold foil and sequential numbering to 750.

COMPLETE SET (6) 10.00 25.00
NBA1 Dwight Howard 6.00 15.00
NBA2 Luol Deng 2.50 6.00
NBA3 Ben Gordon 2.50 6.00
NBA4 Chris Duhon 2.00 5.00
NBA5 Josh Smith 3.00 8.00
NBA6 Andre Iguodala 3.00 8.00

1995-96 Upper Deck Chinese Basketball Alliance

Issued only in Taiwan, the 1995-96 Upper Deck Chinese Basketball Alliance set was issued in one series totaling 125 cards. The cards were sold in 10-card packs, and all four teams in the Chinese Basketball Alliance were featured. Each team carries 18 players, with a limit of two foreign players per team. The fronts show white-bordered color action player photos. The backs carry a closeup photo and player information. All text is in Chinese. The four teams represented are Yue Lion (1-16), Hung Kuo (17-34), Tera (35-52), and Luckipar (53-70). Topical subsets or special cards featured are Thousand Times (71-86), 10 Thousand Score (87), Starting Five (88-107), Special Records (108-119), Team Cards (120-123), and Checklists (124-125).

COMPLETE SET (125) 12.00 30.00
1 Chu Chung-Chi .08 .25
2 Lin Chien-Ping .08 .25
3 Roderick James Hannibal .20 .50
4 Tau Song .08 .25
5 Tsi-Fu-Tsi .08 .25
6 Chen Hung-Zung .08 .25
7 Chen Cheng-Sbiun .08 .25
8 Kuo Tien-Lung .08 .25
9 Tungfang Cheieh-Teh .08 .25
10 Li-Yung-Kung .08 .25
11 Hsu Tung-Ching .08 .25
12 Chang Hsien-Ming .08 .25
13 Mark Clark .20 .50
14 Brenton Lloyd Moore .20 .50
15 Arlando F. Bennett .20 .50
16 Christopher Edward Knight .20 .50
17 Tsou Jiunn-San .08 .25
18 Li Chung-Shi .08 .25
19 Liu I-Shang .08 .25
20 Chio Teh-Chih .08 .25
21 Michael Lee Johnson .20 .50
22 Jeng Jyh-Long .08 .25
23 Lo Hsing-Liang .08 .25
24 Huang Chun-Hsiung .08 .25
25 Chang Ya-Tang .08 .25
26 Chu Hao-Ren .08 .25
27 Jye Song .08 .25
28 Stacey Cornilius .20 .50
29 Keith Smith .20 .50
30 Rex Harrison Manu .20 .50
31 Daryl Scott .20 .50
32 Joseph Nathenial Temple .20 .50
33 Laurent Crawford .20 .50
34 David Lewayne Cooke .20 .50
35 Tsou Hai-Zunkg .08 .25
36 Wang Li-Bin .08 .25
37 Bai Ming-Li .08 .25
38 Kofi Kyei .08 .25
39 Lin Chai-Hung .08 .25
40 Chen Chung-Chian .08 .25
41 Li Chi-Chian .08 .25
42 Sun Mao-Shen .08 .25
43 Tzeng Yih-Cho .08 .25
44 Cheyenne Durell Gibson .20 .50
45 Chen Jiunn-Chie .08 .25
46 Kelvin Cornell Allen .20 .50
47 Charng Bing-Hsiang .08 .25
48 Kennard Robison .20 .50
49 David Edward Davies .20 .50
50 Todd Alan Rowe .20 .50
51 Mike Sterner .20 .50
52 Robert Zohn Fife .20 .50
53 Carroll Boudreaux .20 .50
54 Chen Cheng-Kwei .08 .25
55 Hung Chang-Ching .08 .25
56 Yen Chao-Chyun .08 .25
57 Lai Kwo-Hong .08 .25
58 Ko Yiing-Yan .08 .25
59 Gerard Arcement .20 .50
60 Jerry Lew .08 .25
61 Tien Su-Chung .08 .25
62 Chris Collier .20 .50
63 Tzeng Yih-Chin .08 .25
64 DWight Myvett .08 .25
65 Anthony Robert Block .20 .50
66 Lan Chih-Ming .08 .25
67 Lin Shin-Hwa .08 .25
68 Derrell Cunegin .20 .50
69 Harold Boudreaux .20 .50
70 Wu Jye-Wei .08 .25
71 Jerry Lew .08 .25
72 Tsou Jiunn-San .08 .25
73 Derrell Cunegin .20 .50
74 Huang Chun-Hsiung .08 .25
75 Christopher Edward Knight .20 .50
76 Huang Chun-Hsiung .08 .25
77 Joseph Nathenial Temple .20 .50
78 Lo Hsing-Liang .08 .25
79 Hung Chang-Ching .08 .25
80 Tsou Jiunn-San .08 .25
81 Christopher Edward Knight .20 .50
82 David Edward Davies .20 .50
83 Christopher Edward Knight .20 .50
84 Harold Boudreaux .20 .50
85 Arlando F. Bennett .20 .50
86 Arlando F. Bennett .20 .50
87 Tungfang Chieh-Teh .08 .25
88 Arlando F. Bennett .20 .50
89 Christopher Edward Knight .20 .50
90 Tungfang Chieh-Teh .08 .25
91 Li Yung-Kung .08 .25
92 Tsi Fu Tsi .08 .25
93 Tsou Jiunn-San .08 .25
94 Jeng Jyh-Long .08 .25
95 Lo Hsing-Liang .08 .25
96 Rex Harrison Manu .20 .50
97 Stacey Cornilius .20 .50
98 Wang Li-Bin .08 .25
99 Chen Chung-Chian .08 .25
100 Tzeng Tzeng-Cho .08 .25
101 Todd Alan Rowe .20 .50
102 Kennard Robison .20 .50
103 Tzeng Yih-Chin .08 .25
104 Jerry Lew .08 .25
105 Chen Cheng-Kwei .08 .25
106 Dwight Myvett .08 .25
107 Harold Boudreaux .20 .50
108 Dwight Myvett .08 .25
109 Harold Boudreaux .20 .50
110 Todd Alan Rowe .20 .50
111 Jeng Jyh-Long .08 .25
112 Li Chi-Chian .08 .25
113 Harold Boudreaux .20 .50
114 Dwight Myvett .08 .25
115 Tsou Jiunn-San .08 .25
116 Christopher Edward Knight .20 .50
117 Anthony Robert Block .20 .50
118 Rex Harrison Manu .20 .50
119 Rex Harrison Manu .20 .50
120 Yue Lon .08 .25
121 Hung Kuo .08 .25
122 Tera .08 .25
123 Luckipar .08 .25
124 Checklist #1 .08 .25
125 Checklist #2 .08 .25

1995-96 Upper Deck Chinese Alliance MVP's

Randomly inserted in packs, this 9-card set spotlights "most valuable players" in the Chinese Basketball Alliance. The fronts show full-bleed color action photos, except on the right edge where a granite stripe carries the player's name. A gold foil "MVP" emblem adorns the upper right corner. With a smaller inset color photo, the backs presents career summary and statistics.

COMPLETE SET (9) 4.00 10.00
M1 Jeng Jyh-Long .40 1.00
M2 Tsou Jiunn-San .40 1.00
M3 Todd Alan Rowe .75 2.00
M4 Tungfang Chieh-Teh .40 1.00
M5 Arlando F. Bennett .75 2.00
M6 Roderick Nathenial Temple .75 2.00
M7 Joseph Nathenial Temple .40 1.00
M8 Tungfang Chieh-Teh .40 1.00
M9 CBA President .40 1.00

2003 Upper Deck City Heights LeBron James

This LeBron James card was returned to collectors along with any 2003-04 Upper Deck redemption card as an added bonus. Early copies of the card were sent out to dealers who provide valuable product input along with a letter from Upper Deck. The card is done in 3-D lenticular style and places James in front of the Cleveland skyline.

NNO LeBron James 6.00 15.00

2004 Upper Deck Collectibles All-Star Game LeBron James

This card was produced by Upper Deck Collectibles. It is not known how this card was distributed, and each is numbered to 5000.

LJAS LeBron James 2.00 5.00

2002 Upper Deck Collector's Club

Released in March 2002, this set was distributed to members of Upper Deck's Collectors Club as part of their starter kit. Each member received a 20-card kit plus one memorabilia card wrapped in a clear cello wrapper along with an Upper Deck baseball cap and a club membership card. Members also received quarterly newsletters with features on upcoming products and sample cards.

COMPLETE SET (21) 10.00 25.00
NBA1 Kobe Bryant 1.25 3.00
NBA2 Allen Iverson .60 1.50
NBA3 Vince Carter 1.00 2.50
NBA4 Jason Kidd .40 1.00
NBA5 Tracy McGrady .50 1.25
NBA6 Pau Gasol .30 .75
NBA7 Kevin Garnett .60 1.50
NBA8 Steve Francis .40 1.00
NBA9 Chris Webber .40 1.00
NBA10 Ray Allen .25 .60
NBA11 Kwame Brown .25 .60
NBA12 Paul Pierce .25 .60
NBA13 Stephon Marbury .25 .60
NBA14 Tim Duncan .50 1.25
NBA15 Shaquille O'Neal .60 1.50
NBA16 Jerry Stackhouse .25 .60
NBA17 Rashard Lewis .15 .40
NBA18 Darius Miles .40 1.00
NBA19 Jamaal Tinsley .40 1.00
NBA20 Michael Jordan 2.00 5.00
KGU Kevin Garnett JSY 6.00 15.00

2010-11 Upper Deck College Colors

COMPLETE SET (15) 6.00 15.00
1 Michael Jordan 2.00 5.00
2 Bill Walton .40 1.00
3 Magic Johnson .75 2.00
4 Hakeem Olajuwon .60 1.50
5 James Worthy .60 1.50

1994 Upper Deck Commemorative Cards

1 1994 Launch Tour/2000 2.00 5.00
Wayne Gretzky
Reggie Jackson
Michael Jordan
Joe Montana

2008 Upper Deck Diamond Club Autographs

These autographed cards were only available to Upper Deck Diamond Club members in 2008. The cards feature hand-numbering on the front. Some are unpriced due to scarcity.

DC3 LeBron James/20 300.00 600.00
DC5 Derrick Rose/30 300.00 600.00
DC6 Michael Beasley/30 100.00 200.00

1997-98 Upper Deck Diamond Vision

This 29-card set features color action player photos taken from actual NBA game footage using the latest cutting-edge technology. The set was distributed in one-card packs with a suggested retail price of $7.99.

COMPLETE SET (29) 30.00 80.00
1 Dikembe Mutombo 1.25 3.00
2 Dana Barros .75 2.00
3 Glen Rice 1.25 3.00
4 Michael Jordan 10.00 25.00
5 Terrell Brandon .75 2.00
6 Michael Finley 1.25 3.00
7 Antonio McDyess 1.00 2.50
8 Grant Hill 2.00 5.00
9 Latrell Sprewell 1.25 3.00
10 Hakeem Olajuwon 1.50 4.00
11 Reggie Miller 1.50 4.00
12 Loy Vaught .75 2.00
13 Shaquille O'Neal 3.00 8.00
14 Alonzo Mourning 1.50 4.00
15 Vin Baker 1.00 2.50
16 Kevin Garnett 2.50 6.00
17 Kerry Kittles .75 2.00
18 Patrick Ewing 1.50 4.00
19 Anfernee Hardaway 2.00 5.00
20 Allen Iverson 2.50 6.00
21 Jason Kidd 2.00 5.00
22 Isaiah Rider .75 2.00
23 Mitch Richmond 1.25 3.00
24 David Robinson 2.00 5.00
25 Gary Payton 1.25 3.00
26 Damon Stoudamire 1.25 3.00
27 Karl Malone 1.50 4.00
28 Shareef Abdur-Rahim 1.25 3.00
29 Chris Webber 1.25 3.00

1997-98 Upper Deck Diamond Vision Signature Moves

Randomly inserted in packs at the rate of one in three, this 29-card set is parallel to the base set. The difference is found in the featured athlete's facsimile signature appearing on these live-action cards. To ascertain individual card values, please refer to the multiplier in the header below coupled with the value of the basic card.

*STARS: .75X TO 2X BASE CARD HI

1997-98 Upper Deck Diamond Vision Dunk Vision

Randomly inserted in packs at the rate of one in 40, this six-card set features borderless color action game photos of spectacular dunks of NBA superstars.

COMPLETE SET (6) 40.00 100.00
D1 Michael Jordan 30.00 80.00
D2 Anfernee Hardaway 6.00 15.00
D3 Shaquille O'Neal 10.00 25.00
D4 Grant Hill 6.00 15.00
D5 Kevin Garnett 8.00 20.00
D6 Hakeem Olajuwon 5.00 12.00

1997-98 Upper Deck Diamond Vision Jordan Highlight Reels

This five-card set was packaged individually with each having an SRP of $9.99. Each 3 1/2" by 5" card features over 20 frames of NBA video footage of various stages of Michael Jordan's career. The cards are numbered on the front - in the upper left-hand corner.

COMPLETE SET (5) 20.00 50.00
COMMON CARD (1-5) 6.00 15.00

1997-98 Upper Deck Diamond Vision Reel Time

Randomly inserted in packs at the rate of one in 500, this one-card set showcases one of Michael Jordan's forays to the hoop in frame-by-frame action imagery during one of the most memorable moments in the NBA.

RT1 Michael Jordan 30.00 80.00

1992 Upper Deck Draft Party Sheets

These 8 1/2" by 11" sheets were given away to attendees of draft day parties hosted by most of the NBA teams. All sheets are dated June 24, 1992, numbered out of 7,000, and feature reproductions of the 1991-92 cards of the top 1992 draft picks: Larry Johnson, Derrick Coleman, Pervis Ellison, Danny Manning, David Robinson and Brad Daugherty. The main differences between the various sheets are the text and logos of the team and corporate sponsor, if any. The sheets are unnumbered and are listed in alphabetical order.

COMPLETE SET (20) 30.00 80.00
COMMON SHEET 2.00 5.00

1993 Upper Deck Draft Party Sheets

These 8 1/2" by 11" sheets were given away to attendees of draft day parties hosted by all 27 NBA teams. All sheets are dated June 30, 1993, numbered out of 7,000, and feature reproductions of the 1992-93 Top Prospect subset cards of the top 1992 draft picks: Shaquille O'Neal, Tom Gugliotta, Alonzo Mourning, Christian Laettner, Jim Jackson and LaPhonso Ellis. The main differences between the various sheets are the text and logos of the team and corporate sponsor, if any. The sheets are unnumbered and are listed in alphabetical order.

COMPLETE SET (27) 60.00 150.00
COMMON SHEET 4.00 10.00

1993-94 Upper Deck Draft Preview Promos

Issued (but never formally released) to promote a new draft picks product, these three draft preview cards measure the standard-size. The fronts feature full-bleed color action photos with the college name airbrushed off the players' jerseys. The player's name appears in a color bar across the bottom of the picture. The backs carry biography, player profile, and statistics.

COMPLETE SET (3) 6.00 15.00
DP1 Shawn Bradley 3.00 8.00
DP2 Calbert Cheaney 3.00 8.00
DP3 Bobby Hurley 1.50 4.00

2007-08 Upper Deck Kevin Durant Promo

KDRC1 Kevin Durant/999 4.00 10.00
KDRC2 Kevin Durant/499 6.00 15.00

1999 Upper Deck Employee Game Jersey

This Michael Jordan card was given to Upper Deck employees as a "Thank You" for the 1999 year. Each card featured a swatch of game-worn jersey. Each card was serially numbered to 275.

NNO Michael Jordan 1000.00 2000.00

2000 Upper Deck Employee Game Jersey

For the second year, Upper Deck gave their employees Game Jerseys as a "Thank You" gift. This year's jersey swatch featured Kobe Bryant, along with Kobe's autograph. The cards were serially numbered out of 300.

KB2000 Kobe Bryant AU/300 500.00 1000.00

2003 Upper Deck Employee LeBron James

These LeBron James cards were sent out by Upper Deck to distributors and other members of the collectible card industry in December 2003 as a holiday card. James is featured in a North Pole Winter League jersey on the non memorabilia card.

LBEC LeBron James JSY/450 100.00 250.00
LBNPL03 LeBron James 4.00 10.00

2006 Upper Deck Employee Quad Jerseys

LJDJSCRB LeBron James 50.00 100.00
Derek Jeter
Sidney Crosby
Reggie Bush

2007 Upper Deck Employee Quad Jerseys

MJKBLJKD Michael Jordan 175.00 350.00
Kobe Bryant
LeBron James
Kevin Durant

1998-99 Upper Deck Encore

Released as a semi-parallel to the 1998-99 Upper Deck set, this 150-card set was issued in six card packs that carried a suggested retail price of $3.99. Each card utilized a special Rainbow Light F/X technology, which differentiated the cards from the regular Upper Deck set. There were several subsets inserted - Michael Jordan cards 91-113 were inserted at one in four, Rookie Watch cards 114-143 were inserted at one in four and Bonus Regular rookie cards 144-150 were inserted at one in eight. A Michael Jordan autograph was also randomly inserted in packs. There were 50 total autographs available.

COMPLETE SET (150) 60.00 120.00
1 Mookie Blaylock .15 .40
2 Dikembe Mutombo .25 .60
3 Steve Smith .20 .50
4 Kenny Anderson .20 .50
5 Antoine Walker .25 .60
6 Ron Mercer .25 .60
7 David Wesley .15 .40
8 Elden Campbell .15 .40
9 Eddie Jones .25 .60
10 Ron Harper .20 .50
11 Toni Kukoc .25 .60
12 Brent Barry .20 .50
13 Shawn Kemp .20 .50
14 Brevin Knight .15 .40
15 Derek Anderson .15 .40
16 Shawn Bradley .15 .40
17 Robert Pack .15 .40
18 Michael Finley .25 .60
19 Antonio McDyess .20 .50
20 Nick Van Exel .20 .50
21 Danny Fortson .15 .40
22 Grant Hill .40 1.00
23 Jerry Stackhouse .25 .60
24 Bison Dele .15 .40
25 Donyell Marshall .15 .40
26 Tony Delk .15 .40
27 Erick Dampier .15 .40
28 John Starks .20 .50
29 Charles Barkley .40 1.00
30 Hakeem Olajuwon .30 .75
31 Othella Harrington .15 .40
32 Scottie Pippen .40 1.00
33 Rik Smits .20 .50
34 Reggie Miller .30 .75
35 Mark Jackson .20 .50
36 Rodney Rogers .15 .40
37 Lamond Murray .15 .40
38 Maurice Taylor .15 .40
39 Kobe Bryant 1.25 3.00
40 Shaquille O'Neal .60 1.50
41 Derek Fisher .25 .60
42 Glen Rice .20 .50
43 Jamal Mashburn .20 .50
44 Alonzo Mourning .20 .50
45 Tim Hardaway .25 .60
46 Ray Allen .30 .75
47 Vinny Del Negro .15 .40
48 Glenn Robinson .20 .50
49 Joe Smith .20 .50
50 Terrell Brandon .15 .40
51 Kevin Garnett .50 1.25
52 Keith Van Horn .25 .60
53 Stephon Marbury .30 .75
54 Jayson Williams .15 .40
55 Patrick Ewing .30 .75
56 Allan Houston .20 .50
57 Latrell Sprewell .25 .60
58 Anfernee Hardaway .40 1.00
59 Horace Grant .20 .50
60 Nick Anderson .15 .40
61 Allen Iverson .50 1.25
62 Matt Geiger .15 .40
63 Theo Ratliff .20 .50
64 Jason Kidd .40 1.00
65 Rex Chapman .15 .40
66 Tom Gugliotta .15 .40
67 Rasheed Wallace .25 .60
68 Arvydas Sabonis .20 .50
69 Damon Stoudamire .25 .60
70 Vlade Divac .25 .60
71 Corliss Williamson .15 .40
72 Chris Webber .25 .60
73 Tim Duncan .50 1.25
74 Sean Elliott .25 .60
75 David Robinson .40 1.00
76 Vin Baker .20 .50
77 Gary Payton .25 .60
78 Detlef Schrempf .25 .60
79 Tracy McGrady .40 1.00
80 John Wallace .15 .40
81 Doug Christie .15 .40
82 Karl Malone .30 .75
83 John Stockton .30 .75
84 Jeff Hornacek .20 .50
85 Bryant Reeves .15 .40
86 Michael Smith .15 .40
87 Shareef Abdur-Rahim .25 .60
88 Juwan Howard .20 .50
89 Rod Strickland .15 .40
90 Mitch Richmond .20 .50
91 Michael Jordan 1.25 3.00
92 Michael Jordan 1.25 3.00
93 Michael Jordan 1.25 3.00
94 Michael Jordan 1.25 3.00
95 Michael Jordan 1.25 3.00
96 Michael Jordan 1.25 3.00
97 Michael Jordan 1.25 3.00
98 Michael Jordan 1.25 3.00
99 Michael Jordan 1.25 3.00
100 Michael Jordan 1.25 3.00
101 Michael Jordan 1.25 3.00
102 Michael Jordan 1.25 3.00
103 Michael Jordan 1.25 3.00
104 Michael Jordan 1.25 3.00
105 Michael Jordan 1.25 3.00
106 Michael Jordan 1.25 3.00
107 Michael Jordan 1.25 3.00
108 Michael Jordan 1.25 3.00
109 Michael Jordan 1.25 3.00
110 Michael Jordan 1.25 3.00
111 Michael Jordan 1.25 3.00
112 Michael Jordan 1.25 3.00
113 Michael Jordan 1.25 3.00
114 Michael Olowokandi RC 1.00 2.50
115 Mike Bibby RC 2.00 5.00
116 Raef LaFrentz RC 1.00 2.50
117 Antawn Jamison RC 2.00 5.00
118 Vince Carter RC 4.00 10.00
119 Robert Traylor RC .75 2.00
120 Jason Williams RC 2.00 5.00
121 Larry Hughes RC 1.50 4.00
122 Dirk Nowitzki RC 5.00 12.00
123 Paul Pierce RC 4.00 10.00
124 Michael Doleac RC .75 2.00
125 Keon Clark RC .75 2.00
126 Michael Dickerson RC .75 2.00
127 Matt Harpring RC 1.00 2.50
128 Bryce Drew RC .75 2.00
129 Pat Garrity RC .75 2.00
130 Roshown McLeod RC .75 2.00
131 Ricky Davis RC 1.25 3.00
132 Peja Stojakovic RC 2.00 5.00
133 Felipe Lopez RC .75 2.00
134 Al Harrington RC 1.25 3.00
135 Ruben Patterson RC .75 2.00
136 Cuttino Mobley RC 1.50 4.00
137 Tyronn Lue RC .75 2.00
138 Brian Skinner RC .75 2.00
139 Nazr Mohammed RC .75 2.00
140 Toby Bailey RC .75 2.00
141 Casey Shaw RC .75 2.00
142 Corey Benjamin RC .75 2.00
143 Rashard Lewis RC 2.00 5.00
144 Jason Williams BON 1.25 3.00
145 Paul Pierce BON 2.50 6.00
146 Vince Carter BON 2.50 6.00
147 Antawn Jamison BON 1.25 3.00
148 Raef LaFrentz BON .60 1.50
149 Mike Bibby BON 1.25 3.00
150 Michael Olowokandi BON .60 1.50
MJ Michael Jordan AU/50 1000.00 2000.00

1998-99 Upper Deck Encore F/X

Randomly inserted into packs, this 150-card set parallels the base set. The cards are serially numbered to 125. To ascertain values for individual cards, please refer to the multiplier in the header below, coupled with the value of individual cards.

COMMON MJ (91-113) 25.00 60.00
*STARS: 12X TO 30X BASE CARD HI
*RCs: 2X TO 5X BASE HI
*BONUS: 3X TO 8X BASE HI
122 Dirk Nowitzki 30.00 80.00
123 Paul Pierce 25.00 60.00

1998-99 Upper Deck Encore Driving Forces

Randomly inserted in packs at one in 23, this 15-card set focuses on offensive superstars. Card backs are numbered with a "F" prefix.

COMPLETE SET (15) 15.00 40.00
*FX CARDS: 2X TO 5X HI COLUMN
FX: STATED PRINT RUN 500 SERIAL #'d SETS
F1 Michael Jordan 8.00 20.00
F2 Kobe Bryant 5.00 12.00
F3 Keith Van Horn 1.00 2.50
F4 Kevin Garnett 2.00 5.00
F5 Tim Duncan 2.00 5.00
F6 Gary Payton 1.00 2.50
F7 Antoine Walker 1.00 2.50
F8 Grant Hill 1.50 4.00
F9 Scottie Pippen 1.50 4.00
F10 Tim Hardaway 1.00 2.50
F11 Reggie Miller 1.25 3.00
F12 Shareef Abdur-Rahim 1.00 2.50
F13 Anfernee Hardaway 1.50 4.00
F14 Allen Iverson 2.00 5.00
F15 Ray Allen 1.25 3.00

1998-99 Upper Deck Encore Intensity

Randomly inserted in packs at one in 11, this 30-card set consists of the league's most intense on-court players. Card backs are numbered with an "I" prefix.

COMPLETE SET (30) 15.00 40.00
I1 Michael Jordan 6.00 15.00
I2 Mitch Richmond .75 2.00
I3 Ron Mercer .60 1.50
I4 Terrell Brandon .50 1.25
I5 Brevin Knight .50 1.25
I6 Rasheed Wallace .75 2.00
I7 Keith Van Horn .75 2.00
I8 Antawn Jamison 2.00 5.00
I9 Antonio McDyess .60 1.50
I10 Allen Iverson 1.50 4.00
I11 Anfernee Hardaway 1.25 3.00
I12 Chris Webber .75 2.00
I13 Lorenzen Wright .50 1.25
I14 Bryant Reeves .50 1.25
I15 Charles Barkley 1.25 3.00
I16 Tracy McGrady 1.25 3.00
I17 Larry Johnson .75 2.00
I18 Jerry Stackhouse .75 2.00
I19 Derrick Coleman .60 1.50
I20 Detlef Schrempf .75 2.00
I21 John Stockton 1.00 2.50
I22 Kobe Bryant 4.00 10.00
I23 Alonzo Mourning 1.00 2.50
I24 Dikembe Mutombo .75 2.00
I25 Jalen Rose .60 1.50
I26 Robert Pack .50 1.25
I27 Tom Gugliotta .50 1.25
I28 Shaquille O'Neal 2.00 5.00
I29 Stephon Marbury 1.00 2.50
I30 David Robinson 1.25 3.00

1998-99 Upper Deck Encore MJ23

Randomly inserted in packs at one in 23, this 20-card set pays tribute to Michael Jordan. Card backs carry a "M" prefix.

COMPLETE SET (20) 60.00 120.00
COMMON CARD (M1-M20) 3.00 8.00
*FX: 10X TO 25X BASE HI
FX: STATED PRINT RUN 23 SERIAL #'d SETS

1998-99 Upper Deck Encore PowerDeck

Randomly inserted in packs at one in 47, this nine-card set features special interactive cards that when loaded in a disk drive, feature game-action footage, sound, photos and career highlights for the players. The cards are not numbered and listed below in alphabetical order.

1 Charles Barkley 5.00 12.00
2 Kobe Bryant 8.00 20.00
3 Vince Carter 6.00 15.00
4 Julius Erving 4.00 10.00
5 Kevin Garnett 4.00 10.00
6 Michael Jordan 12.50 30.00
7 Shaquille O'Neal 4.00 10.00
8 Paul Pierce 4.00 10.00
9 Jason Williams 4.00 10.00

1998-99 Upper Deck Encore Rookie Encore

Randomly inserted into packs at one in 23, this 10-card set features some of the best from the 1998-99 rookie class. Card backs carry a "RE" prefix.

COMPLETE SET (10) 15.00 40.00
*FX: .75X TO 2X HI COLUMN
FX: STATED PRINT RUN 1000 SERIAL #'d SETS
RE1 Jason Williams 2.00 5.00
RE2 Michael Olowokandi 1.00 2.50
RE3 Paul Pierce 4.00 10.00
RE4 Robert Traylor .75 2.00
RE5 Raef LaFrentz 1.00 2.50
RE6 Mike Bibby 2.00 5.00

RE7 Dirk Nowitzki 5.00 12.00
RE8 Antawn Jamison 2.00 5.00
RE9 Larry Hughes 1.50 4.00
RE10 Vince Carter 4.00 10.00

1999-00 Upper Deck Encore

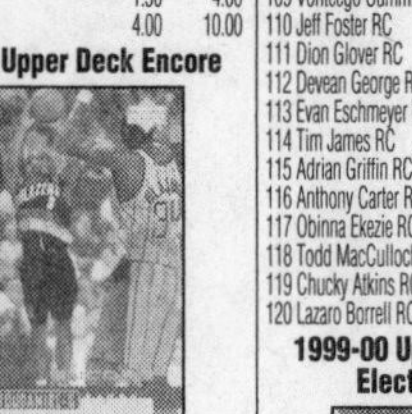

The 1999-00 Upper Deck Encore set was released in late April, 2000 as a 120-card set that featured 90 player cards and 30 rookie cards. The rookies were short printed and serial numbered to 1999. Each pack contained 6-cards and carried a suggested retail price of 3.99.

COMPLETE SET (120) 40.00 100.00
COMPLETE SET w/o RC (90) 10.00 25.00
1 Dikembe Mutombo .30 .75
2 Alan Henderson .20 .50
3 Isaiah Rider .20 .50
4 Kenny Anderson .25 .60
5 Antoine Walker .30 .75
6 Paul Pierce .50 1.25
7 Elden Campbell .20 .50
8 Eddie Jones .30 .75
9 David Wesley .20 .50
10 Hersey Hawkins .20 .50
11 Randy Brown .20 .50
12 Toni Kukoc .30 .75
13 Shawn Kemp .30 .75
14 Bob Sura .20 .50
15 Michael Finley .30 .75
16 Dirk Nowitzki .60 1.50
17 Gary Trent .20 .50
18 Antonio McDyess .25 .60
19 Nick Van Exel .25 .60
20 Raef LaFrentz .25 .60
21 Christian Laettner .25 .60
22 Grant Hill .40 1.00
23 Lindsey Hunter .20 .50
24 Jerry Stackhouse .30 .75
25 John Starks .20 .50
26 Antawn Jamison .30 .75
27 Tony Farmer .20 .50
28 Hakeem Olajuwon .40 1.00
29 Cuttino Mobley .25 .60
30 Charles Barkley .50 1.25
31 Reggie Miller .30 .75
32 Jalen Rose .25 .60
33 Mark Jackson .20 .50
34 Maurice Taylor .20 .50
35 Derek Anderson .20 .50
36 Michael Olowokandi .20 .50
37 Kobe Bryant 1.50 4.00
38 Shaquille O'Neal .75 2.00
39 Glen Rice .30 .75
40 Tim Hardaway .30 .75
41 Alonzo Mourning .40 1.00
42 Ray Allen .30 .75
43 Glenn Robinson .25 .60
44 Sam Cassell .25 .60
45 Tim Thomas .25 .60
46 Kevin Garnett .60 1.50
47 Terrell Brandon .20 .50
48 Keith Van Horn .25 .60
49 Stephon Marbury .25 .60
50 Kendall Gill .20 .50
51 Patrick Ewing .40 1.00
52 Allan Houston .25 .60
53 Latrell Sprewell .30 .75
54 Darrell Armstrong .20 .50
55 John Amaechi RC .30 .75
56 Michael Doleac .20 .50
57 Allen Iverson .60 1.50
58 Theo Ratliff .25 .60
59 Larry Hughes .25 .60
60 Jason Kidd .50 1.25
61 Tom Gugliotta .20 .50
62 Anfernee Hardaway .50 1.25
63 Rasheed Wallace .30 .75
64 Steve Smith .20 .50
65 Damon Stoudamire .20 .50
66 Scottie Pippen .50 1.25
67 Corliss Williamson .20 .50
68 Jason Williams .40 1.00
69 Vlade Divac .30 .75
70 Chris Webber .30 .75
71 Tim Duncan .60 1.50
72 David Robinson .50 1.25
73 Avery Johnson .25 .60
74 Mario Elie .20 .50
75 Gary Payton .30 .75
76 Vin Baker .30 .75
77 Ruben Patterson .20 .50
78 Brent Barry .25 .60
79 Vince Carter .60 1.50
80 Antonio Davis .20 .50
81 Tracy McGrady .50 1.25
82 Karl Malone .40 1.00
83 John Stockton .40 1.00
84 Bryon Russell .20 .50
85 Shareef Abdur-Rahim .25 .60
86 Mike Bibby .30 .75
87 Othella Harrington .20 .50
88 Juwan Howard .25 .60
89 Rod Strickland .20 .50
90 Mitch Richmond .30 .75
91 Elton Brand RC 2.50 6.00
92 Steve Francis RC 2.50 6.00
93 Baron Davis RC 3.00 8.00
94 Lamar Odom RC 3.00 8.00
95 Jonathan Bender RC 1.00 2.50
96 Wally Szczerbiak RC 2.00 5.00
97 Richard Hamilton RC 2.50 6.00
98 Andre Miller RC 2.50 6.00
99 Shawn Marion RC 2.50 6.00
100 Jason Terry RC 2.50 6.00
101 Trajan Langdon RC 1.00 2.50
102 Kenny Thomas RC 1.00 2.50
103 Corey Maggette RC 2.00 5.00
104 William Avery RC 1.00 2.50
105 Ron Artest RC 2.50 6.00
106 Aleksandar Radojevic RC 1.00 2.50
107 James Posey RC 1.00 2.50
108 Quincy Lewis RC 1.00 2.50
109 Vonteego Cummings RC 1.00 2.50
110 Jeff Foster RC 1.00 2.50
111 Dion Glover RC 1.00 2.50
112 Devean George RC 1.00 2.50
113 Evan Eschmeyer RC 1.00 2.50
114 Tim James RC 1.00 2.50
115 Adrian Griffin RC 1.00 2.50
116 Anthony Carter RC 1.00 2.50
117 Obinna Ekezie RC 1.00 2.50
118 Todd MacCulloch RC 1.00 2.50
119 Chucky Atkins RC 1.00 2.50
120 Lazaro Borrell RC 1.00 2.50

1999-00 Upper Deck Encore Electric Currents

Randomly inserted in packs at one in three, this insert set features 20 of the leagues most highly recognized scorers. Card backs carry an "EC" prefix.

COMPLETE SET (20) 5.00 12.00
*F/X: 5X TO 12X BASE HI
F/X: PRINT RUN 150 SERIAL #'d SETS
EC1 Kevin Garnett .75 2.00
EC2 Anfernee Hardaway .60 1.50
EC3 Shareef Abdur-Rahim .30 .75
EC4 Allan Houston .30 .75
EC5 Michael Finley .40 1.00
EC6 Tim Duncan .75 2.00
EC7 Gary Payton .40 1.00
EC8 Kobe Bryant 2.00 5.00
EC9 Derek Anderson .25 .60
EC10 Reggie Miller .40 1.00
EC11 Keith Van Horn .30 .75
EC12 Jason Kidd .60 1.50
EC13 Ray Allen .40 1.00
EC14 Tim Hardaway .40 1.00
EC15 Darrell Armstrong .25 .60
EC16 Antonio McDyess .30 .75
EC17 Eddie Jones .40 1.00
EC18 Paul Pierce .60 1.50
EC19 Stephon Marbury .30 .75
EC20 Chris Webber .40 1.00

1999-00 Upper Deck Encore Future Charge

Randomly inserted in packs at one in six, this insert set features 15 of the NBA's next generation of star players. Card backs carry a "FC" prefix.

COMPLETE SET (15) 4.00 10.00
FC1 Antawn Jamison .50 1.25
FC2 Mike Bibby .50 1.25
FC3 Antoine Walker .50 1.25
FC4 Baron Davis 1.00 2.50
FC5 Jason Terry .75 2.00
FC6 Andre Miller .75 2.00
FC7 Ray Allen .50 1.25
FC8 Wally Szczerbiak .60 1.50
FC9 Raef LaFrentz .40 1.00
FC10 William Avery .30 .75
FC11 Jason Williams .60 1.50
FC12 Michael Olowokandi .30 .75
FC13 Stephon Marbury .40 1.00
FC14 Quincy Lewis .30 .75
FC15 Shawn Marion .75 2.00

1999-00 Upper Deck Encore Game Jerseys

Randomly inserted in packs at one in 300, this insert set features 20-cards that contain pieces of game-worn jerseys of various NBA players. The set also includes autographed game-jersey cards of Michael Jordan, Kevin Garnett, and Kobe Bryant. Card backs are numbered using the players initials. Each autographed card is serial numbered to the specified player's jersey number.

MJ Michael Jordan AU/23 2500.00 4000.00
AIJ Allen Iverson 15.00 40.00
AMJ Andre Miller 8.00 20.00
BDJ Baron Davis 12.50 30.00
GHJ Grant Hill 20.00 50.00
JBJ Jonathan Bender 8.00 20.00
JKJ Jason Kidd 20.00 50.00
JTJ Jason Terry 8.00 20.00
JWJ Jason Williams 15.00 40.00
KBJ Kobe Bryant 60.00 120.00
KGA Kevin Garnett AU/21 175.00 350.00
KGJ Kevin Garnett 20.00 50.00
MCJ Antonio McDyess 8.00 20.00
RHJ Richard Hamilton 8.00 20.00
SFJ Steve Francis 15.00 40.00
SMJ Shawn Marion 10.00 25.00
SOJ Shaquille O'Neal 30.00 80.00
TLJ Trajan Langdon 8.00 20.00
WSJ Wally Szczerbiak 8.00 20.00

1999-00 Upper Deck Encore High Definition

Randomly inserted in packs at one in 15, this insert set features 20 of the most spectacular dunk shots. Card backs carry a "HD" prefix.

COMPLETE SET (20) 15.00 40.00
HD1 Antonio McDyess .75 2.00
HD2 Kevin Garnett 2.00 5.00
HD3 Vince Carter 2.00 5.00
HD4 Shareef Abdur-Rahim .75 2.00
HD5 Stephon Marbury .75 2.00
HD6 Gary Payton 1.00 2.50
HD7 Glenn Robinson .75 2.00
HD8 Kobe Bryant 5.00 12.00
HD9 Antawn Jamison 1.00 2.50
HD10 Chris Webber 1.00 2.50
HD11 Corey Maggette 2.00 5.00
HD12 Shawn Kemp 1.00 2.50
HD13 Derek Anderson .60 1.50
HD14 Michael Finley 1.00 2.50
HD15 Allan Houston .75 2.00
HD16 Anfernee Hardaway 1.50 4.00
HD17 Grant Hill 1.25 3.00
HD18 Shaquille O'Neal 2.50 6.00
HD19 Paul Pierce 1.50 4.00
HD20 Scottie Pippen 1.50 4.00

1999-00 Upper Deck Encore Jamboree

Randomly inserted in packs at one in six, this 15-card insert features some of the most electrifying slam dunkers in the NBA. Card backs carry a "J" prefix.

COMPLETE SET (15) 8.00 20.00
J1 Michael Jordan 5.00 12.00
J2 Karl Malone .75 2.00
J3 Kevin Garnett 1.25 3.00
J4 Antonio McDyess .50 1.25
J5 Shareef Abdur-Rahim .50 1.25
J6 David Robinson 1.00 2.50
J7 Marcus Camby .50 1.25
J8 Kobe Bryant 3.00 8.00
J9 Jason Kidd 1.00 2.50
J10 Tim Duncan 1.25 3.00
J11 Keith Van Horn .50 1.25
J12 Glenn Robinson .50 1.25
J13 Grant Hill .75 2.00
J14 Michael Finley .60 1.50
J15 Vince Carter 1.25 3.00

1999-00 Upper Deck Encore MJ - A Higher Power

Randomly inserted in packs at one in 90, this 10-card insert set honors the greatest player of all time. Card backs carry a "MJ" prefix.

COMPLETE SET (10) 50.00 120.00
COMMON CARD (MJ1-MJ10) 6.00 15.00

1999-00 Upper Deck Encore Upper Realm

Randomly inserted in packs at one in six, this insert set honors 10 of the NBA's most elite players. Card backs carry a "UR" prefix.

COMPLETE SET (10) 4.00 10.00
*F/X: 6X TO 15X HI COLUMN
F/X: PRINT RUN 150 SERIAL #'d SETS
UR1 Kevin Garnett .75 2.00
UR2 Kobe Bryant 2.00 5.00
UR3 Tim Duncan .75 2.00
UR4 Vince Carter .75 2.00
UR5 Gary Payton .40 1.00
UR6 Allen Iverson .75 2.00
UR7 Karl Malone .50 1.25
UR8 Jason Williams .50 1.25
UR9 Scottie Pippen .60 1.50
UR10 Shaquille O'Neal 1.00 2.50

2000-01 Upper Deck Encore

The 2000-01 Upper Deck Encore product was released in May, 2001 and featured a 165-card base set that was broken into tiers as follows: Base Veterans (1-135), and Rookies (136-165) that were serial numbered to 1600. Each pack contained five cards, and carried a suggested retail price of $2.99.

COMPLETE SET w/o RC's 10.00 25.00
1 Brevin Knight .20 .50
2 Lorenzen Wright .20 .50
3 Alan Henderson .20 .50
4 Jason Terry .30 .75
5 Paul Pierce .40 1.00
6 Antoine Walker .25 .60
7 Kenny Anderson .25 .60
8 Tony Battie .20 .50
9 Adrian Griffin .20 .50
10 Derrick Coleman .25 .60
11 David Wesley .20 .50
12 Baron Davis .30 .75
13 Elden Campbell .25 .60
14 Jamal Mashburn .25 .60
15 Elton Brand .30 .75
16 Ron Mercer .20 .50
17 Ron Artest .30 .75
18 Michael Ruffin .20 .50
19 Lamond Murray .20 .50
20 Andre Miller .25 .60
21 Matt Harpring .25 .60
22 Jim Jackson .20 .50
23 Michael Finley .30 .75
24 Dirk Nowitzki .50 1.25
25 Steve Nash .50 1.25
26 Howard Eisley .20 .50
27 Antonio McDyess .25 .60
28 James Posey .20 .50
29 Nick Van Exel .25 .60
30 Raef LaFrentz .20 .50
31 Voshon Lenard .20 .50
32 Jerry Stackhouse .25 .60
33 Ben Wallace .30 .75
34 Michael Curry .20 .50
35 Joe Smith .25 .60
36 Chucky Atkins .20 .50
37 Antawn Jamison .30 .75
38 Larry Hughes .25 .60
39 Chris Mills .20 .50
40 Mookie Blaylock .25 .60
41 Vonteego Cummings .20 .50
42 Steve Francis .30 .75
43 Maurice Taylor .20 .50
44 Hakeem Olajuwon .40 1.00
45 Walt Williams .20 .50
46 Cuttino Mobley .25 .60
47 Reggie Miller .30 .75
48 Jalen Rose .25 .60
49 Austin Croshere .20 .50
50 Travis Best .20 .50
51 Jermaine O'Neal .30 .75
52 Lamar Odom .30 .75
53 Jeff McInnis .20 .50
54 Michael Olowokandi .20 .50
55 Brian Skinner .20 .50
56 Corey Maggette .25 .60
57 Shaquille O'Neal .75 2.00
58 Ron Harper .25 .60
59 Kobe Bryant 1.50 4.00
60 Robert Horry .25 .60
61 Isaiah Rider .25 .60
62 Eddie Jones .30 .75
63 Anthony Carter .20 .50
64 Tim Hardaway .30 .75
65 Brian Grant .20 .50
66 Anthony Mason .20 .50
67 Ray Allen .30 .75
68 Tim Thomas .20 .50
69 Glenn Robinson .25 .60
70 Sam Cassell .25 .60
71 Lindsey Hunter .20 .50
72 Kevin Garnett .60 1.50
73 Wally Szczerbiak .25 .60
74 Terrell Brandon .20 .50
75 Chauncey Billups .30 .75
76 Stephon Marbury .25 .60
77 Keith Van Horn .25 .60
78 Lucious Harris .20 .50
79 Kendall Gill .20 .50
80 Latrell Sprewell .25 .60
81 Marcus Camby .25 .60
82 Larry Johnson .30 .75
83 Allan Houston .25 .60
84 Glen Rice .25 .60
85 Grant Hill .40 1.00
86 Tracy McGrady .50 1.25
87 John Amaechi .20 .50
88 Darrell Armstrong .20 .50
89 Allen Iverson .60 1.50
90 Dikembe Mutombo .30 .75
91 George Lynch .20 .50
92 Aaron McKie .20 .50
93 Eric Snow .25 .60
94 Jason Kidd .50 1.25
95 Tony Delk .20 .50
96 Clifford Robinson .20 .50
97 Tom Gugliotta .20 .50
98 Shawn Marion .30 .75
99 Rasheed Wallace .30 .75
100 Scottie Pippen .50 1.25
101 Steve Smith .25 .60
102 Damon Stoudamire .25 .60
103 Bonzi Wells .25 .60
104 Chris Webber .30 .75
105 Jason Williams .30 .75
106 Peja Stojakovic .30 .75
107 Vlade Divac .25 .60
108 Doug Christie .20 .50
109 Tim Duncan .60 1.50
110 David Robinson .50 1.25
111 Derek Anderson .25 .60
112 Antonio Daniels .20 .50
113 Sean Elliott .25 .60
114 Gary Payton .30 .75
115 Patrick Ewing .40 1.00
116 Vin Baker .25 .60
117 Rashard Lewis .30 .75
118 Vince Carter .60 1.50
119 Alvin Williams .20 .50
120 Antonio Davis .20 .50
121 Charles Oakley .25 .60
122 Karl Malone .40 1.00
123 John Stockton .40 1.00
124 Bryon Russell .20 .50
125 John Starks .20 .50
126 Shareef Abdur-Rahim .25 .60
127 Mike Bibby .30 .75
128 Michael Dickerson .20 .50
129 Grant Long .20 .50
130 Mitch Richmond .25 .60
131 Richard Hamilton .25 .60
132 Chris Whitney .20 .50
133 Jahidi White .20 .50
134 Checklist 1 .08 .25
135 Checklist 2 .08 .25
136 Kenyon Martin RC 3.00 8.00
137 Stromile Swift RC 1.25 3.00
138 Chris Mihm RC 1.25 3.00
139 Marcus Fizer RC 1.25 3.00
140 Darius Miles RC 1.25 3.00
141 Joel Przybilla RC 1.25 3.00
142 Mike Miller RC 2.50 6.00
143 Courtney Alexander RC 1.25 3.00
144 DerMarr Johnson RC 1.25 3.00
145 Stephen Jackson RC 2.00 5.00
146 Jerome Moiso RC 1.25 3.00
147 Keyon Dooling RC 1.25 3.00
148 Erick Barkley RC 1.25 3.00
149 Jason Collier RC 1.25 3.00
150 Jamaal Magloire RC 1.25 3.00
151 DeShawn Stevenson RC 1.50 4.00
152 Hedo Turkoglu RC 2.50 6.00
153 Morris Peterson RC 2.00 5.00
154 Jamal Crawford RC 2.00 5.00
155 Etan Thomas RC 1.25 3.00
156 Quentin Richardson RC 2.00 5.00
157 Mateen Cleaves RC 1.25 3.00
158 Donnell Harvey RC 1.25 3.00
159 Mark Madsen RC 1.25 3.00
160 Desmond Mason RC 1.50 4.00
161 Speedy Claxton RC 1.25 3.00
162 Hanno Mottola RC 1.25 3.00
163 Mamadou N'Diaye RC 1.25 3.00
164 Eduardo Najera RC 1.25 3.00
165 Khalid El-Amin RC 1.25 3.00

2000-01 Upper Deck Encore High Definition

Randomly inserted in packs at one in 16, this 6-card set features player's that are the cornerstones of their teams. Card backs carry a "HD" prefix.

COMPLETE SET (6) 4.00 10.00
HD1 Stephon Marbury .50 1.25
HD2 Steve Francis .60 1.50
HD3 Shaquille O'Neal 1.50 4.00
HD4 Kevin Garnett 1.25 3.00
HD5 Kobe Bryant 3.00 8.00
HD6 Tracy McGrady 1.00 2.50

2000-01 Upper Deck Encore NBA Warm-Ups

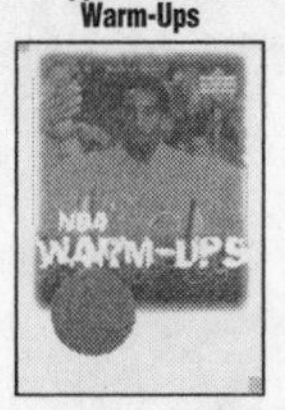

Randomly inserted into packs at one in 8, this 21-card set features swatches of actual game-worn warm-up jerseys. Card backs carry the player's initials followed by the letter "W".

AMW Andre Miller 2.50 6.00
BDW Baron Davis 3.00 8.00
CAW Courtney Alexander 2.00 5.00
CMW Chris Mihm 2.00 5.00
DJW DerMarr Johnson 2.00 5.00
DMW Darius Miles 2.00 5.00
DSW DeShawn Stevenson 2.50 6.00
HMW Hanno Mottola 2.00 5.00
JCW Jamal Crawford 3.00 8.00
JMW Jerome Moiso 2.00 5.00
JSW Jerry Stackhouse 2.50 6.00
KBW Kobe Bryant 12.00 30.00
KDW Keyon Dooling 2.00 5.00
KEW Khalid El-Amin 2.00 5.00
KGW Kevin Garnett 6.00 15.00
KMW Kenyon Martin 5.00 12.00
MAW Corey Maggette 2.50 6.00
MFW Marcus Fizer 2.00 5.00
MMW Mike Miller 4.00 10.00
TMW Tracy McGrady 5.00 12.00
WSW Wally Szczerbiak 2.50 6.00

2000-01 Upper Deck Encore NBA Warm-Ups Autographs

Randomly inserted into packs, this 15-card set features both swatches of actual game-worn warm-up jerseys and an authentic autograph of the depicted player. Card backs carry the player's initials followed by the letter "A". Please note that each of these cards are numbered to 50. Also note that a few players packed out as exchange cards, and must be redeemed no later than 12/05/01.

CMA Chris Mihm/50 8.00 20.00
DJA DerMarr Johnson/50 8.00 20.00
DMA Darius Miles/50 8.00 20.00
DSA DeShawn Stevenson/50 10.00 25.00
JCA Jamal Crawford/50 12.00 30.00
KEA Khalid El-Amin/50 8.00 20.00
KGA Kevin Garnett/21 60.00 120.00
KMA Kenyon Martin/50 20.00 50.00
MFA Marcus Fizer/50 8.00 20.00
MMA Mike Miller/50 15.00 40.00
TMA Tracy McGrady/50 30.00 60.00

2000-01 Upper Deck Encore Performers

Randomly inserted into packs at one in 8, this 12-card set features the league's top performers. Card backs carry a "EP" prefix.

COMPLETE SET (12) 6.00 15.00
EP1 Jason Kidd 1.00 2.50
EP2 Stephon Marbury .50 1.25
EP3 Gary Payton .60 1.50
EP4 Kevin Garnett 1.25 3.00
EP5 Antonio McDyess .50 1.25
EP6 Shareef Abdur-Rahim .50 1.25
EP7 Tim Duncan 1.25 3.00
EP8 Allan Houston .50 1.25
EP9 Kobe Bryant 3.00 8.00
EP10 Andre Miller .50 1.25
EP11 Vince Carter 1.25 3.00
EP12 Ray Allen .60 1.50

2000-01 Upper Deck Encore Powerful Stuff

Randomly inserted in packs at one in 8, this 12-card set highlights some of the more incredible dunks from today's superstars. Card backs carry a "PS" prefix.

COMPLETE SET (12) 8.00 20.00
PS1 Kobe Bryant 3.00 8.00
PS2 Tim Duncan 1.25 3.00
PS3 Allen Iverson 1.25 3.00
PS4 Karl Malone .75 2.00
PS5 Tracy McGrady 1.00 2.50
PS6 Shaquille O'Neal 1.50 4.00
PS7 Vince Carter 1.25 3.00
PS8 Chris Webber .60 1.50
PS9 Eddie Jones .60 1.50
PS10 Kevin Garnett 1.25 3.00
PS11 Elton Brand .60 1.50
PS12 Paul Pierce .75 2.00

2000-01 Upper Deck Encore Star Signatures

Randomly inserted in packs at one in 48, this 37-card insert set features authentic autographs from some of the NBA's elite players. Card backs carry the player's initials as numbering. Please note that a few of the players packed out as exchange cards and must be redeemed no later that 12/05/01.

CA Courtney Alexander 4.00 10.00
CM Chris Mihm 4.00 10.00
CO Corey Maggette 4.00 10.00
CR Jamal Crawford 6.00 15.00
DH Donnell Harvey 4.00 10.00
DJ DerMarr Johnson 4.00 10.00
DM Darius Miles 4.00 10.00
DS DeShawn Stevenson 5.00 12.00
EB Erick Barkley 4.00 10.00
EJ Eddie Jones 12.50 30.00
ET Etan Thomas 4.00 10.00
GP Gary Payton 15.00 30.00
HM Hanno Mottola 4.00 10.00
JA Jamaal Magloire 4.00 10.00
JM Jerome Moiso 4.00 10.00
JO Jermaine O'Neal 6.00 15.00
JP Joel Przybilla 4.00 10.00
JS Jerry Stackhouse 8.00 20.00
KB Kobe Bryant 80.00 160.00
KE Khalid El-Amin 4.00 10.00
KM Kenyon Martin 8.00 20.00
LH Larry Hughes 4.00 10.00
MC Mateen Cleaves 4.00 10.00
MK Mark Madsen 4.00 10.00
MM Mike Miller 8.00 20.00
MN Mamadou N'Diaye 4.00 10.00
MP Morris Peterson 4.00 10.00
RH Richard Hamilton 5.00 12.00
RM Reggie Miller 40.00 100.00
SC Speedy Claxton 4.00 10.00
SF Steve Francis 5.00 12.00
SM Shawn Marion 5.00 12.00
SS Stromile Swift 4.00 10.00
TH Tim Hardaway 8.00 20.00
WS Wally Szczerbiak 5.00 12.00

2000-01 Upper Deck Encore Upper Realm

Randomly inserted in packs at one in 16, this 6-card set features the league's most valuable players. Card backs carry a "UR" prefix.

COMPLETE SET (6) 5.00 12.0
UR1 Shaquille O'Neal 1.50 4.0
UR2 Allen Iverson 1.25 3.0
UR3 Tim Duncan 1.25 3.0
UR4 Kobe Bryant 3.00 8.0
UR5 Chris Webber .60 1.5
UR6 Kevin Garnett 1.25 3.0

2000-01 Upper Deck Encore Vertical Forces

Randomly inserted in packs at one in 16, this 6-card set features the league's most sensational leapers. Card backs carry a "VF" prefix.

COMPLETE SET (6) 4.00 10.0
VF1 Kobe Bryant 3.00 8.0
VF2 Vince Carter 1.25 3.0
VF3 Rashard Lewis .60 1.5
VF4 Chris Webber .60 1.5
VF5 Steve Francis .60 1.5
VF6 Kevin Garnett 1.25 3.0

2005-06 Upper Deck ESPN

Released in September 2005, ESPN consists of 132-cards divided up into 90 veterans and 40 rookies. base cards have borders along the left side and bottom of the card set to match team colors and the ESPN logo and player's name below centered pictures. ESPN was packaged in 24-pack boxes where each pack contains nine cards and carried an initial SRP of $2.99.

COMPLETE SET (132) 15.00 40.0
COMP.SET w/o SP's (90) 6.00 15.0
1 Josh Childress .15 .4
2 Josh Smith .20 .5
3 Al Harrington .15 .4
4 Antoine Walker .15 .4
5 Ricky Davis .15 .4
6 Paul Pierce .25 .6
7 Kareem Rush .12 .3
8 Emeka Okafor .20 .5
9 Gerald Wallace .20 .5
10 Eddy Curry .15 .4
11 Kirk Hinrich .20 .5
12 Ben Gordon .20 .5
13 Drew Gooden .15 .4
14 LeBron James 1.00 2.5
15 Zydrunas Ilgauskas .15 .4
16 Dirk Nowitzki .30 .7
17 Jason Terry .15 .4
18 Josh Howard .15 .4
19 Carmelo Anthony .40 1.0
20 Kenyon Martin .20 .5
21 Andre Miller .15 .4
22 Ben Wallace .20 .5
23 Chauncey Billups .20 .5
24 Richard Hamilton .15 .4
25 Troy Murphy .15 .4
26 Jason Richardson .20 .5
27 Baron Davis .20 .5
28 Tracy McGrady .25 .6
29 Yao Ming .25 .6
30 Juwan Howard .15 .4
31 Jermaine O'Neal .20 .5
32 Reggie Miller .20 .5
33 Ron Artest .20 .5
34 Corey Maggette .15 .4
35 Elton Brand .20 .5
36 Bobby Simmons .12 .3
37 Caron Butler .20 .5
38 Kobe Bryant 1.00 2.5
39 Lamar Odom .20 .5
40 Mike Miller .20 .5
41 Jason Williams .15 .4
42 Pau Gasol .20 .5
43 Dwyane Wade .50 1.2
44 Eddie Jones .15 .4
45 Shaquille O'Neal .40 1.0
46 Desmond Mason .12 .3
47 Maurice Williams .15 .4
48 Michael Redd .20 .5
49 Kevin Garnett .40 1.0
50 Latrell Sprewell .15 .4
51 Sam Cassell .20 .5
52 Vince Carter .30 .7
53 Jason Kidd .30 .7
54 Richard Jefferson .20 .5
55 Dan Dickau .12 .3
56 Jamaal Magloire .12 .3
57 J.R. Smith .20 .5

58 Jamal Crawford .15 .40
59 Stephon Marbury .15 .40
60 Allan Houston .12 .30
61 Dwight Howard .40 1.00
62 Grant Hill .25 .60
63 Steve Francis .20 .50
64 Allen Iverson .30 .75
65 Andre Iguodala .20 .50
66 Chris Webber .20 .50
67 Amare Stoudemire .20 .50
68 Shawn Marion .20 .50
69 Steve Nash .25 .60
70 Damon Stoudamire .15 .40
71 Shareef Abdur-Rahim .15 .40
72 Zach Randolph .15 .40
73 Brad Miller .20 .50
74 Mike Bibby .20 .50
75 Peja Stojakovic .20 .50
76 Manu Ginobili .20 .50
77 Tim Duncan .30 .75
78 Tony Parker .20 .50
79 Rashard Lewis .20 .50
80 Ray Allen .20 .50
81 Luke Ridnour .15 .40
82 Rafer Alston .12 .30
83 Jalen Rose .20 .50
84 Chris Bosh .20 .50
85 Andrei Kirilenko .15 .40
86 Carlos Boozer .20 .50
87 Matt Harpring .15 .40
88 Antawn Jamison .20 .50
89 Gilbert Arenas .20 .50
90 Larry Hughes .15 .40
91 Chris Taft RC .75 2.00
92 Marvin Williams RC 1.00 2.50
93 Chris Paul RC 3.00 8.00
94 Andrew Bogut RC 1.25 3.00
95 Martynas Andriuskevicius RC .75 2.00
96 Louis Williams RC 1.25 3.00
97 C.J. Miles RC 1.00 2.50
98 Gerald Green RC 1.00 2.50
99 Rashad McCants RC .75 2.00
100 Sarunas Jasikevicius RC .75 2.00
101 Andrew Bynum RC 2.50 6.00
102 Raymond Felton RC 1.25 3.00
103 Hakim Warrick RC 1.00 2.50
104 Deron Williams RC 2.00 5.00
105 Daniel Ewing RC .75 2.00
106 Martell Webster RC .75 2.00
107 Johan Petro RC .75 2.00
108 Travis Diener RC .75 2.00
109 Joey Graham RC .75 2.00
110 Antoine Wright RC .75 2.00
111 Ersan Ilyasova RC 1.00 2.50
112 Jason Maxiell RC .75 2.00
113 Linas Kleiza RC .75 2.00
114 Jarrett Jack RC .75 2.00
115 Danny Granger RC 1.50 4.00
116 Monta Ellis RC 1.50 4.00
117 Francisco Garcia RC 1.00 2.50
118 Ryan Gomes RC .75 2.00
119 Wayne Simien RC .75 2.00
120 Von Wafer RC .75 2.00
121 Dijon Thompson RC .75 2.00
122 Nate Robinson RC 1.00 2.50
123 Bracey Wright RC .75 2.00
124 Andray Blatche RC 1.00 2.50
125 Channing Frye RC 1.00 2.50
126 Salim Stoudamire RC .75 2.00
127 Luther Head RC .75 2.00
128 Julius Hodge RC .75 2.00
129 David Lee RC 1.25 3.00
130 Ike Diogu RC .75 2.00
131 Sean May RC .75 2.00
132 Brandon Bass RC 1.00 2.50

2005-06 Upper Deck ESPN 25th Anniversary

Randomly seeded in packs, this 132-card set parallels the base ESPN set enhanced with sequential numbering to 25.
*1-90 25th: 12X TO 30X BASE HI
*91-132 RC 25th: 3X TO 8X BASE HI

2005-06 Upper Deck ESPN ESPY Award Winners

Inserted in packs at the rate of one in one along with the Play of the Day, Highlight Reel, Fast Break and ESPN the Mag inserts, this 20-card set is horizontally designed with a player photo on the left and a picture of the ESPY trophy on the right. Several players have multiple versions, see checklist for details.

COMPLETE SET (20) 15.00 40.00
*25th ANNIV: 6X TO 15X BASE ESPY HI
25th ANNIVERSARY PRINT RUN 25 SETS
AJ Antawn Jamison .40 1.00
CA Carmelo Anthony .75 2.00
EB Elton Brand .40 1.00
GH Grant Hill .50 1.25
KG Kevin Garnett .75 2.00
KV Keith Van Horn .30 .75
LJ LeBron James 2.00 5.00
MF Michael Finley .40 1.00
MJ1 Michael Jordan 2.50 6.00
MJ2 Michael Jordan 2.50 6.00
MJ3 Michael Jordan 2.50 6.00
MJ4 Michael Jordan 2.50 6.00
MJ5 Michael Jordan 2.50 6.00
MJ6 Michael Jordan 2.50 6.00
MJ7 Michael Jordan 2.50 6.00
MJ8 Michael Jordan 2.50 6.00
MJ9 Michael Jordan 2.50 6.00
MJ10 Michael Jordan 2.50 6.00
SO Shaquille O'Neal .75 2.00
TD Tim Duncan .60 1.50

2005-06 Upper Deck ESPN Highlight Reel

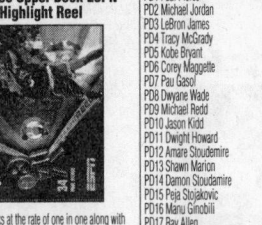

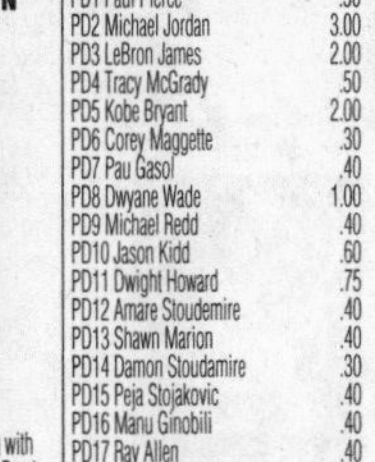

Inserted in packs at the rate of one in one along with the Play of the Day, ESPY Award Winners, Fast Break and ESPN the Mag inserts, this set features a horizontal design with a black Higlight Reel on the left and a player image on the right.

COMPLETE SET (20) 10.00 25.00
*25th ANNIV: 6X TO 15X BASE HI
25th ANNIVERSARY PRINT RUN 25 SETS
HR1 Paul Pierce .50 1.25
HR2 Michael Jordan 3.00 8.00
HR3 LeBron James 2.00 5.00
HR4 Dirk Nowitzki .60 1.50
HR5 Ben Wallace .40 1.00
HR6 Jason Richardson .40 1.00
HR7 Yao Ming .50 1.25
HR8 Jermaine O'Neal .40 1.00
HR9 Kobe Bryant 2.00 5.00
HR10 Dwyane Wade 1.00 2.50
HR11 Vince Carter .60 1.50
HR12 Richard Jefferson .40 1.00
HR13 Baron Davis .40 1.00
HR14 Stephon Marbury .30 .75
HR15 Allen Iverson .60 1.50
HR16 Amare Stoudemire .40 1.00
HR17 Steve Nash .50 1.25
HR18 Tim Duncan .60 1.50
HR19 Ray Allen .40 1.00
HR20 Chris Bosh .40 1.00

2005-06 Upper Deck ESPN Ink

Inserted in packs at the rate of one in 480, this set features NBA Players along with ESPN Personalities. Cards are horizontally designed with player photos on the right side and an centered autographed sticker on the left. SP information for this set was provided by Upper Deck.

AJ Antawn Jamison SP 8.00 20.00
LC Linda Cohn 8.00 20.00

2005-06 Upper Deck ESPN NBA Fast Break

Inserted in packs at the rate of one in one along with the Play of the Day, Highlight Reel, ESPY Award Winners and ESPN the Mag inserts, this 20-card set features a Fast Break logo along the left side of the card in silver foil highlights and full color player action photography.

COMPLETE SET (20) 8.00 20.00
*25th ANNIV: 6X TO 15X BASE HI
25th ANNIVERSARY PRINT RUN 25 SETS
FB1 Antoine Walker .30 .75
FB2 Gary Payton .40 1.00
FB3 Michael Jordan 3.00 8.00
FB4 LeBron James 2.00 5.00
FB5 Carmelo Anthony .75 2.00
FB6 Chauncey Billups .40 1.00
FB7 Richard Hamilton .30 .75
FB8 Jason Richardson .40 1.00
FB9 Yao Ming .50 1.25
FB10 Kobe Bryant 2.00 5.00
FB11 Dwyane Wade 1.00 2.50
FB12 Jason Kidd .60 1.50
FB13 Stephon Marbury .30 .75
FB14 Steve Francis .40 1.00
FB15 Steve Nash .50 1.25
FB16 Mike Bibby .40 1.00
FB17 Tony Parker .40 1.00
FB18 Rashard Lewis .40 1.00
FB19 Andrei Kirilenko .30 .75
FB20 Gilbert Arenas .40 1.00

2005-06 Upper Deck ESPN Plays of the Day

Inserted in packs at the rate of one in one along with the ESPY Award Winners, Highlight Reel, Fast Break and ESPN the Mag inserts, this 20-card set features full color player photos and a border along the bottom of the card with a Plays of the Day logo in silver foil.

COMPLETE SET (20) 6.00 15.00
*25th ANNIV: 6X TO 15X BASE HI
25th ANNIVERSARY PRINT RUN 25 SETS
PD1 Paul Pierce .50 1.25
PD2 Michael Jordan 3.00 8.00
PD3 LeBron James 2.00 5.00
PD4 Tracy McGrady .50 1.25
PD5 Kobe Bryant 2.00 5.00
PD6 Corey Maggette .30 .75
PD7 Pau Gasol .40 1.00
PD8 Dwyane Wade 1.00 2.50
PD9 Michael Redd .40 1.00
PD10 Jason Kidd .60 1.50
PD11 Dwight Howard .75 2.00
PD12 Amare Stoudemire .40 1.00
PD13 Shawn Marion .40 1.00
PD14 Damon Stoudamire .30 .75
PD15 Peja Stojakovic .40 1.00
PD16 Manu Ginobili .40 1.00
PD17 Ray Allen .40 1.00
PD18 Andrei Kirilenko .30 .75
PD19 Carlos Boozer .40 1.00
PD20 Gilbert Arenas .40 1.00

2005-06 Upper Deck ESPN Sports Center Swatches

Found in packs at the rate of one in 12, this 42-card set features an "E" shaped swatch of memorabilia along with color player photos on a card shaded to match the player's team colors.

AM Andre Miller 2.50 6.00
AN Andre Iguodala 3.00 8.00
AS Amare Stoudemire 3.00 8.00
AW Antoine Walker 2.50 6.00
BD Baron Davis 3.00 8.00
BW Ben Wallace 3.00 8.00
CA Carmelo Anthony 6.00 15.00
CB Caron Butler 3.00 8.00
CH Chauncey Billups 3.00 8.00
CM Corey Maggette 2.50 6.00
CW Chris Webber 3.00 8.00
DH Devin Harris 3.00 8.00
DM Desmond Mason 2.00 5.00
DN Dirk Nowitzki 5.00 12.00
EC Eddy Curry 2.50 6.00
ES Eric Snow 2.00 5.00
GA Gilbert Arenas 3.00 8.00
GP Gary Payton 3.00 8.00
JC Josh Childress 2.50 6.00
JH Josh Howard 3.00 8.00
JK Jason Kidd 5.00 12.00
JO Jermaine O'Neal 3.00 8.00
JR Jalen Rose 3.00 8.00
KB Kobe Bryant 10.00 25.00
KG Kevin Garnett 6.00 15.00
KM Kenyon Martin 3.00 8.00
KR Kareem Rush 2.00 5.00
LJ LeBron James 12.50 30.00
LO Lamar Odom 3.00 8.00
LS Latrell Sprewell 2.50 6.00
MJ Michael Jordan 30.00 75.00
PG Pau Gasol 3.00 8.00
PP Paul Pierce 4.00 10.00
RA Ray Allen 3.00 8.00
RM Reggie Miller 3.00 8.00
SF Steve Francis 3.00 8.00
SN Steve Nash 4.00 10.00
SO Shaquille O'Neal 6.00 15.00
ST Sebastian Telfair 2.50 6.00
TD Tim Duncan 5.00 12.00
TM Tracy McGrady 4.00 10.00
YM Yao Ming 4.00 10.00

2005-06 Upper Deck ESPN the Magazine Covers

Inserted in packs at the rate of one in one along with the Play of the Day, Highlight Reel, Fast Break and ESPY Award Winners inserts, this seven card set features colored borders to match the showcased player's team colors along with an image of a memorable ESPN the Magazine cover.

COMPLETE SET (7) 6.00 15.00
*25th ANNIV: 6X TO 15X MAG COV. HI
25th ANNIVERSARY PRINT RUN 25 SETS
BW Ben Wallace .40 1.00
CP Chris Paul 1.50 4.00
DH Dwight Howard .75 2.00
LJ1 LeBron James 2.00 5.00
LJ2 LeBron James 2.00 5.00
MJ1 Michael Jordan 3.00 8.00
MJ2 Michael Jordan 3.00 8.00

2006 Upper Deck Finals

LJ1 LeBron James 2.00 5.00
MJ1 Michael Jordan 4.00 10.00

2007 Upper Deck Finals

FLJ1 LeBron James 2.50 6.00
FMJ1 Michael Jordan 4.00 10.00

2002-03 Upper Deck Finite

Released in December 2002, Upper Deck Finite was issued as a 242-card set divided up as follows: numbers 1-100 are veteran base cards, numbers 101-150 are Major Factors cards and are sequentially numbered to 500, numbers 151-180 are Prominent Powers cards and are sequentially numbered to 250, numbers 181-200 are First Class Finite cards and are sequentially numbered to 25, numbers 201-221 feature rookies and are sequentially numbered to 900, numbers 222-233 also feature rookies and are sequentially numbered to 600, and numbers 234-242 are rookie cards sequentially numbered to 200. Finite was packaged in 10 pack boxes with each pack containing three cards and carried a suggested retail price of $9.99.

COMP.SET w/o SP's (100) 15.00 40.00
1 Shareef Abdur-Rahim .50 1.25
2 Theo Ratliff .40 1.00
3 Glenn Robinson .50 1.25
4 Jason Terry .50 1.25
5 Vin Baker .50 1.25
6 Kedrick Brown .40 1.00
7 Paul Pierce .75 2.00
8 Antoine Walker .50 1.25
9 Tyson Chandler .50 1.25
10 Eddy Curry .50 1.25
11 Jalen Rose .50 1.25
12 Chris Mihm .40 1.00
13 Darius Miles .50 1.25
14 Ricky Davis .50 1.25
15 Michael Finley .60 1.50
16 Raef LaFrentz .50 1.25
17 Steve Nash .75 2.00
18 Dirk Nowitzki 1.00 2.50
19 Nick Van Exel .50 1.25
20 Marcus Camby .50 1.25
21 Juwan Howard .50 1.25
22 James Posey .50 1.25
23 Chauncey Billups .60 1.50
24 Richard Hamilton .50 1.25
25 Ben Wallace .60 1.50
26 Clifford Robinson .40 1.00
27 Gilbert Arenas .60 1.50
28 Antawn Jamison .60 1.50
29 Jason Richardson .60 1.50
30 Eddie Griffin .40 1.00
31 Steve Francis .60 1.50
32 Cuttino Mobley .50 1.25
33 Reggie Miller .60 1.50
34 Jermaine O'Neal .60 1.50
35 Jamaal Tinsley .60 1.50
36 Ron Mercer .40 1.00
37 Elton Brand .60 1.50
38 Andre Miller .50 1.25
39 Lamar Odom .60 1.50
40 Kobe Bryant 3.00 8.00
41 Rick Fox .50 1.25
42 Devean George .40 1.00
43 Shaquille O'Neal 1.50 4.00
44 Shane Battier .60 1.50
45 Pau Gasol .75 2.00
46 Jason Williams .50 1.25
47 LaPhonso Ellis .50 1.25
48 Eddie Jones .50 1.25
49 Brian Grant .50 1.25
50 Ray Allen .60 1.50
51 Tim Thomas .40 1.00
52 Sam Cassell .50 1.25
53 Terrell Brandon .40 1.00
54 Kevin Garnett 1.25 3.00
55 Wally Szczerbiak .50 1.25
56 Marc Jackson .40 1.00
57 Richard Jefferson .60 1.50
58 Jason Kidd 1.00 2.50
59 Kenyon Martin .60 1.50
60 Kerry Kittles .40 1.00
61 Baron Davis .60 1.50
62 Jamal Mashburn .50 1.25
63 David Wesley .40 1.00
64 P.J. Brown .40 1.00
65 Latrell Sprewell .60 1.50
66 Antonio McDyess .50 1.25
67 Allan Houston .50 1.25
68 Tracy McGrady 1.00 2.50
69 Mike Miller .60 1.50
70 Darrell Armstrong .40 1.00
71 Allen Iverson 1.00 2.50
72 Aaron McKie .40 1.00
73 Keith Van Horn .50 1.25
74 Stephon Marbury .50 1.25
75 Shawn Marion .60 1.50
76 Anfernee Hardaway 1.00 2.50
77 Rasheed Wallace .60 1.50
78 Bonzi Wells .50 1.25
79 Scottie Pippen 1.00 2.50
80 Mike Bibby .60 1.50
81 Peja Stojakovic .60 1.50
82 Chris Webber .60 1.50
83 Hedo Turkoglu .60 1.50
84 Tim Duncan 1.25 3.00
85 David Robinson 1.00 2.50
86 Tony Parker .75 2.00
87 Malik Rose .40 1.00
88 Gary Payton .60 1.50
89 Rashard Lewis .60 1.50
90 Brent Barry .40 1.00
91 Desmond Mason .50 1.25
92 Vince Carter 1.00 2.50
93 Morris Peterson .40 1.00
94 Antonio Davis .40 1.00
95 Karl Malone .75 2.00
96 John Stockton .75 2.00
97 Andrei Kirilenko .60 1.50
98 Kwame Brown .40 1.00
99 Jerry Stackhouse .50 1.25
100 Michael Jordan 5.00 12.00
101 Kobe Bryant MF 6.00 15.00
102 Eddie Griffin MF .75 2.00
103 Shawn Marion MF 1.25 3.00
104 Richard Jefferson MF 1.25 3.00
105 Jermaine O'Neal MF 1.25 3.00
106 Allan Houston MF 1.00 2.50
107 Shane Battier MF 1.25 3.00
108 Hedo Turkoglu MF 1.25 3.00
109 Michael Finley MF 1.25 3.00
110 Jamal Mashburn MF 1.00 2.50
111 Rashard Lewis MF 1.25 3.00
112 Tyson Chandler MF 1.00 2.50
113 Terrell Brandon MF .75 2.00
114 Antonio Davis MF .75 2.00
115 Jamaal Tinsley MF .75 2.00
116 Tony Parker MF 1.50 4.00
117 Ray Allen MF 1.25 3.00
118 Rasheed Wallace MF 1.25 3.00
119 Cuttino Mobley MF 1.00 2.50
120 Jason Terry MF 1.00 2.50
121 Mike Miller MF 1.25 3.00
122 Jalen Rose MF 1.00 2.50
123 Morris Peterson MF .75 2.00
124 Ricky Davis MF 1.00 2.50
125 Peja Stojakovic MF 1.25 3.00
126 Gary Payton MF 1.25 3.00
127 Andrei Kirilenko MF 1.25 3.00
128 Tim Duncan MF 2.50 6.00
129 Anfernee Hardaway MF 2.00 5.00
130 Shaquille O'Neal MF 3.00 8.00
131 Latrell Sprewell MF 1.00 2.50
132 Shareef Abdur-Rahim MF 1.00 2.50
133 Steve Nash MF 1.50 4.00
134 Lamar Odom MF 1.25 3.00
135 Antawn Jamison MF 1.25 3.00
136 Reggie Miller MF 1.25 3.00
137 Tim Thomas MF .75 2.00
138 Eddy Curry MF 1.00 2.50
139 Jason Williams MF 1.00 2.50
140 John Stockton MF 1.50 4.00
141 Ben Wallace MF 1.25 3.00
142 Bonzi Wells MF .75 2.00
143 David Robinson MF 2.00 5.00
144 Stephon Marbury MF 1.00 2.50
145 Vince Carter MF 2.00 5.00
146 James Posey MF .75 2.00
147 Wally Szczerbiak MF 1.00 2.50
148 Eddie Jones MF 1.00 2.50
149 Scottie Pippen MF 2.00 5.00
150 Michael Jordan MF 10.00 25.00
151 Kobe Bryant PP 12.00 30.00
152 Pau Gasol PP 3.00 8.00
153 Tim Duncan PP 5.00 12.00
154 Karl Malone PP 3.00 8.00
155 Allan Houston PP 2.00 5.00
156 Steve Nash PP 3.00 8.00
157 Shawn Marion PP 2.50 6.00
158 Jamal Mashburn PP 2.00 5.00
159 Shaquille O'Neal PP 6.00 15.00
160 Reggie Miller PP 2.50 6.00
161 Latrell Sprewell PP 2.50 6.00
162 Peja Stojakovic PP 2.50 6.00
163 Jalen Rose PP 2.00 5.00
164 Kenyon Martin PP 2.50 6.00
165 Baron Davis PP 2.50 6.00
166 Ray Allen PP 2.50 6.00
167 Vince Carter PP 4.00 10.00
168 Rashard Lewis PP 2.50 6.00
169 Steve Francis PP 2.50 6.00
170 Jermaine O'Neal PP 2.50 6.00
171 Shane Battier PP 2.50 6.00
172 Shareef Abdur-Rahim PP 2.00 5.00
173 Michael Finley PP 2.50 6.00
174 John Stockton PP 3.00 8.00
175 Jamaal Tinsley PP 1.50 4.00
176 Wally Szczerbiak PP 2.00 5.00
177 Antawn Jamison PP 2.50 6.00
178 Richard Jefferson PP 2.50 6.00
179 Rasheed Wallace PP 2.50 6.00
180 Michael Jordan PP 25.00 60.00
181 Kobe Bryant FC 80.00 200.00
182 Paul Pierce FC 20.00 50.00
183 Nikoloz Tskitishvili FC 15.00 40.00
184 Kareem Rush FC 15.00 40.00
185 Jason Kidd FC 25.00 60.00
186 Dominique Wilkins FC 20.00 50.00
187 Kevin Garnett FC 30.00 80.00
188 Antoine Walker FC 12.00 30.00
189 Jay Williams FC 20.00 50.00
190 DaJuan Wagner FC 15.00 40.00
191 Caron Butler FC 25.00 60.00
192 Mike Bibby FC 15.00 40.00
193 Mike Miller FC 15.00 40.00
194 Tyson Chandler FC 12.00 30.00
195 Drew Gooden FC 25.00 60.00
196 Kenyon Martin FC 15.00 40.00
197 Marcus Fizer FC 10.00 25.00
198 Nene Hilario FC 20.00 50.00
199 Yao Ming FC 50.00 125.00
200 Michael Jordan FC 125.00 300.00
201 Marko Jaric 1.50 4.00
202 Dan Dickau RC 1.50 4.00
203 Tito Maddox RC 1.50 4.00
204 Predrag Savovic RC 1.50 4.00
205 Robert Archibald RC 1.50 4.00
206 Frank Williams RC 1.50 4.00
207 Ronald Murray RC 1.50 4.00
208 Lonny Baxter RC 1.50 4.00
209 Efthimios Rentzias RC 1.50 4.00
210 Vincent Yarbrough RC 1.50 4.00
211 Gordan Giricek RC 1.50 4.00
212 Carlos Boozer RC 3.00 8.00
213 John Salmons RC 2.00 5.00
214 Manu Ginobili RC 5.00 12.00
215 Roger Mason Jr. RC 1.50 4.00
216 Chris Jefferies RC 1.50 4.00
217 Sam Clancy RC 1.50 4.00
218 Rasual Butler RC 1.50 4.00
219 Dan Gadzuric RC 1.50 4.00
220 Tayshaun Prince RC 2.00 5.00
221 Casey Jacobsen RC 1.50 4.00
222 Qyntel Woods RC 2.00 5.00
223 Jiri Welsch RC 2.00 5.00
224 Curtis Borchardt RC 2.00 5.00
225 Marcus Haislip RC 2.00 5.00
226 Kareem Rush RC 2.00 5.00
227 Fred Jones RC 2.00 5.00
228 Caron Butler RC 3.00 8.00
229 Juan Dixon RC 2.50 6.00
230 Ryan Humphrey RC 2.00 5.00
231 Melvin Ely RC 2.00 5.00
232 Bostjan Nachbar RC 2.00 5.00
233 Jared Jeffries RC 2.00 5.00
234 Jay Williams RC 8.00 20.00
235 Nikoloz Tskitishvili RC 6.00 15.00
236 Chris Wilcox RC 6.00 15.00
237 Drew Gooden RC 10.00 25.00
238 Amare Stoudemire RC 15.00 40.00
239 DaJuan Wagner RC 6.00 15.00
240 Nene Hilario RC 8.00 20.00
241 Mike Dunleavy RC 8.00 20.00
242 Yao Ming RC 20.00 50.00

2002-03 Upper Deck Finite Elements Dual Uniforms

Inserted in packs at the rate of one in 20, this eight card set features a horizontal design with a gray background, small square head shots of the players and two swatches of game used uniforms.

AIJKU Allen Iverson 6.00 15.00
Jason Kidd
JSSFU Joe Smith 5.00 12.00
Steve Francis
KBJRU Kobe Bryant 10.00 25.00
Jason Richardson
KGTBU Kevin Garnett 5.00 12.00
Terrell Brandon
LSCWU Latrell Sprewell 5.00 12.00
Charlie Ward
MJKBU Michael Jordan 50.00 120.00
Kobe Bryant
PPAWU Paul Pierce 8.00 20.00
Antoine Walker
TMMMU Tracy McGrady 6.00 15.00
Mike Miller

2002-03 Upper Deck Finite Elements Dual Warm-Ups

Randomly seeded in packs at the rate of one in four, this 20-card set utilizes the same set design as the Elements Dual Uniforms set but contains swatches of warm ups instead.

AHJJ Anfernee Hardaway 5.00 12.00
Joe Johnson
AIJK Allen Iverson 5.00 12.00
Jason Kidd
BDJM Baron Davis 4.00 10.00
Jamal Mashburn
DNSN Dirk Nowitzki 6.00 15.00
Steve Nash
ECTC Eddy Curry 4.00 10.00
Tyson Chandler
HTMB Hedo Turkoglu 4.00 10.00
Mike Bibby
JRAJ Jason Richardson 4.00 10.00
Antawn Jamison
KBAI Kobe Bryant 10.00 25.00
Allen Iverson
KBTM Kobe Bryant 10.00 25.00
Tracy McGrady
KGWS Kevin Garnett 5.00 12.00
Wally Szczerbiak
KMJS Karl Malone 5.00 12.00
John Stockton
MJKB Michael Jordan 50.00 120.00
Kobe Bryant
PPAW Paul Pierce 5.00 12.00
Antoine Walker
QREB Quentin Richardson 4.00 10.00
Elton Brand
RHKW Richard Hamilton 4.00 10.00
Kwame Brown
SADJ Shareef Abdur-Rahim 4.00 10.00
DerMarr Johnson
SMSM Stephon Marbury 4.00 10.00
Shawn Marion

2002-03 Upper Deck Finite Elements Jerseys

Randomly inserted in packs at the rate of one in ten, this 14-card set utilizes a horizontal card design with full color player photos on the right and swatches of jersey on the left.

BDJ Baron Davis 3.00 8.00
DNJ Dirk Nowitzki 5.00 12.00
EBJ Elton Brand 3.00 8.00
JRJ Jason Richardson 3.00 8.00
JWJ Jay Williams 4.00 10.00
KBJ Kobe Bryant 12.50 30.00
KMJ Karl Malone 4.00 10.00
MJJ Michael Jordan 50.00 120.00
SMJ Stephon Marbury 2.50 6.00

2002-03 Upper Deck Finite Signatures

Randomly inserted, this 27-card set features all sequentially numbered cards-print runs are listed below. Color player photos appear on the left and autographs appear on the right. Eleven players signed for a gold parallel set numbered to ten that is unpriced due to scarcity.

ASA Amare Stoudemire/80 75.00 150.00
AWA Antoine Walker/50 15.00 40.00
CBA Caron Butler/80 30.00 80.00
CWA Chris Wilcox/80 8.00 20.00
DGA Drew Gooden/80 12.00 30.00
DSA DeShawn Stevenson/100 5.00 12.00
DWA DaJuan Wagner/80 8.00 20.00
ETA Etan Thomas/146 5.00 12.00
JJA Jared Jeffries/80 5.00 12.00
JKA Jason Kidd/128 20.00 50.00
JMA Jamaal Magloire/100 5.00 12.00
JTA Jeff Trepagnier/112 5.00 12.00
JWA Jay Williams/80 10.00 25.00
KBA Kobe Bryant 125.00 250.00
KGA Kevin Garnett/25 60.00 150.00
KMA Kenyon Martin/104 10.00 25.00
KRA Kareem Rush/80 10.00 25.00
MBA Mike Bibby/80 10.00 25.00
MEA Melvin Ely/80 5.00 12.00
MFA Marcus Fizer/104 5.00 12.00
MJA Michael Jordan/23 400.00 700.00
MMA Mike Miller/80 10.00 25.00
MOA Jerome Moiso/146 5.00 12.00
NHA Nene Hilario/80 8.00 20.00
PPA Paul Pierce/104 15.00 40.00
TCA Tyson Chandler/80 12.50 30.00
YMA Yao Ming/80 60.00 150.00

2003-04 Upper Deck Finite

Released in late December/early January, Finite is composed of 342 cards. The breakdown of the set is as follows: cards 1-200 are all sequentially numbered and print runs alternate for odd and even cards. The odd numbered card focus on current NBA players and are sequentially numbered to 2999, while the even numbers focus on retired players and are sequentially numbered to 1999. Base cards have borders and full-color player photos are set against a colored grid pattern set to match the team colors. Card numbers 201-236 feature rookie players and are sequentially numbered to 750. Cards 237-242 also feature rookies and are sequentially numbered to 200. Cards 243-292 are designed differently with borders along the top and the bottom, the words Major Factors and sequential numbering to 1000. Cards 293-322 are part of Prominent Powers subset and are sequentially numbered to 500, and cards 323-342 are part of a First Class subset and are sequentially numbered to 50. Upper Deck Finite was packaged in ten pack boxes where packs contained three cards and carried a suggested retail price of $9.99.

1 Shareef Abdur-Rahim .40 1.00
2 Dominique Wilkins 1.00 2.50
3 Theo Ratliff .30 .75
4 Dan Dickau .50 1.25
5 Jason Terry .40 1.00
6 Dion Glover .50 1.25
7 Alan Henderson .30 .75
8 Paul Pierce 1.00 2.50
9 Larry Bird 1.50 4.00
10 Raef LaFrentz .50 1.25
11 Robert Parish .60 1.50
12 Jiri Welsch .50 1.25
13 John Havlicek .50 1.25
14 Vin Baker .50 1.25
15 Jamal Crawford .40 1.00
16 Michael Jordan 6.00 15.00
17 Scottie Pippen .75 2.00
18 Reggie Theus .75 2.00
19 Jalen Rose .40 1.00
20 Tyson Chandler .60 1.50
21 Eddy Curry .40 1.00
22 Dajuan Wagner .50 1.25
23 Lenny Wilkens .50 1.25
24 Carlos Boozer .75 2.00
25 World B. Free .50 1.25
26 Darius Miles .50 1.25
27 Craig Ehlo .30 .75
28 Ricky Davis .60 1.50
29 Dirk Nowitzki .75 2.00
30 Rolando Blackman .75 2.00
31 Steve Nash .60 1.50
32 Tony Delk .50 1.25
33 Antawn Jamison .50 1.25
34 Antoine Walker .75 2.00
35 Michael Finley .50 1.25
36 Andre Miller .60 1.50
37 David Thompson .50 1.25
38 Nene .60 1.50
39 Dan Issel .50 1.25
40 Nikoloz Tskitishvili .50 1.25
41 Alex English .50 1.25
42 Earl Boykins .50 1.25
43 Richard Hamilton .40 1.00
44 Mehmet Okur .60 1.50
45 Ben Wallace .60 1.50
46 Bob Lanier .75 2.00
47 Chauncey Billups .60 1.50
48 Dave Bing .75 2.00
49 Tayshaun Prince .50 1.25
50 Nick Van Exel .60 1.50
51 Erick Dampier .30 .75
52 Jason Richardson .75 2.00
53 Joe Barry Carroll .30 .75
54 Mike Dunleavy .60 1.50
55 Wilt Chamberlain 1.00 2.50
56 Troy Murphy .75 2.00
57 Steve Francis .50 1.25
58 Maurice Taylor .50 1.25
59 Yao Ming 1.00 2.50
60 Robert Reid .75 2.00
61 Cuttino Mobley .40 1.00
62 Moses Malone .75 2.00
63 Eddie Griffin .30 .75
64 Jermaine O'Neal .75 2.00
65 George McGinnis .50 1.25
66 Reggie Miller .60 1.50
67 Clark Kellogg .50 1.25
68 Jamaal Tinsley .50 1.25
69 Al Harrington .40 1.00
70 Ron Artest .75 2.00
71 Elton Brand .50 1.25
72 Corey Maggette .60 1.50
73 Chris Wilcox .30 .75
74 Quentin Richardson .60 1.50
75 Bill Walton .50 1.25
76 Marko Jaric .50 1.25
77 Kobe Bryant 2.50 6.00
78 Kareem Abdul-Jabbar 1.25 3.00
79 Shaquille O'Neal 1.25 3.00
80 Michael Cooper .75 2.00

81 Gary Payton .50 1.25
82 James Worthy 1.00 2.50
83 Karl Malone .60 1.50
84 Pau Gasol .75 2.00
85 Michael Dickerson .30 .75
86 Mike Miller .75 2.00
87 Brevin Knight .30 .75
88 Shane Battier .60 1.50
89 Stromile Swift .30 .75
90 Jason Williams .60 1.50
91 Caron Butler .50 1.25
92 Samaki Walker .50 1.25
93 Eddie Jones .40 1.00
94 Rasual Butler .50 1.25
95 Brian Grant .30 .75
96 Loren Woods .50 1.25
97 Lamar Odom .50 1.25
98 Desmond Mason .60 1.50
99 Sidney Moncrief .50 1.25
100 Toni Kukoc .75 2.00
101 Oscar Robertson .50 1.25
102 Michael Redd .75 2.00
103 Terry Cummings .50 1.25
104 Tim Thomas .50 1.25
105 Kevin Garnett 1.00 2.50
106 Troy Hudson .50 1.25
107 Sam Cassell .40 1.00
108 Latrell Sprewell .60 1.50
109 Michael Olowokandi .30 .75
110 Wally Szczerbiak .60 1.50
111 Jason Kidd .75 2.00
112 Otis Birdsong .75 2.00
113 Kenyon Martin .50 1.25
114 Albert King .50 1.25
115 Richard Jefferson .50 1.25
116 Kerry Kittles .50 1.25
117 Alonzo Mourning .60 1.50
118 Baron Davis .75 2.00
119 Darrell Armstrong .30 .75
120 Jamal Mashburn .60 1.50
121 P.J. Brown .30 .75
122 David Wesley .50 1.25
123 Courtney Alexander .30 .75
124 Jamaal Magloire .50 1.25
125 Allan Houston .40 1.00
126 Willis Reed .75 2.00
127 Keith Van Horn .40 1.00
128 Walt Frazier .75 2.00
129 Antonio McDyess .40 1.00
130 Earl Monroe .75 2.00
131 Kurt Thomas .30 .75
132 Tracy McGrady 1.00 2.50
133 Pat Garrity .30 .75
134 Grant Hill 1.00 2.50
135 Tyronn Lue .30 .75
136 Drew Gooden .60 1.50
137 Juwan Howard .40 1.00
138 Gordan Giricek .50 1.25
139 Allen Iverson .75 2.00
140 Julius Erving 1.50 4.00
141 Glenn Robinson .40 1.00
142 Maurice Cheeks .75 2.00
143 Aaron McKie .30 .75
144 Billy Cunningham .75 2.00
145 Eric Snow .30 .75
146 Stephon Marbury .60 1.50
147 Kevin Johnson .50 1.25
148 Amare Stoudemire 1.25 3.00
149 Larry Nance .50 1.25
150 Shawn Marion .75 2.00
151 Walter Davis .50 1.25
152 Anfernee Hardaway 1.25 3.00
153 Rasheed Wallace .50 1.25
154 Zach Randolph .75 2.00
155 Derek Anderson .30 .75
156 Dale Davis .50 1.25
157 Bonzi Wells .30 .75
158 Jim Paxson .75 2.00
159 Damon Stoudamire .40 1.00
160 Chris Webber .75 2.00
161 Vlade Divac .40 1.00
162 Mike Bibby .75 2.00
163 Bobby Jackson .30 .75
164 Peja Stojakovic .75 2.00
165 Doug Christie .30 .75
166 Brad Miller .75 2.00
167 Tim Duncan .75 2.00
168 Radoslav Nesterovic .50 1.25
169 Tony Parker .50 1.25
170 George Gervin .75 2.00
171 Manu Ginobili .60 1.50
172 Artis Gilmore .75 2.00
173 Ron Mercer .30 .75
174 Ray Allen .75 2.00
175 Spencer Haywood .50 1.25
176 Rashard Lewis .75 2.00
177 Fred Brown .50 1.25
178 Vladimir Radmanovic .50 1.25
179 Jack Sikma .50 1.25
180 Brent Barry .50 1.25
181 Vince Carter .75 2.00
182 Antonio Davis .50 1.25
183 Morris Peterson .30 .75
184 Alvin Williams .50 1.25
185 Chris Jefferies .30 .75
186 Jerome Williams .50 1.25
187 Andrei Kirilenko .50 1.25
188 Pete Maravich 5.00 12.00
189 Matt Harpring .40 1.00
190 Mark Eaton .75 2.00
191 Jarron Collins .30 .75
192 Greg Ostertag .50 1.25
193 Carlos Arroyo .40 1.00
194 Jerry Stackhouse .60 1.50
195 Wes Unseld .50 1.25
196 Gilbert Arenas .75 2.00
197 Larry Hughes .40 1.00
198 Kwame Brown .50 1.25
199 Jeff Malone .30 .75
200 Jared Jeffries .50 1.25
201 Aleksandar Pavlovic RC 2.00 5.00
202 James Lang RC 2.00 5.00
203 Jason Kapono RC 2.00 5.00
204 Luke Walton RC 2.00 5.00
205 Jerome Beasley RC 2.00 5.00
206 Willie Green RC 2.00 5.00
207 Steve Blake RC 2.50 6.00
208 Slavko Vranes RC 2.00 5.00
209 Zaur Pachulia RC 2.00 5.00
210 Travis Hansen RC 2.00 5.00
211 Keith Bogans RC 2.00 5.00
212 Kyle Korver RC 2.50 6.00
213 Brandon Hunter RC 2.00 5.00
214 James Jones RC 2.00 5.00
215 Josh Howard RC 2.00 5.00
216 Leandro Barbosa RC 2.50 6.00
217 Kendrick Perkins RC 3.00 8.00
218 Ndudi Ebi RC 2.00 5.00
219 Brian Cook RC 2.00 5.00
220 Travis Outlaw RC 2.50 6.00
221 Zoran Planinic RC 2.00 5.00
222 Dahntay Jones RC 2.00 5.00
223 Boris Diaw RC 2.50 6.00
224 Zarko Cabarkapa RC 2.00 5.00
225 Troy Bell RC 2.00 5.00
226 Reece Gaines RC 2.00 5.00
227 Luke Ridnour RC 2.50 6.00
228 Chris Kaman RC 2.50 6.00
229 Marcus Banks RC 2.50 6.00
230 Maciej Lampe RC 2.50 6.00
231 David West RC 3.00 8.00
232 Mickael Pietrus RC 2.50 6.00
233 Jarvis Hayes RC 2.50 6.00
234 Mike Sweetney RC 2.50 6.00
235 Kirk Hinrich RC 3.00 8.00
236 Chris Bosh RC 5.00 12.00
237 Nick Collison RC 8.00 20.00
238 T.J. Ford RC 10.00 25.00
239 Dwyane Wade RC 30.00 80.00
240 Carmelo Anthony RC 20.00 50.00
241 Darko Milicic RC 8.00 20.00
242 LeBron James RC 150.00 300.00
243 Michael Jordan MF 6.00 15.00
244 Kobe Bryant MF 4.00 10.00
245 Michael Finley MF .75 2.00
246 Andrei Kirilenko MF .75 2.00
247 Desmond Mason MF .60 1.50
248 Kenyon Martin MF .75 2.00
249 Shaquille O'Neal MF 2.00 5.00
250 Jamal Mashburn MF .60 1.50
251 Jason Terry MF .60 1.50
252 Andre Miller MF .60 1.50
253 Keith Van Horn MF .60 1.50
254 Derek Anderson MF .50 1.25
255 Stephon Marbury MF .60 1.50
256 Glenn Robinson MF .60 1.50
257 Richard Hamilton MF .60 1.50
258 Lamar Odom MF .75 2.00
259 Bonzi Wells MF .50 1.25
260 Wally Szczerbiak MF .60 1.50
261 Alonzo Mourning MF 1.00 2.50
262 Gilbert Arenas MF .75 2.00
263 Mike Bibby MF .75 2.00
264 Antawn Jamison MF .75 2.00
265 Tony Parker MF .75 2.00
266 Reggie Miller MF .75 2.00
267 Vince Carter MF 1.25 3.00
268 Richard Jefferson MF .75 2.00
269 Nene MF .60 1.50
270 Grant Hill MF 1.00 2.50
271 Rashard Lewis MF .75 2.00
272 Shawn Marion MF .75 2.00
273 Morris Peterson MF .50 1.25
274 Chauncey Billups MF .75 2.00
275 Eddie Jones MF .60 1.50
276 Raef LaFrentz MF .50 1.25
277 Jerry Stackhouse MF .60 1.50
278 Pau Gasol MF .75 2.00
279 Darius Miles MF .50 1.25
280 Nick Van Exel MF .60 1.50
281 Gary Payton MF .75 2.00
282 Peja Stojakovic MF .75 2.00
283 Karl Malone MF 1.00 2.50
284 Mike Miller MF .75 2.00
285 Caron Butler MF .75 2.00
286 Cuttino Mobley MF .60 1.50
287 Zach Randolph MF .75 2.00
288 Scottie Pippen MF 1.25 3.00
289 Gordan Giricek MF .50 1.25
290 Ben Wallace MF .75 2.00
291 Manu Ginobili MF 1.00 2.50
292 Vladimir Radmanovic MF .50 1.25
293 Michael Jordan PP 12.00 30.00
294 Kobe Bryant PP 8.00 20.00
295 Vince Carter PP 2.50 6.00
296 Steve Nash PP 2.00 5.00
297 Shaquille O'Neal PP 4.00 10.00
298 Amare Stoudemire PP 2.50 6.00
299 Tracy McGrady PP 2.00 5.00
300 Gary Payton PP 1.50 4.00
301 Chris Bosh PP 3.00 8.00
302 Michael Finley PP 1.50 4.00
303 Caron Butler PP 1.50 4.00
304 Jarvis Hayes PP 1.50 4.00
305 Ben Wallace PP 1.50 4.00
306 Allan Houston PP 1.25 3.00
307 Mike Bibby PP 1.50 4.00
308 Antoine Walker PP 1.50 4.00
309 Dajuan Wagner PP 1.00 2.50
310 Kevin Garnett PP 3.00 8.00
311 Mickael Pietrus PP 1.50 4.00
312 Baron Davis PP 1.50 4.00
313 Paul Pierce PP 2.00 5.00
314 Rasheed Wallace PP 1.50 4.00
315 Chris Webber PP 1.50 4.00
316 Jermaine O'Neal PP 1.50 4.00
317 Shareef Abdur-Rahim PP 1.25 3.00
318 Ray Allen PP 1.50 4.00
319 Peja Stojakovic PP 1.50 4.00
320 Tim Duncan PP 2.50 6.00
321 Gilbert Arenas PP 1.50 4.00
322 Jason Richardson PP 1.50 4.00
323 Dwyane Wade FC 25.00 60.00
324 Gary Payton FC 6.00 15.00
325 Karl Malone FC 8.00 20.00
326 Jason Kidd FC 10.00 25.00
327 Darko Milicic FC 6.00 15.00
328 Steve Francis FC 6.00 15.00
329 Vince Carter FC 10.00 25.00
330 Elton Brand FC 6.00 15.00
331 Amare Stoudemire FC 10.00 25.00
332 Shaquille O'Neal FC 15.00 40.00
333 Carmelo Anthony FC 15.00 40.00
334 Tracy McGrady FC 8.00 20.00
335 Tim Duncan FC 10.00 25.00
336 Chris Webber FC 6.00 15.00
337 Allen Iverson FC 10.00 25.00
338 Dirk Nowitzki FC 10.00 25.00
339 Kevin Garnett FC 12.00 30.00
340 Kobe Bryant FC 30.00 80.00
341 LeBron James FC 150.00 300.00
342 Michael Jordan FC 50.00 125.00

2003-04 Upper Deck Finite Gold

Randomly inserted, this 342-card set parallels the base version enhanced with gold highlights. 1-200 even number singles are sequentially numbered to 100 while 1-200 odd number singles are sequentially numbered to 299. Cards 201-236 are sequentially numbered to 100, cards 237-242 are sequentially numbered to 25, cards 243-292 are sequentially numbered to 50, cards 293-322 are sequentially numbered to 25, and cards 323-342 are sequentially numbered to 10. A Platinum parallel version was also issued and all of these cards are numbered one of one.

*1-200 EVEN SINGLES: 2X TO 5X BASE HI
*1-200 ODD SINGLES: 2X TO 5X BASE HI
*201-228 RC SINGLES: 1.25X TO 3X BASE HI
*229-236 RC SINGLES: 1X TO 2.5X BASE HI
*237-242 RC SINGLES: .6X TO 1.5X BASE HI
*243-292 SINGLES: 3X TO 8X BASE HI
*293-322 SINGLES: 2X TO 5X BASE HI
239 Dwyane Wade 100.00 200.00
242 LeBron James 400.00 700.00

2003-04 Upper Deck Finite Elements Warmups

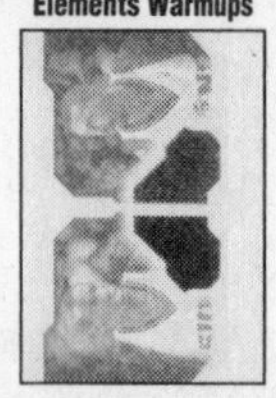

Randomly inserted in packs at the rate of one in four for dual player versions with triple player versions sequentially numbered to 50, this 42-card set utilizes a similar design to its Jerseys counterpart and includes a swatch of game-worn warmup.

FE1 Michael Jordan SP / Kobe Bryant 50.00 100.00
FE2 Antoine Walker / Paul Pierce 4.00 10.00
FE3 Vlade Divac / Gerald Wallace 4.00 10.00
FE4 Allan Houston / Latrell Sprewell 4.00 10.00
FE5 Yao Ming / Steve Francis 5.00 12.00
FE6 Al Harrington / Jonathan Bender 4.00 10.00
FE7 Richard Jefferson / Kenyon Martin 4.00 10.00
FE8 Baron Davis / Jamal Mashburn 4.00 10.00
FE9 Jason Richardson / Gilbert Arenas 4.00 10.00
FE10 Tracy McGrady / Kevin Garnett 6.00 15.00
FE11 Wally Szczerbiak / Joe Smith 4.00 10.00
FE12 Jalen Rose / Eddy Curry 4.00 10.00
FE13 Shawn Marion / Stephon Marbury 4.00 10.00
FE14 Mike Sweetney / Keith Van Horn 4.00 10.00
FE15 Amare Stoudemire / Anfernee Hardaway 5.00 12.00
FE16 Theo Ratliff / Shareef Abdur-Rahim 4.00 10.00
FE17 Josh Howard / Steve Nash 4.00 10.00
FE18 Magic Johnson SP / Julius Erving 20.00 50.00
FE19 John Stockton / Andrei Kirilenko 5.00 12.00
FE20 Darius Miles / Quentin Richardson 4.00 10.00
FE21 Lamar Odom / Elton Brand 4.00 10.00
FE22 Jamaal Tinsley / Reggie Miller 4.00 10.00
FE23 Ben Wallace / Richard Hamilton 4.00 10.00
FE24 Chris Mihm / DaJuan Wagner 4.00 10.00
FE25 David Robinson / Speedy Claxton 5.00 12.00
FE26 Tyson Chandler / Marcus Fizer 4.00 10.00
FE27 Andre Miller / Corey Maggette 4.00 10.00
FE28 Shane Battier / Pau Gasol 4.00 10.00
FE29 Mike Miller / Stromile Swift 4.00 10.00
FE30 Derek Fisher / Kobe Bryant 10.00 25.00
FE31 Jamaal Magloire / Baron Davis / David Wesley 8.00 20.00
FE32 Theo Ratliff / Shareef Abdur-Rahim / Jason Terry 8.00 20.00
FE33 Anfernee Hardaway / Stephon Marbury / Joe Johnson 25.00 60.00
FE34 Tyson Chandler / Marcus Fizer / Eddy Curry 8.00 20.00
FE35 Yao Ming / Cuttino Mobley / James Posey 15.00 40.00
FE36 Allen Iverson / Aaron McKie / Eric Snow 15.00 40.00
FE37 Elton Brand / Corey Maggette / Quentin Richardson 8.00 20.00
FE38 Jalen Rose / Chris Webber / Juwan Howard 25.00 60.00
FE39 Brad Miller / Jermaine O'Neal / Jamaal Tinsley 8.00 20.00
FE40 Chris Bosh / Mike Sweetney / Jarvis Hayes 15.00 30.00
FE41 Mickael Pietrus / Darko Milicic / Dwyane Wade 15.00 30.00
FE42 Kobe Bryant / Michael Jordan / Jason Kidd 100.00 200.00

2003-04 Upper Deck Finite Elements Jerseys

Randomly inserted in packs at the rate of one in 10 for single player jerseys and one in 20 for dual player jerseys, this 42-card set features a horizontal design with full color player photos and a swatch of game-worn jersey.

FJ1 Michael Jordan SP 50.00 100.00
FJ2 Kobe Bryant SP 12.50 30.00
FJ3 Latrell Sprewell 2.50 6.00
FJ4 Dirk Nowitzki 5.00 12.00
FJ5 Paul Pierce 4.00 10.00
FJ6 John Stockton 4.00 10.00
FJ7 Karl Malone 4.00 10.00
FJ8 Grant Hill 4.00 10.00
FJ9 Shawn Marion 3.00 8.00
FJ10 Ray Allen 3.00 8.00
FJ11 Steve Francis 3.00 8.00
FJ12 Steve Nash 4.00 10.00
FJ13 Antoine Walker 3.00 8.00
FJ14 David Robinson 5.00 12.00
FJ15 Yao Ming 6.00 15.00
FJ16 Allen Iverson 5.00 12.00
FJ17 Carmelo Anthony 8.00 20.00
FJ18 LeBron James 30.00 80.00
FJ19 Darko Milicic 3.00 8.00
FJ20 Chris Bosh 6.00 15.00
FJ21 Mike Sweetney 3.00 8.00
FS1 Michael Jordan SP / Kobe Bryant 50.00 120.00
FS2 Allan Houston / Charlie Ward 5.00 12.00
FS3 Latrell Sprewell / Kurt Thomas 5.00 12.00
FS4 Damon Stoudamire / Rasheed Wallace 5.00 12.00
FS5 Jay Williams / Marcus Fizer 5.00 12.00
FS6 Rasho Nesterovic / Wally Szczerbiak 5.00 12.00
FS7 Jason Kidd / Tony Parker 6.00 15.00
FS8 Reggie Miller / Jonathan Bender 5.00 12.00
FS9 Antawn Jamison / Jason Richardson 5.00 12.00
FS10 Lamar Odom / Corey Maggette 5.00 12.00
FS11 Jalen Rose / Eddy Curry 5.00 12.00
FS12 Jermaine O'Neal / Jamaal Tinsley 5.00 12.00
FS13 David Robinson / Tim Duncan 10.00 25.00
FS14 Darius Miles / DaJuan Wagner 5.00 12.00
FS15 Mike Miller / Pau Gasol 5.00 12.00
FS16 Charlie Ward / Kurt Thomas 5.00 12.00
FS17 Kenyon Martin / Richard Jefferson 5.00 12.00
FS18 Ray Allen / Rashard Lewis 5.00 12.00
FS19 Manu Ginobili / Tony Parker 6.00 15.00
FS20 Michael Finley / Dirk Nowitzki 5.00 12.00
FS21 Marcus Fizer / Tyson Chandler 5.00 12.00

2003-04 Upper Deck Finite Signatures

Inserted in packs at the rate of one in 30, this 29-card set features a horizontal design with player photos on the left and a white-out box on the right for a signature. A Gold version was also issued and these cards are sequentially numbered to 10.

AJ Antawn Jamison 5.00 12.00
AM Andre Miller 5.00 12.00
BI Chauncey Billups 6.00 15.00
BO Chris Bosh 20.00 50.00
CA Carmelo Anthony 40.00 100.00
CB Caron Butler 5.00 12.00
CK Chris Kaman 6.00 15.00
DA Darius Miles 5.00 12.00
DJ DerMarr Johnson 5.00 12.00
DM Darko Milicic 6.00 15.00
DW Dwyane Wade 60.00 120.00
GA Gilbert Arenas 8.00 20.00
GP Gary Payton 12.50 30.00
JH Jarvis Hayes 5.00 12.00
JM Jerome Moiso 5.00 12.00
JR Jason Richardson 5.00 12.00
JS Jerry Stackhouse 6.00 15.00
KB Kobe Bryant/100 100.00 200.00
LJ LeBron James/150 400.00 750.00
MB Mike Bibby 6.00 15.00
MJ Michael Jordan/23 300.00 600.00
PP Paul Pierce 12.50 30.00
PS Peja Stojakovic 8.00 20.00
RJ Richard Jefferson 5.00 12.00
SA Shareef Abdur-Rahim 5.00 12.00
SB Shane Battier 5.00 12.00
SF Steve Francis 6.00 15.00
TM Tracy McGrady/100 15.00 40.00
YM Yao Ming 25.00 50.00

2007-08 Upper Deck First Edition

This 230-card set was released in October, 2007. The set was issued through Upper Deck's retail channels and the set was released in 10-card packs which came 36 packs to a box where packs carried an inital SRP of $1.25. The first 200 cards in the set feature NBA veterans while cards numbered 201-230 feature 2007-08 NBA rookies.

COMP.SET w/o RC's (200) 10.00 25.00
1 Austin Croshere .20 .50
2 Devean George .20 .50
3 Devin Harris .30 .75
4 Josh Howard .25 .60
5 Jerry Stackhouse .25 .60
6 Jason Terry .25 .60
7 Rafer Alston .20 .50
8 Shane Battier .25 .60
9 Luther Head .25 .60
10 Juwan Howard .25 .60
11 Tracy McGrady .30 .75
12 Steve Novak .20 .50
13 Rudy Gay .30 .75
14 Eddie Jones .25 .60
15 Kyle Lowry .30 .75
16 Mike Miller .30 .75
17 Damon Stoudamire .25 .60
18 Hakim Warrick .25 .60
19 Brandon Bass .20 .50
20 Tyson Chandler .25 .60
21 Bobby Jackson .20 .50
22 Desmond Mason .20 .50
23 Cedric Simmons .25 .60
24 Peja Stojakovic .30 .75
25 Bruce Bowen .20 .50
26 Michael Finley .30 .75
27 Manu Ginobili .30 .75
28 Tony Parker .30 .75
29 Beno Udrih .20 .50
30 Monta Ellis .30 .75
31 Al Harrington .25 .60
32 Sarunas Jasikevicius .20 .50
33 Stephen Jackson .25 .60
34 Jason Richardson .30 .75
35 Sam Cassell .30 .75
36 Chris Kaman .25 .60
37 Shaun Livingston .20 .50
38 Corey Maggette .25 .60
39 Cuttino Mobley .25 .60
40 Tim Thomas .20 .50
41 Kwame Brown .20 .50
42 Andrew Bynum .40 1.00
43 Jordan Farmar .20 .50
44 Lamar Odom .30 .75
45 Ronny Turiaf .25 .60
46 Luke Walton .20 .50
47 Leandro Barbosa .25 .60
48 Raja Bell .25 .60
49 Boris Diaw .25 .60
50 Shawn Marion .30 .75
51 Amare Stoudemire .30 .75
52 Shareef Abdur-Rahim .25 .60
53 Ron Artest .30 .75
54 Quincy Douby .20 .50
55 Kevin Martin .30 .75
56 Brad Miller .25 .60
57 Allen Iverson .40 1.00
58 Kenyon Martin .30 .75
59 Eduardo Najera .20 .50
60 Nene .25 .60
61 J.R. Smith .30 .75
62 Ricky Davis .25 .60
63 Randy Foye .30 .75
64 Troy Hudson .20 .50
65 Mike James .20 .50
66 Rashad McCants .20 .50
67 Craig Smith .20 .50
68 LaMarcus Aldridge .40 1.00
69 Jarrett Jack .25 .60
70 Jamaal Magloire .20 .50
71 Sergio Rodriguez .20 .50
72 Brandon Roy .40 1.00
73 Martell Webster .25 .60
74 Rashard Lewis .25 .60
75 Luke Ridnour .25 .60
76 Danny Fortson .20 .50
77 Chris Wilcox .20 .50
78 Damien Wilkins .20 .50
79 Ronnie Brewer .25 .60
80 Derek Fisher .25 .60
81 Matt Harpring .25 .60
82 Andrei Kirilenko .25 .60
83 Paul Millsap .25 .60
84 Deron Williams .50 1.25
85 Tony Allen .20 .50
86 Gerald Green .25 .60
87 Al Jefferson .30 .75
88 Wally Szczerbiak .25 .60
89 Allan Ray .20 .50
90 Delonte West .25 .60
91 Hassan Adams .20 .50
92 Richard Jefferson .30 .75
93 Jason Kidd .30 .75
94 Nenad Krstic .20 .50
95 Marcus Williams .20 .50
96 Renaldo Balkman .20 .50
97 Jamal Crawford .25 .60
98 Eddy Curry .20 .50
99 Channing Frye .25 .60
100 Quentin Richardson .25 .60
101 Nate Robinson .30 .75
102 Rodney Carney .20 .50
103 Samuel Dalembert .20 .50
104 Steven Hunter .20 .50
105 Kyle Korver .25 .60
106 Andre Miller .25 .60
107 Shavlik Randolph .20 .50
108 Andrea Bargnani .40 1.00
109 Jose Calderon .25 .60
110 T.J. Ford .25 .60
111 Jorge Garbajosa .25 .60
112 Joey Graham .20 .50
113 Morris Peterson .20 .50
114 Luol Deng .30 .75
115 Ben Gordon .30 .75
116 Kirk Hinrich .30 .75
117 Thabo Sefolosha .30 .75
118 Tyrus Thomas .30 .75
119 Ben Wallace .30 .75
120 Shannon Brown .30 .75
121 Drew Gooden .25 .60
122 Larry Hughes .25 .60
123 Zydrunas Ilgauskas .25 .60
124 Donyell Marshall .20 .50
125 Richard Hamilton .25 .60
126 Amir Johnson .20 .50
127 Antonio McDyess .25 .60
128 Tayshaun Prince .30 .75
129 Rasheed Wallace .30 .75
130 Chris Webber .30 .75
131 Marquis Daniels .20 .50
132 Ike Diogu .20 .50
133 Mike Dunleavy .25 .60
134 Jeff Foster .20 .50
135 Troy Murphy .20 .50
136 Jamaal Tinsley .20 .50
137 Charlie Bell .20 .50
138 Andrew Bogut .30 .75
139 Earl Boykins .20 .50
140 Bobby Simmons .20 .50
141 Charlie Villanueva .30 .75
142 Maurice Williams .25 .60
143 Speedy Claxton .20 .50
144 Solomon Jones .20 .50
145 Tyronn Lue .20 .50
146 Marvin Williams .30 .75
147 Shelden Williams .20 .50
148 Raymond Felton .40 1.00
149 Othella Harrington .20 .50
150 Sean May .20 .50
151 Adam Morrison .30 .75
152 Gerald Wallace .30 .75
153 Udonis Haslem .25 .60
154 Alonzo Mourning .40 1.00
155 Shaquille O'Neal .60 1.50
156 Gary Payton .30 .75
157 Antoine Walker .25 .60
158 Jason Williams .25 .60
159 Carlos Arroyo .25 .60
160 Travis Diener .20 .50
161 Grant Hill .40 1.00
162 Darko Milicic .20 .50
163 Jameer Nelson .25 .60
164 J.J. Redick .30 .75
165 Andray Blatche .20 .50
166 Caron Butler .30 .75
167 Antonio Daniels .20 .50
168 Brendan Haywood .20 .50
169 Antawn Jamison .30 .75
170 DeShawn Stevenson .20 .50
171 Dirk Nowitzki .40 1.00
172 Yao Ming .40 1.00
173 Pau Gasol .30 .75
174 Chris Paul .60 1.50
175 Tim Duncan .50 1.25
176 Baron Davis .30 .75
177 Elton Brand .30 .75
178 Kobe Bryant 1.50 4.00
179 Steve Nash .40 1.00
180 Mike Bibby .30 .75
181 Carmelo Anthony .40 1.00
182 Kevin Garnett .60 1.50
183 Zach Randolph .25 .60
184 Ray Allen .30 .75
185 Carlos Boozer .30 .75
186 Paul Pierce .40 1.00
187 Vince Carter .40 1.00
188 Stephon Marbury .25 .60
189 Andre Iguodala .30 .75
190 Chris Bosh .30 .75
191 Michael Jordan 2.50 6.00
192 LeBron James 1.50 4.00
193 Chauncey Billups .30 .75
194 Jermaine O'Neal .30 .75
195 Michael Redd .30 .75
196 Joe Johnson .30 .75
197 Emeka Okafor .30 .75
198 Dwyane Wade .75 2.00
199 Dwight Howard .50 1.25
200 Gilbert Arenas .30 .75
201 Greg Oden RC .60 1.50
202 Kevin Durant RC 4.00 10.00
203 Al Horford RC .60 1.50
204 Mike Conley Jr. RC .75 2.00
205 Jeff Green RC .60 1.50
206 Marcus Williams RC .50 1.25
207 Corey Brewer RC .60 1.50
208 Brandan Wright RC .50 1.25
209 Joakim Noah RC 1.25 3.00
210 Spencer Hawes RC .50 1.25
211 Acie Law RC .50 1.25
212 Thaddeus Young RC .60 1.50
213 Julian Wright RC .50 1.25
214 Al Thornton RC .50 1.25
215 Rodney Stuckey RC .75 2.00
216 Nick Young RC .75 2.00
217 Sean Williams RC .50 1.25
218 Marco Belinelli RC .50 1.25
219 Javaris Crittenton RC .50 1.25
220 Jason Smith RC .50 1.25
221 Daequan Cook RC .50 1.25
222 Jared Dudley RC .50 1.25
223 Wilson Chandler RC .75 2.00
224 Morris Almond RC .50 1.25
225 Aaron Brooks RC .50 1.25
226 Arron Afflalo RC .60 1.50
227 Alando Tucker RC .50 1.25
228 Petteri Koponen RC .50 1.25
229 Carl Landry RC .50 1.25
230 Gabe Pruitt RC .50 1.25

2007-08 Upper Deck First Edition Gold

*GOLD: .6X TO 1.5X BASE HI
APPROXIMATE ODDS 1:6

2007-08 Upper Deck First Edition All-NBA

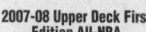

COMPLETE SET (15) 6.00 15.00
APPROXIMATE ODDS 1:8
NBA1 Dirk Nowitzki .75 2.00
NBA2 Tim Duncan 1.00 2.50
NBA3 Amare Stoudemire .60 1.50
NBA4 Steve Nash .75 2.00
NBA5 Kobe Bryant 3.00 8.00
NBA6 LeBron James 3.00 8.00
NBA7 Chris Bosh .60 1.50
NBA8 Yao Ming .75 2.00
NBA9 Gilbert Arenas .60 1.50
NBA10 Tracy McGrady .60 1.50
NBA11 Kevin Garnett 1.25 3.00
NBA12 Carmelo Anthony .75 2.00
NBA13 Dwight Howard 1.00 2.50
NBA14 Dwyane Wade 1.50 4.00
NBA15 Chauncey Billups .60 1.50

2007-08 Upper Deck First Edition Behind the Glass

COMPLETE SET (25) 8.00 20.00
APPROXIMATE ODDS 1:5
BGAI Allen Iverson .40 1.00
BGAS Amare Stoudemire .30 .75
BGBO Carlos Boozer .30 .75
BGBW Ben Wallace .30 .75
BGCA Carmelo Anthony .40 1.00
BGCB Chris Bosh .30 .75
BGCP Chris Paul .60 1.50
BGDH Dwight Howard .50 1.25
BGDN Dirk Nowitzki .40 1.00
BGDW Dwyane Wade .75 2.00
BGGA Gilbert Arenas .30 .75
BGJR Jason Richardson .30 .75
BGKB Kobe Bryant 1.50 4.00
BGKG Kevin Garnett .60 1.50
BGLJ LeBron James 1.50 4.00
BGMA Shawn Marion .30 .75
BGMG Manu Ginobili .30 .75
BGMJ Michael Jordan 2.50 6.00
BGPP Paul Pierce .40 1.00
BGSM Stephon Marbury .25 .60
BGSN Steve Nash .40 1.00
BGSO Shaquille O'Neal .60 1.50
BGTD Tim Duncan .50 1.25
BGTM Tracy McGrady .30 .75
BGYM Yao Ming .40 1.00

2007-08 Upper Deck First Edition Champions of the Court

COMPLETE SET (25) 8.00 20.00
APPROXIMATE ODDS 1:5
CCBR Bill Russell .60 1.50
CCBW Bill Walton .40 1.00
CCCB Chauncey Billups .40 1.00
CCDR Dennis Rodman .60 1.50
CCDW Dwyane Wade 1.00 2.50
CCGM George Mikan .75 2.00
CCHO Hakeem Olajuwon .50 1.25
CCJD Joe Dumars .40 1.00
CCJE Julius Erving .75 2.00
CCJH John Havlicek .40 1.00
CCJO Magic Johnson 1.00 2.50
CCJW James Worthy .50 1.25
CCKA Kareem Abdul-Jabbar .60 1.50
CCKB Kobe Bryant 2.00 5.00
CCLB Larry Bird 1.25 3.00
CCMG Manu Ginobili .40 1.00
CCMJ Michael Jordan 3.00 8.00
CCMM Moses Malone .40 1.00
CCRH Robert Horry .30 .75
CCRO David Robinson .60 1.50
CCSK Steve Kerr .40 1.00
CCSO Shaquille O'Neal .75 2.00
CCTD Tim Duncan .60 1.50
CCTP Tony Parker .40 1.00
CCWC Wilt Chamberlain .75 2.00

2007-08 Upper Deck First Edition Draft Notices

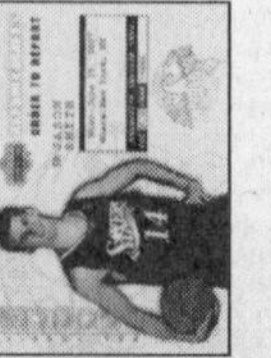

COMPLETE SET (25)	8.00	20.00
APPROXIMATE ODDS 1:5		
DN1 Greg Oden	.50	1.25
DN2 Kevin Durant	3.00	8.00
DN3 Al Horford	.50	1.25
DN4 Mike Conley Jr.	.60	1.50
DN5 Jeff Green	.50	1.25
DN6 Alando Tucker	.40	1.00
DN7 Corey Brewer	.50	1.25
DN8 Brandan Wright	.40	1.00
DN9 Joakim Noah	1.00	2.50
DN10 Spencer Hawes	.40	1.00
DN11 Acie Law	.40	1.00
DN12 Thaddeus Young	.50	1.25
DN13 Julian Wright	.40	1.00
DN14 Al Thornton	.40	1.00
DN15 Rodney Stuckey	.60	1.50
DN16 Nick Young	.60	1.50
DN17 Sean Williams	.40	1.00
DN18 Javaris Crittenton	.40	1.00
DN19 Jason Smith	.40	1.00
DN20 Daequan Cook	.40	1.00
DN21 Jared Dudley	.40	1.00
DN22 Wilson Chandler	.60	1.50
DN23 Morris Almond	.40	1.00
DN24 Aaron Brooks	.40	1.00
DN25 Arron Afflalo	.50	1.25

2007-08 Upper Deck First Edition Kevin Durant Exclusive

COMPLETE SET (6)	6.00	15.00
COMMON CARD (KD1-KD6)	1.50	4.00
RANDOM INSERTS IN PACKS		
AUTOS NOT PRICED DUE TO SCARCITY		

2008-09 Upper Deck First Edition

COMPLETE SET (266)	8.00	20.00
1 Mike Bibby	.15	.40
2 Al Horford	.20	.50
3 Joe Johnson	.20	.50
4 Josh Childress	.15	.40
5 Josh Smith	.20	.50
6 Marvin Williams	.20	.50
7 Eddie House	.12	.30
8 Glen Davis	.15	.40
9 Sam Cassell	.20	.50
10 Kevin Garnett	.40	1.00
11 Rajon Rondo	.25	.60
12 Ray Allen	.20	.50
13 Paul Pierce	.25	.60
14 Adam Morrison	.20	.50
15 Emeka Okafor	.20	.50
16 Gerald Wallace	.20	.50
17 Jared Dudley	.15	.40
18 Jason Richardson	.20	.50
19 Nazr Mohammed	.12	.30
20 Raymond Felton	.15	.40
21 Andres Nocioni	.12	.30
22 Ben Gordon	.20	.50
23 Larry Hughes	.15	.40
24 Joakim Noah	.20	.50
25 Kirk Hinrich	.20	.50
26 Luol Deng	.20	.50
27 Tyrus Thomas	.15	.40
28 Aleksandar Pavlovic	.12	.30
29 Anderson Varejao	.15	.40
30 Daniel Gibson	.20	.50
31 Wally Szczerbiak	.15	.40
32 Ben Wallace	.20	.50
33 LeBron James	1.00	2.50
34 Zydrunas Ilgauskas	.15	.40
35 Jason Kidd	.20	.50
36 Dirk Nowitzki	.25	.60
37 Jason Terry	.15	.40
38 Jerry Stackhouse	.15	.40
39 Jose Barea	.25	.60
40 Josh Howard	.15	.40
41 Allen Iverson	.25	.60
42 Carmelo Anthony	.25	.60
43 J.R. Smith	.20	.50
44 Kenyon Martin	.20	.50
45 Linas Kleiza	.12	.30
46 Marcus Camby	.12	.30
47 Antonio McDyess	.15	.40
48 Chauncey Billups	.20	.50
49 Jason Maxiell	.12	.30
50 Rasheed Wallace	.20	.50
51 Richard Hamilton	.15	.40
52 Rodney Stuckey	.25	.60
53 Tayshaun Prince	.20	.50
54 Al Harrington	.15	.40
55 Baron Davis	.20	.50
56 Kelenna Azubuike	.12	.30
57 Matt Barnes	.12	.30
58 Monta Ellis	.20	.50
59 Stephen Jackson	.15	.40
60 Luis Scola	.15	.40
61 Luther Head	.12	.30
62 Rafer Alston	.12	.30
63 Shane Battier	.15	.40
64 Tracy McGrady	.20	.50
65 Yao Ming	.25	.60
66 Andre Owens	.12	.30
67 Danny Granger	.20	.50
68 Jamaal Tinsley	.12	.30
69 Jermaine O'Neal	.20	.50
70 Kareem Rush	.12	.30
71 Mike Dunleavy	.15	.40
72 Troy Murphy	.12	.30
73 Al Thornton	.15	.40
74 Chris Kaman	.15	.40
75 Corey Maggette	.15	.40
76 Cuttino Mobley	.15	.40
77 Elton Brand	.20	.50
78 Tim Thomas	.12	.30
79 Andrew Bynum	.25	.60
80 Derek Fisher	.15	.40
81 Jordan Farmar	.12	.30
82 Kobe Bryant	1.00	2.50
83 Pau Gasol	.20	.50
84 Lamar Odom	.20	.50
85 Luke Walton	.12	.30
86 Darko Milicic	.12	.30
87 Javaris Crittenton	.12	.30
88 Kyle Lowry	.20	.50
89 Mike Conley Jr.	.15	.40
90 Mike Miller	.20	.50
91 Kwame Brown	.12	.30
92 Rudy Gay	.20	.50
93 Daequan Cook	.12	.30
94 Dorell Wright	.12	.30
95 Dwyane Wade	.40	1.00
96 Jason Williams	.15	.40
97 Ricky Davis	.15	.40
98 Shawn Marion	.20	.50
99 Udonis Haslem	.15	.40
100 Andrew Bogut	.20	.50
101 Charlie Villanueva	.20	.50
102 Desmond Mason	.12	.30
103 Michael Redd	.20	.50
104 Mo Williams	.15	.40
105 Yi Jianlian	.20	.50
106 Al Jefferson	.20	.50
107 Corey Brewer	.15	.40
108 Craig Smith	.12	.30
109 Randy Foye	.20	.50
110 Rashad McCants	.12	.30
111 Ryan Gomes	.12	.30
112 Sebastian Telfair	.12	.30
113 Bostjan Nachbar	.12	.30
114 Devin Harris	.20	.50
115 Josh Boone	.12	.30
116 Nenad Krstic	.12	.30
117 Richard Jefferson	.20	.50
118 Sean Williams	.15	.40
119 Vince Carter	.25	.60
120 David Lee	.15	.40
121 Eddy Curry	.12	.30
122 Jamal Crawford	.15	.40
123 Nate Robinson	.20	.50
124 Quentin Richardson	.15	.40
125 Stephon Marbury	.15	.40
126 Zach Randolph	.15	.40
127 Chris Paul	.30	.75
128 David West	.20	.50
129 Julian Wright	.15	.40
130 Morris Peterson	.12	.30
131 Peja Stojakovic	.20	.50
132 Tyson Chandler	.15	.40
133 Carlos Arroyo	.15	.40
134 Dwight Howard	.40	1.00
135 Hedo Turkoglu	.20	.50
136 J.J. Redick	.20	.50
137 Jameer Nelson	.15	.40
138 Maurice Evans	.12	.30
139 Rashard Lewis	.15	.40
140 Andre Iguodala	.20	.50
141 Andre Miller	.15	.40
142 Jason Smith	.12	.30
143 Louis Williams	.15	.40
144 Samuel Dalembert	.12	.30
145 Thaddeus Young	.15	.40
146 Willie Green	.12	.30
147 Amare Stoudemire	.20	.50
148 Boris Diaw	.12	.30
149 Grant Hill	.25	.60
150 Leandro Barbosa	.15	.40
151 Raja Bell	.15	.40
152 Shaquille O'Neal	.40	1.00
153 Steve Nash	.20	.50
154 Brandon Roy	.20	.50
155 Channing Frye	.15	.40
156 Greg Oden	.20	.50
157 LaMarcus Aldridge	.20	.50
158 Martell Webster	.15	.40
159 Steve Blake	.12	.30
160 Beno Udrih	.12	.30
161 Brad Miller	.15	.40
162 Francisco Garcia	.15	.40
163 John Salmons	.20	.50
164 Kevin Martin	.20	.50
165 Mikki Moore	.12	.30
166 Ron Artest	.20	.50
167 Brent Barry	.12	.30
168 Bruce Bowen	.12	.30
169 Manu Ginobili	.20	.50
170 Michael Finley	.20	.50
171 Robert Horry	.15	.40
172 Tim Duncan	.30	.75
173 Tony Parker	.20	.50
174 Chris Wilcox	.12	.30
175 Damien Wilkins	.12	.30
176 Jeff Green	.15	.40
177 Kevin Durant	.75	2.00
178 Nick Collison	.12	.30
179 Earl Watson	.12	.30
180 Andrea Bargnani	.15	.40
181 Anthony Parker	.12	.30
182 Carlos Delfino	.12	.30
183 Chris Bosh	.20	.50
184 Jamario Moon	.12	.30
185 Jose Calderon	.15	.40
186 T.J. Ford	.12	.30
187 Andrei Kirilenko	.15	.40
188 Carlos Boozer	.20	.50
189 Deron Williams	.20	.50
190 Kyle Korver	.15	.40
191 Mehmet Okur	.12	.30
192 Paul Millsap	.15	.40
193 Ronnie Brewer	.15	.40
194 Antawn Jamison	.20	.50
195 Antonio Daniels	.12	.30
196 Brendan Haywood	.12	.30
197 Caron Butler	.20	.50
198 DeShawn Stevenson	.12	.30
199 Gilbert Arenas	.20	.50
200 Nick Young	.15	.40
201 Spud Webb	.30	.75
202 Bob Cousy	.50	1.25
203 Kevin McHale	.40	1.00
204 Larry Bird	1.00	2.50
205 Dennis Rodman	.50	1.25
206 Michael Jordan	2.50	6.00
207 Isiah Thomas	.30	.75
208 Joe Dumars	.30	.75
209 Nate Thurmond	.30	.75
210 Hakeem Olajuwon	.40	1.00
211 Calvin Murphy	.30	.75
212 Kareem Abdul-Jabbar	.50	1.25
213 Magic Johnson	.75	2.00
214 Oscar Robertson	.30	.75
215 Bill Bradley	.40	1.00
216 Earl Monroe	.30	.75
217 Willis Reed	.30	.75
218 Julius Erving	.60	1.50
219 Clyde Drexler	.40	1.00
220 Bill Walton	.30	.75
221 Maurice Lucas	.30	.75
222 David Robinson	.50	1.25
223 John Stockton	.50	1.25
224 Karl Malone	.40	1.00
225 D.J. Augustin	.60	1.50
226 Brook Lopez	1.00	2.50
227 Jerryd Bayless	.60	1.50
228 Jason Thompson	.60	1.50
229 Brandon Rush	.60	1.50
230 Anthony Randolph	.75	2.00
231 Robin Lopez	.60	1.50
232 Marreese Speights	.60	1.50
233 Roy Hibbert	1.00	2.50
234 Courtney Lee	1.00	2.50
235 J.J. Hickson	.75	2.00
236 Ryan Anderson	1.00	2.50
237 Kosta Koufos	.60	1.50
238 James Gist	.60	1.50
239 Darrell Arthur	.60	1.50
240 Donte Greene	.60	1.50
241 D.J. White	.60	1.50
242 J.R. Giddens	.60	1.50
243 Deron Washington	.60	1.50
244 Joey Dorsey	.60	1.50
245 Mario Chalmers	1.00	2.50
246 DeAndre Jordan	1.25	3.00
247 Luc Richard Mbah A Moute	.60	1.50
248 Kyle Weaver	.60	1.50
249 Sonny Weems	.60	1.50
250 Chris Douglas-Roberts	.60	1.50
251 Sean Singletary	.60	1.50
252 Patrick Ewing Jr.	.60	1.50
253 Shan Foster	.60	1.50
254 Bill Walker	.60	1.50
255 Malik Hairston	.60	1.50
256 Richard Hendrix	.60	1.50
257 DeVon Hardin	.60	1.50
258 Darnell Jackson	.60	1.50
259 Derrick Rose	5.00	12.00
260 Michael Beasley	1.00	2.50
261 O.J. Mayo	1.00	2.50
262 Russell Westbrook	3.00	8.00
263 Kevin Love	2.50	6.00
264 Danilo Gallinari	1.00	2.50
265 Eric Gordon	1.50	4.00
266 Joe Alexander	.60	1.50

2008-09 Upper Deck First Edition Gold

*GOLD: .5X TO 1.25X BASE HI
ONE PER PACK

2008-09 Upper Deck First Edition Chalk Talk

COMPLETE SET (30)	4.00	10.00
APPROXIMATE ODDS 1:2 PACKS		
UNPRICED AUTOS RANDOM INSERTS IN PACKS		
CT1 Joe Johnson	.30	.75
CT2 Paul Pierce	.40	1.00
CT3 Gerald Wallace	.30	.75
CT4 Ben Gordon	.30	.75
CT5 LeBron James	1.50	4.00
CT6 Josh Howard	.25	.60
CT7 Allen Iverson	.40	1.00
CT8 Richard Hamilton	.25	.60
CT9 Stephen Jackson	.25	.60
CT10 Tracy McGrady	.30	.75
CT11 Danny Granger	.30	.75
CT12 Corey Maggette	.25	.60
CT13 Kobe Bryant	1.50	4.00
CT14 Pau Gasol	.30	.75
CT15 Dwyane Wade	.60	1.50
CT16 Yi Jianlian	.30	.75
CT17 Al Jefferson	.30	.75
CT18 Richard Jefferson	.30	.75
CT19 Chris Paul	.50	1.25
CT20 Jamal Crawford	.25	.60
CT21 Dwight Howard	.60	1.50
CT22 Andre Iguodala	.30	.75
CT23 Amare Stoudemire	.30	.75
CT24 LaMarcus Aldridge	.30	.75
CT25 Mike Bibby	.25	.60
CT26 Tony Parker	.30	.75
CT27 Kevin Durant	1.25	3.00
CT28 T.J. Ford	.20	.50
CT29 Deron Williams	.30	.75
CT30 Antawn Jamison	.30	.75

2008-09 Upper Deck First Edition Rookie Standouts

COMPLETE SET (30)	30.00	60.00
RANDOM INSERTS IN PACKS		
RSAR Anthony Randolph	1.25	3.00
RSBL Brook Lopez	1.50	4.00
RSBR Brandon Rush	1.00	2.50
RSBW Bill Walker	1.00	2.50
RSCD Chris Douglas-Roberts	1.00	2.50
RSCL Courtney Lee	1.50	4.00
RSDA D.J. Augustin	1.00	2.50
RSDG Danilo Gallinari	1.50	4.00
RSDR Derrick Rose	8.00	20.00
RSDW D.J. White	1.00	2.50
RSEG Eric Gordon	2.50	6.00
RSJA Joe Alexander	1.00	2.50
RSJB Jerryd Bayless	1.00	2.50
RSJD Joey Dorsey	1.00	2.50
RSJG James Gist	1.00	2.50
RSJH J.J. Hickson	1.25	3.00
RSJT Jason Thompson	1.00	2.50
RSKK Kosta Koufos	1.00	2.50
RSKL Kevin Love	4.00	10.00
RSLM Luc Richard Mbah A Moute	1.00	2.50
RSMB Michael Beasley	1.50	4.00
RSMC Mario Chalmers	1.50	4.00
RSMS Marreese Speights	1.00	2.50
RSOM O.J. Mayo	1.50	4.00
RSPE Patrick Ewing Jr.	1.00	2.50
RSRA Ryan Anderson	1.50	4.00
RSRH Roy Hibbert	1.50	4.00
RSRL Robin Lopez	1.00	2.50
RSRW Russell Westbrook	5.00	12.00
RSSW Sonny Weems	1.00	2.50

2008-09 Upper Deck First Edition Starquest Green

COMPLETE SET (30)	8.00	20.00
ONE PER PACK		
SQ1 Carmelo Anthony	.40	1.00
SQ2 Chauncey Billups	.30	.75
SQ3 Larry Bird	1.00	2.50
SQ4 Chris Bosh	.30	.75
SQ5 Kobe Bryant	1.50	4.00
SQ6 Vince Carter	.40	1.00
SQ7 Baron Davis	.30	.75
SQ8 Tim Duncan	.50	1.25
SQ9 Kevin Durant	1.25	3.00
SQ10 Julius Erving	.60	1.50
SQ11 Walt Frazier	.30	.75
SQ12 Kevin Garnett	.60	1.50
SQ13 Rudy Gay	.30	.75
SQ14 Artis Gilmore	.30	.75
SQ15 Dwight Howard	.60	1.50
SQ16 Allen Iverson	.40	1.00
SQ17 LeBron James	1.50	4.00
SQ18 Al Jefferson	.30	.75
SQ19 Magic Johnson	.75	2.00
SQ20 Michael Jordan	2.50	6.00
SQ21 Shawn Marion	.30	.75
SQ22 Tracy McGrady	.30	.75
SQ23 Yao Ming	.40	1.00
SQ24 Dirk Nowitzki	.40	1.00
SQ25 Shaquille O'Neal	.60	1.50
SQ26 Greg Oden	.30	.75
SQ27 Chris Paul	.50	1.25
SQ28 Brandon Roy	.30	.75
SQ29 Dwyane Wade	.60	1.50
SQ30 Deron Williams	.30	.75

2009-10 Upper Deck First Edition

COMPLETE SET (200)	20.00	50.00
1 Josh Smith	.20	.50
2 Al Horford	.20	.50
3 Mike Bibby	.15	.40
4 Joe Johnson	.20	.50
5 Marvin Williams	.15	.40
6 Kevin Garnett	.40	1.00
7 Paul Pierce	.25	.60
8 Ray Allen	.20	.50
9 Rajon Rondo	.25	.60
10 Kendrick Perkins	.15	.40
11 Raymond Felton	.15	.40
12 Raja Bell	.15	.40
13 D.J. Augustin	.15	.40
14 Gerald Wallace	.20	.50
15 Boris Diaw	.15	.40
16 Emeka Okafor	.20	.50
17 Derrick Rose	.60	1.50
18 Luol Deng	.20	.50
19 Ben Gordon	.20	.50
20 John Salmons	.20	.50
21 Joakim Noah	.20	.50
22 Tyrus Thomas	.15	.40
23 Michael Jordan	1.50	4.00
24 LeBron James	1.00	2.50
25 Mo Williams	.15	.40
26 Ben Wallace	.20	.50
27 Delonte West	.12	.30
28 Zydrunas Ilgauskas	.12	.30
29 Wally Szczerbiak	.15	.40
30 Josh Howard	.15	.40
31 Dirk Nowitzki	.25	.60
32 Jason Kidd	.20	.50
33 Erick Dampier	.12	.30
34 Jason Terry	.15	.40
35 Chauncey Billups	.20	.50
36 Carmelo Anthony	.25	.60
37 Kenyon Martin	.20	.50
38 Nene	.15	.40
39 J.R. Smith	.20	.50
40 Allen Iverson	.25	.60
41 Richard Hamilton	.15	.40
42 Tayshaun Prince	.20	.50
43 Rodney Stuckey	.20	.50
44 Amir Johnson	.12	.30
45 Rasheed Wallace	.20	.50
46 Monta Ellis	.20	.50
47 Stephen Jackson	.15	.40
48 Jamal Crawford	.15	.40
49 Kelenna Azubuike	.12	.30
50 Andris Biedrins	.12	.30
51 Corey Maggette	.15	.40
52 Luis Scola	.15	.40
53 Tracy McGrady	.20	.50
54 Yao Ming	.25	.60
55 Ron Artest	.20	.50
56 Shane Battier	.20	.50
57 Von Wafer	.12	.30
58 T.J. Ford	.12	.30
59 Danny Granger	.20	.50
60 Mike Dunleavy	.12	.30
61 Troy Murphy	.12	.30
62 Jeff Foster	.12	.30
63 Jarrett Jack	.15	.40
64 Eric Gordon	.20	.50
65 Baron Davis	.20	.50
66 Al Thornton	.15	.40
67 Zach Randolph	.15	.40
68 Chris Kaman	.15	.40
69 Kobe Bryant	1.00	2.50
70 Pau Gasol	.20	.50
71 Lamar Odom	.20	.50
72 Derek Fisher	.15	.40
73 Andrew Bynum	.25	.60
74 Sasha Vujacic	.12	.30
75 Trevor Ariza	.12	.30
76 O.J. Mayo	.20	.50
77 Marc Gasol	.20	.50
78 Rudy Gay	.20	.50
79 Darrell Arthur	.15	.40
80 Marko Jaric	.12	.30
81 Mike Conley Jr.	.15	.40
82 Michael Beasley	.20	.50
83 Mario Chalmers	.20	.50
84 Dwyane Wade	.40	1.00
85 Chris Quinn	.12	.30
86 Udonis Haslem	.15	.40
87 Daequan Cook	.12	.30
88 Jermaine O'Neal	.20	.50
89 Luke Ridnour	.15	.40
90 Michael Redd	.20	.50
91 Richard Jefferson	.20	.50
92 Charlie Villanueva	.15	.40
93 Andrew Bogut	.20	.50
94 Ramon Sessions	.15	.40
95 Kevin Love	.30	.75
96 Sebastian Telfair	.12	.30
97 Al Jefferson	.20	.50
98 Randy Foye	.12	.30
99 Mike Miller	.20	.50
100 Devin Harris	.20	.50
101 Vince Carter	.25	.60
102 Yi Jianlian	.15	.40
103 Brook Lopez	.20	.50
104 Chris Douglas-Roberts	.12	.30
105 Eduardo Najera	.12	.30
106 Chris Paul	.30	.75
107 Peja Stojakovic	.20	.50
108 David West	.20	.50
109 Tyson Chandler	.15	.40
110 James Posey	.12	.30
111 Al Harrington	.15	.40
112 Chris Duhon	.12	.30
113 Quentin Richardson	.15	.40
114 David Lee	.15	.40
115 Jared Jeffries	.12	.30
116 Wilson Chandler	.15	.40
117 Danilo Gallinari	.20	.50
118 Russell Westbrook	.30	.75
119 Kevin Durant	.60	1.50
120 Jeff Green	.15	.40
121 Desmond Mason	.12	.30
122 Nick Collison	.12	.30
123 Earl Watson	.12	.30
124 Dwight Howard	.30	.75
125 Courtney Lee	.15	.40
126 Hedo Turkoglu	.20	.50
127 Jameer Nelson	.15	.40
128 Rashard Lewis	.15	.40
129 Mickael Pietrus	.12	.30
130 Elton Brand	.20	.50
131 Andre Miller	.15	.40
132 Andre Iguodala	.20	.50
133 Thaddeus Young	.12	.30
134 Willie Green	.12	.30
135 Samuel Dalembert	.12	.30
136 Jason Richardson	.20	.50
137 Shaquille O'Neal	.40	1.00
138 Steve Nash	.20	.50
139 Grant Hill	.25	.60
140 Amare Stoudemire	.20	.50
141 Leandro Barbosa	.15	.40
142 Robin Lopez	.12	.30
143 Brandon Roy	.20	.50
144 LaMarcus Aldridge	.20	.50
145 Jerryd Bayless	.15	.40
146 Rudy Fernandez	.15	.40
147 Steve Blake	.12	.30
148 Martell Webster	.15	.40
149 Greg Oden	.15	.40
150 Kevin Martin	.20	.50
151 Beno Udrih	.12	.30
152 Francisco Garcia	.15	.40
153 Tim Duncan	.30	.75
154 Tony Parker	.20	.50
155 Manu Ginobili	.20	.50
156 Roger Mason	.12	.30
157 Michael Finley	.20	.50
158 George Hill	.20	.50
159 Chris Bosh	.20	.50
160 Jose Calderon	.15	.40
161 Andrea Bargnani	.15	.40
162 Anthony Parker	.12	.30
163 Deron Williams	.20	.50
164 Carlos Boozer	.20	.50
165 Ronnie Brewer	.15	.40
166 C.J. Miles	.12	.30
167 Mehmet Okur	.12	.30
168 Kyle Korver	.15	.40
169 Andrei Kirilenko	.15	.40
170 Gilbert Arenas	.20	.50
171 Antawn Jamison	.20	.50
172 DeShawn Stevenson	.12	.30
173 Caron Butler	.20	.50
174 Brendan Haywood	.12	.30
175 Nick Young	.15	.40
176 B.J. Mullens RC	.60	1.50
177 Blake Griffin RC	8.00	20.00
178 Brandon Jennings RC	1.25	3.00
179 Chase Budinger RC	.60	1.50
180 DaJuan Summers RC	.60	1.50
181 Darren Collison RC	1.00	2.50
182 DeJuan Blair RC	.75	2.00
183 Earl Clark RC	.60	1.50
184 Eric Maynor RC	.60	1.50
185 Gerald Henderson RC	.60	1.50
186 Taj Gibson RC	.75	2.00
187 Hasheem Thabeet RC	.60	1.50
188 James Harden RC	2.00	5.00
189 Jeff Teague RC	.75	2.00
190 Jonny Flynn RC	.60	1.50
191 Jordan Hill RC	.60	1.50
192 Jrue Holiday RC	1.25	3.00
193 Omri Casspi RC	.60	1.50
194 Austin Daye RC	.60	1.50
195 Sam Young RC	.60	1.50
196 Stephen Curry RC	1.50	4.00
197 Terrence Williams RC	.60	1.50
198 Ty Lawson RC	1.00	2.50
199 Tyler Hansbrough RC	1.00	2.50
200 Tyreke Evans RC	1.50	4.00

2009-10 Upper Deck First Edition Gold

*1-175 GOLD: .75X TO 2X BASE HI		
*176-200 GOLD: .5X TO 1.25X BASE HI		
GOLD CARDS ONE PER PACK		
23 Michael Jordan	4.00	10.00

2009-10 Upper Deck First Edition Behind the Arc

COMPLETE SET (25)	5.00	12.00
INSERT ODDS TWO PER PACK		
BA1 Rashard Lewis	.40	1.00
BA2 Danny Granger	.50	1.25
BA3 Ray Allen	.50	1.25
BA4 Mike Bibby	.40	1.00
BA5 Ben Gordon	.50	1.25
BA6 Roger Mason	.30	.75
BA7 Peja Stojakovic	.50	1.25
BA8 Daequan Cook	.30	.75
BA9 Al Harrington	.40	1.00
BA10 Rudy Fernandez	.40	1.00
BA11 Troy Murphy	.30	.75
BA12 Chauncey Billups	.50	1.25
BA13 Mo Williams	.40	1.00
BA14 Jason Terry	.40	1.00
BA15 O.J. Mayo	.50	1.25
BA16 Hedo Turkoglu	.50	1.25
BA17 Joe Johnson	.50	1.25
BA18 Jamal Crawford	.40	1.00
BA19 J.R. Smith	.50	1.25
BA20 Ron Artest	.50	1.25
BA21 Vince Carter	.60	1.50
BA22 Eddie House	.30	.75
BA23 Quentin Richardson	.40	1.00
BA24 Chris Duhon	.30	.75
BA25 Rasual Butler	.30	.75

2009-10 Upper Deck First Edition Rejected!

COMPLETE SET (25)	6.00	15.00
INSERT ODDS TWO PER PACK		
R1 Dwight Howard	.75	2.00
R2 Ronny Turiaf	.30	.75
R3 Lamar Odom	.50	1.25
R4 Marcus Camby	.30	.75
R5 Tim Duncan	.75	2.00
R6 Emeka Okafor	.50	1.25
R7 Samuel Dalembert	.30	.75
R8 Tyrus Thomas	.40	1.00
R9 Chris Andersen	.75	2.00
R10 Yao Ming	.60	1.50
R11 Kendrick Perkins	.40	1.00
R12 Jermaine O'Neal	.50	1.25
R13 Andrew Bynum	.60	1.50
R14 Al Jefferson	.50	1.25
R15 Danny Granger	.50	1.25
R16 Andris Biedrins	.30	.75
R17 Dwyane Wade	1.00	2.50
R18 Joakim Noah	.50	1.25
R19 Spencer Hawes	.40	1.00
R20 Nene	.40	1.00
R21 Erick Dampier	.30	.75
R22 Ben Wallace	.50	1.25
R23 Shaquille O'Neal	1.00	2.50
R24 Rasheed Wallace	.50	1.25
R25 Josh Smith	.50	1.25

2009-10 Upper Deck First Edition Slam Dunk

COMPLETE SET	15.00	30.00
INSERT ODDS TWO PER PACK		
SD1 Josh Smith	.60	1.50
SD2 Dwight Howard	1.00	2.50
SD3 Nate Robinson	.60	1.50
SD4 Gerald Green	.50	1.25
SD5 LeBron James	3.00	8.00
SD6 Kobe Bryant	3.00	8.00
SD7 Amare Stoudemire	.60	1.50
SD8 Shawn Marion	.60	1.50
SD9 Carmelo Anthony	.75	2.00
SD10 Dwyane Wade	1.25	3.00
SD11 Pau Gasol	.60	1.50
SD12 Andre Iguodala	.60	1.50
SD13 Ben Wallace	.60	1.50
SD14 Richard Jefferson	.60	1.50
SD15 Vince Carter	.75	2.00
SD16 Kenyon Martin	.60	1.50
SD17 Kevin Garnett	1.25	3.00
SD18 Chris Bosh	.60	1.50
SD19 Jason Richardson	.60	1.50
SD20 Tim Duncan	1.00	2.50
SD21 Yao Ming	.75	2.00
SD22 Shaquille O'Neal	1.25	3.00
SD23 Gerald Wallace	.60	1.50
SD24 Tyson Chandler	.50	1.25
SD25 Andrew Bynum	.75	2.00

2009-10 Upper Deck First Edition Star Attractions

COMPLETE SET (25)	15.00	30.00
INSERT ODDS TWO PER PACK		
SA1 Kobe Bryant	3.00	8.00
SA2 LeBron James	3.00	8.00
SA3 Carmelo Anthony	.75	2.00
SA4 Kevin Durant	2.00	5.00
SA5 Tim Duncan	1.00	2.50
SA6 Deron Williams	.60	1.50
SA7 Steve Nash	.60	1.50
SA8 Allen Iverson	.75	2.00
SA9 Chauncey Billups	.60	1.50
SA10 Kevin Garnett	1.25	3.00
SA11 Paul Pierce	.75	2.00
SA12 Jason Kidd	.60	1.50
SA13 Dirk Nowitzki	.75	2.00
SA14 Chris Bosh	.60	1.50
SA15 Vince Carter	.75	2.00
SA16 Michael Redd	.60	1.50
SA17 Brandon Roy	.60	1.50
SA18 Tracy McGrady	.60	1.50
SA19 Chris Paul	1.00	2.50
SA20 Dwight Howard	1.00	2.50
SA21 Danny Granger	.60	1.50
SA22 Kevin Martin	.60	1.50
SA23 Devin Harris	.60	1.50
SA24 Gilbert Arenas	.60	1.50
SA25 Joe Johnson	.60	1.50

2001-02 Upper Deck Flight Team

Released in mid-May 2002, this 240-card set is divided up into 90 veteran cards and 50 different rookies with three versions of each card. The rookie "A" version features a portrait style photo and the word "Portrait" along the right edge of the card, the rookie "B" version features and action photo and the word "Action" along the right edge of the card, and the rookie "C" version features an action photo and the words "Hight Performance" along the right edge of the card. The base design places full color player action photos against a colored background that fades to white at both the top and the bottom of the card. Player names are in big letters and silver foil towards the bottom of the card. The rookie print runs are divided up as follows: Card numbers 91-120 are sequentially numberd to 500 on each version with a combined print run of 1500, card numbers 121-134 are sequentially numbered to 375 on each version for a combined print run of 1125, and card numbers 135-140 are sequentially numbered to 250 on each version for a combined print run of 750. Flight Team was packaged in 14 pack boxes with four cards per pack and carried a suggested retail price of $6.99. Also, a PSA graded version of a rookie card was included as a box-topper in each box.

COMPLETE SET (240)	200.00	400.00
COMP.SET w/o SP's (90)	20.00	40.00
1 Michael Jordan	4.00	10.00
2 Dirk Nowitzki	.50	1.25
3 Antawn Jamison	.30	.75
4 Latrell Sprewell	.25	.60
5 Peja Stojakovic	.30	.75
6 Dikembe Mutombo	.30	.75
7 Jason Williams	.25	.60
8 Kobe Bryant	1.50	4.00
9 Baron Davis	.30	.75
10 Wally Szczerbiak	.25	.60
11 Reggie Miller	.30	.75
12 Marcus Fizer	.20	.50
13 Desmond Mason	.25	.60
14 Glenn Robinson	.25	.60
15 Vince Carter	.50	1.25
16 James Posey	.20	.50
17 Darius Miles	.20	.50
18 Jason Kidd	.50	1.25
19 Anfernee Hardaway	.50	1.25
20 Karl Malone	.40	1.00
21 Kevin Garnett	.60	1.50
22 Shareef Abdur-Rahim	.25	.60
23 Steve Francis	.30	.75
24 Paul Pierce	.40	1.00
25 Mike Miller	.30	.75
26 Tim Duncan	.60	1.50
27 Derek Anderson	.20	.50
28 Eddie Jones	.25	.60
29 Keith Van Horn	.25	.60
30 Chris Mihm	.20	.50
31 Clifford Robinson	.20	.50
32 Gary Payton	.30	.75
33 Courtney Alexander	.20	.50
34 Shaquille O'Neal	.75	2.00
35 Tim Thomas	.20	.50
36 Raef LaFrentz	.20	.50
37 Stromile Swift	.20	.50
38 Stephon Marbury	.25	.60
39 Morris Peterson	.20	.50
40 Donyell Marshall	.20	.50
41 Kenny Thomas	.20	.50
42 Juwan Howard	.25	.60
43 Tracy McGrady	.50	1.25
44 Kenny Anderson	.25	.60
45 Larry Hughes	.25	.60
46 Allan Houston	.25	.60
47 Chris Webber	.30	.75
48 Andre Miller	.25	.60
49 Corey Maggette	.25	.60
50 Sam Cassell	.25	.60
51 Steve Smith	.25	.60
52 Jamal Mashburn	.25	.60
53 Al Harrington	.25	.60
54 Brian Grant	.20	.50
55 Rasheed Wallace	.30	.75
56 Rick Fox	.25	.60
57 Jason Terry	.30	.75
58 Rashard Lewis	.30	.75
59 Joe Smith	.25	.60
60 Michael Dickerson	.20	.50
61 Michael Finley	.30	.75
62 Danny Fortson	.20	.50
63 Allen Iverson	.60	1.50
64 Richard Hamilton	.25	.60
65 Antonio McDyess	.25	.60
66 David Wesley	.20	.50
67 Ben Wallace	.30	.75
68 Mike Bibby	.30	.75
69 Antonio Davis	.20	.50
70 Cuttino Mobley	.25	.60
71 Lamond Murray	.20	.50
72 Antoine Walker	.25	.60
73 Jermaine Oâ€™Neal	.30	.75
74 Alonzo Mourning	.40	1.00
75 Shawn Marion	.30	.75
76 John Stockton	.40	1.00
77 Marcus Camby	.25	.60
78 Derek Fisher	.25	.60
79 DerMarr Johnson	.20	.50
80 Aaron McKie	.20	.50
81 David Robinson	.50	1.25
82 Steve Nash	.50	1.25
83 Ray Allen	.30	.75
84 Elton Brand	.30	.75
85 Kenyon Martin	.30	.75
86 Bonzi Wells	.20	.50
87 Grant Hill	.40	1.00
88 Terrell Brandon	.20	.50
89 Toni Kukoc	.25	.60
90 Jerry Stackhouse	.25	.60
91A Tierre Brown RC	.75	2.00
91B Tierre Brown RC	.75	2.00
91C Tierre Brown RC	.75	2.00
92A Jamison Brewer RC	.75	2.00
92B Jamison Brewer RC	.75	2.00
92C Jamison Brewer RC	.75	2.00
93A Antonis Fotsis RC	.75	2.00
93B Antonis Fotsis RC	.75	2.00
93C Antonis Fotsis RC	.75	2.00
94A Mike James RC	.75	2.00
94B Mike James RC	.75	2.00
94C Mike James RC	.75	2.00
95A Primoz Brezec RC	.75	2.00
95B Primoz Brezec RC	.75	2.00
95C Primoz Brezec RC	.75	2.00

96A Jeryl Sasser RC	.75	2.00
96B Jeryl Sasser RC	.75	2.00
96C Jeryl Sasser RC	.75	2.00
97A DeSagana Diop RC	.75	2.00
97B DeSagana Diop RC	.75	2.00
97C DeSagana Diop RC	.75	2.00
98A Mengke Bateer RC	.75	2.00
98B Mengke Bateer RC	.75	2.00
98C Mengke Bateer RC	.75	2.00
99A Gerald Wallace RC	1.25	3.00
99B Gerald Wallace RC	1.25	3.00
99C Gerald Wallace RC	1.25	3.00
100A Kenny Satterfield RC	.75	2.00
100B Kenny Satterfield RC	.75	2.00
100C Kenny Satterfield RC	.75	2.00
101A Ruben Boumtje-Boumtje RC	.75	2.00
101B Ruben Boumtje-Boumtje RC	.75	2.00
101C Ruben Boumtje-Boumtje RC	.75	2.00
102A Brian Scalabrine RC	.75	2.00
102B Brian Scalabrine RC	.75	2.00
102C Brian Scalabrine RC	.75	2.00
103A Oscar Torres RC	.75	2.00
103B Oscar Torres RC	.75	2.00
103C Oscar Torres RC	.75	2.00
104A Jarron Collins RC	.75	2.00
104B Jarron Collins RC	.75	2.00
104C Jarron Collins RC	.75	2.00
105A Jeff Trepagnier RC	.75	2.00
105B Jeff Trepagnier RC	.75	2.00
105C Jeff Trepagnier RC	.75	2.00
106A Brendan Haywood RC	1.00	2.50
106B Brendan Haywood RC	1.00	2.50
106C Brendan Haywood RC	1.00	2.50
107A Vladimir Radmanovic RC	.75	2.00
107B Vladimir Radmanovic RC	.75	2.00
107C Vladimir Radmanovic RC	.75	2.00
108A Loren Woods RC	.75	2.00
108B Loren Woods RC	.75	2.00
108C Loren Woods RC	.75	2.00
109A Terence Morris RC	.75	2.00
109B Terence Morris RC	.75	2.00
109C Terence Morris RC	.75	2.00
110A Kirk Haston RC	.75	2.00
110B Kirk Haston RC	.75	2.00
110C Kirk Haston RC	.75	2.00
111A Earl Watson RC	.75	2.00
111B Earl Watson RC	.75	2.00
111C Earl Watson RC	.75	2.00
112A Brandon Armstrong RC	.75	2.00
112B Brandon Armstrong RC	.75	2.00
112C Brandon Armstrong RC	.75	2.00
113A Zach Randolph RC	2.00	5.00
113B Zach Randolph RC	2.00	5.00
113C Zach Randolph RC	2.00	5.00
114A Bobby Simmons RC	.75	2.00
114B Bobby Simmons RC	.75	2.00
114C Bobby Simmons RC	.75	2.00
115A Alton Ford RC	.75	2.00
115B Alton Ford RC	.75	2.00
115C Alton Ford RC	.75	2.00
116A Predrag Drobnjak RC	.75	2.00
116B Predrag Drobnjak RC	.75	2.00
116C Predrag Drobnjak RC	.75	2.00
117A Michael Bradley RC	.75	2.00
117B Michael Bradley RC	.75	2.00
117C Michael Bradley RC	.75	2.00
118A Samuel Dalembert RC	1.00	2.50
118B Samuel Dalembert RC	1.00	2.50
118C Samuel Dalembert RC	1.00	2.50
119A Gilbert Arenas RC	1.25	3.00
119B Gilbert Arenas RC	1.25	3.00
119C Gilbert Arenas RC	1.25	3.00
120A Kedrick Brown RC	.75	2.00
120B Kedrick Brown RC	.75	2.00
120C Kedrick Brown RC	.75	2.00
121A Trenton Hassell RC	1.00	2.50
121B Trenton Hassell RC	1.00	2.50
121C Trenton Hassell RC	1.00	2.50
122A Zeljko Rebraca RC	1.00	2.50
122B Zeljko Rebraca RC	1.00	2.50
122C Zeljko Rebraca RC	1.00	2.50
123A Jason Collins RC	1.00	2.50
123B Jason Collins RC	1.00	2.50
123C Jason Collins RC	1.00	2.50
124A Will Solomon RC	1.00	2.50
124B Will Solomon RC	1.00	2.50
124C Will Solomon RC	1.00	2.50
125A Joseph Forte RC	1.00	2.50
125B Joseph Forte RC	1.00	2.50
125C Joseph Forte RC	1.00	2.50
126A Steven Hunter RC	1.00	2.50
126B Steven Hunter RC	1.00	2.50
126C Steven Hunter RC	1.00	2.50
127A Eddy Curry RC	1.50	4.00
127B Eddy Curry RC	1.50	4.00
127C Eddy Curry RC	1.50	4.00
128A Troy Murphy RC	1.50	4.00
128B Troy Murphy RC	1.50	4.00
128C Troy Murphy RC	1.50	4.00
129A Shane Battier RC	2.00	5.00
129B Shane Battier RC	2.00	5.00
129C Shane Battier RC	2.00	5.00
130A Tyson Chandler RC	1.50	4.00
130B Tyson Chandler RC	1.50	4.00
130C Tyson Chandler RC	1.50	4.00
131A Joe Johnson RC	2.50	6.00
131B Joe Johnson RC	2.50	6.00
131C Joe Johnson RC	2.50	6.00
132A Richard Jefferson RC	2.00	5.00
132B Richard Jefferson RC	2.00	5.00
132C Richard Jefferson RC	2.00	5.00
133A Eddie Griffin RC	1.00	2.50
133B Eddie Griffin RC	1.00	2.50
133C Eddie Griffin RC	1.00	2.50
134A Rodney White RC	1.00	2.50
134B Rodney White RC	1.00	2.50
134C Rodney White RC	1.00	2.50
135A Andrei Kirilenko RC	3.00	8.00
135B Andrei Kirilenko RC	3.00	8.00
135C Andrei Kirilenko RC	3.00	8.00
136A Tony Parker RC	5.00	12.00
136B Tony Parker RC	5.00	12.00
136C Tony Parker RC	5.00	12.00
137A Jamaal Tinsley RC	1.50	4.00
137B Jamaal Tinsley RC	1.50	4.00
137C Jamaal Tinsley RC	1.50	4.00
138A Pau Gasol RC	4.00	10.00
138B Pau Gasol RC	4.00	10.00
138C Pau Gasol RC	4.00	10.00
139A Jason Richardson RC	2.50	6.00
139B Jason Richardson RC	2.50	6.00
139C Jason Richardson RC	2.50	6.00
140A Kwame Brown RC	1.25	3.00
140B Kwame Brown RC	1.25	3.00
140C Kwame Brown RC	1.25	3.00

2001-02 Upper Deck Flight Team Copper

Randomly seeded in packs, this 240-card set parallels the base Flight Team set enhanced with copper foil highlights. Each card is sequentially numbered to 125.

*COPPER STARS: 5X TO 12X BASE CARD HI
*COPPER RC/500: 2X TO 5X BASE CARD HI
*COPPER RC/375: 1.5X TO 4X BASE CARD HI
*COPPER RC/250: 1.25X TO 3X BASE CARD HI

1 Michael Jordan	40.00	70.00

2001-02 Upper Deck Flight Team Gold

Randomly seeded in packs, this 240-card set parallels the base Flight Team set enhanced with gold foil highlights. Each card is sequentially numbered to 50.

*GOLD STARS: 10X TO 25X BASE CARD HI
*GOLD RC/500: 4X TO 10X BASE CARD HI
*GOLD RC/350: 3X TO 8X BASE CARD HI
*GOLD RC/250: 2.5X TO 6X BASE CARD HI

1 Michael Jordan	60.00	120.00

2001-02 Upper Deck Flight Team 2 the Air

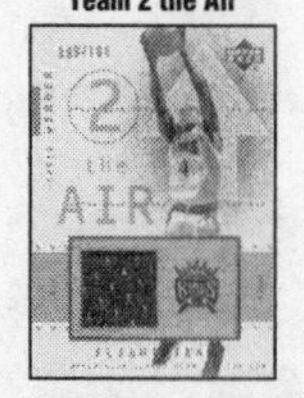

Randomly seeded in packs, this six card set features a full color player action photo on the top of the card and a swatch of a game jersey and a swatch of game floor on the bottom of the card. The jersey swatch is embedded in the left side of the floor swatch, and the floor swatch has the player's team logo engraved in it. Each card is sequentially numbered to 100. A gold version sequentially numbered to 10 was also inserted in packs.

2AI Allen Iverson	12.00	30.00
2CW Chris Webber	8.00	20.00
2KB Kobe Bryant	30.00	80.00
2KG Kevin Garnett	12.00	30.00
2MC Tracy McGrady	10.00	25.00
2MJ Michael Jordan	75.00	150.00

2001-02 Upper Deck Flight Team Flight Patterns

Randomly inserted in packs at the rate of one in 14, this 24-card set features full color player action photos and an arrow shaped swatch of a game worn jersey where the arrow is pointing to the right. A gold version sequentially numbered to 125 was also issued.

*GOLD: .75X TO 2X FLT.PAT HI

AH Anfernee Hardaway	6.00	15.00
AJ Antawn Jamison	4.00	10.00
AL Al Harrington	3.00	8.00
AM Andre Miller	3.00	8.00
BD Baron Davis	4.00	10.00
BR Bryon Russell	2.50	6.00
CM Corey Maggette	3.00	8.00
DG Devean George	2.50	6.00
DM Desmond Mason	3.00	8.00
DS DeShawn Stevenson	2.50	6.00
GH Grant Hill	5.00	12.00
JK Jason Kidd	6.00	15.00
JM Jamal Mashburn	3.00	8.00
JS Jerry Stackhouse	3.00	8.00
JT Jason Terry	4.00	10.00
KE Kedrick Brown	4.00	10.00
KV Keith Van Horn	3.00	8.00
KW Kwame Brown	4.00	10.00
LO Lamar Odom	4.00	10.00
MF Marcus Fizer	2.50	6.00
MP Morris Peterson	2.50	6.00
QR Quentin Richardson	3.00	8.00
SH Shawn Marion	4.00	10.00
WS Wally Szczerbiak	3.00	8.00

2001-02 Upper Deck Flight Team Key Signatures

Seeded in packs, this 15-card set features a horizontal card design with a colored background to match the featured player's team colors. Each card is sequentially numbered to 100 and has a player photo on the right side of the card and an authentic player signature on the left side.

BAS Brandon Armstrong/100	6.00	15.00
CWS Kenyon Martin/100	10.00	25.00
ECS Eddy Curry/100	10.00	25.00
JKS Jason Kidd/100	20.00	50.00
JRS Jason Richardson/100	12.00	30.00
JTS Jamaal Tinsley/100	8.00	20.00
KBS Kobe Bryant/100	100.00	200.00
KGS Kevin Garnett/100	30.00	80.00
KWS Kwame Brown/100	6.00	15.00
MJS Michael Jordan/23	400.00	800.00
RJS Richard Jefferson/100	12.00	30.00
SDS Samuel Dalembert/100	8.00	20.00
TCS Tyson Chandler/100	10.00	25.00
TMS Troy Murphy/100	10.00	25.00
TPS Tony Parker/100	25.00	60.00

2001-02 Upper Deck Flight Team Superstar Flight Patterns

Randomly inserted in packs, this 24-card set features full color player action photos and an arrow shaped swatch of a game worn jersey where the arrow is pointing to the left. Each card is sequentially numbered to 100. A Gold version sequentially numbered to 25 was also inserted.

*GOLD: 1.25X TO 3X HI

AI Allen Iverson	12.00	30.00
CW Chris Webber	6.00	15.00
KB Kobe Bryant	30.00	80.00
KG Kevin Garnett	12.00	30.00
MC Tracy McGrady	10.00	25.00
MJ Michael Jordan	75.00	150.00

2001-02 Upper Deck Flight Team UD Jersey Jams

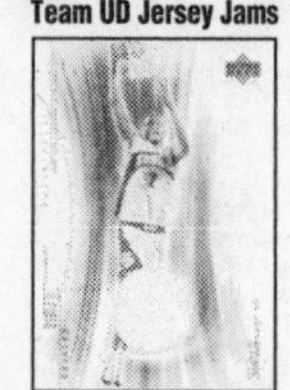

Inserted in packs at the rate of one in 19, this 24-card set centers player action photography and a circular swatch of a game jersey. Backgrounds are rainbow colored, and the left and right sides are white. A Gold version sequentially numbered to 50 was also issued.

*GOLD: 1.25X TO 3X JSY JAM HI

AWJ Antoine Walker	3.00	8.00
BDJ Baron Davis	4.00	10.00
DMJ Darius Miles	2.50	6.00
ECJ Eddy Curry	6.00	15.00
EGJ Eddie Griffin	4.00	10.00
GRJ Glenn Robinson	3.00	8.00
JKJ Jason Kidd	6.00	15.00
JRJ Jason Richardson	8.00	20.00
JSJ Jeryl Sasser	4.00	10.00
KBJ Kobe Bryant	15.00	40.00
KGJ Kevin Garnett	8.00	20.00
KMJ Karl Malone	5.00	12.00
LOJ Lamar Odom	4.00	10.00
MJJ Michael Jordan	30.00	80.00
PPJ Paul Pierce	5.00	12.00
RJJ Richard Jefferson	8.00	20.00
RLJ Rashard Lewis	4.00	10.00
SAJ Shareef Abdur-Rahim	3.00	8.00
SFJ Steve Francis	4.00	10.00
SHJ Steven Hunter	4.00	10.00
SMJ Stephon Marbury	3.00	8.00
TCJ Tyson Chandler	6.00	15.00
TMJ Troy Murphy	6.00	15.00
WSJ Wally Szczerbiak	3.00	8.00

1993 Upper Deck French McDonald's

The 1993 Upper Deck McDonald's French set consists of 40 standard-size cards. The three-card foil packs were made available to McDonald's customers in France only, during September and October of 1993. The packs were distributed free to customers who purchased a "Menu Basket Meal", consisting of a Big Mac, large fries and a Coke, and valued at 5.50. Two million packs were produced, with 28,000 randomly inserted cards carrying the words "Slam Dunk". This insert entitled the customer to win an official Spalding basketball. One unique feature of this set is the wrappers were printed in French, while the cards were printed in both French and English. The front design was the same as the regular issue 1991-92 Upper Deck set, with color player photos, bordered below and on the right by a hardwood basketball court design. The player's name appears beneath the photo, while the team name is printed vertically along the right side. The team logo appears in the lower right corner. The backs display a second color player photo as well as biographical and statistical information.

COMPLETE SET (40)	15.00	40.00
1 Charles Barkley	2.00	5.00
2 Muggsy Bogues	.60	1.50
3 Derrick Coleman	.30	.75
4 Brad Daugherty	.20	.50
5 Vlade Divac	.40	1.00
6 Clyde Drexler	1.50	4.00
7 Joe Dumars	.75	2.00
8 Pervis Ellison	.20	.50
9 Patrick Ewing	.75	2.00
10 Horace Grant	.40	1.00
11 Tim Hardaway	.50	1.25
12 Derek Harper	.30	.75
13 Hersey Hawkins	.30	.75
14 Larry Johnson	.40	1.00
15 Michael Jordan	6.00	15.00
16 Shawn Kemp	.60	1.50
17 Reggie Lewis	.30	.75
18 Karl Malone	2.00	5.00
19 Moses Malone	.40	1.00
20 Danny Manning	.40	1.00
21 Sarunas Marciulionis	.40	1.00
22 Reggie Miller	1.00	2.50
23 Chris Mullin	.60	1.50
24 Dikembe Mutombo	.75	2.00
25 Hakeem Olajuwon	.75	2.00
26 Robert Parish	.60	1.50
27 Scottie Pippen	1.50	4.00
28 Mark Price	.60	1.50
29 Glen Rice	.60	1.50
30 Mitch Richmond	.75	2.00
31 David Robinson	2.00	5.00
32 Detlef Schrempf	.60	1.50
33 Rony Seikaly	.40	1.00
34 Scott Skiles	.40	1.00
35 Rik Smits	.40	1.00
36 John Stockton	2.50	6.00
37 Isiah Thomas	1.25	3.00
38 Doug West	.40	1.00
39 Dominique Wilkins	2.50	6.00
40 James Worthy	1.50	4.00

1994 Upper Deck French McDonald's Team

This 33-card standard-size set was sponsored by McDonald's restaurants and corresponds to the schedule cards (210-236) from the 1993-94 Upper Deck regular series. The cards were available in three-card foil packs, and a six-card hologram set was randomly inserted throughout the packs. The fronts are identical to the regular series cards, while the backs differ insofar as they were redesigned to accommodate bilingual (French and English) text. Two other distinctive features of the back are the card number (1-27) and the holographic anti-counterfeiting mark in the shape of McDonald's golden arches.

COMPLETE SET (33)	60.00	150.00
COMP.TEAM CARD SET (27)	6.00	15.00
COMP.HOLOGRAM SET (6)	50.00	125.00
1 Atlanta Hawks Group	.20	.50
2 Boston Celtics Group	.20	.50
3 Charlotte Hornets Group	.20	.50
4 Chicago Bulls Michael Jordan	1.50	4.00
5 Cleveland Cavs Mark Price	.20	.50
6 Dallas Mavericks Jim Jackson	.40	1.00
7 Denver Nuggets Group	.20	.50
8 Detroit Pistons Isiah Thomas	.40	1.00
9 Golden State Warriors Group	.20	.50
10 Houston Rockets Hakeem Olajuwon	.30	.75
11 Indiana Pacers Rik Smits	.20	.50
12 Los Angeles Clippers Group	.20	.50
13 Los Angeles Lakers Group	.20	.50
14 Miami Heat Group	.20	.50
15 Milwaukee Bucks Group	.20	.50
16 Minnesota Timberwolves Group	.20	.50
17 New Jersey Nets Kenny Anderson	.20	.50
18 New York Knicks Group	.20	.50
19 Orlando Magic Shaquille O'Neal	.75	2.00
20 Philadelphia 76'ers Hersey Hawkins	.20	.50
21 Phoenix Suns Charles Barkley Cedric Ceballos	.30	.75
22 Portland Trail Blazers Group	.20	.50
23 Sacramento Kings Mitch Richmond	.40	1.00
24 San Antonio Spurs David Robinson Sean Elliott	.30	.75
25 Seattle Supersonics Gary Payton Shawn Kemp	.30	.75
26 Utah Jazz Group	.20	.50
27 Washington Bullets Group	.20	.50
28H Hakeem Olajuwon Hologram	6.00	15.00
29H Michael Jordan Hologram	40.00	100.00
30H Charles Barkley Hologram	8.00	20.00
31H Shawn Kemp Hologram	4.00	10.00
32H Patrick Ewing Hologram	5.00	12.00
33H Ron Harper Hologram	2.00	5.00

1998-99 Upper Deck Game Call

Sold at various retail outlets including Kay-Bee toy stores, this set features a picture of Michael Jordan with a built-in speaker on the back of the card that plays the call of Michael Jordan's 1998 Game 6 and NBA Finals winning shot. While we have five cards checklisted, so far we've only been able to confirm the existance of card number MJ5. If you have any information regarding the first four cards, please email us at basketballmag@beckett.com.

COMMON CARD	4.00	10.00

1999 Upper Deck Kevin Garnett Santa Game Jersey

This one card was sent out as a Christmas card by Upper Deck to various dealers and media outlets. The oversized card features a swatch of a red felt Christmas hat worn by Garnett. The card back features a message from Richard McWilliam and carries a "HH" prefix.

HH2 Kevin Garnett	20.00	50.00

2002-03 Upper Deck Generations

Released in late November 2002, Upper Deck Generations was issued as a 234-card set with UD basketball's first stab at a pack within a pack. Each "pack" actually contained another pack, the outside was the New School pack which features glossy cards and the inside pack was the Old School pack which featured rougher cardboard cards. Generations breaks down as follows: numbers 1-50 were extra glossy veteran cards, numbers 51-92 are glossy RC cards sequentially numbered to 999, numbers 93-192 feature retired players on non-glossy cardboard, and cards 193-234 feature both single and dual player cards, both rookie year players and retired veterans. Cards 193-234 are sequentially numbered to 999. Generations was packaged in 18-pack boxes where packs contained five cards and carried a suggested retail price of $4.99.

COMP.SET w/o SP's (150)	25.00	60.00
1 Shareef Abdur-Rahim	.25	.60
2 Paul Pierce	.40	1.00
3 Antoine Walker	.25	.60
4 Jalen Rose	.25	.60
5 Tyson Chandler	.25	.60
6 Darius Miles	.20	.50
7 Dirk Nowitzki	.50	1.25
8 Steve Nash	.40	1.00
9 James Posey	.20	.50
10 Richard Hamilton	.25	.60
11 Ben Wallace	.30	.75
12 Antawn Jamison	.30	.75
13 Jason Richardson	.30	.75
14 Steve Francis	.30	.75
15 Eddie Griffin	.20	.50
16 Reggie Miller	.30	.75
17 Jamaal Tinsley	.20	.50
18 Elton Brand	.30	.75
19 Andre Miller	.25	.60
20 Kobe Bryant	1.50	4.00
21 Shaquille O'Neal	.75	2.00
22 Pau Gasol	.40	1.00
23 Shane Battier	.30	.75
24 Alonzo Mourning	.40	1.00
25 Ray Allen	.30	.75
26 Kevin Garnett	.60	1.50
27 Wally Szczerbiak	.25	.60
28 Jason Kidd	.50	1.25
29 Kenyon Martin	.30	.75
30 Jamal Mashburn	.25	.60
31 Baron Davis	.30	.75
32 Latrell Sprewell	.25	.60
33 Tracy McGrady	.50	1.25
34 Allen Iverson	.50	1.25
35 Stephon Marbury	.25	.60
36 Shawn Marion	.30	.75
37 Rasheed Wallace	.30	.75
38 Bonzi Wells	.20	.50
39 Chris Webber	.30	.75
40 Mike Bibby	.30	.75
41 Tim Duncan	.60	1.50
42 Tony Parker	.40	1.00
43 Gary Payton	.30	.75
44 Rashard Lewis	.30	.75
45 Vince Carter	.50	1.25
46 Morris Peterson	.20	.50
47 Karl Malone	.40	1.00
48 John Stockton	.40	1.00
49 Michael Jordan	3.00	8.00
50 Jerry Stackhouse	.25	.60
51 Yao Ming RC	5.00	12.00
52 Jay Williams RC	2.00	5.00
53 Mike Dunleavy RC	2.00	5.00
54 Drew Gooden RC	2.50	6.00
55 Nikoloz Tskitishvili RC	1.50	4.00
56 DaJuan Wagner RC	1.50	4.00
57 Nene Hilario RC	2.00	5.00
58 Chris Wilcox RC	1.50	4.00
59 Amare Stoudemire RC	4.00	10.00
60 Caron Butler RC	2.50	6.00
61 Jared Jeffries RC	1.50	4.00
62 Melvin Ely RC	1.50	4.00
63 Marcus Haislip RC	1.50	4.00
64 Fred Jones RC	1.50	4.00
65 Bostjan Nachbar RC	1.50	4.00
66 Jiri Welsch RC	1.50	4.00
67 Juan Dixon RC	2.00	5.00
68 Curtis Borchardt RC	1.50	4.00
69 Ryan Humphrey RC	1.50	4.00
70 Kareem Rush RC	1.50	4.00
71 Qyntel Woods RC	1.50	4.00
72 Casey Jacobsen RC	1.50	4.00
73 Tayshaun Prince RC	2.00	5.00
74 Predrag Savovic RC	1.50	4.00
75 Frank Williams RC	1.50	4.00
76 John Salmons RC	2.00	5.00
77 Chris Jefferies RC	1.50	4.00
78 Dan Dickau RC	1.50	4.00
79 Marcus Taylor RC	1.50	4.00
80 Roger Mason RC	1.50	4.00
81 Robert Archibald RC	1.50	4.00
82 Vincent Yarbrough RC	1.50	4.00
83 Dan Gadzuric RC	1.50	4.00
84 Carlos Boozer RC	3.00	8.00
85 Tito Maddox RC	1.50	4.00
86 Rod Grizzard RC	1.50	4.00
87 Ronald Murray RC	1.50	4.00
88 Marko Jaric	1.50	4.00
89 Lonny Baxter RC	1.50	4.00
90 Sam Clancy RC	1.50	4.00
91 Matt Barnes RC	2.00	5.00
92 Jamal Sampson RC	1.50	4.00
93 Oscar Robertson	.60	1.50
94 Moses Malone	.30	.75
95 Earl Monroe	.30	.75
96 Pete Maravich	1.25	3.00
97 Artis Gilmore	.30	.75
98 Julius Erving	.60	1.50
99 Nate Archibald	.30	.75
100 Wes Unseld	.30	.75
101 Willis Reed	.30	.75
102 Jo Jo White	.30	.75
103 Isiah Thomas	.30	.75
104 Bill Sharman	.30	.75
105 Wilt Chamberlain	.60	1.50
106 Bob Cousy	.50	1.25
107 Tom Heinsohn	.30	.75
108 Terry Cummings	.30	.75
109 John Havlicek	.40	1.00
110 Bob Pettit	.30	.75
111 Drazen Petrovic	.30	.75
112 Dan Roundfield	.30	.75
113 David Thompson	.30	.75
114 Bobby Jones	.30	.75
115 Clyde Lovellette	.30	.75
116 Rick Barry	.30	.75
117 K.C. Jones	.30	.75
118 Lionel Hollins	.30	.75
119 Bob Lanier	.30	.75
120 Al Attles	.30	.75
121 Jack Sikma	.30	.75
122 George McGinnis	.30	.75
123 Quinn Buckner	.30	.75
124 Magic Johnson	1.00	2.50
125 Larry Bird	1.00	2.50
126 Cliff Hagan	.30	.75
127 Jerry Lucas	.30	.75
128 Ricky Pierce	.30	.75
129 Walter Davis	.30	.75
130 Danny Ainge	.30	.75
131 Reggie Theus	.30	.75
132 Darryl Dawkins	.40	1.00
133 Tom Chambers	.30	.75
134 M.L. Carr	.30	.75
135 Kelly Tripucka	.30	.75
136 George Gervin	.40	1.00
137 Robert Parish	.40	1.00
138 Mitch Kupchak	.30	.75
139 Lou Hudson	.30	.75
140 Bill Cartwright	.30	.75
141 Lafayette Lever	.30	.75
142 Kevin Loughery	.30	.75
143 Hal Greer	.30	.75
144 Jamaal Wilkes	.30	.75
145 Alvan Adams	.30	.75
146 Thomas Sanders	.30	.75
147 Cazzie Russell	.30	.75
148 Austin Carr	.30	.75
149 Gail Goodrich	.30	.75
150 Billy Knight	.30	.75
151 Dave Bing	.30	.75
152 Bill Walton	.30	.75
153 Sam Jones	.30	.75
154 Swen Nater	.30	.75
155 Bobby Dandridge	.30	.75
156 Junior Bridgeman	.30	.75
157 Paul Silas	.30	.75
158 John Kerr	.30	.75
159 Phil Chenier	.30	.75
160 Alex English	.30	.75
161 Geoff Petrie	.30	.75
162 Walt Bellamy	.30	.75
163 Don Nelson	.30	.75
164 Byron Scott	.30	.75
165 Harvey Catchings	.30	.75
166 Edward Macauley	.30	.75
167 John Drew	.30	.75
168 Detlef Schrempf	.30	.75
169 Rolando Blackman	.30	.75
170 Dave DeBusschere	.30	.75
171 Marvin Barnes	.30	.75
172 Elgin Baylor	.30	.75
173 Cedric Maxwell	.30	.75
174 Vern Mikkelsen	.30	.75
175 Larry Brown	.30	.75
176 Rick Mahorn	.30	.75
177 Dolph Schayes	.30	.75
178 Kevin McHale	.40	1.00
179 Clark Kellogg	.30	.75
180 Otis Birdsong	.30	.75
181 Michael Cooper	.30	.75
182 Mike Dunleavy	.30	.75
183 Spencer Haywood	.30	.75
184 Larry Nance	.30	.75
185 Maurice Lucas	.30	.75
186 Fred Brown	.30	.75
187 Jerry West	.40	1.00
188 Joe Barry Carroll	.30	.75
189 Dave Cowens	.30	.75
190 Sidney Moncrief	.30	.75
191 Kiki Vandeweghe	.30	.75
192 Walt Frazier	.30	.75
193 Yao Ming Wilt Chamberlain	4.00	10.00
194 Jay Williams Julius Erving	2.50	6.00
195 Mike Dunleavy Jr. Mike Dunleavy Sr.	2.50	6.00
196 Drew Gooden John Havlicek	3.00	8.00
197 Nikoloz Tskitishvili Kevin McHale	1.50	4.00
198 DaJuan Wagner Oscar Robertson	1.50	4.00
199 Nene Hilario Kiki Vandeweghe	2.50	6.00
200 Chris Wilcox	1.50	4.00
201 Amare Stoudemire George McGinnis	5.00	12.00
202 Caron Butler Willis Reed	2.50	6.00
203 Jared Jeffries Larry Bird	2.00	5.00
204 Melvin Ely Elgin Baylor	1.50	4.00
205 Marcus Haislip Kareem Abdul-Jabbar	1.50	4.00
206 Fred Jones K.C. Jones	1.50	4.00
207 Bostjan Nachbar	1.50	4.00
208 Jiri Welsch	1.50	4.00
209 Juan Dixon	2.00	5.00
210 Curtis Borchardt	1.50	4.00
211 Ryan Humphrey Bob Lanier	1.50	4.00
212 Kareem Rush Walt Frazier	1.50	4.00
213 Qyntel Woods Jamaal Wilkes	1.50	4.00
214 Casey Jacobsen Tom Chambers	1.50	4.00
215 Tayshaun Prince Byron Scott	2.00	5.00
216 Predrag Savovic Drazen Petrovic	1.50	4.00
217 Frank Williams	1.50	4.00
218 John Salmons Elgin Baylor	1.50	4.00
219 Chris Jefferies Walter Davis	1.50	4.00
220 Dan Dickau	1.50	4.00
221 Marcus Taylor Oscar Robertson	1.50	4.00
222 Roger Mason Jo Jo White	1.50	4.00
223 Robert Archibald Sidney Moncrief	1.50	4.00
224 Vincent Yarbrough Earl Monroe	1.50	4.00
225 Dan Gadzuric Bill Walton	1.50	4.00
226 Carlos Boozer Robert Parish	3.00	8.00
227 Tito Maddox	1.50	4.00
228 Rod Grizzard George Gervin	1.50	4.00
229 Ronald Murray Lafayette Lever	1.50	4.00
230 Marko Jaric	1.50	4.00
231 Lonny Baxter	1.50	4.00
232 Sam Clancy Wes Unseld	1.50	4.00
233 Matt Barnes	2.00	5.00
234 Jamal Sampson	1.50	4.00

2002-03 Upper Deck Generations All-Time Authentics

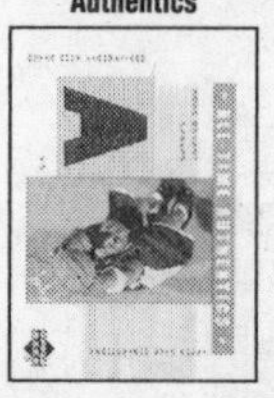

Randomly inserted in packs at the rate of one in 18 Old School, this 27-card set features a horizontal design on which player photos appear on the right and an "A" shaped swatch of game worn material appears on the left.

AMA Alonzo Mourning	5.00	12.00
BCA Bob Cousy	8.00	20.00
BWA Bill Walton	6.00	15.00
CDA Clyde Drexler	5.00	12.00
DRA David Robinson	6.00	15.00
GPA Gary Payton	4.00	10.00
JEA Julius Erving Blue	15.00	30.00
JE2A Julius Erving White	15.00	30.00
JKA Jason Kidd	6.00	15.00
JSA John Stockton	5.00	12.00
KAA Kareem Abdul-Jabbar	8.00	20.00
KBA Kobe Bryant	15.00	30.00
KMA Karl Malone	5.00	12.00
LBA Larry Bird	12.00	30.00
MCA Kevin McHale	5.00	12.00
MGA Magic Johnson Yellow	8.00	20.00
MG2A Magic Johnson White	8.00	20.00
MJA Michael Jordan Warm	60.00	150.00
MJ2A Michael Jordan Shirt	60.00	150.00
MRA Mitch Richmond	4.00	10.00
ORA Oscar Robertson	10.00	25.00
RBA Rick Barry	5.00	12.00
RMA Reggie Miller	4.00	10.00
SPA Scottie Pippen	15.00	30.00
TAA Nate Archibald Green	4.00	10.00
TA2A Nate Archibald White	4.00	10.00
WCA Wilt Chamberlain	30.00	80.00

2002-03 Upper Deck Generations All-Time Dual Autographs

Inserted randomly in Old School packs, this 10-card set is also horizontally designed with a player in the top left corner and one in the bottom right corner next to authentic player autographs. Each card is sequentially numbered to 25.

DT/GG David Thompson George Gervin	25.00	60.00
DW/JR Dominique Wilkins Jason Richardson	60.00	120.00
EB/KM Elgin Baylor Kenyon Martin	25.00	60.00
KA/TC Kareem Abdul-Jabbar Tyson Chandler	100.00	200.00
LB/MM Larry Bird Mike Miller	150.00	300.00
MG/JK Magic Johnson Jason Kidd	150.00	300.00

MJ/KB Michael Jordan 600.00 1000.00
Kobe Bryant
WF/DJ Walt Frazier 25.00 60.00
DerMarr Johnson

2002-03 Upper Deck Generations All-Time Dual Jerseys

Inserted in Old School packs, this seven card set is utilizes the same design as the All-Time Dual Autographs insert set with player photos pushed closer to the middle of the card and two swatches of memorabilia on the left and right side of the card.

JEALI Julius Erving 30.00 60.00
Allen Iverson
JELBJ Julius Erving 60.00 150.00
Larry Bird
MGLBJ Magic Johnson 40.00 100.00
Larry Bird
MJJEJ Michael Jordan 100.00 250.00
Julius Erving
MJKBJ Michael Jordan 150.00 300.00
Kobe Bryant
MJMGJ Michael Jordan 60.00 150.00
Magic Johnson
WCBRJ Wilt Chamberlain 100.00 200.00
Bill Russell

2002-03 Upper Deck Generations Reel Time Jersey

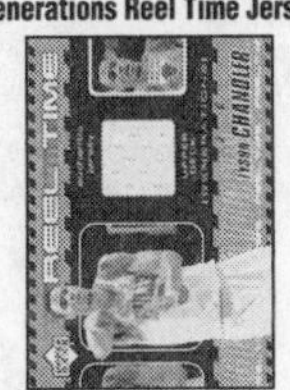

Inserted in packs at the rate of one in 18 New School, this 20-card set has blueish-silver borders along the top and bottom, a black strip throught the middle of the horozontal design-left to right, full color player photos on the left and a swatch of game worn memorabilia on the right.

AIJ Allen Iverson 5.00 12.00
AWJ Antoine Walker 2.50 6.00
BDJ Baron Davis 3.00 8.00
CWJ Chris Webber 3.00 8.00
DNJ Dirk Nowitzki 5.00 12.00
EBJ Elton Brand 3.00 8.00
JKJ Jason Kidd 5.00 12.00
JOJ Jermaine O'Neal 3.00 8.00
JSJ Jerry Stackhouse 2.50 6.00
KBJ Kobe Bryant 12.50 30.00
KGJ Kevin Garnett 6.00 15.00
KMJ Kenyon Martin 3.00 8.00
MBJ Mike Bibby 3.00 8.00
MCJ Antonio McDyess 2.50 6.00
MJJ Michael Jordan 75.00 150.00
PPJ Paul Pierce 4.00 10.00
SFJ Steve Francis 3.00 8.00
SMJ Stephon Marbury 2.50 6.00
TCJ Tyson Chandler 2.50 6.00
TMJ Tracy McGrady 5.00 12.00

2002-03 Upper Deck Generations Signature Classics

Inserted in packs at the rate of one in 54 Old School, this 26-card set uses a horizontal design with red borders along the top and bottom of the card, a centered player portrait photo along the top and an authentic player autograph.

AES Alex English 8.00 20.00
BCS Bob Cousy 20.00 50.00
BWS Bill Walton 12.50 30.00
BYS Byron Scott 8.00 20.00
CDS Clyde Drexler 20.00 50.00
DTS David Thompson 8.00 20.00
DWS Dominique Wilkins 20.00 50.00
EBS Elgin Baylor 12.50 30.00
GGS George Gervin 10.00 25.00
JES Julius Erving 75.00 150.00
JHS John Havlicek 15.00 40.00
JMS Jerome Moiso 4.00 10.00
KAS Kareem Abdul-Jabbar 30.00 80.00
LBS Larry Bird 75.00 150.00
MGS Magic Johnson 60.00 120.00
MJS Michael Jordan 350.00 650.00
MMS Mike Miller 5.00 12.00
NAS Nate Archibald 8.00 20.00
QRS Quentin Richardson 4.00 10.00
RBS Rick Barry 10.00 25.00
RMS Ron Mercer 4.00 10.00
SAS Shareef Abdur-Rahim 6.00 15.00
TBS Terrell Brandon 4.00 10.00
WFS Walt Frazier 8.00 20.00

1996 Upper Deck German Kellogg's

This 40-card set was packaged three per German Kellogg's Frosties or Chocos box. The cards are similar in design to the 1995-96 Upper Deck American cards. The only difference is the cards lack the gold foil on the player's name. Card backs are identical to the American release.

COMPLETE SET (40) 40.00 100.00
CHECKLIST (NNO) .75 2.00
1 Jerry Stackhouse 3.00 8.00
2 Clifford Robinson 1.50 4.00
3 Glenn Robinson 2.50 6.00
4 Chris Webber 3.00 8.00
5 Dennis Rodman 5.00 12.00
6 Scottie Pippen 4.00 10.00
7 Toni Kukoc 2.50 6.00
8 Dan Majerle 2.50 6.00
9 Dino Radja 2.00 5.00
10 Loy Vaught 1.50 4.00
11 Bryant Reeves 1.50 4.00
12 Stacey Augmon 2.00 5.00
13 Kevin Willis 1.50 4.00
14 Muggsy Bogues 2.00 5.00
15 John Stockton 3.00 8.00
16 Karl Malone 3.00 8.00
17 Mitch Richmond 2.50 6.00
18 Charles Oakley 2.00 5.00
19 Nick Van Exel 2.50 6.00
20 Anfernee Hardaway 4.00 10.00
21 Horace Grant 2.00 5.00
22 Jason Kidd 4.00 10.00
23 Ed O'Bannon 1.50 4.00
24 Dikembe Mutombo 2.50 6.00
25 Dale Davis 1.50 4.00
26 Derrick McKey 1.50 4.00
27 Mark Jackson 2.50 6.00
28 Rik Smits 2.00 5.00
29 Grant Hill 4.00 10.00
30 Damon Stoudamire 2.50 6.00
31 Clyde Drexler 3.00 8.00
32 Hakeem Olajuwon 3.00 8.00
33 Detlef Schrempf 2.50 6.00
34 Gary Payton 2.50 6.00
35 Hersey Hawkins 1.50 4.00
36 Sam Perkins 1.50 4.00
37 David Robinson 4.00 10.00
38 Charles Barkley 4.00 10.00
39 Christian Laettner 2.00 5.00
40 B.J. Armstrong 1.50 4.00

1999-00 Upper Deck Gold Reserve

The 1999-00 Upper Deck Gold Reserve product was released as a retail-only product in late March,2000. The 270-card set features 240 player cards and a 30-card rookie subset that is serial numbered to 3500. Each pack contained 10-cards and carried a suggested retail price of 2.99.

COMPLETE SET (270) 60.00 120.00
COMPLETE SET w/o RC (240) 15.00 40.00
1 Roshown McLeod .20 .50
2 Dikembe Mutombo .30 .75
3 Alan Henderson .20 .50
4 Chris Crawford .20 .50
5 Jim Jackson .25 .60
6 Isaiah Rider .20 .50
7 Lorenzen Wright .20 .50
8 Bimbo Coles .20 .50
9 Kenny Anderson .25 .60
10 Antoine Walker .30 .75
11 Paul Pierce .50 1.25
12 Vitaly Potapenko .20 .50
13 Dana Barros .20 .50
14 Calbert Cheaney .20 .50
15 Pervis Ellison .20 .50
16 Eric Williams .20 .50
17 Toby Bailey .25 .60
18 Elden Campbell .20 .50
19 Eddie Jones .30 .75
20 David Wesley .20 .50
21 Derrick Coleman .25 .60
22 Ricky Davis .25 .60
23 Anthony Mason .20 .50
24 Todd Fuller .20 .50
25 Brad Miller .30 .75
26 Corey Benjamin .20 .50
27 Randy Brown .20 .50
28 Dickey Simpkins .20 .50
29 Toni Kukoc .30 .75
30 Fred Hoiberg .20 .50
31 Hersey Hawkins .20 .50
32 Will Perdue .20 .50
33 Chris Anstey .20 .50
34 Shawn Kemp .30 .75
35 Wesley Person .20 .50
36 Brevin Knight .20 .50
37 Bob Sura .20 .50
38 Danny Ferry .20 .50
39 Lamond Murray .20 .50
40 Cedric Henderson .20 .50
41 Andrew DeClercq .20 .50
42 Michael Finley .30 .75
43 Shawn Bradley .20 .50
44 Dirk Nowitzki .60 1.50
45 Erick Strickland .20 .50
46 Cedric Ceballos .20 .50
47 Hubert Davis .20 .50
48 Robert Pack .20 .50
49 Gary Trent .20 .50
50 Antonio McDyess .25 .60
51 Nick Van Exel .25 .60
52 Chauncey Billups .30 .75
53 Bryant Stith .20 .50
54 Raef LaFrentz .25 .60
55 Ron Mercer .25 .60
56 George McCloud .20 .50
57 Roy Rogers .20 .50
58 Keon Clark .20 .50
59 Grant Hill .40 1.00
60 Lindsey Hunter .20 .50
61 Jerry Stackhouse .30 .75
62 Terry Mills .20 .50
63 Michael Curry .20 .50
64 Christian Laettner .25 .60
65 Jerome Williams .20 .50
66 Loy Vaught .20 .50
67 John Starks .30 .75
68 Antawn Jamison .30 .75
69 Erick Dampier .25 .60
70 Jason Caffey .20 .50
71 Terry Cummings .20 .50
72 Donyell Marshall .25 .60
73 Chris Mills .20 .50
74 Tony Farmer .20 .50
75 Adonal Foyle .20 .50
76 Hakeem Olajuwon .40 1.00
77 Cuttino Mobley .25 .60
78 Charles Barkley .50 1.25
79 Bryce Drew .20 .50
80 Shandon Anderson .20 .50
81 Kelvin Cato .20 .50
82 Walt Williams .20 .50
83 Carlos Rogers .20 .50
84 Reggie Miller .30 .75
85 Jalen Rose .25 .60
86 Mark Jackson .30 .75
87 Dale Davis .20 .50
88 Chris Mullin .30 .75
89 Al Harrington .30 .75
90 Rik Smits .20 .50
91 Sam Perkins .20 .50
92 Austin Croshere .20 .50
93 Maurice Taylor .20 .50
94 Tyrone Nesby RC .20 .50
95 Michael Olowokandi .20 .50
96 Eric Piatkowski .25 .60
97 Troy Hudson .25 .60
98 Derek Anderson .25 .60
99 Eric Murdock .20 .50
100 Brian Skinner .20 .50
101 Kobe Bryant 1.50 4.00
102 Shaquille O'Neal .75 2.00
103 Glen Rice .30 .75
104 Robert Horry .30 .75
105 Ron Harper .20 .50
106 Derek Fisher .30 .75
107 Rick Fox .30 .75
108 A.C. Green .30 .75
109 Tim Hardaway .30 .75
110 Alonzo Mourning .40 1.00
111 P.J. Brown .20 .50
112 Dan Majerle .30 .75
113 Jamal Mashburn .25 .60
114 Voshon Lenard .20 .50
115 Clarence Weatherspoon .20 .50
116 Rex Walters .20 .50
117 Ray Allen .30 .75
118 Glenn Robinson .25 .60
119 Sam Cassell .25 .60
120 Robert Traylor .20 .50
121 J.R. Reid .20 .50
122 Ervin Johnson .20 .50
123 Danny Manning .20 .50
124 Tim Thomas .25 .60
125 Kevin Garnett .60 1.50
126 Sam Mitchell .20 .50
127 Dean Garrett .20 .50
128 Bobby Jackson .25 .60
129 Radoslav Nesterovic .30 .75
130 Terrell Brandon .20 .50
131 Joe Smith .20 .50
132 Anthony Peeler .20 .50
133 Keith Van Horn .25 .60
134 Stephon Marbury .25 .60
135 Kendall Gill .20 .50
136 Scott Burrell .20 .50
137 Jayson Williams .20 .50
138 Jamie Feick RC .20 .50
139 Kerry Kittles .20 .50
140 Johnny Newman .20 .50
141 Patrick Ewing .40 1.00
142 Allan Houston .25 .60
143 Latrell Sprewell .30 .75
144 Larry Johnson .30 .75
145 Marcus Camby .25 .60
146 Chris Childs .20 .50
147 Kurt Thomas .20 .50
148 Charlie Ward .20 .50
149 Darrell Armstrong .20 .50
150 Matt Harpring .25 .60
151 Michael Doleac .20 .50
152 Bo Outlaw .20 .50
153 Tariq Abdul-Wahad .20 .50
154 John Amaechi RC .30 .75
155 Ben Wallace .30 .75
156 Monty Williams .20 .50
157 Allen Iverson .60 1.50
158 Theo Ratliff .20 .50
159 Larry Hughes .25 .60
160 Eric Snow .20 .50
161 George Lynch .20 .50
162 Tyrone Hill .20 .50
163 Billy Owens .20 .50
164 Aaron McKie .20 .50
165 Jason Kidd .50 1.25
166 Clifford Robinson .20 .50
167 Tom Gugliotta .20 .50
168 Luc Longley .20 .50
169 Anfernee Hardaway .50 1.25
170 Rex Chapman .20 .50
171 Oliver Miller .20 .50
172 Rodney Rogers .20 .50
173 Rasheed Wallace .30 .75
174 Arvydas Sabonis .25 .60
175 Damon Stoudamire .25 .60
176 Brian Grant .20 .50
177 Scottie Pippen .50 1.25
178 Detlef Schrempf .25 .60
179 Steve Smith .20 .50
180 Jermaine O'Neal .30 .75
181 Bonzi Wells .20 .50
182 Jason Williams .40 1.00
183 Vlade Divac .30 .75
184 Peja Stojakovic .30 .75
185 Lawrence Funderburke .20 .50
186 Chris Webber .30 .75
187 Nick Anderson .20 .50
188 Darrick Martin .20 .50
189 Corliss Williamson .20 .50
190 Tim Duncan .60 1.50
191 Sean Elliott .30 .75
192 David Robinson .50 1.25
193 Mario Elie .20 .50
194 Avery Johnson .25 .60
195 Terry Porter .20 .50
196 Malik Rose .20 .50
197 Jaren Jackson .20 .50
198 Gary Payton .30 .75
199 Vin Baker .20 .50
200 Rashard Lewis .30 .75
201 Jelani McCoy .20 .50
202 Brent Barry .25 .60
203 Horace Grant .25 .60
204 Vernon Maxwell UER .25 .60
Listed as 294, should be 204
205 Ruben Patterson .20 .50
206 Vince Carter .60 1.50
207 Doug Christie .25 .60
208 Kevin Willis .20 .50
209 Dee Brown .20 .50
210 Antonio Davis .20 .50
211 Tracy McGrady .50 1.25
212 Dell Curry .20 .50
213 Charles Oakley .25 .60
214 Karl Malone .40 1.00
215 John Stockton .40 1.00
216 Howard Eisley .20 .50
217 Bryon Russell .20 .50
218 Greg Ostertag .20 .50
219 Jeff Hornacek .25 .60
220 Olden Polynice .20 .50
221 Adam Keefe .20 .50
222 Shareef Abdur-Rahim .25 .60
223 Mike Bibby .30 .75
224 Felipe Lopez .20 .50
225 Cherokee Parks .20 .50
226 Michael Dickerson .20 .50
227 Othella Harrington .20 .50
228 Bryant Reeves .20 .50
229 Brent Price .20 .50
230 Michael Smith .20 .50
231 Juwan Howard .25 .60
232 Rod Strickland .20 .50
233 Chris Whitney .20 .50
234 Tracy Murray .20 .50
235 Mitch Richmond .30 .75
236 Aaron Williams .20 .50
237 Isaac Austin .20 .50
238 Kobe Bryant CL 1.50 4.00
239 Michael Jordan CL 2.50 6.00
240 Kevin Garnett CL .60 1.50
241 Elton Brand RC 2.00 5.00
242 Steve Francis RC 2.50 6.00
243 Baron Davis RC 2.50 6.00
244 Lamar Odom RC 2.50 6.00
245 Jonathan Bender RC .75 2.00
246 Wally Szczerbiak RC 1.50 4.00
247 Richard Hamilton RC 2.00 5.00
248 Andre Miller RC 2.00 5.00
249 Shawn Marion RC 2.00 5.00
250 Jason Terry RC 2.00 5.00
251 Trajan Langdon RC .75 2.00
252 Aleksandar Radojevic RC .75 2.00
253 Corey Maggette RC 1.50 4.00
254 William Avery RC .75 2.00
255 Ron Artest RC 2.00 5.00
256 Cal Bowdler RC .75 2.00
257 James Posey RC .75 2.00
258 Quincy Lewis RC .75 2.00
259 Dion Glover RC .75 2.00
260 Jeff Foster RC .75 2.00
261 Kenny Thomas RC .75 2.00
262 Devean George RC .75 2.00
263 Tim James RC .75 2.00
264 Vonteego Cummings RC .75 2.00
265 Jumaine Jones RC .75 2.00
266 Scott Padgett RC .75 2.00
267 Rodney Buford RC .75 2.00
268 Adrian Griffin RC .75 2.00
269 Anthony Carter RC .75 2.00
270 Eddie Robinson RC .75 2.00

1999-00 Upper Deck Gold Reserve Gold Mine

Randomly inserted in packs at one in 11, this 15-card insert set features some of the NBA's greatest players. Card backs carry a "R" prefix.

COMPLETE SET (15) 10.00 25.00
R1 Kobe Bryant 3.00 8.00
R2 Vince Carter 1.25 3.00
R3 Steve Francis 1.50 4.00
R4 Kevin Garnett 1.25 3.00
R5 Elton Brand 1.50 4.00
R6 Gary Payton .60 1.50
R7 Lamar Odom 2.00 5.00
R8 Grant Hill .75 2.00
R9 Jason Williams .75 2.00
R10 Shareef Abdur-Rahim .50 1.25
R11 Tim Duncan 1.25 3.00
R12 Keith Van Horn .50 1.25
R13 Tim Hardaway .60 1.50
R14 Karl Malone .75 2.00
R15 Shaquille O'Neal 1.50 4.00

1999-00 Upper Deck Gold Reserve Gold Strike

Randomly inserted in packs at one in four, this insert set features 15 of the NBA's rising stars. Card backs carry a "GS" prefix.

COMPLETE SET (15) 6.00 15.00
GS1 Kevin Garnett .75 2.00
GS2 Kobe Bryant 2.00 5.00
GS3 Tim Duncan .75 2.00
GS4 Adrian Griffin .40 1.00
GS5 Lamar Odom 1.25 3.00
GS6 Jason Kidd .60 1.50
GS7 Wally Szczerbiak .75 2.00
GS8 Stephon Marbury .30 .75
GS9 Shaquille O'Neal 1.00 2.50
GS10 Elton Brand 1.00 2.50
GS11 Allen Iverson .75 2.00
GS12 Shawn Marion 1.00 2.50
GS13 Jason Williams .50 1.25
GS14 Antonio McDyess .30 .75
GS15 Vince Carter .75 2.00

1999-00 Upper Deck Gold Reserve UD Authentics

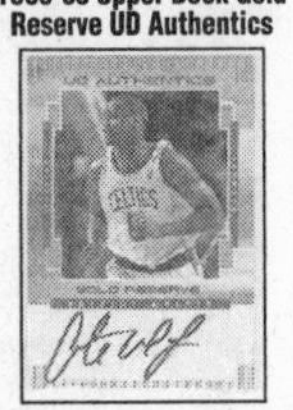

Randomly inserted in packs at one in 480, this 10-card insert set features autographed cards of some of the hottest players in the NBA. Card backs are numbered using the player's initials.

AH Anfernee Hardaway 50.00 125.00
AW Antoine Walker 3.00 8.00
BD Baron Davis 10.00 25.00
JB Jonathan Bender 3.00 8.00
JT Jason Terry 8.00 20.00
KB Kobe Bryant 150.00 325.00
KG Kevin Garnett 100.00 200.00
RH Richard Hamilton 8.00 20.00
SF Steve Francis 8.00 20.00
WS Wally Szczerbiak 6.00 15.00

2009 Upper Deck Goodwin Champions Preview

RANDOM INSERTS IN PACKS
GCP8 Michael Jordan 6.00 15.00

2009 Upper Deck Goodwin Champions

COMMON CARD (1-150) .15 .40
COMMON NIGHT 5.00 12.00
COMMON SP (151-190) 1.25 3.00
151-190 STATED ODDS 1:2 HOBBY
COMMON SUPER SP (191-210) 1.50 4.00
191-210 STATED ODDS 1:10 HOBBY
PLATES RANDOMLY INSERTED
PLATE PRINT RUN 1 SET PER COLOR
BLACK-CYAN-MAGENTA-YELLOW ISSUED
NO PLATE PRICING DUE TO SCARCITY
24 O.J. Mayo .40 1.00
61 Michael Beasley .40 1.00
73 LeBron James 1.50 4.00
111 Kevin Garnett .60 1.50
114 Michael Jordan 1.00 2.50
143 Derrick Rose .75 2.00

2009 Upper Deck Goodwin Champions Mini

COMPLETE SET (192) 75.00 150.00
*MINI 1-150: 1X TO 2.5X BASIC
APPX.MINI ODDS ONE PER PACK
PLATES RANDOMLY INSERTED
PLATE PRINT RUN 1 SET PER COLOR
BLACK-CYAN-MAGENTA-YELLOW ISSUED
NO PLATE PRICING DUE TO SCARCITY

2009 Upper Deck Goodwin Champions Mini Black Border

*MINI BLK 1-150: 1.5X TO 4X BASE
*MINI BLK 211-252: .75X TO 2X MINI
RANDOM INSERTS IN PACKS

2009 Upper Deck Goodwin Champions Mini Foil

*MINI FOIL 1-150: 3X TO 8X BASE
*MINI FOIL 211-252: 1.5X TO 4X MINI
RANDOM INSERTS IN PACKS
ANNCD PRINT RUN OF 88 TOTAL SETS

2009 Upper Deck Goodwin Champions Autographs

STATED ODDS 1:20 HOBBY
EXCHANGE DEADLINE 8/31/2011
GK Kevin Garnett/25 * 50.00 100.00
MJ Michael Jordan/23 * 500.00 700.00

2009 Upper Deck Goodwin Champions Memorabilia

STATED ODDS 1:10 HOBBY
EXCHANGE DEADLINE 8/31/2011
DR Derrick Rose 5.00 12.00
KG Kevin Garnett 5.00 12.00
LJ LeBron James 12.50 30.00
MB Michael Beasley 3.00 8.00
MJ Michael Jordan/50 * 30.00 60.00
OM O.J. Mayo 3.00 8.00

2011 Upper Deck Goodwin Champions

COMP.SET w/o VAR (210) 40.00 80.00
COMP.SET w/o SP's (150) 10.00 25.00
COMMON SP (151-190) 1.00 2.50
151-190 SP ODDS 1:3 HOBBY
COMMON SP (191-210) 1.50 4.00
191-210 SP ODDS 1:12 HOBBY
COMMON VARIATION SP 4.00 10.00
2 John Havlicek .25 .60
6 LeBron James 1.25 3.00
7 Rick Barry .25 .60
8 Walt Frazier .25 .60
23A Michael Jordan 1.50 4.00
23B Michael Jordan Lightning SP 12.50 30.00
33 Cynthia Cooper .30 .75
35 Hakeem Olajuwon .30 .75
37 Larry Bird .60 1.50
44 Alonzo Mourning .30 .75
45 John Stockton .40 1.00
53 Bill Laimbeer .25 .60
54 Dennis Rodman .40 1.00
55 Bill Walton .25 .60
60 Bill Russell .40 1.00
88 Jerry West .30 .75
90 Magic Johnson .60 1.50
100 Candace Parker .40 1.00
105 David Robinson .40 1.00
106 Tim Hardaway .25 .60
111 Derrick Rose .60 1.50
114 Greg Monroe .40 1.00
115 James Worthy .30 .75
121 Russell Westbrook .30 .75
135 Anfernee Hardaway .60 1.50
137 Chris Paul .40 1.00
138 Julius Erving .50 1.25
143 Derrick Favors .50 1.25
145 Clyde Drexler .30 .75
147A Grant Hill .25 .60
147B Grant Hill Lightning SP 4.00 10.00
149 DeMarcus Cousins .75 2.00
207 James Naismith SP 1.50 4.00

2011 Upper Deck Goodwin Champions Mini

*1-150 MINI: 1X TO 2.5X BASIC
1-150 MINI ODDS 1:4 HOBBY
COMMON CARD (211-231) .60 1.50
211-231 MINI ODDS 1:13 HOBBY
PRINTING PLATES RANDOMLY INSERTED
PLATE PRINT RUN 1 SET PER COLOR
BLACK-CYAN-MAGENTA-YELLOW ISSUED
NO PLATE PRICING DUE TO SCARCITY

2011 Upper Deck Goodwin Champions Mini Black

*1-150 MINI BLACK: 1.2X TO 3X BASIC
1-150 MINI BLACK ODDS 1:13 HOBBY
*211-231 MINI BLK: .6X TO 1.5X BASIC MINI
211-231 MINI BLACK ODDS 1:46 HOBBY

2011 Upper Deck Goodwin Champions Mini Foil

*1-150 MINI FOIL: 2.5X TO 6X BASIC
1-150 ANNCD PRINT RUN OF 89
*211-231 MINI FOIL : 1X TO 2.5X BASIC MINI
211-231 ANNCD PRINT RUN OF 178
PRINT RUNS PROVIDED BY UD
23 Michael Jordan 20.00 50.00

2011 Upper Deck Goodwin Champions Autographs

GROUP A ODDS 1:1577 HOBBY
GROUP B ODDS 1:729 HOBBY
GROUP C ODDS 1:339 HOBBY
GROUP D ODDS 1:246 HOBBY
GROUP E ODDS 1:72 HOBBY
GROUP F ODDS 1:35 HOBBY
OVERALL AUTO ODDS 1:20 HOBBY
EXCHANGE DEADLINE 6/7/2013
BL Bill Laimbeer E 4.00 10.00
BW Bill Walton C 10.00 25.00
CP Candace Parker E 6.00 15.00
DR David Robinson A 50.00 125.00
GH Grant Hill A 75.00 200.00
LB Larry Bird A 75.00 150.00
LJ LeBron James C 150.00 250.00
MA Magic Johnson A 75.00 150.00
MJ Michael Jordan C 500.00 700.00
OL Hakeem Olajuwon A 30.00 80.00
PA Chris Paul B 10.00 25.00
RD Derrick Rose A 75.00 150.00
RO Dennis Rodman B 50.00 100.00
TH Tim Hardaway E 8.00 20.00

2011 Upper Deck Goodwin Champions Figures of Sport

COMP.SET w/o SP's (14) 10.00 25.00
COMMON CARD (1-14) .60 1.50
1-14 STATED ODDS 1:21 HOBBY
15-18 SP ODDS 1:300 HOBBY
FS1 LeBron James 3.00 8.00
FS15 Michael Jordan SP 6.00 15.00

2011 Upper Deck Goodwin Champions Memorabilia

GROUP A ODDS 1:14,613 HOBBY
GROUP B ODDS 1:179 HOBBY
GROUP C ODDS 1:31 HOBBY
GROUP D ODDS 1:22 HOBBY
NO GROUP A PRICING AVAILABLE
AM Alonzo Mourning C 4.00 10.00
CD Clyde Drexler B 5.00 12.00
CP Chris Paul D 3.00 8.00
DR David Robinson B 4.00 10.00
GH Grant Hill C 4.00 10.00
JL Julius Erving B 4.00 10.00
JO Magic Johnson C 4.00 10.00
LB Larry Bird C 6.00 15.00
LJ LeBron James C 5.00 12.00
MJ Michael Jordan C 20.00 50.00
OL Hakeem Olajuwon C 4.00 10.00
RD Dennis Rodman B 8.00 20.00
RO Derrick Rose B 4.00 10.00
RW Russell Westbrook D 3.00 8.00

2011 Upper Deck Goodwin Champions Memorabilia Dual

GROUP A ODDS 1:87,680 HOBBY
GROUP B ODDS 1:8768 HOBBY
GROUP C ODDS 1:2923 HOBBY
GROUP D ODDS 1:877 HOBBY
GROUP E ODDS 1:585 HOBBY
NO GROUP A PRICING AVAILABLE
LJ LeBron James E 10.00 25.00
MJ Michael Jordan D 20.00 50.00

2012 Upper Deck Goodwin Champions

COMP.SET w/o VAR (210) 25.00 50.00
COMP.SET w/o SP's (150) 10.00 25.00
151-190 SP ODDS 1:3 HOBBY, BLASTER
191-210 SP ODDS 1:12 HOBBY, BLASTER
4A Hakeem Olajuwon .30 .75
4B Hakeem Olajuwon 6.00 15.00
Bill Clinton SP
5A Magic Johnson .50 1.25
5B Magic Johnson/Bill Walton 6.00 15.00
Larry Bird SP
7 Chris Singleton .40 1.00
17 Grant Hill .25 .60
23 Elgin Baylor .30 .75
40 Bill Walton .25 .60
41 Alonzo Mourning .25 .60
44 Chris Paul .40 1.00
47A Karl Malone .30 .75
47B Karl Malone 6.00 15.00
Hulk Hogan
Dennis Rodman SP
57 Bobby Hurley .15 .40
58 Oscar Robertson .25 .60
63 David Robinson .40 1.00
76 Christian Laettner .20 .50
83 Steve Nash .30 .75
88 Larry Bird .60 1.50
90 Clyde Drexler .30 .75
94 Adrian Dantley .15 .40
106 Jackie Stiles .15 .40
112 Norris Cole .40 1.00
114 Jimmer Fredette .30 .75
116 Jason Kidd .30 .75
118 LeBron James 1.00 2.50
120 Kawhi Leonard .40 1.00
123A Michael Jordan 1.50 4.00
123B Michael Jordan
Julius Erving SP
126 Larry Johnson .20 .50
135 Dominique Wilkins .20 .50
138 Sam Cassell .15 .40
162 Alec Burks SP 1.00 2.50
167 Tristan Thompson SP 1.00 2.50

2012 Upper Deck Goodwin Champions Mini

*1-150 MINI: 1X TO 2.5X BASIC CARDS
1-150 MINI STATED ODDS 1:2 HOBBY, BLASTER
211-231 MINI ODDS 1:2 HOBBY, BLASTER

2012 Upper Deck Goodwin Champions Mini Foil

*1-150 MINI FOIL: 2.5X TO 6X BASIC
1-150 MINI FOIL ANNCD. PRINT RUN 99
*211-231 MINI FOIL: 1X TO 2.5X BASIC MINI
211-231 MINI FOIL ANNCD. PRINT RUN 199

2012 Upper Deck Goodwin Champions Mini Green

*1-150 MINI GREEN: 1.25X TO 3X BASIC
*211-231 MINI GREEN: .6X TO 1.5X BASIC MINI
TWO MINI GREEN PER HOBBY BOX
ONE MINI GREEN PER BLASTER

2012 Upper Deck Goodwin Champions Autographs

GROUP A ODDS 1:1,977
GROUP B ODDS 1:353
GROUP C ODDS 1:264
GROUP D ODDS 1:185
GROUP E ODDS 1:82
GROUP F ODDS 1:36
OVERALL AUTO ODDS 1:20
EXCHANGE DEADLINE 7/12/2014
ACL Christian Laettner B 10.00 25.00
ACP Chris Paul A 20.00 40.00
ADW Dominique Wilkins B EXCH 12.00 30.00
AJF Jimmer Fredette C 12.00 30.00
AJK Jason Kidd B 15.00 40.00
AJS Jackie Stiles F 4.00 10.00
ALJ LeBron James A 150.00 250.00
AMJ Michael Jordan A 350.00 500.00
ASC Sam Cassell C 6.00 15.00

2012 Upper Deck Goodwin Champions Memorabilia

GROUP A ODDS 1:10,631
GROUP B ODDS 1:4,784
GROUP C ODDS 1:302
GROUP D ODDS 1:118
GROUP E ODDS 1:36
GROUP F ODDS 1:23
MAM Alonzo Mourning F 5.00 12.00
MBW Bill Walton D 4.00 10.00
MCP Chris Paul F 3.00 8.00
MDR David Robinson F 3.00 8.00
MHO Hakeem Olajuwon F 4.00 10.00
MJO Magic Johnson E 5.00 12.00
MLB Larry Bird D 6.00 15.00
MLJ LeBron James D 6.00 15.00
MMJ Michael Jordan D 15.00 40.00

2012 Upper Deck Goodwin Champions Memorabilia Dual

GROUP A ODDS 1:95,680
GROUP B ODDS 1:31,893
GROUP C ODDS 1:2,514
GROUP D ODDS 1:1,306
GROUP E ODDS 1:520
NO PRICING ON GROUP A
M2DR David Robinson D 8.00 20.00
M2LJ LeBron James E 10.00 25.00
M2MJ Michael Jordan D 30.00 60.00

2012 Upper Deck Goodwin Champions Sport Royalty Autographs

Cards have a 2010 copyright on the back.
GROUP A ODDS 1:15,947
GROUP B ODDS 1:7,973
GROUP C ODDS 1:4,932
ABW Bill Walton C 30.00 60.00
ADN Don Nelson A
AEB Elgin Baylor A
AHO Hakeem Olajuwon B
ASN Steve Nash B
AYM Yao Ming B

2007 Upper Deck Goudey Sport Royalty

ONE PER HOBBY BOX LOADER
DS Dean Smith 2.00 5.00
JW John Wooden 3.00 8.00
KB Kobe Bryant 6.00 15.00
KD Kevin Durant 5.00 12.00
LJ LeBron James 15.00 40.00
MJ Michael Jordan 20.00 50.00

2007 Upper Deck Goudey Sport Royalty Autographs

STATED ODDS TWO PER CASE
FOUND IN HOBBY BOX LOADER PACKS
JW John Wooden 100.00 200.00
KD Kevin Durant 150.00 250.00
LJ LeBron James 250.00 400.00

2008 Upper Deck Goudey

COMP.SET w/o HIGH #s (200) 20.00 50.00
COMMON CARD (1-200) .20 .50

COMMON ROOKIE (1-200) .30 .75
COMMON SP (201-230) 2.00 5.00
COMMON SP (231-250) 1.50 4.00
COMMON SP (251-270) 2.00 5.00
COMMON CARD (271-300) 2.00 5.00
COMMON CARD (301-330) 3.00 8.00
279 Cynthia Cooper SR SP 2.00 5.00
288 Julius Erving SR SP 2.50 6.00
299 Magic Johnson SR SP 3.00 8.00
300 Michael Jordan SR SP 3.00 8.00
307 Kobe Bryant SR SP 5.00 12.00
308 Kevin Durant SR SP 5.00 12.00
312 Larry Bird SR SP 6.00 15.00
313 LeBron James SR SP 6.00 15.00

2008 Upper Deck Goudey Mini Black Backs

*BLACK 1-200: .75X TO 2X GRN 1-200
*BLACK RC 1-200: .75X TO 2X GRN RC 1-200
*BLACK SP 201-250: .75X TO 2X GRN 201-250
*BLACK SP 251-270: .5X TO 1.2X GRN 251-270
*BLACK SR 271-330: .5X TO 1.2X GRN 271-330
RANDOM INSERTS IN PACKS
STATED PRINT RUN 34 SER.#'d SETS
300 Michael Jordan SR 20.00 50.00
307 Kobe Bryant SR 6.00 15.00

2008 Upper Deck Goudey Mini Blue Backs

*BLUE 1-200: 1.5X TO 4X BASIC 1-200
*BLUE RC 1-200: 1X TO 2.5X BASIC RC 1-200
*BLUE 201-270: .6X TO 1.5X BASIC SP 201-270
*BLUE 271-330: .6X TO 1.5X BASIC SR 201-270
RANDOM INSERTS IN PACKS

2008 Upper Deck Goudey Mini Green Backs

RANDOM INSERTS IN PACKS
STATED PRINT RUN 88 SER.#'d SETS
279 Cynthia Cooper SR 2.50 6.00
288 Julius Erving SR 3.00 8.00
299 Magic Johnson SR 4.00 10.00
300 Michael Jordan SR 12.50 30.00
307 Kobe Bryant SR 4.00 10.00
308 Kevin Durant SR 4.00 10.00
312 Larry Bird SR 5.00 12.00
313 LeBron James SR 10.00 25.00

2008 Upper Deck Goudey Mini Red Backs

*RED 1-200: 1X TO 2.5X BASIC 1-200
*RED RC 1-200: .75X TO 2X BASIC RC 1-200
*RED 201-270: .5X TO 1.2X BASIC SP 201-270
*RED 271-330: .5X to 1.2X BASIC SR 271-330
RANDOM INSERTS IN PACKS

2008 Upper Deck Goudey Hit Parade of Champions

RANDOM INSERTS IN PACKS
4 Bill Russell 1.25 3.00
14 Kobe Bryant 2.50 6.00
16 Larry Bird 2.00 5.00
17 LeBron James 3.00 8.00
18 Magic Johnson 1.25 3.00
21 Michael Jordan 4.00 10.00

2008 Upper Deck Goudey Sport Royalty Autographs

OVERALL AUTO ODDS 1:18 HOBBY
ASTERISK EQUALS PARTIAL EXCHANGE
EXCHANGE DEADLINE 7/17/2010
CC Cynthia Cooper 10.00 25.00

2009 Upper Deck Goudey

COMPLETE SET (300) 200.00 300.00
COMP.SET w/o SP's (200) 20.00 50.00
COMMON CARD (1-200) .20 .50
COMMON RC (1-200) .40 1.00
COMMON SP (201-300) 2.00 5.00
APPX.SP ODDS 201-220 1:9 HOBBY
APPX.SP ODDS 221-260 1:6 HOBBY
APPX.SP ODDS 261-300 1:6 HOBBY
256 Paul Pierce SR SP 3.00 8.00
257 Jerry West SR SP 3.00 8.00
258 Larry Bird SR SP 3.00 8.00
259 John Havlicek SR SP 2.50 6.00
260 Michael Jordan SR SP 5.00 12.00

2009 Upper Deck Goudey Mini Green Back

*GREEN 1-200: 1.2X TO 3X BASIC
*GREEN RC 1-200: .6X TO 1.5X BASIC
COMMON CARD (201-300) .75 2.00
APPROX.ODDS 1:6 HOBBY
256 Paul Pierce SR 2.50 6.00
257 Jerry West SR 3.00 8.00
258 Larry Bird SR 6.00 15.00
259 John Havlicek SR 2.00 5.00
260 Michael Jordan SR 6.00 15.00

2009 Upper Deck Goudey Mini Navy Blue Back

*BLUE 1-200: 1.5X TO 4X BASIC
*BLUE RC 1-200: .75X TO 2X BASIC
*BLUE: 201-300: .6X TO 1.5X MINI GREEN
APPROX.ODDS 1:9 HOBBY

2009 Upper Deck Goudey Sport Royalty Autographs

OVERALL AUTO ODDS 1:18 HOBBY
EXCHANGE DEADLINE 4/1/2011
BS Bill Sharman 15.00 40.00
JH John Havlicek 125.00 250.00
JO Michael Jordan 600.00 900.00
JW Jerry West 75.00 150.00
LB Larry Bird 30.00 60.00

2009 Upper Deck Griffey-Jordan

RANDOM INSERTS IN PACKS
KGMJ Ken Griffey Jr. 15.00 40.00
Michael Jordan

1998 Upper Deck Hardcourt

The 1998 Upper Deck Hardcourt hobby-only set was issued in one series totalling 90 cards. The 4-card packs retail for $5.99 each. The cards feature 32-point stock with a "wood" designed background. The set contains the topical subset: Rookie Experience (71-90). A bonus Michael Jordan card was also included in packs (#23a) at a reported rate of one in every two boxes. Also included, was a 5" by 7" Michael Jordan jumbo card. It was included one per box.

COMPLETE SET (90) 40.00 75.00
1 Kobe Bryant 3.00 8.00
2 Donyell Marshall .40 1.00
3 Bryant Reeves .40 1.00
4 Keith Van Horn .60 1.50
5 David Robinson 1.00 2.50
6 Nick Anderson .40 1.00
7 Nick Van Exel .50 1.25
8 David Wesley .40 1.00
9 Alonzo Mourning .75 2.00
10 Shawn Kemp .60 1.50
11 Maurice Taylor .40 1.00
12 Kenny Anderson .50 1.25
13 Jason Kidd 1.00 2.50
14 Marcus Camby .50 1.25
15 Tim Hardaway .60 1.50
16 Damon Stoudamire .60 1.50
17 Detlef Schrempf .60 1.50
18 Dikembe Mutombo .60 1.50
19 Charles Barkley 1.00 2.50
20 Ray Allen .75 2.00
21 Ron Mercer .50 1.25
22 Shawn Bradley .40 1.00
23 Michael Jordan 5.00 12.00
23A Michael Jordan Special 8.00 20.00
24 Antonio McDyess .50 1.25
25 Stephon Marbury .75 2.00
26 Rik Smits .50 1.25
27 Michael Stewart .40 1.00
28 Steve Smith .50 1.25
29 Glenn Robinson .50 1.25
30 Chris Webber .60 1.50
31 Antoine Walker .60 1.50
32 Eddie Jones .60 1.50
33 Mitch Richmond .60 1.50
34 Kevin Garnett 1.25 3.00
35 Grant Hill 1.00 2.50
36 John Stockton .75 2.00
37 Allan Houston .50 1.25
38 Bobby Jackson .50 1.25
39 Sam Cassell .50 1.25
40 Allen Iverson 1.25 3.00
41 LaPhonso Ellis .40 1.00
42 Lorenzen Wright .40 1.00
43 Gary Payton .60 1.50
44 Patrick Ewing .75 2.00
45 Scottie Pippen 1.00 2.50
46 Hakeem Olajuwon .75 2.00
47 Glen Rice .60 1.50
48 Antonio Daniels .40 1.00
49 Jayson Williams .40 1.00
50 Juwan Howard .50 1.25
51 Reggie Miller .75 2.00
52 Joe Smith .50 1.25
53 Shaquille O'Neal 1.50 4.00
54 Dennis Rodman 1.25 3.00
55 Vin Baker .50 1.25
56 Rod Strickland .40 1.00
57 Anfernee Hardaway 1.00 2.50
58 Zydrunas Ilgauskas .60 1.50
59 Chris Mullin .60 1.50
60 Rasheed Wallace .60 1.50
61 Shareef Abdur-Rahim .60 1.50
62 Tom Gugliotta .40 1.00
63 Tim Duncan 1.25 3.00
64 Michael Finley .60 1.50
65 Jim Jackson .40 1.00
66 Chauncey Billups .75 2.00
67 Jerry Stackhouse .60 1.50
68 Jeff Hornacek .50 1.25
69 Clyde Drexler .75 2.00
70 Karl Malone .75 2.00
71 Tim Duncan RE 1.25 3.00
72 Keith Van Horn RE .60 1.50
73 Chauncey Billups RE .75 2.00
74 Antonio Daniels RE .40 1.00
75 Tony Battie RE .50 1.25
76 Ron Mercer RE .50 1.25
77 Tim Thomas RE .60 1.50
78 Tracy McGrady RE 1.00 2.50
79 Danny Fortson RE .40 1.00
80 Derek Anderson RE .40 1.00
81 Maurice Taylor RE .40 1.00
82 Kelvin Cato RE .40 1.00
83 Brevin Knight RE .40 1.00
84 Bobby Jackson RE .50 1.25
85 Rodrick Rhodes RE .40 1.00
86 Anthony Johnson RE .40 1.00
87 Cedric Henderson RE .40 1.00
88 Chris Anstey RE .40 1.00
89 Michael Stewart RE .40 1.00
90 Zydrunas Ilgauskas RE .60 1.50
NNO Michael Jordan Jumbo 4.00 10.00

1998 Upper Deck Hardcourt Home Court Advantage

Randomly inserted in packs at a rate of one in four, this 90-card set parallels the basic set. The cards feature blue foil across the card front and the actual card is on wood paper stock. To ascertain values on individual cards, please refer to the multiplier in the header below, coupled with the value of the base card.
*STARS: .75X TO 2X BASE CARD HI

1998 Upper Deck Hardcourt Home Court Advantage Plus

Randomly inserted in packs, this 90-card set parallels the basic set. The front features gold foil writing across the card front with the cards printed on wood paper stock. The cards are also serially numbered to 500 on the card back. To ascertain values on individual cards, please refer to the multiplier in the header below, coupled with the value of the base card.
*STARS: 4X TO 10X BASE CARD HI

1998 Upper Deck Hardcourt High Court

Randomly inserted into packs, this 30-card set features some of the high-flying performers in the NBA. The cards are producd on wood paper stock with a silver logo titled "High Court" in the lower left corner. The cards are serially numbered to 1300 in gold foil on the card front.

H1 Dikembe Mutombo 3.00 8.00
H2 Ron Mercer 2.50 6.00
H3 Glen Rice 3.00 8.00
H4 Scottie Pippen 5.00 12.00
H5 Shawn Kemp 3.00 8.00
H6 Michael Finley 3.00 8.00
H7 LaPhonso Ellis 2.00 5.00
H8 Grant Hill 5.00 12.00
H9 Erick Dampier 2.00 5.00
H10 Hakeem Olajuwon 4.00 10.00
H11 Chris Mullin 3.00 8.00
H12 Lamond Murray 2.00 5.00
H13 Kobe Bryant 15.00 40.00
H14 Tim Hardaway 3.00 8.00
H15 Ray Allen 4.00 10.00
H16 Stephon Marbury 4.00 10.00
H17 Keith Van Horn 3.00 8.00
H18 Allan Houston 2.50 6.00
H19 Anfernee Hardaway 5.00 12.00
H20 Allen Iverson 6.00 15.00
H21 Antonio McDyess 2.50 6.00
H22 Rasheed Wallace 3.00 8.00
H23 Mitch Richmond 3.00 8.00
H24 Tim Duncan 6.00 15.00
H25 Gary Payton 3.00 8.00
H26 Chauncey Billups 4.00 10.00
H27 John Stockton 4.00 10.00
H28 Shareef Abdur-Rahim 3.00 8.00
H29 Juwan Howard 2.50 6.00
H30 Michael Jordan 25.00 60.00

1998 Upper Deck Hardcourt Jordan Holding Court Red

Randomly inserted into packs, this 30-card set features a duel-player, double-wood card. The cards feature 40-point stock. Each card features Michael Jordan on one side and one of 29 other NBA superstars on the other. The base set features the title of the set and the Upper Deck logo in red foil. The cards are serially numbered to 2300.

*BRONZE: 1.5X TO 4X HI COLUMN
BRONZE: PRINT RUN 230 SERIAL #'d SETS
UNPRICED GOLD PARALLEL SERIAL #'d TO 1
J1 Steve Smith 2.50 6.00
Michael Jordan
J2 Antoine Walker 3.00 8.00
Michael Jordan
J3 Glen Rice 3.00 8.00
Michael Jordan
J4 Scottie Pippen 6.00 15.00
Michael Jordan
J5 Shawn Kemp 4.00 10.00
Michael Jordan
J6 Michael Finley 4.00 10.00
Michael Jordan
J7 Bobby Jackson 2.50 6.00
Michael Jordan
J8 Grant Hill 6.00 15.00
Michael Jordan
J9 Jim Jackson 2.00 5.00
Michael Jordan
J10 Charles Barkley 5.00 12.00
Michael Jordan
J11 Reggie Miller 4.00 10.00
Michael Jordan
J12 Lorenzen Wright 2.00 5.00
Michael Jordan
J13 Kobe Bryant 20.00 50.00
Michael Jordan
J14 Tim Hardaway 3.00 8.00
Michael Jordan
J15 Glenn Robinson 2.50 6.00
Michael Jordan
J16 Kevin Garnett 6.00 15.00
Michael Jordan
J17 Keith Van Horn 3.00 8.00
Michael Jordan
J18 Patrick Ewing 4.00 10.00
Michael Jordan
J19 Anfernee Hardaway 6.00 15.00
Michael Jordan
J20 Allen Iverson 8.00 20.00
Michael Jordan
J21 Jason Kidd 5.00 12.00
Michael Jordan
J22 Damon Stoudamire 3.00 8.00
Michael Jordan
J23 Mitch Richmond 3.00 8.00
Michael Jordan
J24 Tim Duncan 8.00 20.00
Michael Jordan
J25 Gary Payton 3.00 8.00
Michael Jordan
J26 Chauncey Billups 4.00 10.00
Michael Jordan
J27 Karl Malone 4.00 10.00
Michael Jordan
J28 Shareef Abdur-Rahim 3.00 8.00
Michael Jordan
J29 Chris Webber 6.00 15.00
Michael Jordan
J30 Michael Jordan 20.00 50.00
Michael Jordan

1998 Upper Deck Hardcourt Jordan Holding Court Silver

Randomly inserted into packs, this 30-card set features a duel-player, double-wood card. The cards feature 40-point stock. Each card features Michael Jordan on one side and one of 29 other NBA superstars on the other. The base set features the title of the set and the Upper Deck logo in silver foil. The cards are serially numbered to 23.

*SILVER: 5X TO 12X BASE HI
STATED PRINT RUN 23 SETS
J13 Kobe Bryant 600.00 1100.00
Michael Jordan
J20 Allen Iverson 125.00 300.00
Michael Jordan
J30 Michael Jordan 600.00 1000.00
Michael Jordan

1999-00 Upper Deck Hardcourt

Released in late 1999, this set consisted of 90 player cards, which included 60 veterans and 30 rookies. The cards came five to a pack with a suggested retail price of $4.99. The 30-card rookie subset was inserted at one in four packs. Also inserted in packs was a Michael Jordan floor card, which was serially numbered to 50 and a Wilt Chamberlain floor card, which was serially numbered to 100. They are listed at the end of the set.

COMPLETE SET (90) 30.00 80.00
COMPLETE SET w/o RC (60) 10.00 25.00
1 Dikembe Mutombo .40 1.00
2 Alan Henderson .25 .60
3 Antoine Walker .40 1.00
4 Paul Pierce .60 1.50
5 Eddie Jones .40 1.00
6 Elden Campbell .25 .60
7 Toni Kukoc .40 1.00
8 Randy Brown .25 .60
9 Shawn Kemp .40 1.00
10 Brevin Knight .25 .60
11 Michael Finley .40 1.00
12 Dirk Nowitzki .75 2.00
13 Antonio McDyess .30 .75
14 Nick Van Exel .30 .75
15 Grant Hill .50 1.25
16 Jerry Stackhouse .40 1.00
17 Antawn Jamison .40 1.00
18 John Starks .40 1.00
19 Hakeem Olajuwon .50 1.25
20 Scottie Pippen .60 1.50
21 Reggie Miller .40 1.00
22 Jalen Rose .30 .75
23 Maurice Taylor .25 .60
24 Michael Olowokandi .25 .60
25 Shaquille O'Neal 1.00 2.50
26 Kobe Bryant 2.00 5.00
27 Tim Hardaway .40 1.00
28 Alonzo Mourning .50 1.25
29 Glenn Robinson .30 .75
30 Ray Allen .40 1.00
31 Kevin Garnett .75 2.00
32 Terrell Brandon .25 .60
33 Stephon Marbury .30 .75
34 Keith Van Horn .30 .75
35 Latrell Sprewell .40 1.00
36 Allan Houston .30 .75
37 Patrick Ewing .50 1.25
38 Darrell Armstrong .25 .60
39 Bo Outlaw .25 .60
40 Allen Iverson .75 2.00
41 Larry Hughes .30 .75
42 Jason Kidd .60 1.50
43 Tom Gugliotta .25 .60
44 Brian Grant .25 .60
45 Damon Stoudamire .40 1.00
46 Jason Williams .50 1.25
47 Vlade Divac .40 1.00
48 Tim Duncan .75 2.00
49 David Robinson .60 1.50
50 Avery Johnson .30 .75
51 Gary Payton .40 1.00
52 Vin Baker .40 1.00
53 Vince Carter .75 2.00
54 Tracy McGrady .60 1.50
55 Karl Malone .50 1.25
56 John Stockton .50 1.25
57 Shareef Abdur-Rahim .30 .75
58 Mike Bibby .40 1.00
59 Juwan Howard .30 .75
60 Mitch Richmond .40 1.00
61 Elton Brand RC 1.50 4.00
62 Jason Terry RC 1.50 4.00
63 Kenny Thomas RC .60 1.50
64 Jonathan Bender RC .60 1.50
65 Aleksandar Radojevic RC .60 1.50
66 Galen Young RC .60 1.50
67 Baron Davis RC 2.00 5.00
68 Corey Maggette RC 1.25 3.00
69 Dion Glover RC .60 1.50
70 Scott Padgett RC .60 1.50
71 Steve Francis RC 1.50 4.00
72 Richard Hamilton RC 1.50 4.00
73 James Posey RC .60 1.50
74 Jumaine Jones RC .60 1.50
75 Chris Herren RC .60 1.50
76 Andre Miller RC 1.50 4.00
77 Lamar Odom RC 2.00 5.00
78 Wally Szczerbiak RC 1.25 3.00
79 William Avery RC .60 1.50
80 Devean George RC .60 1.50
81 Trajan Langdon RC .60 1.50
82 Cal Bowdler RC .60 1.50
83 Kris Clack RC .60 1.50
84 Tim James RC .60 1.50
85 Shawn Marion RC 1.50 4.00
86 Ryan Robertson RC .60 1.50
87 Quincy Lewis RC .60 1.50
88 Vonteego Cummings RC .60 1.50
89 Obinna Ekezie RC .60 1.50
90 Jeff Foster RC .60 1.50
GF1 Michael Jordan Floor/50 250.00 500.00
GF6 Wilt Chamberlain Floor/100 100.00 200.00

1999-00 Upper Deck Hardcourt Baseline Grooves Rainbow

Randomly inserted in packs, this 90-card set is a parallel of the base set. The cards feature rainbow foil and are serially numbered to 500. To ascertain values on individual cards, please refer to the multiplier in the header, coupled with the value of the base card.
*STARS: 2.5X TO 6X BASE CARD HI
*RCs: .75X TO 2X BASE HI

1999-00 Upper Deck Hardcourt Baseline Grooves Silver

Randomly inserted in packs, this 90-cards set parallels the base set. The cards are featured on wood stock with silver foil and are serially numbered to 50. To ascertain values on individual cards, please refer to the multiplier in the header, coupled with the value of the base card.
*STARS: 15X TO 40X BASE CARD HI
*RCs: 5X TO 12X BASE HI
26 Kobe Bryant 150.00 300.00

1999-00 Upper Deck Hardcourt Court Authority

Randomly inserted in packs at one in 99, this 10-card set captures the players with the most dynamic on court moves in the NBA. Card backs carry an "A" prefix.

COMPLETE SET (10) 40.00 80.00
A1 Tim Duncan 6.00 15.00
A2 Vince Carter 6.00 15.00
A3 Allen Iverson 6.00 15.00
A4 Jason Williams 4.00 10.00
A5 Kevin Garnett 6.00 15.00
A6 Keith Van Horn 2.50 6.00
A7 Jason Kidd 5.00 12.00
A8 Grant Hill 4.00 10.00
A9 Antoine Walker 3.00 8.00
A10 Michael Jordan 25.00 60.00

1999-00 Upper Deck Hardcourt Court Forces

Randomly inserted in packs at one in eight, this 10-card set highlights some of the top newcomers to the NBA. Card backs carry a "CF" prefix.

COMPLETE SET (10) 3.00 8.00
CF1 Shareef Abdur-Rahim .40 1.00
CF2 Scottie Pippen .75 2.00
CF3 Latrell Sprewell .50 1.25
CF4 Tim Hardaway .50 1.25
CF5 Shaquille O'Neal 1.25 3.00
CF6 Mike Bibby .50 1.25
CF7 Allen Iverson 1.00 2.50
CF8 John Stockton .60 1.50
CF9 Michael Finley .50 1.25
CF10 Reggie Miller .50 1.25

1999-00 Upper Deck Hardcourt Legends of the Hardcourt

Randomly inserted in packs at one in 19, this 10-card set takes a look back in time at some of the NBA's all time greatest players. Card backs carry a "L" prefix.

COMPLETE SET (10) 12.50 30.00
L1 Michael Jordan 10.00 25.00
L2 Elgin Baylor 1.25 3.00
L3 Kevin McHale 1.50 4.00
L4 Julius Erving 2.50 6.00
L5 Larry Bird 4.00 10.00
L6 George Gervin 1.25 3.00
L7 Bob Cousy 2.00 5.00
L8 John Havlicek 1.50 4.00
L9 Jerry West 1.50 4.00
L10 Walt Frazier 1.25 3.00

1999-00 Upper Deck Hardcourt MJ Records Almanac

Randomly inserted in packs at one in 19, this 10-card set takes a look inside the numbers at some of the amazing records MJ broke during his career. Card backs carry a "J" prefix.

COMPLETE SET (10) 20.00 50.00
COMMON CARD (J1-J10) 2.50 6.00

1999-00 Upper Deck Hardcourt New Court Order

Randomly inserted in packs at one in three, this 20-card set features current and future NBA stars on 32-point laminated card stock. Card backs carry a "NC" prefix.

COMPLETE SET (20) 5.00 12.00
NC1 Vince Carter .75 2.00
NC2 Allan Houston .30 .75
NC3 Paul Pierce .60 1.50
NC4 Eddie Jones .40 1.00
NC5 Antawn Jamison .40 1.00
NC6 Mike Bibby .40 1.00
NC7 Tim Duncan .75 2.00
NC8 Kobe Bryant 2.00 5.00
NC9 Maurice Taylor .25 .60
NC10 Darrell Armstrong .25 .60
NC11 Stephon Marbury .30 .75
NC12 Gary Payton .40 1.00
NC13 Brian Grant .25 .60
NC14 Jason Williams .50 1.25
NC15 Shareef Abdur-Rahim .30 .75
NC16 Damon Stoudamire .40 1.00
NC17 Keith Van Horn .30 .75
NC18 Tom Gugliotta .25 .60
NC19 Antonio McDyess .30 .75
NC20 Ray Allen .40 1.00

1999-00 Upper Deck Hardcourt Power in the Paint

Randomly inserted in packs at one in six, this 12-card set is die cut and features the top big men in the NBA. Card backs carry a "P" prefix.

COMPLETE SET (12) 3.00 8.00
P1 Antoine Walker .50 1.25
P2 Karl Malone .60 1.50
P3 Hakeem Olajuwon .60 1.50
P4 David Robinson .75 2.00
P5 Antonio McDyess .40 1.00
P6 Shawn Kemp .50 1.25
P7 Glenn Robinson .40 1.00
P8 Juwan Howard .40 1.00
P9 Patrick Ewing .60 1.50
P10 Alonzo Mourning .60 1.50
P11 Antawn Jamison .50 1.25
P12 Dikembe Mutombo .50 1.25

2000-01 Upper Deck Hardcourt

The 2000-01 Upper Deck Hardcourt product was released in September,2000 and featured a 102-card base set that was broken into tiers as follows: 60 Base Veterans (1-60), and 42 Rookie cards (61-102) that are individually serial numbered to 900. Each pack contained five cards and carried a suggested retail price of $4.99.

COMPLETE SET w/o RC (60) 10.00 25.00
1 Dikembe Mutombo .30 .75
2 Jason Terry .30 .75
3 Antoine Walker .25 .60
4 Paul Pierce .40 1.00
5 Eddie Jones .30 .75
6 Baron Davis .30 .75
7 Elton Brand .30 .75
8 Ron Artest .30 .75
9 Andre Miller .25 .60
10 Shawn Kemp .30 .75
11 Dirk Nowitzki .50 1.25
12 Michael Finley .30 .75
13 Antonio McDyess .25 .60
14 Nick Van Exel .25 .60
15 Grant Hill .40 1.00
16 Jerry Stackhouse .25 .60
17 Antawn Jamison .30 .75
18 Larry Hughes .25 .60
19 Steve Francis .30 .75
20 Hakeem Olajuwon .40 1.00
21 Reggie Miller .30 .75
22 Jalen Rose .25 .60
23 Lamar Odom .30 .75
24 Eric Piatkowski .20 .50
25 Shaquille O'Neal .75 2.00
26 Kobe Bryant 1.50 4.00
27 Alonzo Mourning .40 1.00
28 Jamal Mashburn .25 .60
29 Ray Allen .30 .75
30 Glenn Robinson .25 .60
31 Kevin Garnett .60 1.50
32 Wally Szczerbiak .25 .60
33 Keith Van Horn .25 .60
34 Stephon Marbury .25 .60
35 Allan Houston .25 .60
36 Latrell Sprewell .25 .60
37 Darrell Armstrong .20 .50
38 Ron Mercer .20 .50
39 Allen Iverson .60 1.50
40 Toni Kukoc .25 .60
41 Jason Kidd .50 1.25
42 Anfernee Hardaway .50 1.25
43 Shawn Marion .30 .75
44 Scottie Pippen .50 1.25
45 Damon Stoudamire .25 .60
46 Chris Webber .30 .75
47 Jason Williams .30 .75
48 Tim Duncan .60 1.50
49 David Robinson .50 1.25
50 Gary Payton .30 .75
51 Vin Baker .25 .60
52 Rashard Lewis .30 .75
53 Tracy McGrady .50 1.25
54 Vince Carter .60 1.50
55 Karl Malone .40 1.00
56 John Stockton .40 1.00
57 Shareef Abdur-Rahim .25 .60
58 Mike Bibby .30 .75
59 Mitch Richmond .25 .60
60 Richard Hamilton .25 .60
61 Kenyon Martin RC 4.00 10.00
62 Marcus Fizer RC 1.50 4.00
63 Chris Mihm RC 1.50 4.00
64 Chris Porter RC 1.50 4.00
65 Stromile Swift RC 1.50 4.00
66 Morris Peterson RC 1.50 4.00
67 Quentin Richardson RC 2.50 6.00
68 Courtney Alexander RC 1.50 4.00
69 Scoonie Penn RC 1.50 4.00
70 Mateen Cleaves RC 1.50 4.00
71 Erick Barkley RC 1.50 4.00
72 A.J. Guyton RC 1.50 4.00
73 Darius Miles RC 1.50 4.00
74 DerMarr Johnson RC 1.50 4.00
75 Hedo Turkoglu RC 3.00 8.00
76 Hanno Mottola RC 1.50 4.00
77 Mike Miller RC 3.00 8.00
78 Desmond Mason RC 2.00 5.00
79 Mark Madsen RC 1.50 4.00
80 Eduardo Najera RC 1.50 4.00
81 Speedy Claxton RC 1.50 4.00
82 Joel Przybilla RC 1.50 4.00
83 Brian Cardinal RC 1.50 4.00
84 Khalid El-Amin RC 1.50 4.00
85 Etan Thomas RC 1.50 4.00
86 Corey Hightower RC 1.50 4.00
87 Dan Langhi RC 1.50 4.00
88 Michael Redd RC 4.00 10.00
89 Pete Mickeal RC 1.50 4.00
90 Mamadou N'Diaye RC 1.50 4.00
91 Jerome Moiso RC 1.50 4.00
92 Chris Carrawell RC 1.50 4.00
93 Jason Collier RC 1.50 4.00
94 Keyon Dooling RC 1.50 4.00
95 Mark Karcher RC 1.50 4.00
96 Jamaal Magloire RC 1.50 4.00
97 Jason Hart RC 1.50 4.00
98 Jabari Smith RC 1.50 4.00
99 Donnell Harvey RC 1.50 4.00
100 Lavor Postell RC 1.50 4.00
101 Eddie House RC 1.50 4.00
102 Dan McClintock RC 1.50 4.00

2000-01 Upper Deck Hardcourt Court Authority

Randomly inserted in packs at one in 15, this 15-card set features the league's most dominant players. Card backs carry a "CA" prefix.

COMPLETE SET (15) 12.50 30.00
CA1 Kobe Bryant 4.00 10.00
CA2 Allen Iverson 1.50 4.00
CA3 Gary Payton .75 2.00
CA4 Tim Duncan 1.50 4.00
CA5 Kevin Garnett 1.50 4.00
CA6 Steve Francis .75 2.00
CA7 Vince Carter 1.50 4.00
CA8 Shaquille O'Neal 2.00 5.00
CA9 Jason Kidd 1.25 3.00
CA10 Karl Malone 1.00 2.50
CA11 Shareef Abdur-Rahim .60 1.50
CA12 Grant Hill 1.00 2.50
CA13 Reggie Miller .75 2.00
CA14 Keith Van Horn .60 1.50
CA15 John Stockton 1.00 2.50

2000-01 Upper Deck Hardcourt Court Forces

Randomly inserted in packs at one in 12, this 11-card set focuses on players who are the best all-around threats on the floor today. Card backs carry a "C" prefix.

COMPLETE SET (11) 4.00 10.00
C1 Elton Brand .50 1.25
C2 Steve Francis .50 1.25
C3 Allan Houston .40 1.00
C4 Lamar Odom .50 1.25
C5 Andre Miller .40 1.00
C6 Jason Williams .50 1.25
C7 Ron Mercer .30 .75
C8 Kobe Bryant 2.50 6.00
C9 Kevin Garnett 1.00 2.50
C10 Jerry Stackhouse .40 1.00
C11 Latrell Sprewell .40 1.00

2000-01 Upper Deck Hardcourt Floor Leaders

Randomly inserted in packs at one in seven, this 20-card set showcases the most respected leaders on the

NBA hardwood. Card backs carry a "FL" prefix.
COMPLETE SET (20) 6.00 15.00
FL1 Kobe Bryant 2.50 6.00
FL2 Eddie Jones .50 1.25
FL3 Kevin Garnett 1.00 2.50
FL4 Andre Miller .40 1.00
FL5 Keith Van Horn .40 1.00
FL6 Allan Houston .40 1.00
FL7 Larry Hughes .40 1.00
FL8 Jason Williams .50 1.25
FL9 Tracy McGrady .75 2.00
FL10 Shawn Kemp .50 1.25
FL11 Stephon Marbury .40 1.00
FL12 Glenn Robinson .40 1.00
FL13 Mike Bibby .50 1.25
FL14 Baron Davis .50 1.25
FL15 Scottie Pippen .75 2.00
FL16 David Robinson .75 2.00
FL17 Paul Pierce .60 1.50
FL18 Wally Szczerbiak .40 1.00
FL19 Jalen Rose .40 1.00
FL20 Lamar Odom .50 1.25

2000-01 Upper Deck Hardcourt Game Floor

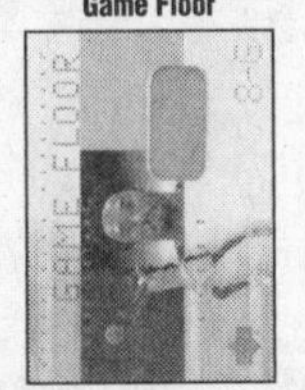

Randomly inserted in packs at one in 15, this 25-card set features a real piece of the floor that the player played on. Card backs are numbered by the player's initials. Four players also autographed versions of the floor, which were numbered to the player's jersey. Those players were Kobe Bryant, Kevin Garnett, Karl Malone and Michael Jordan.

AHF Anfernee Hardaway 5.00 12.00
AIF Allen Iverson 6.00 15.00
ALF Allan Houston 2.50 6.00
AMF Alonzo Mourning 4.00 10.00
AWF Antoine Walker 2.50 6.00
CWF Chris Webber 3.00 8.00
DRF David Robinson 6.00 15.00
EJF Eddie Jones 3.00 8.00
GHF Grant Hill 4.00 10.00
GPF Gary Payton 3.00 8.00
JKF Jason Kidd 5.00 12.00
KBF Kobe Bryant 10.00 25.00
KGA Kevin Garnett AU/21 150.00 300.00
KGF Kevin Garnett 6.00 15.00
KMA Karl Malone AU/32 150.00 300.00
KMF Karl Malone 4.00 10.00
MCF Antonio McDyess 2.50 6.00
MFF Michael Finley 3.00 8.00
MJA Michael Jordan AU/23 600.00 1200.00
RAF Ray Allen 3.00 8.00
RGF Reggie Miller 3.00 8.00
RMF Ron Mercer 2.00 5.00
RWF Rasheed Wallace 3.00 8.00
SAF Shareef Abdur-Rahim 2.50 6.00
SMF Stephon Marbury 2.50 6.00
SOF Shaquille O'Neal 8.00 20.00
SPF Scottie Pippen 5.00 12.00
THF Tim Hardaway 3.00 8.00

2000-01 Upper Deck Hardcourt Night Court

Randomly inserted in packs at one in 15, this 15-card set features players who always hold court whenever they are in the game. Card backs carry a "NC" prefix.

COMPLETE SET (15) 10.00 25.00
NC1 Kevin Garnett 1.50 4.00
NC2 Tim Duncan 1.50 4.00
NC3 Larry Hughes .60 1.50
NC4 Elton Brand .75 2.00
NC5 Kobe Bryant 4.00 10.00
NC6 Anfernee Hardaway 1.25 3.00
NC7 Tracy McGrady 1.25 3.00
NC8 Antonio McDyess .60 1.50
NC9 Paul Pierce 1.00 2.50
NC10 Lamar Odom .75 2.00
NC11 Chris Webber .75 2.00
NC12 Ray Allen .75 2.00
NC13 Allan Houston .60 1.50
NC14 Wally Szczerbiak .60 1.50
NC15 Alonzo Mourning 1.00 2.50

2000-01 Upper Deck Hardcourt Thriller Instinct

Randomly inserted in packs at one in 12, this 11-card set features players who put a scare into opposing coaches on a nightly basis. Card backs carry a "TI" prefix.

COMPLETE SET (11) 4.00 10.00
TI1 Kevin Garnett 1.00 2.50
TI2 Vince Carter 1.00 2.50
TI3 Shawn Marion .50 1.25
TI4 Stephon Marbury .40 1.00
TI5 Antawn Jamison .50 1.25
TI6 Jason Williams .50 1.25
TI7 Michael Finley .50 1.25
TI8 Kobe Bryant 2.50 6.00
TI9 Richard Hamilton .40 1.00
TI10 Reggie Miller .50 1.25
TI11 Elton Brand .50 1.25

2000-01 Upper Deck Hardcourt UD Authentics

Randomly inserted in packs at one in 100, this 24-card set features authentic autographs from NBA stars. Card backs are numbered using the player's initials.

AH Anfernee Hardaway 30.00 80.00
AI Allen Iverson 30.00 80.00
AM Andre Miller 5.00 12.00
BD Baron Davis 6.00 15.00
DM Darius Miles 5.00 12.00
DS Damon Stoudamire 6.00 15.00
GP Gary Payton 25.00 60.00
JM Jerome Moiso 5.00 12.00
JR Jalen Rose 5.00 12.00
JS Jerry Stackhouse 6.00 15.00
KB Kobe Bryant 80.00 200.00
KG Kevin Garnett 30.00 80.00
KM Karl Malone 80.00 160.00
LH Larry Hughes 5.00 12.00
MC Antonio McDyess 6.00 15.00
MF Marcus Fizer 5.00 12.00
MF Michael Finley 8.00 20.00
PP Paul Pierce 10.00 25.00
QR Quentin Richardson 8.00 20.00
RA Ray Allen 20.00 40.00
SA Shareef Abdur-Rahim 5.00 12.00
SF Steve Francis 6.00 15.00
TH Tim Hardaway 10.00 25.00
WS Wally Szczerbiak 5.00 12.00

2001-02 Upper Deck Hardcourt

Released in late October of 2001, this 121 card set consists of 91 veterans and 30 rookies with three different versions each. The versions are broken down into bronze, silver and gold, with each having: On Court, Off Court, and High Court. Rookies 91-100 are serial #'d to 1000 on each version for a total print run of 3000, 101-110 are serial #'d to 600 on each version for a total print run 1800, and 111-120 are serial #'d 300 on each version for a total print run of 900. Card backgrounds are slightly embossed and resemble the wooden floor of a basketball court, and both player action and portrait photos appear on the fronts. Hardcourt was packaged in 15 pack boxes where packs contained five cards and carried a suggested retail price of $4.99.

COMP.SET w/o SP's (90) 25.00 50.00
1 Jason Terry .40 1.00
2 DerMarr Johnson .25 .60
3 Toni Kukoc .30 .75
4 Antoine Walker .30 .75
5 Paul Pierce .50 1.25
6 Kenny Anderson .30 .75
7 Jamal Mashburn .30 .75
8 Baron Davis .40 1.00
9 David Wesley .25 .60
10 Ron Artest .40 1.00
11 Jamal Crawford .30 .75
12 Ron Mercer .25 .60
13 Andre Miller .40 1.00
14 Lamond Murray .25 .60
15 Matt Harpring .30 .75
16 Michael Finley .40 1.00
17 Dirk Nowitzki .60 1.50
18 Steve Nash .60 1.50
19 Antonio McDyess .30 .75
20 Nick Van Exel .30 .75
21 James Posey .25 .60
22 Jerry Stackhouse .30 .75
23 Chucky Atkins .25 .60
24 Mateen Cleaves .25 .60
25 Antawn Jamison .40 1.00
26 Larry Hughes .30 .75
27 Marc Jackson .25 .60
28 Steve Francis .40 1.00
29 Maurice Taylor .25 .60
30 Cuttino Mobley .30 .75
31 Reggie Miller .40 1.00
32 Jalen Rose .30 .75
33 Jermaine O'Neal .40 1.00
34 Darius Miles .25 .60
35 Lamar Odom .30 .75
36 Elton Brand .40 1.00
37 Kobe Bryant 2.00 5.00
38 Shaquille O'Neal 1.00 2.50
39 Derek Fisher .30 .75
40 Robert Horry .30 .75
41 Alonzo Mourning .50 1.25
42 Eddie Jones .30 .75
43 Brian Grant .25 .60
44 Anthony Mason .25 .60
45 Ray Allen .40 1.00
46 Glenn Robinson .30 .75
47 Tim Thomas .30 .75
48 Kevin Garnett .75 2.00
49 Wally Szczerbiak .30 .75
50 Terrell Brandon .25 .60
51 Anthony Peeler .25 .60
52 Jason Kidd .60 1.50
53 Kenyon Martin .40 1.00
54 Stephen Jackson .30 .75
55 Latrell Sprewell .30 .75
56 Allan Houston .30 .75
57 Glen Rice .30 .75
58 Tracy McGrady .60 1.50
59 Darrell Armstrong .25 .60
60 Mike Miller .40 1.00
61 Allen Iverson .75 2.00
62 Dikembe Mutombo .40 1.00
63 Aaron McKie .25 .60
64 Stephon Marbury .30 .75
65 Shawn Marion .40 1.00
66 Tom Gugliotta .25 .60
67 Rasheed Wallace .40 1.00
68 Scottie Pippen .60 1.50
69 Damon Stoudamire .30 .75
70 Chris Webber .40 1.00
71 Mike Bibby .40 1.00
72 Peja Stojakovic .40 1.00
73 Tim Duncan .75 2.00
74 David Robinson .60 1.50
75 Derek Anderson .25 .60
76 Gary Payton .40 1.00
77 Rashard Lewis .40 1.00
78 Desmond Mason .30 .75
79 Vince Carter .60 1.50
80 Morris Peterson .25 .60
81 Antonio Davis .25 .60
82 Karl Malone .50 1.25
83 John Stockton .50 1.25
84 Donyell Marshall .25 .60
85 Bryant Reeves .25 .60
86 Jason Williams .30 .75
87 Stromile Swift .25 .60
88 Richard Hamilton .30 .75
89 Courtney Alexander .25 .60
90 Chris Whitney .25 .60
91A Kenny Satterfield ON RC 1.50 4.00
91B Kenny Satterfield OFF RC 1.50 4.00
91C Kenny Satterfield HI RC 1.50 4.00
92A Jeff Trepagnier ON RC 1.50 4.00
92B Jeff Trepagnier OFF RC 1.50 4.00
92C Jeff Trepagnier HI RC 1.50 4.00
93A Michael Wright ON RC 1.50 4.00
93B Michael Wright OFF RC 1.50 4.00
93C Michael Wright HI RC 1.50 4.00
94A Terence Morris ON RC 1.50 4.00
94B Terence Morris OFF RC 1.50 4.00
94C Terence Morris HI RC 1.50 4.00
95A Omar Cook ON RC 1.50 4.00
95B Omar Cook OFF RC 1.50 4.00
95C Omar Cook HI RC 1.50 4.00
96A Gilbert Arenas ON RC 2.50 6.00
96B Gilbert Arenas OFF RC 2.50 6.00
96C Gilbert Arenas HI RC 2.50 6.00
97A Joseph Forte ON RC 1.50 4.00
97B Joseph Forte OFF RC 1.50 4.00
97C Joseph Forte HI RC 1.50 4.00
98A Jamaal Tinsley ON RC 2.00 5.00
98B Jamaal Tinsley OFF RC 2.00 5.00
98C Jamaal Tinsley HI RC 2.00 5.00
99A Samuel Dalembert ON RC 2.00 5.00
99B Samuel Dalembert OFF RC 2.00 5.00
99C Samuel Dalembert HI RC 2.00 5.00
100A Gerald Wallace ON RC 2.50 6.00
100B Gerald Wallace OFF RC 2.50 6.00
100C Gerald Wallace HI RC 2.50 6.00
101A Brendan Haywood ON RC 2.50 6.00
101B Brendan Haywood OFF RC 2.50 6.00
101C Brendan Haywood HI RC 2.50 6.00
102A Richard Jefferson ON RC 4.00 10.00
102B Richard Jefferson OFF RC 4.00 10.00
102C Richard Jefferson HI RC 4.00 10.00
103A Michael Bradley ON RC 2.00 5.00
103B Michael Bradley OFF RC 2.00 5.00
103C Michael Bradley HI RC 2.00 5.00
104A Loren Woods ON RC 2.00 5.00
104B Loren Woods OFF RC 2.00 5.00
104C Loren Woods HI RC 2.00 5.00
105A Jeryl Sasser ON RC 2.00 5.00
105B Jeryl Sasser OFF RC 2.00 5.00
105C Jeryl Sasser HI RC 2.00 5.00
106A Jason Collins ON RC 2.00 5.00
106B Jason Collins OFF RC 2.00 5.00
106C Jason Collins HI RC 2.00 5.00
107A Kirk Haston ON RC 2.00 5.00
107B Kirk Haston OFF RC 2.00 5.00
107C Kirk Haston HI RC 2.00 5.00
108A Steven Hunter ON RC 2.00 5.00
108B Steven Hunter OFF RC 2.00 5.00
108C Steven Hunter HI RC 2.00 5.00
109A Troy Murphy ON RC 3.00 8.00
109B Troy Murphy OFF RC 3.00 8.00
109C Troy Murphy HI RC 3.00 8.00
110A Vladimir Radmanovic ON RC 2.00 5.00
110B Vladimir Radmanovic OFF RC 2.00 5.00
110C Vladimir Radmanovic HI RC 2.00 5.00
111A Rodney White ON RC 4.00 10.00
111B Rodney White OFF RC 4.00 10.00
111C Rodney White HI RC 4.00 10.00
112A Kedrick Brown ON RC 4.00 10.00
112B Kedrick Brown OFF RC 4.00 10.00
112C Kedrick Brown HI RC 4.00 10.00
113A Joe Johnson ON RC 10.00 25.00
113B Joe Johnson OFF RC 10.00 25.00
113C Joe Johnson HI RC 10.00 25.00
114A Eddie Griffin ON RC 4.00 10.00
114B Eddie Griffin OFF RC 4.00 10.00
114C Eddie Griffin HI RC 4.00 10.00
115A Shane Battier ON RC 8.00 20.00
115B Shane Battier OFF RC 8.00 20.00
115C Shane Battier HI RC 8.00 20.00
116A Eddy Curry ON RC 6.00 15.00
116B Eddy Curry OFF RC 6.00 15.00
116C Eddy Curry HI RC 6.00 15.00
117A Jason Richardson ON RC 8.00 20.00
117B Jason Richardson OFF RC 8.00 20.00
117C Jason Richardson HI RC 8.00 20.00
118A DeSagana Diop ON RC 4.00 10.00
118B DeSagana Diop OFF RC 4.00 10.00
118C DeSagana Diop HI RC 4.00 10.00
119A Tyson Chandler ON RC 6.00 15.00
119B Tyson Chandler OFF RC 6.00 15.00
119C Tyson Chandler HI RC 6.00 15.00
120A Kwame Brown ON RC 4.00 10.00
120B Kwame Brown OFF RC 4.00 10.00
120C Kwame Brown HI RC 4.00 10.00
121 Michael Jordan 6.00 15.00

2001-02 Upper Deck Hardcourt Exclusives

Seeded in packs, this 181-card set parallels the base Upper Deck Hardcourt set with rainbow holofoil highlights. Each card is sequentially numbered to 25.

*STARS: 20X TO 50X BASE CARD HI
*ROOKIES 91-100: 3X TO 8X BASE CARD HI
*ROOKIES 101-110: 2.5X TO 6X HI
*ROOKIES 111-120: 1.25X TO 3X HI

2001-02 Upper Deck Hardcourt Fantastic Floor

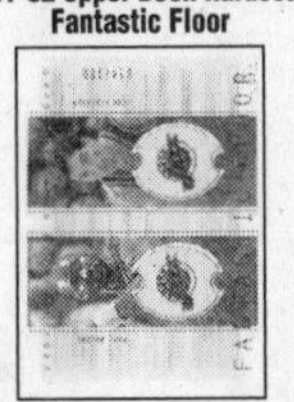

Randomly inserted in packs, this 22-card set features both player portrait style photos and swatches of NBA court. The court swatches have the respective player's team logo burned into them and each card is sequentially numbered to 100.

AHLS Allan Houston 8.00 20.00
Latrell Sprewell
AITM Allen Iverson 15.00 40.00
Tracy McGrady
CWPS Chris Webber 12.00 30.00
Predrag Stojakovic
EJTH Eddie Jones 8.00 20.00
Tim Hardaway
GPRLDM Gary Payton 15.00 30.00
Rashard Lewis
Desmond Mason
JMBD Jamal Mashburn 8.00 20.00
Baron Davis
JSMC Jerry Stackhouse 8.00 20.00
Mateen Cleaves
KBAI Kobe Bryant 20.00 50.00
Allen Iverson
KBDM Kobe Bryant 20.00 50.00
Darius Miles
KBKG Kobe Bryant 25.00 60.00
Kevin Garnett
KBRL Kobe Bryant 20.00 50.00
Rashard Lewis
KBSF Kobe Bryant 20.00 50.00
Steve Francis
KGTBWS Kevin Garnett 15.00 40.00
Terrell Brandon
Wally Szczerbiak
KMJS Karl Malone 20.00 40.00
John Stockton
MCNV Antonio McDyess 8.00 20.00
Nick Van Exel
MFDNSN Michael Finley 15.00 30.00
Dirk Nowitzki
Steve Nash
MJKBKG Michael Jordan 100.00 200.00
Kobe Bryant
Kevin Garnett
PPAW Paul Pierce 10.00 25.00
Antoine Walker
RAGR Ray Allen 8.00 20.00
Glenn Robinson
RMJOJB Reggie Miller 12.50 30.00
Jermaine O'Neal
Jonathan Bender
RWSPDS Rasheed Wallace 10.00 25.00
Scottie Pippen
Damon Stoudamire
TMMM Tracy McGrady 10.00 25.00
Mike Miller

2001-02 Upper Deck Hardcourt UD Game Film/Floor

Randomly seeded in packs at the rate of one in 15, this 30-card set features player portrait style photos, a swatch of NBA floor with the player's team logo burned into it, and a piece of film with a game photo on it.

AIF Allen Iverson 8.00 20.00
BDF Baron Davis 4.00 10.00
CWF Chris Webber 4.00 10.00
DAF Darius Miles 2.50 6.00
DMF Desmond Mason 3.00 8.00
DRF David Robinson 6.00 15.00
EJF Eddie Jones 3.00 8.00
JMF Jamal Mashburn 3.00 8.00
JSF Jerry Stackhouse 3.00 8.00
JTF Jason Terry 4.00 10.00
KBF Kobe Bryant 15.00 40.00
KEF Kenyon Martin 4.00 10.00
KGF Kevin Garnett 8.00 20.00
KMF Karl Malone 5.00 12.00
LSF Latrell Sprewell 3.00 8.00
MAF Shawn Marion 4.00 10.00
MCF Antonio McDyess 3.00 8.00
MFF Michael Finley 4.00 10.00
MMF Mike Miller 4.00 10.00
MPF Morris Peterson 2.50 6.00
PPF Paul Pierce 5.00 12.00
PSF Peja Stojakovic 4.00 10.00
RAF Ray Allen 4.00 10.00
RMF Reggie Miller 4.00 10.00
SFF Steve Francis 4.00 10.00
SJF Stephen Jackson 3.00 8.00
TMF Tracy McGrady 6.00 15.00

2001-02 Upper Deck Hardcourt UD Game Floor

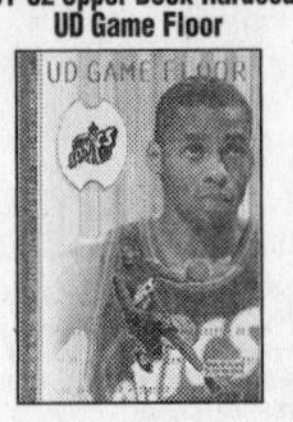

Randomly inserted in packs at the rate of one in 15, this 27-card set features a "court" background and player portrait style photos. The swatch of NBA court is burned with the featured player's team logo.

AI Allen Iverson 5.00 12.00
BD Baron Davis 2.50 6.00
CW Chris Webber 2.50 6.00
DA Darius Miles 1.50 4.00
DM Desmond Mason 2.00 5.00
DR David Robinson 4.00 10.00
EJ Eddie Jones 2.00 5.00
JM Jamal Mashburn 2.00 5.00
JS Jerry Stackhouse 2.00 5.00
JT Jason Terry 2.50 6.00
KB Kobe Bryant 10.00 25.00
KE Kenyon Martin 2.50 6.00
KG Kevin Garnett 5.00 12.00
KM Karl Malone 3.00 8.00
LS Latrell Sprewell 2.00 5.00
MA Shawn Marion 2.50 6.00
MC Antonio McDyess 2.00 5.00
MF Michael Finley 2.50 6.00
MM Mike Miller 2.50 6.00
MP Morris Peterson 1.50 4.00
PP Paul Pierce 3.00 8.00
PS Peja Stojakovic 2.50 6.00
RA Ray Allen 2.50 6.00
RM Reggie Miller 2.50 6.00
SF Steve Francis 2.50 6.00
SJ Stephen Jackson 2.00 5.00
TM Tracy McGrady 4.00 10.00

2001-02 Upper Deck Hardcourt UD Game Floor Autographs

Inserted one in 150, this 12-card set features two player photos along the right side of the card, one in action, and one portrait; and a piece of game used floor in the upper left hand corner of the card with each player's team logo etched into it. Cards contain authentic player autographs.

DAA Darius Miles 8.00 20.00
DMA Desmond Mason 8.00 20.00
JMA Jamal Mashburn 10.00 25.00
JSA Jerry Stackhouse 10.00 25.00
KBA Kobe Bryant 100.00 200.00
KEA Kenyon Martin 10.00 25.00
KGA Kevin Garnett 30.00 80.00
MCA Antonio McDyess 10.00 25.00
MMA Mike Miller 10.00 25.00
MPA Morris Peterson 6.00 15.00
PPA Paul Pierce 15.00 40.00
RAA Ray Allen 20.00 50.00

2002-03 Upper Deck Hardcourt

Released in late September 2002, Upper Deck Hardcourt boasts a 135-card base set divided up into 90 veteran player cards and 45 rookie cards. The rookie cards were divided up into three tiers as follows: Hardcourt Futures Level III includes card numbers 91-120 where each card is sequentially numbered to 1999, Hardcourt Futures Level II includes card numbers 121-129 where each card is sequentially numbered to 1299, and Hardcourt Futures Level I includes card numbers 130-135 where each card is sequentially numbered to 799. Base card feature full color player action photos set on a true background with a white strip along the right side of the card running from top to bottom. The rookie cards have "wood" borders along the top and bottom of the card and the words, Hardcourt Futures. Each rookie card is sequentially numbered. Upper Deck Hardcourt was issued in 15 pack boxes with packs containing five card and carried a suggested retail price of $4.99.

COMP.SET w/o SP's (90) 20.00 50.00
1 Shareef Abdur-Rahim .30 .75
2 Glenn Robinson .30 .75
3 Jason Terry .30 .75
4 Antoine Walker .30 .75
5 Paul Pierce .50 1.25
6 Kedrick Brown .25 .60
7 Jalen Rose .30 .75
8 Eddy Curry .30 .75
9 Tyson Chandler .30 .75
10 Marcus Fizer .25 .60
11 Lamond Murray .25 .60
12 Darius Miles .25 .60
13 Chris Mihm .25 .60
14 Dirk Nowitzki .60 1.50
15 Michael Finley .40 1.00
16 Steve Nash .50 1.25
17 James Posey .25 .60
18 Juwan Howard .30 .75
19 Kenny Satterfield .25 .60
20 Jerry Stackhouse .30 .75
21 Clifford Robinson .25 .60
22 Ben Wallace .40 1.00
23 Antawn Jamison .40 1.00
24 Jason Richardson .40 1.00
25 Gilbert Arenas .40 1.00
26 Steve Francis .40 1.00
27 Cuttino Mobley .30 .75
28 Eddie Griffin .25 .60
29 Reggie Miller .40 1.00
30 Jermaine O'Neal .40 1.00
31 Jamaal Tinsley .25 .60
32 Elton Brand .40 1.00
33 Andre Miller .30 .75
34 Lamar Odom .40 1.00
35 Kobe Bryant 2.00 5.00
36 Shaquille O'Neal 1.00 2.50
37 Derek Fisher .30 .75
38 Devean George .25 .60
39 Pau Gasol .50 1.25
40 Jason Williams .30 .75
41 Shane Battier .40 1.00
42 Alonzo Mourning .50 1.25
43 Eddie Jones .30 .75
44 Brian Grant .25 .60
45 Ray Allen .40 1.00
46 Tim Thomas .25 .60
47 Sam Cassell .30 .75
48 Kevin Garnett .75 2.00
49 Wally Szczerbiak .30 .75
50 Terrell Brandon .25 .60
51 Jason Kidd .60 1.50
52 Richard Jefferson .40 1.00
53 Dikembe Mutombo .40 1.00
54 Jamal Mashburn .30 .75
55 Baron Davis .40 1.00
56 David Wesley .25 .60
57 Allan Houston .30 .75
58 Latrell Sprewell .30 .75
59 Antonio McDyess .30 .75
60 Tracy McGrady .60 1.50
61 Mike Miller .40 1.00
62 Darrell Armstrong .25 .60
63 Allen Iverson .60 1.50
64 Keith Van Horn .30 .75
65 Aaron McKie .25 .60
66 Stephon Marbury .30 .75
67 Shawn Marion .40 1.00
68 Anfernee Hardaway .60 1.50
69 Rasheed Wallace .40 1.00
70 Damon Stoudamire .30 .75
71 Scottie Pippen .60 1.50
72 Chris Webber .40 1.00
73 Mike Bibby .40 1.00
74 Peja Stojakovic .40 1.00
75 Tim Duncan .75 2.00
76 David Robinson .60 1.50
77 Tony Parker .50 1.25
78 Gary Payton .40 1.00
79 Rashard Lewis .40 1.00
80 Desmond Mason .30 .75
81 Vince Carter .60 1.50
82 Morris Peterson .25 .60
83 Antonio Davis .25 .60
84 Karl Malone .50 1.25
85 John Stockton .50 1.25
86 Andrei Kirilenko .40 1.00
87 Richard Hamilton .30 .75
88 Michael Jordan 3.00 8.00
89 Chris Whitney .25 .60
90 Kwame Brown .25 .60
91 Efthimios Rentzias RC 1.25 3.00
92 Marko Jaric 1.25 3.00
93 Jiri Welsch RC 1.25 3.00
94 Carlos Boozer RC 2.50 6.00
95 Fred Jones RC 1.25 3.00
96 Sam Clancy RC 1.25 3.00
97 Predrag Savovic RC 1.25 3.00
98 Frank Williams RC 1.25 3.00
99 Rod Grizzard RC 1.25 3.00
100 Casey Jacobsen RC 1.25 3.00
101 Jamal Sampson RC 1.25 3.00
102 Lonny Baxter RC 1.25 3.00
103 Darius Songaila RC 1.25 3.00
104 Tito Maddox RC 1.25 3.00
105 Chris Owens RC 1.25 3.00
106 Juan Dixon RC 1.50 4.00
107 Chris Jefferies RC 1.25 3.00
108 Dan Dickau RC 1.25 3.00
109 Manu Ginobili RC 3.00 8.00
110 Tamar Slay RC 1.25 3.00
111 Matt Barnes RC 1.50 4.00
112 Vincent Yarbrough RC 1.25 3.00
113 Bostjan Nachbar RC 1.25 3.00
114 Dan Gadzuric RC 1.25 3.00
115 Robert Archibald RC 1.25 3.00
116 Ryan Humphrey RC 1.25 3.00
117 Tayshaun Prince RC 1.50 4.00
118 John Salmons RC 1.50 4.00
119 Steve Logan RC 1.25 3.00
120 Melvin Ely RC 1.25 3.00
121 Nikoloz Tskitishvili RC 1.50 4.00
122 Qyntel Woods RC 1.50 4.00
123 Marcus Haislip RC 1.50 4.00
124 Nene Hilario RC 2.00 5.00
125 Amare Stoudemire RC 4.00 10.00
126 Jared Jeffries RC 1.50 4.00
127 Kareem Rush RC 1.50 4.00
128 Chris Wilcox RC 1.50 4.00
129 Curtis Borchardt RC 1.50 4.00
130 Drew Gooden RC 3.00 8.00
131 Mike Dunleavy RC 2.50 6.00
132 DaJuan Wagner RC 2.00 5.00
133 Caron Butler RC 3.00 8.00
134 Yao Ming RC 6.00 15.00
135 Jay Williams RC 1.25 3.00

2002-03 Upper Deck Hardcourt Autographs

Randomly seeded in packs at the rate of one in 30, this 21-card set also showcases the base Hardcourt set design with a "cut signature" signed on plastic in place of the white strip from the base set. Information received from Upper Deck suggests the following players are short printed: Jerry Stackhouse, Kobe Bryant, Kevin Garnett, Marcus Fizer, and Wally Szczerbiak. The Michael Jordan card is sequentially numbered to 23.

AJC Alvin Jones 4.00 10.00
CAC Courtney Alexander 4.00 10.00
GAC Gilbert Arenas 8.00 20.00
HMC Hanno Mottola 4.00 10.00
JMC Jamaal Magloire 4.00 10.00
JRC Jason Richardson 6.00 15.00
JSC Jerry Stackhouse SP 10.00 25.00
JTC Jamaal Tinsley 4.00 10.00
KBC Kobe Bryant SP 125.00 250.00
KGC Kevin Garnett SP 40.00 100.00
KMC Kenyon Martin 6.00 15.00
KSC Kenny Satterfield 4.00 10.00
LHC Larry Hughes 4.00 10.00
LMC Lamond Murray 4.00 10.00
MFC Marcus Fizer SP 4.00 10.00
MJC Michael Jordan/23 500.00 800.00
MMC Mike Miller 6.00 15.00
QRC Quentin Richardson 4.00 10.00
RWC Rodney White 4.00 10.00
TCC Tyson Chandler 6.00 15.00
WSC Wally Szczerbiak SP 10.00 25.00

2002-03 Upper Deck Hardcourt UD Game Floor

Randomly inserted in packs at the rate of one in 15, this 11-card set showcases a horizontal design with full color player action photos on the right and a swatch of game used floor on the left. Each floor swatch has the featured player's team logo burned into it. Information received from Upper Deck suggests that the Michael Jordan card is short printed.

JKF Jason Kidd 4.00 10.00
JSF Jerry Stackhouse 2.00 5.00
KBF Kobe Bryant 8.00 20.00
KGF Kevin Garnett 5.00 12.00
MJF Michael Jordan SP 25.00 60.00
MMF Mike Miller 2.50 6.00
PPF Paul Pierce 3.00 8.00
PSF Peja Stojakovic 2.50 6.00
RLF Rashard Lewis 2.50 6.00
SFF Steve Francis 2.50 6.00
SMF Stephon Marbury 2.00 5.00

2002-03 Upper Deck Hardcourt UD Game Floor Metallics

Randomly seeded in packs at the rate of one in 150, this 15-card set parallels the design of the base Hardcourt UD Game Floor insert set enhanced with "metal" surrounding the floor swatch. Information received from Upper Deck suggests the following players are short printed: Kobe Bryant and Michael Jordan.

AIM Allen Iverson 8.00 20.00
AWM Antoine Walker 4.00 10.00
CWM Chris Webber 6.00 15.00
DNM Dirk Nowitzki 8.00 20.00
KBM Kobe Bryant SP 40.00 100.00
KGM Kevin Garnett 10.00 25.00
LSM Latrell Sprewell 4.00 10.00
MFF Michael Finley 5.00 12.00
MJM Michael Jordan SP 100.00 250.00
RAM Ray Allen 5.00 12.00
RLM Rashard Lewis 5.00 12.00
SFM Steve Francis 5.00 12.00
SHM Shawn Marion 5.00 12.00
SMM Stephon Marbury 4.00 10.00
TMN Tracy McGrady 8.00 20.00

2002-03 Upper Deck Hardcourt UD Game Floor/Film

Randomly inserted in packs at the rate of one in 30, this 10-card set features a full color player action photo on the left, and swatch of game used floor in the middle, and a swatch of film with an in-action game photo. Information received from Upper Deck suggests the following players are short printed: Kobe Bryant and Michael Jordan.

AIFF Allen Iverson 5.00 12.00
CWFF Chris Webber 3.00 8.00
DNFF Dirk Nowitzki 5.00 12.00
JKFF Jason Kidd 5.00 12.00
KBFF Kobe Bryant SP 12.50 30.00
KGFF Kevin Garnett 6.00 15.00
MJFF Michael Jordan SP 30.00 80.00
RLFF Rashard Lewis 3.00 8.00
SFFF Steve Francis 3.00 8.00
TMFF Tracy McGrady 5.00 12.00

2002-03 Upper Deck Hardcourt UD Game Jersey Metallics

Randomly inserted in packs at the rate of one in 300, this 15-card set is similar to the Hardcourt UD Game Floor Metallics. The design is opposite, however, placing the player photo on the left and the swatch of jersey surrounded by "metal" on the right. Information from Upper Deck suggests several players are short printed. Those players appear below with print run numbers.

AIJ Allen Iverson/75 25.00 60.00
AMJ Andre Miller 5.00 12.00
CWJ Chris Webber/75 25.00 60.00
DMJ Darius Miles 4.00 10.00
EBJ Elton Brand 6.00 15.00
JKJ Jason Kidd 10.00 25.00
KBJ Kobe Bryant/50 100.00 200.00
KGJ Kevin Garnett 12.00 30.00
KMJ Karl Malone 8.00 20.00
MCJ Antonio McDyess 5.00 12.00
MJJ Michael Jordan/23 175.00 350.00
MMJ Mike Miller 6.00 15.00
PPJ Paul Pierce 8.00 20.00
SMJ Stephon Marbury 5.00 12.00
TMJ Tracy McGrady/75 25.00 60.00

2003-04 Upper Deck Hardcourt

Released in late September 2003, Hardcourt features a 132-card set divided up into 90 base veteran cards, 36 rookie cards sequentially numbered to 1999 (cards 91-126) and six rookie cards sequentially numbered to 799. Base cards have white circles in the upper right and lower left hand corner with player photos in the middle and rookie cards place player photos in the middle of colorful backgrounds set to match the player's team colors. Hardcourt was packaged in 15-pack boxes with five cards per pack which carried a suggested retail price of $4.99.

COMP.SET w/o SP's (100) 15.00 40.00
1 Shareef Abdur-Rahim .25 .60
2 Jason Terry .25 .60
3 Glenn Robinson .25 .60
4 Paul Pierce .40 1.00
5 Antoine Walker .30 .75
6 Vin Baker .20 .50
7 Jalen Rose .25 .60
8 Tyson Chandler .25 .60
9 Michael Jordan 2.50 6.00
10 DaJuan Wagner .20 .50
11 Ricky Davis .25 .60
12 Darius Miles .20 .50
13 Dirk Nowitzki .50 1.25
14 Michael Finley .30 .75
15 Steve Nash .40 1.00
16 Nene .25 .60
17 Marcus Camby .25 .60
18 Nikoloz Tskitishvili .20 .50
19 Richard Hamilton .25 .60
20 Ben Wallace .30 .75
21 Tayshaun Prince .30 .75
22 Antawn Jamison .30 .75
23 Jason Richardson .30 .75
24 Gilbert Arenas .30 .75
25 Steve Francis .30 .75
26 Yao Ming .60 1.50
27 Eddie Griffin .20 .50
28 Reggie Miller .30 .75
29 Jamaal Tinsley .20 .50
30 Jermaine O'Neal .30 .75
31 Elton Brand .30 .75
32 Andre Miller .25 .60
33 Lamar Odom .30 .75
34 Kobe Bryant 1.50 4.00
35 Gary Payton .30 .75
36 Shaquille O'Neal .75 2.00
37 Karl Malone .40 1.00
38 Pau Gasol .30 .75
39 Shane Battier .25 .60
40 Mike Miller .30 .75
41 Eddie Jones .25 .60
42 Rasual Butler .20 .50
43 Caron Butler .30 .75
44 Michael Redd .30 .75
45 Joe Smith .25 .60
46 Desmond Mason .25 .60
47 Kevin Garnett .60 1.50
48 Wally Szczerbiak .25 .60
49 Sam Cassell .25 .60
50 Jason Kidd .50 1.25
51 Richard Jefferson .30 .75
52 Alonzo Mourning .40 1.00
53 Baron Davis .30 .75
54 Jamal Mashburn .25 .60
55 Jamaal Magloire .20 .50
56 Allan Houston .25 .60
57 Antonio McDyess .25 .60
58 Latrell Sprewell .25 .60
59 Tracy McGrady .40 1.00
60 Grant Hill .40 1.00
61 Drew Gooden .25 .60
62 Allen Iverson .50 1.25
63 Keith Van Horn .25 .60
64 Kenny Thomas .20 .50
65 Stephon Marbury .25 .60
66 Shawn Marion .30 .75
67 Amare Stoudemire .50 1.25
68 Rasheed Wallace .30 .75
69 Bonzi Wells .20 .50
70 Damon Stoudamire .25 .60
71 Chris Webber .30 .75
72 Mike Bibby .30 .75
73 Peja Stojakovic .30 .75
74 Bobby Jackson .20 .50
75 Tim Duncan .50 1.25
76 David Robinson .50 1.25
77 Tony Parker .30 .75
78 Manu Ginobili .40 1.00
79 Ray Allen .30 .75
80 Rashard Lewis .30 .75
81 Reggie Evans .20 .50
82 Vince Carter .50 1.25
83 Morris Peterson .20 .50
84 Antonio Davis .20 .50
85 Matt Harpring .25 .60
86 John Stockton .40 1.00
87 Andrei Kirilenko .30 .75
88 Jerry Stackhouse .25 .60
89 Kwame Brown .20 .50
90 Larry Hughes .25 .60
91 Kirk Hinrich RC 2.50 6.00
92 T.J. Ford RC 2.50 6.00
93 Mike Sweetney RC 2.00 5.00
94 Jarvis Hayes RC 2.00 5.00
95 Mickael Pietrus RC 2.00 5.00
96 Nick Collison RC 2.00 5.00
97 Marcus Banks RC 2.00 5.00
98 Luke Ridnour RC 2.50 6.00
99 Reece Gaines RC 2.00 5.00
100 Troy Bell RC 2.00 5.00
101 Zarko Cabarkapa RC 2.00 5.00
102 David West RC 2.50 6.00
103 Aleksandar Pavlovic RC 2.00 5.00
104 Dahntay Jones RC 2.00 5.00
105 Boris Diaw RC 2.50 6.00
106 Zoran Planinic RC 2.00 5.00
107 Travis Outlaw RC 2.50 6.00
108 Brian Cook RC 2.00 5.00
109 Carlos Delfino RC 2.50 6.00
110 Ndudi Ebi RC 2.00 5.00
111 Kendrick Perkins RC 3.00 8.00
112 Leandro Barbosa RC 2.50 6.00
113 Josh Howard RC 2.00 5.00
114 Maciej Lampe RC 2.00 5.00
115 Jason Kapono RC 2.00 5.00
116 Luke Walton RC 2.00 5.00
117 Jerome Beasley RC 2.00 5.00
118 Sofoklis Schortsanitis RC 2.00 5.00
119 Kyle Korver RC 2.50 6.00
120 Travis Hansen RC 2.00 5.00
121 Steve Blake RC 2.50 6.00
122 Slavko Vranes RC 2.00 5.00
123 Zaur Pachulia RC 2.00 5.00
124 Keith Bogans RC 2.00 5.00
125 Matt Bonner RC 2.50 6.00
126 Maurice Williams RC 3.00 8.00
127 Chris Kaman RC 5.00 12.00
128 Dwyane Wade RC 15.00 40.00
129 Chris Bosh RC 8.00 20.00
130 Carmelo Anthony RC 10.00 25.00
131 Darko Milicic RC 4.00 10.00
132 LeBron James RC 40.00 100.00

2003-04 Upper Deck Hardcourt Clear Commemoratives Autographs

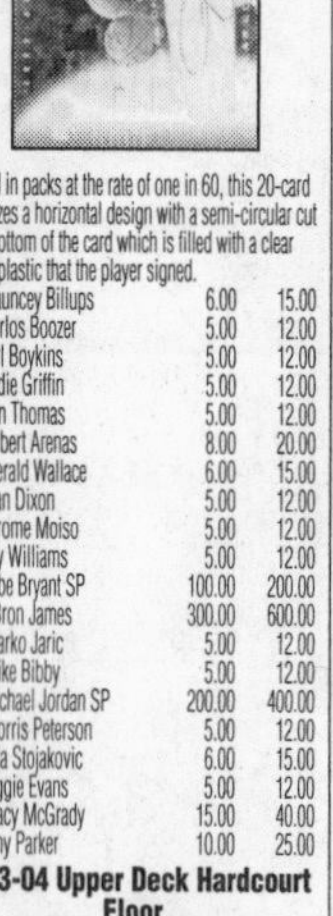

Inserted in packs at the rate of one in 60, this 20-card set utilizes a horizontal design with a semi-circular cut in the bottom of the card which is filled with a clear acetate plastic that the player signed.

BIA Chauncey Billups 6.00 15.00
CBA Carlos Boozer 5.00 12.00
EBA Earl Boykins 5.00 12.00
EGA Eddie Griffin 5.00 12.00
ETA Etan Thomas 5.00 12.00
GAA Gilbert Arenas 8.00 20.00
GWA Gerald Wallace 6.00 15.00
JDA Juan Dixon 5.00 12.00
JMA Jerome Moiso 5.00 12.00
JWA Jay Williams 5.00 12.00
KBA Kobe Bryant SP 100.00 200.00
LJA LeBron James 300.00 600.00
MAA Marko Jaric 5.00 12.00
MBA Mike Bibby 5.00 12.00
MJA Michael Jordan SP 200.00 400.00
MPA Morris Peterson 5.00 12.00
PSA Peja Stojakovic 6.00 15.00
REA Reggie Evans 5.00 12.00
TMA Tracy McGrady 15.00 40.00
TPA Tony Parker 10.00 25.00

2003-04 Upper Deck Hardcourt Floor

Inserted in packs at the rate of one in 30, this 27-card set places full color player action photos on each card with a star-shaped swatch of game-used floor in the lower right-hand corner.

AIF Allen Iverson 4.00 10.00
CWF Chris Webber 2.50 6.00
DRF David Robinson 4.00 10.00
GHF Grant Hill 4.00 10.00
GPF Gary Payton 2.50 6.00
GRF Glenn Robinson 2.00 5.00
JKF Jason Kidd 4.00 10.00
JMF Jamal Mashburn 2.00 5.00
JOF Jermaine O'Neal 2.50 6.00
JSF Jerry Stackhouse 2.00 5.00
JSF John Stockton 3.00 8.00
KBF Kobe Bryant 12.00 30.00
KGF Kevin Garnett 5.00 12.00
KMF Karl Malone 3.00 8.00
LJF LeBron James 12.00 30.00
LSF Latrell Sprewell 2.00 5.00
MJF Michael Jordan 25.00 60.00
RAF Ray Allen 2.50 6.00
RMF Reggie Miller 2.50 6.00
RWF Rasheed Wallace 2.50 6.00
SAF Shareef Abdur-Rahim 2.00 5.00
SMF Steve Nash 3.00 8.00
SMF Stephon Marbury 2.00 5.00
SOF Shaquille O'Neal 6.00 15.00
SPF Scottie Pippen 4.00 10.00
TDF Tim Duncan 4.00 10.00
TMF Tracy McGrady 3.00 8.00

2003-04 Upper Deck Hardcourt Floor/Fabric Combos

Randomly seeded in packs at the rate of one in 60, this 20-card set is vertically desiged with full-color player action photos. Centered towards the bottom of the card is a swatch of game-used floor with an embedded jersey swatch on the left side.

AIFF Allen Iverson 10.00 25.00
CWFF Chris Webber 6.00 15.00
DRFF David Robinson 10.00 25.00
GHFF Grant Hill 8.00 20.00
GPFF Gary Payton 6.00 15.00
JKFF Jason Kidd 10.00 25.00
JOFF Jermaine O'Neal 6.00 15.00
JSFF John Stockton 8.00 20.00
KBFF Kobe Bryant 20.00 50.00
KMFF Karl Malone 8.00 20.00
LJFF LeBron James 100.00 200.00
LSFF Latrell Sprewell 5.00 12.00
MJFF Michael Jordan 75.00 150.00
RAFF Ray Allen 6.00 15.00
SAFF Shareef Abdur-Rahim 5.00 12.00
SMFF Stephon Marbury 5.00 12.00
SNFF Steve Nash 8.00 20.00
SPFF Scottie Pippen 10.00 25.00
TDFF Tim Duncan 10.00 25.00
TMFF Tracy McGrady 8.00 20.00

2003-04 Upper Deck Hardcourt Hardwood Commemoratives

Inserted at the rate of one in 300, this 14-card set is horizontally desiged with a large swatch of game-used floor appearing centered towards the bottom. A dual swatch version was also produced, featuring two players, and these cards are sequentially numbered to 8. Please note that all SP's in the set were announced by Upper Deck.

AMAF Antonio McDyess 8.00 20.00
AWAF Antoine Walker 8.00 20.00
CBAF Chauncey Billups 8.00 20.00
DRAF David Robinson 30.00 80.00
DWAF Dominique Wilkins 15.00 40.00
JBAF LeBron James SP 400.00 600.00
JKAF Jason Kidd 25.00 60.00
JRAF Jalen Rose 8.00 20.00
JSAF Jerry Stackhouse 8.00 20.00
KBAF Kobe Bryant SP 100.00 200.00
KGAF Kevin Garnett SP 50.00 120.00
TMAF Tracy McGrady SP 25.00 60.00

2003-04 Upper Deck Hardcourt Heart of a Champion

Randomly inserted, this 15-card set traces the career of Michael Jordan with a design similar to that of the base Hardcourt cards. Several different versions of this set were inserted in packs. Cards numbers 1-15 were inserted at the rate of one in 23. Silver card numbers 1-15 were inserted at the rate of one in 60, and Gold card numbers 1-15 were inserted at the rate of one in 180.

COMPLETE SET (15) 20.00 50.00
COMMON MJ (1-15) 3.00 8.00
COMMON GOLD (1-15) 12.00 30.00

2003-04 Upper Deck Hardcourt LeBron James Floor

Randomly inserted at the rate of one in 15, this 12-card set features a horizontal design with photos on the right spanning LeBron's High School to the Pros career and a circular swatch of floor on the left.

COMMON CARD (LB1-LB12) 8.00 20.00

2004-05 Upper Deck Hardcourt

Released in October 2004, Upper Deck Hardcourt boasts a 132-card base set where cards 1-90 feature veteran players, cards 91-96 feature rookies serially numbered to 999 and cards 97-132 feature rookies serially numbered to 1999. Hardcourt was packaged in 15-pack boxes where each pack contained five cards and carried a suggested retail price of $4.99.

COMP.SET w/o SP's (90) 15.00 40.00
1 Boris Diaw .25 .60
2 Antoine Walker .30 .75
3 Al Harrington .25 .60
4 Jiri Welsch .20 .50
5 Paul Pierce .40 1.00
6 Ricky Davis .25 .60
7 Gerald Wallace .30 .75
8 Eddie House .20 .50
9 Jason Kapono .20 .50
10 Tyson Chandler .25 .60
11 Eddy Curry .25 .60
12 Kirk Hinrich .30 .75
13 Jeff McInnis .20 .50
14 Dajuan Wagner .20 .50
15 LeBron James 2.00 5.00
16 Michael Finley .30 .75
17 Dirk Nowitzki .50 1.25
18 Marquis Daniels .20 .50
19 Kenyon Martin .30 .75
20 Carmelo Anthony .60 1.50
21 Nene .25 .60
22 Ben Wallace .30 .75
23 Richard Hamilton .25 .60
24 Rasheed Wallace .30 .75
25 Mike Dunleavy .25 .60
26 Jason Richardson .30 .75
27 Derek Fisher .25 .60
28 Tracy McGrady .40 1.00
29 Tyronn Lue .20 .50
30 Yao Ming .60 1.50
31 Jermaine O'Neal .30 .75
32 Reggie Miller .30 .75
33 Stephen Jackson .25 .60
34 Corey Maggette .25 .60
35 Elton Brand .30 .75
36 Marko Jaric .20 .50
37 Karl Malone .40 1.00
38 Kobe Bryant 1.50 4.00
39 Lamar Odom .30 .75
40 James Posey .20 .50
41 Mike Miller .30 .75
42 Pau Gasol .30 .75
43 Dwyane Wade 1.00 2.50
44 Eddie Jones .25 .60
45 Shaquille O'Neal .75 2.00
46 Desmond Mason .25 .60
47 Michael Redd .30 .75
48 T.J. Ford .25 .60
49 Kevin Garnett .60 1.50
50 Latrell Sprewell .25 .60
51 Sam Cassell .25 .60
52 Jason Kidd .50 1.25
53 Aaron Williams .20 .50
54 Richard Jefferson .30 .75
55 Baron Davis .30 .75
56 Jamaal Magloire .20 .50
57 Jamal Mashburn .30 .75
58 Allan Houston .25 .60
59 Jamal Crawford .25 .60
60 Stephon Marbury .25 .60
61 Hedo Turkoglu .30 .75
62 Steve Francis .30 .75
63 Cuttino Mobley .25 .60
64 Allen Iverson .50 1.25
65 Glenn Robinson .25 .60
66 Kenny Thomas .20 .50
67 Amare Stoudemire .40 1.00
68 Quentin Richardson .25 .60
69 Shawn Marion .30 .75
70 Darius Miles .20 .50
71 Shareef Abdur-Rahim .25 .60
72 Zach Randolph .25 .60
73 Chris Webber .30 .75
74 Mike Bibby .30 .75
75 Peja Stojakovic .30 .75
76 Manu Ginobili .40 1.00
77 Tim Duncan .50 1.25
78 Tony Parker .30 .75
79 Rashard Lewis .30 .75
80 Ray Allen .30 .75
81 Ronald Murray .20 .50
82 Chris Bosh .30 .75
83 Jalen Rose .25 .60
84 Vince Carter .50 1.25
85 Andrei Kirilenko .25 .60
86 Carlos Arroyo .25 .60
87 Carlos Boozer .30 .75
88 Gilbert Arenas .30 .75
89 Jarvis Hayes .20 .50
90 Antawn Jamison .30 .75
91 Dwight Howard RC 8.00 20.00
92 Emeka Okafor RC 4.00 10.00
93 Ben Gordon RC 3.00 8.00
94 Shaun Livingston RC 2.50 6.00
95 Devin Harris RC 4.00 10.00
96 Josh Childress RC 2.50 6.00
97 Luol Deng RC 3.00 8.00
98 Andre Iguodala RC 3.00 8.00
99 Luke Jackson RC 2.00 5.00
100 Andris Biedrins RC 2.50 6.00
101 Sebastian Telfair RC 2.00 5.00
102 Josh Smith RC 3.00 8.00
103 Rafael Araujo RC 2.00 5.00
104 Robert Swift RC 2.00 5.00
105 Kris Humphries RC 2.00 5.00
106 Al Jefferson RC 3.00 8.00
107 Kirk Snyder RC 2.00 5.00
108 J.R. Smith RC 2.50 6.00
109 Dorell Wright RC 3.00 8.00
110 Jameer Nelson RC 2.50 6.00
111 Pavel Podkolzine RC 2.00 5.00
112 Justin Reed RC 2.00 5.00
113 Sergei Monia RC 2.00 5.00
114 Delonte West RC 2.50 6.00
115 Tony Allen RC 2.50 6.00
116 Kevin Martin RC 2.50 6.00
117 Sasha Vujacic RC 2.00 5.00
118 Beno Udrih RC 2.00 5.00
119 David Harrison RC 2.00 5.00
120 Anderson Varejao RC 2.50 6.00
121 Jackson Vroman RC 2.00 5.00
122 Peter John Ramos RC 2.00 5.00
123 Lionel Chalmers RC 2.00 5.00
124 Donta Smith RC 2.00 5.00
125 Andre Emmett RC 2.00 5.00
126 Antonio Burks RC 2.00 5.00
127 Royal Ivey RC 2.00 5.00
128 Chris Duhon RC 2.00 5.00
129 Trevor Ariza RC 2.00 5.00
130 Ha Seung-Jin RC 2.00 5.00
131 Romain Sato RC 2.00 5.00
132 Rickey Paulding RC 2.00 5.00

2004-05 Upper Deck Hardcourt Clear Commemorative Autographs

Inserted in packs at the rate of one in 60, this 18-card set is horizontally designed and has a die-cut area where a clear piece of plastic was inserted with the featured players autograph.

SP INFO PROVIDED BY UPPER DECK
AH Al Harrington 5.00 12.00
AK Andrei Kirilenko 6.00 15.00
AM Andre Miller 5.00 12.00
CH Chauncey Billups 8.00 20.00
CM Corey Maggette 5.00 12.00
DR Dennis Rodman 40.00 100.00
GA Gilbert Arenas 6.00 15.00
JR Jason Richardson 5.00 12.00
KB Kobe Bryant SP 125.00 225.00
KG Kevin Garnett SP 40.00 100.00
LJ LeBron James SP 125.00 300.00
LO Lamar Odom 8.00 20.00
MJ Michael Jordan SP 400.00 600.00
PS Peja Stojakovic 8.00 20.00
RJ Richard Jefferson 5.00 12.00
TM Tracy McGrady SP 15.00 40.00
ZO Alonzo Mourning 15.00 40.00
ZR Zach Randolph 6.00 15.00

2004-05 Upper Deck Hardcourt Engraved Endorsements

Inserted in packs at the rate of one in 300, this 18-card set features engraved likenesses of the players on a wood card along with an autograph.

SP INFO PROVIDED BY UPPER DECK
AI Andre Iguodala 40.00 100.00
AM Alonzo Mourning 40.00 100.00
AS Amare Stoudemire 30.00 80.00
BD Baron Davis 15.00 40.00
CA Carmelo Anthony 50.00 100.00
CB Carlos Boozer 15.00 40.00
DH Dwight Howard 80.00 200.00
JK Jason Kidd 40.00 80.00
JR Jason Richardson 15.00 40.00
KB Kobe Bryant SP 150.00 300.00
KG Kevin Garnett SP 80.00 160.00
LJ LeBron James SP 200.00 350.00
LO Lamar Odom 15.00 40.00
MJ Michael Jordan SP 500.00 800.00
PP Paul Pierce 20.00 50.00
RM Reggie Miller 60.00 120.00
TM Tracy McGrady SP 50.00 100.00
YM Yao Ming 50.00 120.00

2004-05 Upper Deck Hardcourt Hardwood Commemoratives

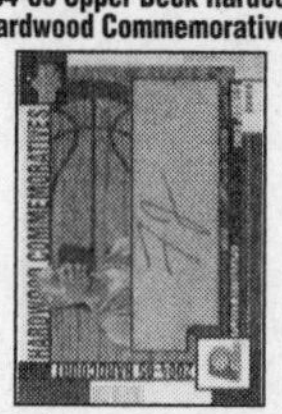

Randomly inserted in packs at the rate of one in 60, this 21-card set places player photos along with an autographed swatch of wood.

SP INFO PROVIDED BY UPPER DECK
AJ Antawn Jamison 5.00 12.00
AS Amare Stoudemire 10.00 25.00
BD Baron Davis 5.00 12.00
BO Carlos Boozer 5.00 12.00
CA Carmelo Anthony 25.00 60.00
DA Darius Miles 5.00 12.00
DW Dwyane Wade 40.00 100.00
FJ Fred Jones 5.00 12.00
GW Gerald Wallace 5.00 12.00
JA Jalen Rose 5.00 12.00
JK Jason Kidd 20.00 50.00
JS Jerry Stackhouse 5.00 12.00
KB Kobe Bryant SP 125.00 225.00
KG Kevin Garnett SP 40.00 100.00
LJ LeBron James 125.00 250.00
MJ Michael Jordan SP 400.00 700.00
PG Pau Gasol 8.00 20.00
RH Richard Hamilton 5.00 12.00
RJ Richard Jefferson 5.00 12.00
SA Shareef Abdur-Rahim 5.00 12.00
SC Sam Cassell 5.00 12.00

2004-05 Upper Deck Hardcourt Hardwood Commemoratives Dual

Inserted in packs at the rate of one in 300, this 18-card set parallels the design of the Hardwood Commemoratives insert but places two players and two autographs on each card.

SP INFO PROVIDED BY UPPER DECK
AM Carmelo Anthony SP / Andre Miller 25.00 60.00
BH Chauncey Billups / Richard Hamilton 15.00 40.00
BS Mike Bibby / Peja Stojakovic 15.00 40.00
GB Pau Gasol / Shane Battier 20.00 50.00
GC Kevin Garnett SP / Sam Cassell 60.00 150.00
JA Antawn Jamison / Gilbert Arenas 15.00 40.00
JB LeBron James SP / Carlos Boozer 200.00 350.00
JJ LeBron James SP / Michael Jordan 500.00 1000.00
KS Andrei Kirilenko / John Stockton 125.00 250.00
MH Reggie Miller / Al Harrington 40.00 100.00
MR Desmond Mason / Michael Redd 15.00 40.00
OW Lamar Odom / Dwyane Wade 60.00 120.00
PR Gary Payton / Kareem Rush 20.00 50.00
RJ Jason Richardson / Fred Jones 15.00 40.00
RM Zach Randolph / Shareef Abdur-Rahim 15.00 40.00
SH Jerry Stackhouse / Juwan Howard 15.00 40.00
SM Amare Stoudemire / Shawn Marion 15.00 40.00

2004-05 Upper Deck Hardcourt Materials

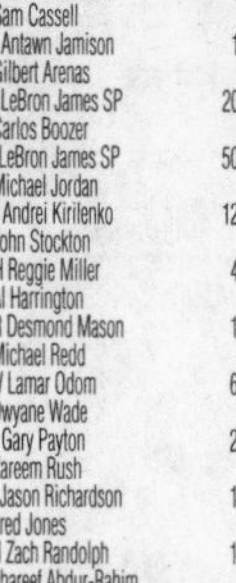

Inserted in packs at the rate of one in 15, this 42-card set places player images on the top of the card and an "M" shaped swatch of memorabilia on the bottom. A combos version with a swatch of wood was also inserted at the rate of one in 15.

*COMBO SINGLES: .6X TO 1.5X BASE JSY HI
SP INFO PROVIDED BY UPPER DECK
AI Allen Iverson 4.00 10.00
AJ Antawn Jamison 2.50 6.00
AK Andrei Kirilenko 2.00 5.00
AS Amare Stoudemire 3.00 8.00
BD Baron Davis 2.50 6.00
BW Ben Wallace 2.50 6.00
CA Carmelo Anthony 5.00 12.00
CB Carlos Boozer 2.50 6.00
DN Dirk Nowitzki 4.00 10.00
DW Dwyane Wade 8.00 20.00
EB Elton Brand 2.50 6.00
EG Manu Ginobili 3.00 8.00
GA Gilbert Arenas 2.50 6.00
JC Jamal Crawford 2.00 5.00
JK Jason Kidd 4.00 10.00
JM Jamaal Magloire 2.00 5.00
JO Jermaine O'Neal 2.50 6.00
JR Jason Richardson 2.50 6.00
JT Jason Terry 2.00 5.00
KB Kobe Bryant SP 10.00 25.00
KG Kevin Garnett 5.00 12.00
LJ LeBron James 10.00 25.00
LO Lamar Odom 2.50 6.00
MB Mike Bibby 2.50 6.00
MJ Michael Jordan SP 30.00 80.00
PG Pau Gasol 2.50 6.00
PP Paul Pierce 3.00 8.00
PS Peja Stojakovic 2.50 6.00
RA Ray Allen 2.50 6.00
RJ Richard Jefferson 2.50 6.00
RM Reggie Miller 2.50 6.00
SA Shareef Abdur-Rahim 2.00 5.00
SF Steve Francis 2.50 6.00
SH Shawn Marion 2.50 6.00
SM Stephon Marbury 2.00 5.00
SN Steve Nash 3.00 8.00
SO Shaquille O'Neal 6.00 15.00
TD Tim Duncan 4.00 10.00
TM Tracy McGrady 3.00 8.00
TP Tony Parker 2.50 6.00
YM Yao Ming 5.00 12.00
ZR Zach Randolph 2.00 5.00

2005-06 Upper Deck Hardcourt

Released in late September, Hardcourt boasts a 137 card base set where cards 1-90 feature veterans and 91-140 feature rookies sequentially numbered to 1750. Base cards have wood grain borders on the left and the right, full-color player photos set on backgrounds set to match team colors and silver foil highlights. Hardcourt was packaged in 15-pack boxes of five cards each and carried a SRP of $4.99.

COMP.SET w/o SP's (90) 15.00 40.00
1 Tony Delk .20 .50
2 Josh Smith .30 .75
3 Al Harrington .25 .60
4 Antoine Walker .25 .60
5 Gary Payton .30 .75
6 Paul Pierce .40 1.00
7 Kareem Rush .20 .50
8 Emeka Okafor .30 .75
9 Primoz Brezec .20 .50
10 Eddy Curry .25 .60
11 Kirk Hinrich .30 .75
12 Ben Gordon .30 .75
13 Drew Gooden .25 .60
14 LeBron James 1.50 4.00
15 Zydrunas Ilgauskas .25 .60
16 Dirk Nowitzki .50 1.25
17 Jason Terry .25 .60
18 Jerry Stackhouse .25 .60
19 Carmelo Anthony .60 1.50
20 Kenyon Martin .30 .75
21 Earl Boykins .20 .50
22 Ben Wallace .30 .75
23 Chauncey Billups .30 .75
24 Richard Hamilton .25 .60
25 Troy Murphy .25 .60
26 Jason Richardson .30 .75
27 Baron Davis .30 .75
28 Tracy McGrady .40 1.00
29 Yao Ming .40 1.00
30 Juwan Howard .25 .60
31 Jermaine O'Neal .30 .75
32 Stephen Jackson .25 .60
33 Ron Artest .30 .75
34 Corey Maggette .25 .60
35 Elton Brand .30 .75
36 Bobby Simmons .20 .50
37 Caron Butler .30 .75
38 Kobe Bryant 1.50 4.00
39 Lamar Odom .30 .75
40 Mike Miller .30 .75
41 Jason Williams .25 .60
42 Pau Gasol .30 .75
43 Dwyane Wade .75 2.00
44 Eddie Jones .25 .60
45 Shaquille O'Neal .60 1.50
46 Desmond Mason .20 .50
47 Maurice Williams .25 .60
48 Michael Redd .30 .75
49 Kevin Garnett .60 1.50
50 Latrell Sprewell .25 .60
51 Sam Cassell .30 .75
52 Vince Carter .50 1.25
53 Jason Kidd .50 1.25
54 Richard Jefferson .30 .75
55 Dan Dickau .20 .50
56 Jamaal Magloire .20 .50
57 J.R. Smith .30 .75
58 Jamal Crawford .25 .60
59 Stephon Marbury .25 .60
60 Allan Houston .20 .50
61 Dwight Howard .60 1.50
62 Grant Hill .40 1.00
63 Steve Francis .30 .75
64 Allen Iverson .50 1.25
65 Andre Iguodala .30 .75
66 Chris Webber .30 .75
67 Amare Stoudemire .30 .75
68 Shawn Marion .30 .75
69 Steve Nash .40 1.00
70 Damon Stoudamire .25 .60
71 Shareef Abdur-Rahim .25 .60
72 Zach Randolph .25 .60
73 Mike Bibby .30 .75
74 Peja Stojakovic .30 .75
75 Brad Miller .30 .75
76 Manu Ginobili .30 .75
77 Tim Duncan .50 1.25
78 Tony Parker .30 .75
79 Rashard Lewis .30 .75
80 Ray Allen .30 .75
81 Ronald Murray .20 .50
82 Rafer Alston .20 .50
83 Jalen Rose .30 .75
84 Chris Bosh .30 .75
85 Andrei Kirilenko .25 .60
86 Carlos Boozer .30 .75
87 Matt Harpring .25 .60
88 Antawn Jamison .30 .75
89 Gilbert Arenas .30 .75
90 Larry Hughes .25 .60
91 Linas Kleiza RC 2.00 5.00
92 Julius Hodge RC 2.00 5.00
93 David Lee RC 3.00 8.00
94 Sarunas Jasikevicius RC 2.00 5.00
95 Jason Maxiell RC 2.00 5.00
96 Luther Head RC 2.00 5.00
97 Brandon Bass RC 2.50 6.00
98 Ricky Sanchez RC 2.00 5.00
99 Ersan Ilyasova RC 2.50 6.00
100 Andray Blatche RC 2.50 6.00
101 Sean May RC 2.00 5.00
102 Ike Diogu RC 2.00 5.00
103 Nate Robinson RC 2.50 6.00
105 Bracey Wright RC 2.00 5.00
106 Daniel Ewing RC 2.00 5.00
107 Salim Stoudamire RC 2.00 5.00
108 Dijon Thompson RC 2.00 5.00
109 Danny Granger RC 4.00 10.00
110 Raymond Felton RC 3.00 8.00
111 Louis Williams RC 3.00 8.00
112 Channing Frye RC 2.50 6.00
113 Francisco Garcia RC 2.50 6.00
114 Ryan Gomes RC 2.00 5.00
115 Travis Diener RC 2.00 5.00
116 Jarrett Jack RC 2.00 5.00
118 Von Wafer RC 2.00 5.00
119 C.J. Miles RC 2.50 6.00
120 Lawrence Roberts RC 2.00 5.00
121 Amir Johnson RC 2.00 5.00
122 Monta Ellis RC 4.00 10.00
123 Martell Webster RC 2.00 5.00
124 Johan Petro RC 2.00 5.00
126 Andrew Bynum RC 6.00 15.00
127 Martynas Andriuskevicius RC 2.00 5.00
128 Charlie Villanueva RC 2.50 6.00
129 Antoine Wright RC 2.00 5.00
130 Joey Graham RC 2.00 5.00
131 Wayne Simien RC 2.00 5.00
132 Hakim Warrick RC 2.50 6.00
133 Gerald Green RC 2.50 6.00
134 Marvin Williams RC 2.50 6.00
135 Deron Williams RC 5.00 12.00
136 Rashad McCants RC 2.00 5.00
137 Yaroslav Korolev RC 2.00 5.00
138 Chris Taft RC 2.00 5.00
139 Chris Paul RC 8.00 20.00
140 Andrew Bogut RC 3.00 8.00

2005-06 Upper Deck Hardcourt Hardwood Signatures

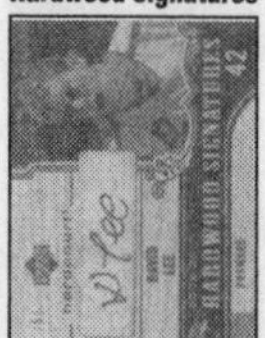

Inserted in packs, this 42-card set is horizontally designed with a wood grain background, player photos on the left and an autograph on a swatch of wood

entered on the left. Cards are serially numbered to either 50 or 25.
UNPRICED DUAL PRINT RUN 10 SETS
AB Andrew Bogut/50 12.00 30.00
AK Andrei Kirilenko/50 8.00 20.00
CA Carmelo Anthony/25 30.00 80.00
CF Channing Frye/50 10.00 25.00
CJ C.J. Miles/50 10.00 25.00
CP Chris Paul/50 100.00 200.00
CV Charlie Villanueva/50 10.00 25.00
DG Danny Granger/50 15.00 40.00
DH Dwight Howard/50 20.00 50.00
DL David Lee/50 12.00 30.00
DT Dijon Thompson/50 8.00 20.00
DW Deron Williams/50 50.00 100.00
GG Gerald Green/50 10.00 25.00
HW Hakim Warrick/50 10.00 25.00
ID Ike Diogu/50 8.00 20.00
JK Jason Kidd/50 20.00 50.00
JR J.R. Smith/50 10.00 25.00
KH Kirk Hinrich/50 8.00 20.00
KK Kyle Korver/50 8.00 20.00
LH Luther Head/50 8.00 20.00
LJ LeBron James/25 125.00 250.00
LO Lamar Odom/50 10.00 25.00
MA Martynas Andriuskevicius/50 8.00 20.00
MD Marquis Daniels/50 8.00 20.00
ME Monta Ellis/50 20.00 50.00
MR Michael Redd/50 15.00 40.00
MW Marvin Williams/50 10.00 25.00
PP Paul Pierce/50 12.50 30.00
RF Raymond Felton/50 12.00 30.00
RM Rashad McCants/50 8.00 20.00
SE Sean May/50 8.00 20.00
SN Steve Nash/25 100.00 200.00
SS Salim Stoudamire/50 8.00 20.00
TA Tony Allen/50 8.00 20.00
WE Martell Webster/50 8.00 20.00
WS Wayne Simien/50 8.00 20.00

2005-06 Upper Deck Hardcourt Materials

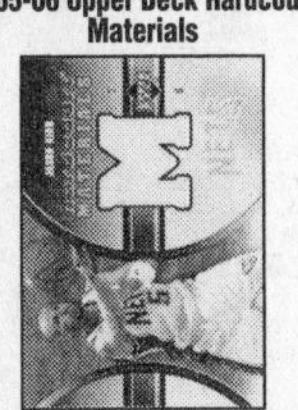

Inserted in packs at the rate of one in 15, this horizontally designed set places player photos on the left and an "M" shaped swatch of memorabilia on the right.
*MAT/WOOD: .6X TO 1.5X BASE MAT HI
AH Al Harrington 2.50 6.00
AK Andrei Kirilenko 2.50 6.00
AN Andre Iguodala 3.00 8.00
BD Baron Davis 3.00 8.00
BG Ben Gordon 3.00 8.00
BM Brad Miller 3.00 8.00
BW Ben Wallace 3.00 8.00
CB Carlos Boozer 3.00 8.00
CH Chris Bosh 3.00 8.00
CM Corey Maggette 2.50 6.00
DF Derek Fisher 2.50 6.00
DG Drew Gooden 2.50 6.00
DH Dwight Howard 6.00 15.00
DM Desmond Mason 2.50 6.00
GA Gilbert Arenas 3.00 8.00
GP Gary Payton 3.00 8.00
GW Gerald Wallace 3.00 8.00
JC Jamal Crawford 2.50 6.00
JH Josh Howard 3.00 8.00
JK Jason Kidd 5.00 12.00
JM Jamaal Magloire 2.00 5.00
JR Jalen Rose 2.00 5.00
KB Kobe Bryant 12.50 30.00
KD Keyon Dooling 2.00 5.00
KG Kevin Garnett 5.00 12.00
KK Kyle Korver 2.50 6.00
LJ LeBron James 12.50 30.00
MB Mike Bibby 3.00 8.00
MJ Michael Jordan 25.00 60.00
PG Pau Gasol 3.00 8.00
PP Paul Pierce 4.00 10.00
PS Peja Stojakovic 3.00 8.00
QR Quentin Richardson 2.50 6.00
RJ Richard Jefferson 3.00 8.00
RM Ronald Murray 2.00 5.00
SB Shane Battier 2.50 6.00
SF Steve Francis 3.00 8.00
SM Stephon Marbury 2.50 6.00
SN Steve Nash 4.00 10.00
TA Tony Allen 2.00 5.00
TM Tracy McGrady 4.00 10.00
YM Yao Ming 4.00 10.00

2005-06 Upper Deck Hardcourt Materials/Wood Autographs

Inserted randomly in packs, this 42-card set parallels the Materials/Wood set enhanced with an autograph sticker and sequential numbering to 50.
AH Al Harrington/50 8.00 20.00
AK Andrei Kirilenko/50 8.00 20.00
AN Andre Iguodala/50 25.00 60.00
BD Baron Davis/50 10.00 25.00
BG Ben Gordon/50 25.00 60.00
BM Brad Miller/50 8.00 20.00
BW Ben Wallace/50 20.00 50.00
CH Chris Bosh/50 15.00 40.00
CM Corey Maggette/50 8.00 20.00
DF Derek Fisher/50 10.00 25.00
DG Drew Gooden/50 8.00 20.00
DH Dwight Howard/50 20.00 50.00
DM Desmond Mason/50 8.00 20.00
GA Gilbert Arenas/50 12.50 30.00
GP Gary Payton/50 15.00 40.00
JH Josh Howard/50 8.00 20.00
JK Jason Kidd/50 15.00 40.00
JM Jamaal Magloire/50 8.00 20.00
KD Keyon Dooling/50 8.00 20.00
KG Kevin Garnett/50 40.00 100.00
KK Kyle Korver/50 12.50 30.00
LJ LeBron James/25 150.00 300.00
MB Mike Bibby/50 8.00 20.00
MJ Michael Jordan/25 350.00 650.00
PG Pau Gasol/50 12.50 30.00
PP Paul Pierce/50 12.50 30.00
PS Peja Stojakovic/50 12.50 30.00
QR Quentin Richardson/50 8.00 20.00
RJ Richard Jefferson/50 8.00 20.00
RM Ronald Murray/50 8.00 20.00
SB Shane Battier/50 8.00 20.00
SM Stephon Marbury/50 12.50 30.00
SN Steve Nash/50 50.00 120.00
TA Tony Allen/50 8.00 20.00
TM Tracy McGrady/25 40.00 100.00
YM Yao Ming/25 40.00 100.00

2005-06 Upper Deck Hardcourt Rookie Jerseys

Inserted randomly in packs, this 30-card set is horizontally designed with a player photo on the left and an "R" shaped swatch of memorabilia on the right. Each card is sequentially numbered to 250.
UNPRICED JSY AU PRINT RUN 15 SETS
*JSY/WOOD/250: .6X TO 1.5X BASE JSY HI
*JSY/WOOD/99: .5X TO 1.25X BASE JSY HI
JSY/WOOD PRINT RUN 50 SER.#'d SETS
92J Julius Hodge/250 3.00 8.00
93J David Lee/250 5.00 12.00
95J Jason Maxiell/250 3.00 8.00
96J Luther Head/250 3.00 8.00
97J Brandon Bass/250 4.00 10.00
100J Andray Blatche/250 4.00 10.00
101J Sean May/250 3.00 8.00
103J Nate Robinson/250 4.00 10.00
106J Daniel Ewing/250 3.00 8.00
107J Salim Stoudamire/250 3.00 8.00
109J Danny Granger/250 6.00 15.00
110J Raymond Felton/250 5.00 12.00
111J Louis Williams/250 5.00 12.00
112J Channing Frye/250 4.00 10.00
113J Francisco Garcia/250 4.00 10.00
114J Ryan Gomes/250 3.00 8.00
116J Jarrett Jack/250 3.00 8.00
119J C.J. Miles/250 4.00 10.00
123J Martell Webster/250 3.00 8.00
128J Charlie Villanueva/250 4.00 10.00
129J Antoine Wright/250 3.00 8.00
130J Joey Graham/250 3.00 8.00
131J Wayne Simien/250 3.00 8.00
132J Hakim Warrick/250 4.00 10.00
133J Gerald Green/250 4.00 10.00
134J Marvin Williams/99 5.00 12.00
135J Deron Williams/99 10.00 25.00
136J Rashad McCants/99 4.00 10.00
139J Chris Paul/99 12.00 30.00
140J Andrew Bogut/99 6.00 15.00

2005-06 Upper Deck Hardcourt Signatures

Inserted in packs at the rate of one in 15, this 90-card set features both veteran and rookie players on a card with borders along the left and right, a player photo centered at the top and an autograph sticker centered along the bottom. Short Print information for this set was provided by Upper Deck.
AI Andre Iguodala 6.00 15.00
AK Andrei Kirilenko 4.00 10.00
AM Antonio McDyess 4.00 10.00
AN Andrew Bogut SP 8.00 20.00
AV Anderson Varejao 4.00 10.00
AW Antoine Wright 4.00 10.00
BI Andris Biedrins 4.00 10.00
BU Beno Udrih 4.00 10.00
BY Andrew Bynum 15.00 40.00
CD Chris Duhon 4.00 10.00
CF Channing Frye 5.00 12.00
CJ C.J. Miles 5.00 12.00
CM Corey Maggette 4.00 10.00
CP Chris Paul SP 40.00 100.00
CT Chris Taft 4.00 10.00
CU Cuttino Mobley 4.00 10.00
CV Charlie Villanueva 5.00 12.00
DA David Harrison 4.00 10.00
DD Dan Dickau 4.00 10.00
DF Derek Fisher 6.00 15.00
DH Dwight Howard 15.00 40.00
DL David Lee 6.00 15.00
DM Desmond Mason 4.00 10.00
DO Dorell Wright 4.00 10.00
DT Dijon Thompson 4.00 10.00
DW Delonte West 4.00 10.00
FE Raymond Felton 6.00 15.00
FG Francisco Garcia 5.00 12.00
FV Fran Vazquez 4.00 10.00
GA Gilbert Arenas 5.00 12.00
GG Gerald Green 5.00 12.00
GR Danny Granger 8.00 20.00
GW Gerald Wallace 5.00 12.00
HS Ha Seung-Jin 4.00 10.00
HW Hakim Warrick 6.00 15.00
JA Jalen Rose 5.00 12.00
JC Jamal Crawford 4.00 10.00
JM Jamaal Magloire 4.00 10.00
JN Jameer Nelson 6.00 15.00
JO Joey Graham 4.00 10.00
JP Johan Petro 4.00 10.00
JR J.R. Smith 4.00 10.00
JU Justin Reed 4.00 10.00
JW Jason Williams 12.50 30.00
KD Keyon Dooling 4.00 10.00
KK Kyle Korver 4.00 10.00
KR Kareem Rush 4.00 10.00
KS Kirk Snyder 4.00 10.00
LF Luis Flores 4.00 10.00
LH Luther Head 4.00 10.00
LJ LeBron James 125.00 300.00
LU Luke Jackson 4.00 10.00
MA Martynas Andriuskevicius 4.00 10.00
MC Rashad McCants 4.00 10.00
ME Monta Ellis 10.00 25.00
MJ Michael Jordan SP 300.00 600.00
MP Morris Peterson 4.00 10.00
MW Marvin Williams SP 10.00 25.00
NO Andres Nocioni 4.00 10.00
NR Nate Robinson 10.00 25.00
PA Pavel Podkolzin 4.00 10.00
PB Primoz Brezec 4.00 10.00
QR Quentin Richardson 4.00 10.00
RA Rafael Araujo 4.00 10.00
RG Ryan Gomes 4.00 10.00
RO Robert Traylor 4.00 10.00
RT Ronny Turiaf 6.00 15.00
SM Sean May 4.00 10.00
SN Steve Nash SP 75.00 150.00
SS Salim Stoudamire 4.00 10.00
ST Sebastian Telfair 4.00 10.00
TA Trevor Ariza 4.00 10.00
TK Toni Kukoc 10.00 25.00
TO Travis Outlaw 4.00 10.00
UH Udonis Haslem 4.00 10.00
VK Viktor Khryapa 4.00 10.00
WI Maurice Williams 4.00 10.00
WS Wayne Simien 4.00 10.00
YM Yao Ming SP 20.00 50.00
AU Stacey Augmon 4.00 10.00

2006-07 Upper Deck Hardcourt

Released in mid September 2006, Hardcourt features a 150-card base set where cards 1-100 picture veteran players, cards 101-135 picture rookies sequentially numbered to 1750 and cards 136-150 picture rookies along with an autograph sticker and sequential numbering to 399. Hardcourt is packaged in 15-pack boxes of five cards each and carried an initial suggested retail price of $4.99. Also included in each box is a game floor card of either Michael Jordan or LeBron James.
COMP.SET w/o SP's (100) 15.00 40.00
UNPRICED GOLD PRINT RUN ONE SET
1 Joe Johnson .30 .75
2 Salim Stoudamire .20 .50
3 Marvin Williams .30 .75
4 Dan Dickau .20 .50
5 Paul Pierce .40 1.00
6 Wally Szczerbiak .25 .60
7 Raymond Felton .40 1.00
8 Emeka Okafor .30 .75
9 Gerald Wallace .30 .75
10 Tyson Chandler .25 .60
11 Luol Deng .30 .75
12 Ben Gordon .30 .75
13 Michael Jordan 2.50 6.00
14 Drew Gooden .25 .60
15 Larry Hughes .25 .60
16 Zydrunas Ilgauskas .25 .60
17 LeBron James 1.50 4.00
18 Erick Dampier .20 .50
19 Devin Harris .30 .75
20 Dirk Nowitzki .50 1.25
21 Jason Terry .25 .60
22 Carmelo Anthony .40 1.00
23 Earl Boykins .20 .50
24 Marcus Camby .25 .60
25 Kenyon Martin .25 .60
26 Chauncey Billups .30 .75
27 Richard Hamilton .25 .60
28 Antonio McDyess .25 .60
29 Ben Wallace .30 .75
30 Baron Davis .30 .75
31 Derek Fisher .25 .60
32 Troy Murphy .20 .50
33 Jason Richardson .30 .75
34 Luther Head .25 .60
35 Tracy McGrady .40 1.00
36 Yao Ming .40 1.00
37 Danny Granger .30 .75
38 Jermaine O'Neal .30 .75
39 Peja Stojakovic .30 .75
40 Elton Brand .30 .75
41 Sam Cassell .30 .75
42 Chris Kaman .25 .60
43 Shaun Livingston .20 .50
44 Kwame Brown .20 .50
45 Kobe Bryant 1.50 4.00
46 Andrew Bynum .50 1.25
47 Shane Battier .25 .60
48 Pau Gasol .30 .75
49 Mike Miller .30 .75
50 Hakim Warrick .25 .60
51 Shaquille O'Neal .60 1.50
52 Dwyane Wade .75 2.00
53 Jason Williams .25 .60
54 Andrew Bogut .25 .60
55 T.J. Ford .20 .50
56 Jamaal Magloire .20 .50
57 Michael Redd .30 .75
58 Ricky Davis .25 .60
59 Kevin Garnett .60 1.50
60 Rashad McCants .30 .75
61 Vince Carter .40 1.00
62 Richard Jefferson .30 .75
63 Jason Kidd .50 1.25
64 Desmond Mason .20 .50
65 Chris Paul .60 1.50
66 J.R. Smith .30 .75
67 Jamal Crawford .25 .60
68 Channing Frye .25 .60
69 Stephon Marbury .25 .60
70 Quentin Richardson .25 .60
71 Dwight Howard .50 1.25
72 Darko Milicic .20 .50
73 Jameer Nelson .25 .60
74 Andre Iguodala .30 .75
75 Allen Iverson .40 1.00
76 Chris Webber .30 .75
77 Shawn Marion .30 .75
78 Steve Nash .40 1.00
79 Amare Stoudemire .30 .75
80 Zach Randolph .25 .60
81 Sebastian Telfair .20 .50
82 Martell Webster .30 .75
83 Ron Artest .30 .75
84 Mike Bibby .30 .75
85 Brad Miller .30 .75
86 Tim Duncan .50 1.25
87 Manu Ginobili .30 .75
88 Tony Parker .30 .75
89 Ray Allen .30 .75
90 Danny Fortson .20 .50
91 Rashard Lewis .30 .75
92 Chris Bosh .30 .75
93 Joey Graham .20 .50
94 Charlie Villanueva .30 .75
95 Carlos Boozer .30 .75
96 Andrei Kirilenko .25 .60
97 Deron Williams .50 1.25
98 Gilbert Arenas .30 .75
99 Caron Butler .30 .75
100 Antawn Jamison .30 .75
101 Adam Morrison RC 2.00 5.00
102 Randy Foye RC 2.00 5.00
103 Rudy Gay RC 2.50 6.00
104 Patrick O'Bryant RC 1.50 4.00
105 Saer Sene RC 1.50 4.00
106 J.J. Redick RC 2.00 5.00
107 Hilton Armstrong RC 1.50 4.00
108 Thabo Sefolosha RC 2.00 5.00
109 Cedric Simmons RC 1.50 4.00
110 Shawne Williams RC 1.50 4.00
111 Tarence Kinsey RC 1.50 4.00
112 Quincy Douby RC 1.50 4.00
113 Renaldo Balkman RC 1.50 4.00
114 Josh Boone RC 1.50 4.00
115 Kyle Lowry RC 2.00 5.00
116 Shannon Brown RC 2.50 6.00
117 Jordan Farmar RC 1.50 4.00
118 Joel Freeland RC 1.50 4.00
119 Paul Davis RC 1.50 4.00
120 P.J. Tucker RC 1.50 4.00
121 Craig Smith RC 1.50 4.00
122 Bobby Jones RC 1.50 4.00
123 David Noel RC 1.50 4.00
124 Denham Brown RC 1.50 4.00
125 James Augustine RC 1.50 4.00
126 Daniel Gibson RC 2.00 5.00
127 Allan Ray RC 1.50 4.00
128 Alexander Johnson RC 1.50 4.00
129 Dee Brown RC 1.50 4.00
130 Paul Millsap RC 2.50 6.00
131 Leon Powe RC 1.50 4.00
132 Ryan Hollins RC 1.50 4.00
133 Mike Gansey RC 1.50 4.00
134 Hassan Adams RC 1.50 4.00
135 Will Blalock RC 1.50 4.00
136 Andrea Bargnani AU RC 8.00 20.00
137 LaMarcus Aldridge AU RC 12.00 30.00
138 Tyrus Thomas AU RC 6.00 15.00
139 Shelden Williams AU RC 5.00 12.00
140 Brandon Roy AU RC 12.00 30.00
141 Ronnie Brewer AU RC 6.00 15.00
142 Rodney Carney AU RC 5.00 12.00
143 Rajon Rondo AU RC 25.00 60.00
144 Marcus Williams AU RC 5.00 12.00
145 Kevin Pittsnogle AU RC 5.00 12.00
146 Maurice Ager AU RC 5.00 12.00
147 Mardy Collins AU RC 5.00 12.00
148 James White AU RC 5.00 12.00
149 Steve Novak AU RC 5.00 12.00
150 Solomon Jones AU RC 5.00 12.00

2006-07 Upper Deck Hardcourt Copper

*1-100 COPPER: 1X TO 2.5X BASE HI
*101-135 COPPER: .6X TO 1.5X BASE HI
*136-150 COPPER: .2X TO .5X BASE HI
COPPER PRINT RUN 199 SER.#'d SETS

2006-07 Upper Deck Hardcourt Silver

*1-100 SILVER: 2.5X TO 6X BASE HI
*101-135 SILVER: 1.25X TO 3X BASE HI
*136-150 SILVER: .4X TO 1X BASE HI
PRINT RUN 50 SER.#'d SETS

2006-07 Upper Deck Hardcourt Debut Jerseys

PRINT RUN 199 SER.#'d SETS
AR Allan Ray 3.00 8.00
BA Renaldo Balkman 3.00 8.00
BJ Bobby Jones 3.00 8.00
CS Cedric Simmons 3.00 8.00
DB Dee Brown 3.00 8.00
HA Hilton Armstrong 3.00 8.00
JB Josh Boone 3.00 8.00
JF Jordan Farmar 3.00 8.00
JW James White 3.00 8.00
KL Kyle Lowry 4.00 10.00
MA Maurice Ager 3.00 8.00
MC Mardy Collins 3.00 8.00
MW Marcus Williams 3.00 8.00
PD Paul Davis 3.00 8.00
PO Patrick O'Bryant 3.00 8.00
QD Quincy Douby 3.00 8.00
RB Ronnie Brewer 4.00 10.00
RC Rodney Carney 3.00 8.00
RG Rudy Gay 5.00 12.00
RR Rajon Rondo 8.00 20.00
SB Shannon Brown 5.00 12.00
SJ Solomon Jones 3.00 8.00
SN Steve Novak 3.00 8.00
SW Shawne Williams 3.00 8.00

2006-07 Upper Deck Hardcourt Debut Jerseys 2

PRINT RUN 99 SER.#'d SETS
JR J.J. Redick 5.00 12.00
KP Kevin Pittsnogle 4.00 10.00
LA LaMarcus Aldridge 10.00 25.00
RF Randy Foye 5.00 12.00
TT Tyrus Thomas 5.00 12.00
WS Shelden Williams 4.00 10.00

2006-07 Upper Deck Hardcourt Game Floor

COMMON JORDAN 12.50 30.00
COMMON LEBRON 6.00 15.00
COMMON JORDAN/LEBRON 25.00 60.00
STATED ODDS ONE PER BOX
JORDAN/LEBRON PRINT RUN 99 SER.#'d SETS
AUTO PRINT RUN 23 SER.#'d SETS
25 Michael Jordan / LeBron James 25.00 60.00
26 Michael Jordan / LeBron James 25.00 60.00
27 Michael Jordan / LeBron James 25.00 60.00
29 Michael Jordan AU/23 300.00 600.00
30 LeBron James AU/23 150.00 350.00

2006-07 Upper Deck Hardcourt Heart of a Champion Autographs

APPROXIMATE ODDS ONE PER BOX
AA Alex Acker 4.00 10.00
AJ Al Jefferson 4.00 10.00
BB Brent Barry 8.00 20.00
BO Bruce Bowen 4.00 10.00
CA Carmelo Anthony SP 20.00 50.00
CB Chauncey Billups 6.00 15.00
CH Chuck Hayes 4.00 10.00
CM Cuttino Mobley 4.00 10.00
CP Chris Paul 25.00 60.00
DJ Dwayne Jones 4.00 10.00
DW Deron Williams 15.00 40.00
GG George Gervin 8.00 20.00
HW Hakim Warrick 6.00 15.00
JA Jarrett Jack 4.00 10.00
JG Joey Graham 4.00 10.00
KA Kareem Abdul-Jabbar SP 50.00 120.00
KD Keyon Dooling 4.00 10.00
ME Maurice Evans 4.00 10.00
NR Nate Robinson 5.00 12.00
QR Quentin Richardson 4.00 10.00
RF Raymond Felton 8.00 20.00
RT Ronny Turiaf 12.50 30.00
RW Robert Whaley 4.00 10.00
SK Steve Kerr 12.50 30.00
SP Sam Perkins 6.00 15.00
TD Travis Diener 4.00 10.00
TF T.J. Ford 4.00 10.00

2006-07 Upper Deck Hardcourt Materials

APPROXIMATE ODDS ONE PER BOX
AI Andre Iguodala 2.50 6.00
AS Amare Stoudemire 2.50 6.00
BR Kwame Brown 2.00 5.00
CA Carmelo Anthony 3.00 8.00
CB Caron Butler 2.50 6.00
CM Corey Maggette 2.00 5.00
CW Chris Webber 2.50 6.00
DG Drew Gooden 2.00 5.00
DH Dwight Howard SP 4.00 10.00
DM Desmond Mason 1.50 4.00
DN Dirk Nowitzki 4.00 10.00
EB Elton Brand 2.50 6.00
EC Eddy Curry 2.00 5.00
FJ Fred Jones 2.00 5.00
GA Gilbert Arenas 2.50 6.00
JM Jeff McInnis 2.00 5.00
JR Jason Richardson 2.50 6.00
JS J.R. Smith 2.50 6.00
KB Kobe Bryant 8.00 20.00
KG Kevin Garnett 5.00 12.00
KH Kirk Hinrich 2.50 6.00
KK Kyle Korver 2.50 6.00
LH Larry Hughes 2.00 5.00
LJ LeBron James 10.00 25.00
LW Luke Walton 2.50 6.00
MG Manu Ginobili 2.50 6.00
MJ Michael Jordan SP 25.00 60.00
MS Mike Sweetney 2.00 5.00
NE Nene 2.00 5.00
PG Pau Gasol 2.50 6.00
PS Peja Stojakovic 2.50 6.00
QR Quentin Richardson 2.00 5.00
RA Ray Allen 2.50 6.00
RH Richard Hamilton 2.00 5.00
RJ Richard Jefferson 2.50 6.00
SD Samuel Dalembert 2.00 5.00
SN Steve Nash 3.00 8.00
SO Shaquille O'Neal 5.00 12.00
TD Tim Duncan 4.00 10.00
TP Tony Parker 3.00 8.00
WS Wally Szczerbiak 2.00 5.00
ZI Zydrunas Ilgauskas 2.00 5.00

2006-07 Upper Deck Hardcourt Materials Dual

PRINT RUN 50 SER.#'d SETS
BG Elton Brand / Kevin Garnett 4.00 10.00
BH Chris Bosh / Dwight Howard 5.00 12.00
BM Kobe Bryant / Tracy McGrady 10.00 25.00
DP Tim Duncan / Tony Parker 10.00 25.00
DR Baron Davis / Jason Richardson 4.00 10.00
GN Kevin Garnett / Dirk Nowitzki 6.00 15.00
GV Devean George / Sasha Vujacic 4.00 10.00
HW Richard Hamilton / Ben Wallace 4.00 10.00
JA LeBron James / Carmelo Anthony 20.00 50.00
JJ Michael Jordan / LeBron James 40.00 100.00
KC Jason Kidd / Vince Carter 6.00 15.00
MM Tracy McGrady / Yao Ming 8.00 20.00
MO Yao Ming / Shaquille O'Neal 10.00 25.00
MS Shawn Marion / Amare Stoudemire 5.00 12.00
NM Steve Nash / Stephon Marbury 5.00 12.00
SM Wally Szczerbiak / Jeff McInnis 4.00 10.00
SO Peja Stojakovic / Jermaine O'Neal 4.00 10.00
WI Chris Webber / Andre Iguodala 4.00 10.00

2000 Upper Deck Hawaii

These cards were issued by Upper Deck and given away at the Kit Young annual conference in Hawaii in 2000. These cards feature autographs of four athletes Upper Deck brought over to the conference. Each player signed a card serial numbered to 500. The card featuring all four players signed was not included in the factory set, but 100 cards featuring all four players were also signed and distributed. Two Kit Young cards were also included with the factory sets.
COMPLETE SET (6) 160.00 400.00
DR Julius Erving AU 60.00 150.00
GAU Julius Erving AU/100 200.00 400.00
Gordie Howe AU
Joe Namath AU
Tom Seaver AU

2004 Upper Deck Hawaii Trade Conference LeBron James Room Key

NNO LeBron James 12.50 30.00

2007 Upper Deck Hawaii Trade Conference

COMPLETE SET (13) 15.00 40.00
12 LeBron James 3.00 8.00
13 Michael Jordan 5.00 12.00

1999-00 Upper Deck HoloGrFX

Released for the first time by Upper Deck, this premiere set contained 90 cards. Intended as a retail-only release, each pack contained three-cards and carried a suggested retail price of $1.99.
COMPLETE SET (90) 20.00 50.00
COMPLETE SET w/o RC (60) 8.00 20.00
1 Dikembe Mutombo .30 .75
2 Alan Henderson .20 .50
3 Antoine Walker .30 .75
4 Paul Pierce .50 1.25
5 Eddie Jones .30 .75
6 David Wesley .20 .50
7 Dickey Simpkins .20 .50
8 Toni Kukoc .30 .75
9 Shawn Kemp .30 .75
10 Zydrunas Ilgauskas .25 .60
11 Michael Finley .30 .75
12 Cedric Ceballos .20 .50
13 Antonio McDyess .25 .60
14 Nick Van Exel .25 .60
15 Grant Hill .40 1.00
16 Bison Dele .20 .50
17 Jerry Stackhouse .30 .75
18 Antawn Jamison .30 .75
19 John Starks .30 .75
20 Scottie Pippen .50 1.25
21 Charles Barkley .50 1.25
22 Hakeem Olajuwon .40 1.00
23 Reggie Miller .30 .75
24 Rik Smits .30 .75
25 Michael Olowokandi .20 .50
26 Maurice Taylor .20 .50
27 Shaquille O'Neal .75 2.00
28 Kobe Bryant 1.50 4.00
29 Tim Hardaway .30 .75
30 Alonzo Mourning .40 1.00
31 Ray Allen .30 .75
32 Glenn Robinson .25 .60
33 Kevin Garnett .60 1.50
34 Terrell Brandon .20 .50
35 Stephon Marbury .25 .60
36 Keith Van Horn .25 .60
37 Allan Houston .25 .60
38 Latrell Sprewell .30 .75
39 Bo Outlaw .20 .50
40 Darrell Armstrong .20 .50
41 Allen Iverson .60 1.50
42 Larry Hughes .25 .60
43 Jason Kidd .50 1.25
44 Tom Gugliotta .20 .50
45 Damon Stoudamire .30 .75
46 Rasheed Wallace .30 .75
47 Jason Williams .40 1.00
48 Chris Webber .30 .75
49 Tim Duncan .60 1.50
50 David Robinson .50 1.25
51 Gary Payton .30 .75
52 Vin Baker .30 .75
53 Vince Carter .60 1.50
54 Tracy McGrady .50 1.25
55 John Stockton .40 1.00
56 Karl Malone .40 1.00
57 Mike Bibby .30 .75
58 Shareef Abdur-Rahim .25 .60
59 Juwan Howard .25 .60
60 Mitch Richmond .30 .75
61 Elton Brand RC 1.00 2.50
62 Lamar Odom RC 1.25 3.00
63 Kenny Thomas RC .40 1.00
64 Scott Padgett RC .40 1.00
65 Trajan Langdon RC .40 1.00
66 James Posey RC .40 1.00
67 Shawn Marion RC 1.00 2.50
68 Chris Herren RC .40 1.00
69 Tim James RC .40 1.00
70 Evan Eschmeyer RC .40 1.00
71 Corey Maggette RC .75 2.00
72 Richard Hamilton RC 1.00 2.50
73 Baron Davis RC 1.25 3.00
74 Galen Young RC .40 1.00
75 Dion Glover RC .40 1.00
76 Jumaine Jones RC .40 1.00
77 Wally Szczerbiak RC .75 2.00
78 Andre Miller RC 1.00 2.50
79 Devean George RC .40 1.00
80 Obinna Ekezie RC .40 1.00
81 Steve Francis RC 1.00 2.50
82 Jason Terry RC 1.00 2.50
83 Quincy Lewis RC .40 1.00
84 Ryan Robertson RC .40 1.00
85 William Avery RC .40 1.00
86 Aleksandar Radojevic RC .40 1.00
87 Jonathan Bender RC .40 1.00
88 Cal Bowdler RC .40 1.00
89 Venteggo Cummings RC .40 1.00
90 Jeff Foster RC .40 1.00

1999-00 Upper Deck HoloGrFX AUSome

Randomly inserted in packs at one in 12, this 90-card set parallels the base set. The cards feature gold ink. To ascertain values on individual cards, please refer to the multiplier in the header, coupled with the value of the base card.
*STARS: 1.5X TO 4X HI COLUMN
*RCs: .75X TO 2X HI

1999-00 Upper Deck HoloGrFX HoloFame

Randomly inserted in packs at one in 17, this nine-card set features NBA standouts already in or bound for the Hall of Fame. Card backs carry a "HF" prefix.
COMPLETE SET (9) 15.00 30.00
*GOLD: 1.5X TO 4X HI COLUMN
GOLD: STATED ODDS 1:210
HF1 Michael Jordan 10.00 25.00
HF2 Julius Erving 2.00 5.00
HF3 Larry Bird 3.00 8.00
HF4 George Gervin 1.00 2.50
HF5 Tim Duncan 2.00 5.00
HF6 Kevin Garnett 2.00 5.00
HF7 Kobe Bryant 8.00 20.00
HF8 Jason Williams 1.25 3.00
HF9 Vince Carter 2.00 5.00

1999-00 Upper Deck HoloGrFX Maximum Jordan

Randomly inserted in packs at one in 34, this six-card set features cards that highlight each one of MJ's six championship seasons. Card backs carry a "MJ" prefix.
COMPLETE SET (6) 12.50 25.00
COMMON CARD (MJ1-MJ6) 2.50 6.00
COMMON GOLD 20.00 50.00
GOLD: STATED ODDS 1:431

1999-00 Upper Deck HoloGrFX NBA 24-7

Randomly inserted in packs at one in three, this 15-card set features the most exciting players in the NBA, 24 hours a day, seven days a week. Card backs carry a "N" prefix.
COMPLETE SET (15) 4.00 10.00
*GOLD: 2.5X TO 6X HI COLUMN
GOLD: STATED ODDS 1:105
N1 Tim Duncan .60 1.50
N2 Allen Iverson .60 1.50
N3 Vince Carter .60 1.50
N4 Kevin Garnett .60 1.50
N5 Shaquille O'Neal .75 2.00
N6 Shareef Abdur-Rahim .25 .60
N7 Jason Williams .40 1.00
N8 Kobe Bryant 1.50 4.00
N9 Grant Hill .40 1.00
N10 Antoine Walker .30 .75
N11 Stephon Marbury .25 .60
N12 Antonio McDyess .25 .60
N13 Jason Kidd .50 1.25
N14 Keith Van Horn .25 .60
N15 Karl Malone .40 1.00

1999-00 Upper Deck HoloGrFX NBA Shoetime

Randomly inserted in packs at one in 431, this 19-card set features pieces of game-used shoes by today's top NBA players. Card backs are numbered by the player's initials.
AIS Allen Iverson 20.00 50.00
BRS Bryon Russell 6.00 15.00
CBS Charles Barkley 20.00 50.00
CWS Chris Webber 10.00 25.00
DMS Dikembe Mutombo 10.00 25.00
DRS David Robinson 20.00 50.00
GHS Grant Hill 15.00 40.00
GPS Gary Payton 15.00 40.00
JKS Jason Kidd 15.00 40.00
JMS Jamal Mashburn 8.00 20.00
JSS John Stockton 12.00 30.00
KBS Kobe Bryant 50.00 125.00
KMA Karl Malone AU/32 200.00 400.00
KMS Karl Malone 12.00 30.00
MJA Michael Jordan AU/23 2500.00 4000.00
MJS Michael Jordan 80.00 200.00
PES Patrick Ewing 12.00 30.00
SMS Stephon Marbury 8.00 20.00
SOS Shaquille O'Neal 25.00 60.00
SPS Scottie Pippen 20.00 50.00
THS Tim Hardaway 10.00 25.00

1999-00 Upper Deck HoloGrFX UD Authentics

Randomly inserted in packs at one in 431, this 21-card set autographs from 21 of the brightest stars in the NBA. Card backs carry the player's initials.
AJ Antawn Jamison 6.00 15.00
BD Baron Davis 12.00 30.00
BG Brian Grant 4.00 10.00
CM Corey Maggette 8.00 20.00
DA Darrell Armstrong 4.00 10.00
JO Michael Jordan 2000.00 3000.00
JS Jerry Stackhouse 6.00 15.00
JT Jason Terry 10.00 25.00
LH Larry Hughes 8.00 20.00
MB Mike Bibby 6.00 15.00
MF Michael Finley 8.00 20.00
MK Mark Jackson 5.00 12.00
MT Maurice Taylor 4.00 10.00
RD Richard Hamilton 10.00 25.00
RH Wally Szczerbiak 8.00 20.00
RL Raef LaFrentz 4.00 10.00
RT Robert Traylor 4.00 10.00
SF Steve Francis 10.00 25.00
SM Sam Mack 4.00 10.00
TG Tom Gugliotta 4.00 10.00
SHM Shawn Marion 10.00 25.00

1993-94 Upper Deck Holojams

This set of 36 standard-size "Lithogram" cards features Upper Deck's picks for the NBA's best slam-dunkers. The boxed set, which was available only at hobby stores at a suggested price of 24.95, includes one player from each NBA team (1-27) plus nine rookies (28-36). A mail-in card for a storage album for the set was included. The checklist card carried the production number out of a total 127,800 sets produced. The borderless fronts feature two pictures of the player, a foreground photo in full-color lithography and a second holographic photo. Cards of the rookies feature a single photo, with the player in full-color and the background printed as a hologram. The player's name and position, along with the Holojam logo, are printed near the bottom. The multicolored back features a small closeup of the player, along with career highlights. The cards are numbered on the back with an "H" prefix.
COMP. FACT SET (38) 10.00 25.00
H1 Dominique Wilkins .20 .50
H2 Dee Brown .08 .25
H3 Alonzo Mourning .40 1.00
H4 Michael Jordan 4.00 10.00
H5 Brad Daugherty .08 .25
H6 Jim Jackson .08 .25
H7 Dikembe Mutombo .08 .25
H8 Terry Mills .08 .25
H9 Billy Owens .08 .25
H10 Hakeem Olajuwon .50 1.25
H11 Reggie Miller .15 .40
H12 Ron Harper .08 .25
H13 James Worthy .15 .40
H14 Harold Miner .08 .25
H15 Blue Edwards .08 .25
H16 Doug West .08 .25
H17 Derrick Coleman .08 .25
H18 Patrick Ewing .20 .50
H19 Shaquille O'Neal 2.00 5.00
H20 Clarence Weatherspoon .08 .25
H21 Charles Barkley .50 1.25
H22 Clyde Drexler .20 .50
H23 Walt Williams .08 .25
H24 David Robinson .50 1.25
H25 Shawn Kemp .40 1.00
H26 Karl Malone .75 2.00
H27 Tom Gugliotta .15 .40
H28 Chris Webber 2.50 6.00
H29 Shawn Bradley .15 .40
H30 Anfernee Hardaway 2.00 5.00
H31 Jamal Mashburn .50 1.25
H32 Isaiah Rider .50 1.25
H33 Rodney Rogers .08 .25
H34 Lindsey Hunter .08 .25
H35 Doug Edwards .08 .25
H36 George Lynch .08 .25
NNO Checklist .08 .25
NNO Album mail-in card .08 .25

1997 Upper Deck Holojams

Singles from this 20-card set were available in an Upper Deck re-pack at Wal-Mart stores towards the end of Summer 1997. A single gold Holojam was issued (visible from inside the packaging) along with two 1996-97 Collector's Choice Series 2 retail packs and two 1996-97 Upper Deck Series 2 retail packs for $9.97. The card fronts contain full bleed holographic in-action player images, and a small color photo of the player. The right side of the card bears the words "Holojam" and "ninety-seven" along with an Upper Deck logo, the player's name, team name, and team logo. The backs contain two more photos and a short description of the player.
COMPLETE SET (20) 125.00 250.00
1 Michael Jordan 40.00 100.00
2 Juwan Howard 2.50 6.00
3 Shaquille O'Neal 8.00 20.00
4 Kevin Garnett 6.00 15.00
5 Allen Iverson 10.00 25.00
6 Glen Rice 3.00 8.00
7 Hakeem Olajuwon 4.00 10.00
8 Patrick Ewing 4.00 10.00
9 Karl Malone 4.00 10.00
10 Reggie Miller 4.00 10.00
11 Shawn Kemp 3.00 8.00
12 Alonzo Mourning 4.00 10.00
13 Grant Hill 5.00 12.00
14 Kobe Bryant 40.00 100.00
15 Stephon Marbury 6.00 15.00
16 Vin Baker 2.50 6.00
17 Latrell Sprewell 3.00 8.00
18 Scottie Pippen 5.00 12.00
19 Shareef Abdur-Rahim 5.00 12.00
20 Anfernee Hardaway 5.00 12.00

2001-02 Upper Deck Honor Roll

Released in late march of 2002, this 130-card set us divided up into 90 veteran cards and 40 rookie cards. Base cards have colored backgrounds to match the featured player's jersey and silver foil highlights. Full color player photos are centered with a semi-circle black and white background. The rookie cards have the same design with a gold background, gold foil highlights, and the word "rookie" centered at the bottom. The rookie print runs are broken down as follows: card numbers 91-120 are sequentially numbered to 2499, and card numbers 121-130 are sequentially numbered to 1000. Honor Roll was packaged in 24-pack boxes where each pack contained five cards and carried a suggested retail price of $2.99.
COMPLETE SET (130) 125.00 250.00
COMP.SET w/o SP's (90) 12.50 30.00
1 Shareef Abdur-Rahim .25 .60
2 Jason Terry .30 .75
3 Dion Glover .20 .50
4 Paul Pierce .40 1.00
5 Antoine Walker .25 .60
6 Kenny Anderson .25 .60
7 Baron Davis .30 .75
8 Jamal Mashburn .25 .60
9 David Wesley .20 .50
10 Ron Mercer .20 .50
11 Brad Miller .30 .75
12 Andre Miller .25 .60
13 Lamond Murray .20 .50
14 Chris Mihm .20 .50
15 Michael Finley .30 .75
16 Dirk Nowitzki .50 1.25
17 Steve Nash .50 1.25
18 Juwan Howard .25 .60
19 Nick Van Exel .25 .60
20 Raef LaFrentz .25 .60
21 Antonio McDyess .25 .60
22 James Posey .25 .60
23 Jerry Stackhouse .25 .60
24 Clifford Robinson .20 .50
25 Ben Wallace .30 .75
26 Antawn Jamison .30 .75
27 Larry Hughes .25 .60
28 Steve Francis .30 .75
29 Cuttino Mobley .25 .60
30 Glen Rice .25 .60
31 Reggie Miller .30 .75
32 Jalen Rose .30 .75
33 Jermaine O'Neal .30 .75
34 Darius Miles .30 .75
35 Elton Brand .30 .75
36 Lamar Odom .30 .75
37 Corey Maggette .25 .60
38 Kobe Bryant 1.50 4.00
39 Shaquille O'Neal .75 2.00
40 Rick Fox .25 .60
41 Lindsey Hunter .20 .50
42 Stromile Swift .20 .50
43 Jason Williams .25 .60
44 Alonzo Mourning .40 1.00
45 Eddie Jones .25 .60
46 Anthony Carter .25 .60
47 Brian Grant .20 .50
48 Ray Allen .30 .75
49 Glenn Robinson .25 .60
50 Sam Cassell .25 .60
51 Kevin Garnett .60 1.50
52 Terrell Brandon .20 .50
53 Wally Szczerbiak .25 .60
54 Joe Smith .25 .60
55 Jason Kidd .50 1.25
56 Kenyon Martin .30 .75
57 Allan Houston .25 .60
58 Latrell Sprewell .25 .60
59 Marcus Camby .25 .60
60 Mark Jackson .25 .60
61 Tracy McGrady .50 1.25
62 Grant Hill .40 1.00
63 Mike Miller .30 .75
64 Allen Iverson .60 1.50
65 Dikembe Mutombo .30 .75
66 Aaron McKie .20 .50
67 Stephon Marbury .25 .60
68 Shawn Marion .30 .75
69 Anfernee Hardaway .50 1.25
70 Tom Gugliotta .20 .50
71 Rasheed Wallace .30 .75
72 Damon Stoudamire .25 .60
73 Derek Anderson .20 .50
74 Chris Webber .30 .75
75 Mike Bibby .30 .75
76 Peja Stojakovic .30 .75
77 Tim Duncan .60 1.50
78 David Robinson .50 1.25
79 Steve Smith .25 .60
80 Gary Payton .30 .75
81 Rashard Lewis .30 .75
82 Desmond Mason .25 .60
83 Vince Carter .50 1.25
84 Morris Peterson .20 .50
85 Antonio Davis .20 .50
86 Karl Malone .40 1.00
87 John Stockton .40 1.00
88 Donyell Marshall .20 .50
89 Richard Hamilton .25 .60
90 Michael Jordan 5.00 12.00
91 Andrei Kirilenko RC 2.50 6.00
92 Gilbert Arenas RC 1.50 4.00
93 Earl Watson RC 1.00 2.50
94 Terence Morris RC 1.00 2.50
95 Kedrick Brown RC 1.00 2.50
96 Zach Randolph RC 2.50 6.00
97 Joe Johnson RC 2.50 6.00
98 Brandon Armstrong RC 1.00 2.50
99 DeSagana Diop RC 1.00 2.50
100 Joseph Forte RC 1.00 2.50
101 Brendan Haywood RC 1.25 3.00
102 Samuel Dalembert RC 1.25 3.00
103 Jason Collins RC 1.00 2.50
104 Michael Bradley RC 1.00 2.50
105 Gerald Wallace RC 1.50 4.00
106 Tierre Brown RC 1.00 2.50
107 Troy Murphy RC 1.50 4.00
108 Alton Ford RC 1.00 2.50
109 Vladimir Radmanovic RC 1.00 2.50
110 Ruben Boumtje-Boumtje RC 1.00 2.50
111 Bobby Simmons RC 1.00 2.50
112 Oscar Torres RC 1.00 2.50
113 Jeryl Sasser RC 1.00 2.50
114 Loren Woods RC 1.00 2.50
115 Shane Battier RC 2.00 5.00
116 Jamison Brewer RC 1.00 2.50
117 Richard Jefferson RC 2.00 5.00
118 Pau Gasol RC 3.00 8.00
119 Damone Brown RC 1.00 2.50
120 Rodney White RC 1.00 2.50
121 Kwame Brown JSY RC 6.00 15.00
Kevin Garnett JSY
122 Tyson Chandler JSY RC 6.00 15.00
Darius Miles JSY
123 Eddy Curry JSY RC 8.00 20.00
Karl Malone JSY
124 Jason Richardson JSY RC 10.00 25.00
Kobe Bryant JSY
125 Tony Parker JSY RC 12.50 30.00
Jason Kidd JSY
126 Eddie Griffin JSY RC 5.00 12.00
Anfernee Hardaway JSY
127 Kirk Haston JSY RC 4.00 10.00
Jamal Mashburn JSY
128 Jamaal Tinsley JSY RC 4.00 10.00
Andre Miller JSY
129 Trenton Hassell JSY RC 4.00 10.00
Marcus Fizer JSY
130 Steven Hunter JSY RC 6.00 15.00
Tracy McGrady JSY

2001-02 Upper Deck Honor Roll All-NBA Authentic Jerseys

Seeded in packs at the rate of one in 88, this 19-card set features a horizontal design with a full color player action photo on the right, and a swatch of a game jersey on the left. The photo and jersey are centered on the card by two silver stripes outside of which are white borders with the brand name, Honor Roll, and the set name running from top to bottom.
1 Kobe Bryant 20.00 50.00
2 Allen Iverson 8.00 20.00
3 Tracy McGrady 6.00 15.00
4 Andre Miller 3.00 8.00
5 Darius Miles 2.50 6.00
6 Baron Davis 4.00 10.00
7 Kevin Garnett 8.00 20.00
8 John Stockton 5.00 12.00
9 Ron Mercer 2.50 6.00
10 Shareef Abdur-Rahim 3.00 8.00
11 Dikembe Mutombo 4.00 10.00
12 Lamar Odom 4.00 10.00
13 Ray Allen 4.00 10.00
14 Mike Miller 4.00 10.00
15 Marcus Fizer 2.50 6.00
16 Toni Kukoc 3.00 8.00
17 Stephon Marbury 3.00 8.00
18 Jason Kidd 6.00 15.00
19 Karl Malone 5.00 12.00

2001-02 Upper Deck Honor Roll All-NBA Authentics Jerseys Combos

Randomly seeded in packs at the rate of one in 240, this nine card set utilizes the same base design as the single jersey version with two players and two swatches of jersey.
1 Kobe Bryant 25.00 60.00
Kevin Garnett
2 Kobe Bryant 30.00 80.00
Allen on
3 Baron Davis 5.00 12.00
Andre Miller
4 Jason Kidd 8.00 20.00
Kenyon Martin
5 Karl Malone 10.00 25.00
John Stockton
6 Elton Brand 6.00 15.00
Kevin Garnett
7 Grant Hill 5.00 12.00
Mike Miller
8 Stephon Marbury 5.00 12.00
Shawn Marion
9 Shareef Abdur-Rahim 5.00 12.00
Jason Terry

2001-02 Upper Deck Honor Roll Fab Five All-Stars

Randomly inserted in packs at the rate of one in 24, this 10-card set features color player photos set against a red background with the bottom third of the card containing a stripe with the player's name and team name. The bottom of the card is in white, and and has the set names in silver foil. All the Fab Five insert sets share the same design.
COMPLETE SET (10) 15.00 30.00
1 Tim Duncan 1.50 4.00
2 Chris Webber .75 2.00
3 Kevin Garnett 1.50 4.00
4 Kobe Bryant 4.00 10.00
5 Shaquille O'Neal 2.00 5.00
6 Vince Carter 1.25 3.00
7 Allen Iverson 1.50 4.00
8 Tracy McGrady 1.25 3.00
9 Latrell Sprewell .60 1.50
10 Michael Jordan 6.00 15.00

2001-02 Upper Deck Honor Roll Fab Five Rookies

Randomly inserted in packs at the rate of one in 24, this 10-card set shares the same set design as the Fab Five All-Stars set with gold backgrounds instead of red.
COMPLETE SET (10) 10.00 25.00
1 Tony Parker 3.00 8.00
2 Jamaal Tinsley 1.00 2.50
3 Pau Gasol 2.50 6.00
4 Jason Richardson 1.50 4.00
5 Kwame Brown .75 2.00
6 Shane Battier 1.50 4.00
7 Eddie Griffin .75 2.00
8 Eddy Curry 1.25 3.00
9 Andrei Kirilenko 2.00 5.00
10 Joe Johnson 2.00 5.00

2001-02 Upper Deck Honor Roll Fab Five Scorers

Randomly inserted in packs at the rate of one in 24, this 10-card set shares the same set design as the Fab Five All-Stars set with gold backgrounds instead of red.
COMPLETE SET (10) 15.00 30.00
1 Michael Jordan 6.00 15.00
2 Kobe Bryant 4.00 10.00
3 Vince Carter 1.25 3.00
4 Shaquille O'Neal 2.00 5.00
5 Dirk Nowitzki 1.25 3.00
6 Tim Duncan 1.50 4.00
7 Kevin Garnett 1.50 4.00
8 Paul Pierce 1.00 2.50
9 Shareef Abdur-Rahim .60 1.50
10 Jerry Stackhouse .60 1.50

2001-02 Upper Deck Honor Roll Fab Floor Autographs

Seeded in packs at the rate of one in 480, this eight card set features full color player action photos on the right side of the card, and an oval swatch of floor on the left containing authentic player autographs. The card backgrounds are gold and cards are highlighted with gold foil.
1 Kobe Bryant 125.00 250.00
2 Michael Jordan 300.00 600.00
3 Kevin Garnett 40.00 80.00
4 Wally Szczerbiak 8.00 20.00
5 Darius Miles 8.00 20.00
6 Antoine Walker 8.00 20.00
7 Andre Miller 8.00 20.00
8 Jason Kidd 25.00 60.00

2001-02 Upper Deck Honor Roll Fab Floor Duos

Randomly seeded in packs at the rate of one in 96, this 17-card set features a horizontal card design with players on both the left and right side of the card and circular swatches of NBA court in the middle. Each swatch is engraved with the respective player's team logo.
1 Kobe Bryant 40.00 100.00
Michael Jordan
2 Kobe Bryant 15.00 30.00
Kevin Garnett
3 Antonio McDyess 4.00 10.00
Shawn Marion
4 Jason Terry 4.00 10.00
DerMarr Johnson
5 Kevin Garnett 5.00 12.00
Rashard Lewis
6 Kevin Garnett 5.00 12.00
Terrell Brandon
7 Kevin Garnett 5.00 12.00
Darius Miles
8 Stephon Marbury 4.00 10.00
Shawn Marion
9 Michael Finley 6.00 15.00
Dirk Nowitzki
10 Antoine Walker 6.00 15.00
Paul Pierce
11 Rasheed Wallace 4.00 10.00
Derek Anderson
12 Ray Allen 4.00 10.00
Glenn Robinson
13 Jerry Stackhouse 4.00 10.00
Rasheed Wallace
14 Latrell Sprewell 4.00 10.00
Allan Houston
15 David Robinson 6.00 15.00
Dikembe Mutombo
16 Baron Davis 4.00 10.00
Jamal Mashburn
17 Gary Payton 4.00 10.00
Desmond Mason

2001-02 Upper Deck Honor Roll Fab Floor Triples

Randomly inserted in packs at the rate of one in 240, this five card set features three players and three swatches of game used court. Each swatch of court is engraved with the featured player's team logo.
1 Kobe Bryant 60.00 150.00
Kevin Garnett
Michael Jordan
2 Kobe Bryant 15.00 30.00
Kevin Garnett
Kenyon Martin
3 Kevin Garnett 6.00 15.00
Wally Szczerbiak
Terrell Brandon
4 Glenn Robinson 6.00 15.00
Ray Allen
Tim Thomas
5 Reggie Miller 6.00 15.00
Jermaine O'Neal
Johnathon Bender

2002-03 Upper Deck Honor Roll

This 135-card standard-size set was issued in five-card packs which were packaged 24 packs to a box. Cards numbered 1 through 90 feature veterans. Cards card 91 through 105 feature rookie cards along with a game-used jersey swatch and those cards were numbered to a stated print run of 499 serial numbered sets. Cards numbered 106 through 135 feature other rookie cards and those cards were issued to a stated print run of 1999 serial numbered sets.
COMP.SET w/o SP's (90) 12.50 30.00
1 Glenn Robinson .25 .60
2 Shareef Abdur-Rahim .25 .60
3 Jason Terry .25 .60
4 Paul Pierce .40 1.00
5 Antoine Walker .25 .60
6 Tony Delk .20 .50
7 Jalen Rose .25 .60
8 Tyson Chandler .25 .60
9 Eddy Curry .25 .60
10 Darius Miles .20 .50
11 Zydrunas Ilgauskas .25 .60
12 Ricky Davis .25 .60
13 Dirk Nowitzki .50 1.25
14 Michael Finley .30 .75
15 Steve Nash .40 1.00
16 Raef LaFrentz .20 .50
17 Eduardo Najera .20 .50
18 Rodney White .25 .60
19 Juwan Howard .25 .60
20 Chris Whitney .20 .50
21 Ben Wallace .30 .75
22 Richard Hamilton .25 .60
23 Chauncey Billups .30 .75
24 Chucky Atkins .20 .50
25 Jason Richardson .30 .75
26 Antawn Jamison .30 .75
27 Gilbert Arenas .30 .75
28 Steve Francis .30 .75
29 Cuttino Mobley .25 .60
30 Jermaine O'Neal .30 .75
31 Reggie Miller .30 .75
32 Jamaal Tinsley .25 .60
33 Andre Miller .25 .60
34 Elton Brand .30 .75
35 Quentin Richardson .25 .60
36 Shaquille O'Neal .75 2.00
37 Kobe Bryant 1.50 4.00
38 Robert Horry .25 .60
39 Shane Battier .30 .75
40 Pau Gasol .40 1.00
41 Stromile Swift .20 .50
42 Eddie Jones .25 .60
43 Brian Grant .20 .50
44 Malik Allen .20 .50
45 Ray Allen .30 .75
46 Tim Thomas .20 .50
47 Kevin Garnett .60 1.50
48 Wally Szczerbiak .25 .60
49 Jason Kidd .50 1.25
50 Kenyon Martin .30 .75
51 Richard Jefferson .30 .75
52 Baron Davis .30 .75
53 Jamal Mashburn .25 .60
54 David Wesley .20 .50
55 P.J. Brown .20 .50
56 Allan Houston .25 .60
57 Latrell Sprewell .25 .60
58 Kurt Thomas .25 .60
59 Tracy McGrady .50 1.25
60 Grant Hill .40 1.00
61 Mike Miller .30 .75
62 Allen Iverson .50 1.25
63 Keith Van Horn .30 .75
64 Aaron McKie .20 .50
65 Shawn Marion .30 .75
66 Stephon Marbury .25 .60
67 Rasheed Wallace .30 .75
68 Derek Anderson .20 .50
69 Bonzi Wells .20 .50
70 Mike Bibby .30 .75
71 Chris Webber .30 .75
72 Peja Stojakovic .30 .75
73 Hedo Turkoglu .30 .75
74 Tim Duncan .60 1.50
75 David Robinson .50 1.25
76 Tony Parker .40 1.00
77 Gary Payton .30 .75
78 Rashard Lewis .30 .75
79 Brent Barry .20 .50
80 Desmond Mason .20 .50
81 Vince Carter .50 1.25
82 Antonio Davis .20 .50
83 Morris Peterson .20 .50
84 John Stockton .40 1.00
85 Karl Malone .40 1.00
86 Andrei Kirilenko .30 .75
87 Matt Harpring .25 .60
88 Jerry Stackhouse .25 .60
89 Kwame Brown .20 .50
90 Michael Jordan 2.50 6.00
91 Ryan Humphrey JSY RC 3.00 8.00
92 Juan Dixon JSY RC 4.00 10.00
93 Fred Jones JSY RC 3.00 8.00
94 Marcus Haislip JSY RC 3.00 8.00
95 Melvin Ely JSY RC 3.00 8.00
96 Jared Jeffries JSY RC 3.00 8.00
97 Caron Butler JSY RC 5.00 12.00
98 Amare Stoudemire JSY RC 8.00 20.00
99 Chris Wilcox JSY RC 3.00 8.00
100 Nene Hilario JSY RC 4.00 10.00
101 Dajuan Wagner JSY RC 3.00 8.00
102 Nikoloz Tskitishvili JSY RC 3.00 8.00
103 Drew Gooden JSY RC 5.00 12.00
104 Jay Williams JSY RC 4.00 10.00
105 Yao Ming JSY RC 10.00 25.00
106 Mike Dunleavy RC 2.00 5.00
107 Bostjan Nachbar RC 1.50 4.00
108 Jiri Welsch RC 1.50 4.00
109 Rasual Butler RC 1.50 4.
110 Kareem Rush RC 1.50 4.
111 Qyntel Woods RC 1.50 4.
112 Casey Jacobsen RC 1.50 4.
113 Tayshaun Prince RC 2.00 5.
114 Frank Williams RC 1.50 4.
115 John Salmons RC 2.00 5.
116 Chris Jefferies RC 1.50 4.
117 Dan Dickau RC 1.50 4.
118 Juaquin Hawkins RC 1.50 4.
119 Roger Mason RC 1.50 4.
120 Robert Archibald RC 1.50 4.(
121 Vincent Yarbrough RC 1.50 4.(
122 Dan Gadzuric RC 1.50 4.(
123 Carlos Boozer RC 3.00 8.
124 Tito Maddox RC 1.50 4.
125 Gordan Giricek RC 1.50 4.(
126 Ronald Murray RC 1.50 4.
127 Lonny Baxter RC 1.50 4.(
128 Pat Burke RC 1.50 4.(
129 Manu Ginobili RC 4.00 10.(
130 Predrag Savovic RC 1.50 4.(
131 Marko Jaric 1.50 4.(
132 Efthimios Rentzias RC 1.50 4.(
133 J.R. Bremer RC 1.50 4.(
134 Igor Rakocevic RC 1.50 4.(
135 Tamar Slay RC 1.50 4.(

2002-03 Upper Deck Honor Roll Award Performances

Issued at a stated rate of one in 12, this 14 card set features players who are in competition for major NBA awards.
COMPLETE SET (14) 10.00 25.0
AP1 Kobe Bryant 3.00 8.0
AP2 Tim Duncan 1.25 3.0
AP3 Eddie Jones .50 1.2
AP4 Steve Francis .60 1.5
AP5 Shareef Abdur-Rahim .50 1.2
AP6 Rasheed Wallace .60 1.5
AP7 Shaquille O'Neal 1.50 4.0
AP8 Rashard Lewis .60 1.5
AP9 Ray Allen .60 1.5
AP10 Pau Gasol .75 2.0
AP11 Elton Brand .60 1.5
AP12 Ben Wallace .60 1.5
AP13 Andre Miller .50 1.2
AP14 Michael Jordan 5.00 12.0

2002-03 Upper Deck Honor Roll Dual Jerseys

Issued at a stated rate of one in 240, this 12 card set featurs game-used jersey cards from two players (usually from the same team) with something in common.
AWPP Antoine Walker 6.00 15.00
Paul Pierce
BDJM Baron Davis 6.00 15.00
Jamal Mashburn
CWMB Chris Webber 6.00 15.00
Mike Bibby
DNSN Dirk Nowitzki 8.00 20.00
Steve Nash
JKKM Jason Kidd 8.00 20.00
Kenyon Martin
JRAJ Jason Richardson 6.00 15.00
Antawn Jamison
KBAI Kobe Bryant 15.00 40.00
Allen Iverson
KMJS Karl Malone 10.00 25.00
John Stockton
MJKB Michael Jordan SP 50.00 120.00
Kobe Bryant
SMSM Stephon Marbury 6.00 15.00
Shawn Marion
TMKG Tracy McGrady 12.50 30.00
Kevin Garnett
YMJW Yao Ming 10.00 25.00
Jay Williams

2002-03 Upper Deck Honor Roll Dual Warm-ups

Issued at a stated rate of one in 48, these 16 cards feature two swatches of NBA "warm-up" material on them.
AWPP Antoine Walker 5.00 12.00
Paul Pierce
BDJM Baron Davis 4.00 10.00
Jamal Mashburn
CWMB Chris Webber 4.00 10.00
Mike Bibby
DNSN Dirk Nowitzki 5.00 12.00
Steve Nash

DRTP David Robinson 6.00 15.00
Tony Parker
EBAM Elton Brand 4.00 10.00
Andre Miller
GPRL Gary Payton 4.00 10.00
Rashard Lewis
JKKM Jason Kidd 5.00 12.00
Kenyon Martin
JRAJ Jason Richardson 4.00 10.00
Antawn Jamison
KBKG Kobe Bryant 15.00 40.00
Kevin Garnett
KGWS Kevin Garnett 5.00 12.00
Wally Szczerbiak
KMJS Karl Malone 5.00 12.00
John Stockton
MJKB Michael Jordan SP 50.00 120.00
Kobe Bryant
SBSS Shane Battier 4.00 10.00
Stromile Swift
SMSM Stephon Marbury 4.00 10.00
Shawn Marion
TMMM Tracy McGrady 5.00 12.00
Mike Miller

2002-03 Upper Deck Honor Roll Popular Acclaim

Issued at a stated rate of one in 12, these 14 cards feature some of the most popular NBA players.

COMPLETE SET (14) 12.50 30.00
PA1 Michael Jordan 5.00 12.00
PA2 Shaquille O'Neal 1.50 4.00
PA3 Shane Battier .60 1.50
PA4 Michael Finley .60 1.50
PA5 Vince Carter 1.00 2.50
PA6 Darius Miles .40 1.00
PA7 Peja Stojakovic .60 1.50
PA8 Kobe Bryant 3.00 8.00
PA9 Tracy McGrady 2.00 5.00
PA10 Jalen Rose .50 1.25
PA11 Allen Iverson 1.00 2.50
PA12 Jay Williams .75 2.00
PA13 Drew Gooden 1.00 2.50
PA14 Shawn Marion .60 1.50

2002-03 Upper Deck Honor Roll Principals Autograph Jerseys

Issued at a stated rate of one in 480, these 20 cards feature not only game-used jersey swatches but authentic autographs of the featured players. Some of the players were issued in shorter supply and where noted we have put the announced print run next to the player's name. In addition, some players did not return their signed cards in time for the promotion and those cards were issued as exchange cards.

AWAJ Antoine Walker 15.00 40.00
CJAJ Chris Jefferies 10.00 25.00
DAAJ Dan Gadzuric 10.00 25.00
DGAJ Drew Gooden 20.00 50.00
DSAJ DeShawn Stevenson 10.00 25.00
JKAJ Jason Kidd 40.00 100.00
JWAJ Jay Williams 12.50 30.00
KGAJ0 Kevin Garnett/21 100.00 200.00
KMAJ Kenyon Martin 12.50 30.00
MFAJ Marcus Fizer 10.00 25.00
MJAJ Michael Jordan/23 400.00 800.00
MMAJ Mike Miller 10.00 25.00
PPAJ0 Paul Pierce 25.00 60.00
PSAJ Peja Stojakovic 25.00 60.00
SMAJ Shawn Marion 15.00 40.00
TPAJ Tayshaun Prince 15.00 40.00

2002-03 Upper Deck Honor Roll Signature Class

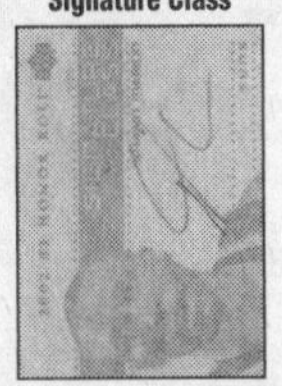

Issued at a stated rate of one in 480, these 12 cards feature authentic autographs from leading NBA players. A few players signed a very limited number of cards and we have put the announced print run next to the player's name in our checklist. In addition, Antoine Walker and Michael Jordan did not return their cards in time for inclusion in this product and those cards were issued as exchange cards.

AWS Antoine Walker 10.00 25.00
ETS Etan Thomas 6.00 15.00
JKS Jason Kidd 30.00 80.00
JMS Jerome Moiso 6.00 15.00
KBS Kobe Bryant/25 150.00 300.00
KMS Kenyon Martin 10.00 25.00
MFS Marcus Fizer 6.00 15.00
MJS Michael Jordan/23 400.00 800.00
MMS Mike Miller 6.00 15.00
SMS Shawn Marion 12.50 30.00

2002-03 Upper Deck Honor Roll Signature Class Duals

Randomly inserted into packs, these six cards feature signatured from two leading NBA players. These cards were issued to a stated print run of 25 serial numbered sets and no pricing is available due to market scarcity.

KBKG Kobe Bryant 200.00 400.00
Kevin Garnett
MJKB Michael Jordan 600.00 1200.00
Kobe Bryant
PPAW Paul Pierce 75.00 150.00
Antoine Walker
YMJW Yao Ming 100.00 200.00
Jay Williams

2002-03 Upper Deck Honor Roll Superstar Tributes

Issued at a stated rate of one in 24, these seven cards feature tributes to seven of the best NBA players.

COMPLETE SET (7) 10.00 25.00
ST1 Kobe Bryant 4.00 10.00
ST2 Michael Jordan 6.00 15.00
ST3 Steve Francis .75 2.00
ST4 Vince Carter 1.25 3.00
ST5 Allen Iverson 1.25 3.00
ST6 Tim Duncan 1.50 4.00
ST7 Shaquille O'Neal 2.00 5.00

2002-03 Upper Deck Honor Roll Tremendous Talents

Issued at a stated rate of one in 24, these seven cards feature players who have shown more talent than many of their NBA contemporaries during their career.

COMPLETE SET (7) 10.00 25.00
TT1 Jay Williams 1.00 2.50
TT2 Tim Duncan 1.50 4.00
TT3 Kobe Bryant 4.00 10.00
TT4 Yao Ming 2.50 6.00
TT5 Mike Bibby .75 2.00
TT6 Vince Carter 1.25 3.00
TT7 Michael Jordan 6.00 15.00

2002-03 Upper Deck Honor Roll Triple Warm-ups

Issued at a stated rate of one in 120, these eight cards feature three "warm-up" swatches from NBA players.

1 Andre Miller 8.00 20.00
Elton Brand
Michael Olowokandi
2 Chris Webber 25.00 60.00
Kobe Bryant
Paul Pierce *
3 Dirk Nowitzki 15.00 40.00
Michael Finley
Steve Nash
4 Jamal Mashburn 8.00 20.00
Baron Davis
David Wesley
5 John Stockton 8.00 20.00
Karl Malone
Andrei Kirilenko
6 Kenyon Martin 8.00 20.00
Jason Kidd
Richard Jefferson
7 Tracy McGrady 15.00 40.00
Kobe Bryant
Jason Richardson *
8 Wally Szczerbiak 8.00 20.00
Joe Smith
Terrell Brandon

2003-04 Upper Deck Honor Roll

Released in January 2004, Honor Roll boasts a 123-card set divided up into 90 veteran player cards, 15 rookie cards sequentially numbered to 2999 (numbers 91-105) and 24 Rookie Jersey cards sequentially numbered to 499. Base cards feature a split design with color on the right and a centered player photo. Please note that the rookie jerseys are event worn, not game worn. Honor Roll was packaged in 24-pack boxes where packs contained five cards and carried a suggested retail price of $2.99.

COMP.SET w/o SP's (90) 15.00 40.00
1 Shareef Abdur-Rahim .25 .60
2 Dan Dickau .20 .50
3 Jason Terry .25 .60
4 Raef LaFrentz .20 .50
5 Vin Baker .20 .50
6 Paul Pierce .40 1.00
7 Antonio Davis .20 .50
8 Scottie Pippen .50 1.25
9 Jamal Crawford .25 .60
10 Dajuan Wagner .20 .50
11 Ricky Davis .25 .60
12 Darius Miles .20 .50
13 Dirk Nowitzki .50 1.25
14 Antoine Walker .30 .75
15 Steve Nash .40 1.00
16 Michael Finley .30 .75
17 Nikoloz Tskitishvili .20 .50
18 Andre Miller .25 .60
19 Nene .25 .60
20 Chauncey Billups .30 .75
21 Richard Hamilton .25 .60
22 Ben Wallace .30 .75
23 Clifford Robinson .20 .50
24 Jason Richardson .30 .75
25 Mike Dunleavy .25 .60
26 Yao Ming .60 1.50
27 Cuttino Mobley .25 .60
28 Steve Francis .30 .75
29 Jermaine O'Neal .30 .75
30 Reggie Miller .30 .75
31 Al Harrington .25 .60
32 Elton Brand .30 .75
33 Corey Maggette .25 .60
34 Quentin Richardson .25 .60
35 Kobe Bryant 1.50 4.00
36 Karl Malone .40 1.00
37 Gary Payton .30 .75
38 Shaquille O'Neal .75 2.00
39 Pau Gasol .30 .75
40 Jason Williams .25 .60
41 Mike Miller .30 .75
42 Lamar Odom .30 .75
43 Eddie Jones .25 .60
44 Caron Butler .30 .75
45 Michael Redd .30 .75
46 Desmond Mason .25 .60
47 Tim Thomas .20 .50
48 Latrell Sprewell .25 .60
49 Kevin Garnett .60 1.50
50 Wally Szczerbiak .25 .60
51 Richard Jefferson .30 .75
52 Kenyon Martin .30 .75
53 Jason Kidd .50 1.25
54 Jamal Mashburn .25 .60
55 Baron Davis .30 .75
56 Jamaal Magloire .20 .50
57 Allan Houston .25 .60
58 Antonio McDyess .25 .60
59 Keith Van Horn .25 .60
60 Grant Hill .40 1.00
61 Drew Gooden .25 .60
62 Tracy McGrady .40 1.00
63 Glenn Robinson .25 .60
64 Allen Iverson .50 1.25
65 Eric Snow .20 .50
66 Amare Stoudemire .50 1.25
67 Stephon Marbury .25 .60
68 Shawn Marion .30 .75
69 Derek Anderson .20 .50
70 Damon Stoudamire .25 .60
71 Rasheed Wallace .30 .75
72 Peja Stojakovic .30 .75
73 Chris Webber .30 .75
74 Mike Bibby .30 .75
75 Bobby Jackson .20 .50
76 Tony Parker .30 .75
77 Tim Duncan .50 1.25
78 Manu Ginobili .40 1.00
79 Vladimir Radmanovic .20 .50
80 Ray Allen .30 .75
81 Rashard Lewis .30 .75
82 Morris Peterson .20 .50
83 Vince Carter .50 1.25
84 Jalen Rose .25 .60
85 Andrei Kirilenko .30 .75
86 Matt Harpring .25 .60
87 Greg Ostertag .20 .50
88 Gilbert Arenas .30 .75
89 Larry Hughes .25 .60
90 Jerry Stackhouse .25 .60
91 Kirk Hinrich RC 2.00 5.00
92 T.J. Ford RC 2.00 5.00
93 Nick Collison RC 1.50 4.00
94 Kendrick Perkins RC 2.50 6.00
95 Leandro Barbosa RC 2.00 5.00
96 Josh Howard RC 1.50 4.00
97 Jason Kapono RC 1.50 4.00
98 Jerome Beasley RC 1.50 4.00
99 Travis Hansen RC 1.50 4.00
100 Steve Blake RC 2.00 5.00
101 Willie Green RC 1.50 4.00
102 Zaur Pachulia RC 1.50 4.00
103 Keith Bogans RC 1.50 4.00
104 Kyle Korver RC 2.00 5.00
105 Brandon Hunter RC 1.50 4.00
106 LeBron James JSY RC 40.00 100.00
107 Darko Milicic JSY RC 4.00 10.00
108 Carmelo Anthony JSY RC 10.00 25.00
109 Chris Bosh JSY RC 8.00 20.00
110 Dwyane Wade JSY RC 15.00 40.00
111 Chris Kaman JSY RC 5.00 12.00
112 Mike Sweetney JSY RC 4.00 10.00
113 Jarvis Hayes JSY RC 4.00 10.00
114 Mickael Pietrus JSY RC 4.00 10.00
115 Marcus Banks JSY RC 4.00 10.00
116 Luke Ridnour JSY RC 5.00 12.00
117 Reece Gaines JSY RC 4.00 10.00
118 Troy Bell JSY RC 4.00 10.00
119 Zarko Cabarkapa JSY RC 4.00 10.00
120 David West JSY RC 5.00 12.00
121 Aleksandar Pavlovic JSY RC 4.00 10.00
122 Dahntay Jones JSY RC 4.00 10.00
123 Boris Diaw JSY RC 5.00 12.00
124 Zoran Planinic JSY RC 4.00 10.00
125 Travis Outlaw JSY RC 5.00 12.00
126 Brian Cook JSY RC 4.00 10.00
127 Ndudi Ebi JSY RC 4.00 10.00
128 Maciej Lampe JSY RC 4.00 10.00
129 Slavko Vranes JSY RC 4.00 10.00
130 Luke Walton JSY RC 4.00 10.00

2003-04 Upper Deck Honor Roll Gold

Randomly seeded, this 108-card set parallels the base set enhanced with gold highlights and sequential numbering to 100 for cards 1-90 and numbering to 25 for the rookie players.

*GOLD 1-90: 4X TO 10X BASE HI
*GOLD 91-105 RCs: 2X TO 5X BASE HI

2003-04 Upper Deck Honor Roll Jersey Autographs Gold

*GOLD: 1X TO 2.5X BASE HI
PRINT RUN 25 SERIAL #'d SETS
106 LeBron James 600.00 1000.00
108 Carmelo Anthony 100.00 200.00
109 Chris Bosh 50.00 120.00
110 Dwyane Wade 250.00 500.00

2003-04 Upper Deck Honor Roll Award Performers

Randomly inserted at one in 12, this 14-card set features a horizontal design with the player on one side set to a circular background of the team's colors. A gold version of this set was also issued and those cards are sequentially numbered to 100.

COMPLETE SET (14) 10.00 25.00
*GOLD SINGLES: 2.5X TO 6X BASE HI
AP1 LeBron James 4.00 10.00
AP2 Peja Stojakovic .40 1.00
AP3 Yao Ming .75 2.00
AP4 Gilbert Arenas .40 1.00
AP5 Jermaine O'Neal .40 1.00
AP6 Amare Stoudemire .60 1.50
AP7 Kobe Bryant 2.00 5.00
AP8 Jason Kidd .60 1.50
AP9 Vince Carter .60 1.50
AP10 Shaquille O'Neal 1.00 2.50
AP11 Michael Jordan 3.00 8.00
AP12 Caron Butler .40 1.00
AP13 Ben Wallace .40 1.00
AP14 Elton Brand .40 1.00

2003-04 Upper Deck Honor Roll Dual Warm Ups

Inserted at one in 48, this 21-card set features a horizontal design with two player photos along the top and two swatches of warm up. A Gold version of this set was also issued and those cards are sequentially numbered to 100.

*GOLD SINGLES: .6X TO 1.5X BASE HI
1 Allen Iverson 5.00 12.00
Eric Snow
2 Andre Miller 4.00 10.00
Nene
3 Darko Milicic 4.00 10.00
Richard Hamilton
4 Caron Butler 8.00 20.00
Dwyane Wade
5 Eddy Curry 4.00 10.00
Tyson Chandler
6 Jason Kidd 4.00 10.00
Kenyon Martin
7 Baron Davis 4.00 10.00
Jamaal Magloire
8 Jamaal Tinsley 4.00 10.00
Jermaine O'Neal
9 Gilbert Arenas 4.00 10.00
Jason Richardson
10 Jason Terry 4.00 10.00
Shareef Abdur-Rahim
11 Kobe Bryant 12.50 30.00
Gary Payton
12 Kevin Garnett 5.00 12.00
Wally Szczerbiak
13 Karl Malone 5.00 12.00
Devean George
14 John Stockton 30.00 80.00
Michael Jordan
15 DaJuan Wagner 4.00 10.00
Darius Miles
16 Paul Pierce 4.00 10.00
Antoine Walker
17 Mike Bibby 4.00 10.00
Richard Jefferson
18 Dirk Nowitzki 5.00 12.00
Steve Nash
19 Tracy McGrady 5.00 12.00
Drew Gooden
20 Tim Duncan 5.00 12.00
Tony Parker
21 Chris Wilcox 4.00 10.00
Steve Francis

2003-04 Upper Deck Honor Roll Popular Acclaim

Inserted at one in 12, this 14-card set is vertically designed with a player photo on the right and a silver bar with the set name along the left. A gold version of this set was issued also, and those cards are sequentially numbered to 50.

COMPLETE SET (14) 8.00 20.00
*GOLD SINGLES: 2.5X TO 6X BASE HI
PA1 Kobe Bryant 2.00 5.00
PA2 Ray Allen .40 1.00
PA3 Shawn Marion .40 1.00
PA4 Steve Francis .40 1.00
PA5 Dajuan Wagner .25 .60
PA6 Steve Nash .50 1.25
PA7 LeBron James 5.00 12.00
PA8 Carmelo Anthony 1.00 2.50
PA9 Paul Pierce .50 1.25
PA10 Gary Payton .40 1.00
PA11 Richard Jefferson .40 1.00
PA12 Michael Jordan 3.00 8.00
PA13 Baron Davis .40 1.00
PA14 Shaquille O'Neal 1.00 2.50

2003-04 Upper Deck Honor Roll Principals

Randomly seeded at the rate of one in 480, this 21-card set features a horizontal design with both a player photo and a circular swatch of game used memorabilia.

BA Marcus Banks 8.00 20.00
CA Carmelo Anthony 60.00 150.00
CH Chris Bosh 30.00 80.00
CM Corey Maggette 8.00 20.00
DG Drew Gooden 8.00 20.00
DM Darko Milicic 10.00 25.00
DR David Robinson 40.00 100.00
DW Dajuan Wagner 8.00 20.00
GA Gilbert Arenas 10.00 25.00
JH Jarvis Hayes 8.00 20.00
JK Jason Kidd 25.00 60.00
JM Jerome Moiso 8.00 20.00
LJ LeBron James 400.00 800.00
MB Mike Bibby 12.50 30.00
MJ Michael Jordan/23 400.00 800.00
RJ Richard Jefferson 8.00 20.00
SF Steve Francis 10.00 25.00
TO Travis Outlaw 10.00 25.00
WA0 Dwyane Wade 100.00 200.00
YM Yao Ming 30.00 80.00

2003-04 Upper Deck Honor Roll Signature Class

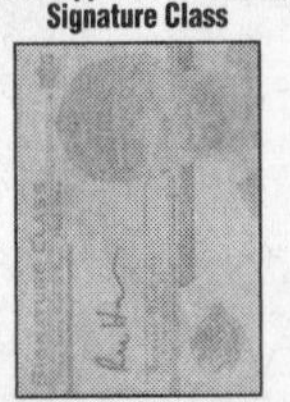

Inserted at one in 480, this 12-card set is horizontally designed with a black and white player portrait on the right and an autograph on the left. Dual signature versions featuring two players were also inserted. Dual cards are sequentially numbered to 15.

SC1 Jerome Moiso 8.00 20.00
SC2 Cuttino Mobley 8.00 20.00
SC3 Richard Hamilton 10.00 25.00
SC4 Andre Miller 8.00 20.00
SC5 Mickael Pietrus 8.00 20.00
SC6 Luke Ridnour 10.00 25.00
SC8 Jarvis Hayes 8.00 20.00
SC9 Ndudi Ebi 8.00 20.00
SC10 LeBron James 500.00 900.00
SC12 Kobe Bryant 150.00 300.00

2003-04 Upper Deck Honor Roll Superstar Tributes

Inserted at one in 24, this seven card set features a "framed" portrait photo of the player centered on a split background where to top of the card is white and the bottom matches the player's team colors. A gold version was inserted as well and these cards are sequentially numbered to five.

COMPLETE SET (7) 10.00 25.00
ST1 Michael Jordan 6.00 15.00
ST2 Dirk Nowitzki 1.25 3.00
ST3 LeBron James 8.00 20.00
ST4 Kobe Bryant 4.00 10.00
ST5 Kevin Garnett 1.50 4.00
ST6 Tracy McGrady 1.00 2.50
ST7 Carmelo Anthony 2.00 5.00

2003-04 Upper Deck Honor Roll Tremendous Talents

Inserted at one in 24, this seven card set places a full-color player action phot on the right and a silver top-to-bottom design on the left. A Gold version of the set was also produced and these cards are sequentially numbered to 25.

COMPLETE SET (7) 8.00 20.00
*GOLD: 3X TO 8X BASE HI
TT1 Tim Duncan 1.25 3.00
TT2 Shaquille O'Neal 2.00 5.00
TT3 Kobe Bryant 4.00 10.00
TT4 Allen Iverson 1.25 3.00
TT5 Vince Carter 1.25 3.00
TT6 Chris Webber .75 2.00
TT7 LeBron James 8.00 20.00

2003-04 Upper Deck Honor Roll Triple Warm Ups

Inserted in packs at the rate of one in 144, this 21-card set places three players and three swatches of warm up on the card front. A Gold version of the set was also produced and those cards are sequentially numbered to 25.

*GOLD: .75X TO 2X BASE HI
1 Allen Iverson 8.00 20.00
Aaron McKie
Eric Snow
2 Antawn Jamison 6.00 15.00
Gilbert Arenas
Jason Richardson
3 DaJuan Wagner 6.00 15.00
Carlos Boozer
Darius Miles
4 Dirk Nowitzki 10.00 25.00
Michael Finley
Steve Nash
5 Chris Wilcox 6.00 15.00
Elton Brand
Melvin Ely
6 Eddy Curry 6.00 15.00
Jalen Rose
Jay Williams
7 Kobe Bryant 25.00 60.00
Gary Payton
Karl Malone
8 Shareef Abdur-Rahim 6.00 15.00
Glenn Robinson
Jason Terry
9 Jason Kidd 8.00 20.00
Kenyon Martin
Richard Jefferson
10 Brendan Haywood 6.00 15.00
Larry Hughes
Jason Richardson
11 Allan Houston 6.00 15.00
Dikembe Mutombo
Slavko Vranes
12 Amare Stoudemire 8.00 20.00
Stephon Marbury
Shawn Marion
13 Michael Jordan 40.00 100.00
John Stockton
Kobe Bryant
14 Lamar Odom 6.00 15.00
Quentin Richardson
Corey Maggette
15 Mike Miller 6.00 15.00
Shane Battier
Pau Gasol
16 Gerald Wallace 6.00 15.00
Peja Stojakovic
Mike Bibby
17 Desmond Mason 6.00 15.00
Ray Allen
Joe Smith
18 Darko Milicic 6.00 15.00
Chauncey Billups
Richard Hamilton
19 Tim Duncan 12.50 30.00
Tony Parker
Radoslav Nesterovic
20 Kobe Bryant 15.00 40.00
Kevin Garnett
Tracy McGrady
21 Baron Davis 6.00 15.00
Stephon Marbury
Steve Francis

2012 Upper Deck Industry Summit Signature Icons Autographs

LAS VEGAS INDUSTRY SUMMIT EXCLUSIVE
LVLJ LeBron James/25

2001-02 Upper Deck Inspirations

Released in late June of 2002, Upper Deck Inspirations features a 140-card set divided up as follows: cards 1-90 showcase full color player action photos with an orange and black marble background. The left border of the card is a solid orange line, and the right border features orange and black non-embossed basketball texturing. The Upper Deck Inspirations logo appears in the lower left hand corner. Cards 91-106 contain pictures of both a rookie player and a veteran player and are sequentially numbered to 2249. These vertical-style cards have a green backdrop on the right side where a portrait style photo of the veteran player appears along with the corresponding name, while the left side of the card contains a full color action photo of the featured rookie. The rookie name appears along the left hand side of the card. Cards 107-109 feature the same card design as the previous numbers, but are enhanced with player autographs and are sequentially numbered to 275. Cards 104-106 contain veteran player autographs only, and cards 107-109 contain rookie player autographs only. Cards 110-116 once again features the same card design with both rookie and veteran autographs, and are sequentially numbered to 1149. Cards 117-124 have a blue background and showcase a portrait style head shot of both players, the veteran player on the right and the rookie player on the left. These cards feature rookie jerseys only, which are cut in the shape of the letter "R." Each card is sequentially numbered to 1500, and card number 118 is a short print, sequentially numbered to 525. Cards 125-140 feature the same design as the previous rookie jerseys, but have jersey swatches from both rookies and veterans. The rookie jerseys are once again cut in an "R" shape, while the veteran swatches are cut in an "S" shape. Card numbers 141T-180T feature draft picks from the 2002-03 NBA Draft in New York. These cards were originally issued as redemptions, and are sequentially numbered as follows: 141T-152T #'d to 2999, 153T-164T #'d to 2699, 165T to 176T #'d to 1999, and 177T to 182T #'d to 499. Upper Deck inspirations also marks the first draft redemption cards in basketball that were redeemable online at www.upperdeck.com.

COMP.SET w/o SP's (90) 15.00 40.00
1 Shareef Abdur-Rahim .25 .60
2 Jason Terry .30 .75
3 Dion Glover .20 .50
4 Antoine Walker .25 .60
5 Paul Pierce .40 1.00
6 Larry Bird 1.00 2.50
7 Baron Davis .30 .75
8 Jamal Mashburn .25 .60
9 David Wesley .20 .50
10 Elden Campbell .20 .50
11 Jalen Rose .25 .60
12 Marcus Fizer .20 .50
13 Andre Miller .25 .60
14 Lamond Murray .20 .50
15 Chris Mihm .20 .50
16 Dirk Nowitzki .50 1.25
17 Steve Nash .50 1.25
18 Michael Finley .30 .75
19 Nick Van Exel .25 .60
20 Raef LaFrentz .20 .50
21 Antonio McDyess .25 .60
22 Juwan Howard .25 .60
23 Tim Hardaway .30 .75
24 James Posey .20 .50
25 Jerry Stackhouse .25 .60
26 Ben Wallace .30 .75
27 Isiah Thomas .30 .75
28 Antawn Jamison .30 .75
29 Larry Hughes .25 .60
30 Steve Francis .30 .75
31 Moses Malone .30 .75
32 Reggie Miller .30 .75
33 Jermaine O'Neal .30 .75
34 Elton Brand .30 .75
35 Darius Miles .20 .50
36 Lamar Odom .30 .75
37 Quentin Richardson .25 .60
38 Kobe Bryant 1.50 4.00
39 Shaquille O'Neal .75 2.00
40 Derek Fisher .25 .60
41 Devean George .20 .50
42 Stromile Swift .20 .50
43 Jason Williams .25 .60
44 Alonzo Mourning .40 1.00
45 Eddie Jones .25 .60
46 Anthony Carter .20 .50
47 Ray Allen .30 .75
48 Sam Cassell .25 .60
49 Glenn Robinson .25 .60
50 Tim Thomas .20 .50
51 Oscar Robertson .40 1.00
52 Kevin Garnett .60 1.50
53 Wally Szczerbiak .25 .60
54 Terrell Brandon .20 .50
55 Chauncey Billups .30 .75
56 Jason Kidd .50 1.25
57 Kenyon Martin .30 .75
58 Latrell Sprewell .25 .60
59 Allan Houston .25 .60
60 Marcus Camby .25 .60
61 Kurt Thomas .20 .50
62 Grant Hill .40 1.00
63 Mike Miller .30 .75
64 Tracy McGrady .50 1.25
65 Allen Iverson .60 1.50
66 Julius Erving .60 1.50
67 Bobby Jones .30 .75
68 Stephon Marbury .25 .60
69 Shawn Marion .30 .75
70 Anfernee Hardaway .50 1.25
71 Rasheed Wallace .30 .75
72 Bill Walton .30 .75
73 Chris Webber .30 .75
74 Peja Stojakovic .30 .75
75 Mike Bibby .30 .75
76 Tim Duncan .60 1.50

77 David Robinson .50 1.25
78 George Gervin .30 .75
79 Gary Payton .30 .75
80 Rashard Lewis .30 .75
81 Desmond Mason .25 .60
82 Vince Carter .50 1.25
83 Morris Peterson .20 .50
84 Antonio Davis .20 .50
85 Hakeem Olajuwon .40 1.00
86 Karl Malone .40 1.00
87 John Stockton .40 1.00
88 Donyell Marshall .20 .50
89 Richard Hamilton .25 .60
90 Michael Jordan 4.00 10.00
91 Zeljko Rebraca RC 2.00 5.00
Shaquille O'Neal
92 Oscar Robertson 2.00 5.00
Oscar Torres RC
93 Reggie Miller 2.00 5.00
Jamison Brewer RC
94 Peja Stojakovic 2.00 5.00
Predrag Drobnjak RC
95 Mengke Bateer RC 2.00 5.00
Wang Zhi-Zhi
96 Jerry West 2.00 5.00
Willie Solomon RC
97 Tim Duncan 2.00 5.00
Malik Allen RC
98 Walt Frazier 2.00 5.00
Damone Brown RC
99 Shawn Marion 2.00 5.00
Alton Ford RC
100 Toni Kukoc 2.00 5.00
Antonis Fotsis RC
101 Bill Walton 5.00 12.00
Zach Randolph RC
102 Stephon Marbury 2.00 5.00
Joe Crispin RC
103 Wes Unseld 2.00 5.00
Bobby Simmons RC
104 Jason Kidd AU 12.50 30.00
Jamaal Tinsley RC
105 Kevin Garnett AU 20.00 50.00
Pau Gasol RC
106 Kobe Bryant AU 50.00 100.00
Shane Battier RC
107 Vince Carter 6.00 15.00
Jeff Trepagnier AU RC
108 Julius Erving 8.00 20.00
Kwame Brown AU RC
109 Tim Duncan 8.00 20.00
Eddy Curry AU RC
110 Lamar Odom AU 6.00 15.00
Eddie Griffin AU RC
111 Courtney Alexander AU 6.00 15.00
Earl Watson AU RC
112 Morris Peterson AU 10.00 25.00
Gilbert Arenas AU RC
113 Kenyon Martin AU 6.00 15.00
Brian Scalabrine AU RC
114 Tyson Chandler AU RC 10.00 25.00
Marcus Fizer AU
115 Corey Maggette AU 6.00 15.00
Ruben Boumtje-Boumtje AU RC
116 Jarron Collins AU RC 6.00 15.00
Mark Madsen AU
117 Vince Carter 4.00 10.00
Joseph Forte JSY RC
118 Antawn Jamison 6.00 15.00
Troy Murphy JSY SP RC
119 Kenyon Martin 4.00 10.00
Brandon Armstrong JSY RC
120 Steve Francis 4.00 10.00
Terence Morris JSY RC
121 Grant Hill 4.00 10.00
Steven Hunter JSY RC
122 Alonzo Mourning 4.00 10.00
Vladimir Radmanovic JSY RC
123 Brendan Haywood JSY RC 8.00 20.00
Shaquille O'Neal
124 Samuel Dalembert JSY RC 5.00 12.00
Moses Malone
125 Wally Szczerbiak JSY 5.00 12.00
Primoz Brezec JSY RC
126 Peja Stojakovic JSY 5.00 12.00
Michael Bradley JSY RC
127 Anfernee Hardaway JSY 8.00 20.00
Joe Johnson JSY RC
128 Loren Woods JSY RC 5.00 12.00
Theo Ratliff JSY
129 Chris Webber JSY 6.00 15.00
Gerald Wallace JSY RC
130 Antoine Walker JSY 5.00 12.00
Kedrick Brown JSY RC
131 Baron Davis JSY 5.00 12.00
Jamison Brewer JSY RC
132 Dirk Nowitzki JSY 10.00 25.00
Andrei Kirilenko JSY RC
133 Joe Smith JSY 5.00 12.00
Alton Ford JSY RC
134 John Stockton JSY 6.00 15.00
Joseph Crispin JSY RC
135 Karl Malone JSY 6.00 15.00
Rodney White JSY RC
136 Tracy McGrady JSY 6.00 15.00
Jeryl Sasser JSY RC
137 Elton Brand JSY 6.00 15.00
Jason Collins JSY RC
138 Kobe Bryant JSY 20.00 50.00
Richard Jefferson JSY RC
139 Allen Iverson JSY 15.00 40.00
Tony Parker JSY RC
140 Michael Jordan JSY 40.00 100.00
Jason Richardson JSY RC
141 Ronald Murray XRC 2.50 6.00
142 Pat Burke XRC 2.50 6.00
143 Manu Ginobili XRC 6.00 15.00
144 Gordan Giricek XRC 2.50 6.00
145 Tito Maddox XRC 2.50 6.00
146 Tamar Slay XRC 2.50 6.00
147 Rasual Butler XRC 2.50 6.00
148 Carlos Boozer XRC 5.00 12.00
149 Dan Gadzuric XRC 2.50 6.00
150 Vincent Yarbrough XRC 2.50 6.00
151 Robert Archibald XRC 2.50 6.00
152 Roger Mason XRC 2.50 6.00
153 Jamal Sampson XRC 2.50 6.00
154 Sam Clancy XRC 2.50 6.00
155 Dan Dickau XRC 2.50 6.00
156 Chris Jefferies XRC 2.50 6.00
157 John Salmons XRC 3.00 8.00
158 Frank Williams XRC 2.50 6.00
159 Lonny Baxter XRC 2.50 6.00
160 Tayshaun Prince XRC 3.00 8.00
161 Casey Jacobsen XRC 2.50 6.00
162 Qyntel Woods XRC 2.50 6.00
163 Kareem Rush XRC 2.50 6.00
164 Ryan Humphrey XRC 2.50 6.00
165 Curtis Borchardt XRC 3.00 8.00
166 Juan Dixon XRC 4.00 10.00
167 Jiri Welsch XRC 3.00 8.00
168 Bostjan Nachbar XRC 3.00 8.00
169 Fred Jones XRC 3.00 8.00
170 Marcus Haislip XRC 3.00 8.00
171 Melvin Ely XRC 3.00 8.00
172 Jared Jeffries XRC 3.00 8.00
173 Caron Butler XRC 5.00 12.00
174 Amare Stoudemire XRC 8.00 20.00
175 Chris Wilcox XRC 3.00 8.00
176 Nene Hilario XRC 4.00 10.00
177 Dajuan Wagner XRC 6.00 15.00
178 Nikoloz Tskitishvili XRC 6.00 15.00
179 Drew Gooden XRC 10.00 25.00
180 Mike Dunleavy XRC 8.00 20.00
181 Jay Williams XRC 8.00 20.00
182 Yao Ming XRC 20.00 50.00

2001-02 Upper Deck Inspirations Hardwood Imagery

Randomly inserted in packs at the rate of one in 47, this 21-card set features a small color player action photo on a large swatch of floor that takes up approximately 80% of the card front. Engraved in the wood swatch is the featured player's name, number, position, as well as the Upper Deck Inspirations logo. The top and bottom card borders are flat black, and the little bit of cardboard border left exposed by the swatch is printed on to look like wood.

COMPLETE SET (21) 100.00 200.00
AL Allen Iverson 6.00 15.00
AM Andre Miller 2.50 6.00
CW Chris Webber 3.00 8.00
DM Darius Miles 2.00 5.00
DN Dirk Nowitzki 5.00 12.00
JK Jason Kidd 5.00 12.00
JS Jerry Stackhouse 2.50 6.00
KB Kobe Bryant 15.00 40.00
KG Kevin Garnett 6.00 15.00
KM Kenyon Martin 3.00 8.00
MF Michael Finley 3.00 8.00
MJ Michael Jordan 25.00 60.00
MM Mike Miller 3.00 8.00
MP Morris Peterson 2.00 5.00
PP Paul Pierce 4.00 10.00
RA Ray Allen 3.00 8.00
SA Shareef Abdur-Rahim 2.50 6.00
SF Steve Francis 3.00 8.00
SH Shawn Marion 3.00 8.00
SM Stephon Marbury 2.50 6.00
TM Tracy McGrady 5.00 12.00

2001-02 Upper Deck Inspirations Hardwood Imagery Combo

Randomly inserted in packs at the rate of one in 47, this 21-card set features two small color player action photos on a large swatch of floor that takes up approximately 80% of the card front. Engraved in the wood swatch is the featured player's names, numbers, positions, as well as the Upper Deck Inspirations logo. The top and bottom card borders are flat black, and the little bit of cardboard border left exposed by the swatch is printed on to look like wood.

COMPLETE SET (21) 150.00 300.00
AH/LS Latrell Sprewell 4.00 10.00
Allan Houston
AI/SF Steve Francis 6.00 15.00
Allen Iverson
BD/JM Jamal Mashburn 4.00 10.00
Baron Davis
EJ/BG Eddie Jones 4.00 10.00
Brian Grant
JK/KM Jason Kidd 5.00 12.00
Kenyon Martin
KB/JK Kobe Bryant 10.00 25.00
Jason Kidd
KB/JS Jerry Stackhouse 10.00 25.00
Kobe Bryant
KB/KG Kobe Bryant 12.50 30.00
Kevin Garnett
KG/CW Kevin Garnett 5.00 12.00
Chris Webber
KG/WS Wally Szczerbiak 5.00 12.00
Kevin Garnett
KM/JS Karl Malone 6.00 15.00
John Stockton
LO/QR Lamar Odom 4.00 10.00
Quentin Richardson
MF/DN Michael Finley 5.00 12.00
Dirk Nowitzki
MJ/KB Michael Jordan 40.00 100.00
Kobe Bryant
PP/AW Antoine Walker 6.00 15.00
Paul Pierce
RA/GR Ray Allen 4.00 10.00
Glenn Robinson
RM/JO Reggie Miller 4.00 10.00
Jerrmaine O'Neal
RW/SP Scottie Pippen 6.00 15.00
Rasheed Wallace
SA/DJ Shareef Abdur-Rahim 4.00 10.00
DerMarr Johnson
SM/SM Stephon Marbury 4.00 10.00
Shawn Marion
TM/DM Tracy McGrady 6.00 15.00
Darius Miles

2001-02 Upper Deck Inspirations Like Mike

Randomly inserted in packs at the rate of one in 576, this 5-card set features the same card design as the double swatch jersey rookies from the base Upper Deck Inspirations. Lil' Bow Wow appears on the left side of the card with an "R" shaped jersey worn in the filming of "Like Mike," and a veteran player appears on the right side of the card with an "S" shaped jersey. Also included in this set is a Lil' Bow Wow autographed card sequentially numbered to 100. This auto'd card features an action photo, a portrait photo, and a cut signature.

LBW Bow Wow AU/100 50.00 100.00
LBWAI Allen Iverson 10.00 25.00
Bow Wow JSY
LBWCW Chris Webber 10.00 25.00
Bow Wow JSY
LBWGP Gary Payton 10.00 25.00
Bow Wow JSY
LBWJK Jason Kidd 10.00 25.00
Bow Wow JSY

2002-03 Upper Deck Inspirations

Released in July 2003, this set was Upper Deck's last 2002-03 Product. The 197-card set is divided up as follows: Numbers 1-90 are base veteran cards, numbers 91-104 feature dual player rookie cards with one veteran and one rookie and are inserted at the rate of one in 12, numbers 105-110 are dual player cards as well with a swatch from a rookie player and a swatch from a veteran player, these cards are sequentially numbered to 325, numbers 111-127 are also dual jersey cards with the same format as cards 105-110 and are sequentaily numbered to 1500, numbers 128-133 feature one rookie player autograph and one veteran autograph and are sequentially numbered to 275, numbers 134-139 are the same format as cards 128-133 and are sequentially numbered to 1600, numbers 140-149 are autographed by the rookie and sequentially numbered to 1600, and the remaining cards in the set were draft pick redemption cards for the players drawn in the 2003 NBA Draft. The Draft Pick cards breakdown as follows: Cards 156-161 are sequentially numbered to 499, cards 162-167 are sequentially numbered to 799, cards 168-175 are sequentially numbered to 1499, and cards 176-197 are sequentially numbered to 2999. Inspirations was packaged in 24-pack boxes where packs contained five cards and carried a suggested retail price of $4.99.

COMP.SET w/o SP's (90) 12.50 30.00
1 Shareef Abdur-Rahim .25 .60
2 Jason Terry .25 .60
3 Glenn Robinson .25 .60
4 Paul Pierce .40 1.00
5 Antoine Walker .25 .60
6 Bill Russell .50 1.25
7 Vin Baker .25 .60
8 Jalen Rose .25 .60
9 Tyson Chandler .25 .60
10 Eddy Curry .25 .60
11 Ricky Davis .25 .60
12 Zydrunas Ilgauskas .25 .60
13 Darius Miles .20 .50
14 Dirk Nowitzki .50 1.25
15 Michael Finley .30 .75
16 Steve Nash .40 1.00
17 Nick Van Exel .25 .60
18 Rodney White .20 .50
19 Juwan Howard .25 .60
20 Richard Hamilton .25 .60
21 Ben Wallace .30 .75
22 Isiah Thomas .30 .75
23 Antawn Jamison .30 .75
24 Jason Richardson .30 .75
25 Gilbert Arenas .30 .75
26 Steve Francis .30 .75
27 Eddie Griffin .20 .50
28 Cuttino Mobley .25 .60
29 Reggie Miller .30 .75
30 Jamaal Tinsley .20 .50
31 Jermaine O'Neal .30 .75
32 Elton Brand .30 .75
33 Andre Miller .25 .60
34 Lamar Odom .30 .75
35 Kobe Bryant 1.50 4.00
36 Shaquille O'Neal .75 2.00
37 Wilt Chamberlain .60 1.50
38 Derek Fisher .25 .60
39 Pau Gasol .40 1.00
40 Shane Battier .30 .75
41 Stromile Swift .20 .50
42 Eddie Jones .25 .60
43 Alonzo Mourning .40 1.00
44 Travis Best .20 .50
45 Gary Payton .30 .75
46 Sam Cassell .25 .60
47 Desmond Mason .25 .60
48 Kevin Garnett .60 1.50
49 Wally Szczerbiak .25 .60
50 Joe Smith .25 .60
51 Jason Kidd .50 1.25
52 Richard Jefferson .30 .75
53 Kenyon Martin .30 .75
54 Baron Davis .30 .75
55 Jamal Mashburn .25 .60
56 David Wesley .20 .50
57 Allan Houston .25 .60
58 Antonio McDyess .25 .60
59 Latrell Sprewell .25 .60
60 Tracy McGrady .50 1.25
61 Grant Hill .40 1.00
62 Pat Garrity .20 .50
63 Allen Iverson .50 1.25
64 Julius Erving .60 1.50
65 Stephon Marbury .25 .60
66 Shawn Marion .30 .75
67 Anfernee Hardaway .50 1.25
68 Rasheed Wallace .30 .75
69 Derek Anderson .20 .50
70 Scottie Pippen .50 1.25
71 Chris Webber .30 .75
72 Mike Bibby .30 .75
73 Peja Stojakovic .30 .75
74 Hedo Turkoglu .30 .75
75 Tim Duncan .60 1.50
76 David Robinson .50 1.25
77 Tony Parker .40 1.00
78 Ray Allen .30 .75
79 Rashard Lewis .30 .75
80 Brent Barry .20 .50
81 Voshon Lenard .20 .50
82 Vince Carter .50 1.25
83 Morris Peterson .20 .50
84 Antonio Davis .20 .50
85 Karl Malone .40 1.00
86 John Stockton .40 1.00
87 Andrei Kirilenko .30 .75
88 Jerry Stackhouse .25 .60
89 Michael Jordan 2.50 6.00
90 Kwame Brown .20 .50
91 Roger Mason RC 1.50 4.00
Michael Jordan
92 Junior Harrington RC 1.25 3.00
Alex English
93 Mike Dunleavy Jr. RC 1.50 4.00
Rick Barry
94 Robert Archibald RC 1.25 3.00
Stromile Swift
95 Tito Maddox RC 1.25 3.00
Steve Francis
96 Juaquin Hawkins RC 1.25 3.00
Moses Malone
97 Mike Batiste RC 1.25 3.00
Jason Williams
98 Ken Johnson RC 1.25 3.00
Alonzo Mourning
99 Smush Parker RC 1.25 3.00
Darius Miles
100 Pat Burke RC 1.25 3.00
Shaquille O'Neal
101 Raul Lopez RC 1.25 3.00
John Stockton
102 Chris Owens RC 1.25 3.00
Shane Battier
103 Mike Wilks RC 1.25 3.00
Earl Boykins
104 Antoine Rigadeau RC 1.25 3.00
Dirk Nowitzki
105 Caron Butler JSY RC 8.00 20.00
Kevin Garnett JSY
106 Dajuan Wagner JSY RC 6.00 15.00
Allen Iverson JSY
107 Kareem Rush JSY RC 8.00 20.00
Kobe Bryant JSY
108 Nene Hilario JSY RC 8.00 20.00
Tim Duncan JSY
109 Melvin Ely JSY RC 4.00 10.00
Elton Brand JSY
110 Ryan Humphrey JSY RC 4.00 10.00
Tracy McGrady JSY
111 Marco Jaric 3.00 8.00
Andre Miller
112 Fred Jones JSY RC 3.00 8.00
Reggie Miller JSY
113 Lonny Baxter JSY RC 3.00 8.00
Joe Smith JSY
114 J.R. Bremer JSY RC 3.00 8.00
Paul Pierce JSY
115 Carlos Boozer JSY RC 6.00 15.00
Grant Hill JSY
116 Predrag Savovic JSY RC 3.00 8.00
Vlade Divac JSY
117 Mehmet Okur JSY RC 4.00 10.00
Hedo Turkoglu JSY
118 Jannero Pargo JSY RC 3.00 8.00
Derek Fisher JSY
119 Cezary Trybanski JSY RC 3.00 8.00
Stromile Swift JSY
120 Ronald Murray JSY RC 6.00 15.00
Rashard Lewis JSY
121 Reggie Evans JSY RC 3.00 8.00
Ray Allen JSY
122 Rasual Butler JSY RC 3.00 8.00
Eddie Jones JSY
123 Jamal Sampson JSY RC 3.00 8.00
Shareef Abdur-Rahim JSY
124 Igor Rakocevic JSY RC 3.00 8.00
Terrell Brandon JSY
125 Tamar Slay JSY RC 3.00 8.00
Richard Jefferson JSY
126 Efthmios Rentzias JSY RC 3.00 8.00
Keith Van Horn JSY
127 Vincent Yarbrough JSY RC 3.00 8.00
Juwan Howard JSY
128A Jay Williams AU RC 75.00 150.00
Kobe Bryant AU
128B Jay Williams AU RC 250.00 500.00
Michael Jordan AU
129 Drew Gooden AU RC 20.00 50.00
Kevin Garnett AU
130 Amare Stoudemire AU RC 20.00 50.00
Shawn Marion AU
131 Nikoloz Tskitishvili AU RC 6.00 15.00
Peja Stojakovic AU
132 Yao Ming AU RC 50.00 120.00
Wang Zhi Zhi AU
133 Juan Dixon AU RC 10.00 25.00
Jason Kidd AU
134 Jared Jeffries AU RC 6.00 15.00
Jerry Stackhouse AU
135 Marcus Haislip AU 6.00 15.00
Kenyon Martin AU
136 Jiri Welsch AU RC 6.00 15.00
Jason Richardson AU
137 John Salmons AU RC 6.00 15.00
Gerald Wallace AU
138 Manu Ginobili AU RC 25.00 60.00
Tony Parker AU
138B Manu Ginobili AU 25.00 60.00
Tony Parker AU
139 Dan Dickau AU RC 6.00 15.00
Mike Bibby AU
140 Sam Clancy AU RC 3.00 8.00
Julius Erving
141 Qyntel Woods AU RC 3.00 8.00
Rasheed Wallace
142 Frank Williams AU RC 3.00 8.00
Allan Houston
143 Casey Jacobsen AU RC 3.00 8.00
Anfernee Hardaway
144 Bostijan Nachbar AU RC 3.00 8.00
Tim Duncan
145 Dan Gadzuric AU RC 3.00 8.00
Shaquille O'Neal
146 Gordon Giricek AU RC 3.00 8.00
Tracy McGrady
147 Curtis Borchardt AU RC 3.00 8.00
Karl Malone
148 Tayshaun Prince AU RC 6.00 15.00
Antoine Walker
149 Chris Wilcox AU RC 3.00 8.00
Vince Carter
156 LeBron James XRC 60.00 150.00
157 Darko Milicic XRC 5.00 12.00
158 Carmelo Anthony XRC 12.00 30.00
159 Chris Bosh XRC 10.00 25.00
160 Dwyane Wade XRC 20.00 50.00
161 Chris Kaman XRC 6.00 15.00
162 Kirk Hinrich XRC 5.00 12.00
163 T.J. Ford XRC 5.00 12.00
164 Mike Sweetney XRC 4.00 10.00
165 Jarvis Hayes XRC 4.00 10.00
166 Mickael Pietrus XRC 4.00 10.00
167 Nick Collison XRC 4.00 10.00
168 Marcus Banks XRC 3.00 8.00
169 Luke Ridnour XRC 4.00 10.00
170 Reece Gaines XRC 3.00 8.00
171 Troy Bell XRC 3.00 8.00
172 Zarko Cabarkapa XRC 3.00 8.00
173 David West XRC 4.00 10.00
174 Aleksandar Pavlovic XRC 3.00 8.00
175 Dahntay Jones XRC 3.00 8.00
176 Boris Diaw XRC 2.50 6.00
177 Zoran Planinic XRC 2.00 5.00
178 Travis Outlaw XRC 2.50 6.00
179 Brian Cook XRC 2.00 5.00
180 Udonis Haslem XRC 2.50 6.00
181 Ndudi Ebi XRC 2.00 5.00
182 Kendrick Perkins XRC 3.00 8.00
183 Leandro Barbosa XRC 2.50 6.00
184 Josh Howard XRC 2.00 5.00
185 Maciej Lampe XRC 2.00 5.00
186 Jason Kapono XRC 2.00 5.00
190 Luke Walton XRC 2.00 5.00
191 Jerome Beasley XRC 2.00 5.00
192 Travis Hansen XRC 2.00 5.00
193 Steve Blake XRC 2.50 6.00
194 Slavko Vranes XRC 2.00 5.00
195 Keith Bogans XRC 2.00 5.00
196 Willie Green XRC 2.00 5.00
197 Zaur Pachulia XRC 2.00 5.00

2002-03 Upper Deck Inspirations Rookie Holofoil

These holofoil variations to the XRC Draft Exchange cards were only featured in the first 50 cards printed out of the serial numbering run, for example on LeBron James, cards 1-50 feature holofoil and cards 51-499 feature gold foil. These parallel cards carry the exact same serial numbering as the base XRC exchange cards, but feature holofoil instead of the standard gold foil on the card front and numbering.

*HOLO 156-161: .75X TO 2X BASE HI
*HOLO 162-167: 1X TO 2.5X BASE HI
*HOLO 168-175: 1.25X TO 3X BASE HI
*HOLO 176-197: 2X TO 5X BASE HI
156A LeBron James 300.00 600.00
160A Dwyane Wade 125.00 250.00

1991-92 Upper Deck International Award Winner Holograms

The 1991-92 Upper Deck International Hologram set features nine standard-size holograms depicting league leaders in various statistical categories and honoring award winners such as Sixth Man, Rookie of the Year, and Defensive Player of the Year. The cards were randomly inserted into approximately 1:10 packs in both Italian and Spanish packs. The borderless fronts feature holographic cut-out images of the player against a game-action photo of the player. The player's name and award are displayed at the bottom. The backs are blank. The cards are unnumbered and checklisted below in alphabetical order.

COMPLETE SET (9) 5.00 12.00
1 Derrick Coleman .20 .50
2 Michael Jordan MVP 2.00 5.00
3 Michael Jordan Scoring 2.00 5.00
4 Hakeem Olajuwon .60 1.50
5 Alvin Robertson .08 .25
6 David Robinson .60 1.50
7 Dennis Rodman .60 1.50
8 Detlef Schrempf .20 .50
9 John Stockton .60 1.50

1991-92 Upper Deck International Italian

The Italian version of this 200-card standard-size set, which features white-bordered glossy color player action shots on the fronts. The cards were sold in ten-card packs (30 packs per box). Much like the 1991-92 American issues, each card front has the player's name and position displayed below the photo within a simulated hardwood floor strip. This strip continues up the right side and carries the player's team name in a team color. The team logo appears in the bottom right corner. The back is adorned by another player picture that covers the right two-thirds of the back. The horizontal remaining third carries the player's 1991-92 stats, and player highlights in both Italian and English. Card numbers 1 and 2 are East and West All-Star checklists, respectively, and they begin the All-Star subset, comprising the East All-Stars (3-14) and the West All-Stars (15-27). There are three art cards (106-108), cards of the Italian National Team (109-118), the Spanish National Team (119-130), and each NBA team has a logo card (131-157). There are also 1992 NBA Playoffs cards (158-169), NBA Finals (170-177), Cards on Collecting (178-183), and World Stars (184-199), which feature NBA stars born outside the United States. This product has been made available to the U.S. market through closeouts.

COMPLETE SET (200) 10.00 25.00
1 Checklist .50 1.25
East All-Stars
2 Checklist .20 .50
West All-Stars
3 Isiah Thomas AS .25 .60
4 Michael Jordan AS .75 2.00
5 Scottie Pippen AS .25 .60
6 Charles Barkley AS .30 .75
7 Patrick Ewing AS .25 :60
8 Michael Adams AS .07 .20
9 Dennis Rodman AS .25 .60
10 Reggie Lewis AS .07 .20
11 Joe Dumars AS .15 .40
12 Mark Price AS .15 .40
13 Brad Daugherty AS .07 .20
14 Kevin Willis AS .07 .20
15 Clyde Drexler AS .25 .60
16 Magic Johnson AS .30 .75
17 Chris Mullin AS .15 .40
18 Karl Malone AS .25 .60
19 David Robinson AS .25 .60
20 Tim Hardaway AS .20 .50
21 Jeff Hornacek AS .15 .40
22 John Stockton AS .30 .75
23 Dikembe Mutombo AS .20 .50
24 Hakeem Olajuwon AS .20 .50
25 James Worthy AS .20 .50
26 Otis Thorpe AS .07 .20
27 Dan Majerle AS .15 .40
28 Stacey Augmon .15 .40
29 Dominique Wilkins .40 1.00
30 Rumeal Robinson .07 .20
31 Rick Fox .20 .50
32 Reggie Lewis .15 .40
33 Kevin McHale .20 .50
34 Robert Parish .15 .40
35 Muggsy Bogues .15 .40
36 Larry Johnson .20 .50
37 Kendall Gill .20 .50
38 Michael Jordan 1.50 4.00
39 Scottie Pippen .30 .75
40 Horace Grant .15 .40
41 Mark Price .15 .40
42 Brad Daugherty .07 .20
43 Doug Smith .07 .20
44 Derek Harper .15 .40
45 Dikembe Mutombo .25 .60
46 Reggie Williams .07 .20
47 Isiah Thomas .25 .60
48 Joe Dumars .20 .50
49 Bill Laimbeer .15 .40
50 Dennis Rodman .25 .60
51 Chris Mullin .20 .50
52 Tim Hardaway .20 .50
53 Sarunas Marciulionis .07 .20
54 Billy Owens .15 .40
55 Hakeem Olajuwon .20 .50
56 Otis Thorpe .15 .40
57 Reggie Miller .30 .75
58 Vern Fleming .07 .20
59 Detlef Schrempf .15 .40
60 Rik Smits .15 .40
61 Danny Manning .15 .40
62 Ron Harper .15 .40
63 James Worthy .20 .50
64 Vlade Divac .15 .40
65 Byron Scott .15 .40
66 Sam Perkins .15 .40
67 Magic Johnson .40 1.00
68 Rony Seikaly .07 .20
69 Glen Rice .30 .75
70 Alvin Robertson .07 .20
71 Moses Malone .20 .50
72 Doug West .07 .20
73 Felton Spencer .07 .20
74 Derrick Coleman .15 .40
75 Drazen Petrovic .40 1.00
76 Patrick Ewing .30 .75
77 Charles Oakley .07 .20
78 Scott Skiles .15 .40
79 Dennis Scott .15 .40
80 Manute Bol .07 .20
81 Johnny Dawkins .07 .20
82 Hersey Hawkins .15 .40
83 Tom Chambers .15 .40
84 Kevin Johnson .20 .50
85 Dan Majerle .15 .40
86 Clyde Drexler .30 .75
87 Terry Porter .07 .20
88 Kevin Duckworth .07 .20
89 Mitch Richmond .20 .50
90 Spud Webb .15 .40
91 Terry Cummings .15 .40
92 David Robinson .30 .75
93 Sean Elliott .15 .40
94 Shawn Kemp .15 .40
95 Ricky Pierce .07 .20
96 Eddie Johnson .07 .20
97 Gary Payton .20 .50
98 Karl Malone .30 .75
99 John Stockton .30 .75
100 Checklist .07 .20
101 Jeff Malone .07 .20
102 Mark Eaton .07 .20
103 Michael Adams .07 .20
104 Bernard King .15 .40
105 Pervis Ellison .07 .20
106 Magic's Moment ART .20 .50
107 Michael Jordan ART .75 2.00
108 Stacey Augmon ART .07 .20
109 Ferdinando Gentile INT .07 .20
110 Walter Magnifico INT .08 .25
111 Alberto Rossini INT .07 .20
112 Carlton Myers INT .07 .20
113 Riccardo Pittis INT .07 .20
114 Antonello Riva INT .08 .25
115 Ario Costa INT .07 .20
116 Davide Cantarello INT .07 .20
117 Alberto Vianini INT .07 .20
118 Claudio Coldebella INT .07 .20
119 Juan Antonio San SNT .07 .20
120 Javier Fernandez SNT .07 .20
121 Jose A. Arcega SNT .07 .20
122 Juan Antonio SNT .07 .20
123 Jordi Villacampa SNT .07 .20
124 Enrique Andreu SNT .07 .20
125 Jose Antonio Montero SNT .07 .20
126 Rafael Jofresa SNT .07 .20
127 Jose Biriukov SNT .07 .20
128 Santiago Aldama SNT .07 .20
129 Alberto Herreros SNT .07 .20
130 Andres Jimenez SNT .07 .20
131 Hawks Logo .07 .20
132 Celtics Logo .07 .20
133 Hornets Logo .07 .20
134 Bulls Logo .15 .40
135 Cavaliers Logo .07 .20
136 Mavericks Logo .07 .20
137 Nuggets Logo .07 .20
138 Pistons Logo .07 .20
139 Warriors Logo .07 .20
140 Rockets Logo .07 .20
141 Pacers Logo .07 .20
142 Clippers Logo .07 .20
143 Lakers Logo .07 .20
144 Heat Logo .07 .20
145 Bucks Logo .07 .20
146 Timberwolves Logo .07 .20
147 Nets Logo .07 .20
148 Knicks Logo .07 .20
149 Magic Logo .07 .20
150 76ers Logo .07 .20
151 Suns Logo .07 .20
152 Trail Blazers Logo .07 .20
153 Kings Logo .07 .20
154 Spurs Logo .07 .20
155 Supersonics Logo .07 .20
156 Jazz Logo .07 .20
157 Bullets Logo .07 .20
158 Michael Jordan .75 2.00
Rony Seikaly PO
159 Kevin McHale .15 .40
Dale Davis PO
160 Cavaliers .07 .20
Nets PO
161 Patrick Ewing .15 .40
Joe Dumars PO
162 Kevin Duckworth PO .07 .20
163 John Stockton PO .20 .50
164 Tim Hardaway .15 .40
Ricky Pierce PO
165 Kevin Johnson .15 .40
Sean Elliott PO
166 New York Knicks .60 1.50
Scottie Pippen
Michael Jordan PO
167 Brad Daugherty PO .07 .20
168 Terry Porter .07 .20
Kevin Johnson PO
169 Shawn Kemp .20 .50
Karl Malone PO
170 Scottie Pippen .15 .40
Larry Nance PO
171 Clyde Drexler .20 .50
Jeff Malone PO
172 Michael Jordan FIN .75 2.00
173 Clifford Robinson FIN .07 .20
174 Clyde Drexler .60 1.50
Michael Jordan FIN
175 Clyde Drexler FIN .20 .50
176 Michael Jordan FIN .75 2.00
177 Michael Jordan FIN .75 2.00
178 Michael Jordan COC .75 2.00
179 Drazen Petrovic COC .30 .75
180 Magic Johnson COC .30 .75
181 Michael Jordan COC .75 2.00
182 Sarunas Marciulionis COC .07 .20
183 Rik Smits COC .07 .20
184 Rumeal Robinson WS .07 .20
185 Luc Longley WS .15 .40
186 Vlade Divac WS .15 .40
187 Rik Smits WS .07 .20
188 Drazen Petrovic WS .15 .40
189 Detlef Schrempf WS .07 .20
190 Dominique Wilkins WS .15 .40
191 Sarunas Marciulionis WS .07 .20
192 Rick Fox WS .15 .40
193 Patrick Ewing WS .15 .40
194 Manute Bol WS .07 .20
195 Steve Kerr WS .07 .20
196 Dikembe Mutombo WS .15 .40
197 Hakeem Olajuwon WS .20 .50
198 Rony Seikaly WS .07 .20
199 Carl Herrera WS .07 .20
200 Checklist Card .07 .20

1991-92 Upper Deck International Spanish

The Spanish version of this 200-card standard-size set, which features white-bordered glossy color player action shots on the fronts. The cards were sold in ten-card packs (30 packs per box). Much like the 1991-92 American issues, each card front has the player's name and position displayed below the photo within a simulated hardwood floor strip. This strip continues up the right side and carries the player's team name in a team color. The team logo appears in the bottom right corner. The back is adorned by another player picture that covers the right two-thirds of the back. The horizontal remaining third carries the player's 1991-92 stats, and player highlights in both Spanish and English. Card numbers 1 and 2 are East and West All-Star checklists, respectively, and they begin the All-Star subset, comprising the East All-Stars (3-14) and the West All-Stars (15-27). There are three art cards (106-108), cards of the Italian National Team (109-118), the Spanish National Team (119-130), and each NBA team has a logo card (131-157). There are also 1992 NBA Playoffs cards (158-169), NBA Finals (170-177), Cards on Collecting (178-183), and World Stars (184-199), which feature NBA stars born outside the United States. This product has been made available to the U.S. market through closeouts.

COMPLETE SET (200) 10.00 25.00
SPANISH: SAME VALUE AS ITALIAN

1992-93 Upper Deck International French

The 1992-93 Upper Deck International French basketball set consists of 255 standard-size cards. The fronts feature color action player photos with white borders. The team name is gold-foil stamped across the top of the picture. The border design at the bottom carries the player's name and position, and consists of a team-colored stripe that shades from one team color to the other with diagonal stripes within the larger stripe. The entire design is edged in gold foil. The right end is off-set slightly by the Upper Deck logo. The backs show an action player photo in a vertical layout on the left. The right side is horizontal and displays statistics printed on a ghosted NBA logo. The player's profile is printed in English and French. Within the set are the following subsets: NBA All-Stars (1-25), "In Your Face" 1993 Slam Dunk Competition (26-34), All-Division Team (35-54), Rookie Standouts (55-74), Foreign Exchange (75-85), and Fanimation (86-90). This product has been made available the U.S. market through closeouts.

COMPLETE SET (255) 15.00 40.00
1 Brad Daugherty CL .07 .20
Mark Price
Larry Nance
2 Scottie Pippen AS .40 1.00
3 Larry Johnson AS .15 .40
4 Shaquille O'Neal AS 1.50 4.00
5 Michael Jordan AS 1.00 2.50
6 Isiah Thomas AS .30 .75
7 Brad Daugherty AS .07 .20
8 Joe Dumars AS .25 .60
9 Patrick Ewing AS .40 1.00
10 Larry Nance AS .08 .25
11 Mark Price AS .08 .25
12 Detlef Schrempf AS .07 .20
13 Dominique Wilkins AS .40 1.00
14 Karl Malone AS .40 1.00
15 Charles Barkley AS .40 1.00
16 David Robinson AS .40 1.00
17 John Stockton AS .40 1.00
18 Clyde Drexler AS .40 1.00
19 Sean Elliott AS .10 .30
20 Tim Hardaway AS .08 .25
21 Shawn Kemp AS .30 .75
22 Dan Majerle AS .20 .50

3 Danny Manning AS .07 .20
4 Hakeem Olajuwon AS .40 1.00
5 Terry Porter AS .07 .20
6 Harold Miner FACE .07 .20
7 David Benoit FACE .07 .20
8 Cedric Ceballos FACE .07 .20
9 Mahmoud Abdul-Rauf FACE .07 .20
0 Tim Perry FACE .07 .20
1 Kenny Smith FACE .08 .25
2 Clarence Weatherspoon FACE .07 .20
3 Michael Jordan FACE 1.00 2.50
4 Dominique Wilkins FACE .40 1.00
5 Shaquille O'Neal AD 1.50 4.00
6 Derrick Coleman AD .07 .20
7 Glen Rice AD .20 .50
8 Reggie Lewis AD .08 .25
9 Kenny Anderson AD .07 .20
0 Brad Daugherty AD .07 .20
1 Dominique Wilkins AD .40 1.00
2 Larry Johnson AD .15 .40
3 Michael Jordan AD 1.00 2.50
4 Mark Price AD .08 .25
5 David Robinson AD .40 1.00
6 Karl Malone AD .40 1.00
7 Sean Elliott AD .10 .30
8 John Stockton AD .40 1.00
9 Derek Harper AD .07 .20
50 Kevin Duckworth AD .25 .60
51 Chris Mullin AD .15 .40
52 Charles Barkley AD .40 1.00
53 Tim Hardaway AD .08 .25
54 Clyde Drexler AD .40 1.00
55 Adam Keefe RS .07 .20
56 Alonzo Mourning RS .60 1.50
57 Sean Rooks RS .07 .20
58 LaPhonso Ellis RS .07 .20
59 Latrell Sprewell RS .40 1.00
60 Robert Horry RS .40 1.00
61 Malik Sealy RS .10 .30
62 Anthony Peeler RS .07 .20
63 Harold Miner RS .07 .20
64 Anthony Avent RS .07 .20
65 Todd Day RS .07 .20
66 Lee Mayberry RS .07 .20
67 Christian Laettner RS .30 .75
68 Tom Gugliotta RS .40 1.00
69 Shaquille O'Neal RS 1.50 4.00
70 Clarence Weatherspoon RS .07 .20
71 Richard Dumas RS .07 .20
72 Walt Williams RS .07 .20
73 Lloyd Daniels RS .07 .20
74 Hubert Davis RS .07 .20
75 Manute Bol FE .07 .20
76 Vlade Divac FE .08 .25
77 Patrick Ewing FE .40 1.00
78 Sarunas Marciulionis FE .10 .30
79 Dikembe Mutombo FE .20 .50
80 Hakeem Olajuwon FE .40 1.00
81 Detlef Schrempf FE .07 .20
82 Rony Seikaly FE .07 .20
83 Rik Smits FE .07 .20
84 Kiki Vandeweghe FE .08 .25
85 Dominique Wilkins FE .40 1.00
86 Michael Jordan FAN 1.00 2.50
87 Larry Bird FAN .50 1.25
88 Karl Malone FAN .40 1.00
89 Dikembe Mutombo FAN .20 .50
90 Michael Jordan FAN 1.00 2.50
Larry Bird
91 Stacey Augmon .07 .20
92 Mookie Blaylock .08 .25
93 Duane Ferrell .07 .20
94 Paul Graham .07 .20
95 Adam Keefe .07 .20
96 Jon Koncak .07 .20
97 Dominique Wilkins .40 1.00
98 Kevin Willis .07 .20
99 Alaa Abdelnaby .07 .20
100 Dee Brown .07 .20
101 Sherman Douglas .07 .20
102 Rick Fox .15 .40
103 Reggie Lewis .08 .25
104 Xavier McDaniel .07 .20
105 Robert Parish .15 .40
106 Ed Pinckney .07 .20
107 Muggsy Bogues .15 .40
108 Dell Curry .07 .20
109 Kenny Gattison .07 .20
110 Kendall Gill .08 .25
111 Larry Johnson .15 .40
112 Alonzo Mourning .75 2.00
113 Johnny Newman .07 .20
114 David Wingate .07 .20
115 B.J. Armstrong .15 .40
116 Bill Cartwright .08 .25
117 Horace Grant .15 .40
118 Michael Jordan 2.00 5.00
119 Stacey King .07 .20
120 John Paxson .15 .40
121 Scottie Pippen .60 1.50
122 Scott Williams .07 .20
123 John Battle .07 .20
124 Terrell Brandon .10 .30
125 Brad Daugherty .07 .20
126 Craig Ehlo .07 .20
127 Larry Nance .15 .40
128 Mark Price .20 .50
129 Gerald Wilkins .07 .20
130 Hot Rod Williams .07 .20
131 Walter Bond .07 .20
132 Terry Davis .07 .20
133 Derek Harper .15 .40
134 Donald Hodge .07 .20
135 Brian Howard .07 .20
136 Jim Jackson .75 2.00
137 Sean Rooks .07 .20
138 Doug Smith .07 .20
139 LaPhonso Ellis .20 .50
140 Mahmoud Abdul-Rauf .07 .20
141 Marcus Liberty .07 .20
142 Todd Lichti .07 .20
143 Mark Macon .07 .20
144 Dikembe Mutombo .25 .60
145 Robert Pack .07 .20
146 Reggie Williams .07 .20
147 Mark Aguirre .08 .25
148 Joe Dumars .25 .60
149 Gerald Glass .07 .20
150 Bill Laimbeer .15 .40
151 Terry Mills .07 .20
152 Olden Polynice .07 .20
153 Dennis Rodman .40 1.00
154 Isiah Thomas .30 .75
155 Victor Alexander .07 .20
156 Chris Gatling .07 .20
157 Tim Hardaway .15 .40
158 Tyrone Hill .07 .20
159 Sarunas Marciulionis .10 .30
160 Chris Mullin .25 .60
161 Billy Owens .07 .20
162 Latrell Sprewell .40 1.00
163 Scott Brooks .07 .20
164 Matt Bullard .07 .20
165 Sleepy Floyd .07 .20
166 Robert Horry .40 1.00
167 Vernon Maxwell .07 .20
168 Hakeem Olajuwon .40 1.00
169 Kenny Smith .08 .25
170 Otis Thorpe .08 .25
171 Dale Davis .07 .20
172 Vern Fleming .07 .20
173 Reggie Miller .30 .75
174 Sam Mitchell .07 .20
175 Pooh Richardson .07 .20
176 Detlef Schrempf .08 .25
177 Malik Sealy .10 .30
178 Rik Smits .08 .25
179 Gary Grant .07 .20
180 Ron Harper .30 .75
181 Mark Jackson .30 .75
182 Danny Manning .08 .25
183 Ken Norman .07 .20
184 Stanley Roberts .07 .20
185 Loy Vaught .07 .20
186 John Williams .07 .20
187 Elden Campbell .07 .20
188 Doug Christie .10 .30
189 Vlade Divac .20 .50
190 A.C. Green .20 .50
191 Anthony Peeler .07 .20
192 Byron Scott .20 .50
193 Sedale Threatt .07 .20
194 James Worthy .30 .75
195 Bimbo Coles .07 .20
196 Kevin Edwards .07 .20
197 Grant Long .07 .20
198 Harold Miner .07 .20
199 Glen Rice .30 .75
200 John Salley .08 .25
201 Rony Seikaly .07 .20
202 Brian Shaw .07 .20
203 Frank Brickowski .07 .20
204 Todd Day .07 .20
205 Blue Edwards .07 .20
206 Eric Murdock .07 .20
207 Christian Laettner .30 .75
208 Luc Longley .08 .25
209 Chuck Person .07 .20
210 Doug West .07 .20
211 Kenny Anderson .08 .25
212 Derrick Coleman .08 .25
213 Chris Morris .07 .20
214 Rumeal Robinson .07 .20
215 Patrick Ewing .40 1.00
216 Charles Oakley .08 .25
217 Doc Rivers .15 .40
218 John Starks .08 .25
219 Nick Anderson .08 .25
220 Shaquille O'Neal 5.00 12.00
221 Scott Skiles .25 .60
222 Manute Bol .07 .20
223 Hersey Hawkins .08 .25
224 Jeff Hornacek .25 .60
225 Danny Ainge .15 .40
226 Charles Barkley .40 1.00
227 Richard Dumas .07 .20
228 Kevin Johnson .15 .40
229 Dan Majerle .20 .50
230 Clyde Drexler .40 1.00
231 Terry Porter .07 .20
232 Clifford Robinson .10 .30
233 Buck Williams .08 .25
234 Mitch Richmond .25 .60
235 Lionel Simmons .07 .20
236 Spud Webb .15 .40
237 Walt Williams .07 .20
238 Antoine Carr .07 .20
239 Vinny Del Negro .07 .20
240 Sean Elliott .15 .40
241 David Robinson .40 1.00
242 Eddie Johnson .07 .20
243 Shawn Kemp .30 .75
244 Derrick McKey .07 .20
245 Ricky Pierce .07 .20
246 Mark Eaton .07 .20
247 Jeff Malone .07 .20
248 Karl Malone .40 1.00
249 John Stockton .40 1.00
250 Michael Adams .07 .20
251 Rex Chapman .07 .20
252 Pervis Ellison .07 .20
253 Tom Gugliotta .40 1.00
254 Michael Jordan .40 1.00
Checklist 1-128
255 Michael Jordan .40 1.00
Checklist 129-255

1992-93 Upper Deck International French Award Winner Holograms

The 1992-93 Upper Deck International French Award Winner Hologram standard-size set features nine holograms depicting league leaders in various statistical categories and honoring award winners such as top Sixth Man, Rookie of the Year, Defensive Player of the Year, and Most Valuable Player. The borderless fronts feature holographic cut-out images of the player against a game-action photo of the player. The player's name and award are displayed at the bottom. The backs carry vertical, color player photos. A light blue plaque-style panel contains information about the player and the award won in English and the corresponding foreign language. The cards are numbered on the back with a "EB" prefix.

COMPLETE SET (9) 6.00 15.00
1 Michael Jordan 3.00 8.00
Scoring
2 John Stockton 1.25 3.00
Steals
3 Dennis Rodman 1.25 3.00
Rebounds
4 Detlef Schrempf .20 .50
Sixth Man
5 Larry Johnson .40 1.00
Rookie of the Year
6 David Robinson .75 2.00
Blocked Shots
7 David Robinson .75 2.00
Def. Player of Year
8 John Stockton 1.25 3.00
Assists
9 Michael Jordan 3.00 8.00
Most Valuable Player

1992-93 Upper Deck International Italian

The 1992-93 Upper Deck International Italian basketball set consists of 255 standard-size cards. The fronts feature color action player photos with white borders. The team name is gold-foil stamped across the top of the picture. The border design at the bottom carries the player's name and position, and consists of a team-colored stripe that shades from one team color to the other with diagonal stripes within the larger stripe. The entire design is edged in gold foil. The right end is off-set slightly by the Upper Deck logo. The backs show an action player photo in a vertical layout on the left. The right side is horizontal and displays statistics printed on a ghosted NBA logo. The player's profile is printed in English and Italian. Within the set are the following subsets: NBA All-Stars (1-25), "In Your Face" 1993 Slam Dunk Competition (26-34), All-Division Team (35-54), Rookie Standouts (55-74), Foreign Exchange (75-85), and Fanimation (86-90). This product has been made available the U.S. market through closeouts.

COMPLETE SET (255) 15.00 40.00
*ITALIAN: SAME VALUE AS FRENCH

1992-93 Upper Deck International Italian Award Winner Holograms

The 1992-93 Upper Deck International Italian Award Winner Hologram standard-size set features nine holograms depicting league leaders in various statistical categories and honoring award winners such as top Sixth Man, Rookie of the Year, Defensive Player of the Year, and Most Valuable Player. The borderless fronts feature holographic cut-out images of the player against a game-action photo of the player. The player's name and award are displayed at the bottom. The backs carry vertical, color player photos. A light blue plaque-style panel contains information about the player and the award won in English and the corresponding foreign language. The cards are numbered on the back with a "EB" prefix.

COMPLETE SET (9) 6.00 15.00
*ITALIAN: SAME VALUE AS FRENCH

1992-93 Upper Deck International Spanish

The 1992-93 Upper Deck International Spanish basketball set consists of 255 standard-size cards. The fronts feature color action player photos with white borders. The team name is gold-foil stamped across the top of the picture. The border design at the bottom carries the player's name and position, and consists of a team-colored stripe that shades from one team color to the other with diagonal stripes within the larger stripe. The entire design is edged in gold foil. The right end is off-set slightly by the Upper Deck logo. The backs show an action player photo in a vertical layout on the left. The right side is horizontal and displays statistics printed on a ghosted NBA logo. The player's profile is printed in English and Spanish. Within the set are the following subsets: NBA All-Stars (1-25), "In Your Face" 1993 Slam Dunk Competition (26-34), All-Division Team (35-54), Rookie Standouts (55-74), Foreign Exchange (75-85), and Fanimation (86-90). This product has been made available the U.S. market through closeouts.

COMPLETE SET (255) 15.00 40.00
*SPANISH: SAME VALUE AS FRENCH

1992-93 Upper Deck International Spanish Award Winner Holograms

The 1992-93 Upper Deck International Spanish Award Winner Hologram standard-size set features nine holograms depicting league leaders in various statistical categories and honoring award winners such as top Sixth Man, Rookie of the Year, Defensive Player of the Year, and Most Valuable Player. The borderless fronts feature holographic cut-out images of the player against a game-action photo of the player. The player's name and award are displayed at the bottom. The backs carry vertical, color player photos. A light blue plaque-style panel contains information about the player and the award won in English and the corresponding foreign language. The cards are numbered on the back with a "EB" prefix.

COMPLETE SET (9) 6.00 15.00
*SPANISH: SAME VALUE AS FRENCH

1993-94 Upper Deck International French

This 195-card set is similar in design to the 1993-94 American issue. The cards were distributed in France, Germany, Italy and Spain. Cards were issued in 10-card packs (30 packs per box). Cards 166-175 are Mr. June subset cards. 176-180 are Signature Moves subset cards. 181-192 are Flight Team subset cards. 193-195 are Checklists. Its believed that all of the subset cards are tougher to pull from packs than the regular issue cards. This product was made available to the U.S. market through closeouts.

COMPLETE SET (195) 12.00 30.00
1 Stacey Augmon .05 .15
2 Chris Mills .08 .25
3 Joe Dumars .30 .75
4 Grant Long .05 .15
5 Robert Horry .20 .50
6 Rod Strickland .08 .25
7 Frank Brickowski .05 .15
8 Ricky Pierce .05 .15
9 Dan Majerle .20 .50
10 Dell Curry .05 .15
11 Derek Harper .08 .25
12 Anthony Avent .05 .15
13 Vern Fleming .05 .15
14 Dee Brown .05 .15
15 Kevin Johnson .20 .50
16 Clifford Robinson .08 .25
17 Doc Rivers .15 .40
18 Doug West .05 .15
19 Michael Adams .05 .15
20 Sherman Douglas .05 .15
21 Harold Miner .05 .15
22 John Williams .05 .15
23 Michael Jordan 2.00 5.00
24 Jim Jackson .20 .50
25 Glen Rice .20 .50
26 Jeff Hornacek .25 .60
27 Derrick Coleman .08 .25
28 Sam Perkins .20 .50
29 Willie Anderson .05 .15
30 Rumeal Robinson .05 .15
31 Blue Edwards .05 .15
32 Sarunas Marciulionis .15 .40
33 Clyde Drexler .50 1.25
34 Shawn Bradley .20 .50
35 Ron Harper .20 .50
36 Chris Morris .05 .15
37 Brad Daugherty .05 .15
38 Duane Ferrell .05 .15
39 Chuck Person .05 .15
40 Todd Day .05 .15
41 Sedale Threatt .05 .15
42 Xavier McDaniel .05 .15
43 Kevin Willis .05 .15
44 Chris Mullin .30 .75
45 Terrell Brandon .08 .25
46 Kenny Smith .15 .40
47 Malik Sealy .08 .25
48 John Starks .08 .25
49 Dino Radja .05 .15
50 David Robinson .60 1.50
51 John Salley .08 .25
52 Danny Ainge .25 .60
53 Sam Cassell .40 1.00
54 Latrell Sprewell .25 .60
55 Dikembe Mutombo .20 .50
56 Doug Edwards .05 .15
57 A.C. Green .20 .50
58 Otis Thorpe .05 .15
59 Antoine Carr .05 .15
60 Tim Legler .05 .15
61 Don MacLean .05 .15
62 Horace Grant .15 .40
63 John Stockton .60 1.50
64 Muggsy Bogues .25 .60
65 Rex Chapman .20 .50
66 Stanley Roberts .05 .15
67 Walt Williams .05 .15
68 Dominique Wilkins .30 .75
69 Brent Price .05 .15
70 Lloyd Daniels .05 .15
71 Mark Price .20 .50
72 Sean Elliott .20 .50
73 Scottie Pippen .60 1.50
74 Rodney Rogers .08 .25
75 Charles Barkley .60 1.50
76 Kevin Gamble .05 .15
77 Lionel Simmons .05 .15
78 Dennis Rodman .40 1.00
79 Jeff Malone .05 .15
80 Larry Johnson .25 .60
81 Armon Gilliam .05 .15
82 Chris Dudley .05 .15
83 Bryant Stith .05 .15
84 Mark Jackson .30 .75
85 Paul Graham .05 .15
86 Calbert Cheaney .08 .25
87 Clarence Weatherspoon .05 .15
88 Isiah Thomas .40 1.00
89 Scott Brooks .05 .15
90 Mitch Richmond .30 .75
91 Kendall Gill .15 .40
92 Robert Parish .20 .50
93 Karl Malone .50 1.25
94 Rik Smits .05 .15
95 Rex Walters .05 .15
96 Oliver Miller .05 .15
97 Hersey Hawkins .15 .40
98 Vinny Del Negro .05 .15
99 Spud Webb .20 .50
100 Chris Webber 1.25 3.00
101 Moses Malone .25 .60
102 Hubert Davis .05 .15
103 Gary Payton .40 1.00
104 Mahmoud Abdul-Rauf .05 .15
105 Larry Nance .15 .40
106 Bobby Hurley .15 .40
107 David Benoit .05 .15
108 Danny Manning .08 .25
109 Pervis Ellison .05 .15
110 Anthony Peeler .05 .15
111 Tim Hardaway .20 .50
112 Detlef Schrempf .15 .40
113 Hakeem Olajuwon .40 1.00
114 Elden Campbell .05 .15
115 Charles Smith .05 .15
116 B.J. Armstrong .15 .40
117 Dennis Scott .05 .15
118 LaPhonso Ellis .05 .15
119 Isaiah Rider .08 .25
120 Tim Perry .05 .15
121 Lindsey Hunter .08 .25
122 Anthony Bowie .05 .15
123 Micheal Williams .05 .15
124 Gerald Wilkins .05 .15
125 Tom Chambers .15 .40
126 Vincent Askew .05 .15
127 Vernon Maxwell .05 .15
128 Nick Van Exel .40 1.00
129 Buck Williams .15 .40
130 Alonzo Mourning .30 .75
131 Loy Vaught .05 .15
132 Shaquille O'Neal 1.00 2.50
133 Derrick McKey .05 .15
134 Kenny Anderson .08 .25
135 Bill Cartwright .15 .40
136 Nick Anderson .05 .15
137 Billy Owens .05 .15
138 Anfernee Hardaway .75 2.00
139 Terry Mills .05 .15
140 John Paxson .15 .40
141 Charles Oakley .05 .15
142 Steve Smith .20 .50
143 Johnny Dawkins .05 .15
144 Thurl Bailey .05 .15
145 Jamal Mashburn .75 2.00
146 Terry Porter .08 .25
147 Duane Causwell .05 .15
148 Reggie Miller .40 1.00
149 Shawn Kemp .20 .50
150 James Worthy .30 .75
151 Scott Skiles .20 .50
152 Donald Hodge .05 .15
153 Christian Laettner .20 .50
154 Vin Baker .15 .40
155 Doug Christie .05 .15
156 Tyrone Corbin .05 .15
157 Toni Kukoc .40 1.00
158 Ken Norman .05 .15
159 Randy White .05 .15
160 Rony Seikaly .05 .15
161 Tom Gugliotta .08 .25
162 Vlade Divac .20 .50
163 Eric Murdock .05 .15
164 Pooh Richardson .05 .15
165 Patrick Ewing .40 1.00
166 Michael Jordan 2.00 5.00
A Steal
167 Michael Jordan 2.00 5.00
High Five
168 Michael Jordan 2.00 5.00
Finals MVP
169 Michael Jordan 2.00 5.00
35 Points
170 Michael Jordan 2.00 5.00
Three-Point King
171 Michael Jordan 2.00 5.00
Back-To-Back
172 Michael Jordan 2.00 5.00
55-Point Game
173 Michael Jordan 2.00 5.00
Scoring Avg.
174 Michael Jordan 2.00 5.00
Third Straight MVP
175 Michael Jordan 2.00 5.00
Mr. June Checklist
176 Michael Jordan SM 2.00 5.00
177 Shawn Kemp SM .20 .50
178 Karl Malone SM .50 1.25
179 Clyde Drexler SM .40 1.00
180 Tim Hardaway SM .20 .50
181 Charles Barkley FT .40 1.00
182 Cedric Ceballos FT .05 .15
183 Derrick Coleman FT .05 .15
184 Clyde Drexler FT .40 1.00
185 Larry Johnson FT .15 .40
186 Shawn Kemp FT .20 .50
187 Harold Miner FT .05 .15
188 Alonzo Mourning FT .30 .75
189 Shaquille O'Neal FT .50 1.25
190 Scottie Pippen FT .40 1.00
191 Clarence Weatherspoon FT .05 .15
192 Dominique Wilkins FT .30 .75
193 Kenny Anderson .05 .15
Xavier McDaniel CL
194 Doug West .15 .40
James Worthy CL
195 Reggie Miller .40 1.00
Joe Dumars CL

1993-94 Upper Deck International German

This 195-card set is similar in design to the 1993-94 American issue. The cards were distributed in France, Germany, Italy and Spain. Cards were issued in 10-card packs (30 packs per box). Cards 166-175 are Mr. June subset cards. 176-180 are Signature Moves subset cards. 181-192 are Flight Team subset cards. 193-195 are Checklists. Its believed that all of the subset cards are tougher to pull from packs than the regular issue cards. This product was made available to the U.S. market through closeouts.

COMPLETE SET (195) 12.00 30.00
*GERMAN: SAME VALUE AS FRENCH

1993-94 Upper Deck International German Triple Double

Randomly inserted at a rate of one in five packs, these ten cards parallel the 1993-94 American Triple Double inserts.

COMPLETE SET (10) 5.00 12.00
*GERMAN: SAME VALUE AS FRENCH

1993-94 Upper Deck International Italian

This 195-card set is similar in design to the 1993-94 American issue. The cards were distributed in France, Germany, Italy and Spain. Cards were issued in 10-card packs (30 packs per box). Cards 166-175 are Mr. June subset cards. 176-180 are Signature Moves subset cards. 181-192 are Flight Team subset cards. 193-195 are Checklists. Its believed that all of the subset cards are tougher to pull from packs than the regular issue cards. This product was made available to the U.S. market through closeouts.

COMPLETE SET (195) 12.00 30.00
*ITALIAN: SAME VALUE AS FRENCH

1993-94 Upper Deck International Italian Triple Double

Randomly inserted at a rate of one in five packs, these ten cards parallel the 1993-94 American Triple Double inserts.

COMPLETE SET (10) 5.00 12.00
*ITALIAN: SAME VALUE AS FRENCH

1993-94 Upper Deck International Spanish

This 195-card set is similar in design to the 1993-94 American issue. The cards were distributed in France, Germany, Italy and Spain. Cards were issued in 10-card packs (30 packs per box). Cards 166-175 are Mr. June subset cards. 176-180 are Signature Moves subset cards. 181-192 are Flight Team subset cards. 193-195 are Checklists. Its believed that all of the subset cards are tougher to pull from packs than the regular issue cards. This product was made available to the U.S. market through closeouts.

COMPLETE SET (195) 12.00 30.00
*SPANISH: SAME VALUE AS FRENCH

1993-94 Upper Deck International Spanish Triple Double

Randomly inserted at a rate of one in five packs, these ten cards parallel the 1993-94 American Triple Double inserts.

COMPLETE SET (10) 5.00 12.00
*SPANISH: SAME VALUE AS FRENCH

1993-94 Upper Deck International French Triple Double

Randomly inserted at a rate of one in five packs, these nine cards parallel the 1993-94 American Triple Double inserts, with the only exception being the #TD10 Detlef Schrempf, who exists in the Italian and Spanish parallel, but not the French.

COMPLETE SET (9) 5.00 12.00
TD1 Charles Barkley 1.00 2.50
TD2 Michael Jordan 3.00 8.00
TD3 Scottie Pippen 1.25 3.00
TD4 Micheal Williams .20 .50
TD5 Mark Jackson .40 1.00
TD6 Kenny Anderson .20 .50
TD7 Larry Johnson .30 .75
TD8 Dikembe Mutombo .30 .75
TD9 Rumeal Robinson .20 .50

1996-97 Upper Deck Italian Stickers

This set features a design similar to the American 1996-97 Collector's Choice set. Each sticker measures 2" by 4". In addition to player stickers, each team's logo is featured individually or on a dual-numbered sticker. A sticker album was also available and priced at the end of the set.

COMPLETE SET (186) 15.00 40.00
1 NBA Logo .10 .25
2 Western Conference Logo .10 .25
3 Eastern Conference Logo .10 .25
4 Golden State Warriors Logo .10 .25
5 B.J. Armstrong .10 .25
6 Joe Smith .12 .30
7 Donyell Marshall .10 .25
8 Rony Seikaly .12 .30
9 Chris Mullin .15 .40
10 Los Angeles Clippers Logo .10 .25
11 Rodney Rogers .10 .25
12 Brent Barry .12 .30
13 Lamond Murray .10 .25
14 Pooh Richardson .10 .25
15 Loy Vaught .10 .25
16 Los Angeles Lakers Logo .10 .25
17 Cedric Ceballos .10 .25
18 George Lynch .10 .25
19 Eddie Jones .15 .40
20 Anthony Peeler .10 .25
21 Nick Van Exel .15 .40
22 Phoenix Suns Logo .10 .25
23 Charles Barkley .25 .60
24 Wayman Tisdale .10 .25
25 Wesley Person .10 .25
26 A.C. Green .15 .40
27 Danny Manning .12 .30
28 Portland Trail Blazers Logo .10 .25
29 Harvey Grant .10 .25
30 Aaron McKie .10 .25
31 Gary Trent .10 .25
32 Buck Williams .10 .25
33 Clifford Robinson .10 .25
34 Sacramento Kings Logo .10 .25
35 Billy Owens .10 .25
36 Brian Grant .12 .30
37 Tyus Edney .10 .25
38 Olden Polynice .10 .25
39 Mitch Richmond .15 .40
40 Seattle Supersonics Logo .10 .25
41 Nate McMillan .10 .25
42 Vincent Askew .10 .25
43 Hersey Hawkins .10 .25
44 Detlef Schrempf .15 .40
45 Shawn Kemp .15 .40
46 Dallas Mavericks Logo .10 .25
47 Tony Dumas .10 .25
48 Jim Jackson .10 .25
49 Loren Meyer .10 .25
50 Jamal Mashburn .12 .30
51 Jason Kidd .25 .60
52 Denver Nuggets Logo .10 .25
53 Mahmoud Abdul-Rauf .10 .25
54 Antonio McDyess .15 .40
55 Tom Hammonds .10 .25
56 Dale Ellis .10 .25
57 LaPhonso Ellis .10 .25
58 Houston Rockets Logo .10 .25
59 Hakeem Olajuwon .20 .50
60 Mario Elie .10 .25
61 Robert Horry .12 .30
62 Chucky Brown .10 .25
63 Clyde Drexler .20 .50
64 Minnesota Timberwolves Logo .10 .25
65 Kevin Garnett .40 1.00
66 Terry Porter .10 .25
67 Sam Mitchell .10 .25
68 Tom Gugliotta .10 .25
69 Isaiah Rider .12 .30
70 San Antonio Spurs Logo .10 .25
71 Avery Johnson .12 .30
72 Vinny Del Negro .10 .25
73 Sean Elliott .15 .40
74 Will Perdue .10 .25
75 David Robinson .25 .60
76 Utah Jazz Logo .10 .25
77 Jeff Hornacek .12 .30
78 Chris Morris .10 .25
79 Antoine Carr .10 .25
80 Karl Malone .20 .50
81 John Stockton .20 .50
82 Vancouver Grizzlies Logo .10 .25
83 Shareef Abdur-Rahim .30 .75
84 Blue Edwards .10 .25
85 Bryant Reeves .10 .25
86 Lawrence Moten .10 .25
87 Greg Anthony .10 .25
88 Michael Jordan 1.25 3.00
Bulls Victory Tour
89 Michael Jordan 1.25 3.00
Bulls Victory Tour
90 Michael Jordan 1.25 3.00
Bulls Victory Tour
91 Michael Jordan 1.25 3.00
Bulls Victory Tour
92 Scottie Pippen .25 .60
Bulls Victory Tour
93 Luc Longley .10 .25
Bulls Victory Tour
94 Luc Longley .10 .25
Bulls Victory Tour
95 Toni Kukoc .15 .40
Bulls Victory Tour
96 Toni Kukoc .15 .40
Bulls Victory Tour
97 Atlanta Hawks Logo .10 .25
98 Grant Long .10 .25
99 Mookie Blaylock .10 .25
100 Christian Laettner .12 .30
101 Ken Norman .10 .25
102 Stacey Augmon .12 .30
103 Charlotte Hornets Logo .10 .25
104 Dell Curry .10 .25
105 Scott Burrell .10 .25
106 Matt Geiger .10 .25
107 Muggsy Bogues .12 .30
108 Glen Rice .15 .40
109 Chicago Bulls Logo .10 .25
110 Steve Kerr .12 .30
111 Dennis Rodman .30 .75
112 Scottie Pippen .25 .60
113 Luc Longley .10 .25
114 Michael Jordan 1.25 3.00
115 Cleveland Cavaliers Logo .10 .25
116 Terrell Brandon .10 .25
117 Bobby Phills .10 .25
118 Tyrone Hill .10 .25
119 Bob Sura .10 .25
120 Danny Ferry .10 .25
121 Detroit Pistons Logo .10 .25
122 Joe Dumars .15 .40
123 Theo Ratliff .10 .25
124 Lindsey Hunter .10 .25
125 Terry Mills .10 .25
126 Grant Hill .25 .60
127 Indiana Pacers Logo .10 .25
128 Derrick McKey .10 .25
129 Eddie Johnson .10 .25
130 Travis Best .10 .25
131 Mark Jackson .15 .40
132 Rik Smits .12 .30
133 Milwaukee Bucks Logo .10 .25
134 Vin Baker .12 .30
135 Shawn Respert .10 .25
136 Sherman Douglas .10 .25
137 Johnny Newman .10 .25
138 Glenn Robinson .15 .40
139 Toronto Raptors Logo .10 .25
140 Sharone Wright .10 .25
141 Zan Tabak .10 .25
142 Doug Christie .10 .25
143 Damon Stoudamire .15 .40
144 Oliver Miller .10 .25
145 Boston Celtics Logo .10 .25
146 Dana Barros .10 .25
147 Rick Fox .10 .25
148 David Wesley .10 .25
149 Eric Williams .10 .25
150 Dee Brown .10 .25
151 Miami Heat Logo .10 .25
152 Rex Chapman .10 .25
153 Kurt Thomas .10 .25
154 Keith Askins .10 .25
155 Walt Williams .10 .25
156 Alonzo Mourning .20 .50
157 New Jersey Nets Logo .10 .25
158 Kendall Gill .10 .25
159 Jayson Williams .10 .25
160 Kevin Edwards .10 .25
161 Shawn Bradley .10 .25
162 Ed O'Bannon .10 .25
163 New York Knicks Logo .10 .25
164 Gary Grant .10 .25
165 J.R. Reid .10 .25
166 Charles Oakley .12 .30
167 John Starks .12 .30
168 Patrick Ewing .20 .50
169 Orlando Magic Logo .10 .25
170 Nick Anderson .10 .25
171 Brian Shaw .10 .25
172 Anfernee Hardaway .25 .60
173 Dennis Scott .10 .25
174 Shaquille O'Neal .40 1.00
175 Philadelphia 76ers Logo .10 .25
176 Allen Iverson .75 2.00
177 Rex Walters .10 .25
178 Clarence Weatherspoon .10 .25
179 Jerry Stackhouse .20 .50
180 Derrick Coleman .12 .30
181 Washington Bullets Logo .10 .25
182 Calbert Cheaney .10 .25
183 Chris Webber .20 .50
184 Tim Legler .10 .25
185 Gheorghe Muresan .10 .25
186 Rasheed Wallace .20 .50
NNO Sticker Album 1.50 4.00

1996-97 Upper Deck Italian Stickers Eurostar

This 10-card sticker set was inserted into packs of 1996-97 Upper Deck Italian Stickers. This set focuses on ten European players who made it to the NBA. Card fronts are similar to the basic set except the borders are silver and in the top left of the card contains the word "Eurostar". Card backs are numbered with a "ES" prefix.

COMPLETE SET (10) 1.50 4.00
ES1 Sasha Danilovic .20 .50
ES2 Vlade Divac .30 .75
ES3 Toni Kukoc .30 .75
ES4 Gheorghe Muresan .20 .50
ES5 Dino Radja .25 .60
ES6 Arvydas Sabonis .25 .60
ES7 Detlef Schrempf .30 .75
ES8 Rik Smits .25 .60
ES9 Zan Tabak .20 .50
ES10 George Zidek .20 .50

1996 Upper Deck Jordan Metal

COMPLETE SET (6) 20.00 50.00
COMMON CARD (1-6) 5.00 12.00
*ORANGE: .5X TO 1.25X BASE HI

1994 Upper Deck Jordan Rare Air

The Michael Jordan Rare Air Tribute set consists of 90 standard-size cards, combining Walter Iooss, Jr. photography with other classic shots from Jordan's career. The set was sold exclusively in a factory box with a suggested retail price of $19.99. Each set included two 3 3/8" by 7 7/8" cards featuring black-and-white action shots highlighted by a red tint stripe. In addition, each set had a serial number out of 30,000. One gold foil-stamped set was included in every 12-set case for the hobby only. The fronts feature full- bleed color photos, capturing Jordan both on and off the court. Set subtitles are silver foil-stamped on the fronts. The "Rare Air" cards (1-50) have pictures taken directly from the best-selling book Rare Air, by Michael Jordan and Walter Iooss Jr. The "Out Takes" cards (51-60) feature pictures from Iooss' personal collection that were never released. Finally, the "MJ, Decade of Dominanace" cards (61- 90) highlight Jordan's incredible accomplishments during his NBA career. The backs present personal commentary by Iooss and/or Jordan, or highlights from Jordan's career.

COMPLETE SET (90) 15.00 40.00
1 Michael Jordan .40 1.00
(Close-up with white robe)
2 Michael Jordan .40 1.00
(Close-up profile)
3 Michael Jordan .20 .50
(Michael's shooting form)
4 Michael Jordan .08 .25
(Close-up of his left hand)
5 Michael Jordan .20 .50
(Entering onto court in Orlando)
6 Michael Jordan .20 .50
(Lifting weights)
7 Michael Jordan .20 .50
(Driving car to Chicago Stadium)
8 Michael Jordan .20 .50
(Sitting in visitor's locker room in Miami Arena)
9 Michael Jordan .20 .50
(Relaxing on trainer's table)
10 Michael Jordan .20 .50
(Listening to pre-game instructions)
11 Michael Jordan .20 .50
(Readying himself for action on the floor)
12 Michael Jordan .20 .50
(Greeted by teammates during pre-game introductions)
13 Michael Jordan .08 .25
(Pre-game huddle with Chicago teammates)
14 Michael Jordan .20 .50
(Performing final pre-game rituals)
15 Michael Jordan .08 .25
(Close-up look at his feet)
16 Michael Jordan .40 1.00
(Stealing a pass intended for A.C. Green)
17 Michael Jordan .20 .50
(Guarding James Worthy)
18 Michael Jordan .40 1.00
(Greeted in mid-air by Shaquille O'Neal)
19 Michael Jordan .20 .50
(Slaming another one home during a game in Chicago Stadium)
20 Michael Jordan .20 .50
(Pippen with hand on Michael's head during playoff game)
21 Michael Jordan .08 .25
(Facing reporters in locker room after game)
22 Michael Jordan .40 1.00
(Heading to locker room after game at Chicago Stadium)
23 Michael Jordan .40 1.00
(Listening to questions from reporters)
24 Michael Jordan .20 .50
(Sleeping on the bus)
25 Michael Jordan .20 .50
(Boarding plane after bus ride to airport)
26 Michael Jordan .20 .50
(Settling into seat on team's private airplane)
27 Michael Jordan .08 .25
(Treating sprained ankle in hotel room)
28 Michael Jordan .20 .50
(Getting rest and relaxation on road trip)
29 Michael Jordan .20 .50
(Peering out of car window)
30 Michael Jordan .20 .50
(Enjoying game of cards)
31 Michael Jordan .20 .50
(Shooting pool)
32 Michael Jordan .20 .50
(Caring for golf clubs)
33 Michael Jordan .40 1.00
(Preparing to drive shot onto green)
34 Michael Jordan .40 1.00
(Sizing up a putt)
35 Michael Jordan .08 .25
(Calling home from golf course)
36 Michael Jordan .20 .50
(Sitting by window taking time out)
37 Michael Jordan .40 1.00
(Close-up view, chin resting in hand)
38 Michael Jordan .40 1.00
(Wearing uniform, enjoying 1993 baseball All-Star Game)
39 Michael Jordan .20 .50
(Shaving head)
40 Michael Jordan .20 .50
(Wearing warm-ups, standing outside locker room)
41 Michael Jordan .20 .50
(Passing to Horace Grant in game against Atlanta)
42 Michael Jordan .20 .50
(Preparing to shoot free throw in playoff game against Atlanta)
43 Michael Jordan .20 .50
(Driving lane between New York's John Starks and Doc Rivers)
44 Michael Jordan .20 .50
(Standing next to Charles Barkley during game)
45 Michael Jordan .20 .50
(Celebrating third NBA Championship)
46 Michael Jordan .40 1.00
(Celebrating third NBA Championship, arms outstretched)
47 Michael Jordan .20 .50
(Celebrating with team in locker
48 Michael Jordan .40 1.00
(Holding up three fingers, representing three NBA titles)
49 Michael Jordan .08 .25
(Michael with a special friend)
50 Michael Jordan .40 1.00
(Close-up shot from back)
51 Michael Jordan .08 .25
(Head bowed, hand on brow)
52 Michael Jordan .08 .25
(Palming basketball)
53 Michael Jordan .20 .50
(Lifting weights with curl bar)
54 Michael Jordan .20 .50
(Sitting in weight training room)
55 Michael Jordan .20 .50
(Resting on sofa beside telephone)
56 Michael Jordan .20 .50
(Signing sports cards)
57 Michael Jordan .20 .50
(Boarding team bus)
58 Michael Jordan .20 .50
(In black sports car, outside Chicago Stadium)
59 Michael Jordan .20 .50
(In locker room before game)
60 Michael Jordan .20 .50
(Michael at free throw line, shot from above)
61 Michael Jordan .40 1.00
(Close-up with ball, orange background)
62 Michael Jordan .40 1.00
(Winning NBA Slam Dunk Championship)
63 Michael Jordan .40 1.00
(Cheering on sidelines)
64 Michael Jordan .40 1.00
(Preparing to shoot free throw)
65 Michael Jordan .40 1.00
(Defensive posture)
66 Michael Jordan .20 .50
Efficient Scorer
67 Michael Jordan .20 .50
(In mid-air preparing to dunk)
68 Michael Jordan .20 .50
(Signing autographs for fans)
69 Michael Jordan .20 .50
(A multi-mirror image)
70 Michael Jordan .20 .50
(Playing wheel chair basketball with child)
71 Michael Jordan .20 .50
(Watching a game on TV)
72 Michael Jordan .40 1.00
(Scoring over opponent)
73 Michael Jordan .20 .50
(Jordan defended by Mark West and Charles Barkley)
74 Michael Jordan .20 .50
(Dunking over Patrick Ewing)
75 Michael Jordan .40 1.00
(Driving baseline)
76 Michael Jordan .40 1.00
(Fighting for rebound position)
77 Michael Jordan .20 .50
(Shooting over Scott Skiles)
78 Michael Jordan .40 1.00
(Defending against Orlando Magic player)
79 Michael Jordan .20 .50
(Driving past Vlade Divac)
80 Michael Jordan .20 .50
(Shooting jump shot over Orlando Magic players)
81 Michael Jordan .20 .50
(Shooting lay up around Patrick Ewing)
82 Michael Jordan .20 .50
(Shooting jump shot over outstretched arms)
83 Michael Jordan .40 1.00
(Driving down court)
84 Michael Jordan .20 .50
(In mid-air during game against Nets)
85 Michael Jordan .40 1.00
(Dribbling past New York defender)
86 Michael Jordan .20 .50
(Positioning for rebound against Phoenix)
87 Michael Jordan .20 .50
(Shooting jump shot over Dan Majerle)
88 Michael Jordan .40 1.00
(Fingerroll lay up against Phoenix)
89 Michael Jordan .40 1.00
(Shooting jump shot over Gerald Wilkins)
90 Michael Jordan .20 .50
(In warm-ups shot from above)
NNO Michael Jordan Promo 5.00 12.00
NNO Michael Jordan .40 1.00
Passing Ball
NNO Jordan Under Backboard .40 1.00

1996 Upper Deck Kellogg's Space Jam

Inserted into German Kellogg's products, this single card features Michael Jordan and Tweety on the card front.

3 Michael Jordan 6.00 15.00

2007 Upper Deck Kevin Durant Team Upper Deck

This card features Kevin Durant as a Longhorn, dribbling the ball, with a congratulatory message on the card back welcoming him to the Upper Deck Spokesmen family.

KD1 Kevin Durant 8.00 20.00
Pictured as Longhorn w/ball

2000 Upper Deck Lakers Championship Jumbos

This 10-card set was released by Upper Deck shortly after the L.A. Lakers won the NBA Championship during the 1999/00 season. The set features ten postcard sized cards, as well as, two special inserts. The inserts included a Kobe Bryant jersey card (1:100) and a Kobe Bryant autographed game jersey card (1:1250). Each pack contained 4 cards and carried a suggested retail price of $20.00.

COMP. FACT SET (10) 12.00 30.00
1 Shaquille O'Neal 3.20 8.00
2 Kobe Bryant 4.00 10.00
3 Glen Rice .80 2.00
4 A.C. Green .80 2.00
5 Ron Harper .80 2.00
6 Robert Horry .40 1.00
7 Derek Fisher .40 1.00
8 Rick Fox .40 1.00
9 Kobe Bryant 4.80 12.00
10 Team Photo 4.00 10.00
NNO Kobe Bryant JSY/100 100.00 250.00

2000 Upper Deck Lakers Master Collection

The 2000 Upper Deck Lakers Master Collection was released in July,2000, and featured a 25-card base set, one mystery pack, ten game-used jersey cards, one Forum Floor card, and one Wilt Chamberlain warm-up card. The set originally sold for the suggest price of $3000. There were only 300 Master Collections produced.

COMPLETE SET (25) 200.00 400.00
1 Magic Johnson 25.00 60.00
2 Wilt Chamberlain 20.00 50.00
3 Kareem Abdul-Jabbar 15.00 40.00
4 Jerry West 10.00 25.00
5 Elgin Baylor 6.00 15.00
6 James Worthy 6.00 15.00
7 Byron Scott 5.00 12.00
8 Kurt Rambis 4.00 10.00
9 Michael Cooper 4.00 10.00
10 Norm Nixon 4.00 10.00
11 Gail Goodrich 4.00 10.00
12 Jamaal Wilkes 4.00 10.00
13 A.C. Green 4.00 10.00
14 Kobe Bryant 30.00 80.00
15 Shaquille O'Neal 30.00 80.00
16 Glen Rice 4.00 10.00
17 Derek Fisher 4.00 10.00
18 Robert Horry 4.00 10.00
19 Rick Fox 4.00 10.00
20 Ron Harper 4.00 10.00
21 Chick Hearn 10.00 25.00
22 Phil Jackson 6.00 15.00
23 Pat Riley 5.00 12.00
24 Mitch Kupchak 4.00 10.00
25 L.A. Forum 4.00 10.00

2000 Upper Deck Lakers Master Collection Fabulous Forum Floor Cards

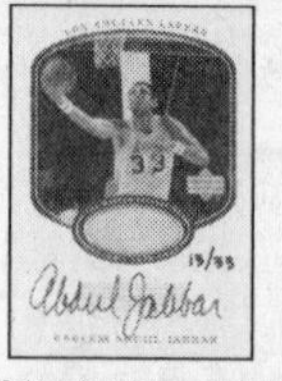

This 6-card set was released in the 2000 Upper Deck Lakers Master Collection. Each Master Collection included one of the six game-used Forum Floor cards. These cards are individually serial numbered to 50. Card backs carry the player's initials as numbering.

EBJ Elgin Baylor 50.00 100.00
EJF Magic Johnson 150.00 300.00
JWF Jerry West 75.00 150.00
KAF Kareem Abdul-Jabbar 150.00 300.00
WCF Wilt Chamberlain 125.00 250.00
WOJ James Worthy 50.00 100.00

2000 Upper Deck Lakers Master Collection Game Jerseys

This 10-card game-used jersey set was included in the 2000 Upper Deck Laker's Master collection. Each Master Collection incuded all 10-cards, and each card is serial numbered to 300. Card backs carry the player's initials.

COMPLETE SET (10) 750.00 1500.00
AGJ A.C. Green 20.00 50.00
BSJ Byron Scott 30.00 80.00
EJJ Magic Johnson 200.00 400.00
JWJ Jerry West 75.00 150.00
KAJ Kareem Abdul-Jabbar 50.00 120.00
KBJ Kobe Bryant 200.00 400.00
MCJ Michael Cooper 25.00 60.00
RHJ Robert Horry 30.00 80.00
SOJ Shaquille O'Neal 200.00 400.00
WOJ James Worthy 40.00 100.00

2000 Upper Deck Lakers Master Collection Mystery Pack Inserts

Mystery Packs were inserted at a rate of one per Master Collection. The mystery packs included one autographed game-used memorabilia card from players such as Kobe Bryant, Elgin Baylor, Magic Johnson, Jerry West, Kareem Abdul-Jabbar, and James Worthy. Card backs carry the player's initials as numbering.

EBAF Elgin Baylor FF/22 200.00 400.00
EJAF Magic Johnson FF/32 500.00 1000.00
EJAJ Magic Johnson JSY/32 500.00 1000.00
JWAF Jerry West FF/44 250.00 500.00
JWAJ Jerry West JSY/44 250.00 500.00
KAAF Kareem Abdul-Jabbar FF/33 250.00 500.00
KAAJ Kareem Abdul-Jabbar JSY/33250.00 500.00
WOAJ James Worthy JSY/42 75.00 150.00

2000 Upper Deck Lakers Master Collection Warm-Ups

This card was inserted into Laker Master Collections at a rate of one per set. The card features a swatch from a game-used Wilt Chamberlain warm-up jersey. Card back carries the player's initials.

WCW Wilt Chamberlain 100.00 200.00

2003 Upper Deck LeBron James Box Set

Released in October 2003, this 32-card box set features an array of photographs of LeBron James ranging from on-court to studio posed. Each card has the Upper Deck logo in the top right corner and a LeBron James Box Set logo with a caption along the bottom in gold foil. Two oversized cards were inserted on top of the three rows of base set cards. Autographs serially numbered to 23 were also randomly inserted in boxes which carried a suggested retail price of $19.99.

COMPLETE SET (30) 15.00 40.00
COMMON JAMES (1-30) .75 2.00
COMMON JUMBO (LJ1-LJ2) .75 2.00
LJ1A LeBron James AU/23 300.00 600.00
LJ2A LeBron James AU/23 300.00 600.00

2004 Upper Deck LeBron James Freshman Season

COMPLETE SET (90) 20.00 40.00
COMMON CARD (1-90) .40 1.00

2001-02 Upper Deck Legends

This 132-card base set was issued in July of 2001. The set includes 90 veteran and retired legends and 42 draft pick redemption cards. The redemptions were available starting in September 2001. The standard sized set features both black and white and color photography for players. The left side of the card is white and fades into a gray basketball background then the picture, while the right side has a colored border and the players name. All cards have silver foil highlights and rookies break down as follows: card numbers 91-110 are sequentially numberd to 3250, card numbers 111-125 are sequentially numbered to 1999, and card numbers 126-132 are sequentially numbered to 500. Cards were packaged in 25-pack boxes with packs containing five cards and carrying a suggested retail price of $4.99. Please notice that these cards read 2000-01 in foil along the top; however, were issued after the 2001 draft with that rookie class inserted as redemptions so is listed with the rest of the 2001-02 sets.

COMP.SET w/o SP's (90) 10.00 25.00
NOTE CARDS READ 2000-01
1 Michael Jordan 2.00 5.00
2 Wilt Chamberlain .50 1.25
3 Karl Malone .30 .75
4 Steve Francis .25 .60
5 George McGinnis .25 .60
6 Julius Erving .50 1.25
7 Alonzo Mourning .30 .75
8 Kobe Bryant 1.25 3.00
9 Glen Rice .20 .50
10 Mitch Kupchak .25 .60
11 Isiah Thomas .25 .60
12 Rick Barry .25 .60
13 Moses Malone .25 .60
14 Larry Bird .75 2.00
15 Vince Carter .40 1.00
16 Jamaal Wilkes .25 .60
17 John Havlicek .30 .75
18 Elgin Baylor .25 .60
19 Dave Bing .25 .60
20 Steve Smith .25 .60
21 Kevin Garnett .50 1.25
22 Hakeem Olajuwon .30 .75
23 Walt Bellamy .25 .60
24 Kevin McHale .30 .75
25 Kareem Abdul-Jabbar .40 1.00
26 Chris Webber .25 .60
27 Tom Heinsohn .25 .60
28 Walt Frazier .25 .60
29 Ron Boone .25 .60
30 Gary Payton .25 .60
31 Wes Unseld .25 .60
32 Magic Johnson .75 2.00
33 David Thompson .25 .60
34 Maurice Lucas .25 .60
35 Paul Pierce .30 .75
36 Dikembe Mutombo .25 .60
37 Gail Goodrich .25 .60
38 Bob Lanier .25 .60
39 Chris Mullin .25 .60
40 Allen Iverson .50 1.25
41 Sam Jones .25 .60
42 James Worthy .30 .75
43 Cedric Maxwell .25 .60
44 George Gervin .25 .60
45 Earl Monroe .25 .60
46 Lenny Wilkens .25 .60
47 Tracy McGrady .40 1.00
48 Walter Davis .25 .60
49 Stephon Marbury .20 .50
50 Bob Cousy .40 1.00
51 Spencer Haywood .25 .60
52 Dave Cowens .25 .60
53 Scottie Pippen .40 1.00
54 Hal Greer .25 .60
55 Kiki Vandeweghe .25 .60
56 Paul Silas .25 .60
57 Elton Brand .25 .60
58 John Stockton .30 .75
59 Shareef Abdur-Rahim .20 .50
60 Reggie Miller .30 .75
61 Nate Thurmond .25 .60
62 Billy Cunningham .25 .60
63 Patrick Ewing .30 .75
64 Nate Archibald .25 .60
65 Tim Duncan .50 1.25
66 Lafayette Lever .25 .60
67 Willis Reed .25 .60
68 Ray Allen .25 .60
69 Jo Jo White .25 .60
70 Pete Maravich .75 2.00
71 Grant Hill .30 .75
72 Jerry West .30 .75
73 George Karl .25 .60
74 Bill Sharman .25 .60
75 Dave DeBusschere .25 .60
76 Tim Hardaway .25 .60
77 Bill Walton .25 .60
78 Jerry Lucas .25 .60
79 Antonio McDyess .20 .50
80 Robert Parish .25 .60
81 Shaquille O'Neal .60 1.50
82 Bill Russell .40 1.00
83 Clyde Drexler .30 .75
84 Dolph Schayes .25 .60
85 K.C. Jones .25 .60
86 Bob Pettit .25 .60
87 Jason Kidd .40 1.00
88 Mitch Richmond .25 .60
89 Oscar Robertson .30 .75
90 David Robinson .40 1.00
91 Bobby Simmons RC 1.50 4.00
92 Jamison Brewer RC 1.50 4.00
93 Earl Watson RC 1.50 4.00
94 Kenny Satterfield RC 1.50 4.00
95 Zeljko Rebraca RC 1.50 4.00
96 Damone Brown RC 1.50 4.00
97 Ruben Boumtje-Boumtje RC 1.50 4.00
98 Brian Scalabrine RC 1.50 4.00
99 Terence Morris RC 1.50 4.00
100 Willie Solomon RC 1.50 4.00
101 Primoz Brezec RC 1.50 4.00
102 Gilbert Arenas RC 2.50 6.00
103 Trenton Hassell RC 1.50 4.00
104 Loren Woods RC 1.50 4.00
105 Tony Parker RC 6.00 15.00
106 Jamaal Tinsley RC 2.00 5.00
107 Samuel Dalembert RC 2.00 5.00
108 Gerald Wallace RC 2.50 6.00
109 Andrei Kirilenko RC 4.00 10.00
110 Brandon Armstrong RC 1.50 4.00
111 Jeryl Sasser RC 3.00 8.00
112 Joseph Forte RC 3.00 8.00
113 Brendan Haywood RC 4.00 10.00
114 Zach Randolph RC 8.00 20.00
115 Jason Collins RC 3.00 8.00
116 Michael Bradley RC 3.00 8.00
117 Kirk Haston RC 3.00 8.00
118 Steven Hunter RC 3.00 8.00
119 Troy Murphy RC 5.00 12.00
120 Richard Jefferson RC 6.00 15.00
121 Vladimir Radmanovic RC 3.00 8.00
122 Kedrick Brown RC 3.00 8.00
123 Joe Johnson RC 8.00 20.00
124 Rodney White RC 3.00 8.00
125 DeSagana Diop RC 3.00 8.00
126 Eddie Griffin RC 4.00 10.00
127 Shane Battier RC 8.00 20.00
128 Jason Richardson RC 8.00 20.00
129 Eddy Curry RC 6.00 15.00
130 Pau Gasol RC 12.00 30.00
131 Tyson Chandler RC 6.00 15.00
132 Kwame Brown RC 4.00 10.00

2001-02 Upper Deck Legends Fiorentino Collection

Randomly inserted in packs at a rate of 1:15, this 15-card insert set features portrait paintings of the showcased player by James Fiorentino. Cards are enhanced with silver foil highlights.

COMPLETE SET (15) 15.00 40.00
F1 Michael Jordan 6.00 15.00
F2 Larry Bird 2.50 6.00
F3 Magic Johnson 2.50 6.00
F4 Julius Erving 1.50 4.00
F5 Bill Russell 1.25 3.00
F6 Jerry West 1.00 2.50
F7 Oscar Robertson 1.00 2.50
F8 Wilt Chamberlain 1.50 4.00
F9 Kareem Abdul-Jabbar 1.25 3.00
F10 Isiah Thomas .75 2.00
F11 George Gervin .75 2.00
F12 Elgin Baylor .75 2.00
F13 Bob Cousy 1.25 3.00
F14 Pete Maravich 2.50 6.00
F15 John Havlicek 1.00 2.50

2001-02 Upper Deck Legends Fiorentino Collection Autographs

Randomly inserted in packs, this 11-card set parallels the base design of the Legendary Signatures set, but rather than having a photo, these cards are drawn in charcoal. Each card has an announced print number and they are listed below.

JH John Havlicek/17* 15.00 40.00
JW Jerry West/44* 80.00 200.00
KA Kareem Abdul-Jabbar/33* 100.00 200.00
LB Larry Bird/33* 250.00 500.00
MA Magic Johnson/32* 150.00 300.00

2001-02 Upper Deck Legends Generations

This nine-card insert set was randomly inserted in packs at a rate of 1:24, and features two players on the front of each card, one on the left and the other on the right. Each card is enhanced with silver foil highlights.

COMPLETE SET (9) 15.00 40.00
G1 Michael Jordan 6.00 15.00
Kobe Bryant
G2 Oscar Robertson 2.50 6.00
Jason Kidd
G3 Walt Frazier 2.50 6.00
Ray Allen
G4 Elvin Hayes 2.50 6.00
Kevin Garnett
G5 Moses Malone 4.00 10.00
Tim Duncan
G6 Bob Lanier 2.50 6.00
David Robinson
G7 George Gervin 2.50 6.00
Tracy McGrady
G8 Nate Archibald 2.50 6.00
Steve Francis
G9 Michael Jordan 3.00 8.00
Vince Carter

2001-02 Upper Deck Legends Legendary Floor

Randomly inserted in packs at a rate of 1:23, this 29-card insert set features a full color player portrait photo on the right and a swatch of court on the left. These cards are horizontally designed and are highlighted with silver foil.

AIF Allen Iverson 6.00 15.00
AMF Alonzo Mourning 4.00 10.00
CWF Chris Webber 3.00 8.00
DAF David Robinson 5.00 12.00
DJF Julius Erving 10.00 25.00
GHF Grant Hill 4.00 10.00
HOF Hakeem Olajuwon 4.00 10.00
ITF Isiah Thomas 3.00 8.00
JHF John Havlicek 8.00 20.00
JKF Jason Kidd 5.00 12.00
JSF John Stockton 4.00 10.00
JWF James Worthy 3.00 8.00
KAF Kareem Abdul-Jabbar 12.50 30.00
KBF Kobe Bryant 15.00 40.00
KGF Kevin Garnett 6.00 15.00
KMF Karl Malone 4.00 10.00
LBF Larry Bird 15.00 40.00
MAF Magic Johnson 15.00 40.00
MJF Michael Jordan 25.00 60.00
MMF Moses Malone 10.00 25.00
PEF Patrick Ewing 4.00 10.00
PMF Pete Maravich 25.00 60.00
RMF Reggie Miller 3.00 8.00
SFF Steve Francis 3.00 8.00
SMF Stephon Marbury 2.50 6.00
SPF Scottie Pippen 6.00 15.00
THF Tim Hardaway 3.00 8.00
TMF Tracy McGrady 6.00 15.00
WCF Wilt Chamberlain 25.00 60.00

2001-02 Upper Deck Legends Legendary Floor Autographs

Seeded in packs, this 10-card set parallels the design of the base Legendary Floor set enhanced with authentic player autographs. Each card is sequentially numbered to 100, except for Michael Jordan who is numbered to 23.

DRAF Julius Erving/100 60.00 150.00
JHAF John Havlicek/100 50.00 120.00
KAAF Kareem Abdul-Jabbar/100 60.00 150.00
KBAF Kobe Bryant/100 125.00 300.00
KGAF Kevin Garnett/100 50.00 120.00
LBAF Larry Bird/100 100.00 200.00
MAAF Magic Johnson/100 80.00 160.00
MJAF Michael Jordan/23 600.00 1200.00
MMAF Moses Malone/100 30.00 80.00
SFAF Steve Francis/100 30.00 80.00

2001-02 Upper Deck Legends Legendary Jerseys

Randomly inserted in packs at a rate of 1:23, this 28-card set utilizes the same design as the Legendar Floor set and has player jerseys on the left side of the card.

AIJ Allen Iverson 10.00 25.00
BRJ Bill Russell 20.00 50.00
BWJ Bill Walton 6.00 15.00
CDJ Clyde Drexler 10.00 25.00
DAJ David Robinson 8.00 20.00
DDJ Dave DeBusschere 8.00 20.00
DRJ Julius Erving 15.00 40.00
EMJ Earl Monroe 6.00 15.00
GGJ George Gervin 6.00 15.00
GHJ Grant Hill 6.00 15.00
ITJ Isiah Thomas 8.00 20.00
JHJ John Havlicek 10.00 25.00
JSJ John Stockton 6.00 15.00
JWJ Jerry West 10.00 25.00
KAJ Kareem Abdul-Jabbar 12.50 30.00
KBJ Kobe Bryant 12.50 30.00
KGJ Kevin Garnett 8.00 20.00
KMJ Karl Malone 6.00 15.00
LBJ Larry Bird 15.00 40.00
MAJ Magic Johnson 10.00 25.00
MCJ Kevin McHale 6.00 15.00
MJJ Michael Jordan 60.00 120.00
MJ/DRJ Michael Jordan 75.00 150.00
Julius Erving
MJ/KBJ Michael Jordan 100.00 200.00
Kobe Bryant
MJ/LBJ Michael Jordan 80.00 200.00
Larry Bird
PEJ Patrick Ewing 6.00 15.00
RPJ Robert Parish 6.00 15.00
SPJ Scottie Pippen 6.00 15.00

2001-02 Upper Deck Legends Legendary Jerseys Autographs

Randomly seeded in packs, this 15-card set parallels the design of the base Legendary Jerseys set enhanced with authentic player autographs. Most of the cards are sequentially numbered to 50, except for those that are listed below with numbers after the player's name.

SOME UNPRICED DUE TO SCARCITY
BRAJ Bill Russell/50 300.00 600.00
DDAJ Dave DeBusschere/50 40.00 100.00
DRAJ Julius Erving/50 150.00 300.00
EMAJ Earl Monroe/50 40.00 100.00
GGAJ George Gervin/50 40.00 100.00
JWAJ Jerry West/50 125.00 250.00
KAAJ Kareem Abdul-Jabbar/50 100.00 200.00
KBAJ Kobe Bryant/50 200.00 400.00
KGAJ Kevin Garnett/50 75.00 150.00
LBAJ Larry Bird/50 200.00 400.00
MAAJ Magic Johnson/50 200.00 400.00
MJAJ Michael Jordan/23 1000.00 2000.00

2001-02 Upper Deck Legends Legendary Signatures

This 31-card insert set was randomly inserted in packs at a rate of 1:71, this 31-card set features authentic player autographs. Full color player photos are set on the top half of the card and are surrounded by a "cloud" background which fades to gold at the card edges. The bottom of the card showcases the autograph. Two dual-player cards were issued with this set featuring Michael Jordan with Julius Erving and Kobe Bryant. Three cards are suspected short prints, Steve Francis, Larry Bird, and Julius Erving.

BR Bill Russell 500.00 700.00
BS Bill Sharman 8.00 20.00
DR Julius Erving SP 100.00 200.00
DT David Thompson 6.00 15.00
EB Elgin Baylor 15.00 40.00
EM Earl Monroe 10.00 25.00
GG George Gervin 12.00 30.00
JH John Havlicek 15.00 40.00
JW Jerry West 25.00 60.00
KA Kareem Abdul-Jabbar 50.00 100.00
KV Kiki Vandeweghe 6.00 15.00
LB Larry Bird SP 250.00 500.00
MA Magic Johnson 75.00 150.00
MM Moses Malone 10.00 25.00
NA Nate Archibald 10.00 25.00
OR Oscar Robertson 50.00 120.00
SF Steve Francis SP 10.00 25.00
WR Willis Reed 10.00 25.00

2001-02 Upper Deck Legends Record Producers

Randomly inserted in packs at a rate of 1:24, this 9-card insert set takes a look at some of the most important milestones on the NBA record books. Base cards contain full color action photos, gold borders on the left and right, and silver foil highlights.

COMPLETE SET (9) 10.00 25.00
RP1 Michael Jordan 6.00 15.00
RP2 John Stockton 1.00 2.50

RP3 Reggie Miller .75 2.00
RP4 Oscar Robertson 1.00 2.50
RP5 Hakeem Olajuwon 1.00 2.50
RP6 Elgin Baylor .75 2.00
RP7 Karl Malone 1.00 2.50
RP8 Kobe Bryant 4.00 10.00
RP9 Jerry West 1.00 2.50

2001-02 Upper Deck Legends Yearbook

This 9-card insert set was randomly inserted in packs at a rate of 1:24. The retro set captures memorable NBA moments of several NBA stars. Player photos are set agains a silver and black background with white borders.

COMPLETE SET (9) 10.00 25.00
Y1 Michael Jordan 6.00 15.00
Y2 Kobe Bryant 4.00 10.00
Y3 Walt Frazier .75 2.00
Y4 Pete Maravich 2.50 6.00
Y5 Clyde Drexler 1.00 2.50
Y6 Bob Lanier .75 2.00
Y7 Bill Russell 1.25 3.00
Y8 Bill Walton .75 2.00
Y9 Kevin Garnett 1.50 4.00

2003-04 Upper Deck Legends

Released in late June 2004, Upper Deck Legends boasts a 150-card base set divided up into 90 veteran player cards, 35 rookie cards sequentially numbered to 1999 (cards 91-125), 10 rookie cards sequentially numbered to 999 (cards 126-135) and 15 draft pick redemption cards with stated odds of one in 24. Legends was packaged in 24-pack boxes with packs containing five cards and carried a suggested retail price of $4.99. Each box contained an assortment of 16 Legends and eight Legends Retro packs, where Legends came out of the packs with LeBron James on them and Retro out of the Michael Jordan packs

COMP.SET w/o SP's (90) 12.50 30.00
1 Bob Sura .20 .50
2 Stephen Jackson .25 .60
3 Jason Terry .25 .60
4 Ricky Davis .25 .60
5 Jiri Welsch .20 .50
6 Paul Pierce .40 1.00
7 Eddy Curry .25 .60
8 Jamal Crawford .25 .60
9 Tyson Chandler .25 .60
10 Dajuan Wagner .20 .50
11 Carlos Boozer .30 .75
12 Zydrunas Ilgauskas .25 .60
13 Dirk Nowitzki .50 1.25
14 Antoine Walker .30 .75
15 Steve Nash .40 1.00
16 Michael Finley .30 .75
17 Jon Barry .20 .50
18 Andre Miller .25 .60
19 Nene .25 .60
20 Rasheed Wallace .30 .75
21 Richard Hamilton .25 .60
22 Ben Wallace .30 .75
23 Erick Dampier .20 .50
24 Jason Richardson .30 .75
25 Nick Van Exel .25 .60
26 Yao Ming .60 1.50
27 Cuttino Mobley .25 .60
28 Steve Francis .30 .75
29 Jermaine O'Neal .30 .75
30 Reggie Miller .30 .75
31 Ron Artest .30 .75
32 Elton Brand .30 .75
33 Corey Maggette .25 .60
34 Quentin Richardson .25 .60
35 Kobe Bryant 1.50 4.00
36 Karl Malone .40 1.00
37 Gary Payton .30 .75
38 Shaquille O'Neal .75 2.00
39 Pau Gasol .30 .75
40 Bonzi Wells .20 .50
41 Mike Miller .30 .75
42 Lamar Odom .30 .75
43 Eddie Jones .25 .60
44 Caron Butler .30 .75
45 Keith Van Horn .25 .60
46 Desmond Mason .25 .60
47 Michael Redd .30 .75
48 Latrell Sprewell .25 .60
49 Kevin Garnett .60 1.50
50 Sam Cassell .25 .60
51 Richard Jefferson .30 .75
52 Kenyon Martin .30 .75
53 Jason Kidd .50 1.25
54 Jamal Mashburn .25 .60
55 Baron Davis .30 .75
56 David Wesley .20 .50
57 Allan Houston .25 .60
58 Stephon Marbury .25 .60
59 Kurt Thomas .20 .50
60 Juwan Howard .25 .60
61 Drew Gooden .25 .60
62 Tracy McGrady .40 1.00
63 Zendon Hamilton RC .30 .75
64 Allen Iverson .50 1.25
65 Eric Snow .20 .50
66 Amare Stoudemire .50 1.25
67 Joe Johnson .30 .75
68 Shawn Marion .30 .75
69 Zach Randolph .30 .75
70 Darius Miles .20 .50
71 Shareef Abdur-Rahim .25 .60
72 Peja Stojakovic .30 .75
73 Chris Webber .30 .75
74 Mike Bibby .30 .75
75 Brad Miller .30 .75
76 Tony Parker .30 .75
77 Tim Duncan .50 1.25
78 Manu Ginobili .40 1.00
79 Ronald Murray .20 .50
80 Ray Allen .30 .75
81 Rashard Lewis .30 .75
82 Donyell Marshall .20 .50
83 Vince Carter .50 1.25
84 Jalen Rose .25 .60
85 Andrei Kirilenko .30 .75
86 Matt Harpring .25 .60
87 Carlos Arroyo .25 .60
88 Gilbert Arenas .30 .75
89 Larry Hughes .25 .60
90 Jerry Stackhouse .25 .60
91 Devin Brown RC 2.00 5.00
92 Ronald Dupree RC 2.00 5.00
93 Alex Garcia RC 2.00 5.00
94 Udonis Haslem RC 2.50 6.00
95 Maurice Williams RC 3.00 8.00
96 Brandon Hunter RC 2.00 5.00
97 Keith Bogans RC 2.00 5.00
98 Willie Green RC 2.00 5.00
99 Zaza Pachulia RC 2.00 5.00
100 Zarko Cabarkapa RC 2.00 5.00
101 Kyle Korver RC 2.50 6.00
102 Luke Walton RC 2.00 5.00
103 Maciej Lampe RC 2.00 5.00
104 Josh Howard RC 2.00 5.00
105 Kendrick Perkins RC 3.00 8.00
106 Ndudi Ebi RC 2.00 5.00
107 Jerome Beasley RC 2.00 5.00
108 Brian Cook RC 2.00 5.00
109 Travis Outlaw RC 2.50 6.00
110 Zoran Planinic RC 2.00 5.00
111 Boris Diaw RC 2.50 6.00
112 Steve Blake RC 2.50 6.00
113 Aleksandar Pavlovic RC 2.00 5.00
114 David West RC 2.50 6.00
115 Mike Sweetney RC 2.00 5.00
116 Troy Bell RC 2.00 5.00
117 Reece Gaines RC 2.00 5.00
118 Marcus Banks RC 2.00 5.00
119 Dahntay Jones RC 2.00 5.00
120 Chris Kaman RC 2.50 6.00
121 Mickael Pietrus RC 2.00 5.00
122 Luke Ridnour RC 2.50 6.00
123 Jason Kapono RC 2.00 5.00
124 Marquis Daniels RC 2.00 5.00
125 Travis Hansen RC 2.00 5.00
126 Leandro Barbosa RC 3.00 8.00
127 Nick Collison RC 2.50 6.00
128 Kirk Hinrich RC 3.00 8.00
129 T.J. Ford RC 3.00 8.00
130 Jarvis Hayes RC 2.50 6.00
131 Dwyane Wade RC 10.00 25.00
132 Chris Bosh RC 5.00 12.00
133 Carmelo Anthony RC 6.00 15.00
134 Darko Milicic RC 2.50 6.00
135 LeBron James RC 25.00 60.00
136 Dwight Howard XRC 10.00 25.00
137 Emeka Okafor XRC 5.00 12.00
138 Ben Gordon XRC 4.00 10.00
139 Shaun Livingston XRC 3.00 8.00
140 Devin Harris XRC 5.00 12.00
141 Josh Childress XRC 3.00 8.00
142 Luol Deng XRC 5.00 12.00
143 Rafael Araujo XRC 3.00 8.00
144 Andre Iguodala XRC 5.00 12.00
145 Luke Jackson XRC 3.00 8.00
146 Andris Biedrins XRC 4.00 10.00
147 Robert Swift XRC 3.00 8.00
148 Sebastian Telfair XRC 3.00 8.00
149 Kris Humphries XRC 3.00 8.00
150 Al Jefferson XRC 5.00 12.00

2003-04 Upper Deck Legends Throwback

This set breaks down very similarly to the base Upper Deck Legends set but instead features retired players on cards 1-90. Rookie players, numbers 91-135 are sequentially numbered to 100, and draft exchanges were inserted at one in 380.

COMP.SET w/o SP's 20.00 50.00
*TB 91-125: .5X TO 1.25X BASE HI
*TB 126-135: .4X TO 1X BASE HI
*TB 136-150: 1.25X TO 3X BASE HI
1 Dominique Wilkins .50 1.25
2 Spud Webb .50 1.25
3 Danny Ainge .40 1.00
4 Larry Bird 1.25 3.00
5 John Havlicek .40 1.00
6 Bob Cousy .60 1.50
7 Bill Russell .60 1.50
8 Kevin McHale .50 1.25
9 Dave Cowens .50 1.25
10 Dennis Johnson .40 1.00
11 K.C. Jones .40 1.00
12 Robert Parish .50 1.25
13 Nate Archibald .40 1.00
14 Michael Jordan 3.00 8.00
15 Dennis Rodman .50 1.25
16 Bill Cartwright .40 1.00
17 Spencer Haywood .40 1.00
18 World B. Free .40 1.00
19 Rolando Blackman .40 1.00
20 Walt Bellamy .40 1.00
21 Dan Issel .40 1.00
22 David Thompson .40 1.00
23 Alex English .40 1.00
24 Dave Bing .40 1.00
25 Isiah Thomas .40 1.00
26 Bill Laimbeer .40 1.00
27 Bob Lanier .40 1.00
28 Vinnie Johnson .40 1.00
29 M.L. Carr .40 1.00
30 Cazzie Russell .40 1.00
31 Rick Barry .40 1.00
32 Chris Mullin .50 1.25
33 Nate Thurmond .40 1.00
34 Gail Goodrich .40 1.00
35 Kenny Smith .40 1.00
36 George McGinnis .40 1.00
37 Clark Kellogg .40 1.00
38 Michael Cage .40 1.00
39 Wilt Chamberlain .75 2.00
40 Magic Johnson 1.25 3.00
41 Kurt Rambis .50 1.25
42 James Worthy .50 1.25
43 Jamaal Wilkes .40 1.00
44 Kareem Abdul-Jabbar .60 1.50
45 George Mikan .75 2.00
46 Elgin Baylor .40 1.00
47 Michael Cooper .40 1.00
48 Pat Riley .50 1.25
49 Alonzo Mourning .50 1.25
50 Rony Seikaly .40 1.00
51 Ricky Pierce .40 1.00
52 Terry Cummings .40 1.00
53 Oscar Robertson .40 1.00
54 Sidney Moncrief .40 1.00
55 Darryl Dawkins .50 1.25
56 Otis Birdsong .40 1.00
57 Jerry Lucas .40 1.00
58 Dave DeBusschere .50 1.25
59 Patrick Ewing .50 1.25
60 Willis Reed .40 1.00
61 Walt Frazier .40 1.00
62 Earl Monroe .40 1.00
63 Donald Royal .40 1.00
64 Moses Malone .40 1.00
65 Julius Erving .75 2.00
66 Maurice Cheeks .40 1.00
67 Billy Cunningham .40 1.00
68 Kevin Johnson .40 1.00
69 Tom Chambers .40 1.00
70 Larry Nance .40 1.00
71 Walter Davis .40 1.00
72 Maurice Lucas .40 1.00
73 Paul Westphal .50 1.25
74 Bill Walton .40 1.00
75 Jim Paxson .40 1.00
76 Clyde Drexler .50 1.25
77 Reggie Theus .40 1.00
78 Nate McMillan .40 1.00
79 David Robinson .60 1.50
80 Artis Gilmore .40 1.00
81 George Gervin .40 1.00
82 Fred Brown .40 1.00
83 Detlef Schrempf .40 1.00
84 Jack Sikma .40 1.00
85 Lenny Wilkens .40 1.00
86 Pete Maravich 1.25 3.00
87 John Stockton .50 1.25
88 Darrell Griffith .40 1.00
89 Wes Unseld .40 1.00
90 Elvin Hayes .40 1.00
131 Dwyane Wade 15.00 40.00
135 LeBron James 30.00 80.00

2003-04 Upper Deck Legends Championship Numbers Autographs

Randomly seeded, this 35-card set features a picture and an autograph of each player and all cards are sequentially numbered to the jersey number that player wore while winning an NBA Championship.

SOME NOT PRICED DUE TO SCARCITY
BL Bill Laimbeer/40 25.00 60.00
BS Bill Sharman/21 15.00 40.00
CD Chuck Daly/80 30.00 60.00
CM Cedric Maxwell/31 15.00 40.00
CO Michael Cooper/21 25.00 60.00
CR Cazzie Russell/33 12.50 30.00
CU Billy Cunningham/80 25.00 60.00
DC Dave Cowens/18 20.00 50.00
DR David Robinson/50 50.00 120.00
GM George Mikan/99 125.00 250.00
JW James Worthy/42 75.00 150.00
KJ K.C. Jones/25 15.00 40.00
KJ K.C. Jones/80 12.50 30.00
KR Kurt Rambis/31 25.00 60.00
LB Larry Bird/33 125.00 250.00
MA Magic Johnson/32 75.00 150.00
MJ Michael Jordan/90 300.00 600.00
PR Pat Riley/80 30.00 80.00
RO Dennis Rodman/91 60.00 150.00
RP Robert Parish/80 20.00 50.00
WI Jamaal Wilkes/52 12.50 30.00
WR Willis Reed/19 40.00 100.00
WU Wes Unseld/41 12.50 30.00

2003-04 Upper Deck Legends Championship Teammates Dual Autographs

Randomly inserted, this 18-card set pairs two players from the same championship team, one on the top and one on the bottom, along with a small head photo and an authentic autograph. Each card is sequentially numbered to 25.

UNPRICED TRIPLE PRINT RUN 5 SER.#'d SETS
BT Bob Cousy 30.00 80.00
  Tommy Heinsohn
BW Larry Bird 125.00 250.00
  Bill Walton
CC Billy Cunningham 25.00 60.00
  Maurice Cheeks
CR Bob Cousy 200.00 350.00
  Bill Russell
EC Julius Erving 50.00 120.00
  Maurice Cheeks
FR Walt Frazier 25.00 60.00
  Willis Reed
JH K.C. Jones 25.00 60.00
  Tommy Heinsohn
JS K.C. Jones 40.00 100.00
  Bill Sharman
JW Magic Johnson 150.00 300.00
  James Worthy
RF Cazzie Russell 40.00 100.00
  Walt Frazier
RR Pat Riley 30.00 80.00
  Kurt Rambis
TL Isiah Thomas 30.00 80.00
  Bill Lambeer
WJ Bill Walton 25.00 60.00
  Dennis Johnson
WP Bill Walton 40.00 100.00
  Robert Parish
WR James Worthy 40.00 100.00
  Kurt Rambis

2003-04 Upper Deck Legends Hall of Fame Induction Ink

Randomly inserted with all other autographed cards at the combined rate of one in eight, this six-card set features HOF greats, both from the NBA and elsewhere. Each card has a photo on the right and a vertical cut signature on the left.

DM Dino Meneghin 25.00 50.00
EL Earl Lloyd 25.00 60.00
JW James Worthy 30.00 80.00
LB Leon Barmore 15.00 40.00
ML Meadowlark Lemon 40.00 80.00
RP Robert Parish 15.00 40.00

2003-04 Upper Deck Legends Legendary Inscriptions

Limited to 100 copies per, each of these cards is horizontally designed with a small player photo and an autograph along with a special inscription.

AG Artis Gilmore A-Train 20.00 50.00
BC Bob Cousy Cooz 50.00 120.00
BW Bill Walton Big Red 25.00 60.00
CM Cedric Maxwell Cornbread 20.00 50.00
DA David Robinson Admiral 80.00 160.00
DC Dave Cowens Big Red 20.00 50.00
DD Darryl Dawkins Chocolate Thunder 20.00 50.00
DD1 Darryl Dawkins Love Tron 20.00 50.00
DG Darrell Griffith Dr. Dunkenstein 20.00 50.00
DJ Dennis Johnson DJ 30.00 80.00
DT David Thompson Skywalker 20.00 50.00
EH Elvin Hayes The Big E 20.00 50.00
GG George Gervin The Iceman 25.00 60.00
GM George Mikan Mr. Basketball 250.00 450.00
IT Isiah Thomas Zeke 40.00 100.00
JA Jamaal Wilkes Silk 20.00 50.00
JE Julius Erving Dr. J 60.00 150.00
JS John Salley Spider 20.00 50.00
JW James Worthy Big Game James 40.00 100.00
KR Kurt Rambis Clark Kent 20.00 50.00
MA Magic Johnson Magic 100.00 200.00
MC Michael Cooper Coop 20.00 50.00
MO Maurice Cheeks Mo 20.00 50.00
RP Robert Parish Chief 40.00 100.00
SW Anthony Webb Spud 20.00 50.00
WF Walt Frazier Clyde 30.00 80.00
WR Willis Reed The Captain 30.00 80.00
ZO Alonzo Mourning Zo 40.00 100.00

2003-04 Upper Deck Legends Legendary Signatures

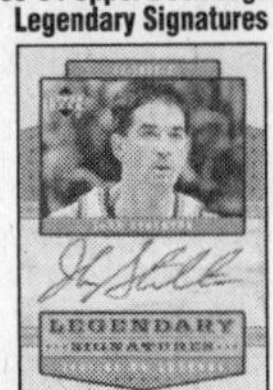

Inserted with all other autographed cards with the combined odds of one in eight, this 40-card set features a photo of each player and an autograph. Please note that SP information was provided by Upper Deck. Michael Cooper has two autograph versions-one is just a signature while the other contains the inscription "Coop."

AG Artis Gilmore 8.00 20.00
AM Alonzo Mourning 15.00 40.00
BC Bob Cousy 20.00 50.00
BL Bill Laimbeer 8.00 20.00
BR Bill Russell SP 100.00 200.00
BS Bill Sharman 8.00 20.00
BW Bill Walton 10.00 25.00
CD Chuck Daly 20.00 40.00
CR Cazzie Russell 8.00 20.00
CU Billy Cunningham 50.00 120.00
DA David Robinson SP 40.00 80.00
DC Dave Cowens 8.00 20.00
DD Darryl Dawkins 8.00 20.00
DG Darrell Griffith 8.00 20.00
DJ Dennis Johnson 25.00 60.00
DR Dennis Rodman 40.00 100.00
DT David Thompson 8.00 20.00
EH Elvin Hayes 8.00 20.00
GG George Gervin 8.00 20.00
GM George Mikan 125.00 250.00
IT Isiah Thomas 20.00 50.00
JA Jamaal Wilkes 8.00 20.00
JE Julius Erving SP 50.00 120.00
JS John Stockton SP 60.00 150.00
JW James Worthy 25.00 60.00
KC K.C. Jones 10.00 25.00
KR Kurt Rambis 10.00 25.00
LB Larry Bird SP 100.00 200.00
MA Magic Johnson SP 60.00 150.00
MC Michael Cooper 8.00 20.00
MC1 Michael Coop Cooper 8.00 20.00
MJ Michael Jordan SP 400.00 700.00
MO Maurice Cheeks 8.00 20.00
PE Patrick Ewing 75.00 150.00
PR Pat Riley 20.00 40.00
RP Robert Parish 12.50 30.00
SW Spud Webb 8.00 20.00
TH Tommy Heinsohn 10.00 25.00
WF Walt Frazier 10.00 25.00
WR Willis Reed 10.00 25.00
WU Wes Unseld 10.00 25.00

2003-04 Upper Deck Legends Rookie Impressions Dual Autographs

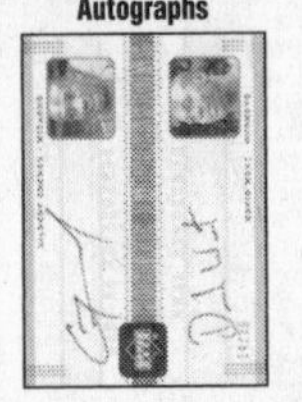

Randomly seeded, this 12-card set features a rookie and a veteran on a horizontally designed card with small head-shot photos and authentic autographs. Each card is sequentially numbered to 25.

AJJH Antawn Jamison 20.00 50.00
  Josh Howard
GADA Gilbert Arenas 20.00 50.00
  David West
GPTB Gary Payton 20.00 50.00
  Troy Bell
JDSB Juan Dixon 20.00 50.00
  Steve Blake
JKMB Jason Kidd 40.00 100.00
  Marcus Banks
JRMP Jason Richardson 20.00 50.00
  Mickael Pietrus
KBDW Kobe Bryant 400.00 700.00
  Dwyane Wade
KGCB Kevin Garnett 75.00 200.00
  Chris Bosh
LBDM Larry Bird 125.00 250.00
  Darko Milicic
MJLJ Michael Jordan 2500.00 4000.00
  LeBron James
TMCA Tracy McGrady 100.00 200.00
  Carmelo Anthony
YMCK Yao Ming 40.00 100.00
  Chris Kaman

2003-04 Upper Deck Legends Signs of a Future Legend

Inserted along with all other autograph cards at the rate of one in eight, this 36-card set places a photo of the player on the right and a vertical signature on the left.

AK Andrei Kirilenko 6.00 15.00
AM Andre Miller 4.00 10.00
AS Amare Stoudemire 12.50 30.00
BC Brian Cook 4.00 10.00
BD Boris Diaw 5.00 12.00
BO Carlos Boozer 5.00 12.00
CA Carmelo Anthony SP 25.00 60.00
CB Chris Bosh SP 15.00 40.00
CH Chauncey Billups 6.00 15.00
DA David West 5.00 12.00
DM Darko Milicic SP 8.00 20.00
DW Dajuan Wagner 4.00 10.00
DY Dwyane Wade 75.00 150.00
EG Manu Ginobili 15.00 40.00
FJ Fred Jones 4.00 10.00
GA Gilbert Arenas 8.00 20.00
GP Gary Payton SP 15.00 40.00
JA Jalen Rose 5.00 12.00
JH Josh Howard 4.00 10.00
JK Jason Kidd SP 12.50 30.00
JR Jason Richardson 4.00 10.00
KB Keith Bogans 4.00 10.00
KG Kevin Garnett SP 30.00 80.00
KK Kyle Korver 5.00 12.00
KR Kareem Rush 4.00 10.00
LB Leandro Barbosa 5.00 12.00
LJ LeBron James SP 250.00 450.00
LR Luke Ridnour 5.00 12.00
LW Luke Walton 4.00 10.00
ML Maciej Lampe 4.00 10.00
NH Nene 4.00 10.00
RH Richard Hamilton 4.00 10.00
RJ Richard Jefferson 6.00 15.00
SC Sam Cassell 6.00 15.00
TM Tracy McGrady SP 20.00 50.00
YM Yao Ming SP 25.00 60.00

2000 Upper Deck Legends Master Collection

The 2000 Upper Deck Legends Master Collection was released in late 2000, and featured an 18-card base set, one mystery pack, one Warm-Up card, five Autographs, and one Floor card packaged in a wooden box with a certificate of authenticity. There were only 200 Master Collections produced.

COMPLETE SET (18) 400.00 800.00
1 Michael Jordan 125.00 300.00
2 Bill Russell 25.00 60.00
3 Magic Johnson 50.00 125.00
4 Larry Bird 50.00 125.00
5 Julius Erving 30.00 80.00
6 Wilt Chamberlain 30.00 80.00
7 Jerry West 20.00 50.00
8 Bill Walton 15.00 40.00
9 Bob Cousy 25.00 60.00
10 John Havlicek 20.00 50.00
11 Elgin Baylor 15.00 40.00
12 Oscar Robertson 20.00 50.00
13 Walt Frazier 15.00 40.00
14 George Gervin 15.00 40.00
15 Pete Maravich 50.00 125.00
16 Isiah Thomas 15.00 40.00
17 Moses Malone 15.00 40.00
18 Rick Barry 15.00 40.00

2000 Upper Deck Legends Master Collection Legendary Floor

This 2-card game-used floor set was included in the 2000 Upper Deck Legends Master collection. Each Master Collection incuded one of the two cards, and each card is serial numbered to 100. Card backs carry the player's initials.

COMPLETE SET (2) 100.00 200.00
COMMON CARD (F1-F2) 60.00 120.00

2000 Upper Deck Legends Master Collection Living Legends Autographs

This 20-card autograph set was included in the 2000 Upper Deck Legends Master collection. Each Master Collection incuded a set of 5 of these cards, and each card is serial numbered to 50. Card backs carry the player's initials.

BL1 Bill Russell 125.00 250.00
BL2 Bill Russell 125.00 250.00
BL3 Bill Russell 125.00 250.00
BL4 Bill Russell 125.00 250.00
EL1 Magic Johnson 60.00 120.00
EL2 Magic Johnson 60.00 120.00
EL3 Magic Johnson 60.00 120.00
EL4 Magic Johnson 60.00 120.00
JL1 Julius Erving 60.00 120.00
JL2 Julius Erving 60.00 120.00
JL3 Julius Erving 60.00 120.00
JL4 Julius Erving 60.00 120.00
LL1 Larry Bird 100.00 200.00
LL2 Larry Bird 100.00 200.00
LL3 Larry Bird 100.00 200.00
LL4 Larry Bird 100.00 200.00
ML1 Michael Jordan 600.00 1000.00
ML2 Michael Jordan 600.00 1000.00
ML3 Michael Jordan 600.00 1000.00
ML4 Michael Jordan 600.00 1000.00

2000 Upper Deck Legends Master Collection Mystery Pack Inserts

Mystery Packs were inserted at a rate of one per Master Collection. The mystery packs included one game-used memorabilia card from players such as Michael Jordan, Magic Johnson, Larry Bird, and Bill Russell, and Julius Erving. Card backs carry the player's initials as numbering.

EJA Magic Johnson Floor AU/32 80.00 160.00
DR/EJ Julius Erving 50.00 100.00
  Magic Johnson Jsy/37

2000 Upper Deck Legends Master Collection Warm-Ups

This card was inserted into Legends Master Collections at a rate of one per set. The card features a swatch from a game-used Wilt Chamberlain warm-up jersey. Card back carries the player's initials. Stated print run of 200 serial numbered sets.

WC1 Wilt Chamberlain 50.00 100.00

2003 Upper Deck Lego Sports

Released in eight different packs of three, these cards were produced by Upper Deck in conjunction with Lego. The three packs were issued in the following configurations: #3560 Ray Allen, Tim Duncan, and Pau Gasol. #3561 Antoine Walker, Shaquille O'Neal and Tony Parker. #3562 Gary Payton, Dirk Nowitzki, and Vince Carter. #3563 Toni Kukoc, Jason Kidd, and Kobe Bryant. #3564 Allen Iverson, Steve Francis, and Karl Malone. #3565 Paul Pierce, Jerry Stackhouse, and Steve Nash. #3566 Jalen Rose, Peja Stojakovic and Kevin Garnett. #3567 Tracy McGrady, Chris Webber and Allen Houston. Each package contains three cards, three lego figures and three stands where both the figure and card can be set up. Each three-card pack contained on gold card verson. The gold cards are differentiated by gold foil and embossing on the card front.

COMPLETE SET (24) 6.00 15.00
*GOLD: .75X TO 2X BASE HI
2 Ray Allen .40 1.00
4 Shaquille O'Neal .75 2.00
5 Antoine Walker .40 1.00
6 Tony Parker .40 1.00
7 Vince Carter .40 1.00
8 Dirk Nowitzki .50 1.25
10 Kobe Bryant 2.00 5.00
11 Jason Kidd .50 1.25
12 Toni Kukoc .40 1.00
13 Allen Iverson .50 1.25
14 Tracy McGrady .50 1.25
15 Karl Malone .50 1.25
16 Paul Pierce .40 1.00
17 Jerry Stackhouse .40 1.00
18 Steve Nash .50 1.25
19 Kevin Garnett .60 1.50
21 Jalen Rose .40 1.00
22 Chris Webber .40 1.00
23 Steve Francis .40 1.00
24 Allan Houston .40 1.00

2008-09 Upper Deck Lineage

This set was released on April 1, 2009. The base set consists of 233 cards. Cards 1-200 feature veterans, and cards 201-233 are rookies.

COMP.SET w/o RCs (200) 20.00 40.00
1 Bill Russell .50 1.25
2 Sam Jones .40 1.00
3 Oscar Robertson .30 .75
4 Kareem Abdul-Jabbar .50 1.25
5 Julius Erving .60 1.50
6 George Gervin .40 1.00
7 Bill Walton .30 .75
8 Robert Parish .30 .75
9 Larry Bird 1.00 2.50
10 Magic Johnson .75 2.00
11 Isiah Thomas .30 .75
12 James Worthy .30 .75
13 Dominique Wilkins .40 1.00
14 Clyde Drexler .40 1.00
15 John Stockton .50 1.25
16 Hakeem Olajuwon .40 1.00
17 Michael Jordan 2.50 6.00
18 Tom Chambers .30 .75
19 Adrian Dantley .30 .75
20 David Robinson .50 1.25
21 Shaquille O'Neal .60 1.50
22 Alonzo Mourning .40 1.00
23 Jason Kidd .30 .75
24 Grant Hill .40 1.00
25 Rasheed Wallace .30 .75
26 Kevin Garnett .60 1.50
27 Bruce Bowen .20 .50
28 Steve Nash .30 .75
29 Marcus Camby .20 .50
30 Derek Fisher .25 .60
31 Ben Wallace .30 .75
32 Allen Iverson .40 1.00
33 Ray Allen .30 .75
34 Brad Miller .25 .60
35 Kobe Bryant 1.50 4.00
36 Jermaine O'Neal .30 .75
37 Tim Duncan .50 1.25
38 Chauncey Billups .30 .75
39 Tracy McGrady .30 .75
40 Zydrunas Ilgauskas .25 .60
41 Javaris Crittenton .20 .50
42 Antawn Jamison .30 .75
43 Vince Carter .40 1.00
44 Peja Stojakovic .30 .75
45 Paul Pierce .40 1.00
46 Mike Bibby .25 .60
47 Dirk Nowitzki .40 1.00
48 Rashard Lewis .25 .60
49 Al Harrington .25 .60
50 Andre Miller .25 .60
51 Wally Szczerbiak .25 .60
52 Jason Terry .25 .60
53 Richard Hamilton .25 .60
54 Shawn Marion .30 .75
55 Elton Brand .30 .75
56 Baron Davis .30 .75
57 Lamar Odom .30 .75
58 Corey Maggette .25 .60
59 Ron Artest .30 .75
60 Morris Peterson .20 .50
61 Desmond Mason .20 .50
62 Kenyon Martin .30 .75
63 Stephen Jackson .25 .60
64 Hedo Turkoglu .30 .75
65 Michael Redd .30 .75
66 Mike Miller .30 .75
67 Jamal Crawford .25 .60
68 Quentin Richardson .25 .60
69 Keyon Dooling .20 .50
70 DeShawn Stevenson .20 .50
71 Jamaal Tinsley .20 .50
72 Shane Battier .25 .60
73 Earl Watson .20 .50
74 Richard Jefferson .30 .75
75 Pau Gasol .30 .75
76 Jason Richardson .30 .75
77 Andrei Kirilenko .25 .60
78 Joe Johnson .30 .75
79 Zach Randolph .25 .60
80 Gilbert Arenas .30 .75
81 Tony Parker .30 .75
82 Gerald Wallace .30 .75
83 Tyson Chandler .25 .60
84 Eddy Curry .20 .50
85 Manu Ginobili .30 .75
86 Marko Jaric .20 .50
87 Mehmet Okur .20 .50
88 John Salmons .30 .75
89 Tayshaun Prince .30 .75
90 Caron Butler .30 .75
91 Yao Ming .40 1.00
92 Mike Dunleavy .25 .60
93 Samuel Dalembert .20 .50
94 Carlos Boozer .30 .75
95 Chris Wilcox .20 .50
96 Nene .25 .60
97 Amare Stoudemire .30 .75
98 Steve Blake .20 .50
99 Luke Walton .20 .50
100 Josh Howard .25 .60
101 Keith Bogans .20 .50
102 Udonis Haslem .25 .60
103 David West .30 .75
104 Kirk Hinrich .30 .75
105 Kyle Korver .25 .60
106 Willie Green .20 .50
107 Dwyane Wade .60 1.50
108 Boris Diaw .20 .50
109 Chris Kaman .25 .60
110 Leandro Barbosa .25 .60
111 Mo Williams .25 .60
112 Chris Bosh .30 .75
113 Carmelo Anthony .40 1.00
114 Kendrick Perkins .25 .60
115 LeBron James 1.50 4.00
116 Andres Nocioni .20 .50
117 Damien Wilkins .20 .50
118 Jameer Nelson .25 .60
119 Beno Udrih .20 .50
120 Chris Duhon .20 .50
121 Anderson Varejao .25 .60
122 Emeka Okafor .30 .75
123 Kevin Martin .30 .75
124 Devin Harris .30 .75
125 T.J. Ford .20 .50
126 Ben Gordon .30 .75
127 Andre Iguodala .30 .75
128 Sasha Vujacic .20 .50
129 Al Jefferson .30 .75
130 Luol Deng .30 .75
131 J.R. Smith .30 .75
132 Josh Smith .30 .75
133 Dwight Howard .60 1.50
134 Fabricio Oberto .20 .50
135 Jose Calderon .25 .60

136 Francisco Garcia .25 .60
137 Hakim Warrick .25 .60
138 Luther Head .20 .50
139 Jason Maxiell .20 .50
140 Danny Granger .30 .75
141 David Lee .25 .60
142 Chuck Hayes .20 .50
143 Jarrett Jack .25 .60
144 Raymond Felton .25 .60
145 Deron Williams .30 .75
146 Rashad McCants .20 .50
147 Andrew Bogut .30 .75
148 Brandon Bass .20 .50
149 Chris Paul .50 1.25
150 Shaun Livingston .20 .50
151 Monta Ellis .30 .75
152 Marvin Williams .30 .75
153 Louis Williams .25 .60
154 Martell Webster .25 .60
155 Andrew Bynum .40 1.00
156 Randy Foye .30 .75
157 Shelden Williams .20 .50
158 Leon Powe .20 .50
159 Rodney Carney .20 .50
160 Jose Barea .40 1.00
161 Brandon Roy .30 .75
162 Josh Boone .20 .50
163 Ronnie Brewer .25 .60
164 LaMarcus Aldridge .30 .75
165 Andrea Bargnani .25 .60
166 Rajon Rondo .40 1.00
167 Daniel Gibson .30 .75
168 Kyle Lowry .30 .75
169 Sergio Rodriguez .20 .50
170 Tyrus Thomas .25 .60
171 Rudy Gay .30 .75
172 Jordan Farmar .20 .50
173 Luis Scola .25 .60
174 Jamario Moon .20 .50
175 Carl Landry .20 .50
176 Al Thornton .25 .60
177 C.J. Watson .20 .50
178 Adam Morrison .30 .75
179 Acie Law .25 .60
180 Morris Almond .20 .50
181 Joakim Noah .30 .75
182 Nick Young .25 .60
183 Arron Afflalo .20 .50
184 Jared Dudley .25 .60
185 Glen Davis .25 .60
186 Corey Brewer .25 .60
187 Marco Belinelli .20 .50
188 Ramon Sessions .25 .60
189 Rodney Stuckey .40 1.00
190 Al Horford .30 .75
191 Jeff Green .25 .60
192 Sean Williams .25 .60
193 Daequan Cook .20 .50
194 Julian Wright .25 .60
195 Brandan Wright .25 .60
196 Mike Conley Jr. .25 .60
197 Yi Jianlian .30 .75
198 Thaddeus Young .25 .60
199 Kevin Durant 1.25 3.00
200 Greg Oden .30 .75
201 Derrick Rose RC 10.00 25.00
202 Michael Beasley RC 1.25 3.00
203 O.J. Mayo RC 1.25 3.00
204 Russell Westbrook RC 4.00 10.00
205 Kevin Love RC 3.00 8.00
206 Danilo Gallinari RC 1.25 3.00
207 Eric Gordon RC 2.00 5.00
208 Joe Alexander RC .75 2.00
209 D.J. Augustin RC .75 2.00
210 Brook Lopez RC 1.25 3.00
211 Jerryd Bayless RC .75 2.00
212 Jason Thompson RC .75 2.00
213 Brandon Rush RC .75 2.00
214 Anthony Randolph RC 1.00 2.50
215 Robin Lopez RC .75 2.00
216 Marreese Speights RC .75 2.00
217 Roy Hibbert RC 1.25 3.00
218 J.J. Hickson RC 1.00 2.50
219 Ryan Anderson RC 1.25 3.00
220 George Hill RC 1.25 3.00
221 Darrell Arthur RC .75 2.00
222 Donte Greene RC .75 2.00
223 D.J. White RC .75 2.00
224 J.R. Giddens RC .75 2.00
225 Walter Sharpe RC .75 2.00
226 Mario Chalmers RC 1.25 3.00
227 Sonny Weems RC .75 2.00
228 Chris Douglas-Roberts RC .75 2.00
229 Sean Singletary RC .75 2.00
230 Luc Richard Mbah A Moute RC .75 2.00
231 Bill Walker RC .75 2.00
232 Marc Gasol RC 1.25 3.00
233 Rudy Fernandez RC 1.00 2.50

2008-09 Upper Deck Lineage SE

*1-200 VETS: 1.25X TO 3X BASE HI
*201-233 ROOKIES: .6X TO 1.5X BASE HI
RANDOM INSERTS IN PACKS

2008-09 Upper Deck Lineage 15,000 Point Club

COMBINED AUTO ODDS 1:12
15AD Adrian Dantley 6.00 15.00
15AE Alex English 6.00 15.00
15AG Artis Gilmore 6.00 15.00
15BA Rick Barry 10.00 25.00
15GG George Gervin 8.00 20.00
15GR Glen Rice 6.00 15.00
15HO Hakeem Olajuwon 10.00 25.00
15KA Kareem Abdul-Jabbar 40.00 100.00
15KG Kevin Garnett 40.00 75.00
15MJ Michael Jordan 300.00 500.00
15RP Robert Parish 6.00 15.00
15SJ Sam Jones 10.00 25.00
15TC Tom Chambers 6.00 15.00
15VC Vince Carter 30.00 60.00

2008-09 Upper Deck Lineage Collection

COMBINED AUTO ODDS 1:12
LCAD Adrian Dantley 5.00 12.00
LCAM Alonzo Mourning 150.00 300.00
LCBA B.J. Armstrong 6.00 15.00
LCBD Brad Daugherty 6.00 15.00
LCDR David Robinson 40.00 100.00
LCGR Glen Rice 6.00 15.00
LCHG Horace Grant 20.00 50.00
LCHO Hakeem Olajuwon 25.00 60.00
LCIT Isiah Thomas 10.00 25.00
LCJO Michael Jordan 300.00 500.00
LCJS John Stockton 125.00 250.00
LCMB Muggsy Bogues 6.00 15.00
LCME Mark Eaton 5.00 12.00
LCMJ Magic Johnson 30.00 60.00
LCMM Moses Malone 8.00 20.00
LCMP Mark Price 12.00 30.00
LCSA John Salley 6.00 15.00
LCSP Sam Perkins 8.00 20.00
LCSW Spud Webb 6.00 15.00
LCTC Terry Cummings 5.00 12.00
LCTO Tom Chambers 5.00 12.00
LCVD Vlade Divac 6.00 15.00

2008-09 Upper Deck Lineage Flight Team

COMBINED AUTO ODDS 1:12
FTAI Andre Iguodala 6.00 15.00
FTAT Al Thornton 8.00 20.00
FTBD Baron Davis 15.00 30.00
FTDH Dwight Howard 20.00 40.00
FTDM Desmond Mason 5.00 12.00
FTDS DeShawn Stevenson 5.00 12.00
FTGG Gerald Green 5.00 12.00
FTJA Joe Alexander 5.00 12.00
FTJR J.R. Giddens 5.00 12.00
FTKB Kobe Bryant 100.00 200.00
FTLJ LeBron James 125.00 250.00
FTLM Luc Richard Mbah A Moute 5.00 12.00
FTRG Rudy Gay 6.00 15.00
FTRJ Richard Jefferson 5.00 12.00
FTSM J.R. Smith 8.00 20.00
FTSW Sean Williams 5.00 12.00
FTTP Tayshaun Prince 5.00 12.00
FTWE Sonny Weems 5.00 12.00

2008-09 Upper Deck Lineage Mr. June

COMPLETE SET (23) 30.00 60.00
COMMON CARD 1.50 4.00

2008-09 Upper Deck Lineage Rookie Standouts

COMPLETE SET (54) 30.00 60.00
RANDOM INSERTS IN PACKS
RS1 Derrick Rose 6.00 15.00
RS2 Michael Beasley 1.25 3.00
RS3 O.J. Mayo 1.25 3.00
RS4 Russell Westbrook 4.00 10.00
RS5 Kevin Love 3.00 8.00
RS6 Danilo Gallinari 1.25 3.00
RS7 Eric Gordon 2.00 5.00
RS8 Joe Alexander .75 2.00
RS9 D.J. Augustin .75 2.00
RS10 Brook Lopez 1.25 3.00
RS11 Jerryd Bayless .75 2.00
RS12 Jason Thompson .75 2.00
RS13 Brandon Rush .75 2.00
RS14 Anthony Randolph 1.00 2.50
RS15 Robin Lopez .75 2.00
RS16 Marreese Speights .75 2.00
RS17 Roy Hibbert 1.25 3.00
RS18 Luc Richard Mbah A Moute .75 2.00
RS19 Mario Chalmers 1.25 3.00
RS20 Javale McGee 1.25 3.00
RS21 Anthony Morrow .75 2.00
RS22 Darrell Arthur .75 2.00
RS23 Nicolas Batum 1.25 3.00
RS24 Ryan Anderson 1.25 3.00
RS25 Bobby Brown .50 1.25
RS26 J.J. Hickson 1.00 2.50
RS27 Sun Yue 1.00 2.50
RS28 DeMarcus Nelson .50 1.25
RS29 Courtney Lee 1.25 3.00
RS30 Kosta Koufos .75 2.00
RS31 Donte Greene .75 2.00
RS32 Mike Taylor .75 2.00
RS33 Roko Leni Ukic .75 2.00
RS34 Anthony Tolliver .50 1.25
RS35 Darnell Jackson .75 2.00
RS36 Alexis Ajinca .75 2.00
RS37 Goran Dragic 1.25 3.00
RS38 Chris Douglas-Roberts .75 2.00
RS39 Sean Singletary .75 2.00
RS40 Kyle Weaver .75 2.00
RS41 Bill Walker .75 2.00
RS42 DeAndre Jordan 1.50 4.00
RS43 Rob Kurz .50 1.25
RS44 Rudy Fernandez 1.00 2.50
RS45 George Hill 1.25 3.00
RS46 Greg Oden .75 2.00
RS47 Marc Gasol 1.25 3.00
RS48 Louis Amundson .50 1.25
RS49 Nathan Jawai .75 2.00
RS50 Othello Hunter .75 2.00
RS51 Walter Sharpe .75 2.00
RS52 Joey Dorsey .75 2.00
RS53 J.R. Giddens .75 2.00
RS54 Jawad Williams .75 2.00

2008-09 Upper Deck Lineage SE Die Cut Autographs

COMBINED AUTO ODDS 1:12
2 Sam Jones 15.00 40.00
3 Oscar Robertson 50.00 125.00
4 Kareem Abdul-Jabbar 40.00 80.00
5 Julius Erving 50.00 120.00
6 George Gervin 8.00 20.00
8 Robert Parish 6.00 15.00
10 Magic Johnson 30.00 80.00
12 James Worthy 40.00 80.00
13 Dominique Wilkins 40.00 100.00
17 Michael Jordan 350.00 550.00
18 Tom Chambers 5.00 12.00
19 Adrian Dantley 4.00 10.00
20 David Robinson 50.00 125.00
23 Jason Kidd 20.00 50.00
26 Kevin Garnett 50.00 100.00
27 Bruce Bowen 4.00 10.00
28 Steve Nash 30.00 60.00
30 Derek Fisher 6.00 15.00
33 Ray Allen 20.00 40.00
36 Jermaine O'Neal 12.00 30.00
38 Chauncey Billups 8.00 20.00
41 Javaris Crittenton 4.00 10.00
43 Vince Carter 30.00 60.00
45 Paul Pierce 30.00 60.00
49 Al Harrington 4.00 10.00
57 Lamar Odom 6.00 15.00
58 Corey Maggette 6.00 15.00
59 Ron Artest 6.00 15.00
65 Michael Redd 4.00 10.00
68 Quentin Richardson 4.00 10.00
74 Richard Jefferson 4.00 10.00
78 Joe Johnson 6.00 15.00
84 Eddy Curry 4.00 10.00
89 Tayshaun Prince 4.00 10.00
90 Caron Butler 15.00 40.00
94 Carlos Boozer 5.00 12.00
97 Amare Stoudemire 15.00 30.00
100 Josh Howard 8.00 20.00
103 David West 4.00 10.00
105 Kyle Korver 4.00 10.00
108 Boris Diaw 4.00 10.00
109 Chris Kaman 4.00 10.00
110 Leandro Barbosa 4.00 10.00
112 Chris Bosh 20.00 40.00
115 LeBron James 200.00 325.00
118 Jameer Nelson 4.00 10.00
119 Beno Udrih 4.00 10.00
120 Chris Duhon 4.00 10.00
121 Anderson Varejao 5.00 12.00
126 Ben Gordon 6.00 15.00
127 Andre Iguodala 6.00 15.00
128 Sasha Vujacic 6.00 15.00
129 Al Jefferson 5.00 12.00
130 Luol Deng 4.00 10.00
131 J.R. Smith 6.00 15.00
133 Dwight Howard 20.00 40.00
136 Francisco Garcia 4.00 10.00
139 Jason Maxiell 4.00 10.00
140 Danny Granger 6.00 15.00
141 David Lee 6.00 15.00
143 Jarrett Jack 4.00 10.00
144 Raymond Felton 4.00 10.00
145 Deron Williams 8.00 20.00
148 Brandon Bass 4.00 10.00
149 Chris Paul 40.00 100.00
150 Shaun Livingston 4.00 10.00
152 Marvin Williams 4.00 10.00
153 Louis Williams 4.00 10.00
155 Andrew Bynum 20.00 40.00
156 Randy Foye 4.00 10.00
157 Shelden Williams 4.00 10.00
161 Brandon Roy 10.00 25.00
162 Josh Boone 4.00 10.00
163 Ronnie Brewer 5.00 12.00
165 Andrea Bargnani 5.00 12.00
166 Rajon Rondo 8.00 20.00
167 Daniel Gibson 6.00 15.00
168 Kyle Lowry 4.00 10.00
170 Tyrus Thomas 8.00 20.00
171 Rudy Gay 5.00 12.00
172 Jordan Farmar 6.00 15.00
173 Luis Scola 4.00 10.00
175 Carl Landry 4.00 10.00
176 Al Thornton 6.00 15.00
180 Morris Almond 4.00 10.00
183 Arron Afflalo 4.00 10.00
184 Jared Dudley 4.00 10.00
185 Glen Davis 6.00 15.00
188 Ramon Sessions 5.00 12.00
189 Rodney Stuckey 6.00 15.00
191 Jeff Green 6.00 15.00
192 Sean Williams 4.00 10.00
193 Daequan Cook 4.00 10.00
194 Julian Wright 4.00 10.00
199 Kevin Durant 100.00 200.00
201 Derrick Rose 100.00 200.00
203 O.J. Mayo 20.00 50.00
204 Russell Westbrook 75.00 150.00
205 Kevin Love 40.00 100.00
206 Danilo Gallinari 10.00 25.00
207 Eric Gordon 20.00 50.00
208 Joe Alexander 5.00 12.00
209 D.J. Augustin 5.00 12.00
210 Brook Lopez 8.00 20.00
211 Jerryd Bayless 5.00 12.00
212 Jason Thompson 5.00 12.00
213 Brandon Rush 5.00 12.00
214 Anthony Randolph 10.00 25.00
215 Robin Lopez 5.00 12.00
216 Marreese Speights 5.00 12.00
217 Roy Hibbert 8.00 20.00
218 J.J. Hickson 6.00 15.00
219 Ryan Anderson 8.00 20.00
220 George Hill 8.00 20.00
221 Darrell Arthur 5.00 12.00
222 Donte Greene 5.00 12.00
223 D.J. White 5.00 12.00
224 J.R. Giddens 5.00 12.00
225 Walter Sharpe 5.00 12.00
226 Mario Chalmers 8.00 20.00
227 Sonny Weems 5.00 12.00
228 Chris Douglas-Roberts 5.00 12.00
229 Sean Singletary 5.00 12.00
230 Luc Richard Mbah A Moute 5.00 12.00
231 Bill Walker 10.00 25.00
233 Rudy Fernandez 10.00 25.00

1999-00 Upper Deck MJ Master Collection

The 99/00 Upper Deck MJ Master Collection set was released to hobby dealers in late 1999 as a 26-card box set. The set included a 23-card base set that was limited to 500 serial-numbered sets. The box set also included an autographed Michael Jordan card, a jersey card of Michael Jordan, and one mystery pack that contained either an MJ autograph, a MJ game uniform card, a MJ shoe card, a MJ final floor card, or a 1 of 1 Michael Jordan card.
COMP.FACT SET (23) 200.00 500.00
COMMON CARD (1-23) 15.00 40.00

1999-00 Upper Deck MJ Master Collection Game Jerseys

This insert was randomly inserted into the 99/00 MJ Master Collection box set. The five-card set features swatches from actual game-used Michael Jordan jerseys. The five-card set was limited to 100 serial-numbered sets. Card backs carry a "MJGJ" prefix.
COMMON CARD (MJGJ1-5) 200.00 500.00

1999-00 Upper Deck MJ Master Collection Mystery Pack Inserts

This insert was randomly inserted into the 99/00 MJ Master Collection box set. The "mystery packs" were inserted at one per box set, and contained either a 1 of 1 Michael Jordan card, a MJ final floor card, a MJ shoe card, or a MJ game-used uniform card. Several cards are not priced due to scarcity.
M1 Michael Jordan 150.00 300.00
5x7 Floor/54
MJGS1 Michael Jordan Shoe/223 150.00 300.00
MJGU1 Michael Jordan Uniform/200150.00 300.00

1999-00 Upper Deck MJ Master Collection Signature Performances

This insert was randomly inserted into the 99/00 MJ Master Collection box set. The set features 10 autographed cards of Michael Jordan. This insert was limited to 50 serial-numbered sets. Card backs carry a "MJ" prefix.
COMMON CARD (MJ1-MJ10) 300.00 800.00

1998 Upper Deck MJ Sticker Collection

COMPLETE SET (138) 25.00 50.00
COMMON STICKER (1-138) .60 1.50

1998 Upper Deck MJ Sticker Collection Stickers

COMPLETE SET (38) 6.00 15.00
COMMON STICKER (1-38) .60 1.50

2001-02 Upper Deck MJ Tributes MJ Milestones

Randomly inserted in late season UD products, MJ Tributes MJ Milestones featuers photos of Michael Jordan coupled with a swatch of jersey and an authentic autograph. Each card is squentially numbered to 30. These cards were originally issued as exchanges, and were inserted in the following products: Card number M1 in Upper Deck Honor Roll, M2 and M3 in Upper Deck Playmakers, M4 and M5 in SP Authentic, M6 and M7 in Upper Deck Flight Team, and M8 and M9 in Upper Deck Inspirations.
COMMON CARD (M1-M7) 400.00 700.00

2001-02 Upper Deck MJ Tributes Portrait of a Champion

Randomly insereted in the following brands, Upper Deck Honor Roll, Upper Deck Playmakers, SP Authentic, Upper Deck Flight Team, and Upper Deck Inspirations, this set features jerseys from different points in Michael Jordan's career along with autographs. These cards were initially issued as exchanges, and each card is squentially numbered to 23.
COMMON CARD 400.00 700.00

2001-02 Upper Deck MJ's Back

This 90-card set was inserted in with the majority of Upper Deck's 2001-02 Basketball releases. Cards were issued in special three-card bonus packs which were found at the top of UD's product boxes. Each card features a photo of Michael Jordan with a border along the left side of the card, and "MJ's Back" in silver foil highlights. Full color action photos are set against a silver and white backdrop. Packs were inserted chronologically in these brands: Upper Deck Hardcourt, Upper Deck Series 1, Upper Deck Ovation, Upper Deck Sweet Shot, and Upper Deck Series 2.
COMMON CARD (MJ1-MJ90) 2.00 5.00

2001-02 Upper Deck MJ's Back 23 Karat Gold

Randomly inserted in MJ's Back Bonus Packs, this 90-card set parallels the base Upper Deck MJ's Back set enhanced with a gold foil shift from the base silver, and cards are sequentially numbered to 23.
COMMON CARD 75.00 150.00

2001-02 Upper Deck MJ's Back Jerseys

Randomly inserted in MJ's Back bonus packs, this five card set features a photo of Michael Jordan and traces his way from college to the pros to his comeback with the Wizards with commemorative swatches of each of these jerseys. Each card is sequentially numbered to 100. Dual Jerseys were also issued and feature two jersey swatches and sequential numbering to 50.
COMMON CARD (CC1-CC5) 150.00 300.00

2001-02 Upper Deck MJ's Back Jerseys Autographs

Randomly inserted in MJ's Back packs, this five card set parallels the base MJ's Jerseys set enhanced with a Michael Jordan Autograph and sequential numbering to 23.
COMMON CARD (1-5) 500.00 900.00

2001-02 Upper Deck MJ's Back Jerseys Dual

Randomly inserted in Upper Deck MJ's Back Bonus Packs, this five card set feautes a small picture of Michael Jordan in the upper right hand corner of the card with two swatches of jerseys beneath which, the logos of the teams those jerseys are from appear. Each card is sequentially numbered to 50.
COMMON CARD (CCD1-CCD5) 200.00 400.00

2001-02 Upper Deck MJ's Back Jerseys Dual Autographs

Randomly inserted in Upper Deck MJ's Back Bonus Packs, this five card set parallels the base MJ's Back Jerseys Dual enhanced with authentic Michael Jordan autographs. Each card is sequentially numbered to 23.
COMMON CARD (1-5) 500.00 1000.00

2001-02 Upper Deck MJ's Back Jerseys Triple

Randomly inserted in Upper Deck MJ's Back Bonus Packs, this set features a single card with three swatches of jersey on it. Design is similar to the Jerseys Dual set, and the card sequentially numbered to 25.
UNPRICED TRIPLE AU PRINT RUN 10 SETS
CCT1 Michael Jordan 300.00 600.00

2001-02 Upper Deck MJ's Back Jerseys Quad

Randomly inserted in Upper Deck MJ's Back Bonus Packs, this set features a single card with four swatches of jersey on it. Design is similar to the Jerseys Dual set, and the card sequentially numbered to 23.
UNPRICED QUAD AU PRINT RUN 5 SETS
CCQ1 Michael Jordan 500.00 800.00

1998 Upper Deck MJx

This Michael Jordan only set was released in 5 card packs which carried a suggested retail price of $4.40. The 135 card set was broken up into different themes, with different insertion rates. Cards 1-45 were "MJ Timeline 1st Half" and were inserted at two per pack. Cards 46-55 were "1st Quarter Highlights" and were inserted at one in 17. Cards 56-65 were "2nd Quarter Highlights" and were inserted at one in 12. Cards 66-110 were "MJ Timeline 2nd Half" and were inserted at two per pack. Cards 111-120 were "3rd Quarter Highlights" and inserted at one in 7. Cards 121-130 were "4th Quarter Highlights" and inserted one per pack. The last five cards, 131-135, were "The Best of Times" and inserted one in 23.
COMPLETE SET (135) 100.00 200.00
COMMON CARD (1-45) .20 .50
COMMON CARD (46-55) 5.00 12.00
COMMON CARD (56-65) 4.00 10.00
COMMON CARD (66-110) .20 .50
COMMON CARD (111-120) 2.50 6.00
COMMON CARD (121-130) .40 1.00
COMMON CARD (131-135) 6.00 15.00
A1 Michael Jordan AU/50 1500.00 3000.00
GC1 Michael Jordan Warmups 150.00 300.00
GC2 Michael Jordan Shoes 150.00 300.00

1998 Upper Deck MJx Live

Randomly inserted into packs, this 30-card set features up close and personal interview excerpts from Michael Jordan. The cards are serially numberd to 100.
COMMON CARD (1-30) 40.00 100.00

1998 Upper Deck MJx Timepieces Red

Randomly inserted in packs, this 90-card set is a semi-parallel of the base set. This set parallels both the 45 Timeline 1st Half cards and the 45 Timeline 2nd Hald cards. The cards feature die cutting on both sides of the card and are serially numbered to 2300.
COMPLETE SET (90) 125.00 250.00
COMMON CARD 2.50 5.00

1998 Upper Deck MJx Timepieces Bronze

Randomly inserted in packs, this 90-card set is a semi-parallel of the base set. This set parallels both the 45 Timeline 1st Half cards and the 45 Timeline 2nd Hald cards. The cards feature die cutting on both sides of the card and are serially numbered to 230.
COMMON CARD 15.00 40.00

1998 Upper Deck MJx Timepieces Gold

Randomly inserted in packs, this 90-card set is a semi-parallel of the base set. This set parallels both the 45 Timeline 1st Half cards and the 45 Timeline 2nd Hald cards. The cards feature die cutting on both sides of the card and are serially numbered to 23.
COMMON CARD 75.00 200.00

2003 Upper Deck Magazine

As a bonus to buyers of the Upper Deck magazine produced by Krause Publications late in 2003, a nine-card perforated sheet featuring players basically signed to Upper Deck exclusives was included. When the cards were perforated, these cards measured the standard size. Please note that all of these cards have a "UD" prefix.
COMPLETE SET (9) 8.00 20.00
UD1 Lebron James 2.50 6.00
UD3 Darko Milicic .75 2.00
UD8 Michael Jordan 1.25 3.00

1991-92 Upper Deck McDonald's/Paris

This 11-card set was issued by Upper Deck to highlight their involvement in the McDonald's Open held in Paris, France on October 18-19, 1991. The McDonald's Open features four leading international basketball teams, including the Los Angeles Lakers and three European teams. A special 11" by 8 1/2" commemorative sheet (not included in set price) and card packs, containing five Laker player cards and a special hologram card, were distributed to fans attending the event. The front design was the same as the regular issue cards, featuring a full color player photo with a wooden basketball court border on the right and bottom of the picture. The backs have a different color action photo and brief biography of the player in French. The cards are numbered on the back.
COMPLETE SET (11) 3.00 8.00
M1 Elden Campbell .40 1.00
M2 Vlade Divac .40 1.00
M3 A.C. Green .40 1.00
M4 Magic Johnson 2.50 6.00
M5 Sam Perkins .40 1.00
M6 Byron Scott .40 1.00
M7 Tony Smith .20 .50
M8 Terry Teagle .20 .50
M9 James Worthy .60 1.50
M10 Checklist .20 .50
NNO Hologram Card .20 .50
NNO Byron Scott 4.00 10.00
James Worthy
A.C. Green
Magic Johnson
Sam Perkins
Vlade Divac

1992-93 Upper Deck McDonald's

Produced by Upper Deck, this 103-card set was issued for McDonald's NBA Fantasy promotion, which began on March 5, 1993 and continued while supplies lasted. Three-card foil packs were available at participating McDonald's restaurants free with the purchase of an Extra Value Meal, or for 59 cents with the purchase of any other menu item. Each three-card pack contained either two player cards and an instant-win NBA fantasy card, or simply three player cards. In the Boston, Chicago, Cleveland, Orlando, and Los Angeles areas, packs featured one special regional player card from the home team. A pack in these areas contained two regular player cards and a local team player card. In addition to meeting Michael Jordan and serving as an honorary ballperson at the 1994 NBA All-Star Game in Minneapolis, many winners received a fantasy NBA contract, special momento jersey, and one-day NBA salary. Over one million other prizes were also available. The cards measure the standard size (2 1/2" by 3 1/2"). The fronts display color action player photos with white borders. The player's name and team name appear in team color-coded bars at the bottom of the picture that intersect a basketball icon that carries the team logo. The Future Force cards, showcasing top rookies, have a special emblem in the upper left corner and the player's name and position on a gray bar. The backs have a second color photo as well as biography and statistics. The Upper Deck foil emblem on the backs takes the shape of the McDonald's golden arches. The cards are numbered on the back and arranged alphabetically according to team names. The set is divided into established NBA stars (P1-P42) and a Future Force subset (P43-P50). The team sets are numbered within themselves and are prefixed with letter abbreviations for the city. A Michael Jordan Hologram was also randomly inserted into all forms of the foil packs. Also, there were some factory sets (master sets containing everything) that were made available for the winner redemption prizes.
COMPLETE SET (103) 25.00 60.00
COMPLETE FACT.SET (103) 25.00 60.00
COMPLETE NAT.SET (50) 4.00 10.00
COMPLETE BOST SET (10) 3.00 8.00
COMPLETE CHI SET (12) 6.00 15.00
COMPLETE CLE SET (10) 1.50 4.00
COMPLETE LA SET (10) 3.00 8.00
COMPLETE ORL SET (10) 5.00 12.00
P1 Dominique Wilkins .20 .50
P2 Reggie Lewis .05 .15
P3 Kevin McHale .10 .30
P4 Larry Johnson .10 .30
P5 Michael Jordan 1.50 4.00
P6 Horace Grant .08 .25
P7 Brad Daugherty .05 .15
P8 Mark Price .08 .25
P9 Derek Harper .08 .25
P10 Dikembe Mutombo .10 .30
P11 Joe Dumars .10 .30
P12 Isiah Thomas .20 .50
P13 Tim Hardaway .10 .30
P14 Chris Mullin .10 .30
P15 Hakeem Olajuwon .15 .40
P16 Otis Thorpe .05 .10
P17 Detlef Schrempf .05 .10
P18 Reggie Miller .20 .50
P19 Ron Harper .08 .25
P20 Danny Manning .08 .25
P21 James Worthy .15 .40
P22 Sam Perkins .08 .25
P23 Rony Seikaly .05 .05
P24 Steve Smith .08 .25
P25 Alvin Robertson .05 .15
P26 Derrick Coleman .05 .10
P27 Drazen Petrovic .25 .60
P28 Patrick Ewing .20 .50
P29 Scott Skiles .08 .25
P30 Hersey Hawkins .05 .10
P31 Dan Majerle .08 .25
P32 Kevin Johnson .08 .25
P33 Clyde Drexler .20 .50
P34 Terry Porter .05 .05
P35 Spud Webb .05 .10
P36 Antoine Carr .05 .05
P37 David Robinson .20 .50
P38 Shawn Kemp .20 .50
P39 Ricky Pierce .05 .05
P40 Karl Malone .20 .50
P41 John Stockton .25 .60
P42 Michael Adams .05 .05
P43 Shaquille O'Neal 1.25 3.00
P44 Alonzo Mourning .50 1.25
P45 Christian Laettner .40 1.00
P46 LaPhonso Ellis .05 .15
P47 Walt Williams .08 .25
P48 Todd Day .05 .15
P49 Clarence Weatherspoon .08 .25
P50 Tom Gugliotta .30 .75
BT1 Dee Brown .20 .50
BT2 Sherman Douglas .20 .50
BT3 Rick Fox .25 .60
BT4 Kevin Gamble .20 .50
BT5 Joe Kleine .20 .50
BT6 Reggie Lewis .40 1.00
BT7 Xavier McDaniel .20 .50
BT8 Kevin McHale 1.00 2.50
BT9 Robert Parish .75 2.00
BT10 Ed Pinckney .20 .50
CH1 B.J. Armstrong .20 .50
CH2 Bill Cartwright .20 .50
CH3 Horace Grant .30 .75
CH4 Michael Jordan 5.00 12.00
CH5 Stacey King .20 .50
CH6 Rodney McCray .20 .50
CH7 John Paxson .20 .50
CH8 Will Perdue .20 .50
CH9 Scottie Pippen 1.50 4.00
CH10 Trent Tucker .20 .50
CH11 Corey Williams .20 .50
CH12 Scott Williams .20 .50
CL1 John Battle .20 .50
CL2 Terrell Brandon .40 1.00
CL3 Brad Daugherty .20 .50
CL4 Craig Ehlo .20 .50
CL5 Danny Ferry .20 .50
CL6 Larry Nance .30 .75
CL7 Mark Price .30 .75
CL8 Mike Sanders .20 .50
CL9 Gerald Wilkins .20 .50
CL10 Hot Rod Williams .30 .75
LA1 Elden Campbell .30 .75
LA2 Duane Cooper .20 .50
LA3 Vlade Divac .40 1.00
LA4 James Edwards .20 .50
LA5 A.C. Green .40 1.00
LA6 Anthony Peeler .40 1.00
LA7 Sam Perkins .40 1.00
LA8 Byron Scott .40 1.00
LA9 Sedale Threatt .20 .50
LA10 James Worthy .75 2.00
OR1 Nick Anderson .40 1.00
OR2 Anthony Bowie .20 .50
OR3 Terry Catledge .20 .50
OR4 Greg Kite .20 .50
OR5 Shaquille O'Neal 4.00 10.00
OR6 Jerry Reynolds .20 .50
OR7 Donald Royal .20 .50
OR8 Dennis Scott .40 1.00
OR9 Scott Skiles .30 .75
OR10 Jeff Turner .20 .50
NNO Michael Jordan Holo 5.00 12.00

1999 Upper Deck Michael Jordan Athlete of the Century

Released as a 90-card set, this Upper Deck product is a Michael Jordan tribute, and only contains images of him. Each pack contained five cards and carried a suggested retail price of $4.99.
COMPLETE SET (90) 20.00 50.00
COMMON CARD (1-90) .40 1.00
MC1 Master Collection .40 1.00
MJSS1 Michael Jordan AU/23 3000.00 6000.00
MJSS2 Michael Jordan AU/23 3000.00 6000.00

1999 Upper Deck Michael Jordan Athlete of the Century Gold

Randomly inserted in packs, this 90-card set parallels the base set featuring gold foil. The cards are serially numbered to 50.
COMMON CARD (1-90) 40.00 100.00

1999 Upper Deck Michael Jordan Athlete of the Century Elevation

Randomly inserted in packs at one in 11, this 16-card set takes the form of a timeline, reliving Jordan's ascension to the 29,277 point plateau. Card backs carry an EL prefix.
COMPLETE SET (16) 20.00 50.00
COMMON CARD (EL1-16) 2.00 5.00

1999 Upper Deck Michael Jordan Athlete of the Century Extreme Air

Randomly inserted in packs at one in 144, this 15-card set uses Ionix technology to bring MJ's aerial moves to live. Card backs carry an EA prefix.
COMPLETE SET (15) 250.00 450.00
COMMON CARD (EA1-15) 15.00 40.00

1999 Upper Deck Michael Jordan Athlete of the Century High Class

Randomly inserted in packs at one in 11, this six-card set highlights Jordan's off-court contributions as a role model. Card backs carry a HC prefix.
COMPLETE SET (6) 7.50 15.00
COMMON CARD (HC1-HC6) 1.50 4.00

1999 Upper Deck Michael Jordan Athlete of the Century MJ Phenomenon

Randomly inserted in packs at one in 72, this 15-card set captures some of Jordan's greatest action shots thoroughout his career. Card backs carry a P prefix.
COMPLETE SET (15) 60.00 150.00
COMMON CARD (P1-P15) 6.00 15.00

1999 Upper Deck Michael Jordan Athlete of the Century The Jordan Era

Randomly inserted in packs at one in five, this 20-card set features each card relating to a specific moment in Jordan's career along with a current world trend at that point in time. Card backs carry a JE prefix.
COMPLETE SET (20) 15.00 40.00
COMMON CARD (JE1-20) 1.50 4.00

1999 Upper Deck Michael Jordan Athlete of the Century Total Dominance

Randomly inserted in packs at one in 23, this 20-card set focuses on how Jordan dominated the NBA during his thirteen year NBA career. Card backs carry a TD prefix.
COMPLETE SET (20) 50.00 120.00
COMMON CARD (TD1-20) 3.00 8.00

1999 Upper Deck Michael Jordan Athlete of the Century Upper Deck Remembers

Randomly inserted in packs at one in 23, this 10-card set features the most memorable MJ cards ever produced by Upper Deck beginning with his first card from the 91-92 season. Card backs carry a UD prefix.
COMPLETE SET (10) 15.00 40.00
COMMON CARD (UD1-10) 2.50 6.00

1999 Upper Deck Michael Jordan Career

Sold exclusively in 60-card box sets, these cards measure the standard size and look at Jordan's career, from the early years, through retirement. Each set also contained one of six blow-up cards. Those are listed at the end of the base set and carry a "CC" prefix.
COMP. FACT SET (60) 20.00 50.00
COMMON CARD (1-60) .40 1.00

1998 Upper Deck Michael Jordan Career Collection

Released as a boxed set, this 60-card set focuses on the early years of Michael Jordan's career - 1984-1993. The set breaks down into several themes: A Michael Jordan Upper Deck rookie card (if they had produced cards at that time), Pictures of Excellence, Spectacular Stats and MJ Retro.
COMP.FACT SET (60) 12.00 30.00
COMMON CARD (1-60) .40 1.00
1 Michael Jordan Rookie Card 1.25 3.00
20 Michael Jordan Spectacular Stats 90-91 .60 1.50
21 Michael Jordan Spectacular Stats 1993 .60 1.50
22 Michael Jordan Spectacular Stats 92-93 .60 1.50
23 Michael Jordan Spectacular Stats 89-90 .60 1.50
24 Michael Jordan Spectacular Stats 1991 .60 1.50
25 Michael Jordan Spectacular Stats 88-89 .60 1.50
26 Michael Jordan Spectacular Stats 87-88 .60 1.50
27 Michael Jordan Spectacular Stats 1988 .60 1.50
28 Michael Jordan Spectacular Stats 86-87 .60 1.50

1997 Upper Deck Michael Jordan Championship Journals

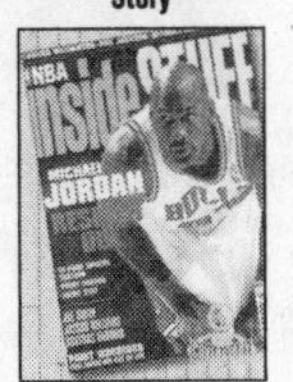

This special boxed set features Michael Jordan reviewing his championship seasons. This 24-card set was oversized (3 1/2" by 5") and each card depicted a special moment from Jordan's career with his comments on the card back about that moment. Also included in each set is a special limited edition card of Jordan (to 5,000). Fifty of these cards were autographed and randomly inserted into sets. The suggested retail price for the set was $19.99.
COMP.FACT SET (25) 12.00 30.00
COMMON CARD (1-24) .60 1.50
NNO Michael Jordan Special Card/5000 2.00 5.00
NNO Michael Jordan Special Card - AU/50 1000.00 2500.00

1998 Upper Deck Michael Jordan Gatorade

This set was released in 1998 as a 12-postcard sized set by Upper Deck. The set was distributed by Gatorade. Each card features a black facimile autograph.
COMPLETE SET (12) 10.00 25.00
COMMON CARD (1-12) 1.20 3.00

1999 Upper Deck Michael Jordan Gatorade

Released by Upper Deck in conjunction with Gatorade, this six card postcard sized set features highlights from each of Michael Jordan's six championships. Card design mirrors that of 1997-98 Upper Deck and each card features a facsimile Michael Jordan autograph along the bottom of the card.
COMPLETE SET (6) 10.00 25.00
COMMON CARD (MJ1-MJ6) 2.50 6.00

2008-09 Upper Deck Michael Jordan Legacy Collection

COMMON CARD 1.50 4.00

2008-09 Upper Deck Michael Jordan Legacy Collection Memorabilia

COMMON CARD (1-100) 60.00 150.00
STATED PRINT RUN 23 SER.#'d SETS

2009-10 Upper Deck Michael Jordan Legacy Collection

COMPLETE SET (50) 8.00 20.00
COMP.FAC.SET (51) 10.00 25.00
COMMON CARD (1-50) .40 1.00

2009-10 Upper Deck Michael Jordan Legacy Collection Gold

This 100-card set was issued in complete box set form, with a limited box run of 30,000 serially numbered boxes.
COMPLETE SET (100) 100.00 200.00
COMMON CARD (1-100) 1.25 3.00
97 Michael Jordan 86-87 Reprint 10.00 25.00

2009-10 Upper Deck Michael Jordan Legacy Collection Oversized

COMPLETE SET (10) 15.00 30.00
COMMON CARD (MJ1-MJ10) 2.00 5.00
ONE PER FACTORY SET

1998 Upper Deck Michael Jordan Living Legend

The 1998 Upper Deck Michael Jordan Living Legend product was released during the 1998-99 season and features a 165-card base set that highlights Michael Jordan's NBA career. The product also had Micheal Jordan autographs and game-used jersey cards randomly inserted into packs.
COMPLETE SET (165) 50.00 100.00
COMMON CARD (1-165) .40 1.00
MJ1 Michael Jordan AU/50 3000.00 4000.00

1998 Upper Deck Michael Jordan Living Legend Cover Story

Randomly inserted in packs at a rate of one in 14, this 8-card set features a few of the many magazine covers that Jordan has graced. Each card is numbered with a "C" prefix.
COMPLETE SET (8) 12.50 30.00
COMMON CARD (C1-C8) 2.00 5.00

1998 Upper Deck Michael Jordan Living Legend Game Action Red

Randomly inserted in packs, this 30-card set features several memorable moments of Jordan game action. This first tier features red-foil on the outside of the card and is serially numbered to 2300. Card backs are numbered with a "G" prefix.
COMPLETE SET (30) 100.00 250.00
COMMON CARD (G1-G30) 4.00 10.00

1998 Upper Deck Michael Jordan Living Legend Game Action Silver

Randomly inserted in packs, this 30-card set features several memorable moments of Jordan game action. This second tier features silver-foil on the outside of the card and is serially numbered to 230. Card backs are numbered with a "G" prefix.
COMMON CARD (G1-G30) 25.00 60.00

1998 Upper Deck Michael Jordan Living Legend Game Action Gold

Randomly inserted in packs, this 30-card set features several memorable moments of Jordan game action. This third tier features gold-foil on the outside of the card and is serially numbered to 23. Card backs are numbered with a "G" prefix.
COMMON CARD (G1-G30) 100.00 250.00

1998 Upper Deck Michael Jordan Living Legend In-Flight

Randomly inserted in packs at a rate of one in five, this 15-card set features shots of Jordan in-flight. Each card back carries an "IF" prefix.
COMPLETE SET (15) 10.00 25.00
COMMON CARD (IF1-IF15) .75 2.00

1995 Upper Deck Michael Jordan Milk Caps

COMPLETE SET (54) 15.00 30.00
COMMON POG .40 1.00

1995 Upper Deck Michael Jordan Milk Caps Slammers

COMPLETE SET (45) 25.00 50.00
COMMON SLAMMER (S1-S45) .75 2.00

1999 Upper Deck Michael Jordan Retirement

Released in a 23-card box set, these 3 1/2" by 5" cards commemorate the amazine basketball career of Michael Jordan.
COMP.FACT SET (23) 10.00 25.00
COMMON CARD (1-23) .75 2.00

1997 Upper Deck Michael Jordan Tribute

COMPLETE SET (90) 30.00 75.00
COMP.VISIONS SET (30) 10.00 25.00
COMP.IMPRESSIONS SET (30) 10.00 25.00
COMP.REFLECTIONS SET (30) 10.00 25.00
COMMON CARD (1-90) .40 1.00

1996-97 Upper Deck Folz Minis

This 48-card set features miniature version of the cards used in Collector's Choice sets. The cards were available via Folz Vending Machines at Toys R Us stores and other retailers. The first six cards feature foil and are designated as such in the checklist.
COMPLETE SET (48) 250.00 500.00
1 Michael Jordan FOIL 30.00 80.00
2 Anfernee Hardaway FOIL 12.00 30.00
3 Shawn Kemp FOIL 8.00 20.00
4 Shaquille O'Neal FOIL 20.00 50.00
5 Grant Hill FOIL 12.00 30.00
6 Hakeem Olajuwon FOIL 10.00 25.00
7 Mookie Blaylock 2.00 5.00
8 Antoine Walker 6.00 15.00
9 Anthony Mason 2.00 5.00
10 Scottie Pippen 5.00 12.00
11 Terrell Brandon 2.00 5.00
12 Samaki Walker 3.00 8.00
13 LaPhonso Ellis 2.00 5.00
14 Joe Dumars 3.00 8.00
15 Latrell Sprewell 3.00 8.00
16 Charles Barkley 5.00 12.00
17 Reggie Miller 4.00 10.00
18 Brent Barry 2.50 6.00
19 Eddie Jones 3.00 8.00
20 Tim Hardaway 3.00 8.00
21 Vin Baker 2.50 6.00
22 Stephen Marbury 8.00 20.00
23 Kendall Gill 2.00 5.00
24 Patrick Ewing 4.00 10.00
25 Horace Grant 2.50 6.00
26 Allen Iverson 15.00 40.00
27 Kevin Johnson 3.00 8.00
28 Kenny Anderson 2.50 6.00
29 Olden Polynice 2.00 5.00
30 Sean Elliott 3.00 8.00
31 Gary Payton 3.00 8.00
32 Marcus Camby 5.00 12.00
33 John Stockton 4.00 10.00
34 Shareef Abdur-Rahim 6.00 15.00
35 Juwan Howard 2.50 6.00
36 Dikembe Mutombo 3.00 8.00
37 Glen Rice 3.00 8.00
38 Dennis Rodman 6.00 15.00
39 Antonio McDyess 3.00 8.00
40 Rik Smits 2.50 6.00
41 Nick Van Exel 3.00 8.00
42 Alonzo Mourning 4.00 10.00
43 Glenn Robinson 3.00 8.00
44 Larry Johnson 3.00 8.00
45 Dennis Scott 2.00 5.00
46 Jerry Stackhouse 4.00 10.00
47 Sam Perkins 2.00 5.00
48 Chris Webber 4.00 10.00

1999-00 Upper Deck MVP

The premier set of Upper Deck MVP consisted of 220 cards. The cards came in 10 card packs that carried a suggested retail price of $1.59. The set features 178 base cards, 30 MJ Exclusive cards, 10 rookie cards and two checklists.
COMPLETE SET (220) 20.00 40.00
1 Dikembe Mutombo .20 .50
2 Steve Smith .12 .30
3 Mookie Blaylock .12 .30
4 Alan Henderson .12 .30
5 LaPhonso Ellis .12 .30
6 Grant Long .12 .30
7 Kenny Anderson .15 .40
8 Antoine Walker .20 .50
9 Ron Mercer .15 .40
10 Paul Pierce .30 .75
11 Vitaly Potapenko .12 .30
12 Dana Barros .12 .30
13 Elden Campbell .12 .30
14 Eddie Jones .20 .50
15 David Wesley .12 .30
16 Bobby Phills .12 .30
17 Derrick Coleman .15 .40
18 Ricky Davis .20 .50
19 Toni Kukoc .20 .50
20 Brent Barry .15 .40
21 Ron Harper .12 .30
22 Kornell David RC .20 .50
23 Mark Bryant .12 .30
24 Dickey Simpkins .12 .30
25 Shawn Kemp .20 .50
26 Derek Anderson .12 .30
27 Brevin Knight .12 .30
28 Andrew DeClercq .12 .30
29 Zydrunas Ilgauskas .15 .40
30 Cedric Henderson .12 .30
31 Shawn Bradley .12 .30
32 A.C. Green .20 .50
33 Gary Trent .12 .30
34 Michael Finley .20 .50
35 Dirk Nowitzki .40 1.00
36 Steve Nash .30 .75
37 Antonio McDyess .15 .40
38 Nick Van Exel .15 .40
39 Chauncey Billups .20 .50
40 Danny Fortson .12 .30
41 Eric Washington .12 .30
42 Raef LaFrentz .15 .40
43 Grant Hill .25 .60
44 Bison Dele .12 .30
45 Lindsey Hunter .12 .30
46 Jerry Stackhouse .20 .50
47 Don Reid .12 .30
48 Christian Laettner .15 .40
49 John Starks .20 .50
50 Antawn Jamison .20 .50
51 Erick Dampier .12 .30
52 Donyell Marshall .12 .30
53 Chris Mills .12 .30
54 Bimbo Coles .12 .30
55 Charles Barkley .30 .75
56 Hakeem Olajuwon .25 .60
57 Scottie Pippen .30 .75
58 Othella Harrington .12 .30
59 Bryce Drew .12 .30
60 Michael Dickerson .12 .30
61 Rik Smits .20 .50
62 Reggie Miller .20 .50
63 Mark Jackson .20 .50
64 Antonio Davis .12 .30
65 Jalen Rose .15 .40
66 Dale Davis .12 .30
67 Chris Mullin .20 .50
68 Maurice Taylor .12 .30
69 Lamond Murray .12 .30
70 Rodney Rogers .12 .30
71 Darrick Martin .12 .30
72 Michael Olowokandi .12 .30
73 Tyrone Nesby RC .20 .50
74 Kobe Bryant 1.00 2.50
75 Shaquille O'Neal .50 1.25
76 Robert Horry .20 .50
77 Glen Rice .20 .50
78 J.R. Reid .12 .30
79 Rick Fox .12 .30
80 Derek Fisher .20 .50
81 Tim Hardaway .20 .50
82 Alonzo Mourning .25 .60
83 Jamal Mashburn .15 .40
84 P.J. Brown .12 .30
85 Terry Porter .12 .30
86 Dan Majerle .20 .50
87 Ray Allen .20 .50
88 Vinny Del Negro .12 .30
89 Glenn Robinson .15 .40
90 Dell Curry .12 .30
91 Sam Cassell .15 .40
92 Robert Traylor .12 .30
93 Kevin Garnett .40 1.00
94 Terrell Brandon .12 .30
95 Joe Smith .15 .40
96 Sam Mitchell .12 .30
97 Anthony Peeler .12 .30
98 Bobby Jackson .15 .40
99 Keith Van Horn .15 .40
100 Stephon Marbury .15 .40
101 Jayson Williams .12 .30
102 Kendall Gill .12 .30
103 Kerry Kittles .12 .30
104 Scott Burrell .12 .30
105 Patrick Ewing .25 .60
106 Allan Houston .15 .40
107 Latrell Sprewell .20 .50
108 Larry Johnson .20 .50
109 Marcus Camby .15 .40
110 Charlie Ward .12 .30
111 Anfernee Hardaway .30 .75
112 Darrell Armstrong .12 .30
113 Nick Anderson .12 .30
114 Horace Grant .15 .40
115 Isaac Austin .12 .30
116 Matt Harpring .15 .40
117 Michael Doleac .12 .30
118 Allen Iverson .40 1.00
119 Theo Ratliff .15 .40
120 Matt Geiger .12 .30
121 Larry Hughes .15 .40
122 Tyrone Hill .12 .30
123 George Lynch .12 .30
124 Jason Kidd .30 .75
125 Tom Gugliotta .12 .30
126 Rex Chapman .12 .30
127 Clifford Robinson .12 .30
128 Luc Longley .12 .30
129 Danny Manning .12 .30
130 Rasheed Wallace .20 .50
131 Arvydas Sabonis .15 .40
132 Damon Stoudamire .20 .50
133 Brian Grant .12 .30
134 Isaiah Rider .12 .30
135 Walt Williams .12 .30
136 Jim Jackson .15 .40
137 Jason Williams .25 .60
138 Vlade Divac .20 .50
139 Chris Webber .20 .50
140 Corliss Williamson .12 .30
141 Peja Stojakovic .20 .50
142 Tariq Abdul-Wahad .12 .30
143 Tim Duncan .40 1.00
144 Sean Elliott .20 .50
145 David Robinson .30 .75
146 Mario Elie .12 .30
147 Avery Johnson .15 .40
148 Steve Kerr .15 .40
149 Gary Payton .20 .50
150 Vin Baker .20 .50
151 Detlef Schrempf .15 .40
152 Hersey Hawkins .12 .30
153 Dale Ellis .12 .30
154 Olden Polynice .12 .30
155 Vince Carter .40 1.00
156 John Wallace .12 .30
157 Doug Christie .15 .40
158 Tracy McGrady .30 .75
159 Kevin Willis .12 .30
160 Charles Oakley .15 .40
161 Karl Malone .25 .60
162 John Stockton .25 .60
163 Jeff Hornacek .15 .40
164 Bryon Russell .12 .30
165 Howard Eisley .12 .30
166 Shandon Anderson .12 .30
167 Shareef Abdur-Rahim .15 .40
168 Mike Bibby .20 .50
169 Bryant Reeves .12 .30
170 Felipe Lopez .12 .30
171 Cherokee Parks .12 .30
172 Michael Smith .12 .30
173 Juwan Howard .15 .40
174 Rod Strickland .12 .30
175 Mitch Richmond .20 .50
176 Otis Thorpe .12 .30
177 Calbert Cheaney .12 .30
178 Tracy Murray .12 .30
179 Michael Jordan .75 2.00
180 Michael Jordan .75 2.00
181 Michael Jordan .75 2.00
182 Michael Jordan .75 2.00
183 Michael Jordan .75 2.00
184 Michael Jordan .75 2.00
185 Michael Jordan .75 2.00
186 Michael Jordan .75 2.00
187 Michael Jordan .75 2.00
188 Michael Jordan .75 2.00
189 Michael Jordan .75 2.00
190 Michael Jordan .75 2.00
191 Michael Jordan .75 2.00
192 Michael Jordan .75 2.00
193 Michael Jordan .75 2.00
194 Michael Jordan .75 2.00
195 Michael Jordan .75 2.00
196 Michael Jordan .75 2.00
197 Michael Jordan .75 2.00
198 Michael Jordan .75 2.00
199 Michael Jordan .75 2.00
200 Michael Jordan .75 2.00
201 Michael Jordan .75 2.00
202 Michael Jordan .75 2.00
203 Michael Jordan .75 2.00
204 Michael Jordan .75 2.00
205 Michael Jordan .75 2.00
206 Michael Jordan .75 2.00
207 Michael Jordan .75 2.00
208 Michael Jordan .75 2.00
209 Elton Brand RC .75 2.00
210 Steve Francis RC .75 2.00
211 Baron Davis RC 1.00 2.50
212 Wally Szczerbiak RC .60 1.50
213 Richard Hamilton RC .75 2.00
214 Andre Miller RC .75 2.00
215 Jason Terry RC .75 2.00
216 Corey Maggette RC .60 1.50
217 Shawn Marion RC .75 2.00
218 Lamar Odom RC 1.00 2.50
219 Michael Jordan CL .75 2.00
220 Michael Jordan CL .75 2.00
S1 Michael Jordan PROMO 1.25 3.00

1999-00 Upper Deck MVP Silver Script

Randomly inserted in packs at one in two, this 220-card set parallels most of the base set. The cards feature a silver signature of that particular player on the front. To ascertain values on individual cards, please refer to the multipliers in the header below, coupled with the value of the base card.
COMMON MJ (179-208/CL) 2.00 5.00
*STARS: 1.5X TO 4X BASE CARD HI
*RCs: .75X TO 2X BASE HI
S1 Michael Jordan PROMO 2.00 5.00

1999-00 Upper Deck MVP Gold Script

Randomly inserted in hobby packs, this 220-card set parallels most of the base set. The cards feature a gold signature of that particular player on the front. The cards are serially numbered to 100. To ascertain values on individual cards, please refer to the multipliers in the header below, coupled with the value of the base card.
COMMON MJ (179-208/CL) 20.00 50.00
*STARS: 15X TO 40X BASE CARD HI
*RCs: 6X TO 15X BASE HI

1999-00 Upper Deck MVP Super Script

Randomly inserted in hobby packs, this 220-card set parallels most of the base set. The cards feature a holographic signature of that particular player on the front. The cards are serially numbered to 25. To ascertain values on individual cards, please refer to the multipliers in the header, coupled with the value of the base card.
COMMON MJ (179-208/CL) 60.00 150.00
*STARS: 50X TO 120X BASE CARD HI
*RCs: 15X TO 40X BASE HI
161 Karl Malone 40.00 100.00

1999-00 Upper Deck MVP 21st Century NBA

Randomly inserted in packs at one in 13, this 10-card set features some of the key players in the NBA who are poised to become the next superstars of the league. Card backs carry a "N" prefix.
COMPLETE SET (10) 4.00 10.00
N1 Jason Williams .60 1.50
N2 Paul Pierce .75 2.00
N3 Antoine Walker .50 1.25
N4 Keith Van Horn .40 1.00
N5 Allen Iverson 1.00 2.50
N6 Antawn Jamison .50 1.25
N7 Kobe Bryant 2.50 6.00
N8 Shareef Abdur-Rahim .40 1.00
N9 Stephon Marbury .40 1.00
N10 Grant Hill .60 1.50

1999-00 Upper Deck MVP Draw Your Own Trading Card

Randomly inserted in packs at one in two, this 26-card set features the winning cards from Upper Deck's Draw Your Own Trading Card contest. The following cards do not exist: W11, W15, W19 and W27. Card backs carry a "W" prefix.
COMPLETE SET (26) 5.00 12.00
W1 Michael Jordan .75 2.00
W2 Grant Hill .12 .30
W3 Kobe Bryant .50 1.25
W4 Michael Jordan .75 2.00
W5 Glen Rice .10 .25
W6 Michael Jordan .75 2.00
W7 David Robinson .15 .40
W8 Grant Hill .12 .30
W9 Stephon Marbury .07 .20
W10 Michael Jordan .75 2.00
W12 Charles Barkley .15 .40
W13 Antoine Walker .10 .25
W14 Shaquille O'Neal .25 .60
W16 Michael Jordan .75 2.00
W17 Stephon Marbury .07 .20
W18 Michael Jordan .75 2.00
W20 Allen Iverson .20 .50
W21 Michael Jordan .75 2.00
W22 Shareef Abdur-Rahim .07 .20
W23 Reggie Miller .10 .25
W24 Karl Malone .12 .30
W25 Christian Laettner .07 .20
W26 John Stockton .12 .30
W28 Michael Jordan .75 2.00
W29 Michael Jordan .75 2.00
W30 Michael Jordan .75 2.00

1999-00 Upper Deck MVP Dynamics

Randomly inserted in packs at one in 27, this six-card set features some of the most collectible players in the NBA. Card backs carry a "D" prefix.
COMPLETE SET (6) 8.00 20.00
D1 Michael Jordan 6.00 15.00
D2 Kobe Bryant 4.00 10.00
D3 Grant Hill 1.00 2.50
D4 Shareef Abdur-Rahim .60 1.50
D5 Kevin Garnett 1.50 4.00
D6 Vince Carter 1.50 4.00

1999-00 Upper Deck MVP Electrifying

Randomly inserted in packs at one in nine, this 15-card set focuses on players who bring NBA crowds to their feet. Card backs carry an "E" prefix.
COMPLETE SET (15) 4.00 10.00
E1 Shaquille O'Neal 1.25 3.00
E2 Steve Smith .30 .75
E3 Toni Kukoc .50 1.25
E4 Ron Mercer .40 1.00
E5 Damon Stoudamire .50 1.25
E6 Tim Hardaway .50 1.25
E7 Paul Pierce .75 2.00
E8 Jason Kidd .75 2.00
E9 Stephon Marbury .40 1.00
E10 Terrell Brandon .30 .75
E11 Reggie Miller .50 1.25
E12 Ray Allen .50 1.25
E13 Maurice Taylor .30 .75
E14 Chris Webber .50 1.25
E15 Charles Barkley .75 2.00

1999-00 Upper Deck MVP Game-Used Souvenirs

Randomly inserted in hobby packs only at one in 131, this 15-card set features a piece of a game-used basketball in each card. The cards are numbered on the back according to the player's initials. Two cards were also autographed: Anfernee Hardaway (card AH-A) and Karl Malone (KM). Those cards are listed below with an "AU" designation.
AHS Anfernee Hardaway 8.00 20.00
AJS Antawn Jamison 4.00 10.00
AMS Antonio McDyess 3.00 8.00
GPS Gary Payton 4.00 10.00
JKS Jason Kidd 6.00 15.00
JWS Jason Williams 5.00 12.00
KBS Kobe Bryant 15.00 40.00
KGS Kevin Garnett 8.00 20.00
KMA Karl Malone AU/32 250.00 500.00
KMS Karl Malone 5.00 12.00
MBS Mike Bibby 4.00 10.00
MFS Michael Finley 4.00 10.00
MOS Michael Olowokandi 2.50 6.00
SOS Shaquille O'Neal 10.00 25.00

SPS Scottie Pippen	6.00	15.00
TDS Tim Duncan	8.00	20.00

1999-00 Upper Deck MVP Jam Time

Randomly inserted in packs at one in six, this 14-card set features some of the best aerial artists of the NBA. Card backs carry a "JT" prefix.

COMPLETE SET (14)	3.00	8.00
JT1 Michael Jordan	2.50	6.00
JT2 Alonzo Mourning	.40	1.00
JT3 Shawn Kemp	.30	.75
JT4 Juwan Howard	.25	.60
JT5 Chris Webber	.30	.75
JT6 Tim Duncan	.60	1.50
JT7 Keith Van Horn	.25	.60
JT8 Eddie Jones	.30	.75
JT9 Michael Finley	.30	.75
JT10 Anfernee Hardaway	.50	1.25
JT11 Antonio McDyess	.25	.60
JT12 Charles Barkley	.50	1.25
JT13 Latrell Sprewell	.30	.75
JT14 Hakeem Olajuwon	.40	1.00

1999-00 Upper Deck MVP Jordan MVP Moments

Randomly inserted in packs at one in 27, this 14-card set relives all of Michael Jordan's MVP honors from his regular season awards to his All-Star game and post-season highlights. Card backs carry a "MJ" prefix.

COMMON CARD (MJ1-MJ14)	3.00	8.00

1999-00 Upper Deck MVP MVP Theatre

Randomly inserted in packs at one in nine, this 15-card set takes a look at the players that will be battling it out for the MVP award for years to come. Card backs carry a "M" prefix.

COMPLETE SET (15)	5.00	12.00
M1 Karl Malone	.60	1.50
M2 Tom Gugliotta	.30	.75
M3 Shaquille O'Neal	1.25	3.00
M4 Mitch Richmond	.50	1.25
M5 David Robinson	.75	2.00
M6 Gary Payton	.50	1.25
M7 Allen Iverson	1.00	2.50
M8 Glenn Robinson	.40	1.00
M9 Antoine Walker	.50	1.25
M10 Hakeem Olajuwon	.60	1.50
M11 Patrick Ewing	.60	1.50
M12 Antonio McDyess	.40	1.00
M13 Tim Hardaway	.50	1.25
M14 Scottie Pippen	.75	2.00
M15 Anfernee Hardaway	.75	2.00

1999-00 Upper Deck MVP ProSign

Randomly inserted in retail packs at one in 144, this 16-card set features autographs from NBA players. The cards are numbered on the back by initial.

CH Charlie Ward	4.00	10.00
CW Clarence Weatherspoon	4.00	10.00
DA Darrell Armstrong	4.00	10.00
DF Derek Fisher	8.00	20.00
IA Isaac Austin	4.00	10.00
JJ Jim Jackson	4.00	10.00
JK Jaren Jackson	4.00	10.00
JR Jalen Rose	8.00	20.00
MD Michael Dickerson	4.00	10.00
MJ Michael Jordan/23	600.00	1000.00
NV Nick Van Exel	6.00	15.00
RT Robert Traylor	4.00	10.00
SA Stacey Augmon	4.00	10.00
TC Terry Cummings	4.00	10.00
TR Theo Ratliff	4.00	10.00
VC Vince Carter	20.00	50.00

2000-01 Upper Deck MVP

The 2000-01 Upper Deck MVP product was released in late August, 2000, and featured a 220-card base set that was broken into tiers as follows: Base Veterans (1-188), Checklists (189-190), and Rookies (191-220). Each pack contained 10 cards, and carried a suggested retail price of $1.59.

COMPLETE SET (220)	20.00	40.00
1 Dikembe Mutombo	.20	.50
2 Jason Terry	.20	.50
3 Jim Jackson	.12	.30
4 Alan Henderson	.12	.30
5 Roshown McLeod	.12	.30
6 Bimbo Coles	.12	.30
7 Lorenzen Wright	.12	.30
8 Antoine Walker	.15	.40
9 Paul Pierce	.25	.60
10 Kenny Anderson	.15	.40
11 Adrian Griffin	.12	.30
12 Vitaly Potapenko	.12	.30
13 Dana Barros	.12	.30
14 Eric Williams	.12	.30
15 Eddie Jones	.20	.50
16 Eddie Robinson	.12	.30
17 Ricky Davis	.15	.40
18 Elden Campbell	.12	.30
19 Derrick Coleman	.15	.40
20 David Wesley	.12	.30
21 Baron Davis	.20	.50
22 Elton Brand	.20	.50
23 Ron Artest	.20	.50
24 Hersey Hawkins	.12	.30
25 Chris Carr	.12	.30
26 Corey Benjamin	.12	.30
27 Will Perdue	.12	.30
28 Andre Miller	.15	.40
29 Shawn Kemp	.12	.30
30 Wesley Person	.12	.30
31 Lamond Murray	.12	.30
32 Bob Sura	.12	.30
33 Andrew DeClercq	.12	.30
34 Dirk Nowitzki	.30	.75
35 Michael Finley	.20	.50
36 Cedric Ceballos	.12	.30
37 Shawn Bradley	.12	.30
38 Erick Strickland	.12	.30
39 Hubert Davis	.12	.30
40 Antonio McDyess	.15	.40
41 Raef LaFrentz	.12	.30
42 Keon Clark	.12	.30
43 Nick Van Exel	.15	.40
44 James Posey	.12	.30
45 Chris Gatling	.12	.30
46 George McCloud	.12	.30
47 Grant Hill	.25	.60
48 Jerry Stackhouse	.15	.40
49 Lindsey Hunter	.12	.30
50 Christian Laettner	.12	.30
51 Jerome Williams	.12	.30
52 Terry Mills	.12	.30
53 Antawn Jamison	.20	.50
54 Donyell Marshall	.12	.30
55 Chris Mills	.12	.30
56 Larry Hughes	.15	.40
57 Mookie Blaylock	.15	.40
58 Vonteego Cummings	.12	.30
59 Steve Francis	.20	.50
60 Shandon Anderson	.12	.30
61 Cuttino Mobley	.15	.40
62 Hakeem Olajuwon	.25	.60
63 Walt Williams	.12	.30
64 Kelvin Cato	.12	.30
65 Reggie Miller	.20	.50
66 Austin Croshere	.12	.30
67 Rik Smits	.12	.30
68 Jalen Rose	.15	.40
69 Dale Davis	.12	.30
70 Jonathan Bender	.12	.30
71 Michael Olowokandi	.12	.30
72 Lamar Odom	.20	.50
73 Tyrone Nesby	.12	.30
74 Eldrick Bohannon RC	.20	.50
75 Eric Piatkowski	.12	.30
76 Shaquille O'Neal	.50	1.25
77 Kobe Bryant	1.00	2.50
78 Robert Horry	.15	.40
79 Ron Harper	.15	.40
80 Rick Fox	.15	.40
81 Derek Fisher	.20	.50
82 Devean George	.12	.30
83 Alonzo Mourning	.25	.60
84 Clarence Weatherspoon	.12	.30
85 Anthony Carter	.12	.30
86 P.J. Brown	.12	.30
87 Tim Hardaway	.20	.50
88 Jamal Mashburn	.12	.30
89 Voshon Lenard	.12	.30
90 Ray Allen	.20	.50
91 Glenn Robinson	.15	.40
92 Tim Thomas	.12	.30
93 Sam Cassell	.15	.40
94 Robert Traylor	.12	.30
95 Ervin Johnson	.12	.30
96 Danny Manning	.12	.30
97 Kevin Garnett	.40	1.00
98 Wally Szczerbiak	.15	.40
99 Terrell Brandon	.12	.30
100 William Avery	.12	.30
101 Anthony Peeler	.12	.30
102 Radoslav Nesterovic	.12	.30
103 Dean Garrett	.12	.30
104 Keith Van Horn	.15	.40
105 Kerry Kittles	.12	.30
106 Stephon Marbury	.15	.40
107 Evan Eschmeyer	.12	.30
108 Jim McIlvaine	.12	.30
109 Lucious Harris	.12	.30
110 Jamie Feick	.12	.30
111 Allan Houston	.15	.40
112 Latrell Sprewell	.15	.40
113 Patrick Ewing	.25	.60
114 Chris Childs	.12	.30
115 Marcus Camby	.15	.40
116 Charlie Ward	.12	.30
117 Larry Johnson	.20	.50
118 Darrell Armstrong	.12	.30
119 Corey Maggette	.15	.40
120 Ron Mercer	.12	.30
121 Pat Garrity	.12	.30
122 Chucky Atkins	.12	.30
123 Ben Wallace	.20	.50
124 Michael Doleac	.12	.30
125 Allen Iverson	.40	1.00
126 Matt Geiger	.12	.30
127 Eric Snow	.12	.30
128 Toni Kukoc	.15	.40
129 Theo Ratliff	.12	.30
130 George Lynch	.12	.30
131 Jason Kidd	.30	.75
132 Tom Gugliotta	.12	.30
133 Rodney Rogers	.12	.30
134 Shawn Marion	.20	.50
135 Clifford Robinson	.12	.30
136 Kevin Johnson	.15	.40
137 Anfernee Hardaway	.30	.75
138 Scottie Pippen	.30	.75
139 Damon Stoudamire	.15	.40
140 Arvydas Sabonis	.15	.40
141 Jermaine O'Neal	.20	.50
142 Bonzi Wells	.12	.30
143 Rasheed Wallace	.20	.50
144 Detlef Schrempf	.15	.40
145 Chris Webber	.20	.50
146 Vlade Divac	.15	.40
147 Peja Stojakovic	.20	.50
148 Jason Williams	.20	.50
149 Corliss Williamson	.12	.30
150 Nick Anderson	.12	.30
151 Jon Barry	.12	.30
152 Tim Duncan	.40	1.00
153 David Robinson	.30	.75
154 Avery Johnson	.15	.40
155 Terry Porter	.15	.40
156 Mario Elie	.12	.30
157 Jaren Jackson	.12	.30
158 Steve Kerr	.12	.30
159 Gary Payton	.20	.50
160 Vin Baker	.15	.40
161 Brent Barry	.12	.30
162 Horace Grant	.15	.40
163 Ruben Patterson	.12	.30
164 Rashard Lewis	.20	.50
165 Tracy McGrady	.30	.75
166 Charles Oakley	.15	.40
167 Doug Christie	.12	.30
168 Antonio Davis	.12	.30
169 Vince Carter	.40	1.00
170 Kevin Willis	.12	.30
171 Karl Malone	.25	.60
172 John Stockton	.25	.60
173 Bryon Russell	.12	.30
174 Quincy Lewis	.12	.30
175 Olden Polynice	.12	.30
176 Jacque Vaughn	.12	.30
177 Shareef Abdur-Rahim	.15	.40
178 Michael Dickerson	.12	.30
179 Bryant Reeves	.12	.30
180 Mike Bibby	.20	.50
181 Othella Harrington	.12	.30
182 Felipe Lopez	.12	.30
183 Mitch Richmond	.15	.40
184 Richard Hamilton	.15	.40
185 Jahidi White	.12	.30
186 Aaron Williams	.12	.30
187 Juwan Howard	.15	.40
188 Rod Strickland	.15	.40
189 Kobe Bryant CL	1.00	2.50
190 Kevin Garnett CL	.40	1.00
191 Kenyon Martin RC	.50	1.25
192 Marcus Fizer RC	.20	.50
193 Chris Mihm RC	.20	.50
194 Stromile Swift RC	.20	.50
195 Morris Peterson RC	.30	.75
196 Quentin Richardson RC	.30	.75
197 Courtney Alexander RC	.20	.50
198 Soonie Penn RC	.20	.50
199 Mateen Cleaves RC	.20	.50
200 Erick Barkley RC	.20	.50
201 A.J. Guyton RC	.20	.50
202 Darius Miles RC	.20	.50
203 DerMarr Johnson RC	.20	.50
204 Jerome Moiso RC	.20	.50
205 Jamaal Magloire RC	.20	.50
206 Hanno Mottola RC	.20	.50
207 Mike Miller RC	.40	1.00
208 Desmond Mason RC	.25	.60
209 Chris Carrawell RC	.20	.50
210 Eduardo Najera RC	.20	.50
211 Speedy Claxton RC	.20	.50
212 Joel Przybilla RC	.20	.50
213 Mark Madsen RC	.20	.50
214 Khalid El-Amin RC	.20	.50
215 Etan Thomas RC	.20	.50
216 Jason Collier RC	.20	.50
217 Jason Hart RC	.20	.50
218 Michael Redd RC	.50	1.25
219 Keyon Dooling RC	.20	.50
220 Mamadou N'Diaye RC	.20	.50

2000-01 Upper Deck MVP Silver Script

Randomly inserted in packs at one in two, this 220-card set parallels the base set. The cards feature a silver signature of that particular player on the front. To ascertain values on individual cards, please refer to the multipliers in the header below, coupled with the value of the base card.

*STARS: 1.25X TO 3X VALUE
*RCs: .75X TO 2X VALUE

2000-01 Upper Deck MVP Gold Script

Randomly inserted in hobby packs, this 220-card set parallels the base set. The cards feature a gold signature of that particular player on the front. The cards are serially numbered to 100. To ascertain values on individual cards, please refer to the multipliers in the header below, coupled with the value of the base card.

*STARS: 12X TO 30X BASE CARD HI
*RCs: 8X TO 20X BASE CARD HI

77 Kobe Bryant	40.00	100.00
189 Kobe Bryant CL	40.00	100.00

2000-01 Upper Deck MVP Super Script

Randomly inserted in hobby packs, this 220-card set parallels the base set. The cards feature a holographic signature of that particular player on the front. The cards are serially numbered to 25. To ascertain values on individual cards, please refer to the multiplier in the header, coupled with the value of the base card.

*STARS: 50X TO 120X BASE CARD HI
*RCs: 20X TO 50X BASE CARD HI

2000-01 Upper Deck MVP Dynamics

Randomly inserted into packs at one in 28, this 20-card insert features players that are "dynamic" on the court. Card backs carry a "D" prefix.

COMPLETE SET (20)	15.00	40.00
D1 Shaquille O'Neal	2.50	6.00
D2 Allen Iverson	2.00	5.00
D3 Paul Pierce	1.25	3.00
D4 Scottie Pippen	1.50	4.00
D5 Lamar Odom	1.00	2.50
D6 Kobe Bryant	5.00	12.00
D7 Gary Payton	1.00	2.50
D8 Antonio McDyess	.75	2.00
D9 Stephon Marbury	.75	2.00
D10 Alonzo Mourning	1.25	3.00
D11 Vince Carter	2.00	5.00
D12 Jason Kidd	1.50	4.00
D13 Michael Finley	1.00	2.50
D14 Chris Webber	1.00	2.50
D15 Anfernee Hardaway	1.50	4.00
D16 Kevin Garnett	2.00	5.00
D17 Jason Williams	1.00	2.50
D18 Allan Houston	.75	2.00
D19 Elton Brand	1.00	2.50
D20 Karl Malone	1.25	3.00

2000-01 Upper Deck MVP Electrifying

Randomly inserted into packs at one in nine, this 10-card set features players that "electrify" the competition. Card backs carry an "E" prefix.

COMPLETE SET (10)	2.00	5.00
E1 Kevin Garnett	.60	1.50
E2 Stephon Marbury	.25	.60
E3 Damon Stoudamire	.25	.60
E4 Jalen Rose	.25	.60
E5 Latrell Sprewell	.25	.60
E6 Eddie Jones	.30	.75
E7 Wally Szczerbiak	.25	.60
E8 Kobe Bryant	1.50	4.00
E9 Shawn Marion	.30	.75
E10 Mike Bibby	.30	.75

2000-01 Upper Deck MVP Game-Used Souvenirs

Randomly inserted into hobby packs at one in 130, this 28-card set features game-used basketball cards from some of the best players in the NBA, this set includes names such as Allen Iverson, Kobe Bryant, and Kevin Garnett. Please note that these cards use the player's initials as numbering. Two players that were supposed to be included, did not get produced - Shareef Abdur-Rahim and Shawn Marion. A 12-card autographed set was also produced where each card is sequentially numbered to 25.

AHS Allan Houston	3.00	8.00
AIS Allen Iverson	8.00	20.00
AJS Antawn Jamison	4.00	10.00
AMS Andre Miller	3.00	8.00
ANS Anfernee Hardaway	6.00	15.00
EJS Eddie Jones	4.00	10.00
GPS Gary Payton	4.00	10.00
JKS Jason Kidd	6.00	15.00
JWS Jason Williams	4.00	10.00
KBS Kobe Bryant	15.00	40.00
KGS Kevin Garnett	8.00	20.00
KMS Karl Malone	5.00	12.00
LHS Larry Hughes	3.00	8.00
MBS Mike Bibby	4.00	10.00
MCS Antonio McDyess	3.00	8.00
MFS Michael Finley	4.00	10.00
PPS Paul Pierce	5.00	12.00
RAS Ron Artest	4.00	10.00
RHS Richard Hamilton	3.00	8.00
RMS Reggie Miller	4.00	10.00
RWS Rasheed Wallace	4.00	10.00
RYS Ray Allen	5.00	12.00
SFS Steve Francis	4.00	10.00
SMS Stephon Marbury	3.00	8.00
SOS Shaquille O'Neal	10.00	25.00
SPS Scottie Pippen	6.00	15.00
TMS Tracy McGrady	6.00	15.00
WSS Wally Szczerbiak	3.00	8.00

2000-01 Upper Deck MVP Game-Used Souvenirs Autographs

Randomly inserted into packs, this 12-card set features autographed game-used basketball cards from some of the best players in the NBA, this set includes names such as Allen Iverson, Kobe Bryant, and Kevin Garnett. Please note that these cards use the player's initials as numbering.

ANA Anfernee Hardaway	75.00	150.00
KBA Kobe Bryant	150.00	300.00
KGA Kevin Garnett	100.00	200.00
KMA Karl Malone	125.00	250.00
LHA Larry Hughes	25.00	60.00
MBA Mike Bibby	25.00	60.00
MCA Antonio McDyess	25.00	60.00
PPA Paul Pierce	40.00	100.00
RHA Richard Hamilton	30.00	80.00
RYA Ray Allen	50.00	120.00
SFA Steve Francis	30.00	80.00
WSA Wally Szczerbiak	25.00	60.00

2000-01 Upper Deck MVP Theatre

Randomly inserted into packs at one in 14, this 10-card set features players that put on a "show" everytime that step onto the court. Card backs carry a "M" prefix.

COMPLETE SET (10)	3.00	8.00
M1 Kobe Bryant	2.00	5.00
M2 Alonzo Mourning	.50	1.25
M3 Reggie Miller	.40	1.00
M4 Chris Webber	.40	1.00
M5 John Stockton	.50	1.25
M6 Vince Carter	.75	2.00
M7 Richard Hamilton	.30	.75
M8 Hakeem Olajuwon	.50	1.25
M9 Kevin Garnett	.75	2.00
M10 David Robinson	.60	1.50

2000-01 Upper Deck MVP MVPerformers

Randomly inserted into packs at one in 28, this 11-card insert features MVP caliber players. Card backs carry a "P".

COMPLETE SET (11)	5.00	12.00
P1 Kobe Bryant	3.00	8.00
P2 Antawn Jamison	.60	1.50
P3 John Stockton	.75	2.00
P4 Andre Miller	.50	1.25
P5 Latrell Sprewell	.50	1.25
P6 Jason Williams	.60	1.50
P7 Kevin Garnett	1.25	3.00
P8 Lamar Odom	.60	1.50
P9 Allan Houston	.50	1.25
P10 Keith Van Horn	.50	1.25
P11 Antoine Walker	.50	1.25

2000-01 Upper Deck MVP ProSign

Randomly inserted in retail packs at one in 216, this 18-card set features autographs from NBA players. The cards are numbered on the back by initial. A gold version sequentially numbered to 25 was also issued.

AH Anfernee Hardaway	30.00	80.00
CB Calvin Booth	4.00	10.00
DA Darrell Armstrong	4.00	10.00
DS Damon Stoudamire	10.00	25.00
GP Gary Payton	20.00	40.00
JR Jalen Rose	10.00	25.00
KA Karl Malone	40.00	80.00
KB Kobe Bryant	100.00	200.00
KG Kevin Garnett	40.00	100.00
LH Larry Hughes	6.00	15.00
MB Mike Bibby	6.00	15.00
MD Antonio McDyess	6.00	15.00
PP Paul Pierce	15.00	40.00
RA Ray Allen	15.00	40.00
SA Shareef Abdur-Rahim	8.00	20.00
SF Steve Francis	6.00	15.00
WS Wally Szczerbiak	5.00	12.00

2000-01 Upper Deck MVP ProSign Gold

Randomly inserted in packs, this 18-card set parallels the 2000-01 Prosign autographs, and are serial numbered to 25. The cards are numbered on the back by initial.

*GOLD: .75X TO 2X HI
STATED PRINT RUN 25 SERIAL #'d SETS

MJ Michael Jordan	1000.00	2000.00

2000-01 Upper Deck MVP World Jam

Randomly inserted into packs at one in five, this 20-card insert features players that have mastered the art of the "slam-dunk". Card backs carry a "WJ" prefix.

COMPLETE SET (20)	4.00	10.00
WJ1 Kobe Bryant	1.50	4.00
WJ2 Vince Carter	.60	1.50
WJ3 Steve Francis	.30	.75
WJ4 Keith Van Horn	.25	.60
WJ5 Rasheed Wallace	.30	.75
WJ6 Corey Maggette	.25	.60
WJ7 Kevin Garnett	.60	1.50
WJ8 Larry Hughes	.25	.60
WJ9 Tim Duncan	.60	1.50
WJ10 Alonzo Mourning	.40	1.00
WJ11 Chris Webber	.30	.75
WJ12 Shareef Abdur-Rahim	.25	.60
WJ13 Lamar Odom	.30	.75
WJ14 Ron Mercer	.20	.50
WJ15 Rashard Lewis	.30	.75
WJ16 Michael Dickerson	.20	.50
WJ17 Jerry Stackhouse	.25	.60
WJ18 Latrell Sprewell	.25	.60
WJ19 Shawn Kemp	.30	.75
WJ20 Elton Brand	.30	.75

2001-02 Upper Deck MVP

This 220-card base set includes 188 veterans, 30 rookies and 2 checklist cards. The set was issued in August of 2001. There are 24 packs per box; 8 cards per pack and a SRP of $1.99 per pack. The standard sized card features a color action shot of the featured player set within white borders. Black tags are found on the top and bottom of the card with the player's name on the bottom black tag.

COMPLETE SET (220)	20.00	40.00
1 Jason Terry	.20	.50
2 Alan Henderson	.12	.30
3 Toni Kukoc	.15	.40
4 Hanno Mottola	.12	.30
5 Theo Ratliff	.15	.40
6 DerMarr Johnson	.12	.30
7 Paul Pierce	.25	.60
8 Antoine Walker	.15	.40
9 Bryant Stith	.12	.30
10 Kenny Anderson	.15	.40
11 Vitaly Potapenko	.12	.30
12 Eric Williams	.12	.30
13 Jamal Mashburn	.15	.40
14 David Wesley	.12	.30
15 Baron Davis	.20	.50
16 Elden Campbell	.12	.30
17 P.J. Brown	.12	.30
18 Jamaal Magloire	.12	.30
19 Eddie Robinson	.12	.30
20 Elton Brand	.20	.50
21 Ron Mercer	.12	.30
22 Fred Hoiberg	.12	.30
23 Jamal Crawford	.15	.40
24 Ron Artest	.20	.50
25 Marcus Fizer	.12	.30
26 Andre Miller	.15	.40
27 Lamond Murray	.12	.30
28 Jim Jackson	.12	.30
29 Chris Mihm	.12	.30
30 Matt Harpring	.15	.40
31 Chris Gatling	.12	.30
32 Michael Finley	.20	.50
33 Steve Nash	.30	.75
34 Dirk Nowitzki	.30	.75
35 Juwan Howard	.15	.40
36 Howard Eisley	.12	.30
37 Eduardo Najera	.15	.40
38 Wang Zhizhi	.15	.40
39 Antonio McDyess	.15	.40
40 Nick Van Exel	.15	.40
41 Raef LaFrentz	.12	.30
42 James Posey	.12	.30
43 George McCloud	.12	.30
44 Voshon Lenard	.12	.30
45 Jerry Stackhouse	.15	.40
46 Chucky Atkins	.12	.30
47 Corliss Williamson	.12	.30
48 Joe Smith	.15	.40
49 Mateen Cleaves	.12	.30
50 Ben Wallace	.20	.50
51 Antawn Jamison	.20	.50
52 Marc Jackson	.12	.30
53 Larry Hughes	.15	.40
54 Bob Sura	.12	.30
55 Chris Porter	.12	.30
56 Vonteego Cummings	.12	.30
57 Steve Francis	.20	.50
58 Hakeem Olajuwon	.25	.60
59 Cuttino Mobley	.15	.40
60 Maurice Taylor	.12	.30
61 Shandon Anderson	.12	.30
62 Walt Williams	.12	.30
63 Moochie Norris	.12	.30
64 Reggie Miller	.20	.50
65 Jalen Rose	.15	.40
66 Jermaine O'Neal	.20	.50
67 Austin Croshere	.12	.30
68 Travis Best	.12	.30
69 Al Harrington	.15	.40
70 Jonathan Bender	.12	.30
71 Darius Miles	.15	.40
72 Corey Maggette	.15	.40
73 Lamar Odom	.20	.50
74 Quentin Richardson	.15	.40
75 Keyon Dooling	.12	.30
76 Jeff McInnis	.12	.30
77 Eric Piatkowski	.12	.30
78 Kobe Bryant	1.00	2.50
79 Shaquille O'Neal	.50	1.25
80 Rick Fox	.15	.40
81 Derek Fisher	.15	.40
82 Robert Horry	.15	.40
83 Ron Harper	.15	.40
84 Brian Shaw	.12	.30
85 Alonzo Mourning	.25	.60
86 Eddie Jones	.15	.40
87 Tim Hardaway	.20	.50
88 Anthony Mason	.12	.30
89 Brian Grant	.12	.30
90 Anthony Carter	.12	.30
91 Bruce Bowen	.12	.30
92 Ray Allen	.20	.50
93 Glenn Robinson	.15	.40
94 Sam Cassell	.15	.40
95 Tim Thomas	.12	.30
96 Ervin Johnson	.12	.30
97 Joel Przybilla	.12	.30
98 Kevin Garnett	.40	1.00
99 Terrell Brandon	.12	.30
100 Wally Szczerbiak	.15	.40
101 Chauncey Billups	.20	.50
102 LaPhonso Ellis	.12	.30
103 Anthony Peeler	.12	.30
104 Stephon Marbury	.15	.40
105 Keith Van Horn	.15	.40
106 Kenyon Martin	.20	.50
107 Kendall Gill	.12	.30
108 Lucious Harris	.12	.30
109 Stephen Jackson	.15	.40
110 Latrell Sprewell	.15	.40
111 Allan Houston	.15	.40
112 Marcus Camby	.15	.40
113 Mark Jackson	.15	.40
114 Glen Rice	.15	.40
115 Kurt Thomas	.12	.30
116 Tracy McGrady	.30	.75
117 Darrell Armstrong	.12	.30
118 Mike Miller	.20	.50
119 Grant Hill	.25	.60
120 Pat Garrity	.12	.30
121 John Amaechi	.12	.30
122 Allen Iverson	.40	1.00
123 Dikembe Mutombo	.20	.50
124 Aaron McKie	.12	.30
125 Tyrone Hill	.12	.30
126 George Lynch	.12	.30
127 Eric Snow	.12	.30
128 Matt Geiger	.12	.30
129 Jason Kidd	.30	.75
130 Shawn Marion	.20	.50
131 Tony Delk	.12	.30
132 Rodney Rogers	.12	.30
133 Tom Gugliotta	.12	.30
134 Anfernee Hardaway	.30	.75
135 Rasheed Wallace	.20	.50
136 Damon Stoudamire	.15	.40
137 Arvydas Sabonis	.15	.40
138 Scottie Pippen	.30	.75
139 Steve Smith	.15	.40
140 Stacey Augmon	.12	.30
141 Bonzi Wells	.15	.40
142 Jason Williams	.15	.40
143 Chris Webber	.20	.50
144 Peja Stojakovic	.20	.50
145 Doug Christie	.15	.40
146 Scot Pollard	.12	.30
147 Hedo Turkoglu	.20	.50
148 Vlade Divac	.15	.40
149 Tim Duncan	.40	1.00
150 David Robinson	.30	.75
151 Antonio Daniels	.12	.30
152 Sean Elliott	.12	.30
153 Derek Anderson	.15	.40
154 Avery Johnson	.12	.30
155 Malik Rose	.12	.30
156 Gary Payton	.20	.50
157 Rashard Lewis	.15	.40
158 Patrick Ewing	.25	.60
159 Vin Baker	.15	.40
160 Emanual Davis	.12	.30
161 Desmond Mason	.15	.40
162 Vince Carter	.30	.75
163 Morris Peterson	.15	.40
164 Antonio Davis	.12	.30
165 Keon Clark	.12	.30
166 Chris Childs	.12	.30
167 Charles Oakley	.15	.40
168 Alvin Williams	.12	.30
169 Dell Curry	.12	.30
170 Karl Malone	.25	.60
171 John Stockton	.25	.60
172 Donyell Marshall	.12	.30
173 John Starks	.12	.30
174 Bryon Russell	.12	.30
175 David Benoit	.12	.30
176 Jacque Vaughn	.12	.30
177 Shareef Abdur-Rahim	.15	.40
178 Mike Bibby	.20	.50
179 Michael Dickerson	.12	.30
180 Bryant Reeves	.12	.30
181 Grant Long	.12	.30
182 Stromile Swift	.12	.30
183 Richard Hamilton	.15	.40
184 Tyrone Nesby	.12	.30
185 Jahidi White	.12	.30
186 Chris Whitney	.12	.30
187 Courtney Alexander	.12	.30
188 Christian Laettner	.12	.30
189 Kobe Bryant CL	.50	1.25
190 Kevin Garnett CL	.20	.50
191 Vladimir Radmanovic RC	.40	1.00
192 Alvin Jones RC	.40	1.00
193 Tyson Chandler RC	.60	1.50
194 Omar Cook RC	.40	1.00
195 Kedrick Brown RC	.40	1.00
196 DeSagana Diop RC	.40	1.00
197 Eddie Griffin RC	.40	1.00
198 Zach Randolph RC	1.00	2.50
199 Eddy Curry RC	.60	1.50
200 Jeryl Sasser RC	.40	1.00
201 Gerald Wallace RC	.60	1.50
202 Jamaal Tinsley RC	.50	1.25
203 Kirk Haston RC	.40	1.00
204 Terence Morris RC	.40	1.00
205 Jarron Collins RC	.40	1.00
206 Joseph Forte RC	.40	1.00
207 Kenny Satterfield RC	.40	1.00
208 Michael Wright RC	.40	1.00
209 Jason Richardson RC	.75	2.00
210 Michael Bradley RC	.40	1.00
211 Gilbert Arenas RC	.60	1.50
212 Jeff Trepagnier RC	.40	1.00
213 Samuel Dalembert RC	.50	1.25
214 Troy Murphy RC	.60	1.50
215 Rodney White RC	.40	1.00
216 Joe Johnson RC	1.00	2.50
217 Richard Jefferson RC	.75	2.00
218 Kwame Brown RC	.40	1.00
219 Jason Collins RC	.40	1.00
220 Steven Hunter RC	.40	1.00

2001-02 Upper Deck MVP Airborne

Randomly inserted in packs at a rate of one in 24, this seven card set shows player's in top flight mode set against a purple sky background with silver foil highlights outlining and surround the photo, and gold foil highlights on the Upper Deck MVP Logo, the set name, and the player's name.

COMPLETE SET (7) 5.00 12.00
A1 Kobe Bryant 3.00 8.00
A2 Vince Carter 1.00 2.50
A3 Baron Davis .60 1.50
A4 Kevin Garnett 1.25 3.00
A5 Tracy McGrady 1.00 2.50
A6 Shaquille O'Neal 1.50 4.00
A7 Desmond Mason .50 1.25

2001-02 Upper Deck MVP Authentic Kobe

Randomly inserted in hobby packs only at a rate of one in 288, this insert set showcases Kobe Bryant. The collection is comprised of six different card types: Authentic Kobe Autograph (numbered to 100); Authentic Kobe Warm-up; Authentic Kobe Shooting Shirt, Authentic Kobe Game Floor, Authentic Kobe Autographed Game Floor (numbered to 8), and Authentic Kobe Autograph Gold (numbered to 8).

COMMON AU (KBA1-KBA2) 100.00 200.00
COMMON FLOOR (KBF1-KBF8) 10.00 25.00
KBW Kobe Bryant Warm-up 8.00 20.00
KBSS Kobe Bryant Shirt 8.00 20.00

2001-02 Upper Deck MVP Basketball Diary

Randomly inserted in packs at a rate of one in 12, this 14-card set photos players in full color with foil borders on three sides and gold foil highlights.

COMPLETE SET (14) 6.00 15.00
BD1 Alonzo Mourning .60 1.50
BD2 Wang Zhizhi .40 1.00
BD3 Chris Webber .50 1.25
BD4 Paul Pierce .60 1.50
BD5 Kevin Garnett 1.00 2.50
BD6 Dirk Nowitzki .75 2.00
BD7 Marc Jackson .30 .75
BD8 Kobe Bryant 2.50 6.00
BD9 Ray Allen .50 1.25
BD10 Tracy McGrady .75 2.00
BD11 Jerry Stackhouse .40 1.00
BD12 Kenyon Martin .50 1.25
BD13 Rasheed Wallace .50 1.25
BD14 Steve Francis .50 1.25

2001-02 Upper Deck MVP Game Night Gear

Randomly inserted in hobby packs at a rate of one in 96, this 19-card set features a full color player photo and a swatch of a game used jersey. Jason Kidd appeared on the original checklist but his card was never produced

AIG Allen Iverson 6.00 15.00
AJG A.J. Guyton 2.00 5.00
BCG Brian Cardinal 2.00 5.00
CMG Chris Mihm 2.00 5.00
COG Corey Maggette 2.50 6.00
DAG Darrell Armstrong 2.00 5.00
DGG Dean Garrett 2.00 5.00
DHG Donnell Harvey 2.00 5.00
IRG Isaiah Rider 2.00 5.00
JAG John Amaechi 2.00 5.00
JSG Jerry Stackhouse 2.50 6.00
KBG Kobe Bryant 15.00 40.00
KGG Kevin Garnett 6.00 15.00
KVG Keith Van Horn 2.50 6.00
LMG Lamond Murray 2.00 5.00
MAG Marcus Camby 2.50 6.00
MCG Antonio McDyess 2.50 6.00
RMG Ron Mercer 2.00 5.00
WSG Wally Szczerbiak 2.50 6.00

2001-02 Upper Deck MVP Game Night Gear Autographs

Randomly inserted in hobby packs, this 10-card set parallels the base design of the Game Night Gear cards enhanced with authentic player autographs. Each card is sequentially numbered to 100.

CMA Chris Mihm 8.00 20.00
COA Corey Maggette 8.00 20.00
DAA Darrell Armstrong 8.00 20.00
DHA Donnell Harvey 8.00 20.00
JSA Jerry Stackhouse 12.50 30.00
KBA Kobe Bryant 125.00 250.00
KGA Kevin Garnett 25.00 60.00
LMA Lamond Murray 8.00 20.00
MCA Antonio McDyess 8.00 20.00
WSA Wally Szczerbiak 8.00 20.00

2001-02 Upper Deck MVP Respect the Game

This 14-card insert set was randomly inserted in packs at a rate of one in 12, this 14-card set places full color player action photos on an all holo-foil background. The borders are white except for a square in each corner of holofoil, and cards are enhanced with gold and sliver foil highlights.

COMPLETE SET (14) 8.00 20.00
RG1 Kobe Bryant 3.00 8.00
RG2 Gary Payton .60 1.50
RG3 Tim Duncan 1.25 3.00
RG4 Lamar Odom .60 1.50
RG5 Vince Carter 1.00 2.50
RG6 Eddie Jones .50 1.25
RG7 Kevin Garnett 1.25 3.00
RG8 Jamal Mashburn .50 1.25
RG9 Michael Finley .60 1.50
RG10 Shaquille O'Neal 1.50 4.00
RG11 Latrell Sprewell .50 1.25
RG12 Steve Francis .60 1.50
RG13 Reggie Miller .60 1.50
RG14 Ray Allen .60 1.50

2001-02 Upper Deck MVP Souvenirs

Randomly inserted in hobby packs only at a rate of one in 96, this 19-card set features full color player photography set on a white and silver background. Each card is enhanced with silver foil highlights and a swatch of game used material. A Gold version sequentially numbered to 50 was also issued.

*GOLD: 1.25X TO 3X SOUVENIR HI
AJ Antawn Jamison 4.00 10.00
AM Andre Miller 3.00 8.00
CW Chris Webber 6.00 15.00
DM Darius Miles 2.50 6.00
DR David Robinson 6.00 15.00
JK Jason Kidd 6.00 15.00
JS Jerry Stackhouse 3.00 8.00
JT Jason Terry 4.00 10.00
KB Kobe Bryant 20.00 50.00
KG Kevin Garnett 8.00 20.00
KM Karl Malone 5.00 12.00
MC Antonio McDyess 3.00 8.00
MF Michael Finley 4.00 10.00
RH Richard Hamilton 3.00 8.00
RM Ron Mercer 2.50 6.00
SF Steve Francis 4.00 10.00
SH Shawn Marion 4.00 10.00
SM Stephon Marbury 3.00 8.00
TB Terrell Brandon 2.50 6.00

2001-02 Upper Deck MVP Souvenirs Combos

Randomly inserted in hobby packs only at a rate of one in 288, this nine card set utilizes the same design as the MVP Souvenirs set but switches the card to a horizontal design. Each card features two players and two swatches of game used memorabilia. A Gold version sequentially numbered to 50 was also issued.

*GOLD: 1X TO 2.5X COMBO HI
AWPP Antoine Walker 10.00 25.00
  Paul Pierce
BDJM Baron Davis 8.00 20.00
  Jamal Mashburn
DMQRCM Darius Miles 8.00 20.00
  Quentin Richardson
  Corey Maggette
DRDA David Robinson 8.00 20.00
  Derek Anderson
JKSM Jason Kidd 10.00 25.00
  Shawn Marion
KBDM Kobe Bryant 12.50 30.00
  Darius Miles
KBKG Kobe Bryant 20.00 50.00
  Kevin Garnett
KMJS Karl Malone 15.00 40.00
  John Stockton
SMKMKV Stephon Marbury 8.00 20.00
  Kenyon Martin
  Keith Van Horn

2001-02 Upper Deck MVP Watch

Randomly inserted in packs at a rate of one in 24, this seven card set features full color player photos in holofoil set against a non-foil background. The right side of the card features a one-color player photo and gold foil highlights.

COMPLETE SET (7) 6.00 15.00
M1 Shaquille O'Neal 1.50 4.00
M2 Vince Carter 1.00 2.50
M3 Chris Webber .60 1.50
M4 Karl Malone .75 2.00
M5 Kevin Garnett 1.25 3.00
M6 Kobe Bryant 3.00 8.00
M7 Tim Duncan 1.25 3.00

2002-03 Upper Deck MVP

Released in late August 2002, Upper Deck MVP boasts a 220-card base set divided up into 190 veteran cards and 30 rookie cards. Base card design consists of full-color player action phototgraphy set against a colored background set to match his team's colors. This colored background fades into a white border. MVP was packaged in 24-pack boxes where each pack contained eight cards and carried a suggested retail price of $1.99.

COMPLETE SET (220) 20.00 50.00
1 Shareef Abdur-Rahim .15 .40
2 Jason Terry .15 .40
3 Toni Kukoc .15 .40
4 DerMarr Johnson .12 .30
5 Nazr Mohammed .12 .30
6 Theo Ratliff .12 .30
7 Dion Glover .12 .30
8 Paul Pierce .25 .60
9 Antoine Walker .15 .40
10 Kenny Anderson .15 .40
11 Tony Delk .12 .30
12 Eric Williams .12 .30
13 Rodney Rogers .12 .30
14 Jamal Mashburn .15 .40
15 Baron Davis .20 .50
16 David Wesley .12 .30
17 Elden Campbell .12 .30
18 P.J. Brown .12 .30
19 Jamaal Magloire .12 .30
20 Stacey Augmon .12 .30
21 Jalen Rose .15 .40
22 Marcus Fizer .12 .30
23 Tyson Chandler .15 .40
24 Trenton Hassell .12 .30
25 Eddy Curry .15 .40
26 Travis Best .12 .30
27 Andre Miller .15 .40
28 Lamond Murray .12 .30
29 Ricky Davis .15 .40
30 Zydrunas Ilgauskas .15 .40
31 Jumaine Jones .12 .30
32 Chris Mihm .12 .30
33 Dirk Nowitzki .30 .75
34 Michael Finley .20 .50
35 Steve Nash .25 .60
36 Nick Van Exel .15 .40
37 Raef LaFrentz .12 .30
38 Adrian Griffin .12 .30
39 Avery Johnson .15 .40
40 Marcus Camby .15 .40
41 Juwan Howard .15 .40
42 James Posey .12 .30
43 Ryan Bowen .12 .30
44 Donnell Harvey .12 .30
45 Voshon Lenard .12 .30
46 Jerry Stackhouse .15 .40
47 Clifford Robinson .12 .30
48 Chucky Atkins .12 .30
49 Ben Wallace .20 .50
50 Jon Barry .12 .30
51 Corliss Williamson .12 .30
52 Antawn Jamison .20 .50
53 Jason Richardson .20 .50
54 Danny Fortson .12 .30
55 Gilbert Arenas .20 .50
56 Bob Sura .12 .30
57 Troy Murphy .20 .50
58 Steve Francis .20 .50
59 Cuttino Mobley .15 .40
60 Eddie Griffin .12 .30
61 Kenny Thomas .12 .30
62 Moochie Norris .12 .30
63 Kelvin Cato .12 .30
64 Glen Rice .15 .40
65 Reggie Miller .20 .50
66 Jermaine O'Neal .20 .50
67 Ron Mercer .12 .30
68 Jamaal Tinsley .12 .30
69 Al Harrington .15 .40
70 Ron Artest .20 .50
71 Austin Croshere .12 .30
72 Elton Brand .20 .50
73 Darius Miles .12 .30
74 Lamar Odom .20 .50
75 Quentin Richardson .15 .40
76 Corey Maggette .15 .40
77 Jeff McInnis .12 .30
78 Michael Olowokandi .12 .30
79 Kobe Bryant 1.00 2.50
80 Shaquille O'Neal .50 1.25
81 Derek Fisher .15 .40
82 Rick Fox .15 .40
83 Robert Horry .15 .40
84 Devean George .12 .30
85 Samaki Walker .12 .30
86 Pau Gasol .25 .60
87 Jason Williams .15 .40
88 Shane Battier .20 .50
89 Stromile Swift .12 .30
90 Lorenzen Wright .12 .30
91 Tony Massenburg .12 .30
92 Eddie Jones .15 .40
93 Alonzo Mourning .25 .60
94 Brian Grant .12 .30
95 Anthony Carter .12 .30
96 LaPhonso Ellis .15 .40
97 Jim Jackson .12 .30
98 Ray Allen .20 .50
99 Glenn Robinson .15 .40
100 Sam Cassell .15 .40
101 Tim Thomas .12 .30
102 Anthony Mason .12 .30
103 Joel Przybilla .12 .30
104 Ervin Johnson .12 .30
105 Kevin Garnett .40 1.00
106 Wally Szczerbiak .15 .40
107 Chauncey Billups .20 .50
108 Terrell Brandon .12 .30
109 Marc Jackson .12 .30
110 Joe Smith .15 .40
111 Jason Kidd .30 .75
112 Keith Van Horn .15 .40
113 Kenyon Martin .20 .50
114 Kerry Kittles .12 .30
115 Richard Jefferson .20 .50
116 Jason Collins .12 .30
117 Todd MacCulloch .12 .30
118 Allan Houston .15 .40
119 Latrell Sprewell .15 .40
120 Kurt Thomas .12 .30
121 Antonio McDyess .15 .40
122 Othella Harrington .12 .30
123 Clarence Weatherspoon .12 .30
124 Tracy McGrady .30 .75
125 Mike Miller .20 .50
126 Darrell Armstrong .12 .30
127 Grant Hill .25 .60
128 Horace Grant .15 .40
129 Steven Hunter .12 .30
130 Allen Iverson .30 .75
131 Dikembe Mutombo .20 .50
132 Aaron McKie .12 .30
133 Derrick Coleman .15 .40
134 Eric Snow .12 .30
135 Matt Harpring .15 .40
136 Stephon Marbury .15 .40
137 Shawn Marion .20 .50
138 Joe Johnson .20 .50
139 Anfernee Hardaway .30 .75
140 Iakovos Tsakalidis .12 .30
141 Tom Gugliotta .12 .30
142 Bo Outlaw .12 .30
143 Rasheed Wallace .20 .50
144 Damon Stoudamire .15 .40
145 Scottie Pippen .30 .75
146 Ruben Patterson .12 .30
147 Derek Anderson .12 .30
148 Dale Davis .12 .30
149 Bonzi Wells .12 .30
150 Chris Webber .20 .50
151 Peja Stojakovic .20 .50
152 Mike Bibby .20 .50
153 Doug Christie .12 .30
154 Vlade Divac .15 .40
155 Bobby Jackson .12 .30
156 Hedo Turkoglu .20 .50
157 Tim Duncan .40 1.00
158 David Robinson .30 .75
159 Steve Smith .15 .40
160 Tony Parker .25 .60
161 Antonio Daniels .12 .30
162 Charles Smith .12 .30
163 Bruce Bowen .12 .30
164 Gary Payton .20 .50
165 Rashard Lewis .20 .50
166 Vin Baker .15 .40
167 Brent Barry .12 .30
168 Desmond Mason .15 .40
169 Vladimir Radmanovic .12 .30
170 Vince Carter .30 .75
171 Morris Peterson .12 .30
172 Antonio Davis .12 .30
173 Hakeem Olajuwon .25 .60
174 Alvin Williams .12 .30
175 Jerome Williams .12 .30
176 Keon Clark .12 .30
177 Karl Malone .25 .60
178 John Stockton .25 .60
179 Donyell Marshall .12 .30
180 Andrei Kirilenko .20 .50
181 Bryon Russell .12 .30
182 Jarron Collins .12 .30
183 DeShawn Stevenson .12 .30
184 Michael Jordan 1.50 4.00
185 Richard Hamilton .15 .40
186 Kwame Brown .12 .30
187 Chris Whitney .12 .30
188 Tyronn Lue .12 .30
189 Brendan Haywood .12 .30
190 Jahidi White .12 .30
191 DaJuan Wagner RC .50 1.25
192 Jay Williams RC .60 1.50
193 Yao Ming RC 1.50 4.00
194 Drew Gooden RC .75 2.00
195 Chris Jefferies RC .50 1.25
196 Casey Jacobsen RC .50 1.25
197 Juan Dixon RC .60 1.50
198 Melvin Ely RC .50 1.25
199 Curtis Borchardt RC .50 1.25
200 John Salmons RC .60 1.50
201 Carlos Boozer RC 1.00 2.50
202 Fred Jones RC .50 1.25
203 Frank Williams RC .50 1.25
204 Jamal Sampson RC .50 1.25
205 Dan Dickau RC .50 1.25
206 Marcus Haislip RC .50 1.25
207 Jared Jeffries RC .50 1.25
208 Amare Stoudemire RC 1.25 3.00
209 Caron Butler RC .75 2.00
210 Qyntel Woods RC .50 1.25
211 Kareem Rush RC .50 1.25
212 Ryan Humphrey RC .50 1.25
213 Jiri Welsch RC .50 1.25
214 Mike Dunleavy RC .60 1.50
215 Tayshaun Prince RC .60 1.50
216 Nene Hilario RC .60 1.50
217 Nikoloz Tskitishvili RC .50 1.25
218 Bostjan Nachbar RC .50 1.25
219 Efthimios Rentzias RC .50 1.25
220 Rod Grizzard RC .50 1.25

2002-03 Upper Deck MVP Classic

Randomly inserted in packs at the rate of one in two, this 220-card set parallels the base set enhanced with a green border along the left side of the card and silver foil highlights.

*CLASSIC: .5X TO 1.25X BASE CARD HI

2002-03 Upper Deck MVP Classic Black

Randomly seeded in packs, this 220-card set paralells the base MVP set enhanced with black borders around the picture and gold borders along the edges of the card. Each card is sequentially numbered to 50 on the front.

*BLACK: 10X TO 25X BASE CARD HI

2002-03 Upper Deck MVP Gold

Randomly inserted in packs, this 220-card set parallels the base MVP set enhanced with a gold border along the left side of the card. Each card is sequentially numbered to 100.

*GOLD: 8X TO 20X BASE CARD HI
79 Kobe Bryant 25.00 60.00
184 Michael Jordan 60.00 120.00

2002-03 Upper Deck MVP Air Apparent

Inserted in packs at the rate of one in 24, this seven card set centers full color player action photography on a card enhanced with silver foil highlights. The Air Apparent logo is centered along the bottom of the card.

COMPLETE SET (7) 5.00 12.00
1 Kobe Bryant 4.00 10.00
2 Kevin Garnett 1.50 4.00
3 Darius Miles .50 1.25
4 Vince Carter 1.25 3.00
5 Tracy McGrady 1.25 3.00
6 Rashard Lewis .75 2.00
7 Jason Richardson .75 2.00

2002-03 Upper Deck MVP Basketball Diary

Inserted in packs at the rate of one 12, this 14-card set showcases a date where the featured player compiled some type of incredible statistic. The top of the card features full color action photo separated towards the bottom third by silver foil and the statistic.

COMPLETE SET (14) 8.00 20.00
1 Michael Jordan 4.00 10.00
2 Kobe Bryant 2.50 6.00
3 Kevin Garnett 1.00 2.50
4 Dirk Nowitzki .75 2.00
5 Shaquille O'Neal 1.25 3.00
6 Pau Gasol .60 1.50
7 Stephon Marbury .40 1.00
8 Jerry Stackhouse .40 1.00
9 Steve Francis .50 1.25
10 Jason Richardson .50 1.25
11 Elton Brand .50 1.25
12 Vince Carter .75 2.00
13 Jamaal Tinsley .30 .75
14 Tim Duncan 1.00 2.50

2002-03 Upper Deck MVP East Side West Side Shooting Shirt

Inserted in packs, this six card set features a horizontal card design with two players. On the far left side of the card front is a player from the Eastern Conference, and on the far right side is a player from the Western conference. Two swatches of shooting shirt appear towards the middle, and each card is sequentially numbered to 100.

BD/SM Baron Davis 15.00 40.00
  Stephon Marbury
JK/JS Jason Kidd 40.00 80.00
  John Stockton
KW/CW Kenyon Martin 25.00 60.00
  Chris Webber
MJ/KB Michael Jordan 125.00 300.00
  Kobe Bryant
PP/SH Paul Pierce 25.00 60.00
  Shawn Marion
RH/PS Richard Hamilton 15.00 40.00
  Peja Stojakovic

2002-03 Upper Deck MVP Materials Combo

Inserted in packs at the rate of one in 144, this six card set showcases a player with a swatch of both a shooting shirt and a warm up. The design places players in action in the center of the card with an oval design around him and the swatches on either side of the picture.

1 Chris Webber 8.00 20.00
2 Kobe Bryant 40.00 100.00
3 Kevin Garnett 15.00 40.00
4 Lamar Odom 8.00 20.00
5 Michael Jordan 100.00 250.00
6 Wally Szczerbiak 6.00 15.00

2002-03 Upper Deck MVP Materials Shooting Shirt

Inserted in packs at the rate of one in 72, this 12-card set places a full color player action photo on the left against a background set to match team colors and a square swatch of shooting shirt on the right.

AKS Andrei Kirilenko 4.00 10.00
AWS Antoine Walker 3.00 8.00
DJS DerMarr Johnson 2.50 6.00
EBS Elton Brand 4.00 10.00
JSS Jeryl Sasser 2.50 6.00
KBS Kobe Bryant 15.00 40.00
MBS Mike Bibby 4.00 10.00
MJS Michael Jordan 60.00 150.00
MPS Morris Peterson 2.50 6.00
SHS Shawn Marion 4.00 10.00
SMS Stephon Marbury 3.00 8.00

2002-03 Upper Deck MVP Materials Warm Up

Inserted in packs at the rate of one in 48, this 12-card set places a full color player action photo on the right against a background set to match team colors and a square swatch of shooting shirt on the left.

ADW Antonio Davis 2.00 5.00
BDW Baron Davis 3.00 8.00
BHW Brendan Haywood 2.00 5.00
DNW Dirk Nowitzki 5.00 12.00
GRW Glenn Robinson 2.50 6.00
KBW Kobe Bryant 12.00 30.00
KGW Kevin Garnett 6.00 15.00
KMW Karl Malone 4.00 10.00
KVW Keith Van Horn 2.50 6.00
MCW Antonio McDyess 2.50 6.00
MJW Michael Jordan 40.00 100.00
SAW Shareef Abdur-Rahim 2.50 6.00

2002-03 Upper Deck MVP Moments

Randomly seeded in packs at the rate of one in 24, this seven card set showcases top NBA players on a bordered card. Action photos are centered, and the card front is enhanced with silver foil highlights.

COMPLETE SET (7) 8.00 20.00
1 Shaquille O'Neal 1.50 4.00
2 Jason Kidd 1.00 2.50
3 Allen Iverson 1.00 2.50
4 Tim Duncan 1.25 3.00
5 Michael Jordan 5.00 12.00
6 Kevin Garnett 1.25 3.00
7 Kobe Bryant 3.00 8.00

2002-03 Upper Deck MVP Prosign

Randomly inserted in packs at the rate of one in 288, this 28-card set fatures a player photo on the left, his number on the right over which an authentic player autograph appears.

1 Brandon Armstrong 5.00 12.00
2 Corey Maggette 6.00 15.00
3 DerMarr Johnson 5.00 12.00
4 Eddie Griffin 5.00 12.00
5 Gilbert Arenas 10.00 25.00
6 Hanno Mottola 5.00 12.00
7 Jeff Trepagnier 5.00 12.00
8 Jamaal Magloire 5.00 12.00
9 Jason Richardson 10.00 25.00
12 Kobe Bryant 75.00 150.00
13 Kenyon Martin 15.00 40.00
17 Michael Bradley 5.00 12.00
18 Marcus Fizer 5.00 12.00
20 Terence Morris 5.00 12.00
21 Paul Pierce 20.00 50.00
22 Richard Jefferson 10.00 25.00
25 Samuel Dalembert 5.00 12.00
26 Tyson Chandler 10.00 25.00

2002-03 Upper Deck MVP Rising to the Occasion

Inserted in packs at the rate of one in 12, this 14-card set features a full color player action photo towards the left and a colored background to match team colors containing a player portrait style photo on the right. Each card is enhanced with silver foil higlights.

COMPLETE SET (14) 8.00 20.00
1 Kobe Bryant 2.50 6.00
2 Kevin Garnett 1.00 2.50
3 Michael Jordan 4.00 10.00
4 Paul Pierce .60 1.50
5 Shawn Marion .50 1.25
6 Jason Kidd .75 2.00
7 Peja Stojakovic .50 1.25
8 Tim Duncan 1.00 2.50
9 Shaquille O'Neal 1.25 3.00
10 Steve Francis .50 1.25
11 Ray Allen .50 1.25
12 Latrell Sprewell .40 1.00
13 Darius Miles .30 .75
14 Vince Carter .75 2.00

2002-03 Upper Deck MVP Triple Dimension

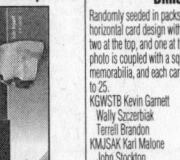

Randomly seeded in packs, this six card set features a horizontal card design with three players on each card, two at the top, and one at the bottom. Each player photo is coupled with a square swatch of game memorabilia, and each card is sequentially numbered to 25.

KGWSTB Kevin Garnett 25.00 60.00
  Wally Szczerbiak
  Terrell Brandon
KMJSAK Karl Malone 30.00 80.00
  John Stockton
  Andrei Kirilenko
MJKBKG Michael Jordan 150.00 300.00
  Kobe Bryant
  Kevin Garnett
TMMMGH Tracy McGrady 30.00 80.00
  Mike Miller
  Grant Hill

2003-04 Upper Deck MVP

Released as a 230-card set, MVP is divided up into 200 base veteran cards and 30 rookie cards. Base cards feature white borders and colored backgrounds with "MVP" appearing towards the top of the card. Several different parallels were issued for this set. A Gold version is highlighted with gold foil and sequentially numbered to 100. A Silver version was inserted at the rate of one in two for the veterans and one in 24 for the rookies, and a Black version sequentially numbered to 25 exists as well. MVP was packaged in 24-pack boxes where packs contained eight cards and carried a suggested retail price of $1.99.

COMPLETE SET (230) 20.00 50.00
1 Shareef Abdur-Rahim .15 .40
2 Jason Terry .15 .40
3 Terrell Brandon .12 .30
4 Alan Henderson .12 .30
5 Dan Dickau .12 .30
6 Theo Ratliff .12 .30
7 Dion Glover .12 .30
8 Paul Pierce .25 .60
9 Antoine Walker .20 .50
10 Eric Williams .12 .30
11 Tony Delk .12 .30
12 J.R. Bremer .12 .30

13 Vin Baker .12 .30
14 Jalen Rose .15 .40
15 Marcus Fizer .12 .30
16 Tyson Chandler .15 .40
17 Jamal Crawford .15 .40
18 Eddy Curry .15 .40
19 Scottie Pippen .30 .75
20 Darius Miles .12 .30
21 Dajuan Wagner .12 .30
22 Ricky Davis .15 .40
23 Zydrunas Ilgauskas .15 .40
24 Carlos Boozer .20 .50
25 Chris Mihm .12 .30
26 Dirk Nowitzki .30 .75
27 Michael Finley .20 .50
28 Steve Nash .25 .60
29 Nick Van Exel .15 .40
30 Raef LaFrentz .12 .30
31 Eduardo Najera .12 .30
32 Shawn Bradley .12 .30
33 Marcus Camby .15 .40
34 Vincent Yarbrough .12 .30
35 Rodney White .12 .30
36 Nene Hilario .15 .40
37 Nikoloz Tskitishvili .12 .30
38 Shammond Williams .12 .30
39 Richard Hamilton .15 .40
40 Clifford Robinson .12 .30
41 Chauncey Billups .20 .50
42 Ben Wallace .20 .50
43 Elden Campbell .12 .30
44 Corliss Williamson .12 .30
45 Antawn Jamison .20 .50
46 Jason Richardson .20 .50
47 Danny Fortson .12 .30
48 Speedy Claxton .12 .30
49 Mike Dunleavy .15 .40
50 Troy Murphy .20 .50
51 Steve Francis .20 .50
52 Cuttino Mobley .15 .40
53 Eddie Griffin .12 .30
54 Yao Ming .40 1.00
55 Maurice Taylor .12 .30
56 Kelvin Cato .12 .30
57 Glen Rice .12 .30
58 Reggie Miller .20 .50
59 Jermaine O'Neal .20 .50
60 Scot Pollard .12 .30
61 Jamaal Tinsley .12 .30
62 Al Harrington .15 .40
63 Ron Artest .20 .50
64 Danny Ferry .20 .50
65 Elton Brand .20 .50
66 Andre Miller .15 .40
67 Lamar Odom .20 .50
68 Quentin Richardson .15 .40
69 Corey Maggette .15 .40
70 Chris Wilcox .12 .30
71 Marko Jaric .12 .30
72 Kobe Bryant 1.00 2.50
73 Shaquille O'Neal .50 1.25
74 Derek Fisher .15 .40
75 Karl Malone .25 .60
76 Gary Payton .20 .50
77 Devean George .12 .30
78 Kareem Rush .12 .30
79 Pau Gasol .20 .50
80 Jason Williams .15 .40
81 Shane Battier .15 .40
82 Stromile Swift .12 .30
83 Lorenzen Wright .12 .30
84 Mike Miller .20 .50
85 Eddie Jones .15 .40
86 Ken Johnson .12 .30
87 Brian Grant .12 .30
88 Anthony Carter .12 .30
89 Rasual Butler .12 .30
90 Caron Butler .20 .50
91 Marcus Haislip .12 .30
92 Toni Kukoc .20 .50
93 Joe Smith .15 .40
94 Tim Thomas .12 .30
95 Anthony Mason .12 .30
96 Joel Przybilla .12 .30
97 Desmond Mason .15 .40
98 Kevin Garnett .40 1.00
99 Wally Szczerbiak .15 .40
100 Troy Hudson .12 .30
101 Michael Olowokandi .12 .30
102 Kendall Gill .12 .30
103 Sam Cassell .15 .40
104 Jason Kidd .30 .75
105 Kenyon Martin .20 .50
106 Alonzo Mourning .25 .60
107 Kerry Kittles .12 .30
108 Richard Jefferson .20 .50
109 Jason Collins .12 .30
110 Dikembe Mutombo .20 .50
111 Jamal Mashburn .15 .40
112 Baron Davis .20 .50
113 David Wesley .12 .30
114 Kenny Anderson .15 .40
115 P.J. Brown .12 .30
116 Jamaal Magloire .12 .30
117 George Lynch .12 .30
118 Courtney Alexander .12 .30
119 Allan Houston .15 .40
120 Keith Van Horn .15 .40
121 Kurt Thomas .12 .30
122 Antonio McDyess .15 .40
123 Othella Harrington .12 .30
124 Clarence Weatherspoon .12 .30
125 Tracy McGrady .25 .60
126 Drew Gooden .15 .40
127 Tyronn Lue .12 .30
128 Pat Garrity .12 .30
129 Grant Hill .25 .60
130 Gordan Giricek .12 .30
131 Juwan Howard .15 .40
132 Allen Iverson .30 .75
133 Glenn Robinson .15 .40
134 Aaron McKie .12 .30
135 Derrick Coleman .15 .40
136 Eric Snow .12 .30
137 Kenny Thomas .12 .30
138 Stephon Marbury .15 .40
139 Shawn Marion .20 .50
140 Joe Johnson .20 .50
141 Anfernee Hardaway .30 .75
142 Amare Stoudemire .30 .75
143 Casey Jacobsen .12 .30
144 Tom Gugliotta .12 .30
145 Bo Outlaw .12 .30
146 Rasheed Wallace .20 .50
147 Damon Stoudamire .15 .40
148 Jeff McInnis .12 .30
149 Ruben Patterson .12 .30
150 Derek Anderson .12 .30
151 Dale Davis .12 .30
152 Bonzi Wells .12 .30
153 Chris Webber .20 .50
154 Peja Stojakovic .20 .50
155 Mike Bibby .20 .50
156 Doug Christie .12 .30
157 Vlade Divac .15 .40
158 Bobby Jackson .12 .30
159 Brad Miller .20 .50
160 Keon Clark .12 .30
161 Tim Duncan .30 .75
162 David Robinson .30 .75
163 Steve Smith .12 .30
164 Tony Parker .20 .50
165 Hedo Turkoglu .20 .50
166 Radoslav Nesterovic .12 .30
167 Manu Ginobili .25 .60
168 Ron Mercer .12 .30
169 Ray Allen .20 .50
170 Rashard Lewis .20 .50
171 Antonio Daniels .12 .30
172 Brent Barry .12 .30
173 Predrag Drobnjak .12 .30
174 Vladimir Radmanovic .12 .30
175 Vince Carter .30 .75
176 Morris Peterson .12 .30
177 Antonio Davis .12 .30
178 Chris Jefferies .12 .30
179 Lindsey Hunter .12 .30
180 Alvin Williams .12 .30
181 Jerome Williams .12 .30
182 Jerome Moiso .12 .30
183 Greg Ostertag .12 .30
184 John Stockton .25 .60
185 Matt Harpring .15 .40
186 Andrei Kirilenko .20 .50
187 Calbert Cheaney .12 .30
188 Jarron Collins .12 .30
189 DeShawn Stevenson .12 .30
190 Michael Jordan 1.50 4.00
191 Jerry Stackhouse .15 .40
192 Kwame Brown .12 .30
193 Larry Hughes .15 .40
194 Gilbert Arenas .20 .50
195 Brendan Haywood .12 .30
196 Juan Dixon .12 .30
197 Jahidi White .12 .30
198 Etan Thomas .12 .30
199 Michael Jordan CL 1.00 2.50
200 Michael Jordan CL 1.00 2.50
201 LeBron James RC 6.00 15.00
202 Darko Milicic RC .60 1.50
203 Carmelo Anthony RC 1.50 4.00
204 Chris Bosh RC 1.25 3.00
205 Dwyane Wade RC 2.50 6.00
206 Chris Kaman RC .75 2.00
207 Kirk Hinrich RC .75 2.00
208 T.J. Ford RC .75 2.00
209 Mike Sweetney RC .60 1.50
210 Jarvis Hayes RC .60 1.50
211 Mickael Pietrus RC .60 1.50
212 Nick Collison RC .60 1.50
213 Marcus Banks RC .60 1.50
214 Luke Ridnour RC .75 2.00
215 Reece Gaines RC .60 1.50
216 Troy Bell RC .60 1.50
217 Zarko Cabarkapa RC .60 1.50
218 David West RC .75 2.00
219 Aleksandar Pavlovic RC .60 1.50
220 Dahntay Jones RC .60 1.50
221 Boris Diaw-Riffiod RC .75 2.00
222 Zoran Planinic RC .60 1.50
223 Travis Outlaw RC .75 2.00
224 Brian Cook RC .60 1.50
225 Carlos Delfino RC .75 2.00
226 Ndudi Ebi RC .60 1.50
227 Kendrick Perkins RC 1.00 2.50
228 Leandro Barbosa RC .75 2.00
229 Josh Howard RC .60 1.50
230 Maciej Lampe RC .60 1.50

2003-04 Upper Deck MVP Black

Randomly inserted, this 230-card set parallels the base MVP set enhanced with sequential numbering to 25.
*BLACK SINGLES: 15X TO 40X BASE HI
*BLACK RCs: 6X TO 15X BASE HI
190 Michael Jordan 100.00 200.00
199 Michael Jordan CL 100.00 200.00
200 Michael Jordan CL 100.00 200.00
201 LeBron James 150.00 300.00

2003-04 Upper Deck MVP Gold

Sequentially numbered to 100, this 230-card set parallels the base MVP set enhanced with gold foil highlights.
*GOLD SINGLES: 6X TO 15X BASE CARD HI
*GOLD CL: 12X TO 30X BASE CARD HI
*GOLD RCs: 4X TO 10X BASE CARD HI

2003-04 Upper Deck MVP Silver

Inserted at the rate of one in two for cards 1-200 and one in 24 for cards 201-230, this 230-card set parallels the base MVP set enhanced with silver foil highlights.
*SINGLES: .75X TO 2X BASE CARD HI

2003-04 Upper Deck MVP Basketball Diary

Randomly inserted at the rate of one in 12, this 14-card set places a full-color player photo on a card that has a border along the right edge. A Platinum parallel version of this set was also issued where cards are sequentilly numbered to 100.
COMPLETE SET (14) 10.00 25.00
*PLATINUM: 4X TO 10X BASE HI
BD1 Yao Ming .75 2.00
BD2 Michael Jordan 3.00 8.00
BD3 Kevin Garnett .75 2.00
BD4 Jason Richardson .40 1.00
BD5 Jason Kidd .60 1.50
BD6 Peja Stojakovic .40 1.00
BD7 Gilbert Arenas .40 1.00
BD8 Kobe Bryant 2.00 5.00
BD9 Tim Duncan .60 1.50
BD10 Ray Allen .60 1.50
Gary Payton
BD11 Vince Carter .60 1.50
BD12 Amare Stoudemire .60 1.50
BD13 LeBron James 4.00 10.00
BD14 Tim Duncan 1.00 2.50
David Robinson

2003-04 Upper Deck MVP Combo Materials

Randomly seeded at the rate of one in 144, this eight card set combines two players on a horizontal design where one player is on the top, the other on the bottom along with a swatch of game used material from each.
DMRJ Dikembe Mutombo 6.00 15.00
Richard Jefferson SP
DRTP David Robinson 10.00 25.00
Tony Parker
JSKM John Stockton 10.00 25.00
Karl Malone
JSRH Jerry Stackhouse 6.00 15.00
Richard Hamilton SP
JWEC Jay Williams 6.00 15.00
Eddy Curry
KBMJ Kobe Bryant 75.00 150.00
Michael Jordan SP
SHSM Shawn Marion 6.00 15.00
Stephon Marbury
WSTB Wally Szczerbiak 6.00 15.00
Terrell Brandon

2003-04 Upper Deck MVP Materials Shirts

Inserted at the rate of one in 72, this 12-card set places a player action photo on the right side of the card and a star-shaped swatch of memorabilia on the left.
AKSS Andrei Kirilenko SP 2.50 6.00
CWSS Chris Webber 2.50 6.00
DASS Darrell Armstrong 2.00 5.00
EBSS Elton Brand 2.50 6.00
GWSS Gerald Wallace 2.50 6.00
JKSS Jason Kidd SP 4.00 10.00
JOSS Jermaine O'Neal 2.50 6.00
KBSS Kobe Bryant SP 8.00 20.00
MJSS Michael Jordan SP 60.00 120.00
RMSS Reggie Miller 2.50 6.00
SASS Shareef Abdur-Rahim 2.00 5.00
TCSS Tyson Chandler 2.00 5.00

2003-04 Upper Deck MVP Materials Warmups

Inserted in packs at the rate of one in 48, this 11-card set is horizontally designed with a player photo on the right and a swatch of memorabilia on the left.
AMWU Antonio McDyess 2.00 5.00
CMWU Corey Maggette 2.00 5.00
GAWU Gilbert Arenas 2.50 6.00
JFWU Joseph Forte 2.00 5.00
JMWU Jamaal Magloire 2.00 5.00
JWWU Jay Williams 2.00 5.00
KBWU Kobe Bryant SP 8.00 20.00
KGWU Kevin Garnett 5.00 12.00
MJWU Michael Jordan SP 50.00 120.00
RAWU Ray Allen 2.50 6.00
TKWU Toni Kukoc 2.50 6.00

2003-04 Upper Deck MVP Monumental Moments

Inserted at the rate of one in 24, this seven card set places full-color player action photo among gold foil highlights. A Platinum parallel was also produced with cards sequentially numbered to five.
MM1 Kobe Bryant 3.00 8.00
MM2 Michael Jordan 5.00 12.00
MM3 Tim Duncan 1.00 2.50
MM4 Ben Wallace .60 1.50
MM5 Bobby Jackson .40 1.00
MM6 David Robinson 1.00 2.50
MM7 Amare Stoudemire 1.00 2.50

2003-04 Upper Deck MVP ProSign

Inserted at the rate of one in 288, this 40-card set is horizontally desiged with player photos on the left and a vertically stuck autographed sticker on the right.
AJ Antawn Jamison 8.00 20.00
AS Amare Stoudemire 15.00 40.00
BI Chauncey Billups 10.00 25.00
CB Carlos Boozer 4.00 10.00
CK Chris Kaman SP 10.00 25.00
CM Cuttino Mobley 4.00 10.00
DD Dan Dickau 4.00 10.00
DG Dan Gadzuric 4.00 10.00
DJ DerMarr Johnson 4.00 10.00
DW Dajuan Wagner 4.00 10.00
EB Earl Boykins 4.00 10.00
EG Eddie Griffin 4.00 10.00
ET Etan Thomas 4.00 10.00
GI Manu Ginobili/20 15.00 40.00
GO Drew Gooden 5.00 12.00
HA Richard Hamilton SP 12.50 30.00
JD Juan Dixon 4.00 10.00
JM Jerome Moiso 4.00 10.00
JS Jerry Stackhouse 10.00 25.00
KB Kobe Bryant/25 100.00 200.00
LJ LeBron James/23 600.00 1000.00
MA Corey Maggette 4.00 10.00
MP Morris Peterson 6.00 15.00
PP Paul Pierce/34 20.00 50.00
PS Peja Stojakovic SP 8.00 20.00
RE Reggie Evans 4.00 10.00
RH Ryan Humphrey 4.00 10.00
SB Shane Battier 4.00 10.00
SM Shawn Marion/31 15.00 40.00
TP Tony Parker 12.50 30.00
YM Yao Ming/25 30.00 80.00

2003-04 Upper Deck MVP Rising to the Occasion

Inserted at the rate of one in 12, this 14-card set features full-color player action photos centered between borders on the right and left side of the card. A Gold parallel version of this set was also produced with cards sequentially numbered to 250.
COMPLETE SET (14) 10.00 25.00
*GOLD: 1.5X TO 4X BASE HI
RO1 Kobe Bryant 2.50 6.00
RO2 LeBron James 5.00 12.00
RO3 Michael Jordan 4.00 10.00
RO4 Desmond Mason .40 1.00
RO5 Richard Jefferson .50 1.25
RO6 Vince Carter .75 2.00
RO7 Shaquille O'Neal 1.25 3.00
RO8 Yao Ming 1.00 2.50
RO9 Tracy McGrady .60 1.50
RO10 Jason Richardson .50 1.25
RO11 Rashard Lewis .50 1.25
RO12 Caron Butler .50 1.25
RO13 Baron Davis .50 1.25
RO14 Amare Stoudemire .75 2.00

2003-04 Upper Deck MVP Sportsnut Fantasy

Inserted at the rate of one in three, this 90-card set places full-color player photos on a gray background with borders on both the left and right of the card. Each card has a scratch off box on the front for use at www.upperdeck.com's Sport Nut Fantasy Game website.
COMPLETE SET (90) 20.00 50.00
SN1 Shareef Abdur-Rahim .30 .75
SN2 Jason Terry .30 .75
SN3 Glenn Robinson .30 .75
SN4 Theo Ratliff .25 .60
SN5 Antoine Walker .40 1.00
SN6 Paul Pierce .50 1.25
SN7 Jalen Rose .30 .75
SN8 Eddy Curry .30 .75
SN9 Tyson Chandler .30 .75
SN10 Dajuan Wagner .25 .60
SN11 Darius Miles .25 .60
SN12 Zydrunas Ilgauskas .30 .75
SN13 Michael Finley .40 1.00
SN14 Steve Nash .50 1.25
SN15 Dirk Nowitzki .60 1.50
SN16 Nene Hilario .30 .75
SN17 Juwan Howard .30 .75
SN18 Marcus Camby .30 .75
SN19 Richard Hamilton .30 .75
SN20 Ben Wallace .40 1.00
SN21 Chauncey Billups .40 1.00
SN22 Danny Fortson .25 .60
SN23 Antawn Jamison .40 1.00
SN24 Jason Richardson .40 1.00
SN25 Gilbert Arenas .40 1.00
SN26 Yao Ming .75 2.00
SN27 Steve Francis .40 1.00
SN28 Reggie Miller .40 1.00
SN29 Jermaine O'Neal .40 1.00
SN30 Brad Miller .40 1.00
SN31 Elton Brand .40 1.00
SN32 Michael Olowokandi .25 .60
SN33 Andre Miller .30 .75
SN34 Kobe Bryant 2.00 5.00
SN35 Shaquille O'Neal 1.00 2.50
SN36 Pau Gasol .40 1.00
SN37 Mike MIller .40 1.00
SN38 Lorenzen Wright .25 .60
SN39 Alonzo Mourning .50 1.25
SN40 Eddie Jones .30 .75
SN41 Caron Butler .40 1.00
SN42 Gary Payton .40 1.00
SN43 Dan Gadzuric .25 .60
SN44 Sam Cassell .30 .75
SN45 Kevin Garnett .75 2.00
SN46 Radoslav Nesterovic .25 .60
SN47 Jason Kidd .60 1.50
SN48 Kenyon Martin .40 1.00
SN49 Dikembe Mutombo .40 1.00
SN50 Baron Davis .40 1.00
SN51 Jamaal Magloire .25 .60
SN52 Jamal Mashburn .30 .75
SN53 Latrell Sprewell .30 .75
SN54 Allan Houston .30 .75
SN55 Kurt Thomas .25 .60
SN56 Tracy McGrady .50 1.25
SN57 Drew Gooden .30 .75
SN58 Grant Hill .50 1.25
SN59 Allen Iverson .60 1.50
SN60 Todd MacCulloch .25 .60
SN61 Amare Stoudemire .60 1.50
SN62 Stephon Marbury .30 .75
SN63 Shawn Marion .40 1.00
SN64 Rasheed Wallace .40 1.00
SN65 Damon Stoudamire .30 .75
SN66 Dale Davis .25 .60
SN67 Vlade Divac .30 .75
SN68 Mike Bibby .40 1.00
SN69 Peja Stojakovic .40 1.00
SN70 Chris Webber .40 1.00
SN71 Tim Duncan .60 1.50
SN72 Tony Parker .40 1.00
SN73 Ray Allen .40 1.00
SN74 Vladimir Radmanovic .25 .60
SN75 Rashard Lewis .40 1.00
SN76 Vince Carter .60 1.50
SN77 Antonio Davis .25 .60
SN78 Karl Malone .50 1.25
SN79 Andrei Kirilenko .40 1.00
SN80 Jerry Stackhouse .30 .75
SN81 Kwame Brown .25 .60
SN82 Nick Collison .40 1.00
SN83 Jarvis Hayes .40 1.00
SN84 Mike Sweetney .40 1.00
SN85 Dwyane Wade 1.50 4.00
SN86 T.J. Ford .50 1.25
SN87 Chris Bosh .75 2.00
SN88 Darko Milicic .40 1.00
SN89 Carmelo Anthony 1.00 2.50
SN90 LeBron James 4.00 10.00

2003-04 Upper Deck MVP Tribute to Greatness

Randomly inserted in packs, this seven-card set follows the career of Michael Jordan. A Platinum version of the set was issued as well with cards sequentially numbered to 50.
COMMON CARD (MJ1-MJ7) 2.50 6.00
COMMON PLAT. (MJ1-MJ7) 25.00 60.00

2008-09 Upper Deck MVP

This set was released on September 30, 2008. The base set consists of 258 cards. Cards 1-200 feature veterans, cards 201-240 are rookies, and cards 241-260 feature legends. Rookies were inserted at one per pack and Legends at one in two packs.
COMPLETE SET (258) 30.00 60.00
COMP.SET w/o SPs (200) 10.00 25.00
UNPRICED SUPER SCRIPT PRINT RUN ONE SET
1 Joe Johnson .20 .50
2 Marvin Williams .20 .50
3 Acie Law .15 .40
4 Al Horford .20 .50
5 Mike Bibby .15 .40
6 Josh Smith .20 .50
7 Kendrick Perkins .15 .40
8 Glen Davis .15 .40
9 Rajon Rondo .25 .60
10 Ray Allen .20 .50
11 Paul Pierce .25 .60
12 Kevin Garnett .40 1.00
13 Adam Morrison .20 .50
14 Raymond Felton .15 .40
15 Jason Richardson .20 .50
16 Emeka Okafor .20 .50
17 Gerald Wallace .20 .50
18 Tyrus Thomas .15 .40
19 Andres Nocioni .12 .30
20 Joakim Noah .20 .50
21 Luol Deng .20 .50
22 Kirk Hinrich .20 .50
23 Ben Gordon .20 .50
24 Zydrunas Ilgauskas .15 .40
25 Anderson Varejao .15 .40
26 Ben Wallace .20 .50
27 Daniel Gibson .20 .50
28 LeBron James 1.00 2.50
29 Wally Szczerbiak .15 .40
30 Dirk Nowitzki .25 .60
31 Josh Howard .15 .40
32 Jason Kidd .20 .50
33 Jerry Stackhouse .15 .40
34 Jason Terry .15 .40
35 Brandon Bass .12 .30
36 Allen Iverson .25 .60
37 Carmelo Anthony .25 .60
38 Marcus Camby .12 .30
39 Kenyon Martin .20 .50
40 J.R. Smith .20 .50
41 Linas Kleiza .12 .30
42 Chauncey Billups .20 .50
43 Richard Hamilton .15 .40
44 Tayshaun Prince .20 .50
45 Rasheed Wallace .20 .50
46 Rodney Stuckey .25 .60
47 Jason Maxiell .12 .30
48 Baron Davis .20 .50
49 Monta Ellis .20 .50
50 Al Harrington .15 .40
51 Stephen Jackson .15 .40
52 Marco Belinelli .12 .30
53 Yao Ming .25 .60
54 Tracy McGrady .20 .50
55 Luis Scola .15 .40
56 Rafer Alston .12 .30
57 Shane Battier .15 .40
58 Mike Dunleavy .15 .40
59 Danny Granger .20 .50
60 Jermaine O'Neal .20 .50
61 Jamaal Tinsley .12 .30
62 David Harrison .12 .30
63 Elton Brand .20 .50
64 Chris Kaman .15 .40
65 Corey Maggette .15 .40
66 Al Thornton .15 .40
67 Cuttino Mobley .15 .40
68 Tim Thomas .12 .30
69 Kobe Bryant 1.00 2.50
70 Pau Gasol .20 .50
71 Andrew Bynum .25 .60
72 Jordan Farmar .12 .30
73 Luke Walton .12 .30
74 Lamar Odom .20 .50
75 Rudy Gay .20 .50
76 Kyle Lowry .20 .50
77 Mike Conley Jr. .15 .40
78 Mike Miller .20 .50
79 Hakim Warrick .15 .40
80 Dwyane Wade .40 1.00
81 Shawn Marion .20 .50
82 Ricky Davis .15 .40
83 Jason Williams .15 .40
84 Daequan Cook .12 .30
85 Michael Redd .20 .50
86 Maurice Williams .15 .40
87 Yi Jianlian .20 .50
88 Charlie Villanueva .20 .50
89 Andrew Bogut .20 .50
90 Al Jefferson .20 .50
91 Rashad McCants .12 .30
92 Corey Brewer .15 .40
93 Randy Foye .20 .50
94 Ryan Gomes .12 .30
95 Richard Jefferson .20 .50
96 Vince Carter .25 .60
97 Josh Boone .12 .30
98 Bostjan Nachbar .12 .30
99 Sean Williams .15 .40
100 Chris Paul .30 .75
101 David West .20 .50
102 Peja Stojakovic .20 .50
103 Tyson Chandler .15 .40
104 Morris Peterson .12 .30
105 Julian Wright .15 .40
106 Jamal Crawford .15 .40
107 Zach Randolph .15 .40
108 Stephon Marbury .15 .40
109 Eddy Curry .12 .30
110 Nate Robinson .20 .50
111 David Lee .15 .40
112 Dwight Howard .40 1.00
113 Hedo Turkoglu .20 .50
114 Rashard Lewis .15 .40
115 Jameer Nelson .15 .40
116 Keith Bogans .12 .30
117 Carlos Arroyo .15 .40
118 Andre Iguodala .20 .50
119 Andre Miller .15 .40
120 Willie Green .12 .30
121 Samuel Dalembert .12 .30
122 Reggie Evans .12 .30
123 Thaddeus Young .15 .40
124 Amare Stoudemire .20 .50
125 Steve Nash .20 .50
126 Leandro Barbosa .15 .40
127 Shaquille O'Neal .40 1.00
128 Grant Hill .25 .60
129 Raja Bell .15 .40
130 Brandon Roy .20 .50
131 LaMarcus Aldridge .20 .50
132 Travis Outlaw .15 .40
133 Martell Webster .15 .40
134 Greg Oden .20 .50
135 Jarrett Jack .15 .40
136 Kevin Martin .20 .50
137 Ron Artest .20 .50
138 Brad Miller .15 .40
139 John Salmons .20 .50
140 Mikki Moore .12 .30
141 Francisco Garcia .15 .40
142 Manu Ginobili .20 .50
143 Tim Duncan .30 .75
144 Tony Parker .20 .50
145 Michael Finley .20 .50
146 Bruce Bowen .12 .30
147 Damon Stoudamire .15 .40
148 Kevin Durant .75 2.00
149 Chris Wilcox .12 .30
150 Jeff Green .15 .40
151 Damien Wilkins .12 .30
152 Earl Watson .12 .30
153 Chris Bosh .20 .50
154 Jose Calderon .15 .40
155 T.J. Ford .12 .30
156 Andrea Bargnani .15 .40
157 Jamario Moon .12 .30
158 Jason Kapono .12 .30
159 Carlos Boozer .20 .50
160 Deron Williams .20 .50
161 Kyle Korver .15 .40
162 Andrei Kirilenko .15 .40
163 Ronnie Brewer .15 .40
164 Mehmet Okur .12 .30
165 Gilbert Arenas .20 .50
166 Caron Butler .20 .50
167 Antawn Jamison .20 .50
168 DeShawn Stevenson .12 .30
169 Brendan Haywood .12 .30
170 Nick Young .15 .40
171 Joe Johnson .20 .50
172 Kevin Garnett .40 1.00
173 Gerald Wallace .20 .50
174 Luol Deng .20 .50
175 LeBron James 1.00 2.50
176 Dirk Nowitzki .25 .60
177 Carmelo Anthony .25 .60
178 Chauncey Billups .20 .50
179 Monta Ellis .20 .50
180 Tracy McGrady .20 .50
181 Danny Granger .20 .50
182 Chris Kaman .15 .40
183 Kobe Bryant 1.00 2.50
184 Rudy Gay .20 .50
185 Dwyane Wade .40 1.00
186 Michael Redd .20 .50
187 Al Jefferson .20 .50
188 Vince Carter .25 .60
189 Chris Paul .30 .75
190 Zach Randolph .15 .40
191 Dwight Howard .40 1.00
192 Andre Iguodala .20 .50
193 Steve Nash .20 .50
194 Brandon Roy .20 .50
195 Kevin Martin .20 .50
196 Tim Duncan .30 .75
197 Kevin Durant .75 2.00
198 Chris Bosh .20 .50
199 Deron Williams .20 .50
200 Antawn Jamison .20 .50
201 Derrick Rose RC 5.00 12.00
202 Michael Beasley RC 1.00 2.50
203 O.J. Mayo RC 1.00 2.50
204 Russell Westbrook RC 3.00 8.00
205 Kevin Love RC 2.50 6.00
206 Danilo Gallinari RC 1.00 2.50
207 Eric Gordon RC 1.50 4.00
208 Joe Alexander RC .60 1.50
209 D.J. Augustin RC .60 1.50
210 Brook Lopez RC 1.00 2.50
211 Jerryd Bayless RC .60 1.50
212 Jason Thompson RC .60 1.50
213 Brandon Rush RC .60 1.50
214 Anthony Randolph RC .75 2.00
215 Robin Lopez RC .60 1.50
216 Marreese Speights RC .60 1.50
217 Roy Hibbert RC 1.00 2.50
218 Courtney Lee RC 1.00 2.50
219 J.J. Hickson RC .75 2.00
220 Ryan Anderson RC 1.00 2.50
221 Kosta Koufos RC .60 1.50
223 Darrell Arthur RC .60 1.50
224 Donte Greene RC .60 1.50
225 D.J. White RC .60 1.50
226 Bill Walker RC .60 1.50
227 James Gist RC .60 1.50
228 Joey Dorsey RC .60 1.50
229 Mario Chalmers RC 1.00 2.50
230 DeAndre Jordan RC 1.25 3.00
231 Luc Richard Mbah A Moute RC .60 1.50
232 Kyle Weaver RC .60 1.50
233 Sonny Weems RC .60 1.50
234 Chris Douglas-Roberts RC .60 1.50
235 Sean Singletary RC .60 1.50
236 Patrick Ewing Jr. RC .60 1.50
237 Darnell Jackson RC .60 1.50
238 Maarty Leunen RC .60 1.50
240 Deron Washington RC .60 1.50
241 Spud Webb 1.00 2.50
242 Larry Bird 3.00 8.00
243 Bill Russell 1.50 4.00
244 Kevin McHale 1.25 3.00
245 Michael Jordan 8.00 20.00
246 Scottie Pippen 1.50 4.00
247 Joe Dumars 1.00 2.50
248 Isiah Thomas 1.00 2.50
249 Hakeem Olajuwon 1.25 3.00
250 Magic Johnson 2.50 6.00
251 Wilt Chamberlain 2.00 5.00
252 Kareem Abdul-Jabbar 1.50 4.00
253 Oscar Robertson 1.00 2.50
254 Pete Maravich 3.00 8.00
255 Patrick Ewing 1.25 3.00
256 Willis Reed 1.00 2.50
257 Julius Erving 2.00 5.00
258 David Robinson 1.50 4.00
259 Karl Malone 1.25 3.00
260 John Stockton 1.50 4.00

2008-09 Upper Deck MVP Gold Script

*GOLD 1-200: 3X TO 8X BASE HI
*GOLD 201-240: 1.25X TO 3X BASE HI
*GOLD 241-260: 1.25X TO 3X BASE
PRINT RUN 100 SER.#'d SET
28 LeBron James 12.00 30.00
69 Kobe Bryant 12.00 30.00
175 LeBron James 12.00 30.00
183 Kobe Bryant 12.00 30.00
245 Michael Jordan 30.00 80.00

2008-09 Upper Deck MVP Silver Script

*SILVER: .6X TO 1.5X BASE HI
OVERALL PARALLEL ODDS 1:4

2008-09 Upper Deck MVP Game Night Souvenirs

STATED ODDS 1:36
*PATCHES: .75X TO 2X BASE HI
PATCH PRINT RUN 25 SER.#'d SETS
GNAB Andris Biedrins 2.00 5.00
GNAI Allen Iverson 4.00 10.00
GNAK Andrei Kirilenko 2.50 6.00
GNAM Adam Morrison 3.00 8.00
GNAW Antoine Walker 2.50 6.00
GNBB Brent Barry 2.00 5.00
GNBC Brian Cook 2.00 5.00
GNBD Boris Diaw 2.00 5.00
GNBO Andrew Bogut 3.00 8.00
GNCM Corey Maggette 2.50 6.00
GNCS Cedric Simmons 2.50 6.00
GNDG Drew Gooden 2.50 6.00
GNDH Devin Harris 3.00 8.00
GNDM Dikembe Mutombo 3.00 8.00
GNDN Dirk Nowitzki 4.00 10.00
GNDW Delonte West 2.50 6.00
GNEB Elton Brand 3.00 8.00
GNGH Grant Hill 6.00 15.00
GNGW Gerald Wallace 3.00 8.00

GNJH Josh Howard 2.50 6.00
GNJJ Joe Johnson 3.00 8.00
GNJK Jason Kidd 3.00 8.00
GNJN Jameer Nelson 2.50 6.00
GNJO Jermaine O'Neal 3.00 8.00
GNJP Johan Petro 2.00 5.00
GNJR Jason Richardson 3.00 8.00
GNJT Jamaal Tinsley 2.00 5.00
GNKG Kevin Garnett 6.00 15.00
GNKM Kenyon Martin 3.00 8.00
GNLJ LeBron James 10.00 25.00
GNMA Donyell Marshall 2.00 5.00
GNMB Mike Bibby 2.50 6.00
GNMG Manu Ginobili 3.00 8.00
GNMR Michael Redd 3.00 8.00
GNPG Pau Gasol 3.00 8.00
GNPS Peja Stojakovic 3.00 8.00
GNRW Rasheed Wallace 3.00 8.00
GNSO Shaquille O'Neal 6.00 15.00
GNZR Zach Randolph 2.50 6.00

2008-09 Upper Deck MVP Kobe MVP

COMMON CARD (KB1-100) 1.50 4.00
STATED ODDS 1:2

2008-09 Upper Deck MVP Kobe MVP White

COMMON CARD (1-100) 2.50 6.00
INSERTED APPROXIMATELY ONE PER BOX

2008-09 Upper Deck MVP SE

*STARS: 1X TO 2.5X BASE HI
*RCs: .4X TO 1X BASE HI
RANDOM INSERTS IN RETAIL PACKS

2008-09 Upper Deck MVP Signatures Required

STATED ODDS 1:288
SRAO Kelenna Azubuike 5.00 12.00
Patrick O'Bryant
SRAS Arron Afflalo 8.00 20.00
Rodney Stuckey
SRAT Alando Tucker 5.00 12.00
Morris Almond
SRAW Hilton Armstrong 5.00 12.00
Julian Wright
SRBA Corey Brewer 5.00 12.00
Arron Afflalo
SRBJ LeBron James 100.00 225.00
Kobe Bryant
SRBL Acie Law 6.00 15.00
Mike Bibby
SRBP Tony Parker 15.00 40.00
Chauncey Billups
SRCW Javaris Crittenton 5.00 12.00
Mario West
SRDD Jermareo Davidson 6.00 15.00
Jared Dudley
SRDG Kevin Durant 75.00 150.00
Jeff Green
SRDH Al Horford 75.00 150.00
Kevin Durant
SRDS Kevin Durant 75.00 150.00
Luis Scola
SRGS Taurean Green 5.00 12.00
D.J. Strawberry
SRHG Larry Hughes 10.00 25.00
Aaron Gray
SRHH Dwight Howard 20.00 40.00
Al Horford
SRHW Marvin Williams 15.00 30.00
Al Horford
SRIS Jason Smith 6.00 15.00
Andre Iguodala
SRJG Taurean Green 5.00 12.00
Bobby Jones
SRJL Jason Smith 5.00 12.00
Louis Williams
SRJW Maurice Williams 5.00 12.00
Richard Jefferson
SRKB Ronnie Brewer 8.00 20.00
Kyle Korver
SRKW Chris Kaman 6.00 15.00
Sean Williams
SRLB Carl Landry 6.00 15.00
Aaron Brooks
SRLS Carl Landry 8.00 20.00
Luis Scola
SRNC Demetris Nichols 5.00 12.00
JamesOn Curry
SRNL Steve Novak 6.00 15.00
Carl Landry
SRNS Amare Stoudemire 40.00 100.00
Steve Nash
SROW Sean Williams 5.00 12.00
Patrick O'Bryant
SRPW Deron Williams 30.00 80.00
Chris Paul
SRRP Gabe Pruitt 10.00 25.00
Rajon Rondo
SRSS Spencer Hawes 8.00 20.00
Shelden Williams
SRSW Sean Williams 5.00 12.00
Cheikh Samb
SRTL Carl Landry 15.00 30.00
Alando Tucker
SRWH Louis Williams 5.00 12.00
Herbert Hill
SRWS Ramon Sessions 5.00 12.00
Maurice Williams

2008-09 Upper Deck MVP Star Combos

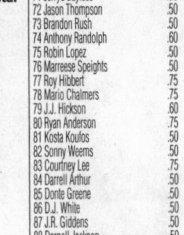

STATED ODDS 1:84
*PATCH: 1.25X TO 3X BASE HI
PATCH PRINT RUN 25 SER.#'d SETS
SCBJ Joe Johnson 4.00 10.00
Mike Bibby
SCBM Corey Maggette 4.00 10.00
Elton Brand
SCCN Brian Cook 4.00 10.00
Jameer Nelson
SCCR Zach Randolph 4.00 10.00
Eddy Curry
SCGD Drew Gooden 4.00 10.00
Luol Deng
SCGK Andrei Kirilenko 6.00 15.00
Kevin Garnett
SCGN Kevin Garnett 6.00 15.00
Dirk Nowitzki
SCHD Grant Hill 8.00 20.00
Boris Diaw
SCIA Allen Iverson 6.00 15.00
Carmelo Anthony
SCJB LeBron James 25.00 50.00
Kobe Bryant
SCKH Devin Harris 4.00 10.00
Jason Kidd
SCKN Dirk Nowitzki 5.00 12.00
Jason Kidd
SCMB Dikembe Mutombo 4.00 10.00
Shane Battier
SCMO Shaquille O'Neal 6.00 15.00
Shawn Marion
SCOG Pau Gasol 8.00 20.00
Lamar Odom
SCRB Andrew Bogut 4.00 10.00
Michael Redd
SCRM Adam Morrison 4.00 10.00
Jason Richardson
SCTO Jermaine O'Neal 4.00 10.00
Jamaal Tinsley
SCWP Rasheed Wallace 4.00 10.00
Tayshaun Prince
SCWS Peja Stojakovic 4.00 10.00
David West

2008-09 Upper Deck MVP Victory

COMPLETE SET (90) 25.00 50.00
RANDOM INSERTS IN RETAIL PACKS
*ULTIMATE: .6X TO 1.5X VICTORY HI
ULTIMATE STATED ODDS 1:2 HOBBY
1 Joe Johnson .30 .75
2 Al Horford .30 .75
3 Paul Pierce .40 1.00
4 Kevin Garnett .60 1.50
5 Jason Richardson .30 .75
6 Gerald Wallace .30 .75
7 Luol Deng .30 .75
8 Ben Gordon .30 .75
9 Ben Wallace .30 .75
10 LeBron James 1.50 4.00
11 Dirk Nowitzki .40 1.00
12 Jason Kidd .40 1.00
13 Allen Iverson .40 1.00
14 Carmelo Anthony .40 1.00
15 Chauncey Billups .30 .75
16 Richard Hamilton .25 .60
17 Baron Davis .30 .75
18 Stephen Jackson .25 .60
19 Yao Ming .40 1.00
20 Tracy McGrady .30 .75
21 Danny Granger .30 .75
22 Jermaine O'Neal .30 .75
23 Chris Kaman .25 .60
24 Corey Maggette .25 .60
25 Kobe Bryant 1.50 4.00
26 Pau Gasol .30 .75
27 Rudy Gay .30 .75
28 Mike Conley Jr. .25 .60
29 Dwyane Wade .60 1.50
30 Shawn Marion .30 .75
31 Michael Redd .30 .75
32 Maurice Williams .25 .60
33 Al Jefferson .30 .75
34 Rashad McCants .20 .50
35 Richard Jefferson .30 .75
36 Vince Carter .40 1.00
37 Chris Paul .50 1.25
38 David West .25 .60
39 Jamal Crawford .25 .60
40 Zach Randolph .30 .75
41 Dwight Howard .60 1.50
42 Rashard Lewis .25 .60
43 Andre Iguodala .25 .60
44 Andre Miller .25 .60
45 Amare Stoudemire .30 .75
46 Steve Nash .30 .75
47 Brandon Roy .30 .75
48 Greg Oden .30 .75
49 Kevin Martin .30 .75
50 Ron Artest .30 .75
51 Tim Duncan .50 1.25
52 Tony Parker .50 1.25
53 Kevin Durant 1.25 3.00
54 Jeff Green .25 .60
55 Chris Bosh .30 .75
56 Jose Calderon .25 .60
57 Carlos Boozer .30 .75
58 Deron Williams .30 .75
59 Gilbert Arenas .30 .75
60 Antawn Jamison .30 .75
61 Derrick Rose 4.00 10.00
62 Michael Beasley .75 2.00
63 O.J. Mayo .75 2.00
64 Russell Westbrook 2.50 6.00
65 Kevin Love 2.00 5.00
66 Danilo Gallinari .75 2.00
67 Eric Gordon 1.25 3.00
68 Joe Alexander .50 1.25
69 D.J. Augustin .50 1.25
70 Brook Lopez .75 2.00
71 Jerryd Bayless .50 1.25
72 Jason Thompson .50 1.25
73 Brandon Rush .50 1.25
74 Anthony Randolph .60 1.50
75 Robin Lopez .50 1.25
76 Marreese Speights .50 1.25
77 Roy Hibbert .75 2.00
78 Mario Chalmers .75 2.00
79 J.J. Hickson .60 1.50
80 Ryan Anderson .75 2.00
81 Kosta Koufos .50 1.25
82 Sonny Weems .50 1.25
83 Courtney Lee .75 2.00
84 Darrell Arthur .50 1.25
85 Donte Greene .50 1.25
86 D.J. White .50 1.25
87 J.R. Giddens .50 1.25
88 Darnell Jackson .50 1.25
89 Chris Douglas-Roberts .50 1.25
90 Patrick Ewing Jr. .50 1.25

1992-93 Upper Deck MVP Holograms

This 38-card standard-size hologram set consists of Upper Deck's selection of the MVP on each of the NBA's 27 teams (1-27) plus nine "Future MVPs" (28-36) focusing on player's who could become their team's MVP in the near future. Just 138,000 individually numbered sets were produced, and they were available only through hobby dealers and select retail outlets beginning in mid-May. The fronts display a color, action cut-out photo and a holographic inset photo set against a background of geometric shapes in gray, black, and the team's colors. On team color-coded panels with gray geometric shapes, the backs carry player profiles. Included in the set is a card that carries instructions for ordering a matching display album.

COMP. FACT SET (38) 12.50 30.00
1 Dominique Wilkins .15 .40
2 Reggie Lewis .08 .25
3 Larry Johnson .40 1.00
4 Michael Jordan 4.00 10.00
5 Mark Price .08 .25
6 Derek Harper .08 .25
7 Dikembe Mutombo .15 .40
8 Isiah Thomas .15 .40
9 Chris Mullin .15 .40
10 Hakeem Olajuwon .50 1.25
11 Reggie Miller .30 .75
12 Danny Manning .08 .25
13 James Worthy .15 .40
14 Glen Rice .30 .75
15 Alvin Robertson .08 .25
16 Chuck Person .08 .25
17 Derrick Coleman .08 .25
18 Patrick Ewing .30 .75
19 Scott Skiles .08 .25
20 Hersey Hawkins .08 .25
21 Charles Barkley .50 1.25
22 Clyde Drexler .30 .75
23 Mitch Richmond .30 .75
24 David Robinson .50 1.25
25 Shawn Kemp .75 2.00
26 Karl Malone .50 1.25
27 Pervis Ellison .08 .25
28 Lloyd Daniels .08 .25
29 Todd Day .08 .25
30 Tom Gugliotta 1.00 2.50
31 Robert Horry .50 1.25
32 Christian Laettner .75 2.00
33 Harold Miner .08 .25
34 Alonzo Mourning 1.50 4.00
35 Shaquille O'Neal 4.00 10.00
36 Walt Williams .30 .75
NNO Checklist .08 .25
NNO Album Offer Card .08 .25

2009 Upper Deck Mystery Iconic Cuts Redemption

AUTOS ISSUED VIA EXCH CARD

2000 Upper Deck NBA Card Clips

These minature card clips were released by Upper Deck in early December, 2000. Each card measures 2" wide by 2.75" long. Cards featured are minature versions of the 2000-01 Upper Deck MVP base cards.

COMPLETE SET (58) 25.00 50.00
1 Dikembe Mutombo 1.00 2.50
2 Lorenzen Wright .50 1.25
3 Antoine Walker .50 1.25
4 Kenny Anderson .50 1.25
5 Elden Campbell .50 1.25
6 Baron Davis 1.25 3.00
7 Elton Brand 1.00 2.50
8 Ron Mercer .50 1.25
9 Andre Miller .50 1.25
10 Chris Mihm .50 1.25
11 Michael Finley .60 1.50
12 Dirk Nowitzki 2.00 5.00
13 Antonio McDyess .50 1.25
14 Nick Van Exel .50 1.25
15 Jerry Stackhouse .50 1.25
16 Mateen Cleaves .50 1.25
17 Antawn Jamison .50 1.25
18 Larry Hughes .50 1.25
19 Steve Francis .60 1.50
20 Hakeem Olajuwon 1.00 2.50
21 Reggie Miller 1.25 3.00
22 Jalen Rose .50 1.25
23 Michael Olowokandi .50 1.25
24 Lamar Odom 1.00 2.50
25 Shaquille O'Neal 2.50 6.00
26 Kobe Bryant 4.00 10.00
27 Alonzo Mourning 1.00 2.50
28 Tim Hardaway .50 1.25
29 Ray Allen 1.25 3.00
30 Glenn Robinson .50 1.25
31 Kevin Garnett 2.50 6.00
32 Wally Szczerbiak .50 1.25
33 Keith Van Horn .50 1.25
34 Stephon Marbury .60 1.50
35 Allan Houston .50 1.25
36 Latrell Sprewell .50 1.25
37 Grant Hill 1.25 3.00
38 Tracy McGrady 1.50 4.00
39 Allen Iverson 1.50 4.00
40 Toni Kukoc .50 1.25
41 Jason Kidd 1.50 4.00
42 Anfernee Hardaway .50 1.25
43 Scottie Pippen 1.50 4.00
44 Rasheed Wallace 1.00 2.50
45 Chris Webber 1.25 3.00
46 Jason Williams .50 1.25
47 Tim Duncan 2.00 5.00
48 David Robinson 2.00 5.00
49 Gary Payton .50 1.25
50 Vin Baker .50 1.25
51 Charles Oakley .50 1.25
52 Vince Carter 2.00 5.00
53 Karl Malone 1.50 4.00
54 John Stockton 1.50 4.00
55 Shareef Abdur-Rahim .50 1.25
56 Bryant Reeves .50 1.25
57 Mitch Richmond .50 1.25
58 Juwan Howard .50 1.25

2007-08 Upper Deck NBA Rookie Box Set

COMPLETE SET (30) 10.00 25.00
AUTOS RANDOMLY INSERTED
1 Arron Afflalo .60 1.50
2 Morris Almond .50 1.25
3 Corey Brewer .60 1.50
4 Aaron Brooks .50 1.25
5 Wilson Chandler .75 2.00
6 Mike Conley Jr. .75 2.00
7 Daequan Cook .50 1.25
8 Javaris Crittenton .50 1.25
9 Glen Davis .75 2.00
10 Jared Dudley .50 1.25
11 Kevin Durant 4.00 10.00
12 Nick Fazekas .50 1.25
13 Jeff Green .60 1.50
14 Taurean Green .50 1.25
15 Spencer Hawes .60 1.50
16 Al Horford .60 1.50
17 Acie Law .50 1.25
18 Josh McRoberts .50 1.25
19 Joakim Noah 1.25 3.00
20 Greg Oden .60 1.50
21 Gabe Pruitt .50 1.25
22 D.J. Strawberry .50 1.25
23 Rodney Stuckey .75 2.00
24 Al Thornton .50 1.25
25 Alando Tucker .50 1.25
26 Sean Williams .50 1.25
27 Brandan Wright .50 1.25
28 Julian Wright .50 1.25
29 Nick Young .75 2.00
30 Thaddeus Young .60 1.50

2000 Upper Deck National Kobe Bryant

This 10-card set was sold at the 2000 National Convention in Anaheim, CA in July, 2000. The set features 10 Kobe Bryant cards. Card backs carry a "KB" prefix.

COMPLETE SET (10) 12.00 30.00
COMMON CARD (KB1-KB10) 1.00 2.50

2002 Upper Deck National Convention

N13 Kobe Bryant 1.25 3.00
N14 Kevin Garnett .60 1.50
N15 Michael Jordan CL 1.50 4.00

2004 Upper Deck National Convention

STATED PRINT RUN 500 SER.#'d SETS
TN1 LeBron James 4.00 10.00
TN2 Kobe Bryant 4.00 10.00
TN3 Michael Jordan 5.00 12.00
TN18 Kevin Garnett 3.00 8.00
TN19 Carmelo Anthony 2.50 6.00

2004 Upper Deck National Convention LeBron James Fan Favorite

STATED PRINT RUN 100 SER.#'d SETS
FF1 LeBron James 10.00 25.00
FF2 LeBron James 10.00 25.00
FF3 LeBron James 10.00 25.00
FF4 LeBron James 10.00 25.00

2004 Upper Deck National Convention VIP

VIP1 LeBron James 6.00 15.00
VIP2 Michael Jordan 8.00 20.00

2005 Upper Deck National Convention

Upper Deck produced this set and distributed it at the 2005 National Sport Collectors Convention in Chicago. The set includes famous Chicago area athletes from a variety of sports with the title "The National" printed on the cardfronts. The company made the cards available to collectors via a wrapper redemption program at their show booth and each card was serial numbered to 750-copies. Some players also signed just 5-cards which are not priced due to scarcity.

STATED PRINT RUN 750 SER.#'d SETS
UNPRICED AUTO PRINT RUN 5
CL3 Michael Jordan 5.00 12.00

2005 Upper Deck National Convention VIP

Upper Deck produced this set and distributed it to special VIP package members attending the 2005 National Sport Collectors Convention in Chicago. The set includes famous athletes from a variety of sports with the title "The National" printed on the cardfronts along with a "VIP" stamp.

VIP1 Michael Jordan 8.00 20.00
VIP2 LeBron James 8.00 20.00

2006 Upper Deck National NBA

COMPLETE SET (3) 5.00 12.00
PRINT RUN 500 SER.#'d SETS
NBA1 Michael Jordan 3.00 8.00
NBA2 LeBron James 2.50 6.00
NBA3 Chris Paul 1.25 3.00

2006 Upper Deck National Southern California

COMPLETE SET (6) 5.00 12.00
SoCal1 Elton Brand .75 2.00

2006 Upper Deck National NBA VIP

COMPLETE SET (6) 6.00 15.00
1 Michael Jordan 3.00 8.00
2 LeBron James 2.50 6.00
3 Chris Bosh 1.25 3.00
4 Yao Ming 1.25 3.00
5 Tim Duncan 1.25 3.00
6 Chris Paul 1.25 3.00

2007 Upper Deck National Convention

NTL5 Kobe Bryant 1.00 2.50
NTL6 Michael Jordan 1.50 4.00
NTL7 LeBron James 1.25 3.00

2007 Upper Deck National Convention VIP

VIP5 Kobe Bryant 1.50 4.00
VIP6 Michael Jordan 2.50 6.00
VIP7 LeBron James 2.00 5.00

2008 Upper Deck National Convention

NAT4 Kobe Bryant 1.25 3.00
NAT6 Michael Jordan 2.00 5.00
NAT9 LeBron James 1.25 3.00

2008 Upper Deck National Convention VIP

CARDS FEATURE VIP LOGO ON FRONT
NAT4 Kobe Bryant 3.00 8.00
NAT6 Michael Jordan 5.00 12.00
NAT9 LeBron James 3.00 8.00

2009 Upper Deck National Convention

NC6 LeBron James 1.25 3.00
NC7 LeBron James 1.25 3.00
NC8 Mo Williams .40 1.00
NC13 Derrick Rose .75 2.00
NC18 Kobe Bryant 1.25 3.00
NC21 Michael Jordan 2.00 5.00
NC22 Paul Pierce .60 1.50

2009 Upper Deck National Convention VIP

VIP3 LeBron James 2.50 6.00
VIP8 Michael Jordan 4.00 10.00

2010 Upper Deck National Convention

COMPLETE SET (20) 15.00 40.00
NSC1 Michael Jordan 3.00 8.00
NSC5 Julius Erving 2.00 5.00
NSC6 LeBron James 3.00 8.00
NSC14 Alonzo Mourning 1.25 3.00
NSC19 David Robinson 1.25 3.00

2010 Upper Deck National Convention Autographs

STATED PRINT RUN 9-90
NALJ LeBron James/23 125.00 250.00
NAMJ Michael Jordan/23 300.00 600.00

2010 Upper Deck National Convention VIP

COMPLETE SET (6) 6.00 15.00
VIP3 LeBron James 3.00 8.00
VIP5 Michael Jordan 3.00 8.00

2011 Upper Deck National Convention

NSCC1 Michael Jordan 2.00 5.00
NSCC3 Derrick Rose 1.25 3.00
NSCC15 LeBron James 1.25 3.00
NSCC19 B.J. Armstrong .75 2.00

2011 Upper Deck National Convention Autographs

NSCCLJ LeBron James/15 125.00 250.00

2011 Upper Deck National Convention VIP

1 Michael Jordan 1.50 4.00
4 LeBron James 1.00 2.50

2012 Upper Deck National Convention

NSCC1 Michael Jordan 3.00 8.00
NSCC3 Alonzo Mourning 2.00 5.00
NSCC16 LeBron James 2.00 5.00

2012 Upper Deck National Convention Autographs

STATED PRINT RUN 1-35
NSCCLJ LeBron James/15 150.00 300.00

2012 Upper Deck National Convention VIP

3 LeBron James 2.00 5.00
5 Michael Jordan 4.00 10.00

2004 Upper Deck Naxcom LeBron James

Produced by Upper Deck in conjunction with Naxcom, this LeBron James cards was given away to new members of Naxcom's website as a promotion. Each card pictures LeBron in a gray suit and comes sealed in a tamper-proof screw down case.

NNO LeBron James 10.00 25.00

1997 Upper Deck Nestle Crunch Time

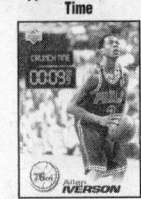

Produced by Upper Deck and Nestle, this 40-card set measures the standard size and was inserted in four-card packs in special Nestle Crunch bars. The set focuses on players who either made a clutch shot down the stretch of a 1996-97 NBA game to win the game or seal the victory for his team. Card fronts feature a color action shot of the player against a black and white crowd background. The player's name and team logo are at the bottom. Each card front also features a digital timer. Card backs are numbered with a "CT" prefix.

COMPLETE SET (40) 8.00 20.00
CT1 Kenny Anderson .30 .75
CT2 Arvydas Sabonis .30 .75
CT3 Elliot Perry UER .25 .60
Misp. Elliott
CT4 Chris Webber .40 1.00
CT5 Michael Jordan 4.00 10.00
CT6 Terrell Brandon .25 .60
CT7 Rick Fox .25 .60
CT8 Brent Barry .30 .75
CT9 Bryant Reeves .25 .60
CT10 Steve Smith .30 .75
CT11 Mookie Blaylock .25 .60
CT12 Christian Laettner .30 .75
CT13 Tim Hardaway .40 1.00
CT14 Voshon Lenard .25 .60
CT15 Dan Majerle .40 1.00
CT16 Glen Rice .40 1.00
CT17 Dell Curry .25 .60
CT18 Karl Malone .50 1.25
CT19 John Stockton .50 1.25
CT20 Mitch Richmond .40 1.00
CT21 Patrick Ewing .50 1.25
CT22 Kobe Bryant 3.00 8.00
CT23 Eddie Jones .40 1.00
CT24 Anfernee Hardaway .60 1.50
CT25 Rony Seikaly .30 .75
CT26 Chris Gatling .25 .60
CT27 Kendall Gill .25 .60
CT28 Dale Ellis .25 .60
CT29 Reggie Miller .50 1.25
CT30 Terry Mills .25 .60
CT31 Damon Stoudamire .40 1.00
CT32 Clyde Drexler .50 1.25
CT33 Allen Iverson .75 2.00
CT34 Jerry Stackhouse .40 1.00
CT35 Hersey Hawkins .25 .60
CT36 Gary Payton .40 1.00
CT37 Carl Herrera .25 .60
CT38 Rex Chapman .25 .60
CT39 Tom Gugliotta .25 .60
CT40 Latrell Sprewell .40 1.00

1996 Upper Deck Nestle Slam Dunk

This 40-card set was issued by Upper Deck and inserted with Nestle Crunch bars and features the design of the 1996-97 Collector's Choice series. The exception is card fronts contain the phrase "Slam Dunk Series" in brown-orange at the bottom. Card backs are numbered X of 40.

COMPLETE SET (40) 8.00 20.00
1 Grant Long .25 .60
2 Scott Burrell .25 .60
3 Ron Harper .30 .75
4 Michael Jordan 4.00 10.00
5 Scottie Pippen .60 1.50
6 Bobby Phills .25 .60
7 Tyrone Hill .25 .60
8 Tony Dumas .25 .60
9 LaPhonso Ellis .25 .60
10 Antonio McDyess .40 1.00
11 Theo Ratliff .30 .75
12 Joe Smith .30 .75
13 Rodney Rogers .25 .60
14 Brent Barry .30 .75
15 Cedric Ceballos .25 .60
16 Eddie Jones .40 1.00
17 Vlade Divac .40 1.00
18 Anthony Peeler .25 .60
19 Kurt Thomas .25 .60
20 Vin Baker .30 .75
21 Kevin Garnett 1.00 2.50
22 Shawn Bradley .25 .60
23 Ed O'Bannon .25 .60
24 Nick Anderson .25 .60
25 Clarence Weatherspoon .25 .60
26 Jerry Stackhouse .50 1.25
27 Charles Barkley .60 1.50
28 Gary Trent .25 .60
29 Brian Grant .30 .75
30 Olden Polynice .25 .60
31 Will Perdue .25 .60
32 Vincent Askew .25 .60
33 Doug Christie .25 .60
34 Chris Morris .25 .60
35 Chris Webber .50 1.25
36 Grant Hill .60 1.50
37 Alonzo Mourning .50 1.25
38 Dee Brown .25 .60
39 Shawn Kemp .40 1.00
40 Rasheed Wallace .50 1.25

1997 Upper Deck Nestle Slam Dunk

This 40-card set was issued by Upper Deck and inserted with Nestle Crunch bars. Card fronts contain a borderless action photo with the word "Slam" on the left of the card and the word "Dunk" on the right. The player's name is listed at the bottom. Card backs are numbered X of 40.

COMPLETE SET (40) 8.00 20.00
1 Chris Webber .40 1.00
2 Shawn Kemp .40 1.00
3 Dikembe Mutombo .40 1.00
4 Alonzo Mourning .50 1.25
5 Marcus Camby .40 1.00
6 Otis Thorpe .25 .60
7 Antonio McDyess .30 .75
8 Vin Baker .30 .75
9 Kevin Garnett .75 2.00
10 Patrick Ewing .50 1.25
11 Shareef Abdur-Rahim .40 1.00
12 Antoine Walker .40 1.00
13 Joe Smith .30 .75
14 Glen Rice .40 1.00
15 Juwan Howard .30 .75
16 Eddie Jones .40 1.00
17 Karl Malone .50 1.25
18 Bryant Reeves .25 .60
19 Anfernee Hardaway .60 1.50
20 LaPhonso Ellis .25 .60
21 Kerry Kittles .25 .60
22 Michael Jordan 3.00 8.00
23 Latrell Sprewell .40 1.00
24 Olden Polynice .25 .60
25 Rik Smits .30 .75
26 Glenn Robinson .30 .75
27 Loy Vaught .25 .60
28 Jim Jackson .25 .60
29 Horace Grant .30 .75
30 Allen Iverson .75 2.00
31 Clifford Robinson .25 .60
32 Isaiah Rider .25 .60
33 Clyde Drexler .50 1.25
34 Sean Elliott .40 1.00
35 Eric Williams .25 .60
36 Larry Johnson .40 1.00
37 Anthony Mason .25 .60
38 Terrell Brandon .25 .60
39 Reggie Miller .50 1.25
40 Kevin Johnson .40 1.00

1997 Upper Deck Nestle Slam Dunk Contestants

This set was randomly inserted into packs of special Slam Dunk Nestle Crunch bars and features all of the participants from the 1996-97 Slam Dunk contest at the All-Star game.

COMPLETE SET (6) 25.00 60.00
CC1 Kobe Bryant 25.00 60.00
Champion
CC2 Chris Carr 3.00 8.00
CC3 Michael Finley 5.00 12.00
CC4 Darvin Ham 3.00 8.00
CC5 Bob Sura 3.00 8.00
CC6 Ray Allen 6.00 15.00

1994 Upper Deck Nintendo Chaos in the Windy City

This perforated card was available through Game Pro Magazine and does not have a card number on back.

NNO Michael Jordan 40.00 100.00

1994 Upper Deck Nothing But Net

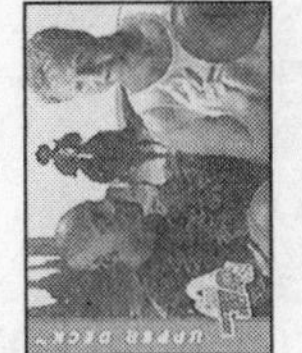

This 15-card standard-size set captures scenes from McDonald's "Nothing but Net" commercials featuring Larry Bird, Michael Jordan, and Charles Barkley. The horizontal fronts feature full-bleed color shots except on the left side, where a gold stripe carries "Upper Deck" in white lettering. A special McDonald's logo appears in the lower left corner. In a film strip design, the back carries four copies of the front picture as well as the dialogue between the players. The cards are numbered on the back "X of 15" in the upper left corner. Also produced was a jumbo-size version of this set distributed only in WalMart. WalMart originally offered complete standard-sized "Nothing But Net" sets along with one jumbo-sized card in a special package for 5.00. Jumbo cards are valued at five times the values listed below.

COMPLETE SET (15) 5.00 12.00
1 Larry Bird 1.00 2.50
Michael Jordan
(I've got an idea)
2 Charles Barkley .40 1.00
(Can I play)
3 Over the Grand Canyon .20 .50
4 Off your face .20 .50
(Mt. Rushmore)
5 Michael Jordan .75 2.00
(Through the window off the floor)
6 Larry Bird .75 2.00
(Nothing but Net)
7 Michael Jordan 1.00 2.50
Larry Bird

(Watch this shot)
8 Charles Barkley .30 .75
(Hey, can I play)
9 Michael Jordan 1.00 2.50
Larry Bird
(No)
10 Charles Barkley .30 .75
(The Shark)
11 Charles Barkley .30 .75
(Please...Pretty Please)
12 Larry Bird .75 2.00
Michael Jordan
Charles Barkley
(No)
13 Michael Jordan .75 2.00
(I'm hungry ...)
14 Larry Bird .60 1.50
(Play ya to see who buys)
15 McDonald's Logo in .08 .25
Outer Space

1998-99 Upper Deck Ovation

The 1998-99 Upper Deck Ovation set was released in early 1999 as an 80-card set that was broken into tiers as follows: 70 Base Veterans (1-70), 10 Rookies (71-80). Each pack carried a suggested retail of $2.99.

COMPLETE SET (80) 25.00 60.00
COMPLETE SET w/o RC (70) 12.00 30.00
1 Steve Smith .30 .75
2 Dikembe Mutombo .40 1.00
3 Antoine Walker .40 1.00
4 Ron Mercer .30 .75
5 Glen Rice .40 1.00
6 Bobby Phills .25 .60
7 Michael Jordan 3.00 8.00
8 Toni Kukoc .40 1.00
9 Dennis Rodman .75 2.00
10 Scottie Pippen .60 1.50
11 Shawn Kemp .40 1.00
12 Derek Anderson .25 .60
13 Brevin Knight .25 .60
14 Michael Finley .40 1.00
15 Shawn Bradley .25 .60
16 LaPhonso Ellis .25 .60
17 Bobby Jackson .30 .75
18 Grant Hill .60 1.50
19 Jerry Stackhouse .40 1.00
20 Donyell Marshall .25 .60
21 Erick Dampier .25 .60
22 Hakeem Olajuwon .50 1.25
23 Charles Barkley .60 1.50
24 Reggie Miller .50 1.25
25 Chris Mullin .40 1.00
26 Rik Smits .30 .75
27 Maurice Taylor .25 .60
28 Lorenzen Wright .25 .60
29 Kobe Bryant 2.00 5.00
30 Eddie Jones .40 1.00
31 Shaquille O'Neal 1.00 2.50
32 Alonzo Mourning .50 1.25
33 Tim Hardaway .40 1.00
34 Jamal Mashburn .30 .75
35 Ray Allen .50 1.25
36 Terrell Brandon .25 .60
37 Glenn Robinson .30 .75
38 Kevin Garnett .75 2.00
39 Tom Gugliotta .25 .60
40 Stephon Marbury .50 1.25
41 Keith Van Horn .40 1.00
42 Kerry Kittles .25 .60
43 Jayson Williams .25 .60
44 Patrick Ewing .50 1.25
45 Allan Houston .30 .75
46 Larry Johnson .40 1.00
47 Anfernee Hardaway .60 1.50
48 Nick Anderson .25 .60
49 Allen Iverson .75 2.00
50 Joe Smith .30 .75
51 Tim Thomas .40 1.00
52 Jason Kidd .60 1.50
53 Antonio McDyess .30 .75
54 Damon Stoudamire .40 1.00
55 Isaiah Rider .25 .60
56 Rasheed Wallace .40 1.00
57 Tariq Abdul-Wahad .25 .60
58 Corliss Williamson .25 .60
59 Tim Duncan .75 2.00
60 David Robinson .60 1.50
61 Vin Baker .30 .75
62 Gary Payton .40 1.00
63 Chauncey Billups .50 1.25
64 Tracy McGrady .60 1.50
65 Karl Malone .50 1.25
66 John Stockton .50 1.25
67 Shareef Abdur-Rahim .40 1.00
68 Bryant Reeves .25 .60
69 Juwan Howard .30 .75
70 Rod Strickland .25 .60
71 Michael Olowokandi RC 1.00 2.50
72 Mike Bibby RC 2.00 5.00
73 Raef LaFrentz RC 1.00 2.50
74 Antawn Jamison RC 2.00 5.00
75 Vince Carter RC 4.00 10.00
76 Robert Traylor RC .75 2.00
77 Jason Williams RC 2.00 5.00
78 Larry Hughes RC 1.50 4.00
79 Dirk Nowitzki RC 5.00 12.00
80 Paul Pierce RC 4.00 10.00
BK1 Michael Jordan 750.00 1500.00
Game Used Basketball Card/90

1998-99 Upper Deck Ovation Gold

Randomly inserted in packs, this 80-card set parallels the base set. The cards feature serial numbering to 1000 on the card front. Cards 71-80 were available via redemption only. To ascertain card values, please use the multiplier provided in the header below, coupled with the value of the base card.

*STARS: 2.5X TO 6X BASE CARD HI
*RCs: .75X TO 2X BASE HI
75 Vince Carter 15.00 40.00
79 Dirk Nowitzki 15.00 40.00

1998-99 Upper Deck Ovation Future Forces

Randomly inserted into packs at a rate of one in 29, this 20-card set focuses on young players who have the ability to make a high impact. The card fronts feature a silver border, while the card backs are numbered with a "F" prefix.

COMPLETE SET (20) 30.00 80.00
F1 Tim Duncan 4.00 10.00
F2 Keith Van Horn 2.00 5.00
F3 Kobe Bryant 10.00 25.00
F4 Tracy McGrady 3.00 8.00
F5 Maurice Taylor 1.25 3.00
F6 Shareef Abdur-Rahim 2.00 5.00
F7 Kevin Garnett 4.00 10.00
F8 Brevin Knight 1.25 3.00
F9 Ron Mercer 1.50 4.00
F10 Tim Thomas 2.00 5.00
F11 Antoine Walker 2.00 5.00
F12 Michael Finley 2.00 5.00
F13 Grant Hill 3.00 8.00
F14 Jerry Stackhouse 2.00 5.00
F15 Erick Dampier 1.25 3.00
F16 Lorenzen Wright 1.25 3.00
F17 Ray Allen 2.50 6.00
F18 Stephon Marbury 2.50 6.00
F19 Allen Iverson 4.00 10.00
F20 Damon Stoudamire 2.00 5.00

1998-99 Upper Deck Ovation Jordan Rules

Randomly inserted into packs at different levels, this 15-card set focuses on Jordan's dominant play during his NBA career showing why he "rules". The first tier (cards J1-J5) feature a bronze background and were inserted at one in 23. The second tier (cards J6-J10) feature a silver background are were inserted at one in 45. The last tier (cards J11-J15) feature a die cut gold background and were inserted at a rate of one in 99. Card backs feature a "J" prefix.

COMMON CARD (J1-J5) 6.00 15.00
COMMON CARD (J6-J10) 10.00 25.00
COMMON CARD (J11-J15) 15.00 40.00

1998-99 Upper Deck Ovation Superstars of the Court

Randomly inserted in packs at a rate of one in two, this 20-card set features the top stars who dominate the court. The cards feature a holofoil background on the front, and are numbered with a "C" prefix.

COMPLETE SET (20) 10.00 25.00
C1 Michael Jordan 3.00 8.00
C2 Tim Duncan .75 2.00
C3 Grant Hill .60 1.50
C4 Karl Malone .50 1.25
C5 Dennis Rodman .75 2.00
C6 Hakeem Olajuwon .50 1.25
C7 Keith Van Horn .40 1.00
C8 Kobe Bryant 2.00 5.00
C9 Jason Kidd .60 1.50
C10 Stephon Marbury .50 1.25
C11 Reggie Miller .50 1.25
C12 Damon Stoudamire .40 1.00
C13 Tracy McGrady .60 1.50
C14 Scottie Pippen .60 1.50
C15 Vin Baker .30 .75
C16 Shaquille O'Neal 1.00 2.50
C17 Anfernee Hardaway .60 1.50
C18 Charles Barkley .60 1.50
C19 Kevin Garnett .75 2.00
C20 Antoine Walker .40 1.00

1999-00 Upper Deck Ovation

The second year for Ovation was released as a 90-card base set, containing 60 veterans and 30 rookies. Each card had the look and feel of an actual basketball, with the color photo in the middle of the front. The rookie subset cards were inserted at one in four packs.

COMPLETE SET (90) 30.00 80.00
COMPLETE SET w/o RC (60) 10.00 25.00
1 Dikembe Mutombo .40 1.00
2 Alan Henderson .25 .60
3 Antoine Walker .40 1.00
4 Paul Pierce .60 1.50
5 David Wesley .25 .60
6 Eddie Jones .40 1.00
7 Toni Kukoc .40 1.00
8 Randy Brown .25 .60
9 Shawn Kemp .40 1.00
10 Zydrunas Ilgauskas .30 .75
11 Michael Finley .40 1.00
12 Dirk Nowitzki .75 2.00
13 Nick Van Exel .30 .75
14 Antonio McDyess .30 .75
15 Grant Hill .50 1.25
16 Jerry Stackhouse .40 1.00
17 Antawn Jamison .40 1.00
18 John Starks .40 1.00
19 Hakeem Olajuwon .50 1.25
20 Charles Barkley .60 1.50
21 Cuttino Mobley .30 .75
22 Reggie Miller .40 1.00
23 Rik Smits .40 1.00
24 Maurice Taylor .25 .60
25 Michael Olowokandi .25 .60
26 Kobe Bryant 2.00 5.00
27 Shaquille O'Neal 1.00 2.50
28 Tim Hardaway .40 1.00
29 Alonzo Mourning .50 1.25
30 Glenn Robinson .30 .75
31 Ray Allen .40 1.00
32 Kevin Garnett .75 2.00
33 Joe Smith .30 .75
34 Stephon Marbury .30 .75
35 Keith Van Horn .30 .75
36 Patrick Ewing .50 1.25
37 Latrell Sprewell .50 1.25
38 Darrell Armstrong .25 .60
39 Bo Outlaw .25 .60
40 Allen Iverson .75 2.00
41 Larry Hughes .40 1.00
42 Jason Kidd .60 1.50
43 Anfernee Hardaway .60 1.50
44 Brian Grant .25 .60
45 Damon Stoudamire .40 1.00
46 Jason Williams .50 1.25
47 Chris Webber .40 1.00
48 Tim Duncan .75 2.00
49 David Robinson .50 1.25
50 Sean Elliott .40 1.00
51 Gary Payton .40 1.00
52 Vin Baker .40 1.00
53 Vince Carter .75 2.00
54 Tracy McGrady .60 1.50
55 Karl Malone .50 1.25
56 John Stockton .50 1.25
57 Shareef Abdur-Rahim .30 .75
58 Mike Bibby .40 1.00
59 Juwan Howard .30 .75
60 Mitch Richmond .40 1.00
61 Elton Brand RC 1.50 4.00
62 Steve Francis RC 1.50 4.00
63 Baron Davis RC 2.00 5.00
64 Lamar Odom RC 2.00 5.00
65 Jonathan Bender RC .60 1.50
66 Wally Szczerbiak RC 1.25 3.00
67 Richard Hamilton RC 1.50 4.00
68 Andre Miller RC 1.50 4.00
69 Shawn Marion RC 1.50 4.00
70 Jason Terry RC 1.50 4.00
71 Trajan Langdon RC .60 1.50
72 Aleksandar Radojevic RC .60 1.50
73 Corey Maggette RC 1.25 3.00
74 William Avery RC .60 1.50
75 Galen Young RC .60 1.50
76 Chris Herren RC .60 1.50
77 Cal Bowdler RC .60 1.50
78 James Posey RC .60 1.50
79 Quincy Lewis RC .60 1.50
80 Dion Glover RC .60 1.50
81 Jeff Foster RC .60 1.50
82 Kenny Thomas RC .60 1.50
83 Devean George RC .60 1.50
84 Tim James RC .60 1.50
85 Vonteego Cummings RC .60 1.50
86 Jumaine Jones RC .60 1.50
87 Scott Padgett RC .60 1.50
88 Obinna Ekezie RC .60 1.50
89 Ryan Robertson RC .60 1.50
90 Evan Eschmeyer RC .60 1.50
MJS Michael Jordan AU/23 1500.00 2200.00

1999-00 Upper Deck Ovation Standing Ovation

Randomly inserted in packs, this 90-card set parallels the base set. The cards feature a silver foil and are serially numbered to 50. To ascertain values on individual cards, please refer to the multiplier in the header, coupled with the value of the base card.

*STARS: 20X TO 50X BASE CARD HI
*RCs: 4X TO 10X BASE HI

1999-00 Upper Deck Ovation A Piece of History

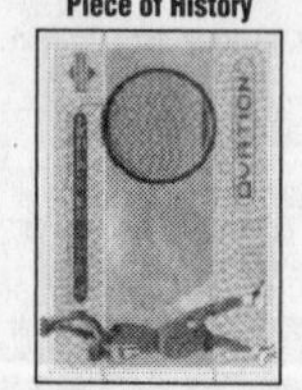

Randomly inserted in packs at one in 352, this 14-card set features an actual piece of a game-used basketball on the corresponding player's card. There was only 4,560 total cards available. The cards are numbered on the back by the players initials.

AM Andre Miller 8.00 20.00
BD Baron Davis 10.00 25.00
HO Hakeem Olajuwon 8.00 20.00
JB Jonathan Bender 3.00 8.00
JS John Stockton 8.00 20.00
JW Jason Williams 8.00 20.00
KB Kobe Bryant 30.00 80.00
KG Kevin Garnett 12.00 30.00
KM Karl Malone 8.00 20.00
RH Richard Hamilton 8.00 20.00
RM Reggie Miller 15.00 40.00
SF Steve Francis 8.00 20.00
SM Shawn Marion 8.00 20.00
WS Wally Szczerbiak 6.00 15.00

1999-00 Upper Deck Ovation A Piece of History Autographs

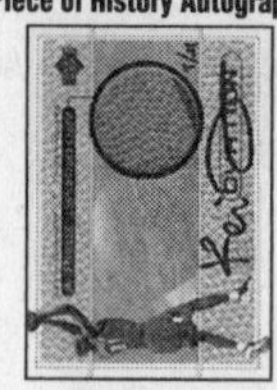

Randomly inserted in packs, this six-card set features authentic signatures on the player's A Piece of History insert card. The cards are numbered to the player's jersey number.

KGA Kevin Garnett/21 200.00 400.00
KMA Karl Malone/32 200.00 400.00
RHA Richard Hamilton/32 60.00 120.00
SMA Shawn Marion/31 60.00 120.00

1999-00 Upper Deck Ovation Curtain Calls

Randomly inserted in packs at one in nine, this 10-card set focuses on some of the most collectible players in the NBA and their accomplishments during the 98-99 season. Card backs carry a "CC" prefix.

COMPLETE SET (10) 3.00 8.00
CC1 Hakeem Olajuwon .60 1.50
CC2 Karl Malone .60 1.50
CC3 Latrell Sprewell .50 1.25
CC4 Allen Iverson 1.00 2.50
CC5 Tim Hardaway .50 1.25
CC6 Shaquille O'Neal 1.25 3.00
CC7 Jason Kidd .75 2.00
CC8 Charles Barkley .75 2.00
CC9 Antonio McDyess .40 1.00
CC10 Gary Payton .50 1.25

1999-00 Upper Deck Ovation Lead Performers

Randomly inserted in packs at one in nine, this 10-card set highlights players who are known for their leadership skills on the floor. Card backs carry a "LP" prefix.

COMPLETE SET (10) 5.00 12.00
LP1 Tim Duncan 1.00 2.50
LP2 Kevin Garnett 1.00 2.50
LP3 Keith Van Horn .40 1.00
LP4 Shareef Abdur-Rahim .40 1.00
LP5 Antoine Walker .50 1.25
LP6 Shaquille O'Neal 1.25 3.00
LP7 Grant Hill .60 1.50
LP8 Kobe Bryant 2.50 6.00
LP9 Allen Iverson 1.00 2.50
LP10 Jason Williams .60 1.50

1999-00 Upper Deck Ovation MJ Center Stage

Randomly inserted in packs at varying levels, this 15-card set focuses on Michael Jordan at his best. Cards CS1-CS5 contained silver foil and were inserted at one in nine. Cards CS6-CS10 contained gold foil and were inserted at one in 39. Finally, cards CS11-CS15 contained rainbow foil and were inserted at one in 99. Card backs carry a "CS" prefix.

COMMON CARD (CS1-CS5) 2.00 5.00
COMMON CARD (CS6-CS10) 4.00 10.00
COMMON CARD (CS11-CS15) 8.00 20.00

1999-00 Upper Deck Ovation Premiere Performers

Randomly inserted in packs at one in 19, this 10-card set showcases the top rookies for the 1999-2000 season. Card backs carry a "PP" prefix.

COMPLETE SET (10) 4.00 10.00
PP1 Elton Brand .75 2.00
PP2 Steve Francis .75 2.00
PP3 Baron Davis 1.00 2.50
PP4 Lamar Odom 1.00 2.50
PP5 Jonathan Bender .30 .75
PP6 Wally Szczerbiak .60 1.50
PP7 Richard Hamilton .75 2.00
PP8 Andre Miller .75 2.00
PP9 Shawn Marion .75 2.00
PP10 Jason Terry .75 2.00

1999-00 Upper Deck Ovation Spotlight

Randomly inserted in packs at one in three, this 10-card set spotlights some of the top young stars in the NBA. Card backs carry an "OS" prefix.

COMPLETE SET (10) 2.50 6.00
OS1 Kevin Garnett .60 1.50
OS2 Antawn Jamison .30 .75
OS3 Kobe Bryant 1.50 4.00
OS4 Shareef Abdur-Rahim .25 .60
OS5 Keith Van Horn .25 .60
OS6 Vince Carter .60 1.50
OS7 Stephon Marbury .25 .60
OS8 Paul Pierce .50 1.25
OS9 Tim Duncan .60 1.50
OS10 Jason Williams .40 1.00

1999-00 Upper Deck Ovation Superstar Theatre

Randomly inserted in packs at one in 19, this 20-card set features the NBA's best performers. Card backs carry a "ST" prefix.

COMPLETE SET (20) 30.00 60.00
ST1 Michael Jordan 10.00 25.00
ST2 Vince Carter 2.50 6.00
ST3 Kevin Garnett 2.50 6.00
ST4 Paul Pierce 2.00 5.00
ST5 Jason Williams 1.50 4.00
ST6 Tim Duncan 2.50 6.00
ST7 Allen Iverson 2.50 6.00
ST8 Antawn Jamison 1.25 3.00
ST9 Kobe Bryant 6.00 15.00
ST10 Grant Hill 1.50 4.00
ST11 Antoine Walker 1.25 3.00
ST12 Tracy McGrady 2.00 5.00
ST13 Shareef Abdur-Rahim 1.00 2.50
ST14 Stephon Marbury 1.00 2.50
ST15 Jason Kidd 2.00 5.00
ST16 Shaquille O'Neal 3.00 8.00
ST17 Tim Hardaway 1.25 3.00
ST18 Keith Van Horn 1.00 2.50
ST19 Gary Payton 1.25 3.00
ST20 Karl Malone 1.50 4.00

2000-01 Upper Deck Ovation

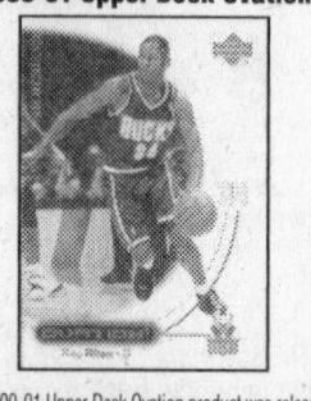

The 2000-01 Upper Deck Ovation product was released in December,2000. The product featured a 90-card base set that was broken into tiers as follows: 60 Base Veterans (1-60), and 30 Rookies (61-90) that were individually serial numbered to 2000. Each pack contained 5 cards, and carried a suggested retail price of $2.99.

COMPLETE SET w/o RC (60) 10.00 25.00
1 Dikembe Mutombo .30 .75
2 Jim Jackson .20 .50
3 Paul Pierce .40 1.00
4 Antoine Walker .25 .60
5 Derrick Coleman .25 .60
6 Baron Davis .30 .75
7 Elton Brand .30 .75
8 Ron Artest .30 .75
9 Lamond Murray .20 .50
10 Andre Miller .25 .60
11 Michael Finley .30 .75
12 Dirk Nowitzki .50 1.25
13 Antonio McDyess .25 .60
14 Nick Van Exel .25 .60
15 Jerry Stackhouse .25 .60
16 Jerome Williams .20 .50
17 Larry Hughes .25 .60
18 Antawn Jamison .30 .75
19 Steve Francis .30 .75
20 Hakeem Olajuwon .40 1.00
21 Reggie Miller .30 .75
22 Jalen Rose .25 .60
23 Lamar Odom .25 .60
24 Michael Olowokandi .20 .50
25 Shaquille O'Neal .75 2.00
26 Kobe Bryant 1.50 4.00
27 Alonzo Mourning .40 1.00
28 Anthony Carter .20 .50
29 Ray Allen .30 .75
30 Tim Thomas .30 .75
31 Kevin Garnett .60 1.50
32 Wally Szczerbiak .25 .60
33 Stephon Marbury .25 .60
34 Keith Van Horn .25 .60
35 Allan Houston .25 .60
36 Latrell Sprewell .25 .60
37 Grant Hill .40 1.00
38 Tracy McGrady .50 1.25
39 Allen Iverson .60 1.50
40 Toni Kukoc .25 .60
41 Jason Kidd .50 1.25
42 Anfernee Hardaway .50 1.25
43 Rasheed Wallace .30 .75
44 Scottie Pippen .50 1.25
45 Damon Stoudamire .25 .60
46 Chris Webber .30 .75
47 Jason Williams .30 .75
48 Tim Duncan .60 1.50
49 David Robinson .50 1.25
50 Gary Payton .30 .75
51 Brent Barry .20 .50
52 Rashard Lewis .30 .75
53 Vince Carter .60 1.50
54 Antonio Davis .20 .50
55 Karl Malone .40 1.00
56 John Stockton .40 1.00
57 Shareef Abdur-Rahim .25 .60
58 Mike Bibby .30 .75
59 Mitch Richmond .25 .60
60 Richard Hamilton .25 .60
61 Kenyon Martin RC 3.00 8.00
62 Stromile Swift RC 1.25 3.00
63 Darius Miles RC 1.25 3.00
64 Marcus Fizer RC 1.25 3.00
65 Mike Miller RC 2.50 6.00
66 DerMarr Johnson RC 1.25 3.00
67 Chris Mihm RC 1.25 3.00
68 Jamal Crawford RC 2.00 5.00
69 Joel Przybilla RC 1.25 3.00
70 Keyon Dooling RC 1.25 3.00
71 Jerome Moiso RC 1.25 3.00
72 Etan Thomas RC 1.25 3.00
73 Courtney Alexander RC 1.25 3.00
74 Mateen Cleaves RC 1.25 3.00
75 Jason Collier RC 1.25 3.00
76 Hedo Turkoglu RC 2.50 6.00
77 Desmond Mason RC 1.50 4.00
78 Quentin Richardson RC 2.00 5.00
79 Jamaal Magloire RC 1.25 3.00
80 Speedy Claxton RC 1.25 3.00
81 Morris Peterson RC 1.25 3.00
82 Donnell Harvey RC 1.25 3.00
83 DeShawn Stevenson RC 1.50 4.00
84 Mamadou N'Diaye RC 1.25 3.00
85 Erick Barkley RC 1.25 3.00
86 Mark Madsen RC 1.25 3.00
87 A.J. Guyton RC 1.25 3.00
88 Khalid El-Amin RC 1.25 3.00
89 Eddie House RC 1.25 3.00
90 Chris Porter RC 1.25 3.00

2000-01 Upper Deck Ovation Standing Ovation

Randomly inserted into packs, this 90-card set is a complete parallel of the Ovation base set. Each card is individually serial numbered to 50. To ascertain values on individual cards, please refer to the multiplier in the header, coupled with the value of the base card.

*STARS: 20X TO 50X BASE CARD HI
*RCs: 1.5X TO 4X BASE CARD HI

2000-01 Upper Deck Ovation A Piece of History

Randomly inserted into packs at one in 120, this 28-card set features game-used ball and shoe cards. Please note that five of these cards are autographed, and are serial numbered to the respective player's jersey number. Card backs are numbered using the player's initials.

AHB Anfernee Hardaway 10.00 25.00
AIB Allen Iverson 12.00 30.00
ALB Alonzo Mourning 8.00 20.00
AMB Andre Miller 5.00 12.00
BDB Baron Davis 6.00 15.00
CWS Chris Webber Shoe 10.00 25.00
GPB Gary Payton 6.00 15.00
JSB Jerry Stackhouse 5.00 12.00
JWB Jason Williams 6.00 15.00
KBB Kobe Bryant Ball 20.00 50.00
KBC Kobe Bryant 125.00 250.00
Ball-Shoe/25
KBS Kobe Bryant Shoe 20.00 50.00
KGA Kevin Garnett AU/21 125.00 250.00
KGB Kevin Garnett Ball 12.00 30.00
KGC Kevin Garnett 50.00 100.00
Ball-Shoe/25
KGS Kevin Garnett Shoe 12.50 30.00
KMS Karl Malone Shoe 12.50 30.00
LHB Larry Hughes 5.00 12.00
MFB Michael Finley 6.00 15.00
MJA Michael Jordan AU/23 900.00 1500.00
MJS Michael Jordan Shoe 100.00 225.00
PPB Paul Pierce 8.00 20.00
RAB Ray Allen 6.00 15.00
SAB Shareef Abdur-Rahim 5.00 12.00
SOS Shaquille O'Neal Shoe 15.00 40.00
SPB Scottie Pippen 8.00 20.00
WSB Wally Szczerbiak 5.00 12.00

2000-01 Upper Deck Ovation Center Stage

Randomly inserted into packs at one in 19, this 10-card insert features players that that take center stage when the game is on the line. Card backs carry a "CS" prefix. Please note that these cards were produced with bronze foil stamping.

COMPLETE SET (10) 6.00 15.00
STATED ODDS 1:19
*SILVER: 2X TO 5X BASE CARD HI
SILVER: PRINT RUN 200 SERIAL #'d SETS
*GOLD: 12X TO 30X BASE CARD HI
GOLD: PRINT RUN 25 SERIAL #'d SETS
CS1 Kevin Garnett 1.25 3.00
CS2 Tim Duncan 1.25 3.00
CS3 Lamar Odom .60 1.50
CS4 Jason Kidd 1.00 2.50
CS5 Vince Carter 1.25 3.00
CS6 Alonzo Mourning .75 2.00
CS7 Elton Brand .60 1.50
CS8 Chris Webber .60 1.50
CS9 Anfernee Hardaway 1.00 2.50
CS10 Kobe Bryant 3.00 8.00

2000-01 Upper Deck Ovation Lead Performers

Randomly inserted into packs at one in 12, this 11-card insert features players that lead their teams to victory. Card backs carry a "LP" prefix.

COMPLETE SET (11) 6.00 15.00
LP1 Shaquille O'Neal 1.25 3.00
LP2 Vince Carter 1.00 2.50
LP3 Kevin Garnett 1.00 2.50
LP4 Allen Iverson 1.00 2.50
LP5 Jason Kidd .75 2.00
LP6 Elton Brand .50 1.25
LP7 Gary Payton .50 1.25
LP8 Kobe Bryant 2.50 6.00
LP9 Steve Francis .50 1.25
LP10 Stephon Marbury .40 1.00
LP11 Tim Duncan 1.00 2.50

2000-01 Upper Deck Ovation Spotlight

Randomly inserted into packs at one in seven, this 20-card insert spotlights some of the most talented players in the NBA. Card backs carry an "OS" prefix.

COMPLETE SET (20) 6.00 15.00
OS1 Kobe Bryant 2.50 6.00
OS2 Larry Hughes .40 1.00
OS3 Andre Miller .40 1.00
OS4 Michael Finley .50 1.25
OS5 Ray Allen .50 1.25
OS6 Latrell Sprewell .50 1.25
OS7 Jalen Rose .40 1.00
OS8 Antonio McDyess .40 1.00
OS9 Karl Malone .60 1.50
OS10 Paul Pierce .60 1.50
OS11 Shareef Abdur-Rahim .40 1.00
OS12 Chris Webber .60 1.50
OS13 Stephon Marbury .40 1.00
OS14 Scottie Pippen .75 2.00
OS15 Lamar Odom .40 1.00
OS16 Alonzo Mourning .60 1.50
OS17 Kevin Garnett 1.00 2.50
OS18 Anfernee Hardaway .75 2.00
OS19 Jason Williams .50 1.25
OS20 Rasheed Wallace .50 1.25

2000-01 Upper Deck Ovation Super Signatures

Randomly inserted in packs at one in 200, this 15-card set features signatures from some of the top stars in the NBA. The card backs are numbered by the player's initials.

AH Anfernee Hardaway 30.00 60.00
CA Courtney Alexander 4.00 10.00
CM Chris Mihm 4.00 10.00
DA Darrell Armstrong 4.00 10.00
DM DerMarr Johnson 4.00 10.00
JP Joel Przybilla 4.00 10.00
JR Jalen Rose 6.00 15.00
KB Kobe Bryant 100.00 200.00
KG Kevin Garnett 30.00 80.00
KY Kenyon Martin 8.00 20.00
LH Larry Hughes 8.00 20.00
MF Marcus Fizer 4.00 10.00
SA Shareef Abdur-Rahim 6.00 15.00
SM Shawn Marion 6.00 15.00
SS Stromile Swift 4.00 10.00

2000-01 Upper Deck Ovation Super Signatures Gold

Randomly inserted into packs, this 15-card insert is a complete parallel of the Super Signatures insert. Please note that these cards have gold foil stamping on the card front and are individually serial numbered to the respective player's jersey number.

SOME UNPRICED DUE TO SCARCITY
KG Kevin Garnett/21 150.00 300.00
LH Larry Hughes/20 30.00 80.00

2000-01 Upper Deck Ovation Superstar Theatre

Randomly inserted into packs at one in 12, this 11-card insert features players that put on a show when they walk onto the court. Card backs carry a "S" prefix.

COMPLETE SET (11) 6.00 15.00
S1 Kobe Bryant 2.50 6.00
S2 Vince Carter 1.00 2.50
S3 Jason Kidd .75 2.00
S4 Steve Francis .50 1.25
S5 Reggie Miller .50 1.25
S6 Tim Duncan 1.00 2.50
S7 Kevin Garnett 1.00 2.50
S8 Gary Payton .50 1.25
S9 Elton Brand .50 1.25
S10 Allen Iverson 1.00 2.50
S11 Shaquille O'Neal 1.25 3.00

2000-01 Upper Deck Ovation UD Authentics Rookie Exclusives

Randomly inserted in packs, this three-card set features autographs from the 2000-01 rookie class. Each player is numbered with their initials.

JP Joel Przybilla 3.00 8.00
MC Mateen Cleaves 3.00 8.00
MP Morris Peterson 3.00 8.00

2001-02 Upper Deck Ovation

This 180-card base set includes 90 veterans and 90 rookies. The rookie players can be found in six different versions. Level 1: 20 Profile cards sequentially #'d to 625; Level 1: 20 Stat cards sequentially #'d to 625; Level 1: 20 Scouting Report cards sequentially #'d to 625; Level 2: 10 Profile cards sequentially #'d to 250; Level 2: 10 Stat cards sequentially #'d to 250; and Level 2: 10 Scouting Report cards sequentially #'d to 250. Base cards feature full color player action photos and bronze highlights. Ovation was packaged in five card packs with boxes containing 20 packs.

COMP.SET w/o SP's (90) 20.00 40.00
1 Jason Terry .30 .75
2 DerMarr Johnson .20 .50
3 Shareef Abdur-Rahim .25 .60
4 Paul Pierce .40 1.00
5 Antoine Walker .25 .60
6 Kenny Anderson .25 .60
7 Jamal Mashburn .25 .60
8 David Wesley .20 .50
9 Baron Davis .30 .75
10 Ron Mercer .20 .50
11 Marcus Fizer .20 .50
12 Ron Artest .30 .75
13 Andre Miller .25 .60
14 Lamond Murray .20 .50
15 Chris Mihm .20 .50
16 Michael Finley .30 .75
17 Steve Nash .50 1.25
18 Dirk Nowitzki .50 1.25
19 Antonio McDyess .25 .60
20 Nick Van Exel .25 .60
21 Raef LaFrentz .20 .50
22 Jerry Stackhouse .25 .60
23 Chucky Atkins .20 .50
24 Corliss Williamson .20 .50
25 Antawn Jamison .30 .75
26 Chris Porter .20 .50
27 Larry Hughes .25 .60
28 Steve Francis .30 .75
29 Cuttino Mobley .25 .60
30 Maurice Taylor .20 .50
31 Reggie Miller .30 .75
32 Jalen Rose .25 .60
33 Jermaine O'Neal .30 .75
34 Darius Miles .20 .50
35 Corey Maggette .25 .60
36 Lamar Odom .30 .75
37 Elton Brand .30 .75
38 Kobe Bryant 1.50 4.00
39 Shaquille O'Neal .75 2.00
40 Rick Fox .25 .60
41 Derek Fisher .25 .60
42 Stromile Swift .20 .50
43 Michael Dickerson .20 .50
44 Jason Williams .25 .60
45 Alonzo Mourning .40 1.00
46 Eddie Jones .25 .60
47 Anthony Carter .20 .50
48 Ray Allen .30 .75
49 Glenn Robinson .25 .60
50 Sam Cassell .25 .60
51 Kevin Garnett .60 1.50
52 Terrell Brandon .20 .50
53 Wally Szczerbiak .25 .60
54 Joe Smith .25 .60
55 Kenyon Martin .30 .75
56 Keith Van Horn .25 .60
57 Jason Kidd .50 1.25
58 Latrell Sprewell .25 .60
59 Allan Houston .25 .60
60 Marcus Camby .25 .60
61 Tracy McGrady .50 1.25
62 Mike Miller .30 .75
63 Grant Hill .40 1.00
64 Allen Iverson .60 1.50
65 Dikembe Mutombo .30 .75
66 Aaron McKie .20 .50
67 Stephon Marbury .25 .60
68 Shawn Marion .30 .75
69 Tom Gugliotta .20 .50
70 Rasheed Wallace .30 .75
71 Damon Stoudamire .25 .60
72 Bonzi Wells .20 .50
73 Chris Webber .30 .75
74 Peja Stojakovic .30 .75
75 Mike Bibby .30 .75
76 Tim Duncan .60 1.50
77 David Robinson .50 1.25
78 Antonio Daniels .20 .50
79 Gary Payton .30 .75
80 Rashard Lewis .30 .75
81 Desmond Mason .25 .60
82 Vince Carter .50 1.25
83 Morris Peterson .20 .50
84 Antonio Davis .20 .50
85 Karl Malone .40 1.00
86 John Stockton .40 1.00
87 Donyell Marshall .20 .50
88 Richard Hamilton .25 .60
89 Courtney Alexander .20 .50
90 Michael Jordan 6.00 15.00
91A Jeff Trepagnier P RC 1.25 3.00
91B Jeff Trepagnier S RC 1.25 3.00
91C Jeff Trepagnier SR RC 1.25 3.00
92A Pau Gasol P RC 4.00 10.00
92B Pau Gasol S RC 4.00 10.00
92C Pau Gasol SR RC 4.00 10.00
93A Will Solomon P RC 1.25 3.00
93B Will Solomon S RC 1.25 3.00
93C Will Solomon SP RC 1.25 3.00
94A Gilbert Arenas P RC 2.00 5.00
94B Gilbert Arenas S RC 2.00 5.00
94C Gilbert Arenas SR RC 2.00 5.00
95A Andrei Kirilenko P RC 3.00 8.00
95B Andrei Kirilenko S RC 3.00 8.00
95C Andrei Kirilenko SR RC 3.00 8.00
96A Jamaal Tinsley P RC 1.50 4.00
96B Jamaal Tinsley S RC 1.50 4.00
96C Jamaal Tinsley SR RC 1.50 4.00
97A Samuel Dalembert P RC 1.50 4.00
97B Samuel Dalembert S RC 1.50 4.00
97C Samuel Dalembert SR RC 1.50 4.00
98A Gerald Wallace P RC 2.00 5.00
98B Gerald Wallace S RC 2.00 5.00
98C Gerald Wallace SR RC 2.00 5.00
99A Brandon Armstrong P RC 1.25 3.00
99B Brandon Armstrong S RC 1.25 3.00
99C Brandon Armstrong SR RC 1.25 3.00
100A Jeryl Sasser P RC 1.25 3.00
100B Jeryl Sasser S RC 1.25 3.00
100C Jeryl Sasser SR RC 1.25 3.00
101A Joseph Forte P RC 1.25 3.00
101B Joseph Forte S RC 1.25 3.00
101C Joseph Forte SR RC 1.25 3.00
102A Brendan Haywood P RC 1.50 4.00
102B Brendan Haywood S RC 1.50 4.00
102C Brendan Haywood SR RC 1.50 4.00
103A Zach Randolph P RC 3.00 8.00
103B Zach Randolph S RC 3.00 8.00
103C Zach Randolph SR RC 3.00 8.00
104A Jason Collins P RC 1.25 3.00
104B Jason Collins S RC 1.25 3.00
104C Jason Collins SR RC 1.25 3.00
105A Michael Bradley P RC 1.25 3.00
105B Michael Bradley S RC 1.25 3.00
105C Michael Bradley SR RC 1.25 3.00
106A Kirk Haston P RC 1.25 3.00
106B Kirk Haston S RC 1.25 3.00
106C Kirk Haston SR RC 1.25 3.00
107A Steven Hunter P RC 1.25 3.00
107B Steven Hunter S RC 1.25 3.00
107C Steven Hunter SR RC 1.25 3.00
108A Troy Murphy P RC 2.00 5.00
108B Troy Murphy S RC 2.00 5.00
108C Troy Murphy SR RC 2.00 5.00
109A Richard Jefferson P RC 2.50 6.00
109B Richard Jefferson S RC 2.50 6.00
109C Richard Jefferson SR RC 2.50 6.00
110A Vladimir Radmanovic P RC 1.25 3.00
110B Vladimir Radmanovic S RC 1.25 3.00
110C Vladimir Radmanovic SR RC 1.25 3.00
111A Kedrick Brown P RC 2.50 6.00
111B Kedrick Brown S RC 2.50 6.00
111C Kedrick Brown SR RC 2.50 6.00
112A Joe Johnson P RC 6.00 15.00
112B Joe Johnson S RC 6.00 15.00
112C Joe Johnson SR RC 6.00 15.00
113A Rodney White P RC 2.50 6.00
113B Rodney White S RC 2.50 6.00
113C Rodney White SR RC 2.50 6.00
114A DeSagana Diop P RC 2.50 6.00
114B DeSagana Diop S RC 2.50 6.00
114C DeSagana Diop SR RC 2.50 6.00
115A Eddie Griffin P RC 2.50 6.00
115B Eddie Griffin S RC 2.50 6.00
115C Eddie Griffin SR RC 2.50 6.00
116A Shane Battier P RC 5.00 12.00
116B Shane Battier S RC 5.00 12.00
116C Shane Battier SR RC 5.00 12.00
117A Jason Richardson P RC 5.00 12.00
117B Jason Richardson S RC 5.00 12.00
117C Jason Richardson SR RC 5.00 12.00
118A Eddy Curry P RC 4.00 10.00
118B Eddy Curry S RC 4.00 10.00
118C Eddy Curry SR RC 4.00 10.00
119A Tyson Chandler P RC 4.00 10.00
119B Tyson Chandler S RC 4.00 10.00
119C Tyson Chandler SR RC 4.00 10.00
120A Kwame Brown P RC 2.50 6.00
120B Kwame Brown S RC 2.50 6.00
120C Kwame Brown SR RC 2.50 6.00

2001-02 Upper Deck Ovation MJ UNC Memorabilia

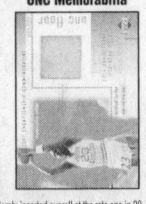

Randomly inserted overall at the rate one in 20, this five card set features a piece of UNC game used memorabilia from Michael Jordan's college days. Several of the cards are sequentially numbered and autographed versions exist also.

MJF1 Michael Jordan Floor 10.00 25.00
MJF2 Michael Jordan Floor 10.00 25.00
MJF3 Michael Jordan Floor 10.00 25.00
MJF4 Michael Jordan Floor 10.00 25.00
MJF5 Michael Jordan Floor 10.00 25.00
MJJ1 Michael Jordan JSY/82 75.00 150.00
MJC1 Michael Jordan Floor-JSY/82 125.00 250.00
MJFA Michael Jordan Floor AU/23 500.00 800.00
MJJA Michael Jordan JSY AU/23 700.00 1200.00
MJCA M.Jordan Flr-JSY AU/23 1000.00 1500.00

2001-02 Upper Deck Ovation Superstar Warm-Ups

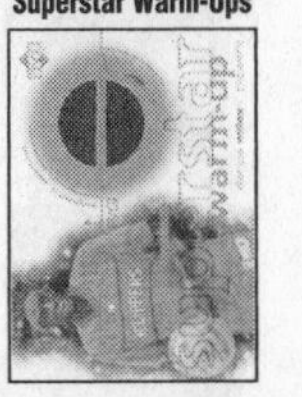

Randomly iinserted in packs at one in 20, this 29 card set features a piece of warm-up jersey on the corresponding player's card. The cards are numbered on back with the player's initials. Photos appear on the left side of the card, while a circular jersey swatch appears on the right.

AM Andre Miller 2.50 6.00
AW Antoine Walker 2.50 6.00
BD Baron Davis 3.00 8.00
CM Corey Maggette 2.50 6.00
DA Darrell Armstrong 2.00 5.00
DJ DerMarr Johnson 2.00 5.00
DM Darius Miles 2.00 5.00
DN Dirk Nowitzki 5.00 12.00
GH Grant Hill 4.00 10.00
HM Hanno Mottola 2.00 5.00
JA Jamaal Magloire 2.00 5.00
JM Jamal Mashburn 2.50 6.00
JS Joe Smith 2.50 6.00
KB Kobe Bryant 15.00 40.00
KD Keyon Dooling 2.00 5.00
KG Kevin Garnett 6.00 15.00
KM Karl Malone 4.00 10.00
MC Antonio McDyess 2.50 6.00
MF Michael Finley 3.00 8.00
MO Michael Olowokandi 2.00 5.00
MP Morris Peterson 2.00 5.00
PP Paul Pierce 4.00 10.00
QR Quentin Richardson 2.50 6.00
RH Richard Hamilton 2.50 6.00
RM Ron Mercer 2.00 5.00
SM Shawn Marion 3.00 8.00
ST John Stockton 4.00 10.00
TB Terrell Brandon 2.00 5.00
WS Wally Szczerbiak 2.50 6.00

2001-02 Upper Deck Ovation Superstar Warm-Ups Autographs

Randomly inserted in packs at one in every 240, this eight card set parallels the base Superstar Warmups set enhanced with authentic player autographs.

DAS Darrell Armstrong 5.00 12.00
DMS Darius Miles 5.00 12.00
HMS Hanno Mottola 5.00 12.00
JMS Jamal Mashburn 6.00 15.00
KBS Kobe Bryant 100.00 200.00
KGS Kevin Garnett 25.00 60.00
MPS Morris Peterson 5.00 12.00
QRS Quentin Richardson 5.00 12.00

2001-02 Upper Deck Ovation Tremendous Trios

Randomly inserted one in 240, this 6 card set features cards with three game-used jersey swatches from three different players. Two player photos appear on both the right and left side of this horizontally designed card with a jersey swatch centered from the single player pictured on the bottom. The two jersey swatches from the top players appear directly below them.

AJLHMA Antawn Jamison 8.00 20.00
Larry Hughes
Marc Jackson
BDJMDW Baron Davis 8.00 20.00
Jamal Mashburn
David Wesley
KGTBWS Kevin Garnett 8.00 20.00
Terrell Brandon
Wally Szczerbiak
MJKBKG Michael Jordan 60.00 150.00
Kobe Bryant
Kevin Garnett
RMRAJC Ron Mercer 8.00 20.00
Ron Artest
Marcus Fizer
TMGHMM Tracy McGrady 10.00 25.00
Grant Hill
Mike Miller

2002-03 Upper Deck Ovation

This 134 card standard-size set was issued in five card packs which came 24 to a box. Cards numbered 1-90 feature veterans. Cards 91 through 99 feature 3 cards each of Kevin Garnett, Kobe Bryant and Michael Jordan. The Garnett cards were issued to a stated print run of 2999 cards while the Kobe cards were issued to a stated print run of 1999 cards and the Jordan cards to a stated print run of 499 cards. Cards numbered 100 through 119 feature rookies and were issued to a stated print run of 2999 cards while rookie cards numbered 120 through 134 were issued to a stated print run of 1999 sets.

COMP.SET w/o SP's (90) 20.00 50.00
1 Shareef Abdur-Rahim .25 .60
2 Jason Terry .25 .60
3 Glenn Robinson .25 .60
4 Paul Pierce .40 1.00
5 Antoine Walker .25 .60
6 Vin Baker .25 .60
7 Jalen Rose .25 .60
8 Tyson Chandler .25 .60
9 Eddy Curry .25 .60
10 Marcus Fizer .20 .50
11 Darius Miles .20 .50
12 Lamond Murray .20 .50
13 Chris Mihm .20 .50
14 Dirk Nowitzki .50 1.25
15 Michael Finley .30 .75
16 Steve Nash .40 1.00
17 Marcus Camby .25 .60
18 Juwan Howard .25 .60
19 James Posey .20 .50
20 Jerry Stackhouse .25 .60
21 Ben Wallace .30 .75
22 Clifford Robinson .20 .50
23 Antawn Jamison .30 .75
24 Jason Richardson .30 .75
25 Gilbert Arenas .30 .75
26 Steve Francis .30 .75
27 Eddie Griffin .20 .50
28 Cuttino Mobley .25 .60
29 Jermaine O'Neal .30 .75
30 Reggie Miller .30 .75
31 Jamaal Tinsley .20 .50
32 Elton Brand .30 .75
33 Andre Miller .25 .60
34 Lamar Odom .30 .75
35 Kobe Bryant 1.50 4.00
36 Shaquille O'Neal .75 2.00
37 Derek Fisher .25 .60
38 Devean George .20 .50
39 Pau Gasol .40 1.00
40 Shane Battier .30 .75
41 Jason Williams .25 .60
42 Alonzo Mourning .40 1.00
43 Eddie Jones .25 .60
44 Brian Grant .20 .50
45 Ray Allen .30 .75
46 Tim Thomas .20 .50
47 Sam Cassell .25 .60
48 Kevin Garnett .60 1.50
49 Wally Szczerbiak .25 .60
50 Terrell Brandon .20 .50
51 Jason Kidd .50 1.25
52 Kenyon Martin .30 .75
53 Richard Jefferson .30 .75
54 Jamal Mashburn .25 .60
55 Baron Davis .30 .75
56 David Wesley .20 .50
57 Latrell Sprewell .25 .60
58 Allan Houston .25 .60
59 Antonio McDyess .25 .60
60 Tracy McGrady .50 1.25
61 Mike Miller .30 .75
62 Darrell Armstrong .20 .50
63 Allen Iverson .50 1.25
64 Eric Snow .20 .50
65 Aaron McKie .20 .50
66 Stephon Marbury .25 .60
67 Shawn Marion .30 .75
68 Anfernee Hardaway .50 1.25
69 Rasheed Wallace .30 .75
70 Bonzi Wells .20 .50
71 Scottie Pippen .50 1.25
72 Chris Webber .30 .75
73 Mike Bibby .30 .75
74 Peja Stojakovic .30 .75
75 Tim Duncan .60 1.50
76 David Robinson .50 1.25
77 Tony Parker .40 1.00
78 Gary Payton .30 .75
79 Rashard Lewis .30 .75
80 Desmond Mason .25 .60
81 Vince Carter .50 1.25
82 Morris Peterson .20 .50
83 Antonio Davis .20 .50
84 Karl Malone .40 1.00
85 John Stockton .40 1.00
86 Andrei Kirilenko .30 .75
87 Michael Jordan 2.50 6.00
88 Richard Hamilton .25 .60
89 Chris Whitney .20 .50
90 Kwame Brown .20 .50
91 Kevin Garnett/2999 2.50 6.00
92 Kevin Garnett/2999 2.50 6.00
93 Kevin Garnett/2999 2.50 6.00
94 Kobe Bryant/1999 5.00 12.00
95 Kobe Bryant/1999 5.00 12.00
96 Kobe Bryant/1999 5.00 12.00
97 Michael Jordan/499 15.00 40.00
98 Michael Jordan/499 15.00 40.00
99 Michael Jordan/499 15.00 40.00
100 Fred Jones RC 2.50 6.00
101 Jamal Sampson RC 2.50 6.00
102 John Salmons RC 3.00 8.00
103 Jiri Welsch RC 2.50 6.00
104 Dan Gadzuric RC 2.50 6.00
105 Vincent Yarbrough RC 2.50 6.00
106 Juan Dixon RC 3.00 8.00
107 Efthimios Rentzias RC 2.50 6.00
108 Predrag Savovic RC 2.50 6.00
109 Rod Grizzard RC 2.50 6.00
110 Bostjan Nachbar RC 2.50 6.00
111 Marko Jaric 2.50 6.00
112 Tayshaun Prince RC 3.00 8.00
113 Chris Jefferies RC 2.50 6.00
114 Casey Jacobsen RC 2.50 6.00
115 Carlos Boozer RC 5.00 12.00
116 Frank Williams RC 2.50 6.00
117 Dan Dickau RC 2.50 6.00
118 Ryan Humphrey RC 2.50 6.00
119 Melvin Ely RC 2.50 6.00
120 Nene Hilario RC 4.00 10.00
121 Nikoloz Tskitishvili RC 3.00 8.00
122 Marcus Haislip RC 3.00 8.00
123 Qyntel Woods RC 3.00 8.00
124 Caron Butler RC 5.00 12.00
125 Amare Stoudemire RC 8.00 20.00
126 Curtis Borchardt RC 3.00 8.00
127 Chris Wilcox RC 3.00 8.00
128 Drew Gooden RC 5.00 12.00
129 Jared Jeffries RC 3.00 8.00
130 Kareem Rush RC 3.00 8.00
131 Mike Dunleavy RC 4.00 10.00
132 Yao Ming RC 10.00 25.00
133 DaJuan Wagner RC 3.00 8.00
134 Jay Williams RC 4.00 10.00

2002-03 Upper Deck Ovation Authentics Shooting Shirt

Issued at a stated rate of one in 144, these 13 cards feature pieces of "shirts" worn by leading NBA players. A Gold parallel sequentially numbered to 15 was also inserted in packs.

AIS Allen Iverson 6.00 15.00
CWS Chris Webber 4.00 10.00
DJS DerMarr Johnson 2.50 6.00
ECS Eddy Curry 3.00 8.00
JES Jerry Stackhouse 3.00 8.00
JSS John Stockton 5.00 12.00
KBS Kobe Bryant 20.00 50.00
KGS Kevin Garnett 8.00 20.00
KWS Kwame Brown 2.50 6.00
MBS Mike Bibby 4.00 10.00
PSS Peja Stojakovic 4.00 10.00
SAS Shareef Abdur-Rahim 3.00 8.00
SMS Stephon Marbury 3.00 8.00

2002-03 Upper Deck Ovation Authentics Uniform

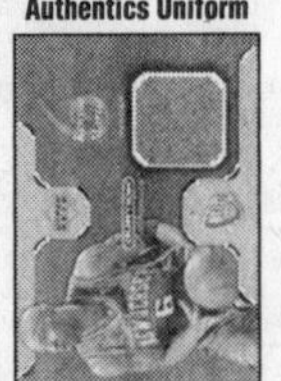

Issued at a stated rate of one in 72, these 13 cards feature swatches of game-worn uniforms. A Gold parallel sequentially numbered to 25 was also inserted in packs.

*GOLD: 1.25X TO 3X BASE HI
AHU Anfernee Hardaway 5.00 12.00
AIU Allen Iverson 5.00 12.00
BDU Baron Davis 3.00 8.00
CMU Corey Maggette 2.50 6.00
DMU Darius Miles 2.00 5.00
DNU Dirk Nowitzki 5.00 12.00
DSU DeShawn Stevenson 2.00 5.00
KBU Kobe Bryant 15.00 40.00
KEU Kenyon Martin 3.00 8.00
KGU Kevin Garnett 6.00 15.00
KMU Karl Malone 4.00 10.00
RFU Rick Fox 2.50 6.00
RLU Rashard Lewis 3.00 8.00

2002-03 Upper Deck Ovation Authentics Warm-Ups

Issued at a stated rate of one in 24, these 18 cards feature authentic swatches of NBA "warm-up" material. A Gold parallel sequentially numbered to 100 was also inserted in packs.

*GOLD: .75X TO 2X WARM UP HI
AWW Antoine Walker 2.50 6.00
BDW Baron Davis 3.00 8.00
CMW Corey Maggette 2.50 6.00
EBW Elton Brand 3.00 8.00
JKW Jason Kidd 5.00 12.00
JMW Jamal Mashburn 2.50 6.00
KBW Kobe Bryant 15.00 40.00
KGW Kevin Garnett 6.00 15.00
KMW Kenyon Martin 3.00 8.00
KWW Kwame Brown 2.00 5.00
LOW Lamar Odom 3.00 8.00
MAW Karl Malone 4.00 10.00
MBW Mike Bibby 3.00 8.00
MJW Michael Jordan 50.00 120.00
MMW Mike Miller 3.00 8.00
QRW Quentin Richardson 2.50 6.00
RJW Richard Jefferson 3.00 8.00
SMW Stephon Marbury 2.50 6.00

2002-03 Upper Deck Ovation Authentics Warm-Ups Dual

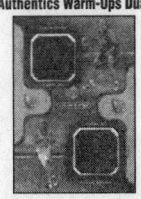

Inserted at a stated rate of one in 144, these 18 cards feature two swatches of NBA "Warm-Up" material. In most of the cases the swatches feature teammates but occassionally they feature players who have something in common. A Gold parallel sequentially numbered to 50 was also inserted in packs.

*GOLD: .75X TO 2X WARM UP DUAL HI
AH/LS Allan Houston 6.00 15.00
Latrell Sprewell
AM/LM Andre Miller 6.00 15.00
Lamond Murray
BD/JM Baron Davis 6.00 15.00
Jamal Mashburn
CM/DM Corey Maggette 6.00 15.00
Darius Miles
CW/PS Peja Stojakovic 10.00 25.00
Chris Webber
EC/MF Eddy Curry 6.00 15.00
Marcus Fizer
KB/KG Kobe Bryant 15.00 40.00
Kevin Garnett
KB/MJ Kobe Bryant 60.00 150.00
Michael Jordan
KG/KW Kevin Garnett 10.00 25.00
Kwame Brown
KG/TB Kevin Garnett 10.00 25.00
Terrell Brandon
KG/WS Kevin Garnett 10.00 25.00
Wally Szczerbiak
KM/AK Karl Malone 6.00 15.00
Andrei Kirilenko
KM/RJ Kenyon Martin 6.00 15.00
Richard Jefferson
LO/QR Lamar Odom 6.00 15.00
Quentin Richardson
PP/AW Paul Pierce 10.00 25.00
Antoine Walker
SA/JT Shareef Abdur-Rahim 6.00 15.00
Jason Terry
SM/SH Stephon Marbury 6.00 15.00
Shawn Marion
WS/TB Wally Szczerbiak 6.00 15.00
Terrell Brandon

2002-03 Upper Deck Ovation Authentics Warm-Ups Triple

Issued at a stated rate of one in 288, these six cards feature three swatches of NBA "Warm-Up" material. Again, the swatches come either from teammates or from players with something in common. A Gold parallel sequentially numbered to 25 was also inserted in packs.

*GOLD: .75X TO 2X BASE HI
BGK Kobe Bryant 30.00 80.00
Kevin Garnett
Jason Kidd
BJG Kobe Bryant 100.00 250.00
Michael Jordan
Kevin Garnett
CFC Eddy Curry 10.00 25.00
Marcus Fizer
Tyson Chandler
GSB Kevin Garnett 15.00 40.00
Wally Szczerbiak
Terrell Brandon
MBO Darius Miles 10.00 25.00
Elton Brand
Lamar Odom
WSB Chris Webber 20.00 50.00
Peja Stojakovic
Mike Bibby

2002-03 Upper Deck Ovation Signatures

Inserted at a stated rate of one in 96, these 16 cards feature authentic autographs from NBA Players. There is one card signed by Michael Jordan, Kobe Bryant and Kevin Garnett and that card was printed to a stated print run of 25 serial numbered sets. Fifteen players signed for a gold parallel set that is sequentially numbered to 10.

CA Courtney Alexander 4.00 10.00
CM Chris Mihm 4.00 10.00
DM Darius Miles 4.00 10.00
GA Gilbert Arenas 10.00 25.00
HM Hanno Mottola 4.00 10.00
JP Joel Przybilla 4.00 10.00
JR Jason Richardson 6.00 15.00
JS Jerry Stackhouse 6.00 15.00
KS Kenny Satterfield 4.00 10.00
LW Loren Woods 4.00 10.00
MF Marcus Fizer 4.00 10.00
QR Quentin Richardson 4.00 10.00
TC Tyson Chandler 6.00 15.00
TM Terence Morris 4.00 10.00
ZZ Wang ZhiZhi 8.00 20.00
OS1 Michael Jordan/25 700.00 1200.00
Kobe Bryant
Kevin Garnett

2006-07 Upper Deck Ovation

Issued in mid September, Upper Deck Ovation utilizes an embossed card stock and pictures veteran players on cards 1-90 and rookie players on cards 91-132 which are sequentially numbered to 999. On-card rookie autographs are available in the Gold parallel. Ovation is packaged in 18-pack boxes of five cards each and carried an initial suggested retail price of $4.99.

COMP.SET w/o SP's (90) 20.00 50.00
1 Joe Johnson .40 1.00
2 Marvin Williams .40 1.00
3 Paul Pierce .50 1.25
4 Wally Szczerbiak .30 .75
5 Raymond Felton .50 1.25
6 Emeka Okafor .40 1.00
7 Gerald Wallace .40 1.00
8 Tyson Chandler .30 .75
9 Ben Gordon .40 1.00
10 Michael Jordan 3.00 8.00
11 Drew Gooden .30 .75
12 Zydrunas Ilgauskas .30 .75
13 LeBron James 2.00 5.00
14 Devin Harris .40 1.00
15 Dirk Nowitzki .60 1.50
16 Jason Terry .30 .75
17 Carmelo Anthony .50 1.25
18 Marcus Camby .30 .75
19 Kenyon Martin .40 1.00
20 Chauncey Billups .40 1.00
21 Richard Hamilton .30 .75
22 Ben Wallace .40 1.00
23 Baron Davis .40 1.00
24 Jason Richardson .40 1.00
25 Luther Head .30 .75
26 Tracy McGrady .50 1.25
27 Yao Ming .50 1.25
28 Austin Croshere .25 .60
29 Jermaine O'Neal .40 1.00
30 Peja Stojakovic .40 1.00
31 Elton Brand .40 1.00
32 Sam Cassell .40 1.00
33 Cuttino Mobley .30 .75
34 Kwame Brown .25 .60
35 Kobe Bryant 2.00 5.00
36 Lamar Odom .40 1.00
37 Pau Gasol .40 1.00
38 Mike Miller .40 1.00
39 Damon Stoudamire .30 .75
40 Shaquille O'Neal .75 2.00
41 Wayne Simien .25 .60
42 Dwyane Wade 1.00 2.50
43 Andrew Bogut .40 1.00
44 T.J. Ford .30 .75
45 Michael Redd .40 1.00
46 Ricky Davis .30 .75
47 Kevin Garnett .75 2.00
48 Rashad McCants .25 .60
49 Vince Carter .50 1.25
50 Richard Jefferson .40 1.00
51 Jason Kidd .60 1.50
52 Desmond Mason .25 .60
53 Chris Paul .75 2.00
54 J.R. Smith .40 1.00
55 Steve Francis .40 1.00
56 Stephon Marbury .30 .75
57 Nate Robinson .40 1.00
58 Dwight Howard .60 1.50
59 Darko Milicic .25 .60
60 Jameer Nelson .30 .75
61 Andre Iguodala .40 1.00
62 Allen Iverson .50 1.25
63 Chris Webber .40 1.00
64 Boris Diaw .30 .75
65 Shawn Marion .40 1.00
66 Steve Nash .50 1.25
67 Zach Randolph .30 .75
68 Sebastian Telfair .25 .60
69 Ron Artest .40 1.00
70 Mike Bibby .40 1.00
71 Bonzi Wells .25 .60
72 Tim Duncan .60 1.50
73 Manu Ginobili .40 1.00
74 Tony Parker .40 1.00
75 Ray Allen .40 1.00
76 Rashard Lewis .40 1.00
77 Luke Ridnour .30 .75
78 Chris Bosh .40 1.00
79 Joey Graham .25 .60
80 Charlie Villanueva .40 1.00
81 Carlos Boozer .40 1.00
82 Andrei Kirilenko .30 .75
83 Gilbert Arenas .40 1.00
84 Antawn Jamison .40 1.00
85 Josh Childress .30 .75
86 Al Jefferson .40 1.00
87 Derek Fisher .30 .75
88 Juan Dixon .25 .60
89 Deron Williams .60 1.50
90 Caron Butler .40 1.00
91 Tyrus Thomas RC 2.00 5.00
92 Adam Morrison RC 2.00 5.00
93 LaMarcus Aldridge RC 4.00 10.00
94 Rudy Gay RC 2.50 6.00
95 Andrea Bargnani RC 2.50 6.00

96 Rodney Carney RC 1.50 4.00
97 Will Blalock RC 1.50 4.00
98 Brandon Roy RC 4.00 10.00
99 Patrick O'Bryant RC 1.50 4.00
100 Randy Foye RC 2.00 5.00
101 Ronnie Brewer RC 2.00 5.00
102 Mardy Collins RC 1.50 4.00
103 Shelden Williams RC 1.50 4.00
104 J.J. Redick RC 2.00 5.00
105 Hilton Armstrong RC 1.50 4.00
106 Marcus Williams RC 1.50 4.00
107 Rajon Rondo RC 6.00 15.00
108 Cedric Simmons RC 1.50 4.00
109 Alexander Johnson RC 1.50 4.00
110 Jordan Farmar RC 1.50 4.00
111 Maurice Ager RC 1.50 4.00
112 Renaldo Balkman RC 1.50 4.00
113 Leon Powe RC 1.50 4.00
114 Saer Sene RC 1.50 4.00
115 Paul Millsap RC 2.50 6.00
116 Josh Boone RC 1.50 4.00
117 Steve Novak RC 1.50 4.00
118 Daniel Gibson RC 2.00 5.00
119 Hassan Adams RC 1.50 4.00
120 Kyle Lowry RC 2.00 5.00
121 James White RC 1.50 4.00
122 Dee Brown RC 1.50 4.00
123 Shawne Williams RC 1.50 4.00
124 P.J. Tucker RC 1.50 4.00
125 Craig Smith RC 1.50 4.00
126 Paul Davis RC 1.50 4.00
127 Solomon Jones RC 1.50 4.00
128 Denham Brown RC 1.50 4.00
129 Thabo Sefolosha RC 2.00 5.00
130 Quincy Douby RC 1.50 4.00
131 Joel Freeland RC 1.50 4.00
132 Ryan Hollins RC 1.50 4.00

2006-07 Upper Deck Ovation Gold

*1-90 GOLD: 2X TO 5X BASE HI
*91-132 GOLD NON AU: 1.25X TO 3X BASE HI
PRINT RUN 99 SER.#'d SETS
91 Tyrus Thomas AU 10.00 25.00
93 LaMarcus Aldridge AU 20.00 50.00
94 Rudy Gay AU 12.00 30.00
95 Andrea Bargnani AU 12.00 30.00
96 Rodney Carney AU 8.00 20.00
98 Brandon Roy AU 20.00 50.00
99 Patrick O'Bryant AU 8.00 20.00
100 Randy Foye AU 10.00 25.00
101 Ronnie Brewer AU 10.00 25.00
102 Mardy Collins AU 8.00 20.00
103 Shelden Williams AU 8.00 20.00
105 Hilton Armstrong AU 8.00 20.00
106 Marcus Williams AU 8.00 20.00
107 Rajon Rondo AU 30.00 80.00
108 Cedric Simmons AU 8.00 20.00
110 Jordan Farmar AU 8.00 20.00
111 Maurice Ager AU 8.00 20.00
112 Renaldo Balkman AU 8.00 20.00
115 Paul Millsap AU 12.00 30.00
116 Josh Boone AU 8.00 20.00
117 Steve Novak AU 8.00 20.00
119 Hassan Adams AU 8.00 20.00
120 Kyle Lowry AU 10.00 25.00
121 James White AU 8.00 20.00
123 Shawne Williams AU 8.00 20.00
124 P.J. Tucker AU 8.00 20.00
125 Craig Smith AU 8.00 20.00
127 Solomon Jones AU 8.00 20.00
128 Denham Brown AU 8.00 20.00
130 Quincy Douby AU 8.00 20.00
132 Ryan Hollins AU 8.00 20.00

2006-07 Upper Deck Ovation Apparel

APPROXIMATE ODDS 1:18
*GOLD: .6X TO 1.5X BASE JSY HI
GOLD PRINT RUN 50 SER.#'d SETS
AB Andrew Bynum 4.00 10.00
AI Andre Iguodala 2.50 6.00
AK Andrei Kirilenko 2.00 5.00
AS Amare Stoudemire 2.50 6.00
BC Brian Cook 2.00 5.00
BD Baron Davis 2.50 6.00
BH Brendan Haywood 2.00 5.00
BU Beno Udrih 2.00 5.00
CW Chris Wilcox 2.00 5.00
DG Drew Gooden 2.00 5.00
DN Dirk Nowitzki 4.00 10.00
EC Eddy Curry 2.00 5.00
GA Gilbert Arenas 2.50 6.00
HO Julius Hodge 2.00 5.00
JH Josh Howard 2.00 5.00
JM Jeff McInnis 2.00 5.00
JO Jermaine O'Neal 2.00 5.00
JR Jason Richardson 2.50 6.00
JT Jamaal Tinsley 2.00 5.00
KB Kobe Bryant SP 8.00 20.00
KG Kevin Garnett 5.00 12.00
KK Kyle Korver 2.00 5.00
LJ LeBron James SP 10.00 25.00
LK Linas Kleiza 2.00 5.00
LW Luke Walton 2.00 5.00
MG Manu Ginobili 2.50 6.00
MJ Michael Jordan SP 20.00 50.00
MS Mike Sweetney 2.00 5.00
PG Pau Gasol 2.50 6.00
RA Ray Allen 2.50 6.00
RH Richard Hamilton SP 2.00 5.00
RL Rashard Lewis 2.50 6.00
SC Sam Cassell 2.50 6.00
SL Shaun Livingston 2.00 5.00
SM Shawn Marion 2.50 6.00
TC Tyson Chandler 2.00 5.00
TD Tim Duncan 4.00 10.00
TP Tony Parker 2.50 6.00
VC Vince Carter 3.00 8.00
WS Wally Szczerbiak 2.00 5.00
ZI Zydrunas Ilgauskas 2.00 5.00

2006-07 Upper Deck Ovation Center Stage

COMPLETE SET (12) 4.00 10.00
APPROXIMATE ODDS 1:9
AS Amare Stoudemire .60 1.50
BM Brad Miller .60 1.50
BW Ben Wallace .60 1.50
CF Channing Frye .50 1.25
CK Chris Kaman .50 1.25
DH Dwight Howard 1.00 2.50
MC Marcus Camby .50 1.25
MO Mehmet Okur .40 1.00
SO Shaquille O'Neal 1.25 3.00
YM Yao Ming .75 2.00
ZI Zydrunas Ilgauskas .50 1.25

2006-07 Upper Deck Ovation Leading Performers

COMPLETE SET (20) 10.00 25.00
APPROXIMATE ODDS 1:9
AI Allen Iverson .75 2.00
BG Ben Gordon .60 1.50
CB Chauncey Billups .60 1.50
CP Chris Paul 1.25 3.00
DH Dwight Howard 1.00 2.50
DN Dirk Nowitzki 1.00 2.50
DW Dwyane Wade 1.50 4.00
EB Elton Brand .60 1.50
EO Emeka Okafor .60 1.50
KB Kobe Bryant 3.00 8.00
KG Kevin Garnett 1.25 3.00
LJ LeBron James 3.00 8.00
MA Shawn Marion .60 1.50
MJ Michael Jordan 5.00 12.00
PP Paul Pierce .75 2.00
SM Stephon Marbury .50 1.25
SN Steve Nash .75 2.00
SO Shaquille O'Neal 1.25 3.00
TM Tracy McGrady .75 2.00
YM Yao Ming .75 2.00

2006-07 Upper Deck Ovation Spotlight Signature

APPROXIMATE ODDS 1:18
*GOLD: .75X TO 2X BASE HI
GOLD PRINT RUN 25 SER.#'d SETS
AA Alex Acker 4.00 10.00
AB Andrew Bogut SP 5.00 12.00
AJ Al Jefferson 4.00 10.00
AN Andrea Bargnani SP 10.00 25.00
BA Brent Barry 6.00 15.00
BB Brandon Bass 4.00 10.00
BD Baron Davis 4.00 10.00
BJ Bobby Jackson 4.00 10.00
BK Bernard King 8.00 20.00
BO Bruce Bowen 4.00 10.00
BR Brandon Roy 12.00 30.00
BS Bobby Simmons 4.00 10.00
BW Bill Walton 10.00 25.00
CA Carmelo Anthony 12.50 30.00
CB Carlos Boozer 4.00 10.00
CD Chris Duhon 4.00 10.00
CM Cuttino Mobley 4.00 10.00
CP Chris Paul 20.00 50.00
CS Cedric Simmons 4.00 10.00
CT Chris Taft 4.00 10.00
DJ Dwayne Jones 4.00 10.00
DM Desmond Mason 4.00 10.00
DS DeShawn Stevenson 4.00 10.00
DT Dijon Thompson 4.00 10.00
EI Ersan Ilyasova 4.00 10.00
FO Randy Foye 10.00 25.00
HA Hilton Armstrong 4.00 10.00
HW Hakim Warrick 4.00 10.00
ID Ike Diogu SP 4.00 10.00
JK Jarrett Jack 4.00 10.00
JO Amir Johnson 4.00 10.00
JR Jalen Rose 4.00 10.00
JS J.R. Smith 4.00 10.00
KB Kwame Brown 4.00 10.00
KD Keyon Dooling 4.00 10.00
KH Kirk Hinrich 6.00 15.00
LA LaMarcus Aldridge 10.00 25.00
LJ LeBron James SP 150.00 300.00
LR Lawrence Roberts 4.00 10.00
MC Mardy Collins 4.00 10.00
MD Marquis Daniels 4.00 10.00
ME Maurice Evans 4.00 10.00
MJ Michael Jordan SP 250.00 500.00
MW Marvin Williams 4.00 10.00
NR Nate Robinson 4.00 10.00
PO Patrick O'Bryant 4.00 10.00
PP Paul Pierce SP 8.00 20.00
PS Peja Stojakovic 4.00 10.00
QR Quentin Richardson 4.00 10.00
RB Ronnie Brewer 12.50 30.00
RC Rodney Carney 4.00 10.00
RF Raymond Felton 5.00 12.00
RG Rudy Gay 8.00 20.00
RI Luke Ridnour 4.00 10.00
RJ Richard Jefferson 4.00 10.00
RM Rashad McCants 4.00 10.00
RR Rajon Rondo 15.00 40.00
RT Ronny Turiaf 6.00 15.00
SC Speedy Claxton 4.00 10.00
SJ James Singleton 4.00 10.00
SK Steve Kerr 10.00 25.00
SL Shaun Livingston 4.00 10.00
SS Stromile Swift 4.00 10.00
SW Shelden Williams 4.00 10.00
TF T.J. Ford 4.00 10.00
TT Tyrus Thomas 8.00 20.00
VC Vince Carter 12.50 30.00
VR Vladimir Radmanovic 4.00 10.00
VW Von Wafer 4.00 10.00
WI Marcus Williams 4.00 10.00
WR Bracey Wright 4.00 10.00
YK Yaroslav Korolev 4.00 10.00
YM Yao Ming SP 12.50 30.00

2006-07 Upper Deck Ovation Superstar Theatre

COMPLETE SET (10) 8.00 20.00
APPROXIMATE ODDS 1:9
BR Bill Russell 1.25 3.00
JE Julius Erving 1.25 3.00
JO Magic Johnson 1.50 4.00
KA Kareem Abdul-Jabbar 1.00 2.50
KB Kobe Bryant 3.00 8.00
LJ LeBron James 3.00 8.00
MJ Michael Jordan 5.00 12.00
SN Steve Nash .75 2.00
SO Shaquille O'Neal 1.25 3.00
TM Tracy McGrady .75 2.00

2001-02 Upper Deck Playmakers

Released in March 2002, this 145-card base set features standard-size cards with full color action shots on the fronts. The set includes 100 veteran cards, 30 rookie red-level cards, numbers 101-130 which are sequentially numbered to 1999, and 15 rookie blue-level cards, numbers 131-145 which are sequentially numbered to 999. Playmakers was packaged in 24-pack boxes with five cards per pack and carried a suggested retail of $2.99. Each Playmaker's box also contained an Upper Deck Bobble Head Doll.

COMPLETE SET (145) 100.00 200.00
COMP.SET w/o SP's (100) 20.00 40.00
1 Shareef Abdur-Rahim .25 .60
2 Dion Glover .20 .50
3 Jason Terry .30 .75
4 Toni Kukoc .25 .60
5 Theo Ratliff .20 .50
6 Paul Pierce .40 1.00
7 Antoine Walker .25 .60
8 Baron Davis .30 .75
9 Jamal Mashburn .25 .60
10 Ron Mercer .20 .50
11 Brad Miller .30 .75
12 Marcus Fizer .20 .50
13 Andre Miller .25 .60
14 Chris Mihm .20 .50
15 Lamond Murray .20 .50
16 Michael Finley .30 .75
17 Dirk Nowitzki .50 1.25
18 Steve Nash .50 1.25
19 Tim Hardaway .25 .60
20 Antonio McDyess .25 .60
21 Nick Van Exel .25 .60
22 Raef LaFrentz .25 .60
23 Jerry Stackhouse .25 .60
24 Clifford Robinson .20 .50
25 Ben Wallace .30 .75
26 Antawn Jamison .30 .75
27 Larry Hughes .25 .60
28 Danny Fortson .20 .50
29 Steve Francis .30 .75
30 Cuttino Mobley .25 .60
31 Kenny Thomas .20 .50
32 Jalen Rose .30 .75
33 Reggie Miller .30 .75
34 Jermaine O'Neal .30 .75
35 Darius Miles .30 .75
36 Elton Brand .30 .75
37 Corey Maggette .25 .60
38 Quentin Richardson .25 .60
39 Kobe Bryant 1.50 4.00
40 Shaquille O'Neal .75 2.00
41 Mitch Richmond .25 .60
42 Derek Fisher .25 .60
43 Lindsey Hunter .20 .50
44 Stromile Swift .25 .60
45 Jason Williams .25 .60
46 Michael Dickerson .20 .50
47 Eddie Jones .25 .60
48 Alonzo Mourning .40 1.00
49 Anthony Carter .20 .50
50 Brian Grant .20 .50
51 Glenn Robinson .25 .60
52 Ray Allen .30 .75
53 Sam Cassell .25 .60
54 Tim Thomas .20 .50
55 Anthony Mason .20 .50
56 Kevin Garnett .60 1.50
57 Wally Szczerbiak .25 .60
58 Terrell Brandon .20 .50
59 Joe Smith .25 .60
60 Jason Kidd .50 1.25
61 Kenyon Martin .30 .75
62 Allan Houston .25 .60
63 Latrell Sprewell .25 .60
64 Marcus Camby .25 .60
65 Mark Jackson .25 .60
66 Kurt Thomas .20 .50
67 Tracy McGrady .50 1.25
68 Grant Hill .40 1.00
69 Mike Miller .30 .75
70 Allen Iverson .60 1.50
71 Dikembe Mutombo .30 .75
72 Aaron McKie .20 .50
73 Stephon Marbury .25 .60
74 Shawn Marion .30 .75
75 Anfernee Hardaway .50 1.25
76 Tom Gugliotta .20 .50
77 Rasheed Wallace .30 .75
78 Derek Anderson .20 .50
79 Bonzi Wells .20 .50
80 Chris Webber .30 .75
81 Peja Stojakovic .30 .75
82 Mike Bibby .30 .75
83 Doug Christie .20 .50
84 Tim Duncan .60 1.50
85 David Robinson .50 1.25
86 Antonio Daniels .20 .50
87 Steve Smith .25 .60
88 Gary Payton .30 .75
89 Rashard Lewis .30 .75
90 Desmond Mason .25 .60
91 Vince Carter .50 1.25
92 Morris Peterson .20 .50
93 Antonio Davis .20 .50
94 Hakeem Olajuwon .40 1.00
95 Karl Malone .40 1.00
96 John Stockton .40 1.00
97 Donyell Marshall .20 .50
98 Michael Jordan 4.00 10.00
99 Courtney Alexander .20 .50
100 Richard Hamilton .25 .60
101 Jeryl Sasser RC 1.00 2.50
102 DeSagana Diop RC 1.00 2.50
103 Alvin Jones RC 1.00 2.50
104 Gerald Wallace RC 1.50 4.00
105 Kenny Satterfield RC 1.00 2.50
106 Ruben Boumtje-Boumtje RC 1.00 2.50
107 Brian Scalabrine RC 1.00 2.50
108 Oscar Torres RC 1.00 2.50
109 Jarron Collins RC 1.00 2.50
110 Jeff Trepagnier RC 1.00 2.50
111 Brendan Haywood RC 1.25 3.00
112 Vladimir Radmanovic RC 1.00 2.50
113 Loren Woods RC 1.00 2.50
114 Terence Morris RC 1.00 2.50
115 Kirk Haston RC 1.00 2.50
116 Earl Watson RC 1.00 2.50
117 Brandon Armstrong RC 1.00 2.50
118 Zach Randolph RC 2.50 6.00
119 Bobby Simmons RC 1.00 2.50
120 Alton Ford RC 1.00 2.50
121 Trenton Hassell RC 1.00 2.50
122 Damone Brown RC 1.00 2.50
123 Michael Bradley RC 1.00 2.50
124 Zeljko Rebraca RC 1.00 2.50
125 Jason Collins RC 1.00 2.50
126 Samuel Dalembert RC 1.25 3.00
127 Gilbert Arenas RC 1.50 4.00
128 Willie Solomon RC 1.00 2.50
129 Joseph Forte RC 1.00 2.50
130 Steven Hunter RC 1.00 2.50
131 Andrei Kirilenko RC 4.00 10.00
132 Eddy Curry RC 2.50 6.00
133 Tony Parker RC 6.00 15.00
134 Troy Murphy RC 2.50 6.00
135 Shane Battier RC 3.00 8.00
136 Kedrick Brown RC 1.50 4.00
137 Tyson Chandler RC 2.50 6.00
138 Jamaal Tinsley RC 2.00 5.00
139 Pau Gasol RC 5.00 12.00
140 Joe Johnson RC 4.00 10.00
141 Jason Richardson RC 3.00 8.00
142 Richard Jefferson RC 3.00 8.00
143 Eddie Griffin RC 1.50 4.00
144 Rodney White RC 1.50 4.00
145 Kwame Brown RC 1.50 4.00

2001-02 Upper Deck Playmakers PC Game Jersey

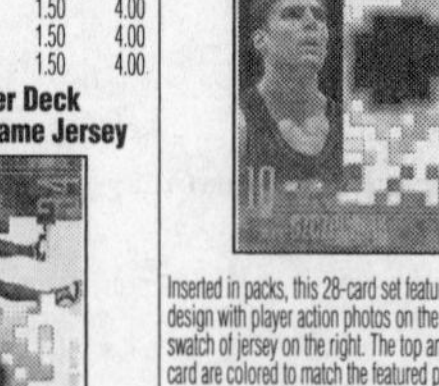

This 27-card insert set comes with pieces of game-used jerseys on standard-size cards. Solid colored player portraits with jagged borders appear on the right side of this horizontally designed card in color's to match the featured player's team, with a matching color stripe along the right side and a swatch of a jersey in the center on a colored "cube" background. Each card is sequentially numbered to 350. Fourteen players also appear in a parallel Autographed set sequentially numbered to 10 and a Gold version sequentially numbered to 100.

*GOLD: .75X TO 2X BASE JSY HI
AIJ Allen Iverson 6.00 15.00
AJJ Antawn Jamison 3.00 8.00
BDJ Baron Davis 3.00 8.00
CWJ Chris Webber 3.00 8.00
DEJ Desmond Mason 2.50 6.00
DMJ Darius Miles 2.00 5.00
DNJ Dirk Nowitzki 5.00 12.00
ECJ Eddy Curry 5.00 12.00
EGJ Eddie Griffin 3.00 8.00
GWJ Gerald Wallace 5.00 12.00
JJJ Joe Johnson 8.00 20.00
JKJ Jason Kidd 5.00 12.00
JRJ Jason Richardson 6.00 15.00
JSJ John Stockton 4.00 10.00
JTJ Jamaal Tinsley 4.00 10.00
KBJ Kobe Bryant 15.00 40.00
KEJ Kedrick Brown 3.00 8.00
KGJ Kevin Garnett 6.00 15.00
KMJ Karl Malone 4.00 10.00
KWJ Kwame Brown 3.00 8.00
LOJ Lamar Odom 3.00 8.00
MAJ Kenyon Martin 3.00 8.00
MMJ Mike Miller 3.00 8.00
PPJ Paul Pierce 4.00 10.00
SHJ Steven Hunter 3.00 8.00
SMJ Stephon Marbury 2.50 6.00
TMJ Tracy McGrady 5.00 12.00

2001-02 Upper Deck Playmakers PC Shooting Shirt

Randomly inserted in packs, this 26-card set uses a similar design to the base Player's Club Game Jerseys set except the player portrait is on the left side of the horizontally designed card in black and white. A matching stripe appears on the right edge of the card and player shooting shirts are centered on the card. Each card is sequentially numbered to 350 and contains silver foil highlights. 10 Players appear in an autographed parallel set sequentially numbered to 25 and 16 players appear in a gold set sequentially numbered to 150.

*GOLD: .75X TO 2X BASE SHIRT HI
AIS Allen Iverson 5.00 12.00
AKS Andrei Kirilenko 6.00 15.00
DMS Desmond Mason 2.00 5.00
EGS Eddie Griffin 2.50 6.00
JAS Jamaal Magloire 1.50 4.00
JES Jerry Stackhouse 2.00 5.00
JSS Joe Smith 2.00 5.00
JTS Jason Terry 2.50 6.00
KBS Kobe Bryant 12.00 30.00
KDS Keyon Dooling 1.50 4.00
KGS Kevin Garnett 5.00 12.00
KMS Karl Malone 3.00 8.00
KWS Kwame Brown 2.50 6.00
MFS Michael Finley 2.50 6.00
MOS Michael Olowokandi 1.50 4.00
NVS Nick Van Exel 2.00 5.00
PGS Pau Gasol 8.00 20.00
SBS Shane Battier 5.00 12.00
SSS Stromile Swift 1.50 4.00
TBS Terrell Brandon 1.50 4.00
TCS Tyson Chandler 4.00 10.00
TIS Jamaal Tinsley 3.00 8.00
TMS Tracy McGrady 4.00 10.00
VBS Vin Baker 2.00 5.00
WSS Wally Szczerbiak 2.00 5.00
ZRS Zach Randolph 6.00 15.00

2001-02 Upper Deck Playmakers PC Shooting Shirt Autographs

This 10-card insert set is standard-size and features both autographs and pieces of authentic shooting shirts worn by top NBA veterans and rookies. The design is similar to the base Shooting Shirt insert set but enhanced with player autographs and a foil shift from the base silver to gold. Cards are sequentially numbered to 25.

JEAS Jerry Stackhouse 12.50 30.00
KBAS Kobe Bryant 150.00 300.00
KGAS Kevin Garnett 50.00 120.00
MJAS Michael Jordan 300.00 500.00
TCAS Tyson Chandler 25.00 60.00
TIAS Jamaal Tinsley 15.00 40.00
WSAS Wally Szczerbiak 15.00 40.00

2001-02 Upper Deck Playmakers PC Warm Up

Inserted in packs, this 28-card set features a vertical design with player action photos on the left side and a swatch of jersey on the right. The top and bottom of the card are colored to match the featured player's team colors and are highlighted with silver foil. Each card is sequentially numbered to 350. A Gold version sequentially numbered to 250 was also issued

*GOLD: .6X TO 1.5X WARMUP HI
AHW Allan Houston 2.00 5.00
ALW Al Harrington 2.00 5.00
AMW Andre Miller 2.00 5.00
AWW Antoine Walker 2.00 5.00
CMW Corey Maggette 2.00 5.00
DNW Dirk Nowitzki 4.00 10.00
DRW David Robinson 4.00 10.00
ECW Eddy Curry 4.00 10.00
GHW Grant Hill 3.00 8.00
GPW Gary Payton 2.50 6.00
JAW Jamaal Magloire 1.50 4.00
JBW Jonathan Bender 1.50 4.00
JMW Jamal Mashburn 2.00 5.00
JSW Joe Smith 2.00 5.00
KBW Kobe Bryant 12.00 30.00
KGW Kevin Garnett 5.00 12.00
KMW Kenyon Martin 2.50 6.00
LSW Latrell Sprewell 2.00 5.00
MCW Antonio McDyess 2.00 5.00
MFW Michael Finley 2.50 6.00
MPW Morris Peterson 1.50 4.00
PPW Paul Pierce 3.00 8.00
RYW Ray Allen 2.50 6.00
STW John Stockton 3.00 8.00
TBW Terrell Brandon 1.50 4.00
TCW Tyson Chandler 4.00 10.00
TMW Tracy McGrady 4.00 10.00
WSW Wally Szczerbiak 2.00 5.00

2001-02 Upper Deck Playmakers PC Warm Up Autographs

Seeded in packs, this 10-card set parallels the design of the base Warm Ups set enhanced with a foil shift from silver to gold, authentic player autographs, and sequential numbering to 50.

AMAW Andre Miller 12.50 30.00
CMAW Corey Maggette 12.50 30.00
KBAW Kobe Bryant 125.00 250.00
KGAW Kevin Garnett 40.00 100.00
MPAW Morris Peterson 12.50 30.00
PPAW Paul Pierce 30.00 60.00
TBAW Terrell Brandon 12.50 30.00
WSAW Wally Szczerbiak 12.50 30.00

2001-02 Upper Deck Playmakers Playmaker Dolls

Inserted in boxes as a topper, this 26-card set features plastic bobble head dolls. Both home and away uniform versions are available for each player.

APMAIH Allen Iverson H 8.00 20.00
APMAIR Allen Iverson A 8.00 20.00
APMECH Eddy Curry H 6.00 15.00
APMECR Eddy Curry A 6.00 15.00
APMEGH Eddie Griffin H 6.00 15.00
APMEGR Eddie Griffin A 6.00 15.00
APMJEH Julius Erving H 12.50 30.00
APMJER Julius Erving A 12.50 30.00
APMJJH Joe Johnson H 6.00 15.00
APMJJR Joe Johnson A 6.00 15.00
APMJRH Jason Richardson H 6.00 15.00
APMJRR Jason Richardson A 6.00 15.00
APMKBH Kwame Brown H 6.00 15.00
APMKBR Kwame Brown A 6.00 15.00
APMKGH Kevin Garnett H 8.00 20.00
APMKGR Kevin Garnett A 8.00 20.00
APMTCH Tyson Chandler H 6.00 15.00
APMTCR Tyson Chandler A 6.00 15.00
APMTMH Tracy McGrady H 8.00 20.00
APMTMR Tracy McGrady A 8.00 20.00
PMKMH Kenyon Martin H 6.00 15.00
PMKMR Kenyon Martin A 6.00 15.00
PMKOBH Kobe Bryant H 10.00 25.00
PMKOBR Kobe Bryant A 10.00 25.00
PMLSH Latrell Sprewell H 6.00 15.00
PMLSR Latrell Sprewell A 6.00 15.00

2001-02 Upper Deck Playmakers Playmaker Dolls Autographs

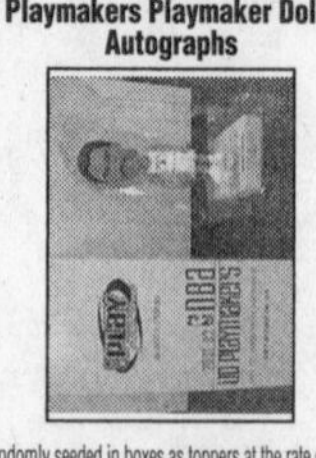

Randomly seeded in boxes as toppers at the rate of one in 336, this 20-bobble-head set parallels the base Playmaker Dolls set enhanced with a foil sticker containing an authentic player autograph. Each home autograph doll is numbered to the featured player's jersey number. Only Julius Erving features limited numbering on the road autograph doll.

HOME VERSIONS SERIALLY #'d BELOW
APMEGR Eddie Griffin 15.00 40.00
APMJJR Joe Johnson 30.00 80.00
APMJRH Jason Richardson/23 75.00 150.00
APMJRR Jason Richardson 25.00 60.00
APMKGA Kevin Garnett 40.00 100.00
APMKMR Kenyon Martin 15.00 40.00
APMKOBR Kobe Bryant 100.00 200.00
APMTCR Tyson Chandler 20.00 50.00

2001-02 Upper Deck Playmakers Triple Overtime

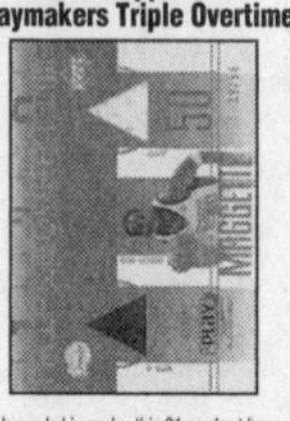

Randomly seeded in packs, this 21-card set has a similar design to the other memorabilia sets. Each card features a swatch of a jersey, a warm-up, and a shooting shirt. Each card is sequentially numbered to 50.

AHOT Anfernee Hardaway 30.00 80.00
CMOT Corey Maggette 15.00 40.00
DMOT Darius Miles 12.00 30.00
ECOT Eddy Curry 30.00 80.00
EGOT Eddie Griffin 20.00 50.00
GWOT Gerald Wallace 30.00 80.00
JAOT Jason Terry 20.00 50.00
JKOT Jason Kidd 20.00 50.00
JSOT Joe Smith 15.00 40.00
KBOT Kobe Bryant 100.00 250.00
KGOT Kevin Garnett 40.00 100.00
KMOT Karl Malone 25.00 60.00
KWOT Kwame Brown 20.00 50.00
MMOT Mike Miller 20.00 50.00
NAOT Steve Nash 30.00 80.00
SAOT Shareef Abdur-Rahim 15.00 40.00
SMOT Stephon Marbury 15.00 40.00
SSOT Stromile Swift 12.00 30.00
TBOT Terrell Brandon 12.00 30.00
TCOT Tyson Chandler 30.00 80.00
WSOT Wally Szczerbiak 15.00 40.00

2003-04 Upper Deck Phenomenal Beginning LeBron James

Released by Upper Deck in January 2004, this 20-card set was packaged with all cards, 1-20, and one bonus gold card. The gold cards parallel the design of the base set enhanced with a gold color shift on the border. The set was issued with a $9.99 SRP.

COMPLETE SET 8.00 20.00
*GOLD: 2X TO 5X BASE HI
GOLD: ONE PER BOX
*GOLD 100: 6X TO 15X BASE HI
LJ LeBron James AU/23 600.00 1000.00

1999 Upper Deck PowerDeck Athletes of the Century

These CD-Rom cards featuring four of the most prominent athletes of the 20th century were issued by Upper Deck in one boxed set. The cards are inserted into a computer and display various highlights of the player's career and his stats and other information.

COMPLETE SET (4) 8.00 20.00
2 Michael Jordan 3.00 8.00

2007-08 Upper Deck Premier

Released in April 2008, Upper Deck Premier is packaged in single packs only of five cards each and carried an initial SRP of $300. The base set boasts 136 cards and features veteran and retired players sequentially numbered to 99 on cards 1-94, rookies sequentially numbered to 99 on cards 95-100 and jersey autograph rookies sequentially numbered to 199 on cards 101-136.

1 Bill Russell 3.00 8.00
2 Larry Bird 6.00 15.00
3 Paul Pierce 2.50 6.00
4 Ray Allen 2.00 5.00
5 Al Harrington 1.50 4.00
6 Baron Davis 2.00 5.00
7 Rick Barry 2.00 5.00
8 Earl Monroe 2.00 5.00
9 Eddy Curry 1.25 3.00
10 Stephon Marbury 1.50 4.00
11 Chauncey Billups 2.00 5.00
12 Dave Bing 2.00 5.00
13 Richard Hamilton 1.50 4.00
14 Kobe Bryant 10.00 25.00
15 Luke Walton 1.25 3.00
16 Magic Johnson 5.00 12.00
17 Kevin Martin 2.00 5.00
18 Mike Bibby 2.00 5.00
19 Ron Artest 2.00 5.00
20 Bob Pettit 2.50 6.00
21 Joe Johnson 2.00 5.00
22 Josh Smith 2.00 5.00
23 Josh Childress 2.00 5.00
24 Andre Miller 1.50 4.00
25 Julius Erving 4.00 10.00
26 Elvin Hayes 2.00 5.00
27 Caron Butler 2.00 5.00
28 Gilbert Arenas 2.00 5.00
29 Ben Gordon 2.00 5.00
30 Ben Wallace 2.00 5.00
31 Michael Jordan 30.00 80.00
32 Allen Iverson 2.50 6.00
33 Carmelo Anthony 2.50 6.00
34 Marcus Camby 1.25 3.00
35 Hakeem Olajuwon 2.50 6.00
36 Tracy McGrady 2.50 6.00
37 Yao Ming 2.50 6.00
38 Jamaal Tinsley 1.25 3.00
39 Jermaine O'Neal 2.00 5.00
40 Mike Dunleavy 1.50 4.00
41 Jason Kidd 2.00 5.00
42 Richard Jefferson 2.00 5.00
43 Vince Carter 2.50 6.00
44 Chris Wilcox 1.25 3.00
45 Delonte West 1.50 4.00
46 Detlef Schrempf 2.00 5.00
47 Andrew Bogut 2.00 5.00
48 Michael Redd 2.00 5.00
49 Oscar Robertson 2.00 5.00
50 Amare Stoudemire 2.00 5.00
51 Grant Hill 2.50 6.00
52 Shawn Marion 2.00 5.00
53 Steve Nash 2.50 6.00
54 Brad Daugherty 2.00 5.00
55 Larry Hughes 1.50 4.00
56 LeBron James 10.00 25.00
57 Cuttino Mobley 1.50 4.00
58 Elton Brand 2.00 5.00
59 Sam Cassell 2.00 5.00
60 Brandon Roy 2.50 6.00
61 Clyde Drexler 2.50 6.00
62 LaMarcus Aldridge 2.50 6.00
63 Sean Elliott 2.00 5.00
64 George Gervin 2.00 5.00
65 Tim Duncan 3.00 8.00
66 Tony Parker 2.00 5.00
67 Carlos Boozer 2.00 5.00
68 Deron Williams 3.00 8.00
69 Karl Malone 2.50 6.00
70 Mehmet Okur 1.25 3.00
71 Dirk Nowitzki 2.50 6.00
72 Jason Terry 1.50 4.00
73 Josh Howard 1.50 4.00
74 Alonzo Mourning 2.50 6.00
75 Dwyane Wade 5.00 12.00
76 Shaquille O'Neal 4.00 10.00

77 Chris Paul 4.00 10.00
78 David West 2.00 5.00
79 Tyson Chandler 1.50 4.00
80 Kevin Garnett 4.00 10.00
81 Randy Foye 2.00 5.00
82 Al Jefferson 2.00 5.00
83 Dwight Howard 3.00 8.00
84 Jameer Nelson 1.50 4.00
85 Rashard Lewis 1.50 4.00
86 Darko Milicic 1.25 3.00
87 Mike Miller 2.00 5.00
88 Pau Gasol 2.00 5.00
89 Andrea Bargnani 2.50 6.00
90 Chris Bosh 2.00 5.00
91 T.J. Ford 1.50 4.00
92 Emeka Okafor 2.00 5.00
93 Gerald Wallace 2.00 5.00
94 Jason Richardson 2.00 5.00
95 Yi Jianlian RC 6.00 15.00
96 Marco Belinelli RC 4.00 10.00
97 Greg Oden RC 5.00 12.00
98 Brandan Wright RC 4.00 10.00
99 Nick Young RC 6.00 15.00
100 Thaddeus Young RC 5.00 12.00
101 Kevin Durant JSY AU RC 250.00 450.00
102 Al Horford JSY AU RC 8.00 20.00
103 Mike Conley Jr. JSY AU RC 10.00 25.00
104 Jeff Green JSY AU RC 8.00 20.00
105 Corey Brewer JSY AU RC 8.00 20.00
106 Joakim Noah JSY AU RC 15.00 40.00
107 Spencer Hawes JSY AU RC 6.00 15.00
108 Acie Law JSY AU RC 6.00 15.00
109 Julian Wright JSY AU RC 6.00 15.00
110 Al Thornton JSY AU RC 6.00 15.00
111 Rodney Stuckey JSY AU RC 10.00 25.00
112 Sean Williams JSY AU RC 6.00 15.00
113 Javaris Crittenton JSY AU RC 6.00 15.00
114 Jason Smith JSY AU RC 6.00 15.00
115 Daequan Cook JSY AU RC 6.00 15.00
116 Jared Dudley JSY AU RC 6.00 15.00
117 Wilson Chandler JSY AU RC 10.00 25.00
118 Morris Almond JSY AU RC 6.00 15.00
119 Arron Afflalo JSY AU RC 8.00 20.00
120 Alando Tucker JSY AU RC 6.00 15.00
121 Carl Landry JSY AU RC 6.00 15.00
122 Gabe Pruitt JSY AU RC 6.00 15.00
124 Nick Fazekas JSY AU RC 6.00 15.00
125 Glen Davis JSY AU RC 10.00 25.00
126 Jermareo Davidson JSY AU RC 6.00 15.00
127 Josh McRoberts JSY AU RC 6.00 15.00
129 Adam Haluska JSY AU RC 6.00 15.00
131 Stephane Lasme JSY AU RC 6.00 15.00
132 Dominic McGuire JSY AU RC 6.00 15.00
133 Aaron Gray JSY AU RC 6.00 15.00
134 Taurean Green JSY AU RC 6.00 15.00
135 Demetris Nichols JSY AU RC 6.00 15.00
136 D.J. Strawberry JSY AU RC 6.00 15.00
137 Aaron Brooks JSY AU RC 6.00 15.00
138 Herbert Hill JSY AU RC 6.00 15.00
139 Chris Richard JSY AU RC 6.00 15.00

2007-08 Upper Deck Premier Attractions Autographs Jerseys

PRINT RUN 50 SER.#'d SETS
PAAD Adrian Dantley 10.00 25.00
PAAI Andre Iguodala 8.00 20.00
PAAJ Al Jefferson 8.00 20.00
PAAM Alonzo Mourning 20.00 50.00
PABD Baron Davis 8.00 20.00
PABG Ben Gordon 8.00 20.00
PACM Corey Maggette 8.00 20.00
PACP Chris Paul 40.00 75.00
PADR Dennis Rodman 30.00 80.00
PADW Deron Williams 15.00 30.00
PAHO Hakeem Olajuwon 20.00 40.00
PAJO Michael Jordan 300.00 550.00
PAJW James Worthy 20.00 50.00
PAKB Kobe Bryant 125.00 250.00
PALJ LeBron James 100.00 200.00
PAMJ Magic Johnson 50.00 100.00
PAPA Tony Parker 15.00 30.00
PAPR Pat Riley 15.00 40.00
PARG Rudy Gay 10.00 25.00
PASN Steve Nash 30.00 60.00
PATP Tayshaun Prince 8.00 20.00
PAVC Vince Carter 20.00 40.00
PAWE Jerry West 30.00 80.00

2007-08 Upper Deck Premier Draft Mates Autographs

PRINT RUN 15 SER.#'d SETS
DMAR Brandon Roy 25.00 60.00
LaMarcus Aldridge
DMBC Mike Conley Jr. 25.00 50.00
Corey Brewer
DMBF Chris Bosh 15.00 40.00
T.J. Ford
DMBN Kobe Bryant 125.00 250.00
Steve Nash
DMBV Rick Barry 25.00 50.00
Dick Van Arsdale
DMCJ Vince Carter 30.00 60.00
Antawn Jamison
DMDG Kevin Durant 125.00 300.00
Jeff Green
DMDH Kevin Durant 125.00 300.00
Al Horford
DMGI Andre Iguodala 25.00 50.00
Ben Gordon
DMHJ Dwight Howard 30.00 60.00
Al Jefferson
DMJA LeBron James 125.00 250.00
Carmelo Anthony
DMJO Michael Jordan 450.00 750.00
Hakeem Olajuwon
DMKM Steve Kerr 15.00 30.00
Danny Manning
DMNH Joakim Noah 40.00 75.00
Al Horford
DMPH Paul Pierce 25.00 60.00
Al Harrington
DMRS Jack Sikma 15.00 30.00
Tree Rollins
DMSB Rodney Stuckey 15.00 30.00
Marco Belinelli

2007-08 Upper Deck Premier Exclusivity Autographs

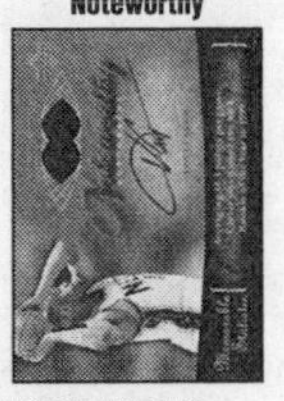

PRINT RUN 25 SER.#'d SETS
EXAH Al Horford 12.50 30.00
EXJG Jeff Green 12.50 30.00
EXJN Joakim Noah 25.00 60.00
EXKB Kobe Bryant 100.00 200.00
EXKD Kevin Durant 125.00 250.00
EXKG Kevin Garnett 40.00 80.00
EXLJ LeBron James 100.00 200.00
EXMC Mike Conley Jr. 12.50 30.00
EXMJ Michael Jordan 250.00 500.00

2007-08 Upper Deck Premier First Round Phenoms Autographs

PRINT RUN 6 TO 50 SER.#'d SETS
SOME UNPRICED DUE TO SCARCITY
FPBI Larry Bird/33 40.00 80.00
FPCA Carmelo Anthony/50 15.00 40.00
FPDA Brad Daugherty/50 15.00 40.00
FPHG Horace Grant/50 15.00 40.00
FPHO Hakeem Olajuwon/34 15.00 40.00
FPJO Magic Johnson/32 50.00 100.00
FPJS John Stockton/12 50.00 100.00
FPKB Kobe Bryant/24 100.00 200.00
FPLJ LeBron James/23 100.00 200.00
FPMJ Michael Jordan/23 300.00 550.00
FPMO Alonzo Mourning/50 15.00 40.00
FPPA Tony Parker/50 15.00 40.00
FPPP Paul Pierce/50 15.00 40.00
FPSN Steve Nash/50 25.00 50.00
FPVC Vince Carter/50 15.00 40.00
FPWF Walt Frazier/50 15.00 40.00
FPYM Yao Ming/50 15.00 40.00

2007-08 Upper Deck Premier Franchise Faces Autographs

PRINT RUN 24 TO 50 SER.#'d SETS
FFAM Alonzo Mourning/50 20.00 50.00
FFBG Ben Gordon/50 10.00 25.00
FFBR Brandon Roy/50 10.00 25.00
FFCA Carmelo Anthony/50 25.00 60.00
FFDR David Robinson/50 25.00 50.00
FFDW Deron Williams/50 12.50 30.00
FFHO Hakeem Olajuwon/34 15.00 40.00
FFJE Julius Erving/50 30.00 80.00
FFJO Magic Johnson/32 50.00 100.00
FFJW Jerry West/50 50.00 100.00
FFKB Kobe Bryant/24 100.00 200.00
FFLB Larry Bird/33 50.00 100.00
FFLJ LeBron James/23 100.00 200.00
FFPA Tony Parker/50 12.50 30.00
FFPP Paul Pierce/50 10.00 25.00
FFRB Rick Barry/50 10.00 25.00
FFTM Tracy McGrady/50 12.50 30.00
FFWF Walt Frazier/50 12.50 30.00
FFWU Wes Unseld/50 12.50 30.00
FFYM Yao Ming/50 15.00 30.00

2007-08 Upper Deck Premier Impressions

PRINT RUN 50 SER.#'d SETS
UNPRICED COPPER PRINT RUN ONE SET
PIAA Arron Afflalo 6.00 15.00
PIAH Al Horford 6.00 15.00
PICL Carl Landry 5.00 12.00
PIDC Daequan Cook 5.00 12.00
PIGD Glen Davis 8.00 20.00
PIGP Gabe Pruitt 5.00 12.00
PIJN Joakim Noah 20.00 50.00
PIJW Julian Wright 5.00 12.00
PIKD Kevin Durant 100.00 200.00
PIMB Marco Belinelli 5.00 12.00
PIRS Rodney Stuckey 8.00 20.00
PISW Sean Williams 5.00 12.00
PIWC Wilson Chandler 8.00 20.00

2007-08 Upper Deck Premier Impressions Gold

PRINT RUN 25 SER.#'d SETS
PIAH Al Horford 10.00 25.00
PIAL Acie Law 8.00 20.00
PICB Corey Brewer 10.00 25.00
PICL Carl Landry 8.00 20.00
PIDC Daequan Cook 8.00 20.00
PIJN Joakim Noah 30.00 80.00
PIKD Kevin Durant 150.00 300.00
PIWC Wilson Chandler 12.00 30.00

2007-08 Upper Deck Premier Noteworthy

PRINT RUNS LISTED IN CHECKLIST
UNPRICED COPPER PRINT RUN ONE SET
NWBG Ben Gordon/48 10.00 25.00
NWBI Larry Bird/60 40.00 100.00
NWBR Brandon Roy/29 15.00 30.00
NWCP Chris Paul/35 40.00 75.00
NWDR David Robinson/71 25.00 60.00
NWDT David Thompson/73 8.00 20.00
NWEB Elgin Baylor/71 15.00 40.00
NWHO Hakeem Olajuwon/51 20.00 40.00
NWJE Al Jefferson/32 8.00 20.00
NWJW Jerry West/63 25.00 60.00
NWKB Kobe Bryant/81 100.00 200.00
NWLA LaMarcus Aldridge/30 12.50 30.00
NWLH Larry Hughes/44 10.00 25.00
NWLJ LeBron James/56 100.00 200.00
NWMJ Michael Jordan/69 250.00 450.00
NWPP Paul Pierce/50 12.50 30.00
NWPR Tayshaun Prince/33 10.00 25.00
NWRB Rick Barry/64 10.00 25.00
NWRG Rudy Gay/31 8.00 20.00
NWSN Steve Nash/42 30.00 80.00
NWTM Tracy McGrady/62 10.00 25.00
NWTP Tony Parker/38 15.00 30.00
NWVC Vince Carter/51 12.50 30.00

2007-08 Upper Deck Premier Noteworthy Gold

PRINT RUN 25 SER.#'d SETS
NWBI Larry Bird 50.00 120.00
NWBR Brandon Roy 15.00 30.00
NWCP Chris Paul 40.00 75.00
NWDR David Robinson 40.00 80.00
NWDT David Thompson 10.00 25.00
NWEB Elgin Baylor 20.00 50.00
NWHO Hakeem Olajuwon 20.00 50.00
NWJW Jerry West 40.00 75.00
NWKB Kobe Bryant 125.00 300.00
NWLJ LeBron James 125.00 250.00
NWPP Paul Pierce 15.00 40.00
NWRG Rudy Gay 10.00 25.00
NWSN Steve Nash 30.00 80.00
NWTM Tracy McGrady 12.50 30.00
NWTP Tony Parker 15.00 40.00
NWVC Vince Carter 15.00 40.00

2007-08 Upper Deck Premier Opening Night Autographs Jerseys

PRINT RUN 25 SER.#'d SETS
ONAD Kevin Durant 150.00 300.00
Carmelo Anthony
ONAJ Al Jefferson 20.00 40.00
Carmelo Anthony
ONBM Kobe Bryant 125.00 225.00
Tracy McGrady
ONBP Mike Bibby 40.00 80.00
Chris Paul
ONBW Mike Bibby 10.00 25.00
Julian Wright
ONCG Mardy Collins 10.00 25.00
Daniel Gibson
ONCT Vince Carter 30.00 60.00
Tyrus Thomas
ONDM Baron Davis 15.00 30.00
Corey Maggette
ONHN Dwight Howard 20.00 50.00
David Noel
ONHT Al Thornton 10.00 25.00
Al Harrington
ONJF LeBron James 80.00 160.00
Nick Fazekas
ONKH Kirk Hinrich 25.00 50.00
Jason Kidd
ONMB Bruce Bowen 25.00 50.00
Josh McRoberts
ONMC Yao Ming 25.00 50.00
Javaris Crittenton
ONND Kevin Durant 150.00 250.00
Steve Nash
ONNW Joakim Noah 20.00 40.00
Sean Williams
ONPC Tony Parker 20.00 40.00
Mike Conley Jr.
ONPR Tony Parker 25.00 50.00
Brandon Roy
ONSC Rodney Stuckey 15.00 40.00
Daequan Cook

2007-08 Upper Deck Premier Pairings Autographs

PRINT RUN 20 SER.#'d SETS
PPAR Brandon Roy 25.00 50.00
LaMarcus Aldridge
PPAS Rodney Stuckey 15.00 30.00
Arron Afflalo
PPBD Baron Davis 15.00 30.00
Marco Belinelli
PPBN Steve Nash 125.00 225.00
Kobe Bryant
PPCG Jeff Green 20.00 40.00
Mike Conley Jr.
PPCM Vince Carter 30.00 80.00
Tracy McGrady
PPDB Baron Davis 15.00 30.00
Rick Barry
PPDP Mark Price 20.00 50.00
Brad Daugherty
PPFD Walt Frazier 15.00 30.00
Louie Dampier
PPGN Ben Gordon 15.00 40.00
Joakim Noah
PPHB Al Horford 25.00 50.00
Corey Brewer
PPHG Dwight Howard 25.00 50.00
Ben Gordon
PPJB Larry Bird 100.00 200.00
Magic Johnson
PPJE Michael Jordan 300.00 600.00
Julius Erving
PPJJ Michael Jordan 500.00 850.00
LeBron James
PPKA B.J. Armstrong 15.00 30.00
Steve Kerr
PPKC Jason Kidd 40.00 75.00
Vince Carter
PPLC Mike Conley Jr. 15.00 30.00
Kyle Lowry
PPMO Hakeem Olajuwon 30.00 60.00
Yao Ming
PPND Kevin Durant 150.00 300.00
Joakim Noah
PPPP Morris Peterson 40.00 75.00
Chris Paul
PPRR Dennis Rodman 60.00 120.00
David Robinson
PPTN Tyrus Thomas 20.00 50.00
Joakim Noah
PPWH Al Horford 30.00 60.00
Dominique Wilkins
PPWP Bill Walton 20.00 40.00
Robert Parish

2007-08 Upper Deck Premier Patches Dual Gold

PRINT RUN 9 TO 50 SER.#'d SETS
SOME UNPRICED DUE TO SCARCITY
UNPRICED AUTO PRINT RUN 10 TO 23 SETS
UNPRICED SPECTRUM PRINT RUN ONE SET
AA Arron Afflalo/25 8.00 20.00
AT Al Thornton/25 6.00 15.00
CA Carmelo Anthony/25 8.00 20.00
CP Chris Paul/25 12.00 30.00
DC Daequan Cook/25 6.00 15.00
DE Deron Williams/25 10.00 25.00
DN David Noel/25 4.00 10.00
DR David Robinson/25 10.00 25.00
JE Julius Erving/25 12.00 30.00
JS Jason Smith/25 6.00 15.00
JW Jerry West/25 15.00 30.00
KB Kobe Bryant/25 30.00 80.00
LJ LeBron James/25 20.00 50.00
PA Tony Parker/25 6.00 15.00
PP Paul Pierce/25 8.00 20.00
SN Steve Nash/25 8.00 20.00
ST John Stockton/25 10.00 25.00
SW Sean Williams/25 6.00 15.00
VC Vince Carter/25 8.00 20.00

2007-08 Upper Deck Premier Patches Dual Silver

STATED PRINT RUN ONE TO 52 SER.#'d SETS
SOME UNPRICED DUE TO SCARCITY
AT Al Thornton/12 8.00 20.00
DR David Robinson/50 10.00 25.00
JS Jason Smith/14 8.00 20.00
JW Jerry West/44 15.00 30.00
KB Kobe Bryant/24 25.00 60.00
LJ LeBron James/23 25.00 60.00
PP Paul Pierce/34 10.00 25.00
SN Steve Nash/13 10.00 25.00
ST John Stockton/12 12.00 30.00
SW Sean Williams/51 6.00 15.00
TC Tom Chambers/42 6.00 15.00

2007-08 Upper Deck Premier Patches Dual Silver Spectrum

PRINT RUN 15 SER.#'d SETS
AA Arron Afflalo 10.00 25.00
CA Carmelo Anthony 10.00 25.00
DE Deron Williams 12.00 30.00
DR David Robinson 12.00 30.00
JC Javaris Crittenton 8.00 20.00
JS Jason Smith 8.00 20.00
JW Jerry West 20.00 40.00
KB Kobe Bryant 30.00 80.00
LJ LeBron James 25.00 60.00
SB Shannon Brown 8.00 20.00
SN Steve Nash 10.00 25.00
ST John Stockton 12.00 30.00
SW Sean Williams 8.00 20.00
TC Tom Chambers 8.00 20.00
VC Vince Carter 10.00 25.00

2007-08 Upper Deck Premier Patches Triple Silver

PRINT RUN 35 SER.#'d SETS
UNPRICED SILVER SPEC.PRINT RUN 5 SETS
UNPRICED GOLD PRINT RUN 10 SETS
UNPRICED GOLD AUTO PRINT RUN 5 SETS
UNPRICED GOLD SPEC.PRINT RUN ONE SET
AL Acie Law 6.00 15.00
CP Chris Paul 12.00 30.00
DR David Robinson 10.00 25.00
DU Kevin Durant 40.00 80.00
GR Jeff Green 8.00 20.00
JE Julius Erving 12.00 30.00
JN Joakim Noah 15.00 40.00
JS John Stockton 10.00 25.00
KB Kobe Bryant 20.00 50.00
KG Kevin Garnett 12.00 30.00
LJ LeBron James 20.00 50.00
MC Mike Conley Jr. 10.00 25.00
PP Paul Pierce 8.00 20.00
PR Tayshaun Prince 6.00 15.00
RS Rodney Stuckey 10.00 25.00
SN Steve Nash 8.00 20.00
TP Tony Parker 6.00 15.00
VC Vince Carter 8.00 20.00
WE Jerry West 15.00 30.00

2007-08 Upper Deck Premier Penmanship Autographs

PRINT RUN 50 SER.#'d SETS
UNPRICED COPPER PRINT RUN ONE SET
AH Al Horford 10.00 25.00
AJ Antawn Jamison 6.00 15.00
AM Alonzo Mourning 20.00 50.00
AT Al Thornton 8.00 20.00
BA B.J. Armstrong 10.00 25.00
BR Brandon Roy 12.00 30.00
CA Carmelo Anthony 20.00 50.00
CL Clyde Lovellette 15.00 40.00
CO Corey Brewer 6.00 15.00
CP Chris Paul 30.00 80.00
DR Dennis Rodman 25.00 50.00
DW Deron Williams 20.00 40.00
EO Emeka Okafor 6.00 15.00
GR Glen Rice 15.00 40.00
HO Horace Grant 20.00 40.00
JE Al Jefferson 6.00 15.00
JG Jeff Green 6.00 15.00
JN Joakim Noah 15.00 40.00
JO Magic Johnson 40.00 80.00
KB Kobe Bryant 150.00 275.00
KD Kevin Durant 150.00 275.00
LA LaMarcus Aldridge 12.50 30.00
LB Larry Bird 50.00 100.00
LJ LeBron James 150.00 275.00
MJ Michael Jordan 250.00 450.00
OL Hakeem Olajuwon 15.00 40.00
PA Tony Parker 10.00 25.00
PP Paul Pierce 20.00 40.00
RG Rudy Gay 6.00 15.00
RO David Robinson 30.00 60.00
RR Rajon Rondo 30.00 60.00
RS Rodney Stuckey 6.00 15.00
RU Bill Russell 125.00 250.00
SK Steve Kerr 8.00 20.00
TM Tracy McGrady 15.00 30.00
TP Tayshaun Prince 6.00 15.00
TT Tyrus Thomas 8.00 20.00
VC Vince Carter 20.00 40.00
WE Jerry West 30.00 80.00
WF Walt Frazier 10.00 25.00
WI Dominique Wilkins 20.00 50.00
WO James Worthy 20.00 50.00
WT Wayman Tisdale 15.00 40.00
WU Wes Unseld 15.00 40.00
YM Yao Ming 20.00 40.00

2007-08 Upper Deck Premier Penmanship Autographs Gold

PRINT RUNS LISTED IN CHECKLIST
SOME UNPRICED DUE TO SCARCITY
AH Al Horford/15 15.00 40.00
AM Alonzo Mourning/33 40.00 80.00
BA B.J. Armstrong/11 60.00 120.00
CA Carmelo Anthony/15 25.00 60.00
HO Horace Grant/54 20.00 50.00
JE Al Jefferson/25 8.00 20.00
JO Magic Johnson/32 75.00 150.00
JW Julian Wright/32 10.00 25.00
KB Kobe Bryant/24 200.00 400.00
KD Kevin Durant/35 175.00 350.00
LB Larry Bird/33 75.00 150.00
LJ LeBron James/23 175.00 350.00
MC Mike Conley Jr./11 25.00 50.00
MJ Michael Jordan/23 400.00 700.00
OL Hakeem Olajuwon/34 25.00 60.00
PP Paul Pierce/34 20.00 40.00
RG Rudy Gay/22 10.00 25.00
RO David Robinson/50 30.00 60.00
SK Steve Kerr/25 12.50 30.00
VC Vince Carter/15 25.00 50.00
WE Jerry West/44 40.00 75.00
WO James Worthy/42 20.00 50.00
YM Yao Ming/11 25.00 50.00

2007-08 Upper Deck Premier Preeminence

PRINT RUN 50 SER.#'d SETS
UNPRICED COPPER PRINT RUN ONE SET
PEAI Andre Iguodala 6.00 15.00
PEBR Brandon Roy 8.00 20.00
PECP Chris Paul 20.00 50.00
PEDW Deron Williams 10.00 25.00
PEJE Al Jefferson 5.00 12.00
PEKB Kobe Bryant 100.00 200.00
PEMJ Magic Johnson 40.00 80.00
PERG Rudy Gay 8.00 20.00
PESK Steve Kerr 8.00 20.00
PETP Tayshaun Prince 5.00 12.00
PEVC Vince Carter 12.50 30.00
PEWT Wayman Tisdale 6.00 15.00
PEYM Yao Ming 15.00 40.00

2007-08 Upper Deck Premier Preeminence Gold

PRINT RUN 25 SER.#'d SETS
PEAI Andre Iguodala 10.00 25.00
PEBR Brandon Roy 15.00 30.00
PECP Chris Paul 40.00 75.00
PEKB Kobe Bryant 150.00 300.00
PEMJ Magic Johnson 60.00 120.00
PERG Rudy Gay 12.50 30.00
PESK Steve Kerr 12.50 30.00
PETC Tyson Chandler 8.00 20.00
PETP Tayshaun Prince 8.00 20.00
PETT Tyrus Thomas 8.00 20.00
PEVC Vince Carter 15.00 40.00

2007-08 Upper Deck Premier Rare Patches Dual Gold

PRINT RUN 15 SER.#'d SETS
UNPRICED SPECTRUM PRINT RUN ONE SET
*SILVER PATCH: .4X TO 1X BASE HI
SILVER PRINT RUN 25 SER.#'d SETS
UNPRICED SILVER SPEC.PRINT RUN 10 SETS
AC Al Horford 8.00 20.00
Corey Brewer
AG Ray Allen 25.00 50.00
Kevin Garnett
AH Ray Allen 8.00 20.00
Richard Hamilton
AS Arron Afflalo 8.00 20.00
Rodney Stuckey
BB Shane Battier 10.00 25.00
Carlos Boozer
BJ Kobe Bryant 40.00 75.00
LeBron James
BM Desmond Mason 8.00 20.00
Andrew Bogut
BN Kobe Bryant 20.00 40.00
Steve Nash
DG Kevin Durant 40.00 80.00
Jeff Green
DJ John Stockton 15.00 30.00
Deron Williams
DM Tim Duncan 15.00 30.00
Yao Ming
DR Clyde Drexler 20.00 40.00
David Robinson
GI Ben Gordon 8.00 20.00
Andre Iguodala
GJ Kevin Garnett 20.00 40.00
Al Jefferson
GN Aaron Gray 8.00 20.00
Joakim Noah
HB Richard Hamilton 8.00 20.00
Chauncey Billups
HL Al Horford 10.00 25.00
Acie Law
IA Allen Iverson 20.00 40.00
Carmelo Anthony
IN Allen Iverson 15.00 30.00
Dirk Nowitzki
JB Magic Johnson 20.00 40.00
Larry Bird
JD LeBron James 50.00 125.00
Kevin Durant
JJ Michael Jordan 100.00 250.00
LeBron James
JW Antawn Jamison 8.00 20.00
Luke Walton
KM Jason Kidd 8.00 20.00
Stephon Marbury
PD Gabe Pruitt 8.00 20.00
Glen Davis
PH Paul Pierce 8.00 20.00
Kirk Hinrich
PR Chris Paul 15.00 30.00
Brandon Roy
PW Chris Paul 10.00 25.00
Julian Wright
SH Amare Stoudemire 15.00 40.00
Dwight Howard
WD Gerald Wallace 8.00 20.00
Jared Dudley
WN Ben Wallace 8.00 20.00
Joakim Noah
WW Rasheed Wallace 8.00 20.00
Ben Wallace
YS Thaddeus Young 8.00 20.00
Jason Smith

2007-08 Upper Deck Premier Rare Patches Triple Silver

PRINT RUN 15 SER.#'d SETS
UNPRICED SILVER SPEC.PRINT RUN 5 SETS
UNPRICED GOLD PRINT RUN 10 SETS
UNPRICED GOLD SPEC.PRINT RUN ONE SET
ASH Arron Afflalo 12.50 30.00
Rodney Stuckey
Richard Hamilton
BFC Javaris Crittenton 20.00 40.00
Kobe Bryant
Jordan Farmar
BGJ Kobe Bryant 50.00 100.00
Kevin Garnett
LeBron James
BNI Allen Iverson 30.00 60.00
Kobe Bryant
Steve Nash
BPW Chris Paul 20.00 50.00
Chauncey Billups
Deron Williams
DGC Mike Conley Jr. 40.00 75.00
Kevin Durant
Jeff Green
DGO Shaquille O'Neal 25.00 50.00
Kevin Garnett
Tim Duncan
DPG Tony Parker 20.00 50.00
Manu Ginobili
Tim Duncan
JJB Larry Bird 100.00 200.00
Michael Jordan
Magic Johnson
MRL David Lee 12.50 30.00
Zach Randolph
Stephon Marbury
NHB Al Horford 25.00 50.00
Corey Brewer
Joakim Noah
NHH Dirk Nowitzki 15.00 40.00
Josh Howard
Devin Harris
OGR David Robinson 25.00 50.00
Kevin Garnett
Hakeem Olajuwon
PAG Kevin Garnett 50.00 100.00
Ray Allen
Paul Pierce
WSD John Stockton 40.00 100.00
Jerry West
Clyde Drexler

2007-08 Upper Deck Premier Rare Remnants Quad

PRINT RUN 50 SER.#'d SETS
AGDG Kevin Durant 12.00 30.00
Jeff Green
Ray Allen
Kevin Garnett
AGPD Glen Davis 8.00 20.00
Kevin Garnett
Gabe Pruitt
Ray Allen
ARPA LaMarcus Aldridge 8.00 20.00
Brandon Roy
Hilton Armstrong
Chris Paul
DNSA Dirk Nowitzki 10.00 25.00
Tim Duncan
Carmelo Anthony
Amare Stoudemire
GCMM Kevin Garnett 20.00 50.00
Vince Carter
Tracy McGrady
Shawn Marion
GJGB LeBron James 12.50 30.00
Daniel Gibson
Drew Gooden
Shannon Brown
HDGT Ben Gordon 6.00 15.00
Kirk Hinrich
Luol Deng
Tyrus Thomas
JABW LeBron James 50.00 100.00
Carmelo Anthony
Chris Bosh
Dwyane Wade
JEJB Larry Bird 60.00 150.00
Magic Johnson
Michael Jordan
Julius Erving
KCJW Richard Jefferson 6.00 15.00
Vince Carter
Jason Kidd
Sean Williams
KJHO LeBron James 25.00 50.00
Shaquille O'Neal
Dwight Howard
Jason Kidd
MWOC Shaquille O'Neal 10.00 25.00
Dwyane Wade
Daequan Cook
Alonzo Mourning
NGHB Joakim Noah 8.00 20.00
Al Horford
Corey Brewer
Taurean Green
SDRR David Robinson 25.00 50.00
Dennis Rodman
John Stockton
Clyde Drexler
YHSI Thaddeus Young 6.00 15.00
Jason Smith
Andre Iguodala
Herbert Hill

2007-08 Upper Deck Premier Rare Remnants Quad Gold

PRINT RUN 25 SER.#'d SETS
UNPRICED SPECTRUM PRINT RUN ONE SET
UNPRICED SILVER SPEC.PRINT RUN 10 SETS
AGDG Kevin Durant 20.00 50.00
Jeff Green

Ray Allen
Kevin Garnett
ARPA LaMarcus Aldridge 10.00 25.00
Brandon Roy
Hilton Armstrong
Chris Paul
DNSA Dirk Nowitzki 15.00 30.00
Tim Duncan
Carmelo Anthony
Amare Stoudemire
GCMM Kevin Garnett 20.00 40.00
Vince Carter
Tracy McGrady
Shawn Marion
GJGB LeBron James 20.00 40.00
Daniel Gibson
Drew Gooden
Shannon Brown
HDGT Ben Gordon 10.00 25.00
Kirk Hinrich
Luol Deng
Tyrus Thomas
JABW LeBron James 50.00 120.00
Carmelo Anthony
Chris Bosh
Dwyane Wade
KJHO LeBron James 25.00 60.00
Shaquille O'Neal
Dwight Howard
Jason Kidd
YHSI Thaddeus Young 10.00 25.00
Jason Smith
Andre Iguodala
Herbert Hill

2007-08 Upper Deck Premier Rare Remnants Triple

PRINT RUN 99 SER.#'d SETS
ASB Arron Afflalo 4.00 10.00
Rodney Stuckey
Chauncey Billups
BAH Ron Artest 4.00 10.00
Spencer Hawes
Mike Bibby
BGJ Kobe Bryant 12.50 30.00
Kevin Garnett
LeBron James
BMA Kobe Bryant 10.00 25.00
Tracy McGrady
Carmelo Anthony
BNI Allen Iverson 12.00 30.00
Kobe Bryant
Steve Nash
BPW Chris Paul 6.00 15.00
Chauncey Billups
Deron Williams
CBH Vince Carter 6.00 15.00
Chris Bosh
Dwight Howard
DGO Shaquille O'Neal 8.00 20.00
Kevin Garnett
Tim Duncan
JAB LeBron James 8.00 20.00
Carmelo Anthony
Chris Bosh
JCS Josh Smith 5.00 12.00
Joe Johnson
Josh Childress
JDM LeBron James 12.50 30.00
Kevin Durant
Tracy McGrady
JEB Michael Jordan 30.00 80.00
Larry Bird
Julius Erving
JHB Al Harrington 4.00 10.00
Antawn Jamison
Carlos Boozer
JJJ LeBron James 30.00 60.00
Michael Jordan
Magic Johnson
KWS John Stockton 8.00 20.00
Andrei Kirilenko
Deron Williams
MMB Tracy McGrady 6.00 15.00
Yao Ming
Aaron Brooks
MNW Deron Williams 6.00 15.00
Dirk Nowitzki
Tracy McGrady
MSO Shaquille O'Neal 10.00 25.00
Amare Stoudemire
Yao Ming
NHB Joakim Noah 6.00 15.00
Al Horford
Corey Brewer
NMS Steve Nash 6.00 15.00
Amare Stoudemire
Shawn Marion
OGR David Robinson 8.00 20.00
Hakeem Olajuwon
Kevin Garnett
TAB Andrea Bargnani 4.00 10.00
Tyrus Thomas
LaMarcus Aldridge

2007-08 Upper Deck Premier Rare Remnants Triple Gold

PRINT RUN 50 SER.#'d SETS
UNPRICED SPECTRUM PRINT RUN ONE SET
ASB Arron Afflalo 5.00 12.00
Rodney Stuckey
Chauncey Billups
BAH Ron Artest 5.00 12.00
Spencer Hawes
Mike Bibby
BGJ Kobe Bryant 20.00 50.00
Kevin Garnett
LeBron James
BMA Kobe Bryant 12.50 30.00
Tracy McGrady
Carmelo Anthony
BNI Allen Iverson 15.00 40.00
Kobe Bryant
Steve Nash
BPW Chris Paul 8.00 20.00
Chauncey Billups
Deron Williams
CBH Vince Carter 8.00 20.00
Chris Bosh
Dwight Howard
DGO Shaquille O'Neal 10.00 25.00
Kevin Garnett
Tim Duncan
JAB LeBron James 10.00 25.00
Carmelo Anthony
Chris Bosh
JCS Josh Smith 6.00 15.00
Joe Johnson
Josh Childress
JDM LeBron James 15.00 40.00
Kevin Durant
Tracy McGrady
JEB Michael Jordan 40.00 100.00
Larry Bird
Julius Erving
JHB Al Harrington 5.00 12.00
Antawn Jamison
Carlos Boozer
JJJ LeBron James 40.00 100.00
Michael Jordan
Magic Johnson
KWS John Stockton 10.00 25.00
Andrei Kirilenko
Deron Williams
MMB Tracy McGrady 8.00 20.00
Yao Ming
Aaron Brooks
MNW Deron Williams 8.00 20.00
Dirk Nowitzki
Tracy McGrady
MSO Shaquille O'Neal 12.50 30.00
Amare Stoudemire
Yao Ming
NHB Joakim Noah 8.00 20.00
Al Horford
Corey Brewer
NMS Steve Nash 8.00 20.00
Amare Stoudemire
Shawn Marion
OGR David Robinson 10.00 25.00
Hakeem Olajuwon
Kevin Garnett
TAB Andrea Bargnani 5.00 12.00
Tyrus Thomas
LaMarcus Aldridge

2007-08 Upper Deck Premier Rare Remnants Triple Silver Spectrum

PRINT RUN 25 SER.#'d SETS
ASB Arron Afflalo 6.00 15.00
Rodney Stuckey
Chauncey Billups
BAH Ron Artest 6.00 15.00
Spencer Hawes
Mike Bibby
BGJ Kobe Bryant 25.00 60.00
Kevin Garnett
LeBron James
BMA Kobe Bryant 20.00 40.00
Tracy McGrady
Carmelo Anthony
BPW Chris Paul 10.00 25.00
Chauncey Billups
Deron Williams
CBH Vince Carter 10.00 25.00
Chris Bosh
Dwight Howard
DGO Shaquille O'Neal 15.00 30.00
Kevin Garnett
Tim Duncan
JAB LeBron James 15.00 40.00
Carmelo Anthony
Chris Bosh
JCS Josh Smith 8.00 20.00
Joe Johnson
Josh Childress
JDM LeBron James 25.00 60.00
Kevin Durant
Tracy McGrady
JEB Michael Jordan 50.00 125.00
Larry Bird
Julius Erving
JHB Al Harrington 6.00 15.00
Antawn Jamison
Carlos Boozer
JJJ LeBron James 75.00 200.00
Michael Jordan
Magic Johnson
KWS John Stockton 15.00 30.00
Andrei Kirilenko
Deron Williams
MMB Tracy McGrady 10.00 25.00
Yao Ming
Aaron Brooks
MNW Deron Williams 10.00 25.00
Dirk Nowitzki
Tracy McGrady
MSO Shaquille O'Neal 15.00 40.00
Amare Stoudemire
Yao Ming
NHB Joakim Noah 10.00 25.00
Al Horford
Corey Brewer
NMS Steve Nash 10.00 25.00
Amare Stoudemire
Shawn Marion
OGR David Robinson 15.00 30.00
Hakeem Olajuwon
Kevin Garnett
TAB Andrea Bargnani 6.00 15.00
Tyrus Thomas
LaMarcus Aldridge

2007-08 Upper Deck Premier Remnants Quad

STATED PRINT RUN ONE TO 99 SER.#'d SETS
SOME UNPRICED DUE TO SCARCITY
DR David Robinson/89 8.00 20.00
JE Julius Erving/76 8.00 20.00
JS John Stockton/84 6.00 15.00
KB Kobe Bryant/96 10.00 25.00
KG Kevin Garnett/95 8.00 20.00
SN Steve Nash/96 5.00 12.00
TC Tom Chambers/81 4.00 10.00
VC Vince Carter/98 5.00 12.00
WE Jerry West/60 8.00 20.00

2007-08 Upper Deck Premier Remnants Quad Autographs

PRINT RUN 25 SER.#'d SETS
AH Al Horford 20.00 40.00
AM Andre Miller 8.00 20.00
BD Boris Diaw 8.00 20.00
CA Carmelo Anthony 25.00 60.00
CB Corey Brewer 15.00 30.00
CP Chris Paul 40.00 80.00
DU Kevin Durant 175.00 350.00
JE Julius Erving 40.00 80.00
JN Joakim Noah 25.00 60.00
JS John Stockton 50.00 100.00
LJ LeBron James 250.00 400.00
MC Mike Conley Jr. 12.00 30.00
RS Rodney Stuckey 15.00 40.00
SN Steve Nash 30.00 80.00
VC Vince Carter 25.00 50.00
WE Jerry West 40.00 80.00

2007-08 Upper Deck Premier Remnants Quad Gold

PRINT RUN 50 SER.#'d SETS
UNPRICED SPECTRUM PRINT RUN ONE SET
UNPRICED SILVER SPEC.PRINT RUN 10 SETS
CA Carmelo Anthony 6.00 15.00
CP Chris Paul 10.00 25.00
DR David Robinson 8.00 20.00
DU Kevin Durant 25.00 60.00
GR Jeff Green 6.00 15.00
JE Julius Erving 10.00 25.00
JN Joakim Noah 12.00 30.00
JS John Stockton 8.00 20.00
JW Julian Wright 5.00 12.00
KB Kobe Bryant 20.00 50.00
LJ LeBron James 15.00 40.00
MC Mike Conley Jr. 8.00 20.00
TC Tom Chambers 5.00 12.00
TP Tony Parker 5.00 12.00
VC Vince Carter 6.00 15.00
WE Jerry West 8.00 20.00

2007-08 Upper Deck Premier Remnants Triple

PRINT RUN 99 SER.#'d SETS
*GOLD: .5X TO 1.25X BASE HI
GOLD PRINT RUN 50 SER.#'d SETS
*SILVER SPEC: .6X TO 1.5X BASE HI
SILVER SPEC.PRINT RUN 25 SETS
UNPRICED GOLD SPEC.PRINT RUN ONE SET
AT Al Thornton 3.00 8.00
CP Chris Paul 6.00 15.00
DC Daequan Cook 3.00 8.00
DE Deron Williams 5.00 12.00
KB Kobe Bryant 10.00 25.00
LJ LeBron James 12.00 30.00
SN Steve Nash 4.00 10.00
SW Sean Williams 3.00 8.00
TP Tayshaun Prince 3.00 8.00
VC Vince Carter 4.00 10.00

2007-08 Upper Deck Premier Remnants Triple Autographs

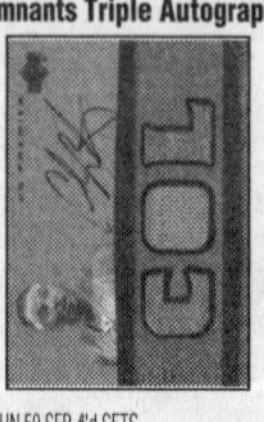

PRINT RUN 50 SER.#'d SETS
AA Arron Afflalo 6.00 15.00
AB Aaron Brooks 6.00 15.00
AM Andre Miller 6.00 15.00
BD Boris Diaw 6.00 15.00
CA Carmelo Anthony 25.00 60.00
CM Corey Maggette 6.00 15.00
CP Chris Paul 30.00 60.00
DC Daequan Cook 6.00 15.00
DE Deron Williams 10.00 25.00
DR David Robinson 40.00 80.00
JE Julius Erving 40.00 80.00
JW Jerry West 30.00 80.00
KB Kobe Bryant 125.00 250.00
LJ LeBron James 125.00 250.00
PA Tony Parker 15.00 40.00
PP Paul Pierce 12.00 30.00
SN Steve Nash 25.00 60.00
ST John Stockton 40.00 75.00
SW Sean Williams 6.00 15.00
TP Tayshaun Prince 8.00 20.00
VC Vince Carter 20.00 40.00
WC Wilson Chandler 10.00 25.00

2007-08 Upper Deck Premier Rookies Autographs Jerseys Copper

PRINT RUN 99 SER.#'d SETS
*BLUE: .6X TO 1.5X COPPER HI
BLUE PRINT RUN 25 SER.#'d SETS
*GREEN: .5X TO 1.25X COPPER
GREEN PRINT RUN 49 SER.#'d SETS
UNPRICED GOLD PRINT RUN ONE SET
UNPRICED RED PRINT RUN 15 SER.#'d SETS
101 Kevin Durant 250.00 450.00
102 Al Horford 8.00 20.00
103 Mike Conley Jr. 10.00 25.00
104 Jeff Green 8.00 20.00
105 Corey Brewer 8.00 20.00
106 Joakim Noah 15.00 40.00
107 Spencer Hawes 6.00 15.00
108 Acie Law 6.00 15.00
109 Julian Wright 6.00 15.00
110 Al Thornton 6.00 15.00
111 Rodney Stuckey 10.00 25.00
112 Sean Williams 6.00 15.00
113 Javaris Crittenton 6.00 15.00
114 Jason Smith 6.00 15.00
115 Daequan Cook 6.00 15.00
116 Jared Dudley 6.00 15.00
117 Wilson Chandler 10.00 25.00
118 Morris Almond 6.00 15.00
119 Arron Afflalo 8.00 20.00
120 Alando Tucker 6.00 15.00
121 Carl Landry 6.00 15.00
122 Gabe Pruitt 6.00 15.00
125 Glen Davis 10.00 25.00
126 Jermareo Davidson 6.00 15.00
129 Adam Haluska 6.00 15.00
133 Aaron Gray 6.00 15.00
134 Taurean Green 6.00 15.00
135 Demetris Nichols 6.00 15.00
136 D.J. Strawberry 6.00 15.00
137 Aaron Brooks 6.00 15.00
138 Herbert Hill 6.00 15.00
139 Chris Richard 6.00 15.00

2007-08 Upper Deck Premier Stitchings Patches

PRINT RUN 50 SER.#'d SETS
STITCHINGS PATCH FEATURE TEAM LOGO
*ALT LOGO: .4X TO 1X BASE HI
ALT LOGO PRINT RUN 50 SETS
*GOLD: .4X TO 1X BASE HI
GOLD PRINT RUN 25 SETS
*GOLD ALT: .4X TO 1X BASE HI
GOLD ALT PRINT RUN 25 SETS
UNPRICED AUTO PRINT RUN 5 SETS
UNPRICED AUTO ALT PRINT RUN ONE SET
UNPRICED COPPER PRINT RUN 10 SETS
UNPRICED COPPER ALT PRINT RUN 10 SETS
PSAB Aaron Brooks 8.00 20.00
PSAH Al Horford 8.00 20.00
PSAI Allen Iverson 10.00 25.00
PSAN Carmelo Anthony 10.00 25.00
PSAS Amare Stoudemire 10.00 25.00
PSAT Al Thornton 8.00 20.00
PSBA Andrea Bargnani 8.00 20.00
PSBB Bill Bradley 8.00 20.00
PSBG Ben Gordon 8.00 20.00
PSBM Bob McAdoo 10.00 25.00
PSBO Chris Bosh 8.00 20.00
PSBR Bill Russell 12.50 30.00
PSBW Bill Walton 8.00 20.00
PSCA Carlos Arroyo 10.00 25.00
PSCB Carlos Boozer 8.00 20.00
PSCD Clyde Drexler 8.00 20.00
PSCH Wilt Chamberlain 10.00 25.00
PSCO Corey Brewer 8.00 20.00
PSCP Chris Paul 10.00 25.00
PSDC Daequan Cook 8.00 20.00
PSDE Dennis Rodman 20.00 40.00
PSDH Dwight Howard 10.00 25.00
PSDN Dirk Nowitzki 10.00 25.00
PSDR David Robinson 12.50 30.00
PSDW Deron Williams 8.00 20.00
PSEJ Magic Johnson 12.50 30.00
PSEM Earl Monroe 8.00 20.00
PSEO Emeka Okafor 8.00 20.00
PSGG George Gervin 10.00 25.00
PSGO Greg Oden 8.00 20.00
PSGR Gerald Green 8.00 20.00
PSHO Hakeem Olajuwon 10.00 25.00
PSIT Isiah Thomas 10.00 25.00
PSJD Jared Dudley 8.00 20.00
PSJG Jeff Green 8.00 20.00
PSJH John Havlicek 10.00 25.00
PSJK Jason Kidd 10.00 25.00
PSJO Jermaine O'Neal 8.00 20.00
PSJS Jason Smith 8.00 20.00
PSJW Jerry West 12.50 30.00
PSKB Kobe Bryant 25.00 60.00
PSKD Kevin Durant 15.00 40.00
PSKG Kevin Garnett 12.50 30.00
PSKH Kirk Hinrich 8.00 20.00
PSKM Karl Malone 8.00 20.00
PSLA LaMarcus Aldridge 8.00 20.00
PSLB Larry Bird 15.00 40.00
PSLD Luol Deng 8.00 20.00
PSLJ LeBron James 15.00 40.00
PSMB Marco Belinelli 8.00 20.00
PSMC Kevin McHale 8.00 20.00
PSMG Manu Ginobili 10.00 25.00
PSMJ Michael Jordan 60.00 150.00
PSMM Moses Malone 8.00 20.00
PSNO Joakim Noah 8.00 20.00
PSNY Nick Young 8.00 20.00
PSOR Oscar Robertson 10.00 25.00
PSPP Paul Pierce 8.00 20.00
PSPS Peja Stojakovic 8.00 20.00
PSPW Paul Westphal 8.00 20.00
PSRE Willis Reed 10.00 25.00
PSRF Randy Foye 8.00 20.00
PSRG Rudy Gay 8.00 20.00
PSRO Brandon Roy 8.00 20.00
PSRP Robert Parish 10.00 25.00
PSRR Rajon Rondo 10.00 25.00
PSRS Rodney Stuckey 8.00 20.00
PSSH Spencer Hawes 8.00 20.00
PSSN Steve Nash 10.00 25.00
PSSO Shaquille O'Neal 12.50 30.00
PSST John Stockton 8.00 20.00
PSTD Tim Duncan 12.50 30.00
PSTM Tracy McGrady 8.00 20.00
PSTT Tyrus Thomas 8.00 20.00
PSTU Alando Tucker 8.00 20.00
PSTY Thaddeus Young 8.00 20.00
PSVC Vince Carter 10.00 25.00
PSWA Dwyane Wade 12.50 30.00
PSWC Wilson Chandler 8.00 20.00
PSWF Walt Frazier 10.00 25.00
PSWI Dominique Wilkins 10.00 25.00
PSWR Brandan Wright 8.00 20.00
PSYM Yao Ming 10.00 25.00

2007-08 Upper Deck Premier Trios Autographs

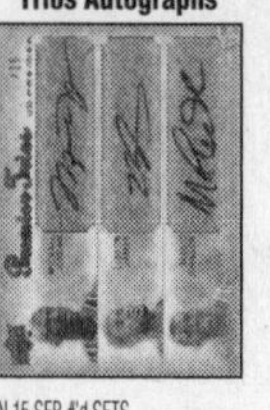

PRINT RUN 15 SER.#'d SETS
HGN Kirk Hinrich 40.00 75.00
Joakim Noah
Ben Gordon
JFB Randy Foye 15.00 40.00
Al Jefferson
Corey Brewer
JJJ Michael Jordan 400.00 800.00
LeBron James
Magic Johnson
KCW Sean Williams 100.00 200.00
Jason Kidd
Vince Carter
MLB Carl Landry 30.00 60.00
Aaron Brooks
Tracy McGrady
OHJ Al Jefferson 40.00 75.00
Emeka Okafor
Dwight Howard
PAG Kevin Garnett 250.00 500.00
Paul Pierce
Ray Allen
RFD Pat Riley 40.00 75.00
Walt Frazier
Louie Dampier
SDG Kevin Durant 100.00 200.00
Jeff Green
Lonnie Shelton
TAG Tyrus Thomas 25.00 50.00
LaMarcus Aldridge
Rudy Gay
WHL Al Horford 30.00 60.00
Acie Law
Shelden Williams

2008-09 Upper Deck Premier

This set was released on March 11, 2009. The base set consists of 130 cards.

1-94 PRINT RUN 99 SER.#'d SETS
95-100 PRINT RUN 99 SER.#'d SETS
95-130 PRINT RUN 199 SER.#'d SETS
1 Kevin Garnett 4.00 10.00
2 Paul Pierce 2.50 6.00
3 Ray Allen 2.00 5.00
4 Larry Bird 6.00 15.00
5 Stephen Jackson 1.50 4.00
6 Monta Ellis 2.00 5.00
7 Mitch Richmond 2.00 5.00
8 Stephon Marbury 1.50 4.00
9 Jamal Crawford 1.50 4.00
10 Patrick Ewing 2.50 6.00
11 Chauncey Billups 2.00 5.00
12 Rasheed Wallace 2.00 5.00
13 Isiah Thomas 2.00 5.00
14 Kobe Bryant 10.00 25.00
15 Pau Gasol 2.00 5.00
16 Magic Johnson 5.00 12.00
17 Elgin Baylor 2.00 5.00
18 Kevin Martin 2.00 5.00
19 Beno Udrih 1.25 3.00
20 Oscar Robertson 2.00 5.00
21 Joe Johnson 2.00 5.00
22 Al Horford 2.00 5.00
23 Dominique Wilkins 2.50 6.00
24 Andre Iguodala 2.00 5.00
25 Elton Brand 2.00 5.00
26 Julius Erving 4.00 10.00
27 Wilt Chamberlain 4.00 10.00
28 Gilbert Arenas 2.00 5.00
29 Antawn Jamison 2.00 5.00
30 Elvin Hayes 2.00 5.00
31 Ben Gordon 2.00 5.00
32 Luol Deng 2.00 5.00
33 Michael Jordan 30.00 60.00
34 Scottie Pippen 3.00 8.00
35 Allen Iverson 2.50 6.00
36 Carmelo Anthony 2.50 6.00
37 Alex English 2.00 5.00
38 Tracy McGrady 2.00 5.00
39 Yao Ming 2.50 6.00
40 Hakeem Olajuwon 2.50 6.00
41 T.J. Ford 1.25 3.00
42 Danny Granger 2.00 5.00
43 Mike Dunleavy 1.50 4.00
44 Yi Jianlian 2.00 5.00
45 Vince Carter 2.50 6.00
46 Buck Williams 2.00 5.00
47 Kevin Durant 8.00 20.00
48 Jeff Green 1.50 4.00
49 Detlef Schrempf 2.00 5.00
50 Richard Jefferson 2.00 5.00
51 Andrew Bogut 2.00 5.00
52 Kareem Abdul-Jabbar 3.00 8.00
53 Steve Nash 2.00 5.00
54 Shaquille O'Neal 4.00 10.00
55 Kevin Johnson 2.00 5.00
56 LeBron James 10.00 25.00
57 Daniel Gibson 2.00 5.00
58 Mark Price 3.00 8.00
59 Baron Davis 2.00 5.00
60 Chris Kaman 1.50 4.00
61 World B. Free 2.00 5.00
62 Brandon Roy 2.00 5.00
63 LaMarcus Aldridge 2.00 5.00
64 Clyde Drexler 2.50 6.00
65 Tim Duncan 3.00 8.00
66 Tony Parker 2.00 5.00
67 David Robinson 3.00 8.00
68 Deron Williams 2.00 5.00
69 Carlos Boozer 2.00 5.00
70 Karl Malone 2.50 6.00
71 John Stockton 3.00 8.00
72 Dirk Nowitzki 2.50 6.00
73 Jason Kidd 2.00 5.00
74 Rolando Blackman 2.00 5.00
75 Dwyane Wade 4.00 10.00
76 Alonzo Mourning 2.50 6.00
77 Tim Hardaway 2.00 5.00
78 Chris Paul 3.00 8.00
79 David West 2.00 5.00
80 Larry Johnson 2.00 5.00
81 Al Jefferson 2.00 5.00
82 Corey Brewer 1.50 4.00
83 Dwight Howard 4.00 10.00
84 Hedo Turkoglu 2.00 5.00
85 Nick Anderson 2.00 5.00
86 Rudy Gay 2.00 5.00
87 Hakim Warrick 1.50 4.00
88 Mike Conley Jr. 1.50 4.00
89 Chris Bosh 2.00 5.00
90 Jermaine O'Neal 2.00 5.00
91 Jose Calderon 1.50 4.00
92 Emeka Okafor 2.00 5.00
93 Gerald Wallace 2.00 5.00
94 Raymond Felton 1.50 4.00
95 Courtney Lee RC 4.00 10.00
96 Chris Douglas-Roberts RC 2.50 6.00
97 Patrick Ewing Jr. RC 2.50 6.00
98 Alexis Ajinca RC 2.50 6.00
99 Bill Walker RC 2.50 6.00
100 Sonny Weems RC 2.50 6.00
101 Derrick Rose JSY AU RC 200.00 400.00
102 Michael Beasley JSY AU RC 15.00 40.00
103 O.J. Mayo JSY AU RC 15.00 40.00
104 Russell Westbrook JSY AU RC 50.00 125.00
105 Kevin Love JSY AU RC 50.00 120.00
106 Patrick Ewing Jr. JSY AU RC 5.00 12.00
107 Eric Gordon JSY AU RC 20.00 50.00
108 Joe Alexander JSY AU RC 5.00 12.00
109 D. J. Augustin JSY AU RC 5.00 12.00
110 Brook Lopez JSY AU RC 8.00 20.00
111 Jerryd Bayless JSY AU RC 5.00 12.00
112 Jason Thompson JSY AU RC 5.00 12.00
113 Brandon Rush JSY AU RC 5.00 12.00
114 Anthony Randolph JSY AU RC 6.00 15.00
115 Robin Lopez JSY AU RC 5.00 12.00
116 Marreese Speights JSY AU RC 5.00 12.00
117 Chris Douglas-Roberts JSY AU RC5.00 12.00
118 Javale McGee JSY AU RC 8.00 20.00
119 J.J. Hickson JSY AU RC 6.00 15.00
120 Ryan Anderson JSY AU RC 8.00 20.00
121 Kosta Koufos JSY AU RC 5.00 12.00
122 George Hill JSY AU RC 8.00 20.00
123 Darrell Arthur JSY AU RC 5.00 12.00
124 Donte Greene JSY AU RC 5.00 12.00
125 Sonny Weems JSY AU RC 5.00 12.00
126 J.R. Giddens JSY AU RC 5.00 12.00
127 Walter Sharpe JSY AU RC 5.00 12.00
128 Joey Dorsey JSY AU RC 5.00 12.00
129 Mario Chalmers JSY AU RC 10.00 25.00
130 DeAndre Jordan JSY AU RC 10.00 25.00

2008-09 Upper Deck Premier Attractions Autographs Jerseys

STATED PRINT RUN 25 SER.#'d SETS
ATAD Adrian Dantley 8.00 20.00
ATAH Al Horford 8.00 20.00
ATAJ Al Jefferson 6.00 15.00
ATAM Louis Amundson 6.00 15.00
ATBG Ben Gordon 10.00 25.00
ATBR Brandon Roy 15.00 30.00
ATBY Andrew Bynum 15.00 40.00
ATCB Carlos Boozer 6.00 15.00
ATCL Carl Landry 6.00 15.00
ATJA Antawn Jamison 6.00 15.00
ATJB Josh Boone 6.00 15.00
ATJE Julius Erving 35.00 75.00
ATJF Jordan Farmar 8.00 20.00
ATJO Michael Jordan 300.00 600.00
ATKB Kobe Bryant 200.00 350.00
ATKD Kevin Durant 125.00 250.00
ATLA LaMarcus Aldridge 10.00 25.00
ATLB Larry Bird 50.00 120.00
ATLJ LeBron James 150.00 300.00
ATMP Mark Price 25.00 60.00
ATMR Micheal Ray Richardson 6.00 15.00
ATPP Paul Pierce 20.00 40.00
ATRB Renaldo Balkman 6.00 15.00
ATRG Rudy Gay 8.00 20.00
ATRJ Richard Jefferson 6.00 15.00
ATRP Robert Parish 10.00 25.00
ATSA Stacey Augmon 6.00 15.00
ATSV Sasha Vujacic 10.00 25.00
ATSW Sean Williams 6.00 15.00
ATTC Tom Chambers 6.00 15.00
ATWE Spud Webb 12.50 30.00

2008-09 Upper Deck Premier Classmates Autographs

STATED PRINT RUN 50 SER.#'d SETS
CLASS01 Tony Parker 15.00 30.00
Richard Jefferson
CLASS03 David West 8.00 20.00
Luke Walton
CLASS04 Dwight Howard 15.00 40.00
Emeka Okafor
CLASS07 Kevin Durant 50.00 120.00
Al Horford
CLASS70 Bob Lanier 15.00 30.00
Rudy Tomjanovich
CLASS86 John Salley 25.00 50.00
Mark Price
CLASS87 Kenny Smith 15.00 30.00
Muggsy Bogues
CLASS88 Tito Horford 8.00 20.00
Steve Kerr

2008-09 Upper Deck Premier Consumate Masters Autographs

STATED PRINT RUN 15 SER.#'d SETS
UNPRICED SILVER PRINT RUN ONE SET
CMBP Bob Pettit 20.00 40.00
CMBR Bill Russell 125.00 250.00
CMCA Adrian Dantley 15.00 30.00
CMCP Chris Paul 50.00 100.00
CMDH Dwight Howard 30.00 60.00
CMDR Dennis Rodman 40.00 100.00
CMGR Glen Rice 15.00 30.00
CMHO Hakeem Olajuwon 25.00 50.00
CMJK Jason Kidd 30.00 60.00
CMJO Michael Jordan 450.00 650.00
CMJS John Stockton 50.00 125.00
CMKB Kobe Bryant 200.00 400.00
CMLJ LeBron James 200.00 400.00
CMMB Muggsy Bogues 15.00 30.00
CMMJ Magic Johnson 50.00 100.00
CMMR Micheal Ray Richardson 15.00 30.00

2008-09 Upper Deck Premier Foursome Autographs

STATED PRINT RUN 10 SER.#'d SETS
P4BOJA Kobe Bryant 250.00 500.00
Lamar Odom
Magic Johnson
Kareem Abdul-Jabbar
P4BWWH Mike Bibby 100.00 200.00
Spud Webb
Dominique Wilkins
Al Horford
P4PGBP Paul Pierce 200.00 400.00
Kevin Garnett
Larry Bird
Robert Parish
P4WBPJ David West 150.00 300.00
Muggsy Bogues
Chris Paul
Larry Johnson

2008-09 Upper Deck Premier Franchise Faces Autographs

STATED PRINT RUN 25 TO 50 SER.#'d SETS
UNPRICED SILVER PRINT RUN ONE SET
FFAD Adrian Dantley/50 8.00 20.00
FFAH Al Horford/25 6.00 15.00
FFAM Alonzo Mourning/25 30.00 60.00
FFCW Chet Walker/25 6.00 15.00
FFGI Artis Gilmore/50 8.00 20.00
FFJO Michael Jordan/25 300.00 450.00
FFKB Kobe Bryant/25 175.00 300.00
FFKD Kevin Durant/25 125.00 250.00
FFKG Kevin Garnett/25 50.00 125.00
FFLJ LeBron James/25 175.00 300.00
FFSW Spud Webb/25 6.00 15.00
FFTP Tony Parker/25 8.00 20.00
FFWF Walt Frazier/25 10.00 25.00

2008-09 Upper Deck Premier Head to Head Autographs Jerseys

STATED PRINT RUN 25 SER.#'d SETS
H2HBJ LeBron James 300.00 600.00
Kobe Bryant
H2HBK Andrew Bynum 20.00 40.00
Chris Kaman
H2HGB Rudy Gay 15.00 30.00
Shane Battier
H2HHH Dwight Howard 25.00 50.00
Al Horford
H2HJA Al Jefferson 20.00 40.00
LaMarcus Aldridge
H2HMC Tyson Chandler 15.00 30.00
Brad Miller
H2HWB Luke Walton 15.00 30.00
Bruce Bowen

2008-09 Upper Deck Premier Impressions Autographs

STATED PRINT RUN 50 SER.#'d SETS
UNPRICED SILVER PRINT RUN ONE SET
PIAA Alexis Ajinca 5.00 12.00
PIAR Anthony Randolph 6.00 15.00
PIBL Brook Lopez 8.00 20.00
PIBR Brandon Rush 5.00 12.00
PIDG Danilo Gallinari 12.50 30.00
PIDW D.J. White 5.00 12.00
PIGH George Hill 8.00 20.00
PIJA Joe Alexander 5.00 12.00

PIJB Jerryd Bayless 5.00 12.00
PIJH J.J. Hickson 6.00 15.00
PIJM Javale McGee 8.00 20.00
PIJT Jason Thompson 5.00 12.00
PIMC Mario Chalmers 8.00 20.00
PIMS Marreese Speights 5.00 12.00
PIRA Ryan Anderson 8.00 20.00
PIRH Roy Hibbert 8.00 20.00
PIRL Robin Lopez 5.00 12.00
PIRW Russell Westbrook 50.00 125.00

2008-09 Upper Deck Premier Pairings Autographs

STATED PRINT RUN 25 SER.#'d SETS
P2AR LaMarcus Aldridge 30.00 60.00
Brandon Roy
P2DJ LeBron James 300.00 500.00
Kevin Durant
P2FR Walt Frazier 15.00 30.00
Micheal Ray Richardson
P2GB Kobe Bryant 225.00 325.00
Kevin Garnett
P2GC Rudy Gay 15.00 30.00
Mike Conley Jr.
P2HH Al Horford 10.00 25.00
Tito Horford
P2JJ Michael Jordan 450.00 750.00
LeBron James
P2JW Antawn Jamison 10.00 25.00
David West
P2ML Muggsy Bogues 75.00 200.00
Larry Johnson
P2PA Ray Allen 50.00 120.00
Paul Pierce
P2PS John Salley 15.00 30.00
Tayshaun Prince
P2SD Kenny Smith 20.00 40.00
Clyde Drexler
P2SV J.R. Smith 10.00 25.00
Sasha Vujacic

2008-09 Upper Deck Premier Penmanship Autographs

STATED PRINT RUN 50 SER.#'d SETS
UNPRICED SILVER PRINT RUN ONE SET
PENAE Alex English 5.00 12.00
PENAH Al Harrington 5.00 12.00
PENBD Bob Dandridge 8.00 20.00
PENBL Bob Lanier 6.00 15.00
PENBM Brad Miller 5.00 12.00
PENCH Cliff Hagan 8.00 20.00
PENCK Chris Kaman 5.00 12.00
PENDA Brad Daugherty 5.00 12.00
PENDF Derek Fisher 6.00 15.00
PENDO Don Ohl 8.00 20.00
PENDR Dennis Rodman 40.00 70.00
PENDV Dick Van Arsdale 6.00 15.00
PENEM Ed Macauley 20.00 40.00
PENGI Artis Gilmore 10.00 25.00
PENGR Glen Rice 20.00 40.00
PENHO Tito Horford 5.00 12.00
PENJP Jim Paxson 6.00 15.00
PENKB Kobe Bryant 150.00 275.00
PENLH Lou Hudson 5.00 12.00
PENPA John Paxson 10.00 25.00
PENPF Phil Ford 6.00 15.00
PENRG Richie Guerin 5.00 12.00
PENRH Rod Hundley 20.00 40.00
PENRS Ralph Sampson 6.00 15.00
PENSJ Sam Jones 15.00 30.00
PENSM Slater Martin 10.00 25.00
PENTC Terry Cummings 6.00 15.00
PENTD Terry Dischinger 8.00 20.00
PENTR Tree Rollins 6.00 15.00

2008-09 Upper Deck Premier Preeminence Autographs

STATED PRINT RUN 25 SER.#'d SETS
UNPRICED SILVER PRINT RUN ONE SET
PEAB Andrew Bynum 20.00 40.00
PEAD Adrian Dantley 6.00 15.00
PEAG Artis Gilmore 8.00 20.00
PEAH Al Horford 6.00 15.00
PEAJ Al Jefferson 6.00 15.00
PEAL Joe Alexander 6.00 15.00
PEAT Al Thornton 6.00 15.00
PEBA B.J. Armstrong 8.00 20.00
PEBR Brandon Roy 25.00 50.00
PECW Chet Walker 6.00 15.00
PEDC Daequan Cook 6.00 15.00
PEDW David West 6.00 15.00
PEEG Eric Gordon 20.00 50.00
PEJA Antawn Jamison 6.00 15.00
PEJO Michael Jordan 300.00 550.00
PEKB Kobe Bryant 125.00 250.00
PEKD Kevin Durant 50.00 125.00
PEKG Kevin Garnett 50.00 120.00
PELE LeBron James 150.00 300.00
PELJ Larry Johnson 30.00 60.00
PELW Luke Walton 10.00 25.00
PEMP Mark Price 35.00 70.00
PEMR Micheal Ray Richardson 6.00 15.00
PEPM Paul Millsap 6.00 15.00
PERG Rudy Gay 6.00 15.00
PERJ Richard Jefferson 6.00 15.00
PERS Ramon Sessions 6.00 15.00
PERU Brandon Rush 6.00 15.00
PESK Steve Kerr 10.00 25.00
PESV Sasha Vujacic 8.00 20.00
PESW Spud Webb 8.00 20.00
PETK Toni Kukoc 20.00 40.00
PETP Tayshaun Prince 8.00 20.00

2008-09 Upper Deck Premier Rare Patch Dual

STATED PRINT RUN 15 TO 50 SER.#'d SETS
RP2AW LeBron James/50 30.00 80.00
Carmelo Anthony
RP2BD Kobe Bryant/50 25.00 60.00
Kevin Durant
RP2BJ LeBron James/50 45.00 90.00
Kobe Bryant
RP2CM Kevin Martin/40 10.00 25.00
Vince Carter
RP2DO Shaquille O'Neal/50 20.00 40.00
Tim Duncan
RP2EW Brandan Wright/50 8.00 20.00
Monta Ellis
RP2GG Kevin Garnett/50 15.00 30.00
Pau Gasol
RP2GN Dirk Nowitzki/50 25.00 50.00
Kevin Garnett
RP2GT Ben Gordon/50 8.00 20.00
Tyrus Thomas
RP2HW Grant Hill/50 25.00 60.00
Luke Walton
RP2IA Allen Iverson/50 15.00 30.00
Carmelo Anthony
RP2IB Andre Iguodala/50 8.00 20.00
Corey Brewer
RP2JA LaMarcus Aldridge/50 8.00 20.00
Al Jefferson
RP2JD Kevin Durant/50 30.00 60.00
LeBron James
RP2LM Rashard Lewis/15 15.00 30.00
Shawn Marion
RP2MB Andrew Bogut/50 8.00 20.00
Desmond Mason
RP2MP Pau Gasol/50 10.00 25.00
Manu Ginobili
RP2MS Alonzo Mourning/50 15.00 30.00
Amare Stoudemire
RP2NG Jeff Green/50 8.00 20.00
Joakim Noah
RP2NP Steve Nash/30 20.00 40.00
Chris Paul
RP2PA Paul Pierce/50 15.00 30.00
Ray Allen
RP2RB Andrew Bogut/50 8.00 20.00
Michael Redd
RP2RC Quentin Richardson/50 8.00 20.00
Eddy Curry
RP2SH Amare Stoudemire/50 15.00 30.00
Dwight Howard
RP2TH Jason Terry/50 8.00 20.00
Josh Howard
RP2WJ Kevin Garnett/50 30.00 60.00
LeBron James
RP2YW Brandan Wright/50 8.00 20.00
Thaddeus Young

2008-09 Upper Deck Premier Rare Patch Rookies Dual

STATED PRINT RUN 25 SER.#'d SETS
R2RAG Eric Gordon 10.00 25.00
D.J. Augustin
R2RAK Kosta Koufos 6.00 15.00
Darrell Arthur
R2RAL Ryan Anderson 15.00 40.00
Courtney Lee
R2RBL Michael Beasley 10.00 25.00
Kevin Love
R2RBR Derrick Rose 25.00 50.00
Michael Beasley
R2RDS Walter Sharpe 6.00 15.00
Joey Dorsey
R2RDW Kyle Weaver 8.00 20.00
Chris Douglas-Roberts
R2RGB Eric Gordon 10.00 25.00
Jerryd Bayless
R2RGH George Hill 8.00 20.00
Donte Greene
R2RJE DeAndre Jordan 6.00 15.00
Patrick Ewing Jr.
R2RLL Brook Lopez 10.00 25.00
Robin Lopez
R2RMR Derrick Rose 20.00 50.00
O.J. Mayo
R2RRT Jason Thompson 10.00 25.00
Anthony Randolph

2008-09 Upper Deck Premier Rare Patch Rookies Triple

STATED PRINT RUN 15 SER.#'d SETS
R3RABJ Michael Beasley 20.00 40.00
D.J. Augustin
DeAndre Jordan
R3RABM Michael Beasley 10.00 25.00
D.J. Augustin
Javale McGee
R3RARB D.J. Augustin 8.00 20.00
Jerryd Bayless
Brandon Rush
R3RBLK Kevin Love 8.00 20.00
Jerryd Bayless
Kosta Koufos
R3RBWW Jerryd Bayless 8.00 20.00
Kyle Weaver
Sonny Weems
R3RGEA Joe Alexander 8.00 20.00
Donte Greene
Patrick Ewing Jr.
R3RGGT Jason Thompson 8.00 20.00
Eric Gordon
Donte Greene
R3RGLA Kevin Love 15.00 40.00
Eric Gordon
Joe Alexander
R3RHAS Joe Alexander 8.00 20.00
J.J. Hickson
Walter Sharpe
R3RLDA Brook Lopez 8.00 20.00
Ryan Anderson
Chris Douglas-Roberts
R3RMBL O.J. Mayo 10.00 25.00
Kevin Love
Jerryd Bayless
R3RMBR Derrick Rose 30.00 60.00
Michael Beasley
O.J. Mayo
R3RMEH O.J. Mayo 10.00 25.00
George Hill
Patrick Ewing Jr.
R3RRAC Brandon Rush 10.00 25.00
Darrell Arthur
Mario Chalmers
R3RRDD Derrick Rose 25.00 50.00
Joey Dorsey
Chris Douglas-Roberts
R3RRDS Derrick Rose 20.00 40.00
Walter Sharpe
Joey Dorsey
R3RRLT Brook Lopez 15.00 30.00
Jason Thompson
Anthony Randolph
R3RRWS Marreese Speights 15.00 30.00
Anthony Randolph
Sonny Weems
R3RWAL Robin Lopez 10.00 25.00
Ryan Anderson
Kyle Weaver

2008-09 Upper Deck Premier Rare Patch Triple

STATED PRINT RUN 10 TO 15 SER.#'d SETS
RPTBGJ LeBron James 80.00 160.00
Kobe Bryant
Kevin Garnett
RPTBOG Kobe Bryant 40.00 80.00
Pau Gasol
Lamar Odom
RPTDGR Tim Duncan 60.00 120.00
Manu Ginobili
David Robinson
RPTDLT Isiah Thomas 30.00 60.00
Bill Laimbeer
Joe Dumars
RPTHDG Kirk Hinrich 15.00 30.00
Luol Deng
Ben Gordon
RPTHMS John Stockton 40.00 80.00
Karl Malone
Jeff Hornacek
RPTIMA Allen Iverson 20.00 50.00
Carmelo Anthony
Kenyon Martin
RPTJAW Chris Bosh/10 40.00 80.00
Carmelo Anthony
LeBron James
RPTJBJ LeBron James 125.00 250.00
Michael Jordan
Kobe Bryant
RPTJPR Michael Jordan 225.00 325.00
Scottie Pippen
Dennis Rodman
RPTKNH Dirk Nowitzki 15.00 30.00
Josh Howard
Jason Kidd
RPTNDH Kevin Durant 20.00 50.00
Al Horford
Joakim Noah
RPTNSO Amare Stoudemire 60.00 120.00
Shaquille O'Neal
Steve Nash
RPTPAG Ray Allen 60.00 120.00
Kevin Garnett
Paul Pierce
RPTWJG Zydrunas Ilgauskas 30.00 80.00
LeBron James
Daniel Gibson
RPTWMW Dominique Wilkins 15.00 30.00
Spud Webb
Moses Malone

2008-09 Upper Deck Premier Rare Remnants Quad Patch

STATED PRINT RUN 5 TO 25 SER.#'d SETS
UNPRICED UD LOGO PRINT RUN 10 SETS
RR4AJ LeBron James/25 25.00 50.00
Carmelo Anthony
RR4BD Kobe Bryant/25 30.00 80.00
Kevin Durant
RR4BF Carlos Boozer/25 8.00 20.00
Channing Frye
RR4BJ LeBron James/25 60.00 120.00
Kobe Bryant
RR4BK Andrei Kirilenko/25 6.00 15.00
Shane Battier
RR4CM Kevin Martin/25 15.00 30.00
Vince Carter
RR4DD Jermareo Davidson/25 6.00 15.00
Jared Dudley
RR4GG Kevin Garnett/25 15.00 30.00
Pau Gasol
RR4GN Dirk Nowitzki/25 30.00 60.00
Kevin Garnett
RR4GT Ben Gordon/25 8.00 20.00
Tyrus Thomas
RR4HD Kirk Hinrich/25 6.00 15.00
Luol Deng
RR4HW Grant Hill/15 60.00 120.00
Luke Walton
RR4IA Allen Iverson/25 15.00 30.00
Carmelo Anthony
RR4IB Andre Iguodala/25 6.00 15.00
Corey Brewer
RR4JD Kevin Durant/25 25.00 60.00
LeBron James
RR4JS Joe Johnson/25 8.00 20.00
Josh Smith
RR4KP Tony Parker/25 10.00 25.00
Jason Kidd
RR4LM Rashard Lewis/25 10.00 25.00
Shawn Marion
RR4MB Andrew Bogut/25 6.00 15.00
Desmond Mason
RR4MH Dikembe Mutombo/25 40.00 75.00
Dwight Howard
RR4MS Alonzo Mourning/25 20.00 40.00
Amare Stoudemire
RR4MW Corey Maggette/25 6.00 15.00
Brandan Wright
RR4NP Steve Nash/25 20.00 40.00
Chris Paul
RR4NS Jason Smith/25 10.00 25.00
Joakim Noah
RR4PA Paul Pierce/25 15.00 30.00
Ray Allen
RR4PM Pau Gasol/25 15.00 30.00
Manu Ginobili
RR4RC Quentin Richardson/25 6.00 15.00
Eddy Curry
RR4TH Jason Terry/25 6.00 15.00
Josh Howard
RR4WM Kenyon Martin/25 6.00 15.00
Rasheed Wallace
RR4YW Brandan Wright/25 6.00 15.00
Thaddeus Young

2008-09 Upper Deck Premier Rare Remnants Triple Patch

STATED PRINT RUN 35 TO 50 SER.#'d SETS
RR3AI Allen Iverson 8.00 20.00
RR3AJ Al Jefferson 6.00 15.00
RR3AK Andrei Kirilenko 5.00 12.00
RR3BG Ben Gordon 6.00 15.00
RR3BR Brandon Roy 6.00 15.00
RR3BU Caron Butler 6.00 15.00
RR3BW Brandan Wright 5.00 12.00
RR3CB Carlos Boozer/35 6.00 15.00
RR3CM Corey Maggette 5.00 12.00
RR3DG Danny Granger 6.00 15.00
RR3DM Dikembe Mutombo 8.00 20.00
RR3DN Dirk Nowitzki 8.00 20.00
RR3EB Elton Brand 6.00 15.00
RR3GH Grant Hill 20.00 40.00
RR3IG Andre Iguodala 6.00 15.00
RR3JA Antawn Jamison 6.00 15.00
RR3JK Jason Kidd 6.00 15.00
RR3JN Joakim Noah 6.00 15.00
RR3JT Jason Terry 5.00 12.00
RR3KA Kelenna Azubuike 4.00 10.00
RR3KB Kobe Bryant 25.00 50.00
RR3KD Kevin Durant 15.00 40.00
RR3KG Kevin Garnett 12.00 30.00
RR3KH Kirk Hinrich 6.00 15.00
RR3KK Kyle Korver 5.00 12.00
RR3KM Kenyon Martin 6.00 15.00
RR3LD Luol Deng 6.00 15.00
RR3LJ LeBron James 25.00 50.00
RR3LW Luke Walton 4.00 10.00
RR3MA Kevin Martin 6.00 15.00
RR3MC Mike Conley Jr. 5.00 12.00
RR3MG Manu Ginobili 6.00 15.00
RR3MR Michael Redd 6.00 15.00
RR3PG Pau Gasol 6.00 15.00
RR3PS Peja Stojakovic 6.00 15.00
RR3RA Ray Allen 6.00 15.00
RR3RL Rashard Lewis 5.00 12.00
RR3RW Rasheed Wallace 6.00 15.00
RR3SM Shawn Marion 6.00 15.00
RR3SN Steve Nash 6.00 15.00
RR3SO Shaquille O'Neal 12.00 30.00
RR3TD Tim Duncan 10.00 25.00
RR3TM Tracy McGrady 6.00 15.00
RR3VC Vince Carter 8.00 20.00

2008-09 Upper Deck Premier Rare Remnants Triple Patch NBA Logo

*NBA LOGO: .5X TO 1.25X BASE HI
STATED PRINT RUN 25 SER.#'d SETS
RR3AB Andrea Bargnani 6.00 15.00
RR3AH Al Harrington 6.00 15.00
RR3AS Amare Stoudemire 8.00 20.00
RR3CA Carmelo Anthony 10.00 25.00
RR3DH Dwight Howard 15.00 40.00
RR3GH Grant Hill 40.00 80.00
RR3GI Daniel Gibson 8.00 20.00
RR3JH Josh Howard 6.00 15.00
RR3JJ Joe Johnson 8.00 20.00
RR3JR Jason Richardson 8.00 20.00
RR3PP Paul Pierce 10.00 25.00
RR3SB Shane Battier 6.00 15.00
RR3TT Tyrus Thomas 6.00 15.00

2008-09 Upper Deck Premier Remnants Quad

STATED PRINT RUN 50 SER.#'d SETS
*CONFERENCE: .4X TO 1X BASE HI
CONFERENCE PRINT RUN 25 SETS
UNPRICED INITIAL PRINT RUN 10 SETS
PR4AR Andrew Bogut 4.00 10.00
Richard Jefferson
PR4BD Kobe Bryant 25.00 60.00
Kevin Durant
PR4BF Carlos Boozer 4.00 10.00
Channing Frye
PR4BJ LeBron James 30.00 60.00
Kobe Bryant
PR4BP Chauncey Billups 6.00 15.00
Chris Paul
PR4BW Josh Boone 4.00 10.00
Sean Williams
PR4DB Baron Davis 4.00 10.00
Chauncey Billups
PR4DD Jermareo Davidson 4.00 10.00
Jared Dudley
PR4EC Vince Carter 10.00 25.00
Julius Erving
PR4FB Andrew Bynum 10.00 25.00
Jordan Farmar
PR4FR Walt Frazier 5.00 12.00
Micheal Ray Richardson
PR4GC Rudy Gay 4.00 10.00
Mike Conley Jr.
PR4GT Ben Gordon 4.00 10.00
Tyrus Thomas
PR4HH Dwight Howard 5.00 12.00
Al Horford
PR4HL Acie Law 4.00 10.00
(Al Horford
PR4IB Andre Iguodala 4.00 10.00
Corey Brewer
PR4JA LaMarcus Aldridge 4.00 10.00
Al Jefferson
PR4JB Michael Jordan 40.00 80.00
Kobe Bryant
PR4JD Kevin Durant 20.00 40.00
LeBron James
PR4JH Antawn Jamison 4.00 10.00
Al Harrington
PR4JR Oscar Robertson 25.00 60.00
Michael Jordan
PR4KW Bill Walton 4.00 10.00
Chris Kaman
PR4LB Carl Landry 6.00 15.00
Aaron Brooks
PR4LM Rashard Lewis 4.00 10.00
Shawn Marion
PR4MA Tracy McGrady 6.00 15.00
Carmelo Anthony
PR4MG Chris Mullin 4.00 10.00
Daniel Gibson
PR4ML Magic Johnson 25.00 50.00
Larry Bird
PR4MO Yao Ming 5.00 12.00
Emeka Okafor
PR4MS Alonzo Mourning 8.00 20.00
Amare Stoudemire
PR4MT Corey Maggette 4.00 10.00
Al Thornton
PR4ND Glen Davis 6.00 15.00
Joakim Noah
PR4NK Steve Nash 10.00 25.00
Jason Kidd
PR4NP Steve Nash 10.00 25.00
Chris Paul
PR4PA Paul Pierce 10.00 25.00
Ray Allen
PR4RC Quentin Richardson 4.00 10.00
Eddy Curry
PR4RJ Oscar Robertson 25.00 50.00
LeBron James
PR4RM Dennis Rodman 6.00 15.00
Moses Malone
PR4WG Darrell Griffith 4.00 10.00
Deron Williams
PR4WR Brandon Roy 6.00 15.00
Deron Williams

2008-09 Upper Deck Premier Remnants Triple

STATED PRINT RUN 99 SER.#'d SETS
PR3AB Andrew Bynum 4.00 10.00
PR3AM Alonzo Mourning 5.00 12.00
PR3AS Amare Stoudemire 3.00 8.00
PR3AT Al Thornton 2.50 6.00
PR3BD Baron Davis 3.00 8.00
PR3BR Brandon Roy 3.00 8.00
PR3CA Carmelo Anthony 4.00 10.00
PR3CB Chauncey Billups 3.00 8.00
PR3CM Corey Maggette 2.50 6.00
PR3CP Chris Paul 5.00 12.00
PR3DG Darrell Griffith 3.00 8.00
PR3DH Dwight Howard 6.00 15.00
PR3DR Dennis Rodman 6.00 15.00
PR3DW Deron Williams 3.00 8.00
PR3HO Hakeem Olajuwon 6.00 15.00
PR3JE Julius Erving 6.00 15.00
PR3JK Jason Kidd 3.00 8.00
PR3JO Michael Jordan 30.00 80.00
PR3KB Kobe Bryant 15.00 40.00
PR3KD Kevin Durant 12.00 30.00
PR3KG Kevin Garnett 6.00 15.00
PR3LB Larry Bird/89 10.00 25.00
PR3LJ LeBron James 15.00 40.00
PR3MJ Magic Johnson 8.00 20.00
PR3MU Chris Mullin 3.00 8.00
PR3ON Jermaine O'Neal 3.00 8.00
PR3OR Oscar Robertson 6.00 15.00
PR3PE Patrick Ewing 6.00 15.00
PR3PP Paul Pierce 4.00 10.00
PR3RA Ray Allen 3.00 8.00
PR3RJ Richard Jefferson 3.00 8.00
PR3RR Rajon Rondo 4.00 10.00
PR3SM Shawn Marion 3.00 8.00
PR3SN Steve Nash 3.00 8.00
PR3TM Tracy McGrady 3.00 8.00
PR3VC Vince Carter 4.00 10.00
PR3WF Walt Frazier 3.00 8.00
PR3YM Yao Ming 4.00 10.00

2008-09 Upper Deck Premier Remnants Triple City

STATED PRINT RUN 50 SER.#'d SETS
PR3AB Andrew Bynum 5.00 12.00
PR3AH Al Horford 4.00 10.00
PR3AI Andre Iguodala 4.00 10.00
PR3AJ Antawn Jamison 4.00 10.00
PR3AL Acie Law 3.00 8.00
PR3AM Alonzo Mourning 6.00 15.00
PR3AS Amare Stoudemire 4.00 10.00
PR3AT Al Thornton 3.00 8.00
PR3BD Baron Davis 4.00 10.00
PR3BG Ben Gordon 4.00 10.00
PR3BO Carlos Boozer 4.00 10.00
PR3BR Brandon Roy 4.00 10.00
PR3CA Carmelo Anthony 5.00 12.00
PR3CB Chauncey Billups 4.00 10.00
PR3CL Carl Landry 2.50 6.00
PR3CM Corey Maggette 3.00 8.00
PR3CP Chris Paul 6.00 15.00
PR3DG Darrell Griffith 4.00 10.00
PR3DH Dwight Howard 8.00 20.00
PR3DR Dennis Rodman 8.00 20.00
PR3DW Deron Williams 4.00 10.00
PR3HO Hakeem Olajuwon 8.00 20.00
PR3JE Julius Erving 8.00 20.00
PR3JF Al Jefferson 4.00 10.00
PR3JK Jason Kidd 4.00 10.00
PR3JO Michael Jordan 40.00 100.00
PR3KB Kobe Bryant 20.00 50.00
PR3KD Kevin Durant 15.00 40.00
PR3KG Kevin Garnett 8.00 20.00
PR3LA LaMarcus Aldridge 4.00 10.00
PR3LB Larry Bird 12.00 30.00
PR3LJ LeBron James 20.00 50.00
PR3MC Mike Conley Jr. 3.00 8.00
PR3MJ Magic Johnson 10.00 25.00
PR3MU Chris Mullin 4.00 10.00
PR3ON Jermaine O'Neal 4.00 10.00
PR3OR Oscar Robertson 8.00 20.00
PR3PE Patrick Ewing 8.00 20.00
PR3PP Paul Pierce 5.00 12.00
PR3QR Quentin Richardson 3.00 8.00
PR3RA Ray Allen 5.00 12.00
PR3RG Rudy Gay 4.00 10.00
PR3RJ Richard Jefferson 4.00 10.00
PR3RR Rajon Rondo 5.00 12.00
PR3SM Shawn Marion 4.00 10.00
PR3SN Steve Nash 4.00 10.00
PR3TM Tracy McGrady 4.00 10.00
PR3VC Vince Carter 5.00 12.00
PR3WF Walt Frazier 4.00 10.00
PR3YM Yao Ming 5.00 12.00

2008-09 Upper Deck Premier Remnants Triple Position

PRINT RUN 25 SER.#'d SETS
PR3AB Andrew Bynum 6.00 15.00
PR3AH Al Horford 5.00 12.00
PR3AI Andre Iguodala 5.00 12.00
PR3AJ Antawn Jamison 5.00 12.00
PR3AL Acie Law 4.00 10.00
PR3AM Alonzo Mourning 15.00 30.00
PR3AS Amare Stoudemire 5.00 12.00
PR3AT Al Thornton 4.00 10.00
PR3BD Baron Davis 5.00 12.00
PR3BG Ben Gordon 5.00 12.00
PR3BO Carlos Boozer 5.00 12.00
PR3BR Brandon Roy 5.00 12.00
PR3CA Carmelo Anthony 6.00 15.00
PR3CB Chauncey Billups 5.00 12.00
PR3CL Carl Landry 3.00 8.00
PR3CM Corey Maggette 4.00 10.00
PR3CP Chris Paul 8.00 20.00
PR3DG Darrell Griffith 5.00 12.00
PR3DH Dwight Howard 10.00 25.00
PR3DR Dennis Rodman 12.00 30.00
PR3DW Deron Williams 5.00 12.00
PR3HO Hakeem Olajuwon 10.00 25.00
PR3JE Julius Erving 10.00 25.00
PR3JF Al Jefferson 5.00 12.00
PR3JK Jason Kidd 5.00 12.00
PR3JO Michael Jordan 60.00 150.00
PR3KB Kobe Bryant 25.00 60.00
PR3KD Kevin Durant 20.00 50.00
PR3KG Kevin Garnett 10.00 25.00
PR3LA LaMarcus Aldridge 5.00 12.00
PR3LB Larry Bird 15.00 40.00
PR3LJ LeBron James 25.00 60.00
PR3MC Mike Conley Jr. 4.00 10.00
PR3MJ Magic Johnson 12.00 30.00
PR3MU Chris Mullin 5.00 12.00
PR3ON Jermaine O'Neal 5.00 12.00
PR3OR Oscar Robertson 10.00 25.00
PR3PE Patrick Ewing 10.00 25.00
PR3PP Paul Pierce 6.00 15.00
PR3QR Quentin Richardson 4.00 10.00
PR3RA Ray Allen 5.00 12.00
PR3RG Rudy Gay 5.00 12.00
PR3RJ Richard Jefferson 5.00 12.00
PR3RR Rajon Rondo 6.00 15.00
PR3SM Shawn Marion 5.00 12.00
PR3SN Steve Nash 5.00 12.00
PR3TM Tracy McGrady 5.00 12.00
PR3VC Vince Carter 6.00 15.00
PR3WF Walt Frazier 5.00 12.00
PR3YM Yao Ming 6.00 15.00

2008-09 Upper Deck Premier Rookies Autographs Jerseys 75

STATED PRINT RUN 75 SER.#'d SETS
UNPRICED JERSEY 15 PRINT RUN 15 SETS
UNPRICED JERSEY 1 PRINT RUN ONE SET
101 Derrick Rose 225.00 450.00
102 Michael Beasley 20.00 50.00
103 O.J. Mayo 20.00 50.00
104 Russell Westbrook 50.00 125.00
105 Kevin Love 50.00 120.00
106 Patrick Ewing Jr. 5.00 12.00
107 Eric Gordon 20.00 50.00
108 Joe Alexander 5.00 12.00
109 D.J. Augustin 5.00 12.00
110 Brook Lopez 8.00 20.00
111 Jerryd Bayless 5.00 12.00
112 Jason Thompson 5.00 12.00
113 Brandon Rush 5.00 12.00
114 Anthony Randolph 6.00 15.00
115 Robin Lopez 5.00 12.00
116 Marreese Speights 5.00 12.00
117 Chris Douglas-Roberts 5.00 12.00
118 Javale McGee 8.00 20.00
119 J.J. Hickson 6.00 15.00
120 Ryan Anderson 8.00 20.00
121 Kosta Koufos 5.00 12.00
122 George Hill 8.00 20.00
123 Darrell Arthur 5.00 12.00
124 Donte Greene 5.00 12.00
125 Sonny Weems 5.00 12.00
126 J.R. Giddens 5.00 12.00
127 Walter Sharpe 5.00 12.00
128 Joey Dorsey 5.00 12.00
129 Mario Chalmers 8.00 20.00
130 DeAndre Jordan 10.00 25.00

2008-09 Upper Deck Premier Stitchings

STATED PRINT RUN 50 SER.#'d SETS
*STITCH 25: .5X TO 1.25X BASE
STITCH 5 UNPRICED DUE TO SCARCITY
STITCH 1 UNPRICED DUE TO SCARCITY
AUTO 5 UNPRICED DUE TO SCARCITY
AUTO 1 UNPRICED DUE TO SCARCITY
PSAC Austin Carr 6.00 15.00
PSAH Al Horford 6.00 15.00
PSAI Allen Iverson 15.00 30.00
PSAM Alonzo Mourning 15.00 30.00
PSAS Amare Stoudemire 6.00 15.00
PSAT Al Thornton 6.00 15.00
PSBB Bill Bradley 6.00 15.00
PSBC Billy Cunningham 15.00 30.00
PSBP Bob Pettit 6.00 15.00
PSBR Bill Russell 20.00 40.00
PSBS Bill Sharman 15.00 30.00
PSBW Bill Walton 8.00 20.00
PSCA Carmelo Anthony 6.00 15.00
PSCD Clyde Drexler 10.00 25.00
PSCM Calvin Murphy 6.00 15.00
PSCO Bob Cousy 8.00 20.00
PSCP Chris Paul 6.00 15.00
PSDA D.J. Augustin 6.00 15.00
PSDB Dave Bing 10.00 25.00
PSDC Dave Cowens 10.00 25.00
PSDD Dave DeBusschere 6.00 15.00
PSDE Dennis Rodman 10.00 25.00
PSDG Darrell Griffith 6.00 15.00
PSDH Dwight Howard 10.00 25.00
PSDN Dirk Nowitzki 10.00 25.00
PSDR David Robinson 10.00 25.00
PSDS Dolph Schayes 10.00 25.00
PSDT David Thompson 10.00 25.00
PSDW Dominique Wilkins 8.00 20.00
PSEB Elgin Baylor 6.00 15.00
PSEG Eric Gordon 8.00 20.00
PSEH Elvin Hayes 6.00 15.00
PSEM Earl Monroe 12.00 30.00
PSGA Danilo Gallinari 6.00 15.00
PSGG George Gervin 8.00 20.00
PSGH Grant Hill 30.00 60.00
PSGM George Mikan 15.00 30.00
PSGO Greg Oden 6.00 15.00
PSHG Hal Greer 6.00 15.00
PSHO Hakeem Olajuwon 8.00 20.00
PSIT Isiah Thomas 6.00 15.00
PSJA LeBron James 25.00 50.00
PSJB Jerryd Bayless 6.00 15.00
PSJD Joe Dumars 8.00 20.00
PSJE Julius Erving 15.00 40.00
PSJH John Havlicek 8.00 20.00
PSJK Jason Kidd 8.00 20.00
PSJL Jerry Lucas 8.00 20.00
PSJO Michael Jordan 60.00 150.00
PSJS John Stockton 15.00 30.00
PSJW James Worthy 6.00 15.00
PSKA Kareem Abdul-Jabbar 10.00 25.00
PSKB Kobe Bryant 25.00 50.00
PSKD Kevin Durant 12.00 30.00
PSKG Kevin Garnett 15.00 30.00
PSKL Kevin Love 8.00 20.00
PSKM Karl Malone 8.00 20.00
PSLB Larry Bird 15.00 30.00
PSLJ Larry Johnson 10.00 25.00
PSLW Lenny Wilkens 6.00 15.00
PSMB Michael Beasley 8.00 20.00
PSMC Kevin McHale 10.00 25.00
PSMJ Magic Johnson 15.00 40.00
PSMM Moses Malone 6.00 15.00
PSMU Chris Mullin 6.00 15.00
PSNA Nate Archibald 10.00 25.00
PSNT Nate Thurmond 8.00 20.00
PSOA Charles Oakley 6.00 15.00
PSOM O.J. Mayo 8.00 20.00
PSOR Oscar Robertson 6.00 15.00
PSPE Patrick Ewing 10.00 25.00
PSPG Pau Gasol 10.00 25.00
PSPM Pete Maravich 50.00 100.00
PSPP Paul Pierce 15.00 30.00
PSPR Pat Riley 8.00 20.00
PSRA Ray Allen 6.00 15.00
PSRB Rick Barry 6.00 15.00
PSRD Derrick Rose 25.00 50.00
PSRO Brandon Roy 6.00 15.00
PSRP Robert Parish 8.00 20.00
PSRS Ralph Sampson 6.00 15.00
PSRW Russell Westbrook 10.00 25.00
PSSJ Sam Jones 10.00 25.00
PSSN Steve Nash 10.00 25.00
PSSO Shaquille O'Neal 15.00 30.00
PSSP Scottie Pippen 20.00 40.00
PSTD Tim Duncan 10.00 25.00
PSTM Tracy McGrady 6.00 15.00
PSVC Vince Carter 10.00 25.00
PSWA Dwyane Wade 8.00 20.00
PSWC Wilt Chamberlain 12.00 30.00
PSWE Jerry West 15.00 30.00
PSWF Walt Frazier 6.00 15.00
PSWR Willis Reed 8.00 20.00
PSWU Wes Unseld 6.00 15.00
PSR08 Derrick Rose 15.00 30.00
Michael Beasley
O.J. Mayo
PSBBOY Isiah Thomas 8.00 20.00
Dennis Rodman
Bill Laimbeer
Joe Dumars
PSBSTN Larry Bird 20.00 40.00
Bill Russell
John Havlicek
Bob Cousy
PSSHOW Magic Johnson 20.00 40.00
Kareem Abdul-Jabbar
James Worthy
Michael Cooper

2008-09 Upper Deck Premier Trios Autographs

STATED PRINT RUN 15 SER.#'d SETS
P3TD Russell Westbrook 175.00 350.00
Kevin Durant
D.J. White
P3BLA Michael Beasley 40.00 100.00
Kevin Love
Joe Alexander
P3BVB Kobe Bryant 125.00 250.00
Andrew Bynum
Sasha Vujacic
P3HDS Kevin Durant 75.00 150.00
Al Horford
Luis Scola
P3IND Brandon Rush 30.00 60.00
Danny Granger
Roy Hibbert
P3JJJ Michael Jordan 500.00 800.00
Magic Johnson
LeBron James
P3LRD Bill Laimbeer 50.00 100.00
Dennis Rodman
Adrian Dantley
P3MEM Derrick Rose 60.00 120.00
Joey Dorsey
Chris Douglas-Roberts
P3MTW Corey Brewer 30.00 60.00
Kevin Love
Al Jefferson
P3PAG Ray Allen 175.00 350.00
Kevin Garnett
Paul Pierce
P3RBM Derrick Rose 150.00 300.00
Michael Beasley
O.J. Mayo
P3SHJ Amare Stoudemire 40.00 80.00
Dwight Howard
Al Jefferson
P3WGA Russell Westbrook 60.00 150.00
Eric Gordon
D.J. Augustin
P3BLAZ Jerryd Bayless 30.00 80.00
Brandon Roy
LaMarcus Aldridge
P3GRIZ Mike Conley Jr. 40.00 80.00
O.J. Mayo
Rudy Gay
P3HEAT Michael Beasley 40.00 100.00
Mario Chalmers
Daequan Cook
P3UCLA Russell Westbrook 75.00 200.00
Kevin Love
Luc Richard Mbah A Moute

2004-05 Upper Deck Pro Sigs

Released in December 2004, this 120-card set features veteran players on cards 1-90 and rookie players on cards 91-120. This set is also referred to as Diamond Collection and is sometimes difficult to find the listing. Pro Sigs was packaged in 24-pack boxes where packs contained six cards a carried a SRP of $2.99.

COMP.SET w/o SP's 8.00 20.00
1 Antoine Walker .25 .60
2 Al Harrington .20 .50
3 Boris Diaw .20 .50
4 Paul Pierce .30 .75
5 Ricky Davis .20 .50
6 Gary Payton .25 .60
7 Jahidi White .15 .40
8 Jason Kapono .15 .40
9 Gerald Wallace .25 .60
10 Eddy Curry .20 .50
11 Kirk Hinrich .25 .60
12 Tyson Chandler .20 .50
13 LeBron James 1.50 4.00
14 Dajuan Wagner .15 .40
15 Drew Gooden .20 .50
16 Dirk Nowitzki .40 1.00
17 Michael Finley .25 .60
18 Jerry Stackhouse .20 .50
19 Carmelo Anthony .50 1.25
20 Andre Miller .20 .50
21 Kenyon Martin .25 .60
22 Chauncey Billups .25 .60
23 Rasheed Wallace .25 .60
24 Ben Wallace .25 .60
25 Derek Fisher .20 .50
26 Jason Richardson .25 .60
27 Mike Dunleavy .20 .50
28 Yao Ming .50 1.25
29 Jim Jackson .15 .40
30 Tracy McGrady .30 .75
31 Jermaine O'Neal .25 .60
32 Reggie Miller .25 .60
33 Ron Artest .25 .60
34 Elton Brand .25 .60
35 Corey Maggette .20 .50
36 Kerry Kittles .15 .40
37 Kobe Bryant 1.25 3.00
38 Chris Mihm .15 .40
39 Lamar Odom .25 .60
40 Pau Gasol .25 .60
41 Jason Williams .20 .50
42 Bonzi Wells .15 .40
43 Shaquille O'Neal .60 1.50
44 Dwyane Wade .75 2.00
45 Eddie Jones .20 .50

46 Michael Redd .25 .60
47 Desmond Mason .20 .50
48 T.J. Ford .20 .50
49 Latrell Sprewell .20 .50
50 Kevin Garnett .50 1.25
51 Sam Cassell .20 .50
52 Richard Jefferson .25 .60
53 Aaron Williams .15 .40
54 Jason Kidd .40 1.00
55 Jamal Mashburn .25 .60
56 Baron Davis .25 .60
57 Jamaal Magloire .15 .40
58 Allan Houston .20 .50
59 Jamal Crawford .20 .50
60 Stephon Marbury .20 .50
61 Cuttino Mobley .20 .50
62 Kelvin Cato .15 .40
63 Steve Francis .25 .60
64 Glenn Robinson .20 .50
65 Allen Iverson .40 1.00
66 Samuel Dalembert .15 .40
67 Amare Stoudemire .30 .75
68 Steve Nash .30 .75
69 Shawn Marion .25 .60
70 Shareef Abdur-Rahim .20 .50
71 Damon Stoudamire .20 .50
72 Zach Randolph .20 .50
73 Peja Stojakovic .25 .60
74 Chris Webber .25 .60
75 Mike Bibby .25 .60
76 Tony Parker .25 .60
77 Tim Duncan .40 1.00
78 Manu Ginobili .30 .75
79 Ronald Murray .15 .40
80 Ray Allen .25 .60
81 Rashard Lewis .25 .60
82 Chris Bosh .25 .60
83 Vince Carter .40 1.00
84 Jalen Rose .20 .50
85 Andrei Kirilenko .20 .50
86 Carlos Boozer .25 .60
87 Carlos Arroyo .20 .50
88 Gilbert Arenas .25 .60
89 Jarvis Hayes .15 .40
90 Antawn Jamison .25 .60
91 Dwight Howard RC 3.00 8.00
92 Emeka Okafor RC 1.50 4.00
93 Ben Gordon RC 1.25 3.00
94 Shaun Livingston RC 1.00 2.50
95 Devin Harris RC 1.50 4.00
96 Josh Childress RC 1.00 2.50
97 Luol Deng RC 1.50 4.00
98 Rafael Araujo RC 1.00 2.50
99 Andre Iguodala RC 1.50 4.00
100 Luke Jackson RC 1.00 2.50
101 Andris Biedrins RC 1.25 3.00
102 Robert Swift RC 1.00 2.50
103 Sebastian Telfair RC 1.00 2.50
104 Kris Humphries RC 1.00 2.50
105 Al Jefferson RC 1.50 4.00
106 Kirk Snyder RC 1.00 2.50
107 Josh Smith RC 1.50 4.00
108 J.R. Smith RC 1.25 3.00
109 Dorell Wright RC 1.50 4.00
110 Jameer Nelson RC 1.25 3.00
111 Pavel Podkolzine RC 1.00 2.50
112 Viktor Khryapa RC 1.00 2.50
113 Sergei Monia RC 1.00 2.50
114 Delonte West RC 1.25 3.00
115 Tony Allen RC 1.25 3.00
116 Kevin Martin RC 1.25 3.00
117 Sasha Vujacic RC 1.00 2.50
118 Beno Udrih RC 1.00 2.50
119 David Harrison RC 1.00 2.50
120 Lionel Chalmers RC 1.00 2.50

2004-05 Upper Deck Pro Sigs Gold

Inserted in packs at the rate of one in 24 for cards 1-90 and sequentially numbered to 100 for cards 91-120, this 120-card set parallels the base Pro Sigs set enhanced with gold foil highlights.
*1-90 GOLD SINGLES: 2X TO 5X BASE HI
*91-120 GOLD RC's: 1.25X TO 3X BASE HI

2004-05 Upper Deck Pro Sigs Silver

*1-90 SILVER SINGLES: .75X TO 2X BASE HI
*91-120 SILVER RCs: .6X TO 1.5X BASE HI

2004-05 Upper Deck Pro Sigs Pro Signs

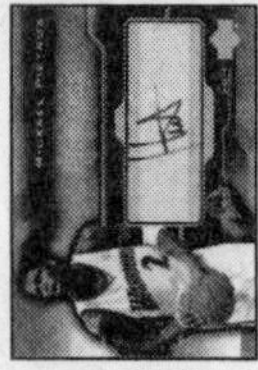

Inserted in packs at the rate of one in 170, this 58-card set is horizontally designed with player images on the left and sticker autographs on the right.
SP INFO PROVIDED BY UPPER DECK
AB Antonio Burks 4.00 10.00
AH Al Harrington 4.00 10.00
AK Andrei Kirilenko 6.00 15.00
BB Brent Barry 5.00 12.00
BH Brandon Hunter 4.00 10.00
CE Cedric Maxwell 4.00 10.00
CL Clyde Drexler SP 20.00 50.00
CM Corey Maggette 4.00 10.00
CR Jamal Crawford 4.00 10.00
DD Dan Dickau 4.00 10.00
DJ Dahntay Jones 4.00 10.00
DY Dwyane Wade SP 50.00 100.00
FE Francisco Elson 4.00 10.00
GA Gilbert Arenas SP 8.00 20.00
GG Gordan Giricek 4.00 10.00
GR Glenn Robinson 4.00 10.00
GW Gerald Wallace 4.00 10.00
JB Jerome Beasley SP 4.00 10.00
JD Juan Dixon 4.00 10.00
JH Josh Howard 4.00 10.00
JJ James Jones 4.00 10.00
JM Jerome Moiso 4.00 10.00
JO Jon Barry 4.00 10.00
JS John Salley 6.00 15.00
JW Jamaal Wilkes 4.00 10.00
KB Kobe Bryant SP 125.00 225.00
KK Kyle Korver 5.00 12.00
KR Kareem Rush 4.00 10.00
LJ LeBron James SP 100.00 200.00
LO Lamar Odom SP 10.00 25.00
LR Luke Ridnour 6.00 15.00
MB Marcus Banks 4.00 10.00
MD Marquis Daniels 4.00 10.00
MI Darko Milicic SP 6.00 15.00
MP Mickael Pietrus 4.00 10.00
MW Maurice Williams 4.00 10.00
NH Nene 4.00 10.00
PB Primoz Brezec 4.00 10.00
RG Reece Gaines 4.00 10.00
RH Richard Hamilton 8.00 20.00
RM Reggie Miller SP 50.00 100.00
SB Steve Blake 4.00 10.00
TO Travis Outlaw 4.00 10.00
TS Theron Smith 4.00 10.00
WG Willie Green 4.00 10.00
WZ Wang Zhizhi 6.00 15.00
ZC Zarko Cabarkapa 4.00 10.00
ZO Zoran Planinic 4.00 10.00
ZP Zaza Pachulia 4.00 10.00

2004-05 Upper Deck Pro Sigs Pro Signs Gold

Serially numbered to the featured player's jersey number and randomly inserted in packs, this 58-card set parallels the Pro Signs insert and is enhanced with gold highlights.
SOME NOT PRICED DUE TO SCARCITY
AK Andrei Kirilenko/47 8.00 20.00
BB Brent Barry/32 20.00 50.00
BH Brandon Hunter/56 5.00 12.00
CL Clyde Drexler/22 40.00 100.00
DJ Dahntay Jones/30 5.00 12.00
DM Desmond Mason/24 8.00 20.00
FE Francisco Elson/56 5.00 12.00
GR Glenn Robinson/31 6.00 15.00
JB Jerome Beasley/24 5.00 12.00
JB2 Jon Barry/20 5.00 12.00
JJ James Jones/33 5.00 12.00
JK Jason Kapono/25 5.00 12.00
JS John Salley/22 10.00 25.00
JW Jamaal Wilkes/52 6.00 15.00
KG Kevin Garnett/21 50.00 100.00
KK Kyle Korver/26 12.50 30.00
KR Kareem Rush/21 5.00 12.00
LJ LeBron James/23 250.00 500.00
MA Magic Johnson/32 75.00 150.00
MJ Michael Jordan/23 400.00 700.00
MS Mike Sweetney/50 5.00 12.00
MW Maurice Williams/25 5.00 12.00
NH Nene/31 8.00 20.00
PB Primoz Brezec/27 5.00 12.00
RH Richard Hamilton/32 12.50 30.00
RM Reggie Miller/31 40.00 100.00
WG Willie Green/33 5.00 12.00
ZP Zaza Pachulia/27 6.00 15.00

2004-05 Upper Deck Pro Sigs Pro Signs Rookies

Inserted in packs randomly at the rate of one in 30, this 42-card set parallels the design of the Pro Signs insert set but focuses on the rookies.
*GOLD: 1.25X TO 3X BASE HI
GOLD PRINT RUN 25 SER.#'d SETS
AE Andre Emmett 4.00 10.00
AI Andre Iguodala 6.00 15.00
AL Al Jefferson Big Al 6.00 15.00
AV Anderson Varejao 5.00 12.00
BG Ben Gordon 5.00 12.00
BI Andris Biedrins 5.00 12.00
BS Blake Stepp 4.00 10.00
BU Antonio Burks 4.00 10.00
CD Chris Duhon 4.00 10.00
DA David Harrison 4.00 10.00
DE Delonte West 5.00 12.00
DH Devin Harris 6.00 15.00
DH Dwight Howard 25.00 60.00
DO Dorell Wright 6.00 15.00
DS Donta Smith 4.00 10.00
HS Ha Seung-Jin 4.00 10.00
JC Josh Childress 4.00 10.00
JN Jameer Nelson 5.00 12.00
JR J.R. Smith 5.00 12.00
JR2 Justin Reed 4.00 10.00
JV Jackson Vroman 4.00 10.00
KH Kris Humphries 4.00 10.00
KM Kevin Martin 5.00 12.00
KS Kirk Snyder 4.00 10.00
LC Lionel Chalmers 4.00 10.00
LD Luol Deng 6.00 15.00
LU Luke Jackson 4.00 10.00
MF Matt Freije 4.00 10.00
PP Pavel Podkolzine 4.00 10.00
PR Peter John Ramos 4.00 10.00
PS Pape Sow 4.00 10.00
RA Rafael Araujo 4.00 10.00
RI Royal Ivey 4.00 10.00
RS Robert Swift 4.00 10.00
SL Shaun Livingston 4.00 10.00
ST Sebastian Telfair 4.00 10.00
SV Sasha Vujacic 4.00 10.00
TA Tony Allen 5.00 12.00
TP Tim Pickett 4.00 10.00
TR Trevor Ariza 4.00 10.00
UD Beno Udrih 4.00 10.00
VK Viktor Khryapa 4.00 10.00

2009 Upper Deck Prominent Cuts

COMPLETE SET (60) 30.00 60.00
3 Bill Bradley .40 1.00
4 Jim Bunning .40 1.00
37 Kevin Johnson .40 1.00
43 Kevin Garnett .60 1.50
45 LeBron James 2.00 5.00
47 Michael Jordan 4.00 10.00
60 Dave Bing .40 1.00

2009 Upper Deck Prominent Cuts Cut Signatures

OVERALL CUT SIGN. ODDS ONE PER BOX
STATED PRINT RUN B/WN 1-118
PCCN C.M. Newton/22 50.00 100.00
PCGM George Mikan/107 75.00 150.00
PCIT Isiah Thomas/50 20.00 40.00
PCLC Lou Carnesecca/18 20.00 50.00
PCHOU Bob Houbregs/24 25.00 50.00
PCRED Red Auerbach/99 75.00 150.00
PCMARV Marv Harshman/35 20.00 40.00
PCWILT Wilt Chamberlain/15 500.00 1000.00

2000-01 Upper Deck Pros and Prospects

The 2000-01 Upper Deck Pros & Prospects product was released in September,2000 as a 120-card set. The base set features 90 veterans, and 30 rookies (each serial numbered to 999). Please note that the Kenyon Martin and Marcus Fizer rookies are jersey cards.
COMPLETE SET (120) 75.00 150.00
COMP.SET w/o RC (90) 10.00 25.00
1 Dikembe Mutombo .30 .75
2 Alan Henderson .20 .50
3 Jim Jackson .20 .50
4 Paul Pierce .40 1.00
5 Kenny Anderson .25 .60
6 Antoine Walker .25 .60
7 Baron Davis .30 .75
8 Derrick Coleman .25 .60
9 David Wesley .20 .50
10 Elton Brand .30 .75
11 Ron Artest .30 .75
12 Hersey Hawkins .20 .50
13 Andre Miller .25 .60
14 Lamond Murray .20 .50
15 Shawn Kemp .30 .75
16 Michael Finley .30 .75
17 Dirk Nowitzki .50 1.25
18 Cedric Ceballos .20 .50
19 Antonio McDyess .25 .60
20 Nick Van Exel .25 .60
21 Raef LaFrentz .20 .50
22 Christian Laettner .20 .50
23 Jerry Stackhouse .25 .60
24 Lindsey Hunter .20 .50
25 Antawn Jamison .30 .75
26 Larry Hughes .25 .60
27 Chris Mills .20 .50
28 Steve Francis .30 .75
29 Hakeem Olajuwon .40 1.00
30 Shandon Anderson .20 .50
31 Reggie Miller .30 .75
32 Jonathan Bender .20 .50
33 Jalen Rose .25 .60
34 Lamar Odom .30 .75
35 Michael Olowokandi .20 .50
36 Tyrone Nesby .30 .75
37 Kobe Bryant 1.50 4.00
38 Shaquille O'Neal .75 2.00
39 Ron Harper .25 .60
40 Robert Horry .25 .60
41 Alonzo Mourning .40 1.00
42 P.J. Brown .20 .50
43 Jamal Mashburn .25 .60
44 Ray Allen .30 .75
45 Glenn Robinson .25 .60
46 Sam Cassell .25 .60
47 Kevin Garnett .60 1.50
48 Wally Szczerbiak .25 .60
49 Terrell Brandon .20 .50
50 William Avery .20 .50
51 Stephon Marbury .25 .60
52 Keith Van Horn .25 .60
53 Kerry Kittles .20 .50
54 Latrell Sprewell .25 .60
55 Allan Houston .25 .60
56 Patrick Ewing .40 1.00
57 Darrell Armstrong .20 .50
58 Pat Garrity .20 .50
59 Michael Doleac .20 .50
60 Allen Iverson .60 1.50
61 Theo Ratliff .20 .50
62 Tyrone Hill .20 .50
63 Jason Kidd .50 1.25
64 Anfernee Hardaway .50 1.25
65 Shawn Marion .30 .75
66 Scottie Pippen .50 1.25
67 Rasheed Wallace .30 .75
68 Damon Stoudamire .25 .60
69 Bonzi Wells .20 .50
70 Chris Webber .30 .75
71 Peja Stojakovic .30 .75
72 Jason Williams .30 .75
73 Tim Duncan .60 1.50
74 David Robinson .50 1.25
75 Terry Porter .25 .60
76 Gary Payton .30 .75
77 Rashard Lewis .30 .75
78 Vin Baker .25 .60
79 Vince Carter .60 1.50
80 Doug Christie .20 .50
81 Antonio Davis .20 .50
82 Karl Malone .40 1.00
83 John Stockton .40 1.00
84 Bryon Russell .20 .50
85 Shareef Abdur-Rahim .25 .60
86 Mike Bibby .30 .75
87 Michael Dickerson .20 .50
88 Mitch Richmond .25 .60
89 Richard Hamilton .25 .60
90 Juwan Howard .25 .60
91 Kenyon Martin JSY RC 12.00 30.00
92 Stromile Swift RC 2.00 5.00
93 Darius Miles RC 2.00 5.00
94 Marcus Fizer JSY RC 4.00 10.00
95 Mike Miller RC 4.00 10.00
96 DerMarr Johnson RC 2.00 5.00
97 Chris Mihm RC 2.00 5.00
98 Chris Porter RC 2.00 5.00
99 Joel Przybilla RC 2.00 5.00
100 Keyon Dooling RC 2.00 5.00
101 Jerome Moiso RC 2.00 5.00
102 Etan Thomas RC 2.00 5.00
103 Courtney Alexander RC 2.00 5.00
104 Mateen Cleaves RC 2.00 5.00
105 Jason Collier RC 2.00 5.00
106 Dan Langhi RC 2.00 5.00
107 Desmond Mason RC 2.50 6.00
108 Quentin Richardson RC 3.00 8.00
109 Jamaal Magloire RC 2.00 5.00
110 Speedy Claxton RC 2.00 5.00
111 Morris Peterson RC 2.00 5.00
112 Donnell Harvey RC 2.00 5.00
113 Hanno Mottola RC 2.00 5.00
114 Mamadou N'Diaye RC 2.00 5.00
115 Erick Barkley RC 2.00 5.00
116 Mark Madsen RC 2.00 5.00
117 A.J. Guyton RC 2.00 5.00
118 Khalid El-Amin RC 2.00 5.00
119 Lavor Postell RC 2.00 5.00
120 Eddie House RC 2.00 5.00

2000-01 Upper Deck Pros and Prospects ProActive

Randomly inserted in packs at one in six, this 10-card set focuses on the best performers in the NBA. Card backs carry a "PA" prefix.
COMPLETE SET (10) 3.00 8.00
PA1 Kobe Bryant 1.50 4.00
PA2 Kevin Garnett .60 1.50
PA3 Vince Carter .60 1.50
PA4 Jason Kidd .50 1.25
PA5 Steve Francis .30 .75
PA6 Chris Webber .30 .75
PA7 Shaquille O'Neal .75 2.00
PA8 Larry Hughes .25 .60
PA9 Gary Payton .30 .75
PA10 Allen Iverson .60 1.50

2000-01 Upper Deck Pros and Prospects ProMotion

Randomly inserted in packs at one in six, this 10-card set features rookie players being "promoted" to the NBA. Card backs carry a "PM" prefix.
COMPLETE SET (10) 2.50 6.00
PM1 Darius Miles .40 1.00
PM2 Stromile Swift .40 1.00
PM3 Marcus Fizer .40 1.00
PM4 Kenyon Martin 1.00 2.50
PM5 Courtney Alexander .40 1.00
PM6 Keyon Dooling .40 1.00
PM7 DerMarr Johnson .40 1.00
PM8 Chris Mihm .40 1.00
PM9 Chris Porter .40 1.00
PM10 Mike Miller .75 2.00

2000-01 Upper Deck Pros and Prospects Signature Jerseys

Randomly inserted in packs at one in 96, this 18-card set featured swatches of authentic game-worn jerseys and autographs from top players. Card backs are numbered by the player's initials.
AH Anfernee Hardaway 30.00 60.00
AW Antoine Walker 6.00 15.00
BD Baron Davis 8.00 20.00
CM Corey Maggette 6.00 15.00
DS Damon Stoudamire 8.00 20.00
GP Gary Payton 12.50 30.00
GR Glenn Robinson 6.00 15.00
KB Kobe Bryant 150.00 300.00
KG Kevin Garnett 30.00 60.00
KM Karl Malone 100.00 250.00
MB Mike Bibby 8.00 20.00
MF Michael Finley 15.00 30.00
PP Paul Pierce 15.00 40.00
SA Shareef Abdur-Rahim 8.00 20.00
TB Terrell Brandon 6.00 15.00
VB Vin Baker 6.00 15.00
WA William Avery 6.00 15.00
WS Wally Szczerbiak 6.00 15.00

2000-01 Upper Deck Pros and Prospects Signature Jerseys Level 2

Randomly inserted in packs, this 10-card set is a semi-parallel to the Signature Jersey insert. Selected players have had sequential numbering added to the card, numbered to their jersey. Card backs carry the player's initials. Lower print run players are listed, but unpriced.
CM2 Corey Maggette/50 20.00 50.00
KG2 Kevin Garnett/21 125.00 250.00
KM2 Karl Malone/32 300.00 500.00
MJ2 Michael Jordan/23 1200.00 2000.00

2000-01 Upper Deck Pros and Prospects Star Command

Randomly inserted in packs at one in 12, this 12-card set focuses on the most exciting and powerful players in the league. Card backs carry a "SC" prefix.
COMPLETE SET (12) 8.00 20.00
SC1 Kobe Bryant 3.00 8.00
SC2 Vince Carter 1.25 3.00
SC3 Allen Iverson 1.25 3.00
SC4 Shaquille O'Neal 1.50 4.00
SC5 Chris Webber .60 1.50
SC6 Karl Malone .75 2.00
SC7 Lamar Odom .60 1.50
SC8 Jason Kidd 1.00 2.50
SC9 Steve Francis .60 1.50
SC10 Kevin Garnett 1.25 3.00
SC11 Larry Hughes .50 1.25
SC12 Gary Payton .60 1.50

2000-01 Upper Deck Pros and Prospects Star Futures

Randomly inserted in packs at one in 12, this 10-card set focuses on some of the premier prospects from the 2000 Draft. Card backs carry a "SF" prefix.
COMPLETE SET (10) 5.00 12.00
SF1 Kenyon Martin 1.50 4.00
SF2 Keyon Dooling .60 1.50
SF3 Chris Porter .60 1.50
SF4 Courtney Alexander .60 1.50
SF5 Darius Miles .60 1.50
SF6 Mike Miller 1.25 3.00
SF7 Mateen Cleaves .60 1.50
SF8 Stromile Swift .60 1.50
SF9 Marcus Fizer .60 1.50
SF10 DerMarr Johnson .60 1.50

2000-01 Upper Deck Pros and Prospects UD Authentics Rookie Exclusives

Randomly inserted into packs, this 3-card insert features autographs from top draft-packs. Each card is serial numbered to 200. Card backs carry the players initials as numbering.
CM Chris Mihm 5.00 12.00
ET Etan Thomas 5.00 12.00
JP Joel Przybilla 5.00 12.00

2001-02 Upper Deck Pros and Prospects

This 131-card base set was issued in August of 2001. The set comes in 24 packs per box; 5 cards per pack; and a SRP of $4.99 per pack. The 131 base cards are broken down as follows: 90 veteran cards where full color action photography is framed by silver foil highlights and white borders, and 31 rookie cards which utilize the same design as the veterans but photos from the NBA draft. Card numbers 91-125 are sequentially numbered to 1000, and card numbers 126-131 are sequentially numbered to 350.
COMP.SET w/o SP's (90) 10.00 25.00
1 Jason Terry .30 .75
2 Toni Kukoc .25 .60
3 DerMarr Johnson .20 .50
4 Paul Pierce .40 1.00
5 Antoine Walker .25 .60
6 Kenny Anderson .25 .60
7 Jamal Mashburn .25 .60
8 Baron Davis .30 .75
9 David Wesley .20 .50
10 Elton Brand .30 .75
11 Ron Mercer .20 .50
12 Jamal Crawford .25 .60
13 Andre Miller .25 .60
14 Lamond Murray .20 .50
15 Chris Mihm .20 .50
16 Michael Finley .30 .75
17 Wang ZhiZHi .25 .60
18 Dirk Nowitzki .50 1.25
19 Antonio McDyess .25 .60
20 Nick Van Exel .25 .60
21 Raef LaFrentz .20 .50
22 Jerry Stackhouse .25 .60
23 Joe Smith .25 .60
24 Mateen Cleaves .20 .50
25 Antawn Jamison .30 .75
26 Marc Jackson .20 .50
27 Larry Hughes .25 .60
28 Steve Francis .30 .75
29 Maurice Taylor .20 .50
30 Hakeem Olajuwon .40 1.00
31 Reggie Miller .30 .75
32 Jermaine O'Neal .30 .75
33 Jalen Rose .25 .60
34 Lamar Odom .30 .75
35 Darius Miles .20 .50
36 Quentin Richardson .25 .60
37 Kobe Bryant 1.50 4.00
38 Shaquille O'Neal .75 2.00
39 Derek Fisher .25 .60
40 Rick Fox .25 .60
41 Alonzo Mourning .40 1.00
42 Eddie Jones .25 .60
43 Tim Hardaway .30 .75
44 Brian Grant .20 .50
45 Ray Allen .30 .75
46 Glenn Robinson .25 .60
47 Tim Thomas .20 .50
48 Kevin Garnett .60 1.50
49 Terrell Brandon .20 .50
50 Wally Szczerbiak .25 .60
51 Chauncey Billups .30 .75
52 Stephon Marbury .25 .60
53 Kenyon Martin .30 .75
54 Keith Van Horn .25 .60
55 Allan Houston .25 .60
56 Latrell Sprewell .25 .60
57 Glen Rice .25 .60
58 Tracy McGrady .50 1.25
59 Mike Miller .30 .75
60 Darrell Armstrong .20 .50
61 Allen Iverson .60 1.50
62 Dikembe Mutombo .30 .75
63 Aaron McKie .20 .50
64 Jason Kidd .50 1.25
65 Shawn Marion .30 .75
66 Tom Gugliotta .20 .50
67 Rasheed Wallace .30 .75
68 Damon Stoudamire .25 .60
69 Scottie Pippen .50 1.25
70 Peja Stojakovic .30 .75
71 Jason Williams .25 .60
72 Chris Webber .30 .75
73 Tim Duncan .60 1.50
74 Derek Anderson .20 .50
75 David Robinson .50 1.25
76 Gary Payton .30 .75
77 Rashard Lewis .30 .75
78 Desmond Mason .25 .60
79 Vince Carter .50 1.25
80 Morris Peterson .20 .50
81 Antonio Davis .20 .50
82 Karl Malone .40 1.00
83 John Stockton .40 1.00
84 Donyell Marshall .20 .50
85 Shareef Abdur-Rahim .25 .60
86 Mike Bibby .30 .75
87 Stromile Swift .20 .50
88 Richard Hamilton .25 .60
89 Courtney Alexander .20 .50
90 Chris Whitney .20 .50
91 Ruben Boumtje-Boumtje RC 2.00 5.00
92 Sean Lampley RC 2.00 5.00
93 Ken Johnson RC 2.00 5.00
94 Earl Watson RC 2.00 5.00
95 Jamaal Tinsley RC 2.50 6.00
96 Damone Brown RC 2.00 5.00
97 Michael Wright RC 2.00 5.00
98 Alvin Jones RC 2.00 5.00
99 Omar Cook RC 2.00 5.00
100 Jarron Collins RC 2.00 5.00
101 Brian Scalabrine RC 2.00 5.00
102 Jeryl Sasser RC 2.00 5.00
103 Samuel Dalembert RC 2.50 6.00
104 Terence Morris RC 2.00 5.00
105 Will Solomon RC 2.00 5.00
106 Kirk Haston RC 2.00 5.00
107 Richard Jefferson RC 4.00 10.00
108 Jason Collins RC 2.00 5.00
109 Troy Murphy RC 3.00 8.00
110 Gerald Wallace RC 3.00 8.00
111 Shane Battier RC 4.00 10.00
112 Jeff Trepagnier RC 2.00 5.00
113 Brandon Armstrong RC 2.00 5.00
114 Loren Woods RC 2.00 5.00
115 Joseph Forte RC 2.00 5.00
116 Michael Bradley RC 2.00 5.00
117 Joe Johnson RC 5.00 12.00
118 Gilbert Arenas RC 3.00 8.00
119 Ousmane Cisse RC 2.00 5.00
120 Kenny Satterfield RC 2.00 5.00
121 Vladimir Radmanovic RC 2.00 5.00
122 DeSagana Diop RC 2.00 5.00
123 Kedrick Brown RC 2.00 5.00
124 Trenton Hassell RC 2.00 5.00
125 Steven Hunter RC 2.00 5.00
126 Rodney White RC 4.00 10.00
127 Eddy Curry RC 6.00 15.00
128 Jason Richardson RC 8.00 20.00
129 Tyson Chandler RC 6.00 15.00
130 Eddie Griffin RC 4.00 10.00
131 Kwame Brown RC 4.00 10.00

2001-02 Upper Deck Pros and Prospects Rookie Memorabilia

Inserted in packs, this six card set parallels the last six cards in the base Pros and Prospects set. These cards utilize the same design and are enhanced with a swatch of shoe. Each card is sequentially numbered to 350.
126 Rodney White Shoe 5.00 12.00
127 Eddy Curry Shoe 8.00 20.00
128 Jason Richardson Shoe 10.00 25.00
129 Tyson Chandler Shoe 8.00 20.00
130 Eddie Griffin Shoe 5.00 12.00
131 Kwame Brown Shoe 5.00 12.00

2001-02 Upper Deck Pros and Prospects Alley-Oop Team-Ups

This 10-card insert set is sequentially numbered to 100. Each card features two swatches of game-used jersey in the shape of an arrow from some of the league's best alley-oop combinations. Player photos are set on either side of the card on this horizontal design with the two player's team logo in the center. A Gold version sequentially numbered to 25 was also issued.
*GOLD: 1.25X TO 3X BASE HI
BDJM Baron Davis / Jamal Mahburn 8.00 20.00
CPAJ Chris Porter / Antawn Jamison 8.00 20.00
DATM Darrell Armstrong / Tracy McGrady 10.00 25.00
GPRL Gary Payton / Rashard Lewis 8.00 20.00
JSKM John Stockton / Karl Malone 25.00 50.00
KGKB Kevin Garnett / Kobe Bryant 20.00 50.00
NVAM Nick Van Exel / Antonio McDyess 8.00 20.00
PPAW Paul Pierce / Antoine Walker 10.00 25.00
QRDM Quentin Richardson / Darius Miles 8.00 20.00
TBKG Terrell Brandon / Kevin Garnett 8.00 20.00

2001-02 Upper Deck Pros and Prospects All-Star Team-Ups

Randomly inserted in packs at a rate of one in 192, this 10-card insert set features two swatches of 2001 NBA All-Star Weekend-used memorabilia from two different NBA All-Stars. Each player is pictured on one side of the card on this horizontal design, and centered between them is the 2001 All-Star game logo. A Gold version sequentially numbered to 25 was also issued.
*GOLD: 1.25X TO 3X BASE HI
ADDM Antonio Davis / Dikembe Mutombo 8.00 20.00
AHLS Allan Houston / Latrell Sprewell 12.50 30.00
AIKB Allen Iverson / Kobe Bryant 30.00 80.00
CWAM Chris Webber / Antonio McDyess 10.00 25.00
DRKG David Robinson / Kevin Garnett 10.00 25.00
JKGP Jason Kidd / Gary Payton 8.00 20.00
JSRW Jerry Stackhouse / Rasheed Wallace 8.00 20.00
KMMF Karl Malone / Michael Finley 8.00 20.00
RAGR Ray Allen / Glenn Robinson 8.00 20.00
TMSM Tracy McGrady / Stephon Marbury 10.00 25.00

2001-02 Upper Deck Pros and Prospects Game Jerseys

Randomly inserted in packs at a rate of one in 24, this 26-card set features a full color player action photo on the right side of the card and a swatch of jersey on the left. Each card is highlighted with silver foil, and the player's number appears below the swatch on the non-autographed versions rendering counterfeit Autographed versions impossible to make out of base insert versions. A Gold version sequentially numbered to 75 was also issued.
*GOLD: 1X TO 2.5X JSY HI
AI Allen Iverson 8.00 20.00
AJ Antawn Jamison 4.00 10.00
AW Antoine Walker 3.00 8.00
CM Chris Mihm 2.50 6.00
CO Corey Maggette 3.00 8.00
DA Darrell Armstrong 2.50 6.00
DC Derrick Coleman 3.00 8.00
DM Darius Miles 2.50 6.00
GR Glen Rice 3.00 8.00
HM Hanno Mottola 2.50 6.00
JC Jamal Crawford 3.00 8.00
JM Jerome Moiso 2.50 6.00
JS John Stockton 5.00 12.00
KA Kenny Anderson 3.00 8.00
KB Kobe Bryant 12.00 30.00
KG Kevin Garnett 8.00 20.00
KV Keith Van Horn 3.00 8.00
LM Lamond Murray 2.50 6.00
MA Desmond Mason 3.00 8.00
MO Michael Olowokandi 2.50 6.00
MP Morris Peterson 2.50 6.00
RL Raef LaFrentz 2.50 6.00
RM Ron Mercer 2.50 6.00
SS Stromile Swift 2.50 6.00
TB Terrell Brandon 2.50 6.00
WA William Avery 2.50 6.00

2001-02 Upper Deck Pros and Prospects Game Jerseys Autographs

Randomly inserted in packs at a rate of one in 192, this 11-card set features the same design as the base Game Jerseys insert set with a different player photo and gold foil highlights instead of silver foil highlights. Unlike the Non-autographed version, these cards do not have the player's number below the jersey swatch, and this is where the authentic autographs appear. A Gold version of this set was also issued with cards sequentially numbered to 50.
*GOLD: .6X TO 1.5X BASE AU HI
AWA Antoine Walker 8.00 20.00
CMA Chris Mihm 6.00 15.00
COA Corey Maggette 8.00 20.00
DAA Darrell Armstrong 6.00 15.00
DMA Darius Miles 6.00 15.00
KBA Kobe Bryant 125.00 250.00
LMA Lamond Murray 6.00 15.00
MPA Morris Peterson 6.00 15.00
SSA Stromile Swift 6.00 15.00
TBA Terrell Brandon 6.00 15.00
KGA Kevin Garnett 25.00 60.00

2001-02 Upper Deck Pros and Prospects ProActive

Seeded in packs at the rate of one in 23, this 10-card set showcases full color player action photos against a hexagonal color background. Each card has silver foil highlights and white borders along the top, bottom and right side of the card.
COMPLETE SET (10) 8.00 20.00

PA1 Kobe Bryant 4.00 10.00
PA2 Vince Carter 1.25 3.00
PA3 Tim Duncan 1.50 4.00
PA4 Ray Allen .75 2.00
PA5 Michael Finley .75 2.00
PA6 Paul Pierce 1.00 2.50
PA7 Latrell Sprewell .60 1.50
PA8 Steve Francis .75 2.00
PA9 Kevin Garnett 1.50 4.00
PA10 Eddie Jones .60 1.50

2001-02 Upper Deck Pros and Prospects ProMotion

Randomly inserted in packs at a rate of one in 18, this 12-card set features full color player action photos with brightly colored backgrounds with "shadows" of the player and silver foil highlights.
COMPLETE SET (12) 8.00 20.00
PM1 Kevin Garnett 1.25 3.00
PM2 Chris Webber .60 1.50
PM3 Michael Finley .60 1.50
PM4 Tim Duncan 1.25 3.00
PM5 Ray Allen .60 1.50
PM6 Jamal Mashburn .50 1.25
PM7 Antonio McDyess .50 1.25
PM8 Kobe Bryant 3.00 8.00
PM9 Latrell Sprewell .50 1.25
PM10 Vince Carter 1.00 2.50
PM11 Shaquille O'Neal 1.50 4.00
PM12 Karl Malone .75 2.00

2001-02 Upper Deck Pros and Prospects Star Command

Randomly inserted in packs at a rate of one in 23, this 10-card set shows players in action set against a colorful background. Each card contains silver foil highlights, and the the set name and player name appear on the right side of the card.
COMPLETE SET (10) 10.00 25.00
SC1 Allen Iverson 1.50 4.00
SC2 Steve Francis .75 2.00
SC3 Kevin Garnett 1.50 4.00
SC4 Vince Carter 1.25 3.00
SC5 Kobe Bryant 4.00 10.00
SC6 Tim Duncan 1.50 4.00
SC7 Chris Webber .75 2.00
SC8 Tracy McGrady 1.25 3.00
SC9 Darius Miles .50 1.25
SC10 Shaquille O'Neal 2.00 5.00

2001-02 Upper Deck Pros and Prospects Star Futures

Randomly inserted in packs at the rate of one in 23, this 10-card set focuses on rookie players. Full color player photos are set against a criss-cross colored cubed background.
COMPLETE SET (10) 12.00 30.00
SF1 Eddy Curry 2.00 5.00
SF2 Rodney White 1.25 3.00
SF3 Tyson Chandler 2.00 5.00
SF4 Steven Hunter 1.25 3.00
SF5 Eddie Griffin 1.25 3.00
SF6 Kwame Brown 1.25 3.00
SF7 DeSagana Diop 1.25 3.00
SF8 Troy Murphy 2.00 5.00
SF9 Joe Johnson 3.00 8.00
SF10 Jason Richardson 2.50 6.00

1993-94 Upper Deck Pro View

This 110-card standard-size set was distributed in 5-card packs (48 per box) that included 3-D glasses with which to see the 3-D effect. Fronts feature white-bordered color player action shots, with the player's name appearing within a vertical ghosted strip on the left. The back carries a color player action shot on the left, with career highlights horizontally printed alongside on the right. The set closes with the following subsets: 3-D Playground Legends (71-79), 3-D Rookie (80-88) and 3-D Jams (89-108). Rookie Cards of note include Vin Baker, Anfernee Hardaway, Jamal Mashburn and Chris Webber.
COMPLETE SET (110) 15.00 30.00
1 Karl Malone .40 1.00
2 Chuck Person .10 .30
3 Latrell Sprewell .40 1.00
4 Dominique Wilkins .15 .40
5 Reggie Miller .15 .40
6 Vlade Divac .12 .30
7 Otis Thorpe .12 .30
8 Patrick Ewing .12 .30
9 Ron Harper .12 .30
10 Brad Daugherty .12 .30
11 Robert Parish .12 .30
12 Glen Rice .12 .30
13 Kevin Johnson .12 .30
14 Christian Laettner .12 .30
15 Ricky Pierce .12 .30
16 Joe Dumars .15 .40
17 James Worthy .20 .50
18 John Stockton .25 .60
19 Robert Horry .12 .30
20 John Starks .12 .30
21 Danny Manning .12 .30
22 Alonzo Mourning .20 .50
23 Michael Jordan 2.00 5.00
24 Hakeem Olajuwon .25 .60
25 Scott Skiles .12 .30
26 Stacey Augmon .12 .30
27 Mitch Richmond .15 .40
28 Derrick Coleman .12 .30
29 Jeff Malone .12 .30
30 Larry Johnson .15 .40
31 Sam Perkins .12 .30
32 Shaquille O'Neal .75 2.00
33 Walt Williams .12 .30
34 Doug West .12 .30
35 Mark Price .12 .30
36 Rony Seikaly .12 .30
37 Michael Adams .12 .30
38 Anthony Peeler .12 .30
39 Larry Nance .12 .30
40 Shawn Kemp .15 .40
41 Terry Porter .12 .30
42 Dan Majerle .12 .30
43 Dennis Rodman .20 .50
44 Isiah Thomas .15 .40
45 Spud Webb .12 .30
46 Pooh Richardson .12 .30
47 Tim Hardaway .15 .40
48 Derek Harper .12 .30
49 Pervis Ellison .12 .30
50 Xavier McDaniel .12 .30
51 Jeff Hornacek .12 .30
52 Ken Norman .12 .30
53 LaPhonso Ellis .12 .30
54 Charles Barkley .25 .60
55 Tom Gugliotta .15 .40
56 Clifford Robinson .12 .30
57 Mark Jackson .12 .30
58 Mahmoud Abdul-Rauf .12 .30
59 Todd Day .12 .30
60 Kenny Anderson .12 .30
61 Jim Jackson .12 .30
62 Chris Mullin .15 .40
63 Scottie Pippen .50 1.25
64 Dikembe Mutombo .12 .30
65 Sean Elliott .12 .30
66 Clarence Weatherspoon .12 .30
67 Chris Morris .12 .30
68 Clyde Drexler .20 .50
69 Dennis Scott .12 .30
70 David Robinson .25 .60
71 Larry Johnson PL .12 .30
72 Chris Webber PL .75 2.00
73 Alonzo Mourning PL .12 .30
74 Lloyd Daniels PL .12 .30
75 Derrick Coleman PL .12 .30
76 Tim Hardaway PL .12 .30
77 Isiah Thomas PL .12 .30
78 Chris Mullin PL .12 .30
79 Shaquille O'Neal PL .40 1.00
80 Shawn Bradley RC .12 .30
81 Chris Webber RC 1.25 3.00
82 Jamal Mashburn RC .30 .75
83 Anfernee Hardaway RC 1.25 3.00
84 Calbert Cheaney RC .12 .30
85 Vin Baker RC .30 .75
86 Isaiah Rider RC .20 .50
87 Lindsey Hunter RC .12 .30
88 Bobby Hurley RC .12 .30
89 Dominique Wilkins 3DJ .12 .30
90 Charles Barkley 3DJ .15 .40
91 Michael Jordan 3DJ 1.00 2.50
92 Derrick Coleman 3DJ .12 .30
93 Scottie Pippen 3DJ .25 .60
94 Karl Malone 3DJ .15 .40
95 Larry Johnson 3DJ .12 .30
96 Cedric Ceballos 3DJ .12 .30
97 David Robinson 3DJ .15 .40
98 Patrick Ewing 3DJ .12 .30
99 Clarence Weatherspoon 3DJ .12 .30
100 Alonzo Mourning 3DJ .12 .30
101 Stacey Augmon 3DJ .12 .30
102 Shaquille O'Neal 3DJ .40 1.00
103 Clyde Drexler 3DJ .12 .30
104 Shawn Kemp 3DJ .12 .30
105 Harold Miner 3DJ .12 .30
106 Chris Webber 3DJ .75 2.00
107 Dikembe Mutombo 3DJ .12 .30
108 Doug West 3DJ .12 .30
109 Michael Jordan CL .12 .30
110 Michael Jordan CL .12 .30

2004-05 Upper Deck R-Class

Released in January 2005, R-Class was a retail product which would seem has replaced the MVP brand. The set consists of veterans for cards 1-90 and rookies for cards 91-132, inserted at the rate of two per pack. R-Class was packaged in 24-pack boxes where packs contained eight cards and carried a SRP of $2.99.
COMPLETE SET (132) 20.00 50.00
COMP.SET w/o RC's (90) 8.00 20.00
1 Antoine Walker .25 .60
2 Al Harrington .20 .50
3 Boris Diaw .20 .50
4 Paul Pierce .30 .75
5 Gary Payton .25 .60
6 Jiri Welsch .15 .40
7 Gerald Wallace .25 .60
8 Jason Kapono .15 .40
9 Brandon Hunter .15 .40
10 Eddy Curry .20 .50
11 Kirk Hinrich .25 .60
12 Tyson Chandler .20 .50
13 LeBron James 1.50 4.00
14 Dajuan Wagner .15 .40
15 Zydrunas Ilgauskas .20 .50
16 Dirk Nowitzki .40 1.00
17 Michael Finley .25 .60
18 Jason Terry .20 .50
19 Andre Miller .20 .50
20 Carmelo Anthony .50 1.25
21 Kenyon Martin .25 .60
22 Chauncey Billups .25 .60
23 Rasheed Wallace .25 .60
24 Ben Wallace .25 .60
25 Speedy Claxton .15 .40
26 Jason Richardson .25 .60
27 Mike Dunleavy .20 .50
28 Yao Ming .50 1.25
29 Tracy McGrady .30 .75
30 Juwan Howard .20 .50
31 Jermaine O'Neal .25 .60
32 Reggie Miller .25 .60
33 Ron Artest .25 .60
34 Elton Brand .25 .60
35 Corey Maggette .20 .50
36 Marko Jaric .15 .40
37 Kobe Bryant 1.25 3.00
38 Devean George .15 .40
39 Lamar Odom .25 .60
40 Pau Gasol .25 .60
41 Jason Williams .20 .50
42 Bonzi Wells .15 .40
43 Shaquille O'Neal .60 1.50
44 Dwyane Wade .75 2.00
45 Eddie Jones .20 .50
46 Michael Redd .25 .60
47 Desmond Mason .20 .50
48 T.J. Ford .20 .50
49 Latrell Sprewell .20 .50
50 Kevin Garnett .50 1.25
51 Sam Cassell .20 .50
52 Richard Jefferson .25 .60
53 Aaron Williams .15 .40
54 Jason Kidd .40 1.00
55 Jamal Mashburn .25 .60
56 Baron Davis .25 .60
57 Jamaal Magloire .15 .40
58 Allan Houston .20 .50
59 Jamal Crawford .20 .50
60 Stephon Marbury .20 .50
61 Steve Francis .25 .60
62 Kelvin Cato .15 .40
63 Cuttino Mobley .20 .50
64 Glenn Robinson .20 .50
65 Allen Iverson .40 1.00
66 Willie Green .15 .40
67 Amare Stoudemire .30 .75
68 Quentin Richardson .20 .50
69 Steve Nash .30 .75
70 Shareef Abdur-Rahim .20 .50
71 Damon Stoudamire .20 .50
72 Zach Randolph .20 .50
73 Peja Stojakovic .25 .60
74 Chris Webber .25 .60
75 Mike Bibby .25 .60
76 Tony Parker .25 .60
77 Tim Duncan .40 1.00
78 Manu Ginobili .30 .75
79 Ronald Murray .15 .40
80 Ray Allen .25 .60
81 Rashard Lewis .25 .60
82 Chris Bosh .25 .60
83 Vince Carter .40 1.00
84 Jalen Rose .20 .50
85 Andrei Kirilenko .20 .50
86 Carlos Boozer .25 .60
87 Carlos Arroyo .20 .50
88 Gilbert Arenas .25 .60
89 Jarvis Hayes .15 .40
90 Antawn Jamison .25 .60
91 Dwight Howard RC 2.00 5.00
92 Emeka Okafor RC 1.00 2.50
93 Ben Gordon RC .75 2.00
94 Shaun Livingston RC .60 1.50
95 Devin Harris RC 1.00 2.50
96 Josh Childress RC .60 1.50
97 Luol Deng RC 1.00 2.50
98 Andre Iguodala RC 1.00 2.50
99 Luke Jackson RC .60 1.50
100 Andris Biedrins RC .75 2.00
101 Sebastian Telfair RC .60 1.50
102 Josh Smith RC 1.00 2.50
103 Rafael Araujo RC .60 1.50
104 Robert Swift RC .60 1.50
105 Kris Humphries RC .60 1.50
106 Al Jefferson RC 1.00 2.50
107 Kirk Snyder RC .60 1.50
108 J.R. Smith RC .75 2.00
109 Dorell Wright RC 1.00 2.50
110 Jameer Nelson RC .75 2.00
111 Pavel Podkolzine RC .60 1.50
112 Bernard Robinson RC .60 1.50
113 Yuta Tabuse RC 1.25 3.00
114 Delonte West RC .75 2.00
115 Tony Allen RC .75 2.00
116 Kevin Martin RC .75 2.00
117 Sasha Vujacic RC .60 1.50
118 Beno Udrih RC .60 1.50
119 David Harrison RC .60 1.50
120 Anderson Varejao RC .75 2.00
121 Jackson Vroman RC .60 1.50
122 Peter John Ramos RC .60 1.50
123 Lionel Chalmers RC .60 1.50
124 Donta Smith RC .60 1.50
125 Andre Emmett RC .60 1.50
126 Antonio Burks RC .60 1.50
127 Royal Ivey RC .60 1.50
128 Chris Duhon RC .60 1.50
129 Trevor Ariza RC .60 1.50
130 Tim Pickett RC .60 1.50
131 Romain Sato RC .60 1.50
132 Nenad Krstic RC .60 1.50

2004-05 Upper Deck R-Class Gold

Randomly seeded in packs, this 132-card set parallels the base set enhanced with gold foil highlights and sequential numbering to 150 for cards 1-90 and 50 for cards 91-132. A Platinum parallel was also inserted where cards 1-90 are serially numbered to 25 and cards 91-132 are serially numbered to 10.
*1-90 GOLD: 2X TO 5X BASE HI
*91-132 GOLD: 2.5X TO 6X BASE RC HI

2004-05 Upper Deck R-Class Platinum

Randomly seeded in packs, this 132-card set parallels the base set enhanced with platinum foil highlights and sequential numbering to 25 for cards 1-90 and 10 for cards 91-132.
*1-90 PLATINUM: 8X TO 20X BASE HI

2004-05 Upper Deck R-Class R-Tifacts

Inserted in packs at the rate of one in 18, this 42-card set features a player photo on the right and a swatch of memorabilia on the left.
SP INFO PROVIDED BY UPPER DECK
AH Allan Houston 2.00 5.00
AK Andrei Kirilenko 2.00 5.00
AS Amare Stoudemire 3.00 8.00
BC Brian Cook 2.00 5.00
BD Baron Davis 2.50 6.00
BI Chauncey Billups 2.50 6.00
BM Brad Miller 2.50 6.00
BO Carlos Boozer 2.50 6.00
CA Carmelo Anthony 5.00 12.00
CB Caron Butler 2.50 6.00
CM Corey Maggette 2.00 5.00
DG Drew Gooden 2.00 5.00
DN Dirk Nowitzki 4.00 10.00
DW Dajuan Wagner 2.00 5.00
EC Eddy Curry 2.00 5.00
EG Manu Ginobili 3.00 8.00
ES Eric Snow 2.00 5.00
GA Gilbert Arenas 2.50 6.00
GP Gary Payton 2.50 6.00
JC Jamal Crawford 2.00 5.00
JM Jamaal Magloire 2.00 5.00
JO Jermaine O'Neal 2.50 6.00
JT Jason Terry 2.00 5.00
KB Kobe Bryant 8.00 20.00
KG Kevin Garnett 5.00 12.00
KM Karl Malone 3.00 8.00
LJ LeBron James 10.00 25.00
MF Michael Finley 2.50 6.00
MJ Michael Jordan SP 25.00 60.00
MP Morris Peterson 1.50 4.00
PP Paul Pierce 3.00 8.00
QR Quentin Richardson 2.00 5.00
RJ Richard Jefferson 2.50 6.00
RM Reggie Miller 2.50 6.00
SD Samuel Dalembert 2.00 5.00
SM Shawn Marion 2.50 6.00
SS Steve Smith 2.00 5.00
ST Stephon Marbury 2.00 5.00
TC Tyson Chandler 2.00 5.00
TM Tracy McGrady 3.00 8.00
VD Vlade Divac 2.00 5.00
WS Wally Szczerbiak 2.00 5.00

2004-05 Upper Deck R-Class R-Tifacts Dual

Seeded randomly at the rate of one in 36, this 30-card set places two players along with two swatches of memorabilia on the card front.
SP INFO PROVIDED BY UPPER DECK
AH Gilbert Arenas / Brendan Haywood 4.00 10.00
AM Carmelo Anthony / Andre Miller 5.00 12.00
BJ Kobe Bryant SP / LeBron James 25.00 60.00
BM Elton Brand / Corey Maggette 4.00 10.00
CC Eddy Curry / Tyson Chandler 4.00 10.00
CW Brian Cook / Luke Walton 4.00 10.00
DG Tim Duncan / Manu Ginobili 10.00 25.00
DM Baron Davis / Jamaal Magloire 4.00 10.00
FM Steve Francis / Cuttino Mobley 4.00 10.00
GM Pau Gasol / Mike Miller 4.00 10.00
GS Kevin Garnett / Wally Szczerbiak 6.00 15.00
HB David Harrison / Chauncey Billups 4.00 10.00
HW Al Harrington / Antoine Walker 4.00 10.00
JJ LeBron James SP / Michael Jordan 30.00 80.00
KB Andre Kirilenko / Carlos Boozer 4.00 10.00
KJ Nenad Krstic / Richard Jefferson 4.00 10.00
KK Kobe Bryant / Karl Malone 8.00 20.00
MF Tracy McGrady / Steve Francis 6.00 -15.00
ML Ronald Murray / Rashard Lewis 4.00 10.00
MR Shawn Marion / Quentin Richardson 4.00 10.00
MS Stephon Marbury / Mike Sweetney 4.00 10.00
NF Dirk Nowitzki / Michael Finley 5.00 12.00
OH Shaquille O'Neal / Udonis Haslem 6.00 15.00
PP Paul Pierce / Gary Payton 5.00 12.00
PR Morris Peterson / Jason Richardson 4.00 10.00
RF Jason Richardson / Derek Fisher 4.00 10.00
RM Quentin Richardson / Darius Miles 4.00 10.00
SJ Amare Stoudemire / Joe Johnson 5.00 12.00
TO Jamal Tinsley / Jermaine O'Neal 4.00 10.00
WS Chris Webber / Peja Stojakovic 5.00 12.00

2004-05 Upper Deck R-Class R-Tifacts Triple

Randomly inserted in packs, this 12-card set features three players along with three swatches of memorabilia. Each card is sequentially numbered to 25.
JJB LeBron James / Michael Jordan / Kobe Bryant 125.00 250.00
MGB Tracy McGrady / Kevin Garnett / Kobe Bryant 20.00 50.00

2004-05 Upper Deck R-Class R-Tifacts Signatures

Limited to 50 serially numbered copies, this 35-card set includes a player photo, a swatch of memorabilia and an autograph.
AB Andris Biedrins 10.00 25.00
AI Andre Iguodala 12.00 30.00
AJ Al Jefferson 12.00 30.00
AV Anderson Varejao 10.00 25.00
BG Ben Gordon 10.00 25.00
DA David Harrison 8.00 20.00
DE Devin Harris 12.00 30.00
DF Derek Fisher 8.00 20.00
DH Dwight Howard 100.00 200.00
DO Dorell Wright 12.00 30.00
DW Delonte West 10.00 25.00
JA Jamal Crawford 10.00 25.00
JN Jameer Nelson 10.00 25.00
JR J.R. Smith 10.00 25.00
JS Josh Smith 12.00 30.00
KB Kobe Bryant 100.00 200.00
KH Kris Humphries 8.00 20.00
KM Kevin Martin 10.00 25.00
KS Kirk Snyder 8.00 20.00
LC Lionel Chalmers 8.00 20.00
LJ LeBron James 150.00 300.00
LU Luke Jackson 8.00 20.00
MJ Michael Jordan 400.00 600.00
NK Nenad Krstic 8.00 20.00
RA Rafael Araujo 8.00 20.00
ST Sebastian Telfair 8.00 20.00
TA Tony Allen 10.00 25.00
YT Yuta Tabuse 20.00 50.00

2004-05 Upper Deck R-Class Signatures

Randomly seeded at the rate of one in 480, this 42-card set features full color player photos on the right of the card and an autograph up the left side.
SP INFO PROVIDED BY UPPER DECK
AI Andre Iguodala 10.00 25.00
JR J.R. Smith 8.00 20.00
KG Kevin Garnett SP 25.00 60.00
LJ LeBron James SP 125.00 250.00

2008-09 Upper Deck Radiance

COMP.SET w/o RCs (90) 125.00 250.00
1-90 PRINT RUN 299 SER.#'d SETS
91-110 RC PRINT RUN 299 SER.#'d SETS
101-120 RC PRINT RUN 99 SER.#'d SETS
1 LaMarcus Aldridge 1.50 4.00
2 Ray Allen 1.50 4.00
3 Carmelo Anthony 2.00 5.00
4 Ron Artest 1.50 4.00
5 Brandon Bass 1.00 2.50
6 Chauncey Billups 1.50 4.00
7 Carlos Boozer 1.50 4.00
8 Chris Bosh 1.50 4.00
9 Elton Brand 1.50 4.00
10 Kobe Bryant 12.00 30.00
11 Caron Butler 1.50 4.00
12 Andrew Bynum 2.00 5.00
13 Jose Calderon 1.25 3.00
14 Marcus Camby 1.00 2.50
15 Vince Carter 2.00 5.00
16 Tyson Chandler 1.25 3.00
17 Wilson Chandler 1.25 3.00
18 Mike Conley Jr. 1.25 3.00
19 Jamal Crawford 1.25 3.00
20 Eddy Curry 1.00 2.50
21 Baron Davis 1.50 4.00
22 Luol Deng 1.50 4.00
23 Michael Jordan 25.00 60.00
24 Tim Duncan 2.50 6.00
25 Kevin Durant 6.00 15.00
26 Monta Ellis 1.50 4.00
27 T.J. Ford 1.00 2.50
28 Francisco Garcia 1.25 3.00
29 Kevin Garnett 3.00 8.00
30 Rudy Gay 1.50 4.00
31 Manu Ginobili 1.50 4.00
32 Ben Gordon 1.50 4.00
33 Danny Granger 1.50 4.00
34 Devin Harris 1.50 4.00
35 Al Horford 1.50 4.00
36 Dwight Howard 3.00 8.00
37 Andre Iguodala 1.50 4.00
38 Allen Iverson 2.00 5.00
39 Stephen Jackson 1.25 3.00
40 LeBron James 12.00 30.00
41 Antawn Jamison 1.50 4.00
42 Al Jefferson 1.50 4.00
43 Richard Jefferson 1.50 4.00
44 Yi Jianlian 1.50 4.00
45 Jason Kidd 1.50 4.00
46 Andrei Kirilenko 1.25 3.00
47 David Lee 1.25 3.00
48 Corey Maggette 1.25 3.00
49 Shawn Marion 1.50 4.00
50 Kenyon Martin 1.50 4.00
51 Kevin Martin 1.50 4.00
52 Desmond Mason 1.00 2.50
53 Tracy McGrady 1.50 4.00
54 Brad Miller 1.25 3.00
55 Mike Miller 1.50 4.00
56 Yao Ming 2.00 5.00
57 Jamario Moon 1.00 2.50
58 Alonzo Mourning 2.00 5.00
59 Steve Nash 1.50 4.00
60 Joakim Noah 1.50 4.00
61 Dirk Nowitzki 2.00 5.00
62 Shaquille O'Neal 3.00 8.00
63 Greg Oden 1.50 4.00
64 Lamar Odom 1.50 4.00
65 Tony Parker 1.50 4.00
66 Chris Paul 2.50 6.00
67 Paul Pierce 2.00 5.00
68 Tayshaun Prince 1.50 4.00
69 Michael Redd 1.50 4.00
70 Jason Richardson 1.50 4.00
71 Brandon Roy 1.50 4.00
72 Luis Scola 1.25 3.00
73 Ramon Sessions 1.25 3.00
74 Josh Smith 1.50 4.00
75 Amare Stoudemire 1.50 4.00
76 Rodney Stuckey 2.00 5.00
77 Al Thornton 1.25 3.00
78 Hedo Turkoglu 1.50 4.00
79 Dwyane Wade 3.00 8.00
80 Ben Wallace 1.50 4.00
81 Gerald Wallace 1.50 4.00
82 Rasheed Wallace 1.50 4.00
83 David West 1.50 4.00
84 Chris Wilcox 1.00 2.50
85 Deron Williams 1.50 4.00
86 Louis Williams 1.25 3.00
87 Marvin Williams 1.50 4.00
88 Mo Williams 1.25 3.00
89 Brandan Wright 1.25 3.00
90 Thaddeus Young 1.25 3.00
91 Joe Alexander AU RC 5.00 12.00
92 Mario Chalmers AU RC 8.00 20.00
93 Joey Dorsey AU RC 5.00 12.00
94 Darrell Arthur AU RC 5.00 12.00
95 Rudy Fernandez AU RC 6.00 15.00
96 Marc Gasol AU RC 8.00 20.00
97 J.R. Giddens AU RC 5.00 12.00
98 Donte Greene AU RC 5.00 12.00
99 Roy Hibbert AU RC 8.00 20.00
100 J.J. Hickson AU RC 6.00 15.00
101 George Hill AU RC 8.00 20.00
102 Robin Lopez AU RC 5.00 12.00
103 Anthony Randolph AU RC 8.00 20.00
104 Brandon Rush AU RC 5.00 12.00
105 Walter Sharpe AU RC 5.00 12.00
106 Marreese Speights AU RC 5.00 12.00
107 Jason Thompson AU RC 5.00 12.00
108 Kyle Weaver AU RC 5.00 12.00
109 Sonny Weems AU RC 5.00 12.00
110 D.J. White AU RC 5.00 12.00
81RC D.J. Augustin AU RC 10.00 25.00
82RC Jerryd Bayless AU RC 10.00 25.00
83RC Michael Beasley AU RC 15.00 40.00
84RC Danilo Gallinari AU RC 15.00 40.00
85RC Eric Gordon AU RC 25.00 60.00
86RC Brook Lopez AU RC 15.00 40.00
87RC Kevin Love AU RC 75.00 150.00
88RC O.J. Mayo AU RC 15.00 40.00
89RC Derrick Rose AU RC 300.00 500.00
90RC Russell Westbrook AU RC 75.00 150.00

2008-09 Upper Deck Radiance AU Standard

STATED PRINT RUN 10 TO 25 SER.#'d SETS
SOME UNPRICED DUE TO SCARCITY
AUAG Artis Gilmore/25 10.00 25.00
AUAH Al Horford/25 6.00 15.00
AUBR Brandon Roy/25 10.00 25.00
AUCL Carl Landry/25 15.00 30.00
AUCP Chris Paul/25 40.00 80.00
AUDA D.J. Augustin/25 6.00 15.00
AUDH Dwight Howard/25 25.00 50.00
AUDR Derrick Rose/25 150.00 400.00
AUEG Eric Gordon/25 25.00 60.00
AUGG George Gervin/25 12.00 30.00
AUJA Joe Alexander/25 6.00 15.00
AUJB Jerryd Bayless/25 8.00 20.00
AUJG J.R. Giddens/25 6.00 15.00
AULJ LeBron James/23 200.00 400.00
AULW Luke Walton/25 8.00 20.00
AUMA Morris Almond/25 6.00 15.00
AUMB Michael Beasley/25 15.00 40.00
AUMJ Michael Jordan/23 250.00 500.00
AUOM O.J. Mayo/25 15.00 40.00
AUPP Paul Pierce/25 20.00 50.00
AURF Rudy Fernandez/25 10.00 25.00
AURR Rajon Rondo/25 20.00 50.00
AURW Russell Westbrook/25 40.00 100.00
AUSW Sonny Weems/25 6.00 15.00
AUTC Tom Chambers/25 6.00 15.00

2008-09 Upper Deck Radiance Auto Focus

APPROXIMATE ODDS 1:6
AFBE Marco Belinelli 6.00 15.00
AFCL Carl Landry 10.00 25.00
AFDH Dwight Howard SP 20.00 50.00
AFDR Derrick Rose SP 150.00 350.00
AFDW Deron Williams 15.00 40.00
AFGH George Hill 8.00 20.00
AFJG J.R. Giddens 6.00 15.00
AFKB Kobe Bryant SP 125.00 225.00
AFKG Kevin Garnett SP 75.00 150.00
AFLJ LeBron James SP 250.00 500.00
AFMB Michael Beasley 15.00 40.00
AFMC Mario Chalmers 8.00 20.00
AFMJ Michael Jordan 300.00 600.00
AFOM O.J. Mayo SP 15.00 40.00
AFRF Rudy Fernandez 8.00 20.00
AFRR Rajon Rondo 15.00 30.00

2008-09 Upper Deck Radiance Auto Focus Dual

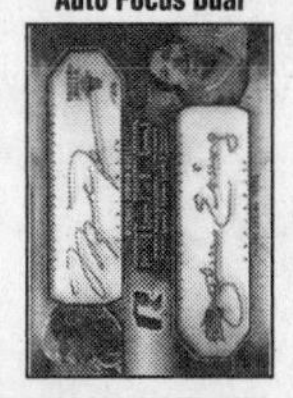

STATED PRINT RUN 10 TO 25 SER.#'d SETS
UNPRICED TRIPLE PRINT RUN 5 TO 10 SETS
AFDBF Jordan Farmar/25 / Andrew Bynum 40.00 100.00
AFDCC Daequan Cook/25 / Mario Chalmers 15.00 40.00
AFDDH Kevin Durant/25 / Al Horford 50.00 120.00
AFDJB Larry Bird/25 / Magic Johnson 200.00 350.00
AFDJE Michael Jordan/25 / Julius Erving 300.00 600.00
AFDMB O.J. Mayo/25 / Michael Beasley 30.00 60.00
AFDPG Kevin Garnett/25 / Paul Pierce 100.00 200.00
AFDRH Brandon Rush/25 / Roy Hibbert 15.00 40.00

2008-09 Upper Deck Radiance Diplomatic Autographs

APPROXIMATE ODDS 1:3
DIAD Adrian Dantley 5.00 12.00
DICD Clyde Drexler 20.00 40.00
DIDG Donte Greene 5.00 12.00
DIDH Dwight Howard SP 20.00 50.00
DIDR David Robinson SP 25.00 60.00
DIDW D.J. White 5.00 12.00
DIJC Javaris Crittenton 5.00 12.00
DIJK Jason Kidd SP 20.00 40.00
DIJO Magic Johnson 30.00 80.00
DIKB Kobe Bryant SP 125.00 225.00
DIKG Kevin Garnett 40.00 80.00
DILJ LeBron James 100.00 200.00
DIMB Michael Beasley SP 20.00 40.00
DIMJ Michael Jordan 300.00 600.00
DIMP Mark Price 20.00 40.00
DIRF Randy Foye 5.00 12.00
DIRH Richard Hendrix 5.00 12.00
DIRJ Richard Jefferson 5.00 12.00
DITP Tayshaun Prince 5.00 12.00
DIVC Vince Carter 25.00 50.00

2008-09 Upper Deck Radiance Inked

STATED PRINT RUN 10 TO 99 SER.#'d SETS
IAL Acie Law/99 5.00 12.00
IBE Michael Beasley/99 12.50 30.00
ICW C.J. Watson/99 5.00 12.00
IDE Deron Williams/99 10.00 25.00
IDG Donte Greene/99 5.00 12.00
IEC Eddy Curry/99 5.00 12.00
IGH George Hill/99 10.00 25.00
IJF Jordan Farmar/99 5.00 12.00
IJS Josh Smith/99 5.00 12.00
ILA LaMarcus Aldridge/99 8.00 20.00
ILJ LeBron James/23 200.00 400.00
IMB Mike Bibby/99 5.00 12.00
IMW Mo Williams/99 15.00 30.00
IQR Quentin Richardson/99 5.00 12.00
IRB Ronnie Brewer/99 5.00 12.00
ISM J.R. Smith/99 5.00 12.00
ITT Tyrus Thomas/99 8.00 20.00
IWE David West/99 5.00 12.00

2008-09 Upper Deck Radiance Marks Dual

STATED PRINT RUN 10 TO 50 SER.#'d SETS
SOME UNPRICED DUE TO SCARCITY
DMBW Deron Williams/50 / Carlos Boozer 20.00 40.00
DMCB Daequan Cook/50 / Michael Beasley 15.00 30.00
DMGF Rudy Fernandez/50 / Marc Gasol 20.00 40.00

DMGM O.J. Mayo/50 20.00 40.00
Rudy Gay
DMGR Ben Gordon/50 100.00 225.00
Derrick Rose
DMPG Kevin Garnett/50 50.00 120.00
Paul Pierce
DMSA Walter Sharpe/50 8.00 20.00
Arron Afflalo
DMSW J.R. Smith/50 8.00 20.00
Sonny Weems

2008-09 Upper Deck Radiance Name Tag Autographs

APPROXIMATE ODDS 1:3
NTAA Alexis Ajinca 4.00 10.00
NTBW Bill Walker 4.00 10.00
NTDA D.J. Augustin SP 8.00 20.00
NTDR Derrick Rose SP 125.00 250.00
NTDW D.J. White 4.00 10.00
NTGH George Hill 5.00 12.00
NTGR Donte Greene 4.00 10.00
NTJB Jerryd Bayless SP 6.00 15.00
NTJJ J.J. Hickson 5.00 12.00
NTJM Javale McGee 5.00 12.00
NTJT Jason Thompson 4.00 10.00
NTKL Kevin Love SP 20.00 50.00
NTLM Luc Richard Mbah A Moute 4.00 10.00
NTMB Michael Beasley 12.50 30.00
NTMC Mario Chalmers 5.00 12.00
NTMT Mike Taylor 4.00 10.00
NTOM O.J. Mayo SP 20.00 40.00
NTRF Rudy Fernandez 8.00 20.00
NTRH Roy Hibbert 5.00 12.00
NTRW Russell Westbrook SP 25.00 60.00
NTSS Sean Singletary 4.00 10.00
NTSW Sonny Weems 4.00 10.00
NTWS Walter Sharpe 4.00 10.00

2008-09 Upper Deck Radiance Signature Flight

APPROXIMATE ODDS 1:3
SFAB Aaron Brooks 4.00 10.00
SFAT Al Thornton SP 6.00 15.00
SFDH Dwight Howard SP 25.00 50.00
SFDT David Thompson 6.00 15.00
SFDW Dominique Wilkins SP 15.00 30.00
SFJF Jordan Farmar SP 4.00 10.00
SFJG J.R. Giddens 4.00 10.00
SFKB Kobe Bryant SP 100.00 200.00
SFLJ LeBron James 100.00 200.00
SFMJ Michael Jordan 200.00 400.00
SFQR Quentin Richardson SP 4.00 10.00
SFRB Ronnie Brewer 4.00 10.00
SFSS Stromile Swift SP 5.00 12.00
SFSW Sonny Weems 4.00 10.00
SFTM Tracy McGrady 12.00 30.00
SFTP Tayshaun Prince SP 5.00 12.00
SFWE Spud Webb SP 5.00 12.00

2008-09 Upper Deck Radiance Sweet Shot Autographs

APPROXIMATE ODDS 1:6
SSAA Arron Afflalo 4.00 10.00
SSBB Bruce Bowen 15.00 30.00
SSBG Ben Gordon SP 15.00 30.00
SSBM Brad Miller 4.00 10.00
SSBO Andrew Bogut 5.00 12.00
SSCB Carlos Boozer 4.00 10.00
SSCM Corey Maggette SP 6.00 15.00
SSCP Chris Paul 20.00 50.00
SSCS Cedric Simmons 4.00 10.00
SSDG Danny Granger 6.00 15.00
SSDH Dwight Howard SP 25.00 60.00
SSGD Glen Davis 8.00 20.00
SSGI Daniel Gibson SP 5.00 12.00
SSGP Gabe Pruitt 4.00 10.00
SSHA Devin Harris 6.00 15.00
SSJB Josh Boone 4.00 10.00
SSKV Kiki Vandeweghe SP 5.00 12.00
SSLA LaMarcus Aldridge SP 8.00 20.00
SSMA Morris Almond 4.00 10.00
SSMW Marvin Williams 4.00 10.00
SSNR Nate Robinson 4.00 10.00
SSRB Ronnie Brewer SP 6.00 15.00
SSSB Shannon Brown 4.00 10.00
SSSK Steve Kerr 6.00 15.00
SSTP Tony Parker 10.00 25.00

2008-09 Upper Deck Radiance Writing Samples

STATED PRINT RUN 50 SER.#'d SETS
WSAB Arron Afflalo 10.00 25.00
Marco Belinelli
WSBH Shane Battier 25.00 60.00
Dwight Howard
WSDA Kevin Durant 50.00 120.00
D.J. Augustin
WSGR George Hill 20.00 50.00
Roy Hibbert
WSGS George Gervin 10.00 25.00
Rodney Stuckey
WSGW Glen Davis 35.00 75.00
Larry Johnson
WSLL Brook Lopez 15.00 30.00
Robin Lopez
WSLP Bill Laimbeer 10.00 25.00
Tayshaun Prince
WSLW Russell Westbrook 100.00 200.00
Kevin Love
WSPG Kevin Garnett 50.00 120.00
Paul Pierce
WSRC Brandon Rush 15.00 30.00
Mario Chalmers
WSWR Jamaal Wilkes 20.00 50.00
Dennis Rodman

1999-00 Upper Deck Retro

The debut release of Retro contained 110-cards, combining legends of the NBA with current NBA stars and new rookies.
COMPLETE SET (110) 20.00 40.00
UNPRICED PLATINUM SERIAL #'d TO 1
1 Michael Jordan 2.00 5.00
2 John Havlicek .30 .75
3 Antawn Jamison .25 .60
4 Chris Webber .25 .60
5 Maurice Taylor .15 .40
6 Kevin Garnett .50 1.25
7 Walter Davis .25 .60
8 Kobe Bryant 1.25 3.00
9 Tim Duncan .50 1.25
10 Karl Malone .30 .75
11 Larry Bird .75 2.00
12 Juwan Howard .20 .50
13 Bill Walton .25 .60
14 Bob Cousy .40 1.00
15 Dave DeBusschere .25 .60
16 Toni Kukoc .25 .60
17 Allan Houston .20 .50
18 Grant Hill .30 .75
19 Rik Smits .25 .60
20 Glenn Robinson .20 .50
21 Dave Cowens .25 .60
22 Isaac Austin .15 .40
23 Derek Anderson .15 .40
24 Tracy McGrady .40 1.00
25 Nate Thurmond .25 .60
26 Dikembe Mutombo .25 .60
27 Oscar Robertson .30 .75
28 Antonio McDyess .20 .50
29 Jamaal Wilkes .20 .50
30 Eddie Jones .25 .60
31 Nick Van Exel .20 .50
32 Reggie Miller .25 .60
33 David Thompson .30 .75
34 Ray Allen .25 .60
35 Anfernee Hardaway .40 1.00
36 Brian Grant .15 .40
37 Allen Iverson .50 1.25
38 Vince Carter .50 1.25
39 Mitch Richmond .25 .60
40 Kareem Abdul-Jabbar .40 1.00
41 Alonzo Mourning .30 .75
42 Jonathan Bender RC .30 .75
43 Scottie Pippen .40 1.00
44 George Gervin .25 .60
45 Shawn Kemp .25 .60
46 Dave Bing .25 .60
47 John Starks .25 .60
48 Earl Monroe .25 .60
49 Stephon Marbury .20 .50
50 Cedric Maxwell .25 .60
51 Tom Gugliotta .15 .40
52 David Robinson .40 1.00
53 Shareef Abdur-Rahim .20 .50
54 Elvin Hayes .25 .60
55 Wilt Chamberlain .50 1.25
56 Willis Reed .25 .60
57 Kevin McHale .30 .75
58 Elden Campbell .15 .40
59 Steve Smith .15 .40
60 Brent Barry .20 .50
61 Jerry Stackhouse .25 .60
62 Otis Birdsong .25 .60
63 Michael Olowokandi .15 .40
64 Joe Smith .20 .50
65 Tim Thomas .20 .50
66 Rick Barry .25 .60
67 Jason Williams .30 .75
68 Julius Erving .50 1.25
69 John Stockton .30 .75
70 Cal Bowdler RC .30 .75
71 Nate Archibald .25 .60
72 Elgin Baylor .25 .60
73 Ron Mercer .20 .50
74 Damon Stoudamire .25 .60
75 Jerry West .30 .75
76 Michael Finley .25 .60
77 Charles Barkley .40 1.00
78 Shaquille O'Neal .60 1.50
79 Paul Pierce .40 1.00
80 Keith Van Horn .20 .50
81 Jason Kidd .40 1.00
82 Gary Payton .25 .60
83 James Worthy .30 .75
84 Mike Bibby .25 .60
85 Bill Russell .40 1.00
86 Wes Unseld .25 .60
87 Robert Parish .25 .60
88 Walt Frazier .25 .60
89 Antoine Walker .25 .60
90 Steve Nash .40 1.00
91 Moses Malone .25 .60
92 Hakeem Olajuwon .30 .75
93 Tim Hardaway .25 .60
94 Patrick Ewing .30 .75
95 Vin Baker .25 .60
96 Trajan Langdon RC .25 .60
97 Ron Artest RC .75 2.00
98 James Posey RC .30 .75
99 Shawn Marion RC .75 2.00
100 Jumaine Jones RC .30 .75
101 William Avery RC .30 .75
102 Corey Maggette RC .60 1.50
103 Andre Miller RC .75 2.00
104 Jason Terry RC .75 2.00
105 Wally Szczerbiak RC .60 1.50
106 Richard Hamilton RC .75 2.00
107 Elton Brand RC .75 2.00
108 Baron Davis RC 1.00 2.50
109 Steve Francis RC .75 2.00
110 Lamar Odom RC 1.00 2.50

1999-00 Upper Deck Retro Gold

Randomly inserted in packs, this 110-card set parallels the base set. The cards are serially numbered to 250. To ascertain values on individual cards, please refer to the multiplier in the header below, coupled with the value of the base card.
*STARS: 6X TO 15X BASE CARD HI
*RCs: 3X TO 8X BASE HI

1999-00 Upper Deck Retro Distant Replay

Randomly inserted in packs at one in 11, this 10-card set features some of the early heroes of the NBA and their most memorable accomplishments. Card backs feature a "D" prefix.
COMPLETE SET (10) 12.50 25.00
*PARALLEL: 2.5X TO 6X HI COLUMN
PARALLEL: PRINT RUN 100 SERIAL #'d SETS
D1 Michael Jordan 6.00 15.00
D2 Kareem Abdul-Jabbar 1.25 3.00
D3 Bill Russell 1.25 3.00
D4 Julius Erving 1.50 4.00
D5 George Gervin .75 2.00
D6 Moses Malone .75 2.00
D7 Larry Bird 2.50 6.00
D8 Jerry West 1.00 2.50
D9 Oscar Robertson 1.00 2.50
D10 Elgin Baylor .75 2.00

1999-00 Upper Deck Retro Epic Jordan

Randomly inserted in packs at one in 23, this 10-card set takes you inside Jordan's amazing career. Card backs carry a "J" prefix.
COMPLETE SET (10) 20.00 50.00
COMMON CARD (J1-J10) 2.50 6.00

1999-00 Upper Deck Retro Epic Jordan Parallel

Randomly inserted in packs, this 10-card set parallels the Epic Jordan insert. The cards are serially numbered to 50. Card backs carry a "J" prefix. To ascertain values on individual cards, please refer to the multiplier in the header below, coupled with the value of the base insert.
COMMON CARD (J1-J10) 40.00 100.00

1999-00 Upper Deck Retro Fast Forward

Randomly inserted at one in 23, this 15-card set takes a look into the future of basketball and the next superstars of the NBA. Card backs carry a "F" prefix.
COMPLETE SET (15) 15.00 40.00
F1 Kevin Garnett 2.00 5.00
F2 Kobe Bryant 5.00 12.00
F3 Keith Van Horn .75 2.00
F4 Allen Iverson 2.00 5.00
F5 Vince Carter 2.00 5.00
F6 Paul Pierce 1.50 4.00
F7 Shareef Abdur-Rahim .75 2.00
F8 Jason Williams 1.25 3.00
F9 Tim Duncan 2.00 5.00
F10 Shaquille O'Neal 2.50 6.00
F11 Scottie Pippen 1.50 4.00
F12 Anfernee Hardaway 1.50 4.00
F13 Antawn Jamison 1.00 2.50
F14 Antonio McDyess .75 2.00
F15 Stephon Marbury .75 2.00

1999-00 Upper Deck Retro Inkredible

Randomly inserted in packs at one in 23, this 24-card set features authentic autographs of current and past NBA greats. Card backs are numbered by the player's initial.
AH Anfernee Hardaway 50.00 120.00
AJ Antawn Jamison 6.00 15.00
BC Bob Cousy 25.00 60.00
BG Brian Grant 5.00 12.00
BR Bill Russell 350.00 650.00
CA Cory Alexander 5.00 12.00
DA Darrell Armstrong 5.00 12.00
EH Elvin Hayes 8.00 20.00
ES Eric Snow 5.00 12.00
GG George Gervin 10.00 25.00
GR Glen Rice 10.00 25.00
JH John Havlicek 15.00 40.00
JR Jalen Rose 8.00 20.00
JW Jerry West 25.00 60.00
MB Mookie Blaylock 5.00 12.00
MJ Mark Jackson 8.00 20.00
MT Maurice Taylor 5.00 12.00
NA Nate Archibald 10.00 25.00
RL Raef LaFrentz 5.00 12.00
RT Robert Traylor 5.00 12.00
TK Toni Kukoc 12.00 30.00
VC Vince Carter 15.00 40.00
WC Wilt Chamberlain 1500.00 2300.00
WF Walt Frazier 12.50 30.00

1999-00 Upper Deck Retro Inkredible Level 2

Randomly inserted in packs, this 26-card set features autographs of current and past NBA stars. Each card is hand-numbered to the player's jersey number. Cards with shorter print runs are listed but not priced below.
BG Brian Grant/44 20.00 50.00
ES Eric Snow/20 20.00 50.00
GG George Gervin/44 30.00 60.00
GR Glen Rice/41 40.00 75.00
JH John Havlicek/17 75.00 150.00
JW Jerry West/44 100.00 225.00
MJ Michael Jordan/23 1700.00 2500.00
MT Maurice Taylor/23 20.00 50.00
RL Raef LaFrentz/45 20.00 50.00
RT Robert Traylor/54 20.00 50.00
VC Vince Carter/15 75.00 150.00

1999-00 Upper Deck Retro Lunchboxes

These 11 lunchboxes served as the boxes in which the 1999-00 Upper Deck Retro product shipped out in. The lunchboxes picture Larry Bird, Michael Jordan, and Julius Erving.
1 Larry Bird 6.00 15.00
2 Julius Erving 6.00 15.00
3 Julius Erving 6.00 15.00
Larry Bird
4 Michael Jordan #1 6.00 15.00
5 Michael Jordan #2 6.00 15.00
6 Michael Jordan #3 6.00 15.00
7 Michael Jordan 6.00 15.00
Larry Bird
8 Michael Jordan 6.00 15.00
Julius Erving
9 Michael Jordan #1 6.00 15.00
Michael Jordan #2
10 Michael Jordan #1 6.00 15.00
Michael Jordan #3
11 Michael Jordan #2 6.00 15.00
Michael Jordan #3

1999-00 Upper Deck Retro Old School/New School

Randomly inserted in packs at one in three, this 30-card set highlights some of the top hoop stars of yesterday and today in two unique card designs. Card backs carry a "S" prefix.
COMPLETE SET (30) 12.50 30.00
*PARALLEL: 2X TO 5X HI COLUMN
PARALLEL: PRINT RUN 500 SERIAL #'d SETS
S1 Michael Jordan 3.00 8.00
S2 Wilt Chamberlain .75 2.00
S3 Oscar Robertson .50 1.25
S4 Julius Erving .75 2.00
S5 George Gervin .40 1.00
S6 John Havlicek .50 1.25
S7 Elgin Baylor .40 1.00
S8 Earl Monroe .40 1.00
S9 Jerry West .50 1.25
S10 Larry Bird 1.25 3.00
S11 Elvin Hayes .40 1.00
S12 Moses Malone .40 1.00
S13 Bill Walton .40 1.00
S14 Kareem Abdul-Jabbar .60 1.50
S15 Bill Russell .60 1.50
S16 Kobe Bryant 2.00 5.00
S17 Allen Iverson .75 2.00
S18 Stephon Marbury .30 .75
S19 Shaquille O'Neal 1.00 2.50
S20 Kevin Garnett .75 2.00
S21 Keith Van Horn .30 .75
S22 Jason Williams .50 1.25
S23 Paul Pierce .60 1.50
S24 Vince Carter .75 2.00
S25 Tim Duncan .75 2.00
S26 Antoine Walker .40 1.00
S27 Shareef Abdur-Rahim .30 .75
S28 Ray Allen .40 1.00
S29 Anfernee Hardaway .60 1.50
S30 Grant Hill .50 1.25

2004-05 Upper Deck Rivals Box Set

COMPLETE SET (30) 8.00 20.00
COMMON LEBRON (1-13) .60 1.50
COMMON CARMELO (14-26) .30 .75
COMMON DUAL (27-30) .40 1.00
AUTO'S NOT PRICED DUE TO SCARCITY
KCLJ LeBron James Jumbo 1.25 3.00

2004-05 Upper Deck Rivals Box Set Gold

*GOLD SINGLES: 1.25X TO 3X BASE HI

2004-05 Upper Deck Rivals Box Set Platinum

LEBRON PRINT RUN 23 SER.#'d SETS
CARMELO PRINT RUN 15 SER.#'d SETS
NOT PRICED DUE TO SCARCITY
COMMON COMBO (27-30) 40.00 100.00
COMBO PRINT RUN 38 SER.#'d SETS

2005-06 Upper Deck Rookie Debut

Released in September of 2005, Rookie Debut features the first live autographs and rookie cards from an NBA licensed products. The base set contains 150 cards where numbers 1-100 picture veterans and numbers 101-150 picture rookies. Base cards have full color action photography on the fronts and a colored line and banner in team colors with the player's name and team logo. Rooki cards employ a slightly different design where the word, "Rookie" is prominently displayed. Rookie Debut was packaged in 28-pack boxes of six cards each and carried a SRP of $2.99.
COMPLETE SET (150) 40.00 80.00
COMP.SET w/o RC's (100) 15.00 40.00
1 Tony Delk .15 .40
2 Josh Smith .25 .60
3 Al Harrington .20 .50
4 Antoine Walker .25 .60
5 Ricky Davis .20 .50
6 Paul Pierce .30 .75
7 Kareem Rush .15 .40
8 Emeka Okafor .25 .60
9 Primoz Brezec .15 .40
10 Eddy Curry .20 .50
11 Kirk Hinrich .25 .60
12 Ben Gordon .25 .60
13 Luol Deng .25 .60
14 Drew Gooden .20 .50
15 LeBron James 1.25 3.00
16 Zydrunas Ilgauskas .20 .50
17 Dirk Nowitzki .40 1.00
18 Jason Terry .25 .60
19 Josh Howard .25 .60
20 Michael Finley .25 .60
21 Carmelo Anthony .50 1.25
22 Kenyon Martin .25 .60
23 Andre Miller .20 .50
24 Earl Boykins .15 .40
25 Ben Wallace .25 .60
26 Chauncey Billups .25 .60
27 Richard Hamilton .20 .50
28 Tayshaun Prince .25 .60
29 Troy Murphy .25 .60
30 Jason Richardson .25 .60
31 Baron Davis .25 .60
32 Tracy McGrady .30 .75
33 Yao Ming .30 .75
34 Juwan Howard .20 .50
35 Jermaine O'Neal .25 .60
36 Stephen Jackson .20 .50
37 Ron Artest .25 .60
38 Corey Maggette .25 .60
39 Elton Brand .25 .60
40 Bobby Simmons .15 .40
41 Caron Butler .25 .60
42 Kobe Bryant 1.25 3.00
43 Lamar Odom .25 .60
44 Mike Miller .25 .60
45 Jason Williams .25 .60
46 Pau Gasol .25 .60
47 Stromile Swift .15 .40
48 Dwyane Wade .60 1.50
49 Eddie Jones .25 .60
50 Shaquille O'Neal .50 1.25
51 Desmond Mason .15 .40
52 Maurice Williams .20 .50
53 Michael Redd .25 .60
54 Kevin Garnett .50 1.25
55 Latrell Sprewell .25 .60
56 Sam Cassell .25 .60
57 Vince Carter .40 1.00
58 Jason Kidd .40 1.00
59 Richard Jefferson .25 .60
60 Dan Dickau .15 .40
61 Jamaal Magloire .15 .40
62 J.R. Smith .25 .60
63 Jamal Crawford .20 .50
64 Stephon Marbury .20 .50
65 Allan Houston .15 .40
66 Dwight Howard .50 1.25
67 Grant Hill .30 .75
68 Steve Francis .25 .60
69 Allen Iverson .40 1.00
70 Andre Iguodala .25 .60
71 Chris Webber .25 .60
72 Kyle Korver .20 .50
73 Amare Stoudemire .25 .60
74 Shawn Marion .25 .60
75 Steve Nash .30 .75
76 Quentin Richardson .20 .50
77 Damon Stoudamire .20 .50
78 Shareef Abdur-Rahim .20 .50
79 Zach Randolph .25 .60
80 Brad Miller .25 .60
81 Mike Bibby .25 .60
82 Peja Stojakovic .25 .60
83 Cuttino Mobley .20 .50
84 Manu Ginobili .25 .60
85 Tim Duncan .40 1.00
86 Tony Parker .25 .60
87 Rashard Lewis .25 .60
88 Ray Allen .25 .60
89 Luke Ridnour .20 .50
90 Vladimir Radmanovic .15 .40
91 Rafer Alston .15 .40
92 Jalen Rose .25 .60
93 Chris Bosh .25 .60
94 Andrei Kirilenko .25 .60
95 Carlos Boozer .25 .60
96 Matt Harpring .25 .60
97 Antawn Jamison .25 .60
98 Gilbert Arenas .25 .60
99 Larry Hughes .20 .50
100 Jarvis Hayes .15 .40
101 Andrew Bogut RC 1.25 3.00
102 Chris Taft RC .75 2.00
103 Chris Paul RC 3.00 8.00
104 Martynas Andriuskevicius RC .75 2.00
105 Amir Johnson RC .75 2.00
106 Andrew Bynum RC 2.50 6.00
107 Gerald Green RC 1.00 2.50
108 Rashad McCants RC .75 2.00
109 Fran Vazquez RC .75 2.00
110 Ike Diogu RC .75 2.00
111 Raymond Felton RC 1.25 3.00
112 Hakim Warrick RC 1.00 2.50
113 Deron Williams RC 2.00 5.00
114 Daniel Ewing RC .75 2.00
115 Sean May RC .75 2.00
116 Johan Petro RC .75 2.00
117 Erazem Lorbek RC .75 2.00
118 Joey Graham RC .75 2.00
119 Antoine Wright RC .75 2.00
120 Ronny Turiaf RC .75 2.00
121 Linas Kleiza RC .75 2.00
122 Alex Acker RC .75 2.00
123 Jarrett Jack RC .75 2.00
124 Danny Granger RC 1.50 4.00
125 Francisco Garcia RC 1.00 2.50
126 Ryan Gomes RC .75 2.00
127 Wayne Simien RC .75 2.00
128 Robert Whaley RC .75 2.00
129 Dijon Thompson RC .75 2.00
130 Nate Robinson RC 1.00 2.50
131 Brandon Bass RC 1.00 2.50
132 Andray Blatche RC 1.00 2.50
133 Channing Frye RC 1.00 2.50
134 Salim Stoudamire RC .75 2.00
135 Luther Head RC .75 2.00
136 Julius Hodge RC .75 2.00
137 David Lee RC 1.25 3.00
138 Travis Diener RC .75 2.00
139 Marvin Williams RC 1.00 2.50
140 Lawrence Roberts RC .75 2.00
141 C.J. Miles RC 1.00 2.50
142 Ricky Sanchez RC .75 2.00
143 Bracey Wright RC .75 2.00
144 Jason Maxiell RC .75 2.00
145 Uros Slokar RC .75 2.00
146 Martell Webster RC .75 2.00
147 Orien Greene RC .75 2.00
148 Charlie Villanueva RC 1.00 2.50
149 Monta Ellis RC 1.50 4.00
150 Von Wafer RC .75 2.00

2005-06 Upper Deck Rookie Debut Blue

Randomly seeded in packs, this 150-card set parallels the base set enhanced with blue foil shifts and each card is sequentially numbered to 150. Other parallel inserts are Gold sequentially numbered to 50, Silver sequentially numbered to 100 and Spectrum sequentially numbered to 25. Each different version has corresponding foil highlights on the card.
*1-100 BLUE: 2X TO 5X BASE HI
*101-150 RC BLUE: .6X TO 1.5X BASE HI

2005-06 Upper Deck Rookie Debut Gold

Randomly seeded in packs, this 150-card set parallels the base set enhanced with blue foil shifts and each card is sequentially numbered to 50.
*1-100 GOLD: 5X TO 12X BASE HI
*101-150 RC GOLD: 1.5X TO 4X BASE HI

2005-06 Upper Deck Rookie Debut Silver

Randomly seeded in packs, this 150-card set parallels the base set enhanced with silver foil shifts and each card is sequentially numbered to 100.
*1-100 SILVER: 3X TO 8X BASE HI
*101-150 RC SILVER: 1X TO 2.5X BASE HI

2005-06 Upper Deck Rookie Debut Spectrum

Randomly seeded in packs, this 150-card set parallels the base set enhanced with silver foil shifts and each card is sequentially numbered to 25.
*1-100 SPEC: 8X TO 20X BASE HI
101-150 SPEC: 2X TO 5X BASE HI

2005-06 Upper Deck Rookie Debut Draft Duos

Randomly inserted in packs, this 24-card set features a horizontal design with two rookie player pictures and two sticker autographs. Each card is sequentially numbered to 75.
BT Andrew Bogut/75 20.00 50.00
Chris Taft
EB Andre Emmett/75 8.00 20.00
Antonio Burks
EM Monta Ellis/75 15.00 40.00
C.J. Miles
FM Raymond Felton/75 20.00 50.00
Rashad McCants
FS Channing Frye/75 12.50 30.00
Salim Stoudamire
GG Ryan Gomes/75 20.00 50.00
Danny Granger
HN Dwight Howard/75 75.00 150.00
Jameer Nelson
JA LeBron James/25 300.00 600.00
Carmelo Anthony
LG David Lee/75 15.00 40.00
Francisco Garcia
PU Pavel Podkolzin/75 8.00 20.00
Beno Udrih
PW Chris Paul/75 100.00 200.00
Deron Williams
RD Kareem Rush/75 8.00 20.00
Dan Dickau
RW Justin Reed/75 12.50 30.00
Delonte West
TH Dijon Thompson/75 8.00 20.00
Julius Hodge
TS Ronny Turiaf/75 12.50 30.00
Wayne Simien
VD Fran Vazquez/75 8.00 20.00
Travis Diener
WM Marvin Williams/75 20.00 50.00
Sean May
WV Hakim Warrick/75 25.00 60.00
Charlie Villanueva
WW Antoine Wright/75 8.00 20.00
Martell Webster

2005-06 Upper Deck Rookie Debut Hotagraphs

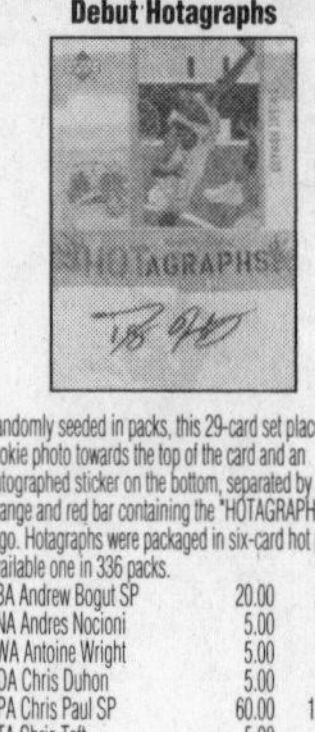

Randomly seeded in packs, this 29-card set places a rookie photo towards the top of the card and an autographed sticker on the bottom, separated by an orange and red bar containing the "HOTAGRAPHS" logo. Hotagraphs were packaged in six-card hot packs available one in 336 packs.
ABA Andrew Bogut SP 20.00 50.00
ANA Andres Nocioni 5.00 12.00
AWA Antoine Wright 5.00 12.00
CDA Chris Duhon 5.00 12.00
CPA Chris Paul SP 60.00 120.00
CTA Chris Taft 5.00 12.00
CVA Charlie Villanueva 6.00 15.00
DEA Daniel Ewing 5.00 12.00
DHA Dwight Howard 15.00 40.00
FVA Fran Vazquez 5.00 12.00
GGA Gerald Green SP 8.00 20.00
HWA Hakim Warrick 6.00 15.00
JGA Joey Graham 5.00 12.00
JHA Julius Hodge 5.00 12.00
JNA Jameer Nelson 5.00 12.00
JRA J.R. Smith 5.00 12.00
LHA Luther Head 5.00 12.00
LJA LeBron James SP 150.00 300.00
MAA Martell Webster 5.00 12.00
MWA Marvin Williams SP 10.00 25.00
RFA Raymond Felton 8.00 20.00
RGA Ryan Gomes 5.00 12.00
RMA Rashad McCants 5.00 12.00
RTA Ronny Turiaf 8.00 20.00
SMA Sean May SP 6.00 15.00
SSA Salim Stoudamire 5.00 12.00

2005-06 Upper Deck Rookie Debut Ink

Inserted at the rate of one in 14, this 74-card set employs similar design elements to the base set along with photos and sticker autographs. Several players were shortprinted, information that was provided directly from Upper Deck.
AB Andrew Bogut SP 12.50 30.00
AE Andre Emmett 5.00 12.00
AJ Al Jefferson 5.00 12.00
AN Antonio Burks 5.00 12.00
AV Anderson Varejao 5.00 12.00
AW Antoine Wright 5.00 12.00
BI Andris Biedrins 5.00 12.00
BL Andray Blatche 6.00 15.00
BR Bernard Robinson 5.00 12.00
BU Beno Udrih 5.00 12.00
BW Bracey Wright 5.00 12.00
BY Andrew Bynum 15.00 40.00
CD Chris Duhon 5.00 12.00
CF Channing Frye 6.00 15.00
CJ C.J. Miles 5.00 12.00
CP Chris Paul SP 50.00 120.00
CT Chris Taft 5.00 12.00
CV Charlie Villanueva 6.00 15.00
DA Danny Granger 10.00 25.00
DD Dan Dickau 5.00 12.00
DE Daniel Ewing 5.00 12.00
DH Dwight Howard 12.50 30.00
DL David Lee 8.00 20.00
DT Dijon Thompson 5.00 12.00
DW Deron Williams SP 20.00 40.00
ED Erik Daniels 5.00 12.00
FG Francisco Garcia 6.00 15.00
FV Fran Vazquez 5.00 12.00
GG Gerald Green 6.00 15.00
HS Ha Seung-Jin 5.00 12.00
HW Hakim Warrick 6.00 15.00
ID Ike Diogu 5.00 12.00
JE John Edwards 5.00 12.00
JH Julius Hodge 5.00 12.00
JJ Jarrett Jack 5.00 12.00
JM Jason Maxiell 5.00 12.00
JN Jameer Nelson 5.00 12.00
JP Johan Petro 5.00 12.00
JR J.R. Smith 5.00 12.00
JU Justin Reed 5.00 12.00
KD Keyon Dooling 5.00 12.00
KS Kirk Snyder 5.00 12.00
LC Lionel Chalmers 5.00 12.00
LF Luis Flores 5.00 12.00
LH Luther Head 5.00 12.00
LJ LeBron James SP 125.00 250.00
MA Martynas Andriuskevicius 5.00 12.00
MD Marquis Daniels 5.00 12.00
ME Monta Ellis 10.00 25.00
MG Michael Gelabale 5.00 12.00
ML Martell Webster 5.00 12.00
MR Michael Redd SP 8.00 20.00
MW Marvin Williams SP 10.00 25.00
NO Andres Nocioni 5.00 12.00
NR Nate Robinson 6.00 15.00
PP Pavel Podkolzin 5.00 12.00
RA Rafael Araujo 5.00 12.00
RF Raymond Felton 8.00 20.00
RG Ryan Gomes 5.00 12.00
RI Royal Ivey 5.00 12.00
RM Rashad McCants 5.00 12.00
RT Ronny Turiaf 8.00 20.00
SM Sean May 5.00 12.00
SS Salim Stoudamire 5.00 12.00
ST Sebastian Telfair 5.00 12.00
TD Travis Diener 5.00 12.00
UH Udonis Haslem 5.00 12.00

Viktor Khryapa 5.00 12.00
Delonte West 5.00 12.00
Maurice Williams 5.00 12.00
Wayne Simien 5.00 12.00

2005-06 Upper Deck Rookie Debut Sizzling Swatches

Inserted as four-card memorabilia hot packs at the rate of one in 168, this 42-card set employs a horizontal design with player images on the right and a circle swatch of memorabilia on the left.

Allen Iverson 4.00 10.00
Antawn Jamison 2.50 6.00
Amare Stoudemire 2.50 6.00
Ben Gordon 2.50 6.00
Ben Wallace 2.50 6.00
Carmelo Anthony 5.00 12.00
Chris Bosh 2.50 6.00
Chris Webber 2.50 6.00
Devin Harris 2.50 6.00
Dwight Howard 5.00 12.00
Dirk Nowitzki 4.00 10.00
Gilbert Arenas 2.50 6.00
Gary Payton 2.50 6.00
Andre Iguodala 2.50 6.00
Jason Richardson 2.50 6.00
Josh Childress 2.00 5.00
Jason Kidd 4.00 10.00
J.R. Smith 2.50 6.00
Josh Smith 2.50 6.00
Kobe Bryant 8.00 20.00
Kevin Garnett 5.00 12.00
Luol Deng 2.50 6.00
LeBron James 10.00 25.00
Michael Finley 2.50 6.00
Manu Ginobili 2.50 6.00
Michael Jordan 40.00 100.00
Pau Gasol 2.50 6.00
Paul Pierce 3.00 8.00
Peja Stojakovic 2.50 6.00
Ray Allen 2.50 6.00
Richard Hamilton 2.00 5.00
Richard Jefferson 2.50 6.00
Rashard Lewis 2.50 6.00
Steve Francis 2.50 6.00
Shawn Marion 2.50 6.00
Steve Nash 3.00 8.00
Shaquille O'Neal 5.00 12.00
Stephon Marbury 2.00 5.00
Tim Duncan 4.00 10.00
Tracy McGrady 3.00 8.00
Tony Parker 2.50 6.00
Yao Ming 3.00 8.00

2005-06 Upper Deck Rookie Debut Threads

Randomly seeded at one in 28, this 90-card set also utilizes a horizontal design with some similar design attributes to the base set. Player images appear on the right of the card, while a square swatch of memorabilia appears on the left.

Allan Houston 2.00 5.00
Allen Iverson 4.00 10.00
Andrei Kirilenko 2.00 5.00
Rafer Alston 2.00 5.00
Andre Miller 2.00 5.00
Antonio McDyess 2.00 5.00
Ron Artest 2.50 6.00
Amare Stoudemire 2.50 6.00
Antoine Walker 2.00 5.00
Brian Cook 2.00 5.00
Baron Davis 2.50 6.00
Brad Miller 2.50 6.00
Chris Bosh 2.50 6.00
Caron Butler 2.50 6.00
Ben Wallace 2.50 6.00
Carmelo Anthony 5.00 12.00
Carlos Boozer 2.50 6.00
Chauncey Billups 2.50 6.00
Chris Kaman 2.50 6.00
Corey Maggette 2.00 5.00
Cuttino Mobley 2.00 5.00
Chris Webber 2.50 6.00
Dan Dickau 2.00 5.00
Derek Fisher 2.00 5.00
Devean George 2.00 5.00
Darko Milicic 2.00 5.00
Dirk Nowitzki 4.00 10.00
Donyell Marshall 2.00 5.00
Drew Gooden 2.00 5.00
Damon Stoudamire 2.00 5.00
Elton Brand 2.50 6.00
Eddy Curry 2.00 5.00
Andre Iguodala 2.50 6.00
Grant Hill 3.00 8.00
Gary Payton 2.50 6.00
Glenn Robinson 2.00 5.00
Gerald Wallace 2.50 6.00
Anfernee Hardaway 6.00 15.00
Josh Howard 2.50 6.00
Hedo Turkoglu 2.50 6.00
Andre Iguodala 2.50 6.00
Jason Richardson 2.50 6.00
Jamal Crawford 2.00 5.00
Jarvis Hayes 2.00 5.00
Joe Johnson 2.50 6.00
Jason Kidd 4.00 10.00
Jermaine O'Neal 2.50 6.00
Jalen Rose 2.50 6.00
Jamal Tinsley 2.00 5.00
KB Kobe Bryant 8.00 20.00
KG Kevin Garnett 5.00 12.00
KK Kyle Korver 2.00 5.00
KM Kenyon Martin 2.50 6.00
KR Kareem Rush 2.00 5.00
KT Kurt Thomas 2.00 5.00
KW Kwame Brown 2.00 5.00
LJ LeBron James 10.00 25.00
LO Lamar Odom 2.50 6.00
LW Luke Walton 2.00 5.00
MA Marko Jaric 2.00 5.00
MB Mike Bibby 2.50 6.00
MF Michael Finley 2.50 6.00
MG Manu Ginobili 2.50 6.00
MJ Michael Jordan 40.00 100.00
MO Morris Peterson 1.50 4.00
MP Mickael Pietrus 2.00 5.00
MR Michael Redd 2.50 6.00
NH Nene 2.00 5.00
NV Nick Van Exel 2.50 6.00
PG Pau Gasol 2.50 6.00
PP Paul Pierce 3.00 8.00
PS Peja Stojakovic 2.50 6.00
QR Quentin Richardson 2.00 5.00
RA Ray Allen 2.50 6.00
RH Richard Hamilton 2.00 5.00
RJ Richard Jefferson 2.50 6.00
RL Rashard Lewis 2.50 6.00
RW Rasheed Wallace 2.50 6.00
SF Steve Francis 2.50 6.00
SM Shawn Marion 2.50 6.00
SN Steve Nash 3.00 8.00
SO Shaquille O'Neal 5.00 12.00
ST Stephon Marbury 2.00 5.00
TC Tyson Chandler 2.00 5.00
TD Tim Duncan 4.00 10.00
TE Jason Terry 2.00 5.00
TM Tracy McGrady 3.00 8.00
TP Tony Parker 2.50 6.00
WE Bonzi Wells 2.00 5.00
WI Chris Wilcox 2.00 5.00

2006-07 Upper Deck Rookie Debut

Released in late September 2006, Rookie Debut base cards place full-color player photos on cards designed with a colored strip along the right side of the card to match team colors and a run sheet of player information along the bottom. Veteran players are pictured on card numbers 1-100 and rookies on cards 101-146. Rookie Debut is packaged in 28-pack boxes of six cards each and carried an initial suggested retail price of $2.99.

COMPLETE SET (146) 40.00 80.00
COMP.SET w/o SP's (100) 12.50 30.00
1 Josh Childress .20 .50
2 Joe Johnson .25 .60
3 Marvin Williams .25 .60
4 Gerald Green .20 .50
5 Al Jefferson .25 .60
6 Paul Pierce .30 .75
7 Raymond Felton .30 .75
8 Emeka Okafor .25 .60
9 Gerald Wallace .25 .60
10 Tyson Chandler .20 .50
11 Luol Deng .25 .60
12 Ben Gordon .25 .60
13 Larry Hughes .20 .50
14 Zydrunas Ilgauskas .20 .50
15 LeBron James 1.25 3.00
16 Devin Harris .25 .60
17 Josh Howard .20 .50
18 Dirk Nowitzki .40 1.00
19 Jason Terry .25 .60
20 Carmelo Anthony .30 .75
21 Marcus Camby .20 .50
22 Kenyon Martin .25 .60
23 Chauncey Billups .25 .60
24 Richard Hamilton .20 .50
25 Tayshaun Prince .25 .60
26 Ben Wallace .25 .60
27 Baron Davis .25 .60
28 Troy Murphy .15 .40
29 Jason Richardson .25 .60
30 Rafer Alston .15 .40
31 Tracy McGrady .30 .75
32 Stromile Swift .15 .40
33 Yao Ming .30 .75
34 Jermaine O'Neal .25 .60
35 Peja Stojakovic .25 .60
36 Jamaal Tinsley .15 .40
37 Elton Brand .25 .60
38 Sam Cassell .25 .60
39 Chris Kaman .20 .50
40 Kobe Bryant 1.25 3.00
41 Devean George .15 .40
42 Ronny Turiaf .20 .50
43 Pau Gasol .25 .60
44 Mike Miller .25 .60
45 Damon Stoudamire .20 .50
46 Shaquille O'Neal .50 1.25
47 Gary Payton .25 .60
48 Dwyane Wade .60 1.50
49 Andrew Bogut .25 .60
50 T.J. Ford .20 .50
51 Jamaal Magloire .15 .40
52 Michael Redd .25 .60
53 Ricky Davis .20 .50
54 Kevin Garnett .50 1.25
55 Rashad McCants .15 .40
56 Vince Carter .30 .75
57 Richard Jefferson .25 .60
58 Jason Kidd .40 1.00
59 P.J. Brown .15 .40
60 Desmond Mason .15 .40
61 Chris Paul .50 1.25
62 J.R. Smith .25 .60
63 Steve Francis .25 .60
64 Channing Frye .25 .60
65 Stephon Marbury .20 .50
66 Nate Robinson .25 .60
67 Grant Hill .30 .75
68 Dwight Howard .40 1.00
69 Jameer Nelson .20 .50
70 Darko Milicic .15 .40
71 Andre Iguodala .25 .60
72 Allen Iverson .30 .75
73 Kyle Korver .20 .50
74 Chris Webber .25 .60
75 Boris Diaw .20 .50
76 Shawn Marion .25 .60
77 Steve Nash .30 .75
78 Amare Stoudemire .25 .60
79 Juan Dixon .15 .40
80 Joel Przybilla .15 .40
81 Sebastian Telfair .15 .40
82 Shareef Abdur-Rahim .20 .50
83 Ron Artest .25 .60
84 Mike Bibby .25 .60
85 Tim Duncan .40 1.00
86 Manu Ginobili .25 .60
87 Robert Horry .20 .50
88 Tony Parker .25 .60
89 Ray Allen .25 .60
90 Rashard Lewis .25 .60
91 Luke Ridnour .20 .50
92 Chris Bosh .25 .60
93 Jose Calderon .20 .50
94 Charlie Villanueva .25 .60
95 Carlos Boozer .25 .60
96 Andrei Kirilenko .20 .50
97 Deron Williams .40 1.00
98 Gilbert Arenas .25 .60
99 Antawn Jamison .25 .60
100 Caron Butler .25 .60
101 Tyrus Thomas RC .75 2.00
102 Adam Morrison RC .75 2.00
103 LaMarcus Aldridge RC 1.50 4.00
104 Rudy Gay RC 1.00 2.50
105 Andrea Bargnani RC 1.00 2.50
106 Rodney Carney RC .60 1.50
107 Mike Gansey RC .60 1.50
108 Brandon Roy RC 1.50 4.00
109 Patrick O'Bryant RC .60 1.50
110 Randy Foye RC .75 2.00
111 Ronnie Brewer RC .75 2.00
112 Mardy Collins RC .60 1.50
113 Shelden Williams RC .60 1.50
114 J.J. Redick RC .75 2.00
115 Hilton Armstrong RC .60 1.50
116 Marcus Williams RC .60 1.50
117 Rajon Rondo RC 2.50 6.00
118 Cedric Simmons RC .60 1.50
119 Ryan Hollins RC .60 1.50
120 Jordan Farmar RC .60 1.50
121 Maurice Ager RC .60 1.50
122 Renaldo Balkman RC .60 1.50
123 Leon Powe RC .60 1.50
124 Solomon Jones RC .60 1.50
125 Bobby Jones RC .60 1.50
126 Josh Boone RC .60 1.50
127 Saer Sene RC .60 1.50
128 Daniel Gibson RC .75 2.00
129 Hassan Adams RC .60 1.50
130 Kyle Lowry RC .75 2.00
131 Shannon Brown RC 1.00 2.50
132 Dee Brown RC .60 1.50
133 Shawne Williams RC .60 1.50
134 P.J. Tucker RC .60 1.50
135 Craig Smith RC .60 1.50
136 Paul Davis RC .60 1.50
137 Allan Ray RC .60 1.50
138 Denham Brown RC .60 1.50
139 Chris Quinn RC .60 1.50
140 Joel Freeland RC .60 1.50
141 James Augustine RC .60 1.50
142 Thabo Sefolosha RC .75 2.00
143 Quincy Douby RC .60 1.50
144 James White RC .60 1.50
145 David Noel RC .60 1.50
146 Steve Novak RC .60 1.50

2006-07 Upper Deck Rookie Debut Bronze

*1-100 BRONZE: 2.5X TO 6X BASE HI
*101-146 BRONZE: 1.25X TO 3X BASE HI
BRONZE PRINT RUN 100 SER.#'d SETS

2006-07 Upper Deck Rookie Debut Gold

*1-100 GOLD: 8X TO 20X BASE HI
*101-146 GOLD: 6X TO 15X BASE HI
GOLD PRINT RUN 10 SER.#'d SETS

2006-07 Upper Deck Rookie Debut Platinum

*1-100 PLATINUM: 2X TO 5X BASE HI
*101-146 PLATINUM: 1X TO 2.5X BASE HI
STATED PRINT RUN 150 SER.#'d SETS

2006-07 Upper Deck Rookie Debut Silver

*1-100 SILVER: 3X TO 8X BASE HI
*101-146 SILVER: 2X TO 5X BASE HI
SILVER PRINT RUN 50 SER.#'d SETS

2006-07 Upper Deck Rookie Debut Draft Duos

COMPLETE SET (25) 20.00 50.00
APPROXIMATE ODDS 1:20
BA Elton Brand / Ron Artest 1.50 4.00
BH Mike Bibby / Larry Hughes 1.50 4.00
BJ Chauncey Billups / Bobby Jackson 1.50 4.00
BP Carlos Boozer / Tayshaun Prince 1.50 4.00
BW Andrew Bogut / Marvin Williams 1.50 4.00
CB Tyson Chandler / Kwame Brown 1.50 4.00
DH Baron Davis / Richard Hamilton 1.50 4.00
DS Keyon Dooling / DeShawn Stevenson 1.50 4.00
EK Daniel Ewing / Yaroslav Korolev 1.50 4.00
FM Raymond Felton / Sean May 1.50 4.00
FV Channing Frye / Charlie Villanueva 1.50 4.00
GD Ben Gordon / Chris Duhon 1.50 4.00
IC Andre Iguodala / Josh Childress 2.00 5.00
JA LeBron James / Carmelo Anthony 4.00 10.00
JJ Joe Johnson / Richard Jefferson 1.50 4.00
KH Kyle Korver / Kirk Hinrich 1.50 4.00
LS Shaun Livingston / J.R. Smith 1.50 4.00
NJ Jameer Nelson / Al Jefferson 1.50 4.00
OH Emeka Okafor / Dwight Howard 2.00 5.00
PC Paul Pierce / Vince Carter 2.50 6.00
PW Chris Paul / Deron Williams 3.00 8.00
RH Luke Ridnour / Kirk Hinrich 1.50 4.00
RS Vladimir Radmanovic / Bobby Simmons 1.50 4.00
SR Quentin Richardson / Stromile Swift 1.50 4.00
WH Hakim Warrick / Luther Head 1.50 4.00

2006-07 Upper Deck Rookie Debut Draft Duos Autographs

STATED PRINT RUN 5 TO 25 SER.#'d SETS
SOME UNPRICED DUE TO SCARCITY
BH Mike Bibby / Larry Hughes 12.50 30.00
BW Andrew Bogut / Marvin Williams 12.50 30.00
CB Tyson Chandler / Kwame Brown 10.00 25.00
DS Keyon Dooling / DeShawn Stevenson 10.00 25.00
EK Daniel Ewing / Yaroslav Korolev 10.00 25.00
FM Raymond Felton / Sean May 12.50 30.00
JJ Joe Johnson / Richard Jefferson 10.00 25.00
LS Shaun Livingston / J.R. Smith 10.00 25.00
PW Chris Paul / Deron Williams 40.00 100.00
RS Vladimir Radmanovic / Bobby Simmons 10.00 25.00
SR Quentin Richardson / Stromile Swift 10.00 25.00

2006-07 Upper Deck Rookie Debut Ink

APPROXIMATE ODDS 1:20
*GOLD: .75X TO 2X BASE HI
GOLD PRINT RUN 25 SER.#'d SETS
AB Andrea Bargnani 6.00 15.00
AD Hassan Adams 4.00 10.00
BJ Bobby Jones 4.00 10.00
BR Brandon Roy 10.00 25.00
CS Cedric Simmons 4.00 10.00
DB Dee Brown 4.00 10.00
DE Denham Brown 4.00 10.00
DG Daniel Gibson 5.00 12.00
DN David Noel 4.00 10.00
HA Hilton Armstrong 4.00 10.00
JA James Augustine 4.00 10.00
JB Josh Boone 4.00 10.00
JF Jordan Farmar 4.00 10.00
JW James White 4.00 10.00
KL Kyle Lowry 5.00 12.00
LA LaMarcus Aldridge 10.00 25.00
MA Maurice Ager 4.00 10.00
MC Mardy Collins 4.00 10.00
MW Marcus Williams 4.00 10.00
PD Paul Davis 4.00 10.00
PO Patrick O'Bryant 4.00 10.00
PT P.J. Tucker 4.00 10.00
QD Quincy Douby 4.00 10.00
RB Ronnie Brewer 5.00 12.00
RC Rodney Carney 4.00 10.00
RF Randy Foye 5.00 12.00
RG Rudy Gay 6.00 15.00
RH Ryan Hollins 4.00 10.00
RR Rajon Rondo 20.00 50.00
SJ Solomon Jones 4.00 10.00
SM Craig Smith 4.00 10.00
SN Steve Novak 4.00 10.00
SW Shelden Williams 4.00 10.00
TS Thabo Sefolosha 5.00 12.00
TT Tyrus Thomas 5.00 12.00

2006-07 Upper Deck Rookie Debut Materialization

APPROXIMATE ODDS 1:12
AB Andrew Bynum 4.00 10.00
AI Andre Iguodala 2.50 6.00
AS Amare Stoudemire 2.50 6.00
BL Andray Blatche 2.00 5.00
BO Andrew Bogut 2.50 6.00
BR Kobe Bryant 8.00 20.00
CA Carmelo Anthony SP 3.00 8.00
CB Chris Bosh 2.50 6.00
CM Corey Maggette 2.00 5.00
CP Chris Paul 5.00 12.00
CV Charlie Villanueva 2.50 6.00
CW Chris Webber 2.50 6.00
DG Danny Granger 2.50 6.00
DH Dwight Howard 4.00 10.00
DM Donyell Marshall 2.00 5.00
DN Dirk Nowitzki 4.00 10.00
DS Damon Stoudamire 2.00 5.00
EB Elton Brand 2.50 6.00
FG Francisco Garcia 2.00 5.00
GE Devean George 2.00 5.00
GW Gerald Wallace SP 2.50 6.00
HO Julius Hodge 2.00 5.00
ID Ike Diogu 2.00 5.00
JG Joey Graham 2.00 5.00
JJ Joe Johnson 2.50 6.00
JK Jason Kidd 4.00 10.00
JM Jamaal Magloire 2.00 5.00
JO Jermaine O'Neal 2.50 6.00
JP Johan Petro 2.00 5.00
KB Kwame Brown 2.00 5.00
KG Kevin Garnett 5.00 12.00
KM Kenyon Martin 2.50 6.00
KT Kurt Thomas 2.00 5.00
LH Larry Hughes 2.00 5.00
LJ LeBron James 10.00 25.00
MA Desmond Mason 2.00 5.00
MC Jeff McInnis 2.00 5.00
MJ Michael Jordan SP 30.00 80.00
MR Michael Redd 2.50 6.00
MS Mike Sweetney 2.00 5.00
MW Martell Webster 2.00 5.00
PG Pau Gasol 2.50 6.00
PP Paul Pierce 3.00 8.00
PS Peja Stojakovic 2.50 6.00
RJ Richard Jefferson 2.50 6.00
RM Rashad McCants 2.00 5.00
SD Samuel Dalembert 2.00 5.00
SF Steve Francis 2.50 6.00
SH Shawn Marion 2.50 6.00
SM Sean May 1.50 4.00
SO Shaquille O'Neal 5.00 12.00
SS Stromile Swift 2.00 5.00
TC Tyson Chandler 2.00 5.00
TD Tim Duncan 4.00 10.00
TM Tracy McGrady SP 3.00 8.00
TP Tony Parker 2.50 6.00
VC Vince Carter 3.00 8.00
WS Wally Szczerbiak 2.00 5.00
YM Yao Ming 3.00 8.00
ZI Zydrunas Ilgauskas 2.00 5.00

2003-04 Upper Deck Rookie Exclusives

Released in February 2004, Rookie Exclusives boasts a 60-card set where the first 30 are rookie cards and the last 30 are veterans. Each card places a full-color player action photo on a color background with borders on the left right and bottom of the card. Rookie Exclusives was packaged in 28-pack boxes where packs contained six cards and carried a suggested retail price of $2.99.

COMPLETE SET (60) 12.50 30.00
1 LeBron James RC 5.00 12.00
2 Darko Milicic RC .40 1.00
3 Carmelo Anthony RC 1.00 2.50
4 Chris Bosh RC .75 2.00
5 Dwyane Wade RC 1.50 4.00
6 Chris Kaman RC .50 1.25
7 Jarvis Hayes RC .40 1.00
8 Mickael Pietrus RC .40 1.00
9 Marcus Banks RC .40 1.00
10 Luke Ridnour RC .50 1.25
11 Reece Gaines RC .40 1.00
12 Troy Bell RC .40 1.00
13 Zarko Cabarkapa RC .40 1.00
14 David West RC .50 1.25
15 Aleksandar Pavlovic RC .40 1.00
16 Dahntay Jones RC .40 1.00
17 Boris Diaw RC .50 1.25
18 Zoran Planinic RC .40 1.00
19 Travis Outlaw RC .50 1.25
20 Brian Cook RC .40 1.00
21 Ndudi Ebi RC .40 1.00
22 Kendrick Perkins RC .60 1.50
23 Leandro Barbosa RC .50 1.25
24 Josh Howard RC .40 1.00
25 Maciej Lampe RC .40 1.00
26 Jason Kapono RC .40 1.00
27 Luke Walton RC .40 1.00
28 Travis Hansen RC .40 1.00
29 Steve Blake RC .50 1.25
30 Slavko Vranes RC .40 1.00
31 Darius Miles .12 .30
32 Tony Parker .20 .50
33 Chauncey Billups .20 .50
34 Carlos Boozer .20 .50
35 Richard Hamilton .15 .40
36 Jamaal Tinsley .12 .30
37 Tracy McGrady .25 .60
38 Manu Ginobili .25 .60
39 Andre Miller .15 .40
40 Richard Jefferson .15 .40
41 Paul Pierce .25 .60
42 Peja Stojakovic .20 .50
43 Jason Richardson .20 .50
44 Shawn Marion .20 .50
45 Antawn Jamison .20 .50
46 Reggie Evans .12 .30
47 Earl Boykins .12 .30
48 Corey Maggette .15 .40
49 Cuttino Mobley .15 .40
50 Shane Battier .15 .40
51 Shareef Abdur-Rahim .15 .40
52 Chris Wilcox .12 .30
53 Steve Francis .20 .50
54 Mike Bibby .20 .50
55 Morris Peterson .12 .30
56 Nene .15 .40
57 Juan Dixon .12 .30
58 Yao Ming .40 1.00
59 Kobe Bryant 1.00 2.50
60 Michael Jordan 1.50 4.00

2003-04 Upper Deck Rookie Exclusives Gold

Randomly seeded, this set parallels the base set enhanced with gold foil highlights and sequential numbering to 100.

*1-30 RCs: 3X TO 8X BASE CARD HI
*31-60 SINGLES: 5X TO 12X BASE CARD HI
1 LeBron James 60.00 150.00

2003-04 Upper Deck Rookie Exclusives Variation

Randomly inserted at the rate of one in 12, this 60-card set parallels the design of the base set along with the first 30 cards and have brown backgrounds. Several new players were added for the 31-60 cards. A Variation Super set was also produced where cards are sequentially numbered to 10.

*1-30 RCs: 1X TO 2.5X BASE CARD HI
31 Allen Iverson .75 2.00
32 Dirk Nowitzki .75 2.00
33 Steve Nash .60 1.50
34 Richard Hamilton .40 1.00
35 Shaquille O'Neal 1.25 3.00
36 Jamaal Tinsley .60 1.50
37 Tim Duncan .75 2.00
38 Stephon Marbury .40 1.00
39 Caron Butler .50 1.25
40 Paul Pierce .60 1.50
41 Amare Stoudemire .75 2.00
42 Gary Payton .50 1.25
43 Karl Malone .60 1.50
44 Ben Wallace .50 1.25
45 Antoine Walker .50 1.25
46 Kenyon Martin .50 1.25
47 Latrell Sprewell .40 1.00
48 Rasheed Wallace .50 1.25
49 Chris Webber .50 1.25
50 Ray Allen .50 1.25
51 Jermaine O'Neal .50 1.25
52 Chris Wilcox .30 .75
53 Kevin Garnett 1.00 2.50
54 Pau Gasol .50 1.25
55 Jason Kidd .75 2.00
56 Jason Terry .40 1.00
57 Dajuan Wagner .30 .75
58 Yao Ming 1.00 2.50
59 Kobe Bryant 2.50 6.00
60 Michael Jordan 4.00 10.00

2003-04 Upper Deck Rookie Exclusives Autographs

Inserted at the rate of one in 28 Hobby and one in 1000 Retail, this 59-card set parallels the base set enhanced with authentic player autographs. Please note that card A36 was not released.

A1 LeBron James SP 250.00 450.00
A2 Darko Milicic 4.00 10.00
A3 Carmelo Anthony SP 50.00 120.00
A4 Chris Bosh 15.00 40.00
A5 Dwyane Wade 50.00 120.00
A6 Chris Kaman 5.00 12.00
A7 Jarvis Hayes 4.00 10.00
A8 Mickael Pietrus 4.00 10.00
A9 Marcus Banks 4.00 10.00
A10 Luke Ridnour 5.00 12.00
A11 Reece Gaines 4.00 10.00
A12 Troy Bell 4.00 10.00
A13 Zarko Cabarkapa 4.00 10.00
A14 David West 5.00 12.00
A15 Aleksandar Pavlovic 4.00 10.00
A16 Dahntay Jones 4.00 10.00
A17 Boris Diaw 5.00 12.00
A18 Zoran Planinic 4.00 10.00
A19 Travis Outlaw 5.00 12.00
A20 Brian Cook 4.00 10.00
A21 Ndudi Ebi 4.00 10.00
A22 Kendrick Perkins 6.00 15.00
A23 Leandro Barbosa 6.00 15.00
A24 Josh Howard 4.00 10.00
A25 Maciej Lampe 4.00 10.00
A26 Jason Kapono 4.00 10.00
A27 Luke Walton 4.00 10.00
A28 Travis Hansen 4.00 10.00
A29 Steve Blake 5.00 12.00
A30 Slavko Vranes 4.00 10.00
A31 Darius Miles 4.00 10.00
A32 Tony Parker 8.00 20.00
A33 Chauncey Billups 6.00 15.00
A34 Carlos Boozer 6.00 15.00
A35 Richard Hamilton 5.00 12.00
A37 Tracy McGrady 15.00 40.00
A38 Manu Ginobili 10.00 25.00
A39 Andre Miller 4.00 10.00
A40 Richard Jefferson 4.00 10.00
A41 Paul Pierce 12.00 30.00
A42 Peja Stojakovic 8.00 20.00
A43 Jason Richardson 6.00 15.00
A44 Shawn Marion 6.00 15.00
A45 Antawn Jamison 4.00 10.00
A46 Reggie Evans 4.00 10.00
A47 Earl Boykins 4.00 10.00
A48 Corey Maggette 4.00 10.00
A49 Cuttino Mobley 4.00 10.00
A50 Shane Battier 5.00 12.00
A51 Shareef Abdur-Rahim 4.00 10.00
A52 Chris Wilcox 4.00 10.00
A53 Steve Francis 6.00 15.00
A54 Mike Bibby 4.00 10.00
A55 Morris Peterson 4.00 10.00
A56 Nene 4.00 10.00
A57 Juan Dixon 4.00 10.00
A58 Yao Ming 25.00 60.00
A59 Kobe Bryant 100.00 200.00
A60 Michael Jordan 400.00 700.00

2003-04 Upper Deck Rookie Exclusives Jerseys

Inserted at one in 28 Hobby and one in 14 Retail, this 60-card set parallels the base set enhanced with a swatch of jersey in the shape of the letters RE. The jerseys used for the rookie players are event used, while the veterans are game used.

J1 LeBron James 30.00 80.00
J2 Darko Milicic 2.50 6.00
J3 Carmelo Anthony 6.00 15.00
J4 Chris Bosh 5.00 12.00
J5 Dwyane Wade 10.00 25.00
J6 Chris Kaman 3.00 8.00
J7 Jarvis Hayes 2.50 6.00
J8 Mickael Pietrus 2.50 6.00
J9 Marcus Banks 2.50 6.00
J10 Luke Ridnour 3.00 8.00
J11 Reece Gaines 2.50 6.00
J12 Troy Bell 2.50 6.00
J13 Zarko Cabarkapa 2.50 6.00
J14 David West 3.00 8.00
J15 Aleksandar Pavlovic 2.50 6.00
J16 Dahntay Jones 2.50 6.00
J17 Boris Diaw 3.00 8.00
J18 Zoran Planinic 2.50 6.00
J19 Travis Outlaw 3.00 8.00
J20 Brian Cook 2.50 6.00
J21 Ndudi Ebi 2.50 6.00
J22 Kendrick Perkins 4.00 10.00
J23 Leandro Barbosa 3.00 8.00
J24 Josh Howard 2.50 6.00
J25 Maciej Lampe 2.50 6.00
J26 Jason Kapono 2.50 6.00
J27 Luke Walton 2.50 6.00
J28 Travis Hansen 2.50 6.00
J29 Steve Blake 3.00 8.00
J30 Slavko Vranes 2.50 6.00
J31 Darius Miles 2.50 6.00
J32 Tony Parker 2.50 6.00
J33 Chauncey Billups 2.50 6.00
J34 Carlos Boozer SP 4.00 10.00
J35 Richard Hamilton 2.00 5.00
J36 Jamaal Tinsley 2.00 5.00
J37 Tracy McGrady 3.00 8.00
J38 Manu Ginobili 3.00 8.00
J39 Andre Miller 2.00 5.00
J40 Richard Jefferson 2.50 6.00
J41 Paul Pierce 3.00 8.00
J42 Peja Stojakovic 2.50 6.00
J43 Jason Richardson 2.50 6.00
J44 Shawn Marion 2.50 6.00
J45 Antawn Jamison 2.50 6.00
J46 Reggie Evans 2.00 5.00
J47 Earl Boykins 2.00 5.00
J48 Corey Maggette 2.00 5.00
J50 Shane Battier 2.00 5.00
J51 Shareef Abdur-Rahim 2.00 5.00
J52 Chris Wilcox 2.00 5.00
J53 Steve Francis 2.50 6.00
J54 Mike Bibby 2.50 6.00
J55 Morris Peterson 1.50 4.00
J56 Nene 2.00 5.00
J57 Juan Dixon 2.00 5.00
J58 Yao Ming 5.00 12.00
J59 Kobe Bryant 10.00 25.00
J60 Michael Jordan 30.00 80.00

2003-04 Upper Deck Rookie Exclusives Jerseys Variation

Inserted in Hobby packs at the rate of one in 28 and retail at the rate of one in 14, this 24-card set is a partial parallel of the jerseys set with the backgrounds shifted from color to brown.

J24 Mike Sweetney 2.50 6.00
J31 Allen Iverson 4.00 10.00
J32 Dirk Nowitzki 4.00 10.00
J33 Steve Nash 3.00 8.00
J35 Shaquille O'Neal 6.00 15.00
J37 Tim Duncan 4.00 10.00
J38 Stephon Marbury 2.00 5.00
J39 Caron Butler 2.50 6.00
J41 Amare Stoudemire 4.00 10.00
J42 Gary Payton 2.50 6.00
J43 Karl Malone 3.00 8.00
J44 Ben Wallace 2.50 6.00
J45 Antoine Walker SP 2.50 6.00
J46 Kenyon Martin 2.50 6.00
J47 Latrell Sprewell 2.50 6.00
J48 Rasheed Wallace SP 2.50 6.00
J49 Chris Webber 2.50 6.00
J50 Ray Allen SP 4.00 10.00
J51 Jermaine O'Neal 2.50 6.00
J53 Kevin Garnett 5.00 12.00
J54 Pau Gasol 2.50 6.00
J55 Jason Kidd 4.00 10.00
J56 Jason Terry 2.00 5.00
J57 Dajuan Wagner 2.00 5.00

2003-04 Upper Deck Rookie Exclusives Superstar Exclusives

Randomly inserted, this 100-card set is designed completely differently than the other inserts. Full-color player photos appear on the right and a the words, Superstar Exclusives, appear in gold foil from top to bottom on the left. Each card is sequentially numbered to 100.

EX1 Tracy McGrady 4.00 10.00
EX2 Dajuan Wagner 2.00 5.00
EX3 Allen Iverson 5.00 12.00

EX4 Caron Butler 3.00 8.00
EX5 Jason Kidd 5.00 12.00
EX6 Kenyon Martin 3.00 8.00
EX7 Lamar Odom 3.00 8.00
EX8 Kobe Bryant 15.00 40.00
EX9 T.J. Ford 4.00 10.00
EX10 Wally Szczerbiak 2.50 6.00
EX11 Yao Ming 6.00 15.00
EX12 Kirk Hinrich 4.00 10.00
EX13 Steve Nash 4.00 10.00
EX14 Baron Davis 3.00 8.00
EX15 Carmelo Anthony 8.00 20.00
EX16 Pau Gasol 3.00 8.00
EX17 Amare Stoudemire 5.00 12.00
EX18 Reggie Miller 3.00 8.00
EX19 Sam Cassell 2.50 6.00
EX20 Gary Payton 3.00 8.00
EX21 Kevin Garnett 6.00 15.00
EX22 Reece Gaines 3.00 8.00
EX23 LeBron James 30.00 80.00
EX24 Andre Miller 2.50 6.00
EX25 Rasheed Wallace 3.00 8.00
EX26 Darius Miles 2.00 5.00
EX27 Peja Stojakovic 3.00 8.00
EX28 Paul Pierce 4.00 10.00
EX29 Nick Collison 3.00 8.00
EX30 Dahntay Jones 3.00 8.00
EX31 Darko Milicic 3.00 8.00
EX32 Richard Hamilton 2.50 6.00
EX33 Scottie Pippen 5.00 12.00
EX34 Shaquille O'Neal 8.00 20.00
EX35 Jarvis Hayes 3.00 8.00
EX36 Tony Parker 3.00 8.00
EX37 Nick Van Exel 2.50 6.00
EX38 Maciej Lampe 3.00 8.00
EX39 Jalen Rose 2.50 6.00
EX40 Ray Allen 3.00 8.00
EX41 Dirk Nowitzki 5.00 12.00
EX42 Elton Brand 3.00 8.00
EX43 Jermaine O'Neal 3.00 8.00
EX44 Brian Grant 2.00 5.00
EX45 Jason Richardson 3.00 8.00
EX46 Allan Houston 2.50 6.00
EX47 Tim Thomas 2.00 5.00
EX48 Glenn Robinson 2.50 6.00
EX49 Nene 2.50 6.00
EX50 Corey Maggette 2.50 6.00
EX51 Richard Jefferson 3.00 8.00
EX52 Mickael Pietrus 3.00 8.00
EX53 Stephon Marbury 2.50 6.00
EX54 Mike Miller 3.00 8.00
EX55 Bonzi Wells 2.00 5.00
EX56 Boris Diaw 4.00 10.00
EX57 Manu Ginobili 4.00 10.00
EX58 Steve Francis 3.00 8.00
EX59 Jamal Mashburn 2.50 6.00
EX60 Mike Bibby 3.00 8.00
EX61 Tony Delk 2.00 5.00
EX62 Troy Bell 3.00 8.00
EX63 Dwyane Wade 12.00 30.00
EX64 Karl Malone 4.00 10.00
EX65 Desmond Mason 2.50 6.00
EX66 Antawn Jamison 3.00 8.00
EX67 Vince Carter 5.00 12.00
EX68 Eddie Jones 2.50 6.00
EX69 Gordan Giricek 2.00 5.00
EX70 Ben Wallace 3.00 8.00
EX71 Latrell Sprewell 2.50 6.00
EX72 Leandro Barbosa 4.00 10.00
EX73 Jamaal Tinsley 2.00 5.00
EX74 Travis Outlaw 4.00 10.00
EX75 Jason Terry 2.50 6.00
EX76 Quentin Richardson 2.50 6.00
EX77 Morris Peterson 2.00 5.00
EX78 Cuttino Mobley 2.50 6.00
EX79 Rashard Lewis 3.00 8.00
EX80 Jerry Stackhouse 2.50 6.00
EX81 Michael Finley 3.00 8.00
EX82 Antoine Walker 3.00 8.00
EX83 Shawn Marion 3.00 8.00
EX84 Gilbert Arenas 3.00 8.00
EX85 Marcus Banks 3.00 8.00
EX86 Tim Duncan 5.00 12.00
EX87 Brian Cook 3.00 8.00
EX88 Chauncey Billups 3.00 8.00
EX89 Andrei Kirilenko 3.00 8.00
EX90 Shareef Abdur-Rahim 2.50 6.00
EX91 Antonio McDyess 2.50 6.00
EX92 Chris Bosh 6.00 15.00
EX93 Ron Artest 3.00 8.00
EX94 David West 4.00 10.00
EX95 Chris Webber 3.00 8.00
EX96 Ricky Davis 2.50 6.00
EX97 Vladimir Radmanovic 2.00 5.00
EX98 Nikoloz Tskitishvili 2.00 5.00
EX99 Drew Gooden 2.50 6.00
EX100 Zach Randolph 3.00 8.00

1993-94 Upper Deck SE

This 225-card standard-size set was distributed in 12-card hobby East, hobby West, retail and 10-card magazine retail packs. There are 36 packs per box. Card fronts feature color player action shots that are borderless, except on the left, where a strip carries the player's name in gold foil along with his position and a vertically distorted black-and-white version of the action shot. The player's team name appears in vertical gold-foil lettering near the right edge. The back carries a color player action photo, with his name, position, and brief biography appearing in stripes across the top. Statistics and career highlights are displayed horizontally in a ghosted panel on the left. The set closes with the following topical subsets: NBA All-Star Weekend Highlights (181-198) and Team Headlines (199-225). Two Michael Jordan insert cards are a Kilroy card (JK1) and a retirement tribute card (MJR1). These were inserted at a rate of 1 in 72 packs. Rookie Cards of note in this set include Vin Baker, Anfernee Hardaway, Jamal Mashburn, Nick Van Exel and Chris Webber.

COMPLETE SET (225) 7.50 15.00
1 Scottie Pippen .40 1.00
2 Todd Day .01 .05
3 Detlef Schrempf .05 .15
4 Chris Webber RC 1.25 3.00
5 Michael Adams .01 .05
6 Loy Vaught .01 .05
7 Doug West .01 .05
8 A.C. Green .05 .15
9 Anthony Mason .05 .15
10 Clyde Drexler .10 .30
11 Popeye Jones RC .01 .05
12 Vlade Divac .05 .15
13 Armon Gilliam .01 .05
14 Hersey Hawkins .05 .15
15 Dennis Scott .01 .05
16 Bimbo Coles .01 .05
17 Blue Edwards .01 .05
18 Negele Knight .01 .05
19 Dale Davis .01 .05
20 Isiah Thomas .10 .30
21 Latrell Sprewell .30 .75
22 Kenny Smith .01 .05
23 Bryant Stith .01 .05
24 Terry Porter .01 .05
25 Spud Webb .05 .15
26 John Battle .01 .05
27 Jeff Malone .01 .05
28 Olden Polynice .01 .05
29 Kevin Willis .01 .05
30 Robert Parish .05 .15
31 Kevin Johnson .05 .15
32 Shaquille O'Neal .60 1.50
33 Willie Anderson .01 .05
34 Micheal Williams .01 .05
35 Steve Smith .10 .30
36 Rik Smits .05 .15
37 Pete Myers .01 .05
38 Oliver Miller .01 .05
39 Eddie Johnson .01 .05
40 Calbert Cheaney RC .05 .15
41 Vernon Maxwell .01 .05
42 James Worthy .10 .30
43 Dino Radja RC .01 .05
44 Derrick Coleman .05 .15
45 Reggie Williams .01 .05
46 Dale Ellis .01 .05
47 Clifford Robinson .05 .15
48 Doug Christie .05 .15
49 Ricky Pierce .01 .05
50 Sean Elliott .05 .15
51 Anfernee Hardaway RC 1.00 2.50
52 Dana Barros .01 .05
53 Reggie Miller .10 .30
54 Brian Williams .01 .05
55 Otis Thorpe .05 .15
56 Jerome Kersey .01 .05
57 Larry Johnson .10 .30
58 Rex Chapman .01 .05
59 Kevin Edwards .01 .05
60 Nate McMillan .01 .05
61 Chris Mullin .10 .30
62 Bill Cartwright .01 .05
63 Dennis Rodman .25 .60
64 Pooh Richardson .01 .05
65 Tyrone Hill .01 .05
66 Scott Brooks .01 .05
67 Brad Daugherty .01 .05
68 Joe Dumars .10 .30
69 Vin Baker RC .30 .75
70 Rod Strickland .05 .15
71 Tom Chambers .01 .05
72 Charles Oakley .05 .15
73 Craig Ehlo .01 .05
74 LaPhonso Ellis .01 .05
75 Kevin Gamble .01 .05
76 Shawn Bradley RC .10 .30
77 Kendall Gill .05 .15
78 Hakeem Olajuwon .20 .50
79 Nick Anderson .05 .15
80 Anthony Peeler .01 .05
81 Wayman Tisdale .01 .05
82 Danny Manning .05 .15
83 John Starks .05 .15
84 Jeff Hornacek .05 .15
85 Victor Alexander .01 .05
86 Mitch Richmond .10 .30
87 Mookie Blaylock .05 .15
88 Harvey Grant .01 .05
89 Doug Smith .01 .05
90 John Stockton .10 .30
91 Charles Barkley .20 .50
92 Gerald Wilkins .01 .05
93 Mario Elie .01 .05
94 Ken Norman .01 .05
95 B.J. Armstrong .01 .05
96 John Williams .01 .05
97 Rony Seikaly .01 .05
98 Sean Rooks .01 .05
99 Shawn Kemp .20 .50
100 Danny Ainge .05 .15
101 Terry Mills .01 .05
102 Doc Rivers .05 .15
103 Chuck Person .01 .05
104 Sam Cassell RC .50 1.25
105 Kevin Duckworth .01 .05
106 Dan Majerle .05 .15
107 Mark Jackson .05 .15
108 Steve Kerr .05 .15
109 Sam Perkins .05 .15
110 Clarence Weatherspoon .01 .05
111 Felton Spencer .01 .05
112 Greg Anthony .01 .05
113 Pete Chilcutt .01 .05
114 Malik Sealy .01 .05
115 Horace Grant .05 .15
116 Chris Morris .01 .05
117 Xavier McDaniel .01 .05
118 Lionel Simmons .01 .05
119 Dell Curry .01 .05
120 Moses Malone .10 .30
121 Lindsey Hunter RC .10 .30
122 Buck Williams .01 .05
123 Mahmoud Abdul-Rauf .01 .05
124 Rumeal Robinson .01 .05
125 Chris Mills RC .10 .30
126 Scott Skiles .01 .05
127 Derrick McKey .01 .05
128 Avery Johnson .01 .05
129 Harold Miner .01 .05
130 Frank Brickowski .01 .05
131 Gary Payton .20 .50
132 Don MacLean .01 .05
133 Thurl Bailey .01 .05
134 Nick Van Exel RC .40 1.00
135 Matt Geiger .01 .05
136 Stacey Augmon .01 .05
137 Sedale Threatt .01 .05
138 Patrick Ewing .10 .30
139 Tyrone Corbin .01 .05
140 Jim Jackson .05 .15
141 Christian Laettner .05 .15
142 Robert Horry .05 .15
143 J.R. Reid .01 .05
144 Eric Murdock .01 .05
145 Alonzo Mourning .20 .50
146 Sherman Douglas .01 .05
147 Tom Gugliotta .10 .30
148 Glen Rice .05 .15
149 Mark Price .01 .05
150 Dikembe Mutombo .10 .30
151 Derek Harper .05 .15
152 Karl Malone .20 .50
153 Byron Scott .05 .15
154 Reggie Jordan RC .01 .05
155 Dominique Wilkins .10 .30
156 Bobby Hurley RC .05 .15
157 Ron Harper .05 .15
158 Bryon Russell RC .10 .30
159 Frank Johnson .01 .05
160 Toni Kukoc RC .50 1.25
161 Lloyd Daniels .01 .05
162 Jeff Turner .01 .05
163 Muggsy Bogues .05 .15
164 Chris Gatling .01 .05
165 Kenny Anderson .05 .15
166 Elmore Spencer .01 .05
167 Jamal Mashburn RC .30 .75
168 Tim Perry .01 .05
169 Antonio Davis RC .15 .40
170 Isaiah Rider RC .25 .60
171 Dee Brown .01 .05
172 Walt Williams .01 .05
173 Elden Campbell .01 .05
174 Benoit Benjamin .01 .05
175 Billy Owens .01 .05
176 Andrew Lang .01 .05
177 David Robinson .20 .50
178 Checklist 1 .01 .05
179 Checklist 2 .01 .05
180 Checklist 3 .01 .05
181 Shawn Bradley ASW .05 .15
182 Calbert Cheaney ASW .01 .05
183 Toni Kukoc ASW .10 .30
184 Popeye Jones ASW .01 .05
185 Lindsey Hunter ASW .05 .15
186 Chris Webber ASW .60 1.50
187 Bryon Russell ASW .05 .15
188 A.Hardaway ASW .50 1.25
189 Nick Van Exel ASW .10 .30
190 P.J.Brown ASW .05 .15
191 Isaiah Rider ASW .10 .30
192 Chris Mills ASW .05 .15
193 Antonio Davis ASW .05 .15
194 Jamal Mashburn ASW .10 .30
195 Dino Radja ASW .01 .05
196 Sam Cassell ASW .10 .30
197 Isaiah Rider ASW SD .10 .30
198 Mark Price LDS .01 .05
199 Stacey Augmon TH .01 .05
200 Celtics Team TH .01 .05
201 Eddie Johnson TH .01 .05
202 Scottie Pippen TH .20 .50
203 Brad Daugherty TH .01 .05
204 Jamal Mashburn TH .10 .30
205 Dikembe Mutombo TH .05 .15
206 Lindsey Hunter TH .05 .15
207 Chris Webber TH .40 1.00
208 Rockets Team TH .01 .05
209 Derrick McKey TH .01 .05
210 Danny Manning TH .01 .05
211 Doug Christie TH .05 .15
212 Glen Rice TH .01 .05
213 Todd Day TH .01 .05
Ken Norman TH
Vin Baker TH
Jon Barry TH
214 Isaiah Rider TH .10 .30
215 Kenny Anderson TH .01 .05
216 Patrick Ewing TH .05 .15
217 Anfernee Hardaway TH .30 .75
218 Moses Malone TH .05 .15
219 Kevin Johnson TH .01 .05
220 Clifford Robinson TH .01 .05
221 Wayman Tisdale TH .01 .05
222 David Robinson TH .10 .30
223 Sonics Team TH .01 .05
224 John Stockton TH .05 .15
225 Don MacLean TH .01 .05
JK1 Johnny Kilroy 6.00 15.00
(Michael Jordan)
MJR1 Michael Jordan 3.00 8.00
Retirement Card

1993-94 Upper Deck SE Electric Court

This 225-card set parallels that of the 1993-94 Upper Deck SE. The only difference in design is an "Electric Court" logo that appears on the fronts and the thicker stock that these cards feature. These cards were distributed one per 12-card hobby East, hobby West and retail pack and two per 10-card magazine pack. Please refer to the multipliers provided below (coupled with the prices of the corresponding regular issue cards) to ascertain values.ersion of the action shot. The player's team name appears in vertical gold-foil lettering near the right edge. The Electric Court set name appears in prismatic silver foil lettering near the bottom. The back carries a color player action photo, with his name, position, and brief biography appearing in stripes across the top. Statistics and career highlights are displayed horizontally in a ghosted panel on the left.

COMPLETE SET (225) 25.00 50.00
*STARS: .75X TO 2X BASE CARD HI
*RCs: .6X TO 1.5X BASE HI

1993-94 Upper Deck SE Electric Court Gold

Randomly inserted in hobby East, hobby West and retail packs at a rate of one in 36, this is a parallel set to '93-94 Upper Deck SE. The Electric Gold set name appears in gold foil lettering near the bottom. To ascertain values on individual cards, please refer to the multiplier in the header, coupled with the value of the base card.

*STARS: 8X TO 20X BASE CARD HI
*RCs: 5X TO 12X BASE HI

1993-94 Upper Deck SE Behind the Glass

Randomly inserted in 12-card retail packs at a rate of one in 30, cards from this 15-card standard-size set capture some of the NBA's best dunkers from the unique camera angle behind the backboard glass. A gold-foil "Behind the Glass Trade Card" was randomly inserted in hobby packs at a rate of one in 360. The collector could redeem the card for the complete 15-card "Behind the Glass" set. The redemption deadline was August 31, 1994. The borderless front features a color player action shot on a gold metallic finish. The player's name and position appear vertically along the right side. The back features a color player action shot on the right side with career highlights appearing alongside on the left.

COMPLETE SET (15) 15.00 40.00
G1 Shawn Kemp 1.00 2.50
G2 Patrick Ewing .60 1.50
G3 Dikembe Mutombo .60 1.50
G4 Charles Barkley 1.00 2.50
G5 Hakeem Olajuwon 1.00 2.50
G6 Larry Johnson .60 1.50
G7 Chris Webber 4.00 10.00
G8 John Starks .30 .75
G9 Kevin Willis .08 .25
G10 Scottie Pippen 2.00 5.00
G11 Michael Jordan 8.00 20.00
G12 Alonzo Mourning 1.00 2.50
G13 Shaquille O'Neal 3.00 8.00
G14 Shawn Bradley .60 1.50
G15 Ron Harper .30 .75
NNO Expired BHG Trade .60 1.50
NNO Redeemed BHG Trade .08 .25

1993-94 Upper Deck SE Die Cut All-Stars

In these two 15-card insert standard-size sets, Upper Deck saluted a selection of current and potential future all-stars. The cards were available in East hobby and West hobby packs at a rate of one in 30 packs. Hobby dealers in the East received cases containing players from the Eastern conference, while hobby dealers in the West received cases containing players from the Western conference. These die-cut cards were inserted in hobby packs only. This unique card design features a partial gold-foil border at the top only. Centered is a color player action photo. The player's name and team appear in red vertical lettering along the left side. The back features brief statistics. Each set is sequenced in alphabetical team order.

COMPLETE SET (30) 140.00 275.00
COMP.EAST SET (15) 65.00 125.00
COMP.WEST SET (15) 75.00 150.00
E1 Dominique Wilkins 3.00 8.00
E2 Alonzo Mourning 6.00 15.00
E3 B.J. Armstrong 1.25 3.00
E4 Scottie Pippen 8.00 20.00
E5 Mark Price 1.25 3.00
E6 Isiah Thomas 3.00 8.00
E7 Harold Miner 1.25 3.00
E8 Vin Baker 4.00 10.00
E9 Kenny Anderson 2.00 5.00
E10 Derrick Coleman 2.00 5.00
E11 Patrick Ewing 5.00 12.00
E12 Anfernee Hardaway 12.50 30.00
E13 Shaquille O'Neal 15.00 40.00
E14 Shawn Bradley 3.00 8.00
E15 Calbert Cheaney 2.00 5.00
W1 Jim Jackson 2.50 6.00
W2 Jamal Mashburn 6.00 15.00
W3 Dikembe Mutombo 4.00 10.00
W4 Latrell Sprewell 6.00 15.00
W5 Chris Webber 15.00 40.00
W6 Hakeem Olajuwon 6.00 15.00
W7 Danny Manning 2.50 6.00
W8 Nick Van Exel 8.00 20.00
W9 Isaiah Rider 6.00 15.00
W10 Charles Barkley 8.00 20.00
W11 Clyde Drexler 6.00 15.00
W12 Mitch Richmond 3.00 8.00
W13 David Robinson 10.00 25.00
W14 Shawn Kemp 6.00 15.00
W15 Karl Malone 8.00 20.00

1993-94 Upper Deck SE USA Trade

This 24-card standard-size set was only available by exchanging the Upper Deck SE USA Trade card (random insert at one in 360 packs) before August 31, 1994. The set previewed the USA Basketball set that was released in the summer of 1994. The cards depict the 12 players selected by USA Basketball for "Dream Team II" plus Tim Hardaway, who was originally selected to the team was unable to participate due to injury, and 11 from the original Dream Team. Each card features a borderless color player action shot on its front. The player's name and position appear in white lettering within red and blue stripes near the bottom. The words "Exchange Set" in vertical gold-foil lettering and the gold-foil Upper Deck logo appear at the upper left. On a background of the American flag, the back carries a posed color shot of the player in his USA uniform and career highlights. The cards are numbered on the back with a "USA" prefix.

COMPLETE SET (24) 20.00 40.00
1 Charles Barkley 1.00 2.50
2 Larry Bird 2.50 6.00
3 Clyde Drexler .60 1.50
4 Patrick Ewing .60 1.50
5 Michael Jordan 6.00 15.00
6 Christian Laettner .30 .75
7 Karl Malone 1.00 2.50
8 Chris Mullin .60 1.50
9 Scottie Pippen 2.00 5.00
10 David Robinson 1.00 2.50
11 John Stockton .60 1.50
12 Dominique Wilkins .60 1.50
13 Isiah Thomas .60 1.50
14 Dan Majerle .30 .75
15 Steve Smith .60 1.50
16 Alonzo Mourning 1.00 2.50
17 Shawn Kemp 1.00 2.50
18 Larry Johnson .60 1.50
19 Tim Hardaway .60 1.50
20 Joe Dumars .60 1.50
21 Mark Price .20 .50
22 Derrick Coleman .30 .75
23 Reggie Miller .60 1.50
24 Shaquille O'Neal 3.00 8.00
NNO Expired USA Trade Card .40 1.00
NNO Red. USA Trade Card .08 .25

1991-92 Upper Deck Sheets

Upper Deck produced commemorative sheets that were given away during the 1991-92 season at selected games or events. Each sheet measures approximately 8 1/2" by 11" and is printed on card stock. The sheets have an Upper Deck stamp indicating the production run and an individual number. The design typically features Upper Deck card reproductions or artwork. The backs are blank. The sheets are unnumbered and listed in chronological order.

COMPLETE SET (14) 60.00 150.00
1 Number 1 Draft Choices 4.00 10.00
June 26, 1991 (12,000)
Number One Picks
Patrick Ewing
Brad Daugherty
David Robinson
Danny Manning
Pervis Ellison
Derrick Coleman
2 12th National Sports 2.00 5.00
Collectors Convention
July 4, 1991 (65,000)
Brad Daugherty
David Robinson
Danny Manning
Pervis Ellison
Derrick Coleman
Larry Johnson
3 Philadelphia Sports 4.00 10.00
Heroes *
Oct. 17, 1991 (21,500)
Charles Barkley
Mike Schmidt
Rick Tocchet
Reggie White
4 McDonald's Open 4.00 10.00
Paris, France
Oct. 18-19, 1991 (59,000)
James Worthy
Byron Scott
A.C. Green
Magic Johnson
Sam Perkins
Vlade Divac
5 Detroit Pistons vs. 3.00 8.00
Nov. 27, 1991 (38,500)
Joe Dumars
Dennis Rodman
Mark Aguirre
Bill Laimbeer
John Salley
Isiah Thomas
6 All-Star Weekend 8.00 20.00
Orlando, Florida
Feb. 7-9, 1992 (22,000)
7 1971-72 World Champion 8.00 20.00
Feb. 26, 1992 (22,000)/(20th Anniversary)
Wilt Chamberlain
Bill Sharman CO
Jerry West
Pat Riley
Jim McMillian
Gail Goodrich
8 New York Knicks 3.00 8.00
vs. Minnesota Timberwolves
Feb. 29, 1992 (19,000)
Kiki Vandeweghe
Patrick Ewing
Charles Oakley
Gerald Wilkins
John Starks
Anthony Mason
Xavier McDaniel
Mark Jackson
9 Detroit Pistons 3.00 8.00
vs. Los Angeles Clippers
March 31, 1992 (38,500)
Bill Laimbeer
John Salley
Isiah Thomas
Orlando Woolridge
Dennis Rodman
Joe Dumars
10 1992 NCAA Final Four 8.00 20.00
Championship Coaches
April 4-6, 1992 (68,000)
John Wooden
Dean Smith
Adolph Rupp
Bob Knight
11 Hoop It Up 4.00 10.00
San Jose, California
June 6-7, 1992 (15&000)
Sarunas Marciulonis
Billy Owens
Tim Hardaway
Victor Alexander
Chris Gatling
Chris Mullin
12 Battle of the 4.00 10.00
Basketball Stars
Undated (10,000)
Reportedly issued 6/20/92
Charles Smith
Dominique Wilkins
Pervis Ellison
Kenny Smith
Isiah Thomas
Mitch Richmond
Pooh Richardson
Tim Hardaway
13 Upper Deck Commemorates 6.00 15.00
the NBA Draft
June 24, 1992 (15,000)
Larry Johnson
Kenny Anderson
Billy Owens
Dikembe Mutombo
Steve Smith
Doug Smith
Luc Longley
Mark Macon
14 1992 USA Basketball 8.00 20.00
Team/(80,000)
Issued June 1992

1992-93 Upper Deck Sheets

Upper Deck produced commemorative sheets that were given away during the 1992-93 season at selected events and games. Each sheet measures approximately 8 1/2" by 11" and is printed on card stock. The sheets have an Upper Deck stamp indicating the production run and an individual number. The backs are blank. The sheets are unnumbered and listed in chronological order.

COMPLETE SET (10) 50.00 125.00
1 Utah Jazz 4.00 10.00
Stay in School
Undated (67,000)
Issued Oct. 1992
David Benoit
Karl Malone
Mark Eaton
Jeff Malone
Mike Brown
John Stockton
Jay Humphries
Tyrone Corbin
2 Cleveland Cavaliers 3.00 8.00
Jan. 12, 1993 (30,000)
Larry Nance
Hot Rod Williams
Mark Price
Brad Daugherty
Craig Ehlo
John Battle
3 Larry Bird Salute 10.00 25.00
(Retirement Ceremony,
Boston Garden)
Feb. 4, 1993 (25,000)
(Alan Studt artwork)
4 All-Star Weekend 1.25 3.00
Autograph Sheet/(Upper Deck Trading Card
and Memorabilia Show
Feb. 19-21, 1993 (75,000)
(Picture of Salt Lake
City with mountains in
background)
5 All-Star Heroes 8.00 20.00
Feb. 19-21, 1993 (10,000)
Jerry West
John Havlicek
Elgin Baylor
Dave Cowens
6 Milwaukee Bucks 6.00 15.00
25th Anniversary
Undated (13,000)
Reportedly issued 3/3/93
Jon McGlocklin
Sidney Moncrief
Oscar Robertson
Kareem Abdul-Jabbar
Bob Lanier
Brian Winters
Junior Bridgeman
7 Atlanta Hawks 6.00 15.00
Undated (10,000)
Reportedly issued
March 25, 1993
Stacey Augmon
Mookie Blaylock
Duane Ferrell
Adam Keefe
Dominique Wilkins
Kevin Willis
8 Upper Deck Salutes 10.00 25.00
April 20. 1993 (22.500)
Bill Cartwright
Michael Jordan
John Paxson
Scottie Pippen
B.J. Armstrong
Horace Grant
9 AT and T Long Distance 5.00 12.00
Shootout
Undated (22,500)
Reportedly issued 6/93
Dan Majerle
Mark Price
Terry Porter
Dana Barros
Kenny Smith
B.J. Armstrong
Reggie Miller
10 Upper Deck Commemorates 8.00 20.00
the NBA Draft/(1992 Top Draft Choices)
June 30, 1993 (22,000)
Shaquille O'Neal
Alonzo Mourning
Christian Laettner
Jim Jackson
LaPhonso Ellis
Tom Gugliotta
Walt Williams
Todd Day

1993-94 Upper Deck Sheets

Upper Deck produced commemorative sheets that were given away during the 1993-94 season at selected events and games. Each sheet measures approximately 8 1/2" by 11" and is printed on card stock. The sheets have an Upper Deck stamp indicating the production run and an individual number. The backs are blank. The sheets are unnumbered and listed in chronological order.

COMPLETE SET (8) 25.00 60.00
1 1993 National Conv. 4.00 10.00
Chicago, Illinois
July 20-25, 1993
Michael Jordan
2 1993 McDonald's Open 4.00 10.00
October 21,1993
Danny Ainge
Dan Majerle
Oliver Miller
Charles Barkley
Kevin Johnson
Mark West
Negele Knight
Cedric Ceballos
3 Chicago Bulls 6.00 15.00
Nov.13, 1993 (22,000)
John Paxson
B.J. Armstrong
Corie Blount
Scottie Pippen
Bill Cartwright
Horace Grant
4 Upper Deck Salutes 4.00 10.00
NBA Standouts
All-Star Weekend
Undated (30,000)
Issued Feb. 1994
Harold Miner
Patrick Ewing
Hakeem Olajuwon
Alonzo Mourning
Jim Jackson
Derrick Coleman
5 Upper Deck All-Star 1.25 3.00
Autograph Sheet
All-Star Weekend
Undated (20,000)
Issued Feb. 1994
6 SE Preview 5.00 12.00
Undated (16,000)
Issued March 1994
Shawn Bradley
Shaquille O'Neal
LaPhonso Ellis
Jamal Mashburn
Chris Webber
Calbert Cheaney
7 1994 NBA All-Rookie 4.00 10.00
Team
No Date (40,000)
Chris Webber
Isaiah Rider
Jamal Mashburn
Vin Baker
Anfernee Hardaway
8 Upper Deck Salutes 5.00 12.00
NBA Draft Picks
June 29, 1994 (25,000)
Chris Webber
Shawn Bradley
Anfernee Hardaway
Jamal Mashburn
Isaiah Rider
Calbert Cheaney

1994-95 Upper Deck Sheets

These commemorative sheets were given away during the 1994-95 season at selected events and games. Each sheet measures 8 1/2" by 11" and is printed on card stock. The sheets have an Upper Deck seal indicating the production run and serial number.

COMPLETE SET (4) 12.00 30.00
1 Series Two NBA 3.00 8.00
Basketball Cards/(Promo sheet)
Shawn Kemp (Predictor)
Scottie Pippen
Shaquille O'Neal
Shawn Kemp (Slam Dunk)
Bobby Hurley
Jason Kidd
2 Upper Deck Predictor 4.00 10.00
Series Cards
No date (12,000)
Shawn Kemp
Patrick Ewing
Kevin Willis
Mookie Blaylock
Tim Hardaway
Glenn Robinson
3 Upper Deck Salutes 4.00 10.00
Michael Jordan
Jewel
No date (50,000)
4 1995 NBA Draft 5.00 12.00
Grant Hill
Juwan Howard
Jason Kidd
Donyell Marshall
Glenn Robinson
Sharone Wright
No date(5,000 issued)

1995-96 Upper Deck Sheets

The first commemorative sheet was given away during the 1996 NBA draft. It measures 8 1/2" by 11" and is printed on card stock. It has an Upper Deck seal indicating the production run and serial number. The second sheet commemorates the 1995-96 Chicago Bulls Championship team. The sheet measures 8 1/2" by 11" and is serially numbered out of 7210.

COMPLETE SET (2) 8.00 20.00
1 1996 NBA Draft 6.00 15.00
Kevin Garnett
Antonio McDyess
Bryant Reeves
Joe Smith
Jerry Stackhouse
Rasheed Wallace
2 1996 NBA Champions 6.00 15.00
Randy Brown
Toni Kukoc
Dickey Simpkins
Ron Harper
Luc Longley
John Salley
Michael Jordan
Steve Kerr
Jud Buechler
Scottie Pippen
Bill Wennington
Jason Caffey
James Edwards
Jack Haley
Dennis Rodman

2000-01 Upper Deck Slam

Debuting in November, 2000, this 100-card set featured an all-acetate look. The set contained 60 veterans, 30 rookies serially numbered to 2500 and 10 rookies serially numbered to 900. Please note that a Kevin Garnett promo card was issued to dealers and to members of the media prior to the release of the product. The card is listed below as card "P21".

COMPLETE SET w/o RC (60) 8.00 20.00
1 Dikembe Mutombo .30 .75
2 Jim Jackson .20 .50
3 Paul Pierce .40 1.00
4 Antoine Walker .25 .60
5 Eddie Jones .30 .75
6 Baron Davis .30 .75
7 Derrick Coleman .25 .60
8 Elton Brand .30 .75
9 Ron Artest .30 .75
10 Andre Miller .25 .60
11 Shawn Kemp .25 .60
12 Michael Finley .30 .75
13 Dirk Nowitzki .50 1.25
14 Antonio McDyess .25 .60
15 James Posey .20 .50
16 Jerry Stackhouse .25 .60
17 Jerome Williams .20 .50
18 Larry Hughes .25 .60
19 Antawn Jamison .30 .75
20 Steve Francis .30 .75
21 Hakeem Olajuwon .40 1.00
22 Reggie Miller .30 .75
23 Jalen Rose .25 .60
24 Lamar Odom .30 .75
25 Michael Olowokandi .20 .50
26 Shaquille O'Neal .75 2.00
27 Kobe Bryant 1.50 4.00
28 Alonzo Mourning .40 1.00
29 Jamal Mashburn .25 .60
30 Ray Allen .30 .75
31 Glenn Robinson .25 .60
32 Kevin Garnett .60 1.50
33 Wally Szczerbiak .25 .60
34 Stephon Marbury .25 .60
35 Keith Van Horn .25 .60
36 Latrell Sprewell .25 .60
37 Allan Houston .25 .60
38 Darrell Armstrong .20 .50
39 Ron Mercer .20 .50
40 Allen Iverson .60 1.50
41 Toni Kukoc .25 .60
42 Jason Kidd .50 1.25
43 Anfernee Hardaway .50 1.25
44 Shawn Marion .30 .75
45 Scottie Pippen .50 1.25
46 Rasheed Wallace .30 .75
47 Chris Webber .30 .75
48 Vlade Divac .25 .60
49 Tim Duncan .60 1.50
50 David Robinson .50 1.25
51 Gary Payton .30 .75
52 Rashard Lewis .30 .75
53 Vince Carter .60 1.50
54 Doug Christie .20 .50
55 Karl Malone .40 1.00
56 Bryon Russell .20 .50
57 Shareef Abdur-Rahim .25 .60
58 Michael Dickerson .20 .50
59 Juwan Howard .25 .60
60 Richard Hamilton .25 .60
61 Jerome Moiso RC 1.00 2.50
62 Etan Thomas RC 1.00 2.50
63 Courtney Alexander RC 1.00 2.50
64 Mateen Cleaves RC 1.00 2.50
65 Jason Collier RC 1.00 2.50
66 Hedo Turkoglu RC 4.00 10.00
67 Desmond Mason RC 1.25 3.00
68 Quentin Richardson RC 1.50 4.00
69 Jamaal Magloire RC 1.00 2.50
70 Speedy Claxton RC 1.00 2.50
71 Morris Peterson RC 1.00 2.50
72 Donnell Harvey RC 1.00 2.50
73 Ira Newble RC 1.00 2.50
74 Mamadou N'Diaye RC 1.00 2.50
75 Erick Barkley RC 1.00 2.50
76 Mark Madsen RC 1.00 2.50
77 Dan Langhi RC 1.00 2.50
78 A.J. Guyton RC 1.00 2.50
79 Olumide Oyedeji RC 2.00 5.00
80 Eddie House RC 2.00 5.00
81 Eduardo Najera RC 2.00 5.00
82 Lavor Postell RC 2.00 5.00
83 Hanno Mottola RC 2.00 5.00
84 Chris Carrawell RC 2.00 5.00
85 Michael Redd RC 5.00 12.00
86 Jabari Smith RC 2.00 5.00
87 Jason Hart RC 2.00 5.00
88 Corey Hightower RC 1.00 2.50
89 Chris Porter RC 1.00 2.50
90 Justin Love RC 2.00 5.00
91 Kenyon Martin RC 2.50 6.00
92 Stromile Swift RC 1.00 2.50
93 Darius Miles RC 1.00 2.50
94 Marcus Fizer RC 1.00 2.50
95 Mike Miller RC 2.00 5.00
96 DerMarr Johnson RC 1.00 2.50
97 Chris Mihm RC 1.00 2.50
98 Jamal Crawford RC 1.50 4.00
99 Joel Przybilla RC 1.00 2.50
100 Keyon Dooling RC 1.00 2.50
P21 Kevin Garnett 1.00 2.50

2000-01 Upper Deck Slam Extra Strength Silver

Randomly inserted in packs, this 100-card set parallels the base set. The cards feature silver foil and were serially numbered to 500. To ascertain values on individual cards, please refer to the multiplier in the header, coupled with the value of the base card.

*STARS: 3X TO 8X BASE CARD HI
*RCs/2500: .5X TO 1.25X BASE CARD HI
*RCs/900: .25X TO .6X BASE CARD HI

2000-01 Upper Deck Slam Extra Strength Gold

Randomly inserted in packs, this 100-card set parallels the base set. The cards feature gold foil and were serially numbered to 25. To ascertain values on individual cards, please refer to the multiplier in the header, coupled with the value of the base card.

*STARS: 25X TO 60X BASE CARD HI
*RCs/2500: 4X TO 10X BASE CARD HI
*RCs/900: 2X TO 5X BASE CARD HI

2000-01 Upper Deck Slam Air Styles

Randomly inserted in packs at one in nine, this nine-card set showcased some of the extraordinary techniques of the top jammers. Card backs carry an "AS" prefix.

COMPLETE SET (9) 4.00 10.00
AS1 Kevin Garnett 1.00 2.50
AS2 Vince Carter 1.00 2.50
AS3 Gary Payton .50 1.25
AS4 Steve Francis .50 1.25
AS5 Shareef Abdur-Rahim .40 1.00
AS6 Allen Iverson 1.00 2.50
AS7 Elton Brand .50 1.25
AS8 Kobe Bryant 2.50 6.00
AS9 Scottie Pippen .75 2.00

2000-01 Upper Deck Slam Air Supremacy

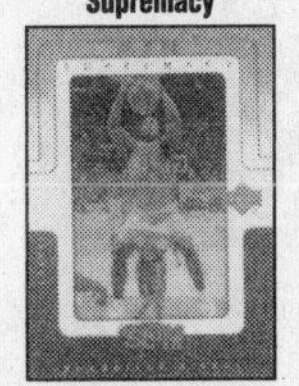

Randomly inserted in packs at one in 18, this six-card set pays tribute to the top players in the NBA. Card backs carry a "S" prefix.

COMPLETE SET (6) 5.00 12.00
S1 Kobe Bryant 3.00 8.00
S2 Vince Carter 1.25 3.00
S3 Shaquille O'Neal 1.50 4.00
S4 Allen Iverson 1.25 3.00
S5 Steve Francis .60 1.50
S6 Kevin Garnett 1.25 3.00

2000-01 Upper Deck Slam Flight Gear

Randomly inserted in packs at one in 108, this 14-card set features an authentic swatch from a game-used jersey on a see-through card. Card backs are numbered by the player's initials. Two autographed versions were also included, Kobe Bryant numbered to eight and Kevin Garnett numbered to 21. The Kobe Bryant card is not priced due to scarcity.

KB2G Kobe Bryant 15.00 40.00
KG2G Kevin Garnett 6.00 15.00
AIG Allen Iverson 6.00 15.00
AMG Alonzo Mourning 4.00 10.00
DRG David Robinson 5.00 12.00
GPG Gary Payton 3.00 8.00
KBG Kobe Bryant 15.00 40.00
KGA Kevin Garnett AU/21 60.00 150.00
KGG Kevin Garnett 6.00 15.00
KMG Karl Malone 4.00 10.00
MJG Michael Jordan/23 250.00 500.00
SAG Shareef Abdur-Rahim 2.50 6.00
SOG Shaquille O'Neal 8.00 20.00
THG Tim Hardaway 3.00 8.00
WSG Wally Szczerbiak 2.50 6.00

2000-01 Upper Deck Slam Power Windows

Randomly inserted in packs at one in 18, this six-card set captures some of the best moves to the hoop, featuring pictures from behind the glass. Card backs carry a "PW" prefix.

COMPLETE SET (6) 5.00 12.00
PW1 Shaquille O'Neal 1.50 4.00
PW2 Kevin Garnett 1.25 3.00
PW3 Karl Malone .75 2.00
PW4 Kobe Bryant 4.00 10.00
PW5 Elton Brand .60 1.50
PW6 Vince Carter 1.25 3.00

2000-01 Upper Deck Slam Signature Slams

Randomly inserted in packs at one in 108, this nine-card set features autographs of some of the top dunkers in the game. The cards are numbered by the player initials.

AH Anfernee Hardaway 25.00 60.00
AJ Antawn Jamison 8.00 20.00
AM Andre Miller 8.00 20.00
BD Baron Davis 8.00 20.00
KB Kobe Bryant 100.00 200.00
KG Kevin Garnett 40.00 100.00
RA Ray Allen 12.50 30.00
TM Tracy McGrady 15.00 40.00
WS Wally Szczerbiak 8.00 20.00

2000-01 Upper Deck Slam Slam Exam

Randomly inserted in packs at one in six, this nine-card set highlights jams by the top NBA stars. Card backs carry a "SE" prefix.

COMPLETE SET (9) 3.00 8.00
SE1 Kobe Bryant 2.00 5.00
SE2 Kevin Garnett .75 2.00
SE3 Anfernee Hardaway .60 1.50
SE4 Lamar Odom .40 1.00
SE5 Michael Finley .40 1.00
SE6 Latrell Sprewell .30 .75
SE7 Larry Hughes .30 .75
SE8 Chris Webber .40 1.00
SE9 Antonio McDyess .30 .75

2000-01 Upper Deck Slam UD Authentics

Randomly inserted in packs, this three-card set features autographs from the 2000-01 rookie class. The cards feature a congratulatory message on the back.

DH Donnell Harvey 4.00 10.00
JM Jamaal Magloire 4.00 10.00
MN Mamadou N'Diaye 4.00 10.00

2005-06 Upper Deck Slam

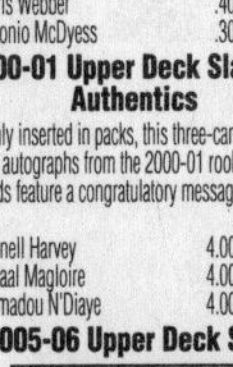

Released in September 2005, Upper Deck Slam features a 120 card set where cards 1-90 picture veterans and cards 91-120 picture rookies. Base cards have white borders along the left and right with highlights to match team colors and a Upper Deck Slam logo along the bottom. Slam is packaged in 24-pack boxes where packs contain six cards and upon release, carried a SRP of $1.99.

COMPLETE SET (120) 15.00 40.00
COMP.SET w/o SP's 6.00 15.00
1 Tony Delk .12 .30
2 Josh Smith .20 .50
3 Al Harrington .15 .40
4 Antoine Walker .15 .40
5 Gary Payton .20 .50
6 Paul Pierce .25 .60
7 Kareem Rush .12 .30
8 Emeka Okafor .20 .50
9 Primoz Brezec .12 .30
10 Eddy Curry .15 .40
11 Kirk Hinrich .20 .50
12 Ben Gordon .20 .50
13 Drew Gooden .15 .40
14 LeBron James 1.00 2.50
15 Zydrunas Ilgauskas .15 .40
16 Dirk Nowitzki .30 .75
17 Jason Terry .15 .40
18 Michael Finley .20 .50
19 Carmelo Anthony .40 1.00
20 Kenyon Martin .20 .50
21 Earl Boykins .12 .30
22 Ben Wallace .20 .50
23 Chauncey Billups .20 .50
24 Richard Hamilton .15 .40
25 Troy Murphy .15 .40
26 Jason Richardson .20 .50
27 Baron Davis .20 .50
28 Tracy McGrady .25 .60
29 Yao Ming .25 .60
30 Juwan Howard .15 .40
31 Jermaine O'Neal .20 .50
32 Stephen Jackson .15 .40
33 Ron Artest .20 .50
34 Corey Maggette .15 .40
35 Elton Brand .20 .50
36 Bobby Simmons .12 .30
37 Caron Butler .20 .50
38 Kobe Bryant 1.00 2.50
39 Lamar Odom .20 .50
40 Mike Miller .20 .50
41 Jason Williams .15 .40
42 Pau Gasol .20 .50
43 Dwyane Wade .50 1.25
44 Eddie Jones .15 .40
45 Shaquille O'Neal .40 1.00
46 Desmond Mason .12 .30
47 Maurice Williams .15 .40
48 Michael Redd .20 .50
49 Kevin Garnett .40 1.00
50 Latrell Sprewell .15 .40
51 Sam Cassell .20 .50
52 Vince Carter .30 .75
53 Jason Kidd .30 .75
54 Richard Jefferson .20 .50
55 Dan Dickau .12 .30
56 Jamaal Magloire .12 .30
57 J.R. Smith .20 .50
58 Jamal Crawford .15 .40
59 Stephon Marbury .15 .40
60 Allan Houston .12 .30
61 Dwight Howard .40 1.00
62 Grant Hill .25 .60
63 Steve Francis .20 .50
64 Allen Iverson .30 .75
65 Andre Iguodala .20 .50
66 Chris Webber .20 .50
67 Amare Stoudemire .20 .50
68 Shawn Marion .20 .50
69 Steve Nash .25 .60
70 Damon Stoudamire .15 .40
71 Shareef Abdur-Rahim .15 .40
72 Zach Randolph .15 .40
73 Mike Bibby .20 .50
74 Peja Stojakovic .20 .50
75 Brad Miller .20 .50
76 Manu Ginobili .20 .50
77 Tim Duncan .30 .75
78 Tony Parker .20 .50
79 Rashard Lewis .20 .50
80 Ray Allen .20 .50
81 Ronald Murray .12 .30
82 Rafer Alston .12 .30
83 Jalen Rose .20 .50
84 Chris Bosh .20 .50
85 Andrei Kirilenko .15 .40
86 Carlos Boozer .20 .50
87 Matt Harpring .15 .40
88 Antawn Jamison .20 .50
89 Gilbert Arenas .20 .50
90 Larry Hughes .15 .40
91 Andrew Bogut RC 1.00 2.50
92 Martynas Andriuskevicius RC .60 1.50
93 Chris Paul RC 2.50 6.00
94 Deron Williams RC 1.50 4.00
95 Luther Head RC .60 1.50
96 Chris Taft RC .60 1.50
97 David Lee RC 1.00 2.50
98 Gerald Green RC .75 2.00
99 Andrew Bynum RC 2.00 5.00
100 Rashad McCants RC .60 1.50
101 Raymond Felton RC 1.00 2.50
102 Danny Granger RC 1.25 3.00
103 Johan Petro RC .60 1.50
104 Antoine Wright RC .60 1.50
105 Channing Frye RC .75 2.00
106 Joey Graham RC .60 1.50
107 Wayne Simien RC .60 1.50
108 Monta Ellis RC 1.25 3.00
109 Charlie Villanueva RC .75 2.00
110 Martell Webster RC .60 1.50
111 C.J. Miles RC .75 2.00
112 Hakim Warrick RC .75 2.00
113 Ike Diogu RC .60 1.50
114 Jarrett Jack RC .60 1.50
115 Nate Robinson RC .75 2.00
116 Francisco Garcia RC .75 2.00
117 Sarunas Jasikevicius RC .60 1.50
118 Salim Stoudamire RC .60 1.50
119 Marvin Williams RC .75 2.00
120 Sean May RC .60 1.50

2005-06 Upper Deck Slam Dunk Swatches

Inserted in packs at the rate of one in 24, this 30-card set utilizes a horizontal design where player photos appear on the right and an arrow-shaped swatch of memorabilia appears on the left.

AK Andrei Kirilenko 2.00 5.00
BB Bruce Bowen 2.00 5.00
BR Bryon Russell 2.00 5.00
CB Carlos Boozer 2.50 6.00
CH Chris Bosh 2.50 6.00
DG Devean George 2.00 5.00
DN Dirk Nowitzki 4.00 10.00
DW Dajuan Wagner 2.00 5.00
JK Jason Kidd 4.00 10.00
JO Jermaine O'Neal 2.50 6.00
JR Jason Richardson 2.50 6.00
KB Kobe Bryant 8.00 20.00
KG Kevin Garnett 5.00 12.00
KR Kareem Rush 2.00 5.00
KT Kurt Thomas 2.00 5.00
LJ LeBron James 8.00 20.00
ME Stanislav Medvedenko 2.00 5.00
MJ Michael Jordan SP 25.00 60.00
MR Malik Rose 2.00 5.00
RJ Richard Jefferson 2.50 6.00
SF Steve Francis 2.50 6.00
SM Shawn Marion 2.50 6.00
SN Steve Nash 3.00 8.00
SO Shaquille O'Neal 5.00 12.00
ST Stephon Marbury 2.00 5.00
TD Tim Duncan 4.00 10.00
TM Tracy McGrady 3.00 8.00
UH Udonis Haslem 2.00 5.00
WS Wally Szczerbiak 2.00 5.00
YM Yao Ming 3.00 8.00

2005-06 Upper Deck Slam Signature Slams

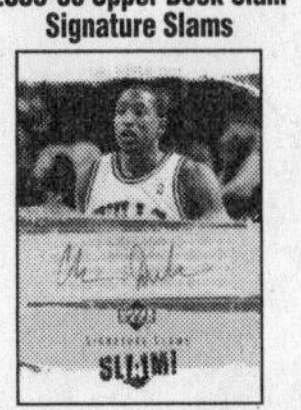

Inserted at the rate of one in 480, this 30-card set features a player photo shaded to match team colors on the top and a centered autograph sticker in the middle.

AI Andre Iguodala 8.00 20.00
AJ Antawn Jamison 5.00 12.00
BM Brad Miller 5.00 12.00
BU Beno Udrih 5.00 12.00
CD Chris Duhon 5.00 12.00
CW Chris Wilcox 5.00 12.00
DM Desmond Mason 5.00 12.00
DW Dorell Wright 5.00 12.00
JR J.R. Smith 5.00 12.00
JW Jason Williams 10.00 25.00
LJ LeBron James 100.00 200.00
MJ Michael Jordan SP 350.00 650.00
MP Morris Peterson 5.00 12.00
PP Paul Pierce SP 10.00 25.00
RJ Richard Jefferson 5.00 12.00
SN Steve Nash SP 50.00 120.00

2005-06 Upper Deck Slam Target Jerseys

RANDOM INSERTS IN TARGET PACKS
HC21 Austin Croshere 2.00 5.00
HC22 Brendan Haywood 2.00 5.00
HC23 Darius Songaila 2.00 5.00
HC24 Grant Hill 3.00 8.00
HC25 Jameer Nelson 2.00 5.00
HC26 Jason Richardson 2.50 6.00
HC27 Jason Terry 2.00 5.00
HC28 Josh Howard 2.50 6.00
HC29 Kelvin Cato 2.00 5.00
HC30 Kevin Martin 2.50 6.00
HC31 Lamar Odom 2.50 6.00
HC32 LeBron James 10.00 25.00
HC33 Malik Rose 2.00 5.00
HC34 Marcus Camby 2.00 5.00
HC35 Mike Sweetney 1.50 4.00
HC36 Peja Stojakovic 2.50 6.00
HC37 Reggie Miller 2.50 6.00
HC38 Tayshaun Prince 2.50 6.00
HC39 Yao Ming 3.00 8.00
HC40 Zydrunas Ilgauskas 2.00 5.00

1996 Upper Deck Space Jam

COMPLETE SET (106) 4.00 10.00
1 Bugs Bunny .01 .05
2 Lola Bunny .01 .05
3 Daffy Duck .01 .05
4 Porky Pig .01 .05
5 Elmer Fudd .01 .05
6 Tasmanian Devil .01 .05
7 Sylvester .01 .05
8 Tweety .01 .05
9 Granny .01 .05
10 Wile E. Coyote .01 .05
11 Road Runner .01 .05
12 Pepe Le Pew .01 .05
13 Marvin the Martian .01 .05
14 Yosemite Sam .01 .05
15 Speedy Gonzales .01 .05
16 Foghorn Leghorn .01 .05
17 Sniffles .01 .05
18 Witch Hazel .01 .05
19 Michael Jordan w Stan Podolak 1.25 3.00
20 Minion .01 .05
21 Charles Barkley .25 .60
22 Muggsy Bogues .15 .40
23 Michael Jordan 1.25 3.00
24 Bertie & Hubie .01 .05
25 Swackhammer .01 .05
26 Bang .01 .05
27 Bupkus .01 .05
28 Blanko .01 .05
29 Pound .01 .05
30 Nawt .01 .05
31 Bugs' Latest Creation .01 .05
32 The Ducktor .01 .05
33 Trying to be Terrible .01 .05
34 The Rabbit is Revealed Michael Jordan .01 .05
35 The Book of Bugs .01 .05
36 Daffy the Demolisher .01 .05
37 An Alien Crash Landing .01 .05
38 The Monstars Meet Their Match .01 .05
39 The Mean Team .01 .05
40 Analyzing the Competition .01 .05
41 Porky Solicits a Souvenir .01 .05
42 A Paranormal Experience .01 .05
43 Michael Jordan 1.25 3.00
44 It's Monstar Time .01 .05
45 Half-Time Heartbreak .01 .05
46 Bang .01 .05
47 Bupkus .01 .05
48 Blanko .01 .05
49 Pound .01 .05
50 Nawt .01 .05
51 Michael Jordan 1.25 3.00
52 Michael Jordan From Golf Clubs to Fan Club .01 .05
53 Michael Jordan 1.25 3.00
54 Double Agent .01 .05
55 A High-Flyin Monstars-Cryin Jam .01 .05
56 A Scary Stare from Air .01 .05
57 Bugs Bunny Busses a Bull .01 .05
58 Pepe Kisses One off the Glass .01 .05
59 Nice Butt .01 .05
60 Michael Jordan 1.25 3.00
61 Bugs Bunny .01 .05
62 Lola Bunny .01 .05
63 Daffy Duck .01 .05
64 Porky Pig .01 .05
65 Elmer Fudd .01 .05
66 Tasmanian Devil .01 .05
67 Sylvester .01 .05
68 Tweety .01 .05
69 Granny .01 .05
70 Wile E. Coyote .01 .05
71 Road Runner .01 .05
72 Pepe Le Pew .01 .05
73 Marvin the Martian .01 .05
74 Yosemite Sam .01 .05
75 Speedy Gonzales .01 .05
76 Foghorn Leghorn .01 .05
77 Sniffles .01 .05
78 Witch Hazel .01 .05
79 Stan Podolak .01 .05
80 Minion .01 .05
81 Michael Jordan 1.25 3.00
82 Muggsy Bogues .15 .40
83 Michael Jordan 1.25 3.00
84 Hubie & Bertie .01 .05
85 Swackhammer .01 .05
86 Bang .01 .05
87 Bupkus .01 .05
88 Michael Jordan 1.25 3.00
89 Pound .01 .05
90 Nawt .01 .05
91 Pondering Their Plight .01 .05
92 The Monstars Toss An Airball .01 .05
93 Hopping To The Hoop .01 .05
94 Anybody In There? .01 .05
95 Bottom's Up .01 .05
96 Checking Out The Competition .01 .05
97 We're Going To Be Slaves .01 .05
98 Snooping For Some Sneakers .01 .05
99 Looking For Something Looney .01 .05
100 We Gotta Believe In Ourselves .01 .05
101 Naughty Little Nerdlucks .01 .05
102 Boo .01 .05
103 The Ultimate Game .01 .05
104 Taking Back Their Talent .01 .05
105 Love Is In The Hare .01 .05
SJ1 Michael Jordan w Bugs Bunny PROMO 1.25 3.00

1996 Upper Deck Space Jam Scratchers

COMPLETE SET (3) 2.00 5.00
COMMON CARD 1.25 3.00

2004 Upper Deck Sportsfest

These cards were issued in groups of five over the course of three days at the 2004 Sportsfest card show in Chicago. Collectors would receive a group of 5 each day in exchange for 10 Upper Deck card wrappers that carried and SRP valued of $2.99 or higher. A 16th card was issued as an exchange card good for the first pick in the 2004 NBA draft.

STATED PRINT RUN 500 SER.#'d SETS
SF1 LeBron James 5.00 12.00
SF2 Kobe Bryant 5.00 12.00
SF3 Michael Jordan 5.00 12.00

2005 Upper Deck Sportsfest

COMPLETE SET (6) 8.00 20.00
UNPRICED AUTO PRINT RUN 5 SETS
NBA1 LeBron James 2.50 6.00
NBA2 Kobe Bryant 2.50 6.00
NBA3 Michael Jordan 5.00 12.00
NBA4 Kevin Garnett 1.50 4.00
NBA5 Yao Ming 1.25 3.00
NBA6 Steve Nash 1.25 3.00

2006 Upper Deck Sportsfest

COMPLETE SET (3) 7.50 15.00
NBA1 Michael Jordan 4.00 10.00
NBA2 LeBron James 3.00 8.00
NBA3 Chris Paul 2.00 5.00

2007 Upper Deck Sportsfest

UNPRICED AUTO PRINT RUN 3 TO 5 SETS
SF7 Kevin Durant 10.00 25.00
SF8 Michael Jordan 2.50 6.00
SF9 LeBron James 2.00 5.00

2008 Upper Deck Sportsfest

COMPLETE SET (12) 15.00 40.00
UNPRICED AUTO PRINT RUN 5 SETS
SF2 Michael Jordan 2.50 6.00
SF8 Kobe Bryant 2.00 5.00
SF11 LeBron James 2.00 5.00

2003-04 Upper Deck Standing O

Issued in October 2003, Standing O features a 126-card base set where veterans comprise cards 1-84 and rookies are showcased on cards 85-126 and inserted at the rate of one in four. Base cards have white borders and set a full-color player photo against a basketball background. Rookie cards do not have borders, rather a colored background that is set on top of a basketball image and bleeds to the edges. Standing O was packaged in 24-pack boxes where packs contained four cards and carried a suggested retail price of $1.99.

COMP.SET w/o SP's 15.00 40.00
1 Shareef Abdur-Rahim .25 .60
2 Jason Terry .25 .60
3 Theo Ratliff .20 .50
4 Paul Pierce .40 1.00
5 Antoine Walker .30 .75
6 Vin Baker .20 .50
7 Jalen Rose .25 .60
8 Tyson Chandler .25 .60
9 Michael Jordan 2.50 6.00
10 Dajuan Wagner .20 .50
11 Zydrunas Ilgauskas .25 .60
12 Darius Miles .20 .50
13 Dirk Nowitzki .50 1.25
14 Michael Finley .30 .75
15 Steve Nash .40 1.00
16 Nene .25 .60
17 Rodney White .20 .50
18 Richard Hamilton .25 .60
19 Ben Wallace .30 .75
20 Chauncey Billups .30 .75
21 Nick Van Exel .25 .60
22 Jason Richardson .30 .75
23 Mike Dunleavy .25 .60
24 Steve Francis .30 .75
25 Yao Ming .60 1.50
26 Cuttino Mobley .25 .60
27 Reggie Miller .30 .75
28 Jamaal Tinsley .20 .50
29 Jermaine Oâ€™Neal .30 .75
30 Elton Brand .30 .75
31 Corey Maggette .25 .60
32 Quentin Richardson .25 .60
33 Kobe Bryant 1.50 4.00
34 Shaquille O'Neal .75 2.00
35 Gary Payton .30 .75
36 Karl Malone .40 1.00
37 Pau Gasol .30 .75
38 Mike Miller .30 .75
39 Eddie Jones .25 .60
40 Brian Grant .20 .50
41 Caron Butler .30 .75
42 Michael Redd .30 .75
43 Joe Smith .25 .60
44 Desmond Mason .25 .60
45 Kevin Garnett .60 1.50
46 Latrell Sprewell .25 .60
47 Sam Cassell .25 .60
48 Jason Kidd .50 1.25
49 Richard Jefferson .30 .75
50 Alonzo Mourning .40 1.00
51 Baron Davis .30 .75
52 Jamal Mashburn .25 .60
53 Jamaal Magloire .20 .50
54 Allan Houston .25 .60
55 Antonio McDyess .25 .60
56 Keith Van Horn .25 .60
57 Tracy McGrady .40 1.00
58 Juwan Howard .25 .60
59 Drew Gooden .25 .60
60 Allen Iverson .50 1.25
61 Glenn Robinson .25 .60
62 Stephon Marbury .25 .60
63 Shawn Marion .30 .75
64 Amare Stoudemire .50 1.25
65 Rasheed Wallace .30 .75
66 Bonzi Wells .20 .50
67 Chris Webber .30 .75
68 Mike Bibby .30 .75
69 Peja Stojakovic .30 .75
70 Tim Duncan .50 1.25
71 David Robinson .50 1.25
72 Tony Parker .30 .75
73 Ray Allen .30 .75
74 Rashard Lewis .30 .75
75 Reggie Evans .20 .50
76 Vince Carter .50 1.25
77 Morris Peterson .20 .50
78 Antonio Davis .20 .50
79 Jarron Collins .20 .50
80 John Stockton .40 1.00
81 Andrei Kirilenko .30 .75
82 Jerry Stackhouse .25 .60
83 Gilbert Arenas .30 .75
84 Larry Hughes .25 .60
85 LeBron James RC 15.00 40.00
86 Darko Milicic RC 1.50 4.00
87 Carmelo Anthony RC 4.00 10.00
88 Chris Bosh RC 3.00 8.00
89 Dwyane Wade RC 6.00 15.00
90 Chris Kaman RC 2.00 5.00
91 Kirk Hinrich RC 2.00 5.00
92 T.J. Ford RC 2.00 5.00
93 Mike Sweetney RC 1.50 4.00
94 Jarvis Hayes RC 1.50 4.00
95 Mickael Pietrus RC 1.50 4.00
96 Nick Collison RC 1.50 4.00
97 Marcus Banks RC 1.50 4.00
98 Luke Ridnour RC 2.00 5.00
99 Reece Gaines RC 1.50 4.00
100 Troy Bell RC 1.50 4.00
101 Zarko Cabarkapa RC 1.50 4.00
102 David West RC 2.00 5.00
103 Aleksandar Pavlovic RC 1.50 4.00
104 Dahntay Jones RC 1.50 4.00
105 Boris Diaw RC 2.00 5.00
106 Zoran Planinic RC 1.50 4.00
107 Travis Outlaw RC 2.00 5.00
108 Brian Cook RC 1.50 4.00
109 Carlos Delfino RC 2.00 5.00
110 Ndudi Ebi RC 1.50 4.00
111 Kendrick Perkins RC 2.50 6.00
112 Leandro Barbosa RC 2.00 5.00
113 Josh Howard RC 1.50 4.00
114 Maciej Lampe RC 1.50 4.00
115 Jason Kapono RC 1.50 4.00
116 Luke Walton RC 1.50 4.00
117 Jerome Beasley RC 1.50 4.00
118 Willie Green RC 1.50 4.00
119 Kyle Korver RC 2.00 5.00
120 Travis Hansen RC 1.50 4.00
121 Steve Blake RC 2.00 5.00
122 Slavko Vranes RC 1.50 4.00
123 Zaur Pachulia RC 1.50 4.00
124 Keith Bogans RC 1.50 4.00
125 Theron Smith RC 1.50 4.00
126 Brandon Hunter RC 1.50 4.00

2003-04 Upper Deck Standing O Die Cuts/Embossed

Inserted at the rate of one per pack for the veterans and one in 24 for the rookies, this 126-card set parallels the base set in die-cut format. Rookie cards are also embossed.

*SINGLES: .75X TO 2X BASE CARD HI
*RCs: .4X TO 1X BASE CARD HI

2003-04 Upper Deck Standing O Graphs

Randomly inserted, this 21-card set places player action photos on the right and leaves space for the authentic player autograph.

Card	Low	High
BI Chauncey Billups SP	10.00	25.00
BO Carlos Boozer	8.00	20.00
DJ DerMarr Johnson	4.00	10.00
ET Etan Thomas	4.00	10.00
GA Gilbert Arenas SP	12.50	30.00
KB Kobe Bryant SP	100.00	225.00
LJ LeBron James SP	400.00	700.00
MJ Michael Jordan/23	400.00	600.00
MP Morris Peterson	4.00	10.00
RE Reggie Evans SP	4.00	10.00
RL Rashard Lewis	15.00	40.00
TM Tracy McGrady/25	20.00	50.00

2003-04 Upper Deck Standing O Swatches

Card	Low	High
AVAILABLE VIA REDEMPTION CARDS		
AIPH Allen Iverson	5.00	12.00
CBPH Caron Butler	3.00	8.00
CWPH Chris Webber	3.00	8.00
DNPH Dirk Nowitzki	5.00	12.00
GHPH Grant Hill	5.00	12.00
JKPH Jason Kidd	5.00	12.00
JOPH Jermaine O'Neal	3.00	8.00
JSPH John Stockton	4.00	10.00
KBPH Kobe Bryant	12.50	30.00
KGPH Kevin Garnett	6.00	15.00
KMPH Kenyon Martin	3.00	8.00
LSPH Latrell Sprewell	2.50	6.00
MJPH Michael Jordan	60.00	120.00
PPPH Paul Pierce	4.00	10.00
SAPH Amare Stoudemire	5.00	12.00
SMPH Stephon Marbury	2.50	6.00
SNPH Steve Nash	4.00	10.00
SPPH Scottie Pippen	5.00	12.00
TDPH Tim Duncan	5.00	12.00
TMPH Tracy McGrady	4.00	10.00
YMPH Yao Ming	6.00	15.00

1991-92 Upper Deck Stay in School Sheets

Upper Deck produced commemorative sheets that were given away at 1991-92 Stay In School events around the country. Orlando was the 1992 All-Star Game city and hosted the nationally televised Stay in School Jam. Each sheet measures approximately 5" by 7" and is printed on card stock. All sheets except Orlando have an Upper Deck stamp indicating the production run of 3,000 and an individual number. The production run for Orlando was 45,000. The design features Stay In School spokesman Bob Lanier and the logo of the team hosting the session, except for Orlando where a photo of Magic player Otis Smith replaces the logo. The backs are blank. The sheets are unnumbered and listed in alphabetical order. Despite the small quantity produced, these sheets do not have much demand because of the lack of subject matter.

Card	Low	High
COMPLETE SET (10)	15.00	40.00
1 Boston Celtics	2.50	6.00
2 Charlotte Hornets	2.50	6.00
3 Chicago Bulls	2.50	6.00
4 Detroit Pistons	2.50	6.00
5 Houston Rockets	2.50	6.00
6 Miami Heat	2.50	6.00
7 New Jersey Nets	2.50	6.00
8 Orlando Magic DP	.75	2.00
9 Portland Trail Blazers	2.50	6.00
10 San Antonio Spurs	2.50	6.00

2003 Upper Deck Top Prospects LeBron James Promos

Given away in Rosemont, Illinois on June 27-29 at the Collector's Universe Sportsfest show, card number P3 was LeBron James' first issue by a major manufacturer. A total of 4000 LeBron cards were mixed in randomly with other promo cards which were handed out at the Upper Deck show display. Three-packs containing all of the cards were handed out at the National Collector's Convention in Atlantic City, NJ on July 25th, 26th, and 27th. These packages were shrink-wrapped in clear plastic.

Card	Low	High
COMPLETE SET (3)	10.00	25.00
COMMON CARD (P1-P3)	4.00	10.00

1999 Upper Deck Tribute to Michael Jordan

This set was released in 1999 by Upper Deck, and features 30 cards that highlight Michael Jordan's career.

Card	Low	High
COMP. FACT SET (30)	10.00	25.00
COMMON CARD (1-30)	.40	1.00

2004-05 Upper Deck Trilogy

Released in May 2005, Upper Deck Trilogy boasts a 150-card set where cards 1-100 feature veteran players and cards 101-140 feature rookies serially numbered to 999 and cards 141-150 feature rookies serially numbered to 499. All of the rookies are printed on UD's patented plexi-glass and were covered with a tan tape to avoid scratches. Trilogy was packaged in nine card packs of five cards each and carried a SRP of $29.99.

Card	Low	High
COMP.SET w/o SP's (100)	60.00	150.00
UNPRICED SPECTRUM PRINT RUN 10 SETS		
1 Antoine Walker	.75	2.00
2 Al Harrington	.60	1.50
3 Boris Diaw	.60	1.50
4 Paul Pierce	1.00	2.50
5 Ricky Davis	.60	1.50
6 Gary Payton	.75	2.00
7 Gerald Wallace	.75	2.00
8 Emeka Okafor RC	1.25	3.00
9 Keith Bogans	.50	1.25
10 Eddy Curry	.60	1.50
11 Kirk Hinrich	.75	2.00
12 Michael Jordan	6.00	15.00
13 LeBron James	5.00	12.00
14 Dajuan Wagner	.50	1.25
15 Jeff McInnis	.50	1.25
16 Drew Gooden	.60	1.50
17 Dirk Nowitzki	1.25	3.00
18 Michael Finley	.75	2.00
19 Jerry Stackhouse	.60	1.50
20 Jason Terry	.60	1.50
21 Kenyon Martin	.75	2.00
22 Andre Miller	.60	1.50
23 Carmelo Anthony	1.50	4.00
24 Nene	.60	1.50
25 Chauncey Billups	.75	2.00
26 Rasheed Wallace	.75	2.00
27 Ben Wallace	.75	2.00
28 Richard Hamilton	.60	1.50
29 Derek Fisher	.60	1.50
30 Jason Richardson	.75	2.00
31 Mike Dunleavy	.60	1.50
32 Yao Ming	1.50	4.00
33 Tracy McGrady	1.00	2.50
34 Juwan Howard	.60	1.50
35 Jermaine O'Neal	.75	2.00
36 Reggie Miller	.75	2.00
37 Ron Artest	.75	2.00
38 Jamaal Tinsley	.50	1.25
39 Elton Brand	.75	2.00
40 Corey Maggette	.60	1.50
41 Marko Jaric	.50	1.25
42 Kerry Kittles	.50	1.25
43 Kobe Bryant	4.00	10.00
44 Caron Butler	.75	2.00
45 Lamar Odom	.75	2.00
46 Brian Cook	.50	1.25
47 Pau Gasol	.75	2.00
48 Jason Williams	.60	1.50
49 Bonzi Wells	.50	1.25
50 Shaquille O'Neal	2.00	5.00
51 Dwyane Wade	2.50	6.00
52 Eddie Jones	.60	1.50
53 Michael Redd	.75	2.00
54 Desmond Mason	.60	1.50
55 Maurice Williams	.60	1.50
56 Latrell Sprewell	.60	1.50
57 Kevin Garnett	1.50	4.00
58 Sam Cassell	.60	1.50
59 Troy Hudson	.50	1.25
60 Vince Carter	1.25	3.00
61 Richard Jefferson	.75	2.00
62 Jason Kidd	1.25	3.00
63 P.J. Brown	.50	1.25
64 Baron Davis	.75	2.00
65 Jamaal Magloire	.50	1.25
66 Allan Houston	.60	1.50
67 Jamal Crawford	.60	1.50
68 Stephon Marbury	.60	1.50
69 Grant Hill	1.00	2.50
70 Cuttino Mobley	.60	1.50
71 Steve Francis	.75	2.00
72 Glenn Robinson	.60	1.50
73 Allen Iverson	1.25	3.00
74 Willie Green	.50	1.25
75 Amare Stoudemire	1.00	2.50
76 Steve Nash	1.00	2.50
77 Quentin Richardson	.60	1.50
78 Shawn Marion	.75	2.00
79 Shareef Abdur-Rahim	.60	1.50
80 Damon Stoudamire	.60	1.50
81 Zach Randolph	.60	1.50
82 Darius Miles	.50	1.25
83 Peja Stojakovic	.75	2.00
84 Chris Webber	.75	2.00
85 Mike Bibby	.75	2.00
86 Tony Parker	.75	2.00
87 Tim Duncan	1.25	3.00
88 Manu Ginobili	1.00	2.50
89 Ronald Murray	.50	1.25
90 Ray Allen	.75	2.00
91 Rashard Lewis	.75	2.00
92 Chris Bosh	.75	2.00
93 Rafer Alston	.50	1.25
94 Jalen Rose	.60	1.50
95 Andrei Kirilenko	.60	1.50
96 Carlos Arroyo	.60	1.50
97 Carlos Boozer	.75	2.00
98 Gilbert Arenas	.75	2.00
99 Jarvis Hayes	.50	1.25
100 Antawn Jamison	.75	2.00
101 Rafael Araujo RC	3.00	8.00
102 Luke Jackson RC	3.00	8.00
103 Andris Biedrins RC	4.00	10.00
104 Robert Swift RC	3.00	8.00
105 Kris Humphries RC	3.00	8.00
106 Al Jefferson RC	5.00	12.00
107 Kirk Snyder RC	3.00	8.00
108 Josh Smith RC	5.00	12.00
109 Dorell Wright RC	5.00	12.00
110 Jameer Nelson RC	4.00	10.00
111 Pavel Podkolzine RC	3.00	8.00
112 Andres Nocioni RC	3.00	8.00
113 Luis Flores RC	3.00	8.00
114 Delonte West RC	4.00	10.00
115 Tony Allen RC	4.00	10.00
116 Kevin Martin RC	4.00	10.00
117 Sasha Vujacic RC	3.00	8.00
118 Beno Udrih RC	3.00	8.00
119 David Harrison RC	3.00	8.00
120 Anderson Varejao RC	4.00	10.00
121 Jackson Vroman RC	3.00	8.00
122 Peter John Ramos RC	3.00	8.00
123 Lionel Chalmers RC	3.00	8.00
124 Donta Smith RC	3.00	8.00
125 Andre Emmett RC	3.00	8.00
126 Antonio Burks RC	3.00	8.00
127 Royal Ivey RC	3.00	8.00
128 Chris Duhon RC	3.00	8.00
129 Nenad Krstic RC	3.00	8.00
130 Justin Reed RC	3.00	8.00
131 Pape Sow RC	3.00	8.00
132 Trevor Ariza RC	3.00	8.00
133 Tim Pickett RC	3.00	8.00
134 Bernard Robinson RC	3.00	8.00
135 John Edwards RC	3.00	8.00
136 Damien Wilkins RC	3.00	8.00
137 Romain Sato RC	3.00	8.00
138 Matt Freije RC	3.00	8.00
139 D.J. Mbenga RC	3.00	8.00
140 Yuta Tabuse RC	6.00	15.00
141 Dwight Howard RC	12.00	30.00
142 Emeka Okafor	6.00	15.00
143 Ben Gordon RC	5.00	12.00
144 Shaun Livingston RC	4.00	10.00
145 Devin Harris RC	6.00	15.00
146 Josh Childress RC	4.00	10.00
147 Luol Deng RC	6.00	15.00
148 Andre Iguodala RC	6.00	15.00
149 Sebastian Telfair RC	4.00	10.00
150 J.R. Smith RC	5.00	12.00
P23 Carmelo Anthony PROMO	2.00	5.00

2004-05 Upper Deck Trilogy Gold

Randomly inserted in packs, this 100-card set parallels the base Trilogy set enhanced with sequential numbering to 100. A Spectrum version was also inserted and those cards are serially numbered to 10.
*GOLD SINGLES: 1.25X TO 3X BASE HI

2004-05 Upper Deck Trilogy Rookie Premiere Crystal

Randomly inserted in packs, this 50-card set parallels the rookie cards from the base set enhanced with sequential numbering to 25.
*101-140 RCs: 1.25X TO 3X BASE HI
*141-150 RCs: 1X TO 2.5X BASE HI

2004-05 Upper Deck Trilogy Auto Focus

Inserted in packs at the rate of one in nine, this 40-card set was printed on UD's plexi-glass and contains an autograph of the featured player. A pink Crystal parallel was also inserted and those cards are numbered to 25.

Card	Low	High
AI Andre Iguodala	8.00	20.00
AJ Al Jefferson	8.00	20.00
AK Andrei Kirilenko	6.00	15.00
AL Ray Allen	15.00	40.00
AS Amare Stoudemire	15.00	30.00
BD Baron Davis	6.00	15.00
BG Ben Gordon	6.00	15.00
CA Carmelo Anthony SP	20.00	40.00
DE Devin Harris	8.00	20.00
DH Dwight Howard SP	40.00	100.00
DW Dorell Wright	8.00	20.00
JC Josh Childress	5.00	12.00
JK Jason Kidd SP	15.00	30.00
JN Jameer Nelson	6.00	15.00
JR J.R. Smith	6.00	15.00
JS Josh Smith	8.00	20.00
KB Kobe Bryant SP	100.00	200.00
KG Kevin Garnett SP	30.00	60.00
KH Kris Humphries	5.00	12.00
KI Kirk Hinrich	8.00	20.00
KS Kirk Snyder	5.00	12.00
LD Luol Deng	10.00	25.00
LJ LeBron James SP	125.00	250.00
LU Luke Jackson	5.00	12.00
MB Mike Bibby	5.00	12.00
MJ Michael Jordan SP	300.00	600.00
PG Pau Gasol	10.00	25.00
PP Paul Pierce	10.00	25.00
PS Peja Stojakovic	6.00	15.00
RA Rafael Araujo	5.00	12.00
RH Richard Hamilton	6.00	15.00
RS Robert Swift	5.00	12.00
SH Shawn Marion	6.00	15.00
SL Shaun Livingston	5.00	12.00
SM Stephon Marbury SP	12.00	30.00
ST Sebastian Telfair	5.00	12.00
TA Tony Allen	6.00	15.00
TM Tracy McGrady SP	12.00	30.00
WE Delonte West	6.00	15.00
YM Yao Ming	20.00	50.00

2004-05 Upper Deck Trilogy Auto Focus Crystal

Randomly inserted in packs, this 40-card set parallels the Auto Focus insert on a pink glass stock and is sequentially numbered to 25.
*CRYSTAL: 1X TO 2.5X BASE HI

Card	Low	High
KB Kobe Bryant	150.00	300.00
LJ LeBron James	150.00	300.00
MJ Michael Jordan	300.00	600.00
TM Tracy McGrady	25.00	60.00

2004-05 Upper Deck Trilogy One Two Combo Clearcut Autographs

Limited to 25 serially numbered copies, this 14-card set is printed on plastic and features two players along with their autographs.

Card	Low	High
AM Carmelo Anthony	30.00	80.00
Andre Miller		
CS Josh Childress	20.00	50.00
Josh Smith		
DG Luol Deng	40.00	100.00
Ben Gordon		
DS Baron Davis	20.00	50.00
J.R. Smith		
HJ Dwight Howard	300.00	500.00
LeBron James		
HN Dwight Howard	100.00	200.00
Jameer Nelson		
JB LeBron James	400.00	600.00
Kobe Bryant		
JJ Michael Jordan	600.00	1000.00
LeBron James		
KH Andrei Kirilenko	20.00	50.00
Kris Humphries		
KJ Jason Kidd	40.00	100.00
Richard Jefferson		
MC Stephon Marbury	25.00	60.00
Jamal Crawford		
MM Yao Ming	100.00	200.00
Tracy McGrady		
PB Paul Pierce	100.00	200.00
Larry Bird		
SM Amare Stoudemire	40.00	100.00
Shawn Marion		

2004-05 Upper Deck Trilogy Signature Swatches

Randomly inserted in packs, this 30-card set is horizontally designed and features a player image on the left, a swatch of memorabilia in the upper-right corner in the shape of "SS", and the player's signature beneath the swatch. Each card is serially numbered to 25.

Card	Low	High
AI Andre Iguodala	20.00	50.00
AJ Al Jefferson	20.00	50.00
AK Andrei Kirilenko	15.00	40.00
AS Amare Stoudemire	30.00	80.00
BD Baron Davis	12.00	30.00
BG Ben Gordon	15.00	40.00
CA Carmelo Anthony	50.00	120.00
DE Devin Harris	20.00	50.00
DH Dwight Howard	125.00	250.00
JC Josh Childress	12.00	30.00
JK Jason Kidd	25.00	60.00
JN Jameer Nelson	15.00	40.00
JR J.R. Smith	15.00	40.00
JS Josh Smith	20.00	50.00
KB Kobe Bryant	150.00	300.00
KG Kevin Garnett	75.00	150.00
KH Kris Humphries	12.00	30.00
KS Kirk Snyder	12.00	30.00
LD Luol Deng	20.00	50.00
LJ LeBron James	175.00	350.00
LO Lamar Odom	15.00	40.00
LU Luke Jackson	12.00	30.00
MB Mike Bibby	12.00	30.00
MJ Michael Jordan	400.00	650.00
PG Pau Gasol	12.00	30.00
PP Paul Pierce	25.00	60.00
SL Shaun Livingston	12.00	30.00
SM Stephon Marbury	25.00	60.00
ST Sebastian Telfair	12.00	30.00
TM Tracy McGrady	40.00	100.00

2004-05 Upper Deck Trilogy Signs of Stardom

Seeded randomly in packs at the rate of one in three, this 50-card set is horizontally designed with gold foil highlights, player images on the left, and an autograph in a white-out box on the right.

Card	Low	High
AE Andre Emmett	5.00	12.00
AI Andre Iguodala	8.00	20.00
AJ Al Jefferson	8.00	20.00
AK Andrei Kirilenko	6.00	15.00
AL Ray Allen	15.00	40.00
AS Amare Stoudemire	12.50	30.00
AV Anderson Varejao	6.00	15.00
BD Baron Davis	5.00	12.00
BG Ben Gordon	6.00	15.00
BM Brad Miller	5.00	12.00
BU Beno Udrih	5.00	12.00
CA Carmelo Anthony SP	20.00	50.00
CD Chris Duhon	5.00	12.00
DA David Harrison	5.00	12.00
DE Devin Harris	8.00	20.00
DH Dwight Howard SP	15.00	40.00
DW Dorell Wright	8.00	20.00
JC Josh Childress	5.00	12.00
JK Jason Kidd SP	12.50	30.00
JM Jamaal Magloire	5.00	12.00
JN Jameer Nelson	6.00	15.00
JR J.R. Smith	6.00	15.00
JS Josh Smith	8.00	20.00
JV Jackson Vroman	5.00	12.00
KB Kobe Bryant SP	100.00	200.00
KG Kevin Garnett SP	30.00	80.00
KH Kris Humphries	5.00	12.00
KI Kirk Hinrich	10.00	25.00
KM Kevin Martin	6.00	15.00
KS Kirk Snyder	5.00	12.00
LC Lionel Chalmers	5.00	12.00
LD Luol Deng	8.00	20.00
LJ LeBron James SP	150.00	300.00
LO Lamar Odom	6.00	15.00
LU Luke Jackson	5.00	12.00
MB Mike Bibby	5.00	12.00
MJ Michael Jordan SP	350.00	500.00
PG Pau Gasol	8.00	20.00
PP Paul Pierce	10.00	25.00
RA Rafael Araujo	5.00	12.00
RH Richard Hamilton	6.00	15.00
SH Shawn Marion	6.00	15.00
SL Shaun Livingston	5.00	12.00
SM Stephon Marbury	10.00	25.00
ST Sebastian Telfair	5.00	12.00
SV Sasha Vujacic	5.00	12.00
TA Tony Allen	6.00	15.00
TM Tracy McGrady SP	20.00	40.00
TR Trevor Ariza	5.00	12.00
WE Delonte West	6.00	15.00

2004-05 Upper Deck Trilogy Swatches of Stardom

Randomly seeded in packs and serially numbered to 50, this 42-card set is horizontally designed with a player image on the left and an oversized jersey swatch on the right in the shape of "SS."

Card	Low	High
AI Allen Iverson	8.00	20.00
AK Andrei Kirilenko	4.00	10.00
AS Amare Stoudemire	6.00	15.00
BD Baron Davis	5.00	12.00
BG Ben Gordon	6.00	15.00
BK Bernard King	5.00	12.00
BR Bill Russell	20.00	50.00
BW Ben Wallace	5.00	12.00
CA Carmelo Anthony	10.00	25.00
DE Devin Harris	8.00	20.00
DH Dwight Howard	15.00	40.00
DN Dirk Nowitzki	8.00	20.00
EB Elton Brand	5.00	12.00
JC Josh Childress	5.00	12.00
JE Julius Erving	20.00	40.00
JK Jason Kidd	8.00	20.00
JN Jameer Nelson	6.00	15.00
JO Jermaine O'Neal	5.00	12.00
JR J.R. Smith	6.00	15.00
JS Josh Smith	8.00	20.00
KB Kobe Bryant	25.00	60.00
KG Kevin Garnett	10.00	25.00
LB Larry Bird	35.00	75.00
LD Luol Deng	8.00	20.00
LJ LeBron James	40.00	100.00
MA Magic Johnson	20.00	50.00
MJ Michael Jordan	150.00	300.00
PG Pau Gasol	5.00	12.00
PP Paul Pierce	6.00	15.00
PS Peja Stojakovic	5.00	12.00
RM Reggie Miller	8.00	20.00
SF Steve Francis	5.00	12.00
SH Shawn Marion	5.00	12.00
SL Shaun Livingston	5.00	12.00
SM Stephon Marbury	4.00	10.00
SN Steve Nash	6.00	15.00
SO Shaquille O'Neal	20.00	50.00
ST Sebastian Telfair	5.00	12.00
TD Tim Duncan	8.00	20.00
TM Tracy McGrady	6.00	15.00
WF Walt Frazier	8.00	20.00
YM Yao Ming	10.00	25.00

2004-05 Upper Deck Trilogy The Cutting Edge

Randomly inserted in packs at the rate of one in three, this 42-card set features player photos on the right and a swatch of memorabilia in the lower left.

Card	Low	High
AE Andre Emmett	2.50	6.00
AI Allen Iverson	4.00	10.00
AJ Al Jefferson	4.00	10.00
AN Andre Iguodala	4.00	10.00
AS Amare Stoudemire	3.00	8.00
BD Baron Davis SP	2.50	6.00
BG Ben Gordon	3.00	8.00
CA Carmelo Anthony	5.00	12.00
CD Chris Duhon	2.50	6.00
DE Devin Harris	4.00	10.00
DH Dwight Howard	8.00	20.00
DN Dirk Nowitzki	4.00	10.00
JA Jason Richardson	2.50	6.00
JC Josh Childress	2.50	6.00
JK Jason Kidd	4.00	10.00
JN Jameer Nelson	3.00	8.00
JR J.R. Smith	3.00	8.00
JS Josh Smith	4.00	10.00
KB Kobe Bryant SP	10.00	25.00
KG Kevin Garnett SP	6.00	15.00
KH Kris Humphries	2.50	6.00
KM Kevin Martin	3.00	8.00
KS Kirk Snyder	2.50	6.00
LD Luol Deng	4.00	10.00
LJ LeBron James SP	15.00	40.00
LU Luke Jackson	2.50	6.00
MB Mike Bibby	2.50	6.00
MJ Michael Jordan SP	40.00	100.00
PP Paul Pierce	3.00	8.00
PS Peja Stojakovic	2.50	6.00
RA Ray Allen	2.50	6.00
RJ Richard Jefferson	2.50	6.00
SA Shareef Abdur-Rahim	2.00	5.00
SL Shaun Livingston	2.50	6.00
SM Stephon Marbury	2.00	5.00
SO Shaquille O'Neal SP	6.00	15.00
ST Sebastian Telfair	2.50	6.00
TA Tony Allen	3.00	8.00
TD Tim Duncan	4.00	10.00
TM Tracy McGrady	3.00	8.00
WE Delonte West	3.00	8.00
YM Yao Ming	5.00	12.00

2004-05 Upper Deck Trilogy TriMarks I

Limited to 35 serially numbered copies, this 29-card set is printed on plastic and features three players along with their autographs.

Card	Low	High
CARDS WITH ASTERISK ISSUED AS EXCH		
UNPRICED TRIMARKS II PRINT RUN 10 SETS		
AMS Ray Allen	30.00	80.00
Ronald Murray		
Robert Swift		
ART Shareef Abdur-Rahim	30.00	80.00
Zach Randolph		
Sebastian Telfair		
BMM Mike Bibby	50.00	100.00
Brad Miller		
Kevin Martin		
BOR Kobe Bryant	125.00	250.00
Lamar Odom		
Kareem Rush		
CSI Josh Childress	30.00	80.00
Josh Smith		
Royal Ivey		
DWK Baron Davis	125.00	225.00
Jason Williams		
Jason Kidd		
GDH Ben Gordon	125.00	250.00
Luol Deng		
Kirk Hinrich		
GEB Pau Gasol	30.00	80.00
Andre Emmett		
Antonio Burks		
HCS Al Harrington	60.00	120.00
Josh Childress		
Josh Smith		
HGL Dwight Howard	150.00	300.00
Ben Gordon		
Shaun Livingston		
HHD Josh Howard	40.00	100.00
Devin Harris		
Marquis Daniels		
HJB Dwight Howard	500.00	900.00
LeBron James		
Kobe Bryant		
HMB Richard Hamilton	30.00	80.00
Chauncey Billups		
Darko Milicic		
IBJ Andre Iguodala	30.00	80.00
Mike Bibby		
Richard Jefferson		
JAR Antawn Jamison	30.00	80.00
Gilbert Arenas		
Peter John Ramos		
JJV LeBron James	250.00	400.00
Luke Jackson		
Anderson Varejao		
JWA Al Jefferson	60.00	150.00
Delonte West		
Tony Allen		
KHS Andrei Kirilenko	30.00	80.00
Kris Humphries		
Kirk Snyder		
MCA Stephon Marbury	30.00	80.00
Jamal Crawford		
Trevor Ariza		
MLC Corey Maggette	30.00	80.00
Shaun Livingston		
Lionel Chalmers		
MSP Jamaal Magloire	30.00	80.00
J.R. Smith		
Tim Pickett		
NTL Jameer Nelson	30.00	80.00
Sebastian Telfair		
Shaun Livingston		
OVR Lamar Odom	30.00	80.00
Sasha Vujacic		
Kareem Rush		
PUS Tony Parker	40.00	100.00
Ben Udrih		
Romain Sato		
RFB Jason Richardson	30.00	80.00
Derek Fisher		
Andris Biedrins		
RMK Michael Redd	50.00	120.00
Desmond Mason		
Toni Kukoc		
RPA Jalen Rose	30.00	80.00
Morris Peterson		
Rafael Araujo		
SBM Peja Stojakovic	60.00	120.00
Mike Bibby		
Brad Miller		
SMV Amare Stoudemire	75.00	150.00
Shawn Marion		
Jackson Vroman		

2005-06 Upper Deck Trilogy

Card	Low	High
COMP.SET w/o SP's (90)	25.00	60.00
1 Josh Smith	1.00	2.50
2 Josh Childress	.75	2.00
3 Al Harrington	.75	2.00
4 Paul Pierce	1.25	3.00
5 Ricky Davis	.75	2.00
6 Al Jefferson	1.00	2.50
7 Emeka Okafor	1.00	2.50
8 Gerald Wallace	1.00	2.50
9 Kareem Rush	.60	1.50
10 Michael Jordan	8.00	20.00
11 Luol Deng	1.00	2.50
12 Ben Gordon	1.00	2.50
13 LeBron James	5.00	12.00
14 Larry Hughes	.75	2.00
15 Donyell Marshall	.60	1.50
16 Dirk Nowitzki	1.50	4.00
17 Josh Howard	1.00	2.50
18 Jason Terry	.75	2.00
19 Carmelo Anthony	2.00	5.00
20 Kenyon Martin	1.00	2.50
21 Andre Miller	.75	2.00
22 Chauncey Billups	1.00	2.50
23 Richard Hamilton	.75	2.00
24 Ben Wallace	1.00	2.50
25 Jason Richardson	1.00	2.50
26 Baron Davis	1.00	2.50
27 Troy Murphy	.75	2.00
28 Yao Ming	1.25	3.00
29 Tracy McGrady	1.25	3.00
30 Stromile Swift	.60	1.50
31 Ron Artest	1.00	2.50
32 Jermaine O'Neal	1.00	2.50
33 Fred Jones	.60	1.50
34 Elton Brand	1.00	2.50
35 Shaun Livingston	.60	1.50
36 Corey Maggette	.75	2.00
37 Kobe Bryant	5.00	12.00
38 Kwame Brown	.60	1.50
39 Lamar Odom	1.00	2.50
40 Pau Gasol	1.00	2.50
41 Shane Battier	.75	2.00
42 Mike Miller	1.00	2.50
43 Shaquille O'Neal	2.00	5.00
44 Dwyane Wade	2.50	6.00
45 Udonis Haslem	.75	2.00
46 Michael Redd	1.00	2.50
47 Maurice Williams	.75	2.00
48 Desmond Mason	.60	1.50
49 Kevin Garnett	2.00	5.00
50 Wally Szczerbiak	.75	2.00
51 Marko Jaric	.60	1.50
52 Jason Kidd	1.50	4.00
53 Vince Carter	1.50	4.00
54 Richard Jefferson	1.00	2.50
55 Jamaal Magloire	.60	1.50
56 J.R. Smith	1.00	2.50
57 Speedy Claxton	.60	1.50
58 Stephon Marbury	.75	2.00
59 Jamal Crawford	.75	2.00
60 Quentin Richardson	.75	2.00
61 Steve Francis	1.00	2.50
62 Dwight Howard	2.00	5.00
63 Grant Hill	1.25	3.00
64 Allen Iverson	1.50	4.00
65 Kyle Korver	.75	2.00
66 Chris Webber	1.00	2.50
67 Steve Nash	1.25	3.00
68 Amare Stoudemire	1.00	2.50
69 Shawn Marion	1.00	2.50
70 Sebastian Telfair	.75	2.00
71 Zach Randolph	.75	2.00
72 Travis Outlaw	.75	2.00
73 Peja Stojakovic	1.00	2.50
74 Mike Bibby	1.00	2.50
75 Brad Miller	1.00	2.50
76 Tim Duncan	1.50	4.00
77 Manu Ginobili	1.00	2.50
78 Tony Parker	1.00	2.50
79 Ray Allen	1.00	2.50
80 Rashard Lewis	1.00	2.50
81 Luke Ridnour	.75	2.00
82 Chris Bosh	1.00	2.50
83 Morris Peterson	.60	1.50
84 Jalen Rose	1.00	2.50
85 Carlos Boozer	1.00	2.50
86 Matt Harpring	.75	2.00
87 Andrei Kirilenko	.75	2.00
88 Antawn Jamison	1.00	2.50
89 Gilbert Arenas	1.00	2.50
90 Caron Butler	1.00	2.50
91 Sarunas Jasikevicius RC	3.00	8.00
92 Alex Acker RC	3.00	8.00
93 Amir Johnson RC	3.00	8.00
94 Lawrence Roberts RC	3.00	8.00
95 Dijon Thompson RC	3.00	8.00
96 Orien Greene RC	3.00	8.00
97 Robert Whaley RC	3.00	8.00
98 Ryan Gomes RC	3.00	8.00
99 Andray Blatche RC	4.00	10.00
100 Yaroslav Korolev RC	3.00	8.00
101 Bracey Wright RC	3.00	8.00
102 Louis Williams RC	5.00	12.00
103 Martynas Andriuskevicius RC	3.00	8.00
104 Chris Taft RC	3.00	8.00
105 Monta Ellis RC	6.00	15.00
106 Von Wafer RC	3.00	8.00
107 Travis Diener RC	3.00	8.00
108 Ersan Ilyasova RC	4.00	10.00
109 Arvydas Macijauskas RC	3.00	8.00
110 C.J. Miles RC	4.00	10.00
111 Brandon Bass RC	4.00	10.00
112 Daniel Ewing RC	3.00	8.00
113 Salim Stoudamire RC	3.00	8.00
114 David Lee RC	5.00	12.00
115 Wayne Simien RC	3.00	8.00
116 Jason Maxiell RC	3.00	8.00
117 Johan Petro RC	3.00	8.00
118 Luther Head RC	3.00	8.00
119 Francisco Garcia RC	4.00	10.00
120 Jarrett Jack RC	3.00	8.00
121 Nate Robinson RC	4.00	10.00
122 Julius Hodge RC	3.00	8.00
123 Hakim Warrick RC	4.00	10.00
124 Gerald Green RC	4.00	10.00
125 Danny Granger RC	6.00	15.00
126 Joey Graham RC	3.00	8.00
127 Antoine Wright RC	3.00	8.00
128 Rashad McCants RC	3.00	8.00
129 Sean May RC	3.00	8.00
130 Linas Kleiza RC	3.00	8.00
131 Andrew Bynum RC	12.00	30.00
132 Ike Diogu RC	4.00	10.00
133 Channing Frye RC	5.00	12.00
134 Charlie Villanueva RC	5.00	12.00

5 Martell Webster RC 4.00 10.00
6 Raymond Felton RC 6.00 15.00
7 Chris Paul RC 15.00 40.00
8 Deron Williams RC 10.00 25.00
9 Marvin Williams RC 5.00 12.00
0 Andrew Bogut RC 6.00 15.00

2005-06 Upper Deck Trilogy Auto Focus

PPROXIMATELY ONE PER BOX
B Andrew Bogut 8.00 20.00
N Andrew Bynum 15.00 40.00
W Antoine Wright 5.00 12.00
G Ben Gordon 6.00 15.00
F Channing Frye 6.00 15.00
P Chris Paul 50.00 120.00
G Danny Granger 10.00 25.00
H Dwight Howard 20.00 50.00
O Emeka Okafor 6.00 15.00
G Francisco Garcia 6.00 15.00
G George Gervin 12.50 30.00
O Hakeem Olajuwon SP 20.00 50.00
D Ike Diogu 5.00 12.00
T Isiah Thomas 12.50 30.00
A Jarrett Jack 5.00 12.00
J Joe Johnson 6.00 15.00
P Johan Petro 5.00 12.00
R J.R. Smith SP 8.00 20.00
B Kwame Brown 5.00 12.00
D Keyon Dooling 5.00 12.00
A Larry Bird SP 60.00 120.00
B LeBron James 150.00 300.00
MA Magic Johnson SP 50.00 120.00
MJ Michael Jordan SP 400.00 700.00
MR Michael Redd 5.00 12.00
MW Marvin Williams 6.00 15.00
NR Nate Robinson 8.00 20.00
PP Paul Pierce 12.50 30.00
RF Raymond Felton 8.00 20.00
RH Richard Hamilton 6.00 15.00
RM Rashad McCants 5.00 12.00
SE Sean May 5.00 12.00
SJ Sarunas Jasikevicius 5.00 12.00
SM Stephon Marbury 10.00 25.00
SP Scottie Pippen SP 100.00 200.00
TM Tracy McGrady SP 15.00 40.00
VR Vladimir Radmanovic 5.00 12.00
WF Walt Frazier 12.00 30.00
WS Wayne Simien 5.00 12.00
YM Yao Ming SP 20.00 50.00

2005-06 Upper Deck Trilogy DuoMarks

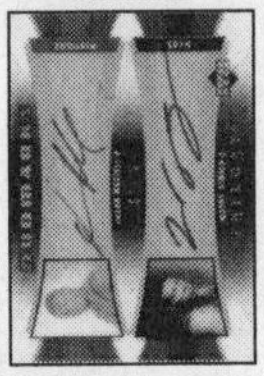

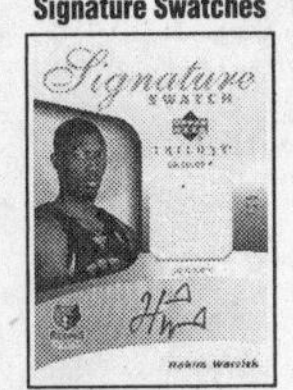

PRINT RUN 25 TO 75 SER.#'d SETS
AW Carmelo Anthony/25 25.00 60.00
Hakim Warrick
BF Andrew Bogut/25 25.00 60.00
Channing Frye
BP Andrew Bynum/75 15.00 40.00
Johan Petro
BS Bernard King/75 15.00 40.00
Stephon Marbury
CD Zarko Cabarkapa/75 10.00 25.00
Ike Diogu
CK Vince Carter/75 60.00 120.00
Jason Kidd
DR Marquis Daniels/75 10.00 25.00
Quentin Richardson
GH Ben Gordon/75 15.00 40.00
Kirk Hinrich
GW Danny Granger/75 10.00 25.00
Hakim Warrick
HE Luther Head/75 10.00 25.00
Daniel Ewing
HS Kirk Hinrich/75 12.50 30.00
Wayne Simien
HW Dwight Howard/75 20.00 50.00
Marvin Williams
IW Andre Iguodala/75 12.50 30.00
Louis Williams
JA Magic Johnson/25 100.00 225.00
Kareem Abdul-Jabbar
JC Joe Johnson/75 10.00 25.00
Josh Childress
JG Al Jefferson/75 10.00 25.00
Orien Greene
JJ Michael Jordan/25 600.00 1000.00
LeBron James
KH Linas Kleiza/75 10.00 25.00
Julius Hodge
LB David Lee/75 10.00 25.00
Brandon Bass
LE Shaun Livingston/75 10.00 25.00
Daniel Ewing
MM Sean May/75 10.00 25.00
Rashad McCants
MS Jason Maxiell/75 10.00 25.00
Wayne Simien
MY Tracy McGrady/25 50.00 120.00
Yao Ming
NB Steve Nash/25 75.00 150.00
Chauncey Billups
ND Jameer Nelson/75 10.00 25.00
Travis Diener
PB Tayshaun Prince/75 25.00 60.00
Chauncey Billups

PG Paul Pierce/75 15.00 40.00
Gerald Green
PR Scottie Pippen/25 250.00 450.00
Dennis Rodman
PW Chris Paul/25 50.00 100.00
Marvin Williams
RG David Robinson/25 100.00 200.00
George Gervin
RJ Nate Robinson/75 12.50 30.00
Jarrett Jack
SP J.R. Smith/75 30.00 80.00
Chris Paul
SS Damon Stoudamire/75 10.00 25.00
Salim Stoudamire
SW John Stockton/25 75.00 200.00
Deron Williams
VG Charlie Villanueva/75 15.00 30.00
Joey Graham
WF Deron Williams/75 25.00 60.00
Raymond Felton
WG Martell Webster/75 12.50 30.00
Gerald Green
WH Antoine Wright/75 10.00 25.00
Julius Hodge
WJ Martell Webster/75 10.00 25.00
Jarrett Jack

2005-06 Upper Deck Trilogy One Two Combo Clearcut Autographs

PRINT RUN 50 SER.#'d SETS
UNPRICED 1-2-3 AUTO PRINT RUN 10 SETS
BP Larry Bird 100.00 250.00
Robert Parish
BV Chris Bosh 40.00 100.00
Charlie Villanueva
BW Andrew Bogut 25.00 60.00
Marvin Williams
FM Raymond Felton 15.00 40.00
Sean May
GH Ben Gordon 25.00 60.00
Kirk Hinrich
GW Pau Gasol 15.00 40.00
Hakim Warrick
HB Richard Hamilton 30.00 75.00
Chauncey Billups
HJ Dwight Howard 25.00 60.00
Al Jefferson
JJ LeBron James 700.00 1000.00
Michael Jordan
JP Al Jefferson 20.00 50.00
Paul Pierce
KW Jason Kidd 15.00 40.00
Antoine Wright
MH Tracy McGrady 25.00 60.00
Luther Head
PW Chris Paul 100.00 200.00
Deron Williams
RB Michael Redd 30.00 60.00
Andrew Bogut
RM Quentin Richardson 15.00 40.00
Stephon Marbury
SP J.R. Smith 40.00 75.00
Chris Paul
TB Isiah Thomas 20.00 50.00
Chauncey Billups
TJ Sebastian Telfair 15.00 40.00
Jarrett Jack
VG Charlie Villanueva 15.00 40.00
Joey Graham
WF Deron Williams 25.00 60.00
Raymond Felton

2005-06 Upper Deck Trilogy Signature Swatches

UNPRICED PATCH PRINT RUN 15 SETS
UNPRICED DUAL PRINT RUN 15 SETS
UNPRICED DUAL PATCH PRINT RUN 5 SETS
AB Andrew Bogut 25.00 60.00
AW Antoine Wright 15.00 40.00
BG Ben Gordon 25.00 60.00
CF Channing Frye 20.00 50.00
CP Chris Paul 125.00 250.00
CV Charlie Villanueva 20.00 50.00
DG Danny Granger 30.00 80.00
DH Dwight Howard 40.00 80.00
DW Deron Williams 100.00 175.00
FG Francisco Garcia 20.00 50.00
HW Hakim Warrick 20.00 50.00
ID Ike Diogu 15.00 40.00
JG Joey Graham 15.00 40.00
JH Julius Hodge 15.00 40.00
JJ Jarrett Jack 15.00 40.00
JK Jason Kidd 30.00 80.00
JM Jason Maxiell 15.00 40.00
LH Luther Head 15.00 40.00
MA Martell Webster 15.00 40.00
MJ Michael Jordan 500.00 800.00
MW Marvin Williams 20.00 50.00
NR Nate Robinson 20.00 50.00
PG Pau Gasol 20.00 50.00
PP Paul Pierce 20.00 50.00
RF Raymond Felton 25.00 60.00
RM Rashad McCants 15.00 40.00
SM Sean May 15.00 40.00

TM Tracy McGrady 30.00 80.00
YM Yao Ming 60.00 150.00

2005-06 Upper Deck Trilogy Signs of Stardom

APPROXIMATELY TWO PER BOX
AB Andrew Bogut 6.00 15.00
AJ Antawn Jamison 4.00 10.00
AL Al Jefferson 4.00 10.00
AN Andrew Bynum 12.00 30.00
AW Antoine Wright 4.00 10.00
BD Baron Davis 5.00 12.00
BJ Bobby Jackson 4.00 10.00
BM Brad Miller 4.00 10.00
BS Bobby Simmons 4.00 10.00
CA Carmelo Anthony SP 20.00 40.00
CF Channing Frye 5.00 12.00
CH Chauncey Billups 8.00 20.00
CJ C.J. Miles 5.00 12.00
CP Chris Paul 40.00 100.00
CT Chris Taft SP 4.00 10.00
DE Daniel Ewing 4.00 10.00
DG Danny Granger 8.00 20.00
DH Dwight Howard 10.00 25.00
DL David Lee 6.00 15.00
DM Donyell Marshall 4.00 10.00
FG Francisco Garcia 5.00 12.00
GG Gerald Green 5.00 12.00
ID Ike Diogu 4.00 10.00
JA Jamaal Magloire 4.00 10.00
JG Joey Graham 4.00 10.00
JH Julius Hodge 4.00 10.00
JJ Jarrett Jack 4.00 10.00
JK Jason Kidd SP 10.00 25.00
JM Jason Maxiell 4.00 10.00
JP Johan Petro 4.00 10.00
JR J.R. Smith 4.00 10.00
LH Luther Head 4.00 10.00
LJ LeBron James SP 150.00 300.00
LK Linas Kleiza 4.00 10.00
LO Lamar Odom 5.00 12.00
MJ Michael Jordan SP 300.00 500.00
MR Michael Redd 5.00 12.00
MW Marvin Williams 5.00 12.00
NR Nate Robinson 5.00 12.00
PP Paul Pierce 8.00 20.00
RF Raymond Felton 6.00 15.00
RH Richard Hamilton 6.00 15.00
RM Rashad McCants 4.00 10.00
SE Sean May 4.00 10.00
SM Stephon Marbury SP 6.00 15.00
SP Speedy Claxton 4.00 10.00
SS Salim Stoudamire 4.00 10.00
ST Stromile Swift 4.00 10.00
TC Tyson Chandler 4.00 10.00
TM Tracy McGrady 10.00 25.00
TP Tayshaun Prince 8.00 20.00
WS Wayne Simien 4.00 10.00
YK Yaroslav Korolev 4.00 10.00

2005-06 Upper Deck Trilogy Swatches of Stardom

PRINT RUN 50 SER.#'d SETS
AB Andrew Bogut 6.00 15.00
AW Antonie Wright 4.00 10.00
BK Bernard King 6.00 15.00
CD Clyde Drexler 12.50 30.00
CF Channing Frye 5.00 12.00
CP Chris Paul 15.00 40.00
CV Charlie Villanueva 5.00 12.00
DG Danny Granger 8.00 20.00
DH Dwight Howard 8.00 20.00
DW Deron Williams 10.00 25.00
FG Francisco Garcia 5.00 12.00
GG Gerald Green 5.00 12.00
HK Hakeem Olajuwon 8.00 20.00
HW Hakim Warrick 5.00 12.00
ID Ike Diogu 4.00 10.00
IT Isiah Thomas 6.00 15.00
JG Joey Graham 4.00 10.00
JH Julius Hodge 4.00 10.00
JJ Jarrett Jack 4.00 10.00
JM Jason Maxiell 4.00 10.00
JO John Stockton 12.50 30.00
JS Jamal Sampson 4.00 10.00
JW James Worthy 15.00 40.00
KB Kobe Bryant 15.00 40.00
KG Kevin Garnett 8.00 20.00
KM Kevin McHale 10.00 25.00
LB Larry Bird 20.00 50.00
LH Luther Head 4.00 10.00
LJ LeBron James 20.00 50.00
MA Magic Johnson 15.00 40.00
MJ Michael Jordan 100.00 200.00
MW Marvin Williams 5.00 12.00
NR Nate Robinson 5.00 12.00
PM Pete Maravich 100.00 200.00
RF Raymond Felton 6.00 15.00
RM Rashad McCants 4.00 10.00
SM Sean May 4.00 10.00
TM Tracy McGrady 5.00 12.00
WE Martell Webster 4.00 10.00
WS Wayne Simien 4.00 10.00
YM Yao Ming 8.00 20.00

2005-06 Upper Deck Trilogy The Cutting Edge

APPROXIMATELY TWO PER BOX
AB Andrew Bogut 4.00 10.00
AI Andre Iguodala 2.50 6.00
AJ Antawn Jamison 2.50 6.00
AS Amare Stoudemire 2.50 6.00
AW Antoine Wright 2.50 6.00
BW Ben Wallace 2.50 6.00
CA Carmelo Anthony 5.00 12.00
CF Channing Frye 3.00 8.00
CP Chris Paul 8.00 20.00
CV Charlie Villanueva 3.00 8.00
CW Chris Webber 2.50 6.00
DE Deron Williams 6.00 15.00
DG Danny Granger 5.00 12.00
DH Dwight Howard 5.00 12.00
DN Dirk Nowitzki 4.00 10.00
EB Elton Brand 2.50 6.00
GA Gilbert Arenas SP 2.50 6.00
ID Ike Diogu 2.50 6.00
JG Joey Graham 2.50 6.00
JK Jason Kidd SP 4.00 10.00
JO Jermaine O'Neal 2.50 6.00
JR Jason Richardson 2.50 6.00
JS J.R. Smith 2.50 6.00
KB Kobe Bryant 8.00 20.00
KG Kevin Garnett 5.00 12.00
KM Kenyon Martin 2.50 6.00
LJ LeBron James 10.00 25.00
MA Martell Webster 2.50 6.00
MJ Michael Jordan SP 30.00 80.00
MW Marvin Williams 3.00 8.00
PP Paul Pierce 3.00 8.00
RF Raymond Felton 4.00 10.00
RJ Richard Jefferson SP 2.50 6.00
RM Rashad McCants 2.50 6.00
SE Sean May 2.50 6.00
SF Steve Francis 2.50 6.00
SH Shawn Marion 2.50 6.00
SM Stephon Marbury 2.00 5.00
SO Shaquille O'Neal 5.00 12.00
TD Tim Duncan 4.00 10.00
TM Tracy McGrady 3.00 8.00
YM Yao Ming 3.00 8.00

2005-06 Upper Deck Trilogy TriMarks

PRINT RUN 10 TO 40 SER.#'d SETS
SOME UNPRICED DUE TO SCARCITY
AGJ Tony Allen 15.00 40.00
Gerald Green
Al Jefferson
BGV Chris Bosh 20.00 50.00
Joey Graham
Charlie Villanueva
DBT Ike Diogu 15.00 40.00
Andris Biedrins
Chris Taft
DDT Baron Davis 15.00 40.00
Ike Diogu
Chris Taft
DEB Chris Duhon 15.00 40.00
Daniel Ewing
Carlos Boozer
FFK Walt Frazier 30.00 80.00
Channing Frye
Bernard King
FLR Channing Frye 40.00 80.00
David Lee
Nate Robinson
GJA Danny Granger 30.00 80.00
Sarunas Jasekevicius
Ron Artest
GJW Pau Gasol 25.00 60.00
Bobby Jackson
Hakim Warrick
GOV Ben Gordon 40.00 100.00
Emeka Okafor
Charlie Villanueva
JBM Jarrett Jack 25.00 60.00
Chris Bosh
Stephon Marbury
KJW Jason Kidd 25.00 50.00
Richard Jefferson
Antoine Wright
MME Corey Maggette 15.00 40.00
Cuttino Mobley
Daniel Ewing
MMF Rashad McCants 25.00 50.00
Sean May
Raymond Felton
MRR Stephon Marbury 25.00 60.00
Nate Robinson
Quentin Richardson
OBW Lamar Odom 30.00 60.00
Andrew Bynum
Von Wafer
OMF Emeka Okafor 20.00 50.00
Sean May
Raymond Felton
PSB Chris Paul 50.00 120.00
J.R. Smith
Brandon Bass
RSM Michael Redd 20.00 50.00
Bobby Simmons
Desmond Mason

TRL Isiah Thomas 100.00 200.00
Dennis Rodman
Bill Laimbeer
WBG Martell Webster 25.00 60.00
Andrew Bynum
Gerald Green
WBP Ben Wallace 60.00 120.00
Chauncey Billups
Tayshaun Prince
WPM Bill Walton 40.00 80.00
Robert Parish
Cedric Maxwell

2006-07 Upper Deck Trilogy

Upper Deck Trilogy was released in mid June 2007 and features a 140-card base set where cards 1-60 picture veteran players, cards 61-90 showcase a horizontal card design with three players from the same team pictured, cards 91-98 picture rookies on a horizontally designed acetate card sequentially numbered to 299 and cards 99-140 picture rookies on the same design and are sequentially numbered to 499. Trilogy is packaged in nine-pack boxes of five cards each and carried an initial suggested retail price of $10.00 per pack. Each box of Trilogy contains three rookies, three autographs and three memorabilia cards.

COMP.SET w/o SP's (90) 20.00 50.00
UNPRICED GOLD PRINT RUN 10 SETS
1 Joe Johnson .75 2.00
2 Marvin Williams .75 2.00
3 Paul Pierce 1.00 2.50
4 Wally Szczerbiak .60 1.50
5 Emeka Okafor .75 2.00
6 Raymond Felton 1.00 2.50
7 Ben Wallace .75 2.00
8 Kirk Hinrich .75 2.00
9 Ben Gordon .75 2.00
10 LeBron James 4.00 10.00
11 Larry Hughes .60 1.50
12 Dirk Nowitzki 1.25 3.00
13 Jason Terry .60 1.50
14 Carmelo Anthony 1.00 2.50
15 Andre Miller .60 1.50
16 Chauncey Billups .75 2.00
17 Richard Hamilton .60 1.50
18 Jason Richardson .75 2.00
19 Baron Davis .75 2.00
20 Yao Ming 1.00 2.50
21 Tracy McGrady 1.00 2.50
22 Jermaine O'Neal .75 2.00
23 Al Harrington .60 1.50
24 Elton Brand .75 2.00
25 Sam Cassell .75 2.00
26 Kobe Bryant 4.00 10.00
27 Lamar Odom .75 2.00
28 Pau Gasol .75 2.00
29 Dwyane Wade 2.00 5.00
30 Shaquille O'Neal 1.50 4.00
31 Michael Redd .75 2.00
32 Andrew Bogut .75 2.00
33 Kevin Garnett 1.50 4.00
34 Mike James .50 1.25
35 Vince Carter 1.00 2.50
36 Jason Kidd 1.25 3.00
37 Richard Jefferson .75 2.00
38 Chris Paul 1.50 4.00
39 David West .75 2.00
40 Stephon Marbury .60 1.50
41 Steve Francis .75 2.00
42 Dwight Howard 1.25 3.00
43 Jameer Nelson .60 1.50
44 Allen Iverson 1.00 2.50
45 Chris Webber .75 2.00
46 Steve Nash 1.00 2.50
47 Shawn Marion .75 2.00
48 Zach Randolph .60 1.50
49 Mike Bibby .75 2.00
50 Ron Artest .75 2.00
51 Tim Duncan 1.25 3.00
52 Tony Parker .75 2.00
53 Ray Allen .75 2.00
54 Rashard Lewis .75 2.00
55 Chris Bosh .75 2.00
56 T.J. Ford .60 1.50
57 Mehmet Okur .50 1.25
58 Andrei Kirilenko .60 1.50
59 Gilbert Arenas .75 2.00
60 Antawn Jamison .75 2.00
61 Josh Childress .75 2.00
Speedy Claxton
Josh Smith
62 Al Jefferson .75 2.00
Delonte West
Sebastian Telfair
63 Gerald Wallace .75 2.00
Primoz Brezec
Brevin Knight
64 Andres Nocioni 1.25 3.00
Luol Deng
P.J. Brown
65 Drew Gooden .75 2.00
Zydrunas Ilgauskas
Donyell Marshall
66 Josh Howard 1.25 3.00
Jerry Stackhouse
Devin Harris
67 Kenyon Martin 1.25 3.00
Marcus Camby
J.R. Smith
68 Rasheed Wallace 1.25 3.00
Tayshaun Prince
Nazr Mohammed
69 Troy Murphy .75 2.00
Mike Dunleavy
Ike Diogu
70 Rafer Alston .75 2.00
Shane Battier
Bonzi Wells
71 Danny Granger .75 2.00
Jamaal Tinsley
Mike Dunleavy
72 Chris Kaman .75 2.00
Corey Maggette
Shaun Livingston
73 Smush Parker 1.25 3.00
Vladimir Radmanovic
Kwame Brown
74 Mike Miller .75 2.00
Damon Stoudamire
Hakim Warrick
75 Antoine Walker 1.25 3.00
Udonis Haslem
Jason Williams
76 Charlie Villanueva .75 2.00
Ruben Patterson
Maurice Williams
77 Ricky Davis .75 2.00
Trenton Hassell
Mark Blount
78 Nenad Krstic .75 2.00
Jason Collins
Clifford Robinson
79 Tyson Chandler .75 2.00
Peja Stojakovic
Desmond Mason
80 Eddy Curry .75 2.00
Jamal Crawford
Channing Frye
81 Darko Milicic 1.00 2.50
Hedo Turkoglu
Grant Hill
82 Andre Iguodala .75 2.00
Kyle Korver
Samuel Dalembert
83 Amare Stoudemire 1.25 3.00
Boris Diaw
Raja Bell
84 Jarrett Jack .75 2.00
Zach Randolph
Martell Webster
85 Brad Miller 1.00 2.50
Shareef Abdur-Rahim
Kevin Martin
86 Manu Ginobili 1.50 4.00
Michael Finley
Bruce Bowen
87 Luke Ridnour .75 2.00
Chris Wilcox
Nick Collison
88 Morris Peterson .75 2.00
Joey Graham
Jose Calderon
89 Carlos Boozer 1.25 3.00
Deron Williams
Gordan Giricek
90 Caron Butler .75 2.00
Etan Thomas
DeShawn Stevenson
91 Shelden Williams RC 3.00 8.00
92 Tyrus Thomas RC 4.00 10.00
93 Rudy Gay RC 5.00 12.00
94 Randy Foye RC 4.00 10.00
95 Rodney Carney RC 3.00 8.00
96 LaMarcus Aldridge RC 8.00 20.00
97 Brandon Roy RC 8.00 20.00
98 Andrea Bargnani RC 5.00 12.00
99 Solomon Jones RC 2.00 5.00
100 Rajon Rondo RC 8.00 20.00
101 Allan Ray RC 2.00 5.00
102 Thabo Sefolosha RC 2.50 6.00
103 Shannon Brown RC 3.00 8.00
104 Maurice Ager RC 2.00 5.00
105 Patrick O'Bryant RC 2.00 5.00
106 Steve Novak RC 2.00 5.00
107 Shawne Williams RC 2.00 5.00
108 Paul Davis RC 2.00 5.00
109 Jordan Farmar RC 2.00 5.00
110 Kyle Lowry RC 2.50 6.00
111 David Noel RC 2.00 5.00
112 Craig Smith RC 2.00 5.00
113 Marcus Williams RC 2.00 5.00
114 Josh Boone RC 2.00 5.00
115 Hilton Armstrong RC 2.00 5.00
116 Cedric Simmons RC 2.00 5.00
117 Renaldo Balkman RC 2.00 5.00
118 Mardy Collins RC 2.00 5.00
119 Bobby Jones RC 2.00 5.00
120 Quincy Douby RC 2.00 5.00
121 Saer Sene RC 2.00 5.00
122 P.J. Tucker RC 2.00 5.00
123 Jorge Garbajosa RC 2.00 5.00
124 Ronnie Brewer RC 2.50 6.00
125 Dee Brown RC 2.00 5.00
126 Leon Powe RC 2.00 5.00
127 Ryan Hollins RC 2.00 5.00
128 Adam Morrison RC 2.50 6.00
129 Daniel Gibson RC 2.50 6.00
130 Pops Mensah-Bonsu RC 2.00 5.00
131 Yakhouba Diawara RC 2.00 5.00
132 Will Blalock RC 2.00 5.00
133 Alexander Johnson RC 2.00 5.00
134 Damir Markota RC 2.00 5.00
135 Hassan Adams RC 2.00 5.00
136 Marcus Vinicius RC 2.00 5.00
137 James Augustine RC 2.00 5.00
138 J.J. Redick RC 2.50 6.00
139 Sergio Rodriguez RC 2.00 5.00
140 Paul Millsap RC 3.00 8.00

2006-07 Upper Deck Trilogy Blue

*1-60 BLUE: .75X TO 2X BASE HI
1-60 BLUE PRINT RUN 66 SER.#'d SETS
*61-90 BLUE: 1.25X TO 3X BASE HI
*91-98 BLUE: .75X TO 2X BASE HI
*99-140 BLUE: 1.25X TO 3X BASE HI
61-140 BLUE PRINT RUN 33 SER.#'d SETS

2006-07 Upper Deck Trilogy Auto Focus

APPROXIMATE ODDS ONE PER BOX
AFAB Andrea Bargnani 10.00 25.00
AFAI Andre Iguodala 6.00 15.00
AFBG Ben Gordon 6.00 15.00
AFBO Chris Bosh 10.00 25.00
AFBR Brandon Roy 12.00 30.00
AFCA Carmelo Anthony 15.00 40.00
AFCP Chris Paul 15.00 40.00
AFCS Cedric Simmons 5.00 12.00
AFJB Josh Boone 5.00 12.00
AFJF Jordan Farmar 5.00 12.00
AFJK Jason Kidd 10.00 25.00
AFJW James White 5.00 12.00
AFLA LaMarcus Aldridge 12.00 30.00
AFLJ LeBron James SP 150.00 300.00
AFMB Mike Bibby 5.00 12.00
AFMC Mardy Collins 5.00 12.00
AFMJ Michael Jordan SP 300.00 600.00
AFMW Marcus Williams 5.00 12.00
AFPP Paul Pierce 12.00 30.00
AFQD Quincy Douby 5.00 12.00
AFRB Renaldo Balkman 5.00 12.00
AFRC Rodney Carney 5.00 12.00
AFRF Randy Foye 6.00 15.00
AFRG Rudy Gay 8.00 20.00
AFRH Richard Hamilton 6.00 15.00
AFRJ Richard Jefferson 5.00 12.00
AFRO Ronnie Brewer 6.00 15.00
AFRR Rajon Rondo 20.00 50.00
AFSB Shannon Brown 8.00 20.00
AFSN Steve Nash SP 60.00 120.00
AFSR Sergio Rodriguez 5.00 12.00
AFSS Saer Sene 5.00 12.00
AFSW Shawne Williams 5.00 12.00
AFTS Thabo Sefolosha 6.00 15.00
AFTT Tyrus Thomas 6.00 15.00
AFWI Shelden Williams 5.00 12.00
AFYM Yao Ming 20.00 50.00

2006-07 Upper Deck Trilogy Generations Future Memorabilia

APPROXIMATE ODDS ONE PER BOX
*PATCHES: .6X TO 1.5X BASE HI
PATCH PRINT RUN 50 SER.#'d SETS
FMAB Andrea Bargnani 4.00 10.00
FMAR Allan Ray 2.50 6.00
FMBJ Bobby Jones 2.50 6.00
FMBR Ronnie Brewer 3.00 8.00
FMCS Cedric Simmons 2.50 6.00
FMHA Hilton Armstrong 2.50 6.00
FMJB Josh Boone 2.50 6.00
FMJG Jorge Garbajosa 2.50 6.00
FMJR J.J. Redick 3.00 8.00
FMJW James White 2.50 6.00
FMKL Kyle Lowry 3.00 8.00
FMLA LaMarcus Aldridge 6.00 15.00
FMMC Mardy Collins 2.50 6.00
FMMW Marcus Williams 2.50 6.00
FMPD Paul Davis 2.50 6.00
FMPO Patrick O'Bryant 2.50 6.00
FMPT P.J. Tucker 2.50 6.00
FMQD Quincy Douby 2.50 6.00
FMRB Renaldo Balkman 2.50 6.00
FMRC Rodney Carney 2.50 6.00
FMRF Randy Foye 3.00 8.00
FMRG Rudy Gay 4.00 10.00
FMRO Brandon Roy 6.00 15.00
FMSB Shannon Brown 4.00 10.00
FMSJ Solomon Jones 2.50 6.00
FMSS Saer Sene 2.50 6.00
FMSW Shawne Williams 2.50 6.00
FMTT Tyrus Thomas 3.00 8.00
FMWB Will Blalock 2.50 6.00
FMWI Shelden Williams 2.50 6.00

2006-07 Upper Deck Trilogy Generations Future Signatures

APPROXIMATE ODDS ONE PER BOX
UNPRICED TRIO PRINT RUN 3 SETS
FSAB Andrea Bargnani 10.00 25.00
FSAR Allan Ray 4.00 10.00
FSBR Brandon Roy 12.00 30.00
FSCS Cedric Simmons 4.00 10.00
FSDN David Noel 4.00 10.00
FSHA Hilton Armstrong 4.00 10.00
FSJB Josh Boone 4.00 10.00
FSJF Jordan Farmar 4.00 10.00
FSKL Kyle Lowry 5.00 12.00
FSLA LaMarcus Aldridge 10.00 25.00
FSMA Maurice Ager 4.00 10.00
FSMC Mardy Collins 4.00 10.00
FSPD Paul Davis 4.00 10.00
FSPO Patrick O'Bryant 4.00 10.00
FSQD Quincy Douby 4.00 10.00
FSRB Renaldo Balkman 4.00 10.00
FSRC Rodney Carney 4.00 10.00
FSRF Randy Foye 5.00 12.00
FSRG Rudy Gay 6.00 15.00
FSRO Ronnie Brewer 5.00 12.00
FSRR Rajon Rondo 20.00 50.00
FSSB Shannon Brown 6.00 15.00
FSSM Craig Smith 4.00 10.00
FSSN Steve Novak 4.00 10.00
FSSS Saer Sene 4.00 10.00
FSSW Shawne Williams 4.00 10.00
FSTS Thabo Sefolosha 5.00 12.00
FSTT Tyrus Thomas 5.00 12.00
FSWI Shelden Williams 4.00 10.00

2006-07 Upper Deck Trilogy Generations Past and Future Memorabilia

PRINT RUN 50 SER.#'d SETS
PFMBB Larry Bird 15.00 30.00
Andrea Bargnani
PFMBE Mark Eaton 5.00 12.00
Ronnie Brewer
PFMDA Adrian Dantley 5.00 12.00
Maurice Ager
PFMDB Clyde Drexler 8.00 20.00
Shannon Brown
PFMDC Darryl Dawkins 5.00 12.00
Rodney Carney
PFMEW Julius Erving 8.00 20.00
Shawne Williams
PFMFB Walt Frazier 5.00 12.00
Renaldo Balkman
PFMGW George Gervin 5.00 12.00
James White
PFMJA Jo Jo White 5.00 12.00
Allan Ray
PFMJW Magic Johnson 8.00 20.00
Marcus Williams
PFMKB Bernard King 5.00 12.00
Ronnie Brewer
PFMKC Karl Malone 6.00 15.00
Cedric Simmons
PFMMD Kevin McHale 5.00 12.00
Paul Davis
PFMMF Earl Monroe 6.00 15.00
Randy Foye
PFMMJ Moses Malone 5.00 12.00
Solomon Jones
PFMMN James Worthy 6.00 15.00
David Noel
PFMMR Chris Mullin 8.00 20.00
J.J. Redick
PFMMS Karl Malone 8.00 20.00
Craig Smith
PFMMT Pete Maravich 30.00 80.00
Tyrus Thomas
PFMON Hakeem Olajuwon 5.00 12.00
Steve Novak
PFMRJ David Robinson 6.00 15.00
Solomon Jones
PFMRS Dennis Rodman 10.00 25.00
Thabo Sefolosha
PFMSB John Stockton 20.00 40.00
Dee Brown
PFMTD Reggie Theus 5.00 12.00
Quincy Douby
PFMWE Sean Elliott 8.00 20.00
James White
PFMWF Jerry West 10.00 25.00
Jordan Farmar
PFMWG James Worthy 6.00 15.00
Rudy Gay
PFMWL Spud Webb 5.00 12.00
Kyle Lowry

2006-07 Upper Deck Trilogy Generations Past and Future Signatures

PRINT RUN 33 SER.#'d SETS
PFSAL Nate Archibald 8.00 20.00
Kyle Lowry
PFSAR Alvin Robertson 8.00 20.00
Ronnie Brewer
PFSBR Dee Brown 15.00 40.00
Rajon Rondo
PFSDB Darryl Dawkins 8.00 20.00
Josh Boone
PFSEH Mark Eaton 8.00 20.00
Ryan Hollins
PFSEW Wayman Tisdale 8.00 20.00
Shawne Williams
PFSFF Walt Frazier 20.00 50.00
Randy Foye
PFSGG George Gervin 10.00 25.00
Rudy Gay
PFSHA Elvin Hayes 15.00 30.00
LaMarcus Aldridge
PFSJC Bobby Jones 8.00 20.00
Rodney Carney
PFSKA Steve Kerr 10.00 25.00
Hassan Adams
PFSMM Adrian Dantley 15.00 30.00
Paul Millsap
PFSMN Bob McAdoo 15.00 40.00
David Noel
PFSMR Michael Ray Richardson 8.00 20.00
Renaldo Balkman
PFSMS Xavier McDaniel 8.00 20.00
Saer Sene
PFSPA Robert Parish 10.00 25.00
Hilton Armstrong
PFSRB David Robinson 60.00 120.00
Andrea Bargnani
PFSRM Alvin Robertson 15.00 30.00
Damir Markota
PFSRT Dennis Rodman 30.00 80.00
Tyrus Thomas
PFSSF Byron Scott 20.00 40.00
Jordan Farmar
PFSSN Ralph Sampson 8.00 20.00
Steve Novak
PFSTD Reggie Theus 8.00 20.00
Quincy Douby
PFSTO Nate Thurmond 8.00 20.00
Patrick O'Bryant
PFSWR Bill Walton 30.00 80.00
Brandon Roy
PFSWW Spud Webb 10.00 25.00
Shelden Williams

2006-07 Upper Deck Trilogy Generations Past and Present Memorabilia

PRINT RUN 50 SER.#'d SETS
PPMAM Earl Monroe 6.00 15.00
Carmelo Anthony
PPMBP Larry Bird 15.00 30.00
Paul Pierce
PPMCM Tom Chambers 15.00 30.00
Shawn Marion
PPMCO Wilt Chamberlain 30.00 80.00
Shaquille O'Neal
PPMDM Clyde Drexler 20.00 40.00
Tracy McGrady
PPMDR Adrian Dantley 5.00 12.00
Michael Redd
PPMEK Mark Eaton 6.00 15.00
Andrei Kirilenko
PPMFH Walt Frazier 8.00 20.00
Richard Hamilton
PPMJB Magic Johnson 20.00 40.00
Kobe Bryant
PPMJJ Michael Jordan 60.00 120.00
LeBron James
PPMKA Bernard King 5.00 12.00
Gilbert Arenas
PPMKE Kevin McHale 5.00 12.00
Elton Brand
PPMKJ Steve Kerr 5.00 12.00
Richard Jefferson
PPMMA Chris Mullin 10.00 25.00
Ron Artest
PPMMB Karl Malone 8.00 20.00
Carlos Boozer
PPMMH Moses Malone 6.00 15.00
Dwight Howard
PPMMI Pete Maravich 40.00 80.00
Allen Iverson
PPMMN Pete Maravich 75.00 150.00
Steve Nash
PPMOM Hakeem Olajuwon 6.00 15.00
Yao Ming
PPMRB Oscar Robertson 12.00 30.00
Andrew Bogut
PPMRD David Robinson 20.00 40.00
Tim Duncan
PPMRK Oscar Robertson 15.00 30.00
Jason Kidd
PPMRO Pat Riley 8.00 20.00
Lamar Odom
PPMRW Dennis Rodman 10.00 25.00
Ben Wallace
PPMTB Reggie Theus 5.00 12.00
Mike Bibby
PPMTG Reggie Theus 6.00 15.00
Ben Gordon
PPMWA Jerry West 20.00 40.00
Ray Allen
PPMWH Jo Jo White 8.00 20.00
Kirk Hinrich
PPMWP Spud Webb 8.00 20.00
Chris Paul

2006-07 Upper Deck Trilogy Generations Past and Present Signatures

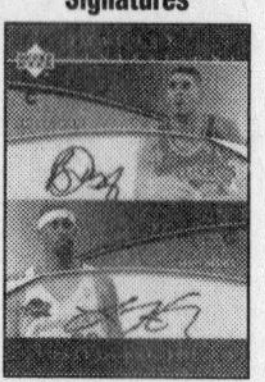

PRINT RUN 33 SER.#'d SETS
PPSAA Nate Archibald 10.00 25.00
Gilbert Arenas
PPSAC Alvin Robertson 10.00 25.00
Charlie Bell
PPSAG B.J. Armstrong 15.00 30.00
Ben Gordon
PPSBA Dee Brown 8.00 20.00
Tony Allen
PPSBC Michael Cooper 20.00 40.00
Andrew Bynum
PPSBP Muggsy Bogues 30.00 80.00
Chris Paul
PPSDC Dennis Rodman 30.00 80.00
Chauncey Billups
PPSDH Brad Daugherty 8.00 20.00
Larry Hughes
PPSDO Darryl Dawkins 15.00 30.00
Jermaine O'Neal
PPSEB Mark Eaton 15.00 30.00
Carlos Boozer
PPSEJ Sean Elliott 15.00 30.00
Richard Jefferson
PPSEK Mark Eaton 8.00 20.00
Chris Kaman
PPSHK Connie Hawkins 15.00 40.00
Kyle Korver
PPSJA Michael Jordan 325.00 550.00
Carmelo Anthony
PPSJN Michael Ray Richardson 8.00 20.00
Channing Frye
PPSJW Bobby Jones 8.00 20.00
Marvin Williams
PPSKB Steve Kerr 40.00 75.00
Brent Barry
PPSLP Bill Laimbeer 20.00 40.00
Tayshaun Prince
PPSME Bob McAdoo 20.00 40.00
Daniel Ewing
PPSMR Xavier McDaniel 15.00 30.00
Luke Ridnour
PPSMT Reggie Theus 8.00 20.00
Brad Miller
PPSMW Xavier McDaniel 15.00 30.00
Damien Wilkins
PPSPP Robert Parish 20.00 40.00
Paul Pierce
PPSSM Ralph Sampson 30.00 60.00
Yao Ming
PPSSV Kiki Vandeweghe 8.00 20.00
J.R. Smith
PPSTB Reggie Theus 10.00 25.00
Mike Bibby
PPSTM Wayman Tisdale 8.00 20.00
Brad Miller
PPSWW Spud Webb 10.00 25.00
Marvin Williams

2006-07 Upper Deck Trilogy Generations Past Memorabilia

APPROXIMATE ODDS ONE PER BOX
*PATCHES: .75X TO 2X BASE HI
PATCH PRINT RUN 50 SER.#'d SETS
PMAD Adrian Dantley 4.00 10.00
PMBK Bernard King 4.00 10.00
PMBL Bill Laimbeer 4.00 10.00
PMCD Clyde Drexler 5.00 12.00
PMCM Chris Mullin 4.00 10.00
PMDR Dennis Rodman 6.00 15.00
PMGG George Gervin 4.00 10.00
PMHO Hakeem Olajuwon 5.00 12.00
PMJE Julius Erving 8.00 20.00
PMJH Jeff Hornacek 4.00 10.00
PMJO Magic Johnson 10.00 25.00
PMJS John Stockton 6.00 15.00
PMKA Kareem Abdul-Jabbar 6.00 15.00
PMKM Kevin McHale 5.00 12.00
PMLB Larry Bird 12.00 30.00
PMME Mark Eaton 4.00 10.00
PMMJ Michael Jordan 25.00 60.00
PMMM Moses Malone 4.00 10.00
PMOR Oscar Robertson 6.00 15.00
PMPR Pat Riley 5.00 12.00
PMRO David Robinson 6.00 15.00
PMRT Reggie Theus 4.00 10.00
PMSK Steve Kerr 4.00 10.00
PMSW Spud Webb 4.00 10.00
PMTC Tom Chambers 4.00 10.00
PMWE Jerry West 8.00 20.00
PMWF Walt Frazier 4.00 10.00
PMWH Jo Jo White 4.00 10.00

2006-07 Upper Deck Trilogy Generations Past Present and Future Memorabilia

PRINT RUN 33 SER.#'d SETS
UNPRICED AUTO PRINT RUN 3 SETS
UNPRICED AUTO MEM PRINT RUN 3 SETS
PPFMBAG Larry Bird 15.00 30.00
Carmelo Anthony
Rudy Gay
PPFMCWS Tom Chambers 6.00 15.00
Damien Wilkins
Saer Sene
PPFMDIC Darryl Dawkins 6.00 15.00
Andre Iguodala
Rodney Carney
PPFMDMB Clyde Drexler 20.00 40.00
Tracy McGrady
Shannon Brown
PPFMDMJ Darryl Dawkins 6.00 15.00
Andre Miller
Bobby Jones
PPFMDNA Adrian Dantley 10.00 25.00
Dirk Nowitzki
Maurice Ager
PPFMGJS George Gervin 20.00 50.00
LeBron James
Thabo Sefolosha
PPFMGLT George Gervin 6.00 15.00
Rashard Lewis
P.J. Tucker
PPFMJBF Magic Johnson 20.00 40.00
Kobe Bryant
Jordan Farmar
PPFMKGS Steve Kerr 10.00 25.00
Ben Gordon
Thabo Sefolosha
PPFMKMC Bernard King 6.00 15.00
Stephon Marbury
Mardy Collins
PPFMLOB Bill Laimbeer 8.00 20.00
Emeka Okafor
Josh Boone
PPFMMBA Karl Malone 6.00 15.00
Chris Bosh
Hilton Armstrong
PPFMMDS Kevin McHale 10.00 25.00
Tim Duncan
Craig Smith
PPFMMHW Moses Malone 6.00 15.00
Dwight Howard
Shelden Williams
PPFMMIR Earl Monroe 15.00 30.00
Allen Iverson
Brandon Roy
PPFMMOT Pete Maravich 75.00 150.00
Shaquille O'Neal
Tyrus Thomas
PPFMOMN Hakeem Olajuwon 8.00 20.00
Yao Ming
Steve Novak
PPFMRGA David Robinson 25.00 50.00
Kevin Garnett
LaMarcus Aldridge
PPFMRNR Oscar Robertson 20.00 40.00
Steve Nash
Rajon Rondo
PPFMRWT Dennis Rodman 10.00 25.00
Ben Wallace
Tyrus Thomas
PPFMSWB John Stockton 40.00 80.00
Deron Williams
Dee Brown
PPFMWAR Jerry West 30.00 60.00
Ray Allen
Brandon Roy
PPFMWBB Bill Walton 8.00 20.00
Andrew Bogut
Andrea Bargnani
PPFMWCN James Worthy 10.00 25.00
Vince Carter
David Noel
PPFMWJW James Worthy 6.00 15.00
Richard Jefferson
Shawne Williams
PPFMWPL Spud Webb 10.00 25.00
Chris Paul
Kyle Lowry
PPFMWPR Jo Jo White 6.00 15.00
Paul Pierce
Rajon Rondo

2006-07 Upper Deck Trilogy Generations Past Signatures

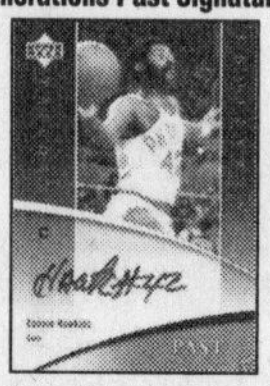

APPROXIMATE ODDS ONE PER BOX
UNPRICED TRIO PRINT RUN 3 SETS
PSAD Adrian Dantley 5.00 12.00
PSAJ Avery Johnson 6.00 15.00
PSAR Alvin Robertson 5.00 12.00
PSBA B.J. Armstrong 8.00 20.00
PSBJ Bobby Jones 6.00 15.00
PSBL Bill Laimbeer 10.00 25.00
PSBM Bob McAdoo 10.00 25.00
PSBS Byron Scott 12.50 30.00
PSCH Connie Hawkins 6.00 15.00
PSDB Dee Brown 5.00 12.00
PSDD Darryl Dawkins 10.00 25.00
PSEH Elvin Hayes 8.00 20.00
PSGG George Gervin 10.00 25.00
PSKV Kiki Vandeweghe 5.00 12.00
PSMB Muggsy Bogues 10.00 25.00
PSME Mark Eaton 5.00 12.00
PSMJ Michael Jordan 300.00 500.00
PSML Maurice Lucas 5.00 12.00
PSRP Robert Parish 10.00 25.00
PSRS Ralph Sampson 5.00 12.00
PSRT Reggie Theus 5.00 12.00
PSWT Wayman Tisdale 5.00 12.00
PSXM Xavier McDaniel 5.00 12.00

2006-07 Upper Deck Trilogy Generations Present and Future Memorabilia

PRINT RUN 50 SER.#'d SETS
PRFMAR Ray Allen 4.00 10.00
Allan Ray
PRFMBD Elton Brand 4.00 10.00
Paul Davis
PRFMBF Andrew Bynum 5.00 12.00
Jordan Farmar
PRFMBG Chris Bosh 6.00 15.00
Jorge Garbajosa
PRFMBN Shane Battier 4.00 10.00
Steve Novak
PRFMBT Chris Bosh 5.00 12.00
P.J. Tucker
PRFMFB Channing Frye 4.00 10.00
Renaldo Balkman
PRFMGS Kevin Garnett 5.00 12.00
Craig Smith
PRFMIJ Andre Iguodala 4.00 10.00
Bobby Jones
PRFMJN Antawn Jamison 4.00 10.00
David Noel
PRFMKW Jason Kidd 6.00 15.00
Marcus Williams
PRFMLS Rashard Lewis 4.00 10.00
Saer Sene
PRFMMC Stephon Marbury 4.00 10.00
Mardy Collins
PRFMMQ Mike Bibby 4.00 10.00
Quincy Douby
PRFMNA Dirk Nowitzki 6.00 15.00
Maurice Ager
PRFMNR Jameer Nelson 4.00 10.00
J.J. Redick
PRFMOA Emeka Okafor 4.00 10.00
Hilton Armstrong
PRFMPJ Pau Gasol 10.00 25.00
Jorge Garbajosa
PRFMPR Paul Pierce 8.00 20.00
Rajon Rondo
PRFMPW Tony Parker 5.00 12.00
James White
PRFMRA Zach Randolph 5.00 12.00
LaMarcus Aldridge
PRFMRO Jason Richardson 4.00 10.00
Patrick O'Bryant
PRFMWB Deron Williams 15.00 30.00
Dee Brown
PRFMWT Ben Wallace 10.00 25.00
Tyrus Thomas
PRFMWW Marvin Williams 4.00 10.00
Shelden Williams

2006-07 Upper Deck Trilogy Generations Present and Future Signatures

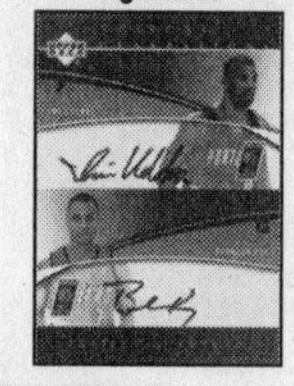

PRINT RUN 33 SER.#'d SETS
PRFSAR Tony Allen 6.00 15.00
Allan Ray
PRFSBB Chauncey Billups 8.00 20.00
Will Blalock
PRFSBD Mike Bibby 8.00 20.00
Quincy Douby
PRFSBM Charlie Bell 6.00 15.00
Damir Markota
PRFSBS Renaldo Balkman 6.00 15.00
Wayne Simien
PRFSCA Chris Bosh 20.00 40.00
Andrea Bargnani
PRFSCJ Josh Childress 6.00 15.00
Solomon Jones
PRFSFA LaMarcus Aldridge 15.00 40.00
T.J. Ford
PRFSGS Ben Gordon 20.00 40.00
Thabo Sefolosha
PRFSGT Ben Gordon 15.00 40.00
Tyrus Thomas
PRFSIC Andre Iguodala 8.00 20.00
Rodney Carney
PRFSJA Richard Jefferson 8.00 20.00
Hassan Adams
PRFSJF Mike James 8.00 20.00
Randy Foye
PRFSJR Ime Udoka 30.00 60.00
Brandon Roy
PRFSKD Chris Kaman 10.00 25.00
Paul Davis
PRFSMB Brad Miller 6.00 15.00
Josh Boone
PRFSMF Chris Mihm 8.00 20.00
Jordan Farmar
PRFSMN Yao Ming 20.00 40.00
Steve Novak
PRFSMS Rashad McCants 8.00 20.00
Craig Smith
PRFSOO Jermaine O'Neal 6.00 15.00
Patrick O'Bryant
PRFSPA Morris Peterson 6.00 15.00
Maurice Ager
PRFSPR Paul Pierce 20.00 50.00
Rajon Rondo
PRFSRS Luke Ridnour 6.00 15.00
Saer Sene
PRFSSS Peja Stojakovic 8.00 20.00
Cedric Simmons
PRFSWA Deron Williams 20.00 40.00
James Augustine
PRFSWW Marvin Williams 6.00 15.00
Shelden Williams

2006-07 Upper Deck Trilogy Generations Present Memorabilia

APPROXIMATE ODDS ONE PER BOX
*PATCHES: 1X TO 2.5X BASE HI
PATCH PRINT RUN 50 SER.#'d SETS
PRMAI Andre Iguodala 2.50 6.00
PRMAJ Antawn Jamison 2.50 6.00
PRMAK Andrei Kirilenko 2.50 6.00
PRMBD Baron Davis 2.00 5.00
PRMCB Chauncey Billups 2.50 6.00
PRMDH Dwight Howard 4.00 10.00
PRMDN Dirk Nowitzki 4.00 10.00
PRMEO Emeka Okafor 2.50 6.00
PRMGA Gilbert Arenas 2.50 6.00
PRMJK Jason Kidd 4.00 10.00
PRMKB Kobe Bryant 10.00 25.00
PRMKG Kevin Garnett 5.00 12.00
PRMLH Larry Hughes 2.00 5.00
PRMLJ LeBron James 10.00 25.00
PRMLO Lamar Odom 2.50 6.00
PRMMB Mike Bibby 2.50 6.00
PRMMP Morris Peterson 1.50 4.00
PRMMR Michael Redd 2.50 6.00
PRMPG Pau Gasol 2.50 6.00
PRMRH Richard Hamilton 2.00 5.00
PRMRL Rashard Lewis 2.50 6.00
PRMSL Shaun Livingston 2.00 5.00
PRMSM Shawn Marion 2.50 6.00
PRMSN Steve Nash 3.00 8.00
PRMSO Shaquille O'Neal 5.00 12.00
PRMTD Tim Duncan 4.00 10.00
PRMTM Tracy McGrady 3.00 8.00
PRMTP Tayshaun Prince 2.50 6.00
PRMVC Vince Carter 3.00 8.00
PRMYM Yao Ming 3.00 8.00

2006-07 Upper Deck Trilogy Generations Present Signatures

APPROXIMATE ODDS ONE PER BOX
UNPRICED TRIO PRINT RUN 3 SETS
PRSAH Al Harrington 4.00 10.00
PRSBG Ben Gordon 8.00 20.00
PRSBM Brad Miller 4.00 10.00
PRSCD Chris Duhon 4.00 10.00
PRSCK Chris Kaman 4.00 10.00
PRSCM Chris Mihm 4.00 10.00
PRSDW Damien Wilkins 4.00 10.00
PRSGG Gerald Green 4.00 10.00
PRSGW Gerald Wallace 4.00 10.00
PRSJC Josh Childress 4.00 10.00
PRSJH Julius Hodge 4.00 10.00
PRSJS James Singleton 4.00 10.00
PRSLJ LeBron James 125.00 250.00
PRSMJ Mike James 4.00 10.00
PRSMP Morris Peterson 4.00 10.00
PRSMW Marvin Williams 5.00 12.00
PRSRJ Richard Jefferson 4.00 10.00
PRSRM Rashad McCants 4.00 10.00
PRSSL Shaun Livingston 4.00 10.00
PRSTP Tayshaun Prince 6.00 15.00

2006-07 Upper Deck Trilogy Signs of Stardom Dual

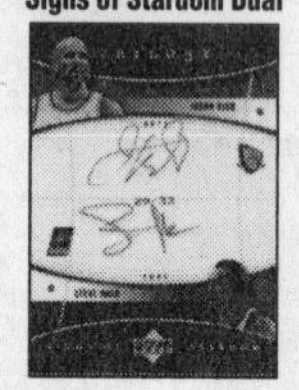

PRINT RUN 33 SER.#'d SETS
SOSAR LaMarcus Aldridge 40.00 100.00
Brandon Roy
SOSBB Andrea Bargnani 20.00 40.00
Chris Bosh
SOSBC Renaldo Balkman 8.00 20.00
Mardy Collins
SOSCM Tracy McGrady 200.00 300.00
Vince Carter
SOSFH Jordan Farmar 10.00 25.00
Ryan Hollins
SOSFO Raymond Felton 10.00 25.00
Emeka Okafor
SOSGL Rudy Gay 10.00 25.00
Kyle Lowry
SOSHB Chauncey Billups 20.00 40.00
Richard Hamilton
SOSHG Ben Gordon 12.00 30.00
Kirk Hinrich
SOSJJ Michael Jordan 700.00 1200.00
LeBron James
SOSJP Richard Jefferson 8.00 20.00
Tayshaun Prince
SOSKI Andre Iguodala 8.00 20.00
Kyle Korver
SOSNK Jason Kidd 75.00 150.00
Steve Nash
SOSOM Patrick O'Bryant 8.00 20.00
Paul Millsap
SOSPA Paul Pierce 30.00 80.00
Carmelo Anthony
SOSRD Ronnie Brewer 10.00 25.00
Dee Brown
SOSRR Rajon Rondo 15.00 40.00
Allan Ray
SOSSA Hilton Armstrong 8.00 20.00
Cedric Simmons
SOSSF Craig Smith 10.00 25.00
Randy Foye
SOSSP Chris Paul 20.00 40.00
Peja Stojakovic
SOSSR Saer Sene 8.00 20.00
Sergio Rodriguez
SOSTS Tyrus Thomas 25.00 60.00
Thabo Sefolosha
SOSWB Marcus Williams 10.00 25.00
Josh Boone
SOSWJ Shelden Williams 8.00 20.00
Solomon Jones
SOSWW Shawne Williams 8.00 20.00
James White

2003-04 Upper Deck Triple Dimensions

Released in April 2004, Triple Dimensions is a 132-card set divided up into 90 base veteran cards (numbers 1-90), 36 rookie cards sequentially numbered to 1999 (numbers 91-126) and six rookie cards sequentially numbered to 999 (numbers 127-132). Base cards place a full-color player action photo on a card that has a ball background on the top and the bottom. Rookie cards are horizontally designed with a player photo on the left and a mirror-like hologram image in the shape of an "R" on the right. Triple Dimensions was packaged in 18-pack boxes where packs contained five cards and carried a suggested retail price of $4.99.

COMP.SET w/o SP's (90) 12.50 30.00
1 Jason Terry .25 .60
2 Theo Ratliff .20 .50
3 Shareef Abdur-Rahim .25 .60
4 Raef LaFrentz .20 .50
5 Vin Baker .20 .50
6 Paul Pierce .40 1.00
7 Eddy Curry .25 .60
8 Tyson Chandler .25 .60
9 Antonio Davis .20 .50
10 Dajuan Wagner .20 .50
11 Zydrunas Ilgauskas .25 .60
12 Carlos Boozer .30 .75
13 Steve Nash .40 1.00
14 Antoine Walker .30 .75
15 Dirk Nowitzki .50 1.25
16 Michael Finley .30 .75
17 Andre Miller .25 .60
18 Nene .25 .60
19 Earl Boykins .20 .50
20 Ben Wallace .30 .75
21 Chauncey Billups .30 .75
22 Richard Hamilton .25 .60
23 Mike Dunleavy .25 .60
24 Jason Richardson .30 .75
25 Nick Van Exel .25 .60
26 Cuttino Mobley .25 .60
27 Yao Ming .60 1.50
28 Steve Francis .30 .75
29 Reggie Miller .30 .75
30 Jamaal Tinsley .20 .50
31 Jermaine O'Neal .30 .75
32 Corey Maggette .25 .60
33 Elton Brand .30 .75
34 Quentin Richardson .25 .60
35 Shaquille O'Neal .75 2.00
36 Kobe Bryant 1.50 4.00
37 Karl Malone .40 1.00
38 Gary Payton .30 .75
39 Mike Miller .30 .75
40 Pau Gasol .30 .75
41 Shane Battier .25 .60
42 Eddie Jones .25 .60
43 Caron Butler .30 .75
44 Lamar Odom .30 .75
45 Desmond Mason .25 .60
46 Tim Thomas .30 .75
47 Michael Redd .30 .75
48 Latrell Sprewell .25 .60
49 Kevin Garnett .60 1.50
50 Wally Szczerbiak .25 .60
51 Kenyon Martin .30 .75
52 Jason Kidd .50 1.25
53 Richard Jefferson .30 .75
54 Jamal Mashburn .25 .60
55 Baron Davis .30 .75
56 Jamaal Magloire .20 .50
57 Stephon Marbury .25 .60
58 Allan Houston .25 .60
59 Keith Van Horn .25 .60
60 Drew Gooden .25 .60
61 Tracy McGrady .40 1.00
62 Gordan Giricek .20 .50
63 Glenn Robinson .25 .60
64 Allen Iverson .50 1.25
65 Eric Snow .20 .50
66 Antonio McDyess .25 .60
67 Amare Stoudemire .50 1.25
68 Shawn Marion .30 .75
69 Zach Randolph .30 .75
70 Rasheed Wallace .30 .75
71 Damon Stoudamire .25 .60
72 Mike Bibby .30 .75
73 Chris Webber .30 .75
74 Peja Stojakovic .30 .75
75 Brad Miller .30 .75
76 Tony Parker .30 .75
77 Tim Duncan .50 1.25
78 Manu Ginobili .40 1.00
79 Rashard Lewis .30 .75
80 Ray Allen .30 .75
81 Vladimir Radmanovic .20 .50
82 Morris Peterson .20 .50
83 Vince Carter .50 1.25
84 Jalen Rose .25 .60
85 Andrei Kirilenko .30 .75
86 Matt Harpring .25 .60
87 Carlos Arroyo .25 .60
88 Jerry Stackhouse .25 .60
89 Gilbert Arenas .30 .75
90 Larry Hughes .25 .60
91 Udonis Haslem RC 2.50 6.00
92 Brandon Hunter RC 2.00 5.00
93 Maurice Williams RC 3.00 8.00
94 Keith Bogans RC 2.00 5.00
95 Zaur Pachulia RC 2.00 5.00
96 Willie Green RC 2.00 5.00
97 Kyle Korver RC 2.50 6.00
98 James Jones RC 2.00 5.00
99 Steve Blake RC 2.50 6.00
100 Travis Hansen RC 2.00 5.00
101 Jerome Beasley RC 2.00 5.00
102 Luke Walton RC 2.50 6.00
103 Jason Kapono RC 2.00 5.00
104 Maciej Lampe RC 2.00 5.00
105 Josh Howard RC 2.50 6.00
106 Leandro Barbosa RC 2.50 6.00
107 Kendrick Perkins RC 3.00 8.00
108 Ndudi Ebi RC 2.00 5.00
109 Brian Cook RC 2.00 5.00
110 Travis Outlaw RC 2.50 6.00
111 Zoran Planinic RC 2.00 5.00
112 Boris Diaw RC 2.50 6.00
113 Dahntay Jones RC 2.00 5.00
114 Aleksandar Pavlovic RC 2.50 6.00
115 David West RC 2.50 6.00
116 Zarko Cabarkapa RC 2.00 5.00
117 Troy Bell RC 2.00 5.00
118 Reece Gaines RC 2.00 5.00
119 Luke Ridnour RC 2.50 6.00
120 Marcus Banks RC 2.00 5.00
121 Nick Collison RC 2.00 5.00
122 Mickael Pietrus RC 2.00 5.00
123 Mike Sweetney RC 2.00 5.00
124 Chris Kaman RC 2.00 5.00
125 T.J. Ford RC 2.50 6.00
126 Kirk Hinrich RC 2.50 6.00
127 Jarvis Hayes RC 2.50 6.00
128 Dwyane Wade RC 10.00 25.00
129 Chris Bosh RC 5.00 12.00
130 Carmelo Anthony RC 6.00 15.00
131 Darko Milicic RC 2.50 6.00
132 LeBron James RC 25.00 60.00

2003-04 Upper Deck Triple Dimensions Slam Hologram

Consisting of the first 100 serially numbered copies of the rookie cards, this 42-card parallel set features a

ifferent background hologram showing the player in a lam dunk pose.
*91-132 SLAM HOLO: .75X TO 2X BASE HI

2003-04 Upper Deck Triple Dimensions 3-D Jerseys

All of the memorabilia card designs from Triple Dimensions are similar. Each includes a color photo of the featured player and a swatch of game used jersey. A Patch version was also made and these cards are sequentially numbered to 25.
*PATCH: 2X TO 5X BASE HI
PATCH PRINT RUN 25 SER.#'d SETS
J1 Ray Allen 3.00 8.00
J2 Allen Iverson 5.00 12.00
J3 Jason Richardson 3.00 8.00
J4 Shareef Abdur-Rahim 2.50 6.00
J5 Jason Kidd 5.00 12.00
J6 Steve Nash 4.00 10.00
J7 Richard Jefferson 3.00 8.00
J8 Manu Ginobili 4.00 10.00
J9 Shaquille O'Neal 8.00 20.00
J10 Shawn Marion 3.00 8.00
J11 Kenyon Martin 3.00 8.00
J12 Gilbert Arenas 3.00 8.00
J13 LeBron James 30.00 80.00
J14 Richard Hamilton 2.50 6.00
J15 Dajuan Wagner 2.00 5.00
J16 Kobe Bryant 10.00 25.00
J17 Tracy McGrady 4.00 10.00
J18 Andrei Kirilenko 3.00 8.00
J19 Reggie Miller 3.00 8.00
J20 Steve Francis 3.00 8.00
J21 Carmelo Anthony 8.00 20.00
J22 Lamar Odom 3.00 8.00
J23 Tim Duncan/120 5.00 12.00
J24 Stephon Marbury 2.50 6.00
J25 Yao Ming 6.00 15.00
J26 Chauncey Billups 3.00 8.00
J27 Chris Webber 3.00 8.00
J28 Baron Davis 3.00 8.00
J29 Elton Brand 3.00 8.00
J30 Bonzi Wells 2.00 5.00
J31 Caron Butler 3.00 8.00
J32 Jermaine O'Neal 3.00 8.00
J33 Paul Pierce 4.00 10.00
J34 Wally Szczerbiak 2.50 6.00
J35 Gary Payton 3.00 8.00
J36 Michael Jordan 40.00 80.00
J37 Tony Parker 3.00 8.00
J38 Michael Finley 3.00 8.00
J39 Rashard Lewis 3.00 8.00
J40 Amare Stoudemire 5.00 12.00
J41 Dirk Nowitzki 5.00 12.00
J42 Kevin Garnett 6.00 15.00

2003-04 Upper Deck Triple Dimensions 3-D Warmups

Randomly seeded in packs, this 47-card set features both a player color photo and a swatch of warmup. Each card is sequentially numbered to 999. Upon release, card number W21 was not issued.
*SHOOT.SHIRTS: .5X TO 1.25X WARM HI
SHIRTS PRINT RUN 499 SER.#'d SETS
W1 Ray Allen 2.50 6.00
W2 Allen Iverson 4.00 10.00
W3 Jason Richardson 2.50 6.00
W4 Shareef Abdur-Rahim 2.00 5.00
W5 Jason Kidd 4.00 10.00
W6 Steve Nash 3.00 8.00
W7 Richard Jefferson 2.50 6.00
W8 Manu Ginobili 3.00 8.00
W9 Shaquille O'Neal 6.00 15.00
W10 Shawn Marion 2.50 6.00
W11 Kenyon Martin 2.50 6.00
W12 Gilbert Arenas 2.50 6.00
W13 LeBron James 25.00 60.00
W14 Richard Hamilton 2.00 5.00
W15 Dajuan Wagner 2.00 5.00
W16 Kobe Bryant 8.00 20.00
W17 Tracy McGrady 3.00 8.00
W18 Andrei Kirilenko 3.00 8.00
W19 Reggie Miller 2.50 6.00
W20 Steve Francis 2.50 6.00
W22 Lamar Odom 2.50 6.00
W23 Tim Duncan 4.00 10.00
W24 Stephon Marbury 2.00 5.00
W25 Yao Ming 5.00 12.00
W26 Chauncey Billups 2.50 6.00
W27 Chris Webber 2.50 6.00
W28 Baron Davis 2.50 6.00
W29 Elton Brand 2.50 6.00
W30 Jamal Mashburn 2.00 5.00
W31 Caron Butler 2.50 6.00
W32 Jermaine O'Neal 2.50 6.00
W33 Paul Pierce 3.00 8.00
W34 Wally Szczerbiak 2.00 5.00
W35 Gary Payton 2.50 6.00
W36 Michael Jordan 25.00 60.00
W37 Tony Parker 2.50 6.00
W38 Michael Finley 2.50 6.00
W39 Rashard Lewis 2.50 6.00
W40 Amare Stoudemire 4.00 10.00
W41 Dirk Nowitzki 4.00 10.00
W42 Kevin Garnett 5.00 12.00
W43 Jason Terry 2.00 5.00
W44 Eddy Curry 2.00 5.00
W45 Corey Maggette 2.00 5.00
W46 Quentin Richardson 2.00 5.00
W47 Karl Malone 3.00 8.00
W48 Peja Stojakovic 2.50 6.00

2003-04 Upper Deck Triple Dimensions Reflections

Inserted at the rate of one per pack, this 90-card set places full-color player photos on an all foil background. Several different versions of the set were released as well. An Amethyst foil parallel is sequentially numbered to 300, and Emerald foil parallel is sequentially numbered to 100, a Gold foil parallel is sequentially numbered to 50, a Ruby foil parallel is sequentially numbered to 500, a Sapphire foil parallel is sequentially numbered to 10 and a Titanium foil parallel is sequentially numbered to 1.
*AMETHYST: 1.5X TO 4X BASE REF.HI
*EMERALD: 2.5X TO 6X BASE REF.HI
*RUBY: 1X TO 2.5X BASE REF.HI
1 Rasheed Wallace .50 1.25
2 Jason Terry .40 1.00
3 Paul Pierce .60 1.50
4 Ricky Davis .40 1.00
5 Michael Jordan 4.00 10.00
6 Eddy Curry .40 1.00
7 Kirk Hinrich .60 1.50
8 Jamal Crawford .40 1.00
9 Scottie Pippen .75 2.00
10 LeBron James 8.00 20.00
11 Carlos Boozer .50 1.25
12 Dajuan Wagner .30 .75
13 Dirk Nowitzki .75 2.00
14 Steve Nash .60 1.50
15 Antoine Walker .50 1.25
16 Josh Howard .50 1.25
17 Carmelo Anthony 1.50 4.00
18 Andre Miller .40 1.00
19 Nene .40 1.00
20 Ben Wallace .50 1.25
21 Darko Milicic .50 1.25
22 Chauncey Billups .50 1.25
23 Jason Richardson .50 1.25
24 Nick Van Exel .40 1.00
25 Steve Francis .50 1.25
26 Yao Ming 1.00 2.50
27 Cuttino Mobley .40 1.00
28 Jermaine O'Neal .50 1.25
29 Al Harrington .40 1.00
30 Reggie Miller .50 1.25
31 Kobe Bryant 2.50 6.00
32 Shaquille O'Neal 1.25 3.00
33 Gary Payton .50 1.25
34 Karl Malone .60 1.50
35 Elton Brand .50 1.25
36 Chris Kaman .60 1.50
37 Corey Maggette .40 1.00
38 Pau Gasol .50 1.25
39 Troy Bell .50 1.25
40 Jason Williams .40 1.00
41 Dwyane Wade 3.00 8.00
42 Lamar Odom .50 1.25
43 Eddie Jones .40 1.00
44 T.J. Ford .60 1.50
45 Michael Redd .50 1.25
46 Desmond Mason .40 1.00
47 Kevin Garnett 1.00 2.50
48 Latrell Sprewell .50 1.25
49 Ndudi Ebi .50 1.25
50 Kenyon Martin .50 1.25
51 Jason Kidd .75 2.00
52 Richard Jefferson .50 1.25
53 Baron Davis .50 1.25
54 David West .60 1.50
55 Stephon Marbury .50 1.25
56 Allan Houston .40 1.00
57 Kurt Thomas .30 .75
58 Tracy McGrady .60 1.50
59 Keith Bogans .50 1.25
60 Drew Gooden .40 1.00
61 Allen Iverson .75 2.00
62 Glenn Robinson .40 1.00
63 Leandro Barbosa .60 1.50
64 Amare Stoudemire .75 2.00
65 Shawn Marion .50 1.25
66 Shareef Abdur-Rahim .40 1.00
67 Zach Randolph .50 1.25
68 Travis Outlaw .60 1.50
69 Darius Miles .50 1.25
70 Peja Stojakovic .50 1.25
71 Chris Webber .50 1.25
72 Brad Miller .50 1.25
73 Mike Bibby .50 1.25
74 Bobby Jackson .30 .75
75 Tim Duncan .75 2.00
76 Tony Parker .50 1.25
77 Manu Ginobili .60 1.50
78 Ray Allen .50 1.25
79 Nick Collison .50 1.25
80 Luke Ridnour .60 1.50
81 Chris Bosh 1.00 2.50
82 Vince Carter .75 2.00
83 Jalen Rose .50 1.25
84 Donyell Marshall .30 .75
85 Andrei Kirilenko .50 1.25
86 Carlos Arroyo .40 1.00
87 Jarvis Hayes .50 1.25
88 Jerry Stackhouse .40 1.00
89 Gilbert Arenas .50 1.25
90 Larry Hughes .40 1.00

2003-04 Upper Deck Triple Dimensions Reflections Gold

Randomly seeded, this 90-card set is a parallel to the Reflections insert enhanced with Gold foil and is sequentially numbered to 50.
*GOLD SINGLES: 4X TO 10X BASE REF.HI
10 LeBron James 150.00 300.00
17 Carmelo Anthony 25.00 60.00
41 Dwyane Wade 60.00 150.00
81 Chris Bosh 15.00 40.00

2003-04 Upper Deck Triple Dimensions Standout Sigs

Randomly inserted in packs, this 69-card set places full-color player photos on a card with green borders along the top and the bottom, gold foil highlights and a white-out oval towards the bottom of the card for an authentic autograph. Unless specified in the checklist, these cards are sequentially numbered to 100. Card 21, Steve Franics, was not produced.
1 Kobe Bryant/25 125.00 250.00
2 Kevin Garnett/25 75.00 150.00
3 LeBron James/25 600.00 1000.00
4 Carmelo Anthony/25 75.00 200.00
5 Michael Jordan/25 400.00 700.00
7 Tracy McGrady/25 25.00 60.00
8 Amare Stoudemire/25 25.00 60.00
9 Darko Milicic/25 30.00 80.00
12 Luke Walton 6.00 15.00
13 Reggie Evans 6.00 15.00
14 Lamar Odom 10.00 25.00
15 Reggie Miller 50.00 120.00
16 Gerald Wallace 6.00 15.00
17 Dahntay Jones 6.00 15.00
18 Boris Diaw 8.00 20.00
19 Wang ZhiZhi 10.00 25.00
20 Jalen Rose 6.00 15.00
22 Alonzo Mourning 20.00 50.00
23 Dan Dickau 6.00 15.00
24 Antawn Jamison 6.00 15.00
25 Brent Barry 6.00 15.00
26 Cuttino Mobley 6.00 15.00
27 Luke Ridnour 8.00 20.00
28 Chris Wilcox 6.00 15.00
29 Carlos Boozer 6.00 15.00
30 Gordan Giricek 6.00 15.00
31 Chris Kaman 8.00 20.00
32 Josh Howard 6.00 15.00
33 Leandro Barbosa 8.00 20.00
34 Jon Barry 6.00 15.00
35 Shawn Marion 6.00 15.00
36 Kendrick Perkins 10.00 25.00
37 Chris Bosh 15.00 40.00
38 Travis Outlaw 8.00 20.00
39 Antonio McDyess 6.00 15.00
40 Drew Gooden 6.00 15.00
41 Peja Stojakovic 6.00 15.00
42 Chauncey Billups 10.00 25.00
43 Darius Miles 6.00 15.00
44 Marko Jaric 6.00 15.00
45 Corey Maggette 6.00 15.00
46 Dajuan Wagner 6.00 15.00
47 Andre Miller 6.00 15.00
48 Shane Battier 6.00 15.00
49 Reece Gaines 6.00 15.00
50 Troy Bell 6.00 15.00
51 Morris Peterson 6.00 15.00
52 Richard Hamilton 6.00 15.00
53 Mike Sweetney 6.00 15.00
54 Michael Pietrus 6.00 15.00
55 Tony Parker 10.00 25.00
56 Marcus Banks 6.00 15.00
57 Eddy Curry 6.00 15.00
58 Brian Cook 6.00 15.00
59 Maciej Lampe 6.00 15.00
60 Zoran Planinic 6.00 15.00
61 Paul Pierce 12.50 30.00
62 Jason Kidd 15.00 40.00
63 Richard Jefferson 6.00 15.00
64 Mike Bibby 6.00 15.00
65 Gilbert Arenas 8.00 20.00
66 Earl Boykins 6.00 15.00
67 Dwyane Wade 100.00 200.00
68 David West 8.00 20.00
69 Desmond Mason 6.00 15.00
70 Jerry Stackhouse 8.00 20.00

2002 Upper Deck Twizzlers

5 Alonzo Mourning 1.00 2.50
6 Alonzo Mourning 1.00 2.50

1996 Upper Deck U.S. Olympic

This multisport product was issued in June 1996, prior to the Centennial Olympic Games in Atlanta. Packs of 10 standard-size cards had a suggested retail price of $1.99. The set contains the following subsets: U.S. Olympic Moments (1-90), Future Champions (91-120) and Passing the Torch (121-135).
COMPLETE SET (135) 8.00 20.00
11 Michael Jordan 1.25 3.00
12 Larry Bird .40 1.00
93 Anfernee Hardaway .30 .75
134 Michael Jordan .60 1.50
Anfernee Hardaway

1996 Upper Deck U.S. Olympic Reflections of Gold

These cards were inserted in packs at a rate of 1:5. The photos are rendered in a bright metallic fashion on the fronts.
COMPLETE SET (10) 8.00 20.00
STATED ODDS 1:5
RG1 Michael Jordan 6.00 15.00

1996 Upper Deck U.S. Olympic Reflections of Gold Signatures

These cards were distributed exclusively via mail-in redemption cards, which were inserted at a rate of 1:79 packs. Each redemption card identified which athlete's signature card it represented. There was an expiration date of Dec. 31, 1996. The Jordan card is extremely scarce; probably 25 or less were signed, and some never were redeemed. Kristi Yamaguchi apparently did not participate in this promotion.
COMPLETE SET (9) 3000.00 5000.00
STATED ODDS 1:79
RG1 Michael Jordan 2500.00 5000.00

1996 Upper Deck U.S. Olympic Reign of Gold Holograms

These hologram cards were inserted at a rate of 1:17 packs. Each of the five athletes in this set have won multiple gold medals.
COMPLETE SET (5) 6.00 15.00
STATED ODDS 1:17
RN1 Michael Jordan 6.00 15.00

1994 Upper Deck USA

These 90 standard-size cards honor the '94 Team USA players. Cards were distributed in 10-card packs. Each foil box contained 36 packs. The borderless fronts feature color posed and action player shots. The player's name and position appear in red, white, and blue bars near the bottom. The card's subtitle appears vertically in gold-foil lettering near the left edge, information for which appears on the back.
COMPLETE SET (90) 10.00 25.00
1 Derrick Coleman .08 .25
2 Derrick Coleman .08 .25
3 Derrick Coleman .08 .10
4 Derrick Coleman .08 .25
5 Derrick Coleman .08 .25
6 Derrick Coleman .08 .25
7 Joe Dumars .08 .25
8 Joe Dumars .08 .25
9 Joe Dumars .08 .25
10 Joe Dumars .08 .25
11 Joe Dumars .08 .25
12 Joe Dumars .08 .25
13 Tim Hardaway .10 .30
14 Tim Hardaway .10 .30
15 Tim Hardaway .10 .30
16 Tim Hardaway .10 .30
17 Tim Hardaway .10 .30
18 Tim Hardaway .10 .30
19 Larry Johnson .10 .30
20 Larry Johnson .10 .30
21 Larry Johnson .10 .30
22 Larry Johnson .10 .30
23 Larry Johnson .10 .30
24 Larry Johnson .10 .30
25 Shawn Kemp .15 .40
26 Shawn Kemp .15 .40
27 Shawn Kemp .15 .40
28 Shawn Kemp .15 .40
29 Shawn Kemp .15 .40
30 Shawn Kemp .15 .40
31 Dan Majerle .08 .25
32 Dan Majerle .08 .25
33 Dan Majerle .08 .25
34 Dan Majerle .08 .25
35 Dan Majerle .08 .25
36 Dan Majerle .08 .25
37 Reggie Miller .10 .30
38 Reggie Miller .10 .30
39 Reggie Miller .10 .30
40 Reggie Miller .10 .30
41 Reggie Miller .10 .30
42 Reggie Miller .10 .30
43 Alonzo Mourning .15 .40
44 Alonzo Mourning .15 .40
45 Alonzo Mourning .15 .40
46 Alonzo Mourning .15 .40
47 Alonzo Mourning .15 .40
48 Alonzo Mourning .15 .40
49 Shaquille O'Neal .40 1.00
50 Shaquille O'Neal .40 1.00
51 Shaquille O'Neal .40 1.00
52 Shaquille O'Neal .40 1.00
53 Shaquille O'Neal .40 1.00
54 Shaquille O'Neal .40 1.00
55 Mark Price .08 .25
56 Mark Price .08 .25
57 Mark Price .08 .25
58 Mark Price .08 .25
59 Mark Price .08 .25
60 Mark Price .08 .25
61 Steve Smith .08 .25
62 Steve Smith .08 .25
63 Steve Smith .08 .25
64 Steve Smith .08 .25
65 Steve Smith .08 .25
66 Steve Smith .08 .25
67 Isiah Thomas .10 .30
68 Isiah Thomas .10 .30
69 Isiah Thomas .10 .30
70 Isiah Thomas .10 .30
71 Isiah Thomas .10 .30
72 Isiah Thomas .10 .30
73 Dominique Wilkins .10 .30
74 Dominique Wilkins .10 .30
75 Dominique Wilkins .10 .30
76 Dominique Wilkins .10 .30
77 Dominique Wilkins .10 .30
78 Dominique Wilkins .10 .30
79 Jennifer Azzi 1.25 3.00
80 Daedra Charles .60 1.50
81 Lisa Leslie 1.50 4.00
82 Katrina McClain .60 1.50
83 Dawn Staley 1.25 3.00
84 Sheryl Swoopes 1.50 4.00
85 Michael Jordan ATG 85 1.00 2.50
86 Larry Bird ATG 86 .30 .75
87 Jerry West ATG 87 .25 .60
88 Adrian Dantley ATG 88 .08 .25
89 Cheryl Miller ATG 89 1.50 4.00
90 Henry Iba ATG 90 .08 .25
CK1 Checklist 1 .08 .25
CK2 Checklist 2 .08 .25

1994 Upper Deck USA Gold Medal

Inserted one per '94 Upper Deck USA pack, these gold cards are identical to the regular issues except for the Upper Deck Gold Medal logos appearing on the fronts. The cards are numbered on the back. Please refer to the multipliers provided below (coupled with the prices of the corresponding regular issue cards) to ascertain value.
COMPLETE SET (90) 20.00 50.00
*STARS: 1X TO 2.5X HI COLUMN

1994 Upper Deck USA Chalk Talk

Randomly inserted in Upper Deck USA packs at a rate of one in 35, the Chalk Talk set consists of 14 standard-size cards. Card fronts include a small hologram of Don Nelson who is also quoted on the back in reference to the player on the card. The card fronts are full-bleed on one side with a gray border on the other that contains the player's name. In addition to Nelson's quote, a small photo of him and a larger photo of the player appear on the back.
COMPLETE SET (14) 10.00 25.00
CT1 Derrick Coleman .75 2.00
CT2 Joe Dumars 1.00 2.50
CT3 Tim Hardaway 1.00 2.50
CT4 Larry Johnson 1.00 2.50
CT5 Shawn Kemp 1.25 3.00
CT6 Dan Majerle .75 2.00
CT7 Reggie Miller 1.00 2.50
CT8 Alonzo Mourning 1.50 4.00
CT9 Shaquille O'Neal 6.00 15.00
CT10 Mark Price .40 1.00
CT11 Steve Smith .75 2.00
CT12 Isiah Thomas 1.00 2.50
CT13 Dominique Wilkins 1.00 2.50
CT14 Kevin Johnson .75 2.00

1994 Upper Deck USA Follow Your Dreams Assists

Randomly inserted at a rate of one in 14 packs, these 42 standard-size game-prize cards feature borderless color player action shots on front. The cards are broken into three 14-card sets that are distinguished by categories: assists, rebounds and scoring. The category appears on gold foil stamping on the front that appears in on one side along with the player's name. The back carries the rules for playing the game. Briefly, each game card depicts one of the 14 players from the '94 USA Dream Team. Each card also designates the player as either a "Top Scorer," "Top Rebounder," or "Top Assists." The player that led Dream Team II in either of these categories could have that specific card redeemed by the collector for a 14-card set of that category. Kevin Johnson's Assists card and Shaquille O'Neal's Rebounds and Scoring cards qualified as the three exchange cards. The redemption deadline for the three cards was November 30, 1994. Card values below are for any of the three sets.
COMPLETE SET (14) 6.00 15.00
*REBOUNDS/SCORING: EQUAL VALUE
*EXCHANGE SETS: EQUAL VALUE
1 Derrick Coleman .40 1.00
2 Joe Dumars .60 1.50
3 Tim Hardaway .60 1.50
4 Kevin Johnson .40 1.00
5 Larry Johnson .40 1.00
6 Shawn Kemp .75 2.00
7 Dan Majerle .40 1.00
8 Reggie Miller .60 1.50
9 Alonzo Mourning 1.00 2.50
10 Shaquille O'Neal 4.00 10.00
11 Mark Price .20 .50
12 Steve Smith .40 1.00
13 Isiah Thomas .60 1.50
14 Dominique Wilkins .60 1.50

1994 Upper Deck USA Jordan's Highlights

Randomly inserted at a rate of one in 35 packs, the five-card standard-size set features action photos of Michael Jordan representing the United States during international play. A facsimile autograph in gold foil lettering appears near the bottom. On back, the American flag is used as a backdrop to highlights and statistics that pertain to action on the front.
COMPLETE SET (5) 15.00 40.00
COMMON JORDAN (JH1-JH5) 5.00 12.00

1996 Upper Deck USA

This 62-card, skip-numbered set features the first 10 team members of the 1996 men's and complete 1996 USA women's basketball teams. The cards were released during the summer of 1996. Each pack contained twelve cards and sold for a suggested retail price of $2.29. Each box contained 32 packs. The entire set features die-cut cards and gold foil stamping.
COMPLETE SET (62) 8.00 20.00
1 Anfernee Hardaway .15 .40
2 Anfernee Hardaway .15 .40
3 Anfernee Hardaway .15 .40
4 Anfernee Hardaway .15 .40
5 Grant Hill .15 .40
6 Grant Hill .15 .40
7 Grant Hill .15 .40
8 Grant Hill .15 .40
9 Karl Malone .12 .30
10 Karl Malone .12 .30
11 Karl Malone .12 .30
12 Karl Malone .12 .30
13 Reggie Miller .12 .30
14 Reggie Miller .12 .30
15 Reggie Miller .12 .30
16 Reggie Miller .12 .30
17 Shaquille O'Neal .25 .60
18 Shaquille O'Neal .25 .60
19 Shaquille O'Neal .25 .60
20 Shaquille O'Neal .25 .60
21 Hakeem Olajuwon .12 .30
22 Hakeem Olajuwon .12 .30
23 Hakeem Olajuwon .12 .30
24 Hakeem Olajuwon .12 .30
25 Scottie Pippen .15 .40
26 Scottie Pippen .15 .40
27 Scottie Pippen .15 .40
28 Scottie Pippen .15 .40
29 David Robinson .15 .40
30 David Robinson .15 .40
31 David Robinson .15 .40
32 David Robinson .15 .40
33 Glenn Robinson .10 .25
34 Glenn Robinson .10 .25
35 Glenn Robinson .10 .25
36 Glenn Robinson .10 .25
37 John Stockton .12 .30
38 John Stockton .12 .30
39 John Stockton .12 .30
40 John Stockton .12 .30
49 Anfernee Hardaway .15 .40
50 Grant Hill .15 .40
51 Karl Malone .12 .30
52 Reggie Miller .12 .30
53 Shaquille O'Neal .25 .60
54 Hakeem Olajuwon .12 .30
55 Scottie Pippen .15 .40
56 David Robinson .15 .40
57 Glenn Robinson .10 .25
58 John Stockton .12 .30
61 Jennifer Azzi 1.00 2.50
62 Ruthie Bolton-Holifield 1.00 2.50
63 Teresa Edwards .75 2.00
64 Lisa Leslie 1.50 4.00
65 Rebecca Lobo 1.25 3.00
66 Katrina McClain .40 1.00
67 Nikki McCray 1.00 2.50
68 Carla McGhee .40 1.00
69 Dawn Staley 1.00 2.50
70 Katy Steding .40 1.00
71 Sheryl Swoopes 2.00 5.00
72 Tara VanDerveer CO .40 1.00
NNO USA Trade Card .08 .25
Expired

1996 Upper Deck USA Exchange Set

This 10-card set was available through a special USA Update Trade card and features Charles Barkley (#'s 41-44 and 59) and Mitch Richmond (#'s 45-48 and 60) to finish off the set. This card was randomly seeded into one in every ten packs. The expiration of the trade card was October 31, 1996.
COMPLETE SET (10) .75 2.00
41 Charles Barkley .15 .40
42 Charles Barkley .15 .40
43 Charles Barkley .15 .40
44 Charles Barkley .15 .40
45 Mitch Richmond .10 .25
46 Mitch Richmond .10 .25
47 Mitch Richmond .10 .25
48 Mitch Richmond .10 .25
59 Charles Barkley .15 .40
60 Mitch Richmond .10 .25

1996 Upper Deck USA Follow Your Dreams

Randomly inserted in packs at a rate of one in 6, this 11-card insert set features the first 10 members selected to the team, plus a special "Field Card" representing Charles Barkley, Gary Payton and Mitch Richmond. Card front designs featured a full-color player cut out set against a red and white striped background. If a collector had the card of the USAB 1996 Olympics scoring leader, a 12-card gold commemorative set was awarded; collectors with second place scoring leader cards received a 12-card silver commemorative set. The expiration date for the exchange was October 31, 1996.
COMPLETE SET (11) 5.00 12.00
F1 Anfernee Hardaway 1.00 2.50
F2 Grant Hill 1.00 2.50
F3 Karl Malone .75 2.00
F4 Reggie Miller W .75 2.00
F5 Shaquille O'Neal 1.50 4.00
F6 Hakeem Olajuwon .75 2.00
F7 Scottie Pippen 1.00 2.50
F8 David Robinson W 1.00 2.50
F9 Glenn Robinson .60 1.50
F10 John Stockton .75 2.00
F11 Field Card .20 .50

1996 Upper Deck USA Follow Your Dreams Exchange Set

This 12-card exchange set was redeemable by mailing in winning cards of either Reggie Miller or David Robinson. The set contained cards for Charles Barkley, Mitch Richmond and Gary Payton - who were not available in the regular set. It was Gary Payton's only Olympic card.
COMPLETE SET (12) 8.00 20.00
FD1 Charles Barkley 1.25 3.00
FD2 David Robinson 1.25 3.00
FD3 Reggie Miller 1.00 2.50
FD4 Scottie Pippen 1.25 3.00
FD5 Grant Hill 1.25 3.00
FD6 Mitch Richmond .75 2.00
FD7 Shaquille O'Neal 2.00 5.00
FD8 Anfernee Hardaway 1.25 3.00
FD9 Karl Malone 1.00 2.50
FD10 Gary Payton .75 2.00
FD11 Hakeem Olajuwon 1.00 2.50
FD12 John Stockton 1.00 2.50

1996 Upper Deck USA Anfernee Hardaway American Made

Randomly inserted in packs at a rate of one in 56, this 4-card die cut insert set focuses on Orlando guard Penny Hardaway. Each card looks at a particular aspect of Hardaway's abilities - scoring, defense, smoothness and versatility.
COMPLETE SET (4) 10.00 25.00
COMMON CARD (A1-A4) 3.00 8.00

1996 Upper Deck USA Michael Jordan American Made

Randomly inserted in packs at a rate of one in 55, this 4-card die cut insert set looks at basketball legend Michael Jordan. Each card focuses on a particular part of Jordan's game - scoring, defense, desire and leadership.
COMPLETE SET (4) 30.00 80.00
COMMON CARD (M1-M4) 10.00 25.00

1996 Upper Deck USA SP Career Statistics

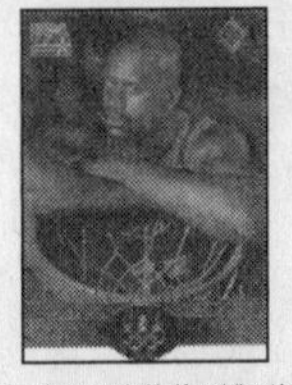

Inserted one in every pack, this 10-card die cut insert set features a card of each 1996 USAB player outlining their career stats and accomplishments. Each card is printed on premium stock and features Upper Deck's special silver "Light F/X" technology.
COMPLETE SET (10) 2.50 6.00
*GOLD: 3X TO 8X HI COLUMN
GOLD STATED ODDS 1:27 PACKS
S1 Anfernee Hardaway .60 1.50
S2 Grant Hill .60 1.50
S3 Karl Malone .50 1.25
S4 Reggie Miller .50 1.25
S5 Shaquille O'Neal 1.00 2.50
S6 Hakeem Olajuwon .50 1.25
S7 Scottie Pippen .60 1.50
S8 David Robinson .60 1.50
S9 Glenn Robinson .40 1.00
S10 John Stockton .50 1.25
S11 Charles Barkley .60 1.50
S12 Mitch Richmond .40 1.00

1999-00 Upper Deck Victory

Released by Upper Deck, this 440-card set was released as a retail-only product. Each pack contained 12-cards and carried a suggested retail price of $.99. There were no inserts in Victory, but the set contained the following subsets: Check It Out (33 cards), Rookie Flashback (20 cards), Dynamite Dunks (30 cards), Court Catalysts (15 cards), Power Corps (15 cards), Scoring Circle (15 cards), Jordan's Greatest Hits (50 cards) and 10 Rookie Exchange cards.
COMPLETE SET (440) 35.00 60.00
1 Dikembe Mutombo CL .15 .40
2 Steve Smith .10 .25
3 Dikembe Mutombo .15 .40
4 Ed Gray .10 .25
5 Alan Henderson .10 .25
6 LaPhonso Ellis .10 .25
7 Roshown McLeod .10 .25
8 Bimbo Coles .10 .25
9 Chris Crawford .10 .25
10 Anthony Johnson .10 .25
11 Antoine Walker CL .15 .40
12 Kenny Anderson .12 .30
13 Antoine Walker .15 .40
14 Greg Minor .10 .25
15 Tony Battie .10 .25
16 Ron Mercer .12 .30
17 Paul Pierce .25 .60
18 Vitaly Potapenko .10 .25
19 Dana Barros .10 .25
20 Walter McCarty .10 .25
21 Elden Campbell CL .10 .25
22 Elden Campbell .10 .25
23 Eddie Jones .15 .40
24 David Wesley .10 .25
25 Bobby Phills .10 .25
26 Derrick Coleman .10 .25

27 Anthony Mason .10 .25
28 Brad Miller .15 .40
29 Eldridge Recasner .10 .25
30 Ricky Davis .15 .40
31 Toni Kukoc CL .15 .40
32 Michael Jordan 1.25 3.00
33 Brent Barry .12 .30
34 Randy Brown .10 .25
35 Keith Booth .10 .25
36 Kornel David RC .20 .50
37 Mark Bryant .10 .25
38 Toni Kukoc .15 .40
39 Rusty LaRue .10 .25
40 Brevin Knight CL .10 .25
41 Shawn Kemp .15 .40
42 Wesley Person .10 .25
43 Johnny Newman .10 .25
44 Derek Anderson .10 .25
45 Brevin Knight .10 .25
46 Bob Sura .10 .25
47 Andrew DeClercq .10 .25
48 Zydrunas Ilgauskas .12 .30
49 Danny Ferry .10 .25
50 Steve Nash CL .25 .60
51 Michael Finley .15 .40
52 Robert Pack .10 .25
53 Shawn Bradley .10 .25
54 John Williams .10 .25
55 Hubert Davis .10 .25
56 Dirk Nowitzki .30 .75
57 Steve Nash .25 .60
58 Chris Anstey .10 .25
59 Erick Strickland .10 .25
60 Nick Van Exel CL .12 .30
61 Antonio McDyess .12 .30
62 Nick Van Exel .12 .30
63 Bryant Stith .10 .25
64 Chauncey Billups .15 .40
65 Danny Fortson .10 .25
66 Eric Williams .10 .25
67 Eric Washington .10 .25
68 Raef LaFrentz .12 .30
69 Johnny Taylor .10 .25
70 Jerry Stackhouse CL .15 .40
71 Grant Hill .20 .50
72 Lindsey Hunter .10 .25
73 Bison Dele .10 .25
74 Loy Vaught .10 .25
75 Jerome Williams .10 .25
76 Jerry Stackhouse .15 .40
77 Christian Laettner .12 .30
78 Jud Buechler .10 .25
79 Don Reid .10 .25
80 Antawn Jamison CL .15 .40
81 John Starks .15 .40
82 Antawn Jamison .15 .40
83 Adonal Foyle .10 .25
84 Jason Caffey .10 .25
85 Donyell Marshall .10 .25
86 Chris Mills .10 .25
87 Tony Delk .10 .25
88 Mookie Blaylock .10 .25
89 Charles Barkley CL .25 .60
90 Hakeem Olajuwon .20 .50
91 Scottie Pippen .25 .60
92 Charles Barkley .25 .60
93 Bryce Drew .10 .25
94 Cuttino Mobley .12 .30
95 Othella Harrington .10 .25
96 Matt Maloney .10 .25
97 Michael Dickerson .10 .25
98 Matt Bullard .10 .25
99 Jalen Rose CL .12 .30
100 Reggie Miller .15 .40
101 Rik Smits .15 .40
102 Jalen Rose .12 .30
103 Antonio Davis .10 .25
104 Mark Jackson .15 .40
105 Sam Perkins .10 .25
106 Travis Best .10 .25
107 Dale Davis .10 .25
108 Chris Mullin .15 .40
109 Michael Olowokandi CL .10 .25
110 Maurice Taylor .10 .25
111 Tyrone Nesby RC .20 .50
112 Lamond Murray .10 .25
113 Darrick Martin .10 .25
114 Michael Olowokandi .10 .25
115 Rodney Rogers .10 .25
116 Eric Piatkowski .12 .30
117 Lorenzen Wright .10 .25
118 Brian Skinner .10 .25
119 Kobe Bryant CL .75 2.00
120 Kobe Bryant .75 2.00
121 Shaquille O'Neal .40 1.00
122 Derek Fisher .15 .40
123 Tyronn Lue .10 .25
124 Travis Knight .10 .25
125 Glen Rice .15 .40
126 Derek Harper .12 .30
127 Robert Horry .15 .40
128 Rick Fox .10 .25
129 Tim Hardaway CL .15 .40
130 Tim Hardaway .15 .40
131 Alonzo Mourning .20 .50
132 Keith Askins .10 .25
133 Jamal Mashburn .12 .30
134 P.J. Brown .10 .25
135 Clarence Weatherspoon .10 .25
136 Terry Porter .10 .25
137 Dan Majerle .15 .40
138 Voshon Lenard .10 .25
139 Ray Allen CL .15 .40
140 Ray Allen .15 .40
141 Vinny Del Negro .10 .25
142 Glenn Robinson .12 .30
143 Dell Curry .10 .25
144 Sam Cassell .12 .30
145 Haywoode Workman .10 .25
146 Armon Gilliam .10 .25
147 Robert Traylor .10 .25
148 Chris Gatling .10 .25
149 Kevin Garnett CL .30 .75
150 Kevin Garnett .30 .75
151 Malik Sealy .10 .25
152 Radoslav Nesterovic .15 .40
153 Joe Smith .12 .30
154 Sam Mitchell .10 .25
155 Dean Garrett .10 .25
156 Anthony Peeler .10 .25
157 Tom Hammonds .10 .25
158 Bobby Jackson .12 .30
159 Jayson Williams CL .10 .25
160 Keith Van Horn .12 .30
161 Stephon Marbury .12 .30
162 Jayson Williams .10 .25
163 Kendall Gill .10 .25
164 Kerry Kittles .10 .25
165 Jamie Feick RC .20 .50
166 Scott Burrell .10 .25
167 Lucious Harris .10 .25
168 Marcus Camby CL .12 .30
169 Patrick Ewing .20 .50
170 Allan Houston .12 .30
171 Latrell Sprewell .15 .40
172 Kurt Thomas .10 .25
173 Larry Johnson .15 .40
174 Chris Childs .10 .25
175 Marcus Camby .12 .30
176 Charlie Ward .10 .25
177 Chris Dudley .10 .25
178 Bo Outlaw CL .10 .25
179 Anfernee Hardaway .25 .60
180 Darrell Armstrong .10 .25
181 Nick Anderson .12 .30
182 Horace Grant .12 .30
183 Isaac Austin .10 .25
184 Matt Harpring .12 .30
185 Michael Doleac .10 .25
186 Bo Outlaw .10 .25
187 Allen Iverson CL .30 .75
188 Allen Iverson .30 .75
189 Theo Ratliff .10 .25
190 Matt Geiger .10 .25
191 Larry Hughes .12 .30
192 Tyrone Hill .10 .25
193 George Lynch .10 .25
194 Eric Snow .12 .30
195 Aaron McKie .10 .25
196 Harvey Grant .10 .25
197 Jason Kidd CL .25 .60
198 Jason Kidd .25 .60
199 Tom Gugliotta .10 .25
200 Rex Chapman .10 .25
201 Clifford Robinson .10 .25
202 Luc Longley .10 .25
203 Danny Manning .10 .25
204 Pat Garrity .10 .25
205 George McCloud .10 .25
206 Toby Bailey .10 .25
207 Brian Grant CL .10 .25
208 Rasheed Wallace .15 .40
209 Arvydas Sabonis .12 .30
210 Damon Stoudamire .12 .30
211 Brian Grant .10 .25
212 Isaiah Rider .10 .25
213 Walt Williams .10 .25
214 Jim Jackson .12 .30
215 Greg Anthony .10 .25
216 Stacey Augmon .12 .30
217 Vlade Divac CL .15 .40
218 Jason Williams .20 .50
219 Vlade Divac .15 .40
220 Chris Webber .15 .40
221 Nick Anderson .10 .25
222 Peja Stojakovic .15 .40
223 Tariq Abdul-Wahad .10 .25
224 Vernon Maxwell .12 .30
225 Lawrence Funderburke .12 .30
226 Jon Barry .12 .30
227 David Robinson CL .25 .60
228 Tim Duncan .30 .75
229 Sean Elliott .10 .25
230 David Robinson .25 .60
231 Mario Elie .10 .25
232 Avery Johnson .12 .30
233 Steve Kerr .12 .30
234 Malik Rose .10 .25
235 Jaren Jackson .10 .25
236 Vin Baker CL .15 .40
237 Gary Payton .15 .40
238 Vin Baker .12 .30
239 Detlef Schrempf .10 .25
240 Hersey Hawkins .10 .25
241 Dale Ellis .10 .25
242 Rashard Lewis .15 .40
243 Billy Owens .10 .25
244 Aaron Williams .10 .25
245 Vince Carter CL .30 .75
246 Vince Carter .30 .75
247 John Wallace .10 .25
248 Doug Christie .12 .30
249 Tracy McGrady .25 .60
250 Kevin Willis .10 .25
251 Michael Stewart .10 .25
252 Dee Brown .10 .25
253 John Thomas .10 .25
254 Alvin Williams .10 .25
255 Karl Malone CL .20 .50
256 Karl Malone .20 .50
257 John Stockton .20 .50
258 Jacque Vaughn .10 .25
259 Bryon Russell .10 .25
260 Howard Eisley .10 .25
261 Greg Ostertag .10 .25
262 Adam Keefe .10 .25
263 Todd Fuller .10 .25
264 Mike Bibby CL .12 .30
265 Shareef Abdur-Rahim .12 .30
266 Mike Bibby .15 .40
267 Bryant Reeves .10 .25
268 Felipe Lopez .10 .25
269 Cherokee Parks .10 .25
270 Michael Smith .10 .25
271 Tony Massenburg .10 .25
272 Rodrick Rhodes .10 .25
273 Juwan Howard CL .12 .30
274 Juwan Howard .12 .30
275 Rod Strickland .10 .25
276 Mitch Richmond .15 .40
277 Otis Thorpe .10 .25
278 Calbert Cheaney .10 .25
279 Tracy Murray .10 .25
280 Ben Wallace .15 .40
281 Terry Davis .10 .25
282 Michael Jordan RF 1.25 3.00
283 Reggie Miller RF .15 .40
284 Dikembe Mutombo RF .15 .40
285 Patrick Ewing RF .20 .50
286 Allan Houston RF .12 .30
287 Danny Manning RF .10 .25
288 Jalen Rose RF .12 .30
289 Rasheed Wallace RF .15 .40
290 Jerry Stackhouse RF .15 .40
291 Damon Stoudamire RF .15 .40
292 Kenny Anderson RF .12 .30
293 Shawn Kemp RF .15 .40
294 Vlade Divac RF .15 .40
295 Larry Johnson RF .15 .40
296 Jamal Mashburn RF .12 .30
297 Ron Harper RF .10 .25
298 Steve Smith RF .10 .25
299 Kendall Gill RF .10 .25
300 Chris Mullin RF .15 .40
301 Robert Horry RF .15 .40
302 Dikembe Mutombo DD .15 .40
303 Ron Mercer DD .12 .30
304 Eddie Jones DD .15 .40
305 Toni Kukoc DD .15 .40
306 Derek Anderson DD .10 .25
307 Shawn Bradley DD .10 .25
308 Danny Fortson DD .10 .25
309 Bison Dele DD .10 .25
310 Antawn Jamison DD .15 .40
311 Scottie Pippen DD .25 .60
312 Reggie Miller DD .15 .40
313 Maurice Taylor DD .15 .40
314 Glen Rice DD .15 .40
315 Alonzo Mourning DD .20 .50
316 Glenn Robinson DD .12 .30
317 Anthony Peeler DD .10 .25
318 Kerry Kittles DD .10 .25
319 Latrell Sprewell DD .15 .40
320 Darrell Armstrong DD .10 .25
321 Larry Hughes DD .12 .30
322 Tom Gugliotta DD .10 .25
323 Brian Grant DD .10 .25
324 Chris Webber DD .15 .40
325 David Robinson DD .25 .60
326 Vin Baker DD .12 .30
327 Vince Carter DD .30 .75
328 Bryon Russell DD .10 .25
329 Felipe Lopez DD .10 .25
330 Juwan Howard DD .12 .30
331 Michael Jordan DD 1.25 3.00
332 Jason Kidd CC .25 .60
333 Rod Strickland CC .10 .25
334 Stephon Marbury CC .15 .40
335 Gary Payton CC .15 .40
336 Mark Jackson CC .15 .40
337 John Stockton CC .20 .50
338 Brevin Knight CC .10 .25
339 Bobby Jackson CC .12 .30
340 Nick Van Exel CC .12 .30
341 Tim Hardaway CC .15 .40
342 Darrell Armstrong CC .10 .25
343 Avery Johnson CC .12 .30
344 Mike Bibby CC .15 .40
345 Damon Stoudamire CC .15 .40
346 Jason Williams CC .20 .50
347 Allen Iverson PC .30 .75
348 Kobe Bryant PC .75 2.00
349 Karl Malone PC .20 .50
350 Keith Van Horn PC .12 .30
351 Kevin Garnett PC .30 .75
352 Antoine Walker PC .15 .40
353 Tim Duncan PC .30 .75
354 Scottie Pippen PC .25 .60
355 Paul Pierce PC .25 .60
356 Michael Finley PC .15 .40
357 Shaquille O'Neal PC .40 1.00
358 Grant Hill PC .20 .50
359 Jason Williams PC .20 .50
360 Antonio McDyess PC .12 .30
361 Shareef Abdur-Rahim PC .12 .30
362 Allen Iverson SC .30 .75
363 Shaquille O'Neal SC .40 1.00
364 Karl Malone SC .20 .50
365 Shareef Abdur-Rahim SC .12 .30
366 Keith Van Horn SC .12 .30
367 Tim Duncan SC .30 .75
368 Gary Payton SC .15 .40
369 Stephon Marbury SC .12 .30
370 Antonio McDyess SC .12 .30
371 Grant Hill SC .20 .50
372 Kevin Garnett SC .30 .75
373 Shawn Kemp SC .15 .40
374 Kobe Bryant SC .75 2.00
375 Michael Finley SC .15 .40
376 Vince Carter SC .30 .75
377 Checklist .10 .25
378 Checklist .10 .25
379 Checklist .10 .25
380 Checklist .10 .25
431 Elton Brand RC .50 1.25
432 Steve Francis RC .50 1.25
433 Baron Davis RC .60 1.50
434 Lamar Odom RC .60 1.50
435 Wally Szczerbiak RC .40 1.00
436 Richard Hamilton RC .50 1.25
437 Andre Miller RC .50 1.25
438 Shawn Marion RC .50 1.25
439 Jason Terry RC .50 1.25
440 Corey Maggette RC .40 1.00
NNO Michael Jordan Jsy Entry .75 2.00

2000-01 Upper Deck Victory

Released in October 2000, this 330-card set is the lower-end Upper Deck brand, targeted at kids. The set contained 231 regular player cards, 20 rookies, 29 leader cards and 50 FLY2K cards, featuring Kobe Bryant and Kevin Garnett.

COMPLETE SET (330) 30.00 60.00
1 Dikembe Mutombo .15 .40
2 Jim Jackson .10 .25
3 Jason Terry .15 .40
4 Roshown McLeod .10 .25
5 Alan Henderson .10 .25
6 Bimbo Coles .10 .25
7 Dion Glover .10 .25
8 Lorenzen Wright .10 .25
9 Paul Pierce .20 .50
10 Kenny Anderson .12 .30
11 Antoine Walker .15 .40
12 Adrian Griffin .10 .25
13 Vitaly Potapenko .10 .25
14 Dana Barros .10 .25
15 Eric Williams .10 .25
16 Calbert Cheaney .10 .25
17 Derrick Coleman .10 .25
18 Eddie Jones .15 .40
19 Anthony Mason .10 .25
20 Elden Campbell .10 .25
21 Eddie Robinson .10 .25
22 David Wesley .10 .25
23 Baron Davis .15 .40
24 Ricky Davis .12 .30
25 Elton Brand .15 .40
26 Ron Artest .12 .30
27 Chris Carr .10 .25
28 Fred Hoiberg .10 .25
29 Hersey Hawkins .10 .25
30 Dickey Simpkins .10 .25
31 Corey Benjamin .10 .25
32 Matt Maloney .10 .25
33 Shawn Kemp .15 .40
34 Lamond Murray .10 .25
35 Wesley Person .10 .25
36 Andre Miller .12 .30
37 Bob Sura .10 .25
38 Andrew DeClercq .10 .25
39 Brevin Knight .10 .25
40 Earl Boykins RC .75 2.00
41 Michael Finley .15 .40
42 Dirk Nowitzki .25 .60
43 Cedric Ceballos .10 .25
44 Robert Pack .10 .25
45 Erick Strickland .10 .25
46 Sean Rooks .10 .25
47 Shawn Bradley .10 .25
48 Steve Nash .25 .60
49 Antonio McDyess .12 .30
50 Nick Van Exel .12 .30
51 Keon Clark .10 .25
52 Raef LaFrentz .10 .25
53 James Posey .10 .25
54 Chris Gatling .10 .25
55 George McCloud .10 .25
56 Bryant Stith .10 .25
57 Jerry Stackhouse .12 .30
58 Lindsey Hunter .10 .25
59 Christian Laettner .10 .25
60 Jerome Williams .10 .25
61 Michael Curry .10 .25
62 Loy Vaught .10 .25
63 Eric Montross .10 .25
64 Grant Hill .20 .50
65 Antawn Jamison .15 .40
66 Chris Mills .10 .25
67 Vonteego Cummings .10 .25
68 Larry Hughes .12 .30
69 Donyell Marshall .10 .25
70 Mookie Blaylock .12 .30
71 Erick Dampier .10 .25
72 Jason Caffey .10 .25
73 Steve Francis .15 .40
74 Shandon Anderson .10 .25
75 Hakeem Olajuwon .20 .50
76 Walt Williams .10 .25
77 Kenny Thomas .10 .25
78 Carlos Rogers .10 .25
79 Bryce Drew .10 .25
80 Kelvin Cato .10 .25
81 Reggie Miller .15 .40
82 Austin Croshere .10 .25
83 Rik Smits .10 .25
84 Jalen Rose .12 .30
85 Dale Davis .10 .25
86 Jonathan Bender .10 .25
87 Travis Best .10 .25
88 Chris Mullin .15 .40
89 Lamar Odom .15 .40
90 Tyrone Nesby .15 .40
91 Michael Olowokandi .12 .30
92 Eric Piatkowski .12 .30
93 Jeff McInnis .10 .25
94 Brian Skinner .10 .25
95 Pete Chilcutt .10 .25
96 Eric Murdock .10 .25
97 Shaquille O'Neal .40 1.00
98 Kobe Bryant .75 2.00
99 Ron Harper .12 .30
100 Robert Horry .12 .30
101 Rick Fox .12 .30
102 Derek Fisher .15 .40
103 Tyronn Lue .12 .30
104 Devean George .12 .30
105 Alonzo Mourning .20 .50
106 Jamal Mashburn .12 .30
107 Anthony Carter .10 .25
108 P.J. Brown .10 .25
109 Clarence Weatherspoon .10 .25
110 Otis Thorpe .10 .25
111 Voshon Lenard .10 .25
112 Tim Hardaway .15 .40
113 Ray Allen .15 .40
114 Glenn Robinson .12 .30
115 Sam Cassell .12 .30
116 Robert Traylor .10 .25
117 Ervin Johnson .10 .25
118 Scott Williams .10 .25
119 Tim Thomas .10 .25
120 Vinny Del Negro .10 .25
121 Kevin Garnett .30 .75
122 Wally Szczerbiak .12 .30
123 Terrell Brandon .10 .25
124 Dean Garrett .10 .25
125 William Avery .10 .25
126 Sam Mitchell .10 .25
127 Radoslav Nesterovic .10 .25
128 Anthony Peeler .10 .25
129 Stephon Marbury .12 .30
130 Keith Van Horn .12 .30
131 Kerry Kittles .10 .25
132 Lucious Harris .10 .25
133 Evan Eschmeyer .10 .25
134 Jamie Feick .10 .25
135 Jim McIlvaine .10 .25
136 Kendall Gill .10 .25
137 Allan Houston .12 .30
138 Marcus Camby .12 .30
139 Latrell Sprewell .15 .40
140 Patrick Ewing .20 .50
141 Larry Johnson .15 .40
142 Charlie Ward .10 .25
143 Chris Childs .10 .25
144 John Wallace .10 .25
145 Darrell Armstrong .10 .25
146 Corey Maggette .12 .30
147 Pat Garrity .10 .25
148 John Amaechi .10 .25
149 Matt Harpring .12 .30
150 Michael Doleac .10 .25
151 Ron Mercer .10 .25
152 Chucky Atkins .10 .25
153 Allen Iverson .30 .75
154 Matt Geiger .10 .25
155 Eric Snow .10 .25
156 Tyrone Hill .10 .25
157 Theo Ratliff .10 .25
158 George Lynch .10 .25
159 Kevin Ollie .10 .25
160 Toni Kukoc .10 .25
161 Jason Kidd .25 .60
162 Anfernee Hardaway .25 .60
163 Rodney Rogers .10 .25
164 Shawn Marion .15 .40
165 Clifford Robinson .10 .25
166 Tom Gugliotta .10 .25
167 Luc Longley .10 .25
168 Randy Livingston .10 .25
169 Scottie Pippen .25 .60
170 Steve Smith .12 .30
171 Damon Stoudamire .12 .30
172 Bonzi Wells .10 .25
173 Jermaine O'Neal .15 .40
174 Arvydas Sabonis .12 .30
175 Rasheed Wallace .15 .40
176 Detlef Schrempf .12 .30
177 Jason Williams .12 .30
178 Chris Webber .15 .40
179 Peja Stojakovic .15 .40
180 Vlade Divac .12 .30
181 Lawrence Funderburke .10 .25
182 Tony Delk .10 .25
183 Jon Barry .10 .25
184 Tim Duncan .30 .75
185 Sean Elliott .12 .30
186 Terry Porter .10 .25
187 David Robinson .25 .60
188 Samaki Walker .10 .25
189 Malik Rose .10 .25
190 Jaren Jackson .10 .25
191 Steve Kerr .10 .25
192 Gary Payton .15 .40
193 Brent Barry .10 .25
194 Vin Baker .12 .30
195 Horace Grant .12 .30
196 Ruben Patterson .10 .25
197 Vernon Maxwell .10 .25
198 Shammond Williams .10 .25
199 Rashard Lewis .15 .40
200 Tracy McGrady .25 .60
201 Charles Oakley .12 .30
202 Doug Christie .10 .25
203 Antonio Davis .10 .25
204 Vince Carter .30 .75
205 Kevin Willis .10 .25
206 Dell Curry .10 .25
207 Dee Brown .10 .25
208 Karl Malone .20 .50
209 John Stockton .20 .50
210 Bryon Russell .10 .25
211 Olden Polynice .10 .25
212 Jacque Vaughn .10 .25
213 Greg Ostertag .10 .25
214 Quincy Lewis .10 .25
215 Armon Gilliam .10 .25
216 Shareef Abdur-Rahim .12 .30
217 Michael Dickerson .10 .25
218 Mike Bibby .15 .40
219 Bryant Reeves .10 .25
220 Othella Harrington .10 .25
221 Grant Long .10 .25
222 Felipe Lopez .10 .25
223 Obinna Ekezie .10 .25
224 Mitch Richmond .12 .30
225 Richard Hamilton .12 .30
226 Tracy Murray .10 .25
227 Jahidi White .10 .25
228 Aaron Williams .10 .25
229 Juwan Howard .12 .30
230 Rod Strickland .10 .25
231 Isaac Austin .10 .25
232 Dikembe Mutombo VL .07 .20
233 Antoine Walker VL .05 .15
234 Derrick Coleman VL .05 .15
235 Elton Brand VL .07 .20
236 Shawn Kemp VL .05 .15
237 Michael Finley VL .07 .20
238 Antonio McDyess VL .05 .15
239 Grant Hill VL .07 .20
240 Antawn Jamison VL .07 .20
241 Steve Francis VL .07 .20
242 Jalen Rose VL .05 .15
243 Lamar Odom VL .07 .20
244 Shaquille O'Neal VL .20 .50
245 Alonzo Mourning VL .07 .20
246 Ray Allen VL .07 .20
247 Kevin Garnett VL .15 .40
248 Stephon Marbury VL .05 .15
249 Allan Houston VL .05 .15
250 Darrell Armstrong VL .05 .15
251 Allen Iverson VL .15 .40
252 Jason Kidd VL .12 .30
253 Rasheed Wallace VL .07 .20
254 Chris Webber VL .07 .20
255 Tim Duncan VL .15 .40
256 Gary Payton VL .07 .20
257 Vince Carter VL .15 .40
258 Karl Malone VL .07 .20
259 Shareef Abdur-Rahim VL .05 .15
260 Mitch Richmond VL .05 .15
261 Kenyon Martin RC .60 1.50
262 Marcus Fizer RC .25 .60
263 Chris Mihm RC .25 .60
264 Stromile Swift RC .25 .60
265 Keyon Dooling RC .25 .60
266 Morris Peterson RC .25 .60
267 Quentin Richardson RC .40 1.00
268 Courtney Alexander RC .25 .60
269 Desmond Mason RC .30 .75
270 Mateen Cleaves RC .25 .60
271 Erick Barkley RC .25 .60
272 A.J. Guyton RC .25 .60
273 Darius Miles RC .50 1.25
274 DerMarr Johnson RC .25 .60
275 Joel Przybilla RC .25 .60
276 Hanno Mottola RC .25 .60
277 Mike Miller RC .50 1.25
278 Donnell Harvey RC .25 .60
279 Speedy Claxton RC .25 .60
280 Khalid El-Amin RC .25 .60

2003-04 Upper Deck Victory

Released in August 2003, Victory boasts a 230-card set divided up into several different subsets as follows: cards 1-100 feature veteran players and have black borders and full-color action photos, cards 101-130 are Rookie Orientation rookie cards with player photos set on a gold foil background and inserted at the rate of one in two. Cards 131, 132 and 133 were not issued upon release. Cards 134-161 showcase NBA All-Stars on a green background and are inserted at the rate of one in eight. Cards 162-181 feature clutch shooters on a bronze foil background and are inserted at the rate of one in ten. Cards 182-201 are point of difference cards and have a blue foil background are inserted at the rate of one in ten. Cards 202-211 are AKA cards on green foil with the player's nickname and inserted at the rate of one in 20. Cards 212-226 feature Monster Jams from players and are inserted at the rate of one in 35. Cards 227-233 feature Michael Jordan and higlight his career and are inserted at the rate of one in 35. Victory was packaged in 36-pack boxes where packs contained six cards and carried a suggested retail price of $0.99. A Michael Jordan Promotional card was also issued and is card #300. It is not included in the set price and listed at the end.

COMP.SET w/o SP's (100) 6.00 15.00
1 Shareef Abdur-Rahim .12 .30
2 Jason Terry .12 .30
3 Glenn Robinson .12 .30
4 Paul Pierce .20 .50
5 Antoine Walker .15 .40
6 J.R.Bremer .10 .25
7 Vin Baker .10 .25
8 Jalen Rose .12 .30
9 Tyson Chandler .12 .30
10 Eddy Curry .12 .30
11 Jay Williams .10 .25
12 DaJuan Wagner .10 .25
13 Ricky Davis .12 .30
14 Zydrunas Ilgauskas .12 .30
15 Darius Miles .10 .25
16 Dirk Nowitzki .25 .60
17A Michael Finley .15 .40
17B Jermaine O'Neal .15 .40
18 Steve Nash .20 .50
19 Nick Van Exel .12 .30
20 Rodney White .10 .25
21 Juwan Howard .12 .30
22 Marcus Camby .12 .30
23 Nene Hilario .12 .30
24 Richard Hamilton .12 .30
25 Ben Wallace .15 .40
26 Cliff Robinson .12 .30
27 Antawn Jamison .15 .40
28 Jason Richardson .15 .40
29 Gilbert Arenas .15 .40
30 Mike Dunleavy .12 .30
31 Steve Francis .15 .40
32 Eddie Griffin .10 .25
33 Cuttino Mobley .12 .30
34 Yao Ming .30 .75
35 Reggie Miller .15 .40
36 Jamaal Tinsley .10 .25
38 Elton Brand .15 .40
39 Andre Miller .12 .30
40 Lamar Odom .15 .40
41 Kobe Bryant .75 2.00
42 Shaquille O'Neal .40 1.00
43 Derek Fisher .12 .30
44 Pau Gasol .15 .40
45 Shane Battier .12 .30
46 Mike Miller .15 .40
47 Eddie Jones .12 .30
48 Alonzo Mourning .20 .50
49 Caron Butler .15 .40
50 Gary Payton .15 .40
51 Desmond Mason .12 .30
52 Sam Cassell .12 .30
53 Toni Kukoc .15 .40
54 Kevin Garnett .30 .75
55 Wally Szczerbiak .12 .30
56 Joe Smith .12 .30
57 Jason Kidd .25 .60
58 Richard Jefferson .15 .40
59 Kenyon Martin .15 .40
60 Baron Davis .15 .40
61 Jamal Mashburn .12 .30
62 Jamaal Magloire .10 .25
63 Allan Houston .12 .30
64 Antonio McDyess .12 .30
65 Latrell Sprewell .12 .30
66 Tracy McGrady .20 .50
67 Grant Hill .20 .50
68 Drew Gooden .12 .30
69 Gordan Giricek .10 .25
70 Allen Iverson .25 .60
71 Keth Van Horn .12 .30
72 Aaron McKie .10 .25
73 Stephon Marbury .12 .30
74 Shawn Marion .15 .40
75 Anfernee Hardaway .25 .60
76 Amare Stoudemire .25 .60
77 Rasheed Wallace .15 .40
78 Derek Anderson .10 .25
79 Scottie Pippen .25 .60
80 Chris Webber .15 .40
81 Mike Bibby .15 .40
82 Peja Stojakovic .15 .40
83 Hedo Turkoglu .15 .40
84 Tim Duncan .25 .60
85 David Robinson .25 .60
86 Tony Parker .15 .40
87 Manu Ginobili .20 .50
88 Ray Allen .15 .40
89 Rashard Lewis .15 .40
90 Reggie Evans .10 .25
91 Alvin Williams .10 .25
92 Vince Carter .25 .60
93 Morris Peterson .10 .25
94 Antonio Davis .10 .25
95 Karl Malone .20 .50
96 John Stockton .20 .50
97 Andrei Kirilenko .15 .40
98 Jerry Stackhouse .12 .30
99 Kwame Brown .10 .25
100 Michael Jordan 1.25 3.00
101 Lebron James SP RC 6.00 15.00
102 Darko Milicic RC .60 1.50
103 Carmelo Anthony RC 1.50 4.00
104 Chris Bosh RC 1.25 3.00
105 Dwyane Wade RC 2.50 6.00
106 Chris Kaman RC .75 2.00
107 Kirk Hinrich RC .75 2.00
108 T.J. Ford RC .75 2.00
109 Mike Sweetney RC .60 1.50
110 Jarvis Hayes RC .60 1.50
111 Mickael Pietrus RC .60 1.50
112 Nick Collison RC .60 1.50
113 Marcus Banks RC .60 1.50
114 Luke Ridnour RC .75 2.00
115 Reece Gaines RC .60 1.50
116 Troy Bell RC .60 1.50
117 Zarko Cabarkapa RC .60 1.50
118 David West RC .75 2.00
119 Aleksandar Pavlovic RC .60 1.50
120 Dahntay Jones RC .60 1.50
121 Boris Diaw RC .75 2.00
122 Zoran Planinic RC .60 1.50
123 Travis Outlaw RC .75 2.00
124 Brian Cook RC .60 1.50
125 Carlos Delfino RC .75 2.00
126 Ndudi Ebi RC .60 1.50
127 Kendrick Perkins RC 1.00 2.50
128 Leandro Barbosa RC .75 2.00
129 Josh Howard RC .60 1.50
130 Luke Walton RC .60 1.50
134 Michael Jordan AS 5.00 12.00
135 Kobe Bryant AS 3.00 8.00
136 Kevin Garnett AS 1.25 3.00
137 Yao Ming AS 1.25 3.00
138 Vince Carter AS 1.00 2.50
139 Dirk Nowitizki AS 1.00 2.50
140 Antoine Walker AS .60 1.50
141 Chris Webber AS .60 1.50
142 Ben Wallace AS .60 1.50
143 Tracy McGrady AS .75 2.00
144 Jason Kidd AS 1.00 2.50
145 Steve Francis AS .60 1.50
146 Gary Payton AS .60 1.50
147 Peja Stojakovic AS .60 1.50
148 Brad Miller AS .60 1.50
149 Shawn Marion AS .60 1.50
150 Zydrunas Ilgauskas AS .50 1.25
151 Stephon Marbury AS .50 1.25
152 Jermaine O'Neal AS .60 1.50
153 Desmond Mason AS .50 1.25
154 Jeson Richardson AS .60 1.50
155 Tony Parker AS .60 1.50
156 Tim Duncan AS 1.00 2.50
157 Jamal Mashburn AS .50 1.25
158 Allen Iverson AS 1.00 2.50
159 Shaquille O'Neal AS 1.50 4.00
160 Paul Pierce AS .75 2.00
161 Steve Nash AS .75 2.00
162 Michael Jordan CS 5.00 12.00
163 Mike Bibby CS .60 1.50
164 Jay Williams CS .40 1.00
165 Richard Hamilton CS .50 1.25
166 Jerry Stackhouse CS .50 1.25
167 Peja Stojakovic CS .60 1.50
168 Reggie Miller CS .60 1.50
169 Robert Horry CS .50 1.25
170 Tim Duncan CS 1.00 2.50
171 Jalen Rose CS .50 1.25
172 Jason Richardson CS .60 1.50
173 Allen Iverson CS 1.00 2.50
174 Tracy McGrady CS .75 2.00
175 Paul Pierce CS .75 2.00
176 Dirk Nowitzki CS 1.00 2.50
177 Baron Davis CS .60 1.50
178 Latrell Sprewell CS .50 1.25
179 John Stockton CS .75 2.00
180 Ray Allen CS .60 1.50
181 Kobe Bryant CS 3.00 8.00
182 Mike Bibby POD .60 1.50
183 Earl Boykins POD .40 1.00
184 John Stockton POD .75 2.00
185 Alvin Williams POD .40 1.00
186 Darrell Armstrong POD .40 1.00
187 Tony Parker POD .60 1.50
188 Gary Payton POD .60 1.50
189 Jalen Rose POD .50 1.25
190 Jason Williams POD .50 1.25
191 Derek Fisher POD .50 1.25
192 Steve Nash POD .75 2.00
193 Jamaal Tinsley POD .40 1.00
194 Andre Miller POD .50 1.25
195 Baron Davis POD .60 1.50
196 Steve Francis POD .60 1.50
197 DaJuan Wagner POD .40 1.00
198 Stephon Marbury POD .50 1.25
199 Jason Kidd POD 1.00 2.50
200 Chauncey Billups POD .60 1.50
201 Jay Williams POD .40 1.00
202 Allen Iverson AKA 1.50 4.00
203 Steve Francis AKA 1.00 2.50
204 Kenyon Martin AKA 1.00 2.50
205 Vince Carter AKA 1.50 4.00
206 Lebron James AKA 10.00 25.00
207 Julius Erving AKA 2.00 5.00
208 Tracy McGrady AKA 1.25 3.00
209 Jason Richardson AKA 1.00 2.50
210 Earvin Johnson AKA 3.00 8.00
211 Michael Jordan AKA 8.00 20.00
212 Michael Jordan MJ 8.00 20.00
213 Kobe Bryant MJ 5.00 12.00
214 Richard Jefferson MJ 1.00 2.50
215 Desmond Mason MJ .75 2.00
216 Vince Carter MJ 1.50 4.00
217 Amare Stoudemire MJ 1.50 4.00
218 Yao Ming MJ 2.00 5.00
219 Elton Brand MJ 1.00 2.50
220 Kevin Garnett MJ 2.00 5.00
221 Shaquille O'Neal MJ 2.50 6.00
222 Lebron James HR 10.00 25.00
223 Kobe Bryant HR 5.00 12.00
224 Richard Jefferson HR 1.00 2.50
225 Yao Ming HR 2.00 5.00
226 Amare Stoudemire HR 1.50 4.00
227 Michael Jordan HR 6.00 15.00
228 Michael Jordan FL 6.00 15.00
229 Michael Jordan FL 6.00 15.00
230 Michael Jordan FL 6.00 15.00
231 Michael Jordan FL 6.00 15.00
232 Michael Jordan FL 6.00 15.00
233 Michael Jordan FL 6.00 15.00
300 Michael Jordan Promotional Card 4.00 10.00

2003-04 Upper Deck Victory Parallel

Randomly inserted, this 230-card set parallels the base set enhanced with sequential numbering. Cards 1-100 are numbered one of one's and cards 101-130 are sequentially numbered to 25. 134-230 cards are sequentially numbered to 100.
*101-133 RCs: 5X TO 12X BASE HI
*134-201 SINGLES: 2.5X TO 6X BASE HI
*202-226 SINGLES: 1.5X TO 4X BASE HI
COMMON JORDAN (227-233) 30.00 80.00
101 Lebron James 100.00 250.00

1993-94 Upper Deck Walmart Jumbos

These jumbo size (3 1/2" by 5") cards were available in blister packs at Walmart. Each pack consisted of a retail foil pack, a team set (ten team sets in all were offered), and two jumbo cards, one of which was a player from the team set. The advertising insert indicates that only one jumbo card was included per repack, but a gold foil sticker on the blister packs states that each repack "contains 2 jumbo cards." The jumbo cards are oversized versions of the regular cards, and both regular series cards and subset cards are featured. The cards are numbered on the back as they are in the regular series.

COMPLETE SET (28) 30.00 75.00
32 Shawn Kemp 1.00 2.50
48 Ron Harper .30 .75
64 Mitch Richmond .75 2.00
154 Glen Rice .75 2.00
195 Reggie Miller .75 2.00
243 Kenny Anderson .30 .75
361 Isaiah Rider 1.00 2.50
382 Anfernee Hardaway 4.00 10.00
391 LaPhonso Ellis .40 1.00
483 Chris Webber 5.00 12.00
485 Shawn Bradley .75 2.00
486 Jamal Mashburn 2.00 5.00
487 Calbert Cheaney .60 1.50
490 Vin Baker 2.50 6.00
492 Lindsey Hunter .60 1.50
497 Nick Van Exel 2.50 6.00
AN5 Mark Price .30 .75
AN8 Patrick Ewing .75 2.00
FT2 Charles Barkley 1.25 3.00
FT4 Dee Brown .20 .50
FT7 Clyde Drexler .75 2.00
FT13 Karl Malone 2.00 5.00
FT15 Alonzo Mourning .60 1.50
LT3 Shaquille O'Neal 3.00 8.00
TM1 Dominique Wilkins .30 .75
TM4 Scottie Pippen 2.50 6.00
TM10 Hakeem Olajuwon 1.25 3.00
TM24 David Robinson 1.25 3.00

2010 Upper Deck World of Sports

COMPLETE SET (375) 100.00 150.00
COMP.SET w/o SPs (300) 30.00 60.00
1 LeBron James 1.50 4.00
2 Yao Ming .25 .60
3 Brandon Roy .15 .40
4 Russell Westbrook .25 .60
5 Derrick Rose .40 1.00
6 Bill Russell .25 .60
7 Bobby Hurley .15 .40
8 Christian Laettner .15 .40
9 Danny Ferry .15 .40
10 Bill Walton .15 .40
11 Jerry West .25 .60
12 Rick Barry .15 .40
13 Steve Alford .15 .40
14 Calbert Cheaney .15 .40
15 Larry Johnson .15 .40
16 John Havlicek .25 .60
17 Tim Hardaway .15 .40
18 Dennis Rodman .25 .60
19 Bill Laimbeer .15 .40
20 Mateen Cleaves .15 .40
21 Magic Johnson .25 .60
22 Larry Bird .40 1.00
23 Michael Jordan 2.00 5.00
24 Craig Brackins .15 .40
25 Gani Lawal .15 .40
26 James Anderson .15 .40
27 Sherron Collins .15 .40
28 Stanley Robinson .15 .40
29 Trevor Booker .15 .40
30 Devin Ebanks .15 .40
31 Aubrey Coleman .15 .40
32 Ekpe Udoh .25 .60
33 Solomon Alabi .15 .40
34 Jarvis Varnado .15 .40
35 Jerome Jordan .15 .40
36 Luke Babbitt .15 .40
37 Terrico White .15 .40
38 DeMarcus Cousins .75 2.00
39 Hassan Whiteside .15 .40
40 Da'Sean Butler .15 .40
41 Derrick Favors .40 1.00
42 Damion James .15 .40
43 Gordon Hayward .25 .60
44 Paul George .25 .60
45 Dexter Pittman .15 .40
46 Luke Harangody .15 .40
47 Jordan Crawford .15 .40
48 Manny Harris .25 .60
49 Quincy Pondexter .15 .40
50 Scottie Reynolds .15 .40
51 Elliot Williams .15 .40
52 Brian Zoubek .15 .40
53 Xavier Henry .25 .60
54 A.J. Ogilvy .15 .40
55 Armon Johnson .15 .40
56 Cole Aldrich .25 .60
57 Deon Thompson .15 .40
58 Donald Williams .15 .40
59 Sam Cassell .15 .40
60 Toni Kukoc .15 .40
331 Xavier Henry SP 2.00 5.00
332 DeMarcus Cousins SP 1.00 2.50
333 Derrick Favors SP 1.00 2.50
334 Damion James SP 1.00 2.50
335 Luke Harangody SP 1.00 2.50
336 LeBron James SP 2.00 5.00
337 Michael Jordan SP 3.00 8.00
338 Larry Bird SP 1.50 4.00
339 Magic Johnson SP 1.00 2.50
340 Dennis Rodman SP 1.00 2.50
345 Tubby Smith SP 1.00 2.50
346 Gary Williams SP 1.00 2.50
347 Matt Painter SP 1.00 2.50
348 Jamie Dixon SP 1.00 2.50
349 Mark Few SP 1.00 2.50
350 Steve Alford SP 1.00 2.50
351 Bruce Pearl SP 1.00 2.50
352 Mike Montgomery SP 1.00 2.50
353 Steve Fisher SP 1.00 2.50
354 Bo Ryan SP 1.00 2.50
355 Jeff Capel III SP 1.00 2.50
356 Bobby Cremins SP 1.00 2.50
357 Rick Majerus SP 1.00 2.50
358 Sean Miller SP 1.00 2.50
359 Jim Boeheim SP 1.00 2.50
360 Dana Altman SP 1.00 2.50
361 Tom Crean SP 1.00 2.50
362 Roy Williams SP 1.00 2.50
363 Jim Calhoun SP 1.00 2.50
364 Tom Izzo SP 1.00 2.50
365 Ben Howland SP 1.00 2.50
366 Billy Donovan SP 1.00 2.50
367 Bill Self SP 1.00 2.50
368 Thad Matta SP 1.00 2.50
369 Bob Huggins SP 1.00 2.50
370 John Beilein SP 1.00 2.50
371 Homer Drew SP 1.00 2.50
372 Jay Wright SP 1.00 2.50
373 Bruce Weber SP 1.00 2.50
374 Mike Brey SP 1.00 2.50
375 Seth Greenberg SP 1.00 2.50

2010 Upper Deck World of Sports All-Sport Apparel Memorabilia

STATED ODDS ONE PER BOX
ASA1 LeBron James 8.00 20.00
ASA2 Michael Jordan 25.00 50.00
ASA3 Yao Ming 5.00 12.00
ASA4 Brandon Roy 4.00 10.00
ASA5 Russell Westbrook 5.00 12.00
ASA6 Derrick Rose 6.00 15.00
ASA8 Hakeem Olajuwon 6.00 15.00
ASA9 Julius Erving 5.00 12.00
ASA10 Magic Johnson 6.00 15.00
ASA11 Alonzo Mourning 5.00 12.00
ASA12 Bill Walton 4.00 10.00
ASA13 David Robinson 5.00 12.00
ASA14 Xavier Henry 4.00 10.00

2010 Upper Deck World of Sports All-Sport Apparel Memorabilia Autographs

OVERALL AUTO ODDS TWO PER BOX
STATED PRINT RUN 25 SER.#'d SETS
ASA1 LeBron James 125.00 250.00
ASA2 Michael Jordan 300.00 600.00
ASA3 Yao Ming 20.00 50.00
ASA4 Brandon Roy 12.00 30.00
ASA5 Russell Westbrook 40.00 80.00
ASA6 Derrick Rose 75.00 150.00
ASA7 Clyde Drexler 20.00 50.00
ASA8 Hakeem Olajuwon 25.00 60.00
ASA9 Julius Erving 40.00 80.00
ASA11 Alonzo Mourning 25.00 60.00
ASA13 David Robinson 40.00 100.00
ASA15 Greg Monroe 12.00 30.00

2010 Upper Deck World of Sports Autographs

OVERALL AUTO ODDS TWO PER BOX
1 LeBron James 125.00 200.00
2 Yao Ming 12.00 30.00
3 Brandon Roy 6.00 15.00
4 Russell Westbrook 12.00 30.00
5 Derrick Rose 40.00 100.00
6 Bill Russell 50.00 100.00
7 Bobby Hurley 5.00 12.00
9 Danny Ferry 5.00 12.00
10 Bill Walton 15.00 30.00
11 Jerry West 30.00 60.00
12 Rick Barry 10.00 25.00
13 Steve Alford 6.00 15.00
14 Calbert Cheaney 5.00 12.00
17 Tim Hardaway 6.00 15.00
18 Dennis Rodman 15.00 40.00
19 Bill Laimbeer 5.00 12.00
20 Mateen Cleaves 5.00 12.00
22 Larry Bird 40.00 80.00
23 Michael Jordan 250.00 400.00
24 Craig Brackins 5.00 12.00
26 James Anderson 6.00 15.00
27 Sherron Collins 10.00 25.00
28 Stanley Robinson 5.00 12.00
29 Trevor Booker 5.00 12.00
32 Ekpe Udoh 5.00 12.00
33 Solomon Alabi 5.00 12.00
35 Jerome Jordan 5.00 12.00
36 Luke Babbitt 5.00 12.00
38 DeMarcus Cousins 20.00 50.00
39 Hassan Whiteside 5.00 12.00
40 Da'Sean Butler 6.00 15.00
41 Derrick Favors 10.00 25.00
43 Gordon Hayward 10.00 25.00
44 Paul George 6.00 15.00
45 Dexter Pittman 5.00 12.00
47 Jordan Crawford 5.00 12.00
49 Quincy Pondexter 10.00 25.00
50 Scottie Reynolds 5.00 12.00
51 Elliot Williams 5.00 12.00
52 Brian Zoubek 6.00 15.00
53 Xavier Henry 6.00 15.00
54 A.J. Ogilvy 5.00 12.00
55 Armon Johnson 5.00 12.00
56 Cole Aldrich 10.00 25.00
58 Donald Williams 10.00 25.00
59 Sam Cassell 6.00 15.00
331 Xavier Henry 5.00 12.00
332 DeMarcus Cousins 15.00 40.00
333 Derrick Favors 10.00 25.00
336 LeBron James 125.00 175.00
337 Michael Jordan 250.00 400.00
338 Larry Bird 40.00 80.00
340 Dennis Rodman 15.00 40.00
345 Tubby Smith 10.00 25.00
346 Gary Williams 30.00 60.00
347 Matt Painter 10.00 25.00
348 Jamie Dixon 15.00 30.00
349 Mark Few 10.00 25.00
350 Steve Alford 6.00 15.00
351 Bruce Pearl 10.00 25.00
352 Mike Montgomery 6.00 15.00
354 Bo Ryan 15.00 40.00
355 Jeff Capel III 6.00 15.00
356 Bobby Cremins 10.00 25.00
358 Sean Miller 6.00 15.00
359 Jim Boeheim 10.00 25.00
360 Dana Altman 6.00 15.00
361 Tom Crean 10.00 25.00
362 Roy Williams 25.00 50.00
363 Jim Calhoun 15.00 40.00
364 Tom Izzo 15.00 40.00
365 Ben Howland 6.00 15.00
366 Billy Donovan 10.00 25.00
367 Bill Self 20.00 40.00
368 Thad Matta 25.00 50.00
369 Bob Huggins 20.00 40.00
370 John Beilein 10.00 25.00
372 Jay Wright 15.00 40.00
373 Bruce Weber 6.00 15.00
374 Mike Brey 20.00 40.00
375 Seth Greenberg 6.00 15.00

2010 Upper Deck World of Sports Clear Competitors

STATED ODDS ONE PER BOX
STATED PRINT RUN 550 SER.#'d SETS
CC1 LeBron James 6.00 15.00
CC2 Yao Ming 3.00 8.00
CC3 Magic Johnson 4.00 10.00
CC4 Larry Bird 5.00 12.00
CC5 Derrick Rose 5.00 12.00
CC6 DeMarcus Cousins 5.00 12.00
CC7 Derrick Favors 3.00 8.00
CC8 Xavier Henry 4.00 10.00
CC9 Anfernee Hardaway 4.00 10.00
CC10 Tom Izzo 3.00 8.00
CC11 Roy Williams 5.00 12.00
CC12 Jim Boeheim 3.00 8.00

2011 Upper Deck World of Sports

COMPLETE SET (400) 75.00 150.00
COMP.SET w/o SPs (300) 25.00 60.00
33 LeBron James 1.25 3.00
34 DeMarcus Cousins .40 1.00
35 Michael Jordan 2.00 5.00
36 Scottie Reynolds .15 .40
37 Quincy Pondexter .15 .40
38 Rick Fox .15 .40
39 Cole Aldrich .25 .60
40 Al-Farouq Aminu .15 .40
41 Stanley Robinson .15 .40
42 Sherron Collins .25 .60
43 Jerome Jordan .15 .40
44 Jarvis Varnado .15 .40
45 James Anderson .15 .40
46 Gani Lawal .15 .40
47 Ekpe Udoh .15 .40
48 Devin Ebanks .15 .40
49 Craig Brackins .15 .40
50 Larry Johnson .15 .40
51 Brook Lopez .15 .40
52 Eric Bledsoe .15 .40
53 Mark A. Jackson .15 .40
54 Steve Nash .25 .60
55 Manny Harris .15 .40
56 John Starks .15 .40
57 John Stockton .25 .60
58 Bill Walton .15 .40
59 Anfernee Hardaway .15 .40
60 Tim Hardaway .15 .40
61 Jimmer Fredette .15 .40
62 Toni Kukoc .25 .60
63 Candace Parker .15 .40
64 Jackie Stiles .15 .40
65 Steve Alford .15 .40
66 Bobby Cremins .15 .40
67 Bruce Pearl .15 .40
68 Mike Montgomery .15 .40
69 Mike Brey .15 .40
70 Thad Matta .15 .40
71 Bo Ryan .15 .40
72 Steve Fisher .15 .40
73 Bob Huggins .15 .40
74 Jay Wright .15 .40
75 Ben Howland .15 .40
76 Gary Williams .15 .40
77 Mark Few .15 .40
78 Jeff Capel III .15 .40
79 John Beilein .15 .40
80 Jim Calhoun .15 .40
81 Sean Miller .15 .40
82 Dana Altman .15 .40
83 Seth Greenberg .15 .40
84 Homer Drew .15 .40
85 Matt Painter .15 .40
86 Bruce Weber .15 .40
87 Tom Crean .15 .40
88 Rick Majerus .15 .40
311 Chris Paul SP 1.00 2.50
312 Derrick Rose SP 1.50 4.00
313 Alonzo Mourning SP 1.00 2.50
314 Magic Johnson SP 1.00 2.50
315 David Robinson SP 1.00 2.50
316 Walt Frazier SP 1.00 2.50
317 Hakeem Olajuwon SP 1.00 2.50
318 Clyde Drexler SP 1.00 2.50
319 Christian Laettner SP 1.00 2.50
320 Greg Monroe SP 1.00 2.50
321 LeBron James SP 1.50 4.00
322 Michael Jordan SP 2.00 5.00
323 Julius Erving SP 1.25 3.00
324 Tom Izzo SP 1.00 2.50
325 Billy Donovan SP 1.00 2.50
326 Jamie Dixon SP 1.00 2.50
327 Bill Self SP 1.00 2.50
328 Tubby Smith SP 1.00 2.50
329 Jim Boeheim SP 1.00 2.50

2011 Upper Deck World of Sports Athletes of the World Autographs

OVERALL AUTO/MEM ODDS 3 PER BOX
AWKG Kevin Garnett 20.00 40.00
AWYM Yao Ming 12.00 30.00

2011 Upper Deck World of Sports Autographs

33 LeBron James B 100.00 175.00
34 DeMarcus Cousins B 25.00 60.00
35 Michael Jordan B 350.00 500.00
41 Stanley Robinson C 4.00 10.00
43 Jerome Jordan C 4.00 10.00
45 James Anderson A 4.00 10.00
46 Gani Lawal C 4.00 10.00
47 Ekpe Udoh B 4.00 10.00
49 Craig Brackins C 4.00 10.00
50 Larry Johnson B 15.00 40.00
51 Brook Lopez B 5.00 12.00
52 Eric Bledsoe B 15.00 40.00
54 Steve Nash B 25.00 60.00
57 John Stockton A 40.00 100.00
58 Bill Walton A 10.00 25.00
60 Tim Hardaway B 6.00 15.00
61 Jimmer Fredette B 25.00 60.00
62 Toni Kukoc B 12.00 30.00
64 Jackie Stiles C 6.00 15.00
65 Steve Alford C 5.00 12.00
66 Bobby Cremins C 4.00 10.00
67 Bruce Pearl C 4.00 10.00
68 Mike Montgomery (Coach) C 4.00 10.00
69 Mike Brey C 6.00 15.00
70 Thad Matta C 10.00 25.00
71 Bo Ryan C 8.00 20.00
72 Steve Fisher C 5.00 12.00
73 Bob Huggins C 12.00 30.00
74 Jay Wright B 4.00 10.00
76 Gary Williams C 15.00 40.00
77 Mark Few B 6.00 15.00
78 Jeff Capel III C 5.00 12.00
79 John Beilein C 6.00 15.00
80 Jim Calhoun B 8.00 20.00
81 Sean Miller C 4.00 10.00
82 Dana Altman C 4.00 10.00
83 Seth Greenberg C 6.00 15.00
84 Homer Drew C 4.00 10.00
85 Matt Painter C 5.00 12.00
86 Bruce Weber C 4.00 10.00
87 Tom Crean C 10.00 25.00
88 Rick Majerus C 4.00 10.00
312 Derrick Rose A 75.00 150.00
318 Clyde Drexler A 15.00 40.00
321 LeBron James A 100.00 175.00
322 Michael Jordan B 350.00 450.00
324 Tom Izzo A 15.00 40.00
325 Billy Donovan A 12.00 30.00
326 Jamie Dixon B 4.00 10.00
327 Bill Self B 25.00 50.00
328 Tubby Smith B 4.00 10.00

2011 Upper Deck World of Sports Evolution Video Cards

EVO1 Michael Jordan 150.00 250.00
EVO2 Chris Paul 15.00 40.00
EVO3 Alonzo Mourning 50.00 100.00

1988-89 Warriors Smokey

The 1988-89 Smokey Golden State Warriors set contains four 5" by 8" (approximately) cards featuring color action photos. The card backs feature a large fire safety cartoon and minimal player information. The cards are unnumbered and are ordered below alphabetically. The set was sponsored by the California Department of Forestry and Fire Protection and the Bureau of Land Management. The player's name, number, and position are overprinted in the lower right corner of each obverse.

COMPLETE SET (4) 12.00 30.00
1 Winston Garland 2.00 5.00
2 Chris Mullin 10.00 20.00
3 Ralph Sampson 3.00 8.00
4 Larry Smith 2.00 5.00

1971-72 Warriors Team Issue

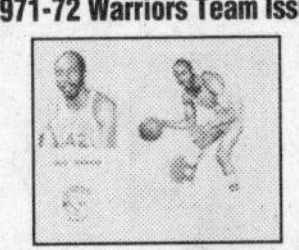

This 1971-72 Golden State Warriors set consists of 13 team-issued photos, each measuring approximately 10" by 8 1/8". The fronts feature one black-and-white posed action player photograph on the right side, and a smaller black-and-white player portrait in the top left corner. The player's name appears under the photo, with the team logo in the lower left. The backs are blank. The photos are unnumbered and checklisted below in alphabetical order. The set's date is based on the fact that Odis Allison and Vic Bartolome only played in 1971-72.

COMPLETE SET (13) 40.00 80.00
1 Odis Allison 1.50 4.00
2 Al Attles 5.00 10.00
3 Jim Barnett 2.00 5.00
4 Vic Bartolome 1.50 4.00
5 Joe Ellis 2.00 5.00
6 Nick Jones 1.50 4.00
7 Clyde Lee 2.00 5.00
8 Jeff Mullins 5.00 10.00
9 Bob Portman 1.50 4.00
10 Cazzie Russell 6.00 12.00
11 Nate Thurmond 10.00 20.00
12 Bill Turner 1.50 4.00
13 Ron(Fritz) Williams 2.00 5.00

1993-94 Warriors Topps/Safeway

Issued in four perforated five-card strips (the fifth card being the coupon card), these 16 standard-size cards were distributed at Safeway stores in the Bay Area. The white-bordered fronts display color action player photos with a team-color-coded inner border three quarters of the way down the left side and curving along the bottom of the picture. The player's name is printed in white script at the lower left with the team name appearing on a team-color-coded bar at the very bottom. The horizontal backs carry a close-up player photo on one side, with complete NBA statistics, biography, and career highlights on a beige panel on the other side. The cards are numbered on the back with a "GS" prefix. Reportedly there were 162 Safeway stores from Northern California and Nevada involved with the promotion which ran from Jan. 19 through Apr. 12. Shoppers were to obtain a coupon from the store's photo department and redeem it at the customer service window for their free cards. In addition, 8,000 four-card strips were handed out at Warrior games (Jan. 26, Feb 19, Mar. 15, and Apr. 14.) to promote the offer. It has been reported that of the 162 Safeway stores, 100 were given 1,000 of each strip; while the remaining stores recieved 785 of each strip.

COMPLETE SET (16) 3.00 8.00
1 Chris Mullin .40 1.00
2 Byron Houston .08 .25
3 Chris Gatling .20 .50
4 Don Nelson CO .20 .50
5 Nate Thurmond LEGEND .40 1.00
6 Chris Webber 1.50 4.00
7 Latrell Sprewell .60 1.50
8 Jeff Grayer .08 .25
9 Al Attles LEGEND .20 .50
10 Tim Hardaway .60 1.50
11 Jud Buechler .08 .25
12 Victor Alexander .08 .25
13 Keith Jennings .08 .25
14 Sarunas Marciulionis .30 .75
15 Billy Owens .20 .50
16 Avery Johnson .30 .75

1994-95 Warriors Topps/Safeway

Produced by Topps, this sets consists of three 5-card perforated strips that measure 12 1/2" by 3 1/2". After perforation, the cards measure the standard size, and the fifth slot on each strip features either a Kellogg's Pop-Tarts Minis coupon or a Safeway film-developing coupon. Most of the cards are identical to their regular issue counterparts; several cards appear to produced just for this set (Jennings and Lanier). Note also that the cards are numbered as one series with "GS" prefixes, and several of the card numbers (as noted below) are misnumbered.

COMPLETE SET (12) 2.50 6.00
GS1 Tim Hardaway .60 1.50
GS2 Victor Alexander .08 .25
GS3 Latrell Sprewell .60 1.50
(Numbered GS13 on back)
GS4 Rod Higgins .08 .25
(Numbered GS16 on back)
GS5 Chris Mullin .40 1.00
GS6 Clifford Rozier .08 .25
GS7 Chris Gatling .20 .50
GS8 Keith Jennings .08 .25
GS9 Rony Seikaly .08 .25
GS10 Carlos Rogers .08 .25
GS11 Ricky Pierce .08 .25
(Numbered 267 on back)
GS12 Bob Lanier CO .40 1.00

1995-96 Warriors Topps/Safeway

Produced by Topps, this set consists of three 5-card perforated strips that measure 12 1/2" by 3 1/2". After perforation, the cards measure the standard size. Each strip contains four player cards and one Kodak or Kellogg's advertising card. Most of the player cards are identical to their corresponding regular-issue 1995-96 Topps cards, except for the card numbering each of which is a ssigned a GS prefix and numbered as a twelve card series. The cards were regionally distributed in California in early 1996 at participating Safeway stores.

COMPLETE SET (15) 2.00 5.00
GS1 Chris Gatling .08 .25
GS2 Donyell Marshall .20 .50
GS3 Tim Hardaway .60 1.50
GS4 Rick Adelman CO .20 .50
GS5 B.J. Armstrong .15 .40
GS6 Jon Barry .15 .40
GS7 Latrell Sprewell .40 1.00
GS8 Joe Smith .75 2.00
GS9 Jerome Kersey .08 .25
GS10 Rony Seikaly .08 .25
GS11 Chris Mullin .40 1.00
GS12 Clifford Rozier .08 .25
NNO Kellogg's Ad Card 2 .08 .25
NNO Kellogg's Ad Card 1 .08 .25
NNO Kodak Ad Card .08 .25

1992 Washington Little Sun

Produced by Little Sun and distributed by Snyder's Bakery of Spokane, Washington, this eight-card multi-sport standard-size set features former and current athletes from the state of Washington. The cards were available for eight weeks beginning Sept. 14. One card per week was inserted into loaves of Snyder's Premium White and Roman Meal bread. During the promotion, a total of 80,000 of each card were distributed. The bakery also made a donation to the Scholarship Fund of the Tacoma Athletic Commission in the names of the athletes included in the set. The sports represented in the set are baseball (1, 6), football (2, 8), basketball (3), bowling (4), skiing (5), and mountain climbing (7).

COMPLETE SET (8) 3.00 8.00
3 Doug Christie .60 1.50

1924 Willard's Chocolates Sports Champions V122

42 Edmonton Grads
Women's Basketball

1996-98 Worldcom Calling Cards

1 Michael Jordan 10 minutes Black Uniform 2.50 6.00
2 Michael Jordan 10 minutes Red Uniform 2.50 6.00
3 Michael Jordan 30 minutes Black Uniform 4.00 10.00
4 Michael Jordan 10 minutes Rayovac 2.50 6.00
5 Michael Jordan 5 minutes Red Uniform 2.00 5.00
6 Michael Jordan 5 minutes Cologne Ad 2.00 5.00
7 Michael Jordan 60 minutes Black Uniform 4.00 10.00
10 Michael Jordan 5 dollars Limited Edition 4.00 10.00

1951 Wheaties

The cards in this six-card set measure approximately 2 1/2" by 3 1/4". Cards of the 1951 Wheaties set are actually the backs of small individual boxes of Wheaties. The cards are waxed and depict three baseball players, one football player, one basketball player, and one golfer. They are occasionally found as complete boxes, which are worth 50 percent more than the prices listed below. The catalog designation for this set is F272-3. The cards are blank-backed and unnumbered; they are numbered below in alphabetical order for convenience.

COMPLETE SET (6) 300.00 600.00
3 George Mikan BK 100.00 200.00

1952 Wheaties

The cards in this 60-card set measure 2" by 2 3/4". The 1952 Wheaties set of orange, blue and white, unnumbered cards was issued in panels of eight or ten cards on the backs of Wheaties cereal boxes. Each player appears in an action pose, designated in the checklist with an "A", and as a portrait, listed in the checklist with a "B". The catalog designation is F272-4. The cards are blank-backed and unnumbered, but have been assigned numbers below using a sport prefix (BB- baseball, BK- basketball, FB- football, G-Golf, OT- other).

COMPLETE SET (60) 600.00 1000.00
BK1A Bob Davies 12.50 20.00
BK1B Bob Davies 12.50 20.00
BK2A George Mikan 75.00 125.00
BK2B George Mikan 75.00 125.00
BK3A Jim Pollard 10.00 25.00
BK3B Jim Pollard 10.00 25.00

2005 WNBA Promo Sheet

Given out to distributors, this six-card promo sheet debuts the new look of the 2005 WNBA set. The sheet contains six cards, three on top and three on bottom and is perforated.

NNO Diana Taurase 4.00 10.00
Swin Case
Sue Bird
Asjha Jones
Nykesha Sales
Svetlana Abrosimova

2005 WNBA

COMPLETE SET (110) 10.00 25.00
1 Seattle Storm TC 1.25 3.00
2 LaToya Thomas .15 .40
3 Crystal Robinson .15 .40
4 Chasity Melvin .15 .40
5 Dawn Staley .40 1.00
6 Svetlana Abrosimova .15 .40
7 Houston Comets TC .60 1.50
8 Wendy Palmer-Daniel .40 1.00
9 Betty Lennox .30 .75
10 Lisa Leslie .75 2.00
11 Margo Dydek .25 .60
12 Vickie Johnson .25 .60
13 Charlotte Sting TC .60 1.50
14 Ayana Walker .15 .40
15 Shannon Johnson .15 .40
16 Tangela Smith .15 .40
17 Michelle Snow .20 .50
18 Chandi Jones .15 .40
19 Adrienne Goodson .15 .40
20 Lauren Jackson .75 2.00
21 Elaine Powell .15 .40
22 Minnesota Lynx TC .60 1.50
23 La'Keshia Frett .15 .40
24 Allison Feaster .20 .50
25 Lindsay Whalen .40 1.00
26 DeMya Walker .15 .40
27 Tamecka Dixon .25 .60
28 Kelly Miller .15 .40
29 San Antonio Silver Stars TC .60 1.50
30 Tina Thompson .50 1.25
31 Tamika Williams .20 .50
32 Doneeka Hodges RC .25 .60
33 Kelly Mazzante .25 .60
34 Shameka Christon .15 .40
35 Sheryl Swoopes 1.00 2.50
36 Nicole Powell .20 .50
37 Indiana Fever TC .60 1.50
38 Alicia Thompson .15 .40
39 Kristen Rasmussen .15 .40
40 Diana Taurasi 1.00 2.50
41 Elena Baranova .40 1.00
42 Taj McWilliams-Franklin .15 .40
43 Nakia Sanford RC .30 .75
44 Tamika Whitmore .15 .40
45 Katie Smith .50 1.25
46 Phoenix Mercury TC .60 1.50
47 Tully Bevilaqua .15 .40
48 Tari Phillips .15 .40
49 Charlotte Smith-Taylor .15 .40
50 Sue Bird 1.25 3.00
51 Natalie Williams .30 .75
52 Connecticut Sun TC .75 2.00
53 Bernadette Ngoyisa RC .30 .75
54 Anna DeForge .15 .40
55 Becky Hammon .75 2.00
56 Sacramento Monarchs TC .60 1.50
57 Mwadi Mabika .15 .40
58 Asjha Jones .20 .50
59 Kamila Vodichkova .15 .40
60 Yolanda Griffith .50 1.25
61 Deanna Jackson .15 .40
62 Le'Coe Willingham RC .25 .60
63 Gwen Jackson .15 .40
64 Erin Buescher .15 .40
65 Alana Beard .30 .75
66 New York Liberty TC .60 1.50
67 Helen Darling .15 .40
68 Dominique Canty .25 .60
69 Marie Ferdinand .15 .40
70 Tamika Catchings .40 1.00
71 Kara Lawson .30 .75
72 Vanessa Hayden .15 .40
73 Nikki McCray .40 1.00
74 Washington Mystics TC .60 1.50
75 Ruth Riley .25 .60
76 Penny Taylor .25 .60
77 Ticha Penicheiro .40 1.00
78 Katie Douglas .25 .60
79 Janeth Arcain .15 .40
80 Swin Cash .30 .75
81 Kelly Schumacher .15 .40
82 Detroit Shock TC .60 1.50
83 Plenette Pierson .15 .40
84 Sheri Sam .15 .40
85 Chamique Holdsclaw 1.00 2.50
86 Delisha Milton-Jones .15 .40
87 Nicole Ohlde .15 .40
88 Edna Campbell .20 .50
89 Tammy Sutton-Brown .15 .40
90 Nikki Teasley .15 .40
91 Ann Wauters .20 .50
92 Janell Burse .15 .40
93 Kristi Harrower .15 .40
94 Murriel Page .20 .50
95 Cheryl Ford .25 .60
96 Christi Thomas .15 .40
97 Brooke Wyckoff .25 .60
98 Barbara Farris .15 .40
99 Mandisa Stevenson RC .30 .75
100 Nykesha Sales .25 .60
101 Jurgita Streimikyte .15 .40
102 Amber Jacobs RC .25 .60
103 Coco Miller .15 .40
104 Iziane Castro Marques .15 .40
105 Deanna Nolan .15 .40
106 Los Angeles Sparks TC .60 1.50
107 Rebekkah Brunson .15 .40
108 Checklist 1 .15 .40
109 Checklist 2 .15 .40
110 Checklist 3 .15 .40
P1 Diana Taurasi PROMO 2.50 6.00
P1A Becky Hammon Binder 4.00 10.00

2005 WNBA Autographs

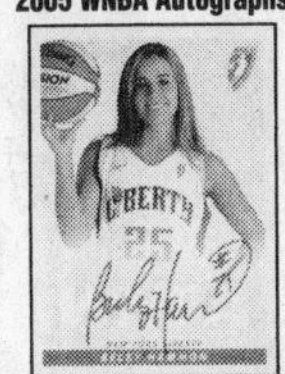

AB Adia Barnes Trophy 5.00 12.00
AB1 Alana Beard Posed 6.00 15.00
AB2 Alana Beard Action 6.00 15.00
AD Anne Donovan CO 10.00 25.00
AT Alicia Thompson Trophy 5.00 12.00
BH1 Becky Hammon Posed 15.00 40.00
BH2 Becky Hammon Action 15.00 40.00
BH3 Becky Hammon Dress 15.00 40.00
BL Betty Lennox Trophy 6.00 15.00
CC1 Cynthia Cooper 12.50 30.00
DA1 Lauren Jackson AU
Sue Bird AU
DS1 Dawn Staley Posed 8.00 20.00
DS2 Dawn Staley Action 8.00 20.00
DT1 Diana Taurasi Posed 20.00 50.00
DT2 Diana Taurasi Action 20.00 50.00
DT3 Diana Taurasi Dress 20.00 50.00
JB Janell Burse Trophy 5.00 12.00
KS1 Katie Smith Posed 10.00 25.00
KS2 Katie Smith Action 10.00 25.00
KS3 Katie Smith Dress 10.00 25.00
KV Kamila Vodichkova Trophy 5.00 12.00
LJ1 Lauren Jackson Trophy 20.00 50.00
LJ2 Lauren Jackson Action 20.00 50.00
LL1 Lisa Leslie Yellow 12.50 30.00
LL2 Lisa Leslie Black 12.50 30.00
LL3 Lisa Leslie Dress 12.50 30.00
NS1 Nykesha Sales Action 5.00 12.00
NS2 Nykesha Sales Dress 5.00 12.00
NT1 Nikki Teasley Posed 5.00 12.00
NT2 Nikki Teasley Action 5.00 12.00
NT3 Nikki Teasley Dress 5.00 12.00
SB1 Sue Bird Trophy 25.00 60.00
SB2 Sue Bird Posed 25.00 60.00
SB3 Sue Bird Action 25.00 60.00
SC1 Swin Cash Posed 6.00 15.00
SC2 Swin Cash Action 6.00 15.00
SC3 Swin Cash Dress 6.00 15.00
SE Simone Edwards Trophy 5.00 12.00
SJ1 Shannon Johnson Action 5.00 12.00
SJ2 Shannon Johnson Dress 5.00 12.00
SS Sheri Sam Trophy 5.00 12.00
TB Tully Bevilaqua Trophy 5.00 12.00
TC1 Tamika Catchings Posed 8.00 20.00
TC2 Tamika Catchings Action 8.00 20.00
TC3 Tamika Catchings Dress 8.00 20.00
YG1 Yolanda Griffith Press 6.00 15.00
YG2 Yolanda Griffith Action 6.00 15.00

2005 WNBA Jerseys

Inserted in packs at the rate of one in 80, this 12-card set features numbers R1-R10 in packs, #AR1 and AR2 as autographed and numbered distributor promos, #DR1 Sue Bird/Lauren Jackson as a random case topper, and a Becky Hammon card available through a mail-in offer for the Rittenhouse Archives binder for storing 2005 WNBA cards.

R1 Lisa Leslie 6.00 15.00
R2 Lauren Jackson 20.00 50.00
R3 Tina Thompson 4.00 10.00
R4 Diana Taurasi 10.00 25.00
R5 Sue Bird 10.00 25.00
R6 Yolanda Griffith 4.00 10.00
R7 Tamika Catchings 4.00 10.00
R8 Swin Cash 6.00 15.00
R9 Nikki Teasley 6.00 15.00
R10 Nykesha Sales 4.00 10.00
AR1 Lisa Leslie AU/299 25.00 60.00
AR2 Diana Taurasi AU/99 125.00 250.00
DR1 Sue Bird 20.00 50.00
Lauren Jackson Topper
NNO Becky Hammon Archives 8.00 20.00

2005 WNBA League Leaders

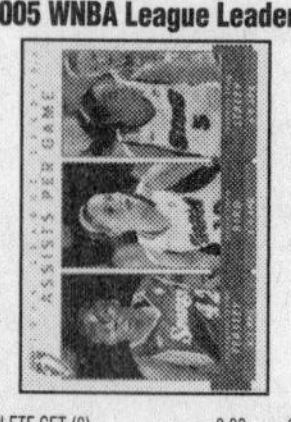

COMPLETE SET (8) 8.00 20.00
LL1 Lauren Jackson 2.00 5.00
Tina Thompson
Lisa Leslie
LL2 Nikki Teasley 3.00 8.00
Sue Bird
Dawn Staley
LL3 Lisa Leslie 2.00 5.00
Cheryl Ford
Michelle Snow
LL4 Yolanda Griffith 1.25 3.00
Nykesha Sales
Alana Beard
LL5 Lisa Leslie 2.00 5.00
Tammy Sutton-Bron
Lauren Jackson
LL6 Katie Smith 1.25 3.00
Tamika Johnson
Cheryl Miller
LL7 Charlotte Smith-Taylor 1.00 2.50
Elena Baranova
Gwen Jackson
LL8 Tamika Williams 2.00 5.00
Yolana Griffith
Lisa Leslie

2005 WNBA Playoffs

STATED ODDS 1:7
P1 Conn. def. Wash 2-1 .75 2.00
P2 NY def. LA 2-1 .75 2.00
P3 Sacram. def. LA 2-1 .75 2.00
P4 Seattle def. Minn. 2-0 .75 2.00
P5 Conn. def. NY 2-0 .75 2.00
P6 Seattle def. Sacram 2-1 1.25 3.00
P7 Conn. Win Game 1 .75 2.00
P8 Seattle Ties it Up 1.25 3.00
P9 Seattle Reigns 1.25 3.00

2005 WNBA Rookies

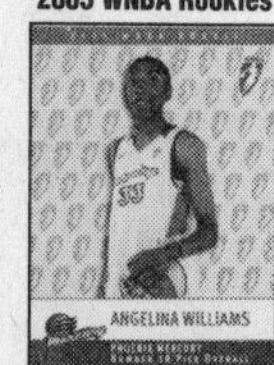

COMPLETE SET (33) 250.00 450.00
STATED PRINT RUN 333 SER.#'d SETS
RC1 Janel McCarville 10.00 25.00
RC2 Tan White 10.00 25.00
RC3 Sandora Irvin 10.00 25.00
RC4 Kendra Wecker 10.00 25.00
RC5 Sancho Lyttle 8.00 20.00
RC6 Temeka Johnson 8.00 20.00
RC7 Kara Braxton 10.00 25.00
RC8 Katie Feenstra 10.00 25.00
RC9 Kristin Haynie 15.00 40.00
RC10 Loree Moore 8.00 20.00
RC11 Kristen Mann 8.00 20.00
RC12 Tanisha Wright 8.00 20.00
RC13 Shyra Ely 10.00 25.00
RC14 Roneeka Hodges 8.00 20.00
RC15 Yolanda Paige 10.00 25.00
RC16 Jacqueline Batteast 10.00 25.00
RC17 Angelina Williams 8.00 20.00
RC18 Chelsea Newton 12.00 30.00
RC19 Jessica Moore 10.00 25.00
RC20 Ashley Battle 10.00 25.00
RC21 Belinda Snell 8.00 20.00
RC22 Laurie Koehn 8.00 20.00
RC23 Caity Matter 8.00 20.00
RC24 Cathrine Kraayeveld 8.00 20.00
RC25 Edwige Lawson 8.00 20.00
RC26 Francesca Zara 8.00 20.00
RC27 Jamie Carey 8.00 20.00
RC28 Jenni Benningfield 8.00 20.00
RC29 Laura Summerton 8.00 20.00
RC30 Miao Li Jie 8.00 20.00
RC31 Natalia Vodopyanova 8.00 20.00
RC32 Sui Fei Fei 8.00 20.00
RC33 Suzy Batkovic 8.00 20.00

2005 WNBA Team Leaders

COMPLETE SET (13) 8.00 20.00
STATED ODDS 1:8
TL1 Allison Feaster .75 2.00
Dawn Staley
Tammy Sutton-Brown
TL2 Nykesha Sales .75 2.00
Lindsey Whalen
Taj McWilliams-Franklin
TL3 Swin Case .60 1.50
Nichole Powell
Cheryl Ford
TL4 Tina Thompson 2.00 5.00
Sheryl Swoopes
Michelle Snow
TL5 Tamika Catchings .75 2.00
TL6 Lisa Leslie 1.50 4.00
Nikki Teasley
Lisa Leslie
TL7 Katie Smith 1.00 2.50
Helen Darling
Tamika Williams
TL8 Becky Hammon 1.50 4.00
Elena Baranova
TL9 Diana Taurasi 2.00 5.00
Penny Taylor
Diana Taurasi
TL10 Yolanda Griffith 1.00 2.50
Ticha Penicheiro
Yolanda Griffith
TL11 Latoya Thomas .30 .75
Shannon Johnson
Adrienne Goodson
TL12 Lauren Jackson 2.50 6.00
Sue Bird
Lauren Jackson
TL13 Chamique Holdsclaw 2.00 5.00
Alana Beard
Chamique Holdsclaw

2006 WNBA

COMPLETE SET (1-110) 10.00 25.00
1 Sacramento Monarchs TC .60 1.50
2 Lindsay Whalen .40 1.00
3 Tamika Whitmore .15 .40
4 Tangela Smith .15 .40
5 Alana Beard .30 .75
6 Chicago Sky TC .60 1.50
7 Vickie Johnson .25 .60
8 Kelly Schumacher .15 .40
9 Plenette Pierson .15 .40
10 Sheryl Swoopes 1.00 2.50
11 Los Angeles Sparks TC 1.00 2.50
12 Katie Douglas .25 .60
13 Nicole Ohlde .15 .40
14 Anna DeForge .15 .40
15 Swin Cash .30 .75
16 Kelly Miller .15 .40
17 Kara Lawson .30 .75
18 Shameka Christon .15 .40
19 Dominique Canty .25 .60
20 Sue Bird 1.25 3.00
21 Detroit Shock TC .75 2.00
22 Margo Dydek .25 .60
23 Shannon Johnson .15 .40
24 Chandi Jones .15 .40
25 Cheryl Ford .25 .60
26 Katie Feenstra .20 .50
27 Ashley Battle .20 .50
28 Tammy Sutton-Brown .15 .40
29 Deanna Jackson .15 .40
30 Yolanda Griffith .50 1.25
31 Minnesota Lynx TC .60 1.50
32 Asjha Jones .20 .50
33 Nicole Powell .20 .50
34 Sancho Lyttle .15 .40
35 Nykesha Sales .25 .60
36 LaToya Thomas .15 .40
37 Nikki Teasley .15 .40
38 Kara Braxton .20 .50
39 Rebekkah Brunson .15 .40
40 Lauren Jackson .75 2.00
41 Phoenix Mercury TC .75 2.00
42 Brooke Wyckoff .25 .60
43 Betty Lennox .30 .75
44 Tan White .20 .50
45 Dawn Staley .40 1.00
46 Washington Mystics TC .60 1.50
47 Svetlana Abrosimova .15 .40
48 Mandisa Stevenson .15 .40
49 Chantelle Anderson .15 .40
50 Deanna Nolan .15 .40
51 Indiana Fever TC .60 1.50
52 Le'coe Willingham .15 .40
53 Stacey Dales .25 .60
54 Tully Bevilaqua .15 .40
55 Ruth Riley .25 .60
56 Janell Burse .15 .40
57 Doneeka Hodges .15 .40
58 Stacey Lovelace .25 .60
59 Hamchetou Maiga-Ba .15 .40
60 Tamika Catchings .40 1.00
61 New York Liberty TC 1.00 2.50
62 Jamie Carey .15 .40
63 Delisha Milton-Jones .15 .40
64 Elaine Powell .15 .40
65 Laurie Koehn .15 .40
66 Allison Feaster .20 .50
67 Shyra Ely .20 .50
68 Ticha Penicheiro .40 1.00
69 Laura Summerton .15 .40
70 Diana Taurasi 1.00 2.50
71 Seattle Storm TC 1.25 3.00
72 Kristin Haynie .25 .60
73 Iziane Castro Marques .15 .40
74 Tamika Williams .20 .50
75 Marie Ferdinand .15 .40
76 Belinda Snell .15 .40
77 Mwadi Mabika .15 .40
78 Loree Moore .15 .40
79 Crystal Robinson .15 .40
80 Taj McWilliams-Franklin .15 .40
81 Houston Comets TC .60 1.50
82 Kendra Wecker .20 .50
83 Janel McCarville .20 .50
84 Kristen Mann .15 .40
85 Chamique Holdsclaw 1.00 2.50
86 Tanisha Wright .15 .40
87 Kamila Vodichkova .15 .40
88 Christi Thomas .15 .40
89 Chasity Melvin .15 .40
90 Lisa Leslie .75 2.00
91 Tina Thompson .50 1.25
92 Connecticut Sun TC .75 2.00
93 Erin Buescher .15 .40
94 Chelsea Newton .25 .60
95 Katie Smith .50 1.25
96 Temeka Johnson .15 .40
97 Sheri Sam .15 .40
98 Wendy Palmer .40 1.00
99 DeMya Walker .15 .40
100 Becky Hammon .75 2.00
101 Charlotte Sting TC .60 1.50
102 Charlotte Smith .15 .40
103 Cathrine Kraayeveld .15 .40
104 Tamecka Dixon .25 .60
105 Michelle Snow .20 .50
106 Vanessa Hayden .15 .40
107 San Antonio Silver Stars TC .60 1.50
108 Checklist 1 .15 .40
109 Checklist 2 .15 .40
110 Checklist 3 .15 .40

2006 WNBA All-Star Jerseys

APPROXIMATELY ONE PER BOX
RE1 Alana Beard 3.00 8.00
RE2 Swin Cash 3.00 8.00
RE3 Tamika Catchings 4.00 10.00
RE4 Cheryl Ford 2.50 6.00
RE5 Becky Hammon 8.00 20.00
RE6 Taj McWilliams-Franklin 2.50 6.00
RE7 Deanna Nolan 2.50 6.00
RE8 Ruth Riley 2.50 6.00
RE9 Nykesha Sales 2.50 6.00
RW1 Sue Bird 12.00 30.00
RW2 Marie Ferdinand 2.50 6.00
RW3 Yolanda Griffith 5.00 12.00
RW4 Chamique Holdsclaw 6.00 15.00
RW5 Lauren Jackson 8.00 20.00
RW6 Lisa Leslie 8.00 20.00
RW7 Katie Smith 5.00 12.00
RW8 Michelle Snow 2.50 6.00
RW9 Sheryl Swoopes 6.00 15.00
RE10 Dawn Staley 4.00 10.00
RE11 Ann Wauters 2.50 6.00
RW10 Diana Taurasi 10.00 25.00
RW11 DeMya Walker 2.50 6.00

2006 WNBA Autographs

APPROXIMATELY TWO PER BOX
1 Temeka Johnson Action 5.00 12.00
2 Temeka Johnson ROY 5.00 12.00
3 Chelsea Newton 5.00 12.00
4 Katie Feenstra Action 5.00 12.00
5 Katie Feenstra Close Up 5.00 12.00
6 Tan White 5.00 12.00
7 Janel McCarville 5.00 12.00
8 Kara Braxton 5.00 12.00
9 Yolanda Griffith MVP 8.00 20.00
10 Yolanda Griffith Champs 8.00 20.00
11 Kristin Haynie 5.00 12.00
12 Rebekkah Brunson 5.00 12.00
13 Nicole Powell 5.00 12.00
14 Olympia Scott-Richardson 5.00 12.00
15 Erin Buescher 5.00 12.00
16 DeMya Walker 5.00 12.00
17 Kara Lawson 6.00 15.00
18 Ticha Penicheiro 8.00 20.00
19 Hamchetou Maiga 5.00 12.00
20 Chelsea Newton 5.00 12.00
21 John Whisenant 5.00 12.00
22 Sue Bird Assists 25.00 60.00
23 Sue Bird Action 25.00 60.00
24 Sue Bird Glamour 25.00 60.00
25 Marie Ferdinand Action 5.00 12.00
26 Marie Ferdinand Glamour 5.00 12.00
27 Anna DeForge Action 5.00 12.00
28 Anna DeForge Glamour 5.00 12.00
29 Diana Taurasi Action 15.00 40.00
30 Diana Taurasi Glamour 15.00 40.00
31 Becky Hammon Career 15.00 40.00
32 Becky Hammon Action 15.00 40.00
33 Becky Hammon Glamour 15.00 40.00
34 Nicole Ohlde 5.00 12.00
35 Svetlana Abrosimova 5.00 12.00
36 Chamique Holdsclaw Portrait 8.00 20.00
37 Chamique Holdsclaw Glamour 8.00 20.00
38 Tamika Catchings Defensive 8.00 20.00
39 Tamika Catchings Glamour 8.00 20.00
40 Tamika Catchings 2nd Team 8.00 20.00
41 Michelle Snow Action 5.00 12.00
42 Michelle Snow Glamour 5.00 12.00
43 Sheryl Swoopes AS MVP 8.00 20.00
44 Sheryl Swoopes WNBA 1st Team 8.00 20.00
45 Sheryl Swoopes MVP 8.00 20.00
46 Sheryl Swoopes Glamour 8.00 20.00
47 Deanna Nolan Glamour 5.00 12.00
48 Deanna Nolan Action 5.00 12.00
49 Ruth Riley Glamour 5.00 12.00
50 Ruth Riley Action 5.00 12.00
51 Cheryl Ford Glamour 5.00 12.00
52 Cheryl Ford Action 5.00 12.00
53 Taj McWilliams Award 5.00 12.00
54 Taj McWilliams Action 5.00 12.00
55 Taj McWilliams Glamour 5.00 12.00
56 Lindsey Whalen Album 10.00 25.00

2006 WNBA League Leaders

COMPLETE SET (9) 8.00 20.00
APPROXIMATELY TWO PER BOX
LL1 Sheryl Swoopes 2.00 5.00
Lauren Jackson
Chamique Holdsclaw
LL2 Sue Bird 2.50 6.00
Temeka Johnson
Lindsay Whalen
LL3 Cheryl Ford 1.50 4.00
Lauren Jackson
Tamika Catchings
LL4 Tamika Catchings 2.00 5.00
Sheryl Swoopes
Lisa Leslie
LL5 Margo Dydek 1.50 4.00
Vanessa Hayden
Lisa Leslie
LL6 Becky Hammon 1.50 4.00
Janeth Arcain
Betty Lennox
LL7 Laurie Koehn .60 1.50
Doneeka Hodges
Kara Lawson
LL8 Michelle Snow .40 1.00
Ann Wauters
DeMya Walker
LL9 Cheryl Ford 1.50 4.00
Lauren Jackson

2006 WNBA Patches

PRINT RUN 250 SER.#'d SETS
P1 Sheryl Swoopes 20.00 50.00
P2 Sue Bird 25.00 60.00
P3 Yolanda Griffith 10.00 25.00
P4 Lauren Jackson 15.00 40.00
P5 Deanna Nolan 3.00 8.00
P6 Tamika Catchings 8.00 20.00
P7 Diana Taurasi 20.00 50.00
P8 Taj McWilliams-Franklin 3.00 8.00
P9 Lisa Leslie 15.00 40.00
P10 Becky Hammon 15.00 40.00

2006 WNBA Playoffs

COMPLETE SET (10) 5.00 12.00
APPROXIMATELY SIX PER BOX
P1 Eastern Semi-Finals .75 2.00
P2 Eastern Semi-Finals .75 2.00
P3 Western Semi-Finals .75 2.00
P4 Western Semi-Finals .75 2.00
P5 Eastern Finals .75 2.00
P6 Western Finals .75 2.00
P7 WNBA Finals .75 2.00
P8 WNBA Finals .75 2.00
P9 WNBA Finals .75 2.00
P10 WNBA Finals .75 2.00

2006 WNBA Rookies

PRINT RUN 333 SER.#'d SETS
RC1 Seimone Augustus 20.00 50.00
RC2 Cappie Pondexter 12.00 30.00
RC3 Monique Currie 8.00 20.00
RC4 Sophia Young 8.00 20.00
RC5 Lisa Willis 5.00 12.00
RC6 Candice Dupree 10.00 25.00
RC7 Shona Thorburn 5.00 12.00
RC8 Tamara James 5.00 12.00
RC9 La'Tangela Atkinson 5.00 12.00
RC10 Tye'sha Fluker 5.00 12.00
RC11 Barbara Turner 8.00 20.00
RC12 Sherill Baker 5.00 12.00
RC13 Kim Smith 5.00 12.00
RC14 Ann Strother 12.00 30.00
RC15 Shanna Zolman 12.00 30.00
RC16 Nikki Blue 6.00 15.00
RC17 Mistie Williams 6.00 15.00
RC18 Megan Mahoney 15.00 40.00
RC19 Erin Phillips 12.00 30.00
RC20 Liz Shimek 5.00 12.00
RC21 LaToya Bond 5.00 12.00
RC22 Ambrosia Anderson 5.00 12.00
RC23 Scholanda Dorrell 5.00 12.00
RC24 Jennifer Lacy 5.00 12.00
RC25 Megan Duffy 6.00 15.00
RC26 Crystal Smith 5.00 12.00
RC27 Anastasia Hostaki 5.00 12.00
RC28 Emmeline Ndongue 5.00 12.00
RC29 Yelena Leuchanka 5.00 12.00
RC30 Kasha Terry 5.00 12.00
RC31 Brandi Davis 5.00 12.00
RC32 Christelle N'Garsanet 5.00 12.00
RC33 Brittany Wilkins 5.00 12.00
RC34 Zane Teilane 5.00 12.00

2006 WNBA Team Leaders

COMPLETE SET (13) 5.00 12.00
APPROXIMATELY FIVE PER BOX
L1 Tangela Smith .50 1.25
Dawn Staley
Tammy Sutton-Brown
L2 Nykesha Sales .50 1.25
Lindsay Whalen
Taj McWilliams-Franklin
L3 Deanna Nolan .30 .75
Deanna Nolan
Cheryl Ford
L4 Sheryl Swoopes 1.25 3.00
Sheryl Swoopes
Michelle Snow
L5 Tamika Catchings .50 1.25
Tamika Catchings
Tamika Catchings
L6 Chamique Holdsclaw 1.25 3.00
Nikki Teasley
Lisa Leslie
L7 Katie Smith .60 1.50
Kristi Harrower
Nicole Ohlde
L8 Becky Hammon 1.00 2.50
Becky Hammon
Elena Baranova
L9 Diana Taurasi 1.25 3.00
Diana Taurasi
Kamila Vodichkova
L10 DeMya Walker .60 1.50
Ticha Penicheiro
Yolanda Griffith
L11 Marie Ferdinand .50 1.25
Shannon Johnson
Wendy Palmer-Daniel
L12 Lauren Jackson 1.50 4.00
Sue Bird
Lauren Jackson
L13 Alana Beard .40 1.00
Temeka Johnson
Chasity Melvin

2006 WNBA Toppers

RANDOM INSERTS IN BOXES
NNO Yolanda Griffith JSY AU 12.00 30.00
NNO Sheryl Swoops JSY AU/150 12.00 30.00
NNO Tan White JSY 6.00 15.00
Katie Feenstra JSY
NNO Temeka Johnson JSY AU/150 8.00 20.00

2007 WNBA

COMPLETE SET (90) 8.00 20.00
COMMON CARD (1-90) .20 .50
1 Diana Taurasi 1.25 3.00
2 Marie Ferdinand-Harris .20 .50
3 Megan Mahoney .50 1.25
4 Chasity Melvin .20 .50
5 Lauren Jackson 1.00 2.50
6 Tammy Sutton-Brown .20 .50
7 Nicole Ohlde .20 .50
8 Dominique Canty .30 .75
9 Alana Beard .40 1.00
10 Tina Thompson .60 1.50
11 Janell Burse .20 .50
12 Asjha Jones .25 .60
13 Kelly Miller .20 .50
14 Tamika Catchings .50 1.25
15 Kara Braxton .25 .60
16 Erika DeSouza RC .30 .75
17 Erin Thorn RC .20 .50
18 Tamika Whitmore .20 .50
19 Seimone Augustus .60 1.50
20 Erin Buescher .20 .50
21 Nicole Powell .25 .60
22 Mwadi Mabika .20 .50
23 Cappie Pondexter .40 1.00
24 Stacey Dales .30 .75
25 Temeka Johnson .20 .50
26 Nikki Teasley .20 .50
27 Katie Douglas .30 .75
28 Sheryl Swoopes 1.25 3.00
29 Anna DeForge .20 .50
30 Monique Currie .25 .60
31 Kelly Schumacher .20 .50
32 Becky Hammon 1.00 2.50
33 Tangela Smith .20 .50
34 Jia Perkins RC .30 .75
35 DeMya Walker .20 .50
36 DeLisha Milton-Jones .20 .50
37 Chamique Holdsclaw 1.25 3.00
38 Kelly Mazzante .30 .75
39 Tan White .25 .60
40 Penny Taylor .30 .75
41 Cheryl Ford .30 .75
42 Ebony Hoffman .25 .60
43 Vickie Johnson .30 .75
44 Loree Moore .20 .50
45 Candice Dupree .30 .75
46 Deanna Nolan .20 .50
47 Nakia Sanford .25 .60
48 Cathrine Kraayeveld .20 .50
49 Hamchetou Maiga-Ba .20 .50
50 Nykesha Sales .30 .75
51 Amber Jacobs .20 .50
52 Kara Lawson .40 1.00
53 Shannon Johnson .20 .50
54 Taj McWilliams-Franklin .20 .50
55 Sue Bird 1.50 4.00
56 Laurie Koehn .20 .50
57 Barbara Farris .20 .50
58 Tari Phillips .20 .50
59 Swin Cash .40 1.00
60 Jamie Carey .20 .50
61 Kristen Mann .20 .50
62 Sherill Baker .20 .50
63 Lindsay Whalen .50 1.25
64 Yolanda Griffith .60 1.50
65 Shanna Zolman Crossley .40 1.00
66 Tully Bevilaqua .20 .50
67 Chelsea Newton .30 .75
68 Katie Smith .60 1.50
69 K.B. Sharp .20 .50
70 Iziane Castro Marques .20 .50
71 Rebekkah Brunson .20 .50
72 Sophia Young .25 .60
73 Shameka Christon .20 .50
74 Christi Thomas .20 .50
75 Coco Miller .20 .50
76 Plenette Pierson .20 .50
77 Ruth Riley .30 .75
78 Scholanda Robinson RC .30 .75
79 Murriel Page .25 .60
80 Ashley Battle .25 .60
81 Michelle Snow .25 .60
82 Betty Lennox .40 1.00
83 LaToya Thomas .20 .50
84 Katie Feenstra .25 .60
85 Kendra Wecker .25 .60
86 Margo Dydek .30 .75
87 Ticha Penicheiro .50 1.25
88 Kayte Christensen .20 .50
89 Lecoe Willingham .20 .50
90 Lisa Leslie 1.00 2.50

2007 WNBA Parallel

*PARALLEL: 2X TO 5X BASE HI
PRINT RUN 333 SER.#'d SETS

2007 WNBA 3-Case Incentive

1 Nancy Lieberman 6.00 15.00
Ann Meyers AU

2007 WNBA All-WNBA Team

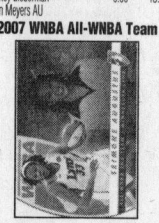

PRINT RUN 100 SER.#'d SETS
T01 Lisa Leslie 25.00 60.00
T02 Tamika Catchings 12.00 30.00
T03 Diana Taurasi 30.00 80.00
T04 Lauren Jackson 25.00 60.00
T05 Katie Douglas 8.00 20.00
T06 Alana Beard 10.00 25.00
T07 Cheryl Ford 8.00 20.00
T08 Taj McWilliams-Franklin 5.00 12.00
T09 Seimone Augustus 15.00 40.00
T10 Sheryl Swoopes 30.00 80.00

2007 WNBA Autographs

APPROXIMATE ODDS THREE PER BOX
1 Seimone Augustus 12.00 30.00
2 Cheryl Ford 6.00 15.00
3 Plenette Pierson 4.00 10.00
4 Kara Braxton 5.00 12.00
5 Angelina Williams 4.00 10.00
6 Jacqueline Batteast 5.00 12.00
7 Bill Laimbeer 8.00 20.00
8 Cheryl Miller 10.00 25.00
9 Ann Meyers 10.00 25.00
10 Sherill Baker 4.00 10.00
11 Shanna Zolman Crossley 8.00 20.00
12 Cappie Pondexter 8.00 20.00
13 Barbara Turner 5.00 12.00
14 Scholanda Robinson 6.00 15.00
15 Jennifer Lacy 4.00 10.00
17 Brooke Wyckoff 6.00 15.00
18 Katie Douglas 6.00 15.00
19 Asjha Jones 5.00 12.00
20 Le'coe Willingham 4.00 10.00
21 Margo Dydek 6.00 15.00
22 Tamika Whitmore 4.00 10.00
23 Sophia Young 5.00 12.00
24 Kristen Mann 4.00 10.00
25 Amber Jacobs 4.00 10.00
26 Shameka Christon 4.00 10.00
27 Cathrine Kraayeveld 4.00 10.00
28 Kelly Schumacher 4.00 10.00
29 Kendra Wecker 5.00 12.00
30 Chasity Melvin 4.00 10.00
31 Nakia Sanford 5.00 12.00
32 Jia Perkins 6.00 15.00
33 Dominique Canty 6.00 15.00
34 Candice Dupree 6.00 15.00
35 Mwadi Mabika 4.00 10.00
36 Katie Smith 10.00 25.00
37 Swin Cash 8.00 20.00
38 Ruth Riley 6.00 15.00
39 Elaine Powell 4.00 10.00
40 Deanna Nolan 4.00 10.00
MC Monique Currie 4.00 10.00
MT Mike Thibault 4.00 10.00
DMJ DeLisha Milton-Jones 4.00 10.00

2007 WNBA Highlights

COMPLETE SET (9) 10.00 25.00
RANDOM INSERTS IN PACKS
H1 Lisa Leslie Notches 5,000th Point 2.50 6.00
H2 2006 All-Star Game .75 2.00
H3 Diana Taurasi 47 Points 3.00 8.00
H4 Diana Taurasi Scoring Mark 3.00 8.00
H5 Seimone Augustus RC Scoring 1.50 4.00
H6 Cheryl Ford Rebound Total .75 2.00
H7 Van Chancellor 200 Wins .75 2.00
H8 Detroit Shock WNBA Title .75 2.00
H9 Lisa Leslie Ties Swoopes MVP 2.50 6.00

2007 WNBA League Leaders

COMPLETE SET (9) 8.00 20.00
RANDOM INSERTS IN PACKS
LL1 Diana Taurasi 2.00 5.00
Seimone Augustus
Lisa Leslie
LL2 Nikki Teasley 2.50 6.00
Temeka Johnson
Sue Bird
LL3 Cheryl Ford 1.50 4.00
Taj McWilliams-Franklin
Lisa Leslie
LL4 Tamika Catchings 2.00 5.00
Tully Bevilaqua
Sheryl Swoopes
LL5 Margo Dydek 1.50 4.00
Tammy Sutton-Brown
Lauren Jackson
LL6 Becky Hammon 1.50 4.00
Katie Smith
Lindsay Whalen
LL7 Erin Thorn .30 .75
DeLisha Milton-Jones
Dawn Staley
LL8 Erin Buescher 1.50 4.00
Lauren Jackson
Bernadette Ngoyisa
LL9 Cheryl Ford 1.50 4.00
Lisa Leslie
Taj McWilliams-Franklin

2007 WNBA Rookies

PRINT RUN 444 SER.#'d SETS
RC01 Lindsey Harding 4.00 10.00
RC02 Jessica Davenport 4.00 10.00
RC03 Armintie Price 4.00 10.00
RC04 Noelle Quinn 5.00 12.00
RC05 Tiffany Jackson 6.00 15.00
RC06 Bernice Mosby 5.00 12.00
RC07 Katie Gearlds 6.00 15.00
RC08 Ashley Shields 3.00 8.00
RC09 Alison Bales 6.00 15.00
RC10 Carla Thomas 4.00 10.00
RC11 Ivory Latta 6.00 15.00
RC12 Kamesha Hairston 3.00 8.00
RC13 Dee Davis 3.00 8.00
RC14 Eshaya Murphy 4.00 10.00
RC15 Shay Doron 8.00 20.00
RC16 Camille Little 3.00 8.00
RC17 Stephanie Raymond 3.00 8.00
RC18 Amy Sanders 3.00 8.00
RC19 Kathrin Ress 4.00 10.00
RC20 Sidney Spencer 10.00 25.00

C21 Cori Chambers 4.00 10.00
C22 Martina Weber 3.00 8.00
C23 Gillian Goring 3.00 8.00
C24 Claire Coggins 5.00 12.00
C25 Navonda Moore 4.00 10.00
C26 Marta Fernandez 3.00 8.00
C27 Lindsay Bowen 3.00 8.00

2008 WNBA

COMPLETE SET (90) 8.00 20.00
COMP.ARCHIVE BOX SET 625.00 825.00
1 Lauren Jackson 1.00 2.50
2 Jia Perkins .20 .50
3 Swin Cash .40 1.00
4 Tina Thompson .60 1.50
5 Katie Douglas .30 .75
6 Taj McWilliams-Franklin .20 .50
7 Nicole Ohlde .20 .50
8 Shameka Christon .20 .50
9 Nicole Powell .25 .60
10 Diana Taurasi 1.25 3.00
11 Yolanda Griffith .60 1.50
12 Nikki Blue .25 .60
13 Cathrine Kraayeveld .20 .50
14 Jamie Carey .20 .50
15 Deanna Nolan .20 .50
16 Sidney Spencer .50 1.25
17 Rebekkah Brunson .20 .50
18 Tamecka Dixon .30 .75
19 Becky Hammon 1.00 2.50
20 Tamika Catchings .50 1.25
21 Alana Beard .40 1.00
22 Betty Lennox .40 1.00
23 Tangela Smith .20 .50
24 Asjha Jones .25 .60
25 Temeka Johnson .20 .50
26 Elaine Powell .20 .50
27 Michelle Snow .25 .60
28 Marie Ferdinand-Harris .20 .50
29 Noelle Quinn .30 .75
30 Candice Dupree .30 .75
31 Kelly Miller .20 .50
32 Kara Lawson .40 1.00
33 Monique Currie .25 .60
34 Barbara Turner .25 .60
35 Katie Smith .60 1.50
36 Janel McCarville .25 .60
37 Katie Feenstra .25 .60
38 Tan White .25 .60
39 Tiffany Jackson .30 .75
40 Stacey Lovelace .30 .75
41 Kristen Rasmussen .20 .50
42 Nakia Sanford .25 .60
43 Murriel Page .25 .60
44 Helen Darling .20 .50
45 Seimone Augustus .60 1.50
46 Brooke Wyckoff .30 .75
47 Tammy Sutton-Brown .20 .50
48 Iziane Castro .20 .50
49 Ticha Penicheiro .50 1.25
50 Cappie Pondexter .40 1.00
51 Mwadi Mabika .20 .50
52 Erin Thorn .20 .50
53 Kim Smith .20 .50
54 Keisha Brown RC .30 .75
55 Lindsay Whalen .50 1.25
56 Alison Bales .40 1.00
57 Tamika Whitmore .20 .50
58 Sancho Lyttle .20 .50
59 Chasity Melvin .20 .50
60 Cheryl Ford .30 .75
61 Loree Moore .20 .50
62 Camille Little .20 .50
63 Le'coe Willingham .20 .50
64 Jessica Davenport .25 .60
65 DeLisha Milton-Jones .20 .50
66 Katie Gearlds .40 1.00
67 Shanna Crossley RC .40 1.00
68 Tamika Raymond RC .30 .75
69 Kara Braxton .25 .60
70 Sheryl Swoopes 1.25 3.00
71 Erika DeSouza .20 .50
72 Coco Miller .20 .50
73 Ivory Latta .40 1.00
74 Ruth Riley .30 .75
75 Armintie Price .25 .60
76 Erin Buescher .20 .50
77 Plenette Pierson .20 .50
78 Chelsea Newton .30 .75
79 Vickie Johnson .30 .75
80 Lisa Leslie 1.00 2.50
81 Tully Bevilaqua .20 .50
82 Nykesha Sales .30 .75
83 Lindsey Harding .25 .60
84 Sophia Young .25 .60
85 Adrian Williams-Strong .20 .50
86 Shannon Johnson .20 .50
87 Dominique Canty .30 .75
88 Anna DeForge .20 .50
89 Kelly Mazzante .30 .75
90 Sue Bird 1.50 4.00
P1 All-Star Team Promo 2.00 5.00
P2 Candace Parker Promo 25.00 50.00

2008 WNBA 3-Case Incentive

TP Diana Taurasi AU 20.00 50.00
Cappie Pondexter

2008 WNBA Autographs

APPROXIMATE ODDS 1:12
AM Ann Meyers-Drysdale 3.00 8.00
AP Armintie Price 3.00 8.00
AS Ann Strother 5.00 12.00
BH Becky Hammon 12.00 30.00
CL Camille Little 2.50 6.00
CL Crystal Langhorne 5.00 12.00
CP Candace Parker 25.00 60.00
CP Cappie Pondexter 5.00 12.00
CW Candice Wiggins 10.00 25.00
DT Diana Taurasi 15.00 40.00
ET Erin Thorn 2.50 6.00
JD Jessica Davenport 3.00 8.00
JD Jennifer Derevjanik 2.50 6.00
JL Jennifer Lacy 2.50 6.00
KM Kelly Miller 2.50 6.00
KM Kelly Mazzante 4.00 10.00
KS Kelly Schumacher 2.50 6.00
LH Laura Harper 2.50 6.00
LH Lindsey Harding 3.00 8.00
LJ Lauren Jackson 12.00 30.00
LM Loree Moore 2.50 6.00
LW Lindsay Whalen 6.00 15.00
NL Nancy Lieberman 8.00 20.00
NQ Noelle Quinn 4.00 10.00
OS Olympia Scott 2.50 6.00
SF Sylvia Fowles 8.00 20.00
SS Sidney Spencer 6.00 15.00
TJ Tiffany Jackson 4.00 10.00
TS Tangela Smith 2.50 6.00

2008 WNBA Case Topper

BALL PRINT RUN 250 SER.#'d SETS
2Q 2006 AS Game 2nd Quarter Ball 8.00 20.00
3Q 2006 AS Game 3rd Quarter Ball 8.00 20.00
NNO Kendra Wecker AU 4.00 10.00
NNO Monique Currie AU 4.00 10.00

2008 WNBA Relics

PRINT RUN 444 SER.#'d SETS
AS1 Cheryl Ford 2.50 6.00
AS2 Tamika Catchings 4.00 10.00
AS3 Anna DeForge 2.50 6.00
AS4 Deanna Nolan 2.50 6.00
AS5 Kara Braxton 2.50 6.00
AS6 Katie Douglas 3.00 8.00
AS7 Asjha Jones 2.50 6.00
AS8 Alana Beard 3.00 8.00
AS9 DeLisha Milton-Jones 2.50 6.00
AS10 Candice Dupree 2.50 6.00
AS11 Tammy Sutton-Brown 2.50 6.00
AS12 Diana Taurasi 8.00 20.00
AS13 Becky Hammon 8.00 20.00
AS14 Tina Thompson 4.00 10.00
AS15 Lauren Jackson 8.00 20.00
AS16 Yolanda Griffith 4.00 10.00
AS17 Taj McWilliams-Franklin 2.50 6.00
AS18 Seimone Augustus 8.00 20.00
AS19 Penny Taylor 4.00 10.00
AS20 Sophia Young 2.50 6.00
AS21 Cappie Pondexter 3.00 8.00
AS22 Kara Lawson 3.00 8.00
PM1 Cappie Pondexter 5.00 12.00
PM2 Diana Taurasi 15.00 40.00
PM3 Penny Taylor 4.00 10.00
PM4 Tangela Smith 4.00 10.00
PM5 Kelly Miller 4.00 10.00
PM6 Kelly Schumacher 4.00 10.00
PM7 Kelly Mazzante 4.00 10.00
PM8 Belinda Snell 4.00 10.00
RR1 Candace Parker
RR2 Sylvia Fowles
RR3 Candice Wiggins

2008 WNBA Rookies

PRINT RUN 444 SER.#'d SETS
R01 Candace Parker 30.00 80.00
R02 Sylvia Fowles 10.00 25.00
R03 Candice Wiggins 12.00 30.00
R04 Alexis Hornbuckle 8.00 20.00
R05 Matee Ajavon 4.00 10.00
R06 Crystal Langhorne 6.00 15.00
R07 Essence Carson 5.00 12.00
R08 Tamera Young 3.00 8.00
R09 Amber Holt 5.00 12.00
R10 Laura Harper 3.00 8.00
R11 Tasha Humphrey 3.00 8.00
R12 Ketia Swanier 3.00 8.00
R13 LaToya Pringle 3.00 8.00
R14 Erlana Larkins 4.00 10.00
R15 Charde Houston 5.00 12.00
R16 Nicky Anosike 8.00 20.00
R17 Jolene Anderson 5.00 12.00
R18 Khadijah Whittington 3.00 8.00
R19 Crystal Kelly 3.00 8.00
R20 Sandrine Gruda 3.00 8.00
R21 Shannon Bobbitt 3.00 8.00
R22 Brooke Smith 3.00 8.00
R23 Leilani Mitchell 3.00 8.00
R24 Erica White 3.00 8.00
R25 Kerri Gardin 3.00 8.00
R26 Olayinka Sanni 3.00 8.00
R27 Quianna Chaney 3.00 8.00
R28 Morenike Atunrase 3.00 8.00
R29 A'Quonesia Franklin 3.00 8.00

2008 WNBA USAB Womens National Team

STATED PRINT RUN 667 SER.#'d SETS
STATED PRINT RUN 444 SER.#'d SETS
G1 Seimone Augustus 2.00 5.00
G2 Sue Bird 5.00 12.00
G3 Tamika Catchings 1.50 4.00
G4 Sylvia Fowles 3.00 8.00
G5 Kara Lawson 1.25 3.00
G6 Lisa Leslie 3.00 8.00
G7 DeLisha Milton-Jones .60 1.50
G8 Candace Parker 10.00 25.00
G9 Cappie Pondexter 1.25 3.00
G10 Katie Smith 2.00 5.00
G11 Diana Taurasi 4.00 10.00
G12 Tina Thompson 2.00 5.00
USAB1 Candace Parker 8.00 20.00
Sylvia Fowles
Candice Wiggins
USAB2 Diana Taurasi 4.00 10.00
Sue Bird
Swin Cash
USAB3 Michelle Snow 2.00 5.00
Tamika Catchings
Kara Lawson
USAB4 Seimone Augustus 3.00 8.00
Cheryl Ford
Sheryl Swoopes
USAB5 Katie Smith 2.00 5.00
Jessica Davenport
Katie Douglas
USAB6 Alana Beard 2.00 5.00
Delisha Milton-Jones
Loree Moore
USAB7 Janel McCarville 2.00 5.00
Asjha Jones
Lindsay Whalen
USAB8 Lisa Leslie 2.50 6.00
Tina Thompson
Taj McWilliams-Franklin
USAB9 Rebekkah Brunson 2.00 5.00
Lindsey Harding
Cappie Pondexter

2009 WNBA 1

COMPLETE BOX SET (17) 45.00 90.00
STATED PRINT RUN 399 SER.#'d SETS
1 Diana Taurasi 4.00 10.00
Cappie Pondexter
Tangela Smith
4 Michelle Snow 1.25 3.00
Ivory Latta
Tamera Young
7 Deanna Nolan 2.00 5.00
Katie Smith
Plenette Pierson
10 Candace Parker 4.00 10.00
Lisa Leslie
DeLisha Milton-Jones
13 Jia Perkins 1.50 4.00
Candice Dupree
Sylvia Fowles
16 Asjha Jones 1.50 4.00
Lindsay Whalen
Tamika Whitmore
19 Lauren Jackson 5.00 12.00
Sue Bird
Camille Little
22 Alana Beard 1.25 3.00
Monique Currie
Tasha Humphrey
25 Katie Douglas 1.50 4.00
Tamika Catchings
Tammy Sutton-Brown
28 Janel McCarville 1.25 3.00
Shameka Christon
Cathrine Kraayeveld
31 Nicole Powell 1.25 3.00
Kara Lawson
Rebecca Brunson
34 Seimone Augustus 2.00 5.00
Candice Wiggins
Nicky Anosike
37 Becky Hammon 3.00 8.00
Sophia Young
Ann Wauters
NNO Candace Parker 4.00 10.00
Lisa Leslie
Header Card

2009 WNBA 1 Autographs

INSERTED IN SERIES 1 BOX SET
CP Candace Parker 25.00 60.00
MA Matee Ajavon 4.00 10.00
NA Nicky Anosike 4.00 10.00

2009 WNBA 2 Rookies

COMPLETE BOX SET 45.00 90.00
PRINT RUN 499 SER.#'d SETS
BOX SET INCLUDES FIVE AUTOS
1 Angel McCoughtry 6.00 15.00
2 Marissa Coleman 5.00 12.00
3 Kristi Toliver 5.00 12.00
4 Renee Montgomery 3.00 8.00
5 DeWanna Bonner 3.00 8.00
6 Briann January 3.00 8.00
7 Courtney Paris 3.00 8.00
8 Kia Vaughn 3.00 8.00
9 Quanitra Holligsworth 3.00 8.00
10 Chante Black 3.00 8.00
11 Shavonte Zellous 3.00 8.00
12 Ashley Walker 3.00 8.00
13 Lindsay Wisdom-Hylton 4.00 10.00

2009 WNBA 2 Rookies Autographs

INSERTED IN SERIES 2 BOX SET
AM Angel McCoughtry 6.00 15.00
CP Courtney Paris 3.00 8.00
KT Kristi Toliver 5.00 12.00
MC Marissa Coleman 5.00 12.00
RM Renee Montgomery 3.00 8.00

2009 WNBA 3 All-Stars

COMPLETE BOX SET 60.00 120.00
BOX SET INCL. 4 RCs AND 5 AUTOS
AS1 Sue Bird 5.00 12.00
Katie Douglas
AS2 Becky Hammon 4.00 10.00
Alana Beard
AS3 Tina Thompson 2.50 6.00
Sylvia Fowles
AS4 Swin Cash 1.25 3.00
Candice Dupree
AS5 Lauren Jackson 3.00 8.00
Tamika Catchings
AS6 Diana Taurasi 4.00 10.00
Asjha Jones
AS7 Nicky Anosike 2.00 5.00
Katie Smith
AS8 Cappie Pondexter 1.25 3.00
Erika DeSouza
AS9 Nicole Powell 1.25 3.00
Shameka Christon
AS10 Sophia Young 1.25 3.00
Jia Perkins
AS11 Charde Houston 1.25 3.00
Sancho Lyttle

2009 WNBA 3 Rookies

PRINT RUN 499 SER.#'d SETS
RC14 Megan Frazee 4.00 10.00
RC15 Anete Jekobsone 3.00 8.00
RC16 Rashanda McCants 4.00 10.00
RC17 Shalee Lehning 6.00 15.00

2009 WNBA 3 Rookies Autographs

INSERTED IN SERIES 3 BOX SET
BJ Briann January 4.00 10.00
CB Chante Black 4.00 10.00
DB DeWanna Bonner 4.00 10.00
MF Megan Frazee 5.00 12.00
QH Quanitra Hollingsworth 4.00 10.00
SZ Shavonte Zellous 4.00 10.00

2009 WNBA Autographs Three-Set Incentive

ANNOUNCED PRINT RUN 133 SETS
CP Candace Parker MVP 30.00 80.00

2010 WNBA

COMPLETE SET (36) 15.00 40.00
COMPLETE FACT.BOX 45.00 90.00
ANNOUNCED PRINT RUN 675 SETS
1 Angel McCoughtry 1.00 2.50
Iziane Castro-Marques
2 Sancho Lyttle 1.25 3.00
Alison Bales
3 Erika de Souza .75 2.00
Armintie Price
4 Shameka Christon 1.00 2.50
Dominique Canty
5 Sylvia Fowles 1.25 3.00
Jia Perkins
6 Cathrine Kraayeveld .60 1.50
Erin Thorn
7 Asjha Jones .75 2.00
Tan White
8 Kara Lawson 1.25 3.00
Sandrine Gruda
9 Renee Montgomery .60 1.50
Anete Jekabsone-Zogota
10 Tamika Catchings 1.50 4.00
Ebony Hoffman
11 Katie Douglas 1.00 2.50
Tammy Sutton-Brown
12 Briann January .75 2.00
Eshaya Murphy
13 Candace Parker 4.00 10.00
Tina Thompson
14 DeLisha Milton-Jones 1.25 3.00
Betty Lennox
15 Noelle Quinn 1.00 2.50
Kristi Toliver
16 Seimone Augustus 2.00 5.00
Nicky Anosike
17 Charde Houston 2.00 5.00
Candice Wiggins
18 Lindsay Whalen 1.50 4.00
Rashanda McCants
19 Cappie Pondexter 1.25 3.00
Janel McCarville
20 Essence Carson 1.00 2.50
Taj McWilliams-Franklin
21 Nicole Powell .75 2.00
Leilani Mitchell
22 Diana Taurasi 4.00 10.00
Tangela Smith
23 Candice Dupree 1.00 2.50
Penny Taylor
24 DeWanna Bonner .60 1.50
Temeka Johnson
25 Sophia Young .75 2.00
Michelle Snow
26 Becky Hammon 3.00 8.00
Ruth Riley
27 Edwige Lawson-Wade 4.00 10.00
Chamique Holdsclaw
28 Sue Bird 5.00 12.00
Swin Cash
29 Lauren Jackson 3.00 8.00
Tanisha Wright
30 Camille Little .60 1.50
Le'coe Willingham
31 Kara Braxton 1.25 3.00
Shanna Crossley
32 Chante Black .60 1.50
Scholanda Robinson
33 Alexis Hornbuckle 1.25 3.00
Amber Holt
34 Katie Smith 2.00 5.00
Lindsey Harding
35 Crystal Langhorne 1.00 2.50
Marissa Coleman
36 Monique Currie .75 2.00
Nakia Sanford

2010 WNBA Autographs

TWO RANDOM AUTOS PER SET
AH Ashley Houts 4.00 10.00
DM Danielle McCray 4.00 10.00
MW Monica Wright 6.00 15.00
TC Tina Charles 12.00 30.00

2010 WNBA Diana Taurasi MVP Bonus

RANDOM INSERTS IN SETS
NNO Diana Taurasi MVP/250 8.00 20.00

2010 WNBA Rookies

COMPLETE SET (12) 60.00 120.00
PRINT RUN 250 SER.#'d SETS
FOUR RANDOM ROOKIES PER SET
R1 Tina Charles 15.00 40.00
R2 Monica Wright 8.00 20.00
R3 Kelsey Griffin 8.00 20.00
R4 Epiphanny Prince 6.00 15.00
R5 Jayne Appel 8.00 20.00
R6 Jacinta Monroe 5.00 12.00
R7 Andrea Riley 5.00 12.00
R8 Alison Lacey 5.00 12.00
R9 Jene Morris 6.00 15.00
R10 Natasha Lacy 6.00 15.00
R11 Kalana Greene 6.00 15.00
R12 Marion Jones 10.00 25.00

2011 WNBA

STATED PRINT RUN 225 SER.#'d SETS
1 Diana Taurasi 8.00 20.00
2 Cappie Pondexter 2.50 6.00
3 Angel McCoughtry 2.00 5.00
4 Candace Parker 8.00 20.00
5 Lauren Jackson 6.00 15.00
6 Tamika Catchings 3.00 8.00
7 Sylvia Fowles 2.50 6.00
8 Iziane Castro-Marques 1.25 3.00
9 Seimone Augustus 4.00 10.00
10 Tina Thompson 4.00 10.00
11 Crystal Langhorne 2.00 5.00
12 Penny Taylor 2.50 6.00
13 Candice Dupree 2.00 5.00
14 Tina Charles 3.00 8.00
15 DeLisha Milton-Jones 1.25 3.00
16 Sophia Young 1.50 4.00
17 Becky Hammon 6.00 15.00
18 Monique Currie 1.50 4.00
19 Swin Cash 2.50 6.00
20 Candice Wiggins 4.00 10.00
21 Katie Douglas 2.00 5.00
22 Renee Montgomery 1.25 3.00
23 Sancho Lyttle 1.25 3.00
24 Lindsay Whalen 3.00 8.00
25 Ivory Latta 2.00 5.00
26 Erika DeSouza 1.25 3.00
27 Lindsey Harding 1.50 4.00
28 DeWanna Bonner 1.25 3.00
29 Scholanda Robinson 1.25 3.00
30 Charde Houston 2.00 5.00
31 Matee Ajavon 1.50 4.00
32 Rebekkah Brunson 1.25 3.00
33 Monica Wright 2.00 5.00
34 Sue Bird 10.00 25.00
35 Asjha Jones 1.50 4.00
36 Jia Perkins 1.25 3.00
37 Taj McWilliams-Franklin 1.25 3.00
38 Michelle Snow 1.50 4.00
39 Noelle Quinn 2.00 5.00
40 Camille Little 1.25 3.00
41 Tan White 1.50 4.00
42 Kara Braxton 1.50 4.00
43 Epiphanny Prince 1.50 4.00
44 Plenette Pierson 1.25 3.00
45 Kelsey Griffin 2.00 5.00
46 Katie Smith 4.00 10.00
47 Leilani Mitchell 1.25 3.00
48 Nicole Powell 1.50 4.00
49 Tangela Smith 1.25 3.00
50 Temeka Johnson 1.25 3.00
51 Tanisha Wright 1.25 3.00
52 Nicky Anosike 2.00 5.00
53 Dominique Canty 2.00 5.00
54 Marie Ferdinand-Harris 1.25 3.00
55 Essence Carson 2.00 5.00
56 Amber Holt 2.00 5.00
57 Kristi Toliver 1.50 4.00
58 Kelly Miller 1.25 3.00
59 Kara Lawson 2.50 6.00
60 Tammy Sutton-Brown 1.25 3.00
61 Ebony Hoffman 1.50 4.00
62 Ticha Penicheiro 3.00 8.00
63 Sheryl Swoopes 4.00 10.00

2011 WNBA 3-Box Incentive Autographs

NNO Tina Charles/55 50.00 120.00

2011 WNBA Autographs

STATED ODDS THREE PER PACK
NNO CARDS LISTED BY INITIALS
AH Amber Harris 3.00 8.00
AM Angel McCoughtry 6.00 15.00
CP Cappie Pondexter 3.00 8.00
CV Courtney Vandersloot 8.00 20.00
DR Danielle Robinson 4.00 10.00
DT Diana Taurasi 10.00 25.00
JM1 Jene Morris 3.00 8.00
JM2 Jacinta Monroe 3.00 8.00
JP Jeanette Pohlen 5.00 12.00
JT Jasmine Thomas 3.00 8.00
KG1 Kelsey Griffin 5.00 12.00
KG2 Kalana Greene 3.00 8.00
KP Kayla Pedersen 4.00 10.00
MM1 Maya Moore 40.00 80.00
MM2 Maya Moore VAR 100.00 200.00
Dressed, holding jersey
PT Penny Taylor 8.00 20.00
TP Ta'Shia Phillips 3.00 8.00
VD Victoria Dunlap 3.00 8.00

2011 WNBA Rookies

STATED PRINT RUN 225 SER.#'d SETS
R1 Maya Moore 30.00 80.00
R2 Elizabeth Cambage 8.00 20.00
R3 Courtney Vandersloot 6.00 15.00
R4 Amber Harris 6.00 15.00
R5 Jantel Lavender 5.00 12.00
R6 Danielle Robinson 6.00 15.00
R7 Kayla Pedersen 6.00 15.00
R8 Ta'Shia Phillips 5.00 12.00
R9 Jeanette Pohlen 6.00 15.00
R10 Victoria Dunlap 5.00 12.00
R11 Jasmine Thomas 5.00 12.00
R12 Danielle Adams 6.00 15.00

2012 WNBA

COMPLETE FACT.SET (111) 60.00 150.00
COMPLETE SET (96) 30.00 80.00
ANNOUNCED PRINT RUN 400 SETS
1 Angel McCoughtry 1.50 4.00
2 Armintie Price 1.25 3.00
3 Cathrine Kraayeveld 1.00 2.50
4 Ketia Swanier 1.00 2.50
5 Lindsey Harding 1.25 3.00
6 Sancho Lyttle 1.00 2.50
7 Yelena Leuchanka 1.00 2.50
8 Courtney Vandersloot 1.25 3.00
9 Epiphanny Prince 1.25 3.00
10 Eshaya Murphy 1.25 3.00
11 Le'coe Willingham 1.00 2.50
12 Ruth Riley 1.50 4.00
13 Swin Cash 2.00 5.00
14 Sylvia Fowles 2.00 5.00
15 Tamera Young 1.00 2.50
16 Ticha Penicheiro 2.50 6.00
17 Allison Hightower RC 1.50 4.00
18 Asjha Jones 1.25 3.00
19 Danielle McCray 1.00 2.50
20 Kalana Greene 1.25 3.00
21 Kara Lawson 2.00 5.00
22 Mistie Mims RC 1.50 4.00
23 Renee Montgomery 1.00 2.50
24 Tan White 1.25 3.00
25 Tina Charles 2.50 6.00
26 Briann January 1.00 2.50
27 Erin Phillips 2.00 5.00
28 Jeanette Pohlen 1.25 3.00
29 Jessica Davenport 1.25 3.00
30 Katie Douglas 1.50 4.00
31 Shavonte Zellous 1.00 2.50
32 Tamika Catchings 2.50 6.00
33 Tammy Sutton-Brown 1.00 2.50
34 Alana Beard 2.00 5.00
35 Candace Parker 6.00 15.00
36 Delisha Milton-Jones 1.00 2.50
37 Ebony Hoffman 1.25 3.00
38 Jantel Lavender 1.00 2.50
39 Kristi Toliver 1.25 3.00
40 Marissa Coleman 1.25 3.00
41 Candice Wiggins 3.00 8.00
42 Jessica Adair RC 1.50 4.00
43 Lindsay Whalen 2.50 6.00
44 Maya Moore 6.00 15.00
45 Monica Wright 1.50 4.00
46 Rebekkah Brunson 1.00 2.50
47 Seimone Augustus 3.00 8.00
48 Taj McWilliams-Franklin 1.00 2.50
49 Cappie Pondexter 2.00 5.00
50 DeMya Walker 1.00 2.50
51 Essence Carson 1.50 4.00
52 Kara Braxton 1.25 3.00
53 Kelly Miller 1.00 2.50
54 Kia Vaughn 1.00 2.50
55 Leilani Mitchell 1.00 2.50
56 Nicole Powell 1.25 3.00
57 Plenette Pierson 1.00 2.50
58 Alexis Gray-Lawson RC 1.50 4.00
59 Alexis Hornbuckle 2.00 5.00
60 Candice Dupree 1.50 4.00
61 Charde Houston 1.50 4.00
62 DeWanna Bonner 1.00 2.50
63 Diana Taurasi 6.00 15.00
64 Nakia Sanford 1.25 3.00
65 Becky Hammon 5.00 12.00
66 Danielle Adams 1.25 3.00
67 Danielle Robinson 1.25 3.00
68 Jayne Appel 1.50 4.00
69 Jia Perkins 1.00 2.50
70 Shameka Christon 1.00 2.50
71 Sophia Young 1.25 3.00
72 Tangela Smith 1.00 2.50
73 Ann Wauters 1.25 3.00
74 Camille Little 1.00 2.50
75 Ewelina Kobryn RC 1.50 4.00
76 Katie Smith 3.00 8.00
77 Lauren Jackson 5.00 12.00
78 Sue Bird 8.00 20.00
79 Tanisha Wright 1.00 2.50
80 Tina Thompson 3.00 8.00
81 Chante Black 1.00 2.50
82 Ivory Latta 1.50 4.00
83 Courtney Paris 1.00 2.50
84 Jennifer Lacy 1.00 2.50
85 Kayla Pedersen 1.25 3.00
86 Liz Cambage 1.50 4.00
87 Scholanda Dorrell 1.00 2.50
88 Temeka Johnson 1.00 2.50
89 Ashley Robinson 1.00 2.50
90 Crystal Langhorne 1.50 4.00
91 Shannon Bobbitt 1.00 2.50
92 Jasmine Thomas 1.00 2.50
93 Matee Ajavon 1.25 3.00
94 Michelle Snow 1.25 3.00
95 Monique Currie 1.25 3.00
96 Noelle Quinn 1.50 4.00
NNO Nnemkadi Ogwumike AU 10.00 25.00

2012 WNBA Rookies

COMPLETE SET (14) 20.00 50.00
ANNOUNCED PRINT RUN 400 SETS
R1 Nnemkadi Ogwumike 5.00 12.00
R2 Shekinna Stricklen 4.00 10.00
R3 Devereaux Peters 4.00 10.00
R4 Glory Johnson 5.00 12.00
R5 Shenise Johnson 2.50 6.00
R6 Samantha Prahalis 6.00 15.00
R7 Kelley Cain 4.00 10.00
R8 Natalie Novosel 5.00 12.00
R9 Sasha Goodlett 2.50 6.00
R10 Riquna Williams 2.50 6.00
R11 Avery Warley 2.50 6.00
R12 Tiffany Hayes 4.00 10.00
R13 Aneika Henry 2.50 6.00
R14 April Sykes 2.50 6.00

1995 Women's Basketball Association

Produced by Fair Play Inc., this set consists of nineteen player cards and eight schedule cards of the Women's Basketball Association. The player cards present the 1994 WBA All-Stars. Measuring the standard size, the player card fronts feature full-bleed color action photos. The player's name is printed in a stripe across the bottom. Either "American Conference" or "National Conference" is printed vertically in red block lettering along the right edge. The backs carry a color closeup photo, biography, and professional and college statistics. The schedule cards show the team logo on the front and the schedule on the back.

COMPLETE SET (27) 4.00 10.00
1 Checklist .20 .50
2 Lightning Mitchell DIR .20 .50
3 Sarah Campbell .20 .50
4 Lisa Carlsen .20 .50
5 Joy Champ .20 .50
6 Cledella Evans .20 .50
7 Crystal Flint .20 .50
8 Robbie Garcia .20 .50
9 Kay Kay Hart .20 .50
10 Petra Jackson .20 .50
11 Patrice Marshall .20 .50
12 Evette Ott .20 .50
13 Lynn Page .20 .50
14 Lisa Sandbothe .20 .50
15 Danielle Shareef .20 .50
16 Lisa Tate .20 .50
17 Diana Vines .20 .50
18 Tammy Williams .20 .50
19 Cynthia Wilson .20 .50
L1 Kansas City Mustangs .08 .25
L2 Chicago Twisters .08 .25
L3 St. Louis River Queens .08 .25
L4 Kentucky Marauders .08 .25
L5 Memphis Blues .08 .25
L6 Minnesota Stars .08 .25
L7 Nebraska Express .08 .25
L8 Oklahoma Flames .08 .25

1993 World University Games

This 10-card set features borderless photos of various sporting events at the World University Games in Buffalo in 1993. The backs display two different ways the collector could win prizes in two different scratch-off games. The cards are unnumbered and checklisted below alphabetically according to the sport pictured on the card front.

COMPLETE SET (10) 1.20 3.00
2 Basketball .10 .25

1993 XXV Jogos Olimpicos

This 84-card set commemorates medal winners from the 1992 XXV Olympics in Barcelona. The cards measure 2 11/16" by 3 7/8", have rounded corners, and are printed on thin cardboard stock. The fronts feature full-bleed color action photos, with the event, player's name, and country in one of the corners. The back is divided into two registers.The top register consists of a 1993 calendar, while the bottom lists the three medal winners' names, countries, and their winning scores or times. All text is in Portuguese. NBA stars Scottie Pippen (77) and Magic Johnson (78) are featured in this set.

COMPLETE SET (84) 25.00 60.00
77 Scottie Pippen 3.00 8.00
78 Magic Johnson 5.00 12.00

1996-97 Z-Force

The inaugural edtion of SkyBox Z-Force has a total of 200 cards. The eight-card hobby and retail packs carry a suggested retail price of $2.49 each. Card fronts contain an action shot of the player against an "explosive-type" background. The player's name is in block letters at the top of the card and the SkyBox Z-Force logo is outlined in gold foil along the bottom right of the card. Card backs contain a hardwood floor design in the background with a player shot over it. Statistical and biographical information is also located on the back. The cards are grouped alphabetically within teams. The series two cards feature the same graphics as series one, but a thicker card stock. A Grant Hill Total Z card was inserted in series two packs at a rate of one in 900 packs. The card is a one-shot leather card. Series two packs also featured a 10-card redemption for a full set of the 1996-97 SkyBox Autographics program. The tough card number was card #5. Also, a non-numbered two-card promo sheet was also issued for the first series which features a basic card of Grant Hill and Jerry Stackhouse. For the second series, a Grant Hill promo was released that mirrored his regular issue card bearing the words "Promotion Sample" on the front and back. The two promos are listed below at the end of the set.

COMPLETE SET (200) 20.00 40.00
COMPLETE SERIES 1 (100) 10.00 20.00
COMPLETE SERIES 2 (100) 10.00 20.00
1 Mookie Blaylock .12 .30
2 Alan Henderson .12 .30
3 Christian Laettner .15 .40
4 Steve Smith .15 .40
5 Rick Fox .12 .30
6 Dino Radja .15 .40
7 Eric Williams .12 .30
8 Muggsy Bogues .15 .40
9 Larry Johnson .20 .50
10 Glen Rice .20 .50
11 Michael Jordan 1.50 4.00
12 Toni Kukoc .20 .50
13 Scottie Pippen .30 .75
14 Dennis Rodman .40 1.00
15 Terrell Brandon .12 .30
16 Bobby Phills .12 .30
17 Bob Sura .12 .30
18 Jim Jackson .12 .30
19 Jason Kidd .30 .75
20 Jamal Mashburn .15 .40
21 George McCloud .12 .30
22 Mahmoud Abdul-Rauf .12 .30
23 Antonio McDyess .20 .50
24 Dikembe Mutombo .20 .50
25 Joe Dumars .20 .50
26 Grant Hill .30 .75
27 Allan Houston .15 .40
28 Otis Thorpe .12 .30
29 Chris Mullin .20 .50
30 Joe Smith .15 .40
31 Latrell Sprewell .20 .50
32 Sam Cassell .15 .40
33 Clyde Drexler .25 .60
34 Robert Horry .15 .40
35 Hakeem Olajuwon .25 .60
36 Travis Best .12 .30
37 Dale Davis .12 .30
38 Reggie Miller .25 .60
39 Rik Smits .15 .40
40 Brent Barry .15 .40
41 Loy Vaught .12 .30
42 Brian Williams .12 .30
43 Cedric Ceballos .12 .30
44 Eddie Jones .20 .50
45 Nick Van Exel .20 .50
46 Tim Hardaway .20 .50
47 Alonzo Mourning .25 .60
48 Kurt Thomas .12 .30
49 Walt Williams .12 .30
50 Vin Baker .15 .40
51 Glenn Robinson .20 .50
52 Kevin Garnett .50 1.25
53 Tom Gugliotta .12 .30
54 Isaiah Rider .15 .40
55 Shawn Bradley .12 .30
56 Chris Childs .12 .30
57 Jayson Williams .12 .30
58 Patrick Ewing .25 .60
59 Anthony Mason .12 .30
60 Charles Oakley .15 .40
61 Nick Anderson .12 .30
62 Horace Grant .15 .40
63 Anfernee Hardaway .30 .75
64 Shaquille O'Neal .50 1.25
65 Dennis Scott .12 .30
66 Jerry Stackhouse .25 .60
67 Clarence Weatherspoon .12 .30
68 Charles Barkley .30 .75
69 Michael Finley .25 .60
70 Kevin Johnson .20 .50
71 Clifford Robinson .12 .30
72 Arvydas Sabonis .15 .40
73 Rod Strickland .12 .30
74 Tyus Edney .12 .30
75 Brian Grant .15 .40
76 Billy Owens .12 .30
77 Mitch Richmond .20 .50
78 Vinny Del Negro .12 .30
79 Sean Elliott .20 .50
80 Avery Johnson .15 .40
81 David Robinson .30 .75
82 Hersey Hawkins .12 .30
83 Shawn Kemp .20 .50
84 Gary Payton .20 .50
85 Detlef Schrempf .20 .50
86 Doug Christie .12 .30
87 Damon Stoudamire .20 .50
88 Sharone Wright .12 .30
89 Jeff Hornacek .15 .40
90 Karl Malone .25 .60
91 John Stockton .25 .60
92 Greg Anthony .12 .30
93 Bryant Reeves .12 .30
94 Byron Scott .15 .40
95 Juwan Howard .15 .40
96 Gheorghe Muresan .12 .30
97 Rasheed Wallace .25 .60
98 Chris Webber .25 .60
99 Checklist .12 .30
100 Checklist .12 .30
101 Dikembe Mutombo .20 .50
102 Dee Brown .12 .30
103 Dell Curry .12 .30
104 Vlade Divac .20 .50
105 Anthony Mason .12 .30
106 Robert Parish .20 .50
107 Oliver Miller .12 .30
108 Eric Montross .12 .30
109 Ervin Johnson .12 .30
110 Stacey Augmon .15 .40
111 Charles Barkley .30 .75
112 Jalen Rose .15 .40
113 Rodney Rogers .12 .30
114 Shaquille O'Neal .50 1.25
115 Dan Majerle .20 .50
116 Kendall Gill .12 .30
117 Khalid Reeves .12 .30
118 Allan Houston .15 .40
119 Larry Johnson .20 .50
120 John Starks .15 .40
121 Rony Seikaly .15 .40
122 Gerald Wilkins .12 .30
123 Michael Cage .12 .30
124 Derrick Coleman .15 .40
125 Sam Cassell .15 .40
126 Danny Manning .15 .40
127 Robert Horry .15 .40
128 Kenny Anderson .15 .40
129 Isaiah Rider .15 .40
130 Rasheed Wallace .25 .60
131 Mahmoud Abdul-Rauf .12 .30
132 Vernon Maxwell .12 .30
133 Dominique Wilkins .25 .60
134 Hubert Davis .12 .30
135 Popeye Jones .12 .30
136 Anthony Peeler .12 .30
137 Tracy Murray .12 .30
138 Rod Strickland .12 .30
139 Shareef Abdur-Rahim RC .40 1.00
140 Ray Allen RC .75 2.00
141 Shandon Anderson RC .20 .50
142 Kobe Bryant RC 4.00 10.00
143 Marcus Camby RC .30 .75
144 Erick Dampier RC .20 .50
145 Emanual Davis RC .20 .50
146 Tony Delk RC .20 .50
147 Todd Fuller RC .20 .50
148 Darvin Ham RC .20 .50
149 Othella Harrington RC .20 .50
150 Shane Heal RC .20 .50
151 Allen Iverson RC 1.00 2.50
152 Dontae' Jones RC .20 .50
153 Kerry Kittles RC .20 .50
154 Priest Lauderdale RC .20 .50
155 Matt Maloney RC .20 .50
156 Stephon Marbury RC .50 1.25
157 Walter McCarty RC .20 .50
158 Steve Nash RC 1.00 2.50
159 Jermaine O'Neal RC .50 1.25
160 Ray Owes RC .20 .50
161 Vitaly Potapenko RC .20 .50
162 Roy Rogers RC .20 .50
163 Antoine Walker RC .40 1.00
164 Samaki Walker RC .20 .50
165 Ben Wallace RC 1.00 2.50
166 John Wallace RC .20 .50
167 Jerome Williams RC .20 .50
168 Lorenzen Wright RC .20 .50
169 Vin Baker ZUP .15 .40
170 Charles Barkley ZUP .30 .75
171 Patrick Ewing ZUP .25 .60
172 Michael Finley ZUP .25 .60
173 Kevin Garnett ZUP .50 1.25
174 Anfernee Hardaway ZUP .30 .75
175 Grant Hill ZUP .30 .75
176 Juwan Howard ZUP .15 .40
177 Jim Jackson ZUP .12 .30
178 Eddie Jones ZUP .20 .50
179 Michael Jordan ZUP 1.50 4.00
180 Shawn Kemp ZUP .20 .50
181 Jason Kidd ZUP .30 .75
182 Karl Malone ZUP .25 .60
183 Antonio McDyess ZUP .20 .50
184 Reggie Miller ZUP .25 .60
185 Alonzo Mourning ZUP .25 .60
186 Hakeem Olajuwon ZUP .25 .60
187 Shaquille O'Neal ZUP .50 1.25
188 Gary Payton ZUP .20 .50
189 Mitch Richmond ZUP .20 .50
190 Clifford Robinson ZUP .12 .30
191 David Robinson ZUP .30 .75
192 Glenn Robinson ZUP .20 .50
193 Dennis Rodman ZUP .40 1.00
194 Joe Smith ZUP .15 .40
195 Jerry Stackhouse ZUP .25 .60
196 John Stockton ZUP .25 .60
197 Damon Stoudamire ZUP .20 .50
198 Chris Webber ZUP .25 .60
199 Checklist (101-157) .12 .30
200 Checklist (158-200/ins.) .12 .30
NNO Grant Hill PROMO .75 2.00
NNO Grant Hill .75 2.00
Jerry Stackhouse PROMO
NNO Grant Hill Total Z 8.00 20.00

1996-97 Z-Force Z-Cling

Inserted one per series one pack, this 100-card set is a semi-parallel to the regular set. The card fronts are identical to the basic issue, but the card backs are blank outside of the player's name and the card number. 96 of the original 100 cards are parallels. The exceptions are Shaquille O'Neal, which has him in a Laker uniform on the parallel, the Byron Scott card (#94), which was never issued and the two checklist cards. The Byron Scott card and the two checklists were replaced with the following rookies: Ray Allen (#R1), Stephon Marbury (#R2) and Shareef Abdur-Rahim (#R3), thus making the set complete at 100 cards. To ascertain values of individual cards, please refer to the multiplier in the header, coupled with the value of the basic card.

COMPLETE SET (100) 15.00 40.00
*Z-CLING: .75X TO 2X BASIC
64 Shaquille O'Neal 2.00 5.00
Lakers uniform
R1 Ray Allen 2.50 6.00
R2 Stephon Marbury 1.50 4.00
R3 Shareef Abdur-Rahim 1.25 3.00

1996-97 Z-Force Big Men on the Court

Randomly inserted in series two packs at a rate of one in 240, this 10-card die-cut set feature some of the leagues top players. The cards are printed with silver foil with the insert set name "Big Men on the Court" in the background.

COMPLETE SET (10) 300.00 600.00
1 Charles Barkley 20.00 50.00
2 Anfernee Hardaway 20.00 50.00
3 Grant Hill 20.00 50.00
4 Michael Jordan 250.00 450.00
5 Shawn Kemp 15.00 40.00
6 Alonzo Mourning 15.00 40.00
7 Hakeem Olajuwon 20.00 50.00
8 Shaquille O'Neal 30.00 80.00
9 Scottie Pippen 25.00 60.00
10 David Robinson 20.00 50.00

1996-97 Z-Force Big Men on the Court Z-peat

Randomly inserted in series two packs at a rate of one in 1,120, this 10-card set parallels the Big Men on the Court regular insert. These cards have the same die-cut design, but use gold foil rather that silver. Card fronts also have the name "Z-peat" on them to further distinguish between the two sets. To ascertain values on individual cards, please refer to the multiplier in the header below, coupled with the value of the base card.

*STARS: .75X TO 2X HI COLUMN
4 Michael Jordan 600.00 1000.00

1996-97 Z-Force Little Big Men

Randomly inserted in series two retail packs only at a rate of one in 36, this 10-card set focuses on some of the NBA's smaller superstars. Card fronts contain buildings in the background on silver foil.

COMPLETE SET (10) 20.00 40.00
1 Kenny Anderson 2.00 5.00
2 Mookie Blaylock 1.50 4.00
3 Muggsy Bogues 2.00 5.00
4 Terrell Brandon 1.50 4.00
5 Allen Iverson 6.00 15.00
6 Avery Johnson 2.00 5.00
7 Kevin Johnson 2.50 6.00
8 Stephon Marbury 3.00 8.00
9 Gary Payton 2.50 6.00
10 Nick Van Exel 2.50 6.00

1996-97 Z-Force Slam Cam

Randomly inserted in series one hobby and retail packs at a rate of one in 240, this nine-card set features some of the top slam dunkers in the game. Card fronts contain a kaleidoscopic color background with an action photo laid on top. The player's name and the set name "Slam Cam" are loctated above the photo. Card backs are horizontal with the set name in the background with another action shot of the player. The cards are numbered with a "SC" prefix.

COMPLETE SET (9) 175.00 350.00
SC1 Clyde Drexler 12.00 30.00
SC2 Michael Finley 12.00 30.00
SC3 Anfernee Hardaway 15.00 40.00
SC4 Grant Hill 15.00 40.00
SC5 Michael Jordan 125.00 250.00
SC6 Shawn Kemp 10.00 25.00
SC7 Karl Malone 12.00 30.00
SC8 Antonio McDyess 10.00 25.00
SC9 Shaquille O'Neal 25.00 60.00

1996-97 Z-Force Swat Team

Randomly inserted in series one hobby packs only at a rate of one in 72, this 9-card set features some of the leagues best blockers. Card front backgrounds are prismatic with the logo "Swat Team" designed into it. An action shot of the player is laid on top with their names directly underneath. Card backs contain the same type background as the front, without the prismatic foil. The cards are numbered with a "ST" prefix.

COMPLETE SET (9) 40.00 80.00
ST1 Patrick Ewing 5.00 12.00
ST2 Kevin Garnett 10.00 25.00
ST3 Alonzo Mourning 5.00 12.00
ST4 Dikembe Mutombo 4.00 10.00
ST5 Hakeem Olajuwon 5.00 12.00
ST6 Shaquille O'Neal 10.00 25.00
ST7 David Robinson 6.00 15.00
ST8 Dennis Rodman 8.00 20.00
ST9 Joe Smith 3.00 8.00

1996-97 Z-Force Vortex

Randomly inserted in series one retail packs only at a rate of one in 36, this 15-card set features embossed card fronts with a swirl background. The action shot of the player is located in the middle of the card with the player's name in gold foil block letters directly below. Card backs are horizontal with a similar background and have a brief commentary along with another action shot. The cards are numbered as "Vortex/X".

COMPLETE SET (15) 50.00 120.00
V1 Charles Barkley 5.00 12.00
V2 Anfernee Hardaway 5.00 12.00
V3 Grant Hill 5.00 12.00
V4 Juwan Howard 2.50 6.00
V5 Michael Jordan 30.00 80.00
V6 Jason Kidd 5.00 12.00
V7 Reggie Miller 4.00 10.00
V8 Gary Payton 3.00 8.00
V9 Scottie Pippen 5.00 12.00
V10 Mitch Richmond 3.00 8.00
V11 Glenn Robinson 3.00 8.00
V12 Arvydas Sabonis 2.50 6.00
V13 Jerry Stackhouse 4.00 10.00
V14 John Stockton 4.00 10.00
V15 Damon Stoudamire 3.00 8.00

1996-97 Z-Force Zebut

Randomly inserted in series two hobby packs only at a rate of one in 24, this 20-card set features embossed and printed on silver foil. The set focuses on first year players from the 96-97 class.

COMPLETE SET (20) 50.00 100.00
1 Shareef Abdur-Rahim 3.00 8.00
2 Ray Allen 6.00 15.00
3 Kobe Bryant 20.00 50.00
4 Marcus Camby 2.50 6.00
5 Erick Dampier 1.50 4.00
6 Todd Fuller 1.50 4.00
7 Othella Harrington 1.50 4.00
8 Allen Iverson 8.00 20.00
9 Kerry Kittles 1.50 4.00
10 Priest Lauderdale 1.50 4.00
11 Stephon Marbury 4.00 10.00
12 Steve Nash 8.00 20.00
13 Jermaine O'Neal 4.00 10.00
14 Ray Owes 1.50 4.00
15 Vitaly Potapenko 1.50 4.00
16 Roy Rogers 1.50 4.00
17 Antoine Walker 3.00 8.00
18 Samaki Walker 1.50 4.00
19 John Wallace 1.50 4.00
20 Lorenzen Wright 1.50 4.00

1996-97 Z-Force Zebut Z-peat

Randomly inserted in series two hobby packs only at a rate of one in 240, this 20-card set parallels the Zebut insert. The only difference with the parallel is the cards are printed on gold foil rather that silver. Card fronts also have the name "Z-peat" on them to further distinguish between the two sets. To ascertain values on individual cards, please refer to the multiplier in the header below, coupled with the value of the base card.

*ZPEAT: 1.5X TO 4X BASE HI
3 Kobe Bryant 100.00 250.00

1996-97 Z-Force Zensations

Randomly inserted in all series two packs at a rate of one in six, this 20-card set features a foil-stamped background and focuses on veterans and rookies. Card fronts feature the player spotlighted.

COMPLETE SET (20) 10.00 25.00
1 Shareef Abdur-Rahim 1.00 2.50
2 Ray Allen 2.00 5.00
3 Nick Anderson .50 1.25
4 Vin Baker .60 1.50
5 Mookie Blaylock .50 1.25
6 Calbert Cheaney .50 1.25
7 Kevin Garnett 2.00 5.00
8 Horace Grant .60 1.50
9 Tim Hardaway .75 2.00
10 Allen Iverson 2.50 6.00
11 Avery Johnson .60 1.50
12 Kevin Johnson .75 2.00
13 Danny Manning .60 1.50
14 Stephon Marbury 1.25 3.00
15 Jamal Mashburn .60 1.50
16 Glen Rice .75 2.00
17 Isaiah Rider .60 1.50
18 Latrell Sprewell .75 2.00
19 Rod Strickland .50 1.25
20 Nick Van Exel .75 2.00

1997-98 Z-Force

This 210-card set was issued in two series, distributed in eight-card packs with a suggested retail price of $1.59. The fronts feature borderless color action player photos printed on 14 pt. card stock with gold foil stamping and UV coating. The player's name is written vertically down the side in different foil colors. The backs carry another player photo and player information.

COMPLETE SET (210) 12.50 25.00
COMPLETE SERIES 1 (110) 5.00 10.00
COMPLETE SERIES 2 (100) 7.50 15.00
1 Anfernee Hardaway .25 .60
2 Mitch Richmond .15 .40
3 Stephon Marbury .20 .50
4 Charles Barkley .25 .60
5 Juwan Howard .12 .30
6 Avery Johnson .12 .30
7 Rex Chapman .10 .25
8 Antoine Walker .15 .40
9 Nick Van Exel .12 .30
10 Tim Hardaway .15 .40
11 Clarence Weatherspoon .10 .25
12 John Stockton .20 .50
13 Glenn Robinson .12 .30
14 Anthony Mason .10 .25
15 Latrell Sprewell .15 .40
16 Kendall Gill .10 .25
17 Terry Mills .10 .25
18 Mookie Blaylock .10 .25
19 Michael Finley .15 .40
20 Gary Payton .15 .40
21 Kevin Garnett .30 .75
22 Clyde Drexler .20 .50
23 Michael Jordan 1.25 3.00
24 Antonio McDyess .12 .30
25 Nick Anderson .10 .25
26 Patrick Ewing .20 .50
27 Anthony Peeler .10 .25
28 Doug Christie .10 .25
29 Bobby Phills .10 .25
30 Kerry Kittles .10 .25
31 Reggie Miller .20 .50
32 Karl Malone .20 .50
33 Grant Hill .25 .60
34 Shaquille O'Neal .40 1.00
35 Loy Vaught .10 .25
36 Kenny Anderson .12 .30
37 Wesley Person .10 .25
38 Jamal Mashburn .12 .30
39 Christian Laettner .12 .30
40 Shawn Kemp .15 .40
41 Glen Rice .15 .40
42 Vin Baker .12 .30
43 Popeye Jones .10 .25
44 Derrick Coleman .12 .30
45 Rik Smits .12 .30
46 Dale Ellis .10 .25
47 Rod Strickland .10 .25
48 Mark Price .15 .40
49 Toni Kukoc .15 .40
50 David Robinson .25 .60
51 John Wallace .10 .25
52 Samaki Walker .10 .25
53 Shareef Abdur-Rahim .15 .40
54 Rodney Rogers .10 .25
55 Dikembe Mutombo .15 .40
56 Rony Seikaly .12 .30
57 Matt Maloney .10 .25
58 Chris Webber .15 .40
59 Robert Horry .12 .30
60 Rasheed Wallace .15 .40
61 Jeff Hornacek .12 .30
62 Walt Williams .10 .25
63 Detlef Schrempf .15 .40
64 Dan Majerle .15 .40
65 Dell Curry .10 .25
66 Scottie Pippen .25 .60
67 Greg Anthony .10 .25
68 Mahmoud Abdul-Rauf .10 .25
69 Cedric Ceballos .10 .25
70 Terrell Brandon .10 .25
71 Arvydas Sabonis .12 .30
72 Malik Sealy .10 .25
73 Dean Garrett .10 .25
74 Joe Dumars .15 .40
75 Joe Smith .12 .30
76 Shawn Bradley .10 .25
77 Gheorghe Muresan .10 .25
78 Dale Davis .10 .25
79 Bryant Stith .10 .25
80 Lorenzen Wright .10 .25
81 Chris Childs .10 .25
82 Bryon Russell .10 .25
83 Steve Smith .12 .30
84 Jerry Stackhouse .15 .40
85 Hersey Hawkins .10 .25
86 Ray Allen .20 .50
87 Dominique Wilkins .20 .50
88 Kobe Bryant .75 2.00
89 Tom Gugliotta .10 .25
90 Dennis Scott .10 .25
91 Dennis Rodman .30 .75
92 Bryant Reeves .10 .25
93 Vlade Divac .15 .40
94 Jason Kidd .25 .60
95 Mario Elie .10 .25
96 Lindsey Hunter .10 .25
97 Olden Polynice .10 .25
98 Allan Houston .12 .30
99 Alonzo Mourning .20 .50
100 Allen Iverson .30 .75
101 LaPhonso Ellis .10 .25
102 Bob Sura .10 .25
103 Chris Mullin .15 .40
104 Sam Cassell .12 .30
105 Eric Williams .10 .25
106 Antonio Davis .10 .25
107 Marcus Camby .15 .40
108 Isaiah Rider .10 .25
109 Checklist .10 .25
110 Checklist .10 .25
111 Tim Duncan RC 1.00 2.50
112 Joe Smith .12 .30
113 Shawn Kemp .15 .40
114 Terry Mills .10 .25
115 Jacque Vaughn RC .15 .40
116 Ron Mercer RC .20 .50
117 Brian Williams .10 .25
118 Rik Smits .12 .30
119 Eric Williams .10 .25
120 Tim Thomas RC .30 .75
121 Damon Stoudamire .15 .40
122 God Shammgod RC .15 .40
123 Tyrone Hill .10 .25
124 Elden Campbell .10 .25
125 Keith Van Horn RC .30 .75
126 Brian Grant .10 .25
127 Antonio McDyess .12 .30
128 Darrell Armstrong .10 .25
129 Sam Perkins .10 .25
130 Chris Mills .10 .25
131 Reggie Miller .20 .50
132 Chris Gatling .10 .25
133 Ed Gray RC .15 .40
134 Hakeem Olajuwon .20 .50
135 Chris Webber .15 .40
136 Kendall Gill .10 .25
137 Wesley Person .10 .25
138 Derrick Coleman .12 .30
139 Dana Barros .10 .25
140 Dennis Scott .10 .25
141 Paul Grant RC .15 .40
142 Scott Burrell .10 .25
144 Austin Croshere RC .15 .40
145 Maurice Taylor RC .15 .40
146 Kevin Johnson .15 .40
147 Tony Battie RC .20 .50
148 Tariq Abdul-Wahad RC .15 .40
149 Johnny Taylor RC .15 .40
150 Allen Iverson .30 .75
151 Terrell Brandon .10 .25
152 Derek Anderson RC .15 .40
153 Calbert Cheaney .10 .25
154 Jayson Williams .10 .25
155 Rick Fox .10 .25
156 John Thomas RC .15 .40
157 David Wesley .10 .25
158 Bobby Jackson RC .20 .50
159 Kelvin Cato RC .15 .40
160 Vinny Del Negro .10 .25
161 Adonal Foyle RC .15 .40
162 Larry Johnson .15 .40
163 Brevin Knight RC .15 .40
164 Rod Strickland .10 .25
165 Rodrick Rhodes RC .15 .40
166 Scot Pollard RC .15 .40
167 Sam Cassell .12 .30
168 Jerry Stackhouse .15 .40
169 Mark Jackson .15 .40
170 John Wallace .10 .25
171 Horace Grant .12 .30
172A Vin Baker .12 .30
172B Tracy McGrady ERR RC .75 2.00
173 Eddie Jones .15 .40
174 Kerry Kittles .10 .25
175 Antonio Daniels RC .15 .40
176 Alan Henderson .10 .25
177 Sean Elliott .15 .40
178 John Starks .12 .30
179 Chauncey Billups RC .60 1.50
180 Juwan Howard .12 .30
181 Bobby Phills .10 .25
182 Latrell Sprewell .15 .40
183 Jim Jackson .10 .25
184 Danny Fortson RC .15 .40
185 Zydrunas Ilgauskas .15 .40
186 Clifford Robinson .10 .25
187 Chris Mullin .15 .40
188 Greg Ostertag .10 .25
189 Antoine Walker ZUP .15 .40
190 Michael Jordan ZUP 1.25 3.00
191 Scottie Pippen ZUP .25 .60
192 Dennis Rodman ZUP .30 .75
193 Grant Hill ZUP .25 .60
194 Clyde Drexler ZUP .20 .50
195 Kobe Bryant ZUP .75 2.00
196 Shaquille O'Neal ZUP .40 1.00
197 Alonzo Mourning ZUP .20 .50
198 Ray Allen ZUP .20 .50
199 Kevin Garnett ZUP .30 .75
200 Stephon Marbury ZUP .20 .50
201 Anfernee Hardaway ZUP .25 .60
202 Jason Kidd ZUP .25 .60
203 David Robinson ZUP .25 .60
204 Gary Payton ZUP .15 .40
205 Marcus Camby ZUP .15 .40
206 Karl Malone ZUP .20 .50
207 John Stockton ZUP .20 .50
208 Shareef Abdur-Rahim ZUP .15 .40
209 Charles Barkley CL .25 .60
210 Gary Payton CL .15 .40

1997-98 Z-Force Rave

Randomly inserted in both series hobby packs only, this 208-card set is a hobby parallel version of the basic set. Less than 399 of this set were produced and are sequentially numbered. The cards are differentiated on the front by the silver "prismatic" foil in the player's name and the "Z-Force" logo. To ascertain values on individual cards, please refer to the multiplier in the header below, coupled with the value of the base card.

*STARS: 25X TO 60X BASE CARD HI
*RCs: 12X TO 30X BASE HI
23 Michael Jordan 250.00 500.00
88 Kobe Bryant 100.00 250.00
190 Michael Jordan ZUP 150.00 400.00

1997-98 Z-Force Super Rave

Randomly inserted in series two hobby packs only, this 100-card set parallels the series two set. The cards are serially numbered to 50.

*STARS: 100X TO 250X VALUE
*RCs: 50X TO 125X VALUE
111 Tim Duncan 250.00 500.00
135 Chris Webber 60.00 150.00
190 Michael Jordan ZUP 3000.00 4500.00
192 Dennis Rodman ZUP 175.00 350.00
194 Clyde Drexler ZUP 80.00 200.00
195 Kobe Bryant ZUP 600.00 1000.00

1997-98 Z-Force Big Men on Court

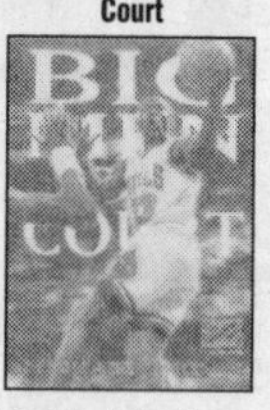

Randomly inserted in series two packs at a rate of one in 288, this 15-card set features some of the best players on the court. The cards are produced on special multi-dimensional thermo-plastic card stock.

COMPLETE SET (15) 1000.00 1500.00
1 Shareef Abdur-Rahim 20.00 50.00
2 Kobe Bryant 175.00 350.00
3 Marcus Camby 20.00 50.00
4 Tim Duncan 40.00 100.00
5 Kevin Garnett 40.00 100.00
6 Anfernee Hardaway 30.00 80.00
7 Grant Hill 30.00 80.00
8 Allen Iverson 40.00 100.00
9 Michael Jordan 350.00 650.00
10 Shawn Kemp 20.00 50.00
11 Stephon Marbury 25.00 60.00
12 Shaquille O'Neal 50.00 125.00
13 Scottie Pippen 40.00 100.00
14 Dennis Rodman 50.00 120.00
15 Antoine Walker 20.00 50.00

1997-98 Z-Force Boss

Randomly inserted in series one packs at a rate of one in six, this 20-card set features color action player photos of top players on the court. The card fronts feature a photo of the player embossed against a hardwood floor background. The backs carry player information.

COMPLETE SET (20) 12.00 30.00
*SUPER BOSS: 1.25X TO 3X BASE BOSS
SUPER BOSS: SER.1 STATED ODDS 1:36 H/R
1 Shareef Abdur-Rahim .50 1.25
2 Ray Allen .60 1.50
3 Kobe Bryant 2.50 6.00
4 Marcus Camby .50 1.25
5 Kevin Garnett 1.00 2.50
6 Anfernee Hardaway .75 2.00
7 Grant Hill .75 2.00
8 Allen Iverson 1.00 2.50
9 Eddie Jones .60 1.50
10 Michael Jordan 4.00 10.00
11 Shawn Kemp .50 1.25
12 Kerry Kittles .50 1.25
13 Stephon Marbury .60 1.50
14 Shaquille O'Neal 1.25 3.00
15 Hakeem Olajuwon .60 1.50
16 Scottie Pippen .75 2.00
17 Dennis Rodman 1.00 2.50
18 Joe Smith .40 1.00
19 Damon Stoudamire .50 1.25
20 Antoine Walker .50 1.25

1997-98 Z-Force Fast Track

Randomly inserted in series one packs at a rate of one in 24, this 12-card set features color action photos of players who are on the road to NBA stardom. Card fronts contain a yellow background with the title "Fast Track" having a felt-feel. The backs carry player information.

COMPLETE SET (12) 12.00 30.00
1 Ray Allen 1.50 4.00
2 Kobe Bryant 6.00 15.00
3 Marcus Camby 1.25 3.00
4 Juwan Howard 1.00 2.50
5 Eddie Jones 1.25 3.00
6 Kerry Kittles .75 2.00
7 Antonio McDyess 1.00 2.50
8 Joe Smith 1.00 2.50
9 Jerry Stackhouse 1.25 3.00
10 Damon Stoudamire 1.25 3.00
11 Antoine Walker 1.25 3.00
12 Chris Webber 1.25 3.00

1997-98 Z-Force Limited Access

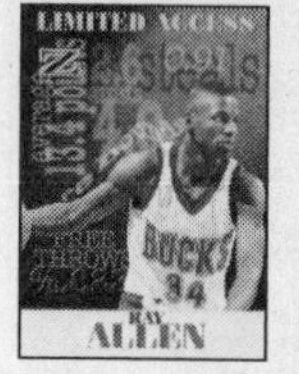

Randomly inserted in series one retail packs only at a rate of one in 18, this 10-card set features color player photos on a bi-fold card with in-depth statistical analysis.

COMPLETE SET (10) 15.00 40.00
1 Shareef Abdur-Rahim 1.25 3.00
2 Ray Allen 1.50 4.00
3 Charles Barkley 2.00 5.00
4 Anfernee Hardaway 2.00 5.00
5 Juwan Howard 1.00 2.50
6 Michael Jordan 10.00 25.00
7 Stephon Marbury 1.50 4.00
8 Shaquille O'Neal 3.00 8.00
9 Dennis Rodman 2.50 6.00
10 Antoine Walker 1.25 3.00

1997-98 Z-Force Quick Strike

Randomly inserted in series two packs at a rate of one in 96, this 12-card set focuses on players who can light up the scoreboard in the blink of an eye. Card fronts feature holofoil backing on clear plastic stock.

COMPLETE SET (12) 50.00 120.00
1 Shareef Abdur-Rahim 4.00 10.00
2 Anfernee Hardaway 6.00 15.00
3 Grant Hill 6.00 15.00
4 Allen Iverson 8.00 20.00
5 Michael Jordan 40.00 100.00
6 Stephon Marbury 5.00 12.00
7 Hakeem Olajuwon 5.00 12.00
8 Scottie Pippen 6.00 15.00
9 Damon Stoudamire 4.00 10.00
10 Keith Van Horn 4.00 10.00
11 Antoine Walker 4.00 10.00
12 Chris Webber 4.00 10.00

1997-98 Z-Force Rave Reviews

Randomly inserted in series one packs at a rate of one in 288, this 12-card set features color action photos of players who generate incredible numbers on the court and continually make the headlines. The backs carry player information.

COMPLETE SET (12) 300.00 550.00
1 Shareef Abdur-Rahim 12.00 30.00
2 Kevin Garnett 25.00 60.00
3 Anfernee Hardaway 20.00 50.00
4 Grant Hill 20.00 50.00
5 Allen Iverson 25.00 60.00
6 Michael Jordan 150.00 325.00
7 Shawn Kemp 15.00 40.00
8 Stephon Marbury 15.00 40.00
9 Shaquille O'Neal 30.00 80.00
10 Hakeem Olajuwon 15.00 40.00
11 Scottie Pippen 20.00 50.00
12 Dennis Rodman 25.00 60.00

997-98 Z-Force Slam Cam

Randomly inserted in series two packs at a rate of one in 36, this 12-card set featues NBA players who play their game above the rim. The card fronts feature a black and white film footage background on plastic stock.

COMPLETE SET (12) 40.00 70.00
1 Kobe Bryant 8.00 20.00
2 Marcus Camby 1.50 4.00
3 Tim Duncan 5.00 12.00
4 Kevin Garnett 3.00 8.00
5 Michael Jordan 12.00 30.00
6 Shawn Kemp 1.50 4.00
7 Karl Malone 2.00 5.00
8 Antonio McDyess 1.25 3.00
9 Shaquille O'Neal 4.00 10.00
10 Joe Smith 1.25 3.00
11 Jerry Stackhouse 1.50 4.00
12 Chris Webber 1.50 4.00

1997-98 Z-Force Star Gazing

Randomly inserted in series two retail packs at a rate of one in 18, this 15-card set features some of the NBA's best against a dark foil-board background.

COMPLETE SET (15) 30.00 60.00
1 Shareef Abdur-Rahim 1.50 4.00
2 Kobe Bryant 8.00 20.00
3 Marcus Camby 1.50 4.00
4 Kevin Garnett 3.00 8.00
5 Anfernee Hardaway 2.50 6.00
6 Grant Hill 2.50 6.00
7 Allen Iverson 3.00 8.00
8 Stephon Marbury 2.00 5.00
9 Hakeem Olajuwon 2.00 5.00
10 Shaquille O'Neal 4.00 10.00
11 Scottie Pippen 2.50 6.00
12 Dennis Rodman 3.00 8.00
13 Damon Stoudamire 1.50 4.00
14 Keith Van Horn 1.50 4.00
15 Antoine Walker 1.50 4.00

1997-98 Z-Force Total Impact

Randomly inserted in series one packs at a rate of one in 48, this 12-card set features color action photos of players who can hurt their opponents with their many skills. Card fronts carry a player shot against a diffracting foil background. The backs carry player information.

COMPLETE SET (12) 20.00 50.00
1 Kobe Bryant 8.00 20.00
2 Marcus Camby 1.50 4.00
3 Kevin Garnett 3.00 8.00
4 Grant Hill 2.50 6.00
5 Allen Iverson 3.00 8.00
6 Eddie Jones 1.50 4.00
7 Shawn Kemp 1.50 4.00
8 Kerry Kittles 1.00 2.50
9 Hakeem Olajuwon 2.00 5.00
10 Scottie Pippen 2.50 6.00
11 Joe Smith 1.25 3.00
12 Chris Webber 1.50 4.00

1997-98 Z-Force Zebut

Randomly inserted in series two packs at a rate of one in 24, this 12-card set features rookie phenoms who are destined for the NBA spotlight. Each player is set against a spotlight with a 100% die cut foil background

COMPLETE SET (12) 6.00 15.00
1 Derek Anderson .40 1.00
2 Tony Battie .50 1.25
3 Chauncey Billups 1.50 4.00
4 Austin Croshere .40 1.00
5 Antonio Daniels .40 1.00
6 Tim Duncan 2.50 6.00
7 Danny Fortson .40 1.00
8 Tracy McGrady 2.00 5.00
9 Ron Mercer .50 1.25
10 Tariq Abdul-Wahad .40 1.00
11 Tim Thomas .75 2.00
12 Keith Van Horn .75 2.00

1997-98 Z-Force Zensations

Randomly inserted in series two packs at a rate of one in six, this 25-card set features die cut, mulit-colored cards showcasing the league's marquee players.

COMPLETE SET (25) 6.00 15.00
1 Ray Allen .60 1.50
2 Vin Baker .40 1.00
3 Charles Barkley .75 2.00
4 Clyde Drexler .60 1.50
5 Patrick Ewing .60 1.50
6 Juwan Howard .40 1.00
7 Eddie Jones .50 1.25
8 Shawn Kemp .50 1.25
9 Jason Kidd .75 2.00
10 Kerry Kittles .30 .75
11 Karl Malone .60 1.50
12 Antonio McDyess .40 1.00
13 Hakeem Olajuwon .60 1.50
14 Gary Payton .50 1.25
15 Glen Rice .50 1.25
16 Mitch Richmond .50 1.25
17 David Robinson .75 2.00
18 Dennis Rodman 1.00 2.50
19 Joe Smith .40 1.00
20 Latrell Sprewell .50 1.25
21 Jerry Stackhouse .50 1.25
22 John Stockton .60 1.50
23 Damon Stoudamire .50 1.25
24 Rasheed Wallace .50 1.25
25 Chris Webber .50 1.25

1992 ACC Tournament Champs

This 40-card boxed set was offered by the Atlantic Coast Conference in conjunction with Spectator Sports Services. It features 36 championship teams from 1954 to 1989, including 19 NCAA Final Four teams and three national championship teams. Only 10,000 of this first edition set were produced, with the set number indicated on a sequentially numbered gold card of authenticity. Also each set includes a randomly inserted bonus card, which is a duplicate of one of the championship team cards but portrays the official ACC seal in gold foil. The standard-size cards display on the front reproductions of the original black and white or color team photos as taken during the respective ACC championship seasons. The information presented on the backs includes a synopsis of the championship game, the box score, a listing of players and coaches appearing in the team photo, and the winner of the MVP award of the ACC Tournament. There are a number of noteworthy inclusions in the photos that have increased demand somewhat for some of the cards; these are noted parenthetically in the checklist below.

COMPLETE SET (40) 8.00 20.00
1 '54 NC State Wolfpack .20 .50
2 '55 NC State Wolfpack .20 .40
3 '56 NC State Wolfpack .20 .40
4 '57 UNC Tar Heels .20 .40
5 '58 Maryland Terrapins .20 .40
6 '59 NC State Wolfpack .20 .40
7 '60 Duke Blue Devils .20 .40
8 '61 Wake Forest .25 .60
Demon Deacons
(Billy Packer)
9 '62 Wake Forest .25 .60
Demon Deacons
(Billy Packer)
10 '63 Duke Blue Devils .20 .50
11 '64 Duke Blue Devils .20 .40
12 '65 NC State Wolfpack .20 .40
13 '66 Duke Blue Devils .20 .40
14 '67 UNC Tar Heels .20 .40
15 '68 UNC Tar Heels .20 .40
16 '69 UNC Tar Heels .20 .40
17 '70 NC State Wolfpack .20 .40
18 '71 SC Gamecocks .20 .40
19 '72 UNC Tar Heels .20 .40
20 '73 NC State Wolfpack .20 .50
21 '74 NC State Wolfpack .40 1.00
22 '75 UNC Tar Heels .20 .40
23 '76 Virginia Cavaliers .20 .40
24 '77 UNC Tar Heels .20 .40
25 '78 Duke Blue Devils .20 .40
26 '79 UNC Tar Heels .20 .40
27 '80 Duke Blue Devils .20 .40
28 '81 UNC Tar Heels .20 .50
29 '82 UNC Tar Heels 5.00 12.00
(Michael Jordan)
30 '83 NC State Wolfpack .40 1.00
(Coach Jim Valvano)
31 '84 Maryland Terrapins 1.25 3.00
(Len Bias)
32 '85 Georgia Tech .40 1.00
Yellow Jackets
(Mark Price)
33 '86 Duke Blue Devils .40 1.00
34 '87 NC State Wolfpack .20 .50
35 '88 Duke Blue Devils .40 1.00
36 '89 UNC Tar Heels .20 .50
NNO '91 FSU Joins ACC .20 .50
NNO Original ACC Seal .20 .40
NNO Revised ACC Seal .20 .40
(With Florida State)
NNO Certificate of .20 .40
Authenticity

1992 ACC Tournament Champs Gold

1 '54 NC State Wolfpack 1.50 4.00
2 '55 NC State Wolfpack 1.50 4.00
3 '56 NC State Wolfpack 1.50 4.00
4 '57 UNC Tar Heels 1.50 4.00
5 '58 Maryland Terrapins 1.50 4.00
6 '59 NC State Wolfpack 1.50 4.00
7 '60 Duke Blue Devils 1.50 4.00
8 '61 Wake Forest 2.50 6.00
Demon Deacons
(Billy Packer)
9 '62 Wake Forest 2.50 6.00
Demon Deacons
(Billy Packer)
10 '63 Duke Blue Devils 1.50 4.00
11 '64 Duke Blue Devils 1.50 4.00
12 '65 NC State Wolfpack 1.50 4.00
13 '66 Duke Blue Devils 1.50 4.00
14 '67 UNC Tar Heels 2.00 5.00
15 '68 UNC Tar Heels 2.00 5.00
16 '69 UNC Tar Heels 2.00 5.00
17 '70 NC State Wolfpack 1.50 4.00
18 '71 SC Gamecocks 1.50 4.00
19 '72 UNC Tar Heels 3.00 8.00
20 '73 NC State Wolfpack 3.00 8.00
21 '74 NC State Wolfpack 3.00 8.00
22 '75 UNC Tar Heels 2.50 6.00
23 '76 Virginia Cavaliers 1.50 4.00
24 '77 UNC Tar Heels 2.00 5.00
25 '78 Duke Blue Devils 2.00 5.00
26 '79 UNC Tar Heels 2.00 5.00
27 '80 Duke Blue Devils 2.00 5.00
28 '81 UNC Tar Heels 2.00 5.00
29 '82 UNC Tar Heels 25.00 60.00
(Michael Jordan)
30 '83 NC State Wolfpack 3.00 8.00
(Coach Jim Valvano)
31 '84 Maryland Terrapins 5.00 12.00
(Len Bias)
32 '85 Georgia Tech 5.00 12.00
Yellow Jackets
(Mark Price)
33 '86 Duke Blue Devils 3.00 8.00
34 '87 NC State Wolfpack 3.00 8.00
35 '88 Duke Blue Devils 5.00 12.00
36 '89 UNC Tar Heels 3.00 8.00

1993 Air Force Smokey

This set was produced to honor current and past Air Force Academy athletes and athletic traditions. These 16 standard-size cards feature on their fronts color player action shots set within gray borders with white diagonal stripes. The player's name and position appear on the left side underneath the photo. The team name and logo appear above the photo. The plain white back carries the player's name and position at the top, followed by a Smokey safety tip, and the player's career highlights. The cards are unnumbered and checklisted below in alphabetical order.

COMPLETE SET (16) 6.00 15.00
6 Reggie Minton BK CO .30 .75

1994 Air Force Smokey

Similar to the 1993 release, this set was produced to honor current and past Air Force Academy athletes and athletic traditions. These 16 standard-size cards feature on their fronts color player action shots set within gray borders with white diagonal stripes. The player's name and position appear on the left side underneath the photo with the team name and logor above the photo. The cards are unnumbered and checklisted below in alphabetical order.

COMPLETE SET (16) 6.00 15.00
3 Ray Dudley BK .30 .75
6 Reggie Minton CO BK .30 .75

1996-97 Alabama Schedules

This three card set features full color schedules picturing two players plus coach David Hobbs. The schedules were distributed for free at home games and at sponsor businesses like Texaco gas and Winn Dixie super markets.

COMPLETE SET (3) .60 1.50
1 Anthony Brown .20 .50
2 David Hobbs CO .30 .75
3 Wade Kaiser .20 .50

1992-93 Alabama-Birmingham

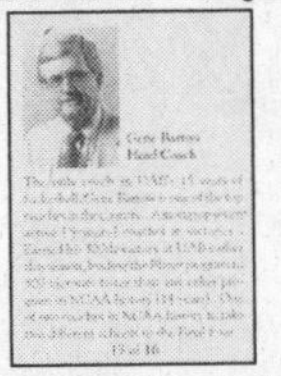

This 16-card set was issued in two eight-card perforated sheets consisting of standard-size cards. The fronts feature color action and posed player photos on a black card face. Two team color-coded horizontal stripes intersect the black border about one-third of the way from the top. The team logo is printed in golden yellow at the lower left edge. The player's name, team position, and number are printed on a golden yellow bar at the bottom of the picture. The white backs carry a black-and-white head shot of the player in the upper left. A brief biography appears to the right of the head shot while below is a player profile.

COMPLETE SET (16) 4.00 10.00
1 Reginald Allen .20 .50
2 Jeremy Bearden .20 .50
3 Carlos Browning .20 .50
4 Willie Chapman .20 .50
5 Patrick Craft .20 .50
6 Travis Harper .20 .50
7 Frank Haywood .20 .50
8 Nigel Hodges .20 .50
9 Corey Jackson .20 .50
10 Stanley Jackson .75 2.00
11 Carter Long .20 .50
12 Robert Shannon .60 1.50
13 Clarence Thrash .20 .50
14 George Wilkerson .20 .50
15 Gene Bartow CO .75 2.00
16 Willie Chapman .40 1.00
Stanley Jackson
George Wilkerson

1993-94 Alabama-Birmingham

This set consists of 14 standard-size cards. The fronts feature white-bordered color action and posed player photos. The team name appears in yellow and green lettering at the top; the player's name, position, and uniform number appear at the bottom. The while backs have the player's name and position centered at the top, with the career highlights below.

COMPLETE SET (14) 4.00 10.00
1 Gene Bartow CO .75 2.00
2 Frank Haywood .20 .50
3 Reginald Allen .20 .50
4 Carlos Browning .20 .50
5 George Wilkerson .20 .50
6 Clarence Thrash .20 .50
7 Robert Shannon 1.50 4.00
guarded by Anfernee Hardaway
8 Carter Long .20 .50
9 Corey Jackson .20 .50
10 Jeremy Bearden .20 .50
11 Chad Jones .20 .50
12 Travis Harper .20 .50
13 Blazer Seniors .40 1.00
Reginald Allen
Frank Haywood
Carter Long
Robert Shannon
Clarence Thrash
George Wilkerson
14 Checklist .20 .50

1998 AMA Kentucky Legends

This 36-card set was released by AMA in 1998, the set features some of the University of Kentucky's all-time great players.

COMPLETE SET (36) 8.00 20.00
1 Rupp Arena .25 .60
2 Team CL .25 .60
3 Cliff Barker .25 .60
4 Ralph Beard .40 1.00
5 Jerry Bird .25 .60
6 Rex Chapman .50 1.25
7 Johnny Cox .25 .60
8 Louie Dampier .40 1.00
9 John DeMoisey .25 .60
10 Billy Evans .25 .60
11 Richie Farmer .25 .60
12 Jack Givens .40 1.00
13 Phil Grawemeyer .30 .75
14 Kevin Grevey .50 1.25
15 Alex Groza .40 1.00
16 Cliff Hagan .60 1.50
17 Joe Hall .60 1.50
18 Vernon Hatton .25 .60
19 Basil Hayden .25 .60
20 Dan Issel .50 1.25
21 Wallace Jones .25 .60
22 Kyle Macy .40 1.00
23 Jamal Mashburn .75 2.00
24 Cotton Nash .40 1.00
25 Frank Ramsey .40 1.00
26 Pat Riley .75 2.00
27 Kenny Rollins .25 .60
28 Gayle Rose .25 .60
29 Layton Rouse .25 .60
30 Adolph Rupp 1.50 3.00
31 Forest Sale .25 .60
32 Jeff Sheppard .25 .60
33 Orlando Smith .25 .60
34 Carey Spicer .25 .60
35 Lou Tsioropoulos .40 1.00
36 Antoine Walker .75 2.00

1980-81 Arizona

This 19-card standard-size set was co-sponsored by Golden Eagle Distributors and the Tucson Police Department. The cards feature on the fronts color posed close-up photos, with the players in uniform and holding a basketball in their hands. The pictures are full-bleed on three sides, with the player's name and number in the bottom white border. The backs have biographical information, a discussion or definition of an aspect of basketball, and a safety message. The cards are unnumbered and checklisted below in alphabetical order. The two SP cards (Cook and Mosebar) are very difficult to find as they were pulled from the set before the set went into general distribution.

COMPLETE SET (19) 75.00 150.00
1 John Belobraydic 1.25 3.00
2 Russell Brown 1.25 3.00
3 Jeff Collins 1.25 3.00
4 Greg Cook SP 40.00 80.00
5 Ron Davis 1.25 3.00
6 Robbie Dosty 1.25 3.00
7 Mike Frink ACO 1.25 3.00
8 Len Gordy ACO 1.50 4.00
9 Mike Green ACO 1.25 3.00
10 Jack Magno 1.25 3.00
11 Donald Mellon 1.25 3.00
12 Charles Miller 1.25 3.00
13 David Mosebar SP 25.00 50.00
14 Frank Smith 1.25 3.00
15 John Smith 1.25 3.00
16 Fred Snowden CO 1.50 4.00
17 Harvey Thompson 1.25 3.00
18 Ernie Valenzuela 1.25 3.00
19 Ricky Walker 1.50 4.00

1981-82 Arizona

#22 • GREG COOK

This 20-card set measures approximately 2 5/8" by 3 5/8". It is sponsored by Golden Eagle Distributors. A posed color photo appears on the front of the card, with the name and uniform number underneath the picture. The back of the card provides basic biographical information, a discussion or definition of an aspect of basketball, and a safety message. The cards have been arranged and numbered alphabetically in the checklist below.

COMPLETE SET (20) 16.00 40.00
1 Ken Atkins CO 1.00 2.50
2 John Belobraydic 55 1.00 2.50
3 Brock Brunkhorst 10 1.00 2.50
4 Jeff Collins 24 1.00 2.50
5 Greg Cook 22 2.00 5.00
6 Len Gordy CO 1.25 3.00
7 Gary J. Heintz CO 1.00 2.50
8 Keith Jackson 21 1.00 2.50
9 Mark Jung 33 1.00 2.50
10 Jack Magno 41 1.00 2.50
11 Donald Mellon 35 1.00 2.50
12 Charles Miller 52 1.00 2.50
13 Pete Murphy 15 1.00 2.50
14 Kevin Roundfield 44 1.00 2.50
(Misspelled Ronndfield)
15 Frank Smith 31 1.00 2.50
16 Fred Snowden CO 1.50 4.00
17 Ernest Taylor-Harris 32 1.00 2.50
18 Harvey Thompson 34 1.00 2.50
19 John Vlahogeorge 14 1.00 2.50
20 Ricky Walker 12 1.25 3.00

1983-84 Arizona

This 18-card set was cosponsored by the Tucson Police Department and Golden Eagle Distributors. The cards measure approximately 2 1/4" by 3 3/4". The fronts feature borderless posed color player photos, with the player's name and uniform number in the white stripe beneath the picture. The Beard and Haskin cards differ from the others in having the 1983-84 basketball schedule printed on the front. The backs present player profile, a discussion or definition of some aspect of basketball, and a safety message. The cards are unnumbered and checklisted below in alphabetical order, with the uniform number after the player's name. Among the players in the set is Steve Kerr, who would later go on to a career in the NBA.

COMPLETE SET (18) 20.00 35.00
1 Van Beard 54 .60 1.50
2 Ricky Byrdsong ACO 1.50 4.00
3 Brock Brunkhorst 10 .60 1.50
4 Ken Burmeister ACO .60 1.50
5 Troy Cooke 20 .60 1.50
6 Ken Ensor 22 .60 1.50
7 David Haskin 24 .60 1.50
8 Keith Jackson 21 .60 1.50
9 Steve Kerr 25 6.00 15.00
10 Lute Olson CO 5.00 12.00
11 Eddie Smith 14 .60 1.50
12 Michael Tait 11 .60 1.50
13 Greg Taylor 52 .60 1.50
14 Harvey Thompson 34 .60 1.50
15 Scott Thompson ACO .60 1.50
16 Pete Williams 32 1.00 2.50
17 Andy Woodtli 44 .60 1.50
18 Scott Thompson ACO 3.00 8.00
Lute Olson CO
Ricky Byrdsong ACO
Ken Burmeister ACO

1984-85 Arizona

This 16-card set measures approximately 2 1/4" by 3 3/4". It is jointly sponsored by the Tucson Police Department and Golden Eagle Distributors. The front of the card features a posed color photo of the player on the top portion, and the name and uniform number underneath the picture. The back of the card gives basic biographical information (including the player's nickname where appropriate), a discussion or definition of an aspect of basketball, and a safety message. Among the players in the set is Steve Kerr, who would later go on to a career in the NBA.

COMPLETE SET (16) 10.00 25.00
1 Brock Brunkhorst 10 .50 1.25
2 Ken Burmeister ACO 1.00 2.50
3 Ricky Byrdsong ACO .75 2.00
4 John Edgar 50 .50 1.25
5 Bruce Fraser 22 .50 1.25
6 David Haskin 24 .50 1.25
7 Keith Jackson 21 .50 1.25
8 Rolf Jacobs 13 .50 1.25
9 Steve Kerr 25 5.00 12.00
10 Craig McMillan 20 .50 1.25
11 Lute Olson CO 4.00 10.00
12 Eddie Smith 14 .50 1.25
13 Morgan Taylor 34 .50 1.25
14 Scott Thompson CO .50 1.25
15 Joe Turner 33 .50 1.25
16 Pete Williams 32 .50 1.25

1985-86 Arizona

This 14-card set measures approximately 2 1/4" by 3 3/4". It is jointly sponsered by the Tucson Police Department and Golden Eagle Distributors. The front of the card features a posed color photo of the player on the top portion and the name and uniform number underneath the picture. The back of the card gives basic biographical information, a discussion or definition of an aspect of basketball and a safety message. This set includes future NBA players and TV analysts Sean Elliott and Steve Kerr as well as major league star outfielder Kenny Lofton.

COMPLETE SET (14) 30.00 60.00
1 Anthony Cook 00 .75 2.00
2 Eric Cooper 21 .40 1.00
3 Brian David 34 .40 1.00
4 John Edgar 50 .40 1.00
5 Sean Elliott 32 8.00 20.00
6 Bruce Fraser 22 .40 1.00
7 David Haskin 24 .40 1.00
8 Rolf Jacobs 13 .40 1.00
9 Steve Kerr 25 4.00 10.00
10 Kenny Lofton 11 12.50 30.00
11 Craig McMillan 20 .40 1.00
12 Lute Olson CO 3.00 8.00
13 Joe Turner 33 .40 1.00
14 Bruce Wheatley 45 .40 1.00

1986-87 Arizona

COMPLETE SET (12) 25.00 50.00
1 Jud Buechler 2.00 5.00
2 Anthony Cook .60 1.50
3 Brian David .40 1.00
4 Sean Elliott 6.00 15.00
5 Bruce Fraser .40 1.00
6 Steve Kerr 3.00 8.00
7 Kenny Lofton 8.00 20.00
8 Harvey Mason .40 1.00
9 Craig McMillan .40 1.00
10 Lute Olson CO 2.50 6.00
11 Tom Tolbert 4.00 10.00
12 Joe Turner .40 1.00

1987-88 Arizona

COMPLETE SET (14) 20.00 40.00
1 Jud Buechler 35 1.25 3.00
2 Anthony Cook 00 .60 1.50
3 Brian David 34 .40 1.00
4 Sean Elliott 32 5.00 12.00
5 Mark Georgeson 34 .40 1.00
6 Steve Kerr 25 2.50 6.00
7 Kenny Lofton 11 6.00 15.00
8 Harvey Mason 44 .40 1.00
9 Craig McMillan 20 .40 1.00
10 Matt Muehlebach 44 .60 1.50
11 Lute Olson CO 2.00 5.00
12 Sean Rooks 23 1.50 4.00
13 Tom Tolbert 23 2.50 6.00
14 Joe Turner 33 .40 1.00

1988-89 Arizona

MATT OTHICK #12

This 13-card set measures approximately 2 1/4" by 3 3/4". The set was jointly sponsored by the Tucson Police Department and Golden Eagle Distributors; some sets have been found however without the Golden Eagle logo. The front of the card features a posed color photo of the player on the top portion, and the name and uniform number underneath the picture. The back of the card gives basic biographical information, a discussion or definition of an aspect of basketball, and a safety message. NBA players Jud Buechler, Sean Elliott (misspelled Elliot), and Sean Rooks are included in this set as well as Cleveland Indians star outfielder Kenny Lofton. The cards are unnumbered and are checklisted below in alphabetical order, with the uniform number after the player's name.

COMPLETE SET (13) 10.00 25.00
1 Jud Buechler 35 1.25 3.00
2 Anthony Cook 00 .60 1.50
3 Ron Curry 33 .40 1.00
4 Brian David 34 .40 1.00
5 Sean Elliott 32 UER 4.00 10.00
(Misspelled Elliot)
6 Mark Georgeson 45 .40 1.00
7 Kenny Lofton 11 5.00 12.00
8 Harvey Mason 44 .40 1.00
9 Matt Muehlebach 24 .60 1.50
10 Lute Olson CO 2.00 5.00
11 Matt Othick 12 .60 1.50
12 Sean Rooks 42 1.25 3.00
13 Wayne Womack 30 .60 1.50

1989-90 Arizona

CHRIS MILLS #42

This 14-card set was cosponsored by the Tucson Police Department and Golden Eagle Distributors. The cards measure approximately 2 1/4" by 3 3/4". The fronts feature borderless posed color player photos, with the player's name and uniform number in the white stripe beneath the picture. The backs present player profile, a discussion or definition of some aspect of basketball, and a safety message. The cards are unnumbered and checklisted below in alphabetical order, with the uniform number after the player's name. The key cards in the set are Chris Mills, Sean Rooks, and Brian Williams.

COMPLETE SET (14) 8.00 20.00
1 Jud Buechler 35 1.00 2.50
2 Brian David 34 .40 1.00
3 Kevin Flanagan 51 .40 1.00
4 Deron Johnson 23 .40 1.00
5 Harvey Mason 44 .40 1.00
6 Chris Mills 42 3.00 8.00
7 Matt Muehlebach 24 .60 1.50
8 Lute Olson CO 2.00 5.00
9 Matt Othick 12 .60 1.50
10 Sean Rooks 45 1.25 3.00
11 Casey Schmidt 11 .40 1.00
12 Ed Stokes 41 .60 1.50
13 Brian Williams 21 2.50 6.00
14 Wayne Womack 30 .40 1.00

1990-91 Arizona

This 13-card set was cosponsored by the Tucson Police Department and Golden Eagles Distributors. The cards measure approximately 2 1/4" by 3 5/8". The fronts feature borderless posed color photos shot in front of the basketball goal. Each player is dressed in a dark blue jersey and is holding a basketball at his right side. The backs carry player profile, a discussion or definition of some aspect of basketball, and a safety message. The cards are unnumbered and checklisted below in alphabetical order. The key cards in this set are Chris Mills, Khalid Reeves, Sean Rooks, and Brian Williams.

COMPLETE SET (13) 10.00 25.00
1 Tony Clark .40 1.00
2 Kevin Flanagan .40 1.00
3 Deron Johnson .40 1.00
4 Chris Mills 2.50 6.00
5 Matt Muehlebach .60 1.50
6 Lute Olson CO 1.50 4.00
7 Matt Othick .60 1.50
8 Khalid Reeves 2.00 5.00
9 Sean Rooks 1.00 2.50
10 Casey Schmidt .40 1.00
11 Ed Stokes .60 1.50
12 Brian Williams 2.00 5.00
13 Wayne Womack .40 1.00

1990-91 Arizona Collegiate Collection Promos

This ten-card standard size set was produced by Collegiate Collection and features some of the great players of Arizona over the past few years. This set involves players of different sports and we have added a two-letter abbreviation next to the person's name to indicate what sport is pictured on the card. The back of the card either has statistical or biographical information about the player during their college career.

COMPLETE SET (10) 2.00 5.00
2 Steve Kerr BK .40 1.00
3 Lute Olson CO BK/(Watch Visible) .40 1.00
5 Lute Olson CO BK .40 1.00
9 Sean Elliott BK .75 2.00

1990-91 Arizona Collegiate Collection

This 125-card standard-size was produced by Collegiate Collection. We've included a sport initial (B-baseball, K-basketball, F-football) for players in the top collected sports.

COMPLETE SET (125) 5.00 12.00
1 Steve Kerr K .20 .50
2 Sean Elliott K .40 1.00
4 Lute Olson CO K .20 .50
11 Warren Rustand K .05 .15
13 Steve Strong K .05 .15
17 Fred Snowden CO K .05 .15
21 Larry Demic K .05 .15
28 Steve Kerr K .20 .50
33 Anthony Cook K .05 .15
38 Sean Elliott K .40 1.00
39 Alan Zinter K .05 .15
40 Russell Brown K .05 .15
57 Pete Williams K .05 .15
64 Al Fleming K .05 .15
71 Joe Tofflemire K .05 .15
79 Kenny Lofton K 1.00 2.50
85 Sean Elliott K .40 1.00
88 Morris Udall K .10 .25
92 Eddie Smith K .05 .15
93 Steve Kerr K .20 .50
94 Dwight Taylor K .05 .15
97 Bob Elliott K .05 .15
99 Joe Nehls K .05 .15
103 Lute Olson CO K .30 .75
106 Bob Elliott K .05 .15
110 Sean Elliott K .40 1.00
118 J.F.(Pop) McKale CO K .05 .15
121 Ken Lofton K 1.00 2.50

1990-91 Arizona State Collegiate Collection Promos

This ten-card standard size set was issued by Collegiate Collection to honor some of the leading athletes in all sports played at Arizona State. The front features a full-color photo while the back of the card has information or statistical information about the player featured. To help identify the player there is a two-letter abbreviation of the athlete's sport next to the player's name.

COMPLETE SET (10) 1.50 4.00
2 Fat Lever BK .20 .50
5 Byron Scott BK .30 .75
6 Sam Williams BK .05 .15

1990-91 Arizona State Collegiate Collection

This 200-card standard-size mulit-sport set was produced by Collegiate Collection. We've included a sport initial (B-baseball, K-basketball, F-football, WK-women's basketball) for players in the top collected sports. The key card is one of the few cards featuring all-time Baseball great Barry Bonds in a college uniform.

COMPLETE SET (200) 6.00 15.00
4 Sam Williams K .05 .15
8 Byron Scott K .20 .50
9 Fat Lever K .07 .20
12 Lionel Hollins K .07 .20

15 Kurt Nimphius K .05 .15
18 Scott Lloyd K .05 .15
23 Chris Beasley K .05 .15
26 Steve Beck K .05 .15
31 Alton Lister K .07 .20
33 Fat Lever K .07 .20
41 Mark Landsberger K .05 .15
44 Paul Williams K .05 .15
64 Byron Scott K .15 .40
102 Bobby Winkles CO K .08 .25
128 Ned Wulk CO K .05 .15
154 Joe Caldwell K .05 .15
161 Art Becker K .05 .15
184 Freddie Lewis K .05 .15

1987-88 Arizona State

Sponsored by the Valley of the Sun Kiwanis Club and "Our Quest: Their Best", this 22-card standard-size was produced by Sports Marketing Inc. The cards feature Arizona State athletes from various sports. The fronts have action color player photos against a white background. A maroon and wider yellow stripe appear below the picture, with the yellow stripe containing the player's name and sport. The words "Arizona State" are printed in maroon block letters above the photo and are underlined by a yellow stripe printed with the word "University". The Sun Devils mascot in the lower right corner rounds out the front. The backs are white with maroon print and include a player profile and a community service announcement from Sparky, the mascot. Sponsors' logos appear at the bottom. The sports represented are basketball, swimming, baseball, football, softball, track, gymnastics, tennis, and volleyball. The cards are unnumbered and checklisted below in alphabetical order.

COMPLETE SET (22) 8.00 20.00
1 Mark Becker BK .40 1.00
4 Mark Carlino BK .40 1.00
7 Mike Davies BK .40 1.00
15 Shamona Mosley BK .40 1.00
18 Steve Patterson CO BK .75 2.00
21 Arthur Thomas BK .40 1.00

1982-83 Arkansas

This 16-card set measures standard card size, 2 1/2" by 3 1/2". The card set was sponsored by Tom Kamerling's Sports Magazine. The black and white posed photo on the card's front is enclosed by a red border. The Arkansas Razorback logo appears above the photo, and the player's name, position, height, college classification, and hometown below the photo. The back features the 1982-83 game schedule. Future NBA players included in this set are Joe Kleine, Alvin Robertson, and Darrell Walker. The cards are numbered for convenience in the checklist below alphabetically by subject.

COMPLETE SET (16) 25.00 60.00
1 Charles Balentine 1.50 4.00
2 Darryl Bedford 1.25 3.00
3 Robert Brannon 1.25 3.00
4 Willie Cutts 1.25 3.00
5 Keenan DeBose 1.25 3.00
6 Carey Kelly 1.25 3.00
7 Robert Kitchen 1.25 3.00
8 Joe Kleine 6.00 15.00
9 Ricky Norton 1.50 4.00
10 Eric Poerschke 1.25 3.00
11 Mike Ratliff 1.25 3.00
12 Alvin Robertson 6.00 15.00
13 John Snively 1.25 3.00
14 Eddie Sutton CO 6.00 15.00
15 Leroy Sutton 1.25 3.00
16 Darrell Walker 6.00 15.00

1989-90 Arkansas

This 24-card basketball standard-size set commemorates the 1989-90 Arkansas Razorbacks' appearance in the Final Four. The fronts feature action player photos. The player's name appears in a diagonal bar across the lower right corner. The words "1990 Final Four" are printed in a similar diagonal bar at the upper left corner of the picture. The title "Arkansas" is printed in bold lettering across the top of the card. The backs carry biographical information, player profile, and anti-drug messages in the form of "Tips from the Razorbacks."

COMPLETE SET (24) 20.00 50.00
1 Nolan Richardson CO 3.00 8.00
2 Clyde Fletcher .40 1.00
3 Larry Marks .40 1.00
4 Mario Credit .60 1.50
5 Warren Linn .40 1.00
6 Ernie Murry .40 1.00
7 Darrell Hawkins .40 1.00
8 Cannon Whitby .40 1.00
9 Ron Huery .60 1.50
10 Lenzie Howell .60 1.50
11 Lee Mayberry 2.00 5.00
12 Todd Day 2.50 6.00
13 Arlyn Bowers .40 1.00
14 Shawn Davis .40 1.00
15 Lee Mayberry 2.00 5.00
16 Lenzie Howell .60 1.50
17 Lee Mayberry 1.50 4.00
18 Todd Day 2.50 6.00
19 Nolan Richardson CO 3.00 8.00
20 SWC Classic Champs .60 1.50
21 Barnhill Arena .60 1.50
22 Todd Day 2.50 6.00
23 Oliver Miller 2.00 5.00
24 Edgar Anderson ACO 1.50 4.00
Nolan Richardson CO

1991 Arkansas Collegiate Collection

This 100-card multi-sport standard-size set was produced by Collegiate Collection. The fronts features a mixture of black and white or color player photos with black borders. The player's name is included in a black stripe below the picture. In a horizontal format the backs present biographical information, career summary, or statistics on a white background. Unless noted below, all players are from the sport of football.

COMPLETE SET (100) 6.00 15.00
3 Sidney Moncrief BK .20 .50
15 Tony Brown BK .07 .20
20 Keith Wilson BK .07 .20
35 Scott Hastings BK .05 .15
38 Joe Kleine BK .07 .20
44 Marvin Delph BK .07 .20
51 Alvin Robertson BK .07 .20
66 Martin Terry BK .10 .30
67 Andrew Lang BK .08 .25
69 Ron Brewer BK .07 .20
80 Ron Huery BK .07 .20
85 Darrell Walker BK .10 .30

1991-92 Arkansas Collegiate Collection

This 25-card standard-size set was produced by Collegiate Collection. The fronts display either action or posed color player photos, with rounded corners and black borders. The player's name appears in a red stripe below the picture. The horizontally oriented backs have biography, statistics, and career summary, superimposed over a gray razorback. The cards are numbered on the back and generally arranged in alphabetical order. The key cards in the set are Todd Day, Lee Mayberry, and Oliver Miller.

COMPLETE SET (25) 10.00 25.00
1 Nolan Richardson CO 2.50 6.00
2 Ray Biggers .40 1.00
3 Ken Biley .40 1.00
4 Shawn Davis .40 1.00
5 Todd Day 2.00 5.00
6 Clyde Fletcher .40 1.00
7 Darrell Hawkins .60 1.50
8 Warren Linn .40 1.00
9 Elmer Martin .40 1.00
10 Lee Mayberry 1.25 3.00
11 Clint McDaniel 1.00 2.50
12 Oliver Miller 2.00 5.00
13 Isaiah Morris 1.25 3.00
guarded by Larry Johnson
14 Davor Rimac .40 1.00
15 Robert Shepherd .40 1.00
16 Roosevelt Wallace .60 1.50
17 Alfred Warren .40 1.00
18 Barnhill Arena .40 1.00
19 Mike Anderson ACO .40 1.00
20 Brad Dunn ACO .40 1.00
21 Wayne Stehlik ACO .40 1.00
22 Nolan Richardson III .40 1.00
Volunteer Assistant CO
23 Ernie Murry .40 1.00
Graduate Assistant CO
24 Team Photo .75 2.00
25 Director Card .40 1.00
Checklist

1992-93 Arkansas

This 15-card set measures the standard size and features color action player photos bordered on the left or right edge by a gray stripe containing the team name. The player's name appears in red lettering on a white stripe at the bottom. The horizontal backs feature close-up player pictures with shadow box borders. The white background is printed with a profile of the player. The school logo and biographical information appear at the top. The cards are numbered on the back. The set contains the first card of Corliss Williamson.

COMPLETE SET (15) 6.00 15.00
1 Nolan Richardson CO 1.00 2.50
2 Dwight Stewart .60 1.50
3 Ken Biley .30 .75
4 Craig Tyson .30 .75
5 Corey Beck .75 2.00
6 Darrell Hawkins .40 1.00
7 Scotty Thurman 1.25 3.00
8 Warren Linn .30 .75
9 Davor Rimac .30 .75
10 Robert Shepherd .30 .75
11 Roger Crawford .30 .75
12 Corliss Williamson 2.00 5.00
13 Elmer Martin .30 .75
14 Clint McDaniel .60 1.50
15 Ray Biggers .30 .75

1993-94 Arkansas

Issued to commemorate the inaugural season of Arkansas' Walton Arena, these 18 standard-size cards feature on their fronts red-bordered color action shots of the 1993-94 NCAA champion Razorbacks. The player's name appears in gold-colored lettering within one of the photo's corners. A gray panel on the red-bordered back carries another color player action shot at its upper left, followed by Coach Nolan Richardson's comments on the player, and previous season highlights. The player's name, position, class, and major appear in white lettering within the bottom red margin. The cards are unnumbered and checklisted below in alphabetical order. There were two versions of this set produced. The first printing indicates "Walton Arena Inaugural Season" and the second printing indicates "1994 NCAA Champs". Some premiums have been seen for the slightly more difficult to obtain "Walton" set.

COMPLETE SET (18) 6.00 15.00
1 Corey Beck .60 1.50
2 Ray Biggers .20 .50
3 Ken Biley .20 .50
4 Roger Crawford .20 .50
5 Al Dillard .30 .75
6 Elmer Martin .20 .50
7 Clint McDaniel .40 1.00
8 Nolan Richardson CO 1.00 2.50
9 Davor Rimac .20 .50
10 Darnell Robinson 1.25 3.00
11 Dwight Stewart .40 1.00
12 Scotty Thurman 1.25 3.00
13 Corliss Williamson 2.00 5.00
14 Lee Wilson .60 1.50
15 Mike Anderson ACO .25 .60
Brad Dunn ACO
Wayne Stehlik ACO
Nolan Richardson III ACO
16 Team Card .30 .75
17 Walton Arena .30 .75
18 Title Card .20 .50

1994-95 Arkansas Tickets

This set of 18 tickets features the 1994-95 Arkansas Razorbacks. Each ticket measures 1 1/2" by 5" and shows evidence of perforation on all four sides. (The set is also known to exist as an uncut sheet.) The tickets divide into two portions: the top portion and the bottom 1 3/8" perforated tab. The tabs have the admission price, day of the week, date of game, and are numbered Event 1-18. Inside gold borders, the top portion displays a color photo with a 1994 National Champions banner draped across the top of the picture. The location of the game ("Bud Walton Arena") and the opponent are printed in the bottom gold border. The back consists of an advertisement from Coca-Cola and Subway and an offer to receive a free medium Coke with the purchase of a sandwich. The tickets are numbered according to the event and are checklisted below accordingly. Ticket #1 shows President Bill Clinton congratulating Nolan Richardson. Ticket #13 features Corliss Williamson, who was drafted by the Sacramento Kings in the 1995 NBA Draft.

COMPLETE SET (18) 4.00 10.00
1 Nolan Richardson CO 1.50 4.00
Bill Clinton PRES
2 John Engskov .20 .50
3 Reggie Merritt .20 .50
4 Natl Championship Trophy .20 .50
5 Kareem Reed .40 1.00
6 Lee Wilson .30 .75
7 Elmer Martin .20 .50
8 Landis Williams .20 .50
9 Nolan Richardson CO 1.25 3.00
10 Davor Rimac .20 .50
11 Darnell Robinson .40 1.00
12 Corey Beck .40 1.00
13 Corliss Williamson 1.50 4.00
14 Scotty Thurman .40 1.00
15 Dwight Stewart .30 .75
16 Clint McDaniel .30 .75
17 Reggie Garrett .20 .50
18 Alex Dillard .30 .75

1987-88 Auburn

This 16-card standard-size set was issued by Auburn University and includes members from different sports programs. Reportedly only 5,000 sets were made by McDag Productions, and the cards were distributed by the Opelika, Alabama police department. The cards feature color player photos on white card stock. The backs present safety tips for children. The last three cards of the set feature "Tiger Greats," former Auburn athletes Bo Jackson, Rowdy Gaines, and Chuck Person. The key card in the set is Frank Thomas. The sports represented in this set are football (1, 3, 5, 11-13, 16), basketball (4, 6, 9-10, 14), baseball (2), and swimming (15). A card of Bo Jackson playing Football has been recently discovered. Since very few of these cards are known it is not considered part of the complete set.

COMPLETE SET (16) 70.00 175.00
4 Sonny Smith CO BK .60 1.50
6 Joe Ciampi BK .60 1.50
9 Jeff Moore BK .60 1.50
10 Vickie Orr BK .60 1.50
14 Chuck Person BK 4.00 10.00

1992-93 Auburn

This 14-card standard size set was produced by Collegiate Products. The fronts feature a mix of posed and action photos with a dark blue stripe on the left side displaying the school name. Along the bottom edge within a white stripe is the player's name in orange print. The horizontal backs carry a color head shot with black shadow box borders, school logo, biography, career summary and statistics. The set features the first card of Wesley Person.

COMPLETE SET (14) 4.00 10.00
1 Tommy Joe Eagles CO .30 .75
2 Aubrey Wiley .30 .75
3 Wesley Person 2.50 6.00
4 Aaron Swinson .40 1.00
5 Ronnie Battle .30 .75
6 Cameron Boozer .30 .75
7 Reggie Gallon .20 .50
8 Leonard Smith .20 .50
9 Rod Joyce .20 .50
10 Byron Bell .20 .50
11 Pat Burke .20 .50
12 Mark Hutton .20 .50
13 Shawn Stuart .20 .50
14 Lance Weems .30 .75

1987-88 Baylor

This 17-card standard-size set was sponsored by the Hillcrest Baptist Medical Center, the Waco Police Department, and the Baylor University Department of Public Safety. The cards represent several sports: baseball (1-3), basketball (4-6), track (7-10), and football (11-17). The front feature color action shots of the players on white card stock. At the top the words "Baylor Bears 1987-88" are printed between the Hillcrest and Baylor University logos. Player information is given below the picture. The back has more logos, brief career summaries, and "Bear Briefs," which consist of instructional sports information and an anti-drug or crime message.

COMPLETE SET (17) 12.00 30.00
4 Micheal Williams 3.00 8.00
5 Darryl Middleton .75 2.00
6 Gene Iba CO .75 2.00

1989-90 Baylor

This 15-card standard-size set was issued compliments of the Waco Tribune-Herald. Inside white and green borders, the fronts feature posed color player photos shot against a yellow background. The player's name, position, and number are printed in the wider bottom border. The horizontal backs present biography, player profile, and collegiate statistics. The cards are unnumbered and checklisted below in alphabetical order. The most important card is that of David Wesley, a 1993-94 NBA rookie.

COMPLETE SET (15) 6.00 15.00
1 Kelvin Chalmers .40 1.00
2 Toby Christian .40 1.00
3 Julius Denton .40 1.00
4 Joey Fatta .40 1.00
5 Mitch Fogle .40 1.00
6 Michael Hobbs .40 1.00
7 Alex Holcombe .40 1.00
8 Melvin Hunt .40 1.00
9 Gene Iba CO .75 2.00
10 Ivan Jones .40 1.00
11 Dennis Lindsey .40 1.00
12 Tim Schumacher .40 1.00
13 David Wesley 3.00 8.00
14 Brian Zvonocek .40 1.00
15 Team photo .40 1.00

1990-91 Baylor

This 16-card set, sponsored by the Waco Tribune-Herald, highlights the 1990-91 Baylor Bears basketball team. The fronts have player close-up shots inside a green border. The rest of the card is white and green including the Baylor University logo in the bottom right corner. The backs are green and white as well with "Baylor Basketball 1990-91" inside a green border on the side. The player biographies and statistics are also included horizontally on the back. The cards are unnumbered and checklisted below in alphabetical order.

COMPLETE SET (16) 6.00 15.00
1 Ulises Asprilla .40 1.00
2 Herb Baker .40 1.00
3 Kelvin Chalmers .40 1.00
4 Toby Christian .40 1.00
5 Joey Fatta .40 1.00
6 David Hamilton .40 1.00
7 Alex Holcombe .40 1.00
8 Melvin Hunt .40 1.00
9 Gene Iba CO .75 2.00
10 Anthony Lewis .40 1.00
11 Dennis Lindsey .40 1.00
12 Tim Schumacher .40 1.00
13 Willie Sublett .40 1.00
14 Joe Tanksley .40 1.00
15 David Wesley 2.00 5.00
16 Brian Zvonocek .40 1.00
17 Baylor Bear CL .40 1.00

1972-73 Bradley Schedules

These five schedule cards measure approximately 2 1/2" by 3 3/4" and are printed on heavy cardboard stock. Each card shows a black and white photo of a player on the front with a Bradley schedule for the 1972-73 basketball season on the back. The cards have rounded corners; on the front, the player's name appears on a white stripe beneath the posed black-and-white player photo.

COMPLETE SET (5) 40.00 80.00
1 Sam Allen 10.00 20.00
2 Mark Dohner 10.00 20.00
3 Dave Klobucher 10.00 20.00
4 Seymour Reed 12.50 25.00
5 Doug Shank 10.00 20.00

1982-83 Bradley

This 16 card set measures approximately 3 1/2" by 2 1/8". The full color fronts feature a mix of posed and action shots. The backs have some limited biographical information. A variety of local sponsors helped produce these cards. Some cards do not have sponsor stamping on the back.

COMPLETE SET (16) 6.00 15.00
1 Tony Barrone ACO 1.00 2.50
2 Roosevelt Davison .40 1.00
3 Jay Eck ACO .40 1.00
4 Melvin Harden .40 1.00
5 Rudy Keeling ACO .40 1.00
6 Booker Johnson .40 1.00
7 Pat Marshall .40 1.00
8 Eddie Mathews .40 1.00
9 Barney Mines .40 1.00
10 Willie Scott .40 1.00
11 Franz Smith .40 1.00
12 Dick Versace CO 1.50 4.00
13 Anthony Webster .40 1.00
14 Greg Willie .40 1.00
15 Boise Winters .40 1.00
16 Arena .40 1.00

1985-86 Bradley

This 56-card standard-size set was made as a playing card set, complete with rounded corners and playing-card finish. Most of the fronts feature white-bordered black-and-white photos of great Bradley Braves players from the past. The player's name and distinction appear on the border beneath the photo, and the card number and suit appear in the top left, and again, but inverted, in the bottom right. The back has the Bradley Braves name and logo in a pink field edged in red and bordered in white. Also on the back, "75 Memorable Years" is printed in red. The cards are listed below as they appear on the cards, with suffixes (C, D, H and S) representing the suits (Clubs, Diamonds, Hearts and Spades); the numbers 11, 12 and 13 representing Jacks, Queens and Kings, respectively; and JK denoting Jokers.

COMPLETE SET (56) 16.00 40.00
C1 Chet Walker 2.00 5.00
C2 Al Smith .60 1.50
C3 Mike Owens .40 1.00
C4 Tom Les .40 1.00
C5 1950-51 Team Photo .60 1.50
C6 Jack Brickhouse ANN 1.25 3.00
Mark Holtz ANN
Tom Kelly ANN
Vince Lloyd ANN
Dave Snell ANN
Bob Starr ANN
C7 Levern Tart .60 1.50
C8 Chuck Orsborn CO .40 1.00
C9 Willie Scott .40 1.00
C10 1956-57 Team Photo .60 1.50
C11 Forddy Anderson CO .40 1.00
C12 1963-64 Team Photo .60 1.50
C13 1981-82 Team Photo .60 1.50
D1 Gene Morse .40 1.00
D2 Joe Stowell CO .40 1.00
D3 Steve Kuberski .75 2.00
D4 L.C. Bowen .40 1.00
D5 Bobby Humbles .40 1.00
D6 Joe Allen ACO .75 2.00
Tony Barone ACO
Chuck Buescher ACO
Mark Dohner ACO
Ron Harris ACO
Rudy Keeling ACO
D7 Journal Star Writers .40 1.00
Gary Childs
Kenneth Jones
Paul King
Dick Lien
Max Siebel
Phil Theobald
Lefty Tyler
D8 Harry Wilcoxen .40 1.00
D9 Joe Billy McDade .40 1.00
D10 Ron Ferguson CO .40 1.00
D11 Mitchell Anderson .75 2.00
D12 1979-80 Team Photo .60 1.50
D13 Joe Allen .60 1.50
H1 Paul Unruh .75 2.00
H2 Voise Winters .40 1.00
H3 PA Announcers .40 1.00
Frank Busone
Paul Herzog
Bob Loy
H4 Ken Brown ANN .40 1.00
Lorne Brown ANN
Frank Busone ANN
Mort Cantor ANN
H5 1965-66 Team Photo .60 1.50
H6 Joe Strawder .40 1.00
H7 Chiefs Club Presidents .40 1.00
Grant Bush
Mort Cantor
Ed Erhgott
Henry Holling
Keith Holloway
Grant Mathey
Paul Unruh
H8 Marcel DeSouza .75 2.00
H9 1959-60 Team Photo .60 1.50
H10 Shellie McMillon .75 2.00
H11 Gene Melchiorre .60 1.50
H12 Bradley's Famous Five .60 1.50
H13 A.J. Robertson CO .40 1.00
S1 Bob Carney .40 1.00
S2 Ray Ramsey .40 1.00
S3 Barney Cable .75 2.00
S4 Dutch Meinen CO .40 1.00
S5 All-Stars Who .75 2.00
Toured Brazil
Jim Caruthers
Mike Davis
Mark Dohner
Tom Les
Seymour Reed
S6 Bradley Area .40 1.00
Automobile Sponsors
Joe McCarthy
Dick Miller
Neil Norton
John Pearl
Mickey Smith
Bill and Ken Schaffnit
S7 B Club Presidents .40 1.00
Ron Baurer
Larry Cowling
Jack Heintzman
Glen McCullough
Bill Ridgely
William Robertson
Carl Traficana
S8 Bobby Joe Mason 1.25 3.00
S9 Dick Versace CO 1.25 3.00
S10 Stan Albeck 1.25 3.00
S11 Roger Phegley .75 2.00
S12 Jack Brickhouse 1.25 3.00
HOF broadcaster
S13 1949-50 Team Photo .60 1.50
JK Peoria Civic Center .40 1.00
JK 1985-86 Schedule .40 1.00
NNO Joker .40 1.00
Peoria Civic Center
NNO Schedule card .40 1.00

1987-88 Bradley Schedules

Sponsored by Cheddar's, this 16-card schedule set was produced for the Bradley Braves 1987-88 season. Each schedule (when flat) features a coupon on the front left half and a player photo on the right half. The back features the Bradley Braves schedule on the left half and the Chiefs Club Promotional Events on the right. The cards measure 4 1/4" by 5 1/2". The cards are not numbered and listed below alphabetically.

COMPLETE SET (16) 5.00 12.00
1 Stan Albeck CO 1.25 3.00
2 Steve Bayless .30 .75
3 Scott Becoue .30 .75
4 Len Bertolini .30 .75
5 Deon Butler .30 .75
6 Mike Cash .30 .75
7 Hersey Hawkins 3.00 8.00
8 Luke Jackson .30 .75
9 Greg Jones .30 .75
10 Anthony Manuel .30 .75
11 Bruce Mordini .30 .75
12 Donald Powell .30 .75
13 Jay Schell .30 .75
14 Jerry Thomas .30 .75
15 Trevor Trimpe .30 .75
16 Paul Wilson .30 .75

1990-91 Bradley

Co-sponsored by Kodacolor and Peoria Camera Shop, this 25-card standard-size set was issued in five five-card perforated strips. One strip was given away at each of five home games. The fronts feature red-bordered color player posed and action shots on the fronts, except for a couple "Brave of the Past" cards, which sport black-and-white photos. The player's name, jersey number, and position appear in white beneath his picture, and the Bradley logo is displayed in the upper left. The plain white back has the player's name, jersey number and position, along with a brief biography and the Bradley logo, at the top. A short section that contains career highlights and stats lies beneath, and the Kodak logo at the bottom rounds out the back. The cards are unnumbered and checklisted below in alphabetical order.

COMPLETE SET (25) 12.00 30.00
1 Stan Albeck CO 1.00 2.50
2 James Bailey .40 1.00
3 Mark Bailey .40 1.00
4 Andy Bastock .40 1.00
5 Scott Behrends .40 1.00
6 Duane Broussard .40 1.00
7 Kwame Brown .40 1.00
8 Adam Carl .40 1.00
9 Mark Dietrich .40 1.00
10 Marty Gillespie CO .40 1.00
11 James Hamilton .40 1.00
12 Hersey Hawkins 5.00 12.00
13 Xanthus Houston .60 1.50
14 Paul Lee .40 1.00
15 Jim Les 1.25 3.00
16 Mo McHone ACO .60 1.50
17 Roger Phegley .60 1.50
18 Sean Smith .40 1.00
19 Maurice Stovall .40 1.00
20 Curtis Stuckey .60 1.50
21 Paul Unruh .60 1.50
22 Chet Walker 2.50 6.00
23 Charles White .40 1.00
24 Tom Wilson .40 1.00
25 Tony Wysinger .40 1.00

1993-94 Bradley

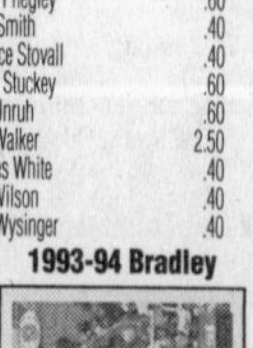

Sponsored by Peoria Downtown Kiwanis Club, this 18-card standard-size set features the 1993-94 Bradley Braves. The fronts feature color player photos with white borders. The player's name and position appear on the bottom of the card on team color-coded stripes. The horizontal backs have another small color player photo, with short biography and accomplishments. Platinum sponsors are printed in a red rectangle, gold sponsors in a gray rectangle.

COMPLETE SET (18) 5.00 12.00
1 Checklist .20 .50
2 Duane Broussard .20 .50
3 Jim Molinari .30 .75
4 Duane Broussard ACO .20 .50
Pat Donahue ACO
Rob Judson ACO
5 Marcus Pollard .20 .50
6 Roger Suchy .20 .50
7 David Winslow .20 .50
8 Dwayne Funches .20 .50
9 Rick Harris .20 .50
10 Deon Jackson .30 .75
11 Chad Kleine .20 .50
12 Billy Wright .30 .75
13 James Baptist .20 .50
14 Kerry Burrell .20 .50
15 Anthony Parker 1.25 3.00
16 Aaron Zobrist .20 .50
17 Jim Les 1.25 3.00
Hersey Hawkins
Bradley Alumni
in the NBA
18 Dave Snell ANN .20 .50
Joe Stowell ANN
Jim Watson ANN

1994-95 Bradley

Sponsored by Peoria Downtown Kiwanis Club, this 18-card standard-size set features the 1994-95 Bradley Braves. On a simulated wooden background, the fronts feature tilted color action player photos. The player's name and position appear at the bottom on red stripes. The horizontal backs carry a small black-and-white player photo, along with short biography and accomplishments. Platinum sponsors are printed in a red rectangle, gold sponsors in a gray rectangle.

COMPLETE SET (18) 3.00 8.00
1 Checklist .20 .50
Bob Carney
Joe Allen
2 Jim Molinari CO .30 .75
3 Duane Broussard ACO .20 .50
Pat Donahue ACO
Rob Judson ACO
4 David Winslow .20 .50
5 Aaron Zobrist .20 .50
6 Billy Wright .30 .75
7 Marcus Samuels .20 .50
8 Anthony Parker 1.00 2.50
9 Kerry Burrell .20 .50
10 Chad Kleine .20 .50
11 Dwayne Funches .20 .50
12 Deon Jackson .40 1.00
guarded by Brent Barry
13 Mbaukwu Nwaogwugwu .20 .50
14 James Baptist .20 .50
15 Adebayo Akinkunle .20 .50
16 Ben Coupet .20 .50
17 Dave Snell ANN .20 .50
Joe Stowell ANN
Jim Watson ANN
18 Marcus Pollard .20 .50

1995-96 Bradley

Sponsored by Peoria Downtown Kiwanis Club, this 18-card standard-size set features the 1995-96 Bradley Braves. The fronts have color action player photos set on a red background. The player's name appears in a white oval below the picture, and their position is listed in white below the oval. The horizontal backs carry a small colored action photo with a short biography and accomplishments. Platinum sponsors are listed with white type in a red oval, and below the oval in red print are gold sponsors.

COMPLETE SET (18) 3.00 8.00
1 Checklist .60 1.50
Banquet
Hall of Fame
Gene Gathers
Chet Walker
2 Jim Molinari CO .30 .75
3 Duane Broussard ACO .20 .50
Pat Donahue ACO
Rob Judson ACO
4 Deon Jackson .30 .75
5 Chad Kleine .20 .50
6 Billy Wright .30 .75
7 Dwayne Funches .20 .50
8 Mbaukwu Nwaogwugwu .20 .50
9 Anthony Parker 1.00 2.50
10 Ben Coupet .20 .50
11 Kerry Burrell .20 .50
12 Aaron Zobrist .20 .50
13 James Baptist .20 .50
14 Adebayo Akinkunle .20 .50
15 Marcus Samuels .20 .50

6 Gavin Schairer .20 .50
7 Jim Watson ANN .20 .50
Dave Snell ANN
Joe Stowell ANN
8 Kiwanis Builder Award .30 .75
Billy Wright

1987-88 BYU

This 25-card standard-size set was issued by Brigham Young University. Reportedly only 20,000 sets were produced, and each set was numbered from 1 to 20,000 on the back of every card. The player cards feature color photos, while the team photo card is sepia-toned. The cards have a blue border, with the BYU logo in the lower right corner. Popular players on the team are featured on two cards, one action shot and one portrait. The backs have biographical and statistical information, as well as the card number.

COMPLETE SET (25) 5.00 12.00
1 Michael Smith .75 2.00
2 BYU Header card .40 1.00
3 Jim Usevitch .20 .50
4 Nathan Call .20 .50
5 Brian Taylor .20 .50
6 Ladell Andersen CO .40 1.00
7 Roger Reid .40 1.00
8 Carl Ingersoll .20 .50
9 Jeff Chatman .30 .75
10 Team Photo .60 1.50
11 Mike Herring .20 .50
12 Chris Lynch .20 .50
13 Steve Schreiner .20 .50
14 Gary Trost .30 .75
15 David Lynch .20 .50
16 Brian Taylor .30 .75
17 Andy Toolson .60 1.50
18 Jim Usevitch .20 .50
19 Vince Bryan .20 .50
20 Mark Clausen .20 .50
21 Alan Astle .20 .50
22 Nathan Call .20 .50
23 Jeff Chatman .30 .75
24 Marty Haws .30 .75
25 Michael Smith .75 2.00

1988-89 BYU

This 25-card set measures the standard size. Five thousand sets were printed, and the set serial number appears on a cardboard tag attached to the clear plastic package. The fronts feature color action and posed player photos with white borders. A light blue bar area below the picture contains the player's name, height, weight, classification, and position. The BYU logo is in the lower right corner. The season year is printed in black and superimposed at the upper left corner of the photo. The horizontal backs of card numbers 1-17 present statistics, and player information under the following categories: personal, high school, BYU, and Coach Ladell Andersen's comments on the player. The content of the backs of card numbers 18-24 is listed below.

COMPLETE SET (25) 4.00 10.00
1 Team Photo .60 1.50
2 Michael Smith .75 2.00
3 Alan Framton .20 .50
4 Alan Astle .20 .50
5 Mike Herring .20 .50
6 Mark Heslop .20 .50
7 Steve Andrus .20 .50
8 Steve Schreiner .20 .50
9 Andy Toolson UER .40 1.00
(Misspelled Toolsen)
10 Vince Bryan .20 .50
11 Marty Haws .30 .75
12 Kevin Santiago .20 .50
13 David Wolfe .20 .50
14 John Fish .20 .50
15 Carl Ingersoll ACO .20 .50
16 Roger Reid ACO .30 .75
17 Ladell Andersen CO .40 1.00
18 Alan Astle .20 .50
19 Marty Haws .30 .75
20 Michael Smith .40 1.00
(Coaching records on back)
21 Michael Smith .40 1.00
22 Marty Haws .30 .75
23 Andy Toolson UER .40 1.00
(BYU basketball statistics on back; misspelled Toolsen)
24 Marty Haws .30 .75
25 Title Card .30 .75

1990-91 BYU Shawn Bradley

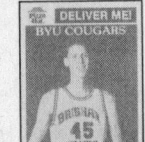

Sponsored by Pizza Hut, this black and white, over-sized card (2 7/8" x 4 1/4") features star center and eventual number two overall draft pick Shawn Bradley. The black and white back features information on Bradley and a basketball tip. The best information known is that there are at least two other cards in this set, but no specifics are known. It may be part of a larger set and it's likely that it was distributed at home games and or with pizza delivery.

1 Shawn Bradley 3.00 8.00

1989-90 California

This 16-card standard-size set was jointly sponsored by the USDA Forest Service, California Dept. of Forestry and Fire Protection, and USDI Bureau of Land Management. On a white card face, the fronts feature either posed or action color player photos. Yellow stripes edge the photo above and below, and a blue shadow border runs along the right side of the picture. The backs carry biography, player profile, and a fire prevention cartoon starring Smokey the Bear. The cards are unnumbered and checklisted below in alphabetical order.

COMPLETE SET (16) 12.00 30.00
1 Rich Branham .75 2.00
2 Andrew Brigham .75 2.00
3 DeShon Brown .75 2.00
4 Lou Campanelli CO 1.50 4.00
5 John Carty .75 2.00
6 Gary Colson ACO 1.25 3.00
7 Ryan Drew .75 2.00
8 Bill Elleby .75 2.00
9 Roy Fisher 1.25 3.00
10 Sean Harrell .75 2.00
11 Brian Hendrick 1.25 3.00
12 Eric McDonough .75 2.00
13 Andre Reyes .75 2.00
14 Keith Smith .75 2.00
15 Bryant Walton .75 2.00
16 Jeff Wulburn ACO .75 2.00

1994-95 California

This 16 card standard-size set was sponsored by Power Bar. The front features a full bleed, full color action photo with the player's name written vertically on the left side in white letters. There is a yellow "Cal" emblem in the upper-right hand corner. The backs have a blue border with four blue diamonds. Inside the border, the player's biography, player profile, and Power Bar logo are found. The cards are unnumbered and checklisted below in alphabetical order.

COMPLETE SET (16) 8.00 20.00
1 Monty Buckley .20 .50
2 Randy Duck .60 1.50
3 Tremaine Fowlkes 1.25 3.00
4 Jelani Gardner .75 2.00
5 Tony Gonzalez 4.00 10.00
6 Alfred Grigsby .30 .75
7 Ryan Jamison .20 .50
8 Sean Marks .20 .50
9 Anwar McQueen .20 .50
10 K.J. Roberts .20 .50
11 Michael Stewart 1.00 2.50
12 Todd Bozeman CO .60 1.50
13 Billy Kennedy ACO .20 .50
Kurtis Townsend ACO
Charles Payne ACO
14 Oski (Mascot) .20 .50
15 Team Photo .30 .75
16 Team Photo .30 .75

1996-97 California

This 10-card set was released at California during the 1996-97 season. These cards were sponsored by the California Highway Patrol, and feature many of the players from that season's team. The set is not numbered and is listed below in alphabetical order.

COMPLETE SET (10) 6.00 15.00
1 Randy Duck .40 1.00
2 Tony Gonzalez 3.00 8.00
3 Ed Gray 1.25 3.00
4 Alfred Grigsby .20 .50
5 Sean Jackson .20 .50
6 Kenyon Jones .20 .50
7 Sean Marks .20 .50
8 Prentice McGruder .20 .50
9 Anwar McQueen .20 .50
10 Michael Stewart .75 2.00

1996-97 California Women

This 10-card set was released at California during the 1996-97 season. These cards were sponsored by the California Highway Patrol, and feature many of the players from that season's team. The set is not numbered and is listed below in alphabetical order.

COMPLETE SET (10) 3.00 8.00
1 Patrycja Czepiec .30 .75
Tatiana Dmitrieva
2 Elke Snijder .30 .75
Lexy Tamony
3 Sherrise Smith .30 .75
Kobie Kennon
4 Geneva McDaniel .30 .75
Paige Bowie
5 Mary Scotty .30 .75
Liz Rizzo
6 Jamilla Churchill .30 .75
Jennie Leander
7 Marie Folsom .30 .75
Angie Wong
8 Marianne Stanley 1.25 3.00
Barbara Thaxton
Marie Christian
9 Team Photo .30 .75
10 Team Photo .30 .75

1990-91 California State Women

This 17-card standard size set was sponsored by Smokey. The cards are unnumbered and checklisted below in alphabetical order.

COMPLETE SET (17) 2.50 6.00
1 Ann Brewster .20 .50
2 Alice Cole .20 .50
3 Nicole Coupland .20 .50
4 Kristy Cox .20 .50
5 Lori Cox .20 .50
6 Keli Floyd .20 .50
7 Melinda Levering .20 .50
8 Julie Mack .20 .50
9 Stacy McClelland .20 .50
10 Lisa Minturn .20 .50
11 Heather Moulton .20 .50
12 Nicole Perry .20 .50
13 Sherri Renfrow .20 .50
14 Kellie Rhoads .20 .50
15 Carol Schoenmann .20 .50
16 Tricia Stilwell .20 .50
17 Kelly Walund .20 .50

1994-95 Cassville HS

This 30-card set measures the standard size and features the men's (111-118, 129-135) and women's (112-128) basketball teams. Just 500 sets were produced. The fronts feature color action player shots with the school name on a green stripe at the bottom. The cards are numbered on the back with #111-135 as the team set and #147-151 being special edition singles. In black print on a gray background, the backs carry the player's name, sport, activities, a positive image point, and the slogan "Youth for a Positive Self Image." The team's best player was Sam Okey, who signed with the University of Wisconsin.

COMPLETE SET (30) 8.00 20.00
111 Scott Uppena .20 .50
112 Chris Koopman .20 .50
John Koopman
113 John Koopman .20 .50
114 Chris Koopman .20 .50
115 Tim Ackerman .20 .50
Todd Ackerman
116 Tim Ackerman .20 .50
117 Todd Ackerman .20 .50
118 Marty Riedl .20 .50
119 Katie Koopman .20 .50
120 Maureen White .20 .50
121 Jaime Hochhausen .20 .50
122 Annie Klein .20 .50
123 Sara Wunderlin .20 .50
124 Laura Uppena .20 .50
125 Jessica Kartman .20 .50
126 Carolyn Hughes .20 .50
127 Jane Tennessen .40 1.00
128 Jason Schulting CO .20 .50
129 Jeff Adrian .20 .50
130 Tom Tennessen .20 .50
131 T. J. Whyte .20 .50
132 Kris Willis .20 .50
133 Dennis Uppena CO .75 2.00
134 Adam Ploessl .20 .50
135 Sam Okey 1.25 3.00
147 Sam Okey 1.25 3.00
148 Sam Okey 1.25 3.00
149 Sam Okey 1.25 3.00
150 Sam Okey 1.25 3.00
151 Sam Okey 1.25 3.00

1992-93 Cincinnati

This 14-card standard-size set features full-bleed action color player photos. A diagonal gray stripe across one of the top corners contains the word "Cincinnati". A white bar near the bottom displays the player's name in red print. The horizontal backs feature small, color close-ups, and the player's name and biographical information. The major portion of the back is devoted to a player profile and statistics. The cards are unnumbered and checklisted below in alphabetical order. The set features the first card of Nick Van Exel.

COMPLETE SET (14) 5.00 12.00
1 Corie Blount 1.00 2.50
2 Curtis Bostic .40 1.00
3 LaZelle Durden .40 1.00
4 David Evans .20 .50
5 Darrick Ford .20 .50
6 Terrance Gibson .20 .50
7 Keith Gregor .30 .75
8 Mike Harris .30 .75
9 Bob Huggins CO 1.25 3.00
10 Allen Jackson .20 .50
11 John Jacobs .20 .50
12 Erick Martin .30 .75
13 Terry Nelson .30 .75
14 Nick Van Exel 3.00 8.00

1993-94 Cincinnati

This 18-card standard-size set features the 1993-94 Cincinnati Bearcats. Inside bright red borders, the fronts feature color player cutouts on a screened maroon background. Printed in red lettering at the top in the background is "Cincinnati Bearcats"; the player's name is printed in gold next to the cutout. Inside a bright red border on a gray panel, the horizontal backs carry a color head shot, player profile, and statistics. The cards are unnumbered and checklisted below in alphabetical order.

COMPLETE SET (18) 5.00 12.00
1 Corie Blount 2.00 5.00
Nick Van Exel
Bearcats in the Pros
2 Curtis Bostic .40 1.00
3 Darnell Burton .40 1.00
4 LaZelle Durden .40 1.00
5 David Evans .20 .50
6 Damon Flint .40 1.00
7 Keith Gregor .20 .50
8 Mike Harris .20 .50
9 Larry Harrison ACO .20 .50
Steve Moeller ACO
John Loyer ACO
10 Bob Huggins CO .75 2.00
11 John Jacobs .20 .50
12 Jackson Julson .20 .50
13 Dontonio Wingfield 1.00 2.50
14 Brian Wolf .20 .50
15 Marko Wright .20 .50
16 The Shoemaker Center .20 .50
17 Cincinnati in the NCAA Tournament .20 .50
18 Title Card .20 .50

1988-89 Clemson

This 16-card standard-size set was sponsored by Carolina Pride, and its company logo appears in the upper right corner of the card face. The fronts feature color head and shoulders player photos on a white card face. Player identification is given in the border below the picture. The cards are unnumbered and checklisted below in alphabetical order. Key cards in the set include Elden Campbell and Dale Davis.

COMPLETE SET (16) 12.00 30.00
1 Colby Brown .40 1.00
2 Donnell Bruce .40 1.00
3 Elden Campbell 5.00 12.00
4 Marion Cash .40 1.00
5 Dale Davis 5.00 12.00
6 Cliff Ellis CO 1.25 3.00
7 Derrick Forrest .40 1.00
8 Len Gordy ACO .40 1.00
9 Eugene Harris ACO .40 1.00
10 Kirkland Howling .40 1.00
11 Ricky Jones .40 1.00
12 Tim Kincaid .40 1.00
13 Rod Mitchell .40 1.00
14 Jerry Pryor .40 1.00
15 David Young .40 1.00
16 Logo Card .20 .50

1989-90 Clemson

This 16-card set was sponsored by Carolina Pride, and its company logo appears in the lower left corner of the card face as well as on the back. The cards were issued on an unperforated sheet with four rows of four cards; after cutting, the cards measure the standard size. The fronts feature color head and shoulders player photos on a white card face. Blue borders on the bottom and right of the picture form a shadow. The school and team names are printed in orange and blue above the picture, with an orange pawprint in the upper right corner. Player identification is given in the blue border below the picture. The backs have biographical information, player evaluation, and basketball advice in the form of "Tips from the Tigers." The cards are unnumbered and checklisted below in alphabetical order, with the uniform number after the player's name. Key cards in the set include Elden Campbell and Dale Davis.

COMPLETE SET (16) 10.00 25.00
1 Colby Brown 44 .40 1.00
2 Donnell Bruce 14 .40 1.00
3 Wayne Buckingham 42 .40 1.00
4 Elden Campbell 41 4.00 10.00
5 Marion Cash 12 .40 1.00
6 Dale Davis 34 4.00 10.00
7 Cliff Ellis CO .75 2.00
8 Derrick Forrest 13 .40 1.00
9 Len Gordy CO .40 1.00
10 Eugene Harris CO .40 1.00
11 Kirkland Howling 4 .40 1.00
12 Ricky Jones 25 .40 1.00
13 Zlatko Josic 32 .40 1.00
14 Shawn Lastinger 15 .40 1.00
15 Sean Tyson 22 .40 1.00
16 David Young 11 .40 1.00

1990-91 Clemson

This 16-card standard-size set was issued by Carolina Pride. The orange color front of the card has an action color photo in the middle, with black text on each of its four sides. The back of each card includes basic biographical information and a basketball tip. The cards are numbered for convenience in the checklist below alphabetically by subject. The key card in the set is Dale Davis.

COMPLETE SET (16) 6.00 15.00
1 Andre Bovain 31 .40 1.00
2 Colby Brown 44 .40 1.00
3 Donnell Bruce 14 .40 1.00
4 Eric Burks 24 .40 1.00
5 Dale Davis 34 3.00 8.00
6 Cliff Ellis CO .60 1.50
7 Len Gordy ACO .40 1.00
8 Eugene Harris ACO .40 1.00
9 Steve Harris 13 .60 1.50
10 Ricky Jones 25 .75 2.00
11 Shawn Lastinger 15 .40 1.00
12 Jimmy Mason 10 .40 1.00
13 Tyrone Paul 32 .40 1.00
14 Sean Tyson 22 .40 1.00
15 Joey Watts 20 .40 1.00
16 David Young 11 .40 1.00

1990-91 Clemson Collegiate Collection Promos

This ten-card standard-size set was issued by Collegiate Collection to honor some of the great athletes who played at Clemson. The front of the card features a full-color photo of the person featured while the back of the card has details about the person pictured. As this set is a multi-sport set we have used a two-letter identification of the sport next to the person's name.

COMPLETE SET (10) 1.50 4.00
C1 Tree Rollins BK .30 .75

1990-91 Clemson Collegiate Collection

This 200-card standard-size set was produced by Collegiate Collection. We've included a sport initial (B-baseball, K-basketball, F-football, G-Golf; WK-women's basketball) for players in the top collected sports.

COMPLETE SET (200) 6.00 15.00
3 Wayne(Tree) Rollins K .08 .25
6 Larry Nance K .20 .50
8 Horace Grant K .40 1.00
12 Bobby Conrad K .07 .20
17 Elden Campbell K .20 .50
24 Vincent Hamilton K .05 .15
29 Tigers Win Classic K .05 .15
35 Murray Jarman K .05 .15
40 Grayson Marshall K .05 .15
43 Billy Williams K .05 .15
59 Randy Mazey B .05 .15
68 Butch Zatezalo K .05 .15
74 Michael Tait K .05 .15
76 Horace Wyatt K .05 .15
80 Tigers with ACC Title K .05 .15
92 Cliff Ellis CO K .07 .20
97 Derrick Forrest K .05 .15
114 Bill Foster CO K .07 .20
125 Kirk Howling K .05 .15
135 Littlejohn Coliseum K .05 .15
148 Jim Davis WK .05 .15
149 Jim Brennan K .05 .15
154 Andie Tribble WK .05 .15
157 Choppy Patterson K .05 .15
166 Tommy Mahaffey K .08 .25
168 Bill Yarborough K .05 .15
172 Jerry Pryor K .05 .15
177 Richie Mahaffey K .05 .15
185 Mary Ann Cubelic WK .05 .15
188 Randy Mahaffey K .05 .15
191 Karen Ann Jenkins WK .05 .15
192 Bobbie Mims WK .05 .15
193 Janet Knight WK .05 .15
199 Donnie Mahaffey K .05 .15

1990-91 Clemson Women

This 16-card standard-size set was sponsored by Carolina Pride and features Clemson's Lady Tigers basketball team, who made it to the round of sixteen in the 1990 NCAA tournament. The cards are printed on thin card stock. The fronts feature color action player photos enclosed by full-bleed orange borders. The top has 1990 NCAA Sweet Sixteen in black; the sides display the school and team names; and the bottom carries player information. The backs present biography, career summary, and "Tips from the Lady Tigers" which consist of anti-drug and alcohol messages. The cards are unnumbered and checklisted below in alphabetical order.

COMPLETE SET (16) 2.50 6.00
1 Kerry Boyatt .20 .50
2 Shandy Bryan .20 .50
3 Jim Davis CO .30 .75
4 Jackie Farmer .20 .50
5 Donna Forrest .20 .50
6 Shanna Howard .20 .50
7 Courtney Johnson .20 .50
8 Jackie Mattress .20 .50
9 Melissa Miller .20 .50
10 Angie Peters .20 .50
11 Dana Puckett .20 .50
12 Peggy Sells .20 .50
13 Kim Stephens .20 .50
14 Cheron Wells .20 .50
15 Imani Wilson .20 .50
16 Title Card .20 .50
The Davis Era

1992-93 Clemson Schedules

These ten cards measure approximately 2 1/4" by 3 1/2" and feature color action shots on their orange-bordered fronts. The white backs carry the various sport schedules in orange and black lettering. The name of the player depicted on the front appears at the bottom of the back. The cards are unnumbered and checklisted below in alphabetical order.

COMPLETE SET (11) 1.50 4.00
1 Kerry Boyatt-Hall .20 .50
Women's Basketball
9 Chris Whitney BK .30 .75

1910 College Athlete Felts B-33

Issued as a cigarette redemption premium, most prominently by Egyptiene Cigarettes, but also other companies also probably offered these as premiums. Many of the backs have a listing on the reverse side listing a factory and district number. Although 10 different sports are included in this series, we are only listing the colleges in which basketball figures are known to exist. Although these are not numbered, we are putting these in alphabetical order for convenience.

COMPLETE SET 2000.00 3300.00
1 Amherst 50.00 100.00
2 Army 75.00 150.00
3 Brown 75.00 150.00
4 Bucknell 50.00 100.00
5 California 50.00 100.00
6 Chicago 50.00 100.00
7 Colgate 50.00 100.00
8 Colorado 50.00 100.00
9 Columbia 75.00 150.00
10 Cornell 75.00 150.00
11 Dartmouth 75.00 150.00
12 Harvard 100.00 200.00
13 Johns Hopkins 60.00 120.00
14 Knox 50.00 100.00
15 Michigan 75.00 150.00
16 Navy 50.00 100.00
17 Oregon 50.00 100.00
18 Pennsylvania 75.00 150.00
19 Princeton 100.00 200.00
20 Rutgers 50.00 100.00
21 St Louis 50.00 100.00
22 Stanford 100.00 200.00
23 Syracuse 50.00 100.00
24 Trinity 50.00 100.00
25 Tufts 50.00 100.00
26 Utah 50.00 100.00
27 Vermont 50.00 100.00
28 Williams 60.00 120.00
29 Wisconsin 50.00 100.00
30 Yale 100.00 200.00

1990 Collegiate Collection Say No to Drugs

This multi-sport set was released by Collegiate Collection for the "Say No To Drugs, Yes to Life" campaign. Each card is essentially a re-issue of a standard card from one of the college team sets along with a different card number and different copyright line.

COMPLETE SET (6) 5.00 12.00
NC1 Michael Jordan 3.00 8.00

1995-96 Colorado

COMPLETE SET (16) 6.00 15.00
3 Martice Moore .40 1.00
4 Chauncey Billups 5.00 12.00
5 Howard Frier .40 1.00
11 Leroy Carter .40 1.00
12 Matt Daniel .40 1.00
13 Charlie Melvin .40 1.00
21 Devon Gilchrist .40 1.00
23 Jamie Miller .40 1.00
31 Fred Edmonds .40 1.00
32 Mack Tuck .40 1.00
40 Ted Kritza .40 1.00
42 Greg Jensen .40 1.00
44 Charles Thompson .40 1.00
45 Dennis Griffin .40 1.00
NNO Colorado Title Card .40 1.00
NNO Joe Harrington CO .40 1.00

1990-91 Connecticut

This 16-card set was sponsored by Petro Pantry food stores, WTIC 1080 radio, and Citgo. The cards were issued in four strips of four cards each; after perforation, they measure the standard size. The front features a color action player photo on a dark blue background. In white lettering the team name appears above the picture. Player information is given below the picture, sandwiched between sponsors' logos. The back has biographical information, career summary, and "Husky Rap," which consists of an anti-drug or alcohol message. A Huskie's logo at the bottom completes the card back. The cards are unnumbered and are checklisted below in alphabetical order, with the uniform number after the player's name. Key cards in the set include Scott Burrell and Chris Smith.

COMPLETE SET (16) 6.00 15.00
1 Scott Burrell 24 1.50 4.00
2 Jim Calhoun CO 2.50 6.00
3 Dan Cyrulik 55 .40 1.00
4 Lyman DePriest 23 .40 1.00
5 Shawn Ellison 32 .40 1.00
guarding Vin Baker
6 John Gwynn 15 .30 .75
7 Gilad Katz 10 .30 .75
8 Oliver Macklin 11 .30 .75
9 Steve Pikiell 21 .30 .75
10 Tim Pikiell 31 .30 .75
11 Rod Sellers 22 .40 1.00
12 Chris Smith 13 1.25 3.00
13 Marc Suhr 30 .30 .75
14 Toraino Walker 42 .40 1.00
15 Murray Williams 20 .30 .75
16 Jonathan (Mascot) .30 .75

1991-92 Connecticut Legends

This 16-card standard-size set was sponsored by Petro Pantry Food Stores and WTIC-1080. It was issued in four stripes with four cards each and features outstanding players and coaches from the University of Connecticut. The fronts feature a mix of black, white or color player photos. The pictures are bordered by white on the top and the sides, with the words "Connecticut Basketball Legends" printed in dark blue in these white borders. Sponsor logos and the player's name appear in the bottom dark blue border. In blue print on white, the backs present biography, career summary, and "Husky Rap," which consists of anti-drug and alcohol messages. The cards are unnumbered and checklisted below in alphabetical order. The key card in the set is Cliff Robinson.

COMPLETE SET (16) 5.00 12.00
1 Wes Bialosuknia .20 .50
2 Jim Calhoun CO 1.25 3.00
3 Walt Dropo .60 1.50
4 Phil Gamble .20 .50
5 Tate George .40 1.00
6 Hugh Greer CO .20 .50
7 Tony Hanson .20 .50
8 Nadav Henefeld .40 1.00
9 Toby Kimball .20 .50
10 Mike McKay .20 .50
11 Art Quimby .20 .50
12 Clifford Robinson 2.00 5.00
13 Dee Rowe CO .20 .50
14 John Thomas .20 .50
15 Corny Thompson .40 1.00
16 UConn Field House .20 .50

1991-92 Connecticut

This 16-card standard-size set was sponsored by Petro Pantry Food Stores and Citgo. The fronts are accented in the team's colors (dark blue and white) and have color action player photos. The top of the pictures is curved to resemble an archway, and the school and team names follow the curve of the arch. In dark blue print on white, the backs have biography, career summary, and "Husky Rap," which consist of anti-drug and alcohol messages. The cards are unnumbered and checklisted below in alphabetical order. The key card in the set is Donyell Marshall's first card.

COMPLETE SET (16) 5.00 12.00
1 Rich Ashmeade .20 .50
2 Scott Burrell 1.25 3.00
3 Jeff Calhoun .30 .75
4 Dan Cyrulik .30 .75
5 Brian Fair .30 .75
6 Rudy Johnson .20 .50
7 Gilad Katz .30 .75
8 Oliver Macklin .20 .50
9 Donny Marshall 1.25 3.00
10 Donyell Marshall 2.50 6.00
11 Kevin Ollie .40 1.00
12 Tim Pikiell .20 .50
13 Rod Sellers .30 .75
14 Chris Smith .75 2.00
15 Toraino Walker .30 .75
16 Nantambu Willingham .20 .50

1992-93 Connecticut

Issued in a perforated sheet, these 16 standard-size cards feature on their fronts color player action shots that are borderless on the right and bottom, blue-bordered on the left and top. The player's name, position, and class appear in white lettering within the blue border on the left. The white backs carry a black-and-white head shot at the upper left. The player's uniform number, name, class, and position appear alongside; career highlights appear below. The cards are unnumbered and checklisted below in alphabetical order.

COMPLETE SET (16) 12.50 30.00
1 Scott Burrell 1.50 4.00
2 Jeff Calhoun .60 1.50
3 Jim Calhoun CO 2.00 5.00
4 Covington Cormier .60 1.50
5 Steve Emt .60 1.50
6 Brian Fair .60 1.50
7 Eric Hayward .60 1.50
8 Rudy Johnson .60 1.50
9 Travis Knight 2.50 6.00
10 Oliver Macklin .60 1.50
11 Donny Marshall 1.00 2.50
12 Donyell Marshall 3.00 8.00
13 Kevin Ollie .60 1.50
14 Nantambu Willingham .60 1.50
15 Howie Dickenman ACO .60 1.50

Dave Leitao ACO		
Glen Miller ACO		
16 Cheerleaders	.75	2.00

1993-94 Connecticut

Issued in a perforated sheet, these 16 standard-size cards feature on their fronts color player action shots that are borderless on the right and top, blue-bordered on the left and bottom. The player's name and uniform number appear in white lettering within the blue border on the bottom. The horizontal white backs carry a black-and-white head shot at the upper left and the player's career highlights appear to the right. A ghosted Huskies logo forms the background. The cards are unnumbered and checklisted below in alphabetical order. Ray Allen's first card is in this set.

COMPLETE SET (16)	15.00	40.00
1 Ray Allen	10.00	25.00
2 Jeff Calhoun	.20	.50
3 Jim Calhoun CO	2.00	5.00
4 Brian Fair	.30	.75
5 Eric Hayward	.20	.50
6 Ruslan Inyatkin	.20	.50
7 Rudy Johnson	.20	.50
8 Kirk King	.30	.75
9 Travis Knight	1.25	3.00
10 Donny Marshall	.75	2.00
11 Donyell Marshall	2.00	5.00
12 Kevin Ollie	.40	1.00
13 Doron Sheffer	.75	2.00
14 Marcus Thomas	.20	.50
15 Nantambu Willingham	.20	.50
16 Howie Dickenman ACO	.20	.50
Dave Leitao ACO		
Glen Miller ACO		

1993-94 Connecticut Women

Issued in a perforated sheet, these 16 standard-size cards feature on their fronts color player action shots that are borderless on the right and top, blue-bordered on the left and bottom. The player's name and uniform number appear in white lettering within the blue border on the bottom. The horizontal white backs carry a black-and-white head shot at the upper left and the player's career highlights appear to the right. A ghosted Huskies logo forms the background. The cards are unnumbered and checklisted below in alphabetical order. This set contains the first card of Rebecca Lobo, who led the Lady Huskies to an undefeated, national championship season, and later played for the gold medal-winning 1996 USA team. Also included in this set are Jennifer Rizzotti and Kara Wolters, key members of the national championship team.

COMPLETE SET (16)	20.00	50.00
1 Geno Auriemma CO	6.00	15.00
2 Carla Berube	1.00	2.50
3 Kim Better	.75	2.00
4 Tonya Boone	.75	2.00
5 The Connecticut Fans	.75	2.00
6 Jamelle Elliott	.75	2.00
7 Colleen Healy	.75	2.00
8 Jonathan the Husky Dog (Mascot)	.75	2.00
9 Rebecca Lobo	6.00	15.00
10 Shea Matlock	.75	2.00
11 Sue Mayo	.75	2.00
12 Jennifer Rizzotti	5.00	12.00
13 Missy Rose	.75	2.00
14 Pam Webber	1.00	2.50
15 Kara Wolters	5.00	12.00
16 Chris Dailey ACO	.75	2.00
Meghan Pattyson ACO		
Wendy Davis ACO		

1994-95 Connecticut

This 10" by 14" perforated sheet was sponsored by First Fidelity. After perforation, the cards measure the standard size. The fronts feature color action player photos that are superposed over the top dark blue stripes that carry the school and year. Another dark blue stripe cuts across the bottom and provides player information. The horizontal backs show a black-and-white closeup, biography, and player profile. The cards are unnumbered and checklisted below in alphabetical order. Notable players are Donny Marshall and Ray Allen.

COMPLETE SET (16)	12.50	30.00
1 Ray Allen	6.00	15.00
2 Jim Calhoun CO	2.00	5.00
3 Uri Cohen-Mintz	.40	1.00
4 Brian Fair	.40	1.00
5 Eric Hayward	.40	1.00
6 Ruslan Inyatkin	.40	1.00
7 Rudy Johnson	.40	1.00
8 Kirk King	.40	1.00
9 Travis Knight	1.50	4.00
10 Donny Marshall	.75	2.00
11 Kevin Ollie	.60	1.50
12 Doron Sheffer	.75	2.00
13 Justin Srb	.40	1.00
14 Marcus Thomas	.40	1.00
15 Nantambu Willingham	.40	1.00
16 Greg Yeomens	.40	1.00

1995-96 Connecticut

Sponsored by First Union Bank, this 16-card set was issued as a perforated sheet. The sheets were given out at Connecticut home games during the 1995-96 season. When broken up, the individual cards measure the standard 2 1/2" by 3 1/2". The fronts display color, action photos surrounded by a dark blue border. The back are black and white, featuring a small player head shot and biographical information. The cards are unnumbered and checklisted below in alphabetical order. Add a 10% premium for complete sets in their original uncut sheet format.

COMPLETE SET (16)	10.00	25.00
1 Ray Allen	5.00	12.00
2 Jim Calhoun CO	2.00	5.00
3 Dion Carson	.40	1.00
4 Kyle Chapman	.40	1.00
5 Eric Hayward	.40	1.00
6 Ruslan Inyatkin	.40	1.00
7 Rudy Johnson	.40	1.00
8 Rashamel Jones	1.00	2.50
9 Pete Kane	.40	1.00
10 Kirk King	.50	1.25
11 Antric Klaiber	.40	1.00
12 Travis Knight	1.25	3.00
13 Predrag Materic	.40	1.00
14 Rickey Moore	.50	1.25
15 Doron Sheffer	.50	1.25
16 Justin Srb	.40	1.00

1996-97 Connecticut

This 16-card set was released at the University of Connecticut during the 1996-97 season. These cards were sponsored by First Union, and feature many of the players from that season's team. The set is not numbered and is listed below in alphabetical order.

COMPLETE SET (16)	15.00	35.00
1 Jim Calhoun CO	1.50	4.00
2 Dion Carson	.30	.75
3 Kyle Chapman	.30	.75
4 Kevin Freeman	.75	2.00
5 Sam Funches	.30	.75
6 Richard Hamilton	10.00	25.00
7 Monquencio Hardnett	.30	.75
8 Ruslan Inyatkin	.30	.75
9 Rashamel Jones	.75	2.00
10 Kirk King	.30	.75
11 Antric Klaiber	.30	.75
12 Michael LeBlanc	.30	.75
13 Pete McCann	.30	.75
14 Ricky Moore	.75	2.00
15 Mike Smith	.30	.75
16 Jake Voskuhl	1.50	4.00

1997-98 Connecticut

This 16-card set was released at the University of Connecticut during the 1997-98 season. These cards were sponsored by First Union, and feature many of the players from that season's team. The set is not numbered and is listed below in alphabetical order.

COMPLETE SET (16)	8.00	20.00
1 Jeff Cybart	.20	.50
2 Khalid El-Amin	1.00	2.50
3 Kevin Freeman	.75	2.00
4 Richard Hamilton	6.00	15.00
5 Monquencio Hardnett	.20	.50
6 E.J. Harrison	.20	.50
7 Rashamel Jones	.75	2.00
8 Antric Klaiber	.20	.50
9 Rickey Moore	.60	1.50
10 Albert Mouring	.20	.50
11 Jake Voskuhl	1.00	2.50
12 Souleymane Wane	.20	.50
13 Jim Calhoun CO	1.25	3.00
14 Karl Hobbs ACO	.20	.50
15 Dave Leitao ACO	.20	.50
16 Tom Moore ACO	.20	.50

1997-98 Connecticut Women

This 16-card set was released at the University of Connecticut during the 1997-98 season. These cards were sponsored by First Union, and feature many of the players from that season's team. The set is not numbered and is listed below in alphabetical order.

COMPLETE SET (16)	8.00	20.00
1 Geno Auriemma CO	3.00	8.00
2 Tihana Abrlic	.20	.50
3 Svetlana Abrosimova	2.00	5.00
4 Jean Clark	.20	.50
5 Amy Duran	.40	1.00
6 Courtney Gaine	.20	.50
7 Marci Glenney	.20	.50
8 Stacy Hansmeyer	.20	.50
9 Kelley Hunt	.20	.50
10 Shea Ralph	1.00	2.50
11 Nykesha Sales	3.00	8.00
12 Paige Sauer	.60	1.50
13 Kelly Schumacher	.20	.50
14 Rita Williams	1.00	2.50
15 Chris Dailey ACO	.20	.50
16 Tonya Cartloza	.20	.50
Jamelle Elliot CO		

1998-99 Connecticut

This 20-card set was released at the University of Connecticut during the 1998-99 season. These cards were sponsored by First Union, and feature many of the players from that season's team. The set is not numbered and is listed below in alphabetical order.

COMPLETE SET (20)	10.00	25.00
1 Beau Archibald	.20	.50
2 Justin Brown	.20	.50
3 Ajou Ajou Deng	.20	.50
4 Khalid El-Amin	.75	2.00
5 Kevin Freeman	.75	2.00
6 Richard Hamilton	6.00	15.00
7 E.J. Harrison	.20	.50
8 Rashamel Jones	.75	2.00
9 Antric Klaiber	.20	.50
10 Ricky Moore	.60	1.50
11 Albert Mouring	.20	.50
12 Edmund Saunders	.20	.50
13 Jake Voskuhl	.75	2.00
14 Souleymane Wane	.20	.50
15 Jim Calhoun CO	1.25	3.00
16 Karl Hobbs ACO	.20	.50
17 Dave Leitao ACO	.20	.50
18 Tom Moore ACO	.20	.50
19 Harry A. Gampel Pavillion	.20	.50
20 Hartford Civic Center	.20	.50

1998-99 Connecticut Women

This 19-card set was released at the University of Connecticut during the 1998-99 season. These cards were sponsored by First Union, and feature many of the players from that season's team. The set is not numbered and is listed below in alphabetical order. Sue Bird's first ever card is in this set.

COMPLETE SET (19)	8.00	20.00
1 Geno Auriemma CO	2.00	5.00
2 Tihana Abrlic	.20	.50
3 Svetlana Abrosimova	2.00	5.00
4 Sue Bird	6.00	15.00
5 Swintayla Cash	2.50	6.00
6 Marci Czel	.20	.50
7 Amy Duran	.30	.75
8 Courtney Gaine	.20	.50
9 Marci Glenney	.20	.50
10 Stacy Hansmeyer	.20	.50
11 Asjha Jones	.20	.50
12 Shea Ralph	.75	2.00
13 Kelly Schumacher	.20	.50
14 Keirsten Walters	.20	.50
15 Tamika Williams	.60	1.50
16 Chris Dailey ACO	.20	.50
17 Tonya Cardoza ACO	.20	.50
18 Jamelle Elliott ACO	.20	.50
19 Rita Williams ACO	.75	2.00

1999-00 Connecticut

This 18 card standard-size set features members of the then defending National Champion Uconn Huskies. The full-bleed borders feature glossy fronts with the players name on the bottom. The backs have a portrait, some biographical information as well as career highlights. As the cards are not numbered, we have put them in alphabetical order.

COMPLETE SET (18)	6.00	15.00
1 Beau Archibald	.20	.50
2 Justin Brown	.20	.50
3 Jim Calhoun CO	1.25	3.00
4 Marcus Cox	.20	.50
5 Ajou Deng	.20	.50
6 Khalid El-Amin	.75	2.00
7 Kevin Freeman	.60	1.50
8 Karl Hobbs ACO	.20	.50
9 Dave Leitao ACO	.20	.50
10 Tom Moore ACO	.20	.50
11 Albert Mouring	.40	1.00
12 Tony Robertson	.20	.50
13 Edmund Saunders	.20	.50
14 Jake Voskuhl	.75	2.00
15 Soulemane Wane	.20	.50
16 Brett Watson	.20	.50
17 Doug Wrenn	.20	.50
18 Big Blue and Johnathan Mascots	.20	.50

1999-00 Connecticut Women

This 18 card standard-size set features members of the then defending National Champion Uconn Huskies. The full-bleed borders feature glossy fronts with the players name on the bottom. The backs have a portrait, some biographical information as well as career highlights. As the cards are not numbered, we have put them in alphabetical order.

COMPLETE SET (18)	8.00	20.00
1 Svetlana Abrosimova	1.25	3.00
2 Geno Auriemma CO	1.50	4.00
3 Sue Bird	4.00	10.00
4 Tonya Cardoza	.20	.50
5 Swin Cash	1.50	4.00
6 Marci Czel	.20	.50
7 Chris Dailey ACO	.20	.50
8 Jamelle Elliott	.20	.50
9 Stacy Hansmeyer	.20	.50
10 Kennitrya Johnson	.20	.50
11 Ashja Jones	.75	2.00
12 Shea Ralph	.75	2.00
13 Christine Rigby	.20	.50
14 Paige Sauer	.20	.50
15 Kelly Schumacher	.40	1.00
16 Keirsten Walters	.20	.50
17 Tamika Williams	.20	.50
18 Big Blue and Johnathan Mascots	.20	.50

1991-92 David Lipscomb

This 30-card standard-size set features the David Lipscomb University Bison basketball team. Inside a black border, color player cut-outs are superimposed on a geometric background that fades between pink and purple. The bottom purple bar carries the school logo and the player's name. The backs present a black-and-white head shot, biography, statistics, and player profile in the form of "Coaches Comments."

COMPLETE SET (30)	5.00	12.00
1 Chuck Ross	.20	.50
2 Shannon Terry	.20	.50
3 Rob Browne	.20	.50
4 Greg Eubanks	.20	.50
5 Greg Thompson	.20	.50
6 Brian Ayers	.20	.50
7 Lyndell Goldston	.20	.50
8 Jerry Meyer	.20	.50
9 Mark Campbell	.20	.50
10 Michael Green	.20	.50
11 John Pierce	.20	.50
12 Daniel Dennison	.20	.50
13 Malcolm Montgomery	.20	.50
14 Kevin Dixon	.20	.50
15 Andy McQueen	.20	.50
16 Lee Anderson	.20	.50
17 Adam Pierce	.20	.50
18 Thomas Lanier	.20	.50
19 Paul Rogers ACO	.20	.50
20 Gene Barnett ACO	.20	.50
21 Robert Sain ACO	.20	.50
22 Jon Fouss ACO	.20	.50
23 Greg Brown ACO	.20	.50
24 Todd Fouss ACO	.20	.50
25 Robert Butler ACO	.20	.50
26 Chris Snoddy TR	.20	.50
27 Jonathan Seamon ADM	.20	.50
28 Mike Roller ACO	.20	.50
29 Ralph Turner ACO	.20	.50
30 Don Meyer CO	.20	.50

1992-93 David Lipscomb

This 30-card standard-size set features the David Lipscomb University Bison basketball team. Inside a black border, color player cut-outs are superimposed on a geometric background that fades between pink and purple. The bottom purple bar carries the school logo and the player's name. The backs present a black-and-white head shot, biography, statistics, and player profile in the form of "Coaches Comments."

COMPLETE SET (30)	5.00	12.00
1 Chuck Ross	.20	.50
2 Shannon Terry	.20	.50
3 Rob Browne	.20	.50
4 Greg Eubanks	.20	.50
5 Greg Thompson	.20	.50
6 Brian Ayers	.20	.50
7 Lyndell Goldston	.20	.50
8 Jerry Meyer	.20	.50
9 Mark Campbell	.20	.50
10 Michael Green	.20	.50
11 John Pierce	.20	.50
12 Daniel Dennison	.20	.50
13 Malcolm Montgomery	.20	.50
14 Kevin Dixon	.20	.50
15 Andy McQueen	.20	.50
16 Lee Anderson	.20	.50
17 Adam Pierce	.20	.50
18 Thomas Lanier	.20	.50
19 Paul Rogers ACO	.20	.50
20 Gene Barnett ACO	.20	.50
21 Robert Sain ACO	.20	.50
22 Jon Fouss ACO	.20	.50
23 Greg Brown ACO	.20	.50
24 Todd Fouss ACO	.20	.50
25 Robert Butler ACO	.20	.50
26 Chris Snoddy TR	.20	.50
27 Jonathan Seamon ADM	.20	.50
28 Mike Roller ACO	.20	.50
29 Ralph Turner ACO	.20	.50
30 Don Meyer CO	.20	.50

1983-84 Dayton

This 20-card standard-size set of Dayton Flyers was sponsored by Blue Shield and television Channel 7. The front features borderless blue-tinted posed player photos, with the player's name above and team name below in red lettering on white card stock. The horizontally oriented backs are printed in blue and provide biographical information and the sponsors' logos. The cards are unnumbered and are checklisted below in alphabetical order. There was a 21st card in the set which was pulled from the set just prior to mass distribution due to the fact that the player quit the team.

COMPLETE SET (20)	8.00	20.00
1 Jack Butler ACO and Dan Hipsher ACO	.40	1.00
2 Roosevelt Chapman	2.00	5.00
3 Dan Christie	.40	1.00
4 Dave Colbert	.40	1.00
5 Rory Dahlinghaus	.40	1.00
6 Don Donoher CO	.75	2.00
7 Damon Goodwin	.40	1.00
8 Anthony Grant	.40	1.00
9 Ted Harris	.40	1.00
10 Mike Hartsock	.40	1.00
11 Paul Hawkins	.40	1.00
12 Mick Hubert	.40	1.00
13 Don Hughes	.40	1.00
14 Larry Schellenberg	.40	1.00
15 Jim Shields	.40	1.00
16 Sedric Toney	1.25	3.00
17 Jeff Tressler	.40	1.00
18 Ed Young	.40	1.00
19 Jeff Zern	.40	1.00
20 Flyer Fan Card	.40	1.00

1986-87 DePaul Playing Cards

This rather unattractive set of playing cards was issued to honor Ray Meyer, who retired fifth on the all-time list of most career victories for Division I coaches. The cards measure the standard size. The fronts feature posed or action black and white photos that span Meyer's career and his teams. The backs are turquoise with a white border and white lettering. At the top is a DePaul Blue Demons logo in white, then the school name, and in the lower half of the card is a head shot of Ray Meyer in a heart-shaped opening. At the bottom the coach's name is given along with the words "42 Memorable Years." Numerical values have been assigned to all the cards (ace equals 1; jack equals 11, etc.). The cards are listed according to suits as follows: hearts (H), clubs (C), diamonds (D), and spades (S). The two jokers are listed at the end.

COMP. FACT SET (54)	20.00	50.00
C1 Coach of the Year 1944	.40	1.00
C2 Frank Blum and Jim Lamkin	.30	.75
C3 Bill Robinzine and Ron Sobieszcyk	.50	1.25
C4 Howie Carl	.40	1.00
C5 McKinley Cowsen	.30	.75
C6 M.C. Thompson	.30	.75
C7 Emmette Bryant	.40	1.00
C8 NIT Tournament 1963	.40	1.00
C9 Tom Meyer	.30	.75
C10 Starting Five 1965-66	.40	1.00
C11 Dave Mills	.30	.75
C12 400th Victory Celebration	.40	1.00
C13 Joey Meyer	.50	1.25
D1 Basketball Hall of Fame	.40	1.00
D2 Jim Mitchem	.30	.75
D3 Mark Aguirre	1.25	3.00
D4 Gary Garland	.40	1.00
D5 Final Four NCAA 1978-79	.40	1.00
D6 Curtis Watkins	.30	.75
D7 Joe Ponsetto	.30	.75
D8 Ray and Digger Phelps	.75	2.00
D9 Ron Norwood	.30	.75
D10 Dave Corzine	.50	1.25
D11 Ray and Al McGuire	1.25	3.00
D12 Bill Robinzine Jr.	.50	1.25
D13 500th Victory	.40	1.00
H1 Ray Meyer	1.50	4.00
H2 1st Team (1942)	.40	1.00
H3 Dick Triptow	.30	.75
H4 1st NIT Championship 1945	1.25	3.00
H5 George Mikan	5.00	12.00
H6 NIT Starting Five 1945	1.25	3.00
H7 Ed Mikan and Whitey Kachan	.75	2.00
H8 Early Great Team	.60	1.50
H9 George Mikan and Bill Donato	2.50	6.00
H10 Bato Govedarica	.30	.75
H11 1948 Team	.40	1.00
H12 Ray Meyer	.40	1.00
Marge Meyer and Family		
H13 Dick Heise	.30	.75
S1 700th Victory	.40	1.00
S2 Jerry McMillan	.40	1.00
S3 Last Home Game	.30	.75
S4 Rosemont Horizon	.30	.75
S5 Ray and Joey	.75	2.00
S6 Terry Cummings turns pro	1.00	2.50
S7 Terry Cummings	1.25	3.00
S8 No. 1 Basketball Family	.40	1.00
S9 Last Game at Alumni Hall	.40	1.00
S10 Mark Aguirre and Clyde Bradshaw	.60	1.50
S11 Mark Aguirre and Terry Cummings	1.25	3.00
S12 1979-80 Team	.40	1.00
S13 1979-80 Team Clowning	.40	1.00
xx Joker Card	.30	.75
Year by year record		
xx Joker Card Milestones	.30	.75

1987-88 Duke

This 13-card standard-size set features the Duke Blue Devils basketball team. A special logo cover card was also released, but is not considered part of the complete set. This set features members of the semi-finalists of the 1988 NCAA Tournament. The set is sponsored by Adolescent Care Unit and Glaxo and their company names are on the top of the card. Underneath their names is the Blue Devils' identification. The full-color players photo is in the middle of the card and on the bottom of the card is the players name, uniform number, and position. The back has basic biographical information about the players along with both a basketball and a anti-crime or drug message. Some of the key players in the set include NBA players Danny Ferry and Alaa Abdelnaby in addition to the first card of Duke coach Mike Krzyzewski. The set was produced by Sports Marketing of Seattle, Washington. The cards are numbered for convenience in the checklist below according to the player's uniform number.

COMPLETE SET (13)	20.00	50.00
13 Joe Cook	.75	2.00
14 Quin Snyder	2.50	6.00
21 Robert Brickey	1.00	2.50
22 Greg Koubek	1.25	3.00
30 Alaa Abdelnaby	1.50	4.00
31 Kevin Strickland	.75	2.00
33 John Smith	.75	2.00
35 Danny Ferry	3.00	8.00
42 George Burgin	.75	2.00
44 Phil Henderson	1.50	4.00
45 Clay Buckley	.75	2.00
55 Billy King	.75	2.00
xx Mike Krzyzewski CO	10.00	25.00
NNO Logo Cover Card	8.00	20.00

1988-89 Duke

This 13-card standard-size set featuring the Duke Blue Devils was sponsored by Adolescent CareUnit, Glaxo, and local law enforcement agencies. On a royal blue card face, the fronts show color action player photos enclosed by gray border stripes. Sponsor logos and the team name appear above the picture, while the player's name, jersey number, and position are given below it. In addition to sponsor acknowledgments, the backs carry player profile and "Tips from the Blue Devils," which consist of anti-drug and alcohol messages. The cards are unnumbered and checklisted below in alphabetical order. The key card in the set is the first card of Christian Laettner.

COMPLETE SET (13)	40.00	100.00
1 Alaa Abdelnaby	2.00	5.00
2 Robert Brickey	1.50	4.00
3 Clay Buckley	1.50	4.00
4 George Burgin	1.50	4.00
5 Brian Davis	2.00	5.00
6 Danny Ferry	4.00	10.00
7 Phil Henderson	2.00	5.00
8 Greg Koubek	2.00	5.00
9 Mike Krzyzewski CO	8.00	20.00
10 Christian Laettner	25.00	60.00
11 Crawford Palmer	1.50	4.00
12 John Smith	1.50	4.00
13 Quin Snyder	3.00	8.00

1988-89 East Carolina

Sponsored by Pizza Hut, this six-card standard-size set features 1988-89 East Carolina Pirates basketball players. On a white card face, the color action photos are bordered on three sides by team color-coded (purple and mustard) borders. Player information appears in the bottom purple border. The backs carry a player profile and "Tips from the Pirates" which consist of anti-drug or alcohol messages. There were four other football cards produced by East Carolina that are sometimes considered part of this set.

COMPLETE SET (6)	6.00	15.00
1 Gus Hill	.75	2.00
2 Kenny Murphy	.75	2.00
3 Jeff Kelly	.75	2.00
4 Mike Steele CO	.75	2.00
5 Reed Lose	.75	2.00
6 Blue Edwards	3.00	8.00

1989-90 East Tennessee State

Sponsored by Shoney's and East Tennessee State University, this 12-card standard-size set features color action shots of the players. The backs carry biographical information, statistics, and public service messages. The cards are unnumbered and checklisted below in alphabetical order.

COMPLETE SET (12)	6.00	15.00
1 Greg Dennis	.75	2.00
2 Major Geer	.60	1.50
3 Keith (Mister) Jennings	1.50	4.00
4 Chad Keller	.30	.75
5 Avery Marshall	.30	.75
6 Jerry Pelphrey	.60	1.50
Robert Spears		
James Jacobs		
Darell Jones		
7 Les Robinson CO	1.25	3.00
8 Marty Story	.60	1.50
9 Calvin Talford	1.00	2.50
10 Alvin West	.30	.75
11 Michael Woods	.30	.75
12 East Tennessee State	.60	1.50

1990-91 East Tennessee State

Sponsored by Shoney's and East Tennessee State University, this 14-card standard-size set features color shots of the players posed against a blue studio background. The card backs carry biographical information, statistics, and public service messages. The cards are unnumbered and checklisted below in alphabetical order.

COMPLETE SET (14)	5.00	12.00
1 Jeff Lebo ACO	.50	1.25
Grafton Young ACO		
John Shulman ACO		
Ed Howat ACO		
2 Eric Palmer	.50	1.25
Trazel Silvers		
Moe Hayes		
3 Greg Dennis	.60	1.50
4 Rodney English	.50	1.25
5 Major Geer	.50	1.25
6 Keith(Mister) Jennings	.75	2.00
7 Darell Jones	.30	.75
8 Alan LeForce CO	.50	1.25
9 Jerry Pelphrey	.50	1.25
10 Robert Spears	.30	.75
11 Marty Story	.50	1.25
12 Calvin Talford	.75	2.00
13 Alvin West	.30	.75
14 Michael Woods	.30	.75

1991-92 East Tennessee State

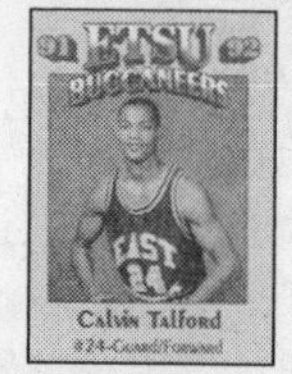

Sponsored by Shoney's and East Tennessee State University, this 15-card standard-size set features color shots of the players posed against a blue studio background. The card face is orange-yellow and is printed with the player's name, jersey number, and position at the bottom. The year, school, and team names appear at the top. The backs carry biographical information, statistics, and public service messages. The cards are unnumbered and checklisted below in alphabetical order.

COMPLETE SET (15)	4.00	10.00
1 Grafton Young ACO	.40	1.00
Ed Howat ACO		
John Shulman ACO		
Jeff Lebo ACO		
2 Greg Dennis	.40	1.00
3 Rodney English	.40	1.00
4 Moe Hayes	.30	.75
Loren Riddick		
5 Damien Hodge	.30	.75
Justin McClellan		
Reece Dudley		
Leslie Brunn		
6 Darell Jones	.30	.75
7 Alan LeForce CO	.60	1.50
8 Jason Niblett	.40	1.00
9 Eric Palmer	.30	.75
10 Jerry Pelphrey	.40	1.00
11 Trazel Silvers	.40	1.00
12 Southern Conference Trophy and Ball	.40	1.00
13 Robert Spears	.30	.75
14 Marty Story	.40	1.00
15 Calvin Talford	.60	1.50

1992-93 East Tennessee State

Sponsored by Shoney's, the ETSU Department of Public Safety, and East Tennessee State University, this 14-card standard-size set features the 1992-93 East Tennessee State men's basketball team. Ten thousand sets and 500 uncut sheets were reportedly produced. The cards are printed on thin card stock and feature posed color player photos on the fronts. The pictures have irregular edges that make it appear as though they have been revealed by tearing through the blue border. The ETSU letters appear at the top in yellow, and the team name, the Buccaneers, is shown just below in white. The player's name, position, and jersey number are shown in white at the bottom. The white back displays the player's name in white letters within a black bar. A brief biography and stats are placed beneath. At the bottom, safety advice provided by the ETSU Department of Public Safety, and the ETSU and Shoney's logos, round out the card. The cards are unnumbered and checklisted below in alphabetical order.

COMPLETE SET (14)	4.00	10.00
1 Leslie Brunn	.30	.75
2 Robert Doggett	.40	1.00
Geoff Herman		
Tony Patterson		
3 Darell Jones	.30	.75
4 Alan LeForce CO	.60	1.50
5 Alan LeForce CO (Cutting down net)	.60	1.50
6 Justin McClellan	.30	.75

7 Jason Niblett .40 1.00
8 Jay Nidiffer ACO .30 .75
John Shulman ACO
Grafton Young ACO
9 Eric Palmer .30 .75
10 Jerry Pelphrey .40 1.00
11 Andy Pennington .30 .75
Phil Powe
12 Trazel Silvers .40 1.00
13 Robert Spears .30 .75
14 Team Photo .40 1.00

1993-94 East Tennessee State

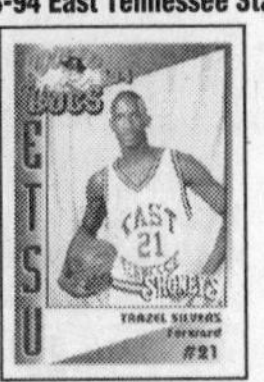

Sponsored by Shoney's, the ETSU Department of Public Safety, and East Tennessee State University, this 15-card standard-size set features the 1993-94 East Tennessee State Men's Basketball team. The cards are printed on thin card stock and the fronts carry posed color player photos. The team logo is in the top left corner with player's name, position, and jersey number at the bottom right below the picture. The backs have biographical information and statistics with an anti-drug message and sponsor logos below. The cards are unnumbered and checklisted below in alphabetical order.

COMPLETE SET (15) 4.00 10.00
1 Leslie Brunn .30 .75
2 Robert Doggett .40 1.00
3 Junior Floyd .30 .75
4 Geoff Herman .30 .75
5 Corrie Johnson .30 .75
Mike Biggs
6 Darell Jones .30 .75
7 Alan LeForce CO .60 1.50
8 Justin McClellan .30 .75
9 Tony Patterson .30 .75
10 Andy Pennington .30 .75
11 Shahid Perkins .30 .75
12 Phil Powe .30 .75
13 Trazel Silvers .30 .75
14 Steve Snell ACO .30 .75
John Shulman ACO
Jay Nidiffer ACO
Jerry Pelphrey ACO
15 Chris Timmerman .30 .75
James Abrams

1992-93 Eastern Illinois

This 12-card standard-size set was sponsored by the Coles County Law Enforcement Agencies and area businesses. The cards feature posed, color player photos with red, white, and blue borders. The player's names are printed at the bottom in the margin, and the school logo appears in the lower right corner. Two players are featured on some of the cards. The backs display public service messages and biographical information within white boxes on a light blue background.

COMPLETE SET (12) 5.00 12.00
1 Rick Samuels CO .40 1.00
and Assistants
2 Team Photo .60 1.50
3 Michael Slaughter .60 1.50
Johnny Hernandez
4 Steve Weemer .40 1.00
Steven Nichols
5 Andre Rodriguez .60 1.50
Louis Jordan
6 Kurt Corner .40 1.00
Walter Graham
7 Troy Collier .60 1.50
Derrick Landrus
8 C.J. Williams .40 1.00
Darrell Young
9 Eric West .60 1.50
10 Curtis Leib .60 1.50
11 Derek Kelley .60 1.50
12 Billy Panther .40 1.00
(Mascot)

1986-87 Emporia State

Sponsored by B and K Nostalgia, this eighteen-card set was issued in two uncut unperforated sheets. If the cards were cut, they would measure the standard size. The fronts feature black-and-white player portraits inside a black frame with white outer borders. The top of the pictures is curved to resemble an archway, and the team name follows the curve of the arch on a yellow background. Player information appears in a yellow stripe below the pictures. The backs carry biography, statistics, or career summary. The cards are unnumbered and checklisted below in alphabetical order.

COMPLETE SET (18) 12.00 30.00
1 Eric Anderson .75 2.00
Bill Pitko
2 Cardell Armstrong .75 2.00
3 Jim Biggs .75 2.00
4 Gary Birch .75 2.00
5 Marvin Chatman .75 2.00
6 Jon Cramer .75 2.00
7 Johnny Craven .75 2.00
8 Dale Cushinberry .75 2.00
9 Dennis Fort .75 2.00
10 Derrick Howse .75 2.00
11 John Hughes .75 2.00
12 Mark Lackey .75 2.00
13 Brian Robinson .75 2.00
14 Ron Slaymaker CO .75 2.00
Hornets Logo
15 Chris Sparks .75 2.00
16 Ryan Sprecker .75 2.00
17 Craig Stromgren .75 2.00
18 Bob Yonke .75 2.00

1993-94 Evansville

The 1993-94 University of Evansville Purple Aces consists of 16 standard-size cards. The cards are printed on thin card stock. The white-bordered fronts carry a mix of posed and action color photos. In the upper left corner within a basketball icon are the school initials and the year of the set. Below the photo on team color-coded bars are the player's name and school name. The backs display a head shot of the player with player profile, biography, and statistics on a purple speckled background. The cards are unnumbered and checklisted below in alphabetical order.

COMPLETE SET (16) 3.00 8.00
1 Jermaine Ball .40 1.00
guarded by Sam Cassell
2 Todd Cochenour .20 .50
3 Jim Crews CO .40 1.00
4 Andy Elkins .60 1.50
5 Mark Hisle .30 .75
6 Reed Jackson .20 .50
7 Brent Kell .20 .50
8 Jeff Layden .20 .50
9 Toby Madison .20 .50
10 Arad McCutchan CO .20 .50
11 Chris Quinn .20 .50
12 Carl Reeder .20 .50
13 Scott Sparks .20 .50
14 Ace Purple (Mascot) .20 .50
15 Ace-Ettes .20 .50
16 Cheerleaders .20 .50

1982-83 Fairfield

This 18-card standard-size set for Fairfield University was produced by Big League Cards. The front features a posed color photo enframed by black and red borders, with the player's name, the university, and a basketball logo below the picture. The back gives biographical information.

COMPLETE SET (18) 6.00 15.00
1 Jay Byrne .40 1.00
2 Vin Cazzetta .60 1.50
3 Pete DeBisschop .40 1.00
4 Joe DeSantis CO .60 1.50
5 Tony George .40 1.00
6 Craig Golden .40 1.00
7 Bobby Hurt .60 1.50
8 Ed Janka CO .40 1.00
9 Jerry Johnson .40 1.00
10 John Leonard .40 1.00
11 Terry O'Connor .60 1.50
12 Tim O'Toole .40 1.00
13 Brendan Potter .60 1.50
14 Ron Ross CO .60 1.50
15 Greg Schwartz .40 1.00
16 Don Wilson .40 1.00
17 Pat Yerina .40 1.00
18 Fairfield Stags .60 1.50

1993 FCA Final Four

This seven-card standard-size set was packaged in a cello pack by the Fellowship of Christian Athletes for distribution at Final Four viewing parties. The color player photos on the fronts are accented on three sides by a thin pink stripe; the card face itself shades from purple to white as one moves toward the bgottom. The FCA logo, featuring a cross with two olive branches, is superimposed in the upper left corner, while the player's name and position are printed beneath the picture. On a purple background, the backs carry a close-up photo, biography, and the player's testimony.

COMPLETE SET (7) 3.00 8.00
1 Steve Alford .75 2.00
2 John Wooden CO 1.50 4.00
3 Bobby Jones 1.00 2.50
4 Rod Foster .60 1.50
5 Keith Erickson .75 2.00
NNO Cover Card .20 .50
NNO Order Form .20 .50

1988-89 Florida

This 14-card standard-size set was sponsored by University Athletic Association in conjunction with Burger King. The front features a color action shot of an athlete engaging in the particular sport highlighted on the card. The pictures are outlined by a thin black border on white card stock. The Burger King and the Gators' logo round out the card face. The back provides additional information on the sport as well as an anti-drug or crime message.

COMPLETE SET (14) 6.00 15.00
3 Men's Basketball 2.00 5.00

1990-91 Florida State Collegiate Collection

This 200-card standard-size set by Collegiate Collection features past and current athletes of Florida State University from a variety of sports.

COMPLETE SET (200) 6.00 15.00
107 Jeff Hogan BK .05 .15
109 Dick Artmeier BK .05 .15
116 Gary Schull BK .05 .15
123 Rowland Garrett BK .05 .15
131 Dave Cowens BK .20 .50
147 Hugh Durham BK .07 .20
183 Ron King BK .05 .15
192 Paul Wernke BK .05 .15
194 Dave Fedor BK .05 .15

1992-93 Florida State

This 80-card multi-sport standard-size set features "Seminole Superstars" from various Florida State teams. The sports represented are golf (1-3), tennis (4-8), swimming and diving (9-14), track and field (15-21), softball (22-25), basketball (26-28, 39-42), volleyball (29-31), baseball (32-38), basketball (39-43), and football (44-75).

COMPLETE SET (80) 15.00 30.00
26 Marynell Meadors CO BK .02 .10
27 Allison Peercy BK .07 .20
28 Ursula Woods BK .07 .20
39 Pat Kennedy CO BK .20 .50
40 Sam Cassell BK 3.20 8.00
41 Rodney Dobard BK .07 .20
42 Chuck Graham BK .07 .20
43 Charlie Ward BK 3.20 8.00

1985-86 Fort Hays State

As indicated on the bottom of the reverse, this rather unattractive 18-card standard-size set was sponsored by K-Bob's Steakhouse. Each set was accompanied by a coupon redeemable at K-Bob's Steakhouse. The cards are printed on thin card stock. The fronts feature black and white head shots framed by black borders on a white card face. A yellow diagonal bar in the upper right corner carries the college letters while the player's name appears beneath the photo in a yellow stripe. The backs have a Tiger pawprint in the upper left corner and present biography, statistics, and career summary. The cards are unnumbered and checklisted below in alphabetical order.

COMPLETE SET (18) 3.00 8.00
1 Tyree Allen .20 .50
2 Joe Anderson .20 .50
3 Troy Applegate .20 .50
Student Coach
4 Kale Barton .20 .50
5 Bruce Brawner .20 .50
6 Fred Campbell .40 1.00
7 Craig Cox CO .20 .50
8 Thomas Hardnett .20 .50
9 Archie Johnson .20 .50
10 David Lackey .20 .50
11 Greg Lackey CO .20 .50
12 Raymond Lee .20 .50
13 Mike Miller .20 .50
14 Bill Morse CO .20 .50
15 Ron Morse .20 .50
16 Cedric Williams .20 .50
17 Team Photo .40 1.00
18 Title Card .40 1.00

1989 Fresno State Women

This three-card 3" by 5" set was sponsored by Smokey. The cards are not numbered and checklisted below in alphabetical order.

COMPLETE SET (3) 1.25 3.00
1 Ginger Connolly .40 1.00
Softball
2 RaeAnn Pifferini .75 2.00
Gina LoPiccolo
Basketball
3 Margie Wright .40 1.00
Julie Smith
Softball

1989-90 Fresno State

This 16-card standard-size set was sponsored by the USDA Forest Service, several other federal agencies, and Grandy's restaurants. The fronts feature either posed or action color player photos with a white card face background. The school name appears in red lettering above the picture, with the team name in the blue stripe just below it. Red and blue stripes appear below the picture, overlayed by the Smokey and Grandy's logos. The back has brief biographical information and a fire prevention cartoon starring Smokey the Bear. The cards are unnumbered and are checklisted below in alphabetical order, with the uniform number after the player's name.

COMPLETE SET (16) 4.00 10.00
1 Ron Adams CO .40 1.00
2 Bijou Baly 15 .40 1.00
3 Dave Barnett 12 .40 1.00
4 Tod Bernard 33 .60 1.50
5 Chris Henderson 25 .40 1.00
6 Wilbert Hooker 30 .60 1.50
7 Pasi Lahtinen 3 .40 1.00
8 Dimitri Lambrecht 32 .40 1.00
9 Sammie Lindsey 50 .40 1.00
10 Joey Paglierani 00 .40 1.00
11 Todd Peebles 23 .40 1.00
12 Pat Riddlesprigger 34 .40 1.00
13 Sammy Taylor 22 .40 1.00
14 Carlo Williams 44 .40 1.00
15 Rey Young 54 .40 1.00
16 Greg Zuffelato 24 .40 1.00

1990-91 Fresno State

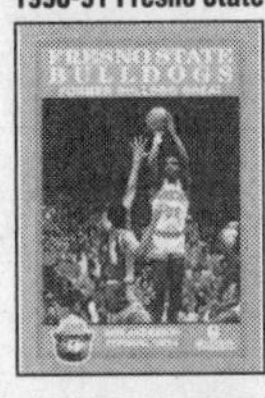

This 16-card standard-size set was sponsored by Grandy's. The front features a color action photo enframed by a blue border on red background, with the player's name, position, and years below the photo, as well as a picture of Smokey the Bear in the left hand corner and a Grandy's logo in the right. The back has biographical information and a public service announcement (with cartoon) concerning wildfire prevention. Ron Anderson of the Philadelphia 76ers is included in this set. The cards are numbered for convenience in the checklist below according to alphabetical order of the player's name.

COMPLETE SET (16) 4.00 10.00
1 Ron Anderson 1.00 2.50
2 Dave Barnett 12 .30 .75
3 Tod Bernard 33 .40 1.00
4 Tyrone Bradley .30 .75
5 Gary Colson CO .75 2.00
6 Carl Ray Harris 11 .40 1.00
7 Doug Harris 20 .30 .75
8 Wilbert Hooker 30 .40 1.00
9 Dimitri Lambrecht 32 .30 .75
10 Sammie Lindsey 50 .30 .75
11 Michael Pearson 3 .30 .75
12 Pat Riddlesprigger 34 .30 .75
13 Sammy Taylor 22 .30 .75
14 Rey Young 54 .30 .75
15 Fresno State Mascot .30 .75
16 Selland Arena .30 .75

1981-82 Georgetown

This set contains 20 cards measuring approximately 2 5/8" by 4 1/8" featuring the Georgetown Hoyas. The fronts of the cards have a blue border. Backs contain safety tips with black print on white card stock. The set was sponsored by the District of Columbia Police Dept. and Safeway. The cards are numbered below by "Tip Number" as listed on the card back. The key card in the set is the first card of NBA superstar Patrick Ewing.

COMPLETE SET (20) 30.00 80.00
1 Jack the Bulldog (Mascot) .60 1.50
2 Elvado Smith .60 1.50
3 Eric Smith .75 2.00
4 Patrick Ewing 30.00 70.00
5 Anthony Jones .75 2.00
6 Bill Martin .75 2.00
7 Bill Stein ACO .60 1.50
8 Norman Washington .60 1.50
Grad. Asst. Coach
9 Ed Spriggs .75 2.00
10 Eric(Sleepy) Floyd 3.00 8.00
11 Gene Smith .75 2.00
12 Fred Brown 1.50 4.00
13 Mike Hancock .60 1.50
14 Kurt Kaull .60 1.50
15 Ed Meyers .60 1.50
16 Ron Blaylock .60 1.50
17 David Blue .60 1.50
18 John Thompson CO 5.00 12.00
19 Ralph Dalton .75 2.00
20 Hoyas Team 1981-1982 3.00 8.00

1982-83 Georgetown

This set contains 15 cards measuring approximately 2 5/8" by 4 1/8" featuring the Georgetown Hoyas. The fronts of the cards have a blue border. Backs contain safety tips with black print on white card stock. The cards are numbered below by "Tip Number" as listed on the card back. The set was sponsored by the District of Columbia Police Dept. and Games Production, Inc. The key card in the set is Patrick Ewing.

COMPLETE SET (15) 15.00 35.00
1 John Thompson CO 3.00 7.00
2 Patrick Ewing 10.00 20.00
3 David Dunn .40 1.00
4 Ralph Dalton .60 1.50
5 Fred Brown .75 2.00
6 Horace Broadnax .60 1.50
7 David Blue .40 1.00
8 Michael Jackson .75 2.00
(listed as Center
on card front)
9 David Wingate 2.00 5.00
10 Vadi Smith .40 1.00
11 Gene Smith .60 1.50
12 Victor Morris .60 1.50
13 Bill Martin .60 1.50
14 Kurt Kaull .40 1.00
15 Anthony Jones .60 1.50

1983-84 Georgetown

This set contains 15 cards measuring approximately 2 5/8" by 4 1/8" featuring the Georgetown Hoyas. Backs contain safety tips. The set was sponsored by the District of Columbia Police Dept. and Coca Cola. This set features the Hoya team that won the 1983-84 NCAA Championship. The key cards in the set are Patrick Ewing and the first card of NBA guard Reggie Williams.

COMPLETE SET (15) 10.00 25.00
1 John Thompson CO 2.00 5.00
2 Hoya 1983-84 Team 2.00 5.00
3 Michael Jackson .60 1.50
4 Bill Martin .60 1.50
5 Jack the Bulldog .40 1.00
Hoya Mascot
6 Gene Smith .60 1.50
7 Fred Brown .60 1.50
8 Horace Broadnax .60 1.50
9 Victor Morris .40 1.00
10 Patrick Ewing 6.00 15.00
11 Ralph Dalton .60 1.50
12 Michael Graham .60 1.50
13 Clifton Dairsow .60 1.50
14 David Wingate 1.25 3.00
15 Reggie Williams 1.50 4.00

1984-85 Georgetown

This set contains 14 cards each measuring approximately 2 5/8" by 4 1/8" featuring the Georgetown Hoyas. Fronts of the cards make reference to Georgetown's National Championship the year before. This set was sponsored by the District of Columbia Police Dept. and Coca Cola. Backs contain safety tips and are written in black ink with a red accent. The cards are numbered for convenience in the checklist below according to alphabetical order of the player's name. The key card in the set is Patrick Ewing.

COMPLETE SET (14) 10.00 25.00
1 John Thompson CO 1.50 4.00
2 Horace Broadnax .60 1.50
3 Ralph Dalton .60 1.50
4 Patrick Ewing 5.00 12.00
5 Kevin Floyd .40 1.00
6 Ron Highsmith .60 1.50
7 Michael Jackson .60 1.50
8 Bill Martin .60 1.50
9 Grady Mateen .40 1.00
10 Perry McDonald .60 1.50
11 Reggie Williams 1.00 2.50
12 David Wingate .75 2.00
13 NCAA Championship .40 1.00
Trophy
14 Team Photo 1.50 4.00

1985-86 Georgetown

The 1985-86 Georgetown Hoyas set contains 16 cards measuring approximately 2 1/2" by 4". There are 13 player cards, plus one coach card, one team picture card, and one mascot card. The card fronts feature color photos and fascimile signatures. Each card back has one basketball tip and one safety tip. The cards are numbered for convenience in the checklist below according to alphabetical order of the player's name.

COMPLETE SET (16) 3.00 8.00
1 1985-86 Hoyas .20 .50
Team Photo
2 John Thompson CO 1.25 3.00
3 Horace Broadnax .30 .75
4 Ralph Dalton .30 .75
5 Johnathan Edwards .30 .75
6 Hoyas Mascot .20 .50
7 Ronnie Highsmith .20 .50
8 Jaren Jackson .75 2.00
9 Michael Jackson .30 .75
10 Grady Mateen .20 .50
11 Perry McDonald .30 .75
12 Victor Morris .20 .50
13 Charles Smith .40 1.00
14 Reggie Williams .75 2.00
15 David Wingate .75 2.00
16 Bobby Winston .20 .50

1986-87 Georgetown

The 1986-87 Georgetown Hoyas set contains 14 cards measuring approximately 2 1/2" by 4". There are 12 player cards, plus one coach card and one team picture card. The card fronts have color photos, and each card back has one basketball tip and one safety tip. The cards are numbered for convenience in the checklist below according to alphabetical order of the player's name.

COMPLETE SET (14) 3.00 8.00
1 1986-87 Hoyas .40 1.00
2 John Thompson CO 1.25 3.00
3 Anthony Allen .20 .50
4 Dwayne Bryant .20 .50
5 Johnathan Edwards .30 .75
6 Ben Gillery .20 .50
7 Ronnie Highsmith .20 .50
8 Jaren Jackson .60 1.50
9 Sam Jefferson .20 .50
10 Perry McDonald .30 .75
11 Charles Smith .30 .75
12 Mark Tillmon .30 .75
13 Reggie Williams .60 1.50
14 Bobby Winston .20 .50

1987-88 Georgetown

The 1987-88 Georgetown Hoyas set contains 16 cards measuring approximately 2 1/2" by 4". There are 14 player cards, plus one coach card and one team picture card. The card fronts have color photos, and each card back has one basketball tip and one safety tip. The cards are numbered for convenience in the checklist below according to alphabetical order of the player's name.

COMPLETE SET (16) 3.00 8.00
1 1987-88 Hoyas .30 .75
2 John Thompson CO .75 2.00
3 Anthony Allen .20 .50
4 Dwayne Bryant .20 .50
5 Johnathan Edwards .30 .75
6 Ben Gillery .20 .50
7 Ronnie Highsmith .20 .50
8 Jaren Jackson .40 1.00
9 Sam Jefferson .20 .50
10 Johnny Jones .20 .50
11 Tom Lang .20 .50
12 Perry McDonald .30 .75
13 Charles Smith .30 .75
14 Mark Tillmon .30 .75
15 Anthony Tucker .20 .50
16 Bobby Winston .20 .50

1988-89 Georgetown

The 1988-89 Georgetown Hoyas set contains 17 cards measuring approximately 2 1/2" by 4". There are 14 player cards, plus one coach card, one team picture card and one mascot card. The card fronts have color photos, and each card back has one safety tip. The cards are numbered for convenience in the checklist below according to alphabetical order of the player's name. The set features the first cards of future NBA Lottery picks and star centers Alonzo Mourning and Dikembe Mutombo.

COMPLETE SET (17) 15.00 40.00
1 1988-89 Hoyas 2.00 5.00
2 John Thompson CO 1.25 3.00
3 Anthony Allen .20 .50
4 Dwayne Bryant .30 .75
5 Johnathan Edwards .30 .75
6 Ronnie Thompson .20 .50
7 Milton Bell .40 1.00
8 Jaren Jackson .40 1.00
9 Sam Jefferson .20 .50
10 Johnny Jones .20 .50
11 Alonzo Mourning 8.00 20.00
12 John Turner .30 .75
13 Charles Smith .30 .75
14 Mark Tillmon .30 .75
15 Dikembe Mutombo 6.00 15.00
16 Bobby Winston .20 .50
17 McGruff The Crime Dog .20 .50
and Jack The Bulldog

1989-90 Georgetown

The 1989-90 Georgetown Hoyas set contains 17 cards measuring approximately 2 1/2" by 4". The front has a posed color photo of the player, enclosed by a blue border on the top and a gray one below. The back is printed in blue and red ink and has a safety tip from McGruff the Crime Dog. The cards are numbered below by "Tip Number" as listed on the card back. The key cards in the set feature Alonzo Mourning and Dikembe Mutombo.

COMPLETE SET (17) 2.50 6.00
1 1989-90 Hoyas .40 1.00
2 John Thompson CO .40 1.00
3 Anthony Allen .08 .25
4 Dwayne Bryant .08 .25
5 David Edwards .08 .25
6 Ronny Thompson .08 .25
7 Milton Bell .20 .50
8 Kayode Vann .08 .25
9 Sam Jefferson .08 .25
10 Johnny Jones .08 .25
11 Alonzo Mourning 1.25 3.00
12 Mike Sabol .08 .25
13 Michael Tate .20 .50
14 Mark Tillmon .20 .50
15 Dikembe Mutombo 1.00 2.50
16 Antoine Stoudamire .08 .25
17 McGruff The Crime Dog .08 .25
and Jack the Bulldog

1990-91 Georgetown

The 1990-91 Georgetown Hoyas set contains 15 cards measuring approximately 2 1/2" by 4". The front has a posed color photo of the player, enclosed by gray borders above and below. The back is printed in blue and red ink and has a safety tip from McGruff the Crime Dog. The cards are numbered below by "Tip Number" as listed on the card back. The key cards in the set feature Alonzo Mourning and Dikembe Mutombo.

COMPLETE SET (15) 2.50 6.00
1 1990-91 Hoyas .40 1.00
Team Photo
2 Kayode Vann .08 .25
4 Antoine Stoudamire .08 .25
5 Alonzo Mourning 1.00 2.50
6 Ronny Thompson .08 .25
7 Dikembe Mutombo .75 2.00
8 Charles Harrison .08 .25
9 Brian Kelly .08 .25
10 Robert Churchwell .20 .50
11 Joey Brown .20 .50
12 Vladimir Bosanac .08 .25
13 Lamont Morgan .08 .25
14 John Thompson CO .40 1.00
15 McGruff The Crime Dog .08 .25
and Jack The Bulldog

1991 Georgetown Collegiate Collection

This 100-card standard-size set was produced by Collegiate Collection. The fronts feature color player photos, with dark blue borders and the player's name in the gray stripe below the picture. The horizontally oriented backs present biographical information, career summary, or statistics on a white background with dark blue lettering and borders.

COMPLETE SET (100) 6.00 15.00
1 John Thompson CO .20 .50
2 Patrick Ewing .40 1.00
3 Eric(Sleepy) Floyd .10 .30
4 Reggie Williams .15 .40
5 John Duren .07 .20
6 Craig Shelton .10 .30
7 Charles Smith .10 .30
8 Michael Jackson .08 .25
9 Jaren Jackson .10 .30
10 David Wingate .10 .30
11 Mark Tillmon .08 .25
12 Fred Brown .08 .25
13 Kurt Kaull .07 .15
14 Ron Highsmith .07 .15
15 Dwayne Bryant .07 .15
16 Michael Jackson .08 .25
17 Al Dutch .07 .15
18 Jim Barry .07 .20
19 Ralph Dalton .07 .20
20 1984 NCAA Champs .15 .40
21 Craig Esherick .07 .15
22 Bobby Winston .07 .15
23 Bill Martin .07 .20
24 Horace Broadnax .07 .20
25 John Thompson CO .20 .50
26 Dwayne Bryant .07 .15
27 Tom Lang .07 .20
28 Perry McDonald .07 .20
29 Reggie Williams .15 .40
30 Patrick Ewing .40 1.00
31 Patrick Ewing .40 1.00
32 Perry McDonald .07 .20
33 Sam Jefferson .07 .20
34 Michael Jackson .08 .25
35 Anthony Allen .07 .15
36 Mike Riley .07 .15
37 John Duren .07 .20
38 Mark Tillmon .08 .25
39 Mike Frazier .07 .15
40 Eric Smith .07 .20
41 Ed Spriggs .07 .20
42 Johnathan Edwards .07 .20
43 Derrick Jackson .07 .20

44 Mike Hancock	.07	.15
45 Tom Scales	.07	.15
46 David Blue	.07	.15
47 Charles Smith	.10	.30
48 John Thompson CO	.20	.50
49 Patrick Ewing	.40	1.00
50 Al Dutch	.07	.15
51 Eric (Sleepy) Floyd	.10	.30
52 Craig Shelton	.10	.30
53 Reggie Williams	.15	.40
53 Tom Lang	.07	.15
54 Michael Jackson	.08	.25
55 Patrick Ewing	.40	1.00
56 Bill Thomas	.07	.15
57 Ed Hopkins	.07	.15
58 John Thompson CO	.20	.50
59 Jon Smith	.07	.15
60 Merlin Wilson	.07	.15
61 Gene Smith	.07	.20
62 Johnny Jones	.07	.15
63 Senior Night	.07	.15
64 Eric (Sleepy) Floyd	.10	.30
65 Reggie Williams	.15	.40
66 Steve Martin	.07	.15
67 Mark Gallagher	.07	.15
68 Mike McDermont	.07	.15
69 Greg Brooks	.07	.15
70 Larry Long	.07	.15
71 Felix Yeoman	.07	.15
72 Lonnie Duren	.07	.15
73 Terry Fenlon	.07	.15
74 Steve Martin	.07	.15
75 Fred Brown	.08	.25
76 Bill Lynn	.07	.15
77 Patrick Ewing	.40	1.00
78 Mike Laska	.07	.15
79 Paul Tagliabue	.40	1.00
80 Don Weber	.07	.15
81 Jaren Jackson	.10	.30
82 1982 NCAA Finalists	.10	.30
83 1985 NCAA Finalists	.10	.30
84 Jim Brown	.07	.15
85 Jim Christy	.07	.15
86 Tim Mercier	.07	.15
87 Joe Missett	.07	.20
88 Charlie Adrian	.07	.15
89 John Thompson CO	.20	.50
90 Craig Esherick	.07	.15
91 Dennis Cesar	.07	.15
92 Ken Pichette	.07	.15
93 Charlie Adrian	.07	.15
94 Mike Laughna	.07	.15
95 Tommy O'Keefe	.07	.15
96 Merlin Wilson	.07	.15
97 Craig Shelton	.10	.30
98 Derrick Jackson	.07	.15
99 Mike Riley	.07	.15
100 Director Card	.07	.15

1991-92 Georgetown

The 1991-92 Georgetown Hoyas police set contains 18 cards measuring approximately 2 1/2" by 4". The fronts carry a posed player photo enclosed by a white border. The year and team name appear in a purple stripe above the picture, while player information is printed in a gray stripe beneath the picture. In blue and red ink, the backs carry "Kids and Cops" safety tips (from McGruff the Crime Dog), a list of sponsor names, the McGruff logo, and the Coke logo. The cards are numbered by the safety tips on the back. The key card in the set features Alonzo Mourning.

COMPLETE SET (18)	2.50	6.00
1 Team Photo	.40	1.00
2 Robert Churchwell	.20	.50
3 Charles Harrison	.08	.25
4 Joey Brown	.20	.50
5 Alonzo Mourning	1.25	3.00
6 Ronny Thompson	.08	.25
7 Vladimir Bosanac	.08	.25
8 Pascal Fleury	.08	.25
9 Brian Kelly	.08	.25
10 Lamont Morgan	.08	.25
11 Kevin Millen	.08	.25
12 Don Reid	.40	1.00
13 Derrick Patterson	.08	.25
14 Lonnie Harrell	.08	.25
15 Irvin Church	.20	.50
16 John Jacques	.08	.25
17 McGruff The Crime Dog	.08	.25
Jack The Bulldog		
18 John Thompson CO	.40	1.00

1992-93 Georgetown

This 16-card set measures approximately 2 1/2" by 4" and was sponsored by the National Crime Prevention Council, Coca-Cola, and local police departments. The cards feature posed color player photos with white borders. A dark purple stripe across the top of the photo contains the words "1992-93 Hoyas" in white lettering. A gray stripe at the bottom displays the player's name and basic biographical information. The backs are white and carry "Kids and Cops" public service tips from the Hoyas. The cards are numbered on the back by the tip number.

COMPLETE SET (16)	2.00	5.00
1 Team Photo	.30	.75
2 John Thompson CO	.40	1.00
3 Duane Spencer	.08	.25
4 Derrick Patterson	.08	.25
5 Vladimir Bosanac	.08	.25
6 Don Reid	.40	1.00
7 Othella Harrington	.75	2.00
8 John Jacques	.08	.25
9 Irvin Church	.20	.50
10 Joey Brown	.20	.50
11 Robert Churchwell	.20	.50
12 Lonnie Harrell	.08	.25
13 Eric Micoud	.08	.25
14 Lamont Morgan	.08	.25
15 Kevin Millen	.08	.25
16 Jack the Bulldog	.08	.25
Mascot		
McGruff the Crime Dog		

1993-94 Georgetown

The 1993-94 Georgetown Hoyas set consists of 16 cards measuring approximately 2 1/2" by 4". The cards are printed on thin card stock. The white-bordered fronts carry posed color player photos. Above the photo the team name and year is reversed out of a blue bar. Below the photo the player's name and bio are reversed out of a gray bar. The backs have a Kids and Cops safety tip printed in navy and red. The cards are unnumbered and checklisted below in alphabetical order.

COMPLETE SET (16)	2.00	5.00
1 Team Photo	.30	.75
2 John Thompson CO	.40	1.00
3 Joey Brown	.20	.50
4 John Jacques	.08	.25
5 Vladimir Bosanac	.08	.25
6 Robert Churchwell	.20	.50
7 Eric Micoud	.08	.25
8 Lamont Morgan	.08	.25
9 Kevin Millen	.08	.25
10 George Butler	.20	.50
11 Othella Harrington	.60	1.50
12 Cheikh Dia	.30	.75
13 Duane Spencer	.20	.50
14 Don Reid	.30	.75
15 Irvin Church	.20	.50
16 McGruff Crime Dog	.08	.25
Jack the Bulldog		

1994-95 Georgetown

The 1994-95 Georgetown Hoyas set was sponsored by the National Crime Prevention Council, various law enforcement agencies, as well as Nissan and Coca-Cola. The cards measure 2 1/2" by 4". Inside white borders, the fronts feature posed player portraits, in which the players are dressed in coat-and-tie. Above the photo the team name and year are reversed out in a blue bar. Below the photo the player's name and bio are reversed on in a gray bar. The backs are printed in navy and red and have Kids & Cops safety tips. The cards are numbered on the back by tip. Allen Iverson's first card is in this set.

COMPLETE SET (16)	12.50	30.00
1 Team Photo	.40	1.00
2 John Thompson CO	.40	1.00
3 John Jacques	.08	.25
4 Boubacar Aw	.30	.75
5 Allen Iverson	10.00	25.00
6 Irvin Church	.20	.50
7 Kevin Millen	.08	.25
8 George Butler	.08	.25
9 Jerry Nichols	.30	.75
10 Othella Harrington	.40	1.00
11 Cheikh Dia	.30	.75
12 Jerome Williams	1.50	4.00
13 Eric Myles	.08	.25
14 Jahidi White	.75	2.00
15 Don Reid	.30	.75
16 McGruff The Crime Dog	.08	.25
And Jack The Bulldog		

1996-97 Georgetown

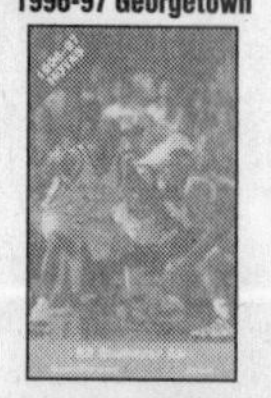

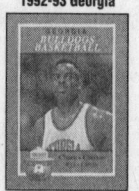

This set was sponsored by the National Crime Prevention Council, various law enforcement agencies, as well as Nissan and Coca-Cola. The cards measure 2 1/2" by 4". The fronts feature posed player portraits, in which the players are dressed in coat-and-tie or an action photo . In the top left corner of the photo the team name and year are in white on a black diagonal bar. Below the photo, the player's name and bio are in a gray bar. The backs are printed in navy and red and have Kids & Cops safety tips. The sponsors names and a few logos are represented as well. The cards are numbered on the back by tip.

COMPLETE SET (18)	4.00	10.00
1 Team Photo	.40	1.00
2 Joseph Touomou	.20	.50
3 Daymond Jackson	.20	.50
4 Dean Berry	.20	.50
5 Brendan Gaughan	.20	.50
6 Cheikh Ya-Ya Dia	.30	.75
7 Shernard Long	.20	.50
8 Boubacar Aw	.30	.75
9 Rhese Gibson	.20	.50
10 Jerry Nichols	.20	.50
11 Ed Sheffey	.20	.50
12 Godwin Owinje	.20	.50
13 Jahidi White	.40	1.00
14 Jameel Watkins	.20	.50
15 Victor Page	.75	2.00
16 Shamel Jones	.30	.75
17 John Thompson CO	.40	1.00
18 Law Enforcement Agencies	.20	.50
Group Photo		

1989-90 Georgia

This 12-card standard-size set was sponsored by the USDA Forest Service and other agencies. The fronts feature color action photos on a white card face. The school name appears in red lettering across the top. The team name and player identification are given in white lettering on a black bar above and below the picture, with the Smokey icon in the lower left corner. The backs carry biographical information as well as a fire prevention cartoon starring Smokey. The cards are unnumbered and checklisted below in alphabetical order.

COMPLETE SET (12)	6.00	15.00
1 Neville Austin	.40	1.00
2 Arlando Bennett	.40	1.00
3 Rod Cole	.40	1.00
4 Hugh Durham CO	1.25	3.00
5 Litterial Green	1.25	3.00
6 Pat Hamilton	.40	1.00
7 Mike Harron	.40	1.00
8 Lemuel Howard	.40	1.00
9 Alec Kessler	1.00	2.50
10 Jody Patton	.40	1.00
11 Elmore Spencer	.75	2.00
12 Marshall Wilson	.40	1.00

1990-91 Georgia

This 16-card standard-size set was sponsored by the USDA Forest Service in conjunction with several other federal agencies. The cards feature on fronts color action photos bordered in red. Inside the border the school name and player identification are given in gray stripes above and below the picture, with the Smokey icon in the lower left corner. The background color outside the red border varies from card to card, ranging from black to gray. The back presents either career statistics or summary, as well as a fire prevention cartoon starring Smokey. The cards are unnumbered and are checklisted below in alphabetical order, with the uniform number after the player's name.

COMPLETE SET (16)	6.00	15.00
1 Neville Austin 35	.40	1.00
2 Arlando Bennett 32	.40	1.00
3 Charles Claxton 33	.75	2.00
4 Rod Cole 22	.40	1.00
5 Bernard Davis 23	.40	1.00
6 Hugh Durham CO	1.00	2.50
7 Shaun Golden 10	.40	1.00
8 Litterial Green 11	1.00	2.50
9 Antonio Harvey 34	1.00	2.50
10 Lem Howard 25	.40	1.00
11 Marcel Kon 51	.40	1.00
12 Jody Patton 12	.40	1.00
13 Kendall Rhine 15	.40	1.00
14 Reggie Tinch 24	.40	1.00
15 Marshall Wilson 44	.60	1.50
guarded by Dennis Scott		
16 1990-91 Bulldogs	.75	2.00
Team Photo		

1992-93 Georgia

Sponsored by the USDA Forest Service and the state forestry agency, this 16-card standard-size set was issued as a perforated sheet consisting of four rows of four cards each. On a red card face, the fronts feature posed and action color player photos. A white frame encloses the pictures as well as player information. A Smokey the Bear logo at the lower left rounds out the front. The backs carry biographical information and a fire prevention cartoon starring Smokey. The cards are unnumbered and checklisted below in alphabetical order.

COMPLETE SET (16)	6.00	15.00
1 Shandon Anderson	2.50	6.00
2 Terrell Bell	.40	1.00
3 Arlando Bennett	.30	.75
4 Dathon Brown	.30	.75
5 Charles Claxton	.75	2.00
6 Bernard Davis	.30	.75
7 Shaun Golden	.30	.75
8 Cleveland Jackson	.30	.75
9 Steve Jones	.30	.75
10 Kris Nordholz	.30	.75
11 Brian Peterson	.30	.75
12 Kendall Rhine	.40	1.00
13 Pertha Robinson	.40	1.00
14 Carlos Strong	.40	1.00
15 Chris Tiger	.30	.75
16 Ty Wilson	.30	.75

1993-94 Georgia

Sponsored by the USDA Forest Service and the state forestry agency, this 16-card standard size set was issued as a perforated sheet consisting of four rows of four cards each. On a red card face, the fronts feature posed and action color player photos. The team name is printed above the photo, with the player's name, number and position below. The team logo and Smokey's 50th year anniversary logo complete the fronts. The backs carry the player's name and number and a fire prevention cartoon starring Smokey. The cards are unnumbered and checklisted below in alphabetical order.

COMPLETE SET (16)	5.00	12.00
1 Shandon Anderson	1.50	4.00
2 Terrell Bell	.40	1.00
3 Dathon Brown	.30	.75
4 Charles Claxton	.60	1.50
5 Bernard Davis	.30	.75
6 Melvin Drake	.30	.75
7 Hugh Durham CO	.60	1.50
8 Cleveland Jackson	.30	.75
9 Steve Jones	.30	.75
10 Kris Nordholz	.30	.75
11 Brian Peterson	.30	.75
12 Pertha Robinson	.40	1.00
13 Carlos Strong	.40	1.00
14 Chris Tiger	.30	.75
15 Ty Wilson	.30	.75
16 Team Photo	.40	1.00

1988-89 Georgia Tech

This 12-card standard-size set was sponsored by Nike, whose company name appears on both sides of the card. Sets were given out to fans attending a certain Georgia Tech home game during the 1988-89 season. The fronts feature either posed or action color photos, with a gold border on the left and dark blue borders on the bottom and right of the picture. The backs have biographical information and a tip from the Yellow Jackets consisting of an anti-drug message. The key cards in the set are Tom Hammonds, Brian Oliver, and Dennis Scott. The cards are numbered for convenience alphabetically by player's name in the checklist below.

COMPLETE SET (12)	8.00	20.00
1 Maurice Brittain 52	.40	1.00
2 Karl Brown 5	.75	2.00
3 Bobby Cremins CO	2.50	6.00
4 Brian Domalik 12	.40	1.00
5 Tom Hammonds 20	1.50	4.00
6 Johnny McNeil 44	.75	2.00
7 James Munlyn 24	.40	1.00
8 Brian Oliver 13	.75	2.00
9 Willie Reese 31	.40	1.00
10 Dennis Scott 4	2.00	5.00
11 Anthony Sherrod 42	.75	2.00
12 David Whitmore 23	.40	1.00

1989-90 Georgia Tech

This 20-card standard-size set was sponsored by the Atlanta City Police Department and produced by Coca-Cola. The cards were distributed in the Atlanta area by the Police Athletic League; reportedly 10,000 sets were distributed. The fronts feature either posed or action color photos on a white card stock. The backs have biographical information and a tip from the Yellow Jackets consisting of an anti-drug message. The cards are numbered for convenience alphabetically by player's name in the checklist below. Key cards in the set include the three Kenny Andersons, two Dennis Scotts, Matt Geiger and Malcolm Mackey's first card.

COMPLETE SET (20)	7.00	14.00
1 Kenny Anderson 12	1.25	3.00
(Portrait)		
2 Kenny Anderson 12	1.25	3.00
(Free Throw)		
3 Kenny Anderson 12	1.25	3.00
(Jump Shot)		
4 Rod Balanis 34	.20	.50
5 Darryl Barnes 15	.20	.50
6 Brian Black 23	.20	.50
7 Karl Brown 5	.30	.75
8 Bobby Cremins CO	.60	1.50
9 Brian Domalik 3	.20	.50
10 Matt Geiger 52	.75	2.00
11 Malcolm Mackey 32	.30	.75
12 Johnny McNeil 44	.30	.75
13 James Munlyn 24	.20	.50
14 Ivano Newbill 33	.30	.75
15 Brian Oliver 13	.40	1.00
16 Dennis Scott 4	.75	2.00
(Free Throw)		
17 Dennis Scott 4	.75	2.00
(Shooting)		
18 Greg White 14	.20	.50
19 Team Photo	.40	1.00
20 Lethal Weapon 3	.60	1.50
Brian Oliver		
Dennis Scott		
Kenny Anderson		

1990-91 Georgia Tech

This 20-card standard-size set was sponsored by the Atlanta City Police Department and Coca-Cola, and the latter sponsor's logos appear in the upper right corner of the card face as well as at the bottom of the back. It is reported that 10,000 sets were issued in two lots: the first 5,000 went out to the housing projects and kids in the Atlanta Police Athletic Program, and the second lot was offered to the general public. The front features a borderless color action photo of the player on white card stock. The team name appears in gold lettering above the picture, with player information in black lettering below the picture. The back has brief biographical information and "Tips from the Yellow Jackets," which consist of various public service announcements. The cards are unnumbered and are checklisted below in alphabetical order. Key cards in the set include the three Kenny Andersons, two Malcolm Mackeys, and Jon Barry's first card.

COMPLETE SET (20)	4.00	10.00
1 Kenny Anderson 12	1.00	2.50
(Shooting lay-up)		
2 Kenny Anderson 12	1.00	2.50
(Driving past defender)		
3 Kenny Anderson 12	1.00	2.50
(Dribbling)		
4 Rod Balanis 34	.20	.50
5 Darryl Barnes 15	.20	.50
6 Jon Barry 14	1.00	2.50
7 Brian Black 23	.20	.50
8 Bobby Cremins CO	.60	1.50
9 Brian Domalik 3	.20	.50
10 James Gaddy 10	.20	.50
11 Todd Harlicka 30	.20	.50
12 Bryan Hill 11	.30	.75
13 Matt Geiger 52	.60	1.50
14 Brian Gemberling 41	.20	.50
15 Malcolm Mackey 32	.30	.75
16 Malcolm Mackey 32	.30	.75
17 James Munlyn 24	.20	.50
18 Ivano Newbill 33	.30	.75
19 Greg White 31	.20	.50
20 Team Photo	.40	1.00

1991 Georgia Tech Collegiate Collection

This 200-card set is standard sized. The fronts have a blue border with color action shots on each one. The school name and logo are found across the top border of the card. The featured player's name is found along the bottom border set against a yellow-gold background. The backs carry a small bio of the player and his/her statistics.

COMPLETE SET (200)	4.00	10.00
2 Ida Neal BK	.05	.15
3 Lenny Horton BK	.05	.15
4 Dennis Scott BK	.10	.25
6 Dolores Bootz BK	.05	.15
9 LeeAnn Woodhull BK	.05	.15
15 Tom Hammonds BK	.05	.15
17 Cindy Cochran BK	.05	.15
24 Tory Ehle BK	.05	.15
26 Brook Steppe BK	.07	.20
30 Brian Oliver BK	.05	.15
33 Craig Neal BK	.05	.15
35 Duane Ferrell BK	.05	.15
40 Marielle Walker BK	.05	.15
42 Yvon Joseph BK	.05	.15
46 Karl Brown BK	.05	.15
58 John Salley BK	.20	.50
60 Sheila Wagner BK	.05	.15
91 Bonnie Tate BK	.05	.15
109 Pete Silas BK	.05	.15
122 Mark Price BK	.20	.50
124 Bobby Cremins BK CO	.07	.20
134 Bruce Dalrymple BK	.05	.15
135 Johnny McNeil BK	.05	.15
141 Scott Petway BK	.05	.15
158 Kate Brandt BK	.05	.15
159 Melvin Dold BK	.05	.15
160 Tico Brown BK	.05	.15
167 Jim Caldwell BK	.05	.15
168 Buddy Blemker BK	.05	.15
170 Roger Kaiser BK	.05	.15
176 Bobby Kimmel BK	.05	.15
177 Phil Wagner BK	.05	.15
178 Jim Wood BK	.05	.15
179 Rich Yunkus BK	.07	.20

1991-92 Georgia Tech

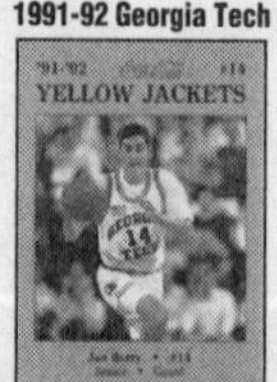

This 15-card standard-size set was sponsored by Coca-Cola in conjunction with Atlanta Police Athletic League. The fronts feature glossy color player photos on a gold card face. The year, Coke logo, jersey number, and team name appear above the picture, while player information is given below it. The backs carry biographical information and "Tips from the Yellow Jackets," which consist of safety tips. The cards are unnumbered and checklisted below in alphabetical order. Key cards in the set include the first cards of Travis Best and James Forrest.

COMPLETE SET (15)	6.00	15.00
1 Rod Balanis	.20	.50
2 Darryl Barnes	.20	.50
3 Drew Barry	1.25	3.00
4 Jon Barry	.75	2.00
5 Travis Best	1.50	4.00
6 Bobby Cremins CO	.60	1.50
7 James Forrest	.60	1.50
8 James Gaddy	.20	.50
9 Matt Geiger	.60	1.50
10 Todd Harlicka	.20	.50
11 Bryan Hill	.30	.75
12 Malcolm Mackey	.40	1.00
13 Ivano Newbill	.30	.75
14 Fred Vinson	.30	.75
15 Greg White	.20	.50

1992-93 Georgia Tech

This 15-card standard-size set features color action player photos. A mustard border on one side of the card carries the school name. A white bar at the bottom contains the player's name in mustard print. This bar intersects the mustard border at one of the lower corners. The horizontal backs feature black-and-white portraits with shadow borders in the upper left corner. The player's name, biography, statistics, and a personal profile fills the remainder of the back.

COMPLETE SET (15)	3.00	8.00
1 Bobby Cremins CO	.60	1.50
2 Bryan Hill	.30	.75
3 James Gaddy	.20	.50
4 Ivano Newbill	.30	.75
5 Malcolm Mackey	.30	.75
6 Rod Balanis	.20	.50
7 Travis Best	1.25	3.00
8 Fred Vinson	.30	.75
9 Darryl Barnes	.20	.50
10 James Forrest	.40	1.00
11 Todd Harlicka	.20	.50
12 Drew Barry	.60	1.50
13 Keith Kenney	.20	.50
14 John Kelly	.20	.50
15 Martice Moore	.40	1.00

1991-92 Hawaii-Hilo

This 15-card set measures 2 1/4 " by 3 1/2" and is sponsored by Mauna Loa. The fronts feature posed player shots framed with a thin purple inner border and a thin red outer border on a blue background. The player's name and position run along the right side of the photo. The backs carry the player's name, position and jersey number on a white stripe at the top with biographical information, career summary, and statistics below on a blue background. The cards are unnumbered and checklisted below in alphabetical order.

COMPLETE SET (15)	10.00	25.00
1 Steve Armstrong	.75	2.00
2 Darren Buchanan	.75	2.00
3 Jason Cabral	.75	2.00
4 Chris Dane	.75	2.00
5 Jeff Garner	.75	2.00
6 Russ Harper	.75	2.00
7 Warren Harrell	.75	2.00
8 Mike Helm	.75	2.00
9 Paul Lee	.75	2.00
10 Jim Malinchak	.75	2.00
11 Cris Murphy	.75	2.00
12 Brett Nesland	.75	2.00
13 Mike Pollock	.75	2.00
14 Dwayne Sarver	.75	2.00
15 Booker Waugh	.75	2.00

1992-93 Hawaii-Hilo

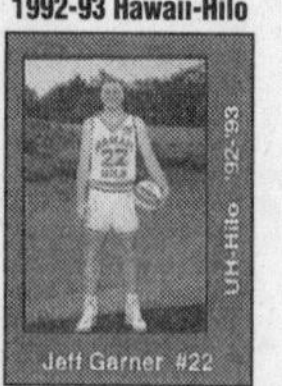

This 15-card set measures the standard size. The fronts feature posed color shots with a red border. The player's name and jersey number are listed at the bottom. The backs carry a small black-and-white player's portrait in the upper left corner with biographical information on a white background. The cards are unnumbered and checklisted below in alphabetical order.

COMPLETE SET (15)	8.00	20.00
1 Dan Androff	.60	1.50
2 Tyro Banks	.60	1.50
3 Fred Crawford	.60	1.50
4 Jerome Facione	.60	1.50
5 Jeff Garner	.60	1.50
6 Eddie Hayward	.60	1.50
7 Paul Lee	.60	1.50
8 Tim Lovejoy ACO	.60	1.50
9 Brett Nesland	.60	1.50
10 Mike Redwood	.60	1.50
11 Dwayne Sarver	.60	1.50
12 Mike Seawright	.60	1.50
13 Mike Van Staveren	.60	1.50
14 Bob Wilson CO	.60	1.50
15 Syrus Yarbrough	.60	1.50

1921 Holy Cross

This set was issued around 1922 and features cards of coaches and team captains for various Holy Cross University sports. The six cards measrue roughly 2 1/2" by 3 3/4" and were issued inside a "wrap-around" style folder that included a photo of the football team. Each card is blankbacked and was printed on thick cream colored stock.

COMPLETE SET (7)	100.00	200.00
4 McLaughlin BK	10.00	20.00

1992-93 Houston

This 28-card standard-size set was produced by Motion Sports Inc. The fronts feature posed, color player photos with black borders. A red bar at the top contains the player's name, while the school name appears in a similar red bar at the bottom. The backs carry biographical information and player profiles on white semi-transparent panels. The panels are set against an action photo of the player that is visible through the panel.

COMPLETE SET (29)	10.00	25.00
1 Pat Foster CO	.20	.50
(Close up)		
2 Bo Outlaw	2.50	6.00
3 Jessie Drain	.08	.25
4 Derrick Smith	.08	.25
5 Craig Lillie	.20	.50
6 Tyrone Evans	.08	.25
7 Rafael Carrasco	.08	.25
8 Brandon Rollins	.08	.25
9 David Diaz	.08	.25
10 Jermaine Johnson	.08	.25
11 Darrell Grayson	.08	.25
12 Anthony Goldwire	1.00	2.50
13 Lloyd Wiles	.08	.25
14 Pat Foster CO	.20	.50
(Standing)		
15 Tommy Jones ACO	.08	.25
16 Alvin Brooks ACO	.08	.25
17 Team Photo	.20	.50
18 Game of Century	.40	1.00
Houston vs. UCLA		
19 Otis Birdsong	.40	1.00
20 Elvin Hayes	2.00	5.00
21 Hakeem Olajuwon	2.00	5.00
22 Clyde Drexler	2.00	5.00
23 Guy V. Lewis	.75	2.00
Former CO		
24 1968 UPI and AP	.20	.50
25 Cougar Pride	.08	.25
26 Ad Card Motion Sports	.08	.25
NNO Front Card	.08	.25
NNO Back Card	.08	.25
NNO Checklist	.08	.25

1990 Idaho Women

COMPLETE SET (12)	3.00	8.00
1 Julie Balch	.40	1.00
2 Jennifer Ballenger	.40	1.00
3 Hettie DeJong	.40	1.00
4 Sabrina Dial	.40	1.00
5 Kortnie Edwards	.40	1.00
6 Brenda Kuehlthau	.40	1.00
7 Sherri Lathen	.40	1.00
8 Andi McCarthy	.40	1.00
9 Kelly Moeller	.40	1.00
10 Sherry Peterson	.40	1.00
11 Erina Queen	.40	1.00
12 Krista Smith	.40	1.00

1994-95 IHSA Boys A State Tournament

Produced by Roox Limited Corporation, this set presents the final sixteen Boys A teams that participated in the Illinois High School Association March Madness Tournament. Just 1,000 sets of each team was produced at tournament time. Measuring the standard size, the borderless fronts feature a mix of color or black-and-white action or posed player photos. A gold-shaded bar across the top carries the player's name with the words "March Madness '95" in a brighter, thin yellow bar below it. The horizontal backs carry the player's name and high school; in addition, his position, height, weight, and class are printed across a faded picture of a basketball. Each set came with a title card, which is not included in the listing below. The school name is given first, followed by the city or township (where appropriate) in parentheses. Numbering errors or inconsistencies abound--some are not in order, some are out of sequence, some are missing, and some are duplicated. For example, #184-195 (except for #186) are duplicated. Both sets of numbers are used for Tabernacle Christian and Unity High School. #193 is duplicated under Unity High School.

COMPLETE SET (215)	25.00	60.00
1 Neal Cotts	.15	.40
2 Richard Douglas	.15	.40
3 John Flick	.15	.40
4 Chad Kerksick	.15	.40
5 Jason Kunz	.15	.40
6 Duane Roth	.15	.40
7 Parnell Roulds	.15	.40
8 Adam Schieppe	.15	.40
9 Eric Schwehr	.15	.40
10 Justin Tarver	.30	.75
11 Steve Walraven	.15	.40
12 DeMarcus Walter	.15	.40
13 Mike Schaefer	.15	.40
14 Steve St. Jules	.15	.40
15 Jim Ward	.15	.40
16 Matt Becker	.15	.40

17 Brad Bryan .15 .40
18 Duane Goebel .15 .40
19 Scott Huegen .15 .40
20 Kurt Kalmer .15 .40
21 Jeff Kehrer .15 .40
22 Nathan Kreke .15 .40
23 Glenn Lammers .15 .40
24 Troy Pingsterhaus .15 .40
25 Brett Schulte .15 .40
26 Bob Tebbe .15 .40
27 Luke Woltering .15 .40
28 Adam Zieren .15 .40
29 Clayton Arnett .15 .40
30 Tyson Bottom .15 .40
31 Andy Brannan .15 .40
32 Brian Clough .15 .40
33 Blake Cunningham .15 .40
34 Derek Freand .15 .40
35 Ben Goetten .15 .40
36 Ryan Graner .15 .40
37 Brian Hires .15 .40
38 Matt Hoots .15 .40
39 Adam Price .15 .40
40 Matt Ruyle .15 .40
41 Daryl Schnelten .15 .40
42 Mark Tepen .15 .40
43 Dan Walker .15 .40
44 Josh Allen .15 .40
45 Eric Glass .15 .40
46 Kyle Herring .15 .40
47 Charlie Holland .15 .40
48 Damon Lampley .15 .40
49 Robert Neal .15 .40
50 Martin Nicholes .15 .40
51 Dale Overstreet UER .15 .40
(Card misnumbered as 581)
52 C.R. Rath .15 .40
53 Brandon Reynolds .15 .40
54 Jared Sperling .15 .40
55 Brad Vineyard .15 .40
56 Daniel Wenzel .15 .40
57 Brock Billings .15 .40
59 Peter Craig .15 .40
61 Heath Hall .15 .40
62 Jimmy Harris .15 .40
63 Marty Hull .15 .40
65 Rusty Lynch .15 .40
67 Kirk Mosley .15 .40
68 Ryan Pulliam .15 .40
70 Jason Stotts .15 .40
71 Joe Wilson .15 .40
72 Neil Banwart .15 .40
73 Brandon Branson .15 .40
74 Kevin Dyer .15 .40
75 Derric Eisenmann .15 .40
76 Chris Fowler .15 .40
77 Ryan Hiviley .15 .40
78 Jeff Howard .15 .40
79 Ryan Martin .15 .40
80 Matt Mougey .15 .40
81 Jeff Peterson .15 .40
82 Cory Richmond .15 .40
83 Tim Sinclair .15 .40
84 Dustin Sullivan .15 .40
85 Kendall Welch .15 .40
86 Matt Wills .15 .40
87 Jonah Batambuze .15 .40
88 Jason Graf .15 .40
89 D.J. Hubbard .15 .40
90 Nathan Hubbard .15 .40
91 Kevin Jones .15 .40
92 Andy Matthews .15 .40
93 Matt McClintock .15 .40
94 Jason Naffziger .15 .40
95 Kurt Olson .15 .40
96 Eric Schlipf .15 .40
97 Nitai Spiro .15 .40
98 Jeremy Stanton .15 .40
99 Darrin York .15 .40
100 Bryan Butt .15 .40
101 Mark Churchill .15 .40
102 Nathan DeBaillie .15 .40
103 Mark Gannon .15 .40
104 Jamie Hixson .15 .40
105 Chris John .15 .40
106 Ryan Jones .15 .40
107 Aaron Kunert .15 .40
108 Jason Larson .15 .40
109 Tim Shields .15 .40
110 Josh Talley .15 .40
111 Brandon Welborn .15 .40
112 Justin Welborn .15 .40
113 Ryan Westlund .15 .40
114 Jarred Wilson .15 .40
115 Scott Cornelis .15 .40
116 Dan Coyne-Logan .15 .40
117 Mike Coyne-Logan .15 .40
118 Tim Dinneen .15 .40
119 Matt Gripp .15 .40
120 Shawn Keeven .15 .40
121 Ryan Kelly .15 .40
122 Charlie Manis .15 .40
123 Brian Moran .15 .40
124 Steve Sottos .15 .40
125 Tony Stock .15 .40
126 Brian Trapkus .15 .40
127 Pat Voss .15 .40
128 Chris Watson .15 .40
129 Pat Watson .15 .40
130 Josh Anderson .15 .40
131 Marc Carlson .15 .40
132 Tyson Erdelac .15 .40
133 Scott Frank .15 .40
134 Erik Frykholm .15 .40
135 Sam Glomp .15 .40
136 Andre Green .15 .40
137 Anthony Harris .15 .40
138 John Harris .15 .40
139 Bret Holmertz .15 .40
140 Dan Jameson .15 .40
141 Neil Kessman .15 .40
142 Bob Lindwall .15 .40
143 Shannon Tripplett .15 .40
144 Rich Beyers .15 .40
145 Jim Brix .15 .40
149 Kevin Herdes .15 .40
150 Roger Jones .15 .40
151 Harlan Kennell .15 .40
152 Alex Miller .15 .40
153 Aaron Rohdemann .15 .40
154 Ryan Shambo .15 .40
155 Ben Short .15 .40
156 Mike Steers .15 .40
157 Todd Wilderman .15 .40
158 Derek Williams .15 .40
159 Eric Roley .15 .40
160 Ryan Cox .15 .40
161 Brock Friese .15 .40
162 Mark Giertz .15 .40
163 Phil Manhart .15 .40
164 Scott Meers .30 .75
165 Christian Merriman .15 .40
166 Patrick Merriman .15 .40
167 Ryan Moomaw .15 .40
168 Craig Ogle .15 .40
170 Brock Vonderheide .15 .40
171 Ben Commare .15 .40
172 Peter Doetschman .15 .40
173 Brian Duffy .15 .40
174 Jake Engler .15 .40
175 Trevor Gartner .15 .40
176 Scott Gengler .15 .40
177 Greg Johnson .15 .40
178 Pat Keller .15 .40
179 Peter Knaub .15 .40
180 Matt Lowry .15 .40
181 Jake Nauman .15 .40
182 Matt Pavesich .15 .40
183 Gary Anderson .15 .40
184 Ricky Brown .15 .40
184 Brian Cardinal .15 .40
185 Kendall Caples .15 .40
185 C.J. Franks .15 .40
186 Sterling Chears .15 .40
187 Vincent Dawkins .15 .40
187 Jacques LeFaivre .15 .40
188 Roosevelt Deanes .15 .40
188 Lyndon Mumm .15 .40
189 Ephraim Eaddy .15 .40
189 Brad Siuts .15 .40
190 Hiawatha Griffin .15 .40
190 Eric Stevens .15 .40
191 Philip Johnson .15 .40
191 Eric Tempel .15 .40
192 Craig Jones .15 .40
192 Zach Trimble .15 .40
193 John Jones .15 .40
193 Brady Allison .15 .40
193 Matt VanNote .15 .40
194 Reginald Jones .15 .40
194 Ryan Rich .15 .40
195 Jamell McLaurin .15 .40
195 John Hausman .15 .40
196 Thaddeus Bates .15 .40
321 Derrick York .15 .40
323 Dustin Rothrock .15 .40
341 Adam Law .15 .40
342 PJ McKinney .15 .40
343 Jed Cryder .15 .40
344 Jabari Harrell .15 .40
345 Brad Punke .15 .40
346 Zeno Weems .15 .40
347 Matt Scott .15 .40
348 Joe Mann .15 .40
349 Steve Becker .15 .40
350 Aaron Sovern .15 .40
351 Nathan Thompson .15 .40
352 Josh Wayne .15 .40
353 Julian Harrell .15 .40
354 Mark Allen .15 .40

1994-95 IHSA Boys A Slam Dunk

This 65-card set features those players who participated in the slam dunk competition at the state tournament. Five hundred of each card were printed. The fronts feature a small color or black-and-white, posed or action player photo in a thin red frame on a blue background. The player's name is printed in white on a purple stripe below the picture. The set title is printed up the right and across the top with a basketball between the words in the top right. The horizontal backs carry the player's name in white on a black stripe with his high school below along with the player's height, class, and what college he would like to attend or career highlights. The March Madness logo appears at the right. Cards are numbered consecutively except the last card is numbered 106 instead of 66 and is a duplicate of card 65.

COMPLETE SET (65) 8.00 20.00
1 Charles Adams .15 .40
2 Ricky Brown .15 .40
3 Jeff Averkamp .15 .40
4 Tim Cavinder .15 .40
5 Phil Durkin .15 .40
6 Robert Hahn .15 .40
7 Mike Hawks .15 .40
8 Jason Peake .15 .40
9 Damiano Scalera .15 .40
10 James Gast .15 .40
11 Bryan Zotz .15 .40
12 Mike Tyler .15 .40
13 Tim West .15 .40
14 Jim Vance .15 .40
15 Tom Pshak .15 .40
16 Tommy Sawyer .15 .40
17 Derek Crabill .15 .40
18 Rick Lawson .15 .40
19 Brian Shaw .15 .40
20 Joel Hubbard .15 .40
21 Josh Born .15 .40
22 Jamie Reel .15 .40
23 Shawn Lade .15 .40
24 Jeff Peterson .15 .40
25 Josh Pistole .15 .40
26 Josh Jones .15 .40
27 A.J. Strum .15 .40
28 Kale Sellers .15 .40
29 Andy Ellet .15 .40
30 Chad Brecunier .15 .40
31 Eric Esker .15 .40
32 Marty Hull .15 .40
33 Matt Alepra .15 .40
34 Mark Rasmussen .15 .40
35 Robert Clark .15 .40
36 Damon Lampley .15 .40
37 Trevor Hiel .15 .40
38 Greg McDanel .15 .40
39 Todd Stewart .15 .40
40 William Newton .15 .40
41 Cory Eshleman .15 .40
42 Jackson Jones .15 .40
43 Tim Volpert .15 .40
44 Tony Zook .15 .40
45 Thomas Robinson .15 .40
46 Matt Gunier .15 .40
47 Ronnie Kammes .15 .40
48 Ryan Ashley .15 .40
49 Michael Glover .15 .40
50 Chris Prather .15 .40
51 Brandon Merchalnt .15 .40
52 Duane Roth .15 .40
53 Dusty Johnson .15 .40
54 Jason Ogorzaly .15 .40
55 Jeremy Browne .15 .40
56 Derrick DeWilde .15 .40
57 Brian Miller .15 .40
58 Alan Loy .15 .40
59 Kris Stoneking .15 .40
60 Michael Klinger .15 .40
61 Shea Banning .15 .40
62 James Gast .15 .40
63 David Cerven .15 .40
64 Alvin Valentine .15 .40
65 Andre Williams .15 .40
106 Andre Williams .15 .40

1994-95 IHSA Boys A 3-Point Showdown

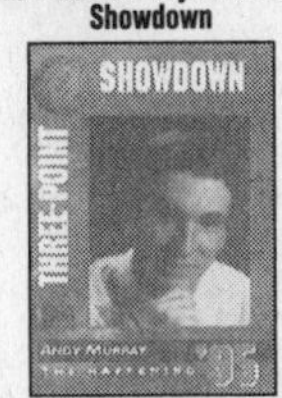

This 52-card set features those players who participated in the 3-point showdown at the state tournament. Five hundred of each card were printed. Measuring the standard size, the fronts feature a small color or black-and-white, posed or action player photo in a thin red frame on a blue background. The player's name is printed in white on a purple stripe below the picture. The set title is printed down the left and at the top with a basketball between the words in the top left. The horizontal backs carry the player's name in white on a black stripe with his high school below along with the player's height, class, and what college he would like to attend or some career highlights. The March Madness logo appears at the right. The title card is not included in the listing below. Some card numbers are out of sequence; some numbers are skipped. Two cards are not numbered.

COMPLETE SET (52) 8.00 20.00
1 Mike Abner .15 .40
2 Rob Buckley .15 .40
3 Mike Cox .15 .40
4 Corey Fox .15 .40
5 Ryan Fritch .15 .40
6 Drazen Jozic .15 .40
7 Muamer Karamovic .15 .40
9 Josh Komnick .15 .40
10 Steven Lester .15 .40
11 Mike Martin .15 .40
13 Patrick Presser .15 .40
14 Willie Reinburg .15 .40
15 Torey Rein .15 .40
16 Douglas Scott .15 .40
17 Michael Sommer .15 .40
18 Tom Stirnaman .15 .40
19 Brian Tackitt .15 .40
20 Josh Williams .15 .40
21 Joe Whitmore .15 .40
22 Andy Murray .15 .40
23 Luke Williams .15 .40
24 Michael Torman .15 .40
25 Michael Siegfried .15 .40
26 Aaron Sovern .15 .40
27 Scot Kent .15 .40
31 Guy Kuhn .15 .40
32 Dru McCulley .15 .40
33 Tony Merlie .15 .40
35 Eric Sherrier .15 .40
36 Bill Heisler .15 .40
37 Tony Hartman .15 .40
38 Ryan Hammer .15 .40
39 Chad Hammond .15 .40
40 David Griffiths .15 .40
41 Brent Fowler .15 .40
42 Chad Fulton .15 .40
43 Adam Crenshaw .15 .40
44 Ryan Clark .15 .40
45 Jason Clark .15 .40
46 Brian Ball .15 .40
47 Brent Baker .15 .40
48 Michael Arroyo .15 .40
52 Jeremy Lansaw .15 .40
53 John Harris .15 .40
54 Jacob Mundell .15 .40
55 Josh Menser .15 .40
56 Nick Pestka .15 .40
66 Troy Kemmerling .15 .40
67 Matt Morris .15 .40
302 J.C. Murray .15 .40
NNO Ryan Knuppel .15 .40
NNO Eric Schwehr .15 .40

1994-95 IHSA Boys AA State Tournament

Produced by Roox Limited Corporation, this set presents the final sixteen Boys AA teams that participated in the Illinois High School Association March Madness Tournament. Just 1,000 sets of each team were produced at tournament time. Measuring the standard size, the borderless fronts feature a mix of color or black-and-white, action or posed player photos. A gold-shaded bar across the top carries the player's name with the words "March Madness '95" in a brighter, thin yellow bar below it. The horizontal backs carry the player's name and high school; in addition, his position, height, weight, and class are printed across a faded picture of a basketball. Each set came with a title card, which is not included in the listing below. The set is checklisted below according to school. Some numbers are not used in this set, and there are two of #101 and #106. Some cards have no photos because they were unavailable. This set includes the first cards of Kevin Garnett, drafted by the Minnesota Timberwolves with the fifth pick in the 1995 NBA Draft. His high school teammate, Ronnie Fields (227), was first team all-state in basketball. Other athletes who will play sports at the collegiate level are Antonio "Chico" Brown (64; Illinois football); Tai Streets (106; Michigan football); Gary Bell (108; Notre Dame football); Willie Coleman (139; Bradley basketball); and Monte Jenkins (172; Southern Illinois basketball).

COMPLETE SET (328) 50.00 125.00
1 Mike Becker .20 .50
1 Josh Veith .20 .50
2 Brad Bowsher .20 .50
3 Rob Brynjelsen .20 .50
4 Todd Dahlstrom .20 .50
5 Robert Davis .20 .50
6 Tom Honeycutt .20 .50
7 Chris Jacobs .20 .50
8 Steve Koliopoulos .20 .50
9 Dan Korvas .20 .50
10 Zach Maddox .20 .50
11 Jason McKinney .20 .50
12 Steve Nelson .20 .50
13 Chris Nowinski .20 .50
14 Joe Potocnic .20 .50
15 Brent Prorok .20 .50
16 Michael White .20 .50
17 Paul Wolf .20 .50
18 John Wotal .20 .50
19 Hector Barnes .20 .50
20 Durius Cunningham .20 .50
21 Corey Dagley .20 .50
22 Chuck Garrett .20 .50
23 Rick Garrett .20 .50
24 Mark Hamilton .20 .50
25 Tyrone Jones .20 .50
26 Justin Knolhoff .20 .50
27 Andre Marshall .20 .50
28 Ivan McPhail .20 .50
29 Ewin Meeks .20 .50
30 Ty Moss .20 .50
31 Chad Schnitker .20 .50
32 Luke Sharp .20 .50
33 Brett Skort .20 .50
34 Kimonie Evans .75 2.00
35 Jerry Harris .20 .50
36 Kevin Thornton .20 .50
37 Jason Price .20 .50
38 Nick Irvin .20 .50
39 John Smith .20 .50
40 Marcel O'Neal .20 .50
41 Jason Garcia .20 .50
42 Keith Coley .20 .50
43 Chris Worrell .20 .50
44 Rodderick Thompson .20 .50
45 Artis James .20 .50
46 Alvin Robinson .20 .50
47 Darius Hampton .20 .50
48 Matt Horner .20 .50
49 Mark Wiggins .20 .50
50 Mike Valentine .20 .50
51 Andrew LeCrone .20 .50
52 Eric Norberg .20 .50
53 Milo Moreland .20 .50
54 Harry Beck .20 .50
55 Ed Precht .20 .50
56 Antwan Cuble .20 .50
57 Marty Mulcrone .20 .50
58 Matt Koch .20 .50
59 Doug Meyers .20 .50
60 Steve Rogala .20 .50
61 Andy Mitchell .20 .50
62 Erasmus Balfour .20 .50
63 Mark Allaria .20 .50
64 Antonio Brown .40 1.00
65 Derek Cowan .20 .50
66 Jim Dougherty .20 .50
67 Maurice Douglas .20 .50
68 Eric Ess .20 .50
69 John Harris .20 .50
70 Tom Hofeditz .20 .50
71 Anthony Jumper .20 .50
72 Steffan Nicholson .20 .50
73 Joe Semith .20 .50
74 Mark Thomas .20 .50
75 Stacy Vaughn .20 .50
76 Dwight Woods .20 .50
77 Chris Wright .20 .50
78 Joe Bongratz .20 .50
79 Eric Bradley .20 .50
80 Joel Dangel .20 .50
81 Damion Forrest .20 .50
82 Maurice Foster .20 .50
83 Chris Hayes .20 .50
85 Brian Jaworski .20 .50
86 Ryan Kelver .20 .50
87 Ted Makela .20 .50
88 Joe Merrick .20 .50
89 David Moo .20 .50
90 Luke Moo .20 .50
92 Darnell Smith .20 .50
93 Carlton DeBose .20 .50
94 Denard Eaves .20 .50
95 Melvin Ely 4.00 10.00
96 Corey Harris .20 .50
97 Napoleon Harris .20 .50
98 Erik Herring .20 .50
99 James Johnson .20 .50
100 Chauncey Jones .20 .50
101A Richard King .20 .50
(Running down court)
101B Richard King .20 .50
(In action against other team)
102 Nick Love .20 .50
103 Antwaan Randle El .20 .50
104 Curtis Randle El .20 .50
105 Maurice Scott .20 .50
106A Tai Streets 3.00 8.00
(Crashing the boards)
106B Tai Streets 3.00 8.00
(different shot)
107 Chip Bates .20 .50
108 Gary Bell .40 1.00
109 Eric Breuer .20 .50
110 Dwayne Edmon .20 .50
111 Adrice Edwards .20 .50
112 John Ford .20 .50
113 Paul Forsythe .20 .50
114 Joel House .20 .50
115 Michael Mines .20 .50
116 Blowery Moody .20 .50
117 Rory O'Connell .20 .50
118 Eric Patnoudes .20 .50
119 Paul Purcell .20 .50
120 Kevin Raub .20 .50
121 Oku Satcher .20 .50
122 Erik Walton .20 .50
123 Tim Barrett .20 .50
125 Peter Carroll .20 .50
127 James Dombkiewicz .20 .50
128 Bill Donlon .20 .50
129 Michael Downes .20 .50
130 Sean Eggert .20 .50
131 Gabe Frank .20 .50
132 Joe Hein .20 .50
133 Stu Katz .20 .50
134 Jon Moeller .20 .50
135 Doug Rosen .20 .50
136 Adam Schimel .20 .50
138 Tim Caldwell .20 .50
139 Willie Coleman .75 2.00
140 Kahil Gayton .20 .50
141 Marcus Griffin .20 .50
142 Darrell Ivory .20 .50
143 Dewayne Johnson .20 .50
144 Sergio McClain .20 .50
145 Charles Russell .20 .50
146 Willie Simmons .20 .50
148 Sean Walls .20 .50
149 Jeff Walraven .20 .50
150 Ivan Watson .20 .50
151 Frank Williams .20 .50
152 Willie Williams .20 .50
168 L.T. Boyd .20 .50
169 Josh Elston .20 .50
170 Heith Gadient .20 .50
171 Cory Jenkins .20 .50
172 Monte Jenkins .75 2.00
173 Mike King .20 .50
174 Pete Mickeal .20 .50
175 Andy Milton .20 .50
176 Matt Quinones .20 .50
177 Larry Stevens .20 .50
178 Tymon Vesey .20 .50
179 Marlon White .20 .50
180 Brad Wilson .20 .50
181 Luke Woods .20 .50
183 Ricky Boone .20 .50
184 Dexter Gipson .20 .50
185 Pat Hand .20 .50
187 Walter Hill .20 .50
188 Craig Hopson .20 .50
189 Jon Luchetti .20 .50
190 Ryan Melling .20 .50
192 Charlie Newman .20 .50
193 Ryan Peterson .20 .50
195 Jeremy Warner .20 .50
196 Ali Azim .20 .50
197 Steve Ball .20 .50
198 Garrett Beatty .20 .50
199 Schaun Catey .20 .50
200 Kevin DePiazza .20 .50
201 Cameron Deppe .20 .50
202 Casey Dodson .20 .50
203 Mike Gullickson .20 .50
204 Daryl Kowalski .20 .50
205 Phillip Krahenbuhl .20 .50
206 Chris Levandowski .20 .50
207 Ryan Lindgren .20 .50
208 Lynwood Schambach .20 .50
209 Matt Wasinger .20 .50
210 Chris Wright .20 .50
211 Marcus Betts .20 .50
212 Ron Blanchard .20 .50
213 Gregory Bryant .20 .50
214 Danny Cassell .20 .50
215 Rubin Conway .20 .50
216 Marcus Crump .20 .50
217 Ian Dent .20 .50
218 Jim Devereux .20 .50
219 Mike Gadomski .20 .50
220 Richard James .20 .50
221 Aaron McIntosh .20 .50
222 Derrick Mims .20 .50
223 Ted Moore .20 .50
224 Justin Papuga .20 .50
225 Rob Walls .20 .50
226 Kevin Garnett 25.00 60.00
227 Ronnie Fields 2.00 5.00
228 Michael Wright .40 1.00
229 Jonathon Washington .20 .50
230 Charles Johnson .20 .50
231 Maurice Woodfork .20 .50
233 Jerome McBride .20 .50
234 Daniel Sierra .20 .50
235 Miguel Estrada .20 .50
236 Jamal Rome .20 .50
(Misnumbered 237)
237 Frank Smith .20 .50
(Identical to 238)
238 Frank Smith .20 .50
(Identical to 237)
342 Tory Hickman .20 .50
343 Brandon Douglas .20 .50
344 Brian Trowbridge .20 .50
345 Jim Flynn .20 .50
346 Loren Wallace CO .20 .50
Tim Wallace ACO
Jeff Wallace ACO
347 Brett Douglas .20 .50
348 Kendall Davis .20 .50
349 Mike Reddington .20 .50
350 Cory VonderHaar .20 .50
351 Adam Requet .20 .50
352 Ryan Stanton .20 .50
353 Kyle Cartmill .20 .50
354 Everette Abbey .20 .50

1994-95 IHSA Boys AA State Tournament Garnett Special Edition

Issued after the original 330-card IHSA Boys AA State Tournament set, these two Kevin Garnett cards feature the current NBA wunderkind during his high school days in Chicago.

COMPLETE SET (2) 70.00 130.00
COMMON CARD (239-240) 30.00 65.00

1994-95 IHSA Boys AA 3-Point Showdown

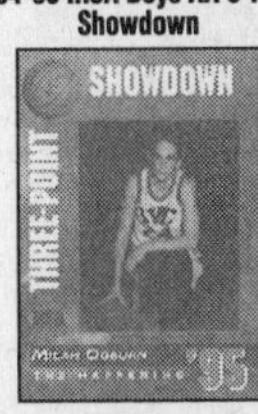

This 60-card set features those players who participated in the 3-point showdown at the state tournament. Five hundred of each card were printed. Measuring the standard size, the fronts feature a small color or black-and-white, posed or action player photo in a thin red frame on a blue background. The player's name is printed in white on a purple stripe below the picture. The set title is printed down the left and at the top with a basketball between the words in the top left. The horizontal backs carry the player's name in white on a black stripe with his high school below along with the player's height, class, and what college he would like to attend or career highlights. The March Madness logo appears at the right. The title card is not included in the listing below. Card number 10, 59, 60, 62, and 63 were not produced. One card was not numbered.

COMPLETE SET (60) 8.00 20.00
1 Marcus Blossom .15 .40
2 Durwood McCoy .15 .40
3 Brad Mann .15 .40
4 Brett Nishibayashi .15 .40
5 Micah Ogburn .15 .40
6 Matt Wasinger .15 .40
7 Ray Hooks .15 .40
8 Charlie McKenna .15 .40
9 Steve Dahl .15 .40
11 Nick Sanchez .15 .40
12 Greg Gilberg .15 .40
13 Brian Sims .15 .40
14 Steven Wennstrom .15 .40
15 Tony Alvarado .15 .40
16 Josh Suter .30 .75
17 Dave Zell .15 .40
18 Ali Ali .15 .40
19 Ryan Naughton .15 .40
20 Frederick Smith .15 .40
21 Greg Moog .15 .40
22 Dominic Catalano .15 .40
23 Brad Fuller .15 .40
24 David Mikes .15 .40
25 Jon Heider .15 .40
26 Korey Coon .15 .40
27 Michael Mines .15 .40
28 Mark Richardson .15 .40
29 Kyle Breden .15 .40
30 Danny Nicholas .15 .40
31 Todd Meggos .15 .40
32 Chris Johnston .15 .40
33 Jasper Mallory .15 .40
34 Cordell Henry .15 .40
35 Adam Riva .15 .40
36 Alfonzo Lewis .15 .40
37 Luke Windy .15 .40
38 Bob Castelli .15 .40
39 Jeff Peterson .15 .40
40 Arthur Stapleton .15 .40
41 Darius Wesley .15 .40
42 Matt Boudeman .15 .40
43 Kevin Casey .15 .40
44 John Lackaff .15 .40
45 Tom Schmidt .15 .40
46 Mike Pryor .15 .40
47 Mike Geurin .15 .40
48 Bob Tolone .15 .40
49 Jonathan Daniels .15 .40
50 John Mackinson .15 .40
51 Tarise Bryson .15 .40
52 Jeremy Lansaw .15 .40
53 John Harris .15 .40
54 Jacob Mundell .15 .40
55 Josh Menser .15 .40
56 Nick Pestka .15 .40
57 Brandon Frerichs .15 .40
58 Donya Jackson .15 .40
61 Adrian Diaz .15 .40
64 Danyell Cresswell .15 .40
NNO Chris Bereziak .15 .40

1994-95 IHSA Girls A State Tournament

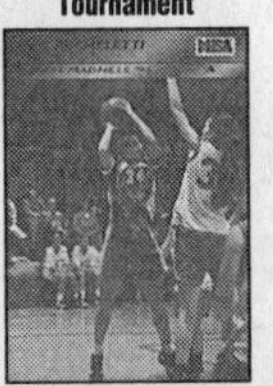

Produced by Roox Limited Corporation, this set presents the final sixteen Girls A teams that participated in the Illinois High School Association March Madness Tournament. Just 1,000 sets of each team was produced at tournament time. Measuring the standard size, the borderless fronts feature a mix of color or black-and-white, action or posed player photos. A gold-shaded bar across the top carries the player's name with the words "March Madness '95" in a brighter, thin yellow bar below it. The horizontal backs carry the player's name and high school; in addition, her position, height, weight, and class are printed across a faded picture of a basketball. Each set came with a title card, which is not included in the listing below. The set is checklisted below according to school. Numbering errors abound--some numbering is out of sequence or card numbers are omitted altogether. Some cards have no photos because they were unavailable for the player whose name is on the card.

COMPLETE SET (195) 20.00 50.00
29 Michelle Donahoo .15 .40
30 Leslie Dumstorff .15 .40
31 Sara Evans .15 .40
32 Heather Fruend .15 .40
33 Danielle Funderburk .15 .40
34 Kristin Hustedde .15 .40
35 Tara Kell .15 .40
36 Erin Knuf .15 .40
37 Racheal Nelson .15 .40
38 Shannon Pollmann .15 .40
39 Courtney Smith .15 .40
40 Amy Allison .15 .40
43 Lindsay Fecht .15 .40
45 Cassie Kinnamon .15 .40
46 Andrea Livingston .15 .40
49 Alisha Nagel .15 .40
52 Koula Toubekis .15 .40
53 Sabrina Bannister .15 .40
54 Ladonna Barton .15 .40
55 Lawanda Burras .15 .40
56 Christina Evans .15 .40
57 Sabrina Minter .15 .40
58 Latrice Payne .15 .40
59 Latrice Ray .15 .40
60 Whitney Wells .15 .40
61 Quinlora Smith .15 .40
62 Tondalaya Wilson .15 .40
115 Lindsey Armstrong .15 .40
116 Heather Cassady .15 .40
117 Jacey Cook .15 .40
118 Melissa Cotter .15 .40
119 Jessi Davis .15 .40
120 Stephanie Donovan .15 .40
121 Tracie Gramkow .15 .40
122 Sara Harlan .15 .40
123 Stephanie Marino .15 .40
124 Lisa Nicoll .15 .40
125 Kari Singer .15 .40
126 Jaima Stowell .15 .40
128 Sara Urban .15 .40
172 Corrie Allan .15 .40
173 Randi Anderson .15 .40
174 Theresa Bertolino .15 .40
175 Kami Derganc .15 .40
176 Margo Girardi .15 .40
177 Kara Joyce .15 .40
178 Celia Jubelt .15 .40
179 Laura Mansholt .15 .40
180 Jodi Ottersburg .15 .40
181 Kristine Polo .15 .40
182 Deneisch Reiniesch .15 .40
183 Alisha Saracco .15 .40
184 Angie Thompson .15 .40
185 Wendy Wolff .15 .40
186 Anna Banks .15 .40
187 Kelly Cartwright .15 .40
188 Rachyl Clayton .15 .40
189 Jaylyn Crabb .15 .40
190 Ricki DeArmon .15 .40
191 Amanda Duggins .15 .40
192 Dawn Halverson .15 .40
193 Alisha Logan .15 .40
194 Chrystal Milligan .15 .40
195 Amy Molinarolo .15 .40
196 Audrey Murphy .15 .40
197 Traci Richerson .15 .40
198 Jessica Stafford .15 .40
199 Tory Teckenbrock .15 .40
200 Erin Watson .15 .40
230 Monica Blyenberg .15 .40
231 Kristen Bruinsma .15 .40
232 Linda DeJong .15 .40
233 Suzanne DeJong .15 .40
234 Kim DeYoung .15 .40
235 Karri Hamstra .15 .40
237 Jennifer Huizenga .15 .40
238 Jennifer Kreykes .15 .40
239 Jill Scott .15 .40
240 Nicole Terpstra .15 .40
241 Becky Vugteveen .15 .40
286 Julie Abell .15 .40
287 Kim Beer .15 .40
288 Shanda Cushing .15 .40
289 Laura Dwyer .15 .40
290 Jenelle Halm .15 .40
291 Hilary Hamer .15 .40
292 Lisa Hendrickson .15 .40
293 Meredith Jackson .15 .40
294 Courtney Jones .15 .40
295 Nikki McCleary .15 .40
296 Erin Micheletti .15 .40
297 Christine O'Connor .15 .40
327 Nicki Bradford .15 .40
328 Cali Broege .15 .40
329 Stacy Ditzler .15 .40
330 Stephanie Fransen .15 .40
331 Kara Hillmer .15 .40
332 Kendra Hillmer .15 .40
333 Kelley Hofmaster .15 .40
334 Jody Knoup .15 .40
335 Kim Koehn .15 .40
336 Cari Pacey .15 .40
337 Elaine Smielewski .15 .40
338 Jocelyn Stiefel .15 .40
339 Sara Thompson .15 .40
340 Tiffany Gallamore .15 .40
341 Shannon Hoyt .15 .40
342 Julie Knuffman .15 .40
344 Susan Laws .15 .40
345 Julie Ludwig .15 .40
346 Robyn Martin .15 .40
347 Dana Schutte .15 .40
348 Deanna Schutte .15 .40
349 Becky Smith .15 .40
350 Michelle Sulewski .15 .40
351 Deanna Venvertloh .15 .40
352 Abbey Williams .15 .40
353 Angie Zanger .15 .40
354 Hope Almy .15 .40

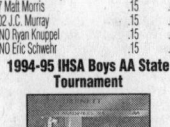

355 Jennie Baird .15 .40
356 Cindy Cheney .15 .40
357 Jill Cheney .15 .40
358 Karen Davis .15 .40
359 Brandi Heleine .15 .40
360 Kasi High .15 .40
361 Lisa Hillary .15 .40
363 Laine Kistler .15 .40
364 Angela Pryle .15 .40
365 Billy Reagan .15 .40
366 Amy Thompson .15 .40
367 Jamie Todd .15 .40
368 Lisa Holley .15 .40
369 Amy Johnson .15 .40
370 Trish Kazak .15 .40
371 Lisa Kuppler .15 .40
372 Stephanie Morphey .15 .40
373 Jacqui Powers .15 .40
374 Amy Reiss .15 .40
375 Cori Stahl .15 .40
376 Leanne Stinson .15 .40
377 LeAnne Stout .15 .40
379 Haylie Behmer .15 .40
380 Brianne Bennett .15 .40
381 Michelle Fager .15 .40
382 Jennifer Harms .15 .40
383 Lea Horii .15 .40
384 Mandey Johnson .15 .40
385 Shelley Johnson .15 .40
386 Angie Patzner .15 .40
387 Jill Schwitters .15 .40
388 Elizabeth Stout .15 .40
389 Jill Tyler .15 .40
390 Katie Tyler .15 .40
391 Erin York .15 .40
392 Gina Bloemer .15 .40
393 Karla Campbell .15 .40
394 Sara Gebben .15 .40
395 Karen Kroeger .15 .40
396 Marcia Meyer .15 .40
397 Amy Niebrugge .15 .40
398 Maria Niebrugge .15 .40
399 Sarah Niebrugge .15 .40
400 Elizabeth Ordner .15 .40
401 Emily Probst .15 .40
402 Kari Probst .15 .40
403 Christina Sehy .15 .40
404 Monica Tegeler .15 .40
405 Kim Walk .15 .40
406 Crystal Worman .15 .40
407 Stormy Young .15 .40
408 Sherry Austin .15 .40
409 Jennifer Bales .15 .40
410 Alicia Brown .15 .40
411 Carissa Brown .15 .40
412 Kristy Duncan .15 .40
413 Katie Edgecombe .15 .40
414 Julie Farr .15 .40
415 Amy Friend .15 .40
416 Stacey Garner .15 .40
417 Leslie Harris .15 .40
418 Chrissy Kunz .15 .40
419 Amanda Park .15 .40
420 Carrie Wickline .15 .40
423 Amy Anderson .15 .40
424 Hilary Anderson .15 .40
425 Lynette Carlson .15 .40
427 Laura Curry .15 .40
428 Kindel McLaughlin .15 .40
429 Shanna Metzler .15 .40
430 Tara Miller .15 .40
431 Jodie Peterson .15 .40
432 Rachel Peterson .15 .40
433 April Schultz .15 .40
436 Laura Bearrows .15 .40
443 Corrie Allan .15 .40

1994-95 IHSA Girls A 3-Point Showdown

This 64-card set features those players who participated in the 3-point showdown at the state tournament. Five hundred of each card were printed. The fronts feature a small color or black-and-white, posed or action player photo in a thin red frame on a blue background. The player's name is printed in white on a purple stripe below the picture. The set title is printed down the left and at the top with a basketball between the words in the top left. The horizontal backs carry the player's name in white on a black stripe with his high school below along with the player's height, class, and what college he would like to attend or career highlights. The March Madness logo appears at the right.

COMPLETE SET (64) 6.00 15.00
1 Missy Barrett .15 .40
2 Ami Beck .15 .40
3 Kristi Bosman .15 .40
4 Nicole Brinker .15 .40
5 Trudy Brooks .15 .40
6 Amanda Colgan .15 .40
7 Patty Conover .15 .40
8 Kami Dergane .15 .40
9 Heather Downing .15 .40
10 Bethany Ellis .15 .40
11 Jill Gomric .15 .40
12 Alicia Granger .15 .40
13 Liza Gualandi .15 .40
14 Stacie Hall .15 .40
15 Erin Henderson .15 .40
16 Heather Holsapple .15 .40
17 Shannon Huff .15 .40
18 Kim Jones .15 .40
19 Ning Kongrut .15 .40
20 Kari Koonce .15 .40
21 Megan Linke .15 .40
22 Traci Lloyd .15 .40
23 Kimberly Lowe .15 .40
24 Ashley Mathias .15 .40
25 Paula Meeker .15 .40
26 Kendra Meyer .15 .40
27 Crystal Miller .15 .40
28 Bridget Monahan .15 .40
29 Dobee Oros .15 .40
30 Heidi Ott .15 .40
31 Cari Pacey .15 .40
32 Jenny Pansa .15 .40
33 Melissa Piper .15 .40
34 Michelle Plack .15 .40
35 Stephanie Rolf .15 .40
36 Maggie Ross .15 .40
37 Kelli Ryan .15 .40
38 Mary Saline .15 .40
39 Kimberly Shafer .15 .40
40 Kelly Slaughter .15 .40
41 Mandy Snell .15 .40
42 Shavon Ellen Sork .15 .40
43 Kimberly Stephenson .15 .40
44 Laura Stucker .15 .40
45 Jody Turrell .15 .40
46 Jesse Weber .15 .40
47 Cathy Wells .15 .40
48 Laurie Zawila .15 .40
49 Lisa Dolan .15 .40
50 Amber Grubbs .15 .40
51 Jessica Kittel .15 .40
52 Amanda White .15 .40
53 Sarah Hunt .15 .40
54 Valerie Lepper .15 .40
55 Gina Fisher .15 .40
56 Brooke Moyer .15 .40
57 Addie Ahlemeyer .15 .40
58 Kris Slavin .15 .40
59 Melanie Mueller .15 .40
60 Melissa Signa .15 .40
61 Alisha Logan .15 .40
62 Teara Backens .15 .40
63 Erin Murphy .15 .40
64 Meredith Jackson .15 .40

1994-95 IHSA Girls AA State Tournament

Produced by Roox Limited Corporation, this set presents the final sixteen Girls AA teams that participated in the Illinois High School Association March Madness Tournament. Just 1,000 sets of each team was produced at tournament time. Measuring the standard size, the borderless fronts feature a mix of color or black-and-white, action or posed player photos. A gold-shaded bar across the top carries the player's name with the words "March Madness '95" in a brighter, thin yellow bar below it. The horizontal backs carry the player's name and high school; in addition, her position, height, weight, and class are printed across a faded picture of a basketball. Each set came with a title card, which is not included in the listing below. The set is checklisted below according to school. Numbering errors and inconsistencies abound--some are out of sequence; others are duplicated; and some are omitted. For example, cards 15 and 16 are out of order and so are cards numbered 436, 437, 438, 439, and 445. Cards 162 and 168 are duplicated with different players and pictures on each card. The Jerseyville High School set, numbered 201-214, is duplicated with the second set having the same but better quality photos. Cards numbers 220 and 221 have the same photo, but two different players' names on them. Some cards have no photos because they were unavailable. This set includes the first card of Dominique Canty (102), a high school All-American who signed to play basketball at Univ. of Alabama. Her teammates, Danielle Scott (113; Coppin State) and Jacqui Jones (107; Alabama), have also signed to play college basketball. Finally, the Lincolnshire team, featuring Tamika and Tauja Catchings (245-46), was ranked #3 in the USA Today final national poll.

COMPLETE SET (227) 25.00 60.00
1 Kathy Fioresi .15 .40
2 Dana Hellgren .15 .40
3 Julie Janota .15 .40
4 Anna Johnson .15 .40
5 Mary Beth Johnson .15 .40
6 Karly Kirkpatrick .15 .40
7 Melissa Parker .15 .40
8 Kim Pompa .15 .40
9 Cathy Ptasnik .15 .40
10 Leslie Schock .15 .40
11 Suzy Smith .15 .40
12 Karisa Turek .15 .40
13 Rachel Voss .15 .40
14 Tina Wenckaitis .15 .40
15 Nykisha Barefield .15 .40
16 Samantha Cartwright .15 .40
17 Sheila Ahern .15 .40
18 Tanisha Brewer .15 .40
19 Cherise Compobasso .15 .40
20 Kate Harker .15 .40
21 Lisa Holman .15 .40
22 Christina Jost .15 .40
23 Stacy Kondziolka .15 .40
24 Kelly Ludy .15 .40
25 Kelly Murman .15 .40
26 Anne Sudlow .15 .40
27 Diana Wendell .15 .40
28 Karen Zygowicz .15 .40
63 Cheri Buchanan .15 .40
64 Jill Fagan .15 .40
65 Andrea Gunnell .15 .40
66 Valerie Kobel .15 .40
67 Jenny Linane .15 .40
68 Katie McAlinden .15 .40
69 Anne McDonald .15 .40
70 Mary Moravek .15 .40
71 Katie Morrissey .15 .40
72 Jeanene Novick .15 .40
73 Katie Schumacher .15 .40
75 Karen Siska .15 .40
76 Karen Valentas .15 .40
77 Trish Watson .15 .40
78 Latasha Love .15 .40
79 Lakendra Moffett .15 .40
80 Kilah Moore .15 .40
81 Michelle Roberts .15 .40
82 Virginia Sellers .15 .40
83 Lori Shelby .15 .40
84 Janelle Tabor .15 .40
85 Stephanie Wallace .15 .40
86 Jenny Accardo .15 .40
87 Amy Anderson .15 .40
88 Tara Babich .15 .40
89 Ann Brophy .15 .40
90 Melissa Collins .15 .40
91 Michelle Foley .15 .40
92 Beth Gawlinski .15 .40
93 Jackie Geraci .15 .40
94 Julie Johnson .15 .40
95 Lauren Manczko .15 .40
96 Mfary Ellen O'Grady .15 .40
97 Kristen Rezny .15 .40
98 Sara Shrader .15 .40
99 Erin Stafford .15 .40
100 Krista Thomas .15 .40
101 Marcella Barry .15 .40
102 Dominique Canty .75 2.00
103 Shereena Clarke .15 .40
104 Deon Cooper .15 .40
105 Clarissa Flores .15 .40
106 Yolanda Howard .15 .40
107 Jaqui Jones .60 1.50
108 Terica Keaton .15 .40
109 Lawanda McCants .15 .40
110 Kimberly Moore .15 .40
111 Danielle Pinkston .15 .40
112 Natasha Pointer .15 .40
113 Danielle Scott .60 1.50
129 Sandi Andersen .15 .40
130 Stefanie Boerema .15 .40
131 Kristi Bosman .15 .40
132 Beth Boven .15 .40
133 Anna Christen .15 .40
134 Laurie Decker .15 .40
135 Cheryl Kooima .15 .40
136 Marisa Kottke .15 .40
137 Becky Lanenga .15 .40
138 Heidi Rimpila .15 .40
139 Siira Rimpila .15 .40
140 Lora Vandenberg .15 .40
141 Stephanie Webber .15 .40
142 Nicole Wieringa .15 .40
143 Katie Zeilstra .15 .40
144 Kristine Abramowski .15 .40
145 Kim Brock .15 .40
146 Betsy Byers .15 .40
147 Tracy Clay .15 .40
148 Amy Coleman .15 .40
149 Jenny Crouse .15 .40
150 Emily Dale .15 .40
151 Tanya Deutscher .15 .40
152 Heather Dittmar .15 .40
153 Melissa Meyers .15 .40
154 Emily Stadel .15 .40
155 Colleen Stebbins .15 .40
156 Lindsay Werntz .15 .40
157 Bonny Apsey .15 .40
158 Jennifer Bulkeley .15 .40
160 Angie Galyean .15 .40
161 Heidi Gengenbacher .15 .40
162 Jenny Cirimotich .15 .40
162 Kathy Kelley .15 .40
163 Steph Latham .15 .40
164 Julie Lofing .15 .40
165 Gina Miller .15 .40
167 Ami Pendry .15 .40
168 Stefanie Mitchell .15 .40
168 Mandy Rinker .15 .40
169 Molly Watson .15 .40
170 Sara Wood .15 .40
171 Jen Wright .15 .40
201 Beth Bear .15 .40
202 Lori Breitweiser .15 .40
203 Julie Carroll .15 .40
204 Brieanna Coffman .15 .40
205 Becky Cox .15 .40
206 Paula Hawkins .15 .40
207 Jara Hellrung .15 .40
208 Michelle Jarman .15 .40
209 Karla Krueger .15 .40
210 Amy Mortensen .15 .40
211 Katie Mortensen .15 .40
212 Kristen Norton .15 .40
213 Jana Shortal .15 .40
214 Amanda Vaughn .15 .40
216 Jennifer Buell .15 .40
217 Kelly Byrne .15 .40
218 Lashonda Clay .15 .40
219 Jamie Hankus .15 .40
220 Katie Maley .15 .40
221 Kelly Maley .15 .40
222 Alicia Mesi .15 .40
223 Amanda Miller .15 .40
224 Kim Nischik .15 .40
225 Ellen Sauser .15 .40
226 Aubrey Sekal .15 .40
227 Jamie Selip .15 .40
228 Beth Walse .15 .40
229 Kate Walse .15 .40
242 Aarin Bartelt .15 .40
243 Ashley Campbell .15 .40
244 Kimberly Carter .15 .40
245 Tamika Catchings 5.00 12.00
246 Tauja Catchings 2.00 5.00
247 Amy Chaness .15 .40
248 Kelly Cole .15 .40
249 Katie Coleman .15 .40
250 Tricia DeClark .15 .40
251 Rebekah Ford .15 .40
252 Noelle Mendenwaldt .15 .40
253 Christy Miller .15 .40
254 Felice Rosenzwig .15 .40
255 Carolyn Roth .15 .40
256 Jamie Smith .15 .40
257 Jennifer Warkins .15 .40
258 Laura Boyer .15 .40
259 Amanda Ely .15 .40
260 Kristen Hamman .15 .40
261 Jessica Jackson .15 .40
262 Jennifer Klein .15 .40
263 Kari Kuefler .15 .40
264 Jenny Leigh .15 .40
265 Liz Luthman .15 .40
266 Jamila Minnicks .15 .40
267 Heather Ory .15 .40
268 Suzie Rizek .15 .40
269 Alicia Stewart .15 .40
270 Tjunia(T.J.) Williams .15 .40
271 Sara Eggleston .15 .40
272 Jaime Gray .15 .40
273 Samantha Hardwick .15 .40
274 Missi Keeley .15 .40
275 Jackie Kopp .15 .40
276 Abby Lewis .15 .40
277 Katy McCain .15 .40
278 Jill McDaniel .15 .40
279 Kelly Moore .15 .40
280 Sara Mozingo .15 .40
281 Jenny Reeves .15 .40
282 Jenny Schmidt .15 .40
283 Kristy Schutz .15 .40
284 Sparkle Thornton .15 .40
298 Kim Bugel .15 .40
299 Laura Castelloni .15 .40
300 Maureen Enright .15 .40
301 Becky Gorecki .15 .40
302 Nora Hogueisson .15 .40
303 Tina LaCombe .15 .40
304 Meggan MacFarlane .15 .40
305 Jenny Malone .15 .40
306 Trisha Monahan .15 .40
307 Jean Nagler .15 .40
308 Amy Novak .15 .40
309 Julie Ricci .15 .40
310 Jenny Sosnowski .15 .40
311 Jill Turner .15 .40
312 Jodi Williams .15 .40
313 Kim Anderson .15 .40
314 Dixie Brazelton .15 .40
315 Missi Clark .15 .40
316 Katie Cutright .15 .40
317 Angi Dewitt .15 .40
318 Bessie Fulk .15 .40
319 Erin Hutchinson .15 .40
320 Randi Johnson .15 .40
321 Adrienne Kraemer .15 .40
322 Erin McNary .15 .40
323 Danette Pine .15 .40
324 Denise Pine .15 .40
325 Shelby Strow .15 .40
326 Emily Stuck .15 .40
436 Tammy Cartwright .15 .40
437 Vanessa Harris .15 .40
438 Danyell Humphries .15 .40
439 Quatoya Johnson .15 .40
445 Laurie Schumacher .15 .40

1994-95 IHSA Girls AA 3-Point Showdown

This 56-card features those players who participated in the 3-point showdown at the state tournament. Five hundred of each card were printed. The fronts feature a small colored or black-and-white, posed or action player photo in a thin red frame on a blue background. The player's name is printed in white on a purple stripe below the picture. The set title is printed down the left and at the top with a basketball between the words in the top left. The horizontal backs carry the player's name in white on a black stripe with his high school below along with the player's height, class, and what college he would like to attend or career highlights. The March Madness logo appears at the right. Photos were not available and thus omitted on several cards.

COMPLETE SET (56) 6.00 15.00
65 Stacy Albrecht .15 .40
66 Michelle Allured .15 .40
67 Tamika Coleman .15 .40
68 Latavia Davis .20 .50
69 Manali Doshi .15 .40
70 Bessie Jo Fulk .15 .40
71 Mackenzie Goebel .15 .40
72 Danielle Green .15 .40
73 Andrea Gunnell .15 .40
74 K.C. Hammond .15 .40
75 Esther Henigan .15 .40
76 Keesha Humphrey .15 .40
77 Holly Johnson .15 .40
78 Jaime Johnson .15 .40
79 Yulonda Jones .15 .40
80 GeGe King .15 .40
81 Tammie Krysh .15 .40
82 Maggie Lamb .15 .40
83 Roz Leeck .15 .40
84 Jenny Lindemann .15 .40
85 Karen Niebrugge .15 .40
86 Denise Pavichevich .15 .40
87 Lisa Perales .15 .40
88 Stacey Pohar .15 .40
89 Holly Palombi .15 .40
90 Tania Price .15 .40
91 Michelle Roof .15 .40
92 Daryl Schaffeld .15 .40
93 Jennifer Sciortino .15 .40
94 Anne Sudlow .15 .40
95 Amanda Vaughn .15 .40
96 Beth Walse .15 .40
97 Jodi Williams .15 .40
98 Carly Zilligen .15 .40
99 Kameelah Morgan .15 .40
100 Anne Mucci .15 .40
101 Denise McMillan .15 .40
102 Jaime Maurer .15 .40
103 Anne McDonald .15 .40
104 Jaime Lynn Burandt .15 .40
105 Shannon O'Neill .15 .40
106 Jenny Schmidt .15 .40
107 Jaime Gray .15 .40
108 Amanda Cavitt .15 .40
109 Jill Carpenter .15 .40
110 Trish Ackerman .15 .40
111 Crystal Tarr .15 .40
112 Danielle Moles .15 .40
113 Laura Valente .15 .40
114 Kelly Gilbert .15 .40
115 Monique Daniel .15 .40
116 Erin Backman .15 .40
117 Nicole LaBuhn .15 .40
118 Wakeelah Ross .15 .40
119 Vanessa Johnson .15 .40
120 Melissa Frawley .15 .40

1994-95 IHSA Historic Record Holders

This 30-card set commemorates outstanding performances in Illinois state basketball tournaments. Five hundred of each card were printed. The fronts feature action or posed player photos in hues of brown which blend into the brown background. The player's name is printed on a black nameplate below the year when they set the record. The March Madness logo is at the bottom. The horizontal backs carry the player's name, height, position, school attended, record set, and state tournament statistics. This set includes past NBA star Dave Robisch and current NBA star LaPhonso Ellis.

COMPLETE SET (30) 6.00 15.00
62 Fernando Bunch .20 .50
63 Sandy Braun .20 .50
64 Brent Carmichael .20 .50
65 Walter Downing .20 .50
66 Mike Duff .20 .50
67 Jim Edmondson .20 .50
68 LaPhonso Ellis 1.25 3.00
69 Jo Jo Johnson .20 .50
70 Dale Kelley .20 .50
71 Jim Lazenby .20 .50
72 Nora Lewis .20 .50
73 Matt Maton .20 .50
74 Chris Payne .20 .50
75 Courtney Porter .20 .50
76 Dave Robisch .60 1.50
77 Johnny Selvie .40 1.00
78 Jay Shidler .40 1.00
79 Cathy Shoup .20 .50
80 Marty Simmons .20 .50
81 Gary Tidwell .20 .50
82 Tammy Van Oppen .20 .50
83 Kevin Washington .20 .50
84 Connie Erickson .20 .50
85 Lori Fitzjarrald .20 .50
86 Dee Dee Franklin .20 .50
87 Shannon Hickenbottom .20 .50
88 Cammy Hudson .20 .50
89 Tina Hutchinson .20 .50
90 Cindy Kaufmann .20 .50
91 Jamie Brandon .40 1.00

1980-81 Illinois

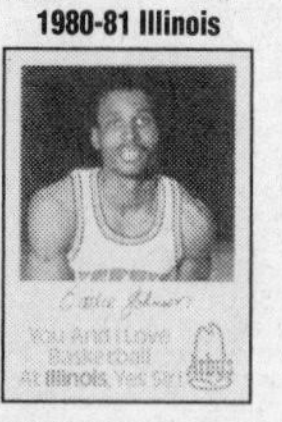

This 15-card standard-size set was sponsored by Arby's Restaurants and features players of the 1980-81 Fighting Illini squad. The player's signature and an Arby's advertisement appear below a color posed photo of the player. The horizontally oriented back provides biographical and statistical information. The cards are numbered for convenience alphabetically in the checklist below. Key cards in the set include the first cards of NBA veterans Derek Harper and Eddie Johnson.

COMPLETE SET (15) 15.00 30.00
1 Kevin Bontemps .40 1.00
2 James Griffin .40 1.00
3 Derek Harper 7.50 15.00
4 Lou Henson CO 1.50 4.00
5 Derek Holcomb .75 2.00
6 Eddie Johnson 6.00 12.00
7 Bryan Leonard .40 1.00
8 Dick Nagy ACO .40 1.00
9 Perry Range .40 1.00
10 Quinn Richardson .40 1.00
11 Mark Smith .40 1.00
12 Neale Stoner .40 1.00
13 Craig Tucker .40 1.00
14 Tony Yates ACO .75 2.00
15 Team Photo 1.50 4.00

1981-82 Illinois

This 16-card standard-size set was sponsored by Arby's Restaurants and features players of the 1981-82 Fighting Illini squad. The player's signature and an Arby's advertisement appear below a color posed photo of the player. The horizontally oriented back provides biographical and statistical information. Lou Henson's last name is misspelled on the back of his card (Hensen). The cards are numbered for convenience alphabetically in the checklist below. The key card in the set is Derek Harper.

COMPLETE SET (16) 8.00 20.00
1 Kevin Bontemps .40 1.00
2 Jay Daniels .40 1.00
3 James Griffin .40 1.00
4 Derek Harper 4.00 10.00
5 Lou Henson CO UER 1.25 3.00
(Misspelled Hensen on card back)
6 Dan Klier .40 1.00
7 Bryan Leonard .40 1.00
8 Dee Maras .40 1.00
9 George Montgomery .40 1.00
10 Dick Nagy ACO .40 1.00
11 Perry Range .40 1.00
12 Quinn Richardson .40 1.00
13 Craig Tucker .40 1.00
14 Anthony Welch .60 1.50
15 Tony Yates ACO .60 1.50
16 Team Photo .75 2.00

1992-93 Illinois

Produced by Flying Color Graphics Inc., this 16-card standard-size set was sponsored by Pepsi. This set features both basketball players from the University of Illinois. The fronts display color, action player photos with an orange stripe down the left side and a dark blue stripe across the bottom. The school name is reversed out in dark blue in the orange stripe, while the player's name is printed in orange in the dark blue stripe. The backs are white and carry biographical information, the sponsor logo, and a public service message. The cards are unnumbered and checklisted below alphabetically.

COMPLETE SET (16) 4.00 10.00
1 Robert Bennett .08 .25
2 Rennie Clemons .40 1.00
3 Jimmy Collins ACO .20 .50
4 Mark Coomes ACO .08 .25
5 Marc Davidson .08 .25
6 Chris Gandy .08 .25
7 Lou Henson CO 1.25 3.00
8 Chief Illiniwek .08 .25
(Mascot)
9 Andy Kaufmann .40 1.00
10 Richard Keene .20 .50
11 Tom Michael .60 1.50
guarded by Jalen Rose
12 Dick Nagy ACO .08 .25
13 Brooks Taylor .08 .25
14 Deon Thomas .60 1.50
15 T.J. Wheeler .20 .50
16 Assembly Hall .20 .50

1992-93 Illinois Women's

Produced by Flying Color Graphics Inc., this 16-card standard-size set was sponsored by Pepsi. This set features female basketball players from the University of Illinois. The fronts display color, action player photos with an orange stripe down the left side and a dark blue stripe across the bottom. The school name is reversed out in dark blue in the orange stripe, while the player's name is printed in orange in the dark blue stripe. The backs are white and carry biographical information, the sponsor logo, and a public service message. Though they share similar card front designs, the women's cards have different backs than the men's backs. The cards are unnumbered and checklisted below alphabetically.

COMPLETE SET (16) 1.25 3.00
1 Tonya Booker .08 .25
2 Anita Clinton .08 .25
3 Mandy Cunningham .08 .25
4 Merimartha Cunningham .08 .25
5 Cindy Dilger .08 .25
6 Kris Dupps .08 .25
7 Jill Estey .08 .25
8 Keila Flagg .08 .25
9 Cindi Hanna .08 .25
10 Jackie Hemann .08 .25
11 Bridget Inman .08 .25
12 Vicki Klingler .08 .25
13 Kathy Lindsey CO .08 .25
14 Lolita Platt .08 .25
15 Robbyn Preacely .08 .25
16 Connie Ruholl .08 .25

1986-87 Indiana Greats I

This 42-card standard-size set is the first series of the All-Time Greats of Indiana University. The cards were sponsored by Bank One of Indiana. The fronts present a mixture of black and white or color photos, posed and action. The horizontally-oriented backs have biographical and statistical information on the player, with the card number in the upper right hand corner. The key card in the set is the first card of Indiana coach Bobby Knight.

COMPLETE SET (42) 6.00 15.00
1 Bobby Knight CO 2.00 5.00
2 Walt Bellamy 1.00 2.50
3 Pete Obremskey .08 .25
4 Jim Wisman .08 .25
5 Frank Radovich .08 .25
6 Ted Kitchel .08 .25
7 Don Schlundt .40 1.00
8 Uwe Blab .20 .50
9 Lou Watson .08 .25
10 Bobby Masters .08 .25
11 Steve Redenbaugh .08 .25
12 Bob Wilkerson .25 .60
13 Kent Benson .60 1.50
14 Everett Dean .40 1.00
15 Rick Ford .08 .25
16 Hallie Bryant .08 .25
17 Dan Dakich .20 .50
18 Sam Gee .08 .25
19 George McGinnis 1.00 2.50
20 John Ritter .08 .25
21 Jon McGlocklin .40 1.00
22 Landon Turner .40 1.00
23 Gary Long .08 .25
24 Jim Crews .40 1.00
25 Steve Downing .40 1.00
26 Vern Huffman .20 .50
27 Ernie Andres .08 .25
28 Charles Hodson .08 .25
29 Jerry Thompson .08 .25
30 Tom Abernethy .20 .50
31 Tom Bolyard .08 .25
32 Jimmy Rayl .40 1.00
33 John Laskowski .20 .50
34 Archie Dees .20 .50
35 Joby Wright .40 1.00
36 Gary Greiger .08 .25
37 Randy Wittman .40 1.00
38 Steve Green .08 .25
39 Erv Inniger .08 .25
40 Steve Risley .08 .25
41 Bill DeHeer .08 .25
42 Checklist Card .20 .50

1987-88 Indiana Greats II

This 42-card standard-size set is the second series of the All-Time Greats of Indiana University. The cards were sponsored by Bank One of Indiana. The fronts present a mixture of black and white or color photos, posed and action. The horizontally oriented backs have biographical and statistical information on the player, with the card number in the upper right hand corner. The back of the checklist card contains an offer to buy either Series I or II for 10.00 from the Big Red Gift Center. The key card in the set features NBA superstar Isiah Thomas.

COMPLETE SET (42) 10.00 25.00
1 Steve Alford's .75 2.00
Farewell
2 Bob Dro .08 .25
3 Butch Joyner .08 .25
4 Bobby Leonard .30 .75
5 Branch McCracken CO .40 1.00
with Walt Bellamy
6 Ray Tolbert .40 1.00
7 Wayne Radford .20 .50
8 Earl Schneider .08 .25
9 Jim Strickland .08 .25
10 Al Harden .08 .25
11 Bob Menke .08 .25
12 Steve Alford .75 2.00
13 Mike Woodson .40 1.00
14 Tom Van Arsdale .75 2.00
Dick Van Arsdale
15 Wally Choice .08 .25
16 Charlie Hall .08 .25
17 Indiana Coach Legend .40 1.00
18 Stew Robinson .20 .50
19 Dynamic Duo .40 1.00
20 Steve Alford .75 2.00
21 Quinn Buckner .60 1.50
22 Bob Knight .40 1.00
Everett Dean
23 Winston Morgan .08 .25
24 1975-76 Seniors .40 1.00
25 Jim Thomas .20 .50
26 Vern Payne .08 .25
27 Scott May .60 1.50
28 Dave Porter .08 .25
29 Dick Farley .08 .25
30 Isiah Thomas 3.00 8.00
31 Butch Carter .20 .50
32 Burke Scott .08 .25
33 Jack Johnson .08 .25
34 Charley Kraak .08 .25
35 Marv Huffman .08 .25
36 Steve Bouchie .08 .25
37 Bobby Knight .75 2.00
38 Bill Garrett .08 .25
39 Jerry Bass .08 .25
40 Jay McCreary .08 .25
41 Ken Johnson .08 .25
42 Checklist Card .20 .50
(Send-in offer on back)

1991-92 Indiana Magazine Insert

The premiere issue of Hoosier College Basketball (November, 1991) featured 12 cards (nine on an unperforated sheet and three additional cards on an attached strip). The production run was reportedly 5,000 sets. The sheet is unperforated; if the cards were cut, they would measure approximately the standard size. The glossy color player photos appear on a jet black card face and are framed by narrow gold-foil border stripes. The player's name is printed in gold-foil lettering beneath the picture. The backs carry biographical information, jersey number, and player profile. The cards are unnumbered and checklisted below in alphabetical order. Key cards in the set include Damon Bailey, Calbert Cheaney, Greg Graham, and Alan Henderson. Reportedly an additional 100 sets were made with red borders; these sell at a 3X to 4X multiple of the regular gold-border cards. According to sources in the hobby, due to licensing issues, the NCAA recalled a good deal of these sets after release.

COMPLETE SET (12)	10.00	25.00
1 Eric Anderson	1.50	4.00
2 Damon Bailey	3.00	8.00
3 Calbert Cheaney	3.00	8.00
4 Brian Evans	2.00	5.00
5 Greg Graham	1.50	4.00
6 Pat Graham	1.50	4.00
7 Alan Henderson	2.50	6.00
8 Bobby Knight CO	2.50	6.00
9 Pat Knight	1.50	4.00
10 Jamal Meeks	.75	2.00
11 Matt Nover	1.50	4.00
12 Chris Reynolds	.75	2.00

1992-93 Indiana

This 18-card standard-size set was produced by Phipps Sports Marketing, Inc. Inside red borders, the fronts display color action player photos against a background of a basketball. The player's name and number are printed vertically in block lettering to the left of the picture. A "1992-1993 Hoosiers" emblem at the lower right corner rounds out the front. On the same basic background, the horizontal backs carry a color headshot, biography, career summary, and statistics on a panel that shades from white to rose. The cards are unnumbered and checklisted below in alphabetical order, with non-player cards listed at the end.

COMPLETE SET (18)	6.00	15.00
1 Damon Bailey	.75	2.00
2 Calbert Cheaney	1.50	4.00
3 Brian Evans	.75	2.00
4 Greg Graham	.30	.75
5 Pat Graham	.30	.75
6 Alan Henderson	1.50	4.00
7 Bob Knight CO	1.50	4.00
8 Pat Knight	.75	2.00
9 Todd Leary	.20	.50
10 Todd Lindeman	.30	.75
11 Matt Nover	.40	1.00
12 Chris Reynolds	.20	.50
13 Malcolm Sims	.20	.50
14 Assembly Hall	.30	.75
15 Dan Dakich ACO Norm Ellenberger ACO Ron Felling ACO	.20	.50
16 Team Photo	.40	1.00
17 The Knight Era	.30	.75
18 Title Card	.20	.50

1993-94 Indiana

Produced by Phipps Sports Marketing, Inc., this 18-card standard-size set features the Indiana Hoosiers. Inside red borders, the fronts display color action or posed player photos. The player's name is printed inside the photo, while the words "1993-94 Indiana Hoosiers Basketball" appear under the photo. Printed vertically in block lettering to the left inside the picture is "Indiana". Inside red borders, the backs carry a color player portrait, along with player name, number, biography and statistics, and career summary. The cards are unnumbered and checklisted below in alphabetical order.

COMPLETE SET (18)	5.00	12.00
1 Damon Bailey	.60	1.50
2 Robbie Eggers	.20	.50
3 Brian Evans	.60	1.50
4 Robert Foster	.20	.50
5 Pat Graham	.30	.75
6 Steve Hart	.20	.50
7 Alan Henderson	1.00	2.50
8 Bob Knight CO	1.00	2.50
9 Pat Knight	.60	1.50
10 Todd Leary	.20	.50
11 Todd Lindeman	.30	.75
12 Richard Mandeville	.20	.50
13 Sherron Wilkerson	.30	.75
14 Team Photo	.30	.75
15 Dan Dakich ACO Ron Felling ACO Norm Ellenberger ACO Tim Garl ACO	.20	.50
16 Assembly Hall	.30	.75
17 Chris Reynolds Matt Nover Greg Graham Calbert Cheaney The Class of 1993	.60	1.50
18 Title Card	.20	.50

1994-95 Indiana

14 card set, blank white backs, fronts have a red border and a wood-like rectangle with red streaks and color action photos in them. "Hoosiers" is written vertically on either the right or left side of the card in the wood-like colored font. The players name and personal data are found in white at the bottom of the card.

COMPLETE SET (14)	2.00	5.00
1 Bob Knight CO Brian Evans	.60	1.50
2 Robbie Eggers	.20	.50
3 Brian Evans	.40	1.00
4 Steve Hart	.20	.50
5 Alan Henderson	.40	1.00
6 Michael Hermon	.20	.50
7 Rob Hodgson	.20	.50
8 Pat Knight	.40	1.00
9 Todd Lindeman	.40	1.00
10 Richard Mandeville	.20	.50
11 Charlie Miller	.20	.50
12 Andrae Patterson	.60	1.50
13 Neil Reed	.60	1.50
14 Sherron Wilkerson	.40	1.00

1982-83 Indiana State

This multi-sport set was sponsored by the First National Bank of Terre Haute, 7-Up, and WTHI/TV Channel 10. The cards measure approximately 2 5/8" by 4 1/8". On a bright blue card face, the fronts feature black and white player photos enclosed by a white border. A white diagonal stripe appears beneath the picture, with a drawing of the Sycamores' mascot and the words "Sycamore Rampage." The backs have brief biographical information, a quote about the player, a safety tip, and sponsor logos. Sports represented in this set include wrestling (1), basketball (2-3, 4-10, 12), football (11), and gymnastics (13). Olympic athletes included in the set are Bruce Baumgartner and Kurt Thomas. The key card in the set is NBA superstar Larry Bird. The cards are unnumbered and checklisted below in alphabetical order.

9 Larry Bird BK	40.00	100.00
13 Terry Braun BK	1.25	3.00
20 Myron Christian BK	1.25	3.00
22 Al Cole BK	1.25	3.00
29 Rick Fields BK	1.25	3.00
31 Mark Golden BK	1.25	3.00
48 Jeff McComb BK	1.25	3.00
53 Scott Mugg BK	1.25	3.00
61 Dave Schellhase CO BK	1.25	3.00
64 James Smith BK	1.25	3.00

1987-88 Iowa

This 15-card standard-size set features Iowa Hawkeyes and was sponsored by Nike. The cards are unnumbered and are listed below in alphabetical order by subject. The set features the first card of B.J. Armstrong.

COMPLETE SET (15)	8.00	20.00
1 B.J. Armstrong	5.00	12.00
2 Curtis Cuthbert	.40	1.00
3 Rodell Davis	.60	1.50
4 Brian Garner	.40	1.00
5 Kent Hill	.40	1.00
6 Ed Horton	.60	1.50
7 Les Jepsen	1.25	3.00
8 Mark Jewell	.40	1.00
9 Bill Jones	.40	1.00
10 Al Lorenzen	.40	1.00
11 Roy Marble	.75	2.00
12 Jeff Moe	.40	1.00
13 Michael Morgan	.40	1.00
14 Mike Reaves	.40	1.00
15 Brig Tubbs	.40	1.00

1990-91 Iowa

This 14-card set was issued by the University of Iowa and sponsored by radio station KCRG Country 1600. The fronts display color portraits of the player within a black border. The players are photographed out of uniform. Below the photo is a basketball icon in the lower left corner with the player's name, team number, and position printed in black on a yellow bar. The horizontal white backs list the 1990-91 Iowa basketball schedule. The KCRG 1600 radio station logo appears in the upper right corner. The cards are unnumbered and checklisted below alphabetically.

COMPLETE SET (14)	6.00	15.00
1 Val Barnes	1.25	3.00
2 Jim Bartels	.40	1.00
3 Philip Chime	.40	1.00
4 Rodell Davis	.75	2.00
5 Acie Earl	2.00	5.00
6 Wade Lookingbill	.40	1.00
7 Paul Lusk	.40	1.00
8 James Moses	.75	2.00
9 Troy Skinner	.40	1.00
10 Kevin Smith	.40	1.00
11 Chris Street	2.00	5.00
12 Brig Tubbs	.40	1.00
13 Jay Webb	.40	1.00
14 James Winters	.40	1.00

1991-92 Iowa

This 15-card standard-size set is printed on thin card stock. The fronts feature color player photos, with a gold and black parquet floor border. Player information appears in the black stripe at the bottom of the card face, while the school logo appears in an orange basketball at the lower left corner. In a horizontal format, the backs carry a black and white head shot and a player profile. The cards are unnumbered and checklisted below in alphabetical order. The key cards in the set feature Acie Earl and Chris Street.

COMPLETE SET (15)	5.00	12.00
1 Val Barnes	.40	1.00
2 Jim Bartels	.30	.75
3 Phil Chime	.30	.75
4 Rodell Davis	.40	1.00
5 Acie Earl	1.50	4.00
6 Wade Lookingbill	.30	.75
7 Paul Lusk	.30	.75
8 Russ Millard	.60	1.50
9 James Moses	.40	1.00
10 Troy Skinner	.30	.75
11 Kevin Smith	.30	.75
12 Chris Street	1.50	4.00
13 Brig Tubbs	.30	.75
14 Jay Webb	.30	.75
15 James Winters	.30	.75

1992-93 Iowa

This 13-card standard-size set features color, action and posed player photos. The pictures are set against a black panel in the upper left corner. The player's first name appears in the lower black margin. A white stripe just below the panel contains the player's last name in reverse type. An orange-yellow border runs along the bottom and up the right side of the card. This border contains the player's classification, school, and the team name. The horizontal backs are white and carry biographical information, statistics, and a public service message from Herky, the mascot. The cards are unnumbered and checklisted below in alphabetical order.

COMPLETE SET (13)	4.00	10.00
1 Val Barnes	.40	1.00
2 Jim Bartles	.30	.75
3 Fred Brown Jr.	.30	.75
4 Acie Earl	1.00	2.50
5 Mon'ter Glasper	.40	1.00
6 Wade Lookingbill	.30	.75
7 Russ Millard	.40	1.00
8 Kenyon Murray	.40	1.00
9 Kevin Skillett	.30	.75
10 Kevin Smith	.30	.75
11 Chris Street	1.25	3.00
12 Jay Webb	.30	.75
13 James Winters	.30	.75

1992-93 Iowa Women

Sponsored by Wendy's restaurants, this is a 13-card standard-size set. The fronts feature color player portraits tilted slightly the left and resting on a golden background. The player's name and the team name are printed above the picture. The sponsor's logo appears on a white box at the lower left corner, while the uniform number appears in an orange basketball at the lower right corner. In a horizontal format, the backs carry biographical and statistical information. The cards are unnumbered and checklisted below in alphabetical order.

COMPLETE SET (13)	4.00	10.00
1 Laurie Aaron	.20	.50
2 Karen Clayton	.20	.50
3 Virgie Dillingham	.20	.50
4 Toni Foster	1.25	3.00
5 Andrea Harmon	.20	.50
6 Tia Jackson	1.25	3.00
7 Antonia Macklin	.20	.50
8 Cathy Marx	.20	.50
9 Jenny Noll	.20	.50
10 C.Vivian Stringer CO	1.50	4.00
11 Molly Tideback	.20	.50
12 Necole Tunsil	.20	.50
13 Arneda Yarbrough	.20	.50

1993-94 Iowa

The 1993-94 University of Iowa basketball set consists of 11 standard-size cards printed on thin card stock. The glossy fronts display color action and posed player photos with a black shadow box border. The player's name and team number are printed within the border below the photo. The picture is placed at an angle over a black-and-white parquet basketball court background. The word "Hawkeyes" is printed across the top in gold lettering. The team logo is printed in the lower right corner. The horizontal light yellow backs have the school name printed in ghosted yellow lettering. The player's biography, profile, statistics, and a black-and-white head shot complete the back. The set includes a card in memory of Chris Street, the Iowa player tragically killed in a car accident during the 1992-93 season. The cards are unnumbered and checklisted below in alphabetical order.

COMPLETE SET (11)	4.00	10.00
1 Jim Bartels	.20	.50
2 John Carter	.20	.50
3 Mon'ter Glasper	.30	.75
4 Chris Kingsbury	.75	2.00
5 Russ Millard	.40	1.00
6 Kenyon Murray	.30	.75
7 Jess Settles	.75	2.00
8 Kevin Skillett	.20	.50
9 Chris Street MEM	1.25	3.00
10 James Winters	.20	.50
11 Andre Woolridge	.75	2.00

1993-94 Iowa Women

Sponsored by Wendy's restaurants, this 13-card set measures the standard-size. The fronts feature posed color player portraits tilted slightly to the left and resting on gray and yellow backgrounds. The player's name and uniform number appear below the picture. The yellowish backs carry biographical and statistical information. The cards are unnumbered and checklisted below in alphabetical order.

COMPLETE SET (13)	3.00	8.00
1 Karen Clayton	.20	.50
2 Virgie Dillingham	.20	.50
3 Simone Edwards	.20	.50
4 Andrea Harmon	.20	.50
5 Tia Jackson	1.00	2.50
6 Susan Koering	.20	.50
7 Antonia Macklin	.20	.50
8 Cathy Marx	.20	.50
9 Jenny Noll	.20	.50
10 Erinn Reed	.20	.50
11 C.Vivian Stringer CO	1.50	4.00
12 Necole Tunsil	.20	.50
13 Arneda Yarbrough	.20	.50

1994-95 Iowa

Sponsored by Norwest Banks, Coca-Cola and 1040 WHO Des Moines, this 13-card set measures the standard size. The fronts feature color, action and posed, player photos framed by white borders. Across the bottom, the player's name, his number and the words "94-95 Iowa Basketball" are printed in team color-coded bars that intersect an orange basketball at the lower right corner. On a white background, the horizontal backs carry a black-and-white player head shot, biography, a player profile in an "Iowa Item" feature, and complete statistics. The cards are unnumbered and checklisted below in alphabetical order.

COMPLETE SET (13)	4.00	10.00
1 Jim Bartels	.20	.50
2 Ryan Bowen	.20	.50
3 John Carter	.20	.50
4 Mon'ter Glasper	.30	.75
5 Herky (Mascot)	.20	.50
6 Chris Kingsbury	.75	2.00
7 Kent McCausland	.20	.50
8 Kenyon Murray	.30	.75
9 Jess Settles	.75	2.00
10 Kevin Skillett	.20	.50
11 Andre Woolridge	.75	2.00
12 Black and Gold Blowout	.20	.50
13 Carver-Hawkeye Arena	.30	.75

1995-96 Iowa

This 14-card set was released at the University of Iowa during the 1995-96 season. The set features many of the players from that year's team. This set was produced by Partners In Excellence. Please note that these cards are not numbered and are listed below in alphabetical order.

COMPLETE SET (14)	4.00	10.00
1 Ryan Bowen	.30	.75
2 Trey Bullet	.30	.75
3 Mon'ter Glasper	.30	.75
4 Greg Helmers	.30	.75
5 Chris Kingsbury	.30	.75
6 J.R. Koch	.40	1.00
7 Kent McCausland	.30	.75
8 Russ Millard	.30	.75
9 Kenyon Murray	.30	.75
10 Alvin Robinson	.30	.75
11 Guy Rucker	.30	.75
12 Jess Settles	.75	2.00
13 Andre Woolridge	.60	1.50
14 Herky MASCOT	.30	.75

1996-97 Iowa

This 13-card set was released at the University of Iowa during the 1996-97 season. The set features many of the players from that season's team. This set was produced by Partners In Excellence. Please note that these cards are not numbered and are listed below in alphabetical order.

COMPLETE SET (13)	4.00	10.00
1 Ryan Bowen	.30	.75
2 Marcelo Gomes	.30	.75
3 Greg Helmers	.30	.75
4 J.R. Koch	.40	1.00
5 Ryan Luehrsmann	.30	.75
6 Kent McCausland	.30	.75
7 Alvin Robinson	.30	.75
8 Guy Rucker	.30	.75
9 Jess Settles	1.00	2.50
10 Vernon Simmons	.30	.75
11 Andre Woolridge	.60	1.50
12 Herky MASCOT	.30	.75
13 Hawkeye Sports.com	.30	.75

1997-98 Iowa

This 13-card set was released at the University of Iowa during the 1997-98 season. The set features many of the players from that season's team. This set was produced by Partners In Excellence. Please note that these cards are not numbered and are listed below in alphabetical order.

COMPLETE SET (13)	5.00	12.00
1 Jason Bauer	.20	.50
2 Ryan Bowen	.20	.50
3 Ricky Davis	4.00	9.00
4 Marcelo Gomes	.20	.50
5 Greg Helmers	.20	.50
6 J.R. Koch	.20	.50
7 Ryan Luehrsmann	.20	.50
8 Kent McCausland	.20	.50
9 Darryl Moore	.20	.50
10 Dean Oliver	.20	.50
11 Guy Rucker	.20	.50
12 Jess Settles	.75	2.00
13 Vernon Simmons	.20	.50

1999-00 Iowa

This 15-card set was released at the University of Iowa during the 1999-2000 season. The set features many of the players from that season's team. Please note that these cards are not numbered and are listed below in alphabetical order.

COMPLETE SET	1.25	3.00
1 Steve Alford CO	.75	2.00
2 Joe Fermino	.15	.40
3 Kyle Galloway	.15	.40
4 Marcelo Gomez	.15	.40
5 Rob Griffin	.15	.40
6 Duez Henderson	.15	.40
7 Ryan Hogan	.15	.40
8 Jacob Jaacks	.15	.40
9 Ryan Luehrsmann	.15	.40
10 Dean Oliver	.15	.40
11 Jason Price	.15	.40
12 Antonio Ramos	.15	.40
13 Jason Smith	.15	.40
14 Rod Thompson	.15	.40
15 John Carl Williams	.15	.40

2000-01 Iowa

This 14-card set was released at the University of Iowa during the 2000-01 season. The set features many of the players from that season's team. Please note that these cards are not numbered and are listed below in alphabetical order.

COMPLETE SET	1.50	4.00
1 Steve Alford CO	.75	2.00
2 Brody Boyd	.15	.40
3 Reggie Evans	.30	.75
4 Joe Fermino	.15	.40
5 Ryan Hogan	.15	.40
6 Duez Henderson	.15	.40
7 Dean Oliver	.15	.40
8 Luke Recker	.15	.40
9 Jared Reiner	.15	.40
10 Cortney Scott	.15	.40
11 Jason Smith	.15	.40
12 Sean Sonderleiter	.15	.40
13 Rod Thompson	.15	.40
14 Glen Worley	.15	.40

2001-02 Iowa

This 16-card set was released at the University of Iowa during the 2001-02 season. The set features many of the players from that season's team. Please note that these cards are not numbered and are listed below in alphabetical order.

COMPLETE SET	1.50	4.00
1 Steve Alford CO	.75	2.00
2 Brody Boyd	.15	.40
3 Reggie Evans	.30	.75
4 Erek Hansen	.15	.40
5 Duez Henderson	.15	.40
6 Ryan Hogan	.15	.40
7 Chauncey Leslie	.15	.40
8 Pierre Pierce	.15	.40
9 Luke Recker	.25	.60
10 Jared Reiner	.15	.40
11 Cortney Scott	.15	.40
12 Marcellus Sommerville	.15	.40
13 Sean Sonderleiter	.15	.40
14 Rod Thompson	.15	.40
15 Glen Worley	.15	.40
16 Big 10 Tourney Winners	.15	.40

2002-03 Iowa

This 12-card set was released at the University of Iowa during the 2002-03 season. The set features many of the players from that season's team. This set was produced by Partners In Excellence. Please note that these cards are not numbered and are listed below in alphabetical order.

COMPLETE SET	1.50	4.00
1 Steve Alford CO	.75	2.00
2 Brody Boyd	.15	.40
3 Jack Brownlee	.15	.40
4 Greg Brunner	.15	.40
5 Jeff Horner	.15	.40
6 Josh Kimm	.15	.40
7 Chauncey Leslie	.15	.40
8 Pierre Pierce	.15	.40
9 Jared Reiner	.15	.40
10 Sean Sonderleiter	.15	.40
11 Kurt Spurgeon	.15	.40
12 Glen Worley	.15	.40

1988-89 Jacksonville

This 15-card set was co-sponsored by Blue Cross and Blue Shield of Florida, The Jacksonville Sheriff's Office, and the Jacksonville Say No To Drugs Coalition. The cards measure approximately 2 1/2" by 4 1/2", and one inch of the length of the card consists of a tab containing a coupon for one free child's admission to a regular season basketball game. The white-bordered fronts feature action color photos with a yellow bar above and below the picture. The player's name, team number, and position are printed below. The white backs are borderless and carry biography, career highlights, and anti-drug messages. The Blue Cross and Blue Shield of Florida logo is printed in the lower left corner. The Dolphins' home schedule appears on the tab portion at the bottom. The cards are unnumbered and checklisted below alphabetically.

COMPLETE SET (15)	10.00	25.00
1 Ken Aldrich	.40	1.00
2 Tyrone Boykin	.75	2.00
3 Dee Brown	6.00	15.00
4 Sean Byrd	.40	1.00
5 Jim Cavanaugh	.40	1.00
6 Steve Gilbert	.40	1.00
7 Rich Haddad CO	.40	1.00
8 Willie Ivery	.40	1.00
9 Pat Laguerre	.40	1.00
10 Reggie Law	.75	2.00
11 Adrian Simmons	.75	2.00
12 Chris Slocum	.40	1.00
13 Curtis Taylor	.40	1.00
14 JU-D2 (Mascot)	.40	1.00
15 Team Photo	1.50	4.00

1989-90 Jacksonville Classic

Showcasing the 1969-70 team that was the NCAA runner-up, this eight-card standard-size set was sponsored by Blue Cross and Blue Shield of Florida, the Jacksonville Sheriff's Office, and the Clay County Sheriff's Office. The cards are printed on a thin paper stock. The fronts carry sepia-toned action photos with a green outer border and a gold inner border. On a gold diagonal bar in the upper left corner are the words "Classic Card". The Jacksonville University Dolphins is printed above the photo and the player's name is printed on a gold bar below. The white backs list biographical information and NCAA career highlights. The Blue Cross and Blue Shield of Florida logo is printed in the lower left corner. The cards are unnumbered and checklisted below alphabetically.

COMPLETE SET (8)	8.00	20.00
1 Mike Blevins	.75	2.00
2 Pembrook Burrows	.75	2.00
3 Chip Dublin	.75	2.00
4 Artis Gilmore	4.00	10.00
5 Rod McIntyre	.75	2.00
6 Rex Morgan	.75	2.00
7 Greg Nelson	.75	2.00
8 Vaughn Wedeking	.75	2.00

1989-90 Jacksonville

This 13-card standard-size set was sponsored by Blue Cross Blue Shield of Florida in conjunction with the Jacksonville and Clay County Sheriff's Offices. Each card has a perforated coupon at the bottom good for one free child's general admission ticket to any regular season home game when accompanied by a paying adult. The fronts display a mix of action and posed color photos enclosed by a yellow border on a green card face. The team name appears in yellow block lettering at the top while the team logo and player's name appears in the bottom yellow border. The backs feature biography, player profile, and an anti-drug message between black bands. Sponsor logos and names round out the back. The cards are unnumbered and checklisted below in alphabetical order. The key card in the set is Dee Brown.

COMPLETE SET (13)	8.00	20.00
1 Tyrone Boykin	.40	1.00
2 Dee Brown	5.00	12.00
3 Sean Byrd	.40	1.00
4 Chris Capers	.75	2.00
5 Steve Gilbert	.40	1.00
6 Rich Haddad	.40	1.00
7 Tabarris Hamilton and Alonzo Harris	.40	1.00
8 Willie Ivery	.40	1.00
9 Reggie Law	.40	1.00
10 Jerome McDuffie and Danny Tirado	.40	1.00
11 Al Powell and Kent Shafer	.40	1.00
12 Curtis Taylor	.40	1.00
13 Team Photo	1.50	4.00

1991-92 James Madison

The 1991-92 James Madison basketball set was sponsored by the USDA Forest Service, the state forestry service, and James Madison University. The standard-size cards are printed on thin card stock. The fronts display a mix of color posed and action player photos, enclosed by purple borders and accented by mustard stripes above and below. The school name, player's name, number, and position appear in the mustard stripes. In black print on white card stock, the backs have brief biographical information, a fire prevention cartoon starring Smokey, and sponsor acknowledgments. The cards are unnumbered and checklisted below alphabetically by player's last name.

COMPLETE SET (12)	4.00	10.00
1 Troy Bostic	.40	1.00
2 Paul Carter	.40	1.00
3 Jeff Chambers	.40	1.00
4 Vladimir Cuk	.40	1.00
5 Kent Culuko	.60	1.50
6 William Davis	.40	1.00
7 Lefty Driesell CO	1.50	4.00
8 Bryan Edwards	.60	1.50
9 Gerry Lancaster	.40	1.00
10 Keith Peoples	.40	1.00
11 Clayton Ritter	.40	1.00
12 Michael Venson	.60	1.50

1992-93 James Madison

This 12-card standard-size set was sponsored by the USDA Forest Service and state forestry agencies. The fronts feature color, action player photos on a purple card face. Above and below the photo are orange-yellow border stripes containing the team name and the player's name and position. The photo and borders are accented by a gray shadow border. The backs are white with black print and carry limited player information and a wildfire prevention cartoon. The cards are unnumbered and checklisted below in alphabetical order.

COMPLETE SET (12)	3.00	8.00
1 Paul Carter	.30	.75
2 Jeff Chambers	.30	.75
3 Vladimir Cuk	.30	.75
4 Kent Culuko	.40	1.00
5 William Davis	.30	.75
6 Duke Dog (Mascot)	.30	.75
7 Lefty Driesell CO	1.25	3.00
8 Bryan Edwards	.40	1.00
9 Channing McGuffin	.30	.75
10 Clayton Ritter	.30	.75
11 Michael Venson	.40	1.00
12 Travis Wells	.30	.75

1993-94 James Madison

The 1993-94 University of James Madison basketball set consists of 13 standard-size cards. Fronts display color action and posed player photos with a yellow border with white diagonal stripes. The player's name and position are printed below the photo to the right of the Smokey 50th logo. The team name and logo are centered above the photo. The player's biography is centered at the top of the plain back with a Smokey saftey tip below. The cards are unnumbered and checklisted below in alphabetical order.

COMPLETE SET (13)	3.00	8.00
1 Vladimir Cuk	.20	.50
2 Ryan Culicerto	.20	.50
3 Kent Culuko	.30	.75
4 Lefty Driesell CO	1.25	3.00
5 Dennis Leonard	.20	.50
6 Charles Lott	.20	.50
7 Darren McLinton	.20	.50
8 Clayton Ritter	.20	.50
9 Kareem Robinson	.20	.50
10 Louis Rowe	.20	.50
11 Michael Venson	.30	.75
12 Emeka Wilson	.20	.50
13 Duke Dog (Mascot)	.20	.50

1994-95 James Madison

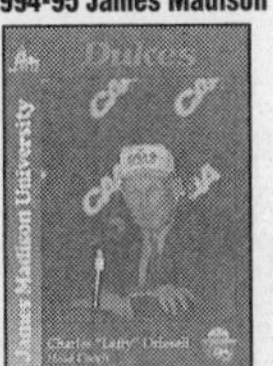

This 16-card set was issued on a 10" by 14" perforated sheet with four rows of four cards. When the cards are separated, they measure the standard size. The set is sponsored by the USDA Forest Service and the state forestry agency. The fronts display color action and posed player photos with player's name, position, jersey number and Smokey logo below the photo in the violet border. The backs carry player information above a Smokey cartoon and a fire prevention safety tip. The cards are unnumbered and checklisted below in alphabetical order.

COMPLETE SET (16) 3.00 8.00
1 Lamont Boozer .20 .50
2 Eric Carpenter .20 .50
3 Cheerleaders .20 .50
4 James Colemano .20 .50
5 Ryan Culicerto .20 .50
6 Kent Culuko .30 .75
7 Charles Driesell CO (Lefty) 1.25 3.00
8 Duke Dog (Mascot) .20 .50
9 Duke Dog (Mascot) .20 .50
Smokey Bear
10 Dennis Leonard .20 .50
11 Charles Lott .20 .50
12 Darren McLinton .20 .50
13 James Pelham .20 .50
14 Kareem Robinson .20 .50
15 Louis Rowe .20 .50
16 Heath Smith .20 .50

1987-88 Kansas

This 16-card set was sponsored by Nike and issued on an unperforated sheet with four rows of four cards. After cutting, they measure the standard size. The fronts feature a mix of posed and action color player photos on a white card face. Above the picture appears the team name, year, and the Nike logo. The picture is bordered by red on the left and by dark blue on the right and bottom. The Jayhawk logo appears in the lower left corner, with player identification in the blue border below the picture. The backs have biographical information, player evaluation, and basketball advice in the form of "Tips from the Jayhawks." The cards are unnumbered and checklisted below in alphabetical order, with the uniform number after the player's name. This set features the team that won the 1987-88 NCAA Championship as well as the first card of NBA star Danny Manning.

COMPLETE SET (16) 20.00 40.00
1 Sean Alvarado 52 .40 1.00
2 Scooter Barry 10 2.00 5.00
3 Marvin Branch 54 .40 1.00
4 Larry Brown CO 4.00 10.00
5 Jeff Gueldner 33 .40 1.00
6 Keith Harris 45 .40 1.00
7 Otis Livingston 12 .40 1.00
8 Mike Maddox 32 .40 1.00
9 Danny Manning 25 8.00 20.00
10 Archie Marshall 23 .40 1.00
11 Mike Masucci 44 .40 1.00
12 Lincoln Minor 11 .40 1.00
13 Milt Newton 21 .75 2.00
14 Chris Piper 24 .75 2.00
15 Kevin Pritchard 14 1.25 3.00
16 Mark Randall 42 1.25 3.00

1989-90 Kansas

This 16-card standard-size set was licensed to Leesley by the University of Kansas. The cards feature on the fronts color action player shots, with white and black borders on dark blue background. The player's name is given below the picture, with the Jayhawk team logo on an orange basketball in the lower right corner. The backs present biographical information and a player profile. The cards are numbered on the back in continuation of the Kansas Football card set. The set features the first cards of Adonis Jordan and coach Roy Williams.

COMPLETE SET (16) 8.00 20.00
41 Frequent Flyers Poster .60 1.50
42 Jeff Gueldner .30 .75
43 Freeman West .30 .75
44 Rick Calloway .40 1.00
45 Mark Randall .75 2.00
46 Mike Maddox .40 1.00
47 Alonzo Jamison .60 1.50
48 Kevin Pritchard .75 2.00
49 Terry Brown .30 .75
50 Kirk Wagner .30 .75
51 Pekka Markkanen .30 .75
52 Sean Tunstall .30 .75
53 Macolm Nash .30 .75
54 Todd Alexander .30 .75
55 Adonis Jordan 1.50 4.00
56 Roy Williams CO 4.00 10.00
NNO Title Card .30 .75

1991-92 Kansas

This 18-card standard-size set features on the fronts either posed or action color photos, enclosed by red and blue borders. The player's position appears in a gray stripe on the right side of the picture, while his name is printed in gray stripe beneath the picture. The horizontally oriented backs carry a black and white head shot, biography, and player profile. The cards are unnumbered and checklisted below in alphabetical order. The key cards in the set feature Alonzo Jamison, Adonis Jordan, Greg Ostertag, and Rex Walters.

COMPLETE SET (18) 6.00 15.00
1 Lane Czaplinski .30 .75
2 Ben Davis .75 2.00
3 Greg Gurley .30 .75
4 Alonzo Jamison .60 1.50
5 David Johanning .30 .75
6 Adonis Jordan 1.00 2.50
7 Macolm Nash .30 .75
8 Greg Ostertag 1.50 4.00
9 Eric Pauley .40 1.00
10 Sean Pearson .40 1.00
11 Calvin Rayford .40 1.00
12 Patrick Richey .30 .75
13 Richard Scott .40 1.00
14 Rex Walters 1.50 4.00
15 Roy Williams CO 2.50 6.00
16 Steve Woodberry .75 2.00
17 The O-Zone .40 1.00
Alonzo Jamison
18 Team Photo .40 1.00
Checklist

1992-93 Kansas

This 16-card standard-size set features color, posed and action player photos with red and blue borders. Also featured in this set is an art card of former Kansas player, Danny Manning. The player's name appears in a light gray bar at the bottom, while his position is contained in a light gray vertical bar running down the right edge. Though the design is identical to the previous year's issue, these cards are easily distinguished by the "92-93" year indication in the upper left corner. The horizontal backs carry biographical information, statistics, and a player profile. The cards are unnumbered and checklisted below in alphabetical order.

COMPLETE SET (16) 5.00 12.00
1 Matt Doherty ACO .40 1.00
Steve Robinson ACO
Kevin Stallings ACO
2 Greg Gurley .20 .50
3 Darrin Hancock .60 1.50
4 Adonis Jordan .75 2.00
5 Danny Manning Art 1.25 3.00
6 Greg Ostertag 1.00 2.50
7 Eric Pauley .30 .75
8 Sean Pearson .30 .75
9 Calvin Rayford .30 .75
10 Patrick Richey .20 .50
11 Richard Scott .30 .75
12 Rex Walters .75 2.00
13 Rex Walters .75 2.00
Eric Pauley
Adonis Jordan
14 Roy Williams CO 1.50 4.00
15 Steve Woodberry .40 1.00
16 Team Photo .30 .75

1993-94 Kansas

The 1993-94 Kansas University set consists of 17 standard-size cards. The fronts consist of full color action photos bleeding off the top, right, and left sides. Below the photo is a blue bar with the player's name reversed out and his position in red. The mascot and year is printed to the left. The white backs have a black-and-white player head shot in the upper left. The player's name and bio are printed in blue centered at the top with the team mascot to the right. The player's autograph is centered below the bio with the his career highlights below. The cards are unnumbered and checklisted below in alphabetical order. The set features the first card of Jacque Vaughn.

COMPLETE SET (17) 6.00 15.00
1 Greg Gurley .20 .50
2 Greg Ostertag 1.25 3.00
3 Sean Pearson .30 .75
4 Scot Pollard 1.50 4.00
5 Nick Proud .75 2.00
Jason Kidd in background
6 Calvin Rayford .20 .50
7 Patrick Richey .20 .50
8 Richard Scott .30 .75
9 Jacque Vaughn 1.50 4.00
10 Blake Weichbrodt .20 .50
11 T.J. Whatley .20 .50
12 B.J. Williams .60 1.50
13 Roy Williams CO 1.50 4.00
14 Steve Woodberry .30 .75
15 Assistant Coaches .40 1.00
Matt Doherty
Joe Holladay
Steve Robinson

2009-10 Kansas

COMPLETE SET (8) 15.00 40.00
1 Cole Aldrich 4.00 10.00
2 Sherron Collins 4.00 10.00
3 Brady Morningstar 4.00 10.00
4 Marcus Morris 6.00 15.00
5 Markieff Morris 6.00 15.00
6 Thomas Robinson 4.00 10.00
7 Bill Self CO 2.00 5.00
8 Jeff Withey 4.00 10.00

1996-97 Kansas Schedules

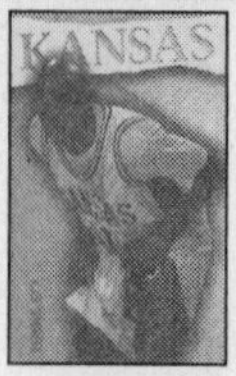

Unlike previous seasons where all seniors were pictured together on one schedule, Kansas University decided to honor their talented 1996-97 seniors by featuring each on his own schedule. The set is highlighted by the inclusion of All-American candidate and NBA guard Jacques Vaughn. These schedules were distributed for free at 1996-97 home games. The schedules are unnumbered on back and have been checklisted below alphabetically for convenience.

COMPLETE SET (4) 1.50 4.00
1 Jerod Haase .08 .25
2 Scot Pollard .75 2.00
3 Jacque Vaughn .75 2.00
4 B.J. Williams .08 .25

1987-88 Kansas State

This cards from this set measure 2 1/2" by 3 1/2" and feature posed or game action shots. The set was sponsered by The Saint Mary Hospital. Card backs have the player's biographical information and an anti-drug message. The cards are not numbered and listed below alphabetically.

COMPLETE SET (14) 30.00 80.00
1 Charles Bledsoe 1.25 3.00
2 Fabio de Almedia 1.25 3.00
3 Carlos Diggins 1.25 3.00
4 Mark Dobbins 1.25 3.00
5 Buster Glover 1.25 3.00
6 Steve Henson 2.50 6.00
7 Lon Kruger CO 3.00 8.00
8 Fred McCoy 1.25 3.00
9 Ron Meyer 1.25 3.00
10 Mark Nelson 1.25 3.00
11 John Rettiger 1.25 3.00
12 Mitch Richmond 20.00 50.00
13 William Scott 1.25 3.00
14 Willie the Wildcat Mascot 1.25 3.00

1997-98 Kansas State Legends

This 20-card set was produced by the Blind Tiger Brewery during the 1997-98 season at Kansas State University. This set features some of the greatest players to ever play for Kansas State University.

COMPLETE SET (20) 8.00 20.00
1 Ernie Barrett .30 .75
2 Rolando Blackman 1.00 2.50
3 Bob Boozer .75 2.00
4 Mike Evans .40 1.00
5 Steve Henson .40 1.00
6 Lon Kruger .40 1.00
7 Dick Kuostman .30 .75
8 Ed Nealy .40 1.00
9 Mitch Richmond 2.00 5.00
10 Howard Shannon .30 .75
11 Willie Murrell .30 .75
12 Jack Gardner .30 .75
13 Jack Hartman .30 .75
14 Tex Winter .60 1.50
15 Elliot Hatcher .30 .75
16 Askia Jones .30 .75
17 Eddie Elder .30 .75
18 Jack Parr .40 1.00
19 Rick Harman .30 .75
20 Team Photo .40 1.00

1998-99 Kansas State

This 16-card set was released at Kansas State University during the 1998-99 season, the set features many of the players from that year's team. Please not that this set is unnumbered and is listed below in alphabetical order.

COMPLETE SET (16) 6.00 15.00
1 Team Photo .40 1.00
2 Willie the Wildcat MASCOT .40 1.00
3 Tom Asbury CO .60 1.50
4 Manny Dies .40 1.00
5 Chris Griffin .40 1.00
6 Cortez Groves .40 1.00
7 Jay Heidrick .40 1.00
8 Josh Kimm .40 1.00
9 Tony Kitt .40 1.00
10 Joe Leonard .40 1.00
11 Ayome May .40 1.00
12 Josh Reid .40 1.00
13 Travis Reynolds .40 1.00
14 Shawn Rhodes .40 1.00
15 David Ries .40 1.00
16 Ty Simms .40 1.00

2010-11 Kansas State

COMPLETE SET (17) 3.00 8.00
1 Freddy Asprilla .40 1.00
2 Jordan Henriquez-Roberts .40 1.00
3 Martavious Irving .40 1.00
4 Wally Judge .40 1.00
5 Curtis Kelly .40 1.00
6 Frank Martin CO .40 1.00
7 Rodney McGruder .40 1.00
8 Juevol Myles .40 1.00
9 Victor Ojeleye .40 1.00
10 Devon Peterson .40 1.00
11 Alex Potuzak .40 1.00
12 Jacob Pullen .40 1.00
13 Nick Russell .40 1.00
14 Jamar Samuels .40 1.00
15 Shane Southwell .40 1.00
16 Will Spradling .40 1.00
17 Nino Williams .40 1.00

2011-12 Kansas State

COMPLETE SET (16) 6.00 15.00
1 Adrian Diaz .60 1.50
2 Thomas Gipson .60 1.50
3 Jordan Henriquez .60 1.50
4 Martavious Irving .60 1.50
5 Jeremy Jones .60 1.50
6 Omari Lawrence .60 1.50
7 Rodney McGruder .60 1.50
8 Shawn Meyer .60 1.50
9 Victor Ojeleye .60 1.50
10 Angel Rodriguez .60 1.50
11 Brian Rohleder .60 1.50
12 Jamar Samuels .60 1.50
13 Shane Southwell .60 1.50
14 Will Spradling .60 1.50
15 James Watson .60 1.50
16 Nino Williams .60 1.50

2011-12 Kansas State Women

COMPLETE SET (13) 4.00 10.00
1 Branshea Brown .40 1.00
2 Heidi Brown .40 1.00
3 Chantay Caron .40 1.00
4 Brittany Chambers .40 1.00
5 Jalana Childs .40 1.00
6 Julianne Chisholm .40 1.00
7 Tasha Dickey .40 1.00
8 Katya Leick .40 1.00
9 Emma Ostermann .40 1.00
10 Haley Texada .40 1.00
11 Mariah White .40 1.00
12 Stephanie Wittman .40 1.00
13 Ashia Woods .40 1.00

1976-77 Kentucky Schedules

This 12-card set features schedule cards each measuring approximately 2 1/4" by 3 3/4". The fronts display borderless dark blue-tinted player photos. Player information is given in the white stripe below the picture. On white backgrounds in dark blue lettering, the backs carry the 1976-77 basketball schedule. The cards are unnumbered and checklisted below in alphabetical order. These schedule cards were passed out individually at games by booster clubs.

COMPLETE SET (12) 15.00 30.00
1 Dwane Casey 2.00 5.00
2 Truman Claytor 1.50 4.00
3 Jack Givens 2.50 6.00
4 Merion Haskins .75 2.00
5 Larry Johnson 1.25 3.00
6 James Lee 1.50 4.00
7 Kyle Macy 3.00 8.00
8 Mike Phillips 1.50 4.00
9 Rick Robey 2.50 6.00
10 Jay Shidler 1.50 4.00
11 Tim Stephens 1.25 3.00
12 LaVon Williams 1.25 3.00

1977-78 Kentucky

This 22-card set measures 2 1/2" by 3 3/4" and was produced by Wildcat News. The front features a black and white action photo with a royal blue border on white card stock. The player cards have the Wildcat logo, year, and the card number (in a basketball) across the top of the card face. The player's name and position appear below the picture. The back has a black and white head shot of the player in the upper right corner, with biographical and statistical information filling in the remainder of the space. This set features early cards of Kyle Macy and Rick Robey, who later played with different NBA teams. This set features the team that won the 1977-78 NCAA Championship.

COMPLETE SET (22) 22.50 45.00
1 Ralph Beard 2.50 6.00
Kenny Rollins
Wah Wah Jones
Alex Groza
Cliff Barker
Adolph Rupp CO
2 Joe Hall's First .75 2.00
UK Team (Team Photo)
3 1975 NCAA Runners-Up .75 2.00
(Team photo in plaid blazers)
4 1977-78 Wildcats .75 2.00
5 Leonard Hamilton CO 1.25 3.00
6 Joe Dean CO .40 1.00
7 Joe B. Hall CO 1.25 3.00
8 Dick Parsons CO .75 2.00
9 Scott Courts .40 1.00
10 Chuck Aleksinas .75 2.00
11 LaVon Williams .75 2.00
12 Chris Gettelfinger .40 1.00
13 Dwane Casey 1.25 3.00
14 Fred Cowan .75 2.00
15 Kyle Macy 3.00 8.00
16 Tim Stephens .40 1.00
17 James Lee 1.25 3.00
18 Jay Shidler 1.25 3.00
19 Rick Robey 2.00 5.00
20 Truman Claytor .75 2.00
21 Jack Givens 2.50 6.00
22 Mike Phillips .75 2.00

1977-78 Kentucky Schedules

This 19-card set features schedule cards each measuring approximately 2 1/4" by 3 3/4". These schedule cards were passed out individually at games by booster clubs. The fronts display borderless dark blue-tinted player photos. Player information is given in the white stripe below the picture. On white backgrounds in dark blue lettering, the backs carry the 1977-78 basketball schedule. Included in this set is a second card of head coach Joe B. Hall featuring a full-bleed color photo. The cards are unnumbered and checklisted below in alphabetical order.

COMPLETE SET (19) 20.00 40.00
1 Chuck Aleksinas 1.25 3.00
2 Dwane Casey 1.50 4.00
3 Truman Claytor 1.25 3.00
4 Scott Courts .75 2.00
5 Fred Cowan 1.25 3.00
6 Joe Dean ACO .75 2.00
7 Joe B. Hall CO 1.25 3.00
(Blue tint photo)
8 Joe B. Hall CO 1.25 3.00
(Color photo)
9 Leonard Hamilton ACO 1.25 3.00
10 Chris Gettelfinger .75 2.00
11 Jack Givens 2.00 5.00
12 James Lee 1.50 4.00
13 Kyle Macy 2.50 6.00
14 Dick Parsons ACO .75 2.00
15 Mike Phillips 1.25 3.00
16 Rick Robey 2.00 5.00
17 Jay Shidler 1.25 3.00
18 Tim Stephens .75 2.00
19 LaVon Williams .75 2.00

1978-79 Kentucky

This 22-card set was produced by Wildcat News and sponsored by Food Town. The cards were originally given out one per week at the participating grocery stores. The cards measure approximately 2 1/2" by 3 3/4". The front features a black and white action photo, with the Wildcat logo, year, and the card number (in a basketball) to the left of the picture. The player's name and position appear below the picture, and a royal blue border outlines the card face. The back has a black and white head shot of the player in the upper right corner, with biographical and statistical information filling in the remainder of the space. This set features an early card of Kyle Macy, who later played in the NBA.

COMPLETE SET (22) 7.50 15.00
1 Homeward Bound .60 1.50
(Joe B. Hall and wife)
2 Jack Givens .60 1.50
Mike Phillips
Rick Robey
James Lee
3 Moment of Glory .75 2.00
(Jack Givens)
4 Cliff Hagan's .75 2.00
Hall of Fame Induction
5 1978-79 Wildcats .60 1.50
Team Photo
6 1978 NCAA Champions .60 1.50
Team Photo
7 Dwight Anderson .75 2.00
8 Clarence Tillman .30 .75
9 Chuck Verderber .60 1.50
10 Dwane Casey .75 2.00
11 Truman Claytor .60 1.50
12 Tim Stephens .30 .75
13 Kyle Macy 1.50 4.00
14 LaVon Williams .60 1.50
15 Jay Shidler .60 1.50
16 Freddie Cowan .60 1.50
17 Chuck Aleksinas .60 1.50
18 Chris Gettelfinger .30 .75
19 Joe B. Hall CO .75 2.00
20 Dick Parsons ACO .60 1.50
21 Leonard Hamilton ACO .60 1.50
22 Joe Dean ACO .30 .75

1978-79 Kentucky Schedules

This 16-card set features schedule cards each measuring approximately 2 1/4" by 3 3/4". These schedule cards were passed out individually at games by booster clubs. The fronts feature borderless dark blue-tinted player photos. Player information is given in the white stripe below the picture. In dark blue lettering on a white background, the backs have the 1978-79 basketball schedule. The cards are unnumbered and checklisted below in alphabetical order.

COMPLETE SET (16) 15.00 30.00
1 Chuck Aleksinas .75 2.00
2 Dwight Anderson 1.25 3.00
3 Dwane Casey 1.25 3.00
4 Truman Claytor 1.25 3.00
5 Fred Cowan .75 2.00
6 Joe Dean ACO .75 2.00
7 Chris Gettelfinger .75 2.00
8 Joe B. Hall CO 1.25 3.00
9 Leonard Hamilton ACO 1.25 3.00
10 Kyle Macy 1.50 4.00
11 Dick Parsons ACO .75 2.00
12 Jay Shidler 1.25 3.00
13 Tim Stephens .75 2.00
14 Clarence Tillman .75 2.00
15 Chuck Verderber 1.25 3.00
16 LaVon Williams .75 2.00

1979-80 Kentucky

This 22-card set was sponsored by Food Town. The cards measures approximately 2 1/2" by 3 3/4". The front features a black and white action photo, with the player's name printed vertically to the right of the picture. The card number (in a basketball), the year, and the Wildcat logo appear at the bottom of the card face. A royal blue border outlines the card face. The back has a black and white head shot of the player in the upper right corner, with biographical information filling in the remainder of the space. This set features cards of Kyle Macy, Sam Bowie, and Dirk Minniefield, who later played with different NBA teams.

COMPLETE SET (22) 10.00 20.00
1 1979-1980 Wildcats .40 1.00
Team Photo
2 Kyle Macy 1.25 3.00
3 Jay Shidler .40 1.00
4 LaVon Williams .40 1.00
5 Chris Gettelfinger .30 .75
6 Fred Cowan .40 1.00
7 Dwight Anderson .60 1.50
8 Bo Lanter .30 .75
9 Chuck Verderber .30 .75
10 Dirk Minniefield 1.00 2.50
11 Sam Bowie 2.50 6.00
12 Charles Hurt .75 2.00
13 Derrick Hord .60 1.50
14 Tom Heitz .30 .75
15 Joe Dean CO .30 .75
16 Leonard Hamilton CO .60 1.50
17 Dick Parsons CO .40 1.00
18 Joe B. Hall CO .60 1.50
19 Rupp Arena .30 .75
20 Kyle Macy .75 2.00
Pan Am Gold Medalist
(Schedule on back)
21 Sam Bowie .75 2.00
Tom Heitz
Derrick Hord
Charles Hurt
Dirk Minniefield
22 Kyle Macy .75 2.00
LaVon Williams
Jay Shidler

1979-80 Kentucky Schedules

This 17-card set features schedule cards each measuring approximately 2 1/4" by 3 3/4". These schedule cards were passed out individually at games by booster clubs. The fronts feature borderless dark blue-tinted player photos. Player information is given in the white stripe below the picture. In dark blue lettering, the backs have the 1979-80 basketball schedule. The cards are unnumbered and checklisted below in alphabetical order.

COMPLETE SET (17) 10.00 20.00
1 Dwight Anderson .75 2.00
2 Sam Bowie 2.00 5.00
3 Fred Cowan .40 1.00
4 Joe Dean ACO .40 1.00
5 Chris Gettelfinger .40 1.00
6 Joe B. Hall CO .60 1.50
7 Leonard Hamilton ACO .60 1.50
8 Tom Heitz .40 1.00
9 Derrick Hord .75 2.00
10 Charles Hurt .75 2.00
11 Bo Lanter .40 1.00
12 Kyle Macy 1.25 3.00
13 Dirk Minniefield 1.25 3.00
14 Dick Parsons ACO .40 1.00
15 Jay Shidler .60 1.50
16 Chuck Verderber .40 1.00
17 LaVon Williams .40 1.00

1980-81 Kentucky Schedules

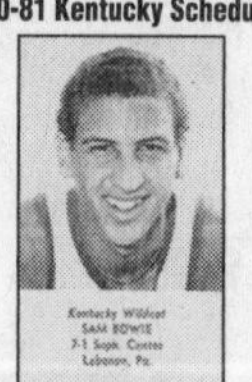

This 16-card set features schedule cards each measuring approximately 2 1/4" by 3 3/4". These schedule cards were passed out individually at games by booster clubs. The fronts feature borderless dark blue-tinted player photos. Player information is given in the white stripe below the picture. In dark blue lettering, the backs have the 1980-81 basketball schedule. The only color photo in this set is of head coach Joe B. Hall. The cards are unnumbered and checklisted below in alphabetical order.

COMPLETE SET (16) 10.00 20.00
1 Dicky Beal .40 1.00
2 Bret Bearup .40 1.00
3 Sam Bowie 1.50 4.00
4 Fred Cowan .40 1.00
5 Joe Dean ACO .40 1.00
6 Chris Gettelfinger .40 1.00
7 Joe B. Hall CO .60 1.50
8 Leonard Hamilton ACO .60 1.50
9 Tom Heitz .40 1.00
10 Derrick Hord .60 1.50
11 Charles Hurt .60 1.50
12 Bo Lanter .40 1.00
13 Jim Master .75 2.00
14 Dirk Minniefield .75 2.00
15 Melvin Turpin 1.25 3.00
16 Chuck Verderber .40 1.00

1981-82 Kentucky Schedules

This 17-card set features schedule cards each measuring approximately 2 1/4" by 3 3/4". These schedule cards were passed out individually at games by booster clubs. The card fronts feature a borderless black and white player photo with a dark blue tint. Player information is given in the white stripe below the picture. In dark blue lettering the back has the 1981-82 basketball schedule. The only color photo in this set is of head coach Joe B. Hall. These unnumbered cards are ordered below alphabetically by subject's name.

COMPLETE SET (17) 8.00 20.00
1 Mike Ballenger .40 1.00
2 Dicky Beal .40 1.00
3 Butch Bearup .40 1.00
4 Sam Bowie 1.50 4.00
5 Bob Chambers ACO .40 1.00
6 Joe Dean ACO .40 1.00
7 Joe B. Hall CO .60 1.50
8 Leonard Hamilton ACO .40 1.00
9 Tom Heitz .40 1.00
10 Derrick Hord .60 1.50
11 Charles Hurt .60 1.50
12 Bo Lanter .40 1.00
13 Jim Master .60 1.50
14 Troy McKinley .40 1.00
15 Dirk Minniefield .75 2.00
16 Melvin Turpin .75 2.00
17 Chuck Verderber .40 1.00

1981-82 Kentucky Women

This 15-card set was released during the 1981-82 season at the University of Kentucky. The set features all of the members of the Kentucky Women's basketball team. Please note that each card back carries a team schedule for the 1981-82 season.

COMPLETE SET (15) 5.00 12.00
1 Dottie Berry CO .40 1.00
2 Lisa Collins .40 1.00
3 Lori Edgington .40 1.00
4 Tayna Fogle .40 1.00
5 Terry Hall CO .40 1.00
6 Patty Jo Hedges .40 1.00
7 Lynnette Lewis .40 1.00
8 Kathy Lokie .40 1.00
9 Donna Martin .40 1.00
10 Terri Naiser .40 1.00
11 Lynn Norenberg TR .40 1.00
12 Grace Odrick .40 1.00
13 Jody Runge .40 1.00
14 Diane Stephens .40 1.00
15 Lea Wise .40 1.00

1982-83 Kentucky Schedules

This 17-card set features schedule cards each measuring approximately 2 1/4" by 3 1/4". The card fronts feature a borderless black and white player photo with a dark blue tint. Player information is given in the white stripe below the picture. In dark blue lettering the back has the 1982-83 basketball schedule. These unnumbered cards are ordered below alphabetically by player's name.

COMPLETE SET (17) 8.00 20.00
1 Dicky Beal .40 1.00
2 Bret Bearup .40 1.00
3 Sam Bowie 1.25 3.00
4 Bob Chambers ACO .40 1.00
5 Joe Dean ACO .40 1.00
6 Joe B. Hall CO .75 2.00
7 Leonard Hamilton ACO .40 1.00
8 Roger Harden .40 1.00
9 Tom Heitz .40 1.00
10 Derrick Hord .60 1.50
11 Charles Hurt .60 1.50
12 Todd May .40 1.00
13 Jim Master .60 1.50
14 Troy McKinley .40 1.00
15 Dirk Minniefield .75 2.00
16 Melvin Turpin .75 2.00
17 Kenny Walker 1.50 4.00

1983-84 Kentucky Schedules

This 17-card set features schedule cards each measuring approximately 2 1/4" by 3 1/4". The card fronts feature a borderless black and white player photo with a dark blue tint. Player information is given in the white stripe below the picture. In dark blue lettering the back has the 1983-84 basketball schedule. These unnumbered cards are ordered below alphabetically by player's name.

COMPLETE SET (17) 8.00 20.00
1 Paul Andrews .40 1.00
2 Dicky Beal .40 1.00
3 Bret Bearup .40 1.00
4 Winston Bennett .75 2.00
5 James Blackmon .60 1.50
6 Sam Bowie 1.25 3.00
7 Joe B. Hall CO .60 1.50
8 Leonard Hamilton ACO .60 1.50
9 Hatfield .40 1.00
10 Tom Heitz .40 1.00
11 John Kelly .40 1.00
12 Jim Master .60 1.50
13 Todd May .40 1.00
14 Troy McKinley .40 1.00
15 Melvin Turpin .75 2.00
16 Kenny Walker .75 2.00
17 Todd Ziegler .40 1.00

1984-85 Kentucky Schedules

This 16-card set features schedule cards each measuring approximately 2 1/4" by 3 3/4". The card fronts feature a borderless black and white player photo with a dark blue tint. Player information is given in the white stripe below the picture. In dark blue lettering the back has the 1984-85 basketball schedule. These unnumbered cards are ordered below alphabetically by player's name.

COMPLETE SET (16) 6.00 15.00
1 Joe B. Hall CO .60 1.50
2 Leonard Hamilton ACO .60 1.50
3 John Kelly ACO .40 1.00
4 Hatfield .40 1.00
5 Troy McKinley .40 1.00
6 Leroy Byrd .40 1.00
7 Todd Ziegler .40 1.00
8 Rob Lock .40 1.00
9 James Blackmon .40 1.00
10 Cedric Jenkins .60 1.50
11 Richard Madison .40 1.00
12 Butch Bearup .40 1.00
13 Kenny Walker .75 2.00
14 Ed Davender .40 1.00
15 Roger Harden .40 1.00
16 Paul Andrews .40 1.00

1988 Kentucky Soviet Program Insert

This 18-card set was issued as an insert in the U.S. AAU All-Stars vs. Soviet Junior Nationals official program for the game played at Memorial Coliseum in Lexington, KY, May 14, 1988. The set is the only one printed during the Russian Junior team's U.S. tour. The cards were issued in two panels; after perforation, the cards measure approximately 2 1/2" by 3 1/2". The front features a mix of posed or action, black and white player photos, with a light blue background and thin black border on white card stock. A 1888-1988 AAU/USA 100th anniversary emblem is superimposed at the left corner of the photo. Player information appears below the picture in the lower left corner. An AAU/Soviet tour emblem in the lower right corner rounds out the card face. The back has a black and white head shot of the player in the upper left corner. Biographical information appears in a light blue-tinted box, with high school statistics at the bottom. The cards are numbered on the back. The set features the first cards of Damon Bailey, Allan Houston, Shawn Kemp, Don McLean, and Chris Mills.

COMPLETE SET (18) 50.00 100.00
1 Checklist 1.25 3.00
2 Scott Davenport CO .75 2.00
3 Keith Adkins .75 2.00
4 Mike Allen .75 2.00
5 Damon Bailey 3.00 8.00
6 Scott Boley .75 2.00
7 David DeMarcus .75 2.00
8 Richie Farmer 1.50 4.00
9 Travis Ford 2.00 5.00
10 Pat Graham 1.50 4.00
11 Robbie Graham .75 2.00
12 Allan Houston 25.00 50.00
13 Shawn Kemp 20.00 50.00
14 Don MacLean 4.00 10.00
15 Kenneth Martin .75 2.00
16 Chris Mills 5.00 12.00
17 Derrick Miller .75 2.00
18 Sean Woods 1.50 4.00

1988-89 Kentucky Collegiate Collection

The 1988-89 University of Kentucky Wildcats set contains 269 standard-sized cards featuring "Kentucky's Finest" basketball players. This set was issued in eight-card cello packs. The fronts have deep blue and white borders. The backs have various statistical and biographical information.

COMPLETE SET (269) 12.00 30.00
1 Adolph Rupp CO .30 .75
2 Cliff Hagan .20 .50
3 Frank Ramsey .15 .40
4 Ralph Beard .15 .40
5 Alex Groza .15 .40
6 Wallace Jones .15 .40
7 Dan Issel .30 .75
8 Cotton Nash .15 .40
9 Kevin Grevey .15 .40
10 Kyle Macy .15 .40
11 Kenny Walker .15 .40
12 Louie Dampier .15 .40
13 Vernon Hatton .15 .40
14 Johnny Cox .15 .40
15 Jack Givens .15 .40
16 Bill Spivey .15 .40
17 Pat Riley .40 1.00
18 Ellis Johnson .15 .40
19 Forest Sale .15 .40
20 Kenny Rollins .15 .40
21 Sam Bowie .15 .40
22 John DeMoisey .15 .40
23 Leroy Edwards .15 .40
24 Lee Huber .15 .40
25 Rick Robey .15 .40
26 Bob Burrow .15 .40
27 Cliff Barker .15 .40
28 Bernie Opper .15 .40
29 Ralph Carlisle .15 .40
30 Joe B. Hall CO .15 .40
31 Bob Brannum .15 .40
32 Jack Parkinson .15 .40
33 Jack Tingle .15 .40
34 Joe Holland .15 .40
35 Jim Line .15 .40
36 Bobby Watson .15 .40
37 Bill Evans .15 .40
38 Bill Lickert .15 .40
39 Larry Conley .15 .40
40 Eddie Sutton .15 .40
41 Larry Steele .15 .15
42 Tom Parker .15 .10
43 Shelby Linville .15 .10
44 Lou Tsioropoulos .15 .15
45 Gayle Rose .15 .15
46 Jim Andrews .15 .10
47 Ed Davender .15 .15
48 Winston Bennett .15 .20
49 Willie Rouse .15 .10
50 Mike Pratt .15 .15
51 Harry C. Lancaster .15 .15
52 Dirk Minniefield .15 .20
53 Russell Rice .15 .10
54 Carey Spicer .15 .10
55 Paul McBrayer .15 .10
56 Burgess Carey .15 .10
57 Ermal Allen .15 .15
58 Dale Barnstable .15 .10
59 Kenton Campbell .15 .10
60 Guy Strong .15 .10
61 Lucian Whitaker .15 .10
62 Bennie Coffman .15 .10
63 C.M. Newton .15 .30
64 Walt Hirsch .15 .10
65 John Brewer .15 .15
66 Phil Grawemeyer .15 .10
67 John Crigler .15 .10
68 Gerry Calvert .15 .10
69 Ed Beck .15 .10
70 Jerry Bird .15 .10
71 Harold Ross .15 .40
72 Adrian Smith .15 .15
73 Don Mills .15 .10
74 Ned Jennings .15 .10
75 Sid Cohen .15 .10
76 Dickie Parsons .15 .10
77 Larry Pursiful .15 .10
78 Herky Rupp .15 .15
79 Charles Ishmael .15 .10
80 Jim McDonald .15 .10
81 Terry Mobley .15 .10
82 Tommy Kron .15 .15
83 Randy Embry .15 .10
84 Steve Clevenger .15 .10
85 Jim LeMaster .15 .10
86 Basil Hayden .15 .10
87 Cliff Berger .15 .10
88 Jim Dinwiddie .15 .15
89 Randy Pool .15 .10
90 Terry Mills .15 .15
91 Bob McCowan .15 .10
92 Mike Casey .15 .15
93 Kent Hollenbeck .15 .10
94 Scotty Baesler .15 .10
95 Phil Argento .15 .10
96 John R. Adams .15 .10
97 Larry Stamper .15 .10
98 Ray Edelman .15 .10
99 Ronnie Lyons .15 .10
100 G.J. Smith .15 .10
101 Jerry Hale .15 .10
102 Bob Guyette .15 .10
103 Mike Flynn .15 .15
104 Jimmy Dan Connor .15 .15
105 Larry Johnson .15 .15
106 Joey Holland .15 .10
107 Reggie Warford .15 .10
108 Merion Haskins .15 .10
109 James Lee .15 .15
110 Dwane Casey .15 .25
111 Truman Claytor .15 .15
112 LaVon Williams .15 .15
113 Jay Shidler .15 .15
114 Fred Cowan .15 .15
115 Dwight Anderson .15 .25
116 Chuck Verderber .15 .15
117 Bo Lanter .15 .10
118 Charles Hurt .15 .15
119 Derrick Hord .15 .15
120 Tom Heitz .15 .10
121 Dicky Beal .15 .15
122 Bret Bearup .15 .15
123 Melvin Turpin .15 .20
124 Jim Master .15 .15
125 Troy McKinley .15 .10
126 Roger Harden .15 .15
127 James Blackmon .15 .15
128 Leroy Byrd .15 .15
129 Cedric Jenkins .15 .15
130 Rob Lock .15 .15
131 Richard Madison .15 .15
132 Cawood Ledford .15 .20
133 '47-'48 Team .15 .20
134 '48-'49 Team .15 .20
135 '50-'51 Team .15 .20
136 '57-'58 Team .15 .20
137 '77-'78 Team .15 .20
138 Stan Key .15 .10
139 Mike Phillips .15 .15
140 Joe B. Hall CO .15 .25
141 Mike Flynn .15 .15
142 Thad Jaracz .15 .15
143 Larry Conley .15 .30
144 Rex Chapman .20 .50
145 Pat Riley .40 1.00
146 Melvin Turpin .15 .20
147 Kenny Walker .15 .25
148 Wallace Jones .15 .15
149 Alex Groza .15 .40
150 Mike Pratt .15 .15
151 Cliff Barker .15 .15
152 Jim Andrews .15 .10
153 Kenny Walker .15 .25
154 Kevin Grevey .15 .20
155 Kyle Macy .15 .30
156 Jim Line .15 .10
157 Pat Riley .40 1.00
158 Larry Steele .15 .15
159 Jack Givens .15 .25
160 Ed Davender .15 .15
161 Ralph Beard .15 .40
162 Vernon Hatton .15 .10
163 Frank Ramsey .15 .40
164 Bob Burrow .15 .10
165 Sam Bowie .15 .30
166 Dan Issel .30 .75
167 Rick Robey .15 .20
168 Winston Bennett .15 .20
169 Louie Dampier .15 .20
170 Gayle Rose .15 .15
171 Cliff Hagan .20 .50
172 Cotton Nash .15 .25
173 Mike Pratt .15 .15
174 Richard Madison .15 .15
175 Kyle Macy .15 .30
176 Rob Lock .15 .15
177 Larry Johnson .15 .15
178 Cedric Jenkins .15 .15
179 Dan Issel .30 .75
180 Charles Hurt .15 .15
181 Cliff Hagan .20 .50
182 Wallace Jones .15 .15
183 Roger Harden .15 .15
184 Bob Guyette .15 .10
185 Kevin Grevey .15 .20
186 Jack Givens .15 .25
187 Ed Davender .15 .15
188 Jimmy Dan Connor .15 .15
189 Fred Cowan .15 .15
190 Larry Conley .15 .30
191 Leroy Byrd .15 .15
192 Sam Bowie .15 .30
193 James Blackmon .15 .15
194 Winston Bennett .15 .20
195 Dicky Beal .15 .15
196 Jim Andrews .15 .10
197 Kenny Walker .15 .25
198 Pat Riley .40 1.00
199 Frank Ramsey .15 .40
200 Truman Claytor .15 .15
201 Dwane Casey .15 .25
202 Rex Chapman .20 .50
203 Jim Master .15 .15
204 Mike Phillips .15 .15
205 Dirk Minniefield .15 .20
206 Jimmy Dan Connor .15 .15
207 Bill Lickert .15 .10
208 Leroy Byrd .15 .15
209 Mike Pratt .15 .15
210 Rob Lock .15 .40
211 Dickie Parsons .15 .10
212 Frank Ramsey .15 .40
213 Adolph Rupp CO .30 .75
214 G.J. Smith .15 .10
215 Rick Robey .15 .20
216 James Blackmon .15 .15
217 Mike Casey .15 .15
218 LaVon Williams .15 .15
219 Larry Pursiful .15 .10
220 Terry Mobley .15 .10
221 Kyle Macy .15 .30
222 Larry Conley .15 .30
223 Dirk Minniefield .15 .20
224 Jim Master .15 .40
225 Jerry Bird .15 .10
226 Dan Issel .30 .75
227 Larry Johnson .15 .15
228 Bret Bearup .15 .15
229 Ronnie Lyons .15 .10
230 James Lee .15 .15
231 Don Mills .15 .10
232 Truman Claytor .15 .15
233 Rex Chapman .20 .50
234 Fred Cowan .15 .15
235 Truman Claytor .15 .15
236 Dicky Beal .15 .15
237 Larry Johnson .15 .15
238 John R. Adams .15 .10
239 Sam Bowie .15 .30
240 Thad Jaracz .15 .15
241 Phil Argento .15 .10
242 Cedric Jenkins .15 .15
243 Charles Hurt .15 .15
244 Charles Hurt .15 .15
245 Cliff Hagan .20 .50
246 Kent Hollenbeck .15 .10
247 Wallace Jones .15 .15
248 Roger Harden .15 .15
249 Bob Guyette .15 .10
250 Richard Madison .15 .15
251 Kevin Grevey .15 .20
252 Jack Givens .15 .25
253 Tommy Kron .15 .15
254 Derrick Hord .15 .15
255 Tom Heitz .15 .10
256 Cliff Hagan .20 .50
257 Louie Dampier .15 .20
258 Jimmy Dan Connor .15 .15
259 Dwane Casey .15 .25
260 Cliff Hagan .20 .50
261 Walt Hirsch .15 .10
262 Merion Haskins .15 .10
263 Roger Harden .15 .15
264 Bob Guyette .15 .10
265 Phil Grawemeyer .15 .10
266 Jay Shidler .15 .15
267 Jim Dinwiddie .15 .15
268 Fred Cowan .15 .15
269 Leroy Byrd .15 .15

1988-89 Kentucky Big Blue

This 18-card set was issued as an insert in the Summer 1989 Volume 3, Number 2 issue of Oscar Combs' Big Blue Basketball magazine. The cards honor Kentucky players for various outstanding achievements. The cards were issued in two panels; after perforation, the cards measure approximately 2 1/2" by 3 1/2". In a horizontal format, the front features a color action player photo, with blue and black borders on white card stock. The name of the award appears in white lettering in the upper left corner of the photo, with the player's name in a white box in the lower left corner. The back has a black and white head shot of the player in the upper left corner. Biographical information appears in a light blue-tinted box. The cards are numbered on the back, and we have listed the award below after the player's name.

COMPLETE SET (18) 9.00 18.00
1 Sean Sutton .30 .75
Leadership
2 Chris Mills 1.50 4.00
Most Valuable Player
3 Mike Scott .30 .75
Outstanding Senior
4 Richie Farmer .60 1.50
Best Free Throw Percentage
5 Derrick Miller .30 .75
Fewest Turnovers
6 Chris Mills 1.50 4.00
Freshman Leadership
7 Mike Scott .30 .75
Scholastic
8 Sean Sutton .30 .75
Most Assists
9 Chris Mills 1.50 4.00
Most Rebounds
10 LeRon Ellis .60 1.50
Leading Scorer
11 Reggie Hanson .60 1.50
Best Defender
12 Deron Feldhaus .60 1.50
110 Percent Award
13 Sean Sutton and .60 1.50
Leron Ellis
Sacrifice Award
14 LeRon Ellis .60 1.50
Best Field Goal Percentage
15 Sean Sutton .30 .75
Best Three-pt. Field Goal Percentage
16 Reggie Hanson .60 1.50
Most Steals
17 Eddie Sutton CO .75 2.00
18 Checklist Card UER .30 .75
(Misspelled sacrifice as sacrafice)

1989-90 Kentucky Big Blue

This perforated 18-card set was issued as an insert in the Winter 1990 Volume 3,, Number 4 issue of Oscar Combs' Big Blue Basketball magazine. The cards honor Kentucky players for various outstanding achievements. The cards were issued in two panels; after perforation, the cards measure approximately 2 1/2" by 3 1/2". The front features a color action player photo, with dark blue and black borders on white card stock. The name of the award is written vertically in an orange bar to the left of the picture, while the player's name appears in a gray bar above the picture. The back has a black and white head shot of the player in the upper left corner. Biographical information appears in a blue-tinted box. The cards are numbered on the back, beginning with 19 in continuation of the numbering of the previous year's issue. The award is listed below after the player's name.

COMPLETE SET (18) 8.00 20.00
19 Checklist Card .30 .75
20 Richie Farmer .60 1.50
Best FT Shooter
21 Reggie Hanson .60 1.50
Most Rebounds
22 Deron Feldhaus .60 1.50
Fewest Turnovers
23 Billy Donovan ACO 1.25 3.00
Herb Sendek ACO
Tubby Smith ACO
Ralph Willard ACO
24 Deron Feldhaus .60 1.50
Mr. Hustle Award
25 Reggie Hanson .60 1.50
Leadership
26 John Pelphrey .60 1.50
Student Athlete
27 Derrick Miller .30 .75
Outstanding Senior
28 Deron Feldhaus .60 1.50
Most Improved
29 Happy Chandler 1.25 3.00
Fan of the Year
30 John Pelphrey .60 1.50
Best Playmaker
31 Reggie Hanson .60 1.50
John Pelphrey
Mr. Deflection
32 Reggie Hanson .60 1.50
Most Valuable
33 Deron Feldhaus .60 1.50
Best FG Shooter
34 Sean Woods .30 .75
Most Assists
35 Derrick Miller .30 .75
Leading Scorer
36 Rick Pitino 2.00 5.00
Coach of the Year

1989-90 Kentucky Big Blue Team of the 80's

This perforated 18-card set was issued as an insert in the Spring 1990 Volume 4, Number 1 issue of Oscar Combs' Big Blue Basketball magazine. The cards honor outstanding Kentucky players for the decade of the 1980's. The cards were issued in two panels; after perforation, the cards measure approximately 2 1/2" by 3 1/2". The front features a color action player photo, on a light blue background that washes out as one moves from top to bottom. A thin black border outlines this blue background. The player's name appears in black lettering above the picture. The left lower corner of the photo is cut out, and in the triangular-shaped area appears a basketball icon and the pro team(s) played for. The back is blue tinted, and it has a black and white head shot of the player on the left side, with biographical information around the picture and career college statistics on the bottom. The cards are numbered on the back, beginning with 37 in continuation of the numbering of the previous year's issue.

COMPLETE SET (18) 8.00 20.00
37 Checklist Card .30 .75
38 Kyle Macy .75 2.00
39 Rex Chapman 1.25 3.00
40 Kenny Walker .75 2.00
41 Winston Bennett .50 1.25
42 Melvin Turpin .50 1.25
43 Sam Bowie 1.00 2.50
44 Dicky Beal .30 .75
45 Dirk Minniefield .50 1.25
46 Jim Master .50 1.25
47 Rob Lock .30 .75
48 Chris Mills 1.00 2.50
49 Roger Harden .30 .75
50 Jay Shidler .50 1.25
51 LeRon Ellis .50 1.25
52 Fred Cowan .30 .75
53 Derrick Hord .50 1.25
54 Joe Hall CO 1.25 3.00
Eddie Sutton CO
Rick Pitino CO

1989-90 Kentucky Schedules

This seven-card multi-sport set features schedule cards each measuring approximately 2 1/4" by 3 3/4". These schedule cards were passed out individually at games by booster clubs. The fronts feature full-bleed color action photos, some horizontally, some vertically oriented. The name "Kentucky" appears in either blue or white letters across the top of the card face on most cards. The backs carry the 1989-90 schedules for the respective sports. The cards are unnumbered and checklisted below with the named individuals listed first.

COMPLETE SET (7) 2.50 6.00
2 Rick Pitino CO BK 1.60 4.00

1990 Kentucky Class A High School All-Stars

This 18-card set was issued as an insert in the Kentucky All "A" Classic official program (produced by Wildcat News) for the state tournament played at Memorial Coliseum in Lexington, KY, February 7-10, 1990. The set consists of a checklist card, a special card honoring current Lexington mayor Scotty Baesler as a "Class A Great" player of the past, and 16 cards honoring the coaches' preseason choices for best players in each of the sixteen regions. The cards were issued in two panels; after perforation, the cards measure approximately 2 1/2" by 3 1/2". The front features a mix of posed or action, black and white player photos, with a peach color background and thin blue border on white card stock. Below the picture, the region number and player's name appears in a gray stripe, with player information further below in the right corner. A Kentucky shaped emblem in the lower left corner rounds out the card face. The back has a black and white head shot of the player in the upper left corner. Biographical information appears in a peach-tinted box, with high school statistics on the bottom. The cards are numbered on the back.

COMPLETE SET (18) 4.00 10.00
1 Checklist Card .40 1.00
2 Scott Baesler .40 1.00
3 Eugene Alexander .30 .75
4 Sergio Luyk .40 1.00
5 Chris Knight .30 .75
6 Chris Huffman .40 1.00
7 Shannon Phillips .30 .75
8 Glen Wathen .30 .75
9 Jason Hagan .30 .75
10 Bryan Milburn .40 1.00
11 Andre McClendon .30 .75
12 Chris Harrison .40 1.00
13 Daniel Swintosky .40 1.00
14 Jamie Cromer .30 .75
15 Mo Hollingsworth .30 .75
16 Jeff Moore .40 1.00
17 Jody Thompson .30 .75
18 Mike Helton .30 .75

1990 Kentucky Soviet Program Insert

This 18-card set was issued in two panels inside the AAU/Soviet Tour program (produced by Wildcat News) for the game played in Memorial Coliseum at Lexington, Kentucky, on May 15, 1990. After perforation, the cards measure approximately 2 1/2" by 3 1/2" and showcase the Kentucky AAU All-Stars. The fronts feature a mix of action or posed, black and white player photos, with red borders on a white and blue diagonally-striped background. The words "Ky. AAU All-Stars" appear in blue lettering in white stripe above the picture; the player's name is presented in the same format below the picture. The backs have black and white head shots of the player in the upper left corners. In a lavender colored box, they present career summaries, with high school statistics appearing at the bottom of the card. The cards are numbered on the back in the upper right corners. The key card in the set is the first card of NBA Lottery Pick Jamal Mashburn.

COMPLETE SET (18) 20.00 35.00
1 Checklist Card .40 1.00
2 Kentucky .40 1.00
USSR rosters
3 Jim Lankster .40 1.00
4 Paul Bingham .40 1.00
5 James Crutcher .40 1.00
6 Jason Eitutis .40 1.00
7 Greg Glass .40 1.00
8 Arlando Johnson .40 1.00
9 Gimel Martinez .60 1.50
10 Jamal Mashburn 10.00 25.00
11 Jeff Moore .40 1.00
12 Dwayne Morton 1.50 4.00
13 Keith Peel .40 1.00
14 Andy Penick .40 1.00
15 Daniel Swintosky .40 1.00
16 Jody Thompson .40 1.00
17 Carlos Toomer .40 1.00
18 Kelly Wells .40 1.00

1990-91 Kentucky Big Blue 18

This rather unattractive perforated 18-card set was issued as an insert in Oscar Combs' Big Blue Basketball magazine. After perforation, the cards measure approximately 2 5/8" by 3 5/8." The fronts display a mix of action and posed color head shots enclosed by a white border. The player's name appears in black lettering in a yellow bar at the top flanked by a basketball to the left. In a horizontal format, the backs have blue and white reverse lettering and carry a black and white head shot, a Fun Fact, and a "Coach Pitino Sez" feature. The cards are numbered on the back. The key card in the set features NBA Lottery Pick Jamal Mashburn.

COMPLETE SET (18) 8.00 20.00
1 Johnathon Davis .30 .75
2 Reggie Hanson .30 .75
3 Richie Farmer .60 1.50
4 Deron Feldhaus .30 .75
5 John Pelphrey .60 1.50
6 Sean Woods .30 .75
7 Todd Bearup .20 .50
8 Junior Braddy .20 .50
9 Jeff Brassow .30 .75
10 Gimel Martinez .30 .75
11 Jamal Mashburn 4.00 10.00
12 Henry Thomas .20 .50
13 Carlos Toomer .20 .50
14 Travis Ford .60 1.50
15 Rick Pitino CO 1.50 4.00
16 UK Cracks Top 10 .20 .50
17 UK 93, U of L 85 .20 .50
18 Checklist Card .20 .50

1990-91 Kentucky Big Blue Dream Team/Award Winners

This perforated 18-card set was issued as an insert in the Spring 1991 Volume 5, Number 1 issue of Oscar Combs' Big Blue Basketball magazine. The cards were issued in two panels of nine cards each. After perforation, the cards measure approximately 2 9/16" by 3 5/8". The cards are numbered 19-36, in continuation of an 18-card insert set of 1990-91 Kentucky players in an earlier issue of Big Blue Basketball. The fronts feature a color action photo enclosed by a white border. A blue box in the upper left corner indicates whether the player belongs to the Dream Team (19-26), which consists the most impressive opponents faced during the season as voted by the captains on the Kentucky squad, or is an Award Winner (28-36). The player's name appears in a color stripe at the bottom of the picture. Within a light blue border, the backs show a black and white head shot and a career summmary presented in the format of a newspaper article. The cards are numbered on the back. Reportedly only 7,500 sets were produced. The key cards in the set are NBA superstar Shaquille O'Neal and NBA stars Allan Houston and Jamal Mashburn. The O'Neal card is his very first trading card and the only card issued of him during his LSU collegiate career. "B" Versions of this set are available also. This version mirrors the cards found in the Big Blue Magazine, but are unperforated and were machine cut with a print run of about 1,200 sets.

COMPLETE SET (18) 40.00 100.00
19 Shaquille O'Neal 15.00 30.00
LSU
19B Shaquille O'Neal 40.00 80.00
Unperforated
20 Allan Houston 2.50 6.00
Tennessee
20B Allan Houston 6.00 15.00
Unperforated
21 Calbert Cheaney 1.50 4.00
Indiana
21B Calbert Cheaney 4.00 10.00
Unperforated
22 Rick Fox 2.00 5.00
North Carolina
22B Rick Fox 4.00 10.00
Unperforated
23 Litterial Green .60 1.50
Georgia
23B Litterial Green 1.25 3.00
Unperforated
24 Bobby Knight CO 1.25 3.00
Indiana
24B Bobby Knight CO 2.00 5.00
Unperforated
25 Dean Smith CO 1.50 4.00
North Carolina
25B Dean Smith CO 2.50 6.00
Unperforated
26 Freedom Hall .30 .75
26B Freedom Hall .60 1.50
Unperforated
27 Checklist .30 .75
27B Checklist .60 1.50
Unperforated
28 Richie Farmer .60 1.50
28B Richie Farmer .75 2.00
Unperforated
29 Jamal Mashburn 2.50 6.00
29B Jamal Mashburn 6.00 15.00
Unperforated
30 Jeff Brassow .30 .75
30B Jeff Brassow .60 1.50
Unperforated
31 Todd Bearup .30 .75
31B Todd Bearup .60 1.50
Unperforated
32 Sean Woods .60 1.50
32B Sean Woods .75 2.00
Unperforated
33 Deron Feldhaus .60 1.50
33B Deron Feldhaus .75 2.00
Unperforated
34 John Pelphrey .60 1.50
34B John Pelphrey .75 2.00
Unperforated
35 Reggie Hanson .60 1.50
35B Reggie Hanson .75 2.00
Unperforated
36 Rick Pitino CO 1.00 2.50
36B Rick Pitino CO 1.50 4.00
Unperforated

1990-91 Kentucky Women Schedules

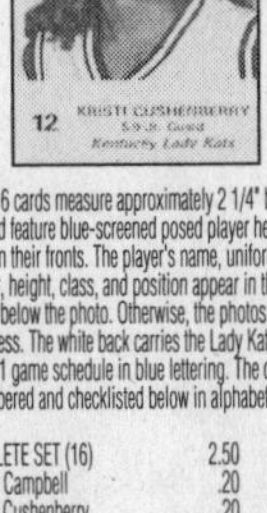

These 16 cards measure approximately 2 1/4" by 3 3/4" and feature blue-screened posed player head shots on their fronts. The player's name, uniform number, height, class, and position appear in the white margin below the photo. Otherwise, the photos are borderless. The white back carries the Lady Kats' 1990-91 game schedule in blue lettering. The cards are unnumbered and checklisted below in alphabetical order.

COMPLETE SET (16) 2.50 6.00
1 Kayla Campbell .20 .50
2 Kristi Cushenberry .20 .50
3 Mia Daniel .20 .50
4 Tracye Davis .20 .50

5 Tedra Eberhart	.20	.50
6 Jennifer Gray	.20	.50
7 Sharon Fanning CO	.20	.50
8 Jamie Hobgood	.20	.50
9 Christe Jordan	.20	.50
10 Karen Killen	.20	.50
11 Pattresa Leonard	.20	.50
12 Tiundra Love	.20	.50
13 Stacy McIntyre	.20	.50
14 Jocelyn Mills	.20	.50
15 Cathy Proctor	.20	.50
16 Rebekah Reasor	.20	.50

1991-92 Kentucky Big Blue 20

This 20-card set was issued as inserts in the Summer 1991 Volume 5, Number 2, and Fall 1991 Volume 5, Number 3 issues of Oscar Combs' Big Blue Basketball magazine. Each issue had two insert sheets: an 8 1/2" by 11" photo and a sheet of player cards. After perforation, the player cards measure 2 9/16" by 3 5/8." The horizontally oriented fronts feature a color head shot to the left of the Wildcats' logo. A blue stripe traverses the top of the card face, while the player's name appears in a short red stripe at the lower right corner. The backs are vertically oriented and display black and white action photos. The cards are numbered on the back. The key card in the set features NBA Lottery Pick Jamal Mashburn.

COMPLETE SET (20)	8.00	20.00
1 John Pelphrey	.40	1.00
2 Deron Feldhaus	.30	.75
3 Richie Farmer	.40	1.00
4 Jeff Brassow	.30	.75
5 Junior Braddy	.20	.50
6 Sean Woods	.30	.75
7 Gimel Martinez	.30	.75
8 Travis Ford	.40	1.00
9 Dale Brown	.30	.75
10 Chris Harrison	.20	.50
11 Carlos Toomer	.20	.50
12 Jamal Mashburn	4.00	10.00
13 Rick Pitino CO	1.25	3.00
14 Aminu Timberlake	.20	.50
15 Andre Riddick	.60	1.50
16 Bernadette Locke-Mattox Asst. CO	.40	1.00
17 Billy Donovan ACO	1.50	4.00
18 Herb Sendek ACO	.30	.75
NNO Wildcat Seniors	1.00	2.50
NNO Team Photo	1.50	4.00

1992-93 Kentucky Schedules

Sponsored by McDonald's, this ten-card multi-sport schedule features schedule cards each measuring 2 1/4" by 3 1/2". These schedule cards were passed out individually at games by booster clubs. The fronts feature a mix of color and black-and-white action player photos. Card numbers 1 and 2 are folded in the middle. The backs (or the insides) carry the 1992-93 schedules for the respective sports. The sponsor's logo appears either on the front or on the back. The cards are unnumbered and checklisted below in alphabetical order, with the schedule cards not featuring athletes listed at the end.

COMPLETE SET (10)	2.50	6.00
4 Jamal Mashburn BK	1.20	3.00
5 Stacey Reed Women's Basketball schedule	.10	.25
8 Basketball schedule	.20	.50

1993-94 Kentucky

The 1993-94 University of Kentucky set contains 18 standard-size cards. The light blue-bordered fronts feature a mix of posed and action color photos. The team nickname, "Cats," appears across the top of the photo in simulated polished metal. The player's name is printed in blue and white script and appears in a lower corner. The set name is printed in the lower border. The blue-bordered horizontal backs carry a second player photo in a narrow vertical box on the left side. Player profile, statistics, biography, team number, and logo are printed on a ghosted photo of a basketball court. The cards are unnumbered and checklisted below in alphabetical order. The set could originally be purchased through the mail for 9.25 plus 2.00 for shipping and handling.

COMPLETE SET (18)	7.00	14.00
1 Jeff Brassow	.20	.50
2 Tony Delk	1.50	4.00
3 Rodney Dent	.30	.75
4 Anthony Epps	.75	2.00
5 Travis Ford	.30	.75
6 Chris Harrison	.20	.50
7 Bill Keightley EQ MG	.20	.50
8 Gimel Martinez	.30	.75
9 Walter McCarty	1.50	4.00
10 Rick Pitino CO	.75	2.00
11 Jared Prickett	.30	.75
12 Rodrick Rhodes	1.00	2.50
13 Andre Riddick	.30	.75
14 Jeff Sheppard	.30	.75
15 Delray Brooks ACO Shaun Brown ACO Billy Donovan ACO Bernadette Locke-Mattox ACO	1.25	3.00
16 1993 SEC Champions	.40	1.00
17 Team Photo Card	.30	.75
18 Title Card	.20	.50

1993-94 Kentucky Schedules

4 Men's Basketball Gimel Martinez Rodney Dent Travis Ford Jeff Brassow	.20	.50
5 Jennifer Gray Kayla Campbell Tedra Eberhart Christe Jordan Women's Basketball	.20	.50

1997-98 Kentucky Women

This set was released for the University of Kentucky Women's Basketball during the 1997-98 season. The set features cards of all of the players and coaches on a purple bordered card courtesy of Mildred White.

COMPLETE SET (20)	2.50	6.00
1 Leah Berki	.20	.50
2 Lisa Byington	.20	.50
3 Megan Chawansky	.20	.50
4 Mary Connolly	.20	.50
5 Amber DeWall	.20	.50
6 Kristina Divjak	.20	.50
7 Becky Fisher	.20	.50
8 Clarissa Flores	.20	.50
9 Anne Giblin	.20	.50
10 Chala Holland	.20	.50
11 Shannon McGarrigle	.20	.50
12 Leslie Schock	.20	.50
13 Tami Sears	.20	.50
14 Candace Wrenn	.20	.50
15 Dana Leonard	.20	.50
16 Team Photo	.20	.50
17 Don Perrelli CO	.30	.75
18 Robin Garrett Amy Backus Jennifer Kiefer	.20	.50
19 Wildcat Seniors	.20	.50
20 Wildcat Freshmen	.20	.50

1998-99 Kentucky Schedules

This three-card set features the 1998-99 Kentucky team schedule cards that were passed out during Kentucky home games.

COMPLETE SET (3)	1.50	4.00
1 Heshimu Evans	.40	1.00
2 Scott Padgett	1.25	3.00
3 Wayne Turner	.40	1.00

1987 Kentucky Bluegrass State Games

This 24-card set of standard size cards was co-sponsored by Coca-Cola and Valvoline, and their company logos appear on the bottom of the card face. The card sets were originally given out by the Kentucky county sheriff's departments and the Kentucky Highway Patrol. Reportedly about 350 sets were given to the approximately 120 counties in the state of Kentucky. One card per week was given out from May 25 to October 19, 1987. Once all 22 of the numbered cards were collected, they could be turned in to a local sheriff's department for prizes. The front features a color action player photo, on a blue card face with a white outer border. The player's name and the "Champions Against Drugs" insignia appear below the picture. The back has a anti-drug or alcohol tip on a gray background, with white border. The set commemorates Kentucky's hosting of the 1987 Bluegrass State Games and was endorsed by Governor Martha Layne Collins in Kentucky's Champions Against Drugs Crusade for Youth. The set features stars from a variety of sports as well as public figures. The two cards in the set numbered "SC" for special card were not distributed with the regular cards; they were produced in smaller quantities than the 22 numbered cards. The set features the first card of NBA superstar David Robinson. Reportedly the Robinson cards were distributed at the March 1987 Kentucky Boy's State High School Tournament in Rupp Arena, when David Robinson was in attendance.

COMPLETE SET (24)	25.00	60.00
2 Kenny Walker K	.30	.75
4 Dan Issel K	1.60	4.00
7 Melvin Turpin K Sam Bowie	.60	1.50
8 Darrell Griffith K	.60	1.50
9 Winston Bennett K	.30	.75
15 Jim Master K	.30	.75
16 Kyle Macy K	.40	1.00
17 Pervis Ellison K	.60	1.50
18 Dale Baldwin K	.20	.50
21 Rex Chapman K	1.60	4.00
SC Billy Packer SP K	4.00	10.00
SC David Robinson SP K	16.00	40.00

1985-86 LSU

This 16-card standard-size set was sponsored by LSU, Baton Rouge General Medical Center, Chemical Dependency Unit of Baton Rouge, and various law enforcement agencies and produced by McDag Productions. The General and the Chemical Dependency Unit logos adorn the top of the observe and the bottom of the reverse. The cards are unnumbered and we have checklisted them in alphabetical order. Since this set includes athletes from two different sports, we have indicated the sport after the player's name (B for baseball; BK for basketball). The set features Major League Baseball slugger Joey (Albert) Belle and other future Major Leaguers Mark Guthrie and Jeff Reboulet.

COMPLETE SET (16)	10.00	25.00
3 Ricky Blanton BK	.40	1.00
4 Dale Brown BK CO	1.20	3.00
5 Ollie Brown BK	.20	.50
11 Don Redden BK	.20	.50
12 Derrick Taylor BK	.20	.50
13 Jose Vargas BK	.20	.50
14 John Williams BK	1.00	2.50
15 Nikita Wilson BK	.40	1.00
16 Anthony Wilson BK	.20	.50

1987-88 LSU

This 16-card standard-size set was sponsored by LSU, Baton Rouge General Medical Center, Chemical Dependency Unit of Baton Rouge, and various law enforcement agencies and was produced by McDag Productions. The General and the Chemical Dependency Unit logos adorn the bottom of both sides of the card. Six thousand sets were printed, and they were distributed by participating police agencies in the Baton Rouge area. The fronts feature borderless action or posed color photos of the players on white card stock. The upper left and right corners give the school name and player information. The backs have additional player information and "Tips from the Tigers", which consist of anti-drug or alcohol messages. This set includes athletes from basketball (1-7, 16) and baseball (8-15). Of special interest is card number 16, issued in memory of the late Pete Maravich, the all-time leading scorer in college basketball history. The set features the first card of Ben McDonald.

COMPLETE SET (16)	15.00	40.00
1 Dale Brown BK CO	1.20	3.00
2 Ricky Blanton BK	.60	1.50
3 Jose Vargas BK	.40	1.00
4 Fess Irvin BK	.60	1.50
5 Darryl Joe BK	.40	1.00
6 Bernard Woodside BK	.40	1.00
7 Neboisha Bukumirovich BK	.40	1.00
16 Pete Maravich BK MEM	12.00	30.00

1988-89 LSU

This 16-card standard-size set was sponsored by LSU, Baton Rouge General Medical Center, Chemical Dependency Unit of Baton Rouge, and various law enforcement agencies and was produced by McDag Productions. The General Medical Center and Chemical Dependency Unit logos adorn the bottom of both sides of the card. The cards were distributed in the Baton Rouge area by participating law enforcement agencies, the Medical Center, and the Chemical Dependency Unit. This set features athletes from basketball (1-8) and baseball (9-16). This set includes early cards of Chris Jackson, who played in the NBA, and of Ben McDonald, who pitched for the USA Olympic Baseball Team and the Baltimore Orioles.

COMPLETE SET (16)	5.00	12.00
1 Ricky Blanton	.40	1.00
2 Dale Brown CO	.80	2.00
3 Wayne Simms	.20	.50
4 Chris Jackson	1.60	4.00
5 Kyle McKenzie	.20	.50
6 Lyle Mouton	.60	1.50
7 Vernel Singleton	.40	1.00
8 Russell Grant	.20	.50
9 Skip Bertman CO	.40	1.00

1990 LSU Collegiate Collection

This 200-card standard-size multi-sport set was produced by Collegiate Collection. Although a few color photos are included, the front features mostly black and white player photos, with borders in the team's colors of gold and purple. Unless noted below, all are football subjects.

COMPLETE SET (200)	6.00	15.00
1 Pete Maravich BK	2.00	5.00
2 Chris Jackson BK	.20	.50
4 Ricky Blanton BK	.10	.25
6 Joe Dean BK	.07	.20
11 Dale Brown CO BK	.15	.40
14 John Williams BK	.10	.25
18 Chris Jackson BK	.10	.25
22 Glenn Hansen BK	.05	.15
25 Leonard Mitchell BK	.05	.15
32 Ethan Martin BK	.05	.15
33 Julie Gross WBK	.05	.15
35 Eddie Palubinskas BK	.05	.15
37 Frank Brian BK	.05	.15
40 Howard Carter BK	.07	.20
42 Nikita Wilson BK	.07	.20
46 DeWayne Scales BK	.05	.15
50 Durand Macklin BK	.07	.20
53 Joyce Walker WBK	.05	.15
54 Bobby Lowther BK	.05	.15
55 Al Sanders BK	.05	.15
58 George Nattin BK	.05	.15
61 Maree Jackson WBK	.05	.15
62 Sparky Wade BK	.05	.15
65 Al Green BK	.05	.15
71 Dick Maile BK	.05	.15
74 Pete Maravich BK	2.00	5.00
91 Chris Jackson BK	.20	.50
98 Jerry Reynolds BK	.10	.25
136 Kenny Higgs BK	.05	.15
138 Bob Pettit BK	.30	.75
154 Pete Maravich Center BK	.20	.50
165 Buddy Blair BK	.05	.15
171 Joe Bill Padcock BK	.05	.15
189 Chris Jackson BK	.20	.50
190 Chris Jackson BK	.20	.50
196 Howard Carter BK	.07	.20
197 Glenn Hansen BK	.05	.15
198 Durand Macklin BK	.07	.20

1993-94 LSU

This 16-card standard-size set was produced by McDag Productions Inc. The fronts feature color action player photos framed by yellowish-orange borders. "LSU Tigers" and "1993-94" are printed in purple in the top border. The player's name, position, and uniform number are printed in purple in the bottom border, immediately to the right of an orange basketball icon. In purple print on a white background, the horizontal backs present biographical information and player profile. This set features the first card of Randy Livingston, a highly-touted two-time Parade magazine Prep All-American who was red-shirted during his first year due to a knee injury. The cards are unnumbered and checklisted below in alphabetical order.

COMPLETE SET (16)	3.00	8.00
1 Doug Annison	.20	.50
2 David Bosley	.20	.50
3 Dale Brown CO	.75	2.00
4 Jamie Brandon	.30	.75
5 Lenear Burns	.20	.50
6 Clarence Ceasar	.30	.75
7 Sean Gipson	.20	.50
8 Ronnie Henderson	.75	2.00
9 Glover Jackson	.20	.50
10 Randy Livingston	1.00	2.50
11 Andre Owens	.30	.75
12 Roman Roubtchenko	.20	.50
13 Brandon Titus	.20	.50
14 Mike the Tiger The Tiger	.20	.50
15 Mike the Tiger The Mascot	.20	.50
16 Cheerleaders	.20	.50

1988-89 LSU All-Americas

Produced by McDag Productions, this 16-card standard-size set was sponsored by LSU, Baton Rouge General Medical Center, Chemical Dependency Unit of Baton Rouge, and various law enforcement agencies. The General Medical Center and Chemical Dependency Unit logos adorn the bottom of both sides of the card. This set showcases athletes from basketball (1-2), baseball (3-5), track (6), volleyball (7), football (8-15) and golf (16). This set includes early cards of Chris Jackson, who was selected in the first round of the NBA draft by the Denver Nuggets, and of Ben McDonald, who was selected first by the Baltimore Orioles.

COMPLETE SET (16)	5.00	12.00
1 Chris Jackson	1.60	4.00
2 Durand(Rudy) Macklin	.40	1.00

1989-90 Louisiana Tech

This 16-card set measures the standard size and features members of the men's (1-8) and women's (9-16) basketball teams. The fronts feature close-up photos with red and white borders. Above the picture is a gray box containing the school name and year. Below the photo is a sky blue box that displays the player's name, jersey number, and position. The backs carry limited player information and a wildfire prevention cartoon. The cards are unnumbered and checklisted below in alphabetical order within each team. This set features the first card of Venus Lacy, a member of the gold medal-winning 1996 USA team.

COMPLETE SET (16)	6.00	15.00
1 Eldon Bowman	.20	.50
2 P.J. Brown	3.00	8.00
3 Dickie Crawford	.20	.50
4 Anthony Dade	.40	1.00
5 Reggie Gibbs	.20	.50
6 Jo Jo Goldsmith	.20	.50
7 Brett Guillory	.20	.50
8 Roosevelt Powell	.20	.50
9 Barbara Bolden	.40	1.00
10 Sheila Ethridge	.20	.50
11 Cara Gullion	.20	.50
12 Shantel Hardison	.20	.50
13 Venus Lacy	1.25	3.00
14 Annie Lockett	.20	.50
15 Sebrena Smith	.20	.50
16 Pam Wells	.40	1.00

1981-82 Louisville

This 31-card set was sponsored by Pepsi, the Louisville Area Chamber of Commerce, and Greater Louisville Police Departments. The cards measure approximately 2 5/8" by 4 1/8" and are printed in thin card stock. On a red card face, the fronts show black and white player photos enclosed by a white border. Player information and the words "Cardinal Spirit" appear beneath the picture. The backs include a safety tip, a definition or discussion of an aspect of basketball, and sponsor logos. The cards are numbered on the back by the tip number.

COMPLETE SET (31)	30.00	55.00
1 Charles Jones	1.00	2.50
2 Rodin's The Thinker	.60	1.50
3 1981-82 Schedule	.60	1.50
4 Bill Olsen ATH DIR and family	.60	1.50
5 Coaching Staff	1.00	2.50
6 Lancaster Gordon	1.25	3.00
7 Donald C. Swain PRES	.60	1.50
8 Scooter McCray	1.25	3.00
9 Cheerleaders	.60	1.50
10 Marty Pulliam	.60	1.50
11 Derek Smith	2.50	6.00
12 Jack Tennant ANN and Van Vance ANN	1.00	2.50
13 Jerry Eaves	1.00	2.50
14 Greg Deuser	.60	1.50
15 Manuel Forrest	1.00	2.50
16 Danny Mitchell	.60	1.50
17 Team Photo Men's team	2.00	5.00
18 Jerry May TR Rudy Ellis Dir. Sports Medicine	.60	1.50
19 Poncho Wright	1.00	2.50
20 James Jeter	.60	1.50
21 Cardinal Bird Mascot	.60	1.50
22 Milt Wagner	2.00	5.00
23 Denny Crum CO and 1981-82 Freshman	2.00	5.00
24 Team Photo Women's Team	.60	1.50
25 Wiley Brown	1.00	2.50
26 Kent Jones	.60	1.50
27 Denny Crum CO and Returning Starters	2.00	5.00
28 Darrell Griffith U of L Professional Basketball Players	3.00	8.00
29 Denny Crum CO	3.00	8.00
30 Rodney McCray	2.00	5.00
NNO Logo Card SP	15.00	30.00

1983-84 Louisville

This 20-card set consists of oversized cards measuring approximately 7" by 5". On the left portion the front features a borderless color action photo, measuring 4" by 5". On the remaining portion, a head shot of the player, player information (in white lettering), and a Cardinal logo appear on a red background. The back of the cards presents biographical information, career summary, and statistics in a two-column format, along with the player's autograph. The cards are unnumbered and checklisted below in alphabetical order.

COMPLETE SET (20)	15.00	40.00
1 Denny Crum CO	4.00	10.00
2 Manuel Forrest	.75	2.00
3 Lancaster Gordon	1.50	4.00
4 Darrell Griffith	4.00	10.00
5 Jeff Hall	.75	2.00
6 James Jeter	.75	2.00
7 Charles Jones	.75	2.00
8 Kent Jones	.75	2.00
9 Mark McSwain	.75	2.00
10 Danny Mitchell	2.50	6.00
11 Will Olliges	.75	2.00
12 Barry Sumpter	1.50	4.00
13 Billy Thompson	1.50	4.00
14 Robbie Valentine	1.50	4.00
15 Milt Wagner	2.50	6.00
16 Chris West	.75	2.00
17 Bobby Dotson ACO Wade Houston ACO Jerry Jones ACO	.75	2.00
18 Cheerleaders	1.50	4.00
19 Pep Band	.75	2.00
20 Freedom Hall Home of the Cardinals	1.50	4.00

1988-89 Louisville Collegiate Collection

The 1988-89 University of Louisville Cardinals basketball set contains 194 standard-sized cards featuring "Louisville's Finest" basketball players. The fronts have red and white borders. The backs have various statistical and biographical information. This set was issued in eight-card cello packs.

COMPLETE SET (194)	6.00	15.00
1 Denny Crum CO	.15	.40
2 Wes Unseld	.20	.50
3 Darrell Griffith	.10	.30
4 John Dromo	.07	.20
5 Bernard (Peck) Hickman	.07	.20
6 Butch Beard	.10	.30
7 Herbert Crook	.07	.20
8 Milt Wagner	.07	.20
9 Lancaster Gordon	.07	.20
10 Billy Thompson	.07	.20
11 Rodney McCray	.08	.25
12 Scooter McCray	.07	.15
13 Wade Houston	.07	.15
14 Jerry Jones	.07	.05
15 Derek Smith	.07	.15
16 Tony Branch	.07	.10
17 Wesley Cox	.07	.10
18 Manuel Forrest	.07	.10
19 Jerry Eaves	.07	.10
20 1980 NCAA Champs	.08	.25
21 Junior Bridgeman	.07	.15
22 Jeff Hall	.07	.10
23 Charles Jones	.07	.10
24 Rick Wilson	.07	.05
25 The Cardinal Bird	.07	.05
26 Wiley Brown	.07	.10
27 Charlie Tyra	.07	.10
28 Phil Rollins	.07	.05
29 James Jeter	.07	.05
30 Poncho Wright	.07	.05
31 Vladimir Gastevich	.07	.05
32 Terry Howard	.07	.05
33 Mark McSwain	.07	.10
34 Ricky Gallon	.07	.05
35 1975 NCAA Final Four	.07	.10
36 1972 NCAA Final Four	.07	.10
37 Mike Lawhon	.07	.05
38 Bill Bunton	.07	.10
39 Roger Burkman	.07	.05
40 Henry Bacon	.07	.05
41 Larry Williams	.07	.05
42 Phil Bond	.07	.05
43 Bobby Brown	.07	.05
44 Charles Jones	.07	.10
45 Mike Grosso	.07	.05
46 Freedom Hall	.07	.15
47 Fred Holden	.07	.05
48 1948 NAIB Champs	.07	.10
49 Glen Combs	.07	.10
50 Jadie Frazier	.07	.05
51 Marty Pulliam	.07	.05
52 Eddie Whitehead	.07	.05
53 Bobby Turner	.07	.05
54 Will Olliges	.07	.20
55 Eddie Creamer	.07	.05
56 Corky Cox	.07	.05
57 Bob Lochmueller	.07	.05
58 Jeff Hall	.07	.10
59 Al Vilcheck	.07	.05
60 Jim Morgan	.07	.05
61 Jim Price	.07	.10
62 Ron Thomas	.07	.10
63 Bobby Dotson	.07	.05
64 Jerry Eaves	.07	.10
65 1956 NIT Champs	.07	.10
66 John Reuther	.07	.05
67 Ron Hawley	.07	.05
68 Kent Jones	.07	.05
69 1983 NCAA Final Four	.07	.15
70 1982 NCAA Final Four	.07	.15
71 1959 Louisville	.07	.10
72 Fred Sawyer	.07	.05
73 Kenny Reeves	.07	.05
74 Chris West	.07	.05
75 Dick Peloff	.07	.05
76 Allen Murphy	.07	.05
77 John Prudhoe	.07	.05
78 Mike Abram	.07	.05
79 Bud Olsen	.07	.05
80 Ron Rubenstein	.07	.05
81 Gerald Moreman	.07	.05
82 Chuck Noble	.07	.05
83 Bill Darragh	.07	.05
84 Jerry Dupont	.07	.05
85 Danny Mitchell	.07	.05
86 John Turner	.07	.05
87 Daryl Cleveland	.07	.05
88 Greg Deuser	.07	.05
89 Don Goldstein	.07	.05
90 Marv Selvy	.07	.05
91 Dave Gilbert	.07	.05
92 Tommy Finnegan	.07	.05
93 Joe Liedtke	.07	.05
94 Jack Coleman	.07	.05
95 Dennis Clifford	.07	.05
96 Robbie Valentine	.07	.05
97 Ron Rooks	.07	.05
98 The Coaching Staff	.07	.15
99 Denny Crum CO	.15	.40
100 Manuel Forrest	.07	.10
101 Darrell Griffith	.10	.30
102 Wesley Cox	.07	.10
103 Wes Unseld	.20	.50
104 John Dromo	.07	.10
105 Peck Hickman	.07	.10
106 Butch Beard	.10	.30
107 Herbert Crook	.07	.15
108 Milt Wagner	.07	.20
109 Lancaster Gordon	.07	.20
110 Billy Thompson	.07	.20
111 Rodney McCray	.08	.25
112 Scooter McCray	.07	.15
113 Derek Smith	.07	.15
114 Tony Branch	.07	.10
115 Manuel Forrest	.07	.10
116 Jerry Eaves	.07	.10
117 Jeff Hall	.07	.10
118 Charles Jones	.07	.10
119 Rick Wilson	.07	.05
120 Wiley Brown	.07	.10
121 Charlie Tyra	.07	.10
122 Phil Rollins	.07	.05
123 Poncho Wright	.07	.05
124 Terry Howard	.07	.05
125 Mark McSwain	.07	.10
126 Ricky Gallon	.07	.05
127 Mike Lawhon	.07	.05
128 Roger Burkman	.07	.05
129 Henry Bacon	.07	.05
130 Larry Williams	.07	.05
131 Phil Bond	.07	.05
132 Stanley Bunton	.07	.05
133 Fred Holden	.07	.05
134 Marty Pulliam	.07	.05
135 Bobby Turner	.07	.05
136 Will Olliges	.07	.05
137 Al Vilcheck	.07	.05
138 Jim Price	.07	.10
139 Chris West	.07	.05
140 Allen Murphy	.07	.05
141 Mike Abram	.07	.05
142 Danny Mitchell	.07	.05
143 John Turner	.07	.05
144 Daryl Cleveland	.07	.05
145 Don Goldstein	.07	.05
146 Marv Selvy	.07	.05
147 Dave Gilbert	.07	.05
148 Joe Liedtke	.07	.05
149 Robbie Valentine	.07	.05
150 Tony Branch	.07	.10
151 Manuel Forrest	.07	.10
152 Jerry Eaves	.07	.10
153 Rick Wilson	.07	.05
154 Jeff Hall	.07	.10
155 Charles Jones	.07	.10
156 Derek Smith	.07	.15
157 Scooter McCray	.07	.15
158 Robbie Valentine	.07	.05
159 Mike Abram	.07	.05
160 Rodney McCray	.08	.25
161 Roger Burkman	.07	.05
162 Henry Bacon	.07	.05
163 Mike Lawhon	.07	.05
164 Ricky Gallon	.07	.05
165 Billy Thompson	.08	.20
166 Milt Wagner	.07	.20
167 Lancaster Gordon	.07	.20
168 Butch Beard	.10	.30
169 Herbert Crook	.07	.15
170 Wes Unseld	.20	.50
171 Wesley Cox	.07	.10
172 Darrell Griffith	.10	.30
173 Denny Crum CO	.15	.40
174 Mark McSwain	.07	.10
175 Wiley Brown	.07	.10
176 Will Olliges	.07	.05
177 Phil Bond	.07	.05
178 Phil Bond	.07	.05
179 Wiley Brown	.07	.10
180 Mark McSwain	.07	.10
181 Denny Crum CO	.15	.40
182 Darrell Griffith	.10	.30
183 Wesley Cox	.07	.20
184 Peck Hickman CO	.07	.10
185 Lancaster Gordon	.07	.20
186 Billy Thompson	.07	.20
187 Rodney McCray	.08	.25
188 Stanley Bunton	.07	.05
189 Henry Bacon	.07	.05
190 Scooter McCray	.07	.15
191 Derek Smith	.07	.15
192 Jerry King	.07	.05
193 Van Vance and Jock Sutherland	.07	.05
194 Bill Olsen	.07	.05

1991-92 Louisville Schedules

Sponsored by UL/Cellular One, this three-card set features schedule cards each measuring approximately 4 1/2" by 3 1/2". The fronts, which carry a Cellular One advertisement on the left portion and a full-bleed color action player photo on the right, can be folded in the middle. The inside pages carry the 1991-92 basketball schedule and identify the senior pictured. The cards are unnumbered and checklisted below in alphabetical order.

COMPLETE SET (3)	.60	1.50
1 Cornelius Holden	.20	.50
2 Everick Sullivan	.30	.75
3 Jason McClendon	.20	.50

1992-93 Louisville

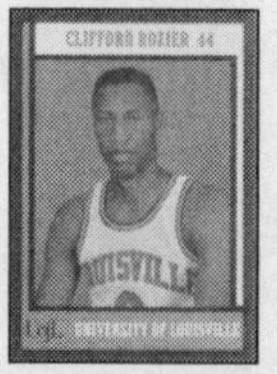

Produced by Motion Sports, this 31-card standard-size set features posed and action color player photos. The top and right edge of the picture is accented by an L-shaped white border design containing the player's name. The bottom and left edge is accented by a red L-shaped border design containing the university name. The entire card front is framed by a thin black border. The backs display career summary on a ghosted panel superimposed on a basketball arena scene. Some sets also included a value coupon that could be redeemed at the Cardinal athletic offices for one free set of basketball trading cards; a total of 50 sets were given away in this manner. Some uncut press sheets were also offered to the public for 20.00 plus 2.00 for shipping and handling.

COMPLETE SET (31)	6.00	15.00
1 Denny Crum CO	1.25	3.00
2 NCAA Championship	.20	.50
3 Brian Hopgood	.08	.25
4 Clifford Rozier	1.00	2.50
5 Keith LeGree	.20	.50
6 Tick Rogers	.20	.50
7 Jimmy King	.08	.25
8 Brian Kiser	.08	.25
9 Doug Calhoun	.08	.25
10 Mike Case	.08	.25
11 James Brewer	.08	.25
12 Dwayne Morton	.60	1.50
13 Greg Minor	1.00	2.50
14 Troy Smith	.08	.25
15 Robby Wine	.08	.25
16 Derwin Webb	.08	.25
17 Brian Hopgood	.08	.25
18 Keith LeGree	.20	.50
19 Mike Case	.08	.25
20 James Brewer	.08	.25
21 Dwayne Morton	.60	1.50
22 Greg Minor	1.00	2.50
23 Troy Smith	.08	.25
24 Derwin Webb	.08	.25
25 Seniors Mike Case Troy Smith Derwin Webb James Brewer	.08	.25
26 Cardinal Mascot	.08	.25
27 Denny Crum CO 500th Career Victory	1.00	2.50
28 Ad Card Motion Sports	.08	.25
DC1 Denny Crum Promo	.40	1.00
DC2 Denny Crum Comm 4-inch x 9-inch honoring his 500th win	1.00	2.50
NNO Title Card	.08	.25
NNO Back Card	.08	.25
NNO Card Directory	.08	.25

1992-93 Louisville Schedules

Sponsored by Storer Cable Communications, this five-card set features schedule cards each measuring approximately 4 1/2" by 3 1/2". The fronts, which carry a Storer Cable Communications advertisement on the left portion and a full-bleed color action player photo on the right, can be folded in the middle. The insides carry the 1992-93 basketball schedule and identify the senior pictured. The cards are unnumbered and checklisted below in alphabetical order.

COMPLETE SET (5)	.80	2.00
1 James (Boo) Brewer	.20	.50
2 Mike Case	.20	.50
3 Neil Knox	.20	.50
4 Troy Smith	.20	.50
5 Derwin Webb	.20	.50

1993-94 Louisville

This 20-card standard-size set was produced by Collect-A-Sport, College Division. The fronts feature color action player photos inside white borders. A red marbleized bar at the bottom of the picture carries the player's name, position, and team logo. On a white back, two red marbleized panels present biography and player profile respectively. The cards are unnumbered and checklisted below in alphabetical order.
COMPLETE SET (20) 6.00 15.00
1 Doug Calhoun .20 .50
2 Denny Crum CO 1.00 2.50
3 Jimmy King .20 .50
4 Brian Kiser .30 .75
5 Greg Minor .75 2.00
6 Dwayne Morton .40 1.00
7 Jason Osborne .20 .50
8 Tick Rogers .30 .75
9 Clifford Rozier .75 2.00
10 Matt Simons .20 .50
11 Alvin Sims .30 .75
12 Beau Zach Smith .20 .50
13 DeJuan Wheat 1.25 3.00
14 Robby Wine .20 .50
15 Larry Gay ACO .30 .75
Jerry Jones ACO
Scooter McCray ACO
16 Greg Minor .60 1.50
Doug Calhoun
Dwayne Morton
17 Greg Minor .60 1.50
Doug Calhoun
Dwayne Morton
18 Team Photo .30 .75
19 Freedom Hall .30 .75
20 Title Card .20 .50

1993-94 Louisville Schedules

Sponsored by BellSouth Mobility, this three-card set features schedule cards each measuring approximately 4 1/2" by 3 1/2". The fronts, which carry a BellSouth Mobility advertisement on the left portion and a full-bleed color action player photo on the right, can be folded in the middle. The inside pages carry the 1993-94 basketball schedule and identify the senior pictured. The cards are unnumbered and checklisted below in alphabetical order.
COMPLETE SET (3) .80 2.00
1 Jody Martin .20 .50
2 Greg Minor .40 1.00
3 Dwayne Morton .30 .75

1994-95 Louisville Schedules

Sponsored by BellSouth Mobility, this three-card set features schedule cards each measuring approximately 4 1/2" by 3 1/2". (The cards fold in the middle to measure 2 1/4" by 3 1/2".) The fronts feature full-bleed color action player photos. The inside pages carry the 1994-95 women's (1) or men's (2-3) basketball schedule and identify the player pictured. The backs carry a BellSouth Mobility advertisement. The cards are unnumbered and checklisted below in alphabetical order.
COMPLETE SET (3) .80 2.00
1 Kristin Mattox .20 .50
2 Jason Osborne .30 .75
3 DeJuan Wheat .40 1.00

2011 Lowe's Senior Class

This 11-card set was made available at the 2011 College All-Star Game.
COMPLETE SET (11) 20.00 50.00
1 Shane Battier TRIB 3.00 8.00
2 Devon Beitzel 3.00 8.00
3 Dodie Dunson 3.00 8.00
4 Jimmer Fredette 3.00 8.00
5 Matt Howard 3.00 8.00
6 Cameron Jones 3.00 8.00
7 Jon Leuer 3.00 8.00
8 David Lighty 3.00 8.00
9 E'Twaun Moore 3.00 8.00
10 Tyrel Reed 3.00 8.00
11 Kyle Singler 3.00 8.00

2012 Lowe's Senior Class

This 11-card set was made available at the 2012 College All-Star Game.
COMPLETE SET (11) 20.00 50.00
1 William Buford 3.00 8.00
2 Jimmer Fredette TRIB 3.00 8.00
3 Ashton Gibbs 3.00 8.00
4 Draymond Green 3.00 8.00
5 Mick Hedgepeth 3.00 8.00
6 Robbie Hummel 3.00 8.00
7 Quinn McDowell 3.00 8.00
8 Ronald Nored 3.00 8.00
9 Zach Novak 3.00 8.00
10 Zach Rosen 3.00 8.00
11 Tyler Zeller 3.00 8.00

1986-87 Maine

This 14-card set of Maine Black Bears is part of a "Kids and Kops" promotion, and one card was printed each Saturday in the Bangor Daily News. The cards measure approximately 2 1/2" by 4". The cards were to be collected from any participating plice officer. Once five cards had been collected (including card number 1), they could be turned in at a police station for a University of Maine ID card, which permitted free admission to selected university activities. When all 14 cards had been collected, they could be turned in at a police station to register for the Grand Prize drawing (bicycle) and to pick up a free "Kids and Kops" tee-shirt. The backs have tips in the form of an anti-drug or alcohol message and logos of Burger King, University of Maine and Pepsi across the bottom. With the exception of the rules card, the cards are numbered on the back.
COMPLETE SET (14) 6.00 15.00
3 Amadou Coco Barry BK .40 1.00
9 Jim Boylen BK .40 1.00
13 Matt Rossignol BK .40 1.00
NNO Matt Rossignol BK .40 1.00
Kids and Kops Rules

1987-88 Maine

This 14-card set of Maine Black Bears is part of a "Kids and Kops" promotion, and one card was printed each Saturday in the Bangor Daily News. The cards measure approximately 2 1/2" by 4". The cards were to be collected from any participating police officer. Once five cards had been collected (including card number 1), they could be turned in at a police station for a University of Maine ID card, which permitted free admission to selected university activities. When all 14 cards had been collected, they could be turned in at a police station to register for the Grand Prize drawing (bicycle) and to pick up a free "Kids and Kops" tee-shirt. The backs have tips in the form of an anti-drug or alcohol message and logos of Burger King, University of Maine, and Pepsi across the bottom. With the exception of the rules card, the cards are numbered on the back. Sports represented in this set include hockey (2), basketball (3, 9, 13), tennis (4), baseball (5), swimming (6), soccer (7), track (8), football (10), field hockey (11), and softball (12).
COMPLETE SET (14) 6.00 15.00
1 Bananas (Mascot) and 2.00 5.00
K.C. Jones CO BK
3 Matt Rossignol BK .40 1.00
9 Elizabeth(Liz) Coffin BK .40 1.00
13 Amadou Coco Barry BK .40 1.00
NNO Matt Rossignol BK .40 1.00
Kids and Kops Rules

1982-83 Marquette

This 16-card set measures the standard card size, 2 1/2" by 3 1/2", and was issued in conjunction with Lite Beer. The front of the card features a black and white action photo inside an "arrowhead" against a pale yellow background, surrounded by the player's name, height, and position, with the team name ("Warriors") emblazoned across the bottom. The back has biographical and statistical information. The set also features the first card of NBA veteran Glenn "Doc" Rivers.
COMPLETE SET (16) 6.00 15.00
1 Ric Cobb ACO .50 1.25
2 Dwayne(DJ) Johnson .30 .75
3 Mandy Johnson .30 .75
4 Vic Lazzaretti .30 .75
5 Rick Majerus ACO 3.00 8.00
6 Marc Marotta .30 .75
7 Lloyd Moore .30 .75
8 Paul Newman .30 .75
9 Tom Pipines .30 .75
10 Hank Raymonds CO .75 2.00
11 Terry Reason .30 .75
12 Doc Rivers 4.00 10.00
13 Terrell Schlundt .50 1.25
14 Don Smolinski .30 .75
15 Kerry Trotter .30 .75
xx Title Card .50 1.25

1991-92 Marquette

Sponsored by Cyganiak Planning Inc., this 17-card set measures the standard size. The cards show signs of perforation on their sides and feature color action player photos on their fronts. The photo is framed by a thin yellow line and set on a white card face. The player's name and jersey number appear in black print at the top. His height and classification appear below the picture. An emblem in the lower left corner commemorates the 75th year of Marquette basketball. The backs carry biographical information, high school or college highlights, and statistics. The cards are unnumbered and checklisted below in alphabetical order. This set features the first card of William Gates, one of two players featured in the critically acclaimed 1995 documentary film Hoop Dreams.
COMPLETE SET (17) 6.00 15.00
1 Craig Aamot .40 1.00
2 Ron Curry .40 1.00
3 William Gates 1.50 4.00
star of the movie Hoop Dreams
4 Damon Key .40 1.00
5 Robb Logterman .40 1.00
6 Amal McCaskill .75 2.00
7 Jim McIlvaine 1.25 3.00
8 Tony Miller .20 .50
9 Kevin O'Neill CO .75 2.00
10 Ben Peavy .20 .50
11 Shannon Smith .20 .50
12 Jay Zulauf .40 1.00
13 Team Photo .60 1.50
14 Ron Curry .60 1.50
Jim McIlvaine
Damon Key
15 Building on a Great .40 1.00
Tradition(Team photo at
construction site)
16 Bradley Center .20 .50
17 Sponsor Card .20 .50

1992-93 Marquette

This 17-card set was issued on 4 perforated strips. When the cards are separated, they measure the standard size. This set was sponsored by Cyganiak Planning Inc. The fronts feature color action player photos on a white background. The player's name is above the photo and the team and sponsor logos along with the player's position and jersey number are below. The backs carry the player's name, biographical information and career highlights in blue print on a white background. The cards are unnumbered and checklisted below in alphabetical order. Among the players in the set are NBA center Jim McIlvaine and William Gates, star of the acclaimed documentary Hoop Dreams.
COMPLETE SET (17) 5.00 12.00
1 Craig Aamot .40 1.00
2 Ron Curry .40 1.00
3 Roney Eford .40 1.00
4 William Gates 1.00 2.50
5 Damon Key .40 1.00
6 Robb Logterman .40 1.00
7 Amal McCaskill .60 1.50
8 Jim McIlvaine 1.00 2.50
9 Tony Miller .20 .50
10 Kevin O'Neill CO .75 2.00
11 Ben Peavy .20 .50
12 Adam Schabes .20 .50
13 Shannon Smith .20 .50
14 Dwaine Streater .20 .50
15 Jay Zulauf .40 1.00
16 Team Photo .40 1.00
Roster
17 Sponsor Card .20 .50

1994-95 Marquette

Sponsored by Cyganiak Planning Inc., this 17-card set was issued on 4 perforated strips. When the cards are separated, they measure the standard size. The fronts feature color action player photos on a gold background. The player's name is above the photo and the team and sponsor logos are below. The backs carry the player's name, jersey number, biographical information and career highlights in blue print on a white background. The cards are unnumbered and checklisted below in alphabetical order. William Gates, featured in the movie Hoop Dreams, is included in this set.
COMPLETE SET (17) 5.00 12.00
1 Faisal Abraham .40 1.00
2 Chris Crawford .40 1.00
3 Mike Deane CO .30 .75
4 Roney Eford .40 1.00
5 William Gates .75 2.00
6 Aaron Hutchins .75 2.00
7 Abel Joseph .30 .75
8 Shane Littles .30 .75
9 Zack McCall .30 .75
10 Amal McCaskill .75 2.00
11 Tony Miller .30 .75
12 Anthony Pieper .40 1.00
13 Richard Shaw .30 .75
14 Dwaine Streater .30 .75
15 1969-70 Team Photo .40 1.00
1970 NIT Champions
16 Team Photo .40 1.00
1994-95 Roster
17 Sponsor Card .20 .50

1995-96 Marquette

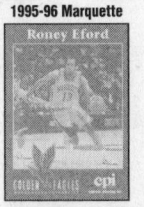

Sponsored by Cyganiak Planning Inc., this 20-card set was issued on 4 perforated strips. When the cards are separated, they measure the standard size. The fronts feature color action player photos on a blue background. The player's name is above the photo and the team and sponsor logos are below. The backs carry the player's name, jersey number, biographical information and career highlights in blue print on a white background. The cards are unnumbered and checklisted below in alphabetical order.
COMPLETE SET (20) 5.00 12.00
1 Faisal Abraham .30 .75
2 Mike Bargen .30 .75
3 Chris Crawford .30 .75
4 Mike Deane CO .40 1.00
5 Roney Eford .40 1.00
6 Mark Harris .30 .75
7 Aaron Hutchins .75 2.00
8 Abel Joseph .30 .75
9 Jarrod Lovette .30 .75
10 Zack McCall .30 .75
11 Amal McCaskill .75 2.00
12 Anthony Pieper .40 1.00
13 John Polonowski .30 .75
14 Bob Riley .30 .75
15 Dwaine Streater .30 .75
16 Team Photo .40 1.00
1995-96 Roster
17 Sponsor Card .20 .50
18 Sponsor Card .20 .50
19 Sponsor Card .20 .50
20 Sponsor Card .20 .50

2009-10 Marquette

COMPLETE SET (4) 4.00 10.00
1 Sheet 1 1.50 4.00
David Cubillan
Robert Frozena
Darius Johnson-Odom
Hank Raymonds
Spirit Card
2 Sheet 2 1.50 4.00
Buzz Williams
Dwight Buycks
Erik Williams
Al McGuire
Sixth Man
3 Sheet 3 2.00 5.00
Lazar Hayward
Jimmy Butler
Chris Otule
Youssoupha Mbao
Team Card
4 Sheet 4 1.50 4.00
Maurice Acker
Joseph Fulce
Junior Cadougan
Marquette Seniors
Pep Band

2011-12 Marquette

COMPLETE SET (4) 4.00 10.00
1 Sheet 1 1.50 4.00
Jae Crowder
Jamil Wilson
Derrick Wilson
Tony Benford
Pep Band
2 Sheet 2 1.50 4.00
Darius Johnson-Odom
Davante Gardner
Jake Thomas
Buzz Williams
Team Card
3 Sheet 3 1.50 4.00
Chris Otule
Jamail Jones
Todd Mayo
Scott Monarch
Sixth Man
4 Sheet 4 1.50 4.00
Junior Cadougan
Vander Blue
Juan Anderson
Aki Collins
Spirit Card

1984 Marshall Playing Cards

Produced by Triangle Productions, Inc., this All-Time Greats boxed-set of playing cards is reported to have been issued in conjunction with old-timer games. The set originally sold for 2.00 and could be purchased at the Marshall University bookstore. The cards measure approximately 2 1/4" by 3 1/2" and have rounded corners. The fronts feature black-and-white posed or action shots, with coach or player identification below the picture. The backs are green on white and display the Marshall University logo and the phrase All Time Greats.-- The cards are checklisted in playing card order by suits and numbers are assigned to Aces (1), Jacks (11), Queens (12), and Kings (13). The jokers are unnumbered and listed at the end.
COMP. FACT SET (54) 12.00 30.00
C1 Stewart Way CO .20 .50
C2 Jim Davidson .20 .50
C3 Tom Langfitt .20 .50
C4 Bill Hall .20 .50
C5 Bill Toothman .20 .50
C6 Gene James .20 .50
C7 Bob Koontz .20 .50
C8 Andy Tonkovich .20 .50
C9 Danny D'Antoni .40 1.00
C10 Paul Underwood .20 .50
C11 Walt Walowac .20 .50
C12 Cebe Price .20 .50
C13 John Milhoan .20 .50
D1 Ellis Johnson CO .20 .50
D2 Walt Walowac .20 .50
D3 George Stone .30 .75
D4 Charlie Slack .20 .50
D5 Mike D'Antoni 2.00 5.00
D6 Jules Rivlin .20 .50
D7 Danny D'Antoni .40 1.00
D8 Greg White .20 .50
D9 Ken Labanowski .20 .50
D10 Bob Burgess .20 .50
D11 Bob Allen .20 .50
D12 Leo Byrd .20 .50
D13 Hal Greer 2.00 5.00
H1 Stu Aberden CO .20 .50
H2 Stu Aberden CO .20 .50
(Same picture as H1)
H3 Bob Daniels CO .20 .50
H4 Bunny Gibson .30 .75
H5 Cebe Price .20 .50
H6 Carl Tacy CO .30 .75
H7 Stewart Way CO .20 .50
H8 Ellis Johnson CO .20 .50
H9 Cam Henderson CO .60 1.50
H10 Mike D'Antoni 2.00 5.00
H11 Bob Daniels CO .20 .50
H12 Jules Rivlin .20 .50
H13 Russell Lee .40 1.00
S1 Cam Henderson CO .60 1.50
S2 Ken Labanowski .20 .50
S3 Greg White .20 .50
S4 Randy Noll .20 .50
S5 Bob Redd .20 .50
S6 George Stone .30 .75
S7 Bunny Gibson .30 .75
S8 Bob Wright .20 .50
S9 Charlie Slack .20 .50
S10 Russell Lee .40 1.00
S11 Carl Tacy CO .30 .75
S12 Leo Byrd .20 .50
S13 Hal Greer 2.00 5.00
NNO Joker .20 .50
Marshall University
NNO Joker .20 .50
Triangle Productions

1988 Marshall Women

Originally a 20-card set sponsored by Ashland Oil, these standard-size cards were made available by Marshall University for a $20 donation to the Lady Herd basketball program. Two seasons later, a twenty-first card was issued, that of Lady Herd coach Judy Southard. The fronts display a mix of black-and-white or color action photos. The pictures are full-bleed and accented by a white picture frame. The Lady Herd logo and the year are printed on each front. On a white background in green print, the backs present a player profile or summary of the event commemorated. The cards are unnumbered and checklisted below in chronological order. The set includes a card of professional lady golfer Tammie Green, who was on the 1994 U.S. Solheim Cup team.
COMPLETE SET (21) 5.00 12.00
1 1907 Team Picture .40 1.00
2 Donna Lawson CO .40 1.00
Judy Southard CO
3 Beverly Duckwyler .20 .50
4 1971-72 Team .20 .50
5 Jody Lambert .20 .50
6 Brenda Dennis .20 .50
7 Agnes Wheeler .20 .50
8 Gullickson Hall Action .20 .50
9 Mary Lopez .20 .50
10 Stephanie Austin .40 1.00
Agnes Wheeler
Mary Lopez
Kim Williams
Kathy Baker
Donna Lawson CO
11 Tammie Green 1.25 3.00
12 Saundra Fullen .40 1.00
Thea Garland
Becky Williamson
Paula Hatten
Deanna Carter
13 Lisa Prunner .20 .50
14 Barb McConnell .20 .50
15 Tywands Abercrombie .40 1.00
Karla May
Karen Pelphrey
Debbie Van Liew
16 Karen Pelphrey .20 .50
17 Tammy Wiggins .20 .50
18 Chris Laslo .20 .50
19 The Challenge .20 .50
20 Kim Lewis .20 .50
21 Judy Southard CO .40 1.00

1988-89 Maryland

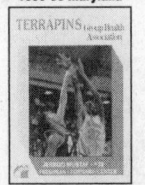

This set consists of 12 cards, measuring the standard card size 2 1/2" by 3 1/2". The company name of the sponsor, Group Health Association, appears in the right corner on the front of the card. The action color photo on the front is bordered on three sides by Maryland's colors (red and yellow), with the player's name, uniform number, classification, and position listed below the photo. The Terrapin logo in the lower left hand corner completes the front of the card. The back includes biographical information and a basketball tip. For convenience the cards are ordered and numbered below in alphabetical order. The set features first cards of future NBA players Jerrod Mustaf and Walt Williams.
COMPLETE SET (12) 6.00 15.00
1 Vincent Broadnax .30 .75
2 Dave Dickerson .30 .75
3 John Johnson SP 1.25 3.00
4 Matt Kaluzienski .30 .75
5 Mitch Kasoff .30 .75
6 Cedric Lewis .40 1.00
7 Jesse Martin .30 .75
8 Tony Massenburg 2.00 5.00
9 Jerrod Mustaf .75 2.00
10 Greg Nared SP 1.25 3.00
11 Bob Wade CO .30 .75
12 Walt Williams 3.00 8.00

1989 McNeese State

This 16-card standard-size set was sponsored by the Behavioral Health Unit of Lake Charles Memorial Hospital, and the sponsor's logo appears at the bottom of both sides of the card. This set was produced by McDag Productions. The front features a color posed player photo, with the McNeese logo and player information in the upper corners. The back presents biographical information and "Tips from The Cowboys," which consist of mental health tips. Sports represented in this set include basketball (1-6, 9-12), softball (7), golf (8), and baseball (13-15). Card number 13 Steve Boulet was missing from a number of sets and is believed to be somewhat tougher to find than other cards in the set.
COMPLETE SET (16) 4.00 10.00
1 Kevin Williams BK .30 .75
2 Terry Griggley BK .20 .50
3 Tab Harris BK .20 .50
4 Chandra Davis BK .40 1.00
5 Tom McGrath BK .20 .50
6 Angie Perry BK .40 1.00
9 Michael Cutright BK .40 1.00
10 Anthony Pullard BK .60 1.50
11 Mark Thompson BK .20 .50
12 Kim Turner BK .20 .50

1992-93 Memphis State

This 15-card standard-size set features color action player photos bordered on the left or right edge by a blue stripe containing the words "Memphis State." The player's name appears in blue lettering on a white stripe at the bottom. The horizontal backs feature close-up player pictures with shadow box borders. The white background is printed with a profile of the player. The school logo and biographical information appear at the top. Reportedly less than 10,000 sets were produced.
COMPLETE SET (15) 5.00 12.00
1 Larry Finch CO .40 1.00
2 Kelvin Allen .20 .50
3 Anthony Douglas .20 .50
4 Anfernee Hardaway 3.00 8.00
5 Chris Haynes .20 .50
6 Leon Mitchell .20 .50
7 Marcus Nolan .20 .50
8 Billy Smith .20 .50
9 David Vaughn .75 2.00
10 Sidney Coles .20 .50
11 Jerrell Horne .20 .50
12 Rodney Newsom .40 1.00
13 Team Photo .75 2.00
14 The Pyramid .20 .50
15 Tom II (Mascot) .20 .50

1993 Memphis Sheriff Anfernee Hardaway

This one standard-size card was issued by the Millington County Police Departement and features Memphis State player Anfernee "Penny" Hardaway. The front features Hardaway in a "keep the dream" uniform and he is identified on the left. The back has vital statistics and a safety tip.
1 Anfernee Hardaway 3.00 8.00

1993-94 Memphis State

This 16-card standard-size set (2 1/2 by 3 1/2") has fronts composed of color action and posed player photos inset in gray borders. Below the photo are the player's name and position with the team logo to the left. The back has a color player head shot in the upper left. The player's number is in the upper right while the team logo, player's name and bio are centered at the top. Career highlights follow below. The cards are unnumbered and checklisted below in alphabetical order.
COMPLETE SET (16) 4.00 10.00
1 Larry Finch CO .40 1.00
2 David Vaughn .75 2.00
3 Jerrell Horne .20 .50
4 Leon Mitchell .20 .50
5 Sidney Coles .20 .50
6 Rob Forrest .20 .50
7 Jason Fox .20 .50
8 Rodney Newsom .40 1.00
9 Marcus Nolan .20 .50
10 Chris Garner .60 1.50
11 Deuce Ford .20 .50
12 Cedric Henderson .60 1.50
13 Johnny Miller .20 .50
14 Michael Simmons .20 .50
15 Jason Smith .20 .50
16 Justin Wimmer .20 .50

1994-95 Memphis State

Produced by The 7th Inning, this 17-card standard-size set features the 1994-95 University of Memphis men's basketball team (formerly Memphis State). The fronts show full-bleed color action photos. The player's name and number are printed vertically in blue on a white bar along the left edge. The bar intersects the school logo at the lower left corner. The horizontal backs carry player profile on the left and a color closeup photo on the right. The cards are unnumbered and checklisted below in alphabetical order. David Vaughn, drafted by the NBA in the first round, is included in this set.
COMPLETE SET (16) 5.00 12.00
1 Larry Finch CO .30 .75
2 Deuce Ford .20 .50
3 Rob Forrest .20 .50
4 Jason Fox .20 .50
5 Chris Garner .40 1.00
6 Cedric Henderson .40 1.00
7 Mingo Johnson .30 .75
8 Leon Mitchell .20 .50
9 Rodney Newsom .30 .75
10 Marcus Nolan .20 .50
11 Jason Smith .20 .50
12 David Vaughn .60 1.50
13 Michael Wilson .30 .75
14 Justin Wimmer .20 .50
15 Lorenzen Wright 2.50 6.00
16 Team Photo .30 .75

1993-94 Miami

Given away in four-card perforated strips at University of Miami games, these 20 cards measure approximately 2 1/2" by 3 5/8". The fronts feature color player action shots with black and green borders highlighted by orange basketballs. The player's name appears in orange lettering above the photo; his position and jersey number appear below the photo. The plain white backs carry the player's name, uniform number, height, weight, and hometown at the top, followed below by a bilingual description of his style of play. The Bumble Bee sponsor logo at the bottom rounds out the card. The cards are unnumbered and checklisted below in alphabetical order.
COMPLETE SET (20) 6.00 15.00
1 Will Davis .40 1.00
2 Adam Dusewicz .40 1.00
Chris Parker
Anthony Rosa
3 Steven Edwards .60 1.50
4 Alex Fraser .40 1.00
5 Steve Frazier .60 1.50
6 Michael Gardner .40 1.00
7 Leonard Hamilton CO .75 2.00
8 Tshombe High .40 1.00
9 Jamal Johnson .40 1.00
10 Pat Lawrence .40 1.00
11 Torey McCormick .40 1.00
12 Lorenzo Pearson .40 1.00
13 Constantin Popa .60 1.50
14 Steve Rich .60 1.50
15 Brad Timpf .40 1.00
16 Thad Fitzpatrick ACO .40 1.00
Scott Howard ACO
Mike Jaskulski ACO
17 Free Ticket Offer .20 .50
18 Free Ticket Offer .20 .50
19 Free Ticket Offer .20 .50
20 Checklist .20 .50

1994-95 Miami

Sponsored by Bumble Bee, this 20-card, unperforated sheet measures 10 1/2" by 18" and consists of five rows of four cards each. The first three cards in each row are player cards, while the fourth card is a "Buy One, Get One Free" ticket offer for a particular game. One row (or strip) of cards was given away at five different University of Miami games. On a black and orange card face, the fronts feature color action player shots with the player's name and uniform number in orange and green stencil lettering. The backs carry biography, player profile (in English and Spanish), and different answers to the question "What advice would you give young basketball players wanting to play at the collegiate level?" The cards are unnumbered and checklisted below in alphabetical order.
COMPLETE SET (20) 3.00 8.00
1 Chuck Barker .20 .50
David Isles
Jaime Waggoner
2 Will Davis .20 .50
3 Mitchell Dunn .20 .50
4 Steven Edwards .30 .75
5 Alex Fraser .20 .50
6 Steve Frazier .30 .75
7 Leonard Hamilton CO .60 1.50
8 Scott Howard ACO .08 .25
Mike Jaskulski ACO
Silas McKinnie ACO
9 Torey McCormick .20 .50
10 Kevin Norris .20 .50
11 Lorenzo Pearson .30 .75
12 Constantin Popa .30 .75
13 Steve Rich .30 .75
14 Anthony Rosa .20 .50
15 Brad Timpf .20 .50
16 Team Photo .30 .75
17 Free Ticket Offer CL .08 .25
18 Free Ticket Offer .08 .25
19 Free Ticket Offer .08 .25
20 Free Ticket Offer .08 .25

1997 Miami (OH) Cradle of Coaches

This set was produced by American Marketing Associates and features coaching greats from the University of Miami in Ohio. Football is the focus of the set although it also contains a few coaches from other sports as noted below. The cards are

unnumbered and checklisted below in alphabetical order.
COMPLETE SET (19) 8.00 20.00
7 Wayne Embry BK .80 2.00
11 Darrell Hedric BK .40 1.00
17 Richard Shrider BK .40 1.00

1988-89 Michigan

This 16-card standard-size set was sponsored by Nike and distributed at Michigan Wolverine games during the 1988-89 season. The front features a color action photo, with a yellow border on the left side and purple borders on the right and below. The sponsor logo appears in the upper right corner, and player information is given in the bottom border. The back has biographical information and an anti-drug tip. The cards are unnumbered and are checklisted below in alphabetical order. The set features first cards of NBA players Sean Higgins, Terry Mills, Glen Rice, Rumeal Robinson, and Loy Vaught.
COMPLETE SET (16) 20.00 50.00
1 Demetrius Calip .75 2.00
2 Bill Frieder CO 1.50 4.00
3 Mike Griffin .40 1.00
4 Sean Higgins 1.50 4.00
5 Mark Hughes .40 1.00
6 Marc Koenig .40 1.00
7 Terry Mills 3.00 8.00
8 J.P. Oosterbaan .40 1.00
9 Rob Pelinka 1.50 4.00
10 Glen Rice 10.00 25.00
11 Eric Riley 1.50 4.00
12 Rumeal Robinson 3.00 7.00
13 Chris Seter .40 1.00
14 Kirk Taylor .40 1.00
15 Loy Vaught 4.00 10.00
16 James Voskuil 1.25 3.00

1989 Michigan

This 17-card set measures approximately 2 3/8" by 4" and is numbered on the back. The set features members of the 1989 Michigan Wolverines NCAA Championship basketball team. The front features a color photo, and the school and team name are printed in the school's colors (purple and yellow) on the top of the card. Below the photo appears the team logo (lower left hand corner) and the player's name. The back has biographical information (black lettering on white card stock). Future NBA players Sean Higgins, Terry Mills, Glen Rice, Rumeal Robinson, and Loy Vaught are featured in this set.
COMPLETE SET (17) 10.00 25.00
1 Steve Fisher CO 1.00 2.50
2 Brian Dutcher .30 .75
3 Kirk Taylor .30 .75
4 Chris Seter .30 .75
5 Glen Rice 3.00 8.00
6 Rob Pelinka 1.00 2.50
7 Rumeal Robinson 1.25 3.00
8 Terry Mills 1.25 3.00
9 Demetrius Calip .60 1.50
10 James Voskuil .60 1.50
11 Loy Vaught 1.50 4.00
12 J.P. Oosterbaan .30 .75
13 Sean Higgins .75 2.00
14 Marc Koenig .30 .75
15 Mark Hughes .30 .75
16 Eric Riley .75 2.00
17 Mike Griffin .30 .75

1991 Michigan

This 56-card multi-sport standard-size set was issued by College Classics. The fronts feature a mix of color or black and white player photos. This set features a card of Gerald Ford, center for the Wolverine football squad from 1932-34. Ford autographed 200 of his cards, one of which was to be included in each of the 200 cases of 50 sets. A letter of authenticity on Gerald Ford stationery accompanies each Ford autographed card. No price has been established for the Ford signed card. The cards are unnumbered and we have checklisted them below according to alphabetical order.
COMPLETE SET (56) 6.00 15.00
5 Marty Bodnar BK .02 .10
7 M.C. Burton BK .02 .10
15 Diane Dietz BK .02 .10
27 Phil Hubbard BK .30 .75
36 Tim McCormick BK .08 .25
43 Richard Rellford BK .02 .10
45 Cazzie Russell BK .30 .75
52 Rudy Tomjanovich BK .60 1.50

1992-93 Michigan

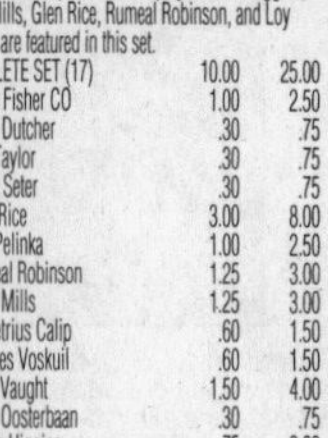

This 15-card set measures the standard size (2 1/2" by 3 1/2") and features color action player photos bordered on one side by a navy blue stripe containing the word "Michigan." The cards were produced by College Classics and were originally available from the M Den at Yost and Crisler Arenas for around 7.00. The player's name appears in yellow print on a white bar at the bottom. The horizontal backs are white and display a shadow bordered close-up picture, the player's name, and a player profile. The cards are numbered on the back. This set contains the cards of Michigan's "Fab Five", Juwan Howard, Ray Jackson, Jimmy King, Jalen Rose, and Chris Webber.
COMPLETE SET (15) 5.00 12.00
1 Steve Fisher CO .40 1.00
2 Jason Bossard .20 .50
3 Juwan Howard 1.25 3.00
4 Eric Riley .30 .75
5 Jalen Rose 1.50 4.00
6 Michael Talley .30 .75
7 James Voskuil .30 .75
8 Chris Webber 2.50 6.00
9 Ray Jackson .40 1.00
10 Jimmy King .40 1.00
11 Rob Pelinka .40 1.00
12 Leon Derricks .20 .50
13 Dugan Fife .30 .75
14 Checklist .20 .50
15 Sean Dobbins .20 .50

1990-91 Michigan State Collegiate Collection 20

This 20-card standard-size set was produced by Collegiate Collection and features the 1990-91 Michigan State Spartan basketball team. The fronts display color action player photos, bordered in white and green, and with the corners of the pictures cut off. In green print on a white background, the backs have biography, statistics, and player profile. This set features an early card of NBA guard Steve Smith.
COMPLETE SET (20) 8.00 20.00
1 Jud Heathcote CO 2.00 5.00
2 Matt Hofkamp .30 .75
3 Parish Hickman .60 1.50
4 Matt Steigenga .60 1.50
5 Dwayne Stephens .30 .75
6 Jon Zulauf .30 .75
7 Shawn Respert 2.00 5.00
8 Jeff Casler .30 .75
9 Steve Smith 5.00 12.00
10 Andy Penick .30 .75
11 Mark Montgomery .60 1.50
12 Kris Weshinskey .30 .75
13 Jack Breslin Center .30 .75
14 Spartan Captains 2.00 5.00
Steve Smith
Matt Steigenga
15 Brian Gregory CO .30 .75
16 Jim Boylen CO .30 .75
17 Stan Joplin CO .40 1.00
18 Tom Izzo CO 3.00 8.00
19 Mike Peplowski 1.00 2.50
20 Team Photo 1.00 2.50

1990-91 Michigan State Collegiate Collection Promos

This ten-card standard size set features some of the great athletes from Michigan State History. Most of the cards in the set feature an action photograph on the front of the card along with either statistical or biographical information on the back of the card. Since this set involves more than one sport we have put a two-letter abbreviation to indicate the sport played.
COMPLETE SET (10) 1.50 4.00
4 Magic Johnson BK 1.00 2.50
9 Gregory Kelser BK .20 .50
10 Kip Miller HK .10 .30

1990-91 Michigan State Collegiate Collection 200

This 200-card standard-size set was produced by Collegiate Collection. The fronts feature black and white shots for earlier players or color shots for later players, with borders in the team's colors white and green. Since most cards are football, we've noted below which cards feature other sports. Although some players were famous in others sports, like Kirk Gibson and Steve Garvey, they do have football cards in this set.
COMPLETE SET (200) 6.00 15.00
46 Jerry West .05 .15
62 Amo Bessone CO BK .05 .15
101 Michael Robinson BK .05 .15
102 Jack Quiggle BK .05 .15
103 Robert Anderegg BK .05 .15
112 Gregory Kelser BK .07 .20
119 Kevin Willis BK .08 .25
123 Jay Vincent BK .05 .15
128 Johnny Green BK .08 .25
131 Magic Johnson BK .40 1.00
132 Gregory Kelser BK .07 .20
133 Magic Johnson BK .40 1.00
140 Scott Skiles BK .08 .25
148 Sam Vincent BK .05 .15
152 Scott Skiles BK .08 .25
159 Jud Heathcote CO BK .08 .25
161 Pete Newell CO BK .08 .25
163 Kevin Willis BK .08 .25
170 Ralph Simpson BK .07 .20
171 Terry Furlow BK .05 .15
178 Jud Heathcote CO BK .08 .25
179 Kevin Willis BK .08 .25
182 Magic Johnson BK .40 1.00
186 Magic Johnson BK .40 1.00
189 Magic Johnson BK .40 1.00
191 Gus Ganakas .05 .15
192 Jay Vincent BK .05 .15
194 Magic Johnson BK .40 1.00
198 Sam Vincent BK .05 .15
199 Terry Donnelly BK .05 .15

1998-99 Michigan State Legends

This set, features leading players in Michigan State history. The full bleed cards feature a player's photo on one side with a solid border in Michigan State's colors on the other side. The backs feature player information about the career at Michigan State. Since these cards are unnumbered, we have sequenced them in alphabetical order.
COMPLETE SET (36) 6.00 15.00
1 Bob Anderegg .30 .75
2 Chet Aubuchon .30 .75
3 Rickey Ayala .30 .75
4 Bob Chapman .30 .75
5 Bill Curtis .30 .75
6 Al Ferrari .30 .75
7 Terry Furlow .40 1.00
8 Pete Gent .40 1.00
9 Johnny Green .40 1.00
10 Lindsay Hairston .30 .75
11 Tom Izzo CO 1.25 3.00
12 Darryl Johnson .30 .75
13 Magic Johnson 3.00 8.00
14 Gregory Kelser .75 2.00
15 Bill Kilgore .30 .75
16 Lee Lafayette .30 .75
17 Julius McCoy .30 .75
18 Mark Montgomery .30 .75
19 Lance Olson .30 .75
20 Mike Peplowski .30 .75
21 Jack Quiggle .30 .75
22 Shawn Respert .60 1.50
23 Mike Robinson .30 .75
24 Steve Smith 1.00 2.50
25 Ralph Simpson .40 1.00
26 Scott Skiles .75 2.00
27 Eric Snow .75 2.00
28 Matt Steigenga .30 .75
29 Jay Vincent .40 1.00
30 Sam Vincent .60 1.50
31 Horace Walker .30 .75
32 Stan Washington .30 .75
33 Title Card .30 .75
34 Team CL .30 .75
35 Breslin Center .30 .75
36 Jenison Field House .30 .75

2003 Michigan State TK Legacy

COMPLETE SET (27) 12.00 30.00
B1 Greg Kelser BK .50 1.25
B2 Brad Van Pelt BK .50 1.25
B3 Mike Brkovich BK .40 1.00
B4 Ron Charles BK .50 1.25
B5 Gary Ganakas BK .40 1.00
BC1 Jud Heathcote CO BK .50 1.25
BC2 Gus Ganakas CO BK .40 1.00

2003 Michigan State TK Legacy All-Americans

COMPLETE SET (6) 7.50 15.00
STATED ODDS 1:14
BAA1 Greg Kelser BK .75 2.00

2003 Michigan State TK Legacy Autographs

OVERALL AUTO STATED ODDS 1:1
SB1 Greg Kelser BK 6.00 15.00
SB2 Mike Brkovich BK 6.00 15.00
SB3 Ron Charles BK 6.00 15.00
SB4 Gary Ganakaas BK 6.00 15.00
SB5 Jud Heathcote BK 6.00 15.00
SB6 Gus Ganakas BK 6.00 15.00
SB7 Brad Van Pelt BK 6.00 15.00

2003 Michigan State TK Legacy Historical Links Autographs

DOUBLE AUTO STATED ODDS 1:31
TRIPLE AUTO STATED ODDS 1:100
HL3 Jud Heathcote 20.00 40.00
Greg Kelser BK/200

2003 Michigan State TK Legacy National Champions Autographs

STATED ODDS 1:5
1979A Greg Kelser BK 7.50 15.00
1979B Jud Heathcote BK 7.50 15.00
1979C Mike Brkovich BK 7.50 15.00
1979D Ron Charles BK 7.50 15.00

2003 Michigan State TK Legacy Retired Numbers

STATED ODDS 1:38
STATED PRINT RUN 300 SER.#'d SETS
BRN1 Greg Kelser BK 1.50 4.00

1991-92 Minnesota

Sponsored by Hardee's restaurants, this 17-card standard-size set features posed and action color player photos on an orange-yellow card face. The picture is offset, and the player's name runs down the left edge of the card. The sponsor logo appears at the bottom. The backs carry biographical information and player profile within an orange-yellow outlined box. The cards are unnumbered and checklisted below in alphabetical order.
COMPLETE SET (17) 6.00 15.00
1 Randy Carter .30 .75
2 Chris Clark .20 .50
3 David Grim .30 .75
4 Clem Haskins CO .60 1.50
5 Dana Jackson .20 .50
6 Chad Kolander .30 .75
7 Jon Laster .20 .50
8 Voshon Lenard 3.00 8.00
9 Bob Martin .75 2.00
10 Arriel McDonald .60 1.50
11 Josh Nichols .20 .50
12 Ernest Nzigamasabo .20 .50
13 Townsend Orr .30 .75
14 Robert Roe .20 .50
15 Nate Tubbs .20 .50
16 Jayson Walton .30 .75
17 Ryan Wolf .20 .50

1992-93 Minnesota

Sponsored by the University of Minnesota's Department of Men's Intercollegiate Athletics, this 17-card set measures the standard size and features color action player photos. A gray border stripe at the top contains the words "University of Minnesota" while a bright yellow bar near the bottom is printed in red with the player's name. The horizontal backs display a small, close-up player picture with a yellow shadow border. The card face is white and includes player profile information. The player's name appears at the top right in burgundy lettering.
COMPLETE SET (17) 4.00 10.00
1 Clem Haskins CO .60 1.50
2 Milton Barnes ACO .20 .50
Dan Kosmoski ACO
Dave Thorson ACO
3 Kevin Baker .20 .50
4 Randy Carter .30 .75
5 David Grim .30 .75
6 Dana Jackson .20 .50
7 Chad Kolander .30 .75
8 Voshon Lenard 1.50 4.00
9 Arriel McDonald .30 .75
10 Ernest Nzigamasabo .20 .50
11 Townsend Orr .30 .75
12 Robert Roe .20 .50
13 Nate Tubbs .20 .50
14 Jayson Walton .30 .75
15 David Washington .20 .50
16 Trevor Winter .20 .50
17 Ryan Wolf .20 .50

1993-94 Minnesota

The 1993-94 University of Minnesota set consists of 18 standard-size cards. The set was produced by Phipps Sports Marketing. The team color-bordered fronts feature a mix of posed and action color photos. Along the wider left border are the words "Golden Gophers" in simulated gold lettering. The player's name appears in one corner and the school logo is in another. The horizontal backs are also bordered in team colors and carry a black-and-white head shot at the upper left. The player's biography, profile, and statistics are printed on a ghosted cartoon of the team mascot. The cards are unnumbered and checklisted below in alphabetical order. There have been reports that the Lenard card may have been reprinted.
COMPLETE SET (18) 4.00 10.00
1 Kevin Baker .20 .50
2 Randy Carter .30 .75
3 Hosea Crittenden .20 .50
4 David Grim .30 .75
5 Clem Haskins CO .60 1.50
6 Chad Kolander .30 .75
7 Voshon Lenard 1.25 3.00
8 Arriel McDonald .30 .75
9 Ernest Nzigamasabo .20 .50
10 Townsend Orr .30 .75
11 John Thomas .75 2.00
12 Jayson Walton .30 .75
13 David Washington .20 .50
14 Sean Whitlock .20 .50
15 Trevor Winter .20 .50
16 Ryan Wolf .20 .50
17 1993 NIT Champions .30 .75
Milton Barnes ACO
Dan Kosmoski ACO
Dave Thorson ACO
18 Title Card .20 .50

1994-95 Minnesota

This 17-card set of the University of Minnesota Basketball Team measures the standard size and is sponsored by Hardee's. The fronts feature action color photos with red variegated borders. The team name, player's name, position, and team logo are printed in the wider left border. The backs carry biography, profile, and statistics. The cards are unnumbered and checklisted below in alphabetical order.
COMPLETE SET (17) 3.00 8.00
1 Hosea Crittenden .20 .50
2 David Grim .30 .75
3 Eric Harris .20 .50
4 Clem Haskins CO .60 1.50
5 Sam Jacobson .75 2.00
6 Chad Kolander .30 .75
7 Voshon Lenard 1.00 2.50
8 Townsend Orr .30 .75
9 John Thomas .60 1.50
10 Jayson Walton .30 .75
11 Micah Watkins .20 .50
12 Darrell Whaley .20 .50
13 Trevor Winter .20 .50
14 Ryan Wolf .20 .50
15 Williams Arena/(The Barn) .20 .50
16 Coaching Staff .20 .50
Milton Barnes ACO
Larry Davis ACO
Bill Brown ACO
17 Title Card .20 .50

1996-97 Minnesota

This 17-card standard size set was produced by Collect-A-Sport for the 1996-97 Gophers basketball team and was sponsored by Coca Cola. The fronts have full color player action photographs inside a border that is maroon on the left half, and white on the right. The players name and jersey number appear on the top right hand corner of the card. Minnesota's logo is in maroon and white in the bottom left corner, and a Coca Cola logo is "cut" into the photo in the middle of the right side. The backs give the player's biography, Minnesota statistics and are mostly white with some maroon. A large maroon "M" appears in the middle along with the words "Big Ten Conference." The cards are unnumbered and listed below in alphabetical order.
COMPLETE SET (17) 9.00 18.00
1 Russ Archambault .20 .50
2 Eric Harris .20 .50
3 Bobby Jackson 4.00 10.00
4 Sam Jacobson .60 1.50
5 Courtney James .30 .75
6 Quincy Lewis .75 2.00
7 Kevin Lodge .20 .50
8 Kyle Sanden .20 .50
9 Aaron Stauber .20 .50
10 Jason Stanford .20 .50
11 Jermaine Stanford .20 .50
12 Miles Tarver .20 .50
13 Charles Thomas .30 .75
14 John Thomas .60 1.50
15 Trevor Winter .20 .50
16 Coaching Staff .20 .50
Bill Brown ACO
Hosea Crittenden SACO
Charles Cunningham
Larry Davis ACO
Brent Haskins AIDE
Clem Haskins CO
17 Title Card CL .30 .75

1984-85 Minnesota-Duluth

Measuring 2 1/2" by 3 1/2", this 20-card set features players from the men's basketball team. The fronts feature color photos, with a player action shot, the mascot, and the player's name, number and position. The backs feature vitals and player information. The cards are numbered.
COMPLETE SET (20) 6.00 15.00
1 David Thompson .40 1.00
2 Todd Leyse .40 1.00
3 Rich Hirstein .40 1.00
4 Alan Wimes .40 1.00
5 Todd Lind .40 1.00
6 Kraig Erickson .40 1.00
7 Jerry Brockhaus .40 1.00
8 Jeff Guidinger .40 1.00
9 John Podominick .40 1.00
10 Tom Hutton .40 1.00
11 Kendall Kelly .40 1.00
12 Tod Kowalczyk .40 1.00
13 Robby Peterson .40 1.00
14 David Asplund .40 1.00
15 Bernie Lindner .40 1.00
Student Asst. Coach
16 Dale Race .40 1.00
Head Coach
17 Butch Koronen ACO .40 1.00
Chris Neumann ACO
Bill DeVinney - TR
18 U.M.D. Bulldog Team Photo .40 1.00
19 David Thompson IA .40 1.00
20 Alan Wimes IA .40 1.00

1985-86 Minnesota-Duluth

Measuring 2 1/2" by 3 1/2", this 18-card set features players from the men's basketball team. The fronts feature color photos, with a player action shot, a posed shot in a circle, and the player's name, number and position. The backs feature vitals and player information. The cards are numbered.
COMPLETE SET (18) 6.00 15.00
1 Kendall Kelly .40 1.00
2 Bernie Lindner .40 1.00
3 Jerry Brockhaus .40 1.00
4 Lonnie Schock .40 1.00
5 Tom Hutton .40 1.00
6 Dave Asplund .40 1.00
7 Jeff Vandenberg .40 1.00
8 Tod Kowalczyk .40 1.00
9 Jeff Guidinger .40 1.00
10 Steve Geels .40 1.00
11 Rich Hirstein .40 1.00
12 Jim Olson .40 1.00
13 Alan Wimes .40 1.00
14 David Thompson .40 1.00
15 Jim Hill .40 1.00
16 Dale Race CO .40 1.00
17 Butch Kuronen ACO .40 1.00
18 Cheerleaders .40 1.00

1985-86 Minnesota-Duluth Women

Measuring 2 1/2" by 3 1/2", this 18-card set features players from the women's basketball team. The fronts feature color photos, with a player action shot, a posed shot in a circle, and the player's name, number and position. The backs feature vitals and player information. The cards are numbered.
COMPLETE SET (18) 8.00 20.00
1 85-86 UMD Team Photo .60 1.50
2 Mary Zgonc .60 1.50
3 Brenda Kuczmarski .60 1.50
4 Julie Hay .60 1.50
5 Mary Hannula .60 1.50
6 Lori Ogren .60 1.50
7 Carmen Kuntz .60 1.50
8 Suzanne Peterson .60 1.50
9 Denise Holm .60 1.50
10 Sarah Halsey .60 1.50
11 Laura Lackner .60 1.50
12 Mindy Boorman .60 1.50
13 Lisa Muehlbauer .60 1.50
14 Carolyn Neumann .60 1.50
15 Sue Anderson .60 1.50
16 Chris Beal .60 1.50
17 Lisa Bogatzki .60 1.50
18 Bonnie Jacobon MG .60 1.50
Amy Jaeger - ACO
Dee Dee Schreier - TR
Karen Stromme - CO

1988-89 Missouri

This 16-card standard-size set of Missouri Tigers was sponsored by Kodak, KMIZ-17 TV, and Columbia Photo. The cards were originally issued in four-card sheets. The front features a color photo, with borders above and below in the school's colors (black and yellow). The player's name, uniform number, classification, and position appear below the picture, with a tiger pawprint in the lower left hand corner. Biographical information and "tips for better sports pictures" are provided on the card backs. The first three panels of cards were given out at games between Missouri and Oklahoma State (January 21), Nebraska (February 19), and Colorado. The final panel was available at Columbia Photo and Video sometime after March 4. For convenience the cards are ordered and numbered alphabetically by player's name. The set features the first cards of NBA players Anthony Peeler and Doug Smith.
COMPLETE SET (16) 15.00 40.00
1 Nathan Buntin .75 2.00
2 Derrick Chievous PRO 1.50 4.00
3 Greg Church .75 2.00
4 Jamal Coleman .75 2.00
5 Jim Horton .75 2.00
6 Byron Irvin 1.50 4.00
7 Gary Leonard 1.50 4.00
8 John McIntyre .75 2.00
9 Anthony Peeler 4.00 10.00
10 Mike Sandbothe .75 2.00
11 Doug Smith 1.50 4.00
12 Norm Stewart CO 2.00 5.00
13 Steve Stipanovich 1.50 4.00
14 Jon Sundvold PRO 1.50 4.00
15 Bradd Sutton .75 2.00
16 Mike Wawrzyniak .75 2.00

1989-90 Missouri

This 16-card standard-size set was originally issued on three four-card sheets and sponsored by Kodak, Jiffy Lube, and Columbia Photo and Video. The front has an action color photo, with borders in the school's colors (yellow and black). The player's name, classification, and position appear below the card, with a tiger pawprint in the lower left hand corner. The back has biographical information and a tip for better sports pictures. For convenience the cards are ordered and numbered alphabetically by player's name. The set features cards of NBA players Anthony Peeler and Doug Smith.
COMPLETE SET (16) 10.00 25.00
1 Nathan Buntin 22 .40 1.00
2 John Burns 33 .40 1.00
3 Jamal Coleman 32 .40 1.00
4 Lee Coward 4 .40 1.00
5 Larry Drew 1.25 3.00
6 Travis Ford 5 .75 2.00
7 Chris Heller 41 .75 2.00
8 Jim Horton 13 .40 1.00
9 John McIntyre 23 .40 1.00
10 Anthony Peeler 44 3.00 8.00
11 Todd Satalowich 54 .40 1.00
12 Doug Smith 34 1.25 3.00
13 Norm Stewart CO 1.50 4.00
14 Steve Stipanovich 1.25 3.00
15 Bradd Sutton 35 .40 1.00
16 Jeff Warren 45 .40 1.00

1990-91 Missouri

This 16-card set was issued in four four-card strips and given away at four non-conference games last season. The standard-size cards are similar in design to the previous year's issue, with color action photos bordered in the school's colors (yellow and black). One difference is that "Missouri Tigers" appears in white rather than yellow lettering. The backs contain biographical information and Missouri Basketball Fun Facts. The cards are unnumbered and checklisted below in alphabetical order. The set features cards of NBA players Anthony Peeler and Doug Smith as well as the first cards of Melvin Booker and Jevon Crudup.
COMPLETE SET (16) 8.00 20.00
1 Melvin Booker 1.25 3.00
2 John Brown .75 2.00
Tiger of the Past
3 John Burns .40 1.00
4 Jamal Coleman .40 1.00
5 Jevon Crudup .75 2.00
6 Derek Dunham .40 1.00
7 Lamont Frazier .40 1.00
8 Jed Frost .40 1.00
9 Chris Heller .40 1.00
10 Jim Horton .40 1.00
11 Anthony Peeler 2.50 6.00
12 Doug Smith .75 2.00
13 Reggie Smith .40 1.00
14 Willie Smith .75 2.00
Tiger of the Past
15 Norm Stewart CO 1.25 3.00
16 Jeff Warren .40 1.00

1991-92 Missouri

This 16-card set was sponsored by Coca-Cola, Farm Bureau Insurance, and Columbia Photo. The production run was reportedly limited to 9,000 sets, with eight cards per perforated sheet. One sheet was given away at the February 23 home game against Oklahoma State, while the second sheet was given out at the March 4 game against Oklahoma. In total, 7,000 sets were distributed at home games; the rest of the sets were given to the sponsors. The standard size (2 1/2" by 3 1/2") cards have on the fronts color action photos enclosed by white and black borders, with the words "Mizzou Tigers" inscribed above the picture. The player's name appears beneath the picture, with his jersey number in a basketball at the lower right corner. The backs have biographical information, player profile, and "Tips for Better Sports Pictures." The cards are unnumbered and checklisted below in alphabetical order. The key card in the set is Anthony Peeler.
COMPLETE SET (16) 9.00 18.00
1 Kim Anderson .60 1.50
Tiger of the Past
2 Melvin Booker .75 2.00
3 John Burns .30 .75
4 Jamal Coleman .30 .75
5 Jevon Crudup .60 1.50
6 Derek Dunham .30 .75
7 Lamont Frazier .30 .75
8 Ricky Frazier .60 1.50
Tiger of the Past
9 Jed Frost .30 .75
10 Chris Heller .30 .75
11 Steve Horton .30 .75
12 Anthony Peeler 1.50 4.00
13 Chris Smith .30 .75
14 Reggie Smith .30 .75
15 Norm Stewart CO .75 2.00
16 Jeff Warren .30 .75

1992-93 Missouri

his 16-card set was sponsored by Coca-Cola, KOMU-V, Columbia Photo, and the University of Missouri-Columbia Hearnes Center. The set was issued in four-card perforated strips. The fronts of these standard-size cards display color action photos framed by white and black borders, with the words "Mizzou Tigers" printed above the picture. The player's name appears beneath the picture with his jersey number in a basketball at the lower right corner. The backs carry biographical information, a player profile, and "Tips for Better Sports Pictures." The card are unnumbered and checklisted below in alphabetical order.

COMPLETE SET (16) 5.00 12.00
1 Mark Atkins .30 .75
2 Melvin Booker .75 2.00
3 John Burns .30 .75
4 Jevon Crudup .60 1.50
5 Derek Dunham .30 .75
6 Marlo Finner .30 .75
7 Lamont Frazier .30 .75
8 Jed Frost .30 .75
9 Chris Heller .30 .75
10 Steve Horton .30 .75
11 Derrick Johnson .30 .75
12 Reggie Smith .30 .75
13 Norm Stewart CO .75 2.00
14 Jon Sundvold .60 1.50
15 Chip Walther .30 .75
16 Jeff Warren .30 .75

1993-94 Missouri

This 16-card set was sponsored by Modern Business Systems, Inc. and Ford. The perforated set was issued in two eight-card strips. The fronts feature color action player photos framed by a thin, yellow, white and black border. The words "Mizzou Tigers" are printed above the picture with the player's name and jersey number below. The white backs carry biographical information and player profile with the sposors' logos at the bottom. The cards are unnumbered and checklisted below in alphabetical order.

COMPLETE SET (16) 5.00 12.00
1 Mark Atkins .30 .75
2 Melvin Booker .75 2.00
3 Jevon Crudup .60 1.50
4 Marlo Finner .30 .75
5 Lamont Frazier .30 .75
6 Jed Frost .30 .75
7 Derek Grimm .30 .75
8 Chris Heller .30 .75
9 Derrick Johnson .30 .75
10 Paul O'Liney .30 .75
11 Reggie Smith .30 .75
12 Norm Stewart CO .60 1.50
13 Jason Sutherland .30 .75
14 Kelly Thames .60 1.50
15 Chip Walther .30 .75
16 Julian Winfield .60 1.50

1995-96 Missouri

This 16-card set was sponsored by Pizza Hut, Subway, and Radio Station 96.7 KCMQ. The perforated set was issued in two six-card sheets and one four-card strip. The fronts feature color action player photos framed by a thin yellow, white, and black borders. The words "Mizzou Tigers" are printed above the picture with the player's name and jersey number below. The white backs carry biographical information and player profile with sponsors' logos at the bottom. The cards are unnumbered and checklisted below in alphabetical order.

COMPLETE SET (16) 4.00 10.00
1 Danny Allouche .30 .75
2 Scott Combs .30 .75
3 Desmond Ferguson .30 .75
4 Derek Grimm .30 .75
5 Sammie Haley .40 1.00
6 Simeon Haley .40 1.00
7 Monte Hardge .30 .75
8 Kendrick Moore .30 .75
9 L. Dee Murdock .30 .75
10 Dustin Reeve .30 .75
11 Norm Stewart CO .60 1.50
12 Jason Sutherland .30 .75
13 Corey Tate .30 .75
14 Kelly Thames .40 1.00
15 Chip Walther .30 .75
16 Julian Winfield .40 1.00

1989-90 Montana Smokey

COMPLETE SET (12) 5.00 10.00
1 Cheryl Brandell .40 1.00
Women's basketball
5 K.C. McGowan .40 1.00
Men's basketball
6 Lisa McLeod .40 1.00
Women's basketball
7 Jean McNulty .40 1.00
Women's basketball
9 John Reckard .40 1.00
Men's basketball
10 Tony Reed .40 1.00
Men's basketball
12 Wayne Tinkle .40 1.00
Men's basketball

1992-93 Montana

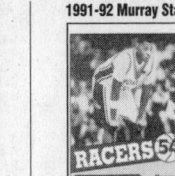

Sponsored by Taco Bell, these 20 standard-size cards feature color player action shots on their white-bordered fronts. The player's name, position, and the sponsor logo appear in black lettering within the wide lower margin. The black-and-white backs carry the player's name and uniform number at the top, followed below by his height, position, biography, and college highlights. The cards are unnumbered and checklisted below in alphabetical order.

COMPLETE SET (20) 6.00 15.00
1 Guy Bonner .30 .75
2 Nate Covill .30 .75
3 Brandon Dade .30 .75
4 Travis DeCuire .30 .75
5 Israel Evans .30 .75
6 Don Hedge .30 .75
7 Don Holst ACO .30 .75
8 Gary Kane .30 .75
9 Matt Kempfert .60 1.50
10 Josh Lacheur .30 .75
11 Jeremy Lake .40 1.00
12 Kevin McLeod ACO .30 .75
13 Paul Perkins .30 .75
14 Shawn Samuelson .60 1.50
15 Chris Spoja .40 1.00
16 Blaine Taylor CO .30 .75
17 Scott Tharp .30 .75
18 Kirk Walker .30 .75
19 Leroy Washington ACO .30 .75
20 Title Card .30 .75

1997 Montana

COMPLETE SET (23) 15.00 25.00
18 Brandon Dade BK .50 1.25
19 Brent Smith BK .50 1.25
20 Chris Spoja BK .50 1.25
21 Kirk Walker BK .50 1.25
22 Greta Koss WBK .50 1.25

1990-91 Montana State

This 16-card set was sponsored by the USDA Forest Service and other agencies. The cards measure slightly shorted than standard size (2 1/2" by 3 7/16"). The school name appears above the picture while the player's name appears beneath it. The backs carry player information, biographical data, and cartoons depicting a fire safety message. The cards are unnumbered and checklisted below in alphabetical order within sex; the men's team are listed as card numbers 1-8 and the women's team are listed as card numbers 9-16.

COMPLETE SET (16) 6.00 15.00
1 Willard Dean .75 2.00
2 Todd Dickson .60 1.50
3 Chris Herriford .60 1.50
4 Allen Lightfoot .60 1.50
5 Johnny Mack .75 2.00
6 Dave Moritz .60 1.50
7 Johnny Perkins .75 2.00
8 Greg Powell .60 1.50
9 Alaina Bauer .40 1.00
10 Debbie Cober .40 1.00
11 Sarah Flock .40 1.00
12 Sandy Neiss and .60 1.50
Susan Neiss
13 Terri Ross .40 1.00
14 Judy Spoelstra CO .60 1.50
15 Karen Weeter .40 1.00
16 Anna Wheery .40 1.00

1990-91 Murray State

This 16-card set was sponsored by The Pro Image, a sporting goods store in Paducah, Kentucky. The production run was reportedly limited to 2,000 sets, with only 1,000 of these being distributed as sets. The other 1,000 sets were given away as singles. Moreover, 45 uncut and numbered sheets were produced. The cards measure approximately 2 1/4" by 3 1/4" and are printed on thin card stock. The fronts feature black and white action or posed photos enclosed by full-bleed canary yellow borders. "Murray State Basketball," the player's name, and the sponsor logo appear on the front in blue ink. The horizontally oriented backs have biography, statistics, and player profile. The cards are numbered in the upper right corner.

COMPLETE SET (16) 5.00 12.00
1 Paul King .20 .50
2 Doug Gold .20 .50
3 Donald Overstreet .20 .50
4 Greg Coble .20 .50
5 John Jackson .20 .50
6 Popeye Jones 2.00 5.00
7 Donnie Langhi .20 .50
8 Terry Birdsong .20 .50
9 Scott Adams .20 .50
10 Frank Allen .20 .50
11 Scott Sivills .20 .50
12 Cedric Gumm .40 1.00
13 Jerry Wilson .20 .50
14 Jason Karem .20 .50
15 Coaching Staff .40 1.00
Steve Newton CO
Craig Morris ACO
James Holland ACO
16 Team Photo .60 1.50

1991-92 Murray State

This 17-card set was sponsored by The Pro Image, a sporting goods store in Paducah, Kentucky. The production run was limited to 1,500 sets, with 1,000 of these being distributed as sets and the rest as singles. Moreover, 35 uncut sheets were produced. The cards measure 2 1/2" by 3 1/2" and are printed on thin card stock. The fronts feature black and white action photos enclosed by white borders. The team name "Racers" appears in a blue diagonal toward the bottom of the card; the stripe intersects a basketball icon, which has the player's uniform number. The sponsor logo and player's name round out the card face and are printed on a yellow background immediately below the stripe. The backs have biography and player profile on a white background enclosed by blue borders. The cards are numbered on the back.

COMPLETE SET (17) 4.00 10.00
1 Scott Adams .20 .50
2 Popeye Jones 1.50 4.00
3 Frank Allen .40 1.00
4 Maurice Cannon .40 1.00
5 Jamal Evans .20 .50
6 Darren Hill .20 .50
7 Michael Hunt .20 .50
8 Rafeal Peterson .20 .50
9 Scott Sivills .20 .50
10 Bo Walden .20 .50
11 Craig Gray .20 .50
12 Cedric Gumm .40 1.00
13 Jerry Wilson .20 .50
14 Scott Edgar CO .20 .50
15 Ken Roth ACO .20 .50
16 Eddie Fields ACO .20 .50
17 Team Photo .60 1.50

1992-93 Murray State

Sponsored by The Pro Image (Paducah, Kentucky), this 17-card standard-size set features black-and-white action player photos with thin royal blue borders. The pictures are set on a white card face and are accented by an orange-yellow stripe down the left side. The stripe carries the player's name and the school and team name in royal blue print. The backs display biographical information on a yellow panel and a career summary on the remaining white portion. The cards are unnumbered and checklisted below in alphabetical order.

COMPLETE SET (17) 3.00 8.00
1 Frank Allen .30 .75
2 Tony Bailey .20 .50
3 Marcus Brown .75 2.00
4 Lawrence Bussell .20 .50
5 Maurice Cannon .30 .75
6 Scott Edgar CO .30 .75
7 Cedric Gumm .30 .75
8 Antwan Hoard .20 .50
9 Michael Hunt .20 .50
10 Michael James .20 .50
11 Jeremy Park .20 .50
12 Scott Sivills .20 .50
13 Kenneth Taylor .20 .50
14 Antoine Teague .20 .50
15 Bo Walden .20 .50
16 Jerry Wilson .20 .50
17 Team Photo .60 1.50

1984-85 Nebraska

This 31-card multi-sport set was distributed by the Lincoln Police Department. The cards measure approximately 2 1/4" by 3 5/8" and are printed on thin card stock. The sports represented are football (1-10), volleyball (11-12), gymnastics (13-15), basketball (16-19), baseball (20-24, 26, 28, 30), and track (25, 27, 29, 31).

COMPLETE SET (31) 20.00 40.00
16 Dave Hoppen BK 1.25 3.00
17 Debra Powell BK .40 1.00
18 Ronnie Smith BK .80 2.00
19 Angie Miller BK .40 1.00

1985 Nebraska All Stars Cereal

COMPLETE SET (25) 125.00 250.00
7 Lyle Nannen 6.00 12.00
10 Stuart Lantz 6.00 12.00
11 Ron Simmons 6.00 12.00

1985-86 Nebraska

This 37-card multi-sport set measuring 2 1/2" by 4" has on the fronts color action and posed player photos enclosed by a red border. The sports represented are football (2-11), volleyball (12, 14), gymnastics (13, 15-17), track (18, 20, 29-30), basketball (19, 21, 23, 26), baseball (20-24, 31-37), and swimming (22, 24, 27-28). The cards are numbered on the back. The key cards in the set are NBA draftee Rich King and NFL running back Tom Rathman.

COMPLETE SET (37) 20.00 40.00
23 Dave Hoppen .80 2.00
36 Rich King 1.00 2.50

1986-87 Nebraska

This 30-card multi-sport set was distributed by the Lincoln Police Department. The cards measure approzimately 2 1/2" by 4" and are printed on thin card stock.

COMPLETE SET (30) 20.00 35.00
11 Tisha Delaney .50 1.25
12 Brian Carr .50 1.25
13 Angie Miller .50 1.25
14 Bill Jackman .50 1.25
15 Maurtice Ivy .50 1.25
16 Anthony Bailous .50 1.25

1987-88 Nebraska

This 26-card multi-sport set was distributed by the Lincoln Police Department. The cards measure approximately 2 1/2" by 4" and is printed on this cardboard stock.

COMPLETE SET (26) 20.00 35.00
10 Virginia Stahr .50 1.25
14 Stephanie Bolli .50 1.25
16 Amy Stephens .50 1.25

1988-89 Nebraska

COMPLETE SET (32) 12.50 30.00
16 Eric Johnson .40 1.00
17 Amy Stephens .40 1.00
18 Pete Manning .40 1.00
19 Kim Harris .40 1.00
20 Richard Van Poelgeest .40 1.00
21 Amy Bullock .40 1.00

1989-90 Nebraska

This 33-card multi-sport set measures approximately 2 1/2" by 4" and is printed on thin cardboard stock. The fronts feature color player action photos on a red card face. In black lettering the words "89-90 Huskers" appear over the picture, while the player's name and other information are printed beneath the picture. The backs carry "Husker Tips," which consist of comments about the players combined with crime prevention tips. Sponsor names and logos at the bottom round out the back.

COMPLETE SET (33) 10.00 25.00
20 Ray Richardson .40 1.00
21 Ann Halsne .40 1.00
22 Clifford Scales .60 1.50
23 Kelly Hubert .40 1.00
24 Richard Van Poelgeest .40 1.00
25 Kim Yancey .40 1.00

1990-91 Nebraska

This 28-card set was sponsored by the National Bank of Commerce, the University of Nebraska-Lincoln, and the Lincoln Police Department. Sponsors' logos at the bottom round out the back. The sports represented in this set are football (2-13), volleyball (14-15), wrestling (16), gymnastics (17-20), basketball (21-24), softball (25, 27), and baseball (26, 28). The key cards in the set are these players with NFL experience: Mike Croel, Bruce Pickens, and Kenny Walker.

COMPLETE SET (28) 12.50 30.00
21 Clifford Scales .40 1.00
22 Ann Halsne .40 1.00
23 Carl Hayes .40 1.00
24 Kelly Hubert .40 1.00

1991-92 Nebraska

COMPLETE SET (22) 10.00 25.00
13 Danny Lee CO .40 1.00
14 Carl Hayes .40 1.00
15 Carol Russell .40 1.00
16 Eric Piatkowski 1.25 3.00
17 Karen Jennings .40 1.00
18 DaPreis Owens .40 1.00
19 Sue Hesch .40 1.00

1992-93 Nebraska

This 27-card multisport set was sponsored by the National Bank of Commerce, the University of Nebraska-Lincoln, and the Lincoln Police Department. The cards measure approximately 2 5/8" by 3 1/2" and are printed on thin card stock. Sponsor names and logos round out the back. The sports represented are football (1-9), women's volleyball (10, 11), basketball (12-17), gymnastics (18-20), track and field, (21-22) and baseball (23-27).

COMPLETE SET (27) 10.00 25.00
16 Eric Piatkowski 1.50 4.00

1993-94 Nebraska

This 25-card multisport standard-size set was jointly sponsored by the National Bank of Commerce, the Lincoln Police Department, and the university. The cards are unnumbered and checklisted below alphabetically within sport as follows: football (1-9), basketball (men [10-11]; women [12-13]), gymnastics (14-17), baseball (18-19), women's softball (20-21), volleyball (22-23), and wrestling (24-25).

COMPLETE SET (25) 10.00 25.00
11 Eric Piatkowski 1.25 3.00

1994-95 Nebraska

This 21-card multi-sport set was jointly sponsored by Union Bank, the Lincoln Police Department and the university. The unnumbered, attractive, full color cards are slightly wider than standard size and printed on very thin stock. Several sports are featured and are listed below alphabetically within sport as follows: baseball (1-2), men's basketball (3-4), women's basketball (5-6), football (7-14), men's gymnastics (15-16), women's gymnastics (17-18), softball (19) and women's volleyball (20-21). Future NBA player Erick Strickland has his first card in this set.

COMPLETE SET (21) 10.00 25.00
3 Jaron Boone .75 2.00
4 Erick Strickland 1.50 4.00
5 Emily Thompson .40 1.00
6 Tanya Upthegrove .40 1.00

1995-96 Nebraska

This 21-card multisport set was jointly sponsored by National Bank, Lincoln Police Department and the university. The unnumbered, full-color cards are slightly wider than standard size and feature bold red borders on front. The set contains several sports and is checklisted below alphabetically within sport as follows: men's basketball (1-3), women's basketball (4-6), football (7-13), men's gymnastics (14), women's soccer (15), women's swimming (16), women's volleyball (17-20) and wrestling (21). The set contains early cards of football players Tommy Frazier and Brook Berringer as well as an early card of NBA player Erick Strickland.

COMPLETE SET (21) 12.00 30.00
1 Jaron Boone .60 1.50
2 Erick Strickland 1.20 3.00
3 Tom Wald .30 .75
4 Pyra Aarden .30 .75
5 Anna DeForge .30 .75
6 Kate Galligan .30 .75

1995-96 Nebraska Schedules

Each of these attractive full color schedules features a different senior from the 1995-96 team. The set is highlighted by the inclusion of NBA guard Erick Strickland. The schedules were distributed for free at home games throughout the 1995-96 season.

COMPLETE SET (3) .75 2.00
1 Jaron Boone .20 .50
2 Erick Strickland .60 1.50
3 Tom Wald .08 .25

1996-97 Nebraska

This 21-card standard-size set was produced by Nebraska and features athletes from all sports. The set features primarily football players, but a variety of other sports as well. We've included initials after each player's name that represent the sport in which they played.

COMPLETE SET (21) 10.00 20.00
11 Bernard Garner BK .40 1.00
12 Mikki Moore BK 1.25 3.00
15 Anna DeForge BK 1.00 2.50
16 LaToya Doage BK .40 1.00

1996-97 Nebraska Schedules

Each of these attractive full color schedules features an action photo of one of the three different seniors from the 1996-97 team. The schedules were distributed for free at Nebraska home games throughout the 1996-97 season.

COMPLETE SET (3) .40 1.00
1 Bernard Garner .08 .25
2 Tyronn Lue .60 1.50
3 Mikki Moore .40 1.00

1997-98 Nebraska

This 21-card standard-size set featured players who were seniors at Nebraska. The set features primarily football players, but a variety of other sports as well. We've included initials after each player's name that represent the sport in which they played.

COMPLETE SET (21) 10.00 20.00
11 Tyronn Lue BK 1.00 2.50
12 Venson Hamilton BK .40 1.00
16 Anna DeForge BK 1.00 2.50

1998-99 Nebraska

This 21-card set was sponsored by Union Bank and Trust Co, University of Nebraska-Lincoln and the Lincoln Police Department. Each includes a color photo of the player surrounded by a red and gray border with the the year "98 and '99" printed on the front. The unnumbered backs are a simple black print on white card stock. The set features primarily football players, but a variety of other sports as well. We've included initials after each player's name that represent the sport in which they played.

COMPLETE SET (21) 10.00 20.00
6 Venson Hamilton BK .30 .75
14 Andy Markowski BK .30 .75
15 Cori McDill W-BK .30 .75
21 Monet Williams BK .30 .75

1999-00 Nebraska

This 19-card set was sponsored by Union Bank and Trust Co, University of Nebraska-Lincoln and the Lincoln Police Department. The set features a variety of sports and we have the put an appropriate initial after each player's name.

COMPLETE SET (19) 6.00 12.00
8 Nicole Kubik W-BK .20 .50
14 Charlie Rogers BK .20 .50

2000-01 Nebraska

This 20-card standard-size features star athletes from Nebraska. The set features primarily football players, but a variety of other sports as well. We've included initials after each player's name that represent the sport in which they played.

COMPLETE SET (20) 8.00 20.00
6 Cookie Blecher BK .60 1.50
7 Amanda Went BK .60 1.50

1988-89 New Mexico

This 18-card set was sponsored by Drug Emporium and KGGM-TV (Channel 13). The cards measure the standard size (2 1/2" by 3 1/2"). The fronts feature color posed player photos enclosed by white borders. Sponsor logos and the words "Lobos 88-89" appear above the picture, while player information is given below the picture. The cards are unnumbered and checklisted below in alphabetical order.

COMPLETE SET (18) 12.00 30.00
1 Doug Ash ACO .40 1.00
2 Willie Banks .75 2.00
3 Dave Bliss CO .40 1.00
4 Scott Duncan ACO .40 1.00
5 Rob Loeffel .40 1.00
6 Luc Longley 5.00 12.00
7 Marvin McBurrows .40 1.00
8 John McCullough ACO .75 2.00
9 Darrell McGee .40 1.00
10 Kurt Miller .40 1.00
11 Chriss O'Gorman .40 1.00
12 Rob Robbins .75 2.00
13 Tony Steffen .40 1.00
14 Charlie Thomas .75 2.00
15 Chris Tower .40 1.00
16 Donnie Walker .40 1.00
17 Mike Winters .40 1.00
Graduate Assistant
18 The Pit .75 2.00
University Arena

1989-90 New Mexico

This 18-card set was sponsored by Drug Emporium and KGGM-TV (Channel 13). The cards measure the standard size (2 1/2" by 3 1/2"). The fronts feature color posed player photos enclosed by white borders. Sponsor logos and the words "Lobos 89-90" appear above the picture, while player information is given below the picture. The cards are unnumbered and checklisted below in alphabetical order.

COMPLETE SET (18) 10.00 25.00
1 Doug Ash ACO .40 1.00
2 Willie Banks .75 2.00
3 Dave Bliss CO .40 1.00
4 Scott Duncan ACO .40 1.00
5 J.J. Griego .40 1.00
6 Samie Liberatore .40 1.00
7 Luc Longley 4.00 10.00
8 Marvin McBurrows .40 1.00
9 John McCullough ACO .40 1.00
10 Andre McGee .40 1.00
11 Darrell McGee .40 1.00
12 Kurt Miller .40 1.00
13 Rob Newton .40 1.00
14 Rob Robbins .75 2.00
15 Omar Sierra .40 1.00
16 Tony Steffen .40 1.00
17 Donnie Walker .40 1.00
18 Mike Winters .40 1.00

1990-91 New Mexico

This 17-card standard-size set was sponsored by Arby's restaurants and KGGM-TV (Channel 13). The fronts feature color posed player photos enclosed by white borders. Sponsor logos and the words "Lobos 90-91" appear above the picture, while player information is given below the picture. The cards are unnumbered and checklisted below in alphabetical order.

COMPLETE SET (17) 12.00 30.00
1 Doug Ash ACO .30 .75
2 Willie Banks .60 1.50
3 Dave Bliss CO .30 .75
4 Paul Graham ACO .30 .75
5 Khari Jaxon .60 1.50
6 Luc Longley 2.50 6.00
7 Marvin McBurrows .30 .75
8 Vladimir McCrary .30 .75
9 John McCullough ACO .30 .75
10 Lance Milford .30 .75
11 Kurt Miller .30 .75
12 Rob Newton .30 .75
13 George Powdrill SP 6.00 15.00
14 Rob Robbins .60 1.50
15 Jimmy Taylor .30 .75
16 Ike Williams .60 1.50
17 The Pit .60 1.50
University Arena

1991-92 New Mexico

This 18-card set was sponsored by Arby's restaurants and KGGM-TV (Channel 13). It is reported that 10,000 sets were printed, and two to four cards per week were given away at Arby's restaurants in the Albuquerque area. The cards measure the standard size. The fronts feature color posed player photos enclosed by white borders. Sponsor logos and the words "Lobos 91-92" appear above the picture, while player information is given below the picture. The cards are unnumbered and checklisted below in alphabetical order.

COMPLETE SET (18) 4.00 10.00
1 Doug Ash ACO .20 .50
2 Willie Banks .40 1.00
3 Dave Bliss CO .20 .50
4 Paul Graham ACO .20 .50
5 J.J. Griego .20 .50
6 Brian Hayden .20 .50
7 Trent Heffner .20 .50
8 Khari Jaxon .40 1.00
9 Lewis Lamar .20 .50
10 Steve Logan .40 1.00
11 Vladimir McCrary .20 .50
12 John McCullough ACO .20 .50
13 Andre McGee .20 .50
14 Lance Milford .20 .50
15 Scott Pritchett .20 .50
16 Will Scott .20 .50
17 Eric Thomas .20 .50
18 Ike Williams .40 1.00

1992-93 New Mexico

This 16-card set issued in two-card perforated strips was sponsored by First National Bank in Albuquerque. A total of 15,000 sets were produced according to information on the reverse. The cards measure standard size (2 1/2" by 3 1/2"). The white-bordered fronts feature color action player shots with a red banner superimposed on the upper portion of the photo. Within the red banner in white lettering appears the team name, with the season dates printed in white below. A basketball icon in the lower right corner carries the player's name and across the bottom edge a green stripe contains the set sponsors: First National Bank in Albuquerque and radio station KRQE. The white backs carry biography and college statistics. The cards are unnumbered and checklisted below in alphabetical order.

COMPLETE SET (16) 3.00 8.00
1 Dave Bliss CO .60 1.50
2 Greg Brown .20 .50
3 J.J. Griego .20 .50
4 Brian Hayden .20 .50
5 Trent Heffner .20 .50
6 Khari Jaxon .40 1.00
7 Corey Jenkins .20 .50
8 Lewis LaMar .20 .50
9 Lobo Lucy and Louie .20 .50
(Mascots)
10 Steve Logan .20 .50
11 Lance Milford .20 .50
12 Canonchet Neves .20 .50
13 Mike Powers .20 .50
Sports Director
14 Eric Thomas .20 .50
15 Ike Williams .40 1.00
16 Frank Willis .20 .50

1992-93 New Mexico State

This 13-card set measures the standard size (2 1/2" by 3 1/2") and features color action player photos bordered on one side by a gray stripe containing the words "New Mexico State." The player's name appears in maroon print on a white bar at the bottom. The horizontal backs are white and display a shadow bordered close-up picture, the player's name, and a player profile. The cards are numbered on the back.

COMPLETE SET (13) 3.00 8.00
1 Neil McCarthy CO .75 2.00
2 Ron Putzi .20 .50
3 Eric Traylor .40 1.00
4 Tracey Ware .30 .75
5 Marc Thompson .30 .75
6 David Lofton .20 .50
7 D.J. Jackson .30 .75
8 Corey Rogers .30 .75
9 Cliff Reed .20 .50
10 Ron Coleman .20 .50
11 Juriad Hughes .20 .50
12 James Dockery .40 1.00
13 Sam Crawford .75 2.00

1993-94 New Mexico State

This 18-card standard size (2 1/2" by 3 1/2") set. The fronts feature full bleed color posed player shots. In the lower right side there is a red color bar with the team name reversed out which overlaps a black color bar whick has the players name reversed out. The white backs have as a color player head shot in the upper left. The player'a player's name and bio are centered at the top. A player profile follow below. The cards numbered and listed below.

COMPLETE SET (18) 4.00 10.00
1 Ron Coleman .20 .50
2 James Dockery .30 .75
3 D.J. Jackson .20 .50
4 Corey Rogers .30 .75
5 Chris Lopez .20 .50
6 Mike Schutz .20 .50
7 Dwain Bradberry .20 .50
8 William Howze .20 .50
9 Lance Jackson .20 .50
10 Paul Jarrett .20 .50
11 Keith Johnson .20 .50
12 Skip McCoy .20 .50
13 Johnny Selvie .30 .75
14 Rodney Walker .30 .75
15 Thomas Wyatt .30 .75
16 Pistol Pete (Mascot) .20 .50
17 Dr. James Halligan PR .20 .50
18 Neil McCarthy CO .75 2.00

1996-97 New Mexico State

This 14-card set was offered at New Mexico State University during the 1996-97 season. The set was produced by White Sands Federal Credit Union.

COMPLETE SET (14) 3.00 8.00
1 Charles Gosa .30 .75
2 Antoine Hubbard .30 .75
3 Chris Lopez .30 .75
4 Louis Richardson .30 .75
5 Carl Laws .30 .75
6 Maurice Lawson .30 .75
7 Aaron Brodt .30 .75
8 Denmark Reid .30 .75
9 Joaquin Chavez .30 .75
10 Bostjan Leban .30 .75
11 Rhoute Davis .30 .75
12 Douminic Ellison .30 .75
13 Neil McCarthy CO .40 1.00
14 Team Card .30 .75

1988 New Mexico State Greats

This 12-card multi-sport set was sponsored by the Charter Hospital of Santa Teresa. The cards measure approximately 2 5/8" by 4" and are printed on thin cardboard stock. On a white background with a dark red border on three sides, the fronts feature black-and-white posed or action player photos and player information. The backs have brief biographical and statistical information, a cartoon of Chum and a public service announcement. The logo and address of the sponsor round out the backs. The cards are unnumbered and checklisted below in alphabetical order.

COMPLETE SET (12) 9.00 18.00
3 Jimmy Collins BK 1.00 2.50
4 Steve Colter BK .75 2.00
7 Sam Lacey BK 1.25 3.00

1973-74 North Carolina Playing Cards

This 54-card standard-size set features North Carolina players. The set is designed like a playing card set and has rounded corners. On a white background, the fronts feature black-and-white player photos, with the player's name printed below. The backs are blue on white and carry the team name and logo. The cards are checklisted in playing card order by suits and numbers are assigned to Aces (1), Jacks (11), Queens (12), and Kings (13).

COMP. FACT SET (54) 75.00 150.00
1C 1956-57 National Champs .75 2.00
1D Bobby Jones 4.00 10.00
1H Homer Rice DIR .75 2.00
1S Dean Smith CO 20.00 35.00
2C Bob Lewis .75 2.00
2D Dave Hanners .75 2.00
2H Jerry Vayda 1.25 3.00
2S James Smith .75 2.00
3C Dennis Wuycik .75 2.00
3D Billy Chambers .75 2.00
3H Steve Previs .75 2.00
3S Bruce Buckley .75 2.00
4C Billy Cunningham 5.00 10.00
4D Mickey Bell .75 2.00
4H Dick Grubar .75 2.00
4S Tommy LaGarde 1.25 3.00
5C Lee Shaffer .75 2.00
5D Charles Waddell .75 2.00
5H Rusty Clark .75 2.00
5S John Kuester .75 2.00
6C Hook Dillon .75 2.00
6D Brad Hoffman .75 2.00
6H Joe Quigg .75 2.00
6S Tony Shaver .75 2.00
7C York Larese 1.50 4.00
7D Ray Hite .75 2.00
7H Tommy Kearns 1.25 3.00
7S Eddie Fogler 2.00 5.00
8C Jim Jorden .75 2.00
8D Walter Davis 5.00 12.00
8H Bill Bunting .75 2.00
8S Bill Guthridge 5.00 12.00
9C Doug Moe 3.00 8.00
9D Ed Stahl .75 2.00
9H Larry Brown 5.00 12.00
9S 1971-72 Third Nationally .75 2.00
10C Pete Brennan 1.50 4.00
10D Mitch Kupchak 3.00 8.00
10H Bill Chamberlain .75 2.00
10S 1970-71 NIT Champs .75 2.00
11C Charlie Scott 3.00 8.00
11D John O'Donnell .75 2.00
11H Robert McAdoo 6.00 15.00
11S 1968-69 ACC Champs .75 2.00
12C Larry Miller 2.50 6.00
12D Ray Harrison .75 2.00
12H Lailee McNair .75 2.00
12S 1967-68 Second Nationally 1.25 3.00
13C Lennie Rosenbluth 2.50 6.00
13D Darrell Elston .75 2.00
13H George Karl 4.00 10.00
13S 1966-67 ACC Champs 1.25 3.00
JK Bell Tower .75 2.00
JK Old Well .75 2.00

1974-75 North Carolina Schedules

This three-card set was issued by the University of North Carolina. Each card measures approximately 2 3/8" by 3 1/2". The fronts feature full-bleed close-up color player photos, with the player's name and jersey number at the bottom of the card. The backs list the 1974-75 varsity basketball schedule. The cards are unnumbered and checklisted below in alphabetical order.

COMPLETE SET (3) 7.50 15.00
1 Mickey Bell 2.00 5.00
2 Brad Hoffman 2.00 5.00
3 Ed Stahl 2.00 5.00

1975-76 North Carolina Schedules

This three-card set was issued by the University of North Carolina. Each card measures approximately 2 3/8" by 3 1/2". The fronts feature full-bleed close-up color player photos, with the player's name and jersey number at the bottom of the card. The backs list the 1975-76 varsity basketball schedule. The cards are unnumbered and checklisted below in alphabetical order.

COMPLETE SET (3) 7.50 15.00
1 Bill Chambers 1.50 4.00
2 Dave Hanners 1.50 4.00
3 Mitch Kupchak 5.00 10.00

1976-77 North Carolina Schedules

This five-card set was issued by the University of North Carolina. Each card measures approximately 2 3/8" by 3 1/2". The fronts feature full-bleed close-up color player photos, with the player's name and jersey number at the bottom of the card. The backs list the 1976-77 varsity basketball schedule. The cards are unnumbered and checklisted below in alphabetical order.

COMPLETE SET (5) 12.50 25.00
1 Bruce Buckley 1.25 3.00
2 Woody Coley 1.25 3.00
3 Walter Davis 5.00 10.00
4 John Kuester 1.50 4.00
5 Tommy LaGarde 2.50 6.00

1977-78 North Carolina Schedules

This three-card set was issued by the University of North Carolina. Each card measures approximately 2 3/8" by 3 1/2". The fronts feature full-bleed close-up color player photos, with the player's name and jersey number at the bottom of the card. The backs list the 1977-78 varsity basketball schedule. The cards are unnumbered and checklisted below in alphabetical order.

COMPLETE SET (3) 5.00 10.00
1 Geoff Crompton 1.25 3.00
2 Phil Ford 2.50 6.00
3 Tom Zaliagiris 1.25 3.00

1978-79 North Carolina Schedules

This three-card set was issued by the University of North Carolina. Each card measures approximately 2 3/8" by 3 1/2". The fronts feature full-bleed close-up color player photos, with the player's name and jersey number at the bottom of the card. The backs list the 1978-79 varsity basketball schedule. The cards are unnumbered and checklisted below in alphabetical order.

COMPLETE SET (3) 4.00 8.00
1 Dudley Bradley 1.50 4.00
2 Ged Doughton 1.25 3.00
3 Randy Wiel 1.25 3.00

1979-80 North Carolina Schedules

This five-card set was issued by the University of North Carolina. Each card measures approximately 2 3/8" by 3 1/2". The fronts feature full-bleed close-up color player photos, with the player's name and jersey number at the bottom of the card. The backs list the 1979-80 varsity basketball schedule. The cards are unnumbered and checklisted below in alphabetical order.

COMPLETE SET (5) 6.00 12.00
1 Dave Colescott .75 2.00
2 Mike O'Koren 1.50 4.00
3 John Virgil .75 2.00
4 Jeff Wolf 1.25 3.00
5 Rich Yonakor 1.25 3.00

1980-81 North Carolina Schedules

These four cards were apparently issued by the Athletic Department of the University of North Carolina. Each card measures approximately 2 3/8" by 3 3/8". The fronts feature full-bleed close-up color photos, with the player's name and jersey number at the bottom of the card face. The backs list the 1980-81 varsity basketball schedule. The cards are unnumbered and checklisted below in alphabetical order.

COMPLETE SET (4) 3.00 6.00
1 Pete Budko .60 1.50
2 Eric Kenny .60 1.50
3 Mike Pepper .60 1.50
4 Al Wood 1.25 3.00

1981-82 North Carolina Schedules

These three cards were apparently issued by the Athletic Department of the University of North Carolina. Each card measures approximately 2 3/8" by 3 3/8". The fronts feature full-bleed close-up color photos, with the player's name and jersey number at the bottom of the card face. The backs list the 1981-82 varsity basketball schedule. The cards are unnumbered and checklisted below in alphabetical order.

COMPLETE SET (3) 2.00 5.00
1 Jeb Barlow .60 1.50
2 Jimmy Black .75 2.00
3 Chris Brust .60 1.50

1982-83 North Carolina Schedules

Measuring approximately 2 3/8" by 3 1/2", this card was issued by the University of North Carolina. The front features a full-bleed color portrait with the player's name and jersey number at the bottom of the card. The back lists the 1982-83 varsity basketball schedule. The card is unnumbered.

1 Jimmy Braddock .60 1.50

1983-84 North Carolina Schedules

This three-card set was issued by the University of North Carolina. Each card measures approximately 2 3/8" by 3 1/2". The fronts feature full-bleed close-up color player photos, with the player's name and jersey number at the bottom of the card. The backs list the 1983-84 varsity basketball schedule. The cards are unnumbered and checklisted below in alphabetical order.

COMPLETE SET (3) 3.00 8.00
1 Matt Doherty .75 2.00
2 Cecil Exum .60 1.50
3 Sam Perkins 2.50 6.00

1984-85 North Carolina Schedules

This three-card set was issued by the University of North Carolina. Each card measures approximately 2 3/8" by 3 1/2". The fronts feature full-bleed close-up color player photos, with the player's name and jersey number at the bottom of the card. The backs list the 1984-85 varsity basketball schedule. The cards are unnumbered and checklisted below in alphabetical order.

COMPLETE SET (3) 1.50 4.00
1 Timo Makkonen .40 1.00
2 Cliff Morris .40 1.00
3 Buzz Peterson .75 2.00

1985-86 North Carolina Schedules

This four-card set was issued by the University of North Carolina. Each card measures approximately 2 3/8" by 3 1/2". The fronts feature full-bleed close-up color player photos, with the player's name and jersey number at the bottom of the card. The backs list the 1985-86 varsity basketball schedule. The cards are unnumbered and checklisted below in alphabetical order.

COMPLETE SET (4) 2.50 6.00
1 Brad Daugherty 1.50 4.00
2 Jimmy Daye .40 1.00
3 Steve Hale .40 1.00
4 Warren Martin .40 1.00

1986-87 North Carolina

This 13-card set was sponsored by Adolescent CareUnit, Alamance Health Services, and various police departments. The cards measure the standard size (2 1/2" by 3 1/2"). The front features a posed color head-and-shoulders shot of the player on a white card face. In black lettering, the Adolescent Care Unit logo, the school name, and year appear above the picture. The player's name and number are given below, sandwiched between the team name. The back is printed in black on white card stock and presents biographical information and "Tips from the Tar Heels," which consist of anti-drug and alcohol messages. The cards are unnumbered and checklisted below by uniform number. The set features the first cards of NBA players Kenny Smith, J.R. Reid, and Scott Williams.

COMPLETE SET (13) 9.00 18.00
3 Jeff Denny .40 1.00
14 Jeff Lebo 1.00 2.50
20 Steve Bucknall .60 1.50
21 Michael Norwood .40 1.00
24 Joe Wolf 1.00 2.50
30 Kenny Smith 2.50 6.00
32 Pete Chilcutt 1.25 3.00
33 Ranzino Smith .60 1.50
34 J.R. Reid 1.25 3.00
35 Dave Popson .75 2.00
42 Scott Williams 1.25 3.00
43 Curtis Hunter .60 1.50
45 Marty Hensley .40 1.00

1986-87 North Carolina Schedules

This five-card set was issued by the University of North Carolina. Each card measures approximately 2 3/8" by 3 1/2". The fronts feature full-bleed close-up color player photos, with the player's name and jersey number at the bottom of the card. The backs list the 1986-87 varsity basketball schedule. The cards are unnumbered and checklisted below in alphabetical order.

COMPLETE SET (5) 2.50 6.00
1 Curtis Hunter .40 1.00
2 Mike Norwood .30 .75
3 Dave Popson .60 1.50
4 Kenny Smith 1.25 3.00
5 Joe Wolf .60 1.50

1987-88 North Carolina

This 12-card standard-size set was sponsored by Adolescent CareUnit, Alamance Health Services, and various police departments. The front features a posed color head-and-shoulders shot of the player on a white card face. In black lettering, the Adolescent CareUnit and Blue Cross/Blue Shield logos appear above the picture. In contrast to the previous year's issue, these cards have "Tar Heels" printed in large blue type above the picture. The player's name and number are given below, sandwiched between two blue basketballs. The back is printed in black on white card stock and presents biographical information and "Tips from the Tar Heels," which consist of anti-drug and alcohol messages. The cards are unnumbered and checklisted below by uniform number. The set features the first card of NBA player Rick Fox.

COMPLETE SET (12) 9.00 18.00
34 J.R. Reid 1.25 3.00
42 Scott Williams 1.00 2.50
44 Rick Fox 4.00 9.00

1987-88 North Carolina Schedules

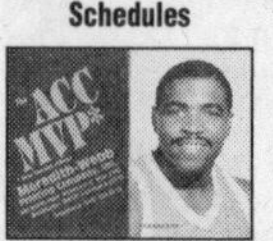

Sponsored by the Meredith-Webb Printing Company, this schedule card measures approximately 2 1/4" by 3 1/2" when folded. The front features a full-bleed close-up color player photo, with the player's name at the bottom of the card face. The inside lists the 1987-88 varsity basketball schedule. The back carries the sponsor's logo and address in gold lettering on a brown background. The card is unnumbered.

1 Ranzino Smith .30 .75

1988-89 North Carolina

This 15-card standard-size set was sponsored by Adolescent CareUnit, Alamance Health Services, and local law enforcement agencies. The fronts feature a color action photo of the player, with black borders on a medium blue card face. In black lettering, the Adolescent CareUnit and Blue Cross/Blue Shield logos appear within the border above the picture. These cards have "Tar Heels" printed in large white type above the picture. The player's name and number are given below, with the letters "NC" superimposed over one another in the lower left corner. The back is printed in black on white card stock and presents biographical information and "Tips from the Tar Heels," which consist of anti-drug and alcohol messages. The cards are unnumbered and checklisted below by uniform number. The Defense card is mysteriously listed on the back as '87 and '88 in the upper corners.

COMPLETE SET (15) 8.00 20.00
3 Jeff Denny .40 1.00
14 Jeff Lebo .60 1.50
20 Steve Bucknall .40 1.00
21 King Rice .60 1.50
22 Kevin Madden .40 1.00
32 Pete Chilcutt 1.25 3.00
34 J.R. Reid 1.00 2.50
42 Scott Williams 1.25 3.00
44 Rick Fox 3.00 7.00
45 Marty Hensley .40 1.00
NNO Dean Smith CO 3.00 7.00
NNO Teamwork .40 1.00
NNO Defense .60 1.50
(Scott Williams and Jeff Lebo defending)
NNO The Fast Break .60 1.50
(King Rice dribbling)
NNO A Fun Game 1.25 3.00
(bench scene with Rick Fox and Scott Williams)

1988-89 North Carolina Schedules

Sponsored by Hardee's, this three-card set features schedule cards that fold in the middle. Each card measures approximately 2 1/4" by 3 1/2" when folded. The fronts feature full-bleed close-up color player photos, with the player's name at the bottom of the card face. The insides list the 1988-89 varsity basketball schedule. The backs carry the sponsor's advertisement showing a color photo of a hamburger, with the Hardee's logo and the slogan "We're out to win you over" below. The cards are unnumbered and checklisted below in alphabetical order.

COMPLETE SET (3) 1.20 3.00
1 Steve Bucknall .40 1.00
2 Jeff Lebo .60 1.50
3 David May .30 .75

1989-90 North Carolina Collegiate Collection

This 200-card standard-size set was produced by Collegiate Collection and sponsored by Coca-Cola, and the Coke logo appears in the lower left corner on the card face. The fronts feature a mix of black and white photos for earlier players and color for later ones, with rounded corners and powder blue borders. The pictures are superimposed over a powder blue and white diagonally striped card face, with a powder blue outer border. The top reads "North Carolina's Finest," and the school logo appears in the upper right corner. The horizontally oriented backs are printed in powder blue on white and present biographical information, career summaries, or statistics. Many numbers can be found without the trademark notation on the card front, i.e., missing the circled R under the Tar heel logo. Collegiate Collection also issued a Gold version of this set in a special binder, with an individually numbered certificate indicating that 1,000 sets were produced. The Gold cards have gold foil trim surrounding the photos.

COMPLETE SET (200) 8.00 20.00
*GOLD SINGLES: 3X TO 8X BASE CARD HI
1 Dean Smith .20 .50
2 Dean Smith .20 .50
3 Dean Smith .20 .50
4 Dean Smith .20 .50
5 Dean Smith .20 .50
6 Dean Smith .20 .50
7 Phil Ford .08 .25
8 Phil Ford .08 .25
9 Phil Ford .08 .25
10 Phil Ford .08 .25
11 Phil Ford .08 .25
12 Phil Ford .08 .25
13 Michael Jordan .75 2.00
14 Michael Jordan .75 2.00
15 Michael Jordan .75 2.00
16 Michael Jordan .75 2.00
17 Michael Jordan .75 2.00
18 Michael Jordan .75 2.00
19 James Worthy .10 .30
20 James Worthy .10 .30
21 James Worthy .10 .30
22 James Worthy .10 .30
23 James Worthy .10 .30
24 Larry Miller .08 .10
25 Larry Miller .08 .10
26 Larry Miller .08 .10
27 Larry Miller .08 .10
28 Charlie Scott .08 .25
29 Charlie Scott .08 .25
30 Charlie Scott .08 .25
31 Charlie Scott .08 .25
32 Sam Perkins .08 .25
33 Sam Perkins .08 .25
34 Sam Perkins .08 .25
35 Sam Perkins .08 .25
36 Sam Perkins .08 .25
37 Billy Cunningham .08 .25
38 Billy Cunningham .08 .25
39 Billy Cunningham .08 .25
40 Billy Cunningham .08 .25
41 Lennie Rosenbluth .08 .25
42 Lennie Rosenbluth .08 .25
43 Lennie Rosenbluth .08 .25
44 Bobby Jones .08 .25
45 Bobby Jones .08 .25
46 Bobby Jones .08 .25
47 Mitch Kupchak .08 .10
48 Mitch Kupchak .08 .10
49 Mitch Kupchak .08 .10
50 1980-81 Tar Heels .08 .10
51 Walter Davis .08 .25
52 Walter Davis .08 .25
53 Walter Davis .08 .25
54 Walter Davis .08 .25
55 Mike O'Koren .08 .10
56 Mike O'Koren .08 .10
57 Mike O'Koren .08 .10
58 Mike O'Koren .08 .10
59 The Huddle .08 .05
60 Larry Brown .08 .25
61 Billy Cunningham .08 .25
62 Matt Doherty .08 .10
63 Phil Ford .08 .25
64 Doug Moe .08 .25
65 Michael Jordan 1.00 2.50
66 Kenny Smith .08 .25
67 Kenny Smith .08 .25
68 Kenny Smith .08 .25
69 Bob Lewis .08 .05
70 Bob Lewis .08 .05
71 Bob Lewis .08 .05
72 Charlie Scott .08 .25
73 Sam Perkins .08 .25
74 Doug Moe .08 .25
75 Doug Moe .08 .25
76 Bob McAdoo .08 .25
77 Bob McAdoo .08 .25
78A Pete Brennan ERR .08 .05
(No trademark on back)
78B Pete Brennan COR .08 .05
79 Pete Brennan .08 .05
80 J.R. Reid .08 .15
81 J.R. Reid .08 .15
82 J.R. Reid .08 .15
83 Tommy Kearns .08 .10
84 Tommy Kearns .08 .10
85 John Dillon .08 .05
86 The Smith Center .08 .05
87 Dick Grubar .08 .05
88 Dick Grubar .08 .05
89 Rusty Clark .08 .05
90 Rusty Clark .08 .05
91 Bill Bunting .08 .05
92 Bill Bunting .08 .05
93 Jimmy Black .08 .10
94 Jimmy Black .08 .10
95 Five Tournament Titles .08 .10
96 UNC Cheerleaders .08 .10
97 Bobby Jones .08 .25
98 J.R. Reid .08 .15
99 Frank McGuire .08 .25
100 1957 NCAA Champions .08 .10
101 Bill Guthridge .08 .25
102 York Larese .08 .10
103 York Larese .08 .10
104 Frank McGuire .08 .25
105 Bones McKinney .08 .25
106 Larry Miller .08 .10
107 Kenny Smith .08 .25
108 Steve Previs .08 .05
109 Steve Previs .08 .05
110 Larry Brown .08 .25
111 Larry Brown .08 .25
112 Eddie Fogler .08 .25
113 Eddie Fogler .08 .25
114 James Worthy .10 .30
115 Bob McAdoo .08 .25
116 UNC Basketball .08 .05
117 UNC Basketball .08 .25
118 Cartwright Carmichael .08 .05
119 Steve Hale .08 .05
120 Steve Hale .08 .05
121 Joe Quigg .08 .10
122 Joe Quigg .08 .10
123 Bob Cunningham .08 .05
124 Bob Cunningham .08 .05
125 Jim Delaney .08 .05
126 Bones McKinney .08 .25
127 Jerry Vayda .08 .05
128 Matt Doherty .08 .10
129 Matt Doherty .08 .10
130 Bob Paxton .08 .05
131 Dave Chadwick .08 .05
132 Dave Hanners .08 .05
133 Jim Jordan .08 .05
134 Jeff Lebo .08 .10
135 Jeff Lebo .08 .10
136 Lee Shaffer .08 .10
137 Lee Shaffer .08 .10
138 Joe Wolf .08 .10
139 Joe Wolf .08 .10
140 Warren Martin .08 .05
141 Warren Martin .08 .05
142 Carmichael Auditorium .08 .05
143 Jim Hudock .08 .05
144 Darrell Elston .08 .05
145 Brad Hoffman .08 .05
146 Harvey Salz .08 .05
147 Dave Colescott .08 .25
148 Ed Stahl .08 .05
149 Joe Brown .08 .05
150 Gerald Tuttle .08 .05
151 Richard Tuttle .08 .05
152 Tony Radovich .08 .05
153 Dave Popson .08 .10
154 Donnie Walsh .08 .05
155 Rich Yonakor .08 .10
156 Jeff Wolf .08 .05
157 Pete Budko .08 .05
158 Randy Wiel .08 .05
159 Tom Gauntlett .08 .05
160 Mike Pepper .08 .05
161 Jim Braddock .08 .10
162 Yogi Poteet .08 .05
163 Charlie Shaffer .08 .05
164 Lee Dedmon .08 .05
165 Bob Bennett .08 .05
166 Ray Hite .08 .05
167 Tom Zaliagiris UER .08 .05
(Tim on front)
168 Kim Huband .08 .05
169 Ranzino Smith .08 .05
170 Donn Johnston .08 .05
171 Dale Gipple .08 .05
172 Curtis Hunter .08 .05
173 John Yokley .08 .05
174 Bryan McSweeney .08 .05
175 John O'Donnell .08 .05
176 Hugh Donahue .08 .05
177 1968-69 Tar Heels .08 .10
178 Bruce Buckley .08 .05
179 Ray Respess .08 .05
180 Buzz Peterson .08 .10
181 Mike Cooke .08 .05
182 Mickey Bell .08 .05
183 John Virgil .08 .05
184 Charles Waddell .08 .05
185 Mark Mirken .08 .05
186 Ralph Fletcher .08 .05
187 1971-72 ACC Champs .08 .10
188 Ged Doughton .08 .05
189 Bill Chambers .08 .05
190 Bill Chambers .08 .05
191 James Daye .08 .05
192 Jeb Barlow .08 .05
193 Chris Brust .08 .05
194 Eric Kenny .08 .05
195 1970-71 NIT Champs .08 .10
196 Don Eggleston .08 .05
197 Ricky Webb .08 .05
198 Jim Frye .08 .05
199 Timo Makkonen .08 .05
200 1982 NCAA Champions .08 .10

1989-90 North Carolina Schedules

Sponsored by Hardee's, this five-card set features schedule cards that fold in the middle. Each card measures approximately 2 1/4" by 3 1/2" when folded. The fronts feature full-bleed close-up color player photos, with the player's name at the bottom of the card. The insides list the 1989-90 varsity basketball schedule. The backs carry the words "1989-90 UNC Basketball Schedule" in black letters, the sponsor's logo in red letters, and the slogan "We're out to win you over." The cards are unnumbered and checklisted below in alphabetical order.

COMPLETE SET (5) 1.50 4.00
1 Jeff Denny .20 .50
2 John Greene .20 .50
3 Marty Hensley .20 .50
4 Kevin Madden .30 .75
5 Scott Williams .75 2.00

1990-91 North Carolina Collegiate Collection Promos

This ten-card set features various sports stars of North Carolina from recent years. Since this set features athletes from more than one sport we have put a two letter abbreviation next to the player's name which identifies the sport he plays. This set includes a Michael Jordan card. All the cards in the set feature full-color photos of the athletes on the front along with either a biography or statistics of the players pictured on the card.

COMPLETE SET (10) 3.00 8.00
NC1 Michael Jordan BK 2.50 6.00
NC3 Steve Hale BK .08 .25
NC5 Matt Doherty BK .08 .25
NC7 Sam Perkins BK .40 1.00
NC9 Kenny Smith BK .40 1.00

1990-91 North Carolina Schedules

Sponsored by Hardee's, this three-card set features schedule cards that fold in the middle. Each card measures approximately 2 1/4" by 3 1/2" when folded. The fronts feature full-bleed close-up color player photos, with the player's name at the bottom of the card face. The insides list the 1990-91 varsity basketball schedule. The backs carry the words "1990-91 UNC Basketball Schedule" and the sponsor's logo in black letters on a white background. The cards are unnumbered and checklisted below in alphabetical order.

COMPLETE SET (3) 1.50 4.00
1 Pete Chilcutt .30 .75
2 Rick Fox 1.50 4.00
3 King Rice .20 .50

1991-92 North Carolina Schedules

Sponsored by Hardee's, this one-card set is a schedule card that can be folded in the middle. It measures approximately 2 1/8" by 3 1/2" when folded. The front features a full-bleed close-up color player photo, with the player's name at the bottom of the card face. The inside lists the 1991-92 men's basketball schedule. The card is unnumbered. There also exists a Knox card which carries the women's basketball schedule.

COMPLETE SET (1) .80 2.00
1 Hubert Davis .75 2.00

1992-93 North Carolina Schedules

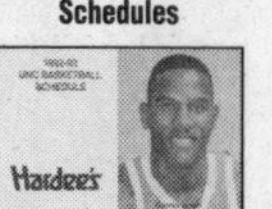

Sponsored by Hardee's, this five-card set features schedule cards each measuring the standard size when folded in the middle. The fronts feature glossy full-bleed color player photos of seniors with their names across the bottom of the picture. The insides carry the 1992-93 men's basketball schedule. On white backgrounds, the backs have the words "1992-93 UNC Basketball Schedule" and the sponsor's logo. The cards are unnumbered and checklisted below in alphabetical order.

COMPLETE SET (5) 1.00 2.50
1 Scott Cherry .20 .50
2 George Lynch .40 1.00
3 Henrik Rodl .20 .50
4 Travis Stephenson .20 .50
5 Matt Wenstrom .20 .50

1995-96 North Carolina Schedules

Continuing the tradition of featuring all of the seniors from each year's team, the 1995-96 UNC schedule set is highlighted by the inclusion of scrappy Dante Calabria. As is typical with UNC skeds, these skeds feature a close-up, full color, posed shot of each player. The skeds were distributed for free at 1996-97 home games. Though they are unnumbered on back, we've checklisted them below alphabetically for convenience.

COMPLETE SET (3) .40 1.00
1 Dante Calabria .30 .75

2 Clyde Lynn .08 .25
3 David Neal .08 .25

1996-97 North Carolina Schedules

The 1996-97 UNC skeds features the typical theme of honoring each senior with his own schedule. This year's set is highlighted by the inclusion of NBA draftee Serge Zwikker. Each schedule features a full color, posed shot. The schedules were distributed for free at 1996-97 home games. Though unnumbered, we've checklisted them below in alphabetical order for convenience.

COMPLETE SET (3) .40 1.00
1 Charlie McNairy .08 .25
2 Webb Tyndall .08 .25
3 Serge Zwikker .40 1.00

1997-98 North Carolina Schedules

The 1997-98 UNC skeds features the typical theme of honoring each senior with his own schedule. Each schedule features a full color, posed shot. The schedules were distributed for free at 1997-98 home games. The schedules were sponsered by Hardee's. Though unnumbered, we've checklisted them below in alphabetical order for convenience.

COMPLETE SET (2) .40 1.00
1 Makhtar Ndiaye .20 .50
2 Shammond Williams .20 .50

1973-74 North Carolina State Playing Cards

This 54-card standard size set features former North Carolina State University All-America players and team photos of ACC champions. The set is designed like a playing card set and has rounded corners and black-and-white photos on white backgrounds. The backs are red on white and display the N.C. State mascot and have the words "Pack Power" printed above the mascot and "Wolfpack Country" printed below in red outlined block letters. Since the set is similar to a playing card deck, it is checklisted below as if it were a playing card set. In the checklist C means Clubs, D means Diamonds, H means Hearts, S means Spades, and JK means Joker. The cards are checklisted in playing card order by suits and numbers are assigned to Aces (1), Jacks (11), Queens (12), and Kings (13). The jokers are unnumbered and listed at the end.

COMP.FACT SET (54) 50.00 120.00
C1 Willis Casey AD .40 1.00
C2 Ken Gehring .40 1.00
C3 Steve Smith .75 2.00
C4 Dwight Johnson .40 1.00
C5 Jerry Hunt .40 1.00
C6 Tommy Burleson 2.00 5.00
C7 John Richter .40 1.00
C8 Lou Pucillo .40 1.00
C9 Vic Molodet .40 1.00
C10 Ronnie Shavlik .40 1.00
C11 Bob Speight .40 1.00
C12 Sammy Ranzino .40 1.00
C13 Dick Dickey .40 1.00
D1 Everett Case CO 1.25 3.00
D2 1965 ACC Champs .75 2.00
D3 1959 ACC Champs .75 2.00
D4 1956 ACC Champs .75 2.00
D5 1955 ACC Champs .75 2.00
D6 1954 ACC Champs .75 2.00
D7 1953 Dixie Classic Champs .75 2.00
D8 1952 S.C. Champs .75 2.00
D9 1951 S.C. Champs .75 2.00
D10 1950 S.C. Champs .75 2.00
D11 1949 S.C. Champs .75 2.00
D12 1948 S.C. Champs .75 2.00
D13 1947 S.C. Champs .75 2.00
H1 Tommy Burleson 2.00 5.00
H2 Bruce Dayhuff .40 1.00
H3 Bill Lake .40 1.00
H4 Mike Buurma .40 1.00
H5 Greg Hawkins .40 1.00
H6 Craig Kuszmaul .40 1.00
H7 Mark Moeller .40 1.00
H8 Phil Spence .40 1.00
H9 Steve Nuce .75 2.00
H10 Moe Rivers .75 2.00
H11 Tim Stoddard .75 2.00
H12 Monte Towe 1.50 4.00
H13 David Thompson 10.00 25.00
S1 Norm Sloan CO 4.00 10.00
S2 Vann Williford .75 2.00
S3 Jo Ann Sloan .40 1.00
S4 Everett Case CO 1.25 3.00
The Old Gray Fox Does It Again
S5 Tommy Burleson 2.00 5.00
Monte Towe
S6 Three All-Americans/1973 5.00 12.00
Tommy Burleson
Monte Towe
David Thompson
S7 David Thompson 10.00 25.00
S8 David Thompson 10.00 25.00
S9 1970 ACC Champs .75 2.00
S10 1973 ACC Champs 1.25 3.00
S11 Sam Esposito ACO .75 2.00
S12 Art Musselman ACO .40 1.00
S13 Eddie Bierderbach ACO .40 1.00
JK Pack Power .75 2.00
JK Reynolds Coliseum .75 2.00

1987-88 North Carolina State

This 15-card standard-size set commemorates the Wolfpack's 1987 ACC title. It was sponsored by Adolescent CareUnit, IBM, and local police agencies. The sets were distributed at a home game and by police officers. Most fans in attendance at the home game only received 14 cards, because Sean Green transferred after the cards were printed and his cards were removed from the set. A small number of his cards still made their way to the general public. The fronts feature either posed or action color photos on a white card face, with a drop border in red on the bottom and right side of picture. The school name in red and ACC Champions in black appear above the picture, while the player's name is printed in white in the bottom red drop border. The backs carry biography, career summary, and "Tips from the Wolfpack," which consist of anti-drug or alcohol messages. The cards are unnumbered and checklisted below in alphabetical order. The set features the first card of coach Jim Valvano.

COMPLETE SET (15) 10.00 25.00
1 Chucky Brown 1.50 4.00
2 Chris Corchiani 1.50 4.00
3 Brian D'Amico .30 .75
4 Vinny Del Negro 2.00 5.00
5 Sean Green SP 1.50 4.00
6 Brian Howard .50 1.25
7 Quinton Jackson .30 .75
8 Avie Lester .50 1.25
9 Rodney Monroe 1.00 2.50
10 Kenny Poston .30 .75
11 Charles Shackleford .50 1.25
12 Bryon Tucker .30 .75
13 Jim Valvano CO 3.00 8.00
14 Kelsey Weems .30 .75
15 Team Photo .75 2.00

1988-89 North Carolina State

This 16-card standard size (2 1/2" by 3 1/2") set was sponsored by Adolescent CareUnit, IBM, and local police agencies. The sets were given away at a home game and by local police officers. On a white card face, the fronts feature action or posed color photos enclosed by a black drop border on the left and red drop borders on the right and bottom of the picture. A Wolfpack logo appears in the lower left corner while player information appears in the bottom red drop border. The backs carry biography, player profile, and "Tips from the Wolfpack," which consist of anti-drug or alcohol messages. The cards are unnumbered and checklisted below in alphabetical order. The set features the first card of NBA player Tom Gugliotta.

COMPLETE SET (16) 8.00 20.00
1 Chucky Brown 52 1.25 3.00
2 Chris Corchiani 13 1.25 3.00
3 Brian D'Amico 54 .30 .75
4 Tom Gugliotta 24 4.00 10.00
5 Mickey Hinnant 3 .30 .75
6 Brian Howard 22 .60 1.50
7 James Knox 23 .30 .75
8 David Lee 25 .30 .75
9 Avie Lester 32 .30 .75
10 Rodney Monroe .60 1.50
11 Kenny Poston 30 1.25 3.00
12 Jim Valvano CO 2.50 6.00
13 Kelsey Weems 11 .60 1.50
14 Mr. and Mrs. Wuf .30 .75
Mascots
15 Kay Yow CO 1.25 3.00
Women's Basketball
16 Women's Team .60 1.50

1989 North Carolina State Collegiate Collection

This 200-card standard-size set was produced by Collegiate Collection and sponsored by Coca-Cola, and the Coke logo appears in the lower left corner on the card face. The fronts feature a mix of black and white photos for earlier players and color for later ones, with rounded corners and red borders. The pictures are superimposed over a red and white diagonally-striped card face, with a red outer border. The top reads "N.C. State's Finest," and the school logo appears in the upper right corner. The horizontally oriented backs are printed in red on white and present biographical information, career summaries, or statistics.

COMPLETE SET (200) 10.00 25.00
1 Rick Anheuser .07 .15
2 Rick Anheuser .07 .15
3 Rick Anheuser .07 .15
4 Pete Auksel .07 .15
5 Pete Auksel .07 .15
6 Pete Auksel .07 .15
7 Clyde Austin .07 .20
8 Clyde Austin .07 .20
9 Clyde Austin .07 .20
10 Thurl Bailey .10 .30
11 Thurl Bailey .10 .30
12 Thurl Bailey .10 .30
13 Eddie Bartels .07 .15
14 Eddie Bartels .07 .15
15 Eddie Bartels .07 .15
16 Alvin Battle .07 .15
17 Alvin Battle .07 .15
18 Alvin Battle .07 .15
19 William Bell .07 .15
20 William Bell .07 .15
21 Eddie Bierderbach .07 .15
22 Eddie Bierderbach .07 .15
23 Eddie Bierderbach .07 .15
24 Dick Braucher .07 .15
25 Dick Braucher .07 .15
26 Dick Braucher .07 .15
27 Chucky Brown .08 .25
28 Chucky Brown .08 .25
29 Chucky Brown .08 .25
30 Vic Bubas .08 .25
31 Vic Bubas .08 .25
32 Tom Burleson .10 .30
33 Tom Burleson .10 .30
34 Tom Burleson .10 .30
35 Charles Shackleford .07 .20
36 Charles Shackleford .07 .20
37 Charles Shackleford .07 .20
38 Terry Shackleford .07 .15
39 Ronnie Shavlik .07 .15
40 Ronnie Shavlik .07 .15
41 Ronnie Shavlik .07 .15
42 Jon Garwood Speaks .07 .15
43 Jon Garwood Speaks .07 .15
44 Jon Garwood Speaks .07 .15
45 Craig Watts .07 .15
46 Phil Spence .07 .15
47 Phil Spence .07 .20
48 Phil Spence .07 .15
49 Tim Stoddard .08 .25
50 Tim Stoddard .08 .25
51 Tim Stoddard .08 .25
52 Glenn Joseph Sudhop .07 .15
53 Glenn Joseph Sudhop .07 .15
54 Glenn Joseph Sudhop .07 .15
55 Joe Cafferky .07 .15
56 Joe Cafferky .07 .15
57 Larry Wosley .07 .15
58 Kenny Carr .08 .25
59 Kenny Carr .08 .25
60 Kenny Carr .08 .25
61 Horace McKinney .10 .30
62 John Richter .07 .15
63 Warren Cartier .07 .15
64 Paul Coder .07 .15
65 Paul Coder .07 .15
66 Paul Coder .07 .15
67 Bill Kretzer .07 .15
68 Darnell Adell .07 .15
69 Gary Stokan .07 .15
70 Pete Coker .07 .15
71 Dereck Whittenburg .08 .25
72 Pete Coker .07 .15
73 Craig Davis .07 .15
74 Smedes York .07 .15
75 Craig Davis .07 .15
76 Dick Dickey .07 .15
77 Dick Dickey .07 .15
78 Dick Dickey .07 .15
79 Tommy Dinardo .07 .15
80 Tommy Dinardo .07 .15
81 Vann Williford .07 .15
82 Bob Distefano .07 .15
83 Dan Englehardt .07 .15
84 Dan Englehardt .07 .15
85 Gary Stokan .07 .15
86 Smedes York .07 .15
87 Vann Williford .07 .15
88 Vinny Del Negro .10 .30
89 Vinny Del Negro .10 .30
90 Vinny Del Negro .10 .30
91 Larry Larkins .07 .15
92 Larry Larkins .07 .15
93 Larry Larkins .07 .15
94 Larry Larkins .07 .15
95 Sidney Lowe .08 .25
96 Sidney Lowe .08 .25
97 Ernest Myers .07 .15
98 Ernest Myers .07 .15
99 Ernest Myers .07 .15
100 Checklist 1-100 .07 .15
101 Hal Blondeau .07 .15
102 Les Robinson .10 .30
103 Nate McMillan .10 .30
104 Nate McMillan .10 .30
105 Nate McMillan .10 .30
106 Charles G. Nevitt .08 .25
107 Charles G. Nevitt .08 .25
108 Charles G. Nevitt .08 .25
109 Quinton Leonard .07 .15
110 Bruce Hoadley .07 .15
111 Les Robinson .10 .30
112 Bruce Hoadley .07 .15
113 Emmett Lay .07 .15
114 Emmett Lay .07 .15
115 Larry Worsley .07 .15
116 Harold Thompson .07 .15
117 Harold Thompson .07 .15
118 Harold Thompson .07 .15
119 Howard Turner .07 .15
120 Mike O'Neal Warren .07 .15
121 Mike O'Neal Warren .07 .15
122 Kenny Matthews .07 .15
123 Anthony Warren .07 .15
124 Anthony Warren .07 .15
125 Vann Williford .07 .15
126 Raymond Walters .07 .15
127 Raymond Walters .07 .15
128 Raymond Walters .07 .15
129 Craig T. Watts .07 .15
130 Larry Worsley .07 .15
131 Craig T. Watts .07 .15
132 Spud Webb .15 .40
133 Spud Webb .15 .40
134 Spud Webb .15 .40
135 Ray Hodgdon .07 .15
136 Herb Applebaum .07 .15
137 Bill Kretzer .07 .15
138 Charles Whitney .07 .20
139 Charles Whitney .07 .20
140 Charles Whitney .07 .20
141 Dereck Whittenburg .08 .25
142 Dereck Whittenburg .08 .25
143 Tom Mattocks .07 .15
144 Tom Mattocks .07 .15
145 Tom Mattocks .07 .15
146 Mark Moeller .07 .15
147 Mark Moeller .07 .15
148 Mark Moeller .07 .15
149 Cheerleader .07 .15
Mascot
150 Quentin Jackson .07 .15
151 Quentin Jackson .07 .15
152 Steve Nuce .07 .15
153 Steve Nuce .07 .15
154 Steve Nuce .07 .15
155 Scott Parzych .07 .15
156 Scott Parzych .07 .15
157 Scott Parzych .07 .15
158 Dan Wherry .07 .15
159 Hal Blondeau .07 .15
160 Dan Wherry .07 .15
161 Mascots .07 .15
162 Max Perry .07 .15
163 Max Perry .07 .15
164 David Thompson .30 .75
165 David Thompson .30 .75
166 David Thompson .30 .75
167 Monte Towe .08 .25
168 Monte Towe .08 .25
169 Monte Towe .08 .25
170 Press Maravich .07 .20
171 Terry Gannon .08 .25
172 Nick Pond .07 .15
173 Lou Pucillo .07 .15
174 Ray Hodgdon .07 .15
175 Darnell Adell .07 .15
176 Herb Applebaum .07 .15
177 Max Perry .07 .15
178 John Richter .07 .20
179 Kenny Poston .07 .20
180 Terry Gannon .08 .25
181 Pete Coker .07 .15
182 Quentin Jackson .07 .15
183 Jim Rezinger .07 .15
184 Kenny Poston .07 .20
185 Rick Hoot .07 .15
186 Everett Case .08 .25
187 Everett Case .08 .25
188 Everett Case .08 .25
189 Kenny Matthews .07 .15
190 Reynolds Stadium .07 .20
191 Jim Valvano CO .20 .50
192 Jim Valvano CO .20 .50
193 Jim Valvano CO .20 .50
194 Cheerleaders .07 .20
195 Ray Hodgdon .07 .15
196 Lou Pucillo .07 .15
197 Kenny Poston .07 .20
198 Everett Case .08 .25
199 Reynolds Coliseum .07 .15
200 Checklist 101-200 .07 .15

1989-90 North Carolina State

This 16-card set of standard-size cards was sponsored by Hardee's WPTF/680 AM radio, and IBM; these company logos adorn the top of observe and the bottom of the reverse. The front features a color action player photo, with red borders on the top, right, and for most of the bottom. The school name and player identification is given in the top and bottom borders, with the year "1989-90" in the lower left corner. The back has biographical information and "Tips from the Wolfpack," which consist of anti-drug messages. The cards are unnumbered and are checklisted below in alphabetical order, with the uniform number after the player's name. The set features a card of NBA player Tom Gugliotta.

COMPLETE SET (16) 6.00 15.00
1 Chris Corchiani 13 .60 1.50
2 Brian D'Amico 54 .30 .75
3 Bryant Feggins 34 .60 1.50
4 Tom Gugliotta 24 3.00 8.00
5 Mickey Hinnant 3 .30 .75
6 Brian Howard 22 .60 1.50
7 Jamie Knox 23 .30 .75
8 David Lee 25 .30 .75
9 Avie Lester 32 .30 .75
10 Rodney Monroe 21 .60 1.50
11 Andrea Stinson 32 2.00 5.00
12 Kevin Thompson 42 .60 1.50
13 Jim Valvano CO 2.00 5.00
14 Roland Whitley 15 .30 .75
15 Wuf (Mascot) .30 .75
16 Kay Yow 1.25 3.00
Women's Coach

1990-91 North Carolina State

This 16-card standard size set was cosponsored by IBM and Nabisco Brands. Reportedly 2500 sets were given away at Youth Night before a home game, and an equal number of sets were distributed by local police officers. On a white card face, the fronts feature action or posed color photos enclosed by a red border. The school name appears above the picture, while player information is provided beneath the picture. A Wolfpack logo appears in the lower right corner in a circle. The backs carry biography and player profile, with anti-drug and alcohol messages in a black box. The cards are unnumbered and checklisted below in alphabetical order. The key card in the set features NBA player Tom Gugliotta.

COMPLETE SET (16) 6.00 15.00
1 Migjen Bakalli .30 .75
2 Chris Corchiani .60 1.50
3 Bryant Feggins .30 .75
4 Adam Fletcher .30 .75
5 Tom Gugliotta 3.00 8.00
6 Jamie Knox .30 .75
7 David Lee .30 .75
8 Marc Lewis .30 .75
9 Rodney Monroe .60 1.50
10 Anthony Robinson .30 .75
11 Les Robinson CO .60 1.50
12 Andrea Stinson 1.50 4.00
13 Kevin Thompson .60 1.50
14 Kay Yow CO 1.25 3.00
Women's Basketball
15 Celebrating a Victory .30 .75
Paul Campion
Chris Ritter
Tim Thompson
16 Mr. Wuf (Mascot) .30 .75

1991-92 North Carolina State

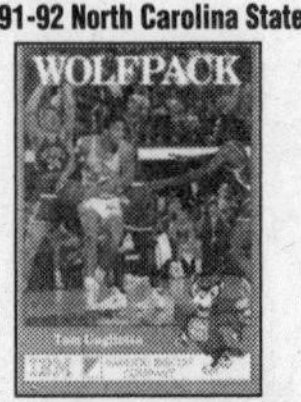

This 16-card standard size set was cosponsored by IBM and Nabisco Biscuit Company. The print run was limited to 5,000 sets, and the sets were given away at Youth Night and distributed by the local police department. The fronts feature action color player photos enclosed by a red border. The team name is superimposed in white lettering at the top of the picture, while the player's name, Wolfpack logo, and sponsor names appear at the bottom of the card face. In a horizontal format, the backs carry a black and white mug shot, biography, career highlights, and anti-drug messages in a black box. The cards are unnumbered and checklisted below in alphabetical order. The key card in the set features NBA player Tom Gugliotta.

COMPLETE SET (16) 5.00 12.00
1 Migjen Bakalli .30 .75
2 Mark Davis .60 1.50
3 Bryant Feggins .30 .75
4 Adam Fletcher .30 .75
5 Tom Gugliotta 2.50 6.00
6 Jamie Knox .30 .75
7 Marc Lewis .30 .75
8 Curtis Marshall .30 .75
9 Lakista McCuller .30 .75
10 Victor Newman .30 .75
11 Anthony Robinson .30 .75
12 Les Robinson CO .60 1.50
13 Donnie Seale .30 .75
14 Kevin Thompson .60 1.50
15 Mr. Wuf (Mascot) .30 .75
16 Reynolds Coliseum .60 1.50

1992-93 North Carolina State

This 16-card set features the 1992-93 North Carolina State Wolfpack. The fronts display color action photos with team color-coded borders. The backs provide a closeup shot and player information. The cards are unnumbered and checklisted below in alphabetical order.

COMPLETE SET (16) 4.00 10.00
1 Migjen Bakalli .30 .75
2 Mark Davis .60 1.50
3 Todd Fuller 1.50 4.00
4 Jamie Knox .30 .75
5 Chuck Kornegay .60 1.50
6 Bill Kretzer .30 .75
7 Marc Lewis .30 .75
8 Curtis Marshall .30 .75
9 Lakista McCuller .30 .75
10 Victor Newman .30 .75
11 Les Robinson CO .60 1.50
12 Donnie Seale .30 .75
13 Kevin Thompson .30 .75
14 Marcus Wilson .30 .75
15 Mr. Wuf (Mascot) .30 .75
16 Coaching Staff .30 .75

1993-94 North Carolina State

This 16-card set features the 1993-94 North Carolina State Wolfpack. The fronts display color action photos with team color-coded borders. The backs provide a closeup shot and player information. The cards are unnumbered and checklisted below in alphabetical order.

COMPLETE SET (16) 5.00 12.00
1 Greg Clucas .30 .75
2 Ricky Daniels .30 .75
3 Mark Davis .60 1.50
4 Bryant Feggins .30 .75
5 Todd Fuller 1.00 2.50
6 Jeremy Hyatt .60 1.50
7 Bill Kretzer .30 .75
8 Marc Lewis .30 .75
9 Lakista McCuller .30 .75
10 Curtis Marshall .30 .75
11 Les Robinson CO .60 1.50
12 Lewis Sims .30 .75
13 Jason Sutton .30 .75
14 Marcus Wilson .30 .75
15 Mr. Wuf (Mascot) .30 .75
16 Coaching Staff .30 .75

1994-95 North Carolina State

This 16-card set features the 1994-95 North Carolina State Wolfpack. The fronts display color action photos with team color-coded borders. The backs provide a closeup shot and player information. The cards are unnumbered and checklisted below in alphabetical order.

COMPLETE SET (16) 4.00 10.00
1 Ishua Benjamin .60 1.50
2 Ricky Daniels .30 .75
3 Mark Davis .40 1.00
4 Bryant Feggins .30 .75
5 Todd Fuller .75 2.00
6 Clint(CC) Harrison .30 .75
7 Jeremy Hyatt .60 1.50
8 Bill Kretzer .30 .75
9 Lakista McCuller .30 .75
10 Curtis Marshall .30 .75
11 Al Pinkins .30 .75
12 Geoff Richards .30 .75
13 Les Robinson CO .60 1.50
14 Jason Sutton .30 .75
15 Marcus Wilson .30 .75
16 Coaching Staff .30 .75

1997-98 North Carolina State

This 17-card standard size set, highlighting the 1996-97 Wolfpack basketball team, was produced by Action Graphics in conjunction with Sears Roebuck and The National Association of Basketball Coaches. The card fronts have color action photos transposed over a red sea of fans background within a black border. "Wolfpack Basketball" is written in cursive at the top and an Action Graphics logo can be found at the bottom. The black and white horizontal backs carry player biographies and career high NC State statistics through January 1997. The right side dawns a close-up photo and anti-drug advice. The cards are numbered out of 16, but there was also a cover card that gives information on how to support the Coaches vs. Cancer Program.

COMPLETE SET (17) 3.00 8.00
1 Team Photo CL .40 1.00
2 Herb Sendek CO .20 .50
3 John Groce ACO .20 .50
Larry Harris ACO
Sean Miller ACO
4 Ishua Benjamin .40 1.00
5 Luke Buffum .20 .50
6 Justin Gainey .20 .50
7 Clint C.C. Harrison .20 .50
8 Jeremy Hyatt .40 1.00
9 Andre McCullum .60 1.50
10 Steve Norton .20 .50
11 Al Pinkins .20 .50
12 Danny Strong .40 1.00
13 Jason Sutton .20 .50
14 Damon Thornton .40 1.00
15 Tim Wells .20 .50
16 Mr. Wuf (Mascot) .20 .50
NNO Sears Coaches vs. Cancer .20 .50
Cover Card

1991-92 North Dakota

COMPLETE SET (12) 6.00 12.00
1 Whitney Meier .20 .50
Greg Johnson
David Vonesh
men's basketball
2 Marty McDermott .20 .50
Chris Gardner
Scott Guldseth
men's basketball
3 Ben Jacobson .20 .50
Steve McAndrew
David Robertson
men's basketball
4 Jonathon Marshall .20 .50
Mike Wiskus
Broderick Powell
men's basketball
5 Todd Johnson .20 .50
Mark Sipple
James Baird
men's basketball
6 Men's Basketball Team Photo .20 .50
7 Women's Basketball Team Photo .20 .50
8 Darcy Deutsch .20 .50
Tracey Pudenz
Jenny Walter
women's basketball
9 Heidi Kasprowicz .20 .50
Misty Langseth
Shea Smirl
women's basketball
10 Maria Oistad .20 .50
Heidi Meyer
Emily Shilhanek
women's basketball

1997-98 Northwestern Women

This 20-card set was released at Northwestern University during the 1997-98 season. The set features player cards from that season's team. These cards are not numbered, and are listed below in alphabetical order. Please note that these cards were issued as singles, and were not distributed as complete team sets.

COMPLETE SET (20) 4.00 10.00
1 Team Photo .20 .50
2 Don Perrelli CO .75 2.00
3 Robin Garrett .20 .50
Amy Backus
Jennifer Kiefer CO
4 Lisa Byington .20 .50
Mary Connolly
Amber DeWall
Shannon McGarrigle
Candace Wrenn
5 Becky Fisher .20 .50
Clarissa Flores
Chala Holland
Dana Leonard
Tami Sears
6 Leah Berki .20 .50
7 Lisa Byington .20 .50
8 Megan Chawansky .20 .50
9 Mary Connolly .20 .50
10 Amber DeWall .20 .50
11 Kristina Divjak .20 .50
12 Becky Fisher .20 .50
13 Clarissa Flores .20 .50
14 Anne Giblin .20 .50
15 Chala Holland .20 .50
16 Dana Leonard .20 .50
17 Shannon McGarrigle .20 .50
18 Leslie Schock .20 .50
19 Tami Sears .20 .50
20 Candace Wrenn .20 .50

1998-99 Northwestern Women

Released as a 16-card set, the cards measure standard size and feature photos of the 1998-99 Northwestern Women's basketball team. The cards are not numbered and listed below in alphabetical order.

COMPLETE SET (16) 2.50 6.00
1 Leah Berki .20 .50
2 Megan Chawansky .20 .50
3 Kristina Divjak .20 .50
4 Becky Fisher .20 .50
5 Clarissa Flores .20 .50
6 Anne Giblin .20 .50
7 Chala Holland .20 .50
8 Sara Jurek .20 .50
9 Dana Leonard .20 .50
10 Shannon McGarrigle .20 .50
11 Billee Russell .20 .50
12 Leslie Schock .20 .50
13 Tami Sears .20 .50
14 Team Photo .20 .50
15 Don Perrelli CO .30 .75
16 Robin Garrett ACO .20 .50
Amy Backus ACO
Jennifer Kiefer ACO

1988 Notre Dame Smokey

This 14-card standard size set was sponsored by the U. S. Forestry Service. The front features a color action photo, with orange and green borders on a purple background. The back has biographical information (or a schedule) and a fire prevention cartoon starring Smokey the Bear. These unnumbered cards are ordered alphabetically within type for convenience. Ricky Watters is featured in this set.

COMPLETE SET (14) 14.00 35.00
15 Women's Basketball .60 1.50

1990-91 Notre Dame

This 58 card standard-size set is a retrospective on famous and outstanding players at Notre Dame. The cards are numbered as "X of 58"; the Anson card is unnumbered and is the only baseball player featured and is not considered part of the set On the front of the cards, older players appear in black and white photos while newer players appear in color. These current players have been highlighted in the checklist below with the word "NEW" after each name. The photos are enframed by a black line on a white background, with the school name and the Notre Dame logo (upper right hand corner) above the photo, and the player's name below. The card backs provide biographical information, including the player's position and the team they played on. Past and present NBA players included are Gary Brokaw, Austin Carr, Adrian Dantley, LaPhonso Ellis (his first card), Bill Hanzlik, Tom Hawkins, Toby Knight, Bill Laimbeer, John Paxson, David Rivers, John Shumate, Kelly Tripucka, and Orlando Woolridge.

COMPLETE SET (59) 10.00 25.00
CAP ANSON NOT INCLUDED IN SET
1 Richard (Digger) Phelps NEW .75 2.00
2 Collis Jones .20 .50
3 Dick Rosenthal .20 .50
4 Tim Singleton NEW .30 .75
5 Austin Carr .40 1.00
6 Kevin O'Shea .20 .50
7 Keith Tower NEW .40 1.00
8 Tom Hawkins .40 1.00
9 Leo Barnhorst .30 .75
10 John Shumate .40 1.00
11 Donald Royal .40 1.00
12 Edward(Moose) Krause .20 .50
13 Bill Laimbeer .75 2.00
14 Adrian Dantley .75 2.00
15 Keith Robinson .20 .50
16 Edward(Monk) Malloy .20 .50
17 Leo Klier .20 .50
18 Rich Branning .20 .50
19 Don(Duck) Williams .20 .50
20 Kevin Ellery NEW .30 .75
21 Eddie Smith .20 .50
22 Ken Barlow .40 1.00
23 LaPhonso Ellis NEW 2.00 5.00
24 John Nyikos .20 .50
25 Daimon Sweet NEW .60 1.50
26 Jack Stephens .20 .50
27 Orlando Woolridge .75 2.00
28 Noble Kizer .20 .50
29 John Smyth .20 .50
30 John Paxson .75 2.00
31 Paul Nowak .20 .50
32 Elmer Bennett NEW .60 1.50
33 Toby Knight .20 .50
34 Dave Batton .20 .50
35 Bob Whitmore .20 .50
36 David Rivers .40 1.00
37 Gary Brokaw .40 1.00
38 Gary Novak .20 .50

39 Lloyd Aubrey .20 .50
40 Robert Faught .20 .50
41 Raymond Scanlan .20 .50
42 Bill Hanzlik .40 1.00
43 Vince Boryla .30 .75
44 Eddie Riska .20 .50
45 Dwight Clay .20 .50
46 Bruce Flowers .25 .60
47 Ray Meyer .75 2.00
48 Monty Williams NEW 1.00 2.50
49 John Moir .20 .50
50 Bill Hassett .20 .50
51 Bob Arnzen .20 .50
52 Robert Rensberger .20 .50
53 Larry Sheffield .20 .50
54 Kelly Tripucka .40 1.00
55 Ron Reed .40 1.00
56 George Ireland .20 .50
57 Tracy Jackson .40 1.00
58 Walt Sahm .20 .50
NNO Adrian(Cap) Anson 1.25 3.00

1996-97 Notre Dame Schedules

Featuring a surprisingly lively design, highlighted by full color action photos framed by gold borders and dark blue text, cards from this schedule set feature all three seniors from the 1996-97 team. The schedules were distributed for free at home games throughout the 1996-97 season. The schedules are unnumbered on back and have been checklisted below alphabetically for convenience.

COMPLETE SET (3) .30 .75
1 Matt Gotsch .08 .25
2 Ardmore White .08 .25
3 Marcus Young .08 .25

1991 Oklahoma State Collegiate Collection

This 100-card multi-sport standard-size set was produced by Collegiate Collection. We've cataloged players from the top three sports using these initials: B-baseball, K-basketball, and F-football.

COMPLETE SET (100) 6.00 15.00
1 Henry Iba K .08 .25
8 1945 NCAA Basketball Champions K .05 .15
40 John Starks K .20 .50
49 Jess(Cob) Rennick K .05 .15
80 Gale McArthur K .05 .15
99 Eddie Sutton K .08 .25

1999-00 Oklahoma State

This fifteen-card standard-size set was issued to commemorate the 1999-2000 Oklahoma State care. It was issued in a sheet of 16 cards, which when perforated, measures the standard size for each card. Since these cards are unnumbered, we have sequenced them in alphabetical order. This set was sponsored by Oklahoma Gas and Electric.

COMPLETE SET (15) 6.00 15.00
1 Joe Adkins .20 .50
2 Glendon Alexander .20 .50
3 Zac Cazzelle .20 .50
4 Nate Fleming .20 .50
5 Doug Gottlieb .40 1.00
6 Fredrik Jonzen .20 .50
7 Jason Keep .20 .50
8 Daniel Lawson .20 .50
9 Desmond Mason 4.00 10.00
10 Brian Montonati .20 .50
11 Rodney Sooter .20 .50
12 Eddie Sutton CO 1.25 3.00
13 Alex Webber .20 .50
14 Andre Williams .20 .50
15 Gallagher-Iba Arena .20 .50

1991-92 Ohio State

This 15-card standard-size set was produced by College Classics of Columbus, Ohio. The cards were sold in the university bookstore and at a souvenir shop in St. John Arena. The cards were sold through April 30, and the print run was limited by the number of sets requested by the bookstore. It is reported that more than 10,000 sets were sold in the first four weeks. The fronts features either action or posed color player photos enclosed by red and gray borders. The player's name is printed in a gray stripe beneath the picture, while his position appears in a gray stripe along the right side of the picture. The school logo appears at the top right of the photo. In a horizontal format, the backs carry a color head shot, school logo, biography, career summary, and statistics. The cards are unnumbered and checklisted below in alphabetical order. The key card in the set features NBA player Jim Jackson.

COMPLETE SET (15) 6.00 15.00
1 Randy Ayers CO .40 1.00
2 Mark Baker .40 1.00
3 Tom Brandewie .20 .50
4 Jamaal Brown .20 .50
5 Alex Davis .20 .50
6 Rickey Dudley .75 2.00
7 Doug Etzler .20 .50
8 Lawrence Funderburke 1.25 3.00
9 Steve Hall .20 .50
10 Jim Jackson 3.00 8.00
11 Chris Jent 1.25 3.00
12 Jimmy Ratliff .20 .50
13 Joe Reid .20 .50
14 Bill Robinson .20 .50
15 Jamie Skelton .40 1.00

1992-93 Ohio State

This 15-card set measures the standard size (2 1/2" by 3 1/2") and was available through the Ohio State Department of Athletics, the Arena Shop, and its affiliated bookstores. The fronts feature color action player photos bordered on the left or right edge by a gray stripe containing the school name. The player's name appears in red lettering on a gray stripe at the bottom. The horizontal backs feature close-up player pictures with gray shadow box borders. The white background is printed with a profile of the player. The school logo and biographical information appear at the top. The cards are numbered on the back.

COMPLETE SET (15) 5.00 12.00
1 Randy Ayers CO .40 1.00
2 Derek Anderson 2.50 6.00
3 Tom Brandewie .20 .50
4 Alex Davis .20 .50
5 Rickey Dudley 1.00 2.50
6 Gerald Eaker .20 .50
7 Doug Etzler .20 .50
8 Lawrence Funderburke .75 2.00
9 Charles Macon .20 .50
10 Jimmy Ratliff .20 .50
11 Greg Simpson .40 1.00
12 Jamie Skelton .40 1.00
13 Antonio Watson .20 .50
14 Nate Wilbourne .20 .50
15 Otis Winston .20 .50

1992-93 Ohio State Women

This 16-card set features the 1992-93 Ohio State Lady Buckeyes. The cards measure the standard size. The fronts feature color action photos; the backs provide biography and statistics. The cards are unnumbered and checklisted below in alphabetical order. This set includes the first card of Katie Smith.

COMPLETE SET (16) 5.00 12.00
1 Alysiah Bond .20 .50
2 Audrey Burcy .20 .50
3 Nancy Darsch CO .20 .50
4 Kelly Fergus .20 .50
5 Stacie Howard .20 .50
6 Erin Ingwersen .20 .50
7 Gigi Jackson .20 .50
8 Adrienne Johnson .40 1.00
9 Nikki Keyton .20 .50
10 Lisa Negri .20 .50
11 Averrill Roberts .20 .50
12 Lisa Sebastian .20 .50
13 Katie Smith 3.00 8.00
14 Lavona Turner .20 .50
15 Big Bear (Sponsor card) .20 .50
16 820 WOSU-AM (Sponsor card) .20 .50

1993-94 Ohio State

This is a 12-card standard size set. The gray-bordered fronts feature color action player shots with a series of basketballs apearing to bounce along the bottom of the photo. Above the photo is the players name printed in red with a black drop shadow. Below the photo the players number is printed in red and their position is printed on top in black. The white backs carry a player head shot with the biography to the right and the player profile below. The cards are numbered and checklisted below. Card number 2 was never issued.

COMPLETE SET (12) 4.00 10.00
1 Randy Ayers CO .60 1.50
3 Jamie Skelton .40 1.00
4 Jimmy Ratliff .20 .50
5 Derek Anderson 1.50 4.00
6 Doug Etzler .20 .50
7 Charles Macon .20 .50
8 Greg Simpson .40 1.00
9 Antonio Watson .20 .50
10 Rickey Dudley .75 2.00
11 Gerald Eaker .20 .50
12 Nate Wilbourne .20 .50
13 Otis Winston .20 .50

1993-94 Ohio State Women

This 16-card set features the 1993-94 Ohio State Lady Buckeyes. The cards measure the standard size. The fronts feature color action photos; the backs provide biography and statistics. The cards are unnumbered and checklisted below in alphabetical order. This set includes the second card of Katie Smith.

COMPLETE SET (16) 4.00 10.00
1 Marcie Alberts .20 .50
2 Alysiah Bond .20 .50
3 Nancy Darsch CO .20 .50
4 Kelly Fergus .20 .50
5 Stacie Howard .20 .50
6 Erin Ingwersen .20 .50
7 Gigi Jackson .20 .50
8 Adrienne Johnson .30 .75
9 Lisa Negri .20 .50
10 Katie Smith 2.50 6.00
11 Marlene Stollings .20 .50
12 Amy Turner .20 .50
13 Lavona Turner .20 .50
14 Team Photo .30 .75
15 Big Bear (Sponsor card) .20 .50
16 1460 WBNS-AM (Sponsor card) .20 .50

1994-95 Ohio State Women

This set consists of 16 standard-size cards. Inside white borders, the fronts feature color action player photos. Player information is printed on a bar that is superposed on a basketball-and-hardwood floor design. On a ghosted version of the school logo, the backs carry biography and player profile. The cards are unnumbered and checklisted below in alphabetical order, with nonplayer cards listed at the end.

COMPLETE SET (16) 3.00 8.00
1 Marcie Alberts .20 .50
2 Alysiah Bond .20 .50
3 Peggy Evans .20 .50
4 Kelly Fergus .20 .50
5 Tiffany Glosson .20 .50
6 Erin Ingwersen .20 .50
7 GiGi Jackson .20 .50
8 Adrienne Johnson .25 .60
9 Lisa Negri .20 .50
10 Katie Smith 2.00 5.00
11 Marlene Stollings .20 .50
12 Amy Turner .20 .50
13 Melissa McFerrin ACO Nancy Darsch CO Nikita Lowry ACO .20 .50
14 1994-95 OSU Buckeyes Go Bucks! .20 .50
15 Big Bear (Sponsor card) .20 .50
16 1460 WBNS-AM Radio (Sponsor Card) .20 .50

1997-98 Ohio State

This 22-card set is unnumbered and listed below in alphabetical order. The cards feature top athletes from both men's and women's sports at Ohio State.

COMPLETE SET (22) 4.00 10.00
1 Roslyn Barker BK .20 .50
17 Jason Singleton BK .20 .50

2000-01 Ohio State

Released by Ohio State in conjunction with Honda, this 16-card set was released as a sheet. The card backgrounds are read and feature a basketball design and the card backs showcase player photos and biographies.

COMPLETE SET (16) 1.25 3.00
COMPLETE SHEET 2.00 5.00
3 Sean Connolly .15 .40
4 Brent Darby .15 .40
10 Doylan Robinson .15 .40
13 Brian Brown .15 .40
14 Velimir Radinovic .15 .40
21 Boban Savovic .15 .40
23 Ryan Heflin .15 .40
24 Shaun Smith .15 .40
31 Kel Frazier .15 .40
32 Ken Johnson .15 .40
33 Zach Williams .15 .40
34 Cobe Ocokoljic .15 .40
43 Will Dudley .15 .40
44 Tim Martin .15 .40
NNO Mascot .15 .40
NNO Jim O'Brien .75 2.00

2006-07 Ohio State

Produced by Ohio State and sponsored by Gatorade, this 12-player sheet measures 10x12" and each player's card is standard sized and surrounded by perforation lines.

COMPLETE SHEET 20.00 40.00
NNO Danny Peters .75 2.00
NNO Mark Titus .75 2.00
NNO Kyle Madsen .75 2.00
NNO Matt Terwilliger .75 2.00
NNO Daequan Cook 2.00 5.00
NNO Othello Hunter .75 2.00
NNO Ivan Harris .75 2.00
NNO David Lighty .75 2.00
NNO Jamar Butler 2.00 5.00
NNO Mike Conley Jr. 4.00 10.00
NNO Ron Lewis .75 2.00
NNO Greg Oden 8.00 20.00

1992-93 Ohio Valley Conference ATG

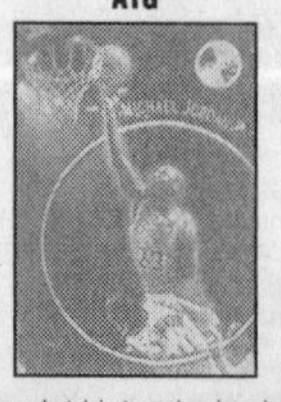

These two perforated sheets were issued as an insert in the 1993 Ohio Valley Conference Basketball Tourney Program and feature stars of the past who played in the Ohio Valley Conference. Each sheet consists of nine cards, each measuring approximately 2 5/8" by 3 1/2". The fronts feature black-and-white action player photos on a white card face. In green, the Ohio Valley Conference logo appears in the left corner above the picture, while the words "Stars of the Past" appear in the right corner on a green panel. The player's name is printed in a white stripe below the picture, and the school he attended in a green stripe immediately below. The backs carry biography, statistics, and career summary. The cards are unnumbered and checklisted below in alphabetical order.

COMPLETE SET (18) 6.00 15.00
1 John (Sonny) Allen .60 1.50
2 Jim Baechtold .40 1.00
3 Jerry Beck .40 1.00
4 Tom Chilton .40 1.00
5 Howard Crittenden .40 1.00
6 Jimmy Hagan .40 1.00
7 Steve Hamilton .60 1.50
8 Clem Haskins 1.00 2.50
9 Joe Jakubick .40 1.00
10 Ronald(Popeye) Jones .75 2.00
11 Tom Marshall .40 1.00
12 Jeff Martin .40 1.00
13 Anthony Mason 1.50 4.00
14 Jim McDonald .60 1.50
15 Brett Roberts .40 1.00
16 Kenny Sidwell .40 1.00
17 James (Fly) Williams .75 2.00
18 Stars of the Past Checklist Card (OVC Dream Team) .60 1.50

1991-92 Oklahoma State

Produced by Motion Sports, this 57-card set features the Oklahoma State Cowboys basketball team. Two sets were available: 1) a team-issued set (no more than 5,000 sets produced); and 2) a limited edition "Signature Series" set of 8" by 10" photos autographed by all players and coaches, and encased in an 8" by 10" leather binder (originally sold for 99.95). The regular set was sold to the public at all home games and through the Student Union Bookstore. The cards measure the standard size (2 1/2" by 3 1/2"). The fronts of card numbers 1-25 display a full-color head shot of the player on a screened red background enframed by a black border. The player's name appears in a gray-to-red screened band at the top of the photo while the school name and sponsor's name (Johnsons) appear in a red band at the bottom. Card numbers 28-32 have on the fronts action photos of seniors on the squad. The last major section of the set consists of card numbers 37-54. These cards are similar to SkyBox in design, with color action player photos cut out and superimposed over a background of computer-generated graphics and geometric shapes. The player information on the backs of all cards is superimposed over ghosted OSU campus scenes. The cards are numbered on the back.

COMPLETE SET (57) 10.00 25.00
1 Earl Jones .08 .25
2 Corey Williams .20 .50
3 Jason Turk .08 .25
4 Binky Triplett .08 .25
5 Sean Sutton .20 .50
6 Darwyn Alexander .08 .25
7 Sean Walker .08 .25
8 Terry Collins .08 .25
9 Byron Houston .50 1.25
10 Randy Davis .08 .25
11 Scott Sutton .08 .25
12 Brooks Thompson .75 2.00
13 Mike Philpott .08 .25
14 Cornell Hatcher .08 .25
15 Milton Brown .08 .25
16 Sean Pell .08 .25
17 Von Bennett .08 .25
18 Bryant Reeves 1.50 4.00
19 Steve Anthis ACO .08 .25
20 Scott Streller ACO .08 .25
21 Russ Pennell ACO .08 .25
22 Eddie Sutton CO 1.25 3.00
23 Rob Evans ACO .08 .25
24 Bill Self ACO .08 .25
25 Pistol Pete (Mascot) .08 .25
26 Eddie Sutton CO 1.25 3.00
27 Trophies .08 .25
28 Cornell Hatcher .08 .25
29 Byron Houston .50 1.25
30 Corey Williams .20 .50
31 Sean Sutton .20 .50
32 Darwyn Alexander .08 .25
33 Eddie Sutton CO Henry Iba CO 1.25 3.00
34 Team Photo .40 1.00
35 Mike Johnson John Johnson -Basketball Sponsors .08 .25
36 Scott Sutton Sean Sutton Eddie Sutton CO .40 1.00
37 Milton Brown .08 .25
38 Earl Jones .08 .25
39 Terry Collins .08 .25
40 Von Bennett .08 .25
41 Byron Houston .50 1.25
42 Darwyn Alexander .08 .25
43 Mike Philpott .08 .25
44 Sean Pell .08 .25
45 Bryant Reeves 1.50 4.00
46 Randy Davis .08 .25
47 Cornell Hatcher .08 .25
48 Jason Turk .08 .25
49 Sean Sutton .20 .50
50 Sean Walker .08 .25
51 Sean Walker .08 .25
52 Binky Triplett .08 .25
53 Corey Williams .20 .50
54 Brooks Thompson .75 2.00
NNO Ad Card Motion Sports .08 .25
NNO Card Directory CL .08 .25
NNO Title Card .08 .25

2002-03 Oregon

These 24 cards feature members of both the men's and women's Oregon basketball team. The cards feature the an action photo with the player's name on the bottom. The back features some personal information as well as some blurbed information. Since these cards are unnumbered, we have sequenced them in alphabetical order by first men's and then the women's team.

COMPLETE SET 6.00 15.00
1 Jay Anderson .30 .75
2 Ian Crosswhite .30 .75
3 Jame Davis .30 .75
4 Brian Helquist .30 .75
5 Luke Jackson 1.25 3.00
6 Robert Johnson .30 .75
7 Andre Joseph .30 .75
8 Brandon Lincoln .30 .75
9 Luke Ridnour 2.50 6.00
10 Matt Short .30 .75
11 Tyler York .30 .75
12 Adam Zahn Jordan Kent .30 .75
13 Andrea Bills .30 .75
14 Brandi Davis .30 .75
15 Alissa Edwards .30 .75
16 Carolyn Ganes .30 .75
17 Kedzie Gunderson .30 .75
18 Cathrine Kraayeveld .30 .75
19 Corrie Mizusawa .30 .75
20 Yadili Okwumabua .30 .75
21 Kourtney Shreve .30 .75
22 Kayla Steen .30 .75
23 Amy Taylor .30 .75
24 Chelsea Wagner .30 .75

1996-97 Oregon Women

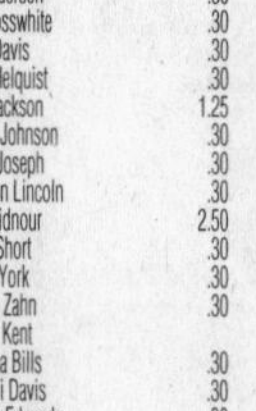

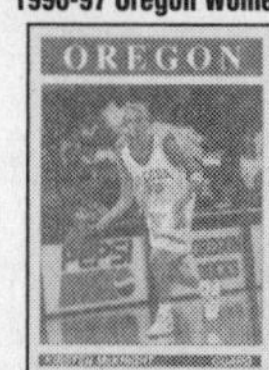

Sponsored by Pepsi, this 12-card set was issued on a perforated sheet with three columns and four rows. When separated, the cards are standard size with white backgrounds and color action photos on the front. The school name is written in white inside a green rectangle at the top of the card. The backs are white stock with black print stating the players' position, year, and hometown followed by the previous year's highlights. The university and Pepsi logo are found at the bottom of the card. The cards are unnumbered so listed below in alphabetical order.

COMPLETE SET (12) 4.00 10.00
1 Mendy Benson .30 .75
2 Betty Ann Boeving .30 .75
3 Lisa Bowyer .30 .75
4 Adrianne Boyer .60 1.50
5 Sonja Curtis .30 .75
6 Cindie Edamura .30 .75
7 Sandie Edwards .30 .75
8 Renae Fegent .60 1.50
9 Kirsten McKnight .30 .75
10 Jenny Mowe .30 .75
11 Elsa Oliveira .30 .75
12 Jody Runge CO .30 .75

1989-90 Oregon State

This 16-card set was printed on thin cardboard stock and issued in one sheet; after perforation, the cards measure approximately 3" by 4 1/16". The set may also have been issued as single unperforated cards. It is reported that some autographed sets were available in limited quantities. The front features a black and white action player photo, with white borders. The player's name appears in an orange and black basketball superimposed in the upper left corner. The player's name and position appear below the picture in a black stripe. In orange lettering, the team name "Beavers" is printed, with an oversized B–. The backs are printed in orange and black, and present a black and white head shot as well as biographical and statistical information. The cards are unnumbered and are checklisted below in alphabetical order, with the uniform number after the player's name. There are two variations of the Teo Alibegovic card. This set includes the first card of Gary Payton, who was chosen as the second pick by Seattle in the 1990 NBA draft, as well as 1993 NBA draftee Scott Haskin.

COMPLETE SET (16) 12.00 30.00
1 Teo Alibegovic 12 .20 .50
2 Jim Anderson CO .40 1.00
3 Karl Anderson 22 .40 1.00
4 Will Brantley 25 .40 1.00
5 Bob Cavell 4 .20 .50
6 Allan Celestine 40 .20 .50
7 Kevin Grant 11 .20 .50
8 Kevin Harris 14 .20 .50
9 Scott Haskin 44 .75 2.00
10 Earl Martin 24 .20 .50
11 Lamont McIntosh 33 .20 .50
12 Charles McKinney 23 .40 1.00
13 Gary Payton 20 10.00 25.00
14 Chris Rueppell 21 .20 .50
15 Travis Stel 13 .20 .50
16 Jim Anderson CO .40 1.00

1990-91 Oregon State

The 1990-91 Oregon State basketball set was issued on a perforated sheet, with three rows of six cards each. After perforation, the cards measure approximately 2 1/2" by 3 1/2". Reportedly 2,000 perforated sheets were produced. This set includes a card of Brent Barry, son of HOFer Rick Barry. On an orange background enclosed by white and black borders, the fronts feature black and white player photos inside an oval design. Player information appears beneath the picture. In orange and black print, the backs carry biography, career summary, and statistics. The cards are unnumbered and checklisted below in alphabetical order. The key cards in the set feature Brent Barry and Scott Haskin.

COMPLETE SET (18) 6.00 15.00
1 Teo Alibegovic .20 .50
2 Jim Anderson CO .40 1.00
3 Karl Anderson .20 .50
4 Brent Barry 3.00 8.00
5 Will Brantley .20 .50
6 Bob Cavell .20 .50
7 Allan Celestine .20 .50
8 Canaan Chatman .20 .50
9 Kevin Harris .20 .50
10 Scott Haskin .60 1.50
11 Mario Jackson .20 .50
12 Charles McKinney .20 .50
13 Henrik Ringmar .20 .50
14 Tony Ross .20 .50
15 Chris Rueppell .20 .50
16 Chad Scott .40 1.00
17 Travis Stel .20 .50
18 Fred Boyd ACO Andy McClouskey ACO Jim Shaw ACO Brent Wilder ACO .20 .50

1991-92 Oregon State

The 1991-92 Oregon State basketball set was issued on a perforated sheet, with three rows of six cards each. After perforation, the cards measure approximately 2 1/2" by 3 1/2". On a white card face, the fronts feature black and white player photos enclosed by black and orange borders. The player's name appears beneath the picture, while the words "Oregon State 1991-92" are printed in a box at the upper right corner of the picture. The backs present biography and career highlights. The cards are unnumbered and checklisted below in alphabetical order. Reportedly 2,000 perforated sheets were produced. No complete autographed sheets exist; Earnest Killum died two days before the sets were completed.

COMPLETE SET (18) 6.00 15.00
1 Jim Anderson CO .40 1.00
2 Kareem Anderson .60 1.50
3 Karl Anderson .20 .50
4 Brent Barry 2.50 6.00
5 Freddie Boyd ACO .20 .50
6 David Brown .20 .50
7 Canaan Chatman .20 .50
8 Kevin Harris .20 .50
9 Scott Haskin .60 1.50
10 Mario Jackson .20 .50
11 Earnest Killum .60 1.50
12 David Lawson .20 .50
13 Andy McClouskey ACO .20 .50
14 Charles McKinney .20 .50
15 Ray Ross .20 .50
16 Chad Scott .40 1.00
17 Pat Strickland .20 .50
18 Brent Wilder ACO .20 .50

1992-93 Oregon State

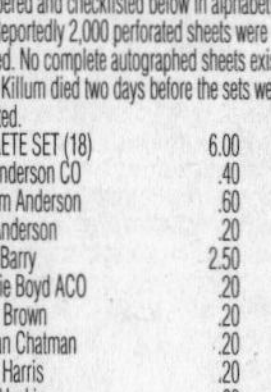

These standard-size cards were available in a perforated sheet consisting of three rows with six cards per row. The fronts feature black-and-white action player photos inside a white border. The left and bottom edge of the pictures is edged by black stripes carrying "Oregon State 1992-93" and the player's name. The horizontal backs have a black-and-white head shot, biography, career highlights, and career statistics. The cards are unnumbered and checklisted below in alphabetical order.

COMPLETE SET (18) 5.00 12.00
1 Jim Anderson CO .40 1.00
2 Kareem Anderson .40 1.00
3 Brent Barry 2.50 6.00
4 David Brown .20 .50
5 Jerohn Brown .40 1.00
6 Kevin Harris (Dribbling ball) .20 .50
7 Kevin Harris (Lay up) .20 .50
8 Scott Haskin (Blocking shot) .40 1.00
9 Scott Haskin (Shooting hook shot) .40 1.00
10 Mustapha Hoff .20 .50
11 David Lawson .20 .50
12 Charles McKinney (Looking down court) .20 .50
13 Charles McKinney (Looking at ball while dribbling) .20 .50
14 Brandon Peterson .20 .50
15 Chad Scott .40 1.00
16 Pat Strickland .20 .50
17 Ibou Thioune .20 .50
18 J.D. Vetter .20 .50

1993-94 Oregon State

The 1993-94 Oregon State basketball set was issued on a perforated sheet, with four rows of three cards each. After perforation, the cards measure approximately 3" by 4". The fronts feature color posed and action player photos with white borders. The team name is printed above the photo, with the player's name, number and the team logo below, all in team colors. The backs carry a short biography, career highlights and a fire prevention cartoon starring Smokey. The cards are unnumbered and checklisted below in alphabetical order.

COMPLETE SET (12) 5.00 12.00
1 Kareem Anderson .60 1.50
2 Brent Barry 2.00 5.00
3 Sonny Benjamin .60 1.50
4 Jelani Boline .40 1.00
5 David Brown .40 1.00
6 Jerohn Brown .40 1.00
7 Stephane Brown .60 1.50
8 David Drakeford .40 1.00
9 Dwayne Franklin .40 1.00
10 Mustapha Hoff .40 1.00
11 Brandon Peterson .40 1.00
12 J.D. Vetter .40 1.00

1995-96 Pacific

Produced by High Step, this 2-card set was available at the University of Pacific during the 1995-96 school year.

COMPLETE SET (2) .40 1.00
21 Adam Jacobsen .20 .50
31 Charles Jones .20 .50

1996-97 Pacific

Produced by High Step, this card was available through the University of Pacific during the 1996-97 school year.

NNO Bob Thomason CO .25 .60

1997-98 Pacific

55 Michael Olowokandi .40 1.00

1992 Penn State Winter Sports

This 16-card standard-size set was sponsored by The Second Mile, the Jostens Foundation, KMart, and Penn State Intercollegiate Athletics. The cards are printed on thin card stock. A diagonal cuts across the card face, separating the top white portion from the bottom blue portion. The color player photos are superimposed on this background and are tilted slightly to the left. The backs have career summary, Nittany Lion Tips in the form of player quotes, and sponsor logos. The cards are unnumbered and checklisted below.

COMPLETE SET (16) 6.00 15.00
2 Monroe Brown .40 1.00
5 Dave Degitz .40 1.00
7 Dana Eikenberg .40 1.00
9 Kathy Phillips .40 1.00
12 Susan Robinson .40 1.00

1994 Penn State Winter Sports

This 25-card standard-size set was sponsored by The Second Mile, Penn State Intercollegiate Athletics and Keystone Real Estate. The cards are printed on thin card stock. The card fronts feature a thin red border with a light blue border inside. A white triangle at the top of the card features the Penn State name, while another white triangle at the bottom feature the player's name and class or position. The color player photos are featured in the middle of the card. The backs have career summary and Nittany Lion Tips in the form of player quotes. The cards are unnumbered and checklisted below.

COMPLETE SET (25) 5.00 12.00
3 John Amaechi .80 2.00
4 Greg Bartram .20 .50
7 Carla Coleman .20 .50
12 Katina Mack .20 .50
14 Missy Masley .20 .50

16 Tina Nicholson .20 .50
20 Glenn Sekunda .40 1.00
23 Donovan Williams .20 .50

1996 Penn State Winter Sports

This 25-card set was sponsored by The Second Mile and Penn State Intercollegiate Athletics. The set covers men's and women's basketball, men's and women's gymnastics and men's wrestling. Each team is given five cards. The full-color cards measure the standard size and are printed on thin non-coated stock. The cards are unnumbered and checklisted below in alphabetical order.

COMPLETE SET (25) 6.00 15.00
4 Kim Calhoun .30 .75
6 Dan Earl .80 2.00
8 Matt Gaudio .30 .75
14 Pete Lisickey .80 2.00
Calvin Booth
15 Tiffany Longworth .30 .75
16 Katina Mack .30 .75
20 Tina Nicholson .30 .75
21 Angie Potthoff .30 .75
23 Glenn Sekunda .40 1.00
24 Phil Williams .30 .75

2002 Penn State Winter Sports

The set is unnumbered and listed below in alphabetical order.

COMPLETE SET (25) 8.00 20.00
2 Rashana Barnes BK .40 1.00
5 Jennifer Brenden BK .40 1.00
6 Jessica Brungo BK .40 1.00
10 Ndu Egekeze BK .40 1.00
12 Ken Krimell BK .40 1.00
13 Kelly Mazzante BK .40 1.00
18 Tyler Smith BK .40 1.00
20 Jamaal Tate BK .40 1.00
22 Courtney Upshaw BK .40 1.00
25 Brandon Watkins BK .40 1.00

2003 Penn State Winter Sports

COMPLETE SET (25) 8.00 20.00
4 Jenny Brenden BK .40 1.00
5 Jessica Brungo BK .40 1.00
6 Sharif Chambliss BK .40 1.00
9 Ndu Egekeze BK .40 1.00
11 Kelly Mazzante BK .40 1.00
18 Jessica Strom BK .40 1.00
19 Jamaal Tate BK .40 1.00
23 B.J. Vossekul BK .40 1.00
24 Brandon Watkins BK .40 1.00
25 Tanisha Wright BK .40 1.00

2008 Penn State Winter Sports

COMPLETE SET (25) 5.00 10.00
2 Geary Claxton BK .40 1.00
3 Jamelle Cornley BK .40 1.00
6 Kamela Gissendanner WBK .30 .75
7 Tyra Grant WBK .30 .75
9 Brandon Hassell BK .40 1.00
13 Rashida Mark WBK .30 .75
15 Danny Morrissey BK .40 1.00
16 Brianne O'Rourke WBK .30 .75
24 Mike Walker BK .40 1.00
25 Mashea Williams WBK .30 .75

1989-90 Pittsburgh

This 12-card set featuring members of the Pittsburgh Panthers basketball team was sponsored by Foodland; each card measures the standard size. The front features an action color photo enframed by orange border on blue background. Above the photo appears the school's name "Panthers" (in orange print), player's name, jersey number, classification, and position. The sponsor's name is found below the photo. The back is filled with biographical information, a basketball tip from the Panthers, and an anti-drug message. The set is unnumbered and checklisted below in alphabetical order.

COMPLETE SET (12) 2.50 6.00
1 Rod Brookin .30 .75
2 Pat Cavanaugh .20 .50
3 Paul Evans CO .30 .75
4 Gilbert Johnson .30 .75
5 Bobby Martin .30 .75
6 Jason Matthews .20 .50
7 Sean Miller .40 1.00
8 Darren Morningstar .40 1.00
9 Pitt Panther/(team mascot) .20 .50
10 Darelle Porter .20 .50
11 Brian Shorter .40 1.00
12 Travis Ziegler .20 .50

1990-91 Pittsburgh

This 12 card standard-size set was sponsored by Foodland. The front features a borderless color action photo of the player, with "Panthers" written in blue letter on white above the picture. Two color stripes appear below the picture; in the blue one appears the player's name and number, while in the thicker orange one appears the sponsor's logo. A basketball icon superimposed over these two bars at the left completes the card face. The back has biographical information, a tip from the Pittsburgh Panthers in the form of an anti-drug or alcohol message, and the sponsor's logo. The cards are unnumbered and are checklisted them below in alphabetical order, with uniform number after the player's name.

COMPLETE SET (12) 2.50 6.00
1 Antoine Jones 21 .20 .50
2 Gandhi Jordan 4 .30 .75
3 Bobby Martin 55 .30 .75
4 Jason Matthews 22 .20 .50
5 Chris McNeal 24 .20 .50
6 Jermaine Morgan 42 .20 .50
7 Sean Miller 3 .30 .75
8 Darren Morningstar 33 .30 .75
9 Omo Moses 44 .20 .50
10 Darelle Porter 20 .20 .50
11 Ahmad Shareef 13 .20 .50
12 Brian Shorter 00 .30 .75

1991-92 Providence

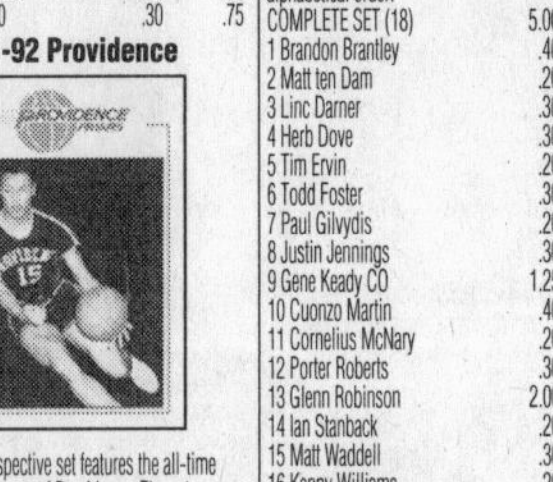

This 24-card retrospective set features the all-time great basketball players of Providence. The sets were originally available direct from the school for 7.00 postpaid. The set was produced by Ballpark Cards, and each card measures the standard size. The fronts feature a mix of black and white action or posed player photos enclosed by an orange border. The words "Providence Friars" appear at the top superimposed over an orange basketball. In black lettering on a gray background, the horizontally oriented backs have collegiate statistics, pro stints, and awards received. The card numbers appear in a circle at the bottom right.

COMPLETE SET (24) 6.00 15.00
1 Joseph Mullaney CO .40 1.00
2 Dave Gavitt CO .40 1.00
3 Rick Pitino CO 1.00 2.50
4 Rick Barnes CO .30 .75
5 Team Photo .30 .75
1973 Friars
6 Team Photo .30 .75
1987 Friars
7 Lenny Wilkens 1.50 4.00
8 John Egan .20 .50
9 Jim Hadnot .30 .75
10 Vinny Ernst .20 .50
11 Ray Flynn .30 .75
12 John Thompson .75 2.00
13 Mike Riordan .40 1.00
14 Jimmy Walker .30 .75
15 Jim Larranaga .20 .50
16 Ernie DiGregorio .75 2.00
17 Marvin Barnes 1.25 3.00
18 Kevin Stacom .30 .75
19 Joe Hassett .20 .50
20 Bruce Campbell .20 .50
21 Otis Thorpe 1.00 2.50
22 Billy Donovan .40 1.00
23 Eric Murdock .60 1.50
24 Checklist Card .20 .50

1992-93 Purdue

Produced by Phipps Sports Marketing Inc., this 18-card set measures the standard size and features color, action player photos with gold and black borders. The player's name and jersey number are superimposed on the photo in the lower right corner. The horizontal backs carry a small, close-up picture along with biographical information, career highlights, and statistics. The backs are pale yellow-orange. The cards are unnumbered and checklisted below in alphabetical order. The set features the first card of Glenn Robinson.

COMPLETE SET (18) 6.00 15.00
1 Brandon Brantley .30 .75
2 Linc Darner .30 .75
3 Herb Dove .30 .75
4 Todd Foster .30 .75
5 Justin Jennings .30 .75
6 Gene Keady CO 2.00 5.00
7 Cuonzo Martin .60 1.50
8 Cornelius McNary .20 .50
9 Matt Painter .30 .75
10 Porter Roberts .30 .75
11 Glenn Robinson 2.50 6.00
12 Tim Spiker .20 .50
13 Ian Stanback .20 .50
14 Matt Waddell .40 1.00
15 Bruce Weber ACO 1.50 4.00
Frank Kendrick ACO
Gene Keady CO
Gary Johnson TR
Tom Reiter ACO
16 Kenny Williams .20 .50
17 Mackey Arena .30 .75
18 Title Card .20 .50
(Checklist)

1993-94 Purdue

Produced by Phipps Sports Marketing Inc., the funds generated from the sale of this 18-card standard-size set benefitted the Purdue University Athletic Scholarship Fund. It could be ordered from the John Purdue Club for 7.00. The fronts feature a mix of posed and action color player photos inside gold borders. In the wider right margin, the player's name is printed vertically in script and overlays the team name in ghosted block lettering. The bottom border of the picture is formed by the school name in variegated gold lettering. On a ghosted panel featuring a basketball, the back presents a black-and-white head shot, biography, career highlights, and statistics. The cards are unnumbered and checklisted below in alphabetical order.

COMPLETE SET (18) 5.00 12.00
1 Brandon Brantley .40 1.00
2 Matt ten Dam .20 .50
3 Linc Darner .30 .75
4 Herb Dove .30 .75
5 Tim Ervin .20 .50
6 Todd Foster .30 .75
7 Paul Gilvydis .20 .50
8 Justin Jennings .30 .75
9 Gene Keady CO 1.25 3.00
10 Cuonzo Martin .40 1.00
11 Cornelius McNary .20 .50
12 Porter Roberts .30 .75
13 Glenn Robinson 2.00 5.00
14 Ian Stanback .20 .50
15 Matt Waddell .30 .75
16 Kenny Williams .30 .75
17 Larry Leverenz ACO 1.25 3.00
Jay Price ACO
Gene Keady CO
Frank Kendrick ACO
Bruce Weber ACO
18 Title card .20 .50

1993-94 Purdue Women

Produced by Phipps Sports Marketing Inc., the funds generated from the sale of this 18-card standard-size set benefitted the Purdue University Athletic Scholarship Fund. It could be ordered from the John Purdue Club for 7.00. The fronts feature a mix of posed and action color player photos inside gold borders. In the wider right margin, the player's name is printed vertically in script and overlays the team name in ghosted block lettering. The bottom border of the picture is formed by the school name in variegated gold lettering. On a ghosted panel featuring a basketball, the back presents a black-and-white head shot, biography, career highlights, and statistics. The cards are unnumbered and checklisted below in alphabetical order.

COMPLETE SET (17) 5.00 12.00
1 Melina Griffin .30 .75
2 Andrea Hildebrand .30 .75
3 Jennifer Jacoby .40 1.00
4 Leslie Johnson 1.00 2.50
5 Tonya Kirk .30 .75
6 Cindy Lamping .40 1.00
7 Shannon Lindsey .30 .75
8 Stacey Lovelace .40 1.00
9 Danielle McCulley .30 .75
10 Jannon Roland .40 1.00
11 Nicki Taggart .30 .75
12 Lin Dunn CO .60 1.50
13 Tracy Brown MG .30 .75
Tammi Hoffman MG
Angie Brown MG
14 Sarah Sharp ACO .30 .75
Dallas Boychuk ACO
MaCelle Joseph ACO
15 1993-94 Boiler Makers .30 .75
16 Mackey Arena .30 .75
17 Title card .30 .75

2000 Purdue Legends

COMPLETE SET (36) 10.00 25.00
1 Mark Atkinson .25 .60
2 Chad Austin .25 .60
3 Joe Barry Carroll .30 .75
4 Russell Cross .25 .60
5 Terry Dischinger .40 1.00
6 Keith Edmonson .30 .75
7 Bob Ford .25 .60
8 Mel Garland .25 .60
9 John Garrett .25 .60
10 Herman Gilliam .30 .75
11 Paul Hoffman .40 1.00
12 Walter Jordan .25 .60
13 Gene Keady CO .75 2.00
14 Billy Keller .60 1.50
15 Frank Kendrick .25 .60
16 Troy Lewis .25 .60
17 Cuonzo Martin .40 1.00
18 Willie Merriweather .25 .60
19 Brad Miller .75 2.00
20 Todd Mitchell .25 .60
21 Rick Mount .60 1.50
22 Charles Murphy .75 2.00
23 Eugene Parker .25 .60
24 Bruce Parkinson .25 .60
25 Glenn Robinson .75 2.00
26 Jim Rowinski .25 .60
27 Stephen Scheffler .30 .75
28 Dave Schellhase .25 .60
29 Joe Sexson .25 .60
30 Jerry Sichting .40 1.00
31 Everette Stephens .30 .75
32 Matt Waddell .30 .75
33 Brian Walker .25 .60
34 John Wooden 1.25 3.00
35 Jewell Young .25 .60
36 Logo CL .25 .60

1910 Richmond College Silks S23

These colorful silks were issued around 1910 by Richmond Straight Cut Cigarettes. Each measures roughly 4" by 5 1/2" and are often called "College Flag, Seal, Song, and Yell" due to the content found on each one. More importantly to most sports collectors is the image found in the lower right hand bottom corner. A few feature a mainstream sports' subject such as a generic player or piece of equipment, while most include a realistic image of the school's mascot or image of the founder or the school's namesake.

28 Oberlin BK Player 75.00 150.00
32 Rochester Basketball 60.00 120.00

2003-06 Saint Vincent-Saint Mary High School

Released by the Saint Vincent-Saint Mary's high school book store, this oversized post card (3.5" x 5.25") features a team photo on the front and the words, "2002-03 National Champion/State Champion" in green letters along the bottom. It was announced that 10,000 total green versions of the team card were printed. The card back lists the players in the photo and team statistics from the season. Also present is a silver hologram with a background circle and a serial number starting with the letter A. Each card also came with a certificate of authenticity from St.V-St.M bookstore with the corresponding serial number. This green version came with a green COA. Gold and Ruby versions were also printed and the "2002-03 National Champion/State Champion" on the bottom front of the card appears in gold or red depending on the version and a gold serial numbered hologram is attached to the card back along with a separate COA from the school with a matching gold hologram. 2300 copies of the Gold and 2003 copies of the Ruby version were printed. A LeBron James football card and three basketball cards dated 1999 to 2002 showed up on the secondary market sometime during or after 2005.

*GOLD: .5X TO 1.2X BASE HI
*RUBY: .6X TO 1.5X BASE HI
3 LeBron James 2001 Football 8.00 20.00
5 Team Photo 10.00 25.00
Willie McGee
Brandon Weems
Dru Joyce III
Marcus Johnson
Corey Jones
Mike Snowbarger CO
Dru Joyce HCO
Tim Marks
Sian Cotton
LeBron James
Romeo Travis
Preston Sims
Lee Cotton CO
Steve Culp CO
1a LeBron James 1999-00 8.00 20.00
2a LeBron James 2000-01 8.00 20.00
6a LeBron James 2001-02 8.00 20.00

2005-06 San Diego State

Produced by High Step in conjunction with the San Diego State Alumni Association, this 15-card set was available on the campus during the 2005-06 school year.

COMPLETE SET (15) 3.00 8.00
0 Tommy Johnson .20 .50
1 Brandon Heath .60 1.50
3 Chris Walton .30 .75
5 Travis Hanour .20 .50
11 Tyler Smith .20 .50
15 John Sharper .20 .50
20 Trimaine Davis .20 .50
21 Matt Thomas .20 .50
24 Tim McGrath .20 .50
30 Chris Lamb .20 .50
31 Jared Ines .20 .50
33 Chris Manker .20 .50
42 Marcus Slaughter .20 .50
50 Mohamed Camara .20 .50
NNO Steve Fisher CO .50 1.25

2006-07 San Diego State

Produced by High Step, this 13-card set was available through San Diego State during the 2006-07 school year.

COMPLETE SET (13) 3.00 8.00
1 Mohamed Camara .20 .50
2 Trimaine Davis .20 .50
3 Mohamed Abukar .20 .50
4 Brandon Heath .75 2.00
5 Brett Hoerner .20 .50
6 Tim McGrath .20 .50
7 Chris Lamb .20 .50
8 Marcus Slaughter .20 .50
9 John Sharper .20 .50
10 Matt Thomas .20 .50
11 Kyle Spain .20 .50
12 Richie Williams .20 .50
13 Steve Fisher CO .60 1.50

1990-91 San Jose State

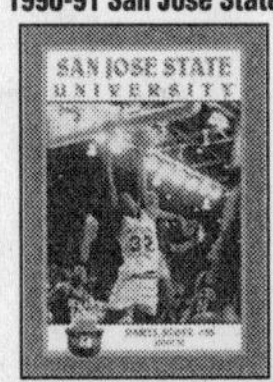

This nine-card set was printed in the same style as the 1990 San Jose football set. The cards measure 2 1/2" by 3 1/2" and are printed on thin white stock. The fronts feature color action player photos. The picture is enframed by an orange border on a blue background. The backs provide player information and have a fire prevention cartoon starring Smokey the Bear. The cards are unnumbered and are checklisted below in alphabetical order with non-player cards listed at the end.

COMPLETE SET (9) 2.50 6.00
1 Troy Batiste .40 1.00
2 Terry Cannon .40 1.00
3 Robert Dunlap .40 1.00
4 Kevin Logan .40 1.00
5 Stan Morrison CO .60 1.50
6 Daryl Scott .40 1.00
7 Charles Terrell .60 1.50
8 Event Center .40 1.00
9 Smokey Bear .40 1.00

1991 South Carolina Collegiate Collection

This 200-card set measures standard sized and features cards of all-time great South Carolina athletes. The fronts have a black border with color action shots on each one. The school name and logo are found across the top border of the card. The featured player's name is found along the bottom border set against a red background. The backs carry a small bio of the player and his/her statistics.

COMPLETE SET (200) 5.00 12.00
1 Frank McGuire BK CO .20 .50
3 Alex English BK .20 .50
5 Kevin Darmody BK .05 .15
9 Linwood Moye BK .05 .15
24 Karlton Hilton BK .05 .15
26 Zam Fredrick BK .05 .15
35 Alex English BK .20 .50
38 Jimmy Hawthorne BK .05 .15
62 Jack Thompson BK .05 .15
64 Kevin Joyce BK .08 .25
68 Cedrick Hordges BK .05 .15
73 Grady Wallace BK .05 .15
78 Tom Riker BK .08 .25
80 Bobby Cremins BK .20 .50
85 Gary Gregor BK .05 .15
90 Ronnie Collins BK .05 .15
99 Joe Smith BK .05 .15
106 Jack Gilloon BK .05 .15
125 Mike Doyle BK .05 .15
126 Brad Jergenson BK .05 .15
143 John Hudson BK .05 .15
150 Mike Brittain BK .05 .15
156 Art Whisnant BK .05 .15
157 Jim Slaughter BK .05 .15
158 Skip Harlicka BK .05 .15
178 Ray Pericola BK .05 .15

1987-88 Southern

This 16-card standard-size set was sponsored by McDonald's, Southern University, and local law enforcement agencies, and was produced by McDag Productions. The McDonald's logo appears at the bottom of both sides of the card. The front features a mix of action or posed, black and white player photos. The pictures are bordered in turquoise on the sides, yellow above, and white below. The school name and player information appear in black lettering in the yellow border. A picture of the school mascot in the lower right corner rounds out the card face. The back presents biographical information, Jag Facts, and "Tips from The Jaguars" in the form of an anti-drug message. The sports represented in this set are football (1-3, 14-16) and basketball (4-13). The key cards in the set feature the first cards of NBA player Avery Johnson and NFL player Gerald Perry.

COMPLETE SET (16) 5.00 12.00
4 Ben Jobe CO BK .40 1.00
5 Daryl Battles BK .20 .50
6 Patrick Garner BK .20 .50
7 Avery Johnson BK 3.20 8.00
8 Rodney Washington BK .20 .50
9 Kevin Florent BK .20 .50
10 Dervynn Johnson BK .20 .50
11 Claudene Stovall BK .20 .50
12 Michelle Currie BK .20 .50
13 Gibbie Phillips BK .20 .50

1990-91 Southern Cal

This 20-card standard-size set was sponsored by the USDA Forest Service in conjunction with several other agencies. The cards have color action shots, with orange borders on a maroon card face with the words "USC Trojans" above the player's picture and his name, uniform number, school year, and position underneath his picture. The back has two Trojan logos at the top and features a player profile and a fire prevention cartoon starring Smokey. The cards are unnumbered and checklisted below in alphabetical order, with the uniform number after the player's name. Cards 1-2 and 12 feature basketball rather than football players and are so indicated by BKB. The checklist card in the set lists the football players but not the basketball players. The set features the first cards of NFL running back Ricky Ervins and NBA guard Robert Pack.

COMPLETE SET (20) 8.00 20.00
1 Calvin Banks BKB .60 1.50
2 Ronnie Coleman BKB .30 .75
12 Robert Pack BKB 2.00 5.00

1991 Southern Cal College Classics

Produced by College Classics Inc., this 100-card standard-size set honors former Trojan Athletes of various sports. Most players are football, other sports are designated in the listings below. The complete set comes with a blank-backed white card that carries the set's production number out of a total of 20,000 produced. In addition, 1,400 cards autographed by John Naber, Ron Fairly, Tom Seaver, Charles White, Dave Stockton, Mike Garrett, Anthony Davis, and Fred Lynn were randomly inserted throughout 1,000 of these sets. Since these cards rarely appear in the secondary marketplace, they are not priced.

COMPLETE SET (100) 10.00 25.00
6 Bill Sharman BK .30 .75
20 John Block BK .02 .10
42 Wayne Carlander BK .02 .10
52 Bob Boyd CO BK .02 .10
54 John Lambert BK .02 .10
75 Paul Westphal BK .40 1.00

1987-88 Southern Mississippi

This 14-card set, measuring 2 3/8" by 3 1/2", was co-sponsored by Deposit Guaranty National Bank and Coca-Cola, and their company names appear at the bottom corners on the front. The front has a posed action photo on a yellow background; two cards of the set feature two players. Player's names and team logo surmount the photo. The back presents biographical information and the card number.

COMPLETE SET (14) 8.00 20.00
1 The Freshmen .60 1.50
2 The Coaches .60 1.50
3 Casey Fisher .60 1.50
4 Derrek Hamilton .60 1.50
5 Randolph Keys 1.50 4.00
6 John White .60 1.50
7 D.J. and Allen .60 1.50
D.J. Bowe and
Allen Chapman
8 The Browns .60 1.50
John Brown and
Willie Brown
9 Jurado Hinton .60 1.50
10 Jay Ladner .60 1.50
11 Randy Pettus .60 1.50
12 Jimmy Smith .60 1.50
13 Roger Boyd .60 1.50
14 The Team 1.25 3.00

1994-95 Southwest Missouri St. Women

This 14-card Women's set measures the standard size and was produced by Springfield News-Leader and Southwest Missouri State University Athletic Program. The fronts feature posed color player photos framed by rose-colored borders. The player's name, position, and jersey number are printed in the border below the picture. The backs carry biographical information, statistics, and career highlights. The sponsor logos are at the bottom. The cards are unnumbered and checklisted below in alphabetical order.

COMPLETE SET (14) 5.00 12.00
1 Marsha Burton .40 1.00
2 Lisa Davies .40 1.00
3 Latanya Davis .40 1.00
4 Shannon Gage .40 1.00
5 Kindra Garst .40 1.00
6 Marla Harrison .40 1.00
7 Julie Howard .40 1.00
8 Charitee Longstreth .40 1.00
9 Lisa Moore .40 1.00
10 Courtney Murdock .40 1.00
11 Donease Smith .40 1.00
12 Stephanie Thurman .40 1.00
13 Richelle Winn .40 1.00
14 Team Photo .40 1.00

1996-97 Southwest Missouri State

This 13-card set was released at Southwest Missouri State University during the 1996-97. The set features all of the players from that years team. Each card is unnumbered and is listed below in alphabetical order.

COMPLETE SET (13) 4.00 10.00
1 Steve Alford CO 1.25 3.00
2 Kevin Ault .30 .75
3 Ryan Bettenhausen .30 .75
4 Coleco Buie .30 .75
5 JoJo Dabbs .30 .75
6 Tony Davis .30 .75
7 William Fontleroy .30 .75
8 Josh Hotz .30 .75
9 Ben Kandlbinder .30 .75
10 Omar Lincoln .30 .75
11 Omar Lincoln .30 .75
12 Monte Marsh .30 .75
13 Team Photo .30 .75

1986-87 Southwestern Louisiana

This 16-card standard-size set was sponsored by the Chemical Dependency Unit of Acadiana in Lafayette, the University of Southwest Louisiana, and local law enforcement agencies and was produced by McDag Productions. Only 3,500 sets were produced. The cards were distributed by the CDU adolescent program and by law enforcement officers.The front features borderless color action player photos, on white card stock with black lettering. The CDU logo and the words "USL Ragin' Cajuns" appear on the top of the card, with player information below the picture. The back has biographical information and "Tips from the Ragin' Cajuns" which encourage children to avoid drug use. Sports represented in this set include basketball (1, 4, 9, 11, 15), baseball (2, 5, 8, 16), softball (7, 14), track (3), and tennis (6, 10, 12-13). The cards are unnumbered and we have checklisted them below in alphabetical order. The set includes a card of high jumper Hollis Conway, who competed for the 1992 United States Olympic team at Barcelona.

COMPLETE SET (16) 4.00 10.00
1 Stephen Beene .30 .75
4 Teena Cooper .30 .75
9 Brian Jolivette .30 .75
11 Rodney McNeil .30 .75
15 Randal Smith .30 .75

1987-88 Southwestern Louisiana

This 16-card standard-size set was sponsored by CDU of Acadiana in Lafayette, University of Southwestern Louisiana, and local law enforcement agencies. The fronts display color action player photos on a white card face. The CDU logo, school logo, and year appear above the picture, while player information is given below the picture. The backs carry player profile, advertisements, and "Tips From the Ragin' Cajuns," which consist of anti-drug and alcohol messages. Sports represented in this set include men's basketball (1-4), women's basketball (5-6), tennis (7-8), men's baseball (9-12), women's softball (14-16), and track (13). The set includes a card of high jumper Hollis Conway, who competed for the 1992 United States Olympic team at Barcelona. .

COMPLETE SET (16) 5.00 12.00
1 Randal Smith BK .30 .75
2 Earl Watkins BK .30 .75
3 Kevin Brooks BK .60 1.50
4 Stephen Beene BK .30 .75
5 Kim Perrot BK 2.40 6.00
6 Teena Cooper BK .30 .75

1979-80 St. Bonaventure

This 18-card set measures the standard size, 2 1/2" by 3 1/2". The front features a sepia-toned photo with the player's name above and jersey number in a basketball logo at upper right hand corner; the team name "Bonnies" appears below the photo. The photo is also enframed by a thin brown border on white card stock. The back is filled with biographical and statistical information. The set is ordered below alphabetically for convenience. At time of issue, a collector could order this set from St Bonaventure for $1.

COMPLETE SET (18) 20.00 40.00
1 Earl Belcher 25 1.50 4.00
2 Dan Burns 41 1.25 3.00
3 Bruno DeGiglio 24 1.25 3.00
4 Jim Elenz 10 1.25 3.00
5 Lacey Fulmer 20 1.25 3.00
6 Delmar Harrod 52 1.25 3.00
7 Alfonza Jones 12 1.25 3.00
8 Mark Jones 11 1.50 4.00
9 Bill Kalbaugh CO 1.25 3.00
10 Lloyd Praedel 44 1.25 3.00
11 Pat Rodgers 35 1.25 3.00
12 Bob Sassone CO 1.25 3.00
13 Jim Satalin CO 1.25 3.00
14 Mark Spencer 15 1.25 3.00
15 Eric Stover 40 1.25 3.00
16 Shawn Waterman 33 1.25 3.00
17 Brian West 30 1.25 3.00
18 Title Card 2.00 5.00

1985-86 Stanford Schedules

Measuring 3 1/2" by 4 1/2", this 16-card set features schedules for the 1985-86 Stanford basketball team. The schedules are in color (despite the black and white photo above) and the right-half features a player photo with his name, height, weight, position and collegiate status underneath. The left-half features an advertisement from Miller. The back features ticket information and the actual schedule. These are not numbered and listed below in alphabetical order.

COMPLETE SET (16) 1.00 2.50
1 Steve Brown .08 .25
2 Derek Bruton .08 .25
3 Greg Butler .08 .25
4 Andy Fischer .08 .25
5 Neil Johnson .08 .25
6 Earl Koberlein .08 .25
7 Todd Lichti .60 1.50
8 Bryan McSweeney .08 .25
9 Scott Meinert .08 .25
10 John Paye .08 .25
11 Keith Ramee .08 .25
12 Eric Reveno .08 .25
13 Terry Taylor .08 .25
14 Novlan Whitsitt .08 .25
15 John Williams .30 .75
16 Howard Wright .08 .25

1994-95 Stanford Schedules

Mixing elements of traditional trading cards and pocket schedules, cards from this set feature members of the 1994-95 men's and women's Stanford Cardinal. The cards are believed to have been distributed at Cardinal home games during the 1994-95 season. Because they carry no numbers on back, we've listed the set below in the order we discovered them. The set is highlighted by a freshman season card of future NBA guard Brevin Knight.

COMPLETE SET (7) 1.50 4.00
1 Dion Cross .40 1.00
guarded by Jason Kidd
2 David Harbour .40 1.00
guarded by Jason Kidd
3 Brevin Knight .75 2.00
4 Bart Lammerson .30 .75

5 Todd Manley	.08	.25
6 Vanessa Nygaard	.08	.25
7 Andy Poppink	.08	.25
8 Darren Allaway	.08	.25
9 Warren Gravely	.08	.25
10 David Harbour	.08	.25
11 Rich Jackson	.08	.25

1995-96 Stanford Women

Issued by High Step, this 12-card set was available through Stanford during the 1995-96 school year.

COMPLETE SET (12)	2.50	6.00
0 Olympia Scott	.10	.30
4 Amy Wustefeld	.10	.30
10 Jamila Wideman	.15	.40
13 Vanessa Nygaard	.75	2.00
15 Regan Freuen	.10	.30
21 Charmin Smith	.15	.40
23 Bobbie Kelsey	.10	.30
30 Kate Starbird	1.25	3.00
32 Chandra Benton	.10	.30
33 Tara Harrington	.10	.30
34 Naome Mulitauaopele	.10	.30
44 Heather Owen	.10	.30

1996-97 Stanford

This 16-card set, produced by High Step Trading Cards, pays tribute to the 1996-97 Stanford men's basketball team. The card fronts have black backgrounds with a color action photo (except for Madsen in black and white) underneath the school name which is written in large red type at the top. The card backs, in black and white, contain basic player biographies and university statistics. For some unknown reason, two Brevin Knights cards were produced. The backs carry identical information; however, one card front shows him passing, and the other going to the hoop. The cards are unnumbered and listed below in alphabetical order.

COMPLETE SET (16)	8.00	20.00
1 Rich Jackson	.20	.50
2 Brevin Knight Charging	1.50	4.00
3 Brevin Knight Passing	1.50	4.00
4 Arthur Lee	.75	2.00
5 Mark Madsen	2.00	5.00
6 Ryan Mendez	.40	1.00
7 Mike Montgomery CO	1.25	3.00
8 David Moseley	.20	.50
9 Peter Sauer	.40	1.00
10 Mark Seaton	.40	1.00
11 Mark Thompson	.20	.50
12 Kamba Tshionyi	.20	.50
13 Peter Van Elswyk	.20	.50
14 Kris Weems	.40	1.00
15 Karl Wente	.20	.50
16 Tim Young	1.00	2.50

1996-97 Stanford Women

Produced by High Step, this 16-card set was available through Stanford during the 1996-97 school year.

COMPLETE SET (16)	4.00	10.00
0 Olympia Scott	.10	.30
4 Melody Peterson	.10	.30
5 Christina Batastini	.10	.30
10 Jamila Wideman	.20	.50
13 Vanessa Nygaard	.75	2.00
14 Yvonne Gbalazeh	.10	.30
15 Regan Freuen	.10	.30
20 Milena Flores	.20	.50
21 Charmin Smith	.75	2.00
30 Kate Starbird	1.00	2.50
32 Chandra Benton	.10	.30
33 Tara Harrington	.10	.30
34 Naomi Mulitauaopele	.15	.40
44 Heather Owen	.15	.40
NNO Tara VanDerveer CO	.40	1.00
NNO Team Card Schedule	.40	1.00

1997-98 Stanford

This collegiate set measures the standard-size was sponsered by Pepsi and produced by High Step. Card fronts feature a bordered action photo with the school name in a maroon bar across the top and the player's name in light-yellow at the bottom. Card backs feature the player's bio and statistics. The cards are numbered by jersey on the card back.

COMPLETE SET (14)	8.00	20.00
3 Kris Weems	.40	1.00
4 Michael McDonald	.20	.50
5 Peter Sauer	.40	1.00
21 David Moseley	.20	.50
31 Jarron Collins	1.50	4.00
32 Ryan Mendez	.20	.50
33 Jason Collins	1.50	4.00
35 Kamba Tshionyi	.20	.50
40 Peter Van Elswyk	.20	.50
44 Mark Seaton	.40	1.00
45 Mark Madsen	1.50	4.00
55 Tim Young	.75	2.00
NNO 1997-98 Schedule	.20	.50
NNO Mike Montgomery CO	.75	2.00

1997-98 Stanford Women

Produced by High Step and sponsored by Pepsi, this 17-card set was available through Stanford during the 1997-98 school year.

COMPLETE SET (17)	4.00	10.00
0-Olympia Scott	.10	.30
4 Melody Peterson	.10	.30
5 Christina Batastini	.10	.30
13 Vanessa Nygaard	.75	2.00
14 Yvonne Gbalazeh	.10	.30
15 Regan Freuen	.10	.30
20 Milena Flores	.25	.60
24 Kristin Folkl	.75	2.00
31 Karesa Granderson	.10	.30
32 Chandra Benton	.10	.30
33 Sarah Dimson	.10	.30
34 Naomi Mulitauaopele	.75	2.00
44 Heather Owen	.75	2.00
53 Carolyn Moos	.10	.30
55 Naila Moseley	.10	.30
NNO Tara VanDerveer CO	.40	1.00
NNO Team Card Schedule	.40	1.00

1998-99 Stanford

Produced by High Step, this 16-card set was offered at Stanford University during the 1998-99 season. The set was produced by Pepsi Cola. Please note that the set is not numbered and is listed in alphabetical order below.

COMPLETE SET (16)	9.00	18.00
1 Jarron Collins	1.25	3.00
2 Jason Collins	1.25	3.00
3 Alex Gelbard	.20	.50
4 Tony Giovacchini	.20	.50
5 Arthur Lee	.75	2.00
6 Kyle Logan	.20	.50
7 Mark Madsen	1.25	3.00
8 Michael McDonald	.20	.50
9 Ryan Mendez	.40	1.00
10 Mike Montgomery CO	.75	2.00
11 David Moseley	.20	.50
12 Peter Sauer	.20	.50
13 Mark Seaton	.20	.50
14 Kris Weems	.20	.50
15 Tim Young	.75	2.00
16 The Stanford Tree	.20	.50

1998-99 Stanford Women

Produced by High Step and sponsored by Pepsi, this 14-card set was available through Stanford during the 1998-99 school year.

COMPLETE SET (14)	2.00	5.00
1 Christina Batastini	.10	.30
2 Sarah Dimson	.10	.30
3 Bethany Donaphin	.20	.50
4 Cori Enghusen	.10	.30
5 Milena Flores	.20	.50
6 Regan Freuen	.10	.30
7 Yvonne Gbalazeh	.10	.30
8 Karesa Granderson	.10	.30
9 Enjoli Izidor	.10	.30
10 Carolyn Moos	.10	.30
11 Naila Moseley	.10	.30
12 Lauren St. Clair	.10	.30
13 Tara VanDerveer CO	.40	1.00
14 Lindsey Yamasaki	.10	.30

2000-01 Stanford

This 16 card set was sponsored by Pepsi and featured NCAA championship contender Stanford. Since these cards are unnumbered we have sequenced them in alphabetical order.

COMPLETE SET (16)	9.00	18.00
1 Julius Barnes	.20	.50
2 Tyler Besecker	.20	.50
3 Curtis Borchardt	.20	.50
4 Jarron Collins	1.25	3.00
5 Jason Collins	1.25	3.00
6 Justin Davis	.20	.50
7 Tony Giovacchini	.20	.50
8 Casey Jacobsen	2.00	5.00
9 Teyo Johnson	1.25	3.00
10 Joe Kirchofer	.20	.50
11 Kyle Logan	.20	.50
12 Matt Lottich	.20	.50
13 Mike McDonald	.20	.50
14 Ryan Mendez	.20	.50
15 Mike Montgomery CO	.75	2.00
16 Nick Robinson	.20	.50

2000-01 Stanford Women

Produced by High Step and sponsored by Pepsi, this 14-card set was available through Stanford during the 1996-97 school year.

COMPLETE SET (14)	2.50	6.00
0 Chelsea Trotter	.20	.40
10 Becky Bonner	.20	.40
11 Jamie Carey	.40	1.00
14 Nicole Powell	.60	1.50
22 Enjoli Izidor	.20	.40
24 Susan King	.20	.40
25 Lindsey Yamasaki	.40	1.00
32 Katie Denny	.20	.40
33 Sarah Dimson	.20	.40
41 Bethany Donaphin	.40	1.00
42 Lauren St. Clair	.20	.40
51 Cori Enghusen	.20	.40
53 Carolyn Moos	.20	.40
NNO Tara VanDerveer CO	.40	1.00

2001-02 Stanford Women

Produced by High Step, this 16-card set was available through Stanford during the 2001-02 school year.

COMPLETE SET (8)	1.50	4.00
5 Kelley Suminski	.20	.40
22 Enjoli Izidor	.20	.40
25 Lindsey Yamasaki	.60	1.50
33 Sebnem Kimyacioglu	.20	.40
34 T'Nae Thiel	.20	.40
44 Azella Perryman	.20	.40
51 Cori Enghusen	.20	.40
NNO Karen Middleton ACO	.20	.50

2002-03 Stanford Women

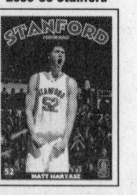

COMPLETE SET (13)	3.00	8.00
0 Chelsea Trotter	.15	.40
2 Krista Rappahahn	.15	.40
4 Clare Bodensteiner	.15	.40
5 Kelley Suminski	.15	.40
14 Nicole Powell	.60	1.50
21 Shelley Nweke	.15	.40
22 Eziamaka Okafor	.30	.75
24 Susan King	.15	.40
32 Katie Denny	.15	.40
33 Sebnem Kimyacioglu	.15	.40
34 T'Nae Thiel	.15	.40
44 Azella Perryman	.15	.40
NNO Tara VanDerveer CO	.60	1.50

2003-04 Stanford

COMPLETE SET (13)	3.00	8.00
0 Joe Kirchofer	.20	.50
1 Josh Childress	1.25	3.00
10 Tim Morris	.20	.50
11 Chris Hernandez	.20	.50
20 Dan Grunfeld	.20	.50
21 Nick Robinson	.20	.50
22 Justin Davis	.20	.50
32 Jason Haas	.20	.50
33 Matt Lottich	.20	.50
42 Rob Little	.20	.50
44 Fred Washington	.20	.50
52 Matt Haryasz	.20	.50
NNO Mike Montgomery CO	.75	2.00

2003-04 Stanford Women

Produced by High Step in conjunction with Pepsi, this 15-card set was available through the school during the 2003-04 school year.

COMPLETE SET (15)	3.00	8.00
0 Chelsea Trotter	.15	.40
2 Krista Rappahahn	.15	.40
4 Clare Bodensteiner	.15	.40
5 Kelley Suminski	.15	.40
14 Nicole Powell	.60	1.50
21 Shelley Mweke	.15	.40
22 Eziamaka Okafor	.30	.75
24 Susan King Borchardt	.15	.40
30 Brooke Smith	.15	.40
32 Katie Denny	.15	.40
33 Sebnem Kimyacioglu	.15	.40
34 T'Nae Thiel	.15	.40
43 Kristen Newlin	.15	.40
44 Azella Perryman	.15	.40
NNO Tara VanDerveer CO	.60	1.50

2004-05 Stanford

Produced by High Step and sponsored by Pepsi, this 15-card set was available through Stanford during the 2004-05 school year.

COMPLETE SET (15)	2.50	6.00
1 Mark Bradford	.20	.50
2 Kenny Brown	.20	.50
3 Dan Grunfeld	.20	.50
4 Taj Finger	.20	.50
5 Jason Haas	.20	.50
6 Matt Haryasz	.20	.50
7 Chris Hernandez	.20	.50
8 Trent Johnson	.20	.50
9 Rob Little	.20	.50
10 Evan Moore	.20	.50
11 Tim Morris	.20	.50
12 Peter Prowitt	.20	.50
13 Nick Robinson	.20	.50
14 Fred Washington	.20	.50
15 Carlton Weatherby	.20	.50

2004-05 Stanford Women

Produced by High Step in conjunction with Pepsi, this 17-card set was available through Stanford during the 2004-05 school year.

COMPLETE SET (17)	2.50	6.00
2 Krista Rappahahn	.15	.40
3 Markisha Coleman	.15	.40
4 Clare Bodensteiner	.15	.40
5 Kelley Suminski	.15	.40
11 Candice Wiggins	.15	.40
12 Christy Titchenal	.15	.40
13 Cissy Pierce	.15	.40
21 Shelley Nweke	.15	.40
22 Eziamaka Okafor	.30	.75
24 Susan King Borchardt	.15	.40
30 Brooke Smith	.15	.40
33 Sebnem Kimyacioglu	.15	.40
34 T'Nae Thiel	.15	.40
42 Jessica Elway	.15	.40
43 Kristen Newlin	.15	.40
44 Azella Perryman	.15	.40
NNO Tara VanDerveer	.40	1.00

2005-06 Stanford

Produced by High Step in conjunction with Pepsi, this 14-card set was available through Stanford during the 2005-06 school year.

COMPLETE SET (14)	2.50	6.00
1 Kenny Brown	.20	.50
2 Taj Finger	.20	.50
3 Anthony Goods	.20	.50
4 Dan Grunfeld	.20	.50
5 Jason Haas	.20	.50
6 Matt Haryasz	.20	.50
7 Chris Hernandez	.20	.50
8 Lawrence Hill	.20	.50
9 Mitch Johnson	.20	.50
10 Tim Morris	.20	.50
11 Peter Prowitt	.20	.50
12 Fred Washington	.20	.50
13 Carlton Weatherby	.20	.50
14 Trent Johnson	.20	.50

2005-06 Stanford Women

Produced by High Step and sponsored by Pepsi, this 14-card set was available through Stanford during the 2005-06 school year.

COMPLETE SET (14)	2.00	5.00
1 Krista Rappahahn	.15	.40
2 Markisha Coleman	.15	.40
3 Clare Bodensteiner	.15	.40
4 Candice Wiggins	.15	.40
5 Christy Titchenal	.15	.40
6 Cissy Pierce	.15	.40
7 Shelley Nweke	.15	.40
8 Eziamaka Okafor	.15	.40
9 Rosalyn Gold-Onwude	.15	.40
10 Brooke Smith	.15	.40
11 Morgan Clyburn	.15	.40
12 Jillian Harmon	.15	.40
13 Kristen Newlin	.15	.40
14 Tara VanDerveer	.60	1.50

1988-89 Syracuse

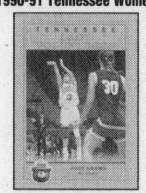

This 12-card standard-size set was sponsored by Louis Rich; their company logo appears on the bottom of the reverse. The front features a posed color photo of the player, shot from waist up on a blue background. The lettering and border on the card face are orange on white card stock. The back has biographical information and career summary, and "The Orangemen Say" feature, which consists of an anti-drug or alcohol message. The cards are unnumbered and are checklisted below in alphabetical order. Future NBA players showcased in this set include Derrick Coleman, Sherman Douglas, David Johnson, and Billy Owens.

COMPLETE SET (12)	15.00	40.00
1 Jim Boeheim CO	5.00	12.00
2 Derrick Coleman	5.00	12.00
3 Sherman Douglas	3.00	8.00
4 Herman Harried	.75	2.00
5 Dave Johnson	1.50	4.00
6 Rich Manning	.75	2.00
7 Billy Owens	3.00	8.00
8 Matt Roe	1.25	3.00
9 Erik Rogers	.75	2.00
10 Anthony Scott	.75	2.00
11 Dave Siock	.75	2.00
12 Stephen Thompson	1.50	4.00

1989-90 Syracuse

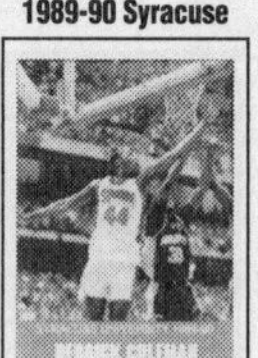

This 15-card set was sponsored by Pepsi, Y94FM radio, and Burger King. The cards measure approximately 2 5/8" by 3 1/2" and are numbered on the back. The action color photo on the front is outlined by orange border on white background. Below the photo in an orange bar appears the school's name, year, and the player's name in white lettering. The back has biographical information and a brief anti-drug message. Several players have two cards in this set: Derrick Coleman, Stephen Thompson, and Billy Owens.

COMPLETE SET (15)	3.00	8.00
1 Derrick Coleman 44	1.00	2.50
2 LeRon Ellis 25	.30	.75
3 Rich Manning 34	.20	.50
4 Stephen Thompson 32	.30	.75
5 Michael Edwards 5	.20	.50
6 Dave Johnson 23	.30	.75
7 Billy Owens 30	1.00	2.50
8 Conrad McRae 13	.20	.50
9 Jim Boeheim CO	.60	1.50
10 Stephen Thompson 32	.30	.75
11 Mike Hopkins 33	.20	.50
12 Tony Scott 40	.20	.50
13 Billy Owens 30	1.00	2.50
14 Erik Rogers 41	.20	.50
15 Derrick Coleman 44	1.00	2.50

1988-89 Tennessee

This 12-card set features members of the Tenessee Volunteers basketball team and measures the standard card size, 2 1/2" by 3 1/2". The front features a color action photo; above and below appear orange and gray lettering and borders. The Smokey the Bear logo in the lower left hand corner completes the front. The back gives brief biographical information and a public service announcement (illustrated with cartoon) concerning wildfire prevention. The set is checklisted below according to uniform number.

COMPLETE SET (12)	8.00	20.00
11 Clarence Swearengen	1.25	3.00
23 Greg Bell	1.25	3.00
24 Rickey Clark	.40	1.00
25 Travis Henry	.40	1.00
31 Dyron Nix	1.25	3.00
33 Mark Griffin	.40	1.00
34 Ronnie Reese	.40	1.00
50 Doug Roth	.40	1.00
51 Ian Lockhart	1.25	3.00
xx Don Devoe CO	1.25	3.00
xx Smokey The Hound (Mascot)	.40	1.00
xx Thompson-Boling Arena	1.25	3.00

1990-91 Tennessee Women

This 16-card standard-size set was sponsored by the USDA Forest Service and the state forestry agency. The fronts feature color action player photos, with a turquoise border on an orange background. Within the border, the team's name is printed above the picture, with the player's name, jersey number, and position below. The Smokey the Bear logo in the lower left corner rounds out the card face. The backs have two Lady Volunteers logos at the top, brief biographical information, and a fire prevention cartoon starring Smokey. The cards are unnumbered and checklisted below in alphabetical order.

COMPLETE SET (16)	10.00	25.00
1 Jody Adams	.50	1.25
2 Nikki Caldwell	.50	1.25
3 Tamara Carver	.50	1.25
4 Kelli Casteel	.50	1.25
5 Daedra Charles	1.50	4.00
6 Regina Clark	.50	1.25
7 Mickie DeMoss ACO	.50	1.25
8 Peggy Evans	.50	1.25
9 Lisa Harrison	.50	1.25
10 Debbie Hawhee	.50	1.25
11 Dena Head	1.00	2.50
12 Marlene Jeter	.50	1.25
13 Pat Summitt CO	5.00	12.00
14 Holly Warlick ACO	.50	1.25
15 Thompson-Boling Arena	.50	1.25
16 Smokey (Mascot)	.40	1.00

1991-92 Tennessee Women

COMPLETE SET (18)	15.00	30.00
1 Jody Adams	.50	1.25
2 Nikki Caldwell	.50	1.25
3 Kelli Casteel	.50	1.25
4 Regina Clark	.50	1.25
5 Mickie DeMoss ACO	.50	1.25
6 Rochone Dilligard	.50	1.25
7 Peggy Evans	.50	1.25
8 Lisa Harrison	.75	2.00
9 Debbie Hawhee	.50	1.25
10 Dena Head	.50	1.25
11 Marlene Jeter	.50	1.25
12 Dana Johnson	.50	1.25
13 Nikki McCray	4.00	10.00
14 Pat Summitt CO	4.00	10.00
15 Vonda Ward	.50	1.25
16 Holly Warlick ACO	.50	1.25
17 Tiffany Woosley	.50	1.25
18 Smokey (Mascot)	.40	1.00

1992-93 Tennessee Women

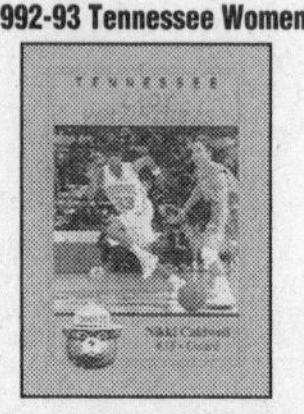

This 16-card standard-size set was sponsored by the USDA Forest Service and the state forestry agency. The fronts feature color action player photos, with a turquoise border on an orange background. Within the border, the team's name is printed above the picture, with the player's name, number, and position below. The Smokey the Bear logo in the lower left corner completes the card face. The backs have two Lady Volunteers logos at the top, brief biographical information, and a fire prevention cartoon starring Smokey. The cards are unnumbered and checklisted below in alphabetical order. This set features the first card of Nikki McCray, a member of the gold medal-winning 1996 USA team.

COMPLETE SET (16)	8.00	20.00
1 Jody Adams	.30	.75
2 Nikki Caldwell	.30	.75
3 Latina Davis	.75	2.00
4 Mickie DeMoss ACO	.30	.75
5 Rachone Dilligard	.30	.75
6 Peggy Evans	.30	.75
7 Lisa Harrison	.30	.75
8 Dana Johnson	.30	.75
9 Michelle Johnson	.30	.75
10 Nikki McCray	4.00	10.00
11 Pat Summitt CO	2.00	5.00
12 Pam Tanner ACO	.30	.75
13 Vonda Ward	.30	.75
14 Holly Warlick ACO	.30	.75
15 Tiffany Woosley	1.25	3.00
16 Cheerleaders	.30	.75

1993-94 Tennessee Women

This 16-card standard-size set was sponsored by the USDA Forest Service and the state forestry agency. On an orange background with white stripes, the fronts feature color action player photos. The team name is printed above the photo, with the player's name, number and position below. The team logo and Smokey's 50th year anniversary logo complete the fronts. The backs carry two Lady Volunteers logos at the top, the player's name and number, and a fire prevention cartoon starring Smokey. The cards are unnumbered and checklisted below in alphabetical order.

COMPLETE SET (16)	6.00	15.00
1 Nikki Caldwell	.20	.50
2 Abby Conklin	.40	1.00
3 Latina Davis	.40	1.00
4 Mickie DeMoss ACO	.20	.50
5 Rachone Dilligard	.20	.50
6 Dana Johnson	.20	.50
7 Michelle Marciniak	.40	1.00
8 Nikki McCray	2.50	6.00
9 Carolyn Peck ACO	.20	.50
10 Tanika Smith	.20	.50
11 Pat Summitt CO	1.50	4.00
12 Pashen Thompson	.40	1.00
13 Vonda Ward	.20	.50
14 Holly Warlick ACO	.20	.50
15 Tiffany Woosley	.75	2.00
16 The Cheerleaders	.20	.50

1994-95 Tennessee Women

This 16-card set was issued on a 10" by 14" perforated sheet with four rows of four cards. When the cards are separated, they measure the standard size. The set is sponsored by the USDA Forest Service and the state forestry agency. The fronts display color action and posed player photos with player's name, position, jersey number and Smokey logo below the photo in the orange border. The backs carry the player's name, jersey number, school year, and position at the top above a Smokey cartoon and a fire prevention safety tip. The cards are unnumbered and checklisted below in alphabetical order.

COMPLETE SET (16)	5.00	12.00
1 Abby Conklin	.40	1.00
2 Latina Davis	.40	1.00
3 Mickie DeMoss ACO	.20	.50
4 Dana Johnson	.20	.50
5 Tiffani Johnson	.60	1.50
6 Brynae Laxton	.20	.50
7 Michelle Marciniak	.60	1.50
8 Nikki McCray	1.50	4.00
9 Laurie Milligan	.20	.50
10 Carolyn Peck ACO	.20	.50
11 Tanika Smith	.20	.50
12 Pat Summitt CO	1.50	4.00
13 Pashen Thompson	.40	1.00
14 Vonda Ward	.20	.50
15 Holly Warlick ACO	.20	.50
16 Tiffany Woosley	.60	1.50

1998-99 Tennessee

This set was released for the University of Tennessee Men's Basketball team during the 1998-99 season. The 16-card set features all of the team's players and coaches.

COMPLETE SET (16)	2.50	6.00
1 Krystal Title Card	.20	.50
2 Team Photo	.20	.50
3 Del Baker	.20	.50
4 C.J. Black	.20	.50
5 Vegas Davis	.20	.50
6 Aaron Green	.20	.50
7 Jerry Green CO	.30	.75
8 Tony Harris	.20	.50
9 Torrey Harris	.20	.50
10 Charles Hathaway	.20	.50
11 Rashard Lee	.20	.50
12 Isiah Victor	.20	.50
13 John Ward	.20	.50
14 Brandon Wharton	.20	.50
15 Vincent Yarbrough	.40	1.00
16 The 6th Man	.20	.50

2010-11 Tennessee

COMPLETE SET (18)	6.00	15.00
1 Josh Bone	.40	1.00
2 John Fields	.40	1.00
3 Melvin Goins	.40	1.00
4 Trae Golden	.40	1.00
5 Kenny Hall	.40	1.00
6 Tobias Harris	2.00	5.00
7 Scotty Hopson	.40	1.00
8 Allan Houston HON	.60	1.50
9 Michael Hubert	.40	1.00
10 Jeronne Maymon	.40	1.00
11 Skylar McBee	.40	1.00
12 Jordan McRae	.40	1.00
13 Bruce Pearl CO	.40	1.00
14 Steven Pearl	.40	1.00
15 Tyler Summitt	.40	1.00
16 Cameron Tatum	.40	1.00
17 Brian Williams	.40	1.00
18 Renaldo Woolridge	.40	1.00

2011-12 Tennessee Women

COMPLETE SET (12)	10.00	25.00
1 Briana Bass	.75	2.00
2 Vicki Baugh	.75	2.00
3 Cierra Burdick	.75	2.00
4 Isabelle Harrison	.75	2.00

Glory Johnson .75 2.00
Alicia Manning 1.25 3.00
Ariel Massengale .75 2.00
Meighan Simmons .75 2.00
Taber Spani .75 2.00
Shekinna Stricklen .75 2.00
Pat Summitt CO 4.00 10.00
Kamiko Williams .75 2.00

1999-00 Tennessee Multi-Ad

OMPLETE SET (16) 4.00 10.00
Krystal Card .20 .50
Tennessee Volunteers .20 .50
Del Baker .20 .50
C.J. Black .20 .50
Vegas Davis .20 .50
Jerry Green CO .40 1.00
Jenis Grindstaff .20 .50
Marcus Haislip .75 2.00
Tony Harris .20 .50
0 Charles Hathaway .20 .50
Jon Higgins .20 .50
Ron Slay .75 2.00
Isiah Victor .20 .50
Harris Walker .20 .50
Terrence Woods .20 .50
Vincent Yarbrough .20 .50

1991-92 Tennessee Tech

his 16-card standard size (2 1/2" by 3 1/2") set was sponsored by Little Caesar's Pizza and features posed color player photos. Within a violet border, a bright yellow frame around the picture contains the player's name and jersey number. The backs are white with violet print and present the player's name, classification, position, hometown, and a player profile. A violet dot-pattern circle at the upper left contains the jersey number. The sponsor's name appears at the top. The cards are unnumbered and checklisted below in alphabetical order.

OMPLETE SET (16) 4.00 10.00
John Best .40 1.00
Mitch Cupples .40 1.00
Damon Davis .40 1.00
John Dykstra .40 1.00
Charles Edmonson .40 1.00
Frank Harrell CO .40 1.00
Clyde Hopkins .40 1.00
Maurice Houston .40 1.00
P.J. Mays .40 1.00
Eric Mitchell .40 1.00
Jesse Nayadley .40 1.00
Donnie Paulk .40 1.00
Ronnie Robinson .40 1.00
Van Usher .40 1.00
Rob West .40 1.00
6 Wade Wester .40 1.00

1992-93 Tennessee Tech

his 18-card standard-size (2 1/2" by 3 1/2") set was sponsored by Little Caesar's Pizza. The fronts feature posed color player photos inside a thin black frame on a purple card face. In yellow lettering, the words "Tennessee Tech" overlay the bottom of the picture. The player's number is printed on the left and his name on the right side below the picture. On a yellow background in black lettering, the backs carry the sponsor's logo at the top, the uniform number in a big circle in the upper left corner, with biographical, statistical, and personal information filling in the remainder of the space. The cards are unnumbered and checklisted below in alphabetical order.

OMPLETE SET (18) 3.00 8.00
John Best .30 .75
Greg Bibb .30 .75
Carlos Carter .30 .75
Chad Crouch .30 .75
Mitch Cupples .30 .75
Charley Dean .30 .75
John Dykstra .30 .75
Carlos Floyd .30 .75
Maurice Houston .30 .75
0 David Ingram .30 .75
1 Trent McCracken .30 .75
2 Eric Mitchell .30 .75
3 Jesse Nayadley .30 .75
4 Brian Riggins .30 .75
5 Earl Smith .30 .75
6 Rob West .30 .75
7 Wade Wester .30 .75
8 Team Leaders .30 .75
Angelo Volpe PRES
Frank Harrell CO

1993-94 Tennessee Tech

This 18-card standard-size set was sponsored by Little Caesars' Pizza. The fronts feature posed color player photos with yellow borders. The player's name and uniform number appear in white lettering within purple bars at the bottom of the photo. The white backs carry the player's uniform number, name, and biography at the top, followed below by his class, position, hometown, statistics, and college highlights, all in purple lettering. The cards are unnumbered and checklisted below in alphabetical order.

COMPLETE SET (18) 3.00 8.00
1 Greg Bibb .30 .75
2 Dennis Buckley .30 .75
3 Marc Burnett .40 1.00
'93 Inductee HOF
4 Carlos Carter .30 .75
5 Lorenzo Coleman .60 1.50
6 Chad Crouch .30 .75
7 Charley Dean .30 .75
8 Carlos Floyd .30 .75
9 Maurice Houston .30 .75
10 David Ingram .30 .75
11 Reggie Mayo .30 .75
12 Eric Mitchell .30 .75
13 Jesse Nayadley .30 .75
14 Earl Smith .30 .75
15 Chris Turner .30 .75
16 Steve Taylor .30 .75
Distinguished Career
17 Rob West .30 .75
18 Eblen Center (Arena) .30 .75

1994-95 Tennessee Tech

This 18-card set measures the standard size. The fronts feature posed color player photos with purple borders. The player's name appears in white lettering at the bottom below the team logo. The lavender backs carry the uniform number, name, biography, class, position, statistics and college highlights all in purple lettering. The cards are unnumbered and checklisted below in alphabetical order.

COMPLETE SET (18) 3.00 8.00
1 Greg Bibb .30 .75
2 Carlos Carter .30 .75
3 Lorenzo Coleman .40 1.00
4 Romain Coleman .30 .75
5 Chad Crouch .30 .75
6 Theron Curry .30 .75
7 Carlos Floyd .30 .75
8 Marc Glanton .30 .75
9 Eric Mitchell .30 .75
10 Jesse Nayadley .30 .75
11 Ricky Norris .30 .75
12 Lance Parr .30 .75
13 Kenneth Smith .30 .75
14 Chris Turner .30 .75
15 Frank Harrell CO .30 .75
Kevin Bray ACO
Bob Eskew ACO
Jason Craighead MG
Susan Fitzpatrick SECY
16 Loyal Fans .30 .75
Johnny Donnelly
17 Gene Davidson ANN .30 .75
Eldon Burgess ANN
18 Chad Smith MG .30 .75
Timmy Rogers MG
Phil Dennis MG

1996-97 Tennessee Tech Schedules

Though they'll certainly win no awards for outstanding achievement in card design, these four unsightly purple pocket schedules nonetheless present part of the collecting universe for die-hard Golden Eagle basketball fans. The set features all of the seniors from the 1996-97 team, including Lorenzo Coleman, one of the nation's more talented big men. These schedules were distributed free at various home games throughout the season. The skeds are unnumbered andhave been checklisted below alphabetically for convenience.

COMPLETE SET (4) .75 2.00
1 Lorenzo Coleman .60 1.50
2 Jason Embry .08 .25
3 Chris Turner .08 .25
4 Curtis Wiggins .08 .25

1990 Texas

Financed by the MOSHANA Foundation and distributed by local law enforcement agencies, this 32-card multi-sport set measures 2 1/2" by 3 1/2" and is printed on thin card stock. The fronts display color action player photos inside a black frame on a white card face. The team name appears in a black bar above the picture, while the player's name and position are printed in the wider bottom border. The backs feature biographical information, player profile, and "A Texas Tip" in the form of anti-drug or alcohol messages. The sports represented are golf (1, 19), basketball (2-4, 8, 25-26, 29, 30), track and field (5-6, 15, 23), tennis (7, 28), baseball (9-10, 16, 32), swimming and diving (11, 13, 20-21), volleyball (12, 14, 18, 31), and football (17, 22, 24, 27). The cards are unnumbered and checklisted below in alphabetical order.

COMPLETE SET (32) 8.00 20.00
2 Susan Anderson BK .30 .75
3 Ellen Bayer BK .30 .75
4 Lance Blanks BK .60 1.50
8 Jody Conradt CO BK .80 2.00
25 Travis Mays BK .60 1.50
26 Lyssa McBride BK .40 1.00
29 George Muller BK .30 .75
30 Tom Penders CO BK .80 2.00

1991 Texas A&M Collegiate Collection

This 100 card standard-size multi-sport set was produced by Collegiate Collection. Although a few color photos are included, the front features mainly black and white player photos with borders in the team's colors. All cards are of football players unless noted.

COMPLETE SET (100) 5.00 10.00
8 John Beasley BK .05 .15
15 Lisa Langston BK .01 .05
30 John Thornton BK .01 .05
49 Barry Davis BK .01 .05
53 Dave Goff BK .01 .05
55 Lynn Hickey CO BK .01 .05
63 James H. Heitmann BK .01 .05
78 Lisa L.J. Jordon BK .01 .05
87 Lisa Herner BK .01 .05
88 Traci Thomas BK .01 .05
97 Yvonne Hill BK .01 .05

1994-95 Texas A&M

Sponsored by Star Tel Long Distance Telephone Service, this 20-card multi-sport set was issued in five 12 1/2" by 3 1/2" strips. The strips are not perforated; however, if the cards were cut, they would measure the standard size. The set is subdivided as follows: men's baseball (1-5), men's basketball (6-10), women's basketball (11-15), and women's volleyball (16-20). The fronts feature posed or action player photos with the sport and sponsor name in the right border. The backs carry a caption on the photo on a maroon background with the sponsor name at the bottom. The cards are unnumbered and checklisted below in alphabetical order within the sport.

6 Tony Barone CO BK .75 2.00
Porter Moser ACO
Mitch Buonaguro ACO
Frank Haith ACO
7 Kyle Kessel BK .40 1.00
Waseem Ali
Quinton James
Chris Oney
John Stevens
Dario Que
8 Jimmy Smith BK .40 1.00
Chris Pulliams
John Stevens
Chris LeBlanc/1994-95 Schedule
9 Roy Wills BK .75 2.00
Damon Johnson
Tony McGinnis
Corey Henderson
Joe Wilbert
John
11 Carey Owens BK .40 1.00
Sutton Helvey
Kim Linder
12 Christy Lake BK .40 1.00
Shanae Ford
Marianne Miller
Lana Tucker/1994-95 Schedule
13 Juniors and Seniors BK .40 1.00
Angel Spinks
Martha McClelland
Kelly Cerny
Debbie B
14 Coaches .40 1.00
Angela Taylor ACO
Kristy Sims ACO
Candi Harvey CO
Lisa Jordon A

1992-93 Texas Tech Women

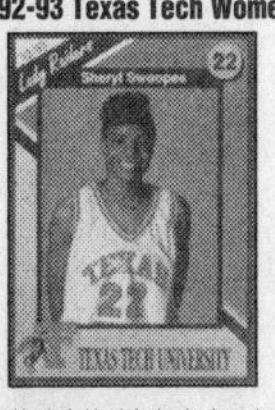

Sponsored by the Lubbock Avalanche-Journal and other local businesses, this 19-card set measures the standard size and is printed on thin card stock. The fronts display posed, color photos of the Lady Raiders, the 1992-93 Southwest Conference and NCAA Champions. The pictures are framed by a thin black line and set on a card face that is divided diagonally by a black stripe. The upper portion is red, while the lower portion is gray. The player's name is printed above the photo in the black border. The set year is in the upper left corner. The backs carry biographical information, statistics, and sponsor logos. The cards are unnumbered and checklisted below in alphabetical order. The key card in the set is Sheryl Swoopes, who started for the gold medal-winning 1996 USA team and is considered to be among the best female basketball players of all time.

COMPLETE SET (19) 10.00 25.00
1 Michi Atkins .60 1.50
2 Cynthia Clinger .30 .75
3 Nikki Heath .30 .75
4 Noel Johnson .30 .75
5 Diana Kersey .30 .75
6 Krista Kirkland .30 .75
7 Kim Pruitt .30 .75
8 Raider Red (Mascot) .30 .75
9 Roger Reding ACO .30 .75
10 Stephanie Scott .30 .75
11 Marsha Sharp CO 1.00 2.50
12 Sheryl Swoopes 8.00 20.00
13 Michelle Thomas .30 .75
14 Linden Weese ACO .30 .75
15 Terri Weldon .30 .75
Graduate Assistant
16 Melinda White .30 .75
17 Checklist .30 .75
18 Sponsor Card .30 .75
19 Texas Tech Sign .30 .75

1992-93 Texas Tech Women NCAA Champs

Sponsored by United Supermarket, this 25-card standard-size set commemorates the 1993 Lady Raiders National Championship team. The fronts feature color action photos with a red inner border and a black pebble grain outer border. The player's name, position and number appear on a light gray bar at the bottom. The backs carry a black-and-white portrait with biographical information, career summary and statistics on a gray background. This set features several cards of Sheryl Swoopes, who started for the gold medal-winning 1996 USA team and is considered to be among the best female basketball players of all time.

COMPLETE SET (25) 12.00 30.00
1 Trophy Card .40 1.00
2 Diana Kersey .20 .50
3 Nikki Heath .20 .50
4 Stephanie Scott .20 .50
5 Krista Kirkland .20 .50
6 Sheryl Swoopes 6.00 15.00
7 Noel Johnson .20 .50
8 Janice Farris .20 .50
9 Kim Pruitt .20 .50
10 Cynthia Clinger .20 .50
11 Michelle Thomas .20 .50
12 Melinda White .20 .50
13 Michi Atkins .40 1.00
14 Marsha Sharp CO .75 2.00
15 Linden Weese ACO .20 .50
16 Roger Reding ACO .20 .50
17 Terri Weldon .20 .50
Graduate Assistant
18 Jeannine McHaney DIR .20 .50
19 SWC Championship .40 1.00
20 National Semifinals .40 1.00
Michi Atkins
21 National Finals 2.00 5.00
Sheryl Swoopes
22 Emotional Finish 2.00 5.00
Sheryl Swoopes
Krista Kirkland
23 1992-93 Season Record .20 .50
Krista Kirkland
Sheryl Swoopes
Cynthia Clinger
24 Sheryl Swoopes 2.00 5.00
Player of the Year
Records and Accolades
25 Team Photo CL .40 1.00

1990-91 UCLA

This 40-card set was produced by Collegiate Collection and features the men's and women's basketball teams. The standard size (2 1/2" by 3 1/2") cards feature on the fronts a mix of posed or action color player photos (with rounded corners), with a thin black border on royal blue background. While the school name appears above the picture in yellow lettering, the player's name appears in black lettering in a yellow stripe below the picture. The UCLA and Collegiate Collection logos at the top complete the card face. The horizontally oriented backs provide brief biography, statistics, and the card number, all within a royal blue border. Due to a production error, the Keith Owens card incorrectly depicts Destah Owens. A coupon was included in the set to exchange for a free replacement card. Note that the back of the corrected card differs from the regular issue in format and color. Men's basketball is represented by cards 1-15 and 35-39; women's basketball by cards 16-34. The set features first cards of Tracy Murray and Ed O'Bannon in addition to an early Don MacLean card.

COMPLETE SET (40) 8.00 20.00
1 Team Photo .40 1.00
2 Tracy Murray 1.25 3.00
3 Ed O'Bannon 1.25 3.00
4 Darrick Martin .60 1.50
5 Mitchell Butler .60 1.50
6 Mike Lanier .08 .25
7 Chris Kenny .08 .25
8A Keith Owens ERR .60 1.50
(Photo actually Destah Owens)
8B Keith Owens COR .75 2.00
9 Dave Paulsell .08 .25
10 Shon Tarver .40 1.00
11 Rodney Zimmerman .08 .25
12 Zan Mason .08 .25
13 Gerald Madkins .75 2.00
14 Don MacLean 1.25 3.00
15 Lou Richie .08 .25
16 Billie Moore CO .30 .75
17 Rehema Stephens .08 .25
18 Nicole Anderson .08 .25
19 Amy Jalewalia .08 .25
20 Pam Walker ACO .08 .25
21 Lynn Kamrath .08 .25
22 Detra Lockhart .08 .25
23 Stacie Gravely .08 .25
24 Laura Collins .08 .25
25 Genevieve Vanoostveen .08 .25
26 Dede Mosman .08 .25
27 Nicole Young .08 .25
28 Dawn Baker .08 .25
29 Melissa Gische .08 .25
30 Rachelle Roulier .08 .25
31 Marcy Tarabochia .08 .25
32 Natalie Williams 2.00 5.00
33 Kathy Olivier ACO .20 .50
34 Mary Hegarty ACO .20 .50
35 Jim Harrick CO .60 1.50
36 Brad Holland ACO .60 1.50
37 Tony Fuller ACO .20 .50
38 Ken Barone ACO .08 .25
39 Mark Gottfried ACO .20 .50
40 Checklist Card .08 .25

1991 UCLA Collegiate Collection

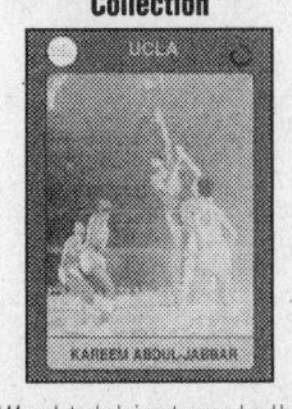

This 144-card standard-size set was produced by Collegiate Collection. The fronts feature a mix of black and white or color player photos, with royal blue borders and the player's name in the yellow stripe below the picture. The horizontally oriented backs present biographical information, career summary, or statistics on a white background with blue lettering and borders.

COMPLETE SET (144) 6.00 15.00
1 John Wooden CO .30 .75
2 Kareem Abdul-Jabbar .30 .75
3 Bill Walton .20 .50
4 Larry Farmer .07 .20
5 Marques Johnson .10 .30
6 Walt Hazzard .08 .25
7 Henry Bibby .20 .50
8 Gail Goodrich .20 .50
9 Jim Harrick .15 .40
10 Kareem Abdul-Jabbar .30 .75
11 Mike Warren .08 .25
12 Gary Maloncon .07 .20
13 James Wilkes .07 .20
14 Kiki Vandeweghe .08 .25
15 1969 NCAA Champs .07 .20
16 Sidney Wicks .08 .25
17 Andre McCarter .07 .20
18 Michael Holton .07 .20
19 Greg Lee .07 .20
20 John Wooden CO .30 .75
21 Gene Bartow CO .07 .20
22 Richard Washington .07 .20
23 Brad Wright .07 .20
24 Pooh Richardson .07 .20
25 Terry Schofield .07 .20
26 Gig Sims .07 .20
27 Darren Daye .07 .20
28 Dave Immel .07 .20
29 Brad Holland .07 .20
30 Bill Walton .20 .50
31 Larry Brown CO .15 .40
32 Kevin Walker .07 .20
33 Kareem Abdul-Jabbar .30 .75
34 Kenny Heitz .07 .20
35 Gary Cunningham .07 .20
36 Lynn Shackelford .07 .20
37 Keith Wilkes .08 .25
38 1975 NCAA Champs .07 .20
39 Raymond Townsend .07 .20
40 Pete Trgovich .07 .20
41 Kelvin Butler .07 .20
42 Ed Sheldrake .07 .20
43 Larry Hollyfield .07 .20
44 Montel Hatcher .07 .20
45 Denise Curry .07 .20
46 Curtis Rowe .08 .25
47 David Meyers .07 .20
48 Lucius Allen .08 .25
49 Kenny Fields .07 .20
50 John Vallely .07 .20
51 John Wooden .20 .50
Neil Wooden
52 Sidney Wicks .10 .30
53 1973 NCAA Champs .07 .20
54 Jack Haley .07 .20
55 Ralph Drollinger .07 .20
56 Don Johnson .07 .20
57 Bill Ellis .07 .20
58 Willie Naulls .07 .20
59 Ron Livingston .07 .20
60 Bill Putnam .07 .20
61 Rod Foster .07 .20
62 Bill Walton .20 .50
63 Roy Hamilton .07 .20
64 Jim Spillane .07 .20
65 Ralph Jackson .07 .20
66 Morris Taft .07 .20
67 Dick Ridgeway .07 .20
68 Dave Minor .07 .20
69 1965 Champs .07 .20
70 Karl Kraushaar .07 .20
71 Craig Jackson .07 .20
72 Kenny Washington .07 .20
73 Keith Wilkes .08 .25
74 Stuart Gray .07 .20
75 John Green .07 .20
76 Doug McIntosh .07 .20
77 Walt Hazzard .08 .25
78 Frank Lubin .07 .20
79 Don Piper .07 .20
80 1967 Champs .07 .20
81 Kenny Booker .07 .20
82 Marques Johnson .10 .30
83 Bill Walton .20 .50
84 1972 Champs .07 .20
85 Steve Patterson .07 .20
86 1964 NCAA Champs .07 .20
87 Alan Sawyer .07 .20
88 Walt Torrence .07 .20
89 Gail Goodrich .20 .50
90 Ralph Bunche .07 .20
91 Swen Nater .08 .25
92 Larry Farmer .07 .20
93 Kareem Abdul-Jabbar .30 .75
94 Mike Sanders .07 .20
95 Niguel Miguel .07 .20
96 Jackie Robinson .60 1.50
97 Dick West .07 .20
98 Rafer Johnson .15 .40
99 John Berberich .07 .20
100 Director Card .07 .20
101 Richard Linthicum .07 .20
102 Chuck Clustka .07 .20
103 John Wooden CO .20 .50
Denny Crum CO
Gary Cunningham CO
104 Jerry Norman .07 .20
105 John Moore .07 .20
106 Trevor Wilson .08 .25
107 David Greenwood .07 .20
108 John Wooden CO .20 .50
J.D.Morgan AD
109 Kareem Abdul-Jabbar .30 .75
110 Ann Meyers .20 .50
111 Denny Crum .20 .50
112 Pierce Works .07 .20
113 Carl Cozens .07 .20
114 George Stanich .07 .20
115 Don Ashen .07 .20
116 David Greenwood .07 .20
117 1971 Team Photo .07 .20
118 Johns Barksdale .07 .20
119 1978 Champion .07 .20
120 John Stanich .07 .20
121 Don Barksdale .07 .20
122 1968 Champs .07 .20
123 Carl Knowles .07 .20
124 Don Bragg .07 .20
125 Ducky Drake .07 .20
126 John Ball .07 .20
127 Pauley Pavilion .07 .20
128 Sam Balter .07 .20
129 A Caddy Works Team .07 .20
130 John Wooden CO .30 .75
131 Fred Goss .07 .20
132 Keith Erickson .08 .25
133 Pete Blackman .07 .20
134 Gail Goodrich .20 .50
135 Kent Miller .07 .20
136 Jack Ketchum .07 .20
137 1970 Team Photo .07 .20
138 Jim Milhorn .07 .20
139 Bill Rankin .07 .20
140 Gary Cunningham .07 .20
141 Bob (Ace) Calkins .07 .20
142 J.D. Morgan AD .07 .20
143 Fred Slaughter .07 .20
144 Director Card .07 .20

1991-92 UCLA

This 21-card set was produced by Collegiate Collection and measures the standard size (2 1/2" by 3 1/2"). The fronts feature color action player photos, with royal blue borders and the player's name in a yellow stripe beneath the picture. The horizontally oriented backs present biographical information, statistics, and career summary on a white background with blue lettering and borders. The cards are numbered on the back in the upper right corner. The set features early cards of Don MacLean, Tracy Murray, and Ed O'Bannon.

COMPLETE SET (21) 6.00 15.00
1 Mike Lanier .20 .50
2 Don MacLean .75 2.00
3 Rodney Zimmerman .20 .50
4 Pauley Pavilion .20 .50
5 Tyus Edney 1.25 3.00
6 Jiri (George) Zidek .75 2.00
7 Brad Holland CO .40 1.00
8 Ed O'Bannon .75 2.00
9 Richard Petruska .30 .75
10 Darrick Martin .40 1.00
11 Tony Fuller CO .20 .50
12 Tracy Murray .75 2.00
13 Gerald Madkins .40 1.00
14 Mitchell Butler .40 1.00
15 Mark Gottfried .20 .50
16 Jim Harrick CO .40 1.00
17 Jonah Naulls .20 .50
18 Steve Lavin CO .60 1.50
19 Steve Elkind .20 .50
20 Shon Tarver .40 1.00
21 Checklist Card .20 .50

1988-89 UNLV

This 12-card standard-size set was produced by Hall of Fame Cards, Inc. Reportedly there were only 10,000 sets produced. The front features a color action shot of the player, trimmed in red borders on a gray card face. The words "Runnin' Rebels" appears in red lettering above the picture, while the school name, player's name, and his position appear below. The back is printed in red and includes biographical information, career statistics at UNLV, and an anti-drug message titled "Rebel Rap." The cards are numbered on the back and checklisted below for convenience. The set features the first cards of NBA players Greg Anthony and Stacey Augmon.

COMPLETE SET (12) 5.00 12.00
1 Stacey Augmon 2.50 6.00
2 Greg Anthony 2.00 5.00
3 Anderson Hunt .75 2.00
4 George Ackles .40 1.00
5 David Butler .75 2.00
6 Clint Rossum .40 1.00
7 Moses Scurry .40 1.00
8 Barry Young .40 1.00
9 James Jones .40 1.00
10 Stacey Cvijanovich .40 1.00
11 Chris Jeter .40 1.00
12 Bryan Emerzian .40 1.00

1989-90 UNLV 7-Eleven

This 14-card standard-size set was sponsored by 7-Eleven, 98.5 KLUC-FM radio, and Nationwide Communications Inc. The cards are printed on very thin card stock. Reportedly more than 25,000 sets were produced and distributed. The fronts feature color action player photos, with black borders on red card face. The team and player's names appear in red lettering in gray boxes above and below the picture respectively. The backs are printed in black on white card stock and provide biographical information and player profile. The cards are unnumbered and are checklisted below in alphabetical order. The set features an early card of NBA star Larry Johnson as well as the first card of coach Jerry Tarkanian.

COMPLETE SET (14) 5.00 12.00
1 Greg Anthony .75 2.00
2 Stacey Augmon 1.25 3.00
3 Travis Bice .40 1.00
4 David Butler .40 1.00
5 Stacey Cvijanovich .20 .50
6 Bryan Emerzian .20 .50
7 Anderson Hunt .40 1.00
8 Chris Jeter .20 .50
9 Larry Johnson 2.00 5.00
10 James Jones .20 .50
11 David Rice .20 .50
12 Moses Scurry .40 1.00
13 Barry Young .20 .50
14 Jerry Tarkanian CO 1.50 4.00

1989-90 UNLV HOF

This 14-card standard-size set was produced by Hall of Fame Cards, Inc. Reportedly 5000 sets were originally produced but an additional 3000 sets were made after UNLV won the NCAA Championship. The card front features a color action player photo outlined by a thin black border. The school name is superimposed at the right upper corner of the picture. The background is red for the top half of the card face and gray for the bottom half. The player's name is printed in red lettering below the picture. In a horizontal format the back has biographical information and the slogan "Say No to Drugs." The set features an early card of NBA star Larry Johnson.

COMPLETE SET (14) 5.00 12.00
1 Stacey Augmon 1.25 3.00
2 Greg Anthony .75 2.00
3 Larry Johnson 2.50 6.00
4 George Ackles .40 1.00
5 Moses Scurry .40 1.00
6 Anderson Hunt .75 2.00
(Hank Gathers visible in background)
7 Travis Bice .40 1.00
8 David Butler .40 1.00
9 Stacey Cvijanovich .20 .50
10 Chris Jeter .20 .50
11 Bryan Emerzian .20 .50
12 James Jones .75 2.00
(Hank Gathers visible in background)
13 Barry Young .20 .50
14 Dave Rice .20 .50

1990-91 UNLV HOF

This 15-card standard-size set was produced by Hall of Fame Cards, Inc. and features the UNLV Runnin' Rebels, the 1990 NCAA national champions. Reportedly only 15,000 sets were produced; each set is individually numbered on card number 4 Anderson Hunt. The fronts feature color action player photos; cards numbered 11-13 feature "Future Rebels" and have posed color photos. All cards have red borders on the top and bottom and white borders on the sides. A red diagonal cuts across the lower right corner of the picture, with the words "1990 Nat'l Champions" in white lettering. The player's name and position are given in white lettering in the bottom red border. The backs have statistical information and the slogan "Say No to Drugs" in either horizontal or vertical formats. The key cards in the set are the two Larry Johnson cards.

COMPLETE SET (15) 4.00 10.00
1 Larry Johnson 1.25 3.00
2 Stacey Augmon .75 2.00
3 Greg Anthony .60 1.50
4 Anderson Hunt .40 1.00
5 Travis Bice .20 .50
6 George Ackles .40 1.00
7 Bryan Emerzian .20 .50
8 Dave Rice .20 .50
9 Chris Jeter .20 .50

10 Anderson Hunt .40 1.00
11 Evric Gray .40 1.00
12 Bobby Joyce .20 .50
13 H. Waldman .40 1.00
14 Larry Johnson 1.25 3.00
15 Runnin' Rebels .40 1.00

1990-91 UNLV Season to Remember

This 15-card standard-size set features the UNLV Runnin' Rebels, who were runner-ups for the 1991 NCAA championship. The front features a color action photo of the player, with a thin black border on dark red background. The school name is superimposed at the right upper corner of the picture, and the player's name is inscribed across the bottom of the picture. In black lettering the words "A Season to Remember" appear below the photo. The back gives biographical and statistical information in a horizontal format, and repeats the words "A Season to Remember," with the team record "34-1." The key card in the set features NBA star Larry Johnson.

COMPLETE SET (15) 3.00 8.00
1 Larry Johnson .75 2.00
2 Stacey Augmon .40 1.00
3 Greg Anthony .40 1.00
4 Anderson Hunt .20 .50
5 Travis Bice .08 .25
6 George Ackles .20 .50
7 Bryan Emerzian .08 .25
8 Dave Rice .08 .25
9 Chris Jeter .08 .25
10 Elmore Spencer .20 .50
11 Evric Gray .20 .50
12 Bobby Joyce .08 .25
13 H. Waldman .20 .50
14 Melvin Love .08 .25
15 Rebel All-Americans .60 1.50
(Anderson Hunt
Greg Anthony
George Ackles
Larry Johnson
Stacey Augmon)

1990-91 UNLV Smokey

This 15-card set was sponsored by the USDA Forest Service in cooperation with other federal agencies. The standard size cards were issued as a set of single cards or as a sheet consisting of four rows of four cards (the 16th slot is blank). The front features a color action player photo, with gray border on dark red background. In black lettering the words "1990-91 UNLV Runnin' Rebels" are printed above the picture, with the player's name and number below. The Smokey the Bear logo in the lower left corner completes the card face. The back presents biographical information and a fire prevention cartoon starring Smokey. The cards unnumbered and we have checklisted them below in alphabetical order, with the jersey number to the right of the name. The key card in the set features NBA star Larry Johnson.

COMPLETE SET (15) 4.00 10.00
1 George Ackles 44 .40 1.00
2 Greg Anthony 50 .60 1.50
3 Stacey Augmon 32 .75 2.00
4 Travis Bice 3 .30 .75
5 Bryan Emerzian 15 .30 .75
6 Evric Gray 23 .40 1.00
7 Anderson Hunt 12 .40 1.00
8 Chris Jeter 53 .30 .75
9 Larry Johnson 4 1.25 3.00
10 Bobby Joyce 42 .30 .75
11 Melvin Love 40 .30 .75
12 Dave Rice 30 .30 .75
13 Elmore Spencer 24 .40 1.00
14 Jerry Tarkanian CO 1.25 3.00
15 H. Waldman 31 .40 1.00

1992-93 UNLV

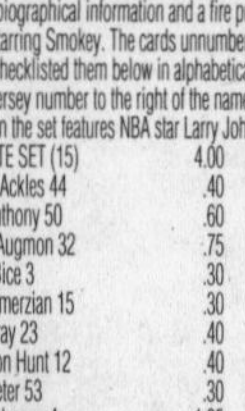

Sponsored by KVBC Channel 3 (Las Vegas) and Centel First Source (phone book), this 16-card set was issued as a perforated sheet that features 14 standard-size player cards and two sponsor cards. The fronts display color, action player photos on a red card face. A gray bar at the bottom contains the player's name, jersey number, and position. A red and gray banner design at the top carries the school and team name, as well as the year. The backs have biographical information, a player profile, and a cartoon of the team mascot. Sponsor logos are printed at the bottom. The cards are unnumbered and checklisted below in alphabetical order.

COMPLETE SET (16) 6.00 15.00
1 Derrick Alesevich .30 .75
2 Dexter Boney .60 1.50
3 Jason Brooks .30 .75
4 Clint Clausen .30 .75
5 Ken Gibson .30 .75
6 Evric Gray .60 1.50
7 Fred Haygood .30 .75
8 Sean Loughran .30 .75
9 Reggie Manuel .30 .75
10 Rollie Massimino CO 1.00 2.50
11 Isaiah (J.R.) Rider 2.50 6.00
12 Damian Smith .30 .75
13 Dedan Thomas .30 .75
14 Lawrence Thomas .30 .75
15 Sponsor Card .30 .75
KVBC Channel 3
16 Sponsor Card .30 .75
Centel First Source

2010-11 Upper Deck North Carolina

COMPLETE SET (183) 60.00 150.00
1 Nathaniel Cartmell .30 .75
2 Cartwright Carmichael .30 .75
3 Monk McDonald .30 .75
4 Jack Cobb .30 .75
5 George Glamack .30 .75
6 Horace Bones McKinney .30 .75
7 Skippy Winstead .30 .75
8 Jerry Vayda .30 .75
9 Frank McGuire .30 .75
10 Lennie Rosenbluth .30 .75
11 Pete Brennan .30 .75
12 Joe Quigg .30 .75
13 York Larese .30 .75
14 Doug Moe .30 .75
15 Larry Brown .30 .75
16 Bobby Lewis .30 .75
17 Rusty Clark .30 .75
18 Dick Grubar .30 .75
19 Charlie Scott .30 .75
20 Jim Delany .30 .75
21 Lee Dedmon .30 .75
22 Bill Chamberlain .30 .75
23 Stephen Previs .30 .75
24 Darrell Elston .30 .75
25 Bobby Jones .40 1.00
26 Bob McAdoo .40 1.00
27 Mitch Kupchak .30 .75
28 Walter Davis .30 .75
29 John Kuester .30 .75
30 Tom LaGarde .30 .75
31 Angela Lumpkin .30 .75
32 Phil Ford .30 .75
33 Marsha Mann .30 .75
34 Mike O'Koren .30 .75
35 Bernadette McGlade .30 .75
36 Dave Colescott .30 .75
37 Al Wood .30 .75
38 Rich Yonakor .30 .75
39 Jennifer Alley .40 1.00
40 James Worthy .60 1.50
41 Matt Doherty .30 .75
42 Sam Perkins .30 .75
43 Michael Jordan 2.00 5.00
44 Buzz Peterson .30 .75
45 Brad Daugherty .30 .75
46 Steve Hale .30 .75
47 Pam Leake .30 .75
48 Kenny Smith .40 1.00
49 Joe Wolf .30 .75
50 J.R. Reid .30 .75
51 Sylvia Hatchell .30 .75
52 Steve Bucknall .30 .75
53 Jeff Lebo .30 .75
54 Kevin Madden .30 .75
55 Scott Williams .30 .75
56 Pete Chilcutt .30 .75
57 Rick Fox .30 .75
58 Hubert Davis .30 .75
59 George Lynch .30 .75
60 Henrik Rodl .30 .75
61 Matt Wenstrom .30 .75
62 Sylvia Crawley .30 .75
63 Eric Montross .30 .75
64 Derrick Phelps .30 .75
65 Tonya Sampson .30 .75
66 Charlotte Smith .30 .75
67 Donald Williams .30 .75
68 Dante Calabria .30 .75
69 Kevin Salvadori .30 .75
70 Marion Jones .40 1.00
71 Jerry Stackhouse .60 1.50
72 Serge Zwikker .30 .75
73 Vince Carter .75 2.00
74 Antawn Jamison .40 1.00
75 Makhtar N'diaye .30 .75
76 Jason Capel .30 .75
77 Kris Lang .30 .75
78 Sean May .30 .75
79 David Noel .30 .75
80 Ty Lawson .60 1.50
81 Ed Davis .60 1.50
82 Roy Williams .60 1.50
83 Dean Smith .75 2.00
84 UNC 1.00 2.50
MSU 1957 Rivalries
85 UNC 1.00 2.50
Kansas 1957 Rivalries
86 Charlie Scott 1.00 2.50
Dave Cowens Rivalries
87 UNC 1.00 2.50
UNLV 1977 Rivalries
88 Larry Nance 1.00 2.50
James Worthy Rivalries
89 UNC 1.00 2.50
Georgetown 1982 Rivalries
90 Horace Grant 2.50 6.00
Michael Jordan Rivalries
91 UNC 1.00 2.50
NC State 1985 Rivalries
92 Danny Ferry 1.00 2.50
Brad Daugherty Rivalries
93 Danny Ferry 1.00 2.50
J.R. Reid Rivalries
94 UNC 1.00 2.50
Oklahoma 1990 Rivalries
95 Christian Laettner 1.00 2.50
Rick Fox Rivalries
96 Christian Laettner 1.00 2.50
Eric Montross Rivalries
97 UNC 1.00 2.50
Michigan 1993 Rivalries
98 UNC 1.00 2.50
Duke 1995 Rivalries
99 UNC 1.00 2.50
Duke 2005 Rivalries
100 UNC 1.00 2.50
Duke Rivalries
101 UNC 1.00 2.50
Duke 2006 Rivalries
102 UNC 1.00 2.50
Duke Rivalries
103 UNC 1.00 2.50
MSU 2009 Rivalries
104 George Glamack AA 1.00 2.50
105 Lennie Rosenbluth AA 1.00 2.50
106 Charlie Scott AA 1.00 2.50
107 Phil Ford AA 1.00 2.50
108 James Worthy AA 1.25 3.00
109 Bob McAdoo AA 1.00 2.50
110 Sam Perkins AA 1.00 2.50
111 Michael Jordan AA 2.50 6.00
112 Pam Leake AA 1.00 2.50
113 Kenny Smith AA 1.00 2.50
114 J.R. Reid AA 1.00 2.50
115 Tonya Sampson AA 1.00 2.50
116 Charlotte Smith AA 1.00 2.50
117 Jerry Stackhouse AA 1.25 3.00
118 Antawn Jamison AA 1.00 2.50
119 Sean May AA 1.00 2.50
120 Marion Jones AA 1.00 2.50
121 Vince Carter AA 1.25 3.00
122 Brad Daugherty AA 1.00 2.50
123 Ty Lawson AA 1.00 2.50
124 Michael Jordan BM 2.00 5.00
125 Bob McAdoo BM .75 2.00
126 Bobby Jones BM .75 2.00
127 UNC 1957 Trophy BM .75 2.00
128 UNC Champ Trophies BM .75 2.00
129 Michael Jordan BM 2.00 5.00
130 Joe Quigg BM .75 2.00
131 Dean Smith BM 1.00 2.50
132 Jerry Stackhouse BM .75 2.00
133 James Worthy BM 1.00 2.50
134 Lee Shaffer BM .75 2.00
135 Michael Jordan BM 2.00 5.00
136 UNC Inside Museum BM .75 2.00
137 Phil Ford BM .75 2.00
138 Walter Davis BM .75 2.00
139 Kenny Smith BM .75 2.00
140 Roy Williams BM 1.00 2.50
141 Eric Montross BM .75 2.00
142 Vince Carter BM 1.00 2.50
143 Tyler Hansbrough BM 1.00 2.50
144 Nathaniel Cartmell TL 1.00 2.50
145 UNC 1.00 2.50
Duke TL
146 Cartwright Carmichael TL 1.00 2.50
147 Jack Cobb TL 1.00 2.50
148 Horace Bones McKinney TL 1.00 2.50
149 Frank McGuire TL 1.00 2.50
150 Pete Brennan TL 1.00 2.50
151 Lennie Rosenbluth TL 1.00 2.50
152 Dean Smith TL 1.25 3.00
153 George Karl TL 1.00 2.50
154 Michael Jordan TL 2.50 6.00
155 Sam Perkins TL 1.00 2.50
156 James Worthy TL 1.25 3.00
157 Donald Williams TL 1.00 2.50
158 Charlotte Smith TL 1.00 2.50
159 Dean Smith TL 1.25 3.00
160 Matt Doherty TL 1.00 2.50
161 Roy Williams TL 1.25 3.00
162 Sean May TL 1.00 2.50
163 Ty Lawson TL 1.00 2.50
164 Michael Jordan JY 1.50 4.00
165 Michael Jordan JY 1.50 4.00
166 Michael Jordan JY 1.50 4.00
167 Michael Jordan JY 1.50 4.00
168 Michael Jordan JY 1.50 4.00
169 Michael Jordan JY 1.50 4.00
170 Michael Jordan JY 1.50 4.00
171 Michael Jordan JY 1.50 4.00
172 Michael Jordan JY 1.50 4.00
173 Michael Jordan JY 1.50 4.00
174 Michael Jordan JY 1.50 4.00
175 Michael Jordan JY 1.50 4.00
176 Michael Jordan JY 1.50 4.00
177 Michael Jordan JY 1.50 4.00
178 Michael Jordan JY 1.50 4.00
179 Michael Jordan JY 1.50 4.00
180 Michael Jordan JY 1.50 4.00
181 Michael Jordan JY 1.50 4.00
182 Michael Jordan JY 1.50 4.00
183 Michael Jordan JY 1.50 4.00
NNO Michael Jordan Banner AU 400.00 600.00

2010-11 Upper Deck North Carolina Autographs

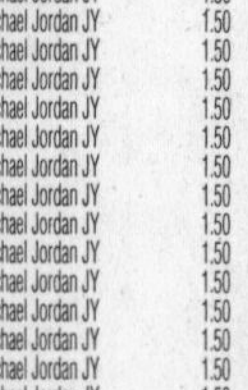

STATED ODDS 1:24 PACKS
UNPRICED SUBSET PRINT RUN ONE TO 3 SETS
7 Skippy Winstead 8.00 20.00
10 Lennie Rosenbluth 15.00 40.00
11 Pete Brennan 8.00 20.00
12 Joe Quigg 8.00 20.00
13 York Larese 8.00 20.00
14 Doug Moe 8.00 20.00
15 Larry Brown 20.00 50.00
16 Bobby Lewis 8.00 20.00
18 Dick Grubar 12.50 30.00
19 Charlie Scott 12.50 30.00
20 Jim Delany 8.00 20.00
21 Lee Dedmon 12.50 30.00
22 Bill Chamberlain 8.00 20.00
23 Stephen Previs 8.00 20.00
24 Darrell Elston 8.00 20.00
25 Bobby Jones 30.00 80.00
26 Bob McAdoo 20.00 50.00
27 Mitch Kupchak 15.00 40.00
28 Walter Davis 10.00 25.00
29 John Kuester 8.00 20.00
31 Angela Lumpkin 8.00 20.00
32 Phil Ford 15.00 40.00
33 Marsha Mann 8.00 20.00
34 Mike O'Koren 10.00 25.00
35 Bernadette McGlade 8.00 20.00
36 Dave Colescott 8.00 20.00
37 Al Wood 8.00 20.00
38 Rich Yonakor 10.00 25.00
39 Jennifer Alley 8.00 20.00
40 James Worthy 75.00 200.00
41 Matt Doherty 12.50 30.00
42 Sam Perkins 50.00 120.00
43 Michael Jordan 500.00 800.00
44 Buzz Peterson 10.00 25.00
45 Brad Daugherty 20.00 50.00
46 Steve Hale 10.00 25.00
47 Pam Leake 8.00 20.00
48 Kenny Smith 25.00 60.00
49 Joe Wolf 8.00 20.00
50 J.R. Reid 30.00 80.00
51 Sylvia Hatchell 10.00 25.00
52 Steve Bucknall 8.00 20.00
53 Jeff Lebo 8.00 20.00
54 Kevin Madden 8.00 20.00
55 Scott Williams 12.50 30.00
56 Pete Chilcutt 10.00 25.00
57 Rick Fox 20.00 50.00
58 Hubert Davis 15.00 40.00
59 George Lynch 8.00 20.00
60 Henrik Rodl 10.00 25.00
61 Matt Wenstrom 10.00 25.00
62 Sylvia Crawley 8.00 20.00
63 Eric Montross 8.00 20.00
64 Derrick Phelps 10.00 25.00
65 Tonya Sampson 8.00 20.00
66 Charlotte Smith 8.00 20.00
67 Donald Williams 12.50 30.00
68 Dante Calabria 10.00 25.00
69 Kevin Salvadori 10.00 25.00
70 Marion Jones 25.00 60.00
71 Jerry Stackhouse 50.00 125.00
72 Serge Zwikker 8.00 20.00
73 Vince Carter 30.00 80.00
74 Antawn Jamison 12.50 30.00
75 Makhtar N'diaye 8.00 20.00
76 Jason Capel 10.00 25.00
77 Kris Lang 8.00 20.00
78 Sean May 8.00 20.00
79 David Noel 10.00 25.00
80 Ty Lawson 100.00 250.00
81 Ed Davis 20.00 50.00
82 Roy Williams 100.00 200.00

2010-11 Upper Deck North Carolina Dream Team 3D

COMPLETE SET (25) 40.00 70.00
STATED ODDS 1:24 PACKS
DT1 Michael Jordan 12.50 30.00
DT2 Jack Cobb 1.50 4.00
DT3 George Glamack 1.50 4.00
DT4 Lennie Rosenbluth 1.50 4.00
DT5 Walter Davis 2.50 6.00
DT6 Marion Jones 2.50 6.00
DT7 Charlie Scott 1.50 4.00
DT8 Bobby Jones 2.00 5.00
DT9 Phil Ford 2.50 6.00
DT10 Mike O'Koren 2.50 6.00
DT11 Al Wood 1.50 4.00
DT12 James Worthy 2.50 6.00
DT13 Sam Perkins 1.50 4.00
DT14 Cartwright Carmichael 1.50 4.00
DT15 Brad Daugherty 2.00 5.00
DT16 Kenny Smith 2.00 5.00
DT17 J.R. Reid 1.50 4.00
DT18 Eric Montross 1.50 4.00
DT19 Charlotte Smith 2.50 6.00
DT20 Jerry Stackhouse 2.50 6.00
DT21 Vince Carter 2.50 6.00
DT22 Antawn Jamison 2.00 5.00
DT23 Sean May 1.50 4.00
DT24 Ty Lawson 2.00 5.00
DT25 Dean Smith 2.50 6.00

2010-11 Upper Deck North Carolina Legendary Numbers 3D

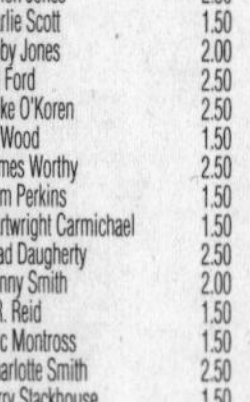

COMPLETE SET (25) 40.00 70.00
STATED ODDS 1:24 PACKS
LN1 Michael Jordan 12.50 30.00
LN2 Ty Lawson 2.00 5.00
LN3 Lennie Rosenbluth 1.50 4.00
LN4 Larry Brown 1.50 4.00
LN5 Vince Carter 2.50 6.00
LN6 George Glamack 1.50 4.00
LN7 Donald Williams 1.50 4.00
LN8 Phil Ford 2.50 6.00
LN9 Buzz Peterson 1.50 4.00
LN10 Eric Montross 1.50 4.00
LN11 Al Wood 1.50 4.00
LN12 Kenny Smith 2.00 5.00
LN13 Sam Perkins 1.50 4.00
LN14 Jack Cobb 1.50 4.00
LN15 Charlie Scott 1.50 4.00
LN16 Antawn Jamison 2.00 5.00
LN17 Bobby Jones 2.00 5.00
LN18 J.R. Reid 1.50 4.00
LN19 George Lynch 1.50 4.00
LN20 Hubert Davis 1.50 4.00
LN21 Sean May 1.50 4.00
LN22 Matt Doherty 1.50 4.00
LN23 Rick Fox 2.00 5.00
LN24 Charlotte Smith 2.50 6.00
LN25 James Worthy 2.50 6.00

2010-11 Upper Deck North Carolina Parallel 50

This 166-card set parallels the base set. The regular cards feature a blue tint and the subsets feature a silver tint. The cards are serially numbered out of 50. To ascertain values for this particular set, please use the base set price times the multiplier listed in the header below.

*1-83 PARALLEL: 8X TO 20X BASE HI
*84-103 PARALLEL: 5X TO 12X BASE HI
*104-123 PARALLEL: 4X TO 10X BASE HI
*124-143 PARALLEL: 5X TO 12X BASE HI
*144-163 PARALLEL: 4X TO 10X BASE HI
*164-183 PARALLEL: 6X TO 15X BASE HI
43 Michael Jordan 25.00 60.00
90 Horace Grant 25.00 60.00
Michael Jordan Rivalries
111 Michael Jordan AA 25.00 60.00
124 Michael Jordan BM 25.00 60.00
129 Michael Jordan BM 25.00 60.00
135 Michael Jordan BM 25.00 60.00
154 Michael Jordan TL 25.00 60.00

1989-90 UTEP

This 24-card standard-size set was sponsored by 7-Together and Drug Emporium and their names are on the top of the card. The team name/subtitle ("Star Miners") is given above the photo, and the player's name and position below it, with black and white photos for older players and color for newer players. Biographical information is on the back. Current and past NBA Stars featured in this set are Nate Archibald and Tim Hardaway (in his first card appearance); also note the presence of a card of Nolan Richardson, who went on to coach the Arkansas Razorbacks. The set is not numbered so the subjects are listed below in alphabetical order by name.

COMPLETE SET (24) 10.00 25.00
1 Nate Archibald 2.00 5.00
2 Jim Barnes .40 1.00
3 Rus Bradburd .20 .50
4 Dallas David .20 .50
5 Antonio Davis 2.00 5.00
6 Ralph Davis .30 .75
7 Norm Ellenberger CO .40 1.00
8 Francis Ezenwa .20 .50
9 Greg Foster .40 1.00
10 Joe Griffin .20 .50
11 Henry Hall .30 .75
12 Tim Hardaway 3.00 8.00
13 Don Haskins CO 1.50 4.00
14 Merle Heimer .20 .50
15 Bobby Joe Hill .30 .75
16 Greg Lackey .20 .50
17 David Lattin .75 2.00
18 Marlon Maxey .40 1.00
19 Mark McCall .20 .50
20 Chris Perez .20 .50
21 Nolan Richardson .75 2.00
22 Arlandis Rush .20 .50
23 Alprentice Stewart .20 .50
24 David Van Dyke .20 .50

1992-93 UTEP

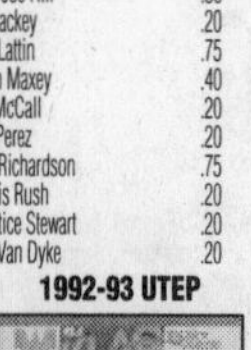

This 14-card standard-size set was sponsored by Whataburger, 95.5 KLAQ radio station, and Major Players. The cards feature color action player photos. The top of the card is accented by an orange stripe that contains sponsor logos. Near the bottom, the player's name appears in orange print in a white bar. The horizontal backs are white and display a shadow-bordered picture in the upper left corner. Biographical information, statistics, and a player profile are presented next to the photo. .

COMPLETE SET (14) 3.00 8.00
1 Don Haskins CO .75 2.00
2 Gym Bice .20 .50
3 Jeff Deal .20 .50
4 Roy Howard .20 .50
5 Johnny Melvin .30 .75
6 John Portis .20 .50
7 Daryl Christopher .20 .50
8 Eddie Rivera .30 .75
9 Ralph Davis .30 .75
10 Bryan Barnes .20 .50
11 Antoine Gillespie .30 .75
12 Hector Gonzalez .20 .50
13 Phil Crocker .20 .50
14 G.Ray Johnson ACO .20 .50
Gary Brewster ACO
Gilbert Miranda
Restricted Earnings CO

1987-88 Vanderbilt

This 14-card set was sponsored by Vanderbilt University Police and Security. The cards measure approximately 2 1/2" by 4". On a white card face, the fronts feature black and white player photos enclosed by black and yellow borders. Player information and the school logo appear in a box below the picture. The backs have biography, a safety tip, and a list of phone numbers to call for a police response. The cards are numbered on the back. Card number 5, Chip Rupp who transfered, was pulled from the sets although perhaps as many as the first 100 sets released included 14 cards, instead of the more typical 13-card sets that are usually found.

COMPLETE SET (14) 25.00 60.00
1 Team Photo 1.50 4.00
2 C.M. Newton CO 1.50 4.00
3 Fred Benjamin .60 1.50
4 Barry Booker .60 1.50
5 Chip Rupp SP 20.00 50.00
6 Scott Laughinghouse .60 1.50
7 Eric Reid .60 1.50
8 Steve Grant .60 1.50
9 Derrick Wilcox .60 1.50
10 Will Perdue 3.00 8.00
11 Frank Kornet 1.25 3.00
12 Charles Mayes .60 1.50
13 Barry Goheen 1.25 3.00
14 Scott Draud .60 1.50

1991-92 Vanderbilt Schedules

This two-card set features schedule cards each measuring approximately 4 1/2" by 3 1/2" when unfolded. The fronts show a full-bleed color player photo, except on the left where a black stripe carries "Vanderbilt 1991-92" in gold lettering. The backs display sponsor advertisements. The inside pages carry the 1991-92 basketball schedule. The cards are unnumbered and checklisted below in alphabetical order.

COMPLETE SET (2) .40 1.00
1 Jade Huntington .20 .50
2 Todd Milholland .20 .50

1982-83 Victoria

Measuring approximately 2 1/8" by 4", this 15-card set was sponsored by Honda City, Weathergard Shop, Factory Sound, CJVI 900 radio, and the Saanich police. On a white card face, the front features posed color action player photos framed by a thin blue border. The wider margin beneath the picture carries the team logo, player identification, and the years (1980, 1981, and 1982) the Vikings won the national championship. The backs present a safety slogan, facsimile autograph, and an offer to see a free game and win a stereo cassette walkman. The sponsor logos at the bottom round out the back. The cards are unnumbered and checklisted below in alphabetical order.

COMPLETE SET (15) 6.00 15.00
1 Dave Bakken .50 1.25
2 Dan Brosseuk .50 1.25
3 Ryan Burles .50 1.25
4 Kelly Dukeshire .50 1.25
5 Quinn Groenhyde .50 1.25
6 Gerald Kazanowski .50 1.25
7 Gregg Kazanowski .50 1.25
8 Tom Narbeshuber .50 1.25
9 Phil Ohl .50 1.25
10 Eli Pasquale .50 1.25
11 Vito Pasquale .50 1.25
12 David Sheehan .50 1.25
13 Ken Shields CO .50 1.25
14 Billy Turney-Loos ACO .50 1.25
15 Craig Higgins ACO .50 1.25

1983-84 Victoria

This 15-card set was sponsored by Sprite, CJVI900 (a radio station), Factory Sound, Sanyo, and the Saanich Police. The cards measure approximately 2 5/8" by 4". On a white card face, the fronts feature posed action photos. The pictures and the player information below them are enclosed by a blue border. The backs have player quotes ("Viking Quotes"), a facsimile autograph, an offer to see a game free and win a stereo cassette walkman, and sponsor logos. The game at which the card holder will be admitted free is noted on the back. The safety slogan "Working together with our youth and the community" rounds out the back. The cards a unnumbered and checklisted below in alphabetical order.

COMPLETE SET (15) 5.00 12.0
1 Cord Clemens .40 1.0
2 Quinn Groenhyde .40 1.0
3 Ian Hyde-Lay ACO .40 1.0
4 Sean Kalinovich .40 1.0
5 Ken Larson .40 1.0
6 John Munro .40 1.0
7 Jamie Newman .40 1.0
8 Phil Ohl .40 1.0
9 Eli Pasquale .40 1.0
10 Dave Sheehan .40 1.0
11 Ken Shields CO .40 1.0
12 Randy Steel .40 1.0
13 Graham Taylor .40 1.0
14 Greg Wiltjer .40 1.0
15 Logo Card .60 1.5
Saanich Police

1984-85 Victoria

This 16-card set was sponsored by Westcoast Saving Credit Union, CJVI-900 (a radio station), Factory Sound and Sanyo, and the Saanich Police. The cards measure approximately 2 5/8" by 4". On a white card face, the fronts feature posed action photos. The pictures and the player information below them are enclosed by a blue border. The backs have player quotes ("Viking Quotes"), a facsimile autograph, an offer to see a game free and win a stereo cassette walkman, and sponsor logos. The game at which the card holder will be admitted free is noted on the back. The safety slogan "Working together with our youth and the community" rounds out the back. The cards a unnumbered and checklisted below in alphabetical order.

COMPLETE SET (16) 5.00 12.0
1 Cord Clemens .40 1.0
2 Jerry Divoky .40 1.0
3 Quinn Groenhyde ACO .40 1.0
4 Shawn Kalinovich .40 1.0
5 Robert Kreke .40 1.0
6 Wade Loukes .40 1.0
7 James Newman .40 1.0
8 Phil Ohl .40 1.0
9 Vito Pasquale .40 1.0
10 Lloyd Scrubb UER .40 1.0
(Name misspelled
Llyod on front)
11 David Sheehan .40 1.0
12 Ken Shields CO .40 1.0
13 Randy Steel .40 1.0
14 Graham Taylor .40 1.0
15 Ellis Whalen .40 1.0
16 Logo Card .60 1.5
Saanich Police

1985-86 Victoria

This 17-card set was sponsored by Pacific Coast Savings Credit Union, Converse, 1200-CKDA, and the Saanich Police. The cards measure approximately 2 5/8" by 4". On a white card face, the fronts feature posed action photos. The pictures and the player information below them are enclosed by a blue border. The backs have player quotes ("Viking Quotes"), a facsimile autograph, an offer to see a game free and win a stereo cassette walkman, and sponsor logos. The game at which the card holder will be admitted free is noted on the back. The safety slogan "Crime prevention is everyone's business" rounds out the back. The card are unnumbered and checklisted below in alphabetical order.

COMPLETE SET (17) 5.00 12.0
1 Maurice Basso .40 1.0
2 Clint Hamilton .40 1.0
3 Fraser Jefferson .40 1.0
4 Tom Johnson .40 1.0
5 Jim Knox .40 1.0
6 David Lescheid .40 1.0
7 Vesa Linnamo .40 1.0
8 David McIntosh .40 1.0
9 Geoff McKay .40 1.0
10 Spencer McKay .40 1.0
11 Rick Mesich .40 1.0
12 Kevin Ottewell .40 1.0
13 Roger Rai .40 1.0
14 Chris Schriek .40 1.0
15 Scott Stinson ACO .40 1.0
16 Guy Vetrie CO .40 1.0
17 Logo Card .60 1.5
Saanich Police

1986-87 Victoria

This set contains 16 cards, each measuring approximately 2 5/8" by 4". The white and blue bordered fronts have posed color player shots. Below the photo are the player's name and biography printed in black. The white backs carry a players quote and copy of their autograph below. The cards are unnumbered and checklisted below in alphabetical order.

COMPLETE SET (16) 5.00 12.00
1 Jerry Divoky .40 1.00
2 Shawn Kalinovich .40 1.00
3 Jay Kenyon .40 1.00
4 Rob Kreke .40 1.00
5 Brian Kruger .40 1.00
6 Wade Loukes .40 1.00
7 Geoff McKay .40 1.00
8 Spencer McKay .40 1.00
9 Steve Mitton .40 1.00
10 Vito Pasquale .40 1.00
11 Alan Phillips .40 1.00
12 Rob Poole .40 1.00
13 Tom Johnson .40 1.00
14 Lloyd Scrubb .40 1.00
15 Ken Shields CO .40 1.00
16 Mark Simpson ACO .40 1.00

1988-89 Victoria

This 16-card set was sponsored by Pacific Coast Savings Credit Union, Converse, 1200-CKDA, and the Saanich Police. The cards were issued on an unperforated sheet; if cut, they would measure approximately 2 5/8" by 4". On a white card face, the fronts feature posed action photos. The pictures and the player information below them are enclosed by a blue border. The backs have player quotes ("Viking Quotes"), a facsimile autograph, an offer to see a game free and win a stereo cassette walkman, and sponsor logos. The game at which the card holder will be admitted free is noted on the back. The safety slogan "Crime prevention is everyone's business" rounds out the back. The cards are unnumbered and checklisted below in alphabetical order.

COMPLETE SET (16) 3.00 8.00
1 Maurice Basso .30 .75
2 Colin Brousson .30 .75
3 Jerry Divoky .30 .75
4 Kevin Harrington .30 .75
5 Tom Johnson .30 .75
6 Daryn Lansdell .30 .75
7 Wade Loukes .30 .75
8 Geoff McKay .30 .75
9 Spencer McKay .30 .75
10 Rick Mesich .30 .75
11 Dale Olson .30 .75
12 Ken Olynyk ACO .30 .75
13 Kevin Ottewell .30 .75
14 Tug Rados .30 .75
15 Ken Shields CO .30 .75
16 Guy Vetrie ACO .30 .75

1988-89 Virginia

This 16-card standard-size set was sponsored by Hardee's Restaurants in conjunction with WINA Radio AM 1070, and their company names appear on the top of the card. The action color photos are surrounded on their sides and bottom by blue and orange thick borders (the school's colors), with the Cavalier logo in the lower left hand corner. The player's name, jersey number, year, and position appear below the photo. The back gives biographical information and Tips from the Cavaliers. The cards are ordered and numbered below according to the alphabetical order of the player's name. The set features a card of Matt Blundin, drafted by the NFL as a quarterback and NBA first-rounder Bryant Stith.

COMPLETE SET (16) 12.50 30.00
1 Brent Bair .75 2.00
2 Matt Blundin 3.00 8.00
3 Mark Cooke .75 2.00
4 John Crotty 3.00 8.00
5 Brent Dabbs .75 2.00
6 Jeff Daniel .75 2.00
7 Terry Holland CO 2.50 6.00
8 Dirk Katstra .75 2.00
9 Richard Morgan .75 2.00
10 Anthony Oliver .75 2.00
11 Bryant Stith 4.00 10.00
12 Kenny Turner .75 2.00
13 Curtis Williams .75 2.00
14 Cheerleaders .75 2.00
15 Coaching Staff .75 2.00
16 Title Card .75 2.00

1991-92 Virginia

This 16-card set was sponsored by Capitol Sports Network, whose logo appears at the top of each card front. The cards are perforated and measure the standard size. The fronts feature posed head and shoulders shots enclosed by white and purple borders. Player identification appears in an orange stripe beneath the picture, and the team logo at the lower left corner rounds out the card face. The backs carry biographical information, career summary, and a player quote. The cards are unnumbered and checklisted below in alphabetical order. Key cards in the set are Chris Havlicek (John's son), NFL running back Terry Kirby, and NBA player Bryant Stith.

COMPLETE SET (16) 10.00 25.00
1 Chris Alexander .40 1.00
2 Cory Alexander 2.50 6.00
3 Yuri Barnes .75 2.00
4 Junior Burrough 1.25 3.00
5 Chris Havlicek .75 2.00
6 Ted Jeffries .75 2.00
7 Derrick Johnson .40 1.00
8 Jeff Jones CO 1.25 3.00
9 Terry Kirby 2.00 5.00
10 Anthony Oliver .75 2.00
11 Cornell Parker .75 2.00
12 Doug Smith .40 1.00
13 Corey Stewart .40 1.00
14 Bryant Stith 2.50 6.00
15 Jason Williford .75 2.00
16 Shawn Wilson .40 1.00

1991-92 Virginia Women

This 16-card set was issued as a perforated sheet and sponsored by McDonald's. After perforation, the cards measure the standard size (2 1/2" by 3 1/2"). On a white card face, the fronts feature a mix of posed or action color player photos enclosed by blue borders. A McDonald's logo with the words "Food Folks and Fun" appears in a bar above the picture, while school logo and player information appear in an orange stripe at the bottom. In black print on white, the backs carry biography, player profile, and an inspirational quote. This set includes the first card of Dawn Staley, who later played point guard for the gold medal-winning 1996 USA team. The cards are unnumbered and checklisted below in alphabetical order.

COMPLETE SET (16) 8.00 20.00
1 Charleata Beale .20 .50
2 Heather Burge .75 2.00
3 Heidi Burge 1.25 3.00
4 Dena Evans 1.25 3.00
5 Chris Lesoravage .20 .50
6 Amy Lofstedt .20 .50
7 Allison Moore .20 .50
8 Tammi Reiss 1.25 3.00
9 Debbie Ryan CO .75 2.00
10 Felicia Santelli .20 .50
11 Audra Smith .20 .50
12 Dawn Staley 3.00 8.00
13 Wendy Toussaint .20 .50
14 Melanee Wagener .20 .50
15 NCAA Midwest Regional .20 .50
16 Virginia vs. NC State .20 .50

1992-93 Virginia

Sponsored by Coca-Cola, this 16-card set was issued as a perforated sheet with four rows of four cards each. After perforation, the cards measure the standard size. On a gradated blue card face, the fronts feature posed or action color player photos. The school name appears above the photo in orange block lettering. The player's name and position appear in a blue bar below the picture. The Coca-Cola emblem is printed at the bottom. The backs carry biographical information and career highlights. The cards are unnumbered and checklisted below in alphabetical order.

COMPLETE SET (16) 5.00 12.00
1 Chris Alexander .20 .50
2 Cory Alexander 1.25 3.00
3 Yuri Barnes .30 .75
4 Junior Burrough .60 1.50
5 Chris Havlicek .30 .75
6 Ted Jeffries .30 .75
7 Cornell Parker .30 .75
8 Doug Smith .20 .50
9 Jason Williford .30 .75
10 Shawn Wilson .20 .50
11 Jeff Jones CO .75 2.00
12 Brian Ellerbe ACO .20 .50
Dennis Wolff ACO
Tom Perrin ACO
13 1980 NIT Champions .30 .75
14 1981 NCAA East .30 .75
Regional Tournament Champions
15 1984 NCAA East .30 .75
Regional Tournament Champions
16 1992 NIT Champions .30 .75

1992-93 Virginia Women

Sponsored by Coca-Cola, this 16-card set was issued as a perforated sheet with four rows of four cards each. After perforation, the cards measure the standard size. On a gradated blue card face, the fronts feature posed or action color player photos. The school name appears above the photo in orange block lettering. The player's name and position appear in a blue bar below the picture. The Coca-Cola emblem is printed at the bottom. The backs carry biographical information and career highlights. The cards are unnumbered and checklisted below in alphabetical order.

COMPLETE SET (16) 5.00 12.00
1 Charleata Beale .20 .50
2 Jenny Boucek .20 .50
3 Heather Burge .60 1.50
4 Heidi Burge .75 2.00
5 Dena Evans 1.00 2.50
6 Jeffra Gausepohl .20 .50
7 Chris Lesoravage .20 .50
8 Amy Lofstedt .20 .50
9 Allison Moore .20 .50
10 Wendy Palmer 2.00 5.00
11 Debbie Ryan CO .75 2.00
12 Kristen Somogyi .20 .50
13 Cheryl Taylor .20 .50
14 Wendy Toussaint .20 .50
15 1992 Atlantic Coast .20 .50
Conference Tournament Champions
16 1992 East Regional .20 .50
Tournament Champions

1993-94 Virginia

These 16 standard-size (2 1/2" by 3 1/2") cards originally were issued in a perforated sheet. The blue-bordered fronts feature color player action and posed photos set within ovals. The player's name and position appear in white lettering at the bottom. The white backs carry the player's name an jersey number in white lettering set on a black stripe at the top. The player's position, height, weight, class, high school, hometown, and career highlights follow below. The cards are unnumbered, but are arranged in alphabetical order on the perforated sheet, except for the coach cards, and are so checklisted below.

COMPLETE SET (16) 5.00 12.00
1 Chris Alexander .20 .50
2 Cory Alexander 1.00 2.50
3 Yuri Barnes .30 .75
4 Mark Bogosh .20 .50
5 Junior Burrough .50 1.25
6 Harold Deane .75 2.00
7 Bobby Graves .20 .50
8 Chris Havlicek .30 .75
9 Cornel Parker .30 .75
10 Mike Powell .20 .50
11 Jamal Robinson .30 .75
12 Maurice Watkins .20 .50
13 Jason Williford .30 .75
14 Shawn Wilson .20 .50
15 Jeff Jones CO .60 1.50
16 Assistant Coaches .20 .50
Brian Ellerbe
Dennis Wolff
Tom Perrin

1993-94 Virginia Women

Sponsored by Cavalier Inn, these 16 standard-size (2 1/2" by 3 1/2") cards originally were issued in a perforated sheet. The blue-bordered fronts feature color player action and posed photos set within ovals. The player's name and position appear in white lettering at the bottom. The white backs carry the player's name an jersey number in white lettering set on a black stripe at the top. The player's position, height, class, hometown, and career highlights follow below. The cards are unnumbered and checklisted below in alphabetical order.

COMPLETE SET (16) 5.00 12.00
1 Charleata Beale .20 .50
2 Jenny Boucek .20 .50
3 Konecka Drakeford .20 .50
4 Tammy Gardner .20 .50
5 Jeffra Gausepohl .20 .50
6 Jackie Glessner .20 .50
7 Chris Lesoravage .20 .50
8 Amy Lofstedt .20 .50
9 Wendy Palmer 1.25 3.00
10 Debbie Ryan CO .75 2.00
11 Tora Suber 1.25 3.00
12 Cheryl Taylor .20 .50
13 Wendy Toussaint .20 .50
14 Dawn Staley's 1.50 4.00
Number Retired
15 NCAA East Regional .20 .50
16 Mascot Day .20 .50

1999-00 Virginia

This set was released for the University of Virginia Men's Basketball during the 1999-00 season. The set features cards of all of the players and coaches on a slightly over-sized white bordered card. The set was produced by Cavalier Sports Cards.

COMPLETE SET (15) 2.00 5.00
1 Willie Dersch .20 .50
2 Stephane Dondon .20 .50
3 Jason Dowling .20 .50
4 Colin Ducharme .20 .50
5 Keith Friel .20 .50
6 Pete Gillen CO .30 .75
7 Adam Hall .20 .50
8 Donald Hand .20 .50
9 Josh Hare .20 .50
10 Cade Lemcke .20 .50
11 Majestic Mapp .20 .50
12 Roger Mason .20 .50
13 Jason Rogers .20 .50
14 Travis Watson .20 .50
15 Chris Williams .20 .50

1999-00 Virginia Women

This set was released for the University of Virginia Women's Basketball during the 1999-00 season. The set features cards of all of the players and coaches on a slightly over-sized white bordered card. The set was produced by Cavalier Sports Cards.

COMPLETE SET (13) 1.50 4.00
1 Anna Crosswhite .20 .50
2 Marcie Dickson .20 .50
3 Lisa Hosac .20 .50
4 Elena Kravchenko .20 .50
5 Schuye Larue .20 .50
6 Chalois Lias .20 .50
7 Dean'na Mitchelson .20 .50
8 Telisha Quarles .20 .50
9 Renee Robinson .20 .50
10 Debbie Ryan CO .30 .75
11 Lauren Swierczek .20 .50
12 Katie Tracy .20 .50
13 Svetlana Volnaya .20 .50

1992-93 Virginia Tech

This 12-card multi-sport set measures the standard size and features full-bleed, color, action player photos. The sports represented in the set are football (1, 2, 5, 10-11), basketball (3, 7-8), baseball (4), soccer (6), and volleyball (9).

COMPLETE SET (12) 5.00 12.00
3 Phyllis Tonkin BK .20 .50
Dayna Sonovick
Tisa Brown
7 Thomas Elliott .20 .50
Jay Purcell
8 Dell Curry 2.40 6.00

1988-89 Wake Forest

This 16-card standard-size set was sponsored by the Adolescent CareUnit of Almanac Health Services, local law enforcement agencies, and Wake Forest University. The cards feature on the front posed color head and shoulders shots, bordered in black on the left and in yellow on the right and below. Player information appears in the bottom yellow border, while the school logo in the lower left corner rounds out the front. The backs present biography, player profile, and "Tips from the Demon Deacons," which consist of anti-drug and alcohol messages. The cards are unnumbered and checklisted below in alphabetical order.

COMPLETE SET (16) 6.00 15.00
1 Tony Black .40 1.00
2 Cal Boyd .40 1.00
3 David Carlyle .40 1.00
4 Darryl Cheeley .40 1.00
5 Sam Ivy .60 1.50
6 Antonio Johnson .60 1.50
7 Daric Keys .40 1.00
8 Chris King 1.00 2.50
9 Ralph Kitley .40 1.00
10 Derrick McQueen .40 1.00
11 Phil Medlin .40 1.00
12 Steve Ray .40 1.00
13 Todd Sanders .40 1.00
14 Robert Siler .40 1.00
15 Bob Staak CO .60 1.50
16 Tom Wise .40 1.00

1991 Washington

This 17-card standard-size (2 1/2" by 3 1/2") set was sponsored by Prime Sports Northwest and TCI Cablevision of Washington. The fronts display color action player photos enframed by purple borders. The school and team name appear above the pictures, while player information is printed in a gold stripe beneath them. The backs have career statistics, an announcement of the Husky KidSports Program, and sponsor logos. The cards are unnumbered and checklisted below in alphabetical order within sex; men's team are given card numbers 1-9 and women's team are numbered 10-17.

COMPLETE SET (17) 5.00 12.00
1 Dion Brown .40 1.00
2 Tim Caviezel .75 2.00
3 James French .40 1.00
4 Mike Hayward .40 1.00
5 Todd Lautenbach .40 1.00
6 Doug Meekins .60 1.50
7 Brent Merritt .40 1.00
8 Lynn Nance CO .60 1.50
9 Quentin Youngblood .40 1.00
10 Tara Davis .30 .75
11 Karen Deden .30 .75
12 Chris Gobrecht CO .30 .75
13 Erika Hardwick .30 .75
14 Jocelyn McIntire .30 .75
15 Laurie Merlino .30 .75
16 Laura Moore .30 .75
17 Dianne Williams .30 .75

1991-92 Washington

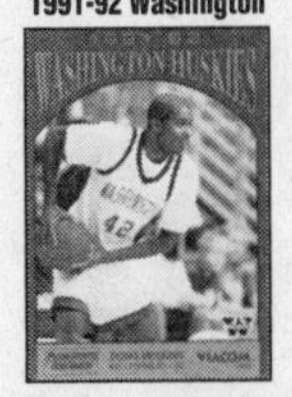

This 17-card standard-size basketball set was sponsored by Prime Sports Northwest and Viacom Cable. The fronts are accented in the team's colors (purple and gold) and have color action player photos. The top of the pictures is curved to resemble an archway, and the team name follows the curve of the arch. Sponsor logos and player identification appear in the gold stripe below the picture. The backs carry statistics (or career summary), an announcement of the Husky KidSports Program, and sponsor logos. The cards are unnumbered and checklisted below in alphabetical order as follows: men's basketball (1-9) and women's basketball (10-17).

COMPLETE SET (17) 5.00 12.00
1 Bryant Boston .40 1.00
2 Tim Caviezel .60 1.50
3 Rich Manning .60 1.50
4 Doug Meekins .40 1.00
5 Chandler Nairn .40 1.00
6 Lynn Nance CO .60 1.50
7 Mark Pope .75 2.00
8 Andy Woods .40 1.00
9 Quentin Youngblood .40 1.00
10 Tara Davis .30 .75
11 Katia Foucade .30 .75
12 Shaunda Greene .30 .75
13 Chris Gobrecht CO .30 .75
14 Erika Hardwick .30 .75
15 Laura Moore .30 .75
16 Jo Shafer .30 .75
17 Dianne Williams .30 .75

2003-04 Washington

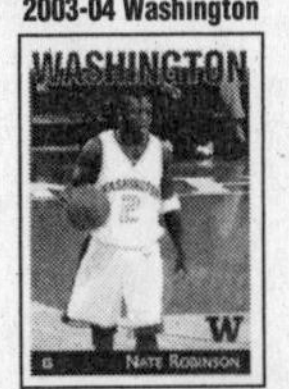

Produced by High Step and printed in conjunction with Red Robin and Pepsi, this 14-card set was available through Washington during the 2003-04 school year.

COMPLETE SET (14) 4.00 10.00
1 C.J. Massingale .20 .50
2 Nate Robinson 1.50 4.00
4 Jeffrey Day .20 .50
5 Will Conroy .60 1.50
15 Bobby Jones .20 .50
20 Curtis Allen .20 .50
24 Doug Wrenn .20 .50
30 Anthony Washington .20 .50
42 Mike Jensen .20 .50
44 Marlon Shelton .20 .50
52 David Hudson .20 .50
55 Ben Devoe .20 .50
20a Lorenzo Romar .30 .75
NNO Lorenzo Romar CO .30 .75

2003-04 Washington Women

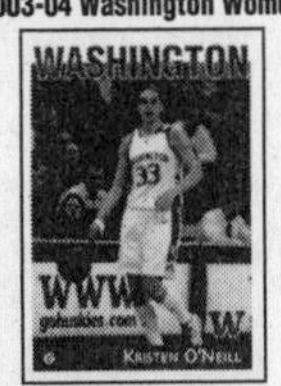

Produced by High Step and sponsored by Red Robin and Pepsi, this 16-card set was available through Washington during the 2003-04 school year.

COMPLETE SET (16) 2.00 5.00
3 Andrea Lalum .15 .40
4 Sarah Keller .15 .40
5 Alicia Heathcote .15 .40
12 Angie Jones .15 .40
13 Giuliana Mendiola .15 .40
15 Nicole Castro .15 .40
20 Kayla Burt .15 .40
21 Erica Schelly .15 .40
22 Loree Payne .15 .40
23 Emily Autrey .15 .40
24 Kellie Dalan .15 .40
25 Jill Bell .15 .40
31 Gioconda Mendiola .15 .40
33 Kristen O'Neill .15 .40
40 Kirsten Brockman .15 .40
44 Cheryl Sorenson .15 .40

1991-92 Washington State

This 12-card standard-size basketball set was sponsored by Prime Sports Northwest and CableVision. The set was issued as an perforated sheet with three rows of four cards each; the first six cards feature the women's basketball team, while the last six cards present the men's team. The fronts are accented in the team's colors (maroon and gray) and have posed and action player photos. The top of the pictures is curved to resemble an archway, and the team name follows the curve of the arch. Sponsor logos and player identification appear in the gray stripe below the picture. The backs carry statistics, player profile, and sponsor advertisements. The cards are unnumbered and checklisted below in alphabetical order as follows: men's basketball (1-6) and women's basketball (7-12).

COMPLETE SET (12) 5.00 12.00
1 Rob Corkrum .60 1.50
2 Ken Critton .60 1.50
3 Eddie Hill .60 1.50
4 Tyrone Maxey .60 1.50
5 Sean Tresvant .60 1.50
6 Joey Warmenhoven .60 1.50
7 Janel Benton .40 1.00
Erika Wheeler
8 Lori Lollis .40 1.00
9 Heather Norman .40 1.00
10 Camille Thompson .40 1.00
Kathy Weber
11 Darla Williamson .40 1.00
12 Team Photo .60 1.50

1996-97 Weber State

This 13-card standard size set was sponsored by Matrix Marketing. The company's logo is found on the bottom of the back of the card. The front features a full color action player photo inside of a black border. The words "Weber Fever" and an orange basketball adorn the top. The bottom has an orange basketball emblem that designates the player's postion. Besides the ball the word "Wildcats" resides in a purple font. The player's name is listed below. The back is black and white, listing the palyer's name at the top within a black box. The player's biography and player profile adorn the back as does the Webber State Logo on the bottom right corner. The cards are unnumbered and listed below in alphabetical order.

COMPLETE SET (13) 2.00 5.00
1 Damien Baskerville .20 .50
2 Ryan Cuff .20 .50
3 Jimmy DeGraffenried .20 .50
4 Bryan Emery .20 .50
5 Joey Haws .20 .50
6 Squirt Hicks .20 .50
7 Eric Ketcham .20 .50
8 Bart McIntire .20 .50
9 Justyn Nielsen .20 .50
10 Andy Smith .20 .50
11 Justin Tebbs .20 .50
12 Women's Basketball Team .20 .50
13 WSU Cheerleaders .20 .50

1977-78 West Virginia Schedules

This set of four schedule cards measures the standard size, 2 1/2" by 3 1/2". Printed on cardboard stock, the fronts show black-and-white action shots or portraits enframed by thick white borders. In team color-coded print, the school name, logo, and "Basketball 1977-78" appear above the pictures, while player information is presented below the pictures. On a white background, the back lists the 1978-78 basketball schedule, again in team color-coded print. The schedule cards are unnumbered and checklisted below in alphabetical order.

COMPLETE SET (4) 4.00 8.00
1 Sid Bostick .75 2.00
2 Dennis Hosey .75 2.00
3 Tommy Roberts .75 2.00
4 Maurice Robinson 1.50 4.00

1978-79 West Virginia Schedules

This set of 15 schedule cards measures approximately 2 5/16" by 3 1/2". Printed on cardboard stock, the fronts show black-and-white closeup player photos enframed by thick white borders. In blue print, the school name and "Basketball '79" appear above the pictures, while player information is presented below the pictures. On a white background, the back lists the 1978-78 basketball schedule, again in blue print. The schedule cards are unnumbered and checklisted below in alphabetical order.

COMPLETE SET (15) 7.50 15.00
1 Gale Catlett CO .75 2.00
2 John Goots .40 1.00
3 Vic Herbert .40 1.00
4 Dennis Hosey .40 1.00
5 Junius Lewis .40 1.00
6 Steve McCune .40 1.00
7 Lowes Moore .75 2.00
8 Noah Moore .40 1.00
9 Greg Nance .40 1.00
10 Dana Perno .40 1.00
11 Mike Richardson .40 1.00
12 Jeff Szczepanski .40 1.00
13 Lanny Van Eman ACO .75 2.00
14 Coaching Staff .40 1.00
15 Eastern Eight Logo .40 1.00

1980-81 Wichita State

This 15-card standard size (2 1/2" by 3 1/2") set was sponsored by Service Auto Glass and the Wichita Police Department. The cards were given away at the Wichita State athletic banquet and also by police officers. The fronts feature a close-up of the player enclosed by a border. The slogan "Love 'Ya Shockers" appears in the upper right corner, while player information is printed beneath the picture. Each card back carries a different safety message and a reminder to call 911. The cards are unnumbered and checklisted below in alphabetical order. Key cards in the set include the first cards of Antoine Carr and Cliff Levingston.

COMPLETE SET (15) 50.00 100.00
1 Antoine Carr 20.00 40.00
2 Mike Denny 1.50 4.00
3 Zarko Djuricic 1.50 4.00
4 James Gibbs 1.50 4.00
5 Jay Jackson 1.50 4.00
6 Mike Jones 1.50 4.00
7 Ozell Jones 4.00 10.00
8 Eric Kuhn 1.50 4.00
9 Cliff Levingston 15.00 30.00
10 Tony Martin 1.50 4.00
11 Karl Papke 1.50 4.00
12 Zoran Rdovic 1.50 4.00
13 Gene Smithson CO 1.50 4.00
14 Randy Smithson 1.50 4.00
15 Team Photo 2.50 6.00

1987-88 Wichita State

This 12-card standard-size set was jointly sponsored by Scholfield Honda, KNSS News Radio (1240 AM), and Riverside Hospital. The fronts show a mix of posed and action color player photos on a white card face. Sponsor logos appear at the top, while player information appears between school logos beneath the picture. The backs carry biography, career summary, "Tips from the Shockers," which consist of anti-drug and alcohol messages. The cards are unnumbered and checklisted below in alphabetical order.

COMPLETE SET (12) 10.00 25.00
1 John Cooper .75 2.00
2 Aaron Davis .75 2.00
3 John Felter .75 2.00
4 Eddie Fogler CO 3.00 8.00
5 Steve Grayer .75 2.00
6 Joe Griffin .75 2.00
7 Paul Guffrovich .75 2.00
8 Tom Kosich .75 2.00
9 Dwayne Praylow .75 2.00
10 Dwight Praylow .75 2.00
11 Sasha Radunovich 2.00 5.00
12 Team Photo 2.00 5.00

1988-89 Wichita State

This 11-card set was jointly sponsored by KWCH TV, KNSS Radio, and Scholfield Auto Dealership, and these sponsors' logos adorn the bottom of the card face. The standard size cards feature posed player photos on the fronts. In the upper left corner the school logo appears inside a circle, while player identification is placed in a rectangle overlaying the bottom edge of the picture. The backs have anti-drug messages. The cards are unnumbered and are checklisted below in alphabetical order. The only player not portrayed in this series is Ricky Bell, who joined the team after the set was composed.

COMPLETE SET (11) 6.00 15.00
1 Keith Bonds .75 2.00
2 John Cooper .75 2.00
3 Aaron Davis .75 2.00
4 Darin Dugger .75 2.00
5 John Felter .75 2.00
6 Steve Grayer .75 2.00
7 Paul Guffrovich .75 2.00
8 Phil Mendelson .75 2.00
9 Dwayne Praylow .75 2.00
10 Dwight Praylow .75 2.00
11 Sasha Radunovich 1.50 4.00

1989-90 Wisconsin

This 14-card set was sponsored by the USDA Forest Service in cooperation with the National Association of State Foresters and BD and A, Inc. The cards were issued on an unperforated sheet with four rows of four cards; two of the cards slots are blacked out where the photo should appear and feature a fire cartoon on their backs. After cutting, the cards measure the standard size (2 1/2" by 3 1/2"). The fronts feature a mix of posed and action color player photos on a white card face. Above the picture appears the school name (in red lettering) and a black stripe. Red and black stripes traverse the card below the picture, with the Smokey logo in the lower left corner and player identification to the right. The backs have biographical information, player evaluation, and a fire prevention cartoon starring Smokey. The cards are unnumbered and checklisted below in alphabetical order.

COMPLETE SET (14)	5.00	12.00
1 Bobby Douglass	.40	1.00
2 John Ellenson	.40	1.00
3 Brian Good	.40	1.00
4 Damon Harrell	.40	1.00
5 Larry Hisle Jr.	.60	1.50
6 Danny Jones	.40	1.00
7 Jason Johnsen	.40	1.00
8 Grant Johnson	.40	1.00
9 Tim Locum	.40	1.00
10 Carlton McGee	.40	1.00
11 Kurt Portmann	.40	1.00
12 Willie Simms	.60	1.50
13 Patrick Tompkins	.40	1.00
14 Steve Yoder CO	.75	2.00

2005-06 Wisconsin

This 16-card set was originally issued in uncut sheet form. The cards are listed below alphabetically.

COMPLETE SET (16)	3.00	8.00
1 Devin Barry	.40	1.00
2 Tanner Bronson	.40	1.00
3 Brian Butch	.40	1.00
4 Morris Cain	.40	1.00
5 Jason Chappell	.40	1.00
6 Michael Flowers	.40	1.00
7 Kevin Gullikson	.40	1.00
8 Joe Krabbenhoft	.40	1.00
9 Marcus Landry	.60	1.50
10 Ray Nixon	.40	1.00
11 Mickey Perry	.40	1.00
12 Bo Ryan CO	.40	1.00
13 Greg Stiemsma	.40	1.00
14 Kammron Taylor	.40	1.00
15 Alando Tucker	.60	1.50
16 Bucky Badger Mascot	.40	1.00

2006-07 Wisconsin

This 18-card set was originally issued in uncut sheet form. The cards are listed below alphabetically.

COMPLETE SET (18)	4.00	10.00
1 Jason Bohannon	.40	1.00
2 Tanner Bronson	.40	1.00
3 Brian Butch	.40	1.00
4 Morris Cain	.40	1.00
5 Jason Chappell	.40	1.00
6 Michael Flowers	.40	1.00
7 J.P. Gavinski	.40	1.00
8 Kevin Gullikson	.40	1.00
9 Trevon Hughes	.40	1.00
10 Joe Krabbenhoft	.40	1.00
11 Marcus Landry	.60	1.50
12 Mickey Perry	.40	1.00
13 Bo Ryan CO	.40	1.00
14 Greg Stiemsma	.40	1.00
15 Kammron Taylor	.40	1.00
16 Alando Tucker	.60	1.50
17 Brett Valentyn	.40	1.00
18 Bucky Badger Mascot	.40	1.00

2007-08 Wisconsin

This 16-card set was originally issued in uncut sheet form. The cards are listed below alphabetically.

COMPLETE SET (16)	3.00	8.00
1 Jason Bohannon	.40	1.00
2 Tanner Bronson	.40	1.00
3 Brian Butch	.40	1.00
4 Morris Cain	.40	1.00
5 Michael Flowers	.40	1.00
6 J.P. Gavinski	.40	1.00
7 Kevin Gullikson	.40	1.00
8 Trevon Hughes	.40	1.00
9 Jim Jarmusz	.40	1.00
10 Joe Krabbenhoft	.40	1.00
11 Marcus Landry	.60	1.50
12 Jon Leuer	.40	1.00
13 Keaton Nankivil	.40	1.00
14 Bo Ryan CO	.40	1.00
15 Greg Stiemsma	.40	1.00
16 Brett Valentyn	.40	1.00

2009-10 Wisconsin

This 16-card set was originally issued in uncut sheet form. The cards are listed below alphabetically.

COMPLETE SET (16)	3.00	8.00
1 Jared Berggren	.40	1.00
2 Jason Bohannon	.40	1.00
3 Mike Bruesewitz	.40	1.00
4 Ryan Evans	.40	1.00
5 Dan Fahey	.40	1.00
6 J.P. Gavinski	.40	1.00
7 Trevon Hughes	.40	1.00
8 Tim Jarmusz	.40	1.00
9 Jon Leuer	.40	1.00
10 Ian Markolf	.40	1.00
11 Keaton Nankivil	.40	1.00
12 Bo Ryan CO	.40	1.00
13 Wquinton Smith	.40	1.00
14 Jordan Taylor	.40	1.00
15 Brett Valentyn	.40	1.00
16 Rob Wilson	.40	1.00

2010-11 Wisconsin

This 18-card set was originally issued in uncut sheet form. The cards are listed below alphabetically.

COMPLETE SET (18)	4.00	10.00
1 Evan Anderson	.40	1.00
2 Jared Berggren	.40	1.00
3 Mike Bruesewitz	.40	1.00
4 Ben Brust	.40	1.00
5 Duje Dukan	.40	1.00
6 Ryan Evans	.40	1.00
7 Dan Fahey	.40	1.00
8 Josh Gasser	.40	1.00
9 J.P. Gavinski	.40	1.00
10 Tim Jarmusz	.40	1.00
11 Jon Leuer	.40	1.00
12 Keaton Nankivil	.40	1.00
13 Bo Ryan CO	.40	1.00
14 Wquinton Smith	.40	1.00
15 Jordan Taylor	.40	1.00
16 Brett Valentyn	.40	1.00
17 Rob Wilson	.40	1.00
18 J.D. Wise	.40	1.00

1991 Wooden Award Winners

This 22-card standard-size set was released by Little Sun of Monrovia, California, to commemorate the John R. Wooden Award. Only 28,000 sets were produced, and the set number is given on the certification card. The set is accompanied by a deluxe card album with two-up plastic sheets to house the cards. The cards chronicle the career of John Wooden and feature all 14 winners (in their college uniforms) of college basketball's most prestigious award. With the exception of some early black and white Wooden photos, the fronts feature borderless color player photos. Each picture is bordered on the left side by a gray stripe, with the Little Sun logo superimposed at the top. A lavender stripe traverses the bottom of the card face and gives a title for that card. The backs have biographical information and full close-ups of each player printed in a blue Mezzo-tint process. John Wooden also signed a select number of card number 1. That price is listed at the bottom of the set and is numbered as "AU1" to not confuse the two cards. It is not considered part of the set.

COMP. FACT SET (22)	4.00	10.00
1 John Wooden 1991	.20	.50
2 Wooden Trophy	.05	.15
3 John Wooden Purdue	.20	.50
4 John Wooden UCLA	.20	.50
5 Wooden Summer Camp	.05	.15
6 Duke Llewellyn	.05	.15
7 Marques Johnson	.08	.25
8 Phil Ford	.08	.25
9 Larry Bird	1.00	2.50
10 Darrell Griffith	.08	.25
11 Danny Ainge	.25	.60
12 Ralph Sampson	.08	.25
13 Michael Jordan	2.00	5.00
14 Chris Mullin	.20	.50
15 Walter Berry	.05	.15
16 David Robinson	.40	1.00
17 Danny Manning	.15	.40
18 Sean Elliott	.20	.50
19 Lionel Simmons	.05	.15
20 Larry Johnson	.20	.50
21 Press Conference 1991	.05	.15
AU1 John Wooden AU	20.00	50.00
NNO Certification of Limited Edition	.05	.15

1991-92 Wright State

This 18-card standard size (2 1/2" by 3 1/2") set was sponsored by Synergy Building Systems Inc. The fronts feature color action player photos that are superimposed over black-green-and-lime geometrically shaped backgrounds inside thin white borders on a yellow background. The team logo and player's name appear on a green stripe below the picture. The horizontal backs carry biography, statistics, uniform number, and the sponsor's logo. The cards are unnumbered and checklisted below in alphabetical order.

COMPLETE SET (18)	6.00	15.00
1 Scott Blair	.40	1.00
2 Lincoln Bramlage	.40	1.00
3 Bill Edwards	.75	2.00
4 Mike Haley II	.40	1.00
5 Sean Hammonds	.60	1.50
6 Rob Haucke	.40	1.00
7 Delme Herriman	.60	1.50
8 Andy Holderman	.60	1.50
9 Chris McGuire	.40	1.00
10 Marcus Mumphrey	.40	1.00
11 Mike Nahar	.60	1.50
12 Renaldo O'Neal	.40	1.00
13 Jon Ramey	.40	1.00
14 Dan Skeoch	.40	1.00
15 Ralph Underhill CO	.60	1.50
16 Jeff Unverferth	.40	1.00
17 Eric Wills	.40	1.00
18 Coaching Staff Ralph Underhill Jim Brown Jack Butler Jim Ehler	.40	1.00

1993-94 Wright State

This is a 18-card standard size (2 1/2" by 3 1/2)" set. The green and yellow bordered fronts have color player action shots siloweted on to a 3-D graphic rendition of the team name. Below the photo is the players name and number printed in green and white. The gray bordered backs carry the players name and number at the top with the bio boxed in below. The cards are unnumbered and checklisted below in alphabetical order.

COMPLETE SET (18)	5.00	12.00
1 Scott Blair	.20	.50
2 Sterling Collins	.20	.50
3 Mike Connor	.20	.50
4 Sean Hammonds	.40	1.00
5 Delme Herriman	.40	1.00
6 Andy Holderman	.40	1.00
7 Rick Martinez	.60	1.50
8 Mike Nahar	.40	1.00
9 Jon Ramey	.20	.50
10 Dan Skeoch	.20	.50
11 Jason Smith	.20	.50
12 Ralph Underhill CO	.40	1.00
13 Rob Welch	.60	1.50
14 Eric Wills	.20	.50
15 Darryl Woods	.40	1.00
16 Assistant Coaches Jim Brown Jack Butler Jim Ehler	.20	.50
17 Mid-Continent Champs	.40	1.00
18 Student Assistants Brad Hess Brian Kelly Tom Rhoades Matt Brown	.20	.50

1994-95 Wright State

Sponsored by Cap'n Bogey's Family Entertainment Center and Fairborn Camera and Video, this 21-card set measures the standard size. The fronts feature borderless color action player photos with the player's name and jersey number printed vertically in a green bar along the left or right side. His position is printed across the bottom of the picture. On a green background, the horizontal backs carry a posed color player photo on the left and player biography and profile on the right. Sponsor logos round out the back.

COMPLETE SET (21)	5.00	12.00
1 Ralph Underhill CO	.40	1.00
2 Quincy Brann	.20	.50
3 Jon Ramey	.20	.50
4 Eric Wills	.20	.50
5 Darryl Woods	.20	.50
6 Delme Herriman	.40	1.00
7 Jason Smith	.20	.50
8 Bilaal Neal	.20	.50
9 Keith Blankenship	.20	.50
10 Mike Conner	.20	.50
11 Rick Martinez	.40	1.00
12 Vitaly Potapenko	1.25	3.00
13 Rob Welch	.40	1.00
14 Thad Burton	.20	.50
15 Antuan Johnson	.20	.50
16 Derek Watkins	.20	.50
17 Jim Brown ACO Jack Butler ACO Jim Ehler ACO	.20	.50
18 Student Assistants Matt Brown Skip Carter Joe Dick Brad Hess Dela Angela Mayho	.20	.50
19 Rowdy Raider (Mascot)	.20	.50
20 Cap'n Bogey	.20	.50
NNO Team Photo	.40	1.00

1994-95 Wyoming

This 16-card set was issued on a 10" by 14" perforated sheet with four rows of four cards. When the cards are separated, they measure the standard size. The set is sponsored by the USDA Forest Service and National Association of State Foresters. The fronts display color posed player photos framed in white and black, with player's name and position below the photo in the gold border. The Smokey logo is centered at the bottom of the picture. The backs carry the player's name and position at the top above a Smokey cartoon and a fire prevention safety tip. Biographical information is below the cartoon. The cards are unnumbered and checklisted below in alphabetical order. The key player in this set is Theo Ratliff, a first-round NBA draft pick.

COMPLETE SET (16)	6.00	15.00
1 Jeff Allen	.40	1.00
2 H.L. Coleman	.40	1.00
3 Chris Haslam	.40	1.00
4 Billy Hessel	.40	1.00
5 Savalious (Sly) Johnson	.40	1.00
6 Pat Kelsey	.40	1.00
7 Theo Ratliff	2.50	6.00
8 Jeron Roberts	.40	1.00
9 Gregg Sawyer	.40	1.00
10 Aaron Smith	.40	1.00
11 Bobby Traylor	.60	1.50
12 LaDrell Whitehead	.40	1.00
13 Alma Mater	.40	1.00
14 Cowboy Joe Song	.40	1.00
15 Team Logo	.40	1.00
16 Team Logo	.40	1.00

1994-95 Wyoming Women

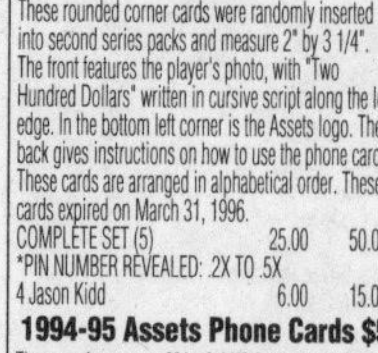

This 16-card set was issued on a 10" by 14" perforated sheet with four rows of four cards. When the cards are separated, they measure the standard size. The set is sponsored by the USDA Forest Service and National Association of State Foresters. The fronts display color posed player photos framed in white and black with player's name and position below the photo in the gold border. The Smokey logo is centered at the bottom of the picture. The backs carry the player's name and position at the top above a Smokey cartoon and a fire prevention safety tip. Biographical information is below the cartoon. The cards are unnumbered and checklisted below in alphabetical order.

COMPLETE SET (16)	2.50	6.00
1 Lauren Andrade	.20	.50
2 Amy Burnett	.20	.50
3 Jesseca Cross	.20	.50
4 Casey Crouch	.20	.50
5 Heather McAdams	.20	.50
6 Laura Pejsa	.20	.50
7 Jennifer Rider	.20	.50
8 Nichole Rider	.20	.50
9 Jennifer Russell	.20	.50
10 Courtney Stapp	.20	.50
11 Jessica Thompson	.20	.50
12 Rebecca Tomlin	.20	.50
13 Alma Mater	.20	.50
14 Cowboy Joe Song	.20	.50
15 Team Logo	.20	.50
16 Team Logo	.20	.50

1994-95 Assets

Produced by Classic, the 1994 Assets set features stars from basketball, hockey, football, baseball, and auto racing. The set was released in two series of 50 cards each. 1,994 cases were produced of each series. This standard-sized card set features a player photo with his name in silver letters on the lower left corner and the Assets logo on the upper right. The back has a color photo on the left side along with a biography on the right side of the card. A Sprint phone card is randomly inserted in each five-card pack.

COMPLETE SET (100)	6.00	15.00
1 Shaquille O'Neal	.20	.50
2 Hakeem Olajuwon	.08	.25
6 Glenn Robinson	.08	.25
10 Alonzo Mourning	.07	.20
14 Jason Kidd	.40	1.00
17 Donyell Marshall	.05	.15
19 Eric Montross	.05	.15
22 Jalen Rose	.15	.40
26 Shaquille O'Neal	.20	.50
27 Hakeem Olajuwon	.08	.25
31 Glenn Robinson	.10	.30
35 Alonzo Mourning	.07	.20
39 Jason Kidd	.40	1.00
42 Donyell Marshall	.05	.15
44 Eric Montross	.05	.15
47 Jalen Rose	.15	.40
50 Glenn Robinson CL	.07	.20
51 Dikembe Mutombo	.05	.15
53 Anfernee Hardaway	.15	.40
54 Isaiah Rider	.05	.15
56 Juwan Howard	.08	.25
58 Jamal Mashburn	.07	.20
69 Eddie Jones	.30	.75
73 Shaquille O'Neal	.20	.50
75 Grant Hill CL	.08	.25
76 Dikembe Mutombo	.05	.15
78 Anfernee Hardaway	.20	.50
79 Isaiah Rider	.05	.15
81 Juwan Howard	.07	.20
83 Jamal Mashburn	.07	.20
94 Eddie Jones	.20	.50
98 Shaquille O'Neal	.20	.50

1994-95 Assets Die Cuts

This 25-card standard-size set was randomly inserted into packs. DC1-10 were included in series one while DC11-25 were included in series two packs. These cards feature the player on the card and the ability to separate the player's photo. The back contains information about the player on the section of the card that is separable.

COMPLETE SET (25)	30.00	80.00
DC1 Shaquille O'Neal	4.00	10.00
DC2 Hakeem Olajuwon	.75	2.00
DC6 Glenn Robinson	1.25	3.00
DC11 Grant Hill	1.25	3.00
DC12 Jason Kidd	4.00	10.00
DC13 Eddie Jones	2.00	5.00
DC20 Isaiah Rider	.60	1.50
DC22 Donyell Marshall	.60	1.50

1994-95 Assets Silver Signature

This 48-card standard-size set was randomly inserted at a rate of four per box. The cards are identical to the first twenty-four cards in the each series, except that these show a silver facsimile autograph on their fronts. The first 24 cards correspond to cards 1-24 in the first series while the second 24 cards correspond to cards 51-74 in the second series.

*SILVER SIGS: 1.2X TO 3X BASIC CARDS

1994-95 Assets Phone Cards $100

These 2" by 3 1/4" rounded corner cards were randomly inserted into packs. These cards were placed into series one packs. The front features the player's photo, with "One Hundred Dollars" written in cursive script along the left edge. The Assets logo is in the bottom left corner. The back gives instructions on how to use the phone card. These cards are listed in alphabetical order. These cards expired on December 1, 1995.

COMPLETE SET (5)	15.00	40.00
*PIN NUMBER REVEALED: .2X TO .5X		
3 Jason Kidd	4.00	10.00
4 Hakeem Olajuwon	3.00	8.00

1994-95 Assets Phone Cards $200

These rounded corner cards were randomly inserted into second series packs and measure 2" by 3 1/4". The front features the player's photo, with "Two Hundred Dollars" written in cursive script along the left edge. In the bottom left corner is the Assets logo. The back gives instructions on how to use the phone card. These cards are arranged in alphabetical order. These cards expired on March 31, 1996.

COMPLETE SET (5)	25.00	50.00
*PIN NUMBER REVEALED: .2X TO .5X		
4 Jason Kidd	6.00	15.00

1994-95 Assets Phone Cards $5

These cards measure 2" by 3 1/4", have rounded corners and were randomly inserted into packs. Cards 1-5 were inserted into first series packs while 6-15 were in second series packs. The front features the player's photo, with "Five Dollars" written in cursive script along the left edge. In the bottom left corner is the Assets logo. The back gives instructions on how to use the phone card. Series one cards expired on December 1, 1995 while second series cards expired on March 31, 1996.

COMPLETE SET (15)	8.00	20.00
*PIN NUMBER REVEALED: .2X TO .5X		
3 Jason Kidd	.75	2.00
4 Hakeem Olajuwon	.50	1.25
10 Jason Kidd	.75	2.00
15 Glenn Robinson	.30	.75

1994-95 Assets Phone Cards One Minute

Measuring 2" by 3 1/4", these cards have rounded corners and were inserted one per pack. Cards 1-24 were in first series packs while 25-48 were included with second series packs. The front features the player's photo and on the side is how long the card is good for. The Assets logo is in the bottom left corner. The back gives instructions on how to use the phone card. The first series cards expired on December 1, 1995 while the second series cards expired on March 31, 1996. The cards with a $2 logo are worth a mulitple of the regular cards. Please refer to the values below for these cards.

COMPLETE SET (48)	7.50	20.00
*PIN NUMB.REVEALED: .2X TO .5X BASIC INS.		
*TWO DOLLAR: .5X TO 1.2X BASIC INSERTS		
11 Jason Kidd	.50	1.25
13 Donyell Marshall	.15	.40
14 Eric Montross	.15	.40
15 Alonzo Mourning	.20	.50
16 Hakeem Olajuwon	.40	1.00
17 Shaquille O'Neal	.75	2.00
19 Glenn Robinson	.20	.50
20 Jalen Rose	.20	.50
31 Anfernee Hardaway	.30	.75
32 Juwan Howard	.30	.75
33 Eddie Jones	.30	.75
34 Jamal Mashburn	.20	.50
39 Dikembe Mutombo	.20	.50
40 Shaquille O'Neal	.75	2.00
44 Isaiah Rider	.15	.40

1995 Assets Gold

This 50-card set measures the standard size. The fronts feature borderless player action photos with the player's name printed in gold at the bottom. The backs carry a portrait of the player with his name, career highlights, and statistics. The Dale Earnhardt card was pulled from circulation early in the product's release. It is considered a Short Print (SP) but is not included in the complete set price.

COMPLETE SET (49)	6.00	15.00
32 Rasheed Wallace	.20	.50
33 Corliss Williamson	.07	.20
34 Tyus Edney	.05	.15
35 Ed O'Bannon	.05	.15
36 Damon Stoudamire	.20	.50
37 Eddie Jones	.08	.25
38 Khalid Reeves	.05	.15
39 Jason Kidd	.30	.75
40 Glenn Robinson	.07	.20
41 Juwan Howard	.07	.20
42 Jamal Mashburn	.07	.20
43 Shaquille O'Neal	.40	1.00
44 Alonzo Mourning	.08	.25
45 Donyell Marshall	.05	.15
46 Jalen Rose	.08	.25
47 Wesley Person	.05	.15
48 Grant Hill	.20	.50
49 Rasheed Wallace CL	.08	.25
NNO Jason Kidd Grant Hill	2.00	5.00
NNO Jason Kidd Grant Hill DC	5.00	12.00

1995 Assets Gold Die Cuts Silver

This 20-card set was randomly inserted in packs at a rate of one in 18. The fronts feature a borderless player color action photo with a diamond-shaped top and the player's action taking place in front of the card name. The backs carry the card name, player's name and career highlights. The cards are numbered on the backs. Gold versions were inserted at a rate of one in 72 packs.

COMPLETE SET (20)	10.00	25.00
*GOLDS: .8X TO 2X SILVERS		
GOLD STATED ODDS 1:72		
SDC2 Shaquille O'Neal	1.50	4.00
SDC4 Glenn Robinson	.50	1.25
SDC6 Grant Hill	.60	1.50
SDC7 Rasheed Wallace	.60	1.50
SDC8 Ed O'Bannon	.40	1.00
SDC14 Jason Kidd	.75	2.00

1995 Assets Gold Printer's Proofs

These parallel cards were randomly seeded at the rate of 1:18 packs. They feature the words "Printer's Proof" on the cardfronts.

*PRINT PROOF: 2X TO 5X BASIC CARDS

1995 Assets Gold Silver Signatures

These parallel cards were inserted one per pack. They feature a silver foil facsimile signature on the cardfronts.

COMP. SILVER SIG SET (50)	15.00	40.00
*SILVER SIGS: .8X TO 2X BASIC CARDS		

1995 Assets Gold Phone Cards $100

This five-card set measures 2 1/8" by 3 3/8". The fronts feature color action player photos with the player's name below. The $100 calling value is printed on the left. The backs carry the instructions on how to use the cards which expired on 7/31/96. The cards are unnumbered and checklisted below in alphabetical order.

*PIN NUMBER REVEALED: HALF VALUE		
2 Jason Kidd	8.00	20.00
4 Rasheed Wallace	6.00	15.00

1995 Assets Gold Phone Cards $2

This 47-card set was randomly inserted in packs and measures 2 1/8" by 3 3/8". The fronts feature color action player photos with the player's name below. The $2 calling value is printed vertically down the left. The backs carry the instructions on how to use the cards which expired on 7/31/96. The cards are unnumbered.

COMPLETE SET (47)	15.00	40.00
*PIN NUMBER REVEALED: HALF VALUE		
32 Rasheed Wallace	.60	1.50
33 Corliss Williamson	.30	.75
34 Tyus Edney	.30	.75
35 Ed O'Bannon	.30	.75
36 Damon Stoudamire	.60	1.50
37 Eddie Jones	.60	1.50
38 Khalid Reeves	.30	.75
39 Jason Kidd	1.00	2.50
40 Glenn Robinson	.40	1.00
41 Juwan Howard	.40	1.00
42 Jamal Mashburn	.30	.75
43 Shaquille O'Neal	1.25	3.00
44 Alonzo Mourning	.40	1.00
45 Donyell Marshall	.30	.75
46 Jalen Rose	.60	1.50
47 Wesley Person	.30	.75

1995 Assets Gold Phone Cards $25

This 5-card set measures 2 1/8" by 3 3/8" and was randomly inserted in packs. The fronts feature color action player photos of two different players with the player's name in gold below each photo. The $25 calling value is printed vertically in gold separating the two players. The backs carry the instructions on how to use the cards which expired on 7/31/96. The cards are unnumbered.

COMPLETE SET (5)	20.00	50.00
*PIN NUMBER REVEALED: HALF VALUE		
3 Glenn Robinson Rasheed Wallace	4.00	10.00
5 Corliss Williamson Ed O'Bannon	3.00	8.00

1995 Assets Gold Phone Cards $5

This 16-card set measures 2 1/8" by 3 3/8" and was randomly inserted in packs. The fronts feature color action player photos with the player's name below. The $5 calling value is printed vertically down the left. The backs carry the instructions on how to use the cards which expired on 7/31/96. The cards are unnumbered. The Microlined versions are inserted at a rate of one in 18 packs versus one in six packs for the basic $5 card.

COMPLETE SET (16)	25.00	60.00
*MICROLINED: .6X TO 1.5X BASIC INSERTS		
STATED ODDS 1:18		
*PIN NUMBER REVEALED: HALF VALUE		
7 Damon Stoudamire	.75	2.00
13 Jason Kidd	1.00	2.50
14 Ed O'Bannon	.50	1.25
15 Shaquille O'Neal	2.00	5.00
16 Glenn Robinson	.60	1.50

1996 Assets

The 1996 Classic Assets was issued in one set totalling 50 cards. This 50-card premium set has a tremendous selection of the top athletes in the world headlines. Each card features action photos, up-to-date statistics and is printed on high-quality, foil-stamped stock. Hot Print cards are parallel cards randomly inserted in Hot Packs and are valued at a multiple of the regular cards below.

COMPLETE SET (50)	5.00	10.00
13 Kevin Garnett	.75	2.00
15 Juwan Howard	.07	.20
16 Eddie Jones	.08	.25
19 Jason Kidd	.15	.40
20 Rebecca Lobo	.08	.25
23 Antonio McDyess	.20	.50
26 Alonzo Mourning	.05	.15
28 Dikembe Mutombo	.07	.20
29 Ed O'Bannon	.05	.15
30 Shaquille O'Neal	.30	.75
31 Hakeem Olajuwon	.08	.25
32 Cherokee Parks	.05	.15
34 Scottie Pippen	.08	.25
37 Glenn Robinson	.05	.15
38 Jalen Rose	.07	.20
42 Joe Smith	.08	.25
43 Jerry Stackhouse	.20	.50
44 Damon Stoudamire	.30	.75
46 Rasheed Wallace	.20	.50
47 Corliss Williamson	.05	.15

1996 Assets A Cut Above

The even cards were randomly inserted in retail packs at a rate of one in eight, and the odd cards were inserted in clear asset packs at a rate of one in 20, this 20-card die-cut set is composed of 10 phone cards and 10 trading cards. The cards have rounded corners except for one which is cut in a straight corner design. The fronts feature a color action player cut-out superimposed over a gray background with the words "cut above" printed throughout and resembled to be cut so it displays a basketball game behind it. The backs carry a color action player photo with the player's name and a short career summary.

COMPLETE SET (20)	20.00	50.00
CA3 Shaquille O'Neal	3.00	8.00
CA5 Scottie Pippen	1.00	2.50
CA9 Jerry Stackhouse	.60	1.50
CA12 Rasheed Wallace	1.00	2.50
CA14 Joe Smith	.60	1.50
CA15 Kevin Garnett	4.00	10.
CA16 Jason Kidd	1.25	3.
CA18 Rebecca Lobo	1.25	3.
CA20 Glenn Robinson	.60	1.

1996 Assets A Cut Above Phone Cards

This 10-card set, which were inserted at a rate of one eight, measures approximately 2 1/8" by 3 3/8" have rounded corners except for one corner which is cut o and made straight. The fronts feature a color action player cut-out superimposed over a gray background with the words "cut above" printed throughout and resembled to be cut so that it displays a game going behind the background. The backs carry the instructions on how to use the card. The cards expire on 1/31/97.

COMPLETE SET (10)	12.50	30.0
*PIN NUMBER REVEALED: HALF VALUE		
2 Shaquille O'Neal	2.50	6.0
3 Scottie Pippen	1.00	2.5
5 Jerry Stackhouse	1.00	2.5
8 Kevin Garnett	4.00	10.0
9 Ed O'Bannon	.50	1.2

1996 Assets Crystal Phone Cards

Randomly inserted in retail packs at a rate of one in 250, this high-tech, 10-card insert set contains clear holographic phone cards worth five minutes of long distance calling time. The cards measure approximately 2 1/8" by 3 3/8" with rounded corners. The fronts display a color action double-image playe cut-out on a clear crystal background with the player' name printed vertically on the side. The backs carry instructions on how to use the card. The cards expire January 31, 1997. Twenty dollar phone cards of these athletes were issued, they are valued as a multiple of the cards below.

COMPLETE SET (10)	20.00	50.0
*PIN NUMBER REVEALED: HALF VALUE		
5 Shaquille O'Neal	2.50	6.0
6 Scottie Pippen	1.00	2.5
8 Jason Kidd	1.25	3.0
9 Joe Smith	.60	1.5
10 Jerry Stackhouse	.75	2.0

1996 Assets Crystal Phone Cards $20

5 Shaquille O'Neal	6.00	15.0
6 Scottie Pippen	2.50	6.0
8 Jason Kidd	3.00	8.0
9 Joe Smith	1.50	4.0
10 Jerry Stackhouse	2.00	5.0

1996 Assets Hot Prints

These parallel cards were randomly seeded in 1996 Assets Hot Packs. Each card is marked Hot Print on th cardfront.

*HOT PRINTS: .8X TO 2X BASIC CARDS

1996 Assets Phone Cards $10

This 10-card set was randomly inserted in packs at a rate of 1 in 20. The cards measure approximately 2 1/8" by 3 3/8" with rounded corners. The fronts displa color action player photos with the player's name in a red bar below. The backs carry the instructions on how to use the cards and the expiration date of 1/31/97.

COMPLETE SET (10)	25.00	60.00
*PIN NUMBER REVEALED: HALF VALUE		
5 Shaquille O'Neal	3.00	8.00
6 Scottie Pippen	2.00	5.00
9 Joe Smith	1.50	4.00
10 Jerry Stackhouse	2.00	5.00

1996 Assets Phone Cards $100

This five card set, randomly inserted in packs, measures approximately 2 1/8" by 3 3/8" with rounded corners. The fronts display color action player photos with the player's name. The backs carry the instructions on how to use the cards and the expiration date of 1/31/97.

COMPLETE SET (5)	40.00	80.00
*PIN NUMBER REVEALED: HALF VALUE		
3 Shaquille O'Neal	8.00	20.00
4 Scottie Pippen	6.00	15.00

1996 Assets Phone Cards $2

This 30-card set was inserted in retail packs at a rate o 1 per pack with a minimum value of $2 per phone card The cards measure approximately 2 1/8" by 3 3/8" with rounded corners. The fronts display color aciton player photos with the player's name in a red bar below. The backs carry the instructions on how to use the cards and the expiration date of 1/31/97. Hot Print Cards parallel cards were randomly inserted in Hot Packs. These cards are valued as a mulitple of the cards below.

COMPLETE SET (30)	12.50	30.00
*$2 CARDS: .6X TO 1.5X $1 CARDS		
*PIN NUMBER REVEALED: HALF VALUE		

1996 Assets Phone Cards $20

This five card set measures approximately 2 1/8" by 3 3/8" with rounded corners and were randomly inserted in retail packs. The fronts display color action player photos with the player's name. The backs carry the instructions on how to use the cards and the expiration date of 1/31/97.

COMPLETE SET (5)	25.00	60.00
*PIN NUMBER REVEALED: HALF VALUE		
2 Scottie Pippen	3.00	8.00
5 Shaquille O'Neal	6.00	15.00

1996 Assets Phone Cards $5

This 20-card set was randomly inserted in retail packs at a rate of 1 in 5. The cards measure approximately 2 1/8" by 3 3/8" with rounded corners. The fronts display color action player photos with the player's name in a red bar below. The backs carry the instructions on how to use the cards and the expiration date of 1/31/97.

COMPLETE SET (20)	30.00	80.00
*PIN NUMBER REVEALED: HALF VALUE		
8 Kevin Garnett	2.00	5.00
9 Jason Kidd	1.00	2.50
11 Shaquille O'Neal	4.00	5.00
12 Hakeem Olajuwon	1.00	2.50
13 Scottie Pippen	1.00	2.50
17 Joe Smith	.60	1.50
18 Jerry Stackhouse	.60	1.50
19 Rasheed Wallace	.40	1.00

1996 Assets Silksations

Randomly inserted in retail packs at a rate of one in 100, this 10-card standard-size set features duplexed fabric-stock with top athletes. The fronts display a color action player cut-out with a two-tone background. The player's name is printed below. The backs carry a head photo of the player made to appear as if it is coming out of a square hole in gold cloth. The player's name and a short career summary are below.

he cards are numbered with a "S" prefix and quenced in alphabetical order.

OMPLETE SET (10)	40.00	80.00
Jason Kidd	5.00	12.00
Shaquille O'Neal	8.00	20.00
Scottie Pippen	4.00	10.00
Joe Smith	2.00	5.00
) Jerry Stackhouse	3.00	8.00

1991 Classic

his 50-card standard-size set of basketball draft picks as produced by Classic Games, Inc. and features 48 ayers picked in the first two rounds of the 1991 NBA raft. A total of 450,000 sets were issued, and each set accompanied by a letter of limited edition. The cards ere only available for sale in these factory-sealed omplete sets with no wax product being produced. he fronts feature a glossy color action photo of each layer. The backs have statistics and biographical iformation. Special cards included in the set are a ommemorative number one draft choice card of Larry ohnson and a "One-on-One" card of Billy Owens am-dunking over Johnson. Three cards were issued s promos for the regular editon set. The player's name ppears below the picture in black lettering. The backs re blank, except for the disclaimer "For Promotional urposes Only." These cards are listed at the end of the egular set.

OMP. FACT SET (50)	2.00	5.00
Larry Johnson	.40	1.00
Billy Owens	.15	.40
Dikembe Mutombo	.40	1.00
Mark Macon	.05	.15
Brian Williams	.15	.40
Greg Anthony	.15	.40
Terrell Brandon	.30	.75
Dale Davis	.30	.75
Anthony Avent	.05	.15
0 Chris Gatling	.15	.40
1 Victor Alexander	.05	.15
2 Kevin Brooks	.05	.15
3 Eric Murdock	.05	.15
4 LeRon Ellis	.05	.15
5 Stanley Roberts	.05	.15
6 Rick Fox	.30	.75
7 Pete Chilcutt	.05	.15
8 Kevin Lynch	.05	.15
9 George Ackles	.05	.15
20 Rodney Monroe	.05	.15
21 Randy Brown	.05	.15
22 Chad Gallagher	.05	.15
23 Donald Hodge	.05	.15
24 Myron Brown	.05	.15
25 Mike Iuzzolino	.05	.15
26 Chris Corchiani	.05	.15
27 Elliot Perry	.05	.15
28 Joe Wylie	.05	.15
29 Jimmy Oliver	.05	.15
30 Doug Overton	.05	.15
31 Sean Green	.05	.15
32 Steve Hood	.05	.15
33 Lamont Strothers	.05	.15
34 Alvaro Teheran	.05	.15
35 Bobby Phills	.15	.40
36 Richard Dumas	.05	.15
37 Keith Hughes	.05	.15
38 Isaac Austin	.15	.40
39 Greg Sutton	.05	.15
40 Joey Wright	.05	.15
41 Anthony Jones	.05	.15
42 Von McDade	.05	.15
43 Marcus Kennedy	.05	.15
44 Larry Johnson UNLV Top Pick	.20	.50
45 Larry Johnson and Billy Owens	.20	.50
46 Anderson Hunt	.05	.15
47 Darrin Chancellor	.05	.15
48 Damon Lopez	.05	.15
49 Thomas Jordan	.05	.15
50 Tony Farmer	.05	.15
NNO Dikembe Mutombo PROMO	.40	1.00
NNO Larry Johnson PROMO	.75	2.00
NNO Billy Owens PROMO	.40	1.00

1991 Classic Autographs

These six certified autograph cards have the same design as the regular issue, except that inside a black frame, the horizontal backs read "Congratulations on receiving this limited edition autographed Classic Draft Pick Card," with the serial number and total production run (1100) written in blue ink near the bottom. The cards are unnumbered and checklisted below in alphabetical order.

1 Victor Alexander	1.25	3.00
2 Anderson Hunt	1.25	3.00
3 Dikembe Mutombo	8.00	20.00
4 Billy Owens	2.00	5.00
5 Stanley Roberts	1.25	3.00
6 Brian Williams	1.25	3.00

1992 Classic Previews

These Classic Basketball Draft Picks preview cards were randomly inserted in the 1992 Classic Football Draft Picks 15-card foil packs. Only 10,000 of each card were produced. The standard-size cards feature on the front glossy color action player photos enclosed by white borders. The Classic logo, player's name, and position appear in a silver stripe beneath the picture. The backs read repeatedly "For Promotional Purposes Only" as well as bearing an advertisement and the Classic logo.

COMPLETE SET (5)	20.00	40.00
1 Shaquille O'Neal	15.00	40.00
2 Alonzo Mourning	3.00	8.00
3 Don MacLean	.40	1.00
4 Walt Williams	.75	2.00
5 Christian Laettner	1.25	3.00

1992 Classic Promos

These standard-size cards feature on the front glossy color action player photos enclosed by white borders. The Classic logo, player's name, and position appear in a silver stripe beneath the picture. The backs have biography, scouting report, and a partially cut out color action photo of the player. Beneath the statistical title line (in the space allotted for statistics), the backs read "For Promotional Purposes Only."

COMPLETE SET (6)	10.00	25.00
1 Shaquille O'Neal	10.00	25.00
2 Alonzo Mourning	2.00	5.00
3 Christian Laettner	.75	2.00
4 Walt Williams	.40	1.00
5 Don MacLean	.20	.50
6 Jimmy Jackson	1.25	3.00

1992 Classic

The 1992 Classic Basketball Draft Picks set contains 100 standard-size cards, including all 54 drafted players. The set features the first nationally distributed 1992 trading card of NBA first overall pick Shaquille O'Neal as well as the only draft cards of second pick Alonzo Mourning and fourth pick Jimmy Jackson. The set also includes a Flashback (95-98) subset. The fronts feature glossy color action photos bordered in white. The player's name appears in a silver stripe beneath the picture, which intersects the Classic logo at the lower left corner. The backs have a second color player photo and present biographical information, complete college statistics, and a scouting report. The cards are numbered on the back. Cards 61-100 were only available in 15-card foil packs as the blister sets contained only cards 1-60. The production run was reportedly 28,000 ten-box cases and 125,000 60-card factory blister sets. The Laettner Bonus Card was inserted one per blister set. Also listed at the end of the set is a Shaquille O'Neal autographed card numbered to 2500. This card was available in a hanging wall plaque from shop at home where it is engraved as Shaquille O'Neal limited edition and the print run of 2500.

COMP.BLISTER SET (61)	6.00	8.00
COMPLETE SET (100)	5.00	10.00
1 Shaquille O'Neal	1.50	4.00
2 Walt Williams	.15	.40
3 Lee Mayberry	.05	.15
4 Tony Bennett	.05	.15
5 Litterial Green	.05	.15
6 Chris Smith	.05	.15
7 Henry Williams	.05	.15
8 Terrell Lowery	.05	.15
9 Radenko Dobras	.05	.15
10 Curtis Blair	.05	.15
11 Randy Woods	.05	.15
12 Todd Day	.15	.40
13 Anthony Peeler	.15	.40
14 Darin Archbold	.05	.15
15 Benford Williams	.05	.15
16 Terrence Lewis	.05	.15
17 James McCoy	.05	.15
18 Damon Patterson	.05	.15
19 Bryant Stith	.15	.40
20 Doug Christie	.15	.40
21 Latrell Sprewell	.25	.60
22 Hubert Davis	.15	.40
23 David Booth	.05	.15
24 David Johnson	.05	.15
25 Jon Barry	.05	.15
26 Everick Sullivan	.05	.15
27 Brian Davis	.05	.15
28 Clarence Weatherspoon	.15	.40
29 Malik Sealy	.15	.40
30 Matt Geiger	.15	.40
31 Jimmy Jackson	.25	.60
32 Matt Steigenga	.05	.15
33 Robert Horry	.15	.40
34 Marlon Maxey	.05	.15
35 Reggie Slater	.05	.15
36 Lucius Davis	.05	.15
37 Chris King	.05	.15
38 Dexter Cambridge	.05	.15
39 Alonzo Jamison	.05	.15
40 Anthony Tucker	.05	.15
41 Tracy Murray	.05	.15
42 Vernel Singleton	.05	.15
43 Christian Laettner	.15	.40
44 Don MacLean	.05	.15
45 Adam Keefe	.05	.15
46 Tom Gugliotta	.15	.40
47 LaPhonso Ellis	.15	.40
48 Byron Houston	.05	.15
49 Oliver Miller	.05	.15
50 Popeye Jones	.05	.15
51 P.J. Brown	.15	.40
52 Eric Anderson	.05	.15
53 Darren Morningstar	.05	.15
54 Isaiah Morris	.05	.15
55 Stephen Howard	.05	.15
56 Reggie Smith	.05	.15
57 Elmore Spencer	.05	.15
58 Sean Rooks	.05	.15
59 Robert Werdann	.05	.15
60 Alonzo Mourning	.40	1.00
61 Steve Rogers	.05	.15
62 Tim Burroughs	.05	.15
63 Ed Book	.05	.15
64 Herb Jones	.05	.15
65 Mik Kilgore	.05	.15
66 Ken Leeks	.05	.15
67 Sam Mack	.05	.15
68 Sean Miller	.05	.15
69 Craig Upchurch	.05	.15
70 Van Usher	.05	.15
71 Corey Williams	.05	.15
72 Duane Cooper	.05	.15
73 Brett Roberts	.05	.15
74 Elmer Bennett	.05	.15
75 Brent Price	.05	.15
76 Daimon Sweet	.05	.15
77 Darrick Martin	.05	.15
78 Gerald Madkins	.05	.15
79 Jo Jo English	.05	.15
80 Alex Blackwell	.05	.15
81 Anthony Dade	.05	.15
82 Matt Fish	.05	.15
83 Byron Tucker	.05	.15
84 Harold Miner	.15	.40
85 Greg Dennis	.05	.15
86 Jeff Roulston	.05	.15
87 Keir Rogers	.05	.15
88 Billy Law	.05	.15
89 Geoff Lear	.05	.15
90 Lambert Shell	.05	.15
91 Elbert Rogers	.05	.15
92 Ron Ellis	.05	.15
93 Predrag Danilovic	.05	.15
94 Calvin Talford	.05	.15
95 Stacey Augmon FB	.05	.15
96 Steve Smith FB	.15	.40
97 Billy Owens FB	.05	.15
98 Dikembe Mutombo FB	.15	.40
99 Checklist 1-50	.05	.15
100 Checklist 51-100	.05	.15
NNO1 Shaquille O'Neal AU/2500	40.00	100.00
NNO2 Christian Laettner BC	.40	1.00
NNO3 Shaquille O'Neal AU/500	60.00	150.00

1992 Classic Gold Promo

This card measures the standard size and features an action color player photo with white borders. The player's name and position are gold foil stamped in a black border stripe at the bottom. The Classic Draft Picks Gold logo overlaps the stripe and the photo at the lower left corner. The white background on the backs displays a vertical action color picture and a scouting report, while the player's name (in a gold stripe), biography, and statistics are printed horizontally. This card can be distinguished by the words "For Promotional Purposes Only" on the back. The card is numbered on the back.

2 Alonzo Mourning	4.00	10.00

1992 Classic Gold

This 101-card standard-size set features all 54 drafted players. Only 8,500 sequentially numbered sets were produced, and each set was packaged in a walnut display case. Each set included an individually numbered Shaquille O'Neal autograph card. The player's name and position are gold foil stamped in a black border stripe at the bottom. To ascertain values for individual cards, please refer to the multiplier in the header, coupled with the value of the base card.

COMP.FACT.SET (101)	70.00	120.00
*GOLD: 2.5X TO 6X BASE CARD HI		
O'NEAL AUTO ONE PER GOLD FACT.SET		
AU Shaquille O'Neal AU/8500	40.00	100.00

1992 Classic LPs

This ten-card set, subtitled "Top Ten Pick", features the top ten picks of the 1992 NBA Draft. These standard size cards were randomly inserted in 1992 Classic Draft Picks 15-card foil packs. The fronts feature glossy color action photos enclosed by white borders. The player's name appears in a silver foil stripe beneath the picture, which intersects the Classic logo at the lower left corner. The production figures "1 of 56,000" and the "Top Ten Pick" emblem at the card top are also silver foil. The horizontally oriented backs have a silver background and feature a second color player photo and player profile. The cards are numbered on the back with an "LP" (limited print) prefix. An 8 1/2" by 11" version of Alonzo Mourning is known to exist.

COMPLETE SET (10)	8.00	20.00
LP1 Shaquille O'Neal	8.00	20.00
LP2 Alonzo Mourning	1.50	4.00
LP3 Christian Laettner	.60	1.50
LP4 Jimmy Jackson	1.00	2.50
LP5 LaPhonso Ellis	.30	.75
LP6 Tom Gugliotta	1.00	2.50
LP7 Walt Williams	.30	.75
LP8 Todd Day	.20	.50
LP9 Clarence Weatherspoon	.20	.50
LP10 Adam Keefe	.08	.25

1992 Classic Magicians

Inserted one per jumbo pack, this 20-card standard-size set features white-bordered color action shots on the fronts. Each card displays the player's name in blue lettering inside a silver foil stripe at the bottom of the photo, with the player's position appearing just beneath inside a black bar, and the Classic logo atop the foil to the left. The silver foil Magician logo in the top right rounds out the front. The backs have narrow-cropped color action photos on their right sides and silver stripes down the left with the player's name. Scouting reports and horizontally oriented biography and stats appear between. Cards 2, 4 and 5 have "91 Flashback" printed in white across the tops of the fronts. The cards are numbered on the back with a "BC" prefix.

COMPLETE SET (20)	2.50	6.00
BC1 Doug Christie	.15	.40
BC2 Billy Owens	.05	.15
BC3 Latrell Sprewell	1.25	3.00
BC4 Stacey Augmon	.05	.15
BC5 Steve Smith	.20	.50
BC6 Jon Barry	.05	.15
BC7 Christian Laettner	.30	.75
BC8 Jimmy Jackson	.50	1.25
BC9 Tracy Murray	.05	.15
BC10 Walt Williams	.15	.40
BC11 Todd Day	.08	.25
BC12 Dave Johnson	.05	.15
BC13 Byron Houston	.05	.15
BC14 Robert Horry	.15	.40
BC15 Harold Miner	.05	.15
BC16 Bryant Stith	.08	.25
BC17 Malik Sealy	.08	.25
BC18 Randy Woods	.05	.15
BC19 Anthony Peeler	.08	.25
BC20 Lee Mayberry	.05	.15

1992 Classic Mutombo Promo

This standard-size card features Dikembe Mutombo. The front has a color action player photo with a bronze-like outer border, and silver and gold inner borders. The player's name appears in a silver bar at the bottom, while the words "Uncirculated - 1 of 5,000" are printed in a silver bar at the top. On a silver background, the back carries information about Dikembe Mutombo and Classic. The card is unnumbered.

1 Dikembe Mutombo	.75	2.00

1992 Classic Show Promos 20

This 20-card standard-size set was issued one card at a time at the various shows throughout the year where Classic maintained a presence or booth. Typically the cards were given out free to attendees while supplies lasted. The cards all read "Promo Card x of 20" prominently on the card back. The cards are done in several different styles depending on the Classic issue that was being promoted by that particular card.

COMPLETE SET (20)	15.00	30.00
1 Billy Owens (1992 Sports Spectacular)	.20	.50
2 Dikembe Mutombo (1992 SportsNet National)	.30	.75
9 Jimmy Jackson (July 1992 Atlanta National)	.40	1.00
11 Shaquille O'Neal (July 1992 Atlanta National)	2.00	5.00
12 Alonzo Mourning (July 1992 Atlanta National)	.80	2.00
13 Christian Laettner (1992 East Coast National)	.30	.75
17 Shaquille O'Neal (1992 Tri-Star St. Louis)	2.00	5.00
20 Harold Miner (1992 Tri-Star Houston)	.20	.50

1992 Classic World Class Athletes

Packaged in a high impact clam shell, this 60-card standard-size set features current and past world class athletes. The production run was 295,000 sets, and an enclosed certificate of limited edition carries the set serial number. A few athletes had autographs randomly inserted into the factory sets. We have noted those cards at the end of our checklist.

COMP.FACT SET (60)	1.60	4.00
2 Carl Lewis Track and Field	.20	.50
47 Carl Lewis Track and Field	.08	.25
48 Carl Lewis Track and Field	.08	.25
49 Carl Lewis Track and Field	.20	.50
50 Carl Lewis Track and Field	.08	.25
51 Carl Lewis Track and Field	.08	.25
52 Carl Lewis Track and Field	.20	.50

1993 Classic Previews

These basketball cards were randomly inserted in 1993 Classic Football Draft Picks foil packs as well as 1993 Classic NFL Pro Line Collection packs. Reportedly 17,500 of each standard-size card were produced and randomly inserted an average of two cards per case, evenly distributed through both products. The fronts feature color player action shots with simulated pinewood borders. The player's name and position appear in a colored stripe at the bottom of the photo. The red-bordered back carries a basketball icon and the number of cards produced. The cards are unnumbered and are checklisted below in alphabetical order.

COMPLETE SET (4)	6.00	15.00
BK1 Chris Webber	4.00	10.00
BK2 Jamal Mashburn	.75	2.00
BK3 Anfernee Hardaway	4.00	10.00
BK4 Allan Houston UER Misspelled Alan	1.50	4.00

1993 Classic

The 1993 Classic Draft Picks set consists of 110 standard-size cards.The production run was limited to 32,500 ten-box cases. The fronts feature color action player photos with simulated pinewood borders. The player's name and position, along with the 1993 Classic Draft Picks logo, appears in a white bar across the base of each picture. The simulated pinewood design continues on the horizontal back. The player's name appears at the top in an ellipse that is of a lighter-colored simulated pinewood. Stats are displayed in a lighter-colored rectangle at the bottom. A narrow-cropped pinewood-bordered player color action shot along the left side rounds out the card. Gold factory sets were produced later.

COMPLETE SET (110)	5.00	10.00
1 Chris Webber	.40	1.00
2 Anfernee Hardaway	.40	1.00
3 Jamal Mashburn	.30	.75
4 Isaiah Rider	.15	.40
5 Vin Baker	.15	.40
6 Rodney Rogers	.15	.40
7 Lindsey Hunter	.15	.40
8 Allan Houston	.15	.40
9 George Lynch	.05	.15
10 Toni Kukoc	.30	.75
11 Ashraf Amaya	.05	.15
12 Mark Bell	.05	.15
13 John Best	.05	.15
14 Corie Blount	.05	.15
15 Dexter Boney	.05	.15
16 Tim Brooks	.05	.15
17 James Bryson	.05	.15
18 Evers Burns	.05	.15
19 Scott Burrell	.05	.15
20 Sam Cassell	.07	.20
21 Derrick Chandler	.05	.15
22 Sam Crawford	.05	.15
23 Ron Curry	.05	.15
24 William Davis	.05	.15
25 Rodney Dobard	.05	.15
26 Tony Dunkin	.05	.15
27 Spencer Dunkley	.05	.15
28 Bill Edwards	.05	.15
29 Bryan Edwards	.05	.15
30 Doug Edwards	.05	.15
31 Chuck Evans	.05	.15
32 Terry Evans	.05	.15
33 Will Flemons	.05	.15
34 Alphonso Ford	.05	.15
35 Brian Gilgeous	.05	.15
36 Josh Grant	.05	.15
37 Evric Gray	.05	.15
38 Geert Hammink	.05	.15
39 Lucious Harris	.05	.15
40 Joe Harvell	.05	.15
41 Antonio Harvey	.05	.15
42 Scott Haskin	.05	.15
43 Brian Hendrick	.05	.15
44 Sascha Hupmann	.05	.15
45 Stanley Jackson	.05	.15
46 Ervin Johnson	.05	.15
47 Adonis Jordan	.05	.15
48 Warren Kidd	.05	.15
49 Malcolm Mackey	.05	.15
50 Rich Manning	.05	.15
51 Chris McNeal	.05	.15
52 Conrad McRae	.05	.15
53 Lance Miller	.05	.15
54 Chris Mills	.15	.40
55 Matt Nover	.05	.15
56 Bo Outlaw	.15	.40
57 Eric Pauley	.05	.15
58 Mike Peplowski	.05	.15
59 Stacey Poole	.05	.15
60 Anthony Reed	.05	.15
61 Eric Riley	.05	.15
62 Darrin Robinson	.05	.15
63 Jackie Robinson	.05	.15
64 James Robinson	.05	.15
65 Bryon Russell	.15	.40
66 Brent Scott	.05	.15
67 Bennie Seltzer	.05	.15
68 Ed Stokes	.05	.15
69 Antoine Stoudamire	.05	.15
70 Dirk Surles	.05	.15
71 Justus Thigpen	.05	.15
72 Kevin Thompson	.05	.15
73 Ray Thompson	.05	.15
74 Gary Trost	.05	.15
75 Nick Van Exel	.07	.20
76 Jerry Walker	.05	.15
77 Rex Walters	.05	.15
78 Leonard White	.05	.15
79 Chris Whitney	.05	.15
80 Steve Worthy	.05	.15
81 Alex Wright	.05	.15
82 Luther Wright	.05	.15
83 Mark Buford	.05	.15
84 Keith Bullock	.05	.15
85 Mitchell Butler	.05	.15
86 Brian Clifford	.05	.15
87 Terry Dehere	.05	.15
88 Acie Earl	.05	.15
89 Greg Graham	.05	.15
90 Angelo Hamilton	.05	.15
91 Thomas Hill	.05	.15
92 Alex Holcombe	.05	.15
93 Khari Jaxon	.05	.15
94 Darnell Mee	.05	.15
95 Sherron Mills	.05	.15
96 Gheorghe Muresan	.15	.40
97 Eddie Rivera	.05	.15
98 Julius Nwosu	.05	.15
99 Richard Petruska	.05	.15
100 Bryan Sallier	.05	.15
101 Harper Williams	.05	.15
102 Ike Williams	.05	.15
103 Byron Wilson	.05	.15
104 Shaquille O'Neal FLB	.15	.40
105 Alonzo Mourning FLB	.15	.40
106 Christian Laettner FLB	.05	.15
107 Jimmy Jackson FLB	.05	.15
108 Harold Miner FLB	.05	.15
109 Checklist 1	.05	.15
110 Checklist 2	.05	.15
PF Chris Webber SPECIAL/60000	.75	2.00
PR1 Chris Webber PROMO	1.25	3.00
NNO Chris Webber DP AU	15.00	40.00

1993 Classic Gold

This 112-card standard-size set parallels the regular Classic Draft basketball set. Only 9,500 sequentially numbered sets were produced, and each set was packaged in a walnut display case. Each set included individually numbered Jamal Mashburn and Chris Webber autograph cards. The player's name and position are gold foil stamped at the bottom. To ascertain values of individual cards, please refer to the multiplier in the header, coupled with the value of the base card.

COMP.FACT.SET (112)	40.00	80.00
*GOLD: 1.5X TO 4X BASIC CARDS		
NNO Jamal Mashburn AU/9500	6.00	15.00
NNO Chris Webber AU/9500	12.50	30.00

1993 Classic Acetate Draft Stars

These five acetate cards were randomly inserted in foil packs. By visually interlocking these cards, the collector created a "Draft Stars" panoramic image featuring Webber, Hardaway, Mashburn, Rider, and Rogers. These visually interlocking clear plastic acetate cards were inserted on an average of three per ten-box case of 1993 Classic Basketball Draft Picks. The cards are unnumbered and checklisted below in alphabetical order.

COMPLETE SET (5)	3.00	8.00
AD1 Anfernee Hardaway	2.00	5.00
AD2 Jamal Mashburn	.40	1.00
AD3 Isaiah Rider	.40	1.00
AD4 Rodney Rogers	.20	.50
AD5 Chris Webber	1.50	4.00

1993 Classic Chromium Draft Stars

Inserted one per jumbo pack, these 20 standard-size cards feature on their metallic fronts borderless color player action shots. The player's name and position appear within the silver bar near the bottom. The horizontal simulated pinewood back carries a narrow-cropped color player action shot on the left. The player's name and biography appear at the top, followed below by a congratulatory message and statistics. The cards are numbered on the back with a "DS" prefix.

COMPLETE SET (20)	2.00	5.00
DS21 Vin Baker	.20	.50
DS22 Terry Dehere	.01	.05
DS23 Sam Cassell	.25	.60
DS24 Doug Edwards	.01	.05
DS25 Greg Graham	.01	.05
DS26 Scott Haskin	.01	.05
DS27 Allan Houston	.30	.75
DS28 Toni Kukoc	.30	.75
DS29 George Lynch	.01	.05
DS30 Jamal Mashburn	.15	.40
DS31 Harold Miner	.01	.05
DS32 Rex Walters	.01	.05
DS33 James Robinson	.01	.05
DS34 Rodney Rogers	.02	.10
DS35 Luther Wright	.01	.05
DS36 Alonzo Mourning	.10	.30
DS37 Anfernee Hardaway	.75	2.00
DS38 Isaiah Rider	.15	.40
DS39 Lindsey Hunter	.07	.20
DS40 Chris Webber	.75	2.00

1993 Classic Chromium Jumbos

These eight oversized (3 1/2 by 5 inches) chromium cards were issued by Classic as bonuses for various retail repackaged products. There are four different cards each of top draft picks Anfernee Hardaway and Chris Webber, using four designs from previously issued Classic Draft sets and insert sets.

COMPLETE SET (8)	6.00	15.00
1 Chris Webber (BK draft)	1.00	2.50
2 Anfernee Hardaway (BK draft)	1.00	2.50
3 Chris Webber (BK draft Illustrated)	1.00	2.50
4 Anfernee Hardaway (BK draft Illustrated)	1.00	2.50
5 Chris Webber (4-Sport LPs)	1.00	2.50
6 Anfernee Hardaway (4-Sport LPs)	1.00	2.50
7 Chris Webber (4-Sport)	1.00	2.50
8 Anfernee Hardaway (4-Sport)	1.00	2.50

1993 Classic Deathwatch Jumbos

Inserted in Classic Deathwatch comic card boxes, these three oversized cards measure approximately 3 1/2" by 5". The fronts feature color player action shots with simulated pinewood borders. The player's name and position appear in black lettering within a gold-foil stripe near the bottom. His NBA team name appears in white cursive lettering in an upper corner. A gold-foil "Traded" or "Drafted" message appears in the other upper corner. The back carries a congratulatory message. The cards are numbered on the back with an "SE" prefix. On a white screened background with the words "Special Edition", the backs give production figures (25,000).

COMPLETE SET (3)	4.00	10.00
SE1 Chris Webber	2.50	6.00
SE2 Jamal Mashburn	.50	1.25
SE3 Anfernee Hardaway	2.50	6.00

1993 Classic Draft Draft Day

This 12-card standard-size set was given away on NBA Draft Day, June 30, 1993. In anticipation of these players being the top draft picks, Classic produced these cards showing the teams (in the upper right corner) who would most likely draft these players. The fronts feature color action player photos with simulated pinewood borders. The player's name and position, along with the 1993 Classic Draft Picks logo, appears in a white bar across the base of each picture. On a white screened background with the words "1993 Draft Day," the backs display the 1993 Classic Draft Picks logo and give the production figures (19,930). The sets were sold through QVC Shopping Network. The cards are unnumbered and checklisted below in alphabetical order.

COMPLETE SET (12)	8.00	20.00
1 Anfernee Hardaway	1.25	3.00
2 Anfernee Hardaway	1.25	3.00
3 Anfernee Hardaway	1.25	3.00
4 Jamal Mashburn	.30	.75
5 Jamal Mashburn	.30	.75
6 Jamal Mashburn	.30	.75
7 Shaquille O'Neal	.75	2.00
8 Rodney Rogers	.20	.50
9 Rodney Rogers	.20	.50
10 Chris Webber	1.50	4.00
11 Chris Webber	1.50	4.00
12 Chris Webber	1.50	4.00

1993 Classic Draft East Coast National

This standard-size card features a borderless color action shot of Jamal Mashburn on its front. The player's name and position appear within a prismatic foil strip near the bottom. The back carries a message about the '93 East Coast National card show. The card is unnumbered.

1 Jamal Mashburn	.75	2.00

1993 Classic Illustrated

Drawn by artist Craig Hamilton, these three standard-size cards display images of basketball superstars and they were reportedly inserted on an average of three per ten-box case. The fronts feature full-bleed artistic portraits of exaggerated action scenes. The player's name and position appear in a white bar across the bottom, and 1993 Classic Draft Picks logo overlays the bar. On a background consisting of a ghosted blow-up of the front portrait, the backs have a narrowly-cropped color player picture and a player profile. The production figures ("1 of 39,000") round out the back. The cards are numbered on the back with an "SS" prefix.

COMPLETE SET (3)	4.00	10.00
SS1 Chris Webber	2.50	6.00
SS2 Jamal Mashburn	.50	1.25
SS3 Anfernee Hardaway	2.50	6.00

1993 Classic LPs

These ten standard-size cards were randomly inserted on an average of two per box of 1993 Classic Basketball Draft Picks. The fronts feature full-bleed color action player photos. The player's name and position appear in a holographic bar at the bottom, with the production run figures ("1 of 74,500") in holographic lettering immediately above. Also the 1993 Classic Draft Picks logo overlays the holographic bar. On a woodgrain-textured silver background, the horizontal backs carry a narrowly-cropped color player picture on the left and a player profile on the right. The player's name appears in a silver foil oval at the top. The cards are numbered on the back with an "LP" prefix.

COMPLETE SET (10)	5.00	12.00
LP1 Chris Webber	2.00	5.00
LP2 Anfernee Hardaway	2.00	5.00
LP3 Jamal Mashburn	.40	1.00
LP4 Isaiah Rider	.40	1.00
LP5 Vin Baker	.50	1.25
LP6 Rodney Rogers	.20	.50
LP7 Lindsey Hunter	.30	.75
LP8 Toni Kukoc	.75	2.00
LP9 Shaquille O'Neal	1.25	3.00
LP10 Alonzo Mourning	.40	1.00

1993 Classic Special Bonus

Issued one per jumbo sheet, these 20 standard-size cards feature on their fronts borderless color player action shots. The player's name and position appear within the gold-foil bar near the bottom. The horizontal simulated pinewood back carries a narrow-cropped color player action shot on the left. The player's name and biography appear at the top, followed below by a scouting report and statistics. The cards are numbered on the back with an "SB" prefix. The Webber card is a special random insert in the sheets.

COMPLETE SET (20)	4.00	10.00
SB1 Chris Webber	1.00	2.50
SB2 Anfernee Hardaway	1.00	2.50
SB3 Jamal Mashburn	.20	.50
SB4 Isaiah Rider	.20	.50
SB5 Rodney Rogers	.05	.15
SB6 Vin Baker	.25	.60
SB7 Lindsey Hunter	.08	.25
SB8 Allan Houston	.40	1.00
SB9 Toni Kukoc	.40	1.00
SB10 Acie Earl	.02	.10
SB11 George Lynch	.02	.10
SB12 Terry Dehere	.02	.10
SB13 Rex Walters	.02	.10

SB14 Harold Miner .02 .10
SB15 Scott Haskin .02 .10
SB16 Doug Edwards .02 .10
SB17 Greg Graham .02 .10
SB18 Christian Laettner .05 .15
SB19 Alonzo Mourning .15 .40
SB20 Shaquille O'Neal .50 1.25
NNO Chris Webber Special 2.00 5.00

1993 Classic Tri-Star Promos

These two standard-siz promo cards were issued in 1993 by Classic for Tri-Star Productions. The fronts display color action photos. The Tri-Star Productions logo is stamped in gold foil near one corner. The player's name appears at the bottom of the photo. The white back carries promo information and has no number.

COMPLETE SET (2) 1.25 3.00
1 Chris Webber 1.25 3.00
2 Jamal Mashburn .40 1.00

1994 Classic Previews

Randomly inserted in 1994 Classic football and ProLine football packs, these five standard-size cards feature color player action shots on their borderless fronts. The player's name and position appear in a black bar near the bottom. The back carries a congratulatory message. The complete set was also available using a redemption card. This offer expired Oct. 1, 1994.

COMPLETE SET (5) 5.00 12.00
BP1 Eric Montross .40 1.00
BP2 Jason Kidd 4.00 10.00
BP3 Yinka Dare .40 1.00
BP4 Glenn Robinson 1.50 4.00
BP5 Clifford Rozier .40 1.00

1994 Classic

These 105 standard-size cards feature borderless color player action shots on their fronts. The player's name and position appear within a black bar near the bottom. The back carries another borderless color player action shot, which is gradually ghosted toward the bottom. The player's name and position appear at the top; statistics and career highlights appear near the bottom. Dick Vitale's facsimile autograph at the lower right rounds out the card. A promotional card of Glenn Robinson was released before the product was live. It is numbered BP1, and the back gives information about the set and its inserts.

COMPLETE SET (100) 5.00 10.00
1 Glenn Robinson .40 1.00
2 Jason Kidd .75 2.00
3 Charlie Ward .15 .40
4 Grant Hill .50 1.25
5 Juwan Howard .15 .40
6 Eric Montross .05 .15
7 Carlos Rogers .05 .15
8 Wesley Person .15 .40
9 Anthony Miller .05 .15
10 Dwayne Morton .05 .15
11 Chris Mills ART .05 .15
12 Jamal Mashburn ART .15 .40
13 Chris Webber ART .15 .40
14 Anfernee Hardaway ART .15 .40
15 Isaiah Rider ART .05 .15
16 Billy McCaffrey .05 .15
17 Steve Woodberry .05 .15
18 Damon Bailey .05 .15
19 Deon Thomas .05 .15
20 Dontonio Wingfield .05 .15
21 Albert Burditt .05 .15
22 Aaron Mckie .05 .15
23 Steve Smith .05 .15
24 Tony Dumas .05 .15
25 Adrian Autry .05 .15
26 Monty Williams .05 .15
27 Askia Jones .05 .15
28 Howard Eisley .15 .40
29 Brian Grant .15 .40
30 Eddie Jones .40 1.00
31 Michael Smith .05 .15
32 Michael Smith .05 .15
33 Clifford Rozier .05 .15
34 Travis Ford .05 .15
35 Jervaughn Scales .05 .15
36 Tracy Webster .05 .15
37 Brooks Thompson .05 .15
38 Jim McIlvaine .05 .15
39 Eric Piatkowski .15 .40
40 Arturas Karnishovas .05 .15
41 Rodney Dent .05 .15
42 Robert Shannon .05 .15
43 Derrick Phelps .05 .15
44 Brian Reese .05 .15
45 Kevin Salvadori .05 .15
46 Shon Tarver .05 .15
47 Anthony Goldwire .05 .15
48 Jamie Watson .05 .15
49 Damon Key .05 .15
50 Kevin Rankin .05 .15
51 Khalid Reeves .05 .15
52 Doremus Benneman .05 .15
53 Sharone Wright .05 .15
54 Melvin Simon .05 .15
55 Andrei Fetisov .05 .15
56 Barry Brown .05 .15
57 B.J. Tyler .05 .15
58 Lawrence Funderburke .05 .15
59 Darrin Hancock .05 .15
60 Gaylon Nickerson .05 .15
61 Jeff Webster .05 .15
62 Derrick Alston .05 .15
63 Kendrick Warren .05 .15
64 Yinka Dare .05 .15
65 Shawnelle Scott .05 .15
66 Patrick Ewing CEN .15 .40
67 Dikembe Mutombo CEN .15 .40
68 Alonzo Mourning CEN .15 .40
69 Shaquille O'Neal CEN .15 .40
70 Hakeem Olajuwon CEN .15 .40
71 Thomas Hamilton .05 .15
72 Joey Brown .05 .15
73 Voshon Lenard .05 .15
74 Donyell Marshall .15 .40
75 Abdul Fox .05 .15
76 Checklist .05 .15
77 Checklist .05 .15
78 Jalen Rose .40 1.00
79 Trevor Ruffin .05 .15
80 Sam Mitchell .05 .15
81 Dick Vitale .15 .40
82 Charlie Ward 2-Sport .15 .40
83 Cornell Parker .05 .15
84 Clayton Ritter .05 .15
85 Carl Ray Harris .05 .15
86 Randy Blocker .05 .15
87 Chuck Graham .05 .15
88 Greg Minor .05 .15
89 Bill Curley .05 .15
90 Harry Moore .05 .15
91 Melvin Booker .05 .15
92 Gary Collier .05 .15
93 Myron Walker .05 .15
94 Jamie Brandon .05 .15
95 Eric Mobley .05 .15
96 Byron Starks .05 .15
97 Antonio Lang .05 .15
98 Jevon Crudup .05 .15
99 Robert Churchwell .05 .15
100 Aaron Swinson .05 .15
101 G. Robinson COMIC SP 1.25 3.00
102 Jason Kidd COMIC SP 1.25 3.00
103 Juwan Howard COMIC SP 1.25 3.00
104 Charlie Ward COMIC SP 1.25 3.00
105 Eric Montross COMIC SP .40 1.00
BP1 Glenn Robinson Promo .40 1.00
PR1 Jason Kidd Promo 1.00 2.50
AU1 Shaquille O'Neal AU/500 50.00 100.00
NNO Shaquille O'Neal Chrome 4.00 10.00

1994 Classic Gold

Inserted one per '94 Classic foil or jumbo pack, the 105 standard-size cards of this parallel set feature borderless color player action shots on their fronts. They are also random inserts in periodical packs. The player's name and position are stamped within a gold-foil bar near the bottom. To ascertain values of individual cards, please refer to the multiplier in the header below, coupled with the value of the base card.

*GOLD: 1.5X TO 4X HI COLUMN

1994 Classic Printer's Proofs

Randomly inserted in early hobby boxes, the 105 standard-size cards comprising this parallel issue are identical in design to the regular '94 Classic Draft set, except for the words "Printer's Proof, 1 of 975" appearing in gold-foil on the front in an upper corner. To ascertain values for individual cards, please refer to the multiplier in the header, coupled with the value of the base card.

*PROOFS: 4X TO 10X BASIC CARDS

1994 Classic Acetate Shaquille O'Neal

This 2 1/2" by 4 3/4" card shows Shaquille O'Neal holding a basketball. According to hobbyists, this card was only available through Home Shopping Network. This card is numbered out of 24,900.

SO1 Shaquille O'Neal 4.00 10.00

1994 Classic BCs

Inserted one per periodical pack, these 25 standard-size cards feature borderless color player action shots on their metallic fronts. The player's name and position appear within a black bar at the lower right. The back carries another borderless color action shot, with the player's biography appearing at the lower right within a ghosted triangle. The cards are numbered on the back with a "BC" prefix.

COMPLETE SET (25) 4.00 10.00
BC1 Glenn Robinson .50 1.25
BC2 Jason Kidd 1.25 3.00
BC3 Grant Hill 1.00 2.50
BC4 Donyell Marshall .15 .40
BC5 Juwan Howard .40 1.00
BC6 Sharone Wright .05 .15
BC7 Brian Grant .40 1.00
BC8 Eric Montross .05 .15
BC9 Eddie Jones 1.00 2.50
BC10 Carlos Rogers .05 .15
BC11 Khalid Reeves .05 .15
BC12 Jalen Rose .60 1.50
BC13 Yinka Dare .05 .15
BC14 Eric Piatkowski .05 .15
BC15 Clifford Rozier .05 .15
BC16 Aaron McKie .05 .15
BC17 Eric Mobley .05 .15
BC18 Tony Dumas .05 .15
BC19 B.J. Tyler .05 .15
BC20 Dickey Simpkins .05 .15
BC21 Bill Curley .05 .15
BC22 Wesley Person .15 .40
BC23 Monty Williams .05 .15
BC24 Greg Minor .05 .15
BC25 Charlie Ward .08 .25
NNO Jason Kidd Chrome 6.00 15.00

1994 Classic Game Cards

Inserted one per jumbo pack, these cards were redeemable for a gold sheet. The cards feature the expression "game card" in red letters down the left side of the front while the rest of the card displays the player's photo and in the bottom right part are the players' name and who drafted them. The back features instructions on how to play and scratch off your cards for the gold sheet prize. Winning cards were redeemable until May 1, 1995.

COMPLETE SET (5) 1.50 2.50
GC1 Glenn Robinson .30 .75
GC2 Jason Kidd .75 2.00
GC3 Juwan Howard .25 .60
GC4 Donyell Marshall .08 .25
GC5 Sharone Wright .05 .15

1994 Classic National Party Autographs

Measuring the standard-size, these cards were signed at a party hosted by Classic during the 15th National Collectors Convention in Houston. Attendees were entitled to have one card signed by one of the three athletes present. The fronts display full-bleed color action shots. The player's name appears in red print on a black bar near the bottom. The player's signature is inscribed across the front in silver ink. On a dark screened background, the backs carry a congratulatory message. The cards are unnumbered and checklisted below in alphabetical order.

COMPLETE SET (4) 15.00 40.00
1 Juwan Howard 6.00 15.00
2 Donyell Marshall 3.00 8.00
3 Jalen Rose 10.00 25.00
4 Jason Kidd 12.50 30.00

1994 Classic Phone Cards $2

1994 Classic Basketball Jumbo is the first Classic trading card product to include Sprint PrePaid Foncards. Randomly inserted at a rate of one in every seven 12-card jumbo packs, each Sprint card provides $2.00 worth of Sprint long distance service. The packs were sold at selected Walmart, Bookland, Sam's and other major retailers. The potential usage of these cards expired on June 30, 1995. The fronts feature a full-color player photo along with the Sprint logo in the upper left corner and the Scoreboard logo in the upper right corner. The bottom of the card features in red lettering the amount the card is worth along with the player's name. The horizontal back features information on how to use the card. The phone cards are unnumbered and checklisted below in alphabetical order.

COMPLETE SET (6) 4.00 10.00
1 Yinka Dare .15 .40
2 Jason Kidd 3.00 8.00
3 Donyell Marshall .25 .60
4 Eric Montross .15 .40
5 Glenn Robinson 1.25 3.00
6 Jalen Rose 1.50 4.00

1994 Classic Picks

This five-card standard-size set was randomly inserted in packs. The fronts feature color-action player cutouts superimposed on a metallized background. The player's name appears on the bottom, while the words "Classic Pick" are printed at the top. On a ghosted background, the backs carry a small color player portrait, along with a short biography and a player profile. 20,000 football and hockey sets were produced while 24,900 basketball and four-sport were produced. The football picks (1-5) were found in the football draft picks packs; the basketball picks (6-10) were in the basketball draft pick packs; the hockey picks (11-15) were in the hockey draft pick packs while the four-sport picks (16-25) were in four-sport packs. We are pricing only the basketball cards in this section.

COMPLETE SET (5) 8.00 20.00
6 Glenn Robinson 1.50 4.00
7 Jason Kidd 4.00 10.00
8 Grant Hill 3.00 8.00
9 Eric Montross .30 .75
10 Juwan Howard 1.25 3.00

1994 Classic ROY Sweepstakes

Randomly inserted in foil and jumbo packs, these 20 standard-size cards feature color action player cutouts on a borderless basketball background. A silhouette of a player appears to the left. The player's name appears within a gold-foil stripe near the bottom. Also in gold foil is the number of cards produced, 6,225. The card of the player selected Rookie of the Year was redeemable for an uncut Vitale's PTPers set sheet as well as a bonus card. This offer expired 7/15/95. The cards are numbered on the back with an "ROY" prefix.

COMPLETE SET (20) 20.00 50.00
1 Glenn Robinson 2.50 6.00
2 Jason Kidd 6.00 15.00
3 Grant Hill 5.00 12.00
4 Sharone Wright .30 .75
5 Juwan Howard 2.00 5.00
6 Monty Williams .30 .75
7 Khalid Reeves .30 .75
8 Eddie Jones 5.00 12.00
9 Clifford Rozier .30 .75
10 Aaron McKie .30 .75
11 Eric Montross .30 .75
12 Askia Jones .30 .75
13 Yinka Dare .30 .75
14 Dontonio Wingfield .30 .75
15 Carlos Rogers .30 .75
16 Eric Piatkowski .30 .75
17 Charlie Ward .50 1.25
18 Deon Thomas .30 .75
19 Dickey Simpkins .30 .75
20 Field Card .50 1.25
Dick Vitale

1994 Classic Vitale's PTPers

Randomly inserted in packs, these 15 standard-size cards feature on their borderless metallic fronts color player action cutouts set on multicolored backgrounds. The player's name appears within a colored stripe across the bottom. The back carries a color player action shot on the right and career highlights on a yellow panel on the left. A color cutout of Dick Vitale and his facsimile autograph at the bottom round out the card. The cards are numbered on the back with a "PTP" prefix.

COMPLETE SET (15) 12.50 30.00
1 Glenn Robinson 1.50 4.00
2 Jason Kidd 4.00 10.00
3 Grant Hill 3.00 8.00
4 Sharone Wright .20 .50
5 Juwan Howard 1.25 3.00
6 Billy McCaffrey .20 .50
7 Khalid Reeves .20 .50
8 Eddie Jones 3.00 8.00
9 Clifford Rozier .20 .50
10 Charlie Ward .30 .75
11 Eric Montross .20 .50
12 Wesley Person .50 1.25
13 Yinka Dare .20 .50
14 Dontonio Wingfield .20 .50
15 Carlos Rogers .20 .50

1994 Classic International Promos

This four-card standard-size set was given away during the International Sportscard and Memorabilia Expo at the Anaheim Convention Center July 19-24, 1994. The fronts display full-bleed color action shots. The player's name appears in red print on a black bar near the bottom. On a dark screened background, the backs carry the logo for the card show. The cards are unnumbered and checklisted below in alphabetical order.

COMPLETE SET (4) 3.00 8.00
4 Grant Hill BK 1.00 2.50

1994 Classic National Promos

This five-card standard-size set was issued to promote the 15th National Sports Collectors Convention in Houston August 4-7, 1994. The fronts display full-bleed color action shots. The player's name appears in red print on a black bar near the bottom. On a dark screened background, the backs carry a gold foil National Convention logo. The Hill card was given out on Exhibitor Preview Night, as noted on its back. The cards are unnumbered and checklisted below in alphabetical order.

COMPLETE SET (5) 6.00 15.00
2 Grant Hill BK 2.00 5.00
3 Jason Kidd BK 1.50 4.00

1995 Classic Previews

This five-card set measures the standard size. Both a hobby and retail set were produced and inserted at a rate of one per box in both the 1995 Classic Assets Gold and 1995 NFL ProLine boxes. This set was also available via a redemption offer in 1995 Images packs. The fronts feature borderless color action player photos with the player's name below. The hobby version has a aqua printer's proof logo while the retail version carries a silver foil signature across the bottom above the player's name. The backs show another player action photo with the player's name, position, biographical information, and career statistics. Sponsors' logos are below. The cards are numbered on the back with prefixes of RP for the retail version and HP for the hobby version.

COMPLETE SET (5) 2.00 5.00
1 Ed O'Bannon .40 1.00
2 Corliss Williamson .40 1.00
3 Joe Smith .75 2.00
4 Rasheed Wallace 1.25 3.00
5 Damon Stoudamire 1.00 2.50

1995 Classic

The 1995 Classic Basketball Rookies set was issued in one series of cards totalling 120 standard-size cards and showcases the best collection of rookie basketball talent. Every card has a unique innovative design with two-color foil stamping. The fronts feature a borderless color action player photo with the player's name across the bottom. The backs carry a color action player shot on the left with the player's name, career highlights, biographical information, and statistics on the right.

COMPLETE SET (120) 4.00 10.00
1 Joe Smith .25 .60
2 Antonio McDyess .30 .75
3 Jerry Stackhouse .40 1.00
4 Rasheed Wallace .40 1.00
5 Kevin Garnett 1.00 2.50
6 Damon Stoudamire .30 .75
7 Shawn Respert .12 .30
8 Ed O'Bannon .12 .30
9 Kurt Thomas .12 .30
10 Gary Trent .12 .30
11 Cherokee Parks .12 .30
12 Corliss Williamson .12 .30
13 Eric Williams .12 .30
14 Brent Barry .20 .50
15 Bob Sura .12 .30
16 Theo Ratliff .20 .50
17 Randolph Childress .12 .30
18 Jason Caffey .12 .30
19 Michael Finley .40 1.00
20 George Zidek .12 .30
21 Travis Best .12 .30
22 Loren Meyer .12 .30
23 David Vaughn .12 .30
24 Sherrell Ford .12 .30
25 Mario Bennett .12 .30
26 Greg Ostertag .12 .30
27 Cory Alexander .12 .30
28 Lou Roe .12 .30
29 Dragan Tarlac .12 .30
30 Terrence Rencher .12 .30
31 Junior Burrough .12 .30
32 Andrew DeClercq .12 .30
33 Jimmy King .12 .30
34 Lawrence Moten .12 .30
35 Frankie King .12 .30
36 Rashard Griffith .12 .30
37 Donny Marshall .12 .30
38 Julius Michalik .12 .30
39 Erik Meeks .12 .30
40 Donnie Boyce .12 .30
41 Eric Snow .12 .30
42 Anthony Pelle .12 .30
43 Troy Brown .12 .30
44 George Banks .12 .30
45 Tyus Edney .12 .30
46 Mark Davis .12 .30
47 Jerome Allen .12 .30
48 Fred Hoiberg .12 .30
49 Constantin Popa .12 .30
50 Erwin Claggett .12 .30
51 Michael McDonald .12 .30
52 Andre Riddick .12 .30
53 Cuonzo Martin .12 .30
54 Don Reid .12 .30
55 James Forrest .12 .30
56 Glen Whisby .12 .30
57 Dwight Stewart .12 .30
58 Jamal Faulkner .12 .30
59 Tom Kleinschmidt .12 .30
60 Donald Williams .12 .30
61 Dan Cross .12 .30
62 Rick Brunson .12 .30
63 Corey Beck .12 .30
64 Lance Hughes .12 .30
65 Bernard Blunt .12 .30
66 Clint McDaniel .12 .30
67 John Amaechi .12 .30
68 Lorenzo Orr .12 .30
69 Randy Rutherford .12 .30
70 Ray Jackson .12 .30
71 Reggie Jackson .12 .30
72 Russell Larson .12 .30
73 Carlin Warley .12 .30
74 James Scott .12 .30
75 Roderick Anderson .12 .30
76 Antoine Gillespie .12 .30
77 Gerald King .12 .30
78 Petey Sessoms .12 .30
79 Steve Payne .12 .30
80 William Gates .12 .30
81 Arthur Agee .12 .30
82 Rebecca Lobo .20 .50
83 Devin Gray .12 .30
84 Scotty Thurman .12 .30
85 Matt Maloney .12 .30
86 Michael Evans .12 .30
87 LaZelle Durden .12 .30
88 Ronnie McMahan .12 .30
89 Ed O'Bannon AW .05 .15
90 Mario Bennett AW .05 .15
91 Randolph Childress AW .05 .15
92 Rasheed Wallace AW .20 .50
93 Lawrence Moten AW .05 .15
94 Shawn Respert AW .05 .15
95 Lou Roe AW .05 .15
96 Damon Stoudamire AW .15 .40
97 Gary Trent AW .05 .15
98 Corliss Williamson AW .05 .15
99 Jerry Stackhouse AW .20 .50
100 Glenn Robinson AR .12 .30
101 Jason Kidd AR .20 .50
102 Juwan Howard AR .12 .30
103 Brian Grant AR .10 .25
104 Eddie Jones AR .15 .40
105 Shaquille O'Neal CA .30 .75
106 Dikembe Mutombo CA .12 .30
107 Alonzo Mourning CA .15 .40
108 Hakeem Olajuwon CA .15 .40
109 Cherokee Parks SS .05 .15
110 Corliss Williamson SS .05 .15
111 Shawn Respert SS .05 .15
112 Bob Sura SS .05 .15
113 Michael Finley SS .20 .50
114 Greg Ostertag SS .05 .15
115 Lou Roe SS .05 .15
116 Loren Meyer SS .05 .15
117 Mario Bennett SS .05 .15
118 Cuonzo Martin SS .05 .15
119 Joe Smith CL .12 .30
120 Jerry Stackhouse CL .20 .50

1995 Classic Foil

Foil versions of the 1995 Classic set have shown up on the secondary market. While not much is known about the manufacturing or distribution of this card, copies are available. The Foil set parallels the basic Classic set enhanced with a metallic foil sheen on the card front.

*FOIL: .75X TO 2X BASE CARD HI

1995 Classic Printer's Proofs

Inserted at a rate of 1 per 18 packs, these 120 standard size cards are the same as the Classic Rookies but with the words "Printer's Proof 1 of 949" across the front. The fronts feature a borderless color action player photo with the player's name across the bottom The backs carry a color action player shot on the left with the player's name, career highlights, biographical information, and statistics on the right. Sponsors' logos are below. The cards are numbered on the back. To ascertain values for individual cards, please refer to the multiplier in the header, coupled with the value of the base card.

*PROOFS: 4X TO 10X BASIC CARDS

1995 Classic Silver Signatures

Randomly inserted in '95 Classic Rookies retail packs, these 120 standard-size cards are similar to the Classic Rookies but with a metallic sheen and a silver signature. The fronts feature a borderless color action player photo with the player's name across the bottom. The backs carry a color action player shot on the left with the player's name, career highlights, biographical information, and statistics on the right. Sponsors' logos are below. To ascertain values for individual cards, please refer to the multiplier in the header below, coupled with the value of the base card.

*SILVER: 2.5X TO 6X BASIC CARDS

1995 Classic Autographs

This set was randomly inserted in boxes of Classic Basketball Rookies at the rate of one to a box. The fronts feature a borderless player action photo with an autograph above the player's printed name. The backs have a congratulations message printed on a background of the bottom view of a basketball net. The Auto Edition autograph cards are not sequentially numbered. They currently have the same value as the cards in the regular rookies packs. Some of the Auto Edition autograph cards are numbered out of 200, these cards were inserted one per box. Ed O'Bannon and Dikembe Mutombo only had Auto Edition cards produced.

1 Joe Smith/1230 2.50 6.00
2 Antonio McDyess/1270 4.00 10.00
2A Antonio McDyess/1975 4.00 10.00
3 Jerry Stackhouse/2370 6.00 15.00
4 Rasheed Wallace/1275 6.00 15.00
6 Damon Stoudamire/1255 4.00 10.00
7 Shawn Respert/1275 1.25 3.00
8A Ed O'Bannon 1.25 3.00
9 Kurt Thomas/3420 1.25 3.00
10 Gary Trent/3465 1.25 3.00
11 Cherokee Parks/2630 1.25 3.00
12 Corliss Williamson/3355 1.25 3.00
13 Eric Williams/2435 1.25 3.00
14 Brent Barry/2690 2.00 5.00
15 Bob Sura/3410 1.25 3.00
16 Theo Ratliff/3310 2.00 5.00
17 Randolph Childress/1260 1.25 3.00
18 Jason Caffey/2500 1.25 3.00
19 Michael Finley/3695 5.00 12.00
19A Michael Finley/5900 4.00 10.00
20 George Zidek/2650 1.25 3.00
21 Travis Best/1990 1.25 3.00
22 Loren Meyer/2920 1.25 3.00
23 David Vaughn/3320 1.25 3.00
24 Sherrell Ford/3635 1.25 3.00
25 Mario Bennett/2620 1.25 3.00
26 Greg Ostertag/2600 1.25 3.00
27 Cory Alexander/3335 1.25 3.00
28 Lou Roe/2845 1.25 3.00
30 Terrence Rencher/3275 1.25 3.00
31 Junior Burrough/3220 1.25 3.00
32 Andrew DeClercq/4080 1.25 3.00
33 Jimmy King/3740 1.25 3.00
34 Lawrence Moten/1715 1.25 3.00
35 Frankie King/3330 1.25 3.00
37 Donny Marshall/4000 1.25 3.00
38 Julius Michalik/3240 1.25 3.00
39 Erik Meeks/3165 1.25 3.00
40 Donnie Boyce/3100 1.25 3.00
41 Eric Snow/3980 1.25 3.00
43 Troy Brown/3340 1.25 3.00
44 George Banks/3240 1.25 3.00
45 Tyus Edney/3600 1.25 3.00
46 Mark Davis/3475 1.25 3.00
47 Jerome Allen/3700 1.25 3.00
48 Fred Hoiberg/4080 1.25 3.00
49 Constantin Popa/3275 1.25 3.00
50 Erwin Claggett/3300 1.25 3.00
52 Andre Riddick/3215 1.25 3.00
53 Cuonzo Martin/3280 1.25 3.00
54 Don Reid/2700 1.25 3.00
57 Dwight Stewart/3445 1.25 3.00
58 Jamal Faulkner/3250 1.25 3.00
59 Tom Kleinschmidt/3250 1.25 3.00
60 Donald Williams/2095 1.25 3.00
61 Dan Cross/3320 1.25 3.00
62 Rick Brunson/3780 1.25 3.00
63 Corey Beck/3155 1.25 3.00
64 Lance Hughes/3500 1.25 3.00
65 Bernard Blunt/3230 1.25 3.00
66 Clint McDaniel/3570 1.25 3.00
67 John Amaechi/3375 1.25 3.00
68 Lorenzo Orr/2870 1.25 3.00
69 Randy Rutherford/3180 1.25 3.00
70 Ray Jackson/3430 1.25 3.00
71 Reggie Jackson/2085 1.25 3.00
72 Russell Larson/3430 1.25 3.00
73 Carlin Warley/3215 1.25 3.00
76 Antoine Gillespie/3320 1.25 3.00
77 Gerald King/3945 1.25 3.00
78 Petey Sessoms/2135 1.25 3.00
79 Steve Payne/3170 1.25 3.00
80 William Gates/3290 1.25 3.00
81 Arthur Agee/3285 1.25 3.00
84 Scotty Thurman/3975 1.25 3.00
85 Matt Maloney/2800 1.25 3.00
86 Michael Evans/3310 1.25 3.00
87 LaZelle Durden/2400 1.25 3.00
88 Ronnie McMahan/3490 1.25 3.00
101 Jason Kidd/300 15.00 40.00
101A Jason Kidd/200 15.00 40.00
102 Juwan Howard/285 6.00 15.00
102A Juwan Howard/200 6.00 15.00
105 Shaquille O'Neal/400 40.00 80.00
105A Shaquille O'Neal/200 40.00 80.00
106A Dikembe Mutombo 6.00 15.00
107 Alonzo Mourning/2550 12.50 30.00

1995 Classic Big Time

This 10-card insert set was randomly inserted into specially marked retail packs of 1995 Classic Basketball Rookies. Each of the ten cards highlights a NBA new-comer who is expected to do well in the "Big Time". The cards are numbered with a "BT" prefix on the back.

COMPLETE SET (10) 8.00 20.00
BT1 Joe Smith 1.00 2.50
BT2 Antonio McDyess 1.25 3.00
BT3 Jerry Stackhouse 1.50 4.00
BT4 Rasheed Wallace 1.50 4.00
BT5 Kevin Garnett 4.00 10.00
BT6 Damon Stoudamire 1.25 3.00
BT7 Shawn Respert .50 1.25
BT8 Ed O'Bannon .50 1.25
BT9 Gary Trent .50 1.25
BT10 Cherokee Parks .50 1.25

1995 Classic Center Stage

Randomly inserted in hobby packs, this 10-card standard-size set captures outstanding college players. The fronts display a color action cut out on a metallic background. Each card is hand-numbered out of 1,750 produced. The backs have a second color photo and a player profile. The cards are numbered with a "CS" prefix.

COMPLETE SET (10) 25.00 60.00
CS1 Joe Smith 3.00 8.00
CS2 Antonio McDyess 4.00 10.00
CS3 Rasheed Wallace 5.00 12.00
CS4 Kevin Garnett 12.00 30.00
CS5 Damon Stoudamire 4.00 10.00
CS6 Ed O'Bannon 1.50 4.00
CS7 Gary Trent 1.50 4.00
CS8 Corliss Williamson 1.50 4.00
CS9 Jerry Stackhouse 5.00 12.00
CS10 Randolph Childress 1.50 4.00

1995 Classic Clear Cuts

The first five cards were randomly inserted in hobby "Hot Boxes," while the second five were included in retail "Hot Boxes." These cards have a color player action cutout superposed on a colored transparent stock that is die cut along the right edge. The backs have the mirror image of the fronts. The hobby cards have a "CCH" prefix while the retail cards have a "CCR" prefix.

COMPLETE SET (10) 40.00 100.00
CCH1 Shaquille O'Neal 10.00 25.00
CCH2 Joe Smith 4.00 10.00
CCH3 Rasheed Wallace 6.00 15.00
CCH4 Kevin Garnett 15.00 40.00
CCH5 Corliss Williamson 2.00 5.00
CCR1 Jason Kidd 6.00 15.00
CCR2 Ed O'Bannon 2.00 5.00
CCR3 Antonio McDyess 5.00 12.00
CCR4 Damon Stoudamire 5.00 12.00
CCR5 Shawn Respert 2.00 5.00

1995 Classic Draft Day

Randomly inserted in retail jumbo packs, this 14-card standard-size set focuses on top NBA draft choices. The fronts feature color action player photos while the backs carry player information.

COMPLETE SET (14) 1.50 4.00
1 Joe Smith .20 .50
2 Joe Smith-Warriors .20 .50
3 Joe Smith .20 .50
4 Rasheed Wallace .30 .75
5 Rasheed Wallace .30 .75
6 Rasheed Wallace .30 .75

Ed O'Bannon .10 .25
Ed O'Bannon .10 .25
Ed O'Bannon .10 .25
0 Corliss Williamson .10 .25
1 Corliss Williamson .10 .25
2 Corliss Williamson .10 .25
3 Jason Kidd .40 1.00
Grant Hill ROY
4 Checklist .10 .25

1995 Classic Draft Day Autographs

RINT RUN 1995 SER.#'d SETS
NO Rasheed Wallace 8.00 20.00

1995 Classic Instant Energy

This 20-card set was randomly inserted at a rate of one per retail jumbo pack. The fronts feature a color action player cut-out on a metallic background of lightning and a basketball court during a game. The player's name, team, and card name appear in an aqua and silver stripe at the bottom. The backs carry another player cut-out on a lightning background with a short career summary.

COMPLETE SET (20) 4.00 10.00
E1 Joe Smith .50 1.25
E2 Antonio McDyess .60 1.50
E3 Jerry Stackhouse .75 2.00
E4 Rasheed Wallace .75 2.00
E5 Kevin Garnett 2.00 5.00
E6 Damon Stoudamire .60 1.50
E7 Shawn Respert .25 .60
E8 Ed O'Bannon .25 .60
E9 Kurt Thomas .25 .60
E10 Gary Trent .25 .60
E11 Cherokee Parks .25 .60
E12 Corliss Williamson .25 .60
E13 Eric Williams .25 .60
E14 Brent Barry .40 1.00
E15 Bob Sura .25 .60
E16 Theo Ratliff .40 1.00
E17 Randolph Childress .25 .60
E18 Jason Caffey .25 .60
E19 Michael Finley .75 2.00
E20 George Zidek .25 .60

1995 Classic Phone Cards $4

This 5-card set, randomly inserted in retail packs, is made up of fully functional phone cards; however, they expired 10/1/96. The fronts contain color photos of the player on a phone-card sized, rounded corner, plastic stock card. The backs contain information on how to use the card. They are individually numbered out of 6334.

COMPLETE SET (5) 8.00 20.00
1 Joe Smith 1.50 4.00
2 Antonio McDyess 2.00 5.00
3 Jerry Stackhouse 2.50 6.00
4 Kevin Garnett 6.00 15.00
5 Rasheed Wallace 2.50 6.00

1995 Classic ROY Candidates

This 5-card insert set was randomly inserted into retail packs of 1995 Classic Basketball Rookies. Each of the five cards highlights a potential NBA Rookie of the Year for the 1995-96 season. (Damon Stoudamire ended up with the trophy, with Jerry Stackhouse as a not-so-distant runner-up.)

COMPLETE SET (5) 2.00 5.00
1 Joe Smith .60 1.50
2 Antonio McDyess .75 2.00
3 Jerry Stackhouse 1.00 2.50
4 Rasheed Wallace 1.00 2.50
5 Damon Stoudamire .75 2.00

1995 Classic ROY Redemptions

Inserted at a rate of 1 per 72 packs, these 20 standard-size cards feature a borderless color player action photo with the player's name above "Rookie of the Year" in gold on the left. The backs carry the player's name and instructions on how to participate in the redemption program. A checklist is listed below the instructions. The cards are numbered with a "ROY" prefix.

COMPLETE SET (20) 12.00 30.00
1 Joe Smith 1.50 4.00
2 Rasheed Wallace 2.50 6.00
3 Ed O'Bannon .75 2.00
4 Antonio McDyess 2.00 5.00
5 Shawn Respert .75 2.00
6 Mario Bennett .75 2.00
7 Jerry Stackhouse 2.50 6.00
8 Cherokee Parks .75 2.00
9 Damon Stoudamire 2.00 5.00
10 Kurt Thomas .75 2.00
11 Randolph Childress .75 2.00
12 Brent Barry 1.25 3.00
13 Corliss Williamson .75 2.00
14 Gary Trent .75 2.00
15 Bob Sura .75 2.00
16 David Vaughn .75 2.00
17 Michael Finley 2.50 6.00
18 Rashard Griffith .75 2.00
19 Lou Roe .75 2.00
20 Field Card .75 2.00

1995 Classic Showtime

Each of these 20 standard-size cards was randomly inserted in retail packs. On a metallic background with color streaks radiating from a row of stage lights, the fronts display a color action player cutout. On a similar design, the backs have a player profile at top and a second color photo at the bottom. Card number S4 was originally going to be Kevin Garnett, but the card does not exist. The cards are numbered with a "S" prefix.

COMPLETE SET (19) 12.00 30.00
S1 Joe Smith 1.50 4.00
S2 Antonio McDyess 2.00 5.00
S3 Rasheed Wallace 2.50 6.00
S5 Shawn Respert .75 2.00
S6 Kurt Thomas .75 2.00
S7 Gary Trent .75 2.00
S8 Cherokee Parks .75 2.00
S9 Eric Williams .75 2.00
S10 Jerry Stackhouse 2.50 6.00
S11 Travis Best .75 2.00
S12 Michael Finley 2.50 6.00
S13 George Zidek .75 2.00
S14 David Vaughn .75 2.00
S15 Mario Bennett .75 2.00
S16 Greg Ostertag .75 2.00
S17 Bob Sura .75 2.00
S18 Lou Roe .75 2.00
S19 Tyus Edney .75 2.00
S20 Jimmy King .75 2.00

1995 Classic Spotlight

Random inserts in auto edition packs, this 10-card set measures the standard size. The fronts display a color action player photo with a blurred background. The player's name and card name round out the front. The backs carry a single player photo with the player's name and a short career summary. The cards are numbered with a "RS" prefix.

COMPLETE SET (10) 5.00 12.00
RS1 Joe Smith .75 2.00
RS2 Antonio McDyess 1.00 2.50
RS3 Jason Kidd 1.25 3.00
RS4 Rasheed Wallace 1.25 3.00
RS5 Kevin Garnett 3.00 8.00
RS6 Damon Stoudamire 1.00 2.50
RS7 Ed O'Bannon .40 1.00
RS8 Shawn Respert .40 1.00
RS9 Kurt Thomas .40 1.00
RS10 Randolph Childress .40 1.00

1995 Classic Stackhouse Showtime

This 5-card insert set was randomly inserted into specially marked retail packs of 1995 Classic Basketball Rookies. Each of the five cards highlights NBA new-comer and ex-Tar Heel, Jerry Stackhouse. The cards are numbered with an "S" prefix on the back.

COMPLETE SET (5) 6.00 15.00
COMMON CARD (S1-S5) 2.00 5.00

1995 Classic National

This 20-card multi-sport set was issued by Classic to commemorate the 16th National Sports Collectors Convention in St. Louis. The set included a certificate of limited edition, with the serial number out of 9,995 sets produced. One thousand Sprint 20-minute phone cards featuring Ki-Jana Carter were also distributed.

COMPLETE SET (20) 8.00 20.00
NC1 Shaquille O'Neal 2.00 5.00
NC7 Glenn Robinson .20 .50
NC9 Jason Kidd 1.00 2.50
NC14 Alonzo Mourning .60 1.50
NC16 Joe Smith .20 .50
NC17 Rasheed Wallace .40 1.00
NC18 Ed O'Bannon .20 .50
NC19 Corliss Williamson .20 .50

1992-93 Classic C3

Limited to only 25,000 members, the Classic Collectors Club (also known as C3) featured two types of memberships: 1) the Presidential Charter membership (5,000), and 2) the Charter membership (20,000). As a bonus, the first 10,000 members received three packs of the bilingual edition of the 1991 Classic Draft Picks Collection. Exclusive to Presidential members were the following: a Brien Taylor autograph card (hand numbered "X/5,000"); an uncut sheet of either 1992 baseball, football, or hockey draft picks; and three special promo cards. In addition to other items (promo cards, T-shirt, newsletter, membership card, and posters), all members received a 30-card standard-size multi-sport set featuring tomorrow's future stars. Each set was accompanied by a certificate of limited edition, giving the set serial number and total production run (25,000). The sports represented are baseball (1-7, 25-27), basketball (8-13), football (14-20), hockey (21-24), track and field (28), and swimming (29).

COMP.FACT SET (30) 6.00 15.00
8 Alonzo Mourning 1.25 3.00
9 Christian Laettner .40 1.00
10 Jimmy Jackson .40 1.00
11 Harold Miner .30 .75
12 Billy Owens .40 1.00
13 Dikembe Mutombo .50 1.25

1993 Classic C3 Promos

Members of the Classic Collectors Club received one standard-size promo card with each newsletter. Although these promo cards have different designs, they share having a "C3" gold foil stamped on their fronts. The production run was 25,000 for each card. The O'Neal card is full-bleed on its front, with a gray stripe running near the left edge. Except for a narrowly-cropped photo, the back has a silver background and presents biography and player profile. The Webber card has simulated pinewood borders on the card front. The simulated pinewood design continues on the horizontal back, which carries brief biography and a narrow-cropped color action shot along the left side.

COMPLETE SET (2) 4.00 10.00
PR1 Shaquille O'Neal 3.00 8.00
PR2 Chris Webber 2.00 5.00

1993-94 Classic C3 Gold Crown Cut Lasercut

Along with the 20-card set checklisted below, the 10,000 members of the 1994 Classic Collectors Gold Crown Club received a 1994 C3 T-shirt, a TONX milk caps collectible sheet, a Classic Games magnet, and a 1994 C3 membership card. In later mailings they also received a 1993 Basketball Draft uncut sheet, a Chris Webber poster, and an autographed card of Jamal Mashburn, along with two promo cards. The sports represented are basketball (1-6), football (7-13), baseball (14-17), and hockey (18-20). The unnumbered checklist carries the set's production number out of the 10,000 produced.

COMPLETE SET (21) 10.00 25.00
1 Chris Webber .75 2.00
2 Anfernee Hardaway .60 1.50
3 Jamal Mashburn .40 1.00
4 Isaiah Rider .40 1.00
5 Rodney Rogers .40 1.00
6 Toni Kukoc .40 1.00

1994 Classic C3 Gold Crown Club

Part of a special issue to Classic Collector's Club members, these standard-size cards feature on their fronts color player action shots that are borderless, except at the bottom, where the player's name appears. His first name is shown at the bottom left within a gray rectangle, which is actually a vertically distorted and ghosted black-and-white player action shot. The last name is shown within a black rectangle edging the bottom right. Another vertically distorted black-and-white player action shot forms a stripe that roughly bisects the back. A color player action shot appears on the left side; the player's name and statistics are shown vertically within white and black panels on the right. As part of the 1994 Classic Collectors Gold Crown Club offer, members also received one of 10,000 individually numbered standard-size white bordered autographed card of Jamal Mashburn. His autograph in blue ink appears across the card face. The back carries the C3 logo and a congratulatory message.

COMPLETE SET (4) 6.00 15.00
CC1 Alonzo Mourning 1.25 3.00
CC4 Donyell Marshall .75 2.00
NNO Jamal Mashburn 6.00 15.00
AUTO/10000

1995 Classic Five Sport

The 1995 Classic Five Sport set was issued in one series of 200 standard-size cards. Cards were issued in 10-card regular packs (SRP $1.99). Boxes contained 36 packs. One autographed card was guaranteed in each pack and one certified autographed card (with an embossed logo) appeared in each box. There were also memorabilia redemption cards included in some packs and were guaranteed in at least one pack per box. The cards are numbered and divided into the five sports as follows: Basketball (1-42), Football (43-92), Baseball (93-122), Hockey (123-160), Racing (161-180), Alma Maters (181-190), Picture Perfect (191-200).

COMPLETE SET (200) 6.00 15.00
1 Joe Smith .15 .40
2 Antonio McDyess .20 .50
3 Jerry Stackhouse .30 .75
4 Rasheed Wallace .30 .75
5 Kevin Garnett 1.00 2.50
6 Damon Stoudamire .15 .40
7 Shawn Respert .05 .15
8 Ed O'Bannon .05 .15
9 Kurt Thomas .08 .25
10 Gary Trent .05 .15
11 Cherokee Parks .05 .15
12 Corliss Williamson .08 .25
13 Eric Williams .05 .15
14 Brent Barry .08 .25
15 Bob Sura .07 .20
16 Theo Ratliff .08 .25
17 Randolph Childress .05 .15
18 Jason Caffey .05 .15
19 Michael Finley .20 .50
20 George Zidek .05 .15
21 Travis Best .05 .15
22 Loren Meyer .05 .15
23 David Vaughn .05 .15
24 Sherrell Ford .05 .15
25 Mario Bennett .05 .15
26 Greg Ostertag .15 .40
27 Cory Alexander .05 .15
28 Lou Roe .05 .15
29 Dragan Tarlac .05 .15
30 Terrence Rencher .05 .15
31 Junior Burrough .05 .15
32 Andrew DeClercq .05 .15
33 Jimmy King .05 .15
34 Lawrence Moten .05 .15
35 Donny Marshall .05 .15
36 Eric Snow .15 .40
37 Anthony Pelle .05 .15
38 Tyus Edney .05 .15
39 Jerome Allen .05 .15
40 Fred Hoiberg .05 .15
41 Constantin Popa .05 .15
42 Rebecca Lobo .15 .40
181 Jerry Stackhouse .15 .40
Jimmy Hitchcock
182 Antonio McDyess .10 .30
Sherman Williams
183 Nomar Garciaparra .40 1.00
Travis Best
184 Andrew DeClercq .07 .20
Ki-Jana Carter
185 Tyrone Wheatley .10 .30
Jimmy King
186 J.J. Stokes .10 .30
Ed O'Bannon
187 Warren Sapp .10 .30
Constantin Popa
189 Eric Williams .05 .15
George Breen
190 Bob Sura .05 .15
Derrick Alexander
192 Hakeem Olajuwon .15 .40
198 Jason Kidd .25 .60
199 Shaquille O'Neal .40 1.00
200 Alonzo Mourning .15 .40

1995 Classic Five Sport Silver Die Cuts

These cards are identical to the regular set with the exception of a die-cut around the balls that are printed on the right side. They were inserted one per regular pack.

COMPLETE SET (200) 12.00 30.00
*SILVER DC: .8X TO 2X BASIC CARDS

1995 Classic Five Sport Autographs

This set was randomly inserted into packs and is a signed version of the basic issue cards. The backs carry a "Congratulations" message stating that it is an autographed 1995 Five Sport Autograph Edition Card with the sport's ball pictured at the bottom. The cards are unnumbered. Many of these autographed cards were later re-issued in 1995-96 Classic Five Sport Signings witha a slightly different cardback that reads "...Received a Limited-Edition Autographed Card." This message is the same one used on the Hot Box Autographs but these Five Sport Signings Autographs are not serial numbered on the back.

*SIGNINGS VERSION: .4X TO 1X
1 Joe Smith 2.00 5.00
2 Antonio McDyess SP 8.00 20.00
4 Rasheed Wallace SP 15.00 30.00
6 Damon Stoudamire SP 8.00 20.00
8 Ed O'Bannon 2.00 5.00
9 Kurt Thomas 2.00 5.00
11 Cherokee Parks 2.00 5.00
14 Brent Barry SP 2.00 5.00
15 Bob Sura 2.00 5.00
16 Theo Ratliff 2.50 6.00
17 Randolph Childress SP 2.00 5.00
19 Michael Finley 3.00 8.00
20 George Zidek 2.00 5.00
24 Sherrell Ford 2.00 5.00
27 Cory Alexander 2.00 5.00
30 Terrence Rencher 2.00 5.00
32 Andrew DeClercq SP 2.00 5.00
35 Donny Marshall 2.00 5.00
36 Eric Snow 2.00 5.00
37 Anthony Pelle 2.00 5.00
38 Tyus Edney 2.00 5.00
39 Jerome Allen 2.00 5.00
40 Fred Hoiberg 2.00 5.00
41 Constantin Popa 2.00 5.00
192 Hakeem Olajuwon 10.00 25.00
198 Jason Kidd SP 15.00 30.00
199 Shaquille O'Neal 40.00 80.00
200 Alonzo Mourning SP 20.00 40.00

1995 Classic Five Sport Autographs Numbered

Cards in this set were issued primarily in 1995-96 Classic Five Sport Signings packs and are essentially a parallel verson of the basic 1995 Classic Five Sport Autographs insert. The only differences are in the hand serial numbering on the cardbacks (of 225 or 295) and the embossing crimp on the card's corner.

2 Antonio McDyess/225 12.50 30.00
4 Rasheed Wallace/225 30.00 60.00
6 Damon Stoudamire/225 15.00 30.00
14 Brent Barry/225 4.00 10.00
19 Michael Finley/225 20.00 40.00
192 Hakeem Olajuwon/225 25.00 50.00
198 Jason Kidd/225 30.00 60.00
199 Shaquille O'Neal/225 40.00 80.00

1995 Classic Five Sport Classic Standouts

Randomly inserted in regular packs at a rate of one in 216, this 10-card standard-size set features both the hot new stars and the established elite of all five sports. Fronts have full-color action player cutouts set against a gold and black foil background. The player's name is printed in gold foil at the top. Backs contain a full-color action shot with the player's name printed in yellow and a career highlights box. The cards are numbered with a "CS" prefix.

COMPLETE SET (10) 15.00 40.00
CS1 Joe Smith 1.25 3.00
CS2 Rebecca Lobo 1.25 3.00
CS6 Jerry Stackhouse 2.00 5.00
CS8 Rasheed Wallace 1.50 4.00

1995 Classic Five Sport Fast Track

Randomly inserted in retail packs, this 20-card standard-size set spotlights the young stars of sports who are fast becoming major stars. Borderless fronts contain a player in full-color action while the rest of the shot is printed in colored foil. Backs have a color action shot in one box and two color separted boxes with the rest of the photo. A player profile appears underneath the photo. The cards are numbered with a "FT" prefix.

COMPLETE SET (20) 15.00 40.00
FT1 Joe Smith .75 2.00
FT3 Jason Kidd 2.50 6.00
FT6 Jerry Stackhouse 1.25 3.00
FT7 Shawn Respert .40 1.00
FT9 Rasheed Wallace .75 2.00
FT10 Ed O'Bannon .50 1.25
FT12 Kevin Garnett 6.00 15.00
FT16 Antonio McDyess 1.25 3.00
FT18 Damon Stoudamire 1.25 3.00
FT20 Corliss Williamson .60 1.50

1995 Classic Five Sport Hot Box Autographs

This set of six autographed standard-sized cards were randomly inserted in Hobby Hot boxes. The cards are nearly identical to the basic Five Sports Autographs with the exception of the hand written serial number on the backs and the slightly different congratulatory message on the back that reads "...Received a Limited-Edition Autographed Card."

4 Jason Kidd/650 10.00 25.00
6 Shaquille O'Neal/655 40.00 80.00

1995 Classic Five Sport On Fire

Ten of the 20-cards in this set were released in Hobby Hot Packs while the other ten were released in retail Hot packs. Fronts have full-color player cutouts set against a flame background with the On Fire logo printed at the bottom. The player's name is printed vertically in white type on the left side. backs feature biography and players's statistics.

COMPLETE SET (20) 30.00 80.00
H2 Joe Smith 2.50 6.00
H6 Rasheed Wallace 2.00 5.00
H7 Jerry Stackhouse 3.00 8.00
H9 Kevin Garnett 6.00 15.00
H10 Rebecca Lobo 2.50 6.00
R1 Jason Kidd 2.50 6.00
R2 Antonio McDyess 2.50 6.00
R3 Hakeem Olajuwon 2.50 6.00
R6 Ed O'Bannon 2.00 5.00

1995 Classic Five Sport Phone Cards $3

The five-card set of $3 Foncards were found one per 72 retail packs. The credit-card size plastic pieces have a borderless front with a full-color action player photo and the $3 emblem printed on the upper right in blue. The player's name is printed in white type vertically on the lower left. The Sprint logo appears on the bottom also. White backs carry information of how to place calls using the card.

COMPLETE SET (5) 4.00 8.00
5 Joe Smith .60 1.50

1995 Classic Five Sport Phone Cards $4

These cards were inserted randomly into packs at a rate of one in 72 and featured the five top prospects or performers of the individual sports. The borderless fronts feature full-color action photos with the athlete's name printed in white across the bottom. The Sprint logo and $4 are printed along the top. White backs contain information about placing calls using the card.

COMPLETE SET (5) 6.00 15.00
4 Jerry Stackhouse 1.00 2.50

1995 Classic Five Sport Previews

Randomly inserted in Classic hockey packs, this five-card standard-size set salutes the leaders and the up-and-coming rookies of the five sports. Borderless fronts have a full-color action shot with gold foil stamp of "preview" and the player's name, school and position printed vertically on the right side of the card. The player's sport's ball (or tire) is printed in a montage on the right. Backs have another full-color action shot and also a biography, statistics and profile. The cards are numbered with a "SP" prefix.

COMPLETE SET (5) 3.00 8.00
SP2 Joe Smith .40 1.00

1995 Classic Five Sport Printer's Proofs

*PRINTER PROOF/75: 4X TO 10X BASIC CARDS
STATED PRINT RUN 795 SETS

1995 Classic Five Sport Record Setters

This 10-card standard-size set was inserted in retail packs and feature the stars and rookies of the five sports. The fronts display full-bleed color action photos; the set title "Record Setters" iin prismatic block lettering appears toward the bottom. On a sepia-tone photo, the backs carry a player profile. The cards are numbered on the back with an "RS" prefix and hand-numbered out of 1250.

COMPLETE SET (10) 12.00 30.00
RS3 Ed O'Bannon .60 1.50
RS5 Joe Smith .75 2.00
RS6 Jerry Stackhouse .75 2.00
RS9 Kevin Garnett 2.50 6.00
RS10 Jeff Gordon 2.50 6.00

1995 Classic Five Sport Red Die Cuts

*RED DIE CUT: 1.2X TO 3X BASIC CARDS
RED DIE CUT STATED ODDS 1:8

1995 Classic Five Sport Strive For Five

This interactive game card set consists of 65 cards to be used like playing cards. Collector's gained a full suit of cards to redeem prizes. The odds of finding the card in packs were one in 10. Fronts are bordered in metallic silver foil and picture the player in full-color action. The cards are numbered on both top and bottom in silver foil and the player's name is printed vertically in silver foil. Backs have green backgrounds with the game rules printed in white type.

COMPLETE SET (65) 12.00 30.00
BK1 Joe Smith .50 1.25
BK2 Gary Trent .20 .50
BK3 Kurt Thomas .20 .50
BK4 Ed O'Bannon .20 .50
BK5 Shawn Respert .20 .50
BK6 Damon Stoudamire .75 2.00
BK7 Kevin Garnett 2.00 5.00
BK8 Rasheed Wallace .60 1.50
BK9 Antonio McDyess .60 1.50
BK10 Hakeem Olajuwon .40 .75
BK11 Jason Kidd .60 1.50
BK12 Rebecca Lobo .50 1.25
BK13 Jerry Stackhouse .50 1.25

1995-96 Classic Five Sport Signings

COMPLETE SET (100) 6.00 15.00
1 Joe Smith .20 .50
2 Antonio McDyess .25 .60
3 Jerry Stackhouse .40 1.00
4 Rasheed Wallace .40 1.00
5 Kevin Garnett 1.25 3.00
6 Damon Stoudamire .20 .50
7 Shawn Respert .07 .20
8 Ed O'Bannon .07 .20
9 Kurt Thomas .10 .30
10 Gary Trent .07 .20
11 Cherokee Parks .07 .20
12 Corliss Williamson .10 .30
13 Eric Williams .07 .20
14 Brent Barry .10 .30
15 Bob Sura .08 .25
16 Randolph Childress .07 .20
17 Michael Finley .25 .60
18 George Zidek .07 .20
19 Travis Best .07 .20
20 David Vaughn .07 .20
21 Mario Bennett .07 .20
22 Greg Ostertag .20 .50
23 Lou Roe .07 .20
24 Junior Burrough .07 .20
25 Andrew DeClercq .07 .20
26 Lawrence Moten .07 .20
27 Donny Marshall .07 .20
28 Tyus Edney .07 .20
29 Jimmy King .07 .20
30 Rebecca Lobo .20 .50
92 Hakeem Olajuwon .20 .50
98 Jason Kidd .30 .75
99 Shaquille O'Neal .50 1.25
100 Alonzo Mourning .20 .50

1995-96 Classic Five Sport Signings Blue Signature

The Blue Signature parallels were randomly inserted in regular Classic Five Sport Hot Boxes and are identical to the regular card with the exception of a blue foil facsimile signature on the front (basic cards feature silver foil signatures).

*BLUE SIGN: 1.5X TO 4X BASIC CARDS

1995-96 Classic Five Sport Signings Red Signature

The Red Signature parallels were randomly inserted in regular Classic Five Sport Hot Boxes and are identical to the regular cards with the exception of a red foil facsimile signature on the front (basic cards feature silver foil signatures).

*RED SIGN: 1.5X TO 4X BASIC CARDS

1995-96 Classic Five Sport Signings Die Cuts

These parallel cards were randomly inserted into one in every four packs. The cards feature a die cut design on the front right edge.

*DIE CUT: .8X TO 2X BASIC CARDS
STATED ODDS 1:4

1995-96 Classic Five Sport Signings Etched in Stone

This 10-card set, printed on 16-point foil board, was randomly inserted in Hot boxes only. Hot boxes were distributed at a rate of 1:5 cases.

1 Shaquille O'Neal 3.00 8.00
2 Jason Kidd 2.00 5.00
3 Scottie Pippen 1.50 4.00
4 Alonzo Mourning 1.50 4.00
10 Hakeem Olajuwon 1.50 4.00

1995-96 Classic Five Sport Signings Freshly Inked

This 30-card set was randomly inserted in 1995 Classic Five Sport Signings packs. The fronts features borderless player color action photos with the player's name printed in gold foil across the bottom. The backs carry an artist's drawing of the player with the player's name at the top.

COMPLETE SET (30) 12.00 30.00
STATED ODDS 1:10
FS1 Joe Smith .75 2.00
FS2 Antonio McDyess 1.00 2.50
FS3 George Zidek .40 1.00
FS4 Ed O'Bannon .40 1.00
FS5 Damon Stoudamire .75 2.00
FS6 Jerry Stackhouse 1.25 3.00
FS7 Cherokee Parks .40 1.00
FS8 Bob Sura .50 1.25
FS9 Rasheed Wallace 1.25 3.00
FS10 Shawn Respert .40 1.00

1991 Classic Four Sport

This 230-card multi-sport standard-size set includes all 200 draft picks players from the four Classic Draft Picks sets (football, baseball, basketball, and hockey), plus an additional 30 draft picks not previously found in these other sets. A subset within the 230 cards consists of five cards highlighting the publicized one-on-one game between Billy Owens and Larry Johnson. As an additional incentive to collectors, Classic randomly inserted over 60,000 autographed cards into the 15-card foil packs; it is claimed that each case should contain two or more autographed cards. The autographed cards feature 61 different players, approximately two-thirds of whom were hockey players. The production run for the English version was 25,000 cases, and a bilingual (French) version of the set was also produced at 20 percent of the English production.

COMPLETE SET (230) 5.00 12.00
1 Larry Johnson .15 .40
Brien Taylor
Russell Maryland
Eric Lindros
134 Terrell Brandon .05 .15
149 Larry Johnson .40 1.00
150 Billy Owens .15 .40
151 Dikembe Mutombo .40 1.00
152 Mark Macon .07 .20
153 Brian Williams .05 .15
154 Terrell Brandon .15 .40
155 Greg Anthony .07 .20
156 Dale Davis .15 .40
157 Anthony Avent .05 .15
158 Chris Gatling .08 .25
159 Victor Alexander .05 .15
160 Kevin Brooks .05 .15
161 Eric Murdock .08 .25
162 LeRon Ellis .05 .15
163 Stanley Roberts .05 .15
164 Rick Fox .20 .50
165 Pete Chilcutt .08 .25
166 Kevin Lynch .05 .15
167 George Ackles .05 .15
168 Rodney Monroe .05 .15
169 Randy Brown .08 .25
170 Chad Gallagher .05 .15
171 Donald Hodge .05 .15
172 Myron Brown .05 .15
173 Mike Iuzzolino .05 .15
174 Chris Corchiani .05 .15
175 Elliot Perry .08 .25
176 Joe Wylie .05 .15
177 Jimmy Oliver .05 .15
178 Doug Overton .05 .15
179 Sean Green .05 .15
180 Steve Hood .05 .15
181 Lamont Strothers .05 .15
182 Alvaro Teheran .05 .15
183 Bobby Phills .08 .25
184 Richard Dumas .05 .15
185 Keith Hughes .05 .15
186 Isaac Austin .08 .25
187 Greg Sutton .05 .15
188 Joey Wright .05 .15
189 Anthony Jones .05 .15
190 Von McDade .05 .15
191 Marcus Kennedy .05 .15
192 Larry Johnson No. 1 Pick .20 .50
193 Classic One on One II .15 .40
194 Anderson Hunt .05 .15
195 Darrin Chancellor .05 .15
196 Damon Lopez .05 .15
197 Thomas Jordan .05 .15
198 Tony Farmer .05 .15
199 Billy Owens No. 3 Pick .15 .40
200 Owens Takes 4-3 Lead .15 .40
(Billy Owens)
201 Johnson Slams for 6-6 Tie .20 .50
(Larry Johnson)
202 Score Tied with :49 Left .15 .40
210 Chris Smith .05 .15
216 Dexter Davis .05 .15
219 Marc Kroon .05 .15

1991 Classic Four Sport Autographs

The 1991 Classic Draft Collection Autograph set consists of 61 standard-size cards. They were randomly inserted throughout the foil packs. Listed after the player's name is how many cards were autographed by that player. An "A" suffix after card number is used here for convenience.

150A Billy Owens/2500 2.50 6.00
151A Dikembe Mutombo/1000 8.00 20.00
153A Brian Williams/1500 2.00 5.00
163A Stanley Roberts/2000 2.00 5.00

1991 Classic Four Sport LPs

This ten-card set was randomly inserted in 1991 Classic Draft Picks Collection foil packs. The cards are distinguished from the regular issue in that nine of them have a silver inner border while one has a gold inner border. A five-card Ismail subset is also to be found within the nine silver-bordered cards. The "1991 Classic Draft Picks" emblem appears as a wine-colored wax seal at the upper left corner. The horizontally oriented backs carry brief comments superimposed over a dusted version of Classic's wax seal emblem. There was also a French parallel set produced.

COMPLETE SET (10) 5.00 12.00
*FRENCH: SAME VALUE
RANDOM INSERTS IN PACKS .40 1.00
LP6 Larry Johnson .75 2.00
LP9 Larry Johnson .75 2.00
Billy Owens

1991 Classic Four Sport French

COMPLETE SET (230) 6.00 15.00
*FRENCH VERSION: .4X TO 1X

1992 Classic Four Sport

The 1992 Classic Draft Picks Collection consists of 325 standard-size cards, featuring the top picks from football, basketball, baseball, and hockey drafts. According to Classic, 40,000 12-box foil cases were produced. Randomly inserted in the 12-card packs were over 100,000 autograph cards from over 50 of the top draft picks from basketball, football, baseball, and hockey, including cards autographed by Shaquille O'Neal, Desmond Howard, Roman Hamrlik, and Phil Nevin. Also inserted in the packs were "Instant Win Giveway Cards" that entitled the collector to the 500,000.00 sports memorabilia giveway that Classic offered in this contest. There was also a factory set produced with gold parallel cards.

COMPLETE SET (325) 6.00 15.00
1 Shaquille O'Neal 1.50 4.00
2 Walt Williams .15 .40
3 Lee Mayberry .05 .15
4 Tony Bennett .05 .15
5 Litterial Green .05 .15
6 Chris Smith .05 .15
7 Henry Williams .05 .15
8 Terrell Lowery .05 .15
9 Curtis Blair .05 .15
10 Randy Woods .05 .15
11 Todd Day .15 .40
12 Anthony Peeler .15 .40
13 Darin Archbold .05 .15
14 Benford Williams .05 .15
15 Damon Patterson .05 .15
16 Bryant Stith .15 .40
17 Doug Christie .15 .40
18 Latrell Sprewell .50 1.25
19 Hubert Davis .15 .40
20 David Booth .05 .15
21 Dave Johnson .05 .15
22 Jon Barry .05 .15
23 Everick Sullivan .05 .15
24 Brian Davis .05 .15
25 Clarence Weatherspoon .15 .40
26 Malik Sealy .15 .40
27 Matt Geiger .15 .40
28 Jimmy Jackson .15 .40
29 Matt Steigenga .05 .15
30 Robert Horry .15 .40
31 Marlon Maxey .05 .15
32 Chris King .05 .15
33 Dexter Cambridge .05 .15
34 Alonzo Jamison .05 .15
35 Anthony Tucker .05 .15
36 Tracy Murray .15 .40
37 Vernel Singleton .05 .15
38 Christian Laettner .15 .40
39 Don MacLean .15 .40
40 Adam Keefe .05 .15
41 Tom Gugliotta .15 .40
42 LaPhonso Ellis .15 .40
43 Byron Houston .05 .15
44 Oliver Miller .05 .15
45 Popeye Jones .05 .15
46 P.J. Brown .15 .40
47 Eric Anderson .05 .15
48 Darren Morningstar .05 .15
49 Isaiah Morris .05 .15
50 Stephen Howard .05 .15

51 Elmore Spencer	.05	.15
52 Sean Rooks	.05	.15
53 Robert Werdann	.05	.15
54 Alonzo Mourning	.40	1.00
55 Steve Rogers	.05	.15
56 Tim Burroughs	.05	.15
57 Herb Jones	.05	.15
58 Sean Miller	.05	.15
59 Corey Williams	.05	.15
60 Duane Cooper	.05	.15
61 Brett Roberts	.05	.15
62 Elmer Bennett	.05	.15
63 Brent Price	.05	.15
64 Daimon Sweet	.05	.15
65 Darrick Martin	.05	.15
66 Gerald Madkins	.05	.15
67 Jo Jo English	.05	.15
68 Matt Fish	.05	.15
69 Harold Miner	.15	.40
70 Greg Dennis	.05	.15
71 Jeff Roulston	.05	.15
72 Keir Rogers	.05	.15
73 Geoff Lear	.05	.15
74 Ron Ellis	.05	.15
75 Predrag Danilovic	.05	.15
258 Chris Smith	.05	.15
303 Reggie Smith	.05	.15
311 Billy Owens FLB	.05	.15
312 Dikembe Mutombo FLB	.15	.40
315 Christian Laettner JWA	.15	.40
316 Harold Miner JWA	.15	.40
317 Jimmy Jackson JWA	.15	.40
318 Shaquille O'Neal JWA	1.00	2.50
319 Alonzo Mourning JWA	.15	.40

1992 Classic Four Sport Gold

Issued in factory set form, these cards parallel the basic Classic Four-Sport set. Each cards features gold foil highlights and are valued as a multiple of the basic Four-Sport cards. The factory sealed set also included an additional "Future Superstars" autographed card. Only 9,500 sequentially numbered factory sets were produced and each was packaged in a walnut display case.

COMP.FACT.SET (326)	60.00	120.00
*GOLD: 1.2X TO 3X BASIC CARDS		
AU Future Superstars AU	30.00	60.00
Phil Nevin		
Shaquille O'Neal		
Desmond Howard		
Roman Hamrlik		
(Certified AUTO/9500)		

1992 Classic Four Sport Autographs

The 1992 Classic Four Sport Autograph set consists of base cards hand signed by the featured player with a congratulatory message on the backs. . They were randomly inserted throughout the foil packs. Each card also included a hand written serial number on the front and the checklist below reflects the quantity of cards each player signed. We've assigned card number according to the player's base card. Jan Caloun and Jan Vopat were not included in the regular set and hence are listed as unnumbered.

1A Shaquille O'Neal/150	150.00	300.00
2 Walt Williams/2550	3.00	8.00
3 Lee Mayberry/2575	2.00	5.00
11 Todd Day/1575	2.50	6.00
25 Clar.Weatherspoon/1575	3.00	8.00
26 Malik Sealy/1575	2.50	6.00
28 Jimmy Jackson/1575	5.00	12.00
36 Tracy Murray/1450	2.50	6.00
38 Christian Laettner/725	10.00	25.00
39 Don MacLean/2575	2.00	5.00
40 Adam Keefe/1575	2.00	5.00
54 Alonzo Mourning/975	40.00	80.00
69 Harold Miner/1475	4.00	10.00

1992 Classic Four Sport BCs

Inserted one per jumbo pack, these 20 bonus cards measure the standard size. The cards are numbered on the dark gray stripe and arranged according to sport as follows: basketball (1-6), hockey (7-12), football (13-17), and baseball (18-20). A randomly inserted Future Superstars card has a picture of all four players on its front, shot against a horizon with dark clouds and lightning; the back indicates that just 10,000 of these cards were produced.

COMPLETE SET (20)	3.00	8.00
BC1 Alonzo Mourning	.08	.25
BC2 Christian Laettner	.08	.25
BC3 Jimmy Jackson	.15	.40
BC4 Tom Gugliotta	.20	.50
BC5 Walt Williams	.08	.25
BC6 Harold Miner	.15	.40

1992 Classic Four Sport LPs

Randomly inserted in foil packs, this 25-card standard-size insert set features full-bleed glossy color action player photos on the fronts. The sports represented are football (1-7, 16), basketball (8-14), baseball (17-21), and hockey (22-25). An 8 1/2" by 11" version of Shaquille O'Neal is known to exist.

LP8 Shaquille O'Neal	3.00	8.00
LP9 Jimmy Jackson	.30	.75
LP10 Alonzo Mourning	.75	2.00
LP11 Christian Laettner	.20	.50
LP12 Harold Miner	.20	.50
LP13 Todd Day	.20	.50
LP14 Kareem Abdul-Jabbar	1.25	3.00
Shaquille O'Neal		
LP15 Phil Nevin	1.50	4.00
Shaquille O'Neal		
Roman Hamrlik		
Desmond Howard		

1992 Classic Four Sport Previews

These five preview standard-size cards were randomly inserted in baseball and hockey draft picks foil packs. According to the backs, just 10,000 of each card were produced. The fronts display the full-bleed glossy color player photos. At the upper right corner, the word "Preview" surmounts the Classic logo. This logo overlays a black stripe that runs down the left side and features the player's name and position. The gray backs have the word "Preview" in red lettering at the top and are accented by short purple diagonal stripes on each side. Between the stripes are a congratulations and an advertisement. The cards are numbered on the back with a "CC" prefix.

COMPLETE SET (5)	6.00	15.00
CC1 Shaquille O'Neal	4.00	10.00
CC5 Alonzo Mourning	1.25	3.00

1992 Classic Four Sport Promos

These five promo cards were packaged in a cello pack and distributed to dealers. The cards measure the standard size (2 1/2" by 3 1/2"). The fronts display the same full-bleed glossy color player photos as the above-mentioned preview cards. They differ in that the Classic logo at the upper left corner is not surmounted by the word Preview." The promo backs have a different design than the preview backs, displaying a second color player photo on the right side as well as biography and player profile in black print on a silver background. The cards are numbered on the back.

COMPLETE SET (5)	6.00	15.00
PR1 Shaquille O'Neal	3.00	8.00
PR5 Alonzo Mourning	1.25	3.00

1993 Classic Four Sport

The 1993 Classic Four-Sport Draft Pick Collection set consists of 325 standard-size cards of the top 1993 draft picks from football, basketball, baseball, and hockey. Just 49,500 sequentially numbered 12-box cases were produced. The set includes two topical subsets: John R. Wooden Award (310-314) and All-Rookie Basketball Team (315-319).

COMPLETE SET (325)	4.00	10.00
1 Chris Webber	.40	1.00
2 Anfernee Hardaway	.40	1.00
3 Jamal Mashburn	.30	.75
4 Isaiah Rider	.15	.40
5 Vin Baker	.08	.25
6 Rodney Rogers	.07	.20
7 Lindsey Hunter	.07	.20
8 Allan Houston	.20	.50
9 George Lynch	.07	.20
10 Toni Kukoc	.20	.50
11 Ashraf Amaya	.05	.15
12 Mark Bell	.05	.15
13 Corie Blount	.05	.15
14 Dexter Boney	.05	.15
15 Tim Brooks	.05	.15
16 James Bryson	.05	.15
17 Evers Burns	.05	.15
18 Scott Burrell	.07	.20
19 Sam Cassell	.15	.40
20 Sam Crawford	.05	.15
21 Ron Curry	.05	.15
22 William Davis	.05	.15
23 Rodney Dobard	.05	.15
24 Tony Dunkin	.05	.15
25 Spencer Dunkley	.05	.15
26 Bryan Edwards	.05	.15
27 Doug Edwards	.05	.15
28 Chuck Evans	.05	.15
29 Terry Evans	.05	.15
30 Will Flemons	.05	.15
31 Alphonso Ford	.05	.15
32 Josh Grant	.05	.15
33 Eric Gray	.05	.15
34 Geert Hammink	.05	.15
35 Joe Harvell	.05	.15
36 Scott Haskin	.05	.15
37 Brian Hendrick	.05	.15
38 Sascha Hupmann	.05	.15
39 Stanley Jackson	.05	.15
40 Ervin Johnson	.15	.40
41 Adonis Jordan	.05	.15
42 Malcolm Mackey	.05	.15
43 Rich Manning	.05	.15
44 Chris McNeal	.05	.15
45 Conrad McRae	.05	.15
46 Lance Miller	.05	.15
47 Chris Mills	.05	.15
48 Matt Nover	.05	.15
49 Charles (Bo) Outlaw	.07	.20
50 Eric Pauley	.05	.15
51 Mike Peplowski	.05	.15
52 Stacey Poole	.05	.15
53 Anthony Reed	.05	.15
54 Eric Riley	.05	.15
55 Darrin Robinson	.05	.15
56 James Robinson	.05	.15
57 Bryon Russell	.07	.20
58 Brent Scott	.05	.15
59 Bennie Seitzer	.05	.15
60 Ed Stokes	.05	.15
61 Antoine Stoudamire	.05	.15
62 Dirk Surles	.05	.15
63 Justus Thigpen	.05	.15
64 Kevin Thompson	.05	.15
65 Ray Thompson	.05	.15
66 Gary Trost	.05	.15
67 Nick Van Exel	.20	.50
68 Jerry Walker	.05	.15
69 Rex Walters	.05	.15
70 Chris Whitney	.05	.15
71 Steve Worthy	.05	.15
72 Luther Wright	.05	.15
73 Mark Buford	.05	.15
74 Mitchell Butler	.05	.15
75 Brian Clifford	.05	.15
76 Terry Dehere	.05	.15
77 Acie Earl	.05	.15
78 Greg Graham	.05	.15
79 Angelo Hamilton	.05	.15
80 Thomas Hill	.05	.15
81 Khari Jaxon	.05	.15
82 Darnell Mee	.05	.15
83 Sherron Mills	.05	.15
84 Gheorghe Muresan	.08	.25
85 Eddie Rivera	.05	.15
86 Richard Petruska	.05	.15
87 Bryan Sallier	.05	.15
88 Harper Williams	.05	.15
89 Ike Williams	.05	.15
90 Byron Wilson	.05	.15
310 John Wooden CO	.30	.75
311 Chris Webber JWA	.30	.75
312 Jamal Mashburn JWA	.15	.40
313 Anfernee Hardaway JWA	.10	.30
314 Terry Dehere JWA	.05	.15
315 Shaquille O'Neal ART	.30	.75
316 Alonzo Mourning ART	.10	.30
317 Christian Laettner ART	.05	.15
318 Jimmy Jackson ART	.05	.15
319 Harold Miner ART	.05	.15
NNO Jamal Mashburn	.75	2.00
Draft Star Mail-In		

1993 Classic Four Sport Gold

This parallel issue to the 1993 Classic Four Sport set consists of 325 Gold foil versions of the regular set, plus four player autograph cards that were inserted into each factory gold set. Each of the four players autographed 3900 cards. Aside from the special gold-foil highlights (such as the ghosted stripe carrying the player's name being offset by gold-foil lines) the cards are identical to the regular 1993 Classic Four Sport base cards.

COMP.FACT.SET (332)	150.00	250.00
*GOLD: 1.5X TO 4X BASIC CARDS		
AU3 Alonzo Mourning AU/3900	15.00	30.00
PR1 Anfernee Hardaway Promo	2.00	5.00

1993 Classic Four Sport Acetates

Randomly inserted throughout the 1993 Classic Four-Sport foil packs, this 12-card standard-size acetate set features on its fronts clear-bordered color player action cutouts set on basketball, football, baseball, or hockey stick backgrounds. The cards are unnumbered but carry letter designations. They are checklisted in the order that spells '93 Rookie Class.

COMPLETE SET (12)	6.00	15.00
1 Chris Webber	1.00	2.50
2 Anfernee Hardaway	.75	2.00
3 Jamal Mashburn	.40	1.00
4 Isaiah Rider	.40	1.00
5 Toni Kukoc	.60	1.50

1993 Classic Four Sport Autographs

Randomly inserted in '93 Classic Four-Sport packs, these standard-size cards feature on their fronts borderless color player action shots. The back carries a congratulatory message. The cards are listed below by their corresponding regular card numbers, except for Jennings and Klippenstein, which are shown as unnumbered cards (NNO) at the end of the checklist since they are not in the regular set. The number of cards each player signed is shown. The Rider card may have been autopenned.

1A Chris Webber/550	40.00	80.00
3A Jamal Mashburn/800	12.50	30.00
4A Isaiah Rider/4100	4.00	10.00
6A Rodney Rogers/4000	4.00	10.00
77A Acie Earl/550	1.50	4.00
310A John Wooden/150	75.00	150.00
315A Shaquille O'Neal/500	25.00	60.00
316A Alonzo Mourning/400	25.00	60.00

1993 Classic Four Sport Chromium Draft Stars

Inserted one per jumbo pack, these 20 standard-size cards feature color player action cutouts on their borderless metallic fronts. The player's name, along with the production number (1 of 80,000), appear vertically in gold foil at the lower left. The cards are numbered on the back with a "DS" prefix.

COMPLETE SET (20)	8.00	20.00
DS41 Chris Webber	.60	1.50
DS42 Anfernee Hardaway	.50	1.25
DS43 Jamal Mashburn	.40	1.00
DS44 Isaiah Rider	.40	1.00
DS45 Toni Kukoc	.30	.75
DS46 Rodney Rogers	.30	.75
DS47 Chris Mills	.30	.75

1993 Classic Four Sport LP Jumbos

Random inserts in hobby boxes, these five oversized cards measure approximately 3 1/2" by 5" and feature on their fronts borderless color player action shots. The player's name, statistics, biography, and career highlights, along with the card's production number out of 8,000 produced, appear on a gray lithic background to the left. The cards are numbered on the back as "X of 5."

COMPLETE SET (5)	12.00	30.00
4 Chris Webber	2.50	6.00
5 Four in One	2.50	6.00

1993 Classic Four Sport LPs

Randomly inserted throughout the 1993 Classic Four-Sport foil packs, this 25-card standard-size set features the hottest draft pick players in 1993. The borderless fronts feature color player action shots. The player's name appears vertically at the lower left. The production number (1 of 63,400) appears in gold foil at the lower right. The cards are numbered on the back with an "LP" prefix.

COMPLETE SET (25)	20.00	40.00
LP1 Four-in-One Card	1.50	4.00
Chris Webber		
Drew Bledsoe		
Alex Rodriguez		
Alexandre Daigle		
LP2 Chris Webber	1.50	4.00
LP3 Anfernee Hardaway	1.00	2.50
LP4 Jamal Mashburn	.75	2.00
LP5 Isaiah Rider	.40	1.00
LP6 Shaquille O'Neal	1.50	4.00
LP7 Toni Kukoc	.60	1.50
LP8 Rodney Rogers	.30	.75
LP9 Lindsey Hunter	.40	1.00

1993 Classic Four Sport C3 Promo

This standard-size promo card was issued in 1993 by Classic for its Classic Collectors Club Members. The front features a full-bleed color action player photo. A ghosted strip runs down the card face near the right edge and carries the player's name and the Classic Four Sport logo in gold foil. The C3 gold foil logo is in the upper left corner. On a rock simulated background, the back carries a brief biography on the left, as well as production figures (25,000). A color player photo along the right edge and the Classic Four Sport Logo on the bottom completes the back. The card is unnumbered.

1 Jamal Mashburn	1.00	2.50

1993 Classic Four Sport MBNA Promos

This two-card set uses Classic's designs from its Four-Sport LPs "Four in One" insert number LP1. Card number 1 reproduces the Chris Webber/Alex Rodriguez side of LP1, card number 2 reproduces the Drew Bledsoe/Alexandre Daigle side. This set was issued exclusively to cardholders of the MBNA/ScoreBoard VISA. The backs contain congratulatory messages, information about the players depicted, and a notation than 10,000 sets were issued. Although the design and copyright reads 1993, these cards probably were first issued in 1994.

1 Chris Webber	4.00	10.00
Alex Rodriguez		

1993 Classic Four Sport McDonald's

Classic produced this 35-card four-sport standard-size set for a promotion at McDonald's restaurants in central and southeastern Pennsylvania, southern New Jersey, Delaware, and central Florida. The cards were distributed in five-card packs. A five-card "limited production" subset was randomly inserted throughout these packs. The promotion also featured instant win cards awarding 2,000 pieces of autographed Score Board memorabilia. An autographed Chris Webber card was also randomly inserted in the packs on a limited basis. The set is arranged according to sports as follows: football (1-10), baseball (11, 26, 31-35), hockey (12-20), and basketball (21-25, 27-30). The cards are numbered on the back in the upper left, and the McDonald's trademark is gold foil stamped toward the bottom.

COMPLETE SET (35)	4.00	10.00
12 Vyacheslav Butsayev	.05	.15
21 Anfernee Hardaway	.50	1.25
22 Jimmy Jackson	.08	.25
23 Christian Laettner	.08	.25
24 Jamal Mashburn	.20	.50
25 Harold Miner	.05	.15
27 Alonzo Mourning	.15	.40
28 Shaquille O'Neal	.60	1.50
29 Clarence Weatherspoon	.05	.15
30 Chris Webber	.50	1.25

1993 Classic Four Sport McDonald's LPs

Measuring the standard size, these five limited production cards were randomly inserted in 1993 Classic McDonald's five-card packs. Chris Webber, the number one pick in the NBA draft, autographed 1,250 of his cards. Printed vertically, and parallel and next to the gold foil band, "1 of 16,750" appears in gold foil. The Classic Four Sport logo appears in the upper right. The cards are numbered on the back in gold foil with an "LP" prefix.

COMPLETE SET (5)	3.00	8.00
LP3 Alonzo Mourning	.30	.75
NNO Chris Webber AU/1250	30.00	60.00

1993 Classic Four Sport Power Pick Bonus

Issued one per jumbo sheet, these 20 standard-size cards feature on their borderless fronts color player action shots, the backgrounds for which are faded to black-and-white. The player's name and the sets production number (1 of 80,000) appear in green-foil cursive lettering near the bottom. The cards are numbered on the back with a "PP" prefix.

COMPLETE SET (20)	10.00	25.00
PP1 Chris Webber	.75	2.00
PP2 Anfernee Hardaway	.60	1.50
PP3 Jamal Mashburn	.60	1.50
PP4 Isaiah Rider	.40	1.00
PP5 Toni Kukoc	.60	1.50
PP6 Rodney Rogers	.40	1.00
PP7 Chris Mills	.40	1.00
NNO Four in One Special	1.50	4.00

1993 Classic Four Sport Previews

Issued as unnumbered inserts in '93 Classic hockey packs, these five cards measure the standard size. The fronts are similar in design to regular 1993 Classic Four-Sport cards. The backs carry a congratulatory message. The cards are unnumbered and checklisted below in alphabetical order.

COMPLETE SET (5)	2.50	6.00
CC4 Chris Webber	1.50	4.00
CC5 Toni Kukoc	.30	.75

1993 Classic Four Sport Tri-Cards

Randomly inserted throughout the 1993 Classic Four-Sport foil packs, this set features five standard-size cards with three players on each card separated by perforations. The cards are numbered on the back with a "TC" prefix.

COMPLETE SET (5)	10.00	25.00
TC1 Anfernee Hardaway	2.50	6.00
TC6 Shaquille O'Neal		
TC11 Chris Webber		
TC5 Drew Bledsoe	3.00	8.00
TC10 Chris Webber		
TC15 Alex Rodriguez		

1994 Classic Four Sport

Featuring top rookies from basketball, baseball, football and hockey, the 1994 Classic Four-Sport set consists of 200 standard-size cards. No more than 25,000 cases were produced. Over 100 players signed 100,000 cards that were randomly inserted four per case. Collectors who found one of 100 Glenn Robinson Instant Winner Cards received a complete Classic Four-Sport autographed card set. Also inserted on an average of one in every five cases were 4,695 hand-numbered 4-in-1 cards featuring all four number 1 picks. Classic's wrapper redemption program offered four levels of participation: 1) bronze-collect 20 wrappers and receive a 4-card Classic Player of the Year set, featuring Grant Hill, Shaquille O'Neal, Emmitt Smith, and Steve Young; 2) silver-collect 30 wrappers and receive the Classic Player of the Year set and a random autograph card; 3) gold-collect 144 wrappers and receive the Classic Player of the Year set and an autograph card by Muhammad Ali; and 4) platinum-collect 216 wrappers and receive the Classic Player of the Year set plus an autograph card by Shaquille O'Neal. The cards are numbered on the back and checklisted below by sport.

COMPLETE SET (200)	6.00	15.00
1 Glenn Robinson	.40	1.00
2 Jason Kidd	.75	2.00
3 Grant Hill	.50	1.25
4 Donyell Marshall	.15	.40
5 Juwan Howard	.15	.40
6 Sharone Wright	.05	.15
7 Billy McCaffrey	.05	.15
8 Brian Grant	.15	.40
9 Eric Montross	.05	.15
10 Eddie Jones	.40	1.00
11 Carlos Rogers	.05	.15
12 Khalid Reeves	.05	.15
13 Jalen Rose	.30	.75
14 Yinka Dare	.05	.15
15 Eric Piatkowski	.15	.40
16 Clifford Rozier	.05	.15
17 Aaron McKie	.08	.25
18 Eric Mobley	.05	.15
19 Tony Dumas	.05	.15
20 B.J. Tyler	.05	.15
21 Dickey Simpkins	.05	.15
22 Bill Curley	.05	.15
23 Wesley Person	.08	.25
24 Monty Williams	.05	.15
25 Greg Minor	.05	.15
26 Charlie Ward	.15	.40
27 Brooks Thompson	.05	.15
28 Deon Thomas	.05	.15
29 Antonio Lang	.05	.15
30 Howard Eisley	.08	.25
31 Rodney Dent	.05	.15
32 Jim McIlvaine	.05	.15
33 Derrick Alston	.05	.15
34 Gaylon Nickerson	.05	.15
35 Michael Smith	.05	.15
36 Andrei Fetisov	.05	.15
37 Dontonio Wingfield	.05	.15
38 Darrin Hancock	.05	.15
39 Anthony Miller	.05	.15
40 Jeff Webster	.05	.15
41 Arturas Karnishovas	.05	.15
42 Gary Collier	.05	.15
43 Shawnelle Scott	.05	.15
44 Damon Bailey	.05	.15
45 Dwayne Morton	.05	.15
46 Jamie Watson	.05	.15
47 Jevon Crudup	.05	.15
48 Melvin Booker	.05	.15
49 Brian Reese	.05	.15
50 Lawrence Funderburke	.05	.15
189 Glenn Robinson JWA	.15	.40
190 Jason Kidd JWA	.30	.75
191 Grant Hill JWA	.25	.60
192 Donyell Marshall JWA	.05	.15
193 Eric Montross JWA	.05	.15
194 Khalid Reeves JWA	.05	.15
195 Jalen Rose JWA	.15	.40
196 Clifford Rozier JWA	.05	.15
197 Damon Bailey JWA	.05	.15
F01 4-in-1	1.00	2.50
Glenn Robinson		
Dan Wilkinson		
Paul Wilson		
Ed Jovanovski		
Number One Draft Picks		
PC1 Shaquille O'Neal	2.00	5.00
$25 Phone Card		

1994 Classic Four Sport Gold

Seeded one per pack and featuring top rookies from basketball, baseball, football and hockey, the 1994 Classic Four-Sport gold set consists of 200 standard-size cards. The player's name and the Classic Four-Sport logo is on the right side of the picture along with the information that this is a gold card.

COMPLETE SET (200)	12.00	30.00
*GOLD: .8X TO 2X BASIC CARDS		

1994 Classic Four Sport Autographs

Randomly inserted in packs at a rate of one in 103, this standard-size set features players from the 1994 Classic Four-Sport set who autographed cards within the set. The fronts feature full-bleed color action player photos. The player's name is gold-foil stamped across the bottom of the picture. The backs have a congratulatory message about receiving an autographed card. Though the cards are unnumbered, we have assigned them the same number as their four-sport regular issue counterpart.

1A Glenn Robinson/1000	6.00	15.00
2A Jason Kidd/1300	10.00	25.00
5A Juwan Howard/940	5.00	12.00
9A Eric Montross/1000	2.50	6.00
11A Carlos Rogers/660	2.00	5.00
13A Jalen Rose/970	6.00	15.00
15A Eric Piatkowski/1090	2.50	6.00
16A Clifford Rozier/900	2.00	5.00
22A Bill Curley/1120	2.00	5.00
23A Wesley Person/1000	2.00	5.00
24A Monty Williams/1100	2.00	5.00
28A Deon Thomas/1090	2.00	5.00
30A Howard Eisley/970	2.50	6.00
32A Jim McIlvaine/965	2.00	5.00
33A Derrick Alston/1050	2.00	5.00
36A Andrei Fetisov/1080	2.00	5.00
39A Anthony Miller/1000	2.00	5.00
40A Jeff Webster/1070	2.00	5.00
41A Arturas Karnishovas/980	2.00	5.00
42A Gary Collier/1000	2.00	5.00
44A Damon Bailey/1050	2.00	5.00
45A Dwayne Morton/1000	2.00	5.00
46A Jamie Watson/1080	2.00	5.00
47A Jevon Crudup/1180	2.00	5.00
49A Brian Reese/960	2.00	5.00

1994 Classic Four Sport BCs

This 20-card bonus standard-size set was inserted one per '94 Classic Four-Sport jumbo packs. The fronts feature full color player photos. The backs carry biographical and statistical information about the player.

COMPLETE SET (20)	6.00	15.00
BC6 Glenn Robinson	.40	1.00
BC7 Jason Kidd	.75	2.00
BC8 Grant Hill	.50	1.25
BC9 Jalen Rose	.30	.75
BC10 Donyell Marshall	.20	.50
BC11 Juwan Howard	.40	1.00
BC12 Khalid Reeves	.20	.50

1994 Classic Four Sport C3 Collector's Club

The cards were issued to members of the 1995 Classic Collectors Club. Each is numbered 1 of 10,000 on the cardbacks and carries a 1995 copyright line. However, the cards are in the design of the 1994 Classic Four Sport set.

C6 Grant Hill	1.50	4.00
NNO Glenn Robinson	.75	2.00

1994 Classic Four Sport Classic Picks

This 10-card standard-size set was randomly inserted in packs at rate of one in 72. The fronts feature full-color action player photos with the player's name and card title below. The backs carry a small player photo, the player's name, biographical information, and career highlights printed over a ghosted photo of the same player.

COMPLETE SET (10)	6.00	15.00
23 Khalid Reeves	.40	1.00
24 Grant Hill	1.50	4.00

1994 Classic Four Sport High Voltage

This 20-card sequentially-numbered standard-size set features the top draft picks. The cards are printed on holographic foil board with a striking design. 2,995 of each even-numbered card and 5,495 of each odd-numbered cards were produced. The cards were inserted on an average of 3 per case and had stated odds of one in 144 hobby packs. The fronts feature the players against a background of lightning while the backs feature a biography on the left side of the card. The right side shows more lightning and the player's photo.

COMPLETE SET (20)	40.00	100.00
HV2 Glenn Robinson SP	5.00	12.00
HV6 Jason Kidd SP	6.00	15.00
HV10 Grant Hill SP	8.00	20.00
HV14 Donyell Marshall SP	2.00	5.00
HV18 Juwan Howard SP	2.50	6.00

1994 Classic Four Sport Phone Cards $1

This set of eight phone cards was randomly inserted in Four-Sport packs. Printed on hard plastic, each card measures 2 1/8" by 3 3/8" and has rounded corners. The fronts display full-bleed color action photos, with the phone time value ($1, $2, $3, $4 or $5) and the player's name printed vertically in red along the right edge. The horizontal backs carry instructions for use of the cards. The cards are unnumbered and checklisted below in alphabetical order. The $3 and $5 cards were inserted into retail packs. The phone cards could be used until November 30, 1995.

COMPLETE SET (8)	3.00	8.00
*TWO DOLLAR: .5X TO 1.2X $1 CARDS		
*THREE DOLLAR: .6X TO 1.5X $1 CARDS		
*FOUR DOLLAR: .8X TO 2X $1 CARDS		
*FIVE DOLLAR: 1X TO 2.5X $1 CARDS		
*PIN NUMBER REVEALED: HALF VALUE		
5 Jason Kidd	1.00	2.50
7 Glenn Robinson	.40	1.00

1994 Classic Four Sport Previews

Randomly inserted in 1994-95 Classic hockey foil packs at a rate of three per case, these five standard-size preview cards show the design of the 1994-95 Classic Four-Sport series. The full-bleed color action photos are gold-foil stamped with the "4-Sport Preview" emblem and the player's name. The backs feature another full-bleed closeup photo, with biography and statistics displayed on a ghosted panel.

COMPLETE SET (5)	6.00	15.00
P3 Grant Hill	2.00	5.00
P4 Jason Kidd	1.50	4.00

1994 Classic Four Sport Printer's Proofs

Randomly inserted in packs and featuring top rookies from basketball, baseball, football and hockey, the 1994 Classic Four-Sport Printer's Proofs set consists of 200 standard-size cards. The information that this is a printer's proof card is directly above the player's name. Both the printer's proof logo and the name of the player are in red.

*PRINT PROOFS: 2.5X TO 6X BASIC CARDS

1994 Classic Four Sport Shaq-Fu Tip Cards

Inserted one in every 18 packs, this 25-card standard-size set features hints and secret clues to play Shaq-Fu, a new video game for Super Nintendo and Sega systems. The fronts feature the title on the left side along with a computerized photo showing on the right 3/4 of the card. The backs are divided between a computer photo on the left side and a description of what the photo means on the right side of he card. The cards are numbered on the back and checklisted below as follows: Character Profiles (SF1-SF12), Special Moves (SF13-SF24), and Secret Tip (SF25). The cards are also licensed throught Electronic Arts and Dolphine Software International.

COMPLETE SET (25)	3.00	8.00
SF1 Shaq	1.00	2.50

1994 Classic Four Sport Tri-Cards

Inserted one in every three cases, this five-card standard-size set features three top running backs, linebackers, hockey centers, pitchers and basketball guards and compares their individual skills. Every card is sequentially-numbered out of 2,695. The horizontal fronts feature the three players equally while the backs gives a brief biography of why the three players are grouped together.

COMPLETE SET (5)	4.00	10.00
TC3 Jalen Rose	1.25	3.00
Jason Kidd		
Khalid Reeves		

1993 Classic Futures Promo

Classic released this promo card in 1993 to spotlight future NBA superstars. The card measures approximately 2 1/2" by 4 3/4". The front features a color action player photo with full-bleed sides. Above and below the photo is a white bar with gold foil lettering. The upper bar carries the set title and the lower bar carries the Classic logo and the player's name and positon. The back has a second action player shot on the left side with a grey panel to the right containing biography and statistics for 1992-93 season. The words "For Promotional Purposes Only" is printed in the middle of the grey panel. The card is unnumbered.

1 Isaiah Rider	.40	1.00

1993 Classic Futures

These 100 cards measure approximately 2 1/2" by 4 3/4" and feature on their fronts color player action shots with backgrounds that have been thrown out of focus. The card has white borders at the top and bottom. The player's name and position appear in gold-foil lettering within the bottom white margin. The same border design is duplicated on the back, which carries a narrow-cropped color player action shot on the left, and biography, career highlights and statistics on the right.

COMPLETE SET (100)	5.00	10.00
1 Chris Webber	1.25	3.00
2 Bill Edwards	.02	.10
3 Anfernee Hardaway	1.25	3.00
4 Bryan Edwards	.02	.10
5 Jamal Mashburn	.25	.60
6 Doug Edwards	.02	.10
7 Isaiah Rider	.25	.60
8 Chuck Evans	.02	.10
9 Vin Baker	.30	.75
10 Terry Evans	.02	.10
11 Rodney Rogers	.07	.20
12 Will Flemons	.02	.10
13 Lindsey Hunter	.10	.30
14 Alphonso Ford	.02	.10
15 Allan Houston	.50	1.25
16 Josh Grant	.02	.10
17 George Lynch	.02	.10
18 Evric Gray	.02	.10
19 Toni Kukoc	.50	1.25
20 Geert Hammink	.02	.10
21 Ashraf Amaya	.02	.10
22 Lucious Harris	.02	.10
23 Mark Bell	.02	.10
24 Joe Harvell	.02	.10
25 Corie Blount	.02	.10
26 Antonio Harvey	.02	.10
27 Dexter Boney	.02	.10
28 Scott Haskin	.02	.10
29 Tim Brooks	.02	.10
30 Brian Hendrick	.02	.10
31 James Bryson	.02	.10
32 Sascha Hupmann	.02	.10
33 Evers Burns	.02	.10
34 Stanley Jackson	.02	.10
35 Scott Burrell	.02	.10
36 Ervin Johnson	.02	.10
37 Sam Cassell	.40	1.00
38 Adonis Jordan	.02	.10
39 Sam Crawford	.02	.10
40 Warren Kidd	.02	.10
41 Ron Curry	.02	.10
42 Malcolm Mackey	.02	.10
43 William Davis	.02	.10
44 Rich Manning	.02	.10
45 Rodney Dobard	.02	.10
46 Chris McNeal	.02	.10
47 Tony Dunkin	.02	.10
48 Conrad McRae	.02	.10
49 Spencer Dunkley	.02	.10
50 Lance Miller	.02	.10
51 Chris Mills	.10	.30
52 Chris Whitney	.02	.10
53 Matt Nover	.02	.10
54 Steve Worthy	.02	.10
55 Bo Outlaw	.07	.20
56 Luther Wright	.02	.10
57 Eric Pauley	.02	.10
58 Mark Buford	.02	.10
59 Mike Peplowski	.02	.10
60 Mitchell Butler	.02	.10
61 Stacey Poole	.02	.10
62 Brian Clifford	.02	.10
63 Anthony Reed	.02	.10
64 Terry Dehere	.02	.10
65 Eric Riley	.02	.10
66 Acie Earl	.02	.10
67 Darrin Robinson	.02	.10
68 Greg Graham	.02	.10
69 James Robinson	.02	.10
70 Angelo Hamilton	.02	.10
71 Bryon Russell	.10	.30
72 Thomas Hill	.02	.10
73 Brent Scott	.02	.10
74 Khari Jaxon	.02	.10
75 Bennie Seltzer	.02	.10
76 Darnell Mee	.02	.10
77 Ed Stokes	.02	.10
78 Sherron Mills	.02	.10
79 Antoine Stoudamire	.02	.10
80 Gheorghe Muresan	.10	.30
81 Dirk Surles	.02	.10
82 Eddie Vivera	.02	.10
83 Justus Thigpen	.02	.10
84 Julius Nwosu	.02	.10
85 Kevin Thompson	.02	.10
86 Richard Petruska	.02	.10
87 Ray Thompson	.02	.10
88 Bryan Sallier	.02	.10
89 Gary Trost	.02	.10
90 Harper Williams	.02	.10
91 Nick Van Exel	.30	.75
92 Ike Williams	.02	.10
93 Jerry Walker	.02	.10
94 Byron Wilson	.02	.10
95 Rex Walters	.02	.10
96 Alex Holcombe	.02	.10
97 Leonard White	.02	.10
98 Alex Wright	.02	.10
99 Checklist 1-50	.02	.10
100 Checklist 51-100	.02	.10
NNO Shaquille O'Neal Acetate	12.50	30.00

1993 Classic Futures LPs

This 1993 Classic Futures Limited Edition five-card set had a production of 29,500. The cards measure approximately 2 1/2" by 4 3/4". The fronts contain full-bleed color action player photos. The player's name is printed in bold lettering within a wide white bar across the lower edge. The white backs have the number of cards produced prominently displayed across the top of the card. Below is biography, career summary and statistics. The player's name is printed at the bottom. The cards are unnumbered and checklisted below in draft order.

COMPLETE SET (5)	6.00	15.00
LP1 Chris Webber	3.00	8.00
LP2 Anfernee Hardaway	3.00	8.00
LP3 Jamal Mashburn	.60	1.50
LP4 Isaiah Rider	.60	1.50
LP5 Toni Kukoc	1.25	3.00

1993 Classic Futures Team

Randomly inserted in packs, these five cards measure approximately 2 1/2" by 4 3/4" and feature on their fronts elliptical color player action shots set on white backgrounds. The player's name and position appear in gold-foil lettering at the bottom. The back carries a

color player action shot at the top and career highlights at the bottom. The cards are numbered on the back with a "CFT" prefix.
COMPLETE SET (5) 8.00 20.00
CFT1 Chris Webber 4.00 10.00
CFT2 Anfernee Hardaway 4.00 10.00
CFT3 Jamal Mashburn .75 2.00
CFT4 Isaiah Rider .75 2.00
CFT5 Toni Kukoc 1.50 4.00

1993 Classic Superheroes

This purple-bordered three-card standard-size subset features the art work of Neal Adams, who has produced sports and comics fantasy cards of various athletes. It s one of two insert sets included (randomly inserted) in Classic's Deathwatch 2,000 110-card set. The horizontal backs carry a color action player photo with a player profile on a purple background.
COMPLETE SET (3) 8.00 20.00
SS1 Shaquille O'Neal 3.00 8.00

1996 Clear Assets

The 1996 Clear Assets set was issued in one series totaling 70 cards. The set features 75 upscale acetate cards of the most collectible athletes from baseball, basketball, football, hockey and auto racing. Also included is the debut appearance by many of the top players entering the 1996 football draft. Release date was April 1996.
COMPLETE SET (70) 6.00 15.00
1 Shaquille O'Neal .60 1.50
2 Hakeem Olajuwon .30 .75
3 Scottie Pippen .30 .75
4 Alonzo Mourning .15 .40
5 Damon Stoudamire .25 .60
6 Jerry Stackhouse .30 .75
7 Joe Smith .25 .60
8 Antonio McDyess .30 .75
9 Rasheed Wallace .20 .50
10 Kevin Garnett 1.50 4.00
11 Shawn Respert .08 .25
12 Ed O'Bannon .10 .30
13 Kurt Thomas .08 .25
14 Gary Trent .10 .30
15 Cherokee Parks .08 .25
16 Corliss Williamson .08 .25
17 Eric Williams .08 .25
18 Brent Barry .08 .25
19 Bob Sura .08 .25
20 Michael Finley .40 1.00
21 Jimmy King .08 .25
22 Jason Kidd .30 .75
23 Dikembe Mutombo .15 .40
24 Greg Ostertag .08 .25
25 Cory Alexander .08 .25
26 Glenn Robinson .10 .30
27 Tyus Edney .08 .25
28 Rebecca Lobo .20 .50

1996 Clear Assets 3X

Randomly inserted in packs at a rate of one in 100, this 10-card set is another first from Classic. The cards resemble triplexed cards with acetate in the middle and an opaque covering.
COMPLETE SET (10) 40.00 100.00
X2 Rasheed Wallace 4.00 10.00
X3 Rebecca Lobo 5.00 12.00
X6 Joe Smith 3.00 8.00
X7 Damon Stoudamire 6.00 15.00
X9 Jerry Stackhouse 4.00 10.00

1996 Clear Assets Phone Cards $1

COMPLETE SET (30) 5.00 12.00
*PIN NUMBER REVEALED: HALF VALUE
$1 CARDS ONE PER RETAIL PACK
*$2 CARDS: .6X TO 1.5X $1 CARDS
ONE PER HOBBY PACK
CARDS EXPIRED 10/1/97
1 Shaquille O'Neal .60 1.50
3 Jerry Stackhouse .25 .60
9 Jason Kidd .15 .40
13 Joe Smith .15 .40
15 Damon Stoudamire .20 .50
17 Hakeem Olajuwon .20 .50
20 Dikembe Mutombo .15 .40
25 Alonzo Mourning .20 .50
28 Rasheed Wallace .20 .50
29 Ed O'Bannon .10 .30
30 Michael Finley .30 .75

1996 Clear Assets Phone Cards $10

Inserted at a rate of 1:30 packs, this 10-card set of acetate phone cards features many of the biggest names in sports. The Sprint phone cards carry expiration dates of 10/1/97.
COMPLETE SET (10) 20.00 50.00
*PIN NUMBER REVEALED:HALF VALUE
1 Shaquille O'Neal 3.00 8.00
6 Joe Smith 1.00 2.50
9 Scottie Pippen 1.25 3.00
10 Jason Kidd 1.50 4.00

1996 Clear Assets Phone Cards $5

Inserted at a rate of 1:10 packs, this 20-card set of acetate phone cards features many of the biggest names in sports. The Sprint phone cards carry expiration dates of 10/1/97.
COMPLETE SET (20) 12.00 30.00
*PIN NUMBER REVEALED:HALF VALUE
1 Shaquille O'Neal 2.00 5.00
3 Jerry Stackhouse .60 1.25
8 Jason Kidd 1.00 2.50
9 Brent Barry .30 .75
11 Joe Smith .30 .75
13 Hakeem Olajuwon .75 2.00
14 Dikembe Mutombo .40 1.00
18 Alonzo Mourning .50 1.25

1995 Collect-A-Card

This 100-card standard-size set features fronts with color action player photos. The player's name is printed vertically in gold foil on the side and his position in silver below. The horizontal backs carry the player's name, position, biographical information, career highlights and statistics.
COMPLETE SET (100) 4.00 10.00
1 Cory Alexander .10 .25
2 Mario Bennett .10 .25
3 Travis Best .10 .25
4 Jason Caffey .10 .25
5 Randolph Childress .10 .25
6 Michael Finley .30 .75
7 Sherrell Ford .10 .25
8 Kevin Garnett .75 2.00
9 Alan Henderson .10 .25
10 Antonio McDyess .25 .60
11 Loren Meyer .10 .25
12 Ed O'Bannon .10 .25
13 Greg Ostertag .10 .25
14 Cherokee Parks .10 .25
15 Theo Ratliff .15 .40
16 Bryant Reeves .10 .25
17 Shawn Respert .10 .25
18 Joe Smith .20 .50
19 Jerry Stackhouse .30 .75
20 Damon Stoudamire .25 .60
21 Bob Sura .10 .25
22 Kurt Thomas .10 .25
23 Gary Trent .10 .25
24 Rasheed Wallace .30 .75
25 Eric Williams .10 .25
26 Corliss Williamson .10 .25
27 George Zidek .10 .25
28 Alan Henderson .10 .25
29 Donnie Boyce .10 .25
30 Cuonzo Martin .10 .25
31 Eric Williams .10 .25
32 Junior Burrough .10 .25
33 Bob Sura .10 .25
34 Donny Marshall .10 .25
35 George Zidek .10 .25
36 Jason Caffey .10 .25
37 Cherokee Parks .10 .25
38 Loren Meyer .10 .25
39 Anthony Pelle .10 .25
40 Theo Ratliff .15 .40
41 Randolph Childress .10 .25
42 Lou Roe .10 .25
43 Andrew DeClercq .10 .25
44 Michael McDonald .10 .25
45 Travis Best .10 .25
46 Fred Hoiberg .10 .25
47 Antonio McDyess .25 .60
48 Constantin Popa .10 .25
49 Kurt Thomas .10 .25
50 Gary Trent .10 .25
51 Eric Snow .10 .25
52 Kevin Garnett .75 2.00
53 Larry Sykes .10 .25
54 Jerome Allen .10 .25
55 Ed O'Bannon .10 .25
56 Jerry Stackhouse .30 .75
57 Michael Finley .30 .75
58 Mario Bennett .10 .25
59 Shawn Respert .10 .25
60 Corliss Williamson .10 .25
61 Tyus Edney .10 .25
62 Cory Alexander .10 .25
63 Sherrell Ford .10 .25
64 Damon Stoudamire .25 .60
65 Jimmy King .10 .25
66 Greg Ostertag .10 .25
67 Bryant Reeves .10 .25
68 Lawrence Moten .10 .25
69 Terrence Rencher .10 .25
70 Corey Beck .10 .25
71 Bryan Collins .10 .25
72 Dan Cross .10 .25
73 Joe Smith .20 .50
74 Michael Hawkins .10 .25
75 Scott Highmark .10 .25
76 Ray Jackson .10 .25
77 Tom Kleinschmidt .10 .25
78 Matt Maloney .10 .25
79 Clint McDaniel .10 .25
80 Julius Michalik .10 .25
81 Paul O'Liney .10 .25
82 Randy Rutherford .10 .25
83 James Scott .10 .25
84 Dwight Stewart .10 .25
85 Scotty Thurman .10 .25
86 Rasheed Wallace .30 .75
87 John Amaechi .10 .25
88 Jamal Faulkner .10 .25
89 Jerry Stackhouse .15 .40
Rasheed Wallace
90 Scotty Thurman .05 .15
Corey Beck
Clint McDaniel
91 Loren Meyer .05 .15
Julius Michalik
Fred Hoiberg
92 Ed O'Bannon .05 .15
Tyus Edney
93 Cory Alexander .05 .15
Junior Burrough
94 Antonio McDyess .12 .30
Jason Caffey
95 Bryant Reeves .05 .15
Randy Rutherford
96 Matt Maloney .05 .15
Jerome Allen
97 Ray Jackson .05 .15
Jimmy King
98 Shawn Respert .05 .15
Eric Snow
99 Andrew DeClercq .05 .15
Dan Cross
100 Checklist (1-100) .05 .15

1995 Collect-A-Card 2 on 1

Randomly inserted in packs at a rate of one in 21, this 10-card set measures the standard size. The fronts display a color action cut-out of a player on a metallic patterned background. The player's name and his school logo are below. The card's name is printed vertically in a wide bar at the side. The backs carry a color action cut-out of another player on the same background with his name below. Sponsors' logos are displayed in a wide bar at the side. The cards are numbered with a "T" prefix.
COMPLETE SET (10) 5.00 12.00
T1 Antonio McDyess 1.00 2.50
Kurt Thomas
T2 Jerry Stackhouse 3.00 8.00
Kevin Garnett
T3 Ed O'Bannon .40 1.00
Corliss Williamson
T4 Michael Finley 1.25 3.00
Mario Bennett
T5 Tyus Edney 1.00 2.50
Damon Stoudamire
T6 Joe Smith 1.25 3.00
Rasheed Wallace
T7 Cherokee Parks .40 1.00
Bryant Reeves
T8 Greg Ostertag .40 1.00
George Zidek
T9 Shawn Respert .40 1.00
Jerome Allen
T10 Sherrell Ford .40 1.00
Randolph Childress

1995 Collect-A-Card 24K Gold

This 4-card set was issued as redemption's at the rate of one per case. Four hundred cards were made of each player. Once redeemed, each card contained 1 gram of .999 pure 24 karat gold.
1 Kevin Garnett 100.00 200.00
2 Ed O'Bannon 40.00 100.00
3 Joe Smith 40.00 100.00
4 Jerry Stackhouse 75.00 150.00

1995 Collect-A-Card Ignition

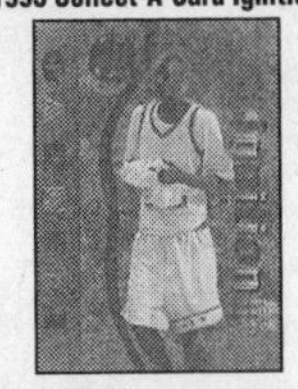

Randomly inserted in packs at a rate of one in 5, this 15-card set measures the standard size. The fronts feature a color action player cut-out on a metallic marble background with the player's name printed vertically in a gold border on one side. The backs carry a small color action player photo with the player's name and small career summary. Card and sponsor logos are below. The cards are numbered with an "I" prefix.
COMPLETE SET (15) 2.50 6.00
I1 Travis Best .20 .50
I2 Randolph Childress .20 .50
I3 Michael Finley .60 1.50
I4 Sherrell Ford .20 .50
I5 Alan Henderson .20 .50
I6 Shawn Respert .20 .50
I7 Jerry Stackhouse .60 1.50
I8 Damon Stoudamire .50 1.25
I9 Bob Sura .20 .50
I10 Gary Trent .20 .50
I11 Kevin Garnett 1.50 4.00
I12 Lou Roe .20 .50
I13 Tyus Edney .20 .50
I14 Fred Hoiberg .20 .50
I15 Jerome Allen .20 .50

1995 Collect-A-Card Liftoff

Randomly inserted in packs at a rate of one in 5, this 15-card set measures the standard size. The fronts feature a color action player cut-out on a patterned silver background. The player's name runs horizontally and vertically on a colored bar. The school logo and card name round out the front. The backs carry a small player photo with the player's name and short career summary. The cards are numbered with a "L" prefix.
COMPLETE SET (15) 1.50 4.00
L1 Cory Alexander .20 .50
L2 Mario Bennett .20 .50
L3 Joe Smith .40 1.00
L4 Constantin Popa .20 .50
L5 Antonio McDyess .50 1.25
L6 Loren Meyer .20 .50
L7 Ed O'Bannon .20 .50
L8 Greg Ostertag .20 .50
L9 Cherokee Parks .20 .50
L10 Theo Ratliff .30 .75
L11 Bryant Reeves .20 .50
L12 Kurt Thomas .20 .50
L13 Eric Williams .20 .50
L14 Corliss Williamson .20 .50
L15 Rasheed Wallace .60 1.50

1995 Collect-A-Card Stackhouse

Randomly inserted in packs, this 5-card set measures the standard size. The fronts display a player action photo in a beige frame on a light blue background. The backs carry a short discription of some phase of Jerry Stackhouse's career. The cards are numbered with a "J" prefix.
COMPLETE SET (5) 4.00 10.00
COMMON CARD (J1-J5) 1.25 3.00

1995 Collect-A-Card Stackhouse Autographs

Randomly inserted in packs, this 5-card set measures the standard size. The fronts display a player action photo in a beige frame on a light blue background. The backs carry a short description of some phase of Jerry Stackhouse's career. The cards are numbered with a "J" prefix.
FH1 Jerry Stackhouse/400 6.00 15.00
FH2 Jerry Stackhouse/275 8.00 20.00
FH3 Jerry Stackhouse/175 10.00 25.00
FH4 Jerry Stackhouse/100 12.50 30.00
FH5 Jerry Stackhouse/50 30.00 60.00

1996 Collector's Edge

The 1996 Collector's Edge Rookie Rage set was issued in one series totaling 50 cards. The card fronts have player photo on a foil, etched background. "Rookie Rage" is written vertically on the left. The backs have a close-up photo and career collegiate statistics. There were two parallel versions to the base set. One die-cut and one gold foil. Both were inserted at the rate of 1 in every 2 retail packs. Also note the prototype card is not included in the number of cards in the complete set or the complete set price.
COMPLETE SET (50) 4.00 10.00
1 Shareef Abdur-Rahim .30 .75
2 Ray Allen .60 1.50
3 Drew Barry .15 .40
4 Terrell Bell .15 .40
5 Joseph Blair .15 .40
6 Kobe Bryant 1.50 4.00
7 Marcus Camby .25 .60
8 Erick Dampier .15 .40
9 Ben Davis .15 .40
10 Tony Delk .15 .40
11 Brian Evans .15 .40
12 Jamie Feick .15 .40
13 Derek Fisher .30 .75
14 Todd Fuller .15 .40
15 Steve Hamer .15 .40
16 Othella Harrington .15 .40
17 Mark Hendrickson .15 .40
18 Reggie Geary .15 .40
19 Allen Iverson .75 2.00
20 Dontae' Jones .15 .40
21 Kerry Kittles .15 .40
22 Travis Knight .15 .40
23 Priest Lauderdale .15 .40
24 Randy Livingston .15 .40
25 Marcus Mann .15 .40
26 Stephon Marbury .40 1.00
27 Walter McCarty .15 .40
28 Amal McCaskill .15 .40
29 Jeff McInnis .15 .40
30 Ryan Minor .20 .50
31 Darnell Robinson .15 .40
32 Steve Nash .75 2.00
33 Moochie Norris .15 .40
34 Jermaine O'Neal .40 1.00
35 Mark Pope .15 .40
36 Vitaly Potapenko .15 .40
37 Shandon Anderson .15 .40
38 Ron Riley .15 .40
39 Roy Rogers .15 .40
40 Malik Rose .20 .50
41 Jason Sasser .15 .40
42 Doron Sheffer .15 .40
43 Ronnie Henderson .15 .40
44 Antoine Walker .30 .75
45 Samaki Walker .15 .40
46 John Wallace .15 .40
47 Jerome Williams .15 .40
48 Lorenzen Wright .15 .40
49 Checklist (1-25) .08 .25
50 Checklist (26-50) .08 .25
P1 Marcus Camby PROMO .60 1.50

1996 Collector's Edge Die Cuts

This 50-card set is an exact parallel of the base set, found one in every two retail packs. The cards are beveled round at the top and in the bottom left corner. "Rookie Rage" is written in gold foil. To ascertain values on individual cards, please refer to the multiplier in the header below, coupled with the value of the base card.
*STARS: .75X TO 2X BASE CARD HI

1996 Collector's Edge Gold

This 50-card set is an exact parallel of the base set, found one in every two retail packs. The cards contain gold foil. To ascertain values on individual cards, please refer to the multiplier in the header below, coupled with the value of the base card.
*STARS: .75X TO 2X BASE CARD HI

1996 Collector's Edge Ice Sculpture

The exact origin of this parallel is unknown - possibly something released after the bankruptcy - but this set parallels the first 48 cards from the regular Collector's Edge set. The cards feature acetate and are die cut.
*ICE: 3X TO 8X BASE HI

1996 Collector's Edge Key Kraze

Randomly inserted in packs at a rate of one in 24 and serially numbered to 3,200, this 24 cards are produced with a "metalized rainbow embossed" front.
COMPLETE SET (24) 25.00 60.00
*DIE CUTS: .4X TO 1X BASE HI
DIE CUTS PRINT RUN 3100 SER.#'d SETS
*GOLD: 1X TO 2.5X KEY KRAZE HI
GOLD PRINT RUN 1000 SER.#'d SETS
1 Shareef Abdur-Rahim 2.00 5.00
2 Ray Allen 4.00 10.00
3 Kobe Bryant 10.00 25.00
4 Marcus Camby 1.50 4.00
5 Erick Dampier 1.00 2.50
6 Tony Delk 1.00 2.50
7 Todd Fuller 1.00 2.50
8 Reggie Geary 1.00 2.50
9 Allen Iverson 5.00 12.00
10 Dontae' Jones 1.00 2.50
11 Kerry Kittles 1.00 2.50
12 Stephon Marbury 2.50 6.00
13 Walter McCarty 1.00 2.50
14 Darnell Robinson 1.00 2.50
15 Steve Nash 5.00 12.00
16 Ben Davis 1.00 2.50
17 Mark Pope 1.00 2.50
18 Roy Rogers 1.00 2.50
19 Ronnie Henderson 1.00 2.50
20 Antoine Walker 2.00 5.00
21 Samaki Walker 1.00 2.50
22 John Wallace 1.00 2.50
23 Jerome Williams 1.00 2.50
24 Lorenzen Wright 1.00 2.50
CK Checklist (1-24) .40 1.00
PR1 Kerry Kittles PROMO .40 1.00

1996 Collector's Edge Key Kraze Factory Set

These cards were only issued via factory sets and instead of the standard serial numbering on the card backs, they state "Factory Set". Please refer to the multipliers in the headers below, coupled with the value of the base insert, for pricing.
*FACTORY SET: .2X TO .5X BASE HI

1996 Collector's Edge Key Kraze Holofoil

Randomly inserted in packs at one in 72 and serially numbered to 2,000, this 24-card set parallels the regular Key Kraze insert. The cards feature holofoil. To ascertain values for individual cards, please refer to the multiplier in the header below, coupled with the value of the base insert.
*HOLOFOIL: .5X TO 1.25X VALUE
PR1 Kerry Kittles PROMO .60 1.50

1996 Collector's Edge Radical Recruits

Randomly inserted in packs at a rate of one in 8 and serially numbered to 6,750, this 24-card set were produced with metalized fronts.
COMPLETE SET (24) 12.00 30.00
*GOLD: 1.5X TO 4X RAD.REC.HI
GOLD PRINT RUN 1,000 SER.#'d SETS
1 Shareef Abdur-Rahim 1.25 3.00
2 Ray Allen 2.50 6.00
3 Kobe Bryant 6.00 15.00
4 Marcus Camby 1.00 2.50
5 Erick Dampier .60 1.50
6 Tony Delk .60 1.50
7 Todd Fuller .60 1.50
8 Allen Iverson 3.00 8.00
9 Dontae' Jones .60 1.50
10 Kerry Kittles .60 1.50
11 Darnell Robinson .60 1.50
12 Stephon Marbury 1.50 4.00
13 Walter McCarty .60 1.50
14 Steve Nash 3.00 8.00
15 Ben Davis .60 1.50
16 Reggie Geary .60 1.50
17 Mark Pope .60 1.50
18 Roy Rogers .60 1.50
19 Ronnie Henderson .60 1.50
20 Antoine Walker 1.25 3.00
21 Samaki Walker .60 1.50
22 John Wallace .60 1.50
23 Jerome Williams .60 1.50
24 Lorenzen Wright .60 1.50
PR1 Allen Iverson PROMO .60 1.50
NNO Checklist (1-24) .20 .50

1996 Collector's Edge Radical Recruits Factory Set

These cards were only issued via factory sets and instead of the standard serial numbering on the card backs, they state "Factory Set". Please refer to the multipliers in the headers below, coupled with the value of the base insert, for pricing.
*FACTORY SET: .2X TO .5X BASE HI

1996 Collector's Edge Radical Recruits Holofoil

Randomly inserted in packs at one in 36 and serially numbered to 2,500, this 24-card set parallels the Radical Recruits insert. The cards feature holofoil. To ascertain values on individual cards, please refer to the multiplier in the header, coupled with the value of the base insert.
*HOLOFOIL: 1.25X TO 3X VALUE
PR1 Allen Iverson PROMO 1.00 2.50

1996 Collector's Edge Time Warp

Randomly inserted in packs at a rate of one in 8 and serially numbered to 12,000, this 12-card set puts one pro legend up against the 1996-97 rookie class.
COMPLETE SET (12) 8.00 20.00
*GOLD: 1.5X TO 4X TIME WARP HI
GOLD STATED PRINT RUN 1,000 SETS
*HOLOFOIL: 1.25X TO 3X TIME WARP HI
HOLOFOIL STATED PRINT RUN 2,500 SETS
1 Shareef Abdur-Rahim .75 2.00
David Thompson
2 Ray Allen 1.50 4.00
Alex English
3 Kobe Bryant 4.00 10.00
Alex English
4 Marcus Camby .60 1.50
Moses Malone
5 Erick Dampier .40 1.00
George Gervin
6 Allen Iverson 2.00 5.00
Isiah Thomas
7 Kerry Kittles .40 1.00
Isiah Thomas
8 Stephon Marbury 1.00 2.50
David Thompson
9 Antoine Walker .75 2.00
Moses Malone
10 Samaki Walker .40 1.00
Walt Frazier
11 John Wallace .40 1.00
George Gervin
12 Lorenzen Wright .40 1.00
Walt Frazier
P1 Antoine Walker .60 1.50
Moses Malone PROMO
NNO Checklist (1-12) .20 .50

1996 Collector's Edge Time Warp Factory Set

These cards were only issued via factory sets and instead of the standard serial numbering on the card backs, they state "Factory Set". Please refer to the multipliers in the headers below, coupled with the value of the base insert, for pricing.
COMPLETE SET (12)
*FACTORY SET: .4X TO 1X BASE HI

1996 Collector's Edge Time Warp Vintage Autographs

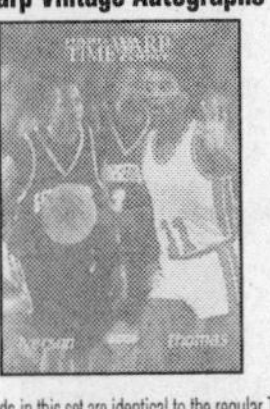

The 6 cards in this set are identical to the regular Time Warp cards, except they are signed by the vintage player in black ink. The card backs are serial numbered with an "AU" prefix and are limited to 1,000 of each card. The set is skip-numbered as each player only signed one version of his two cards in the base set. Cards were randomly inserted into packs.
COMPLETE SET (6) 20.00 50.00
3 Kobe Bryant 3.00 8.00
Alex English AU
5 Erick Dampier 6.00 15.00
George Gervin AU
6 Allen Iverson 5.00 12.00
Isiah Thomas AU
8 Stephon Marbury 3.00 8.00
David Thompson AU
9 Antoine Walker 8.00 20.00
Moses Malone AU
10 Samaki Walker 4.00 10.00
Walt Frazier AU

1997 Collector's Edge Promos

These six cards where issued as promotional cards for the forthcoming 1997 Collector's Edge set. The fronts have player photos and a bronze statue of the player image in the bottom right corner. The backs contain biographical information and 1996-97 statistics. The cards are numbered "PROMO x-6".
COMPLETE SET 3.00 8.00
1 Tim Duncan 2.50 6.00
2 Scottie Pippen .60 1.50
3 Ron Mercer .50 1.25
4 Keith Van Horn .75 2.00
5 Antonio Daniels .40 1.00
6 Kobe Bryant 2.00 5.00

1997 Collector's Edge

This 45-card set features borderless color action photos of both rookies and veterans printed on 16 pt. card stock with gold foil and gloss matte highlights. The backs carry player information.
COMPLETE SET (45) 3.00 8.00
1 Tim Duncan .60 1.50
2 Keith Van Horn .20 .50
3 Kebu Stewart .10 .25
4 Antonio Daniels .10 .25
5 Tony Battie .12 .30
6 Ron Mercer .12 .30
7 Tim Thomas .20 .50
8 Adonal Foyle .10 .25
9 Chauncey Billups .40 1.00
10 Danny Fortson .10 .25
11 Austin Croshere .10 .25
12 Derek Anderson .10 .25
13 Antoine Walker .10 .25
14 Kobe Bryant .50 1.25
15 Shareef Abdur-Rahim .10 .25
16 Stephon Marbury .12 .30
17 Scottie Pippen .15 .40
18 Kelvin Cato .10 .25
19 Scot Pollard .10 .25
20 Paul Grant .10 .25
21 Anthony Parker .10 .25
22 Ed Gray .10 .25
23 Bobby Jackson .12 .30
24 John Thomas .10 .25
25 Charles Smith .10 .25
26 Jacque Vaughn .10 .25
27 Keith Booth .10 .25
28 Charles O'Bannon .10 .25
29 James Collins .10 .25
30 Marc Jackson .10 .25
31 Anthony Johnson .10 .25
32 Jason Lawson .10 .25
33 Alvin Williams .10 .25
34 DeJuan Wheat .10 .25
35 Nate Erdmann .10 .25
36 Olivier Saint-Jean .10 .25
37 Serge Zwikker .10 .25
38 Antoine Walker .10 .25
39 Kobe Bryant .50 1.25
40 Shareef Abdur-Rahim .10 .25
41 Stephon Marbury .12 .30
42 Scottie Pippen .15 .40
43 Checklist 1 .10 .25
44 Checklist 2 .10 .25
45 Checklist 3 .10 .25

1997 Collector's Edge Air Apparent

Randomly inserted in packs at the rate of one in 72, this 15-card set features double color action player images printed on double metal 40 mil card stock with a basketball background. One player image is faded while the other is sharp and bright. The backs carry player information.
COMPLETE SET (15) 25.00 60.00
1 Tim Duncan 12.50 30.00
Scottie Pippen
2 Keith Van Horn 12.50 25.00
Kobe Bryant
3 Olivier St.Jean 2.00 5.00
Shareef Abdur-Rahim
4 Antonio Daniels 2.00 5.00
Stephon Marbury
5 Tony Battie 2.50 6.00
Scottie Pippen
6 Ron Mercer 2.00 5.00
Stephon Marbury
7 Tim Thomas 4.00 10.00
Kobe Bryant
8 Adonal Foyle 2.00 5.00
Shareef Abdur-Rahim
9 Chauncey Billups 2.50 6.00
Stephon Marbury
10 Danny Fortson 2.00 5.00
Scottie Pippen
11 Antoine Walker 2.00 5.00
12 Derek Anderson 5.00 12.00
Kobe Bryant
13 Kelvin Cato 2.00 5.00
Shareef Abdur-Rahim
14 Antoine Walker 2.00 5.00
15 Antoine Walker 2.00 5.00

1997 Collector's Edge Energy

Randomly inserted in packs at the rate of one in 12, this 12-card set features color action player images on an animation card highlighted by a glass-shattering backboard.
COMPLETE SET (12) 4.00 10.00
1 Antonio Daniels .30 .75
2 Austin Croshere .30 .75
3 Charles O'Bannon .30 .75
4 Scot Pollard .30 .75
5 Paul Grant .30 .75
6 Danny Fortson .30 .75
7 Keith Van Horn .60 1.50
8 Kelvin Cato .30 .75
9 Ron Mercer .40 1.00
10 Tim Duncan 2.00 5.00
11 Tim Thomas .60 1.50
12 Chauncey Billups 1.25 3.00
NNO Checklist .30 .75

1997 Collector's Edge Extra

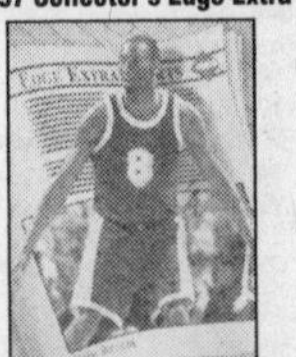

This 12-card insert set features color action photos of top rookies and veterans printed on textured embossed card stock with a newspaper extra edition background. Only 100 of this set were produced and could be obtained by special redemption cards inserted into packs at the rate of one in 48. Only 100 of these redemption cards were also produced.
COMPLETE SET (12) 75.00 150.00
1 Tim Duncan 20.00 50.00
2 Keith Van Horn 6.00 15.00
3 Olivier Saint-Jean 3.00 8.00

4 Antonio Daniels 3.00 8.00
5 Tony Battie 4.00 10.00
6 Ron Mercer 4.00 10.00
7 Tim Thomas 6.00 15.00
8 Antoine Walker 5.00 12.00
9 Kobe Bryant 25.00 60.00
10 Shareef Abdur-Rahim 5.00 12.00
11 Stephon Marbury 6.00 15.00
12 Scottie Pippen 8.00 20.00

1997 Collector's Edge Game Ball

Randomly inserted in packs at the rate of one in 36, this five-card set features color photos of top players with an actual medallion of an authentic game used basketball embedded in each card.

1 Antoine Walker 3.00 8.00
2 Kobe Bryant 10.00 25.00
3 Shareef Abdur-Rahim 3.00 8.00
4 Stephon Marbury 4.00 10.00
5 Scottie Pippen 6.00 15.00

1997 Collector's Edge Hardcourt Force

Randomly inserted in packs at the rate of one in 36, this 25-card set features color player photos printed using metal holofoil technology and forming a puzzle background.

COMPLETE SET (25) 20.00 50.00
1 Chauncey Billups 4.00 10.00
2 Tony Battie 1.25 3.00
3 Tim Duncan 6.00 15.00
4 Paul Grant 1.00 2.50
5 John Thomas 1.00 2.50
6 Scottie Pippen 1.50 4.00
7 Scot Pollard 1.00 2.50
8 Ron Mercer 1.25 3.00
9 Tim Thomas 2.00 5.00
10 Kobe Bryant 5.00 12.00
11 Antonio Daniels 1.00 2.50
12 Kelvin Cato 1.00 2.50
13 Danny Fortson 1.00 2.50
14 Ed Gray 1.00 2.50
15 Derek Anderson 1.00 2.50
16 Bobby Jackson 1.25 3.00
17 Antoine Walker 1.00 2.50
18 Anthony Parker 1.00 2.50
19 Shareef Abdur-Rahim 1.00 2.50
20 Olivier Saint-Jean 1.00 2.50
21 Stephon Marbury 1.25 3.00
22 Keith Van Horn 2.00 5.00
23 Austin Croshere 1.00 2.50
24 Adonal Foyle 1.00 2.50
25 Serge Zwikker 1.00 2.50

1997 Collector's Edge Swoosh

Randomly inserted in packs at the rate of one in 24, this 12-card set features color player images printed on clear acetate, foil-stamped cards viewable from both sides.

COMPLETE SET (12) 8.00 20.00
1 Adonal Foyle .60 1.50
2 Keith Booth .60 1.50
3 Danny Fortson .60 1.50
4 Derek Anderson .60 1.50
5 Jacque Vaughn .60 1.50
6 Keith Van Horn 1.25 3.00
7 Kelvin Cato .60 1.50
8 Ron Mercer .75 2.00
9 Tim Duncan 4.00 10.00
10 Tony Battie .75 2.00
11 Chauncey Billups 2.50 6.00
12 Charles O'Bannon .60 1.50
13 Checklist .60 1.50

1997 Collector's Edge Impulse

The 1997 Collector's Edge Impulse product was released in 1997, and featured a 42-card base set. Each card is diecut, and the top of each card is rounded off to resemble a basketball.

1 Tim Duncan .60 1.50
2 Keith Van Horn .20 .50
3 Kebu Stewart .10 .25
4 Antonio Daniels .10 .25
5 Tony Battie .12 .30
6 Ron Mercer .12 .30
7 Tim Thomas .20 .50
8 Adonal Foyle .10 .25
9 Chauncey Billups .40 1.00
10 Danny Fortson .10 .25
11 Austin Croshere .10 .25
12 Derek Anderson .10 .25
13 Antoine Walker .10 .25
14 Kobe Bryant .50 1.25
15 Shareef Abdur-Rahim .10 .25
16 Stephon Marbury .12 .30
17 Scottie Pippen .15 .40
18 Kelvin Cato .10 .25
19 Scot Pollard .10 .25
20 Paul Grant .10 .25
21 Anthony Parker .10 .25
22 Ed Gray .10 .25
23 Bobby Jackson .12 .30
24 John Thomas .10 .25
25 Charles Smith .10 .25
26 Jacque Vaughn .10 .25
27 Keith Booth .10 .25
28 Charles O'Bannon .10 .25
29 James Collins .10 .25
30 Marc Jackson .10 .25
31 Anthony Johnson .10 .25
32 Jason Lawson .10 .25
33 Alvin Williams .10 .25
34 DeJuan Wheat .10 .25
35 Nate Erdmann .10 .25
36 Olivier Saint-Jean .10 .25
37 Serge Zwikker .10 .25
38 Antoine Walker .10 .25
39 Kobe Bryant .50 1.25
40 Shareef Abdur-Rahim .10 .25
41 Stephon Marbury .12 .30
42 Scottie Pippen .15 .40

1998 Collector's Edge Impulse

The 1998-99 Collector's Edge Impulse set was issued in one series totalling 100 cards. The set contains the topical subsets: All American (33-42), All Rookie (43-50), and Rookie+Veteran (51-100).

COMPLETE SET (100) 7.50 15.00
1 Michael Olowokandi .12 .30
2 Antawn Jamison .25 .60
3 Vince Carter .50 1.25
4 Robert Traylor .10 .25
5 Jason Williams .25 .60
6 Paul Pierce .50 1.25
7 Bonzi Wells .10 .25
8 Keon Clark .10 .25
9 Kobe Bryant CL .30 .75
9B Radoslav Nesterovic .10 .25
10 Pat Garrity .10 .25
11 Ricky Davis .15 .40
12 Tyronn Lue .10 .25
13 Felipe Lopez .10 .25
14 Al Harrington .15 .40
15 Corey Benjamin .10 .25
16 Rashard Lewis .25 .60
17 Jelani McCoy .10 .25
18 Shammond Williams .10 .25
19 DeMarco Johnson .10 .25
20 Korleone Young .10 .25
21 Miles Simon .10 .25
22 Toby Bailey .10 .25
23 J.R. Henderson .10 .25
24 Zendon Hamilton .10 .25
25 Jeff Sheppard .10 .25
26 Kobe Bryant .50 1.25
27 Stephon Marbury .12 .30
28 Tracy McGrady .15 .40
29 Scottie Pippen .15 .40
30 Tim Thomas .10 .25
31 Michael Olowokandi CL .07 .20
32 Antawn Jamison CL .15 .40
33 Michael Olowokandi AA .07 .20
34 Antawn Jamison AA .15 .40
35 Vince Carter AA .30 .75
36 Robert Traylor AA .05 .15
37 Jason Williams AA .15 .40
38 Paul Pierce AA .30 .75
39 Bonzi Wells AA .05 .15
40 Keon Clark AA .05 .15
41 Radoslav Nesterovic AA .05 .15
42 Pat Garrity AA .05 .15
43 Michael Olowokandi AR .07 .20
44 Antawn Jamison AR .15 .40
45 Vince Carter AR .30 .75
46 Robert Traylor AR .05 .15
47 Jason Williams AR .15 .40
48 Paul Pierce AR .30 .75
49 Bonzi Wells AR .05 .15
50 Keon Clark AR .05 .15
51 Paul Pierce / Kobe Bryant .30 .75
52 Paul Pierce / Scottie Pippen .25 .60
53 Antawn Jamison / Stephon Marbury .20 .50
54 Antawn Jamison / Tracy McGrady .20 .50
55 Michael Olowokandi / Tim Thomas .15 .40
56 Michael Olowokandi / Kobe Bryant .30 .75
57 Keon Clark / Scottie Pippen .15 .40
58 Keon Clark / Stephon Marbury .15 .40
59 Pat Garrity / Tracy McGrady .15 .40
60 Pat Garrity / Tim Thomas .15 .40
61 Corey Benjamin / Kobe Bryant .30 .75
62 Corey Benjamin / Scottie Pippen .15 .40
63 Robert Traylor / Stephon Marbury .15 .40
64 Robert Traylor / Tracy McGrady .15 .40
65 Rashard Lewis / Tim Thomas .15 .40
66 Rashard Lewis / Kobe Bryant .30 .75
67 Bonzi Wells / Scottie Pippen .15 .40
68 Bonzi Wells / Stephon Marbury .15 .40
69 J.R.Henderson / Tracy McGrady .15 .40
70 J.R.Henderson / Tim Thomas .15 .40
71 Tobe Bailey / Kobe Bryant .30 .75
72 Toby Bailey / Scottie Pippen .15 .40
73 Tyronn Lue / Stephon Marbury .15 .40
74 Tyronn Lue / Tracy McGrady .15 .40
75 Radoslav Nesterovic / Tim Thomas .15 .40
76 Radoslov Nesterovic / Kobe Bryant .30 .75
77 Miles Simon / Scottie Pippen .15 .40
78 Miles Simon / Stephon Marbury .15 .40
79 Jeff Sheppard / Tracy McGrady .15 .40
80 Jeff Sheppard / Tim Thomas .15 .40
81 Felipe Lopez / Kobe Bryant .30 .75
82 Felipe Lopez / Scottie Pippen .15 .40
83 Shammond Williams / Stephon Marbury .15 .40
84 Shammond Williams / Tracy McGrady .15 .40
85 Zendon Hamilton / Tim Thomas .15 .40
86 Zendon Hamilton / Kobe Bryant .30 .75
87 Jason Williams / Scottie Pippen .20 .50
88 Jason Williams / Stephon Marbury .15 .40
89 Ricky Davis / Tracy McGrady .15 .40
90 Ricky Davis / Tim Thomas .15 .40
91 Korleone Young / Kobe Bryant .30 .75
92 Korleone Young / Scottie Pippen .15 .40
93 Vince Carter / Stephon Marbury .25 .60
94 Vince Carter / Tracy McGrady .30 .75
95 Al Harrington / Tim Thomas .15 .40
96 Al Harrington / Kobe Bryant .30 .75
97 Jelani McCoy / Scottie Pippen .15 .40
98 Jelani McCoy / Stephon Marbury .15 .40
99 DeMarco Johnson / Tracy McGrady .15 .40
100 DeMarco Johnson / Tim Thomas .15 .40

1998 Collector's Edge Impulse Jersey City '99

This 100-card set parallels the base 1998 Collector's Edge Impulse set enhanced on the back, just over the statistical information, with the words "Jersey City '99."

JSY CITY: .75X TO 2X HI COL.

1998 Collector's Edge Impulse Jersey City '99 Gold

This 100-card set parallels the base 1998 Collector's Edge Impulse set enhanced on the back, just over the statistical information, with the words "Jersey City '99." Cards also contain sequential numbering to 5000 in gold foil on the card back as well.

*GOLD: 2X TO 5X HI COL.

1998 Collector's Edge Impulse Jersey City '99 Parallel 50

This 100-card set parallels the base 1998 Collector's Edge Impulse set enhanced on the back, just over the statistical information, with the words "Jersey City '99." Cards also contain sequential numbering to 50 in gold foil on the card back as well.

*SINGLES: 12X TO 30X BASE CARD HI

1998 Collector's Edge Impulse Parallel

Inserted one per pack, this 100-card set parallels the base set, featuring a thicker stock. To ascertain values on individual cards, please refer to the multiplier in the header, coupled with the value of the base card.

*STARS: .75X TO 2X BASE CARD HI

1998 Collector's Edge Impulse KB8

Randomly inserted in packs at one in 36, this five-card set focuses on Kobe Bryant. Cards have a bronze coloring.

COMMON BRONZE (1-5) 2.50 6.00
*SILVER: .6X TO 1.5X BRONZE
SILVER STATED ODDS 1:54
*GOLD: .75X TO 2X BRONZE
GOLD STATED ODDS 1:72
*HOLOFOIL: 1X TO 2.5X BRONZE
HOLOFOIL STATED ODDS 1:90

1998 Collector's Edge Impulse Memorable Moments

Redeemable via an exchange card that was inserted one in 360 packs, this 5-card set features players with a patch of a game-used basketball.

COMPLETE SET (5) 25.00 60.00
1 Kobe Bryant 15.00 40.00
2 Stephon Marbury 4.00 10.00
3 Tracy McGrady 5.00 12.00
4 Scottie Pippen 5.00 12.00
5 Tim Thomas 3.00 8.00

1998 Collector's Edge Impulse Pro Signatures

Randomly inserted in packs at one in 18, this 30-card set features autographs from some of the top rookies from the 1998 NBA Draft, as well as some veterans of the NBA.

1 Antawn Jamison 5.00 12.00
2 Paul Pierce 10.00 25.00
3 Corey Benjamin 2.00 5.00
4 Ricky Davis 3.00 8.00
5 Jason Williams 5.00 12.00
6 Felipe Lopez 2.00 5.00
7 Jelani McCoy 2.00 5.00
8 Vince Carter 12.50 30.00
9 Keon Clark 2.00 5.00
10 Michael Olowokandi 2.50 6.00
11 Robert Traylor 2.00 5.00
12 Bonzi Wells 2.00 5.00
13 Toby Bailey 2.00 5.00
14 Pat Garrity 2.00 5.00
15 Al Harrington 3.00 8.00
16 J.R. Henderson 2.00 5.00
17 DeMarco Johnson 2.00 5.00
18 Zendon Hamilton 2.00 5.00
19 Rashard Lewis 5.00 12.00
20 Tyronn Lue 2.00 5.00
21 Kobe Bryant 50.00 100.00
22 Jeff Sheppard 2.00 5.00
23 Miles Simon 2.00 5.00
24 Shammond Williams 2.00 5.00
25 Korleone Young 2.00 5.00
26 Radoslav Nesterovic 2.00 5.00
27 Stephon Marbury 5.00 12.00
28 Tracy McGrady 8.00 20.00
29 Scottie Pippen 40.00 80.00
30 Tim Thomas 2.00 5.00

1998 Collector's Edge Impulse Swoosh

Randomly inserted at one in 72 packs, this 24-card set featured some of the leading players from the 1998 draft.

COMPLETE SET (24) 25.00 60.00
1L Michael Olowokandi 1.25 3.00
1R Antawn Jamison 2.50 6.00
2L Vince Carter 5.00 12.00
2R Robert Traylor 1.00 2.50
3L Jason Williams 2.50 6.00
3R Paul Pierce 5.00 12.00
4L Keon Clark 1.00 2.50
4R Bonzi Wells 1.00 2.50
5L Kobe Bryant 5.00 12.00
5R Pat Garrity 1.00 2.50
6L Ricky Davis 1.50 4.00
6R Tyronn Lue 1.00 2.50
7L Felipe Lopez 1.00 2.50
7R Al Harrington 1.50 4.00
8L Corey Benjamin 1.00 2.50
8R Rashard Lewis 2.50 6.00
9L Jelani McCoy 1.00 2.50
9R Shammond Williams 1.00 2.50
10L DeMarco Johnson 1.00 2.50
10R Korleone Young 1.00 2.50
11L Miles Simon 1.00 2.50
11R Kobe Bryant 5.00 12.00
12L Stephon Marbury 1.25 3.00
12R Tracy McGrady 1.50 4.00

1998 Collector's Edge Impulse T3

Released as a multi-level set, the first five cards were bronze and inserted at one in 12. The second level, or cards 6-10 were silver and inserted at one in 18. The third level, or cards 11-15 were gold and inserted at one in 36.

COMPLETE SET (15) 10.00 25.00
1 Michael Olowokandi G 1.00 2.50
2 Antawn Jamison G 2.00 5.00
3 Kobe Bryant G 4.00 10.00
4 Scottie Pippen G 1.25 3.00
5 Robert Traylor G .75 2.00
6 Stephon Marbury S .60 1.50
7 Paul Pierce S 2.50 6.00
8 Vince Carter S 2.50 6.00
9 Shammond Williams S .50 1.25
10 Tim Thomas S .50 1.25
11 Bonzi Wells B .40 1.00
12 Tracy McGrady B .60 1.50
13 Rashard Lewis B 1.00 2.50
14 Keon Clark B .40 1.00
15 Corey Benjamin B .40 1.00

1999 Collector's Edge Rookie Rage

The 1999 version of Rookie Rage by Collector's Edge was released as a 50-card set. Each pack carried a suggested retail price of $2.19.

COMPLETE SET (50) 3.00 8.00
1 Ron Artest .25 .60
2 William Avery .10 .25
3 Michael Batiste .10 .25
4 Jonathan Bender .10 .25
5 Roberto Bergersen .10 .25
6 Calvin Booth .10 .25
7 Cal Bowdler .10 .25
8 A.J. Bramlett .10 .25
9 Rodney Buford .10 .25
10 John Celestand .10 .25
11 Kris Clack .10 .25
12 Lonnie Cooper .10 .25
13 Vonteego Cummings .10 .25
14 Baron Davis .30 .75
15 Evan Eschmeyer .10 .25
16 Jeff Foster .10 .25
17 Jelani Gardner .10 .25
18 Devean George .10 .25
19 Dion Glover .10 .25
20 Richard Hamilton .25 .60
21 Venson Hamilton .10 .25
22 Rico Hill .10 .25
23 Tim James .10 .25
24 Jumaine Jones .10 .25
25 J.R. Koch .10 .25
26 Trajan Langdon .10 .25
27 Bobby Lazor .10 .25
28 Melvin Levett .10 .25
29 Quincy Lewis .10 .25
30 Corey Maggette .20 .50
31 Shawn Marion .25 .60
32 B.J. McKie .10 .25
33 Andre Miller .25 .60
34 Lee Nailon .10 .25
35 Ademola Okulaja .10 .25
36 Scott Padgett .10 .25
37 James Posey .10 .25
38 Aleksandar Radojevic .10 .25
39 Michael Ruffin .10 .25
40 Leon Smith .10 .25
41 Jason Terry .25 .60
42 Kenny Thomas .10 .25
43 Tyrone Washington .10 .25
44 Frederic Weis .10 .25
45 Alvin Young .10 .25
46 Kobe Bryant .50 1.25
47 Vince Carter .20 .50
48 Antawn Jamison .10 .25
49 Paul Pierce .15 .40
50 Jason Williams .12 .30

1999 Collector's Edge Rookie Rage Gold

Inserted one per pack, this 50-card set parallels the base set. The cards feature gold foil.

*GOLD: .6X TO 1.5X VALUE

1999 Collector's Edge Rookie Rage HoloGold

Randomly inserted in packs, this 50-card set parallels the base set. The cards feature holofoil around the edges and are serially numbered to 50.

*HOLO: 15X TO 40X VALUE

1999 Collector's Edge Rookie Rage Future Legends

Randomly inserted in packs at one in eight, this 10-card set features top rookies destined to be legends. Card backs carry a "FL" prefix.

COMPLETE SET (10) 2.00 5.00
FL1 Ron Artest .50 1.25
FL2 William Avery .20 .50
FL3 Jonathan Bender .20 .50
FL4 Baron Davis .60 1.50
FL5 Richard Hamilton .50 1.25
FL6 Trajan Langdon .20 .50
FL7 Corey Maggette .40 1.00
FL8 Andre Miller .50 1.25
FL9 Jason Terry .50 1.25
FL10 Frederic Weis .20 .50

1999 Collector's Edge Rookie Rage Game Ball

Randomly inserted in packs at one in 72, this five-card set features pieces of game-used balls in every card.

GB1 Kobe Bryant 12.00 30.00
GB2 Vince Carter 5.00 12.00
GB3 Antawn Jamison 2.50 6.00
GB4 Paul Pierce 4.00 10.00
GB5 Jason Williams 3.00 8.00
GB6 Corey Maggette 5.00 12.00

1999 Collector's Edge Rookie Rage Livin' Large

Randomly inserted in packs at one in 16, this five-card set features top pro player at the top of their game. Card backs carry a "LL" prefix.

COMPLETE SET (5) 1.00 2.50
LL1 Kobe Bryant 1.00 2.50
LL2 Vince Carter .40 1.00
LL3 Antawn Jamison .20 .50
LL4 Paul Pierce .30 .75
LL5 Jason Williams .25 .60

1999 Collector's Edge Rookie Rage Loud and Proud

Randomly inserted in packs at one in 16, this five-card set featues young NBA stars whose game is "loud and proud". Card backs carry a "LP" prefix.

COMPLETE SET (5) 1.00 2.50
LP1 Kobe Bryant 1.00 2.50
LP2 Vince Carter .40 1.00
LP3 Antawn Jamison .20 .50
LP4 Paul Pierce .30 .75
LP5 Jason Williams .25 .60

1999 Collector's Edge Rookie Rage Pro Signatures

Randomly inserted in packs at one in 12, this 50-card set features autographs of each player in the base set.

1 Ron Artest 5.00 12.00
2 William Avery 2.00 5.00
3 Michael Batiste 2.00 5.00
4 Jonathan Bender 2.00 5.00
5 Roberto Bergersen 2.00 5.00
6 Calvin Booth 2.00 5.00
7 Cal Bowdler 2.00 5.00
8 A.J. Bramlett 2.00 5.00
9 Rodney Buford 2.00 5.00
10 John Celestand 2.00 5.00
11 Kris Clack 2.00 5.00
12 Lonnie Cooper 2.00 5.00
13 Vonteego Cummings 2.00 5.00
14 Baron Davis 6.00 15.00
15 Evan Eschmeyer 2.00 5.00
16 Jeff Foster 2.00 5.00
17 Jelani Gardner 2.00 5.00
18 Devean George 2.00 5.00
19 Dion Glover 2.00 5.00
20 Richard Hamilton 5.00 12.00
21 Venson Hamilton 2.00 5.00
22 Rico Hill 2.00 5.00
23 Tim James 2.00 5.00
24 Jumaine Jones 2.00 5.00
25 J.R. Koch 2.00 5.00
26 Trajan Langdon 2.00 5.00
27 Bobby Lazor 2.00 5.00
28 Melvin Levett 2.00 5.00
29 Quincy Lewis 2.00 5.00
30 Corey Maggette 4.00 10.00
31 Shawn Marion 5.00 12.00
32 B.J. McKie 2.00 5.00
33 Andre Miller 5.00 12.00
34 Lee Nailon 2.00 5.00
35 Ademola Okulaja 2.00 5.00
36 Scott Padgett 2.00 5.00
37 James Posey 2.00 5.00
38 Aleksandar Radojevic 2.00 5.00
39 Michael Ruffin 2.00 5.00
40 Leon Smith 2.00 5.00
41 Jason Terry 5.00 12.00
42 Kenny Thomas 2.00 5.00
43 Tyrone Washington 2.00 5.00
44 Frederic Weis 2.00 5.00
45 Alvin Young 2.00 5.00
46 Kobe Bryant/39 75.00 150.00
48 Antawn Jamison 4.00 10.00
49 Paul Pierce 6.00 15.00

1999 Collector's Edge Rookie Rage Successors

Randomly inserted in packs at one in eight, this 10-card set features top rookie players who will suceed in the NBA. Card backs carry a "S" prefix.

COMPLETE SET (10) 2.00 5.00
S1 Ron Artest .50 1.25
S2 William Avery .20 .50
S3 Jonathan Bender .20 .50
S4 Baron Davis .60 1.50
S5 Richard Hamilton .50 1.25
S6 Trajan Langdon .20 .50
S7 Corey Maggette .40 1.00
S8 Andre Miller .50 1.25
S9 Jason Terry .50 1.25
S10 Frederic Weis .20 .50

1991 Courtside

The 1991 Courtside Draft Pix basketball set consists of 45 standard-size cards. All 198,000 sets produced are numbered and distributed as complete sets in their own custom boxes each accompanied by a certificate with a unique serial number. The card front features a color action player photo. The design of the card fronts features a color rectangle (either pearlized red, blue, or green) on a pearlized white background, with two border stripes in the same color intersecting at the upper right corner. The player's name appears at the upper right corner of the card face, with the words "Courtside 1991" at the bottom. The backs reflect the color on the fronts and present stats (biographical), college record (year by year statistics), and player profile. The unnumbered Larry Johnson sendaway card is not included in the complete set price below. Promo versions of all cards in the set are known to exist; they bear a circle-shaped disclaimer reading "Sample Not For Sale" on their back. Single promo cards were given out at the 1991 San Francisco Labor Day show. These promo versions are valued at four times the regualr issue values.

COMP.FACT.SET (45) 1.50 3.00
1 Larry Johnson First Draft Pick .30 .75
2 George Ackles .02 .10
3 Kenny Anderson .20 .50
4 Greg Anthony .05 .15
5 Anthony Avent .02 .10
6 Terrell Brandon .20 .50
7 Kevin Brooks .02 .10
8 Marc Brown .02 .10
9 Myron Brown .02 .10
10 Randy Brown .05 .15
11 Darrin Chancellor .02 .10
12 Pete Chilcutt .05 .15
13 Chris Corchiani .05 .15
14 John Crotty .05 .15
15 Dale Davis .20 .50
16 Marty Dow .02 .10
17 Richard Dumas .02 .10
18 LeRon Ellis .02 .10
19 Tony Farmer .02 .10
20 Roy Fisher .02 .10
21 Rick Fox .20 .50
22 Chad Gallagher .02 .10
23 Chris Gatling .05 .15
24 Sean Green .02 .10
25 Reggie Hanson .02 .10
26 Donald Hodge .02 .10
27 Steve Hood .02 .10
28 Keith Hughes .02 .10
29 Mike Iuzzolino .02 .10
30 Keith Jennings .02 .10
31 Larry Johnson .30 .75
32 Treg Lee .02 .10
33 Cedric Lewis .02 .10
34 Kevin Lynch .02 .10
35 Mark Macon .05 .15
36 Jason Matthews .02 .10
37 Eric Murdock .05 .15
38 Jimmy Oliver .02 .10
39 Doug Overton .02 .10
40 Elliot Perry .05 .15
41 Brian Shorter .02 .10
42 Alvaro Teheran .02 .10
43 Joey Wright .02 .10
44 Joe Wylie .02 .10
45 Larry Johnson POY .30 .75
NNO Larry Johnson SP (Mail-in) .75 2.00

1991 Courtside Autographs

Reportedly, 30,000 autographs were randomly inserted in the 9,900 cases. The cards feature autographs of each player.

1 Larry Johnson First Draft Pick 15.00 40.00
2 George Ackles 4.00 10.00
4 Greg Anthony 8.00 20.00
5 Anthony Avent 4.00 10.00
6 Terrell Brandon 6.00 15.00
7 Kevin Brooks 4.00 10.00
8 Marc Brown 4.00 10.00
9 Myron Brown 4.00 10.00
10 Randy Brown 4.00 10.00
11 Darrin Chancellor 4.00 10.00
12 Pete Chilcutt 4.00 10.00
13 Chris Corchiani 4.00 10.00
14 John Crotty 4.00 10.00
15 Dale Davis 6.00 15.00
16 Marty Dow 4.00 10.00
17 Richard Dumas 4.00 10.00
18 LeRon Ellis 4.00 10.00
19 Tony Farmer 4.00 10.00
20 Roy Fisher 4.00 10.00
21 Rick Fox 8.00 20.00
22 Chad Gallagher 4.00 10.00

3 Chris Gatling	4.00	10.00
4 Sean Green	4.00	10.00
5 Reggie Hanson	4.00	10.00
6 Donald Hodge	4.00	10.00
7 Steve Hood	4.00	10.00
8 Keith Hughes	4.00	10.00
9 Mike Iuzzolino	4.00	10.00
0 Keith Jennings	4.00	10.00
1 Larry Johnson	20.00	40.00
2 Treg Lee	4.00	10.00
3 Cedric Lewis	4.00	10.00
4 Kevin Lynch	4.00	10.00
5 Mark Macon	4.00	10.00
6 Jason Matthews	4.00	10.00
7 Eric Murdock	4.00	10.00
8 Jimmy Oliver	4.00	10.00
9 Doug Overton	4.00	10.00
0 Elliot Perry	4.00	10.00
1 Brian Shorter	4.00	10.00
2 Alvaro Teheran	4.00	10.00
3 Joey Wright	4.00	10.00
4 Joe Wylie	4.00	10.00

1991 Courtside Holograms

These three holograms were issued in a plastic sleeve within a paper envelope. According to information printed on the envelope, 99,000 sets were produced. Each hologram features the player photo against a parquet basketball floor background, with a subtitle at the bottom of the card face. Framed by turquoise borders above and on the right, the backs present stats (biographical), college record (year by year statistics), and profile. The cards are unnumbered and checklisted below in alphabetical order.

COMPLETE SET (3)	1.00	2.50
1 Greg Anthony	.20	.50
2 Larry Johnson	.75	2.00
3 Mark Macon	.10	.30

1992 Courtside Flashback Promo Sheet

The cards, when cut, are standard size, 2 1/2" by 3 1/2". The players are pictured in their college uniforms. The back of the panel states that only 5,000 were printed. The panel's back congratulates them on their gold medal winning performances as a form of Dream Team tie-in. All the card photos are action shots.

1 Courtside Promo Sheet	.75	2.00
Chris Mullin		
St. John's		
Kareem Abdul-Jabbar		
UCLA		
David Robinson		
Navy		
Rick Barry		

1992 Courtside Flashback

As a tribute to 100 years of college basketball, Courtside released this 45-card standard-size set, featuring some of the greatest players and coaches of the sport. It is reported that the production run was 199,000 sets, with 20 sets per individually numbered (from 1 to 9,950) case. Ten thousand autographed cards were randomly included with the sets; the exact number of players who signed is not known, but it is suspected that only a few did not sign. In exchange for the Courtside certificate found within each set, the collector received one of 25,000 promotional strips, featuring Larry Bird, David Robinson, and Kareem Abdul-Jabbar. The front features a color player photo cut out and superimposed on a background consisting of white and either red, green, or blue blocks. The backs carry a second color player photo and a brief career summary. The cards are numbered on the back. A promo version of card 41, Bill Walton, is known; its white back reads "The Big 9 Sports Card Show."

COMP.FACT.SET (45)	2.00	4.00
COMMON CARD (1-45)	.02	.10
1 Tommy Amaker	.02	.10
2 Charles Barkley	.30	.75
3 Rick Barry	.20	.50
4 Larry Bird	.40	1.00
5 Larry Brown CO	.08	.25
6 Quinn Buckner	.02	.10
7 Tom Burleson	.02	.10
8 Austin Carr	.02	.10
9 Phil Ford	.02	.10
10 Andrew Gaze	.08	.25
11 Artis Gilmore	.08	.25
12 Jack Givens	.02	.10
13 Gail Goodrich	.08	.25
14 Kevin Grevey	.02	.10
15 Ernie Grunfeld	.02	.10
16 Elvin Hayes	.20	.50
17 Walt Hazzard	.08	.25
18 Kareem Abdul-Jabbar	.30	.75
19 Marques Johnson	.08	.25
20 John Lucas	.08	.25
21 Kyle Macy	.02	.10
22 Rollie Massimino CO	.02	.10
23 Cedric Maxwell	.02	.10
24 Bob McAdoo	.08	.25
25 Al McGuire CO	.08	.25
26 George Mikan	.30	.75
27 Sidney Moncrief	.08	.25
28 Chris Mullin	.20	.50
29 Calvin Murphy	.08	.25
30 Sam Perkins	.08	.25
31 David Robinson	.20	.50
32 Curtis Rowe	.02	.10
33 Cazzie Russell	.08	.25
34 Charlie Scott	.08	.25
35 Dean Smith CO	.20	.50
36 Jerry Tarkanian CO	.08	.25
37 David Thompson	.08	.25
38 Nate Thurmond	.08	.25
39 Monte Towe	.02	.10
40 Jim Valvano CO	.20	.50
41 Bill Walton	.20	.50
42 Paul Westphal	.08	.25
43 Dereck Whittenburg	.02	.10
44 Sidney Wicks	.02	.10
45 John Wooden CO	.20	.50

1992 Courtside Flashback Autographs

RANDOM INSERTS IN SETS		
1 Tommy Amaker	10.00	25.00
3 Rick Barry	10.00	25.00
4 Larry Bird	50.00	120.00
5 Larry Brown CO	12.50	30.00
6 Quinn Buckner	5.00	12.00
7 Tom Burleson	5.00	12.00
8 Austin Carr	10.00	25.00
9 Phil Ford	5.00	12.00
10 Andrew Gaze	25.00	60.00
11 Artis Gilmore	5.00	12.00
12 Jack Givens	5.00	12.00
13 Gail Goodrich	10.00	25.00
14 Kevin Grevey	3.00	8.00
15 Ernie Grunfeld	5.00	12.00
16 Elvin Hayes	10.00	25.00
17 Walt Hazzard	5.00	12.00
18 Kareem Abdul-Jabbar	25.00	60.00
19 Marques Johnson	6.00	15.00
20 John Lucas	10.00	25.00
21 Kyle Macy	3.00	8.00
22 Rollie Massimino CO	3.00	8.00
23 Cedric Maxwell	5.00	12.00
24 Bob McAdoo	20.00	50.00
25 Al McGuire CO	5.00	12.00
26 George Mikan	75.00	150.00
27 Sidney Moncrief	5.00	12.00
29 Calvin Murphy	8.00	20.00
30 Sam Perkins	5.00	12.00
32 Curtis Rowe	3.00	8.00
33 Cazzie Russell	5.00	12.00
34 Charlie Scott	5.00	12.00
35 Dean Smith CO	40.00	100.00
37 David Thompson	10.00	25.00
38 Nate Thurmond	10.00	25.00
39 Monte Towe	3.00	8.00
40 Jim Valvano CO	100.00	225.00
41 Bill Walton	8.00	20.00
42 Paul Westphal	10.00	25.00
43 Dereck Whittenburg	3.00	8.00
44 Sidney Wicks	3.00	8.00
45 John Wooden CO	75.00	150.00

1991 Front Row

The 1991 Front Row Italian/English Basketball Draft Pick set contains 100 standard-size cards. Each factory set comes with an official certificate of authenticity that bears a unique serial number. This set is distinguished from the American version by size (100 instead of 50 cards), different production quantities (30,000 factory sets and 3,000 wax cases) and a red stripe on the card front. The front design features glossy color action player photos with white borders. The player's name appears in a red stripe beneath the picture. The backs have different smaller color photos (upper right corner) as well as biography, college statistics and achievements superimposed on a gray background with an orange basketball. This set also includes a second (career highlights) card of some players (39-43), a subset devoted to Larry Johnson (44-49) and two "Retrospect" cards (96-97). Italian and Japanese cards are valued the same. Please refer to the multipliers in the header below for foreign cards.

COMPLETE SET (50)	1.25	3.00
COMPLETE ITALIAN SET (100)	1.25	3.00
*ITALIAN AND JAPANESE: SAME VALUE		
1 Larry Johnson	.40	1.00
2 Kenny Anderson	.20	.50
3 Rick Fox	.08	.25
4 Pete Chilcutt	.01	.05
5 George Ackles	.01	.05
6 Mark Macon	.01	.05
7 Greg Anthony	.05	.15
8 Mike Iuzzolino	.01	.05
9 Anthony Avent	.01	.05
10 Terrell Brandon	.30	.75
11 Kevin Brooks	.01	.05
12 Myron Brown	.01	.05
13 Chris Corchiani	.01	.05
14 Chris Gatling	.05	.15
15 Marcus Kennedy	.01	.05
16 Eric Murdock	.01	.05
17 Tony Farmer	.01	.05
18 Keith Hughes	.01	.05
19 Kevin Lynch	.01	.05
20 Chad Gallagher	.01	.05
21 Darrin Chancellor	.01	.05
22 Jimmy Oliver	.01	.05
23 Von McDade	.01	.05
24 Donald Hodge	.01	.05
25 Randy Brown	.01	.05
26 Doug Overton	.01	.05
27 LeRon Ellis	.01	.05
28 Sean Green	.01	.05
29 Elliot Perry	.01	.05
30 Richard Dumas	.01	.05
31 Dale Davis	.08	.25
32 Lamont Strothers	.01	.05
33 Steve Hood	.01	.05
34 Joey Wright	.01	.05
35 Patrick Eddie	.01	.05
36 Joe Wylie	.01	.05
37 Bobby Phills	.05	.15
38 Alvaro Teheran	.01	.05
39 Dale Davis HL	.05	.15
40 Rick Fox HL	.05	.15
41 Terrell Brandon HL	.15	.40
42 Greg Anthony HL	.01	.05
43 Mark Macon HL	.01	.05
44 Larry Johnson HL	.20	.50
45 Larry Johnson	.20	.50
First in the Nation		
46 Larry Johnson	.20	.50
Power		
47 Larry Johnson	.20	.50
A Class Act		
48 Larry Johnson	.20	.50
Flashback		
49 Larry Johnson	.20	.50
Up Close and Personal		
50A Bonus Card	.01	.05
50B Marty Conlon	.01	.05
51 Mike Goodson	.01	.05
52 Drexel Deveaux	.01	.05
53 Sean Muto	.01	.05
54 Keith Owens	.01	.05
55 Joao Viana	.01	.05
56 Chancellor Nichols	.01	.05
57 Charles Thomas	.01	.05
58 Carl Thomas	.01	.05
59 Anthony Blakley	.01	.05
60 Demetrius Calip	.01	.05
61 Dale Turnquist	.01	.05
62 Carlos Funchess	.01	.05
63 Tharon Mayes	.01	.05
64 Andy Kennedy	.01	.05
65 Oliver Taylor	.01	.05
66 David Benoit	.05	.15
67 Gary Waites	.01	.05
68 Corey Crowder	.01	.05
69 Sydney Grider	.01	.05
70 Derek Strong	.01	.05
71 Larry Stewart	.01	.05
72 Matt Roe	.01	.05
73 Cedric Lewis	.01	.05
74 Anthony Houston	.01	.05
75 Steve Bardo	.01	.05
76 Marc Brown	.01	.05
77 Michael Cutright	.01	.05
78 Emanual Davis	.01	.05
79 Paris McCurdy	.01	.05
80 Jackie Jones	.01	.05
81 Mark Peterson	.01	.05
82 Clifford Scales	.01	.05
83 Robert Pack	.05	.15
84 Doug Lee	.01	.05
85 Cameron Burns	.01	.05
86 Tom Copa	.01	.05
87 Clinton Venable	.01	.05
88 Ken Redfield	.01	.05
89 Melvin Newbern	.01	.05
90 Darren Henrie	.01	.05
91 Chris Harris	.01	.05
92 John Crotty	.01	.05
93 Paul Graham	.01	.05
94 Stevie Thompson	.01	.05
95 Clifford Martin	.01	.05
96 Brian Shaw	.05	.15
97 Danny Ferry	.05	.15
98 Doug Loescher	.01	.05
99 Checklist	.01	.05
100 Bonus Card	.01	.05

1991 Front Row Gold

Randomly inserted, these cards carry gold foil. To ascertain values on individual cards, please refer to the multiplier in the header, coupled with the value of the base card.

*GOLD: 1.5X TO 4X BASE CARD HI

1991 Front Row Silver

Randomly inserted, these cards feature silver foil. To ascertain values on individual cards, please refer to the multiplier in the header, coupled with the value of the base card.

*SILVER: .75X TO 2X BASE CARD HI

1991 Front Row Update

Comprising of 50 standard size cards, the update version is a continuation (51-100) of the 50-card Draft Pick set. The checklist to the Draft Pick is identical (with identical values) to the first 50 cards of the Italian/English 100 version. Each set was accompanied by a certificate of authenticity that bears a unique serial number, with the production run reported to be 50,000 sets. The fronts feature glossy color action player photos enclosed by white borders. A basketball backboard and rim with the words "Update 92" appears in the lower left corner, with the player's name and position in a dark green stripe beneath the picture. On a gray background with an orange basketball, the backs carry biography, color close-up photo, statistics, and achievements.

COMPLETE SET (50)	1.25	3.00
51 Billy Owens	.08	.25
52 Dikembe Mutombo	.30	.75
53 Steve Smith	.40	1.00
54 Luc Longley	.08	.25
55 Doug Smith	.01	.05
56 Stacey Augmon	.08	.25
57 Brian Williams	.05	.15
58 Stanley Roberts	.01	.05
59 Rodney Monroe	.01	.05
60 Isaac Austin	.05	.15
61 Rich King	.01	.05
62 Victor Alexander	.01	.05
63 LaBradford Smith	.01	.05
64 Greg Sutton	.01	.05
65 John Turner	.01	.05
66 Joao Viana	.01	.05
67 Charles Thomas	.01	.05
68 Carl Thomas	.01	.05
69 Tharon Mayes	.01	.05
70 David Benoit	.05	.15
71 Corey Crowder	.01	.05
72 Larry Stewart	.01	.05
73 Steve Bardo	.01	.05
74 Paris McCurdy	.01	.05
75 Robert Pack	.05	.15
76 Doug Lee	.01	.05
77 Tom Copa	.01	.05
78 Keith Owens	.01	.05
79 Mike Goodson	.01	.05
80 John Crotty	.01	.05
81 Sean Muto	.01	.05
82 Chancellor Nichols	.01	.05
83 Stevie Thompson	.01	.05
84 Demetrius Calip	.01	.05
85 Clifford Martin	.01	.05
86 Andy Kennedy	.01	.05
87 Oliver Taylor	.01	.05
88 Gary Waites	.01	.05
89 Matt Roe	.01	.05
90 Cedric Lewis	.01	.05
91 Emanual Davis	.01	.05
92 Jackie Jones	.01	.05
93 Clifford Scales	.01	.05
94 Cameron Burns	.01	.05
95 Clinton Venable	.01	.05
96 Ken Redfield	.01	.05
97 Melvin Newbern	.01	.05
98 Chris Harris	.01	.05
99 Bonus Card	.01	.05
100 Checklist	.01	.05

1991 Front Row Update Gold

Randomly inserted, these cards contained gold foil. To ascertain values on individual cards, please refer to the multiplier in the header, coupled with the value of the base card.

*GOLD: 1.25X TO 3X BASE CARD HI

1991 Front Row Update Silver

Randomly inserted, these cards contained silver foil. To ascertain values on individual cards, please refer to the multiplier in the header below, coupled with the value of the base card.

*SILVER: .75X TO 2X BASE CARD HI

1991 Front Row Stacey Augmon

These seven standard-size cards feature seven different action shots of Stacey Augmon. The glossy color photos are enclosed by white borders, while the player's name appears in a purple stripe beneath the picture. Issued with each set, a certificate of authenticity gives the individual serial number of the set and the total production run (25,000). The words "Limited Edition" are gold-foil stamped across the card top. On a gray background with an orange basketball, the horizontally oriented backs summarize Augmon's career. Only card number 7 includes a second photo on its back.

COMPLETE SET (7)	.60	1.50
COMMON CARD (1-7)	.10	.25

1991 Front Row Italian Promos

The American version of the 1991 Front Row Draft Pick set (50) included a bonus card that could be redeemed for two Italian promo cards through a mail-in offer. This promo set consists of ten standard-size cards. The color player photos on the front are bordered in white, and the player's name appears in a red stripe beneath the picture. On a gray background with an orange Front Row basketball logo, the backs read "Italian Promo Card" and "20,000 Ten Card Sets Produced" although the back of the Bonus Card says "50,000 Sets Produced". The cards are unnumbered and checklisted below in alphabetical order.

COMPLETE SET (10)	1.00	2.50
1 Steve Bardo	.08	.25
2 Corey Crowder	.08	.25
3 Danny Ferry	.30	.75
4 Doug Lee	.08	.25
5 Tharon Mayes	.08	.25
6 Robert Pack	.30	.75
7 Brian Shaw	.30	.75
8 Larry Stewart	.08	.25
9 Carl Thomas	.08	.25
10 Charles Thomas	.08	.25

1991 Front Row Larry Johnson

These ten standard-size cards feature different action shots of Larry Johnson. According to Front Row, there were 50,000 sets produced.

COMPLETE SET (10)	1.60	4.00
COMMON CARD (1-10)	.20	.50

1991 Front Row Dikembe Mutombo

These seven standard-size cards feature seven different action shots of Dikembe Mutombo. The glossy color photos are enclosed by white borders, while the player's name appears in a purple stripe beneath the picture. Issued with each set, a certificate of authenticity gives the individual serial number of the set and the total production run (50,000). The words "Limited Edition" are gold-foil stamped across the card top. On a gray background with an orange basketball, the horizontally oriented backs summarize Mutombo's collegiate career. The same set was produced with the Front Row seal and the words "Charter Member" gold-foil stamped on the backs. Again, the certificate of authenticity carries the set serial number and the total production run (20,000).

COMPLETE SET (7)	1.00	2.50
COMMON CARD (1-7)	.16	.40

1991 Front Row Billy Owens

These seven standard-size cards feature seven different action shots of Billy Owens. The glossy color photos are enclosed by white borders, while the player's name appears in a purple stripe beneath the picture. Issued with each set, a certificate of authenticity gives the individual serial number of the set and the total production run (25,000). The words "Limited Edition" are gold-foil stamped across the card top. On a gray background with an orange basketball, the horizontally oriented backs summarize Owens' collegiate career.

COMPLETE SET (7)	.60	1.50
COMMON CARD (1-7)	.10	.25

1991 Front Row Steve Smith

These seven standard-size cards feature seven different action shots of Steve Smith. The glossy color photos are enclosed by white borders, while the player's name appears in a purple stripe beneath the picture. Issued with each set, a certificate of authenticity gives the individual serial number of the set and the total production run (25,000). The words "Limited Edition" are gold-foil stamped across the card top. On a gray background with an orange basketball, the horizontally oriented backs summarize Smith's collegiate career. Only card number 5 includes a second photo on its back.

COMPLETE SET (7)	1.20	3.00
COMMON CARD (1-7)	.20	.50

1991-92 Front Row Premier

The 1991-92 Front Row Premier set contains 120 standard-size cards. No factory sets were made, and the production run was limited to 2,500 waxbox cases, with 360 cards per box. The set included five bonus cards (86, 88, 90, 91, 93) that were redeemable through a mail-in offer for unnamed player cards. The player's name appears in a silver stripe beneath the picture. The backs have biography, statistics, and achievements superimposed on an orange basketball icon.

COMPLETE SET (120)	2.50	6.00
1 Rich King	.01	.05
2 Kenny Anderson	.20	.50
3 Billy Owens	.08	.25
4 Ken Redfield	.01	.05
5 Robert Pack	.05	.15
6 Clinton Venable	.01	.05
7 Tom Copa	.01	.05
8 Rick Fox HL	.05	.15
9 Cameron Burns	.01	.05
10 Doug Lee	.01	.05
11 LaBradford Smith	.01	.05
12 Clifford Scales	.01	.05
13 Mark Peterson	.01	.05
14 Jackie Jones	.01	.05
15 Paris McCurdy	.01	.05
16 Dikembe Mutombo	.30	.75
17 Emanual Davis	.01	.05
18 Michael Cutright	.01	.05
19 Marc Brown	.01	.05
20 Steve Bardo	.01	.05
21 John Turner	.01	.05
22 Anthony Houston	.01	.05
23 Cedric Lewis	.01	.05
24 Matt Roe	.01	.05
25 Larry Stewart	.01	.05
26 Derek Strong	.01	.05
27 Sydney Grider	.01	.05
28 Corey Crowder	.01	.05
29 Gary Waites	.01	.05
30 David Benoit	.05	.15
31 Larry Johnson	.25	.60
32 Oliver Taylor UER	.01	.05
(Chris Corchiani's name on back)		
33 Andy Kennedy	.01	.05
34 Tharon Mayes	.01	.05
35 Carlos Funchess	.01	.05
36 Dale Turnquist	.01	.05
37 Luc Longley	.08	.25
38 Demetrius Calip	.01	.05
39 Anthony Blakley	.01	.05
40 Carl Thomas	.01	.05
41 Charles Thomas	.01	.05
42 Chancellor Nichols	.01	.05
43 Joao Viana	.01	.05
44 Keith Owens	.01	.05
45 Sean Muto	.01	.05
46 Drexel Deveaux	.01	.05
47 Stacey Augmon	.05	.15
48 Mike Goodson	.01	.05
49 Marty Conlon	.01	.05
50 Mark Macon	.01	.05
51 Greg Anthony	.05	.15
52 Dale Davis	.08	.25
53 Isaac Austin	.05	.15
54 Alvaro Teheran	.01	.05
55 Bobby Phills	.05	.15
56 Joe Wylie	.01	.05
57 Patrick Eddie	.01	.05
58 Joey Wright	.01	.05
59 Steve Hood	.01	.05
60 Lamont Strothers	.01	.05
61 Victor Alexander	.01	.05
62 Richard Dumas	.01	.05
63 Elliot Perry	.01	.05
64 Sean Green	.01	.05
65 Rick Fox	.08	.25
66 LeRon Ellis	.01	.05
67 Doug Overton	.01	.05
68 Randy Brown	.01	.05
69 Donald Hodge	.01	.05
70 Von McDade	.01	.05
71 Greg Sutton	.01	.05
72 Jimmy Oliver	.01	.05
73 Terrell Brandon HL	.15	.40
74 Darrin Chancellor	.01	.05
75 Chad Gallagher	.01	.05
76 Kevin Lynch	.01	.05
77 Keith Hughes	.01	.05
78 Tony Farmer	.01	.05
79 Eric Murdock	.01	.05
80 Marcus Kennedy	.01	.05
81 Larry Johnson	.25	.60
82 Stacey Augmon	.08	.25
83 Dikembe Mutombo	.30	.75
84 Steve Smith	.40	1.00
85 Billy Owens UER	.08	.25
86 Bonus Card 1	.01	.05
Stanley Roberts		
87 Brian Shaw	.05	.15
88 Bonus Card 2	.01	.05
Rodney Monroe		
89 LaBradford Smith HL	.01	.05
90 Bonus Card 3	.01	.05
Mark Randall		
91 Bonus Card 4	.05	.15
Brian Williams		
92 Danny Ferry FLB	.05	.15
93 Bonus Card 5	.01	.05
Shawn Vandiver		
94 Doug Smith HL	.01	.05
95 Luc Longley HL	.05	.15
96 Billy Owens HL	.05	.15
97 Steve Smith HL	.20	.50
98 Dikembe Mutombo HL	.15	.40
99 Stacey Augmon HL	.05	.15
100 Larry Johnson HL	.10	.30
101 Chris Gatling	.05	.15
102 Chris Corchiani	.01	.05
103 Myron Brown	.01	.05
104 Kevin Brooks	.01	.05
105 Anthony Avent	.01	.05
106 Steve Smith	.40	1.00
107 Mike Iuzzolino	.01	.05
108 George Ackles	.01	.05
109 Melvin Newbern	.01	.05
110 Robert Pack HL	.01	.05
111 Darren Henrie	.01	.05
112 Chris Harris	.01	.05
113 John Crotty	.01	.05
114 Terrell Brandon	.30	.75
115 Paul Graham	.01	.05
116 Stevie Thompson	.01	.05
117 Clifford Martin	.01	.05
118 Doug Smith	.01	.05
119 Pete Chilcutt	.01	.05
120 Checklist Card	.01	.05

1992 Front Row

The 1992 Front Row Draft Picks basketball set consists of 100 standard-size cards. The set was sold in a cardboard box, and the back panel carries the set serial number and total production run (150,000). The fronts features color action player photos. Teal borders shading from dark to light surround the pictures. A gradated orange vertical bar containing the player's name is superimposed over one side of the photo. The Front Row Draft Picks logo appears below it. The miniature representation of the team mascot appears in the lower left corner. The horizontal backs display biography, collegiate statistics, and career highlights on a teal background with white borders. An orange bar similar to the one on the front runs down the right edge and contains the words "Draft Picks '92". Four cards (90, 92, 96, and 99) have player photos instead of text on their backs.

COMPLETE SET (100)	2.00	5.00
1 Eric Anderson	.01	.05
2 Darin Archbold	.01	.05
3 Woody Austin	.01	.05
4 Mark Baker	.01	.05
5 Jon Barry	.01	.05
6 Elmer Bennett	.01	.05
7 Tony Bennett	.01	.05
8 Alex Blackwell	.01	.05
9 Curtis Blair	.01	.05
10 Ed Book	.01	.05
11 Marques Bragg	.01	.05
12 P.J. Brown	.02	.10
13 Anthony Buford	.01	.05
14 Dexter Cambridge	.01	.05
15 Brian Davis	.01	.05
16 Lucius Davis	.01	.05
17 Todd Day	.02	.10
18 Greg Dennis	.01	.05
19 Radenko Dobras	.01	.05
20 Harold Ellis	.01	.05
21 Chris King	.01	.05
22 Jo Jo English	.01	.05
23 Deron Feldhaus	.01	.05
24 Matt Geiger	.02	.10
25 Lewis Geter	.01	.05
26 George Gilmore	.01	.05
27 Litterial Green	.01	.05
28 Tom Gugliotta	.25	.60
29 Jim Havrilla	.01	.05
30 Robert Horry	.07	.20
31 Stephen Howard	.01	.05
32 Alonzo Jamison	.01	.05
33 David Johnson	.01	.05
34 Herb Jones	.01	.05
35 Popeye Jones	.01	.05
36 Adam Keefe	.01	.05
37 Dan Cyrulik	.01	.05
38 Ken Leeks	.01	.05
39 Ricardo Leonard	.01	.05
40 Gerald Madkins	.01	.05
41 Eric Manuel	.01	.05
42 Marlon Maxey	.01	.05
43 Jim McCoy	.01	.05
44 Oliver Miller	.01	.05
45 Sean Miller	.01	.05
46 Darren Morningstar	.01	.05
47 Isaiah Morris	.01	.05
48 James Moses	.01	.05
49 Doug Christie	.07	.20
50 Damon Patterson	.01	.05
51 John Pelphrey	.01	.05
52 Brent Price	.01	.05
53 Brett Roberts	.01	.05
54 Steve Rogers	.01	.05
55 Sean Rooks	.01	.05
56 Malik Sealy	.02	.10
57 Tom Schurfranz	.01	.05
58 David Scott	.01	.05
59 Rod Sellers	.01	.05
60 Vernel Singleton	.01	.05
61 Reggie Slater	.01	.05
62 Elmore Spencer	.01	.05
63 Chris Smith	.01	.05
64 Latrell Sprewell	.60	1.50
65 Matt Steigenga	.01	.05
66 Bryant Stith	.02	.10
67 Daimon Sweet	.01	.05
68 Craig Upchurch	.01	.05
69 Van Usher	.01	.05
70 Tony Watts	.01	.05
71 Clarence Weatherspoon	.02	.10
72 Robert Werdann	.01	.05
73 Benford Williams	.01	.05
74 Corey Williams	.01	.05
75 Henry Williams	.01	.05
76 Tim Burroughs	.01	.05
77 Erik Wilson	.01	.05
78 Randy Woods	.01	.05
79 Kendall Youngblood	.01	.05
80 Terry Boyd	.01	.05
81 Tracy Murray	.01	.05
82 Reggie Smith	.01	.05
83 Lee Mayberry	.01	.05
84 Matt Fish	.01	.05
85 Hubert Davis	.02	.10
86 Duane Cooper	.01	.05
87 Anthony Peeler	.02	.10
88 Harold Miner	.01	.05
89 Harold Miner	.01	.05
Miner on Dunking		
90 Harold Miner	.01	.05
Action on both sides		
91 Christian Laettner	.15	.40
92 Christian Laettner	.07	.20
Action shot on		
front, portrait on back		
93 Christian Laettner	.07	.20
and Brian Davis		
94 Walt Williams	.07	.20
95 Walt Williams	.02	.10
ACC Terror		
96 Walt Williams	.02	.10
Action shot on		
front, portrait on back		
97 LaPhonso Ellis	.07	.20
98 LaPhonso Ellis	.02	.10
The Ellis File		
99 LaPhonso Ellis	.02	.10
Action shot on		
front, portrait on back		
100 Checklist 1-100	.01	.05
100B Larry Johnson Promo	.75	2.00

1992 Front Row Gold

Randomly inserted in packs, this 100-card set parallels the base set. The cards feature gold foil. To ascertain values on individual cards, please refer to the multiplier in the header, coupled with the value of the base cards.

*GOLD: 1.5X TO 4X BASE CARD HI

1992 Front Row Silver

Randomly inserted in packs, this 100-card set parallels the base set. The cards feature silver foil. To ascertain value on individual cards, please refer to the multiplier in the header, coupled with the value of the base card.

*SILVER: .75X TO 2X BASE CARD HI

1992 Front Row Dream Picks

The 1992 Front Row Dream Picks basketball set contains 100 standard-size cards. The set features five cards each of the top ten players who signed with Front Row from the 1991 NBA Draft and five cards of the top ten from the 1992 draft. The fronts display color action player photos bordered in purple. The player's name appears above the picture in a yellow bar accented by a red shadow border. The Front Row logo appears at the lower right corner in an orange diagonal stripe. The backs are predominantly yellow and present career summary and highlights. The words "Dream Picks" appear in an orange diagonal stripe on the back. The fifth card of each five-card set has a second color player photo on its back.

COMPLETE SET (100)	2.00	5.00
1 Larry Johnson	.08	.25
2 Larry Johnson	.08	.25
3 Larry Johnson	.08	.25
4 Larry Johnson	.08	.25
5 Larry Johnson	.08	.25
6 Dikembe Mutombo	.08	.25
7 Dikembe Mutombo	.08	.25
8 Dikembe Mutombo	.08	.25
9 Dikembe Mutombo	.08	.25
10 Dikembe Mutombo	.08	.25
11 Stacey Augmon	.04	.10
12 Stacey Augmon	.04	.10
13 Stacey Augmon	.04	.10
14 Stacey Augmon	.04	.10
15 Stacey Augmon	.04	.10
16 Billy Owens	.01	.05
17 Billy Owens	.01	.05
18 Billy Owens	.01	.05
19 Billy Owens	.01	.05
20 Billy Owens	.01	.05
21 Clarence Weatherspoon	.01	.05
22 Clarence Weatherspoon	.01	.05
23 Clarence Weatherspoon	.01	.05
24 Clarence Weatherspoon	.01	.05
25 Clarence Weatherspoon	.01	.05
26 Steve Smith	.08	.25
27 Steve Smith	.08	.25
28 Steve Smith	.08	.25
29 Steve Smith	.08	.25
30 Steve Smith	.08	.25
31 Larry Stewart	.01	.05
32 Larry Stewart	.01	.05

33 Larry Stewart .01 .05
34 Larry Stewart .01 .05
35 Larry Stewart .01 .05
36 Rick Fox .01 .05
37 Rick Fox .01 .05
38 Rick Fox .01 .05
39 Rick Fox .01 .05
40 Rick Fox .01 .05
41 Christian Laettner .10 .30
42 Christian Laettner .10 .30
43 Christian Laettner .10 .30
44 Christian Laettner .10 .30
45 Christian Laettner .10 .30
46 Bryant Stith .01 .05
47 Bryant Stith .01 .05
48 Bryant Stith .01 .05
49 Bryant Stith .01 .05
50 Bryant Stith .01 .05
51 Harold Miner .01 .05
52 Harold Miner .01 .05
53 Harold Miner .01 .05
54 Harold Miner .01 .05
55 Harold Miner .01 .05
56 Mark Macon .01 .05
57 Mark Macon .01 .05
58 Mark Macon .01 .05
59 Mark Macon .01 .05
60 Mark Macon .01 .05
61 Adam Keefe .01 .05
62 Adam Keefe .01 .05
63 Adam Keefe .01 .05
64 Adam Keefe .01 .05
65 Adam Keefe .01 .05
66 Tom Gugliotta .20 .50
67 Tom Gugliotta .20 .50
68 Tom Gugliotta .20 .50
69 Tom Gugliotta .20 .50
70 Tom Gugliotta .20 .50
71 Todd Day .01 .05
72 Todd Day .01 .05
73 Todd Day .01 .05
74 Todd Day .01 .05
75 Todd Day .01 .05
76 Walt Williams .04 .10
77 Walt Williams .04 .10
78 Walt Williams .04 .10
79 Walt Williams .04 .10
80 Walt Williams .04 .10
81 Malik Sealy .01 .05
82 Malik Sealy .01 .05
83 Malik Sealy .01 .05
84 Malik Sealy .01 .05
85 Malik Sealy .01 .05
86 Stanley Roberts .01 .05
87 Stanley Roberts .01 .05
88 Stanley Roberts .01 .05
89 Stanley Roberts .01 .05
90 Stanley Roberts .01 .05
91 LaPhonso Ellis .04 .10
92 LaPhonso Ellis .04 .10
93 LaPhonso Ellis .04 .10
94 LaPhonso Ellis .04 .10
95 LaPhonso Ellis .04 .10
96 Terrell Brandon .04 .10
97 Terrell Brandon .04 .10
98 Terrell Brandon .04 .10
99 Terrell Brandon .04 .10
100 Terrell Brandon .04 .10

1992 Front Row Dream Picks Gold

*GOLD: 1.5X TO 4X BASE HI
RANDOM INSERTS IN PACKS

1992 Front Row Dream Picks Silver

*SILVER: ..75X TO 2X BASE HI
RANDOM INSERTS IN PACKS

1992 Front Row Holograms

This three-card standard-size hologram set features close-up player images against graphic art backgrounds. The player's name appears at the bottom in large block letters. The backs carry a small, square color photo in the center of a light blue background with white borders. Biographical information and career achievements are printed in black above and below the picture, respectively. Magenta lettering sets off the player's name printed vertically on each side of the photo. The set comes with a signed certificate of authenticity giving the set serial number and the total production run (50,000).

COMPLETE SET (3) 1.25 3.00
1 Larry Johnson .75 2.00
2 Billy Owens .30 .75
3 Dikembe Mutombo .60 1.50

1992 Front Row Christian Laettner

This set consists of four standard-size cards plus an official certificate of authenticity giving the set serial number and the production run figures (15,000). The fronts feature white-bordered glossy color action photos of Laettner in his Duke uniform. His name appears in white lettering within a dark blue stripe that runs vertically down the left side. Three different design layouts adorn the card backs. The top half of the white-bordered first card has a picture of Laettner glancing up, the bottom half contains a brief description of his Olympic exploits. The backs of card numbers two and four feature full-bleed color action photos of Laettner, with statistics shown in a dark blue rectangle near the bottom of each. The third card's layout is split vertically, with a color action photo of Laettner passing the ball on the left side, and a review of his playoff heroics on the right, all within a white border. The cards are numbered on the back.

COMPLETE SET (4) 1.25 3.00
COMMON CARD (1-4) .40 1.00

1992-93 Front Row Holograms

This 3-card standard size hologram set features close-up player images against an action scene. The horizontal backs contain a color action photo, 1992 collegiate statistics and a Front Row individually numbered holographic strip. The cards are numbered out of 125,000.

COMPLETE SET (3) .60 1.50
1 Christian Laettner .40 1.00
2 Harold Miner .08 .25
3 Walt Williams .20 .50

1992-93 Front Row LJ Pure Gold

This three-card standard-size set comes with a numbered certificate of authenticity carrying the set serial number. Production was limited to 20,000 sets. The cards feature a 23K gold dust stamped border around color action photos of Larry Johnson. The Front Row logo is stamped into the border, as are the words "Pure Gold" at the bottom. The backs feature a small color photo and player information on a light gray background. The player information is printed on the Front Row basketball icon.

COMPLETE SET (3) 4.00 10.00
COMMON CARD (1-3) 1.60 4.00

1993 Front Row LJ Grandmama

This seven-card standard-size captures Larry Johnson's alter ego, Grandmama, who was created to merchandise the new Converse shoes. The production run was 100,000 sets. Inside black borders, the fronts feature color pictures of Grandmama in action from one of the television commercials. The pictures are accented by a red stripe on top and on the right side. The Converse and Front Row logos in opposite corners round out the front. On a pastel blue background with ghosted photo of Grandmama, the backs carry interesting stories on the life of Grandmama.

COMPLETE SET (7) 1.50 4.00
COMMON CARD (G1-G7) .30 .75

1993 Front Row LJ Grandmama Gold

Again teaming up with Converse, the ten-card second edition of the 1993 Front Row Larry Johnson Grandmama set is part of the company's new card line called "The Gold Collection." Production was limited to 5,000 standard-sized sets. The cards feature full-bleed color photos on the fronts. The words "The Gold Collection" are printed in gold foil along the left edge, while "Grandmama" is printed in the same way on a black bar toward the bottom of the picture. The backs have a second full-bleed color photo and, printed on a white rectangle, a quote from Grandmama or a statement extolling her extraordinary roundball skills. The Converse logo appears in the upper left corner.

COMPLETE SET (10) 3.00 8.00
COMMON CARD (1-10) .40 1.00

1997 Genuine Article Previews

This 5-card set was released by Geniune Article to promote their 1997 Genuine Coverage set. The set features some of the NBA's top draft picks of the 1996-97 season. Card backs carry a "BK" prefix.

COMPLETE SET (5) .75 2.00
BK1 Ray Allen .40 1.00
BK2 Allen Iverson .60 1.50
BK3 Kerry Kittles .20 .50
BK4 Antoine Walker .30 .75
BK5 Lorenzen Wright .20 .50

1997 Genuine Article

This 27-card set, produced by The Genuine Article, Inc., came in 7-card packs in 12-pack boxes. The card fronts have color photographs of the player on a hardwood floor background. Under the photo, "Hardwood Signature Series" is written in a gold foil oval. Each pack contained one autograph and one of the following insert sets: Double Cards, Dual Sport Preview, Hometown Heroes, Lottery Connection or Lottery Gems. There is also a Genuine Article "Charlotte Series" product that was produced. Little information is available due to the fact that the company folded around the time this set was printed. Many of these autographed cards have been inexpensively wholesaled via mail order catalogues.

COMPLETE SET (27) 1.50 4.00
1 Derek Anderson UER .10 .25
2 Keith Booth .10 .25
3 Bobby Jackson .12 .30
4 Antonio Daniels .10 .25
5 Harold Deane .10 .25
6 Ya-Ya Dia .05 .15
7 Lee Wilson .05 .15
8 Kebu Stewart .10 .25
9 Adonal Foyle .10 .25
10 Othella Harrington .05 .15
11 Alvin Sims .10 .25
12 Brevin Knight .10 .25
13 Walter McCarty .05 .15
14 Victor Page .10 .25
15 Lorenzen Wright .05 .15
16 Scot Pollard .10 .25
17 Vitaly Potapenko .05 .15
18 Jamal Robinson .05 .15
19 Roy Rogers UER .05 .15
Misspelled Rodgers
20 Shea Seals .10 .25
21 Carmelo Travieso .05 .15
22 Jacque Vaughn .10 .25
23 DeJuan Wheat .10 .25
24 Allen Iverson .20 .50
25 Damon Stoudamire .10 .25
26 Ron Mercer .12 .30
27 Keith Van Horn .20 .50

1997 Genuine Article Autographs

This 27-card is a parallel of the base set. Each player autographed 7500 hand-numbered cards except for Ron Mercer and Keith Van Horn who signed only 200 each. Each autograph, inserted one per pack, has the same card fronts, but the handnumbered backs say who signed the card in the "presence of a representative of The Genuine Article, Inc."

1 Derek Anderson UER 1.50 4.00
2 Keith Booth 1.50 4.00
3 Bobby Jackson 2.00 5.00
4 Antonio Daniels 1.50 4.00
5 Harold Deane 1.50 4.00
6 Ya-Ya Dia 1.00 2.50
7 Lee Wilson 1.00 2.50
8 Kebu Stewart 1.50 4.00
9 Adonal Foyle 1.50 4.00
10 Othella Harrington 1.00 2.50
11 Alvin Sims 1.50 4.00
12 Brevin Knight 1.50 4.00
13 Walter McCarty 1.00 2.50
14 Victor Page 1.50 4.00
15 Lorenzen Wright 1.00 2.50
16 Scot Pollard 1.50 4.00
17 Vitaly Potapenko 1.00 2.50
18 Jamal Robinson 1.00 2.50
19 Roy Rogers UER 1:00 2.50
Misspelled Rodgers
20 Shea Seals 1.50 4.00
21 Carmelo Travieso 1.00 2.50
22 Jacque Vaughn 1.50 4.00
23 DeJuan Wheat 1.50 4.00
25 Damon Stoudamire 1.50 4.00
26 Ron Mercer/200 6.00 15.00
27 Keith Van Horn/200 8.00 20.00
B3 DeJuan Wheat BON/2500 1.50 4.00

1997 Genuine Article Double Cards

This 3-card randomly inserted set highlights some of the youngest professional players in their college uniforms. Each card has a different design and are numbered D1S-D3S on the back.

COMPLETE SET (3) 1.50 4.00
D1S Antoine Walker 1.00 2.50
Ron Mercer
Derek Anderson
D2S Allen Iverson 1.25 3.00
Damon Stoudamire
D3S Ron Mercer .75 2.00
Keith Van Horn

1997 Genuine Article Double Cards Autographs

This 5-card randomly inserted set is an exact parallel on the insert set, except the cards are autographed. The first card is autographed by all three players, and the other two cards were signed by either of the two players on them. Each card is hand numbered of 200 and is numbered D1S-D3S on the back.

D1S Antoine Walker 40.00 80.00
Ron Mercer
Derek Anderson
D3S Ron Mercer 6.00 15.00
D3S Keith Van Horn 8.00 20.00

1997 Genuine Article Hometown Heroes

This 13-card set was randomly inserted and highlights eight different professional players. The card fronts have a photograph of the player in front of a map background of where they are currently playing in the NBA or where they played college ball. Their uniforms have the NBA logos airbrushed out. The card backs are numbered with an "HH" prefix.

COMPLETE SET (13) 3.00 8.00
HH1 Ray Allen .60 1.50
HH2 Ray Allen .60 1.50
HH3 Allen Iverson 1.00 2.50
HH4 Kerry Kittles .30 .75
HH5 Kerry Kittles .30 .75
HH6 Bryant Reeves .30 .75
HH7 Glen Rice .50 1.25
HH8 Damon Stoudamire .50 1.25
HH9 Damon Stoudamire .50 1.25
HH10 Antoine Walker .50 1.25
HH11 Antoine Walker .50 1.25
HH12 Lorenzen Wright .30 .75
HH13 Lorenzen Wright .30 .75

1997 Genuine Article Hometown Heroes Autographs

This 13-card set was randomly inserted and highlights eight different professional players. The card fronts have a photograph of the player in front of a map background of where they are currently playing in the NBA or where they played college ball. Their uniforms have the NBA logos airbrushed out. The card backs are numbered with an "HH" prefix. Each card is autographed and numbered on the back out of 750.

HH1 Ray Allen 8.00 20.00
HH2 Ray Allen 8.00 20.00
HH10 Antoine Walker 6.00 15.00
HH11 Antoine Walker 6.00 15.00

1997 Genuine Article Jumbos

These three jumbo card, measuring 3.5 x 5, are cards that parallel smaller Genuine Article cards except the backs contain a long description of the players pictured on the card fronts. The original distribution of the cards is uncertain; however, they were inexpensively offered through mail order catalogues when Genuine Article disbanded. The back are numbered with a D-prefix.

COMPLETE SET (3) 1.50 4.00
D1 Ron Mercer .60 1.50
Antoine Walker
Derek Anderson (Kentucky's Finest)
D2 Allen Iverson 1.50 4.00
Damon Stoudamire
(Rookie of the Year)
D3 Keith Van Horn .40 1.00
Ron Mercer (Legends of Tomorrow)

1997 Genuine Article Lottery Connection

This randomly inserted, 5-card set highlights some of the younger NBA players in their college uniforms. The fronts have the insert name in the top left corner with a basketball/world icon. Below the full-bleed player photo, the player's last name only appears in a gold foil font. The backs are numbered with a "LC" prefix.

COMPLETE SET (5) 1.50 4.00
LC1 Derek Anderson .60 1.50
LC2 Bobby Jackson .75 2.00
LC3 Brevin Knight .60 1.50
LC4 Jacque Vaughn .60 1.50
LC5 Lorenzen Wright .40 1.00

1997 Genuine Article Lottery Connection Autographs

This randomly inserted, 5-card set highlights some of the younger NBA players in their college uniforms. The fronts have the insert name in the top left corner with a basketball/world icon. Below the full-bleed player photo, the player's last name only appears in a gold foil font. The backs are numbered with a "LC" prefix. The cards are autographed on the front, and numbered out of 3500 on the back.

LC1 Derek Anderson 2.00 5.00
LC2 Bobby Jackson 2.50 6.00
LC3 Brevin Knight 2.00 5.00
LC4 Jacque Vaughn 2.00 5.00
LC5 Lorenzen Wright 1.25 3.00

1997 Genuine Article Lottery Gems

This 5-card insert set, randomly inserted in packs, highlights five of the top picks in the 1997 NBA draft. The fronts picture a color photo of the player inside an oval distorted swirl. The player's name is written gold foil at the bottom . The card backs are numbered with a "LG" prefix.

COMPLETE SET (5) 2.00 5.00
LG1 Antonio Daniels .60 1.50
LG2 Adonal Foyle .60 1.50
LG3 Danny Fortson .60 1.50
LG4 Ron Mercer .75 2.00
LG5 Keith Van Horn 1.25 3.00

1997 Genuine Article Lottery Gems Autographs

This 5-card insert set, randomly inserted in packs, highlights five of the top picks in the 1997 NBA draft. The fronts picture a color photo of the player inside an oval distorted swirl. The player's name is written gold foil at the bottom . The card backs are numbered with a "LG" prefix. The cards are autographed on the front and numbered out of 1500 on the back.

LG2 Adonal Foyle 2.50 6.00
LG3 Danny Fortson 2.50 6.00
LG4 Ron Mercer 3.00 8.00
LG5 Keith Van Horn 5.00 12.00

1993-94 Images Four Sport

These 150 standard-size cards feature on their borderless fronts color player action shots with backgrounds that have been thrown out of focus. On the white background to the left, career highlights, biography and statistics are displayed. Just 6,500 of each card were produced. The set closes with Classic Headlines (128-147) and checklists (148-150). A redemption card inserted one per case entitled the collector to one set of basketball draft preview cards. This offered expired 9/30/94.

COMPLETE SET (150) 6.00 15.00
2 Chris Webber .40 1.00
6 Anfernee Hardaway .30 .75
10 Sherron Mills .08 .25
12 Warren Kidd .08 .25
13 Bryon Russell .15 .40
14 Mike Peplowski .08 .25
18 Doug Edwards .08 .25
22 Darnell Mee .08 .25
27 Corie Blount .08 .25
36 Shaquille O'Neal Rap .50 1.25
40 George Lynch .08 .25
41 Gheorghe Muresan .10 .30
50 Isaiah Rider .10 .30
59 Vin Baker .10 .30
60 Rodney Rogers .08 .25
66 Josh Grant .08 .25
67 Luther Wright .08 .25
68 Allan Houston .25 .60
75 Lindsey Hunter .08 .25
76 Scott Burrell .08 .25
79 Sam Cassell .15 .40
81 Jimmy Jackson .10 .30
84 Chris Mills .08 .25
89 Acie Earl .08 .25
90 Terry Dehere .08 .25
94 James Robinson .08 .25
96 Jamal Mashburn .15 .40
98 Ed Stokes .08 .25
99 Ervin Johnson .08 .25
100 Nick Van Exel .10 .30
109 Rex Walters .08 .25
110 Chris Whitney .08 .25
112 Alonzo Mourning .15 .40
113 Lucious Harris .08 .25
122 Dino Radja .08 .25
123 Harold Miner .08 .25
124 Greg Graham .08 .25
128 Shaquille O'Neal B/W .40 1.00
132 Chris Webber B/W .20 .50
134 Anfernee Hardaway B/W .15 .40
136 Alonzo Mourning BW .15 .40
141 Jamal Mashburn B/W .08 .25
145 Isaiah Rider B/W .08 .25
146 Harold Miner B/W .08 .25
NNO Jamal Mashburn PROMO .75 2.00
NNO BK Preview Redemption .08 .25

1993-94 Images Four Sport Acetates

Randomly inserted in 1993-94 Classic Images packs (four per case; 6,500 of each), these four standard-size clear acetate cards feature color player action cutouts on their fronts.

COMPLETE SET (4) 12.00 30.00
1 Chris Webber 2.00 5.00
4 Hakeem Olajuwon 2.50 6.00

1993-94 Images Four Sport Chrome

Randomly inserted one in every fourteen 1994 Classic Images packs, these 20 limited print (9,750 of each) cards measure the standard size and feature color player action shots on their borderless metallic fronts. The cards are numbered on the back with a "CC" prefix. This set was also available in uncut sheet form as a redeemed prize for the Marshall Faulk M5 card.

COMPLETE SET (20) 15.00 40.00
CC1 Chris Webber 1.25 3.00
CC2 Anfernee Hardaway 1.00 2.50
CC3 Jimmy Jackson .50 1.25
CC4 Nick Van Exel .50 1.25
CC5 Jamal Mashburn .60 1.50
CC6 Isaiah Rider .40 1.00
NNO Uncut Sheet 30.00 80.00

1993-94 Images Four Sport Sudden Impact

Inserted one per '94 Classic Images pack, these 20 gold foil-board cards measure the standard-size. The gold metallic fronts feature borderless color player action shots on backgrounds that have been thrown out of focus. The player's name and position appear in vertical lettering within a black strip across the card near the right edge. The back carries a color player action shot at the top, followed below by career highlights on a white panel. The player's name appears in vertical black lettering within a ghosted action strip at the left edge. The cards are numbered on the back with an "SI" prefix.

COMPLETE SET (20) 4.00 10.00
SI2 Vin Baker .30 .75
SI9 Shaquille O'Neal .75 2.00
SI10 Alonzo Mourning .40 1.00
SI11 Harold Miner .20 .50
SI12 Chris Webber .40 1.00
SI13 Anfernee Hardaway .30 .75
SI14 Jamal Mashburn .30 .75
SI20 Dino Radja .15 .40

1995 Images Four Sport

Printed on 18-point micro-lined foil board, the 1995 Classic Images set consists of 120 standard-size cards, featuring the top draft picks from the four major sports. Classic produced 1,995 sequentially-numbered 16-box hobby cases. This series also features one "Hot Box" in every four cases; each pack in it included at least one card from five insert sets, plus the special Clear Excitement chase cards not found anywhere else, for a total of 24 inserts per Hot Box. There was a promotional card issued, not inserted into '94-95 Assets packs, for Grant Hill numbered HP1. The front is the same as the card in the set, but the back has an orange background and describes the product's features.

COMPLETE SET (120) 6.00 15.00
1 Glenn Robinson .20 .50
2 Jason Kidd .60 1.50
3 Grant Hill .40 1.00
4 Donyell Marshall .10 .30
5 Juwan Howard .20 .50
6 Sharone Wright .10 .30
7 Brian Grant .20 .50
8 Eric Montross .10 .30
9 Eddie Jones .20 .50
10 Carlos Rogers .10 .30
11 Khalid Reeves .10 .30
12 Jalen Rose .20 .50
13 Yinka Dare .10 .30
14 Eric Piatkowski .10 .30
15 Clifford Rozier .10 .30
16 Aaron McKie .10 .30
17 Eric Mobley .10 .30
18 B.J. Tyler .10 .30
19 Dickey Simpkins .10 .30
20 Bill Curley .10 .30
21 Wesley Person .10 .30
22 Monty Williams .10 .30
23 Antonio Lang .10 .30
24 Darrin Hancock .10 .30
25 Michael Smith .10 .30
26 Rodney Dent .10 .30
27 Charlie Ward .30 .75
28 Jim McIlvaine .10 .30
29 Brooks Thompson .10 .30
30 Gaylon Nickerson .10 .30
31 Jamie Watson .10 .30
32 Damon Bailey .10 .30
33 Dontonio Wingfield .10 .30
34 Trevor Ruffin .10 .30
35 Greg Minor .10 .30
36 Dwayne Morton .10 .30
37 Shaquille O'Neal .60 1.50
119 Grant Hill CL .20 .50
HP1 Grant Hill Promo 1.00 2.50

1995 Images Four Sport Classic Performances

Randomly inserted in hobby boxes at a rate of one in every 12 packs, this 20-card standard-size set relives great moments from the careers of 20 top athletes. Each card is numbered out of 4,495. The fronts feature the player against a gold background. The back contains on the left side a description of the great moment and on the right side a color player photo. The cards are numbered with a "CP" prefix.

COMPLETE SET (20) 20.00 50.00
CP1 Glenn Robinson .75 2.00
CP2 Grant Hill 2.00 5.00
CP3 Jason Kidd 2.00 5.00
CP4 Juwan Howard .60 1.50
CP5 Shaquille O'Neal 3.00 8.00
CP6 Alonzo Mourning 1.25 3.00
CP7 Jamal Mashburn .50 1.25

1995 Images Four Sport Clear Excitement

Randomly inserted at a rate of one in every 24 packs in hobby and retail hot boxes (1:1536 over the product run), these two five-card acetate sets each feature five notable athletes from different sports. Cards with the prefix "E" were inserted in hobby hot boxes, while cards with the prefix "C" were found in retail hot boxes. The cards are numbered out of 300.

COMPLETE SET (10) 60.00 150.00
C1 Shaquille O'Neal 12.50 30.00
E1 Grant Hill 6.00 15.00
E4 Hakeem Olajuwon 5.00 12.00

1995 Images Four Sport EP

Randomly inserted in Classic Images boxes these standard-size cards feature a print run of 8000 sets. The fronts feature the player against a silver foil background. The backs contain another player photo and a short bio on the player. The cards are numbered with an "EP" prefix.

EP2 Jason Kidd 1.25 3.00
EP3 Grant Hill 1.00 2.50
EP5 Shaquille O'Neal 2.00 5.00

1995 Images Four Sport Flashbacks

These 10 standard-size cards were randomly inserted into retail boxes at a rate of 1 per 24 packs. The fronts display color action photos, while the backs carry a second photo and player information.

COMPLETE SET (10) 20.00 50.00
TF1 Glenn Robinson 2.50 6.00
TF2 Jason Kidd 3.00 8.00
TF3 Grant Hill 3.00 8.00
TF4 Donyell Marshall 1.50 4.00
TF5 Jamal Mashburn 1.50 4.00
TF6 Eric Montross 1.25 3.00
TF7 Eddie Jones 2.00 5.00
TF8 Alonzo Mourning 2.50 6.00
TF9 Jalen Rose 1.50 4.00
TF10 Shaquille O'Neal 8.00 20.00

1995 Images Four Sport Player of the Year

This four-card standard-size set was obtained through a mail-in wrapper offer, or one set was also included per retail box. The borderless fronts feature a color action player image on a metalic, starburst-look background. The player's name is printed in a black strip at the bottom with the card logo. The backs carry a small color head photo with the player's name, position, and team name below it. A black-and-white player action photo along with the player's statistics round out the back. The cards are numbered with a "POY" prefix.

COMPLETE SET (4) 4.00 10.00
POY3 Grant Hill 1.00 2.50
POY4 Shaquille O'Neal 1.50 4.00

1995 Images Four Sport Previews

Randomly inserted one per 24 packs in second-series '94-95 Assets packs, this five-card standard-size set was issued to promote the Classic Images series. Just 5,000 of each card were produced. The fronts display the player's photo showcased against a metallic background. The backs are devoted on the left side to the player's identification and a note saying you have received a limited edition preview card. The right side of the reverse has a full-color photo of the player and the card is numbered at the upper right corner. The cards are numbered with an "IP" prefix.

COMPLETE SET (5) 6.00 15.00
IP1 Grant Hill 1.00 2.50
IP2 Shaquille O'Neal 2.00 5.00

1999 Jersey City Basketball

COMPLETE SET (50) 3.00 8.00
COMMON CARD (1-50) .05 .15
SEMISTARS .07 .20
UNLISTED STARS .10 .25
1 Michael Olowokandi .05 .15
2 Antawn Jamison .10 .25
3 Vince Carter .20 .50
4 Robert Traylor .05 .15
5 Jason Williams .12 .30
6 Paul Pierce .15 .40
7 Bonzi Wells .05 .15
8 Keon Clark .05 .15
9 Kobe Bryant CL .50 1.25
10 Pat Garrity .05 .15
11 Ricky Davis .07 .20
12 Tyronn Lue .07 .20
13 Felipe Lopez .05 .15
14 Al Harrington .10 .25
15 Corey Benjamin .05 .15
16 Rashard Lewis .10 .25
17 Jelani McCoy .05 .15
18 Shammond Williams .05 .15
19 DeMarco Johnson .05 .15
20 Korleone Young .05 .15
21 Mile Simon .05 .15
22 Toby Bailey .05 .15
23 J.R. Henderson .05 .15
24 Zendon Hamilton .05 .15
25 Jeff Sheppard .05 .15
26 Kobe Bryant .50 1.25
27 Stephon Marbury .07 .20
28 Tracy McGrady .15 .40
29 Scottie Pippen .15 .40
30 Tim Thomas .05 .15
31 Michael Olowokandi CL .05 .15
32 Antawn Jamison CL .10 .25
33 Michael Olowokandi .05 .15
34 Antawn Jamison .10 .25
35 Vince Carter .20 .50
36 Robert Traylor .05 .15
37 Jason Williams .12 .30
38 Paul Pierce .15 .40
39 Bonzi Wells .05 .15
40 Keon Clark .05 .15
41 Kobe Bryant CL .50 1.25
42 Pat Garrity .05 .15
43 Michael Olowokandi .05 .15
44 Antawn Jamison .10 .25
45 Vince Carter .20 .50
46 Robert Traylor .05 .15
47 Jason Williams .12 .30
48 Paul Pierce .15 .40
49 Bonzi Wells .05 .15
50 Keon Clark .05 .15

1999 Jersey City Basketball Gold

*GOLD: .6X TO 1.5X BASE HI

1999 Jersey City Game Gear

STATED ODDS 1:36
1 Kobe Bryant 12.00 30.00
2 Scottie Pippen 4.00 10.00
3 Stephon Marbury 2.00 5.00
4 Tim Thomas 2.00 5.00
5 Tracy McGrady 4.00 10.00

1999 Jersey City Hard Court Time Warp

COMPLETE SET (12) 6.00 15.00
STATED PRINT RUN 1000 TO 12000 SETS
TW1 Shareef Abdur-Rahim .50 1.25
David Thompson
TW2 Ray Allen .60 1.50
Alex English
TW3 Kobe Bryant 3.00 8.00
Alex English
TW4 Marcus Camby .60 1.50
Moses Malone
TW5 Erick Dampier .60 1.50
George Gervin
TW6 Allen Iverson 1.25 3.00
Isiah Thomas
TW7 Kerry Kittles 1.25 3.00
Isiah Thomas
TW8 Stephon Marbury .50 1.25
David Thompson
TW9 Antoine Walker .60 1.50
Moses Malone
TW10 Samaki Walker .60 1.50
Walt Frazier
TW11 John Wallace .60 1.50
George Gervin
TW12 Lorenzen Wright .60 1.50
Walt Frazier

1999 Jersey City Hard Court Time Warp Autographs

STATED PRINT RUN 1000 SETS
ONLY RETIRED SIGNED CARDS
TW2 Ray Allen 6.00 15.00
Alex English AU
TW5 Erick Dampier 8.00 20.00
George Gervin AU
TW6 Allen Iverson 10.00 25.00
Isiah Thomas AU
TW8 Stephon Marbury 6.00 15.00
David Thompson AU
TW9 Antoine Walker 8.00 20.00
Moses Malone AU
TW10 Samaki Walker 8.00 20.00
Walt Frazier AU

1999 Jersey City KB8

COMPLETE SET (5) 2.50 6.00
COMMON CARD (1-5) .75 2.00

1999 Jersey City KB8 Special Edition

COMMON CARD (1-5) 4.00 10.00

1999 Jersey City Markers

COMPLETE SET (15) 2.00 5.00
STATED PRINT RUN 1500 SETS
1 Michael Olowokandi .12 .30
2 Antawn Jamison .20 .50
3 Vince Carter .40 1.00
4 Robert Traylor .12 .30
5 Jason Williams .25 .60
6 Paul Pierce .30 .75
7 Keon Clark .12 .30
8 Pat Garrity .12 .30
9 Jelani McCoy .12 .30
10 Tyronn Lue .15 .40
11 Felipe Lopez .12 .30
12 Al Harrington .20 .50
13 Corey Benjamin .12 .30
14 Kobe Bryant 1.00 2.50
15 Toby Bailey .12 .30

1999 Jersey City Pro Signature Authentics

RANDOM INSERTS IN PACKS
1 Michael Olowokandi 2.00 5.00
2 Antawn Jamison 4.00 10.00
3 Vince Carter 10.00 25.00
4 Robert Traylor 2.00 5.00
5 Jason Williams 3.00 8.00
6 Paul Pierce 6.00 15.00
7 Bonzi Wells 2.00 5.00
8 Keon Clark 2.00 5.00
9 Pat Garrity 2.00 5.00
10 Ricky Davis 2.00 5.00
11 Tyronn Lue 2.00 5.00
12 Felipe Lopez 2.00 5.00
13 Al Harrington 2.00 5.00
14 Corey Benjamin 2.00 5.00
15 Rashard Lewis 3.00 8.00
16 Jelani McCoy 2.00 5.00
17 Shammond Williams 2.00 5.00
18 DeMarco Johnson 2.00 5.00
19 Korleone Young 2.00 5.00
20 Miles Simon 2.00 5.00
21 Toby Bailey 2.00 5.00
22 J.R. Henderson 2.00 5.00
23 Zendon Hamilton 2.00 5.00
24 Jeff Sheppard 2.00 5.00

1996 Pacific Power

This 54-card set highlights 42 draft picks and 12 pre players. Each pack contained three cards. The card fronts have a foil background with player's name written vertically on the left side of the color player photo. The backs have another photo along with a player biography. Also included in the set are a silver (3:37) and platinum (1:721) parallel to the base set. The platinum cards have sky blue foil treament on the card fronts and a PP prefix on the card numbers. Insert sets include Gold Crown Die Cuts, In the Paint and Jump Ball.

COMPLETE SET (54) 8.00 20.00
1 Shareef Abdur-Rahim .50 1.25
2 Ray Allen 1.00 2.50
3 Terrell Bell .25 .60
4 Joseph Blair .25 .60
5 Marcus Brown .25 .60
6 Kobe Bryant 3.00 8.00
7 Marcus Camby .40 1.00
8 Erick Dampier .25 .60
9 Ben Davis .25 .60
10 Tony Delk .25 .60
11 Tyus Edney .15 .40
12 Brian Evans .25 .60
13 Michael Finley .30 .75
14 Derek Fisher .50 1.25
15 Todd Fuller .25 .60
16 Reggie Geary .25 .60
17 Steve Hamer .25 .60
18 Othella Harrington .25 .60

3 Mark Hendrickson .25 .60
) Allen Iverson 1.25 3.00
1 Dontae' Jones .25 .60
2 Jason Kidd .40 1.00
3 Kerry Kittles .25 .60
4 Randy Livingston .25 .60
5 Stephon Marbury .60 1.50
6 Jamal Mashburn .20 .50
7 Walter McCarty .25 .60
8 Amal McCaskill .25 .60
9 Antonio McDyess .25 .60
0 Jeff McInnis .25 .60
1 Russ Millard .25 .60
2 Ryan Minor .30 .75
3 Alonzo Mourning .30 .75
4 Dikembe Mutombo .25 .60
5 Steve Nash 1.25 3.00
6 Moochie Norris .25 .60
7 Ed O'Bannon .15 .40
8 Jermaine O'Neal .60 1.50
9 Mark Pope .25 .60
0 Vitaly Potapenko .25 .60
1 Ron Riley .25 .60
2 Darnell Robinson .25 .60
3 Glenn Robinson .25 .60
4 Roy Rogers .25 .60
5 Jason Sasser .25 .60
6 Doron Sheffer .25 .60
7 Joe Smith .20 .50
8 Damon Stoudamire .25 .60
9 Antoine Walker .50 1.25
50 Samaki Walker .25 .60
51 John Wallace .25 .60
52 Rasheed Wallace .30 .75
53 Jerome Williams .25 .60
54 Lorenzen Wright .25 .60

1996 Pacific Power Platinum

Randomly inserted in packs at one in 721, this 54-card set parallels the base set using Platinum foil. To ascertain values for individual cards, please refer to the multiplier in the header below, coupled with the values from the base set.
*PLATINUM: 25X TO 60X BASE CARD HI

1996 Pacific Power Silver

Randomly inserted in packs at three in 37, this 54-card set parallels the base set using silver foil. To ascertain values on individual cards, please refer to the multiplier in the header below, coupled with the value of the base card.
*SILVER: 4X TO 10X BASE CARD HI

1996 Pacific Power Gold Crown Die Cuts

This 15-card insert set, inserted at a rate of 3:37, follows the same basic design of every other Pacific Gold Crown Die Cuts. A gold crown is die-cut out of the top. Below the player photograph is the player's name in gold foil. The backs have another player photo and a small biography. The cards are numbered with a "GC-" prefix.
COMPLETE SET (15) 20.00 50.00
GC1 Shareef Abdur-Rahim 2.00 5.00
GC2 Ray Allen 4.00 10.00
GC3 Kobe Bryant 10.00 25.00
GC4 Marcus Camby 1.50 4.00
GC5 Erick Dampier 1.00 2.50
GC6 Tony Delk 1.00 2.50
GC7 Allen Iverson 5.00 12.00
GC8 Jason Kidd 1.50 4.00
GC9 Stephon Marbury 2.50 6.00
GC10 Steve Nash 5.00 12.00
GC11 Jermaine O'Neal 2.50 6.00
GC12 Joe Smith .75 2.00
GC13 Damon Stoudamire 1.00 2.50
GC14 Antoine Walker 2.00 5.00
GC15 John Wallace 1.00 2.50

1996 Pacific Power In The Paint

This 20-card insert set was inserted at a rate of 3:37. Each card highlights a pro or college player that spends time in the paint-rebounding or driving. The cards have an action player shot and the player's name is written in a transparent font in large letters behind the player. The backs have another photo and some biographical information. The cards are numbered with a "IP-" prefix.
COMPLETE SET (20) 20.00 50.00
IP1 Shareef Abdur-Rahim 2.00 5.00
IP2 Ray Allen 4.00 10.00
IP3 Kobe Bryant 10.00 25.00
IP4 Marcus Camby 1.50 4.00
IP5 Erick Dampier 1.00 2.50
IP6 Tyus Edney .60 1.50
IP7 Michael Finley 1.25 3.00
IP8 Allen Iverson 5.00 12.00
IP9 Dontae' Jones 1.00 2.50
IP10 Jason Kidd 1.50 4.00
IP11 Stephon Marbury 2.50 6.00
IP12 Antonio McDyess 1.00 2.50
IP13 Dikembe Mutombo 1.00 2.50
IP14 Steve Nash 5.00 12.00
IP15 Ed O'Bannon .60 1.50
IP16 Jermaine O'Neal 2.50 6.00
IP17 Joe Smith .75 2.00
IP18 Damon Stoudamire 1.00 2.50
IP19 Antoine Walker 2.00 5.00
IP20 John Wallace 1.00 2.50

1996 Pacific Power Jump Ball

This 10-card insert set was inserted at a rate of 1:37. The fronts have a gold foil background and a round see-through plastic center that appears you're looking down into the net. A player photo is imprinted on the plastic center. The words "Jump Ball" appear in the bottom right corner next to a small basketball. The backs have another photo. some biographical information and are numbered with the prefix "JB-".
COMPLETE SET (10) 20.00 50.00
JB1 Shareef Abdur-Rahim 2.50 6.00
JB2 Ray Allen 5.00 12.00
JB3 Kobe Bryant 15.00 40.00
JB4 Marcus Camby 2.00 5.00
JB5 Erick Dampier 1.25 3.00
JB6 Allen Iverson 6.00 15.00
JB7 Dontae' Jones 1.25 3.00
JB8 Stephon Marbury 3.00 8.00
JB9 Antoine Walker 2.50 6.00
JB10 Lorenzen Wright 1.25 3.00

1996 Pacific Power Platinum Crown Die Cuts

This mail-in set of five cards resembles the randomly inserted Gold Crown Die Cuts, but the foil is platinum colored. Collectors could receive a complete set by mailing in 18 wrappers and $4.95 to Pacific by 7/31/97.
COMPLETE SET (5) 10.00 25.00
1 Kobe Bryant 8.00 20.00
2 Marcus Camby 1.25 3.00
3 Erick Dampier .75 2.00
4 Allen Iverson 4.00 10.00
5 Steve Nash 4.00 10.00

1996 Pacific Power Regents of Roundball

This 55-card set parallels the base Pacific Power set with a slightly different look where are cards are numbered with an "RR" prefix. The distribution means of this set is still unknown.
*REGENTS: .5X TO 1.25X BASE CARD HI

1994 Pacific Prism Samples

This three-card standard-size set was issued to preview the 1994 Pacific Prism Draft Picks series. The cards were available in both silver and gold prism foil. The gold versions are valued at 1.5X to 2X the prices listed below. The fronts display a player action cutout on a prism foil background. The player's name and the Pacific logo appear in a bar toward the bottom. On a background displaying colorful rays of light emanating from a central point, the horizontal back carries a color player photo, biography, and player profile. On the backs, the cards have the word "SAMPLE" followed by the card number in the upper right corner.
COMPLETE SET (3) 2.00 5.00
1 Glenn Robinson .60 1.50
2 Jason Kidd 1.50 4.00
3 Anfernee Hardaway .60 1.50

1994 Pacific Prisms

This 72-card standard-size set was licensed by Classic Games and produced by Pacific. Just 3,999 individually-numbered cases were produced. Alongside the rookie players are NBA stars: Anfernee Hardaway (21, 69), Jamal Mashburn (31, 70), Harold Miner (35), Isaiah Rider (49), Alonzo Mourning (40, 71), and Dikembe Mutombo (41, 72). The cards were available in both silver and gold prism foil and are printed on 18-point card stock with UV coating on both sides. One prism card was inserted per pack, and each pack also had a "backer" card from either the 20-card Dan Majerle set, checklist cards, or a production information card. The fronts display a player action cutout on a prism foil background. The player's name and the Pacific logo appear in a bar toward the bottom. On a background displaying colorful rays of light emanating from a central point, the horizontal back carries a color player photo, biography, and player profile.
COMPLETE SET (74) 15.00 30.00
1 Derrick Alston .08 .25
2 Adrian Autry .08 .25
3 Damon Bailey .08 .25
4 Melvin Booker .08 .25
5 Joey Brown .08 .25
6 Albert Burditt .08 .25
7 Robert Churchwell .08 .25
8 Gary Collier .08 .25
9 Jevon Crudup .08 .25
10 Bill Curley .40 1.00
11 Yinka Dare .08 .25
12 Rodney Dent .08 .25
13 Tony Dumas .08 .25
14 Howard Eisley .40 1.00
15 Travis Ford .08 .25
16 Lawrence Funderburke .08 .25
17 Anthony Goldwire .08 .25
18 Chuck Graham .08 .25
19 Brian Grant 1.25 3.00
20 Darrin Hancock .08 .25
21 Anfernee Hardaway .40 1.00
22 Carl Ray Harris .08 .25
23 Grant Hill 2.00 5.00
24 Askia Jones .08 .25
25 Eddie Jones 2.00 5.00
26 Arturas Karnishovas .08 .25
27 Damon Key .08 .25
28 Jason Kidd 2.50 6.00
29 Antonio Lang .08 .25
30 Donyell Marshall .75 2.00
31 Jamal Mashburn .40 1.00
32 Billy McCaffrey .08 .25
33 Jim McIlvaine .08 .25
34 Aaron McKie .75 2.00
35 Harold Miner .08 .25
36 Greg Minor .08 .25
37 Eric Mobley .08 .25
38 Eric Montross .40 1.00
39 Dwayne Morton .08 .25
40 Alonzo Mourning .40 1.00
41 Dikembe Mutombo .40 1.00
42 Gaylon Nickerson .08 .25
43 Wesley Person .40 1.00
44 Derrick Phelps .08 .25
45 Eric Piatkowski .40 1.00
46 Kevin Rankin .08 .25
47 Brian Reese .08 .25
48 Khalid Reeves .40 1.00
49 Isaiah Rider .40 1.00
50 Glenn Robinson 2.00 5.00
51 Carlos Rogers .08 .25
52 Jalen Rose 2.00 5.00
53 Clifford Rozier .08 .25
54 Kevin Salvadori .08 .25
55 Jervaughn Scales .08 .25
56 Shawnelle Scott .08 .25
57 Dickey Simpkins .08 .25
58 Michael Smith .08 .25
59 Shon Tarver .08 .25
60 Deon Thomas .08 .25
61 Brooks Thompson .08 .25
62 B.J. Tyler .08 .25
63 Charlie Ward .75 2.00
64 Jamie Watson .08 .25
65 Jeff Webster .08 .25
66 Monty Williams .40 1.00
67 Dontonio Wingfield .08 .25
68 Steve Woodberry .08 .25
69 Anfernee Hardaway .40 1.00
70 Jamal Mashburn .40 1.00
71 Alonzo Mourning .40 1.00
72 Dikembe Mutombo .40 1.00
NNO Pacific Logo .08 .25
NNO Checklist .08 .25

1994 Pacific Prisms Gold

This 72-card standard-size set was inserted at a rate of two per box. The cards were printed on 18-point card stock with UV coating on both sides. The fronts display a player action cutout on a prism foil background. To ascertain values of individual cards, please refer to the multiplier in the header, coupled with the value of the base card.
*GOLD: 1.5X TO 4X VALUE

1994 Pacific Prisms Dan Majerle

This 20-card standard-size insert set highlights Dan Majerle. The fronts feature color action player photos with a white border. Pacific's Crown Collection logo appears in the upper left corner, while the player's name and position are printed in cursive letters in the lower right corner. The white-bordered backs carry another color action player shot with brief player information in the lower right. The cards are numbered on the back as "X of 20".
COMPLETE SET (20) 1.50 3.00
COMMON MAJERLE (1-20) .08 .25

1995 Pacific Prisms

This 54-card set, produced by Pacific Trading Cards, features a borderless color action player photo on the front with the player's name printed on a diagonal stripe in the lower right. The backs carry a small color player photo with the player's name, position, biographical and draft information.
COMPLETE SET (54) 4.00 10.00
1 Joe Smith .40 1.00
2 David Vaughn .20 .50
3 Anthony Pelle .20 .50
4 Sherrell Ford .20 .50
5 Corliss Williamson .20 .50
6 Mario Bennett .20 .50
7 Jason Caffey .20 .50
8 Rick Brunson .20 .50
Erwin Claggett
9 George Zidek .20 .50
10 Eric Snow .20 .50
11 Travis Best .20 .50
12 Theo Ratliff .30 .75
13 Greg Ostertag .20 .50
14 Lou Roe .20 .50
15 Eric Montross .12 .30
16 Hakeem Olajuwon .25 .60
17 Cherokee Parks .20 .50
18 Glenn Robinson .20 .50
19 Hakeem Olajuwon .25 .60
20 Terrence Rencher .20 .50
21 Cory Alexander .20 .50
22 Tyus Edney .20 .50
23 Damon Stoudamire .50 1.25
24 Junior Burrough .20 .50
25 Donny Marshall UER .20 .50
Buck Marshall
26 Brent Barry .30 .75
27 Rasheed Wallace .60 1.50
28 LaZelle Durden .20 .50
29 Jimmy King .20 .50
30 Don Reid .20 .50
31 Loren Meyer .20 .50
32 Joe Smith .40 1.00
33 Cuonzo Martin .20 .50
34 Eddie Jones .25 .60
35 Ed O'Bannon .20 .50
36 Jason Kidd .30 .75
37 Erik Meeks .20 .50
38 Greg Ostertag .20 .50
39 Ed O'Bannon .60 1.50
Rasheed Wallace
40 Eric Williams .20 .50
41 Randolph Childress .20 .50
42 Wesley Person .12 .30
43 Antonio McDyess .50 1.25
44 Andrew DeClercq .20 .50
45 Constantin Popa .20 .50
46 Gary Trent .20 .50
47 Jerome Allen .20 .50
48 Michael Finley .60 1.50
49 Mark Davis .20 .50
50 Shawn Respert .20 .50
51 John Amaechi .20 .50
Corey Beck
52 Rashard Griffith .20 .50
53 Kurt Thomas .20 .50
54 Lawrence Moten .20 .50

1995 Pacific Prisms Blue

Randomly inserted in packs at three in 37, this 54-card set parallels the base set. The cards feature blue foil. To ascertain values for individual cards, please refer to the multiplier in the header below, coupled with the value of the base card.
COMPLETE SET (54) 25.00 60.00
*BLUE: 1.5X TO 4X BASE CARD HI

1995 Pacific Prisms Presidential Gold

Randomly inserted in packs at two in 720, this 54-card set parallels the base set. The cards feature gold foil. To ascertain values of individual cards, please refer to the multiplier in the header below, coupled with the value of the base card.
*GOLD: 20X TO 50X BASE CARD HI

1995 Pacific Prisms Red

Randomly inserted in packs at three in 37, this 54-card set parallels the base set. The cards feature red foil. To ascertain values for individual cards, please refer to the multiplier in the header, coupled with the value of the base card.
COMPLETE SET (54) 25.00 60.00
*RED: 1.5X TO 4X BASE CARD HI

1995 Pacific Prisms Centers of Attention

This 10-card set was randomly inserted in packs and was produced by Pacific Trading Cards with its crystalline technology. The fronts feature a color action player photo with the player's name and a clear backboard in the background. The backs carry the player's name with a discription of the player's ability and a small color player photo.
COMPLETE SET (10) 8.00 20.00
C1 Jason Kidd 1.25 3.00
C2 Antonio McDyess 2.00 5.00
C3 Ed O'Bannon .75 2.00
C4 Hakeem Olajuwon 1.00 2.50
C5 Greg Ostertag .75 2.00
C6 Shawn Respert .75 2.00
C7 Glenn Robinson .75 2.00
C8 Joe Smith 1.50 4.00
C9 Damon Stoudamire 2.00 5.00
C10 Rasheed Wallace 2.50 6.00

1995 Pacific Prisms Gold Crown Die Cuts

This 15-card set was randomly inserted in packs of Draft Pick Prism Basketball Cards. The set features 11 different draft pick players and four current players in their second professional season. The fronts display a color action player photo with the player's name printed in gold foil at the bottom. The top of the card is cut in the shape of a crown with gold foil accents. The backs carry another player photo with the player's name, draft information, and career highlights.
COMPLETE SET (15) 20.00 50.00
DC1 Jason Caffey 1.25 3.00
DC2 Michael Finley 4.00 10.00
DC3 Eddie Jones 1.50 4.00
DC4 Jason Kidd 2.00 5.00
DC5 Antonio McDyess 3.00 8.00
DC6 Ed O'Bannon 1.25 3.00
DC7 Greg Ostertag 1.25 3.00
DC8 Cherokee Parks 1.25 3.00
DC9 Shawn Respert 1.25 3.00
DC10 Glenn Robinson 1.25 3.00
DC11 Joe Smith 2.50 6.00
DC12 Damon Stoudamire 3.00 8.00
DC13 Rasheed Wallace 4.00 10.00
DC14 Eric Williams 1.25 3.00
DC15 Corliss Williamson 1.25 3.00

1995 Pacific Prisms Olajuwon

These cards were randomly inserted in foil packs. Inside an ornate, prismatic gold-foil picture frame, the fronts display color action player photos. Because the set is not licensed by the NBA, team logos have been airbrushed off the pictures. On an orange background displaying a basketball, the backs have "Hakeem Olajuwon The Dream" in large block letters, with a player fact and head shot below.
COMPLETE SET (12) 3.00 8.00
COMMON CARD (1-12) .40 1.00

1995 Pacific Prisms Platinum Crown Die Cuts

This five-card set could be obtained by mailing in 18 wrappers of 1995 Pacific Crown Collection Draft Picks Prism Basketball Cards plus shipping and handling charges to Pacific Trading Cards.
COMPLETE SET (5) 6.00 15.00
P1 Antonio McDyess 3.00 8.00
P2 Ed O'Bannon 1.25 3.00
P3 Greg Ostertag 1.25 3.00
P4 Joe Smith 2.50 6.00
P5 Rasheed Wallace 4.00 10.00

1995 Press Pass

The 1995 Press Pass set consists of 36 regular cards and were issued in three-card packs. Packs contained a regular card, a die-cut card and an insert card. Prime Time Phone cards were inserted in one of every five boxes (36 packs per box). Borderless fronts feature a full-color player cutout set against a photo panel with photo boxes. A gold foil ribbon appears across the bottom with the player's name, draft number and his team in black type. Backs continue with the cutout panel background and a full-color player cutout. A white screened box contains a player biography and statistics which are printed vertically. A blue strip runs along the bottom and has the player's name in white print inside.
COMPLETE SET (36) 5.00 10.00
1 Joe Smith .25 .60
2 Antonio McDyess .30 .75
3 Jerry Stackhouse .40 1.00
4 Rasheed Wallace .40 1.00
5 Kevin Garnett 1.00 2.50
6 Bryant Reeves .12 .30
7 Damon Stoudamire .30 .75
8 Shawn Respert .12 .30
9 Ed O'Bannon .12 .30
10 Kurt Thomas .12 .30
11 Gary Trent .12 .30
12 Cherokee Parks .12 .30
13 Corliss Williamson .12 .30
14 Eric Williams .12 .30
15 Brent Barry .20 .50
16 Theo Ratliff .20 .50
17 Randolph Childress .12 .30
18 Jason Caffey .12 .30
19 Michael Finley .40 1.00
20 George Zidek .12 .30
21 Travis Best .12 .30
22 David Vaughn .12 .30
23 Sherrell Ford .12 .30
24 Mario Bennett .12 .30
25 Lou Roe .12 .30
26 Frankie King .12 .30
27 Rashard Griffith .12 .30
28 Donny Marshall .12 .30
29 Tyus Edney .12 .30
30 Antonio McDyess .25 .60
31 Rasheed Wallace .30 .75
32 Eddie Jones .15 .40
33 Jason Kidd .20 .50
34 Glenn Robinson .12 .30
35 Jalen Rose .15 .40
36 Joe Smith CL .12 .30

1995 Press Pass Die Cuts

Inserted at one per pack, this 36-card set parallels the base set featuring a die cut design. To ascertain values for individual cards, please refer to the multiplier in the header below, coupled with values from the base set.
COMPLETE SET (36) 8.00 20.00
*DIE CUTS: 1X TO 2.5X BASE CARD HI

1995 Press Pass Foil

Randomly inserted in packs at one in nine, this 36-card set parallels the base set using foil treatment. To ascertain values of individual cards, please refer to the multiplier in the header, coupled with the value of the base card.
*FOIL: 4X TO 10X BASE CARD HI

1995 Press Pass Autographs

These autograph cards were randomly seeded in packs. They differ from the regular issue in not having the gold foil across the bottom of the front and bearing an autograph in blue ink.
COMPLETE SET (8) 20.00 50.00
1 Jimmy King 2.00 5.00
2 Antonio McDyess 6.00 15.00
3 Cherokee Parks 2.00 5.00
4 Joe Smith 4.00 10.00
5 Damon Stoudamire 5.00 12.00
6 David Vaughn 2.00 5.00
7 Rasheed Wallace 10.00 25.00
8 Eric Williams 2.00 5.00

1995 Press Pass Pandemonium

Randomly inserted in packs at a rate of one in 18 packs, this nine card standard-size set was printed on Nitrokrome card stock and feature the top nine draft picks. Fronts have colored foil backgrounds and a player action cutout appears in front. The player's last name is printed in a silver foil and his full name is printed in smaller type across the last name. Backs have a full-color action shot and a black strip running vertically down the right side. The player's last name is printed in gray type along the black strip and his full name is printed in smaller white type across that.
COMPLETE SET (9) 6.00 15.00
1 Antonio McDyess 2.00 5.00
2 Ed O'Bannon .75 2.00
3 Shawn Respert .75 2.00
4 Joe Smith 1.50 4.00
5 Damon Stoudamire 2.00 5.00
6 Kurt Thomas .75 2.00
7 Gary Trent .75 2.00
8 Rasheed Wallace 2.50 6.00
9 Corliss Williamson .75 2.00

1995 Press Pass Phone Cards $5

Randomly inserted in packs at one in 36, with the $5 card being the most prevalent, this set of eight cards uses the top draft picks for free phone time. The top three picks, Stackhouse, Smith and McDyess appear on the scarce $1,995 cards. Borderless fronts have two full-color player photos with his name printed vertically on the left side with two stripes on the top and bottom. All printing, including the card value, which appears on the upper right, is gold type. Backs are all white with the rules and instructions for calling printed in black type. $10 and $20 are priced below as multipliers of the $5 cards.
COMPLETE SET (8) 35.00 40.00
*TEN DOLLAR CARDS: .75X TO 2X VALUE
STATED ODDS 1:216
*TWENTY DOLLAR CARDS: 1.5X TO 4X VALUE
STATED ODDS 1:864
1 Kevin Garnett 6.00 15.00
2 Jason Kidd 1.25 3.00
3 Antonio McDyess 2.00 5.00
4 Ed O'Bannon .75 2.00
5 Glenn Robinson .75 2.00
6 Joe Smith 1.50 4.00
7 Jerry Stackhouse 2.50 6.00
8 Rasheed Wallace 2.50 6.00

1995 Press Pass Joe Smith

Randomly inserted in packs at various rates, this set of four standard-size cards focuses on 1995's No. 1 draft pick. The cards were numbered with the prefix "JS" with JS1 being the easiest to find at one in 36 packs. JS2 was inserted in one of 72 packs. JS3 could be found in one of 216 packs and JS4 was scarcest at one in 864. Borderless fronts featured a silver holographic foil background with a player action cutout of Smith in his Maryland uniform. Backs carry a montage of Smith action photos.
COMPLETE SET (4) 12.00 30.00
JS1 Joe Smith .60 1.50
JS2 Joe Smith 1.00 2.50
JS3 Joe Smith 4.00 10.00
JS4 Joe Smith 12.00 30.00

1996 Press Pass

The 1996 Press Pass set was issued in one series totaling 45 cards. The 4-card packs were issued with two bases set cards and two inserts. Over 12,000 autographed were inserted into packs. Also included were random inserts: Acetates, Swish and Net Burner parallels, Jersey Cards, Lottos and Pandemonium.
COMPLETE SET (45) 5.00 12.00
1 Allen Iverson .75 2.00
2 Marcus Camby .25 .60
3 Shareef Abdur-Rahim .30 .75
4 Stephon Marbury .40 1.00
5 Ray Allen .60 1.50
6 Antoine Walker .30 .75
7 Lorenzen Wright .15 .40
8 Kerry Kittles .15 .40
9 Samaki Walker .15 .40
10 Erick Dampier .15 .40
11 Todd Fuller .15 .40
12 Vitaly Potapenko .15 .40
13 Kobe Bryant 1.50 4.00
14 Steve Nash .75 2.00
15 Tony Delk .15 .40
16 Jermaine O'Neal .40 1.00
17 John Wallace .15 .40
18 Walter McCarty .15 .40
19 Dontae' Jones .15 .40
20 Roy Rogers .15 .40
21 Jerome Williams .15 .40
22 Brian Evans .15 .40
23 Travis Knight .15 .40
24 Othella Harrington .15 .40
25 Ryan Minor .20 .50
26 Doron Sheffer .15 .40
27 Jeff McInnis .15 .40
28 Jason Sasser .15 .40
29 Randy Livingston .15 .40
30 Malik Rose .20 .50
31 Jamie Feick .15 .40
32 Mark Pope .15 .40
33 Damon Stoudamire .15 .40
34 Jerry Stackhouse .20 .50
35 Joe Smith .12 .30
36 Michael Finley .20 .50
37 Rasheed Wallace .20 .50
38 Antonio McDyess .15 .40
39 Ray Allen .30 .75
Brevin Knight
Doron Sheffer
40 Walter McCarty .15 .40
Tony Delk
Antoine Walker
Mark Pope
41 Jerome Williams .30 .75
Allen Iverson
Othella Harrington
42 Erick Dampier .12 .30
Dontae' Jones
43 Stephon Marbury .15 .40
Brent Barry
44 Kobe Bryant .75 2.00
Jermaine O'Neal
45 Checklist .12 .30

1996 Press Pass Net Burners

These 45 cards were inserted at the rate of 1 in every 1996 Press Pass pack. The cards are distinguishable by a die cut basketball net with a player photo coming out of the top. The backs do not have a player photo, but contain a small player biography. The cards are numbered "NB x of 45". To ascertain values on individual cards, please refer to the multiplier in the header, coupled with the value of the base card.
COMPLETE SET (45) 12.00 30.00
*STARS: .6X TO 1.5X BASE CARD HI

1996 Press Pass Swisssh

Inserted one per pack, this 45-card set is a parallel of the base set. The cards feature silver foil. To ascertain values on individual cards, please refer to the multiplier in the header, coupled with the value of the base card.
COMPLETE SET (45) 10.00 25.00
*STARS: .6X TO 1.5X BASE CARD HI

1996 Press Pass Acetates

Randomly inserted in hobby packs only at a rate of one in 18, this 9-card set are designed on a see-through plastic card stock. The cards are numbered "F x/9" on the front. Also on the front is a player action shot and the players name written several times in the background. The card backs are blank except for a small copyright notice at the bottom.
COMPLETE SET (9) 10.00 25.00
1 Allen Iverson 5.00 12.00
2 Marcus Camby 1.50 4.00
3 Shareef Abdur-Rahim 2.00 5.00
4 Stephon Marbury 2.50 6.00
5 Ray Allen 4.00 10.00
6 Antoine Walker 2.00 5.00
7 Lorenzen Wright 1.00 2.50
8 Kerry Kittles 1.00 2.50
9 Samaki Walker 1.00 2.50

1996 Press Pass Autographs

This 20-card autograph set were inserted 1:72 packs. The card fronts have the same design as the base set except they bear an autograph of the player. The backs have the player's name and a congratulatory message on receiving the card. The cards are unnumbered and listed below in alphabetical order.

1 Ray Allen	15.00	40.00
2 Kobe Bryant	150.00	300.00
3 Marcus Camby	6.00	15.00
4 Tony Delk	2.00	5.00
5 Brian Evans	2.00	5.00
6 Othella Harrington	2.00	5.00
7 Allen Iverson	40.00	100.00
8 Dontae' Jones	2.00	5.00
9 Travis Knight	2.00	5.00
10 Randy Livingston	2.00	5.00
11 Stephon Marbury	10.00	25.00
12 Walter McCarty	2.00	5.00
13 Steve Nash	20.00	50.00
14 Vitaly Potapenko	2.00	5.00
15 Roy Rogers	2.00	5.00
16 Jason Sasser	2.00	5.00
17 Antoine Walker	8.00	20.00
18 Samaki Walker	2.00	5.00
19 Jerome Williams	2.00	5.00
20 Lorenzen Wright	2.00	5.00

1996 Press Pass Jersey Cards

Randomly inserted in hobby packs at a rate of one in 640 and retail packs at a rate of one in 720, this 4-card set contains actual pieces of a player's game-used jersey. A small piece of the college jersey is in the center of the card above the player's name and the words "Game Used Jersey". The backs have a congratulatory message and are numbered "J x of 4."

J1 Allen Iverson	50.00	125.00
J2 Marcus Camby	15.00	40.00
J3 Ray Allen	40.00	100.00
J4 Shareef Abdur-Rahim	20.00	50.00

1996 Press Pass Lotto

This is a six-card "progressive insert" where each card has a different ratio to be pulled from pack. The cards were available as follows: #1 1:720, #2 1:360, #3 1:180, #4 1:90, #5 1:45, #6 1:36. The cards fronts have silver borders and a picture of the player in front of an orange background. The backs have a picture of the top six picks and are numbers "Lx of 6".

COMPLETE SET (6)	20.00	50.00
1 Allen Iverson	20.00	50.00
2 Marcus Camby	8.00	20.00
3 Shareef Abdur-Rahim	6.00	15.00
4 Stephon Marbury	2.50	6.00
5 Ray Allen	2.00	5.00
6 Antoine Walker	1.00	2.50

1996 Press Pass Pandemonium

Randomly inserted in packs at a rate of one in 12, this 12-card set features some of the hottest players in the college game. Press Pass uses what it calls "NitroKrome" all foil cards. The word "Pandemonium" in very hard to make out, but is jumbled up behind the player photograph on the card fronts. The backs have another player photo and some biographical information. They are also numbered "PM x of 12".

COMPLETE SET (12)	10.00	25.00
1 Shareef Abdur-Rahim	1.50	4.00
2 Ray Allen	3.00	8.00
3 Kobe Bryant	8.00	20.00
4 Marcus Camby	1.25	3.00
5 Erick Dampier	.75	2.00
6 Othella Harrington	.75	2.00
7 Allen Iverson	4.00	10.00
8 Kerry Kittles	.75	2.00
9 Stephon Marbury	2.00	5.00
10 Walter McCarty	.75	2.00
11 Antoine Walker	1.50	4.00
12 John Wallace	.75	2.00

1997 Press Pass

This 45-card set was issued in 4-card packs in 36-pack hobby boxes. The card fronts have full-bleed color player photos and the player's name and Press Pass in gold foil at the bottom. Each hobby box states that is contains on average, two autographs per box. Each pack contained at least two insert cards among the following: All-American, Autographs, Blue Torquers, In Your Face, Jersey Cards, Lotto, Net Burners, One on One and Red Zone.

COMPLETE SET (45)	4.00	10.00
1 Tim Duncan	1.00	2.50
2 Ron Mercer	.20	.50
3 Keith Van Horn	.30	.75
4 Tony Battie	.20	.50
5 Olivier Saint-Jean	.15	.40
6 Tim Thomas	.30	.75
7 Adonal Foyle	.15	.40
8 Tracy McGrady	.75	2.00
9 Antonio Daniels	.15	.40
10 Kelvin Cato	.15	.40
11 Danny Fortson	.15	.40
12 Chauncey Billups	.60	1.50
13 Brevin Knight	.15	.40
14 Jacque Vaughn	.15	.40
15 James Collins	.15	.40
16 Johnny Taylor	.15	.40
17 Derek Anderson	.15	.40
18 Austin Croshere	.15	.40
19 Reggie Freeman	.15	.40
20 Maurice Taylor	.15	.40
21 Shea Seals	.15	.40
22 Anthony Parker	.15	.40
23 John Thomas	.15	.40
24 Kebu Stewart	.15	.40
25 Dedric Willoughby	.15	.40
26 Serge Zwikker	.15	.40
27 Paul Grant	.15	.40
28 Victor Page	.15	.40
29 Bubba Wells	.15	.40
30 Ed Gray	.15	.40
31 Charles O'Bannon	.15	.40
32 Bobby Jackson	.20	.50
33 Keith Booth	.15	.40
34 Eddie Elisma	.15	.40
35 Scot Pollard	.15	.40
36 Harold Deane	.15	.40
37 Jeff Capel	.15	.40
38 Kiwane Garris	.15	.40
39 Charles Smith	.15	.40
40 Alvin Sims	.15	.40
41 Serge Zwikker Tim Duncan Eddie Elisma	.40	1.00
42 Austin Croshere Tim Thomas	.15	.40
43 Tony Battie Jacque Vaughn Chauncey Billups	.20	.50
44 Ron Mercer Derek Anderson	.20	.50
45 Tim Duncan CL	.40	1.00

1997 Press Pass Blue Torquers

This 45-card set is an exact parallel of the base set inserted at one in every retail pack. The foil on the card front bottoms is blue instead of gold. To ascertain values on individual cards, please refer to the multiplier in the header below, coupled with the value of the base card.

*STARS: .6X TO 1.5X BASE CARD HI

1997 Press Pass Red Zone

This 45-card set is an exact parallel of the base set inserted at one in every retail pack. The foil on the card front bottoms is red instead of gold. To ascertain values on individual cards, please refer to the multiplier in the header below, coupled with the value of the base card.

*STARS: .6X TO 1.5X BASE CARD HI

1997 Press Pass All-American

This 12-card set used Press Pass' "NitroKrome" technology. Each card has a foil based background and two photos of the player on the front. The backs have another photo and some biographical information. The cards are numbered "AX of 12".

COMPLETE SET (12)	10.00	25.00
A1 Tim Duncan	4.00	10.00
A2 Keith Van Horn	1.25	3.00
A3 Ron Mercer	.75	2.00
A4 Tracy McGrady	3.00	8.00
A5 Danny Fortson	.60	1.50
A6 Brevin Knight	.60	1.50
A7 Tony Battie	.75	2.00
A8 Jacque Vaughn	.60	1.50
A9 Chauncey Billups	2.50	6.00
A10 Bobby Jackson	.75	2.00
A11 Adonal Foyle	.60	1.50
A12 Shea Seals	.60	1.50

1997 Press Pass Autographs

This 30-card set offers autographs from 30 different NBA rookies. The cards parallel their base set card, but the foil on the bottom is in a yellow font, and the card background has an added white shading to it. The packs have a congratulatory message on receiving the autograph. Some cards were inserted as redemption cards that expired July 30, 1998. The cards are unnumbered and listed below in alphabetical order.

1 Derek Anderson	1.50	4.00
2 Tony Battie	2.00	5.00
3 Chauncey Billups	6.00	15.00
4 Jeff Capel	1.50	4.00
5 Kelvin Cato	1.50	4.00
6 James Collins	1.50	4.00
7 Austin Croshere	1.50	4.00
8 Harold Deane	1.50	4.00
9 Tim Duncan	40.00	100.00
10 Eddie Elisma	1.50	4.00
11 Danny Fortson	1.50	4.00
12 Kiwane Garris	1.50	4.00
13 Paul Grant	1.50	4.00
14 Bobby Jackson	2.00	5.00
15 Brevin Knight	1.50	4.00
16 Tracy McGrady	15.00	40.00
17 Charles O'Bannon	1.50	4.00
18 Anthony Parker	1.50	4.00
19 Scot Pollard	1.50	4.00
20 Olivier Saint-Jean	1.50	4.00
21 Alvin Sims	1.50	4.00
22 Charles Smith	1.50	4.00
23 Kebu Stewart	1.50	4.00
24 Johnny Taylor	1.50	4.00
25 Maurice Taylor	1.50	4.00
26 John Thomas	1.50	4.00
27 Tim Thomas	3.00	8.00
28 Jacque Vaughn	1.50	4.00
29 Bubba Wells	1.50	4.00
30 Serge Zwikker	1.50	4.00

1997 Press Pass In Your Face

Inserted at a rate of 1 per 36 hobby packs, these cards highlight nine different players on a clear acetate-stock card. The cards are numbered on the back with a prefix of "IYF"

COMPLETE SET (9)	10.00	25.00
IYF1 Ron Mercer	1.25	3.00
IYF2 Danny Fortson	1.00	2.50
IYF3 Chauncey Billups	4.00	10.00
IYF4 Maurice Taylor	1.00	2.50
IYF5 Keith Van Horn	2.00	5.00
IYF6 Bobby Jackson	1.25	3.00
IYF7 Tony Battie	1.25	3.00
IYF8 Tim Duncan	6.00	15.00
IYF9 Kelvin Cato	1.00	2.50

1997 Press Pass Jersey Cards

Inserted at the rate of 1 in 612 packs, these cards contain actual pieces of game-worn jerseys from top 1997 NBA draft picks. The cards of Ron Mercer, Keith Van Horn, Tony Battie and Tim Duncan were released later in the Double Threat product.

JC1 Tim Duncan PP	25.00	60.00
JC2 Ron Mercer DT	10.00	25.00
JC3 Keith Van Horn DT	12.50	30.00
JC4 Jacque Vaughn PP	6.00	15.00
BON Tim Duncan DT	40.00	100.00
BON Tony Battie DT	6.00	15.00
BON Chauncey Billups PP	8.00	20.00

1997 Press Pass Lotto

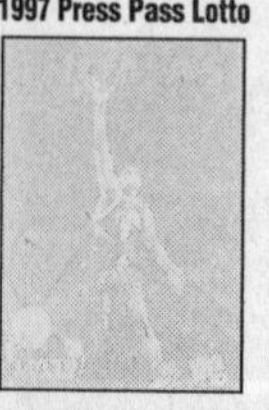

This 7-card set was inserted into packs with progressive ratios that were tougher the lower the card number. The cards have foil background fronts with a player photo, and all players pictured on the back. Each is numbered "LX of 6". The odds for each is as follows: #1 1:720, #2 1:360, #3 1:180, #4 1:90, #5 1:45, #6 1:36. Chauncey Billups was added at the last minute without a card number and was inserted at a rate of one in 360 packs.

COMPLETE SET (7)	25.00	60.00
L1 Tim Duncan	20.00	50.00
L2 Ron Mercer	4.00	10.00
L3 Keith Van Horn	6.00	15.00
L4 Tony Battie	2.50	6.00
L5 Adonal Foyle	2.00	5.00
L6 Tim Thomas	2.50	6.00
NNO Chauncey Billups	5.00	12.00

1997 Press Pass Net Burners

This 36-card all-foil die cut cards were inserted at the rate of one per pack. The fronts have photos of the player in front of a ball and net. The backs have some biographical information and are numbered "NB X of 36".

COMPLETE SET (36)	6.00	15.00
NB1 Tim Duncan	1.50	4.00
NB2 Ron Mercer	.30	.75
NB3 Keith Van Horn	.50	1.25
NB4 Tony Battie	.30	.75
NB5 Scot Pollard	.25	.60
NB6 Tim Thomas	.50	1.25
NB7 Adonal Foyle	.25	.60
NB8 Tracy McGrady	1.25	3.00
NB9 Antonio Daniels	.25	.60
NB10 Kelvin Cato	.25	.60
NB11 Danny Fortson	.25	.60
NB12 Chauncey Billups	1.00	2.50
NB13 Brevin Knight	.25	.60
NB14 Jacque Vaughn	.25	.60
NB15 James Collins	.25	.60
NB16 Alvin Sims	.25	.60
NB17 Derek Anderson	.25	.60
NB18 Austin Croshere	.25	.60
NB19 Reggie Freeman	.25	.60
NB20 Maurice Taylor	.25	.60
NB21 Shea Seals	.25	.60
NB22 Anthony Parker	.25	.60
NB23 Johnny Taylor	.25	.60
NB24 Kebu Stewart	.25	.60
NB25 Dedric Willoughby	.25	.60
NB26 Serge Zwikker	.25	.60
NB27 Olivier Saint-Jean	.25	.60
NB28 Victor Page	.25	.60
NB29 Bubba Wells	.25	.60
NB30 Ed Gray	.25	.60
NB31 Charles O'Bannon	.25	.60
NB32 Bobby Jackson	.30	.75
NB33 Eddie Elisma	.25	.60
NB34 Kiwane Garris	.25	.60
NB35 Keith Booth	.25	.60
NB36 Tim Duncan CL	.60	1.50
NNO Ray Allen Promo	.60	1.50

1997 Press Pass One On One

This 9-card set, inserted at a rate of 1 in 18 packs, highlights one-on-one match-ups of NBA players-to-be. The card fronts picture both players on a silver foil background. The backs talk about what the match-up would be like. Cards are numbered "X of 9".

COMPLETE SET (9)	10.00	25.00
1 Tim Duncan Tony Battie	4.00	10.00
2 Danny Fortson Tim Duncan	4.00	10.00
3 Ron Mercer Tracy McGrady	3.00	8.00
4 Keith Van Horn Tim Thomas	1.25	3.00
5 Antonio Daniels Chauncey Billups	2.50	6.00
6 Adonal Foyle Kelvin Cato	.60	1.50
7 Derek Anderson Ron Mercer	.75	2.00
8 Jacque Vaughn Brevin Knight	.60	1.50
9 Austin Croshere Maurice Taylor	.60	1.50

1998 Press Pass

The 1998 Press Pass set was issued in one series totaling 45 cards and was distributed in four-card packs. The fronts feature full-bleed color player photos. The backs carry player information. Along with the parallel and insert sets that follow this listing, there was a Solo parallel set that was a "One of One" style set where there was only one card produced per base set card. Due to there scarcity, the cards values can not be assessed by our guides.

COMPLETE SET (45)	5.00	10.00
1 Mike Bibby	.40	1.00
2 Nazr Mohammed	.15	.40
3 Raef LaFrentz	.20	.50
4 Vince Carter	.75	2.00
5 Paul Pierce	.75	2.00
6 Michael Olowokandi	.20	.50
7 Larry Hughes	.30	.75
8 Keon Clark	.15	.40
9 Robert Traylor	.15	.40
10 Michael Doleac	.15	.40
11 Pat Garrity	.15	.40
12 Jason Williams	.40	1.00
13 Miles Simon	.15	.40
14 Toby Bailey	.15	.40
15 Bonzi Wells	.15	.40
16 Tyronn Lue	.15	.40
17 Matt Harpring	.20	.50
18 J.R. Henderson	.15	.40
19 Clayton Shields	.15	.40
20 Michael Dickerson	.15	.40
21 Saddi Washington	.15	.40
22 Malcolm Johnson	.15	.40
23 Cory Carr	.15	.40
24 Brad Miller	.40	1.00
25 Mike Jones	.15	.40
26 Brian Skinner	.15	.40
27 Al Harrington	.25	.60
28 Torraye Braggs	.15	.40
29 Corey Louis	.15	.40
30 DeMarco Johnson	.15	.40
31 Anthony Carter	.15	.40
32 Earl Boykins	.15	.40
33 Roshown McLeod	.15	.40
34 Casey Shaw	.15	.40
35 Andrae Patterson	.15	.40
36 Bryce Drew	.15	.40
37 Jeff Sheppard	.15	.40
38 Jahidi White	.15	.40
39 Shammond Williams	.15	.40
40 Ruben Patterson	.15	.40
41 Shammond Williams Vince Carter	.40	1.00
42 Michael Dickerson Miles Simon	.15	.40
43 Raef LaFrentz Paul Pierce	.40	1.00
44 Toby Bailey J.R.Henderson	.15	.40
45 Mike Bibby CL	.15	.40

1998 Press Pass Blue

This 45-card set parallels the base Press Pass set enhanced with blue foil stamping. These cards were available in random retail collector kits.

*BLUE .6X TO 1.5X BASE CARD HI

1998 Press Pass In The Zone

Inserted one in every hobby pack, this 45-card set is a hobby only parallel version of the Press Pass base set. The cards are designated with gold foil stamping instead of silver on the card fronts. To ascertain values on individual cards, please refer to the multiplier in the header, coupled with the value of the base card.

*STARS: .6X TO 1.5X BASE CARD HI

1998 Press Pass Reflectors

Randomly inserted in packs at the rate of one in 90, this 45-card set is a parallel version of the base set printed on holofoil cards with a protective laminate and peel-off covering. To ascertain values on individual cards, please refer to the multiplier in the header, coupled with the value of the base card.

*STARS: 6X TO 15X BASE CARD HI

1998 Press Pass Solos

Randomly inserted in packs, this 45-card set is parallel to the base set and is similar in design. The difference is found in the reflective sheen of the cards. Only one card was produced for each base set card, hence they are not listed,

1998 Press Pass Torquers

Inserted one per every retail pack, this 45-card set is a retail only parallel version of the Press Pass base set. The cards are designated with red foil stamping instead of silver on the card fronts. To ascertain values on individual cards, please refer to the multiplier in the header, coupled with the value of the base card.

*STARS: .6X TO 1.5X BASE CARD HI

1998 Press Pass Autographs

These autographed cards were inserted 1:18 hobby and 1:36 retail packs. Either an autograph or redemption card was inserted. While some players were available via both packs and redemption cards, nine players were only made available via redemption cards: Keon Clark, Bonzi Wells, Paul Pierce, Brian Skinner, Michael Dickerson, Tyronn Lue, Jeff Sheppard, DeMarco Johnson and Miles Simon.

1 Toby Bailey	1.50	4.00
2 Mike Bibby	6.00	15.00
3 Earl Boykins	3.00	8.00
4 Torraye Braggs	1.50	4.00
5 Cory Carr	1.50	4.00
6 Anthony Carter	1.50	4.00
7 Vince Carter	15.00	40.00
8 Keon Clark	1.50	4.00
9 Michael Dickerson	1.50	4.00
10 Michael Doleac	1.50	4.00
11 Bryce Drew	1.50	4.00
12 Pat Garrity	1.50	4.00
13 Matt Harpring	2.00	5.00
14 Al Harrington	2.50	6.00
15 J.R. Henderson	1.50	4.00
16 Larry Hughes	4.00	10.00
17 DeMarco Johnson	1.50	4.00
18 Malcolm Johnson	1.50	4.00
19 Mike Jones	1.50	4.00
20 Raef Lafrentz	2.00	5.00
21 Tyronn Lue	1.50	4.00
22 Roshown McLeod	1.50	4.00
23 Brad Miller	4.00	10.00
24 Nazr Mohammed	1.50	4.00
25 Michael Olowokandi	2.00	5.00
26 Andrae Patterson	1.50	4.00
27 Paul Pierce	10.00	25.00
28 Casey Shaw	1.50	4.00
29 Jeff Sheppard	1.50	4.00
30 Clayton Shields	1.50	4.00
31 Miles Simon	1.50	4.00
32 Brian Skinner	1.50	4.00
33 Robert Traylor	1.50	4.00
34 Saddi Washington	1.50	4.00
35 Bonzi Wells	1.50	4.00
36 Jahidi White	1.50	4.00
37 Jason Williams	6.00	15.00
38 Shammond Williams	1.50	4.00

1998 Press Pass Fastbreak

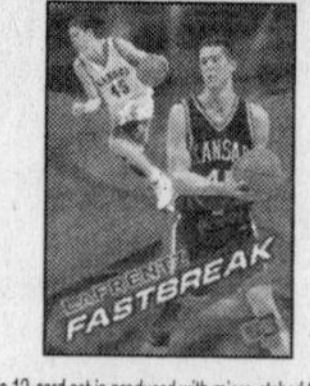

This 12-card set is produced with micro-etched foil technology. Seeded 1:12 packs, card fronts feature two different photographs of the highlighted player. The backs contain another photo and some biographical information. Cards are numbered with a "FB" prefix.

COMPLETE SET (12)	8.00	20.00
FB1 Raef LaFrentz	.75	2.00
FB2 Toby Bailey	.60	1.50
FB3 Mike Bibby	1.50	4.00
FB4 Vince Carter	3.00	8.00
FB5 Paul Pierce	3.00	8.00
FB6 Michael Olowokandi	.75	2.00
FB7 Keon Clark	.60	1.50
FB8 Robert Traylor	.60	1.50
FB9 Michael Doleac	.60	1.50
FB10 Larry Hughes	1.25	3.00
FB11 Pat Garrity	.60	1.50
FB12 Miles Simon	.60	1.50

1998 Press Pass In Your Face

These 9 clear acetate cards were inserted in 1:36 hobby packs only. On a see-through plastic card stock, a player action photo graces the card fronts while the backs are bare save for a copyright line and the card number, prefaced with "IYF".

COMPLETE SET (9)	8.00	20.00
IYF1 Raef LaFrentz	1.00	2.50
IYF2 Mike Bibby	2.00	5.00
IYF3 Michael Dickerson	.75	2.00
IYF4 Paul Pierce	4.00	10.00
IYF5 Pat Garrity	.75	2.00
IYF6 Matt Harpring	1.00	2.50
IYF7 Robert Traylor	.75	2.00
IYF8 Brad Miller	2.00	5.00
IYF9 Vince Carter	4.00	10.00

1998 Press Pass Jersey Cards

Randomly inserted in packs at the rate of one in 720, this five-card set features color player photos with actual game-used jersey pieces from top draft picks embedded in the cards. Card #'s JC1, JC2 and JC3 were only available via redeemed redemption cards inserted into packs at a rate of 1:720 as well. Card JC3, originally Mike Bibby, was replaced by Michael Olowokandi.

JC1 Michael Olowokandi/600	8.00	20.00
JC2 Vince Carter	60.00	120.00
JC3 Mike Bibby Michael Olowokandi	10.00	25.00
JC4 Robert Traylor	6.00	15.00
JC5 Toby Bailey	6.00	15.00

1998 Press Pass Net Burners

Inserted one per pack, this 36-card set features color action player photos printed on all-foil die-cut cards. The backs carry player information.

COMPLETE SET (36)	6.00	15.00
1 Mike Bibby	.60	1.50
2 Nazr Mohammed	.25	.60
3 Raef LaFrentz	.30	.75
4 Vince Carter	1.25	3.00
5 Paul Pierce	1.25	3.00
6 Michael Olowokandi	.30	.75
7 Larry Hughes	.50	1.25
8 Keon Clark	.25	.60
9 Robert Traylor	.25	.60
10 Michael Doleac	.25	.60
11 Pat Garrity	.25	.60
12 Saddi Washington	.25	.60
13 Miles Simon	.25	.60
14 Toby Bailey	.25	.60
15 Bonzi Wells	.25	.60
16 Tyronn Lue	.25	.60
17 Matt Harpring	.30	.75
18 J.R. Henderson	.25	.60
19 Clayton Shields	.25	.60
20 Michael Dickerson	.25	.60
21 DeMarco Johnson	.25	.60
22 Andrae Patterson	.25	.60
23 Cory Carr	.25	.60
24 Torraye Braggs	.25	.60
25 Ruben Patterson	.25	.60
26 Brian Skinner	.25	.60
27 Bryce Drew	.25	.60
28 Shammond Williams	.25	.60
29 Corey Louis	.25	.60
30 Tim Duncan	.50	1.25
31 Keith Van Horn	.25	.60
32 Tim Thomas	.25	.60
33 Derek Anderson	.15	.40
34 Brevin Knight	.15	.40
35 Ron Mercer	.20	.50
36 Roshown McLeod CL	.25	.60
S1 Mike Bibby PROMO	.60	1.50

1998 Press Pass Real Deal Rookies

The nine cards that make up this set are representative of NBA rookies from the 1997-98 season. With the NBA team logos air-brushed out, the card fronts contain two player photos, and the backs contain another photo and rookie year statistics. Card were inserted in 1:18 packs and have an "R" prefix on the card numbers.

COMPLETE SET (9)	5.00	12.00
R1 Tim Duncan	2.00	5.00
R2 Keith Van Horn	1.00	2.50
R3 Tim Thomas	1.00	2.50
R4 Derek Anderson	.60	1.50
R5 Brevin Knight	.60	1.50
R6 Ron Mercer	.75	2.00
R7 Tracy McGrady	1.50	4.00
R8 Danny Fortson	.60	1.50
R9 Maurice Taylor	.60	1.50

1998 Press Pass Super Six

The six players in the set were perceived as six of the best players heading into the 1998 NBA draft. Cards feature dual photo fronts with holofoil technology. The backs contain another player photo and some text that explains why the player made Press Pass' "Superior Six." One card was inserted in every thirty-six packs. Card numbers have a "S" prefix.

COMPLETE SET (6)	6.00	15.00
S1 Raef LaFrentz	.75	2.00
S2 Larry Hughes	1.25	3.00
S3 Mike Bibby	1.50	4.00
S4 Vince Carter	3.00	8.00
S5 Paul Pierce	3.00	8.00
S6 Michael Olowokandi	.75	2.00

1999 Press Pass

The 1999 Press Pass draft pick set was released as a 45-card set. Each box contained 24 packs with five cards per pack. A special Vince Carter card was randomly inserted in packs at one in 480 hobby and one in 720 retail. It is priced at the end of the base set.

COMPLETE SET (45)	4.00	10.00
1 Elton Brand	.30	.75
2 Steve Francis	.30	.75
3 Baron Davis	.40	1.00
4 Lamar Odom	.40	1.00
5 Jonathan Bender	.12	.30
6 Wally Szczerbiak	.25	.60
7 Richard Hamilton	.30	.75
8 Andre Miller	.30	.75
9 Jason Terry	.30	.75
10 Trajan Langdon	.12	.30
11 William Avery	.12	.30
12 Ron Artest	.30	.75
13 Cal Bowdler	.12	.30
14 James Posey	.12	.30
15 Quincy Lewis	.12	.30
16 Jeff Foster	.12	.30
17 Kenny Thomas	.12	.30
18 Devean George	.12	.30
19 Tim James	.12	.30
20 Vonteego Cummings	.12	.30
21 Jumaine Jones	.12	.30
22 Scott Padgett	.12	.30
23 John Celestand	.12	.30
24 Rico Hill	.12	.30
25 Michael Ruffin	.12	.30
26 Chris Herren	.12	.30
27 Evan Eschmeyer	.12	.30
28 Calvin Booth	.12	.30
29 Obinna Ekezie	.12	.30
30 A.J. Bramlett	.12	.30
31 Louis Bullock	.12	.30
32 Lee Nailon	.12	.30
33 Tyrone Washington	.12	.30
34 Lari Ketner	.12	.30
35 Venson Hamilton	.12	.30
36 Roberto Bergersen	.12	.30
37 Rodney Buford	.12	.30
38 Melvin Levett	.12	.30
39 Kris Clack	.12	.30
40 Harold Jamison	.12	.30
41 Heshimu Evans	.12	.30
42 Ademola Okulaja	.12	.30
43 Jamel Thomas	.12	.30
44 Jason Miskiri	.12	.30
45 Elton Brand CL	.30	.75
NNO Vince Carter Special	15.00	40.00

1999 Press Pass Gold Zone

Inserted one per hobby pack, this 45-card set parallels the base set. The cards feature gold foil on the front. To ascertain values on individual cards, please refer to the multiplier in the header, coupled with the value of the base card.

*GOLD: .75X TO 2X BASE CARD HI

1999 Press Pass Reflectors

andomly inserted in packs at one in 90, this 45-card t is a parallel of the base set. The cards feature flective foil on the front. The card backs are serially imbered out of 250. To ascertain values on individual irds, please refer to the multiplier in the header, oupled with the value of the base card.
REFLECTORS: 5X TO 12X BASE CARD HI

1999 Press Pass Torquers

serted one per retail pack, this 45-card set parallels e base set. The cards feature a blue foil on the front. ascertain values on individual cards, please refer to e multiplier in the header, coupled with the value of e base card.
)RQUERS: .75X TO 2X BASE CARD HI

1999 Press Pass Autographs

andomly inserted in hobby packs at one in eight, and etail packs at one in 36, this 40-card set features utographed cards from some of the top draft picks.

Card	Lo	Hi
Elton Brand	4.00	10.00
Steve Francis	4.00	10.00
Baron Davis	5.00	12.00
Lamar Odom	5.00	12.00
Jonathan Bender	1.50	4.00
Wally Szczerbiak	3.00	8.00
Richard Hamilton	4.00	10.00
Andre Miller	4.00	10.00
Jason Terry	4.00	10.00
10 Trajan Langdon	1.50	4.00
11 William Avery	1.50	4.00
12 Ron Artest	4.00	10.00
3 Cal Bowdler	1.50	4.00
14 James Posey	1.50	4.00
15 Quincy Lewis	1.50	4.00
6 Kenny Thomas	1.50	4.00
7 Devean George	1.50	4.00
18 Tim James	1.50	4.00
19 Vonteego Cummings	1.50	4.00
20 John Celestand	1.50	4.00
21 Rico Hill	1.50	4.00
22 Michael Ruffin	1.50	4.00
23 Chris Herren	2.50	6.00
24 Evan Eschmeyer	1.50	4.00
25 Calvin Booth	1.50	4.00
26 A.J. Bramlett	1.50	4.00
27 Louis Bullock	1.50	4.00
28 Lee Nailon	1.50	4.00
29 Tyrone Washington	1.50	4.00
30 Lari Ketner	1.50	4.00
31 Venson Hamilton	1.50	4.00
32 Roberto Bergersen	1.50	4.00
33 Rodney Buford	1.50	4.00
34 Melvin Levett	1.50	4.00
35 Kris Clack	1.50	4.00
36 Harold Jamison	1.50	4.00
37 Heshimu Evans	1.50	4.00
38 Ademola Okulaja	1.50	4.00
39 Jamel Thomas	1.50	4.00
40 Jason Miskiri	1.50	4.00

1999 Press Pass Standout Signatures

Randomly inserted in hobby packs only at one in 120, this 40-card set parallels the Autograph insert. The cards are serially numbered to 100. To ascertain values on individual cards, please refer to the multiplier in the header, coupled with the value of the base card.
*STAND.SIG: .6X TO 1.5X VALUE

1999 Press Pass Courtside

Randomly inserted into retail boxes at a ratio of one in six packs, this 5-card insert features some of the top new talent to enter the NBA.

Card	Lo	Hi
COMPLETE SET (5)	1.25	3.00
1 Steve Francis	.50	1.25
2 Elton Brand	.50	1.25
3 Lamar Odom	.60	1.50
4 Richard Hamilton	.50	1.25
5 Wally Szczerbiak	.40	1.00

1999 Press Pass Crunch Time

Randomly inserted in packs at one in 18, this nine-card set features players who deliver in "crunch time". The cards feature a silver foil front and a "CT" prefix on the back.

Card	Lo	Hi
COMPLETE SET (9)	2.50	6.00
CT1 Elton Brand	.60	1.50
CT2 Steve Francis	.60	1.50
CT3 Baron Davis	.75	2.00
CT4 Lamar Odom	.75	2.00
CT5 Wally Szczerbiak	.50	1.25
CT6 Richard Hamilton	.60	1.50
CT7 Andre Miller	.60	1.50
CT8 Jason Terry	.60	1.50
CT9 William Avery	.25	.60

1999 Press Pass In Your Face

Randomly inserted in hobby packs at one in 24 and retail packs at one in 36, this six-card set features above the rim photos combined with clear acetate. Card backs carry an "IYF" prefix.

Card	Lo	Hi
COMPLETE SET (6)	2.00	5.00
IYF1 Elton Brand	.60	1.50
IYF2 Baron Davis	.75	2.00
IYF3 Andre Miller	.60	1.50
IYF4 Jason Terry	.60	1.50
IYF5 Ron Artest	.60	1.50
IYF6 Kenny Thomas	.25	.60

1999 Press Pass Jersey Cards

Randomly inserted in hobby packs at one in 480 and retail packs at one in 720, this five-card set features cards that contain an actual pierce of a game-used jersey from top 1999 picks. Card backs carry a "JC" prefix and are serially numbered to 300.

Card	Lo	Hi
JC1 Elton Brand	10.00	25.00
JC2 Steve Francis	10.00	25.00
JC3 Lamar Odom	12.00	30.00
JC4 James Posey	4.00	10.00
JC5 Evan Eschmeyer	4.00	10.00

1999 Press Pass Net Burners

Seeded one per pack, this 36-card set features all foil die cut cards.

Card	Lo	Hi
COMPLETE SET (36)	5.00	12.00
NB1 Steve Francis	.50	1.25
NB2 Richard Hamilton	.50	1.25
NB3 Baron Davis	.60	1.50
NB4 Lamar Odom	.60	1.50
NB5 Elton Brand	.50	1.25
NB6 Jason Terry	.50	1.25
NB7 Andre Miller	.50	1.25
NB8 Ron Artest	.50	1.25
NB9 William Avery	.20	.50
NB10 James Posey	.20	.50
NB11 Tim James	.20	.50
NB12 Evan Eschmeyer	.20	.50
NB13 Quincy Lewis	.20	.50
NB14 Scott Padgett	.20	.50
NB15 Jamel Thomas	.20	.50
NB16 Kenny Thomas	.20	.50
NB17 Melvin Levett	.20	.50
NB18 A.J. Bramlett	.20	.50
NB19 Lari Ketner	.20	.50
NB20 Kris Clack	.20	.50
NB21 Lee Nailon	.20	.50
NB22 Vonteego Cummings	.20	.50
NB23 Trajan Langdon	.20	.50
NB24 Wally Szczerbiak	.40	1.00
NB25 Obinna Ekezie	.20	.50
NB26 Rico Hill	.20	.50
NB27 Venson Hamilton	.20	.50
NB28 Michael Ruffin	.20	.50
NB29 Harold Jamison	.20	.50
NB30 Ademola Okulaja	.20	.50
NB31 Chris Herren	.20	.50
NB32 Calvin Booth	.20	.50
NB33 Jonathan Bender	.20	.50
NB34 Rodney Buford	.20	.50
NB35 John Celestand	.20	.50
NB36 Steve Francis CL	.50	1.25

1999 Press Pass On Fire

Randomly inserted in packs at one in 12, this 12-card set features some of the nation's hottest players. The cards are on all foil, microetched Nitrokrome. Card backs carry an "OF" prefix.

Card	Lo	Hi
COMPLETE SET (12)	3.00	8.00
OF1 Elton Brand	.60	1.50
OF2 Steve Francis	.60	1.50
OF3 Baron Davis	.75	2.00
OF4 Lamar Odom	.75	2.00
OF5 Wally Szczerbiak	.50	1.25
OF6 Richard Hamilton	.60	1.50
OF7 Andre Miller	.60	1.50
OF8 Jason Terry	.60	1.50
OF9 William Avery	.25	.60
OF10 Ron Artest	.60	1.50
OF11 James Posey	.25	.60
OF12 Kenny Thomas	.25	.60

1999 Press Pass Y2K

Randomly inserted in hobby packs only at one in 36, this eight-card set features the future stars of the millennium. Card fronts feature a die cut basketball background. Card backs are serially numbered to 2000 and carry a "Y" prefix.

Card	Lo	Hi
COMPLETE SET (8)	5.00	12.00
Y1 Elton Brand	1.00	2.50
Y2 Steve Francis	1.00	2.50
Y3 Baron Davis	1.25	3.00
Y4 Lamar Odom	1.25	3.00
Y5 Wally Szczerbiak	.75	2.00
Y6 Richard Hamilton	1.00	2.50
Y7 Andre Miller	1.00	2.50
Y8 Jason Terry	1.00	2.50

2000 Press Pass

Released in July 2000, this 46-card set features top picks and prospects from the NBA Draft class. Each hobby pack carried five-cards with a suggested retail price of $3.79. Each retail pack carried four-cards with a suggested retail price of $2.99.

Card	Lo	Hi
COMPLETE SET (46)	10.00	25.00
COMPLETE SET w/o SP (40)	5.00	12.00
UNPRICED SOLOS SERIAL #'d TO 1		
1 Chris Mihm CL	.25	.60
2 Chris Mihm	.25	.60
3 Mike Miller	.50	1.25
4 Chris Porter	.25	.60
5 Morris Peterson	.25	.60
6 Darius Miles	.25	.60
7 Jerome Moiso	.25	.60
8 Quentin Richardson	.40	1.00
9 Mateen Cleaves	.25	.60
10 Etan Thomas	.25	.60
11 Scoonie Penn	.25	.60
12 Jason Collier	.25	.60
13 Hanno Mottola	.25	.60
14 Mark Madsen	.25	.60
15 DeShawn Stevenson	.30	.75
16 Dan Langhi	.25	.60
17 Jamaal Magloire	.25	.60
18 Pepe Sanchez	.25	.60
19 Khalid El-Amin	.25	.60
20 Harold Arceneaux	.25	.60
21 Mark Karcher	.25	.60
22 Jason Hart	.25	.60
23 Eddie House	.25	.60
24 Gabe Muoneke	.25	.60
25 Jake Voskuhl	.25	.60
26 Brad Millard	.25	.60
27 Bootsy Thornton	.25	.60
28 Eddie Gill	.25	.60
29 Shaheen Holloway	.25	.60
30 Kevin Freeman	.25	.60
31 Jarrett Stephens	.25	.60
32 Brian Cardinal	.25	.60
33 Brandon Kurtz	.25	.60
34 Elton Brand	.25	.60
35 Steve Francis	.25	.60
36 Lamar Odom	.25	.60
37 Wally Szczerbiak	.25	.60
38 Baron Davis	.25	.60
39 Richard Hamilton	.25	.60
40 Chris Carrawell	.25	.60
41 Chris Mihm PP	.75	2.00
42 Darius Miles PP	.75	2.00
43 Mike Miller PP	1.50	4.00
44 Jerome Moiso PP	.75	2.00
45 Mateen Cleaves PP	.75	2.00
46 Morris Peterson PP	.75	2.00

2000 Press Pass Gold Zone

Inserted one per hobby pack, this 40-card set is a partial parallel to the base set using gold foil, rather than silver. To ascertain values on individual cards, please refer to the multiplier in the header, coupled with the value of the base card.

Card	Lo	Hi
COMPLETE SET (40)	8.00	20.00

*GOLD ZONE: .6X TO 1.5X BASIC CARDS

2000 Press Pass Reflectors

Randomly inserted in packs at one in 72, this 40-card set is a partial parallel of the base set using "reflective" technology. The cards are serially numbered to 500. To ascertain values on individual cards, please refer to the multiplier in the header, coupled with the value of the base card.
*REFLECTORS: 2.5X TO 6X BASE HI

2000 Press Pass Torquers

Inserted one per retail pack, this 40-card set is a partial parallel of the base set using blue foil, rather than silver. To ascertain values on individual cards, please refer to the multiplier in the header, coupled with the value of the base card.

Card	Lo	Hi
COMPLETE SET (40)	8.00	20.00

*TORQUERS: .6X TO 1.5X BASIC CARDS

2000 Press Pass Autographs

Randomly inserted in hobby packs at one in nine and retail packs at one in 36, this set features autographs of top draft picks and stars from the NBA. The cards are not numbered and listed below alphabetically. Card numbers 31 and 32 were issued through various retail re-packs after this product was released

Card	Lo	Hi
1 Elton Brand	4.00	10.00
2 Brian Cardinal	2.00	5.00
3 Mateen Cleaves	2.00	5.00
4 Jason Collier	2.00	5.00
5 Baron Davis	4.00	10.00
6 Keyon Dooling	2.00	5.00
7 Steve Francis	4.00	10.00
8 Eddie Gill	2.00	5.00
9 Jason Hart	2.00	5.00
10 Eddie House	2.00	5.00
11 Dan Langhi	2.00	5.00
12 Mark Madsen	2.00	5.00
13 Jamaal Magloire	2.00	5.00
14 Dan McClintock	2.00	5.00
15 Chris Mihm	2.00	5.00
16 Darius Miles	2.00	5.00
17 Brad Millard	2.00	5.00
18 Mike Miller	4.00	10.00
19 Jerome Moiso	2.00	5.00
20 Hanno Mottola	2.00	5.00
21 Lamar Odom	4.00	10.00
22 Scoonie Penn	2.00	5.00
23 Morris Peterson	2.00	5.00
24 Chris Porter	2.00	5.00
25 Quentin Richardson	3.00	8.00
26 Jarrett Stephens	2.00	5.00
27 DeShawn Stevenson	2.50	6.00
28 Wally Szczerbiak	2.00	5.00
29 Etan Thomas	2.00	5.00
30 Jake Voskuhl	2.00	5.00
31 Shaheen Halloway*	2.00	5.00

2000 Press Pass Breakaway

Inserted one per pack, this 36-card set semi-parallels the base set. Each card is die cut. To ascertain values on individual cards, please refer to the multiplier in the header, coupled with the value of the base card.

Card	Lo	Hi
COMPLETE SET (36)	8.00	20.00
BA1 Mateen Cleaves CL	.40	1.00
BA2 Chris Mihm	.40	1.00
BA3 Mike Miller	.75	2.00
BA4 Chris Porter	.40	1.00
BA5 Morris Peterson	.40	1.00
BA6 Darius Miles	.40	1.00
BA7 Jerome Moiso	.40	1.00
BA8 Quentin Richardson	.60	1.50
BA9 Mateen Cleaves	.40	1.00
BA10 Etan Thomas	.40	1.00
BA11 Scoonie Penn	.40	1.00
BA12 Jason Collier	.40	1.00
BA13 Hanno Mottola	.40	1.00
BA14 Mark Madsen	.40	1.00
BA15 DeShawn Stevenson	.50	1.25
BA16 Dan Langhi	.40	1.00
BA17 Jamaal Magloire	.40	1.00
BA18 Pepe Sanchez	.40	1.00
BA19 Mark Karcher	.40	1.00
BA20 Khalid El-Amin	.40	1.00
BA21 Jason Hart	.40	1.00
BA22 Eddie House	.40	1.00
BA23 Gabe Muoneke	.40	1.00
BA24 Jake Voskuhl	.40	1.00
BA25 Brad Millard	.40	1.00
BA26 Shaheen Holloway	.40	1.00
BA27 Jarrett Stephens	.40	1.00
BA28 Elton Brand	.40	1.00
BA29 Steve Francis	.40	1.00
BA30 Lamar Odom	.40	1.00
BA31 Wally Szczerbiak	.40	1.00
BA32 Baron Davis	.40	1.00
BA33 Richard Hamilton	.40	1.00
BA34 Bootsy Thornton	.40	1.00
BA35 Brian Cardinal	.40	1.00
BA36 Chris Carrawell	.40	1.00

2000 Press Pass In the Paint

Randomly inserted in packs at one in 12, this eight-card set featured some of the premier draft picks who do their work in the paint. Card backs carry an "IP" prefix.

Card	Lo	Hi
COMPLETE SET (8)	3.00	8.00
*DIE CUT: .6X TO 1.5X HI COLUMN		
DIE CUT: STATED ODDS 1:24 H/R		
IP1 Chris Mihm	.60	1.50
IP2 Mateen Cleaves	.60	1.50
IP3 Morris Peterson	.60	1.50
IP4 Jerome Moiso	.60	1.50
IP5 Mike Miller	1.25	3.00
IP6 Darius Miles	.60	1.50
IP7 Jason Collier	.60	1.50
IP8 Etan Thomas	.60	1.50

2000 Press Pass In Your Face

Randomly inserted in packs at one in 28, this six-card set features aerial shots of high-flying draft picks. Card backs carry an "IF" prefix.

Card	Lo	Hi
COMPLETE SET (6)	3.00	8.00
IF1 Chris Mihm	.75	2.00
IF2 Mateen Cleaves	.75	2.00
IF3 Morris Peterson	.75	2.00
IF4 Jerome Moiso	.75	2.00
IF5 Chris Porter	.75	2.00
IF6 Quentin Richardson	1.25	3.00

2000 Press Pass Jersey Cards

Randomly inserted in hobby packs at one in 420 and retail packs at one in 720, this four-card set features a game-used jersey swatch of top draft picks. Each card was serially numbered out of 425.

Card	Lo	Hi
COMPLETE SET (4)	15.00	40.00
JCCM Chris Mihm	5.00	12.00
JCDM Darius Miles	5.00	12.00
JCMC Mateen Cleaves	5.00	12.00
JCMM Mike Miller	10.00	25.00

2000 Press Pass On Fire

Randomly inseted in packs at one in six, this 11-card set features some of the hottest players on microetched foil. Card backs carry an "OF" prefix.

Card	Lo	Hi
COMPLETE SET (11)	4.00	10.00
OF1 Mike Miller	1.00	2.50
OF2 Darius Miles	.50	1.25
OF3 Chris Mihm	.50	1.25
OF4 Quentin Richardson	.75	2.00
OF5 Mateen Cleaves	.50	1.25
OF6 Chris Porter	.50	1.25
OF7 Morris Peterson	.50	1.25
OF8 Khalid El-Amin	.50	1.25
OF9 Jerome Moiso	.50	1.25
OF10 Hanno Mottola	.50	1.25
OF11 Etan Thomas	.50	1.25

2000 Press Pass Power Pick Autographs

Randomly inserted in hobby packs only at one in 269, this six-card set features autographs of the Power Pick subset. The cards are serially numbered to 250. The cards are not numbered and listed below alphabetically.

Card	Lo	Hi
COMPLETE SET (6)	20.00	50.00
1 Mateen Cleaves	4.00	10.00
2 Chris Mihm	4.00	10.00
3 Darius Miles	4.00	10.00
4 Mike Miller	8.00	20.00
5 Jerome Moiso	4.00	10.00
6 Morris Peterson/240	4.00	10.00

2002 Press Pass

Released in August, 2002, this 46-card set showcases 2002 draft picks and college coaches. Hobby product SRP was $3.49 per pack where each pack contained five cards, and boxes contained 24 packs while cases contained 20 boxes. Retail product S.R.P. $2.99 per pack contains four cards per pack, 28 packs per box and 20 boxes per case. Base cards contain full color player action photos and silver foil accents on the player name box and the player's name. There are two versions of the Jay Williams checklist #40, and the last five cards in the set are Power Pick short prints. These cards are inserted in packs at the rate of one in 14.

Card	Lo	Hi
COMPLETE SET (45)	8.00	20.00
1 Matt Barnes	.30	.75
2 Lonny Baxter	.25	.60
3 Carlos Boozer	.50	1.25
4 Curtis Borchardt	.25	.60
5 Chris Christoffersen	.25	.60
6 Sam Clancy	.25	.60
7 Dan Dickau	.25	.60
8 Juan Dixon	.30	.75
9 Mike Dunleavy	.30	.75
10 Dan Gadzuric	.25	.60
11 Drew Gooden	.40	1.00
12 Ryan Humphrey	.25	.60
13 Chris Jefferies	.25	.60
14 Jared Jeffries	.25	.60
15 Jason Jennings	.25	.60
16 Fred Jones	.25	.60
17 Steve Logan	.25	.60
18 Yao Ming	.75	2.00
19 Chris Owens	.25	.60
20 Tayshaun Prince	.30	.75
21 Kareem Rush	.25	.60
22 Predrag Savovic	.25	.60
23 Jamal Sampson	.25	.60
24 Tamar Slay	.25	.60
25 Darius Songaila	.25	.60
26 Amare Stoudemire	.60	1.50
27 Nikoloz Tskitishvili	.25	.60
28 DaJuan Wagner	.25	.60
29 Jiri Welsch	.25	.60
30 Chris Wilcox	.25	.60
31 Jay Williams	.30	.75
32 Frank Williams	.25	.60
33 Vincent Yarbrough	.25	.60
34 Jim Boeheim CO	.40	1.00
35 Jim Calhoun CO	.40	1.00
36 Lute Olson CO	.40	1.00
37 Tubby Smith CO	.40	1.00
38 Gary Williams CO	.75	2.00
39 Roy Williams CO	.40	1.00
40A Jay Williams CL	.25	.60
40B Jay Williams CL	.25	.60
41 Chris Wilcox PP	.75	2.00
42 Kareem Rush PP	.75	2.00
43 Drew Gooden PP	1.25	3.00
44 DaJuan Wagner PP	.75	2.00
45 Jay Williams PP	1.00	2.50

2002 Press Pass Gold Zone

Randomly inserted in Hobby packs at the rate of one in one, this 41-card set parallels the base Press Pass set with a foil shift from silver highlights to gold higlights.
*GOLD: .75X TO 2X BASE CARD HI

2002 Press Pass Red

Randomly inserted in Retail packs, this 41-card set parallels the base set enhanced with red foil highlights.

*RED: .75X TO 2X BASE CARD HI

2002 Press Pass Reflectors

Randomly seeded in packs, this 41-card set parallels the base Press Pass set on a holographic foil card stock. Each card is sequentially numbered to 500.
*REF: 2X TO 5X BASE CARD HI

2002 Press Pass Autographs

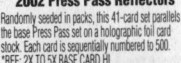

Randomly inserted in packs at a rate of 1:6 (hobby) and 1:14 (retail), this set features signed cards from the 2002 draft prospects and college coaches. The card design features full color action photography, gold ink highlights on the Press Pass logo and player's name, and a diagonal white strip on the bottom third of the card for player autographs. Also priced with this set is a special Jay Williams autograph that was given away at the 2002 National Card Collector's Convention in Chicago. Williams autographed 286 total cards and signed both with his jersey number and without. It is rumored that somewhere in the neighborhood of 200 cards were signed with his jersey number.
*SILVER: .75X TO 2X BASE HI
SILVER PRINT RUN 100 SER.#'d SETS

Card	Lo	Hi
1 Matt Barnes	3.00	8.00
2 Jim Boeheim	5.00	12.00
3 Carlos Boozer	5.00	12.00
4 Curtis Borchardt	2.50	6.00
5 Jim Calhoun	25.00	60.00
6 Chris Christoffersen	2.50	6.00
7 Sam Clancy	2.50	6.00
8 Dan Dickau	2.50	6.00
10 Mike Dunleavy	3.00	8.00
11 Andy Ellis	2.50	6.00
12 Dan Gadzuric	2.50	6.00
13 Drew Gooden	4.00	10.00
14 Lynn Greer	2.50	6.00
15 Ryan Humphrey	2.50	6.00
16 Chris Jefferies	2.50	6.00
17 Jared Jeffries	2.50	6.00
18 Jason Jennings	2.50	6.00
19 Fred Jones	2.50	6.00
20 Yao Ming	12.50	30.00
21 Lute Olson	10.00	25.00
22 Chris Owens	2.50	6.00
23 Tayshaun Prince	3.00	8.00
24 Kareem Rush	2.50	6.00
25 Jamal Sampson	2.50	6.00
26 Predrag Savovic	2.50	6.00
27 Tamar Slay	2.50	6.00
28 Tubby Smith	6.00	15.00
29 Darius Songaila	2.50	6.00
30 Amare Stoudemire	12.50	30.00
31 Nikoloz Tskitishvili	2.50	6.00
32 DaJuan Wagner	2.50	6.00
33 Jiri Welsch	2.50	6.00
34 Chris Wilcox	2.50	6.00
35 Frank Williams	2.50	6.00
36 Gary Williams	10.00	25.00
37 Jay Williams	8.00	20.00
38 Roy Williams	15.00	40.00
39 Vincent Yarbrough	2.50	6.00
NNO Jay Williams SPEC	30.00	60.00

2002 National Convention

2002 Press Pass Big Numbers

Randomly seeded in packs at the rate of one in one, this 27-card set features a horizontal design on an all foil card stock. Two player photos appear on the left, one in color, and one in black and white, and the player's jersey number appears on the right side of the card.

Card	Lo	Hi
COMPLETE SET (27)	6.00	15.00
BN1 Jay Williams CL	.50	1.25
BN2 Carlos Boozer	.75	2.00
BN3 Curtis Borchardt	.40	1.00
BN4 Lonny Baxter	.40	1.00
BN5 Sam Clancy	.40	1.00
BN6 Dan Dickau	.40	1.00
BN7 Juan Dixon	.50	1.25
BN8 Kelly Wise	.40	1.00
BN9 Andy Ellis	.40	1.00
BN10 Dan Gadzuric	.40	1.00
BN11 Drew Gooden	.60	1.50
BN12 Chris Owens	.40	1.00
BN13 Chris Jefferies	.40	1.00
BN14 Jared Jeffries	.40	1.00
BN15 Fred Jones	.40	1.00
BN16 Steve Logan	.40	1.00
BN17 Tayshaun Prince	.50	1.25
BN18 Kareem Rush	.40	1.00
BN19 Jamal Sampson	.40	1.00
BN20 Darius Songaila	.40	1.00
BN21 Nikoloz Tskitishvili	.40	1.00
BN22 DaJuan Wagner	.40	1.00
BN23 Jiri Welsch	.40	1.00
BN24 Chris Wilcox	.40	1.00
BN25 Frank Williams	.40	1.00
BN26 Jay Williams	.50	1.25
BN27 Vincent Yarbrough	.40	1.00

2002 Press Pass Cagers

Randomly inserted in packs at a rate of one in 24, this six card set features an all foil design with full color player action photos set in the middle of a silver fence border. Each player's name is printed in a different color foil.

Card	Lo	Hi
COMPLETE SET (6)	4.00	10.00
C1 Jared Jeffries	1.00	2.50
C2 Frank Williams	1.00	2.50
C3 Drew Gooden	1.50	4.00
C4 DaJuan Wagner	1.00	2.50
C5 Chris Wilcox	1.00	2.50
C6 Jay Williams	1.25	3.00

2002 Press Pass Class of 2002

Randomly inserted in packs at a rate of one in eight, this 12-card set features an all foil card stock with full color player action photos. The top of the card shows about 1/4 of a basketball above the player photo, and the bottom has the same dome shape of the 1/4 basketball but contains a silver embossed portrait of the showcased player along with the player's name.

Card	Lo	Hi
COMPLETE SET (12)	5.00	12.00
CL1 Carlos Boozer	1.25	3.00
CL2 Curtis Borchardt	.60	1.50
CL3 Dan Dickau	.60	1.50
CL4 Dan Gadzuric	.60	1.50
CL5 Drew Gooden	1.00	2.50
CL6 Jared Jeffries	.60	1.50
CL7 Kareem Rush	.60	1.50
CL8 DaJuan Wagner	.60	1.50
CL9 Chris Wilcox	.60	1.50
CL10 Frank Williams	.60	1.50
CL11 Jay Williams	.75	2.00
CL12 Mike Dunleavy	.75	2.00

2002 Press Pass College Jerseys

Randomly inserted in packs at a rate of 1:120 (hobby) and 1:280 (retail). The set contains genuine game-used jersey from the top draft picks of the 2002 class. Each card features a full color player photo, and the jersey swatches are cut in the shape of a tank-top jersey. Each card is sequentially numbered to 425 except Yao Ming which is a short print and was issued originally as an exchange card.

Card	Lo	Hi
COMPLETE SET (8)	40.00	80.00
JCCB1 Carlos Boozer/425	6.00	15.00
JCDG1 Drew Gooden/425	5.00	12.00
JCDG2 Dan Gadzuric/425	3.00	8.00
JCDS Darius Songaila/425	3.00	8.00
JCFJ Fred Jones/425	3.00	8.00
JCJW Jay Williams/425	6.00	15.00
JCSC Sam Clancy/425	3.00	8.00
JCYM Yao Ming/100	25.00	60.00

2002 Press Pass Combo Jerseys

This hobby only set features jersey swatches from current pro's college team and pro team on the same card. A college photo appears in the upper left hand corner while the corresponding college jersey swatch appears below. The upper left hand corner contains a swatch of a pro game used jersey with a pro picture below. Each card is sequentially numbered to 100.

Card	Lo	Hi
CJCM Chris Mihm	4.00	10.00
CJDM Darius Miles	5.00	12.00
CJDS DeShawn Stevenson	4.00	10.00
CJET Etan Thomas	4.00	10.00
CJJMA Jamaal Magloire	4.00	10.00
CJJMO Jerome Moiso	4.00	10.00
CJMMA Mark Madsen	4.00	10.00
CJMMI Mike Miller	8.00	20.00
CJMP Morris Peterson	5.00	12.00
CJQR Quentin Richardson	6.00	15.00

2002 Press Pass Hang Time

Randomly inserted in packs at a rate of one in 12, this nine card set features all foil card stock with full color player action photos. Each player is framed by a dome border with a box towards the bottom of the card containing the player's name.

Card	Lo	Hi
COMPLETE SET (9)	4.00	10.00
*DIE CUTS: .75X TO 2X BASE HI		
DIE CUTS STATED ODDS 1:24		
HT1 Curtis Borchardt	.60	1.50
HT2 Kareem Rush	.60	1.50
HT3 Carlos Boozer	1.25	3.00
HT4 Juan Dixon	.75	2.00
HT5 Drew Gooden	1.00	2.50
HT6 DaJuan Wagner	.60	1.50
HT7 Chris Wilcox	.60	1.50
HT8 Jay Williams	.75	2.00
HT9 Jared Jeffries	.60	1.50

2002 Press Pass Power Pick Autographs

Randomly seeded in packs, this 12-card set utilizes the Power Pick design from the base set enhanced by authentic player autographs. Each card is sequentially numbered to 250.

1 Carlos Boozer 10.00 25.00
2 Curtis Borchardt 4.00 10.00
3 Mike Dunleavy 5.00 12.00
4 Dan Gadzuric 4.00 10.00
5 Drew Gooden 6.00 15.00
6 Jared Jeffries 4.00 10.00
7 Yao Ming 20.00 50.00
8 Tayshaun Prince 5.00 12.00
9 Kareem Rush 4.00 10.00
10 DaJuan Wagner 4.00 10.00
11 Chris Wilcox 4.00 10.00
12 Jay Williams 5.00 12.00

2002 Press Pass Pro Autographs

Randomly inserted in packs at the rate of one in six, this 12-card set features a white background with a square portrait style photo of the showcased player towards the top of the card. Below the photo appears authentic player autographs.

1 Steve Francis 6.00 15.00
2 Mark Madsen 2.50 6.00
3 Jamaal Magloire 2.50 6.00
4 Chris Mihm 2.50 6.00
5 Darius Miles 4.00 10.00
6 Mike Miller 6.00 15.00
7 Jerome Moiso 2.50 6.00
8 Hanno Mottola 2.50 6.00
9 Morris Peterson 2.50 6.00
10 Quentin Richardson 4.00 10.00
11 DeShawn Stevenson 3.00 8.00
12 Etan Thomas 2.50 6.00

2002 Press Pass Pro Jerseys

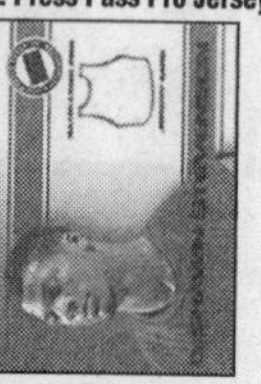

Randomly inserted in packs at a rate of 1:120 Hobby and 1:280 Retail, this 10-card set features full color player portrait photos on the left side of the card and a swatch of a game worn jersey on the right of the card. Each card is sequentially numbered to 300.

PJCCM Chris Mihm 2.00 5.00
PJCDM Darius Miles 3.00 8.00
PJCDS DeShawn Stevenson 2.00 5.00
PJCET Etan Thomas 2.00 5.00
PJCHM Hanno Mottola 2.00 5.00
PJCJM Jamaal Magloire 2.00 5.00
PJCMP Morris Peterson 2.00 5.00
PJCMMA Mark Madsen 2.00 5.00
PJCMMI Mike Miller 5.00 12.00
PJCQR Quentin Richardson 3.00 8.00

2002 Press Pass Pro Shoes

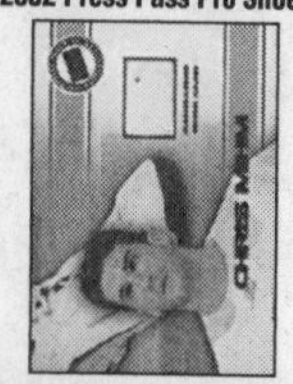

Randomly inserted in Hobby packs, this 10-card set features a full color player portrait photo and a square swatch of a game worn shoe. Each card is sequentially numbered to 40.

SHCM Chris Mihm 5.00 12.00
SHDM Darius Miles 8.00 20.00
SHMMA Mark Madsen 5.00 12.00
SHMP Morris Peterson 5.00 12.00

2002 Press Pass Rookie Chase

Randomly inserted in packs at a rate of one in 24, collectors have a chance to win a complete set of autographed cards from every player in the Press Pass autograph program by sending in eligible cards. There are eleven different players plus a "field card" in the set. Two players are named each November as Rookie of the Month, and the corresponding player card is the winner. If no winner is named, the Field card is the winner.

COMPLETE SET (12) 10.00 25.00
RC1 Carlos Boozer 2.50 6.00
RC2 Curtis Borchardt 1.25 3.00
RC3 Nikoloz Tskitishvili 1.25 3.00
RC4 Chris Jefferies 1.25 3.00
RC5 Drew Gooden 2.00 5.00
RC6 Jared Jeffries 1.25 3.00
RC7 Kareem Rush 1.25 3.00
RC8 DaJuan Wagner 1.25 3.00
RC9 Chris Wilcox 1.25 3.00
RC10 Jay Williams 1.50 4.00
RC11 Frank Williams 1.25 3.00
RC12 Field Card 1.25 3.00

2004 Press Pass

Released in late July, Press Pass boasts "the first look at the 2004-05 Rookies" with a 40 card base set. The cards are borderless with the Press Pass logo in the upper right corner, the player's previous team logo in the lower left and the player's name in the lower right. Both Hobby and Retail packaging with both containing 24 packs of four cards each, Hobby carried a SRP of $3.99 and a Retail SRP of $2.99.

COMPLETE SET (40) 10.00 25.00
COMP.SET w/o SP's (33) 6.00 15.00
1 Tony Allen .40 1.00
2 Rafael Araujo .30 .75
3 Andris Biedrins .40 1.00
4 Andre Brown .30 .75
5 Antonio Burks .30 .75
6 Lionel Chalmers .30 .75
7 Josh Childress .30 .75
8 Luol Deng .50 1.25
9 Chris Duhon .30 .75
10 Andre Emmett .30 .75
11 Desmon Farmer .30 .75
12 Matt Freije .30 .75
13 Ben Gordon .40 1.00
14 Devin Harris .50 1.25
15 David Harrison .30 .75
16 Andre Iguodala .50 1.25
17 Luke Jackson .30 .75
18 Shaun Livingston .30 .75
19 Brandon Mouton .30 .75
20 Emeka Okafor .50 1.25
21 Rickey Paulding .30 .75
22 Tim Pickett .30 .75
23 Justin Reed .30 .75
24 Romain Sato .30 .75
25 Ha Seung-Jin .30 .75
26 J.R. Smith .40 1.00
27 Kirk Snyder .30 .75
28 Blake Stepp .30 .75
29 Robert Swift .30 .75
30 Sebastian Telfair .30 .75
31 Anderson Varejao .40 1.00
32 Damien Wilkins .30 .75
33 Emeka Okafor CL .30 .75
34 Emeka Okafor 1.25 3.00
35 Shaun Livingston .75 2.00
36 Ben Gordon 1.00 2.50
37 Devin Harris 1.25 3.00
38 Andre Iguodala 1.25 3.00
39 Sebastian Telfair .75 2.00
40 Andris Biedrins 1.00 2.50

2004 Press Pass Blue

Randomly inserted in Retail packs at one per, this 33-card set parallels the base set enhanced with blue foil.

*BLUE SINGLES: .75X TO 2X BASE HI

2004 Press Pass Gold

Inserted at one per Hobby pack, this 33-card set parallels the first 33 cards in the base Press Pass set and is enhanced with gold foil highlights.

*GOLD SINGLES: .75X TO 2X BASE HI

2004 Press Pass Reflectors

Randomly inserted in packs, this 33-card set parallels the first 33 cards of the base Press Pass set enhanced with a foil card stock and sequential numbering to 500. A Proofs versions serially numbered to 100 was also inserted.

*REFLECTORS: 1.5X TO 4X BASE HI

2004 Press Pass Reflectors Proofs

Randomly inserted in packs, this 33-card set parallels the first 33 cards of the base Press Pass set enhanced with a foil card stock and sequential numbering to 100.

*REF.PROOF SINGLES: 2.5X TO 6X BASE HI

2004 Press Pass Autographs

Randomly inserted at four per box, this horizontally designed card places a player photo on the right side of the card, an autograph on the left, and a background that is printed in bronze. Several parallel versions of this set were also issued: Blue serially numbered to 50, Gold serially numbered to 100 and Silver serially numbered to 200. These sets also differ in that the card's background appears in the set name's color. Several players have red ink versions of their cards, most of these are unpriced due to scarcity. Print numbers were never released.

RED NOT PRICED DUE TO SCARCITY
*BLUE AU SINGLES: 1.25X TO 3X BASE AU HI
*GOLD AU SINGLES: .6X TO 1.5X BASE AU HI
*SILVER SINGLES: .5X TO 1.25X BASE AU HI
1 Tony Allen 3.00 8.00
2 Rafael Araujo 2.50 6.00
3 Andris Biedrins 3.00 8.00
4 Brian Boddicker 2.50 6.00
5 Andre Brown 2.50 6.00
6 Antonio Burks 2.50 6.00
7 Lionel Chalmers 2.50 6.00
8 Josh Childress 2.50 6.00
9 Luol Deng 4.00 10.00
10 Chris Duhon 2.50 6.00
11 Andre Emmett 2.50 6.00
12 Desmon Farmer 2.50 6.00
13 Matt Freije 2.50 6.00
14 Ben Gordon 6.00 15.00
15 Devin Harris 4.00 10.00
16 David Harrison 2.50 6.00
17 Kris Humphries 2.50 6.00
18 Andre Iguodala 4.00 10.00
19 Luke Jackson 2.50 6.00
20 Shaun Livingston 2.50 6.00
21 James Moore 2.50 6.00
22 Brandon Mouton 2.50 6.00
23 Emeka Okafor 6.00 15.00
24 Rickey Paulding 2.50 6.00
25 Tim Pickett 2.50 6.00
26 Justin Reed 2.50 6.00
27 Romain Sato 2.50 6.00
28 Ha Seung-Jin 2.50 6.00
29 J.R. Smith 3.00 8.00
30 Kirk Snyder 2.50 6.00
31 Pape Sow 2.50 6.00
32 Blake Stepp 2.50 6.00
33 Robert Swift 2.50 6.00
34 Sebastian Telfair 2.50 6.00
35 Anderson Varejao 3.00 8.00
36 Jackson Vroman 2.50 6.00
37 Damien Wilkens 2.50 6.00
38 Carmelo Anthony 20.00 40.00

2004 Press Pass Big Numbers

Inserted one per pack, this 25-card set is horizontally designed with two die-cut basketballs along the left side. Two images of the player, the left in color, the right in color scale, and the player's jersey number appear on the card front.

COMPLETE SET (25) 5.00 12.00
1 Blake Stepp .50 1.25
2 Luke Jackson .50 1.25
3 Rafael Araujo .50 1.25
4 Tim Pickett .50 1.25
5 Tony Allen .60 1.50
6 Robert Swift .50 1.25
7 Andris Biedrins .60 1.50
8 Sebastian Telfair .50 1.25
9 Josh Childress .50 1.25
10 Shaun Livingston .50 1.25
11 Anderson Varejao .60 1.50
12 James Moore .50 1.25
13 Brandon Mouton .50 1.25
14 Andre Emmett .50 1.25
15 Ben Gordon .60 1.50
16 Brian Boddicker .50 1.25
17 Emeka Okafor .75 2.00
18 Devin Harris .75 2.00
19 Desmon Farmer .50 1.25
20 David Harrison .50 1.25
21 Romain Sato .50 1.25
22 J.R. Smith .60 1.50
23 Andre Iguodala .75 2.00
24 Chris Duhon .50 1.25
25 Emeka Okafor CL .75 2.00

2004 Press Pass Game-Used Jerseys

Inserted in packs at the rate of one in 72, this six card memorabilia set places a full-color player image on the left side of the card and a basketball court design on the right containing a rectangular swatch of jersey. Several parallel versions of this set were also released: Gold serially numbered to 200, HoloFoil serially numbered to 50 and Silver serially numbered to 350. Each of the different color versions feature the set name's color as the background.

*GOLD SINGLES: .6X TO 1.5X BASE JSY HI
*HOLO.SINGLES: .75X TO 2X BASE JSY HI
*SILVER SINGLES: .5X TO 1.25X BASE JSY HI
AB Antonio Burks 3.00 8.00
BS Blake Stepp 3.00 8.00
JC Josh Childress 3.00 8.00
LJ Luke Jackson 3.00 8.00
RS Romain Sato 3.00 8.00
SL Shaun Livingston 3.00 8.00

2004 Press Pass Game-Used Shoes

Seeded in packs at the rate of one in 72, this four card set employs the same card design as the jerseys set but has a swatch of game-worn shoe. Several parallels for this set were also produced: Gold featuring gold background highlights is serially numbered to 100 and holofoil features holo background highlights and is sequentially numbered to 50.

*GOLD SINGLES: .75X TO 2X BASE SHOE HI
*HOLO.SINGLES: 1.25X TO 3X BASE SHOE HI
EO Emeka Okafor 6.00 15.00
JS J.R. Smith 5.00 12.00
RS Robert Swift 4.00 10.00
ST Sebastian Telfair 4.00 10.00

2004 Press Pass Hang Time

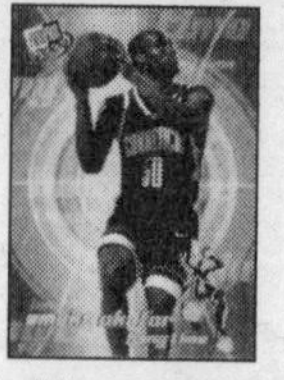

This nine card foil-board set was inserted one in 12 packs and places a full color player action shot against a shiny circle-dominated themed background. The player's name appears in gold foil.

COMPLETE SET (9) 5.00 12.00
1 Ben Gordon 1.00 2.50
2 Andre Iguodala 1.25 3.00
3 Emeka Okafor 1.25 3.00
4 Shaun Livingston .75 2.00
5 Devin Harris 1.25 3.00
6 Sebastian Telfair .75 2.00
7 Josh Childress .75 2.00
8 David Harrison .75 2.00
9 Luke Jackson .75 2.00

2004 Press Pass Lottery Club

Full-color player photos appear on this foil-board set that was inserted in packs at the rate of one in eight. The player's name appears in gold foil along the bottom of the card, and the background consists of 13 numbered basketballs to signify the first 13 lottery picks of the NBA draft.

COMPLETE SET (12) 5.00 12.00
1 Sebastian Telfair .60 1.50
2 Emeka Okafor 1.00 2.50
3 Andre Iguodala 1.00 2.50
4 Shaun Livingston .60 1.50
5 Ben Gordon .75 2.00
6 Devin Harris 1.00 2.50
7 Andris Biedrins .75 2.00
8 Josh Childress .60 1.50
9 J.R. Smith .75 2.00
10 Rafael Araujo .60 1.50
11 Luke Jackson .60 1.50
12 Robert Swift .60 1.50

2004 Press Pass Power Pick Autographs

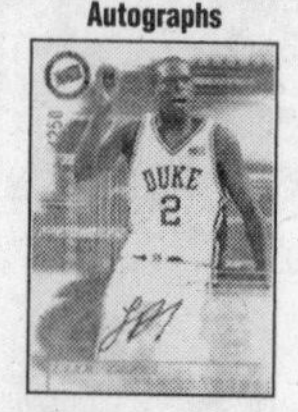

Randomly seeded, this 10-card set places full-color player photos on a background that fades from jersey-matching background color to white. Cards are sequentially numbered to 250 and are autographed.

AB Andris Biedrins 6.00 15.00
AI Andre Iguodala 8.00 20.00
AV Anderson Varejao 6.00 15.00
BG Ben Gordon 8.00 20.00
CD Chris Duhon 5.00 12.00
DH Devin Harris 8.00 20.00
EO Emeka Okafor 6.00 15.00
LD Luol Deng 8.00 20.00
SL Shaun Livingston 5.00 12.00
ST Sebastian Telfair 5.00 12.00

2005 Press Pass

COMPLETE SET (45) 8.00 20.00
1 Deji Akindele .30 .75
2 Kelenna Azubuike .30 .75
3 Brandon Bass .40 1.00
4 Andrew Bogut .50 1.25
5 Will Bynum .50 1.25
6 Taylor Coppenrath .30 .75
7 Drake Diener .30 .75
8 Monta Ellis .60 1.50
9 Daniel Ewing .30 .75
10 Raymond Felton .50 1.25
11 Channing Frye .40 1.00
12 John Gilchrist .30 .75
13 Ryan Gomes .30 .75
14 Joey Graham .30 .75
15 Stephen Graham .30 .75
16 Danny Granger .60 1.50
17 Gerald Green .40 1.00
18 Chuck Hayes .30 .75
19 Luther Head .30 .75
20 Julius Hodge .30 .75
21 Mindaugas Katelynas .30 .75
22 David Lee .50 1.25
23 Sean May .30 .75
24 Rashad McCants .30 .75
25 Ellis Myles .30 .75
26 Chris Paul 1.25 3.00
27 Luke Schenscher .30 .75
28 Wayne Simien .30 .75
29 Chris Taft .30 .75
30 Chris Thomas .30 .75
31 Dijon Thompson .30 .75
32 Fran Vazquez .30 .75
33 Charlie Villanueva .40 1.00
34 Hakim Warrick .40 1.00
35 Martell Webster .30 .75
36 Deron Williams .75 2.00
37 Louis Williams .50 1.25
38 Marvin Williams .40 1.00
39 Antoine Wright .30 .75
40 Bracey Wright .30 .75
41 Sean May .30 .75
Scott May
42 Emeka Okafor 1.00 2.50
Ben Gordon
43 Bruce Weber .75 2.00
44 Roy Williams 1.50 4.00
45 Andrew Bogut CL .40 1.00

2005 Press Pass Blue

*BLUE: .75X TO 2X BASE HI
BLUE STATED ODDS 1:1 RETAIL

2005 Press Pass Gold

*GOLD: .75X TO 2X BASE HI
STATED ODDS 1:1 HOBBY

2005 Press Pass Holo Gold

*HOLO GOLD: 3X TO 8X BASE HI
PRINT RUN 100 SER.#'d SETS

2005 Press Pass Holo Green

*HOLO GREEN: 1.5X TO 4X BASE HI
PRINT RUN 500 SER.#'d SETS

2005 Press Pass Autographs

COMBINED JSY/AU ODDS SIX PER BOX
SP INFO PROVIDED BY PRESS PASS
*BLUE: .75X TO 2X BASE HI
BLUE PRINT RUN 50 SER.#'d SETS
*GOLD: .6X TO 1.5X BASE HI
GOLD PRINT RUN 100 SER.#'d SETS
*SILVER: .5X TO 1.25X BASE HI
SILVER PRINT RUN 200 SER.#'d SETS
AB Andrew Bogut 6.00 15.00
BB Brandon Bass 5.00 12.00
BW Bruce Weber SP 12.50 30.00
CA Carmelo Anthony/100 12.50 30.00
CF Channing Frye 5.00 12.00
CF2 Channing Frye Red 6.00 15.00
CH Chuck Hayes 4.00 10.00
CH2 Chuck Hayes Red 5.00 12.00
CP Chris Paul 20.00 50.00
CT Chris Thomas 4.00 10.00
CT2 Chris Thomas Red CT 5.00 12.00
CT3 Chris Taft 4.00 10.00
CV Charlie Villanueva 5.00 12.00
DA Deji Akindele 4.00 10.00
DA2 Deji Akindele Red 5.00 12.00
DD Drake Diener 4.00 10.00
DE Daniel Ewing 4.00 10.00
DG Danny Granger 8.00 20.00
DG2 Danny Granger Red 10.00 25.00
DL David Lee SP 6.00 15.00
DT Dijon Thompson 4.00 10.00
DW Deron Williams SP 12.50 30.00
EM Ellis Myles 4.00 10.00
FV3 Fran Vazquez FV 4.00 10.00
FV4 Fran Vazquez Red FV 5.00 12.00
GG Gerald Green SP 5.00 12.00
HW Hakim Warrick 5.00 12.00
HW2 Hakim Warrick Red 6.00 15.00
JG Joey Graham 4.00 10.00
JG2 Joey Graham Red 5.00 12.00
JH Julius Hodge 4.00 10.00
JH2 Julius Hodge Red 5.00 12.00
LH Luther Head 4.00 10.00
LH2 Luther Head Red 5.00 12.00
LO Lute Olsen SP 15.00 40.00
LS Luke Schenscher 4.00 10.00
LW Louis Williams 6.00 15.00
MK Mindaugas Katelynas 4.00 10.00
MK2 Mindaugas Katelynas Red 5.00 12.00
MW Marvin Williams 5.00 12.00
RF Raymond Felton 6.00 15.00
RF2 Raymond Felton Red 8.00 20.00
RG Ryan Gomes 4.00 10.00
RM Rashad McCants 4.00 10.00
RW Roy Williams SP 30.00 80.00
SG Stephen Graham 4.00 10.00
SM Sean May 4.00 10.00
TC Taylor Coppenrath 4.00 10.00
WB Will Bynum 4.00 10.00
WS Wayne Simien 4.00 10.00
WS2 Wayne Simien Red 5.00 12.00
MWE Martell Webster 4.00 10.00
MWE2 Martell Webster Red 5.00 12.00
CFAI Channing Frye/200 10.00 25.00
Andre Iguodala
SMSM Sean May/400 6.00 15.00
Scott May
AH Axel Hervelle 4.00 10.00

2005 Press Pass Jerseys

PRINT RUN 600 SER.#'d SETS
*BLUE: .6X TO 1.5X BASE HI
BLUE PRINT RUN 100 SER.#'d SETS
*GOLD: .5X TO 1.25X BASE HI
GOLD PRINT RUN 250 SER.#'d SETS
AB Andrew Bogut 5.00 12.00
CP Chris Paul 12.00 30.00
DE Daniel Ewing 3.00 8.00
DG Danny Granger 6.00 15.00
DL David Lee 5.00 12.00
DT Dijon Thompson 3.00 8.00
SM Sean May 3.00 8.00

2005 Press Pass Old School

COMPLETE SET (25) 10.00 25.00
ONE PER PACK
1 Andrew Bogut 1.00 2.50
2 Taylor Coppenrath .60 1.50
3 Daniel Ewing .60 1.50
4 Raymond Felton 1.00 2.50
5 Channing Frye .75 2.00
6 John Gilchrist .60 1.50
7 Ryan Gomes .60 1.50
8 Joey Graham .60 1.50
9 Danny Granger 1.25 3.00
10 Luther Head .60 1.50
11 Julius Hodge .60 1.50
12 David Lee 1.00 2.50
13 Sean May .60 1.50
14 Rashad McCants .60 1.50
15 Chris Paul 2.50 6.00
16 Luke Schenscher .60 1.50
17 Wayne Simien .60 1.50
18 Chris Taft .60 1.50
19 Chris Thomas .60 1.50
20 Dijon Thompson .60 1.50
21 Charlie Villanueva .75 2.00
22 Hakim Warrick .75 2.00
23 Deron Williams 1.50 4.00
24 Marvin Williams .75 2.00
25 Chris Paul CL 2.50 6.00

2005 Press Pass Power Pick Autographs

PRINT RUN 250 SER.#'d SETS
AB Andrew Bogut 10.00 25.00
CF Channing Frye 8.00 20.00
CP Chris Paul 25.00 60.00
CV Charlie Villanueva 8.00 20.00
DG Danny Granger 12.00 30.00
DW Deron Williams 15.00 40.00
HW Hakim Warrick 8.00 20.00
JH Julius Hodge 6.00 15.00
LH Luther Head 6.00 15.00
MW Marvin Williams 8.00 20.00
RF Raymond Felton 10.00 25.00
RM Rashad McCants 6.00 15.00

2006 Press Pass

Released in July 2006, Press Pass features a 45-card base set picturing 2006-07 rookie players on cards 1-33, 2006-07 rookies in a Power Pick subset on cards 34-38, 2005-06 rookie players on cards 39-42, NCAA Coaches Dean Smith and John Wooden on cards 43 and 44 and Adam Morrison on a checklist card at number 45. Press Pass is packaged in 30-pack boxes of four cards each and carried an initial suggested retail price of $3.99 per pack.

COMPLETE SET (45) 8.00 20.00
1 Maurice Ager .30 .75
2 LaMarcus Aldridge .75 2.00
3 Hilton Armstrong .30 .75
4 James Augustine .30 .75
5 Andrea Bargnani .50 1.25
6 Ronnie Brewer .40 1.00
7 Dee Brown .30 .75
8 Shannon Brown .50 1.25
9 Nick Caner-Medley .30 .75
10 Rodney Carney .30 .75
11 Mardy Collins .30 .75
12 Paul Davis .30 .75
13 Taquan Dean .30 .75
14 Terence Dials .30 .75
15 Randy Foye .40 1.00
16 Mike Gansey .30 .75
17 Rudy Gay .50 1.25
18 Taj Gray .30 .75
19 Kyle Lowry .40 1.00
20 Adam Morrison .40 1.00
21 David Noel .30 .75
22 Patrick O'Bryant .30 .75
23 Kevin Pittsnogle .30 .75
24 Allan Ray .30 .75
25 J.J. Redick .40 1.00
26 Rajon Rondo 1.25 3.00
27 Brandon Roy .75 2.00
28 Curtis Stinson .30 .75
29 Tyrus Thomas .40 1.00
30 P.J. Tucker .30 .75
31 Marcus Williams .30 .75
32 Shawne Williams .30 .75
33 Shelden Williams .30 .75
34 LaMarcus Aldridge PP .75 2.00
35 Adam Morrison PP .40 1.00
36 J.J. Redick PP .40 1.00
37 Brandon Roy PP .75 2.00
38 Tyrus Thomas PP .40 1.00
39 Chris Paul .40 1.00
40 Charlie Villanueva .30 .75
41 Andrew Bogut .30 .75
42 Raymond Felton .40 1.00
43 Dean Smith .60 1.50
44 John Wooden .60 1.50
45 Adam Morrison CL .30 .75

2006 Press Pass Gold

*GOLD: .5X TO 1.25X BASE HI
ONE PER PACK

2006 Press Pass Autographs

APPROXIMATELY FIVE PER BOX
1 Maurice Ager 4.00 10.00
2 LaMarcus Aldridge 10.00 25.00
3 LaMarcus Aldridge Red/92* 10.00 25.00
5 Hilton Armstrong 4.00 10.00
8 James Augustine 4.00 10.00
10 Andrea Bargnani 6.00 15.00
11 Andrea Bargnani Red/116* 10.00 25.00
12 Ronnie Brewer 5.00 12.00
13 Ronnie Brewer Go Hogs Red/24* 10.00 25.00
14 Dee Brown 4.00 10.00
15 Denham Brown 4.00 10.00
20 Shannon Brown 6.00 15.00
23 Nick Caner-Medley 4.00 10.00
24 Nick Caner-Medley Red/74* 4.00 10.00
25 Rodney Carney 4.00 10.00
26 Mardy Collins 4.00 10.00
45 Paul Davis 4.00 10.00
46 Terence Dials 4.00 10.00
47 Terence Dials Red/86* 4.00 10.00
48 Randy Foye 5.00 12.00
49 Randy Foye Foye Wonder/12* 15.00 40.00
50 Mike Gansey 4.00 10.00
60 Rudy Gay 6.00 15.00
61 Taj Gray 4.00 10.00
63 Vincent Grier 4.00 10.00
64 Ryan Hollins 4.00 10.00
65 Damir Markota 4.00 10.00
66 Damir Markota Svetko Red/23* 5.00 12.00
67 Adam Morrison 5.00 12.00
70 David Noel 4.00 10.00
71 Olexsiy Pecherov 4.00 10.00
72 Olexsiy Pecherov Pech Red/14* 5.00 12.00
73 Kevin Pittsnogle 4.00 10.00
75 Chris Quinn 4.00 10.00
76 Chris Quinn Go Irish/23* 5.00 12.00
77 Allan Ray 4.00 10.00
78 Allan Ray Reezy/25* 5.00 12.00
80 Rajon Rondo Blue/Red 15.00 40.00
81 Brandon Roy 10.00 25.00
83 Cedric Simmons 4.00 10.00
84 Dean Smith 30.00 80.00
85 Curtis Stinson 4.00 10.00
87 Tyrus Thomas 5.00 12.00
89 P.J. Tucker 4.00 10.00
90 Shawne Williams 4.00 10.00
91 Shawne Williams Red/143* 5.00 12.00
92 Shelden Williams 4.00 10.00
93 John Wooden 40.00 80.00
94 John Wooden 125.00 250.00
Dean Smith

2006 Press Pass Autographs Blue

*BLUE: .6X TO 1.5X BASE AU HI
38 J.J. Redick 8.00 20.00
45 Curtis Stinson Blue Collar/20* 6.00 15.00

2006 Press Pass Autographs Gold

*GOLD: .5X TO 1.25X BASE AU HI
3 LaMarcus Aldridge Blue/40* 12.00 30.00
24 Terence Dials Go Bucks Red/25* 6.00 15.00
26 Randy Foye Red/43* 6.00 15.00
40 Adam Morrison Go Zags/25* 20.00 40.00
46 J.J. Redick 6.00 15.00

2006 Press Pass Autographs Silver

*SILVER: .5X TO 1.25X BASE AU HI
3 LaMarcus Aldridge Red/77* 12.00 30.00
28 Paul Davis Go State/20* 8.00 20.00
47 Adam Morrison Go Zags/35* 12.50 30.00
53 J.J. Redick 6.00 15.00
60 Tyrus Thomas Blue/39* 12.50 30.00
63 Shawne Williams Blue/39* 8.00 20.00

2006 Press Pass Jerseys

*SILVER: .5X TO 1.25X BASE JSY HI
*GOLD: .5X TO 1.25X BASE JSY HI
*HOLOFOIL: .6X TO 1.5X BASE JSY HI
JCBR Brandon Roy 5.00 12.00
JCKL Kyle Lowry 2.50 6.00
JCLA LaMarcus Aldridge 5.00 12.00
JCRB Ronnie Brewer 2.50 6.00
JCRC Rodney Carney 2.00 5.00
JCRG Rudy Gay 3.00 8.00
JCSB Shannon Brown 3.00 8.00

2006 Press Pass Old School

APPROXIMATELY ONE PER PACK
1 Ronnie Brewer .50 1.25
2 Patrick O'Bryant .40 1.00
3 Hilton Armstrong .40 1.00
4 Rudy Gay .60 1.50
5 Marcus Williams .40 1.00
6 J.J. Redick .50 1.25
7 Shelden Williams .40 1.00
8 Adam Morrison .50 1.25
9 Dee Brown .40 1.00
10 Rajon Rondo 1.50 4.00
11 Taquan Dean .40 1.00
12 Tyrus Thomas .50 1.25
13 Rodney Carney .40 1.00
14 Shawne Williams .40 1.00
15 Shannon Brown .60 1.50
16 Paul Davis .40 1.00
17 David Noel .40 1.00
18 Taj Gray .40 1.00
19 Mardy Collins .40 1.00
20 LaMarcus Aldridge 1.00 2.50
21 Randy Foye .50 1.25
22 Kyle Lowry .50 1.25
23 Brandon Roy 1.00 2.50
24 Kevin Pittsnogle .40 1.00
25 J.J. Redick .50 1.25

2006 Press Pass Power Pick Autographs

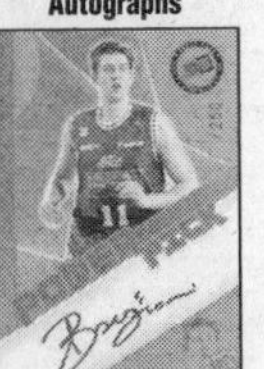

PRINT RUN 250 SER.#'d SETS
1 LaMarcus Aldridge 12.00 30.00
2 Andrea Bargnani 8.00 20.00
3 Ronnie Brewer 6.00 15.00
4 Rodney Carney 5.00 12.00
5 Randy Foye 6.00 15.00
7 Rudy Gay 8.00 20.00
9 Rudy Gay The Kid/21* 15.00 40.00
10 Adam Morrison 6.00 15.00
12 Brandon Roy 12.00 30.00
13 Tyrus Thomas 6.00 15.00
14 Tyrus Thomas T-Time Red/15* 12.50 30.00
15 Shelden Williams 5.00 12.00
16 Shelden Williams Red/96* 5.00 12.00
17 Shelden Williams Landlord/25* 6.00 15.00

2008 Press Pass

COMPLETE SET (65) 10.00 25.00
UNPRICED SOLO PRINT RUN ONE SET
1 D.J. Augustin .30 .75
2 Jerryd Bayless .30 .75
3 Michael Beasley .50 1.25
4 Mario Chalmers .50 1.25
5 Joey Dorsey .30 .75
6 Chris Douglas-Roberts .30 .75
7 Patrick Ewing Jr. .30 .75
8 Shan Foster .30 .75
9 Danilo Gallinari .50 1.25
10 J.R. Giddens .30 .75
11 Eric Gordon .75 2.00
12 Malik Hairston .30 .75
13 DeVon Hardin .30 .75
14 Roy Hibbert .50 1.25
15 J.J. Hickson .40 1.00
16 Darnell Jackson .30 .75
17 Davon Jefferson .30 .75
18 DeAndre Jordan .60 1.50
19 Kosta Koufos .30 .75
20 Courtney Lee .50 1.25
21 Chris Lofton .30 .75
22 Brook Lopez .50 1.25
23 Robin Lopez .30 .75
24 Kevin Love 1.25 3.00
25 O.J. Mayo .50 1.25
26 Candace Parker 3.00 8.00
27 Trent Plaisted .30 .75
28 Anthony Randolph .40 1.00
29 Derrick Rose 2.50 6.00
30 Brandon Rush .30 .75
31 Marreese Speights .30 .75
32 Bryce Taylor .30 .75
33 Sonny Weems .30 .75
34 Russell Westbrook 1.50 4.00
35 D.J. White .30 .75
36 Michael Beasley CL .25 .60
37 Kevin Love CL .60 1.50
38 O.J. Mayo CL .25 .60
39 D.J. Augustin CL .15 .40
40 Jerryd Bayless CL .15 .40
41 Eric Gordon CL .40 1.00
42 D.J. White CL .15 .40
43 Courtney Lee CL .25 .60
44 Shan Foster CL .15 .40
45 Derrick Rose AA 2.50 6.00
46 Brandon Rush AA .30 .75
47 Michael Beasley AA .50 1.25
48 Kevin Love AA 1.25 3.00
49 D.J. Augustin AA .30 .75
50 Candace Parker AA 3.00 8.00
51 Chris Douglas-Roberts AA .30 .75
52 Eric Gordon AA .75 2.00
53 Roy Hibbert AA .50 1.25
54 Brook Lopez AA .50 1.25
55 Brook Lopez 1.00 2.50
Robin Lopez
56 Kevin Love 1.50 4.00
Russell Westbrook
57 Derrick Rose 1.25 3.00
Chris Douglas-Roberts
58 Eric Gordon 1.00 2.50
D.J. White
59 O.J. Mayo 1.00 2.50
Davon Jefferson
60 Brandon Rush 1.00 2.50
Mario Chalmers
61 Derrick Rose PP 2.50 6.00
62 O.J. Mayo PP .50 1.25
63 Michael Beasley PP .50 1.25
64 Kevin Love PP 1.25 3.00
65 Russell Westbrook PP 1.50 4.00

2008 Press Pass Reflectors

*REF: .5X TO 1.25X BASE HI
REFLECTOR STATED ODDS 1:1

2008 Press Pass Reflectors Blue

*BLUE: .6X TO 1.5X BASE HI
RANDOM INSERTS IN RETAIL PACKS

2008 Press Pass Reflectors Holofoil

*HOLO: .75X TO 2X BASE HI
STATED PRINT RUN 250 SER.#'d SETS

2008 Press Pass Reflectors Proofs

*PROOF: 1.25X TO 3X BASE HI
HOLO PRINT RUN 100 SER.#'d SETS

2008 Press Pass Class of 2008

COMPLETE SET (10) 5.00 12.00
STATED ODDS 1:5
CL1 Derrick Rose 4.00 10.00
CL2 O.J. Mayo .75 2.00
CL3 Anthony Randolph .60 1.50
CL4 Brandon Rush .50 1.25
CL5 Russell Westbrook 2.50 6.00
CL6 Eric Gordon 1.25 3.00
CL7 Michael Beasley .75 2.00
CL8 Jerryd Bayless .50 1.25
CL9 Kevin Love 2.00 5.00
CL10 D.J. Augustin .50 1.25

2008 Press Pass Class of 2008 Autographs

STATED PRINT RUN 100 TO 199 SER.#'d SETS
CLAR Anthony Randolph/155 6.00 15.00
CLBL Brook Lopez/155 8.00 20.00
CLBR Brandon Rush/199 5.00 12.00
CLDA D.J. Augustin/155 5.00 12.00
CLDJ DeAndre Jordan/100 10.00 25.00
CLDR Derrick Rose/199 50.00 120.00
CLEG Eric Gordon/199 12.00 30.00
CLJB Jerryd Bayless/107 5.00 12.00
CLKK Kosta Koufos/199 5.00 12.00
CLKL Kevin Love/199 20.00 50.00
CLMB Michael Beasley/199 8.00 20.00
CLOM O.J. Mayo/100 8.00 20.00
CLRW Russell Westbrook/155 30.00 80.00
CLCDR Chris Douglas-Roberts/199 5.00 12.00

2008 Press Pass Game Day Gear Jerseys

STATED PRINT RUN 400 SER.#'d SETS
*GOLD: .5X TO 1.25X BASE JSY
GOLD PRINT RUN 99 SER.#'d SETS
*HOLO: .6X TO 1.5X BASE JSY
HOLO PRINT RUN 50 SER.#'d SETS
GDGAR Anthony Randolph 2.50 6.00
GDGBL Brook Lopez 3.00 8.00
GDGBR Brandon Rush 2.00 5.00
GDGDA D.J. Augustin 2.00 5.00
GDGDR Derrick Rose 8.00 20.00
GDGJD Joey Dorsey 2.00 5.00
GDGRH Roy Hibbert 3.00 8.00
GDGRL Robin Lopez 2.00 5.00
GDGRW Russell Westbrook 6.00 15.00

2008 Press Pass Insider Insight

COMPLETE SET (10) 4.00 10.00
STATED ODDS 1:4
*GOLD: .5X TO 1.25X BASE
RANDOM INSERTS IN PACKS
*FOIL: .6X TO 1.5X BASE
FOIL PRINT RUN 199 SER.#'d SETS
*FOIL GOLD: 1X TO 2.5X BASE
FOIL GOLD PRINT RUN 99 SER.#'d SETS
II1 Michael Beasley .60 1.50
II2 Derrick Rose 3.00 8.00
II3 Jerryd Bayless .40 1.00
II4 Eric Gordon 1.00 2.50
II5 Brook Lopez .60 1.50
II6 Russell Westbrook 2.00 5.00
II7 O.J. Mayo .60 1.50
II8 Kevin Love 1.50 4.00
II9 D.J. Augustin .40 1.00
II10 Brandon Rush .40 1.00

2008 Press Pass Power Picks Autographs

STATED PRINT RUN 100 TO 250 SER.#'d SETS
RED INK: SAME VALUE
PPAR Anthony Randolph/199 8.00 20.00
PPAR1 Anthony Randolph Red 8.00 20.00
PPBL Brook Lopez/199 10.00 25.00
PPBL1 Brook Lopez Red 10.00 25.00
PPBR Brandon Rush/250 6.00 15.00
PPBR1 Brandon Rush Red 6.00 15.00
PPDA D.J. Augustin/199 6.00 15.00
PPDJ DeAndre Jordan/250 12.00 30.00
PPDJ1 DeAndre Jordan Red 12.00 30.00
PPDR Derrick Rose/250 50.00 125.00
PPEG Eric Gordon/250 15.00 40.00
PPJB Jerryd Bayless/250 6.00 15.00
PPKK Kosta Koufos/250 6.00 15.00
PPKK1 Kosta Koufos Red 6.00 15.00
PPKL Kevin Love/250 25.00 60.00
PPKL1 Kevin Love Red 25.00 60.00
PPMB Michael Beasley/250 10.00 25.00
PPOM O.J. Mayo/100 10.00 25.00
PPRW Russell Westbrook/199 30.00 80.00
PPCDR Chris Douglas-Roberts/250 6.00 15.00

2008 Press Pass Primetime Players

COMPLETE SET (10) 5.00 12.00
STATED ODDS 1:5
PT1 Derrick Rose 4.00 10.00
PT2 Brook Lopez .75 2.00
PT3 D.J. Augustin .50 1.25
PT4 Brandon Rush .50 1.25
PT5 Russell Westbrook 2.50 6.00
PT6 Eric Gordon 1.25 3.00
PT7 Michael Beasley .75 2.00
PT8 Jerryd Bayless .50 1.25
PT9 Kevin Love 2.00 5.00
PT10 O.J. Mayo .75 2.00

2008 Press Pass Signings Bronze

PPSAR Anthony Randolph 4.00 10.00
PPSAR1 Anthony Randolph Red 5.00 12.00
PPSBL Brook Lopez 5.00 12.00
PPSBT Brandon Rush 3.00 8.00
PPSBT1 Brandon Rush Red 4.00 10.00
PPSBT2 Bryce Taylor 3.00 8.00
PPSCL Chris Lofton 3.00 8.00
PPSCL Courtney Lee 5.00 12.00
PPSCL1 Courtney Lee Red 6.00 15.00
PPSCP Candace Parker 30.00 60.00
PPSDA D.J. Augustin 3.00 8.00
PPSDG Danilo Gallinari 5.00 12.00
PPSDH DeVon Hardin 3.00 8.00
PPSDJ DeAndre Jordan 6.00 15.00
PPSDR Derrick Rose 40.00 100.00
PPSDW D.J. White 3.00 8.00
PPSEG Eric Gordon 8.00 20.00
PPSEG1 Eric Gordon Red 10.00 25.00
PPSJB Jerryd Bayless 3.00 8.00
PPSJD Joey Dorsey 3.00 8.00
PPSJG J.R. Giddens 3.00 8.00
PPSJG1 J.R. Giddens Red 4.00 10.00
PPSJH J.J. Hickson 4.00 10.00
PPSJH1 J.J. Hickson Red 5.00 12.00
PPSJM James Mays 3.00 8.00
PPSKK Kosta Koufos 3.00 8.00
PPSKL Kevin Love 12.00 30.00
PPSMB Michael Beasley 5.00 12.00
PPSMC Mario Chalmers 5.00 12.00
PPSMH Malik Hairston 3.00 8.00
PPSML Maarty Leunen 3.00 8.00
PPSMS Marreese Speights 3.00 8.00
PPSMS1 Marreese Speights Red 4.00 10.00
PPSOM O.J. Mayo 5.00 12.00
PPSPE Patrick Ewing Jr. 3.00 8.00
PPSPE1 Patrick Ewing Jr. Red 4.00 10.00
PPSRH Roy Hibbert 5.00 12.00
PPSRH1 Roy Hibbert Red 8.00 20.00
PPSRL Robin Lopez 3.00 8.00
PPSRW Russell Westbrook 15.00 40.00
PPSSF Shan Foster 3.00 8.00
PPSSW Sonny Weems 3.00 8.00
PPSSW1 Sonny Weems Red 5.00 12.00
PPSTP Trent Plaisted 3.00 8.00
PPSCDR Chris Douglas-Roberts 3.00 8.00
PPSDJ2 Darnell Jackson 3.00 8.00
PPSDJ3 Darnell Jackson Red 4.00 10.00
PPSDJ4 Davon Jefferson 3.00 8.00

2008 Press Pass Signings Blue

*BLUE: .75X TO 2X BASE AU
PRINT RUN 50 SER.#'d SETS
PPSMB1 Michael Beasley Red 50.00 100.00

2008 Press Pass Signings Gold

*GOLD: .6X TO 1.5X BASE AU
STATED PRINT RUN 75 TO 99 SER.#'d SETS
PPSCP Candace Parker/99 30.00 80.00

2008 Press Pass Signings Silver

*SILVER: .5X TO 1.25X BASE AU
STATED PRINT RUN 67 TO 199 SER.#'d SETS
PPSCP Candace Parker/199 25.00 60.00
PPSDR Derrick Rose/127 60.00 150.00
PPSMB Michael Beasley/125 10.00 25.00
PPSRW Russell Westbrook/100 20.00 50.00
PPSRW1 Russell Westbrook Red 20.00 50.00

2008 Press Pass Teammates Autographs

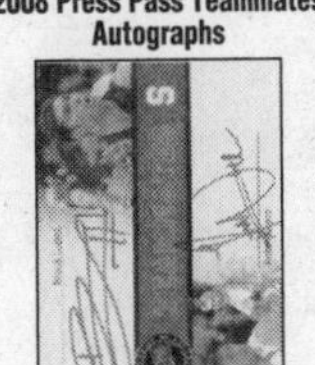

STATED PRINT RUN 25 SER.#'d SETS
TABLRL Brook Lopez 20.00 40.00
Robin Lopez
TAKLRW Kevin Love 40.00 100.00
Russell Westbrook
TADRCDR Derrick Rose 40.00 100.00
Chris Douglas-Roberts

1998 Press Pass Authentics

The Press Pass Authentics set was released during the 1998-99 season and featured many of the NBA's top prospects and young stars.
COMPLETE SET (45) 5.00 10.00
1 Michael Olowokandi .20 .50
2 Mike Bibby .40 1.00
3 Raef LaFrentz .20 .50
4 Vince Carter .75 2.00
5 Robert Traylor .15 .40
6 Jason Williams .40 1.00
7 Larry Hughes .30 .75
8 Paul Pierce .75 2.00
9 Bonzi Wells .15 .40
10 Michael Doleac .15 .40
11 Keon Clark .15 .40
12 Michael Dickerson .15 .40
13 Matt Harpring .20 .50
14 Bryce Drew .15 .40
15 Pat Garrity .15 .40
16 Roshown McLeod .15 .40
17 Brian Skinner .15 .40
18 Tyronn Lue .15 .40
19 Al Harrington .25 .60
20 Sam Jacobson .15 .40
21 Nazr Mohammed .15 .40
22 Ruben Patterson .15 .40
23 Shammond Williams .15 .40
24 Casey Shaw .15 .40
25 DeMarco Johnson .15 .40
26 Miles Simon .15 .40
27 Jahidi White .15 .40
28 Sean Marks .15 .40
29 Toby Bailey .15 .40
30 Andrae Patterson .15 .40
31 Tyson Wheeler .15 .40
32 Cory Carr .15 .40
33 J.R. Henderson .15 .40
34 Torraye Braggs .15 .40
35 Tim Duncan .30 .75
36 Keith Van Horn .15 .40
37 Ron Mercer .12 .30
38 Stephon Marbury .20 .50
39 Ray Allen .20 .50
40 Glen Rice .15 .40
41 Brevin Knight .10 .25
42 Antoine Walker .15 .40
43 Kerry Kittles .10 .25
44 Derek Anderson .10 .25
45 Michael Olowokandi .20 .50

1998 Press Pass Authentics Hang Time

Inserted one per pack, this 45-card set parallels the base set. To ascertain values on individual cards, please refer to the multiplier in the header, coupled with the value of the base card.
*STARS: .6X TO 1.5X BASE CARD HI

1998 Press Pass Authentics Autographs

Randomly inserted in packs at one in eight, this 30-card set features autographs from some of the top stars and rookies of the NBA.
1 Tim Duncan 40.00 80.00
2 Stephon Marbury 5.00 12.00
3 Antoine Walker 5.00 12.00
4 Ray Allen 8.00 20.00
5 Kerry Kittles 1.50 4.00
6 Mike Bibby 6.00 15.00
7 Raef LaFrentz 2.00 5.00
8 Vince Carter 15.00 40.00
9 Robert Traylor 1.50 4.00
10 Jason Williams 6.00 15.00
11 Larry Hughes 4.00 10.00
12 Paul Pierce 10.00 25.00
13 Michael Doleac 1.50 4.00
14 Matt Harpring 2.00 5.00
15 Bryce Drew 1.50 4.00
16 Pat Garrity 1.50 4.00
17 Roshown McLeod 1.50 4.00
18 Brian Skinner 1.50 4.00
19 Tyronn Lue 1.50 4.00
20 Al Harrington 2.50 6.00
21 Sam Jacobson 1.50 4.00
22 Nazr Mohammed 1.50 4.00
23 Ruben Patterson 1.50 4.00
24 Casey Shaw 1.50 4.00
25 DeMarco Johnson 1.50 4.00
26 Sean Marks 1.50 4.00
27 Tyson Wheeler 1.50 4.00
28 Cory Carr 1.50 4.00
29 J.R. Henderson 1.50 4.00
30 Torraye Braggs 1.50 4.00

1998 Press Pass Authentics Full Court Press

Randomly inserted in packs at one in six, this 12-card set features current and future NBA stars who are prominent at both ends of the court. Card backs carry a "FP" prefix.
COMPLETE SET (12) 4.00 10.00
FP1 Paul Pierce 2.00 5.00
FP2 Pat Garrity .40 1.00
FP3 Nazr Mohammed .40 1.00
FP4 Vince Carter 2.00 5.00
FP5 Tim Duncan .75 2.00
FP6 Stephon Marbury .50 1.25
FP7 Ron Mercer .30 .75
FP8 Antoine Walker .40 1.00
FP9 Keith Van Horn .40 1.00
FP10 Michael Olowokandi .50 1.25
FP11 Mike Bibby 1.00 2.50
FP12 Raef LaFrentz .50 1.25

1998 Press Pass Authentics Lottery Club

Randomly inserted at one in 12, this 12-card set features top picks from past NBA Drafts. Card backs carry a "LC" prefix.
COMPLETE SET (12) 8.00 20.00
LC1 Michael Olowokandi .75 2.00
LC2 Tim Duncan 1.25 3.00
LC3 Mike Bibby 1.50 4.00
LC4 Keith Van Horn .60 1.50
LC5 Raef LaFrentz .75 2.00
LC6 Shareef Abdur-Rahim .60 1.50
LC7 Vince Carter 3.00 8.00
LC8 Stephon Marbury .75 2.00
LC9 Ray Allen .75 2.00
LC10 Robert Traylor .60 1.50
LC11 Antoine Walker .60 1.50
LC12 Jason Williams 1.50 4.00

1998 Press Pass Authentics Signed Memorabilia

Randomly inserted in packs at one in 29, this 23-card set features autographed memorabilia from the top rookies of the 1998 NBA Draft, as well as veterans from the NBA. Several items have been too scarce to price, they are listed below for cataloguing purposes.
1B Mike Bibby Mini-BK 15.00 40.00
3 Vince Carter 8X10 20.00 40.00
3A Vince Carter I/O BK 40.00 100.00
3B Vince Carter Mini-BK 25.00 60.00
4 Michael Dickerson 8X10 2.00 5.00
4A Michael Dickerson Plaque 10.00 25.00
5 Michael Doleac 8X10 2.00 5.00
6 Bryce Drew 8X10 2.00 5.00
7 Pat Garrity Plaque 6.00 15.00
8 Matt Harpring 8X10 2.50 6.00
9 Larry Hughes 8X10 4.00 10.00
10 Kerry Kittles 8X10 2.00 5.00
11 Brevin Knight 8X10 2.00 5.00
12 Raef LaFrentz 8X10 4.00 10.00
13 Tyronne Lue 8X10 2.00 5.00
14 Karl Malone Plaque 25.00 60.00
15 Stephon Marbury 8X10 8.00 20.00
16 Nazr Mohammed 8X10 2.00 5.00
17 Michael Olowokandi 8X10 2.50 6.00
18 Paul Pierce Plaque 10.00 25.00
19 David Robinson Plaque 20.00 50.00
20 Brian Skinner 8X10 2.00 5.00
21 Robert Traylor 8X10 2.00 5.00
21A Robert Traylor Plaque 6.00 15.00
22 Keith Van Horn Plaque 6.00 15.00
23 Antoine Walker 8X10 6.00 15.00

1998 Press Pass Authentics Sterling Autographs

Randomly inserted in packs at one in 720, this 21-card set features autographs of some of the top stars and rookies from the NBA.
1 Tim Duncan 60.00 150.00
2 Stephon Marbury 10.00 25.00
3 Mike Bibby 12.00 30.00
4 Raef LaFrentz 4.00 10.00
5 Vince Carter 30.00 80.00
6 Robert Traylor 3.00 8.00
7 Jason Williams 12.00 30.00
8 Larry Hughes 8.00 20.00
9 Paul Pierce 20.00 50.00
10 Michael Doleac 3.00 8.00
11 Matt Harpring 4.00 10.00
12 Bryce Drew 3.00 8.00
13 Pat Garrity 3.00 8.00
14 Roshown Mcleod 3.00 8.00
15 Casey Shaw 3.00 8.00
16 DeMarco Johnson 3.00 8.00
17 Tyronn Lue 3.00 8.00
18 Cory Carr 3.00 8.00
19 J.R. Henderson 3.00 8.00
20 Torraye Braggs 3.00 8.00
21 Al Harrington 5.00 12.00

1999 Press Pass Authentics

Released in four-card packs, this 45-card set features draft picks from the 1999 season.
COMPLETE SET (45) 4.00 10.00
1 Elton Brand .30 .75
2 Steve Francis .30 .75
3 Baron Davis .40 1.00
4 Lamar Odom .40 1.00
5 Jonathan Bender .12 .30
6 Wally Szczerbiak .25 .60
7 Richard Hamilton .30 .75
8 Andre Miller .30 .75
9 Jason Terry .30 .75
10 Trajan Langdon .12 .30
11 William Avery .12 .30
12 Ron Artest .30 .75
13 Cal Bowdler .12 .30
14 James Posey .12 .30
15 Quincy Lewis .12 .30
16 Jeff Foster .12 .30
17 Kenny Thomas .12 .30
18 Devean George .12 .30
19 Tim James .12 .30
20 Vonteego Cummings .12 .30
21 Jumaine Jones .12 .30
22 John Celestand .12 .30
23 Rico Hill .12 .30
24 Michael Ruffin .12 .30
25 Chris Herren .12 .30
26 Evan Eschmeyer .12 .30
27 Calvin Booth .12 .30
28 Obinna Ekezie .12 .30
29 A.J. Bramlett .12 .30
30 Louis Bullock .12 .30
31 Lee Nailon .12 .30
32 Tyrone Washington .12 .30
33 Venson Hamilton .12 .30
34 Roberto Bergersen .12 .30
35 Rodney Buford .12 .30
36 Melvin Levett .12 .30
37 Kris Clack .12 .30
38 Vince Carter .25 .60
39 Jason Williams .15 .40
40 Paul Pierce .20 .50
41 Mike Bibby .15 .40
42 Michael Olowokandi .07 .20
43 Marcus Camby .10 .25
44 Raef LaFrentz .07 .20
45 Vince Carter CL .25 .60

1999 Press Pass Authentics Hang Time

Inserted one per packs, this 45-card set parallels the base set. The cards feature silver foil, rather than the standard gold. To ascertain values on individual cards, please refer to the multiplier in the header, coupled with the value of the base card.
*HANG TIME: .75X TO 2X VALUE

1999 Press Pass Authentics Autographs

Randomly inserted in packs at one in eight, this 33-card set features autographs of the top draft picks. The backs feature a congratulatory message.
*GOLD: .6X TO 1.5X BASIC CARDS
GOLD PRINT RUN 100 SERIAL #'d SETS
1 Elton Brand 4.00 10.00
2 Steve Francis 4.00 10.00
3 Baron Davis 5.00 12.00
4 Lamar Odom 5.00 12.00
5 Wally Szczerbiak 3.00 8.00
6 Richard Hamilton 4.00 10.00
7 Andre Miller 4.00 10.00
8 Jason Terry 4.00 10.00
9 Trajan Langdon 1.50 4.00
10 Ron Artest 4.00 10.00
11 Cal Bowdler 1.50 4.00
12 James Posey 1.50 4.00
13 Quincy Lewis 1.50 4.00
14 Jeff Foster 1.50 4.00
15 Devean George 1.50 4.00
16 Tim James 1.50 4.00
17 Vonteego Cummings 1.50 4.00
18 Jumaine Jones 1.50 4.00
19 John Celestand 1.50 4.00
20 Michael Ruffin 1.50 4.00
21 Chris Herren 2.50 6.00
22 Evan Eschmeyer 1.50 4.00
23 Calvin Booth 1.50 4.00
24 Obinna Ekezie 1.50 4.00
25 A.J. Bramlett 1.50 4.00
26 Louis Bullock 1.50 4.00
27 Lee Nailon 1.50 4.00
28 Tyrone Washington 1.50 4.00
29 Venson Hamilton 1.50 4.00
30 Roberto Bergersen 1.50 4.00
31 Melvin Levett 1.50 4.00
32 Kris Clack 1.50 4.00
33 William Avery 1.50 4.00

1999 Press Pass Authentics Full Court Press

Randomly inserted in packs at one in 12, this 12-card set features future stars who excel on both ends of the court. Card backs carry a "FC" prefix.
COMPLETE SET (12) 3.00 8.00
FC1 Elton Brand .60 1.50
FC2 Steve Francis .60 1.50
FC3 Baron Davis .75 2.00
FC4 Lamar Odom .75 2.00
FC5 Jonathan Bender .25 .60
FC6 Wally Szczerbiak .50 1.25
FC7 Richard Hamilton .60 1.50
FC8 Andre Miller .60 1.50
FC9 Jason Terry .60 1.50
FC10 Trajan Langdon .25 .60
FC11 William Avery .25 .60
FC12 James Posey .25 .60

1999 Press Pass Authentics Lottery Club

Randomly inserted in packs at one in 23, this six-card set six of the hottest draft picks against Nitrokrome. Card backs carry a "LC" prefix.
COMPLETE SET (6) 2.00 5.00
LC1 Elton Brand .60 1.50
LC2 Steve Francis .60 1.50
LC3 Baron Davis .75 2.00
LC4 Lamar Odom .75 2.00
LC5 Jonathan Bender .25 .60
LC6 Wally Szczerbiak .50 1.25

1999 Press Pass Authentics Signed Memorabilia

Inserted one per box, this 46-card set features autographed memorabilia from the top draft picks and some current stars of the NBA. This includes jerseys, basketballs, 8X10 photos and jersey plaques. The items are not numbered, but numbered below for checklisting purposes.
1 William Avery 8X10 4.00 10.00
2 Mike Bibby Plaque 15.00 40.00
3 Calvin Booth 8X10 4.00 10.00
4 Cal Bowdler 8X10 4.00 10.00
5 Elton Brand 8X10 6.00 15.00

5A Elton Brand IO BK 20.00 50.00
5B Elton Brand Jersey 60.00 150.00
5C Elton Brand Mini-BK 15.00 40.00
5D Elton Brand Plaque 12.00 30.00
6 Louis Bullock 8X10 4.00 10.00
7 Vince Carter 8X10 30.00 80.00
7A Vince Carter IO BK 50.00 120.00
8 John Celestand 8X10 4.00 10.00
9 Vonteego Cummings 8X10 4.00 10.00
10 Obinna Ekezie 8X10 4.00 10.00
11 Evan Eschmeyer 8X10 4.00 10.00
11A Evan Eschmeyer Plaque 6.00 15.00
12 Steve Francis 8X10 8.00 20.00
12A Steve Francis IO BK 25.00 60.00
12B Steve Francis Jersey 75.00 150.00
12C Steve Francis Mini-BK 20.00 50.00
12D Steve Francis Plaque 15.00 40.00
13 Ricahrd Hamilton 8X10 6.00 15.00
13A Richard Hamilton IO BK 20.00 50.00
14 Chris Herren 8X10 4.00 10.00
15 Larry Hughes Plaque 10.00 25.00
16 Tim James 8X10 4.00 10.00
17 Jumaine Jones 8X10 4.00 10.00
18 Raef LaFrentz 8X10 4.00 10.00
18A Raef LaFrentz Plaque 6.00 15.00
19 Quincy Lewis 8X10 4.00 10.00
20 Andre Miller 8X10 6.00 15.00
20A Andre Miller Plaque 10.00 25.00
21 Lee Nailon 8X10 4.00 10.00
22 Lamar Odom IO BK 25.00 60.00
22A Lamar Odom Mini-BK 20.00 50.00
22B Lamar Odom Plaque 15.00 40.00
23 Michael Olowokandi IO BK 8.00 20.00
24 James Posey 8X10 4.00 10.00
24A James Posey Plaque 6.00 15.00
25 Michael Ruffin 8X10 4.00 10.00
26 Wally Szczerbiak 8X10 6.00 15.00
26A Wally Szczerbiak IO BK 15.00 40.00
26B Wally Szczerbiak Mini-BK 12.50 30.00
26C Wally Szczerbiak Plaque 10.00 25.00
27 Jason Terry 8X10 6.00 15.00

1999 Press Pass Authentics Team 2000

Randomly inserted in packs at one in five, this 12-card set highlights top draft picks who look to lead their new teams into the new millennium. Card backs carry a "T" prefix.

COMPLETE SET (12) 2.50 6.00
T1 Elton Brand .50 1.25
T2 Steve Francis .50 1.25
T3 Baron Davis .60 1.50
T4 Lamar Odom .60 1.50
T5 Wally Szczerbiak .40 1.00
T6 Richard Hamilton .50 1.25
T7 Andre Miller .50 1.25
T8 Jason Terry .50 1.25
T9 Trajan Langdon .20 .50
T10 Ron Artest .50 1.25
T11 Tim James .20 .50
T12 William Avery .20 .50

1997 Press Pass Double Threat

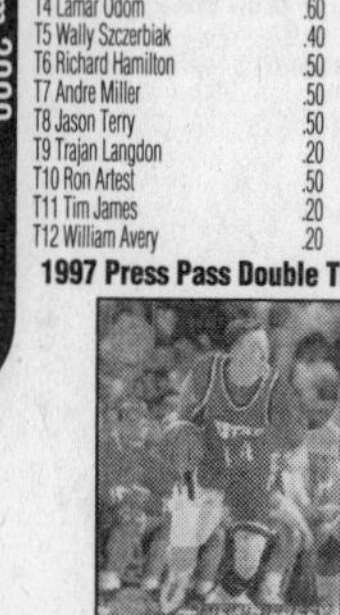

The 1997 Press Pass Double Threat set was issued in one series totalling 45 cards. The fronts feature borderless color action player photos with foil highlights. The backs carry biographical information and career statistics. Cards 34-45 display a photo of both a top veteran and rookie on the same card. A blue-foil parallel version of this base set was also produced as well as a silver-foil hobby only parallel version.

COMPLETE SET (45) 3.00 8.00
1 Tim Duncan 1.00 2.50
2 Keith Van Horn .30 .75
3 Chauncey Billups .60 1.50
4 Antonio Daniels .15 .40
5 Tony Battie .20 .50
6 Ron Mercer .20 .50
7 Tim Thomas .30 .75
8 Adonal Foyle .15 .40
9 Tracy McGrady .75 2.00
10 Danny Fortson .15 .40
11 Olivier Saint-Jean .15 .40
12 Austin Croshere .15 .40
13 Derek Anderson .15 .40
14 Maurice Taylor .15 .40
15 Kelvin Cato .15 .40
16 Brevin Knight .15 .40
17 Johnny Taylor .15 .40
18 Chris Anstey .15 .40
19 Scot Pollard .15 .40
20 Paul Grant .15 .40
21 Anthony Parker .15 .40
22 Ed Gray .15 .40
23 Bobby Jackson .20 .50
24 John Thomas .15 .40
25 Charles Smith .15 .40
26 Jacque Vaughn .15 .40
27 Keith Booth .15 .40
28 Serge Zwikker .15 .40
29 Charles O'Bannon .15 .40
30 Bubba Wells .15 .40
31 Kebu Stewart .15 .40
32 James Collins .15 .40
33 Eddie Elisma .15 .40
34 Tim Duncan .60 1.50
David Robinson
35 Chauncey Billups .40 1.00
Antoine Walker
36 Tony Battie .12 .30
Antonio McDyess
37 Ray Mercer .12 .30
Antoine Walker
38 Antonio Daniels .10 .25
Shareef Abdur-Rahim
39 Danny Fortson .10 .25
Antonio McDyess
40 Jacques Vaughn .12 .30
Karl Malone
41 Adonal Foyle .10 .25
Joe Smith
42 Paul Grant .12 .30
Stephon Marbury
43 Keith Booth .15 .40
Scottie Pippen
44 Charles Smith .12 .30
Alonzo Mourning
45 Tim Duncan .60 1.50
David Robinson CL
NNO Tim Duncan 1.00 2.50
David Robinson PROMO

1997 Press Pass Double Threat Blue

Inserted one per retail pack only, this 45-card set parallels the base set. The cards feature a blue-foil front. To ascertain values on individual cards, please refer to the multiplier in the header, coupled with the value of the base card.

*STARS: .6X TO 1.5X BASE CARD HI

1997 Press Pass Double Threat Retroactive

Inserted one in every pack, this 36-card set features color action photos of top rookies. The backs carry player information and are numbered with an "RA" prefix. To ascertain values on individual cards, please refer to the multiplier in the header, coupled with the value of the base card.

COMPLETE SET (36) 6.00 15.00
*STARS: .5X TO 1.25X BASE CARD HI

1997 Press Pass Double Threat Silver

Inserted one per hobby pack, this 45-card set parallels the base set. The cards feature silver foil on the front. To ascertain values on individual cards, please refer to the multiplier in the header below, coupled with the value of the base card.

*SILVER: .6X TO 1.5X BASE CARD HI

1997 Press Pass Double Threat Autographs

Randomly inserted in hobby packs at the rate of one in 18 and in retail packs at the rate of one in 36, this 30-card set features autographed cards of top players.

1A Tim Duncan 40.00 80.00
2A Keith Van Horn 3.00 8.00
3A Chauncey Billups 6.00 15.00
4A Antonio Daniels 1.50 4.00
5A Tony Battie 2.00 5.00
7A Tim Thomas 3.00 8.00
8A Adonal Foyle 1.50 4.00
9A Tracy McGrady 20.00 50.00
10A Danny Fortson 1.50 4.00
11A Olivier Saint-Jean 1.50 4.00
12A Austin Croshere 1.50 4.00
13A Derek Anderson 1.50 4.00
14A Maurice Taylor 1.50 4.00
15A Kelvin Cato 1.50 4.00
16A Brevin Knight 1.50 4.00
17A Johnny Taylor 1.50 4.00
18A Chris Anstey 1.50 4.00
19A Scot Pollard 1.50 4.00
20A Paul Grant 1.50 4.00
21A Anthony Parker 1.50 4.00
23A Bobby Jackson 2.00 5.00
24A John Thomas 1.50 4.00
25A Charles Smith 1.50 4.00
26A Jacque Vaughn 1.50 4.00
28A Serge Zwikker 1.50 4.00
29A Charles O'Bannon 1.50 4.00
30A Bubba Wells 1.50 4.00
31A Kebu Stewart 1.50 4.00
32A James Collins 1.50 4.00
33A Eddie Elisma 1.50 4.00

1997 Press Pass Double Threat Double Autographs

Randomly inserted in packs, this limited five-card set features autographed color action photos of two top players on the same card. The numbers after the players' names indicate how many of each card were produced and signed.

1 Tim Duncan 200.00 400.00
David Robinson/100
2 Jacques Vaughn 30.00 80.00
Karl Malone/625
3 Tony Battie 8.00 20.00
Antonio McDyess/750
4 Ray Mercer 15.00 40.00
Antoine Walker/250
5 Chauncey Billups 12.00 30.00
Antoine Walker/500

1997 Press Pass Double Threat Double Thread Jerseys

Randomly inserted in packs at the rate of one in 720, this five-card set features color player photos. A different player is pictured on each side with an authentic piece of a game-used jersey of each player embedded in the jersey beside his picture. Only 325 of each card were produced.

DD1 Tim Duncan 60.00 150.00
David Robinson
DD2 Chauncey Billups 15.00 40.00
Antoine Walker
DD3 Ray Mercer 15.00 40.00
Antoine Walker
DD4 Tony Battie 12.50 30.00
Antonio McDyess
DD5 Jacques Vaughn 15.00 40.00
Karl Malone

1997 Press Pass Double Threat Light It Up

Randomly inserted in packs at the rate of one in nine, this 25-card set features color action photos of top players printed on die-cut cards.

COMPLETE SET (25) 10.00 25.00
LU1 Tim Duncan 3.00 8.00
LU2 Keith Van Horn 1.00 2.50
LU3 Chauncey Billups 2.00 5.00
LU4 Antonio Daniels .50 1.25
LU5 Tony Battie .60 1.50
LU6 Ron Mercer .60 1.50
LU7 Tim Thomas 1.00 2.50
LU8 Adonal Foyle .50 1.25
LU9 Tracy McGrady 2.50 6.00
LU10 Danny Fortson .50 1.25
LU11 Olivier Saint-Jean .50 1.25
LU12 Austin Croshere .50 1.25
LU13 Derek Anderson .50 1.25
LU14 Maurice Taylor .50 1.25
LU15 Kelvin Cato .50 1.25
LU16 Brevin Knight .50 1.25
LU17 Alonzo Mourning .60 1.50
LU18 Joe Smith .40 1.00
LU19 Shareef Abdur-Rahim .50 1.25
LU20 Scottie Pippen .75 2.00
LU21 David Robinson .75 2.00
LU22 Karl Malone .60 1.50
LU23 Stephon Marbury .60 1.50
LU24 Antonio McDyess .40 1.00
LU25 Antoine Walker CL .50 1.25

1997 Press Pass Double Threat Lotto

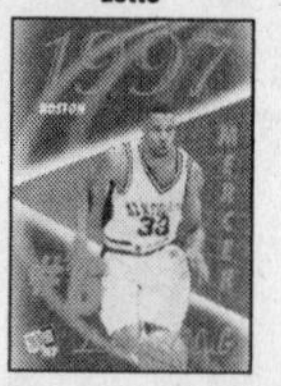

This eight-card "progressive insert" set features color action photos of top lotto picks through the years printed on holofoil cards. The cards were inserted as follows: #1A 1:720, #1B 1:360, #2A 1:180, #2B 1:90, #3A & 3B 1:45, and #4A & 4B 1:36.

COMPLETE SET (8) 40.00 100.00
LC1A Tim Duncan 20.00 50.00
LC1B David Robinson 15.00 40.00
LC2A Keith Van Horn 6.00 15.00
LC2B Antonio McDyess 6.00 15.00
LC3A Antonio Daniels 1.50 4.00
LC3B Stephon Marbury 2.50 6.00
LC4A Ron Mercer 1.50 4.00
LC4B Antoine Walker 2.50 6.00

1997 Press Pass Double Threat Nitrokrome

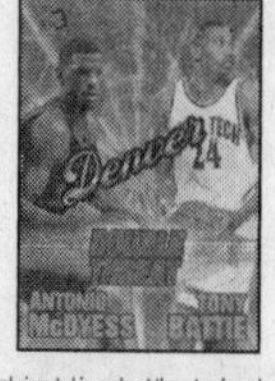

Randomly inserted in packs at the rate of one in 18, this nine-card set features color action player photos of top NBA players and rookies printed on all-foil cards.

COMPLETE SET (9) 6.00 15.00
DT1 Tim Duncan 4.00 10.00
David Robinson
DT2 Jacques Vaughn .75 2.00
Karl Malone
DT3 Tony Battie .75 2.00
Antonio McDyess
DT4 Ron Mercer .75 2.00
Antoine Walker
DT5 Paul Grant .75 2.00
Stephon Marbury
DT6 Chauncey Billups 2.50 6.00
Antoine Walker
DT7 Antonio Daniels .60 1.50
Shareef Abdur-Rahim
DT8 Alonzo Mourning .75 2.00
Charles Smith
DT9 Joe Smith .60 1.50
Adonal Foyle

1997 Press Pass Double Threat Showdown

Randomly inserted in hobby only packs at the rate of one in 36, this six card set features color action photos of a rookie on one side and a veteran on the other printed on canvas card stock.

COMPLETE SET (6) 12.50 30.00
S1 Alonzo Mourning 10.00 25.00
Tim Duncan
S2 Karl Malone 2.00 5.00
Danny Fortson
S3 Joe Smith 2.00 5.00
Tony Battie
S4 Antonio McDyess 3.00 8.00
Keith Van Horn
S5 Scottie Pippen 2.50 6.00
Ron Mercer
S6 David Robinson 2.50 6.00
Adonal Foyle

1998 Press Pass Double Threat

The 1998 Press Pass Double Threat set was issued in one series totalling 45 cards. Special bonus cards were also issued of the top three draft picks. Each card has a special foil treatment and was inserted at one in 180 packs. Those cards are numbered F1 through F3 and are listed at the end of the base set.

COMPLETE SET (45) 5.00 10.00
1 Michael Olowokandi .30 .75
2 Mike Bibby .60 1.50
3 Raef LaFrentz .30 .75
4 Vince Carter 1.25 3.00
5 Robert Traylor .25 .60
6 Jason Williams .60 1.50
7 Larry Hughes .50 1.25
8 Paul Pierce 1.25 3.00
9 Bonzi Wells .25 .60
10 Michael Doleac .25 .60
11 Keon Clark .25 .60
12 Michael Dickerson .25 .60
13 Matt Harpring .30 .75
14 Bryce Drew .25 .60
15 Pat Garrity .25 .60
16 Roshown McLeod .25 .60
17 Brian Skinner .25 .60
18 Tyronn Lue .25 .60
19 Al Harrington .40 1.00
20 Sam Jacobson .25 .60
21 Nazr Mohammed .25 .60
22 Ruben Patterson .25 .60
23 Shammond Williams .25 .60
24 Casey Shaw .25 .60
25 DeMarco Johnson .25 .60
26 Miles Simon .25 .60
27 Jahidi White .25 .60
28 Sean Marks .25 .60
29 Toby Bailey .25 .60
30 Andrae Patterson .25 .60
31 Tyson Wheeler .25 .60
32 Cory Carr .25 .60
33 J.R. Henderson .25 .60
34 Torraye Braggs .25 .60
35 Tim Duncan .50 1.25
36 Keith Van Horn .25 .60
37 Ron Mercer .20 .50
38 Stephon Marbury .30 .75
39 Ray Allen .30 .75
40 Glen Rice .25 .60
41 Tim Thomas .25 .60
42 Antoine Walker .25 .60
43 Kerry Kittles .15 .40
44 Shareef Abdur-Rahim .25 .60
45 Michael Olowokandi CL .30 .75
F1 Michael Olowokandi FOIL 4.00 10.00
F2 Mike Bibby FOIL 8.00 20.00
F3 Raef LaFrentz FOIL 4.00 10.00

1998 Press Pass Double Threat Alley-Oop

Inserted one per hobby pack only, this 45-card set parallels the base set. To ascertain values on individual cards, please refer to the multiplier in the header below, coupled with the value of the base card.

*STARS: .6X TO 1.5X BASE CARD HI

1998 Press Pass Double Threat Torquers

Inserted one per retail pack, this 45-card set is a parallel of regular base set with blue foil treatment. To ascertain values for individual cards, please refer to the multiplier in the headers below, coupled with the value of the base card.

*STARS: .6X TO 1.5X BASE CARD HI

1998 Press Pass Double Threat Double Thread Jerseys

Randomly inserted in packs at one in 720, this three-card set features dual jerseys of current NBA players and draft picks. Card number DT1 was never issued. Cards DT2 and DT4 were only available via trade. Card backs carry a "DT" prefix. Please note that there were only 425 serial numbered sets produced.

DT2 Michael Olowokandi 25.00 60.00
Tim Duncan
DT3 Robert Traylor 10.00 25.00
Keith Van Horn
DT4 Vince Carter 30.00 80.00
Glen Rice

1998 Press Pass Double Threat Dreammates

Inserted in packs at one in 18, this nine-card set features some pairings of "dream" teammates. Each card features a NBA star and a draft pick. Card backs carry a "DM" prefix.

COMPLETE SET (9) 10.00 25.00
DM1 Mike Bibby 2.00 5.00
Tim Duncan
DM2 Michael Olowokandi 1.00 2.50
Stephon Marbury
DM3 Larry Hughes 1.50 4.00
Tim Thomas
DM4 Vince Carter 4.00 10.00
Glen Rice
DM5 Robert Traylor 1.00 2.50
Ray Allen
DM6 Paul Pierce 4.00 10.00
Ron Mercer
DM7 Raef LaFrentz 1.00 2.50
Keith Van Horn
DM8 Michael Dickerson .75 2.00
Antoine Walker
DM9 Jason Williams 2.00 5.00
Shareef Abdur-Rahim
NNO Mike Bibby .75 2.00
Tim Duncan

1998 Press Pass Double Threat Jackpot

Randomly inserted in packs at multi-levels, this eight-card set features the top picks of the draft. Card J1A was inserted at one in 720, card J1B was inserted at one in 360, card J2A was inserted at one in 180, and card J2B was inserted at one in 90. Both cards J3A and J3B were inserted at one in 45, while cards J4A and J4B were inserted at one in 36.

COMPLETE SET (8) 15.00 40.00
J1A Michael Olowokandi 3.00 8.00
J1B Mike Bibby 6.00 15.00
J2A Raef LaFrentz 3.00 8.00
J2B Vince Carter 10.00 25.00
J3A Robert Traylor 1.25 3.00
J3B Jason Williams 2.50 6.00
J4A Larry Hughes 2.00 5.00
J4B Paul Pierce 2.50 6.00

1998 Press Pass Double Threat Player's Club Autographs

Randomly inserted in hobby packs only at one in 360, this 13-card set features autographs of the top draft picks. The cards are serially numbered out of 125. Card backs carry a "PC" prefix.

PC1 Michael Olowokandi 6.00 15.00
PC2 Mike Bibby 12.00 30.00
PC3 Raef LaFrentz 6.00 15.00
PC4 Vince Carter 75.00 150.00
PC5 Robert Traylor 5.00 12.00
PC6 Jason Williams 12.00 30.00
PC7 Larry Hughes 10.00 25.00
PC8 Paul Pierce 25.00 60.00
PC9 Bonzi Wells 5.00 12.00
PC10 Michael Doleac 5.00 12.00
PC11 Keon Clark 5.00 12.00
PC12 Michael Dickerson 5.00 12.00
PC13 Matt Harpring 6.00 15.00

1998 Press Pass Double Threat Retros

Inserted one per pack, this 36-card set is a semi-parallel of the base set. The cards feature a black and white design. Card backs carry a "R" prefix.

COMPLETE SET (36) 8.00 20.00
R1 Michael Olowokandi .30 .75
R2 Mike Bibby .60 1.50
R3 Raef LaFrentz .30 .75
R4 Vince Carter 1.25 3.00
R5 Robert Traylor .25 .60
R6 Jason Williams .60 1.50
R7 Larry Hughes .50 1.25
R8 Paul Pierce 1.25 3.00
R9 Bonzi Wells .25 .60
R10 Michael Doleac .25 .60
R11 Keon Clark .25 .60
R12 Michael Dickerson .25 .60
R13 Matt Harpring .30 .75
R14 Bryce Drew .25 .60
R15 Cory Carr .25 .60
R16 Andrae Patterson .25 .60
R17 Pat Garrity .25 .60
R18 Roshown McLeod .25 .60
R19 Brian Skinner .25 .60
R20 Tyronn Lue .25 .60
R21 Sam Jacobson .25 .60
R22 J.R. Henderson .25 .60
R23 Nazr Mohammed .25 .60
R24 Ruben Patterson .25 .60
R25 Shammond Williams .25 .60
R26 Toby Bailey .25 .60
R27 DeMarco Johnson .25 .60
R28 Miles Simon .25 .60
R29 Jahidi White .25 .60
R30 Tim Duncan .50 1.25
R31 Keith Van Horn .25 .60
R32 Ron Mercer .20 .50
R33 Stephon Marbury .30 .75
R34 Ray Allen .30 .75
R35 Glen Rice .25 .60
R36 Mike Bibby CL .60 1.50

1998 Press Pass Double Threat Rookie Jerseys

Randomly inserted in packs at one in 720, this four-card set features jersey cards of draft picks. Both the Pierce and Dickerson were available via trade cards. Card backs carry a "JC" prefix.

JC1 Raef LaFrentz 6.00 15.00
JC2 Pat Garrity 5.00 12.00
JC3 Paul Pierce 25.00 60.00

1998 Press Pass Double Threat Rookie Script Autographs

Randomly inserted in hobby packs at one in 18 and retail packs at one in 36, this 34-card set features autographs of the 1998 NBA Draft class. Michael Olowokandi, Jason Williams, Keon Clark, Bonzi Wells, Michael Dickerson, Roshown McLeod, Paul Pierce, Miles Simon, Toby Baily and Robert Patterson where only made available via redemption cards. The cards are not numbered and listed below alphabetically.

1 Toby Bailey 1.50 4.00
2 Mike Bibby 6.00 15.00
3 Torraye Braggs 1.50 4.00
4 Cory Carr 1.50 4.00
5 Vince Carter 15.00 40.00
6 Keon Clark 1.50 4.00
7 Michael Dickerson 1.50 4.00
8 Michael Doleac 1.50 4.00
9 Bryce Drew 1.50 4.00
10 Pat Garrity 1.50 4.00
11 Matt Harpring 2.00 5.00
12 Al Harrington 2.50 6.00
13 J.R. Henderson 1.50 4.00
14 Larry Hughes 4.00 10.00
15 Sam Jacobson 1.50 4.00
16 DeMarco Johnson 1.50 4.00
17 Raef LaFrentz 2.00 5.00
18 Tyronn Lue 1.50 4.00
19 Sean Marks 1.50 4.00
20 Roshown McLeod 1.50 4.00
21 Nazr Mohammed 1.50 4.00
22 Michael Olowokandi 2.00 5.00
23 Andrae Patterson 1.50 4.00
24 Ruben Patterson 1.50 4.00
25 Paul Pierce 10.00 25.00
26 Casey Shaw 1.50 4.00
27 Miles Simon 1.50 4.00
28 Brian Skinner 1.50 4.00
29 Robert Traylor 1.50 4.00
30 Bonzi Wells 1.50 4.00
31 Tyson Wheeler 1.50 4.00
32 Jahidi White 1.50 4.00
33 Jason Williams 6.00 15.00
34 Shammond Williams 1.50 4.00

1998 Press Pass Double Threat Two-On-One

Randomly inserted in packs at one in 12, this 12-card set features top combos of NBA stars and draft picks. Each player has an individual card and a combo card. Card backs carry a "TO" prefix.

COMPLETE SET (12) 8.00 20.00
TO1 Raef LaFrentz .75 2.00
TO2 Raef LaFrentz .75 2.00
Keith Van Horn
TO3 Keith Van Horn .60 1.50
TO4 Michael Olowokandi .75 2.00
TO5 Michael Olowokandi 1.25 3.00
Tim Duncan
TO6 Tim Duncan 1.25 3.00
TO7 Mike Bibby 1.50 4.00
TO8 Mike Bibby 1.50 4.00
Stephon Marbury
TO9 Stephon Marbury .75 2.00
TO10 Vince Carter 3.00 8.00
TO11 Vince Carter 3.00 8.00
Antoine Walker
TO12 Antoine Walker .60 1.50

1998 Press Pass Double Threat Veteran Approved Autographs

Randomly inserted in packs at one in 360, this seven-card set features veteran autographs. The following players were only available via trade: Ray Allen, Kerry Kittles, Ron Mercer and Glen Rice. The set is unnumbered and checklisted below in alphabetical order.

1 Ray Allen 8.00 20.00
2 Tim Duncan 40.00 80.00
3 Kerry Kittles 3.00 8.00
4 Stephon Marbury 5.00 12.00
5 Antoine Walker 6.00 15.00

2009 Press Pass Fusion

COMPLETE SET (90) 15.00 40.00
14 Nate Archibald .15 .40
15 DJ Augustin .15 .40
16 Larry Bird .75 2.00
17 Darren Collison .30 .75
18 Stephen Curry .50 1.25
19 Joey Dorsey .30 .75
20 Joe Dumars .15 .40
21 Wayne Ellington .30 .75
22 Jonny Flynn .30 .75
23 Gerald Henderson .30 .75
24 Bobby Hurley .15 .40
25 Brook Lopez .15 .40
26 Robin Lopez .15 .40
27 Jerry Lucas .15 .40
28 Kevin McHale .15 .40
29 Anthony Randolph .15 .40
30 Derrick Rose .30 .75
31 Brandon Rush .15 .40
32 Russell Westbrook .20 .50
33 John Wooden .30 .75
34 James Worthy .15 .40
35 Willis Reed .30 .75
36 Ty Lawson .30 .75
WWJW John Wooden AU/100 75.00 150.00

2009 Press Pass Fusion Bronze

*BRONZE: 1X TO 2.5X BASE
STATED PRINT RUN 150 SER. #'d SETS

2009 Press Pass Fusion Gold

*GOLD: 2X TO 5X BASE
STATED PRINT RUN 50 SER. #'d SETS

2009 Press Pass Fusion Green

*GREEN: 3X TO 8X BASE
STATED PRINT RUN 25 SER. #'d SETS

2009 Press Pass Fusion Silver

*SILVER: 1.25X TO 3X BASE
STATED PRINT RUN 99 SER. #'d SETS

2009 Press Pass Fusion Autographs Gold

STATED PRINT RUN 10-199
EXCHANGE DEADLINE 12/1/10
SSBH Bobby Hurley/199 7.50 15.00
SSDC Darren Collison/198 7.50 15.00
SSGH Gerald Henderson/199 7.50 15.00
SSJD Joe Dumars/42 10.00 25.00
SSJF Jonny Flynn/150 10.00 25.00
SSJL Jerry Lucas/75 7.50 15.00
SSKM Kevin McHale/50 15.00 30.00
SSLB Larry Bird/26 30.00 80.00
SSNA Nate Archibald/50 7.50 15.00
SSSC Stephen Curry/75 15.00 30.00
SSTL Ty Lawson Exchange
SSWE Wayne Ellington/199 7.50 15.00
SSWR Willis Reed/75 10.00 20.00

2009 Press Pass Fusion Autographs Green

STATED PRINT RUN 5-100
EXCHANGE DEADLINE 12/1/2010
SSBH Bobby Hurley/91 10.00 20.00
SSGH Gerald Henderson/99 10.00 20.00
SSJF Jonny Flynn/96 15.00 30.00
SSJL Jerry Lucas/50 15.00 30.00
SSNA Nate Archibald/25 10.00 20.00
SSSC Stephen Curry/50 15.00 30.00
SSTL Ty Lawson/99 20.00 40.00
SSWE Wayne Ellington/99 10.00 20.00
SSWE Wayne Ellington Exchange
SSWR Willis Reed/50 15.00 30.00

2009 Press Pass Fusion Autographs Silver

RANDOM INSERT IN PACKS
EXCHANGE DEADLINE 12/1/2010
SSBH Bobby Hurley 7.50 15.00
SSDC Darren Collison 7.50 15.00
SSGH Gerald Henderson 7.50 15.00
SSJF Jonny Flynn 10.00 25.00
SSNA Nate Archibald 7.50 15.00
SSSC Stephen Curry 10.00 20.00
SSTL Ty Lawson 15.00 30.00
SSWE Wayne Ellington 7.50 15.00
SSWE Wayne Ellington Exchange
SSWR Willis Reed 10.00 20.00

2009 Press Pass Fusion Classic Champions

COMPLETE SET (10) 6.00 15.00
STATED ODDS 1:10
CCH3 Larry Bird 2.50 6.00
CCH8 Joe Dumars .60 1.50
CCH9 Wayne Ellington 1.00 2.50

2009 Press Pass Fusion Classic Champions Autographs Gold

STATED PRINT RUN 15-99
CCHJD Joe Dumars/86 10.00 20.00

CCHLB Larry Bird/25 40.00 80.00
CCHTL Ty Lawson/99 20.00 40.00
CCHWE Wayne Ellington/99 10.00 20.00

2009 Press Pass Fusion Classic Champions Autographs Green

STATED PRINT RUN 10-50
CCHJD Joe Dumars/45 15.00 30.00
CCHLB Larry Bird/15 40.00 100.00
CCHTL Ty Lawson/50 20.00 40.00
CCHWE Wayne Ellington/50 10.00 20.00

2009 Press Pass Fusion Classic Champions Autographs Silver

STATED PRINT RUN 25-199
CCHJD Joe Dumars/100 10.00 20.00
CCHLB Larry Bird/55 40.00 80.00
CCHTL Ty Lawson/199 15.00 30.00
CCHWE Wayne Ellington/199 7.50 15.00

2009 Press Pass Fusion Collegiate Connections

COMPLETE SET (10) 6.00 15.00
STATED ODDS 1:10
CCN1 Kevin McHale .60 1.50
Paul Molitor
CCN3 James Worthy 1.00 2.50
Ty Lawson
CCN5 Bobby Hurley 1.00 2.50
Gerald Henderson
CCN6 Willis Reed .60 1.50
Doug Williams
CCN7 Don Maynard .60 1.50
Nate Archibald
CCN10 John Wooden 1.00 2.50
Karch Kiraly

2009 Press Pass Fusion Collegiate Connections Autographs Gold

STATED PRINT RUN 10-94
CCNDMNA Don Maynard 12.00 30.00
Nate Archibald/94
CCNJWTL James Worthy 20.00 40.00
Ty Lawson/50
CCNWRDW Willis Reed 12.00 30.00
Doug Williams/25

2009 Press Pass Fusion Collegiate Connections Autographs Onyx

STATED PRINT RUN 5-25
EXCHANGE DEADLINE 12/1/10
CCNDMNA Don Maynard 15.00 40.00
Nate Archibald/25
CCNJWTL James Worthy 25.00 50.00
Ty Lawson/25

2009 Press Pass Fusion Cross Training

COMPLETE SET (10) 6.00 15.00
STATED ODDS 1:10
CT4 Dan Gable 1.00 2.50
Kevin McHale

2009 Press Pass Fusion Renowned Rivals

COMPLETE SET (10) 6.00 15.00
STATED ODDS 1:10
RR2 Kevin McHale .60 1.50
James Worthy
RR4 Stephen Curry 2.00 5.00
Ty Lawson
RR6 Jerry Lucas .60 1.50
Willis Reed
RR8 Wayne Ellington 1.00 2.50
Gerald Henderson
RR9 Joe Dumars 2.50 6.00
Larry Bird

2009 Press Pass Fusion Renowned Rivals Autographs Gold

STATED PRINT RUN 10-50
EXCHANGE DEADLINE 12/1/2010
RRJLWR Jerry Lucas 25.00 50.00
Willis Reed EXCH
RRKMJW Kevin McHale 40.00 80.00
James Worthy EXCH
RRSCTL Stephen Curry 30.00 60.00
Ty Lawson

2009 Press Pass Fusion Renowned Rivals Autographs Onyx

STATED PRINT RUN 5-25
EXCHANGE DEADLINE 12/1/10
RRSCTL Stephen Curry 30.00 80.00
Ty Lawson/25

2009 Press Pass Fusion Revered Relics Gold

STATED PRINT RUN 5-50
*HOLOFOIL/25: .5X TO 1.2X BASIC RELIC
RRAR Anthony Randolph 6.00 15.00
RRBR Brandon Rush 6.00 15.00
RRDA DJ Augustin 6.00 15.00
RRRW Russell Westbrook 6.00 15.00
RRBLRL Brook Lopez 6.00 15.00
Robin Lopez
RRDRJD Derrick Rose 6.00 15.00
Joey Dorsey

2009 Press Pass Fusion Revered Relics Silver

STATED PRINT RUN 15-299
RRAR Anthony Randolph/85 4.00 10.00
RRBR Brandon Rush/99 4.00 10.00
RRDA DJ Augustin/99 4.00 10.00
RRRW Russell Westbrook/99 4.00 10.00
RRBLRL Brook Lopez 4.00 10.00
Robin Lopez/99
RRDRJD Derrick Rose 4.00 10.00
Joey Dorsey/299

2009 Press Pass Fusion Timeless Talent

COMPLETE SET (10) 6.00 15.00
STATED ODDS 1:10
TT2 Joe Dumars .60 1.50
TT4 Jonny Flynn 1.00 2.50
TT5 Stephen Curry 2.00 5.00

2009 Press Pass Fusion Timeless Talent Autographs Gold

STATED PRINT RUN 15-99
TTJD Joe Dumars/48 10.00 20.00
TTJF Jonny Flynn/99 15.00 30.00
TTSC Stephen Curry/85 15.00 30.00

2009 Press Pass Fusion Timeless Talent Autographs Green

STATED PRINT RUN 10-50
TTJF Jonny Flynn/50 12.00 30.00
TTSC Stephen Curry/50 20.00 40.00

2009 Press Pass Fusion Timeless Talent Autographs Onyx

STATED PRINT RUN 5-25
TTJF Jonny Flynn/25 15.00 40.00
TTSC Stephen Curry/25 25.00 60.00

2009 Press Pass Fusion Timeless Talent Autographs Silver

STATED PRINT RUN 26-193
TTJD Joe Dumars/74 10.00 20.00
TTJF Jonny Flynn/193 10.00 20.00
TTSC Stephen Curry/100 15.00 30.00

2006 Press Pass National VIP Promos

COMPLETE SET (25) 6.00 15.00
1 Ronnie Brewer .50 1.25
2 Patrick O'Bryant .40 1.00
3 Hilton Armstrong .40 1.00
4 Rudy Gay .60 1.50
5 Marcus Williams .40 1.00
6 J.J. Redick .50 1.25
7 Shelden Williams .40 1.00
8 Adam Morrison .50 1.25
9 Dee Brown .40 1.00
10 Rajon Rondo 1.50 4.00
11 Taquan Dean .40 1.00
12 Tyrus Thomas .50 1.25
13 Rodney Carney .40 1.00
14 Shawne Williams .40 1.00
15 Shannon Brown .60 1.50
16 Paul Davis .40 1.00
17 David Noel .40 1.00
18 Taj Gray .40 1.00
19 Mardy Collins .40 1.00
20 LaMarcus Aldridge 1.00 2.50
21 Randy Foye .50 1.25
22 Kyle Lowry .50 1.25
23 Brandon Roy 1.00 2.50
24 John Pittsnogle .40 1.00
25 J.J. Redick CL .50 1.25

1999 Press Pass SE

Released in four-card packs, this 45-card set features draft picks from the 1999 season. Each hobby pack carried one autograph per pack. The cards are also known as Signature Edition.

COMPLETE SET (45) 4.00 10.00
1 Elton Brand .30 .75
2 Steve Francis .30 .75
3 Baron Davis .40 1.00
4 Lamar Odom .40 1.00
5 Jonathan Bender .12 .30
6 Wally Szczerbiak .25 .60
7 Richard Hamilton .30 .75
8 Andre Miller .30 .75
9 Jason Terry .30 .75
10 Trajan Langdon .12 .30
11 William Avery .12 .30
12 Ron Artest .30 .75
13 Cal Bowdler .12 .30
14 James Posey .12 .30
15 Quincy Lewis .12 .30
16 Jeff Foster .12 .30
17 Kenny Thomas .12 .30
18 Devean George .12 .30
19 Tim James .12 .30
20 Vonteego Cummings .12 .30
21 Jumaine Jones .12 .30
22 John Celestand .12 .30
23 Rico Hill .12 .30
24 Michael Ruffin .12 .30
25 Chris Herren .12 .30
26 Evan Eschmeyer .12 .30
27 Calvin Booth .12 .30
28 Obinna Ekezie .12 .30
29 A.J. Bramlett .12 .30
30 Louis Bullock .12 .30
31 Lee Nailon .12 .30
32 Tyrone Washington .12 .30
33 Venson Hamilton .12 .30
34 Roberto Bergersen .12 .30
35 Rodney Buford .12 .30
36 Melvin Levett .12 .30
37 Kris Clack .12 .30
38 Galen Young .12 .30
39 Lari Ketner .12 .30
40 Eddie Lucas .12 .30
41 Todd MacCulloch .12 .30
42 Francisco Elson .12 .30
43 Vince Carter .25 .60
44 Jason Williams .15 .40
45 Checklist Card .12 .30
NNO Elton Brand PROMO 2.00 5.00

1999 Press Pass SE Alley Oop

Inserted one per hobby pack, this 45-card set parallels the base set. The cards feature silver foil. To ascertain values on individual cards, please refer to the multiplier in the header, coupled with the value of the base card.

*ALLEY-OOP: .75X TO 2X VALUE

1999 Press Pass SE Torquers

Inserted one per retail pack, this 45-card set parallels the base set. The cards feature blue foil. To ascertain values on individual cards, please refer to the multiplier in the header, coupled with the value of the base card.

*TORQUERS: .75X TO 2X VALUE

1999 Press Pass SE Autographs

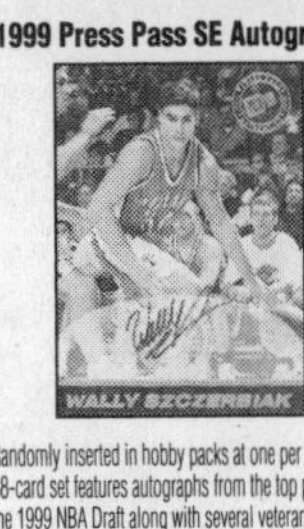

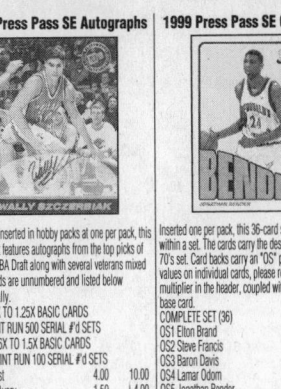

Randomly inserted in hobby packs at one per pack, this 38-card set features autographs from the top picks of the 1999 NBA Draft along with several veterans mixed in. The cards are unnumbered and listed below alphabetically.

*BLUE: .5X TO 1.25X BASIC CARDS
BLUE PRINT RUN 500 SERIAL #'d SETS
*SILVER: .6X TO 1.5X BASIC CARDS
SILVER PRINT RUN 100 SERIAL #'d SETS
1 Ron Artest 4.00 10.00
2 William Avery 1.50 4.00
3 Roberto Bergersen 1.50 4.00
4 Mike Bibby 2.50 6.00
5 Calvin Booth 1.50 4.00
6 Cal Bowdler 1.50 4.00
7 A.J. Bramlett 1.50 4.00
8 Elton Brand 4.00 10.00
9 Louis Bullock 1.50 4.00
10 Marcus Camby 2.50 6.00
11 Vince Carter 12.50 30.00
12 John Celestand 1.50 4.00
13 Baron Davis 5.00 12.00
14 Obinna Ekezie 1.50 4.00
15 Francisco Elson 1.50 4.00
16 Evan Eschmeyer 1.50 4.00
17 Jeff Foster 1.50 4.00
18 Steve Francis 4.00 10.00
19 Devean George 1.50 4.00
20 Richard Hamilton 4.00 10.00
21 Venson Hamilton 1.50 4.00
22 Chris Herren 2.50 6.00
23 Jumaine Jones 1.50 4.00
24 Lari Ketner 1.50 4.00
25 Raef LaFrentz 2.00 5.00
26 Melvin Levett 1.50 4.00
27 Quincy Lewis 1.50 4.00
28 Eddie Lucas 1.50 4.00
29 Todd MacCulloch 1.50 4.00
30 Andre Miller 4.00 10.00
31 Lee Nailon 1.50 4.00
32 Lamar Odom 5.00 12.00
33 Laron Profit 1.50 4.00
34 Wally Szczerbiak 3.00 8.00
35 Jason Terry 4.00 10.00
36 Kenny Thomas 1.50 4.00
37 Tyrone Washington 1.50 4.00
38 Galen Young 1.50 4.00

1999 Press Pass SE In the Bonus

Randomly inserted in packs at ranging odds from 1:12 to 1:144, this eight-card set features the top picks from the 1999 Draft. Card backs carry an "IB" prefix.

COMPLETE SET (8) 8.00 20.00
IB1 Elton Brand 2.00 5.00
IB2 Steve Francis 2.00 5.00
IB3 Baron Davis 2.50 6.00
IB4 Lamar Odom 2.50 6.00
IB5 Wally Szczerbiak 1.50 4.00
IB6 Richard Hamilton 2.00 5.00
IB7 Jason Terry 2.00 5.00
IB8 Trajan Langdon .75 2.00

1999 Press Pass SE Instant Replay

Randomly inserted in packs at one in six, this six-card set features the top players from the draft on microetched foil. Card backs carry an "IR" prefix.

COMPLETE SET (6) 1.50 4.00
IR1 Elton Brand .50 1.25
IR2 Steve Francis .50 1.25
IR3 Baron Davis .60 1.50
IR4 Lamar Odom .60 1.50
IR5 Wally Szczerbiak .40 1.00
IR6 Andre Miller .50 1.25

1999 Press Pass SE Jersey Cards

Randomly inserted in packs at one in 720, this four-card set features an authentic swatch from a game-used jersey. Card backs carry a "JC" prefix and are serially #'d to 300.

JC1 Elton Brand 10.00 25.00
JC2 Steve Francis 10.00 25.00
JC3 Raef LaFrentz 6.00 15.00
JC3A Lamar Odom 12.00 30.00

1999 Press Pass SE Old School

Inserted one per pack, this 36-card set features the set within a set. The cards carry the design of an old time 70's set. Card backs carry an "OS" prefix. To ascertain values on individual cards, please refer to the multiplier in the header, coupled with the value of the base card.

COMPLETE SET (36) 5.00 12.00
OS1 Elton Brand .50 1.25
OS2 Steve Francis .50 1.25
OS3 Baron Davis .60 1.50
OS4 Lamar Odom .60 1.50
OS5 Jonathan Bender .20 .50
OS6 Wally Szczerbiak .40 1.00
OS7 Richard Hamilton .50 1.25
OS8 Andre Miller .50 1.25
OS9 Jason Terry .50 1.25
OS10 Trajan Langdon .20 .50
OS11 William Avery .20 .50
OS12 Ron Artest .50 1.25
OS13 Cal Bowdler .20 .50
OS14 James Posey .20 .50
OS15 Quincy Lewis .20 .50
OS16 Kenny Thomas .20 .50
OS17 Tim James .20 .50
OS18 Vonteego Cummings .20 .50
OS19 Jumaine Jones .20 .50
OS20 John Celestand .20 .50
OS21 Rico Hill .20 .50
OS22 Michael Ruffin .20 .50
OS23 Chris Herren .20 .50
OS24 Evan Eschmeyer .20 .50
OS25 Calvin Booth .20 .50
OS26 Obinna Ekezie .20 .50
OS27 Laron Profit .20 .50
OS28 A.J. Bramlett .20 .50
OS29 Francisco Elson .20 .50
OS30 Louis Bullock .20 .50
OS31 Lee Nailon .20 .50
OS32 Tyrone Washington .20 .50
OS33 Galen Young .20 .50
OS34 Venson Hamilton .20 .50
OS35 Melvin Levett .20 .50
OS36 Checklist Card .20 .50

1999 Press Pass SE Two on One

Randomly inserted in packs at one in 12, this 12-card set featues die cut cards that interlock to form one larger card. Card backs carry a "TO" prefix.

COMPLETE SET (12) 6.00 15.00
TO1A Elton Brand 1.00 2.50
TO1B Elton Brand 1.00 2.50
Vince Carter
TO1C Mike Bibby .40 1.00
TO2A Steve Francis 1.00 2.50
TO2B Steve Francis 1.00 2.50
Mike Bibby
TO2C Vince Carter .75 2.00
TO3A Wally Szczerbiak .75 2.00
TO3B Wally Szczerbiak .75 2.00
Jason Williams
TO3C Jason Williams .50 1.25
TO4A Lamar Odom 1.25 3.00
TO4B Lamar Odom 1.25 3.00
Marcus Camby
TO4C Marcus Camby .30 .75

2000 Press Pass SE

The 2000 Press Pass SE product was released in late September, 2000 and featured a 45-card base set. The set was broken into tiers as follows: 35 Base prospects (1-35), and 10 Rookie Vision (36-45) subset cards. Each pack contained four cards, and each hobby pack carried a $10.99 SRP, while the retail packs carried a $3.49 SRP.

COMPLETE SET (45) 4.00 10.00
1 Mike Miller CL .20 .50
2 Darius Miles .20 .50
3 Mike Miller .40 1.00
4 Chris Mihm .20 .50
5 Keyon Dooling .20 .50
6 Jerome Moiso .20 .50
7 Etan Thomas .20 .50
8 Mateen Cleaves .20 .50
9 Jason Collier .20 .50
10 Quentin Richardson .30 .75
11 Jamaal Magloire .20 .50
12 Morris Peterson .20 .50
13 DeShawn Stevenson .25 .60
14 Mark Madsen .20 .50
15 A.J. Guyton .20 .50
16 Dan Langhi .20 .50
17 Jake Voskuhl .20 .50
18 Khalid El-Amin .20 .50
19 Eddie House .20 .50
20 Hanno Mottola .20 .50
21 Chris Carrawell .20 .50
22 Brian Cardinal .20 .50
23 Mark Karcher .20 .50
24 Jason Hart .20 .50
25 Dan McClintock .20 .50
26 Chris Porter .20 .50
27 Jaquay Walls .20 .50
28 Scoonie Penn .20 .50
29 Pete Mickeal .20 .50
30 Elton Brand .20 .50
31 Steve Francis .20 .50
32 Baron Davis .20 .50
33 Lamar Odom .20 .50
34 Wally Szczerbiak .20 .50
35 Richard Hamilton .20 .50
36 Darius Miles RV .10 .25
37 Mike Miller RV .20 .50
38 Chris Mihm RV .10 .25
39 Keyon Dooling RV .10 .25
40 Jerome Moiso RV .10 .25
41 Etan Thomas RV .10 .25
42 Mateen Cleaves RV .10 .25
43 Jason Collier RV .10 .25
44 Quentin Richardson RV .15 .40
45 Morris Peterson RV .10 .25

2000 Press Pass SE Alley Oop

Inserted into retail packs at one per pack, this 45-card insert is a complete parallel of the Press Pass SE base set. The cards feature gold-stamping on the front of the card. To ascertain values on individual cards, please refer to the multiplier in the header, coupled with the value of the base card.

COMPLETE SET (45) 8.00 20.00
*ALLEY OOP: .75X TO 2X BASIC CARDS

2000 Press Pass SE Autographs

Randomly inserted into packs at one per pack (hobby), and one in 18 (retail), this 36-card insert features authentic autographs from some of the NBA's top young prospects. The cards are not numbered and listed below alphabetically.

*SILVER AU: .5X TO 1.25X HI COLUMN
SILVER AU PRINT RUN 500 SERIAL #'d SETS
1 Elton Brand 4.00 10.00
2 Brian Cardinal 2.00 5.00
3 Chris Carrawell 2.00 5.00
4 Mateen Cleaves 2.00 5.00
5 Jason Collier 2.00 5.00
6 Baron Davis 4.00 10.00
7 Keyon Dooling 2.00 5.00
8 Khalid El-Amin 2.00 5.00
9 Steve Francis 4.00 10.00
10 A.J. Guyton 2.00 5.00
11 Richard Hamilton 5.00 10.00
12 Jason Hart 2.00 5.00
13 Eddie House 2.00 5.00
14 Mark Karcher 2.00 5.00
15 Dan Langhi 2.00 5.00
16 Mark Madsen 2.00 5.00
17 Jamaal Magloire 2.00 5.00
18 Dan McClintock 2.00 5.00
19 Pete Mickeal 2.00 5.00
20 Chris Mihm 2.00 5.00
21 Darius Miles 2.00 5.00
22 Mike Miller 4.00 10.00
23 Jerome Moiso 2.00 5.00
24 Hanno Mottola 2.00 5.00
25 Lamar Odom 4.00 10.00
26 Scoonie Penn 2.00 5.00
27 Morris Peterson 2.00 5.00
28 Chris Porter 2.00 5.00
29 Lavor Postell 2.00 5.00
30 Quentin Richardson 3.00 8.00
31 Jabari Smith 2.00 5.00
32 DeShawn Stevenson 2.50 6.00
33 Wally Szczerbiak 2.00 5.00
34 Etan Thomas 2.00 5.00
35 Jake Voskuhl 2.00 5.00
36 Jaquay Walls 2.00 5.00

2000 Press Pass SE Jersey Cards

Randomly inserted into hobby packs at one in 84 and retail packs at one in 720, this 12-card insert features collegiate level game-used jersey cards of some of the NBA's top prospects. Card backs carry a "JC" prefix.

*NUMBERS: 1.25X TO 3X BASE HI
NUMBERS PRINT RUN 25 SETS
JC1 Mateen Cleaves 5.00 12.00
JC2 Mark Karcher 5.00 12.00
JC3 Mark Madsen 5.00 12.00
JC4 Jamaal Magloire 5.00 12.00
JC5 Chris Mihm 5.00 12.00
JC6 Darius Miles 5.00 12.00
JC7 Mike Miller 10.00 25.00
JC8 Jerome Moiso 5.00 12.00
JC9 Morris Peterson 5.00 12.00
JC10 Quentin Richardson 8.00 20.00
JC11 DeShawn Stevenson 6.00 15.00
JC12 Etan Thomas 5.00 12.00

2000 Press Pass SE Lottery Club

Randomly inserted into packs at one in six, this 6-card insert features some of the NBA's top first round draft picks. Card backs carry a "LC" prefix.

COMPLETE SET (6) 2.00 5.00
LC1 Darius Miles .50 1.25
LC2 Mike Miller 1.00 2.50
LC3 Chris Mihm .50 1.25
LC4 Keyon Dooling .50 1.25
LC5 Jerome Moiso .50 1.25
LC6 Etan Thomas .50 1.25

2000 Press Pass SE Lottery Club Autographs

Randomly inserted into hobby packs, this 6-card insert features authentic autographs from some of the NBA's top first round draft picks. Each card is individually serial nubered to 100.

1 Darius Miles 5.00 12.00
2 Mike Miller 10.00 25.00
3 Chris Mihm 5.00 12.00
4 Keyon Dooling 5.00 12.00
5 Jerome Moiso 5.00 12.00
6 Etan Thomas 5.00 12.00

2000 Press Pass SE Old School

Randomly inserted into packs at one per pack, this 27-card insert features young prospects with a 1970's "old school" design. Card backs carry an "OS" prefix. To ascertain values on individual cards, please refer to the multiplier in the header, coupled with the value of the base card.

COMPLETE SET (27) 6.00 15.00
OS1 Darius Miles .40 1.00
OS2 Mike Miller .75 2.00
OS3 Chris Mihm .40 1.00
OS4 Keyon Dooling .40 1.00
OS5 Jerome Moiso .40 1.00
OS6 Etan Thomas .40 1.00
OS7 Mateen Cleaves .40 1.00
OS8 Jason Collier .40 1.00
OS9 Quentin Richardson .60 1.50
OS10 Jamaal Magloire .40 1.00
OS11 Morris Peterson .40 1.00
OS12 DeShawn Stevenson .50 1.25
OS13 Mark Madsen .40 1.00
OS14 Dan Langhi .40 1.00
OS15 Jake Voskuhl .40 1.00
OS16 Khalid El-Amin .40 1.00
OS17 Eddie House .40 1.00
OS18 Hanno Mottola .40 1.00
OS19 Chris Carrawell .40 1.00
OS20 Brian Cardinal .40 1.00
OS21 Mark Karcher .40 1.00
OS22 Jason Hart .40 1.00
OS23 Chris Porter .40 1.00
OS24 Scoonie Penn .40 1.00
OS25 A.J. Guyton .40 1.00
OS26 Jabari Smith .40 1.00
OS27 Mateen Cleaves CL .40 1.00

2000 Press Pass SE Old School Threads

Randomly inserted into packs, this 2-card insert features swatches from college used game jerseys of Elton Brand and Steve Francis. Card backs carry an "OST" prefix, and each card is individually serial numbered to 50.

OST1 Elton Brand 15.00 40.00
OST2 Steve Francis 15.00 40.00

2000 Press Pass SE Sophomore Sensation

Randomly inserted into hobby/retail packs, this 6-card insert features NBA players that are going into their second year of action. Card backs carry a "SS" prefix. Please note that this insert was tiered, SS1-SS2 were inserted at 1:96 hobby, SS3-SS4 were inserted at 1:48 hobby, SS5-SS6 were inserted at 1:24 hobby, while SS1-SS2 were inserted at 1:192 retail, SS3-SS4 were inserted at 1:96 retail, and SS5-SS6 were inserted at 1:48 retail.

COMPLETE SET (6) 6.00 15.00
SS1 Elton Brand 2.50 6.00
SS2 Steve Francis 2.50 6.00
SS3 Baron Davis 1.25 3.00
SS4 Wally Szczerbiak 1.25 3.00
SS5 Lamar Odom .75 2.00
SS6 Richard Hamilton .75 2.00

2000 Press Pass SE Two on One

Randomly inserted into packs at one in 12, this 12-card insert features die-cut cards that interlock to form one card. Card backs carry a "TO" prefix.

COMPLETE SET (12) 5.00 12.00
TO1A Darius Miles .60 1.50
TO1B Darius Miles 1.00 2.50
Quentin Richardson
TO1C Quentin Richardson 1.00 2.50
TO2A Mateen Cleaves .60 1.50
TO2B Mateen Cleaves .60 1.50
Morris Peterson
TO2C Morris Peterson .60 1.50
TO3A Jerome Moiso .60 1.50
TO3B Baron Davis .60 1.50
Jerome Moiso
TO3C Baron Davis .60 1.50
TO4A Steve Francis .60 1.50
TO4B Elton Brand .60 1.50
Steve Francis
TO4C Elton Brand .60 1.50

1998 SAGE

The 1998 Sage product was released during the 1998-99 season, and featured some of the NBA's top prospects and young superstars. Please note that a 1 of 1 version does exist of the base set.

COMPLETE SET (50) 5.00 12.00
1 Toby Bailey .15 .40
2 Corey Benjamin .15 .40
3 Andrew Betts .15 .40
4 Torraye Braggs .15 .40
5 Corey Brewer .15 .40
6 Kobe Bryant .75 2.00
7 Anthony Carter .15 .40
8 Vince Carter .75 2.00
9 Keon Clark .15 .40
10 Ricky Davis .25 .60
11 Michael Dickerson .15 .40
12 Michael Doleac .15 .40
13 Bryce Drew .15 .40
14 Tremaine Fowlkes .15 .40
15 Pat Garrity .15 .40
16 Zendon Hamilton .15 .40
17 Matt Harpring .20 .50
18 Al Harrington .25 .60
19 J.R. Henderson .15 .40
20 Antawn Jamison .40 1.00
21 DeMarco Johnson .15 .40
22 Charles Jones .15 .40
23 Rashard Lewis .40 1.00
24 Felipe Lopez .15 .40
25 Corey Louis .15 .40
26 Tyronn Lue .15 .40
27 Stephon Marbury .20 .50
28 Sean Marks .15 .40
29 Jelani McCoy .15 .40
30 Tracy McGrady .25 .60
31 Roshown McLeod .15 .40
32 Brad Miller .40 1.00
33 Cuttino Mobley .30 .75
34 Nazr Mohammed .15 .40
35 Makhtar Ndiaye .15 .40
36 Radoslav Nesterovic .15 .40
37 Michael Olowokandi .20 .50
38 Andrae Patterson .15 .40
39 Ruben Patterson .15 .40
40 Paul Pierce .75 2.00
41 Jeff Sheppard .15 .40
42 Miles Simon .15 .40
43 Tim Thomas .15 .40
44 Robert Traylor .15 .40
45 Bonzi Wells .15 .40
46 Tyson Wheeler .15 .40
47 Jahidi White .15 .40
48 Jason Williams .40 1.00
49 Shammond Williams .15 .40
50 Korleone Young .15 .40

1998 SAGE Autographs

Randomly inserted in packs, this 52-card set features autographs from the draft picks in the set. The cards feature a red background. Print runs are listed below.

A1 Toby Bailey/535 1.50 4.00
A2 Corey Benjamin/999 1.50 4.00
A3 Andrew Betts/475 1.50 4.00
A4 Torraye Braggs/890 1.50 4.00
A5 Corey Brewer/999 1.50 4.00
A6 Kobe Bryant/129 50.00 120.00
A7 Anthony Carter/999 1.50 4.00
A8 Vince Carter/479 15.00 40.00

A9 Keon Clark/999 1.50 4.00
A10 Ricky Davis/860 2.50 6.00
A11 Michael Dickerson/999 1.50 4.00
A12 Michael Doleac/549 1.50 4.00
A13 Bryce Drew/999 1.50 4.00
A14 Tremaine Fowlkes/999 1.50 4.00
A15 Pat Garrity/999 1.50 4.00
A16A Zendon Hamilton (Black)/175 1.50 4.00
A16B Zendon Hamilton (Blue)/825 1.50 4.00
A17 Matt Harpring/999 2.00 5.00
A18 Al Harrington/999 2.50 6.00
A19 J.R. Henderson/599 1.50 4.00
A20 Antawn Jamison/909 6.00 15.00
A21 DeMarco Johnson/890 1.50 4.00
A22 Charles Jones/999 1.50 4.00
A23 Rashard Lewis/999 4.00 10.00
A24 Felipe Lopez/999 1.50 4.00
A25 Corey Louis/990 1.50 4.00
A26 Tyronn Lue/999 1.50 4.00
A27 Stephon Marbury/149 8.00 20.00
A28 Sean Marks/999 1.50 4.00
A29 Jelani McCoy/125 2.00 5.00
A30 Tracy McGrady/99 30.00 80.00
A31 Roshown McLeod/970 1.50 4.00
A32 Brad Miller/879 4.00 10.00
A33 Cuttino Mobley/999 3.00 8.00
A34 Nazr Mohammed/739 1.50 4.00
A35 Makhtar Ndiaye/999 1.50 4.00
A36 Radoslav Nesterovic/999 1.50 4.00
A37 Michael Olowokandi/999 2.00 5.00
A38 Andrae Patterson/999 1.50 4.00
A39 Ruben Patterson/690 1.50 4.00
A40 Paul Pierce/199 12.50 30.00
A41 Jeff Sheppard/999 1.50 4.00
A42 Miles Simon/475 1.50 4.00
A43A Tim Thomas (Black)/219 1.50 4.00
A43B Tim Thomas (Blue)/819 1.50 4.00
A44 Robert Traylor/999 1.50 4.00
A45 Bonzi Wells/999 1.50 4.00
A46 Tyson Wheeler/999 1.50 4.00
A47 Jahidi White/459 1.50 4.00
A48 Jason Williams/999 6.00 15.00
A49 Shammond Williams/670 1.50 4.00
A50 Korleone Young/999 1.50 4.00

1998 SAGE Autographs Bronze

Randomly inserted in packs, this 52-card set parallels the regular autograph set. The cards feature a bronze background. Print runs are listed below. To ascertain values on individual cards, please refer to the multiplier in the header, coupled with the value of the base autograph.
*BRONZE AU: .5X TO 1.25X BASE AU

1998 SAGE Autographs Gold

Randomly inserted in packs, this 52-card set parallels the regular autograph set. The cards feature a gold background. Print runs are listed below. To ascertain values on individual cards, please refer to the multiplier in the header, coupled with the value of the base autograph.
*GOLD AU: .75X TO 2X BASE AU

1998 SAGE Autographs Platinum

Randomly inserted in packs, this 52-card set parallels the regular autograph set. The cards feature a platinum background. Print runs are listed below. To ascertain values on individual cards, please refer to the multiplier in the header, coupled with the value of the base autograph. Lower print runs are unpriced.
*PLATINUM AU: 1.5X TO 4X BASE AU
A8 Vince Carter/25 75.00 200.00

1998 SAGE Autographs Silver

Randomly inserted in packs, this 52-card set parallels the regular autograph set. The cards feature a silver background. Print runs are listed below. To ascertain values on individual cards, please refer to the multiplier in the header, coupled with the value of the base autograph.
*SILVER AU: .6X TO 1.5X BASE AU

1999 SAGE

The 1999 version of SAGE was released in three-card packs, which contained one autograph per pack. All autographs were inserted in packs and there were no redemptions. The base set contained 50 cards. .
COMPLETE SET (50) 8.00 20.00
1 Ron Artest .60 1.50
2 William Avery .25 .60
3 Michael Batiste .25 .60
4 Jonathan Bender .25 .60
5 Roberto Bergersen .25 .60
6 Calvin Booth .25 .60
7 Cal Bowdler .25 .60
8 A.J. Bramlett .25 .60
9 Kobe Bryant 1.25 3.00
10 Rodney Buford .25 .60
11 Vince Carter .50 1.25
12 John Celestand .25 .60
13 Kris Clack .25 .60
14 Lonnie Cooper .25 .60
15 Vonteego Cummings .25 .60
16 Baron Davis .75 2.00
17 Francisco Elson .25 .60
18 Evan Eschmeyer .25 .60
19 Jeff Foster .25 .60
20 Devean George .25 .60
21 Dion Glover .25 .60
22 Richard Hamilton .60 1.50
23 Venson Hamilton .25 .60
24 Rico Hill .25 .60
25 Tim James .25 .60
26 Antawn Jamison .25 .60
27 Jumaine Jones .25 .60
28 J.R. Koch .25 .60
29 Trajan Langdon .25 .60
30 Bobby Lazor .25 .60
31 Melvin Levett .25 .60
32 Quincy Lewis .25 .60
33 Corey Maggette .50 1.25
34 Shawn Marion .60 1.50
35 B.J. McKie .25 .60
36 Andre Miller .60 1.50
37 Lee Nailon .25 .60
38 Ademola Okulaja .25 .60
39 Scott Padgett .25 .60
40 Paul Pierce .40 1.00
41 James Posey .25 .60
42 Aleksandar Radojevic .25 .60
43 David Robinson .40 1.00
44 Michael Ruffin .25 .60
45 Leon Smith .25 .60
46 Jason Terry .60 1.50
47 Kenny Thomas .25 .60
48 Tyrone Washington .25 .60
49 Frederic Weis .25 .60
50 Alvin Young .25 .60

1999 SAGE Autographs

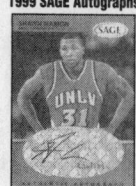

The base, or red, autographs were inserted in packs at one in two. Most players in the 48-card set autographed 999 cards, but some did less. The print runs are listed next to the player's name. Card backs carry an "A" prefix. Cards A24 and A49 do not exist
A1 Ron Artest/699 4.00 10.00
A2 William Avery/999 1.50 4.00
A3 Michael Batiste/999 1.50 4.00
A4 Jonathan Bender/369 1.50 4.00
A5 Roberto Bergersen/999 1.50 4.00
A6 Calvin Booth/999 1.50 4.00
A7 Cal Bowdler/999 1.50 4.00
A8 A.J. Bramlett/999 1.50 4.00
A9 Kobe Bryant/114 40.00 100.00
A10 Rodney Buford/999 1.50 4.00
A11 Vince Carter/39 30.00 80.00
A12 John Celestand/999 1.50 4.00
A13 Kris Clack/999 1.50 4.00
A14 Lonnie Cooper/999 1.50 4.00
A15 Vonteego Cummings/999 1.50 4.00
A16 Baron Davis/339 5.00 12.00
A17 Francisco Elson/999 1.50 4.00
A18 Evan Eschmeyer/999 1.50 4.00
A19 Jeff Foster/999 1.50 4.00
A20 Devean George/999 1.50 4.00
A21 Dion Glover/885 1.50 4.00
A22 Richard Hamilton/899 4.00 10.00
A23 Venson Hamilton/999 1.50 4.00
A25 Tim James/999 1.50 4.00
A26 Antawn Jamison/745 4.00 10.00
A27 Jumaine Jones/999 1.50 4.00
A28 J.R. Koch/999 1.50 4.00
A29 Trajan Langdon/699 1.50 4.00
A30 Bobby Lazor/999 1.50 4.00
A31 Melvin Levett/999 1.50 4.00
A32 Quincy Lewis/999 1.50 4.00
A33 Corey Maggette/464 3.00 8.00
A34 Shawn Marion/789 4.00 10.00
A35 B.J. McKie/999 1.50 4.00
A36 Andre Miller/999 4.00 10.00
A37 Lee Nailon/999 1.50 4.00
A38 Ademola Okulaja/999 1.50 4.00
A39 Scott Padgett/999 1.50 4.00
A41 James Posey/999 1.50 4.00
A42 Aleksandar Radojevic/999 1.50 4.00
A43 David Robinson/113 25.00 60.00
A44 Michael Ruffin/999 1.50 4.00
A45 Leon Smith/999 1.50 4.00
A46 Jason Terry/999 4.00 10.00
A47 Kenny Thomas/999 1.50 4.00
A48 Tyrone Washington/999 1.50 4.00
A50 Alvin Young/999 1.50 4.00

1999 SAGE Autographs Bonus White

Randomly inserted in packs, these 24 autographs were inserted as a bonus. The cards feature the design of the 1998 set, but have a white border. The print runs are listed next to the player. Card backs carry an "A" prefix. Lower print runs are not priced.
A1 Toby Bailey/45 4.00 10.00
A9 Keon Clark/95 4.00 10.00
A11 Michael Dickerson/100 5.00 12.00
A13 Bryce Drew/75 4.00 10.00
A15 Pat Garrity/25 10.00 25.00
A17 Matt Harpring/60 5.00 12.00
A18 Al Harrington/45 10.00 25.00
A23 Rashard Lewis/95 10.00 25.00
A24 Felipe Lopez/100 4.00 10.00
A26 Tyronn Lue/65 4.00 10.00
A33 Cuttino Mobley/85 4.00 10.00
A36 Radoslav Nesterovic/80 4.00 10.00
A37 Michael Olowokandi/90 4.00 10.00
A43 Tim Thomas Blue/20 12.00 30.00
A44 Robert Traylor/85 4.00 10.00
A45 Bonzi Wells/50 10.00 25.00
A50 Korleone Young/90 4.00 10.00

1999 SAGE Autographs Bronze

Randomly inserted in packs at one in four, this 48-card autographed set parallels the base set. Most players autographed 650 cards, but some did less. The print runs are listed next to the player's name. Card backs carry an "A" prefix. Cards A24 and A49 do not exist
*BRONZE AU: .5X TO 1.25X BASIC AU

1999 SAGE Autographs Gold

Randomly inserted in packs at one in 12, this 48-card autographed set parallels the base set. Most players autographed 200 cards, but some did less. The print runs are listed next to the player's name. Card backs carry an "A" prefix. Cards A24 and A49 do not exist. Lower print runs are unpriced.
*GOLD AU: .75X TO 2X BASIC AU
A9 Kobe Bryant/25 200.00 400.00
A43 David Robinson/25 80.00 200.00

1999 SAGE Autographs Platinum

Randomly inserted in packs at one in 46, this 48-card autographed set parallels the base set. Most players autographed 50 cards, but some did less. The print runs are listed next to the player's name. Card backs carry an "A" prefix. Cards A24 and A49 do not exist. Lower print runs are unpriced.
*PLATINUM AU: 1.5X TO 4X BASIC AU

1999 SAGE Autographs Silver

Randomly inserted in packs at one in six, this 48-card autographed set parallels the base set. Most players autographed 400 cards, but some did less. The print runs are listed next to the player's name. Card backs carry an "A" prefix. Cards A24 and A49 do not exist.
*SILVER AU: .6X TO 1.5X BASIC AU

2000 SAGE

The 2000 Sage product was released at the end of October,2000. This set features 50 draft picks and young stars. Each pack contained five cards and carried a suggested retail price of 2.99.
COMPLETE SET (50) 6.00 15.00
1 Dalibor Bagaric .25 .60
2 Vin Baker .25 .60
3 Jonathan Bender .25 .60
4 Primoz Brezec .25 .60
5 Brian Cardinal .25 .60
6 Chris Carrawell .25 .60
7 Eric Coley .25 .60
8 Jason Collier .25 .60
9 Ed Cota .25 .60
10 Schea Cotton .25 .60
11 Baron Davis .25 .60
12 Kaniel Dickens .25 .60
13 Keyon Dooling .25 .60
14 Khalid El-Amin .25 .60
15 Michael Finley .25 .60
16 Kevin Freeman .25 .60
17 Gee Gervin .25 .60
18 Tom Gugliotta .25 .60
19 A.J. Guyton .25 .60
20 Tim Hardaway .25 .60
21 Jason Hart .25 .60
22 Johnny Hemsley .25 .60
23 Shaheen Holloway .25 .60
24 DeeAndre Hulett .25 .60
25 Antawn Jamison .25 .60
26 Marko Jaric .25 .60
27 Larry Johnson .25 .60
28 Michael Jordan .25 .60
29 Dan Langhi .25 .60
30 Lamont Long .25 .60
31 Justin Love .25 .60
32 T.J. Lux .25 .60
33 Desmond Mason .30 .75
34 Antonio McDyess .25 .60
35 Brad Millard .25 .60
36 Gabe Muoneke .25 .60
37 Alonzo Mourning .30 .75
38 Eduardo Najera .25 .60
39 Olumide Oyedeji .25 .60
40 Scoonie Penn .25 .60
41 Scottie Pippen .40 1.00
42 Rodney Rogers .25 .60
43 Pepe Sanchez .25 .60
44 Josip Sesar .25 .60
45 Steve Smith .25 .60
46 Jerry Stackhouse .25 .60
47 Jarrett Stephens .25 .60
48 Hedo Turkoglu .50 1.25
49 Jaquay Walls .25 .60
50 Corliss Williamson .25 .60

2000 SAGE Autographs

Randomly inserted in packs at one in two, this 48-card set features autographs from NBA stars and draft picks. The cards are also known as "red" autographs. Cards 2 and 26 do not exist. Card backs carry an "A" prefix.
A1 Dalibor Bagaric/999 2.00 5.00
A3 Jonathan Bender/369 2.00 5.00
A4 Primoz Brezec/999 2.00 5.00
A5 Brian Cardinal/999 2.00 5.00
A6 Chris Carrawell/999 2.00 5.00
A7 Eric Coley/999 2.00 5.00
A8 Jason Collier/999 2.00 5.00
A9 Ed Cota/999 2.00 5.00
A10 Schea Cotton/999 2.00 5.00
A11 Baron Davis/499 4.00 10.00
A12 Kaniel Dickens/999 2.00 5.00
A13 Keyon Dooling/999 2.00 5.00
A14 Khalid El-Amin/999 2.00 5.00
A15 Michael Finley/179 6.00 15.00
A16 Kevin Freeman/999 2.00 5.00
A17 Gee Gervin/999 2.00 5.00
A18 Tom Gugliotta/299 3.00 8.00
A19 A.J. Guyton/999 2.00 5.00
A20 Tim Hardaway/189 5.00 12.00
A21 Jason Hart/999 2.00 5.00
A22 Johnny Hemsley/999 2.00 5.00
A23 Shaheen Holloway/999 2.00 5.00
A24 DeeAndre Hulett/999 2.00 5.00
A25 Antawn Jamison/369 4.00 10.00
A27 Larry Johnson/299 5.00 12.00
A28 Michael Jordan/999 2.00 5.00
A29 Dan Langhi/999 2.00 5.00
A30 Lamont Long/999 2.00 5.00
A31 Justin Love/999 2.00 5.00
A32 T.J. Lux/999 2.00 5.00
A33 Desmond Mason/999 2.50 6.00
A34 Antonio McDyess/349 4.00 10.00
A35 Brad Millard/999 2.00 5.00
A36 Gabe Muoneke/999 2.00 5.00
A37 Alonzo Mourning/189 12.50 30.00
A38 Eduardo Najera/999 2.00 5.00
A39 Olumide Oyedeji/999 2.00 5.00
A40 Scoonie Penn/999 2.00 5.00
A41 Scottie Pippen/399 20.00 50.00
A42 Rodney Rogers/149 2.50 6.00
A43 Pepe Sanchez/999 2.00 5.00
A44 Josip Sesar/999 2.00 5.00
A45 Steve Smith/319 3.00 8.00
A46 Jerry Stackhouse/369 4.00 10.00
A47 Jarrett Stephens/999 2.00 5.00
A48 Hedo Turkoglu/999 4.00 10.00
A49 Jaquay Walls/999 2.00 5.00
A50 Corliss Williamson/169 3.00 8.00

2000 SAGE Autographs Bonus White

Randomly inserted in packs at one in 135, this 24-card set features "bonus" autographs in last years "style". The cards feature a white background. Lower print run cards are not priced. Card backs carry an "A" prefix.
A1 Ron Artest/40 10.00 25.00
A2 William Avery/40 8.00 20.00
A3 Jonathan Bender/20 8.00 20.00
A7 Cal Bowdler/90 8.00 20.00
A15 Vonteego Cummings/60 8.00 20.00
A20 Devean George/30 8.00 20.00
A27 Jumaine Jones/100 8.00 20.00
A36 Andre Miller/90 10.00 25.00
A39 Scott Padgett/70 8.00 20.00
A41 James Posey/40 8.00 20.00
A42 Aleksandar Radojevic/30 8.00 20.00
A47 Kenny Thomas/40 8.00 20.00

2000 SAGE Autographs Bronze

Randomly inserted in packs at one in four, this 48-card set features autographs from NBA stars and draft picks. Cards 2 and 26 do not exist. Card backs carry an "A" prefix. To ascertain values on individual cards, please refer to the multiplier in the header, coupled with the value of the base autograph.
*BRONZE AU: .5X TO 1.25X BASIC AU

2000 SAGE Autographs Gold

Randomly inserted in packs at one in 12, this 48-card set features autographs from NBA stars and draft picks. Cards 2 and 26 do not exist. Card backs carry an "A" prefix. To ascertain values on individual cards, please refer to the multiplier in the header, coupled with the value of the base autograph.
*GOLD AU: .75X TO 2X BASIC AU

2000 SAGE Autographs Master Edition

Randomly inserted in packs at one in 1,900, this 48-card set features autographs from NBA stars and draft picks. Cards 2 and 26 do not exist. Card backs carry an "A" prefix. Each card is a "one of one".

2000 SAGE Autographs Platinum

Randomly inserted in packs at one in 46, this 48-card set features autographs from NBA stars and draft picks. Cards 2 and 26 do not exist. Card backs carry an "A" prefix. To ascertain values on individual cards, please refer to the multiplier in the header, coupled with the value of the base autograph.
*PLATINUM AU: 1.5X TO 4X BASIC AU

2000 SAGE Autographs Silver

Randomly inserted in packs at one in six, this 48-card set features autographs from NBA stars and draft picks. Cards 2 and 26 do not exist. Card backs carry an "A" prefix. To ascertain values on individual cards, please refer to the multiplier in the header, coupled with the value of the base autograph.
*SILVER AU: .6X TO 1.5X BASIC AU

2000 SAGE Rookie Limited Autographs

Randomly inserted in packs at one in 18, this 24-card set features serial #'d autographs of selected rookies and stars. The cards are numbered out of 500. Card R15 does not exist.
R1 Dalibor Bagaric 3.00 8.00
R2 Jonathan Bender 3.00 8.00
R3 Primoz Brezec 3.00 8.00
R4 Brian Cardinal 3.00 8.00
R5 Chris Carrawell 3.00 8.00
R6 Jason Collier 3.00 8.00
R7 Ed Cota 3.00 8.00
R8 Baron Davis 4.00 10.00
R9 Kaniel Dickens 3.00 8.00
R10 Keyon Dooling 3.00 8.00
R11 Khalid El-Amin 3.00 8.00
R12 A.J. Guyton 3.00 8.00
R13 Jason Hart 3.00 8.00
R14 DeeAndre Hulett 3.00 8.00
R16 Dan Langhi 3.00 8.00
R17 Justin Love 3.00 8.00
R18 Desmond Mason 4.00 10.00
R19 Eduardo Najera 3.00 8.00
R20 Olumide Oyedeji 3.00 8.00
R21 Scoonie Penn 3.00 8.00
R22 Pepe Sanchez 3.00 8.00
R23 Josip Sesar 3.00 8.00
R24 Hedo Turkoglu 6.00 15.00
R25 Jaquay Walls 3.00 8.00

2001 SAGE

Released in August 2001, SAGE features a 36-card set of 2001's top draft packs and rookies. Base cards have a white border along the left side of the card, a full color player photo, and a red strip along the bottom of the card with the player's name. SAGE was packaged so each pack contained either a jersey card or an autographed card, where autographed cards came eight per box, and jersey cards came four per box. Each rookie player's card is numbered one of 3200. SAGE was packaged in 12 box cases with 12 packs per box and three cards per pack.
COMPLETE SET (36) 6.00 15.00
1 Gilbert Arenas .40 1.00
2 Shane Battier .50 1.25
3 Ruben Boumtje-Boumtje .25 .60
4 Bryan Bracey .25 .60
5 Michael Bradley .25 .60
6 Jamison Brewer .25 .60
7 Damone Brown .25 .60
8 Kwame Brown .25 .60
9 Eric Chenowith .25 .60
10 Eddy Curry .40 1.00
11 Samuel Dalembert .30 .75
12 Maurice Evans .25 .60
13 Joseph Forte .25 .60
14 Antonis Fotsis .25 .60
15 Pau Gasol .75 2.00
16 Eddie Griffin .25 .60
17 Trenton Hassell .25 .60
18 Brendan Haywood .30 .75
19 Steven Hunter .25 .60
20 Andre Hutson .25 .60
21 Maurice Jeffers .25 .60
22 Richard Jefferson .50 1.25
23 Ken Johnson .25 .60
24 Alvin Jones .25 .60
25 Sean Lampley .25 .60
26 Troy Murphy .40 1.00
27 Zach Randolph .60 1.50
28 Jason Richardson .50 1.25
29 Jeryl Sasser .25 .60
30 Kenny Satterfield .25 .60
31 Will Solomon .25 .60
32 Jamaal Tinsley .30 .75
33 Gerald Wallace .40 1.00
34 Rodney White .25 .60
35 Loren Woods .25 .60
36 Michael Wright .25 .60

2001 SAGE Authentic Jerseys Red

Randomly seeded in packs, this 21-card set features red borders along the top and the bottom of the card, a full color player photo and an oval swatch of an authentic jersey towards the bottom of the card. Each card is sequentially numbered to 400. Two versions of the Shane Battier card were issued, a blue jersey swatch and a white jersey swatch. These cards are denoted as "A" and "B" verions of card #J2.
*BRONZE: .5X TO 1.25X BASE HI
BRONZE PRINT RUN 300 SER.#'d SETS
*GOLD: .6X TO 1.5X BASE HI
GOLD PRINT RUN 99 SER.#'d SETS
*PLATINUM: 1X TO 2.5X BASE HI
PLATINUM PRINT RUN 25 SER.#'d SETS
*SILVER: .5X TO 1.25X BASE HI
SILVER PRINT RUN 200 SER.#'d SETS
UNPRICED MASTER PRINT RUN ONE SET
J1 Gilbert Arenas 5.00 12.00
J2A Shane Battier Blue 6.00 15.00
J2B Shane Battier White 6.00 15.00
J3 Michael Bradley 3.00 8.00
J4 Damone Brown 3.00 8.00
J5 Kwame Brown 3.00 8.00
J6 Eddy Curry 5.00 12.00
J7 Samuel Dalembert 4.00 10.00
J8 Joseph Forte 3.00 8.00
J9 Eddie Griffin 3.00 8.00
J10 Brendan Haywood 4.00 10.00
J11 Steven Hunter 3.00 8.00
J12 Richard Jefferson 6.00 15.00
J13 Troy Murphy 5.00 12.00
J14 Zach Randolph 8.00 20.00
J15 Jason Richardson 6.00 15.00
J16 Jeryl Sasser 3.00 8.00
J17 Jamaal Tinsley 4.00 10.00
J18 Gerald Wallace 5.00 12.00
J19 Rodney White 3.00 8.00
J20 Loren Woods 3.00 8.00

2001 SAGE Autographs Red

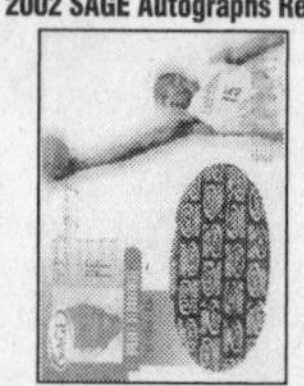

Randomly inserted in packs, this 36-card set features player photos on the right side of the card, a red border on the left side of the card, and a foil oval in the lower left hand corner with an authentic player autograph. These cards are horizontally designed, and each card is sequentially numbered. Print runs are listed below.
*BRONZE: .5X TO 1.25X BASE HI
*GOLD: .75X TO 2X BASE HI
*PLATINUM: 1.5X TO 4X BASE HI
*SILVER: .6X TO 1.5X BASE HI
UNPRICED MASTER PRINT RUN ONE SET
A1 Gilbert Arenas/349 4.00 10.00
A2 Shane Battier/499 5.00 12.00
A3 Ruben Boumtje-Boumtje/699 2.50 6.00
A4 Bryan Bracey/849 2.50 6.00
A5 Michael Bradley/349 2.50 6.00
A6 Jamison Brewer/849 2.50 6.00
A7 Damone Brown/159 2.50 6.00
A8 Kwame Brown/325 2.50 6.00
A9 Eric Chenowith/499 2.50 6.00
A10 Eddy Curry/500 4.00 10.00
A11 Samuel Dalembert/349 3.00 8.00
A12 Maurice Evans/849 2.50 6.00
A13 Joseph Forte/349 2.50 6.00
A14 Antonis Fotsis/849 2.50 6.00
A15 Pau Gasol/349 8.00 20.00
A16 Eddie Griffin/500 2.50 6.00
A17 Trenton Hassell/499 2.50 6.00
A18 Brendan Haywood/349 3.00 8.00
A19 Steven Hunter/349 2.50 6.00
A20 Andre Hutson/549 2.50 6.00
A21 Maurice Jeffers/799 2.50 6.00
A22 Richard Jefferson/699 5.00 12.00
A23 Ken Johnson/159 2.50 6.00
A24 Alvin Jones/599 2.50 6.00
A25 Sean Lampley/999 2.50 6.00
A26 Troy Murphy/349 4.00 10.00
A27 Zach Randolph/349 6.00 15.00
A28 Jason Richardson/349 5.00 12.00
A29 Jeryl Sasser/999 2.50 6.00
A30 Kenny Satterfield/249 2.50 6.00
A31 Will Solomon/599 2.50 6.00
A32 Jamaal Tinsley/349 3.00 8.00
A33 Gerald Wallace/349 4.00 10.00
A34 Rodney White/499 2.50 6.00
A35 Loren Woods/699 2.50 6.00
A36 Michael Wright/999 2.50 6.00

2002 SAGE

Released in August of 2002, Sage consists of 36 draft picks. The base cards place full color player action photos on a true to life background at the bottom of the card which fades into white at the top. The player's name and position appear across the middle of the card, as does the print run for the set. SAGE had a total print run of 2900 sets and was packaged in 12 pack boxes where each pack contained three cards.
COMPLETE SET (36) 8.00 20.00
1 David Anderson .30 .75
2 Robert Archibald .30 .75
3 Matt Barnes .40 1.00
4 Carlos Boozer .60 1.50
5 Curtis Borchardt .30 .75
6 Caron Butler .50 1.25
7 Chris Christoffersen .30 .75
8 Ousmane Cisse .30 .75
9 Sam Clancy .30 .75
10 Dan Dickau .30 .75
11 Melvin Ely .30 .75
12 Dan Gadzuric .30 .75
13 Drew Gooden .50 1.25
14 Rod Grizzard .30 .75
15 Ryan Humphrey .30 .75
16 Casey Jacobsen .30 .75
17 Chris Jefferies .30 .75
18 Jared Jeffries .30 .75
19 Fred Jones .30 .75
20 Tito Maddox .30 .75
21 Yao Ming 1.00 2.50
22 Bostjan Nachbar .30 .75
23 Smush Parker .30 .75
24 Tayshaun Prince .40 1.00
25 Kareem Rush .30 .75
26 Jamal Sampson .30 .75
27 Predrag Savovic .30 .75
28 Darius Songaila .30 .75
29 Amare Stoudemire .75 2.00
30 Nikoloz Tskitishvili .30 .75
31 DaJuan Wagner .30 .75
32 Jiri Welsch .30 .75
33 Frank Williams .30 .75
34 Jay Williams .40 1.00
35 Kelly Wise .30 .75
36 Vincent Yarbrough .30 .75

2002 SAGE Autographs Red

Randomly inserted in packs at the rate of one in two, this 34-card set features a horizontal design where a full color player photo appears on the right and a silver oval sticker with the player's autograph on it appears in the lower left hand corner. The upper right hand corner has the players name and a portrait. This portrait and the trim on the card are red. Each card is sequentially numbered.
*BRONZE: .5X TO 1.25X BASE HI
BRONZE STATED ODDS 1:4
*GOLD: .75X TO 2X BASE HI
GOLD STATED ODDS 1:12
*PLATINUM: 1.5X TO 4X BASE HI
PLATINUM STATED ODDS 1:48
*SILVER: .6X TO 1.5X BASE HI
SILVER STATED ODDS 1:6
UNPRICED MASTER PRINT RUN ONE SET
A1 David Anderson/125 3.00 8.00
A2 Robert Archibald/550 3.00 8.00
A3 Matt Barnes/500 4.00 10.00
A4 Carlos Boozer/440 6.00 15.00
A5 Curtis Borchardt/440 3.00 8.00
A7 Chris Christoffersen/220 3.00 8.00
A8 Ousmane Cisse/550 3.00 8.00
A9 Sam Clancy/440 3.00 8.00
A10 Dan Dickau/440 3.00 8.00
A12 Dan Gadzuric/500 3.00 8.00
A13 Drew Gooden/300 5.00 12.00
A14 Rod Grizzard/500 3.00 8.00
A15 Ryan Humphrey/550 3.00 8.00
A16 Casey Jacobsen/120 3.00 8.00
A17 Chris Jefferies/440 3.00 8.00
A18 Jared Jeffries/440 3.00 8.00
A19 Fred Jones/440 3.00 8.00
A20 Tito Maddox/550 3.00 8.00
A21 Yao Ming/125 25.00 60.00
A22 Bostjan Nachbar/440 3.00 8.00
A23 Smush Parker/125 3.00 8.00
A24 Tayshaun Prince/440 4.00 10.00
A25 Kareem Rush/300 3.00 8.00
A26 Jamal Sampson/440 3.00 8.00
A27 Predrag Savovic/550 3.00 8.00
A28 Darius Songaila/550 3.00 8.00
A29 Amare Stoudemire/440 8.00 20.00
A30 Nikoloz Tskitishvili/550 3.00 8.00
A31 DaJuan Wagner/250 3.00 8.00
A32 Jiri Welsch/440 3.00 8.00
A33 Frank Williams/300 3.00 8.00
A34 Jay Williams/320 8.00 20.00
A35 Kelly Wise/440 3.00 8.00
A36 Vincent Yarbrough/550 3.00 8.00

2002 SAGE Jerseys Red

Randomly inserted in packs at the rate of one in 53, this 10-card set featuers a horizontal design with a portrait style photo of the player on the right side and an oval cut jersey swatch in the lower left hand corner. Each card is sequentially numbered to 99, and the trim by the borders and background through the center of the card are red.
*BRONZE: .5X TO 1.25X BASE HI
BRONZE PRINT RUN 75 SER.#'d SETS
*GOLD: .75X TO 2X BASE HI
GOLD PRINT RUN 25 SER.#'d SETS
*SILVER: .6X TO 1.5X BASE HI
SILVER PRINT RUN 50 SER.#'d SETS
UNPRICED AUTO COMBO PRINT RUN 10 SETS
UNPRICED COMBO PRINT RUN 10 SETS
UNPRICED MASTER PRINT RUN ONE SET
UNPRICED PLATINUM PRINT RUN 10 SETS
ASJ Amare Stoudemire 10.00 25.00
DDJ Dan Dickau 4.00 10.00
DGJ Drew Gooden 6.00 15.00
DWJ DaJuan Wagner 4.00 10.00
FJJ Fred Jones 4.00 10.00
JJJ Jared Jeffries 4.00 10.00
JWJ Jay Williams 5.00 12.00
KRJ Kareem Rush 4.00 10.00
WEJ Jiri Welsch 4.00 10.00
YMJ Yao Ming 12.00 30.00

2004 SAGE

Released late in the summer of 2004, SAGE boasts a 36-card set of the newest draft picks with their slogan, "First cards of the 2004 draft." Base cards have thick white borders framing a player action photo with the player's name centered along the top, the SAGE logo in the lower right and "1 of 2650" appearing in the lower left. Sage was packaged in 12-pack boxes with packs containing three cards each.
COMPLETE SET (36) 6.00 15.00
1 Tony Allen .40 1.00
2 Rafael Araujo .30 .75
3 Brian Boddicker .30 .75
4 Taliek Brown .30 .75
5 Antonio Burks .30 .75
6 Josh Childress .30 .75
7 Luol Deng .50 1.25
8 Marcus Douthit .30 .75
9 Chris Duhon .30 .75
10 Andre Emmett .30 .75
11 Matt Freije .30 .75
12 Ben Gordon .40 1.00
13 Devin Harris .50 1.25
14 David Harrison .30 .75
15 Kris Humphries .30 .75
16 Andre Iguodala .50 1.25
17 Luke Jackson .30 .75
19 Shaun Livingston .30 .75
20 Marcus Moore .30 .75
21 Michel Morandais .30 .75
22 Brandon Mouton .30 .75
23 Emeka Okafor .50 1.25
24 Julius Page .30 .75
25 Rickey Paulding .30 .75
26 Tim Pickett .30 .75
27 Bernard Robinson .30 .75
28 Romain Sato .30 .75
29 Kirk Snyder .30 .75
30 Pape Sow .30 .75
31 Robert Swift .30 .75
32 Diana Taurasi 1.00 2.50
33 Sebastian Telfair .30 .75
34 Beno Udrih .30 .75
35 Jackson Vroman .30 .75
36 Sasha Vujacic .30 .75

2004 SAGE Autographs

Randomly inserted in packs, this 36-card set is horizontally designed and has red borders along the top and the bottom of the card. Player action photos appear on the left, while the trade mark SAGE silver sticker appears on the right with an autograph. Each card is individually numbered to a varying amount.
*BRONZE: .5X TO 1.25X BASE HI
*SILVER: .6X TO 1.5X BASE HI
*GOLD: .75X TO 2X BASE HI
UNPRICED PROOF PRINT RUN 20 SETS
UNPRICED MASTER PRINT RUN ONE SET
A1 Tony Allen/550 5.00 12.00
A2 Rafael Araujo/550 4.00 10.00
A3 Brian Boddicker/560 4.00 10.00
A4 Taliek Brown/560 4.00 10.00
A5 Antonio Burks/790 4.00 10.00
A6 Josh Childress/370 4.00 10.00
A7 Luol Deng/400 6.00 15.00
A8 Marcus Douthit/750 4.00 10.00
A9 Chris Duhon/660 4.00 10.00
A10 Andre Emmett/550 4.00 10.00
A11 Matt Freije/770 4.00 10.00
A12 Ben Gordon/400 6.00 15.00
A13 Devin Harris/400 6.00 15.00
A14 David Harrison/300 4.00 10.00
A15 Kris Humphries/400 4.00 10.00
A16 Andre Iguodala/270 6.00 15.00
A17 Luke Jackson/250 4.00 10.00
A19 Shaun Livingston/400 4.00 10.00
A20 Marcus Moore/770 4.00 10.00

A21 Michel Morandais/770 4.00 10.00
A22 Brandon Mouton/530 4.00 10.00
A23 Emeka Okafor/300 6.00 15.00
A24 Julius Page/520 4.00 10.00
A25 Rickey Paulding/750 4.00 10.00
A26 Tim Pickett/330 4.00 10.00
A27 Bernard Robinson/700 4.00 10.00
A28 Romain Sato/740 4.00 10.00
A29 Kirk Snyder/400 4.00 10.00
A30 Pape Sow/510 4.00 10.00
A31 Robert Swift/400 4.00 10.00
A32 Diana Taurasi/400 10.00 25.00
A33 Sebastian Telfair/600 4.00 10.00
A34 Beno Udrih/400 4.00 10.00
A35 Jackson Vroman/750 4.00 10.00
A36 Sasha Vujacic/400 4.00 10.00

2004 SAGE Jerseys

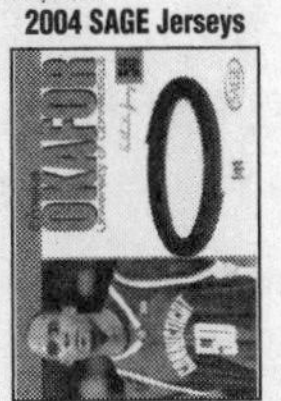

Inserted in packs and sequentially numbered to 99, this 15-card set features a horizontal design with a player photo on the left and an oval swatch of jersey on the right. For the base cards, there are red borders along the top of the card along with the player's last name in red and large block lettering. Several different parallels were produced for this set where the name depicts the color of the borders: Bronze is sequentially numbered to 75, Silver is sequentially numbered to 50, Gold is sequentially numbered to 25, Player's Proof is sequentially numbered to 20, Platinum is sequentially numbered to 10 and Masterpiece one of one's were also produced.

*BRONZE: .5X TO 1.25X JSY HI
BRONZE PRINT RUN 75 SER.#'d SETS
*SILVER: .75X TO 2X JSY HI
SILVER PRINT RUN 50 SER.#'d SETS
*GOLD: 1X TO 2.5X BASE HI
GOLD PRINT RUN 25 SER.#'d SETS
PLAYER PROOF PRINT RUN 20 SETS
UNPRICED AU JSY PRINT RUN 10 SETS
UNPRICED COMBO PRINT RUN 10 SETS
UNPRICED MASTER PRINT RUN 10 SETS
UNPRICED PLATINUM PRINT RUN 10 SETS
J1 Rafael Araujo 3.00 8.00
J2 Josh Childress 3.00 8.00
J3 Luol Deng 5.00 12.00
J4 Chris Duhon 3.00 8.00
J5 Ben Gordon 4.00 10.00
J6 Devin Harris 5.00 12.00
J7 Kris Humphries 3.00 8.00
J8 Andre Iguodala 5.00 12.00
J9 Luke Jackson 3.00 8.00
J10 Shaun Livingston 3.00 8.00
J11 Emeka Okafor 5.00 12.00
J12 Kirk Snyder 3.00 8.00
J13 Robert Swift 3.00 8.00
J14 Diana Taurasi 8.00 20.00
J15 Sebastian Telfair 3.00 8.00

2005 SAGE

COMPLETE SET (30) 4.00 10.00
1 Eddie Basden .25 .60
2 Brandon Bass .30 .75
3 Andrew Bogut .40 1.00
4 Will Bynum .25 .60
5 Travis Diener .25 .60
6 Raymond Felton .40 1.00
7 Channing Frye .30 .75
8 Angelo Gigli .25 .60
9 Joey Graham .25 .60
10 Stephen Graham .25 .60
11 Julius Hodge .25 .60
12 Matt Jones .25 .60
13 Jackie Manuel .25 .60
14 Jason Maxiell .25 .60
15 Sean May .25 .60
16 Rashad McCants .25 .60
17 Josh Pace .25 .60
18 Johan Petro .25 .60
19 Wayne Simien .25 .60
20 Chris Taft .25 .60
21 Dijon Thompson .25 .60
22 Fran Vazquez .25 .60
23 Charlie Villanueva .30 .75
24 Von Wafer .25 .60
25 Hakim Warrick .30 .75
26 Deron Williams .60 1.50
27 Jawad Williams .25 .60
28 Marvin Williams .30 .75
29 Antoine Wright .25 .60
30 Bracey Wright .25 .60

2005 SAGE Autographs Red

*BRONZE: .5X TO 1.25X BASE HI
*SILVER: .6X TO 1.5X BASE HI
*GOLD: .75X TO 2X BASE HI
PLATINUM NOT PRICED DUE TO SCARCITY
UNPRICED PROOF PRINT RUN 20 SETS
UNPRICED MASTER PRINT RUN ONE SET
A1 Eddie Basden/360 4.00 10.00
A2 Brandon Bass/450 5.00 12.00
A3 Andrew Bogut/250 6.00 15.00
A4 Will Bynum/625 4.00 10.00
A5 Travis Diener/540 4.00 10.00
A6 Raymond Felton/250 6.00 15.00
A7 Channing Frye/300 5.00 12.00
A8 Angelo Gigli/210 4.00 10.00
A9 Joey Graham/300 4.00 10.00
A10 Stephen Graham/210 4.00 10.00
A11 Julius Hodge/500 4.00 10.00
A13 Jackie Manuel/425 4.00 10.00
A14 Jason Maxiell/500 4.00 10.00
A15 Sean May/350 4.00 10.00
A16 Rashad McCants/250 4.00 10.00
A17 Josh Pace/450 4.00 10.00
A18 Johan Petro/300 4.00 10.00
A19 Wayne Simien/300 4.00 10.00
A20 Chris Taft/230 4.00 10.00
A21 Dijon Thompson/440 4.00 10.00
A22 Fran Vazquez/270 4.00 10.00
A23 Charlie Villanueva/270 5.00 12.00
A24 Von Wafer/220 4.00 10.00
A25 Hakim Warrick/300 5.00 12.00
A26 Deron Williams/270 10.00 25.00
A27 Jawad Williams/440 4.00 10.00
A28 Marvin Williams/250 5.00 12.00

2002 SAGE Beckett.com Stoudemire Jerseys

Produced by SAGE, and sold exclusively through Beckett.com, this three card set features three different versions of an Amare Stoudemire Jersey card. The Bronze version is sequentially numbered to 299, this silver is numbered to 199, and the gold is numbered to 99. These cards were originally offered as both singles and as a complete set-if the collector wanted all the same serial numbers on each of the three cards. The retail price as sold on Beckett.com was $19.95 for the bronze card, $29.95 for the silver card, $59.95 for the gold card, or the complete three-card set for $79.95

COMPLETE SET (3) 60.00 120.00
1 Amare Stoudemire Bronze/299 12.50 30.00
2 Amare Stoudemire Silver/199 15.00 40.00
3 Amare Stoudemire Gold/99 30.00 80.00

2000 SAGE HIT

The 2000 Sage Hit product was released in October,2000 as a 50-card set. The set features young NBA stars and draft picks. Each pack contained five cards, and carried a suggested retail price of $2.99.

COMPLETE SET (50) 4.00 8.00
1 Baron Davis .20 .50
2 Larry Johnson .20 .50
3 Jerry Stackhouse .20 .50
4 Michael Finley .20 .50
5 Keyon Dooling .20 .50
6 Schea Cotton .20 .50
7 DeeAndre Hulett .20 .50
8 Steve Smith .20 .50
9 Brad Millard .20 .50
10 Tim Hardaway .20 .50
11 Eric Coley .20 .50
12 Scoonie Penn .20 .50
13 Antonio McDyess .20 .50
14 Pepe Sanchez .20 .50
15 Kevin Freeman .20 .50
16 Olumide Oyedeji .20 .50
17 Dan Langhi .20 .50
18 Ed Cota .20 .50
19 Jonathan Bender .20 .50
20 Lamont Long .20 .50
21 Eduardo Najera .20 .50
22 Marko Jaric .20 .50
23 Michael Jordan .20 .50
24 Tom Gugliotta .20 .50
25 A.J. Guyton .20 .50
26 Chris Carrawell .20 .50
27 Jarrett Stephens .20 .50
28 Hedo Turkoglu .40 1.00
29 T.J. Lux .20 .50
30 Jaquay Walls .20 .50
31 Johnny Hemsley .20 .50
32 Alonzo Mourning .25 .60
33 Scottie Pippen .30 .75
34 Desmond Mason .25 .60
35 Brian Cardinal .20 .50
36 Shaheen Holloway .20 .50
37 Khalid El-Amin .20 .50
38 Josip Sesar .20 .50
39 Gabe Muoneke .20 .50
40 Kaniel Dickens .20 .50
41 Antawn Jamison .20 .50
42 Vin Baker .20 .50
43 Justin Love .20 .50
44 Dalibor Bagaric .20 .50
45 Rodney Rogers .20 .50
46 Jason Hart .20 .50
47 Gee Gervin .20 .50
48 Corliss Williamson .20 .50
49 Primoz Brezec .20 .50
50 Jason Collier .20 .50

2000 SAGE HIT NRG

Randomly inserted in packs at one in 1.5, this 50-card set parallels the base set. The cards featured a gold "NRG" stamp on the card front. To ascertain values on individual cards, please refer to the multiplier in the header, coupled with the value of the base card.

COMPLETE SET (50) 7.50 15.00
*NRG: .6X TO 1.5X BASE CARD HI

2000 SAGE HIT Autographs Emerald

Randomly inserted in packs at one in 16, this 48-card set features autographed versions of the base cards.

Cards 22 and 42 do not exist.
*EMERALD CUT: .6X TO 1.5X HI COLUMN
EMERALD CUT: STATED ODDS 1:53
*DIAMOND: .5X TO 1.25X HI COLUMN
DIAMOND: STATED ODDS 1:27
*DIAMOND CUT: .75X TO 2X HI COLUMN
DIAMOND CUT: STATED ODDS 1:160
1 Baron Davis 3.00 8.00
2 Larry Johnson 5.00 12.00
3 Jerry Stackhouse 4.00 10.00
4 Michael Finley 4.00 10.00
5 Keyon Dooling 2.00 5.00
6 Schea Cotton 2.00 5.00
7 DeeAndre Hulett 2.00 5.00
8 Steve Smith 2.50 6.00
9 Brad Millard 2.00 5.00
10 Tim Hardaway 4.00 10.00
11 Eric Coley 2.00 5.00
12 Scoonie Penn 2.00 5.00
13 Antonio McDyess 4.00 10.00
14 Pepe Sanchez 2.00 5.00
15 Kevin Freeman 2.00 5.00
16 Olumide Oyedeji 2.00 5.00
17 Dan Langhi 2.00 5.00
18 Ed Cota 2.00 5.00
19 Jonathan Bender 2.00 5.00
20 Lamont Long 2.00 5.00
21 Eduardo Najera 2.00 5.00
23 Michael Jordan 2.00 5.00
24 Tom Gugliotta 2.50 6.00
25 A.J. Guyton 2.00 5.00
26 Chris Carrawell 2.00 5.00
27 Jarrett Stephens 2.00 5.00
28 Hedo Turkoglu 4.00 10.00
29 T.J. Lux 2.00 5.00
30 Jaquay Walls 2.00 5.00
31 Johnny Hemsley 2.00 5.00
32 Alonzo Mourning 12.00 30.00
33 Scottie Pippen 25.00 60.00
34 Desmond Mason 2.50 6.00
35 Brian Cardinal 2.00 5.00
36 Shaheen Holloway 2.00 5.00
37 Khalid El-Amin 2.00 5.00
38 Josip Sesar 2.00 5.00
39 Gabe Muoneke 2.00 5.00
40 Kaniel Dickens 2.00 5.00
41 Antawn Jamison 4.00 10.00
43 Justin Love 2.00 5.00
44 Dalibor Bagaric 2.00 5.00
45 Rodney Rogers 2.00 5.00
46 Jason Hart 2.00 5.00
47 Gee Gervin 2.00 5.00
48 Corliss Williamson 2.00 5.00
49 Primoz Brezec 2.00 5.00
50 Jason Collier 2.00 5.00

2000 SAGE HIT Draft Flashbacks Emerald

Randomly inserted in packs at one in 80, this 10-card set features veteran players in the flashback theme to their rookie year. The cards were serially numbered to 500. Card backs carry a "D" prefix.

COMPLETE SET (10) 8.00 20.00
*EMERALD CUT: 1.25X TO 3X HI COLUMN
EMERALD CUT: STATED ODDS 1:264
EMERALD CUT: PRINT RUN 150 SETS
*DIAMOND: .6X TO 1.5X HI COLUMN
DIAMOND: STATED ODDS 1:132
DIAMOND: PRINT RUN 300 SETS
*DIAMOND CUT: 2.5X TO 6X HI COLUMN
DIAMOND CUT: STATED ODDS 1:800
DIAMOND CUT: PRINT RUN 50 SETS
D1 Scottie Pippen 1.50 4.00
D2 Larry Johnson 1.00 2.50
D3 Steve Smith 1.00 2.50
D4 Alonzo Mourning 1.25 3.00
D5 Tom Gugliotta 1.00 2.50
D6 Vin Baker 1.00 2.50
D7 Rodney Rogers 1.00 2.50
D8 Jerry Stackhouse 1.00 2.50
D9 Corliss Williamson 1.00 2.50
D10 Antawn Jamison 1.00 2.50

2000 SAGE HIT Prospector Emerald

Randomly inserted in packs at one in 20, this 20-card set features the top draft picks and stars. The cards were serially numbered to 999. Card backs carry a "P" prefix.

COMPLETE SET (20) 8.00 20.00
*EMERALD CUT: .75X TO 2X HI COLUMN
EMERALD CUT: STATED ODDS 1:66
EMERALD CUT: PRINT RUN 300 SETS
*DIAMOND: .5X TO 1.25X HI COLUMN
DIAMOND: STATED ODDS 1:33
DIAMOND: PRINT RUN 600 SETS
*DIAMOND CUT: 2X TO 5X HI COLUMN
DIAMOND CUT: STATED ODDS 1:200
DIAMOND CUT: PRINT RUN 100 SETS
P1 Jonathan Bender .75 2.00
P2 Chris Carrawell .75 2.00
P3 Jason Collier .75 2.00
P4 Baron Davis .75 2.00
P5 Keyon Dooling .75 2.00
P6 Khalid El-Amin .75 2.00
P7 Michael Finley .75 2.00
P8 A.J. Guyton .75 2.00
P9 Tim Hardaway .75 2.00
P10 Jason Hart .75 2.00
P11 Larry Johnson .75 2.00
P12 Dan Langhi .75 2.00
P13 Desmond Mason 1.00 2.50
P14 Antonio McDyess .75 2.00
P15 Alonzo Mourning 1.00 2.50
P16 Eduardo Najera .75 2.00
P17 Scoonie Penn .75 2.00
P18 Scottie Pippen 1.25 3.00
P19 Steve Smith .75 2.00
P20 Jerry Stackhouse .75 2.00

2001 SAGE HIT

Released in August of 2001, this 36-card base set are standard size and set on white bordered cards. The cards feature color action shots of the top 2001 draft picks.. The HIT logo can be found in the upper left-hand corner of the card. On the back of the card there are statistics and in-depth insight on each featured player. SAGE HIT was packaged in 16-box cases with 24-packs per box and four cards per pack. Each pack contained one insert card.

COMPLETE SET (36) 5.00 12.00
1 Kwame Brown .20 .50
2 Michael Wright .20 .50
3 Troy Murphy .30 .75
4 Eddy Curry .30 .75
5 Rodney White .20 .50
6 Loren Woods .20 .50
7 Maurice Jeffers .20 .50
8 Eric Chenowith .20 .50
9 Antonis Fotsis .20 .50
10 Kenny Satterfield .20 .50
11 Jamaal Tinsley .25 .60
12 Sean Lampley .20 .50
13 Richard Jefferson .40 1.00
14 Jamison Brewer .20 .50
15 Steven Hunter .20 .50
16 Pau Gasol .60 1.50
17 Michael Bradley .20 .50
18 Bryan Bracey .20 .50
19 Zach Randolph .50 1.25
20 Brendan Haywood .25 .60
21 Joseph Forte .20 .50
22 Jeryl Sasser .20 .50
23 Jason Richardson .40 1.00
24 Gerald Wallace .30 .75
25 Damone Brown .20 .50
26 Samuel Dalembert .25 .60
27 Will Solomon .20 .50
28 Maurice Evans .20 .50
29 Trenton Hassell .20 .50
30 Gilbert Arenas .30 .75
31 Shane Battier .40 1.00
32 Ken Johnson .20 .50
33 Eddie Griffin .20 .50
34 Andre Hutson .20 .50
35 Alvin Jones .20 .50
36 Ruben Boumtje-Boumtje .20 .50

2001 SAGE HIT Authentic Jerseys

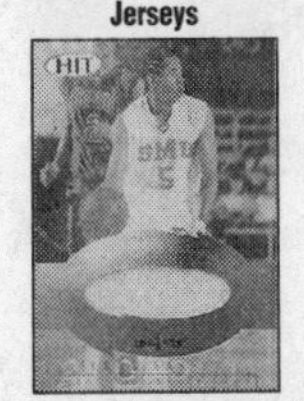

This 21-card insert set is randomly inserted in packs and cards are sequentially numbered to 175. Swatches of jerseys worn by the top 2001 draft picks are featured on the bottom third of the card in an oval shape, and full color player action photos appear above.

J1 Gerald Wallace 8.00 20.00
J2 Gilbert Arenas/175 8.00 20.00
J3 Richard Jefferson 10.00 25.00
J4 Loren Woods 5.00 12.00
J5 Rodney White 5.00 12.00
J6 Steven Hunter 5.00 12.00
J7A Shane Battier Blue 10.00 25.00
J7B Shane Battier White 10.00 25.00
J8 Kwame Brown 5.00 12.00
J9 Jamaal Tinsley 6.00 15.00
J10 Zach Randolph 12.00 30.00
J11 Jason Richardson 10.00 25.00
J12 Joseph Forte 5.00 12.00
J13 Brendan Haywood 6.00 15.00
J14 Troy Murphy 8.00 20.00
J15 Jeryl Sasser 5.00 12.00
J16 Samuel Dalembert 6.00 15.00
J17 Eddie Griffin 5.00 12.00
J18 Damone Brown 5.00 12.00
J19 Eddy Curry 8.00 20.00
J20 Michael Bradley 5.00 12.00

2001 SAGE HIT Autographs

This 36-card insert set is randomly inserted in packs at a rate of 1:6. The set features authentic autographs in a foil logo towards the bottom of the card.

*DIE CUTS: .5X TO 1.25X BASE HI
DIE CUTS PRINT RUN 250 SER.#'d SETS
*RARE CUTS: .75X TO 2X BASE HI
RARE CUTS PRINT RUN 100 SER.#'d SETS
A1 Kwame Brown 2.50 6.00
A2 Michael Wright 2.50 6.00
A3 Troy Murphy 4.00 10.00
A4 Eddy Curry 4.00 10.00
A5 Rodney White 2.50 6.00
A6 Loren Woods 2.50 6.00
A7 Maurice Jeffers 2.50 6.00
A8 Eric Chenowith 2.50 6.00
A9 Antonis Fotsis 2.50 6.00
A10 Kenny Satterfield 2.50 6.00
A11 Jamaal Tinsley 3.00 8.00
A12 Sean Lampley 2.50 6.00
A13 Richard Jefferson 5.00 12.00
A14 Jamison Brewer 2.50 6.00
A15 Steven Hunter 2.50 6.00
A16 Pau Gasol 8.00 20.00
A17 Michael Bradley 2.50 6.00
A18 Bryan Bracey 2.50 6.00
A19 Zach Randolph 6.00 15.00
A20 Brendan Haywood 3.00 8.00
A21 Joseph Forte 2.50 6.00
A22 Jeryl Sasser 2.50 6.00
A23 Jason Richardson 5.00 12.00
A24 Gerald Wallace 4.00 10.00
A25 Damone Brown 2.50 6.00
A26 Samuel Dalembert 3.00 8.00
A27 Will Solomon 2.50 6.00
A28 Maurice Evans 2.50 6.00
A29 Trenton Hassell 2.50 6.00
A30 Gilbert Arenas 4.00 10.00
A31 Shane Battier 5.00 12.00
A32 Ken Johnson 2.50 6.00
A33 Eddie Griffin 2.50 6.00
A34 Andre Hutson 2.50 6.00
A35 Alvin Jones 2.50 6.00
A36 Ruben Boumtje-Boumtje 2.50 6.00

2001 SAGE HIT Rarefied Bronze

Randomly inserted in packs at the rate of one in two, this 36-card set parallels the base set order with a bronze rarefied logo centered along the bottom of the card. Cards have a blue border along the right edge containing the player's name, and are sequentially numbered to 2001.

COMPLETE SET (36) 8.00 20.00
*GOLD: 1.25X TO 3X BASE HI
GOLD PRINT RUN 500 SER.#'d SETS
*SILVER: .6X TO 1.5X BASE HI
SILVER PRINT RUN 999 SER.#'d SETS
R1 Gilbert Arenas .40 1.00
R2 Shane Battier .50 1.25
R3 Michael Bradley .25 .60
R4 Kwame Brown .25 .60
R5 Eddy Curry .40 1.00
R6 Samuel Dalembert .30 .75
R7 Michael Finley .25 .60
R8 Joseph Forte .25 .60
R9 Antonis Fotsis .25 .60
R10 Pau Gasol .75 2.00
R11 Eddie Griffin .25 .60
R12 Tim Hardaway .25 .60
R13 Trenton Hassell .25 .60
R14 Brendan Haywood .30 .75
R15 Steven Hunter .25 .60
R16 Antawn Jamison .25 .60
R17 Richard Jefferson .50 1.25
R18 Desmond Mason .20 .50
R19 Alonzo Mourning .30 .75
R20 Troy Murphy .40 1.00
R21 Scottie Pippen .40 1.00
R22 Zach Randolph .60 1.50
R23 Jason Richardson .50 1.25
R24 Jeryl Sasser .25 .60
R25 Jerry Stackhouse .20 .50
R26 Jamaal Tinsley .30 .75
R27 Gerald Wallace .40 1.00
R28 Rodney White .25 .60
R29 Loren Woods .25 .60
R30 Kwame Brown .25 .60
R31 Pau Gasol .75 2.00
R32 Eddy Curry .40 1.00
R33 Jason Richardson .50 1.25
R34 Shane Battier .50 1.25
R35 Eddie Griffin .25 .60
R36 Rodney White .25 .60

2002 SAGE HIT

Released in late July of 2002, Sage HIT features a 52-card set comprised of the top draft picks of the 2002 season and and several players from the 2001 draft. Base cards feature a full color player photo and a white line towards the bottom below which the HIT logo appears and the player's name. Along the right edge of the card, a small blue fading to white box is present, where the player's position appears. HIT was packaged in 30-pack boxes with packs containing five cards.

COMPLETE SET (52) 6.00 15.00
1 Jared Jeffries .20 .50
2 DaJuan Wagner .20 .50
3 Caron Butler .30 .75
4 Carlos Boozer .40 1.00
5 Yao Ming .60 1.50
6 Curtis Borchardt .20 .50
7 Tito Maddox .20 .50
8 Ryan Humphrey .20 .50
9 Bostjan Nachbar .20 .50
10 Drew Gooden .30 .75
11 Predrag Savovic .20 .50
12 Dan Dickau .20 .50
13 David Andersen .20 .50
14 Lynn Greer .20 .50
15 Rod Grizzard .20 .50
16 Tayshaun Prince .25 .60
17 Smush Parker .20 .50
18 Robert Archibald .20 .50
19 Nikoloz Tskitishvili .20 .50
20 Fred Jones .20 .50
21 Kareem Rush .20 .50
22 Jay Williams .25 .60
23 Matt Barnes .25 .60
24 Jiri Welsch .20 .50
25 Darius Songaila .20 .50
26 Vincent Yarbrough .20 .50
27 Chris Jefferies .20 .50
28 Casey Jacobsen .20 .50
29 Chris Christoffersen .20 .50
30 Frank Williams .20 .50
31 Jamal Sampson .20 .50
32 Amare Stoudemire .50 1.25
33 Melvin Ely .20 .50
34 Dan Gadzuric .20 .50
35 Kelly Wise .20 .50
36 Sam Clancy .20 .50
37 Ousmane Cisse .20 .50
38 Jason Richardson .25 .60
39 Shane Battier .25 .60
40 Gilbert Arenas .25 .60
41 Jamaal Tinsley .20 .50
42 Eddy Curry .20 .50
43 Gerald Wallace .25 .60
44 Richard Jefferson .25 .60
45 Rodney White .20 .50
46 Pau Gasol .30 .75
47 Brendan Haywood .20 .50
48 Kwame Brown .20 .50
49 Troy Murphy .20 .50
50 Zach Randolph .25 .60
51 Eddie Griffin .20 .50
52 Jay Williams CL .20 .50

2002 SAGE HIT 5th Anniversary

Sage HIT 5th Anniversary cards were available in hot packs which were inserted at the rate of one in 15. These hot packs conatain three 5th Anniversary cards and 1 Write Stuff card. The 5th Anniversary cards parallel the base set enhanced with an irridescent foil 5th Anniversary stamp on the card front.

COMPLETE SET (52) 12.50 30.00
*5th ANNIVERSARY: .75X TO 2X BASE CARD HI

2002 SAGE HIT Authentic Jerseys

Randomly seeded in packs at the rate of one in 45, this six card set contains authentic swatches of player worn jerseys. Each card features a full color player photo enhanced with silver foil highlights. The bottom of the card is separated from the picture by a silver foil line, is colored in green, and the player's name appears in white. The jersey swatch is an oval shape in the lower left hand corner, and is also outlined in silver foil.

*RARE: 1X TO 2.5X BASE HI
RARE PRINT RUN 25 SER.#'d SETS
J1 Jay Williams 4.00 10.00
J3 Kareem Rush 3.00 8.00
J4 DaJuan Wagner 3.00 8.00
J5 Jared Jeffries 3.00 8.00
J6 Drew Gooden 5.00 12.00
J7 Amare Stoudemire 8.00 20.00
J8 Yao Ming 10.00 25.00

2002 SAGE HIT Autographs Emerald

Randomly inserted in packs at the rate of one in 10, this 32-card set features full color player photos set above a silver foil area in an oval shape containing authentic player autographs. The Emerald set is the base version, and is distinguished by green highlights around the photo, the player's position, and the player's name along the bottom of the card. The following players do not have emerald autographs: Caron Butler #3, Smush Parker #17, Vincent Yarbrough #26, Casey Jacobsen #28, Frank Williams #30, and Melvin Ely #33

*SILVER: .5X TO 1.25X BASE HI
SILVER STATED ODDS 1:20
H1 Jared Jeffries 3.00 8.00
H2 DaJuan Wagner 3.00 8.00
H4 Carlos Boozer 6.00 15.00
H5 Yao Ming 20.00 50.00
H6 Curtis Borchardt 3.00 8.00
H7 Tito Maddox 3.00 8.00
H8 Ryan Humphrey 3.00 8.00
H9 Bostjan Nachbar 3.00 8.00
H10 Drew Gooden 5.00 12.00
H11 Predrag Savovic 3.00 8.00
H12 Dan Dickau 3.00 8.00
H13 David Andersen 3.00 8.00
H14 Lynn Greer 3.00 8.00
H15 Rod Grizzard 3.00 8.00
H16 Tayshaun Prince 4.00 10.00
H18 Robert Archibald 3.00 8.00
H19 Nikoloz Tskitishvili 3.00 8.00
H20 Fred Jones 3.00 8.00
H21 Kareem Rush 3.00 8.00
H22 Jay Williams 6.00 15.00
H23 Matt Barnes 4.00 10.00
H24 Jiri Welsch 3.00 8.00
H25 Darius Songaila 3.00 8.00
H27 Chris Jefferies 3.00 8.00
H29 Chris Christoffersen 3.00 8.00
H31 Jamal Sampson 3.00 8.00
H32 Amare Stoudemire 8.00 20.00
H34 Dan Gadzuric 3.00 8.00
H35 Kelly Wise 3.00 8.00
H36 Sam Clancy 3.00 8.00
H37 Ousmane Cisse 3.00 8.00

2002 SAGE HIT Autographs Gold

Randomly inserted in packs at the rate of one in 24, this 34-card set parallels the Autographs Emerald set enhanced with an ink shift to gold from the base emerald cards. Each card is sequentially numbered to 250. The following players do not have gold autographs: Caron Butler #3, Vincent Yarbrough #26, and Melvin Ely #33.

*GOLD: .6X TO 1.5X AUTOS EMER HI
H17 Smush Parker 5.00 12.00
H28 Casey Jacobsen 5.00 12.00
H30 Frank Williams 5.00 12.00

2002 SAGE HIT Rarefied Emerald

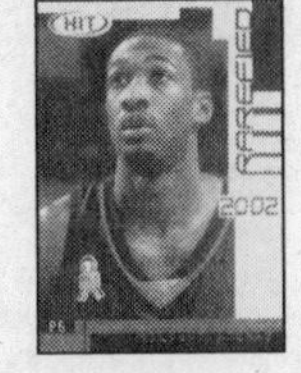

Randomly seeded in packs at the rate of one in two, this 45-card set pictures players in full color with white borders along the top and the right side of the card. The word "Rarefied" and "2002" appear on the right side of the card in emerald foil highlights, as doe the player's name on the bottom, and the team name on the photo.

*SILVER: .5X TO 1.25X BASE CARD HI
R1 David Andersen .40 1.00
R2 Robert Archibald .40 1.00
R3 Gilbert Arenas .40 1.00
R4 Matt Barnes .50 1.25
R5 Shane Battier .40 1.00
R6 Carlos Boozer .75 2.00
R7 Curtis Borchardt .40 1.00
R8 Kwame Brown .40 1.00
R9 Caron Butler .60 1.50
R10 Ousmane Cisse .40 1.00
R11 Sam Clancy .40 1.00
R12 Eddy Curry .40 1.00
R13 Dan Dickau .40 1.00
R14 Melvin Ely .40 1.00
R15 Dan Gadzuric .40 1.00
R16 Pau Gasol .40 1.00
R17 Drew Gooden .60 1.50
R18 Eddie Griffin .40 1.00
R19 Rod Grizzard .40 1.00
R20 Brendan Haywood .40 1.00
R21 Ryan Humphrey .40 1.00
R22 Chris Jefferies .40 1.00
R23 Richard Jefferson .40 1.00
R24 Jared Jeffries .40 1.00
R25 Fred Jones .40 1.00
R26 Tito Maddox .40 1.00
R27 Yao Ming 1.25 3.00
R28 Bostjan Nachbar .40 1.00
R29 Tayshaun Prince .50 1.25
R30 Zach Randolph .40 1.00
R31 Jason Richardson .40 1.00
R32 Kareem Rush .40 1.00
R33 Jamal Sampson .40 1.00
R34 Predrag Savovic .40 1.00
R35 Darius Songaila .40 1.00
R36 Amare Stoudemire 1.00 2.50
R37 Jamaal Tinsley .40 1.00
R38 Nikoloz Tskitishvili .40 1.00
R39 DaJuan Wagner .40 1.00
R40 Gerald Wallace .40 1.00
R41 Jiri Welsch .40 1.00
R42 Rodney White .40 1.00
R43 Frank Williams .40 1.00
R44 Jay Williams .50 1.25
R45 Vincent Yarbrough .40 1.00

2002 SAGE HIT Rarefied Gold Autographs

Randomly inserted in packs at the rate of one in 55, this 42-card set parallels the base design of the Rarefied Emerald set enhanced with a foil shift from the base emerald to gold and a silver oval towards the bottom of the card containing an authentic player autograph. Each card is sequentially numbered to 100. The following players do not have Gold Autographs: Caron Butler #3, Lynn Greer #14, Smush Parker #17, Vincent Yarbrough #26, Casey Jacobsen #28, Chris Christoffersen #29, Melvin Ely #33, Kelly Wise #35, and Troy Murphy #49

G1 Jared Jeffries 6.00 15.00
G2 DaJuan Wagner 6.00 15.00
G4 Carlos Boozer 12.00 30.00
G5 Yao Ming 40.00 100.00
G6 Curtis Borchardt 6.00 15.00
G7 Tito Maddox 6.00 15.00
G8 Ryan Humphrey 6.00 15.00
G9 Bostjan Nachbar 6.00 15.00
G10 Drew Gooden 10.00 25.00
G11 Predrag Savovic 6.00 15.00
G12 Dan Dickau 6.00 15.00
G13 David Andersen 6.00 15.00
G15 Rod Grizzard 6.00 15.00
G16 Tayshaun Prince 8.00 20.00
G17 Drew Gooden 10.00 25.00
G18 Robert Archibald 6.00 15.00
G19 Nikoloz Tskitishvili 6.00 15.00
G20 Fred Jones 6.00 15.00
G21 Kareem Rush 6.00 15.00
G22 Jay Williams 12.50 30.00
G23 Matt Barnes 8.00 20.00
G24 Jiri Welsch 6.00 15.00
G25 Darius Songaila 6.00 15.00
G27 Chris Jefferies 6.00 15.00
G30 Frank Williams 6.00 15.00
G31 Jamal Sampson 6.00 15.00
G32 Amare Stoudemire 15.00 40.00
G34 Dan Gadzuric 6.00 15.00
G36 Sam Clancy 6.00 15.00
G37 Ousmane Cisse 6.00 15.00
G38 Jason Richardson 8.00 20.00
G39 Shane Battier 8.00 20.00
G43 Gerald Wallace 8.00 20.00
G44 Richard Jefferson 8.00 20.00

G45 Rodney White 6.00 15.00
G47 Brendan Haywood 6.00 15.00
G50 Zach Randolph 8.00 20.00

2002 SAGE HIT The Write Stuff

Sage HIT The Write Stuff singles are found one in each Sage HIT hot packs, inserted at the rate of one in 15. This 15-card set features a brown to gray scale. bacground with the featured player's photo and an irridescent foil "The Write Stuff" stamp centered along the bottom. A color player photo appears to the left of the card, and the player's name appears along the left edge of the card.

COMPLETE SET (15) 15.00 40.00
1 Jay Williams 1.50 4.00
2 Drew Gooden 2.00 5.00
3 DaJuan Wagner 1.25 3.00
4 Amare Stoudemire 3.00 8.00
5 Jared Jeffries 1.25 3.00
6 Fred Jones 1.25 3.00
7 Kareem Rush 1.25 3.00
8 Tayshaun Prince 1.50 4.00
9 Dan Dickau 1.25 3.00
10 Caron Butler 2.00 5.00
11 Yao Ming 4.00 10.00
12 Casey Jacobsen 1.25 3.00
13 Melvin Ely 1.25 3.00
14 Nikoloz Tskitishvili 1.25 3.00
15 Carlos Boozer 2.50 6.00

2004 SAGE HIT

Released late in the summer of 2004, SAGE HIT consists of a 50-card base set where the first 36-cards share a similar design that places action photos on a stock that has white and green borders along the right side and bottom, and 19 of the top draft picks on a green bordered Lottery Pick card. SAGE HIT was packaged in 30-pack boxes with packs containing five cards (one insert and four base cards).

COMPLETE SET (50) 6.00 15.00
1 Josh Childress .20 .50
2 Luol Deng .30 .75
3 Diana Taurasi .60 1.50
4 Ben Gordon .25 .60
5 Emeka Okafor .30 .75
6 Brian Boddicker .20 .50
7 Shaun Livingston .20 .50
8 Sasha Vujacic .20 .50
9 Julius Page .20 .50
10 Romain Sato .20 .50
11 Pape Sow .20 .50
12 Robert Swift .20 .50
13 David Harrison .20 .50
14 Andre Emmett .20 .50
15 Beno Udrih .20 .50
16 Kirk Snyder .20 .50
17 Jackson Vroman .20 .50
18 Herve Lamizana .20 .50
19 Antonio Burks .20 .50
20 Marcus Douthit .20 .50
21 Chris Duhon .20 .50
22 Tim Pickett .20 .50
23 Rickey Paulding .20 .50
24 Andre Iguodala .30 .75
25 Tony Allen .25 .60
26 Bernard Robinson .20 .50
27 Brandon Mouton .20 .50
28 Taliek Brown .20 .50
29 Marcus Moore .20 .50
30 Michel Morandais .20 .50
31 Sebastian Telfair .20 .50
32 Kris Humphries .20 .50
33 Luke Jackson .20 .50
34 Devin Harris .30 .75
35 Matt Freije .20 .50
36 Rafael Araujo .20 .50
37 Diana Taurasi LP .60 1.50
38 Emeka Okafor LP .30 .75
39 Ben Gordon LP .25 .60
40 Shaun Livingston LP .20 .50
41 Devin Harris LP .30 .75
42 Josh Childress LP .20 .50
43 Luol Deng LP .30 .75
44 Rafael Araujo LP .20 .50
45 Andre Iguodala LP .30 .75
46 Luke Jackson LP .20 .50
47 Robert Swift LP .20 .50
48 Sebastian Telfair LP .20 .50
49 Kris Humphries LP .20 .50
50 Emeka Okafor CL .20 .50

2004 SAGE HIT Autographs

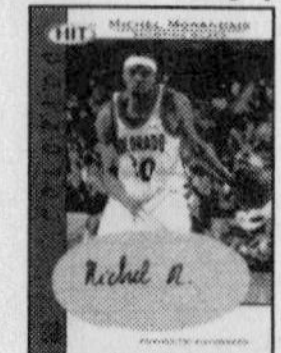

Inserted at the rate of one in 10, this 36-card set has a green border along the left side of the card, full-color player photos and and signature on SAGE's foil sticker along the bottom of the card. Two different autograph versions were issue of this set, Gold features gold highlights and is sequentially numbered to 250, and Silver features silver highlights and can be found one in every 18 packs.

*GOLD: .6X TO 1.5X BASE AU HI
*SILVER: .5X TO 1.25X BASE AU HI
1 Josh Childress 2.50 6.00
2 Luol Deng 4.00 10.00
3 Diana Taurasi 8.00 20.00
4 Ben Gordon 3.00 8.00
5 Emeka Okafor 4.00 10.00
6 Brian Boddicker 2.50 6.00
7 Shaun Livingston 2.50 6.00
8 Sasha Vujacic 2.50 6.00
9 Julius Page 2.50 6.00
10 Romain Sato 2.50 6.00
11 Pape Sow 2.50 6.00
12 Robert Swift 2.50 6.00
13 David Harrison 2.50 6.00
14 Andre Emmett 2.50 6.00
15 Beno Udrih 2.50 6.00
16 Kirk Snyder 2.50 6.00
17 Jackson Vroman 2.50 6.00
18 Herve Lamizana 2.50 6.00
19 Antonio Burks 2.50 6.00
20 Marcus Douthit 2.50 6.00
21 Chris Duhon 2.50 6.00
22 Tim Pickett 2.50 6.00
23 Rickey Paulding 2.50 6.00
24 Andre Iguodala 4.00 10.00
25 Tony Allen 3.00 8.00
26 Bernard Robinson 2.50 6.00
27 Brandon Mouton 2.50 6.00
28 Taliek Brown 2.50 6.00
29 Marcus Moore 2.50 6.00
30 Michel Morandais 2.50 6.00
31 Sebastian Telfair 2.50 6.00
32 Kris Humphries 2.50 6.00
33 Luke Jackson 2.50 6.00
34 Devin Harris 4.00 10.00
35 Matt Freije 2.50 6.00
36 Rafael Araujo 2.50 6.00

2004 SAGE HIT Jerseys

Inserted one per box, this 12-card set has white borders along the left side and bottom of the card that change to green where they meet. Player action photos appear as does an oval swatch of jersey. Premium Swatch versions were also inserted and feature just what the name implies and sequential numbering to 50.

*PREMIUM JSY's: .75X TO 2X BASE JSY HI
JAI Andre Iguodala 5.00 12.00
JBG Ben Gordon 4.00 10.00
JDH Devin Harris 5.00 12.00
JDT Diana Taurasi 8.00 20.00
JEO Emeka Okafor 5.00 12.00
JJC Josh Childress 3.00 8.00
JKH Kris Humphries 3.00 8.00
JLD Luol Deng 5.00 12.00
JLJ Luke Jackson 3.00 8.00
JRS Robert Swift 3.00 8.00
JSL Shaun Livingston 3.00 8.00
JST Sebastian Telfair 3.00 8.00
JTA Tony Allen 4.00 10.00

2004 SAGE HIT Q&A

Inserted at one in two packs, this 36-card set is bordered only on the bottom where in large green foil, the letters "Q" and "A" appear. A silver foil version of this set was also produced and those cards were ineserted at the rate on one in five packs.

COMPLETE SET (36) 8.00 20.00
*SILVER: .6X TO 1.5X BASE HI
Q1 Josh Childress .40 1.00
Q2 Luol Deng .60 1.50
Q3 Diana Taurasi .75 2.00
Q4 Ben Gordon .50 1.25
Q5 Emeka Okafor .60 1.50
Q6 Brian Boddicker .40 1.00
Q7 Shaun Livingston .40 1.00
Q8 Sasha Vujacic .40 1.00
Q9 Julius Page .40 1.00
Q10 Romain Sato .40 1.00
Q11 Pape Sow .40 1.00
Q12 Robert Swift .40 1.00
Q13 David Harrison .40 1.00
Q14 Andre Emmett .40 1.00
Q15 Beno Udrih .40 1.00
Q16 Kirk Snyder .40 1.00
Q17 Jackson Vroman .40 1.00
Q18 Herve Lamizana .40 1.00
Q19 Antonio Burks .40 1.00
Q20 Marcus Douthit .40 1.00
Q21 Chris Duhon .40 1.00
Q22 Tim Pickett .40 1.00
Q23 Rickey Paulding .40 1.00
Q24 Andre Iguodala .60 1.50
Q25 Tony Allen .50 1.25
Q26 Bernard Robinson .40 1.00
Q27 Brandon Mouton .40 1.00
Q28 Taliek Brown .40 1.00
Q29 Marcus Moore .40 1.00
Q30 Michel Morandais .40 1.00
Q31 Sebastian Telfair .40 1.00
Q32 Kris Humphries .40 1.00
Q33 Luke Jackson .40 1.00
Q34 Devin Harris .60 1.50
Q35 Matt Freije .40 1.00
Q36 Rafael Araujo .40 1.00

2004 SAGE HIT Q&A Autographs

Sequentially numbered to 100, this 36-card set parallels the Q&A set but also includes player autographs.

Q1 Josh Childress 5.00 12.00
Q2 Luol Deng 8.00 20.00
Q3 Diana Taurasi 20.00 50.00
Q4 Ben Gordon 6.00 15.00
Q5 Emeka Okafor 8.00 20.00
Q6 Brian Boddicker 5.00 12.00
Q7 Shaun Livingston 5.00 12.00
Q8 Sasha Vujacic 5.00 12.00
Q9 Julius Page 5.00 12.00
Q10 Romain Sato 5.00 12.00
Q11 Pape Sow 5.00 12.00
Q12 Robert Swift 5.00 12.00
Q13 David Harrison 5.00 12.00
Q14 Andre Emmett 5.00 12.00
Q15 Beno Udrih 5.00 12.00
Q16 Kirk Snyder 5.00 12.00
Q17 Jackson Vroman 5.00 12.00
Q18 Herve Lamizana 5.00 12.00
Q19 Antonio Burks 5.00 12.00
Q20 Marcus Douthit 5.00 12.00
Q21 Chris Duhon 5.00 12.00
Q22 Tim Pickett 5.00 12.00
Q23 Rickey Paulding 5.00 12.00
Q24 Andre Iguodala 8.00 20.00
Q25 Tony Allen 6.00 15.00
Q26 Bernard Robinson 5.00 12.00
Q27 Brandon Mouton 5.00 12.00
Q28 Taliek Brown 5.00 12.00
Q29 Marcus Moore 5.00 12.00
Q30 Michel Morandais 5.00 12.00
Q31 Sebastian Telfair 5.00 12.00
Q32 Kris Humphries 5.00 12.00
Q34 Devin Harris 8.00 20.00
Q35 Matt Freije 5.00 12.00
Q36 Rafael Araujo 5.00 12.00

2004 SAGE HIT The Write Stuff

Inserted in packs at one in 15, this 15-card set is horizontally designed with a brown-scale background, irridescent foil letters and a full color player image on the left. On the back the card shows an expert's analysis of the featured player's autograph. An actual player autographed version of this set was also produced, and those cards are sequentially numbered to 25.

COMPLETE SET (15) 10.00 25.00
1 Diana Taurasi 1.50 4.00
2 Emeka Okafor 1.50 4.00
3 Ben Gordon 1.25 3.00
4 Shaun Livingston 1.00 2.50
5 Devin Harris 1.50 4.00
6 Josh Childress 1.00 2.50
7 Luol Deng 1.50 4.00
8 Rafael Araujo 1.00 2.50
9 Andre Iguodala 1.50 4.00
10 Luke Jackson 1.00 2.50
11 Chris Duhon 1.00 2.50
12 Robert Swift 1.00 2.50
13 Sebastian Telfair 1.00 2.50
14 Kris Humphries 1.00 2.50
15 Kirk Snyder 1.00 2.50

2004 SAGE HIT The Write Stuff Autographs

Randomly inserted, this 15-card set parallels the base Write Stuff insert enahnced with player autographs and sequential numbering to 25.

STATED ODDS 1:845
PRINT RUN 25 SER.#'d SETS
5 Devin Harris 20.00 50.00
7 Luol Deng 20.00 50.00
9 Andre Iguodala 20.00 50.00
10 Luke Jackson 12.00 30.00
13 Sebastian Telfair 12.00 30.00

2005 SAGE HIT

COMPLETE SET (53) 6.00 15.00
1 Hakim Warrick .25 .60
2 Raymond Felton .30 .75
3 Charlie Villanueva .25 .60
4 Andrew Bogut .30 .75
5 Deron Williams .50 1.25
6 Fran Vazquez .20 .50
7 Ben Gordon .25 .60
8 Andre Iguodala .30 .75
9 Luol Deng .25 .60
10 Mindaugas Katelynas .20 .50
11 Dijon Thompson .20 .50
12 Angelo Gigli .20 .50
13 David Harrison .20 .50
14 Joey Graham .20 .50
15 Johan Petro .20 .50
16 Kirk Snyder .20 .50
17 Eddie Basden .20 .50
18 Sasha Vujacic .20 .50
19 Robert Swift .20 .50
20 Jawad Williams .20 .50
21 Antoine Wright .20 .50
22 Wayne Simien .20 .50
23 Chris Taft .20 .50
24 Marvin Williams .25 .60
25 Tony Allen .25 .60
26 Julius Hodge .20 .50
27 Donell Taylor .20 .50
28 Beno Udrih .20 .50
29 Stephen Graham .20 .50
30 Brandon Bass .25 .60
31 Sebastian Telfair .20 .50
32 Rashad McCants .20 .50
33 Luke Jackson .20 .50
34 Devin Harris .30 .75
35 Jackie Manuel .20 .50
36 Mile Ilic .20 .50
37 Diana Taurasi .75 2.00
38 Will Bynum .20 .50
39 Chris Duhon .20 .50
40 Bracey Wright .20 .50
41 Josh Childress .20 .50
42 Sean May .20 .50
43 Kris Humphries .20 .50
44 Shaun Livingston .20 .50
45 Channing Frye .25 .60
46 Jason Maxiell .20 .50
47 Josh Pace .20 .50
48 Rafael Araujo .20 .50
49 Matt Jones .20 .50
50 Emeka Okafor .30 .75
51 Robert Whaley .20 .50
52 Von Wafer .20 .50
53 Travis Diener .20 .50

2005 SAGE HIT Autographs

RANDOM INSERTS IN PACKS
*GOLD: .5X TO 1.25X BASE HI
GOLD PRINT RUN 250 SETS
*SILVER: .4X TO 1X BASE HI
A1 Hakim Warrick 4.00 10.00
A2 Raymond Felton 5.00 12.00
A3 Charlie Villanueva 4.00 10.00
A4 Andrew Bogut 5.00 12.00
A5 Deron Williams 8.00 20.00
A6 Fran Vazquez 3.00 8.00
A11 Dijon Thompson 3.00 8.00
A12 Angelo Gigli 3.00 8.00
A14 Joey Graham 3.00 8.00
A15 Johan Petro 3.00 8.00
A17 Eddie Basden 3.00 8.00
A20 Jawad Williams 3.00 8.00
A22 Wayne Simien 3.00 8.00
A23 Chris Taft 3.00 8.00
A24 Marvin Williams 4.00 10.00
A26 Julius Hodge 3.00 8.00
A29 Stephen Graham 3.00 8.00
A30 Brandon Bass 4.00 10.00
A32 Rashad McCants 3.00 8.00
A35 Jackie Manuel 3.00 8.00
A38 Will Bynum 3.00 8.00
A42 Sean May 3.00 8.00
A45 Channing Frye 4.00 10.00
A46 Jason Maxiell 3.00 8.00
A47 Josh Pace 3.00 8.00
A52 Von Wafer 3.00 8.00
A53 Travis Diener 3.00 8.00

2005 SAGE HIT Autographs Gold Reflections

*GOLD REF.: .75X TO 2X BASE AU HI
PRINT RUN 50 TO 100 SER.#'d SETS
7 Ben Gordon/50 10.00 25.00
8 Andre Iguodala/50 8.00 20.00
9 Luol Deng/50 6.00 15.00
34 Devin Harris/50 6.00 15.00
37 Diana Taurasi/50 12.50 30.00
41 Josh Childress/50 5.00 12.00
43 Kris Humphries/50 5.00 12.00
44 Shaun Livingston/50 5.00 12.00
50 Emeka Okafor/50 10.00 25.00

2005 SAGE HIT The Write Stuff

COMPLETE SET (15) 5.00 12.00
RANDOM INSERTS IN PACKS
1 Andrew Bogut .75 2.00
2 Raymond Felton .75 2.00
3 Channing Frye .60 1.50
4 Joey Graham .50 1.25
5 Julius Hodge .50 1.25
6 MattÂ•Jones .50 1.25
7 Sean May .50 1.25
8 Rashad McCants .50 1.25
9 Wayne Simien .50 1.25
10 Fran Vazquez .50 1.25
11 Charlie Villanueva .60 1.50
12 Hakim Warrick .60 1.50
13 Deron Williams 1.25 3.00
14 Marvin Williams .60 1.50
15 Antoine Wright .50 1.25

2005 SAGE HIT The Write Stuff Autographs

STATED PRINT RUN 25 SER.#'d SETS
1 Andrew Bogut 15.00 40.00
2 Raymond Felton 15.00 40.00
3 Channing Frye 12.00 30.00
6 MattÂ•Jones 10.00 25.00
7 Sean May 10.00 25.00
8 Rashad McCants 10.00 25.00
11 Charlie Villanueva 12.00 30.00
13 Deron Williams 25.00 60.00
14 Marvin Williams 12.00 30.00

2005 SAGE HIT Title Series Autographs

PRINT RUN 10 TO 50 SER.#'d SETS
SOME UNPRICED DUE TO SCARCITY
1 Raymond Felton/50 8.00 20.00
2 Jackie Manuel/50 5.00 12.00
5 Jawad Williams/50 5.00 12.00
6 Marvin Williams/50 6.00 15.00
12 Josh Pace/50 5.00 12.00
13 Hakim Warrick/50 6.00 15.00

2005 SAGE HIT Title Trips

COMPLETE SET (36) 15.00 40.00
RANDOM INSERTS IN PACKS
TT1 Raymond Felton .75 2.00
Rashad McCants
Sean May
TT2 Marvin Williams .75 2.00
Jawad Williams
Jackie Manuel
TT3 Raymond Felton .75 2.00
JawadÂ•Williams
Rashad McCants
TT4 Marvin Williams .75 2.00
Sean May
Jackie Manuel
TT5 Raymond Felton .75 2.00
Jackie Manuel
Rashad McCants
TT6 Marvin Williams .75 2.00
Jawad Williams
Rashad McCants
TT7 Raymond Felton .75 2.00
Jackie Manuel
Sean May
TT8 Marvin Williams .75 2.00
Jackie Manuel
Rashad McCants
TT9 Ramond Felton .75 2.00
Rashad McCants
Jawad Williams
TT10 Marvin Williams .75 2.00
Jawad Williams
Sean May
TT11 Raymond Felton .75 2.00
Jawad Williams
Rashad McCants
TT12 Marvin Williams .75 2.00
Rashad McCants
Sean May
TT13 Raymond Felton .75 2.00
Jackie Manuel
Marvin Williams
TT14 Rashad McCants .75 2.00
Jackie Manuel
Sean May
TT15 Raymond Felton .75 2.00
Sean May
Marvin Williams
TT16 Rashad McCants .75 2.00
Jackie Manuel
Jawad Williams
TT17 Raymond Felton .75 2.00
Rashad McCants
Marvin Williams
TT18 Sean May .75 2.00
Jackie Manuel
Jawad Williams
TT19 Raymond Felton .75 2.00
Jawad Williams
Marvin Williams
TT20 Sean May .75 2.00
Jawad Williams
Rashad McCants
TT21 Ben Gordon 1.50 4.00
Emeka Okafor
Diana Taurasi
TT22 Charlie Villanueva 1.00 2.50
Taliek Brown
Emeka Okafor
TT23 Ben Gordon 1.00 2.50
Emeka Okafor
Taliek Brown
TT24 Charlie Villanueva 1.25 3.00
Taliek Brown
Diana Taurasi
TT25 Ben Gordon 1.00 2.50
Charlie Villanueva
Taliek Brown
TT26 Charlie Villanueva 1.50 4.00
Emeka Okafor
Diana Taurasi
TT27 Diana Taurasi 1.25 3.00
Ben Gordon
Taliek Brown
TT28 Ben Gordon 1.50 4.00
Charlie Villanueva
Diana Taurasi
TT29 Emeka Okafor 1.25 3.00
Diana Taurasi
Taliek Brown
TT30 Ben Gordon 1.25 3.00
Emeka Okafor
Charlie Villanueva
TT31 Hakim Warrick 1.00 2.50
Josh Pace
Chris Duhon
TT32 Raymond Felton 1.00 2.50
Ben Gordon
Hakim Warrick
TT33 Marvin Williams 1.00 2.50
Ben Gordon
Hakim Warrick
TT34 Ben Gordon 1.50 4.00
Diana Taurasi
Hakim Warrick
TT35 BenÂ•Gordon 1.25 3.00
Hakim Warrick
Chris Duhon
TT36 DianaÂ•Taurasi 1.25 3.00
Hakim Warrick
Chris Duhon

2002 SAGE National Jerseys

These cards were issued during the National are are serially numbered to 50.

N1 Jay Williams 10.00 25.00
N4 Amare Stoudemire 20.00 50.00

2002 SAGE Pangos Sheets

Given away at Pauley Pavilion, UCLA, on January 4th 2003, this four sheet set features the first card of high school sensation LeBron James. Each sheet features eight players and the SAGE logo coupled with the Pangos Dream Classic 2003 logo. Two versions of these sheets were printed, a Green version and a Gold version. The Green version features a green background with with gold trim around the player's school and position, and around the Pangos logo on the card front. The Gold version features a shift where the background is gold, and the green appears around the school/position box and the logo. 5000 green sheets were produced, 1250 of each, for handing out at the game, and 500 gold, 125 of each, were produced for handing out to the players the sheets featured. LeBron James and Wesley Washington received some sheets, but through a mix-up, the rest were never given to the players. SAGE did, however, give these remaining sheets out with product press releases to dealers and sports card distributors.

1 Sheet 1 15.00 40.00
D.J. Strawberry
Sebastian Telfair
Wesley Washington
DeMarcus Nelson
Header Card
Justin Hawkins
Omar Wilkes
LeBron James
Ekene Ibekwe
2 Sheet 2 15.00 40.00
Dru Joyce III
Sebastian Telfair
Justin Hawkins
DeMarcus Nelson
Aaron Afflalo
D.J. Strawberry
LeBron James
Ekene Ibekwe
3 Sheet 3 15.00 40.00
Wesley Washington
Sebastian Telfair
Harrison Schaen
Ekene Ibekwe
Header Card
Aaron Afflalo
Omar Wilkes
LeBron James
Justin Hawkins
4 Sheet 4 15.00 40.00
DeMarcus Nelson
Sebastian Telfair
Dru Joyce III
D.J. Strawberry
Header Card
Aaron Afflalo
Omar Wilkes
LeBron James
Harrison Schaen

2002 SAGE Pangos Sheets Gold

Given away at Pauley Pavilion, UCLA, on January 4th 2003, this four sheet set features the first card of high school sensation LeBron James. Each sheet features eight players and the SAGE logo, coupled with the Pangos Dream Classic 2003 logo. Two versions of these sheets were printed, a Green version and a Gold version. The Green version features a green background with with gold trim around the player's school and position, and around the Pangos logo on the card front. The Gold version features a shift where the background is gold, and the green appears around the school/position box and the logo. 5000 green sheets were produced, 1250 of each, for handing out at the game, and 500 gold, 125 of each, were produced for handing out to the players the sheets featured. LeBron James and Wesley Washington received some sheets, but through a mix-up, the rest were never given to the players. SAGE did, however, give these remaining sheets out with product press releases to dealers and sports card distributors.

*GOLD: 2X TO 5X HI COLUMN

1994 Score Board Draft Day

Subtitled "Basketball Draft Day," this 13-card standard-size (2 1/2" by 3 1/2") set features some of the top picks in the 1994 NBA draft. Each set included a certificate of limited edition bearing a unique serial number and the production run figures (19,500). The cards are full-bleed except at the bottom, where a color stripe carries the palyer's last name in block lettering. Featuring a player cutout superposed on a background consisting of the appropriate city skyline, the color photos have a metallic sheen to them. The name of the city is printed in a typewriter font and cuts across the middle of the picture in "ticker-tape" fashion. The backs have a player profile and a color headshot. The cards are numbered on the back with a "DD" prefix.

COMPLETE SET (13) 7.20 18.00
DD1 Glenn Robinson (Milwaukee) 1.25 3.00
DD2 Glenn Robinson (Dallas) .60 1.50
DD3 Glenn Robinson (Detroit) .60 1.50
DD4 Jason Kidd (Minneapolis) .40 1.00
DD5 Jason Kidd (Dallas) .40 1.00
DD6 Jason Kidd (Washington) .40 1.00
DD7 Grant Hill (Dallas) .75 2.00
DD8 Grant Hill (Detroit) 1.50 4.00
DD9 Eric Montross (Boston) .08 .25
DD10 Eric Montross (Sacramento) .08 .25
DD11 Juwan Howard (Washington) 1.25 3.00
DD12 Juwan Howard (Philadelphia) .60 1.50
DD13 Checklist .08 .25

1994 Score Board National Promos

Distributed during the 1994 National Sports Collectors Convention, this 20-card standard-size multi-sport set features four subsets: Salute to 1994 Draft Stars (1-5), Centers of Attention (6-9), Texas Heroes (10-13, 20), and Salute to Racing's Greatest (14-18). The borderless fronts feature color action cutouts on multi-colored metallic backgrounds. The players name, position, and team name appear randomly placed on arcs. The borderless backs feature a color head shot on a ghosted backgound. The players name and biography appear at the top with the player's stats and profile at the bottom. The cards are numbered on the back with an "NC" prefix. The sets were given away to attendees at Classic's National Convention Party. Each set included a certificate of authenticity, giving the set serial number out of a total of 9,900 sets produced. There were five different checklist cards created using the fronts of other cards in the set. The complete set price includes only one of the checklist cards.

COMPLETE SET (20) 20.00 40.00
1 Glenn Robinson .40 1.00
2 Jason Kidd 1.25 3.00
3 Donyell Marshall .20 .50
4 Juwan Howard .40 1.00
5 Grant Hill .75 2.00
6 Hakeem Olajuwon .60 1.50
7 Patrick Ewing .60 1.50
8 Dikembe Mutombo .30 .75
9 Alonzo Mourning .60 1.50
13 Hakeem Olajuwon Texas Heroes .60 1.50
20C Hakeem Olajuwon CL .60 1.50

1996 Score Board Draft Day

COMPLETE SET (14) 4.00 10.00
COMMON CARD .20 .50
1A Allen Iverson Philadelphia 1.00 2.50
1B Allen Iverson Vancouver 1.00 2.50
1C Allen Iverson Minnesota 1.00 2.50
3A Stephon Marbury Phoenix .50 1.25
3B Stephon Marbury Minnesota .50 1.25
3C Stephon Marbury Denver .50 1.25
4A Ray Allen Milwaukee .75 2.00
4B Ray Allen Minnesota .75 2.00
4C Ray Allen Dallas .75 2.00
5A Antoine Walker Minnesota .40 1.00
5B Antoine Walker New Jersey .40 1.00
5C Antoine Walker Boston .40 1.00
7 Jason Kidd .30 .75
9 Damon Stoudamire .20 .50

1996 Score Board Frontier Phone Cards

9 Kobe Bryant $100 100.00 200.00

1997 Score Board Draft Day

1A Tim Duncan
1B Tim Duncan
1C Tim Duncan
2A Ron Mercer
2B Ron Mercer
2C Ron Mercer
3A Keith Van Horn
3B Keith Van Horn
3C Keith Van Horn

1996-97 Score Board All Sport PPF

The 1996-97 All Sport Past Present and Future set was issued in two series in six-card packs. The product contains original vintage and rookie cards of the top athletes from baseball, basketball, football and hockey as well as new cards of tomorrow's stars from each sport. Release date for series one was October 1996; series two was February 1997. There was also a gold parallel produced for this set. Series one gold cards were inserted 1:10 packs while series two had gold cards inserted at a 1:5 ratio.

COMPLETE SET (200) 6.00 15.00
1 Shaquille O'Neal .30 .75
2 Scottie Pippen .15 .40
3 Dikembe Mutombo .15 .40
4 Damon Stoudamire .15 .40
5 Brent Barry .07 .20
6 Michael Finley .15 .40
7 Allen Iverson .50 1.25
8 Marcus Camby .15 .40
9 Stephon Marbury .25 .60
10 Antonio McDyess .15 .40
11 Kobe Bryant 1.00 2.50
12 Ray Allen .40 1.00
13 Antoine Walker .30 .75
14 Erick Dampier .07 .20
15 Vitaly Potapenko .07 .20
16 Tony Delk .15 .40
17 John Wallace .15 .40
18 Roy Rogers .07 .20
19 Jerome Williams .15 .40
20 Travis Knight .07 .20
21 Ryan Minor .15 .40
22 Shawn Harvey .07 .20
23 Jason Sasser .07 .20
24 Doron Sheffer .07 .20
25 Malik Rose .15 .40
26 Jermaine O'Neal .08 .25
27 Mark Hendrickson .05 .15
28 Dontae' Jones .07 .20
29 Othella Harrington .15 .40
50 Shaquille O'Neal CL (1-50) .15 .40
80 Allen Iverson .50 1.25
81 Jason Kidd .15 .40
82 Hakeem Olajuwon .15 .40
83 Alonzo Mourning .15 .40
84 Shareef Abdur-Rahim .30 .75
85 Glenn Robinson .15 .40
86 Rasheed Wallace .15 .40
101 Hakeem Olajuwon .15 .40
102 Alonzo Mourning .15 .40
103 Rasheed Wallace .15 .40
104 Glenn Robinson .15 .40
105 Tyus Edney .07 .20
106 Joe Smith .15 .40
107 Jason Kidd .15 .40
108 Shareef Abdur-Rahim .15 .40
109 Kerry Kittles .10 .30
110 Lorenzen Wright .15 .40

111 Samaki Walker .07 .20
112 Todd Fuller .07 .20
113 Steve Nash .30 .75
114 Jamie Feick .07 .20
115 Walter McCarty .07 .20
116 Jeff McInnis .07 .20
117 Derek Fisher .30 .75
118 Moochie Norris .07 .20
119 Joseph Blair .07 .20
120 Steve Hamer .07 .20
121 Randy Livingston .07 .20
122 Ron Riley .07 .20
123 Mark Pope .05 .15
124 Drew Barry .07 .20
125 Brian Evans .07 .20
150 Kobe Bryant CL .50 1.25
179 Allen Iverson .25 .60
180 Antonio McDyess .15 .40
181 Scottie Pippen .15 .40
182 Dikembe Mutombo .15 .40
183 Damon Stoudamire .15 .40
184 Stephon Marbury .15 .40
185 Kobe Bryant .60 1.50
186 Marcus Camby .15 .40

1996-97 Score Board All Sport PPF Gold

*GOLDS: 1.2X TO 3X BASIC CARDS
GOLD STATED ODDS SER.1 1:10/SER.2 1:5

1996-97 Score Board All Sport PPF Retro

Randomly inserted in series one packs at a rate of one in 35, this 10-card set was printed on old-style card stock.

COMPLETE SET (10) 12.00 30.00
R1 Allen Iverson 3.00 8.00
R3 Scottie Pippen 1.50 4.00
R5 Shaquille O'Neal 2.00 5.00
R6 Marcus Camby .60 1.50
R8 Damon Stoudamire .50 1.25

1996-97 Score Board All Sport PPF Revivals

Randomly inserted in series two packs at a rate of one in 35, this 10-card set was printed on old-style card stock.

COMPLETE SET (10) 12.00 30.00
REV1 Allen Iverson 3.00 8.00
REV2 Stephon Marbury 1.50 4.00
REV3 Alonzo Mourning .60 1.50
REV4 Shareef Abdur-Rahim 1.00 2.50
REV5 Kerry Kittles .50 1.25

1996 Score Board Autographed BK

This 50-card set was overshadowed by the autograph (3-4 per box) and memorabilia redemption (1 per box) inserts found in this product. Six base cards found their way into each pack in 16-pack boxes. Each 12 box case was to contain one Shaquille O'Neal autographed memorabilia item, an average of one Allen Iverson autographed memorabilia item, and an average of one game or warm-up jersey. The card fronts have a grainy area on the left or right side of the card next to a color photo of a collegiate player. The backs contain another photo accompanied with collegiate statistics and a small biography.

COMPLETE SET (50) 4.00 10.00
1 Allen Iverson .75 2.00
2 Marcus Camby .25 .60
3 Shareef Abdur-Rahim .30 .75
4 Stephon Marbury .40 1.00
5 Ray Allen .60 1.50
6 Erick Dampier .15 .40
7 Antoine Walker .30 .75
8 John Wallace .15 .40
9 Kerry Kittles .15 .40
10 Lorenzen Wright .15 .40
11 Samaki Walker .15 .40
12 Todd Fuller .15 .40
13 Malik Rose .20 .50
14 Roy Rogers .15 .40
15 Kobe Bryant 1.50 4.00
16 Walter McCarty .15 .40
17 Ryan Minor .20 .50
18 Steve Nash .75 2.00
19 Jermaine O'Neal .40 1.00
20 Vitaly Potapenko .15 .40
21 Mark Pope .15 .40
22 Tony Delk .15 .40
23 Brian Evans .15 .40
24 Reggie Geary .15 .40
25 Dontae' Jones .15 .40
26 Travis Knight .15 .40
27 Priest Lauderdale .15 .40
28 Moochie Norris .15 .40
29 Efthimis Retzias .15 .40
30 Jerome Williams .15 .40
31 Jamie Feick .15 .40
32 Othella Harrington .15 .40
33 Mark Hendrickson .15 .40
34 Chris Robinson .15 .40
35 Randy Livingston .15 .40
36 Marcus Mann .15 .40
37 Darnell Robinson .15 .40
38 Jason Sasser .15 .40
39 Doron Sheffer .15 .40
40 Drew Barry .15 .40
41 Ben Davis .15 .40
42 Steve Hamer .15 .40
43 Ronnie Henderson .15 .40
44 Jeff McInnis .15 .40
45 Scottie Pippen .25 .60
46 Jason Kidd .25 .60
47 Alonzo Mourning .20 .50
48 Hakeem Olajuwon .20 .50
49 Damon Stoudamire .15 .40
50 Allen Iverson CL .40 1.00

1996 Score Board Autographed BK Autographs

Found at the rate of 3 to 4 per 16 pack box, these autographs were hand numbered and signed by 35 different players. Each autograph has a red parallel numbered of 400 and a silver parallel numbered of 325. The values for these parallels are listed below. 1A and 3A were made available via redemption cards only. The following cards do not exist: 7, 9, 11, 12, 19, 24, 25, 27, 29, 36, 41, 43, 45, 46, 47, 48, 49 and 50.

*RED AUTOS: .6X TO 1.5X BASE HI
RED PRINT RUN 240 TO 400 SER.#'d SETS
*SILVER AUTOS: .75X TO 2X BASE HI
SILVER PRINT RUN 325 SER.#'d SETS
1 Allen Iverson 50.00 100.00
2 Marcus Camby 6.00 15.00
3 Shareef Abdur-Rahim 8.00 20.00
3 Stephon Marbury 10.00 25.00
5 Ray Allen 15.00 40.00
6 Erick Dampier 1.50 4.00
8 John Wallace 1.50 4.00
10 Lorenzen Wright 1.50 4.00
13 Malik Rose 2.00 5.00
14 Roy Rogers 1.50 4.00
15 Kobe Bryant 75.00 200.00
16 Walter McCarty 1.50 4.00
17 Ryan Minor 2.00 5.00
18 Steve Nash 20.00 50.00
20 Vitaly Potapenko 1.50 4.00
21 Mark Pope 1.50 4.00
22 Tony Delk 1.50 4.00
23 Brian Evans 1.50 4.00
26 Travis Knight 1.50 4.00
28 Moochie Norris 1.50 4.00
30 Jerome Williams 1.50 4.00
31 Jamie Feick 1.50 4.00
32 Othella Harrington 1.50 4.00
33 Mark Hendrickson 1.50 4.00
34 Chris Robinson 1.50 4.00
35 Randy Livingston 1.50 4.00
37 Darnell Robinson 1.50 4.00
38 Jason Sasser 1.50 4.00
39 Doron Sheffer 1.50 4.00
40 Drew Barry 1.50 4.00
42 Steve Hamer 1.50 4.00
44 Jeff McInnis 1.50 4.00
NNO Derek Fisher 8.00 20.00
NNO Jamal Mashburn/1000 6.00 15.00
NNO Antonio McDyess/995 5.00 12.00
NNO Terrell Bell 1.50 4.00
NNO Shawn Harvey 1.50 4.00
NNO Ron Riley 1.50 4.00

1996 Score Board Autographed BK Pure Performance

Inserted at the rate of 1 in 10 packs, this 30-card set highlights thirty pro and collegiate players. The cards have the insert name embossed on the front in a silver metallic background behind a color player photo. The backs have another player photo and some biographical information. The cards are numbered with a "PP" prefix.

COMPLETE SET (30) 30.00 80.00
*GOLD: .75X TO 2X VALUE
STATED ODDS 1:50
PP1 Allen Iverson 5.00 12.00
PP2 Marcus Camby 1.50 4.00
PP3 Shareef Abdur-Rahim 2.00 5.00
PP4 Stephon Marbury 2.50 6.00
PP5 Ray Allen 4.00 10.00
PP6 Erick Dampier 1.00 2.50
PP7 Antoine Walker 2.00 5.00
PP8 John Wallace 1.00 2.50
PP9 Kerry Kittles 1.00 2.50
PP10 Lorenzen Wright 1.00 2.50
PP11 Samaki Walker 1.00 2.50
PP12 Todd Fuller 1.00 2.50
PP13 Roy Rogers 1.00 2.50
PP14 Kobe Bryant 10.00 25.00
PP15 Walter McCarty 1.00 2.50
PP16 Ryan Minor 1.00 2.50
PP17 Steve Nash 5.00 12.00
PP18 Jermaine O'Neal 2.50 6.00
PP19 Vitaly Potapenko 1.00 2.50
PP20 Tony Delk 1.00 2.50
PP21 Brian Evans 1.00 2.50
PP22 Reggie Geary 1.00 2.50
PP23 Dontae' Jones 1.00 2.50
PP24 Travis Knight 1.00 2.50
PP25 Othella Harrington 1.00 2.50
PP26 Alonzo Mourning 1.25 3.00
PP27 Scottie Pippen 1.50 4.00
PP28 Jason Kidd 1.50 4.00
PP29 Damon Stoudamire 1.25 3.00
PP30 Hakeem Olajuwon 1.25 3.00

1997 Score Board Autographed BK

The 1997-98 Score Board Autographed Basketball set was issued in one series totalling 50 cards and was distributed in five-card packs. The fronts feature color action player photos printed on foil-stamped cards. The backs carry player information.

COMPLETE SET (50) 4.00 10.00
1 Tim Duncan .75 2.00
2 Ron Mercer .15 .40
3 Tracy McGrady .60 1.50
4 Johnny Taylor .12 .30
5 Tim Thomas .25 .60
6 John Thomas .12 .30
7 Scot Pollard .12 .30
8 Brevin Knight .12 .30
9 Keith Booth .12 .30
10 Charles Smith .12 .30
11 Kobe Bryant .60 1.50
12 Kerry Kittles .07 .20
13 Marcus Camby .12 .30
14 Paul Grant .12 .30
15 Damon Stoudamire .12 .30
16 Shareef Abdur-Rahim .12 .30
17 Antonio Daniels .12 .30
18 Stephon Marbury .15 .40
19 Kelvin Cato .12 .30
20 Allen Iverson .25 .60
21 Derek Anderson .12 .30
22 Rasheed Wallace .15 .40
23 Austin Croshere .12 .30
24 Hakeem Olajuwon .15 .40
25 Clyde Drexler .15 .40
26 Adonal Foyle .12 .30
27 Alonzo Mourning .12 .30
28 Ed Gray .12 .30
29 Antonio McDyess .10 .25
30 Ray Allen .15 .40
31 Joe Smith .10 .25
32 Keith Van Horn .25 .60
33 Tony Battie .12 .30
34 Bobby Jackson .15 .40
35 Anthony Parker .12 .30
36 Scottie Pippen .20 .50
37 Chauncey Billups .50 1.25
38 Jacque Vaughn .12 .30
39 Danny Fortson .12 .30
40 Olivier Saint-Jean .12 .30
41 Marc Jackson .12 .30
42 God Shammgod .12 .30
43 Chris Anstey .12 .30
44 DeJuan Wheat .12 .30
45 Serge Zwikker .12 .30
46 Jason Lawson .12 .30
47 Antoine Walker .12 .30
48 Charles O'Bannon .12 .30
49 Kebu Stewart .12 .30
50 Mark Sanford .12 .30

1997 Score Board Autographed BK Tim Duncan

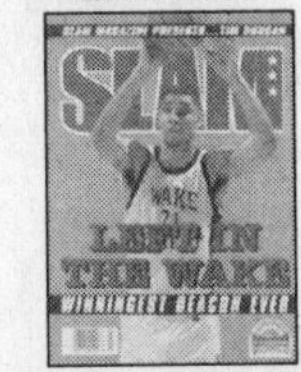

Randomly inserted in packs at one in 18, this 10-card set features a tribute to Tim Duncan, the number one pick of the 1997 NBA Draft.

COMPLETE SET (10) 10.00 25.00
COMMON CARD (SD1-SD10) 1.25 3.00

1997 Score Board Autographed BK Gold Autographs

Randomly inserted one per every 18 hobby only packs, this limited 65-card set features hand-numbered autographed action player photos with gold foil highlights. The numbers after the players' names indicate how many cards they signed.

1 Danya Abrams/266 1.50 4.00
2 Ray Allen/300 12.50 30.00
3 Peter Aluma/300 1.50 4.00
4 Derek Anderson/300 1.50 4.00
5 Chris Anstey/300 1.50 4.00
6 Tunji Awojobi/300 1.50 4.00
7 Tony Battie/291 2.00 5.00
8 Chauncey Billups/300 6.00 15.00
9 Marcus Camby/300 4.00 10.00
10 Kelvin Cato/300 1.50 4.00
11 Lorenzen Coleman/300 1.50 4.00
12 James Collins/300 1.50 4.00
13 Austin Croshere/269 1.50 4.00
14 Erick Dampier/280 1.50 4.00
15 Harold Deane/300 1.50 4.00
16 Tony Delk/295 1.50 4.00
17 Tim Duncan/221 50.00 120.00
18 Eddie Elisma/300 1.50 4.00
19 Nate Erdmann/278 1.50 4.00
20 Derek Fisher/300 3.00 8.00
21 Isaac Fontaine/290 1.50 4.00
22 Danny Fortson/300 1.50 4.00
23 Kiwane Garris/266 1.50 4.00
24 Paul Grant/293 1.50 4.00
25 Steve Hamer/299 1.50 4.00
26 Othella Harrington/300 1.50 4.00
27 Otis Hill/300 1.50 4.00
28 Allen Iverson/45 75.00 150.00
29 Bobby Jackson/288 2.00 5.00
30 Anthony Johnson/300 1.50 4.00
31 Kerry Kittles/300 2.50 6.00
32 Brevin Knight/300 1.50 4.00
33 Travis Knight/300 1.50 4.00
34 Jason Lawson/300 1.50 4.00
35 Quincy Lee/300 1.50 4.00
36 Gordon Malone/296 1.50 4.00
37 Stephon Marbury/300 8.00 20.00
38 Walter McCarty/297 1.50 4.00
39 Antonio McDyess/293 4.00 10.00
40 Tracy McGrady/66 50.00 100.00
40A Tracy McGrady/300 25.00 60.00
41 Alonzo Mourning/300 8.00 20.00
42 Charles O'Bannon/268 1.50 4.00
43 Ed O'Bannon/164 1.50 4.00
44 Anthony Parker/300 1.50 4.00
45 Scot Pollard/300 1.50 4.00
46 Malik Rose/259 1.50 4.00
47 Olivier Saint Jean/300 1.50 4.00
48 Mark Sanford/290 1.50 4.00
49 Shea Seals/300 1.50 4.00
50 Alvin Sims/300 1.50 4.00
51 Charles Smith/300 1.50 4.00
52 Joe Smith/289 2.50 6.00
53 Kebu Stewart/300 1.50 4.00
54 Damon Stoudamire/284 4.00 10.00
55 John Thomas/300 1.50 4.00
56 Tim Thomas/201 3.00 8.00
57 Jacque Vaughn/300 1.50 4.00
58 Antoine Walker/290 6.00 15.00
59 John Wallace/300 2.50 6.00
60 Rasheed Wallace/300 6.00 15.00
61 Reggie Welch/300 1.50 4.00
62 DeJuan Wheat/300 1.50 4.00
63 Alvin Williams/300 1.50 4.00
64 Jerome Williams/300 1.50 4.00
65 Serge Zwikker/282 1.50 4.00

1997 Score Board Autographed BK Platinum Autographs

Randomly inserted one in every nine retail only packs, this 53-card set features autographed color action player photos with platinum foil highlights. Only 200 of each player's card were signed and produced, except for Othella Harrington with only 197 and Charles O'Bannon and Kebu Stewart with 198 each.

1 Shareef Abdur-Rahim 6.00 15.00
2 Danya Abrams 2.00 5.00
3 Chris Anstey 2.00 5.00
4 Peter Aluma 2.00 5.00
5 Tunji Awojobi 2.00 5.00
6 Tony Battie 2.50 6.00
7 Chauncey Billups 8.00 20.00
8 Kelvin Cato 2.00 5.00
9 Lorenzo Coleman 2.00 5.00
10 James Collins 2.00 5.00
11 Austin Croshere 2.00 5.00
12 Harold Deane 2.00 5.00
13 Eddie Elisma 2.00 5.00
14 Nate Erdmann 2.00 5.00
15 Derek Fisher 4.00 10.00
16 Isaac Fontaine 2.00 5.00
17 Danny Fortson 2.00 5.00
18 Kiwane Garris 2.00 5.00
19 Paul Grant 2.00 5.00
20 Steve Hamer 2.00 5.00
21 Othella Harrington/197 2.00 5.00
22 Otis Hill 2.00 5.00
23 Bobby Jackson 2.50 6.00
24 Anthony Johnson 2.00 5.00
25 Brevin Knight 2.00 5.00
26 Travis Knight 2.00 5.00
27 Jason Lawson 2.00 5.00
28 Quincy Lee 2.00 5.00
29 Gordon Malone 2.00 5.00
30 Stephon Marbury 10.00 25.00
31 Walter McCarty 2.00 5.00
32 Charles O'Bannon/198 2.00 5.00
33 Ed O'Bannon 2.00 5.00
34 Anthony Parker 2.00 5.00
35 Scot Pollard 2.00 5.00
36 Malik Rose 2.00 5.00
37 Olivier Saint-Jean 2.00 5.00
38 Mark Sanford 2.00 5.00
39 Shea Seals 2.00 5.00
40 Alvin Sims 2.00 5.00
41 Charles Smith 2.00 5.00
42 Kebu Stewart/198 2.00 5.00
43 John Thomas 2.00 5.00
44 Tim Thomas 4.00 10.00
45 Jacque Vaughn 2.00 5.00
46 Antoine Walker 8.00 20.00
47 John Wallace 3.00 8.00
48 Rasheed Wallace 8.00 20.00
49 Reggie Welch 2.00 5.00
50 DeJuan Wheat 2.00 5.00
51 Alvin Williams 2.00 5.00
52 Jerome Williams 2.00 5.00
53 Serge Zwikker 2.00 5.00

1997 Score Board Autographed BK Silver Autographs

Randomly inserted in hobby and retail packs at the rate of two in nine, this 23-card set features autographed color action player photos with silver-foil highlights.

LP1 Derek Anderson 1.50 4.00
LP2 Danya Abrams 1.50 4.00
LP3 Tony Battie 2.00 5.00
LP4 Chauncey Billups SP 6.00 15.00
LP5 Austin Croshere 1.50 4.00
LP6 Erick Dampier 1.50 4.00
LP7 Danny Fortson 1.50 4.00
LP8 Brevin Knight SP 2.00 5.00
LP9 Tracy McGrady SP 25.00 60.00
LP10 Ed O'Bannon SP 1.50 4.00
LP11 Olivier Saint-Jean 1.50 4.00
LP12 Tim Thomas 3.00 8.00
SS1 Shareef Abdur-Rahim 6.00 15.00
SS2 Ray Allen SP 12.00 30.00
SS3 Kobe Bryant 50.00 100.00
SS4 Marcus Camby SP 4.00 10.00
SS5 Allen Iverson SP 20.00 50.00
SS6 Kerry Kittles SP 2.50 6.00
SS7 Stephon Marbury 4.00 10.00
SS8 Antonio McDyess SP 4.00 10.00
SS9 Alonzo Mourning SP 8.00 20.00
SS10 Damon Stoudamire SP 4.00 10.00
SS11 Antoine Walker 6.00 15.00
SS12 Rasheed Wallace 8.00 20.00

1997 Score Board Autographed BK Trademark Slam

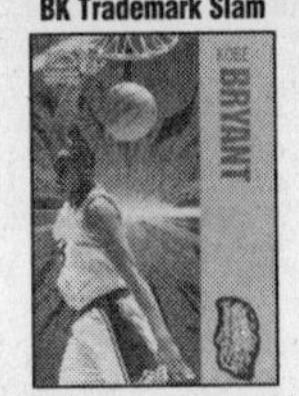

Randomly inserted in packs at the rate of one in eight, this 30-card set features color action player photos representing the greatest dunks in each pictured player's career printed on foil-stamped cards.

COMPLETE SET (30) 10.00 25.00
1 Stephon Marbury .50 1.25
2 Scottie Pippen .60 1.50
3 Antonio McDyess .30 .75
4 Alonzo Mourning .50 1.25
5 Clyde Drexler .50 1.25
6 Joe Smith .30 .75
7 Hakeem Olajuwon .50 1.25
8 Tim Duncan 2.50 6.00
9 Ron Mercer .50 1.25
10 Tracy McGrady 2.00 5.00
11 Paul Grant .40 1.00
12 Tim Thomas .75 2.00
13 John Thomas .40 1.00
14 Scot Pollard .40 1.00
15 Kobe Bryant 2.00 5.00
16 Kerry Kittles .25 .60
17 Marcus Camby .40 1.00
18 Shareef Abdur-Rahim .40 1.00
19 Allen Iverson .75 2.00
20 Derek Anderson .40 1.00
21 Rasheed Wallace .40 1.00
22 Austin Croshere .40 1.00
23 Adonal Foyle .40 1.00
24 Danny Fortson .40 1.00
25 Keith Van Horn .75 2.00
26 Tony Battie .50 1.25
27 Olivier Saint-Jean .40 1.00
28 Kelvin Cato .40 1.00
29 Jason Lawson .40 1.00
30 Antoine Walker .40 1.00

1996-97 Score Board Autographed Collection

Each box of Score Board Autographed Collection contains 16 packs including six cards. The 50-card regular set includes top athletes from all four major team sports. According to Score Board, a total of 1,500 sequentially numbered cases were produced.

COMPLETE SET (50) 5.00 12.00
1 Damon Stoudamire .07 .20
2 Scottie Pippen .15 .40
3 Jason Kidd .15 .40
4 Hakeem Olajuwon .15 .40
5 Alonzo Mourning .15 .40
6 Antonio McDyess .15 .40
7 Allen Iverson .75 2.00
8 Rasheed Wallace .15 .40
9 Glenn Robinson .10 .30
10 Marcus Camby .30 .75
11 Shareef Abdur-Rahim .40 1.00
12 Stephon Marbury .25 .60
13 Kobe Bryant 1.50 4.00
14 Ray Allen .60 1.50
15 Antoine Walker .30 .75
16 Kerry Kittles .10 .30
17 John Wallace .15 .40

1996-97 Score Board Autographed Collection Autographs

Each box of Autographed Collection contains an average of four autographed cards. There are two different varieties: silver foil stamped cards with no individual serial numbering inserted at a rate of 1:7 packs, and Gold foil serial numbered autographs inserted at a rate of 1:16 packs.

2 Shareef Abdur-Rahim 5.00 12.00
3 Ray Allen 6.00 15.00
4 Drew Barry 2.00 5.00
6 Kobe Bryant 50.00 100.00
7 Marcus Camby 3.00 8.00
10 Erick Dampier 1.50 4.00
12 Tony Delk 2.50 6.00
20 Othella Harrington 2.50 6.00
23 Allen Iverson 25.00 50.00
28 Kerry Kittles 2.50 6.00
29 Travis Knight 2.50 6.00
30 Stephon Marbury 8.00 20.00
32 Walter McCarty 2.00 5.00
38 Vitaly Potapenko 2.00 5.00
39 Roy Rogers 2.00 5.00
47 Antoine Walker 4.00 10.00
49 John Wallace 2.50 6.00
50 Jerome Williams 2.50 6.00
52 Lorenzen Wright 2.50 6.00

1996-97 Score Board Autographed Collection Autographs Gold

These Gold foil parallel signed cards were seeded at the rate of 1:16 packs. They are Score Board Certified and individually numbered out of 250, 300 or 350 except for Stepfret Williams.

*UNLISTED GOLD: .6X TO 1.5X BASIC AU
6 Kobe Bryant/300 75.00 150.00
23 Allen Iverson/250 50.00 100.00
47 Antoine Walker/350 8.00 20.00

1996-97 Score Board Autographed Collection Game Breakers

This 30-card insert set was printed on metallic stock and has two versions-- regular and gold. The insertion ratio is 1:10 packs for regular inserts and 1:50 for the gold foil version.

COMPLETE SET (30) 25.00 60.00
*GOLD: .8X TO 2X BASIC INSERTS
GB1 Damon Stoudamire .60 1.50
GB2 Scottie Pippen .75 2.00
GB3 Jason Kidd 1.25 3.00
GB4 Ray Allen 1.25 3.00
GB5 Alonzo Mourning .75 2.00
GB6 Joe Smith .60 1.50
GB7 Allen Iverson 3.00 8.00
GB8 Rasheed Wallace .75 2.00
GB9 Antoine Walker 1.00 2.50
GB10 Marcus Camby 1.50 4.00
GB11 Shareef Abdur-Rahim UER 1.50 4.00
(Front Photo is Mystery Man)
GB12 Stephon Marbury 2.50 3.00
GB13 Kobe Bryant 5.00 12.00

1997-98 Score Board Autographed Collection

The 1998 Autographed Collection set was issued in one series totalling 50 cards with players from baseball, basketball, football and hockey. The product's major draw was an average of five autographed cards and one memorabilia redemption card per 18-pack box. The regular autographs were inserted 1:4.5 packs, the Blue Ribbon autographs were inserted 1:18 packs. The one-per box memorabilia redemption cards were not all redeemed due to the fact that Score Board, Inc. filed for bankruptcy a few months after the product's release. Score Board also released a "Strongbox Collection" that originally retailed for around $125. Each Strongbox included a parallel of this 50 card set, one star player autographed baseball with holder, one star player autographed 8" x 10", one Athletic Excellence card and One Sports City USA card.

COMPLETE SET (50) 5.00 12.00
1 Tim Duncan .50 1.25
5 Allen Iverson .40 1.00
7 Scottie Pippen .15 .40
9 Stephon Marbury .20 .50
14 Keith Van Horn .07 .20
15 Tiki Barber .30 .75
16 Kobe Bryant .75 2.00
18 Tim Thomas .07 .20
20 Hakeem Olajuwon .15 .40
22 Clyde Drexler .15 .40
24 Adonal Foyle .07 .20
25 Alonzo Mourning .15 .40
30 Joe Smith .08 .25
32 Tony Battie .07 .20
37 Chauncey Billups .07 .20
39 Tracy McGrady .40 1.00
41 Antoine Walker .30 .75
45 Ron Mercer .15 .40
47 Antonio Daniels .07 .20
50 Kerry Kittles .15 .40

1997-98 Score Board Autographed Collection Athletic Excellence

These 3 1/2" x 5" cards, were inserted one per Score Board "Strongbox Collection" box that originally retailed for around $125. Each Strongbox also included a parallel of the 1998 Autograph Collection 50 card set, one star player autographed baseball with holder, one star player autographed 8" x 10" and one Sports City USA card. Each card is sequentially numbered out of 750.

COMPLETE SET (12) 10.00 25.00
AE1 Chauncey Billups .75 2.00
AE6 Tim Thomas .75 2.00
AE9 Tim Duncan 3.00 8.00
AE11 Tracy McGrady 2.00 5.00
AE12 Keith Van Horn 1.25 3.00

1997-98 Score Board Autographed Collection Autographs

One autographed card was available in one in every 4.5 Score Board Autograph Collection packs. The cards have a circular player photograph in the middle with a white oval below that includes a player's autograph. The card backs read, "Congratulations! You have received an authentic Score Board autographed card." There was also a Kerry Wood card produced that made its way into the marketplace although it was not inserted into packs. The cards are unnumbered and listed below in alphabetical order.

6 Tony Delk 2.00 5.00
12 Brevin Knight 2.00 5.00
15 Anthony Parker 3.00 8.00
20 Charles Smith 1.50 4.00
21 John Thomas 1.50 4.00
24 Lorenzen Wright 1.50 4.00

1997-98 Score Board Autographed Collection Blue Ribbon Autographs

One Blue Ribbon autographed card was available in one in every 18 Score Board Autograph Collection packs. The cards have a circular player photograph with a blue ribbon border in the middle with a white oval below that includes a player's autograph. The cards are hand numbered out of the amounts listed below in the upper right hand corner. The card backs read, "Congratulations! You have received an authentic Score Board autographed card." The cards are unnumbered and listed below in alphabetical order. A Warrick Dunn card was later released through a home shopping network show. Some Kobe Bryant cards have surfaced in un-signed form and can often be found with forged autographs on the front. No authentic Kobe signed and numbered cards are known although the Congratulations Score Board message is included on the cardbacks.

1 Shareef Abdur-Rahim/570 6.00 15.00
2 Tony Battie/650 2.00 5.00
3 Marcus Camby/675 3.00 8.00
4 Austin Croshere/1350 2.00 5.00
6 Tim Duncan/208 40.00 80.00
7 Danny Fortson/1350 2.00 5.00
9 Kerry Kittles/650 2.00 5.00
10 Stephon Marbury/1300 5.00 12.00
11 Tracy McGrady/670 8.00 20.00
12 Scottie Pippen/90 60.00 120.00
P2 Kobe Bryant Unsigned 6.00 15.00
(no known signed cards exist)

1997-98 Score Board Autographed Collection Sports City USA

These multi-player, city-themed cards were inserted one in nine Autographed Collection packs. There is also a Strongbox parallel found one per Score Board "Strongbox Collection" box that originally retailed for around $125. Each Strongbox also included a parallel of the 1998 Autograph Collection 50 card set, one star player autographed baseball with holder, one star player autographed 8" x 10" and one Athletic Excellence jumbo card.

COMPLETE SET (15) 10.00 25.00
SC1 Adonal Foyle .75 2.00
Joe Smith
Steve Young
SC3 Hakeem Olajuwon .60 1.50
Clyde Drexler
Ricardo Hidalgo
SC4 Kerry Wood .60 1.50
Scottie Pippen
Darnell Autry
SC5 Ray Allen 2.00 5.00
Brett Favre
SC6 Kobe Bryant 2.00 5.00
Adrian Beltre
SC7 Tim Thomas 1.00 2.50
Duce Staley
J.D.Drew
SC8 Alonzo Mourning .50 1.25
Yatil Green
SC9 Joe Thornton .40 1.00
Chauncey Billups
SC12 Wes Helms .40 1.00
Bryan Hanspard
Ed Gray
SC13 Stephon Marbury .40 1.00
Dwayne Rudd
SC14 Jay Payton .75 2.00
Tiki Barber
Keith Van Horn
SC15 Matt Drews .75 2.00
Bryant Westbrook
Scot Pollard

1997-98 Score Board Autographed Collection Sports City USA Strongbox

*STRONGBOX/600: .8X TO 2X BASIC INSERTS

1997-98 Score Board Autographed Collection Strongbox

*STRONGBOX: .8X TO 2X BASIC CARDS

1997 Score Board Players Club

The 70 cards that make-up this set are a grouping from baseball, basketball, football and hockey players. Card fronts are full colored action shots, with professional team names air-brushed out. The card backs contain 1997 projected statistics and biographical information. Along with the number 1 Die-Cuts and Play Back inserts, vintage cards were the major draw to this product. One in 32 packs contained a vintage card from 1909-1979 from any of the four sports. An original Honus Wagner T206 card was offered as a redemption in 1:153,600 packs. Also, one vintage wax pack was available via redemption card in one in every 32 packs.

COMPLETE SET (70) 5.00 12.00
4 Shareef Abdur-Rahim .15 .40
8 Ray Allen .15 .40
9 Derek Anderson .07 .20
15 Tony Battie .07 .20
16 Kobe Bryant .50 1.25
18 Marcus Camby .07 .20
19 Keith Van Horn .07 .20
23 Chauncey Billups .10 .30
24 Scottie Pippen .15 .40
29 Jacque Vaughn .07 .20
30 Tim Thomas .07 .20
31 Clyde Drexler .15 .40
35 Joe Smith .07 .20
36 Antoine Walker .15 .40
40 Hakeem Olajuwon .15 .40
41 Alonzo Mourning .15 .40
43 Stephon Marbury .15 .40
45 Kerry Kittles .07 .20
49 Allen Iverson .25 .60
52 Antonio Daniels .10 .30
55 Olivier Saint-Jean .07 .20
58 Tracy McGrady 1.00 2.50
62 Johnny Taylor .07 .20
64 Austin Croshere .08 .25
66 Brevin Knight .08 .25
68 Ron Mercer .15 .40

1997 Score Board Players Club #1 Die-Cuts

Each player in this 20 card set, inserted one in 32 packs, was at one time selected as a first round selection in the professional draft. The cards are die-cut in the shape of a "1" and have gold foil on the left border. The backs contain pre-professional biographical information and (if applicable) statistics from their last college or minor league season. The card numbers have a "D" prefix.

COMPLETE SET (20) 25.00 60.00
D1 Allen Iverson 4.00 10.00
D5 Hakeem Olajuwon 1.50 4.00
D6 Joe Smith 1.25 3.00
D8 Shareef Abdur-Rahim 1.50 4.00
D9 Stephon Marbury 2.00 5.00
D12 Keith Van Horn 1.25 3.00
D13 Kobe Bryant 8.00 20.00
D14 Chauncey Billups 1.25 3.00
D16 Tim Thomas 1.25 3.00

D17 Tony Battie	1.25	3.00
D20 Antonio Daniels	1.25	3.00

1997 Score Board Players Club Play Backs

This 15-card set highlights stars form all four major U.S. sports. The card fronts have a player photo superimposed on a photo of the player's jersey. To the left is a movie reel design with individual action shots. The backs have another player photograph and biographical information. The cards are numbered with a "PB" prefix.

COMPLETE SET (15)	30.00	80.00
STATED ODDS 1:32		
PB5 Scottie Pippen	2.50	6.00
PB7 Allen Iverson	4.00	10.00
PB9 Marcus Camby	1.50	4.00
PB10 Kobe Bryant	8.00	20.00
PB11 Hakeem Olajuwon	1.50	4.00
PB12 Stephon Marbury	2.00	5.00
PB14 Joe Smith	1.25	3.00
PB15 John Wallace	1.25	3.00

1996 Score Board Rookies

The 1996 Basketball Rookies set was issued in one series totaling 100 cards. The 10-card packs retailed for $1.99 each. Each box contained two original "vintage" rookie cards (1986-1995) from a list of several players. Also in packs were two randomly inserted insert sets: College Jerseys and Die Cuts.

COMPLETE SET (100)	5.00	12.00
1 Allen Iverson	.75	2.00
2 Marcus Camby	.25	.60
3 Stephon Marbury	.40	1.00
4 Shareef Abdur-Rahim	.30	.75
5 Ray Allen	.60	1.50
6 Erick Dampier	.15	.40
7 Antoine Walker	.30	.75
8 John Wallace	.15	.40
9 Kerry Kittles	.15	.40
10 Lorenzen Wright	.15	.40
11 Samaki Walker	.15	.40
12 Todd Fuller	.15	.40
13 Jaron Boone	.15	.40
14 Roy Rogers	.15	.40
15 Kobe Bryant	1.50	4.00
16 Walter McCarty	.15	.40
17 Ryan Minor	.20	.50
18 Steve Nash	.75	2.00
19 Jermaine O'Neal	.40	1.00
20 Vitaly Potapenko	.15	.40
21 Kwame Evans	.15	.40
22 Tony Delk	.15	.40
23 Brian Evans	.15	.40
24 Dion Cross	.15	.40
25 Dontae' Jones	.15	.40
26 Travis Knight	.15	.40
27 Priest Lauderdale	.15	.40
28 Moochie Norris	.15	.40
29 Efthmis Retzias	.15	.40
30 Jerome Williams	.15	.40
31 Jamie Feick	.15	.40
32 Othella Harrington	.15	.40
33 Mark Hendrickson	.15	.40
34 Chris Robinson	.15	.40
35 Randy Livingston	.15	.40
36 Marcus Mann	.15	.40
37 Darnell Robinson	.15	.40
38 Jason Sasser	.15	.40
39 Doron Sheffer	.15	.40
40 Kevin Simpson	.15	.40
41 Joseph Blair	.15	.40
42 Eric Gingold	.15	.40
43 Steve Hamer	.15	.40
44 Ronnie Henderson	.15	.40
45 Jeff McInnis	.15	.40
46 Dante Calabria	.15	.40
47 Martin Muursepp	.15	.40
48 Mark Pope	.15	.40
49 Ron Riley	.15	.40
50 Shandon Anderson	.15	.40
51 Derrick Battie	.15	.40
52 Derek Fisher	.30	.75
53 Kevin Granger	.15	.40
53AU Kevin Granger AU	2.00	5.00
54 Shawn Harvey	.15	.40
55 Bernard Hopkins	.15	.40
56 Raimonds Miglinieks	.15	.40
57 Tim Moore	.15	.40
58 Carlos Strong	.15	.40
59 Chucky Atkins	.15	.40
60 Drew Barry	.15	.40
61 Terrell Bell	.15	.40
62 Donta Bright	.15	.40
63 Marcus Brown	.15	.40
64 William Cunningham	.15	.40
65 Katu Davis	.15	.40
66 Ben Davis	.15	.40
67 Adrian Griffin	.15	.40
68 Darvin Ham	.15	.40
69 Art Long	.15	.40
70 Jerome Lambert	.15	.40
71 Amal McCaskill	.15	.40
72 Mingo Johnson	.15	.40
73 Dametri Hill	.15	.40
74 Michael Lloyd	.15	.40
75 Malik Rose	.20	.50
76 Jeff Nordgaard	.15	.40
77 Duane Simpkins	.15	.40
78 Russ Millard	.15	.40
79 Allen Iverson CL	.40	1.00
80 Marcus Camby CL	.12	.30
81 Allen Iverson AA	.40	1.00
82 Marcus Camby AA	.12	.30
83 Stephon Marbury AA	.20	.50
84 Ray Allen AA	.30	.75
85 Kerry Kittles AA	.07	.20
86 Erick Dampier AA	.07	.20
87 Shareef Abdur-Rahim AA	.15	.40
88 John Wallace AA	.07	.20
89 Lorenzen Wright AA	.07	.20
90 Tony Delk AA	.07	.20
91 Shaquille O'Neal BG	.40	1.00
92 Hakeem Olajuwon BG	.20	.50
93 Joe Smith BG	.12	.30
94 Brent Barry BG	.12	.30
95 Jason Kidd BG	.25	.60
96 Scottie Pippen BG	.25	.60
97 Damon Stoudamire BG	.15	.40
98 Alonzo Mourning BG	.20	.50
99 Rasheed Wallace BG	.20	.50
100 Glenn Robinson BG	.15	.40

1996 Score Board Rookies College Jerseys

Randomly inserted in packs at a rate of one in 10, this 30-card set highlights professional and college athletes on a vertical designed card. The fronts have a photo of the player next to a textured college jersey (not an actual jersey). The backs have another photo and some biographical information. The cards are numbered with a "J" prefix. There was also a Shaquille O'Neal Los Angeles card, inserted one in 432 packs, that tributes his move from the east to west coast. The jersey on this card in not textured. That card is not included in the set price.

COMPLETE SET (30)	15.00	40.00
CJ1 Allen Iverson	3.00	8.00
CJ2 Stephon Marbury	1.50	4.00
CJ3 Marcus Camby	1.00	2.50
CJ4 Ray Allen	2.50	6.00
CJ5 Erick Dampier	.60	1.50
CJ6 John Wallace	.60	1.50
CJ7 Antoine Walker	1.25	3.00
CJ8 Lorenzen Wright	.60	1.50
CJ9 Kerry Kittles	.60	1.50
CJ10 Todd Fuller	.60	1.50
CJ11 Samaki Walker	.60	1.50
CJ12 Roy Rogers	.60	1.50
CJ13 Walter McCarty	.60	1.50
CJ14 Dontae' Jones	.60	1.50
CJ15 Steve Nash	3.00	8.00
CJ16 Jerome Williams	.60	1.50
CJ17 Ryan Minor	.75	2.00
CJ18 Shareef Abdur-Rahim	1.25	3.00
CJ19 Brian Evans	.60	1.50
CJ20 Travis Knight	.60	1.50
CJ21 Mark Hendrickson	.60	1.50
CJ22 Tony Delk	.60	1.50
CJ23 Ronnie Henderson	.60	1.50
CJ24 Drew Barry	.60	1.50
CJ25 Damon Stoudamire	.60	1.50
CJ26 Shaquille O'Neal	1.50	4.00
CJ27 Joe Smith	.50	1.25
CJ28 Jason Kidd	1.00	2.50
CJ29 Alonzo Mourning	.75	2.00
CJ30 Rasheed Wallace	.75	2.00
LA34 Shaquille O'Neal LA	6.00	15.00

1996 Score Board Rookies Die Cuts

Randomly inserted in packs at a rate of one in 50, this 30-card set highlights, in order, the top 29 picks of the 1997 draft. (In addition, Damon Stoudamire was thrown in at the end for good measure.) Each card is die-cut in the shape of a "one". The players name is vertically written in blue on a gold strip on the left of the card next to his photo. The backs have another photo and some information about his place in the draft. The cards are numbered "X of 30".

COMPLETE SET (30)	25.00	60.00
DC1 Allen Iverson	5.00	12.00
DC2 Marcus Camby	1.50	4.00
DC3 Shareef Abdur-Rahim	2.00	5.00
DC4 Stephon Marbury	2.50	6.00
DC5 Ray Allen	4.00	10.00
DC6 Antoine Walker	2.00	5.00
DC7 Lorenzen Wright	1.00	2.50
DC8 Kerry Kittles	1.00	2.50
DC9 Samaki Walker	1.00	2.50
DC10 Erick Dampier	1.00	2.50
DC11 Todd Fuller	1.00	2.50
DC12 Vitaly Potapenko	1.00	2.50
DC13 Kobe Bryant	10.00	25.00
DC14 Shaquille O'Neal	5.00	12.00
DC15 Steve Nash	5.00	12.00
DC16 Tony Delk	1.00	2.50
DC17 Jermaine O'Neal	2.50	6.00
DC18 John Wallace	1.00	2.50
DC19 Walter McCarty	1.00	2.50
DC20 Jason Kidd	3.00	8.00
DC21 Dontae' Jones	1.00	2.50
DC22 Roy Rogers	1.00	2.50
DC23 Efthmis Retzias	1.00	2.50
DC24 Derek Fisher	2.00	5.00
DC25 Martin Muursepp	1.00	2.50
DC26 Jerome Williams	1.00	2.50
DC27 Brian Evans	1.00	2.50
DC28 Priest Lauderdale	1.00	2.50
DC29 Travis Knight	1.00	2.50
DC30 Damon Stoudamire	2.00	5.00
NNO Damon Stoudamire PROMO	.40	1.00

1997 Score Board Rookies

The 1997 Basketball Rookies set was issued in one series totaling 100 cards and was distributed in eight-card packs with a suggested retail price of $2.79. The fronts feature borderless color action player photos. The backs carry player information. Each box of the Hobby-exclusive version contained an average of one vintage card from 50 top players of all time or one original, unopened wax pack from one of the top basketball series ever produced. Redemption cards were inserted for all cards with a book value of more than $200 and for a select few original wax packs. Each box also contained an average of one autographed card signed by a first round pick from the 1994-1997 drafts. These cards were preproduced cards that were signed and stamped with a ScoreBoard seal. The Retail boxes did not contain an autographed card, but contained two vintage cards or packs.

COMPLETE SET (100)	6.00	15.00
1 Tim Duncan	.75	2.00
2 Ron Mercer	.15	.40
3 Marc Jackson	.12	.30
4 Tunji Awojobi	.12	.30
5 Reggie Freeman	.12	.30
6 John Thomas	.12	.30
7 Scot Pollard	.12	.30
8 Brevin Knight	.12	.30
9 Keith Booth	.12	.30
10 Reggie Welch	.12	.30
11 Alvin Sims	.12	.30
12 Victor Page	.12	.30
13 Jason Lawson	.12	.30
14 Paul Grant	.12	.30
15 Kiwane Garris	.12	.30
16 Eddie Elisma	.12	.30
17 Antonio Daniels	.12	.30
18 James Collins	.12	.30
19 Kelvin Cato	.12	.30
20 Peter Aluma	.12	.30
21 Derek Anderson	.12	.30
22 Lorenzo Coleman	.12	.30
23 Austin Croshere	.12	.30
24 Harold Deane	.12	.30
25 Nate Erdmann	.12	.30
26 Adonal Foyle	.12	.30
27 Tony Gonzalez	.12	.30
28 Ed Gray	.12	.30
29 Quincy Lee	.12	.30
30 Charles O'Bannon	.12	.30
31 Shea Seals	.12	.30
32 Keith Van Horn	.25	.60
33 Tony Battie	.15	.40
34 Bobby Jackson	.15	.40
35 Anthony Parker	.12	.30
36 Kebu Stewart	.12	.30
37 Chris Anstey	.12	.30
38 Jacque Vaughn	.12	.30
39 DeJuan Wheat	.12	.30
40 Anthony Johnson	.12	.30
41 Danny Fortson	.12	.30
42 Mark Sanford	.12	.30
43 Jerald Honeycutt	.12	.30
44 Olivier Saint-Jean	.12	.30
45 Chauncey Billups	.50	1.25
46 Isaac Fontaine	.12	.30
47 Otis Hill	.12	.30
48 Tracy McGrady	.60	1.50
49 Johnny Taylor	.12	.30
50 God Shammgod	.12	.30
51 Dedric Willoughby	.12	.30
52 Tim Thomas	.25	.60
53 Alvin Williams	.12	.30
54 Gordon Malone	.12	.30
55 Serge Zwikker	.12	.30
56 Charles Smith	.12	.30
57 Tim Duncan ROY?	.60	1.50
58 Ron Mercer ROY?	.12	.30
59 Keith Van Horn ROY?	.20	.50
60 Tim Thomas ROY?	.20	.50
61 Tim Duncan CL	.60	1.50
62 Tim Duncan AA	.60	1.50
63 Ron Mercer AA	.12	.30
64 Keith Van Horn AA	.20	.50
65 Tony Battie AA	.12	.30
66 Tracy McGrady AA	.50	1.25
67 Danny Fortson AA	.10	.25
68 Brevin Knight AA	.10	.25
69 DeJuan Wheat AA	.10	.25
70 Adonal Foyle AA	.10	.25
71 Jacque Vaughn AA	.10	.25
72 Tim Duncan AA CL	.60	1.50
73 Allen Iverson ART	.20	.50
74 Marcus Camby ART	.10	.25
75 Shareef Abdur-Rahim ART	.10	.25
76 Stephon Marbury ART	.12	.30
77 Ray Allen ART	.12	.30
78 Antoine Walker ART	.10	.25
79 Lorenzen Wright ART	.05	.15
80 Kerry Kittles ART	.05	.15
81 Erick Dampier ART	.05	.15
82 Vitaly Potapenko ART	.05	.15
83 Kobe Bryant ART	.50	1.25
84 Tony Delk ART	.05	.15
85 John Wallace ART	.05	.15
86 Walter McCarty ART	.05	.15
87 Roy Rogers ART	.05	.15
88 Allen Iverson ART CL	.20	.50
89 Rasheed Wallace BD	.10	.25
90 Damon Stoudamire BD	.10	.25
91 Joe Smith BD	.07	.20
92 Glenn Robinson BD	.07	.20
93 Scottie Pippen BD	.15	.40
94 Ed O'Bannon BD	.05	.15
95 Antonio McDyess BD	.07	.20
96 Alonzo Mourning BD	.12	.30
97 Clyde Drexler BD	.12	.30
98 Dikembe Mutombo BD	.10	.25
99 Hakeem Olajuwon BD	.12	.30
100 Scottie Pippen BD CL	.15	.40

1997 Score Board Rookies Dean's List

Randomly inserted in packs at the rate of one in five, this 100-card set is a parallel version of the base set and is distinguished in design by the silver foil stamping. To ascertain values on individual cards, please refer to the multiplier in the header below, coupled with the value of the base card.

COMPLETE SET (100)	12.00	30.00
*STARS: .75X TO 2X BASE VALUE		

1997 Score Board Rookies #1 Die Cuts

Randomly inserted in packs at the rate of one in 36, this 20-card set features color action images of players selected in the first round of the draft and are printed on die-cut foil board around the shape of the number one.

COMPLETE SET (20)	40.00	100.00
1 Tim Duncan	12.00	30.00
2 Tony Battie	2.50	6.00
3 Ron Mercer	2.50	6.00
4 Keith Van Horn	4.00	10.00
5 Antonio Daniels	2.00	5.00
6 Tim Thomas	4.00	10.00
7 Adonal Foyle	2.00	5.00
8 Derek Anderson	2.00	5.00
9 Chauncey Billups	8.00	20.00
10 Tracy McGrady	10.00	25.00
11 Danny Fortson	2.00	5.00
12 Brevin Knight	2.00	5.00
13 Jacque Vaughn	2.00	5.00
14 Austin Croshere	2.00	5.00
15 Stephon Marbury	2.50	6.00
16 Kobe Bryant	10.00	25.00
17 Clyde Drexler	2.50	6.00
18 Scottie Pippen	3.00	8.00
19 Allen Iverson	4.00	10.00
20 Alonzo Mourning	2.50	6.00

1997 Score Board Rookies Traded

Inserted at a rate of 1:36 packs, these cards look identical to the base set cards except they have a glossy finish and have a "Traded to..." stamp on the front. Card numbers are followed by a "T" on the back.

COMPLETE SET (7)	3.00	8.00
19T Kelvin Cato	.75	2.00
32T Keith Van Horn	1.50	4.00
34T Bobby Jackson	1.00	2.50
35T Anthony Parker	.75	2.00
37T Chris Anstey	.75	2.00
41T Danny Fortson	.75	2.00
52T Tim Thomas	1.50	4.00

1997 Score Board Rookies Varsity Club

Randomly inserted in packs at the rate of one in 18, this 20-card set features color photos of the brightest basketball stars printed on foil with an authentic pennant look.

COMPLETE SET (20)	15.00	40.00
VC1 Tim Duncan	6.00	15.00
VC2 Ron Mercer	1.25	3.00
VC3 Keith Van Horn	2.00	5.00
VC4 Tim Thomas	2.00	5.00
VC5 Adonal Foyle	1.00	2.50
VC6 Tony Battie	1.25	3.00
VC7 Antonio Daniels	1.00	2.50
VC8 Kelvin Cato	1.00	2.50
VC9 Charles O'Bannon	1.00	2.50
VC10 Brevin Knight	1.00	2.50
VC11 Danny Fortson	1.00	2.50
VC12 Derek Anderson	1.00	2.50
VC13 Austin Croshere	1.00	2.50
VC14 Tracy McGrady	5.00	12.00
VC15 Jacque Vaughn	1.00	2.50
VC16 God Shammgod	1.00	2.50
VC17 DeJuan Wheat	1.00	2.50
VC18 Danya Abrams	1.00	2.50
VC19 Reggie Freeman	1.00	2.50
VC20 Tony Gonzalez	1.00	2.50

1997 Score Board Talk N' Sports

This product features phone cards with a couple twists, including trivia contests to win memorabilia and to check current sports scores. The 50-card regular set includes stars and prospects from all four major team sports. According to Score Board, a total of 1,500 sequentially numbered cases were produced.

COMPLETE SET (50)	4.00	10.00
24 Clyde Drexler	.15	.40
25 Scottie Pippen	.15	.40
26 Hakeem Olajuwon	.15	.40
27 Alonzo Mourning	.10	.30
28 Joe Smith	.08	.25
29 Antonio McDyess	.07	.20
30 Allen Iverson	.50	1.25
31 Kerry Kittles	.07	.20
32 Stephon Marbury	.15	.40
33 Marcus Camby	.07	.20
34 Ray Allen	.20	.50
35 Shareef Abdur-Rahim	.15	.40
36 Kobe Bryant	.75	2.00
37 Antoine Walker	.15	.40
38 Glenn Robinson	.08	.25
39 Dikembe Mutombo	.10	.30

1997 Score Board Talk N' Sports Essentials

These 10 plastic acetate cards were randomly inserted at a rate of 1:24 Talk N' Sports packs.

COMPLETE SET (10)	25.00	60.00
E2 Scottie Pippen	3.00	8.00
E5 Clyde Drexler	2.50	6.00
E6 Kobe Bryant	8.00	20.00

1997 Score Board Talk N' Sports Phone Cards $1

The $1 phone cards were inserted one per pack. The checklist of this 50-card set parallels the regular set. The phone time on these $1 phone cards could be combined. They expired on 7/31/1998.

COMPLETE SET (50)	8.00	20.00
*PIN NUMBER REVEALED: HALF VALUE		

1997 Score Board Talk N' Sports Phone Cards $10

These $10 phone cards allow users to choose trivia contests to win memorabilia in lieu of the phone time. Entrants who choose the trivia contest forfeit their phone time, but if they answer 9 of 10 questions, they win a baseball bat autographed by one of these six players: Willie Mays, Hank Aaron, Barry Bonds, Ken Griffey Jr., Pete Rose or Chipper Jones. The $10 cards were inserted at a rate of 1:12 packs and expired on 5/20/1998. Each card is sequentially numbered out of 3,960.

COMPLETE SET (10)	12.00	30.00
*PIN NUMBER REVEALED: HALF VALUE		
2 Hakeem Olajuwon	1.25	3.00
9 Clyde Drexler	1.25	3.00
10 Scottie Pippen	2.00	5.00

1997 Score Board Talk N' Sports Phone Cards $20

These $20 phone cards allow users to choose sports updates in lieu of the phone time. The time on the card can be used interchangably for either phone calls or sports updates. The $20 cards were inserted at a rate of 1:36 packs and expired on 7/31/1998. Each card is sequentially numbered out of 1,440.

COMPLETE SET (10)	25.00	60.00
*PIN NUMBER REVEALED: HALF VALUE		
2 Scottie Pippen	3.00	8.00
5 Clyde Drexler	2.50	6.00
6 Kobe Bryant	8.00	20.00

1995 Signature Rookies Auto-Phonex Promo

This card measures approximately 2 1/4" by 3 1/3" and is on a glossy phone card plastic stock. On a black background, two pictures of Jerry Stackhouse in a North Carolina jersey are shown. His name and "1 of 40,000" are printed on the top of the card while "$1,000 Promo" is printed vertically on the left side. The Signatures Rookies Auto Phonex and Sprint logos adorn the bottom. The back is black and white and has a blurb promoting the forthcoming set that was actually never distributed. The word "Promo" is written at the top. The card is unnumbered.

COMPLETE SET (1)	1.20	3.00
NNO Jerry Stackhouse	1.25	3.00

1995 Signature Rookies Club Promos

S4 Wesley Person	.60	1.50

1995 Signature Rookies Sports Slammers Stackers

Printed on 18-point card stock, this set of 40 stackers and 5 slammers POGs combines football and basketball stars in a game. Each pack contained five sports stackers as well as one rule card.

3 Eric Montross BK	.15	.40
8 Brian Grant BK	.15	.40
9 Monty Williams BK	.15	.40
12 Eddie Jones BK	.50	1.25
20 Wesley Person BK	.15	.40
24 Wesley Person BK	.15	.40
27 Eddie Jones BK	.50	1.25
28 Monty Williams BK	.15	.40
31 Eric Montross BK	.15	.40
36 Brian Grant BK	.15	.40
S3 Eric Montross BK Masher	.30	.75
S5 Eddie Jones BK Jammer	.60	1.50

1995 Signature Rookies Autobilia

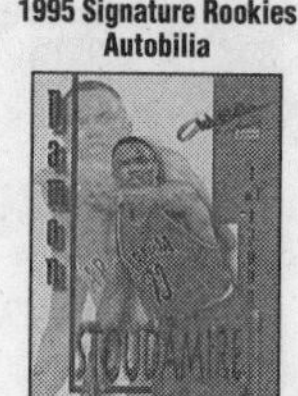

This 30-card set measures the standard size. The fronts feature a small color action player image on a white background with a larger faded duplicate image as a shadow. The player's first name is printed in gold foil down the side with his last name across the bottom. The backs carry the player's name, position, college statistics, biographical information, and player facts on a background of a faded color action player photo. This is a breakdown of memorablia signed: Players signed 1,000 cards, 3,000 photos, 500 pennants, 400 team balls, 350 hats, 24 practice jerseys, and 550 basketballs. Jerry Stackhouse and Kevin Garnett signed 250 Sports Illustrateds.

COMPLETE SET (30)	2.50	6.00
1 Joe Smith	.25	.60
2 Antonio McDyess	.30	.75
3 Jerry Stackhouse	.40	1.00
4 Rasheed Wallace	.40	1.00
5 Kevin Garnett	1.00	2.50
6 Bryant Reeves	.12	.30
7 Damon Stoudamire	.30	.75
8 Shawn Respert	.12	.30
9 Ed O'Bannon	.12	.30
10 Kurt Thomas	.12	.30
11 Gary Trent	.12	.30
12 Cherokee Parks	.12	.30
13 Corliss Williamson	.12	.30
14 Eric Williams	.12	.30
15 Brent Barry	.20	.50
16 Alan Henderson	.12	.30
17 Bob Sura	.12	.30
18 Theo Ratliff	.20	.50
19 Randolph Childress	.12	.30
20 Jason Caffey	.12	.30
21 Michael Finley	.40	1.00
22 George Zidek	.12	.30
23 Travis Best	.12	.30
24 Loren Meyer	.12	.30
25 David Vaughn	.12	.30
26 Sherrell Ford	.12	.30
27 Mario Bennett	.12	.30
28 Greg Ostertag	.12	.30
29 Cory Alexander	.12	.30
NNO Checklist	.12	.30

1995 Signature Rookies Autobilia Autographs

1 Joe Smith	2.50	6.00
2 Antonio McDyess	5.00	12.00
3 Jerry Stackhouse	8.00	20.00
4 Rasheed Wallace	8.00	20.00
5 Kevin Garnett	20.00	50.00
6 Bryant Reeves	1.25	3.00
7 Damon Stoudamire	4.00	10.00
8 Shawn Respert	1.25	3.00
9 Ed O'Bannon	1.25	3.00
10 Kurt Thomas	1.25	3.00
11 Gary Trent	1.25	3.00
12 Cherokee Parks	1.25	3.00
13 Corliss Williamson	1.25	3.00
14 Eric Williams	1.25	3.00
15 Brent Barry	2.00	5.00
16 Alan Henderson	1.25	3.00
17 Bob Sura	1.25	3.00
18 Theo Ratliff	2.00	5.00
19 Randolph Childress	1.25	3.00
20 Jason Caffey	1.25	3.00
21 Michael Finley	6.00	15.00
22 George Zidek	1.25	3.00
23 Travis Best	1.25	3.00
24 Loren Meyer	1.25	3.00
25 David Vaughn	1.25	3.00
26 Sherrell Ford	1.25	3.00
27 Mario Bennett	1.25	3.00
28 Greg Ostertag	1.25	3.00
29 Cory Alexander	1.25	3.00

1995 Signature Rookies Autobilia Garnett

Randomly inserted in packs, this five-card set measures the standard size. The fronts feature two different color action player images on a black background. The player's name, Kevin Garnett, is printed in gold foil on the left. "AutoBilia" is printed in dark pink across the top. The backs carry the card name, player's name, position, career statistics, and a player fact on a background of a player photo.

COMPLETE SET (5)	6.00	15.00
COMMON GARNETT (G1-G5)	1.50	4.00
G4P Kevin Garnett PROMO	4.00	10.00
G5P Kevin Garnett PROMO	4.00	10.00

1995 Signature Rookies Autobilia Stackhouse

Randomly inserted in packs, this five-card set measures the standard size. The fronts feature two different color action player images on a black background. The player's name, Jerry Stackhouse, is printed in gold foil on the left. "AutoBilia" is printed in dark pink across the top. The backs carry the card name, player's name, position, career statistics, and a player fact on a background of a player photo. There were also autographed promo cards available from this set, hand numbered out of 500.

COMPLETE SET (5)	1.50	4.00
COMMON CARD (S1-S5)	.40	1.00
S2AU Jerry Stackhouse Promo Auto/500	8.00	20.00
S4AU Jerry Stackhouse Promo Auto/500	8.00	20.00
S5AU Jerry Stackhouse Promo Auto/500	8.00	20.00

1995 Signature Rookies Draft Day

This 50-card set measures the standard size. The fronts carry a borderless color player action photo with the player's name and a player's silhouette is printed in gold in a faded black stripe at the bottom. The backs carry three small additional action player photos with the player's name, position, biographical information, career highlights, college attended, and statistics. 38,000 of each card was issued.

COMPLETE SET (50)	1.50	4.00
1 Donny Marshall	.10	.25
2 Mario Bennett	.10	.25
3 Dan Cross	.10	.25
4 Devin Gray	.10	.25
5 Dwight Stewart	.10	.25
6 Jerome Allen	.10	.25
7 Travis Best	.10	.25
8 Tyus Edney	.10	.25
9 Mark Davis	.10	.25
10 Michael Finley	.30	.75
11 Gary Trent	.10	.25
12 Julius Michalik	.10	.25
13 Clint McDaniel	.10	.25
14 Sherrell Ford	.10	.25
15 Junior Burrough	.10	.25
16 Bryan Collins	.10	.25
17 Andrew DeClercq	.10	.25
18 Glen Whisby	.10	.25
19 Terrence Rencher	.10	.25
20 Eric Snow	.10	.25
21 Alan Henderson	.10	.25
22 Bob Sura	.10	.25
23 James Forrest	.10	.25
24 Jimmy King	.10	.25
25 Scotty Thurman	.10	.25
26 Matt Maloney	.10	.25
27 Paul O'Liney	.10	.25
28 Lazelle Durden	.10	.25
29 Eric Williams	.10	.25
30 Tom Kleinschmidt	.10	.25
31 Cory Alexander	.10	.25
32 James Scott	.10	.25
33 Michael McDonald	.10	.25
34 Randy Rutherford	.10	.25
35 Donald Williams	.10	.25
36 Kurt Thomas	.10	.25
37 Loren Meyer	.10	.25
38 Donnie Boyce	.10	.25
39 Michael Hawkins	.10	.25
40 Lou Roe	.10	.25
41 Larry Skyes	.10	.25
42 Cuonzo Martin	.10	.25
43 Jason Caffey	.10	.25
44 Scott Highmark	.10	.25
45 Lawrence Moten	.10	.25
46 Anthony Pelle	.10	.25
47 Randolph Childress	.10	.25
48 Ray Jackson	.10	.25
49 Corey Beck	.10	.25
50 Fred Hoiberg	.10	.25
KG Kevin Garnett AU/260	50.00	100.00
NNO Checklist	.10	.25

1995 Signature Rookies Draft Day Signatures

Inserted one per '95 Signature Rookies Draft Day pack, these 50 standard-size cards are the same as 1995 Draft Day only with the player's signature on the front. All 50 players in the set signed 7750 cards. If the cards weren't ready when this product was shipped a "trade coupon" was inserted into the packs. An autograph card or trade coupon was inserted into every pack.

1 Donny Marshall	1.00	2.50
2 Mario Bennett	1.00	2.50

3 Dan Cross 1.00 2.50
4 Devin Gray 1.00 2.50
5 Dwight Stewart 1.00 2.50
6 Jerome Allen 1.00 2.50
7 Travis Best 1.00 2.50
8 Tyus Edney 1.00 2.50
9 Mark Davis 1.00 2.50
10 Michael Finley/1050 4.00 10.00
11 Gary Trent 1.00 2.50
12 Julius Michalik 1.00 2.50
13 Clint McDaniel 1.00 2.50
14 Sherrell Ford 1.00 2.50
15 Junior Burrough 1.00 2.50
16 Bryan Collins 1.00 2.50
17 Andrew DeClercq 1.00 2.50
18 Glen Whisby 1.00 2.50
19 Terrence Rencher 1.00 2.50
20 Eric Snow 1.00 2.50
21 Alan Henderson 1.00 2.50
22 Bob Sura 1.00 2.50
23 James Forrest 1.00 2.50
24 Jimmy King 1.00 2.50
25 Scotty Thurman 1.00 2.50
26 Matt Maloney 1.00 2.50
27 Paul O'Liney 1.00 2.50
28 Lazelle Durden 1.00 2.50
29 Eric Williams 1.00 2.50
30 Tom Kleinschmidt 1.00 2.50
31 Cory Alexander 1.00 2.50
32 James Scott 1.00 2.50
33 Michael McDonald 1.00 2.50
34 Randy Rutherford 1.00 2.50
35 Donald Williams 1.00 2.50
36 Kurt Thomas 1.00 2.50
37 Loren Meyer 1.00 2.50
38 Donnie Boyce 1.00 2.50
39 Michael Hawkins 1.00 2.50
40 Lou Roe 1.00 2.50
41 Larry Skyes 1.00 2.50
42 Cuonzo Martin 1.00 2.50
43 Jason Caffey 1.00 2.50
44 Scott Highmark 1.00 2.50
45 Lawrence Moten 1.00 2.50
46 Anthony Pelle 1.00 2.50
47 Randolph Childress 1.00 2.50
48 Ray Jackson 1.00 2.50
49 Corey Beck 1.00 2.50
50 Fred Hoiberg 1.00 2.50
PROMO Michael Finley/1050 5.00 12.00

1995 Signature Rookies Draft Day Abdul Jabbar

Inserted at a rate of one per 87 packs, these 5 standard-size cards consist of different action portraits of Kareem Abdul Jabbar on the front. All the cards have a black stripe down the left side with his name printed in gold. The backs carry his different career highlights and collegiate stats printed over another color action photo. There is a signed version of each of these cards. Abdul-Jabbar signed 105 of each card.

COMPLETE SET (5) 3.00 8.00
COMMON KAREEM (K1-K5) .75 2.00

1995 Signature Rookies Draft Day Abdul Jabbar Signatures

COMMON CARD (K1-K5) 20.00 50.00
STATED PRINT RUN 105 SERIAL #'d SETS

1995 Signature Rookies Draft Day Draft Gems

Randomly inserted at a rate of 1 per 22 packs, these 10 standard-size cards consist of five player's with two cards each. The fronts feature two different color player action photos. The larger background one is faded while the smaller foreground one is bright. The player's last name is in big gold letters above the bottom of a thin red "L" on the left with his first name printed in red above it. The backs carry the player's name, biographical information, career highlights, statistics, and college printed over a faded color action photo with part of the photo brightly displayed inside a diamond-shaped frame. The cards were announced with a print run of 38,000, are also numbered with a "DG" prefix on the card backs.

COMPLETE SET (10) 4.00 10.00
DG1 Jerry Stackhouse 1.00 2.50
DG2 Jerry Stackhouse 1.00 2.50
DG3 Antonio McDyess .75 2.00
DG4 Antonio McDyess .75 2.00
DG5 Cherokee Parks .30 .75
DG6 Cherokee Parks .30 .75
DG7 Joe Smith .60 1.50
DG8 Joe Smith .60 1.50
DG9 Rasheed Wallace 1.00 2.50
DG10 Rasheed Wallace 1.00 2.50
BP Kevin Garnett PROMO 4.00 10.00
DG2P Jerry Stackhouse PROMO 2.00 5.00

1995 Signature Rookies Draft Day Draft Gems Signatures

Inserted at a rate of 1 per 87 packs, these 10 cards are the same as the 1995 Draft Day Draft Gems cards except for the player's signature on the front. 525 of each card was signed.

DG1 Jerry Stackhouse 10.00 25.00
DG2 Jerry Stackhouse 10.00 25.00
DG3 Antonio McDyess 6.00 15.00
DG4 Antonio McDyess 6.00 15.00
DG5 Cherokee Parks 2.00 5.00
DG6 Cherokee Parks 2.00 5.00
DG7 Joe Smith 4.00 10.00
DG8 Joe Smith 4.00 10.00
DG9 Rasheed Wallace 10.00 25.00
DG10 Rasheed Wallace 10.00 25.00

1995 Signature Rookies Draft Day Reflections

Inserted at a rate of 1 per 18 packs, these 5 cards measure the standard size. The fronts feature borderless player action photos with the player's name and a player silhouette printed in gold in a vertical black stripe on the left. The backs carry the player's name, college, biographical information, career highlights and statistics along with another action player photo and a narrowly-cropped version of the front photo. The cards are numbered with a "R" prefix and have announced numbering out of 15,250.

COMPLETE SET (5) .75 2.00
R1 Brian Grant .30 .75
R2 Wesley Person .25 .60
R3 Eric Montross .25 .60
R4 Juwan Howard .40 1.00
R5 Eddie Jones .50 1.25

1995 Signature Rookies Draft Day Reflections Signatures

Inserted at a rate of 1 per 346 packs, these 5 cards are the same as the 1995 Draft Day Reflections only with the player's signature on the front. Each player signed 250 of these cards.

COMPLETE SET (5) 15.00 40.00
R1 Brian Grant 4.00 10.00
R2 Wesley Person 4.00 10.00
R3 Eric Montross 4.00 10.00
R4 Juwan Howard 6.00 15.00
R5 Eddie Jones 10.00 25.00

1995 Signature Rookies Draft Day Show Stoppers

Inserted at a rate of 1 per 3 packs, these 25 cards measure the standard size. The set consists of five cards each of five different players. The fronts feature color action player photos with a border resembling a roll of film. The player's name is printed in gold in a black bar at the bottom with a gold player silhouette. The backs carry another color action photo, the player's name, position, biographical information, career highlights, college, and statistics over a background of game action. Each card has an announced print run of 11,000.

COMPLETE SET (25) 5.00 12.00
B1 Bryant Reeves .40 1.00
B2 Bryant Reeves .40 1.00
B3 Bryant Reeves .40 1.00
B4 Bryant Reeves .40 1.00
B5 Bryant Reeves .40 1.00
C1 Corliss Williamson .40 1.00
C2 Corliss Williamson .40 1.00
C3 Corliss Williamson .40 1.00
C4 Corliss Williamson .40 1.00
C5 Corliss Williamson .40 1.00
D1 Damon Stoudamire 1.00 2.50
D2 Damon Stoudamire 1.00 2.50
D3 Damon Stoudamire 1.00 2.50
D4 Damon Stoudamire 1.00 2.50
D5 Damon Stoudamire 1.00 2.50
E1 Ed O'Bannon .40 1.00
E2 Ed O'Bannon .40 1.00
E3 Ed O'Bannon .40 1.00
E4 Ed O'Bannon .40 1.00
E5 Ed O'Bannon .40 1.00
S1 Shawn Respert .40 1.00
S2 Shawn Respert .40 1.00
S3 Shawn Respert .40 1.00
S4 Shawn Respert .40 1.00
S5 Shawn Respert .40 1.00
P2 Bryant Reeves
Mail In Promo
P3 Shawn Respert .40 1.00
Mail In Promo

1995 Signature Rookies Draft Day Show Stoppers Signatures

Inserted at a rate of 1 per 18 packs, these 25 cards are the same as the Draft Day Show Stoppers except for the player's signature on the front. 1050 of each card was signed.

B1 Bryant Reeves 2.00 5.00
B2 Bryant Reeves 2.00 5.00
B3 Bryant Reeves 2.00 5.00
B4 Bryant Reeves 2.00 5.00
B5 Bryant Reeves 2.00 5.00
C1 Corliss Williamson 2.00 5.00
C2 Corliss Williamson 2.00 5.00
C3 Corliss Williamson 2.00 5.00
C4 Corliss Williamson 2.00 5.00
C5 Corliss Williamson 2.00 5.00
D1 Damon Stoudamire 5.00 12.00
D2 Damon Stoudamire 5.00 12.00
D3 Damon Stoudamire 5.00 12.00
D4 Damon Stoudamire 5.00 12.00
D5 Damon Stoudamire 5.00 12.00
E1 Ed O'Bannon 2.00 5.00
E2 Ed O'Bannon 2.00 5.00
E3 Ed O'Bannon 2.00 5.00
E4 Ed O'Bannon 2.00 5.00
E5 Ed O'Bannon 2.00 5.00
S1 Shawn Respert 2.00 5.00
S2 Shawn Respert 2.00 5.00
S3 Shawn Respert 2.00 5.00
S4 Shawn Respert 2.00 5.00
S5 Shawn Respert 2.00 5.00

1995 Signature Rookies Draft Day Swat Team

Inserted at a rate of 1 per 3 packs, these 5 cards measure the standard size. The fronts feature borderless color action player photos. The player's name is printed in green above gold sunbeams in the lower right. The backs carry the player's name, position, biographical information, college, career highlights, and statistics. The cards are numbered with a "ST" prefix. Each card has an announced print run of 12,500.

COMPLETE SET (5) .75 2.00
ST1 Tony Maroney .30 .75
ST2 Greg Ostertag .30 .75
ST3 George Zidek .30 .75
ST4 Constantin Popa .30 .75
ST5 Theo Ratliff .50 1.25

1995 Signature Rookies Draft Day Swat Team Signatures

Inserted at a rate of 1 per 18 packs, these 5 cards are identical to the regular Draft Day Swat Team with the exception of the player's autograph and number of signed cards across the front above the player's name. 5,200 of each card was signed.

ST1 Tony Maroney 1.00 2.50
ST2 Greg Ostertag 1.00 2.50
ST3 George Zidek 1.00 2.50
ST4 Constantin Popa 1.00 2.50
ST5 Theo Ratliff 3.00 8.00

1995 Signature Rookies Fame and Fortune

The 1995 Fame and Fortune set was issued in one series totalling 100 cards and featured NBA and NFL draft picks. Cards were distributed in eight-card packs. Five insert card sets were produced with the set and included Collector's Pick, Top 5, Erstad, Star Squad and #1 Pick. The first 48 cards are basketball draft picks and the remaining 52 are football picks. Fronts have full-color action cutout photos with a black background with either a football or basketball. The player's first name is printed in gold foil horizontally while his last name is printed twice vertically in both gold foil and a larger green type on the left side. Backs have another action shot that is seprated with a color screen process. Backs include college statistics, a short biography and a player profile. The set is sequenced in alphabetical order.

COMPLETE SET (100) 5.00 12.00
1 Cory Alexander .07 .20
2 Jerome Allen .07 .20
3 Brent Barry .08 .25
4 Mario Bennett .07 .20
5 Travis Best .08 .25
6 Donie Boyce .07 .20
7 Junior Burrough .07 .20
8 Jason Caffey .08 .25
9 Chris Carr .07 .20
10 Randolph Childress .07 .20
11 Mark Davis .07 .20
12 Andrew DeClerco .07 .20
13 Tyus Edney .08 .25
14 Michael Finley .20 .50
15 Sherell Ford .07 .20
16 Kevin Garnett .60 1.50
17 Alan Henderson .08 .25
18 Fred Hoiberg .07 .20
19 Jimmy King .07 .20
20 Donny Marshall .07 .20
21 Cuonzo Martin .07 .20
22 Michael McDonald .07 .20
23 Anthony McDyess .20 .50
24 Loren Meyer .07 .20
25 Lawrence Moten .07 .20
26 Ed O'Bannon .07 .20
27 Greg Ostertag .08 .25
28 Cherokee Parks .07 .20
29 Anthony Pelle .07 .20
30 Constantin Popa .07 .20
31 Theo Ratliff .08 .25
32 Bryant Reeves .08 .25
33 Don Reid .07 .20
34 Terrance Rencher .07 .20
35 Shawn Respert .07 .20
36 Lou Roe .07 .20
37 Joe Smith .20 .50
38 Eric Snow .08 .25
39 Jerry Stackhouse .30 .75
40 Damon Stoudamire .25 .60
41 Bob Sura .08 .25
42 Kurt Thomas .07 .20
43 Gary Trent .08 .25
44 David Vaughn .07 .20
45 Rasheed Wallace .30 .75
46 Eric Williams .07 .20
47 Corliss Williamson .08 .25
48 George Zidek .07 .20

1995 Signature Rookies Fame and Fortune #1 Pick

Randomly inserted in packs at a rate of three in 16, this five-card set features the No. 1 pick in the NHL, the NFL, The NBA and Major leagues. The No. 5 card pictures all four of the picks. Fronts have a psychedelic background and feature the player in a full-color action cutout. "#1 Pick" appears in a sky blue and green type at the top and the bottom has a gold foil strip that contains the player's name, or names in the case of the #5 card, in raised white letters. Backs continue with the psychedelic background and picture the player or players in action. Player stats and biographies also appear on the back.

COMPLETE SET (5) 1.00 2.50
P4 Joe Smith .20 .50
P5 Brian Berard .30 .75
K-Jana Carter
Darin Erstad
Joe Smith

1995 Signature Rookies Fame and Fortune Collectors Pick

Randomly inserted in packs at a rate of one in 16, this 10-card set highlights the first five NBA picks and the first five NFL picks. Fronts are borderless with white backgrounds with "Collectors" on the top third and "Pick" in a vertically stretched type on the rest of the front. The player is pictured in a full-color action cutout in the foreground. His name is printed vertically in gold foil on the lower left. Backs have a small player head shot, and a faded screen action shot for a background. Player biography, statistics and profile appear on the back.

COMPLETE SET (100) 4.00 10.00
B2 Ed O'Bannon .25 .60
B3 Cherokee Parks .25 .60
B4 Bryant Reeves .30 .75
B7 Joe Smith .30 .75
B8 Jerry Stackhouse 1.00 2.50
B10 Rasheed Wallace 1.00 2.50

1995 Signature Rookies Fame and Fortune Red Hot Rookies

This 10-card set randomly inserted in packs of 1995 Signature Rookies Fame and Fortune. Each card was printed on Red foil stock and include a photo of one football or basketball draft pick from 1995.

COMPLETE SET (10) 5.00 12.00
R2 Jerry Stackhouse .60 1.50
R4 Damon Stoudamire .60 1.50
R6 Kevin Garnett 1.25 3.00
R8 Michael Finley .40 1.00
R10 Joe Smith .20 .50

1995 Signature Rookies Fame and Fortune Top Five

Randomly inserted in packs at a rate of one in four, this five-card set focuses on basketball's '95 draft. "Top Five" is printed in an "L" pattern in red block type with a blue shadow on the front. A full-color action player shot appears also and his name is printed in a backwards "L" pattern in gold type on the top right. A player biography and profile are printed in gold foil on the back against a purple background. A full-color action shot is placed on the right side of the back.

COMPLETE SET (100) 2.50 6.00
T1 Joe Smith .20 .50
T2 Antonio McDyess .40 1.00
T3 Jerry Stackhouse .60 1.50
T4 Rasheed Wallace .60 1.50
T5 Kevin Garnett 1.25 3.00

1994 Signature Rookies Gold Standard

This multi-sport set consists of 100 standard-size cards. The fronts feature color action players photos with a circular gold foil seal at the upper left corner. The player's name appears on a diagonal black stripe edged by yellow. The horizontal backs carry a narrowly-cropped closeup photo and, on a ghosted panel, biography and player profile. The set is subdivided according to sport as follows: basketball (1-25), football (26-50), baseball (51-75), and hockey (76-100). Each sport is sequenced in alphabetical order.

COMPLETE SET (100) 5.00 12.00
1 Derrick Alston .07 .20
2 Damon Bailey .07 .20
3 Bill Curley .07 .20
4 Yinka Dare .07 .20
5 Rodney Dent .07 .20
6 Brian Grant .10 .30
7 Juwan Howard .30 .75
8 Askia Jones .07 .20
9 Eddie Jones .25 .60
10 Donyell Marshall .15 .40
11 Aaron McKie .10 .30
12 Greg Minor .07 .20
13 Eric Montross .07 .20
14 Wesley Person .10 .30
15 Eric Piatkowski .07 .20
16 Jalen Rose .25 .60
17 Clifford Rozier .07 .20
18 Dickey Simpkins .07 .20
19 Deon Thomas .07 .20
20 Brooks Thompson .07 .20
21 B.J. Tyler .07 .20
22 Charlie Ward .10 .30
23 Monty Williams .07 .20
24 Dontonio Wingfield .07 .20
25 Sharone Wright .07 .20

1994 Signature Rookies Gold Standard Facsimile

This 20-card standard-size set was inserted one per pack. The fronts display full-bleed color player photos. A facsimile autograph, the "Gold Standard" seal, and another emblem are gold-foil stamped on the fronts. Also a diagonal line carrying the player's name (also in gold foil) is edged by gold foil stripes. On the left side, the horizontal backs show a narrowly-cropped closeup of the front photo. The remainder of the backs carry biography, statistics, and player profile, all on a ghosted background. In addition to card number, each back carries a serial number.

COMPLETE SET (20) 5.00 12.00
GS9 Juwan Howard .75 2.00
GS12 Eric Montross .60 1.50
GS14 Donyell Marshall .75 2.00
GS16 Sharone Wright .30 .75
GS19 Clifford Rozier .30 .75
GS20 Jalen Rose .60 1.50

1994 Signature Rookies Gold Standard HOF

COMPLETE SET (24) 8.00 20.00
STATED PRINT RUN 20,000 SETS
ISSUED VIA MAIL REDEMPTION
HOF1 Nate Archibald .50 1.25
HOF2 Rick Barry .60 1.50
HOF4 Bob Cousy 1.00 2.50
HOF5 Dave Cowens .50 1.25
HOF6 Dave DeBusschere .60 1.50
HOF8 Walt Frazier .60 1.50
HOF11 Connie Hawkins .50 1.25
HOF12 Elvin Hayes .60 1.50
HOF19 Bob Pettit .50 1.25
HOF22 Bill Walton .75 2.00

1994 Signature Rookies Gold Standard HOF Autographs

Inserted at a rate of one per box, this 24-card standard-sized set is identical to the regular set except for the signatures inscribed across the front and the expression "Hall of Fame" gold-foil stamped at the upper left. Each card is numbered out of 2500. The collector could obtain unsigned versions by mailing in a redemption card that was randomly inserted in packs. These redemption cards are valued at 1/10 the value of the signed cards. The cards are numbered with an "HOF" prefix.

1 Nate Archibald 6.00 15.00
2 Rick Barry 8.00 20.00
4 Bob Cousy 8.00 20.00
5 Dave Cowens 6.00 15.00
6 Dave DeBusschere 30.00 60.00
8 Walt Frazier 8.00 20.00
11 Connie Hawkins 8.00 20.00
12 Elvin Hayes 8.00 20.00
19 Bob Pettit 8.00 20.00
22 Bill Walton 8.00 20.00

1994 Signature Rookies Gold Standard Legends

This five-card standard size set was randomly inserted into packs. This set has great athletes past and presents from all sports. The fronts have the word "Legends" on the top and the player's name on the bottom printed in silver ink against a black background. Meanwhile, the player's photo is shown against a gold background. The backs contains the player's photo on the left quarter with a biography about that player on the remainder of the card.

COMPLETE SET (5) 3.00 8.00
L1 Isiah Thomas .40 1.00
L2 Larry Bird 1.25 3.00

1994 Signature Rookies Gold Standard Promos

COMPLETE SET (5) .75 2.00
ANNOUNCED PRINT RUN 10000
P1 Donyell Marshall .20 .50
P2 Jalen Rose .20 .50

1995 Signature Rookies Kromax Promos

These standard-size promo cards were given away to preview the design of the Kro-Max series. On a purple and black background, the metallic front features a color player cutout. The player's name is printed parallel to the left edge, while the Kro-Max emblem adorns the bottom of the card. On a brightly neon-colored background, the backs carry a player cutout, biography, player profile, and complete collegiate statistics.

COMPLETE SET (2) .40 1.00
P1 Donyell Marshall .30 .75
P2 Juwan Howard .50 1.25

1995 Signature Rookies Kromax

Signature Rookies produced 1,995 eight-box cases, and every box contained one randomly inserted autographed card of a First Round Pick, a Super Acrylium player, or a Flash From the Past star. (SRP $5). Insert sets include Flash From the Past, available one in every six packs, Super Acrylium, which were inserted in the ratio of one every 12 packs, and First Rounders, which were available one every 19 packs. There were no more than 10,000 Super Acrylium and 2,500 First Rounders and Flash From the Past of each player made. Each box of Kro-max included one autograph from one of the three insert sets. One group of players autographed 1,050 each of their cards (Dumas, Montross, Person, Rose, and Rozier). A second group autographed 2,100 each of their cards (Curley, Dare, Grant, Jones, McKie, Piatkowski, Williams, and Wright). The front features the player's name on the left side and the Kromax logo across the bottom of the card. The player's image is in full color, hwile the rest of the scene is a negative print. Backs contain biographical information, a player profile, and college statistics. Members received one of 1,995 uncut sheets, featuring cards 1-40 and accompanied by a certificate of authenticity.

COMPLETE SET (50) 1.25 3.00
1 Donyell Marshall .05 .15
2 Juwan Howard .10 .25
3 Sharone Wright .05 .15
4 Brian Grant .07 .20
5 Eric Montross .05 .15
6 Eddie Jones .12 .30
7 Jalen Rose .12 .30
8 Yinka Dare .05 .15
9 Eric Piatkowski .07 .20
10 Clifford Rozier .05 .15
11 Aaron McKie .05 .15
12 Eric Mobley .05 .15
13 Tony Dumas .05 .15
14 B.J. Tyler .05 .15
15 Dickey Simpkins .05 .15
16 Bill Curley .05 .15
17 Wesley Person .05 .15
18 Monty Williams .05 .15
19 Greg Minor .05 .15
20 Charlie Ward .05 .15
21 Brooks Thompson .05 .15
22 Deon Thomas .05 .15
23 Howard Eisley .05 .15
24 Rodney Dent .05 .15
25 Jim McIlvaine .05 .15
26 Derrick Alston .05 .15
27 Gaylon Nickerson .05 .15
28 Michael Smith .05 .15
29 Andrei Fetisov .05 .15
30 Dontonio Wingfield .05 .15
31 Anthony Miller .05 .15
32 Jeff Webster .05 .15
33 Shawnelle Scott .05 .15
34 Damon Bailey .05 .15
35 Jevon Crudup .05 .15
36 Lawrence Funderburke .05 .15
37 Anthony Goldwire .05 .15
38 Adrian Autry .05 .15
39 Doremus Bennerman .05 .15
40 Melvin Booker .05 .15
41 Dwayne Fontana .05 .15
42 Travis Ford .05 .15
43 Kenny Harris .05 .15
44 Askia Jones .05 .15
45 Jason Kidd .15 .40
46 Bill McCaffrey .05 .15
47 Kevin Rankin .05 .15
48 Melvin Simon .05 .15
49 Glenn Robinson .10 .25
50 Kendrick Warren .05 .15
NNO Checklist .05 .15

1995 Signature Rookies Kromax First Rounders

This 10-card standard-size set is one of three different insert sets randomly seeded in seven-card packs. The First Rounder title is at the lower left corner while the player's name is on the bottom in bright colors. The player's photo is projected in front of a wave effect. 2,500 of each card were produced. The cards are numbered with a "FR" prefix.

COMPLETE SET (10) 4.00 10.00
FR1 Donyell Marshall .60 1.50
FR2 Juwan Howard 1.00 2.50
FR3 Sharone Wright .60 1.50
FR4 Brian Grant .75 2.00
FR5 Eric Montross .60 1.50
FR6 Eddie Jones 1.25 3.00
FR7 Jalen Rose 1.25 3.00
FR8 Yinka Dare .60 1.50
FR9 B.J. Tyler .60 1.50
FR10 Charlie Ward .60 1.50

1995 Signature Rookies Kromax Flash From The Past

This 10-card standard-size set is one of three different insert sets randomly seeded in seven-card packs. Fronts feature former NBA greats in air-brushed uniforms with his name under the photo. Backs contain a player biography. The cards are numbered with a "FP" prefix.

COMPLETE SET (10) 5.00 12.00
FP1 Bob Cousy 1.00 2.50
FP2 Larry Bird 2.00 5.00
FP3 Walt Frazier .60 1.50
FP4 Rick Barry .60 1.50
FP5 Isiah Thomas .60 1.50
FP6 Tiny Archibald .60 1.50
FP7 Dave DeBusschere .60 1.50
FP8 Dave Cowens .60 1.50
FP9 Elvin Hayes .60 1.50
FP10 Kareem Abdul-Jabbar 1.00 2.50

1995 Signature Rookies Kromax Flash From The Past Signatures

All players signed 1,050 of their cards, except for Abdul-Jabbar (1,550), Bird (100), and Thomas (100). The fronts feature former NBA greats in air-brushed uniform with his name underneath. Backs contain a biography about the player pictured and on the bottom the front photo is cropped so the face of the player is shown again. Elvin Hayes (FP9) and Bob Cousy (FP1) did not sign their cards.

FP2 Larry Bird/100 125.00 200.00
FP3 Walt Frazier/1050 6.00 15.00
FP4 Rick Barry/1050 6.00 15.00
FP5 Isiah Thomas/100 15.00 40.00
FP6 Tiny Archibald/1050 6.00 15.00
FP7 Dave DeBusschere/1050 30.00 60.00
FP8 Dave Cowens/1050 6.00 15.00
FP10 Kareem Abdul-Jabbar/1550 25.00 50.00

1995 Signature Rookies Kromax Jumbos

Measuring 3 1/2" by 5", this 10-card set captures some of the 1994 NBA first round draft picks. The players pictured on the fronts stand out on brightly-colored metallic backgrounds. The production figures ("1 of 3,300") are printed in silver along the left edge, while the player's name is printed toward the bottom of the card. On a brightly neon-colored background, the backs carry a player cutout and player profile. Cards number 11 and 12 were only available through a wrapper redemption program. The values on cards numbers 1 through 10 are the same whether they are promo cards or available through the wrapper redemption program.

COMPLETE SET (12) 4.00 10.00
J1 Juwan Howard 1.00 2.50
J2 Donyell Marshall .60 1.50
J3 Sharone Wright .60 1.50
J4 Brian Grant .75 2.00
J5 Eric Montross .60 1.50
J6 Eddie Jones 1.25 3.00
J7 Jalen Rose 1.25 3.00
J8 Yinka Dare .60 1.50
J9 B.J. Tyler .60 1.50
J10 Charlie Ward .60 1.50
J11 Clifford Rozier .60 1.50
J12 Wesley Person .60 1.50

1995 Signature Rookies Kromax Signatures

Five players signed cards for Signature Rookies for inserts in Kromax boxes. The cards are listed below in alphabetical order by player's last name. Next to the players name is how many cards they signed.

1 Bill Curley/2100 1.25 3.00
2 Yinka Dare/2100 1.25 3.00
3 Eric Montross/1050 4.00 10.00
4 Wesley Person/1050 1.25 3.00
5 Sharone Wright/2100 1.25 3.00

1995 Signature Rookies Kromax Super Acrylium Promo

This standard-size promo card was issued to preview the design of the Signature Rookies Acrylium series. Sporting a protective, clear plastic covering, the fronts feature a color action cutout on a silver metallic background. The player's name is printed faintly along the left edge, while the Super Acrylium emblem adorns the lower left corner. The back has a silver cutout that is the mirror image of the front. Just 10,000 cards were produced.

1 Tim Hardaway .40 1.00

1995 Signature Rookies Kromax Super Acrylium

This five-card standard-size set is one of three insert sets randomly seeded in seven-card packs. 10,000 of each card were produced. The fronts feature the player against a plain silver background. The backs allow a collector to see the front of the card.

COMPLETE SET (5) 2.50 6.00
SA1 Scottie Pippen 1.00 2.50
SA2 Tim Hardaway .60 1.50
SA3 Charles Barkley 1.00 2.50
SA4 Dominique Wilkins .75 2.00
SA5 Patrick Ewing .75 2.00

1995 Signature Rookies Kromax Super Acrylium Signatures

Randomly seeded into packs, this five-card set features autographed versions of the regular Super Acrylium cards. The known print runs are listed below. Barkley is not priced due to scarcity.

SA1 Scottie Pippen/33 100.00 250.00
SA2 Tim Hardaway/1050 4.00 10.00
SA4 Dominique Wilkins/1050 6.00 15.00

1995 Signature Rookies Prime

The 1995 Signature Prime basketball set was issued in one series of 45 cards. Five-card packs included a signed card, packed in a sealed plastic case, an insert card, two regular cards and either a checklist card or mail-in offer card. There were 18 packs in each box. Borderless fronts feature the player in a full-color action shot with "Prime" printed vertically in red type on the left side. The player's name is printed in gold foil at the bottom. A full-color action shot appears on the back with the player's biography, profile, and college stats. The set is sequenced in alphabetical order.

COMPLETE SET (45) 3.00 6.00
1 Cory Alexander .10 .25
2 Jerome Allen .10 .25
3 Brent Barry .15 .40
4 Mario Bennett .10 .25
5 Travis Best .10 .25
6 Donnie Boyce .10 .25
7 Junior Burrough .10 .25
8 Jason Caffey .10 .25
9 Chris Carr .10 .25
10 Randolph Childress .10 .25
11 Mark Davis .10 .25
12 Andrew DeClercq .10 .25
13 Tyus Edney .10 .25
14 Michael Finley .30 .75
15 Sherrell Ford .10 .25
16 Kevin Garnett .75 2.00
16P Kevin Garnett PROMO 1.50 4.00
17 Alan Henderson .10 .25
18 Fred Hoiberg .10 .25
19 Jimmy King .10 .25
20 Donny Marshall .10 .25
21 Cuonzo Martin .10 .25
22 Michael McDonald .10 .25
23 Antonio McDyess .25 .60
24 Loren Meyer .10 .25
25 Lawrence Moten .10 .25
26 Ed O'Bannon .10 .25
27 Greg Ostertag .10 .25
28 Cherokee Parks .10 .25
29 Anthony Pelle .10 .25
30 Constantin Popa .10 .25
31 Theo Ratliff .15 .40
32 Bryant Reeves .10 .25
33 Don Reid .10 .25

34 Terrence Rencher .10 .25
35 Shawn Respert .10 .25
36 Lou Roe .10 .25
37 Eric Snow .10 .25
38 Damon Stoudamire .25 .60
39 Bob Sura .10 .25
40 Kurt Thomas .10 .25
41 Gary Trent .10 .25
42 David Vaughn .10 .25
43 Corliss Williamson .10 .25
44 Eric Williams .10 .25
45 George Zidek .10 .25
NNO Checklist .10 .25

1995 Signature Rookies Prime Signatures

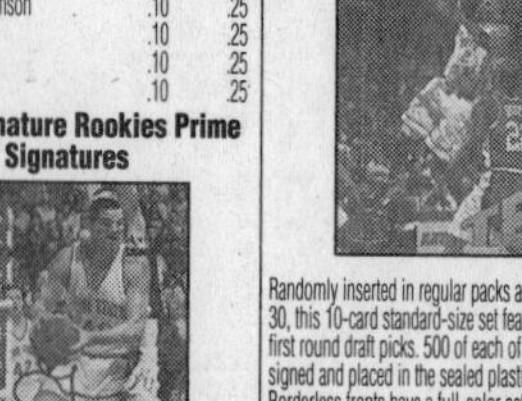

This set represents a signed version of the 1995 SR Signature Prime series. The cards were randomly inserted into packs and each card was numbered out of 3,000. Ed O'Bannon and Jason Caffey did not sign their cards.

1 Cory Alexander 1.25 3.00
2 Jerome Allen 1.25 3.00
3 Brent Barry 2.00 5.00
4 Mario Bennett 1.25 3.00
5 Travis Best 1.25 3.00
6 Donnie Boyce 1.25 3.00
7 Junior Burrough 1.25 3.00
9 Chris Carr 1.25 3.00
10 Randolph Childress 1.25 3.00
11 Mark Davis 1.25 3.00
12 Andrew DeClercq 1.25 3.00
13 Tyus Edney 1.25 3.00
14 Michael Finley 4.00 10.00
15 Sherrell Ford 1.25 3.00
16 Kevin Garnett 15.00 40.00
17 Alan Henderson 1.25 3.00
18 Fred Hoiberg 1.25 3.00
19 Jimmy King 1.25 3.00
20 Donny Marshall 1.25 3.00
21 Cuonzo Martin 1.25 3.00
22 Michael McDonald 1.25 3.00
23 Antonio McDyess 3.00 8.00
24 Loren Meyer 1.25 3.00
25 Lawrence Moten 1.25 3.00
27 Greg Ostertag 1.25 3.00
28 Cherokee Parks 1.25 3.00
29 Anthony Pelle 1.25 3.00
30 Constantin Popa 1.25 3.00
31 Theo Ratliff 2.00 5.00
32 Bryant Reeves 1.25 3.00
33 Don Reid 1.25 3.00
34 Terrence Rencher 1.25 3.00
35 Shawn Respert 1.25 3.00
36 Lou Roe 1.25 3.00
37 Eric Snow 1.25 3.00
38 Damon Stoudamire 3.00 8.00
39 Bob Sura 1.25 3.00
40 Kurt Thomas 1.25 3.00
41 Gary Trent 1.25 3.00
42 David Vaughn 1.25 3.00
43 Corliss Williamson 1.25 3.00
44 Eric Williams 1.25 3.00
45 George Zidek 1.25 3.00

1995 Signature Rookies Prime Hoopla

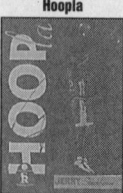

This 5-card set was randomly inserted in football packs. The fronts display a color action cut-out of the player on a metallic, rainbow-colored background. The player's name and card logo is below. The word, "Hoopla" runs vertically on the left. The backs carry another cut-out of the player with his name, position, biographical information, and career summary. The set is numbered with an "H" prefix.

COMPLETE SET (5) 2.00 5.00
H1 Joe Smith .30 .75
H2 Antonio McDyess .40 1.00
H3 Jerry Stackhouse .50 1.25
H4 Rasheed Wallace .50 1.25
H5 Kevin Garnett 1.25 3.00

1995 Signature Rookies Prime Hoopla Signatures

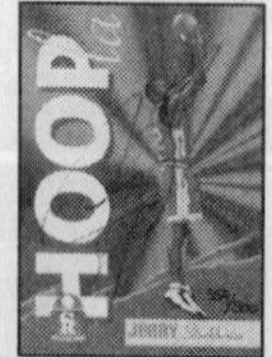

This five-card standard-size set was randomly inserted in football packs at a rate of one in 60. Signed cards (500 of each player) were found only in the football packs. Featuring a full-color player cutout set against a blue, red and silver etched foil background and his signature. "HOOP" is printed in gold vertically with "la" attached to the end. The player's name is printed in red on a gold bar near the bottom. Backs have another full-color action cutout and a screened black-and-white photo for a background. It also contains a player profile, biography and statistics.

H1 Joe Smith 4.00 10.00
H2 Antonio McDyess 8.00 20.00
H3 Jerry Stackhouse 10.00 25.00
H4 Rasheed Wallace 12.50 30.00
H5 Kevin Garnett 30.00 80.00

1995 Signature Rookies Prime Top 10

Randomly inserted in regular packs at a rate of one in 30, this 10-card standard-size set features some 1995 first round draft picks. 500 of each of the 10 cards were signed and placed in the sealed plastic containers. Borderless fronts have a full-color action shot with "TOP" printed at the top of the card and "TEN" printed at the bottom. The player's first name is printed horizontally in white type and his last name is printed in gold foil vertically underneath the first. Backs have another full-color action shot with player stats, biography and a profile. The cards are numbered with a "TT" prefix.

COMPLETE SET (10) 1.50 4.00
TT1 Joe Smith .30 .75
TT2 Antonio McDyess .40 1.00
TT3 Jerry Stackhouse .50 1.25
TT4 Rasheed Wallace .50 1.25
TT5 Kevin Garnett 1.25 3.00
TT6 Bryant Reeves .15 .40
TT7 Damon Stoudamire .40 1.00
TT8 Shawn Respert .15 .40
TT9 Ed O'Bannon .15 .40
TT10 Kurt Thomas .15 .40

1995 Signature Rookies Prime Top 10 Signatures

This set is a signed version of the 1995 SR Signature Prime Top Ten set. The cards were randomly inserted in packs, and each card was numbered out of 1,000.

TT1 Joe Smith 2.50 6.00
TT2 Antonio McDyess 5.00 12.00
TT3 Jerry Stackhouse 6.00 15.00
TT4 Rasheed Wallace 8.00 20.00
TT5 Kevin Garnett 25.00 50.00
TT6 Bryant Reeves 1.25 3.00
TT7 Damon Stoudamire 3.00 8.00
TT8 Shawn Respert 1.25 3.00
TT9 Ed O'Bannon 1.25 3.00
TT10 Kurt Thomas 1.25 3.00

1994 Signature Rookies Tetrad

These 120 standard-size cards feature borderless color player action shots on their fronts. The player's name appears in gold-foil lettering near the bottom. The words "1 of 45,000" appear in vertical gold-foil lettering within a simulated marble column near the left edge. The cards of this four-sport set are numbered on the back in Roman numerals and organized as follows: Football (1-40), Basketball (41-83), Baseball (84-103), and Hockey (104-118).

COMPLETE SET (120) 3.00 8.00
41 Derrick Alston .07 .20
42 Adrian Autry .07 .20
43 Damon Bailey .07 .20
44 Doremus Bennerman .07 .20
45 Melvin Booker .07 .20
46 Jevon Crudup .07 .20
47 Yinka Dare .07 .20
48 Rodney Dent .07 .20
49 Tony Dumas .07 .20
50 Dwayne Fontana .07 .20
51 Travis Ford .07 .20
52 Lawrence Funderburke .07 .20
53 Anthony Goldwire .07 .20
54 Brian Grant .15 .40
55 Kenny Harris .07 .20
56 Juwan Howard UER .15 .40
(Misspelled Juwon)
57 Askia Jones .07 .20
58 Eddie Jones .20 .50
59 Arturas Karnishovas .07 .20
60 Donyell Marshall .15 .40
61 Billy McCaffrey .15 .40
62 Jim McIlvaine .07 .20
63 Aaron McKie .07 .20
64 Greg Minor .07 .20
65 Eric Mobley .07 .20
66 Eric Montross .07 .20
67 Gaylon Nickerson .07 .20
68 Wesley Person .07 .20
69 Eric Piatkowski .15 .40
70 Kevin Rankin .07 .20
71 Shawnelle Scott .07 .20
72 Melvin Simon .07 .20
73 Dickey Simpkins .07 .20
74 Michael Smith .07 .20
75 Stevin Smith .07 .20
76 Deon Thomas .07 .20
77 Brooks Thompson .07 .20
78 B.J. Tyler .07 .20
79 Kendrick Warren .07 .20
80 Jeff Webster .07 .20
81 Monty Williams .07 .20
82 Dontonio Wingfield .07 .20
83 Sharone Wright .07 .20

1994 Signature Rookies Tetrad Autographs

Inserted one card (or trade coupon) per pack, these 117 standard-size autographed cards comprise a parallel set to the regular '94 Tetrad set. Aside from the autographs and each card's numbering out of 7,750 produced, they are identical in design to their regular issue counterparts. The cards of this four-sport set are numbered on the back in Roman numerals and organized as follows: Football (1-40), Basketball (41-83), Baseball (84-103), and Hockey (104-118). Bernard Williams (card number 11) did not sign his cards.

41 Derrick Alston 1.50 4.00
42 Adrian Autry 1.50 4.00
43 Damon Bailey 1.50 4.00
44 Doremus Bennerman 1.50 4.00
45 Melvin Booker 1.50 4.00
46 Jevon Crudup 1.50 4.00
47 Yinka Dare 1.50 4.00
48 Rodney Dent 1.50 4.00
49 Tony Dumas 1.50 4.00
50 Dwayne Fontana 1.50 4.00
51 Travis Ford 1.50 4.00
52 Lawrence Funderburke 1.50 4.00
53 Anthony Goldwire 1.50 4.00
54 Brian Grant 3.00 8.00
55 Kenny Harris 1.50 4.00
56 Juwan Howard UER 3.00 8.00
(Misspelled Juwon)
57 Askia Jones 1.50 4.00
58 Eddie Jones 4.00 10.00
59 Arturas Karnishovas 1.50 4.00
60 Donyell Marshall 2.50 6.00
61 Billy McCaffrey 1.50 4.00
62 Jim McIlvaine 1.50 4.00
63 Aaron McKie 2.50 6.00
64 Greg Minor 1.50 4.00
65 Eric Mobley 1.50 4.00
66 Eric Montross 2.00 5.00
67 Gaylon Nickerson 1.50 4.00
68 Wesley Person 2.00 5.00
69 Eric Piatkowski 2.00 5.00
70 Kevin Rankin 1.50 4.00
71 Shawnelle Scott 1.50 4.00
72 Melvin Simon 1.50 4.00
73 Dickey Simpkins 1.50 4.00
74 Michael Smith 1.50 4.00
75 Stevin Smith 1.50 4.00
76 Deon Thomas 1.50 4.00
77 Brooks Thompson 1.50 4.00
78 B.J. Tyler 1.50 4.00
79 Kendrick Warren 1.50 4.00
80 Jeff Webster 1.50 4.00
81 Monty Williams 1.50 4.00
82 Dontonio Wingfield 1.50 4.00
83 Sharone Wright 1.50 4.00

1994 Signature Rookies Tetrad Flip Cards

Randomly inserted in packs, these five standard-size two-player cards feature a borderless color action shot of one player per side. The player's name appears in gold-foil lettering near the bottom. The words "1 of 7,500" appear in vertical gold-foil lettering within a simulated marble column near the left edge. The cards are numbered on both sides.

COMPLETE SET (5) 10.00 25.00
3 Charlie Ward BK 2.00 5.00
Charlie Ward FB
4 Juwan Howard UER 3.00 8.00
(Misspelled Juwon)
Jalen Rose
5 Glenn Williams UER 1.25 3.00
(Misspelled Glen)
Monty Williams

1994 Signature Rookies Tetrad Flip Cards Autographs

Randomly inserted in packs, this three-card set features two-player cards with a borderless color action shot of one player per side. The player's name appears in gold-foil lettering near the bottom. Each card is autographed. The cards are numbered on both sides.

AU2 Glenn Williams 5.00 12.00
Monty Williams/275
AU3 Charlie Ward 6.00 15.00
FB/BK/275

1994 Signature Rookies Tetrad Previews

Randomly inserted in Signature Rookies Football packs, these seven standard-size cards feature borderless color player action shots on their fronts. The player's name and position appear in gold-foil lettering near the bottom. The words "Promo, 1 of 10,000" appear in vertical gold-foil lettering within a simulated marble column near the left edge. On a ghosted background drawing of a Greek temple, the back carries the player's name, position, team, height and weight, and career highlights. The cards of this multisport set are numbered on the back with a "T" prefix.

COMPLETE SET (7) 1.25 3.00
T1 Eric Montross .08 .25
T5 Charlie Ward .20 .50

1994 Signature Rookies Tetrad Titans

Randomly inserted in packs, these 12 standard-size cards feature borderless color player action shots on their fronts. The player's name appears in gold-foil lettering near the bottom. The words "1 of 10,000" appear in vertical gold-foil lettering within a simulated marble column near the left edge. On a ghosted background drawing of a Greek temple, the back carries the player's name, position, team, height and weight, and career highlights. The cards of this multisport set are numbered on the back in Roman numerals.

COMPLETE SET (12) 3.00 8.00
120 Larry Bird .75 2.00
130 Isiah Thomas UER .50 1.25
(Misspelled Isaiah)

1994 Signature Rookies Tetrad Titans Autographs

Randomly inserted in packs, these 12 standard-size autographed cards comprise a parallel set to the regular 1994 Tetrad Titans set. Aside from the autographs (some cards issued as redemptions in packs) and each card's numbering out of 1,050 produced (except the 2,500 signed O.J. cards), they are identical in design to their regular issue counterparts. The cards of this multisport set are numbered on the back in Roman numerals.

COMPLETE SET (12) 125.00 250.00
120 Larry Bird/1050 40.00 80.00
130 Isiah Thomas/1050 UER 6.00 15.00
(Misspelled Isaiah)

1994 Signature Rookies Tetrad Top Prospects

Randomly inserted in packs, these four standard-size cards feature borderless color player action shots on their fronts. The player's name appears in gold-foil lettering near the bottom. The words "1 of 20,000" appear in vertical gold-foil lettering within a simulated marble column near the left edge. On a ghosted background drawing of a Greek temple, the back carries the player's name, biography, statistics, and career highlights. The cards of this multisport set are numbered on the back in Roman numerals.

COMPLETE SET (4) 1.00 2.50
131 Charlie Ward .30 .75

1994 Signature Rookies Tetrad Top Prospects Autographs

This four-card standard size set was randomly inserted in packs. The fronts feature borderless color player action shots with the player's name in gold-foil lettering near the bottom. The cards are autographed on the fronts. The backs carry the player's name, biography, statistics, and career highlights on a ghosted background drawing of a Greek temple. The cards are numbered on the back in Roman numerals. Other than Shante Carver, the cards are numbered out of 2,000.

131A Charlie Ward 4.00 10.00

1995 Signature Rookies Tetrad

This 76-card standard size set features borderless fronts with color action player photos. The named player stands out on a faded background with his name printed in gold below. The backs carry an elongated color action player photo on one side while a head photo, biographical information, position, college, and career statistics round out the backs.

COMPLETE SET (76) 5.00 12.00
11 Shawn Respert .05 .15
12 Bryant Reeves .08 .25
13 Cherokee Parks .07 .20
14 Greg Ostertag .05 .15
15 Ed O'Bannon .07 .20
16 David Vaughn .05 .15
17 Gary Trent .08 .25
18 Kurt Thomas .08 .25
19 Bob Sura .08 .25
20 Damon Stoudamire .20 .50
21 Brent Barry .08 .25
22 Cory Alexander .05 .15
23 Theo Ratliff .08 .25
24 Loren Meyer .05 .15
25 George Zidek .05 .15
26 Alan Henderson .08 .25
27 Michael Finley .40 1.00
28 Randolph Childress .05 .15
29 Jason Caffey .05 .15
30 Mario Bennett .05 .15
63 Corliss Williamson .08 .25
64 Eric Williams .05 .15
65 Sherell Ford .05 .15

1995 Signature Rookies Tetrad Autographs

SIGS NUMBERED OUT OF 5000
11 Shawn Respert 1.25 3.00
12 Bryant Reeves 2.50 6.00
13 Cherokee Parks 1.50 4.00
14 Greg Ostertag 1.25 3.00
15 Ed O'Bannon 1.50 4.00
16 David Vaughn 1.25 3.00
17 Gary Trent 3.00 8.00
18 Kurt Thomas 1.25 3.00
19 Bob Sura 2.50 6.00
20 Damon Stoudamire 3.00 8.00
21 Brent Barry 1.50 4.00
22 Cory Alexander 1.50 4.00
23 Theo Ratliff 1.50 4.00
24 Loren Meyer 1.25 3.00
25 George Zidek 1.25 3.00
26 Alan Henderson 1.25 3.00
27 Michael Finley 5.00 12.00
28 Randolph Childress 1.25 3.00
29 Jason Caffey 1.25 3.00
30 Mario Bennett 1.25 3.00
63 Corliss Williamson 3.00 8.00
64 Eric Williams 1.25 3.00
65 Sherell Ford 1.25 3.00

1995 Signature Rookies Tetrad Mail-In

This five-card standard size set was available through the mail from Signature Rookies. The set highlights the 1995 first overall draft picks in basketball, football, baseball and hockey. The fronts picture color action photos blended with a fractal-swirling design. In a gold foil stamp, the players name is found vertically on the right, "Mail In" and "#1 Pick" adorn the top and bottom respectively on the left. The back has another color action photo in the upper-right corner. The rest is devoted to a player biography and statistics set on top of the same fractal-swirling design. The cards are numbered with a "P" prefix (P1-P5).

COMPLETE SET (5) 1.50 4.00
P1 Joe Smith .40 1.00
P5 Joe Smith .60 1.50
Ki-Jana Carter
Darin Erstad
Bryan Berard

1995 Signature Rookies Tetrad Previews

This five-card standard-size set was randomly inserted in SR BK autobilia packs. The fronts display borderless color action player photos. The named player stands out on a faded background with his name printed in gold below. The backs carry an elongated color action player photo on one side while a head photo, biographical information, position, college, and career statistics round out the backs.

COMPLETE SET (5) 1.00 2.50
3 Joe Smith .30 .75
4 Jerry Stackhouse .60 1.50

1995 Signature Rookies Tetrad SR Force

This 35-card standard-size set features color action player photos on the front on a white background. Pictures of one foot, the head, and one arm are set out as separate photos on the side of the main picture. The words, "SR Force," are printed in the white border at the top, while the player's name is in gold at the bottom of the picture. The backs carry the same photo as a faded background with photos of the head and parts of one leg. The player's name, position, team, biographical information, and statistics round out the back. The cards are numbered with an "F" prefix.

COMPLETE SET (35) 6.00 15.00
F21 Kevin Garnett .60 1.50
F22 Rasheed Wallace .25 .60
F23 Jerry Stackhouse .25 .60
F24 Antonio McDyess .20 .50
F25 Joe Smith .20 .50

1995 Signature Rookies Tetrad SR Force Autographs

RANDOM INSERTS IN PACKS
F21 Kevin Garnett 10.00 25.00
F22 Rasheed Wallace 5.00 12.00
F23 Jerry Stackhouse 5.00 12.00
F24 Antonio McDyess 4.00 10.00
F25 Joe Smith 3.00 8.00

1995 Signature Rookies Tetrad Titans

This five card standard-size set features borderless fronts with color player action photos on a black background. The player's name is printed at the top with the card name in gold running vertically down the side. The horizontal backs carry another player action photo on a black background with the player's name and a short personal and career summary. The player's position and team round out the back. The cards are numbered with an "T" prefix.

COMPLETE SET (5) 2.00 5.00
T2 Dennis Rodman .60 1.50
T4 Kareem Abdul-Jabbar .75 2.00

1995 Signature Rookies Tetrad Titans Autographs

T2 Dennis Rodman 15.00 40.00
T4 Kareem Abdul-Jabbar 15.00 40.00

1995 Signature Rookies Tetrad Autobilia

The 1995 Signature Rookies Tetrad Autobilia set was issued in one series with a total of 100 cards. The fronts feature a color action player cut-out on a background of a repeated action player photo with the player's name printed in a gold bar at the bottom. The words" Club Set" are printed in gold foil on the fronts as well. The backs carry two player photos with the player's name, position, biographical information, career statistics, and a player fact.

COMPLETE SET (100) 10.00 25.00
*SILVER: .4X TO 1X GOLD
1 Travis Best .30 .75
2 Junior Burrough .08 .25
3 Randolph Childress .08 .25
4 Andrew DeClercq .08 .25
5 Michael Finley .40 1.00
6 Alan Henderson .30 .75
7 Ed O'Bannon .10 .30
8 Cherokee Parks .10 .30
9 Bryant Reeves .15 .40
10 Shawn Respert .08 .25
11 Damon Stoudamire .30 .75
12 Bob Sura .30 .75
13 Scotty Thurman .08 .25
14 Gary Trent .15 .40
15 Corliss Williamson .30 .75
16 Donald Williams .08 .25
17 Eric Williams .08 .25
71 Antonio McDyess .50 1.25
73 Joe Smith .15 .40
74 Jerry Stackhouse .60 1.50
77 Kevin Garnett 1.00 2.50
78 Juwan Howard .30 .75
79 Eddie Jones .30 .75

1995 Signature Rookies Tetrad Autobilia Auto-Phonex Test

This 3-card set was issued in packs of 1995 Signature Rookies Autobilia packs. Each card follows a similar design to the base cards except for the addition of the words 'Auto-Phonex Test Issue' on the left hand side of the cardfronts. The title 'Autobilia' at the top was also replaced with the word Tetrad.

COMPLETE SET (3) 1.25 3.00
T3 Jerry Stackhouse .60 1.50

1995 Signature Rookies Tetrad Autobilia Autographed Cards

These cards are an autographed parallel to the base set. Signature Rookies reported that players signed the following items: 1000 cards, 3000 photos, 500 pennants, 500 hats, 3000 baseballs, 550 basketballs, 1000 footballs. Special items included 100 Darin Erstad signed bats and an undisclosed amount of the following issues: Muhammad Ali signed boxing glove, Joe DiMaggio signed cards, Jaromir Jagr signed hockey stick, Jaromir Jagr signed practice jersey, and Jim Carey signed mask.

1 Travis Best 2.50 6.00
2 Junior Burrough 1.25 3.00
3 Randolph Childress 1.25 3.00
4 Andrew DeClercq 1.25 3.00
5 Michael Finley 6.00 15.00
6 Alan Henderson 3.00 8.00
7 Ed O'Bannon 1.50 4.00
8 Cherokee Parks 1.50 4.00
9 Bryant Reeves 2.50 6.00
10 Shawn Respert 1.25 3.00
11 Damon Stoudamire 3.00 8.00
12 Bob Sura 2.50 6.00
13 Scotty Thurman 1.25 3.00
14 Gary Trent 3.00 8.00
15 Corliss Williamson 3.00 8.00
16 Donald Williams 1.25 3.00
17 Eric Williams 1.25 3.00
71 Antonio McDyess 5.00 12.00
73 Joe Smith 3.00 8.00
74 Jerry Stackhouse 6.00 15.00
77 Kevin Garnett 25.00 50.00
78 Juwan Howard 3.00 8.00
79 Eddie Jones 6.00 15.00

1995 Signature Rookies Tetrad Autobilia Autographed Photos

ANNOUNCED PRINT RUN 3000
1 Travis Best 2.50 6.00
2 Junior Burrough 1.25 3.00
3 Randolph Childress 1.25 3.00
4 Andrew DeClercq 1.25 3.00
5 Michael Finley 6.00 15.00
6 Alan Henderson 1.50 4.00
7 Ed O'Bannon 1.50 4.00
8 Cherokee Parks 1.50 4.00
9 Bryant Reeves 2.50 6.00
10 Shawn Respert 1.25 3.00
11 Damon Stoudamire 3.00 8.00
12 Bob Sura 2.50 6.00
13 Scotty Thurman 1.25 3.00
14 Gary Trent 3.00 8.00
15 Corliss Williamson 3.00 8.00
16 Donald Williams 1.25 3.00
17 Eric Williams 1.25 3.00
71 Antonio McDyess 5.00 12.00
73 Joe Smith 3.00 8.00
74 Jerry Stackhouse 6.00 15.00
77 Kevin Garnett 20.00 40.00
78 Juwan Howard 3.00 8.00
79 Eddie Jones 6.00 15.00

1998 SP Top Prospects

The 1998 SP Top Prospects set was released during the 1998-99 season, and features a 62-card base set broken into tiers as follows: Base Cards (1-40), TP (41-60), and Checklists (61-62).

COMPLETE SET (62) 8.00 20.00
1 Antawn Jamison .75 2.00
2 Vince Carter 1.50 4.00
3 Michael Olowokandi .40 1.00
4 Paul Pierce 1.50 4.00
5 Korleone Young .30 .75
6 Rashard Lewis .75 2.00
7 Miles Simon .30 .75
8 Al Harrington .50 1.25
9 Robert Traylor .30 .75
10 Ansu Sesay .30 .75
11 DeMarco Johnson .30 .75
12 Earl Boykins .30 .75
13 Michael Doleac .30 .75
14 Felipe Lopez .30 .75
15 Cory Carr .30 .75
16 J.R. Henderson .30 .75
17 Michael Dickerson .30 .75
18 Jason Williams .75 2.00
19 Bonzi Wells .30 .75
20 Matt Harpring .40 1.00
21 Pat Garrity .30 .75
22 Ricky Davis .50 1.25
23 Tyronn Lue .30 .75
24 Corey Benjamin .30 .75
25 Jelani McCoy .30 .75
26 Shammond Williams .30 .75
27 Toby Bailey .30 .75
28 Saddi Washington .30 .75
29 Zendon Hamilton .30 .75
30 Steve Wojciechowski .30 .75
31 Nazr Mohammed .30 .75
32 Andrae Patterson .30 .75
33 Ryan Bowen .30 .75
34 Anthony Carter .30 .75
35 Jarod Stevenson .30 .75
36 Casey Shaw .30 .75
37 Brad Miller .75 2.00
38 Charles Jones .30 .75
39 Bryce Drew .30 .75
40 Jeff Sheppard .30 .75
41 Antawn Jamison TP .40 1.00
42 Vince Carter TP .75 2.00
43 Michael Olowokandi TP .20 .50
44 Paul Pierce TP .75 2.00
45 Rashard Lewis TP .40 1.00
46 Robert Traylor TP .15 .40
47 Michael Doleac TP .15 .40
48 Felipe Lopez TP .15 .40
49 Michael Dickerson TP .15 .40
50 Jason Williams TP .40 1.00
51 Bonzi Wells TP .15 .40
52 Matt Harpring TP .20 .50
53 Ricky Davis TP .25 .60
54 Tyronn Lue TP .15 .40
55 Corey Benjamin TP .15 .40
56 Ansu Sesay TP .15 .40
57 Pat Garrity TP .15 .40
58 Shammond Williams TP .15 .40
59 Nazr Mohammed TP .15 .40
60 Bryce Drew TP .15 .40
61 Michael Olowokandi CL .20 .50
62 Antawn Jamison CL .40 1.00

1998 SP Top Prospects President's Edition

Randomly inserted in packs, this 62-card set is a parallel to the base set. The cards are serially numbered to ten.

1998 SP Top Prospects Carolina Heroes

Randomly inserted in packs at one in 11, this 10-card set features top draft players from North Carolina, including four Michael Jordan cards. Card backs carry a "H" prefix.

COMPLETE SET (10) 15.00 40.00
H1 Michael Jordan 4.00 10.00
H2 Michael Jordan 4.00 10.00
H3 Michael Jordan 4.00 10.00
H4 Michael Jordan 4.00 10.00
H5 Antawn Jamison 1.50 4.00
H6 Antawn Jamison 1.50 4.00
H7 Vince Carter 3.00 8.00
H8 Vince Carter 3.00 8.00
H9 Shammond Williams .60 1.50
H10 Shammond Williams .60 1.50

1998 SP Top Prospects Destination Stardom

Randomly inserted in packs at one in 23, this 20-card set focuses on the top player's from the 1998 Draft and their paths to stardom.

COMPLETE SET (20) 30.00 80.00
1 Antawn Jamison 4.00 10.00
2 Vince Carter 8.00 20.00
3 Michael Olowokandi 2.00 5.00
4 Paul Pierce 8.00 20.00
5 Rashard Lewis 4.00 10.00
6 Robert Traylor 1.50 4.00
7 Michael Doleac 1.50 4.00
8 Felipe Lopez 1.50 4.00
9 Pat Garrity 1.50 4.00
10 Michael Dickerson 1.50 4.00
11 Jason Williams 4.00 10.00
12 Bonzi Wells 1.50 4.00
13 Matt Harpring 2.00 5.00
14 Ricky Davis 2.50 6.00
15 Corey Benjamin 1.50 4.00
16 Tyronn Lue 1.50 4.00
17 Al Harrington 2.50 6.00
18 Ansu Sesay 1.50 4.00
19 Nazr Mohammed 1.50 4.00
20 Bryce Drew 1.50 4.00

1998 SP Top Prospects Phi Beta Jordan

Randomly inserted at one in two, this 23-card set features Michael Jordan - and his days at North Carolina. Card backs carry a "J" prefix.

COMPLETE SET (23) 12.00 30.00
COMMON CARD (J1-J23) .75 2.00

1998 SP Top Prospects Vital Signs

Randomly inserted at one in 12, this 19-card set features autographs from some of the top players in the draft. The Michael Jordan autograph was numbered out of 23, and is not considered in the set price.

AH Al Harrington 2.50 6.00
AJ Antawn Jamison 6.00 15.00
AS Ansu Sesay 1.50 4.00
BW Bonzi Wells 1.50 4.00
CC Cory Carr 1.50 4.00
DJ DeMarco Johnson 1.50 4.00
DO Michael Doleac 1.50 4.00
EB Earl Boykins 3.00 8.00
FL Felipe Lopez 1.50 4.00
JR J.R. Henderson 1.50 4.00
JW Jason Williams 6.00 15.00
KY Korleone Young 1.50 4.00
MD Michael Dickerson 1.50 4.00
MH Matt Harpring 2.00 5.00
MJ Michael Jordan/23 1000.00 1800.00
MO Michael Olowokandi 2.00 5.00
MS Miles Simon 1.50 4.00
PP Paul Pierce 15.00 30.00
RL Rashard Lewis 4.00 10.00
RT Robert Traylor 1.50 4.00

1999 SP Top Prospects

This 38-card set was released in August 1999, and features some of the NBA's top draft picks with each shown in his college or high school uniform. The cards were came six per pack with a suggested retail price of $4.99. Cards 8, 15, 19 and 42 were not produced due to a licensing conflict.

COMPLETE SET (38) 4.00 10.00
1 Lee Nailon .15 .40
2 A.J. Bramlett .15 .40
3 Jason Terry .40 1.00
4 Kareem Reid .15 .40
5 Melvin Levett .15 .40
6 Terrell McIntyre .15 .40
7 Trajan Langdon .15 .40
9 Chris Herren .15 .40
10 Shawnta Rogers .15 .40
11 Corey Maggette .30 .75
12 Wayne Turner .15 .40
13 Heshimu Evans .15 .40
14 Bobby Lazor .15 .40
16 Laron Profit .15 .40
17 Ron Artest .40 1.00
18 Tim James .15 .40
20 Louis Bullock .15 .40
21 William Avery .15 .40
22 Quincy Lewis .15 .40
23 Kenny Thomas .15 .40
24 Evan Eschmeyer .15 .40
25 Adrian Peterson .15 .40
26 Keith Carter .15 .40
27 Jelani Gardner .15 .40
28 Baron Davis .50 1.25
29 Jamel Thomas .15 .40

30 B.J. McKie .15 .40
31 Arthur Lee .15 .40
32 Tim Young .15 .40
33 Richard Hamilton .40 1.00
34 Calvin Booth .15 .40
35 Andre Miller .40 1.00
36 Todd MacCulloch .15 .40
37 James Posey .15 .40
38 Lenny Brown .15 .40
39 Scott Padgett .15 .40
40 Venson Hamilton .15 .40
41 Geno Carlisle .15 .40

1999 SP Top Prospects Upper Class

Randomly inserted in packs, this 38-card set parallels the base set. The cards feature a die cut design and are serially numbered to 50. Cards 8, 15, 19 and 42 do not exist.
*UPPER CLASS: 10X TO 25X BASIC CARDS

1999 SP Top Prospects College Legends

Inserted in packs at one in 92, this 10-card set takes a close look at some of the greatest players the college game has ever seen. Card backs contain an "L" prefix.
COMPLETE SET (10) 40.00 80.00
L1 Michael Jordan 10.00 25.00
L2 Michael Jordan 10.00 25.00
L3 Michael Jordan 10.00 25.00
L4 Larry Bird 4.00 10.00
L5 Larry Bird 4.00 10.00
L6 Larry Bird 4.00 10.00
L7 Julius Erving 2.50 6.00
L8 Julius Erving 2.50 6.00
L9 Anfernee Hardaway 2.00 5.00
L10 Anfernee Hardaway 2.00 5.00

1999 SP Top Prospects Jordan's Scrapbook

Randomly inserted in packs at one in 23, this 20-card set focuses on Michael Jordan's career at North Carolina. Card backs carry a "J" prefix.
COMPLETE SET (20) 75.00 150.00
COMMON CARD (J1-J20) 3.00 8.00

1999 SP Top Prospects MJ Flight Mechanics 101

Randomly inserted in packs at one in 4, this 28-card set focuses on 28 top draft picks and provides an introduction into the world of high-flying basketball and what Michael Jordan believes each player will bring to the league. Cards 4 and 25 do not exist. Card backs carry a "FM" prefix.
COMPLETE SET (28) 6.00 15.00
FM1 Jason Terry .75 2.00
FM2 Geno Carlisle .30 .75
FM3 Heshimu Evans .30 .75
FM5 Keith Carter .30 .75
FM6 Trajan Langdon .30 .75
FM7 Ron Artest .75 2.00
FM8 Kenny Thomas .30 .75
FM9 Lenny Brown .30 .75
FM10 Kareem Reid .30 .75
FM11 Shawnta Rogers .30 .75
FM12 Quincy Lewis .30 .75
FM13 Jamel Thomas .30 .75
FM14 James Posey .30 .75
FM15 Lee Nailon .30 .75
FM16 Melvin Levett .30 .75
FM17 Laron Profit .30 .75
FM18 Louis Bullock .30 .75
FM19 Evan Eschmeyer .30 .75
FM20 B.J. McKie .30 .75
FM21 A.J. Bramlett .30 .75
FM22 Wayne Turner .30 .75
FM23 Jelani Gardner .30 .75
FM24 Terrell McIntyre .30 .75
FM26 Venson Hamilton .30 .75
FM27 Andre Miller .75 2.00
FM28 Chris Herren .30 .75
FM29 Adrian Peterson .30 .75
FM30 Tim James .30 .75

1999 SP Top Prospects Vital Signs

Randomly inserted in packs at one in 4, this 39-card set features autograph cards of the league's top draft picks, as well as Michael Jordan. The Jordan cards are limited to 23. Card backs are numbered by the player's name abbreviation.
AB A.J. Bramlett 1.50 4.00
AL Arthur Lee 1.50 4.00
AM Andre Miller 4.00 10.00
AP Adrian Peterson 1.50 4.00
BD Baron Davis 5.00 12.00
BJ B.J. McKie 1.50 4.00
CH Chris Herren 4.00 10.00
DF Damon Frierson 1.50 4.00
DW Donald Watts 1.50 4.00
EE Evan Eschmeyer 1.50 4.00
GC Geno Carlisle 1.50 4.00
GL Gary Lumpkin 1.50 4.00
HE Heshimu Evans 1.50 4.00
JA Michael Jordan/23 400.00 800.00
JG Jelani Gardner 1.50 4.00
JK Jermaine Jackson 1.50 4.00
JP James Posey 1.50 4.00
JT Jamel Thomas 1.50 4.00
KR Kareem Reid 1.50 4.00
KT Kenny Thomas 1.50 4.00
KW Kris Weems 1.50 4.00
LB Lenny Brown 1.50 4.00
LN Lee Nailon 1.50 4.00
LP Laron Profit 1.50 4.00
ML Melvin Levett 1.50 4.00
OE Obinna Ekezie 1.50 4.00
PB Pat Bradley 1.50 4.00
QL Quincy Lewis 1.50 4.00
RB Rasheed Brokenborou 1.50 4.00
RH Richard Hamilton 4.00 10.00
SP Scott Padgett 1.50 4.00
SR Shawnta Rogers 1.50 4.00
TE Jason Terry 4.00 10.00
TJ Tim James 1.50 4.00
TL Trajan Langdon 1.50 4.00
TM Terrell McIntyre 1.50 4.00
TY Tim Young 1.50 4.00
VH Venson Hamilton 1.50 4.00
WT Wayne Turner 3.00 8.00

2000 SP Top Prospects

Released in August 2000, this 50-card set features top prospects from the 2000 NBA Draft. The cards were available in five-card packs that carried a suggested retail price of $4.99. The set contains 45 base cards and five "Famous Firsts" subset cards that were individually serial numbered to 3000.
COMPLETE SET (50) 20.00 40.00
COMPLETE SET w/o SPs (45) 6.00 15.00
1 Kenyon Martin .60 1.50
2 Marcus Fizer .25 .60
3 Michael Redd .60 1.50
4 Desmond Mason .30 .75
5 Corey Hightower .25 .60
6 Erick Barkley .25 .60
7 A.J. Guyton .25 .60
8 Gabe Muoneke .25 .60
9 Khalid El-Amin .25 .60
10 Lavor Postell .25 .60
11 Donnell Harvey .25 .60
12 Terrance Roberson .25 .60
13 Matt Santangelo .25 .60
14 Jarrett Stephens .25 .60
15 Richie Frahm .25 .60
16 Pepe Sanchez .25 .60
17 Jason Collier .25 .60
18 Ed Cota .25 .60
19 Scoonie Penn .25 .60
20 Bootsy Thornton .25 .60
21 Eduardo Najera .25 .60
22 DerMarr Johnson .25 .60
23 Chris Carrawell .25 .60
24 Speedy Claxton .25 .60
25 Jaraan Cornell .25 .60
26 Gee Gervin .25 .60
27 Justin Love .25 .60
28 Joel Przybilla .25 .60
29 Eddie House .25 .60
30 Harold Arceneaux .25 .60
31 Johnny Hemsley .25 .60
32 Courtney Alexander .25 .60
33 Lamont Barnes .25 .60
34 Pete Mickeal .25 .60
35 Brian Cardinal .25 .60
36 Kevin Freeman .25 .60
37 Jason Hart .25 .60
38 Eddie Gill .25 .60
39 Mamadou N'Diaye .25 .60
40 Lamont Long .25 .60
41 Dan Langhi .25 .60
42 Shaheen Holloway .25 .60
43 Eric Coley .25 .60
44 JaRon Rush .25 .60
45 Stromile Swift .25 .60
46 Michael Jordan FF 8.00 20.00
47 Kobe Bryant FF 5.00 12.00
48 Kevin Garnett FF 2.00 5.00
49 Anfernee Hardaway FF 1.50 4.00
50 Kenyon Martin FF 2.50 6.00

2000 SP Top Prospects First Impressions

Randomly inserted in packs at one in five, this 38-card set features autographs of some of the top picks from the 2000 NBA Draft. A congratulatory message is on the back. The cards are numbered by the player's initials.
*GOLD: 2X TO 5X BASIC CARDS
GOLD: PRINT RUN 25 SERIAL #'d SETS
AJ A.J. Guyton 2.00 5.00
BL Bobby Lazor 2.00 5.00
CA Courtney Alexander 2.00 5.00
CC Chris Carrawell 2.00 5.00
CH Corey Hightower 2.00 5.00
CL Calvin Booth 2.00 5.00
DH Donnell Harvey 2.00 5.00
DJ DerMarr Johnson 2.00 5.00
DL Dan Langhi 2.00 5.00
DM Desmond Mason 2.50 6.00
EB Erick Barkley 2.00 5.00
EC Ed Cota 2.00 5.00
EG Eddie Gill 2.00 5.00
EH Eddie House 3.00 8.00
EN Eduardo Najera 2.00 5.00
GG Gee Gervin 2.00 5.00
HA Harold Arceneaux 2.00 5.00
HE Johnny Hemsley 2.00 5.00
JA Jason Collier 2.00 5.00
JC Jaraan Cornell 2.00 5.00
JH Jason Hart 2.00 5.00
JP Joel Przybilla 2.00 5.00
JR JaRon Rush 2.00 5.00
KD Keyon Dooling 2.00 5.00
KE Khalid El-Amin 2.00 5.00
KF Kevin Freeman 2.00 5.00
KM Kenyon Martin 6.00 15.00
LL Lamont Long 2.00 5.00
LP Lavor Postell 2.00 5.00
MF Marcus Fizer 2.00 5.00
MN Mamadou N'Diaye 2.00 5.00
MR Michael Redd 5.00 12.00
MS Matt Santangelo 2.00 5.00
PM Pete Mickeal 2.00 5.00
PS Pepe Sanchez 2.00 5.00
SC Speedy Claxton 2.00 5.00
SP Scoonie Penn 2.00 5.00
SS Stromile Swift 2.00 5.00

2000 SP Top Prospects Future Glory

Randomly inserted in packs at one in 15, this 10-card set focuses on the top draft picks who are bound for the big time. Card backs carry a "F" prefix.
COMPLETE SET (10) 5.00 12.00
F1 Scoonie Penn .60 1.50
F2 Kenyon Martin 1.50 4.00
F3 Marcus Fizer .60 1.50
F4 Chris Carrawell .60 1.50
F5 Donnell Harvey .60 1.50
F6 Erick Barkley .60 1.50
F7 A.J. Guyton .60 1.50
F8 DerMarr Johnson .60 1.50
F9 Desmond Mason .75 2.00
F10 Courtney Alexander .60 1.50

2000 SP Top Prospects Game Jerseys

Randomly inserted in packs at one in 150, this nine-card set features swatches of the players college uniforms. Card backs are numbered by the player's initials. Two autographed Game Jerseys were also inserted, numbered to 25. Those cards are not included in the set price.
CRJ Speedy Claxton 5.00 12.00
DLJ Dan Langhi 5.00 12.00
ECJ Ed Cota 5.00 12.00
JCJ Jason Collier 5.00 12.00
KFJ Kevin Freeman 5.00 12.00
KMA Kenyon Martin AU/25 75.00 150.00
KMJ Kenyon Martin 12.00 30.00
LPJ Lavor Postell 5.00 12.00
MFA Marcus Fizer AU/25 20.00 50.00
MFJ Marcus Fizer 5.00 12.00
PSJ Pepe Sanchez 5.00 12.00

2000 SP Top Prospects Honors Society

Randomly inserted in packs at one in seven, this 12-card set honors college basketball's All-American and All-Conference players. Card backs carry a "H" prefix.
COMPLETE SET (12) 5.00 12.00
H1 Kenyon Martin 1.25 3.00
H2 Marcus Fizer .50 1.25
H3 Courtney Alexander .50 1.25
H4 Chris Carrawell .50 1.25
H5 A.J. Guyton .50 1.25
H6 Desmond Mason .60 1.50
H7 Erick Barkley .50 1.25
H8 Ed Cota .50 1.25
H9 Pepe Sanchez .50 1.25
H10 DerMarr Johnson .50 1.25
H11 Scoonie Penn .50 1.25
H12 Stromile Swift .50 1.25

2000 SP Top Prospects New Wave

Randomly inserted in packs at one in three, this 20-card set features the top picks who are ready for the NBA. Card backs carry a "N" prefix.
COMPLETE SET (20) 5.00 12.00
N1 Kenyon Martin 1.00 2.50
N2 Mamadou N'Diaye .40 1.00
N3 Courtney Alexander .40 1.00
N4 Speedy Claxton .40 1.00
N5 JaRon Rush .40 1.00
N6 Pete Mickeal .40 1.00
N7 Eduardo Najera .40 1.00
N8 Erick Barkley .40 1.00
N9 Scoonie Penn .40 1.00
N10 Desmond Mason .50 1.25
N11 Chris Carrawell .40 1.00
N12 Jason Hart .40 1.00
N13 DerMarr Johnson .40 1.00
N14 Pepe Sanchez .40 1.00
N15 Jarrett Stephens .40 1.00
N16 Ed Cota .40 1.00
N17 Marcus Fizer .40 1.00
N18 A.J. Guyton .40 1.00
N19 Khalid El-Amin .40 1.00
N20 Lavor Postell .40 1.00

1990 Star Pics

This premier edition showcases sixty of college basketball's top pro prospects. The cards were issued exclusively in complete factory set boxes distributed by hobby dealers. The cards measure the standard size. The front features a color action player photo, with the player shown in his college uniform. A white border separates the picture from the surrounding "basketball" background. The player's name appears in an aqua box at the bottom. The back has a head shot of the player in the upper left corner and the card number in a red star in the upper right corner. On a tan-colored basketball court design, the back presents biography, accomplishments, and a mini-scouting report that assesses a player's strengths and weaknesses.
COMP. FACT SET (70) 3.00 6.00
1 Checklist .01 .05
2 David Robinson FLB .40 1.00
3 Antonio Davis .08 .25
4 Steve Bardo .01 .05
5 Jayson Williams .05 .15
6 Alaa Abdelnaby .01 .05
7 Trevor Wilson .01 .05
8 Dee Brown .05 .15
9 Dennis Scott .05 .15
10 Danny Ferry .05 .15
11 Stevie Thompson .01 .05
12 Anthony Bonner .01 .05
13 Keith Robinson .01 .05
14 Sean Higgins .01 .05
15 Bo Kimble .01 .05
16 David Jamerson .01 .05
17 Anthony Pullard .01 .05
18 Phil Henderson .01 .05
19 Mike Mitchell .01 .05
20 Vanderbilt Team .01 .05
21 Gary Payton .60 1.50
22 Tony Massenburg .01 .05
23 Cedric Ceballos .08 .25
24 Dwayne Schintzius .01 .05
25 Bimbo Coles .05 .15
26 Scott Williams .01 .05
27 Willie Burton .01 .05
28 Tate George .01 .05
29 Mark Stevenson .01 .05
30 UNLV Team .01 .05
31 Earl Wise .01 .05
32 Alec Kessler .01 .05
33 Les Jepsen .01 .05
34 Boo Harvey .01 .05
35 Elden Campbell .05 .15
36 Jud Buechler .01 .05
37 Loy Vaught .05 .15
38 Tyrone Hill .05 .15
39 Toni Kukoc .60 1.50
40 Jim Calhoun CO .15 .25
41 Felton Spencer .01 .05
42 Dan Godfread .01 .05
43 Derrick Coleman .08 .25
44 Terry Mills .05 .15
45 Kendall Gill .05 .15
46 A.J. English .01 .05
47 Duane Causwell .01 .05
48 Jerrod Mustaf .01 .05
49 Alan Ogg .01 .05
50 Pervis Ellison .01 .05
51 Matt Bullard .01 .05
52 Melvin Newbern .01 .05
53 Marcus Liberty .01 .05
54 Walter Palmer .01 .05
55 Negele Knight .01 .05
56 Steve Hanson .01 .05
57 Greg Foster .01 .05
58 Brian Oliver .01 .05
59 Travis Mays .01 .05
60 All-Rookie Team .05 .15
61 Steve Scheffler .01 .05
62 Chris Jackson .05 .15
63 Derek Strong .01 .05
64 David Butler .01 .05
65 Kevin Pritchard .01 .05
66 Lionel Simmons .05 .15
67 Gerald Glass .01 .05
68 Tony Harris .01 .05
69 Lance Blanks .01 .05
70 Draft Overview .01 .05

1990 Star Pics Medallion

Only 25,000 of these sets were produced, each carrying it's own serial number. The cards are distinguished by their more glossy feel and gold metallic print. The sets did not contain any autographs. To ascertain values on individual cards, please refer to the multiplier in the header below, coupled with the value of the base card.
COMP.FACT.SET (70) 3.00 8.00
*MEDALLIONS: .5X TO 1.25X BASE CARD HI
NNO Medallion special card .02 .10
Only available as part of Medallion set; numbered 0)

1990 Star Pics Autographs

Randomly inserted in boxes, this set paralled the regular set. Each card contained the player's autograph on the front and a sticker of authenticity on the back. To ascertain values on individual cards, please refer to the multiplier in the header, coupled with the value of the base card.
*AUTOS: 15X TO 40X BASE CARD HI

1991 Star Pics

This 73-card standard-size set was produced by Star Pics, subtitled "Pro Prospects," and features 45 of the 54 players picked in the 1991 NBA draft. The cards were issued exclusively in complete factory set boxes distributed by hobby dealers. The front features a color action photo of player in his college uniform. This picture overlays a black background with a basketball partially in view. The back has a color head shot of the player in the upper left corner and the card number. On a two color jersey background, the back presents biographical information, accomplishments, and a mini scouting report assessing the player's strengths and weaknesses.
COMP.FACT.SET (73) 1.50 3.00
1 Draft Overview .02 .10
2 Derrick Coleman FLB .05 .15
3 Treg Lee .02 .10
4 Rich King .02 .10
5 Kenny Anderson .20 .50
6 John Crotty .05 .15
7 Mark Randall .02 .10
8 Kevin Brooks .02 .10
9 Lamont Strothers .02 .10
10 Tim Hardaway FLB .20 .50
11 Eric Murdock .05 .15
12 Melvin Cheatum .02 .10
13 Pete Chilcutt .05 .15
14 Zan Tabak .02 .10
15 Greg Anthony .05 .15
16 George Ackles .02 .10
17 Stacey Augmon .05 .15
18 Larry Johnson .30 .75
19 Alvaro Teheran .02 .10
20 Reggie Miller FLB .20 .50
21 Steve Smith .30 .75
22 Sean Green .02 .10
23 Johnny Pittman .02 .10
24 Anthony Avent .02 .10
25 Chris Gatling .05 .15
26 Mark Macon .05 .15
27 Joey Wright .02 .10
28 Von McDade .02 .10
29 Bobby Phills .05 .15
30 Larry Fleisher .02 .10
31 Luc Longley .05 .15
32 Jean Derouillere .02 .10
33 Doug Smith .02 .10
34 Chad Gallagher .02 .10
35 Marty Dow .02 .10
36 Tony Farmer .02 .10
37 John Taft .02 .10
38 Reggie Hanson .02 .10
39 Terrell Brandon .20 .50
40 Dee Brown .05 .15
41 Doug Overton .02 .10
42 Joe Wylie .02 .10
43 Myron Brown .02 .10
44 Steve Hood .02 .10
45 Randy Brown .02 .10
46 Chris Corchiani .02 .10
47 Kevin Lynch .02 .10
48 Donald Hodge .02 .10
49 LaBradford Smith .02 .10
50 Shawn Kemp FLB .20 .50
51 Brian Shorter .02 .10
52 Gary Waites .02 .10
53 Mike Iuzzolino .02 .10
54 LeRon Ellis .02 .10
55 Perry Carter .02 .10
56 Keith Hughes .02 .10
57 John Turner .02 .10
58 Marcus Kennedy .02 .10
59 Randy Ayers CO .02 .10
60 All-Rookie Team .02 .10
61 Jackie Jones .02 .10
62 Shaun Vandiver .02 .10
63 Dale Davis .20 .50
64 Jimmy Oliver .02 .10
65 Elliot Perry .05 .15
66 Jerome Harmon .02 .10
67 Darrin Chancellor .02 .10
68 Roy Fisher .02 .10
69 Rick Fox .08 .25
70 Kenny Anderson SPEC .20 .50
71 Richard Dumas .02 .10
72 Checklist .02 .10
NNO Salute/American Flag .02 .10

1991 Star Pics Medallion

A Medallion parallel was issued in set form as a parallel to the base set. The sets do not contain any autographed cards. To ascertain values on individual cards, please refer to the multiplier in the header, coupled with the value of the base card.
SEALED SET (73) 6.00 15.00
*MEDALLION: 1X TO 2.5X BASE CARD HI

1991 Star Pics Autographs

Randomly inserted into sets, these cards featured autographs of the draft picks.
3 Treg Lee 2.00 5.00
4 Rich King 2.00 5.00
5 Kenny Anderson 5.00 12.00
6 John Crotty 2.00 5.00
7 Mark Randall 2.00 5.00
8 Kevin Brooks 2.00 5.00
9 Lamont Strothers 2.00 5.00
11 Eric Murdock 2.00 5.00
12 Melvin Cheatum 2.00 5.00
13 Pete Chilcutt 4.00 10.00
14 Zan Tabak 2.00 5.00
15 Greg Anthony 4.00 10.00
16 George Ackles 2.00 5.00
17 Stacey Augmon 4.00 10.00
18 Larry Johnson 15.00 30.00
19 Alvaro Teheran 2.00 5.00
21 Steve Smith 8.00 20.00
22 Sean Green 2.00 5.00
23 Johnny Pittman 2.00 5.00
24 Anthony Avent 2.00 5.00
25 Chris Gatling 4.00 10.00
26 Mark Macon 2.00 5.00
27 Joey Wright 2.00 5.00
28 Von McDade 2.00 5.00
29 Bobby Phills 5.00 12.00
31 Luc Longley 4.00 10.00
32 Jean Derouillere 2.00 5.00
33 Doug Smith 2.00 5.00
34 Chad Gallagher 2.00 5.00
35 Marty Dow 2.00 5.00
36 Tony Farmer 2.00 5.00
37 John Taft 2.00 5.00
38 Reggie Hanson 2.00 5.00
39 Terrell Brandon 5.00 12.00
40 Dee Brown 4.00 10.00
41 Doug Overton 2.00 5.00
42 Joe Wylie 2.00 5.00
43 Myron Brown 2.00 5.00
44 Steve Hood 2.00 5.00
45 Randy Brown 4.00 10.00
46 Chris Corchiani 4.00 10.00
47 Kevin Lynch 2.00 5.00
48 Donald Hodge 2.00 5.00
49 LaBradford Smith 2.00 5.00
50 Shawn Kemp FLB 4.00 10.00
51 Brian Shorter 2.00 5.00
52 Gary Waites 2.00 5.00
53 Mike Iuzzolino 2.00 5.00
54 LeRon Ellis 2.00 5.00
55 Perry Carter 2.00 5.00
56 Keith Hughes 2.00 5.00
57 John Turner 2.00 5.00
58 Marcus Kennedy 2.00 5.00
59 Randy Ayers CO 4.00 10.00
61 Jackie Jones 2.00 5.00
62 Shaun Vandiver 2.00 5.00
63 Dale Davis 5.00 12.00
64 Jimmy Oliver 2.00 5.00
65 Elliot Perry 4.00 10.00
66 Jerome Harmon 2.00 5.00
67 Darrin Chancellor 2.00 5.00
68 Roy Fisher 2.00 5.00
69 Rick Fox 5.00 12.00
71 Richard Dumas 2.00 5.00

1992 Star Pics

The 1992 Star Pics Pro Prospects Basketball HotPics set contains 90 standard-size cards. The set includes 47 of the 54 players selected in the 1992 NBA Draft as well as some free agents who had a chance to make NBA rosters. Special cards featured in the set include eight StarStats (10, 31, 36, 43, 74, 78, 81, 89), five Flashbacks (30, 40, 50, 60, 70), three Kid cards (33, 68, 83), and two coaches cards (5, 15). Each nine-card foil StarPak included one "Jump At The Chance" game card, with which collectors could win various prizes. The fronts display color action player photos with white borders. The player's position and name are printed vertically in the right border, with the latter in a colored stripe. The Star Pics logo in the lower right corner rounds out the card face. The backs present accomplishments, strengths, weaknesses, and biographical information. A close-up photo appears at the lower right corner inside the Star Pics logo. The unnumbered Bonus card of Steve Smith features a full-bleed color illustration by artist Rip Evans.
COMPLETE SET (90) 2.50 6.00
1 Draft Overview .01 .05
2 Bryant Stith .02 .10
3 Reggie Smith .01 .05
4 Todd Day .02 .10
5 Bob Knight CO .30 .75
6 Darren Morningstar .01 .05
7 Clarence Weatherspoon .02 .10
8 Matt Geiger .01 .05
9 Marlon Maxey .01 .05
10 Christian Laettner SS .07 .20
11 Tony Bennett .01 .05
12 Sean Rooks .01 .05
13 Tom Gugliotta .25 .60
14 Chris King .01 .05
15 Mike Krzyzewski CO .30 .75
16 Sam Mack .02 .10
17 Matt Fish .01 .05
18 Brian Davis .01 .05
19 Oliver Miller .01 .05
20 Damon Sweet .01 .05
21 Eric Anderson .01 .05
22 Henry Williams .01 .05
23 David Johnson .01 .05
24 Duane Cooper .01 .05
25 Lucius Davis .01 .05
26 Matt Steigenga .01 .05
27 Robert Horry .07 .20
28 Brent Price .01 .05
29 Chris Smith .01 .05
30 Vlade Divac FLB .02 .10
31 Adam Keefe SS .01 .05
32 Christian Laettner .15 .40
33 LaPhonso Ellis .07 .20
34 Alex Blackwell .01 .05
35 Popeye Jones .01 .05
36 Walt Williams SS .02 .10
37 Radenko Dobras .01 .05
38 Latrell Sprewell .60 1.50
39 Isaiah Morris .01 .05
40 Horace Grant FLB .02 .10
41 Craig Upchurch .01 .05
42 Alonzo Jamison .01 .05
43 Bryant Stith SS .01 .05
44 Jon Barry .01 .05
45 Litterial Green .01 .05
46 Malik Sealy .02 .10
47 Anthony Peeler .02 .10
48 Dexter Cambridge .01 .05
49 Eric Manuel .01 .05
50 Kendall Gill FLB .02 .10
51 Hubert Davis .02 .10
52 Steve Rogers .01 .05
53 Byron Houston .01 .05
54 Randy Woods .01 .05
55 Elmer Bennett .01 .05
56 Smokey McCovery .01 .05
57 George Gilmore .01 .05
58 Predrag Danilovic .01 .05
59 John Pelphrey .01 .05
60 Dan Majerle FLB .07 .20
61 Elmore Spencer .01 .05
62 Calvin Talford .01 .05
63 David Booth .01 .05
64 Herb Jones .01 .05
65 Benford Williams .01 .05
66 Greg Dennis .01 .05
67 James McCoy .01 .05
68 Clarence Weatherspoon KID .01 .05
69 LaPhonso Ellis .07 .20
70 Sarunus Marciulionis FLB .01 .05
71 Walt Williams .07 .20
72 Lee Mayberry .01 .05
73 Doug Christie .07 .20
74 Jon Barry SS .01 .05
75 Adam Keefe .01 .05
76 Robert Werdann .01 .05
77 P.J. Brown .02 .10
78 Tom Gugliotta SS .10 .30
79 Terrell Lowery .01 .05
80 Tracy Murray .01 .05
81 Clarence Weatherspoon SS .01 .05
82 Melvin Robinson .01 .05
83 Todd Day .01 .05
84 Harold Miner .01 .05
85 Tim Burroughs .01 .05
86 Damon Patterson .01 .05
87 Corey Williams .01 .05
88 Harold Ellis .01 .05
89 LaPhonso Ellis SS .02 .10
90 Checklist .01 .05
NNO Steve Smith ART BC 1.00 2.50

1992 Star Pics Autographs

Redeemable from winning game cards, this set was a parallel to the base set. Each card featured autographs of the draft picks.
2 Bryant Stith 4.00 10.00
3 Reggie Smith 2.00 5.00
4 Todd Day 2.00 5.00
5 Bob Knight CO 15.00 40.00
6 Darren Morningstar 2.00 5.00
7 Clarence Weatherspoon 4.00 10.00
8 Matt Geiger 2.00 5.00
9 Marlon Maxey 2.00 5.00
10 Christian Laettner SS 4.00 10.00
11 Tony Bennett 2.00 5.00
12 Sean Rooks 2.00 5.00
13 Tom Gugliotta 4.00 10.00
14 Chris King 2.00 5.00
15 Mike Krzyzewski CO 75.00 150.00
16 Sam Mack 2.00 5.00
17 Matt Fish 2.00 5.00
18 Brian Davis 2.00 5.00
19 Oliver Miller 2.00 5.00
20 Damon Sweet 2.00 5.00
21 Eric Anderson 2.00 5.00
22 Henry Williams 2.00 5.00
23 David Johnson 2.00 5.00
24 Duane Cooper 2.00 5.00
25 Lucius Davis 2.00 5.00
26 Matt Steigenga 2.00 5.00
27 Robert Horry 40.00 80.00
28 Brent Price 2.00 5.00
29 Chris Smith 2.00 5.00
30 Vlade Divac FLB 6.00 15.00
31 Adam Keefe SS 2.00 5.00
32 Christian Laettner 4.00 10.00
33 LaPhonso Ellis 4.00 10.00
34 Alex Blackwell 2.00 5.00
35 Popeye Jones 2.00 5.00
36 Walt Williams SS 2.00 5.00
37 Radenko Dobras 2.00 5.00
38 Latrell Sprewell 15.00 40.00
39 Isaiah Morris 2.00 5.00
40 Horace Grant FLB 4.00 10.00
41 Craig Upchurch 2.00 5.00
42 Alonzo Jamison 2.00 5.00
43 Bryant Stith SS 2.00 5.00
44 Jon Barry 8.00 20.00
45 Litterial Green 2.00 5.00
46 Malik Sealy 4.00 10.00
47 Anthony Peeler 4.00 10.00
48 Dexter Cambridge 2.00 5.00
49 Eric Manuel 2.00 5.00
50 Kendall Gill FLB 4.00 10.00
51 Hubert Davis 10.00 25.00
52 Steve Rogers 2.00 5.00
53 Byron Houston 2.00 5.00
54 Randy Woods 2.00 5.00
55 Elmer Bennett 2.00 5.00
56 Smokey McCovery 2.00 5.00
57 George Gilmore 2.00 5.00
58 Predrag Danilovic 2.00 5.00
59 John Pelphrey 2.00 5.00
60 Dan Majerle FLB 5.00 12.00
61 Elmore Spencer 2.00 5.00
62 Calvin Talford 2.00 5.00
63 David Booth 2.00 5.00
64 Herb Jones 2.00 5.00
65 Benford Williams 2.00 5.00
66 Greg Dennis 2.00 5.00
67 James McCoy 2.00 5.00
68 Clarence Weatherspoon KID 4.00 10.00
69 LaPhonso Ellis 4.00 10.00
70 Sarunus Marciulionis FLB 2.00 5.00
71 Walt Williams 5.00 12.00
72 Lee Mayberry 2.00 5.00
73 Doug Christie 4.00 10.00
74 Jon Barry SS 4.00 10.00

75 Adam Keefe 5.00 12.00
76 Robert Werdann 2.00 5.00
77 P.J. Brown 4.00 10.00
78 Tom Gugliotta SS 4.00 10.00
79 Terrell Lowery 2.00 5.00
80 Tracy Murray 2.00 5.00
81 Clarence Weatherspoon SS 4.00 10.00
82 Melvin Robinson 2.00 5.00
83 Todd Day 2.00 5.00
84 Harold Miner 10.00 25.00
85 Tim Burroughs 2.00 5.00
86 Damon Patterson 2.00 5.00
87 Corey Williams 2.00 5.00
88 Harold Ellis 2.00 5.00
89 LaPhonso Ellis SS 4.00 10.00

1994-95 Superior Pix Promos

These four standard-size cards were promos for the regular edition 1994-95 Superior Pix Pro Basketball Draft Pix set. The fronts feature full-bleed color action photos, except on the left and bottom where pebble-grain stripes edge the pictures. The player's name is gold foil-stamped in the left pebble-grain stripe. The backs carry a small color player close-up in the upper left corner, and a small action shot in the lower right, along with player biography and profile.

COMPLETE SET (4) 1.50 4.00
1 Glenn Robinson .30 .75
2 Jason Kidd .75 2.00
3 Grant Hill .75 2.00
4 Eddie Jones .50 1.25

1995 Superior Pix

Formerly known as Superior Rookies, this Pro Basketball Draft Pix set consists of 80 standard-size cards. This set was released as a sub-license of Classic. Just 2,995 numbered cases were produced, with 12 boxes per case. Two authentic autographs were inserted in each box; players autographing include Shaquille O'Neal (200), Glenn Robinson (1,500), Jason Kidd (1,500), Dikembe Mutombo (1,000), Alonzo Mourning (1,000), and Jamal Mashburn (1,000). Each case included one autographed card of Robinson or Kidd, as well as one of Mutombo, Mourning or Mashburn. The 8-card packs consist of 7 regular cards and one of 30 1st-round chrome cards (1-26, 74-77). The fronts feature full-bleed color action photos, except on the left and bottom where pebble-grain stripes edge the pictures and have the player's name. The backs carry a small color player close-up in the upper left corner, a small black-and-white player action shot in the lower right, as well as biography and player profile.

COMPLETE SET (80) 2.50 6.00
1 Glenn Robinson .15 .40
2 Jason Kidd .25 .60
3 Grant Hill .25 .60
4 Donyell Marshall .10 .25
5 Juwan Howard .15 .40
6 Sharone Wright .10 .25
7 Brian Grant .12 .30
8 Eric Montross .10 .25
9 Eddie Jones .20 .50
10 Carlos Rogers .10 .25
11 Khalid Reeves .10 .25
12 Jalen Rose .20 .50
13 Yinka Dare .10 .25
14 Eric Piatkowski .12 .30
15 Clifford Rozier .10 .25
16 Aaron McKie .10 .25
17 Eric Mobley .10 .25
18 Tony Dumas .10 .25
19 B.J. Tyler .10 .25
20 Dickey Simpkins .10 .25
21 Bill Curley .10 .25
22 Wesley Person .10 .25
23 Monty Williams .10 .25
24 Greg Minor .10 .25
25 Charlie Ward .10 .25
26 Brooks Thompson .10 .25
27 Sam Mitchell .10 .25
28 Deon Thomas .10 .25
29 Antonio Lang .10 .25
30 Howard Eisley .10 .25
31 Jamie Watson .10 .25
32 Jim McIlvaine .10 .25
33 Jervaughn Scales .10 .25
34 Kendrick Warren .10 .25
35 Melvin Simon .10 .25
36 Albert Burditt .10 .25
37 Robert Shannon .10 .25
38 Kevin Rankin .10 .25
39 Byron Starks .10 .25
40 Askia Jones .10 .25
41 Harry Moore .10 .25
42 Abdul Fox .10 .25
43 Doremus Benneman .10 .25
44 Adrian Autry .10 .25
45 Myron Walker .10 .25
46 Shawnelle Scott .10 .25
47 Tracy Webster .10 .25
48 Billy McCaffrey .10 .25
49 Arturas Karnishovas .10 .25
50 Dwayne Morton .10 .25
51 Anthony Miller .10 .25
52 Damon Bailey .10 .25
53 Lawrence Funderburke .10 .25
54 Darrin Hancock .10 .25
55 Jeff Webster .10 .25
56 Jevon Crudup .10 .25
57 Robert Churchwell .10 .25
58 Damon Key .10 .25
59 Chuck Graham .10 .25
60 Jamie Brandon .10 .25
61 Travis Ford .10 .25
62 Derrick Phelps .10 .25
63 Stevin Smith .10 .25
64 Brian Reese .10 .25
65 Kevin Salvadori .10 .25
66 Steve Woodberry .10 .25
67 Shon Tarver .10 .25
68 Joey Brown .10 .25
69 Melvin Booker .10 .25
70 Carl Ray Harris .10 .25
71 Gaylon Nickerson .10 .25
72 Trevor Ruffin .10 .25
73 Anthony Goldwire .10 .25
74 Shaquille O'Neal .40 1.00
75 Dikembe Mutombo .15 .40
76 Alonzo Mourning .20 .50
77 Jamal Mashburn .15 .40
78 Glenn Robinson .15 .40
79 Grant Hill .25 .60
80 Checklist .10 .25

1995 Superior Pix Gold

Randomly inserted in packs, this 80-card set parallels the base set. The cards feature gold foil. To ascertain values on individual cards, please refer to the multiplier in the header, coupled with the value of the base card.

COMPLETE SET (80) 5.00 12.00
*GOLD: .75X TO 2X BASIC CARDS

1995 Superior Pix Autographs

Formerly known as Superior Rookies, this Pro Basketball Draft Pix Autograph set consists of 38 standard-size cards. Key players who autographed cards include Shaquille O'Neal (200), Glenn Robinson (1,500), Jason Kidd (1,500), Dikembe Mutombo (1,000), Alonzo Mourning (1,000), and Jamal Mashburn (1,000). The fronts feature full-bleed color action photos, except on the left and bottom where pebble-grain stripes edge the pictures and have the player's name. The signature is on the player's photo with the serial number on the bottom of the card. The backs carry a small color player close-up in the upper left corner, and a small black-and-white player action shot in the lower right, along with player biography and profile.

1 Glenn Robinson/1500 6.00 15.00
2 Jason Kidd/1500 10.00 25.00
5 Juwan Howard/1250 4.00 10.00
6 Sharone Wright/2500 .75 2.00
7 Brian Grant/3000 3.00 8.00
8 Eric Montross/2500 .75 2.00
9 Eddie Jones/3000 6.00 15.00
13 Yinka Dare/2000 .75 2.00
14 Eric Piatkowski/2500 2.00 5.00
15 Clifford Rozier/2500 .75 2.00
16 Aaron McKie/3500 .75 2.00
17 Eric Mobley/3000 .75 2.00
18 Tony Dumas/3000 .75 2.00
19 B.J. Tyler/3000 .75 2.00
20 Dickey Simpkins/2000 .75 2.00
21 Bill Curley/3000 .75 2.00
22 Wesley Person/3500 .75 2.00
23 Monty Williams/2500 .75 2.00
24 Greg Minor/2500 .75 2.00
25 Charlie Ward/2500 2.00 5.00
26 Brooks Thompson/2000 .75 2.00
28 Deon Thomas/2700 .75 2.00
30 Howard Eisley/2500 .75 2.00
32 Jim McIlvaine/2600 .75 2.00
40 Askia Jones/3600 .75 2.00
41 Harry Moore/3000 .75 2.00
44 Adrian Autry/2500 .75 2.00
46 Shawnelle Scott/4000 .75 2.00
52 Damon Bailey/3500 .75 2.00
53 Darrin Hancock/2500 .75 2.00
55 Jeff Webster/1250 .75 2.00
57 Robert Churchwell/3000 .75 2.00
61 Travis Ford/3000- .75 2.00
68 Joey Brown/3000 .75 2.00
74 Shaquille O'Neal/200 25.00 60.00
75 Dikembe Mutombo/1000 6.00 15.00
76 Alonzo Mourning/1000 10.00 25.00
77 Jamal Mashburn/1000 6.00 15.00

1995 Superior Pix Chrome

These cards were randomly inserted into packs. These standard-sized cards feature the player in their college uniform. Every player in this insert set was a first round pick in the NBA draft. There was one chrome gold card in each box. The fronts feature a player action cutout against a basketball background. The backs reads "1st round pick" against a basketball background.

COMPLETE SET (30) 4.00 10.00
*GOLD: .75X TO 2X HI COLUMN
1 Glenn Robinson .50 1.25
2 Jason Kidd .75 2.00
3 Grant Hill .75 2.00
4 Donyell Marshall .30 .75
5 Juwan Howard .50 1.25
6 Sharone Wright .30 .75
7 Brian Grant .40 1.00
8 Eric Montross .30 .75
9 Eddie Jones .60 1.50
10 Carlos Rogers .30 .75
11 Khalid Reeves .30 .75
12 Jalen Rose .60 1.50
13 Yinka Dare .30 .75
14 Eric Piatkowski .40 1.00
15 Clifford Rozier .30 .75
16 Aaron McKie .30 .75
17 Eric Mobley .30 .75
18 Tony Dumas .30 .75
19 B.J. Tyler .30 .75
20 Dickey Simpkins .30 .75
21 Bill Curley .30 .75
22 Wesley Person .30 .75
23 Monty Williams .30 .75
24 Greg Minor .30 .75
25 Charlie Ward .30 .75
26 Brooks Thompson .30 .75
27 Dikembe Mutombo .50 1.25
28 Alonzo Mourning .60 1.50
29 Jamal Mashburn .50 1.25
30 Shaquille O'Neal 1.25 3.00

1995 Superior Pix Instant Impact

This 10-card standard-size chrome standard-size set was inserted at a rate of one in every nine packs. Horizontal fronts feature the player in a box for most of the left hand side of the card. Just above the photo is the player's name. The words "Instant Impact" are at the lower right corner. The backs feature a larger version of the front photo on the left side of the card.

COMPLETE SET (10) 3.00 8.00
1 Shaquille O'Neal 1.25 3.00
2 Glenn Robinson .50 1.25
3 Jason Kidd .75 2.00
4 Grant Hill .75 2.00
5 Dikembe Mutombo .50 1.25
6 Alonzo Mourning .60 1.50
7 Jamal Mashburn .50 1.25
8 Juwan Howard .50 1.25
9 Brian Grant .40 1.00
10 Wesley Person .30 .75

1995 Superior Pix Lottery Pick

This 10-card standard-size set was inserted at a rate of one in every 36 packs. The cards are clear acetate and fronts feature the player in their college uniform with the Superior Pix logo in the upper left hand corner and the player's name on the bottom left corner of the card. Since the card is made of clear acetate, the back allows one to see what is on the front from a reverse angle.

COMPLETE SET (10) 6.00 15.00
1 Glenn Robinson 2.00 5.00
2 Jason Kidd 3.00 8.00
3 Grant Hill 3.00 8.00
4 Donyell Marshall 1.25 3.00
5 Juwan Howard 2.00 5.00
6 Sharone Wright 1.25 3.00
7 Brian Grant 1.50 4.00
8 Eric Montross 1.25 3.00
9 Eddie Jones 2.50 6.00
10 Carlos Rogers 1.25 3.00

1995 Ted Williams Promos

These standard-size card were issued to promote the 1995 Ted Williams basketball series. On a partially screened background, the front features a color action photo. Names are printed vertically in team color-coded lettering along the left edge. The back carries an advertisement for the set.

COMPLETE SET (2) 1.25 3.00
P1 Charles Barkley 1.00 2.50
P2 Jason Kidd 1.00 2.50

1995 Ted Williams

The 1995 Ted Williams Draft Pick set consists of 90 standard-size cards, featuring key 1994 draft picks and second-year standouts. 2,999 cases were produced. This set was issued as a sub-license of Classic. These cards were sold in 8-card packs, and each 24-pack box contained either one signature card or a hot pack, which had all inserts. The fronts feature the player's last name in the middle left with the Ted Williams logo in the upper left corner and a silhouette of a basketball player in the lower left side of the card. The backs feature biographical information along with collegiate statistics and a player profile. The first eighty cards are arranged in alphabetical order. The set closes with a Flashback (80-88) subset and checklist cards (89-90).

COMPLETE SET (90) 4.00 10.00
1 Derrick Alston .10 .25
2 Adrian Autry .10 .25
3 Damon Bailey .10 .25
4 Doremus Benneman .10 .25
5 Randy Blocker .10 .25
6 Melvin Booker .10 .25
7 Jamie Brandon .10 .25
8 Barry Brown UER .10 .25
Joey Brown
9 Joey Brown UER .10 .25
Barry Brown
10 Albert Burditt .10 .25
11 Robert Churchwell .10 .25
12 Gary Collier .10 .25
13 Jevon Crudup .10 .25
14 Bill Curley .10 .25
15 Yinka Dare .10 .25
16 Rodney Dent .10 .25
17 Tony Dumas .10 .25
18 Howard Eisley .10 .25
19 Andrei Fetisov .10 .25
20 Travis Ford .10 .25
21 Abdul Fox .10 .25
22 Lawrence Funderburke .10 .25
23 Anthony Goldwire .10 .25
24 Chuck Graham .10 .25
25 Brian Grant .12 .30
26 Thomas Hamilton .10 .25
27 Darrin Hancock .10 .25
28 Carl Ray Harris .10 .25
29 Askia Jones .10 .25
30 Eddie Jones .20 .50
31 Arturas Karnishovas .10 .25
32 Damon Key .10 .25
33 Jason Kidd .25 .60
34 Antonio Lang .10 .25
35 Donyell Marshall .10 .25
36 Billy McCaffrey .10 .25
37 Jim McIlvaine .10 .25
38 Aaron McKie .10 .25
39 Anthony Miller .10 .25
40 Greg Minor .10 .25
41 Eric Mobley .10 .25
42 Eric Montross .10 .25
43 Harry Moore .10 .25
44 Dwayne Morton .10 .25
45 Gaylon Nickerson .10 .25
46 Cornell Parker .10 .25
47 Wesley Person UER .10 .25
48 Derrick Phelps .10 .25
49 Eric Piatkowski .12 .30
50 Kevin Rankin .10 .25
51 Brian Reese .10 .25
52 Khalid Reeves .10 .25
53 Clayton Ritter .10 .25
54 Carlos Rogers .10 .25
55 Jalen Rose .20 .50
56 Clifford Rozier .10 .25
57 Kevin Salvadori .10 .25
58 Jervaughn Scales .10 .25
59 Shawnelle Scott .10 .25
60 Robert Shannon .10 .25
61 Melvin Simon .10 .25
62 Dickey Simpkins .10 .25
63 Michael Smith .10 .25
64 Stevin Smith .10 .25
65 Byron Starks .10 .25
66 Aaron Swinson .10 .25
67 Shon Tarver .10 .25
68 Deon Thomas .10 .25
69 Brooks Thompson .10 .25
70 B.J. Tyler .10 .25
71 Myron Walker .10 .25
72 Charlie Ward .10 .25
73 Kendrick Warren .10 .25
74 Jamie Watson .10 .25
75 Jeff Webster .10 .25
76 Tracy Webster .10 .25
77 Monty Williams .10 .25
78 Dontonio Wingfield .10 .25
79 Steve Woodberry .10 .25
80 Charles Barkley FLB .25 .60
81 Larry Bird FLB .50 1.25
82 Anfernee Hardaway FLB .25 .60
83 Jamal Mashburn FLB .15 .40
84 Chris Mills FB .10 .25
85 Harold Miner FB .10 .25
86 Alonzo Mourning FLB .20 .50
87 Dikembe Mutombo FB .15 .40
88 Rodney Rogers FB .10 .25
89 Checklist (1-45) .10 .25
90 Checklist (46-90) .10 .25

1995 Ted Williams Abdul Jabbar

These 9 standard-size cards were randomly inserted at a rate of one in every sixteen retail packs. The fronts feature full-bleed color action photos, with the player's name in a stripe across the bottom. On a cloudy sky background, the backs describe various highlights from his career. The cards are numbered with a "KAJ" prefix in small gold letters directly under the player's name.

COMPLETE SET (9) 2.50 6.00
COMMON KAREEM (KAJ1-KAJ9) .75 1.00

1995 Ted Williams Co-op

This 9-card standard-size set was randomly inserted at a rate of one in every twelve packs. This set spotlights both NBA superstars (active and retired) and rookies. The fronts feature the player highlighted against a dotted background. The player's name is on the left side of the card. The Ted Williams logo is in the upper left corner while the Classic logo is in the upper right corner. The back carries biography and a player photo. The cards are numbered with a "CO" prefix and are sequenced in alphabetical order.

COMPLETE SET (9) 4.00 10.00
CO1 Charles Barkley .75 2.00
CO2 Larry Bird 1.50 4.00
CO3 Anfernee Hardaway .75 2.00
CO4 Grant Hill .75 2.00
CO5 Jason Kidd .75 2.00
CO6 Pete Maravich 1.50 4.00
CO7 Alonzo Mourning .60 1.50
CO8 Glenn Robinson .50 1.25
CO9 Checklist .40 1.00

1995 Ted Williams Constellation

Randomly inserted in foil packs, this 9-card standard-size set consists of cards from the main set as well as the insert sets. Each card sports the distinctive design of the card series to which it belongs. They differ only in their consecutive numbering C1-C9 on the back. The set is sequenced in alphabetical order.

COMPLETE SET (9) 5.00 12.00
C1 Kareem Abdul-Jabbar 1.25 3.00
C2 Charles Barkley 1.25 3.00
C3 Larry Bird 2.50 6.00
C4 Anfernee Hardaway 1.25 3.00
C5 Juwan Howard .75 2.00
C6 Jason Kidd 1.25 3.00
C7 George Mikan 1.25 3.00
C8 Alonzo Mourning 1.00 2.50
C9 Glenn Robinson .75 2.00

1995 Ted Williams Eclipse

Randomly inserted at a rate of one in every twelve packs, this 9-card standard-size set features NBA legends. The cards show the players in air-brushed professional uniforms with the word "Eclipse" in large red letters on the bottom and the player's name immediately below. The backs carry biographical information. The cards are unnumbered and checklisted below in alphabetical order.

COMPLETE SET (9) 3.00 8.00
EC1 Rick Barry .50 1.25
EC2 Larry Bird 1.50 4.00
EC3 Bob Pettit .50 1.25
EC4 Hal Greer .50 1.25
EC5 Kareem Abdul Jabbar .75 2.00
EC6 Pete Maravich 1.50 4.00
EC7 George Mikan .75 2.00
EC8 Dolph Schayes .50 1.25
EC9 Checklist .20 .50

1995 Ted Williams Gallery

This nine-card standard-size set was randomly inserted at a rate of one in every sixteen packs. The fronts feature a drawing of each player, with both a head-and-shoulder and an action drawing of each player. In the bottom left corner are the words "The Gallery." The backs provide biographical information about the player as well as a blurb about the player in the professional ranks. The cards are numbered with a "G" prefix in the upper left corner and are sequentially numbered at the bottom middle. The cards are sequenced in alphabetical order.

COMPLETE SET (9) 6.00 15.00
G1 Charles Barkley 1.50 4.00
G2 Larry Bird 3.00 8.00
G3 Kareem Abdul Jabbar 1.50 4.00
G4 Walt Frazier 1.00 2.50
G5 Anfernee Hardaway 1.50 4.00
G6 Jamal Mashburn 1.00 2.50
G7 Alonzo Mourning 1.25 3.00
G8 Dikembe Mutombo 1.00 2.50
G9 Checklist .20 .50

1995 Ted Williams Hardwood Legends

This 9-card standard-size set of retired basketball greats as selected by Larry Bird was randomly inserted at a rate of one in every eight regional hobby packs. This set features outstanding duos from New York (1-2), Golden State (3-4), Chicago (5-6), and Boston (7-8). The fronts feature the player in action in airbrushed uniforms while the backs feature biographical information as well as a informational blurb about the player.

COMPLETE SET (9) 1.50 4.00
HL1 Walt Frazier .40 1.00
HL2 Dave DeBusschere .40 1.00
HL3 Rick Barry .40 1.00
HL4 Nate Thurmond .40 1.00
HL5 Artis Gilmore .40 1.00
HL6 Norm Van Lier .40 1.00
HL7 Bill Sharman .40 1.00
HL8 Jo Jo White .40 1.00
HL9 Checklist .20 .50

1995 Ted Williams Royal Court

This 9-card standard-size set was randomly inserted into packs at a rate of one in every twelve packs. This set features some of Charles Barkley's favorite players. The fronts contains a full-color action photo of the player with the Ted Williams Logo in the upper left corner, the player's name in yellow lettering down the left side and a Royal Court of Charles logo in the bottom right corner. The backs present biography and on the right side a sword with the name of the player printed on it.

COMPLETE SET (9) 1.50 4.00
RC1 Anfernee Hardaway .60 1.50
RC2 Harold Miner .25 .60
RC3 Jason Kidd .60 1.50
RC4 Donyell Marshall .25 .60
RC5 Jamal Mashburn .40 1.00
RC6 Juwan Howard .40 1.00
RC7 Alonzo Mourning .50 1.25
RC8 Aaron Swinson .25 .60
RC9 Checklist .08 .25

1995 Ted Williams What's Up

This 12-card standard-size set was randomly inserted at a rate of one in every twelve packs. This set featured some of the star attractions of the 94-5 NBA Rookie Class. The fronts feature a full-bleed player photo. In the upper left corner is the Ted Williams logo while the What's Up logo is in the lower left corner of the card. The name of the player is printed in white in the bottom right corner of the card. The cards are numbered with a "WU" prefix and are sequenced in alphabetical order.

COMPLETE SET (9) 1.50 4.00
WU1 Brian Grant .40 1.00
WU2 Eric Montross .30 .75
WU3 Jason Kidd .75 2.00
WU4 Anthony Miller .30 .75
WU5 Khalid Reeves .30 .75
WU6 Carlos Rogers .30 .75
WU7 Jalen Rose .60 1.50
WU8 Charlie Ward .30 .75
WU9 Checklist .08 .25

2003-04 UD Top Prospects

Released in late July, UD Top Prospects consists of a 60-card set and features draftees from the 2003 NBA draft. Base cards place full color player action photos with a borderless top, bottom and right side along with a white border along the left that reads "Top Prospects." Card backs are green with a scale photo of the player and has the usual player stats on the back. Along with the draftees, both Kobe Bryant and Michael Jordan have appearances in this set. Also of note, UD Top Prospects marks the first live cards for the 2003 draft class, most notably, LeBron James, Carmelo Anthony and Darko Milicic. Top Prospects was packaged in 24-pack boxes where packs contained five cards and carried a suggested retail price of $3.99.

COMPLETE SET (60) 10.00 25.00
1 Michael Jordan 1.25 3.00
2 Kobe Bryant .75 2.00
3 LeBron James 3.00 8.00
4 Darko Milicic .30 .75
5 Carmelo Anthony .75 2.00
6 Pavel Podkolzine .30 .75
7 Maciej Lampe .30 .75
8 Zaur Pachulia .30 .75
9 Viktor Khryapa .30 .75
10 Anderson Varejao .30 .75
11 Chris Kaman .40 1.00
12 Reece Gaines .30 .75
13 Sofoklis Schortsanitis .30 .75
14 Luke Ridnour .40 1.00
15 Zoran Planinic .30 .75
16 Nick Collison .30 .75
17 Boris Diaw .40 1.00
18 Mickael Pietrus .30 .75
19 Travis Hansen .30 .75
20 Zarko Cabarkapa .30 .75
21 Aleksandar Pavlovic .30 .75
22 David West .40 1.00
23 Rick Rickert .30 .75
24 Brian Cook .30 .75
25 Josh Howard .30 .75
26 Jerome Beasley .30 .75
27 Mario Austin .30 .75
28 Brandon Hunter .30 .75
29 Joe Shipp .30 .75
30 Kyle Korver .40 1.00
31 Travis Outlaw .40 1.00
32 Quentin Ross .30 .75
33 Matt Carroll .30 .75
34 Troy Bell .30 .75
35 Dahntay Jones .30 .75
36 Keith Bogans .30 .75
37 Ruben Douglas .30 .75
38 Julius Barnes .30 .75
39 Luke Walton .30 .75
40 Marquis Daniels .30 .75
41 Marcus Banks .30 .75
42 Marcus Hatten .30 .75
43 Jeff Newton .30 .75
44 Ronald Dupree .30 .75
45 James Lang .30 .75
46 Jason Gardner .30 .75
47 Jason Kapono .30 .75
48 Brett Blizzard .30 .75
49 Ebi Ere .30 .75
50 Hollis Price .30 .75
51 Steve Blake .40 1.00
52 Matt Bonner .40 1.00
53 Slavko Vranes .30 .75
54 Kobe Bryant .75 2.00
55 LeBron James 3.00 8.00
56 Darko Milicic .30 .75
57 Carmelo Anthony .75 2.00
58 Michael Jordan 1.25 3.00
59 Kobe Bryant .75 2.00
60 LeBron James 3.00 8.00
P3 LeBron James PROMO 20.00 50.00

2003-04 UD Top Prospects Gold Collection

Randomly seeded in packs, this 60-card set parallels the base set enhanced with gold foil highlights, sequential numbering to 100 along the right side of the card, the words "Gold Collection" along the bottom and a yellow card back.

*GOLD: 5X TO 12X BASE CARD HI

2003-04 UD Top Prospects After School Specials

Randomly inserted in packs at the rate of one in 12, this 14-card set showcases full color action photography of players who made the jump from the NCAA to the NBA. Each photo is framed with a white and blue border along the top and both sides and an all gold foil border along the bottom with the player's alma mater in embossed lettering.

COMPLETE SET (14) 6.00 15.00
AS1 LeBron James 4.00 10.00
AS2 Darko Milicic .40 1.00
AS3 Carmelo Anthony 1.00 2.50
AS4 Luke Ridnour .50 1.25
AS5 David West .50 1.25
AS6 Travis Outlaw .50 1.25
AS7 Chris Kaman .50 1.25
AS8 Marcus Banks .40 1.00
AS9 Reece Gaines .40 1.00
AS10 Hollis Price .40 1.00
AS11 Mario Austin .40 1.00
AS12 Nick Collison .40 1.00
AS13 Travis Hansen .40 1.00
AS14 Josh Howard .40 1.00

2003-04 UD Top Prospects Clashing Colors

Randomly inserted in packs, this five cards set places one player on the top next to a circular swatch of his jersey and one on the bottom. Each card is sequentially numbered to 25.

CCJGJK Jason Gardner 10.00 25.00
Jason Kapono
CCLJCA LeBron James 250.00 400.00
Carmelo Anthony
CCLWJG Luke Walton 12.50 30.00
Jason Gardner
CCLWJK Luke Walton 12.50 30.00
Jason Kapono

2003-04 UD Top Prospects Conference Call

Randomly seeded in packs at the rate of one in 12, this 14-card set places full color action photography between a top and bottom border made to look like a mesh jersey. The player's name appears along the top in gold foil, the player's NCAA conference name appears along the left edge of the card in gold, and the logo for the "Conference Call" insert set is made in embossed gold foil along the bottom of the card.

COMPLETE SET (14) 5.00 12.00
CC1 Carmelo Anthony 1.25 3.00
CC2 Luke Walton .50 1.25
CC3 Dahntay Jones .50 1.25
CC4 Brian Cook .50 1.25
CC5 Chris Kaman .60 1.50
CC6 Rick Rickert .50 1.25
CC7 Reece Gaines .50 1.25
CC8 Hollis Price .50 1.25
CC9 Jason Gardner .50 1.25
CC10 Nick Collison .50 1.25

CC11 Troy Bell .50 1.25
CC12 Mario Austin .50 1.25
CC13 Luke Ridnour .60 1.50
CC14 David West .60 1.50

2003-04 UD Top Prospects Dare to Compare Dual Autographs

Randomly inserted in packs, this six card set features top ranked draft choices paired up on each card with both player's autographs. Each card is sequentially numbered to 25.

DMCA Darko Milicic 50.00 120.00
Carmelo Anthony
DMLJ Darko Milicic 250.00 400.00
LeBron James
LJCA LeBron James 400.00 800.00
Carmelo Anthony
LRLW Luke Ridnour 20.00 50.00
Luke Walton
MJKB Michael Jordan 600.00 1000.00
Kobe Bryant
TFBK Nick Collison 50.00 120.00
Carmelo Anthony

2003-04 UD Top Prospects Foreign Exchange

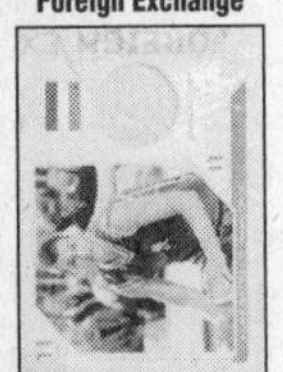

Randomly inserted in packs at the rate of one in 24, this seven card set features players who were drafted out of foreign countries. The set utilizes a horizontal card set up with both a full-color photo of the featured player and a circular gold foil emblem which is embossed with the logo for the Foreign Exchange set.

COMPLETE SET (7) 4.00 10.00
FE1 Darko Milicic 1.00 2.50
FE2 Anderson Varejao 1.00 2.50
FE3 Sofoklis Schortsanitis 1.00 2.50
FE4 Pavel Podkolzine 1.00 2.50
FE5 Mickael Pietrus 1.00 2.50
FE6 Boris Diaw 1.25 3.00
FE7 Aleksandar Pavlovic 1.00 2.50

2003-04 UD Top Prospects Franchise Makers

Randomly seeded in packs, this seven card set utilizes a horizontal card design with a full color player action photo set against a colored checkered background. Each card is sequentially numbered to 25.

FM1 LeBron James 150.00 300.00
FM2 Darko Milicic 8.00 20.00
FM3 Carmelo Anthony 40.00 100.00
FM4 Luke Walton 8.00 20.00
FM5 Pavel Podkolzine 8.00 20.00
FM6 Luke Ridnour 10.00 25.00
FM7 Nick Collison 8.00 20.00

2003-04 UD Top Prospects Higher Achievements

Randomly inserted in packs, this 14-card set places full color action photography on a card design that is borderless on three sides. The bottom of the card has a full border with the set name and gold foil highlights. Each card is sequentially numbered to 50.

HA1 LeBron James 60.00 150.00
HA2 Darko Milicic 6.00 15.00
HA3 Carmelo Anthony 15.00 40.00
HA4 Pavel Podkolzine 6.00 15.00
HA5 Nick Collison 6.00 15.00
HA6 Josh Howard 6.00 15.00
HA7 Chris Kaman 8.00 20.00
HA8 James Lang 6.00 15.00
HA9 Luke Walton 6.00 15.00
HA10 David West 8.00 20.00
HA11 Mario Austin 6.00 15.00
HA12 Rick Rickert 6.00 15.00
HA13 Jerome Beasley 6.00 15.00
HA14 Boris Diaw 8.00 20.00

2003-04 UD Top Prospects Mentors and Learners

Randomly inserted in packs at the rate of one in 24, this seven card set features some of the more talented draft picks paired up with either Michael Jordan or Kobe Bryant. The cards are horizontally designed and place a full color action photo of the draftee on the right and a blue-toned photo of the veteran on the left. All cards have gold foil highlights.

COMPLETE SET (7) 12.50 30.00
ML1 Michael Jordan 8.00 20.00
LeBron James
ML2 Kobe Bryant 2.00 5.00
Luke Ridnour
ML3 Michael Jordan 3.00 8.00
Carmelo Anthony
ML4 Michael Jordan 2.50 5.00
Dahntay Jones
ML5 Kobe Bryant 6.00 15.00
LeBron James
ML6 Michael Jordan 2.00 5.00
James Lang
ML7 Michael Jordan 2.50 6.00
Travis Outlaw

2003-04 UD Top Prospects Report Card

Inserted in packs, this 14-card set places a full color action photo on the left side of the horizontal design and a grading report on the players basketball skills on the right side. Each card contains gold foil highlights and is sequentially numbered to 250.

RC1 LeBron James 20.00 50.00
RC2 Marcus Banks 1.50 4.00
RC3 Carmelo Anthony 4.00 10.00
RC4 David West 2.00 5.00
RC5 Nick Collison 1.50 4.00
RC6 Rick Rickert 1.50 4.00
RC7 Chris Kaman 2.00 5.00
RC8 Luke Walton 1.50 4.00
RC9 Luke Ridnour 2.00 5.00
RC10 Mickael Pietrus 1.50 4.00
RC11 Travis Outlaw 2.00 5.00
RC12 Darko Milicic 1.50 4.00
RC13 Josh Howard 1.50 4.00
RC14 Anderson Varejao 1.50 4.00

2003-04 UD Top Prospects School Colors

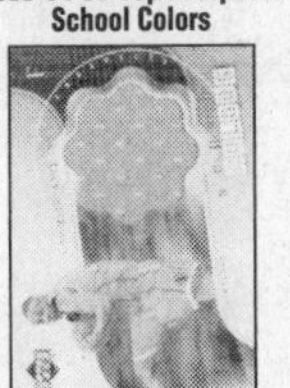

Inserted in packs at the rate of one in 288, this six card set features borders along the top and bottom of the horizonal design. Full color player action photos appear in the middle to the left and a jagged circular swatch of game jersey appears on the right.

SCCA Carmelo Anthony 12.00 30.00
SCJG Jason Gardner 5.00 12.00
SCJK Jason Kapono 5.00 12.00
SCLJ LeBron James 60.00 150.00
SCLW Luke Walton 5.00 12.00
SCMJ Michael Jordan SP 75.00 150.00

2003-04 UD Top Prospects Signs of Success

Randomly inserted in packs at the rate of one in 12, this 53-card set places full-color player photos along the top of the card, a "Signs of Success" logo in the middle and a silver hologram sticker on the bottom featuring the player's autograph.

SSAP Aleksandar Pavlovic 3.00 8.00
SSAV Anderson Varejao 5.00 12.00
SSBB Brett Blizzard 3.00 8.00
SSBC Brian Cook 3.00 8.00
SSBD Boris Diaw 4.00 10.00
SSBE Julius Barnes 3.00 8.00
SSCA Carmelo Anthony 30.00 80.00
SSCK Chris Kaman 4.00 10.00
SSDJ Dahntay Jones 3.00 8.00
SSDM Darko Milicic 3.00 8.00
SSEE Ebi Ere 3.00 8.00
SSHP Hollis Price 3.00 8.00
SSHU Brandon Hunter 3.00 8.00
SSJB Jerome Beasley 3.00 8.00
SSJG Jason Gardner 3.00 8.00
SSJH Josh Howard 3.00 8.00
SSJK Jason Kapono 3.00 8.00
SSJL James Lang 3.00 8.00
SSJN Jeff Newton 3.00 8.00
SSJS Joe Shipp 3.00 8.00
SSKB Keith Bogans 3.00 8.00
SSKB Kobe Bryant 100.00 200.00
SSKK Kyle Korver 4.00 10.00
SSLJ LeBron James 250.00 500.00
SSLR Luke Ridnour 4.00 10.00
SSLW Luke Walton 3.00 8.00
SSMA Mario Austin 3.00 8.00
SSMB Marcus Banks 3.00 8.00
SSMB Matt Bonner 4.00 10.00
SSMC Matt Carroll 3.00 8.00
SSMD Marquis Daniels 3.00 8.00
SSMH Marcus Hatten 3.00 8.00
SSMJ Michael Jordan SP 350.00 600.00
SSML Maciej Lampe 3.00 8.00
SSNC Nick Collison 3.00 8.00
SSPI Mickael Pietrus 3.00 8.00
SSPP Pavel Podkolzine 3.00 8.00
SSQR Quinton Ross 3.00 8.00
SSRD Ronald Dupree 3.00 8.00
SSRD Ruben Douglas 3.00 8.00
SSRG Reece Gaines 3.00 8.00
SSRR Rick Rickert 3.00 8.00
SSSB Steve Blake 4.00 10.00
SSSS Sofoklis Schortsanitis 3.00 8.00
SSSV Slavko Vranes 3.00 8.00
SSTB Troy Bell 3.00 8.00
SSTH Travis Hansen 3.00 8.00
SSTO Travis Outlaw 4.00 10.00
SSVK Viktor Khryapa 3.00 8.00
SSWE David West 4.00 10.00
SSZA Zaur Pachulia 3.00 8.00
SSZC Zarko Cabarkapa 3.00 8.00
SSZP Zoran Planinic 3.00 8.00

1991-92 Ultimate Promo Panel

1 Dmitri Starostenko 1.25 3.00
Popeye
Betty Boop
Bobby Hull
Larry Johnson BK
Pat Falloon
Stan Gelbaugh WLAF

2009-10 Upper Deck Draft Edition

COMPLETE SET (69) 10.00 25.00
UNPRICED PLATINUM PRINT RUN ONE SET
1 A.J. Abrams .20 .50
2 A.J. Price .20 .50
3 Alex Ruoff .20 .50
4 Jimmy Baron SP .40 1.00
5 Alonzo Gee .25 .60
6 Garrett Temple SP .40 1.00
7 Antonio Anderson .20 .50
8 Dionte Christmas .20 .50
9 Austin Daye .20 .50
10 B.J. Mullens .20 .50
11 Ricky Rubio SP 2.00 5.00
12 Ryan Ayers SP .40 1.00
13 Chase Budinger .20 .50
14 Rodrigue Beaubois SP .50 1.25
15 Courtney Fells .20 .50
16 Jack McClinton SP .40 1.00
17 Sam Young SP .40 1.00
18 Cyrus Tate .20 .50
19 Danny Green .30 .75
20 Dar Tucker .20 .50
21 Darren Collison .30 .75
22 B.J. Raymond SP .40 1.00
23 Luke Nevill SP .40 1.00
24 Derrick Brown .20 .50
25 DeMarre Carroll .20 .50
26 Dominic James .20 .50
27 Sergio Llull SP .40 1.00
28 Brandon Costner .20 .50
29 Earl Clark .20 .50
30 Josh Shipp .20 .50
31 Eric Maynor .20 .50
32 Dante Cunningham SP .40 1.00
33 Gerald Henderson .20 .50
34 Stephen Curry SP 1.00 2.50
35 Rasheem Barrett .20 .50
36 Lester Hudson .20 .50
37 Taj Gibson SP .50 1.25
38 Henk Norel .20 .50
39 Jon Brockman .20 .50
40 James Harden .60 1.50
41 James Johnson .20 .50
42 Korvotney Barber SP .40 1.00
43 Ty Lawson SP .60 1.50
44 Jeff Adrien .20 .50
45 Jeff Pendergraph .20 .50
46 Jerel McNeal .20 .50
47 Jeremy Pargo .20 .50
48 Robert Vaden .20 .50
49 Joe Ingles .20 .50
50 Micah Downs .20 .50
51 Jeff Teague .25 .60
52 Jonny Flynn .20 .50
53 Toney Douglas SP .40 1.00
54 Josh Heytvelt .20 .50
55 Jrue Holiday .40 1.00
56 K.C. Rivers .20 .50
57 Daniel Hackett .20 .50
58 Goran Suton SP .40 1.00
59 Lee Cummard .20 .50
60 Leo Lyons .20 .50
61 Connor Atchley .20 .50
62 Tyrese Rice SP .40 1.00
63 Michael Bramos .20 .50
64 Marcus Thornton SP .60 1.50
65 Nando De Colo .20 .50
66 Nick Calathes .20 .50
67 Omri Casspi .20 .50
68 Wesley Matthews SP .60 1.50
B32 Tyler Hansbrough SP .60 1.50
NNO Michael Jordan Redemption 8.00 20.00

2009-10 Upper Deck Draft Edition Blue

*BLUE/99/49: 1.25X TO 3X BASE HI
*BLUE/99/49 SP: .6X TO 1.5X BASE HI
*BLUE/149: .75X TO 2X BASE
*BLUE/149: .4X TO 1X BASE
*BLUE/249: .6X TO 1.5X BASE
*BLUE/249 SP: .4X TO 1X BASE
BLUE PRINT RUN 99 TO 249 SETS

2009-10 Upper Deck Draft Edition Gold

*GOLD: 4X TO 10X BASE HI
*GOLD SP: 2X TO 5X BASE HI
GOLD PRINT RUN 25 SER.#'d SETS

2009-10 Upper Deck Draft Edition Silver

*SILVER: .75X TO 2X BASE HI
*SILVER SP: .4X TO 1X BASE
SILVER PRINT RUN 299 TO 999 SETS

2009-10 Upper Deck Draft Edition Alma Mater

COMPLETE SET (24) 25.00 50.00
RANDOM INSERTS IN PACKS
UNPRICED BLACK PRINT RUN ONE SET
*BLUE: .6X TO 1.5X BASE HI
BLUE PRINT RUN 99 SER.#'d SETS
AMBI Matt Biondi 1.00 2.50
AMBO Tom Bosley 1.00 2.50
AMCL Chuck Liddell 2.50 6.00
AMCP Chris Paul 1.25 3.00
AMDP Dustin Pedroia 1.25 3.00
AMFC Fred Couples 1.00 2.50
AMFI Jennie Finch 2.50 6.00
AMFT Frank Thomas 1.00 2.50
AMJF Jennie Finch 2.50 6.00
AMJO Michael Johnson 1.00 2.50
AMKB Kobe Bryant 4.00 10.00
AMKD Kevin Durant 2.50 6.00
AMKG Kevin Garnett 1.50 4.00
AMLF Lisa Fernandez 1.00 2.50
AMLJ LeBron James 4.00 10.00
AMLO Lorena Ochoa 2.50 6.00
AMMB Michael Biehn 1.00 2.50
AMMJ Michael Jordan 6.00 15.00
AMMP Michael Phelps 2.50 6.00
AMMR Matt Ryan 2.00 5.00
AMNG Natalie Gulbis 2.50 6.00
AMRC Randy Couture 2.00 5.00
AMTB Terry Bradshaw 1.00 2.50
AMTW Tiger Woods 3.00 8.00

2009-10 Upper Deck Draft Edition Alma Mater Autographs

STATED PRINT RUN 10 TO 99 SER.#'d SETS
SOME UNPRICED DUE TO SCARCITY
AMBO Tom Bosley/40 15.00 30.00
AMCL Chuck Liddell/25 100.00 200.00
AMCP Chris Paul/25 25.00 50.00
AMDP Dustin Pedroia/99 20.00 50.00
AMFC Fred Couples/99 20.00 40.00
AMFI Jennie Finch/99 20.00 40.00
AMFT Frank Thomas/25 40.00 100.00
AMJF Jennie Finch/99 20.00 40.00
AMKB Kobe Bryant/24 100.00 200.00
AMKD Kevin Durant/35 75.00 150.00
AMKG Kevin Garnett/25 60.00 120.00
AMLF Lisa Fernandez/99 10.00 25.00
AMLJ LeBron James/23 150.00 300.00
AMLO Lorena Ochoa/99 40.00 80.00
AMMB Michael Biehn/18 10.00 25.00
AMMJ Michael Jordan/23 300.00 500.00
AMMP Michael Phelps/99 150.00 300.00
AMMR Matt Ryan/25 50.00 100.00
AMNG Natalie Gulbis/11 300.00 500.00
AMRC Randy Couture/25 50.00 100.00

2009-10 Upper Deck Draft Edition Alma Mater Green

*GREEN: .75X TO 2X BASE HI
GREEN PRINT RUN 50 SER.#'d SETS
AMCL Chuck Liddell 8.00 20.00
AMMP Michael Phelps 8.00 20.00
AMNG Natalie Gulbis 30.00 60.00
AMRC Randy Couture 6.00 15.00
AMTW Tiger Woods 40.00 100.00

2009-10 Upper Deck Draft Edition Alma Mater Red

*RED: 2X TO 5X BASE HI
RED PRINT RUN 25 SER.#'d SETS
AMCL Chuck Liddell 20.00 40.00
AMMP Michael Phelps 20.00 40.00
AMNG Natalie Gulbis 50.00 100.00
AMRC Randy Couture 20.00 40.00
AMTW Tiger Woods 75.00 150.00

2009-10 Upper Deck Draft Edition Autographs

STATED PRINT RUN 149 TO 999 SER.#'d SETS
UNPRICED BLACK PRINT RUN ONE SET
*BLUE: .75X TO 2X BASE HI
BLUE PRINT RUN 25 SER.#'d SETS
UNPRICED GOLD PRINT RUN 5 SETS
*GREEN: .5X TO 1.25X BASE AU HI
GREEN PRINT RUN 49 TO 249 SER.#'d SETS
1 A.J. Abrams/399 3.00 8.00
3 Alex Ruoff/499 3.00 8.00
4 Jimmy Baron/999 3.00 8.00
5 Alonzo Gee/999 4.00 10.00
6 Garrett Temple/999 3.00 8.00
7 Antonio Anderson/999 3.00 8.00
8 Dionte Christmas/999 3.00 8.00
9 Austin Daye/499 3.00 8.00
10 B.J. Mullens/299 3.00 8.00
11 Ricky Rubio/499 40.00 100.00
12 Ryan Ayers/499 3.00 8.00
13 Chase Budinger/399 3.00 8.00
14 Rodrigue Beaubois/299 4.00 10.00
15 Courtney Fells/999 3.00 8.00
16 Jack McClinton/999 3.00 8.00
17 Sam Young/999 3.00 8.00
18 Cyrus Tate/499 3.00 8.00
19 Danny Green/399 6.00 15.00
20 Dar Tucker/399 3.00 8.00
21 Darren Collison/499 5.00 12.00
22 B.J. Raymond/999 3.00 8.00
23 Luke Nevill/399 3.00 8.00
25 DeMarre Carroll/999 3.00 8.00
26 Dominic James/549 3.00 8.00
28 Brandon Costner/399 3.00 8.00
29 Earl Clark/199 10.00 25.00
30 Josh Shipp/499 3.00 8.00
31 Eric Maynor/349 3.00 8.00
32 Dante Cunningham/899 3.00 8.00
33 Gerald Henderson/499 3.00 8.00
34 Stephen Curry/249 10.00 25.00
35 Rasheem Barrett/499 3.00 8.00
36 Lester Hudson/999 3.00 8.00
38 Henk Norel/999 3.00 8.00
39 Jon Brockman/999 3.00 8.00
40 James Harden/499 10.00 25.00
41 James Johnson/499 3.00 8.00
42 Korvotney Barber/499 3.00 8.00
44 Jeff Adrien/499 3.00 8.00
45 Jeff Pendergraph/199 3.00 8.00
46 Jerel McNeal 3.00 8.00
47 Jeremy Pargo/299 3.00 8.00
48 Robert Vaden/999 3.00 8.00
49 Joe Ingles/399 3.00 8.00
50 Micah Downs/299 3.00 8.00
51 Jeff Teague/499 4.00 10.00
52 Jonny Flynn/499 3.00 8.00
53 Toney Douglas/299 3.00 8.00
54 Josh Heytvelt/999 3.00 8.00
55 Jrue Holiday/499 8.00 20.00
56 K.C. Rivers/499 3.00 8.00
57 Daniel Hackett/999 3.00 8.00
58 Goran Suton/299 3.00 8.00
59 Lee Cummard/399 3.00 8.00
60 Leo Lyons/999 3.00 8.00
61 Connor Atchley/999 3.00 8.00
62 Tyrese Rice/999 3.00 8.00
63 Michael Bramos/999 3.00 8.00
64 Marcus Thornton/999 5.00 12.00
66 Nick Calathes/999 3.00 8.00
67 Omri Casspi/149 3.00 8.00
68 Wesley Matthews/999 5.00 12.00

2009-10 Upper Deck Draft Edition Coaching Legends

COMPLETE SET (3) 3.00 8.00
RANDOM INSERTS IN PACKS
UNPRICED BLACK PRINT RUN ONE SET
*BLUE: .6X TO 1.5X BASE HI
BLUE PRINT RUN 99 SER.#'d SETS
*GREEN: .75X TO 2X BASE HI
GREEN PRINT RUN 50 SER.#'d SETS
*RED: 1.25X TO 3X BASE HI
RED PRINT RUN 25 SER.#'d SETS
CLBD Billy Donovan 2.00 5.00
CLBK Bobby Knight 2.00 5.00
CLJT Jerry Tarkanian 1.50 4.00

2009-10 Upper Deck Draft Edition Coaching Legends Autographs

STATED PRINT RUN 25 TO 50 SER.#'d SETS
CLBD Billy Donovan/50 25.00 60.00
CLBK Bobby Knight/25 30.00 60.00
CLJT Jerry Tarkanian/50 10.00 25.00

2009-10 Upper Deck Draft Edition Draft Class

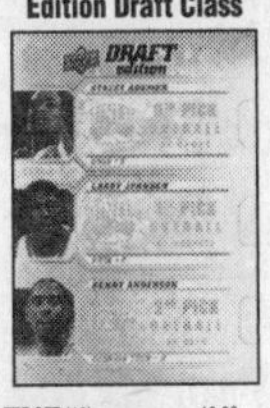

COMPLETE SET (10) 10.00 25.00
APPROXIMATE ODDS 1:8
UNPRICED BLACK PRINT RUN ONE SET
*BLUE: .6X TO 1.5X BASE HI
BLUE PRINT RUN 99 SER.#'d SETS
*GREEN: 1X TO 2.5X BASE HI
GREEN PRINT RUN 50 SER.#'d SETS
*RED: 2X TO 5X BASE HI
RED PRINT RUN 25 SER.#'d SETS
D84 Hakeem Olajuwon 5.00 12.00
John Stockton
Michael Jordan
D87 David Robinson 2.50 6.00
Horace Grant
Kenny Smith
D89 B.J. Armstrong 2.00 5.00
Glen Rice
Vlade Divac
D91 Kenny Anderson 2.00 5.00
Larry Johnson
Stacey Augmon
DARZ Chase Budinger 2.00 5.00
James Harden
Jeff Pendergraph
DCHH Gerald Henderson 2.00 5.00
James Harden
Stephen Curry
DHRC James Harden 2.50 6.00
Ricky Rubio
Stephen Curry
DMFC Eric Maynor 2.50 6.00
Jonny Flynn
Stephen Curry
DRFC Jonny Flynn 4.00 10.00
Ricky Rubio
Stephen Curry
DTHD Lester Hudson 2.00 5.00
Marcus Thornton
Toney Douglas

2009-10 Upper Deck Draft Edition Draft Class Autographs

STATED PRINT RUN 15 TO 60 SER.#'d SETS
SOME UNPRICED DUE TO SCARCITY
D89 B.J. Armstrong/15 40.00 80.00
Glen Rice
Vlade Divac
D91 Kenny Anderson/15 40.00 80.00
Larry Johnson
Stacey Augmon
DARZ Chase Budinger/60 20.00 40.00
James Harden
Jeff Pendergraph
DCHH Gerald Henderson/60 30.00 60.00
James Harden
Stephen Curry
DHRC James Harden/30 125.00 250.00
Ricky Rubio
Stephen Curry
DMFC Eric Maynor/60 30.00 60.00
Jonny Flynn
Stephen Curry
DRFC Jonny Flynn/60 75.00 200.00
Ricky Rubio
Stephen Curry
DTHD Lester Hudson/60 15.00 30.00
Marcus Thornton
Toney Douglas

2009-10 Upper Deck Draft Edition School Ties

COMPLETE SET (13) 7.50 15.00
APPROXIMATE ODDS 1:8
UNPRICED BLACK PRINT RUN ONE SET
*BLUE: .75X TO 2X BASE HI
BLUE PRINT RUN 99 SER.#'d SETS
*GREEN: 1X TO 2.5X BASE HI
GREEN PRINT RUN 50 SER.#'d SETS
*RED: 2X TO 5X BASE HI
RED PRINT RUN 25 SER.#'d SETS
STAH Jrue Holiday 1.50 4.00
Kareem Abdul-Jabbar
STAJ A.J. Abrams 1.00 2.50
Connor Atchley
STCD Sam Cassell 1.00 2.50
Toney Douglas
STGB Jeremy Pargo 1.00 2.50
Micah Downs
STGS Bill Sharman 1.00 2.50
Taj Gibson
STHP James Harden 1.00 2.50
Jeff Pendergraph
STJT Larry Johnson 1.25 3.00
Reggie Theus
STMA Jerel McNeal 1.00 2.50
Wesley Matthews
STMT DeMarre Carroll 1.00 2.50
Leo Lyons
STPT Bob Pettit 1.00 2.50
Marcus Thornton
STTL Connor Atchley 1.50 4.00
Kevin Durant
STUB Darren Collison 1.25 3.00
Josh Shipp
STWF Chris Paul 1.25 3.00
James Johnson

2009-10 Upper Deck Draft Edition School Ties Autographs

STATED PRINT RUN 25 TO 99 SER.#'d SETS
STAH Jrue Holiday/25 30.00 80.00
Kareem Abdul-Jabbar
STAJ A.J. Abrams/99 8.00 20.00
Connor Atchley
STGB Jeremy Pargo/99 10.00 25.00
Micah Downs
STGS Bill Sharman/25 8.00 20.00
Taj Gibson
STHP James Harden/99 12.00 30.00
Jeff Pendergraph
STJT Larry Johnson/25 40.00 100.00
Reggie Theus
STMT DeMarre Carroll/99 8.00 20.00
Leo Lyons
STPT Bob Pettit/25 15.00 40.00
Marcus Thornton
STTL Kevin Durant/25 50.00 120.00
Connor Atchley
STWF Chris Paul/25 30.00 60.00
James Johnson

2009-10 Upper Deck Draft Edition Tournament Titans

COMPLETE SET (15) 10.00 25.00
APPROXIMATE ODDS 1:3
UNPRICED BLACK PRINT RUN ONE SET
*BLUE: .6X TO 1.5X BASE HI
BLUE PRINT RUN 99 SER.#'d SET
*GREEN: 1.5X TO 4X BASE HI
GREEN PRINT RUN 50 SER.#'d SETS
*RED: 2.5X TO 6X BASE HI
RED PRINT RUN 25 SER.#'d SETS
TTBW Bill Walton .60 1.50
TTCP Chris Paul 1.00 2.50
TTDG Darrell Griffith .60 1.50
TTDT David Thompson .75 2.00
TTEB Elgin Baylor .60 1.50
TTGR Glen Rice .60 1.50
TTHO Hakeem Olajuwon .75 2.00
TTIT Isiah Thomas .60 1.50
TTJO Michael Jordan 5.00 12.00
TTJW Jerry West .75 2.00
TTKD Kevin Durant 2.00 5.00
TTMJ Magic Johnson 1.50 4.00
TTSC Stephen Curry 1.50 4.00
TTSY Sam Young .60 1.50
TTTL Ty Lawson 1.00 2.50

2009-10 Upper Deck Draft Edition Tournament Titans Autographs

STATED PRINT RUN 18 TO 25 SER.#'d SETS
TTBW Bill Walton/25 12.50 30.00
TTCP Chris Paul/25 30.00 80.00
TTDG Darrell Griffith/18 20.00 40.00
TTDT David Thompson/25 12.50 30.00
TTEB Elgin Baylor/25 12.50 30.00
TTGR Glen Rice/25 30.00 60.00
TTHO Hakeem Olajuwon/25 30.00 60.00
TTIT Isiah Thomas/25 20.00 40.00
TTJO Michael Jordan/25 300.00 550.00
TTJW Jerry West/25 30.00 60.00
TTKD Kevin Durant/25 75.00 150.00
TTMJ Magic Johnson/25 60.00 120.00
TTSC Stephen Curry/25 25.00 60.00
TTSY Sam Young/25 12.50 30.00

1995 Visions Sample

This sample card was issued to herald the release of Classic's 150-card Vision series. On the fronts, the full-bleed color action photo is ghosted so that the featured player stands out. The player's name and position are stamped in purple foil. The back carries ad copy promoting the series and describing the insert sets. A tag line toward the bottom indicates that this is a sample card for promotional purposes only.

V96 Damon Stoudamire .75 2.00

1995 Visions

The 1995 Classic Basketball Visions was issued in one series totalling 100 standard-size cards. The set was issued in 5-card packs. The fronts feature a borderless color action player photo with the player's name stamped in gold foil across the picture. The word "Visions" appears in silver below the player's name. The backs carry another borderless player action color photo with the player's name, position, biographical and statistical information, and a prediction, or vision, of what will happen to the player in the coming year. The set features the following topical subsets: Clipboard (66-80), Kidd 1-On-1 (81-90) and Shaq 1-On-1 (91-100).

COMPLETE SET (100) 4.00 10.00
1 Joe Smith .25 .60
2 Antonio McDyess .30 .75
3 Jerry Stackhouse .40 1.00
4 Rasheed Wallace .40 1.00
5 Kevin Garnett 1.00 2.50
6 Damon Stoudamire .30 .75
7 Shawn Respert .12 .30
8 Ed O'Bannon .12 .30
9 Kurt Thomas .12 .30
10 Gary Trent .12 .30
11 Cherokee Parks .12 .30
12 Corliss Williamson .12 .30
13 Eric Williams .12 .30
14 Brent Barry .20 .50
15 Bob Sura .12 .30
16 Theo Ratliff .20 .50
17 Randolph Childress .12 .30
18 Jason Caffey .12 .30
19 Michael Finley .40 1.00
20 George Zidek .12 .30
21 Travis Best .12 .30
22 Loren Meyer .12 .30
23 David Vaughn .12 .30
24 Sherrell Ford .12 .30
25 Mario Bennett .12 .30
26 Greg Ostertag .12 .30
27 Cory Alexander .12 .30
28 Lou Roe .12 .30
29 Dragan Tarlac .12 .30
30 Terrence Rencher .12 .30
31 Junior Burrough .12 .30
32 Andrew DeClercq .12 .30
33 Jimmy King .12 .30
34 Lawrence Moten .12 .30
35 Frankie King .12 .30
36 Rashard Griffith .12 .30
37 Donny Marshall .12 .30
38 John Amaechi .12 .30
39 Erik Meeks .12 .30
40 Donnie Boyce .12 .30
41 Eric Snow .12 .30
42 Anthony Pelle .12 .30
43 Troy Brown .12 .30
44 George Banks .12 .30
45 Tyus Edney .12 .30
46 Mark Davis .12 .30
47 Jerome Allen .12 .30
48 Fred Hoiberg .12 .30
49 Constantin Popa .12 .30
50 Michael McDonald .12 .30
51 Chris Carr .12 .30
52 Cuonzo Martin .12 .30
53 Don Reid .12 .30
54 Shaquille O'Neal .30 .75
55 Hakeem Olajuwon .15 .40
56 Alonzo Mourning .15 .40
57 Dikembe Mutombo .12 .30
58 Jason Kidd .20 .50
59 Glenn Robinson .12 .30
60 Juwan Howard .12 .30
61 Brian Grant .10 .25
62 Eddie Jones .15 .40
63 Rebecca Lobo .20 .50
64 Clint McDaniel .12 .30
65 Scotty Thurman .12 .30
66 Joe Smith CB .12 .30
67 Jerry Stackhouse CB .20 .50
68 Rasheed Wallace CB .20 .50

69 Kevin Garnett CB .50 1.25
70 Ed O'Bannon CB .05 .15
71 Gary Trent CB .05 .15
72 Corliss Williamson CB .05 .15
73 Brent Barry CB .10 .25
74 Shaquille O'Neal CB .15 .40
75 Hakeem Olajuwon CB .07 .20
76 Jason Kidd CB .10 .25
77 Eddie Jones CB .07 .20
78 Glenn Robinson CB .05 .15
79 Brian Grant CB .05 .10
80 Rebecca Lobo CB .10 .25
81 Jerry Stackhouse KO .20 .50
82 Damon Stoudamire KO .15 .40
83 Shawn Respert KO .05 .15
84 Brent Barry KO .10 .25
85 Ed O'Bannon KO .05 .15
86 Glenn Robinson KO .05 .15
87 Randolph Childress KO .05 .15
88 Travis Best KO .05 .15
89 Eddie Jones KO .07 .20
90 Tyus Edney KO .05 .15
91 Joe Smith SO .12 .30
92 Antonio McDyess SO .15 .40
93 Rasheed Wallace SO .20 .50
94 Kevin Garnett SO .50 1.25
95 Alonzo Mourning SO .07 .20
96 Kurt Thomas SO .05 .15
97 Cherokee Parks SO .05 .15
98 Corliss Williamson SO .05 .15
99 Hakeem Olajuwon SO .07 .20
100 Shaquille O'Neal SO .15 .40

1995 Visions Effects

The Classic Basketball Visions Effects parallel set was issued in one series totalling 100 standard-size cards. One card was randomly inserted into every 10 packs of Visions cards. The fronts feature a borderless color action player image with a dimensional holographic foil stamp background that makes it appear as if the player is popping off the card. The player's name is stamped in gold foil across the picture. The words "Visions Effects" run vertically down the right side. To ascertain values of individual cards, please refer to the multiplier in the header, coupled with the value of the base card.

COMPLETE SET (100) 25.00 60.00
*EFFECTS: 1.5X TO 4X BASIC CARDS

1995 Visions Hardcourt Skills

This 15-card standard-size set was randomly inserted one to a box and was printed on 24-point grain wood card stock. The fronts feature a cut-out action player photos on a wood background with a basketball at the top and the card logo and player's name at the bottom. The cards are numbered with a "HC" prefix.

COMPLETE SET (15) 15.00 40.00
HC1 Joe Smith 2.00 5.00
HC2 Antonio McDyess 2.50 6.00
HC3 Jerry Stackhouse 3.00 8.00
HC4 Rasheed Wallace 3.00 8.00
HC5 Damon Stoudamire 2.00 5.00
HC6 Shawn Respert 1.00 2.50
HC7 Ed O'Bannon 1.00 2.50
HC8 Jimmy King 1.00 2.50
HC9 Randolph Childress 1.00 2.50
HC10 Shaquille O'Neal 2.50 6.00
HC11 Hakeem Olajuwon 1.25 3.00
HC12 Jason Kidd 1.50 4.00
HC13 Alonzo Mourning 1.25 3.00
HC14 Scottie Pippen 1.50 4.00
HC15 Glenn Robinson 1.00 2.50

1995 Visions Laser Art

This 10-card standard-size set was randomly inserted one every 145 packs. The cards feature a duplexed laser die-cut image on a "fabric" card stock. The fronts display a player's image with a net and basketball background. The player's name is printed in the faded blue border at the bottom. The cards are numbered with a "LA" prefix.

COMPLETE SET (10) 40.00 80.00
LA1 Shaquille O'Neal 5.00 12.00
LA2 Jason Kidd 3.00 8.00
LA3 Alonzo Mourning 2.50 6.00
LA4 Damon Stoudamire 5.00 12.00
LA5 Glenn Robinson 2.00 5.00
LA6 Joe Smith 4.00 10.00
LA7 Jerry Stackhouse 6.00 15.00
LA8 Kevin Garnett 15.00 40.00
LA9 Ed O'Bannon 2.00 5.00
LA10 Rebecca Lobo 3.00 8.00

1996 Visions

The 1996 Classic Visions set consists of 150 standard-size cards. The fronts feature full-bleed color action player photos. The player's position and name are presented in blue foil, while the Classic logo and set title "96 Visions" are stamped in gold foil. The back carries a second color photo, college statistics, biography, and a player fact.

COMPLETE SET (150) 6.00 15.00
1 Shaquille O'Neal .30 .75
2 Scottie Pippen .15 .40
3 Jason Kidd .15 .40
4 Hakeem Olajuwon .15 .40
5 Juwan Howard .15 .40
6 Alonzo Mourning .15 .40
7 Glenn Robinson .15 .40
8 Rasheed Wallace .15 .40
9 Ed O'Bannon .08 .25
10 Joe Smith .08 .25
11 Jerry Stackhouse .15 .40
12 Damon Stoudamire .08 .25
13 Cherokee Parks .08 .25
14 Gary Trent .08 .25
15 Shawn Respert .08 .25
16 Kevin Garnett .40 1.00
17 Kurt Thomas .15 .40
18 Jalen Rose .08 .25
19 Michael Finley .15 .40
20 Jason Caffey .08 .25
21 Randolph Childress .08 .25
22 Tyus Edney .08 .25
23 George Zidek .08 .25
24 Antonio McDyess .15 .40
25 Corliss Williamson .15 .40
26 Theo Ratliff .08 .25
27 Eric Williams .08 .25
28 Dikembe Mutombo .15 .40
29 Lawrence Moten .08 .25
30 Jimmy King .08 .25
31 Donyell Marshall .15 .40
32 Brian Grant .15 .40
33 Sharone Wright .08 .25
34 Eddie Jones .15 .40
35 Greg Ostertag .08 .25
36 Terrence Rencher .08 .25
37 David Vaughn .08 .25
38 Rebecca Lobo .15 .40
121 Shaquille O'Neal .30 .75
125 Scottie Pippen .15 .40
128 Jason Kidd .15 .40
131 Joe Smith .08 .25
132 Rasheed Wallace .15 .40
133 Ed O'Bannon .08 .25
134 Michael Finley .15 .40
135 Jerry Stackhouse .15 .40
136 Tyus Edney .08 .25
137 Damon Stoudamire .08 .25
138 Antonio McDyess .15 .40
139 Kevin Garnett .40 1.00
140 Corliss Williamson .15 .40
V96 Damon Stoudamire .40 1.00
Promo card

1996 Visions Action 21

2 Jerry Stackhouse .20 .50
3 Rasheed Wallace .15 .40

1996 Visions Basketball Update

This 10-card set was intended to update the 1995 Visions basketball draft picks 100-card set. These cards, however, were distributed exclusively as inserts in 1996 Visions multisport packs at a rate of 1:40.

COMPLETE SET (10) 6.00 15.00
U101 Shaquille O'Neal .40 1.00
U102 Jason Kidd .40 1.00
U103 Alonzo Mourning .40 1.00
U104 Damon Stoudamire .20 .50
U105 Glenn Robinson .40 1.00
U106 Joe Smith .20 .50
U107 Jerry Stackhouse .40 1.00
U108 Kevin Garnett .75 2.00
U109 Ed O'Bannon .20 .50
U110 Rebecca Lobo .40 1.00

1996 Visions Signings

The 1996 Visions Signings set consists of 100 standard-size cards. The fronts feature full-bleed color action player photos. The player's position and name are stamped in prismatic foil along with the Classic logo and set title "96 Visions Signings." This set contains standouts from five sports grouped together in this order: basketball, football, hockey, baseball and racing. Cards were distributed in six-card packs. Release date was June 1996. The main allure to this product, in addition to the conventional inserts, were autographed memorabilia redemption cards inserted one per 10 packs.

COMPLETE SET (100) 6.00 15.00
1 Shaquille O'Neal .60 1.50
2 Scottie Pippen .15 .40
3 Jason Kidd .20 .50
4 Hakeem Olajuwon .15 .40
5 Alonzo Mourning .08 .25
6 Glenn Robinson .08 .25
7 Rasheed Wallace .25 .60
8 Ed O'Bannon .08 .25
9 Joe Smith .15 .40
10 Damon Stoudamire .08 .25
11 Cherokee Parks .08 .25
12 Gary Trent .08 .25
13 Shawn Respert .08 .25
14 Kurt Thomas .08 .25
15 Michael Finley .30 .75
16 Jason Caffey .08 .25
17 Randolph Childress .08 .25
18 Tyus Edney .08 .25
19 George Zidek .08 .25
20 Antonio McDyess .20 .50
21 Corliss Williamson .08 .25
22 Theo Ratliff .08 .25
23 Eric Williams .08 .25
24 Brent Barry .08 .25
25 Lawrence Moten .08 .25
26 Bob Sura .08 .25
27 Travis Best .08 .25
28 Terrance Rencher .08 .25

1996 Visions Signings Artistry

This 10-card insert set was printed on thick 24-point stock. Cards were inserted at a rate of 1:60 Vision Signings packs.

COMPLETE SET (10) 20.00 50.00
1 Damon Stoudamire 3.00 8.00
4 Joe Smith 2.00 5.00
7 Jerry Stackhouse 3.00 8.00

1996 Visions Signings Autographs Gold

Certified autographed cards were inserted in Visions Signings packs at an overall rate of 1:12. Some players signed only the silver version while others signed both gold and silver cards. The Gold foil cards were not individually serial numbered. The quantity signed is unknown but assumed to be significantly higher than the corresponding number signed for the silver foil cards. We've listed the unnumbered cards alphabetically.

3 Cory Alexander 1.50 4.00
6 Brent Barry 2.00 5.00
9 Junior Burrough 1.50 4.00
11 Randolph Childress 1.50 4.00
19 Tyus Edney 1.50 4.00
22 Michael Finley 4.00 10.00
29 Fred Hoiberg 2.00 5.00
34 Jason Kidd 8.00 20.00
42 Lawrence Moten 1.50 4.00
43 Alonzo Mourning 6.00 15.00
46 Hakeem Olajuwon 8.00 20.00
47 Shaquille O'Neal 30.00 60.00
50 Scottie Pippen 20.00 40.00
51 Constantin Popa 1.50 4.00
52 Theo Ratliff 4.00 10.00
58 Joe Smith 4.00 10.00
61 Bob Sura 1.50 4.00
72 George Zidek 2.00 5.00

1996 Visions Signings Autographs Silver

Certified autographed cards were inserted in Visions Signings packs at an overall rate of 1:12. Some players signed only silver cards while others signed gold and silver foil cards. The Silver cards were individually serial numbered as noted below. We've listed the unnumbered cards alphabetically.

4 Cory Alexander/375 2.00 5.00
7 Brent Barry/395 2.00 5.00
12 Junior Burrough/395 2.00 5.00
14 Randolph Childress/320 2.00 5.00
22 Tyus Edney/375 2.00 5.00
26 Michael Finley/190 6.00 15.00
33 Fred Hoiberg/395 2.00 5.00
39 Jason Kidd/145 15.00 40.00
48 Lawrence Moten/170 3.00 8.00
49 Alonzo Mourning/405 10.00 25.00
52 Hakeem Olajuwon/270 15.00 40.00
53 Shaquille O'Neal/190 50.00 100.00
56 Scottie Pippen/100 30.00 80.00
57 Constantin Popa/355 2.00 5.00
58 Theo Ratliff/375 6.00 15.00
66 Joe Smith/390 3.00 8.00
69 Bob Sura/385 2.00 5.00
83 George Zidek/365 2.00 5.00

1997 Visions Signings

Score Board's follow-up to the 1996 Visions Signings debut product was released in June 1997. The second-year product had more of a memorabilia emphasis. According to Score Board, 1,700 sequentially numbered cases were produced with five cards per pack, 16 packs per box and 10 boxes per case. Each pack contains either an autographed card or an insert card. The 50-card regular set includes stars and prospects from all four major team sports. Also, one in every two packs contained a gold parallel card to the base set.

COMPLETE SET (50) 5.00 10.00
2 Hakeem Olajuwon .15 .40
3 Glenn Robinson .05 .15
8 Erick Dampier .05 .15
9 Tony Delk .05 .15
10 Steve Nash .30 .75
11 Jerry Stackhouse .15 .40
12 Lorenzen Wright .05 .15
13 Vitaly Potapenko .05 .15
14 Allen Iverson .50 1.25
15 Marcus Camby .05 .15
16 Shareef Abdur-Rahim .05 .15
17 Stephon Marbury .15 .40
18 Ray Allen .25 .60
19 Antoine Walker .15 .40
20 John Wallace .05 .15
21 Kobe Bryant .75 2.00
22 Jermaine O'Neal .08 .25
23 Clyde Drexler .15 .40
24 Scottie Pippen .15 .40
25 Rasheed Wallace .15 .40
26 Joe Smith .08 .25
27 Antonio McDyess .05 .15
28 Alonzo Mourning .05 .15

1997 Visions Signings Gold

COMPLETE SET (50) 10.00 25.00
*GOLD: .8X TO 2X BASIC CARDS
GOLD STATED ODDS 1:2

1997 Visions Signings Artistry

The cards in this 20-card set feature Score Board's "exclusive printing technology" and were inserted at a rate of 1:6 Vision Signings packs.

COMPLETE SET (20) 20.00 40.00
A2 Allen Iverson 3.00 8.00
A3 Marcus Camby 1.00 2.50
A4 Shareef Abdur-Rahim 1.00 2.50
A5 Stephon Marbury 1.00 2.50
A6 Ray Allen 2.00 5.00
A7 Antoine Walker 1.25 3.00
A8 Kobe Bryant 4.00 10.00
A9 Clyde Drexler .60 1.50
A10 Scottie Pippen .60 1.50
A11 Alonzo Mourning .60 1.50

1997 Visions Signings Artistry Autographs

These certified autographed cards feature Score Board's "exclusive printing technology" and were inserted at a rate of 1:18 packs. These 20 cards are autographed parallels of the Artistry insert set.

A2 Allen Iverson 15.00 40.00
A3 Marcus Camby 5.00 12.00
A4 Shareef Abdur-Rahim 8.00 20.00
A5 Stephon Marbury 6.00 15.00
A6 Ray Allen 10.00 25.00
A7 Antoine Walker 12.50 30.00
A8 Kobe Bryant 50.00 100.00
A9 Clyde Drexler 10.00 25.00
A10 Scottie Pippen 15.00 40.00
A11 Alonzo Mourning 8.00 20.00

1997 Visions Signings Autographs

Each 1997 Visions Signings pack contained either an autographed card or an insert card. One in six packs contain a regular autograph card. Four cards, Troy Aikman, Brett Favre, Allen Iverson, and Emmitt Smith were never issued, therefore the complete set only contains 62 cards.

1 Shareef Abdur-Rahim 4.00 10.00
3 Ray Allen 6.00 15.00
7 Dante Calabria 1.50 4.00
10 Erick Dampier 1.50 4.00
11 Tony Delk 1.50 4.00
15 Tyus Edney 1.50 4.00
16 Brian Evans 1.50 4.00
18 Derek Fisher 1.50 4.00
22 Steve Hamer 1.50 4.00
25 Othella Harrington 2.00 5.00
36 Travis Knight 1.50 4.00
39 Stephon Marbury 3.00 8.00
41 Walter McCarty 1.50 4.00
45 Vitaly Potapenko 1.50 4.00
47 Efthimis Rentzias 1.50 4.00
48 Roy Rogers 1.50 4.00
49 Malik Rose 2.00 5.00
54 Kurt Thomas 1.50 4.00
57 Antoine Walker 8.00 20.00
58 John Wallace 1.50 4.00
60 Jerome Williams 1.50 4.00
64 Lorenzen Wright 1.50 4.00

1997 Wheels Rookie Thunder

This 45-card set features color images of top rookie players silhouetted on a multi-color background with silver foil stamping and ultra gloss printed on 24 pt. paper. The backs carry player information. The set contains the following subsets: Take Two (34-39) and Young Guns (40-44).

COMPLETE SET (45) 3.00 8.00
1 Tim Duncan .60 1.50
2 Keith Van Horn .20 .50
3 Chauncey Billups .40 1.00
4 Antonio Daniels .10 .25
5 Tony Battie .12 .30
6 Ron Mercer .12 .30
7 Tim Thomas .20 .50
8 Adonal Foyle .10 .25
9 Tracy McGrady .50 1.25
10 Danny Fortson .10 .25
11 Olivier Saint-Jean .10 .25
12 Austin Croshere .10 .25
13 Derek Anderson .10 .25
14 Maurice Taylor .10 .25
15 Kelvin Cato .10 .25
16 Brevin Knight .10 .25
17 Johnny Taylor .10 .25
18 Chris Anstey .10 .25
19 Scot Pollard .10 .25
20 Paul Grant .10 .25
21 Anthony Parker .10 .25
22 Ed Gray .10 .25
23 Bobby Jackson .12 .30
24 John Thomas .10 .25
25 Charles Smith .10 .25
26 Jacque Vaughn .10 .25
27 Keith Booth .10 .25
28 Serge Zwikker .10 .25
29 Charles O'Bannon .10 .25
30 Bubba Wells .10 .25
31 Kebu Stewart .10 .25
32 James Collins .10 .25
33 Eddie Elisma .10 .25
34 Ron Mercer TT .12 .30
35 Derek Anderson TT .10 .25
36 Scot Pollard TT .10 .25
37 Jacque Vaughn TT .10 .25
38 Bobby Jackson TT .12 .30
39 John Thomas TT .10 .25
40 Chauncey Billups YG .40 1.00
41 Ron Mercer YG .12 .30
42 Tim Thomas YG .20 .50
43 Tracy McGrady YG .50 1.25
44 Maurice Taylor YG .10 .25
45 Checklist .10 .25

1997 Wheels Rookie Thunder Rising Storm

Inserted in hobby packs only at one in 12, this 45-card set parallels the base set. To ascertain values on individual cards, please refer to the multiplier in the header, coupled with the value of the base card
*STARS: 2X TO 5X BASE CARD HI

1997 Wheels Rookie Thunder Storm Front

Randomly inserted in retail packs only at one in 12, this 45-card set parallels the base set. To ascertain values on individual cards, please refer to the multiplier in the header, coupled with the value of the base card.
*STARS: 2X TO 5X BASE CARD HI

1997 Wheels Rookie Thunder Ball

Randomly inserted in packs at the rate of one in 216, this 10-card set features die-cut color player images with a piece of official basketball leather embedded in a micro-ethced foil enhanced background and dual foil stamps.

T1 Tim Duncan 15.00 40.00
T2 Keith Van Horn 5.00 12.00
T3 Chauncey Billups 10.00 25.00
T4 Antonio Daniels 2.50 6.00
T5 Tony Battie 3.00 8.00
T6 Ron Mercer 3.00 8.00
T7 Tim Thomas 5.00 12.00
T8 Adonal Foyle 2.50 6.00
T9 Tracy McGrady 12.00 30.00
T10 Danny Fortson 2.50 6.00

1997 Wheels Rookie Thunder Boomers

Randomly inserted in hobby packs only at the rate of one in 28, this 10-card set features color action photos of top rookies printed on die-cut clear acrylic card stock with flame red and silver foil stamping.

COMPLETE SET (10) 12.50 30.00
TB1 Tim Duncan 6.00 15.00
TB2 Tony Battie 1.25 3.00
TB3 Tracy McGrady 5.00 12.00
TB4 Danny Fortson 1.00 2.50
TB5 Maurice Taylor 1.00 2.50
TB6 Serge Zwikker 1.00 2.50
TB7 Scot Pollard 1.00 2.50
TB8 Charles O'Bannon 1.00 2.50
TB9 Adonal Foyle 1.00 2.50
TB10 Keith Van Horn 2.00 5.00

1997 Wheels Rookie Thunder Double Trouble

Randomly inserted in packs at the rate of one in 42, this two-sided six-card set features different lifelike embossed color player images on each side with silver foil and micro-etching.

COMPLETE SET (6) 20.00 50.00
DT1 Tim Duncan 10.00 25.00
Keith Van Horn
DT2 Chauncey Billups 4.00 10.00
Jacque Vaughn
DT3 Tracy McGrady 6.00 15.00
Ron Mercer
DT4 Bobby Jackson 2.00 5.00
Brevin Knight
DT5 Tim Duncan 6.00 15.00
Tony Battie
DT6 Danny Fortson 3.00 8.00
Tim Thomas

1997 Wheels Rookie Thunder Lights Out

Randomly inserted in packs at the rate of one in 96, this five-card set features color images of top rookie shooters printed with phosphorescent inks that glow in the dark with bright chrome foil stamping.

COMPLETE SET (5) 12.50 30.00
LO1 Chauncey Billups 8.00 20.00
LO2 Keith Van Horn 4.00 10.00
LO3 Tim Duncan 12.00 30.00
LO4 Ron Mercer 2.50 6.00
LO5 Antonio Daniels 2.00 5.00

1997 Wheels Rookie Thunder Shooting Stars

Randomly inserted in packs at the rate of one in 11, this 10-card set features action color images of the top first-year game shooters printed on micro-etched holographic foil with foil stamping.

COMPLETE SET (10) 6.00 15.00
SS1 Chauncey Billups 2.50 6.00
SS2 Tracy McGrady 3.00 8.00
SS3 Brevin Knight .60 1.50
SS4 Austin Croshere .60 1.50
SS5 Derek Anderson .60 1.50
SS6 Jacque Vaughn .60 1.50
SS7 Bobby Jackson .75 2.00
SS8 Tim Duncan 4.00 10.00
SS9 Keith Van Horn 1.25 3.00
SS10 Ron Mercer .75 2.00

1997 Wheels Rookie Thunder Stroke Autographs

Randomly inserted in packs at the rate of one in 32, this 14-card set features color action player images with the player's signature printed on his transparent image in the background.

TS1 Tim Duncan 40.00 100.00
TS2 Keith Van Horn 4.00 10.00
TS3 Chauncey Billups 8.00 20.00
TS4 Antonio Daniels 2.00 5.00
TS5 Tony Battie 2.50 6.00
TS6 Ron Mercer 2.50 6.00
TS7 Adonal Foyle 2.00 5.00
TS8 Olivier Saint-Jean 2.00 5.00
TS9 Jacque Vaughn 2.00 5.00
TS10 Austin Croshere 2.00 5.00
TS11 Derek Anderson 2.00 5.00
TS12 Scot Pollard 2.00 5.00
TS13 Serge Zwikker 2.00 5.00
TS14 Charles O'Bannon 2.00 5.00

1991-92 Wild Card Promos

These two standard-size cards were issued to preview the design of 1991-92 Wild Card basketball issue. Two versions of each card were produced; one was marked with and given out at the 1991 San Francisco Sports Card Expo, while the other version (without the San Francisco Sports Expo emblem) was given to dealers and also available as a random insert in Wild Card College Football foil packs. The color action player photos on the fronts are black-bordered, and colored numbers are displayed in the black border above and to the right of the picture. The backs carry a color headshot, biography, and statistics. The cards are numbered on the back with a "P" prefix. The San Francisco give-away cards are arguably less than valuable than the harder-to-obtain football foil pack insert versions.

COMPLETE SET (2) 1.00 2.50
P1 Larry Johnson .75 2.00
P2 Kenny Anderson .40 1.00

1991-92 Wild Card

The Wild Card Collegiate Basketball set contains 120 standard-size cards. One out of every 100 cards is "Wild", with a numbered stripe to indicate how many cards it can be redeemed for. There are 5, 10, 20, 50, 100, and 1,000 denominations, with the highest numbers the scarcest. Whatever the number, the card can be redeemed for that number of regular cards of the same player, after paying a redemption fee of 4.95 per order. The front design features glossy color action player photos on a black card face, with an orange frame around the picture and different color numbers in the top and right borders. The backs have different shades of purple and a color head shot, biography, and statistics.

COMPLETE SET (120) 2.50 5.00
*5/10/20 STRIPES: 2X TO 5X BASE HI
*50/100 STRIPES: 6X TO 15X BASE HI
*1000 STRIPES: 20X TO 50X BASE CARD HI
1 Larry Johnson .20 .50
First NBA Draft Pick
2 LeRon Ellis .02 .10
3 Alvaro Teheran .02 .10
4 Eric Murdock .08 .25
5A Surprise Card 1 .02 .10
5B Dikembe Mutombo .30 .75
6 Anthony Avent .02 .10
7A Isiah Thomas .20 .50
7B Doug Smith .02 .10
8 Abdul Shamsid-Deen .02 .10
9 Linton Townes .02 .10
10 Joe Wylie .02 .10
11 Cozell McQueen .02 .10
12 David Benoit .08 .25
13 Rodney Monroe .02 .10
14 Dale Davis .20 .50
15 Patrick Ewing .20 .50
16 Greg Anthony .08 .25
17 Robert Pack .08 .25
18 Phil Zevenbergen .02 .10
19 Rick Fox .20 .50
20 Chris Corchiani .08 .25
21 Elliot Perry .08 .25
22 Kevin Brooks .02 .10
23 Mark Macon .08 .25
24 Larry Johnson .30 .75
25 George Ackles .02 .10
26A Surprise Card 5 .02 .10
26B Christian Laettner PROMO .20 .50
27 Andy Fields .02 .10
28 Kevin Lynch .02 .10
29 Graylin Warner .02 .10
30 James Bullock .02 .10
31 Steve Bucknall .02 .10
32 Carl Thomas .02 .10
33 Doug Overton .02 .10
34 Brian Shorter .02 .10
35 Chad Gallagher .02 .10
36 Antonio Davis .08 .25
37 Sean Green .02 .10
38 Randy Brown .08 .25
39 Richard Dumas .02 .10
40 Terrell Brandon .20 .50
41 Marty Embry .02 .10
42 Ronnie Coleman .02 .10
43 King Rice .02 .10
44 Perry Carter .02 .10
45 Andrew Gaze .02 .10
46A Surprise Card 2 .02 .10
46B Billy Owens .08 .25
47A Surprise Card 3 .02 .10
47B Stacey Augmon .08 .25
48 Jimmy Oliver .02 .10
49 Treg Lee .02 .10
50 Ricky Winslow .02 .10
51 Danny Vranes .02 .10
52 Jay Murphy .02 .10
53 Adrian Dantley .08 .25
54 Joe Arlauckas .02 .10
55 Moses Scurry .02 .10
56 Andy Toolson .02 .10
57 Ramon Rivas .02 .10
58 Charles Davis .02 .10
59 Butch Wade .02 .10
60 John Pinone .02 .10
61 Bill Wennington .08 .25
62 Walter Berry .02 .10
63 Terry Dozier .02 .10
64 Mitchell Anderson .02 .10
65 Pace Mannion .02 .10
66 Pete Myers .02 .10
67 Eddie Lee Wilkins .02 .10
68 Mark Hughes .02 .10
69 Darryl Dawkins .08 .25
70 Jay Vincent .02 .10
71 Doug Lee .02 .10
72 Russ Schoene .02 .10
73 Tim Kempton .02 .10
74 Earl Cureton .02 .10
75 Terence Stansbury .02 .10
76 Frank Kornet .02 .10
77 Bob McAdoo .20 .50
78 Haywood Workman .02 .10
79 Vinny Del Negro .08 .25
80 Harold Pressley .02 .10
81 Robert Smith .02 .10
82 Adrian Caldwell .02 .10
83 Scottie Pippen .30 .75
84 John Stockton .10 .30
85 Elwayne Campbell .02 .10
86 Chris Gatling .08 .25
87 Cedric Henderson .02 .10
88 Mike Iuzzolino .02 .10
89 Fennis Dembo .02 .10
90 Darnell Valentine .02 .10
91 Michael Brooks .02 .10
92 Marty Conlon .02 .10
93 Lamont Strothers .02 .10
94 Donald Hodge .02 .10
95 Pete Chilcutt .08 .25
96 Kenny Anderson ERR .20 .50
(1990-87 stats)
96B Kenny Anderson COR .20 .50
(1990-91 stats)
97 Ian Lockhart .02 .10
98A Surprise Card 4 .02 .10
98B Steve Smith .30 .75
99 Larry Lawrence .02 .10
100 Jerome Mincy .02 .10
101 Ben Coleman .02 .10
102 Tom Copa .02 .10
103 Demetrius Calip .02 .10
104 Myron Brown .02 .10
105 Derrick Pope .02 .10
106 Kelvin Upshaw .02 .10
107 Andrew Moten .02 .10
108 Terry Tyler .02 .10
109 Kevin Magee .02 .10
110 Tharon Mayes .02 .10
111 Perry McDonald .02 .10
112 Jose Ortiz .02 .10
113 Rick Mahorn .08 .25
114 David Butler .02 .10
115 Carl Herrera .02 .10
116 Darrell Mickens .02 .10
117 Steve Bardo .02 .10
118 Checklist 1 .02 .10
119 Checklist 2 .02 .10
120 Checklist 3 .02 .10

1991-92 Wild Card Red Hot Rookies

These cards were randomly packed in the Collegiate Basketball foil cases, and they included denomination cards. The cards measure the standard size. The front design features glossy color action player photos on a black card face, with an orange frame around the picture and different color numbers in the top and right borders. The "Red Hot Rookies" emblem in the lower left corner rounds out the card face. The backs have a color close-up photo, biography, and complete college statistics.

COMPLETE SET (10) 5.00 12.00
5/10/20 STRIPES: 1.25X TO 3X VALUE
50/100 STRIPES: 8X to 20X VALUE
1000 STRIPES: 75X TO 150X VALUE
1 Dikembe Mutombo 1.50 4.00
2 Larry Johnson 2.00 5.00
3 Steve Smith 2.00 5.00
4 Billy Owens .50 1.25
5 Mark Macon .20 .50
6 Stacey Augmon UER .50 1.25
7 Victor Alexander .20 .50
8 Mike Iuzzolino .20 .50
9 Rick Fox .50 1.25
10 Terrell Brandon UER 1.50 4.00
(Name misspelled Terrel on card front)

1991-92 Wild Card Redemption Prototypes

This six-card standard-size was intended to preview the forthcoming Wild Card basketball set. By sending in a surprise card from the 1991-92 Wild Card Collegiate set, the collector received a cello pack consisting of a replacement card and two redemption prototype cards. The fronts feature color action player photos with white borders and colored numbers suspended in the top and right borders. The backs feature a color headshot, biography, and statistics. The cards are numbered on the back with a "P" prefix.

COMPLETE SET (6) .80 2.00
P1 LaPhonso Ellis .20 .50
P2 Adam Keefe .05 .15
P3 Robert Horry .20 .50
P4 Bryant Stith .08 .25
P5 Christian Laettner .40 1.00
P6 Malik Sealy .08 .25

1967-77 ABA All-Star Game Programs

1 1967-68 Indiana 75.00 150.00
2 1968-69 Kentucky 80.00 175.00
3 1969-70 Indiana 50.00 100.00
4 1970-71 Carolina 40.00 75.00
5 1971-72 Kentucky 40.00 75.00
6 1972-73 Utah 50.00 100.00
7 1973-74 Virginia 40.00 75.00
8 1974-75 San Antonio 30.00 60.00
9 1975-76 Denver 30.00 60.00

1967-76 ABA All-Star Game Ticket Stubs
1 1967-68 Indiana 60.00 125.00
2 1968-69 Kentucky 75.00 150.00
3 1969-70 Indiana 40.00 75.00
4 1970-71 Carolina 30.00 60.00
5 1971-72 Kentucky 30.00 60.00
6 1972-73 Utah 40.00 75.00
7 1973-74 Virginia 30.00 60.00
8 1974-75 San Antonio 25.00 50.00
9 1975-76 Denver 25.00 50.00

1950-99 NBA All-Star Game Programs
1 1950-51 Boston 200.00 400.00
2 1951-52 Boston 150.00 300.00
3 1952-53 Fort Wayne 150.00 300.00
4 1953-54 New York 150.00 275.00
5 1954-55 New York 150.00 275.00
6 1955-56 Rochester 150.00 300.00
7 1956-57 Boston 150.00 275.00
8 1957-58 St Louis 125.00 250.00
9 1958-59 Detroit 100.00 200.00
10 1959-60 Philadelphia 90.00 175.00
11 1960-61 Syracuse 90.00 175.00
12 1961-62 St Louis 75.00 150.00
13 1962-63 Los Angeles 60.00 125.00
14 1963-64 Boston 75.00 150.00
15 1964-65 St Louis 60.00 125.00
16 1965-66 Cincinnati 60.00 125.00
17 1966-67 San Francisco 60.00 125.00
18 1967-68 New York 50.00 100.00
19 1968-69 Baltimore 50.00 100.00
20 1969-70 Philadelphia 40.00 75.00
21 1970-71 San Diego 50.00 100.00
22 1971-72 Los Angeles 40.00 75.00
23 1972-73 Chicago 40.00 75.00
24 1973-74 Seattle 30.00 60.00
25 1974-75 Phoenix 30.00 60.00
26 1975-76 Philadelphia 25.00 50.00
27 1976-77 Milwaukee 25.00 50.00
28 1977-78 Atlanta 25.00 50.00
29 1978-79 Detroit 15.00 40.00
30 1979-80 Washington 15.00 40.00
31 1980-81 Cleveland 15.00 40.00
32 1981-82 New Jersey 15.00 40.00
33 1982-83 Los Angeles 15.00 40.00
34 1983-84 Denver 15.00 40.00
35 1984-85-Present 15.00 40.00

1950-99 NBA All-Star Game Ticket Stubs
1 1950-51 Boston 150.00 300.00
2 1951-52 Boston 125.00 225.00
3 1952-53 Fort Wayne 125.00 250.00
4 1953-54 New York 100.00 200.00
5 1954-55 New York 100.00 200.00
6 1955-56 Rochester 125.00 225.00
7 1956-57 Boston 100.00 200.00
8 1957-58 St Louis 75.00 150.00
9 1958-59 Detroit 60.00 125.00
10 1959-60 Philadelphia 50.00 100.00
11 1960-61 Syracuse 60.00 125.00
12 1961-62 St Louis 50.00 100.00
13 1962-63 Los Angeles 50.00 100.00
14 1963-64 Boston 50.00 100.00
15 1964-65 St Louis 40.00 75.00
16 1965-66 Cincinnati 40.00 75.00
17 1966-67 San Francisco 40.00 75.00
18 1967-68 New York 40.00 75.00
19 1968-69 Baltimore 40.00 75.00
20 1969-70 Philadelphia 30.00 60.00
21 1970-71 San Diego 30.00 60.00
22 1971-72 Los Angeles 30.00 60.00
23 1972-73 Chicago 30.00 60.00
24 1973-74 Seattle 25.00 50.00
25 1974-75 Phoenix 25.00 50.00
26 1975-76 Philadelphia 15.00 40.00
27 1976-77 Milwaukee 15.00 40.00
28 1977-78 Atlanta 15.00 40.00
29 1978-79 Detroit 15.00 40.00
30 1979-80 Washington 15.00 40.00
31 1980-81 Cleveland 15.00 40.00
32 1981-82 New Jersey 15.00 40.00
33 1982-83 Los Angeles 12.50 30.00
34 1983-84 Denver 12.50 30.00
35 1984-85 - Present 12.50 30.00

1997 All-Star MVPs Basketball
10 Chicago Bulls 10.00 20.00
Steve Kerr
Scottie Pippen
Dennis Rodman
Ron Harper
Toni Kukoc
20 Houston Rockets 10.00 20.00
Mario Elie
Charles Barkley
Clyde Drexler
Hakeem Olajuwon
Kevin Willis
30 Los Angeles Lakers 15.00 30.00
Byron Scott
Nick Van Exel
Robert Horry
Eddie Jones
Kobe Bryant
40 New York Knicks 10.00 20.00
Patrick Ewing
Larry Johnson
Dontae Jones
John Starks
Charles Oakley
50 Seattle Supersonics 10.00 20.00
Sam Perkins
Detlef Schrempf
Shawn Kemp
Gary Payton
Hersey Hawkins

1966 Aurora Sports Model Kits
This set of six plastic models was released in 1966. Each model, when fully assembled, measures approx. 6" high. Prices below are for complete, unbuilt models accompanied by the box. Model kits still in factory wrapped boxes are considered to be Nr-Mt-Mt . Built-up models minus the box are valued at 20 to 50 percent of the Nr-Mt prices below.

6 Jerry West 20.00 50.00

1997-98 Headliners Basketball
This series of figures was produced by Corinthian Marketing. Each figures is 3 1/4" tall. There were 37 pieces that came in two different case assortments. The figures were primarily sold through mass market retail outlets at a suggested retail price of $3.99. There were also special 4-packs released for the positions of guard, forward and center. Those packages are listed below, but are not considered part of the set price. The values listed below refer to unopened packages. The figures are unnumbered and checklisted below in alphabetical order. The complete set includes only the yellow Dennis Rodman hair color variation.

1 Charles Barkley 2.00 5.00
2 Muggsy Bogues FP 2.00 5.00
3 Cedric Ceballos FP 2.00 5.00
4 Clyde Drexler FP 2.50 6.00
5 Patrick Ewing 2.00 5.00
6 Kevin Garnett FP 2.00 5.00
7 Horace Grant 2.00 5.00
8 Anfernee Hardaway 2.00 5.00
9 Grant Hill 2.50 6.00
10 Juwan Howard 2.00 5.00
11 Allen Iverson FP 2.50 6.00
12 Larry Johnson 2.00 5.00
13 Shawn Kemp 2.00 5.00
14 Jason Kidd FP 2.50 6.00
15 Toni Kukoc FP 2.50 6.00
16 Karl Malone 2.50 6.00
17 Jamal Mashburn 2.00 5.00
18 Reggie Miller 2.00 5.00
19 Alonzo Mourning 2.00 5.00
20 Dikembe Mutombo 2.00 5.00
21 Hakeem Olajuwon 2.00 5.00
22 Scottie Pippen 2.50 6.00
23 Bryant Reeves FP 2.00 5.00
24 Mitch Richmond 2.00 5.00
25 Clifford Robinson 2.00 5.00
26 David Robinson 2.00 5.00
27 Glenn Robinson 2.00 5.00
28A Dennis Rodman Green 2.50 6.00
28B Dennis Rodman Orange 2.00 5.00
28C Dennis Rodman Red 2.00 5.00
28D Dennis Rodman Yellow 2.00 5.00
29 Detlef Schrempf FP 2.00 5.00
30 Joe Smith FP 2.00 5.00
31 Rik Smits FP 2.00 5.00
32 Latrell Sprewell FP 2.00 5.00
33 Jerry Stackhouse 2.00 5.00
34 John Stockton FP 2.50 6.00
35 Damon Stoudamire 2.00 5.00
36 Nick Van Exel FP 2.50 6.00
37 Chris Webber FP 2.50 6.00
38 Centers 4-Pack 10.00 18.00
Patrick Ewing
Hakeem Olajuwon
Bryant Reeves
Rik Smits
39 Forwards 4-Pack 10.00 18.00
Charles Barkley
Horace Grant
Grant Hill
Scottie Pippen
40 Future 4-Pack 10.00 18.00
Kevin Garnett
Allen Iverson
Joe Smith
Damon Stoudamire
41 Guards 4-Pack 10.00 18.00
Clyde Drexler
Reggie Miller
Latrell Sprewell
Nick Van Exel

1998-99 Mattel NBA Jams
This 20-figure set was the first basketball release of mini-NBA figures by the Mattel Toy Company and measures approx. 3.5" in height. The figures are featured in action poses, with exaggerated head sculpts, mounted on a base with each player's name. The values listed below refer to unopened packages. The figures are unnumbered and checklisted below in alphabetical order.

1 Shareef Abdur-Rahim 2.50 6.00
2 Vin Baker 2.50 6.00
3 Charles Barkley 2.50 6.00
4 Kobe Bryant 5.00 10.00
5 Kevin Garnett 2.50 6.00
6 Anfernee Hardaway 2.50 6.00
7 Tim Hardaway 2.50 6.00
8 Grant Hill 2.50 6.00
9 Allen Iverson 4.00 8.00
10 Michael Jordan Red 7.50 15.00
11 Michael Jordan White 7.50 15.00
12 Shawn Kemp 2.50 6.00
13 Jason Kidd 2.50 6.00
14 Glen Rice 2.50 6.00
15 David Robinson 2.50 6.00
16 Dennis Rodman 2.50 6.00
17 Rodney Rogers 2.50 6.00
18 Damon Stoudamire 2.50 6.00
19 Steve Smith 2.50 6.00
20 Keith Van Horn 2.50 6.00
21 Antoine Walker 2.50 6.00

1998-99 Mattel NBA Superstars
This 24-figure set was the first basketball release of NBA figures by the Mattel Toy Company. The players are featured in action poses and are accompanied by a standard-size card of each player. The card front has either a posed or action color shot. The back has biographical and statistical information. Key pieces include both Michael Jordan figures as well as Tim Duncan. The values listed below refer to unopened packages. The figures are unnumbered and checklisted below in alphabetical order.

1 Ray Allen 4.00 10.00
2 Vin Baker 3.00 8.00
3 Vin Baker w/CL 3.00 8.00
4 Charles Barkley 4.00 10.00
5 Kobe Bryant 8.00 20.00
6 Tim Duncan 10.00 25.00
7 Kevin Garnett 5.00 12.00
8 Anfernee Hardaway 4.00 10.00
9 Grant Hill 5.00 12.00
10 Allan Houston 3.00 8.00
11 Juwan Howard 3.00 8.00
12 Allen Iverson 12.50 25.00
13 Michael Jordan Red 8.00 20.00
14 Michael Jordan White 8.00 20.00
15 Shawn Kemp 3.00 8.00
16 Jason Kidd 5.00 12.00
17 Jason Kidd w/CL 5.00 12.00
18 Reggie Miller 4.00 10.00
19 Alonzo Mourning 3.00 8.00
20 Dikembe Mutombo 3.00 8.00
21 Scottie Pippen Chicago 5.00 12.00
22 Scottie Pippen Houston 5.00 12.00
23 Glen Rice 3.00 8.00
24 Dennis Rodman Chicago 5.00 12.00
25 Dennis Rodman LA 5.00 12.00
26 Dennis Rodman LA w/CL 5.00 12.00
27 John Stockton 4.00 10.00
28 Keith Van Horn 3.00 8.00
29 Antoine Walker 3.00 8.00

1999-00 Mattel College and Pro Series
These figures were released by the Mattel Toy Company. The figures highlight four players playing in the NBA and show them in both their pro and college uniform. The key figure in the set is Vince Carter appearing in the same year as his first figure. The values listed below refer to unopened packages. The figures are unnumbered and checklisted below in alphabetical order.

1 Vince Carter 10.00 25.00
2 Glen Rice 3.00 8.00
3 Keith Van Horn 3.00 8.00
4 Antoine Walker 3.00 8.00

1999-00 Mattel NBA 13-inch Figures
These figures were released by the Mattel Toy Company. The figures are larger, measuring approx. 13" in height. Each comes with real material for the uniform as well as a small basketball. The values listed below refer to unopened packages. The figures are unnumbered and checklisted below in alphabetical order.

1 Kobe Bryant 15.00 40.00
2 Tim Duncan 10.00 25.00
3 Grant Hill 8.00 20.00
4 Scottie Pippen 8.00 20.00

1999-00 Mattel NBA Maximum Air
This 10-figure set was releases by the Mattel Toy Company that honors Michael Jordan. Each figure is featured in an action pose and comes accompanied by a standard-size card. The card front has either a posed or action color shot. The back has biographical and statistical information. Each of the nine figures in the line are limited edition, 1 of 23,045. A smaller 3 1/2" Platinum JAMS figures with a special card from Upper Deck also is included in the set. The values listed below refer to unopened packages. The figures are unnumbered and checklisted below in alphabetical order.

1 Michael Jordan Silver 3 1/2-inch 10.00 25.00
2 Michael Jordan College POY 10.00 25.00
3 Michael Jordan NBA ROY 10.00 25.00
4 Michael Jordan Play Sensation 10.00 25.00
5 Michael Jordan Champ '91 10.00 25.00
6 Michael Jordan Champ '92 10.00 25.00
7 Michael Jordan Champ '93 10.00 25.00
8 Michael Jordan AS MVP '88 10.00 25.00
9 Michael Jordan AS MVP '96 10.00 25.00
10 Michael Jordan AS MVP '98 10.00 25.00

1999-00 Mattel NBA One-On-One
This 6-figure set was released by the Mattel Toy Company. The figures are smaller in size and come paired together in two's. Each figure comes in an action pose, with exaggerated head sculpts , mounted the same way as the Jams version. The values listed below refer to unopened packages. The figures are unnumbered and checklisted below in alphabetical order.

10 Kobe Bryant 10.00 25.00
Grant Hill
20 Anfernee Hardaway 6.00 15.00
Tim Hardaway
30 Jason Kidd 6.00 15.00
John Stockton
40 Michael Jordan 20.00 50.00
David Robinson
50 Reggie Miller 6.00 15.00
Glen Rice
60 Dennis Rodman 6.00 15.00
Karl Malone

1999-00 Mattel NBA Showcase
This figure was released by the Mattel Toy Company as a tribute to Michael Jordan. Jordan is featured in a couple different uniforms and is accompanied by a standard-size card. The values listed below refer to unopened packages. The figures are unnumbered and checklisted below in alphabetical order.

10 Michael Jordan 20.00 50.00

1999-00 Mattel NBA Superstars
This 25-figure set was the second basketball release of NBA figures by the Mattel Toy Company. The players are featured in action poses and are accompanied by a standard-size card of each player. The card front has either a posed or action color shot. The back has biographical and statistical information. Key first pieces include Vince Carter, Mike Bibby and Antawn Jamison. Other key figures are the Larry Bird and Kobe Bryant Yellow version, both short-printed. Production is limited on each figure to less than 15,000 per figure. The values listed below refer to unopened packages. The figures are unnumbered and checklisted below in alphabetical order.

1 Vin Baker 3.00 8.00
2 Mike Bibby FP 4.00 10.00
3 Larry Bird 10.00 25.00
4 Shawn Bradley 3.00 8.00
5 Kobe Bryant 8.00 20.00
5A Kobe Bryant Yellow 12.00 30.00
6 Vince Carter FP 8.00 20.00
8 Tim Duncan 5.00 12.00
12 Kevin Garnett 5.00 12.00
15 Anfernee Hardaway 3.00 8.00
16 Tim Hardaway 3.00 8.00
17 Grant Hill 4.00 10.00
18 Juwan Howard 3.00 8.00
19 Allen Iverson 8.00 20.00
20 Antawn Jamison FP 6.00 15.00
23 Shawn Kemp 3.00 8.00
25 Raef LaFrentz FP 3.00 8.00
27 Reggie Miller 6.00 15.00
30 Shaquille O'Neal 8.00 20.00
33 Scottie Pippen 3.00 8.00
34 Glen Rice 3.00 8.00
35 David Robinson 5.00 12.00
41 Keith Van Horn 3.00 8.00
42 Antoine Walker 3.00 8.00
44 Jayson Williams 3.00 8.00

1999-00 Mattel NBA Ultra Jams
These figures were released by the Mattel Toy Company. The figures are a larger version of the Jams, with exaggerated head sculpts , measuring approx. 12" in height. Each figure is limited edition and comes with an Ultra JAMS trading card and certificate of Authentication. The values listed below refer to unopened packages. The figures are unnumbered and checklisted below in alphabetical order.

10 Kobe Bryant 8.00 20.00
20 Anfernee Hardaway Orl 3.00 8.00
30 Anfernee Hardaway Phx 3.00 8.00
40 Grant Hill 4.00 10.00
50 Michael Jordan Red 15.00 30.00
60 Michael Jordan Black 15.00 30.00
70 Keith Van Horn 3.00 8.00

1999-00 Mattel PRO Hoops
This 4-figure set was released by the Mattel Toy Company. The players are featured in action poses and are accompanied with basketball and goal. The player has a released action that allows him to shoot a basket. The values listed below refer to unopened packages. The figures are unnumbered and checklisted below in alphabetical order.

10 Tim Duncan 6.00 15.00
20 Anfernee Hardaway 5.00 12.00
30 Grant Hill 6.00 15.00
40 Reggie Miller 5.00 12.00

1999-00 Mattel Shooting Sensations
This 4-figure set was released by the Mattel Toy Company. The players come is super detailed warm-up uniforms and are mounted on a simulated basketball floor. The player comes with a small basketball and has real shooting motion. The values listed below refer to unopened packages. The figures are unnumbered and checklisted below in alphabetical order.

10 Kobe Bryant 20.00 50.00
20 Grant Hill 10.00 25.00
30 Kevin Garnett 10.00 25.00
40 Scottie Pippen 10.00 25.00

1999-00 Mattel Then and Now Collection
These figures were released by the Mattel Toy Company. The figures highlight the careers of Michael Jordan, Kobe Bryant and Dennis Rodman. Each figure shows the player during different stages of their career, in each of the uniforms they wore. The values listed below refer to unopened packages. The figures are unnumbered and checklisted below in alphabetical order.

10 Kobe Bryant 10.00 25.00
20 Michael Jordan 12.00 30.00
30 Dennis Rodman 6.00 15.00

2000 Mattel USA Team
This 12-figure basketball set was produced by the Mattel Toy Company as a tribute to the NBA players playing in the 2000 Olympics. The figures are featured in action poses and are accompanied by a standard-size card of each player. The card front has either a posed or action color shot. The back has biographical and statistical information. Key pieces include Vince Carter and the Team set. The Team Set was produced for and released at Target. The values listed below refer to unopened packages. The figures are unnumbered and checklisted below in alphabetical order.

5 Ray Allen 6.00 15.00
10 Vin Baker 4.00 10.00
20 Vince Carter 8.00 20.00
30 Tim Duncan 8.00 20.00
35 Kevin Garnett 6.00 15.00
40 Tim Hardaway 5.00 12.00
45 Grant Hill 6.00 15.00
50 Allan Houston 5.00 12.00
60 Jason Kidd 6.00 15.00
65 Alonzo Mourning 5.00 12.00
70 Gary Payton 5.00 12.00
80 Steve Smith 5.00 12.00
1000 Team Set 20.00 40.00

2002-03 McFarlane Basketball Series 1-4
The first McFarlane venture into fully-licensed basketball figures, the Series I set features six top players. Series II expanded to include nine players, including First Pieces of Elton Brand, Kwame Brown, Steve Francis, Tracy McGrady, and Dirk Nowitzki. Series III FP's include Baron Davis, Pau Gasol, Paul Pierce, and Rasheed Wallace. A small four-piece Series IV set released in July 2003, featuring FPs of all four NBAers: Jermaine O'Neal, Jalen Rose, Amare Soudemire, and DaJuan Wagner.

BACKBOARD 20.00 35.00
10 Kobe Bryant Yellow 12.00 30.00
11 Kobe Bryant Purple Variant 15.00 40.00
20 Vince Carter White FP 6.00 12.00
21 Vince Carter Purple Variant 15.00 30.00
30 Tim Duncan Black 10.00 25.00
31 Tim Duncan White Variant 20.00 40.00
40 Kevin Garnett White 8.00 20.00
41 Kevin Garnett Blue Variant 15.00 40.00
50 Allen Iverson White 6.00 12.00
Mouth Open
51 Allen Iverson
White Mouth Closed Variant 7.50 15.00
52 Allen Iverson 25.00 50.00
Black Mouth Open Variant
53 Allen Iverson 15.00 30.00
Black Mouth Closed Variant
60 Jason Kidd Blue 7.50 15.00
61 Jason Kidd White Variant 12.50 25.00
100 Ray Allen White 6.00 12.00
101 Ray Allen Purple Variant 15.00 30.00
110 Elton Brand Red FP 6.00 12.00
111 Elton Brand White Variant 15.00 40.00
120 Kwame Brown Blue FP 6.00 12.00
121 Kwame Brown White Variant 15.00 30.00
130 Steve Francis White FP 6.00 12.00
131 Steve Francis Blue Variant 15.00 30.00
140 Antawn Jamison White 6.00 12.00
141 Antawn Jamison Blue Variant 12.50 25.00
150 Tracy McGrady White FP 7.50 15.00
151 Tracy McGrady Blue Variant 15.00 40.00
160 Dirk Nowitzki Blue FP 6.00 15.00
161 Dirk Nowitzki White Variant 15.00 40.00
170 Shaquille O'Neal Yellow 8.00 20.00
171 Shaquille O'Neal Purple Variant 15.00 30.00
180 John Stockton White 6.00 12.00
181 John Stockton Purple Variant 12.50 25.00
200 Mike Bibby White FP 6.00 12.00
201 Mike Bibby 15.00 30.00
Purple NBA Logo Shorts Variant
210 Kobe Bryant Purple 10.00 20.00
211 Kobe Bryant 20.00 40.00
Yellow Short Hair Variant
212 Kobe Bryant 15.00 30.00
Yellow Long Hair Variant
220 Baron Davis White FP 6.00 12.00
221 Baron Davis Blue Variant 12.50 25.00
230 Pau Gasol Black FP 6.00 12.00
231 Pau Gasol White Variant 15.00 30.00
240 Juwan Howard Blue 6.00 12.00
241 Juwan Howard White Variant 12.50 25.00
250 Eddie Jones Red 6.00 12.00
251 Eddie Jones White Variant 12.50 25.00
260 Paul Pierce Green FP 8.00 20.00
261 Paul Pierce White Variant 15.00 30.00
270 Latrell Sprewell White 6.00 12.00
271 Latrell Sprewell Blue Variant 12.50 25.00
280 Rasheed Wallace Black FP 6.00 12.00
281 Rasheed Wallace White Variant 15.00 30.00
300 Jermaine O'Neal Yellow FP 6.00 12.00
301 Jermaine O'Neal White Variant 25.00 50.00
310 Jalen Rose Red FP 6.00 12.00
311 Jalen Rose White Variant 15.00 30.00
320 Amare Stoudemire White FP 6.00 15.00
321 Amare Stoudemire Purple Variant12.00 30.00
330 DaJuan Wagner Red FP 6.00 12.00
331 DaJuan Wagner White Variant 8.00 20.00

2003-04 McFarlane Basketball Series 5-6
Series V debuted in November and was loaded with such superstars as last year's scoring leader Tracy McGrady, defensive player of the year Ben Wallace and rookie phenon LeBron James. First pieces included LeBron James, Yao Ming, Steve Nash and Ben Wallace. Series VI was released in March 2004 and included first pieces of Rookie superstar Carmelo Anthony, Richard Jefferson, Peja Stojakovic and first McFarlane pieces of Gary Payton, Karl Malone (both as Lakers), Michael Finley, and Scottie Pippen (Bulls).

10 Shareef Abdur-Rahim Red 6.00 12.00
12 Shareef Abdur-Rahim 7.50 15.00
White Variant
20 Ray Allen Green 6.00 12.00
22 Ray Allen White Variant 7.50 15.00
30 LeBron James White FP 12.00 30.00
32 LeBron James Red 20.00 50.00
Red Letter Outline Variant
34 LeBron James Red 60.00 100.00
Blue Letter Outline Variant
40 Stephon Marbury White 6.00 12.00
42 Stephon Marbury Purple Variant 7.50 15.00
50 Tracy McGrady White 7.50 15.00
52 Tracy McGrady Blue Variant 10.00 20.00
60 Yao Ming White FP 10.00 20.00
62 Yao Ming Red Variant 10.00 20.00
63 Yao Ming Red 12.50 30.00
with Small Name Variant
70 Steve Nash Blue FP 6.00 12.00
72 Steve Nash White Variant 7.50 15.00
80 Ben Wallace White FP 10.00 20.00
82 Ben Wallace Blue Variant 12.50 25.00
90 Chris Webber White 7.50 15.00
92 Chris Webber Purple Variant 10.00 25.00
100 Carmelo Anthony FP 10.00 20.00
102 Carmelo Anthony White Variant 20.00 50.00
103 Carmelo Anthony White 75.00 150.00
with Blue Headband Variant
110 Tim Duncan 10.00 25.00
112 Tim Duncan Black Variant 15.00 30.00
120 Michael Finley 6.00 12.00
122 Michael Finley Blue Variant
130 Allen Iverson 7.50 15.00
132 Allen Iverson White Variant 15.00 40.00
140 Richard Jefferson FP 6.00 12.00
142 Richard Jefferson Blue Variant 12.50 25.00
150 Karl Malone 10.00 25.00
152 Karl Malone Jazz Variant 12.50 30.00
154 Karl Malone Jazz 20.00 40.00
with Lakers Packaging Variant
160 Gary Payton 7.50 15.00
162 Gary Payton Sonics Variant 12.50 25.00
170 Scottie Pippen 30.00 60.00
172 Scottie Pippen White Variant 25.00 60.00
180 Peja Stojakovic FP 7.50 15.00
182 Peja Stojakovic Purple Variant 20.00 40.00
190 Stephon Marbury Retro Suns 12.50 25.00

2003-04 McFarlane Basketball 3-Inch Duals
10 Shaquille O'Neal 5.00 10.00
Rasheed Wallace
20 LeBron James 8.00 20.00
Paul Pierce
30 Tracy McGrady 5.00 10.00
Dirk Nowitzki
40 Yao Ming 5.00 10.00
Tim Duncan
50 Allen Iverson 6.00 12.00
Chris Webber
60 Ben Wallace Corn Rows 5.00 10.00
Jason Kidd Clean Face
62 Ben Wallace Corn Rows 6.00 12.00
Jason Kidd Beard Variant
64 Ben Wallace Afro 10.00 20.00
Jason Kidd Clean Face Variant

2003-04 McFarlane Basketball 2-Pack
10 Shaquille O'Neal 12.50 25.00
Yao Ming
20 LeBron James 12.50 30.00
Carmelo Anthony
30 Kevin Garnett 12.50 30.00
Ben Wallace

2003-04 McFarlane Basketball NBA All-Star Game Exclusive
STATED PRINT RUN 4000 SETS
10 Shaquille O'Neal 25.00 50.00
Elton Brand

2003 McFarlane Multi-Sport National Convention Exclusive
Sold only at the 2003 National Sports Collector's Convention in Atlantic City (in July of 2003), this set featured New Jersey Net Kenyon Martin and New York Giant Tiki Barber.

20 Kenyon Martin 15.00 25.00

2004-05 McFarlane Basketball Series 7-9
10 Vince Carter 7.00 12.00
11 Vince Carter Red Variant 12.50 25.00
20 Kevin Garnett 7.50 15.00
21 Kevin Garnett White Variant 10.00 25.00
30 LeBron James 10.00 20.00
31 LeBron James White Variant 15.00 30.00
40 Reggie Miller 10.00 20.00
41 Reggie Miller Yellow Variant 15.00 40.00
50 Yao Ming 7.50 15.00
51 Yao Ming White Variant 12.50 25.00
60 Michael Redd FP 7.00 12.00
61 Michael Redd Green Variant 12.50 25.00
70 Ben Wallace 7.50 15.00
71 Ben Wallace 10.00 20.00
Cornrows Variant
72 Ben Wallace White Variant 10.00 20.00
73 Ben Wallace 10.00 20.00
White with Cornrows Variant
80 Jason Williams FP 10.00 20.00
85 Jason Williams White Variant 7.00 12.00
100 Carmelo Anthony White 6.00 12.00
101 Carmelo Anthony Blue Variant 6.00 12.00
110 Allen Iverson White 7.50 15.00
111 Allen Iverson Black Variant 10.00 20.00
120 Jason Kidd White 6.00 12.00
121 Jason Kidd Gray Variant 7.50 15.00
130 Corey Maggette Red FP 6.00 12.00
131 Corey Maggette White Variant 6.00 12.00
140 Stephon Marbury Blue 6.00 12.00
141 Stephon Marbury White Variant 7.50 15.00
150 Shawn Marion White FP 6.00 12.00
151 Shawn Marion Orange Variant 10.00 20.00
160 Lamar Odom Purple FP 15.00 40.00
161 Lamar Odom Yellow Variant 10.00 20.00
170 Shaquille O'Neal Red 10.00 25.00
171 Shaquille O'Neal Black Variant 12.50 25.00
200 Kobe Bryant Yellow 12.00 30.00
201 Kobe Bryant Purple Variant 20.00 50.00
210 Richard Hamilton Blue FP 6.00 15.00
211 Richard Hamilton White Variant 8.00 20.00
220 Grant Hill 6.00 12.00
230 Antawn Jamison 6.00 12.00
240 Dirk Nowitzki 15.00 40.00
250 Emeka Okafor FP 6.00 12.00
260 Jason Richardson FP 6.00 15.00
270 Amare Stoudemire Purple 6.00 15.00
271 Amare Stoudemire Orange Variant10.00 25.00
280 Dwyane Wade Black FP 12.50 30.00
281 Dwyane Wade Red Variant 15.00 40.00

2004-05 McFarlane Basketball 3-Inch Duals
10 Vince Carter 4.00 10.00
Mike Bibby
20 Kevin Garnett 4.00 10.00
Amare Stoudemire
30 Carmelo Anthony 4.00 10.00
Baron Davis
40 Gary Payton 4.00 10.00
Steve Francis
50 Stephon Marbury 4.00 10.00
Michael Finley
60 Scottie Pippen 5.00 12.00
Karl Malone

2004-05 McFarlane Basketball National Convention
10 Allen Iverson 10.00 20.00
20 LeBron James 12.00 30.00

2005-06 McFarlane Basketball Series 10
10 Vince Carter 7.50 15.00
20 Manu Ginobili Black FP 12.00 30.00
21 Manu Ginobili White Variant 7.50 15.00
30 LeBron James Navy 8.00 20.00
31 LeBron James White Variant 10.00 20.00
40 Rashard Lewis 7.50 15.00
50 Tracy McGrady Red 8.00 20.00
51 Tracy McGrady White Variant 8.00 20.00
60 Steve Nash White 7.50 15.00
61 Steve Nash Orange Variant 7.50 15.00
100 Shaquille O'Neal 30.00 60.00
w/Backboard Pack

2005-06 McFarlane Basketball 2-Pack
10 LeBron James 15.00 30.00
Tracy McGrady
20 Rasheed Wallace 15.00 30.00
Ben Wallace

2005-06 McFarlane Basketball 3-Inch
10 Tim Duncan 4.00 8.00
20 Allen Iverson 4.00 10.00
30 LeBron James 6.00 12.00
40 Antawn Jamison 3.00 6.00
50 Richard Jefferson 3.00 6.00
60 Kenyon Martin 3.00 6.00
70 Yao Ming 6.00 10.00
80 Steve Nash 4.00 8.00
90 Jermaine O'Neal 4.00 8.00
100 Peja Stojakovic 3.00 6.00
110 Ben Wallace 3.00 6.00
120 Jason Williams 3.00 6.00

2005-06 McFarlane Basketball 3-Inch Steve Francis
10 Steve Francis 4.00 8.00

2005-06 McFarlane Basketball All-Star Game
10 Carmelo Anthony 10.00 25.00

2005-06 McFarlane Basketball Collector's Club
10 Latrell Sprewell 6.00 15.00
20 Shaquille O'Neal w/backboard 50.00 100.00

2005-06 McFarlane Basketball Legends Series 1
10 Larry Bird Green 8.00 20.00
11 Larry Bird White Variant 10.00 25.00
20 Wilt Chamberlain Phila. 8.00 20.00
21 Wilt Chamberlain 40.00 80.00
Lakers Variant
30 Julius Erving Blue 8.00 20.00
31 Julius Erving White Variant 20.00 50.00
40 Pete Maravich FP Jazz 10.00 25.00
41 Pete Maravich Hawks Variant 20.00 50.00
50 Willis Reed White 8.00 20.00
51 Willis Reed Blue Variant 20.00 40.00
60 Bill Walton Red 10.00 25.00
61 Bill Walton White Variant 20.00 40.00

2005-06 McFarlane Basketball Young Stars
10 Andrei Kirilenko 10.00 20.00
20 J.R. Smith 6.00 15.00
30 Sebastian Telfair 10.00 20.00

2006-07 McFarlane Basketball Series 11-12
10 Carmelo Anthony Pwd.Blue 7.50 15.00
11 Carmelo Anthony Navy Variant 10.00 20.00
20 Ron Artest FP 7.50 15.00
30 Chauncey Billups Blue FP 8.00 20.00
31 Chauncey Billups Red Variant 10.00 25.00
40 Kobe Bryant White 15.00 40.00
41 Kobe Bryant Yellow Variant 20.00 50.00
50 Joe Johnson FP 7.50 15.00
60 Wally Szczerbiak FP 7.50 15.00
100 Gilbert Arenas FP 7.50 15.00
110 Elton Brand 7.50 15.00
120 Allen Iverson 8.00 20.00
130 Tony Parker FP 10.00 25.00
140 Chris Paul Teal FP 8.00 20.00
141 Chris Paul White Variant 15.00 30.00
150 Dwyane Wade White 10.00 25.00
151 Dwyane Wade Red Variant 15.00 30.00
160 Ben Wallace 8.00 20.00
170 Michael Finley Black 15.00 30.00

2006-07 McFarlane Basketball 3-Inch
10 Carmelo Anthony 5.00 10.00
20 Vince Carter 4.00 8.00
30 Michael Finley 4.00 8.00
40 Kevin Garnett 4.00 8.00
50 Allen Iverson 4.00 8.00
60 LeBron James 6.00 12.00
70 Stephon Marbury 4.00 6.00
80 Tracy McGrady 4.00 8.00
90 Dirk Nowitzki 4.00 8.00
100 Shaquille O'Neal 5.00 10.00
110 Amare Stoudemire 4.00 8.00
120 Ben Wallace 4.00 8.00

2006-07 McFarlane Basketball 3-Inch LeBron James
This figure was given away February 6, 2006 at a Cleveland Cavaliers home game.

10 LeBron James 15.00 30.00

2006-07 McFarlane Basketball 3-Inch Ricky Davis
10 Ricky Davis 5.00 10.00

2006-07 McFarlane Basketball Legends Series 2
10 Clyde Drexler Black 7.50 15.00
11 Clyde Drexler White Variant 15.00 30.00
20 Walt Frazier 7.50 15.00
30 Magic Johnson 12.50 30.00
40 Oscar Robertson Celtics 7.50 15.00
41 Oscar Robertson 20.00 35.00
Royals Variant
50 Isiah Thomas White 10.00 20.00
51 Isiah Thomas Blue Variant 15.00 30.00
60 Jerry West 15.00 40.00

2007-08 McFarlane Basketball Series 13-14
10 Chris Bosh FP 7.50 15.00
20 Dwight Howard FP 8.00 20.00
30 LeBron James Red 12.50 25.00
31 LeBron James White Variant 12.50 25.00
40 Shaquille O'Neal 10.00 25.00
50 Paul Pierce White 15.00 30.00
51 Paul Pierce Green Variant 15.00 40.00
60 Jason Terry White FP 7.50 20.00
61 Jason Terry Green Variant 7.50 15.00
100 Carlos Boozer FP 7.50 15.00
110 Kevin Garnett 10.00 20.00
120 Adam Morrison FP 7.50 15.00
121 Adam Morrison Blue Variant 7.50 15.00
130 Steve Nash 7.50 15.00
131 Steve Nash White Variant 10.00 25.00
140 Greg Oden FP 10.00 20.00
150 Tayshaun Prince FP 7.50 15.00
151 Tayshaun Prince White Variant 10.00 20.00

2007-08 McFarlane Basketball 3-Inch
10 Kobe Bryant 6.00 12.00
20 Allen Iverson 4.00 10.00
30 LeBron James 6.00 12.00
40 Steve Nash 4.00 10.00
50 Shaquille O'Neal 4.00 10.00
60 Dwyane Wade 4.00 10.00

2007-08 McFarlane Basketball Legends Series 3
10 Moses Malone Sixers 8.00 20.00
11 Moses Malone Rockets Variant 12.50 25.00
20 Earl Monroe 8.00 20.00
30 David Robinson 10.00 20.00
40 Bill Russell 10.00 20.00
50 Dominique Wilkins Hawks 10.00 25.00
51 Dominique Wilkins 8.00 20.00
All-Star Variant
60 James Worthy Yellow 8.00 20.00
61 James Worthy Purple Variant 12.50 30.00

2008-09 McFarlane Basketball Series 15-16
10 Mike Bibby 7.50 15.00
20 Kobe Bryant 12.50 30.00
30 Vince Carter 10.00 20.00
40 Mike Conley Jr. FP 10.00 20.00
50 Ben Gordon FP 10.00 20.00
60 Desmond Mason FP 10.00 20.00
70 Shaquille O'Neal 10.00 20.00
100 Ray Allen 20.00 50.00
110 Kevin Durant FP 12.00 30.00
120 Andre Iguodala FP 7.50 15.00
130 LeBron James 10.00 20.00
140 Tracy McGrady 7.50 15.00
150 Jermaine O'Neal 7.50 15.00
160 Zach Randolph FP 12.50 25.00

2008-09 McFarlane Basketball Legends Series 4
10 Elgin Baylor 15.00 40.00
20 Larry Bird 12.50 25.00
30 Julius Erving 10.00 20.00
31 Julius Erving Nets Variant 15.00 30.00
40 Patrick Ewing 12.50 30.00
41 Patrick Ewing Blue Variant 12.50 30.00
50 George Gervin 10.00 20.00
60 Spud Webb 10.00 20.00

2009-10 McFarlane Basketball Series 17

10 Kobe Bryant White 12.50 25.00
11 Kobe Bryant 30.00 70.00
Yellow With Trophy/2000 Variant
20 Kevin Garnett 10.00 20.00
21 Kevin Garnett 15.00 40.00
With Trophy/1600 Variant
30 Pau Gasol Yellow 30.00 60.00
31 Pau Gasol 200.00 300.00
Purple/100 Variant
40 LeBron James Yellow 15.00 30.00
41 LeBron James 25.00 60.00
Blue/500 Variant
50 Chris Paul White 10.00 20.00
51 Chris Paul 30.00 60.00
Teal/500 Variant
60 Derrick Rose FP 40.00 100.00
70 Dwyane Wade Black 15.00 30.00
71 Dwyane Wade 40.00 100.00
White/250 Variant

2009-10 McFarlane Basketball Legends Series 5

10 Joe Dumars 7.50 15.00
20 John Havlicek 10.00 20.00
30 Magic Johnson 15.00 40.00
40 Karl Malone 10.00 20.00
41 Karl Malone White Variant 15.00 30.00
50 Dan Majerle 10.00 20.00
60 Hakeem Olajuwon 10.00 20.00
61 Hakeem Olajuwon White Variant 12.50 25.00

2010-11 McFarlane Basketball Series 18

10 Ron Artest 10.00 20.00
11 Ron Artest 12.50 25.00
White/2000 Variant
20 Chauncey Billups 10.00 20.00
30 Kobe Bryant 10.00 25.00
31 Kobe Bryant 30.00 60.00
Purple Sleeve/1000 Variant
40 Kevin Durant 10.00 20.00
50 Kevin Garnett 10.00 20.00
51 Kevin Garnett 12.50 25.00
Green/3000 Variant
60 Dwight Howard 10.00 20.00
70 Jason Kidd 10.00 20.00

2010-11 McFarlane Basketball Series 19

10 Carlos Boozer 10.00 20.00
11 Carlos Boozer 20.00 50.00
White/1000 Variant
20 Chris Bosh 10.00 20.00
21 Chris Bosh 20.00 50.00
Black/1000 Variant
30 LeBron James 12.50 30.00
31 LeBron James 15.00 40.00
Black/2000 Variant
40 Steve Nash 10.00 20.00
41 Steve Nash 25.00 60.00
Latin/500 Variant
50 Shaquille O'Neal 10.00 20.00
60 Rajon Rondo FP 12.50 25.00
61 Rajon Rondo 20.00 50.00
Alt/1000 Variant
70 Amare Stoudemire 10.00 20.00

2010-11 McFarlane Basketball 3-Pack

10 Chris Bosh 40.00 80.00
LeBron James
Dwyane Wade

2011-12 McFarlane Basketball Series 20

10 Carmelo Anthony 10.00 20.00
11 Carmelo Anthony 20.00 50.00
Green Variant
20 Kobe Bryant 12.50 25.00
21 Kobe Bryant 20.00 50.00
Purple/2000 Variant
30 Kevin Durant 10.00 20.00
31 Kevin Durant 20.00 50.00
White/1000 Variant
40 Blake Griffin FP 12.50 25.00
41 Blake Griffin 150.00 250.00
All-Star/100 Variant
50 Derrick Rose 12.50 25.00
51 Derrick Rose 30.00 60.00
Black/2000 Variant
60 John Wall FP 10.00 20.00
70 Dwyane Wade 10.00 20.00
71 Dwyane Wade 40.00 70.00
El Heat Jsy/500 Variant

1988 SLU Basketball

This 85-piece set was issued by Cincinnati-based Kenner Toy Company. The statues feature top National Basketball Association stars in action poses and are accompanied by a standard-size card of each player. The card front has either a posed or action color shot. The back has biographical and statistical information along with a facsimile signature. This was the first Basketball set produced under the Starting Lineup brand. The two main modes of distribution for the '88 Basketball set were regionally issued team cases (12 pieces) and nationally distributed All-Star cases (24 pieces). The All-Star cases consisted of Kareem Abdul-Jabbar (2), Charles Barkley, Larry Bird (3), Patrick Ewing (2), Magic Johnson (3), Michael Jordan (5), Danny Manning, Kevin McHale, Hakeem Olajawon (2), Isiah Thomas (2) and Dominique Wilkins (2). The Utah Jazz team had the lowest print run of any of the teams. The Los Angeles Clippers and Los Angeles Lakers figures came in the same team case, as did the New York Knicks and New Jersey Nets figures. The values listed below refer to unopened packages. The figures are unnumbered and checklisted below in alphabetical order.

ORANGE DISPLAY STAND 25.00 50.00
1988-90 PRICES NM IN PACKAGE
1 Kareem Abdul-Jabbar 10.00 25.00
2 Michael Adams 15.00 40.00
3 Mark Aguirre 20.00 50.00
4 Danny Ainge 15.00 40.00
5 Thurl Bailey 125.00 250.00
6 Charles Barkley 15.00 40.00
7 Walter Berry 15.00 40.00
8 Larry Bird 15.00 40.00
9 Rolando Blackman 20.00 50.00
10 Michael Cage 15.00 40.00
11 Joe Barry Carroll 15.00 40.00
12 Tom Chambers 10.00 25.00
13 Maurice Cheeks 12.00 30.00
14 Michael Cooper 30.00 80.00
15 Terry Cummings 12.00 30.00
16 Adrian Dantley 25.00 60.00
17 Brad Daugherty 12.00 30.00
18 Johnny Dawkins 12.00 30.00
19 Clyde Drexler 25.00 60.00
20 Mark Eaton 100.00 250.00
21 Dale Ellis 20.00 50.00
22 Alex English 20.00 50.00
23 Patrick Ewing 15.00 40.00
24 Sleepy Floyd 20.00 50.00
25 Winston Garland 10.00 25.00
26 Armon Gilliam 15.00 40.00
27 Mike Gminski 12.00 30.00
28 David Greenwood 12.00 30.00
29 Derek Harper 25.00 60.00
30 Ron Harper 25.00 60.00
31 Rod Higgins 12.00 30.00
32 Dennis Hopson 12.00 30.00
33 Jeff Hornacek 20.00 50.00
34 Mark Jackson 10.00 25.00
35 Dennis Johnson 25.00 60.00
36 Eddie Johnson 12.00 30.00
37 Magic Johnson 15.00 40.00
38 Steve Johnson 10.00 25.00
39 Vinnie Johnson 30.00 80.00
40 Michael Jordan 25.00 60.00
41 Bernard King 10.00 25.00
42 Bill Laimbeer 25.00 60.00
43 Lafayette Lever 15.00 40.00
44 Jeff Malone 12.00 30.00
45 Karl Malone 125.00 300.00
46 Moses Malone 25.00 60.00
47 Danny Manning 10.00 25.00
48 Rodney McCray 20.00 50.00
49 Xavier McDaniel 12.00 30.00
50 Kevin McHale 15.00 40.00
51 Derrick McKey 10.00 25.00
52 Reggie Miller 75.00 200.00
53 Sidney Moncrief 20.00 50.00
54 Chris Mullin 15.00 40.00
55 Hakeem Olajuwon 12.00 30.00
56 Robert Parish 20.00 50.00
57 John Paxson 12.00 30.00
58 Sam Perkins 25.00 60.00
59 Chuck Person 10.00 25.00
60 Scottie Pippen 30.00 80.00
61 Terry Porter 12.00 30.00
62 Paul Pressey 15.00 40.00
63 Mark Price 30.00 80.00
64 Doc Rivers 10.00 25.00
65 Alvin Robertson 12.00 30.00
66 Cliff Robinson 12.00 30.00
67 Ralph Sampson 12.00 30.00
68 Danny Schayes 25.00 60.00
69 Jack Sikma 20.00 50.00
70 Kenny Smith 12.00 30.00
71 Steve Stipanovich 20.00 50.00
72 John Stockton 150.00 300.00
73 Isiah Thomas 15.00 40.00
74 LaSalle Thompson 12.00 30.00
75 Otis Thorpe 10.00 25.00
76 Wayman Tisdale 15.00 40.00
77 Kiki Vandeweghe 10.00 25.00
78 Spud Webb 12.00 30.00
79 Dominique Wilkins 15.00 40.00
80 Gerald Wilkins 12.00 30.00
81 Buck Williams 12.00 30.00
82 John Williams 12.00 30.00
83 Reggie Williams 12.00 30.00
84 Kevin Willis 12.00 30.00
85 James Worthy 15.00 40.00

1988-89 SLU Basketball Slam Dunk Red/White Box

This six-piece set was issued by the Cincinnati-based Kenner Toy Company. There are two packaging versions of each piece, a send-a-way and a retail. The first pieces issued came in a white box and were available by sending in five UPC codes. Kenner had many figures leftover from the offer and decided to issue those extra pieces through retail channels in a more colorful red box. These figures first hit retail outlets in late 1989 and early 1990. "Red Box" figures were commonly sold for $9.99 - $12.99 in most retail outlets. The values listed below refer to the unopened "Red Box" version. There is a multiplier for the "White Box" version in the header. The figures are unnumbered and checklisted below in alphabetical order.

*WHITE BOX VERSION: SAME PRICE
1 Larry Bird 50.00 125.00
2 Patrick Ewing 40.00 100.00
3 Magic Johnson 50.00 125.00
4 Michael Jordan 60.00 150.00
5 Isiah Thomas 25.00 60.00
6 Dominique Wilkins 25.00 60.00

1989 SLU Basketball

This five-piece set was issued by Cincinnati-based Kenner Toy Company. The set consist of three Charlotte Hornets and two Cleveland Cavaliers. The Cavaliers figures were distributed in the Cleveland area in a 12-count case with six of each of the two players. The Hornets figures were distributed in the Charlotte area in a 12-count case with Dell Curry (5), Kelly Tripucka (4), and Rex Chapman (3). The figures came in the exact same package as the 1988 figures except for a little flag on the back that says "1989."

1 Rex Chapman 12.00 30.00
2 Dell Curry 10.00 25.00
3 Ron Harper 10.00 25.00
4 Larry Nance 10.00 25.00
5 Kelly Tripucka 10.00 25.00

1989 SLU Legends Series *

The 1989 Legends series focused on legendary players from the sports of Football and Basketball. The figures were carded on a light background card with a player card included.

SET CONSIDERED COMPLETE WITH EITHER UNITAS OR SAYERS VERSION
2 Wilt Chamberlain 15.00 40.00
4 Julius Erving 15.00 40.00
6 John Havlicek 15.00 40.00
7 Oscar Robertson 12.00 30.00

1989 SLU One-On-One *

The 1989 One-On-One series featured baseball, basketball, and football figures in posed action scenes.

5 Charles Barkley 65.00 125.00
Dominique Wilkins
6 Patrick Ewing 30.00 80.00
Kevin McHale
7 Magic Johnson 100.00 250.00
Larry Bird
8 Michael Jordan 125.00 300.00
Isiah Thomas

1990 SLU Basketball

This 17-piece set was issued by Cincinnati-based Kenner Toy Company. The statues feature top National Basketball Association stars in action poses and are accompanied by two cards. The regular card features a posed or action color shot on front. The back has biographical and statistical information along with a facsimile signature. The second card is titled "Rookie Year." The front has an action or posed shot along with a banner in the upper part that has the "Rookie Year" for that particular player. The back features biographical information. Figures were distributed through two different cases assortments (24 pieces) and complete sets were available to the public via a Kenner mail order offer for $119. The two shortest printed figures in the set are Clyde Drexler and Patrick Ewing. The values listed below refer to unopened packages. The figures are unnumbered and checklisted below in alphabetical order.

1 Charles Barkley 10.00 25.00
2 Larry Bird 20.00 50.00
3 Tom Chambers 6.00 15.00
4 Clyde Drexler 15.00 40.00
5 Joe Dumars 8.00 20.00
6 Patrick Ewing 12.00 30.00
7 Magic Johnson 12.00 30.00
8 Michael Jordan 15.00 40.00
9 Karl Malone 15.00 40.00
10 Chris Mullin 8.00 20.00
11 David Robinson 15.00 40.00
12 Byron Scott 12.00 30.00
13 John Stockton 15.00 40.00
14 Isiah Thomas 10.00 25.00
15 Spud Webb 8.00 20.00
16 Dominique Wilkins 10.00 25.00
17 James Worthy 10.00 25.00

1991 SLU Basketball

This 17-piece set was issued by Cincinnati-based Kenner Toy Company. The statues feature top National Basketball Association stars in action poses and are accompanied by standard-size card and a collector coin of each player. The card front has either a posed or action color shot. The back has biographical and statistical information and a facsimile signature. The coin features an embossed player portrait and came in two different variations, steel and aluminum.The steel variation is much tougher to find. Figures were distributed through two different cases assortments (24 pieces) and complete sets were available to the public via a Kenner mail order offer for $109. The two shortest printed figures in the set are Charles Barkley and Patrick Ewing. The values listed below refer to unopened packages. The figures are unnumbered and checklisted below in alphabetical order.

1 Charles Barkley 12.00 30.00
2 Larry Bird 12.00 30.00
3 Derrick Coleman 6.00 15.00
4 Clyde Drexler 10.00 25.00
5 Joe Dumars 6.00 15.00
6 Patrick Ewing 8.00 20.00
7 Kevin Johnson 8.00 20.00
8 Magic Johnson 12.00 30.00
9 Michael Jordan 12.00 30.00
Dunk Pose
10 Michael Jordan 12.00 30.00
Jump Pose
11 Reggie Lewis 10.00 25.00
12 David Robinson 6.00 15.00
13 Dennis Rodman 20.00 50.00
14 Isiah Thomas 6.00 15.00
15 Spud Webb 6.00 15.00
16 Dominique Wilkins 6.00 15.00

1992 SLU Basketball

This 29-piece set was issued by Cincinnati-based Kenner Toy Company. The statues feature top National Basketball Association stars in action poses and are accompanied by standard-size card and a poster of each player. The card front has either a posed or action color shot. The back has biographical and statistical information and a facsimile signature. The poster folds out to be a 11" X 14" shot of the player. Figures were distributed through two different cases assortments (24 pieces). There was one variation in the set. The Magic Johnson figure came in a purple or yellow uniform. The yellow uniform variation is the shortest basketball figure ever produced. It only came in a few of the second cases and it is estimated that there are less than 600 of this piece. The values listed below refer to unopened packages. The figures are unnumbered and checklisted below in alphabetical order.and a poster of each player. The set price doesn't include the yellow Magic Johnson variation.

1 Charles Barkley 15.00 40.00
2 Larry Bird 12.00 30.00
3 Manute Bol 10.00 25.00
4 Dee Brown 8.00 20.00
5 Derrick Coleman 5.00 12.00
6 Vlade Divac 8.00 20.00
7 Clyde Drexler 8.00 20.00
8 Joe Dumars 5.00 12.00
9 Patrick Ewing 10.00 25.00
10 Tim Hardaway 6.00 15.00
11 Kevin Johnson 6.00 15.00
12 Larry Johnson 10.00 25.00
13 Magic Johnson Purple 15.00 40.00
14 Magic Johnson Yellow 60.00 150.00
15 Michael Jordan Regular 25.00 60.00
16 Michael Jordan WrmUps 25.00 60.00
17 Dan Majerle 6.00 15.00
18 Karl Malone 10.00 25.00
19 Reggie Miller 10.00 25.00
20 Chris Mullin 5.00 12.00
21 Dikembe Mutombo 6.00 15.00
22 Hakeem Olajuwon 12.00 30.00
23 John Paxson 5.00 12.00
24 Scottie Pippen 12.00 30.00
25 Mark Price 5.00 12.00
26 David Robinson Regular 8.00 20.00
27 David Robinson WrmUps 8.00 20.00
28 Dennis Rodman 15.00 40.00
29 John Stockton 10.00 25.00
30 Isiah Thomas 6.00 15.00

1992 SLU Basketball Headline Collection

This eight-piece set was the first and only time the Headline Collection series for Basketball was issued by Cincinnati-based Kenner Toy Company. The pieces feature top National Basketball League players action poses. The figures are accompanied by an authentic newspaper article and a high gloss, black base used to insert the article and display the figure. The article is framed and describes a memorable moment from the previous season. The pieces came in 12 count case assortments. The values listed below refer to unopened packages. The figures are unnumbered and listed below in alphabetical order.

1 Charles Barkley 12.00 30.00
2 Larry Bird 15.00 40.00
3 Patrick Ewing 10.00 25.00
4 Magic Johnson 15.00 40.00
5 Michael Jordan 40.00 100.00
6 Dikembe Mutombo 8.00 20.00
7 Scottie Pippen 15.00 40.00
8 David Robinson 10.00 25.00

1993 SLU Basketball

This 29-piece set was issued by Cincinnati-based Kenner Toy Company. The statues feature top National Basketball Association stars in action poses and are accompanied by two standard-size cards. The cards issued are a parallel of the 1992-93 Topps card and of the 1992-93 Stadium Club card. The card fronts have either a posed or action color shot. The back has biographical and statistical information. The only difference between this card and a regular Topps or Stadium Club card is the foil stamped Starting Lineup logo on the front. Figures were distributed through two different cases assortments (24 pieces). The values listed below refer to unopened packages. The figures are unnumbered and checklisted below in alphabetical order.

1 Kenny Anderson 5.00 12.00
2 Stacey Augmon 5.00 12.00
3 Charles Barkley 8.00 20.00
4 Brad Daugherty 5.00 12.00
5 Todd Day 5.00 12.00
6 Clyde Drexler 8.00 20.00
7 Sean Elliott 6.00 15.00
8 Patrick Ewing 8.00 20.00
9 Horace Grant 8.00 20.00
10 Tom Gugliotta 10.00 25.00
11 Tim Hardaway 6.00 15.00
12 Larry Johnson 6.00 15.00
13 Michael Jordan 25.00 60.00
14 Shawn Kemp 8.00 20.00
15 Christian Laettner 8.00 20.00
16 Dan Majerle 5.00 12.00
17 Karl Malone 6.00 15.00
18 Alonzo Mourning 12.00 30.00
19 Dikembe Mutombo 5.00 12.00
20 Shaquille O'Neal 12.00 30.00
21 Scottie Pippen 10.00 25.00
22 Terry Porter 5.00 12.00
23 Mark Price 8.00 20.00
24 Glen Rice 6.00 15.00
25 Mitch Richmond 6.00 15.00
26 David Robinson 6.00 15.00
27 Detlef Schrempf 6.00 15.00
28 John Stockton 6.00 15.00
29 Dominique Wilkins 5.00 12.00

1994 SLU Basketball

This 26-piece set was issued by Cincinnati-based Kenner Toy Company. The statues feature top National Basketball Association stars in action poses and are accompanied by a standard-size Hoops card of each player. The card front has either a posed or action color shot. The back has biographical and statistical information. The cards are a parallel version of the 1993-94 Hoops basketball cards. The appearance of the Starting Lineup logo on the front of the card is the only difference. The figures were distributed in four different 24-count cases. There is one variation in the set. The Dennis Rodman figure came with both blonde hair and red hair. The red hair variation is considerably tougher than the blonde. The values listed below refer to unopened packages. The figures are unnumbered and checklisted below in alphabetical order. The set price doesn't include the red hair Dennis Rodman variation.

1 B.J. Armstrong 5.00 12.00
2 Stacey Augmon 4.00 10.00
3 Charles Barkley 10.00 25.00
4 Shawn Bradley 4.00 10.00
5 Calbert Cheaney 4.00 10.00
6 Derrick Coleman 4.00 10.00
7 Sean Elliott 4.00 10.00
8 LaPhonso Ellis 4.00 10.00
9 Patrick Ewing 5.00 12.00
10 Anfernee Hardaway 15.00 40.00
11 Jim Jackson 5.00 12.00
12 Larry Johnson 4.00 10.00
13 Shawn Kemp 5.00 12.00
14 Karl Malone 6.00 15.00
15 Jamal Mashburn 6.00 15.00
16 Harold Miner 4.00 10.00
17 Alonzo Mourning 4.00 10.00
18 Chris Mullin 4.00 10.00
19 Hakeem Olajuwon 6.00 15.00
20 Shaquille O'Neal 8.00 20.00
21 Scottie Pippen 8.00 20.00
22 David Robinson 6.00 15.00
23 Dennis Rodman 10.00 25.00
Blonde Hair
24 Dennis Rodman 20.00 50.00
Red Hair
25 Latrell Sprewell 10.00 25.00
26 Chris Webber 8.00 20.00
27 Dominque Wilkins 5.00 12.00

1995 SLU Basketball

This 31-piece set was issued by Cincinnati-based Kenner Toy Company. The statues feature top National Basketball Association stars in action poses and are accompanied by a standard-size Hoops card of each player. The card front has either a posed or action color shot. The back has biographical and statistical information. The cards are a parallel version of the 1994-95 Hoops basketball cards. The appearance of the Starting Lineup logo on the front of the card is the only difference. The figures were distributed in two different 16-count cases. The Grant Hill figure was the only piece that could be found in both case assortments. There is one variation in the set. The Horace Grant figure came wearing blue goggles and black goggles. The black goggle variation is the tougher of the two. The values listed below refer to unopened packages. The figures are unnumbered and checklisted below in alphabetical order. The set price doesn't include the black goggle Horace Grant variation and only one of the Hill variations.

1 Charles Barkley 6.00 15.00
2 Muggsy Bogues 5.00 12.00
3 Patrick Ewing 5.00 12.00
4 Horace Grant Blue 6.00 15.00
4B Horace Grant Black 8.00 20.00
5 Anfernee Hardaway 12.00 30.00
6 Grant Hill 8.00 20.00
6B Grant Hill 8.00 20.00
ROY Sticker
7 Jeff Hornacek 5.00 12.00
8 Jim Jackson 4.00 10.00
9 Shawn Kemp 6.00 15.00
10 Jason Kidd 10.00 25.00
11 Tony Kukoc 8.00 20.00
12 Dan Majerle 4.00 10.00
13 Karl Malone 6.00 15.00
14 Reggie Miller 6.00 15.00
15 Eric Montross 4.00 10.00
16 Alonzo Mourning 5.00 12.00
17 Hakeem Olajuwon 8.00 20.00
18 Shaquille O'Neal 10.00 25.00
19 Robert Pack 5.00 12.00
20 Scottie Pippen 8.00 20.00
21 Mark Price 4.00 10.00
22 Clifford Robinson 4.00 10.00
23 David Robinson 6.00 15.00
24 Glenn Robinson 8.00 20.00
25 Steve Smith 6.00 15.00
26 Latrell Sprewell 4.00 10.00
27 John Starks 5.00 12.00
28 Nick Van Exel 8.00 20.00
29 Clarence Weatherspoon 4.00 10.00
30 Chris Webber 6.00 15.00
31 Dominique Wilkins 4.00 10.00

1996-97 SLU Asian Basketball

This 12-piece set was issued by Cincinnati-based Kenner Toy Company. The statues feature top National Basketball Association stars in action poses and are accompanied by a standard-size card of each player. The card front has either a posed or action color shot. The back has biographical and statistical information. This was the first overseas basketball release. The Magic Johnson piece was not supposed to exist - it was only supposed to be a prototype, but some pieces made their way into the cases. The Magic piece is considered part of the regular set. The values listed below refer to unopened packages. The figures are unnumbered and checklisted below in alphabetical order.

1 Charles Barkley 10.00 25.00
2 Sean Elliott 8.00 20.00
3 Anfernee Hardaway 12.00 30.00
4 Grant Hill 12.00 30.00
5 Larry Johnson 8.00 20.00
6 Magic Johnson 125.00 300.00
7 Eddie Jones 12.00 30.00
8 Reggie Miller 8.00 20.00
9 Hakeem Olajuwon 10.00 25.00
10 Shaquille O'Neal 12.00 30.00
11 Scottie Pippen 10.00 25.00
12A Dennis Rodman Green 20.00 50.00
12B Dennis Rodman Yellow 20.00 50.00

1996-97 SLU Basketball Extended

This 8-piece extended set was issued by Cincinnati-based Kenner Toy Company. The statues feature top National Basketball Association stars in action poses and are accompanied by a standard-size card of each player. The card front has either a posed or action color shot. The back has biographical and statistical information. This was the first extended product for the basketball market. The values listed below refer to unopened packages. The figures are unnumbered and checklisted below in alphabetical order. Some of the more popular first pieces from this set include Kobe Bryant and Allen Iverson.

1 Charles Barkley 8.00 20.00
2 Kobe Bryant 15.00 40.00
3 Grant Hill 6.00 15.00
4 Allen Iverson 12.00 30.00
5 Larry Johnson 3.00 8.00
6 Dikembe Mutombo 3.00 8.00
7 Shaquille O'Neal 10.00 25.00
8 Damon Stoudamire 4.00 10.00

1996 SLU Basketball

This 34-piece set was issued by Cincinnati-based Kenner Toy Company. The statues feature top National Basketball Association stars in action poses and are accompanied by a standard-size card of each player. The card front has either a posed or action color shot. The back has biographical and statistical information. There are a couple of variations in the set. The Grant Hill had a regular piece and a finger role special. The finger role is the more popular piece. Dennis Rodman also had three hair variations - green, orange and yellow. The green is slightly tougher than the other two. The values listed below refer to unopened packages. The figures are unnumbered and checklisted below in alphabetical order. The set price includes only one of the Rodman hair variations and the regular Grant Hill. Some of the more popular first pieces from this set include Vin Baker, Kevin Garnett, Juwan Howard, Eddie Jones, Antonio McDyess, Gary Payton, Jerry Stackhouse and Damon Stoudamire.

1 Vin Baker FP 6.00 15.00
2 Charles Barkley 5.00 12.00
3 Clyde Drexler 5.00 12.00
4 Sean Elliott 4.00 10.00
5 Patrick Ewing 5.00 12.00
6 Kevin Garnett FP 12.00 30.00
7 Anfernee Hardaway 6.00 15.00
8A Grant Hill 8.00 20.00
8B Grant Hill Finger Roll 12.00 30.00
9 Tyrone Hill FP 4.00 10.00
10 Juwan Howard FP 8.00 20.00
11 Larry Johnson 5.00 12.00
12 Eddie Jones FP 12.00 30.00
13 Jason Kidd 8.00 20.00
14 Karl Malone 6.00 15.00
15 Jamal Mashburn 5.00 12.00
16 Antonio McDyess FP 8.00 20.00
17 Reggie Miller 5.00 12.00
18 Alonzo Mourning 5.00 12.00
19 Hakeem Olajuwon 5.00 12.00
20 Shaquille O'Neal 6.00 15.00
21 Gary Payton FP 8.00 20.00
22 Scottie Pippen 6.00 15.00
23 Dino Radja FP 4.00 10.00
24 Bryant Reeves FP 4.00 10.00
25 Pooh Richardson FP 4.00 10.00
26 Mitch Richmond 4.00 10.00
27 Clifford Robinson 4.00 10.00
28 David Robinson 5.00 12.00
29 Glenn Robinson 5.00 12.00
30A Dennis Rodman 12.00 30.00
Green Hair Variation
30B Dennis Rodman 12.00 30.00
Orange Hair Variation
30C Dennis Rodman 12.00 30.00
Yellow Hair Variation
31 Joe Smith FP 6.00 15.00
32 Rik Smits FP 6.00 15.00
33 Jerry Stackhouse FP 8.00 20.00
34 Damon Stoudamire FP 6.00 15.00

1997-98 SLU Basketball Extended

This 8-piece extended set was issued by Cincinnati-based Kenner Toy Company. The statues feature top National Basketball Association stars in action poses and are accompanied by a standard-size card of each player. The card front has either a posed or action color shot. The back has biographical and statistical information. This was the second extended product for th[illegible]arket and it was released in two ass[illegible]es listed below refer to unopened packages. The figures are unnumbered and checklisted below in alphabetical order. Some of the more popular first pieces from this set include Tim Duncan and Keith Van Horn.

1 Clyde Drexler 6.00 12.00
2 Tim Duncan FP 20.00 40.00
3 Anfernee Hardaway 6.00 12.00
4 Eddie Jones 10.00 20.00
5 Luc Longley FP 5.00 10.00
6 Anthony Mason FP 3.00 8.00
7 Antonio McDyess 3.00 8.00
8 Keith Van Horn FP 6.00 15.00

1997 SLU Basketball

This 38-piece set was issued by Cincinnati-based Kenner Toy Company. The statues feature top National Basketball Association stars in action poses and are accompanied by a standard-size card of each player. The card front has either a posed or action color shot. The back has biographical and statistical information. The values listed below refer to unopened packages. The figures are unnumbered and checklisted below in alphabetical order. The set is considered complete without the Dennis Rodman retail special.

1 Shareef Abdur-Rahim FP 8.00 20.00
2 Ray Allen FP 8.00 20.00
3 Kenny Anderson 3.00 8.00
4 Vin Baker 3.00 8.00
5 Charles Barkley 4.00 10.00
6 Terrell Brandon FP 5.00 12.00
7 Marcus Camby FP 5.00 12.00
8 Vlade Divac 3.00 8.00
9 Patrick Ewing 3.00 8.00
10 Michael Finley FP 6.00 15.00
11 Kevin Garnett 5.00 12.00
12 Horace Grant 3.00 8.00
13 Tim Hardaway 3.00 8.00
14 Grant Hill 4.00 10.00
15 Allan Houston FP 5.00 12.00
16 Juwan Howard 3.00 8.00
17 Allen Iverson 10.00 25.00
18 Mark Jackson 3.00 8.00
19 Shawn Kemp 3.00 8.00
20 Jason Kidd 5.00 12.00
21 Kerry Kittles FP 5.00 12.00
22 Stephon Marbury FP 8.00 20.00
23 Reggie Miller 4.00 10.00
24 Alonzo Mourning 3.00 8.00
25 Hakeem Olajuwon 4.00 10.00
26 Shaquille O'Neal 5.00 12.00
27 Gary Payton 3.00 8.00
28 Scottie Pippen 5.00 12.00
29 Mitch Richmond 3.00 8.00
30 David Robinson 4.00 10.00
31 Dennis Rodman Special 10.00 25.00
32 Steve Smith 3.00 8.00
33 Latrell Sprewell 3.00 8.00
34 John Stockton 4.00 10.00
35 Damon Stoudamire 4.00 10.00
36 Nick Van Exel 3.00 8.00
37 Loy Vaught FP 3.00 8.00
38 Antoine Walker FP 12.00 30.00
39 Chris Webber 4.00 10.00

1997 SLU Basketball 14-inch Figures

This 5-piece set was distributed in one assortment - six per case. These dolls stand 14" and feature the top NBA stars.

1 Charles Barkley 15.00 40.00
2 Grant Hill 15.00 40.00
3 Shawn Kemp 12.00 30.00
4 Shaquille O'Neal 15.00 40.00
5 Dennis Rodman 15.00 40.00

1997 SLU Basketball Backboard Kings

This 6-piece set was distributed in one assortments and features the first NBA set very similar to the Baseball Stadium Stars. Each figure is 8" and is suspended above a basketball court with facsimile signatures.

1 Charles Barkley 4.00 10.00
2 Grant Hill 4.00 10.00
3 Karl Malone 4.00 10.00
4 Shaquille O'Neal 5.00 12.00
5 Scottie Pippen 4.00 10.00
6 Damon Stoudamire 4.00 10.00

1997 SLU Basketball Classic Doubles

This 7-piece set was distributed in two different assortments. The package features two pieces and highlights some of the best double tandems (both past and present) in the NBA

1 Larry Bird 10.00 25.00
Kevin McHale
2 Wilt Chamberlain 10.00 25.00
Bill Russell
3 Joe Dumars 10.00 25.00
Grant Hill
4 Patrick Ewing 10.00 25.00
Willis Reed
5 Shaquille O'Neal 12.00 30.00
Kareem Abdul-Jabbar
6 Bill Russell 10.00 25.00
Hakeem Olajuwon
7 John Stockton 10.00 25.00
Karl Malone

1998-99 SLU Basketball FAME

The first release of a college based basketball set for the Kenner Company. This 9-piece set was offered in two assortments and featured popular NBA and WNBA stars in their college uniforms. Prices below refer to in-package pieces.

1 Kareem Abdul-Jabbar 6.00 15.00
1A Mike Bibby 5.00 12.00
2 Larry Bird 6.00 15.00
3 Patrick Ewing 3.00 8.00
4 Juwan Howard 3.00 8.00
5 Allen Iverson 8.00 20.00
6 Magic Johnson 5.00 12.00
7 Jason Kidd 30.00 80.00
8 Raef LaFrentz 4.00 10.00
9 Ron Mercer 3.00 8.00
10 Bill Russell 3.00 8.00
11 Sheryl Swoopes 8.00 20.00

1998 SLU Basketball

Produced by the Cincinnati based Kenner, this was the final licensed basketball set for the company. The set includes no first pieces, but does include some of the best players in basketball and one retired player - Magic Johnson. Prices below are for in package pieces. The pieces are not numbered and listed below in alphabetical order.

1 Vin Baker 3.00 8.00
2 Terrell Brandon 3.00 8.00
3 Kobe Bryant 10.00 25.00
4 Patrick Ewing 3.00 8.00
5 Kevin Garnett 5.00 12.00
6 Grant Hill 4.00 10.00
7 Allen Iverson 6.00 15.00
8 Magic Johnson 6.00 15.00
9 Shawn Kemp 3.00 8.00
10 Jason Kidd 4.00 10.00
11 Karl Malone 3.00 8.00
12 Stephon Marbury 3.00 8.00
13 Alonzo Mourning 3.00 8.00
14 Shaquille O'Neal 5.00 12.00
15 Dennis Rodman 5.00 12.00
16 Rik Smits 3.00 8.00

1998 SLU Basketball 12-inch Figures

Released by Kenner, this is the first edition of the 12 inch figures for basketball. The five-piece set was released in one assortment. Prices below refer to in-package pieces.

1 Tim Duncan 10.00 25.00
2 Kevin Garnett 8.00 20.00
3 Juwan Howard 6.00 15.00
4 Allen Iverson 20.00 35.00
5 Glen Rice 6.00 15.00

2000 SLU NCAA March Madness

This 6-figure set was released by the Hasbro Toy Company. The players are featured in action poses and are accompanied by a standard-size card of each player. The card front has either a posed or action color shot. This product was produced and released exclusively for Wal-Mart. The values listed below refer to unopened packages. The figures are unnumbered and checklisted below in alphabetical order.

1 David Robinson 6.00 15.00
2 Jerry Stackhouse 5.00 12.00
3 Sheryl Swoopes 6.00 15.00
4 Isiah Thomas 5.00 12.00
5 Bill Walton 5.00 12.00
6 James Worthy 5.00 12.00

1998 SLU Timeless Legends *

Kenner released its final Timeless Legends series in 1998. The set was released in two different series with series one released in two case assortments and series two in just one. Olympic athletes highlight this set.

2 Larry Bird 6.00 15.00

2000 UDA Playmakers

The 2000 Upper Deck Playmakers were released on the Upper Deck website during the 2000-01 season. These figures are the next generation of "bobbing head dolls". Each figure carries a $9.99 SRP.

1 Larry Bird 10.00 25.00
2 Kobe Bryant 12.00 30.00
3 Vince Carter 12.00 30.00
4 Tim Duncan 20.00 50.00
5 Kevin Garnett 10.00 25.00
6 Grant Hill 10.00 25.00
7 Allen Iverson 10.00 25.00
8 Shaquille O'Neal 10.00 25.00
9 Latrell Sprewell 10.00 25.00

2008-09 Upper Deck Basketball Michael Jordan

10 Michael Jordan 30.00 60.00